HARPER'S DICTIONARY OF

CLASSICAL LITERATURE AND ANTIQUITIES

HARPER'S DICTIONARY OF
CLASSICAL LITERATURE
AND ANTIQUITIES

Edited by

HARRY THURSTON PECK

Illustrated

New York

COOPER SQUARE PUBLISHERS, INC.

1965

published by

Cooper Square Publishers, Inc.

59 Fourth Avenue, New York 3, N. Y.

Library of Congress Catalog Card No. 61-13268

third printing

PRINTED IN THE U.S.A. BY NOBLE OFFSET PRINTERS, INC., NEW YORK 3, N. Y.

VIRO

DOCTISSIMO · ATQVE · HVMANISSIMO

HENRICO · DRISLER · LL · D ·

COLLEGII · COLVMBIAE · QVONDAM · DECANO

LINGVAE . LITTERARVMQVE · GRAECARVM · PROFESSORI · EMERITO

QVI

MIHI · AVXILIVM · CONSILIVMQVE · PETENTI

NVNQVAM · DEFVIT

HOC · OPVS

PIETATIS · AMORIS · VENERATIONIS · TESTIMONIVM

D · D · D·

PREFACE

The purpose of the present volume is to give the student, in a concise and intelligible form, the essential facts concerning those questions that oftenest arise in the study of the life, the literature, the religion, and the art of classical antiquity. Its further purpose is to indicate the sources whence a fuller and more critical knowledge of these subjects can be most readily and most accurately gained.

Until very recently, the study of classical literature was, in all our universities, inseparably linked with the conception of a liberal education. Holding firmly to the dignified traditions of the past, it was accepted as an undisputed fact that the highest type of scholarship, the type best fitted to sustain the supreme test of æsthetic perfection and to be stamped with the final *cachet* that confers distinction, was unattainable if severed from the direct influence and inspiration of the great Hellenic masters whose intellectual activity was imbued with a noble passion for ideal beauty and ideal truth. Of late, the tremendous pressure of material interests from without, and the national eagerness for immediate and tangible results, have bred a new and more utilitarian theory of the academic function; so that the study of ancient life and thought has been deposed from its old supremacy and has been made to take its place beside those subjects of investigation that derive their interest mainly from the appeal which they can make to tastes and motives that are essentially commercial and mechanical.

This revolution in pædagogic theory, with the resulting revolution in the ordering of our university curricula, while it sprang from a false impression of what liberal study really means, and while it is fraught with especial evil to a community such as ours, already far too eager in the pursuit of all material ends, has nevertheless, by way of compensation, not been without a stimulating effect upon the methods and the aims of classical study. It has, to be sure, impaired the value of the university degree that once was everywhere accepted as being the hall-mark of the cultivated gentleman. It has broken down forever the intellectual sympathy that once existed as a powerful bond between all university men—a sympathy based upon absolute identity of training, and one which made them a potent influence in the diffusion of sanity and serenity of thought. It has lowered the whole tone of university life and imported into the academic shades the standards of value, the aims, and the ambitions of the workshop and the counting-room. Yet, nevertheless, the very changes that have narrowed the sphere of classical study and restricted its power for good by releasing from its refining influence the very persons who are most in need of it, have still, within its sphere, compelled it to develop a new and vigorous life, by enabling it to gain in perfection and completeness what it has lost in universality.

The teachers of the classics, under this new system, which takes nothing for granted and ascribes no preëminent value to the study and investigation of the past, have been forced to rouse themselves to a demonstration of that value even from the standpoint of the modern iconoclast. In so doing they have very wisely laid more stress than heretofore upon the intimate relation of the present to the past; they have laboured to bring out the essential modernity of the life of Greece and Rome; and they have dwelt as never before upon the points of resemblance rather than upon the points of difference that exist. Classical teaching has, therefore, gained immensely in vividness and vitality, and its topics of investigation have been at once enlarged and correlated. It is no longer sufficient to dwell upon the linguistic and literary obligations of the modern world to Greece and Rome. It is as necessary as it is entirely possible to show that the religious and the ethical problems of the past are those that still occupy the thought of educated men; that the political and social dangers that confronted the Republics of Hellas and Rome are precisely those that are brooding over the nations of to-day; and that in sociology and economics the student is but a tyro, who has not profoundly studied the *Culturgeschichte* of the two great nations.

Hence it comes about that the study of the classics and of ancient life is to-day far more comprehensive in its scope, far broader in its purpose, far more consciously important in its relation to the whole field of human knowledge, and far more elaborate in its critical apparatus than it ever was before. The classical teacher feels that he must, in studying any side of his subject, avail himself of every possible aid that can be drawn from the investigations of his fellow-specialists in order to give interest and life and richness to his own instruction. If he turn to language, he must draw upon the labours of the epigraphist, the numismatist, the palaeographer; if he deal with art, he must explain its inspiration by the testimony of literature and the history of contemporary life; if he investigate history, he must know the whole intellectual and social environment of the people.

Nor is the appreciation of these things confined to the teacher and the investigator. The younger student of the classics is also becoming more and more alive to the true significance of his work, as with every year more is required of him in the way of special equipment and general information. Even the undergraduate classical courses in our universities and colleges now touch upon many sides of study, and are no longer restricted to the mere reading of ancient authors and the formal study of their language. An early familiarity with the conditions of ancient life is expected and required; some knowledge of art and archæology is a further requisite; and at least a moderate acquaintance with the best and most obvious sources of information is asked of all. It is, therefore, evident that to aid the student in his work, as that work must be pursued under these comparatively new conditions, some manual is needed that shall give him in a simple and intelligible form the most important facts, condensed and summarized and set forth not as isolated bits of information, but in their necessary connection with one another. The present volume is intended as a contribution towards this end.

The information which is given in its articles, arranged under a single alphabet, may be classified under the following general heads:

(1) Biography.—The Dictionary includes articles on all the important personages of classical antiquity in every sphere of effort, whether military, literary,

political, or artistic. The greatest of the Christian Fathers have been added to the list, both because of the general interest of their relation to the history of the Later Empire, and because to the student of language their writings are of marked importance in the study of plebeian Latin and the development of the later dialects of Greek. Among the biographies which the Dictionary contains will be found also those of the great classical scholars and philologists of later times, and extending into our own century, since these represent distinct stages in the development of classical study, and their lives, when taken collectively, give a suggestive outline of the history of Classical Philology. The names of living scholars, for obvious reasons, have been excluded from the list.

(2) MYTHOLOGY.—All the mythological personages whose names appear and reappear in the pages of the Greek and Roman writers are the subjects of separate articles which carefully distinguish the Hellenic myths from those that are essentially Italic, while the relation between them is indicated and the subsequent blending of the two described. In the case of the most famous of the myths the explanatory speculations of the latest schools of comparative mythologists are given, though with caution; and the use of the myths themselves in literature is touched upon, with especial reference to their appearance in the prose and verse of the English classics. A separate general article on Mythology describes briefly the development of the different schools that have endeavoured to explain the folk-lore and religious tradition of the ancients.

(3) GEOGRAPHY.—The names of all countries, provinces, states, cities, and other localities that are mentioned by the most read of the classical writers will be found as separate titles, with a treatment proportionate to the historical importance of the subject and its interest to the student. Numerous maps and diagrams illustrate the geographical information given in the text. The very interesting ethnic questions that arise in this department of the work—as, for example, in the articles *Aegyptus*, *Etruria*, *Scythia*—are briefly noted, with a statement of the views of recent ethnologists and anthropologists, and with bibliographical references to the original sources of information and discussion.

(4) HISTORY.—The principal political events of Greek and Roman history form the subjects of special articles when these topics do not fall under geographical and biographical titles; and even when they do, they are also given as separate captions with cross-references to direct the student to the proper place of treatment.

(5) LITERATURE.—The articles on the great writers of Greek and Roman literature will, it is hoped, be found to be especially complete; and their best-known and most widely read works are noted likewise under distinct titles with cross-references to the leading articles. A very large number of general articles deal also with special phases of literary production, detailing, for example, the history of the Epic, of Lyric Poetry, of Dramatic Literature, of Parody, of the Epigram, of Jokes, of Rhyme, of Satire, of the Anthologies, of the Cento, of the ancient Novel and Romance, of the Alexandrian Canon, of celebrated editions of the classics, of important Codices, of the Renaissance, of Lexicography, of Grammar, and of Rhetoric and Oratory. Everywhere the effect of ancient literature upon the literature of modern times has been noted with particular reference to such of the great modern masterpieces as have derived their suggestion and inspiration directly from the works of Greek and Roman writers. It is believed that this de-

partment of the Dictionary will prove especially attractive to those students who are interested in the study of Comparative Literature; and that it will give to all a fuller sense of the essential unity of man's recorded thought.

(6) Antiquities.—A large portion of the work is devoted to the discussion of subjects relating to the Amusements, Art, Costume, Domestic Life, Law, Music, Numismatics, Philosophy, Religion, and Science of the ancients—a department, in fact, upon which the greatest labour has been expended, as it is the sphere in which the greatest additions to our knowledge of antiquity have been made within the past half-century. It is, indeed, the progress in the field of archæology that has most completely made the older works of reference seem antiquated for the purposes of the modern student. A wealth of new material has of late been presented for scientific investigation. The work of discovery, pursued with increasing intelligence and enthusiasm, has brought to light fresh treasures of ancient art and ornament, and has made plain and in every way intelligible much that before was doubtful and obscure. The investigations of Schliemann, Humann, Dörpfeld, Flinders Petrie, Lanciani, Homolle, and others would alone have made the past three decades a new and brilliant era in the history of classical archæology, even had their discoveries not been supplemented and illustrated by the labours of scholars less known, perhaps, but not less able. Epigraphy, too, in the last fifty years has experienced a marked development. It would be easy to name certain inscriptions whose discovery has given an entirely new meaning to the investigation of ancient life and manners, and especially to the study of Greek and Roman law. Moreover, the literary productiveness of the period in its relation to the study of antiquity has been wonderfully rich in giving a lucid and scientific exposition of these discoveries, and in deducing from them the knowledge which they embody or suggest. It is with these facts in mind that the portion of the work which relates to Archæology proper has been prepared, and it has been the purpose of the Editor to leave no important topic unrecorded, or passed over without at least the most essential information. A number of short general articles take up the subjects that are necessary to an understanding of the collateral sources of information, such as those relating to Epigraphy, Palæography, and Text Criticism; while important bits of special information regarding matters to which reference is frequently made in classical teaching, but for whose explanation the student is too often ignorant where to go, will be found under such titles as Cista Ficoroniana, Choragic Monument, Harpy Monument, Duenos Inscription, Graffiti, Monumentum Adulitanum, Monumentum Ancyranum, Palimpsest, Portland Vase, Tabula Bantina, and very many more.

(7) Language.—It has been thought desirable to provide the student, for purposes of ready reference, with some special information concerning the most important linguistic questions that arise in the study of the classics. Considerations of space have prevented the Editor from elaborating this department of the work and from adding many subjects to an already formidable list. What has been given will, he is assured, be a source of satisfaction to those who use the book. The character of the topics coming under this head can be fairly well indicated by mentioning a few of them, such as Alliteration, the African Latinity, Dialects, Grammar, Grimm's Law, the Indo-European Languages, Onomatopoeia, Philology, the Pronunciation of Greek, the Pronunciation of Latin, Rhotacism, the Sermo Plebeius, and Verner's Law. No work of reference in English that

has to do with classical study has ever included information of this character, and it will be therefore, to American students, a feature that is quite unique.

(8) BIBLIOGRAPHY.—At the end of all of the most important articles a selected bibliography has been appended, including those works that are most famous, most valuable, and most readily accessible to the student who desires to acquire a more special knowledge of the subjects treated. Where such works exist in the English language, these have received the preference over those in foreign tongues. Unfortunately, it is only within the last few years that English and American scholars have begun to put forth monographs in any way comparable with the treatises in which the French and German classicists have long been accustomed to embody the results of their special investigations. Hence, a large proportion of the references are to books and pamphlets in the Continental languages, including many important "programmes" and university dissertations. In no case has an exhaustive bibliography been attempted, but such a selection has been given as will be of the greatest practical assistance.

(9) ILLUSTRATIONS.—A word should be said of the illustrations, of which the Dictionary contains some fifteen hundred. Their insertion has necessarily drawn heavily upon the space at the Editor's disposal; yet he feels that the gain in interest and in intelligibility which they secure far more than compensates for the enhanced brevity which they entail upon the printed text. In the case of material objects, a picture is usually far more intelligible than whole paragraphs of verbal description whose place, in truth, they very efficiently supply. Their sources are in most cases indicated; and the fact that the greater number of them reproduce exactly objects that have come down to us from antiquity gives them an especial interest and value. In some cases, for the clearer comprehension of the original form, restorations by archæologists of distinction, such as Dörpfeld, Bühlmann, Brune, Hoffmann, Wagner, Benvenuti, and Lanciani, have been inserted, and now and then the ideal creations of modern sculptors and painters, such as Canova, Thorwaldsen, Alma-Tadema, and Jalabert, have received a place, as giving a more vivid perception of the essential meaning of a theme.

From what has now been said, it will be evident that the work is, in fact, a Classical Encyclopædia. Were the title not too ambitious, it might perhaps be more correctly described as a Dictionary of Classical Philology, using that term in the sense which it conveys in Germany. It does, indeed, aim to give in a single volume the substance of all the information that it has hitherto been necessary to seek among many books and in many places. The massing of all this material in a single volume and under a single alphabetical arrangement would in itself be an immense gain in convenience to the student who has heretofore been obliged to refer to half a dozen dictionaries for the elucidation of the questions that arise in his daily work; but the advantages of such a consolidation extend far beyond any mere question of convenience. It enables all the topics to be treated in a way that shall show their natural relation to one another and that makes impossible a sense of detachment and isolation. Thus, History illustrates Literature, and Literature explains History; while Art, and Language, and Science are shown in their proper relations to the whole study of ancient life and thought. It has everywhere been the purpose of the Editor to make this intimate connection fully apparent, and every important article in each department refers directly and continually to all the others that in any way have any bearing upon the same subject.

The general articles, such as those on Epigraphy, History, Libraries, Museums, Music, Palæography, Philology, Philosophy, Painting, Sculpture, Numismatics, Religion, and Text Criticism, are meant to give the reader in each case a conspectus of the whole field in an outline which the special articles will enable him to fill in with a more elaborate detail. It is this method of treatment that has made possible the inclusion of so many classes of topics in a volume of moderate size; for each article serves to explain many others, and thus to avoid a tedious and unnecessary repetition.

As may be readily understood, the most difficult question confronting the Editor was the question of proportion. It is unlikely that any two scholars could be found to agree upon the relative importance of the topics presented; and it is, therefore, here that the Editor must expect to receive the greatest amount of criticism. Hence, it is proper to set forth the general principles that have guided him in his work, so that, whether or not they meet with general approval, they may, at any rate, be recognized as definite and consistent. Having in mind the daily needs of the student, it has been the purpose of the Editor to give the fullest treatment to those questions that most frequently arise in one's ordinary reading of the classics, and that are of the greatest practical importance. Thus, the largest assignment of space has been given to articles that deal with ancient literature in all its phases, inasmuch as it is from and through literature that our clearest knowledge of Greek and Roman thought and life has been derived, and because literature has itself been to all succeeding ages the magnet that drew men's minds to the investigation of the past. Historical questions are also quite fully dealt with; while in the department of antiquities those topics that are most closely related to the every-day life of the Greeks and Romans are the ones that have received the preference. Thus, much space is given to describing the dress, the food, the houses, the amusements, the conveniences, the arts, and the religious faith and rites of the two great peoples; far less is assigned to their governmental regulations; while with regard to the minuter points of law, the different *γραφαί* and *δίκαι* and *leges* that one seldom meets outside of the pages of the legal oratory of the ancients, these have usually been allowed to pass with a concise and simple definition. So in Geography, those places that are linked with some great historical event, or that are to us moderns especially interesting because of their importance in the study of archæology, are described with considerable minuteness; but cities and towns and countries that have no such special associations now, and that are known to us only from some casual mention in the pages of Polybius or Strabo or Pomponius Mela, have been merely touched upon with a note or two upon their situation and their relative importance in antiquity. Hence, while the great city of Rhagae has only some twenty lines assigned to it, the description of the little Campanian town of Pompeii occupies a space of nearly seven pages.

Thus the practical needs and the greater convenience of the learner have been everywhere remembered, and to these ends the Editor has occasionally sacrificed considerations of strict consistency when such consistency would render the use of the work less simple, and would secure nothing more valuable than a pedantic uniformity. For instance, in the matter of arrangement, the names of Romans have been placed under the gentile name or the cognomen, according to the respective familiarity of each in English usage: Marcus Tullius Cicero and Gaius

Iulius Caesar are treated under *Cicero* and *Caesar*, but Publius Terentius Afer and Publius Vergilius Maro under *Terentius* and *Vergilius*. The same considerations have guided the Editor in respect to the forms of words that are Greek. When there exists a corresponding Latin form, and when this form is more familiar to the English and American reader than the Greek, it has been given in the title; while in the case of those words that were never Latinized the original is written. Thus, *Thucydides* and *Menelaüs* and *Epaminondas* have been preferred to *Thoukydides* and *Menelaos* and *Epameinondas*; but *Kakosis* is written instead of *Cacosis*. This discrimination has been carried out according to the best judgment of the Editor, who has always made it a rule to avoid what an English scholar has very cleverly described as "the Scylla of *Thoukydides* and the Charybdis of *Samus*." In the orthography, also, it has seemed preferable to go only so far in the direction of scientific exactness as is exemplified by the best texts used in our schools and universities; and therefore the use of the character J has been discarded in Latin words, while the distinction between V and U has been retained. For the greater convenience of the student, again, the usual *index raisonné* at the end of the volume is omitted, and in its stead the English names of the principal topics treated have been inserted in the body of the work and under the single alphabetical arrangement, so that one who wishes to find an article and does not remember the Greek or the Latin title can turn to it in English in its proper alphabetical place and there find the reference to the proper heading. The abundant cross-references will also greatly facilitate the use of the book, and will prove a valuable guide in turning at once to all the collateral branches of a subject.

In the preparation and development of this elaborate scheme, the Editor has been greatly assisted by the advice and suggestions of many eminent scholars, whose encouragement and counsel have been of the utmost service to him at every stage of the work. Unusual value is given to the Dictionary by a number of articles contributed to it by writers whose names are the highest guarantee of the excellence of their work, as standing in each case for special knowledge based upon original study and investigation. It is proper that these contributors should be here mentioned in detail. Professor Frederic D. Allen, of Harvard University, has written the article *Twelve Tables*; Dr. Robert Arrowsmith, formerly of Racine College, the article *Camerarius*; Professor Sidney G. Ashmore, of Union University, the article *P. Terentius Afer*; Professor Franz Bücheler, of the University of Bonn, the article *Umbria*; Professor Edward B. Clapp, of the University of California, the articles *Aeschines*, *Aeschylus*, *Aristoteles*, *Ilium*, *Pronunciation of Greek*, *Syndicus*, *Synegorus*, and *Synthesis*; Dr. Frederic Taber Cooper, of the University of the City of New York, the article *Sermo Plebeius*; the Reverend Charles T. Cruttwell, late of Oxford University, the articles *Quintus Ennius*, *M. Annaeus Seneca*, and *Lucius Annaeus Seneca*; Professor Mortimer Lamson Earle, of Bryn Mawr College, the article *Athenae*; Professor James C. Egbert, Jr., of Columbia University, the articles *Honores* (so much as relates to the *cursus honorum*), *Nomen* (so much as relates to the Roman name), *Papyrus*, *Princeps*, *Principatus*; Professor K. F. Geldner, of the University of Berlin, the article *Persia*; Professor Basil L. Gildersleeve, of the Johns Hopkins University, the article *Pindarus*; Professor Alfred Gudeman, of the University of Pennsylvania, the twenty-one articles on abbreviations given at the beginning of each of the letters of the Greek and Roman alphabets; Dr. Isaac H. Hall, of the Metropolitan Museum of Art in New York City, the article *Cyprus;* Professor A. V. Williams Jackson, of Columbia University, the articles *Rhagae* and *Zoroaster;* Professor Francis W. Kelsey, of the University of Michigan, the articles *Gaius Iulius Caesar*, *Titus Lucretius Carus*, and *Roma;* Professor Rodolfo Lanciani, of the University of Rome, the article *Pompeii;* Professor Charles R. Lanman, of Harvard University, the article *India;* Dr. Charlton T. Lewis, of New York, the article *Lexicon;* Professor Ernest Mondell Pease, of the Stanford University, the article *Satira;* Professor Edward Delavan Perry, of Columbia University, the article *Franz Bopp;* Professor Thomas D. Seymour, of Yale University, the article *Homerus;* Professor Munroe Smith, of Columbia University, the articles *Actio*, *Ius*, *Legatus*, *Lex*, *Magistratus*, *Maiestas*, *Pignus*, *Provincia*, *Senatus;* Professor F. B. Tarbell, of the University of Chicago, the articles *Boulé*, *Mycenae*, *Propylaea*, and *Tiryns*, and a number of architectural definitions; Professor A. F. West, of Princeton University, the article *Liberales Artes;* Professor Benjamin Ide Wheeler, of Cornell University, the articles *Grimm's Law* and *Verner's Law;* and Dr. Clarence H. Young, of Columbia University, the article *Demus*.

For the rest of the Dictionary the Editor is himself responsible; and in making this statement it is proper to give some account of the sources upon which he has drawn and of the extent to which they have been used in the preparation of the articles.

The greater part of the biographical and geographical material is based upon Smith's *Greek and Roman Classical Dictionary* as revised and enlarged and published in this country in 1852 by Professor Charles Anthon and Professor Henry Drisler. Very extensive changes have, however, been made in adapting this material to the purpose of the present work. Statements that subsequent investigations have shown to be inadequate or unfounded have been carefully corrected; a more lively turn has been given to much of the description and characterization; such further information as is now available has been incorporated in the articles; reference to the *loci classici* have been supplied; and to the more important articles a good working bibliography of recent publications in English, French, and German bearing upon the subject has been appended. In the case of authors, the sources of our texts are indicated, the principal editions (including the *editiones principes*) are noted with their dates, and a selection of monographs on the life, style, and subject-matter is given. In many cases, however, the original articles have been wholly rejected as unsatisfactory, and these have been entirely rewritten.

The archæological portion of the Dictionary is based in part, but only in part, upon the edition of Smith's *Dictionary of Greek and Roman Antiquities* as revised by Professor Anthon. Such of this material as has been drawn upon has been very carefully corrected and amplified in the light of our present knowledge, and has been provided also with references to the latest archæological publications. Very valuable to the Editor has been Daremberg and Saglio's *Dictionnaire des Antiquités Grecques et Romaines* for the early portion, and so far as their great work has yet appeared. Baumeister's *Denkmäler des klassischen Alterthums* has also been continually at hand for reference and consultation; as has Bouché-Leclercq's *Institutions Romaines*, with Gilbert's *Greek Constitutional Antiquities* in the German original, and lately in the excellent English version of Messrs.

Brooks and Nicklin published in 1895. Especial mention should be made of the third edition of Sir William Smith's *Dictionary of Greek and Roman Antiquities* (London, 1891), upon which the Editor has continually drawn and from which several important articles* have been wholly or in part condensed. Some useful material has been found in Rich's *Dictionary of Roman and Greek Antiquities* (5th ed., London and New York, 1890). The Becker-Göll revisions of *Charikles* and *Gallus* are frequently cited or referred to under titles relating to the private life of the Greeks and Romans, as are also Marquardt's *Privatleben der Römer* (2d ed., Leipzig, 1886); Friedländer's *Darstellung aus der Sittengeschichte Roms* (6th ed., Leipzig, 1888–90); and Ménard's *Vie Privée des Anciens* (Paris, 1880). For ancient art, of especial use have been the works of Winckelmann, Stark, Overbeck, Westropp, Reber, Murray, Newton, Michaelis, Perry, Krause, Helbig, Woltmann and Woermann, Mau, Middleton, Brunn and Fergusson. For the technical and scientific knowledge of the ancients, Blümner's *Technologie und Terminologie* (Leipzig, 1875–87) has, of course, been of the greatest aid. Some of the general articles are mainly drawn from Seyffert's *Lexikon der klassischen Alterthumskunde* (Leipzig, 1882), though it has, of course, been necessary to add largely to the material found in this excellent but in some respects too elementary work. Here and there the Editor has availed himself of the supplementary matter supplied to these articles of Seyffert by Dr. J. E. Sandys in the English edition made by himself and the late Professor Nettleship—additions so admirable as to induce regret that these distinguished scholars did not supply them in all the articles which they translated. Many useful suggestions in this and other departments of the work were derived from Reinach's *Manuel de Philologie Classique* (Paris, 1883–84), a marvel of encyclopædic knowledge and judicious condensation that has now for twelve years been the philological pemmican of all classical scholars. It would be superfluous to mention the immensely valuable monographs contained in Iwan Müller's *Handbuch der klassischen Altertumswissenchaft.* The Pauly-Wissowa *Real-Encyclopädie der klassischen Altertumswissenchaft* began to appear too late to be used to any extent.

For those articles that deal with the literature of Greece and Rome and those that embody miscellaneous and collateral information, so many works in so many languages have been continually consulted as to render any separate mention of them utterly impossible. Suffice it to say that, besides the great standard authorities in each department, the special monographs of French and German scholars have been frequently referred to, as well as such papers of value as are continually appearing in the archæological and philological journals of England, France, Germany, Italy, and the United States. In preparing the bibliography, much use was naturally made of Engelmann-Preuss, of Professor Hübner's *Grundriss zu Vorlesungen über die römische Litteraturgeschichte* (4th ed., Berlin, 1878), and the same scholar's *Bibliographie der klassischen Altertumswissenchaft* (2d ed., Berlin, 1889), besides the well-known works of Professor J. E. B. Mayor, and the Teuffel-Schwabe-Warr *History of Roman Literature* (London, 1891). In preparing the short biographies of mediæval and modern classical scholars and their works, much help was derived from Pökel's *Schriftstellerlexikon* (1882) and from Professor Alfred Gudeman's excellent *Outlines of the History of Classical Philology* (2d ed., Boston and New York, 1894).

* Especially *Amphitheatrum, Athletae, Bacchanalia, Balneae, Circus, Eleusinia, Fratres Arvales, Theatrum, Vas.*

In drawing upon these and all his other sources, the Editor has allowed himself the very greatest freedom. Whatever he has taken he has used in the way best adapted to secure the end he had in view. When material was, in its original form, precisely suited to his purpose he incorporated it without a change. When change for any reason was desirable, he enlarged, condensed, modified, transposed, or paraphrased according to his conception of what was most needed in the given case; and as the greater part of his work was compilation rather than original exposition, he wishes here to express his very great indebtedness to the many books that have been drawn upon. No acknowledgment can be too full or too comprehensive; and if the completed work be found of service to the student of the classics, this result must be very largely credited to the original sources whence so great a portion of the Dictionary is derived.

The illustrations also come from many places. The various "atlases" published in Germany, especially that of Schreiber, have yielded many; and so have Baumeister's *Denkmäler*, Overbeck's *Pompeii*, and Falke's *Hellas und Rom*. Many, however, are from photographs, for some of which the Editor is indebted to the kindness of the friends who are mentioned in the following paragraph. A good many drawings of minor objects have been taken from Rich; and several from Daremberg and Saglio, and from Guhl and Koner's *Life of the Greeks and Romans*,—a work that has likewise proved of service in other departments of this Dictionary.

Some especial mention is due to those who have in many ways aided in the preparation of the book. To Professor Henry Drisler, whose name is still first among American lexicographers of the classical languages, sincere thanks are due for assistance, information, and advice, as well as for the loan of books from his well-stored private library. To his lamented colleague, Professor Augustus C. Merriam, the Editor is indebted for having read a number of the articles in proof, and for many very valuable suggestions. For a like service, acknowledgments are hereby made to Professors Perry, Jackson, and Egbert. Dr. Robert Arrowsmith assumed the task of translating into English the articles contributed to this work by foreign scholars. Professor Rodolfo Lanciani, Professor Francis W. Kelsey, Professor F. B. Tarbell, and Mr. Henry R. Taylor have been especially kind in furnishing for the Editor's use various photographs, drawings, and diagrams not readily obtainable elsewhere. The publishing-house of Herr Oldenbourg, of Munich, has furnished some of the electrotypes used in Baumeister's *Denkmäler*, and Messrs. Estes and Lauriat of Boston have kindly permitted the reproduction of some of the illustrations from their edition of Duruy's *History of Rome*. The house of Herr Gustav Fock, of Leipzig, has aided greatly in the preparation of the bibliographical portion of the book by furnishing valuable data under this head. Finally, the Editor would be indeed ungrateful were he to abstain from a warm expression of personal indebtedness to his publishers, whose patience and consideration during many unavoidable delays have been as generous as their liberality in carrying out the Editor's plan has been unstinted. It is, in fact, in the cultivated and broad-minded publisher of to-day that one finds the modern type of the Augustan Maecenas, but with a vastness of opportunity and a far-reaching influence such as no ancient ever exercised, for the effective encouragement of literature and learning.

In sending forth at last this volume, to whose preparation he has now for nearly five years devoted every hour that could be spared from other and most arduous duties, the Editor appreciates, far more keenly than when the work began, the enormous difficulties of his task. In bringing together a mass of material requiring at every point so much special knowledge and so much mastery of detail, it is inevitable that what he has done should here and there be open to the charge of inadequacy, of inconsistency, and perhaps of error. Yet it is still his earnest hope that as those most competent to criticise are best able also to appreciate the innumerable perplexities inherent in the undertaking, they will judge his labours as a whole; and that when so regarded, these will be found at least to have done something to promote the comprehensive, intelligent, and sympathetic study of classical antiquity.

Harry Thurston Peck.

Columbia University, New York,
August 1st, 1896.

PREFATORY NOTE TO THE SECOND EDITION

The Editor has availed himself of the opportunity afforded by an early demand for a second edition of this Dictionary to make certain alterations and corrections suggested by a careful reading of the printed sheets. Some additions have been made to the bibliography, some very recent discoveries in archæology have been noted, and such other changes have been introduced as appeared to be feasible and at the same time desirable to make. He wishes here to mention his especial obligation to Professor Alfred Gudeman, of the University of Pennsylvania, who undertook a very thorough examination of the work, bringing to the task a singularly accurate and varied scholarship, and very kindly furnishing the Editor with the notes resulting from this reading. The Editor also thanks those scholars who have discussed the book at length in the columns of the leading critical reviews. If it should appear that he has not in all cases availed himself of the suggestions which have been so thoughtfully commended to him, this is attributable wholly to the fact that a careful consideration of the evidence has sometimes failed to convince him of existing error; for in the sphere of classical study there are found so many questions upon which the best opinion still remains divided as to prevent even the pronouncement of an anonymous reviewer from possessing always the stamp of absolute finality. In conclusion, the Editor desires to express his grateful acknowledgments to the entire body of classical students and instructors who have given to the book so immediate and so warm a welcome.

H. T. P.

July 1st, 1897.

A DICTIONARY

OF

CLASSICAL LITERATURE AND ANTIQUITIES.

A

A, the first letter in both the Greek and Latin alphabets. The principal uses of the letter in abbreviations found in MSS. and inscriptions, or on coins, are given below.

IN GREEK.—Abbreviations of one or even of two letters are of extreme rarity on Greek coins and inscriptions of the pre-Euclidean period; after this time a few instances occur, owing doubtless to Roman influence, their use being chiefly confined to a few Roman proper names, e. g. A=*Αὐλός*, *Αὐρήλιος*, *Ἀντωνῖνος*. With the general introduction of alphabetic numerals, about the beginning of the fifth century B.C., the letter A, *ά*, is also used as a numeral for 1 and 1000 (*͵a*). Cf. S. Reinach, *Traité d'Épigraphie Grecque* (1885), pp. 220 ff. 225 ff.

IN LATIN.—The Romans made an astonishingly extensive use of abbreviations.* Only a very few out of many thousands recorded in the indexes to the *C. I. L.* (ii. 777, iii. 1185, v. 1201, vii. 342, viii. 1103, ix. 795, x. 1165, xii. 945, xiv. 583) can be given here under each letter. On Roman abbreviations in general, cf. R. Mowat, *Bull. Épigraph.* IV. p. 127 ff. (1884); E. Hübner, in Iwan Müller's *Handbuch*, i. 496 ff., 523 ff.; R. Cagnat, *Cours d'Épigraphie Latine* (1889), p. 351 ff.

A = absolvo, written on voting tablets, "I favor acquittal;" hence called *littera salutaris* (Cic. *pro Mur.* vi. 15).

A = antiquo, designates a nay vote in the Roman comitia, in rejection of a proposed change.

A = auditor, or adulescens in some of the MSS. of Cic. *Tusc. Disp.*, to denote one of the interlocutors as opposed to M = Marcus or magister.

A = Aulus, Augustus, Aurelius, Antoninus, Africa, Aprilis, aedilis.

Ɐ = Aurelia (inverted letter always used to designate female names).

A = accipiet, actum, aeternus, annus, annona, ara, armatura, argento, auro, as.

A·A = Aquae, Aponi, Auli duo.

AAGG = Augusti duo.

AAAGGG = Augusti tres.

A·A·A·F·F = aere argento auro flando feriundo.

A·B = a balneis (very frequently for *a* or *ab*), amicus bonus.

A·B·M = amico bene merenti.

A·C = aere collato, armorum custos, a colonia, a commentariis.

A·D = ante diem, ager divisus.

A·D·A = agris dandis adsignandis.

A·D·A·I = agris dandis adsignandis iudicandis.

A·E = actum esse.

A·F·P·R = actum fide Publii Rutilii (Cic. *De Orat.* ii. 69, 280).

A·G·T = Augustus.

A·G·IV·C·P = arborum genera quattuor, cetera privata.

A·H·N·P = ad heredem non pertinet.

A·L = actarius legati, [et si qui] alii liberti [erunt], animo libens, Augusti libertus, arca lata.

A·L·F(P) = animo libente fecit (posuit).

A·O·F·C = amico optimo faciundum curavit.

A·P = aedilicia potestate, animo pio, anno provinciae, a populo, arca publica, argentis pondo, ager publicus.

A·P·R = aerarium populi Romani.

A·P·R·C = anno post Romam conditam.

A·Q·ER·PP = aut qui erunt proximi.

A·Q·E·R·P·P·R·L = ad quem ea res pertinet, pertinebit recte licet.

A·Q·P = a quaestionibus praefecti.

A·S = a sacris, a senatu.

A·S·F (F·C) = a solo fecit, faciundum curavit.

A·V = aediles vici, argenti unciae, ave vale.

A·V·C = anno urbis conditae.

Abacænum. An ancient town of Sicily, west of Messana and south of Tyndaris. See Diod. Sic. xiv. 78, 90.

Abactōres, Abigeatōres, or **Abigei** are terms used to signify those guilty of cattle-stealing (*abigeatus*), which the Roman practice distinguished from ordinary *furtum* (q. v.), when the theft was of a sufficiently serious kind. The stealing of a single horse or ox was *abigeatus*, but to steal less than ten sheep or four pigs was only *furtum*. It was an aggravation of the offence to steal the animals from a pen or other enclosure, or for the *abactor* to carry weapons. The punishment was at the discretion of the magistrate, and ranged from banishment and degradation from rank to penal servitude and death. Cf. *Dig.* 47,

* The original name for these abbreviations seems to have been *litterae singulares* or *singulariae* (cf. Gell. xvii. 9, 1). At a later period *notae* became the more common term (cf. Festus, p. 184: *Nota nunc significat signum ut in pecoribus, tabulis, libris, litterae singulae vel binae*). Valerius Probus wrote an elaborate work *De Notis*, only a part of which has been preserved. In the *Digests* of Justinian *nota* is displaced by the term *sigla*. The word is of doubtful origin. Most scholars regard it as a syncopated form of *sigillum*; others derive it from *singuli*; Mommsen thinks it a mere corruption from *singulares*.

14, *De Abigeis; Cod.* ix. 37; and Rein, *Das Criminalrecht der Röm.* pp. 323–325 (Leips. 1844).

Abactus Venter. See ABORTIO

Abacŭlus (Gr. ἀβακίσκος), diminutive of *abacus* (q. v.), and denoting a tile of marble, glass, etc., used in making ornamental pavements. See MUSIVUM OPUS.

Abăcus (Gr. ἄβαξ, ἀβάκιον). (1) A square plate, especially the stone slab that covers the capital of a column. (2) A dice-board. See DUODECIM SCRIPTA; LATRUNCULI. (3) A mathematician's table strewn with fine sand, on which figures were drawn with a *stilus*. (4) A counting-board, on which sums were worked for private and public accounts. This might be:

(*a*) A tablet with a frame or rim, covered with sand, in which lines or figures could be drawn either with the finger or some pointed instrument; and used in geometry, arithmetic, etc. (Pers. i. 131; *eruditus pulvis*, Cic. *N. D.* ii. 18, 48). The name *arenarius*, applied to the elementary teacher, implies that this sort of abacus was used by school-children.

(*b*) A development of this simple form was the abacus on which ψῆφοι, *calculi*, pebbles or counters, were employed in calculations. It was a board marked off by ridges or grooves (along which balls, counters, or buttons could be moved) into compartments, for the several orders of numbers. We have examples of both Greek and Roman abaci. The Greek abacus figured here is from Salamis, and is of marble, about forty inches long by twenty-eight broad. At a distance of ten inches from one of the sides are marked five parallel lines. At twenty inches' distance from the last of these, eleven others are marked and bisected by a cross

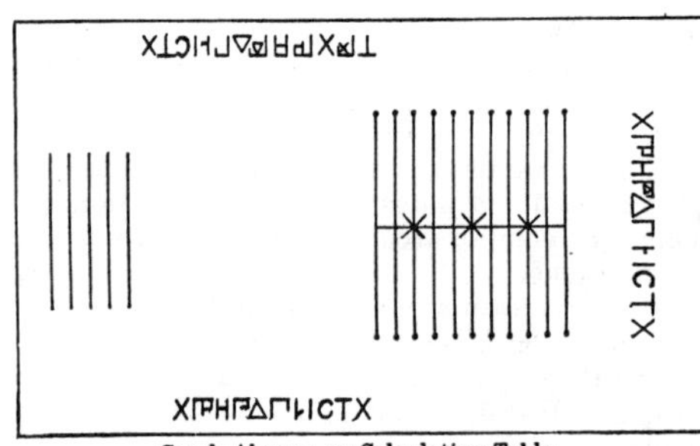

Greek Abacus, or Calculating Table.

line, the point of whose intersection with the third, sixth, and ninth lines is marked by a star. Along three of the sides is arranged a series of characters in the same order, and so as to be read with equal ease whichever way the abacus is turned: the series on one side having two more characters than the others. These characters (⊦ being known as = drachma) gives the following scale, reckoned from the left of ⊦:

⊦	Ꮁ	Δ	⊡	H	⊡	X
1	5	10	50	100	500	1000

These characters are of great antiquity. ⊦ is a mutilated E, initial of ἕν; Ꮁ an old form of Π, i. e. πέντε; Δ obviously represents δέκα, and X χίλιοι; while of the three remaining characters, H is for HEKATON, the old way of writing ἑκατόν, ⊡ is Ꮁ with Δ inscribed, ⊡, Ꮁ with H. The characters on the right of ⊦ are I = obol, C = $\frac{1}{2}$ obol, T = $\frac{1}{4}$ obol, X = χαλκοῦς, $\frac{1}{8}$ obol. The two additional characters in the left-hand series are ⊡ = 5000 (Ꮁ with X inscribed), and T = talent (of 6000 drachmas); so that the lowest and highest money units are at the two ends of the scale.

To understand the use of this abacus, the calculator must be supposed sitting before one of its long sides, and putting counters into the spaces between the marked lines. Each space represents an order of numerals, the space on the right hand being intended for units, the next space for tens, the next for hundreds, and so on. The numbers belonging to the first four of each series are put on that side of the bisecting line which is nearest the calculator; those over five are put beyond it. As five spaces out of the ten would be enough for these purposes, it is conjectured that after the progression of drachmas going up to 5000, a fresh progression of talents began (T = 6000 drachmas), going up to the seventh place (1,000,000). Thus the Greek abacus, like the Roman, which was no doubt derived from it, reckoned up to a million. The fractions of the drachma were reckoned on the five lines at the other end of the slab. It is to an abacus of this kind that Polybius refers, when he compares the ups and downs of court favorites to the ψῆφοι on an ἀβάκιον, which, according to the line in which they are placed, may signify either a talent or a chalcus (Polyb. v. 26, § 13). This comparison is elsewhere attributed to Solon (Diog. Laërt. i. 59).

The Roman abacus (figured here from the Kircherian Museum at Rome) was on the same system.

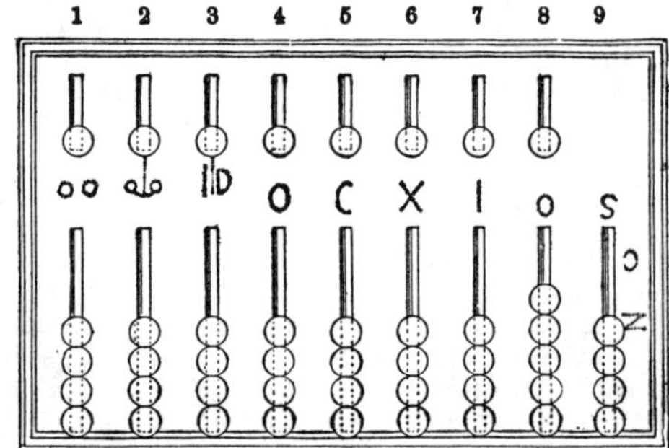

Roman Abacus, or Calculating Table.

It is divided into eight lower and eight higher (somewhat shorter) grooves: there is also a ninth lower groove, without an upper groove to correspond. Four sliding buttons are attached to each lower groove except the eighth, which has five: each upper groove has one button. Between the two sets of grooves the following numbers are marked:

ⅠX̄Ⅰ	CCCIↃↃↃ	CCIↃↃ	CIↃ	C	X	I
1,000,000	100,000	10,000	1000	100	10	1

The units of any other number when not above 4 are marked by moving a corresponding number of buttons along the lower groove upwards, the button in the upper groove = 5. The eighth row was used by reckoning fractions (*aes recurrens*) on the duodecimal system, by ounces, or twelfth of the *as*, and is accordingly marked ○ or ⊖ = uncia: each of its five lower buttons = 1 ounce, and the upper one = 6. Fractions below an ounce were reckoned on the ninth groove, marked:

S	Ↄ	Z or 2
semuncia.	sicilicus.	duella.
$\frac{1}{2}$ oz.	$\frac{1}{4}$ oz.	$\frac{1}{3}$ oz.

See the article LOGISTICA.

(5) The name is also used of a wooden tray or

platter employed in domestic economy. Cf. Plin. *H. N.* xxxvii. § 18 and § 21; Apul. *Met.* ii. 7. (6) A sideboard for vessels, and for offerings to the gods (Boetticher, *Tektonik der Hellenen*, iii. p. 46).

Abacus, sideboard. (Relief in British Museum.)

Abae (Ἄβαι). A city of Phocis, near and to the right of Elatea, towards Opus. The inhabitants had a tradition that their city was founded by Abas, son of Lynceus and Hypermnestra, grandson of Danaus (Paus. 10, 35). It was most probably of Pelasgic origin. Abae was early celebrated for its oracle of Apollo, of greater antiquity than that at Delphi, and hence Apollo is called Abaeus. During the Persian invasion, the army of Xerxes set fire to the temple, and nearly destroyed it; soon after it again gave oracles, though in this dilapidated state, and was consulted for that purpose by an agent of Mardonius (Herod. viii. 134).

Abalienatio. See Mancipium.

Abantes (Ἄβαντες). The ancient inhabitants of Euboea. They are said to have been of Thracian origin, to have first settled in Phocis, where they built Abae (q. v.), and afterwards to have crossed over to Euboea. The Abantes of Euboea assisted in colonizing several of the Ionic cities of Asia Minor.

Abantiădes. A patronymic applied to Perseus (q. v.), Acrisius, and other descendants of Abas (q. v.).

Abantias. (1) Any female descendant of Abas (q. v.), such as Danaë and Atalanta. (2) An ancient name of Euboea. See Abantes.

Abăris (Ἄβαρις). (1) A Hyperborean priest of Apollo, who came from the country about the Caucasus to Greece, while his native land was visited by a plague. His history is entirely mythical: he is said to have taken no earthly food, and to have ridden on an arrow, the gift of Apollo, through the air. (See Müller, *Dorier*, i. 364.) (2) A city of Egypt, east of the Bubastic mouth of the Nile.

Abas (Ἄβας). (1) Son of Metanira, and changed by Demeter into a lizard, because he mocked the goddess when she had come on her wanderings into the house of his mother, and drank eagerly to quench her thirst. (2) Twelfth king of Argos, son of Lynceus and Hypermnestra, grandson of Danaüs, and father of Acrisius and Proetus. When he informed his father of the death of Danaüs, he was rewarded with the shield of his grandfather, which was sacred to Heré. This shield performed various marvels, and the mere sight of it could subdue a river. (See Serv. *ad* Verg. *Aen.* iii. 286). (3) A Latin chief who assisted Aeneas against Turnus, and was killed by Lausus (Verg. *Aen.* x. 170). (4) A river of Albania emptying into the Caspian Sea. (5) A mountain of Armenia Minor, identified by Mannert with Ararat.

Abbreviations. For abbreviations found in MSS. and inscriptions, and on ancient coins, see the articles on the different letters of the alphabet, and also Numismatics; Palaeography.

Abdēra (τὰ Ἄβδηρα). (1) A town of Thrace, near the mouth of the Nestus, which flowed through the town. It was colonized by Timesius of Clazomenae about B.C. 656, and a second time by the inhabitants of Teos in Ionia, who settled there after their own town had been taken by the Persians, B.C. 544. It was the birthplace of Democritus, Hecataeus, Protagoras, Anaxarchus, and other distinguished men; but its inhabitants, notwithstanding, were accounted stupid, and Abderite was a term of reproach. (See Juv. x. 50; Mart. x. 25.) (2) A Punic town of Hispania Baetica, on the sea-coast.

Abderītes (Ἀβδηρίτης) and **Abderīta.** A name generally applied to the "laughing philosopher" Democritus (q. v.), as being a native of Abdera.

Abdērus (Ἄβδηρος). The armour-bearer of Heracles (q. v.), torn in pieces by the mares of Diomedes. The town Abdera was said to have been founded by Heracles in his honour.

Abdicatio. See Magistratus.

Abecedarii Hymni. Hymns containing as many lines as there are letters in the alphabet, each line beginning with a particular letter. An instance is given by St. Augustine in his *Retractationes*, i. 20. See Acrosticha.

Abella or **Avella.** A town of Campania, not far from Nola, founded by the Chalcidians in Euboea. It was celebrated for its apples, whence Vergil calls it *malifera.*

Abgărus (Ἄβγαρος), **Acbărus** (Ἄκβαρος) or **Augărus.** A name common to many rulers of Edessa, the capital of the district of Osrhoëné in Mesopotamia. Of these rulers one is supposed by Eusebius to have been the author of a letter written to Christ, which he found in a church at Edessa and translated from the Syriac. Eusebius (*Eccles. Hist.* i. 13) gives the text of the letter and also of the alleged reply. A translation of both can be found in McClintock and Strong's *Cyclopaedia of Biblical Literature*, s. v. *Abgarus.*

Abia (Ἀβία). (1) A town of Messenia on the Messenian Gulf, and at one time a member of the Achaean League (q. v.). (2) The nurse of Hyllus, in whose honour Cresphontes changed the name of Iré to Abia.

Abigeatōres. See Abactores.

Abigeātus. See Abactores.

Abigei. See Abactores.

Abīla (τὰ Ἄβιλα). (1) A town of Coele-Syria, afterwards called Claudiopolis, and capital of the tetrarchy of Abilené. It is mentioned in the N. T., *Luke*, iii. 1. (2) A mountain of Africa, opposite Gibraltar (Calpé).

Abisăres (Ἀβισάρης). An Indian king who sent embassies to Alexander the Great, and was by him allowed to retain his kingdom with considerable additions. His realm lay beyond the Hydaspes. See Quint. Curt. viii. 12–14; ix. 1.

Ablegmīna (ἀπολεγμοί) were the parts of the victim which were offered to the gods in sacrificing. Other names were *porriciae* and *prosecta.* See Sacrificium; Victima.

Ablecti. See EXTRAORDINARII.

Abnŏba Mons. The range of hills covered by the Black Forest in Germany. See GERMANIA.

Abolla. A rough, thick cloak resembling the Greek *chlamys* (q. v.), and called by Horace (*Ep.* i. 17, 25) *duplex pannus.* It was of foreign origin,

Abolla. (Arch of Septimius Severus.)

and at Rome in imperial times was worn indiscriminately as an outer garment (Juv. iv. 76). With the wealthy it was often of purple (Suet. *Cal.* 35); but it seems to have retained its simple coarseness when adopted by philosophers. It was thus worn by the Cynics, serving alike for day and night clothes (Martial, iv. 53, 5; Hor. *Ep. l. c.*, the same as the τρίβων διπλοῦς, Diog. Laërt. vi. 22). The abolla as worn by soldiers is probably to be recognized in the bas-relief from the arch of Septimius Severus.

Abonitīchos (Ἀβώνου τεῖχος). A town of Paphlagonia, the birthplace of an impostor who assumed the character of Asclepius. See Lucian, *Pseud.* 58.

Aborigĭnes. A name given by the Roman writers to the primitive race, who were thought to have blended with the Siculi, and founded subsequently the nation of the Latins. The name is equivalent to the Greek αὐτόχθονες, as indicating an indigenous race. According to tradition, they dwelt originally around Mount Velino, and Lake Fucinus, extending as far as Carseoli, and towards Reate. This was Cato's account (Dionys. H. ii. 49). The Aborigines are depicted by Sallust and Vergil as savages living in hordes, without manners, law, or agriculture, on the produce of the chase, and on wild fruits. This, however, does not agree with the traces of their towns in the Apennines; but the whole account was, perhaps, little else than an ancient speculation on the progress of mankind from rudeness to civilization. The Aborigines are said to have revered Ianus and Saturn. The latter taught them husbandry, and induced them to choose settled habitations, as the founders of a better way of life. From this ancient race, as has already been remarked, blending with a remnant of the Siculi, the nation of the Latins was said to have sprung; and between Saturn and the time assigned for the Trojan settlement, only three kings of the Aborigines are enumerated — Picus, Faunus, and Latinus. As to the name of this early race, the old and genuine one seems to have been Casci; and the appellation Aborigines was only given them by the later Roman writers. Regarding the historical aborigines of Italy, see ITALIA.

Aborrhas (Ἀβόρρας). A branch of the Euphrates; also written Chaboras, the modern Khabour.

Abortio, Abortus. If we may judge from poets and satirists, it was not an uncommon practice among the Romans to procure abortion (Plaut. *Truc.* 202; Juv. ii. 32; vi. 368). Cicero (*Clu.* 12) relates a case where a testator, leaving his wife pregnant, endeavours to secure the birth of his son by leaving his wife a handsome bequest if his son become heir, and nothing if he does not. Cicero charges Oppianicus with paying the amount contingently bequeathed to the widow, and procuring abortion in order that Oppianicus's son may succeed to the inheritance. A woman at Miletus, who in similar circumstances procured abortion by the use of drugs, was condemned to death in the time of Cicero's proconsulate. It was probably some such dangers that led to the Lex Cornelia, making it a criminal offence to give love-potions or medicines for abortion (Paul. *Sent.* v. 23, 214). All women who procured abortion were, by a rescript of Severus and Caracalla, condemned to exile.

Of the practice and law in Greece still less is known. Lysias in a speech, or declamation, impeached Antigonus for procuring abortion (κατ' Ἀντιγόνου ἀμβλώσεως, *Fragm.* 10, ed. Bait. and Sauppe). Plato recommended it in certain circumstances in his ideal Republic (*Rep.* v. 9, p. 461 c), and so also Aristotle (*Polit.* iv. [vii.] 16).

Abradātas (Ἀβραδάτας). A king of Susa, who submitted with his army to Cyrus, when he learned that his wife, Panthea, who had been made prisoner by the latter, was treated by him with great kindness and humanity. He was subsequently slain in fighting for Cyrus (Xen. *Cyrop.* v. 6).

Abrincatui. A nation of Gaul, dwelling, according to the common opinion, on the western coast, north of the Liger, or Loire, and whose capital, Ingena, is supposed to coincide with Avranches (Pliny, *H. N.* iv. 18).

Abro. (1) An Athenian author, whose work on the festivals of the Greeks is lost. (2) A grammarian of Rhodes of the time of Augustus, and a pupil of Tryphon. (3) An Argive of dissolute and luxurious life, whose name is perpetuated in the proverbial expression Ἄβρωνος βίος (*Abronis vita*) (Suidas, s. h. v.).

Abrocŏmas (Ἀβροκόμας). (1) A son of Darius who accompanied Xerxes against Greece, and was slain at Thermopylae. (2) A satrap of Artaxerxes Mnemon who was sent with an army of 300,000 men to oppose Cyrus on his march into Upper Asia. He burned some boats to prevent Cyrus from crossing the Euphrates, but did not arrive in time for the battle of Cunaxa (Xen. *Anab.* i. 3, § 20; iv. § 3, 5, 18; vii. § 12).

Abrogatio. See LEX.

Abrotŏnum (Ἀβρότονον). An African coast-town lying between the Syrtes. It was founded by the Phœnicians, and subsequently became a Roman colony. It was also called NEAPŎLIS; and with Oea and Leptis Magna formed the so-called African Tripolis (Pliny, *H. N.* v. 4).

Absinthium (ἀψίνθιον). Wormwood.

Absis or **Apsis** (ἁψίς). Literally, a fastening

of any kind. It was applied specially to the joining together of the extremities of a piece of wood, so as to give it the shape of a bow; and hence it came to signify anything of that shape, such as a bow, an arch, or a wheel (Hes. *Op.* 424; Herod. iv. 72.) The next transition of meaning is to anything vaulted (for example, ἡ ὑπουρανία ἀψίς, *the vault of heaven*, Plat. *Phaedr.* 247 B); and in this sense it was adopted in architecture, first, for any building or portion of a building of a circular form, or vaulted (Plin. *Epist.* ii. 17, § 18), and more especially for the circular and vaulted end of a basilica (Paul. Nol. *Ep.* 12). In Christian churches the apse came to mean the end of the choir, where the bishop's throne was placed.

Absolutio. See IUDICIUM.

Abstinendi Beneficium. See HERES.

Absyrtĭdes. Islands at the head of the Adriatic, in the Sinus Flanaticus (Gulf of Quarnero); named, as tradition reported, from Absyrtus the brother of Medea, who, according to one account, was killed here. See ABSYRTUS.

Absyrtus or **Apsyrtus** (Ἄψυρτος). The son of Aeëtes, king of Colchis, whom Medea took with her when she fled with Iason. Being pursued by her father, she murdered her brother, cut his body in pieces, and threw them into the sea, that her father might be detained by gathering the limbs of his child. Tomi, the place where this horror was committed, was believed to have derived its name from τέμνω, "cut." See ARGONAUTAE; MEDEA.

Abus. A river of Britain, now the Humber.

Abūsus. See USUS FRUCTUS.

Abydēnus (Ἀβυδηνός). A pupil of Berosus, who flourished B.C. 268. He wrote in Greek an historical account of the Chaldeans, Babylonians, and Assyrians, some fragments of which have been preserved to us by Eusebius, Cyril, and Syncellus. An important fragment, which clears up some difficulties in Assyrian history, has been discovered in the Armenian translation of the *Chronicon* of Eusebius. See the edition of his fragments by Richter (Leipzig, 1825).

Abȳdos (Ἄβυδος). (1) A town of the Troad on the Hellespont, and a Milesian colony, nearly opposite to Sestos, but a little lower down the stream. The bridge of boats which Xerxes (q. v.) constructed over the Hellespont, B.C. 480, commenced a little higher up than Abydos, and touched the European shore between Sestos and Madytus. (2) A city of Upper Egypt, near the west bank of the Nile; once second only to Thebes, but in Strabo's time (A.D. 14) a small village. It had a temple of Osiris and a Memnonium, both still standing, and an oracle.

Abȳla or **Abĭla.** A mountain in Mauretania forming the eastern extremity of the African coast of the Fretum Gaditanum, or Strait of Gibraltar. This and Mt. Calpé, opposite to it, were called the Columns (or Pillars) of Hercules, from the legend that they were originally a single mountain, and had been torn asunder by Hercules.

Acacius. (1) A disciple of Eusebius, bishop of Caesarea, whom he succeeded in 338 or 340. He was surnamed Μονόφθαλμος (*Luscus*), and wrote a *Life of Eusebius*, not extant; 17 volumes of *Commentaries on Ecclesiastes;* and 6 volumes of *Miscellanies.* Acacius was the leader of the sect called Acacians, who denied the Son to be of the same substance as the Father. (2) A patriarch of Constantinople in 471, who established the superiority of his see over the Eastern bishops. He was a favorite with the Emperor Zeno, who protected him against the Pope. Two letters of his are extant, to Petrus Trullo, and Pope Simplicius. (3) A bishop of Melitené, in Armenia Minor, present at the Council of Ephesus in 431, and who left in the Councils (vol. iii.) a *Homily against Nestorius.* (4) A bishop of Amida, distinguished for piety and charity in having sold church-plate, etc., to redeem 7000 Persian prisoners on the Tigris, in Mesopotamia. His death is commemorated in the Latin Church on April 9th.

Academĭa (Ἀκαδήμεια). (1) A public garden or grove in the suburbs of Athens, about six stadia from the city, named from Academus or Hecademus, who left it to the citizens for gymnastics (Paus. i. 29). It was surrounded with a wall by Hipparchus, adorned with statues, temples, and sepulchres of illustrious men; planted with olive and plane trees, and watered by the Cephissus. The olive-trees, according to Athenian fables, were reared from layers taken from the sacred olive in the Erechtheum, and afforded the oil given as a prize to victors at the Panathenaean festival. Few retreats could be more favorable to philosophy and the Muses. Within this enclosure Plato possessed, as part of his patrimony, a small garden, in which he opened a school for the reception of those inclined to attend his instructions. Hence arose the Academic sect, and hence the term Academy has descended to our times. The appellation *Academia* is frequently used in philosophical writings, especially in Cicero, as indicative of the Academic sect. See PHILOSOPHIA.

Sextus Empiricus enumerates five divisions of the followers of Plato. He makes Plato founder of the first Academy, Arcesilaüs of the second, Carneades of the third, Philo and Charmides of the fourth, Antiochus of the fifth. Cicero recognizes only two Academies, the OLD and NEW, and makes the latter commence as above with Arcesilaus. In enumerating those of the Old Academy, he begins, not with Plato, but Democritus, and gives them in the following order: Democritus, Anaxagoras, Empedocles, Parmenides, Xenophanes, Socrates, Plato, Speusippus, Xenocrates, Polemo, Crates, and Crantor. In the New, or Younger, he mentions Arcesilaüs, Lacydes, Evander, Hegesinus, Carneades, Clitomachus, and Philo (*Acad. Quaest.* iv. 5). If we follow the distinction laid down by Diogenes, and alluded to above, the Old Academy will consist of those followers of Plato who taught the doctrine of their master without mixture or corruption; the MIDDLE will embrace those who, by certain innovations in the manner of philosophizing, in some measure receded from the Platonic system without entirely deserting it; while the NEW will begin with those who relinquished the more obnoxious tenets of Arcesilaüs, and restored, in some measure, the declining reputation of the Platonic school (see PLATO). (2) A villa of Cicero near Puteoli (Pliny, *H. N.* xxxi. 2).

Academĭca or **Academĭcae Quaestiōnes.** A treatise of Cicero, written B.C. 45, originally in two books, named after Catulus and Lucullus, but subsequently in four books. Of the first edition, the second book (*Lucullus*) has come down to us; of the second (*Academica Posteriora*), the first part of the first book, and fragments exist. The Lucullus contains an account of the teachings of Antiochus and Philo regarding knowledge; the beginning of the second edition, besides some general observations, gives a sketch of the history of philosophy from Socrates to Arcesilaüs. An excellent edition of the *Academica*, in English, is that of Reid (1885).

Acadēmus (Ἀκάδημος). A hero, often identified with Cadmus. According to others (Plut. *Thes.* 32), he was an Athenian, who disclosed to Castor and Pollux the place where Theseus had secreted their sister Helen, after having carried her off from Sparta; and is said to have been highly honored, on this account, by the Lacedaemonians. From him the garden of the Academia, presented to the people of Athens, is thought to have been named. See ACADEMIA.

Acaina (ἄκαινα). A measure of length, equivalent to ten Greek feet. It was originally a pointed stick that finally came, like our *rod*, *perch*, or *pole*, and like the German *Stange*, to be used as a measuring-rod. See ACNA.

Acalandrus. A river of Magna Graecia, emptying into the bay of Tarentum.

Acalēphé. A shell-fish, belonging to the genus *urtica*, or sea-nettle.

Acamantis. A name given to Cyprus (q. v.). See ACAMAS.

Acămas (Ἀκάμας). (1) A promontory of Cyprus, northwest of Paphos. It is surmounted by two sugar-loaf summits, and the remarkable appearance which it thus presents to navigators as they approach the island on this side, caused them to give the name of Acamantis to the whole island. (2) A son of Theseus and Phaedra. He was deputed to accompany Diomedé, when the latter was sent to Troy to demand Helen. During his stay at Troy he became the father of Munitus by Laodicea, one of the daughters of Priam. He went to the Trojan War, and was one of the warriors enclosed in the wooden horse. He afterwards led a colony from Athens to Cyprus, where he died.

Acanthis (ἀκανθίς), mentioned by Aristotle, Pliny, and Vergil. The *fringilla spinus* of Linnaeus, called "aberdevine" in England.

Acanthus. (1) In architecture, the name given to the broad leaf used to enrich the capital of the Corinthian column (see COLUMNA). (2) In botany, a name given by the ancients to three different plants, (*a*) in Vergil, a prickly tree, supposed to be holly; (*b*) an Egyptian tree, described by Theophrastus as having pods like those of a bean; and (*c*) an herb, mentioned by Dioscorides, and identical with that which now bears its name.

Acapna, sc. *ligna* (in Greek, ξύλα ἄκαπνα). Firewood specially prepared to burn without smoke, and in great request in antiquity, owing to the defects of the chimneys. It was prepared in three ways: (1) by scorching the wood over a fire, this being known as *ligna cocta;* (2) by soaking in water after removing the bark, and then drying; (3) by smearing with oil-lees (*amurca*), and then exposing to the sun. See Martial, xiii. 15.

Acapnon Mel. Honey taken from the hive without smoking out the bees. Cf. Plin. *H. N.* xi. § 45.

Acarnan and **Amphotĕrus**. The sons of Alcmaeon and Callirrhoë. Their mother, hearing of her husband's murder by Phegeus and his sons, prayed Zeus, who loved her, to let her sons grow up into men at once, so as to avenge their father. This done, they slew the sons of Phegeus at Tegea and himself at Psophis, offered up at Delphi the jewels of Harmonia, which they thus acquired, and then founded a kingdom called after the elder of them Acarnania. See ALPHESIBOEA.

Acarnania (Ἀκαρνανία). A western division of Greece, bounded on the north by the Ambracian Gulf, on the west and southwest by the Ionian Sea, on the northeast by Amphilochia, which is sometimes included in Acarnania, and on the east by Aetolia, from which, at a later time, it was separated by the Achelous. The name of Acarnania does not occur in Homer. In the most ancient times the land was inhabited by the Taphii, Teleboae, and Leleges, and subsequently by the Curetes. At a later time a colony from Argos, said to have been led by Acarnan, settled in the country. In the seventh century B.C. the Corinthians founded several towns on the coast. The Acarnanians first emerge from obscurity at the beginning of the Peloponnesian War, B.C. 431. They were then a rude people, living by piracy and robbery, and they always remained behind the rest of the Greeks in civilization and refinement. They were good slingers, and are praised for their fidelity and courage. The different towns formed a league, which met at Stratus, and subsequently at Thyrium or Leucas.

Acastus (Ἄκαστος). The son of Pelias, king of Iolcos, who joined the Argonautic expedition, though against his father's will, as a friend of Iason. At his father's death he celebrated funeral games which were the theme of ancient poets and artists, and in which Peleus was represented as participating. He took part in the Calydonian boar-hunt. But his wife Astydamia fell in love with Peleus (q. v.), and this brought ruin on the wedded pair. His daughter was Laodamia, renowned for her tender love of Protesilaüs (q. v.).

Acătus, dimin. **Acation** (ἄκατος, ἀκάτιον). (1) A small boat (see NAVIS). (2) In the rigging of a ship, ἀκάτια were small sails, probably stay-sails. (3) A drinking-vessel, shaped like a modern sauce-boat.

Acbărus. See ABGARUS.

Accad. See AKKAD.

Acca Larentia. According to the common tradition, the wife of the herdsman Faustulus, and nurse to Romulus and Remus. See FRATRES ARVALES; LARES; ROMULUS.

Accensi. Properly "supernumeraries," from *accenseo*. The word is used in five senses. (1) A century added to the fifth class of citizens in the Servian classification, and described by Livy (i. 43, 7) as *cornicines, tubicinesque*. Lange, who is now generally followed, takes the name *accensi* as used of the whole fifth class. See COMITIA; EXERCITUS. (2) As a military term, *accensi* denotes the reserve soldiers who, at the time when each soldier had to find his own arms, could provide themselves with nothing better than sticks and stones. From their lack of defensive armor they were known as *velati;* and when any of the regular troops were killed or disabled, the *accensi* took their places, and used their armour and weapons (Varro, *L. L.* vii. 56). They were also known as *ferentarii*. Although after B.C. 352, when the state began to pay its soldiers, the accensi generally secured better weapons, the Column of Trajan shows a soldier armed only with stones. (3) The attendants on the cavalry, who held their spare horses; also the orderlies of the centurions (Varro, *L. L.* v. 82, and Fest. s. v. *Optio*). See CENTURIO. (4) Those attendants upon the magistrates who stood ready to relieve the lictors if necessary. So long as the custom lasted that the two colleagues were preceded by the fasces on alternate days, an accensus attended on the one who did not have the fasces. The duties of these accensi were to summon the people to the Comitia, and to proclaim the third, sixth, and ninth hour of the day in the Comitium. (5) On inscriptions of the time of the Empire mention is made of *accensi velati*, who formed a college of 100 members, charged with the superintendence of the public roads.

Acceptilatio is defined to be a release by mutual interrogation between debtor and creditor, by which each party is exonerated from the same contract. In other words, acceptilatio is the form of words by which a creditor releases his debtor from a debt or obligation, and acknowledges he has received that which in fact he has not received. This release of debt by acceptilatio applies only to such debts as have been contracted by *stipulatio* (q. v.), conformably to a rule of Roman law, that only contracts made by words can be put an end to by words. But the astuteness of the Roman lawyers found a mode of complying with the rule, and at the same time extending the acceptilatio to all kinds and to any number of contracts. This was the invention of Gallus Aquilius, who devised a formula for reducing all and every kind of contracts to the *stipulatio*. This being done, the acceptilatio would immediately apply, inasmuch as the matter was by such formula brought within the general rule of law above mentioned. See NOVATIO.

Accessio. A legal term, by which is expressed the produce or increase of anything, and, at the same time, the notion of such produce or increase becoming the property of him to whom the thing itself belongs. The rule of law was expressed thus: *Accessio cedit principali.* Examples of accessio are contained under the heads of CONFUSIO, etc.

Accipenser. A sturgeon.

Accipĭter. A hawk.

Accius, LUCIUS. See ATTIUS, LUCIUS.

Acclamatio. The public expression of approbation or disapprobation, pleasure or displeasure, by loud acclamations. On many occasions, there appear to have been certain forms of acclamations always used by the Romans; as, for instance, at marriages, *Io Hymen, Hymenaee*, or *Talassio* (explained by Livy); at triumphs, *Io triumphe, Io triumphe;* at the conclusion of plays the last actor called out *Plaudite* to the spectators; orators were usually praised by such expressions as *Bene et praeclare, Belle et festive, Non potest melius*, etc. Other instances of *acclamationes* are given by Ferrarius, in his treatise *De Veterum Acclamationibus et Plausu*, in Graevius *Thesaur. Rom. Antiq.* vol. vi. Cf. also Henzen, *Acta Fratr. Arval.* p. 75. Under the Empire, the manifestation of popular applause in the theatre and circus was reduced to a sort of system. When the emperor entered, the whole audience rose and greeted him in a rhythmic formula. Nero selected a band of 5000 knights and citizens, called *Augustani* or *Augustales*, to be trained in a special form of musical salutation (Suet. *Nero*, 20). The name *acclamationes* was also given to the decrees passed by the Senate in honour of the emperor, as being always carried by acclamation. See the articles FUNUS; MATRIMONIUM; TRIUMPHUS.

Accubatio. The act of reclining at table. See CENA.

Accubitio. See CENA.

Accubĭtum. The name of a couch used for reclining upon at meals, and used at the time of the Empire in place of the *triclinium* (q. v.). It seems to have held any number of guests, and to have been lower and more luxurious than the triclinium. The spreads and pillows were called *accubitalia* (Trebell. Poll. *Claud.* 14).

Accusatio. See CRIMEN; IUDEX; IUDICIUM.

Acé (in Hebrew, *Accho*). A Phœnician seaport town, the modern Acre. The Greeks, having changed the original name into Ἀκή, connected with it the fabulous legend of Heracles having been bitten here by a serpent, and of his having cured (ἀκέομαι) the wound by a certain leaf.

Acerra (λιβανωτίς, λιβανωτρίς). The incense-box used in sacrifices; called by Servius *arca thuralis*.

Horace, enumerating the principal articles necessary in a solemn sacrifice to Iuno, mentions "Flowers and a box full of frankincense." In Vergil, Aeneas worships "with corn and with frankincense from the full acerra" (*Aen.* v. 745).

Pliny, enumerating the principal works of Parrhasius of Ephesus, speaks of a picture representing a priest preparing to sacrifice, with a boy standing beside him, and holding the incense-box and a wreath of flowers. This was, no doubt, a very common and favourite subject for artists of every kind. It frequently occurs in bas-reliefs representing sacrifices, and executed on vases, friezes, and other ancient monuments. It occurs three times on the Columna Traiana at Rome, and once on the Arch of Constantine.

Acerra. (Capitoline Museum.)

The acerra was also, according to Festus, a small altar placed before the dead, on which perfumes were burned: *Acerra, ara quae ante mortuum poni solebat, in qua odores incendebantur.* There was a law in the Twelve Tables which restricted the use of acerrae at funerals (Cic. *De Leg.* ii. 24).

Acesīnes. The Chenâb, a river of India, emptying into the Indus. See HYDASPES.

Acesta. See SEGESTA.

Acestes. A mythical king of Sicily, the friend of Aeneas (Verg. *Aen.* v. 757).

Acetabŭlum (ὀξίς, ὀξύβαφον, ἐμβάφιον). A small shallow vessel originally employed to hold vinegar or sauces into which the food was dipped. It was afterwards employed as a receptacle for salad, wine, honey, and in playing one form of the *cottabus* (q. v.). The accompanying illustration

Dish showing two small Acetabula.

from Daremberg and Saglio s. h. v. shows two acetabula placed one on each side of a sucking pig served up in a lanx. The name is also a Roman measure of capacity in liquid as well as dry measure = ὀξύβαφον, and holding one fourth of the hemina and one eighth of the sextarius.

Acētum (ὄξος). Vinegar. The kinds most in repute among the ancients were the Ægyptian and Cnidian. Pliny gives a full account of the medical properties of vinegar. Among other applications, it was employed when leeches had been introduced into the stomach, or adhered to the larynx. Vinegar was also given in long-standing coughs, just as modern practitioners give oxymels in chronic catarrhs, and it appears to have been thought useful in affections of the ear. ACETUM ITALĬCUM is the proverbial expression for the rude humor of the old Italian, just as *sal Atticum* is used of Greek wit.

Achaea (Ἀχαΐα). (1) The northern coast of the Peloponnesus, originally called Aegialea or Aegialus, i. e. the coast-land, was bounded on the north by the Corinthian Gulf and the Ionian Sea, on the south by Elis and Arcadia, on the west by the Ionian Sea, and on the east by Sicyonia. Respecting its inhabitants, see ACHAEI. (2) A district in Thessaly, which appears to have been the original seat of the Achaei. (3) The Roman province, which included Peloponnesus and northern Greece south of Thessaly. It was formed on the dissolution of the Achaean League (q. v.) in B.C. 146, and hence derived its name.

Achaean League (ACHAĬCUM FOEDUS; τὸ Ἀχαϊκόν). The league or confederation of a number of towns on the northwest coast of Peloponnesus. In speaking of it we must distinguish between two periods. The former, though formed for mutual protection, was mainly of a religious character, whereas the latter was a political confederation to protect the towns against the domination of Macedonia.

(1) *The Earlier League.*—When the Heraclidae took possession of Peloponnesus, a portion of the Achaeans, under Tisamenos, turned northwards and took possession of the northern coast of the peninsula, which was called Αἰγιαλός: the Ionians, who had hitherto occupied that country, sought refuge in Attica and on the west coast of Asia Minor. The country thus occupied by the Achaeans, from whom it derived its name of Achaia, contained twelve towns which had been leagued together even in the time of their Ionian inhabitants. They were governed by the descendants of Tisamenus, until, after the death of King Ogyges, they abolished the kingly rule and established democratic institutions. The time when this happened is not known. In the time of Herodotus (i. 145) the twelve towns of which the league consisted were: Pellene, Aegeira, Aegae, Bura, Helicé, Aegion, Rhypes, Patrae, Pharae, Olenos, Dymé, and Tritaea. After the time of Herodotus, Rhypes and Aegae disappear from the number of the confederate towns, as they had decayed and become deserted (Paus. vii. 23, 25; Strab. viii. p. 387), and Leontion and Cerynea stepped into their place (Polyb. ii. 41). Helicé appears to have been their common place of meeting; but this town, together with Bura, was swallowed up by the sea during an earthquake in B.C. 373, whereupon Aegion was chosen as the place of meeting for the confederates (Strab. viii. p. 384). Of the constitution of this league very little is known; but it is clear that the bond which united the different towns was very loose, and less a political than a religious one. The looseness of the connection among the towns in a political point of view is evident from the fact that some of them acted occasionally quite independent of the rest (Thuc. ii. 9). The confederation generally kept aloof from the troubles of other parts of Greece, on which accordingly it exercised no particular influence down to the time when the league was broken up by the Macedonians. But they were nevertheless highly respected by the other Greek states on account of their honesty, sincerity, and wise moderation. Hence after the battle of Leuctra they were chosen to arbitrate between the Thebans and Lacedaemonians (Polyb. ii. 39). Demetrius, Cassander, and Antigonus Gonatas placed garrisons in some of their towns, while in others they favoured the rising of tyrants. The towns were thus separated from one another, and the whole confederation was gradually destroyed.

(2) *The Later League.*—The ancient confederacy had thus ceased to exist for some time when events took place which in some towns roused the ancient spirit of independence. When in B.C. 281 Antigonus Gonatas attempted to drive Ptolemaeus Ceraunus from the throne of Macedonia, the Achaeans availed themselves of the opportunity of shaking off the Macedonian yoke, and renewing the old confederation. The object, however, was no longer a common worship, but a real political union among the towns. The places which first shook off the yoke of the oppressors were Dymé and Patrae, and the alliance concluded between them was speedily joined by the towns of Tritaea and Pharae (Polyb. ii. 41). One town after another expelled the Macedonian garrisons and tyrants; and when in B.C. 275, Aegion, the head of the ancient league, followed the example of the other towns, the foundation of the new confederation was complete, and the main principles of its constitution were settled, though afterwards many changes and modifications were introduced. The fundamental laws were that henceforth the confederacy should form one inseparable state; that every town which should join it should have equal rights with the others; and that all members in regard to foreign countries should be regarded as dependent, and be bound in every respect to obey the federal government and those officers who were intrusted with the executive (Polyb. ii. 37 foll.). No town, therefore, was allowed to treat with any foreign power without the sanction of the others. Aegion, for religious reasons, was appointed the seat of the government. At Aegion, therefore, the citizens of the various towns met at stated and regular times

to deliberate upon the common affairs of the confederation, and if necessary upon those of any separate town or even of individuals, and to elect the officers of the league. After having thus established a firm union among themselves, the Achaeans zealously exerted themselves in delivering other towns also from their tyrants and oppressors. The league, however, did not acquire any great strength until B.C. 251, when Aratus united Sicyon, his native place, with it, and some years later also gained Corinth for it. Megara, Troezen, and Epidaurus soon followed their example. Afterwards Aratus prevailed upon all the more important towns of Peloponnesus to join the confederacy, and Megalopolis, Argos, Hermioné, Phlius, and others were added to it. In a short time the league thus reached its highest power, for it embraced Athens, Aegina, Salamis, and the whole of Peloponnesus, with the exception of Sparta, Tegea, Orchomenus, Mantinea, and Elis. Greece seemed to revive, and promised to become stronger and more united than ever, but it soon showed that its new power was employed only in self-destruction and its own ruin. The Achaean League might at one time have become a great power, and might have united at least the whole of Peloponnesus into one State; but the original objects of the league were in the course of time so far forgotten that it sought the protection of those against whom it had been formed; and the perpetual discord among its members, the hostility of Sparta, the intrigues of the Romans, and the folly and rashness of the last strategy brought about not only the dissolution and destruction of the confederacy, but the political annihilation of the whole of Greece in the year B.C. 146. (Cf. Schorn, *Gesch. Griechenlands von der Entstehung des aetol. u. achaeischen Bundes*, p. 49 foll. and p. 60 foll.; Drumann, *Ideen zur Gesch. des Verfalls der griech. Staaten*; Thirlwall, *Hist. of Greece*, vol. viii p. 86 foll.; Hertzberg, *Gesch. Griechenlands unter den Römern*, vol. i. [Halle, 1875].)

Achaei (Ἀχαιοί). One of the chief Hellenic races, and, according to tradition, descended from Achaeus, who was the son of Xuthus and Creüsa, and grandson of Hellen. The Achaei originally dwelt in Thessaly, and from thence migrated to Peloponnesus, the whole of which became subject to them with the exception of Arcadia, and the country afterwards called Achaea. As they were the ruling nation in Peloponnesus in the heroic times, Homer frequently gives the name of Achaei to the collective Greeks. On the conquest of Peloponnesus by the Heraclidae and the Dorians, eighty years after the Trojan War, many of the Achaei under Tisamenus, the son of Orestes, left their country and took possession of the northern coast of Peloponnesus, then inhabited by Ionians, whom they expelled from the country, which was henceforth called Achaea. The expelled Ionians migrated to Attica and Asia Minor. The Achaei settled in twelve cities: Pellené, Aegira, Aegae, Bura, Helicé, Aegium, Rhypae, Patrae, Pharae, Olenus, Dymé, and Tritaea. These twelve cities formed a league for mutual defence and protection. The Achaei had little influence in the affairs of Greece till the time of the successors of Alexander. In B.C. 281, the Achaei, who were then subject to the Macedonians, resolved to renew their ancient league for the purpose of shaking off the Macedonian yoke. This was the origin of the celebrated Achaean League (q. v.), which did not, however, obtain much importance till B.C. 251, when Aratus united to it his native town, Sicyon. The example of Sicyon was followed by Corinth and many other towns in Greece, and the league soon became the chief political power in Greece. At length the Achaei declared war against the Romans, who destroyed the league, and thus put an end to the independence of Greece. Corinth, then the chief town of the league, was taken by the Roman general Mummius, in B.C. 146, and the whole of southern Greece made a Roman province under the name of Achaea (q. v.).

Achaeměnes. (1) The ancestor of the Persian kings, who founded the family of the Achaemenidae, which was the noblest family of the Pasargadae, the noblest of the Persian tribes. The Roman poets use the adjective Achaemenius in the sense of Persian. (2) Son of Darius I., was governor of Egypt, and commanded the Egyptian fleet in the expedition of Xerxes against Greece, B.C. 480. He was defeated and killed in battle by Inarus the Libyan, 460 (Herod. vii. 97, 236).

Achaemenĭdes, or Achemenĭdes. A companion of Odysseus, who left him behind in Sicily when he fled from the Cyclops (Verg. *Aen.* iii. 614).

Achaeus. (1) See ACHAEI. (2) A Greek tragic poet of Eretria, born about B.C. 484, a contemporary of Sophocles, and especially famous in the line of satyric drama. He wrote about forty plays, of which only small fragments are preserved. These have been edited by Urlichs (Bonn, 1834).

Achăné (ἀχάνη). A Persian measure equivalent to 45 Attic μέδιμνοι. According to Hesychius, there was also a Boeotian ἀχάνη equivalent to one Attic μέδιμνος. See MEDIMNUS.

Acharistias Diké (ἀχαριστίας δίκη). See KAKOSIS.

Acharnae (Ἀχαρναί). The principal deme of Attica belonging to the tribe Oeneïs, 60 stadia north of Athens, near the foot of Mt. Parnes. The land was fertile, and the population rough and warlike, furnishing at the commencement of the Peloponnesian War 3000 hoplites, or one-tenth of the whole infantry of the republic. The deme gives the name to one of the plays of Aristophanes (q. v.) (Ἀχαρνεῖς), represented B.C. 425.

Achātes. A companion and friend of Aeneas (q. v.) in his wanderings, and styled by Vergil *fidus Achates*, so that his fidelity has become proverbial (*Aen.* i. 188).

Achātes (ἀχάτης). An agate, a precious stone or gem. Theophrastus describes it as a beautiful and rare stone from the river Achates in Sicily, which sold at a high price; but Pliny tells us that in his time it was no longer in esteem, it being then found in many places, of large size and diversified appearance. The ancients distinguished agates into many species, to each of which they gave a name importing its difference from the common agate, whether it were in colour, figure, or texture. Thus they called the red, *haemachates*, which was sprinkled with spots of jasper, or blood-red chalcedony, and now called "dotted agate." The white they termed *leucachates;* the plain yellowish or wax-coloured, *cerachates.*

Achelōüs (Ἀχελῷος). The largest river in Greece. It rises in Mt. Pindus, and flows southward, forming the boundary between Acarnania and Aetolia, and falls into the Ionian Sea opposite the islands called Echinades. It is about 130 miles in length. The god of this river is described as the son of Oceanus and Tethys, and as the eldest of his 3000 brothers. He fought with Heracles for Deïanira, but was conquered in the contest. He then took the form of a bull, but was again overcome by Heracles, who deprived him of one of his horns, which, however, he recovered by giving up the horn of Amalthea (q. v.). According to Ovid (*Met.* x. 87), the Naiads changed the horn which Heracles took from Acheloüs into the horn of plenty. Acheloüs was from the earliest times considered to be a great divinity throughout Greece, and was invoked in prayers and sacrifices. Acheloüs was regarded as the representative of all fresh water; hence we find in Vergil *Acheloïa pocula,* that is, water in general. The Sirens are called Acheloiades, as the daughters of Acheloüs.

Achĕron (Ἀχέρων). The name of several rivers, all of which were, at one time, believed to be connected with the lower world. (1) A river in Thesprotia, in Epirus, which flows through the lake Acherusia into the Ionian Sea. (2) A river in southern Italy, in Bruttii, on which Alexander of Epirus perished. (3) The river of the lower world round which the shades hover, and into which the Pyriphlegethon and Cocytus flow. In late writers the name of Acheron is used to designate the whole of the lower world.

Acherontia. (1) A town in Apulia on the summit of Mt. Vultur. (2) A town on the river Acheron, in Bruttii.

Acherusia. See ACHERON (1).

Achillēis (Ἀχιλλητ̂ς). (1) See HOMERUS. (2) See STATIUS.

Achilles (Ἀχιλλεύς). (1) A son of Earth, to whom Heré fled from the pursuits of Zeus, and who persuaded her to return and marry that deity. (2) The teacher of the centaur Chiron (q. v.). (3) The inventor of the ostracism (q. v). (4) A son of Zeus and Lamia, whose beauty was so great that, in the judgment of Pan, he bore away the prize in every contest. This so offended Aphrodité that she inspired Pan with a fruitless passion for the nymph Echo (q. v.), and further gave him a hideous appearance.

(5) The famous son of Peleus, king of Phthiotis in Thessaly, by Thetis, the sea-deity. According to Lycophron, Thetis became the mother of seven male children by Peleus, six of whom she threw into the fire, because they were not of the same nature with herself, and because the treatment she had received was unworthy of her rank as a goddess. The scholiast on Homer, however, states, that Thetis threw her children into the fire in order to ascertain whether they were mortal or not, the goddess supposing that the fire would consume what was mortal in their natures, while she would preserve what was immortal. The scholiast adds that six of her children perished by this harsh experiment, and that she had, in like manner, thrown the seventh, afterwards named Achilles, into the flames, when Peleus, having beheld the deed, rescued his offspring from this perilous situation. Tzetzes assigns a different motive to Thetis in the case of Achilles. He makes her to have been desirous of conferring immortality upon him, and states that with this view she anointed him with ambrosia during the day, and threw him into fire at evening. Peleus, having discovered the goddess in the act of consigning his child to the flames, cried out with alarm, whereupon Thetis, abandoning the object she had in view, left the court of Peleus and rejoined the nymphs of the ocean. Dictys Cretensis makes Peleus to have rescued Achilles from the fire before any part of his body had been injured but the heel. What has thus far been stated in relation to Achilles, with the single exception of the names of his parents, Peleus and Thetis, is directly at variance with the authority of Homer, and must therefore be regarded as a mere post-Homeric fable. Equally at variance with the account given by the bard is the more popular fiction that Thetis plunged her son into the waters of the Styx, and by that immersion rendered the whole of his body invulnerable, except the heel by which she held him. There are several passages in the *Iliad* which plainly show that the poet does not ascribe to Achilles the possession of any peculiar physical defence against danger.

The care of his education and training was intrusted, according to the common authorities, to the centaur Chiron, and to Phoenix, son of Amyntor. Homer specifically mentions Phoenix as his first instructor. Those, however, who pay more regard in this case to the statements of other writers, make Chiron to have had charge of Achilles first, and to have fed him on the marrow of wild animals; according to Libanius, on that of lions. Calchas having predicted, when Achilles had attained the age of nine years, that Troy could not be taken without him, Thetis, well aware that her son, if he joined that expedition, was destined to perish, sent him disguised in female attire to the court of Lycomedes, king of the island of Scyros, for the purpose of being concealed there. At the court of Lycomedes, he received the name of Pyrrha (Πυρρά, Rufa), from his golden locks, and became the father of Neoptolemus by Deïdamia, one of the monarch's daughters. In this state of concealment Achilles remained until discovered by Odysseus, who came to the island in the disguise of a travelling merchant. The chieftain of Ithaca offered, it seems, various articles of female attire for sale, and mingled with them some pieces of armor. On a sudden blast being given with a trumpet, Achilles discovered himself by seizing upon the arms. The young warrior then joined the army against Troy. This account, however, of the concealment of Achilles is contradicted by the express authority of Homer, who represents him as proceeding directly to the Trojan war from the court of his father. (*Il.* ix. 439.) The Greeks, having made good their landing on the shores of Troas, proved so superior to the enemy as to compel them to seek shelter within their walls. No sooner was this done than the Greeks were forced to turn their principal attention to the means of supporting their numerous forces. A part of the army was therefore sent to cultivate the rich vales of the Thracian Chersonesus, then abandoned by their inhabitants on account of the incursions of the barbarians from the interior. But the Grecian army, being weakened by this separation of its force, could no longer deter the Trojans from again taking the field, nor prevent succour and supplies from being sent into the city. Thus the

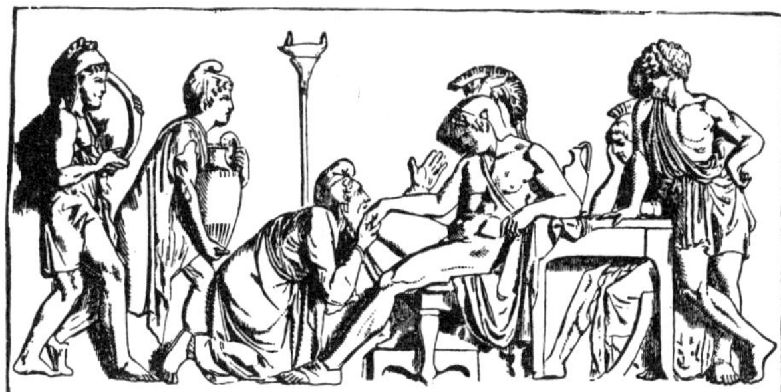

Priam before Achilles. (Relief by Thorwaldsen, Munich.)

siege was protracted to the length of ten years. During a great part of this time, Achilles was employed in lessening the resources of Priam by the reduction of the tributary cities of Asia Minor. With a fleet he ravaged the coasts of Mysia, made frequent disembarkations of his forces, and succeeded eventually in destroying eleven cities. Among the spoils of one, Achilles obtained the beautiful Briseïs, while, at the taking of Thebé, Chryseïs, the daughter of Chryses, a priest of Apollo at Chrysa, became the prize of Agamemnon. A pestilence shortly after appeared in the Grecian camp, and Calchas, encouraged by the proffered protection of Achilles, ventured to attribute it to Agamemnon's detention of the daughter of Chryses, whom her father had endeavored to ransom, but in vain. The monarch, although deeply offended, was compelled at last to surrender his captive; but, as an act of retaliation, and to testify his resentment, he deprived Achilles of Briseïs. Hence arose "the anger of the son of Peleus," on which is based the action of the *Iliad*. Achilles, on his part, withdrew his forces from the contest, and neither prayers nor entreaties, nor direct offers of reconciliation, couched in the most tempting and flattering terms, could induce him to return to the field. The death of his friend Patroclus, however, by the hand of Hector, roused him at length to action and revenge, and a reconciliation having thereupon taken place between the two Grecian leaders, Briseïs was restored. As the arms of Achilles, having been worn by Patroclus, had become the prize of Hector, Hephaestus, at the request of Thetis, fabricated a suit of impenetrable armour for her son. Arrayed in this, Achilles took the field, and after a great slaughter of the Trojans, and a contest with the god of the Scamander, by whose waters he was nearly overwhelmed, he met Hector, chased him thrice around the walls of Troy, and finally slew him by the aid of Athené. According to Homer, Achilles dragged the corpse of Hector at his chariot-wheels thrice round the tomb of Patroclus, and from the language of the poet he would appear to have done this for several days in succession. Vergil, however, makes Achilles to have dragged the body of Hector twice round the walls of Troy. In this it is probable that the Roman poet followed one of the cyclic or else the tragic writers. The corpse of the Trojan hero was at last yielded up to the tears and supplications of Priam, who had come for that purpose to the tent of Achilles, and a truce was granted the Trojans for the performance of the funeral obsequies. Achilles did not long survive his illustrious opponent. According to the more generally received account, as it is given by the scholiast on Lycophron, and also by Dictys Cretensis and Dares Phrygius, Achilles, having become enamoured of Polyxena, the daughter of Priam, signified to the monarch that he would become his ally on condition of receiving her hand in marriage. Priam consented, and the parties having come for that purpose to the temple of the Thymbraean Apollo, Achilles was treacherously slain by Paris, who had concealed himself there, being wounded by him with an arrow in the heel. The ashes of the hero were mingled in a golden urn with those of his friend Patroclus, and were said to repose at Sigaeum.

(5) ACHILLES TATIUS, a native of Alexandria, commonly assigned to the second or third century A.D., but probably much later. He is author of the novel entitled "The Loves of Leucippé and Clitophon" (Τὰ κατὰ Λευκίππην καὶ Κλειτοφῶντα), an interesting and graceful production, though marred by much licentiousness of phrase and allusion. Few works have been so often imitated. A good edition is that by Jacobs (Leipzig, 1821); and the text with a Latin version is given in the *Erotici Scriptores* of the Didot collection edited by Hirschig (Paris, 1856). Eng. trans. by Smith (London, 1855). See NOVELS AND ROMANCES.

Achillēum. A town near the promontory Sigaeum (q. v.) in the Troad, where Achilles was supposed to have been buried.

Achillīdes. Pyrrhus (q. v.), son of Achilles.

Achīvi. The Latin equivalent of Achaei (Ἀχαιοί). See ACHAEI.

Achradīna or **Acradīna.** See SYRACUSAE.

Acidalia. A name applied to Aphrodité from the fountain Acidalius, near Orchomenus, where she was wont to bathe with the Graces.

Acies. See EXERCITUS.

Acilia Calpurnia Lex. See AMBITUS; LEX.

Acilia Lex. See LEX; REPETUNDARUM.

Acilius Glabrio. See GLABRIO.

Acinăces (ἀκινάκης). A Persian sword, short, straight, and thus differing from the Roman *sica*, which was curved. It was worn on the right side, whereas the Greeks and Romans wore their swords on the left. A golden acinaces was frequently given to individuals as a mark of honour. The accompanying illustration is from the bas-relief found

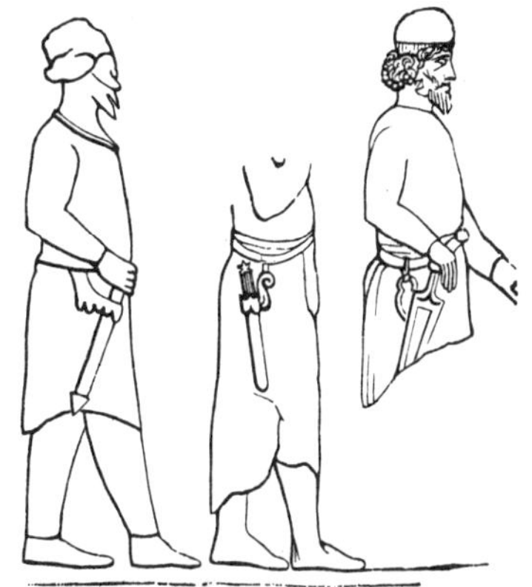

Acinaces, or Persian Sword.

at Persepolis. The god Mithras (q. v.) is frequently represented with the acinaces.

Acis (Ἄκις). The son of Faunus and Symaethis, who was beloved by the nymph Galatea, and slain by Polyphemus, who was jealous of his success. His blood, gushing forth from under the rock with which he had been crushed, was changed by Galatea into the river Acis, or Acinius, at the foot of Mt. Aetna—a story perhaps suggested by the fact that the river in question springs out from under a rock. The legend has suggested a number of fine poems in English, among them Gay's *Song of Polypheme* in his *Acis and Galatea;* J. S. Blackie's *Galatea;* Buchanan's *Polypheme's Passion;* and Procter's *Death of Acis.*

Aciscŭlus. See ASCIA.

Aclis. A kind of dart mentioned by Vergil (*Aen.* vii. 730) as used by the Osci. It had a leathern thong attached to it, so that it might be drawn back again after being thrown.

Acmonĭdes. A name given by Ovid to one of the three Cyclopes (q. v.), called by Vergil Pyracmon, and by other writers Arges.

Acna. See ACTUS.

Acoetes (Ἀκοίτης). A sailor saved by Bacchus for having espoused the cause of the god when the rest of the crew desired to sell him as a slave. The legend will be found narrated under the title DIONYSUS.

Acŏné (ἀκόνη). The whetstone, consisting chiefly of silex and alum.

Acontion (ἀκόντιον). See HASTA.

Acontius (Ἀκόντιος). See CYDIPPÉ.

Acquisitio. A general expression for the acquisition or ownership of property. See IN IURE CESSIO; MANCIPIUM; ACCESSIO; DOMINIUM.

Acrae or **Acra** (Ἄκραι). A town of Sicily, west of Syracuse.

Acraephia (Ἀκραιφία) or **Acraephiae** (Ἀκραιφίαι). A town in Boeotia at Lake Copaïs, in which the Thebans took refuge after their town had been destroyed by Alexander. It contained a temple of Dionysus.

Acrăgas. See AGRIGENTUM.

Acratisma (ἀκράτισμα). The early meal (πρωϊνὸν ἄριστον) of the Greeks, taken immediately on rising, like the first breakfast in France and Germany. It consisted of bread dipped in unmixed wine (ἄκρατος οἶνος), whence the name ἀκράτισμα.

Acratophŏrum (ἀκρατοφόρον). A small vessel for holding wine; a wine-cup. The name is derived from ἄκρᾱτον, "unmixed wine," and φέρω, "to bear." Pollux mentions it in his account of ancient drinking-vessels, and describes it as resting, not on a flat bottom, but on small astragals.

Acrisiōné (Ἀκρισιώνη). Danaë (q. v.), daughter of Acrisius.

Acrisius (Ἀκρίσιος). The son of Abas, king of Argos, by Ocalia, daughter of Mantineus. He was born at the same birth as Proetus, with whom it is said that he quarrelled even in his mother's womb. After many dissensions, Proetus was driven from Argos. Acrisius had Danaë by Eurydicé, daughter of Lacedaemon; and an oracle having declared that he should lose his life by the hand of his grandson, he endeavoured to frustrate the prediction by the imprisonment of his daughter, in order to prevent her becoming a mother. (See DANAË.) His efforts failed of success, and he was eventually killed by Perseus, son of Danaë and Zeus. Acrisius, it seems, had been attracted to Larissa by the reports which had reached him of the prowess of Perseus. At Larissa, Perseus, wishing to show his skill in throwing a quoit, killed an old man who proved to be his grandfather, whom he knew not, and thus the oracle was fulfilled.

Acrītas (Ἀκρείτας). A promontory of Messenia in the Peloponnesus, now Cape Gallo.

Acro, HELENIUS. A Roman grammarian of the end of the second century A.D. He wrote commentaries (now lost) on Terence, Horace, and perhaps Persius. The collection of scholia bearing his name dates from the seventh century. See Gräfenhan, *Geschich. d. class. Philol.* iv. pp. 308–313.

Acroāma (ἀκρόαμα). Properly a musical piece, but also a play, dance, or a recitation, such as were common at meals (Suet. *Vesp.* 19; Pliny, *Ep.* vi. 31, 13). The word also denotes the musicians or actors employed to amuse the guests during an entertainment; and is rarely used of an actor on the stage. See Marquardt, *Röm. Altert.* vii. p. 327; and the article ANAGNOSTAE.

Acroamata. (Millingen, *Peintures*, pl. viii.)

Acroāsis (ἀκρόασις). (1) A literary discourse or lecture. The term (itself of Greek origin) is applied by the Latin writers to a discourse or disputation, by some instructor or professor of an art, to a numerous audience. The corresponding Latin term is *auditio.* (2) It also signifies a place or room where literary men met, a lecture-room.

Acroceraunia. See CERAUNII MONTES.

Acrocorinthus (Ἀκροκόρινθος). A high hill overhanging the city of Corinth, on which was erected a citadel, called also by the same name. This situation was so important a one as to be styled by Philip the fetters of Greece. See CORINTHUS.

Acrolĭthi (ἀκρόλιθοι). Statues, of which the extremities only (head, feet, and hands) were of stone, and the remaining part of the body of bronze or gilded wood (Vitruv. ii. 8, 11).

Acropodium (ἀκροπόδιον). The base or pedestal of a statue, so called from its supporting the extremities or soles of the feet (ἄκρος, πούς).

Acropŏlis (ἀκρόπολις). In nearly all the cities of Greece, which were usually built upon a hill or some natural elevation, there was a kind of tower or citadel, reared upon the highest part, to which the name ἀκρόπολις (upper town) was given. At Rome, the Capitolium (q. v.) was analogous in its purposes to the acropolis of Greek cities.

The Acropolis of Athens was situated on a plateau of rock, about 200 feet in height, 1000 in breadth from east to west, and 460 in length from north to south. It was originally called Cecropia, after Cecrops, the ancestor of the Athenians, whose grave and shrine were shown on the spot. On the north side of the Acropolis was the Erechtheum, the common seat of worship of the ancient gods of Athens, Athené Polias, Hephaestus, Poseidon, and Erechtheus himself, who was said to have founded the sanctuary. His house was possibly northeast of the Erechtheum. Pisistratus, like the ancient kings, had his residence on the Acropolis, and may have added the stylobate to the temple of Athené recently identified, south of the Erechtheum. The walls of the fortress proper were destroyed in the Persian wars, 480 and 479 B.C., and restored by Cimon. But the wall surrounding the foot of the hill, called the Pelasgicon or Pelargicon, and supposed to be a relic of the oldest inhabitants, was left in ruins. Cimon also laid the foundation of a new temple of Athené on the south side of the hill. This temple was begun afresh and completed in the most splendid style by Pericles, and called the Parthenon (q. v.). Pericles at the same time adorned the approach to the west side of the Acropolis with the glorious Propylaea, and began to rebuild the Erechtheum in magnificent style. (See ERECHTHEUM; PROPYLAEA.) There were several other sanctuaries on the Acropolis—that, for instance, of Artemis Brauronia, on the southeastern side of the Propylaea; the beautiful little temple of Athené Niké, to the southwest; and the Pandroseum, adjoining the temple of Erechtheus. There were many altars—that of Zeus Hypatos, for example—and countless statues, among them that of Athené Promachos, with votive offerings. Among the numerous grottos in the rock, one on the north side was dedicated to Pan, another to Apollo. See ATHENAE; and Boetticher, *Die Akropolis von Athen*, w. 36 plates (Berlin, 1888).

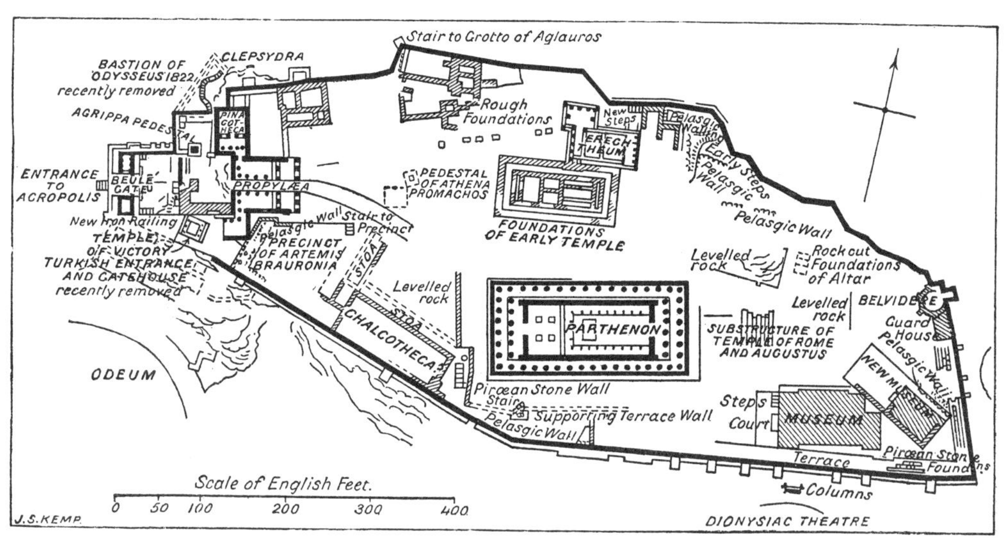

PLAN OF THE ACROPOLIS IN 1889, INCLUDING RESULTS OF THE EXCAVATIONS BEGUN IN 1885.
(Reduced from plan by Messrs. Penrose and Schultz, *Journal of Hellenic Studies*, 1889, pl. viii.)

Acrostĭcha (ἀκρόστιχα). Acrostics, which were popular alike with the Hebrews, Greeks, and Romans. With the Hebrews, in acrostic poetry, the initial letters of the lines or stanzas are made to run over the letters of the alphabet in their order. Twelve Psalms in the Old Testament are so written, the most remarkable being the 119th. One of the most celebrated acrostics in Greek is that contained in the words Ἰησοῦς Χριστὸς Θεοῦ Υἱὸς Σωτήρ, the initial letters of which spell ἰχθύς (fish), whence to the word ἰχθύς a mystical meaning was attached by the early Christians. The Romans borrowed acrostic poetry from the Greeks as early as the time of Ennius, who composed one (Cic. *de Div.* ii. 111). At a later period inscriptional acrostics occur, one of which calls the reader's attention to its character with the line *Inspice, lector, primordia versiculorum* (Wilmanns, 592, 593). The arguments to the Plautine plays are in acrostic lines. When the last letters of the lines spell words, the verse is called *telestic;* when letters in the middle of the lines do so, the verse is *mesostic.* Combinations of acrostic and telestic are found in the *Corp. Inscript. Lat.* v. 1693; of acrostic, mesostic, and telestic, in Flavius Felix (about A.D. 500). See Gerber, *Die Sprache als Kunst*, ii. pp. 262 foll., and the article ABECEDARII HYMNI.

Acroterium (ἀκρωτήριον). A word generally used in the plural, and signifying the extremity of anything. (1) In architecture it is the same as *fastigium* (q. v.), the sloping roof of a building, and also for the ornamental front or gable. A more usual meaning is the pedestals placed on the summit of a pediment to receive statues or other ornamental figures. There were three *acroteria*, one over each angle of the pediment. (2) The extremities of the prow of a vessel, which were usually taken from a conquered vessel as a mark of victory. Hence, the act of so doing is expressed by the verb ἀκρωτηριάζειν. (3) The extremities of a statue, such as the head, feet, hands, wings, etc.

Acrothinion (ἀκροθίνιον). Properly the top of a heap, and hence applied to those parts of the fruits of the earth or of the spoils of war that were offered to the gods.

Acrothōum. A town on the peninsula of Athos in Macedonia. The inhabitants were supposed to live beyond the usual age of man. See Mela, ii. 3.

Acta. (1) The public acts and orders of a Roman magistrate possessing the *ius agendi cum populo*, which, after the expiration of his office, were submitted to the Senate for approval or rejection (Suet. *Iul.* 19, 23). After the death of Iulius Caesar, the triumvirs swore, and compelled all the other magistrates to swear (Dio, xlvii. 48), to observe and maintain all his acta (*in acta iurare*), and hence it became the custom on the accession of each emperor for the new monarch to swear to observe and respect all the acta of his predecessors from Iulius Caesar downwards, with the exception of those who had been branded with infamy after death, such as Nero and Domitian (Tac. *Ann.* iv. 42; Dio, lvi. 33, etc.). The Senate also swore that it would recognize the validity of the acts of the new emperor. Every year all the magistrates upon entering office on the first of January swore approval of the acts of the reigning emperor (Dio, xlvii. 18; liii. 28; Tac. *Ann.* xvi. 22, with the excursus of Lipsius; Dio, lviii. 17; lx. 25).

(2) ACTA SENĀTUS, called also COMMENTARII SENĀTUS (Tac. *Ann.* xv. 74) and ACTA PATRUM (*Ann.* v. 4), containing an account of the various matters brought before the Senate, the opinions of the chief speakers, and the decision of the house. We may infer from a passage of Suetonius (*Iul.* 20.) that the proceedings of the Senate were not usually published till the first consulship of Iulius Caesar, B.C. 59; but under the direction of the presiding magistrate, assisted by certain senators appointed for the purpose, the decrees of the Senate had been written down and recorded in the Aerarium long previously, and the debates on the Catilinarian conspiracy had been widely circulated by Cicero (*Sull.* 14, 15) from notes taken by some friends of his among the senators. Iulius Caesar ordered that the proceedings of the Senate, which had been only occasionally published before, should henceforth be published regularly every day (*senatus acta diurna*) under the authority of the government, from the notes of shorthand writers (Sen. *Mort. Claud.* 9). Augustus forbade the publication of the proceedings of the Senate, but they still continued to be preserved; and one of the senators, who received the title *ab actis senatus*, was chosen by the emperor to compile the account (Tac. *Ann.* v. 4; Spart. *Hadr.* 3; Orelli, *Inscr.* No. 2274, 3186). This office was generally held as an annual one, after the quaestorship (Spart. *Hadr.* 3), but before the praetorship or aedileship. The persons intrusted with this office must not be confounded with the various clerks (*actuarii, servi publici, scribae;* also the *censuales*), who were present in the Senate to take notes of its proceedings, and who were only excluded when the Senate passed a *senatus-consultum tacitum;* that is, when they deliberated on a subject of the greatest importance, respecting which secrecy was necessary or advisable (Capit. *Gord.* 12). It was doubtless from notes and papers of these clerks that the acta were compiled by the senator, who was intrusted with this office. The acta were deposited in the imperial archives (*tabularium*) or in particular departments of the public libraries, to which access could only be obtained by the express permission of the *praefectus urbi.* They were consulted and are frequently referred to by the later historians (e. g. Vopisc. *Prob.* 2; Lamprid. *Sever.* 56; Capitol. *Opil. Macr.* 6), and many extracts from them were published in the Acta Diurna.

(3) ACTA DIURNA. A gazette published daily at Rome by the authority of the government during the later times of the Republic, and under the Empire, corresponding in some measure to our newspapers (Tac. *Ann.* iii. 3; xiii. 31; xvi. 22). In addition to the title *Acta Diurna,* we find them referred to under the names *Diurna, Acta Publica, Acta Urbana, Acta Rerum Urbanarum, Acta Populi,* and they are frequently called simply *Acta.* The Greek writers on Roman history call them *τὰ ὑπομνήματα, τὰ δημόσια ὑπομνήματα, τὰ δημόσια γράμματα,* and *τὰ κοινὰ ὑπομνήματα.* The nature of their contents will be best seen from the following passage of Petronius (cap. 53), where an imitation of them is given by the *actuarius* of Trimalchio: "Actuarius — tanquam acta urbis recitavit: vii. Kal. Sextiles in praedio Cumano, quod est Trimalchionis, nati sunt pueri XXX, puellae XL; sublata in horreum ex area tritici millia modium quingenta; boves domiti quingenti. Eodem die Mithridates servus in crucem actus est, quia Gai nostri genio maledixerat. Eodem die in arcam relatum est, quod collocari non potuit, sestertium centies. Eodem die incendium factum est in hortis Pompeianis, ortum ex aedibus Nastae villici. . . . Iam etiam edicta aedilium recitabantur, et saltuariorum testamenta, quibus Trimalchio cum elogio exheredabatur; iam nomina villicorum et repudiata a circitore liberta in balneatoris contubernio deprehensa; atriensis Baias relegatus; iam reus factus dispensator; et iudicium inter cubicularios actum." From this passage, and from the numerous passages in ancient writers in which the Acta Diurna are quoted (references to which are given by Hübner), it would appear that they usually contained the following matters: (1) The number of births and deaths in the city, an account of the money paid into the treasury from the provinces, and everything relating to the supply of corn. These particulars would be extracted from the *tabulae publicae.* By an ancient regulation, ascribed to Servius Tullius, all births were registered in the Temple of Venus, and all deaths in that of Libitina; and we know that this practice was continued under the Empire, only that at a later time the Temple of Saturn was substituted for that of Venus for the registration of births. (2) Extracts from the Acta Forensia, containing the edicts of magistrates, the testaments of distinguished men, reports of trials, with the names of those who were acquitted and condemned, and likewise a list of the magistrates who were elected. (3) Extracts from the Acta Senatus, especially all the decrees and acclamations (see ACCLAMATIO) in honour of the reigning emperor. (4) A court circular, containing an account of the births, deaths, festivals, and movements of the imperial family. (5) Curious and interesting occurrences, such as prodigies and miracles, the erection of new edifices, the conflagration of buildings, funerals, sacrifices, a list of the various games, and especially amatory tales

and adventures, with the names of the parties. (Cf. Cic. *Ad Fam.* ii. 15.) News of private affairs seems to have been communicated to the official editor by way of advertisement. (Cf. Quint. ix. 3, 17, where a widower speaks of himself as *saucius pectus.*) The fragments of some Acta Diurna have been published by Pighius and Dodwell, but their genuineness is more than doubtful. (Cf. Heinze, *De Spuriis Diurnorum Act. Fragmentis*, Greifswald, 1860.)

It is certain that these acta were published under the authority of the government, but it is not stated under whose superintendence they were drawn up. It is probable, however, that this duty devolved upon the magistrates, who had the care of the *tabulae publicae*, namely, the censors under the Republic (Liv. iv. 8; xliii. 16), and sometimes the quaestors, sometimes the *praefecti aerarii* under the Empire (Tac. *Ann.* xiii. 28). The actual task of compiling them was committed to subordinate officers, called *actuarii* or *actarii*, who were assisted by various clerks, and by reporters (*notarii*), who took down in shorthand the proceedings in the courts, etc. After the acta had been drawn up, they were exposed for a time in some public place in the city *in albo*, where persons could read them and take copies of them. Many scribes, whom Cicero speaks of under the name of *operarii*, made it their business to copy them or make extracts from them for the use of the wealthy in Rome, and especially in the provinces, where they were eagerly sought after and extensively read (Cic. *Ad Fam.* viii. 1; xiii. 8; Tac. *Ann.* xvi. 22). After the acta had been exposed in public for a certain time, they were deposited, like the Acta Senatus, in some of the record offices or the public libraries.

The style of the acta, as appears from the passage in Petronius, was very simple and concise. They contained a bare enumeration of facts, without any attempt at ornament.

Hübner has proved against Becker (*Handbuch*, i. pp. 30 and 32) that these acta were first published in the first consulship of Iulius Caesar. Previous to this time it was common for a MS. chronicle of public events at Rome to be compiled by scribes, and forwarded along with private letters to friends at a distance (Cic. *Ad Fam.* viii. 1, 2, 8, 11; ii. 8; xii. 22; xv. 6. Cf. Hübner, p. 39; Mommsen, *Hist.* iv. 606).

The Acta Diurna are last mentioned by Vopiscus (*Prob.* cap. 2), and probably continued in use to the downfall of the Western Empire. They were never published in Constantinople.

(4) Acta Forensia. These were of two kinds. (*a*) The Romans kept their private accounts with so much accuracy that their books (*accepti et expensi*), bonds (*chirographa*), and contracts (*syngrapha*) were admitted as legal evidence. Frequently witnesses (*pararii*, Sen. *Ben.* ii. 23, § 2) were employed to establish their authenticity. At a later date notaries (*tabelliones*) who had offices (*stationes*) in the public streets drew up these documents, which were ratified by the signature (*subscriptio*) of the parties. A senatus consultum passed under Nero (Suet. *Ner.* 17; Quint. xii. 8, 13; Paul. *Sent. Recept.* v. 25, 6) prescribed the legal form of such documents. See Codex Accepti et Expensi.

(*b*) *Acta iudiciorum* contained the record of all proceedings of the magistrates, alike in contentious and in non-contentious business. The latter included such matters as adoptions, *cessio in iure*, manumissions, the appointment of guardians, and the like. Such magisterial functions could be discharged anywhere, even in the baths or in the streets (*Instit. Iust.* i. 5, 2). Under the Republic there is no evidence of the method of legal attestation in these cases; but under the Empire it was customary for the parties to have a formal statement drawn up by a public official (*acta* or *gesta*), and confirmed by the magistrate (*Instit. Iust.* i. 11, 2, and 12, 8). In the case of contentious business, so long as the *legis actiones* were in use, there was no need of a written record, for the *litis contestatio* was attested by witnesses. On the other hand, when *formulae* came into use, these were necessarily in writing, though the decision of the *iudex* was given *viva voce*. There was a special form of action (*iudicati actio*) against a defendant who denied the existence of a decision given against him. There is evidence of the existence of a record (*acta, Fragm. Vat. Iur.* 112) under the Empire. The *cognitiones extraordinariae* increased the importance of this. But the existence of a written decision was not compulsory before the constitutions of Valentinian, Valens, and Gratian.

(5) Acta Militaria contained an account of the duties, numbers, and expenses of each legion (Veg. ii. 19), and of the amount of property possessed by each soldier (*peculium castrense*). They were probably preserved among the official papers of the several legions. The soldiers who drew up these acta are frequently mentioned in inscriptions and ancient writers under various titles, as *librarius legionis, actuarius* or *actarius legionis, tabularius castrensis.* (Cf. Renier, *Inscriptions Romaines de l'Algérie*, 343, 551, 799.)

See Lipsius, *Excursus ad* Tac. *Ann.* v. 4; Ernesti, *Excursus ad* Suet. *I. Caes.* 20; Schlosser, *Ueber die Quellen der spätern latein. Geschichtschreiber, besonders über Zeitungen*, etc., in the *Archiv für Geschichte*, 1830, pp. 80–106; Prutz, *De Fontibus, quos in conscribendis rebus inde a Tiberio usque ad mortem Neronis gestis auctores veteres secuti videantur* (Halle, 1840); Zell, *Ueber die Zeitungen der Alten* (Freiburg, 1834); Le Clerc, *Des Journaux chez les Romains* (Paris, 1838); Lieberkühn, *De Diurnis Romanorum Actis* (Weimar, 1840); especially Hübner, *De Senatus Populique Romani Actis* (Lips. 1860); Schmidt, *Zeitschr. für Geschichtswissenschaft*, I. (1844), 303; Renssen, *De Diurnis Aliisque Rom. Actis* (1857); and the article in the Pauly-Wissowa *Realencyclopädie.*

Actaeon (Ἀκταίων). A celebrated hunter, son of Aristaeus and Autonoë. Having on one occasion unwittingly seen Artemis while she was bathing, he was changed by the offended goddess into a stag, and was torn in pieces by his own dogs.

Actaeon. (British Museum.)

Actaeus. The first king of Attica. The poets use the word *Actaeus* as an adjective, in the sense of "Attic."

Acté. (1) An ancient name of Attica, found chiefly in the poets. (2) The peninsula between the Strymonic and Singitic gulfs, on which Mt. Athos is situated. The name (ἀκτή) signifies properly any strip of land projecting into the sea.

Acté. The favourite concubine of the Roman emperor Nero. She was originally a slave from Asia Minor, but after Nero became infatuated with her he pretended that she was the descendant of King Attalus, and at one time even thought of marrying her (Suet. *Nero*, 28, 50).

Actia (Ἄκτια). A festival celebrated every three years at Actium in Epirus, with wrestling, horse-racing, and sea-fights, in honour of Apollo. There was a celebrated temple of Apollo at Actium, which

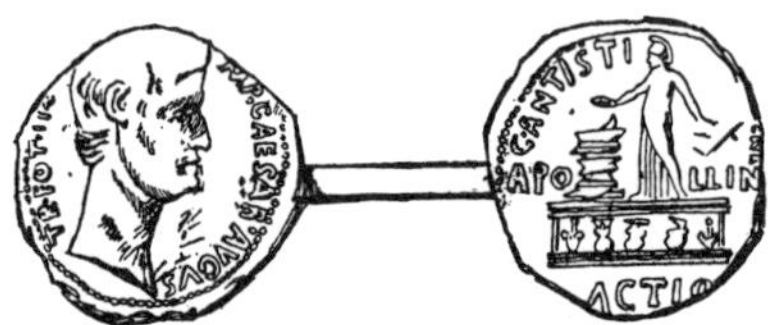

Coin with Worship of the Actian Apollo. (Cabinet de France.)

is mentioned by Thucydides and Strabo. After the defeat of Antony off Actium, Augustus enlarged the temple, and instituted games to be celebrated every four years in commemoration of his victory. See ACTIUM.

Actiăcus. A name given to Apollo as worshipped at Actium (Ovid, *Met.* xiii. 715). See ACTIA.

Actio. See article in Appendix; and JUDICIAL PROCEDURE. For Greek actions, see DIKÉ.

Actis (Ἀκτίς). One of the Heliades (q. v.), or daughters of the Sun.

Actisănes (Ἀκτισάνης). A king of Aethiopia, who conquered Egypt. He was remarkable for his moderation towards his new subjects, as well as for his justice and equity. All the robbers and malefactors, too, were collected from every part of the kingdom, and, having had their noses cut off, were established in Rhinocolura, a city which he had founded for the purpose of receiving them. See Diod. Sic. i. 60.

Actium (now La Punta). A promontory in Acarnania at the mouth of the Ambracian Gulf, off which Augustus gained his celebrated naval victory over Antony and Cleopatra, September 2d, B.C. 31. Here was a temple of Apollo Actiacus or Actius, where the festival Actia had been celebrated. Augustus revived the celebration as a quinquennial feast in honour of his victory, and built Nicopolis (q. v.) on the opposite shore.

The battle of Actium is one of the decisive battles of the world's history, since the stake for which it was fought was nothing less than the lordship of the Roman Empire—that is, of the occidental world. The chances of battle were all in favour of Antony. His troops, encamped on one shore of the gulf, were largely superior to his rival's in both numbers and discipline. He had 100,000 infantry, as against the 80,000 of Octavian (Augustus), an equal force of cavalry (12,000); while his ships not only numbered 500—double the number that Octavian's admiral Agrippa commanded, but were much larger, heavier, and better provided with the engines then in use for discharging missiles. It was, perhaps, this great preponderance of naval force which led Cleopatra, who accompanied Antony, to urge upon him the plan of letting the issue of the war rest upon a naval battle. She herself, with her sixty ships, formed a line behind that of the vessels of Antony.

Marcus Vipsanius Agrippa.

For a long time after the battle began, the light galleys of Octavian made little or no impression upon the massive ships that opposed them; but at last, by a skilful manœuvre, Agrippa forced Antony to extend his line of battle. This done, Agrippa's ships succeeded in breaking through it and darting towards the vessels of Cleopatra. Alarmed at this, the Egyptian queen at once gave the signal for flight, and with her ships put hurriedly to sea. Antony, forgetful that the crisis of the battle had now arrived, recklessly sailed in pursuit of her, leaving his fleet to win or lose as best it might in his absence. Deserted by its commander, it still fought on, but with little heart,

Coin of Antony and Cleopatra.

and by nightfall had been completely routed and destroyed. The troops of Antony were still encamped upon the promontory fronting the forces of Octavian; yet they did not at once give battle, but waited in the hope that their general would return. Seven days passed by, and when he failed to appear, after some hesitation, they surrendered to Octavian and accepted him as their commander, thus making him at a stroke the master of the world.

Actius, LUCIUS. See ATTIUS, LUCIUS.

Actor (Ἄκτωρ). (1) Son of Diomedes, father of Menoetius, and grandfather of Patroclus. (2) A companion of Aeneas, of whose conquered lance Turnus made a boast. This story seems to have given rise to the proverb *Actoris spolium* for any poor spoil (Juv. ii. 100).

Actor. In general, a plaintiff. In a civil or private action, the plaintiff was often called *petitor;* in a public action (*causa publica*) he was called *accusator.* The defendant was called *reus,* both in private and public causes: this term, however, according to Cicero, might signify either party, as indeed we might conclude from the word itself. In a private action the defendant was often called *adversarius,* but either party might be called *adversarius* with respect to the other. (See ACTIO.) A *universitas,* or corporate body, sued and was sued by its *actor* or *syndicus.*

Actor has also the sense of an agent or manager of another's business generally. The *actor publicus* was an officer who had the superintendence or care of slaves and property belonging to the State.

Actor on the stage. See HISTRIO.

Actorĭdes. Patroclus (q. v.). See also MOLIONIDAE.

Actuarii. Shorthand-writers, who took down the speeches in the Senate and the public assemblies. In the debate in the Roman Senate upon the punishment of those who had been concerned in the conspiracy of Catiline, we find the first mention of shorthand-writers, who were employed by Cicero to take down the speech of Cato. See ACTA; NOTAE.

Actuarii Militiae. Officers under the Roman emperors, whose duty it was to keep the accounts of the army, to see that the contractors supplied the soldiers with provisions according to agreement, and to perform other similar duties.

Actus. A Roman measure of length. It formed the basis of the whole system of land measurement. The *actus simplex* or *minimus* was 120 (Roman) feet long and four feet wide. The *actus quadratus* was a square of 120 feet each way = 14,400 square feet (Pliny, *H. N.* xviii. § 9). The actus is an example of the combination of the decimal with the duodecimal system, its length being twelve times the standard *decempeda* (q. v.). The actus was half the *iugerum.* In Hispania Baetica, the *actus quadratus* was called *acna* (also written *agna,* and *agnua*). Cf. Varro, *R. R.* i. 10, § 2.

Acus, dim. **Acicŭla** (βελόνη, βελονίς, ῥαφίς). A needle, a pin.

We may translate acus *a needle,* when we suppose it to have had at one end a hole or eye for the passage of thread; and *a pin,* when, instead of a hole, we suppose it to have had a knob, a small globe, or any other enlarged or ornamental termination (cf. Pollux, vii. 42; x. 136).

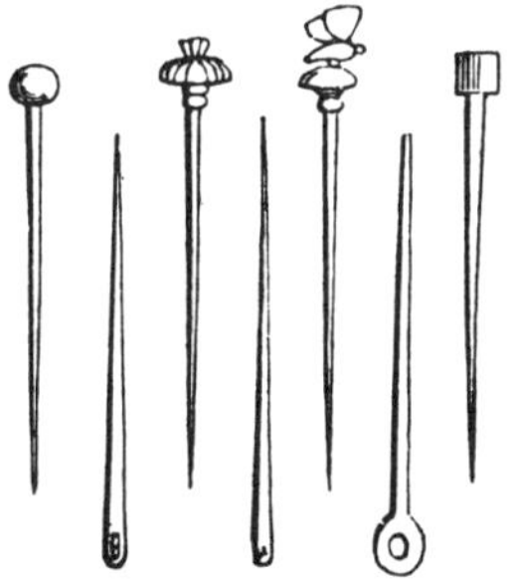

Needles and Pins.

The annexed figures of needles and pins, chiefly taken from originals in bronze, vary in length from an inch and a half to about eight inches.

Pins were made not only of metal, but also of wood, bone, and ivory. Their principal use was to assist in fastening the garments, and more particularly in dressing the hair. The mode of plaiting the hair, and then fastening it with a pin or needle, is shown in the annexed figure of a female head, taken from a marble group which was found at Apt, in the south of France.

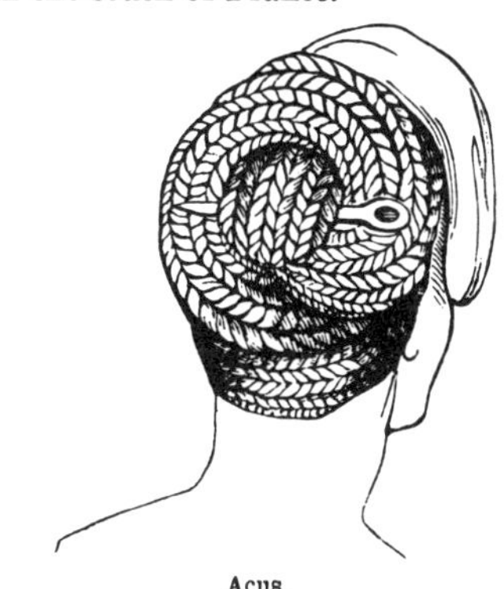

Acus.

The hair-pin was called *acus crinalis* or *acus comatoria* (Petron. 21).

Adămas (ἀδάμας). A name given by the ancients to several hard substances, and among the rest possibly to the diamond. Psellus describes *adamas* as follows: "Its color resembles crystal, and is splendid," which certainly seems appropriate to the diamond. But Pliny (*H. N.* xxxvii. 15), in his account of *adamas,* has evidently confounded the properties of several different minerals, all of which, by their hardness, received from the Greeks the name ἀδάμας. Thus Hesychius applies the name to steel; Pollux to grains of native gold; and Dionysius Periegetes to what was probably fine crystals of quartz. In fact, the ancients knew diamonds, if at all, only in their unpolished state, by which such epithets as "all-resplendent" would scarcely have been suggested. See GEMMA.

Addicti. See NEXI.

Addictio. A legal term meaning the formal award by the praetor or other magistrate of the property in dispute. See Cic. *Verr.* i. 4, 12.

Addix or **Addixis** (ἄδδιξ, ἄδδιξις). A Greek measure, which Hesychius gives as equal to four choenices. See CHOENIX.

Addua. The Adda, a river of Gallia Cisalpina.

Adeia (ἄδεια). When any one in Athens who had not the full privileges of an Athenian citizen, such as a foreigner, a slave, etc., wished to accuse a person of any offence against the people, he was obliged to obtain first permission to do so, which permission was called ἄδεια. An Athenian citizen who had incurred ἀτιμία was also obliged to obtain ἄδεια before he could lay an information against any one. See ATIMIA.

Adelphoe. A play of Terence modelled on the Συναποθνήσκοντες of Diphilus and the Ἀδελφοί of Menander. See TERENTIUS.

Ademptio. See LEGATUM.

Adgnāti. See COGNATIO.

Adgnatio. See HERES; TESTAMENTUM.

Adherbal. See IUGURTHA.

Adiabēnē. A district of Assyria, east of the Tigris, and comprising the more fertile portion of the country. See ASSYRIA.

Aditio Hereditātis. See HERES.

Adiudicatio. See ACTIO.

Adlecti or **Allecti.** (1) Those chosen to fill a vacancy in an office or collegium, and referring oftenest to those chosen to fill up the proper number of the Senate. Under the Empire, the *adlecti*, admitted to the Senate by the emperor, were admitted to a place among the senators who had held the rank of consul, praetor, tribune, or quaestor, according to the emperor's pleasure. These were known as *adlecti inter consulares, praetorios*, etc. (2) Persons admitted to a seat in the council of a *municipium* or *colonia* by a vote of that body were also known as *adlecti*.

Adlector. A provincial tax-collector under the Roman emperors (Orelli, 369).

Adlocutio or **Allocutio.** A speech or address made to his soldiers by an imperator, and corresponding to the modern "general order" or proclamation. See CONTIO.

Admētus (Ἄδμητος). (1) King of Pherae, who sued for Alcestis, the daughter of Pelias. Pelias promised her on condition that he should come in a chariot drawn by lions and boars. This task Admetus performed by the assistance of Apollo. The god tended the flocks of Admetus for nine years, when he was obliged to serve a mortal for having slain the Cyclops. Apollo prevailed upon the Moerae, or Fates, to grant to Admetus deliverance from death if his father, mother, or wife would die for him. Alcestis died in his stead, but was brought back by Heracles from the lower world. See EURIPIDES. (2) King of the Molossians, to whom Themistocles fled for protection when pursued as a party to the treason of Pausanias. See THEMISTOCLES.

Admissio. Reception or audience at the Roman court. At first all visitors were admitted without distinction to the *atria* of their wealthy friends. According to Seneca, C. Gracchus and Livius Drusus were the first to receive some privately and others in a limited number, doubtless for political reasons. Afterwards these distinctions became the rule, and it was the exception for any one to open his doors to all comers. Under the Empire, friends were distinguished as *amici admissionis primae, secundae*, etc. The first alone could enter without delay, and could pay a separate visit. The rest had to await, and sometimes to purchase, the favour of the porter. At the imperial court there was a body of slaves and freedmen acting as the introducers of visitors (*officium admissionis*, Suet. *Vesp.* 14), who were known as *admissionales*. The head of the *officium admissionis* was the *magister admissionum*, subordinate himself to the *magister officiorum*. The *magister admissionum* himself introduced the most exalted visitors; and, at least in the time of Justinian, none were introduced by the *admissionales* but such as were *illustres*.

Admissionāles. See ADMISSIO.

Adonia (Ἀδώνια). A festival celebrated in honour of Adonis (q. v.), and introduced into Greece from the East probably at the time of the wars with Persia. In general the ceremonies lasted two days, the first being the day on which Adonis disappeared (ἀφανισμός), and the second that on which his body was sought (ζήτησις) by the women. The first was a day of mourning, and the second, one of rejoicing and amusement, because on it Adonis was conceived of as returning to life to spend six months with Aphroditê.

Adōnis (Ἄδωνις). (1) A beautiful youth, son of Cinyras, by his daughter Smyrna (q. v.). He was beloved by Aphroditê, but died of a wound which he

Death of Adonis. (Pompeii.)

received from a boar during the chase. The flower anemone sprang from his blood. The grief of the goddess at his death was so great that the gods of the lower world allowed him to spend six months with her on earth, and the remaining six in the shades. (2) A river of Phœnicia, which falls into the Mediterranean below Byblus. Its waters were fabled to flow with blood on the anniversary of the death of Adonis.

Adoptio. (1) At ATHENS adoption (εἰσποίησις or θέσις) took place either in the adopter's lifetime or by will; or again, if a man died childless and intestate, the state interfered to bring into his house the man next entitled by the Attic law of inheritance as heir and adoptive son, so that the race and the religious rites peculiar to it might not die out. None but the independent citizen of respectable character could adopt, and he only while he was as yet without male heirs. If there were daughters, one of them was usually betrothed to the adopted son, and the rest portioned off with dowries. If after that a male heir was born, he and the adopted had equal rights.

(2) At ROME there were two kinds of adoption, both requiring the adopter to be a male and childless: *arrogatio* and adoption proper. The former could only take place where the person to be adopted was independent (*sui iuris*), and his adopter had no prospect of male offspring; at the instance of the pontifex, and after full proof of admissibility, it had to be sanctioned by the Comitia Curiata. (See COMITIA.) Adoption proper applied to those still under paternal rule (*patria potestas*), the father selling his son by formal *mancipatio* (q. v). to the adopter, who then, the paternal power being thus abolished, claimed the son before the court as his own, and the father allowed him to be adjudged to him. By either transaction the person adopted passed completely over into the family and rank of the adopter, and naturally took his

name in full, but with the addition of a second cognomen formed from his own former *nomen gentile* by the suffix *-anus*, e. g. Publius Cornelius Scipio Aemilianus (son of Lucius Aemilius Paulus). Women, too, could be adopted, but not arrogated; neither could they adopt. At the latter end of the Republic we find a testamentary adoption in existence, which at first likewise produced a change of name, but not of status. See NOMEN.

Adoratio (προσκυνησις). (1) A form of worshipping the gods, according to which the worshipper prostrated himself before the statue of the deity, and then kissed his hand and waved it towards the image. While so doing, he moved his whole body around, usually from left to right. Hence, *se convertere* is sometimes used for *adorare* (Livy, v. 21). (2) The *adoratio* paid to the Roman emperors was a form of salutation borrowed from the East, and consisted of prostration on the ground and kissing the feet, knees, or dress of the emperor. Livy speaks of this as *adulatio*. It was not a part of the ordinary etiquette of the court before the time of Diocletian.

Adramyttĭum (Ἀδραμύττειον). A small town of Mysia opposite the island of Lesbos, which suffered severely in the war of the Romans with Mithridates. It is mentioned in the New Test. (Acts, xxvii. 2).

Adrăna. The Eder, a river of Germany flowing into the Fulda near Cassel.

Adrastus (Ἄδραστος). (1) Son of Talaüs of Argos. Being expelled from Argos by Amphiaraüs, he fled to Polybus, king of Sicyon, whom he succeeded on the throne of Sicyon, and instituted the Nemean games. Afterwards he became reconciled to Amphiaraüs, and returned to his kingdom of Argos. He married his two daughters Deïpylé and Argia, the former to Tydeus of Calydon, and the latter to Polynices of Thebes, both fugitives from their native countries. He then prepared to restore Polynices to Thebes, who had been expelled by his brother Eteocles, although Amphiaraüs (q. v.) foretold that all who should engage in the war would perish, with the exception of Adrastus. Thus arose the celebrated war of the "Seven against Thebes," in which Adrastus was joined by six other heroes, viz., Polynices, Tydeus, Amphiaraüs, Capaneus, Hippomedon, and Parthenopaeus. This war ended as unfortunately as Amphiaraüs had predicted, and Adrastus alone was saved by the swiftness of his horse Arion, the gift of Heracles. Ten years afterwards, Adrastus persuaded the six sons of the heroes who had fallen in the war to make a new attack upon Thebes, and Amphiaraüs now promised success. This war is known as the war of the Epigoni (ἐπίγονοι), or descendants. Thebes was taken and razed to the ground. The only Argive hero that fell in this war was Aegialeus, the son of Adrastus: the latter died of grief at Megara on his return to Argos, and was buried in the former city. The legends about Adrastus and the two wars against Thebes furnished ample materials for the epic as well as tragic poets of Greece. (2) Son of the Phrygian king Gordius, having unintentionally killed his brother, fled to Croesus, who received him kindly. While hunting, he accidentally killed Atys, the son of Croesus, and in despair put an end to his own life.

Adria. See HADRIA; MARE SUPERUM.

Adrianopŏlis. See HADRIANOPOLIS.

Adriānus. See HADRIANUS.

Adrogatio or **Arrogatio.** See ADOPTIO.

Adrumētum. See HADRUMETUM.

Adscriptīvi. See ACCENSI (2).

Adsertor. See ASSERTOR.

Adsessor. See ASSESSOR.

Adsignatio or **Assignatio.** See AGER; AGRARIAE LEGES.

Adstipulatio. See OBLIGATIO.

Adstipulātor. See INTERCESSIO.

Aduatŭca or **Aduatŭcum.** A city of Gaul in the territory of the Tungri. See Caes. *B. G.* ii. 29.

Aduatŭci. A people of Gallia Belgica, dwelling between the Scaldis (Scheldt) and the Mosa (Maas).

Adūla Mons. See ALPES.

Adulatio. See ADORATIO.

Adulescens. See INFANS.

Adūlis or **Adūlé** (Ἀδούλη). A city of Aethiopia, on a bay of the Red Sea called Adulitanus Sinus. It fell into the power of the Auxumitae, for whose trade it became the great emporium. Here was found the *Monumentum Adulitanum* (q. v.), a Greek inscription recounting the conquests of Ptolemy Euergetes I. in Asia and Thrace.

Adulterium (μοιχεία). Adultery. (1) GREEK. Among the Athenians, if a man caught another in the act of criminal intercourse with his wife, he might kill him, and the same law held with respect to a concubine (παλλακή). Other punishment was likewise permitted. It appears that at Athens there was no adultery unless a married woman was concerned, and even then there was no adultery if the married woman was a prostitute or one engaged in selling anything in the agora. If the husband chose to bring suit against the adulterer, it was called μοιχείας γραφή. If the adultery was proven, the husband could not condone the offence under penalty of ἀτιμία. (See ATIMIA.) The adulteress was excluded from the temple, and if found there any one might treat her as he pleased, provided he did not kill or mutilate her. (2) ROMAN. The general usages at Rome appear to have been very similar to the Athenian. The Lex Iulia de Adulteriis, passed under Augustus, about B.C. 17, enacted them. By this law, if a husband kept his wife after an act of adultery was known to him, and let the adulterer off, he was guilty of the offence of *lenocinium*. The husband or father in whose power the adulteress was, had sixty days allowed for commencing proceedings against the wife, after which time any other person might prosecute. A woman convicted of adultery was mulcted in half of her dowry and the third part of her property (*bona*), and banished (*relegata*) to some desolate island, such as Seriphos, for instance. The adulterer was mulcted in half his property, and banished in like manner. This law did not inflict the punishment of death on either party; and in those instances under the emperors in which death was inflicted, it must be considered as an extraordinary punishment, and beyond the provisions of the Julian law.

The Julian law permitted the father (both adoptive and natural) to kill the adulterer and adulteress in certain cases, as to which there were several nice distinctions established by the law. If the father killed only one of the parties, he brought himself within the penalties of the Cornelian law *de sicariis*. The husband might kill persons of a certain class, described in the law, whom he caught in the act of adultery with his wife; but he could not kill his wife. The husband, by the fifth chapter of the Julian law, could detain for twenty hours the adulterer whom he had caught in the act, for the purpose of calling in witnesses to prove the adultery. If the wife was divorced for adultery, the husband was entitled to retain part of the dowry. The husband might, if he pleased, take a sum of money from the adulterer by way of compensation, and detain him till he found sureties for the payment. If the alleged adulterer had been unjustly detained, he might bring an action against the husband; and if he gained his cause, he and his sureties were released. If he failed, the law required the sureties to deliver up the adulterer to the husband before the court, to do what he pleased with him, except that he was not to use a knife or dagger. See Rein, *Das Criminalrecht der Römer*.

Adultus. See INFANS.

Adventus. The arrival of an emperor in one of the provinces, an event often commemorated on Roman bronze coins.

Adversaria. A note-book in which the Romans entered memoranda of any importance, especially their accounts of money received and spent (*codex accepti et expensi*), which they afterwards transferred to a ledger. See ACTA.

Adversarius. See ACTOR.

Advocātus. At Rome, under the Republic, a competent friend who gave his advice in a lawsuit and came into court in person, not to speak (the *patronus causae* did that), but to support the cause by his presence. Under the Empire the term was applied to the counsel who pleaded in court in the presence of the parties, for doing which he was allowed, after the time of Claudius, to take a fee. See JUDICIAL PROCEDURE; PATRONUS.

Advocātus Fisci. A Roman official, first appointed by Hadrian, to look after the interests of the imperial treasury. See FISCUS.

Adynăti (ἀδύνατοι). Persons supported by the Athenian State as being unable to earn a livelihood, owing to physical infirmity. Pisistratus first introduced a law for the support of those persons who had been maimed in battle. (See Lysias ὑπὲρ τοῦ ἀδυνάτου.)

Adȳtum. See TEMPLUM.

Aea (Αἶα). A city supposed by the poets to have been the capital of King Aeëtes, on the river Phasis, in Colchis.

Aeacēa (Αἰάκεια). A festival of the Aeginetans in honor of Aeacus (q. v.), the details of which are unknown.

Aeăces. A tyrant of Samos, deposed by Aristagoras, B.C. 500, and restored by the Persians, to whom he had fled, in B.C. 494. See Herod. iv. 138.

Aeacĭdes. A patronymic used of any descendant of Aeacus (q. v.), such as Peleus, Telamon, Phocus, Achilles (q. v.), Pyrrhus, son of Achilles, and Pyrrhus, King of Epirus, who claimed descent from Achilles. See PYRRHUS.

Aeăcus (Αἴακος). Son of Zeus and Aegina, a daughter of the river-god Asopus, born in the island of Aegina, which derived its name from his mother. (See AEGINA.) Some traditions relate that at the birth of Aeacus, Aegina was not yet inhabited, and that Zeus changed the ants of the island into men (Myrmidones), over whom Aeacus ruled. Aeacus was renowned in all Greece for his justice and piety, and after his death became one of the three judges in Hades, the others being Minos and Rhadamanthus. See HADES.

Aeaea (Αἰαίη). (1) Another name for Circé (q. v.), derived from the name of her birthplace, Αἶα. Her son, Telegonus, the reputed founder of Tusculum, is called Aeaeus. (2) A name given to Calypso (q. v.), who was said to live in the island of Aeaea between Italy and Sicily.

Aeantēa (Αἰάντεια). A festival solemnized at Salamis in honour of Aiax, of which no particulars are known.

Aeantēum. A settlement on the coast of Troas near the promontory of Rhoeteum, and famous for the tomb of Aiax and a temple to his memory. The statue of the hero was carried away by Antony and restored by Augustus.

Aeas. A river of Epirus falling into the Ionian Sea.

Aebutia Lex. See LEX.

Aeculānum. A town of the Hirpini in Samnium, just south of Beneventum.

Aedepsus. A town of Euboea, famous for its hot baths in ancient as in modern times.

Aedes. See DOMUS; TEMPLUM.

Aedesius (Αἰδέσιος). A Cappadocian, a Platonic, or more correctly an Eclectic, philosopher, who lived in the fourth century A.D., and was the friend and most distinguished scholar of Iamblichus (q. v.). After the death of his master, the school of Syria was dispersed, and Aedesius, fearing the real or fancied hostility of the Christian emperor Constantine to philosophy, took refuge in divination. An oracle in hexameter verse represented a pastoral life as his only retreat; but his disciples, perhaps calming his fears by a metaphorical interpretation, compelled him to resume his instructions. He settled at Pergamos, where he numbered among his pupils the Emperor Julian. After the accession of the latter to the imperial purple, he invited Aedesius to continue his instructions, but the philosopher, being unequal to the task through age, sent in his stead Chrysanthes and Eusebius, his disciples. See his life by Eunapius.

Aedes Vitiōsae or **Ruinōsae.** See DAMNUM INFECTUM.

Aedicŭla. (1) In the singular, a single room. (2) In the plural, a small house. (3) Oftener a shrine, either attached or unattached to a temple. (4) A niche in the walls of temples or houses containing images of gods or goddesses, like that in the accompanying illustration (Overbeck, *Bildwerke*, pl. xxx. 1).

Aedicula, or Shrine.

Aedīles. At Rome, two sets of magistrates, the Plebeian (*aediles plebis* or *plebeii*) and the Curule (*aediles curules*). (1) The two PLEBEIAN AEDILES were appointed B.C. 494 at the same time with the creation of the tribuneship of the plebs, as servants of the tribunes, and at first probably nominated by them till 471, when, like them and under their presidency, they began to be elected by the whole body of the plebs. They took their name from the temple (*aedes*) of the plebeian goddess Ceres, in which their official archives were kept. Besides the custody of the *plebiscita*, and afterwards of the *senatus consulta*, it was their duty to make arrests at the bidding of the tribunes; to carry out the death-sentences which they passed, by hurling the criminal down from the Tarpeian Rock; to look after the importation of corn; to watch the traffic in the markets; and to organize and superintend the Plebeian and Roman Games. Like the tribunes, they could only be chosen from the body of the plebs, and wore no badge of office, not so much as the *toga praetexta*, even after they became an authority independent of the tribunes. (2) The CURULE AEDILES, from B.C. 366, were taken at first from the patrician body alone, soon after from patricians and plebeians by turns, and lastly from either. Elected yearly in the Comitia Tributa under the presidency of a consul, they were, from the first, officers of the whole people, though low in rank; they sat in the *sella curulis*, from which they took their name, and wore as insignia the *toga praetexta*. As in rank, so in the extent of their powers, they stood above the plebeian aediles, being entitled to exercise civil jurisdiction in market business, where the latter could only impose a fine. The functions of the two were very much alike, comprising: (*a*) the superintendence of trade in the market, where they had to test weights and measures and the quality of goods; to keep down the price of provisions, both by prohibitive measures especially against regraters of corn, and by the purchase and liberal distribution of food (*cura annonae*); and, as regards the money market, to prosecute those who transgressed the laws of usury; (*b*) the care of the streets and buildings within the city and the circuit of a mile outside, by cleansing, paving, and improving the streets, or stirring up those who were bound to do it; by seeing that the street traffic was unimpeded; by keeping in repair the temples, public buildings, and works, such as sewers and aqueducts, and seeing that these latter and the fire apparatus were in working order; (*c*) a superintendence of health and morals, including the inspection of baths, taverns, and brothels, and the putting-down of all that endangered public order and decency, e. g. games of hazard, breaches of sumptuary laws, introduction of foreign religions, etc.; (*d*) the exhibition of games (of which the Roman and Megalensian devolved on the curule, the Plebeian on the plebeian aediles), the supervision of festivities at the *feriae Latinae*, and at games given by private men. The cost of the games given by themselves they defrayed partly out of a sum set apart by the State, but utterly inadequate to the large demands of later times; partly out of the proceeds of fines which were also spent on public buildings, and partly out of their own resources. Thus the aedileship became an expensive luxury, and its enjoyment less and less accessible to men of moderate means. Ambitious men often spent incredible sums in getting up games to win the people's favour, with a view to higher honours, though the aedileship was not necessary as a stepping-stone to these. In Cicero's time the legal age for the curule aedileship was thirty-seven. From B.C. 366 their number was unchanged, till Caesar, in B.C. 44, added two more, the plebeian *aediles cereales*, to whom alone the *cura annonae* and the management of the Ludi Cereales were intrusted. Under the Empire the office of aedile lost much in importance by some of its functions being handed over to separate officers, especially by the transference of its jurisdiction and its control of games to the praetors; and it fell into such contempt that even Augustus had to make a tenure of it, or the tribuneship, a condition of eligibility to the praetorship; and succeeding emperors often had to fill it by compulsion. In the third century A.D. it seems to have died out altogether.

Aedituus, Aeditŭmus (in Gk. νεώκορος, ζάκορος, ὑποζάκορος). A person in charge of a temple, who attended to its general order, and acted as a species of sacristan or cicerone to visitors. In many cases they were women. See Gell. xii. 10.

Aēdon (Ἀηδών). A daughter of Pandareus, wife of Zethus, king of Thebes, and mother of Itylus. Envious of Niobé, the wife of her brother Amphion, who had six sons and six daughters, she resolved to kill the eldest of Niobé's sons, but by mistake slew her own son Itylus. Zeus relieved her grief by changing her into a nightingale, whose melancholy tunes are represented as Aëdon's lamentations for her child.

Aēdon (ἀηδών). One of the names of the nightingale, also known as φιλομήλα and πρόκνη: in Latin, *luscinia*. For one legend, see above.

Aedui or **Haedui**. A powerful people of Gaul, living between the Liger (Loire) and the Arar (Saône), and the first Gallic tribe to form an alliance with the Romans. Their principal town was Bibracté (Autun). See Caes. *B. G.* i. 31 ff.

Aeētes (Αἰήτης). King of Colchis and father of Medea. For the legends connected with his name, see ABSYRTUS; ARGONAUTAE; IASON; MEDEA; PHRIXUS.

Aeētis, Aeetias, Aeëtīné. Patronymics applied to Medea (q. v.), as being the daughter of Aeetes.

Aegae (Αἰγαί). (1) A town in Achaea, with a celebrated temple of Poseidon, originally one of the twelve Achaean towns; but its inhabitants subsequently removed to Aegira. (2) A town in Emathia, in Macedonia, the ancient capital of Macedonia and the burial-place of the Macedonian kings. It was also called Edessa. (3) A town in Euboea, with a celebrated temple of Poseidon, who was hence called Aegaeus. (4) Also AEGAEAE, one of the twelve cities of Aeolis in Asia Minor, north of Smyrna, on the river Hyllus. (5) A seaport town of Cilicia.

Aegaea. An adjective applied to Aphrodité as being worshipped in the Aegean Sea.

Aegaeon (Αἰγαίων). The son of Uranus (Heaven) by Gaea (Earth). Aegaeon and his brothers Gyes or Gyges and Cottus are known under the name of the Uranidae, and are described as huge monsters with 100 arms and 50 heads. Most writers mention the third Uranid under the name of Briareus instead of Aegaeon, which is explained by Homer (*Il.* i. 403), who says that men called him Aegaeon, but the gods Briareus. According to the most ancient tradition, Aegaeon and his brothers conquered the Titans when they made war upon the gods, and secured the victory to Zeus, who thrust the Titans into Tartarus, and placed Aegaeon and his brothers to guard them. Other legends represent Aegaeon as one of the giants who attacked Olympus; and many writers represent him as a marine god living in the Aegaean Sea. See Hesiod, *Theog.* 149, 502, 617, etc.; Apollod. i. i. 1; Hom. *Il.* i. 398 foll.

Aegaeum Mare. The part of the Mediterranean Sea now called the Archipelago. It was bounded on the north by Thrace and Macedonia, on the west by Greece, and on the east by Asia Minor. It contains in its southern part two groups of islands—the Cyclades, which were separated from the coasts of Attica and Peloponnesus by the Myrtoan Sea, and the Sporades, lying off the coasts of Caria and Ionia. The part of the Aegaean which washed the Sporades was called the Icarian Sea, from the island Icaria, one of the Sporades.

Aegaleus (Αἰγάλεως). A mountain in Attica opposite Salamis, from which Xerxes saw the defeat of his fleet, B.C. 480. Cf. Herod. viii. 90.

Aegātes or **Aegūsae** (αἱ Αἰγοῦσσαι). "Goat Islands." The name applied to three islands off the west coast of Sicily, between Drepanum and Lilybaeum, near which the Romans gained a naval victory over the Carthaginians, and thus brought the First Punic War to an end, B.C. 241. The islands were Aegusa or Capraria, Phorbantia, and Hiera.

Agendĭcum. The modern Sens; a town of the Senones, in Gallia Lugdunensis.

Aegesta. See SEGESTA.

Aegestus. See ACESTES.

Aegeus (Αἰγεύς). The son of Pandion, king of Athens, and father of Theseus, whom he begot by Aethra at Troezen. Theseus afterwards came to Athens and restored Aegeus to the throne, of which he had been deprived by his brother Pallas. Having slain Androgeos, son of Minos (q.v.), he was conquered by that king and compelled to send seven youths and seven maidens to Crete once in nine years as victims to the Minotaur. When Theseus set out to free his country from this cruel tax, he agreed in case of success to exchange the black sail of his ship for a white one; but forgetting to do so, Aegeus saw the black sail on the returning vessel, supposed his son lost, and threw himself into the sea, which is thus supposed to have been named *Aegean* after him. He is said to have introduced the worship of Aphroditĕ into Athens, where he himself was honoured with a shrine. See MEDEA; THESEUS; MINOTAUR.

Aegialēa (Αἰγιάλεια). (1) The wife of Diomedĕ, to whom she is said to have been grossly unfaithful during his absence in the Trojan War. (See DIOMEDES.) (2) An island in the Aegean between Cythera and Crete. (3) The earliest name for the country above the north shore of the Peloponnesus.

Aegiălеus (Αἰγιαλεύς). The son of Adrastus, by Amphithea, daughter of Pronax, and a member of the expedition led by the Epigoni against Thebes. He was the only leader slain in this war, as his father was the only one that survived the previous contest. See EPIGONI.

Aegĭdes. A patronymic applied to Theseus, son of Aegeus.

Aegĭla (τὰ Αἴγιλα). A town in Laconia, where Demeter had a temple. Aristomenes, the Messenian leader, endeavoured on one occasion to seize a party of Laconian women who were celebrating here the rites of the goddess. The attempt failed, through the courageous resistance of the women, and Aristomenes himself was taken prisoner. He was released, however, the same night, by Archidamea, the priestess of Demeter, who had before this cherished an affection for him.

Aegilia (Αἰγιλία). (1) An island between Crete and Cythera. (2) An island west of Euboea, opposite Attica.

Aegimius (Αἰγίμιος). A king of the Dorians, reigning in Thessaly, near the range of Pindus. He aided Heracles, according to the Doric legend, in his contest with the Lapithae, and received as a reward the territory from which they were driven. Aegimius is a conspicuous name among the founders of the Doric line, and mention is made by the ancient writers of an epic poem, entitled Αἰγίμιος, which is ascribed by some to Hesiod, by others to Cecrops the Milesian. The posterity of Aegimius formed part of the expedition against the Peloponnesus, and the Doric institutions of Aegimius are spoken of by Pindar as forming the rule or model of government for the Doric race. (Cf. Müller, *Dorier*, vol. ii. p. 12.)

Aegīna (Αἴγινα). (1) A daughter of the river Asopus, carried away by Zeus under the form of an eagle, from Phlius to the island of Oenonĕ. She gave her name to the island. (2) An island in the Sinus Saronicus, near the coast of Argolis. The earliest accounts given by the Greeks make it to have been originally uninhabited, and to have been called, while in this state, by the name of Oenonĕ; for such is evidently the meaning of the fable, which states that Zeus, in order to gratify Aeacus, who was alone there, changed a swarm of ants into men, and thus peopled the island (Pausan. ii, 29, and Apollod. iii. xii. 7). It afterwards took the name of Aegina, from the daughter of the Asopus. But, whoever may have been the earliest settlers on the island, it is evident that its stony and unproductive soil must have driven them at an early period to engage in maritime affairs. Hence they are said to have been the first who coined money for the purpose of commerce, and

Temple of Aegina. (Restoration.)

used regular measures, a tradition which, though no doubt untrue, still points very clearly to their early commercial habits. (See NUMISMATICS.) It is more than probable that their commercial relations caused the people of Aegina to be increased by colonies from abroad, and Strabo expressly mentions Cretans among the foreign inhabitants who had settled there. After the return of the Heraclidae, this island received a Dorian colony from Epidaurus (Pausan. ii. 29), and from this period the Dorians gradually gained the ascendency in it, until at last it became entirely Doric, both in language and form of government. Aegina, for a time, was the maritime rival of Athens, and the competition eventually terminated in open hostilities, in which the Athenians were only able to obtain advantages by the aid of the Corinthians, and by means of intestine divisions among their opponents (Herod. viii. 46, and v. 83). When Darius sent deputies into Greece to demand earth and water, the people of Aegina, partly from hatred towards the Athenians, and partly from a wish to protect their extensive commerce along the coasts of the Persian monarchy, gave these tokens of submission (Herod. vi. 49). For this conduct they were punished by the Spartans. In the war with Xerxes, therefore, they sided with their countrymen, and acted so brave a part in the battle of Salamis as to be able to contest the prize of valour with the Athenians themselves, and to bear it off, as well by the universal suffrages of the confederate Greeks (Herod. viii. 93) as by the declaration of the Pythian oracle. After the termination of the Persian war, however, the strength of Athens proved too great for them. Their fleet of seventy sail was annihilated in a sea-fight by Pericles, and many of the inhabitants were driven from the island, while the remainder were reduced to the condition of tributaries. The fugitives settled at Thyrea in Cynuria, under the protection of Sparta, and it was not until after the battle of Aegos-Potamos, and the fall of Athens, that they were able to regain possession of their native island (Xen. *Hist. Gr.* ii. 2, 5). They never attained, however, to their former prosperity. The situation of Aegina made it subsequently a prize for each succeeding conqueror, until at last it totally disappeared from history. In modern times the island nearly retains its ancient name, being called Aegina or, with a slight corruption, Engia, and is often visited by travellers, being beautiful, fertile, and well cultivated. As far back as the time of Pausanias, the ancient city would appear to have been in ruins. That writer makes mention of some temples that were standing, and of the large theatre built after the model of that in Epidaurus. The most remarkable remnant of antiquity which this island can boast of at the present day is the Temple of Pallas Athené, situated on a mount of the same name, about four hours' distance from the port, and which is supposed to be one of the most ancient temples in Greece, and one of the oldest specimens of the Doric style of architecture. See AEGINETAN SCULPTURES.

Aeginetan Sculptures. The marble pediments of the temple of Athené at Aegina (q. v.), discovered in 1811, restored by Thorwaldsen, and preserved in the Glyptothek at Munich. They are especially valuable as throwing light on the condition of Greek art in the fifth century B.C. See SCULPTURA.

Aeginetārum Feriae (Αἰγινητῶν ἑορτή). A feast in honour of Poseidon, which lasted sixteen days, during which time every family took its meals alone without the attendance of the slaves. Its origin is described by Plutarch (*Quaest. Graec.* 44).

Aegiŏchus (from *αἰγίς* and *ἔχω*). The "aegis-bearer," an epithet applied to Zeus (q. v.). See AEGIS.

Aegīpan (Αἰγίπαν). A poetical appellation of Pan (q. v.), as being the guardian of goats.

Aegiplanctus Mons. A mountain in Megara.

Aegīra (Αἰγεíρα). A city of Achaea near the Corinthian Gulf and northwest of Pellini. See Polyb. iv. 57.

Aegis (*αἰγίς*). The storm-cloud and thunder-cloud of Zeus, imagined in Homer as a shield forged by Hephaestus, blazing brightly and fringed with tassels of gold, and displaying in its centre the awe-inspiring Gorgon's head. When Zeus shakes the aegis, it thunders and lightens, and horror and perdition fall upon those against whom it is lifted. It is borne not only by Zeus "the aegis-bearer," but by his daughter Athené, and occasionally by Apollo. As the same word means a goat-skin, it was explained in later times as the skin of the goat Amalthea (q. v.), which had suckled Zeus in his infancy. At the bidding of the oracle, he drew it over his thunder-shield in the contest with the Giants, and fastened on it the Gorgon's head. When the aegis became a standing attribute of Athené, it was represented as a skin either shaggy or scaly, with a fringe of snakes and the Gorgon's head in the middle, and either serving the goddess as a breast-plate, or hanging behind to screen the back and shoulders, or fastened like a shield on the left arm.

Though the aegis properly belongs to Zeus, it is

West Pediment of the Temple of Aegina.

seldom found in works of art as his attribute. A cameo engraved by Nisus, however, of which a cut

Zeus with the Aegis. (From a Cameo.)

is here given, shows him with the aegis on his left arm.

The Roman emperors also assumed the aegis, intending thereby to exhibit themselves in the character of Iupiter.

Aegisthus (Αἴγισθος). Son of Thyestes and his daughter Pelopia. At his birth he was exposed by his mother, and brought up by shepherds. His uncle, Atreus, husband to Pelopia, found him and brought him to Mycenae, thinking him to be his own son; but Aegisthus and his real father contrived to kill him and seize the sovereignty of the State. This position Aegisthus lost again by his cousin Agamemnon's return from exile; but during that hero's absence at Troy Aegisthus seduced his wife, Clytaemnestra, and with her help slew him treacherously on his return. In the eighth year after this deed Orestes avenged his father's death by slaying Aegisthus. See Agamemnon; Atreus; Clytaemnestra; Orestes; Pelopidae.

Aegium (Αἴγιον). One of the twelve towns of Achaea (q. v.).

Aeglé (Αἴγλη). One of the Hesperides (q. v.), and a name given to several of the nymphs.

Aegles. A Samian wrestler who had been born dumb. Seeing some unlawful measures pursued in a contest, which would deprive him of the prize, his indignation gave him on a sudden the powers of utterance, which had hitherto been denied him, and from this time he spoke with ease. See Aul. Gell. v. 9.

Aeglētes (Αἰγλήτης). A surname of Apollo as the god of day and of the lightning, derived from *αἴγλη*, "splendour." See Apollo.

Aegobolium (*αἰγοβόλιον*). A ceremony of purification in which the candidate was placed in a pit and covered with perforated boards, over which a goat was slain. The blood flowing down into the pit stained its occupant. If a bull was used, the rite was called *taurobolium;* and if a ram, *criobolium.* See Taurobolium.

Aegobŏlus (Αἰγοβόλος). A title given to Bacchus at Potniae in Boeotia, because he had substituted a goat (*αἴξ*) in place of a youth, whom it had formerly been the custom to sacrifice there (Pausan. ix. 8). See Aegobolium.

Aegosăgae. A Gallic tribe who served in the army of Attalus (q. v.). See Polyb. v. 77 foll.

Aegos-Potămos or **Aegos-Potămi** (Αἰγὸς Ποταμός). A small river in the Thracian Chersonesus, on which was a town of the same name. Here the Athenians were totally defeated by the Spartan admiral Lysander in B.C. 405, practically terminating the Peloponnesian War (q. v.), and leading to the capture of Athens.

Aegūsae. See Aegates.

Aegyptium Mare. That part of the Mediterranean which washes the coast of Egypt.

Aegyptus. A country in the northeastern part of Africa; the modern Egypt. The name, in Greek Αἴγυπτος, is perhaps a corruption of *Hakeptah* (City of Ptah), i. e. Memphis. Others explain it with less probability as formed from the Sanskrit *gup*, "to guard"= *âgupta*, "guarded about." In Coptic, as in hieroglyphs, it is called *Kemi* (Black Land) from the colour of the soil. The Jews styled it *Mazor*, "fortified," or in the dual, to denote both Upper and Lower Egypt, *Mizraim.* This name is preserved in the modern Arabic *Misr*—a word applied by the Arabs both to the country and to its capital, Cairo.

Aegyptus was bounded on the north by the Mediterranean; on the east by Palestine, Arabia Petraea, and the Red Sea; on the south by Aethiopia, the division between the two countries being at the First or Little Cataract of the Nile, close to Syené; and on the west by the Great Libyan Desert. From Syené the Nile flows due north for about 500 miles, through a valley whose average breadth is about seven miles, to a point some few miles below Memphis. Here the river divides into branches (seven in ancient times, but now only two), which flow through a low alluvial land, called, from its shape, the Delta, into the Mediterranean. The whole district thus described is periodically laid under water by the overflowing of the Nile from April to October. The river, in subsiding, leaves behind a rich deposit of fine mud, which forms the soil of Egypt. All beyond the reach of the inundation is rock or sand. Hence Egypt was called the "Gift of the Nile." The outlying portions of ancient Egypt consisted of three cultivable valleys (called oases), in the midst of the Western or Libyan Desert.

Ethnology and Civilization.—At the earliest period of which any record has been preserved, Egypt possessed a very high degree of civilization, and one which presupposes many centuries of development. It was the home, too, of a very large population, since during the Fourth Dynasty (about 3600 B.C.) some 100,000 men were employed in constructing the Great Pyramid. At the time of Nero (A.D. 54) the Egyptians numbered 7,800,000; and the population is estimated to have been not much less under the Pharaohs, at which time the towns numbered 1800 as against 3000 under the Ptolemies. The population of modern Egypt Proper in 1882 was 6,806,000. The ancient Egyptians appear to have been of mixed origin, partly Asiatic and partly Nigritic, superimposed upon an aboriginal type, copper-coloured, with high cheek-bones, large lips, thin legs, and large feet. Both these types appear upon the monuments. It is not true, as

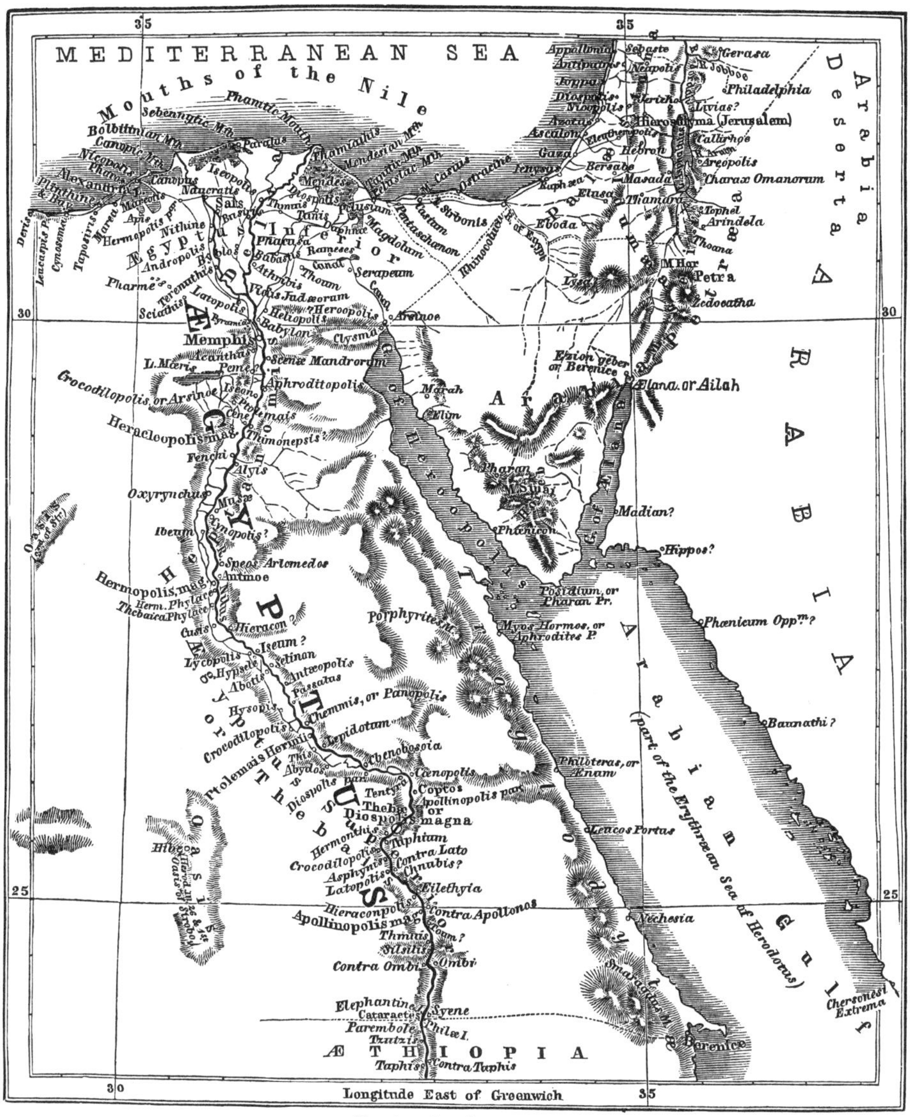

Egypt under the Romans.

stated by the Greek writers, that a caste system prevailed.

As to the knowledge and culture of the ancient Egyptians, it is sufficient to mention certain interesting and significant facts. As early as 4000 B.C., the pyramid-builders possessed a definite system of chronology, a decimal system of numbers, a knowledge of geographical science, of geometry, of astronomy, and probably of chemistry, anatomy, and medicine. Literature dates equally far back, since of this period fragments of the so-called Hermetic Books have come down to us; while Cheops (q. v.) himself was numbered among the authors of Egypt. Architecture and sculpture had attained an extraordinary development, as shown by the remarkably fine specimens of masonry still existing, by the admirably scientific construction of the temples, the elegance of the columns, the chiselled statues of Chephren, and the sculptures found at Meydoun. Egyptian art was rigidly conventional, yet its remains show unusual plastic skill; and in the later centuries, when a freer treatment obtained, the lions and sphinxes evince

Head of Wooden Statue from Bûlak.

much spirit and vigour of execution. The architectural details of the temples were always coloured.

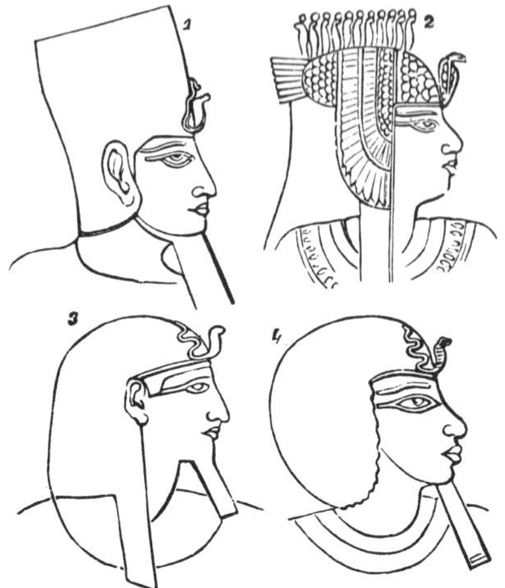

Ancient Profiles (from the Monuments): 1. Egypto-Ethiopian (the Tirhake of Scripture); 2, 4. Ethiopian; 3. Egyptian.

In architecture the vault or arch was known at least 800 years before it can be shown to have been used by the Romans. To transport the huge blocks of stone found in Egyptian structures involved an advanced knowledge of engineering. The mechanical arts also flourished, and many inventions, often regarded as modern, had been made as early as the Fifth Dynasty. The blow-pipe, bellows, and siphons, the saw, chisel, press, balance, harpoon, lever, plough, and adze, were all employed. Razors appear during the Twelfth Dynasty. An opaque kind of glass was made about 3500 B.C., and dated specimens of the reign of Thothmes III. exist. At the same period the potter's wheel and the kiln were known, as well as applications of metallurgy and the use of tin.

Music was cultivated, for the harp and flute were known in the Fourth Dynasty; and later are found the heptachord, pentachord, lyres, drums, trumpets, guitars, and the national instrument, the sistrum (q. v.). Many of these instruments were of considerable size.

Painting was almost as conventional as architecture and sculpture, the colours generally being the primary ones on a white background. The papyri containing rituals often exhibit illuminations like those of the mediæval missals. Frescoes were not unknown; encaustic is found to date back to only a comparatively late period.

In warfare, the Egyptians used shields, cuirasses of leather, helmets, bows, spears, clubs, swords, and axes. In conducting sieges, they employed the *testudo* (q. v.) and scaling-ladders, and appear to have had a knowledge of the principles of mining and counter-mining. Under the Eighteenth Dynasty, war-chariots were introduced, prior to which time the army was composed entirely of infantry. Sea-going vessels were not earlier than B.C. 2500, though galleys and small sailing craft plied on the Nile at a very early period.

Coined money was first introduced by the Persians, previous to which time it is possible that gold circulated in rings or in portions of definite weight. Popular amusements were fencing, juggling, dancing, dice, and bull-fighting.

RELIGION.—The religion of the ancient Egyptians was a pantheistic system, each god, as with the Romans, standing for some special attribute. Each principal divinity is accompanied by a *put*, or retinue of associated gods. As with the Assyrians, the pantheon is grouped in triads, or family groups, each consisting of the parent deity, his wife and sister, and a son. Thus the god Ptah forms a triad with Sekhet or Bast and Imhotep. These triads are often associated with inferior deities to complete the *put*. The worship of many triads was restricted to particular localities; but other triads, such as those of Osiris, Isis, and Horus (all of which see), were adored all over Egypt. The dual conception that embodies the antagonism of good and evil is seen in the opposition of the sun gods to the Great Serpent, Apap, the type of darkness; while Osiris is pitted against Set. On the monuments the gods are generally represented with human bodies but the heads of animals, animals being their living emblems. At the close

Siphons used by the Egyptians.

Colossal Head of a Hyksos King. (Black Granite Sculpture from the Fayûm.)

Egyptian Buffoons.

of the eighteenth dynasty, some foreign deities were admitted into the religious system of Egypt. Among these were Bar (Baal), Ashtarata (Ashtaroth), Ken (Kuin), and Reshpu (Reseph). As with the Greeks and Romans, so with the Egyptians, the gods were conceived as possessed of all the human passions and emotions.

The chief of the Egyptian deities is Ptah, the Opener, the creator of all things, the same as the Phœnician Pataikos. To him belong Sekhet, the Lioness, Bast, Bubastis, the goddess of fire, identified with Artemis. Ptah is depicted as a bow-legged dwarf. His son, Nefer-Tum, wears the lotus on his head. Other gods are Khnum, the ram-headed god of water; Heka, the Frog; Sati, the Sunbeam; Nit, the Shuttle; Khons (Force), the Heracles of Egyptian mythology; Ra, the Sun; Amenra, the hidden power of the Sun; Seb, Time; and Nut, the Firmament. Seb and Nut (Cronos and Rhea) gave birth to Osiris, Isis, Nephthys, Set, and the elder Horus. The myth of Osiris (q. v.) was the Egyptian type of the jugdment and future destiny of man; and all the dead are called by his name. Each deity had its sacred animal, which was regarded as the second life of the deity whom it represented. The most famous of these animals was the Apis, or sacred bull, at Memphis, whose worship was national. See Apis.

Another point of the Egyptian religion was a belief in the transmigration of souls. All who were too impure to be admitted to the Courts of the Sun, or whose bodies when embalmed perished before the end of 3000 years, passed from body to body, having first descended to the lower world. The Sacred Bark in which the mummy was carried over the Nile to its tomb was a type of the Sunboat which would at last bear the purified spirit to Paradise.

The chief remains of Egyptian architecture are religious—tombs, temples, and pyramids—the last-named being royal tombs reared to mark the burial-places of the kings. They are the most ancient of the Egyptian monuments, the next in point of antiquity being the rock-tombs of the Eleventh and Twelfth Dynasties, with their mummy-pits. Later still come the hill-tombs, with a temple before them.

Government.—Ecclesiastical government was in the hands of the high-priests, in conjunction with an inferior hierarchy, overseers, and superintendents of revenues, domains, and gifts. The civil government was carried on by the royal secretaries

Bronze Figure of Apis.

of justice, finance, foreign affairs, and internal administration. The army—at one time numbering some 400,000 men—was officered by nomarchs, colonels, and captains. In the time of Rameses II. there were territorial regiments. Circuit judges administered law.

History.—In the third century B.C., Manetho (q. v.), a priest of Heliopolis, prepared, at the request of King Ptolemy Philadelphus, a history of Egypt from Menes (B.C. 4455) to the conquest of Egypt by Alexander, B.C. 332, a period which he divided into thirty dynasties. The work of Manetho is preserved in the form of epitomes by Iulius Africanus (A.D. 300), Eusebius (q. v.), and Georgius Syncellus (A.D. 800). Much weight is now given to the statements of Manetho, since he undoubtedly had access to the most authentic records of Egypt; and the study of the monumental inscriptions in modern times has served to justify this confidence.

Myth declares Egypt to have been originally governed by a dynasty of divinities—Ptah, Ra, Shu, Seb, Hesiri (Osiris), Set, and Har (Horus)—reigning 13,900 years, and succeeded by demigods who ruled for a further

Temple of Thothmes III. at Karnak.

period of 4000 years. The first purely human monarch of Egypt is said to have been Menes, whose epoch is variously dated by different Egyptologists. Brugsch fixes it at B.C. 4455, and Lepsius at B.C. 3892. No monuments of Menes exist. The seat of his power is said to have been This, near Abydos, and he is believed to have founded Memphis. His dynasty reigned some 250 years, being succeeded by the Second Dynasty, which held sway for 300 years. Under it the worship of sacred animals is asserted to have begun. With the succeeding dynasty (B.C. 3966 according to Brugsch) the monumental history of Egypt commences. The king Senoferu conquered the Sinaitic peninsula and opened the copper-mines of Wady-Maghâra, where his name and portrait may still be seen. The seated figures of Rahotep and his wife Nefert, the oldest statues in the world, date from this reign.

Thoth, the God of Writing.

The Fourth Dynasty lasted 167 years (B.C. 3733–3566). Under it Khufu (Cheops) built the Great Pyramid at Gîzeh; his successor Khafra (Chephrenes) built the second pyramid; and Menkaura (Mycerinus) the third. From this period dates also the famous ritual known as the Book of the Dead, and various works of art.

The Fifth Dynasty comprised nine kings, and lasted some 200 years. The last of the line, Unas, built the truncated pyramid near Sakkara, now called Pharaoh's Seat. See PYRAMIS.

The Sixth Dynasty contains the name of King Pepi, whose general, Una, undertook various wars and expeditions, among them one to Palestine, in which he used negro troops from Nubia. A number of texts belonging to this reign were found in pyramids opened in 1880. It is doubtful whether Queen Nitocris (q. v.), whom Manetho assigns to this dynasty, is an historical personage. Of her, Herodotus relates various interesting stories, and the Arabs believe that she still haunts the third pyramid of Gîzeh, where she is said to have been buried.

From the Seventh to the Twelfth Dynasty, Egyptian history is obscure. One reason, perhaps, is to be found in the fact that the nomarchs or local governors became more and more independent, to the detriment of the importance of the kings. The inscriptions at Siat, recently published by Griffith, show that in the Ninth and Tenth Dynasties, the kings of Egypt waged war against these rebellious nomarchs, especially those of Thebes. These last, under the Tenth Dynasty, began to claim the title of royalty, and did in fact succeed in establishing their claim. More than that, they overran and conquered the whole country after a protracted struggle, so that the Eleventh Dynasty is Theban. Thebes, from being an insignificant provincial town, became the royal capital; and from the time of the Twelfth Dynasty (about B.C. 2500) begins a new period of political unity and intellectual achievement, so that in later times it was regarded as Egypt's Golden Age. Literature flourished, and great material prosperity prevailed. Nubia was conquered as far as the Second Cataract. Besides Thebes, other cities, such as On (Heliopolis), Tanis, and Bubastis, were embellished and enlarged; while the province of Fayûm was gained for agriculture. The excavations of Petrie prove that Amenemhat III. was the Moiris of Herodotus who constructed a great basin for a branch of the Nile flowing into that oasis and losing itself in swamps. In the middle of the basin were found two pyramids with colossal statues surmounting them; and near by, the largest of all the temples of Egypt, the so-called Labyrinth, of which, however, only the foundation stones have been preserved. See LABYRINTHUS.

Between the Thirteenth and the Eighteenth Dynasties there exists a blank. About B.C. 2000, the progress of the kings of Chaldea in Asia, or some other disturbance, sent the Hyksos or "Shepherd Kings" into Lower Egypt. These invaders appear to have been of Tartar race. They carried Memphis by storm, expelled the Theban dynasty, and made the city of Avaris (the later Tanis) their seat. Of these kings, Joseph was probably prime-minister to Apepi at Tanis. His granaries are still visible at Pithom. The Hyksos made some religious changes and tried to replace the worship of Ra by that of Set. They were finally overthrown by the Egyptians of Upper Egypt under Aahmes I. (Amosis), who took Avaris by assault and restored the old religion. The succeeding kings, Amenhotep I., Thothmes I., Thothmes II., and Thothmes III., carried the arms of Egypt far into Ethiopia, Nubia, and Asia, subduing the whole of Syria and part of Mesopotamia. The reign of Thothmes III. is the most brilliant period of Egyp-

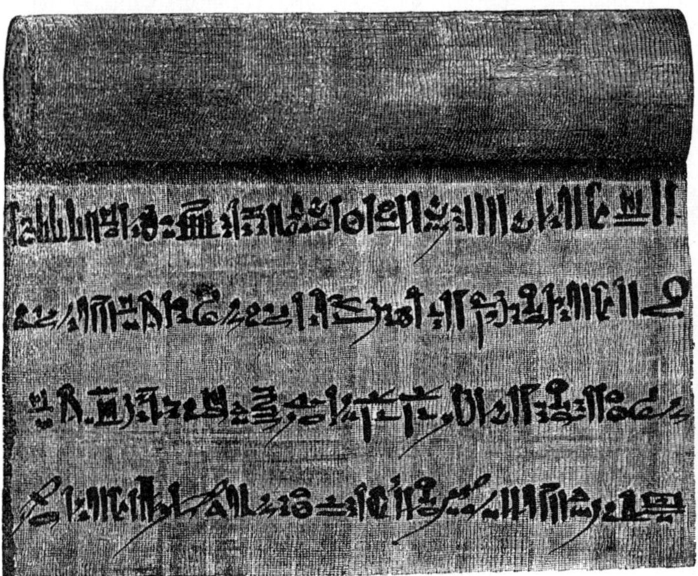

Hieratic Papyrus. (Twentieth Dynasty.)

tian history. To him, Kush and the southern tribes of Ethiopia, the islands, as well as Assyria, Babylonia, Phœnicia, and a good part of Central Asia, paid tribute. Under Amenhotep IV., the capital was removed to Alabastron (Tel-el-Amâri-na), and the monotheistic worship of the sun was allowed to diminish the regard paid to the other deities. The true religion was restored by Harem-hebi (Horus) after a period of some thirty-five years. He was succeeded by Rameses I., who heads a long dynasty. His successor, Seti I. (Sethos), by his victories in Asia, introduced the worship of Baal and Ashtaroth into Egypt. His troops garrisoned Tyre, and Aradus, and Beth-anath in Canaan. Rameses II., son of Seti, defeated the Hittites and took Shaluma, the ancient site of Jerusalem, in a war which lasted four years. A tablet of this monarch has been found near Beyrût in Syria. Rameses II. also reconquered Ethiopia, which had revolted, and established a fleet on the Mediterranean. He it is whose exploits form a basis for the myths woven around the legendary Sesostris (q. v.). His date is about B.C. 1322. His son Meneptah transferred the seat of government to Memphis, and is probably the Pharaoh of the Jewish Exodus.

Rameses III., of the Twentieth Dynasty, waged war with the Philistines, and with some of the maritime tribes of Greece, gaining naval victories in the Mediterranean. His favourite temple and palace were at Medinet Habu. The Ramessids who followed were ended by the high-priests of Thebes, who deposed the last king. A new dynasty from Tanis succeeded, and reigned with little power. Under them, the police ceased trying to protect the tombs of the kings from plunderers, who, in consequence, stole many of the mummies and hid them in an excavation, where they were found in 1881.

Egyptian of the time of the Fifth Dynasty, circa B.C. 3300. (Limestone Statue in the Museum of Ghizeh.)

King Amenembat I., of the Twelfth Dynasty. (Head in Red Granite from the Great Temple of Tanis. Photographed by Mr. W. M. F. Petrie.)

The Twenty-second Dynasty (B.C. 950) was of Libyan origin, probably established by the powerful Libyan body-guard which had become extremely influential. Shoshank I. (the Biblical Shishak) plundered cities in India, and made war upon the Jewish kings Jeroboam and Rehoboam. Under the Twenty-third Dynasty (of Tanis), the unity of the Empire was lost. The different provinces fell away from the central power, and in the Twenty-fourth Dynasty King Bocchoris ruled over Saïs and Memphis alone. Under the Twenty-fifth Dynasty (B.C. 728), the whole of Egypt became an Ethiopian province, and its viceking suffered defeat at the hands of the Assyrians, who, in B.C. 671, under Assar-haddon, conquered Egypt and divided it among tributary princes. (See ASSYRIA.) Many of the Assyrian garrisons were driven out in B.C. 668, and when the Assyrian empire began to decline, Psametik (Psammetichus) of Saïs, descended from the kings of the Twenty-fourth Dynasty, founded a new line with the aid of Greek mercenaries from Ionia and Caria. Under him and his successors, art and learning revived. His successor, Nekao II., began a canal to connect the Red Sea with the Mediterranean, but desisted at the warning of an oracle, having also lost a large number of workmen in the attempt. He it was who defeated Josiah, king of Judah, and conquered Palestine, but was himself defeated by Nebuchadnezzar. In the time of his reign, navigators from Phœnicia first sailed south of the equator. Psammetichus II. warred with the Ethiopians, and was followed by Apries, who was deposed and strangled by Amasis (q. v.), who reigned after him and fostered intercourse with Greece, marrying a Greek wife. He conquered Cyprus, but incurred the enmity of Cambyses (q. v.), second king of the Medes and Persians, who invaded Egypt, and overthrew the son of Amasis at the battle of Pelusium (B.C. 527), thus insuring the conquest of Egypt, which now became a Persian province. Becoming insane, Cambyses committed many barbarous acts, stabbed the sacred bull Apis, and gave himself up to gross debauchery. He was succeeded by Darius I., Xerxes I., and Artaxerxes I., who governed with comparative mildness, but against whom the Egyptians rose in unsuccessful revolt, being aided by the Athenians. The Twenty-eighth (Saïte) Dynasty struggled with varying success against the Persians; the Twenty-ninth maintained a Greek alliance with the same object; but with the Thirtieth, the Persians finally prevailed, and Egypt remained subject to them until the time of Alexander the Great (B.C. 332), who in that year founded Alexandria (q. v.), after having conquered Persia. In B.C. 306, Alexander's general, Ptolemaeus, assumed the title of King of Egypt. His successors transformed Egypt into a Greek kingdom, both the language of the government and of scholarship being Greek. (See ALEXANDRIAN SCHOOL.) The court of the Ptolemies became a centre of learning; and Ptolemy Philadelphus built the famous Museum, founded the great Library, and procured the Septuagint translations of the Hebrew Scriptures. From this time the list of his successors is as follows: Euergetes (246–221 B.C.); Philopator (221–204 B.C.), who persecuted the Jews and warred with Antiochus; Epiphanes (204–180 B.C.); Philometor (180–145 B.C.); Euergetes II. (145–116 B.C.); Ptolemy Soter II. and his mother Cleopatra (116–81 B.C.); Alexander II., Cleopatra Berenicé (81–80 B.C.); Neos Dionysus (80–51 B.C.). Last came the famous Cleopatra (q. v.), the mistress of Antony. After her defeat at the battle of Actium (31 B.C.), Egypt was made a Roman province by Augustus Caesar, under a governor of equestrian rank. See PTOLEMAEUS.

Egypt remained peaceful under Roman rule, except for the conquest of Zenobia (270 A.D.) and the revolt of Firmus (272 A.D.). (See ZENOBIA; FIRMUS.) The most interesting events of this period are, besides the two just mentioned, the visits of Vespasian, Hadrian, and Caracalla to Alexandria; the persecutions of Diocletian (q. v.); the rise of the Gnostics, Manichaeans, and Arians; and the final supremacy of the Christian faith in 379 A.D.

When the Roman Empire was divided in 395 A.D., Egypt went with the Eastern division, and later became one of the great patriarchates of the Church. In 616 A.D., owing to bitter religious feuds, it became a Persian province for twelve years. In the year 639, when the Arabs invaded the country, a native (Coptic) governor was over Egypt, administering it in the name of the Emperor Heraclius. Seeing in the invasion a means for throwing off the rule of the Greeks, he made only a pretended resistance to the Arab chief, 'Amr Ibn el-Asi, who in the year 641 took Alexandria, and made the whole of Egypt a province of the calif Omar.

BIBLIOGRAPHY.—See Wilkinson, *Manners and Customs of the Ancient Egyptians* (1847; new ed. by Birch, 1879); Brugsch, *Recueil des Monuments Egyptiens* (1862–63); Bunsen, *Aegyptens Stelle* (1844–57); Lepsius, *Denkmäler* (1849–74); Sharpe, *History of Egypt* (1846): Mariette, *Monuments of Upper Egypt* (1877); Rawlinson, *History of Ancient Egypt* (1881); Ebers, *Egypt, Historical and Descriptive* (Eng. trans. 2d ed. 1887); Lane-Poole, *Art of the Saracens* (1886); Brugsch Pasha, *Egypt under the Pharaohs* (2d ed. 1861); Erman, *Aegypten* (1885); Lepage-Renouf, *Lectures* (1880); Maspéro, *Life in Ancient Egypt and Assyria* (Engl. trans. 1892); Brimmer, *Egypt* (1892).

For the language, Brugsch's *Grammaire Hiéroglyphique* (1872) may be recommended, and Loret's *Manuel* (1887); with Brugsch's dictionary (1880). Grammars of special periods have been written by Prof. Erman of Berlin. On Egyptian art, see Perrot and Chipiez, *History of Art;* Maspéro, *Archéologie Egyptienne;* Reber, *History of Ancient Art* (Engl. trans. 1882); Lübke, *Geschichte der Kunst*, 11th ed. (1892); Goodyear, *A Grammar of the Lotus* (1892).

Aegyptus (Αἴγυπτος). Son of Belus and twin-brother of Danaüs (q. v.), who subdued the land of the Melampodes, and named it after himself. Ignorant of the fate of his fifty sons, he came to Argos and there died of grief at their death; another account represents his only surviving son as reconciling him to his brother.

Aeinautae (ἀείναυται). Magistrates at Miletus whose custom it was to embark on board ship whenever they had occasion to discuss important business, returning only when the business was completed (Plut. *Quaest. Graec.* 32).

Aeiphygia (ἀειφυγία). See EXSILIUM.

Aeisĭti (ἀείσιτοι). See PRYTANEUM.

Aelāna. The *Elath* of the Jews, a town on the northern arm of the Red Sea, which was in consequence called by the Greeks Αἰλανίτης.

Aelia. A name given to Jerusalem after its restoration by the Roman emperor, Aelius Hadrianus. See HIEROSOLYMA.

Aelia Sentia Lex. See DEDITICII.

Aeliānum Ius. See IURISPRUDENTIA.

Aeliānus. (1) THE TACTICIAN, a Greek writer on war, about 100 A.D., composed a work dedicated to Trajan on the Greek order of battle, with special reference to Macedonian tactics (Τακτικὴ Θεωρία), which is extant both in its original and in an enlarged form. The original used falsely to be attributed to Arrian. See Köchly, *De Libris Tacticis* (1852).

(2) CLAUDIUS AELIĀNUS, called THE SOPHIST, a Roman of Praenesté, who wrote in Greek, lived at Rome in the second century A.D. as a teacher of rhetoric. His surviving works are: (*a*) Twenty insignificant *Peasants' Letters* (Ἀγροικικαὶ Ἐπιστολαί), so called because attributed to Attic peasants; (*b*) *Variae Historiae* (Ποικίλη Ἱστορία) or miscellanies, in fourteen books, some preserved only in extracts; and (*c*) *De Natura Animalium* (Περὶ Ζῴων Ἰδιότητος). The two last-mentioned are copious and valuable collections of all kinds of curiosities in human and animal life. See Lübbe, *De Aeliani Varia Hist.* (1888); and the ed. of the last by Jacobs (1832).

Aelius. A plebeian gens at Rome, divided into the families of Gallus, Lamia, Paetus, and Tubero.

Aëllo (Ἀελλώ). One of the Harpies. See HARPYIAE.

Aemilia. The third daughter of L. Aemilius Paulus (q. v.), wife of Scipio Africanus, and mother of Cornelia, who bore the Gracchi.

Aemilia Via. A Roman road made by M. Aemilius Lepidus, consul in B.C. 187. It continued the Via Flaminia from Ariminum through Bononia, Mutina, and Placentia, to Mediolanum (Milan). See VIAE.

Aemiliānus. The cognomen of P. Cornelius Scipio Africanus Minor, who was the son of L. Aemilius Paulus. See SCIPIO.

Aemilius. The name of a celebrated patrician gens at Rome, for the chief members of which see the articles LEPIDUS; PAULUS; SCAURUS.

Aenaria (also called PITHECŪSA and INARĬMÉ). A volcanic island at the entrance to the Bay of Naples; under it the Roman poets represent Typhoeus (q. v.) as lying. It is the modern Ischia.

Aeneădes. A patronymic applied specifically to Ascanius or Iulus, the son of Aeneas, and generally to those who claimed descent from him, such as Augustus Caesar and the Romans as a race.

Aenēas (Αἰνείας). A Trojan hero, the son of Anchises and Aphroditē, and born on Mount Ida. He was brought up at Dardania, in the house of Alcathoüs, the husband of his sister. At first he took no part in the Trojan war; and it was not till Achilles attacked him on Mount Ida, and drove away his flocks, that he led his Dardanians against the Greeks. Henceforth Aeneas and Hector appear as the great bulwarks of the Trojans against the Greeks. On more than one occasion Aeneas was

Aeneas, followed by Ascanius, and carrying Anchises from burning Troy.

saved in battle by the gods; Aphroditē carried him off when he was wounded by Diomedes, and Poseidon saved him when he was on the point of perishing by the hands of Achilles. Homer makes no allusion to the emigration of Aeneas after the capture of Troy, but, on the contrary, he evidently conceives Aeneas and his descendants as reigning at Troy after the extinction of the house of Priam; but later narratives relate that after the capture of Troy Aeneas withdrew to Mount Ida with his friends and the images of the gods, especially that of Pallas (*Palladium*); and that from thence he crossed over to Europe, and finally settled at Latium in Italy where he became the ancestral hero of the Romans. A description of the wanderings of Aeneas before he reached Latium is given by Vergil in his *Aeneid* (bks. ii.–vi.). After visiting Epirus and Sicily, he was driven by a storm on the coast of Africa, where he met with Dido (q. v.). He then sailed to Latium, where he was hospitably received by Latinus, king of the Aborigines. Here Aeneas founded the town of Lavinium, called after Lavinia, the daughter of Latinus, whom he married. Turnus, to whom Lavinia had been betrothed, made war against Latinus and Aeneas. Latinus fell in the first battle, and Turnus was subsequently slain by Aeneas; whereupon, after the death of Latinus, Aeneas became sole ruler of the Aborigines and Trojans, and both nations were united into one. Soon after this Aeneas fell in battle against the Rutulians, who were assisted by Mezentius, king of the Etruscans. As his body was not found after the battle, it was believed that it had been carried up to heaven, or that he had perished in the river Numicius. The Latins erected a monument to him, with the inscription *To the Father and Native God*. Vergil represents Aeneas as landing in Italy seven years after the fall of Troy, and compresses all the events in Italy, from the landing to the death of Turnus, within the space of twenty days. The story of the descent of the Romans from the Trojans through Aeneas was believed at an early period, but rests on no historical foundation. See TROJAN WAR; VERGILIUS.

Aenēas Silvius. The grandson of Ascanius and great-grandson of Aeneas. His name stands third in the list of the mythical kings of Alba in Latium.

Aeneatōres or **Ahenatōres**. Performers upon wind-instruments in the Roman army, and divided into *bucinatores*, *cornicines*, *tubicines*, *liticines*, and called from the bronze (*aes*) of their instruments.

Aenēid (AENĒIS). The chief Roman epic. See VERGILIUS; EPOS.

Aenesidēmus (Αἰνησίδημος). A skeptic, born at Cnossus, in Crete, who lived a little later than the time of Cicero. He wrote eight books on the doctrines of Pyrrho (q. v.), of which extracts may be found in Photius, *Cod.* 212.

Aeniānes. A Thessalian tribe noted for its frequent migrations, and frequently alluded to by Plutarch in his *Quaestiones Graecae*.

Aenigma (αἴνιγμα) A riddle. The Greeks were especially fond of riddles, the propounding of which even formed a part of some of their semi-religious festivals (see AGRIONIA); and certain persons, such as Theodectes of Phaselis and Aristonymus, owed their celebrity to their cleverness at propounding *aenigmata*. At the symposia especially, the asking and answering of riddles formed a favourite amusement, and those who successfully solved them received a prize in the form of cakes, sweetmeats, wreaths, etc., while the unsuccessful were condemned to swallow a draught of wine sometimes mixed with salt water. Riddles were often written in hexameter verse, and the tragic as well as the comic writers have introduced them into their plays. The most famous riddle of antiquity is perhaps the celebrated one propounded by the Sphinx to Oedipus (q. v.).

The Romans cared little for riddles, though Apuleius wrote a work on the subject (*Liber Ludicrorum et Griphorum*), and mentions several collections of riddles that had been made. (See Athenaeus, x. 457.) A late writer, Symphosius, in the fourth century A.D., wrote a work entitled

Aenigmata Symphosi Scholastici, containing a hundred riddles. The best list of these is in Riese's *Anthologia Lat.*, pp. 187–207; trans. into French by Corpet (Paris, 1868).

Aenobarbus. See AHENOBARBUS.

Aēnum or **Ahēnum**, sc. *vas*. A bronze vessel hung over the fire and used in boiling. The word also designates a dyer's copper; and the boilers that supplied hot water to a bath were also called *aëna*. See BALNEAE.

Aenus. (1) A town in Thrace, near the mouth of the Hebrus, said by Vergil to have been founded by Aeneas. (2) A river in Rhaetia, now the Inn.

Aeŏles or **Aeolii**. One of the chief branches of the Hellenic race, and supposed to be descended from Aeolus, son of Hellen. (See AEOLUS.) They originally lived in Thessaly, subsequently spread over various parts of Greece, and also settled in Aeolis in Asia Minor, and in Lesbos (q. v.).

Aeoliae Insŭlae. A group of islands northeast of Sicily, where Aeolus, the god of the winds, reigned. These islands were also called Hephaestiades or Vulcaniae, because Hephaestus or Vulcan was believed to have his workshop in one of them called Hiera. They were also named Liparenses, from Lipara, the largest of them.

Aeolic Dialect. See DIALECTS.

Aeolĭdes (Αἰολίδης). A patronymic applied to various individuals, of whom the most important are Sisyphus, son of Aeolus; Odysseus, to whom it is given because his mother, Anticlea, was pregnant by Aeolus when she married Laërtes; and Misenus, the follower of Aeneas, who was called so figuratively, from his skill in blowing the trumpet. The feminine form is Aeolis.

Aeŏlis (Αἰολίς) or **Aeolia.** A district in Mysia in Asia Minor, and peopled by Aeolian Greeks. In early times, their twelve most important cities were independent, and formed a league—Cymé, Larissae, Neontichos, Temnus, Cilla, Notium, Aegirusa, Pitane, Aegaeae, Myrina, Grynea, and Smyrna. Those cities were subsequently overcome by Croesus and incorporated in the Persian Empire under Cyrus. See LESBOS.

Aeŏlus (Αἴολος). (1) The ruler of the winds, son of Hippotas and Melanippé, daughter of Chiron. He reigned over the Aeolian Islands, and made his residence at Strongylé, the modern Stromboli. The island was entirely surrounded by a wall of brass, and by smooth, precipitous rocks; and here he dwelt in continual joy and festivity, with his wife and his six sons and as many daughters. The island had no other tenants. The sons and daughters were married to each other, after the fashion set by Zeus and Heré. Odysseus came in the course of his wanderings to the island of Aeolus, and was hospitably entertained there for an entire month. On his departure, he received from Aeolus all the winds but Zephyrus, tied up in a bag of ox-hide. Zephyrus was favourable for his passage homeward. During nine days and nights the ships ran merrily before the wind; on the tenth they were within sight of Ithaca, when Odysseus, who had hitherto held the helm himself, fell asleep. His comrades, who fancied that Aeolus had given him treasure in the bag, opened it: the winds rushed out, and hurried them back to Aeolia. Judging, from what had befallen them, that they were hated by the gods, the ruler of the winds drove them with reproaches from his isle. The name Aeolus has been derived from αἰόλος, "varying," "unsteady," as a descriptive epithet of the winds. (2) A son of Hellen, father of Sisyphus, Cretheus, and Athamas, and the mythic progenitor of the great Aeolic race.

Aeon (αἰών). A term occurring frequently in the philosophical speculations of the Gnostics, who conceived the emanations from Deity to be divided into two classes: the one comprehending all those substantial powers which are contained within the Divine Essence, and which completes the infinite plenitude of the Divine Nature; the other, existing externally with respect to the Divine Essence, and including all finite and imperfect natures. Within the Divine Essence, they, with wonderful ingenuity, imagined a long series of emanative principles, to which they ascribed a real and substantial existence, connected with the first substance as a branch with its root, or a solar ray with the sun. When they began to unfold the mysteries of this system in the Greek language, these Substantial Powers, which they conceived to be comprehended within the πλήρωμα, or Divine Plenitude, they called αἴωνες, aeons. See GNOSTICI.

Aeōra or **Eōra** (αἰώρα, ἑώρα). (1) A festival at Athens accompanied with sacrifices and banquets in commemoration of Erigoné (q. v.). (2) A swing, which was a favourite amusement in Greece, as in modern times. The illustration shows a group engaged in swinging one another.

Aeora, or Swing. (Panofka.)

Aepoliānus. An engraver of precious stones, of the second century A.D.

Aepȳtus (Αἴπυτος). (1) A mythical king of Arcadia, from whom a part of the country was called Aepytis. (2) The younger son of Cresphontes, king of Messenia, and of Meropé, daughter of the Arcadian king Cypselus. When his father and brothers were murdered during an insurrection, Aepytus, who was with his grandfather Cypselus, alone escaped. The throne of Cresphontes was meantime occupied by Polyphontes, who forced Meropé to become his wife. When Aepytus had grown to manhood he returned to his kingdom, and put Polyphontes to death. From him the kings of Messenia were called Aepytidae.

Aequi, Aequicŏli, Aequicŏlae, Aequiculāni. A people of Italy, dwelling in the upper valley of the Anio, in the mountains forming the eastern boundary of Latium, and between the Latini, Sabini, Hernici, and Marsi. In conjunction with the Volsci, who were of the same race, they carried on constant hostilities with Rome, but were finally subdued in B.C. 302. One of their chief seats was Mount Algidus.

Aequi Falisci. See FALERII.

Aequipondium. See LIBRA; TRUTINA.

Aera. See CHRONOLOGY.

Aerarii. By the constitution of Servius Tullius (see CENTURIA), aerarii were citizens who were not settled on land of their own, and therefore not included in any one of the property classes founded on land-ownership. The term was also applied to those standing outside of the tribal union, who were excluded from the right of voting and from military service, and who were bound to pay a poll-tax in proportion to their means. Citizens in the classes and tribes could be expelled from their tribe by the censors in punishment for any fault, and placed among the aerarii. But when the latter were likewise admitted into the tribes (B.C. 308), being enrolled in the city tribes (B.C. 304), which were on that account less esteemed than the country ones, a penal transfer to the aerarii consisted in expulsion from one's proper tribe and removal to one of the city tribes till at least the next census.

Aerarii Tribūni. See AES EQUESTRE; TRIBUNI.

Aerarium (τὸ δημόσιον). The state treasury of Rome, into which flowed the revenues ordinary and extraordinary, and out of which the needful expenses were defrayed. It was kept in the basement of the Temple of Saturn, under the charge of the quaestors. A special reserve fund was the *aerarium sanctius*, in which the proceeds of receipts from the manumission-tax (one twentieth of the freed slave's value) were deposited in gold ingots. When Augustus divided the provinces into senatorial and imperatorial, there were two chief treasuries. (See FISCUS.) The senatorial treasury, which was still kept in the Temple of Saturn, was left under the control of the Senate, but only as a matter of formal right. Practically it passed into the hands of the emperors, who also brought the management of the treasuries under their own eye by appointing, instead of the quaestors, two *praefecti aerarii* taken from those who had served as praetors. Besides this, they diverted into their own *fiscus* all the larger revenues, even those that legally belonged to the aerarium. (See FISCUS.) When in course of time the returns from all the provinces flowed into the imperial treasury, the senatorial aerarium continued to exist as the city treasury. The *aerarium militare* was a pension-fund founded by Augustus in A.D. 6, for disabled soldiers. Its management was intrusted to three *praefecti aerarii militaris*. It was maintained out of the interest on a considerable fund, and the proceeds of the heritage and sale duties. See Marquardt, *Staatsverwaltung*, ii. pp. 293–305.

Aero. A basket of osiers, rushes, or sedge, and used to carry wheat, sand, or earth. See BASCAUDA.

Aërŏpé (Ἀερόπη). The daughter of Catreus, king of Crete, and wife of Plisthenes, the son of Atreus, by whom she became the mother of Agamemnon and Menelaüs. After the death of Plisthenes, Aëropé married Atreus; and her two sons, who were educated by Atreus, were generally believed to be his sons. Aëropé was faithless to Atreus, being seduced by Thyestes. See PELOPIDAE.

Aerūgo. Verdigris. The word is used figuratively of envy. Hor. *S.* i. 4. 101.

Aeruscatōres. Vagrants who made a living by fortune-telling and begging. The Greeks called them ἀγύρται (Gell. xiv. 1). See AGYRTAE.

Aes (χαλκός). Much confusion has arisen from the fact that both Greeks and Romans use only one term for copper and for that mixture of copper and tin which we call bronze. Excepting perhaps gold, copper is the easiest of metals to find and fashion, being found in lumps, and not, like iron, hidden in ore. Hesiod and Lucretius, and ancient writers generally, made the Age of Bronze precede that of Iron, and that they were right is abundantly proved by the excavations of modern times. There seems to have been a time immediately succeeding the Stone Age when implements were beaten out of pure copper, but it did not last long: the custom of adding tin to copper was introduced, and from that time until the close of ancient history, copper unmixed was seldom used for any purpose, various metals being added to it to increase its hardness. Bronze, containing about 12 to 14 per cent. of tin and 88 to 86 per cent. of copper, was made at a very early period in Egypt and Asia. The use of it was introduced into Greece in prehistoric times, probably by the Phœnicians. Tin is not found in Greece, and, in fact, exists in but few parts of Europe: the Phœnicians are supposed to have travelled in search of it as far as Cornwall and India. The likeness of the Greek word for tin (κασσίτερος) to the Sanskrit *kastira* seems to indicate that the original supply of Greek tin came from India. To account, however, for the enormous quantity of tin which in the Bronze Age must have circulated through Europe is not easy.

In Homer's time bronze is the usual material for tripods, vessels, armour of defence, and even spears, though iron was beginning to be used for offensive weapons. It is probable that soon after the Homeric age weapons of bronze fell out of use. This compound, however, continued to be largely employed for utensils of all kinds, for works of art and other purposes. The interior of the treasuries of Mycenae and Orchomenus were lined with bronze; bronze was used in historical times for vessels, candelabra, chariots, for the inscribing of treaties and laws, for personal ornament, and in places for coin. Also all instruments used for religious purposes were made of bronze from motives of religious conservatism. The abundance of copper sufficiently accounts for its general use among the ancients. We have a remarkable result of this fact in the use of χαλκεύς and χαλκεύειν, where working in iron is meant (Hom. *Od.* ix. 391; Aristot. *Poët.* 25). One of the chief sources of copper in antiquity was Cyprus; from the name of that island is derived the Low Latin *cuprum*, and our word copper. The metal was also procured in Euboea, near the town of Chalcis, and in other parts of Greece; also in Campania in Italy, in Germany, and elsewhere. But the most celebrated bronze did not come from those regions, but was an object of special manufacture elsewhere. Two of the most celebrated mixtures were the Delian (Plin. xxxiv. § 9) and the Aeginetan (*l. c.* § 10), which were much used in art. We learn that Myron used the former mixture, Polyclitus the latter. The Delian was reckoned the more precious of these, but still more valuable was the *hepatizon* or liver-coloured bronze, and most valuable of all the Corinthian. With regard to the last-mentioned, a silly story was told that it was produced by a fortuitous mixture of melted metals on the occasion of the burning of Corinth by Mummius. Pliny (xxxiv. § 7) sensibly remarks that this story is absurd, because most of the authors of the highly valued works in Corinthian bronze lived at a much earlier period. A large number of varieties of bronze of various colours were known to the ancients, and it seems that they tinted their statues by making them of a judicious mixture of sorts. Thus we find mention of a bronze Iocasté that was pale, of an Athamas that blushed, and of a Pallas with ruddy cheeks made by Phidias. The ancients also understood the art of hardening the metal by dipping it in water and exposing it to the air. Even in Homer there is one passage (*Od.* ix. 391) which is supposed to allude to this process which recent experiments have proved possible. The mixture of copper and zinc which we call brass was known to the later Greeks and Romans, and by them called *orichalcum* (see Plin. xxxiv. 4). The chief authority as regards the kinds and working of bronze is Pliny (*H. N.* xxxiv.). He distinguishes copper ore into two kinds: *cadmea,* found in Italy and Germany, and *chalcitis* in Cyprus and elsewhere. Of Corinthian bronze (§ 8) he distinguishes three kinds: in the first silver predominates, in the second gold, in the third the metals are balanced and harmonized. Of Cyprian bronze (§ 94) the chief classes are *coronarium,* which is of golden hue when divided into thin layers, and *regulare,* which can be hammered and drawn out into bars and wires. A commoner kind of copper (not Cyprian), called *caldarium,* does not give to the hammer, and is only fit for melting. At Capua they added to copper to make bronze, 10 per cent. of Spanish *plumbum argentarium,* which was made of tin and lead in equal proportions. Pliny states that copper was largely used in medicine (§ 100 foll.), being either mixed with milk or sulphur for external application to wounds, or taken internally, mixed with honey, in order to cause vomiting. For a mass of details of this character we must refer the reader to Pliny himself.

In the early bronze-work of Greece and Etruria, the manufacturing processes were simple. The usual process for utensils and ornaments was to work plates with the hammer into the required shape, fastening them with nails or solder, and beating up a pattern on them in *repoussé* work, the whole being finished with a graving-tool. Small figures were sometimes cast in the lump. When we are told that the Greeks, Rhoecus and Theodorus, first cast in bronze (Pausan. ix. 41, § 1), we must perhaps understand by this that these artists introduced the method of casting statues hollow, not solid, as their predecessors had done. These artists may have lived about the 60th Olympiad, and certainly soon after that time bronze statuary spread with great rapidity over Greece; and indeed bronze continued a favourite material with sculptors until the decay of art. Of the formative process we have a vivid picture on a Greek vase of good period, engraved as the frontispiece to Mr. Murray's *History of Greek Sculpture.* The extraordinary abundance of works of art in bronze, found on almost all ancient sites, especially at Herculaneum and Pompeii, is a notable fact.

Copper as Coin.—In the coinage of the Greeks and Romans copper is seldom unalloyed. A number of analyses made of late years of Greek coins show a proportion of tin of from 10 to 16 per cent., and an occasional 2 to 5 per cent. of lead. Roman *aes signatum* in republican times shows a proportion of 5 to 8 per cent. of tin and 16 to 29 of lead. After the time of Augustus a change was introduced in the composition of Roman coin. Thenceforward sestertii and dupondii were made of brass, that is to say, of a mixture containing 20 per cent. of zinc and 80 of copper; while the asses were made entirely of copper. Money of copper and bronze stood on a very different footing in Italy to that on which it stood in Hellas and Asia. For in western countries, copper was the usual medium of exchange and measure of value; the chief currency consisted in early times of huge ingots of copper stamped with an official type; and when gold and silver came into use, they at first passed merely as the equivalents and representatives of so much copper. In the East, on the other hand, where gold and silver were the true media of exchange, and copper was used only for very small values, it was seldom minted save as money of account. (See NUMISMATICS.) The Ptolemies of Egypt minted copper pieces of full value; and Brandes (*Gewichtswesen,* p. 292) is disposed to think that the early Athenian and other copper money was minted up to full weight for a time. But this was exceptional; and in almost all Hellenic settlements, copper money was a currency of tokens; and the weight of it is consequently most irregular. Copper money was first minted in Greece towards the end of the fifth century, at which period the cities of South Italy, Sicily, and Hellas alike began to strike copper pieces in place of the minute silver coins which had hitherto passed as small change. Conservatives objected to the innovation, as we know from Aristophanes (*Ran.* 725).

Since the most ancient coins in Rome and the old Italian states were made of *aes,* this name was given to money in general, so that Ulpian (Dig. 50, tit. 16, s. 158) says, *Etiam aureos nummos aes dicimus.* (Cf. Hor. *Ars Poët.* 345; *Ep.* i. 7, 23.) For the same reason we have *aes alienum,* meaning debt, and *aera* in the plural, pay to the soldiers (Liv. v. 4; Plin. *H. N.* xxxiv. § 1). The Romans had no other coinage except copper, till B.C. 269, five years before the First Punic War. See AS.

Aesăcus (Αἴσακος). The son of Priam and Alexirrhoë, who fell in love with Hesperia, the daughter of Cebren. While he was pursuing her, she was stung by a viper and died. Aesacus in his grief threw himself into the sea, and was changed by Thetis into an aquatic bird (Ovid, *Met.* xi. 750).

Aesar. (1) An Etruscan word equivalent to the Latin *deus* (Suet. *Octav.* 97). Casaubon connects it with the Gr. *αἶσα,* "fate." (2) A river of Bruttii, near Crotona, in Southern Italy.

Aeschīnes (Αἰσχίνης). (1) A great Athenian orator, born in B.C. 389, the son of Atrometus, a schoolmaster, and Leucothea. The statements of Demosthenes in regard to the disreputable character of his parents are probably groundless. After some experience as a soldier he entered upon the profession of a public clerk, which, however, he soon left to become an actor of indifferent success. But his real talents, aided by his experience of public life gained as a clerk, soon made him prominent when he turned his attention to a political career. In B.C. 348, after the fall of Olynthus, he attracted attention by advocating a general council of the Greek States to concert measures against King Philip. But the failure of the embassy to Arcadia, which he undertook in pursuance of this plan, seems to have so discouraged him that he immediately changed sides, and was thenceforth an adherent of the peace party. In this capacity he played a conspicuous part as a member of the famous embassy to Philip in B. C. 346, preliminary to the peace of Philocrates. The complicated details of these negotiations need not be given here. (See DEMOSTHENES; PHILIP II.) It is sufficient to say that Aeschines was won over by Philip's flattery (there is no proof that he was actually bribed, beyond the partisan statement of Demosthenes), and became convinced that a close alliance with the Macedonian king was the safest

Aeschines the Orator. (National Museum, Naples.)

course for Athens. Almost immediately after the conclusion of the peace, he was indicted by Timarchus, an adherent of Demosthenes, for treasonable conduct, but was triumphantly acquitted. A second accusation, brought by Demosthenes himself in B. C. 343, was more nearly successful, and Aeschines narrowly escaped conviction, after an able defence, in which he was aided by the intercession of Eubulus and Phocion. Aeschines next appears as one of the representatives of Athens at the Amphictyonic Council at Delphi in B. C. 339. Here, as he tells us, he was so enraged by an unjust complaint which the delegates from Amphissa brought against Athens, that he in turn made a vehement counter-attack on the Amphissians for their occupation of the sacred plain of Cirrha. So infuriated were the Amphictyons by his invective that, after burning the buildings of the offending Amphissian settlers, they voted to hold a special meeting of the council to consider what further punishment should be inflicted. Athens and Thebes refused to send delegates to this assembly, and thus became involved in war with Philip and the rest of the Amphictyons—a war which resulted in the fatal battle of Chaeronea and the downfall of Athenian independence.

In stirring up this new conflict, Aeschines certainly played into the hands of Philip, who was awaiting an opportunity for armed interference in the affairs of Central Greece; but here, too, the charge of bribery rests on the unsupported testimony of his bitterest enemy. After the battle of Chaeronea, the party of Aeschines naturally fell into disfavour. He does not figure prominently in public affairs again till B.C. 330, when he made a final effort to defeat his hated rival. An obscure politician named Ctesiphon had in B. C. 336 brought in a bill proposing to confer a golden crown upon Demosthenes for his services to the State. Aeschines raised objection to this on the score of illegality. The case did not come to trial till six years had elapsed, and then each of the orators exhausted every effort to crush his opponent. But Aeschines was the weaker, both in genius and in merit, and, not receiving the fifth part of the votes of the court, he was fined one thousand drachmas, and lost the right of appearing before the people in a similar capacity again. He left Athens and went first to Ephesus and afterwards to Rhodes, where he is said to have opened a school of oratory. He outlived his great opponent and died at Samos at the age of seventy-five.

Only three orations of Aeschines have been preserved, and all of these bear, directly or indirectly, on his quarrel with Demosthenes. Their titles are: (a) *Against Timarchus*, (b) *On the Dishonest Embassy*, (c) *Against Ctesiphon*. The occasion and subject of each have been noticed above. The second of them is generally considered to be the best. In natural gifts of oratory Aeschines was inferior to Demosthenes alone among his contemporaries. He excelled particularly in brilliant narrative, and was also one of the first to win a reputation for extemporaneous speech. He was less careful in his composition than Demosthenes, and was inferior to him in vigour and moral earnestness.

The editions of Schultz (Leipzig, 1865) and Weidner (Berlin, 1872) are among the most important. Richardson's edition of Weidner's *Against Ctesiphon* may be recommended to American readers.

(2) A philosopher of Athens, a pupil of Socrates, after whose death he became a perfumer, but, meeting with little success, went to Sicily and stayed at the court of the tyrant Dionysius until that ruler was expelled. Returning to Athens, he taught philosophy in private for a fee. Besides orations and epistles, he wrote Socratic dialogues on temperance and the other virtues. None of these dialogues remains. Three others that exist and that are ascribed to Aeschines are spurious. They treat (a) of Virtue, (b) of Riches, (c) of Death. Aeschines pretended to have received his dialogues from Xanthippé, the wife of Socrates.

Aeschy̆lus (Αἰσχύλος). The son of Euphorion, born in the Attic deme of Eleusis in the year B.C.

525. The period of his youth and early manhood coincides with the great national struggle which both Asiatic and European Hellas were forced to wage against the barbarians in the first twenty years of the fifth century. In this conflict he played the part of a brave soldier at the battles of Marathon, Salamis, and Plataea, and his works abound in traces of the warlike and patriotic feeling of those stirring days. His brother Cynegirus met an heroic death at Marathon, and another distinguished soldier of Salamis, Aminias, is said to have been of the same family, but this is probably an error. We know little of the youth and education of Aeschylus, but it is certain that he began his career as a tragic poet before the age of thirty years, though his first victory was not gained till 485. About the year 470 he went to Sicily at the invitation of King Hiero of Syracuse. Here he composed his *Aetnaean Women* (Αἰτναῖαι), in honour of the newly founded city of Aetna. His departure from Athens has been ascribed to an indictment by the Athenians for profanation of the mysteries. But it was the policy of Hiero to attract literary men to his brilliant court, and the presence of Aeschylus there needs no more explanation than that of Simonides and Pindar during the same period. Later in his life he visited Sicily a second time, where he met his death in 456. Among the many mythical details with which tradition has surrounded the life of Aeschylus, it is said that he was killed by an eagle letting fall a tortoise upon his bald head, supposing it to be a stone. The high honour in which he was held by the Athenians after his death is shown by the fact that in later times it was made lawful to reproduce his plays in competition for the prize against new tragedies.

Aeschylus. (Capitoline Museum.)

Aeschylus is said to have produced seventy-two, or even ninety dramas, and to have gained the first prize thirteen times. As each poet competed with four plays (three tragedies and a satyric drama), it appears that Aeschylus was successful in more than half of all his contests. Only seven of his tragedies have come down to us. They will be described in what seems to have been their chronological order.

(1) The *Suppliants* (Ἱκέτιδες) takes its name from the chorus representing the fifty daughters of Danaüs fleeing to Argos for protection from the sons of Aegyptus. The prominence of the chorus, the small number of characters, and the absence of a prologue mark this play as the earliest of those of Aeschylus which we have, and consequently the oldest Greek drama extant. Its undeniable merits are much obscured by the very corrupt state of the text.

(2) The *Persians* (Πέρσαι) is unique among the Greek tragedies which we possess in drawing its theme from history rather than from myth. The central point of interest is found in a splendid narrative of the battle of Salamis, but by an artifice of the poet the scene of the play is laid in Susa, and the laments of Atossa and the Persian nobles supply the tragic elements. The *Persians* was produced in B.C. 472, as part of a tetralogy consisting of the *Phineus, Persians, Glaucus ποτνιεύς,* and *Prometheus the Fire-kindler* (πυρκαεύς).

(3) The *Seven against Thebes* (Ἑπτὰ ἐπὶ Θήβας) was produced in B.C. 467, as the third play in a tetralogy of which the remaining pieces were the *Laïus, Oedipus,* and the satyric drama called *The Sphinx.* It includes a magnificent description of the seven Argive champions and their Theban opponents, with the final victory of Thebes, and a hint, at the close, of the Antigoné-motive, afterwards so finely worked out by Sophocles. In this play, as in the *Persians,* the martial spirit of Aeschylus finds ample room for manifestation. Both dramas are "full of war," to quote the words of Aristophanes (*Frogs,* 1021).

(4) The *Prometheus Bound* (Προμηθεὺς δεσμώτης), with its companion pieces the *Prometheus Loosed* (λυόμενος) and the *Prometheus the Fire-bearer* (πυρφόρος), treated the history of the rebellious Titan who steadfastly suffered the wrath of Zeus for his benefactions to mankind. The *Prometheus Bound,* the only play of the trilogy which has come down to us, depicts the hero, fettered to a rock in Scythia, and threatened by Hermes with a penalty still more severe. But he proudly refuses to submit to the will of the new ruler of Olympus, and at the close of the play he is struck by the thunderbolt, and, with the rock to which he is fastened, sinks out of sight. The second play described the final reconciliation and the liberation of Prometheus; while the third (see Westphal's *Proleg. to Aeschylus,* p. 207 foll.) probably celebrated the establishment of Prometheus in Attica as a benignant deity. No Greek tragedy has been more admired than the *Prometheus Bound.* In the grandeur of its action and the sublimity of character displayed, as well as in the exquisite pathos of some of its scenes, it stands almost unequalled. The Prometheus trilogy was probably produced either in B.C. 468 or 466 (Christ), or about ten years earlier (Wecklein).

(5) The trilogy composed of the *Agamemnon* (Ἀγαμέμνων), *Choephori* (Χοηφόροι), and *Eumenides* (Εὐμενίδες), comes last in the list, and is of special interest from the fact that it is the only complete trilogy which is extant from any of the Greek tragedians. In the *Agamemnon* the poet describes the return of the victorious king from Troy, and his murder by Clytaemnestra and her paramour Aegisthus. In the *Choephori,* Orestes, son of Agamemnon, now grown to manhood, returns, and with the help of his friend Pylades avenges the murder of his father by putting to death the guilty pair, and is himself, in turn, driven frantic by the Erinyes. In the *Eumenides* he flees to Athens, where he is tried, and by the advocacy of Apollo and the casting vote of Athené he is acquitted, and the family curse comes to an end. This great trilogy shows the genius of Aeschylus in its loftiest form. Each play is complete in itself, and yet each is but a single act in the

mighty drama of crime, vengeance, and expiation. The *Agamemnon* is the most powerful of the three plays, and probably the greatest work of Aeschylus, if indeed it is not the most impressive tragedy in existence. The trilogy is usually known as the *Oresteia* (Ὀρέστεια), and, with the satyric play *Proteus* (Πρωτεύς), was produced in B.C. 458.

The extant works of Aeschylus show a constant progress in dramatic art. He is said to have added a second actor to the one employed by his predecessors, and in his later plays he adopts, and uses with full mastery, the third actor first introduced by his younger rival, Sophocles. The choral parts, at first the most prominent feature both in extent and importance, gradually give way before the growth of the dialogue. In the scenic effects, too, Aeschylus made many improvements, using extraordinary means to excite wonder or awe. Like Wagner, he was both poet and musician, and, besides training his own choruses, he is said to have taken part as actor in the performances themselves.

The most characteristic feature of his poetry is its grandeur, both of thought and style, though he is none the less master of lyric beauty and tender pathos. His theology is stern and lofty, and pervaded by the idea of a destiny which controls all things, human and divine. But the hereditary curse that brooded over the families of Labdacus and Pelops was always aided in its destructive work by the folly and wickedness of the victims themselves. No poet, in fact, has stated more impressively than Aeschylus the inevitable connection between guilt and punishment. His style, it must be confessed, is sometimes so elevated as to seem almost bombastic, but this apparent fault is the natural result of the poet's mighty current of thought, which could not find vent in the ordinary channels of expression.

All the existing MSS. of Aeschylus are said by W. Dindorf to be derived from the Codex Mediceus (Laurentianus), which dates back to the eleventh century, and contains many valuable scholia taken from the ancient grammarians. It is the chief authority for the *Choephori*, of which, however, the text is in a bad condition. The *Prometheus, Seven against Thebes*, and *Persians* are more fully represented by MSS. than the other plays. Two codices of the fourteenth century (Florentinus and Farnesianus) supply that portion of the *Agamemnon* (lines 295–1026) which is missing from the Codex Mediceus.

The Aldine *editio princeps* (1518) and the edition of Stanley (London, 1663) are worthy of note among the older editions. To these may be added among later works the editions of Hermann (Leipzig, 1852), Kirchhoff (Berlin, 1880), Weil (Leipzig, 1885), and the valuable critical edition of Wecklein-Vitelli (Berlin, 1885). Paley's (London, 1879) is the most convenient English edition of all the plays with notes. Annotated editions of single plays are numerous. Among the more recent are Wecklein's *Oresteia* (Leipzig, 1888), Schneidewin-Heuse's *Agamemnon* (Berlin, 1883), Allen's Wecklein's *Prometheus* (Boston, 1891), Teuffel-Wecklein's *Persians* (Leipzig, 1886), Tucker's *Suppliants* (London, 1889), and Flagg's *Seven against Thebes* (Boston, 1886). Dindorf's *Lexicon Aeschyleum* (Leipzig, 1873) is an indispensable work to the student. The best complete English translation is that of Plumptre; but for the *Agamemnon* and the *Prometheus* we are fortunate in having versions of great excellence by Robert Browning and Mrs. Browning respectively.

Aes circumforaneum. Money borrowed from the *argentarii* (q. v.) who had shops around the Forum.

Aesculapius or **Asclēpius** (Ἀσκληπιός). The god of the medical art. In Homer he is not a divinity, but simply the "blameless physician" whose sons, Machaon and Podalirius, were the physicians in the Greek army. The common story relates that Aesculapius was a son of Apollo and Coronis, and that when Coronis was with child by Apollo she became enamoured of Ischys, an Arcadian. Apollo, informed of this by a raven, killed Coronis and Ischys. When the body of Coronis was to be burnt, the child Aesculapius was saved from the flames, and was brought up by the centaur Chiron, who instructed him in the art of healing and in hunting. There are other tales respecting his birth, according to some of which he was a native of Epidaurus, and this was a common opinion in later times. After he had grown up, he not only cured the sick, but recalled the dead to life. Zeus, fearing lest men might contrive to escape death altogether, killed Aesculapius with his thunderbolt; but, on the request of Apollo, Zeus placed him among the stars. He was married to Epioné, by whom he had the two sons spoken of by Homer, and also other children. The chief seat of the worship of Aesculapius was Epidaurus, where he had a temple surrounded with an extensive grove. Serpents were sacred to him, because they were a symbol of renovation, and were believed to have the power of discovering healing herbs. The cock was sacrificed to him. At Rome the worship of Aesculapius was introduced from Epidaurus in B.C. 293, for the purpose of averting a pestilence. The supposed descendants of Aesculapius were called by the patronymic name of Asclepiadae, and their principal seats were Cos and Cnidus. They were an order or caste of priests, among whom the knowledge of medicine was regarded as a sacred secret, and was transmitted from father to son in these families.

Aesculapius. (Berlin.)

Aescŭlus. A species of trees, commonly ranked in the family of oaks.

Aesēpus. A river rising near Mount Ida, and flowing into the Propontis.

Aes equestré, aes hordearium, aes militaré. Ancient terms for the pay of the Roman soldiers before the regular *stipendium* was introduced. The first denoted the sum given for the purchase of a horse for the eques; the second, the sum paid for the keep of the horse; and the third, the pay of a foot-soldier. See EQUES.

Aesernia. A town of Samnium, made a Roman colony in the First Punic War.

Aes gravé. A term applied to the early Italian bronze or copper coins. See As.

Aesis. A river forming the boundary between Picenum and Umbria.

Aes manuarium. The money won in throwing dice (*manibus collectum*, in which phrase *manus* means a throw). See ALEA; TALI; TESSERAE; PAR IMPAR.

Aes militārē. See AES EQUESTRE.

Aeson (Αἴσων). The son of Cretheus and Tyro, and father of Iason. He was excluded from the throne by his half-brother Pelias. During the absence of Iason on the Argonautic expedition, Pelias attempted to murder Aeson, but the latter put an end to his own life. According to Ovid, Aeson survived the return of the Argonauts, and was made young again by Medea. See ARGONAUTAE; IASON; MEDEA.

Aesōpus (Αἴσωπος). A famous writer of fables, the first author who created an independent class of stories about animals, so that in a few generations his name and person had become typical of that entire class of literature. In course of time, thanks to his plain, popular manner, the story of his own life was enveloped in an almost inextricable tissue of tales and traditions, which represent him as an ugly hunchback and buffoon. In the Middle Ages these were woven into a kind of romance. A Phrygian by birth, and living in the time of the Seven Sages, about B.C. 600, he is said to have been at first a slave to several masters, till Iadmon of Samos set him free. That he next lived at the court of Croesus, and being sent by him on an embassy to Delphi, was murdered by the priests there, is pure fiction. Under his name were propagated in all parts of Greece, at first only by tradition in the mouth of the people, a multitude of prose tales teaching the lessons of life under the guise of fables about animals. We know how Socrates, during his last days in prison, was engaged in turning the fables of Aesop into verse. The first written collection appears to have been made by Demetrius of Phalerum, B.C. 300. The collections of *Aesop's Fables* that have come down to us are, in part, late prose renderings of the version in choliambics by Babrius (q. v.), which still retain here and there a scrap of verse; partly products of the rhetorical schools, and therefore of very different periods and degrees of merit. A good text of the version by Babrius is that of Schneidewin (1865), and of Hartung with German notes and a translation (1858). See also Rutherford's edition of Babrius (London, 1883).

Aesōpus, CLODIUS. A great tragic actor at Rome, a contemporary of Quintus Roscius (q. v.), and, like him, on intimate terms with Cicero. Aesopus appeared upon the stage for the last time at the dedication of Pompey's theatre in B.C. 55. He left a large fortune to his son, who wasted it in luxury and dissipation, on one occasion dissolving a pearl worth $40,000, and swallowing it, in order to outdo the famous exploit of Cleopatra.

Aes rudē. See AS; NUMISMATICS.

Aestii or Aestui. A Slavonic people living on the sea-coast in northeastern Germany (Kurland), and noted for collecting and selling amber, which they called *glaesum* (Tac. *Germ.* 45).

Aestimatio litis. See IUDEX.

Aesŭla. A town of the Aequi, between Praeneste and Tibur.

Aes uxorium. A tax paid by men who reached old age without marrying, and first imposed by the censors in B.C. 403. See LEX IULIA ET PAPIA POPPAEA, p. 942.

Aesymnētes (αἰσυμνήτης, from αἶσα, a just portion). Originally a judge at the games, but later a person whom his fellow-citizens had voluntarily invested with absolute power, so that Dionysius compares the office with the Roman dictatorship. There is but one express instance known of the bestowal of this office, namely, upon Pittacus, in Mitylenē (Dionys. v. 73; Strabo, xiii. 617; Plut. *Solon*, 4; Diog. Laërt. i. 75. See Tittmann, *Griech. Staatsv.* p. 76).

Aetas. See IMPUBES.

Aethalia, Aethălis, or Ilva. An island in the Tuscan Sea, the modern Elba.

Aethalĭdes (Αἰθαλίδης). The son of Hermes and Eupolemia, the herald of the Argonauts. His soul, after many migrations, at length took possession of the body of Pythagoras, in which it still recollected its former migrations. (Apoll. Rh. i. 54.)

Aethiŏpes. A name said to be from αἴθω and ὤψ, but perhaps really a foreign name corrupted, was applied (1) most generally to all black or dark races of men; (2) to all the inhabitants of Inner Africa, south of Mauretania, the Great Desert, and Egypt, from the Atlantic to the Red Sea and Indian Ocean, and to some of the dark races of Asia; and (3) most specifically to the inhabitants of the land south of Egypt, which was called Aethiopia (q. v.).

Aethiopia (Αἰθιοπία). Nubia, Kordofan, Sennaar, Abyssinia. A country of Africa, south of Egypt, the boundary of the countries being at Syenē and the Smaller Cataract of the Nile, and extending on the east to the Red Sea, and to the south and southwest indefinitely, as far apparently as the knowledge of the ancients extended. The people of Aethiopia seem to have been of the Caucasian race, and to have spoken a language allied to the Arabic. Monuments are found in the country closely resembling those of Egypt, but of an inferior style. It was the seat of a powerful monarchy, of which Meroë was the capital. Some traditions made Meroë the parent of Egyptian civilization, while others ascribed the civilization of Aethiopia to Egyptian colonization. So great was the power of the Aethiopians that more than once in its history Egypt was governed by Aethiopian kings. Under the Ptolemies, Graeco-Egyptian colonies established themselves in Aethiopia; but the country was never subdued. The Romans failed to extend their empire over Aethiopia, though they made expeditions into the country, in one of which C. Petronius, prefect of Egypt under Augustus, advanced as far as Napata, and defeated the warrior queen Candacē (B.C. 22). Christianity very early extended to Aethiopia, probably in consequence of the conversion of the treasurer of Queen Candacē. Cf. Acts, viii. 27; and see CANDACĒ.

Aethiŏpis (Αἰθιοπίς). An epic in five books by Arctinus of Miletus, one of the Cyclic poets, said to have been a pupil of Homer. The poem covers the portion of the Trojan War from the death of Hector to the death of Achilles. The heroine is Penthesilea (q. v.). This poem was by some added to the *Iliad* by a modification of the last line. See CYCLIC POETS; EPOS; TROJAN WAR.

Aethra (Αἴθρη). (1) Daughter of Pittheus, king

of Troezen, mother of Theseus by Aegeus or, according to another account, by Poseidon. While Homer merely mentions her as a servant of Helen at Troy, later legend adds that when the Dioscuri took Aphidnae and set free their sister, whom Theseus had carried off, they conveyed Aethra to Sparta as a slave, whence she accompanied Helen to Troy; and that on the fall of that city they brought her grandsons, Acamas and Demophoön, back to Athens. (2) A daughter of Oceanus, by whom Atlas begot the twelve Hyades (q. v.) and a son, Hyas.

Aëtion (Ἀετίων). A Greek painter in the latter half of the fourth century B.C., especially famed for his picture of Alexander the Great's wedding with the beautiful Roxana, B.C. 328. See PICTURA.

Aëtius (Ἀέτιος). (1) Of Amida in Mesopotamia, a Greek physician of the sixth century A.D., who lived at Constantinople as imperial physician in ordinary. He was the author of a great miscellany on pathology and diagnosis in sixteen books. (2) An heresiarch of the fourth century A.D., called by his adversaries "the Atheist." Epiphanius has preserved forty-seven heretical propositions from the work of Aëtius, among them the rejection of the authority of the prophets and apostles; the assertion that the Son of God was not like the Father; the doctrine that faith without works is sufficient; and the claim that the most culpable acts are the necessities of nature. He died A.D. 366. (3) A Roman general born in Moesia towards the end of the fourth century A.D. He led an army of Huns to suppress the usurpation of the emperor John. In A.D. 433 he became consul and general-in-chief, and as such kept back the Western barbarians for twenty years, defeating the Goths, Burgundians, Gauls, and Franks; and at Châlons routed the famous Attila (q. v.) in the year 451. In 454, the emperor Valentinian, jealous of his fame, slew him with his own hand.

Aetna (Αἴτνη). (1) A volcanic mountain in the northeast of Sicily between Tauromenium and Catana. It is said to have derived its name from Aetna, a Sicilian nymph, a daughter of Heaven and Earth. Zeus buried under it Typhon or Enceladus; and in its interior Hephaestus and the Cyclops forged the thunderbolts for Zeus. There were several eruptions of Mount Aetna in antiquity. One occurred in B.C. 475, to which Aeschylus and Pindar probably allude, and another in B.C. 425, which Thucydides says was the third on record since the Greeks had settled in Sicily. (2) A town at the foot of Mount Aetna, on the road to Catana, formerly called Inessa or Innesa. It was founded in B.C. 461 by the inhabitants of Catana, who had been expelled from their own town by the Siculi. They gave the name of Aetna to Inessa, because their own town Catana had been called Aetna by Hiero I.

Aetna. The title of a didactic poem generally ascribed to Lucilius Iunior, the friend of Seneca, though once printed with the minor works of Vergil. It consists of 646 hexameter lines, and describes the mountain, with an account of a former eruption. The poem has been revised, emended, and annotated by H. A. J. Munro (Camb. 1867).

Aetnaea (τὰ Αἴτναια). A festival celebrated in honour of Zeus Aetnaeus, so called from his statue at Mount Aetna. Nothing is known of the details.

Aetolia (Αἰτωλία). A division of Greece, bounded on the west by Acarnania, from which it was separated by the river Acheloüs; on the north by Epirus and Thessaly; on the east by the Ozolian Locrians; and on the south by the entrance to the Corinthian Gulf. It was divided into two parts—Old Aetolia, from the Acheloüs to the Evenus and Calydon; and New Aetolia, or the Acquired, from the Evenus and Calydon to the Ozolian Locrians. On the coast the country is level and fruitful, but in the interior mountainous and unproductive. The mountains contained many wild beasts, and were celebrated in mythology for the hunt of the Calydonian boar. The country was originally inhabited by Curetes and Leleges, but was at an early period colonized by Greeks from Elis, led by the mythical Aetolus (q. v.). The Aetolians took part in the Trojan War, under their king Thoas. They continued for a long time a rude and uncivilized people, living to a great extent by robbery; and even in the time of Thucydides (B.C. 410) many of their tribes spoke a language which was not Greek, and were in the habit of eating raw flesh. They appear to have been early united by a kind of league, but this league first acquired political importance about the middle of the third century B.C., and became a formidable rival to the Macedonian monarchs and the Achaean League. The Aetolians took the side of Antiochus III. against the Romans, and on the defeat of that monarch, B.C. 189, they became virtually the subjects of Rome. On the conquest of the Achaeans, B.C. 146, Aetolia was included in the Roman province of Achaea.

Aetolĭcum Foedus (τὸ κοινὸν τῶν Αἰτωλῶν). A confederation of the Aetolian towns, afterwards joined by other towns and cantons of Greece, and formed in B.C. 338, after the battle of Chaeronea, to counteract the influence of Macedonia in the affairs of Greece. (See ACHAEAN LEAGUE.) Its political existence was destroyed in B.C. 189 by the treaty with Rome by which the Aetolians became Roman subjects.

Aetōlus (Αἰτωλός). The son of Endymion, who founded Elis and Iphianassa. Having accidentally killed Apis, son of Phoroneus, he fled with a band of followers into the country which afterwards was called, in his honour, Aetolia (q. v.). See Apollod. i. 7, 6.

Aëtōma (ἀέτωμα). See FASTIGIUM.

Aĕtos (ἀετός). See AQUILA.

Aex. (1) A rocky island between Tenos and Chios, so called from its having the shape of a goat (αἴξ). (2) The goat Amalthea (q. v.) that suckled Zeus, and became a constellation under the name of Aex.

Afer, GNAEUS DOMITIUS. The preceptor of Quintilian, and an orator of ability, who was born at Nemausus (Nîmes), and died of drunkenness, A.D. 59. He is best remembered as having been an informer under Tiberius, betraying to death Claudia Pulchra and Q. Varus, her son. See Tac. *Ann.* iv. 52; xiv. 19; Quint. v. 7.

Affīnes, Affinĭtas, or **Adfīnes, Adfinĭtas.** Affines are the *cognati* of husband and wife; and the relationship called affinitas can only be the result of a lawful marriage. There are no degrees of affinitas corresponding to those of *cognatio*, though there are terms to express the various kinds of affinitas. The father of a husband is the *socer* of the husband's wife, and the father of a wife is the *socer* of the wife's husband; the term *socrus* expresses the same affinity with respect to the husband's and wife's mothers. A son's wife is *nurus* or daughter-in-law to the son's parents; a wife's husband is *gener* or son-in-law to the wife's parents. See COGNATI.

Thus the *avus, avia—pater, mater*—of the wife become by the marriage, respectively, the *socer magnus, prosocrus*, or *socrus magna—socer, socrus*—of the husband, who becomes with respect to them severally *progener* and *gener*. In like manner, the corresponding ancestors of the husband respectively assume the same names with respect to the son's wife, who becomes with respect to them *pronurus* and *nurus*. The son and daughter of a husband or wife born of a prior marriage are called *privignus* and *privigna* with respect to their step-father or step-mother; and, with respect to such children, the step-father and step-mother are severally called *vitricus* and *noverca*. The husband's brother becomes *levir* with respect to the wife, and his sister becomes *glos* (the Greek γάλως). Marriage was unlawful among persons who had become such affines as above mentioned. A person who had sustained such a *capitis diminutio* as to lose both his freedom and the civitas, lost also all his affines.

Afranius, LUCIUS. The chief master of the *fabula togata*, who flourished about B.C. 100. Taking Menander for his model, he achieved great success in depicting Roman life; and Cicero speaks of him as witty and a master of language. The titles of more than forty of his comedies are known to us; and lines of them have been preserved for us, and can be found in O. Ribbeck's collection. His plays kept possession of the stage until after the time of Nero. (See COMOEDIA.) For criticism, see Ribbeck, *Röm. Dichtung*, i. 204.

Africa (from the Punic *Frigi*, a district on the north coast). A name used by the ancients in two senses, (1) for the whole continent of Africa, and (2) for the portion of North Africa which the Romans erected into a province. (1) In the more general sense, the name was not used by the Greek writers; and its use by the Romans arose from the extension to the whole continent of the name of a part of it. The proper Greek name for the continent is Libya (Λιβύη).

Considerably before the historical period of Greece begins, the Phœnicians extended their commerce over the Mediterranean, and founded several colonies on the north coast of Africa, of which Carthage was the chief. The Greeks knew very little of the country until the foundation of the Dorian colony of Cyrenè (B.C. 620), and the intercourse of Greek travellers with Egypt in the sixth and fifth centuries; and even then their knowledge of all but the part near Cyrenè was derived from the Egyptians and Phœnicians. who sent out some remarkable expeditions to explore the country. A Phœnician fleet sent by the Egyptian Phàraoh Necho (about B.C. 600) was said to have sailed from the Red Sea, around Africa, and so into the Mediterranean: the authenticity of which story is still a matter of dispute. We still possess an authentic account of another expedition, which the Carthaginians despatched under Hanno (q. v.) (about B.C. 510), and which reached a point on the west coast nearly, if not quite, as far as latitude 10° north. In the interior, the Great Desert (Sahara) interposed a formidable obstacle to discovery; but, even before the time of Herodotus, the people on the northern coast told of individuals who had crossed the desert, and had reached a great river flowing towards the east, with crocodiles in it, and black men living on its banks, which, if the story be true, was probably the Niger in its upper course, near Timbuctoo. There were great differences of opinion as to the boundaries of the continent. Some divided the whole world into only two parts, Europe and Asia, but were not agreed to which of these two Libya (i. e. Africa) belonged; and those who recognized three divisions differed again in placing the boundary between Libya and Asia either on the west of Egypt or along the Nile, or at the isthmus of Suez and the Red Sea: the last opinion gradually prevailed. Herodotus divides the inhabitants of Africa into four races: two native, namely, the Libyans and the Ethiopians; and two foreign, namely, the Phœnicians and the Greeks. The Libyans, however, were a Caucasian race; the Ethiopians of Herodotus correspond to our Negro races. The whole of the north of Africa fell successively under the power of Rome, and was finally divided into provinces as follows: (1) AEGYPTUS; (2) LIBYA, including (*a*) Libyae Nomos or Libya Exterior, (*b*) Marmarica, (*c*) Cyrenaïca; (3) AFRICA PROPRIA, the former empire of Carthage; (4) NUMIDIA; (5) MAURETANIA, divided into (*a*) Sitifensis, (*b*) Caesariensis, (*c*) Tingitana: these, with (6) AETHIOPIA, make up the whole of Africa, according to the divisions recognized by the latest of the ancient geographers. The northern district was better known to the Romans than it is to us, and was extremely populous and flourishing. Africa Propria or Provincia, or simply Africa, was the name under which the Romans, after the Third Punic War, B.C. 146, erected into a province the whole of the former territory of Carthage. It extended from the river Musca, on the west, which divided it from Numidia, to the bottom of the Syrtis Minor, on the southeast. It was divided into two districts (*regiones*), namely, (1) Zeugis or Zeugitana, the district round Carthage; (2) Byzacium or Byzacena, south of Zeugitana, as far as the bottom of the Syrtis Minor. It corresponds to the modern regency of Tunis. The province was full of flourishing towns, and was extremely fertile; it furnished Rome with its chief supplies of corn.

In the days of Strabo, the earlier knowledge possessed by the ancients of Africa was little, if at all, improved. The Mediterranean coast and the banks of the Nile were the only ports frequented by the Greeks. Their opinion respecting the continent itself was that it formed a trapezium, or else that the coast from the Columns of Hercules to Pelusium might be considered as the base of a right-angled triangle of which the Nile formed the perpendicular side, extending to Aethiopia and the ocean, while the hypothenuse was the coast comprehended between the extremity of this line and the straits. The apex of the triangle reached beyond the limits of the habitable world, and was consequently regarded as inaccessible. The knowledge of the day respecting the eastern and western coast of Africa appears to have extended no farther than 12° north latitude, or perhaps 12° 30′. The two sides were supposed to approximate, and between the Hesperii Aethiopes to the west and the *cinnamomifera regio* to the east, the distance was supposed to be comparatively small. This intervening space was exposed to excessive heats, according to the common belief, which forbade the traveller's penetrating within its precincts; while, at a little distance beyond, the Atlantic and Indian oceans were brought to unite. The hypothesis which we have here stated made Africa terminate at about one half of its true length, and represented this continent as much smaller than Europe. On the other hand, the opinion of Hipparchus, which united eastern Africa to India, remained for a long period contemned, until Marinus of Tyre and Ptolemy had adopted it. This adoption, however, did not prevent the previous hypothesis from keeping its ground in some measure in the west of Europe, where it contributed to the discovery of the route by the Cape of Good Hope. Africa, according to Pliny (vi. § 33), was three thousand six hundred and forty-eight Roman miles from east to west. The length of the inhabited part of Africa was supposed nowhere to exceed two hundred and fifty Roman miles. Whatever may be the discussions to which the very corrupt state of the Roman numerals in the pages of Pliny are calculated to give rise, one thing is sufficiently evident, that the Romans knew only a third part of Africa. See the article GEOGRAPHIA, with the maps there given.

African Period of Latinity. The period in the history of Latin literature from about 115–180 A.D. was so called because of the fact that many of the prominent writers of this period were natives of Africa, e. g. M. CORNELIUS FRONTO, SEX. IULIUS AFRICANUS, L. APULEIUS, and the Christian writer Q. SEPTIMIUS FLORENS TERTULLIANUS. See SERMO PLEBEIUS.

Africānus. (1) A name given to several of the Scipios for their victories over the Carthaginians. See SCIPIO. (2) See SEXTUS IULIUS.

Afrĭcus. The Roman name for the southwest wind, which the Greeks called λίψ, and given to it because it blew off the coast of Africa.

Agalma (ἄγαλμα). See STATUARIA.

Agamēdes (Ἀγαμήδης). Son of Erginus of Orchomenos, and a famous builder, with his brother Trophonius (q. v.).

Agamemnon (Ἀγαμέμνων). The son of Atreus and brother of Menelaüs. Driven from Mycenae after the murder of Atreus (q. v.) by Thyestes, the two young princes fled to Sparta, where King Tyndareos gave them his daughters in marriage—Clytaemnestra to Agamemnon, and Helen to Menelaüs. While the latter inherited his father-in-law's kingdom, Agamemnon not only drove his uncle out of Mycenae, but so extended his dominions that in the war against Troy for the recovery of Helen the chief command was intrusted to him, as the mightiest prince in Greece. He contributed one hundred ships manned with warriors, besides lending sixty to the Arcadians. (On the immolation of his daughter Iphigenia at Aulis, see IPHIGENIA.) In Homer he is one of the bravest fighters before Troy; yet, by arrogantly refusing to let Chryses, priest of Apollo, ransom his daughter Chryseïs, who had fallen to Agamemnon as the prize of war, he brought a plague on the Grecian host, which he afterwards almost ruined by ruthlessly carrying off Briseïs, the prize of Achilles, who henceforth sulked in his tents and refused to fight. After the fall of Troy, Agamemnon came home with his captive, the princess Cassandra; but at supper he and his comrades were murdered by his wife's lover, Aegisthus, while the queen herself killed Cassandra. Such is Homer's account; the tragic poets make Clytaemnestra, in revenge for her daughter's immolation, throw a net over Agamemnon while bathing, and kill him with the help of Aegisthus. In Homer his children are Iphianassa, Chrysothemis, Laodicé, and Orestes; the later legend puts Iphigenia and Electra in the place of Iphianassa and Laodicé. Agamemnon was worshipped as a hero. His name is the title of a play by Aeschylus (q. v.). See the articles ACHILLES; ORESTES; PELOPIDAE; TROJAN WAR.

Agamemnonĭdes (Ἀγαμεμνονίδης). A patronymic applied to Orestes (q. v.), the son of Agamemnon.

Agamiou Graphé (ἀγαμίου γραφή). An indictment among the Spartans brought against those who married too late or unsuitably; and also against those who did not marry at all. The penalty was ἀτιμία. See ATIMIA; MATRIMONIUM.

Aganippé (Ἀγανίππη). A spring on Mount Helicon, near Thespiae in Boeotia, sacred to the Muses, who were called from it Aganippides. Its water was believed to impart poetic inspiration.

Agasias (Ἀγασίας). A Greek artist of Ephesus, who flourished probably in the first century B.C. The Borghese Gladiator in the Louvre is from his hand. See GLADIATORES.

Agāso. A groom, generally a slave, whose business it was to take care of horses, to drive cattle, or to perform the lowest menial offices.

Agatharchĭdes (Ἀγαθαρχίδης). A Greek grammarian of Cnidos, who lived at Alexandria in the second century B.C. He composed among other historical works one on the successors of Alexander the Great, and a description of the Red Sea in five books. Of both of these, some fragments remain.

Agatharchus (Ἀγάθαρχος). (1) A Greek, the inventor of scene-painting. See Vitruv. vii. *Praef.* and the articles PICTURA; THEATRUM. (2) A Samian painter, the contemporary of Zeuxis, who prided himself on the rapidity of his work, receiving from Zeuxis the famous retort that if Agatharcus painted his works in a short time, he (Zeuxis) painted "for a long time," i. e. for posterity.

Agathias (Ἀγαθίας). A Greek poet and historian of Myrina, in Asia Minor, who was born about A.D. 530, and died about 582. By profession he was a jurist, but in his Κύκλος, a collection of his own and other contemporary poems in eight books, he made a beginning of the Greek Anthology, which still preserves 101 of his epigrams. He also wrote a history of Justinian in five books, in continuation of the work of Procopius (q. v.). See ANTHOLOGY.

Agathŏcles (Ἀγαθοκλῆς). A Sicilian adventurer, born at Thermae, and brought up as a potter at Syracuse. His strength and personal beauty recommended him to Damas, a noble Syracusan, who drew him from obscurity, and on whose death he married his rich widow, and so became one of the wealthiest citizens in Syracuse. His ambitious schemes then developed themselves, and he was driven into exile. After several changes of fortune he collected an army, and was declared sovereign of Syracuse, B.C. 317. In the course of a few years the whole of Sicily which was not under the dominion of Carthage submitted to him. In 310 he was defeated at Himera by the Carthaginians, under Hamilcar, who straightway laid siege to Syracuse, whereupon he formed the bold design of averting the ruin which threatened him by carrying the war into Africa. His successes were most brilliant and rapid. He constantly defeated the troops of Carthage, but was at length summoned from Africa by the affairs of Sicily, where many cities had revolted from him, B.C. 307. These he reduced, after making a treaty with the Carthaginians. He had previously assumed the title of King of Sicily. He afterwards plundered the Lipari Isles, and also carried his arms into Italy, in order to attack the Bruttii. But his last days were embittered by family misfortunes. His grandson Archagathus murdered his son Agathocles, for the sake of succeeding to the crown, and the old king feared that the rest of his family would share his fate. He accordingly sent his wife and her two children to Egypt; and his own death followed almost immediately, in 289, after a reign of twenty-eight years, and in the seventy-second year of his age. Some authors relate an incredible story of his being poisoned by Maeno, an associate of Archagathus. The poison, we are told, was concealed in the quill with which he cleaned his teeth, and reduced him to so frightful a condition that he was placed on the funeral pile and burned while yet living, being unable to give any signs that he was not dead.

Agathodaemon (*ἀγαθοδαίμων*). A friendly disposed spirit of the cornfields and vineyards, to whom libations of unmixed wine were made at meals. See DAEMON ; EVENTUS.

Agathoërgi (*ἀγαθοεργοί*). The five hundred knights who composed the body-guard of the Spartan kings in time of war (Herod. i. 67).

Agăthon (*Ἀγάθων*). An Athenian tragic poet, the friend of Euripides and Plato. He died about B.C. 400.

Agathyrsi (*Ἀγάθυρσοι*). A people in European Sarmatia, on the river Maria (Marosch), in Transylvania, noted for their practice of tattooing their skins.

Agāve (*Ἀγαυή*). Daughter of Cadmus and wife of Echion. She, with other women, in a bacchanalian frenzy, tore to pieces her own son Pentheus (q. v.).

Agdistis (*Ἄγδιστις*). See RHEA.

Agĕla (*ἀγέλη*). An assembly of young men in Crete, who lived together from their eighteenth year till the time of their marriage. An *ἀγέλη* consisted of the sons of the most noble citizens, who were usually under the jurisdiction of the father of the youth who had been the means of collecting the *ἀγέλη*. It was the duty of this person, called *ἀγελάτης*, to superintend the military and gymnastic exercises of the youths (who were called *ἀγελάστοι*), to accompany them to the chase, and to punish them when disobedient. He was accountable, however, to the State, which supported the *ἀγέλαι* at the public expense. All the members of an *ἀγέλη* were obliged to marry at the same time. In Sparta the youths entered the *ἀγέλαι*, usually called *βοῦαι*, at the end of their seventh year. See EDUCATION.

Agelādas (*Ἀγηλάδας*). A Greek artist of the first half of the fifth century B.C., famed for his images of gods and Olympian victors, wrought in metal. His reputation was much enhanced by the fact that Phidias, Myron, and Polyclitus were his pupils. See STATUARIA.

Agēma (*ἄγημα*, from *ἄγω*). The name of a chosen body of troops in the Macedonian army, which generally consisted of horsemen. The agema seems to have varied in number: sometimes it consisted of 150 men, at other times of 300, and in later times it contained as many as 1000 or 2000 men.

Agēnor (*Ἀγήνωρ*). (1) Son of Poseidon and Libyé, king of Phoenicia, brother to Belus, and father of Cadmus and Europa (q. v.).

(2) Son of Antenor by Theano, a priestess of Athené, and one of the bravest heroes of Troy. In Homer he leads the Trojans in storming the Greek intrenchments, rescues Hector when thrown down by Aiax, and even enters the lists with Achilles, but is saved from imminent danger by Apollo. In the post-Homeric legend he dies by the hand of Neoptolemus.

Agenorĭdes (*Ἀγηνορίδης*). A descendant of an Agenor, such as Cadmus, Phineus, and Perseus.

Ageorgiou Diké (*ἀγεωργίου δίκη*). An action which might be brought in the Athenian courts by a landlord against the farmer who had injured his land by neglect or an improper mode of cultivation.

Ager; Ager Publicus. See AGRARIAE LEGES; AGRIMENSORES.

Ager Arcifinius. See AGRIMENSORES.

Ager Decumānus. See AGRIMENSORES.

Ager Limitātus. See AGRIMENSORES.

Ager Quaestorius. See AGRARIAE LEGES.

Ager Religiōsus. See AGRIMENSORES.

Ager Vectigālis. See AGRARIAE LEGES.

Agesander (*Ἀγήσανδρος*). A Greek artist of the school of Rhodes. The celebrated group of the Laocoön is the joint work of Agesander, Athenodorus, and Polydorus. See LAOCOÖN.

Agesilāus (*Ἀγησίλαος*). The name of several kings of Sparta. (1) Agesilaüs who reigned about B.C. 886, and was contemporary with the legislation of Lycurgus. (2) Son of Archidamus II., and succeeded his half-brother Agis II. in B.C. 398, excluding, on the ground of spurious birth, and by the interest of Lysander, his nephew Leotychides. From B.C. 396 to 394 he carried on the war in Asia Minor with great success, but, in the midst of his conquests, was summoned home to defend his country against Thebes, Corinth, and Argos, which had been induced by Artaxerxes to take up arms against Sparta. In the year 394 he met and defeated, at Coronea in Boeotia, the allied forces. During the next four years he regained for his country much of its former supremacy, till at length the fatal battle of Leuctra, B.C. 371, overthrew forever the power of Sparta, and gave the supremacy for a time to Thebes. In 361 he crossed, with a body of Lacedaemonian mercenaries, into Egypt, where he died in the winter of 361–360, after a life of above eighty years and a reign of thirty-eight. In person Agesilaüs was small, mean-looking, and lame, on which last ground objection had been made to his accession, an oracle, curiously fulfilled, having warned Sparta of evils awaiting her under a "lame sovereignty." In his reign, indeed, her fall took place, but not through him, for he was one of the best citizens and generals that Sparta ever had.

Agesipŏlis (*Ἀγησίπολις*). The name of several kings of Sparta. (1) Agesipolis who succeeded his father, Pausanias, while yet a minor, in B.C. 394, and reigned fourteen years. (2) Son of Cleombrotus, reigned one year, B.C. 371. (3) Succeeded Cleomenes in B.C. 220, but was soon deposed by his colleague Lycurgus.

Agetoria. Another name for the CARNEA (q. v.).

Agger (χῶμα), from *ad* and *gero*. A term used in general for a heap or mound of any kind. It was more particularly applied to a mound, usually composed of earth, which was raised around a besieged town, and was gradually increased in breadth and height till it equalled or overtopped the walls. At the siege of Avaricum, Caesar raised

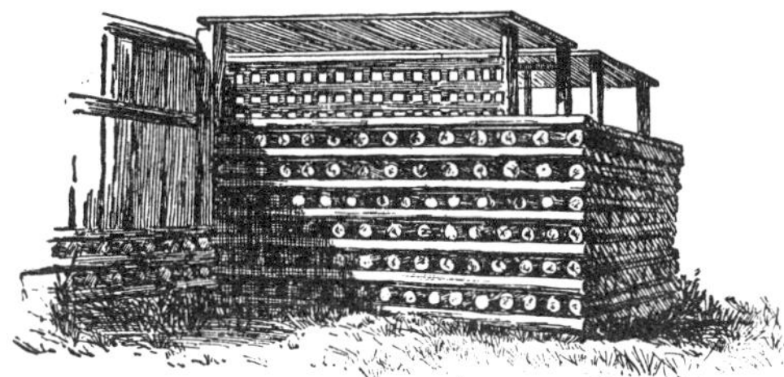

Agger. (From Column of Trajan.)

in twenty-five days an agger 330 feet broad and 80 feet high. The agger was sometimes made not only of earth, but of wood, hurdles, etc., as in the accompanying illustration, whence we read of its being set on fire. The name agger was also applied to the earthen wall surrounding a Roman encampment, composed of the earth dug from the ditch (*fossa*), which was usually nine feet broad and seven feet deep; but if any attack was apprehended, the depth was increased to twelve feet and the breadth to thirteen feet. Sharp stakes were usually fixed upon the agger, which was then called *vallum*. When both words are used (as in Caesar, *agger ac vallum*), the agger means the mound of earth, and the vallum, the sharp stakes which were fixed upon the agger.

Agias (Ἀγίας). See CYCLIC POETS.

Agis (Ἆγις). The name of several kings of Sparta. (1) The son of Eurysthenes, the founder of the family of the Agidae. (2) Son of Archidamus II., reigned B.C. 427-398. He took an active part in the Peloponnesian War, and invaded Attica several times. While Alcibiades was at Sparta he was the guest of Agis, and is said to have seduced his wife Timaea (in consequence of which Leotychides, the son of Agis, was excluded from the throne as illegitimate). (3) Son of Archidamus III., reigned B.C. 338-330. He attempted to overthrow the Macedonian power in Europe while Alexander the Great was in Asia, but was defeated and killed in battle by Antipater in the year 330. (4) Son of Eudamidas II., reigned B.C. 244-240. He attempted to reestablish the institutions of Lycurgus, and to effect a thorough reform in the Spartan state; but he was resisted by his colleague Leonidas II. and the wealthy, was thrown into prison, and there put to death by command of the ephors, along with his mother and grandmother.

Agitatōres. See CIRCUS.

Aglaïa. One of the Graces. See CHARITES.

Agmen. The Roman army on the march. See EXERCITUS.

Agnāti. See COGNATIO.

Agnōmen. See NOMEN

Agonalia, Agonia, or **Agonāles.** A name derived from the old Latin *agonia*, a victim, and given to four festivals in the Roman calendar. (1) A sacrifice to Ianus, on the 9th of January. (2) A sacrifice by the Salii (q. v.) to Mars or Quirinus, on the 17th of March. (3) A sacrifice to Veiovis (q. v.), on the 21st of May. (4) A feast called Septimontium, held on the 11th of December, when a victim was offered on each of the seven hills of Rome. See Huschke, *Das alte röm. Jahr* (1869).

Agōnes (ἀγῶνες). (1) A general term used by the Greeks of the contests at the great national festivals. See OLYMPIA; PYTHIA; NEMEA; ISTHMIA. (2) As a legal term it is used of lawsuits. See TIMEMA.

Agonothĕtae (ἀγωνοθέται). The persons who in the Grecian games decided the disputes and awarded the prizes. See OLYMPIA; PYTHIA; NEMEA; ISTHMIA.

Agŏra (ἀγορά). (1) A word that properly means an assembly of any nature, and is usually employed by Homer for the general assembly of the people. The ἀγορά seems to have been considered an essential part in the constitution of the early Grecian states, since the barbarity and uncivilized condition of the Cyclopes is characterized by their wanting such an assembly. The ἀγορά, though usually convoked by the king—as, for instance, by Telemachus in the absence of his father—appears to have been also summoned at times by some distinguished chieftain, as, for example, by Achilles before Troy. The king occupied the most important seat in these assemblies, and near him sat the nobles, while the people sat or stood in a circle around them. The power and rights of the people in these assemblies have been the subject of much dispute. Platner, Tittmann, and Nitzsch maintain that the people were allowed to speak and vote; while Heeren and Müller think "that the nobles were the only persons who proposed measures, deliberated, and voted, and that the people were only present to hear the debate, and to express their feeling as a body, which expressions might then be noticed by a prince of a mild disposition." The latter view of the question is confirmed by the fact that in no passage in the *Odyssey* is any one of the people represented as taking part in the discussion; while, in the *Iliad*, Odysseus inflicts personal chastisement upon Thersites for presuming

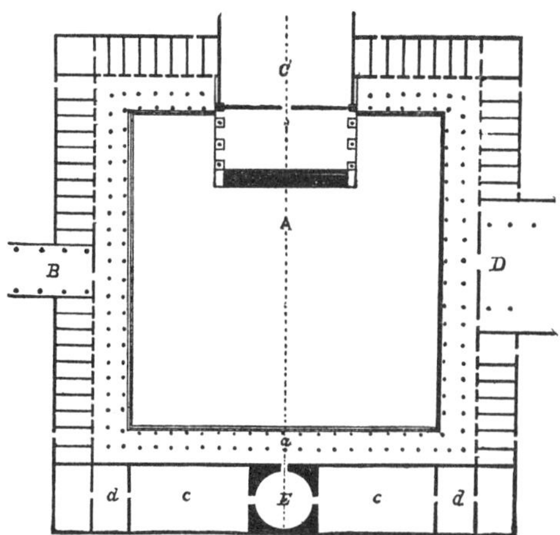

Plan of a Greek Agora, according to Vitruvius.

A, the open court, surrounded by double colonnades and shops; B, tne curia; C, the chief temple, also used as a treasury; D, the basilica, or court of justice; E, the tholus, in connection with the other rooms of the prytaneum, c, d.

to attack the nobles in the ἀγορά. The people appear to have been only called together to hear what had been already agreed upon in the council of the nobles, which is called βουλή and θόωκος, and sometimes even ἀγορά.

Among the Athenians, the proper name for the assembly of the people was ἐκκλησία, and among the Dorians ἁλία. The term ἀγορά was confined at Athens to the assemblies of the phylae and demi. In Crete the original name ἀγορά continued to be applied to the popular assemblies till a late period.

(2) The name ἀγορά was early transferred from the assembly itself to the place in which the assembly was held; and thus it came to be used for the market-place, where goods of all descriptions were bought and sold. The expression ἀγορὰ πλήθουσα, "full market," was used to signify the time from morning to noon, that is, from about nine to twelve o'clock.

The agora in Greek cities corresponds to the Roman forum (q. v.). The chief authorities on the subject are Pausanias and Vitruvius. The accompanying plan (after Vitruvius), taken from Hirt's *Geschichte der Baukunst* (xxi., fig. 1), represents the later form of the agora.

See Boeckh, *Econ. of Athens;* Leake, *Topography of Athens;* Krause, *Hellas*, vol. ii.; Hirt, *Lehre d. Gebäude d. Griechen und Römer*, chap. v.; Wachsmuth, *Hellenische Alterthumskunde;* and Becker-Göll, *Charikles*,4th scene, ii. pp. 177–212.

Agoranŏmi (ἀγορανόμοι). Market-masters. In many Greek towns magistrates somewhat resembling the Roman aediles (q. v.). At Athens ten *agoranomi* were chosen by lot every year, five for the city, and five for the port of Piraeus. They looked especially after the retail trade, gave strangers leave to engage in it, tested weights and measures as well as the quality of goods, confiscating and destroying what was spoiled; they settled disputes between buyers and sellers on the spot, or, if a suit at law was necessary, presided over it. See Boeckh, *Public Econ. of Athens*, pp. 48, 333.

Agrania (ἀγρανία). A festival celebrated at Argos, in memory of one of the daughters of Proetus, who had been afflicted with madness.

Agraphiou Graphé (ἀγραφίου γραφή). The names of all persons at Athens who owed any sum of money to the state were registered by the practores (πράκτορες) upon tablets kept for that purpose in the Temple of Athené on the Acropolis; and hence the expression of being registered on the Acropolis always means indebted to the state. If the name of an individual was improperly erased, he was subject to the action for non-registration (ἀγραφίου γραφή), which was under the jurisdiction of the thesmothetae; but if an individual was not registered, he could only be proceeded against by ἔνδειξις (q. v.), and was not liable to the ἀγραφίου γραφή.

Agrăphou Metallou Graphé (ἀγράφου μετάλλου γραφή). An action brought before the thesmothetae at Athens, against an individual who worked a mine without having previously registered it. The state required that all mines should be registered, because the twenty-fourth part of their produce was payable to the public treasury.

Agrariae Leges (Agrarian Laws). Laws dealing with the distribution of the Roman public land (*ager publicus*), and in general to be described as laws providing for the allotment to the poorer citizens of land belonging to the state, or regulating the tenure on which these lands should be held. Such assignments of land are said to have been made as early as Romulus (Varro, *R. R.* i. 10, 2), but the first agrarian law was that proposed by Sp. Cassius in B.C. 486. The public lands were the result of conquest in war. It was not till towards the end of the Republic that we hear of the state's acquiring territory by the gift of a foreign prince. War in the ancient world made the bodies and belongings of the vanquished the absolute property of the victors. No doubt either policy or pity generally interfered to prevent the full exercise of the power. In Italy especially, the persons were not usually made slaves; but though the conquered community was allowed to exist, it was deprived of part, often of a third part, of its lands. These confiscated lands had sometimes been utterly wasted in war, sometimes were still unhurt and in a state of cultivation, sometimes consisted of moorland and wood. Each kind requires separate treatment.

1. The cultivated lands were dealt with in one, or it may be in all, of four ways.

(*a*) Part was sold by the quaestors, and hence called *agri quaestorii.* According to the Gromatici, the land for this purpose was measured and divided by balks (*limites*) into square plots (*laterculi*), measuring ten *actus* each side, and containing fifty *iugera*, i.e. thirty-one acres, each. As containing one hundred square *actus*, it was sometimes called *centuria.* The earliest instance recorded of a sale was in the case of Pometia, where, although the city was surrendered when about to be stormed, some of the chiefs were slain, some of the husbandmen were sold as slaves, the town was destroyed, and the land sold (Liv. ii. 17). The sale under the spear (*sub hasta*) gave full rights of ownership (Gai. iv. 16). Conquest had extinguished all previous title or claims to the land, and the state would of course give legal effect to its own acts of transfer.

(*b*) Part was given and assigned in full ownership to Roman citizens. This land was duly surveyed, measured, divided by balks into centuries, each containing two hundred *iugera* (one hundred and twenty-five acres), and assigned by lot to Roman citizens. Such land was called *agri dati adsignati.* The oldest assignments were two *iugera* to each man; this formed an hereditament (*heredium*), i.e. he had not the mere use or life interest of the plot, but it passed to his heirs after him. The lots of one hundred men thus formed one century (*cent-uir-ia*). Later on, seven *iugera* were regarded as the normal size of a lot (Plin. *H. N.* xviii. § 18); but, in fact, there was great variety, the amount naturally depending upon the extent of land open to distribution and the number of citizens to share in it. The survey and distribution were effected by a special commission of three, five, or ten men (Cic. *Agr.* ii. 7), called *IIIviri A. D. A.*, i.e. *agris dandis adsignandis.*

(*c*) Part of the confiscated lands were given back to their former owners, and no rent was imposed on these plots.

(*d*) Part was neither sold nor assigned nor restored to the former owners, but let for a rent (*vectigal*), often for long periods to state contractors (*mancipes*), who sublet to the nearest occupiers. Hyginus mentions as long a lease as one hundred years.

2. Besides the cultivated lands still in condition to be sold or let, there were the mountain pastures

and woods. The mountain pastures and woods were often granted (*concessa*) to the old proprietors, or to the municipality, or to the new Roman colony, or reserved to the state; and other tracts of land were often useful as pastures where there were not sufficient farmers to require them as arable land. Sometimes a small rent was required, and then they came under the head of *agri vectigales* (*Grom.* pp. 203, 205). Sometimes strips of wood on the mountain were annexed by the original assignment to the different estates (*fundi*) of private persons. Pastures, in like manner, were sometimes appropriated to individuals, but held *pro indiviso;* or sometimes made common to the whole of the community (*Grom.* p. 48). Appian (*Bell. Civ.* i. 7) says that taxes were laid for the use of the common pastures, both for larger and smaller animals, i. e. horned cattle and sheep. The last was collected by the publicans.

3. Appian says that "the larger part of the lands taken from the conquered had been wasted by war, and uncultivated. As the Romans had no time to distribute it, they gave notice that any one who liked might temporarily work it, paying a tax of a yearly tenth of the seed crops, and a fifth of the plantations" (i. e. fruits; for instance, olives and grapes). There is no other authority for this definite historical statement of a notice and a tax. The Gromatici speak frequently of *agri occupatorii*, i. e. lands belonging to squatters, and explain that it was conquered land occupied by individuals. The word most frequently used to denote this occupation is *possidere;* the occupiers are *possessores;* the lands, *possessiones*—terms which do not, however, imply anything as to the legality of the title by which it is held. But that this sort of occupation was recognized by law is clear from the fact that interference with it by the state was the subject, not of judicial proceedings, but of legislative enactment.

It does not seem probable that any definite arrangement was made in early times for the occupation of public land which was not assigned, or sold, or leased; and the legal claim of the state to deal with it was as incontestable in theory as it was difficult to enforce without the destruction of those reasonable expectations, arising from long use, which are the foundation of the statesman's view of property. It is disputed whether the patricians alone (to the exclusion of the plebeians) had, before the Licinian laws, the right to hold the public land: as a fact, it was probably the case. They were originally, and continued for long to be, the holders of the government, and they were, as a rule, the richest. Now the occupation of tracts of land wasted in war was not a poor Roman's business; it was at a distance; it required capital; and it was insecure, partly from the enemy on the border, and partly from the state's not having assigned it as private property. Neither the peasant nor the small capitalist would find the occupation of such land at a distance from Rome attractive; moreover, he was liable to be called off to serve in war. The rich man could risk something, could employ slave labour, could judge of the political prospects, and have a potential voice in the actions of the state. Such possessions had a natural tendency to accumulate in the hands of the few. The holders added field to field (*continuare agros*), partly by purchase from their poorer neighbours, partly by violence, partly by taking in any vacant land adjoining. Thus were formed the large estates (*latifundia, lati fundi*) which, worked by slaves, drove out, or gave no opening for, free peasants, and, portending the ruin of Italy, roused the Gracchi to their famous legislation.

For some account of the specific agrarian laws, see the articles ROGATIONES LICINIAE; SEMPRONIAE LEGES; THORIA LEX; GRACCHUS.

Agraulia (Ἀγραυλία). An Athenian festival in honour of Agraulos (q. v.), daughter of Cecrops.

Agraulos (Ἄγραυλος). (1) Daughter of Actaeus, first king of Athens, and wife of Cecrops. (2) Daughter of Cecrops and Agraulos, of whom various stories are told. Athené is said to have given Erichthonius in a chest to Agraulos and her sister Hersé, with strict injunctions not to open it; but they disobeyed the command. (See ERICHTHONIUS.) Agraulos was subsequently punished by being changed into a stone by Hermes, because she attempted to prevent the god from entering the house of Hersé, with whom he had fallen in love. Another legend relates that Agraulos threw herself down from the Acropolis because an oracle had declared that the Athenians would conquer if some one would sacrifice himself for his country. The Athenians in gratitude built her a temple on the Acropolis, in which the young Athenians, on receiving their first suit of armour, took an oath that they would always defend their country to the last.

Agrĕtae (ἀγρέται). The name of nine maidens chosen every year in the island of Cos, as priestesses of Athené.

Agriania (ἀγριανία). Probably the same festival as the *agrania* (q. v.), and celebrated in Argos and Thebes.

Agricŏla, GNAEUS IULIUS. A Roman general, who was born June 13th, A.D. 37, at Forum Iulii (Fréjus, in Provence), the son of Iulius Graecinus, who was executed by Calĭgula, and of Iulia Procilla. He received a careful education; he first served in Britain, A.D. 60, under Suetonius Paulinus; was quaestor in Asia in 63; was governor of Aquitania from 74 to 76; and was consul in 77, when he betrothed his daughter to the historian Tacitus, and in the following year gave her to him in marriage. In 78 he received the government of Britain, which he held for seven years, during which time he subdued the whole of the country with the exception of the highlands of Caledonia, and by his wise administration introduced among the inhabitants the language and civilization of Rome. He was recalled in 85 through the jealousy of Domitian, and on his return lived in retirement till his death, in 93, which, according to some, was occasioned by poison administered by order of Domitian. His character is drawn in the brightest colours by his son-in-law Tacitus, whose life of Agricola has come down to us. See TACITUS.

Agricultūra. (1) IN GREECE. Agriculture was a leading industry, at least as early as Homer. The soil was stubborn, fertile plains being comparatively few, and mountains and rocky ground preponderating. But, favoured by a genial climate, agriculture was carried on almost everywhere with a zeal to which the wants of a dense population added their stimulus. That it was regarded as the very groundwork of social life is shown by the fact that its guardian goddess Demeter presided also over wedlock and law. It was looked upon as the most legitimate way of earning a livelihood. It was carried to the highest pitch in the Peloponnesus, where every scrap of cultivable soil was made to yield its crop, as may be seen to this day by the artificial terraces that scarp every mountain-slope. Much care was bestowed on irrigation. Scarcity of water was supplemented by artificial means; provision was made against irregular bursts of mountain torrents by embanking and regulating the natural outlets, while moist lands were channelled and stagnant waters drained. Water was distributed everywhere by ditches and canals, under the supervision of state officials; and laws of ancient date guarded against the unfair use of a watercourse to a neighbour's damage. See EMISSARIUM.

The land was mainly cultivated by slaves and serfs, though field labour was not deemed dishonourable to the freeman, except where law and custom forbade his engaging in any sort of handicraft, as at Sparta. In some countries, especially Arcadia, the old-world plan of every man tilling his field with his own hand remained in force to the latest times; and even eminent statesmen like Philopoemen (q. v.) would not give it up. Four kinds of grain were chiefly grown—wheat, barley, and two kinds of spelt, to all of which the climate allowed two sowings in the year—besides millet, sesame, various leguminous plants, and several sorts of herbage for fodder. With no less diligence was Greek husbandry applied to gardening, especially to the cultivation of the vine. This, while steadily pursued on the mainland, was developed to an extraordinary extent in the islands, most of which, owing to their mountainous character, did not afford their inhabitants sufficient arable soil. In olive-culture no part of Greece competed with Attica, which also produced the best figs, the fruit most widely cultivated. Kitchen-gardening was practised on the largest scale in Boeotia. Considering the enormous consumption of flowers in wreaths, the rearing of them, especially of the rose, lily, narcissus, and violet, must have been a lucrative business, at least in the neighbourhood of great towns. Meadow-farming was of next to no importance, few districts having a soil adapted for it, and such meadows as there were being used for pasture rather than haymaking.

(2) IN ITALY. In Italy also, the existence of the community was regarded as based upon agriculture. This is proved by the practice of marking the site of the future walls of a new town by a furrow drawn with the plough. At Rome especially, the body of irremovable peasantry long formed the core of the commonwealth. In political life the free peasant was the only factor held in account, and accordingly in war the object was to increase the number of free peasants by planting them out on as much of borderland as could be wrested from the enemy. In early times agriculture was thought the only respectable calling in which a Roman citizen could engage; and manual labour was held in high esteem and brought no discredit upon persons of rank and station, even Cato the Censor working in the fields side by side with his slaves.

Husbandry was mainly directed to the raising of grain, the ordinary cereal being at first spelt, till, in the fifth century B.C., wheat began to take a place beside it. They also cultivated barley, millet, and leguminous plants, as well as turnips, greens, and herbs for fodder. On irrigation and drainage the Italians bestowed much pains. They had no lack of grass-lands, either for pasture or haymaking; and from an early time these were artificially watered. The cultivation of the vine and olive extended as that of grains declined; so did the growth of orchard fruit, which, under the late Republic and the early Empire, received a vast expansion both from the improvement of native kinds and the introduction and naturalization of many foreign fruits. In earlier times the prime favourite among fruit trees had been, as in Greece, the nutritious fig. Agriculture proper was ruined by the acquisition of the first extra-Italian possessions, Sicily and Sardinia; for the corn supplied by the provincials as tribute in kind began to be used, not only in provisioning the armies, but in feeding the urban population. (See ANNONA.) As the state, to humour the rabble of Rome, sold this corn at the lowest possible prices, sometimes even below its value, the growth of cereals ceased to be profitable; farmers kept it down to a minimum, and took to cattle-breeding or to raising wine and oil. These branches of industry not only flourished in the face of competition, but, with judicious management, were highly remunerative. The deathblow was given to the Italian peasantry by the increasing employment of slaves and the absorption of small farms in large estates. (See LATIFUNDIUM.) On these, besides the growth of wine, oil, and fruit, the breeding of birds, game, and cattle was carried on, as well as woodcraft and special industries such as pottery, charcoal-burning, and others.

Farming implements, in addition to the plough, or *aratrum* (q. v.), usually drawn by oxen, which was much the same among Greeks and Romans, and always very imperfect, included a great variety of spades, hoes, and mattocks, and among Romans the harrow (*irpex, rastrum*), the use of which among the Greeks is doubted. The season for sowing all cereals was usually autumn. At harvest the stalks were cut with the sickle about half-way down, and the rest left standing as stubble, to be either burned or utilized for manure. The process of threshing was very defective.

See Dickson, *Husbandry of the Ancients* (1788); De la Malle, *Économie Politique des Romains* (1840); Hoskyns, *Hist. of Agriculture* (1849); and the article GEOPONICI.

Agri Decumātes. "Tithe-lands." The name given by the Romans to a part of Germany, east of the Rhine and north of the Danube, which they took possession of when the Germans retired eastward, and which they gave to the Gauls, and subsequently to their own veterans, on the payment of a tenth of the produce (*decuma*). Towards the beginning of the second century A.D. these lands were incorporated in the Roman Empire.

Agrigentum (Ἀκράγας). The modern Girgenti. A city on the south coast of Sicily, about two miles from the sea. It was celebrated for its wealth and populousness, and was one of the most splendid cities of the ancient world. It was founded by a Doric colony from Gela, about B. C. 579; was under the government of the cruel tyrant Phalaris (about 560), and subsequently under that of Theron (488-472). It was destroyed by the Carthaginians (405), and, though rebuilt by Timoleon, never regained its former greatness. It came into the power of the Romans in 210. It was the birthplace of Empedocles. There are still gigantic remains of the ancient city, notably of its temple of Zeus.

Agrimensōres. Land-surveyors; also called *gromatici*, from *groma*, the instrument used in measuring. Under the Roman emperors they formed a collegium. Like the jurisconsults, they had regular schools, and received handsome salaries from the state. Their business was to measure unassigned lands for the state, and ordinary lands for the proprietors, and to fix and maintain boundaries. Their writings on the subject of their art were very numerous; and we have still scientific treatises on the law of boundaries, such as those by Frontinus and Hyginus. They were sometimes vested with judicial power, and were called *spectabiles* and *clarissimi* in the time of Theodosius and Valentinian. As partitioners of land, the agrimensores were the successors of the augurs, and the mode of their *limitatio* was derived from the old augurial method of forming the *templum*. The word *templum*, like the Greek *τέμενος*, simply means a division; its application to signify the vault of the heavens was due to the fact that the directions were always ascertained according to the true cardinal points. At the inauguration of a king or consul, the augur looked towards the east and the person to be inaugurated towards the south. Now, in a case like this, the person to be inaugurated was considered the chief, and the direction in which he looked was the main direction. Thus we find that in the case of land-surveying the augur looked to the south; for the gods were supposed to be in the north, and the augur was considered as looking in the same manner in which the gods looked upon the earth. Hence the main line in land-surveying was drawn from north to south, and was called *cardo*, as corresponding to the axis of the world; the line which cut it was termed *decumanus*, because it made the figure of a cross, like the numeral X. These two lines were produced to the extremity of the ground which was to be laid out, and parallel to these were drawn other lines, according to the size of the quadrangle required. The limits of these divisions were indicated by balks, called *limites*, which were left as high-roads, the ground for them being deducted from the land to be divided. As every sixth was wider than the others, the square bordering upon this would lose *pro tanto*. When land was undivided it was called *arcifinius* or *arcifinalis*, to which class belonged the *ager publicus*. See AGRARIAE LEGES.

Military surveyors were known as *metatores*. In later times the *agrimensor* was called simply *mensor*. Other terms are *finitor*, *decempedator*. *Gromaticus* is properly a professor of the art, and *geometres* a teacher of it.

The writings of the Gromatici which are extant contain short treatises of about the second century after Christ, by Frontinus (embedded in a commentary of a later writer called Agennius Urbicus), by Siculus Flaccus, and by apparently two writers bearing the name of Hyginus; several short mathematical treatises of uncertain date by Balbus, Nipsus, a so-called Boëthius, and others; extracts from official registers, probably of the fifth century, of the colonial and other surveys of lands, chiefly in Italy; lists and descriptions of different kinds of boundary stones; extracts from the Theodosian Code, and one title (x. 1) of Justinian's *Digest*; an obscure and barbarous tract (*casae litterarum*) by one Innocentius, supposed to be school exercises in land-surveying, and some other short pieces. The origin and date of the collection are unknown. Niebuhr awakened modern interest in these writers, and in 1848 Lachmann's critical edition appeared, and superseded all earlier editions. In 1852, a second volume was published, containing essays on the MSS. by Blume, on the text by Lachmann, and on the list of colonies by Mommsen, and an elaborate essay on the whole subject by Rudorff.

Agrimetatio. See AGRIMENSORES.

Agrionia (Ἀγριώνια). A festival celebrated chiefly at Orchomenus, in Boeotia, in honour of Dionysus, surnamed Ἀγριώνιος, i. e. the wild. This festival was solemnized only by women and priests of Dionysus. It consisted of a kind of game, in which the women for a long time acted as if seeking Dionysus, and at last called out to one another that he had escaped to the Muses, and had concealed himself with them. After this they prepared a repast, and, having enjoyed it, amused themselves with solving riddles. This festival was remarkable for a feature which proves its great antiquity. Some virgins, who were descended from the Minyans, and who probably used to assemble around the temple on the occasion, fled, and were followed by the priest armed with a sword, who was allowed to kill the one whom he first caught. This sacrifice of a human being, though originally it must have formed a regular part of the festival, seems to have been avoided in later times. One instance, however, occurred in the days of Plutarch (*Quaest. Graec.* 38). See Müller, *Die Minyer*, p. 166.

Agrippa, MARCUS VIPSANIUS. A Roman general, who was born in B.C. 63, of an obscure family; studied with young Octavius (afterwards the emperor Augustus) at Apollonia, in Illyria, and upon the murder of Caesar, in B.C. 44, was one of the friends of Augustus who advised him to proceed immediately to Rome. In the civil wars which followed, and which terminated in giving Augustus the sovereignty of the Roman world, Agrippa took an active part; and his military abilities contributed greatly to that result. He commanded the fleet of Augustus at the battle of Actium in B.C. 31. He was thrice consul, and in his third consulship, in B.C. 27, he built the Pantheon. In the year 21 he married Iulia, daughter of Augustus. He continued to be employed in various military commands till his death in B.C. 12. By his first wife, Pomponia, Agrippa had Vipsania, married to Tiberius, the successor of Augustus; and by Iulia he had two daughters, Iulia and Agrippina, and three sons, Gaius Caesar, Lucius Caesar, and Agrippa Postumus. The last was banished by Augustus to the island of Planasia, and was put to death by Tiberius, A.D. 14. See portrait on p. 16.

Agrippīna. (1) The daughter of M. Vipsanius Agrippa (q. v.) and of Iulia, the infamous daughter of the emperor Augustus, and married to Germanicus (q. v.), by whom she had nine children, among whom were the emperor Caligula, and Agrippina, the mother of Nero. She was distinguished for her virtues and heroism, and shared all the dangers of her husband's campaigns. On his death, in A.D. 17, she returned to Italy; but the favour with which she was received by the people increased the hatred which Tiberius and his mother, Livia, had long entertained towards her. At length, in A.D. 30, Tiberius banished her to the island of Pandataria, where she died three years afterwards. See the portrait on p. 729. (2) Daughter of Germanicus and Agrippina (supra), and mother of the emperor Nero, was born at Oppidum Ubiorum, afterwards called, in honour of her, Colonia Agrippina, now Cologne. She was beautiful and intelligent, but licentious, cruel, and ambitious. She was first married to Cn. Domitius Ahenobarbus (A.D. 28), by whom she had a son, afterwards the emperor Nero; next to Crispus Passienus; and thirdly to the emperor Claudius (A.D. 49), although she was his niece. In A.D. 50 she prevailed upon Claudius to adopt her son, to the prejudice of his own son Britannicus; and, in order to secure the succession for Nero, she poisoned the emperor in A.D. 54. The young emperor soon became tired of the ascendency of his mother, and, after making several attempts to shake off her authority, he caused her to be assassinated in A.D. 59.

Agronŏmi (ἀγρονόμοι). The country police, whose duties corresponded in most respects to those of the *astynomi* in the city. They appear to have performed nearly the same duties as the *hylori* (ὑλωροί). Aristotle does not inform us in which one of the Greek states they existed. See HYLORI.

Agrotĕras Thysia (Ἀγροτέρας θυσία). A festival celebrated at Athens in honour of Artemis Agrotera (from ἄγρα, chase), in consequence of a vow made during the First Persian War to sacrifice to Artemis as many goats as there should be Persians slain at Marathon. But as the number of Persians slain was so great as to exceed that of the available goats, the Athenians decreed that five hundred goats should be offered every year. This is the account given by Xenophon, but other writers give different legends.

Agrypnis (Ἀγρυπνίς). A nocturnal festival celebrated at Arbela, in Sicily, in honour of Dionysus.

Agyieus (Ἀγυιεύς). See APOLLO.

Agylla. See CAERÉ.

Agyrium (Ἀγύριον). A Sicilian town, the birthplace of the historian Diodorus (q. v.).

Agyrmus (ἀγυρμός). See ELEUSINIA.

Agyrtae (ἀγύρται). Wandering beggars, often claiming the priestly rank, and making their living by fortune-telling and similar arts. They appear to have originated in the East, and finally made their way to Italy, where they received the name of *aeruscatores* (q. v.).

Ahāla, GAIUS SERVILIUS. A Roman who, acting as *magister equitum*, in B.C. 439, slew Spurius Maelius in the Forum, because he refused to appear before the dictator, L. Cincinnatus. For this act, Ahala was tried, but escaped condemnation by a voluntary exile. See MAELIUS.

Ahenobarbus. "Brazen-bearded." A name applied to the members of a noted Roman family, because the Dioscuri (Castor and Pollux) were said to have announced to one of their ancestors, L. Domitius, the victory of the Romans over the Latins at Lake Regillus (B.C. 496), and, in confirmation of the truth of what they told, to have stroked his black hair and beard, which immediately became red. (1) CN. DOMITIUS AHENOBARBUS, consul B.C. 122, conquered the Allobroges in Gaul, at the confluence of the Sulga and Rhodanus. (2) CN. DOMITIUS AHENOBARBUS, tribune of the plebs, B.C. 104, brought forward the law (*Lex Domitia*) by which the election of the priests was transferred from the collegia to the people. The people afterwards elected him Pontifex Maximus out of gratitude. He was consul in 96, and censor in 92, with Licinius Crassus, the orator. (3) L. DOMITIUS AHENOBARBUS, married Porcia, the sister of M. Cato, and was a staunch and courageous supporter of the aristocratical party. He was aedile in B.C. 61, praetor in 58, and consul in 54. On the breaking-out of the civil war in 49 he threw himself into Corfinium, but was compelled by his own troops to surrender to Caesar. He next went to Massilia, and after the surrender of that town repaired to Pompey in Greece. He fell in the battle of Pharsalia (48), where he commanded the left wing, and, according to Cicero's assertion in the second Philippic, by the hand of Antony. (4) CN. DOMITIUS AHENOBARBUS, son of no. 3, was taken with his father at Corfinium (49), was present at the battle of Pharsalia (48), and returned to Italy in 46, when he was pardoned by Caesar. He accompanied Antony in his campaign against the Parthians in 36. He was consul in 32, and deserted to Augustus shortly before the battle of Actium. (5) CN. DOMITIUS AHENOBARBUS, consul A.D. 32, married Agrippina (q. v.), daughter of Germanicus, and was father of the emperor Nero.

Ahēnum. See AENUM.

Ahrens, HEINRICH LUDOLF, philologist, was born June 6th, 1809, at Helmstadt, Germany, and was educated at Göttingen, where he became a privat-docent in 1830. From 1831 to 1845 he was a teacher in the Paedagogium at Ilfeld, leaving it to become head of the Lyceum in Hanover, an office which he filled until 1879. He died at Hanover, Sept. 24th, 1881. His principal works are the treatises, *De Graecae Linguae Dialectis* (Lib. i. *De Dialectis Aeolicis et Pseudo-aeolicis*, 1839; Lib. ii. *De Dialecto Dorico*, 1843); *Griech. Formenlehre des homerischen und attischen Dialekts* (1852); and *Bucolicorum Graecorum Theocriti, Biontis, Moschi Reliquiae*, 2 vols. (1855–59). See DIALECTS.

Aiax (Αἴας). (1) Son of Telamon, king of Salamis, and grandson of Aeacus. Homer calls him Aiax the Telamonian, Aiax the Great, or simply Aiax, whereas the other Aiax, son of Oïleus, is always distinguished from the former by some epithet. He sailed against Troy in twelve ships, and

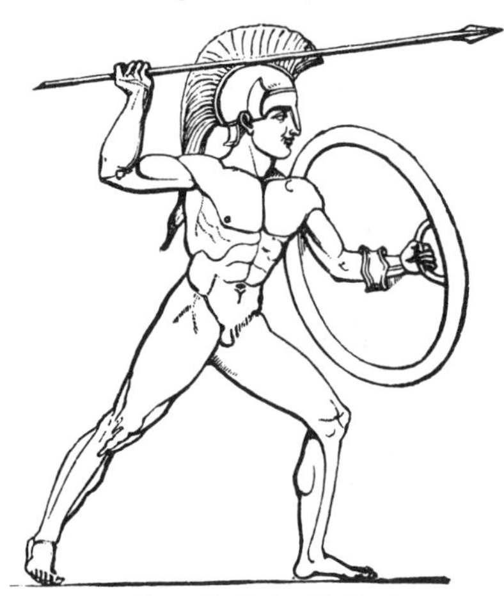

Aiax. (Aeginetan Marbles.)

is represented in the *Iliad* as second only to Achilles in bravery. In the contest for the armour of Achilles he was conquered by Odysseus, and this, says Homer, was the cause of his death. Later poets relate that his defeat by Odysseus threw him into a state of madness; that he rushed from his tent and slaughtered the sheep of the Greek army, fancying they were his enemies; and that at length he put an end to his own life. From his blood there sprang up a purple flower bearing the letters *Ai* (Aἰ) on its leaves, which were at once the initials of his name and expressive of a sigh. Homer does not mention his mistress Tecmessa. (2) Son of Oïleus, king of the Locrians, also called the lesser Aiax, sailed against Troy in forty ships. He is described as small of stature, but skilled in throwing the spear, and, next to Achilles, the most swift-footed among the Greeks. On his return from Troy his vessel was wrecked; he himself safely reached a rock through the assistance of Poseidon; but, as he boasted that he would escape in defiance of the immortals, Poseidon split the rock with his trident, and Aiax was swallowed up by the sea. This is the account of Homer. Others tell us that the anger of Athené was excited against him because on the night of the capture of Troy he violated Cassandra in the temple of the goddess (Lycophron, 360 with schol.).

Aikias Diké (*αἰκίας δίκη*). An action brought at Athens before the Court of the Forty (*οἱ τετταράκοντα*), against any individual who had struck a citizen of the State. Any citizen who had been thus insulted might proceed in two ways against the offending party—either by the *αἰκίας δίκη*, which was a private action, or by the *ὕβρεως γραφή*, which was looked upon in the light of a public prosecution, since the State was considered to be wronged in an injury done to any citizen. It appears to have been a principle of the Athenian law to give an individual who had been injured more than one mode of obtaining redress.

It was necessary to prove (1) that the defendant had struck the plaintiff otherwise than accidentally or in jest; and (2) that the defendant struck the plaintiff first.

In this action, the sum of money to be paid by the defendant as damages was not fixed by the laws; but the plaintiff assessed the amount according to the injury which he thought he had received, and the judges determined on the justice of the claim.

Aïdes (Ἀΐδης). See HADES.

Aïklon (*ἄϊκλον*, *αἶκλον*, or *ἄϊκνον*, *αἶκνον*). (1) A meal in general. Thus Alcman uses *συναίκλιαι* for *συνδείπνια*. (2) The chief dish or course in a meal. The dessert, or after-course, was called *ἐπάϊκλον*.

Aiōra (*αἰώρα*). See AEORA.

Aithousa (*αἴθουσα*). The open portico or veranda of the Homeric house. See DOMUS.

Aitia (Αἴτια). A treatise on Roman manners and customs, written by M. Terentius Varro (q. v.).

Aius Locutius or **Loquens**. A Roman divinity, "the Announcer." A short time before the Gauls took Rome (B.C. 388) a voice was heard at Rome during the silence of night announcing that the Gauls were approaching. The Romans afterwards erected on the spot where the voice had been heard an altar, with a sacred enclosure around it, to Aius Locutius. See Livy, v. 50; Plut. *Camill.* 30.

Akkad or **Accad**. The southeastern division of ancient Babylonia as distinguished from the northwestern division, which was called Sumir. The Akkadians, who appear to have come originally from Elam, were the dominant race in Babylonia at the time of its earliest history, and to them the Assyrians ascribed the civilization of Babylonia, and the invention of the cuneiform writing. There was also a city, Akkad, in the "land of Shinar." See ASSYRIA; BABYLONIA; CUNEIFORM INSCRIPTIONS.

Akoèn Martyrein (*ἀκοὴν μαρτυρεῖν*). Hearsay evidence, which in Athenian law was generally inadmissible. The one general exception to this rule was the attested declaration of a dying person. See EKMARTYRIA.

Ala in a Roman house. See DOMUS, p. 545.

Ala in military language. See ALARII; EXERCITUS.

Alabarches. A Roman official stationed at Alexandria under the Empire. The title is also found in Lycia. See ARABARCHES.

Alabastrothēca (*ἀλαβαστροθήκη*). A holder for bottles, which, having round bottoms, could not stand unsupported (Pollux, x. 121).

Alabastrum or **Alabaster** (*ἀλάβαστρον*, *ἀλάβαστος*). A small tapering or pear-shaped vessel, having no feet, used for holding perfumes and ointments. Such vessels were originally made of alabaster, of which the variety called onyx-alabaster was usually employed for this purpose. It is doubtful, however, whether the vessels were named from the material, or *vice versa*. They are also found of stone and terra-cotta, with a white or cream-coloured ground and black figures. The right-hand illustration shows an alabastrum from Chiusi, carved into female faces above, and having a hole in the crown for pouring out the ointment

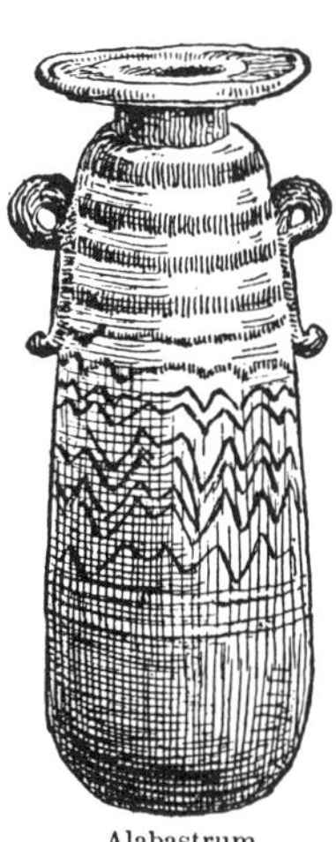
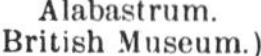
Alabastrum. (British Museum.)

Alabastrum. (Dennis, *Etruria*, i. p. cxxv.)

or perfume (Dennis, *Etruria*, i. p. cxxv.). Other materials were in use—as glass, and even gold (*χρύσεια ἀλάβαστρα*, Theocr. xv. 114). The alabastra usually had no handles, though we sometimes find specimens with them. They are first mentioned by Herodotus (iii. 20). Some of these vessels had a long narrow neck, which was sealed; so that when the woman in the Gospels is said to break the alabaster box of ointment, it appears probable that she only broke the extremity of the neck which was thus closed. (Cf. Becker-Göll, *Gallus*, ii. p. 378).

Alaea (τὰ ἀλαῖα). Games annually celebrated at Tegea in honour of Athené Alea.

Alāni (Ἀλανοί). See SCYTHIA.

Alarīcus (Old German *Al-ric*, i. e. *allrich*). A king of the Visigoths, remarkable as being the first of the barbarian chiefs who entered and sacked the city of Rome, and the first enemy who had appeared before its walls since the time of Hannibal. His first appearance in history is in A.D. 394, when he was invested by Theodosius with the command of the Gothic auxiliaries in his war with Eugenius. In 396, partly from anger at being refused the command of the armies of the Eastern Empire, and partly at the instigation of the minister Rufinus, he invaded and devastated Greece, till by the arrival of Stilicho, in 397, he was compelled to escape to Epirus. He was elected king by his countrymen in 398, having been previously, by the weakness of Arcadius, appointed prefect of Eastern Illyricum. The rest of his life was spent in the two invasions of Italy. The first (400–403), apparently unprovoked, brought him only to Ravenna, and, after a bloody defeat at Pollentia, in which his wife and treasures were taken, and a masterly retreat to Verona, was ended by the treaty with Stilicho, which transferred his services from Arcadius to Honorius, and made him prefect of Western instead of Eastern Illyricum. The second invasion (408–410) was occasioned by delay in fulfilling his demands for pay and for a western province as the future home of his nation, as also by the massacre of the Gothic families in Italy on Stilicho's death. It is marked by the three sieges of Rome, in 408, 409, and 410. The first of these was raised by a promised ransom. The second ended in the unconditional surrender of the city, and in the disposal of the Empire by Alaric to Attalus, till, on discovery of his incapacity, he restored it to Honorius. The third was ended by the treacherous opening of the Salarian Gate, on August 24th, and the sack of the city for six days. It was immediately followed by the occupation of the south of Italy, and the design of invading Sicily and Africa. This intention, however, was frustrated by his death, after a short illness, at Consentia, where he was buried in the bed of the adjacent river Busentinus, and the place of his interment was concealed by the massacre of all the workmen employed on the occasion. The few personal traits that are recorded of him show the true savage humour of a barbarian conqueror. But the impression left upon us by his general character is of a higher order. The real military skill displayed in his escape from Greece and in his retreat to Verona; the wish at Athens to show that he had adopted the use of the bath and the other external forms of civilized life; the moderation and justice which he observed towards the Romans in time of peace; and the humanity which distinguished him during the sack of Rome, all indicate something superior to the mere craft and lawless ambition which he seems to have possessed. See Hodgkin, *Italy and her Invaders* (Oxford, 1880–85).

Alarii were the troops of the allies in the Roman army, and were so called because they were usually stationed in the wings (*alae*). The alarii consisted of both horse and foot soldiers, and were commanded by praefects, in the same manner as the legions were commanded by tribunes. The cavalry of the allies were called *equites alarii*, to distinguish them from the cavalry of the legions (*equites legionarii*); and the infantry-soldiers were called *cohortes alariae*, to distinguish them from the *cohortes legionariae*.

Alastor (Ἀλάστωρ). In Greek mythology, an avenging daemon who dogs the footsteps of the guilty, and avenges upon children the sins of their fathers (Aesch. *Pers.* 354).

Alauda (κόρυδος). The lark. The Fifth Legion from the time of Iulius Caesar down to the third century was known as Alauda from the device of a lark (*alauda*) worn upon the helmets of the soldiers composing it. See Suet. *Iul.* 24.

Alba. (1) ALBA FUCENTIA or FUCENTIS, a town of the Marsi, and subsequently a Roman colony, situated on a lofty rock near the Lake Fucinus, and used by the Romans as a state prison. (2) ALBA LONGA, the most ancient town in Latium, is said to have been built by Ascanius, and to have colonized Rome. It was called Longa from its stretching in a long line down the Alban Mount towards the Alban Lake. It was destroyed by Tullus Hostilius, and was never rebuilt; its inhabitants were removed to Rome. At a later time the surrounding country was studded with the splendid villas of the Roman aristocracy and emperors (e. g. Pompey's and Domitian's), each of which was called Albanum. (3) ALBA POMPEIA, a town in Liguria, colonized by Pompeius Magnus, the birthplace of the emperor Pertinax.

Albania (Ἀλβανία). The southeastern part of what is now Georgia, in Asia, on the west side of the Caspian, extending from the rivers Cyrus and Araxes on the south to Mt. Ceraunius (the east part of the Caucasus) on the north, and bounded on the west by Iberia. It was a fertile plain, abounding in pasture and vineyards; but the inhabitants were fierce and warlike. They were a Scythian tribe, identical with the Alani. The Romans first became acquainted with them at the time of the Mithridatic war, when they encountered Pompey with a large army. Modern geography comprises ancient Albania under two divisions—Daghestan and Leghistan. The name in our own times is applied to the territory which in ancient times was included in Illyria and Epirus.

Albānus Lacus. A small lake, about five miles in circumference, west of the Mons Albanus, between Bovillae and Alba Longa. It is the crater of an extinct volcano, and is many hundred feet deep. The *emissarium* which the Romans bored through the solid rock during the siege of Veii, in order to carry off the superfluous water of the lake, is extant at the present day. See EMISSARIUM.

Albānus Mons was, in its narrower signification, the mountain in Latium on whose declivity the town of Alba Longa was situated. It was the sacred mountain of the Latins, on which the religious festivals of the Latin League were celebrated (*Feriae Latinae*), and on its highest summit was the temple of Iupiter Latiaris, to which the Roman generals ascended in triumph when this honour was denied them in Rome. The Mons Albanus in its wider signification included the Mons Algidus and the mountains about Tusculum.

Albinovānus, C. PEDO. An epic writer of the Augustan Age, the friend of the younger Seneca, who calls him *fabulator elegantissimus*, and quotes him to show his ability as a raconteur. He is also mentioned by Ovid, Martial, and Quintilian. He wrote a *Thebaïs*, and an epic on contemporary history. The elder Seneca (*Suas.* 14) cites twenty-three hexameters of his, describing a storm in the North Sea. See Haube, *Zur Kenntn. des Alb. Ped.* (Fraustadt, 1880).

Albīnus or **Albus Postumius**. The name of a patrician family at Rome, many of the members of which held the highest offices of the State, from the commencement of the Republic to its downfall. The founder of the family was dictator B.C. 498, when he conquered the Latins in the great battle near Lake Regillus (q. v.).

Albīnus, CLODIUS. A governor of Britain at the death of the emperor Commodus (q. v.) in A.D. 192. In order to secure his neutrality, Septimius Severus made him Caesar; but, after Severus had defeated his rivals, he turned his arms against Albinus. A great battle was fought between them at Lugdunum (Lyons), in Gaul, A.D. 197, in which Albinus was defeated and killed.

Albion (Ἀλουΐων). Another name of Britannia (q. v.), and signifying "the white land," from its white cliffs opposite the coast of Gaul. Albion or Albany (the Gaelic form) is now generally believed to have been the early Keltic name of the whole island. The etymology of the word is the same as that of *Alps*. See BRITANNIA.

Albis. The modern Elbe; the most easterly river of Germany with which the Romans were acquainted; nor did they reach its banks until the expedition of Drusus in B.C. 9. The last Roman army that penetrated so far was that commanded by Tiberius in A.D. 5.

Albogalērus. See APEX.

Albŭla. An ancient name of the river Tiber (q. v.). Albula is probably the pure Latin name, and Tiberis the Etruscan. Cf. Verg. *Aen.* viii. 332.

Albŭla Aqua or **Albŭlae Aquae**. Cold sulphurous springs issuing from a small lake about sixteen miles from Rome, and flowing into the Anio. The largest of these springs was known as Albunea. The Romans esteemed the water for its medicinal properties, and used it for both drinking and bathing. Cf. Suet. *Aug.* 82.

Album. (1) A tablet or bulletin-board on which the praetor's edict was inscribed. (See EDICTUM.) It was put up in a public place at Rome, so that all might read it. Some think it to have been a white board with black letters and red titles (*rubricae*); while others hold the board to have been black and the letters white. (2) A list of the members of any public body, as *album senatorium* (Tac. *Ann.* iv. 42). Dio Cassius calls it λεύκωμα.

Albunĕa. See ALBULA AQUA.

Alburnus Mons. A wooded mountain in Lucania behind Paestum.

Alcaeus (Ἀλκαῖος). A famous lyric poet of Mitylenė, in Lesbos, an elder contemporary of Sappho. Towards the end of the seventh century B.C., as the scion of a noble house, he headed the aristocratic party in their contests with the tyrants of his native town, Myrsilus, Melanchrus, and others. Banished from home, he went on romantic expeditions as far as Egypt. When the tyrants were put down, and his former comrade, the wise Pittacus, was called by the people to rule the State, he took up arms against him also as a tyrant in disguise; but, attempting to force his return home, he fell into the power of his opponent, who generously forgave him. Of his further life nothing is known. His poems in the Aeolic dialect, arranged in ten books by the Alexandrians, consisted of hymns, political songs (which formed the bulk of the collection), drinking songs, and love songs, of which we have but a few unsatisfactory fragments. In the opinion of the ancients, his poems were well constructed, while their tone was in harmony with the lofty passion and manly vigour of his character. The alcaic strophe, so much used by his admirer and not unworthy imitator, Horace, is named after him. See Bergk's *Poetae Lyrici* (4th ed. 1878) for the fragments; and Kock, *Alkaeus und Sappho* (1862).

Alcamĕnes (Ἀλκαμένης). A Greek artist of Athens or Lemnos, and a pupil of Phidias, who flourished towards the end of the fifth century B.C. Following his master's ideal tendency, he devoted himself mainly to religious subjects, working like him in various materials, gold and ivory, bronze and marble. His statue of the winner in the Pentathlon was stamped as classic by the epithet of ἐγκρινόμενος, as the *Doryphoros* of Polyclitus was by that of κανών. About B.C. 436 he was employed with Phidias in decorating the temple of Zeus at Olympia. The marble groups of the battle of Centaurs and Lapithae in its western pediment are his work. Of these considerable remains have been brought to light by recent German excavations.

Alcathoüs (Ἀλκάθοος). The son of Pelops and Hippodamia, who obtained as his wife Evaechmé, the daughter of Megareus, by slaying the Cithaeronian lion, and succeeded his father-in-law as king of Megara. He restored the walls of Megara, which is therefore sometimes called Alcathoé by the poets. In this work he was assisted by Apollo. The stone upon which the god used to place his lyre while he was at work was believed, even in late times, to give forth a sound, when struck, similar to that of a lyre.

Alcestis (Ἄλκηστις). See ADMETUS.

Alcibiădes (Ἀλκιβιάδης). The son of Clinias and Dinomaché, born at Athens about B.C. 450, and on the death of his father, in 447, brought up by his relation Pericles. He possessed a beautiful person, transcendent abilities, and great wealth. His youth was disgraced by his amours and debaucheries, and Socrates, who saw his vast capabilities, attempted to win him to the paths of virtue, but in vain. Their intimacy, however, was strengthened by mutual services. At the battle of Potidaea (432) his life was saved by Socrates, and at that of Delium (424) he saved the life of Socrates. After the death of Cleon (422) he became one of the leading politicians, and the head of the war party in opposition to Nicias. In 415 he was appointed, along with Nicias and Lamachus, as commander of the expedition to Sicily. While the preparations for the expedition were going on, there occurred a mysterious mutilation of the busts of the Hermae, which the popular fears connected with an attempt to overthrow the Athenian constitution. Alcibiades was charged with being the ringleader in this attempt. He demanded an investigation before he set sail, but this his enemies would not grant; but he had not been long in Sicily before he was recalled to stand his trial. On his return homeward he managed to escape at Thurii, and thence proceeded to Sparta, where he acted as the avowed enemy of his country. The machinations of his enemy, Agis II., induced him to abandon the Spartans and take refuge with Tissaphernes (412), whose favour he soon gained. Through his influence Tissaphernes deserted the Spartans and professed his willingness to assist the Athenians, who accordingly recalled Alcibiades from banishment in 411. He did not immediately return to Athens, but remained abroad for the next four years, during which the Athenians under his command gained the victories of Cynossema, Abydos, and Cyzicus, and got possession of Chalcedon and Byzantium. In 407 he returned to Athens, where he was received with great enthusiasm, and was appointed commander-in-chief of all the land and sea forces. But the defeat at Notium, occasioned during his absence by the imprudence of his lieutenant, Antiochus, furnished his enemies with a handle against him, and he was superseded in his command (406). He now went into voluntary exile to his fortified domain at Bisanthé, in the Thracian Chersonesus. After the fall of Athens (404) he took refuge with Pharnabazus. He was about to proceed to the court of Artaxerxes, when one night his house was surrounded by a band of armed men and set on fire. He rushed out, sword in hand, but fell, pierced with arrows (404). The assassins were probably either employed by the Spartans or by the brothers of a lady whom Alcibiades had seduced. He left a son by his wife Hippareté named Alcibiades, who never distinguished himself. See Houssaye, *Histoire d'Alcibiade*, 2 vols. (Paris, 1873).

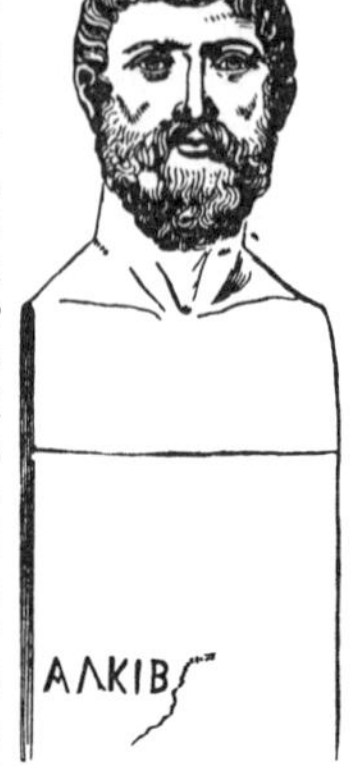

Bust of Alcibiades.

Alcīdes (Ἀλκείδης). A name applied to Heracles (q. v.) as being the grandson of Alceus (or Alcaeus).

Alcimĕdé (Ἀλκιμέδη). The wife of Aeson and mother of Iason (q. v.).

Alcinŏüs (Ἀλκίνοος). The son of Nausithoüs and grandson of Poseidon, celebrated in the *Odyssey* as the ruler of the Phaeacians in the island of Scheria. See PHAEACIA.

Alcĭphron (Ἀλκίφρων). A Greek rhetorician of the second century A.D., author of a collection of 118 fictitious *Letters* in three books. These, written in tolerably pure style and tasteful form, profess to be from sailors, peasants, parasites, and *hetaerae.* They are sketches of character, ingeniously conceived and carried out, which give us a vivid picture of the existing state of culture, especially at Athens. The letters from *hetaerae* are particularly interesting, as their plots are taken from the New Attic Comedy, especially the lost plays of Menander. The text, with a Latin version, is edited by Westermann and Hercher in the Didot collection (Paris, 1856). See NOVELS AND ROMANCES.

Alcithŏé (Ἀλκιθόη). Daughter of Minyas, changed with her sisters into bats, for refusing to join other women of Boeotia in the worship of Dionysus.

Alcmaeon (Ἀλκμαίων). A native of Argos and son of Amphiaraüs (q. v.) and Eriphylé. As his father, in departing on the expedition of the Seven against Thebes, had bound him and his brother Amphilochus, then mere boys, to avenge him on their faithless mother, Alcmaeon refused to take part in the second expedition, that of the Epigoni (q. v.), till he had first fulfilled that filial duty; nevertheless his mother, bribed by Thersander with the garment of Harmonia, persuaded him to go. The real leader at the siege of Thebes, he slew the Theban king, Laodamas, and was the first to enter the conquered city. On returning home, he, at the bidding of the Delphian Apollo, avenged his father by slaying his mother, with, or according to some accounts, without, his brother's help; but immediately, like Orestes, he was set upon by the Furies, and wandered distracted, seeking purification and a new home. Phegeus, of the Arcadian Psophis, half purified him of his guilt, and gave him his daughter Arsinoë or Alphesiboea to wife, to whom he presented the jewels of Harmonia, which he had brought from Argos. But soon the crops failed in the land, and he fell into his distemper again, till, after many wanderings, he arrived at the mouth of the Acheloüs, and there, in an island that had floated up, he found the country promised by the god, which had not existed at the time of his dying mother's curse, and so he was completely cured. He married Acheloüs's daughter, Callirrhoë, by whom he had two sons, Acarnan and Amphoterus (q. v.). Unable to withstand his wife's entreaties that she might have Harmonia's necklace and robe, he went to Phegeus in Arcadia, and begged those treasures of him, pretending that he would dedicate them at Delphi for the perfect healing of his madness. He obtained them; but Phegeus, on learning the truth, set his son to waylay him on the road, and rob him of his treasure and his life. Alcmaeon's sons then avenged their father's death on his murderers. Alcmaeon received divine honours after death, and had a sanctuary at Thebes and a consecrated tomb at Psophis.

Alcmaeonĭdae (Ἀλκμαιωνίδαι). A noble family at Athens, a branch of the family of the Nelidae, who were driven out of Pylus, in Messenia, by the Dorians, and settled at Athens. In consequence of the way in which Megacles, one of the family, treated the insurgents under Cylon (B.C. 612), they brought upon themselves the guilt of sacrilege, and were in consequence banished from Athens about 595 About B.C. 560 they returned from exile, but were again expelled by Pisistratus. In the year 548 they contracted with the Amphictyonic Council to rebuild the temple of Delphi, and obtained great popularity throughout Greece by executing the work in a style of magnificence which much exceeded their engagement. On the expulsion of Hippias in 510, they were again restored to Athens. They now joined the popular party, and Clisthenes, who was at that time the head of the family, gave a new constitution to Athens. See CLISTHENES.

Alcman (Ἀλκμάν, the Doric form of Ἀλκμαίων). The chief lyric poet of Sparta, though by birth a Lydian of Sardis. He was brought to Laconia as a slave when very young, and was emancipated by his master, who discovered his genius. He probably flourished about B.C. 631. He is said to have died, like Sulla, of the *morbus pedicularis.* Alcman is believed by some to have been the inventor of erotic poetry, to which class of verse belong his *Parthenia*, songs sung by choruses of virgins, bridal hymns, and lines in praise of love and wine. The scanty fragments of his poems that remain can be found in Bergk's *Poetae Lyrici Graeci* (4th ed. 1878). The most important fragment is one discovered on an Egyptian papyrus in Paris in 1855.

Alcman was the inventor of the Cretic hexameter. He also used the dactylic, anapaestic, trochaic, and iambic metres. His poems were usually written in strophes. In the Alexandrian Canon his name headed the list of lyric poets. See CANON ALEXANDRINUS.

Alcmēné (Ἀλκμήνη). The daughter of Electryon, king of Mycenae, who promised to marry Amphitryon, provided he avenged the death of her brothers, who had been slain by the sons of Pterelaüs. Amphitryon undertook the task; but, during his absence, Zeus, in the disguise of Amphitryon, visited Alcmené, and, pretending to be her husband, related in what way he had avenged the death of her brothers. Amphitryon himself returned the next day. Alcmené became the mother of Heracles by Zeus, and of Iphicles by Amphitryon.

Alcyŏné (Ἀλκυόνη). (1) The daughter of Aeolus (q. v.) and wife of Ceÿx (q. v.) (2) One of the Pleiades (q. v.).

Alcyonium Mare. The eastern part of the Corinthian Gulf.

Aldobrandini Marriage. See PICTURA.

Alea. Gaming, or playing at a game of chance of any kind. Gaming was looked down upon at Rome, and hence *aleator* was used as a term of reproach (Cic. *in Cat.* ii. 10, 23; *ad Att.* xiv. 5). It was also forbidden by special laws during the times of the Republic and under the emperors (*vetita legibus alea*, Hor. *Carm.* iii. 24, 58; Cic. *Phil.* ii. 23, 56; Ov. *Trist.* ii. 470 foll.; *Dig.* 11, tit. 5). Three such laws occur in the Digest (*l. c.*)—the Leges Titia, Publicia, and Cornelia—and likewise a *senatus consultum* and the praetor's edict; the latter enacting severe penalties on persons compelling others to gamble, and disabling the keepers of gambling-houses from bringing any action for damage or loss against their customers. At what time the two former laws were passed is quite uncertain; but the Lex Cornelia was probably one of the laws of the dictator Sulla, who, we know, made several enactments to check the extravagance and expense of private persons. (See SUMPTUS.) It has been inferred from the *Miles Gloriosus* (ii. 2, 9) that gaming must have been forbidden by law in Plautus's time; but the *lex talaria* (*alearia*, Ritschl) in this passage seems rather to refer to the laws of the game than to any public enactment. Those who were convicted of gaming were condemned to pay four times the sum they had staked (Pseudo-Ascon. *in* Cic. *Div.* § 24, p. 110, ed. Orelli), and became *infames* in consequence. We know that *infamia* (q. v.) was frequently a consequence of a judicial decision; and we may infer that it was so in this case from the expression of Cicero ("Hominem lege, quae est de alea, condemnatum, *in integrum restituit*," Cic. *Phil.* l. c.). Games of chance were, however, tolerated in the month of December at the Saturnalia, a period of general relaxation (Suet. *Aug.* 71); and public opinion allowed old men to amuse themselves in this manner (Cic. *De Sen.* 16, 58). Under the Empire gambling was carried to a great height, and the laws were probably little more than nominal. Many of the early emperors—Augustus, Caligula, Claudius, Vitellius, and Domitian—were very fond of gaming, and set an evil example to their subjects in this matter (Suet. *Aug.* 70, 71; Dio Cass. lix. 22; Suet. *Cal.* 41, *Claud.* 33; Dio Cass. lx. 2; Suet. *Dom.* 21). Professed gamesters made a regular study of their art, and there were treatises on the subject, among which was a book written by the emperor Claudius (Suet. *Claud.* l. c.). All gaming was forbidden finally by Justinian (Cod. 3, tit. 43). See Walter, *Geschichte d. röm. Rechts*, § 763; Rein, *Criminalrecht der Römer*, p. 833; and for an account of the games of chance, the articles PAR IMPAR; TALI; TESSERAE.

Alea (Ἀλέα). A town in Arcadia, south of the Stymphalian Lake, where Athené was worshipped under the name of Alea.

Aleaea or Alaea (Ἀλέαια). A festival held near Tegea in honour of Athené Alea. See HALOTIA.

Alecto (Ἀληκτώ). One of the Furies. See EUMENIDES.

Alectryomantīa (ἀλεκτρυομαντεία). A mode of divination practised by the Greeks. The letters of the alphabet were written in a circle; a grain of wheat or barley was laid upon each letter; and a cock, consecrated or provided for the occasion, was placed within the circle. The required information was obtained by putting together those letters off which the cock picked the grains of corn. To obtain a fuller answer, they laid grains of corn upon the letters a second time, and repeated the process.

Alectryonomachia (ἀλεκτρυονομαχία). The public cock-fight, which was held every year in one of the theatres of Athens. Cock-fights, in general, were exceedingly common among the Greeks and Romans; but the origin of this one in particular, which was sanctioned by the laws of the state, is not known, though Aelian says that when Themistocles marched with his Athenians against the Persians, he saw two cocks fighting against each other, and took the opportunity of addressing his soldiers, reminding them that these cocks were neither fighting for their country nor for the gods, but only for victory. This speech is said to have greatly animated the courage of the Athenians; and, after the war, they commemorated the event which had proved so useful to them by the annual festival in the theatre. (Aelian, *V. H.* ii. 28.)

Aleipterion. See ALIPTAE; BALNEAE, p. 186.

Alemanni, Alamanni, or **Almanni** (German *alle Männer*, "all men"). A confederacy of Germans, consisting of the tribes between the Danube, the Rhine, and the Main. They first came into contact with the Romans in the reign of Caracalla, who assumed the surname of Alemannicus on account of a pretended victory over them (A.D. 214). After this time they continually invaded the Roman dominions, and in the fifth century were in possession of Alsace and of German Switzerland. See GERMANIA.

Aleria or **Alalia.** One of the chief towns of Corsica, on the east of the island, founded by the Phocaeans in B.C. 564, and made a Roman colony by Sulla.

Alēsa. See HALESA.

Alesia. A town of the Mandubii, in Gallia Lugdunensis, and situated on a high hill (now Auxois), which was washed by the two rivers Lutosa (Oze) and Osera (Ozerain). It was taken and destroyed by Caesar in B.C. 52, after a memorable siege.

Aleuădae. See ALEUAS.

Aleuas (Ἀλεύας). A Thessalian, descended from Heracles, who ruled at Larissa. He was the reputed founder of the Aleuadae, a distinguished family of which two branches are mentioned: the Aleuadae and the Scopadae—the former remaining at Larissa, the latter inhabiting Crannon. In the Second Persian War the Aleuadae espoused the Persian cause, and gave aid to Xerxes (B.C. 480) (Herod. vii. 6). After the war, when Leotychides was sent to Thessaly to punish those who had proved disloyal to Greece, the Aleuadae bribed him to a mild course. At a later period, Philip of Macedon found the Aleuadae useful allies.

Alexander (Ἀλέξανδρος). (1) Another name for PARIS (q. v.).

(2) ALEXANDER AETŌLUS, of Pleuron in Aetolia, who flourished about B.C. 280 at Alexandria, where he was employed by Ptolemy in arranging the tragedies and satyric dramas in the great library. He also wrote tragedies, short epics, elegies, and epigrams, of which fragments have been preserved. See Couat, *La Poésie Alexandrine* (Paris, 1882).

(3) ALEXANDER OF APHRODISIAS, in Caria, who flourished about A.D. 200, and is known as Exegetes, or "the expounder," for his exposition of the commentaries of Aristotle. He wrote also original works on Fate, Free Will, and the Soul, which, translated into Latin, were much read and studied in the Middle Ages. See ARISTOTELES.

(4) ALEXANDER OF TRALLES, in Lydia, a Greek physician living at Rome in the sixth century A.D. He made a careful collection of excerpts from the older writers on therapeutics, in twelve books. See MEDICINA.

(5) ALEXANDER OF COTYAEUM, in Phrygia, or, according to Suidas, of Miletus, who flourished in the second century A.D. He took the name of Cornelius Alexander, from his having been a slave of Cornelius Lentulus, who gave him his freedom and made him the instructor to his children. He was surnamed Polyhistor, from the variety and multiplicity of his knowledge. The ancient writers cite one of his works in forty books, each one of which appears to have contained the description of some particular country, and to have had a separate title, such as Αἰγυπτιακά, Καριακά, etc. Pliny often refers to him. It is probable that he was the author of a work entitled Θαυμασίων συναγωγή, "A collection of wonderful things," of which Photius speaks.

Alexander. The name of several kings of Macedonia. See MACEDONIA.

Alexander, known as THE GREAT, son of Philip II., king of Macedon, was born at Pella, B.C. 356. He was educated by Aristotle, who acquired a great influence over his mind and character. He first distinguished himself at the battle of Chaeronea (338), where the victory was mainly owing to his impetuosity and courage. On the murder of Philip (336), he ascended the throne, at the age of twenty, to find himself surrounded by enemies on every side. He first put down rebellion in his own kingdom, and then rapidly marched into Greece. His unexpected activity overawed all opposition; Thebes, which had been most active against him, submitted when he appeared at its gates; and the assembled Greeks at the Isthmus of Corinth elected him to the command against Persia. He now directed his arms against the barbarians of the North, and crossed the Danube (335). A report of his death having reached Greece, the Thebans once more took up arms; but a terrible punishment awaited them. Alexander took Thebes by assault, destroyed all the buildings, with the exception of the house of Pindar, killed most of the inhabitants, and sold the rest as slaves. He now prepared for his great expedition against Persia. In the spring of 334 he crossed the Hellespont with some 35,000 men. Of these 30,000 were foot and 5000 horse, and of the former only 12,000 were Macedonians. Alexander's first engagement with the Persians was on the river Granicus in Mysia (May, 334), where they were entirely defeated by him. In the following year (333) he collected his army at Gordium (q. v.) in Phrygia, where he cut or untied the celebrated Gordian knot, which, it was said, was to be loosened only by the conqueror of Asia. From thence he marched to Issus, on the confines of Syria, where he gained a great victory over Darius, the Persian king. Darius himself escaped, but his mother, wife, and children fell into the hands of Alexander, who treated them with the utmost delicacy and respect. Alexander now directed his arms against the cities of Phoenicia, most of which

Coin representing Alexander the Great as Zeus Ammon.

submitted; but Tyre was not taken till the middle of 332, after an obstinate defence of seven months. He next marched into Egypt, which unresistingly yielded to him. At the beginning of 331 he founded near the mouth of the Nile the city of Alexandria, and about the same time visited the temple of Zeus Ammon, in the desert of Libya, where he was saluted by the priests as the son of Zeus. In the spring of the same year (331) he set out against Darius, who had collected another army. He crossed the Euphrates and the Tigris, and at length met with the immense hosts of Darius, said to have amounted to more than a million of men, in the plains of Gaugamela. The battle was fought in the month of October, 331, and ended in the complete defeat of the Persians. Alexander was now the conqueror of Asia, and began to adopt Persian habits and customs, by which he conciliated the affections of his new subjects. From Arbela he marched to Babylon, Susa, and Persepolis, all of which surrendered to him. He is said to have set fire to the palace of Persepolis, and, according to some accounts, in the revelry of a banquet, at the instigation of Thaïs, an Athenian courtesan. At the beginning of 330, Alexander marched from Persepolis into Media, in pursuit of Darius, whom he followed into Parthia, where the unfortunate king was murdered by Bessus (q. v.), satrap of Bactria. In 329 Alexander crossed the mountains of the Paropamisus (the Hindu Kush), and marched into Bactria against Bessus, who was betrayed to him and put to death. During the next two years he was chiefly engaged in the conquest of Sogdiana. He also crossed the Iaxartes (the Sir), and defeated several Scythian tribes north of that river. By the conquest of a mountain fortress he obtained possession of Roxana, the daughter of the Bactrian chief Oxyartes, whom he made his wife. It was about this time that he killed his friend Clitus in a drunken brawl. He had previously put to death his faithful servant Parmenion, on the charge of treason. In 327 he invaded India, and crossed the Indus, probably near the modern Attock. He met with no resistance till he reached the Hydaspes, where he was opposed by Porus, an Indian king, whom he defeated after a gallant resistance, and took prisoner, subsequently restoring to him his kingdom, and treating him with distinguished honour. He founded a town on the Hydaspes, called Bucephala, in honour of his horse Bucephalus, who died here, after carrying him through many victories. From thence he penetrated as far as the Hyphasis (Garra). This was the farthest point which he reached, for the Macedonians, worn out by long service, and tired

Statue of Alexander the Great. (Naples.)

of the war, refused to advance farther; and Alexander, notwithstanding his entreaties and prayers, was obliged to lead them back. He returned to the Hydaspes, and then sailed down the river with a portion of his troops, while the remainder marched along the banks in two divisions. He finally reached the Indian Ocean about the middle of 326. Nearchus was sent with the fleet to sail along the coast to the Persian Gulf (see NEARCHUS); and Alexander marched with the rest of his forces through Gedrosia, in which country his army suffered greatly from want of water and provisions. He reached Susa at the beginning of 325. Here he allowed himself and his troops some rest from their labours; and anxious to form his European and Asiatic subjects into one people, he assigned Asiatic wives to about eighty of his generals. He himself took a second wife, Barsiné, the eldest daughter of Darius. Towards the close of the year 325 he went to Ecbatana, where he lost his great favourite, Hephaestion. From Ecbatana he marched to Babylon, which he intended to make the capital of his empire, as the best point of communication between his eastern and western dominions. His schemes were numerous and gigantic, but he was cut off in the midst of them, being attacked by a fever, which was probably aggravated by the quantity of wine he had drunk at a banquet given to his principal officers, so that he died, after an illness of eleven days, in the month of May or June, B.C. 323, at the age of thirty-two, after a reign of twelve years and eight months. He appointed no one as his successor, but just before his death gave his ring to Perdiccas. Roxana was with child at the time of his death, and afterwards bore a son who is known by the name of Alexander Aegus (q. v.).

The body of Alexander was interred by Ptolemy in Alexandria, in a golden coffin, and divine honours were paid to him, not only in Egypt, but also in other countries. The sarcophagus in which the coffin was enclosed has been in the British Museum since 1802.

No character in history has afforded matter for more discussion than that of Alexander; and the exact quality of his ambition is to this day a subject of dispute. By some he is regarded as little more than an heroic madman, actuated by the mere desire of personal glory; others give him the honour of vast and enlightened views of policy, embracing the consolidation and establishment of an empire, in which commerce, learning, and the arts should flourish in common with energy and enterprise of every description. Each class of reasoners find facts to countenance their opinion of the mixed character and actions of Alexander. The former quote the wildness of his personal daring, the barren nature of much of his transient mastery, and his remorseless and unnecessary cruelty to the vanquished on some occasions, and capricious magnanimity and lenity on others. The latter advert to facts like the foundation of Alexandria, and other acts indicative of large and prospective views of true policy; and regard his expeditions rather as schemes of discovery and exploration than mere enterprises for fruitless conquest. The truth appears to embrace a portion of both these opinions. Alexander was too much smitten with military glory, and the common self-engrossment of the mere conqueror, to be a great and consistent statesman; while such was the strength of his intellect, and the light opened to him by success, that a glimpse of the genuine sources of lasting greatness could not but break in upon him. The history of Napoleon shows the nature of this mixture of lofty intellect and personal ambition, which has seldom effected much permanent good for mankind in any age.

In person this extraordinary individual was of the middle size, with a neck somewhat awry, but possessed of a fierce and majestic countenance. See Plut. *Alexander;* Arrian, *Exped. Alex.;* Droysen, *Geschichte Alexanders des Grossen* (1877); Freeman's *Historical Essays*, 2d series (1873); and Mahaffy, *Alexander's Empire* (1887).

After many dissensions and bloody wars among themselves, the generals of Alexander laid the foundations of several great empires in the three quarters of the globe. Ptolemy seized Egypt, where he firmly established himself, and where his successors were called Ptolemies, in honour of the founder of their kingdom, which subsisted till the time of Augustus. Seleucus and his posterity reigned in Babylon and Syria. Antigonus at first established himself in Asia Minor, and Antipater

Coin of Alexander the Great.

in Macedonia. The descendants of Antipater were conquered by the successors of Antigonus, who reigned in Macedonia till it was reduced by the Romans in the time of King Perseus. Lysimachus made himself master of Thrace; and Leonatus, who had taken possession of Phrygia, meditated for a while to drive Antipater from Macedonia. Eumenes established himself in Cappadocia, but was soon overpowered by his rival Antigonus, and starved to death. During his lifetime, Eumenes appeared so formidable to the successors of Alexander that none of them dared to assume the title of king.

The element of the wonderful in the campaigns of Alexander, and his tragic death at the height of his power, threw an intensely romantic interest around his figure, so that Alexander soon became the hero of romantic story, scarcely more wonderful than the actual, but growing from age to age with the myth-making spirit which can work as freely in fact as in fiction. The earliest form of the story which we know is the great romance connected with the name of Callisthenes (q. v.), which, under the influence of the popular tradition, arose in Egypt about A.D. 200, and was carried through Latin translations to the West, and through Armenian and Syriac versions to the East. It became widely popular during the Middle Ages, and was worked into poetic form by many writers in French and German. Alberich of Besançon wrote in Middle High German an epic on the subject in the first half of the twelfth century, which was the basis of the German Lamprecht's *Alexanderbuch* (ed. by Hinzel, Halle, 1884), also of the twelfth century. The French poets Lambert li Court and Alexandre de Bernay composed, between 1180 and 1190, a romance of Alexander, the twelve-syllable metre of which gave rise to the name *Alexandrines*. The German poem of Rudolf of Ems was based on the Latin epic of Walter of Châtillon, about 1200, which became henceforward the prevailing form of the story. In contrast with it is the thirteenth-century Old English epic of Alexander (in vol. i. of Weber's *Metrical Romances*, 1810), based on the version of Callisthenes. The story appears also in the East, worked up in conjunction with myths of other nationalities, especially the Persian. It appears in Firdusi, and, among later writers, in Nizami. From the Persians both the substance of the story and its form in poetical treatment have extended to Turks and other Mohammedans, who have interpreted Alexander as the *Dsulkarnein* ("two-horned") of the Korân, and to the Hindus, which last had preserved no independent traditions of Alexander. See Spiegel, *Die Alexandersage bei den Orientalen* (Leip. 1851), and Paul Meyer, *Alexandre le Grand dans la Littérature Française au Moyen-âge* (2 vols. 1886).

Alexander. The name of several kings of Egypt. See PTOLEMAEUS.

Alexander. The name of several kings of Epirus. (1) Surnamed MOLOSSUS, the brother of Olympias, and successor to Arybas. He came into Italy to aid the Tarentines against the Romans, and used to say that while his nephew, Alexander the Great, was warring against women (meaning the effeminate nations of the East), he was fighting against men (Just. xvii. 3; Liv. viii. 17 and 27). He was slain by a Lucanian while crossing the river Acheron in Bruttium (Just. xii. 2). (2) The son of the celebrated Pyrrhus. To avenge the death of his father, who had been slain at Argos, fighting against Antigonus, he seized upon Macedonia, of which the latter was king. He was soon, however, driven out, not only from Macedonia, but also from his own dominions, by Demetrius, son of Antigonus. Taking refuge, on this, among the Acarnanians, he succeeded, by their aid, in regaining the throne of Epirus (Iust. xxvi. 3; id. xxviii. 1; Plut. *Pyrr.* 34).

Alexander. The name of several princes of Iudaea. (1) IANNAEUS, monarch of Iudaea, son of Hyrcanus, and brother of Aristobulus, to whom he succeeded, B.C. 106. He was a warlike prince, and displayed great ability in the different wars in which he was engaged during his reign. Driven from his kingdom by his subjects, who detested him, he took up arms against them, and waged a cruel warfare for the space of six years, slaying upwards of fifty thousand of his foes. Having at last re-entered Jerusalem, he crucified, for the amusement of his concubines, eight hundred of his revolted subjects, and at the same time caused their wives and children to be massacred before their eyes. Being re-established on the throne, he made various conquests in Syria, Arabia, and Idumea, and finally died of intemperance at Jerusalem, B.C. 76, after a reign of twenty-seven years (Josephus, *Ant. Iud.* xvii. 22, etc.).

(2) The son of Aristobulus II., was made prisoner, together with his father, by Pompey, but managed to escape while being conducted to Rome, raised an army, and made some conquests. Hyrcanus, son of Alexander Iannaeus, being then on the throne, solicited the aid of the Romans, and Mark Antony, being sent by Gabinius, defeated Alexander near Jerusalem. After standing a siege for some time in the fortress Alexandreion, he obtained terms of peace; but not long after, having taken up arms for Caesar, who had released his father, he fell into the hands of Metellus Scipio, and was beheaded at Antioch (Josephus, *Ant. Iud.* xiv. 13).

(3) The son of Herod the Great, put to death by his father, along with Aristobulus his brother, on false charges brought against them by Pheroras their uncle, and Salomé their aunt (Josephus, *Ant. Iud.* xvi. 17).

Alexander. The name of several kings of Syria. (1) Surnamed BALAS, a person of low origin, who pretended to be the son of Antiochus IV. Epiphanes, and reigned in Syria B.C. 150–146. He was defeated and dethroned by Demetrius II. Nicator. (2) Surnamed ZEBĪNA or ZABĪNAS, son of a merchant, was set up by Ptolemy Physcon as a pretender to the throne of Syria, B.C. 128. He was defeated by Antiochus Grypus, by whom he was put to death, 122.

Alexander Aegus. The son of Alexander the Great and Roxana, born shortly after the death of his father, in B.C. 323, and acknowledged as the partner of Philip Arrhidaeus in the Empire, under the guardianship of Perdiccas, Antipater, and Polysperchon, in succession. Alexander and his mother, Roxana, were imprisoned by Cassander when he obtained possession of Macedonia in 316, and remained in prison till 311, when they were put to death by Cassander.

Alexander Sevērus. See SEVERUS.

Alexandra (Ἀλεξάνδρα). See CASSANDRA.

Alexandrĭa (Ἀλεξάνδρεια, and in Cicero's time written ALEXANDRĒA). The name of several cities founded by Alexander the Great, and named after him. Of these, the most important are: (1) The capital of Aegyptus (q. v.) under the Ptolemies, ordered by Alexander to be founded in B.C. 332. It was built on the narrow neck of land between the lake Mareotis and the Mediterranean, opposite to the island of Pharos, which was joined to the city by an artificial dike. On this island a great light-house was built in the reign of Ptolemy

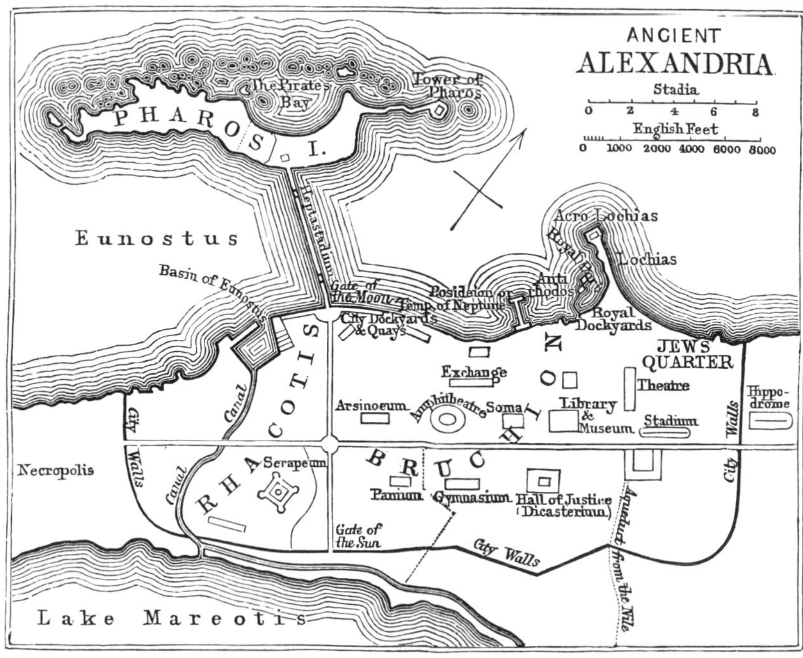

Philadelphus (283). Under the care of the Ptolemies, as the capital of a great kingdom, and commanding by its position all the commerce of Europe with the East, Alexandria soon became the most wealthy and splendid city of the known world. It was celebrated for its magnificent library, founded by the first two Ptolemies. The library suffered severely by fire when Iulius Caesar was besieged in Alexandria, and was finally destroyed by Amrou, the lieutenant of the calif Omar, in A.D. 651. Under the Romans, Alexandria retained its commercial and literary importance, and became also a chief seat of Christianity and theological learning. Its site is now covered by a mass of ruins. Outside the walls, to the south, the column of Diocletian ("Pompey's Pillar") still remains; but the two obelisks known as "Cleopatra's Needles," which once adorned the gate-way of the royal palace, have been removed—one to London in 1878, and one to New York in 1881. The modern city stands on the dike uniting the island of Pharos to the mainland. (2) ALEXANDRIA TROAS, also TROAS simply, on the sea-coast southwest of Troy, was enlarged by Antigonus, hence called Antigonia, but afterwards it resumed its first name. It flourished greatly, both under the Greeks and the Romans; and both Iulius Caesar and Constantine thought of establishing the seat of the Empire in it. (3) ALEXANDRIA AD ISSUM, a seaport at the entrance of Syria, a little south of Issus. (4) In Susiana, afterwards ANTIOCHIA, afterwards CHARAX SPASINI, at the mouth of the Tigris, built by Alexander; destroyed by a flood; restored by Antiochus Epiphanes. It was the birthplace of Dionysius Periegetes and Isidorus Characenus.

Alexandrian Canon. See CANON ALEXANDRINUS.

Alexandrian Library. See BIBLIOTHECA.

Alexandrian Museum. See MUSEUM.

Alexandrian Period. The period of Greek literature, from B.C. 300 to 30, during which Alexandria was the intellectual capital of the Hellenic world. See ALEXANDRIAN SCHOOL.

Alexandrian School. After the decline of liberty and intellectual cultivation in Greece, Alexandria, in Egypt, became the home and centre of science and literature. The time in which it held this position may be divided into two periods—the first including the reigns of the Ptolemies, from B.C. 323 to 30; the second, from B.C. 30 to A.D. 640, or from the fall of the Ptolemaean dynasty to the irruption of the Arabs. During the first period the intellectual activity at Alexandria was mainly of a purely literary or scientific kind; but during the second, partly from Jewish and Christian influences, it developed into the speculative philosophy of the Neo-Platonists (q. v.) and the religious philosophy of the Gnostics. See GNOSTICI.

Ptolemy Soter, the first ruler who introduced and patronized Greek science and literature in Alexandria, was followed by a still more munificent patron, Ptolemy Philadelphus, who regularly established the celebrated Alexandrian Library and Museum, which had been begun by his father. This Museum was somewhat like a modern university, and within its walls learned scholars both lived and taught. (See MUSEUM.) The loss of Greek freedom soon took from Greek thought much of its boldness and originality, but thinkers found substitutes for these in learned research and criticism. They studied grammar, prosody, mythology, astronomy, and medicine, and unfolded their information in long didactic poems in epic form, full of learning, and marked by perfect mastery of verse, but often dull to a degree, and marred by numerous obscure and recondite allusions. Examples of these are the *Argonautica* of Apollonius Rhodius, and the *Alexandra* or *Cassandra* of Lycophron. Other writers of epics were Euphorion, Nicander of Colophon, Dionysius Periegetes, Rhianus, and Oppianus. Many poets employed lyric and elegiac forms for subjects completely unsuited for poetic treatment, which are yet happily expressed in verse. The earliest of the elegiac poets was Philetas of Cos; the greatest, perhaps, Callimachus (q. v.). Among the lyric poets were Phanocles, Hermesianax, Alexander of Aetolia, and Lycophron. Epigrams and dramas were also written, but of the latter scarcely anything has survived beyond the names of the seven tragedians called the Alexandrian Pleiades. Out of the Amoebean verse or bucolic mime—a rudimentary kind of drama—grew the best product of Alexandrian poetry, the idyls of Theocritus (q. v.). Still more active than the poets were the grammarians, to whom it is mainly due that we now possess the masterpieces of Greek literature at all. They were both philologists and littérateurs, who explained things as well as words, and were thus a kind of encyclopædists. Among these the greatest were Zenodotus of Ephesus, Aristophanes of Byzantium, and Aristarchus of Samothrace; only less eminent critics were Alexander of Aetolia, Lycophron, Callimachus, and Eratosthenes. Their chief service consists in having collected the writings then existing, prepared corrected texts, and preserved them for future generations. See TEXTUAL CRITICISM.

The Alexandrian School had a spirit and character altogether different from the previous intellectual life of Greece. From the attention paid to the study of language, it was natural that correctness, purity, and elegance of expression should be especially cultivated; and in these respects many of its writers are distinguished. But what no study and no effort could give—the spirit that animated the earlier Greek poetry—was in most of these works wanting. In place of it, there was displayed greater art in composition; what had formerly been done by genius was now to be done by the rules furnished by criticism. Where imitation and rule thus took the place of inspiration, each generation of disciples became more artificial and lifeless than their masters, until ultimately criticism degenerated into frivolous fault-finding, and both prose and poetry became laboured affectation. Still, for about four centuries, the Alexandrian School was the centre of learning and science in the ancient world. Counting from its origin to its complete extinction, it lasted a thousand years; and its lasting influence upon Latin literature in the Augustan age must not be forgotten. We find it in all the contemporary poets, and notably in Vergil, the greatest poet of the group. See Matter, *Histoire de l'École d'Alexandrie*, 2 vols. (2d ed. Paris, 1840–44); St.-Hilaire, *De l'École d'Alexandrie* (Paris, 1845). Simon, *Histoire de l'École d'Alexandrie*, 2 vols. (Paris, 1844–45); and especially Vacherot, *Histoire Critique de l'École d'Alexandrie*, 3 vols. (Paris, 1846–51).

Alexandrīnum Opus. A kind of mosaic work used for the flooring of rooms, its distinctive character lying in the fact that the pattern was composed of only two colours, e. g. red and black on a white ground, as in the accompanying specimen found at Pompeii in a house. See the article MUSIVUM OPUS.

Alexandrinum Opus. (Pompeii.)

Alexis (Ἄλεξις). One of the most prolific and important writers of the Middle Attic Comedy, and uncle to Menander (q. v.). He was born at Thurii, B.C. 392, and is said to have lived to the age of one hundred and six years, and to have died on the stage with the crown of victory on his head. Some two hundred and forty-five plays are attributed to him, of which numerous extracts are still extant and display both wit and elegance. They are edited by Hirschig (1840). See COMOEDIA.

Alfēnus Varus. A Roman jurist, originally a shoemaker or barber at Cremona. Cf. Horace, *Sat.* i. 3, 130.

Alga. A general name used by the Roman writers of all aquatic plants that, living in the water, are thrown up on the shores or river-banks. See FUCUS.

Algĭdus Mons. A range of mountains in Latium, extending south from Praenesté to Mt. Albanus, cold, but covered with wood, and containing good pasturage. On it was situated the town of Algidum. It was an ancient seat of the worship of Diana. From it the Aequi usually made their incursions into the Roman territory.

Alĭca. A kind of grain resembling spelt, and also known as *zea*. The name is given likewise to a soup or porridge made of this grain, and much relished by the Romans.

Alicŭla. A short cloak coming down to the elbows, worn by boys, and spoken of as worn by boys and huntsmen. Rich derives the name from the resemblance of the garment to wings (*alae*).

Aliēnus Caecīna. See CAECINA.

Alimentarii Pŭeri et Puellae. In the Roman Republic the poorer citizens were assisted by public distributions of corn, oil, and money, which were called *congiaria*. (See CONGIARIUM.) These distributions were not made at stated periods, nor to any but grown-up inhabitants of Rome. The emperor Nero first conceived the notion of extending them, not only to other Italian towns, but also to children (Aurel. Vict. *Epit.* xii. 4); and Trajan appointed them to be made every month, both to orphans and to the children of poor parents. The children who received them were called *pueri et* *puellae alimentarii*, and also (from the emperor) *pueri puellaeque Ulpiani;* and the officers who administered the institution were called *quaestores pecuniae alimentariae, quaestores alimentorum, procuratores alimentorum*, or *praefecti alimentorum.*

A decree of Hadrian (*Dig.* 34, tit. 1, 5, 14) says that boys enjoyed the benefits of this institution up to their eighteenth and girls up to their fourteenth year; and we learn from an inscription (Fabretti, 235, 619) that a boy four years and seven months old had received nine times the ordinary monthly distribution of corn. See Desjardins, *Disp. Hist. de Tabulis Alimentariis.*

Alimentus, L. CINCIUS. A Roman annalist, antiquary, and jurist, who was praetor in Sicily B.C. 209, and wrote, in Greek, several works, of which the best known was his *Annales*, which contained an account of the Second Punic War. See the monograph by Plüss (Bonn, 1865).

Aliphēra (Ἀλίφηρα). A town in Arcadia, on the borders of Elis, south of the river Alpheus. (Polyb. iv. 77.)

Alipĭlus (παρατίλτριος). A slave who attended on bathers to remove the superfluous hair from their bodies. Tweezers (*volsillae*) were used, or depilatory ointment. See Mayor's note on Juv. xi. 157, and the article PSILOTHRUM.

Aliptae (ἀλεῖπται). Persons who anointed the bodies of the athletes. The chief object of this anointing was to close the pores of the body, in order to prevent much perspiration and the weakness consequent thereon. To effect this object, the oil was not simply spread over the surface of the body, but also well rubbed into the skin. The oil was mixed with fine African sand, several jars full of which were found in the baths of Titus. One of these is now in the British Museum. This preparatory anointing was called ἡ παρασκευαστικὴ τρίψις. The athlete was again anointed after the contest, in order to restore the tone of the strained muscles: this anointing was called ἡ ἀποθεραπειά. He then bathed, and had the dust, sweat, and oil scraped off his body by means of an instrument similar to the *strigil* of the Romans, and called στλεγγίς, and afterwards ξύστρα. They were thus a kind of medical trainers, ἰατραλεῖπται. See ATHLETAE.

Among the Romans, the aliptae were slaves. They, too, like the Greek ἀλεῖπται, appear to have attended to their masters' constitution and mode of life. They were also called *unctores.* They used in their operations a kind of scraper called *strigil*, towels (*lintea*), a cruse of oil (*guttus*), which was usually of horn, a bottle (see AMPULLA), and a small vessel called *lenticula.* See BALNEAE.

Alĭso. The modern Elsen; the site of a fortress built by Drusus in B.C. 11, at the junction of the Luppia (Lippe) and the Eliso (Alme). (Dio. Cass. iv. 33.)

Allia, or, less correctly, **Alia.** A small river flowing into the Tiber about eleven miles from Rome. It is memorable for the defeat of the Romans by the Gauls on its banks, July 16th, B.C. 390, or, according to Mommsen, 388. Hence the *dies Alliensis* was an unlucky day in the Roman calendar. See DIES; FASTI; CELTAE.

Allĭfae or **Alĭfae.** A town of the Samnites on the Vulturnus, celebrated for its manufacture of wine flagons; hence called *pocula Allifana.*

Alliteration. Alliteration is the repetition of the same letter or sound, either intentionally or unconsciously introduced to please the ear or to give additional emphasis to the words by making the sound more forceful. When used to any great extent, it is generally characteristic of a primitive literary taste, and is found in verse and prose that have not yet received their final polish. In Anglo-Saxon poetry it is one of the chief means of marking the metrical character of the lines, the important words being distinguished by likeness of sound, as in the following from the *Phoenix:*

"Ne **F**orestes **F**naest, ne **F**yres blaest,
Ne **H**aegles **H**ryre, ne **H**rymes dryre,
Ne **S**unnan haetu, ne **S**incald," etc.

In Greek, alliteration, like assonance and rhyme, plays no important part, because the earliest Greek verse that we possess represents a stage of development in the art of poetry when such crude devices had already been discarded. Only in some few striking passages does alliteration still appear to be a conscious device of the poet, as in the famous line of Sophocles (*Oed. Tyr.* 371), when Oedipus taunts Tiresias with his blindness:

τυφλὸς τά τ' ὦτα τόν τε νοῦν τά τ' ὄμματ' εἶ.

But in Latin of all periods it is an important element of composition and style, less, however, in the Augustan writers than in their predecessors and successors. Ennius has some extraordinary alliterations, the most absurd being his

"O Tite tute Tati, tibi tanta tyranne tulisti!"

found among the fragments of his *Annales.* Plautus uses alliteration with comic effect. Lucretius has a definite system, using *p* and *m* to denote effort, as

"—— magnos manibus divellere montis" (i. 201);

while *v* denotes pity or sorrow, as in the famous line, with its wailing sound,

"Viva videns vivo sepeliri viscera busto" (v 993).

See the articles ONOMATOPOEIA; RHYME; and on the general subject, Buchhold, *De Paromoeoseos apud Veterum Romanorum Poett. Usu* (Leipzig, 1883); Ebrard, *Allit. in d. Lat. Sprache* (Bayreuth, 1882); Boetticher, *De Allitterationis apud Romanos Vi et Usu* (Berlin, 1884); Raebel, *De Usu Adnominationis apud Rom. Poett. Com.* (Halle, 1887); Munro, *Introduct. to Lucretius* (Camb. 1886); Cruttwell, *Hist. of Roman Literature* (1886), pp. 238–239.

Allium. Garlic, said by Horace (*Epod.* iii. 4) to be fit only for reapers. It was a favourite food with Roman soldiers and sailors, and with the Egyptians.

Allobrŏges. A powerful people of Gaul, dwelling between the Rhodanus (Rhone) and the Isara (Isère), as far as the Lacus Lemannus (Lake of Geneva), consequently in the modern Dauphiné and Savoy. Their chief town was Vienna on the Rhone. They were conquered in B.C. 121 by Q. Fabius Maximus Allobrogicus.

Almanac. See FASTI.

Almo. A small river flowing into the Tiber just south of Rome, in whose waters the statues of Cybelé (q. v.) were annually washed. (Ovid, *Fasti*, iv. 337).

Alōa (τὰ ἀλῶα). An Athenian festival celebrated at Eleusis in honour of Dionysus and Demeter, the inventors of the plough and protectors of the fruits of the earth. See A. Mommsen, *Heortologie*, p. 320 foll.

Aloădae (Ἀλωάδαι) or **Aloīdae** (Ἀλωεῖδαι)

Sons of Poseidon by Iphimedia, the wife of Aloeus, son of Canacé and Poseidon; their names were Ephialtes and Otus. They grew every year an ell in breadth and a fathom in length, so that in nine years' time they were thirty-six feet broad and fifty-four feet high. Their strength was such that they chained up the god Ares and kept him in a brazen cask for thirteen months, till their stepmother Eriboea betrayed his whereabouts to Hermes, who came by stealth and dragged his disabled brother out of durance. They threatened to storm heaven itself by piling Ossa on Olympus and Pelion on Ossa, and would have done it, says Homer, had not Apollo slain them with his arrows ere their beards were grown. The later legend represents Ephialtes as in love with Heré, and Otus with Artemis. Another myth represents Artemis as slaying them by craft in the island of Naxos. She runs between them in the form of a hind; they hurl their spears, and wound each other fatally. In the later legend they expiate their sins in the lower world by being bound with snakes to a pillar, back to back, while they are incessantly tormented by the screeching of an owl. On the other hand, they were worshipped as heroes in Naxos, and in the Boeotian Ascra were regarded as the founders of the city and of the worship of the Muses on Mount Helicon.

Aloīdae. See ALOADAE.

Alōeus (Ἀλωεύς). The son of Poseidon and Canacé, who married Iphimedia, the daughter of Tripos. His wife was beloved by Poseidon, by whom she had two sons, Otus and Ephialtes, who are usually called the *Aloadae*, from their reputed father Aloeus. See ALOADAE.

Alogiou graphé (ἀλογίου γραφή). An action which might be brought at Athens before the *logistae* against all ambassadors who failed to pass their accounts when their term of office expired.

Alŏpé (Ἀλόπη). (1) A town of the Opuntian Locris, opposite Euboea. (2) The daughter of Cercyon of Eleusis, and, by Poseidon, mother of Hippothoön (q. v.); after whose birth her father was going to kill her, but the god changed her into a fountain.

Alopĕcé (Ἀλωπεκή). A deme of Attica belonging to the tribe Antiochis.

Alpēnus (Ἀλπηνός). A town of the Epicnemidian Locri, at the entrance of the Pass of Thermopylae.

Alpes (Ἄλπεις). A name derived probably from the Keltic *alb* or *alp*, "a height." The mountains forming the boundary of northern Italy, which were distinguished by the following names. We enumerate them in order from west to east. (1) Alpes Maritimae, the Maritime or Ligurian Alps, from Genua (Genoa), where the Apennines begin, run west as far as the river Varus (Var), and then north to Mt. Vesulus (Monte Viso), one of the highest points of the Alps. (2) Alpes Cottiae or Cottianae, the Cottian Alps (so called from a King Cottius in the time of Augustus), from Monte Viso to Mont Cenis, contained Mt. Matrona, afterwards called Mt. Ianus or Ianua (Mont Genèvre), across which Cottius constructed a road, which became the chief means of communication between Italy and Gaul. (3) Alpes Graiae, also Saltus Graius (the name is probably Keltic, and has nothing to do with Greece), the Graian Alps, from Mont Cenis to the Little St. Bernard inclusive, contained the Iugum Cremonis (le Cramont) and the Centronicae Alpes, apparently the Little St. Bernard and the surrounding mountains. The Little St. Bernard, which is sometimes called Alpis Graia, is probably the pass by which Hannibal crossed the Alps; the road over it, which was improved by Augustus, led to Augusta (Aosta) in the territory of the Salassi. (4) Alpes Penninae, the Pennine Alps, from the Great St. Bernard to the Simplon inclusive, the highest portion of the chain, including Mont Blanc, Monte Rosa, and Mont Cervin. The Great St. Bernard was called Mons Penninus, and on its summit the inhabitants worshipped a deity whom the Romans called Iupiter Penninus. The name is probably derived from the Keltic *pen*, "a height." (5) Alpes Lepontiorum or Lepontiae, the Lepontian or Helvetian Alps, from the Simplon to the St. Gothard. (6) Alpes Rhaeticae, the Rhaetian Alps, from the St. Gothard to the Orteler by the pass of the Stelvio. Mt. Adula is usually supposed to be the St. Gothard. (7) Alpes Tridentinae, the mountains of southern Tyrol, in which the Athesis (Adige) rises, with the pass of the Brenner. (8) Alpes Noricae, the Noric Alps, northeast of the Tridentine Alps, comprising the mountains in the neighbourhood of Salzburg. (9) Alpes Carnicae, the Carnic Alps, east of the Tridentine, and south of the Noric, to Mt. Terglu. (10) Alpes Iuliae, the Julian Alps, from Mt. Terglu to the commencement of the Illyrian or Dalmatian mountains, which are known by the name of the Alpes Pannonicae. The Alpes Iuliae were so called because Iulius Caesar or Augustus constructed roads across them. They are also called Alpes Venetae.

Alphabet (ἄλφα-βῆτα, *alphabētum*). A name given to any collection of graphic representations of sounds, and derived from the names of the first two letters of the Greek alphabet. The word *alphabetum* is not found in early writers. It occurs in Tertullian, *Haeret.* 50, and from his time on. The classical writers used the word *litteratura*, or *litteratura prima* (Tac. *Ann.* xi. 13). Quintilian (i. 1, 24) uses the circumlocution *litterarum nomina et contextum*. (Cf. Juv. xiv. 209.)

The alphabet is the oldest existing monument of civilization. In all, some two hundred varieties have existed, of which only fifty are now in use. They are all modifications of the primitive Phœnician alphabet, itself probably derived from the ideographic signs of the Egyptians. Thus it is seen that all writing in its origin is due to the use of pictures or symbols standing for either things or abstractions. These ultimately became phonographic, representing (1) syllables and (2) elementary sounds. The Greek and Latin alphabets are, of course, of the second class.

I. THE GREEK ALPHABET.—Many Greek alphabets are known from inscriptions on stone or pottery, varying according to the district or the date; but the letters in which Greek literature, properly so called, has descended to us belong to the Ionic alphabet, which, being formally adopted at Athens in B.C. 403, became that generally used by all Hellenes. Like the other Greek alphabets, it is in general identical, in the names, forms, and number of the letters, with the Phœnician or old Semitic alphabet. The Greeks must have obtained their knowledge of it from the trading settlements of the Phœnicians in the Aegean not later than the tenth century B.C. This belief was, indeed, held by the Greeks themselves; for though their legends

ANCIENT ALPHABETS.

Hebrew Names of Letters.	Meaning in English.	English Equivalent.	Egyptian (transliteration). Hieroglyphic.	Hieratic.	Ancient Phœnician.	Old Hebrew.	Square Hebrew.	Old and Later Greek.		Old and Later Latin.	
Aleph	Ox	A					א		A		A
Beth	House	B					ב		B		B
Gimel	Camel	G					ג		Γ		C
Daleth	Door	D					ד		Δ		D
He	Window	H, E					ה		E		E
Vau	Hook	V					ו				F
Zayin	Weapon	Z					ז		Z		Z
Cheth	Fence	Ch					ח		H		H
Teth	Snake	Th					ט		Θ		
Yod	Hand	Y, I, J					י		I		I
Kaph	Bent Hand	C, Ch					כ ך		K		K
Lamed	Ox-goad	L					ל		Λ		L
Mem	Water	M					מ ם		M		M
Nun	Fish	N					נ ן		N		N
Samekh	Post	S					ס		Ξ		
Ayin	Eye	O					ע		O		O
Pe	Mouth	P, Ph					פ ף		Π		P
Tsade	Javelin?	Ts					צ ץ				
Koph	Knot?	K, Q					ק				Q
Resh	Head	R					ר		P		R
Shin	Tooth	Sh					ש		Σ		S
Tau	Sign (Cross)	T, Th					ת		T		T

ascribe the perfection of letters to various individuals, such as Palamedes, and Simonides of Ceos, the actual introduction of the alphabet was almost universally credited to Cadmus (q. v.), a Phœnician settled in Boeotia (Herod. v. 58, 59)—the name Cadmus being undoubtedly the same as the Hebrew *Kadmi*, "an Eastern." Further proof is found in the fact that the names of most of the Greek letters are pure Semitic words. (See the table above.)

Scholars are nearly all agreed that writing was known to the Greeks in the Homeric Age (see *Iliad*, vi. 168), and it is positively stated that lists of victors were kept at Olympia from the year B.C. 776, while we actually possess inscriptions of the seventh century. In the sixth century we hear of geographers, chroniclers, genealogists, legislators, and of schools for teaching the alphabet (Herod. vi. 27), showing that by this period a knowledge of writing must have been very generally diffused. As all Greek alphabets differ from the Phœnician in having characters for the vowels (a striking fact), it is necessary to assume that a knowledge of writing was diffused over Greece from a common centre, and that this diffusion occupied a considerable time. (See Mahaffy, *Greek Literature*, ii. 2, and the same writer in the *Journal of Hellenic Studies*, ii. 162.)

At the date of the oldest Greek inscriptions, the vowels *α*, *ε*, *ο* had been developed out of the Phœnician breath-signs *aleph*, *hé*, and *áyin*; and *ι* and *υ* out of the Phœnician semi-consonants *yod* and *vau*. At this period the writing was still retrograde, i. e. from right to left, after the Semitic fashion. A little later the direction is zigzag, or *boustrophedon* (βουστροφηδόν), "plough-wise," as an ox turns when ploughing, the lines proceeding alternately from right to left and from left to right. In both these styles the writer often began at the bottom of the roll, and wrote each succeeding line above the last. In the sixth century the practice of writing all the lines from left to right was generally adopted. At about the same time two more vowels were evolved—*η* out of the Semitic *cheth*, and *ω* from *ο*. The character *φ* had been differentiated out of *θ*, *χ* out of *κ*, and *ψ* (probably) out of *φ*. The sounds of Ϝ (*vau*) and Q (Semitic *kōph*) began to disappear, and the characters as alphabetic symbols dropped out of use. Up to the third century B.C. only the ordinary capitals were employed, but after this time the more rounded forms known as "uncials" were introduced, together with cursive forms in correspondence. The so-called "minuscules," or small letters, familiar to us in our modern books, were not evolved until the seventh or eighth century A.D. from a combination of uncials and cursives. From a very early date the Greek alphabet showed a tendency to separate into two types—the Eastern, or Ionic, and the Western, or Chalcidian. The final difference between the two will be seen by the following comparison:

Ionic (*Eastern*) *Alphabet.*—Α Β Γ Δ Ε Ζ Η Θ Ι Κ Λ Μ Ν Ξ Ο Π Ρ Σ Τ Υ Φ Χ Ψ Ω.

Chalcidian (*Western*) *Alphabet.*—Α Β Γ Δ Ε F Ζ Η (=h) Θ Ι Κ L Μ Ν Ο Π Q Ρ Σ Τ Υ Χ (=x) Φ Ψ (=kh).

II. The Latin Alphabet.—The Chalcidian or Western Greek alphabet was carried by the Chalcidians to Italy as early as the ninth century B.C. From it in Italy sprang five local Italic alphabets—the Oscan, Umbrian, Etruscan, Faliscan, and Latin. (See Dialects.) As the Latins ultimately attained to the intellectual and political leadership of Italy, the last-named alphabet at last supplanted the other four, and became the only one in general use throughout the Roman Empire, and later of Christendom, thus becoming the prevailing alphabet of the world.

The Latin alphabet, received originally from the Chalcidian Greeks of Cumae in Campania, has adhered more closely than any of the others to the original Phœnician type, discarding only two letters and adding only three. Its archaic character as compared with that of the Ionic Greek alphabet is seen (1) by its retention of the older signs for L and S; (2) by retaining the older value of H; (3) by retaining Ϝ (*vau*) and Q (*kōph*).

At about the year B.C. 100 the letters Y and Z were reintroduced into the Latin alphabet, but are only used in words borrowed from the Greek, in which they express the non-Latin sounds of Υ and Z. Originally the Latin C had the power of G, but later, when K was disused, C took its place and sound, and the new character G was invented (about B.C. 312) to express the sound formerly denoted by C. In abbreviations, however, such as C., Cn., for Gaius, Gnaeus, the character C has its old power and =G. The emperor Claudius (about A.D. 44) tried to introduce three new symbols into the alphabet, as follows: (1) the inverted digamma Ⅎ, to make the consonantal sound of V (i. e. the *w* sound); (2) the character known as anti-sigma Ɔ, to express the sound of the Greek Ψ (*ps* or *bs*); and (3) the sign Ⱶ, to express the sound of the Greek υ, i. e. of French *u*, or German *ü*. These characters never secured any general adoption. The character V was not developed until the tenth century A.D. as distinct from U; and J, as distinct from I, is no older than the fifteenth century. Previously, I and U had been employed as medial and J and V as initial characters to denote the same letters.

As in Greek, so in Latin, cursive forms arose to replace in part the angular forms of the old capital letters. These cursive characters were used chiefly in correspondence and in business, and are best known to us from the *graffiti* found on the walls of Pompeian houses. From the Roman cursive hand our own minuscules were developed.

For further information, see the articles ABBREVIATIONS; BOUSTROPHEDON; EPIGRAPHY; GRAFFITI; LOGISTICA; PALÆOGRAPHY; PRONUNCIATION; TEXTUAL CRITICISM; and the following works: Kirchhoff, *Geschichte des griechischen Alphabets* (Berlin, 1877); Faulmann, *Geschichte der Schrift* (Vienna, 1880); Humphreys, *Origin of the Art of Writing* (London, 1855); and Isaac Taylor, *The Alphabet*, 2 vols. (London, 1883).

Alphesiboea (Ἀλφεσίβοια) or **Arsinŏē** (Ἀρσινόη). Daughter of Phegeus and first wife of Alcmaeon, whom, though unfaithful, she continued to love, and was angry with her brothers for killing him. Her brothers shut her up in a box, and brought her to Agapenor, king of Tegea, pretending that she had killed her husband. Here she came by her end, having compassed her brothers' death by the hand of Alcmaeon's sons.

Alphēus (Ἀλφειός). The chief river of the Peloponnesus, rising in the southeastern part of Arcadia, flowing through Arcadia and Elis, not far from Olympia, and falling into the Ionian Sea. In some parts of its course the river flows underground; and this subterranean descent gave rise to the story about the river-god Alpheus and the nymph Arethusa. The latter, pursued by Alpheus, was changed by Artemis into the fountain of Arethusa in the island of Ortygia at Syracuse; but the god continued to pursue her under the sea, and attempted to mingle his stream with the fountain in Ortygia.

Alpīnus. A name given by Horace to a contemporary poet, supposed to have been M. Furius Bibaculus (q. v.).

Alsium. An ancient Etrurian town near Caere.

Altāre. See ARA.

Althaea (Ἀλθαία). The daughter of Thestius, wife of Oeneus, king of Calydon, mother of Tydeus, Meleager (q. v.), and Deïanira.

Altīnum. A rich trading town of the Veneti, in the north of Italy, at the mouth of the river Silis.

Altis (Ἄλτις). The sacred grove near Olympia (q. v.) in which the Olympic Games were celebrated.

Aluntium (Ἀλόυντιον) or **Haluntium.** A town in northern Sicily celebrated for its wines.

Alus (Ἄλος) or **Halus** (Ἅλος). A town in Phthiotis in Thessaly.

Alūta. See CALCEUS.

Alūtae (ἀλύται). Persons charged with keeping order at the public games of Greece, but mentioned only in connection with the Olympic Games. Elsewhere the officers are called *μαστιγοφόροι*.

Alyattes (Ἀλυάττης). A king of Lydia, who, in B.C. 617, succeeded his father Sadyattes, and was himself succeeded by his son Croesus (Herod. i. 16). The tomb of Alyattes, north of Sardis, near the lake Gygaea, which consisted of a large mound of earth raised upon a foundation of great stones, still exists. It is nearly a mile in circumference.

Alyzia (Ἀλυζία). A town in Acarnania, near the sea, opposite Leucas, containing a temple sacred to Heracles. (Thucyd. vii. 31.)

Amalthēa (Ἀμάλθεια). A figure in Greek mythology. The name was sometimes applied to a goat which suckled the new-born Zeus in Crete, while bees brought him honey, and which was therefore set among the stars by her nursling; sometimes to a nymph who was supposed to possess a miraculous horn, a symbol of plenty, and whose descent was variously given. According to another legend she is the daughter of the Cretan king Melisseus, and brings up the infant god on the milk of a goat, while her sister Melissa (a bee) offers him honey. The horn of the goat is given to her by Zeus, with the promise that she shall always find in it whatever she wishes. From her the cornucopia passed into the possession of the river-god Acheloüs, who exchanged it for his own horn, which Heracles had broken off. It is also assigned to Dionysus, to Plutus, and to other gods of earthly felicity. See CORNU COPIAE; ZEUS.

Amalthēum or **Amalthēa.** A villa of Atticus in Epirus, perhaps originally a shrine of the nymph Amalthea, which Atticus converted into a beautiful summer retreat. Cicero, in imitation, constructed a similar retreat on his estate at Arpinum. Cf. Cic. *Ad Att.* ii.

Amanuensis (*a manu servus*, ὑπογραφεύς). A slave or freedman employed in writing at his master's dictation. The *amanuensis* is not to be confounded with another sort of slave, *ad manum servus*, who was a general factotum, kept ready at hand for any kind of business. Suet. *Nero*, 44.

Amarăcus (ἀμάρακος). A plant, probably the common marjoram.

Amaranthus (ἀμάραντος). The amaranth, or "never-fading," as its name implies. The modern Italians call it *fior di velluto*, or "velvet-flower."

Amarynthia (Ἀμαρύνθια). A festival of Artemis Amarynthia or Amarysia, celebrated originally at Amarynthus, in Euboea, and afterwards at several places in Attica, such as Athmoné. See Strabo, x. p. 448; Pausan. i. 31, § 3.

Amarynthus (Ἀμάρυνθος). A town in Euboea, seven stadia distant from Eretria, and noted for its splendid temple of Artemis, who is hence called Amarynthia or Amarysia.

Amasēnus. A small river in Latium, which, after uniting with the Ufens, falls into the sea between Circeii and Terracina, though the greater part of its waters are lost in the Pontine Marshes.

Amasīa (Ἀμάσεια). The capital of the kings of Pontus, a strongly fortified city on both banks of the river Iris. It was the birthplace of Mithridates the Great and of the geographer Strabo.

Amāsis (Ἄμασις). A king of Egypt, B.C. 570–526, succeeding Apries, whom he dethroned. During his long reign Egypt was in a very prosperous condition, and the Greeks were brought into much closer intercourse with the Egyptians than had existed previously. Both Pythagoras and Solon are said to have visited him. For his alliance with Polycrates, see the article POLYCRATES.

Amastris (Ἄμαστρις). (1) The wife of Xerxes, and mother of Artaxerxes I. She was of a cruel and vindictive character. (Herod. vii. 61.) (2) Also called Amastriné, niece of Darius, the last king of Persia. She married first Craterus; then Dionysius, tyrant of Heraclea in Bithynia, B.C. 322; and last Lysimachus, B.C. 302. She was drowned by her two sons about B.C. 288. (3) A city on the coast of Paphlagonia, built by Amastris after her separation from Lysimachus.

Amāta. The wife of King Latinus, and mother of Lavinia. She opposed the marriage of Lavinia to Aeneas, because she had already promised her to Turnus. When she heard that Turnus had fallen in battle, she hanged herself. (Verg. *Aen.* xii. 603). See AENEAS; TURNUS.

Amăthus (Ἀμαθοῦς). A town on the southern coast of Cyprus, with a celebrated temple of Aphrodité, who was hence called Amathusia. There were copper-mines in the neighbourhood of the town.

Amazŏnes (Ἀμαζόνες) or **Amazonĭdes** (Ἀμαζονίδες). "Breastless." A mythical race of warlike women, who are said to have come from the Caucasus, and to have settled in Asia Minor, about the river Thermodon, where they founded the city Themiscyra. They were governed by a queen, and the female children are said to have had their right breasts cut off that they might use the bow with more ease. They constantly occur in Greek mythology. One of the labours imposed upon Heracles was to take from Hippolyté, the queen of the Amazons, her girdle. (See HERACLES.) In the reign of Theseus they invaded Attica. Towards the end of the Trojan War, they came, under their queen, Penthesilea, to the assistance of Priam; but she was killed by Achilles. In works of art, the Amazons are always represented with two breasts, often on horseback, and in Scythian or Grecian dress, armed with shield, axe, spear, bow, quiver, etc. Phidias, Polyclitus, and Cresilas are among the famous artists in antiquity who made statues of them. The traditional derivation of the word, from ἀ priv. and μαζός, is doubtless fanciful, and is not even supported by ancient works of art, which usually show the breasts unmutilated.

Amazon.

Ambacti. According to Festus, the Gallic name for slaves. They are mentioned by Caesar (*B. G.* vi. 15).

Ambarri. A people of Gaul, dwelling east of the Aedui (q. v.), on the river Arar (Saône).

Ambarvalia. A rural festival among the Romans for the purification (*lustratio*) of the country, and for invoking the blessing of Ceres upon the fruits of the earth. The name is explained by Servius (*ad* Verg. *Ecl.* iii. 77) as given because the victim *ambit arva*.

There were two kinds of Ambarvalia, private and public. The private Ambarvalia are those described by Vergil in detail, and with singular beauty, *Georg.* i. 338 foll. The victims (Cato, *R. R.* 141) were led three times round the cornfields, before the sickle was put in, accompanied by a crowd of merry-makers (*chorus et socii*), the reapers and servants dancing and singing the praises of Ceres, while they offered her libations of milk, honey, and wine. The public Ambarvalia are certainly to be distinguished from the Amburbium (q. v.), but have been identified by several writers (Mommsen, Henzen, Jordan) with the sacrifice of the Fratres Arvales to the Dea Dia. (See FRATRES ARVALES.) Marquardt, who on the whole decides against the identity of the two festivals, observes that the correspondence of time and place is in favour of it, as well as the fact that the *suovetaurilia* were offered at both; but, as he also points out, there is no mention of the Fratres Arvales beating the bounds (*circumire* or *lustrare*). The Ambarvalia at Rome were fixed for May 29; in other parts of Italy the day varied in different districts, but was an immovable feast (*feriae stativae*) in each district. The feast of the Dea Dia, on the other hand, was proclaimed every year; and May 29 might, or might not, coincide with one of the days on which it was held. As regards the locality, the Roman Ambarvalia were performed, according to Strabo, at a spot called Festi, between five and six miles from the city on the way to Alba (Strab. v. p. 230). This spot is identified beyond doubt with the Fossa Cluilia of Livy (i. 23), Dionysius, and Plutarch; the Campus Sacer Horatiorum, where the legendary encounter took place; and the ruins now called Roma Vecchia, on the left-hand side of the Appian Way at the fifth mile-stone (Burn, *Rome and the*

Campagna, p. 416). The Lucus Deae Diae was at about the same distance from Rome, but on a different road, the Via Portuensis, in a southerly, not an easterly, direction. Both were doubtless on the boundary of the Ager Romanus, or original Roman territory; and in this last circumstance we may trace a connection between the festival of the Arvales and the Ambarvalia without assuming that they were identical.

The Ambarvalia furnish one of several instances—the Saturnalia at Christmas being another—of heathen festivals taken up by the Church and adapted to Christian uses. There is a close resemblance to these rites in the ceremonies of the three Rogation Days which precede Ascension Day, occurring nearly at the same time of year. "They were anciently in England called 'Gang-days,' because processions went out on those days; hymns and canticles being sung, and prayers offered at various halting-spots or stations for a blessing on the fruits of the earth." The English custom of "beating the bounds" at Whitsuntide is a relic of a similar rite. See Henzen, *Acta Fratr. Arval.*

Amber. See ELECTRUM.

Ambiāni. A Belgic tribe subdued by Caesar in B.C. 57. Their chief town was Samarobriva or Ambiani (Amiens).

Ambigātus. A king of the Celtae, in the time of Tarquinius Priscus. According to the account given by Livy (v. 34), he sent his two nephews, Sigovesus and Bellovesus, in quest of new settlements, with the view of diminishing the overflowing numbers at home. The two chieftains drew lots respecting their course, and Sigovesus obtianed the route that led towards the Hercynian forest, Bellovesus the road to Italy. What is here stated, however, appears to be a mere legend, owing its origin to the simultaneous emigrations of two hordes of Gallic warriors. See Thierry, *Histoire des Gaulois*, i. 39.

Ambilustrium. See LUSTRATIO.

Ambiŏrix. A Gallic chief of the Eburones, who cut to pieces the Roman troops under Sabinus and Cotta, in B.C. 54. See Caesar, *B. G.* v. 24 and 26.

Ambĭtus. Literally "a going about," and cannot, perhaps, be more nearly expressed than by our word *canvassing*. After the plebs had formed a distinct class at Rome, and when the whole body of the citizens had become very greatly increased, we frequently read, in the Roman writers, of the great efforts which it was necessary for candidates to make in order to secure the votes of the citizens. At Rome, as in every community into which the element of popular election enters, solicitation of votes, and open or secret influence and bribery, were among the means by which a candidate secured his election to the offices of state.

Whatever may be the authority of the piece entitled *Q. Ciceronis de Petitione Consulatus ad M. Tullium Fratrem*, it seems to present a pretty fair picture of those arts and means by which a candidate might lawfully endeavour to secure the votes of the electors, and also some intimation of those means which were not lawful, and which it was the object of various enactments to repress.

A candidate was called *petitor*, and his opponent, with reference to him, *competitor*. A candidate (*candidatus*) was so called from his appearing in the public places, such as the fora and Campus Martius, before his fellow-citizens, in a whitened toga. On such occasions, the candidate was attended by his friends (*deductores*), or followed by the poorer citizens (*sectatores*), who could in no other manner show their good-will or give their assistance. The word *assiduitas* expressed both the continual presence of the candidate at Rome and his continual solicitations. The candidate, in going his rounds or taking his walk, was accompanied by a *nomenclator*, who gave him the names of such persons as he might meet: the candidate was thus enabled to address them by their names—an indirect compliment which could not fail to be generally gratifying to the electors. The candidate accompanied his address with a shake of the hand (*prensatio*). The term *benignitas* comprehended generally any kind of treating, as shows, feasts, etc.

That ambitus, which was the object of several penal enactments, taken as a generic term, comprehended the two species, *ambitus* and *largitiones* (bribery). *Liberalitas* and *benignitas* are opposed by Cicero, as things allowable, to *ambitus* and *largitio*, as things illegal. Money was paid for votes; and in order to insure secrecy and secure the elector, persons called *interpretes* were employed to make the bargain, *sequestres* to hold the money till it was to be paid, and *divisores* to distribute it. The offence of ambitus was a matter which belonged to the *iudicia publica*, and the enactments against it were numerous. Of these the best known are the Lex Aemilia Balbia (B.C. 182); the Lex Cornelia Fulvia (B.C. 159); the Lex Acilia Calpurnia (B.C. 67); the Lex Tullia (B.C. 63); the Lex Aufidia (B.C. 61); the Lex Licinia (B.C. 58); and the Lex Iulia de ambitu under Augustus. The penalties prescribed by these laws varied from exile, and exclusion from the Senate, to money fines. The Lex Licinia made *sodalicium*, or "treating," an offence. By the time of Augustus, ambitus in its proper sense had disappeared, in consequence of the transfer of the elections from the Comitia to the Senate. A list of trials for ambitus under the Republic is given by Rein in his *Criminalrecht der Römer*.

Ambivarĭti. A Gallic people dwelling west of the Mosa (Meuse), near Namur. (Caes. *B. G.* iv. 9.)

Ambivius Turpio, LUCIUS. A popular Roman actor of the time of Terence, in five of whose plays he appeared. See the Didascaliae to the *Andria, Eunuchus, Heauton Timorumenos, Hecyra*, and *Phormio*; also Cic. *De Senect.* 14; and Varro, *L. L.* vii. 30.

Ambracia (Ἀμβρακία). The modern Arta; a town on the left bank of the Arachthus, north of the Ambracian Gulf, and originally included in Acarnania, but afterwards in Epirus. It was colonized by the Corinthians about B.C. 660. Pyrrhus made it the capital of his kingdom, and adorned it with public buildings and statues. At a later time it joined the Aetolian League, was taken by the Romans in B.C. 189, and stripped of its works of art. Its inhabitants were transplanted to the new city of Nicopolis, founded by Augustus after the battle of Actium, B.C. 31.

Ambracius Sinus (Gulf of Arta). A gulf of the Ionian Sea between Epirus and Acarnania, twenty-five miles long and ten wide.

Ambrōnes. A Keltic people defeated by Marius near Aquae Sextiae (Aix) in B.C. 102.

Ambrosia (ἀμβροσία). A name given to anything that confers immortality. (1) The food of the gods, whose drink was nectar (q. v.). Doves are said by Homer to bring ambrosia to Zeus from the far West. (2) The ointment of the gods, which preserved even the dead from decay. (3) The food of the gods' horses.

Ambrosia (τὰ ἀμβρόσια). Festivals observed in Greece in honour of Dionysus. They were held during the month Lenaeon, at the time of the vintage.

Ambrosius. Bishop of Milan in the fourth century, and one of the latest and most distinguished of what are denominated the Fathers of the Christian Church. He was born at Arelaté (Arles), then the metropolis of Gallia Narbonensis, according to some authorities in A.D. 333, according to others, 340. His father was the emperor's lieutenant in that district, and, after his death, Ambrose, who was the youngest of three children, returned with the widow and family to Rome. Here, under the instructions of his mother and his sister Marcellina, who had vowed virginity, he received a highly religious education, and that bias in favour of Catholic orthodoxy by which he was subsequently so much distinguished. Having studied law, he pleaded causes in the court of the praetorian prefect, and was in due time appointed proconsul of Liguria. He thereupon took up his residence at Milan, where a circumstance occurred which produced a sudden change in his fortunes, and transformed him from a civil governor into a bishop. Auxentius, bishop of Milan, the Arian leader in the West, died, and left that see vacant, when a warm contest for the succession ensued between the Arians and Catholics. In the midst of a tumultuous dispute Ambrose appeared in the midst of the assembly, and exhorted them to conduct the election peaceably. At the conclusion of his address a child in the crowd exclaimed, "Ambrose is bishop!" and, whether accidentally or by management, the result throws a curious light upon the nature of the times; for the superstitious multitude, regarding the exclamation as a providential and miraculous suggestion, by general acclamation declared Ambrose to be elected. After various attempts to decline the episcopal office, Ambrose at length entered upon the discharge of its duties, and rendered himself conspicuous by his decided and unremitting opposition to the tenets of Arianism. To his zealous endeavours also was owing the failure of the attempt made by the remains of a pagan party to re-establish the worship of paganism. The strength and ability of Ambrose were such that, although opposed to him on ecclesiastical points, Valentinian and his mother respected his talents, and in moments of political exigency required his assistance. The most conspicuous act on the part of Ambrose was his treatment of Theodosius for the massacre at Thessalonica. The emperor was consigned to a retirement of eight months, and not absolved even then until he had signed an edict, which ordained that an interval of thirty days should pass before any sentence of death, or even of confiscation, should be executed. After having paid the funeral honours to Theodosius, who died soon after obtaining peaceable possession of the entire Roman Empire, the bishop departed from this world, with a composure worthy of his firm character, in the year 397. It is evident that Ambrose was one of those men of great energy of mind and temperament who, in the adoption of a theory or a party, hold no middle course, but act with determination towards the fulfilment of their purposes. Ambrose effected much to advance the Roman Catholic Church to the power to which it afterwards attained.

The writings of this Father are numerous, and the great object of almost all of them was to maintain the faith and discipline of the Catholic Church, while some of them are written to recommend celibacy as the summit of Christian perfection. His best work is the treatise *De Officiis*, on the duties of a Christian priest. His hymns are also very famous, but only four can be proved to be his—"Deus creator omnium," "Aeterne rerum conditor," "Veni redemptor gentium," and "Iam surgit hora tertia." The noble "Te Deum laudamus" was long ascribed to him. He introduced the practice of singing choral hymns arranged antiphonally (*cantus Ambrosianus*). He is probably the author of a Latin version of the *History of the Jewish War* by Josephus, long ascribed to one Hegesippus. The best text of St. Ambrosius is that in Migne's *Patrologia Latina* (4 vols.).

Ambubaiae. Syrian women who gained a living at Rome by singing and dancing in public, often in the Circus. The word comes from the Syrian *ambub*, a flute.

Amburbium or **Amburbiālé.** A sacrifice performed at Rome for the purification of the city, as the Ambarvalia (q. v.) was intended for the purification of the country. See Preller, *Röm. Myth.* p. 372; and SUOVETAURILIA.

Ambustus, FABIUS. (1) MARCUS, pontifex maximus in B.C. 388. His three sons, while acting as ambassadors to the Gauls at Clusium, took part against them in the military operations. The Gauls then demanded them of the Senate, as having violated the law of nations; and on receiving a refusal, marched on Rome. (2) MARCUS, a Roman who was thrice consul (B.C. 360, 356, 354) and dictator (B.C. 351). He conquered the Hernici, Falisci, Tarquinians, and Tiburtes in his consulships. His son was the famous Q. Fabius Maximus Rullianus. See FABIUS.

Ameipsias (Ἀμειψίας). A Greek poet of the Old Comedy, contemporary with Aristophanes, whom he twice overcame. Of his plays only slight fragments remain (Aristoph. *Ran.* 14).

Amentum. See HASTA.

Ameria. An Umbrian town, the birthplace of Sextus Roscius, who was defended by Cicero in his famous oration *Pro Sex. Roscio Amerino.*

Amestrătus. A town of Sicily, near the Halesus. The Romans besieged it for seven months when in the hands of the Carthaginians, but without success. It was taken, however, after a third siege, and razed to the ground, the surviving inhabitants being sold as slaves. Steph. Byz. calls the place *Amestratus;* Diodorus Siculus, *Mystratum;* and Polybius, *Myttistratum.* (Diod. Sic. xxiii. ecl. 9; Polyb. i. 24.)

Amethystus (ἀμέθυστον or -ος). The amethyst, a precious stone of a purple or violet colour, in different degrees of deepness. In modern mineralogy, the name has been applied to two precious stones of essentially different natures: (1) the Oriental amethyst, which is a rare variety of adamantine spar or corundum; and (2) the Occidental or common amethyst. The ancients, on the other hand, reckoned five species, differing in degrees of colour. Their Indian amethyst, to which Pliny assigns the first rank among purple or violet-coloured gems, appears to have been our Oriental species, which is nothing more than a violet-coloured sapphire. We see our amethyst, indeed, plainly indicated in one of the reasons assigned by Pliny for its name, that it does not reach the colour of wine (ἀ, priv., and μέθυ, *wine*), but first fades into violet. He afterwards suggests another, which was the more common derivation, saying that the Magi falsely asserted that these gems were preservative against intoxication (ἀ, priv., and μεθύω, *to intoxicate*). See GEMMA.

Amĭda. A city in Sophené (Armenia Maior), on the upper Tigris.

Amilcar. See HAMILCAR.

Amisia. The Ems, a river of Northern Germany flowing into the North Sea. (Tac. *Ann.* ii. 8.)

Amīsus (Ἀμισός). A large city on the coast of Pontus, called after it Amisenus Sinus, and a favourite residence of Mithridates.

Amiternum. An ancient town of the Sabines, and notable as the birthplace of the historian Sallust.

Amictorium. A linen covering for the breasts of women. See STROPHIUM.

Amictus (ἐπίβλημα). A general term for the outer clothing, as *indutus* for the under clothing. See TUNICA; PALLIUM.

Amma (ἅμμα). A measure of length = forty cubits (πήχεις) or sixty feet (πόδες).

Ammiānus Marcellīnus. The last Roman historian of any importance, born at Antioch, in Syria, about A.D. 330, of noble Grecian descent. After receiving a careful education, he early entered military service, and fought under Julian against the Alemanni and Persians. In the evening of his days he retired to Rome, and about A.D. 390 began his Latin history of the emperors (*Rerum Gestarum Libri*), from Nerva, A.D. 96, to the death of Valens, in thirty-one books. Of these there only remain books xiv.–xxxi., including the period from A.D. 353 to 378, which he relates for the most part as an eye-witness. A heathen himself, he is, nevertheless, fair to the Christians. As his work may be regarded as a continuation of Tacitus, he seems, on the whole, to have taken that writer for his model. He resembles Tacitus in judgment, political acuteness, and love of truth. But he is far inferior in literary culture, though he loves to display his knowledge, especially in describing nations and countries. Latin was a foreign language to him; hence a crudeness and clumsiness of expression, which is made even more repellent by affectation, bombast, and bewildering ornamental imagery. The best edition is by Gardthausen (1875).

Ammon or **Hammon** (Egyptian *Amun*, the hidden or veiled one). A god native to Libya and Upper Egypt. He was represented sometimes in the shape of a ram with enormous curving horns, sometimes in that of a ram-headed man, sometimes as a perfect man standing up or sitting on a throne. On his head were the royal emblems, with two high feathers standing up, the symbols of sovereignty over the upper and under worlds; in his hands were the sceptre and the sign of life. In works of art his figure is coloured blue. Beside him is usually placed Muth (the "mother," the "queen of darkness," as the inscriptions call her), wearing the crown of Upper Egypt or the vulture-skin. His chief temple, with a far-famed oracle, stood in an oasis of the Libyan desert, twelve days' journey from Memphis. Between this oracle and that of Zeus at Dodona a connection is said to have existed from very ancient times, so that the Greeks early identified the Egyptian god with their own Zeus, as the Romans did afterwards with their Iupiter; and his worship found an entrance at several places in Greece—at Sparta, Thebes, and also Athens—whence festal embassies were regularly sent to the Libyan sanctuary. (See THEORIA.) When the oracle was consulted by visitors, the god's symbol, made of emerald and other stones, was carried round by women and girls, to the sound of hymns, on a golden ship hung round with votive cups of silver. His replies were given in tremulous shocks communicated to the bearers, which were interpreted by a priest.

Ammon and Muth.

Ammonĭi (Ἀμμώνιοι). A people of Africa, occupying what is now the Oasis of Siwah. According to Herodotus (ii. 42), the Ammonians were a colony of Egyptians and Ethiopians, speaking a language composed of words taken from both those nations.

Ammonius (Ἀμμώνιος). (1) The preceptor of Plutarch. He taught philosophy and mathematics at Delphi, and lived during the first century of the Christian era, in the reign of Nero, to whom he acted as interpreter when that monarch visited the temple at Delphi. Plutarch makes frequent mention of him in his writings, and particularly in his treatise on the inscription of the Delphic temple. (2) SACCAS or SACCOPHŎRUS (so called because in early life he had been a porter), a celebrated philosopher, who flourished about the beginning of the third century. He was born at Alexandria, of Christian parents, and was early instructed in the catechetical schools established in that city. Here, under the Christian preceptors, Athenagoras, Pantoenus, and Clemens Alexandrinus, he acquired a strong propensity towards philosophical studies, and became exceedingly desirous of reconciling the different opinions which at that time subsisted among philosophers. Porphyry (*ap.* Euseb. *Hist. Ecc.* vi. 19) relates that Ammonius passed over to the legal establishment—that is, apostatized to the pagan religion. Eusebius (l. c.) and Jerome (*De S. E.* c. 55), on the contrary, assert that Ammonius continued in the Christian faith until the end of his life. But it is probable that those Christian fathers refer to another Ammonius, who, in the third century, wrote a *Harmony of the Gospels*, or to some other person of this name, for they refer to the sacred books of Ammonius; whereas Ammonius Saccas, as his pupil Longinus attests, wrote nothing. It is not easy, indeed, to account for the particulars related of this philosopher, but upon the supposition of his having renounced the Christian faith. According to Hierocles (*De Fato*, ap. Phot. *Bibl.* ii. 461, ed. Bekker), Ammonius was induced to adopt the plan of a distinct eclectic school, by a desire of putting an end to those contentions which had so long distracted the philosophical world. Ammonius had many eminent followers and hearers, both pagan and Christian, who all, doubtless, promised themselves much illumination from a preceptor who undertook to collect into a focus all the rays of ancient wisdom. He taught his select disciples certain sublime doctrines and mystical practices, and was called θεοδίδακτος, "the heaven-taught philosopher." These mysteries were communicated to them under a solemn injunction of secrecy. Porphyry relates that Plotinus, with the rest of the disciples of Ammonius, promised not to divulge certain dogmas which they learned in his school, but to lodge them safely in their purified minds. This circumstance accounts for the fact mentioned on the authority of Longinus that he left nothing in writing. Ammonius probably died about the year 243. (3) A Christian writer, a native of Alexandria, who lived about A.D. 250. He wrote a *Harmony of the Gospels*, which Jerome cites with commendation. (4) The son of Hermias, so called for distinction's sake from other individuals of the name, was a native of Alexandria, and a disciple of Proclus. He taught philosophy at Alexandria about the beginning of the sixth century. His system was an eclectic one, embracing principles derived from both Aristotle and Plato. He cannot be regarded as an original thinker: he was very strong, however, in mathematics, and in the study of the exact sciences, which rectified his judgment, and preserved him, no doubt, from the extravagances of the New Platonism. Ammonius has left commentaries on the *Introduction* of Porphyry; on the *Categories* of Aristotle, together with a life of that philosopher; on his treatise *Of Interpretation;* and scholia on the first seven books of the *Metaphysics*. The scholia on the *Metaphysics* have never been edited. (5) A priest of one of the Egyptian temples. He was one of the literary men who fled from Alexandria to Constantinople after the destruction of the pagan temples. There he became, together with Helladius, one of the masters of Socrates, the ecclesiastical writer: this is a fact which appears firmly established, and the reasons alleged by Valckenaer for placing him in the first or second century have been generally considered insufficient. Ammonius has left us a work on Greek synonyms, etc., under the title Περὶ ὁμοίων καὶ διαφόρων λέξεων. It is a production of very inferior merit. Valckenaer's edition (1739) has been reprinted entire, but in a more portable form, at Leipzig (1822), under the care of Schæffer who has added the unedited notes of Kulencamp, and the critical letter of Segaar, addressed to Valckenaer, and published at Utrecht (1776). We have also a treatise of Ammonius, Περὶ ἀκυρολογίας, "On the improper use of words," which has never been printed. (6) A physician of Alexandria, famous from his skill in cutting for the stone—an operation which, according to some, he first introduced. He invented an instrument for crushing the larger calculi while in the bladder. He was accustomed also to make use of caustic applications, especially red arsenic in hemorrhages. See CHIRURGIA.

Amnestia (ἀμνηστία). A word used to describe the arrangement by which offences were *forgotten.* The word is chiefly found used of real or alleged breaches of the laws committed during the conflicts of opposing factions in the Greek republics. A notable amnesty was that arranged at Athens by the mediation of the Spartan king Pausanias, by which the overthrow of the Thirty was brought about, in B.C. 403. See Grote, chap. lxv.; and ADEIA.

Amnīsus (Ἀμνισός). A town in the north of Crete on a river of the same name; the harbour of Cnossus (q. v.). See Apollon. Rhod. iii. 877.

Amnium (ἀμνίον). A basin or vessel in which at the sacrifices the blood of the victims was caught as it fell. (*Odyss.* iii. 444.)

Amnium.

Amoebaea. Verses that answer one another alternately in strophe and antistrophe, as in some of Vergil's *Eclogues*, e. g. the Seventh, Eighth, and Ninth. The amoebaean form prevails also in some of the earlier specimens of Roman verse, as the songs of the Fratres Arvales (q. v.). It is only one of the many manifestations of the Italian liking for dialogue, on which see Teuffel, *Hist. of Rom. Lit.* 3, § 3 (Engl. transl. by Warr [London, 1891]); and Patin, *Études sur la Poésie Latine* (Paris, 1875).

Amor. The god of love. See EROS.

Amōres. A collection of poems by P. Ovidius Naso (q. v.), originally in five books, afterwards reduced to three. They were published in B.C. 13, and are in elegiac verse. They are elegant in form and expression, but extremely licentious in tone.

Amorgīna (τὰ ἀμόργινα). Fine muslin textures made of a flax named from the island Amorgus. See BYSSUS; CARBASUS.

Amorgus (Ἀμοργός). An island, one of the Sporades (q. v.), and the birthplace of the poet Simonides. The Roman emperors used it as a place of banishment.

Ampechŏnē (ἀμπεχόνη). A shawl or scarf worn by Greek women over the *chiton*, or inner garment. See PALLIUM; TUNICA.

Ampelius, LUCIUS. A Roman writer who flourished not earlier than the second century A.D., and wrote a note-book, *Liber Memorialis*, which contains a scanty collection of astronomical, geographical, and historical jottings. Trivial as the book is, a statement in its chapter on the wonders of the world has mainly led to the discovery (in 1878) of the magnificent sculptures of Pergamum, now at Berlin. Ampelius has been edited with notes by Beck (Leipzig, 1826). The best text is that of Wölfflin (Leipzig, 1854).

Amphiarāia (ἀμφιαράϊα). Games celebrated near Oropus in honour of Amphiaraüs (q. v.).

Amphiarāüs (Ἀμφιάραος). An Argive, the son of Oïcles and Hypermnestra, great-grandson of the seer Melampus. In Homer he is a favourite of Zeus and Apollo, alike distinguished as a seer and a hero, who takes part in the Calydonian boar-hunt, in the voyage of the Argonauts, and in the expedition of the Seven against Thebes. Reconciled to Adrastus (q. v.) after a quarrel, and wedded to his sister Eriphylé, he agreed that any future differences between them should be settled by her. She, bribed by Polynices with the fatal necklace of his ancestress Harmonia, insisted on her husband joining the war against Thebes, though he foresaw that it would end fatally for him, and in departing charged his youthful sons Alcmaeon and Amphilochus (q. v.) to avenge his coming death. His wise warnings were unheeded by the other princes; his justice and prudence even brought him into open strife with the savage Tydeus; yet in the fatal closing contest he loyally avenged his death on the Theban Melanippus. In the flight, just as the spear of Periclymenus was descending on him, Zeus interposed to save the pious prophet and make him immortal by cleaving the earth open with his thunderbolt and bidding it swallow up Amphiaraüs, together with his trusty charioteer Baton, like himself a descendant of Melampus. From that time forth, Amphiaraüs was worshipped in various places as an oracular god, especially at Oropus on the frontier of Attica and Boeotia, where he had a temple and a famous oracle for the interpretation of dreams, and where games were celebrated in honour of him.

Amphiclēa (Ἀμφίκλεια). A town of northern Phocis, with a shrine of Dionysus.

Amphicrătes (Ἀμφικράτης). (1) A biographer, who, according to Diogenes Laërtius (*Vit. Aristip.*), was condemned to die by poison. See Athenaeus, xiii. 5. (2) An Athenian orator, who, being banished from his country, retired to Seleucia on the Tigris, and took up his residence there under the protection of Cleopatra, daughter of Mithridates. He starved himself to death, because suspected by this princess of treason.

Amphictўon (Ἀμφικτύων). The son of Deucalion (q. v.) and Pyrrha, and the reputed founder of the Amphictyonic Council. (Herod. vii. 200).

Amphictyŏnes (Ἀμφικτύονες). Literally "those dwelling around," but in a special sense applied to populations which at stated times met at the same sanctuary to keep a festival in common, and to transact common business. The most famous and extensive union of the kind was that called, *par excellence*, the AMPHICTYONIC LEAGUE, whose common sanctuaries were the temple of Pythian Apollo at Delphi, and the temple of Demeter at Anthela, near Pylae or Thermopylae. After Pylae the assembly was named the Pylaean, even when it met at Delphi, and the deputies of the league Pylagorae. The league was supposed to be very ancient, as old even as the name of Hellenes; for its founder was said to be Amphictyon, the son of Deucalion and brother of Hellen, the common ancestor of all Hellenes. (Herod. vii. 200.) It included twelve populations: Malians, Phthians, Aenianes or Oetoeans, Dolopes, Magnetians, Perrhoebians, Thessalians, Locrians, Dorians, Phocians, Boeotians, and Ionians, together with the colonies of each. Though in later times their extent and power were very unequal, yet in point of law they all had equal rights. Besides protecting and preserving those two sanctuaries, and celebrating from the year B.C. 586 onwards the Pythian Games, the league was bound to maintain certain principles of international right, which forbade them, for instance, ever to destroy utterly any city of the league, or to cut off its water, even in time of war. To the assemblies, which met every spring and autumn, each nation sent two ἱερομνήμονες (= wardens of holy things) and several pylagorae. The latter took part in the debates, but only the former had the right of voting. When a nation included several States, these took by turns the privilege of sending deputies. But the stronger states, such as the Ionian Athens or the Dorian Sparta, were probably allowed to take their turn oftener than the rest, or even to send to every assembly. When violations of the sanctuaries or of popular right took place the assembly could inflict fines, or even expulsion; and a State that would not submit to the punishment had a "holy war" declared against it. By such a war the Phocians were expelled B.C. 346, and their two votes given to the Macedonians; but the expulsion of the former was withdrawn because of the glorious part they took in defending the Delphian temple when threatened by the Gauls in B.C. 279, and at the same time the Aetolian community, which had already made itself master of the sanctuary, was acknowledged as a new member of the league. In B.C. 191 the number of members amounted to seventeen, who nevertheless had only twenty-four votes, seven having two votes each, the rest only one. Under the Roman rule the league continued to exist, but its action was now limited to the care of the Delphian temple. It was reorganized by Augustus, who incorporated the Malians, Magnetians, Aenianes, and Pythians with the Thessalians, and substituted for the extinct Dolopes the city of Nicopolis in Acarnania, which he had founded after the battle of Actium. The last notice we find of the league is in the second century A.D. See Freeman, *Hist. of Federal Government* (2d ed. 1893); Tittmann, *Ueber den Bund der Amphictyonen;* Müller, *Dorians;* and Grote, vol. ii. chap. ii.

Amphidromia (ἀμφιδρόμια). At Athens, a family festival at which a new-born infant received religious consecration and its name. The carrying of the child by its nurse around the hearth was the principal part of the ceremony, and from this it is called. (Isaeus, *De Pyrrhi Hered.* § 30.)

Amphilochia (Ἀμφιλοχία). The country of the Amphilochi, an Epirot race, at the east end of the Ambracian Gulf, usually included in Acarnania. Their chief town was Argos Amphilochicum. See AMPHILOCHUS.

Amphilŏchus (Ἀμφίλοχος). The son of Amphiaraüs and Eriphylé, and brother of Alcmaeon (q. v.). He took part in the expedition of the Epigoni against Thebes, assisted his brother in the murder of their mother, and afterwards fought against Troy. Like his father, he was a celebrated seer. He was killed in single combat by Mopsus, who was also a seer, at Mallos, in Cilicia. According to some, he founded Argos Amphilochicum on the Ambracian Gulf.

Amphimallum. See TAPES.

Amphīon (Ἀμφίων). The son of Zeus and Antiopé, and twin-brother of Zethus. They were born on Mt. Cithaeron, and grew up among the shepherds. Having become acquainted with their origin, they marched against Thebes, where Lycus reigned, the husband of their mother, Antiopé, who had married Dircé in her stead. They took the city, and killed Lycus and Dircé because they had treated Antiopé with great cruelty. They put Dircé to death by tying her to a bull, who dragged her about till she perished; and finally threw her body into a fountain, which was from this time called the fountain of Dircé. After they had obtained possession of Thebes, they fortified it by a wall. Amphion had received a lyre from Hermes, on which he played with such magic skill that the stones moved of their own accord and formed the wall. Amphion afterwards married Niobé, who bore him many sons and daughters, all of whom were killed by Apollo and Artemis, whereupon he put an end to his own life. See NIOBÉ.

Amphiorkia or **Amphomosia** (ἀμφιορκία or ἀμφωμοσία). The oath which was taken, both by the plaintiff and the defendant, before the trial of a cause in the Athenian courts, that they would speak the truth. In the ἀνάκρισις, or preliminary investigation, it was called διωμοσία.

Amphipŏlis (Ἀμφίπολις). A town in Macedonia, on the eastern bank of the Strymon, about three miles from the sea. The Strymon flowed almost round the town, nearly forming a circle, whence its name Amphi-polis. It was originally called Ennea Hodoi, the "Nine Ways," and belonged to the Edonians, a Thracian people. It was colonized by the Athenians in B.C. 437, who drove the Edonians out of the place. It was one of the most important of the Athenian possessions in the north of the Aegaean Sea. Hence their indignation when it fell into the hands of Brasidas (B.C. 424), and of Philip (B.C. 358). The port of Amphipolis was Eion. See PHILIPPUS.

Amphippoi (ἄμφιπποι). See DESULTORES.

Amphiprostȳlos (ἀμφιπρόστυλος). See TEMPLUM.

Amphis (Ἄμφις). A Greek comic poet of Athens, contemporary with Plato. His works are lost (Ath. i. 403 foll., Mein.).

Amphissa (Ἄμφισσα). An important town of the Locri Ozolae near Delphi. See SACRED WAR.

Amphithalămus (ἀμφιθάλαμος). A room in the women's quarters of a Greek house, opposite the θάλαμος, and serving probably as a sleeping-room for the grown-up daughters. See DOMUS.

Amphitheātrum (ἀμφιθέατρον). A circular or elliptical building, arranged for the exhibition of combats of gladiators, wild beasts, and for sham sea-fights, all of which constituted the *ludi amphitheatrales*. See LUDI.

The first amphitheatre was probably that of C. Scribonius Curio, which was literally a double theatre, being composed of two wooden theatres placed on pivots, so that they could be turned around, spectators and all, and placed back to back, forming two separate theatres for dramatic exhibits; or face to face, forming an amphitheatre in the ordinary sense of the word. This structure was erected in B.C. 50, and is described by Pliny (*H. N.* xxxvi. § 116). The next was built by Iulius Caesar in B.C. 46, and was also of wood. These edifices were exposed to the danger of destruction by fire, and sometimes, too, proved inadequate to support the weight of the enormous crowds of spectators—often as many as 30,000 to 50,000. It was not until the fourth consulate of Augustus (B.C. 30) that an amphitheatre of stone was erected by Statilius Taurus in the Campus Martius (Suet. *Octav.* 29). This building was the only one of its kind until the erection of the great Flavian amphitheatre. This was carried out in the reigns of Vespasian and Titus, when the *Amphitheatrum Flavium*, which, since the time of Bede, has been known as the Colosseum or Coliseum, arose. An ecclesiastical tradition makes the architect to have been a Christian, one Gaudentius, afterwards a martyr. See Burn, *Rome and the Campagna*, p. 235; Middleton, *Ancient Rome in* 1885, pp. 303 foll.

This marvellous building was commenced by Vespasian (Suet. *Vesp.* 9) early in his reign, and completed by Titus, who dedicated it in the year A.D. 80, on which occasion 5000 animals of various kinds were slaughtered (Suet. *Tit.* 7). He seems not to have added the last story, however, which was done by Domitian, who also caused the ornamental work to be executed. As built by the Flavian emperors, the highest tiers of seats inside, and probably the fourth story, were of wood. Further additions date from a period not earlier than the time of Alexander Severus. (See Burn, p. 235). The name Colosseum was probably given it from the colossus of Nero. No subsequent public amphitheatre was erected in the city of Rome, the little *amphitheatrum castrense*, near the church of S. Croce, being probably intended only for the soldiers of the Guard. See COLOSSUS.

The Colosseum became the spot where prince and people met together to witness those sanguinary exhibitions, the degrading effects of which on the Roman character can hardly be overestimated. It was partially repaired by Antoninus Pius (Capit. *Ant. Pi.* 8). In the reign of Macrinus, on the day of the Vulcanalia, it was struck by lightning, by which the upper rows of benches were consumed, and so much damage was done to other parts of the structure that the games were for some years celebrated in the Stadium (Dio Cass. lxxviii. 25). Its restoration was commenced by Elagabalus, and completed by Alexander Severus. A medal of Gordian III. represents the Colosseum with the legend *Munificentia Gordiani Aug.*, showing that fresh works were undertaken within a few years. It was again struck by lightning in the reign of Decius (Hieron. p. 475), but was soon restored, and the games continued to be celebrated in it down to the sixth century. It is usually stated that, in consequence of the self-devotion of Telemachus, an Asiatic monk, who rushed into the arena to separate the gladiators, and was overwhelmed under a shower of stones, Honorius abolished forever the sacrifices of the gladiators (Theodoret. v. 26); but there is evidence that they were continued even at a later period (Augustin. *Confess.* vi. 8). In later times the amphitheatre has been used sometimes in war as a fortress, and in peace as a quarry; whole palaces, such as the Cancelleria and the Palazzo Farnese, having been built out of its spoils. At length the popes made efforts to preserve it: Sixtus V. attempted to use it as a woollen factory, and to convert the arcades into shops; Clement XI. enclosed the lower arcades; and in 1750 Benedict XIV. consecrated it to the Christians who had been martyred in it. Notwithstanding the damages of time, war, and spoliation, the Flavian Amphitheatre still remains complete enough to give us a fair idea, excepting in some minor details, of the structure and arrangements of this description of building.

The very site of the Flavian Amphitheatre, as of most others, furnishes an example of the prodigal contempt of labour and expense which the Roman emperors displayed in their great works of architecture. The Greeks, in choosing the sites of their theatres, almost always availed themselves of some natural hollow on the side of a hill; but the Roman amphitheatres, with few exceptions, stand upon a plain. The site of the Colosseum was in the

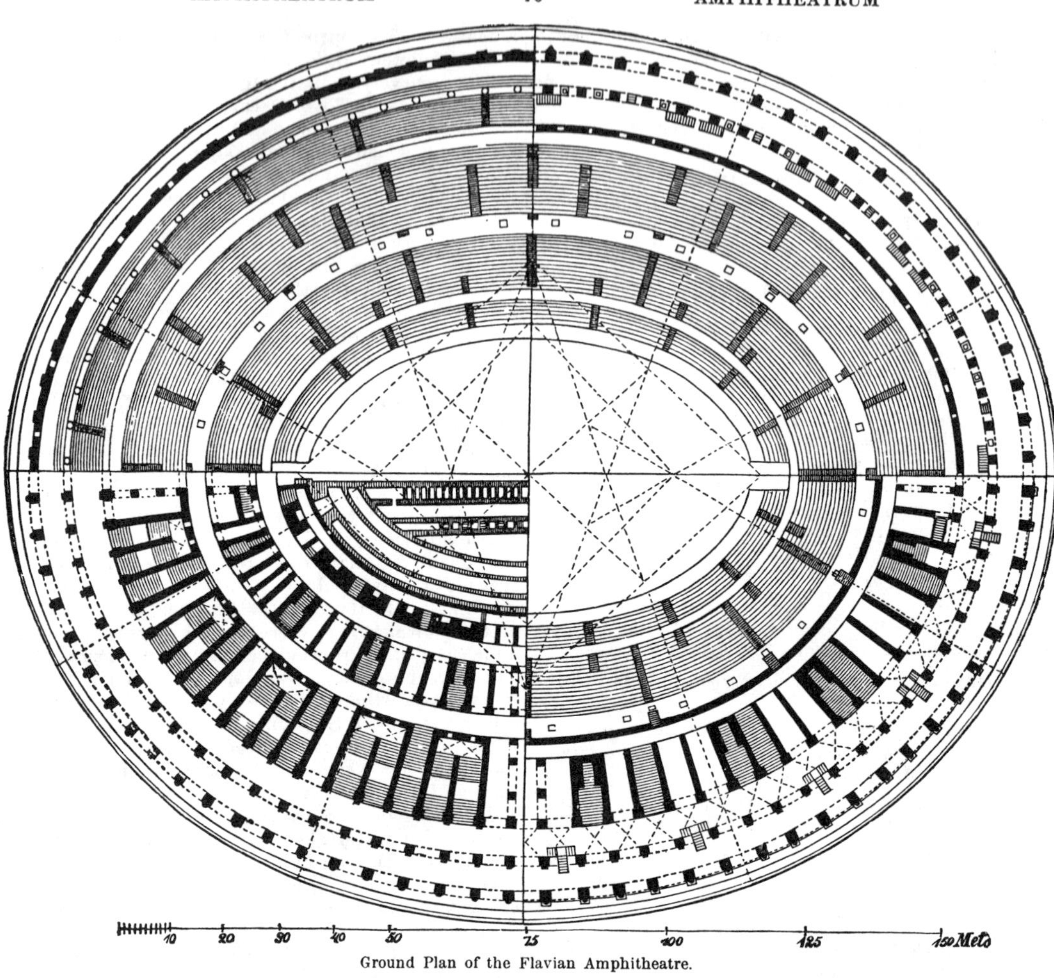

Ground Plan of the Flavian Amphitheatre.

middle of the city, in the valley between the Caelian, the Esquiline, and the Velia, on the marshy ground which was previously the lake of Nero's palace, *stagnum Neronis.*

> "Hic ubi conspicui venerabilis amphitheatri
> Erigitur moles, stagna Neronis erant."
> (Mart. *de Spect.* ii. 5.)

No mere measures can give an adequate conception of this vast structure, the dimensions and arrangements of which were such as to furnish seats for 87,000 spectators, around an arena large enough to afford space for the combats of several hundred animals at once, for the evolutions of mimic sea-fights, and for the exhibition of artificial forests; with passages and staircases to give ingress and egress, without confusion, to the immense mass of spectators, and others for the attendants on the arena; dens for the thousands of victims devoted to destruction; channels for the rapid influx and outlet of water when the arena was used for a *naumachia;* and the means for the removal of the carcases, and the other abominations of the arena. Admirable pictures of the magnitude and magnificence of the amphitheatre and its spectacles are drawn in the *Essays* of Montaigne (iii. 6), and in the latter part of Gibbon's twelfth chapter.

As a general description of the building, the following passage of Gibbon is perfect: "It was a building of an elliptic figure, founded on fourscore arches, and rising, with four successive orders of architecture, to the height of 140 [157] feet. The outside of the edifice was incrusted with marble, and decorated with statues. The slopes of the vast concave which formed the inside were filled and surrounded with sixty or eighty rows of seats, of marble likewise, covered with cushions, and capable of receiving with ease about 80,000 spectators. Sixty-four *vomitories* (for by that name the doors were very aptly distinguished) poured forth the immense multitude; and the entrances, passages, and staircases were contrived with such exquisite skill that each person, whether of the senatorial, the equestrian, or the plebeian order, arrived at his destined place without trouble or confusion. Nothing was omitted which, in any respect, could be subservient to the convenience and pleasure of the spectators. They were protected from the sun and rain by an ample canopy, occasionally drawn over their heads. The air was continually refreshed by the playing of fountains, and profusely impregnated by the grateful scent of aromatics. In the centre of the edifice, the *arena*, or stage, was strewed with the finest sand, and successively assumed the most different forms. At one moment it seemed to rise out of the earth, like the garden of the Hesperides, and was afterwards broken into the rocks and caverns of Thrace. The subterraneous pipes conveyed an inexhaustible supply of water; and what had just before appeared a level plain might be suddenly converted into a wide lake, covered with armed vessels, and replenished with the monsters of the deep. In the decoration of these scenes, the Roman emperors displayed their wealth and liberality; and we read on various occasions that the whole furniture of the amphitheatre consisted either of silver, or of gold, or of amber. The poet who describes the games of Carinus, in the character of a shepherd attracted to the capital by the fame of their magnificence, affirms that the nets designed as a defence against the wild beasts were of gold wire; that the porticos were gilded; and that the *belt* or circle which divided the several ranks of spectators from each other was studded with a precious mosaic of beautiful stones" (really, of glass tesserae in imitation of jewels; cf. ABACULUS).

The annexed woodcut, representing a section, not of an entire amphitheatre, but merely of the exterior wall, and the seats included between that and the arena, will serve to convey an idea of the arrangement of such structures in general. It is that of the Colosseum, and is given upon the authority of Hirt; but it is in some respects conjectural, particularly in the upper part, since no traces of the upper gallery are now remaining. The extreme minuteness of the scale renders it impossible to point out more than the leading form and general disposition of the interior; therefore, as regards the profile of the exterior, merely the heights of the cornices of the different orders are shown, with the figures 1, 2, 3, 4 placed against them respectively.

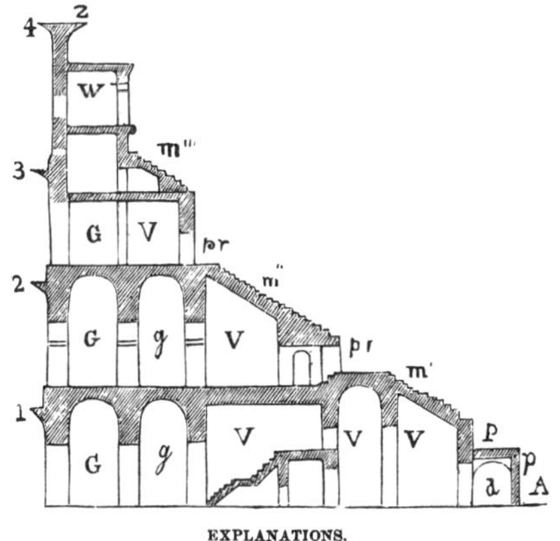

EXPLANATIONS.

A, The arena.
p, The wall or podium enclosing it.
P, The podium itself, on which were chairs or seats for the senators, etc.
m', The first maenianum, or slope of benches, for the equestrian order.
m'', The second maenianum.
m''', The third maenianum, elevated considerably above the preceding one, and appropriated to the pullati.
W, The colonnade, or gallery, which contained seats for women.
Z, The narrow gallery round the summit of the interior, for the attendants who worked the velarium.
pr, *pr*, The praecinctiones, or landings, at the top of the first and second maenianum, in the pavement of which were grated apertures, at intervals, to admit light into the vomitoria beneath them.
V V V V V, Vomitoria.
G G G, The three external galleries through the circumference of the building, open to the arcades of the first three orders of the exterior.
g g, Inner galleries.

Owing to the smallness of the cut, the situation and arrangement of staircases, etc., are not expressed, as such parts could hardly be rendered intelligible except upon a greatly increased scale, and then not in a single section, nor without plans at various levels of the building.

The Colosseum covers altogether about five acres of ground; the transverse, or longer diameter of the external ellipse, is 615 feet, and the conjugate, or shorter one, 510; while those of the interior ellipse, or arena, are 281 and 176 feet respectively. Where it is perfect, the exterior is 157 feet high, and consists of four orders—viz., Doric, Ionic, and Corinthian—in attached three-quarter columns (that is, columns one fourth of whose circumference appears to be buried in the wall behind them), and an upper order of Corinthian pilasters. With the exception of the last, each of these tiers consists of eighty columns, and as many arches between them, forming open galleries throughout the whole circumference of the building; but the fourth has windows instead of large arches, and those are placed only in the alternate inter-columns—consequently, are only forty in number; and this upper portion of the elevation has, both on that account and owing to the comparative smallness of the apertures themselves, an expression of greater solidity than that below. The arches formed open external galleries, with others behind them; besides which there were several other galleries and passages, extending beneath the seats for the spectators, and, together with staircases, affording access to the latter. At present, the seats do not rise higher than the level of the third order of the exterior, or about half its entire height; therefore, the upper part of the edifice appears to have contributed very little, if at all, to its actual capacity for accommodating spectators. Still, though it has never been explained, except by conjecturing that there were upper tiers of seats and galleries (although no remains of them now exist), we must suppose that there existed some very sufficient reason for incurring such enormous expense, and such prodigal waste of material and labour beyond what utility seems to have demanded. This excess of height, so much greater than was necessary, was perhaps, in some measure, with the view that, when the building was covered in with a temporary roofing or awning (*velarium*), as a defence against the sun or rain, it should seem well proportioned as to height; and also, perhaps, in order to allow those who worked the ropes and other mechanism by which the velarium was unrolled or drawn back again, to perform those operations without incommoding the spectators on the highest seats.

With regard to the velarium (q. v.) itself, nothing at all conclusive and satisfactory can now be gathered; and it has occasioned considerable dispute among archæologists how any temporary covering could be extended over the whole of the building. Some have imagined that the velarium extended only over part of the building; but, independent of other objections, it is difficult to conceive how such an extensive surface could have been supported along the extent of its inner edge or circumference. The only thing which affords any evidence as to the mode in which the velarium was fixed is a series of projecting brackets, or corbels, in the uppermost story of the exterior, containing holes or sockets to receive the ends of poles passing through holes in the projection of the cornice, and to which ropes from the velarium were fixed; but the whole of the upper part

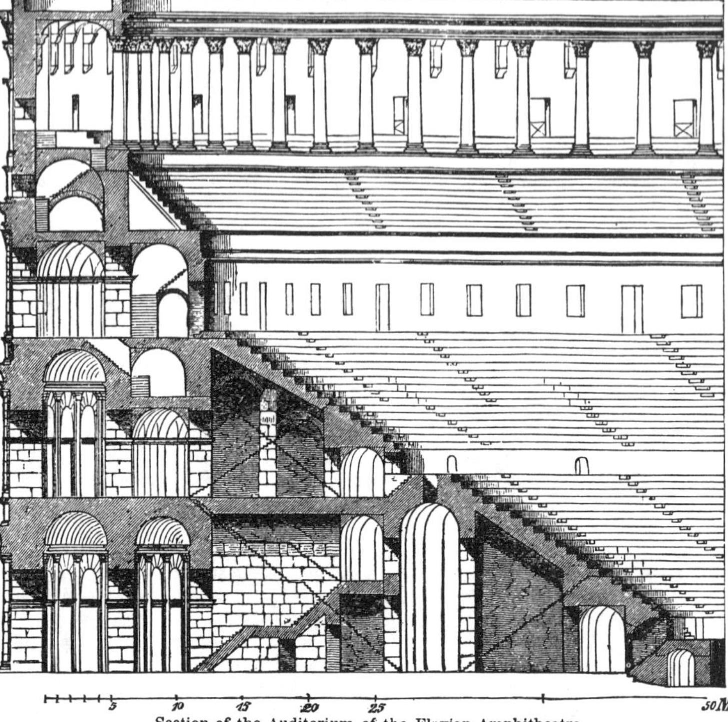

Section of the Auditorium of the Flavian Amphitheatre.

of the interior is now so dismantled as to render it impossible to decide with certainty in what manner the velarium was fastened. The velarium appears usually to have been made of wool, but more costly materials were sometimes employed. When the weather did not permit the velarium to be spread, the Romans used broad-brimmed hats or caps (*petasi*), or a sort of parasol, which was called *umbraculum*, from *umbra*, shade.

The interior of the amphitheatre was divided into three parts—the *arena*, *podium*, and *gradus*. The clear open space in the centre of the amphitheatre was called the arena, because it was covered with sand or sawdust, to prevent the gladiators from slipping and to absorb the blood. The size of the arena was not always the same in proportion to the size of the amphitheatre, but its average proportion was one third of the shorter diameter of the building.

It is now quite clear, since the excavations of 1874–75, that the arena had an actual flooring of boards, covered with sand, and movable. There must have been a souterrain, or vaults, at intervals at least, if not throughout, beneath the arena, as sometimes the animals suddenly issued apparently from beneath the ground (see the annexed illustration), and machinery of different kinds was raised up from below, and afterwards disappeared in the same manner. That there was also some substruction beneath the arena, in some amphitheatres at least, is evident, because the whole arena was, upon particular occasions,

Method of Raising Wild Beasts in the Amphitheatre.

filled with water, and converted into a *naumachia*, where vessels engaged in mimic sea-fights, or else crocodiles and other amphibious animals, were made to attack each other. Nero is said to have frequently entertained the Romans with spectacles and diversions of this kind, which took place immediately after the customary games, and were again succeeded by them; consequently, there must have been not only an abundant supply of water, but mechanical apparatus capable of pouring it in and draining it off again very expeditiously. See NAUMACHIA.

The arena was surrounded by a wall, distinguished by the name of *podium*, although such appellation, perhaps, rather belongs to merely the upper part of it, forming the parapet or balcony before the first or lowermost seats, nearest to the arena. The latter, therefore, was no more than an open oval court, surrounded by a wall about eighteen feet high, measuring from the ground to the top of the parapet; a height considered necessary in order to render the spectators perfectly secure from the attacks of the wild beasts. There were four principal entrances leading into the arena, two at the ends of each axis or diameter of it, to which as many passages led directly from the exterior of the building; besides secondary ones intervening between them, and communicating with the corridors beneath the seats on the podium.

The wall or enclosure of the arena is supposed to have been faced with marble of more or less costliness; besides which there appears to have been, in some instances at least, a sort of network affixed to the top of the podium, consisting of railing, or, rather, open trellis-work of metal. From the mention made of this network by ancient writers, little more can now be gathered respecting it than that, in the time of Nero, such netting, or whatever it might have been, was adorned with gilding and amber—a circumstance that favours the idea of its having been gilt metal-work, with bosses and ornaments of the other material. As a further defence, ditches, called *euripi*, sometimes surrounded the arena.

The term *podium* was also applied to the terrace, or gallery itself, immediately above the lower enclosure, and which was only wide enough to contain two, or at the most three, ranges of movable seats or chairs. This, as being by far the best situation for distinctly viewing the sports in the arena, and also more commodiously accessible than the seats higher up, was the place set apart for senators and other persons of distinction, such as the ambassadors of foreign parts; and it was here, also, that the emperor himself used to sit, in an elevated place called *suggestus* or *cubiculum;* and likewise the person who exhibited the games, on a place elevated like a pulpit or tribunal (*editoris tribunal*). The Vestal Virgins also appear to have had a place allotted to them in the podium, as has been assumed from a passage in Suetonius (*Aug.* 44), though this is only inferential, as the passage relates to an earlier regulation respecting the theatre. Some of these marble seats were carried away in the Middle Ages to be used as episcopal thrones.

Elevation of the Flavian Amphitheatre restored. (Daremberg and Saglio.)

Above the podium were the *gradus*, or seats of the other spectators, which were divided into *maeniana*, or stories. The first *maenianum*, consisting

The Colosseum. (Drawn by Boudier, after Photographs.)

of fourteen rows of stone or marble seats, was appropriated to the equestrian order. The seats appropriated to the senators and equites were covered with cushions (*pulvilli*), which were first used in the time of Caligula. Then, after an interval or space, termed a *praecinctio*, and forming a continued landing-place from the several staircases in it, succeeded the second maenianum, where were the seats called *popularia*, for the third class of spectators, or the *populus*. Behind this was the second praecinctio, bounded by a rather high wall, above which was the third maenianum, where there were only wooden benches for the *pullati*, or common people. The next and last division—namely, that in the highest part of the building—consisted of a colonnade or gallery, where women were allowed to witness the spectacles of the amphitheatre. Some parts of this were also occupied by the pullati. At the very summit was the narrow platform for the men who had to attend to the velarium, and to expand or withdraw the awnings, as there might be occasion. Each maenianum was not only divided from the other by the praecinctio, but was intersected at intervals by spaces for passages left between the seats, called *scalae* or *scalaria;* and the portion between two such passages was called a *cuneus*, because this space gradually widened, like a wedge, from the podium to the top of the building. The entrances to the seats from the outer porticos were called *vomitoria*, because, says Macrobius, *Homines glomeratim ingredientes in sedilia se fundunt.*

Interior of the Colosseum.

There were in the amphitheatre concealed tubes, from which scented liquids were scattered over the audience, and which sometimes issued from statues placed in different parts of the building. (Lucan, ix. 808; Mart. *Spect.* 3.)

The provincial amphitheatres were probably, as a rule, built of wood; but in several of the large cities of the Empire there are important ruins of large amphitheatres of stone, of which the best known are at Verona, Paestum, Pompeii, and Capua, in Italy; at Nîmes, Arles, and Fréjus, in France; at Pola, in Istria; and at Syracuse and Catania, in Sicily.

For an account of the games, combats, etc., held in the amphitheatre, see the articles GLADIATORES; NAUMACHIA; VENATIONES.

On the general subject of amphitheatres, the reader is referred to the following standard works: Lipsius, *De Amphitheatro;* Nibby, *Dell' Anfiteatro Flavio*, a supplement to Nardini, vol. i. p. 233; Fea, *Notizie degli Scavi nell' Anfiteatro Flavio;* Bunsen, *Beschreibung der Stadt Rom*, vol. iii.; Cressy and Taylor, *Architectural Antiquities of Rome;* Stieglitz, *Archäologie der Baukunst;* Hirt, *Geschichte d. Baukunst bei den Alten;* Burn, *Rome and the Campagna;* J. H. Parker, *Archaeology of Rome*, part vii.; Middleton, *Ancient Rome in 1885;* id., *Remains of Ancient Rome* (1892).

Amphitrītê (Ἀμφιτρίτη). A Nereid, wife of Poseidon (q. v.), and mother of Triton (q. v.).

Amphitruo. The title of a comedy of T. Maccius Plautus (q. v.), and differing from the others of his that we possess in being in spirit a burlesque. It is based on the story of Iupiter and Alcmenê, and has been imitated by Molière in French, and Dryden in English. See SATYRIC DRAMA.

Amphitryon or **Amphitruo** (Ἀμφιτρύων). Son of Alcaeus and Hipponomê, husband of Alcmenê, and nominally father of Heracles, who is hence called Amphitryoniades. (See ALCMENÊ.) Amphitryon was slain in a war against Erginus, king of the Minyans.

Amphomosia (ἀμφομοσία). See AMPHIORKIA.

Amphŏra (ἀμφορεύς). A two-handled, big-bellied vessel, usually of clay, with a longish or shortish neck, and a mouth proportioned to the size, sometimes resting firmly on a foot, but often ending in a blunt point, so that in the store-room it had to lean against the wall or be sunk in sand, and, when brought out for use, to be put in a basket, wine-cooler, or hollow stand.

It served to keep oil, honey, and more especially

the wine drawn off from the big fermenting vats. It was fastened with a clay stopper, plastered over with pitch, loam, or gypsum, and had a ticket stating the kind, the year, and the quantity of the wine it contained. The Greek ἀμφορεύς was a

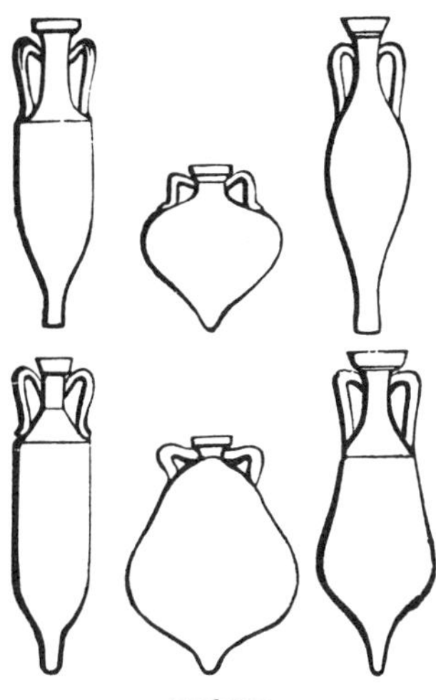

Amphorae.

large liquid measure holding nearly nine gallons (see METRETES); the Roman measure called *amphora* held six gallons and seven pints. See VINUM.

Amphrȳsus (Ἀμφρυσός). A small stream in Thessaly flowing into the Pagasaeus Sinus. On its banks Apollo fed the herds of Admetus (q. v.).

Ampsāga. A river of North Africa flowing past the town of Cirta, and dividing Numidia from Mauritania Sitifensis. (Ptol. iv. 3, § 20.)

Ampsanctus (or **Amsanctus**) **Lacus.** A small lake in Samnium, near Aeculanum, which, by reason of its mephitic vapours, was reputed to be the entrance to the lower world. (Cic. *De Div.* i. 36.)

Ampulla (λήκυθος, βομβύλιος). A tall, slender, narrow-necked vessel, with a handle, used for perfumes, unguents, vinegar, water, and wine (*ampulla potoria*). Lekythi were of constant use at the toilets of Greek ladies. They also held the oil used in anointing the bodies of the dead. The ampulla was used in the Christian Church as a receptacle for the wine and water of the sacrament, and also for holding the consecrated oil or chrism.

Lekythos. (British Museum.)

Amputatio. See IUDICIUM.

Ampyx (Ἄμπυξ). Son of Pelias, husband of Chloris, and father of Mopsus (q. v.), who was hence known as Ampycides.

Ampyx (ἄμπυξ). (1) A frontlet or band worn by Greek ladies to confine the hair; passing around the front of the head and fastened behind. It was often of gold or silver, and adorned with precious stones. Hesychius supposes men

Forms of the Ampyx.

to have worn frontlets in Lydia; and they appear to have been worn also by the Jews. (2) A frontlet worn by horses, and sometimes by elephants, often highly ornamented.

Ampliatio. The Latin term for a delay of verdict pending the production of further evidence in a case not clear to the judges. See COMPERENDINATIO.

Amulētum (περίαπτον, περίαμμα, φυλακτήριον). A charm worn by a human being, or even by an animal, to avert evil or secure good fortune. The word is from the Arabic *hamâlet*, meaning "that which is suspended." Amulets are as old as the Homeric μῶλυ (*Od.* x. 305); but appear to have been introduced into Rome from the East under the early Empire. The word is first used in Pliny (*H. N.* xxxvii. § 124). They consist of gems or stones, metals (e. g. copper, iron, gold); plants (e. g. laurel, hellebore, fig); animals and parts of animals (e. g. the spider, the bat, the dog's gall, the ass's testicles, wolf's fat); parts and secretions of the human body (e. g. the blood of gladiators, the eyetooth of a corpse); and artificial shapes often obscene. These were attached to a chain or belt passed over one shoulder and under the other. See Pliny, *H. N.* Bk. xxxvii.; O. Jahn, *Ueber den bösen Blick* in *Berichte der sächsischen Gesellschaft* (1855); C. W. King, *Precious Stones and Metals;* Marquardt, *Röm. Altert.* vi. p. 104; Labatut in Daremberg and Saglio, s. h. v.; and the articles BULLA; FASCINUM; PHALERAE; MALUS OCULUS.

Amulius. See ROMULUS.

Amussis. A level used in testing the evenness of a surface. See LIBELLA; NORMA; REGULA.

Amȳclae (Ἀμύκλαι). (1) An ancient town of Laconia, on the Eurotas, twenty miles southeast of Sparta. It is said to have been the abode of Tyndarus, and of Castor and Pollux, who are hence called Amyclaei Fratres. After the conquest of Peloponnesus by the Dorians, the Achaeans maintained themselves in Amyclae for a long time; but it was at length taken and destroyed by the Lacedaemonians under Teleclus. Amyclae still continued memorable by the festival of the Hyacinthia celebrated at the place annually, and by the colossal statue of Apollo, who was hence called Amyclaeus. (2) An ancient town of Latium, east of Terracina, on the Sinus Amyclanus, claimed to be an Achaean colony from Laconia. The inhabitants were said to have deserted it on account of its being infested by serpents; whence Vergil speaks of *tacitae Amyclae* (*Aen.* x. 564.)

Amyclīdes. Hyacinthus (q. v.).

Amȳcus (Ἄμυκος). A son of Poseidon; a gigantic king of the Bebrycians on the Bithynian coast, who forced every stranger that landed there to box with him. When the Argonauts wished to draw water from a spring in his country, he forbade them, but was conquered and killed in a match with Polydeuces (Pollux).

Amymōnê (Ἀμυμώνη). The daughter of Danaüs (q. v.), and mother of Nauplius by Poseidon.

Amyntas (Ἀμύντας). (1) A king of Macedonia, who reigned from about B.C. 540 to 500, and was succeeded by his son Alexander I. (2) King of Macedonia, son of Philip, the brother of Perdiccas II., reigned B.C. 393–369, and obtained the crown by the murder of the usurper Pausanias. He carefully cultivated the friendship of Athens. He left by his wife Eurydicê three sons, Alexander, Perdiccas, and the famous Philip, hence called by Ovid, Amyntiades.

Amyntor (Ἀμύντωρ). A king of the Dolopes, and father of Phoenix (q. v.).

Amystis (ἀμυστὶ πίνειν, ἀμυστὶν πίνειν, ἀμυστίζειν), from ἀ and μύω, a draught taken without drawing breath. It was a favourite amusement with the Greeks to try how much they could swallow in this way, and very large quantities are said to have been drunk. Plato (*Symp.* 214 A) represents Socrates and Alcibiades as draining off the contents of a wine-cooler holding eight κοτύλαι, or nearly two quarts; while Alexander the Great is said to have greatly exceeded this amount. Ephippus relates that he succeeded in emptying a vessel containing two χόες, or more than two gallons and a half, and afterwards attempted to drink a second in the same way. This, however, affected him so much as to bring on the illness which resulted in his death. The name was also applied to a kind of vessel adapted for this kind of drinking. (Athen. x. 60, p. 442 foll.; 67, p. 447.)

Amythāon (Ἀμυθάων). A son of Cretheus and Tyro, and father of Bias and Melampus. (*Od.* xi. 235.) See OLYMPIA.

Anabăsis (ἀνάβασις). (1) The title of Xenophon's narrative of the 10,000 Greek troops in the expedition under Cyrus the Younger against his brother Artaxerxes. It is in seven books, of which the first alone deals with the ἀνάβασις, or march up from the coast, the rest relating to the κατάβασις, or retreat and subsequent adventures of the Ten Thousand. (2) The *Anabasis of Alexander*, by Arrianus (q. v.), contains an account of the campaigns of Alexander the Great, written in the second century A.D. Like the *Anabasis* of Xenophon, it is in seven books.

Anăces. See DIOSCURI.

Anacharsis (Ἀνάχαρσις). A Scythian prince, who came to Athens about B.C. 594 to pursue a course of study. He was a friend of Solon and a man of ability. On his return to his native land, he was killed by his brother Saulius. A number of aphorisms were ascribed to him, and he was said to have invented the bellows, the anchor, and the potter's wheel. A number of epistles of later date are falsely attributed to him. See Seneca, *Epist.* xc.

Anacreon (Ἀνακρέων). A famous Greek lyric poet, born about B.C. 550, at Teos, an Ionian town of Asia, whose inhabitants, to escape the threatened yoke of Persia, migrated to Abdera in Thrace, B.C. 540. From Abdera, Anacreon went to the tyrant Polycrates of Samos, after whose death (B.C. 522) he removed to Athens on the invitation of Hipparchus, and lived there, till the fall of the Peisistratidae, on friendly terms with his fellow-poet Simonides, and Xanthippus, the father of Pericles. He is said to have died at Abdera in his eighty-sixth year, choked by the stone of a dried grape. A statue of him stood in the Acropolis at Athens in the guise of an aged minstrel inspired by the wine-god; for Anacreon was regarded as the type of a poet who, in spite of age, paid perpetual homage to wine and love. Love and wine and merry company formed the favourite subjects of his light, sweet, and graceful songs, which were cast in the metres of the Aeolic poets, but composed in the Ionic dialect. Besides fragments of such songs and of elegies, we have also a number of epigrams that bear his name. His songs were largely imitated, and of such imitations we have under his name a collection of about sixty love-songs and drinking-songs of very various (partly much later) dates, and of different degrees of merit. Of these, the renderings by Thomas Moore are unsurpassed in grace and melody. The genuine fragments are contained in Bergk's *Poetae Lyrici Graeci* (4th ed. 1878). Translation edited by Bullen (N. Y. 1893).

Anacrĭsis (ἀνάκρισις). The pleadings preparatory to a trial at Athens, the object of which was to determine, generally, if the action would lie (ἐξετάζουσι δὲ καὶ εἰ ὅλως εἰσάγειν χρή). The magistrates were said ἀνακρίνειν τὴν δίκην, or τοὺς ἀντιδίκους, and the parties ἀνακρίνεσθαι. The process consisted in the production of proofs, of which there were five kinds: (1) the laws; (2) written documents, the production of which by the opposite party might be compelled by a δίκη εἰς ἐμφανῶν κατάστασιν; (3) testimonies of witnesses present (μαρτυρίαι), or affidavits of absent witnesses (ἐκμαρτυρίαι); (4) depositions of slaves extorted by the rack; (5) the oath of the parties. All these proofs were committed to writing, and placed in a box secured by a seal (ἐχῖνος) till they were produced at the trial. The name ἀνάκρισις is given to the pleadings, considered expressly as a written document, in Isaeus. If the evidence produced at the anacrisis was so clear and convincing that there could not remain any doubt, the magistrate could decide the question without sending the cause to be tried before the dicasts: this was called διαμαρτυρία. In this case, the only remedy for the person against whom the decision was given was to bring an action of perjury against the witnesses (ψευδομαρτυρῶν δίκη). These pleadings, like our own, were liable to vexatious delays on the part of the litigants, except in the case of actions concerning merchandise, benefit societies, mines, and dowries, which were necessarily tried within a month from the commencement of the suit, and were therefore called ἔμμηνοι δίκαι. The word ἀνάκρισις is sometimes used of a trial in general (μηδ' εἰς ἄγκρισιν ἐλθεῖν). The archons were the proper officers for the ἀνάκρισις. See Meier and Schömann, *Attische Process;* Platner, *Process und Klagen;* and the articles ARCHON; ANTIGRAPHÉ; ANTOMOSIA.

Anactorium (Ἀνακτόριον). A town of Acarnania, on the Ambracian Gulf.

Anadēma (ἀνάδημα). See MITRA.

Anadesmé (ἀναδέσμη). See MITRA.

Anadikia (ἀναδικία). See EPHESIS.

Anadyomĕné. An epithet of Aphroditê (q. v.).

Anaglypta (ἀνάγλυπτα). See CAELATURA; TOREUTICÉ.

Anagnia. The chief town of the Hernici, in Latium, near which Cicero had a fine estate.

Anagnostae (ἀναγνῶσται). See LECTORES.

Anagōges Diké (ἀναγωγῆς δίκη). If an individual sold a slave who had some secret disease—such, for instance, as epilepsy—without informing the purchaser of the circumstance, it was in the power of the latter to bring an action against the vendor within a certain time, which was fixed by the laws. In order to do this, he had to report (ἀνάγειν) to the proper authorities the nature of the disease; whence the action was called ἀναγωγῆς δίκη. See SERVUS.

Anagogia (ἀναγώγια). A festival celebrated at Eryx in Sicily in honour of Aphroditê. Nine days later, a second festival, the καταγώγια, was celebrated.

Anaïtis ('Αναῖτις). An Armenian goddess, probably to be identified with Aphroditê. Her temple stood in the district of Acilisené, in the territory between the northern and southern branches of the Euphrates. This temple had set apart for it a large tract of land, which was cultivated by male and female slaves (ἱερόδουλοι). It was famous for its riches, and from it Antony in his Parthian expedition carried away an image of the goddess made of solid gold (Pliny, *H. N.* xxxiii. 4). Anaïtis was worshipped also at Zela in Pontus, and in Comana.—Among the Lydians, the name Anaïtis was given to Artemis (Pausan. iii. 16, 8).

Anakeia (ἀνάκεια). A festival of the Dioscuri (q. v.), or Ἄνακες, held at Athens.

Anăkes (Ἄνακες). See DIOSCURI.

Anakleteria (ἀνακλητήρια). The name of a solemnity at which the minority of a young prince was declared at an end, and he assumed the reins of government. The name was chiefly applied to the coming of age of the Ptolemaic kings of Egypt (Polyb. xviii. 38; xxviii. 10).

Anakomĭdé (ἀνακομιδή). The ceremony of returning to his native land the body or ashes of one who had died abroad.

Analemma (ἀνάλημμα). (1) In the plural, walls built on strong foundations. (2) An instrument used to show the different altitudes of the sun at the different periods of the year (Vitruv. ix. 7, 8, § 6, 7). See GNOMON.

Analogists and Anomalists. See PHILOLOGIA.

Anancaeum (ἀναγκαῖον). A large drinking-vessel, whose etymology suggests that the drinker was compelled to empty it at a draught (Plaut. *Rud.* ii. 3, 33). See AMYSTIS.

Anaphlystos ('Ανάφλυστος). A deme of Attica, on the southwestern coast. It belonged to the tribe Antiochis.

Anāpus (Ἄναπος). (1) A river in Sicily flowing into the sea south of Syracuse. (2) A river in Acarnania emptying into the Acheloüs.

Anas. The modern Guadiana; one of the chief rivers of Spain emptying into the ocean. It formed the boundary between Baetica and Lusitania.

Anatokismus (ἀνατοκισμός). See FENUS.

Anaumachiou Graphé (ἀναυμαχίου γραφή). An impeachment of the trierarch who had kept aloof from action while the rest of the fleet was engaged. In a cause of this kind, as in the kindred actions ἀστρατείας, δειλίας, λιπονανυτίου, γιποταξίου, the strategi were naturally the presiding judges. The penalty was ἀτιμία, without confiscation of goods, if we may trust Andocides; whereas on conviction δειλίας or λιποταξίου, the property of the offender was confiscated (Lys. *c. Alcib.* i. § 9).

Anaxagŏras ('Αναξαγόρας). A Greek philosopher, of Clazomenae in Asia Minor, born about B.C. 500. Sprung from a noble family, but wishing to devote himself entirely to science, he gave up his property to his kinsmen, and removed to Athens, where he lived in intimacy with the most distinguished men—above all with Pericles. Shortly before the outbreak of the Peloponnesian War he was charged by the political opponents of Pericles with impiety, i. e. with denying the gods recognized by the State; and, though acquitted through his friend's influence, he felt compelled to emigrate to Lampsacus, where he died soon after, aged seventy-two. He not only had the honour of giving philosophy a home at Athens, where it went on flourishing for quite a thousand years, but he was the first philosopher who, by the side of the material principle, introduced a spiritual, which gives the other life and form. He laid down his doctrine in a work "On Nature" in the Ionic dialect, of which only fragments are preserved. Like Parmenides, he denied the existence of birth or death; the two processes were rather to be described as a mingling and unmingling. The ultimate elements of combination are indivisible, imperishable *primordia* of infinite number, and differing in shape, colour, and taste, called by himself "seeds of things," and by later writers (from an expression of Aristotle) ὁμοιομέρεια, i. e. particles of like kind with each other and with the whole that is made up of them. At first these lay mingled without order; but the divine spirit—νοῦς, pure, passionless reason—set the unarranged matter into motion, and thereby created out of chaos an orderly world. This movement, proceeding from the centre, works on forever, penetrating farther and farther the infinite mass. But the application of the spiritual principle was rather indicated than fully carried out by Anaxagoras: he himself commonly explains phenomena by physical causes, and only when he cannot find these, falls back on the action of divine reason. The fragments of his most important work were edited by Schaubach (1827), and by Schorn (1829). See also Beckel, *Anaxagorae Doctrina de Rebus Animatis* (Münster, 1868), and Ueberweg, *Hist. of Philosophy*, vol. i. pp. 63-67 (Eng. trans., N. Y. 1872). For criticism of Anaxagoras by Lucretius, see the *De Rerum Natura*, i. 830-920.

Anaxagoreia (ἀναξαγόρεια). A day of recreation for the youths at Lampsacus, which took place once every year, in compliance with a wish expressed by Anaxagoras, who, after being expelled from Athens, spent the remainder of his life there.

Anaxandrĭdes ('Αναξανδρίδης). (1) A king of Sparta, who reigned from about B.C. 560 to 520. Having a barren wife whom he would not divorce, the ephors made him take with her a second. By her he had Cleomenes; and after this, by his first wife, Dorieus, Leonidas, and Cleombrotus. (2) A Rhodian Greek poet of the Middle Comedy, who flourished in B.C. 376. He is said to have been the first to make love affairs the theme of comedy. His plays are said to have been characterized by sprightliness and humour, but only fragments of them are now in existence.

Anaxarchus (Ἀνάξαρχος). A philosopher of Abdera, of the school of Democritus, who accompanied Alexander into Asia (B.C. 334). After the death of Alexander (B.C. 323), Anaxarchus was thrown by shipwreck into the power of Nicocreon, king of Cyprus, to whom he had given offence, and who had him pounded to death in a stone mortar.

Anaxarĕté (Ἀναξαρετή). A maiden of Cyprus, treated her lover Iphis with such haughtiness that he hanged himself at her door. She looked with such indifference at the funeral of the youth that Aphroditê changed her into a stone statue.

Anaximander (Ἀναξίμανδρος). A Greek philosopher of Miletus, born B.C. 611, and hence a younger contemporary of Thales and Pherecydes. He lived at the court of Polycrates of Samos, and died B.C. 547. In his philosophy the primal essence, which he was the first to call ἀρχή, was the immortal, imperishable, all-including infinite, a kind of chaos (ἄπειρον), out of which all things proceed, and into which they return. He composed, in the Ionic dialect, a brief and somewhat poetical treatise on his doctrine, which may be regarded as the earliest prose work on philosophy; but only a few sentences out of it are preserved. The advances he had made in physics and astronomy are evidenced by his invention of the sundial, his construction of a celestial globe, and his first attempt at a geographical map. See IONIAN SCHOOL; PHILOSOPHIA.

Anaximĕnes (Ἀναξιμένης). (1) A Greek philosopher of Miletus, a younger contemporary and pupil of Anaximander, who died about B.C. 502. He supposed air to be the fundamental principle, out of which everything arose by rarefaction and condensation. This doctrine he expounded in a work, now lost, written in the Ionic dialect. (2) A Greek sophist of Lampsacus, a favourite of Philip of Macedon and Alexander the Great. He composed orations and historical works, some treating of the actions of those two princes. Of these but little remains. On the other hand, he is the author of the *Rhetoric* dedicated to Alexander, the earliest extant work of this kind, which was once included among the works of Aristotle.

Anaxyrĭdes (ἀναξυρίδες). See BRACAE.

Ancaeus (Ἀγκαῖος). (1) Son of the Arcadian Lycurgus, and father of Agapenor. He was one of the Argonauts, and was killed by the Calydonian boar. (2) Son of Poseidon and Astypalaea, also one of the Argonauts, and the helmsman of the ship Argo after the death of Tiphys.

Anchiălé (Ἀγχιάλη). (1) A town of Thrace, on the Black Sea, near the border of Mysia. (2) A city of Cilicia, near the coast, said to have been founded by Sardanapalus.

Anchīses (Ἀγχίσης). The son of Capys, of the royal house of Troy by both parents, ruler of Dardanus, on Mount Ida. Aphroditê loved him for his beauty, and bore him a son, Aeneas; but having, in spite of her warnings, boasted of her favour, he was (according to various versions of the story) paralyzed, killed, or struck blind by the lightning of Zeus. Vergil represents the disabled chief as borne out of burning Troy on his son's shoulders, and as sharing his wanderings over the sea, and aiding him with his counsel, till they reach Drepanum, in Sicily, where he dies, and is buried on Mount Eryx.

Anchisteia (ἀγχιστεία). See HERES.

Ancīlé. See SALII.

Ancilla. See SERVUS.

Ancōna or **Ancon** (Ἀγκών). A town in Picenum, on the Adriatic Sea, lying in a bend of the coast between two promontories, and hence called *Ancon*, or an "elbow." It was built by the Syracusans in the time of the elder Dionysius, B.C. 392. The Romans made it a colony. It possessed an excellent harbour, completed by Trajan, and was one of the most important seaports of the Adriatic.

Ancŏra (ἄγκυρα). See NAVIS.

Ancus Marcius. The fourth king of Rome. He reigned twenty-four years (B.C. 640–616), and is said to have been the son of Numa's daughter. He took many Latin towns, transported the inhabitants to Rome, and gave them the Aventine to dwell on. These conquered Latins formed the original Plebs. He was succeeded by Tarquinius Priscus. (Livy, i. 32 foll.)

Ancȳra (Ἄγκυρα). (1) A city of Galatia, in Asia Minor, originally the chief city of a Gallic tribe named the Tectosages, who came from the south of France. (See ANCYRANUM MONUMENTUM.) (2) A town in Phrygia Epictetus, on the borders of Mysia.

Ancyrānum Monumentum. The monument at Ancyra (now Angora), a marble wall, of which the greater part is preserved. It belonged to the temple of Augustus at Ancyra, and contained the Latin text of a Greek translation of the report drawn up by that emperor himself on the actions of his reign (*index rerum a se gestarum*). By the terms of his will this report, engraved in bronze, was set up in front of his mausoleum at Rome, and copies were made of it for other temples of Augustus in the provinces. See Perrot, *Exploration Archéologique de la Galatie*, etc.; the fac-simile of the inscription with commentary by Mommsen (Berlin, 1883); and AUGUSTUS, p. 171.

Andabătae. See GLADIATORES.

Andecāvi, **Andegāvi**, or **Andes**. A Gallic people dwelling north of the Liger (Loire), whose chief town was Andes (Angers).

Andes. A village near Mantua, famous as being the birthplace of Vergil.

Andocĭdes (Ἀνδοκίδης). The second in order of time in the roll of great Attic orators. He was born B.C. 439, and belonged by birth to the aristocratic party, but fell out with it in B.C. 415, when he was involved in the famous trial for mutilating the statues of Hermes, and, to save his own and his kinsmen's lives, betrayed his aristocratic accomplices. Having, in spite of the immunity promised him, fallen into partial loss of civic rights, he left Athens, and carried on a profitable trade in Cyprus. After two fruitless attempts to recover his status at home, he was allowed at last, upon the fall of the Thirty Tyrants and the amnesty of B.C. 403, to return to Athens, where he succeeded in repelling renewed attacks, and gaining an honourable position. Sent to Sparta in B.C. 390, during the Corinthian War, to negotiate peace, he brought back the draft of a treaty, for the ratification of which he vainly pleaded in a speech that is still extant. He is said to have been banished in consequence, and to have died in exile. Besides the above-mentioned oration, we have two delivered on his own behalf, one pleading for his recall from banishment, B.C. 410; another against the charge of unlawful participation in the mysteries, B.C. 399; a fourth, against Alcibiades, is spurious. His oratory is plain and artless, and its expressions those of the popular language of the day. A good text is that of Blass (Leipzig, 1880); and C. Müller's, with index (1868). See Blass, *Die attische Beredsamkeit*, 3 vols. (1880).

Andrapodismou Graphé (*ἀνδραποδισμοῦ* or *ἀνδραποδίσεως γραφή*). An action brought before the court of the Eleven (*οἱ ἕνδεκα*), against all persons who carried off slaves from their masters, or reduced free men to a state of slavery. The grammarians mention an oration of Antiphon on this subject, which has not come down to us.

Andrapŏdōn Diké (*ἀνδραπόδων δίκη*). The title of the *διαδικασία* when a property in slaves was the subject of contending claims. The cause belonged to the class of *δίκαι πρός τινα*, and was one of the private suits that came under the jurisdiction of the thesmothetae.

Andreia (*ἀνδρεῖα*). See SYSSITIA.

Andria. A play of Terence, the earliest of his comedies, produced in B.C. 166, when the author was only nineteen years of age. For the story connected with its production, see TERENTIUS.

Andrias (*ἀνδριάς*). See STATUARIA.

Andrŏclus or **Andrŏcles**. The slave of a Roman consul, and sentenced to be exposed to the wild beasts in the circus; but a lion which had been let loose upon him exhibited signs of recognition, and began licking him. Upon inquiry, it appeared that Androclus had run away from his master in Africa; and that, having taken refuge in a cave, a lion entered, went up to him, and held out his paw. Androclus extracted a large thorn which had entered it. Henceforth they lived together for some time, the lion catering for his benefactor. But at last, tired of this savage life, Androclus left the cave, was apprehended by some soldiers, brought to Rome, and condemned to the wild beasts. He was pardoned, and presented with the lion, which he used to lead about the city. (Sen. *Ben.* ii. 19; Gell. v. 14.)

Androgeonia (*Ἀνδρογεώνια*). A festival with games, held every year in the Ceramicus at Athens, in honour of the hero Androgeos, son of Minos, who had overcome all his adversaries in the festive games of the Panathenaea, and was afterwards killed by order of Aegeus (q. v.).

Androgeos (*Ἀνδρόγεως*). A son of Minos, king of Crete, by Pasiphaë. Visiting Athens at the first celebration of the Panathenaea, he won victories over all the champions, when King Aegeus, out of jealousy, sent him to fight the bull of Marathon, which killed him. According to another account he was slain in an ambush. Minos avenged his son by making the Athenians send seven youths and seven maidens every nine years as victims of the Minotaur (q. v.). See THESEUS.

Androlepsia or **Androlepsion** (*ἀνδροληψία* or *ἀνδρολήψιον*). The right of reprisals, a custom recognized by the international law of the Greeks; so that when a citizen of one State had killed a citizen of another, and the countrymen of the former would not surrender him to the relatives of the deceased, it was held lawful to seize upon three, and not more, of the countrymen of the offender, and keep them as hostages till satisfaction was afforded or the homicide given up. The trierarchs and the commanders of the ships of war were the persons intrusted with this office. The property which the hostages had with them at the time of seizure was confiscated, under the name of *σῦλα* or *σῦλαι*.

Andromăché (*Ἀνδρομάχη*). The daughter of Eëtion, king of the Cilician Thebes, and wife of Hector, by whom she had a son, Scamandrius (Astyanax). On the taking of Troy, her son was hurled from the walls of the city, and she herself fell to the share of Neoptolemus (Pyrrhus), the son of Achilles, who took her to Epirus. She afterwards married Helenus, a brother of Hector, who ruled over Chaonia.

Andromăchus (*Ἀνδρόμαχος*). (1) An opulent Sicilian, father of the historian Timaeus. He collected together the inhabitants of the city of Naxos, which Dionysius the tyrant had destroyed, and founded with them Tauromenium. Andromachus, as prefect of the new city, subsequently aided Timoleon in restoring liberty to Syracuse. (Diod. Sic. xvi. 7, 68.) (2) A general of Alexander, to whom Parmenio gave the government of Syria. He was burned alive by the Samaritans, but his death was avenged by Alexander. (Quint. Curt. iv. 5.) (3) A brother-in-law of Seleucus Callinicus. (4) A traitor, who discovered to the Parthians all the measures of Crassus, and, on being chosen guide, led the Roman army into a situation whence there was no mode of escape. (5) A physician of Crete in the age of Nero. He was physician to the emperor, and inventor of the famous medicine, called after him, *theriaca Andromachi*. It was intended at first as an antidote against poisons, but became afterwards a kind of panacea. This medicine enjoyed so high a reputation among the Romans that the emperor Antoninus, at a later period, took some of it every day, and had it prepared every year in his palace. It consisted of sixty-one ingredients, the principal of which were squills, opium, pepper, and dried vipers.

Andromĕda (*Ἀνδρομέδη*). The daughter of Cepheus, king of Aethiopia, and Cassiopea. In consequence of her mother boasting that the beauty of her daughter surpassed that of the Nereids, Poseidon sent a sea-monster to lay waste the country. The oracle of Ammon promised deliverance if Andromeda was given up to the monster, and Cepheus was obliged to chain his daughter to a rock. Here she was found and saved by Perseus, who slew the monster and obtained her as his wife. She had been previously promised to Phineus, and this gave rise to the famous fight of Phineus and Perseus at the wedding, in which the former and all his associates were slain. After her death she was placed among the stars.

Andrōn (*ἀνδρών*). See DOMUS (Greek).

Andronīcus (*Ἀνδρόνικος*). (1) A peripatetic philosopher, a native of Rhodes, who flourished about B.C. 80. He arranged and published the writings of Aristotle, which had been brought to Rome with the library of Apellicon. He commented on many parts of these writings; but no portion of his works has reached us, for the treatise *Περὶ Παθῶν*, and the Paraphrase of the Nicomachean ethics, which have been published under his name, are the productions of another. The treatise *Περὶ Παθῶν* was published by Hösschel in 1593, and was afterwards printed conjointly with the Paraphrase in 1617, 1679, and 1809. The Paraphrase was published by Heinsius in 1607, at Leyden, as an anonymous work (*Incerti Auctoris Paraphrasis*, etc.), and afterwards under the name of *Andronicus of Rhodes*, by the same scholar, in 1617, with the treatise Περὶ Παθῶν added to it. See the dissertations by Littig, *Andronikos von Rhodos* (1891) and by Rösener (1893). (2) CYRRHESTES, an astronomer of Athens, who erected, B.C. 159, an octagonal marble tower in that city to the eight winds, now known as the "Tower of the Winds." On every side of the octagon he caused to be wrought a figure in *relievo*, representing the wind which blew

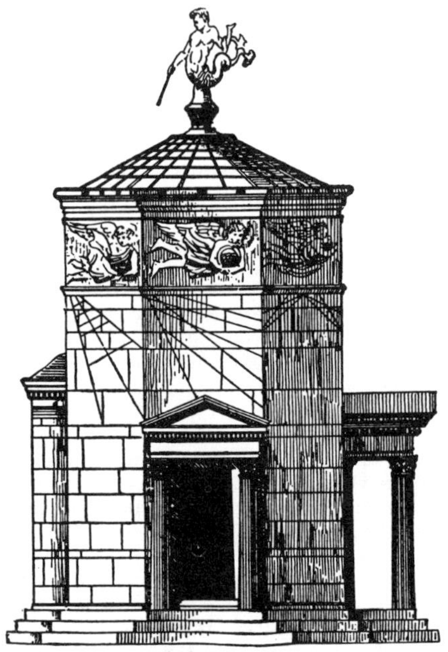

Tower of the Winds.

against that side. The top of the tower was finished with a conical marble, on which he placed a brazen Triton, holding a wand in his right hand. This Triton was so contrived that he turned round with the wind, and always stopped when he directly faced it, pointing with his wand over the figure of the wind at that time blowing. Within the structure was a water-clock, supplied from the fountain in a turret. Beneath the eight figures of the winds lines were traced on the walls of the tower, which, by the shadows cast upon them by styles fixed above, indicated the hour of the day, as the Triton's wand did the quarter of the wind. When the sun did not shine recourse was had to the water-clock within the tower, which building thus supplied both a vane and a chronometer. The structure still stands, though in a damaged state. To the correctness of the sundials Delambre bears testimony, and he describes the series as "the most curious existing monument of the practical gnomonics of antiquity." There are two entrances, facing respectively to the northeast and northwest; each of these openings has a portico supported by two columns. (See Vitruv. i. 6, 4.)

Andronīcus, LIVIUS. See LIVIUS.

Andronītis (ἀνδρωνῖτις). The men's apartments in a Greek house. See DOMUS (Greek).

Andrŏs (Ἄνδρος). The most northerly and one of the largest islands of the Cyclades, southeast of Euboea, twenty-one miles long and eight broad, early attained importance, and colonized Acanthus and Stagira about B.C. 654. It was celebrated for its wine, whence the whole island was regarded as sacred to Dionysus.

Androtion (Ἀνδροτίων). A Greek historian, an Athenian, and a pupil of Isocrates, who was accused of making an illegal proposal, and went into banishment at Megara. We still have the speech composed by Demosthenes for one of the accusers. At Megara he wrote a history of Attica (see ATTHIS) in at least twelve books, one of the best of that class of writings; but only fragments of it have survived.

Anemōnē (ἀνεμώνη). The anemone or windflower.

Angări. See ANGARIA.

Angarīa (ἀγγαρεία). A word borrowed from the Persians, signifying a system of posting which was used among that people, and which, according to Xenophon, was established by Cyrus. Horses were provided at certain distances along the principal roads of the empire; so that couriers (ἄγγαροι), who also of course relieved one another at certain distances, could proceed without interruption both night and day (Herod. viii. 98; iii. 126; Xen. *Cyrop.* viii. 6, § 17). Among the Romans, the word was used to denote compulsory service in forwarding imperial messages. See *Digest*, l. tit. 4, s. 18, §§ 4, 29; and the article CURSUS PUBLICUS.

Angdistis. See RHEA.

Angiportus or **Angiportum.** A narrow lane between two rows of houses, sometimes ending in a *cul-de-sac.* The number of such places seems to have been considerable in ancient Rome, and they were apt to be disreputable (Catull. 58, 4). The form *angiportum* is archaic.

Angli or **Anglii.** A German people on the left bank of the Elbe, who passed over with the Saxons into Britain, which was called after them England—*Engla-land.* Some of them appear to have settled in Angeln, in Schleswig. See SAXONES.

Angothēkē (ἀγγοθήκη). See INCITEGA.

Anguilla. See FLAGRUM.

Anguis. The snake. Among the Romans the snake was the conventional representation of the *genius loci.* (See GENIUS.) Hence figures of serpents were often painted against a wall, as the cross is in modern Italy, and answered the purpose of our sign "Commit no nuisance" (Pers. i. 113). As the emblem of Aesculapius (q. v.), the snake was the sign that hung before the Roman pharmacies, answering to our pestle and mortar. It was also the military ensign of a cohort, being then commonly termed *draco.* See ASPIS; DRACO; GENIUS.

Angustus Clavus. See CLAVUS.

Anicētus. A freedman of Nero, employed by him in many acts of cruelty.

Anīgrus. A small river in the Triphylian Elis, the Minyeius of Homer, flowing into the Ionian Sea, near Samicum. Its waters had a disagreeable smell, in consequence, it is said, of the centaurs having washed in them after they had been wounded by Hercules.

Anio or, anciently, **Anien.** A river rising in the mountains of the Hernici, near Treba, which, after receiving the brook Digentia, forms at Tibur beautiful water-falls, and flows into the Tiber three miles above Rome. The water of the Anio was conveyed to Rome by two aqueducts — the *Anio vetus* and *Anio novus.*

Anius (Ἄνιος). Son of Apollo by Rhoeo or Creüsa, whose father, Staphylus of Naxos, a son of Dionysus and Ariadnè, committed her to the sea in a box. She was carried to Delos, and there gave birth to her son Anius. Apollo taught him divination, and made him his priest and king of Delos. His son Thasus, like Linus and Actaeon, was torn to pieces by dogs, after which no dogs were allowed in the island. His daughters by the nymph Dorippé, being descendants of Dionysus, had the gift of turning anything they pleased into wine, corn, or oil; but when Agamemnon, on his way to Troy, wished to take them from their father by force, Dionysus changed them into doves.

Ankȳlé (ἀγκύλη). See HASTA.

Anna Comnéna. See COMNENA.

Anna Perenna. An ancient Italian goddess, about whose exact attributes the ancients themselves were not clear. She is probably the moon-goddess of the current year, who every month renews her youth, and was therefore regarded as a goddess who bestowed long life, and all that contributes to it. About full moon on the Ides (15th) of March (then the first month of the year), in a grove of fruit trees at the first milestone on the Flaminian Way, the Romans held a feast under the open sky, wishing each other as many years of life as they drank cups of wine. (See Ovid, *Fasti*, iii. 523 foll.) The learned men of the Augustan Age identified Anna with Dido's sister, who, on the death of that queen, had fled from Carthage to Aeneas in Italy; but, having excited Lavinia's jealousy, threw herself into the Numicius.

Annāles. (1) The title of an epic poem by Quintus Ennius (q. v.), in which he aspired to treat the entire history of the Roman people in heroic style. The poem was in eighteen books, arranged as follows: Bk. i., Introduction, Early Traditions, Founding of Rome, Deification of Romulus; bks. ii. and iii., The Regal Period; bk. iv., The Republic down to the burning of Rome by the Gauls; bk. v., The Samnite Wars; bk. vi., The War with Pyrrhus; bk. vii., The First Punic War; bks. viii. and ix., The Second Punic War; bks. x. and xi., The War with Macedonia; bks. xii., xiii. and xiv., The War with Syria; bk. xv., The Campaign of Fulvius Nobilior in Aetolia; bks. xvi., xvii., and xviii., From the Death of Scipio to B.C. 172. (See EPOS.) There remain to us of this great poem only fragments, of which the best edition is that of Vahlen (1854). See also Wordsworth, *Fragments and Specimens of Early Latin* (1874); and Merry (1892). (2) A history by Cornelius Tacitus (q. v.), treating in sixteen books of the Roman Empire from the death of Augustus Caesar to the death of Nero.

Annāles Leges. See LEGES ANNALES.

Annāles Maxĭmi. See PONTIFEX.

Annōna (from *annus*, like *pomona* from *pomum*). A name used (1) for the produce of the year, and hence (2) for provisions in general, especially for the corn which in the latter years of the Republic was collected in the storehouses of the State, and sold to the poor at a cheap rate in times of scarcity; and which under the emperors was distributed to the people gratuitously or given as pay and rewards. (See FRUMENTARIAE LEGES.) (3) For the price of provisions. (4) For a soldier's allowance of provisions for a certain time. It is used also in the plural for yearly or monthly distributions of pay in corn, etc. Similar distributions in money were called *annonae aerariae.* In the plural it also signifies provisions given as the wages of labour.

(5) Annona was anciently worshipped as the goddess who prospered the year's increase. She was represented on an altar in the Capitol as a female with the right arm and shoulder bare, and the rest of the body clothed, holding ears of corn in her right hand, and the cornucopia in her left.

Annŭlus. See ANULUS.

Annus. See CALENDARIUM.

Anquīna (ἀγκοίνα). A collar or ring by which the yard-arm was fastened to the mast of a ship, and called by our sailors a "truss." (Isid. *Orig.* xix. 4, 7.)

Anquisitio. See IUDEX.

Ansa. See HASTA.

Anser. A poet of the Augustan Age, and long considered one of the enemies of Vergil; but of this there is no good evidence, for the line in Verg. *Ecl.* ix. 35 is only traditionally referred to him. He was a writer of erotic poetry. See Unger, *De Ansere Poeta* (Neubrandenb. 1858), and Teuffel, vol. i. p. 453 (Eng. trans. 1891).

Ansibarii. A people of Germany.

Antae (παραστάδες). Square pillars (*quadrae columnae*). They were commonly joined to the side walls of a building, being placed on each side of the door, so as to assist in forming the portico. These terms are seldom found except in the plural, because the purpose served by antae required that, in general, two should be erected corresponding to each other, and supporting the extremities of the same roof. Their position, form, and use will be best understood from the following woodcut, representing a restoration of the front of the

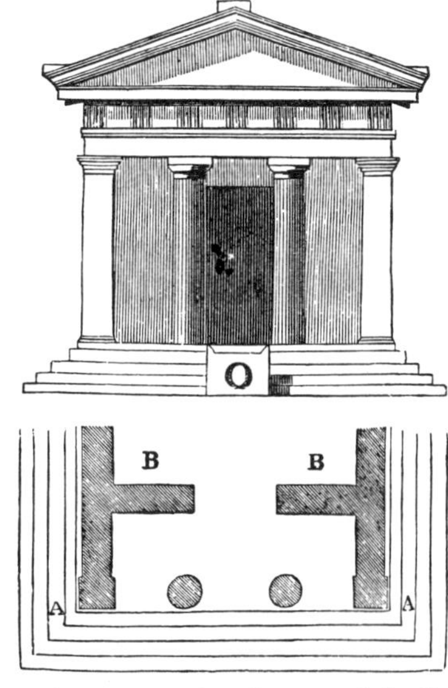

A A, the antae; B B, the cella or ναός: O, the altar

temple of Artemis Propylaea at Eleusis, with a plan of the pronaos, in which A A are the antae.

Antaeopŏlis (Ἀνταίου πόλις). A city of Egypt (Thebaïs) on the eastern bank of the Nile, and one of the chief seats of the worship of Osiris (q. v.). See Diod. Sic. i. 7.

Antaeus (Ἀνταῖος). A giant, the son of Poseidon and Gé (earth). He dwelt in Libya, and his strength was invincible so long as he remained in contact with his mother, Earth. Heracles discovered the source of his strength, lifted him from the earth, and crushed him in the air. On the connection of Antaeus with the Pygmies, see PYGMAEI. The story of Antaeus is given in Apollod. ii. 5.

Antalcĭdas (Ἀνταλκίδας). A Spartan, the son of Leon, and chiefly known by the celebrated treaty concluded with Persia in B.C. 387, usually called the Peace of Antalcidas, since it was the fruit of his diplomacy. According to this treaty all the Greek cities in Asia Minor were to belong to the Persian king. The Athenians were allowed to retain only Lemnos, Imbros, and Scyros; and all the other Greek cities were to be independent. (Xen. *Hist. Graec.* v. 1, § 6.)

Antandrus (Ἄντανδρος). An Aeolian colony on the Adramyttian Gulf, at the foot of Mount Ida.

Anteambulōnes. (1) Slaves who went before their masters to make way for them in a crowd, crying *Date locum domino meo.* See Suet. *Vesp.* 2. (2) Clients who walked before their patrons when the latter appeared in public. See CLIENTES.

Antecenium. See CENA, p. 312.

Antecessōres, called also **Antecursōres.** Roman horse-soldiers, who were accustomed to precede an army on march in order to choose a suitable place for the camp, and to make the necessary provisions for the army. They do not appear to have been merely scouts, like the *speculatores.* This name was also given to the teachers of the Roman law. (*Cod. Iust.* i. 17, 2.)

Antefixa. Terra-cottas exhibiting various ornamental designs, and used in architecture to cover the frieze (*zophorus*) of the entablature.

Antefixa. (British Museum.)

They were probably Etruscan in their origin, and were used by the Greeks. The specimen here given represents Athené superintending the construction of the ship Argo.

Anteia (Ἄντεια). See BELLEROPHON.

Antemnae. A Sabine town, said to have been older than Rome, at the junction of the Anio and the Tiber. It was destroyed by the Romans at an early period. (Verg. *Aen.* vii. 631.)

Antenna (κέρας, κεραία). The yard of a ship. See NAVIS.

Antēnor (Ἀντήνωρ). (1) A Trojan prince related to Priam. He was the husband of Theano, daughter of Cisseus, king of Thrace, and father of nineteen sons, of whom the most known were Polybus, Acamas, Agenor, Polydamas, Helicaon, Archilochus, and Laodocus. He is accused by some of having betrayed his country, not only because he gave a favourable reception to Diomedes, Odysseus, and Menelaüs, when they came to Troy, as ambassadors from the Greeks, to demand the restitution of Helen, but also because he withheld the fact of his recognizing Odysseus, at the time that hero visited the city under the guise of a mendicant (*Od.* iv. 335). After the conclusion of the war Antenor, according to some, migrated with a party of followers into Italy, and built Patavium. According to others, he went with a colony of the Heneti, or Veneti, from Paphlagonia to the shores of the Hadriatic, where the new settlers established themselves in the district called by them Venetia (Liv. i. 1; Plin. iii. 13; Verg. *Aen.* i. 242; Tac. xvi. 21). (2) A statuary, known only as the maker of the original statues of Harmodius and Aristogiton, which were carried off by Xerxes, and restored by Alexander. (Pausan. i. 8.)

Antenorĭdes (Ἀντηνορίδης). A patronymic given to the sons of Antenor.

Antepagmenta. The door-posts, or jambs of a door. See IANUA.

Antepilāni. See PILANI.

Antĕros (Ἀντέρως). The god of requited love, and brother of Eros (q. v.).

Antesignāni. See SIGNUM.

Antestāri. See ACTIO.

Antevorta. See CARMENTA.

Anthēdon (Ἀνθηδών). A city of Boeotia on the shore of the Euripus, celebrated for its wine. Here the Cabiri were worshipped. (Ath. i. p. 31; Pausan. ix. 22.)

Anthēlé (Ἀνθήλη). A small town of Thessaly, in the interval between the river Phoenix and the Straits of Thermopylae, and near the spot where the Asopus flows into the sea. In the immediate vicinity were the temples of Demeter Amphictyonia, that of Amphictyon, and the seats of the Amphictyons. It was one of the two places where the Amphictyonic Council used to meet, the other being Delphi. The place for holding the assembly here was the temple of Demeter. See AMPHICTYONES.

Anthĕmus (Ἀνθεμοῦς) or **Anthemusia.** A city of Mesopotamia, southwest of Edessa, and a little east of the Euphrates. The surrounding district was called by the same name, but was generally included under the name of Osrhoëné.

Anthesphoria (τὰ ἀνθεσφόρια). A flower-festival, principally celebrated in Sicily, in honour of Demeter and Persephoné, in commemoration of the return of Persephoné to her mother in the beginning of spring. It consisted in gathering flowers and twining garlands, because Persephoné had been carried off by Pluto while engaged in this occupation. The women themselves gathered the flowers for the garlands which they wore on the occasion, and it would have been a disgrace to buy the flowers for that purpose. Anthesphoria were also solemnized in honour of other deities, especially in honour of Heré, surnamed 'Ανθεία, at Argos. Aphrodité, too, was worshipped at Cnossus, under the name 'Ανθεία, and has therefore been compared with Flora (q. v.), the Roman deity, as the anthesphoria have been with the Roman festival of the *florifertum*.

Anthesteria. See CALENDARIUM; DIONYSIA.

Anthesterion ('Ανθεστηριών). The name of the eighth Attic month, answering to the end of February and the beginning of March. See CALENDARIUM.

Anthology (ἀνθολογία, *anthologia*). "Garland of flowers." A title now generally given to collections of short poems. Both the Greek and the Latin anthologies are famous.

(1) THE GREEK ANTHOLOGY.—The earliest anthology in Greek was compiled by Meleager of Gadara, about B.C. 60, under the title Στέφανος, or "Garland." It contained poems by the compiler himself and forty six other poets, including Archilochus, Alcaeus, Anacreon, Sappho, and Simonides. Continual additions were made to this collection, and in the tenth century A.D. Constantine Cephalas made a new compilation, as did Maximus Planudes in the fourteenth century. The latter was lacking in literary taste; but his anthology was the only one known to Western Europe until the seventeenth century, when Salmasius, in 1606, found in the library at Heidelberg the much finer collection of Cephalas. The copy made by Salmasius was not, however, published until 1776, when Brunck included it in his *Analecta*. The first critical edition was that of F. Jacobs (13 vols. 1794–1803; revised 1813–17). A good recent edition is that in Didot's *Bibliotheca* (1872), while excellent selections have been made by Weichert and Meineke. See also Thackeray's *Anthologia Graeca*, with notes in English (1877). Translations of parts of the anthology have been made in English by Wrangham, John Sterling, Merivale, and Garnett; but no translations can give any true idea of the terseness, elegance, and sparkle of the original. See Symonds, *Studies of the Greek Poets* (1873); Butler, *Amaranth and Asphodel* (1881); Mackail, *Select Epigrams* (1891); and Finsler, *Gesch. der griech. Anthologie* (1876).

(2) THE LATIN ANTHOLOGY.—Unlike the Greek Anthology, the collection known as the Latin Anthology was wholly made in modern times. The first was the compilation of Scaliger (q. v.), published at Leyden in 1573, entitled *Catalecta Veterum Poetarum*. A second collection was published by Pitthoüs at Paris in 1590; and a still larger one by Peter Burmann (q. v.) in 1759 and 1773. Of this a rearrangement was made by Meyer in 1835. The first critical text of a Latin anthology is that of Riese (1869–70). It contains 942 poems of very unequal merit, but all of interest. See the selections, with notes in English, by Thackeray, *Anthologia Latina* (1878); and the collection by Baehrens, in 5 vols. (1883). See EPIGRAMMA.

Anthrakion (ἀνθράκιον). (1) A species of carbuncle found in the island of Chios. (2) A small portable stove or brazier filled with hot coals.

Anthrax (ἄνθραξ). (1) Coal or charcoal, generally used in the plural ἄνθρακες, like the English "coals" (Aristoph. *Ach.* 34). (2) A precious stone, the carbuncle. (3) Cinnabar.

Anthrēnē (ἀνθρήνη). The hornet, or *vespa crabro*; but also used of the bee (Aristoph. *Nub.* 947).

Anthropophăgi ('Ανθρωποφάγοι). A people of Scythia who fed on human flesh. Herodotus (iv. 106) calls them the Androphagi, and states that they lived in a more savage manner than any other nation, having no public distribution of justice nor established laws. He informs us also that they applied themselves to the breeding of cattle, clothed themselves like the Scythians, and spoke a peculiar language.

Anthylla ("Ανθυλλα). A considerable city of Lower Egypt, near the mouth of the Canopic branch of the Nile, below Naucratis. (Herod. ii. 97.)

Antia Lex. See LEX.

Antias, QUINTUS VALERIUS. A Roman historian who flourished about B.C. 80, and wrote the history of Rome from the earliest times down to those of Sulla. His work was full of exaggerations, but is still, in a way, the most important immediate predecessor of Livy. His history was in at least seventy-five books, for book lxxv. is quoted by Gellius (vi. 9, 17). Livy appears to have drawn upon him largely, for he mentions him by name thirty-five times in the existing books; and in the first decades of his work follows him unhesitatingly. The fragments of the *Annales* may be found in Peter's *Historicorum Reliquiae*, i. 305. See also Nitzsch, *Röm. Annalistik* (1873); and Teuffel, *Hist. of Rom. Lit.* (Eng. trans. 1891).

Anticatōnes. Two pamphlets written by Iulius Caesar in disparagement of Cato the Younger, intended as a reply to the eulogistic utterance of Cicero. Juvenal implies that they were lengthy (vi. 334); Cicero calls them *vituperationes* (*ad Att.* xii. 41); and Pliny (*Epist.* iii. 12) states that in them Caesar accuses Cato of being drunk in the streets. No fragments of them remain, though a MS. of them is said to have been extant in Liège in the sixteenth century. See Roulez, *Revue de l'Instruction Publique en Belgique*, xix. 2.

Anticlēa ('Αντίκλεια). The daughter of Autolycus, wife of Laërtes, and mother of Odysseus. She died of grief at the long absence of her son. (*Odyss.* xi. 85.) It is said that before marrying Laërtes she lived on intimate terms with Sisyphus; whence Odysseus is sometimes called a son of Sisyphus.

Anticrătes ('Αντικράτης). A Spartan who was said to have slain Epaminondas (q. v.) at the battle of Mantinea, and who, in consequence, was richly rewarded by his fellow-countrymen (Plut. *Ages.* 35).

Anticy̆ra ('Αντίκυρα). (1) A town in Phocis, on a bay of the Crissaean Gulf. (2) A town in Thessaly, on the Spercheus, not far from its mouth. Both towns were celebrated for their hellebore, the chief remedy in antiquity for madness: hence the proverb *naviget Anticyram* when a person acted senselessly (Hor. *Sat.* ii. 3. 166).

Antidŏsis (ἀντίδοσις). Literally "an exchange." A term in the language of the Attic courts, peculiarly applied to proceedings under a law which is said to have originated with Solon (Dem. *c. Phaenipp.* init.). It is natural, however, to refer the law to more democratic times; and the orators were in the habit of ascribing to Solon all laws, especially those which they happened to be quoting in a favourable sense. By this law, a citizen nominated to perform a liturgia, such as a trierarchy or choregia, or to rank among the property-tax payers in a class disproportioned to his means, was empowered to call upon any qualified person not so charged to take the office in his stead, or submit to a complete exchange of property—the charge in question, of course, attaching to the first party, if the exchange were finally effected. For these proceedings the courts were opened at a stated time every year by the magistrates that had official cognizance of the particular subject; such as the strategi in cases of trierarchy and rating to the property-taxes, and the archon in those of choregia (Dem. *c. Phaenipp.* p. 1040; Meier, *Att. Process*, p. 471; *προσκαλεῖσθαι τινα εἰς ἀντίδοσιν*, Lysias, *Or.* 24, *pro Inval.* § 10). If the person challenged could prove that he had already discharged the liturgia, or was otherwise lawfully exempted, the magistrates might dismiss the case; otherwise the parties proceeded to a *διαδικασία* or legal award of their respective claims. An oath was taken by both parties that each would deliver to the other, within three days, a correct inventory (*ἀπόφασις*) of their respective properties (Dem. *c. Phaenipp.* p. 1042, § 11); but in practice the time might be extended by consent of the challenger. All immovable and movable property was transferred in the exchange, with the exception of mines, which were exempted from the extraordinary taxes and liturgiae, as being already taxed; and all claims and obligations attached to it, and particularly all debts, were included in the transfer, as may be seen from the speech against Phaenippus.

Professor Mahaffy's remarks on the injustice of this law are by no means too strong: "It seems simply the legislation of the Athenian mob about property which they had never possessed, and did not understand; for the other alternative—that Athenian properties were small or of a simple nature, like our rentals of estates—is refuted by the many descriptions of property in the orators. It is, in fact, inexplicable that any intelligent people should have tolerated such a law, and it is conclusive against the business capacity of the men who tolerated it." See Mahaffy, *Social Life in Greece*, p. 409, 3d ed., and Jebb, *Attic Or.* ii. 135.

Antigĕnes (Ἀντιγένης). A general of Alexander the Great, on whose death he received the satrapy of Susiana and supported Eumenes. On the defeat of the latter, Antigenes was seized and burned alive by his enemy Antigonus, B.C. 316 (Plut. *Alex.* 70).

Antigŏné (Ἀντιγόνη). (1) A daughter of Oedipus by his mother Iocasté, and sister of Ismené and of Eteocles and Polynices. In the tragic story of Oedipus, Antigoné appears as a noble maiden, with a truly heroic attachment to her father and her brothers. When Oedipus had put out his eyes, and was obliged to quit Thebes, he was accompanied by Antigoné, who remained with him till he died at Colonus, and then returned to Thebes. After her two brothers had killed each other in battle, and Creon, the king of Thebes, would not allow Polynices to be buried, Antigoné alone defied the tyrant, and buried the body of her brother. Creon thereupon ordered her to be immured in a subterranean cave, where she killed herself. Her lover, Haemon, the son of Creon, killed himself by her side. A play of Sophocles gets its title from her name. (2) The wife of Peleus (q. v.), who hanged herself from grief at the supposed infidelity of her husband. See PELOPIDAE.

Antigŏnēa (Ἀντιγόνεια). (1) A town in Epirus at the junction of a tributary with the Aous, and near a narrow pass of the Acroceraunian Mountains. (2) A town on the Orontes in Syria, founded by Antigonus as the capital of his empire (B.C. 306); but most of its inhabitants were transferred by Seleucus to Antiochia, which was built in its neighbourhood.

Antigŏnus (Ἀντίγονος). (1) King of Asia, surnamed the ONE-EYED (Μονόφθαλμος or Κύκλωψ), son of Philip of Elymiotis, and father of Demetrius Poliorcetes by Stratonicé. He was one of the generals of Alexander the Great, and in the division of the empire after the death of the latter (B.C. 323) he received the provinces of the Greater Phrygia, Lycia, and Pamphylia. On the death of the regent Antipater, in 319, he aspired to the sovereignty of Asia. In 316 he defeated and put Eumenes to death, after a struggle of nearly three years. He afterwards carried on war, with varying success, against Seleucus, Ptolemy, Cassander, and Lysimachus. After the defeat of Ptolemy's fleet in 306, Antigonus assumed the title of king, and his example was followed by Ptolemy, Lysimachus, and Seleucus. Antigonus and his son Demetrius were at length defeated by Lysimachus at the decisive battle of Ipsus, in Phrygia, in 301. Antigonus fell in the battle, in the eighty-first year of his age. (2) GONATAS, son of Demetrius Poliorcetes, and grandson of the preceding. He assumed the title of king of Macedonia after his father's death in Asia in 283, but he did not obtain possession of the throne till 277. He was driven out of his kingdom by Pyrrhus of Epirus in 273, but recovered it in the following year. He died in 239. He was succeeded by Demetrius II. (3) DOSON (so called because he was always about to give but never did), son of Demetrius of Cyrené, and grandson of Demetrius Poliorcetes. On the death of Demetrius II., in 229, he was left guardian of his son Philip, but married the widow of Demetrius, and became king of Macedonia himself. He supported the Achaean League against Cleomenes, king of Sparta, whom he defeated at Sellasia in 221, and took Sparta. He died 220. (4) A Greek of Carystus, who wrote (about B.C. 240) a summary of curious and interesting facts and fictions regarding natural history. The work is extant in an abbreviated form, and is valuable because of its numerous quotations from lost writings. Ed. by Westermann (Brunswick, 1839). See Köpke, *De Antig. Carystio* (1862).

Antigrăphé (ἀντιγραφή). A term originally signifying the writing put in by the defendant in any cause, whether public or private, in answer to the indictment or bill of the prosecutor. But we find the term employed not only for the answer of the defendant, but also for the statement of the plaintiff (Harpocrat. s. v. ἀντιγραφή: Plato, *Apol. Socr.* p. 27 C; Schömann, *Antiquities*, p. 484). Thus the word "plea," though by no means a coincident term, may be allowed to be a tolerably proximate rendering of ἀντιγραφή. See DIKÉ.

Antigrăpheis (ἀντιγραφεῖς). Checking-clerks, *contrarotulatores.* Efficient checks on the handling of public funds, whether municipal or national, were even more necessary among the Greeks than in modern civilized countries; and the Athenians, with their distrust of official honesty, sought refuge in multiplying such checks. Hence it was the rule in Athenian finance that wherever there was a public officer intrusted with the payment of money, there was by his side an ἀντιγραφεύς, who watched over him and kept duplicate accounts. Thus, it is proved by inscriptions that there was an ἀντιγραφεύς to each deme (*C. I. G.* 100); and a general in the field disposed of his military chest subject to a like control (Dem. *De Chers.* p. 101, § 47). The administrators of sacred funds, such as the treasurers of Delos, were similarly controlled (*Inscr.* 139, 141, 150, 158).

Antilibănus (Ἀντιλίβανος). See Libanus.

Antilŏchus (Ἀντίλοχος). The son of Nestor, who accompanied his father to the Trojan War, and was distinguished among the younger heroes for beauty and bravery. Homer calls him a favourite of Zeus and Poseidon. The dearest friend of Achilles next to Patroclus, he was chosen by the Greeks to break the news to him of his beloved companion's fall. When Memnon attacked the aged Nestor, Antilochus threw himself in his way, and bought his father's safety with his life. He, like Patroclus, was avenged by Achilles, in whose grave-mound the ashes of both friends were laid; even in the lower world Odysseus beheld the three pacing the asphodel meadow, and in after-times the inhabitants of Ilium offered to them jointly the sacrifices due to the dead on the foreland of Sigeum.

Antimăchus (Ἀντίμαχος). A Greek poet and critic of Colophon, an elder contemporary of Plato, about B.C. 400. By his two principal works—the long mythical epic called *Thebaïs* (Quint. x. 1) and a cycle of elegies named after his loved and lost Lydé, and telling of famous lovers parted by death—he became the founder of learned poetry, precursor and prototype of the Alexandrians, who, on account of his learning, assigned him the next place to Homer among epic poets. (See Canon Alexandrinus.) In striving to impart strength and dignity to language by avoiding all that was common, his style became rigid and artificial, and naturally ran into bombast. But we possess only fragments of his works. As a scholar, he is remarkable for having set on foot a critical revision of the Homeric poems. See Homerus.

Antinoēa (τὰ Ἀντινόεια). Annual festivals and quinquennial games instituted by the emperor Hadrian in honour of Antinoüs (q. v.).

Antinomian, The. A name often given to the sophist Hippias of Elis because of his argument against the observance of law (νόμος), which was as follows: Whatever is contrary to nature is an evil: Law forces men to many things that are contrary to their inclinations, and hence to their nature: Law, therefore, is an evīl and should not be respected. See Hippias.

Antinoöpŏlis. See Antinoüs.

Antinoüs. (1) Son of Eupithes of Ithaca, and one of the suitors of Penelopé, was slain by Odysseus. (2) A youth of extraordinary beauty, born at Claudiopolis in Bithynia, was the favourite of the emperor Hadrian, and his companion in all his journeys (Pausan. viii. 9, 7). He was drowned in the Nile, A.D. 122. The grief of the emperor knew no bounds. He enrolled Antinoüs among the gods, caused a temple to be erected to him at Mantinea, and founded the city of Antinoöpolis in honour of him. Beautiful statues and busts of him still exist.

Antiochīa (Ἀντιόχεια). (1) The capital of the Greek kingdom of Syria, and long the chief city of Asia. It stood on the left bank of the Orontes, about twenty miles from the sea, in a beautiful valley. It was built by Seleucus Nicator, about B.C. 300, who called it Antiochia in honour of his father, Antiochus, and peopled it chiefly from the neighbouring city of Antigonia. It was one of the earliest strongholds of the Christian faith; the first place where the Christian name was used (*Acts* xi. 26); and the see of one of the four chief bishops, who were called patriarchs. (2) Antiochia ad Maeandrum, a city of Caria, on the Maeander, built by Antiochus I. (Soter) on the site of the old city of Pythopolis. (3) A city on the borders of Phrygia and Pisidia; built by colonists from Magnesia; made a colony under Augustus, and called Caesarea.

Antiŏchus (Ἀντίοχος). I.—The name of several kings of Syria. (1) Soter (reigned B.C. 280–261), the son of Seleucus I., the founder of the Syrian kingdom of the Seleucidae. He married his stepmother Stratonicé, with whom he had fallen violently in love, and whom his father surrendered to him. He fell in battle against the Gauls in 261. (2) Theos (B.C. 261–246), son and successor of the preceding. The Milesians gave him his surname of Θεός because he delivered them from their tyrant, Timarchus. He carried on war with Ptolemy Philadelphus, king of Egypt, which was brought to a close by his putting away his wife Laodicé, and marrying Berenicé, the daughter of Ptolemy. After the death of Ptolemy he recalled Laodicé, but, in revenge for the insult she had received, she caused Antiochus and Berenicé to be murdered. He was succeeded by his son Seleucus Callinicus. His younger son, Antiochus Hierax, also assumed the crown, and carried on war some years with his brother. (See Berenicé.) (3) The Great (B.C. 223–187), son and successor of Seleucus Callinicus. He carried on war against Ptolemy Philopator, king of Egypt, in order to obtain Coele-Syria, Phoenicia, and Palestine, but was obliged to cede these provinces to Ptolemy, in consequence of his defeat at the battle of Raphia, near Gaza, in 217. He was afterwards engaged for seven years (212–205) in an attempt to regain the eastern provinces of Asia, which had revolted during the reign of Antiochus II.; but, though he met with great success, he found it hopeless to effect the subjugation of the Parthian and Bactrian kingdoms, and accordingly concluded a peace with them. In 198 he conquered Palestine and Coele-Syria, which he afterwards gave as a dowry with his daughter Cleopatra upon her marriage with Ptolemy Epiphanes. He afterwards became involved in hostilities with the Romans, and was urged by Hannibal,

Coin of Antiochus the Great.

who arrived at his court, to invade Italy without loss of time; but Antiochus did not follow his advice. In 192 he crossed over into Greece; and in 191 he was defeated by the Romans at Thermopylae, and compelled to return to Asia. In 190 he was again defeated by the Romans under L. Scipio, at Mount Sipylus, near Magnesia, and compelled to sue for peace, which was granted in 188, on condition of his ceding all his dominions east of Mount Taurus, and paying 15,000 Euboic talents. In order to raise the money to pay the Romans, he attacked a wealthy temple in Elymais, but was killed by the people of the place (187). He was succeeded by his son Seleucus Philopator. (4) EPIPHĂNES (B.C. 175–164), son of Antiochus III., succeeded his brother Seleucus Philopator in 175. He carried on war against Egypt (171–168) with great success; and he was preparing to lay siege to Alexandria in 168, when the Romans compelled him to retire. He endeavoured to root out the Jewish religion and to introduce the worship of the Greek divinities; but this attempt led to a rising of the Jewish people under Mattathias and his heroic sons, the Maccabees, which Antiochus was unable to put down. He attempted to plunder a temple in Elymais in 164, but was repulsed, and died shortly afterwards in a state of raving madness, which the Jews and the Greeks equally attributed to his sacrilegious crimes. His subjects gave him the name of *Epimanes* ("the madman"), in parody of *Epiphanes*. (5) EUPATOR (B.C. 164–162), son and successor of Epiphanes, was nine years old at his father's death. He was dethroned and put to death by Demetrius Soter, the son of Seleucus Philopator. (6) THEOS, son of Alexander Balas. He was brought forward as a claimant to the crown in 144, against Demetrius Nicator, by Tryphon, but he was murdered by the latter, who ascended the throne himself in 142. (7) SIDĒTES (B.C. 137–128), so called from Sidé in Pamphylia, where he was brought up, younger son of Demetrius Soter, succeeded Tryphon. He was defeated and slain in battle by the Parthians in 128. (8) GRYPUS, or Hook-nosed (B.C. 125–96), second son of Demetrius Nicator and Cleopatra. He carried on war for some years with his half-brother, Antiochus Cyzicenus. At length, in 112, the two brothers agreed to share the kingdom between them,—Antiochus Cyzicenus having Coele-Syria and Phœnicia, and Antiochus Grypus the remainder of the provinces. Grypus was assassinated in 96. (9) CYZICĒNUS, from Cyzicus, where he was brought up, brother of Grypus, reigned over Coele-Syria and Phœnicia from 112 to 96, but fell in battle in 95 against Seleucus Epiphanes, son of Grypus. (10) EUSĔBES, son of Cyzicenus, defeated Seleucus Epiphanes, and maintained the throne against the brothers of Seleucus. He succeeded his father in 95. (11) EPIPHĂNES, son of Grypus and brother of Seleucus Epiphanes. He carried on war against Eusebes, but was defeated by the latter, and drowned in the river Orontes. (12) DIONȲSUS, brother of the preceding, held the crown for a short time, but fell in battle against Aretas, king of the Arabians. The Syrians, worn out with the civil broils of the Seleucidae, offered the kingdom to Tigranes, king of Armenia, who united Syria to his own dominions in 83, and held it till his defeat by the Romans in 69. (13) ASIATĬCUS, son of Eusebes, became king of Syria on the defeat of Tigranes by Lucullus in 69; but he was deprived of it in 65 by Pompey, who reduced Syria to a Roman province. In this year the Seleucidae ceased to reign.

II.—Kings of Commagené. (1) A king who made an alliance with the Romans, about B.C. 64. He assisted Pompey with troops in 49, and was attacked by Antony in 38. He was succeeded by Mithridates I. about 31. (2) Succeeded Mithridates I., and was put to death at Rome by Augustus in 29. (3) Succeeded Mithridates II., and died in A.D. 17. Upon his death Commagené became a Roman province, and remained so till A.D. 38. (4) Surnamed EPIPHANES, received his paternal dominion from Caligula in A.D. 38. He assisted the Romans in their wars against the Parthians under Nero, and against the Jews under Vespasian. In 72 he was accused of conspiring with the Parthians against the Romans, was deprived of his kingdom, and retired to Rome, where he passed the remainder of his life.

III.—Literary. OF ASCALON, the founder of the Fifth Academy, was a friend of Lucullus and the teacher of Cicero during his studies at Athens (B.C. 79). See Hoyer, *De Antiocho Ascal.* (1883).

Antiŏpé (Ἀντιόπη). (1) In Homer (*Odyss.* xi. 260) a daughter of the Boeotian river-god Asopus, mother by Zeus of Amphion and Zethus. In later legend her father is Nycteus of Hyria or Hysiae. As he threatened to punish her for yielding to the approaches of Zeus under the form of a satyr, she fled to Epopeus of Sicyon. This king her uncle Lycus killed by order of his brother Nycteus, now dead, and led her back in chains. Arrived on Mount Cithaeron, she gave birth to twins—Amphion by Zeus, Zethus by Epopeus—whom Lycus left exposed upon the mountain. After being long imprisoned and ill-treated by Dircé, the wife of Lycus, she escaped to Cithaeron, and made acquaintance with her sons, whom a shepherd had brought up.

The Farnese Bull. (Naples.)

She made them take a frightful vengeance upon Dircé by tying her to a furious bull, for doing which Dionysus drove her mad, and she wandered through Greece until Phocus, king of Phocis, healed her and made her his wife. (2) An Amazon, sister of Hippolytê the wife of Theseus and mother of Hippolytus (q. v.).

Antipăros (Ἀντίπαρος). A small island opposite Paros, and famous for a grotto of great depth.

Antipăter (Ἀντίπατρος). (1) The son of Iolaüs, a Macedonian. He was first an officer under Philip, and afterwards was raised to the rank of a general under Alexander the Great. When the latter invaded Asia Antipater was appointed governor of Macedonia, and in this station he served his prince with the greatest fidelity. He reduced the Spartans, who had formed a confederacy against the Macedonians; and, having thus secured the tranquillity of Greece, he marched into Asia with a powerful reinforcement for Alexander. After that monarch's death the government of Macedonia and of the other European provinces was allotted to Antipater. He was soon involved in a severe contest with the Grecian states; was defeated by the Athenians, who came against him with an army of 30,000 men and a fleet of 200 ships; and was closely besieged in Lamia, a town of Thessaly. But Leosthenes, the Athenian commander, having been mortally wounded under the walls of the city, and Antipater having received assistance from Craterus, his son-in-law, the fortune of the war was completely changed. The Athenians were routed at Cranon, and compelled to submit at discretion. They were allowed to retain their rights and privileges, but were obliged to deliver up the orators Demosthenes and Hyperides, who had instigated the war, and to receive a Macedonian garrison into the Munychia. Antipater was equally successful in subduing the other States of Greece, who were making a noble struggle for their freedom; but he settled their respective governments with much moderation. In conjunction with Craterus he was the first who attempted to control the growing power of Perdiccas, and after the death of that commander he was invested with all his authority. He exercised this jurisdiction over the other governors with unusual fidelity, integrity, and impartiality, and died in the eightieth year of his age, B.C. 319. At his death he left his son Cassander in a subordinate station; appointed Polysperchon his own immediate successor, and recommended him to the other generals as the fittest person to preside in their councils. Antipater received a learned education, and was the friend and disciple of Aristotle. He appears to have possessed very eminent abilities, and was peculiarly distinguished for his vigilance and fidelity in every trust. It was a saying of Philip, father of Alexander, "I have slept soundly, for Antipater has been awake" (Justin, xi. 12, 13, etc.; Diod. xvii. 18, etc.). (2) The Idumaean, was the father of Herod the Great, and second son of Antipas, governor of Idumaea. He embraced the party of Hyrcanus against Aristobulus, and took a very active part in the contest between the two brothers respecting the office of high-priest in Iudaea. Aristobulus at first, however, succeeded; but when Pompey had deposed him and restored Hyrcanus to the pontifical dignity, Antipater soon became the chief director of affairs in Iudaea, ingratiated himself with the Romans, and used every effort to aggrandize his own family. He gave very effectual aid to Caesar in the Alexandrian War, and the latter in return made him a Roman citizen and procurator of Iudaea. In this latter capacity he exerted himself to restore the ancient Jewish form of government, but was cut off by a conspiracy, the brother of the high-priest having been bribed to give him a cup of poisoned wine. Iosephus makes him to have been distinguished for piety, justice, and love of country (*Ant. Iud.* xiv. 3). (3) A son of Cassander, ascended the throne of Macedonia B.C. 298. He disputed the crown with his brother, Philip IV., and caused his mother, Thessalonica, to be put to death for favouring Philip's side. The two brothers, however, reigned conjointly, notwithstanding this, for three years, when they were dethroned by Demetrius Poliorcetes. Antipater thereupon retired to the court of Lysimachus, his father-in-law, where he ended his days (Justin, xxvi. 1). (4) A native of Tarsus, the disciple and successor of Diogenes the Babylonian, in the Stoic School. He flourished about B.C. 144, and is praised by both Cicero and Seneca as an able supporter of that sect. His chief opponent was Carneades (Cic. *De Off.* iii. 12; Sen. *Ep.* 92). (5) A native of Cyrenê, and one of the Cyrenaic school. He was a disciple of the first Aristippus and the preceptor of Epitimides. (6) A philosopher of Tyre, who wrote a work on duty. He is supposed to have been of the Stoic school. Cicero (*De Orat.* iii. 50) speaks of him as an improvisator. Crassus, into whose mouth the Roman orator puts this remark, might have known the poet when he was quaestor in Macedonia, the same year in which Cicero was born (B.C. 106). Pliny relates (*H. N.* vii. 51) that he had every year a fever on the day of his birth, and that, without ever experiencing any other complaint, he attained to a very advanced age. Some of his epigrams remain, the greater part of which fall under the class of epitaphs (ἐπιτύμβια). (7) A poet of Thessalonica, who flourished towards the end of the last century preceding the Christian era. We have thirty-six of his epigrams remaining. (8) A native of Hierapolis. He was the secretary of Septimius Severus and praefect of Bithynia. He was the preceptor also of Caracalla and Geta, and reproached the former with the murder of his brother.

Antipăter, Lucius Caelius. A Roman historian, and contemporary of C. Gracchus, who wrote *Annales*, containing an account of the Second Punic War, in a highly rhetorical style, but valuable in their substance. The work was in seven books, and dedicated to L. Aelius Stilo. Livy uses it liberally in his third decade; and it appears also to have been drawn upon by Plutarch and Valerius Maximus. See Kranz, *Beitr. z. Quellenkrit. des Val. Max.* (Posen, 1876).

Antiphănes (Ἀντιφάνης). (1) A comic poet of Rhodes, Smyrna, or Carystus, born B.C. 408, of parents in the low condition of slaves. This most prolific writer (he is said to have composed upwards of three hundred dramas), notwithstanding the meanness of his origin, was so popular in Athens that on his decease a decree was passed to remove his remains from Chios to that city, where they were interred with public honours (Suidas, s. v.). (2) A statuary of Argos, the pupil of Pericletus, one of those who had studied under Polycletus.

He flourished about B.C. 400. Several works of this artist are mentioned by Pausanias (x. 9). He formed statues of the Dioscuri and other heroes; and he made also a brazen horse, in imitation of the horse said to have been constructed by the Greeks before Troy. The inhabitants of Argos sent it as a present to Delphi. (3) A poet of Macedonia, nine of whose epigrams are preserved in the Anthology. He flourished between B.C. 100 and the reign of Augustus.

Antiphătes (Ἀντιφάτης). The king of the mythical Laestrygones (q. v.) in Sicily (*Odyss.* x. 106).

Antiphellus (Ἀντίφελλος). See PHELLUS.

Antiphĭlus (Ἀντίφιλος). A Greek painter born in Egypt in the latter half of the fourth century B.C., a contemporary and rival of Apelles; he probably spent the last part of his life at the court of the first Ptolemy. The ancients praise the lightness and dexterity with which he handled subjects of high art, as well as scenes in daily life. Two of his pictures in the latter kind were especially famous, one of a boy blowing a fire, and another of women dressing wool. From his having painted a man named Gryllus (pig) with playful allusions to the sitter's name, caricatures in general came to be called *grylli* (Pliny, *H. N.* xxxv. 114, 138).

Antĭphon (Ἀντιφῶν). The earliest of the ten great Attic orators, born B.C. 480 in Attica, son of the sophist Sophilus, to whom he owed his training. He was the founder of political eloquence as an art, which he taught with great applause in his own school of rhetoric; and he was the first who wrote out speeches for others to deliver in court, though he afterwards published them under his own name. He also played an active part in the politics of his time as a leading member of the oligarchical party, and the real author of the death-blow which was dealt to democracy in B.C. 411 by the establishment of the Council of Four Hundred. He then went as ambassador to Sparta, to purchase peace at any price in the interest of the oligarchy. On the fall of the Four Hundred he was accused of high treason, and, in spite of a masterly defence—the first speech he had ever made in public—was condemned to death B.C. 411. Of the sixty orations attributed to him, only fifteen are preserved—all on trials for murder; but only three of them are about real cases. The rest (named *tetralogies* because every four are the first and second speeches of both plaintiff and defendant on the same subject) are mere exercises. Antiphon's speeches exhibit the art of oratory in its rudimentary stage as regards both substance and form. The best edition is that of Blass (Leipzig, 1881).

Antipŏlis (Ἀντίπολις). The modern Antibes; a town in Gallia Narbonensis on the coast.

Antiquitātum Libri. A work of Varro (q. v.), properly styled *Antiquitates Rerum Humanarum et Divinarum*, in forty-one books—a great monument of Roman learning and a mine for all succeeding writers, being quoted by Pliny, Gellius, and Priscian, and, above all, by St. Augustine in the fifth and seventh books of his treatise *De Civitate Dei.* Of the forty-one books, twenty-five related to profane, and sixteen to sacred, antiquities. See Cruttwell, *Roman Literature*, p. 147 (1886).

Antirrhium (Ἀντίρριον). See RHIUM.

Antisigma (ἀντίσιγμα). An inverted sigma, thus Ͻ. As a symbol it was used by Aristarchus (q. v.) in his criticism of the Homeric text to denote repetitions of the same idea; and by Aristophanes of Byzantium to mark passages that he regarded as spurious. (See Mahaffy, *Hist. of Class. Greek Literature*, vol. i. p. 37.) The same character was added by the emperor Claudius to the Roman alphabet, about A.D. 44, to denote the sound of the Greek ψ (*bs* or *ps*). See Peck, *Latin Pronunciation*, pp. 12, 13 (N. Y. 1890); and the article ALPHABET.

Antissa (Ἄντισσα). A town on the west coast of Lesbos, though formerly on a small island opposite Lesbos, with which it afterwards united.

Antisthĕnes (Ἀντισθένης). A Greek philosopher of Athens, born about B.C. 440, but only a half-citizen, because his mother was a Thracian. He was in his youth a pupil of Gorgias, and himself taught for a time as a sophist, till, towards middle life, he attached himself to Socrates, and became his bosom friend. After the death of Socrates, in B.C. 399, he established a school in the gymnasium Κυνόσαργες, the only one open to persons of half-Athenian descent, whence his followers bore the name of Cynici (Κυνικοί). He lived to the age of seventy. Like Socrates, he regarded virtue as necessary—indeed, alone sufficient—for happiness, and to be a branch of knowledge that could be taught, and that once acquired could not be lost, its essence consisting in freedom from wants by the avoidance of evil (by evil meaning pleasure and desire). Its acquisition needs no dialectic argumentation, only Socratic strength. His pupils, especially the famous Diogenes of Sinopé, degraded his doctrine to cynicism by depreciating all knowledge and despising the current morality of the time. His philosophical and rhetorical works are lost, all but two slight declamations on the contest for the arms of Achilles, the *Aias* and *Odysseus;* and even their genuineness is disputed. They have been edited by A. W. Winckelmann (Zürich, 1842). See also A. Müller, *De Antisthenis Cynici Vita et Scriptis* (Dresden, 1860), and the life by Susemihl (1884).

Antistius Labeo. See LABEO.

Antitaurus (Ἀντίταυρος). Now Ali-dagh; a chain of mountains extending northeast from the range of the Taurus on the southern border of Cappadocia, in the centre of which district it turns and runs east to the Euphrates.

Antium. An ancient town of Latium on a rocky promontory running into the Tuscan Sea. It was founded by the Tyrrhenians and Pelasgians, and was noted for its piracy. It was taken by the Romans in B.C. 468, and a colony was sent thither; but it revolted, was taken a second time by the Romans in 338, was deprived of all its ships, the beaks of which (*rostra*) served to ornament the platform of the speakers in the Roman Forum, and received another Roman colony. In the latter times of the Republic, and under the Empire, it was a favourite residence of many of the Roman nobles and emperors. The emperor Nero was born here, and in the remains of his palace was found the famous statue of the Apollo Belvedere. See APOLLO.

Antlia (ἄντλια). Any contrivance for raising water. Five such machines are mentioned by Vitruvius, x. ch. 4–7; and Lucretius (v. 516) speaks of one like this, in the annexed illustration, which represents a machine still used in the Tyrol. The

Antlia.

antlia with which Martial watered his garden (ix. 19) was nothing more than the pole and bucket still used in Greece, Italy, Egypt, and in some parts of New England.

Antomosia (ἀντωμοσία). A part of the ἀνάκρισις, or preliminary pleadings in an Athenian lawsuit. The term was used of an oath taken by both parties: by the plaintiff, that his complaint was well-founded, and that he was actuated by no improper motives; and by the defendant, that his defence was true. It was also called διωμοσία. The oath might contain either the direct affirmative or negative, in which case it was called εὐθυδικία; or amount to a demurrer or παραγραφή. See ANTIGRAPHÉ; ANACRISIS; DIKÉ; PARAGRAPHÉ; JUDICIAL PROCEDURE.

Antonia. (1) ANTONIA MAIOR, the daughter of M. Antonius and Octavia, wife of L. Domitius Ahenobarbus, and mother of Cn. Domitius, the father of the emperor Nero. (2) MINOR, younger sister of the preceding, wife of Drusus, the brother of the emperor Tiberius, and mother of Germanicus, the father of the emperor Caligula, of Livia or Livilla, and of the emperor Claudius. She died A.D. 38, soon after the accession of her grandson Caligula. She was celebrated for her beauty, virtue, and chastity. (3) The daughter of the emperor Claudius, put to death by Nero, A.D. 66, because she refused to marry him.

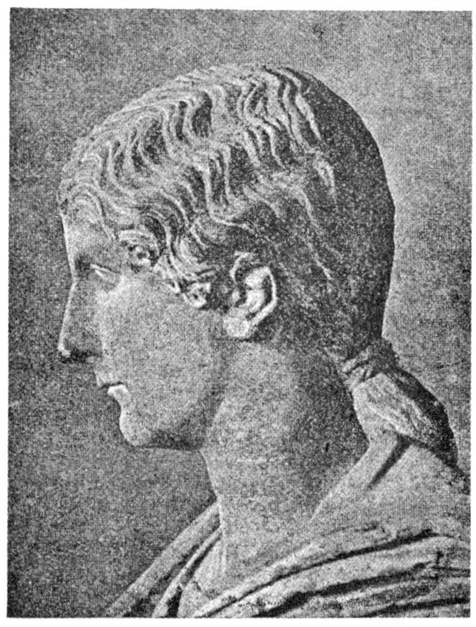

Antonia Minor. (Louvre.)

Antonia Lex. See LEX.

Antonia Turris. A castle on a rock at the northwest corner of the Temple at Jerusalem, originally called Baris, but renamed by Herod the Great in honour of M. Antonius. In it resided the procurator of Iudaea. See Ioseph. *Bell. Iud.* v. 15; and the article HIEROSOLYMA.

Antonīnus. (1) PIUS, or TITUS AURELIUS FULVIUS BOIONIUS ANTONĪNUS, a Roman emperor, A.D. 138–161, born near Lanuvium, A.D. 86, adopted by Hadrian in 138, and succeeded the latter in the same year. The Senate conferred upon him the title of *Pius*, or "the dutifully affectionate," because he persuaded them to grant to his father Hadrian the apotheosis and other honours usually paid to deceased emperors. The reign of Antoninus is almost a blank in history—a blank caused by the suspension for a time of war, violence, and crime. He was one of the best princes that ever mounted a throne, and all his thoughts and energies were dedicated to the happiness of his people. He died in A.D. 161, in his seventy-fifth year. He was succeeded by M. Aurelius, whom he had adopted, when he himself was adopted by Hadrian, and to whom he gave his daughter Faustina in marriage. (2) MARCUS ANNIUS (VERUS) AURELIUS, was born at Rome in the year A.D. 121. Upon the death of Ceionius Commodus, the emperor Hadrian turned his attention towards Marcus Aurelius; but he being then too young for an early assumption of the cares of empire, Hadrian adopted Antoninus Pius, on condition that he in his turn should adopt Marcus Aurelius. His father dying early, the care of his education devolved on his paternal grandfather, Annius Verus, who caused him to receive a general education; but philosophy so early became the object of his ambition that he assumed the philosophic mantle when only twelve years old. The species of philosophy to which he attached himself was the Stoic, as being most connected with morals and the conduct of life; and such was the natural sweetness of his temper that he exhibited none of the pride which sometimes attended the artificial elevation of the Stoic character. This was the more remarkable, as all the honour and power that Antoninus could bestow upon him became his own at an early period, since he was practically associated with him in the administration of the Empire for many years. On his formal accession to the sovereignty his first act was of a kind which at once proved his great disinterestedness; for he immediately took Lucius Verus as his colleague, who had indeed been associated with him by adoption, but who, owing to his defects and vices, had been excluded by Antoninus from the succession, which, at his instigation, the Senate had confined to Marcus Aurelius alone. Notwithstanding their dissimilarity of character, the two emperors reigned conjointly without any disagreement. Verus took the nominal guidance of the war against the Parthians, which was successfully carried on by the lieutenants under him, and during the campaign married Lucilla, the daughter of his colleague. The reign of Marcus Aurelius was more eventful than that of Antoninus. Before the termination of the Parthian War, the Marcomanni and other German tribes began those disturbances which more or less annoyed him for the rest of his life. Against these foes, after the termination of hostilities with Parthia, the two emperors marched; but what was effected during three years' war and negotiation, until the death of Verus, is little known. The sudden decease of that unsuitable colleague by an apoplexy restored to Marcus Aurelius the sole dominion; and for the next five years he carried on the Pannonian War in person, without ever returning to Rome. During these fatiguing campaigns he endured all the hardships incident to a rigorous climate and a military life with a patience and serenity which did the highest honour to his philosophy. Few of the particular actions of this tedious warfare have been fully described; although, owing to conflicting religious zeal, one of them has been exceedingly celebrated. This was the deliverance of the emperor and his army from imminent danger by a victory over the Quadi, in consequence of an extraordinary storm of rain, hail, and lightning, which disconcerted the barbarians, and was, by the conquerors, regarded as miraculous. The emperor and the Romans attributed the timely event to Iupiter Tonans; but the Christians affirmed that God granted this favour on the supplications of the Christian soldiers in the Roman army, who are said to have composed the Twelfth, or Meletine, Legion; and, as a mark of distinction, we are informed by Eusebius that they received from an emperor who persecuted Christianity the title of the "Thundering Legion." The date of this event is fixed by Tillemont as A.D. 174. The general issue of the war was that the barbarians were repressed, but admitted to settle in the territories of the Empire as colonists; and a complete subjugation of the Marcomanni might have followed had not the emperor been recalled by the conspiracy of Avidius Cassius, who assumed the purple in Syria. This usurper was quickly destroyed by a conspiracy among his own officers, and the clemency shown by the emperor to his family was most exemplary. After the suppression of this revolt he made a progress through the East, in which journey he lost his wife Faustina, daughter of Antoninus Pius, a woman as dissolute as she was beautiful, but whose irregularities he never seems to have noticed—a blindness or insensibility that has made him the theme of frequent ridicule. While on this tour he visited Athens, and, like Hadrian, was initiated in the Eleusinian Mysteries. His return to Rome did not take place until after an absence of eight years, and his reception was in the highest degree popular and splendid. After remaining in the capital for nearly two years, and effecting several popular reforms, he was once more called away by the necessity of checking the Marcomanni, and was again successful, but fell ill, at the expiration of two years, at Vindobona, now Vienna. His illness arose from a pestilential disease which prevailed in the army; and it cut him off in the fifty-ninth year of his age and nineteenth of his reign. His death occasioned universal mourning throughout the Empire. Without waiting for the usual decree on the occasion the Roman Senate and people voted him a god by acclamation, and his image was long afterwards regarded with peculiar veneration.

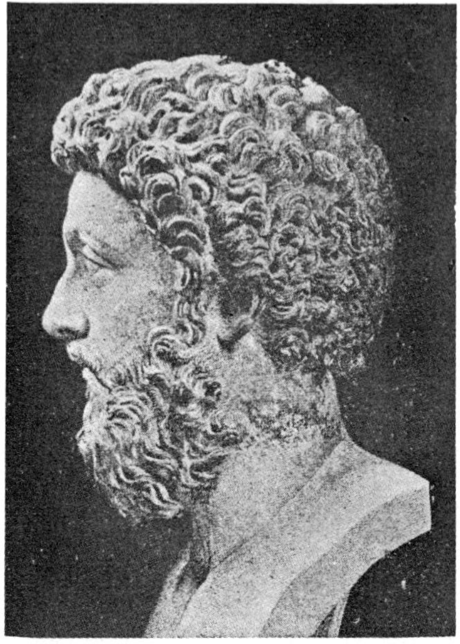

Marcus Aurelius. (Louvre.)

Marcus Aurelius was no friend to the Christians, who were persecuted during the greater part of his reign—an anomaly in a character so universally merciful and clement that may be attributed to an excess of pagan devotion on his part, and still more to the influence of the persons by whom he was surrounded. In all other points of policy and conduct he was one of the most excellent princes on record, both in respect to the salutary regulations he adopted and the temper with which he carried them into practice. Compared with Trajan or Antoninus Pius, he possibly fell short of the manly sense of the one and the simple and unostentatious virtue of the other—philosophy or scholarship on a throne always more or less assuming the appearance of pedantry. The emperor was also himself a writer, and his *Meditations* (Τὰ εἰς ἑαυτόν), in Greek in twelve books, have descended to posterity. They are a collection of maxims and thoughts in the spirit of the Stoic philosophy, which, without much connection or skill in composition, breathe the purest sentiments of piety and benevolence. They were jotted down from time to time in his leisure moments, and largely while he was in camp along the Danube during his campaign against the Marcomanni. His theology, in general, seems pantheistic, the key-note being the doctrine of a "natural unity," including God, nature, and all mankind.

Marcus Aurelius left one son, the brutal Commodus, and three daughters. Among the weaknesses of this good emperor, his too great consideration for his son is deemed one of the most striking; for, although he was unremitting in his endeavours to reclaim him, they were accompanied by much erroneous indulgence, and especially by an early and ill-judged elevation to titles and honours.

Good texts of the *Meditations* are those of Gataker (London, 1697) and Stich (1882). See also the translation, with notes, by Long (1869); the French version by Pierron (1878); Renan's *Marc-Aurèle* (1882); and Watson's *Marcus Aurelius Antoninus* (N. Y., 1884). (3) BASSIĀNUS CARACALLA. (See CARACALLA.) (4) LIBERĀLIS. A mythological writer supposed to have lived in the age of the Antonines, and to have been a freedman of one of them. He wrote a work entitled *A Collection of Metamorphoses* (Μεταμορφωσέων Συναγωγή), in forty-one chapters. Edition by Westermann (Brunswick, 1839). See Oder, *De Antonino Liberali* (1886).

Antonius. (1) MARCUS, the orator, was born B.C. 143; was quaestor in 113; praetor in 104, when he fought against the pirates in Cilicia; consul in 99; and censor in 97. He belonged to Sulla's party, and was put to death by Marius and Cinna, when they entered Rome, in 87; his head was cut off and placed on the Rostra. Cicero mentions him and L. Crassus as the most distinguished orators of their age, and he is introduced as one of the speakers in Cicero's *De Oratore*. (2) MARCUS, surnamed CRETICUS, elder son of the orator, and father of the triumvir, was praetor in B.C. 75, and received the command of the fleet and all the coasts of the Mediterranean, in order to clear the sea of pirates; but he did not succeed in his object, and used his power to plunder the provinces. He died shortly afterwards in Crete, and was called *Creticus* in derision. (3) GAIUS, younger son of the orator and uncle of the triumvir, was expelled from the Senate in B.C. 70, and was the colleague of Cicero in the praetorship (65) and consulship (63). He was one of Catiline's conspirators, but deserted the latter on Cicero's promising him the province of Macedonia. He had to lead an army against Catiline, but, unwilling to fight against his former friend, he gave the command on the day of battle to his legate, M. Petreius. At the conclusion of the war Antony went into his province, which he plundered shamefully; and on his return to Rome in 59 was accused both of taking part in Catiline's conspiracy and of extortion in his province. He was defended by Cicero, but was condemned, and retired to the island of Cephallenia. He was subsequently recalled, probably by Caesar, and was in Rome at the beginning of the year 44. (4) MARCUS, the TRIUMVIR, was the son of Antonius Creticus and Iulia, the sister of Iulius Caesar. He was born about B.C. 83. His father died while he was still young, and he was brought up by Lentulus, who married his mother Iulia, and who was put to death by Cicero in 63 as one of Catiline's conspirators: hence Antony became a personal enemy of Cicero. Antony indulged in his earliest youth in every kind of dissipation, and his affairs soon became deeply involved. In 58, he went to Syria, where he served with distinction under A. Gabinius. In 54, he went to Caesar in Gaul, and by the influence of the latter was elected quaestor (B.C. 52). He now became one of the most active partisans of Caesar. He was tribune of the plebs in 49, and in January fled to Caesar's camp in Cisalpine Gaul, after putting his veto upon the decree of the Senate which deprived Caesar of his command. In 48, Antony was present at the battle of Pharsalia, where he commanded the left wing. In 44, he was consul with Caesar, when he offered him the kingly diadem at the festival of the Lupercalia. After Caesar's murder, on the 15th of March, Antony endeavoured to succeed to his power. He pronounced the speech over Caesar's body, and read his will to the people; and he also obtained the papers and private property of Caesar. But he found a new and unexpected rival in young Octavianus, the adopted son and great-nephew of the dictator, who at first joined the Senate in order to crush Antony. (See AUGUSTUS.) Towards the end of the year Antony proceeded to Cisalpine Gaul, which had been previously granted him by the Senate; but Dec. Brutus refused to surrender the province to Antony, and threw himself into Mutina, where he was besieged by Antony. The Senate approved of the conduct of Brutus, declared Antony a public enemy, and intrusted the conduct of the war against him to Octavianus. Antony was defeated at the battle of Mutina, in April, 43, and was obliged to cross the Alps. Both the consuls, however, had fallen, and the senators now began to show their jealousy of Octavianus. Meantime Antony was joined by Lepidus with a powerful army; Octavianus became

Marcus Antonius.

reconciled to him; and it was agreed that the government of the state should be vested in Antony, Octavianus, and Lepidus, under the title of *Triumviri Republicae Constituendae*, for the next five years. The mutual enemies of each were proscribed, and, in the numerous executions that followed, Cicero, who had attacked Antony in his Philippic Orations, fell a victim to his malice. In 42, Antony and Octavianus crushed the republican party by the battle of Philippi, in which Brutus and Cassius fell. Antony then went to Asia, which he had received as his share of the Roman world. In Cilicia he met with Cleopatra, and followed her to Egypt, a captive to her charms. In 41, Fulvia, the wife of Antony, and his brother, L. Antonius, made war upon Octavianus in Italy. Antony prepared to support his relatives, but the war was brought to a close at the beginning of 40, before Antony could reach Italy. The opportune death of Fulvia facilitated the reconciliation of Antony and Octavianus, which was cemented by the marriage of Antony to Octavia, the sister of Octavianus. Antony remained in Italy till 39, when the triumvirs concluded a peace with Sext. Pompey, and he afterwards went to his provinces in the East. In this year and the following, Ventidius, the lieutenant of Antony, defeated the Parthians. In 37, Antony crossed over to Italy, when the triumvirate was renewed for five years. He then returned to the East, and shortly afterwards sent Octavia back to her brother and surrendered himself entirely to the charms of Cleopatra. In 36, he invaded Parthia, but lost a great number of his troops, and was obliged to retreat. He was more successful in his invasion of Armenia in 34, for he obtained possession of the person of Artavasdes, the Armenian king, and carried him to Alexandria. Antony now laid aside entirely the character of a Roman citizen, and assumed the pomp and ceremony of an Eastern despot. His conduct, and the unbounded influence which Cleopatra had acquired over him, alienated many of his friends and supporters; and Octavianus saw that the time had now come for crushing his rival.

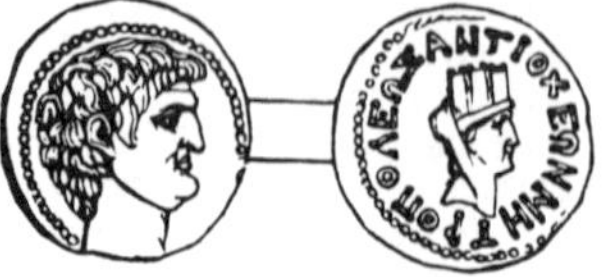

Coin of Antony, struck at Antioch.

Coin of Antony, with Worship of Bacchus and Venus.

The contest was decided by the memorable sea-fight off Actium, September 2d, B.C. 31, in which Antony's fleet was completely defeated. Accompanied by Cleopatra, he fled to Alexandria, where he put an end to his own life in the following year (30), when Octavianus appeared before the city. (5) GAIUS, brother of the triumvir, was praetor in Macedonia in B.C. 44, fell into the hands of M. Brutus in 43, and was put to death by Brutus in 42, to revenge the murder of Cicero. (6) LUCIUS, youngest brother of the triumvir, was consul in B.C. 41, when he engaged in war against Octavianus at the instigation of Fulvia, his brother's wife. He threw himself into the town of Perusia, which he was obliged to surrender in the following year. His life was spared, and he was afterwards appointed by Octavianus to the command of Iberia. (7) MARCUS, elder son of the triumvir by Fulvia, was executed by order of Octavianus, after the death of his father in B.C. 30. (8) IULUS, younger son of the triumvir by Fulvia, was brought up by his step-mother Octavia at Rome, and received great marks of favour from Augustus. He was consul in B.C. 10, but was put to death in the year 2, in consequence of his adulterous intercourse with Iulia, the daughter of Augustus.

Antonius Felix. See FELIX.

Antonius Gnipho. See GNIPHO.

Antonius Musa. See MUSA.

Antonius Primus. See PRIMUS.

Antron (Ἀντρών). A town of Phthiotis in Thessaly, at the entrance to the Sinus Maliacus.

Antyx (ἄντυξ). The rim or border of anything, especially of a shield or chariot. On Greek and

Antyx. (From an Etruscan Tomb.)

Etruscan vases we often see the chariot painted with the antyx much elevated, as in the accompanying illustration. By the figure synecdoche, the word ἄντυξ is sometimes used to denote the whole chariot.

Anūbis (Ἄνουβις). An Egyptian divinity, worshipped in the form of a human being with a jackal's head. The Greeks identified him with their own Hermes, and thus speak of Hermanuphis in the same manner as of Zeus Ammon. His worship was introduced at Rome during the last years of the Republic (Luc. *Tox.* 32).

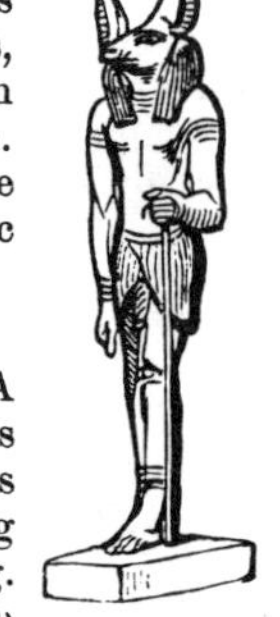

Image of Anubis.

Anŭli Ius. See IUS ANULORUM.

Anŭlus or **Annŭlus** (δακτύλιος). A word derived from the same root as ἀμφί, meaning something which goes round (cf. *annus*), and used for a ring of any kind, especially a finger ring. The old Latin name was *ungulus*. In the earliest times the ring was used, not as an ornament, but as a seal (Macrob. *Sat.* vii. 13, § 12). How ancient the custom of wearing rings among the Greeks was can not be ascertained, though it is certain that in the Homeric poems there are no traces of it. In works of fiction, however, and in those legends in which the customs of later ages are mixed up with those of the earliest times, we find the most ancient heroes described as wearing rings. But it is highly probable that the custom of wearing rings was introduced into Greece from Asia, where it appears to have been almost universal (Herod. i. 195). From Asia Minor to Greece proper the transition of fashion was expeditious, and the signet, now for the first time worn mounted as a finger-ring, came into universal favour among all the Hellenic population. This was a new method for securing the engraved stone; for the original inventors of seal-engraving had worn, and continued to wear down to the very close of their history (even to the date of the Arabian conquest), the cylinder or the conical seal as the ornament of the bracelet or the necklace, etc. We have the express statement of Pliny (*H. N.* xxxiii. 4) that the use of the finger-ring was introduced among the Romans from Greece. (See King, *Handbook of Engraved Gems* [1885], pp. 12, 13.) In the time of Solon seal-rings (σφραγῖδες), as well as the practice of counterfeiting them, seem to have been rather common, for Diogenes Laërtius (i. 57) speaks of a law of Solon which forbade the artist to keep the form of a seal (σφραγίς) which he had sold. There are allusions to counterfeit seals in Aristoph. *Thesm.* 432; and Thuc. i. 132. Rings without precious stones were called ἀπείρονες, ἄπειροι, ἄλιθοι, ἄψηφοι, the name of the gem being ψῆφος or σφραγίς, which was set in a bezel (σφενδόνη, πυελίς, μάνδρα, *funda*, *pala*). In later times rings were worn more as an ornament, and Suidas says (s. v. σφραγίς) that some regularly loaded their hands with rings. Greek women likewise used to wear rings (Aristoph. *Thesm.* frag. 320, 12, Kock), but not so frequently as men. The rings of women appear to have been less costly than those of men, for some are mentioned which were made of amber, ivory, etc. Rings were mostly worn on the left hand and third finger (Gell. x. 10), but also on the little finger (Lucian, *Dial. Merer.* 9, 2). Indeed, Pliny says (*H. N.* xxxiii. 24) that they were worn first on the third, then on the first, and finally on the little finger; and Macrobius (*Sat.* vii. 13, § 15), quoting Ateius Capito, says that originally they were worn on any finger of either hand. But they do not seem to have been ever worn on the middle finger (*digitus infamis*). An Etruscan tomb exhibits rings on the upper joints of the fingers. (See illustration.)

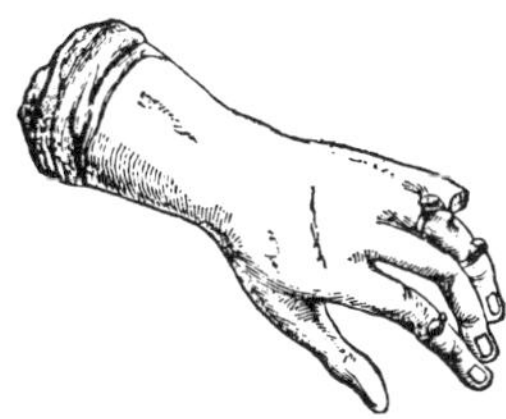
Hand from an Etruscan Tomb, wearing Rings.

The Lacedaemonians are said to have used iron rings at all times (Plin. *H. N.* xxxiii. 9). The law does not appear to have ever attempted in any Greek state to counteract the great partiality for this luxury; and nowhere in Greece does the right of wearing a gold ring appear to have been confined to a particular order or class of citizens.

The custom of wearing rings was believed to have been introduced into Rome by the Sabines, who are described in the early legends as wearing gold rings with precious stones of great beauty (Liv. i. 11). Florus (i. 5) states that it was introduced from Etruria in the reign of Tarquinius Priscus, and Pliny derives it from Greece. At whatever time rings may have become customary at Rome, thus much is certain, that at first they were generally of iron, but often of stone (King, *Antique Gems*, p. 176, ed. 1860); that they were destined for the same purpose as in Greece—namely, to be used as seals; and that every free Roman had a right to use such a ring. This iron ring was used down to the last period of the Republic by such men as loved the simplicity of the good old times, and it retained its place in the ceremony of betrothal. Marius wore an iron ring in his triumph over Iugurtha, and several noble families adhered to the ancient custom, and never wore gold ones (Plin. *H. N.* xxxiii. §§ 12, 21).

Rings with us are mainly associated with marriage, an association borrowed from the Romans. As already mentioned, the *anulus pronubus* was originally of iron, without a stone, and continued to be so even to a late period (Plin. *H. N.* xxxiii. 12); though Tertullian (*Apol.* 6) says the marriage-ring was the one gold ornament that women wore in the olden times. Wedding-rings with precious stones have been found on ancient figures.

Snake-ring. (British Museum.)

The ring of the Roman emperor was a kind of state seal, whose use was sometimes allowed to persons acting as his representatives. The keeping of the imperial seal-ring (*cura anuli*) was intrusted to a special officer.

Different families appear to have had distinct seals like our crests—e. g. Galba's family seal represented a dog leaping from a ship; Pompey's ring bore the device of three trophies; Augustus sealed with a Sphinx, afterwards with a head of Alexander the Great, and finally with his own portrait, as did Hadrian. The Empire, in fact, is the grand era of portraits on gems. In the art of engraving figures upon gems, the ancients far surpass the best work of modern artists. See GEMMA.

Originally, among the Romans, the men only wore one ring and the women none, except that a married woman wore that received at marriage. Later, the love of luxury led both men and women to cover their fingers with rings. In one of the graves at Kertsch, a woman was found with eight rings. Lucian (*Gall.* chap. xii.), ridiculing the rich, speaks of sixteen rings. Martial (xi. 59) tells of a man who wore six on each finger. Some even used different rings for summer and winter, those for the latter season being too heavy for hot weather (Iuv. i. 28, with Schol.). The materials used for rings, as seen by European collections, were iron, lead, zinc, bronze, amber, ivory, silver, and gold. Rings were kept in a box called *dactyliotheca*—a name also applied to a collector of rings. For earrings, see INAURES.

Anxur. See TARRACINA.

Anȳtē (Ἀνύτη). A poetess of Tegea, who versified the oracles of Asclepius at Epidaurus about B.C. 300. Some twenty epigrams are all that remain of her works.

Anȳtus (Ἄνυτος). A wealthy Athenian, the most influential and formidable of the accusers of Socrates, B.C. 399. He was a leading man of the democratical party, and took an active part, along with Thrasybulus, in the overthrow of the Thirty Tyrants. After the death of Socrates, Anytus went into exile to escape the vengeance of the fickle populace, who had repented of what had been done. See Aelian, *V. H.* ii. 13; and the article SOCRATES.

Aŏnes (Ἄονες). An ancient Boeotian race, said to have been so called from Aon, son of Poseidon. Hence the poets frequently use Aonia as equivalent to Boeotia. As Mount Helicon and the fountain Aganippé were in Aonia, the Muses are called Aonides or Aoniae.

Aornis or **Aornos.** A lofty rock in India, taken by Alexander the Great. The Macedonians named it Ἄορνος, as being so high as to be inaccessible even to birds (ἀ + ὄρνις).

Aōüs (Ἀῷος). The chief river of the Greek part of Illyricum rising in Mount Lacmon, and flowing into the Ionian Sea near Apollonia.

Apagōgē (ἀπαγωγή). A technical term of Athenian law, meaning the production of a criminal taken in the act, before the proper magistrate, who then took him into custody, or made him find bail. The name was also given to the document in which the accuser stated the charge. But if the officer was conducted to the spot where the accused was staying the process was called ἐφήγησις.

Apamēa ('Απάμεια). The name of several cities. (1) APAMEA AD ORONTEM, a city of Syria built by Seleucus Nicator on the site of the older city Pella on the river Orontes, and named in honour of his wife Apama. (2) A city in Mesopotamia, of uncertain site. (3) APAMEA CIBŌTUS (Κιβωτός), or AD MAEANDRUM, a great city of Phrygia on the Maeander, just above its union with the Marsyaé. It was built by Antiochus Soter in honour of his mother Apama. The name Κιβωτός ("chest," "coffer"), which appears on some coins of Apamea, is explained generally with reference to the wealth of the city; but certain curious coincidences have been found which some scholars have used in connection with the traditions of the Deluge. The Septuagint and the New Testament speak of the Ark as κιβωτός; and the coins and medals of Apamea show the figure of an ark with two birds above it, one holding a twig. A man and woman stand beside it, and above it is the inscription NOO (ΝΩ). On this, see Mayor's note to Juvenal, i. 82; and the article DEUCALION. (4) APAMEA MYRLĒON in Bithynia. See MYRLEA. (5) A town in Osrhoënê on the left bank of the Euphrates, connected by a pontoon bridge with Zeugma on the opposite bank.

Medal of Apamea Cibotus.

Apateseos tou Demou Graphé (ἀπατήσεως τοῦ δήμου γραφή). A public prosecution at Athens against any one who had misled the people by false statements of fact, quoting imaginary laws, etc. The Senate and the law-courts, as well as the sovereign people, were included in its operation (Dem. *c. Aristocr.* p. 653, § 97). It would seem that it might also be directed against generals who, like Miltiades at Paros, failed in an expedition which they had themselves suggested (Dem. *c. Timoth.* p. 1204, § 67).

Apaturia (ἀπατούρια). The general feast of the phratries (q. v.), held chiefly by Greeks of the Ionian race. At Athens it lasted three days in the month of Pyanepsion (Oct.–Nov.), and was celebrated with sacrificial banquets. On the third day the fathers brought their children born since the last celebration before the members (phrators) assembled at the headquarters of each φρατρία, and, after declaring on oath their legitimate birth, had their names inscribed on the roll of φράτορες. For every child enrolled a sheep or goat was sacrificed, which went to furnish the common feast. On the same day the fathers made their children who were at school give proofs of their progress, especially by reciting passages from poets, and those who distinguished themselves were rewarded with prizes.

Apaulia. See MATRIMONIUM.

Apeleuthĕros (ἀπελεύθερος). See LIBERTUS.

Apelles ('Απελλῆς). The most celebrated of Grecian painters, born, most probably, at Colophon in Ionia, though some ancient writers call him a Coan and others an Ephesian. He was the contemporary of Alexander the Great (B.C. 336–323), who entertained so high an opinion of him that he was the only person whom Alexander would permit to paint his portrait. We are not told when or where he died. Throughout his life Apelles laboured to improve himself, especially in drawing, which he never spent a day without practising. Hence the proverb, *Nulla dies sine linea* (τήμερον οὐδεμίαν γραμμὴν ἤγαγον). Of his portraits, the most celebrated was that of Alexander wielding a thunderbolt; but the most admired of all his pictures was the "Aphroditê Anadyomenê," or Aphroditê rising out of the sea. The goddess was wringing her hair, and the falling drops of water formed a transparent silver veil around her form. The original was Campaspê, a mistress of Alexander. For the painting of Alexander a sum of twenty talents (about $21,600) was paid, and the painting itself was hung in the temple of Diana of Ephesus. He painted also a horse; and, finding that his rivals in the art, who contested the palm with him on this occasion, were about to prevail through unfair means, he caused his own piece and those of the rest to be shown to some horses, and these animals, fairer critics in this case than men had proved to be, neighed at his painting alone. Apelles used to say of his contemporaries that they possessed, as artists, all the requisite qualities except one—namely, grace, and that this was his alone. On one occasion, when contemplating a picture by Protogenes, a work of immense labour, and in which exactness of detail had been carried to excess, he remarked, "Protogenes equals or surpasses me in all things but one—the knowing when to remove his hand from a painting." Apelles was also, as is supposed, the inventor of what artists call glazing. Such, at least, was the opinion of Sir Joshua Reynolds and others. The ingredients probably employed by him for this purpose are given by Jahn, in his *Malerei der Alten*, p. 150. Apelles was accustomed, when he had completed any one of his pieces, to expose it to the view of passengers, and to hide himself behind it in order to hear the remarks of the spectators. On one of these occasions a shoemaker censured the painter for having given one of the slippers of a figure a less number of ties by one than it ought to have had. The next day the shoemaker, emboldened by the success of his previous criticism, began to find fault with a leg, when Apelles indignantly put forth his head, and desired him to confine his decisions to the slipper, "ne supra crepidam iudicaret." Hence arose another common saying, *Ne sutor ultra crepidam* (Pliny, *H. N.* xxxv. 10).

Apellĭcon ('Απελλικῶν). A Peripatetic philosopher, born at Teos in Asia Minor, and one of those to whom we owe the preservation of many of the works of Aristotle. The latter, on his deathbed, confided his works to Theophrastus, his favourite pupil and Theophrastus, by his will, left them to Neleus, who had them conveyed to Scepsis, in Troas, his native city. After the death of Neleus, his heirs, illiterate persons, fearing lest they might fall into the hands of the king of Pergamus, who was enriching in every way his newly-established library, concealed the writings of Aristotle in a cave, where they remained for more than 130 years, and suffered greatly from worms and dampness. At the end of this period Apellicon purchased them for a high price. His wish was to arrange them in proper order, and to fill up the lacunae that were now of frequent occurrence in the manuscripts, in consequence of their neglected state. Being, however, but little versed in philosophy, and possessing still less judgment, he acquitted himself ill in this difficult task, and published the works of the Stagirite full of faults. Subsequently the library of Apellicon fell, among the spoils of Athens, into the hands of Sulla, and was carried to Rome, where the grammarian Tyrannion had access to them. From him copies were obtained by Andronicus of Rhodes, which served for the basis of his arrangement of the works of Aristotle.

Ritter thinks that too much has been made of this story. On its authority it has even been pretended that the works of Aristotle have reached us in a more broken and ill-arranged shape than any other productions of antiquity. He thinks that the story arose out of some laudatory commendations of the edition of Aristotle by Andronicus, and that it is probable, not to say certain, that there were other editions, of the respective merits of which it was possible to make a comparison. At any rate, according to him, the acroamatic works of Aristotle have not reached us solely from the library of Neleus, and consequently it was not necessary to have recourse merely to the restoration by Apellicon, either to complete or retain the lacunae resulting from the deterioration of the manuscripts. See ARISTOTELES.

Apēné (ἀπήνη). A carriage with four wheels, generally drawn by mules. See CURRUS.

Apeniautismos (ἀπενιαυτισμός). See PHONOU DIKÉ.

Apennīnus. A great chain of mountains in Italy, branching off from the Maritime Alps, in the neighbourhood of Genoa, running diagonally from the Ligurian Gulf to the Adriatic, in the vicinity of Ancona; from thence continuing nearly parallel with the latter gulf, as far as the promontory of Garganus, and again inclining to the Maré Inferum, until it finally terminates in the promontory of Leucopetra near Rhegium. The length is about 700 miles (Polyb. ii. 16).

Aper. (1) MARCUS. A Roman orator of the first century A.D. He was a native of Gaul, but spent most of his life at Rome. He is one of the speakers in the *Dialogus* of Tacitus. He died A.D. 85. (2) ARRIUS. A prefect of the Praetorian Guards under the emperor Carus, whom, while ill, he assassinated, pretending that the death had been caused by lightning. The motive of this deed was a desire to secure an election as emperor at the hands of the Guards, and the same ambition also led him to poison Numerianus, the successor of Carus. Falling under suspicion, after successfully accomplishing this crime, Aper was executed by order of Diocletian, whom the soldiery had made emperor. See Aurel. Vict. 38; Vopisc. *Carus*, 8; id. *Numer.* 12 foll.

Aperta Navis. See APHRACTUS.

Apex. A cap of conical form worn by the flamens (see FLAMEN), having a spike of olive-wood at the top, which the word *apex*, in fact, originally denoted. Without it the flamens were not allowed to go into the open air (Gell. x. 15). The Salii likewise wore the apex. The accompanying illustration shows one of the Salii wearing the apex and with a rod in his hand. (See SALII.) The *albogalerus*, or *albus galerus*, was a white cap worn by the *flamen dialis*, made of the skin of a white victim sacrificed to Iupiter, and having the apex fastened to it by an olive twig.

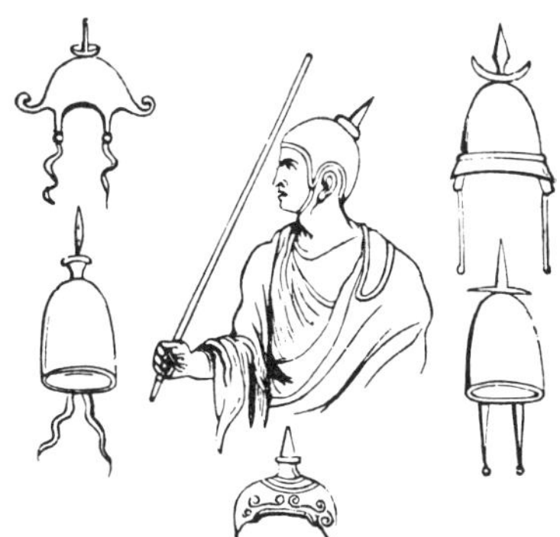

Apices, or Caps worn by the Flamines and Salii.

Aphăca (ἀφάκη). A kind of lentil.

Aphĕtae (ἀφέται). See HELOTAE.

Aphidna (Ἄφιδνα). An Attic deme near Decelea.

Aphlaston (ἄφλαστον). See NAVIS.

Aphormes Diké (ἀφορμῆς δίκη). An action brought against a banker or money-lender to recover funds advanced for the purpose of being employed as banking capital. See PARAKATATHEKÉ.

Aphractus (ἄφρακτος ναῦς), called also *navis aperta*. A ship which had no deck, but was merely covered with planks in the fore and after part, as is represented in the following cut, taken from a coin of Corcyra.

Aphractus.

The ships which had decks were called κατάφρακτοι, and *tectae* or *stratae*. See NAVIS.

Aphrodisia (τὰ Ἀφροδίσια). Festivals celebrated in many towns of Greece in honour of Aphrodité (q. v.). The especial seat of her worship was at Cyprus. No bloody sacrifices were permitted to be offered, but only pure fire, flowers, and incense. The initiated also offered a piece of money to the goddess as a harlot; and received a measure of salt symbolizing the origin of Aphrodité in the sea, and a phallus as expressive of the sexual function.

Aphrodisias (Ἀφροδισιάς). A town of Caria sacred to Aphrodité. See Tac. *Ann.* iii. 62.

Aphrodītē (Ἀφροδίτη; Lat. *Venus*). The Greek goddess of love. Her attributes combine, with Hellenic conceptions, a great many features of Eastern, especially Phœnician, origin, which the Greeks must have grafted upon their native notions in very old times. This double nature appears immediately in the contradictory tales of her origin. To the oldest Greeks she was the daughter of Zeus and Dioné (and is sometimes called by that name herself); yet from a very early time she appears as Aphrogenia, the "foam-born" (see URANUS), as Anadyomené, "she who rises" out of the sea, and steps ashore on Cyprus, which had been colonized by Phœnicians time out of mind; even as far back as Homer she is Cypris, the Cyprian. (See CY-

PRUS.) The same transmarine and Eastern origin of her worship is evidenced by the legend of the island of Cythera, on which she was supposed to have first landed from a sea-shell. Other names applied to her are Pelagia (from Πέλαγος), Anadyomené (as having risen from the water), Erycina (from Mount Eryx in Sicily), Paphia, and Cypris, besides those mentioned below.

Again, the common conception of her as goddess of love limited her agency to the sphere of human life. But she was, at the same time, a power of nature, living and working in the three elements of air, earth, and water. As goddess of the shifting gale and changeful sky, she was Aphrodité Urania (Οὐρανία), the "heavenly," and at many places in Greece and Asia her temples crowned the heights and headlands; for instance, the citadels of Thebes and Corinth, and Mount Eryx in Sicily. As goddess of storm and lightning, she was represented armed, as at Sparta and Cythera; and this, perhaps, explains why she was associated with Ares both in worship and in legend, and worshipped as a goddess of victory.

The moral conception of Aphrodité Urania as goddess of the higher and purer love, especially wedded love and fruitfulness, as opposed to mere sensual lust, was but slowly developed in the course of ages.

As goddess of the sea and maritime traffic, especially of calm seas and prosperous voyages, she was widely worshipped by sailors and fishermen at ports and on sea-coasts, often as the goddess of calm, while Poseidon was the god of disturbance. Next, as regards the life of the earth, she was the goddess of gardens and groves, of spring and its bounties, especially tender plants and flowers, as the rose and myrtle; hence, as the fruitful and bountiful, she was worshipped most of all at that season of the year in which her birth from the sea was celebrated at Paphos in Cyprus. But to this, her time of joyful action, was opposed a season of sorrow, when her creations wither and die—a sentiment expressed in her inconsolable grief for her beloved Adonis (q. v.), the symbol of vegetation perishing in its prime, a myth derived by the Greeks from the Babylonian worship of Adon or Thammuz, and akin to those of Linus, Hyacinthus, and Narcissus. (See Mannhardt Wald- und Feldkulte, 274 [Berlin, 1886].) In the life of gods and men, she showed her power as the golden, sweetly smiling goddess of beauty and love, which she knew how to kindle or to keep away. She outshone all the goddesses in grace and loveliness; in her girdle she wore united all the magic charms that could bewitch the wisest man and subdue the very gods. (See CESTUS.) Her retinue consisted of Eros (Cupid), the Hours, the Graces, Peitho (Persuasion), Pothos and Himeros (personifications of longing and yearning). By uniting the generations in the bond of love, she became a goddess of marriage and family life, and the consequent kinship of the whole community. As such she had formerly been worshipped at Athens under the name of Pandemos (=all the people's), as being a goddess of the whole country. By a regulation of Solon, the name acquired a very different sense, branding her as goddess of prostitution; and then it was that the new and higher meaning was imported into the word Urania. See MERETRIX.

In later times, the worship of Aphrodité as the goddess of mere sensual love made rapid strides, and in particular districts assumed forms more and more immoral, in imitation of the services performed to love-goddesses in the East, especially at Corinth, where large bands of girls were consecrated as slaves to the service of the gods and the practice of prostitution. And later still, the worship of Astarté ("Star"), the Syrian Aphrodité, performed by eunuchs, spread all over Greece. See APHRODISIA; MERETRIX.

In the Greek myths Aphrodité appears occasionally as the wife of Hephaestus. Her love adventures with Ares are notorious. From these sprang Eros and Anteros, Harmonia, the wife of Cadmus, and Deinos and Phobos (Fear and Alarm), attendants on their father. By Anchises she was the mother of Aeneas. The chief seats of her worship were Paphos, Amathus, and Idalion (all in Cyprus), Cnidus in Dorian Asia Minor, Corinth, the island of Cythera, and Eryx in Sicily. As mother of Harmonia, she was a guardian deity of Thebes. Among plants, the myrtle, the rose, and the apple were specially sacred to her as goddess of love; among animals, the ram, he-goat, hare, dove, sparrow, and other creatures of amorous nature (the ram and dove being widely current symbols of great antiquity); as sea-goddess, the swan, mussel, and dolphin; as Urania, the tortoise.

The various myths connected with the name of Aphrodité have inspired many exquisite poems in modern literature. In recent English verse reference may be made to the magnificent Chorus to Aphrodité in Swinburne's *Atalanta in Calydon;* Hake's *Birth of Venus;* Morris's Aphrodité in his *Epic of Hades;* and Rossetti's *Venus Verticordia* and *Venus Victrix.*

In ancient art, in which Aphrodité is one of the favourite subjects, she is represented in a higher or lower aspect, according as the artist's aim was to exhibit Urania or the popular goddess of love. In the earlier works of art she usually appears clothed, but in later ones more or less undraped—either as rising from the sea or leaving the bath, or (as in still later times) merely as an ideal of female beauty. In the course of time the divine element disappeared, and the presentation became more and more ordinary. While the older sculptures show the sturdier forms, the taste of later times leans more and more to softer, weaker outlines. Most renowned in ancient times

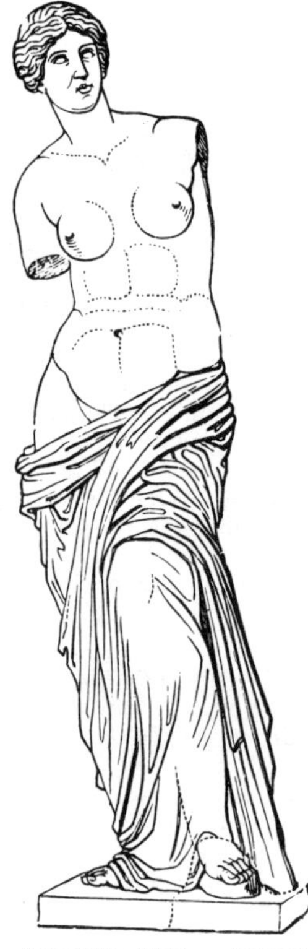

Aphrodité of Melos. (Louvre.)

were the statue at Cnidus by Praxiteles (a copy of which is now at Munich), and the painting of Aphroditê Anadyomenê by Apelles. Of original statues preserved to us, the most famous are the Aphroditê of Melos (see illustration), now at Paris, and that of Capua at Naples, both of which bring out the loftier aspect of the goddess; and the Medicean Venus at Florence, the work of a late Attic sculptor, Cleomenes, in the delicate forms of face and body that pleased a younger age. On the identification of Aphroditê with the Roman goddess of love, see VENUS.

Aphrogeneia (Ἀφρογένεια). "Foam-sprung." An epithet of Aphroditê (q. v.).

Aphthonius (Ἀφθόνιος). A Greek rhetorician of Antioch, about A.D. 400, a pupil of Libanius, who wrote a school-book on the elements of rhetoric, the *Progymnasmata*, much used in schools down to the seventeenth century. This book is really an adaptation of the chapter so named in Hermogenes's *Rhetoric*. A collection of forty fables by Aesop also bears his name.

Aphȳtis (Ἄφυτις). A town in Macedonia containing a celebrated temple and oratory of Zeus Ammon (Pausan. iii. 18.)

Apia. See APIS.

Apicius, MARCUS GAVIUS. A *bon-vivant* of the time of Augustus and Tiberius. He borrowed the name Apicius from an epicure of the republican period, and was himself the author of a cook-book. Though worth a fortune of some $375,000, he became haunted by the fear of starving to death, and so poisoned himself to escape such a fate. The well-known collection of recipes for cooking, in ten books, entitled *De Re Coquinaria*, is of later date, and written by one Apicius Caelius in the third century A.D. The best edition is that of C. Th. Schuch (Heidelberg, 1867), who has added some recipes from a Paris MS. of the seventh century.

Apidănus (Ἀπιδανός). A river in Thessaly flowing into Enipeus, near Pharsalus (Herod. vii. 129).

Apĭna and **Apĭnae.** A small city of Apulia near Trica. *Apina* and *Trica* (*Tricae*) are terms used in Latin of trifles. Cf. Mart. xiv. 1; Plin. *H. N.* iii. 11.

Apiŏla. A town of Italy from whose spoils, taken by Tarquinius Superbus, the Capitolium at Rome was begun (Pliny, *H. N.* iii. 5).

Apion (Ἀπίων). (1) A Greek grammarian of the first century A.D., a pupil of Didymus, and president of the philological school at Alexandria. He also worked for a time at Rome under Tiberius and Claudius. A vain, boastful man, he travelled about the Greek cities, giving popular lectures on Homer. Of his many writings we have only fragments left. The glosses on Homer that bear his name are of later origin; on the other hand, the Homeric lexicon of the sophist Apollonius is based on his genuine Homeric glosses. His bitter complaint, *Against the Jews*, addressed to Caligula at the instance of the Alexandrians, is best known from Iosephus's noble reply to it. See Aul. Gell. v. 14; Sen. *Epist.* 38. (2) See PTOLEMAEUS.

Apis (Ἆπις). (1) Son of Phoroneus and Laodicê, king of Argos, from whom Peloponnesus, and more especially Argos, was called Apia (Pausan. ii. 5). (2) The sacred bull of Memphis, worshipped as a god among the Egyptians. There were certain signs by which he was recognized to be the god. Thus, the body must be black; there must be a square white spot upon the forehead, the figure of an eagle upon the back, a beetle-shaped knot under

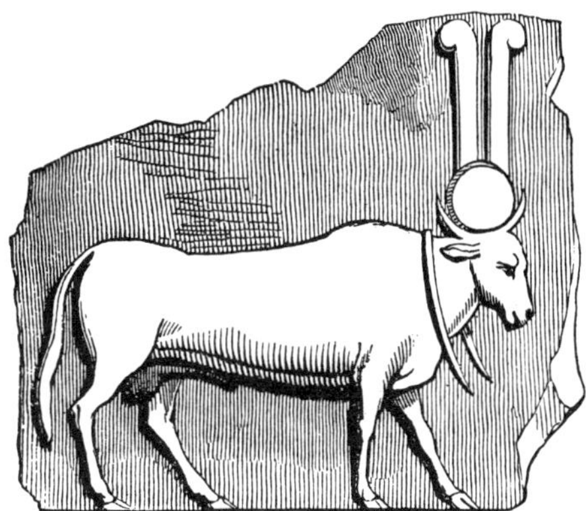

Figure of Apis. (From the Egyptian Monuments.)

the tongue, and a white crescent upon the right side. At Memphis he had a splendid residence, containing extensive walks and courts for his amusement. His birthday, which was celebrated every year, was a day of rejoicing for all Egypt. His death was a season of public mourning, which continued till another sacred bull was discovered by the priests. See OSIRIS.

Apisāon (Ἀπισάων). A Paeonian, the son of Hippasus, who aided Priam at Troy with an army, but was killed by Lycomedes (*Il.* xvii. 348).

Apium (σέλινον). Parsley.

Aplustrê (ἄφλαστον). A wooden ornament on the poop of a ship. See NAVIS.

Apobătes (ἀποβάτης). See DESULTORES.

Apocolocyntōsis (ἀποκολοκύντωσις). "Pumpkinification." A satire on the deification of the emperor Claudius, written after the death of that prince by the younger Seneca. It is the only good example remaining to us of the Satira Menippea (q. v.). Ed. by F. Bücheler (Berlin, 1882).

Apodectae (ἀποδέκται). "Receivers." Public officers at Athens, ten in number, whose principal duty it was to collect the ordinary taxes and distribute them to the separate branches of the administration which were entitled to them (Arist. *Pol.* vi. 8, 1).

Apodidraskinda (ἀποδιδρασκίνδα). The game of hide-and-seek, a favourite among the Greek children. It is represented in a painting found at Herculaneum. See Bekker, *Anecd.* p. 1353.

Apodyterium (ἀποδυτήριον). A room in the Roman bath-houses used for undressing. See BALNEAE.

Apogrăphê (ἀπογραφή). Literally, a "list or register;" but, in the language of the Attic courts, the terms ἀπογράφειν and ἀπογράφεσθαι had three separate applications. (1) Ἀπογραφή was used in reference to an accusation in public matters, more particularly when there were several defendants; the denunciation, the bill of indictment, and enumeration of the accused would in this case be termed apographe, and differ but little, if at all, from the ordinary γραφή. (2) It implied the making of a solemn protest or assertion before a magistrate, to the intent that it might be preserved by him till it was required to be given in evidence. (3) It was a specification of property, said to belong to the state, but actually in the possession of a private person; which specification was made with a view to the confiscation of such property to the state.

Apoikia (ἀποικία). See COLONIA.

Apokeryxis (ἀποκήρυξις). The formal act of disinheriting a son at Athens. See Demos. c. *Boeot. de Nom.* p. 1006, § 39.

Apoleipsis (ἀπόλειψις). See DIVORTIUM.

Apollināres Ludi. See LUDI.

Apollināris, SIDONIUS. See SIDONIUS.

Apollināris, SULPICIUS. See SULPICIUS.

Apollĭnis Promontorium. A promontory in North Africa, forming the west point of the Gulf of Carthage.

Apollo (Ἀπόλλων). Son of Zeus by Leto (Latona), who, according to the legend most widely current, bore him and his twin-sister Artemis at the foot of Mt. Cynthus, in the island of Delos. Apollo appears originally as a god of light, both in its beneficent and its destructive effects; and of light in general, not of the sun only, for to the early Greeks the deity that brought daylight was Helios, with whom it was not till afterwards that Apollo was identified. While the meaning of his name Apollo is uncertain, his epithets of *Phoebus* and *Lycius* clearly mark him as the bright, the life-giving, the former also meaning the pure, the holy; for, as the god of pure light, he is the enemy of darkness, with all its unclean, unhallowed brood. Again, not only the seventh day of the month, his birthday, but the first day of the month, i. e. of each new-born moon, was sacred to him, as it was to Ianus, the Roman god of light; and according to the view that prevailed in many seats of his worship, he withdrew in winter time either to Lycia, or to the Hyperboreans who dwell in perpetual light in the utmost north, and returned in spring to dispel the powers of winter with his beams. When the fable relates that immediately after his birth, with the first shot from his bow he slew the dragon Python (or Delphyné), a hideous offspring of Gaea and guardian of the Delphic oracle, what seems to be denoted must be the spring-god's victory over winter, that filled the land with marsh and mist. As the god of light, his festivals are all in spring or summer, and many of them still plainly reveal in certain features his original attributes. Thus the Delphinia, held at Athens in April, commemorated the calming of the wintry sea after the equinoctial gales, and the consequent reopening of navigation. As this feast was in honour of the god of spring, so was the Thargelia, held at Athens the next month, in honour of the god of summer. That the crops might ripen, he received first-fruits of them, and at the same time propitiatory gifts to induce him to avert the parching heat, so hurtful to fruits and men. About the time of the sun's greatest altitude (July and August), when the god displays his power, both for good and for harm, the Athenians offered him hecatombs, whence the first month of their year was named Hecatomboeon, and the Spartans held their Hyacinthia. (See HYACINTHUS.) In autumn, when the god was ripening the fruit of their gardens and plantations, and preparing for departure, they celebrated the Pyanepsia (q. v.), when they presented him with the first-fruits of harvest.

Apollo gives the crops prosperity, and protection not only against summer heat, but against blight, mildew, and the vermin that prey upon them, such as field-mice and grasshoppers. Hence he was known by special titles in some parts of Asia. He was also a patron of flocks and pastures, and was worshipped in many districts under a variety of names referring to the breeding of cattle. In the story of Hermes (q. v.) stealing his oxen, Apollo is himself the owner of a herd, which he gives up to his brother in exchange for the lyre invented by him. Other ancient legends speak of him as tending the flocks of Laomedon and Admetus, an act afterwards represented as a penalty for a fault. As a god of shepherds he makes love to the nymphs, to Daphné (q. v.), to Coronis (see AESCULAPIUS), and to Cyrené, the mother of Aristaeus, likewise a god of herds. Some forms of his worship and some versions of his story imply that Apollo, like his sister Artemis, was regarded as a protector of tender game and a slayer of rapacious beasts, especially of the wolf, the enemy of flocks, and himself a symbol of the god's power, that now sends mischief, and now averts it. Apollo promotes the health and well-being of man himself. As a god of prolific power, he was invoked at weddings; and as a nurse of tender manhood and trainer of manly youth, to him (as well as the fountain-nymphs) were consecrated the first offerings of the hair of the head. In gymnasia and palaestrae he was worshipped equally with Hermes and Heracles; for he gave power of endurance in boxing, with adroitness and fleetness of foot. As a warlike god and one helpful in fight, the Spartans paid him peculiar honours in their Carneia (q. v.), and in a measure the Athenians in their Boëdromia. Another Athenian festival, the Metageitnia, glorified him as the author of neighbourly union. In many places, but above all at Athens, he was worshipped as Agyieus, the god of streets and highways, whose rude symbol, a conical post with a pointed ending, stood by street-doors and in court-yards, to watch men's exit and entrance, to let in good and keep out evil, and was loaded by the inmates with gifts of honour, such as ribbons, wreaths of myrtle or bay, and the like.

At sea, as well as on land, Apollo was a guide and guardian, and there especially under the name Delphinius, taken from his friend and ally the dolphin, the symbol of the navigable sea. Under this character he was widely worshipped, for the most part with peculiar propitiatory rites, in seaports and on promontories, as that of Actium, and particularly at Athens, being also regarded as a leader of colonies. While he was Ἀλεξίκακος (averter of ills) in the widest sense, he proved his power most especially in times of sickness; for, being god of the hot season, and himself the sender of most epidemics and the dreaded plague, sweeping man swiftly away with his unerring shafts, he could also lend the most effectual aid; so that he and his son Asclepius were revered as the chief gods of healing. As a saviour from epidemics mainly, but also from other evils, the paean (q. v.) was sung in his honour.

In a higher sense also, Apollo was a healer and preserver. From an early time an ethical tinge was given to his purely physical attributes, and the god of light became a god of mental and moral purity, and therefore of order, justice, and legality in human life. As such, he, on the one hand, smote and spared not the insolent offender, Tityus, for instance, the Aloidae, the presumptuous Niobé, and the Greeks before Troy; but, on the other hand, to the guilt-laden soul, turning to him in penitence and supplication, he granted purification from the stain of crime (which was regarded as a disease clouding the mind and crushing the heart), and so he healed the spirit, and readmitted the outcast into civic life and religious fellowship. Of this he had himself set the pattern, when, after slaying the Delphian dragon, he fled from the land, did seven years' menial service to Admetus in atonement for the murder, and, when the time of penance was past, had himself purified in the sacred grove of bay-trees by the Thessalian temple; and not until then did he return to Delphi and enter on his office as prophet of Zeus. Therefore he exacts from all a recognition of the atoning power of penance, in the teeth of the old law of vengeance for blood, which only bred new murders and new guilt. The atoning rites propagated by Apollo's worship, particularly from Delphi, contributed largely to the spread of milder maxims of law, affecting not only individuals, but whole towns and countries. Even without special prompting, the people felt from time to time the need of purification and expiation; and hence certain expiatory rites had from of old been connected with his festivals.

The Pythian Apollo. (Audran, *Proportion du Corps Humain*, pl. 18.)

As the god of light who pierces through all darkness, Apollo is the god of divination, which, however, has in his case a purely ethical significance; for he, as prophet and minister of his father Zeus, makes known his will to men, and helps to further his government in the world. He always declares the truth; but the limited mind of man cannot always grasp the meaning of his sayings. He is the patron of every kind of prophecy, but most especially of that which he imparts through human instruments, chiefly women, while in a state of ecstasy. Great as was the number of his oracles in Greece and Asia, all were eclipsed in fame and importance by that of Delphi (q. v.).

Apollo exercises an elevating and inspiring influence on the mind as god of music, which, though not belonging to him alone any more than atonement and prophecy, was yet pre-eminently his province. In Homer he is represented only as a player on the lyre, while song is the province of the Muses; but in course of time he grows to be the god, as they are the goddesses, of song and poetry, and is therefore Μουσαγέτης (leader of the Muses) as well as master of the choral dance, which goes with music and song. And as the friend of all that beautifies life he is intimately associated with the Graces.

Belvedere Apollo. (Rome, Vatican Museum.)

Standing in these manifold relations to nature and man, Apollo at all times held a prominent position in the religion of the Greeks; and as early as Homer his name is coupled with those of Zeus and Athené, as if between them the three possessed the sum total of divine power. His worship was diffused equally over all the regions in which Greeks were settled; but from remote antiquity he had been the chief god of the Dorians, who were also the first to raise him into a type of moral excellence. The two chief centres of his worship were the island of Delos, his birthplace, where, at his magnificent temple standing by the sea, were held every five years the festive games called Delia, to which the Greek states sent solemn embassies; and Delphi, with its oracle and numerous festivals. (See PYTHIA; THEOXENIA.) Foremost among the seats of his worship in Asia was Patara in Lycia, with a famous oracle.

To the Romans, Apollo became known in the reign of their last king, Tarquinius Superbus, the first Roman who consulted the Delphic oracle, and who also acquired the Sibylline Books (q. v.). By the influence of these writings the worship of Apollo soon became so naturalized among them that in B.C. 431 they built a temple to him as god of healing, from which the expiatory processions (see SUPPLICATIONES) prescribed in the Sibylline Books used to set out. In the Lectisternia (q. v.), first instituted in B.C. 399, Apollo occupies the foremost place. In B.C. 212, during the agony of

Apollo Musagetes. (Osterley Denkm. der alten Kunst, taf. 32.)

the Second Punic War, the Ludi Apollinares were, in obedience to an oracular response, established in honour of him. He was made one of the chief gods of Rome by Augustus, who believed himself to be under his peculiar protection, and ascribed the victory of Actium to his aid; hence he enlarged the old temple of Apollo on that promontory, and decorated it with a portion of the spoils. He also renewed the games held near it, previously every two years, afterwards every four, with gymnastic and artistic contests and regattas on the sea. At Rome he reared a splendid new temple to him near his own house on the Palatine, and transferred the Ludi Saeculares (q. v.) to him and Diana.

The manifold symbols of Apollo correspond with the multitude of his attributes. The commonest is either the lyre or the bow, according as he was conceived as the god of song or as the far-hitting archer. The Delphian diviner, Pythian Apollo, is indicated by the tripod, which was also the favourite offering at his altars. Among plants, the bay, used for purposes of expiation, was early sacred to him. (See DAPHNÉ.) It was planted round his temples, and plaited into garlands of victory at the Pythian Games. The palm-tree was also sacred to him, for it was under a palm-tree that he was born in Delos. Among animals, the wolf, the dolphin, the snow-white and musical swan, the hawk, raven, crow, and snake were under his special protection; the last four in connection with his prophetic functions.

In ancient art he was represented as a long-haired but beardless youth, of tall yet muscular build, and handsome features. Images of him were as abundant as his worship was extensive: there was scarcely an artist of antiquity who did not try his hand upon some incident in the story of Apollo. The ideal type of this god seems to have been fixed chiefly by Praxiteles and Scopas. The most famous statue preserved of him is the Apollo Belvedere in the Vatican, which represents him either as fighting with the Pythian dragon, or with his ægis frightening back the foes who threaten to storm his sanctuary. Other great works, as the Apollo Musagetes in the Vatican, probably from the hand of Scopas, show him as a Citharoedus in the long Ionian robe, or nude. The Apollo Sauroctonus (lizard-killer), copied from a bronze statue by Praxiteles, is especially celebrated for its beauty. It represents a delicate youthful figure leaning against a tree, dart in hand, ready to stab a lizard that is crawling up the tree. It is preserved in bronze at the Villa Albani in Rome, and in marble at Paris.

Apollodōrus (Ἀπολλόδωρος). (1) A Greek poet of the New Comedy, born at Carystus, between B.C. 300 and 260. He wrote forty-seven plays, and won five victories. From him Terence borrowed the plots of his *Phormio* and *Hecyra*. (2) A Greek grammarian and historian of Athens, about B.C. 140, a pupil of Aristarchus and the Stoic Panaetius. He was a most prolific writer on grammar, mythology, geography, and history. Some of his works were written in iambic senarii—e. g. a geography, and the *Chronica*, a condensed enumeration of the most important data in history and literature from the fall of Troy, which he places in B.C. 1183, down to his own time—undoubtedly the most important of ancient works on the subject. Besides fragments, we have under his name a book entitled *Bibliotheca*, a great storehouse of mythological material from the oldest theogonies down to Theseus, and, with all its faults of arrangement and treatment, a valuable aid to our knowledge of Greek mythology. Yet there are grounds for doubting whether it is from his hand at all, or whether it is even an extract from his great work, *On the Gods*, in twenty-four books. A good edition is Hercher's (Berlin, 1874). (3) A Greek painter of Athens, about B.C. 420, the first who graduated light and shade in his pictures, whence he received the name of SCIAGRĂPHUS (shadow-painter). This invention entitled him to be regarded as the founder of a new style, which aimed at producing illusion by pictorial means, and which was carried on further by his younger contemporary Zeuxis (Pliny, *H. N.* xxxv. 60). (4) A Greek architect of Damascus, who lived for a time at Rome, where, among other things, he built Trajan's Forum and Trajan's Column. He was first banished and then put to death under Hadrian, A.D. 129, having incurred that emperor's anger by the freedom of his criticisms. We have a work by him on engines of war, addressed to Hadrian.

Apollonia (Ἀπολλωνία). (1) An important town in Illyria, not far from the mouth of the Aoüs, and sixty stadia from the sea. It was founded by the Corinthians and Corcyraeans, and was equally celebrated as a place of commerce and of learning. Many distinguished Romans, among others the young Octavius, afterwards the emperor Augustus, pursued their studies here. Persons travelling from Italy to Greece and the East usually landed either at Apollonia or Dyrrhacium. (2) A town in Macedonia, on the Via Egnatia, between Thessalonica and Amphipolis, and south of the lake of Bolbé. (3) A town in Thrace, on the Black Sea, a colony of Miletus, which had a celebrated temple of Apollo, from which Lucullus carried away a colossus of this god, and erected it on the Capitol at Rome. (4) A castle or fortified town of the Locri Ozolae, near Naupactus. (5) A town on the northern coast of Sicily. (6) A town in Bithynia, on the lake Apolloniatis, through which the river Rhyndacus flows. (7) A town in Cyrenaica, and the harbour of Cyrené, one of the five towns of the Pentapolis, in Libya; it was the birthplace of Eratosthenes (q. v.).

Apollonia (Ἀπολλώνια). A propitiatory festival solemnized at Sicyon in honour of Apollo and Artemis. See Pausan. ii. 7, § 7.

Apollōnis (Ἀπολλωνίς). A city in Lydia, between Pergamus and Sardis, named after Apollonis, the mother of King Eumenes (q. v.).

Apollonius (Ἀπολλώνιος). (1) APOLLONIUS RHODIUS. A Greek scholar and epic poet of the Alexandrian Age, born at Alexandria about B.C. 260. A pupil of Callimachus, he wrote a long epic, *Argonautica*, in four books, in which, departing from his master's taste for the learned and artificial, he aimed at all the simplicity of Homer. The party of Callimachus rejected the poem, and Apollonius retired in disgust to Rhodes, where his labours as a rhetorician and his newly revised poem won him hearty recognition and even admission to citizenship, whence his surname. Afterwards, returning to Alexandria, he recited his poem once more, and this time with universal applause, so that Ptolemy Epiphanes, in B.C. 196, appointed him to succeed

Eratosthenes as librarian. He probably died during the tenure of this office. His epic poem, which has survived, has a certain simplicity, though falling far short of the naturalness and beauty of Homer. Its uniform mediocrity often makes it positively tedious, though it is constructed with great care, especially in its versification. By the Romans it was much prized, and more than once imitated, as by Varro Atacinus and Valerius Flaccus. A valuable collection of scholia upon it testifies the esteem in which it was held by the learned of old. A good edition is that by Seaton, 1888.

(2) APOLLONIUS OF TRALLES. A Greek sculptor of the school of Rhodes, and joint author with his countryman Tauriscus of the celebrated Dircé group. (See ANTIOPÉ.) Among other artists of the name, the worthiest of mention is APOLLONIUS OF ATHENS, of the first century B.C. From his hand is the Heracles, now only a torso, preserved in the Belvedere at Rome.

(3) APOLLONIUS OF PERGA, in Pamphylia. A Greek mathematician called "the Geometer," who lived at Pergamus and Alexandria in the first century B.C., and wrote a work on Conic Sections in eight books, of which we have only the first four in the original — the fifth, sixth, and seventh in an Arabic translation, and the eighth in extracts. See Schömann, *Apollonius von Perga* (1878).

(4) APOLLONIUS OF TYĂNA, in Cappadocia, the most celebrated of the Neo-Pythagoreans, lived after the middle of the first century A.D. By a severely ascetic life on the supposed principles of Pythagoras, and by pretended miracles, he obtained such a hold upon the multitude that he was worshipped as a god, and set up as a rival to Christ. The account of his life by the elder Philostratus (q. v.) is more romance than history, and offers little to build upon. Having received his philosophical education, and lived in the temple of Asclepius at Aegae till his twentieth year, he divided his patrimony among the poor, and roamed all over the world; he was even said to have reached India and the sources of the Nile. Twice he lived at Rome: first under Nero, until the expulsion of the philosophers; and again in Domitian's reign, when he had to answer a charge of conspiring against the emperor. Smuggled out of Rome during his trial, he continued his life as a wandering preacher of morals and worker of marvels for some years longer, and is said to have died at a great age, the master of a school at Ephesus. Of his alleged writings, eighty-five letters have alone survived. See the work by Pettersch (Berlin, 1879); and *Apollonius Tyanensis* by Göttsching (1889).

(5) APOLLONIUS DYSCŎLUS ("the Surly"). A Greek scholar of Alexandria, where he had received his education, and where he ended his days a member of the Museum, after having laboured as a teacher at Rome under Antoninus Pius, about A.D. 140. He is the father of scientific Grammar, having been the first to reduce it to systematic form. His extant works are the treatises on Pronouns, Adverbs, Conjunctions, and the Syntax of the parts of speech, in four books. He was followed especially by the Latin grammarians, above all by Priscian. See Skrzeczka, *Die Lehre des Apollonius Dyscolus* (1869); and the article PRISCIANUS.

(6) APOLLONIUS THE SOPHIST, of Alexandria. His precise date A.D. is unknown. He was the author of an extant lexicon of Homeric glosses, based on Apion's lost writings. See GLOSSA.

(7) APOLLONIUS OF TYRE, the hero of a Greek romance now lost, composed in Asia Minor, in the third century A.D., on the model of the Ephesian *History of Xenophon*. We have a free Latin version made by a Christian, about the sixth century, probably in Italy, which was much read in the Middle Ages, and translated into Anglo-Saxon, English, French, Italian, Middle-Greek, and German, in prose and verse. Its materials are used in the pseudo-Shakespearian drama of *Pericles, Prince of Tyre*. See Simrock, *Quellen des Shakespeare* (Bonn, 1872); and Hagen, *Der Roman von König Apollonius in seinen verschiedenen Bearbeitungen* (1878).

Apologetĭcum. (1) A treatise of Tertullian composed A.D. 199, addressed to the *praesides imperii*, and containing a defence of the Christians against the charge of disloyalty to the State and to the emperor. The work is perhaps the most vigorous and original of any that its author wrote. Good editions are those of Oehler (Halle, 1849); Kayser (Paderborn, 1865); and of Migne (Paris, 1870). (2) A poem in 1054 lines, by Commodianus (q. v.), composed A.D. 249, and entitled *Carmen Apologeticum adversus Iudaeos et Gentes*. It is written in hexameters that for the most part set all prosody at defiance, and, like English hexameters, follow the accentuation of the popular pronunciation of the day.

Apologia (ἀπολογία). The title of Plato's defence of Socrates, put into the mouth of the latter, and doubtless giving the substance of the speech made by the philosopher before his judges. See PLATO; SOCRATES.

Apomnemoneumăta (ἀπομνημονεύματα). "Reminiscences." The Greek title of Xenophon's memoirs of Socrates, better known by their Latin title *Memorabilia* (q. v.).

Apŏni or **Apŏnus Fons.** Warm medicinal springs, near Patavium, hence called Aquae Patavinae, and much frequented by the sick.

Apopempsis (ἀπόπεμψις). See DIVORTIUM.

Apophăsis (ἀπόφασις). Literally, "a declaration." (1) The proclamation at Athens of the decision which the majority of the judges came to at the end of a trial, and was apparently made by a herald under the direction of the presiding magistrate. The decisions of arbitrators (διαιτηταί) were called by the same name. (2) Such proclamations being generally made on court days, ἀπόφασις came to mean the day on which the trial took place. (3) The word was also employed to indicate the account of a person's property, which was obliged to be given when an *antidosis* (q. v.) was demanded.

Apophŏra (ἀποφορά). This term, which properly means "produce or profit" of any kind, was used at Athens to signify the profit which accrued to masters from their slaves. It thus signified the sum which slaves paid to their masters when they laboured on their own account; and the sum which masters received when they let out their slaves on hire, either for the mines or for any other kind of labour; and also the money which was paid by the state for the use of the slaves who served in the fleet (Xen. *Rep. Ath.* i. 11). The term *apophora* was also applied to the money which was paid by the allied states to Sparta, for the purpose of carrying on the war against the Persians. When Athens acquired the supremacy, these moneys were called φόροι.

Apophorēta. (1) (ἀποφόρητα). Presents which were given to friends at the end of an entertainment, to carry home with them (Petron. 56). Although the name is Greek, the custom is Roman, for Athenaeus expressly tells us that when Cleopatra presented to Antony and his staff the gold and silver dinner service which they had been using at a banquet in Cilicia, she was imitating a Roman usage. Book xiv. of Martial consists of an introductory epigram and 222 distichs, each describing and designed to accompany one of these presents, which range from nuts to works of art and slaves. The first epigram speaks of the Saturnalia as the special time for their distribution. They were also given at weddings (Juv. vi. 203, schol.). (2) (ἀποφορήτη). A utensil mentioned by Isidore as a kind of plate.

Apophrădes Hemĕrai (ἀποφράδες ἡμέραι). Unlucky or unfortunate days (*dies nefasti*), on which no public business, nor any important affairs of any kind, were transacted at Athens. Such were the last three days but one of every month, and the twenty-fifth day of the month Thargelion, on which the Plynteria were celebrated.

Apophthegmăta (ἀποφθέγματα). (1) A collection of pithy sayings gathered together by Cato the Elder. (2) A similar collection made by Iulius Caesar, and spoken of by Suetonius as *Dicta Collectanea*. See Suet. *Iul.* 56; and the article PROVERBIUM.

Aporrhaxis (ἀπόρραξις). The game of "bounce-ball." See PILA.

Aporrhesĕos Diké (ἀπορρήσεως δίκη). The term ἀπόρρησις, "prohibition," has a technical meaning in Attic law in connection with the sale of landed property. Public notice was required to be given of every such sale, for the protection of mortgagees and other creditors; and any one having a claim upon the estate might interdict the sale by an ἀπόρρησις. The vendor, on the other hand, had his remedy against fraudulent or malicious obstruction in an action for damages, called ἀπορρήσεως δίκη.

Aporrhēta (τὰ ἀπόρρητα). Literally, "things forbidden." The word has two peculiar, but widely different, acceptations in the Attic usage. In one of these it implies contraband goods—i. e. those of which the export (not the import) was prohibited. The chief of these were corn (of which there was a steady importation) and articles used in the building and equipment of the fleet. An enumeration of these at different periods of Athenian history is given by Böckh (*P. E.* pp. 53, 54).

In the other sense, it denotes various contumelious epithets, from the application of which both the living and the dead were protected by special laws (Meier, *Att. Process*, p. 482).

Aposphragisma (ἀποσφράγισμα). The device on a signet-ring. See ANULUS.

Apostŏleis (ἀποστολεῖς). Ten commissioners, chosen out of the body of Athenian citizens without distinction of tribes, in order to secure the efficiency and promptitude of a naval expedition (ἀπόστολος) which had been voted. They were thus an extraordinary authority, appointed by decree of the people (Böckh, *Urkunden über das Seewesen*, p. 466; Hudtwalcker, *De Diaetet.* p. 71; Meier and Schömann, *Att. Prozess*, p. 112, with Lipsius's note in the new ed.).

Apothēca (ἀποθήκη). A storehouse or magazine (Thuc. vi. 97) for books (Luc. *Indoct.* 5); a burial-place (id. *Contempl.* 22); but especially a place in the upper part of the house in which the Romans kept their wine in *amphorae*. It was usually above the *fumarium*, since it was thought that the passage of the smoke through the room tended greatly to improve the flavour of the wine. See CELLA; VINUM.

Apotheōsis (ἀποθέωσις, *consecratio*). The enrolment of a human being among the gods, of which the Greeks have an instance as early as Homer, but only in the single case of Leucothea. The oldest notion was that of a bodily removal; then arose the idea of the mortal element being purged away by fire, as in the case of Heracles. There was a kind of deification which consisted in the decreeing of heroic honours to distinguished men after death, which was done from the time of the Peloponnesian War onwards, even in the case of living men. (See HEROS.) The successors of Alexander the Great—both the Seleucidae, and still more the Ptolemies—caused themselves to be worshipped as gods. Of the Romans, whose legend told of the translation of Aeneas and Romulus into heaven, Iulius Caesar was the first who claimed divine honours, if not by building temples to himself, yet by setting his statue among the gods in every sanctuary at Rome and in the Empire, and by having a special flamen assigned to him. The belief in his divinity was confirmed by the comet that shone several months after his death, as long as his funeral games lasted; and under the Second Triumvirate he was formally installed among the deities of Rome, as Divus Iulius, by a decree of the Senate and people. His adopted son and successor Octavianus persistently declined any offer of public worship, but he accepted the title of Augustus (the

Apotheosis of Antoninus Pius and Faustina. (From the Pedestal of the Column of Antoninus Pius.)

consecrated), and allowed his person to be adored in the provinces. On his death the Senate decreed divine honours to him under the title of Divus Augustus, the erection of a temple, the founding of special games, and the establishment of a peculiar priesthood. After this, admission to the number of the Divi, as the deified emperors were called, became a prerogative of the imperial dignity. It was, however, left dependent on a resolution of the Senate, moved in honour of the deceased emperor by his successor. Hence it was not every emperor who obtained it, nor did consecration itself always lead to a permanent worship. Empresses were often consecrated, the first being Augustus's wife Livia as Diva Augusta, and even other members of the imperial house.

The ceremony of Apotheosis, used from the time of Augustus, was the following: After the passing of the Senate's decree a waxen image of the dead, whose body lay hidden below, was exhibited for seven days on an ivory bed of state in the palace, covered with gold-embroidered coverlets; then the bier was borne by knights and senators amid a brilliant retinue, down the Via Sacra to the ancient Forum, where the funeral oration was delivered, and thence to the Campus Martius, where it was deposited in the second of the four stories of a richly decorated funeral pile of pyramidal shape. When the last honours had been performed, the pile was set on fire; and, as it burned up, an eagle soared from the topmost story into the sky, as a symbol of the ascending soul. See Herodian, iv. 3; and the articles AUGUSTALES; MANES.

Apotimēma (ἀποτίμημα). See DOS.

Apotympanismos (ἀποτυμπανισμός). Beating to death with sticks, cudgels, or clubs (τὸ τυμπάνῳ ἀποκτεῖναι, ὅπερ ἐστὶ ξύλον ὥσπερ ῥόπαλον, *Lex. Rhet.* p. 198) which is mentioned as a mode of execution at Athens and elsewhere. See FUSTUARIUM.

Apparitōres. The general name for the free attendants of the magistrates at Rome, as distinguished from the *servi publici*. They received wages (*merces*) from the public treasury, and had places of their own in the theatre and circus (Tac. *Ann.* xvi. 12), doubtless near the magistrates on whom they waited. They were divided into five classes—the ACCENSI, LICTORES, PRAECONES, SCRIBAE, and VIATORES, treated in separate articles.

Appellatio. The Latin term for an appeal to a magistrate to veto the decision of an equal or inferior magistrate. Thus a consul could be appealed to against the other consul, and against all other magistrates except the tribunes; but a tribune against both his colleagues and all other magistrates whatsoever. On the other hand, the *provocatio* (q. v.) under the Republic was an appeal from a magistrate's sentence to the people as supreme judge. During the imperial period the two processes run into one, for the emperor held united in his person both the supreme judicial function and the plenary power of all magistrates, particularly the tribunician veto, so that an appeal to him was at once an *appellatio* and a *provocatio*. This appeal, in our sense of the word, was only permitted in important cases; it had to be made within a short time after sentence was passed, and always addressed to the authority next in order, so that it only reached the emperor if no intermediate authority was competent. If the result was that the disputed verdict was neither quashed nor awarded, but confirmed, the appellant had to pay a fine. As the power of life and death rested with the emperor and the Senate alone, governors of provinces were bound to send to Rome any citizen appealing on a capital charge. See EPHESIS.

Appiānus (Ἀππιανός). A Greek historian of Alexandria, who lived about the middle of the second century A.D. At first he pursued the calling of an advocate at Rome; in later life, on the recommendation of his friend the rhetorician Fronto, he obtained from Antoninus Pius the post of an imperial procurator in Egypt. He wrote an extensive work on the development of the Roman Empire from the earliest times down to Trajan, consisting of a number of special histories of the several periods and the several lands and peoples till the time when they fell under the Roman dominion. Of the twenty-four books of which it originally consisted, only eleven are preserved complete besides the Preface: *Spain* (book vi.), *Hannibal* (vii.), *Carthage* (viii.), *Syria* (xi.), *Mithridates* (xii.), the *Roman Civil Wars* (xiii.-xvii.), and *Illyria* (xxiii.), the rest being lost altogether or only surviving in fragments. Appianus's style is plain and bald, even to dryness, and his historical point of view is purely Roman. The book is a mere compilation, and is disfigured by many oversights and blunders, especially in chronology; nevertheless the use made by the writer of lost authorities lends it considerable worth, and for the history of the Civil Wars it is positively invaluable. The best text is that in Bekker's edition, 2 vols. (Leipzig, 1853).

Appias. A nymph of the Appian Well in the Forum of Iulius Caesar, near the temple of Venus Genetrix, and surrounded by statues of nymphs called Appiades—a name also given to prostitutes living in that vicinity (Ovid, *A. A.* ii. 452).

Appia Via. See VIAE.

Applicatiōnis Ius. See EXSILIUM.

Apries (Ἀπρίης). An Egyptian king, the Pharaoh-Hophra of the Old Testament, who succeeded his father Psammis and reigned B.C. 595-570, being then dethroned and put to death by Amasis (q. v.) (Herod. ii. 161).

Aprosklētos Diké (ἀπρόσκλητος δίκη). If there were insufficient or fraudulent service of the summons (πρόσκλησις) in the case of a suit, the suit was called ἀπρόσκλητος, and dismissed by the magistrate (Dem. *c. Nicostr.* p. 1251, § 15). See DIKÉ; PROSKLESIS.

Aprostasiou Graphé (ἀπροστασίου γραφή). An action at Athens, falling under the jurisdiction of the polemarch, which was brought against those resident aliens who had neglected to provide themselves with a patron (προστάτης). It is probable that the aliens' tax was regularly paid through the προστάτης, and that he was responsible for it; and in that case the default of payment would of itself prove neglect to comply with the provisions of the law. See Meier, *Att. Process*, p. 315.

Apsīnes (Ἀψίνης). A Greek rhetorician of Gadara, who taught at Athens in the first half of the third century A.D., and wrote a valuable treatise on rhetoric, and also a work on the questions usually discussed in the schools of the rhetoricians. These two treatises are printed in the *Rhetores Graeci*, by Walz, ix. p. 534 foll.

Apsis. See ABSIS.

Apsus (Ἄψος). A river in Illyria, flowing into the Ionian Sea (Lucan, v. 461).

Apsȳchon Diké (ἀψυχων δίκη). An action against inanimate objects (ἄψυχα) which had caused the death of a human being. It thus somewhat resembled the English law of deodand, lately abolished. It was tried in the court of the Prytaneum, and, according to Schömann, partook more of the nature of a religious ceremony than a judicial proceeding. If the instruments with which a murder had been committed were captured, and not the murderer himself, these, after the ephetae had pronounced their sentence, were conveyed out of the country by the phylobasileis, or presidents of the four old-Ionic tribes. In the same way were treated such things as had accidentally caused the death of any one. Animals likewise, by which any one had been killed, were here condemned to death, and then conveyed out of the country (Pollux, viii. 111, 120; Dem. *c. Aristocr.* p. 645, § 89; Schömann, *Antiq.* i. 470, E. T.; cf. Plat. *Leg.* ix. 873 E).

Apsyrtus (Ἄψυρτος). See ABSYRTUS.

Aptĕra (Ἄπτερα). A city of Crete about eighty stadia from Cydonia. Its name was said to be derived from the result of a contest in music held at this place between the Sirens and the Muses, when the former, being defeated, were so affected that their wings dropped from their shoulders (Steph. Byzant. s. v. Ἄπτερα).

Apuāni. A Ligurian people, subdued by the Romans and transferred to Samnium in B.C. 180.

Apuleiae Leges. See LEX.

Apuleius, LUCIUS. A Roman writer of the African Period, born at Madaura, in Numidia, about A.D. 130. Having been educated at Carthage, he went to Athens to study philosophy, especially that of Plato; later, he travelled far and wide, everywhere obtaining initiation into the mysteries. For some time he lived in Rome as an advocate. After returning to Africa, he married a lady considerably older than himself, the mother of a friend, Aemilia Pudentilla, whereupon her kinsmen charged him with having won the rich widow's hand by magic, and of having contrived the death of her son—a charge to which he replied with much wit in his oration *De Magia* (earlier than A.D. 161). He afterwards settled down at Carthage, and thence made excursions through Africa, delivering orations or lectures. Of the rest of his life and the year of his death nothing is known. Beside the apology above-mentioned, and a few rhetorical and philosophic writings, another work, his chief one, also survives, which was composed at a ripe age, with hints borrowed from a book of Lucian's. This is a satirical and fantastic moral romance, *Metamorphoseon Libri XI.* (*de Asino Aureo*), the adventures of one Lucius, who is transformed into an ass, and under that disguise has the amplest opportunities of observing, undetected, the preposterous doings of mankind. Then, enlightened by this experience, and with the enchantment taken off him by admission into the mysteries of Osiris, he becomes quite a new man. Of the many episodes interwoven into the story, the most interesting is the beautiful allegorical fairy tale of *Cupid and Psyche*, so much used by later poets and artists. Throughout the book Apuleius paints the moral and religious conditions of his time with much humour and in life-like colours, although his language, while clever, is often affected, bombastic, and disfigured by obsolete and provincial phrases. The *editio princeps* is that published at Rome in 1469; and the most elaborate edition remains that of F. Oudendorp (Leyden, 1786–1823). The *Cupid and Psyche* was translated in 1566 by Adlington, whose version was reprinted (London, 1887), with an introduction by Andrew Lang. Of the *Golden Ass*, as a whole, there is an English translation by Sir G. Head (1851), and of the whole of Apuleius (1853). The best edition of the entire works is that by G. F. Hildebrand (Leipzig, 1842). O. Jahn has edited the *Cupid and Psyche* separately (Leipzig, 1856).

Apuleius Saturnīnus. See SATURNINUS.

Apulia. A district which included, in its widest signification, the whole of the southeast of Italy from the river Frento to the promontory Iapygium. In its narrower sense it was the country east of Samnium, on both sides of the Aufidus, the Daunia and Peucetia of the Greeks; the southeast part was called Calabria by the Romans. The Greeks gave the name of Daunia to the north part of the country from the Frento to the Aufidus, of Peucetia to the country from the Aufidus to Tarentum and Brundusium, and of Iapygia or Messapia to the whole of the remaining southern part; though they sometimes included under Iapygia all Apulia in its widest meaning. The country was very fertile, especially in the neighbourhood of Tarentum, and the mountains afforded excellent pasturage. The population was of a mixed nature: they were for the most part of Illyrian origin, and are said to have settled in the country under the guidance of Iapyx, Daunius, and Peucetius, three sons of an Illyrian king, Lycaon. Subsequently many towns were founded by Greek colonists. The Apulians joined the Samnites against the Romans, and became subject to the latter on the conquest of the Samnites.

Aqua. See AQUAE DUCTUS.

Aquae. The name given by the Romans to many mineral springs and bathing resorts. (1) CUTILIAE, mineral springs in Samnium, near the ancient town of Cutilia, which perished in early times, and east of Reatĕ. There was a celebrated lake in its neighbourhood, with a floating island, which was regarded as the umbilicus or centre of Italy. Vespasian died at this place. (2) PATAVĪNAE. See APONI FONS. (3) SEXTIAE (Aix), a Roman colony in Gallia Narbonensis, founded by Sextius Calvinus, B.C. 122; its mineral waters were long celebrated. Near this place Marius defeated the Teutoni, B.C. 102. (4) STATIELLAE, a town of the Statielli in Liguria, celebrated for its warm baths. (5) MATTIĂCAE, a town of the Mattiaci in Germany, now Wiesbaden. (6) BADĒNAE, a German town, now Baden. (7) PANNONĬCAE, a town in Pannonia, now Baden in Austria.

Aquae Ductus (ὑδραγωγία, ὑδραγωγεῖον, ὑπόνομος). A water-conduit or aqueduct.

(1) GREEK. As nearly all the ancient aqueducts now remaining are of Roman construction, it has been generally imagined that works of this description were entirely unknown to the Greeks. This, however, is an error, since some are mentioned by Pausanias. The Greeks, in fact, at a very early period, had some powers of hydraulic engineering, as is shown by the drainage tunnels of the lake Copaïs, and the similar works of Phaeax at Agrigentum; and we have an instance of a channel for water being carried through a mountain to supply the city of Samos. The height of the mountain was 150 orgyiae (900 Greek feet); the length of the tunnel was seven stadia (seven eighths of a Roman mile, or about 1420 yards); its section was a square of eight Greek feet. The actual channel for the water was cut below this, and was, if the text is right, thirty Greek feet deep and three wide; the water passed through pipes from a copious spring, and was thus brought to the city (Herod. iii. 60). There are still remains of this tunnel. Müller conjectures that the work was one of those executed by Polycrates. Indeed, many of the Greek water-works appear to date from the age of the Tyrants. See EMISSARIUM.

But from early times, the Greeks, where the needs of a city called for it, constructed underground conduits following the undulations of the surface or carried through the hills by tunnels, and closely resembling the earlier Oriental aqueducts, of which they were probably imitations. Thus the conduit which supplied the acropolis of Thebes was attributed to Cadmus, and the canalization of the mountain torrents round Argos to Danaüs. The Greek aqueducts were usually rectangular channels cut in the rock or constructed of solid masonry, but in the Troad we have an instance of one composed of earthenware pipes (Hahn, *Ausgrab. auf der Homer. Pergamus*)

At Athens the rocky part of the city was dependent on cisterns. Two conduits entered the city on the east from the upper course of the Ilissus, which lower down was canalized, and part of its water went to supplement the *Enneakrounos*, below which an underground conduit ran from the river, repeatedly crossing under its bed, and accessible to use by shafts, and finally carried to the Piraeus. Below the Enneakrounos, a stream from Hymettus was carried over the Ilissus into the city. Later, two large conduits were constructed from Lycabettus on the east and west of that mountain. A system of canals from the Cephissus served to irrigate the olive-woods (E. Curtius, *VII Karten von Athen*). Finally, Hadrian, near the end of his reign, built an aqueduct of the Roman type, drawing its water from the Cephissus. Among the finest and best preserved of Greek aqueducts are those of Syracuse, which Thucydides (vi. 100) tells us were laid under ground to bring drinking-water into the city, and which are still in use.

(2) ROMAN. The Romans were in a very different position, with respect to the supply of water, from most of the Greek cities. They at first had recourse to the Tiber and to wells sunk in the city; but the water obtained from those sources was very unwholesome, and must soon have proved insufficient. Consequently, to supply the demands of the public baths and the fullers, and later of the growing population, and later still of the *naumachiae*, they had recourse to public works in order to bring pure water from a considerable distance—from the hills, in fact, which surround the Campagna. The date of the first aqueduct is assigned by Frontinus to the year A.U.C. 441, or B.C. 312 (*De Aquaed. Urb. Rom.* 4); and the number of aqueducts was gradually increased, partly at the public expense and partly by the munificence of individuals, till, in the time of Procopius, they amounted to fourteen; and, even before they were all erected, they might well excite the admiration which Pliny expresses with respect to the Claudian aqueduct (*H. N.* xxxvi. § 123). The Roman aqueducts are among the most magnificent structures of antiquity. Some of these were constructed underground; others, latterly almost all, conveyed the water, often for long distances, in covered channels of brick or stone, over lofty arcades stretching straight through hill and valley. They started from a well-head (*caput aquarum*) and ended in a reservoir (*castellum*), out of which the water ran in Rome into three chambers, lying one above another, the lowest chamber sending it through leaden or clay pipes into the public fountains and basins, the middle one into the great bathing establishments, the uppermost into private houses. Private citizens paid a tax for the water they obtained from these public sources. Under the Republic the construction and repair of aqueducts devolved upon the censors, and their management upon the aediles, but from the time of Augustus, upon a special *curator aquarum*, assisted by a large staff of pipe-masters, fountain-masters, inspectors (*aquarii*), and others, taken partly from the number of the public slaves. The amount of water brought into Rome by its numerous aqueducts, the first of which, the Aqua Appia, was projected B.C. 312, may be estimated from the fact that the four still in use are quite sufficient to supply all the houses, fountains, etc., of modern Rome. In the time of Frontinus (A.D. 97) there were in Rome nine aqueducts, of which four were constructed in the time of the Republic and five under the Empire. These were as follows:

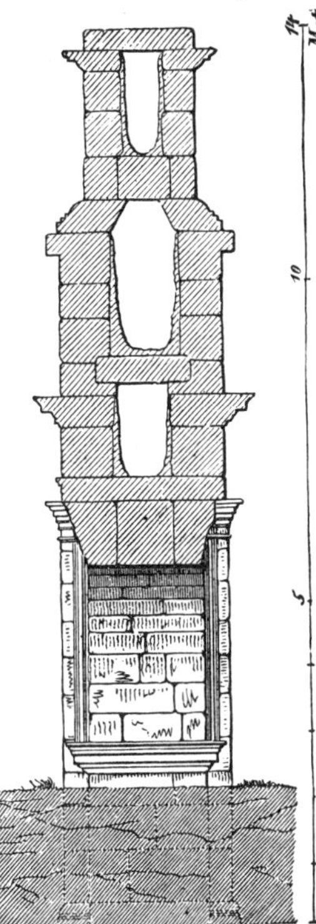

Section of the Aqua Marcia, Tepula, and Iulia, near the Porta San Lorenzo

(1) The AQUA APPIA, begun by the censor Appius Claudius Caecus (q. v.) in B.C. 312. (See Middleton, *Ancient Rome*, p. 466.) Its length was 11,190 *passus*, of which 11,130 were carried under the earth, and the remaining sixty *passus* on arches, from the Porta Capena to the Porta Trigemina, where it ended. See Livy, ix. 29.

(2) The ANIO VETUS, commenced by the censor Manius Curius Dentatus in B.C. 272, the expense of its construction being defrayed out of the spoils taken from Pyrrhus. Its source was in the river Anio, above Tibur, ten Roman miles from the city; but, because of its windings, the actual length was forty-three miles, of which length only 221 *passus* were above ground. There are remains of this aqueduct near the Porta Maggiore.

(3) The AQUA MARCIA, built by the praetor Q. Marcius Rex in B.C. 144, at the cost of 180,000,000 sesterces. It commenced three miles south of the Via Valeria, thirty-six miles from Rome, and its length was some 61,710 *passus*, of which 7463 were above ground, 6935 being on arches. Vitruvius speaks of the excellence of its water as proverbial (viii. 3, § 1). It is still in use.

(4) The AQUA TEPŬLA, built by the censors Cn. Servilius Caepio and L. Cassius Longinus in B.C. 127. It commenced two miles to the right of the tenth mile-stone on the Via Latina. Its water was slightly warm (*tepida*), hence the name *tepula*

applied to it. It was afterwards connected with the Aqua Iulia.

(5) The AQUA IULIA, built by M. Vipsanius Agrippa (q. v.), in B.C. 33, during his aedileship. Its length was 15,426 *passus*, of which 7000 were above ground, partly on arches.

(6) The AQUA VIRGO, also built by Agrippa during his aedileship to supply his baths. (See BALNEAE.) It began near the eighth mile-stone on the Via Collatina, being in length 14,105 *passus*, of which 12,865 were underground. It is still in use.

(7) The AQUA ALSIETĪNA, or AQUA AUGUSTA, built by Augustus. It extended from the Lacus Alsietinus, which lay 6500 *passus* to the right of the fourteenth mile-stone on the Via Claudia, a distance of 22,172 *passus*. Of this length, only 358 *passus* were on arches. Its water was so bad as to be used only for watering gardens and for the *naumachiae*.

(8) The AQUA CLAUDIA, begun by the emperor Caligula in A.D. 38. It began near the thirty-eighth mile-stone on the Via Sublacensis, and furnished excellent water. Its length was 46,406 *passus*, of which 9567 were on arches.

(9) The ANIO NOVUS, the longest of all the aqueducts, being nearly fifty-nine miles in length. It was begun by Caligula in A.D. 38, and finished by Claudius in A.D. 52. Of its length, 9400 feet were above ground, some of its arches being 109 feet high. (See Frontin. 15.) Near the city the Aqua Claudia and the Anio Nova united, forming two channels on the same arches.

It has been calculated that these nine aqueducts supplied the city of Rome with some 332,306,624 gallons of water a day, or about 332 gallons a head. At the present time, forty gallons per head are considered sufficient. After the time of Frontinus two other aqueducts were built.

(10) The AQUA TRAIĀNA, built by Trajan about A.D. 110, and brought from the Lacus Sabatinus to supply the Regio Transtiberina.

(11) The AQUA ALEXANDRĪNA, built by Alexander Severus in A.D. 226 from a spot between Gabii and Lake Regillus, about fourteen miles from Rome, and intended to supply the baths of Severus. There was also

(12) The AQUA CRABRA, originally carried directly through the Circus Maximus from a point near the source of the Aqua Iulia; but its water was so bad that it was abandoned to the people of the Ager Tusculanus, and hence became known as the Aqua Damnata.

See Frontinus, *De Aquaeductibus Urbis Romanae*; Fabretti, *De Aquis et Aquaeductibus Veteris Romae*; Stieglitz, *Archäologie der Baukunst*; Hirt, *Geschichte der Baukunst*; Platner and Bunsen, *Beschreibung der Stadt Rom*; Canina, *Storia dell' Architettura Romana*; Burn, *Rome and the Campagna* (1871); Lanciani, *Topografia di Roma Antica* (1880); Middleton, *Ancient Rome in 1885*; id. *Remains of Ancient Rome* (1892); and the illustration in the article NEMAUSUS.

Aquae Ductus. See SERVITUTES.

Aquae et Ignis Interdictio. See EXSILIUM.

Aquae Haustus. See SERVITUTES.

Aquaelicium or **Aquilicium.** A sacrifice for rain. In times of drought, the Roman matrons, clad in the stola, with bare feet and loosened hair, and the magistrates without their purple robes and with reversed fasces, used to carry in procession a stone which lay outside the Porta Capena near the Temple of Mars, through the city to the Capitol. The name of the stone was *lapis*, or *petra manalis* (Paul. ex Fest. p. 128), i. e. the stone from which water flows.

Aquaemanālis. A ewer used in washing the hands at meals, also called *gutturnium* (Varro ap. Non. 547).

Aquarii and **Aquariŏli.** (1) Slaves who carried water for bathing into the women's apartments. (2) Public officers who attended to the aqueducts. See AQUAE DUCTUS.

Aquĭla. (1) The eagle. See SIGNA MILITARIA. (2) (ἀετός). In architecture, the gable of a house; the pediment of a temple. See FASTIGIUM.

Aquĭla. (1) A native of Sinopé in Asia Minor. He first applied himself to the study of mathematics and architecture; and the emperor Hadrian, according to Saint Epiphanius, made him a superintendent of public buildings, and gave him charge of the restoration and enlargement of Jerusalem, under its new name of Aelia Capitolina. This commission afforded him an opportunity of becoming acquainted with Christianity, which he subsequently embraced, and received the rite of baptism. Becoming afterwards addicted, however, to judicial astrology, he was excommunicated, and then attached himself to Judaism. Aquila is rendered famous by his Greek version of the Old Testament, which he published A.D. 138. It is the first that was made after the Septuagint translation, and appears to have been executed with great care. Aquila's method was to translate word for word, and to express, as far as this could conveniently be done, even the etymological meaning of terms. Although his version was undertaken with the view of opposing and superseding that of the Septuagint, of which last the churches made use after the example of the apostles, still the Fathers found it in general so exact that they often, in preference, drew their texts from it. St. Jerome, who had at first censured it, afterwards praised its exactness. The Hellenistic Jews preferred it also for the use of their synagogues. Some fragments of it are preserved in the *Hexapla* of Origen. Aquila joined to a second edition of his version some Jewish traditions which he had obtained from the rabbi Akiba, his preceptor. This edition was still more favourably received by the Hellenistic Jews than the previous one had been. The emperor Justinian, however, interdicted the reading of it, on the ground that it only made the Jews more stubborn in error. See Clarke, *Succession of Sacred Lit.* i. 44. (2) ROMĀNUS. A Latin rhetorician of the third century A.D., author of a work *De Figuris*. Text by Halm (1863).

Aquilēia. A town in Gallia Transpadana near the head of the Adriatic, founded by the Romans in B.C. 182. It was a strong fortress, and intended to be a barrier against the encroachments of the Northern barbarians. It was taken, however, in A.D. 452 by Attila (q. v.), who destroyed it, the inhabitants escaping to the lagoons of the Adriatic, where subsequently arose the city of Venice.

Aquilius or **Aquillius.** (1) A Roman consul who held office in B.C. 129, finishing the war against Aristonicus, son of Eumenes, king of Pergamus. (2) NEPOS. A general and consul (B.C. 101). He ended the Servile War in Sicily, but in 88 was defeated and taken by Mithridates, who put him to death by pouring molten gold down his throat. See Appian, *Bell. Mithridat.* 26.

Aquillia Via. A Roman road beginning at Capua, and running south through Lucania and Bruttii to Rhegium. See VIAE.

Aquilonia. A town of Samnium, destroyed by the Romans in the Samnite Wars (q. v.).

Aquīnum. A town of the Volsci in Latium, the birthplace of Juvenal. It was celebrated for its purple dye.

Aquitāni. A Gallic people of Iberian or Spanish origin, inhabiting the territory of Aquitania

Aquitania. (1) The country of the Aquitani, extending from the Garumnus (Garonne) to the Pyrenees. (2) A Roman province formed in the reign of Augustus, extending from the Liger (Loire) to the Pyrenees, and bounded on the north by the Mons Cevennus. See GALLIA.

Ara (βωμός, ἐσχάρα). An altar. With reference to these terms, βωμός properly signifies any elevation; ἐσχάρα (Lat. *focus*) means an altar for burnt-offerings; *ara* and *altare* are often used without any distinction, but properly *ara* was a structure of less height than *altare* (*altus*), the latter being erected in honour of the superior gods, and the former to the inferior gods, demigods, and heroes. (Cf. Verg. *Ecl.* v. 65.) Sacrifices to the infernal gods were not offered on altars, but in cavities dug in the ground and known as *scrobes, scrobiculi*, βόθροι, λάκκοι (Festus, s. v. *altaria*).

In early times, and always in sudden emergencies, altars were made of earth, turf, or stones collected on the spot. Otherwise they were built of masonry or brickwork, as shown in the following illustrations.

Altar (Column of Trajan). Etruscan Altar.

Subsequently a base was added (βάσις), and a corresponding projection at the top (ἐσχάρις) to hold the fire. A movable pan or brazier (ἐπίπυρον) sometimes served this purpose. Altars were either square or round.

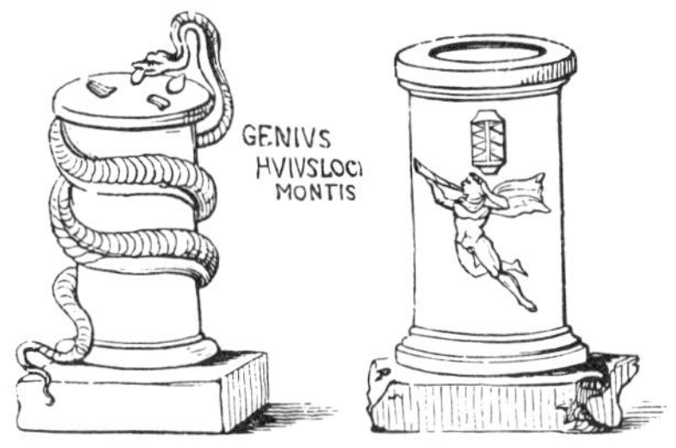

Altar (Herculaneum). Altar (Antium).

Vitruvius directs that altars, though differing in elevation according to the rank of the divinities to whom they were erected, should always be lower than the statues (*simulacra*) before which they were placed. Of the application of this rule we have an example in a medallion on the Arch of Constantine at Rome, shown in the annexed illustration.

Altar with Statue of Apollo (Arch of Constantine).

All altars were places of refuge. The suppliants were considered as placing themselves under the protection of the deities to whom the altars were consecrated; and violence to the unfortunate, even to slaves and criminals, in such circumstances, was regarded as violence towards the deities themselves. It was also the practice among the Greeks to take solemn oaths at altars, either taking hold of the altar or of the statue of the god. Cicero (*pro Balb.* 5, § 12) expressly mentions this as a Greek practice. See K. F. Hermann, *Gottesdienst. Alterth.*, § 17 and § 22.

Arabarches. The governor of Upper Egypt, or the Thebais, under the Roman Empire, this district being often called Arabia (*C. I. G.* 4751). See ALABARCHES.

Arabia (Ἀραβία). A country at the southwestern extremity of Asia, forming a large peninsula, of a sort of hatchet shape, bounded on the west by the Arabicus Sinus (Red Sea), on the south and southeast by the Erythraeum Mare (Gulf of Bab-el-Mandeb and Indian Ocean), and on the northeast by the Persicus Sinus (Persian Gulf). On the north or land side its boundaries were somewhat indefinite, but it seems to have included the whole of the desert country between Egypt and Syria, on the one side, and the banks of the Euphrates on the other. It was divided into three parts. (1) ARABIA PETRAEA, including the triangular piece of land between the two heads of the Red Sea (the peninsula of Mt. Sinai) and the country immediately to the north and northeast, and called from its capital Petra; while the literal signification of the name, "Rocky Arabia," agrees also with the nature of the country. (2) ARABIA DESERTA, including the great Syrian Desert and a portion of the interior of the Arabian peninsula. (3) ARABIA FELIX, consisting of the whole country not included in the two other divisions. The ignorance of the ancients respecting the interior of the peninsula led them to class it with Arabia Felix, although it properly belongs to Arabia Deserta, for it consists of a sandy desert. There is on the west coast a belt of fertile land, which caused the ancients to apply the epithet of Felix to the whole peninsula. The inhabitants of Arabia were of the Semitic race, and hence closely related to the Israelites. The northwest district (Arabia Petraea) was inhabited by the various tribes that constantly appear in Jewish history—the Amalekites, Midianites, Edomites, Moabites, Ammonites, etc. The Greeks and Romans called the inhabitants by the name of Nabathaei, whose capital was Petra. The people of Arabia Deserta were called Arabes Scenitae, from their dwelling in tents, and Arabes Nomadae, from their mode of life. From the earliest known period a considerable traffic was carried on by the people in the north (especially the Nabathaei) by means of caravans, and by those on the south and east coast by sea, in the productions of their own country (chiefly gums, spices, and precious stones), and in those of India and Arabia. The only part of Arabia ever conquered was Arabia Petraea, which became under Trajan a Roman province. Christianity was early introduced into Arabia, where it spread to a great extent, and continued to exist side by side with the old religion, Sabaeism, or the worship of heavenly bodies, and with some admixture of Judaism, until the total revolution produced by the rise of Mohammedanism in A.D. 622.

Arabĭcus Sinus (Ἀραβικὸς κόλπος). The Red Sea; a long, narrow gulf between Africa and Arabia, connected on the south with the Indian Ocean by the Strait of Bab-el-Mandeb, and on the north divided into two heads by the peninsula of Arabia Petraea (Peninsula of Sinai), the eastern of which was called Sinus Aelanites or Aelaniticus (Gulf of Akaba), and the western Sinus Heroöpolites or Heroöpoliticus (Gulf of Suez). Respecting its other name, see ERYTHRAEUM MARE.

Arachné (Ἀράχνη). A Lydian maiden, daughter of Idmon of Colophon, a famous dyer in purple. Arachné excelled in the art of weaving, and, proud of her talent, ventured to challenge Athené to compete with her. The maiden produced a piece of cloth in which the amours of the gods were woven, and as the goddess could find no fault with it she tore the work to pieces. Arachné, in despair, hanged herself. Athené loosened the rope and saved her life, but the rope was changed into a cobweb, and Arachné herself into a spider (ἀράχνη). This fable seems to suggest that man learned the art of weaving from the spider, and that it was invented in Lydia.

Arachosia (Ἀραχωσία). An eastern province of the Persian Empire, bounded on the east by the Indus, and noted for its fertility.

Arachtus or **Aretho**. A river of Epirus, rising in Mt. Lacmon, and flowing into the Sinus Ambracius.

Aracynthus (Ἀράκυνθος). A mountain on the southwestern coast of Aetolia, near Pleuron, sometimes placed in Acarnania, and (erroneously) between Boeotia and Attica.

Arădus (Ἄραδος). An island off the coast of Phœnicia, with a flourishing city, reputed to have been founded by exiles from Sidon. Its harbour, off the mainland, was called Antaradus (Herod. vii. 98).

Araeostȳlos (ἀραιόστυλος). See TEMPLUM.

Arar or **Arăris**. The modern Saône; a river of Gaul, rising in the Vosges and emptying into the Rhodanus (Rhone) at Lugdunum (Lyons).

Aratēa. A name given to the Latin translations of the *Phaenomena* and *Prognostica* of Aratus (q. v.), made by Cicero, Germanicus, and Avienus. The original has been translated into English, with notes, by Poste (1880). Cicero has quoted nearly all of his own version, and there are besides 480 lines extant in a single fragment. We have the version of Germanicus entire, with scholia (ed. princeps, Bologna, 1474, best recent edition by Breysig, Berlin, 1867); and also that of Avienus in 1877 lines (ed. princeps, Venice, 1488). See Schaubach, *De Arati Interpretibus Romanis* (Meiningen, 1817); and the article ARATUS.

Aratēa (τὰ Ἀράτεια). Two sacrifices offered every year at Sicyon in honour of Aratus, a general of the Achaeans, who was honoured as a hero. See Plut. *Arat.* ch. 53.

Arātrum (ἄροτρον). A plough. The annexed illustrations will give a good notion of the various forms of ploughs employed in Greece and in Italy.

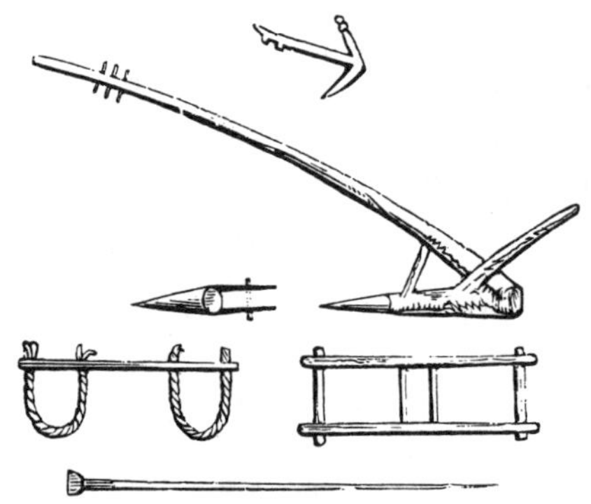

Primitive Forms of the Plough, Yoke, and Goad.

The following representation of a Roman plough is taken from a piece of engraved jasper.

Ancient Plough (Roman).

See the articles AGRICULTURA; IUGUM.

Arātus (Ἄρατος) (1) A Greek poet, of Soli in Cilicia, about B.C. 270, contemporary of Callimachus and Theocritus. At the request of the Macedonian king, Antigonus Gonatas, at whose court he lived as physician, he wrote, without much knowledge of the subject but guided by the works of Eudoxus and Theophrastus, two astronomical poems, *Phaenomena* (Φαινόμενα) and *Prognostica* (Διοσημεῖα) (aspects of the sky and signs of weather). Without genuine poetic inspiration, Aratus manages his intractable material with considerable tact and dignified simplicity. The language, while not always free from stiffness, is choice, and the versification correct. The poems enjoyed a high repute with the general public, as well as with poets and specialists, and the great astronomer Hipparchus wrote a commentary on them in four books. The Romans also took pleasure in reading and translating them—e. g. Cicero, Germanicus, and Avienus. Eng. trans. by Poste (London, 1880). (See ARATEA.) Aratus is mentioned by his contemporary Theocritus in the Sixth and Seventh Idyls, and by St. Paul in his speech (Acts, xvii. 28). Recent edition by Maas. (2) A Greek patriot, born in Sicyon B.C. 273, who expelled from his native state the tyrant Nicocles, and persuaded his countrymen to join the Achaean League, and in 244 secured the adhesion of Corinth. He afterwards had equal success with other States in southern Greece, so that the League became powerful, exciting the jealousy of the Aetolians, who made war upon it, but were defeated by Aratus aided by Antigonus, and for a time by Philip, nephew of Antigonus. This strong alliance overthrew Cleomenes, king of Sparta. Later, however, Aratus incurred the ill-will of Philip, who destroyed him by poison, B.C. 213. See Plut. *Arat.*

Araxes (Ἀράξης). The name of several rivers. (1) In Armenia, rising in Mt. Aba or Abus, joining the Cyrus, and falling with it into the Caspian Sea. The Araxes was proverbial for the force of its current. (2) In Mesopotamia. (3) In Persia, the river on which Persepolis stood, flowing into a salt lake not far below that city. (4) It is doubtful whether the Araxes of Herodotus is the same as the Oxus, Iaxartes, or Volga. (5) The Peneus in Thessaly.

Arbăces (Ἀρβάκης). The founder of the Median Empire, according to Ctesias. He is said to have taken Nineveh in conjunction with Belesis, the Babylonian, and to have destroyed the old Assyrian Empire under the reign of Sardanapalus, B.C. 876. See SARDANAPALUS.

Arbēla (τὰ Ἄρβηλα). A city of Adiabené in Assyria, the headquarters of Darius Codomanus before the last battle in which he was overthrown by Alexander (B.C. 331), which is hence frequently called the battle of Arbela, though it was really fought near Gaugamela, about fifty miles west of Arbela.

Arbĭter. See IUDEX.

Arbĭter, PETRONIUS. See PETRONIUS.

Arbor Infēlix. (1) A tree that was either sterile, or produced black berries and fruit (Plin. *H. N.* xvi. § 108). (2) The cross. See CRUX.

Arbuscŭla. A well-known actress in pantomime of the time of Cicero. Horace alludes to her in I. *Sat.* x. 77.

Arbŭtum (*unedo*, μιμαίκυλον). The fruit of the wild strawberry, or arbutus.

Arbŭtus (κόμαρος). The wild strawberry-tree.

Arbyla (ἀρβύλη). See PERO.

Arca. A city in the northern part of Phœnicia; the birthplace of Alexander Severus.

Arca (κιβωτός). A chest or coffer, is used in several significations, of which the principal are: (1) A chest in which the Romans were accustomed to place their money; and the phrase *ex arca solvere* had the meaning of paying in ready money. These chests were either made of or bound with iron or other metals. The term *arcae* was usually applied to the chests in which the rich kept their money, and was opposed to the smaller *loculi, sacculus*, and *crumena*. (2) The arca was frequently used in later times as equivalent to the *fiscus*—that is, the im-

Roman Arca, or Treasure-chest. (From Pompeii.)

perial treasury. See AERARIUM; FISCUS. (3) The arca also signified the coffin in which persons were buried, or the bier on which the corpse was placed previously to burial. (4) It was also a strong cell made of oak, in which criminals and slaves were confined.

Arcadia (Ἀρκαδία). A country in the middle of the Peloponnesus, surrounded on all sides by mountains, the Switzerland of Greece. The Acheloüs, the greatest river of the Peloponnesus, rises in Arcadia. The northern and eastern parts of the country were barren and unproductive; the western and southern were more fertile, with numerous valleys where corn was grown. The Arcadians regarded themselves as the most ancient people in Greece: the Greek writers call them indigenous and Pelasgians. They were chiefly employed in hunting and in the tending of cattle, whence their worship of Pan, who was especially the god of Arcadia, and of Artemis. They were passionately fond of music, and cultivated it with success. The Arcadians experienced fewer changes than any other people in Greece, and retained possession of their country upon the conquest of the rest of the Peloponnesus by the Dorians. After the Second Messenian War the different towns became independent republics, of which the most important were Mantinea, Tegea, Orchomenus, Psophis, and Pheneus. Like the Swiss, the Arcadians frequently served as mercenaries. The Lacedaemonians made many attempts to obtain possession of parts of Arcadia, but these attempts were finally frustrated by the battle of Leuctra (B.C. 371); and in order to resist all future aggressions on the part of Sparta, the Arcadians, upon the advice of Epaminondas, built the city of Megalopolis. They subsequently joined the Achaean League, and finally became subject to the Romans.

Arcadĭcum Foedus (*κοινόν, τὸ Ἀρκαδικόν*). The Arcadian League, established some time after the battle of Leuctra (B.C. 371), when the victory of Epaminondas had destroyed the supremacy of Sparta in the Peloponnesus and restored the independence of the Arcadian towns. (See Grote, x. pp. 306, 317 foll.) The Arcadian League succeeded in giving unity to the Arcadians for only a short time, however, and its influence soon declined. See MEGALOPOLIS.

Arcadius. Emperor of the East, elder son of Theodosius I., and brother of Honorius (q. v.), who received the Western Empire. Arcadius was both weak and vicious, a tool of favourites, and an inefficient ruler. During his reign Alaric (q. v.)

ravaged the Empire. Arcadius ruled from A.D. 395 to 408.

Arcarius. A person in charge of the money-chest in great houses. See ARCA.

Arcas (Ἄρκας). A king of the Arcadians, and son of Zeus and Callisto (q. v.), from whom Arcadia was supposed to have derived its name (Apollod. iii. 8, 2).

Arcé or **Arcae** (Ἀρκαί). A city of Phœnicia, the birthplace of Alexander Severus.

Arcĕra. A covered carriage or litter, spread with cloths, which was used in ancient times in Rome to carry the aged and infirm, and is mentioned in the Twelve Tables. It is said to have obtained the name of *arcera* on account of its resemblance to an *arca*.

Arcera. (Ginzrot, *Wagen*, Taf. 19, fig. 2.)

Arcesilāus (Ἀρκεσίλαος). (1) Son of Battus, king of Cyrené, who was driven from his kingdom in a sedition, and died B.C. 575. The second of this name died B.C. 550 (Herod. iv. 159). (2) A philosopher, born at Pitané, in Aeolis, the founder of what was termed the Middle Academy. The period of his birth is usually given as B.C. 316. Arcesilaüs at first applied himself to rhetoric, but subsequently passed to the study of philosophy, in which he had for teachers, first Theophrastus, then Crantor the Academician, and probably also Polemo (Diog. Laërt. iv. 24, 29; Cic. *Acad.* i. 9). Besides the instructors above named, Arcesilaüs is also said to have diligently attended the lectures of the Eretrian Menedamus, the Megarian Diodorus, and the sceptic Pyrrho. His love for the quibbling of these individuals has been referred to as the source of his scepticism and his skill in refuting philosophical principles. At the same time it is on all hands admitted that of philosophers Plato was his favourite. He seems to have been sincerely of opinion that his view of things did not differ from the true spirit of the Platonic doctrine; nay, more, that it was perfectly in agreement with those older philosophical teachings, from which, according to the opinion of many, Plato had drawn his own doctrines—namely, those of Socrates, Parmenides, and Heraclitus.

Upon the death of Crantor, the school in the Academy was transferred by a certain Socratides to Arcesilaüs, who here introduced the old Socratic method of teaching in dialogues, although it was rather a corruption than an imitation of the genuine Socratic mode. Arcesilaüs does not appear to have committed his opinions to writing; at least the ancients were not acquainted with any work which could confidently be ascribed to him. Now, as his disciple Lacydes also abstained from writing, the ancients themselves appear to have derived their knowledge of his opinions only from the works of his opponents, of whom Chrysippus was the most eminent. Such a course must naturally be both defective and uncertain, and accordingly we have little that we can confidently advance with respect to his doctrines. According to these statements the results of his opinions would be a perfect scepticism, expressed in the formula that he knew nothing, not even that which Socrates had ever maintained that he knew—namely, his own ignorance (Cic. *Acad.* i. 12). This expression of his opinion implicitly ascribes to Arcesilaüs a full consciousness that he differed in a most important point from the doctrine of Socrates and Plato. But, as the ancients do not appear to have ascribed any such conviction to Arcesilaüs, it seems to be a more probable opinion which imputes to him a desire to restore the genuine Platonic dogma, and to purify it from all those precise and positive determinations which his successors had appended to it. Indeed, one statement expressly declares that the subject of his lecture to his most accomplished scholars was the doctrine of Plato (Cic. *l. c.*); and he would therefore appear to have adopted this formula with a view to meet more easily the objections of the dogmatists. Now if we thus attach Arcesilaüs to Plato, we must suppose him to have been in the same case with many others, and unable to discover in the writings of Plato any fixed and determinate principles of science. The ambiguous manner in which almost every view is therein advanced, and the results of one investigation admitted only conditionally to other inquiries, may perhaps have led him to regard the speculations of Plato in the light of mere shrewd and intelligent conjectures. Accordingly, we are told that Arcesilaüs denied the certainty not only of intellectual, but also of sensuous knowledge (Cic. *De Orat.* iii. 18).

Archelāus (Ἀρχέλαος). (1) A king of Macedonia (B.C. 413–399), who improved the condition of the country and patronized art and literature. (2) See MITHRIDATES. (3) See AEGYPTUS. (4) See PHILOSOPHIA.

Archestrătus (Ἀρχέστρατος). A poet of Gela, in Sicily, who flourished about B.C. 318, and composed the humorous didatic poem Ἡδυπάθεια (Good Cheer), supposed to describe a gastronomic tour round the then known world, with playful echoes of Homer and the dogmatic philosophers. The numerous fragments display much talent and wit. It was imitated in Latin by Ennius (q. v.).

Archias. See LICINIUS ARCHIAS.

Archiāter (ἀρχίατρος). See MEDICUS.

Archidāmus (Ἀρχίδαμος). See SPARTA.

Archilŏchus (Ἀρχίλοχος). A Greek lyric poet, especially eminent as a writer of lampoons. Born at Paros, he was the son of Telesicles by a slave-woman, but was driven by poverty to go with a colony to Thasos in B.C. 640 or 650. From Thasos he was soon driven by want, and by the enmities which his unrestrained passion for invective had drawn upon him. He seems to have roamed restlessly from place to place, until, on his return to Paros, he was slain in a fight by the Naxian, Calondas. Long afterwards, when this man visited the Delphian temple, the god is said to have driven him from his threshold as the slayer of a servant of the Muses, and refused to admit him until he had propitiated the soul of the poet at his tomb—a story which expresses the high value set on his art by the ancients, who placed him on a level with Homer, Pindar, and Sophocles; for Archilochus had an extraordinary poetical genius, which enabled him to invent a large number of new metres, and to manipulate them with the ease of a master. He brought iambic poetry, in particular, to artistic perfection. The many misfortunes of his stormy life had bred in his irritable nature a deeply settled indignation, which in poems perfect in form and alive with force and fury, vented itself in bitter mockery even of his friends, and in merciless, unpardonable abuse of his foes. Such was the effect of his lampoons that Lycambes, who had first promised and then refused him his daughter Neobulé, hanged himself and his family in the despair engendered by the poet's furious attacks. Of his poems, which were written in the Old-Ionic dialect, and taken by Horace for his model in his epodes, only a number of short fragments are preserved. The best text of these will be found in the collection of Bergk.

Archimēdes (Ἀρχιμήδης). A remarkable mathematician and inventor, born at Syracuse in B.C. 287. After spending a long time in travel and study he returned to his native city, and there introduced a great number of inventions, among them the endless screw, first used by him in launching large ships; and the so-called Archimedean screw (*cochlea*), used in draining the fields after the annual inundation of the Nile. During the siege of Syracuse by the Romans (215–212), he invented the catapults which long kept the enemy at bay, being adapted for use at both short and long range. He is said to have set fire to the Roman ships by means of powerful burning-glasses—a story which Buffon in 1777 showed by experiment to be not at all absurd, and which Ball regards as not improbable. He first established the truth that a body plunged in fluid loses as much of its weight as is equal to the weight of an equal volume of the fluid. When Syracuse finally fell, he was slain by the Roman soldiers, who were tempted by the bright metal of his instruments, which they took for gold. Cicero, when quaestor in Sicily (B.C. 75), discovered the tomb of Archimedes (*Tusc. Disp.* v. 23). There still exist nine treatises by him which have been edited with a Latin version, by Heiberg, 3 vols. (Leipzig, 1880–81). See Ball, *Short Hist. of Mathematics*, pp. 59–70 (London, 1888).

Archimīmus (ἀρχίμιμος). See MIMUS.

Architectūra (ἀρχιτεκτονία, ἀρχιτεχτονική). (I.) GREEK.—Of the earliest efforts of the Greeks in architecture we have evidence in the so-called Cyclopean Walls surrounding the castles of kings in the Heroic Age of Tiryns, Argos, Mycenae, and elsewhere. They are of enormous thickness, some being constructed of rude, colossal blocks, whose gaps are filled up with smaller stones; while others are built of stones more or less carefully hewn, their interstices exactly fitting into each other. Gradually they begin to show an approximation to buildings with rectangular blocks. The gates let into these walls are closed at the top either by the courses of stone jutting over from each side till they touch, or by a long straight block laid over the two leaning side-posts. Of the latter kind is the famous Lion Gate at Mycenae (q. v.), so called from its two lions standing with their forefeet on the broad pedestal of a pillar, and remarkable as the oldest specimen of Greek sculpture.

Among the most striking relics of this primitive age are the so-called θησαυροί (treasuries, usually subterranean) of ancient dynasties, the most considerable being the treasure-house of Atreus at Mycenae. (See MYCENAE.) The usual form of

Gate of Thoricos.

these buildings is that of a circular chamber vaulted over by the horizontal courses approaching from all sides till they meet. Thus the vault is not a true arch. The interior seems originally to have been covered with metal plates, thus agreeing with Homer's descriptions of metal as a favourite ornament of princely houses. (See DOMUS.) An open-air building preserved from that age is the supposed Temple of Heré on Mt. Ocha (now Hagios Elias) in Euboea, a rectangle built of regular square blocks, with walls more than a yard thick, two small windows, and a door with leaning posts and a huge lintel in the southern side-wall. The sloping roof is of hewn flag-stones resting on the thickness of the wall and overlapping each other, but the centre is left open as in the hypaethral temples of a later time.

From the simple shape of a rectangular house shut in by blank walls we gradually advance to finer and richer types, formed especially by the introduction of columns detached from the wall and serving to support the roof and ceiling. Even in Homer we find columns in the palaces to support the halls that surround the court-yard and the ceiling of the banqueting-room. The construction of columns (see COLUMNA) received its artistic development first from the Dorians, after their migration into the Peloponnesus about B.C. 1000, next from the Ionians—and from each in a form suitable to their several characters. If the simple, serious character of the Dorians speaks in the Doric order, no less does the lighter, nimbler, and more showy genius of the Ionian race appear in the order named after them. By about B.C. 650, the Ionic style was flourishing side by side with the Doric.

As it was in the construction of temples that architecture had developed her favourite forms, all other public buildings borrowed their artistic character from the temple. (See TEMPLUM.) The structure and furniture of private houses were, during the best days of Greece, kept down to the simplest forms. About B.C. 600, in the Greek islands and on the coast of Asia Minor, we come across the first architects known to us by name. It was then that Rhoecus and Theodorus of Samos, celebrated likewise as inventors of casting in bronze, built the great Temple of Heré in that island, while Chersiphron of Cnosus in Crete, with his son Metagenes, began the Temple of Artemis at Ephesus, one of the seven wonders of the world, which was not finished till one hundred and twenty years after. In Greece Proper a vast temple to Zeus was begun at Athens in the sixth century B.C. (see OLYMPIEUM), and two more at Delphi and Olympia—one of the Corinthian Spintharus, the other by the Elean Libon. Here, and in the western colonies, the Doric style still predominated everywhere. Among the chief remains of this period, in addition to many ruined temples in Sicily, especially at Selinus and Agrigentum, should be mentioned the Temple of Poseidon at Paestum (Posidonia) in South Italy, one of the best preserved and most beautiful relics of antiquity. The patriotic fervour of the Persian Wars created a general expansion of Greek life, in which architecture and the sister art of sculpture were not slow to take a part. In these departments, as in the whole onward movement, a central position was taken by Athens, whose leading statesmen, Cimon and Pericles, lavished the great resources of the state at once in strengthening and beautifying the city. During this period arose a group of masterpieces that still astonish us in their ruins, some in the forms of a softened Doric, others in the Ionic style, which had now found its way into Attica, and was here developed into nobler shapes. The Doric order is represented by the Temple of Theseus; the Propylaea (q. v.), built by Mnesicles; the Parthenon (q. v.), a joint production of Ictinus and Callicrates—while the Erechtheum (q. v.) is the most brilliant creation of the Ionic order in Attica. See ATHENAE.

The progress of the drama to its perfection in this period led to a corresponding improvement in the building of theatres. A stone theatre was begun at Athens even before the Persian Wars, and the Odeum of Pericles served similar purposes. How soon the highest results were achieved in this department, when once the fundamental forms had thus been laid down in outline at Athens, is shown by the theatre at Epidaurus, a work of Polyclitus, unsurpassed, as the ancients testify, by any later theatres in harmony and beauty. Another was built at Syracuse before B.C. 420. Nor is it only in the erection of single buildings that the great advance then made by architecture shows itself. In laying out new towns, or parts of towns, men began to proceed on artistic principles, an innovation due to Hippodamus of Miletus. See THEATRUM.

In the fourth century B.C., owing to the change wrought in the Greek mind by the Peloponnesian War, in place of the pure and even tone of the preceding period, a desire for effect became more and more general, both in architecture and sculpture. The sober Doric style fell into abeyance and gave way to the Ionic, by the side of which a new order, the Corinthian, said to have been invented by the sculptor Callimachus, with its more gorgeous decorations, became increasingly fashionable. In the first half of the fourth century arose what the ancients considered the largest and grandest temple in the Peloponnesus, that of Athené at Tegea, a work of the sculptor and architect Scopas. During the middle of the century another of the "seven wonders," the splendid tomb of Mausolus at Halicarnassus, was constructed. (See MAUSOLEUM.) Many magnificent temples arose in that time. In Asia Minor, the temple at Ephesus, burned down by Herostratus, was rebuilt by Alexander's bold architect Dinocrates. In the islands the ruins of the Temple of Athené at Priené, of Apollo

Porch of the Erechtheum at Athens. (Drawing by Boudier.)

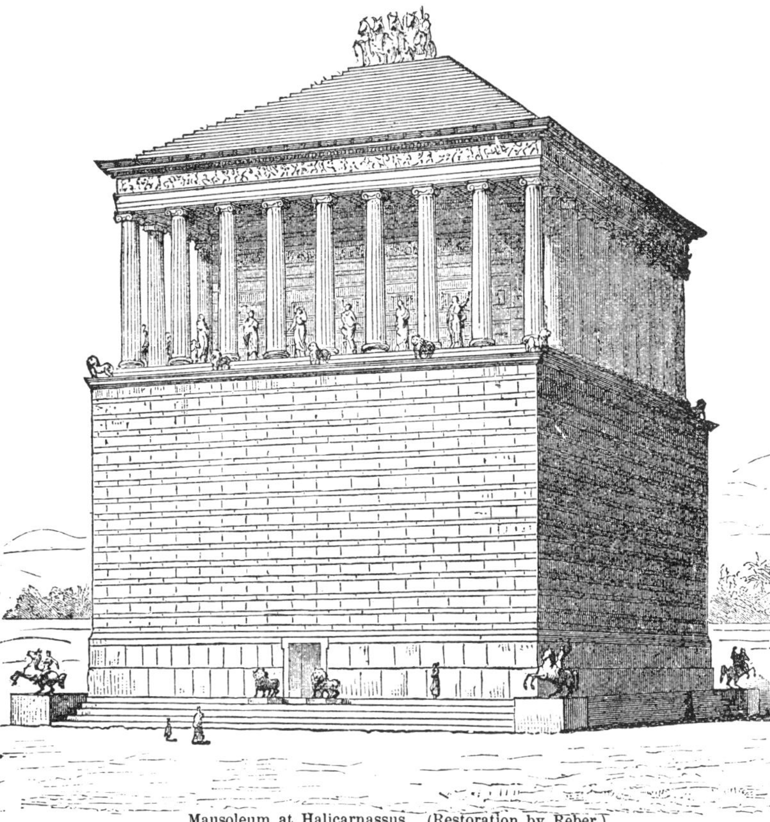
Mausoleum at Halicarnassus. (Restoration by Reber.)

at Miletus, of Dionysus at Teos, and others, even to this day offer a brilliant testimony to their former magnificence. Among Athenian buildings of that age the Monument of Lysicrates (q. v.) is conspicuous for its graceful elegance and elaborate development of the Corinthian style. In the succeeding age, Greek architecture shows its finest achievements in the building of theatres, especially those of Asiatic towns; in the gorgeous palaces of newly built royal capitals; and in general in the luxurious completeness of private buildings. As an important specimen of the last age of Attic architecture may also be mentioned the Tower of the Winds at Athens. See ANDRONICUS.

(II.) ETRUSCAN AND ROMAN. — In architecture, as well as sculpture, the Romans were long under the influence of the Etruscans, who, though not possessing the gift of rising to the ideal, united wonderful activity and inventiveness with a passion for covering their buildings with rich ornamental carving. None of their temples have survived, for they built all the upper parts of wood; but many proofs of their activity in building remain, surviving from various ages, in the shape of tombs and walls. The latter clearly show how they progressed from piling up polygonal blocks in Cyclopean style to regular courses of squared stone. Here and there a building still shows that the Etruscans originally made vaultings by letting horizontal courses jut over, as in the ancient Greek *θησαυροί* above mentioned: on the other hand, some very old gateways, as at Volterra and Perugia, exhibit the true arch of wedge-shaped stones, the introduction of which into Italy is probably due to Etruscan ingenuity, and from the introduction of which a new and magnificent development of architecture takes its rise. The most imposing of ancient Italian arch building is to be seen in the sewers of Rome constructed in the sixth century B.C. See CLOACA.

When all other traces of Etruscan influence were being swept away at Rome by the intrusion of Greek forms of art, especially after the conquest of Greece in the middle of the second century B.C., the Roman architects kept alive in full vigour the Etruscan method of building the arch, which they developed and completed by the inventions of the cross-arch (or groined vault) and the dome. With the arch, which admits of a bolder and more varied management of spaces, the Romans combined, as a decorative element, the columns of the Greek orders. Among these their growing love of pomp gave the preference more and more to the Corinthian, adding to it afterwards a still more gorgeous embellishment in what is called the Roman or Composite capital. Another service rendered by the Romans was the introduction of building in brick. A more vigorous advance in Roman architecture dates from the opening of the third century B.C., when they began making great military roads and aqueducts. In the first half of the second century they built, on Greek models, the first basilica, which, besides its practical utility, served to embellish the Forum. Soon after the middle of the century appeared the first of their more ambitious temples in the Greek style. There is simple grandeur in the ruins of the Tabularium (q. v.), or Record Office, built B.C. 78 on the slope of the Capitol next the Forum. These are among the few remains of Roman republican architecture; but in the last decades of the Republic simplicity gradually disappeared, and men were eager to display a princely pomp in public and private buildings; witness the first stone theatre erected by Pompey as early as B.C. 55. Then all that went before was eclipsed by the vast works undertaken by Caesar — the Theatre, Amphitheatre, Circus, Basilica Iulia, Forum Caesaris with its temple to Venus Genetrix. These were finished by Augustus, under whom Roman architecture seems to have reached its culminating-point. Augustus, aided by his son-in-law Agrippa, a man who understood building, not only

Arch of Titus at Rome.

completed his uncle's plans, but added many magnificent structures—the Forum Augusti with its temple to Mars Ultor, the Theatre of Marcellus with its Portico of Octavia, the Mausoleum, and others. Augustus could fairly boast that "having found Rome a city of brick, he left it a city of marble." The grandest monument of that age, and one of the loftiest creations of Roman art in general, is the Pantheon (q. v.), built by Agrippa, adjacent to, but not connected with, his Thermae, the first of the many works of that kind in Rome. This structure is remarkable as being the only ancient building in Rome of which the walls and arches are now in a complete state of preservation. It was erected by Agrippa in B.C. 27, the original inscription being still retained upon the architrave of its porch. The Pantheon is a circular structure 146 feet and 6 inches in height and inner diameter, with a portico 103 feet long composed of sixteen Corinthian columns, 46 feet in height. Inside the portico at the entrance are two niches which once contained the colossal statues of Agrippa the builder, and of Augustus Caesar. The walls of the building, which are 19 feet thick, support a dome or cupola of vast dimensions, constructed of concrete. At the vertex of the cupola is an opening nearly 30 feet in diameter, lighting the interior.

A still more splendid aspect was imparted to the city by the rebuilding of the old town burned down in Nero's fire, and by the "Golden House" of Nero, a gorgeous pile, the like of which was never seen before, but which was destroyed on the violent death of its creator. The immense and complicated structure, or rather mass of structures, known as the Palace of the Caesars, formed one of the most striking achievements of Roman architectural genius. (See PALATIUM.) It was, as Professor Lanciani puts it, a labyrinth of "endless suites of apartments, halls, terraces, porticoes, crypts, and cellars," having its main approach on the Via Sacra. At its arched entrance was a magnificent quadriga cut from a single block of white marble by Lysias. Beyond was a peristyle of fifty-two fluted columns adorned with a host of exquisite statues representing the Danaïdae, and adjacent to a great library. The magnificence of the palace as a whole may be conjectured from a simple summary of the treasures which we know to have been lavished upon the mere vestibule—a hundred and twenty columns of marble and bronze, statuary, bas-reliefs by Bupalus and Anthermus, a quadriga in gilded bronze, exquisite ivory carvings, hundreds of medallions in gold, silver, and bronze, immense collections of gold and silver plate, gems and cameos, and a colossal bronze statue of Augustus, fifty feet in height. (See Lanciani, *Ancient Rome in the Light of Recent Discoveries*, ch. v.).

Of the luxurious grandeur of private buildings we have ocular proof in the dwelling-houses of Pompeii, a petty country town in comparison with Rome. The progress made under the Flavian emperors is evidenced by Vespasian's amphitheatre, known as the Colosseum, the mightiest Roman ruin in the world; by the ruined Thermae, or Baths, of Titus, and by his triumphal arch, the oldest specimen extant in Rome of this class of monument, itself a creation of the Roman mind. But all previous buildings were surpassed in size and splendour when Trajan's architect, Apollodorus of Damascus, raised the Forum Traianum with its huge Basilica Ulpia and the still surviving Column of Trajan, besides other magnificent structures, including libraries, a great temple, a two-storied gallery, and a triumphal arch. The Basilica had five halls, the central one being 27 yards long, and the whole structure 61 yards wide. It was paved with slabs of rare marble. Only a part of this Forum has yet been excavated, but enough has been brought to light to justify the vivid description of Ammianus Marcellinus (xvi. 10), whose account refers to the time of the emperor Constantine's visit to Rome in the year 356. No less extensive were the works of Hadrian, who, besides adorning Athens with many magnificent buildings, bequeathed to Rome a Temple of Venus and Roma, the most colossal of all Roman temples (see p. 763), and his own Mausoleum (q. v.), the core of which is preserved in the Castle of St.

Colosseum at Rome.

Angelo. While the works of the Antonines already show a gradual decline in architectural feeling, the Triumphal Arch of Severus ushers in the period of decay that set in with the third century. In this closing period of Roman rule the buildings grow more and more gigantic—witness the Baths of Caracalla, those of Diocletian, with his palace at Salona (three miles from Spalatro) in Dalmatia, and the Basilica of Constantine, breathing the last feeble gasp of ancient life. But outside of Rome and Italy, in every part of the enormous Empire to its utmost barbarian borders, bridges, numberless remains of roads and aqueducts and viaducts, ramparts and gateways, palaces, villas, market-places and judgment-halls, baths, theatres, amphitheatres, and temples, attest the versatility, majesty, and solidity of Roman architecture, most of whose creations only the rudest shocks have been able to destroy. See Reber, *Hist. of Ancient Art*, Eng. trans. (N. Y. 1883); Lübke, *Geschichte der Kunst*, vol. i. (new ed. 1891); Fergusson, *Hist. of Architecture*, vol. i. (new ed. 1891); and BALNEAE; DOMUS; PALATIUM; TEMPLUM.

Composite Capital.

Architheōrus (ἀρχιθέωρος). See DELIA.

Archōn (ἄρχων). "Ruler." The Athenian name for the supreme authority established on the abolition of royalty. On the death of the last king, Codrus, B.C. 1068, the headship of the state for life was bestowed on his son Medon and his descendants under the title of Archon. In B.C. 752 their term of office was reduced to ten years; in 714 their exclusive privilege was abolished, and the right to hold the office thrown open to all the nobility, while its duration was diminished to one year; finally in B.C. 683 the power was divided among nine Archons. By Solon's legislation his wealthiest class, the πεντακοσιομέδιμνοι, became eligible to the office; and by Aristides' arrangement after the Persian Wars, it was thrown open to the whole body of citizens, Clisthenes having previously, in the interests of the democracy, substituted the drawing of lots for election by vote. The political power of the office, having steadily decreased with time, sank to nothing when democracy was established; its holders had no longer even the right to deliberate and originate motions, their action being limited to certain priestly and judicial functions, relics of their once regal power.

The titles and duties of the several archons were as follows: (1) Their president, named emphatically Archon or Archon Eponymus (ἄρχων ἐπώνυμος) because the civil year was named after him. He had charge of the Great Dionysia, the Thargelia, the embassies to festivals (θεωρίαι), and the nomination of choregi; also the position of guardian-in-chief, and the power to appoint guardians; the presidency in all suits about family rights (such as questions of divorce or inheritance), and in disputes among the choregi. (2) The Archon Basileus (ἄρχων βασιλεύς), called so because on him devolved certain sacred rites inseparably connected with the name of king. He had the care of the Eleusinian Mysteries, and was obliged therefore to be an initiated person; of the Lenaea and Anthesteria; of gymnastic contests, over which he appointed a superintendent; and of a number of antiquated sacrifices, some of which fell to the share of his wife, the βασίλισσα (queen); and lastly, the position of president in all suits touching religious law, including those trials for murder that came within the jurisdiction of the Ephetae (q. v.). (3) The Archon Polemarchos (ἄρχων πολέμαρχος, leader in war) was originally intrusted with the war department, and as late as the battle of Marathon had the right of voting with the ten generals, and the old royal privilege of commanding the right wing. Afterwards he only had charge of the state sacrifices offered to the gods of war and to the shade of Harmodius; the public funerals of those who fell in war, and the annual feasts in honour of them; and finally, jurisdiction in all questions concerning the personal and family rights of resident aliens (μέτοικοι) and strangers. All this rested on the old assumption that foreigner meant enemy. Each of these three superior archons had two assessors chosen by himself, but responsible. (4) The six Thesmothetae (θεσμοθέται, law-givers) administered justice in all cases not pertaining to the senior archons or some other authority, revised the laws once a year, and superintended the apportioning of public offices by lot. The several archons exercised their jurisdiction at different places in the city; that of the Polemarch alone lay outside the walls. Duties common to all nine were: the yearly appointment by lot of the Heliastae (q. v.), the choice of umpires in the Panathenaea, the holding of elections of the generals and other military officers, jurisdiction in the case of officials suspended or deposed by the people, and latterly even in suits which had previously been subject to the *nautodicae*. (See NAUTODICAE.) If they had discharged their office without blame they entered the Areopagus as members for life. (See AREOPAGUS.) The office of archon lasted even under the Roman rule. See Lugebil, *Zur Geschichte der Staatsverfassung von Athen* (Leipzig, 1871); Meier, *Index Archontum Eponymorum*, etc.

Archōnes (ἀρχώνης). The chief farmer of the taxes at Athens. See TELONES.

Archȳtas (Ἀρχύτας). (1) A musician of Mitylené, mentioned by Diogenes Laërtius as having written a treatise on agriculture. (2) A famous Tarentine astronomer and geometrician, the son of Hestiaeus. He was seven times elected governor of his native city. He is said to have been instrumental in rescuing Plato (q. v.) from the tyrant Dionysius. Many stories are told of his ingenuity. For him is claimed the invention of the screw, of the pulley, and of a wooden pigeon that could fly. He is also reported to have attempted to calculate the number of the grains of sand upon the sea-shore. Only a single fragment of his writings has come down to us in Porphyry. He perished in a shipwreck about B.C. 394. See his life in Diog. Laërt.; Plato, 338 C; and Horace, *Carm.* i. xxviii., with the commentators.

Arcifinius Ager. See AGRIMETATIO; AGRIMENSORES.

Arcitĕnens. An epithet of Apollo as bearing a bow, with which he destroyed the serpent Python.

Arctīnus. See CYCLIC POETS.

Arctos (ἄρκτος). "The Bear." The name of two constellations near the North Pole. (1) THE GREAT BEAR (*Ursa Major*), also called the WAGON (*plaustrum*). The ancient Italian name of this constellation was *Septem Triones*, that is, the Seven Ploughing Oxen, also *Septentrio*, and with the epithet *Maior* to distinguish it from the *Septentrio Minor*, or *Lesser Bear*. (2) THE LESSER or LITTLE BEAR (*Ursa Minor*), likewise called the WAGON and CYNOSURA (dog's tail) from the resemblance of the constellation to the upturned curl of a dog's tail. The constellation before the Great Bear was called *Boötes*, *Arctophylax*, or *Arcturus*. At a later time *Arctophylax* became the general name of the constellation, and the word *Arcturus* was confined to the chief star in it. All these constellations are connected in mythology with the Arcadian nymph Callisto, the daughter of Lycaon. Metamorphosed by Zeus upon the earth into a she-bear, Callisto was pursued by her son Arcas in the chase, and when he was on the point of killing her, Zeus placed them both among the stars—Callisto becoming the Great Bear, and Arcas the Little Bear or Boötes. In the poets the epithets of these stars have constant reference to the family and country of Callisto: thus we find them called *Lycaonis Arctos; Maenalia Arctos* and *Maenalis Ursa* (from Mt. Maenalus in Arcadia); *Erymanthis Ursa* (from Mt. Erymanthus in Arcadia); *Parrhasides Stellae* (from the Arcadian town Parrhasia). (See CALLISTO.) Though most traditions identified Boötes with Arcas, others pronounced him to be Icarus or his daughter Erigonê. Hence the Septentriones are called *Boves Icarii*.

Arctūrus. See ARCTOS.

Arcuballista. A cross-bow. See BALLISTA.

Arcŭla (κιβώτιον). (1) A painter's colour-box (Varro, R. R. iii. 17, 4). (2) A stone coffin. See SEPULCRUM.

Arcŭlum. A kind of porter's knot or pad for carrying burdens on the head. See CESTICILLUS.

Arcŭma or **Arcirma.** A cariole or small carriage to hold one person only (Paul. Diac. p. 14).

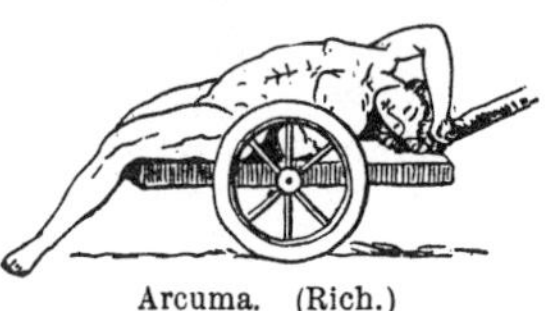

Arcuma. (Rich.)

Arcus (βιός, τόξον). The bow used for shooting arrows. Two kinds of bow were known to antiquity. One consisted of the two horns of the antelope, or an arm of wood similarly shaped, joined by a bridge which served both as a hold for the hand and as a rest for the arrow. The string, made of plaited horse-hair or twisted ox-gut, was fastened to each end (fig. 1). The other, called the Scythian or Parthian bow, was made of a piece of flexible wood, the ends of which were tipped with metal, and bent slightly upwards to hold the string (fig. 2). The arrow (Gr. ὀϊστός, or τόξευμα; Lat. *sagitta*) was made of a stem of reed or light wood, one end furnished with a three-cornered point, sometimes simple and sometimes barbed, the other end with feathers. A notch in the shaft served to place it on the string. The arrows (and sometimes the bow) were kept in a quiver (φαρέτρη, *pharetra*) made of leather, wood, or metal, fitted with a suspender, and sometimes open, sometimes having a lid. The quiver was worn either on the back, according to the Greek manner, or in Oriental fash-

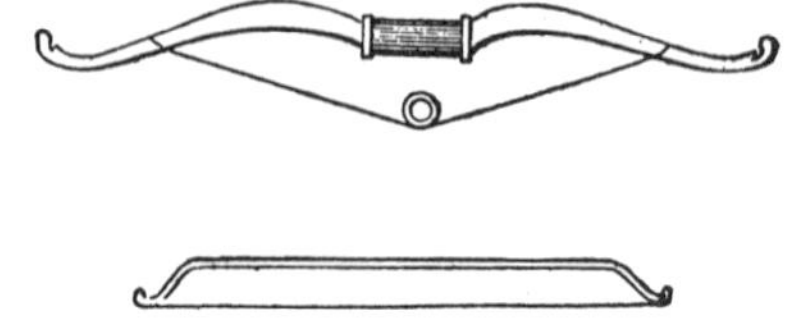

(From *Museum Hunter*. pl. 23 L.)

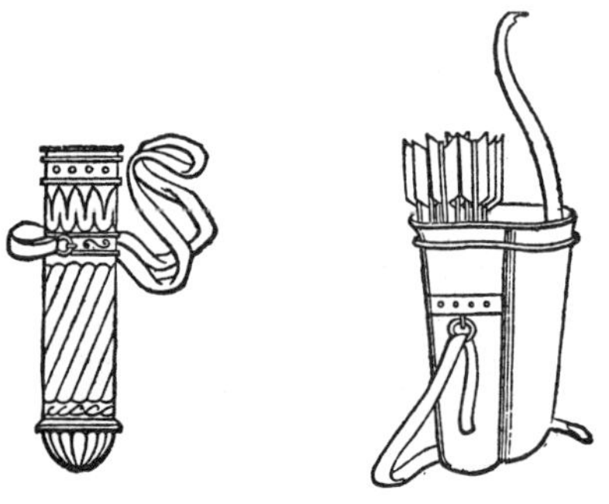

(*Museo Pio Clementino*, iv. tav. xliii.)

Bows and Quivers.

ion, on the left hip. The Cretans had the reputation of being the best archers among the Greeks. They generally served among the light-armed auxiliaries as a special corps. Mounted bowmen were employed by the ancient Athenians (see HIPPEIS); but it was not until after the Punic Wars that

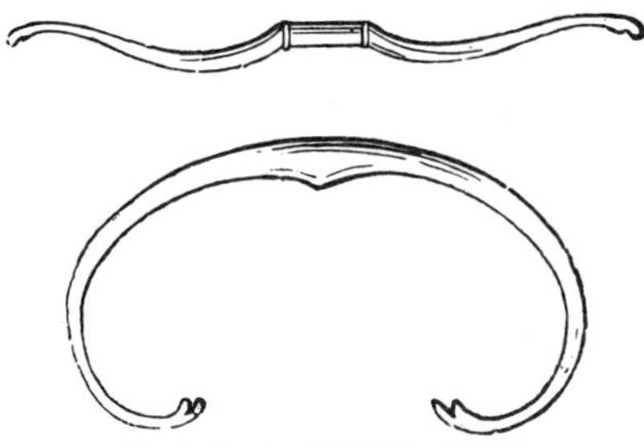

Greek Bows. (Hamilton Vases.)

archers formed a regular part of the Roman army. They were then furnished by the allies, or raised by recruiting, and were mostly taken from Crete and the Balearic Islands. See ARMA.

Arcus (*fornix*, καμάρα). An arch suspended over the head of an aperture, or carried from one side of a wall to another, and serving as the roof or ceiling to the space below. An arch is formed of a series of wedge-like stones or of bricks, supporting each other, and all bound firmly together by the pressure of the centre one upon them, which latter is therefore distinguished by the name of keystone.

It would seem, at first sight, that the arch, as thus defined, and as used by the Romans, was not known to the Greeks in the early periods of their history, otherwise a language so copious as theirs, and of such ready application, would not have wanted a name properly Greek by which to distinguish it. The use of both arches and vaults appears, however, to have been known to them even before the Trojan War, and its use is exemplified in two of the earliest buildings now remaining—the chamber built at Orchomenus by Minyas, king of Boeotia (Pausan. ix. 38), and the treasury of Atreus at Mycenae (Pausan. ii. 16). Both of these works are constructed underground, and each of them consists of a circular chamber formed by regular courses of stones laid horizontally over each other, each course projecting towards the interior, and beyond the one below it, till they meet in an apex over the centre, and thus resemble the inside of a dome. Each of the horizontal courses of stones formed a perfect circle, or two semicircular arches joined together, as the subjoined plan will render evident. See Schliemann, *Mycenae*, p. 43; Leake, *Morea*, ii. 377; and the articles ARCHITECTURA; MYCENAE.

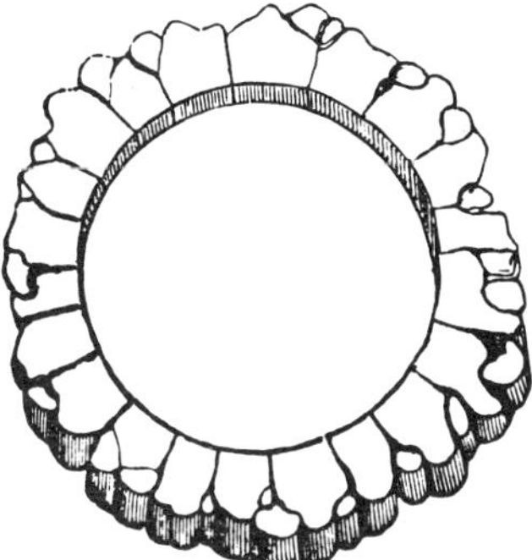

Circular Masonry at Mycenae.

The principle of the construction is that of an arch-shaped mass resisting a great superincumbent weight, and deriving its strength and coherence from the weight itself. Thus it seems that the Greeks did understand the constructive principle on which the arch is formed. They made use of a contrivance, even before the Trojan War, by which they were enabled to gain all the advantages of our archway in making corridors, or hollow galleries, and which in appearance resembled the pointed arch, such as is now termed Gothic. This was effected by cutting away the superincumbent stones in the manner already described, at an angle

• Pointed Arch in the Walls of Tiryns.

of forty-five degrees with the horizon. The mode of construction and appearance of such arches are represented in the annexed drawing of the walls of Tiryns from Sir William Gell's *Argolis*.

The principle of the true arch was known to the Egyptians, but it is remarkable that they did not make use of it in their most massive works (Wilkinson, ii. 299, ed. of 1878). The Assyrians used it in subterranean buildings (Layard, *Nineveh*, i. 167; ii. 260). There are also a few specimens of the true arch in ancient Greece. At Oeniadae, in Acarnania, is a postern of a perfect arch in the polygonal walls of the city (Leake, *Northern Greece*, iii. 560 seq.); and at Xerokampo, in the neighbourhood of Sparta, is a bridge on the true arch-principle (Mure, *Tour in Greece*, ii. 248), though the latter, in the opinion of many archæologists, is of Roman construction (Dennis, *Etruria*, ii. 250 seq.). But these are rare instances; and the Etruscans are the first people who employed the true arch extensively. Hence the use of the arch passed into the architecture of buildings. The Romans probably borrowed it from the Etruscans. Thus the Cloaca Maxima, long held to be the oldest instance of the arch at Rome, and attributed to the Tarquinii (see CLOACA), closely resembles the canal of the Marta (Dennis, *Etruria*, i. 430 seq.) See pp. 373 and 628.

Arcus Triumphālis. A triumphal arch. These arches were peculiar to the Romans, and were usually detached structures built across the principal streets of the city, and, according to the space of their respective localities, consisted of either a single archway, or of a central one for carriages, with two smaller ones on each side for foot-passengers, which sometimes had side communications with the central arch. Sometimes there were two arches of equal height, side by side. Each front was ornamented with trophies and bas-reliefs, which were also placed on the sides of the passages. Both façades had usually columns against the piers, supporting an entablature, surmounted by a lofty attica, on the front of which was the inscription, and on the top of it bronze chariots, war-horses, statues, and trophies. The triumphal arch recalls its original, the city gate, in the concentration of ornament on the façades, while the sides, which in the city gate are buried in the wall, are comparatively plain.

Stertinius is the first upon record who erected anything of the kind. He built an arch in the Forum Boarium, about B.C. 196, and another in the Circus Maximus, each of which was surmounted by gilt statues. Six years afterwards, Scipio Africanus built another on the Clivus Capitolinus, on which he placed seven gilt statues and two figures of horses; and in B.C. 121, Fabius Maximus built a fourth in the Via Sacra, which is called by Cicero the Fornix Fabianus. None of these remain, the Arch of Augustus at Rimini being one of the earliest among those still standing.

There are twenty-one arches recorded by different writers as having been erected in the city of Rome, five of which still remain: (1) ARCUS DRUSI, which was erected to the honour of Claudius Drusus on the Appian Way. (2) ARCUS TITI, at the foot of the Palatine, which was erected to the honour of Titus after his conquest of Iudaea, but does not appear to have been finished till after his death, since in the inscription upon it he is called *Divus*, and is also represented as being carried up to heaven upon an eagle. The bas-re-

Arch of Constantine at Rome.

liefs of this arch represent the spoils from the Temple of Jerusalem carried in triumphal procession. This arch has only a single opening, with two columns of the Roman or Composite order on each side of it. (3) ARCUS SEPTĬMI SEVĒRI, which was erected by the Senate (A.D. 207) at the end of the Via Sacra, in honour of that emperor and his two sons, Caracalla and Geta, on account of his conquest of the Parthians and Arabians. (4) ARCUS GALLIĒNI, erected to the honour of Gallienus by a private individual, M. Aurelius Victor. (5) ARCUS CONSTANTĪNI, which is larger and more profusely ornamented than the Arch of Titus. It has three arches in each front, with columns similarly disposed, and statues on the entablatures over them, which, with the other sculpt-

Arch of Septimius Severus.

ured ornaments, originally decorated the Arch of Trajan.

Arch of Augustus at Aosta.

See Burn, *Rome and the Campagna;* Middleton, *Ancient Rome in 1885;* id. *Remains of Ancient Rome* (1892); and the article ARCHITECTURA.

Ardălus (Ἄρδαλος). A son of Hephaestus, and the reputed inventor of the pipe, whence the Muses, to whom he gave it, are called Ardalides (Pausan. ii. 21).

Ardanion (ἀρδάνιον). A vessel of water placed at the door of a house in which a dead person was lying, in order that those leaving might purify themselves by sprinkling with the water. See Aristoph. *Eccles.* 1033.

Ardea. The chief town of the Rutuli in Latium, situated about three miles from the sea, one of the most ancient places in Italy, and the capital of Turnus. It was conquered and colonized by the Romans B.C. 442 (Livy, iv. 9).

Arduenna Silva. The Ardennes, a vast forest in the northeast of Gaul, extending from the Rhine and the Treviri to the Nervii and Remi, and north as far as the Scheldt (Tac. *Ann.* viii. 42).

Area. Any open space (*purus locus*). (1) A site for a building. (2) The site of a house pulled down in consequence of its owner's treason and devoted to religious uses (Cic. *Ad Att.* iv. 1, 2). (3) An open space in front of a temple, house, sepulchre, or public building. (4) A market-place. (5) A threshing-floor (ἁλῶς).

Area before a Sepulchre. (Villa Corsini, Rome.)

Aregŏnis (Ἀρηγονίς). The mother of Mopsus (q. v.) by Ampyx.

Areiopăgus. See AREOPAGUS.

Arelātē, Arĕlas, or **Arelātum.** Now Arles; a town in Gallia Narbonensis, at the head of the delta of the Rhone, on the left bank, and a Roman colony. The Roman remains at Arles attest the greatness of the ancient city: there are still the ruins of an aqueduct, theatre, amphitheatre, etc.

Aremorĭca. See ARMORICA.

Arēna. (1) Sand, a subject to which Vitruvius (ii. 4) has devoted a chapter. (2) See AMPHITHEATRUM.

Arenarii. Gladiators fighting in the arena. See GLADIATORES.

Areopăgus (Ἄρειος πάγος). The hill of Ares (q. v.). A rocky eminence lying to the west of the Athenian Acropolis. To account for the name, various stories were told. Thus, some said that it was so called from the Amazons, the daughters of Ares, having encamped there when they attacked Athens; others again, as Aeschylus, from the sacrifices there offered by them to that god; while the more received opinion connected the name with the legend of Ares having been brought to trial there by Poseidon for the murder of his son, Halirrhothius (q. v.).

To no legend, however, did the place owe its fame, but rather to the ancient criminal court or council (ἡ ἐν Ἀρείῳ πάγῳ βουλή) which held its sittings there, and sometimes received the name of ἡ ἄνω βουλή, to distinguish it from the Solonian Senate of Four Hundred, or the later Clisthenian Senate of Five Hundred. Solon's legislation raised the Areopagus into one of the most powerful bodies by transferring to it the greater part of the jurisdiction of the Ephetae (q. v.), as well as the supervision of the entire public administration, the conduct of magistrates, the transactions of the popular assembly, religion, laws, morals, and discipline, and giving it power to call even private persons to account for offensive behaviour. See SOLONIAN CONSTITUTION.

Ares (Ἄρης). The Greek name for the god of war, son of Zeus by Heré, whose quarrelsome temper Homer supposes to have passed over to her son so effectively that he delighted in nothing but battle and bloodshed. His insatiable thirst for blood makes him hateful to his father and to all the gods, especially Athené. His favourite haunt

Head of Ares. (Glyptothek, Munich.)

is the land of the wild and warlike Thracians. In form and equipment the ideal of warlike heroes, he advances, according to Homer, now on foot, now in a chariot drawn by magnificent steeds, attended by his equally bloodthirsty sister Eris (strife), his sons Deimos and Phobos (fear and fright), and Enyo, the goddess of battle and waster of cities (he himself being called Enyalios), rushing in blind rage through indiscriminate slaughter. Though fighting on the Trojan side, the bloodshed only is dear to his heart. But his unbridled strength and blind valour turn to his disadvantage, and always bring about his defeat in the presence of Athené, the goddess of ordered battalions; he is also beaten by heroes fighting under her leadership, as by Heracles in the contest with Cycnus, and by Diomede before Troy. And this view of Ares as the bloodthirsty god of battles is, in the main, that of later times also. As early as Homer he is the friend and lover of Aphrodité, who has borne him Eros and Anteros, Deimos and Phobos, as well as Harmonia, wife of Cadmus the founder of Thebes, where both goddesses were worshipped as ancestral deities. He is not named so often as the gods of peace; but, as Ares or Enyalius, he was doubtless worshipped every-

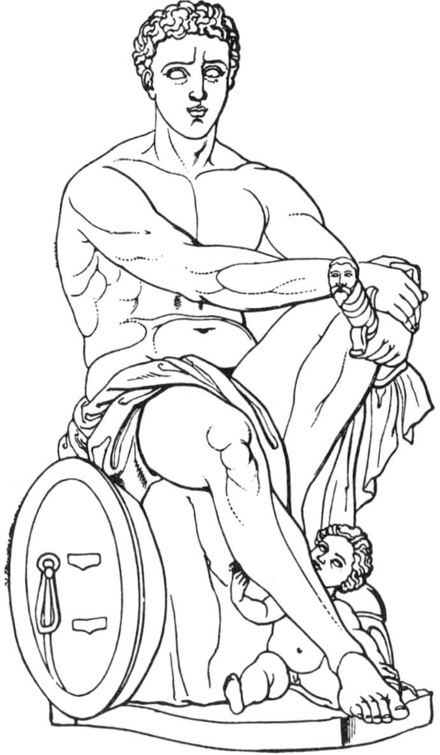

Ares. (Villa Ludovisi, Rome.)

where, notably in Sparta, in Arcadia, and (as the father of Oenomaüs) in Elis. At Sparta young dogs were sacrificed to him under the title of Theritas. At Athens the ancient site of a high court of justice, the Areopagus (q. v.), was consecrated to him. There, in former days, the Olympian gods had sat in judgment on him and absolved him when he had slain Halirrhothius for offering violence to Alcippé, his daughter by Agraulos. His symbols were the spear and the burning torch. Before the introduction of trumpets, two priests of Ares, marching in front of the armies, hurled the torch at the foe as the signal of battle.

In works of art he was represented as a young and handsome man of strong, sinewy frame, his hair in short curls, and a somewhat sombre look in his countenance; in the early style he is bearded and in armour, in the later beardless and with only the helmet on. He is often represented in company with Aphrodité, and their boy Eros, who plays with his father's arms. One of the most famous statues extant is that in the Villa Ludovisi given above, which displays him in an easy resting attitude, with his arms laid aside, and Eros at his feet. On his identification with the Italian Mars, see MARS.

Arestorĭdes. A patronymic applied to Argos (q. v.).

Aretaeus (Ἀρέταιος). A physician of Cappadocia, born near the close of the second century A.D. He was the author of two works, each in four books, on the causes, symptoms, and cure of acute and chronic pains. He wrote in the Ionic dialect with much elegance and clearness; and his treatises show a correctness of understanding with regard to medicine unusual among the ancient writers on this subject. He discourses with especial acuteness of the nerves, of indigestion, and gives an excellent account of diseases of the throat and tonsils. See Mann, *Aretaei Therapia* (1858).

Aretalŏgi (ἀρεταλόγοι). Literally "persons discoursing about virtue." Originally poor stoics or cynics, who, being unable to gain a living by their public lectures, obtained a precarious maintenance at the tables of the rich by their philosophical conversation. The name is generally equivalent to *parasitus* (q. v.) or *scurra*. See Suet. *Aug.* 74.

Arētē (Ἀρήτη). The wife of Alcinoüs (q. v.), king of the Phaeacians, and the protector of Odysseus (q. v.).

Arethūsa (Ἀρέθουσα). (1) One of the Nereids, and nymph of the fountain of the same name in the island of Ortygia, near Syracuse. For the story, see ALPHEUS. (2) One of the Hesperides (q. v.).

Aretīnum. A Roman colony in Etruria (Sil. Ital. v. 123).

Aretium. See ARRETIUM.

Arētus (Ἄρητος). A famous warrior, whose only weapon was an iron club, and who was treacherously slain by Lycurgus, king of Arcadia. See Pausan. viii. 11.

Areus (Ἀρεύς). The name of two kings of Sparta, the first reigning B.C. 309–265; and the second, as a child, about B.C. 264–256.

Argé. A beautiful huntress changed into a stag by Apollo (Hyg. *Fab.* 205).

Argēi. We learn from Livy (i 21) that Numa consecrated places for the celebration of religious services, which were called by the pontifices *argei.* Varro calls them the "chapels of the argei," and says they were twenty-seven in number, distributed in the different districts of the city. We know but little of the particular uses to which they were applied, and that little is unimportant. Thus, we are told that they were solemnly visited on the Liberalia, or festival of Bacchus; and, also, that whenever the flamen Dialis went (*ivit*) to them, he was to adhere to certain observances. They seem also to have been the depositaries of the topographical records. There was a tradition that these *argei* were named from the chieftains who came with Hercules, the Argive, to Rome, and occupied the Capitoline, or, as it was anciently called, Saturnian Hill. See Aul. Gell. x. 16; Varro, *L. L.* v. 45.

The name *argei* was also given to certain figures thrown into the Tiber from the Sublician Bridge, on the Ides of May in every year. This was done by the pontifices, the vestals, the praetors, and other citizens, after the performance of the customary sacrifices. The images were thirty in number, made of bulrushes, and in the form of men. Ovid makes various suppositions to account for the origin of this rite; we can only conjecture that it was a symbolical offering to propitiate the gods, and that the number was a representative either of the thirty patrician curiae at Rome, or perhaps of the thirty Latin townships. See Varro, *L. L.* vii. 44; Ovid. *Fast.* v. 671; and Festus, s. v.

Argentarii (τραπεζῖται). Dealers in money, including money-changers, usurers, and bankers proper. See TRAPEZITAE.

Argenteus. A Roman silver coin, valued at about twelve cents. See NUMISMATICS (Roman).

Argentorātum. The modern city of Strasburg; a Roman municipium in Gallia Belgica, on the Rhine. The Romans had a manufactory of arms here; and here, also, the emperor Julian defeated the Alemanni. In the sixth century we find it called Stratisburgium, whence comes the modern name.

Argentum (ἄργυρος). Silver. The Athenians obtained their silver from the silver mines at Laurium, which were generally regarded as the chief source of the wealth of Athens. We learn from Xenophon that these mines had been worked in remote antiquity; and Xenophon speaks of them as if he considered them inexhaustible. In the time of Demosthenes, however, the profit arising from them had greatly diminished; and in the second century of the Christian era they were no longer worked. The ore from which the silver was obtained was called "silver earth" (ἀργυρῖτις γῆ, or simply ἀργυρῖτις). The same term (*terra*) was also applied to the ore by the Romans, who obtained most of their silver from Spain. See CAELATURA; METALLUM.

The relative value of gold and silver differed considerably at different periods in Greek and Roman history. Herodotus mentions it as 1 to 13; Plato as 1 to 12; Menander as 1 to 10; and Livy as 1 to 10, about B.C. 189. According to Suetonius, Iulius Caesar, on one occasion, exchanged gold for silver in the proportion of 1 to 9; but the most usual proportion under the early Roman emperors was about 1 to 12; and from Constantine to Justinian about 1 to 14, or 1 to 15.

For the use of silver in coinage, see the articles NUMMUS; DENARIUS; DRACHMA, and especially NUMISMATICS.

Argentum Vivum (ἄργυρος χυτός). Quicksilver or mercury. See Pliny, *H. N.* xxxiii. 20.

Arges (Ἄργης). See CYCLOPES.

Argi. See ARGOS.

Argīa (Ἀργεία). The daughter of Adrastus and wife of Polynices (q. v.) (Hyg. *Fab.* 69 and 72). See CREON.

Argias Graphé (ἀργίας γραφή). An action to which any Athenian citizen was liable, according to the old law, if he could not bring evidence that he had some lawful calling. The law was introduced by Draco, who made the penalty of conviction death; Solon re-enacted the law, substituting, however, for the capital punishment a fine of 100 drachmae for the first conviction, and a loss of civic rights (ἀτιμία) if the same person was convicted three times of indolence. According to Iulius Pollux, Draco did not impose a severer punishment than ἀτιμία, and Solon did not punish it at all till the third offence. See Plut. *Sol.* 37; Poll. viii. 42.

Argilētum. A district in Rome, extending from the south of the Quirinal to the Capitoline and the Forum. It was chiefly inhabited by mechanics and booksellers (Mart. i. 4). Varro derives the name from *argilla*, "potter's clay," and some make it *Argi letum*, as referring to the hero Argus (Verg. *Aen.* viii. 346).

Argilla. See CRETA.

Arginūsae (Ἀργινοῦσαι). Three small islands off the coast of Aeolis, opposite Mytilené in Lesbos, celebrated for the naval victory of the Athenians over the Lacedaemonians under Callicratidas, B.C. 406. See PELOPONNESIAN WAR.

Argiphontes (Ἀργειφόντης). "Argus-slayer." An epithet applied to Hermes. See ARGUS.

Argītis. A species of wine, celebrated by Vergil for its durability. It is believed to have been a white wine. See Verg. *Georg.* ii. 99.

Argīvi. See ARGOS.

Argo (Ἀργώ). See ARGONAUTAE.

Argolĭcus Sinus. See ARGOS.

Argŏlis (Ἀργολίς). See ARGOS.

Argonautae (Ἀργοναῦται). A name given to those who sailed in the ship Argo under the lead of Iason (q. v.), son of Aeson, a generation before the Trojan War, to Aea, afterwards identified with Colchis at the eastern end of the Euxine Sea. The expedition was undertaken for the recovery of the golden fleece of the ram on which Phrixus, son of Athamas (q. v.), had fled from his father and Ino, his step-mother, to the court of Aeëtes, king of Aea, a mighty magician. Having been hospitably received by him, and married to his daughter Chalciopé, he had sacrificed the ram, and hung its fleece up in the grove of Ares, where it was guarded by a sleepless dragon. The task of bringing it back was laid upon Iason by his uncle Pelias, son of Poseidon and Tyro, who had deprived his half-brother Aeson of the sovereignty of Iolcus in Thessaly. Aeson, to protect his son from the plots of Pelias, had conveyed him secretly to the centaur Chiron on Mount Pelion, who brought him up until he was twenty years of age. Then Iason came home, and without a shoe on his left foot, having lost it in wading through a mountain torrent, presented himself before Pelias, demanding his father's restoration to his sovereignty. The crafty Pelias, whom an oracle had warned against a one-shoed man, promised on his oath to do what he asked, if Iason would go instead of himself to bring the golden fleece. This task the oracle had imposed upon himself, but he was too old to perform it. Another version of the story is, that Iason, after completing his education with Chiron, preferred to live in the country; that he came, with one shoe on, to a sacrifice that Pelias was offering to Poseidon on the sea-shore; that Pelias asked him what he would do if he were king and had been forewarned of his death at the hand of a subject; and that, upon Iason answering that he would make him bring the golden fleece, Pelias gave him the commission. Heré had put that answer into Iason's mouth, because she regarded him with favour, and wished to punish Pelias for having slain Sidero in her temple. See SALMONEUS.

The vessel for the voyage, the fifty-oared Argo, is said to have been named after its builder Argos, a son of Phrixus after his return to Orchomenus, the home of his fathers. The ship was built of the pines of Pelion under the direction of Athené, like Heré a protectress of Iason, who inserted in the prow a piece of the speaking oak of Dodona. The heroes who, at Iason's call, took part in the expedition (fifty all told, according to the number of the oars), were originally, in the version to which the Minyan family gave currency, Minyans of Iolcos, Orchomenus, Pylos, and other places. Among them were Acastus the son of Pelias, a close friend of Iason; Admetus, Erginus, Euphemus, Periclymenus, and Tiphys. But, as the story spread, all the Greek heroes that could have been living at the time were included among the number of the Argonauts—e. g. Heracles, Castor and Polydeuces, Idas and Lynceus, Calaïs and Zetes the sons of Boreas, Peleus, Tydeus, Meleager, Amphiaraüs, Orpheus, Mopsus and Idmon the prophets of the expedition, and even the huntress Atalanta. Iason takes the command, and Tiphys manages the helm. Setting sail from Pegasae, the port of Iolcos, the Argonauts make the island of Lemnos, where only women dwell, and after some considerable stay there (see HYPSIPYLÉ) go past Samothrace and through the Hellespont to the island of Cyzicus, where they are hospitably received by Cyzicus, the king of the Doliones; but, attempting to proceed, are beaten back by a storm at night, and, being taken by their late friends for pirates, are attacked, and have the ill-fortune to kill their young king. On the coast of Mysia they leave Heracles behind to look for Hylas (q. v.), who has been carried off by nymphs. On the Bithynian shore, Polydeuces vanquishes the Bebrycian king Amycus (q. v.) in a boxing-match. At Salmydessus in Thrace, the blind seer Phineus, whom Calaïs and Zetes had rid of the Harpies, his tormentors, instructs them with regard to the rest of their journey, and especially how to sail through the Symplegades, two floating rocks that clash together at the entrance to the Black Sea. By his advice Iason sends a dove before him, and as she has only her tail-feathers cut off by the colliding rocks, they venture on the feat of rowing the Argo through. By Heré's help, or, according to another account, that of Athené, they do what no man has done before: they pass through, the ship only losing her rudder. Skirting the southern shore of the Pontus, they meet with a friendly reception from Lycus, king of the Maryandini, though here the seer Idmon is killed by a wild boar in hunting, and the helmsman Tiphys dies of a disease, whereupon Ancaeus takes his place. Past the land of the Amazons they come to the island of Aretias, whence they scare away the Stymphalian birds (see HERACLES), and take on board the sons of Phrixus, who had been shipwrecked there on their way to Greece. At length they reach the mouth of the Phasis in the land of the Colchians. Upon Iason's demand, Aeëtes promises to give up the golden fleece, on condition that Iason catches two brazen-hoofed, fire-breathing bulls, yokes them to a brazen plough, and ploughs with them the field of Ares, sows the furrows with dragons' teeth, and overcomes the mail-clad men that are to spring out of them. The hero has given up all hope of success, when Aphrodité kindles in the breast of the king's daughter Medea an irresistible love for the stranger. Medea gives him an ointment to protect him from the fiery breath of the bulls, as well as the strength to harness them, and advises him to throw a stone in among the earth-born giants, who will kill each other. But when all this is done Aeëtes does not give up the fleece. Then Iason, with the help of Medea, whom he promises to take home with him as his wife, throws the dragon that guards it into a sleep, takes it down, and escapes with Medea and his comrades. Aeëtes sends his son Absyrtus in pursuit, whom Iason kills by stratagem. Another story is that Medea takes her little brother Absyrtus with her, cuts him to pieces, and throws the limbs one by one into the sea, so that her father, while pursuing her, might be delayed in picking them up and laying them out.

Athené superintending the Building of the Argo. (Zoëga, Bassi rilievi, tav. 45.)

As to the return of the Argonauts, the legends differ considerably. One of the oldest makes them sail up the Phasis into the river Oceanus, and over that to Libya, where they drag the ship twelve days' journey overland to Lake Tritonis, and get home across the Mediterranean. Other accounts agree with this in substance, while others, again, mix up the older tradition with the adventures of Odysseus. The heroes sail up the Danube into the Adriatic, and are within hail of Corcyra (Corfu) when a storm breaks out, and the piece of oak from Dodona foretells their ruin unless they have the murder of Absyrtus expiated by Circé. Hence they sail up the Eridanus into the Rhone, and so into the Tyrrhenian Sea to the island of Circé, who purifies them. They go past the island of the Sirens, against whose magic the songs of Orpheus protect them. All but Butes (q. v.) pass in safety between Scylla and Charybdis with the help of the gods, and reach the island of the Phaeacians, where Iason marries Medea to evade the sentence of their host Alcinoüs, who, in his capacity as umpire, has given judgment that the girl Medea be delivered up to her Colchian pursuers. Already within sight of the Peloponnesus, a storm drives them into the Libyan Syrtes, whence they carry their ship, saved by divine assistance, to Lake Tritonis. Thence, guided by Triton (see EUPHEMUS) into the Mediterranean, they return by way of Crete to Iolcos.

During their absence Pelias has put to death Aeson and his son Promachus, and Iason's mother has taken her own life. Medea sets to work to avenge them. Before the eyes of Pelias's daughters she cuts up an old he-goat, and by boiling it in a magic caldron restores it to life and youth. Promising in like manner to renew the youth of the aged Pelias, she induces them to kill their father and then leaves them in the lurch. Driven away by Acastus, the son of the murdered king, Iason and Medea take refuge with Creon, king of Corinth. But, after ten years of happy wedlock, Iason resolves to marry Creon's daughter Creüsa, or Glaucé. On this, Medea kills the bride and her father by sending the unsuspecting maiden a poisoned robe and a diadem as a bridal gift, murders her own two sons, Mermerus and Pheres, in her faithless husband's sight, and, escaping in a car drawn by serpents, sent by her grandfather Helios, makes her way to Aegeus, king of Athens. (See MEDEA.) Iason is said to have come by his death through the Argo, which he had set up and consecrated on the Isthmus. One day, when he was lying down to rest under the ship, the stern fell off and killed him.

The legend of the Argonauts is extremely ancient; even Homer speaks of it as universally known. We first find it treated in detail in Pindar; then the Alexandrian poet Apollonius of Rhodes (q. v.) tried to harmonize the various versions, and was followed by the Latin poets Valerius Flaccus, Varro Atacinus, and the late Greek Pseudo-Orpheus. See Roscher, *Ausfürliches Lexicon*, 530–537; A. Lang, *Custom and Myth*, pp. 94–102 (1884); and id. Introduction to Mrs. Hunt's translation of Grimm's *Household Tales* (1884).

Argonautĭca. See APOLLONIUS; VALERIUS FLACCUS; VARRO.

Argos (Ἄργος) is said to have signified, in the language of the Macedonians and Thessalians, a plain, and it may therefore contain the same root as the Latin word *ager*. In Homer we find mention of the Pelasgic Argos—that is, a town or district of Thessaly—and of the Achaean Argos, by which he means sometimes the whole Peloponnesus, sometimes Agamemnon's kingdom of Argos, of which Mycenae was the capital, and sometimes the town of Argos. As Argos frequently signifies the whole Peloponnesus, the most important part of Greece, so the Ἀργεῖοι often occur in Homer as a name of the whole body of the Greeks, in which sense the Roman poets also use *Argivi*.—(1) ARGOS, a district of Peloponnesus, lying between Arcadia and the Aegean Sea, and also called by Greek writers Argia, or Argolicé, or Argolis. Under the Romans ARGŎLIS became the usual name of the country. (2) The chief city of Argolis, about two miles from the sea, on the Sinus Argolicus. It was fabled to have been built by seven Cyclopes from Syria (Eurip. *Iph. in Aul.* 152, 534) for Inachus, the first king. The city was under the especial protection of Heré. Its inhabitants were called Argivi and Argolici—names which are often applied to the whole Greek race. (See HELLAS.) The city is often spoken of in the plural form, *Argi*.

Argos Amphilochĭcum. The chief town of Amphilochia in Acarnania, on the Ambracian Gulf.

Argus (Ἄργος). (1) The son of Zeus and Niobé, and third king of Argos. (2) Called Panoptes, "all-seeing," as having a hundred eyes. He was the son of Agenor, or Arestor, or Inachus. Heré appointed him guardian of the cow into which Io had been metamorphosed; but Hermes, at the command of Zeus, sent him to sleep by the sweet notes of his lute, and then cut off his head. Heré transplanted his eyes to the tail of the peacock, her favourite bird. See IO. (3) The builder of the Argo, son of Phrixus (Apoll. Rhod. i. 112).

Argyraspĭdes (ἀργυράσπιδες). A division of the Macedonian army, who were so called because they carried shields covered with silver plates. They were held in high honour by Alexander the Great, after whose death they went over to Antigonus. Livy mentions them as the royal cohort in the army of Antigonus. The Roman emperor Alexander Severus had in his army a body of men who were called *argyroaspides*. (Lamprid. *Alex. Sev.* 50.)

Argyriou Diké (ἀργυρίου δίκη). A civil suit to compel the defendant to pay over to the plaintiff money in his possession, or for which he was liable.

Argyrĭpa. See ARPI.

Argyrītis (ἀργυρῖτις). See ARGENTUM.

Argyrokopeion (ἀργυροκοπεῖον). The mint at Athens. See MONETA; NUMISMATICS.

Argyrolŏgoi (ἀργυρολόγοι). The ships of the Athenians, ostensibly employed during the Peloponnesian War in levying the regular tribute from the allies; but often engaged in making arbitrary exactions and forced contributions even from neutrals. Cf. Thucyd. iii. 19; iv. 50, 75; Xen. *Hell.* i. 1, 8.

Argўros (ἄργυρος). See ARGENTUM.

Argyrotamiae (ἀργυροταμίαι). The native financial officers of the Greek provinces during the period of Roman rule, and distinguished from the ταμίαι or Roman quaestors. (*C. I. G.* 2787.)

Arīa (Ἀρία and Ἀρεία). The most important of the eastern provinces of the ancient Persian Empire, bounded on the east by the Paropamisadae, on the north by the Margiana and by Hyrcania, on the west by Parthia, and on the south by the desert of Carmania. From Aria was derived the name under which all the eastern provinces were included. See ARIANA; PERSIA.

Ariadné (Ἀριάδνη). The daughter of Minos and Pasiphaë, who fell in love with Theseus when he came to Crete to kill the Minotaur, and gave him a clew of yarn, to help him to find his way back to the light of day after slaying the monster in the Labyrinth. She then escaped with him. Homer represents Ariadné as slain by Artemis in the island of Dia, close to Crete, at the request of Dionysus. But the later legend shifts the scene to the isle of Naxos, where the slumbering Ariadné is deserted by Theseus. On waking, she is in the depths of despair, when Dionysus comes and raises her to the dignity of a god's wife. Zeus grants her immortality, and sets her bridal gift, a crown, among the stars. She received divine honours: at Naxos her festivals were held, now with dismal rites recalling her abandonment, and now with bacchanalian revelry befitting the happy bride of Dionysus. The story of Ariadné has been a favourite subject for artists and poets in all ages.

Sleeping Ariadné. (Vatican.)

At Athens in the autumn they held a joyous festival to her and Dionysus, which Theseus was supposed to have founded on his return from Crete. In Italy, where they identified Dionysus with their wine-god Liber, they also took Ariadné for the wine-goddess Libera (q. v.). See in English, F. Tennyson's *Ariadne*, and Ross's *Ariadne in Naxos*.

Ariadnēa (Ἀριάδνεια). Festivals held in honour of Ariadné in Naxos, and also in Cyprus.

Ariaeus (Ἀριαῖος). The friend of Cyrus, and commander of the left wing of his army at the battle of Cunaxa (q. v.) in B.C. 401. After the death of Cyrus he deserted the Greeks, and thus procured his pardon from King Artaxerxes (Xen. *Anab.* i. 8, 5, etc.).

Ariāna (Ἀριανή). A name derived from Aria (q. v.) and applied to the eastern provinces of the Persian Empire, including Aria, Parthia, the Paropamisadae, Arachosia, Drangiana, Gedrosia, and Carmania. See PERSIA.

Ariarāthes (Ἀριαράθης). The name of several kings of Cappadocia. (1) Son of Ariamnes I., defeated by Perdiccas, and crucified, B.C. 322. Eumenes then obtained possession of Cappadocia. (2) Son of Holophernes, and nephew of Ariarathes I., recovered Cappadocia after the death of Eumenes, 315. He was succeeded by Ariamnes II. (3) Son of Ariamnes II., and grandson of the preceding, married Stratonicé, daughter of Antiochus II., king of Syria. (4) Son of the preceding, reigned 220–162. He married Antiochis, the daughter of Antiochus the Great, and assisted Antiochus in his war against the Romans. After the defeat of Antiochus, Ariarathes sued for peace in 188, which he obtained on favourable terms. (5) Son of the preceding, surnamed Philopator, reigned 163–130. He assisted the Romans in their war against Aristonicus of Pergamus, and fell in this war, B.C. 130. (6) Son of the preceding, reigned 130–96. He married Laodicé, sister of Mithridates VI., king of Pontus, and was put to death by Mithridates. (7) Son of the preceding, also murdered by Mithridates, who now took possession of his kingdom. The Cappadocians rebelled against Mithridates, and placed upon the throne (8) the second son of No. 6; but he was speedily driven out of the kingdom by Mithridates, and shortly afterwards died. (9) Son of Ariobarzanes II., reigned 42–36. He was deposed and put to death by Antony, who appointed Archelaüs as his successor.

Ariaspae (Ἀριάσπαι) or **Agriaspae.** A people in the south part of the Persian province of Drangiana, on the borders of Gedrosia (Arr. *Anab.* iii. 27, 4).

Aricia. Now Riccia; an ancient town of Latium at the foot of the Alban Mount, on the Appian Way, sixteen miles from Rome. It was subdued by the Romans, with the other Latin towns, in B.C. 338, and received the Roman franchise. In its neighbourhood were the celebrated grove and temple of Diana Aricina, on the borders of the Lacus Nemorensis. Diana was worshipped here with barbarous customs; her priest, called Rex Nemorensis, was always a runaway slave, who obtained his office by killing his predecessor in single combat.

This custom is very strikingly alluded to by Macaulay in the following lines:

"From where the witch's fortress
  O'erhangs the dark-blue seas,
From the still, glassy lake that sleeps
  Beneath Aricia's trees—
Those trees in whose dim shadow
  The ghastly priest doth reign,
The priest who slew the slayer,
  And shall himself be slain."

—*Battle of Lake Regillus.*

Aries (κριός). The battering-ram, one of the most effective engines used by the ancients to make a breach in the walls of a besieged town. Originally it consisted of a strong pole, with iron-mounted head, brought up to the wall in earlier

Aries, Battering-ram. (Column of Trajan.)

times by hand, in later times on wheels. In its final form it was constructed in the following manner: A stout beam, sometimes composed of several pieces, and measuring from sixty-five to one hundred feet long or more, was hung by ropes on a strongly mounted horizontal beam, and swung backwards and forwards, so as to loosen the stones of the wall and make it fall. As the engine stood close to the wall, the men working it were sheltered by a roofed shell of boards, called the ram tortoise-shell (*testudo arietina*) and resting on a framework that ran upon wheels. To protect the roof and sides of the shell against fire thrown from the walls, they were coated with raw or well-soaked hides, or other similar contrivances. The loosened stones were picked out of the wall with a strong iron hook at the end of a pole—the wall-sickle (*falx muralis*), as it was called. Single holes were punched in the wall with the wall-borer (*terebra*), a ram with a sharp point, which was pushed forward on rollers.

Battering-ram under shed. *Testudo Arietina.* (Column of Septimius Severus.)

The besieged tried to knock the ram's head off by dropping heavy stones on it, or to catch it in a noose and turn the blow aside or upwards, or to deaden the force of its blows with sand-bags and mats. By the usage of war, a town that wished to secure indulgent treatment must surrender before the ram touched the walls.

Arimaspi (Ἀριμασποί). A people in the north of Scythia, represented as men with only one eye, who fought with the griffins for the possession of the gold in their neighbourhood. The germ of the fable is perhaps to be recognized in the fact that the Ural Mountains abound in gold. See ARISTEAS; AURUM.

Arimazes (Ἀριμάζης or Ἀριομάζης). A powerful Indian prince of Sogdiana, who treated Alexander the Great with much insolence, and who, in consequence, after surrendering, was crucified together with his family (Quint. Curt. vii. 11).

Arĭmi (Ἄριμοι) and **Arĭma** (τὰ Ἄριμα). The names of a mythical people, district, and range of mountains in Asia Minor, which the old Greek poets made the scene of the punishment of the monster Typhoeus (q. v.).

Arimĭnum. Now Rimini; a town in Umbria, at the mouth of the little river Ariminus. It was originally inhabited by Umbrians and Pelasgians, was afterwards in the possession of the Senones, and was colonized by the Romans in B.C. 268, from which time it appears as a flourishing place. After leaving Cisalpine Gaul, it was the first town on the eastern coast of Italy at which a person arrived in Italia proper.

Ariobarzānes (Ἀριοβαρζάνης). I.—KINGS OR SATRAPS OF PONTUS. (1) Betrayed by his son Mithridates to the Persian king, about B.C. 400. (2) Son of Mithridates I., reigned 363–337. He revolted from Artaxerxes in 362, and may be regarded as the founder of the kingdom of Pontus. (3) Son of Mithridates III., reigned 266–240, and was succeeded by Mithridates IV. II.—KINGS OF CAPPADOCIA. (1) Surnamed Philoromaeus, reigned B.C. 93–63, and was elected king by the Cappadocians, under the direction of the Romans. He was several times expelled from his kingdom by Mithridates, but was finally restored by Pompey in 63, shortly before his death. (2) Surnamed Philopator, succeeded his father in 63. (3) Surnamed Eusebes and Philoromaeus, son of No. 2, whom he succeeded about 51. He assisted Pompey against Caesar, who not only pardoned him, but even enlarged his territories. He was slain in B.C. 42 by Cassius.

Arīon. (1) (Ἀρίων). A Greek poet and musician, of Methymna in Lesbos, who flourished about B.C. 625. In the course of a roving life he spent a considerable time at the court of Periander, tyrant of Corinth. Here he first gave the dithyramb (q. v.) an artistic form, and was therefore regarded as the inventor of that style in general. He is best known by the story of his rescue on the back of a dolphin. Returning from a journey through Lower Italy and Sicily, he trusted himself to a crew of Corinthian sailors, who resolved to kill him on the open sea for the sake of his treasures. As a last favour he extorted the permission to sing his songs once more to the lyre, and then to throw himself into the sea. His strains drew a number of dolphins around him, one of which took him on its back, and carried him safe to land at the foot of the foreland of Taenarum. Thence he hastened to Corinth, and convicted the sailors, who were telling Periander that they had left the minstrel safe at Tarentum (Hyg. *Fab.* 194). A bronze statue of a man on a dolphin, which stood on the top of Taenarum, was supposed to be his thank-offering to Poseidon (Herod. i. 24). A hymn of thanksgiving to the god of the sea, preserved under his name, belongs to a later time. (2) (Ἀρείων). A fabulous horse said to have been begotten by Poseidon.

Ariovistus. A German who had conquered a great part of Gaul, but was defeated by Caesar and driven back across the Rhine in B.C. 58 (Caes. *B. G.* Bk. i.).

Aristaenĕtus (Ἀρισταίνετος). A Greek grammarian and rhetorician, of Nicaea in Bithynia, friend of Libanius, who praises him in the highest terms; he was killed in an earthquake at Nicomedia, A.D. 358. His name is erroneously attached to a collection, probably composed in the fifth or sixth century, of erotic Epistles, feeble imitations of Alciphron, loose in tone and declamatory in style. The text and a Latin version are contained in the Didot collection of the *Epistolographi Graeci* (Paris, 1873). See NOVELS AND ROMANCES.

Aristaeus (Ἀρισταῖος). A son of Apollo and Cyrené, was born in Libya. He afterwards went to Thrace, where he fell in love with Eurydicé, the wife of Orpheus. The latter, while fleeing from him, perished by the bite of a serpent; whereupon the Nymphs, in anger, destroyed the bees of Aristaeus. The way in which he recovered his bees is related in the Fourth Georgic of Vergil. After his death he was worshipped as a god, on account of the benefits he had conferred upon mankind. He was regarded as the protector of flocks and shepherds, of vine and olive plantations; he taught men to keep bees, and averted from the fields the burning heat of the sun and other causes of destruction. He is said to have had the care of Dionysus when young.

Aristagŏras (Ἀρισταγόρας). A native of Miletus, brother-in-law of Histiaeus, and left by the latter during his stay at the Persian court in charge of the government of Miletus. Having failed in an attempt upon Naxos (B.C. 501), which he had promised to subdue for the Persians, and fearing the consequences of his failure, he induced the Ionian cities to revolt from Persia. He applied for assistance to the Spartans and Athenians: the former refused, but the latter sent him twenty ships and some troops. In 499 his army captured and burned Sardis, but was finally chased back to the coast. The Athenians now departed; the Persians conquered most of the Ionian cities; and Aristagoras in despair fled to Thrace, where he was slain by the Edonians in 497.

Aristarchus (Ἀρίσταρχος). (1) A Samian mathematician and astronomer at Alexandria, who flourished between B.C. 280 and 264. (2) Of Samothrace, the celebrated grammarian, flourished B.C. 156. He was a pupil of Aristophanes, and founded at Alexandria a grammatical and critical school. At an advanced age he went to Cyprus, where he died at the age of seventy-two, of voluntary starvation, because he was suffering from incurable dropsy. Aristarchus was the greatest critic of antiquity. His labours were chiefly devoted to the Homeric poems, of which he published an edition which has been the basis of the text from his time to the present day. He divided the *Iliad* and *Odyssey* into twenty-four books each. His text of the Homeric poems is substantially the groundwork of our present recensions. It had marginal notes indicating the verses which Aristarchus regarded as spurious or doubtful, and pointing out anything worthy of remark. The meaning of the notes, and the reasons for appending them, were explained in separate commentaries and excursuses, founded on a marvellously minute acquaintance with the language and contents of the Homeric poems and the whole of Greek literature. He was the head of the school of *Aristarcheans,* who continued working on classical texts in his spirit till after the beginning of the Empire. Of his numerous grammatical and exegetical works only fragments remain. An idea of his Homeric studies, and of their character, can best be gathered from the Venetian scholia to the *Iliad,* which are largely founded on extracts from the Aristarcheans Didymus and Aristonicus. See HOMERUS.

Aristeas (Ἀριστέας). An epic poet of Proconnesus, of whose life we have only fabulous accounts. His date is quite uncertain. He is represented as a magician, whose soul could leave and re-enter its body according to its pleasure. He was connected with the worship of Apollo, which he was said to have introduced at Metapontum. He wrote an epic poem on the Arimaspi (q. v.), in three books, from which the pseudo-Longinus quotes. See Herod. iv. 13.

Aristĕrae (Ἀριστεραί). An island on the coast of the Peloponnesus (Pausan. ii. 34).

Aristīdes (Ἀριστείδης). (1) An Athenian, surnamed "the Just," son of Lysimachus, of an ancient and noble family. He fought at the battle of Marathon, B.C. 490; and in the next year, 489, was archon. He was the great rival of Themistocles, and it was through the influence of the latter with the people that he suffered ostracism (q. v.) in 483 or 482. He was still in exile in 480 at the battle of Salamis, where he did good service by dislodging the enemy, with a band raised and armed by himself, from the islet of Psyttalea. He was recalled from banishment after the battle, was appointed general in the following year (479), and commanded the Athenians at the battle of Plataea. In 477, when the allies had become disgusted with the conduct of Pausanias and the Spartans, he and his colleague Cimon had the glory of obtaining for Athens the command of the maritime confederacy (see CONFEDERACY OF DELOS); and to Aristides was by general consent intrusted the task of drawing up its laws and fixing its assessments. The first tribute of four hundred and sixty talents, paid into a common treasury at Delos, bore his name. This is his last recorded act. He probably died in 468, and so poor that he did not leave enough to pay for his funeral. His daughters were portioned by the State, and his son Lysimachus received a grant of land and of money. (2) The author of a licentious romance, in prose, entitled *Milesiaca,* having Miletus for its scene. It was translated into Latin by L. Cornelius Sisenna, a contemporary of Sulla, and became popular with the Romans. The title of his work gave rise to the term "Milesian" as applied to works of fiction. (3) Of Thebes, a celebrated Greek painter, who flourished about B.C. 360–330. His pictures were so much valued that long after his death Attalus, king of Pergamus, offered 600,000 sesterces for one. (4) See THEODORUS. (5) See QUINTILIANUS.

Aristion (Ἀριστίων). A philosopher who, by the influence of Mithridates, made himself tyrant of Athens. He committed suicide, on the capture of Athens by Sulla in B.C. 87.

Aristippus (Ἀρίστιππος). A Greek philosopher, a native of Cyrenê and a pupil of Socrates, after whose death in B.C. 399 he travelled about the Greek cities, imparting instruction for money. He was founder of the Cyrenaic School, or the system of Hedonism (from ἡδονή, pleasure). His doctrine was that as a basis for human knowledge the only things real and true are our sensations, and not the external objects that produce them; that the aim of life is what all living things strive after, pleasure; and that virtue is only so far a good thing as it tends to the production of pleasure. The wise man shows his wisdom in governing his desires; mental training, indeed, being the only thing which can qualify us for real enjoyment. In pleasure there is no difference of kind, only of degree and duration. Aristippus's writings seem to have disappeared early; five letters, in the Doric dialect, which have come down under his name are undoubtedly spurious. See Ueberweg, *Hist. of Philosophy,* pp. 59–98, Eng. trans. (N. Y. 1872); his life by Diogenes Laërtius; and the articles CYRENAICI; EPICURUS; PHILOSOPHIA.

Aristobūlus (Ἀριστόβουλος). A Greek historian, who in his youth accompanied Alexander the Great on his campaigns. In his eighty-fifth year, when living at Cassandrea in Thrace, he wrote a work upon Alexander, in which he recorded his careful observations on geography, ethnography, and natural science. The book is highly praised for its trustworthiness, but only fragments of it have reached us. He and Ptolemy were the chief authorities for Arrian's *Anabasis.*

Aristoclēa (Ἀριστόκλεια). A beautiful woman, who, while offering sacrifice naked, was seen by Strato, who fell violently in love with her, and contended for her so furiously with his rival Callisthenes that she died during the struggle, upon which Strato took his own life, while Callisthenes was never seen again (Plut. *in Amat*).

Aristŏcles (Ἀριστοκλῆς). (1) A Greek artist, and, like his brother Canachus, a sculptor in bronze at Sicyon. He flourished about B.C. 480, and founded a school at Sicyon that lasted for a long time. (2) An Athenian sculptor of the same name and of the same period, author of a relief known as "The Athenian Hoplite," one of the oldest remaining monuments of Attic art. See cut, p. 649.

Aristocratia (ἀριστοκρατία). Literally, "the government of the best." As used by Plato, Aristotle, Polybius, and others, it meant government by a class whose supremacy was founded less on wealth than on personal distinction; whereas government by the wealthy was ὀλιγαρχία. See Arist. *Pol.* iv. 3, 10; Plato *Pol.* p. 301 A; and the articles EUPATRIDAE; GEOMORI; PATRICII.

Aristodēmus (Ἀριστόδημος). (1) A descendant of Heracles, son of Aristomachus, brother of Temenus and Cresphontes, and father of Eurysthenes and Procles. He was killed at Naupactus by a flash of lightning, just as he was setting out on the expedition into the Peloponnesus, and his two sons obtained Sparta, which would have fallen to him. (2) A Messenian, the chief hero in the First Messenian War. He sacrificed his own daughter to save his country. He was afterwards elected king in place of Euphaës; and continued the war against the Spartans, till at length, finding resistance hopeless, he put an end to his life on the tomb of his daughter, about B.C. 723.

Aristogīton (Ἀριστογείτων). See HARMODIUS.

Aristomăchus (Ἀριστομάχος). The son of Cleodemus or Cleodacus, grandson of Hyllus, great-grandson of Heracles, and father of Temenus, Cresphontes, and Aristodemus. He fell in battle when he invaded the Peloponnesus; but his sons were more successful, and conquered the Peloponnesus.

Aristomĕnes (Ἀριστομένης). A Messenian, the hero of the second war with Sparta, who belongs more to legend than to history. He was a native of Andania, and was sprung from the royal line of Aepytus. Tired of the yoke of Sparta, he began the war in B.C. 685. After the defeat of the Messenians, in the third year of the war, Aristomenes retreated to the mountain fortress of Ira, and there maintained the war for eleven years, constantly ravaging the land of Laconia. In one of his incursions the Spartans overpowered him with superior numbers, and, carrying him with fifty of his comrades to Sparta, cast them into the pit where condemned criminals were thrown. The rest perished; but not so Aristomenes, the favourite of the gods; for legends tell how an eagle bore him up on its wings as he fell, and a fox guided him on the third day from the cavern. But the city of Ira, which he had so long successfully defended, fell into the hands of the Spartans, who again became masters of Messenia, B.C. 668. Aristomenes settled at Ialysus, in Rhodes, where he married his daughter to Damagetus, king of Ialysus.

Ariston (Ἀρίστων). (1) Of Chios, a Stoic philosopher, and a disciple of Zeno, who flourished about B.C. 260. (2) A Peripatetic philosopher of Iulis, in the island of Ceos, who succeeded Lycon as head of the Peripatetic school, about B.C. 230.

Ariston (ἄριστον). Breakfast. See CENA; PRANDIUM.

Aristonīcus (Ἀριστόνικος). A natural son of Eumenes II. of Pergamus. Upon the death of his brother Attalus III., B.C. 133, who left his kingdom to the Romans, Aristonicus laid claim to the crown. He defeated in 131 the consul P. Licinius Crassus; but in 130 he was himself defeated and taken prisoner by M. Perperna, was carried to Rome by M'. Aquillus in 129, and was there put to death.

Aristophănes (Ἀριστοφάνης). (1) The greatest writer of Greek comedy. He lived at Athens, B.C. 444–388. His father, Philippus, is said to have been not a native Athenian, but a settler from Rhodes or Egypt, who afterwards acquired citizenship. However this may be, the demagogue Cleon, whose displeasure Aristophanes had incurred, tried to call in question his right to the citizenship. His first comedy appeared in B.C. 427, but was not performed under his own name because of his youth; and several more of his plays were brought upon the stage by Callistratus and Philonides, till in 424 he brought out *The Knights* in his own person. Forty-four of his plays were known to antiquity, though four of them were considered doubtful. Of these we possess eleven, the only complete Greek comedies which have survived, besides the titles and numerous fragments of twenty-six others. The eleven are: (1) *The Acharnians* (Ἀχαρνεῖς), which gained him the victory over Cratinus and Eupolis, B.C. 425, written during the great Peloponnesian War to induce the Athenians to make peace. (2) *The Knights* (Ἱππεῖς) mentioned above, B.C. 424, also crowned with the first prize, and aimed directly against the demagogue Cleon. (3) *The Clouds* (Νεφέλαι), B.C. 423, his most famous and, in his own opinion, his most successful piece, though when played it only won the third prize. We have it now in a second, and apparently unfinished, edition. It is directed against the pernicious influence of the Sophists, as the representative of whom Socrates is attacked. (4) *The Wasps* (Σφῆκες), brought out in B.C. 422, and, like the two following, rewarded with the second prize; it is a satire upon the Athenian passion for lawsuits. (5) *The Peace* (Εἰρήνη), of the year B.C. 421, recommending the conclusion of peace. (6) *The Birds* (Ὄρνιθες), acted in B.C. 414, and exposing the romantic hopes built on the expedition to Sicily. This is unquestionably the happiest production of the poet's genius, and is marked by a careful reserve in the employment of dramatic resource. (7) *The Lysistraté* (Λυσιστράτη), B.C. 411, a Women's Conspiracy to bring about peace; the last of the strictly political plays. (8) *Thesmophoriazusae* (Θεσμοφοριάζουσαι), probably to be dated B.C. 410. It is written against Euripides's dislike of women, for which the women who are celebrating the Thesmophoria drag him to justice. (9) *The Frogs* (Βάτραχοι), which was acted in B.C. 405, and won the first prize. It is a piece sparkling with genius, on the decay of tragic art, the blame of which is laid on Euripides, then recently deceased. (10) *Ecclesiazusae* (Ἐκκλησιάζουσαι), or The National Assembly of Women, B.C. 392. It is levelled against the vain attempts to restore the Athenian state by cut-and-dried constitutions. (11) *Plutus* (Πλοῦτος), or The God of Wealth. The blind god is restored to sight, and better times are brought about. This play was acted first in B.C. 408, then in 388 in a revised form suitable to the time, and dispensing with chorus and parabasis. This play marks the transition to the Middle Comedy. See COMOEDIA.

In the opinion of the ancients, Aristophanes holds a middle place between Cratinus and Eupolis, being neither so rough as the former nor so mild as the latter, but combining the severity of the one with the grace of the other. What was thought of him in his own time is evident from Plato's *Symposium*, where he is numbered among the noblest of men; and an epigram attributed to that philosopher says that the Graces, looking for an enduring shrine, found it in the soul of Aristophanes. He unites understanding, feeling, and fancy in a degree possessed by few poets of antiquity. His keen glance penetrates the many evils of his time and their most hidden causes; his scorn for all that is base, and his patriotic spirit, burning to bring back the grand days of Marathon, urge him on, without respect of persons or regard for self, to drag the faults he sees into daylight, and lash them with stinging sarcasm; while his inexhaustible fancy invents ever new and original materials, which he manipulates with perfect mastery of language and technical skill. If his jokes are often coarse and actually indecent, the fact must be imputed to the character of the Old Comedy and the licentiousness of the Dionysiac festival, during which the plays were acted. No literature has anything to compare with these comedies. Ancient scholars, recognizing their great importance, bestowed infinite pains in commenting on them, and valuable relics of their writings are enshrined in the existing collections of scholia.

The principal MS. of Aristophanes is that of Ravenna, which contains the eleven extant plays. Next in importance is the Codex Venetus Marcianus of nearly the same date, but which lacks the *Acharnians, Thesmophoriazusae, Ecclesiazusae*, and *Lysistraté*. Both of these are probably derived from one Alexandrian archetype. The *editio princeps* of Aristophanes is that of Aldus (Venice, 1498), containing nine plays, to which Junta added two more (1515). The ed. of Invernizzi-Beck contains a collation of the Ravenna MS. Other editions are those of Bekker (1829); Dindorf (5th ed. 1869); Meineke (1860); Blaydes (1886); Holden (5th ed. 1887). Eng. trans. of eight plays by Rudd (1867); of five plays by Frere (1871). There is a complete concordance by Dunbar (1883).

(2) Aristophanes the Grammarian (or Scholar) of Byzantium, born about B.C. 260, went in his early youth to Alexandria, and was there a pupil of Zenodotus and Callimachus. On the death of Apollonius of Rhodes, Aristophanes, when past his sixtieth year, was appointed to be chief librarian, and died at the age of seventy-seven. His fame was eclipsed by that of his pupil Aristarchus, but he still passed for one of the ablest grammarians and critics of antiquity, distinguished by industry, learning, and sound judgment. In addition to the Homeric poems, which formed his favourite study, and of which he was the first to attempt a really critical text, he devoted his labours to Hesiod; the lyric poets, especially Alcaeus and Pindar; and the tragic and comic poets, Aristophanes and Menander in particular. The received introductions to the plays of the tragedians and Aristophanes are in their best parts derived from him. He was also the author of a large and much-quoted work of a lexicographical character, considerable fragments of which still survive. See Homerus; Textual Criticism.

Aristŏphon (Ἀριστόφων). The name of two Attic orators, both contemporaries of Demosthenes. The first (of the deme Azenia) defended the law of Leptines against Demosthenes in B.C. 354. No oration of either Aristophon is extant.

Aristotĕles (Ἀριστοτέλης). A great philosopher, the son of Nicomachus, court physician to Philip II. of Macedon, and born in B.C. 384 at Stagira, a small town in the Thracian Chalcidicé. He received from his father a training in the natural science of the day; but his philosophical education was obtained in Athens, where he was a pupil and companion of Plato during the last twenty years of the latter's life (367–347). His mind was, however, of too exact and unimaginative a type to accept the mystical idealism of Plato's later years, and we find him gradually developing a system of philosophy of his own, distinct from, and often antagonistic to, that of his teacher, whose doctrines he nevertheless always treated with pious respect, even when controverting them. In the later years of his association with Plato and the Academy he began to lecture on his own account, treating especially the subject of rhetoric. At the death of Plato the pre-eminent ability of Aristotle would seem to have designated him to succeed to the leadership of the Academy, but his divergence from his master's teaching was too great to make this possible. At the invitation of his friend Hermeas, ruler of Atarneus and Assos in Mysia, he repaired to his court, where he spent several years, and married his niece and adopted daughter Pythias. His son Nicomachus, however, was the offspring of a later union with Herpyllis, said to have been a slave, but to whom he testifies the warmest gratitude in his will. From 344 to 342 he was again in Athens, but in the latter year he accepted an invitation from King Philip to undertake the oversight of the education of his son Alexander. It is not too fanciful to trace, in the lofty views of the future conqueror, and his passionate love for the Homeric poems, the influence of his three years' association with the great philosopher. Aristotle did not forget, in this influential position, the town of his birth, but obtained from Alexander that Stagira, which had been destroyed by Philip, should be rebuilt. On Alexander's accession to the throne of Macedon in 335, Aristotle removed to Athens, and established his school in the gymnasium known as the Lyceum, from whose shady walks (περίπατοι) his pupils became known as Peripatetics. He is said to have given two classes of lectures: the more abstruse discussions (ἀκροαματικά) in the morning for an inner circle of advanced pupils, and the popular discourses (ἐξωτερικά) in the evening for the general body of lovers of knowledge. At the death of Alexander, in 323, the anti-Macedonian party in Athens recovered a temporary ascendency, and Aristotle was involved in an accusation for impiety, to escape which he fled to Chalcis in Euboea, in order, as he said, "that the Athenians might not for a second time commit a sin against philosophy." Here he died soon after, in 322, of a stomach complaint. A grave recently (1891) excavated at Chalcis, by the explorers of the American School at Athens, is identified with considerable probability as that of Aristotle. His will, perhaps genuine, is preserved to us in Diogenes Laërtius, v. 1. A statuette in the Mattei Palace and a life-size statue in the Villa Spada at Rome reproduce the keen features of the profound thinker. His character, if we may judge from the tone of his writings and from the provisions of his will, was mild and generous; and the slanderous reports found in such writers as Athenaeus may be dismissed as utterly without foundation.

The many-sided activity of Aristotle's mind and his prodigious industry are shown in the extent and variety of his writings, which embraced, according to Diogenes Laërtius, 146 works in 400 books. Another list, which seems to rest on the authority of the Peripatetic Andronicus, who in the time of Cicero published a new edition of Aristotle's works, gives the number of books as 1000.

Head of Aristotle.

The history of his writings, if a widely accepted tradition be true, is a romantic one. After the death of Theophrastus, who had succeeded to the leadership of the Peripatetic School, his library, including the works of Aristotle, is said to have passed into the hands of his pupil Neleus of Scepsis in the Troad. The heirs of Neleus, to protect the books from the literary greed of the Attalids of Pergamus, concealed them in a vault, where they were injured by dampness and the ravages of moths and worms. In this hiding-place they were discovered about the year B.C. 100 by Apellicon (q. v.), a rich book-lover, and conveyed to Athens, whence they were taken to Rome after the capture of Athens by Sulla in B.C. 86. In Rome they soon attracted the attention of scholars, and the new edition then prepared by Andronicus (see above) gave a fresh impetus to the study of Aristotle and of philosophy in general. Strangely enough, the list of works in Diogenes Laërtius, mentioned above, does not seem to contain any of the forty treatises in our Aristotle, and it is not impossible that the whole catalogue is a list of forgeries, compiled at a time when the real works were lost to sight. The greater part of what has come down to us under the name of Aristotle is undoubtedly genuine.

The works of Aristotle fall naturally under three heads: I. Dialogues and other works of a popular character. II. Collections of facts and material for scientific treatment. III. Systematic works. Among his writings of a popular character the only one which we possess of any consequence is the interesting tract *On the Polity of the Athenians*, recently discovered in some Egyptian papyri, and edited by Kenyon under the auspices of the British Museum (London, 1891). It is written in a clear and easy style, and sheds a flood of new light on Athenian political history, and especially on the Constitution in Aristotle's own time. Of the works of the second class nothing worthy of mention has been preserved. The systematic treatises are marked by a severe plainness of style, with none of the golden flow of language which the ancients praised in Aristotle. This may be due to the fact that these works were not, in most cases, published by Aristotle himself or during his lifetime, but were edited after his death, from unfinished MSS., by Eudemus, Nicomachus, or Theophrastus.

Aristotle's systematic treatises may be grouped in several divisions, in accordance with the subjects discussed, as follows: I. Logic. II. Natural Science. III. Psychology and Metaphysics. IV. Ethics. V. Politics. VI. Rhetoric.

I. The writings on the general subject of LOGIC were included by the later Peripatetics under the name of *Organon*, or Instrument, as having to do with reasoning, the chief instrument of dialectic and scientific investigation. They embrace (1) the *Categories* (Κατηγορίαι), treating of the ten fundamental forms of predicating existence (probably not by Aristotle himself, but by one of his pupils). (2) *On Interpretation* (Περὶ Ἑρμηνείας), dealing with the forms and parts of the sentence. (3) *Prior* and *Posterior Analytics* (Ἀναλυτικὰ Πρότερα and Ὕστερα), containing (*a*) the doctrine of scientific proof and (*b*) of cognition or knowledge in general. (4) The *Topics* (Τοπικά), on the art of dialectic. (5) The *Sophistical Refutations* (Σοφιστικοὶ Ἔλεγχοι), an examination of the fallacies of the Sophists, then in such vogue. All of the most important of Aristotle's works in the domain of Logic have come down to us, and they include the most enduring contribution which the great analyst has made to human thought. The science of deductive reasoning has made no essential progress since his day. II. The works in the department of NATURAL SCIENCE are (1) the *Physics* (Φυσικὴ Ἀκρόασις). This is not a treatise on physics in the modern sense of the term, but is happily styled by Hegel the "metaphysics of physics." It treats of the principles of existence, of matter and form, explaining the fundamental conceptions in accordance with which we look at the phenomena of nature. (2) *On the Heavens* (Περὶ Οὐρανοῦ). (3) *On Generation and Decay* (Περὶ Γενέσεως καὶ Φθορᾶς), discussing the pairs of opposites, hot and cold, and wet and dry, and how their different combinations produce the four elements of fire, air, earth, and water. (4) *Meteorology* (Μετεωρολογικά). (5) *Researches about Animals* (Αἱ περὶ τὰ Ζῷα Ἱστορίαι). (6) *On the Parts of Animals* (Περὶ Ζῴων Μορίων). (7) *On the Generation of Animals* (Περὶ Ζῴων Γενέσεως). (8) *On Locomotion of Animals* (Περὶ Πορείας Ζῴων). (9) A number of shorter works are usually classed together under the head of *Parva Naturalia*. They treat of sense and sensation, youth and age, and other phenomena of life. The treatises *On Plants*, *On the Universe*, *On Motion*, *On Respiration*, *On Colour*, *On Physiognomy*, *On Strange Statements*, and the collection of various scientific *Problems*, are all of doubtful authenticity. The above-mentioned works exhibit an astonishing breadth of observation in natural history. The *Researches about Animals* shows an acquaintance with almost five hundred different species, and the observations on the purpose and adaptation of the organs of various creatures are characterized by remarkable insight. III. PSYCHOLOGY AND METAPHYSICS. (1) *On the Soul* (Περὶ τῆς Ψυχῆς). This treatise might fairly be classed with the works on natural science, as it does not deal with psychology in the modern sense, but with the physiology of the vital principle in animals generally. (2) The *Metaphysics* (Μεταφυσικά), as the name indicates, forms the highest step in Aristotle's system, and deals with the first principles of all existence. Here he grapples with the deepest questions of philosophy, but with less clear and satisfactory results than he reaches in many of his discussions. His doctrine of mind (νοῦς), or the godhead, as the power that moves the starry heavens, is not sufficient to account for the structure of the universe or the origin of existing things. IV. ETHICS. The ethical works of Aristotle embrace (1) the *Nicomachean Ethics* ('Ηθικὰ Νικομάχεια); (2) the *Eudemean Ethics* ('Ηθικὰ Εὐδήμεια); (3) the so-called *Magna Moralia* ('Ηθικὰ Μεγάλα). The foundation principles of the Aristotelian system of morals appear alike in all of these works, but it is probable that the first alone is the work of the philosopher himself. He teaches that happiness is the highest good, and that this is found in an activity of the soul in accordance with virtue. Virtue is a permanent state of the soul, and consists in the mean between the too much (ὑπερβολή) and the too little (ἔλλειψις). The *Nicomachean Ethics* is one of the most interesting of Aristotle's works, and his descriptions of some of the virtuous characters (see bk. iv.) are exceedingly impressive. V. POLITICS. Closely connected with the *Ethics* is the *Politics* (Πολιτικά). The best ordering of the State was, to Aristotle's mind, the worthiest problem for the philosopher; and though his treatment of the subject was not brought to a logical conclusion, yet the work contains much valuable information and abounds in interesting remarks. The *Economics* (Οἰκονομικά) is probably the work of some later writer of the Peripatetic School. VI. RHETORIC. The rhetorical works include (1) the *Poetics* (Περὶ Ποιητικῆς), and (2) the *Art of Rhetoric* (Τέχνη 'Ρητορική). The first of these, though insignificant in length, has received more consideration in recent years than almost any other work of the author. The famous definition of tragedy in chap. vi., the discussion of the parts of tragedy in chap. xii., and the distinction between epic and tragic poetry in chap. xxvi. are passages of the greatest interest and value. The celebrated doctrine of the κάθαρσις effected by tragedy (vi. 2) has given rise to much discussion, but has not yet been satisfactorily explained. The doctrine of the three "unities" of tragedy, upon which so much stress has been laid by the French critics, was first promulgated by Aristotle in this work. The *Rhetoric* treats of oratorical proof, and its leading elements, together with an interesting discussion (bk. iii.) of style—all marked by the author's usual clear and exhaustive treatment.

In reviewing the works of Aristotle we are at a loss whether to admire most his vast and accurate observation of nature, his profound acquaintance with the literature of his day, or his deep and penetrating insight, his keen analysis, and his unfailing good sense. In his love for research and his critical tendency he may be regarded as the forerunner of the Alexandrian Age which was soon to open. His style, though so concise as sometimes to be obscure, is often a model of condensed energy, and his occasional illustrations are marvellously appropriate. His influence on the course of human thought since his day has been almost boundless. In antiquity he was the most honoured philosopher, while the early Christian writers compared Plato and Aristotle to Moses and Christ. He was the oracle of the Middle Ages, when his writings, through his followers, the schoolmen, were almost all that saved Europe from utter barbarism. The Arabians, in the reign of the calif Al Mamun (A.D. 813), began to translate his works, which became the foundation of Saracenic culture, and were brought by them to the knowledge of Western Europe through the medium of Latin versions from the Arabic. In Arabic tradition Aristotle is the "wisest man," just as his pupil Ishkander (Alexander) is the hero of warlike fable. The Roman Catholic Church almost canonized him, and his philosophical system, as modified by the great Dominicans Albertus Magnus and Thomas Aquinas, lies at the basis of Catholic theology to-day. But when the Renaissance gave back to Europe the knowledge of Plato, the popularity of Aristotle declined. Plato's perfection of form, and the fact that he wrote for the enlightened public generally, rather than for an inner circle of special students, no doubt contributed to this result. The Reformers, who regarded Aristotle as the bulwark of the Papacy, attacked him bitterly, and by the middle of the eighteenth century he had been almost set aside. It was reserved for the nineteenth century, through the labours of Schleiermacher, Spengel, Brandis, and others, to find the key to the true historical appreciation of the value of Aristotle.

The influence of Aristotle on the vocabulary of modern philosophy is worthy of especial notice. A large number of terms which are in constant use to-day are derived from him, either directly or through the medium of Latin equivalents. Some of these are: *principle* (ἀρχή), *subject* (ὑποκείμενον), *matter* (*materies* = ὕλη), *form*, *end*, *final cause*, *faculty* (δύναμις), *energy*, *category*, *predicament*, *habit*, *mean*, *extreme*, *quintessence*, *metaphysics*, etc.

The great edition of the Prussian Academy (Berlin, 1831–70), in five quarto volumes, contains the text in Bekker's recension (i. and ii.); the Latin translation by Pacius, Argyropylus, Bessario, and others (iii.); the Scholia edited by Brandis (iv.); the fragments, and the Aristotelian Index of Bonitz (v.). A convenient text edition is published in the Teubner Series (Leipzig). Annotated editions of single works are numerous. Among them may be mentioned the *Psychology*, by Trendelenburg (Jena, 1877); the *Metaphysics*, by Schwegler-Bonitz (Bonn, 1848); the *Nicomachean Ethics*, by Ramsauer (Leipzig, 1878); the *Politics*, by Susemihl (Leipzig, 1879); the *Rhetoric*, by Spengel (Leipzig, 1867); the *Poetics*, by Vahlen (Berlin, 1884). Valuable English works are Grant's *Ethics* (London, 1866); Bywater's *Ethics* (Oxford, 1890); Newman's *Politics* (Oxford, 1887); Jowett's *Politics* (Oxford, 1885); Wallace's *Psychology* (Cambridge, 1884); Grote's *Aristotle* (London, 1872). The ancient commentaries of Alexander Aphrodisiensis (A.D. 200) and Simplicius (A.D. 530) are of great importance historically. The *Paraphrases* of Themistius (A.D. 375) are occasionally useful in settling doubtful points in the text. The literal translations in the Bohn Library are of respectable merit.

Aristoxĕnus ('Αριστόξενος). A Greek philosopher and musician, a native of Tarentum, and a pupil of Aristotle. He lived about B.C. 330, and was a prolific writer on various subjects, but most particularly on music. In contrast with the Pythagoreans, who referred everything to the relations of numbers, he regarded music as founded on the difference of tones as perceived by the ear. Of his ʽΑρμονικὰ Στοιχεῖα three books are preserved, but they are neither complete nor in their original shape. They have been edited by Marquard (Berlin, 1869) and Saran (Leipzig, 1893). Only a part of his ʽΡυθμικὰ Στοιχεῖα has survived. See MUSICA.

Arithmetĭca (ἀριθμητική sc. τέχνη). See ABACUS; LOGISTICA; MATHEMATICA.

Arīus (Ἄρειος). A celebrated writer and theologian of Alexandria, who denied the eternal divinity and consubstantiality of the Second Person of the Trinity. Though much persecuted for his heresy, he succeeded in winning the favour of the emperor Constantine, and supplanted his great opponent St. Athanasius. When about to enter the cathedral at Constantinople in triumph, he suddenly died, A.D. 336. From him the sect of the Arians gets its name.

Ariusia (Ἀριουσία). A district on the north coast of Chios, famous for its wine.

Arma, Armatūra (ὅπλα, ἔντεα, τεύχεα). Arms, armour. The weapons of attack and defence employed by the Greeks of historic times are essentially the same as those with which the Homeric heroes appear equipped in an earlier age. The changes gradually introduced, especially after the Persian Wars, tended to make the armour lighter and to give greater power of movement to the combatants. For defensive armour they used a helmet (κόρυς, κυνέη); a cuirass (θώραξ) (see THORAX); a girdle (ζώνη) of leather or felt, covering the lower part of the body, and reaching down to the middle of the thighs. Sometimes this consisted of narrow strips called πτέρυγες (wings) arranged either in single or double rows, and covered with metal. Sometimes it was a complete coat plated with bands of metal. The greaves (κνημῖδες) covered the front part of the legs from the ankles to just above the knee, and consisted of flexible metal plates or leather fastened behind with buckles. The weapons of defence were completed by the shield.

For offensive weapons they had, besides the sword (ξίφος), the lance (δόρυ), five to seven feet long. This was of iron, sometimes broader, sometimes narrower, and sometimes hooked and with an iron joint on the butt end which served to fix the spear more easily in the ground, or could be used as an offensive weapon when the regular head was broken off. The cavalry used a shorter lance (πάλτον) for hurling as well as thrusting; this was much shorter than the Macedonian σάρισσα. The other weapons of attack were javelins (ἀκόντια) of different sizes, the longer kinds of which were hurled by means of a thong, bows and arrows (see ARCUS), and slings. On the equipment of the different kinds of troops, see GYMNETAE; HIPPEIS; HOPLITAE; PELTASTAE.

Among the Romans the full equipment of defensive armour similarly consisted of helmet (*cassis*, *galea*), cuirass (see LORICA), greaves (*ocrea*), and shield (*clipeus, scutum*). With regard to the greaves, it must be noted that in later times the infantry wore them only on the right leg, which was unprotected by the shield.

Besides the sword (*ensis, gladius*), the horse and foot of the legion alike used, as an offensive weapon, the lance (see HASTA). It was only the light-armed troops that fought with javelins and slings. Then the *pilum* (q. v.) was introduced, first for a part and finally for the whole of the legion. This was the missile which the Romans hurled at the commencement of a battle before coming to close quarters with their swords. Bows were not a national weapon with the Romans, and were only used by their allies. See EXERCITUS; LEGIO.

Armamenta. A term more particularly applied to the tackle of a ship. See NAVIS.

Armamentarium (ὁπλοθήκη, σκευοθήκη). A place where *armamenta* (q. v.) were kept. A naval arsenal. A very celebrated one was that in the Piraeus (q. v.), built about B.C. 342–330, and destroyed by Sulla. See Plut. *Sulla*, 14.

Armarium, from a Pompeian Painting. (Rich.)

Armarium. A cupboard, book-case, or closet. In private houses it was usually placed in the *atrium* (q. v.). In an inscription (Orelli, 4549) the word is applied to a sepulchre.

Armenia (Ἀρμενία). A country of Asia, lying between Asia Minor and the Caspian Sea, in a lofty table-land, backed by the chain of the Caucasus, watered by the rivers Cyrus and Araxes, and containing the sources of the Tigris and of the Euphrates, the latter of which divides the country into two unequal parts, which were called Maior and Minor. The people of Armenia were one of the most ancient families of that branch of the human race which is called Caucasian. (See INDO-EUROPEAN LANGUAGES.) They were conquered by the Assyrians and Persians, and were at a later time subject to the Greek kings of Syria. When Antiochus the Great (q. v.) was defeated by the Romans (B.C. 190), the country regained its independence, and was at this period divided into the two kingdoms of Armenia Maior and Minor. Ultimately, Armenia Minor was made a Roman province by Trajan; and Armenia Maior, after being a perpetual object of contention between the Romans and the Parthians, was subjected to the revived Persian Empire by its first king, Artaxerxes, in A.D. 226.

Armilausa. A kind of military tunic worn by foot-soldiers and reaching to the knees. See Mayor on Juv. v. 143; and Ducange, *s. h. v.* (ed. Favre, 1883).

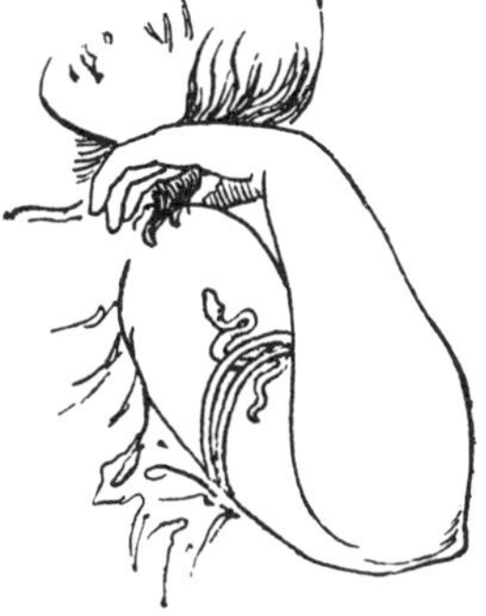

Bracelet. (On Statue of Sleeping Ariadnê in the Vatican.)

Armilla (ψέλεον, ὄφις). A bracelet or armlet. Among the Persians and Medes these ornaments were worn by men, probably as a mark of distinction (Herod. viii. 113); but in Greece they seem to have been confined to women, or to effeminate men. The Greek name ὄφεις (also δράκοντες) was given them because of their serpentine shape.

Bracelets were likewise worn at Rome by ladies of rank, but it was considered a mark of effeminacy for men in an ordinary way to use such feminine ornaments (Suet. *Cal.* 52; *Ner.* 30). They were, however, publicly conferred by a Roman general upon soldiers for deeds of extraordinary merit (Liv. x. 44; Plin. *H. N.* xxxiii. § 37), in which case they were worn as a mark of honour, and probably differed in form from the ordinary ornaments of the kind.

Roman Bracelets.

The cut below shows the Roman military bracelet. The original, which is of pure gold, was found in Cheshire, England.

Roman Military Bracelet.

Armillum. A wine-jug (*urceolus*) used in sacrifices, and carried on the shoulder (*armus*), whence the name.

Armilustrium. A Roman festival for the purification of arms, and celebrated annually on the 19th of October. It marked the end of the campaigning season, as the Quinquatrus marked the beginning of it. See Mommsen, *Inscr. Lat. Ant.* p. 404; and Livy, xxvii. 37.

Arminius. The Latinized form of *Hermann*, "the chieftain." Son of Sigimer, and chief of the tribe of the Cherusci, who inhabited the country to the north of the Hartz Mountains, now forming the south of Hanover and Brunswick. He was born in B.C. 18; and in his youth he led the Cherusci as auxiliaries of the Roman legions in Germany, where he learned the Roman language, was admitted to the freedom of the city, and enrolled among the equites. In A.D. 9, Arminius persuaded his countrymen to rise against the Romans, who were now masters of this part of Germany. His attempt was crowned with success. Quintilius Varus, who was stationed in the country with three legions, was destroyed, with almost all his troops (see VARUS); and the Romans had to relinquish all their possessions beyond the Rhine. In A.D. 14, Arminius had to defend his country against Germanicus. At first he was successful, but Germanicus made good his retreat to the Rhine. It was in the course of this campaign that Thusnelda, the wife of Arminius, fell into the hands of the Romans. In A.D. 16, Arminius was defeated by Germanicus, and his country was probably only saved from subjection by the jealousy of Tiberius, who recalled Germanicus in the following year. At length Arminius aimed at absolute power, and was in consequence cut off by his own relations in the thirty-seventh year of his age, A.D. 19. A colossal statue of Arminius by Bandel was erected in August, 1875, near Detmold in Germany. See Böttger, *Hermann der Cheruskerfürst* (1874), and the article GERMANIA.

Armoracia (*ῥαφανίς*). Horseradish.

Armorĭca or **Aremorĭca.** The name of the northwest coast of Gaul from the Ligeris (Loire) to the Sequana (Seine), derived from the Keltic *ar*, *air*, "upon;" *muir*, *môr*, "the sea." Later, the name was confined to Brittany.

Army. See CASTRA; EXERCITUS; LEGIO; SACRAMENTUM.

Arnê (Ἄρνη). A daughter of Aeolus, who gave her name to two towns, one in Thessaly and the other in Boeotia. Poseidon, under the form of a bull, became her lover (Pausan. ix. 40; Ovid, *Met.* vi. 4).

Arnēis (Ἀρνηΐς). The same as Arnis (q. v.).

Arnis (Ἀρνίς). A festival held by the Argives in August, during which they killed any dog that came into the Agora; hence the name *κυνοφόντις* given to the feast (Athen. iii. p. 99 *e*). The massacre of dogs was probably due to the fear of madness, as was the similar killing of dogs at Rome in the same month, which is, however, usually assigned to their having failed to give notice of the attack of the Gauls on the Capitol. See Pliny, *H. N.* xxix. 59.

Arnobius. An African who won a high reputation as a master of rhetoric at Sicca in Numidia, in the reign of Diocletian. He was at first a heathen and an assailant of Christianity; but on becoming a Christian, to prove the sincerity of his conversion, he wrote (about A.D. 295) the extant work *Adversus Gentes.* This is a superficial and rhetorical defence of Christianity and attack on polytheism, but it is full of instruction with regard to the contemporary heathenism and its various worships. It is contained in seven books. The text is derived from a MS. in Paris of the ninth century, in which the work is entitled *Adversus Nationes.* The *editio princeps* is that of Sabaeus (Rome, 1543). Good editions are those of Hillebrand (Halle, 1844), and Reifferscheid (1875). Eng. trans. in the *Ante-Nicene Library*, vol. xix.

Arnus. The modern Arno; the chief river of Etruria, which, rising in the Apennines, and flowing by Pisae (Pisa), emptied into the Tuscan Sea.

Arŏtoi Hiĕroi (*ἄροτοι ἱεροί*). "Sacred ploughings," three in number, held in Attica in the month Maimacterion (Nov.–Dec.), to commemorate the institution of agriculture. The first ploughing was held at Sciros; the second on the Rarion Plain near Eleusis; the third under the Acropolis. A family of priests known as Βουζύγιοι, a sort of Arval Brotherhood (see FRATRES ARVALES), cared for the sacred plough and oxen. See Schömann, *Griech. Alt.* ii. 266.

Arpi. See ARGYRIPA.

Arpīnum. A town of Latium on the river Fibrenus, originally belonging to the Volscians and afterwards to the Samnites, was a Roman municipium, and received the *ius suffragii*, or right of voting in the Roman Comitia, B.C. 188. It was the birthplace of Marius and Cicero.

Arquītes. See SAGITTARII.

Arra, Arrăbo. An earnest. The word *arrabo* is Semitic, and occurs (ἀρραβών, *LXX.*) in Gen. xxxviii. 17–20, of a ring, bracelets, and staff given as a pledge for the price, and the corresponding verb in Hebrew several times. The Phœnician traders probably brought word and custom to Greece, and Plautus probably followed in this a Greek original. He uses the word for anything given as sign of a bargain being made and as pledge of its fulfilment. The original idea seems to have been a temporary deposit reclaimable on the bargain being fulfilled. The thing thus serving as *arra* ("earnest"—"arles," Scotch; *les arrhes*, French; "erles penny," North-Country English), given on hiring a servant—"Queen's shilling" in enlisting recruits (*Handgeld, Gottesheller, Weinkauf*, in Germany)—might be a mere token or a pledge of some value, as a ring or a piece of money, or might pass into part payment of the price or part delivery of the thing purchased, and, according to any special agreement or custom, might be forfeitable by the party not carrying out his bargain, such forfeit being in lieu of or in addition to other remedies for breach of contract.

Arretium. The modern Arezzo; one of the more important of the twelve cities of Etruria, was situated in the northeast of the country at the foot of the Apennines, and possessed a fertile territory near the sources of the Arnus and the Tiber, producing good wine and corn. It was particularly celebrated for its pottery.

Arrhephoria (τὰ ἀρρηφόρια). A festival which, according to the various ways in which the name is written (for we find ἐρσηφόρια or ἐρρηφόρια), is attributed to different deities. The first form is derived from ἄρρητα, and thus would indicate a festival at which mysterious things were carried about. The other name would point to Ersé or Hersé, who was believed to be a daughter of Cecrops, and whose worship was intimately connected with that of Athené. But, even admitting the latter, we still have sufficient ground for believing that the festival was solemnized, in a higher sense, in honour of Athené. It was held at Athens, in the month of Scitophorion. See Mommsen, *Heortologie*, pp. 443 foll.

Arrhidaeus (Ἀρριδαῖος). The son of Philip of Macedon and a female dancer, Philinna of Larissa. He was of imbecile understanding. On the death of Alexander, B.C. 323, he was elected king under the name of Philip, and in 322 he married Eurydicé. On their return to Macedonia he and his wife were made prisoners and put to death by order of Olympias, in the year 317.

Arria. (1) See PAETUS. (2) See THRASEA.

Arriānus, FLAVIUS. A Greek author, who wrote chiefly on philosophy and history. He was born at Nicomedia in Bithynia, towards the end of the first century A.D., and was a pupil of the Stoic philosopher Epictetus. He lived under the emperors Hadrian, Antoninus Pius, and Marcus Aurelius, enjoying a high reputation for culture and ability, which procured him the citizenship of Rome and Athens, and high offices of state, such as the governorship of Cappadocia under Hadrian, A.D. 136, and the consulship under Antoninus. His last years were spent in his native town, where he filled the office of priest to Demeter, and died at an advanced age. From the likeness of his character to that of the famous Athenian, he was nicknamed "Xenophon Junior." Of his philosophical works we have still the first half (four books) of the *Discourses of Epictetus*, a leading authority for the tenets of that philosopher and the Stoical ethics; and the handbook called the *Encheiridion of Epictetus*, a short manual of morality, which on account of its pithy and practical precepts became a great favourite with Pagans and Christians, had a commentary written on it by Simplicius in the sixth century, and after the revival of learning was long used as a school-book. Of his numerous historical writings we possess the chief one, the *Anabasis of Alexander*, in seven books. This is a complete history of that conqueror from his accession to his death, drawn from the best sources, especially Ptolemy and Aristobulus, and modelled on Xenophon, of whom we are reminded by the very title and the number of books, though it has none of Xenophon's charm. It is the best work on Alexander that has survived from antiquity. To this we should add the *Indica*, a short work on India, written in the Ionic dialect, and especially valuable for its abstract of Nearchus's report of his voyage from the mouth of the Indus to the Persian Gulf; also the description of another coasting voyage, the *Periplus Ponti Euxini*, and a trifling treatise on hunting, the *Cynegeticus*. A work on tactics wrongly ascribed to him is probably from the hand of Aelian the Tactician. Of his other histories—e. g. of the successors of Alexander, of Trajan's battles with the Parthians, of his own native country till its absorption into the Empire, and the campaign against the Alani during his command in Cappadocia—we have only abstracts or fragments. The best edition of the *Anabasis* is that of Krüger (1848). There is an English translation by Chinnock (1893).

Arrogatio. One of the Roman methods of adoption. See ADOPTIO.

Arsăces (Ἀρσάκης). The name of (1) the founder of the Parthian Empire, which was also borne by all his successors, who were hence called the *Arsacidae*. He was of obscure origin, but he induced the Parthians to revolt from Antiochus II., king of Syria, and became the first monarch of the Parthians, about B.C. 250. The events which immediately followed are stated very differently by different historians. He reigned only two years, and was succeeded by his brother Tiridates. (2) TIRIDĀTES, reigned thirty-seven years, B.C. 248–211, and defeated Seleucus Callinicus, the successor of Antiochus II. (3) ARTABĀNUS I., son of the preceding, was attacked by Antiochus III. (the Great), who, however, at length recognized him as king, about 210. (4) PRIAPATIUS, son of the preceding, reigned fifteen years, and left three sons, Phraates, Mithridates, and Artabanus. (5) PHRAATES I. was succeeded by his brother (6) MITHRIDĀTES I., who greatly enlarged the Parthian Empire by his conquests. He defeated Demetrius Nicator, king of Syria, and took him prisoner in 138. He died during the captivity of Demetrius, between 138 and 130. (7) PHRAĀTES II., son of the preceding, defeated and slew in battle Antiochus VII. Sidetes, B.C. 128. Phraates himself was shortly after killed by the Scythians. (8) ARTABĀNUS II., youngest son of No. 4, fell in battle against the Thogarii or Tocharii, apparently after a short reign. (9) MITHRIDĀTES II., son of the preceding, added many nations to the Parthian

Coin of Arsaces VI. (Mithridates I.).

Empire, whence he obtained the surname of Great. He sent an ambassador to Sulla, B.C. 92. (10) MNASCĪRES (?), the successor of the preceding, of whom nothing is known. (11) SANATRŎCES, reigned seven years, and died about B.C. 70. (12) PHRAĀTES III., son of the preceding, lived at the time of the war between the Romans and Mithridates of Pontus, by both of whom he was courted. He was murdered by his two sons, Mithridates and Orodes. (13) MITHRIDĀTES III., son of the preceding, was expelled from the throne on account of his cruelty, and was succeeded by his brother Orodes. (14) ORŌDES I., brother of the preceding, was the Parthian king whose general Surenas defeated Crassus and the Romans, B.C. 53. (See CRASSUS.) After the death of Crassus, Orodes gave the command of the army to his son Pacorus, who invaded Syria both in 51 and 50, but was in each year driven back by Cassius. In 40, the Parthians again invaded Syria, under the command of Pacorus and Labienus, but were defeated in 39 by Ventidius Bassus, one of Antony's legates. In 38, Pacorus once more invaded Syria, but was completely defeated and fell in the battle. This defeat was a severe blow to the aged king, Orodes, who shortly afterwards surrendered the crown to his son Phraates during his lifetime. (15) PHRAĀTES IV. was a cruel tyrant. In 36, Antony invaded Parthia, but was obliged to retreat after losing a great part of his army. A few years afterwards Phraates was driven out of the country by his subjects, and Tiridates proclaimed king in his stead. Phraates, however, was soon restored by the Scythians, and Tiridates fled to Augustus, carrying with him the youngest son of Phraates. Augustus restored his son to Phraates, on condition of his surrendering the Roman standards and prisoners taken in the war with Crassus and Antony. They were given up in 20, and their restoration was celebrated not only by the poets, but by festivals and commemorative monuments. Phraates also sent to Augustus as hostages his four sons. In A.D. 2, Phraates was poisoned by his wife Thermusa and her son Phraataces. (16) PHRAATĂCES reigned only a short time, as he was expelled by his subjects on account of his crimes. The Parthian nobles then elected as king Orodes, who was of the family of the Arsacidae. (17) ORŌDES II. also reigned only a short time, as he was killed by the Parthians on account of his cruelty. Upon his death the Parthians applied to the Romans for Vonones, one of the sons of Phraates IV., who was accordingly granted to them. (18) VONŌNES I., son of Phraates IV., was also disliked by his subjects, who therefore invited Artabanus, king of Media, to take possession of the kingdom. Artabanus drove Vonones out of Parthia, who resided first in Armenia, next in Syria, and subsequently in Cilicia. He was put to death in A.D. 19. (19) ARTABĀNUS III. obtained the Parthian kingdom soon after the expulsion of Vonones, about A.D. 16. Artabanus was involved in hostilities with the Romans, and was expelled more than once by his subjects. (20) GOTARZES succeeded his father, Artabanus III., but was defeated by his brother Bardanes and retired into Hyrcania. (21) BARDĀNES, brother of the preceding, was put to death by his subjects in 47, whereupon Gotarzes again obtained the crown. (22) VONŌNES II. succeeded Gotarzes about 50. His reign was short. (23) VOLOGĒSES I., son of Vonones II. or Artabanus III. Soon after his accession he conquered Armenia, which he gave to his brother Tiridates. He carried on war with the Romans, but was defeated by Domitius Corbulo, and at length made peace with the Romans on condition that Tiridates should receive Armenia as a gift from the Roman emperor. Accordingly Tiridates came to Rome in 63, and obtained from Nero the Armenian crown. (24) PACŎRUS succeeded his father, Vologeses I., and was a contemporary of Domitian and Trajan. (25) CHOSROĒS or OSROĒS succeeded his brother Pacorus during the reign of Trajan. His conquest of Armenia occasioned the invasion of Parthia by Trajan, who stripped it of many of its provinces, and made the Parthians for a time subject to Rome. (See TRAIANUS.) Upon the death of Trajan, in A.D. 117, Hadrian relinquished the conquests of Trajan, and made the Euphrates, as before, the eastern boundary of the Roman Empire. (26) VOLOGĒSES II. succeeded his father, Chosroës, and reigned from about A.D. 122 to 149. (27) VOLOGĒSES III. was defeated by the generals of the emperor Verus, and purchased peace by ceding Mesopotamia to the Romans. From this time to the downfall of the Parthian Empire there is great confusion in the list of kings. The last king of Parthia was ARTABANUS IV., in whose reign the Persians recovered their long-lost independence.

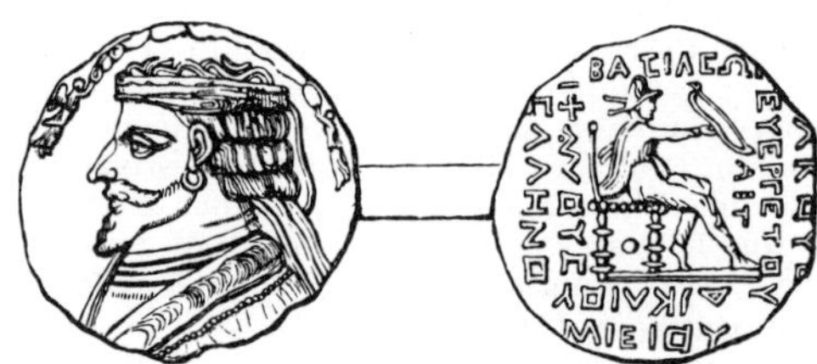

Coin of Parthian Arsacidae.

They were led by Artaxerxes, the son of Sassan, and defeated the Parthians in three great battles, in the last of which Artabanus was taken prisoner and killed, A.D. 226. Thus ended the Parthian Empire of the Arsacidae, after it had existed 476 years. The Parthians were now obliged to submit to Artaxerxes, the founder of the dynasty of the Sassanidae, which continued to reign till A.D. 651. See PARTHIA.

Arsacia (Ἀρσακία). See RHAGAE.

Arsacĭdae. The name of a dynasty of Parthian kings. (See ARSACES.) It was also the name of a dynasty of Armenian kings, who reigned in Armenia from B.C. 149 to A.D. 428.

Ars Amōris or **Ars Amatoria.** A poem on the art of love by P. Ovidius Naso (q. v.), brilliant and licentious, whose immorality was at least the pretence of its author's subsequent banishment by Augustus. It is in three books.

Ars Donāti. The title of a grammar by Aelius

Donatus (q. v.) that was a favourite school-book in the Middle Ages, so that in Old English the word "donat" (Chaucer) is used as a generic term for a grammar.

Arsinŏë (Ἀρσινόη). (1) The daughter of Meleager, and mother of Ptolemy I. of Egypt, by Philip, father of Alexander. During her pregnancy she was married to Lagus. (2) The daughter of Ptolemy I. of Egypt and Berenicé. She married Lysimachus, king of Thrace, who was already advanced in years, by whom she had several children. Lysimachus, setting out for Asia, left her in Macedonia, with two sons, Lysimachus and Philip, a part of the fruits of their union. This monarch having been slain in an expedition, Ptolemy Ceraunus seized on Macedonia, but could not take the city of Cassandria, where Arsinoé had taken refuge with her children. He therefore offered her his hand in marriage, and with much difficulty obtained her consent. But no sooner had he been admitted into the city for the purpose of celebrating the nuptials, than he caused her two sons to be slain, and exiled Arsinoé herself to Samothrace. From this island she soon took her departure to wed Ptolemy Philadelphus, her own brother, the first instance of this kind of union, and which became afterwards so common in the time of the Ptolemies. Although many years older than Ptolemy, she nevertheless inspired him with such a passion that, after her death, he gave her name to one of the nomes of Egypt (Arsinoïtis), and to several cities both in that country and elsewhere. He even gave orders to have a temple erected to her, but his own death and that of the architect prevented the fulfilment of his wishes. It was intended to have had the ceiling of loadstone, and the statue of iron, in order that the latter might appear to be suspended in the air (Plin. *H. N.* xxxiv. 14). (3) A daughter of Lysimachus, king of Thrace, and the earlier wife of Ptolemy Philadelphus. She became by him the mother of Ptolemy III. (Euergetes), Lysimachus, and Berenicé. After Ptolemy's union with Arsinoé, his own sister, she was banished to Coptos. The charge brought against her was a design to overthrow her rival. (4) Daughter of Ptolemy III. and Berenicé, married Ptolemy Philopator, her brother. Her husband subsequently having become enamoured of Agathoclea, and being completely ruled by this woman and her brothers, was induced, at their instigation, to order Arsinoé to be put to death. (5) A daughter of Ptolemy Auletes, proclaimed queen by Ganymedes, when Caesar attacked Alexandria. She was conquered, and brought in triumph to Rome; but, as this proved displeasing to the people, she was set at liberty. Subsequently, at the instigation of her younger sister Cleopatra, she was put to death by the orders of Antony, in the Temple of Artemis at Miletus. See Mahaffy's *Empire of the Ptolemies* (1896).

Arsinŏë (Ἀρσινόη). The name of several cities, each called after one or other of the persons mentioned above. Of these the most important were: (1) In the Nomos Heroöpolites in Lower Egypt, near or upon the head of the Sinus Heroöpolites, or west branch of the Red Sea (Gulf of Suez). It was afterwards called Cleopatra. (2) The chief city of the Nomos Arsinoïtes in Middle Egypt; formerly called Crocodilopolis, from its being the chief seat of the Egyptian worship of the crocodile.

Ars Poetĭca. A poetical epistle written by Q. Horatius Flaccus (q. v.) in hexameters, and addressed to the Pisos. It is best regarded as an expression of his matured views on topics connected with literary studies. It abounds in happy turns of phrase, and is marked throughout its lines by sound sense and excellent literary taste.

Art, ANCIENT. See the articles AES; ARCHITECTURA; AURUM; CAELATURA; COLUMNA; FICTILÉ; GEMMA; NUMISMATICS; PICTURA; STATUARIA.

Artăba (ἀρτάβη). A Persian measure of capacity, much used as a corn-measure, and containing 51 choenices, or 12¾ gallons, nearly (Herod. i. 192).

Artabānus (Ἀρτάβανος). (1) Son of Hystaspes and brother of Darius; is frequently mentioned in the reign of his nephew Xerxes as a wise and frank counsellor. (2) An Hyrcanian, commander of the body-guard of Xerxes, assassinated this king in B.C. 465, but was shortly afterwards killed by Artaxerxes. (3) The name of several kings of Parthia.

Artabāzes (Ἀρταβάζης) or **Artavasdes.** A king of Armenia, the son and successor of Tigranes, who began to reign about B.C. 70. It was principally through his treacherous advice, as to the mode of entering Parthia, that Crassus failed in his expedition against that country. He was subsequently taken by Antony, to whom he had also acted a treacherous part in his Parthian expedition, who led him in triumph at Alexandria. He was put to death, after the battle of Actium, by Cleopatra, who wished to obtain assistance from the king of Media, and therefore sent him the head of Artavasdes, his enemy. The prince appears to have been a very well educated man. He wrote in Greek two historical works, some tragedies, discourses, etc. (Plut. *Anton.* 50, seqq.).

Artaxăta (τὰ Ἀρτάξατα). The chief city of Greater Armenia, and the seat of the kings. It was burned by the Roman Corbulo (q. v.), and when rebuilt by Tiridates was named Neronea, in honour of the emperor Nero. See ARTAXIAS.

Artaxerxes (Ἀρταξέρξης). The name of four Persian kings. (1) Surnamed LONGIMĂNUS, from his right hand being longer than his left, succeeded his father, Xerxes I., and reigned B.C. 465–425. He carried on war against the Egyptians, who were assisted in their revolt by the Athenians. He was succeeded by his son, Xerxes II. (2) Surnamed MNEMON, from his good memory, succeeded his father, Darius II., and reigned B.C. 405–359. Respecting the war between him and his brother Cyrus, see CYRUS. Tissaphernes was appointed satrap of Western Asia in the place of Cyrus, and was actively engaged in wars with the Greeks. Artaxerxes had to carry on frequent wars with tributary princes and satraps, who endeavoured to make themselves independent. Thus he maintained a long struggle against Evagoras of Cyprus, from 385 to 376; and his attempts to recover Egypt were unsuccessful. Towards the end of his reign he put to death his eldest son Darius, who had formed a plot to assassinate him. His last days were still further embittered by the unnatural conduct of his son Ochus, who caused the destruction of two of his brothers, in order to secure the succession for himself. Artaxerxes was succeeded by Ochus, who ascended the throne under the name of Artaxerxes III. (3) Also called OCHUS, reigned B.C. 359–338. By the aid of his Greek generals and mercenaries he reconquered Phœnicia and Egypt. The reins of government were entirely in the hands of the eunuch Bagoas and of Mentor the Rhodian. At last he was poisoned by Bagoas, and was succeeded by his youngest son, Arses. (4) The founder of the dynasty of the Sassanidae. See PERSIA; SASSANIDAE.

Artaxĭas (Ἀρταξίας) or **Artaxes**. The name of three kings of Armenia. (1) The founder of the Armenian kingdom, was one of the generals of Antiochus the Great, but revolted from him about B.C. 188, and became an independent sovereign. Hannibal took refuge at the court of Artaxias, and superintended the building of Artaxata, the capital of Armenia. Artaxias was conquered and taken prisoner by Antiochus IV. Epiphanes, about 165. (2) Son of Artavasdes, was put to death by his own subjects in B.C. 20, and Augustus placed Tigranes on the throne. (3) Son of Polemon, king of Pontus, was proclaimed king of Armenia by Germanicus in A.D. 18. He died about 35.

Artemidōrus (Ἀρτεμίδωρος). (1) THE GEOGRAPHER, a native of Ephesus, who travelled about B.C. 100 through the countries bordering on the Mediterranean and part of the Atlantic coast, and wrote a long work on his researches, the *Γεωγραφούμενα*, in eleven books, as well as an abstract of the same. Of both works, which were much consulted by later geographers, we have only fragments. (2) THE DREAM-INTERPRETER, born at Ephesus at the beginning of the second century A.D., surnamed "the Daldian," from his mother's birthplace, Daldis in Lydia, wrote a work on the interpretation of dreams, the *Ὀνειροκριτικά*, in four books. He had gathered his materials from the works of earlier authors and by oral inquiries during his travels in Asia, Italy, and Greece. The book is an acute exposition of the theory of interpreting dreams, and its practical application to examples systematically arranged according to the several stages of human life. An appendix, counted as a fifth book, gives a collection of dreams that have come true. For the light thrown on the mental condition of antiquity, especially in the second century A.D., and for many items of information on religious rites and myths relating to dreams, these writings are of value. See Reichardt, *De Artemidoro Daldiano* (1893).

Artĕmis (Ἄρτεμις). The virgin daughter of Zeus and Leto (Latona), by the common account born a twin-sister of Apollo, and just before him, at Delos. The Ortygia (see ASTERIA) named in another tradition as her birthplace was interpreted to mean Delos, though several other places where the worship of Artemis had long prevailed put forward pretensions to that name and its mythological renown, especially the well-known island of Ortygia off Syracuse. She, as well as her mother, was worshipped jointly with her brother at Delos, Delphi, and all the most venerable spots where Apollo was honoured. She is armed, as he is, with bow and arrows, which, like him, and often together with him, she wields against monsters and giants; hence the pæan was chanted to her as well as to him. Like those of Apollo, the shafts of Artemis were regarded as the cause of sudden death, especially to maidens and wives. But she was also a beneficent and helpful deity. As Apollo is the luminous god of day, she with her torch is a goddess of light by night, and in course of time becomes identified with all possible goddesses of moon and night. (See SELENÉ; HECATÉ; BENDIS; BRITOMARTIS.) Her proper domain is that of nature, with its hills and valleys, woods, meadows, rivers, and fountains; there, amid her nymphs, herself the fairest and tallest, she is a mighty huntress, sometimes chasing wild animals, sometimes dancing, playing, or bathing with her companions. Her favourite haunt was thought to be the mountains and forests of Arcadia, where, in many spots, she had sanctuaries, consecrated hunting-grounds, and sacred animals. To her, as goddess of the forest and the chase, all beasts of the woods and fields—in fact, all game—were dear and sacred; but her favourite animal was held all over Greece

Diana of Versailles. (Louvre.)

to be the hind. From this sacred animal and the hunting of it, the month which the other Greeks called Artemision or Artemisios (March-April) was named by the Athenians Elaphebolion (Ἐλαφηβολιών), and her festival as goddess of game and hunting, at which deer or cakes in the shape of deer were offered up, Elaphebolia. As goddess of the chase, she had also some influence in war, and the Spartans before battle sought her favour by the gift of a she-goat. Miltiades, too, before the battle of Marathon, had vowed to her as many goats as there should be enemies fallen on the field; but the number proving so great that the vow could not be kept, five hundred goats were sacrificed at each anniversary of the victory in the month of Boedromion. Again, she was much worshipped as the goddess of the moon. At Amarynthus in Euboea the whole island kept holiday to her with processions and prize-fights. At Munychia in Attica, at full moon in the month of Munychion (April-May), large round loaves or cakes, decked all around with lights as a symbol of her own luminary, were borne in procession and presented to her; and at the same time was solemnized the festival of the victory of Salamis in

Cyprus, because on that occasion the goddess had shone in her full glory on the Greeks. An ancient shrine of the Moon-goddess at Brauron in Attica was held in such veneration that the Brauronia, originally a merely local festival, was afterwards made a public ceremony, to which Athens itself sent deputies every five years, and a precinct was dedicated to "Artemis of Brauron" on the Acropolis itself. (See ACROPOLIS.) At this feast the girls between five and ten years of age, clad in saffron-coloured garments, were conducted by their mothers in procession to the goddess and commended to her care; for Artemis is also a protectress of youth, especially those of her own sex. As such she patronized a nurses' festival at Sparta in a temple outside the town, to which little boys were brought by their nurses; while the Ionians at their Apaturia (q. v.) presented her with the hair of boys. Almost everywhere young girls revered the virgin goddess as the guardian of their maiden years, and before marriage they offered up to her a lock of their hair, their girdle, and their maiden garment. She was also worshipped in many parts as the goddess of good repute, especially in youths and maidens, and was regarded as an enemy of all disorderly doings. With her attributes as the goddess of the moon, and as the promoter of healthy development, especially in the female frame, is connected the notion of her assisting in childbirth. (See ILITHYIA.) In early times human sacrifices had been offered to Artemis. A relic of this was the yearly custom observed at Sparta of flogging the boys till they bled at the altar of a deity not unknown elsewhere and named Artemis Orthia (the upright), probably from her stiff posture in the antiquated wooden image. At Sparta, as in other places, the ancient image was looked upon as the same which Iphigenia and Orestes brought away from Tauris (the Crimea)—viz., that of the Tauric Artemis, a Scythian deity who was identified with Artemis because of the human sacrifices common in her worship. The Artemis of Ephesus, too, so greatly honoured by all the Ionians of Asia (Acts, xix. 28), is no Greek divinity, but Asiatic. This is sufficiently shown by the fact that eunuchs were employed in her worship—a practice quite foreign to Greek ideas. The Greek colonists identified her with their own Artemis, because she was goddess of the moon and a power of nature, present in mountains, woods, and marshy places, nourishing life in plants, animals, and men. But, unlike Artemis, she was not regarded as a virgin, but as a mother and foster-mother, as is clearly shown by the multitude of breasts in the effigy. Her worship, frantic and fanatical after the manner of Asia, was traced back to the Amazons. A number of other deities native to Asia were also worshipped by the Greeks under the name of Artemis.

Ancient Representation of the Ephesian Artemis.

Artemis appears in works of art as the ideal of austere maiden beauty—tall of stature, with bow and quiver on her shoulder, or torch in her hand, and generally leading or carrying a hind, or riding in a chariot drawn by hinds. Her commonest character is that of a huntress. In earlier times the figure is fuller and stronger and the clothing more complete; in later works she is represented as more slender and lighter of foot, the hair loose, the dress girt high, the feet protected by the Cretan shoe. The most celebrated of her existing statues is the Diana of Versailles, from Hadrian's villa at Tibur. On the identification of Artemis with the Italian Diana, see DIANA.

Artemisia (Ἀρτεμισία). (1) The daughter of Lygdamis of Halicarnassus, reigned over Halicarnassus, and also over Cos and other adjacent islands. She joined the fleet of Xerxes, when he invaded Greece, with five vessels, the best equipped of the whole fleet after those of the Sidonians; and she displayed so much valour and skill at the battle of Salamis as to elicit from Xerxes the well-known remark that the men had acted like women in the fight and the women like men. The Athenians, indignant that a woman should appear in arms against them, offered a reward of 10,000 drachmae to any one who should take her prisoner. She, however, escaped after the action (Herod. vii. 99; viii. 88, 93). If we are to believe Ptolemy Hephaestion, a writer who mixed up many fables with some truth, Artemisia subsequently conceived an attachment for a youth of Abydos, named Dardanus; but, not meeting with a return for her passion, she put out his eyes while he slept, and then threw herself down from the Lover's Leap at the promontory of Leucaté. (2) Another queen of Caria, not to be confounded with the preceding. She was the daughter of Hecatomnus, king of Caria, and married her brother Mausolus, a species of union sanctioned by the customs of the country. She lost her husband, who was remarkable for personal beauty, B.C. 365, and she became, in consequence, a prey to the deepest affliction. A splendid tomb was erected to his memory, called Mausoleum (Μαυσωλεῖον, scil. μνημεῖον, i. e. "tomb of Mausolus"), and the most noted writers of the day were invited to attend a literary contest, in which ample rewards were to be bestowed on those who should celebrate with most ability the praises of the deceased. Among the individuals who came together on that occasion were, according to Aulus Gellius (x. 18), Theopompus, Theodectes, Naucrites, and even Isocrates. The prize was won by Theopompus. Valerius Maximus and Aulus Gellius relate a marvellous story concerning the excessive grief of Artemisia. They say that she actually mixed the ashes of her husband with water and drank them off (Val. Max. iv. 6). The grief of Artemisia, poignant though it was, did not cause her to neglect the care of her dominions: she conquered the island of Rhodes, and gained possession of some Greek cities on the mainland; and yet it is said that she died of grief two years after the loss of her husband. See MAUSOLEUM.

Artemisia (τὰ Ἀρτεμίσια). Festivals celebrated in honour of Artemis (q. v.) in various parts of Greece in the spring.

Artemisium (Ἀρτεμίσιον). A promontory on the northwestern coast of Euboea, and noted for the naval victory won by the Greeks over the Persians on the same day as the battle of Thermopylae (Herod. vii. 175), in B.C. 480.

Artes Liberāles. See LIBERALES ARTES.

Artiazein (ἀρτιάζειν). See PAR IMPAR.

Artifĭces. Artisans. See COLLEGIUM.

Artȳnoi or **Artȳnai** (ἄρτυνοι, ἄρτυναι). A deliberative and executive council in Argos and Epidaurus, inside the governing aristocracy. See Müller, *Dorier*, ii. 140.

Arundo. See CALAMUS.

Aruns. An Etruscan word which was regarded by the Romans as a proper name, but perhaps signified a younger son in general. (1) Younger brother of Lucumo, i. e. L. Tarquinius Priscus. (2) Younger brother of L. Tarquinius Superbus; was murdered by his wife. (3) Younger son of Tarquinius Superbus; fell in combat with Brutus.

Arūra (ἄρουρα). A Greek measure of surface = 21,904 sq. ft. English. See Hultsch, *Metrol.* p. 38, n. 4; and id. p. 284.

Arusiānus Messius. A Latin grammarian who flourished about A.D. 390, and made an alphabetical collection, for use in schools, of words that admit of various constructions, with examples from Terence, Cicero, Vergil, and Sallust. The title of the collection was *Exempla Elocutionum.* The text is printed in Keil's *Grammatici Latini*, vii. 449. See Gräfenhan, *Geschichte d. class. Philol.* iv. 194–196.

Arūspex. See HARUSPEX.

Arvāles Fratres. See FRATRES ARVALES.

Arx (ἄκρα). A height within the walls of a city. The same city could have several *arces*, as was the case with Rome; but, as there was generally one principal *arx*, the word came to be equivalent to Acropolis (q. v.). At Rome one of the summits of the Capitoline Hill was especially known as the Arx, the German school of topography placing it on the northeast summit (*Arx Caeli*) and the Capitolium (q. v.) on the southwest (Palazzo Caffarelli). At Rome the Arx was the regular place for taking the auspices (Livy, i. 18; x. 7); outside the wall the haruspex turned towards it if it was in sight (Livy, iv. 18). See HARUSPEX.

Aryan Languages. See INDO-EUROPEAN LANGUAGES.

Aryballos (ἀρύβαλλος). A vessel resembling the ampulla or λήκυθος. See AMPULLA.

Arzanēnḗ (Ἀρζανηνή). A district of Armenia Maior, bounded on the south by the Tigris, forming part of Gordyenḗ.

As (*libra*). A pound; the unit of weight among the Romans. See LIBRA; PONDERA.

As. The unit of value in the Roman and Old Italian coinages, and made of copper or bronze. (See AES.) It was originally a pound of copper (*aes grave*), of the value of 16⅔ cents, and was uncoined (*aes rude*). Servius Tullius stamped upon it the figures of animals (hence the term *pecunia*, from *pecus*). In the First Punic War, money being scarce, the *as* was reduced to one sixth of its original weight, and to a value of 2.8 cents. In the Second Punic War it was again reduced, so as to weigh but one ounce, having a value of 1.4 cents. The Lex Papiria (B.C. 191) still further reduced the *as* to half an ounce in weight, and a value of 7.9⅛ mills, which continued the standard weight and value even under the Empire. For a fuller account, see the article NUMISMATICS (Roman).

Asaminthus (ἀσάμινθος, σκαφή, ἔμβασις). A bath-tub used in Homeric times, in which the bather sat while hot water was poured over his head and shoulders. See *Odyss.* x. 361, and the article BALNEAE.

Asander (Ἄσανδρος). (1) Son of Philotas, brother of Parmenio, and one of the generals of Alexander the Great. After the death of Alexander (B.C. 323) he obtained Caria for his satrapy. (2) A general of Pharnaces II., king of Bosporus, whom he put to death in B.C. 17, in hopes of obtaining the kingdom. He was confirmed in the sovereignty by Augustus.

Asbestos or **Amianthus** (ἄσβεστος, ἀμίαντος). A mineral obtained by the ancients from India, Cyprus, and Euboea. It was well adapted for making the wicks of lamps, because indestructible by fire; and hence the Greeks, who used it for this purpose, gave it the name ἄσβεστος, which means inextinguishable. Pausanias mentions that the golden lamp which burned day and night in the temple of Athenḗ Polias at Athens had a wick of this substance.

It was also spun and woven into cloth. Thus manufactured, it was used for napkins (χειρεκμαγεῖα, χειρόμακτρα), which were never washed, but cleansed in a much more effective manner, whenever they required it, by being thrown into the fire.

Another use to which asbestine cloth was applied was to preserve the remains of dead bodies burned in the funeral pile. But the expense of this kind of cloth was so great that it could only be used at the obsequies of persons of the most exalted rank. The testimony of Pliny has been corroborated by the discovery of pieces of the cloth in ancient Roman or Italian sepulchres. The most remarkable specimen of this kind was found at Rome, A.D. 1702, in a marble sarcophagus, enveloping a skull and bones, and in size about five feet by six and a half. It is now in the Vatican.

Ascalăphus (Ἀσκάλαφος). (1) The son of Ares and Astyochḗ, who led, with his brother Ialmenus, the Minyans of Orchomenus against Troy, and was slain by Deïphobus (*Il.* ii. 512). (2) The son of Acheron and Gorgyra or Orphnḗ. When Pluto gave Persephonḗ (Proserpina) permission to return to the upper world, provided she had eaten nothing, Ascalaphus declared that she had eaten part of a pomegranate. Persephonḗ, in revenge, changed him into an owl by sprinkling him with water from the river Phlegethon (Ovid, *Met.* v. 540).

Ascălon (Ἀσκάλων). One of the chief cities of the Philistines, on the coast of Palestine, between Azotus and Gaza.

Ascania (Ἀσκανία). (1) In Bithynia, a great fresh-water lake, at the eastern end of which stood the city of Nicaea. (2) A salt-water lake on the borders of Phrygia and Pisidia.

Ascanius. The son of Aeneas (q. v.) and Creüsa. According to the ordinary account, he accompanied his father to Italy, and, thirty years after the building of Lavinium, founded Alba Longa, where, after his death, his step-brother Silvius reigned. To him, by his name of Iulus, the gens Iulia traced its origin. See TROJAN WAR.

Ascaules (ἀσκαύλης). See TIBIA.

Ascia (σκέπαρνον, τύκος). (1) An adze, used in working wood, as shown in the accompanying illustrations. The left-hand figure represents a ship-carpenter shaping the rib of a vessel with an

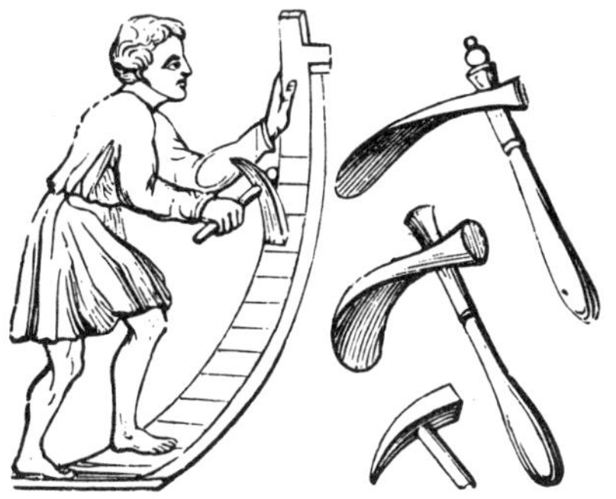

Ascia, or Adze.

ascia. (2) A mason's hammer used in dressing stone. (3) A bricklayer's tool for mixing mortar. (4) A hoe.

Asciburgium. The modern Asburg; an ancient town on the left bank of the Rhine.

Asclepiădes. See AESCULAPIUS.

Asclepiădes (Ἀσκληπιάδης). A Greek poet, a native of Samos, and a younger contemporary of Theocritus. He was the author of thirty-nine epigrams, mostly erotic, in the Greek Anthology. The well-known Asclepiadean metre was perhaps named after him. See ANTHOLOGY.

Asclepiēa (τὰ Ἀσκλεπίεια). Festivals celebrated in places where temples of Asclepius (Aesculapius) existed, and of which the most celebrated was that of Epidaurus, held every fifth year, nine days after the Isthmian Games. See Schol. *ad* Pind. *Nem.* iii. 145; Pausan. ii. 26, § 7.

Asclepiodŏtus (Ἀσκληπιόδοτος). A Greek writer, pupil of the Stoic Posidonius of Rhodes, who died B.C. 51. On the basis of his lectures Asclepiodotus seems to have written the military treatise preserved under his name on the Macedonian military system.

Asclepius (Ἀσκληπιός). See AESCULAPIUS.

Ascolia (τὰ ἀσκώλια). "The leaping upon the leather-bag" was one of the many kinds of amusements in which the Athenians indulged during the Anthesteria and other festivals in honour of Dionysus. The Athenians sacrificed a he-goat to

Ascoliasmus: Dancing on a Wine-skin. (From an Ancient Gem in Krause.)

the god, made a bag out of the skin, smeared it with oil, and then tried to dance upon it (Verg. *Georg.* ii. 384). The various accidents accompanying this attempt afforded great amusement to the spectators. He who succeeded was victor, and received the skin as a reward.

Asconius Pediānus, QUINTUS. A Roman grammarian and historian, probably born at Patavium about the year A.D. 3. He lived latterly at Rome, where he enjoyed the favour of men in high place. During the reigns of Claudius and Nero, having carefully studied the literature of the Ciceronian age, and availing himself of state-papers then existing, he composed for the use of his own sons his valuable historical commentaries on Cicero's orations, of which only those on five orations (*In Pisonem*, *Pro Scauro*, *Pro Milone*, *Pro Cornelio*, *In toga candida*) are preserved, unfortunately in a very fragmentary condition. The commentaries on the Verrine orations, which bear his name, belong probably to the fourth century A.D. They treat chiefly of grammatical points. No other works by Asconius have survived. He died, after twelve years' blindness, about A.D. 88. The *editio princeps* is that published at Venice in 1477. Text in the editions of Cicero by C. G. Schütze and Orelli-Baiter. See Gräfenhan, *Gesch. d. klass. Philol.* iv. 292.

Ascopera, from an Ancient Painting. (Rich.)

Ascopēra (ἀσκοπήρα). A large knapsack of undressed leather carried by travellers on foot (Suet. *Nero*, 45).

Ascos (ἀσκός). (1) A wine-skin. (2) Vessels, such as those shown in the accompanying illustration, used for wine.

Ascoi. (Dennis's *Etruria*.)

Ascra (Ἄσκρα). A town in Boeotia on Mount Helicon, where Hesiod resided, who had removed thither with his father from Cymé in Aeolis, and who is therefore called Ascraeus. See HESIODUS.

Ascŭlum. (1) PICĒNUM, the chief town of Picenum, and a Roman municipium, was destroyed by the Romans in the Social War (B.C. 89), but was afterwards rebuilt. (2) APŬLUM, a town of Apulia in Daunia, on the confines of Samnium, near which Pyrrhus defeated the Romans in the year B.C. 279.

Asdrŭbal (Ἀσδρούβας). See HASDRUBAL.

Asebeias Graphé (ἀσεβείας γραφή). One of the many forms prescribed by the Attic laws for the impeachment of impiety. This crime was apparently as ill-defined at Athens, and therefore as liable to be made the pretext for persecution, as it has been in all other countries in which the civil power has attempted to reach offences so much beyond the natural limits of its jurisdiction. The occasions, however, upon which the Athenian accuser professed to come forward may be classed as, first, breaches of the ceremonial law of public worship; and, secondly, indications of that which in analogous cases of modern times would be called heterodoxy or heresy. The former comprehended encroachment upon consecrated grounds, the plunder or other injury of temples, the violation of asylums, the interruption of sacrifices and festivals, the mutilation of statues of the gods, the introduction of deities not acknowledged by the state, etc.

The heretical delinquencies may be exemplified by the expulsion of Protagoras for writing that "he could not learn whether the gods existed or not"; in the persecution of Anaxagoras—like that of Galileo, in after-times, for impugning the received opinions about the sun—and the condemnation of Socrates for not holding the objects of the public worship to be gods. Any citizen in the enjoyment of free civic rights might bring the accusation, and the Archon Basileus was the magistrate who conducted the examination. The court was the Areopagus (q. v.) or the Heliastic Court. See DICASTES.

If the accuser failed to obtain a fifth of the votes of the dicasts, he forfeited a thousand drachmas, and incurred probably a modified ἀτιμία, though not to the extent of exclusion from office (Demosth. *c. Eubul.* p. 1301, § 28). See Meier, *Att. Prozess;* Schömann, *Antiq.* i. 498.

Asellio, GAIUS (?) SEMPRONIUS. A Roman annalist. He was military tribune in Spain under P. Scipio Africanus in B.C. 133, and wrote a history of Rome from the time of the Punic Wars to the age of the Gracchi, or later.

Asia (Ἀσία). A daughter of Oceanus and Tethys, wife of Iapetus, and mother of Atlas, Epimetheus, and Prometheus (Hes. *Theog.* 359). The name of the continent of Asia is traditionally derived from hers.

Asia (Ἀσία), in the poets **Asis** (Ἀσίς). One of the three great divisions which the ancients made of the known world. It was first used by the Greeks for the western part of Asia Minor, especially the plains watered by the river Caÿster, where the Ionian colonists first settled; and thence, as their geographical knowledge advanced, they extended it to the whole country. The southern part of the continent was supposed to extend much farther to the east than it really does, while to the north and northeast parts, which were quite unknown, much too small an extent was assigned. The different opinions about the boundaries of Asia on the side of Africa are mentioned under AFRICA; on the side of Europe the boundary was formed by the river Tanais (Don), the Palus Maeotis (Sea of Azof), Pontus Euxinus (Black Sea), Propontis (Sea of Marmora), and the Aegean (Archipelago). The most general division of Asia was into two parts, which were different at different times, and known by different names. To the earliest Greek colonists the river Halys, the eastern boundary of the Lydian kingdom, formed a natural division between UPPER and LOWER ASIA; and afterwards the Euphrates was adopted as a more natural boundary. Another division was made by the Taurus into ASIA INTRA TAURUM, i. e. the part of Asia north and northwest of the Taurus, and ASIA EXTRA TAURUM, all the rest of the continent. The division ultimately adopted, but apparently not till the fourth century of our era, was that of ASIA MAIOR and ASIA MINOR. (1) ASIA MAIOR was the part of the continent east of the Tanaïs, the Euxine, an imaginary line drawn from the Euxine to Trapezus (Trebizond), to the Gulf of Issus and the Mediterranean; thus it included the countries of Sarmatia Asiatica, with all the Scythian tribes to the east, Colchis, Iberia, Albania, Armenia, Syria, Arabia, Babylonia, Mesopotamia, Assyria, Media, Susiana, Persia, Ariana, Hyrcania, Margiana, Bactriana, Sogdiana, India, the land of the Sinae, and Serica; respecting which, see the several articles. (2) ASIA MINOR (Anatolia) was the peninsula on the extreme west of Asia, bounded by the Euxine, Aegean, and Mediterranean on the north, west, and south; and on the east by the mountains on the west of the upper course of the Euphrates. It was divided into Mysia, Lydia, and Caria, on the west; Lycia, Pamphylia, and Cilicia, on the south; Bithynia, Paphlagonia, and Pontus, on the north; and Phrygia, Pisidia, Galatia, and Cappadocia, in the centre. (3) ASIA PROPRIA, or simply ASIA, the Roman province formed out of the kingdom of Pergamus, which was bequeathed to the Romans by Attalus III. (B.C. 130), and the Greek cities on the western coast, and the adjacent islands, with Rhodes. It included the districts of Mysia, Lydia, Caria, and Phrygia; and was governed at first by propraetors, afterwards by proconsuls.

Asia Palus (Ἄσιος λειμών). A marsh in Lydia formed by the river Caÿster near its mouth, and noted as the haunt of water-fowl (Hom. *Il.* ii. 470.)

Asiarchae (Ἀσιάρχαι). In the Roman province of Asia, the chief presidents of the religious rites, whose office it was to exhibit games and theatrical amusements every year, in honour of the gods and the Roman emperor, at their own expense, like the Roman aediles.

Asiatic Style of Oratory. The florid style, abounding in tropes and rhetorical display, and thus opposed to the ATTIC STYLE (q. v.). Of the Asiatic School at Rome, Hortensius (q. v.) was the most conspicuous example. See Cicero, *Brutus,* 95.

Asilla (ἀσίλλα). A wooden pole or yoke, held by a man either on his two shoulders, or more

Asilla, or Pole for Carrying Burdens.

Illustration 1 is from a bronze lamp found at Stabiae; No. 2 is from a sardonyx in the Florentine Museum; No. 3 is from a Grecian vase in the Hamilton Collection.

commonly on one shoulder only, and used for carrying burdens.

Asīlus (οἶστρος, *tabanus*). The gad-fly or horse-fly.

Asinaria. A comedy of Plautus (q. v.) with a

farcical plot, taken from the 'Ὀναγός of Demophilos. It was written about B.C. 194.

Asinărus (Ἀσίναρος). A river in eastern Sicily, on which the Athenians were defeated by the Syracusans, B.C. 413, in the Peloponnesian War (q. v.).

Asĭné (Ἀσίνη). (1) A town in Laconia on the sea-coast between Taenarum and Gythium. (2) A town in Argolis, west of Herminoé, built by the Dryopes (q. v.). (3) A town in Messenia.

Asinius Pollio. See POLLIO.

Asōpus (Ἀσωπός). (1) A river in Thessaly rising in Mt. Oeta and emptying into the Sinus Maliacus. (2) A river of Boeotia rising in Mt. Cithaeron and flowing into the Euripus. On its banks the battle of Plataea was fought. (3) A river of Achaea flowing into the Corinthian Gulf near Sicyon. (4) The god of the last-named river, and father of the nymph Aegina (q. v.).

Aspasia (Ἀσπασία). (1) A celebrated woman, a native of Miletus. She came as an adventuress to Athens, in the time of Pericles, and, by the combined charms of her person, manners, and conversation, completely won the affection and esteem of that distinguished statesman. Her station had freed her from the restraints which custom laid on the education of the Athenian matron, and she had enriched her mind with accomplishments which were rare even among men. Her acquaintance with Pericles seems to have begun while he was still united to a lady of high birth, and we can hardly doubt that it was Aspasia who first disturbed this union, although it is said to have been dissolved by mutual consent. But after parting from his wife, who had borne him two sons, Pericles attached himself to Aspasia by the most intimate relation which the laws permitted him to contract with a foreign woman; and she acquired an ascendency over him which soon became notorious, and furnished the comic poets with an inexhaustible fund of ridicule and his enemies with a ground for serious charges. The Samian War was ascribed to her interposition on behalf of her birthplace, and rumours were set afloat which represented her as ministering to the vices of Pericles by the most odious and degrading of offices. There was, perhaps, as little foundation for this report as for a similar one in which Phidias was implicated (Plut. *Pericl.* 13); though among all the imputations brought against Pericles, this is that which it is the most difficult clearly to refute. But we are inclined to believe that it may have arisen from the peculiar nature of Aspasia's private circles, which, with a bold neglect of established usage, were composed not only of the most intelligent and accomplished men to be found at Athens, but also of matrons, who, it is said, were brought by their husbands to listen to her conversation. This must have been highly instructive as well as brilliant, since Plato did not hesitate to describe her as the preceptress of Socrates, and to assert in the *Menexenus* that she both formed the rhetoric of Pericles and composed one of his most admired harangues, the celebrated funeral oration. The innovation, which drew women of free birth and good standing into her company for such a purpose, must, even where the truth was understood, have surprised and offended many, and it was liable to the grossest misconstruction. And if her female friends were sometimes seen watching the progress of the works of Phidias, it was easy, through his intimacy with Pericles, to connect this fact with a calumny of the same kind.

Aspasia. (Vatican.)

There was another rumour still more dangerous, which grew out of the character of the persons who were admitted to the society of Pericles and Aspasia. No persons were more welcome at the house of Pericles than such as were distinguished by philosophical studies, and especially by the profession of new philosophical tenets. The mere presence of Anaxagoras, Zeno, Protagoras, and other celebrated men, who were known to hold doctrines very remote from the religious conceptions of the vulgar, was sufficient to make a circle in which they were familiar pass for a school of impiety. Such were the materials out of which the comic poet Hermippus formed a criminal prosecution against Aspasia. His indictment included two heads: an offence against religion, and that of corrupting Athenian women to gratify the passions of Pericles. The danger was averted; but it seems that Pericles, who pleaded her cause, found need of his most strenuous exertions to save Aspasia, and that he even descended, in her behalf, to tears and entreaties, which no similar emergency of his own could ever draw from him.

After the death of Pericles, Aspasia attached herself to a young man of obscure birth, named Lysicles, who rose through her influence in moulding his character to some of the highest employments in the Republic. (See Plut. *Pericl.;* Xen. *Mem.* ii. 6.) (2) Daughter of Hermotimus, and a native of Phocaea in Asia Minor. She was so remarkable for her beauty that a satrap of Persia carried her off and made her a present to Cyrus the Younger. Her modest deportment soon won the affections of the prince, who lived with her as with a lawful wife. Her name at first was Milto (vermilion), which had been given her in early life on account of the brilliancy of her complexion. Cyrus, however, changed it to Aspasia, calling her thus after the mistress of Pericles. After the death of the prince she fell into the hands of Artaxerxes, who for a long time vainly sought to gain her affections. She only yielded at last to his suit through absolute necessity. When the monarch declared his son Darius his successor, the latter, as it was customary in Persia for an heir to ask a favour of him who had declared him such, requested Aspasia of his father. Aspasia was accordingly sent for, and, contrary to the king's expectation, made choice of Darius. Artaxerxes therefore gave her up, in accordance with established custom, but soon took her away again, and made her a priestess of Artemis at Ecbatana, or of the goddess whom the Persians called Anaïtis. This station required her to pass the rest of her days in chastity (Plut. *Artax.*). Justin, however, says (x. 1) that Artaxerxes made her one of the priestesses of the sun.

Aspendus (Ἄσπενδος). A city of Pamphylia, lying for the most part on a rocky precipice, on the banks of the river Eurymedon. It was a flourishing place even before the expedition of the younger Cyrus (Xen. *Anab.* i. 2, 12). It was here that the Athenian patriot Thrasybulus terminated his life. Being off the coast, he levied contributions from the Aspendians, who, seizing an opportunity when he was on shore, surprised him in his tent at night, and slew him (Xen. *Hist. Gr.* iv. 8).

Asper, AEMILIUS. A Roman grammarian, the author of a commentary on Vergil, now existing in a fragmentary condition, and written probably about A.D. 80. In this he treated systematically Vergil's deviations from ordinary usage in syntax. See Ribbeck's Prolegom. to Vergil, p. 128. Another Asper wrote an *Ars Grammatica*, printed in Keil's *Grammatici Latini*, v. 547.

Asphaltus (ἄσφαλτος). See BITUMEN.

Aspis (ἀσπίς). See CLIPEUS.

Aspis (ἀσπίς). The asp, a species of deadly serpent often mentioned by both Greek and Roman writers. It would seem that several different species of poisonous reptiles were known to the ancients under this common name.

Assarăcus (Ἀσσάρακος). Son of Tros and founder of the collateral line to which Anchises and Aeneas belong in the royal house of Troy. See ANCHISES; AENEAS; DARDANUS.

Assarion (ἀσσάριον). The Greek name for the Latin *as* (q. v.).

Asser. The pole of a litter. See LECTICA.

Assertor or **Adsertor.** Contains the same root as the verb *adserere*, which, when coupled with the word *manu*, signifies to lay hold of a thing, to draw it towards one. Hence the phrase *adserere in libertatem*, or *liberali adserere manu*, applies to him who lays his hand on a person reputed to be a slave, and *asserts* or maintains his freedom. The person who thus maintained the freedom of a reputed slave was called *adsertor*, and by the laws of the Twelve Tables it was enacted in favour of liberty that such *adsertor* should not be called on to give security in the *sacramenti actio* to more than the amount of fifty asses. The person whose freedom was thus claimed was said to be *adsertus*.

Assessor or **Adsessor.** Literally one who sits by the side of another. The consuls, praetors, governors of provinces, and the iudices were often imperfectly acquainted with the law and the forms of procedure, and it was necessary that they should have the aid of those who had made the law their study. These advisers were known as *assessores.* The *praefectus praetorio* and *praefectus urbi*, and other civil and military functionaries, had their assessors. The emperor Alexander Severus gave the assessors a regular salary. See Bethmann-Hollweg, *Der römische Civil-Prozess*, iii. 129, § 141.

Assidui. See LOCUPLETES.

Assignatio. The Latin term for the assignment of public land to citizens or colonies. See AGRARIAE LEGES; COLONIA.

Assus (Ἄσσος). A city in the Troad, on the Adramyttian Gulf, opposite to Lesbos, afterwards called Apollonia; the birthplace of Cleanthes the Stoic.

Assyria (in Greek, Ἀσσυρία; in Assyrian inscriptions called *Assur;* in the Persian, *Athura;* and in the Median, *Assura*). The country properly so called, in the narrowest sense, was a district of Asia, extending along the east side of the Tigris, which divided it on the west and northwest from Mesopotamia and Babylonia, and bounded on the north and east by Mount Niphates and Mount Zagrus, which separated it from Armenia and Media, and on the southeast by Susiana. It was watered by several streams flowing into the Tigris from the east, two of which, the Lycus or Zabatus (Great Zab) and the Caprus or Zabas (Little Zab), divided the country into three parts. The district between the upper Tigris and the Lycus, called Atturia, was probably the most ancient seat of the monarchy, containing the capital, Nineveh or Ninus. The Lycus and the Little Zab bounded the finest portion, called Adiabené. The district southeast of the Little Zab contained the two subdivisions Apolloniatis and Sittacené. In a wider sense the name Assyria was used to designate the whole country watered by the Tigris and Euphrates, including Mesopotamia and Babylonia; and in a still more extended application it meant the whole Assyrian Empire, one of the first great states of which we have any record.

The remarkable fertility of the country enabled it to support a large population; and its great material prosperity, power, and culture are at-

Restoration of an Assyrian Palace. (Reber.)

tested by ancient writers, as well as by the monuments that remain to us in the shape of ruins of cities, extensive canals and water-works, and proofs secured by excavators of the possession of the arts and sciences. At the present day the country is almost a desert; but from Tekrit to Bagdad, and in the vicinity of Nineveh (q. v.), abundant ruins mark the former wealth and splendour of the people.

ETHNOLOGY.—The Assyrians were a branch of the Semitic race, to which the Syrians, Phœnicians, Jews, and Arabs belonged, and which in Chaldaea appears to have supplanted the Scythic or Turanian stock as early as B.C. 2100. Assyria had in the earliest times a close connection with Aethiopia and Arabia. Hence Herodotus speaks of Sennacherib as king of the Arabians as well as of the Assyrians. See BABYLONIA.

LANGUAGE.—The language of the Assyrians is allied to the North Branch of the Semitic family, its vocabulary showing a close affinity to Hebrew and Phœnician. In the fulness of its verbal system and richness of synonyms, however, it resembles the Arabic. The ethnic type of the Assyrians is the Semitic modified by some admixture with Akkadian elements. See AKKAD; CUNEIFORM INSCRIPTIONS.

Assyrian literature is known to us chiefly from the discovery in the palace of Assur-bani-pal, at

Clay Tablet with Cylinder, impressed, from Kouyunjik.

Nineveh, of a library of many thousand tablets collected by that king and his father, Esar-haddon. Duplicate copies of some of these tablets have been found in excavating the Babylonian cities. Of these tablets, many are syllabaries, dictionaries, geographies, and other educational works, often couched in the ancient Akkadian and Sumirian tongues; so that from them, Assyriologists have learned much about the older languages of Chaldaea. The richest literary discoveries, however, have been in the field of poetry and mythology. In 1872 the late Mr. George Smith, of the British Museum, discovered a series of tablets containing an epic in twelve books, one of which relates to the legend of the Deluge, and bears a very striking resemblance to the account given in the Old Testament. In both accounts the Deluge is a punishment for human sins; in both, the builder of an ark gathers into it his family and the beasts of the field; in both, the ark rests upon a mountain; in both, peace between God and man is restored; and in both, a sign of the restoration is the appearance of the rainbow. Many other interesting resemblances to portions of the Book of Genesis are contained in the Assyrian tablets. The hymns and prayers are likewise beautiful and poetic.

Inscribed Tablet impressed with Seals.

RESULTS OF EXCAVATIONS.—Successful excavations have been made by Botta, Layard, Oppert, Rawlinson, Smith, and others, with the result of opening up very many palaces and temples, and bringing to light sculptures covered with inscriptions, and including obelisks, sphinxes, winged lions and bulls, and bas-reliefs of battle-scenes, sieges, hunts, etc. Many smaller objects are no less interesting, such as ornaments, bells, engraved gems, and bronzes. It has been learned that the Assyrians were acquainted with glass; that they employed the arch in building; that they used the lens as a magnifying instrument; and had, among other mechanical appliances, the lever and the roller.

Nebo. (British Museum.)

RELIGION. — The religion of Assyria was simpler than that of the Babylonians, although polytheistic in character. The national deity was Assur, regarded as the founder of the nation. Beside him there are two principal triads, with many minor deities. The first triad is known as the Nature Triad (Anu "the Progenitor," Bel "the Lord of the World," Hea "the Lord of the Sea, Rivers, and Fountains"). The second triad is the Celestial Triad (Sin the Moon-god, Shamas the Sun-god, Istar the Star-goddess). Minor gods are Merodach or Marduk, son of Hea; Nebo the god of learning, who possesses many of the attributes of the Greek Hermes (q. v.); and Nergal and Nusku the war-gods. (See 2 Kings, xvii. 30.)

HISTORY.—Ancient accounts of Assyrian history are those of Berosus (q. v.), a Graeco-Chaldean priest, who wrote at Babylon, where he had access to the inscriptional records, about B.C. 268; of Herodotus; and of Ctesias of Cnidus, physician to the Persian king Artaxerxes Mnemon (B.C. 405). The narrative of Berosus has met with much confirmation from recent excavations and explorations. In the Bible narrative we are told that Nineveh was founded from Babylonia. "Out of that land [Babylonia] he [Nimrod] went forth into Assyria" (Gen. x. 11)—and this statement is fully confirmed by the results of recent explorations. The earliest inscriptions found on the bricks from Assur (Kileh-Shergat), the ancient capital, give to the first rulers of the land the Akkadian title of Patesi, or "high-priest of the city of Assur," and to the city itself the Akkadian name of Pal-bi-ki. The next notice of Assyria does not occur until the Assyrian king Pul, or Tiglath-pileser II., invaded Palestine, and was bought off by Menahem, king of Israel (B.C. 738). In the same reign we find the Jewish king Jehoahaz (Ahaz) becoming a vassal of the court of Assyria, and the tribes beyond Jordan carried away captive (B.C. 734). In B.C. 722, Samaria is captured by Sargon the Tartan, who had usurped the throne from his weak master, Shalmaneser IV. The next reference to Assyria is that of the siege and capture of Jerusalem by Sargon (Isaiah, x., xi., xx.), and the siege of Ashdod (B.C. 712–711). This event is now proved to be distinct from the siege by Sennacherib in B.C. 701, which terminated apparently in a disaster for the Assyrian army. The last mention of Assyria is the record of the murder of Sennacherib by his sons in B.C. 681, and the accession of his faithful son Esar-haddon, the most powerful of all the Assyrian monarchs, for he carried his arms as far as the Mediterranean and conquered Egypt. Little credit is to be attached to the expedition of Holofernes recorded in the apocryphal Book of Judith.

After this the Empire appears to have gradually decayed, until at last, in the reign of Assur-banipal or Sardanapalus, or that of Esar-haddon II. (Sarakos), a league for its destruction was formed between Nabopolassar, governor of Babylon, and Cyaxares, king of Media, which was strengthened by the marriage of Nebuchadnezzar, son of the former, to Nitocris, daughter of the latter. The war and siege are said to have been interrupted by an invasion of the Scythians, which drew off Cyaxares; but at length Nineveh was taken and destroyed about B.C. 605, or, according to Rawlinson, 625. In the time of Darius Hystaspes Assyria rebelled without success in conjunction with Media. In the time of Herodotus the capital had ceased to exist; and when Xenophon passed it the very name was forgotten, though he testifies to the extent of the deserted city, and asserts the height of the ruined walls to be 150 feet. An inconsiderable town seems to have existed on its ruins in the reign of Claudius; and the last notice we have of Nineveh in the classics is in Tacitus.

The fanciful history related by Ctesias is now found to be based on distorted Graeco-Persian traditions; and though the writer managed to make the ancient world give credit to him in preference to Herodotus, his work is now proved to be very untrustworthy. According to him, for thirty generations after Ninyas the kings led a life of luxury and indolence in their palace; the last of them, Sardanapalus, made a vigorous defence against Arbaces, the rebel governor of Media, but, finding it impossible to defend Nineveh, he set fire to his palace, and burned himself with all his treasures. This event took place 1306 years after Ninus. Now, the above account represents Nineveh to have perished nearly three centuries before the real date, which was about B.C. 606, and is utterly incompatible with Scripture. Herodotus assigns to the Empire a duration of 520 years, and Berosus of 526. In order to reconcile these conflicting accounts, historians have supposed that Nineveh was twice destroyed, but this supposition is now generally rejected. However, that part of Nineveh was actually destroyed by fire is proved by the condition of the slabs and statues found in its ruins, which show the action of intense heat.

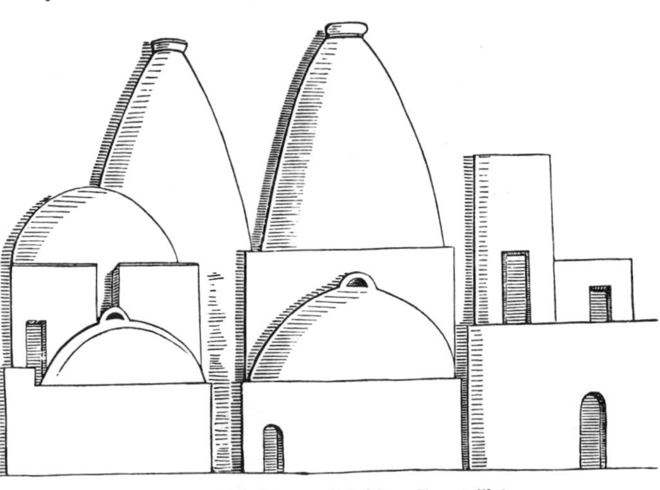

Assyrian Dwellings. (Relief from Kouyunjik.)

BIBLIOGRAPHY.—For Assyrian archæology, see the works of Layard, Oppert, and Smith; Perrot and Chipiez, *Chaldée et Assyrie* (Eng. trans. 1884). For the religion, see Sayce, *Assyria* (1885); Robertson Smith, *Religion of the Semites* (1888); Tiele, *Comparative Hist. of Relig.* (Eng. trans. 1884); Sayce, *Hibbert Lectures* (1887). For the language and literature, see Delitzsch, *Assyrische Grammatik* (Eng. trans. by Kennedy, 1889); id. *Assyrisches Wörterbuch*, vols. i.–iii. (1887); Peiser, *Keilinschriftliche Bibliothek* (1890); Sayce, *Lectures on the Syllabary and Grammar* (1877). For the history, see Rawlinson, *The Five Great Monarchies of the Ancient Eastern World*, 4 vols. (1862–67); Oppert, *Histoire des Empires de Chaldée et d'Assyrie* (1865); Lenormant, *Manuel d'Histoire Ancienne de l'Orient*, 3 vols. (1869); Ménant, *Annales des Rois d'Assyrie* (1874); Maspero, *Histoire Ancienne des Peuples de l'Orient* (4th ed. 1883); Sayce, *Ancient Empires of the East* (1884); id. *Fresh Light from the Ancient Monuments* (1886); Maspero, *Life in Ancient Egypt and Assyria* (Eng. trans. 1892).

Asta. (1) The modern Asti in Piedmont, an inland town of Liguria on the Tanarus, a Roman colony. (2) A town in Hispania Baetica, near Gades, a Roman colony.

Astabŏras (Ἀσταβόρας) and **Astăpus** (Ἀστάπους). Two rivers of Aethiopia, having their sources in the highlands of Abyssinia, and uniting to form the Nile. The land enclosed by them was the island of Meroë (q. v.).

Astăcus (Ἄστακος). A celebrated city of Bithynia, on the Sinus Astacenus, a bay of the Propontis, was a colony from Megara, but afterwards received fresh colonists from Athens, who called the place Olbia. It was destroyed by Lysimachus, but was rebuilt on a neighbouring site by Nicomedes I., who named his new city Nicomedia.

Astarté (Ἀστάρτη). See APHRODITÉ.

Asteria (Ἀστερία). A daughter of the Titan Coeus and the Titanid Phoebé, sister of Leto, and mother of Hecaté by Perses, son of the Titan Crius. She is said to have turned into a quail (ὄρτυξ) and plunged into the sea to escape the advances of Zeus. After her the island of Delos (q. v.) was first called ASTERIA, and later ORTYGIA.

Astĕris (Ἀστερίς) or **Asteria** (Ἀστερία). A small island between Ithaca and Cephallenia.

Astraea (Ἀστραία). The daughter of Zeus and Themis, and goddess of justice, who lived during the Golden Age among men; but when the wickedness of men increased she withdrew to heaven, and was placed among the stars under the name of Virgo. Her sister Pudicitia (Αἰδώς) left the earth along with her (Hyg. *Poet. Astr.* ii. 25).

Astraeus (Ἀστραῖος). A Titan, husband of Eos, and father of the winds and the stars, whence Ovid calls the winds *Astraei fratres.*

Astragălus (ἀστράγαλος). A word which literally signifies that particular bone in the ankles of certain quadrupeds which the Greeks as well as the Romans used for dice and other purposes, as described under the corresponding Latin word TALUS.

As a technical term *astragalus* is used by Vitruvius for a certain moulding (the astragal), which seems to have derived its name from its resemblance to a string or chain of *tali;* and it is, in fact, always used in positions where it seems intended to bind together the parts to which it is applied. It belongs properly to the more highly decorated forms of the Ionic order, in which it appears as a lower edging to the larger mouldings, especially the *echinus* (ovolo), particularly in the capital, as shown in the following wood-cut, which represents an Ionic capital found in the ruins of the temple of Dionysus at Teos. It is also often used in the entablature as an edging to the divisions of the cornice, frieze, and architrave. The lower figure in the illustration represents a portion of the astragal which runs beneath the crowning moulding of the architrave of the Temple of Erechtheus.

Astragalus. (From Ionic Capital.)

The term is also applied to a plain convex moulding of the same sectional outline as the former, but without the division into links, like a *torus* on a small scale.

Astrateias Graphé (ἀστρατείας γραφή). An accusation brought against persons who failed to appear among the troops after they had been enrolled for the campaign by the generals. The court was composed of soldiers, and the generals presided. See EXERCITUS, p. 649.

Astrologia (ἀστρολογία). Equivalent to *astronomia*, a word which is not earlier than Seneca. See ASTRONOMIA.

Astronomia (ἀστρονομία) and **Astrologia** (ἀστρολογία). These terms were at first synonymous expressions among the ancients, both signifying "the science of the stars." But afterwards astrology came to mean that part of the science which deals with the supposed influence of the stars on the destinies of men. Among the Greeks, astronomy, the origin of which they themselves ascribed to the Assyrians, Babylonians, and Egyptians, was for centuries the subject of philosophical speculation without a sufficient groundwork in observation, because mathematics and mechanics had not reached the requisite degree of perfection. The list of observing astronomers opens with Eudoxus of Cnidus in the first half of the fourth century B.C., who assumed that the earth was spherical, and tried to explain the phenomena of the heavens by a complicated theory of concentric spheres. Aristotle, too, maintained and proved the spherical form of the earth, which he took to be the immovable centre of the universe. Astronomy was first raised into a real science after B.C. 300 at Rhodes and Alexandria, in the Museum of which town the first observatory was built; and Aristyllus and Timochares determined the places of the fixed stars with comparative accuracy, though as yet with very rude apparatus. A great step in advance was taken by Aristarchus of Samos, who observed the summer solstice at Alexandria in B.C. 279, maintained the earth's rotation on her axis and revolution round the sun, and made an attempt, by no means contemptible, to ascertain the size and distance of the sun and moon. His successor Eratosthenes also rendered essential service to the progress of the science; thus, he came very near to determining the exact obliquity of the ecliptic. The true founder of scientific astronomy, and the greatest independent observer of antiquity, was Hipparchus of Nicaea (in the second century B.C.), who discovered the precession of the equinoxes, and determined the length of the solar year (at 365 days, 5 hours, 55 minutes, 12 seconds), as well as the time of the moon's revolution, and the magnitude and distances of the heavenly bodies. The last important astronomer of antiquity, and the greatest after Hipparchus, is Claudius Ptolemaeus in the second century A.D. In his chief work, commonly known by its Arabic name of *Almagest*, he digested the discoveries of his predecessors, especially Hipparchus, and his own into a formal system, which passed current all through the Middle Ages. According to it the earth is a sphere resting motionless in the middle of the equally spherical universe, while the sun, moon, planets, and fixed stars roll at various distances around her.

The Romans regarded astronomy as an idle speculation, and gave little attention to it. When Iulius Caesar reformed the Roman calendar he was obliged to bring an astronomer, Sosigenes, from Alexandria to help him.

ASTROLOGY, in the narrower sense of the word, and applied to predictions based upon the observation of the heavenly bodies, arose among the Chaldaeans, and in Greece did not come into vogue until after the time of Alexander the Great. In Rome the professional astrologers were called Chaldaei, or Mathematici, the latter name referring to the astronomical calculations which they made. In the Republican period they were known, but held in utter contempt. In B.C. 139 their unpopularity was so great that they were expelled from Rome and Italy. But in the turbulent times of the civil wars their reputation rose considerably, and still more under the Empire, when the most extensive demands were made upon their science. They were, indeed, repeatedly driven out of Italy and involved in trials for treason (*maiestas*); but this only enhanced the consideration in which they were held, the more so as they were frequently taken into counsel by the emperors and the members of the imperial family. In later times all that the Chaldaeans were forbidden to do was to consult the stars on questions referring to the emperor's life, which was made a criminal offence. The Christian emperors (but none before them) issued many prohibitions against all consultation of astrologers whatever.

In the practice of their art they used calendars written on tablets, in which were set down for every day the motion and relative distances of the stars, whether lucky or unlucky. By another set of tablets they made their calculations of every hour in detail, noting the hour of a person's birth and the relative position of the constellation dominant at the time. In accordance with this they determined the fortunes of him who was born at the hour in question. By a similar process they ascertained the times that were favourable or unfavourable to any undertaking. Among the lucky stars were Iupiter, Venus, and Luna; among the unlucky, Saturn and Mars were the chief. Mercury was lucky or unlucky, according to circumstances.

For an account of ancient astronomy and astrology, the reader is referred to Ball, *Short History of Mathematics* (1888); Lewis, *Astronomy of the Ancients* (1862); Becker, *Handbuch der röm. Alterth.* (1880); Whewell, *History of the Inductive Sciences* (3d ed. 1858); Wolf, *Geschichte der Astronomie* (1877); Delambre, *Histoire de l'Astronomie* (1827); the treatise of Iulius Firmicus in Latin, of Manetho and Ptolemy in Greek; and the Latin poem of Manilius (q. v.), entitled *Astronomica*.

Astŭra. A river in Latium, flowing between Antium and Circeii into the Tyrrhenian Sea. At its mouth it formed a small island, with a town upon it, also called Astura, where Cicero had an estate.

Astŭres. A warlike people in the northwest of Spain, bounded on the east by the Cantabri and Vaccaei, on the west by the Gallaeci, on the north by the ocean, and on the south by the Vettones. Their chief town was Asturica Augusta (Astorga), and they have given their name also to the modern Spanish province of Asturias.

Astyăges (Ἀστυάγης). A son of Cyaxares, and last king of Media (q. v.) who reigned B.C. 594–559, and was deprived of his kingdom by his grandson, Cyrus (q. v.).

Astyănax (Ἀστυάναξ). The son of Hector and Andromachê. After the capture of Troy the Greeks hurled him down from the walls, that he might not restore the kingdom of Troy. See HECTOR.

Astynŏmi (ἀστυνόμοι). The title of ten officers at Athens drawn annually by lot from the ten tribes, five for the city and five for the Piraeus. They formed a kind of city police, responsible for the cleanliness and order of the streets, and probably for the safety of the public buildings. See Böckh, *Publ. Economy of Athens*, p. 203 foll. See, also, AEDILES.

Asylia (ἀσυλία). "Inviolability." (1) The security of person and property enjoyed by ambassadors, heralds, athletes, on their goings to and from the great games, and sometimes to individuals by special favour. See Plut. *Arat.* 28. (2) The right of sanctuary.

Atābŭlus. The name given in Apulia to the sirocco or parching southeast wind, now locally known as *altino*.

Atacīni. A people of Gallia Narbonensis, whose capital was Narbo (Narbonne). They derived their name from the river Atax, now the Aude.

Atacīnus, VARRO. See VARRO.

Atalanta (Ἀταλάντη). A Greek heroine of the type of Artemis (q. v.). There were two slightly different versions of her story, one current in Arcadia and the other in Boeotia.

(1) THE ARCADIAN VERSION. Atalanta, daughter of Zeus and Clymenê, was exposed by her father, who had desired male offspring only. She was suckled by a bear, until she was found and brought up by a party of hunters. Under their care she grew up to be a huntress—keen, swift, and beautiful. She took part in the Calydonian boar-hunt, was the first who struck the boar, and received from Meleager the head and skin of the beast as the prize of victory. (See MELEAGER.) She is also associated with the voyage of the Argonauts. She turned a deaf ear to the entreaties of her numerous suitors; but at last she propitiated the wrath of Aphroditê by returning the faithful love of the beautiful Milanion, who had followed her persistently, and suffered and struggled for her. Their son was Parthenopaeus, one of the Seven against Thebes. Swinburne's poem, *Atalanta in Calydon*, gives a magnificent setting to the story.

(2) THE BOEOTIAN VERSION. Atalanta was the daughter of Schoeneus, son of Athamas, and distinguished for beauty and swiftness of foot. An oracle warned her against marriage, and she accordingly lived a lonely life in the forest. She met the addresses of her suitors by challenging them to race with her, overtaking them in the race and spearing them in the back. She was at length beaten, however, by Hippomenes, who during the race dropped on the ground three golden apples given him by Aphroditê. Atalanta stooped down to pick up the apples, and thus lost the race. Hippomenes forgot to render thanks to Aphroditê, and the goddess in anger caused the pair in their passion to profane the sanctuary of Cybelê, where they were changed into lions. See W. S. Landor's *Hippomenes and Atalanta*.

Atargătis (Ἀτάργατις). See SYRIA DEA.

Atax. A river of Gaul, now the Aude.

Atê (Ἄτη). According to Homer, the daughter of Zeus; according to Hesiod, of Eris (or Strife). She personifies infatuation, the infatuation being generally held to imply guilt as its cause and evil as its consequence. At first she dwelt on Olympus; but after she had entrapped Zeus himself into his rash oath on the occasion of the birth of Heracles (q. v.), he hurled her down to earth. Here she pursues her mission of evil, walking lightly over men's heads, but never touching the ground. Behind her go the Litai (Prayers), the lame, wrinkled, squinting daughters of Zeus. The Litai, if called upon, heal the hurts inflicted by Atê; but they bring fresh evil upon the stubborn. In later times Atê is transformed into an avenger of unrighteousness, like Dikê, the Erinyes, and Nemesis.

Ateius Capĭto, GAIUS. A Roman jurist of the age of Augustus and Tiberius, who was born about B.C. 30, and died about A.D. 22. Unlike his contemporary Antistius Labeo (q. v.), he recommended himself to the ruling powers by his submissive attitude. He was rewarded by many tokens of distinction; among others, by the consulship, to which he was elected in A.D. 5, before attaining the legal age. As a jurist (again unlike Antistius) he represented the conservative tendency, and so became the founder of a special school called the *Sabiniani*, after his pupil Masurius Sabinus, and opposed in its theory of legal interpretation to the radical school of Proculus. See IURISPRUDENTIA.

Ateleia (ἀτέλεια). Immunity from public burdens was enjoyed at Athens by the archons for the time being; by the descendants of certain persons, on whom it had been conferred as a reward for great services, as in the case of Harmodius and Aristogiton; and by the inhabitants of certain foreign States. It was of several kinds: it might be a general immunity (ἀτέλεια ἁπάντων), or a more special exemption, as from custom-duties, from the liturgies, or from providing sacrifices (ἀτέλεια ἱερῶν). Exemption from military service was also called ἀτέλεια.

Atella. The modern Aversa; a town in Campania between Capua and Neapolis, originally inhabited by the Oscans, afterwards a Roman municipium and a colony.

Atellānae Fabŭlae. Plays of a farcical nature; so called from Atella, a town of the Osci in Campania. See COMOEDIA; LITERATURE (Roman).

Aternum. The modern Pescara; a town in central Italy, on the Adriatic, at the mouth of the river Aternus, was the common harbour of the Vestini, Marrucini, and Peligni.

Atestê. The modern Este; a Roman colony in the country of the Veneti in northern Italy.

Athamania (Ἀθαμανία). A mountainous country in the south of Epirus, on the western side of Pindus, of which Argithea was the chief town. The Athamanes were a Thessalian people, who had been driven out of Thessaly by the Lapithae.

Athămas (Ἀθάμας). The son of Aeolus and Enaretê, and king of Orchomenus in Boeotia. At the command of Herê, Athamas married Nephelê, by whom he became the father of Phrixus and Hellê. (See PHRIXUS.) But he was secretly in love with the mortal Ino, the daughter of Cadmus, by whom he begot Learchus and Melicertes. Having thus incurred the anger both of Herê and of Nephelê, Athamas was seized with madness, and in this state killed his own son, Learchus. Ino threw herself with Melicertes into the sea, and both were changed into marine deities—Ino becoming Leucothea, and Melicertes, Palaemon. Athamas, as the murderer of his son, was obliged to flee from Boeotia, and settled in Thessaly. Hence we have Athamantiades, son of Athamas, i. e. Palaemon; and Athamantis, daughter of Athamas, i. e. Hellê.

Athanasius (Ἀθανάσιος). A Christian bishop of the fourth century. He was a native of Egypt, and a deacon of the Church of Alexandria under Alexander the Bishop, whom he succeeded in his dignity A.D. 326. Previous to his obtaining this high office he had been private secretary to Alexander, and had also led for some time an ascetic life with the renowned St. Anthony. Alexander had also taken him to the council at Nice, where he gained the highest esteem of the fathers by the talent which he displayed in the Arian controversy. (See ARIUS.) He had a great share in the decrees passed here, and thereby drew on himself the hatred of the Arians. On his advancement to the prelacy he dedicated all his time and talents to the doctrine of the Trinity, and resolutely refused the request of Constantine for the restoration of Arius to the Catholic communion. In revenge for this refusal, the Arian party brought several accusations against him before the emperor. Of these he was acquitted in the first instance; but, on a new charge of having detained ships at Alexandria, laden with corn for Constantinople, either from conviction or policy, he was found guilty and banished to Gaul. Here he remained in exile eighteen months, or, as some accounts say, upwards of two years, his see in the meantime being unoccupied.

On the death of Constantine he was recalled, and restored to his functions by Constantius; but the Arian party made new complaints against him, and he was condemned by 90 Arian bishops assembled at Antioch. On the opposite side, 100 orthodox bishops, assembled at Alexandria, declared him innocent; and Pope Iulius confirmed this finding, in conjunction with more than 300 bishops assembled at Sardis from the East and West. In consequence of this, he returned a second time to his diocese. But when Constans, emperor of the West, died, and Constantius became master of the whole Empire, the Arians again ventured to rise up against Athanasius. They condemned him in the councils of Arles and Milan, and, as the worthy patriarch refused to listen to anything but an express command of the emperor, when he was one day preparing to celebrate a festival in the church, a body of soldiers suddenly rushed in to make him prisoner. The surrounding priests and monks, however, placed him in security. Athanasius, displaced for a third time, fled into the deserts of Egypt. His enemies pursued him even here, and set a price on his head. To relieve the hermits, who dwelt in these solitary places and who would not betray his retreat, from suffering on his account, he went into those parts of the desert which were entirely uninhabited. He was followed by a faithful servant, who, at the risk of his life, supplied him with the means of subsistence. In this undisturbed spot Athanasius composed many writings, full of eloquence, to strengthen the faith of the believers or expose the falsehoods of his enemies. When Julian the Apostate ascended the throne, he allowed the orthodox bishops to return to their churches. Athanasius, therefore, returned after an absence of six years. The mildness which he exercised towards his enemies was imitated in Gaul, Spain, Italy, and Greece, and restored peace to the Church. But this peace was interrupted by the complaints of the heathen, whose temples the zeal of Athanasius kept always empty. They excited the emperor against him, and he was obliged to fly to the Thebaïs to save his life. The death of the emperor and the accession of Jovian again brought him back; but on Valens becoming emperor eight months after, and the Arians recovering their superiority, he was once more compelled to fly. He concealed himself in the tomb of his father, where he remained four months, until Valens, moved by the pressing entreaties and threats of the Alexandrians, allowed him to return. From this period he remained undisturbed in his office until he died, in A.D. 373.

Of the forty-six years of his official life, he spent twenty in banishment, and the greater part of the remainder in defending the Nicene Creed. Athanasius is one of the greatest men of which the Church can boast. His deep mind, his noble heart, his invincible courage, his living faith, his unbounded benevolence, sincere humility, lofty eloquence, and strictly virtuous life, gained the honour and love of all. His writings are on polemical, historical, and moral subjects. The polemical treat chiefly of the doctrines of the Trinity, the incarnation of Christ, and the divinity of the Holy Spirit. The historical ones are of the greatest importance for the history of the Church. In all his writings the style is distinguished, considering the age in which they were produced, for clearness and moderation. His apology, addressed to the emperor Constantine, is a masterpiece. The creed which bears his name is now generally allowed not to have been his. It was first printed in Greek in 1540, and several times afterwards to 1671. It has been questioned whether this creed was ever received by the Greek and Oriental Churches. In America the Episcopal Church has rejected it. The best edition of Athanasius is in the *Patrologia Graeco-Latina* of Migne (1860). His epistles and some of his orations were translated with notes by J. H. Newman (1842).

Athēnae (Ἀθῆναι). The chief city of Attica. The long southeastern triangle of the northern peninsula of Greece, which terminates in the abrupt promontory of Sunium (mod. Cávo Colónnais), has its most interesting and important division, topographically as well as historically, on the western side, facing the Saronic Gulf. Here, at a point midway between Sunium and the promontory that faces Salamis, the low Cape Zoster terminates the Anhydros range, a lower continuation of Hymettus. The long continuous ridge of Anhydros and Hymettus (1027 metres at its greatest height) extends, in a slightly northeasterly direction, towards the range of Pentelè (Πεντέλη), the ancient Brilessos (Βριλησσός) or Pentelicon (Πεντελικόν sc. ὄρος, Lat. Mons Pentelicus), from which it is separated by the pass through which the modern railway runs southeasterly towards the ancient mines of Laurium, near Sunium. The Pentelicus range (1086.6 metres high) extends northwest and southeast, and forms with Hymettus and Anhydros a well-nigh continuous dividing-wall between the eastern plain of Attica, the Mesogaea (Μεσόγαια), and the middle plain; while the plain of Marathon in the northeast is approachable from the Mesogaea only by a narrow way between Pentelicus and the sea towards Euboea, and from the middle plain by two difficult mountain ways between Pentelicus and Parnes. This last range (1412 metres high) lies to the northwest of Pentelicus and extends nearly east and west. Passable only by way of Decelea (mod. Tatóï) in the east and Phylé in the west, it effectually cuts off Attica from Boeotia. In its furthest extent towards the west, where it continues in the Cithaeron range, it divides the western Attic plain, the Eleusinian, from Boeotia. The middle Attic plain is separated from the Eleusinian by a lower mountain mass, Aegaleos (Αἰγάλεως) or Corydallos (Κορυδαλλός) (467 metres high), which, leaving easy way between itself and Parnes, continues southwest, broken midway by the pass of Daphné, till it terminates in "the rocky brow which looks o'er sea-born Salamis." Within these natural ramparts lies that which we may call *par excellence* the Attic plain, a great V-shaped recess open towards the sea. Its more important internal features, which, taken in connection with its enclosed character on the one hand and its free access to the sea on the other, rendered it an ideal theatre for the development of a Greek state, we must now examine in detail.

From the offshoots of Parnes and Pentelicus in the northeast rises the most considerable waterway of the plain—the Cephissus, which afforded in ancient as in modern times a perennial source of irrigation for the fields of the Attic farmer. As it approaches the sea, below the heights of the city, it seems to have been met by another stream from the east—the Ilissus, which, rising from Hymettus, is in modern times, owing to the denudation of its parent mountain, a much more insignificant stream than in ancient times, hardly more than a dry bed in summer. Hence the difficulty of determining its entire course. The Eridanus mentioned by ancient authors seems to have been a stream from the delicious and wholesome fountain of Kaisariané (Καισαριανή, anc. Κυλλοῦ πήρα), southeast of the sources of the Ilissus, into which the stream emptied east of the city.

Between the Cephissus and the Ilissus, about midway of the plain, a short range of hills, formed like the other heights of the plain of bluish-gray limestone and bearing to-day the name Tourkovoúni

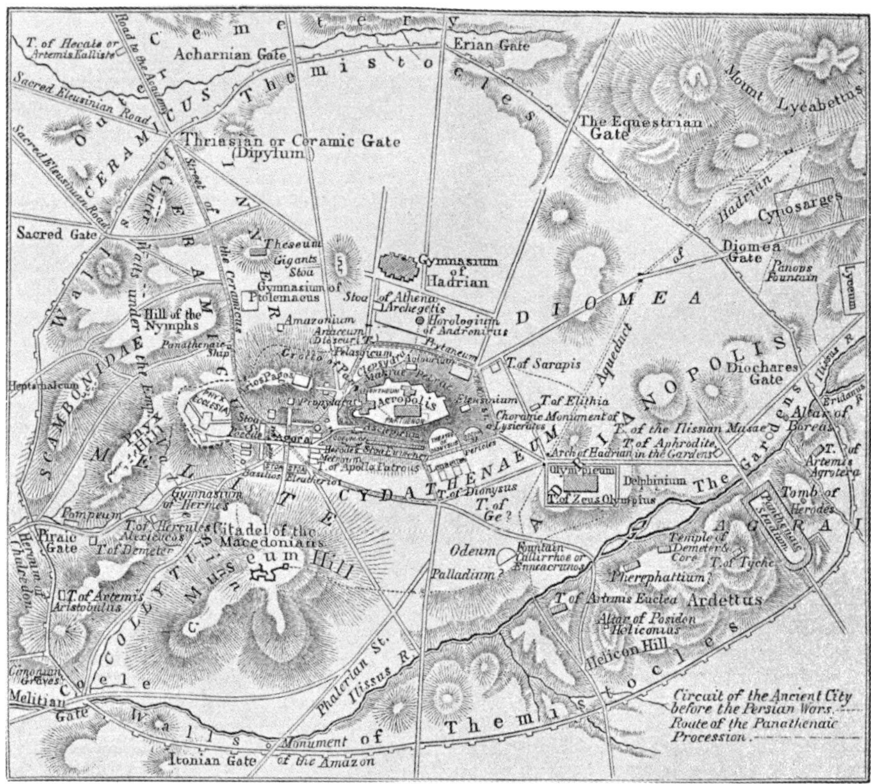

Plan of Athens.

(Τουρκοβούνι, "Turk Mountain," anc. perh. Ἀγχεσμός) (339 metres high), terminates at the southwest in the bold separate peak of Lycabettus (277 metres high), from the pyramidal summit of which, crowned by a chapel of St. George, one commands the most splendid view of the Attic plain, the gulf with its islands, and the Peloponnesian mountains beyond. Some 1000 paces to the southwest of this height, too sharp and steep for habitation, rises a double group of hills of about half the height of Lycabettus. The first and highest of these is the famous Acropolis, the citadel of Athens (156 metres high). Under its western brow lies the lower rock of the Areopagus (Ἄρειος πάγος, "Mars' Hill") (115 metres high). From northwest to south of this extends the group of the Museum (Μουσεῖον, "Muses' Hill"), the Pnyx, and the "Nymphs' Hill" (so called from an inscription), separated by depressions. The highest point is at the southeast extremity of the group, in the summit of the Museum (147 metres high), crowned by the monument of the Syrian Antiochus Philopappus. This triple group of hills seems to have been called collectively in ancient times Pnyx (Πνύξ, "conglomeration").

Lycabettus, the Acropolis, and the Pnyx were

View of the Aeropolis in 1890. (From a photograph.)

manifestly formed by the action of water, which, forcing its way east and west, left the hard blue-gray limestone projecting in three great protuberances, "like bones of a wasted body," as Plato says.

Between four and five English miles southwest of the Acropolis we find as outpost on the sea the rocky peninsula of Acté or Munichia, which, originally an island, like Salamis, was gradually united to the plain by the soil washed from above. North of it lies the secure landlocked harbour of Piraeus (Πειραιεύς); east, the larger open roadstead of Phalerum (Φάληρον), the earlier port of Athens, into which the Cephissus and Ilissus drain, and which is terminated on the southeast by Cape Colias (Κωλιὰς ἄκρα).

If we examine the soil of the plain from the sea inland, we find that the sandy coast is succeeded by a swampy alluvial strip, the Halipedon (Ἁλίπεδον, "salt-plain" or "sea-plain"). This again gives place to the plain proper, which, though "light of soil" and requiring diligent cultivation, is yet the natural home of the olive, and is not ill adapted to the growth of wheat and vegetables. The stony foot-hills above the plain (Φελλεύς) were terraced and utilized for the cultivation of the vine; while the fragrant mountain-plants, particularly of purple Hymettus, furnished pasturage not only for sheep, but for the bees that have made Attic honey proverbial. The fig-tree, too, was made to flourish so well in the plain that Attic figs were as famous as the oil and honey from the same region.

To these resources we must add the abundance of potter's-clay, and the wealth of material for the architect and the sculptor afforded by the quarries of Pentelicus, Hymettus, and Eleusis, as well as by those of the hills of the city and the heights of Piraeus.

In his efforts to wring from the soil its uttermost, the farmer was aided by a climate exceptionally favourable. In the Attic year there are, on the average, not more than thirty-five days on which the sun does not show itself; and though the north winds from snowy Parnes render the winter cold most penetrating, their steady breath by day during the greater part of the year, alternating with the equally steady sea-breeze by night, combined with a wonderful purity and dryness of air, gave to Attica—and still gives to her, though in a less degree—a climate at once physically and mentally exhilarating. Justly, then, might "the children of Erechtheus" be called "blessed of old, and children of the happy gods," "lightly walking through brightest and clearest air," where the goddess of all fertility "irrigated the soil from the streams of ever-flowing Cephissus, and breathed over them temperate breezes."

We turn now to the development of the little city which grew up in the midst of this exceptional environment.

As in the case of other ancient Grecian settlements, so in that of Athens we find an avoidance of immediate proximity to the sea, such as would have been obtained by a settlement on the height of the Piraeus. The natural centre for the development of a town neither remote from the sea nor yet immediately accessible from it—such, too, as to be commanded by a natural asylum in the event of hostile inroads—is afforded, in the case of Athens, by the group of hills below Lycabettus. Not only do we find here a central and isolated position in a plain set apart from the rest of the world by nature, but also, within a narrow compass, arable land with a water-supply, the material for the primitive artisan, and an airy and wholesome position for habitation upon a foundation of native rock, thus leaving the cultivable area unencumbered.

It is not of special moment to us, in tracing the material development of the little community which has done more than any other towards the promotion of civilization, whether we give to the earliest inhabitants any other name than Athenians. The term Pelasgian itself needs interpretation; and, so far as any precise knowledge goes, we might as well regard these early occupants of the "land unsacked" as quite as truly an outgrowth of "the ground itself" as their symbolic cicada. It is evident from the mere consideration of their environment that we must accept the view of Thucydides, that Attica was exceptionally stable in population, and trace, so far as possible, the gradual accretions upon the primitive nucleus, by whatever name we choose to designate it.

The earliest and most permanent traces of human habitation to be found at Athens are the foundations of houses cut in the rock of the group of hills designated by the general name of Pnyx. These are extensive enough to warrant the belief that this region, which in historical times lay waste for the most part, was the seat of a thriving town, according to the conditions of that primitive period. Whether the remarkable rock-cuttings and the semicircular Pelasgic wall upon the hill called *par excellence* Pnyx be the monuments of a prehistoric worship of the primeval god of the sunny sky of Greece as well as of its stormier phenomena, Zeus Hypsistos, or whether we are to see here, as has been the prevailing fashion, the place of the Athenian popular assembly (that which under the former supposition is the altar becoming under the latter the famous bema, from which the orators "shook th' arsenal and fulmin'd over Greece"), to any one who has been upon the ground the extreme antiquity of these imposing works is at once obvious. To the early period under discussion seem to belong also the rock-hewn chambers, one of which is traditionally known as the "Prison of Socrates"—an impossible designation.

We cannot suppose that the inhabitants of this first rock-city, or Cranaä (Κραναά), concerned themselves with the sea, if at all, beyond the demands of their daily existence, which would hardly lead them beyond fishery. It was only enterprising accretions from without that could utilize and develop the entire resources of nature.

Further traces of the early city are to be found in the ancient names, which, attached to the several districts in and about the later city, maintained themselves, not only in the mouth of the people, but in public records, through the entire history of Athens. Among the most certainly distinguishable of these primitive divisions (δῆμοι) is that known, as far back as we can trace, as Ceramicus (Κεραμεικός), so called from the potter's-clay which here furnished abundant material for one of the earliest of human industries. This region stretches northward from the rocky brow of the Areopagus. Melité (Μελίτη) seems to have lain to the south of Ceramicus, and to have embraced the Hill of the Nymphs as well as the Areopagus. Collytus (Κολ-

The Theseum

λυτός) stretched to the northeast of the Acropolis, bordering on the west not only upon Ceramicus, but also upon Melité, as seems proved by a mention of a boundary-stone in Strabo. Diomea (Διόμεια) may be placed next to Collytus, and between the Acropolis and Lycabettus. Ceriadae (Κειριάδαι), within the border of which, just below the precipice of the Nymphs' Hill, lay the depression, formed partly by nature, partly by quarrying, called the Barathrum (Βάραθρον), adjoined Melité on the west; while Coelé (Κοίλη), consonant with its name, occupied the gully between the Hill of the Nymphs and the bed of the Ilissus. The core of these ancient districts is the rock-city in Melité. To the north of Ceramicus, and, apparently, at all times outside the city limits, lay Colonos Hippios, called from its hill (κολωνός).

While the ancient city thus maintained itself in the little inland district just described, those influences were beginning to make themselves felt from the coast which were to govern the destiny of the future state. The Phœnician traders appear to have established their customary trading-posts at an early date not merely on Salamis (which has preserved its Phœnician name), but also on the coast opposite and on the heights of the Piraeus and Phalerum. Ancient rock-cuttings in the citadel of Piraeus seem to attest early settlement there. It was, indeed, such a position as we know, not only from Thucydides, but also from various material remains, to have been most likely to be chosen by these early navigators of the Mediterranean, and mediators between Orient and Occident. To this source, a mixed Oriental coast-settlement in which Phœnicians played the leading part, appears to be due the addition of Aphrodité and Heracles (Astarté and Melkart) to the primitive native worship of Zeus and the Nymphs, "daughters of ægis-holding Zeus," whose cult attached to springs and water-courses. The ritual of these two foreign deities, as carried on in the historical period, certainly points to a very early introduction of their worship. As to the primitive worship of Zeus, reference has already been made to what may, not improbably, be deemed his primeval sanctuary on the Pnyx; concerning a second early seat of his worship, not far removed, we are better informed. Southeast of the Acropolis, above the fountain Callirrhoë and the bed of the Ilissus, was shown in ancient times an opening in the rock into which, according to the legend, the last vestiges of Deucalion's flood had sunk. Here Deucalion was said to have "built the ancient sanctuary of Olympian Zeus," whose worship remained fixed at this spot through all the subsequent history of the city. Cleft rock and spring are fit emblems of the worship of Zeus and his daughters at this spot by the primeval Cranai.

The gradual influences of the influx into Attica, both overland from the north and oversea from the west, may be traced in the gods added to the Athenian pantheon. The Minyan Artemis, the Pelasgic Hermes, the Thracian Ares who gave his name to the Areopagus, Hephaestus the handicraftsman's god, gradually encroached upon the domain of the older cults; while Poseidon gained a seat at Phalerum, and later disputed, according to the legend, the possession of the land with Athené, the intellectual development of the old Oriental mother-goddess, who retained her guardianship of the olive-tree even after she had resigned her care of the fields to Eleusinian Demeter.

The incursions from the north and from the sea, which gradually brought in these new divinities, forced the growing state of the Cranai to take up a securer position on the rock of the Acropolis, which, falling off precipitously on all sides except the west, readily lent itself to the fortifications which the early inhabitants of Greece knew so well how to build, and which we can understand now that the ruins of Tiryns and Mycenae, as well as the Acropolis itself, have been submitted to careful excavation and study. Here, on the top of the rock, which was levelled and provided with retaining-walls, as well as with a surrounding fortification, was established the ancient Polis (Πόλις, a term long retained as the official designation of the Acropolis), the seat of the worship of Zeus Polieus. Here, on the north side, where we now see the ruins of the later Erechtheum, were the old sanctuary of the local daemon Erechtheus and the palace of the royal race of the Cecropid and Erechtheid kings, the foundations of which, as well as of private dwellings of the same epoch, have been traced. Up to this palace led from the north a stairway, unearthed in the recent excavations, and in the enclosure west of the present Erechtheum was the sacred olive-tree, the gift of Athené, and the marble balustrade about the later Ionic temple.

Thus by the sacred olive and the hollow in the rock with its mysterious trident-mark—where the waves could be heard when the south-wind blew—flourished the old priestly and kingly race, hemmed in not only by the wall of the Polis proper, but also, as it seems, by a lower wall enclosing the skirts of the Acropolis, and called from its nine gates Enneapylon (Ἐννεάπυλον), the area within which and below the ramparts of the citadel was known as the Pelargicon (τὸ Πελαργικόν). The main entrance was then, as it has always been perforce, at the west end of the citadel, a fortified way winding up towards the right, the ancient warrior's exposed side, below the bastion of Athené Niké.

The Ionians who immigrated from across the Aegean brought in the Delian Apollo, the god of

Ruins of the Olympieum.

hard by it the tomb of Cecrops, both under the protection of the old local nymph Pandrosos (Cecropium and Pandroseum). Under the northwest brow of the Acropolis, below the "long rocks" (μακραὶ πέτραι), was the grotto of Pan; and still farther to the west, within the modern bastion of Odysseus, a spring called Clepsydra (Κλεψύδρα, "she that hides her water"), popularly supposed to pass underground to Phalerum. This spring was and still is approached from above by a remarkable fortified winding stairway cut in the rock. Under the south face of the Acropolis were a cave and spring, with which the worship of the healer Asclepius came to be associated; and in the southwest spur of the sacred rock, whence Aegeus was said to have flung himself down, Athené was established as goddess of victory (Νίκη), worshipped in an uncouth primitive idol with the sacrifice of a perfect cow, as so beautifully represented on

Ionic colonization and civilization. This new and important factor in the Athenian state established itself south of the Acropolis in what Thucydides regarded as old Athens, in the region called Cydathenaeum (Κυδαθήναιον), extending some 2000 metres around the southeast flank of the Acropolis and up towards Lycabettus. Under the south face of the Acropolis, close to the later Dionysiac Theatre, the northern Dionysus of Eleutherae was established in the Lenaeum, near the sanctuary of the "public" Aphrodité (Ἀφροδίτη πάνδημος). To the south of this seems to have lain the old market-place, the ἀγορά of the Ionic ἄστυ. Here was established the first town-hall—the Prytaneum or Basileum—by which, under the auspices of Themis, the "sceptre-bearing" kings administered justice. The solemn court of murder, so soon as the taking of human life came to be recognized as a state offence, was established on the Areopagus, in a cleft beneath which the Eumenides ("the gracious")—as the avengers of blood, the Erinyes, were here called—were solemnly worshipped. The bodies of the executed, as well as purificatory offerings and offscourings, were thrown into the deep recess of the Barathrum. Thus the highest priesthood was associated with the Acropolis, while the king came down to preside in his political function over the Ionic nobility of Cydathenaeum. The Thesean nobles, true to their Ionic instinct, encouraged closer intercourse with the sea, and Cydathenaeum was linked by a high-road to Phalerum, whence they trafficked abroad; whereas the influence of the Tyrian traders seems to have made itself felt upon the Cranaan city of Melité by a way leading up from the Salaminian Strait.

In the meantime the germ of the later city was rapidly maturing in the industrial settlement northwest of the Acropolis in Ceramicus, which seems to have kept pace in its development with the growing opposition of the lower classes to the encroachments and extortions of the Ionic nobility. After the period of ferment followed by the Solonian legislation, at the opening of the sixth century, came the first great period of the Athenian state—the democratic despotism of the Pisistratidae.

The centre of gravity of the city now shifted to the point at which it remained ever afterwards—to the centre of the settlement of the Ceramicus, which rapidly outgrew in importance the effete Cydathenaeum. Here was established the altar of the Twelve Gods, from which, as from the golden milestone of Rome, distances were reckoned; and here, too, was the focus of Athenian *πολυπραγμοσύνη*. On the Acropolis, Pisistratus probably built the temple of Athené Polias, "the old temple," on the site between the later Parthenon and Erechtheum, where its plan has lately been made out. From this period, too, we date the institution of the great Panathenaea and the carrying of the sacred ship from the outer Ceramicus around and into the citadel. Thus did Pisistratus add new glory to the cult of his patron goddess. Upon the terrace above Callirrhoë, Pisistratus began a great temple to Olympian Zeus, but did not carry out his ambitious design. He also built in, or led an aqueduct from, Callirrhoë, which thus became Enneacrunos (Ἐννεάκρουνος, "the fountain with nine pipes"), and long continued to be, as it had been, the main water supply of the town. The encouragement, if not the introduction, of the Dionysiac worship, which bore such abundant fruit in the succeeding century, seems also to have been an object of especial care to Pisistratus.

Close upon the downfall of the Pisistratidean tyrannis and the struggles of the Clisthenean reform came the Persian wars and the sack of the Acropolis by the barbarians. The remains of the ruined shrines of the pre-Persian period, with curious painted pediments of soft stone, and the statues of Parian marble, executed by artists under the patronage of the Pisistratidae, are among the most precious treasures brought to light by the excavation of the Acropolis.

The wide-reaching schemes of naval empire which sprang from the fertile brain of Themistocles, who fostered the growth of the Athenian navy and first saw the strategic importance of the Piraeus, were destined never to be fully realized. Before the Persian wars, Themistocles had caused the Piraeus to be fully fortified and made a strong naval station, invested with heavy fortress-walls about the citadel of Munichia, and with its harbours (Cantharos, the largest, Munichia, and Zea) narrowed and easily closed. After the devastation of the city, he whose merit it was that he "fastened the city to the Piraeus, the land to the sea," would fain have made the Piraeus the centre of the new city-development—impregnable by land and sea. But the machinations of the Peloponnesians necessitated the hurried fortification of the old site with an effective wall, and thus enabled the conservative party of Aristides and Cimon to carry out their design of maintaining the "wheel-shaped" city about the Acropolis, with a separate port-town and naval station at the Piraeus.

The Themistoclean wall, the successor of older fortifications, passed, as well as can be made out, over the Pnyx hill from the Barathrum to the peak of the Museum, skirted the Ilissus, which lay like a moat without it to the south, curved southeast of the Acropolis, coming around towards the northeast, so as to avoid the foot of Lycabettus, and finally passed from east to west across the plain, taking in the little water-courses from Lycabettus, and finally bending about to the point from which we started. It included Collytus and Diomea, cut Melité in twain, formed an "inner" and an "outer" Ceramicus, and excluded Coelé. The dimensions of the space thus enclosed were about 2000 metres east and west by 1500 metres north and south, the Acropolis lying some 500 metres nearer the south side. Of the gates, we note two in Melité—the Melitid Gate (Μελιτίδες πύλαι) and the "Gate of the Horsemen" (Ἱππάδες πύλαι); then the gate on the south leading to Phalerum (Ἰτωνίαι πύλαι); the Gate of Diochares (Διοχάρους πύλαι) and the Diomean Gate (Διομῆς πύλη) in the east; the Acharnian Gate (Ἀχαρνικὴ πύλη) in the north; and the Dipylon (Δίπυλον), the most important, between the inner and outer Ceramici, where considerable remains of the ancient foundations are still to be seen. South of the last was the Piraic Gate (Πειραϊκὴ πύλη).

To unite the city thus fortified with the Piraeus, the Long Walls were begun, about B.C. 460—a northern, run from the Hill of the Nymphs to Munichia, and a southern, connecting the city with Phalerum. Between these, under Pericles, a second Piraic Wall was built, parallel to the northern, completing the system and linking city and port by a long double fortification—the *σκέλη*, or "legs."

Without and near the gates, particularly the Dipylon, the dead were interred; and public funerals were solemnized over the ashes of military heroes in the outer Ceramicus. Beautiful remains of the tombs of the period succeeding the Periclean, but bearing abundant traces of the Phidian art, have been fortunately preserved to us near the Dipylon, and form one of the most striking monuments of the ancient city.

To the Cimonian period seems to belong the imposing temple, the best preserved of all Greek buildings of classical times, on the hill overlooking the Ceramicus from the west—the so-called Theseum, not improbably to be named the Heracleum.

On the Acropolis, in connection with a new and extensive plan of walling, levelling, and enlargement of area, preparations seem to have been made by Cimon for an imposing new temple on the site now occupied by the Parthenon. Here not only was the irregular edge of the precipice raised and reinforced by a high wall outside the Pelasgian rampart supporting a deep inner grading, but a heavy foundation was built up from the bed-rock as support for a great temple structure, destined not to be completed according to the original design. On the north side, also, the plateau of the Acropolis was built up and walled, drums of columns and portions of architraves being freely used in the construction of the wall, and architectural fragments, inscribed marble tablets, and even statues employed as grading material. The bastion of Niké was also newly fortified. Though the nature of Cimon's whole undertaking was decorative rather than strategic, it might yet be truly said that the Acropolis was walled by the Pelasgians and Cimon.

Pericles, having at his disposal the treasures of the Attic League, which were transferred to Athens (B.C. 454) and apparently kept in the Opisthodomos—as the "ancient" Pisistratidean temple of the Polias, commonly called from its length the Hecatompedon (Ἑκατόμπεδον), and apparently rebuilt, at least in part, on its original site, was henceforth termed—reared upon Cimon's foundation the new and magnificent Doric Parthenon (dedicated B.C. 438). The architecture was intrusted to Ictinus and the sculpture to Phidias, whose chryselephantine statue of the Parthenos adorned the room to which alone the term Parthenon ("the virgin's chamber") strictly applied. The Propylaea (q. v.), a massive ornamental entrance to the Acropolis, in which the Doric and Ionic styles were happily blended, rose under the guidance of the brilliant architect Mnesicles; and, although never completed according to the architect's design, it remained among the greatest wonders of the city.

Of the host of statues of all kinds which fast thronged the Acropolis, particularly during the fifth century—among them the great bronze statue of Athené as champion (πρόμαχος), the bronze figure of the Wooden Horse, the heifer of Myron, and many others mentioned by ancient writers—we can take but passing notice. Their number was constantly increasing down to the times of the Roman Empire.

Some time in the period covered by the first Athenian empire the stately little Ionic temple of Athené Niké seems to have been reared upon the southwest bastion of the Acropolis, and surrounded on three sides with the exquisite marble balustrade, fragments of which are still preserved on the Acropolis.

The new Erechtheum, with its famous porch of the Maidens or Caryatides, was in course of construction at the close of the fifth century. See p. 112.

The agora of the inner Ceramicus, bounded on the south by the abrupt brow of the Areopagus, under which stood the statues of the Eponymi, the namesake-heroes of the ten Clisthenean tribes, seems to have been divided by a line of stone Hermae into a northern and a southern half. About the southern half stood various public buildings, the Council-hall (Βουλευτήριον), the Royal Stoa (Στοὰ Βασίλειος), the Painted Stoa (Στοὰ ποικίλη), the Metroön, the temple of Apollo Patroös, as well as the altar of the Twelve Gods and the statues of the democratic heroes Harmodius and Aristogiton. In its wider extent the agora of Ceramicus is bounded on the west by the hill of the so-called Theseum, and on the east

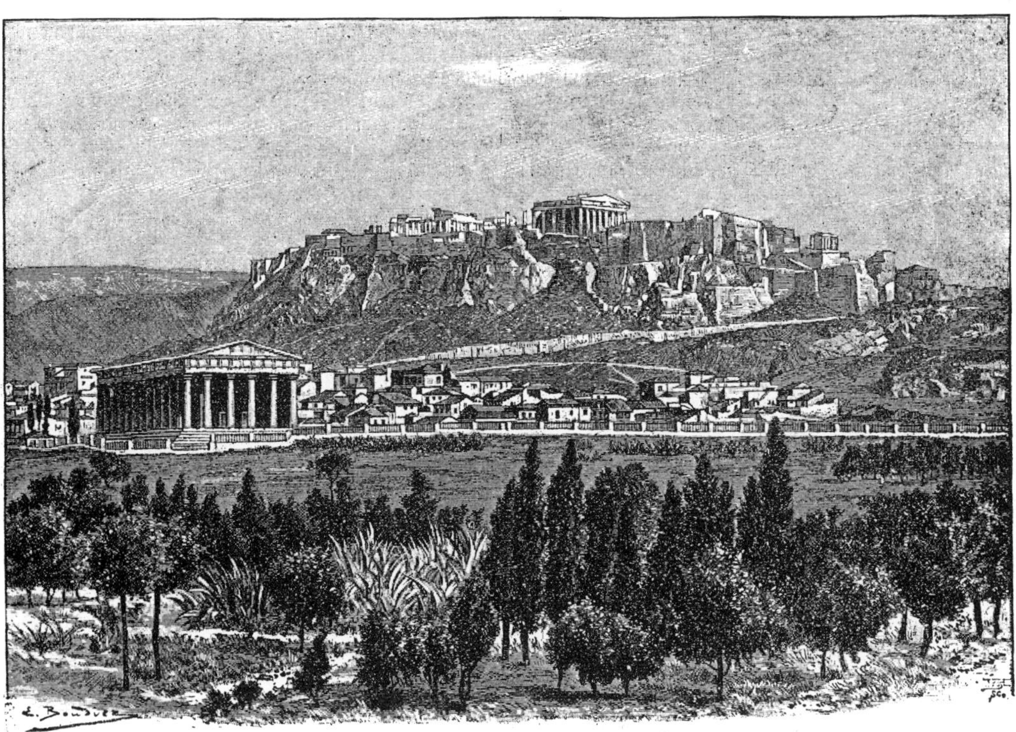

The Acropolis and the Wall of Themistocles.

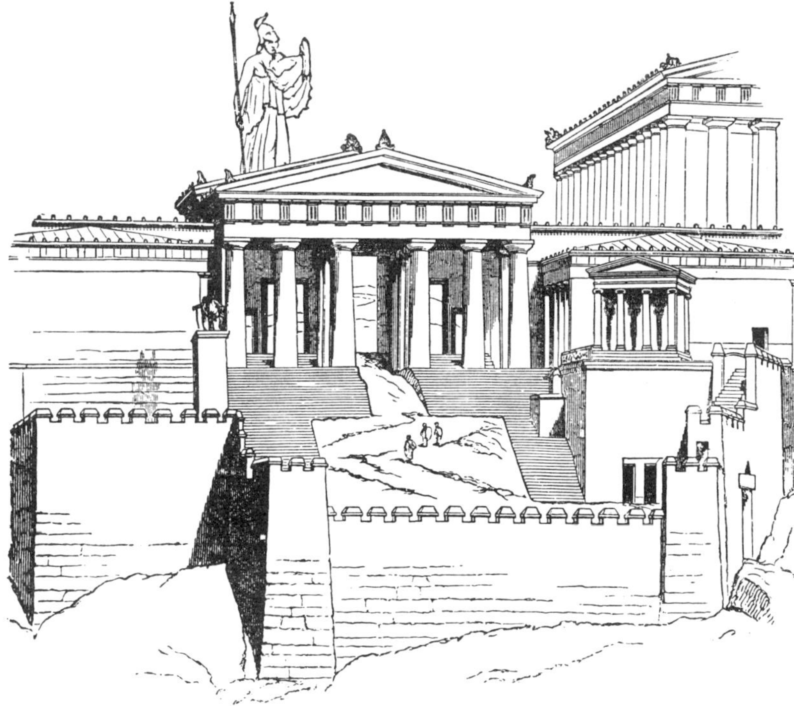

View of the Athenian Propylaea. Restoration. (Reber.)

tion or wealth of their occupants. In this respect the old city seems to have been inferior to the Piraeus, which was better laid out and contained more sumptuous private buildings. At all times, however, in both towns, houses and house-furniture were, for the most part, extremely simple, and the bustling open-air life of the male population was not conducive to private luxury. See DOMUS.

The Long Walls, destroyed at the close of the Peloponnesian War, were re-erected at the birth of the new Athenian empire, under which, and during the

by the gate of Athené Archegetis. Its chief existing monument is the later Stoa of Attalus, king of Pergamos. The mention of these public works needs to be complemented by a word in regard to private structures. The dwelling-houses of the city during the period of Athenian greatness stood in striking contrast with the public structures. Built along narrow, irregular, and ill-kept streets, they gave but little indication of the social posi-

subsequent period of the Hellenistic successors of Alexander, the state received further adornment. Lycurgus completed the great stone theatre within the Lenaeum, overlapping the ancient Orchestra or "dancing-ring," traces of which are still discernible. The Street of the Tripods, winding about the southeastern foot of the Acropolis, is still marked by the delicate choragic monument (q. v.) of Lysicrates (B.C. 334). The Stoa of Eumenes lies

The Acropolis. View Taken from the Olympieum.—Evening Effect.

to the west of the great theatre. The eastern side of the market of Ceramicus is marked by the great stone bazaar of Attalus, previously noticed. Building was carried on by Antiochus Epiphanes till his death (in B.C. 164) upon the site of the old sanctuary of Zeus on the Ilissus, where Hadrian finally reared his colossal Corinthian temple, the few remaining columns of which (the στῦλοι) are one of the most prominent Athenian landmarks. Near it, towards the Acropolis, Hadrian set the gate, still standing, which should separate, according to its inscription, "the Athens of Theseus" from "the Athens of Hadrian." An octagonal tower with water-clock within and weather-vane on the summit, and bearing on its several faces reliefs representing the winds (Horologium or "Tower of the Winds"), was erected by Andronicus Cyrrhestes (q. v.) southeast of the agora, where it still stands. The famous Herodes Atticus built, in honour of his dead wife Regilla, the great Odeum, adjoining the Stoa of Eumenes, under the southwestern slope of the Acropolis. These are among the most prominent monuments of the later Greek and the Graeco-Roman period that still attract the visitor to the ancient site.

The subsequent history of the monuments is one of rapine, defacement, and destruction. The traces of the Valerian wall, forming a great loop north of the Acropolis, and the mediæval and modern fortifications, that have been removed from the approach to the Acropolis, are melancholy witnesses to barbarian invasion, mediæval slavery, and the struggle of reawakening liberty. The archives of the story of the material growth and development of the Athens that has influenced the world had been laid up for a curious posterity long before these structures arose.

BIBLIOGRAPHY.—E. Curtius, *Stadtgeschichte von Athen* (Berlin, 1891) (a most valuable work, containing a full collection of ancient authorities, citations of modern publications, excellent drawings, plans, and maps); art. "Athen" in Baumeister's *Denkmäler des klassischen Alterthums;* "Athen" in Bädeker's *Griechenland* (Eng. trans. 1889). Other works are cited by Curtius. See HELLAS.

Athenaea (Ἀθήναια). An ancient festival originally held in honour of Athené at Athens, and of an agrarian character. See CHALKEIA; PANATHENAEA.

Athenaeum (Ἀθήναιον). The first public educational institution at Rome, built by Hadrian about A.D. 135. The building was in the form of a theatre, and brilliantly fitted up. There rhetoricians and poets held their recitations, and salaried professors gave their lectures in the various branches of general liberal education—philosophy and rhetoric, as well as grammar and jurisprudence. This continued until at least the fifth century A. D.

Athenaeus (Ἀθήναιος). (1) An engineer, and contemporary of Archimedes, who flourished about B.C. 210. He was the author of a work, still preserved, on engines of war (Περὶ Μηχανημάτων).

(2) The Greek scholar, a native of Naucratis in Egypt. He was educated at Alexandria, where he lived from A.D. 170–230. After this he lived at Rome, and there wrote his Δειπνοσοφισταί (or "Banquet of the Learned"), in fifteen books. Of these the first, second, and part of the third are only preserved in a selection made in the eleventh century; the rest survive in a tolerably complete state. The work shows astonishing learning, and contains a number of notices of ancient life which would otherwise have been lost. The author gives us collections and extracts from more than 1500 works (now mostly lost), and by more than 700 writers. His book is thrown into the form of a conversation held in the year A.D. 228 at a dinner given by Larensius, a rich and accomplished Roman, and a descendant of the great antiquarian Varro. Among the guests are the most learned men of the time, including Galen the physician and Ulpian the jurist. The conversation ranges over numberless subjects connected with domestic and social life, manners and customs, trade, art, and science. Among the most valuable things in the book are the numerous passages from prose-writers and poets, especially from the masters of the Middle Comedy. Good editions are those of Dindorf (1827); and Meineke, 4 vols. (1859–67). There is a literal English translation in the Bohn Classical Library, 3 vols. (1854).

Athenagŏras (Ἀθηναγόρας). A Father of the Church, a native of Athens, and in philosophy a Platonist. He wrote a treatise on the doctrine of the resurrection of the body and a defence of the Christians, blending the teachings of the Greek philosophers with those of the Church. He flourished in the second half of the second century.

Athēné (Ἀθήνη) or **Pallas Athēné**. A Greek goddess, identified with the Roman Minerva. According to the story most generally current, she was the daughter of Zeus, who had swallowed his first wife, Metis (Counsel), the daughter of Oceanus, in the fear that she would bring forth a son stronger than himself. Hephaestus (or, according to another version, Prometheus) clave open the head of Zeus with an axe, on which Athené sprang forth in full armour, the goddess of eternal virginity. But her ancient epithet Τριτογένεια (born of Triton, or the roaring flood) points to water—that is, to Oceanus—as the source of her being. Oceanus was, according to Homer, the origin of all things and of all deities. The worship of Athené and the story of her birth were accordingly connected with many brooks and lakes in various regions—especially in Boeotia, Thessalia, and Libya—to which the name Triton was attached.

From the first, Athené took a very prominent place in the Greek popular religion. The Homeric hymns represent her as the favourite of her father, who refuses her nothing. When solemn oaths were to be taken, they joined her name with those of Zeus and Apollo, in a way which shows that the three deities represent the embodiment of all divine authority. With the exception of the two gods just mentioned, there is no other deity whose original character as a power of nature underwent so remarkable an ethical development. Both conceptions of Athené, the natural and the ethical, were intimately connected in the religion of Attica, whose capital, Athens, was named after Athené and was the most important seat of her worship. Athené was originally the maiden daughter of the god of heaven; the clear transparent æther, whose purity is always breaking forth in unveiled brilliancy through the clouds that surround it. As a deity of the sky, she, with Zeus, is the mistress of thunder and lightning. Like Zeus, she carries the aegis (q. v.) with the Gorgon's head, the symbol of the tempest and its terrors. In many statues, accordingly, she is represented as hurling the thunder-bolt. But she also sends down from sky to earth light and warmth and fruitful dew, and with them prosperity to fields and plants. A whole series of fables and usages, belonging especially to the Athenian religion, represent her as the helper and protector of agriculture. The two deities Erechtheus and Erichthonius, honoured in Attica as powers of the fruitful soil, are her foster-children. She was worshipped with Erechtheus in the temple named after him the Erechtheum, the oldest sanctuary on the Athenian Acropolis. The names of her earliest priestesses, the daughters of Cecrops—Aglaurus, Pandrosus, and Hersé—signify the bright air, the dew, and the rain, and are mere personifications of their qualities, of such value to the Athenian territory.

The sowing season was opened in Attica by three sacred services of ploughing. Of these, two were in honour of Athené as inventress of the plough, while the third took place in honour of Demeter. It was Athené, also, who had taught men how to attach oxen to the yoke; above all, she had given them the olive-tree, the treasure of Attica. This tree she had made to grow out of the rock of the citadel, when disputing the possession of the land with Poseidon. Several festivals, having reference to these functions of the goddess, were celebrated in Attica—the Callynteria and Plynteria, the Scirophoria, the Arrhephoria or Hersephoria, and the Oschophoria, which were common to Athené with Dionysus. (See DIONYSIA.) Even her chief feast, the Panathenaea, was originally a harvest festival. It is significant that the presentation of the πέπλος or mantle, the chief offering at the celebration, took place in the sowing season. But afterwards more was made of the intellectual gifts bestowed by the goddess.

Athené was very generally regarded as the goddess of war—an idea which in ancient times was the prevailing one. It was connected with the fact that, like her father, Zeus, she was supposed to be able to send storms and bad weather. In this capacity she appears in story as the true friend of all bold warriors, such as Perseus, Bellerophon, Iason, Heracles, Diomedes, and Odysseus. But her courage is a wise courage, not a blind rashness like that of Ares; and she is always represented, accordingly, as getting the better of him. In this connection she was honoured in Athenian worship mainly as a protector and defender; thus (to take a striking example), she was worshipped on the citadel of Athens under the name of Πρόμαχος, "champion," "protector." But she was also a goddess of victory. As the personification of victory (Athené Niké) she had a second and especial temple on the Athenian Acropolis. (See ACROPOLIS.) And the great statues in the temples represented her, like Zeus, with Niké in her outstretched hand. The occupations of peace, however, formed the main sphere of her activity. Like all the other deities who were supposed to dispense the blessings of nature, she is the protectress of growing children; and, as the goddess of the clear sky and of pure air, she bestows health and keeps off sickness. Further, she is (with Zeus) the patroness of the Athenian φρατρίαι or unions of kinsfolk. At Athens and Sparta she protects the popular and deliberative assemblies; in many places, and especially at Athens, the whole State is under her care (Athené Polias, Poliuchus). Elsewhere she presides over the larger unions of kindred peoples. The festival of Athené Itonia at Coronea was a confederate festival of all Boeotia. Under the title of Παναχαΐς she was worshipped as the goddess of the Achaean League.

Speaking broadly, Athené represents human wit and cleverness, and presides over the whole moral and intellectual side of human life. From her are derived all the productions of wisdom and understanding, every art and science, whether of war or of peace. A number of discoveries, of the most

Athené. (Vatican Museum.)

various kinds, is ascribed to her. It has been already mentioned that she was credited with the invention of the plough and the yoke. She was often associated with Poseidon as the inventress of horse-taming and ship-building. In the Athenian story she teaches Erichthonius to fasten his horses to the chariot. In the Corinthian story she teaches Bellerophon to subdue Pegasus. At Lindus in Rhodes she was worshipped as the goddess who helped Danaüs to build the first fifty-oared ship. In the fable of the Argonauts it is she who instructs the builders of the first ship, the Argo. Even in Homer all the productions of women's art, as of spinning and weaving, are characterized as "works of Athené." Many a Παλλάδιον, or statue of Pallas, bore a spindle and distaff in its left hand. As the mistress and protectress of arts and handiwork, she was worshipped at the Chalkeia, or Feast of Smiths, under the title of Ἐργάνη. Under this name, too, she is mentioned in several inscriptions found on the Acropolis. Her genius covers the field of music and dancing. She is inventor of the flute and the trumpet, as well as of the Pyrrhic war-dance, in which she was said to have been the earliest performer, at the celebration of the victory of the Gods over the Giants.

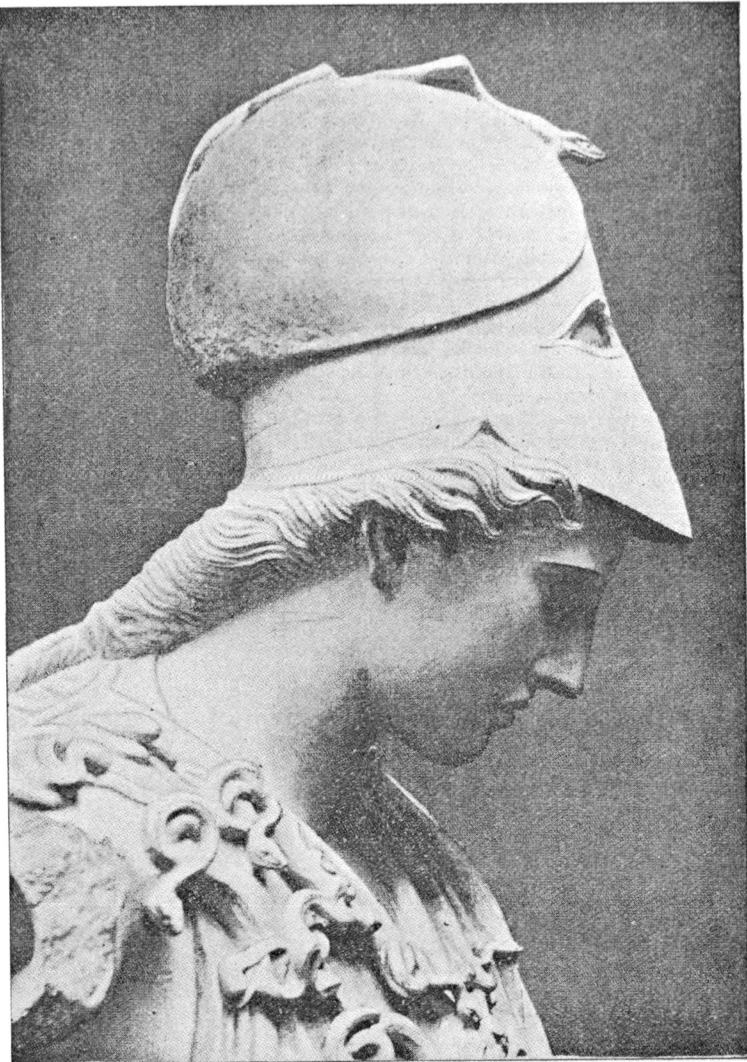

Pallas of Velletri. (Munich.)

It was Phidias (q. v.) who finally fixed the typical representation of Athené in works of art. Among his numerous statues of her, three—the most celebrated—were set up on the Acropolis of Athens. These were: (1) The colossal statue of Athené Parthenos, wrought in ivory and gold, thirty feet in height (with the pedestal), and standing in the Parthenon. (See PARTHENON.) The goddess was represented wearing a long robe falling down to the feet, and on her breast was the aegis with the Gorgon's head. A helmet was on her head; in one hand she bore a Victory, six feet in height, in the other a lance, which leaned against a shield adorned with scenes from the battles of the Amazons with the Giants. (2) The bronze statue of Athené Promachos, erected from the proceeds of the spoils taken at Marathon, and standing between the Propylaea and the Erechtheum. The proportions of this statue were so gigantic that the gleaming point of the lance and the crest of the helmet were visible to seamen on approaching the Piraeus from Sunium. (3) The Lemnian Pallas, so named because it had been dedicated by the Athenian colonists in Lemnos. The attractions of this statue won for it the name of "the Beautiful." Like the second, it was of bronze; being a representation of Athené as the goddess of peace, it was without a helmet. See MINERVA.

Athenodōrus (Ἀθηνόδωρος). (1) A Rhodian sculptor associated with Agesander and Polydorus in producing the famous group of Laocoön (q. v.). (2) Of Tarsus, a Stoic philosopher, surnamed Cordylio, who was keeper of the library at Pergamus, and afterwards removed to Rome, where he lived with M. Cato, at whose house he died. (3) Of Tarsus, a Stoic philosopher, surnamed Cananites, from Cana, in Cilicia, the birthplace of his father. He taught at Apollonia in Epirus, where the young Octavius (subsequently the emperor Augustus) was one of his disciples. He accompanied the latter to Rome, and became one of his intimate friends. On one occasion he is said to have advised the emperor always to repeat the letters of the Greek alphabet before giving way to any impulse of anger.

Athĕsis. The modern Adige or Etsch; a river rising in the Rhaetian Alps. It receives the Atagis (Eisach), flows through upper Italy past Verona, and falls into the Adriatic through many mouths.

Athlētae (ἀθληταί, ἀθλητῆρες). A term in strictness applied to those who contended for prizes (ἆθλα) in the games which required strength, skill, and agility of body, in contradistinction to those who engaged in equestrian and musical contests; though in a general sense it is found extended even to these.

The contests of the athletae were in running, wrestling, boxing, the pentathlon, and the pancratium. Details of these will be found in the separate articles LUCTA; PANCRATIUM; PENTATHLON; PUGILATUS; STADIUM.

In early times in Greece, athletic games were held occasionally at festivals in honour of the gods and heroes, but especially at the funerals of distinguished men; thus in the *Iliad* (xxiii.) games are held at the funeral of Patroclus. But the warriors, as a rule, do not appear to have trained especially for the games; since, as part of their general education, they had been instructed in gymnastics. In this department, Grecian legend told how Heracles, Peleus, and Theseus had been celebrated, as were also Castor and Pollux; but in the Homeric Age there were few who made athletics as such their especial business, though we must not forget the passage (*Od.* viii. 164) where Euryalus reproaches Odysseus as not being "like an athlete." Games were becoming fairly frequent, and the special skill required in the contests was gradually demanding increased application to the different branches of athletics.

In the next age, athletics became the national Hellenic sport, and never ceased to be so till the latest times of the ancient world; for, in the first instance, they satisfied the artistic instinct of the Greeks, as they developed the human frame in strength and beauty. But as it was the national sport, like horse-racing in England, every department tended to become more and more professionalized. The great festivals collected together the greatest concourses of the members of the Hellenic race; and the emulation to succeed before the immense gatherings of their countrymen, and the extravagant honours and rewards bestowed by the cities on their citizens when victorious, rendered victory in the games the most coveted distinction a Greek could acquire; so that every means was resorted to in order to attain the strength and skill necessary for success.

Euripides (*Autol.* Frag. 1) speaks with bitter contempt of the athletes, who, he says, are the greatest of the countless evils of Hellas, who are slaves to their belly, a degenerate lot, useless in war, unable to bear old age or misfortune—for their training is not an ennobling training.

The athletic contests, just as are the "weights" in the ring in this country, were divided into "light" (κοῦφα) and "heavy" (βαρέα) or "violent" (βίαια). See Aristot. *Pol.* v. 4, 7 foll.; Galen. vi. 487, K.; Philostr. *Gymn.* 3.

The training in each of the two main classes became severer and severer as time went on; for more and more striking performances were expected. We hear of a rule that the competitors at Olympia had to swear that they had diligently devoted ten months to the recognized special training in athletics (Pausan. v. 24, 9). This was to maintain that common system of athletic training which prevailed in all Hellenic wrestling-schools. The ordinary gymnastic master who taught the youths bodily exercises as a branch of general education was called παιδοτρίβης, and he who trained those who were intending to compete in the games was the γυμναστής; but this distinction disappeared in later times. The γυμναστής was in constant supervision of his pupils, followed them to the games (Pausan. v. 6, 8), where he made all necessary preparations for their contest, and during the struggle stood by with words of encouragement or reproach (Philostr. *Gymn.* 20). Just as a physician, a trainer required implicit obedience in those for whom he prescribed (Epictet. *Enchir.* 29). Subordinate to him was the ἀλείπτης, who originally, as his name indicates, looked to the anointing of the body; but often, especially in later times, took much more upon himself, became confused with the παιδοτρίβης, and used to prescribe the course of diet to be eaten, and even how it was to be eaten. The diet of athletes is said to have been fresh cheese, dried figs, and wheat; but Dromeus of Stymphalus, or, according to others, a trainer called Pythagoras, introduced a meat diet. However, it is very unlikely that the athletes were ever trained on anything but meat. Pork was the principal meat used, though we find also beef and goat's flesh. Fish was considered bad. They probably drank water and not wine after their exercises, as the latter was dangerous; and they had to abstain from all cakes. The bread they ate was of a particular kind, slightly leavened and hardly baked at all. The usual course was to eat bread for the morning meal and meat for the evening. After the morning meal their exercises continued till the evening, interrupted only by a few intervals (Galen. vi. 168–169). Those who submitted to the severest training (βίαιος τροφή, ἀναγκαιοφαγία, ἀδηφαγία) had to eat enormous masses of meat after the day's exercise: two minae (=2⅝ lbs.) was a very small amount for an athlete, who generally slept it off late into the next day (Galen. i. 28, K.), though we sometimes hear of athletes promoting digestion by walking (Plin. *H. N.* xi. § 283). Many athletes did really eat vast quantities of food; so much, in fact, that their appetite became proverbial (Aristoph. *Pax*, 34).

The exercises which athletes went through were the ordinary ones of the palaestra and those required for the games; though we sometimes find athletes going through exercises which were not departments of competition, merely in order to increase their strength, such as putting heavy weights, bending bars of iron, wrenching back the necks of bulls, knocking suspended bags of sand backwards and forwards by blows of their fists (κωρυκοβολία), and also working with a mattock. The athletes practised, as a rule, each for a separate event. Hence the one-sidedness even of their physical training, and the fact that those who trained for that event which comprised the most varied exertions (such as the pentathlon), were justly considered to have the best-proportioned frames. But sometimes the athletes attempted more than one; for it was considered a great honour to be victorious at Olympia in both wrestling and in the pancratium on the same day. There were only seven such victors besides their mythic predecessor, Heracles. A certain Polites conquered on the same day in the three different kinds of races—the stadion, the diaulos, and the dolichos (Pausan. vi. 13, 3).

Victors in the principal games were called ἱερονῖκαι; those in the separate games, ὀλυμπιονῖκαι, etc.; and those who were successful in all four games were the περιοδονῖκαι. In Roman times, however, we find this latter term applied to celebrated athletes who had been victors in a great number of games, even though they were not the four great ones. Another strange title of distinguished athletes at Rome was παραδοξονίκης, which was strictly applied to those who conquered in both wrestling and the pancratium.

In early times, the athletes used to practise in the gymnasium, where the young men who had made some progress in gymnastics, and were advanced from the palaestra, went through their ordinary unprofessional exercises. In Roman times we find the athletes frequenting the palaestrae, the gymnasia, *xysti* (covered places for use in bad weather), and the stadia. There were also exercising places in the great Roman balneae (q. v.).

Originally the athletes used to contend with a girdle around their loins (διάζωμα, περίζωμα, or simply ζῶμα), according to the custom of the Spartans; but very soon it became the custom to contend naked. It was professional for Roman athletes to wear their hair tied up in a knot called *cirrus*. The Greek as well as the Roman athletes used sometimes to shave off their hair in that tonsure which Aristophanes called "the bowl crop" (σκαφίον, *Thesm.* 838). Further, they occasionally wore a cap (*galericulum*); and as their wonderful style of boxing consisted in swinging round their arms and not striking out straight from the shoulder, they used to wear guards for the ears (ἀμφωτίδες or ἐπωτίδες). For the battered ears of ancient boxers, see Plat. *Protag.* 342 B; Mart. vii. 32, 5.

He who took to the profession of an athlete seldom abandoned it before his thirty-fifth year, which was considered the age at which he was in the prime of manhood; but if he had never won a victory by that time he generally gave up the business. A successful athlete continued to contend in the games till his strength failed (Plut. *Cat. Mai.* 4); and, as might be expected, in many cases, as he advanced in years, became a trainer of younger men: e. g. Iccus (Pausan. vi. 10, 5).

To be an Olympic victor, said Cicero, was esteemed by the Greeks a greater glory than a triumph at Rome. And indeed, the victorious Greek athlete used to have a kind of triumphal entry into the town his victory had ennobled. Surrounded by a large crowd, sometimes with a grand procession of chariots, clad in a purple mantle like a king, he drove into the city through a breach made in the wall for his chariot to pass through—a symbol that cities which possessed such citizens had no need of walls (Plut. *Symp.* ii. 5). Then followed the banquet, during which the victor heard his praises sung by a lyrical chorus and in the verse of the greatest poets of the day. Contests which involved the honour of such a triumphal entry were technically called ἀγῶνες εἰσελαστικοί, which in early times were the four great festivals only; but in Imperial Rome this privilege was extended to other games (Plin. *Epist.* x. 119, 120). Solid material rewards, too, were given. Even as reduced by Solon, the money reward which the Athenians gave the victor in the Olympic games was 500 drachmae, and 100 to the victor in any of the other games; sometimes he received maintenance in the Prytaneum and the honour of the first seat in the assemblies and theatre (προεδρία, Xenophan. *Frag.* 2, 7, ed. Bergk). Statues were often erected to him in his native city and at Olympia. In fact, Plato goes so far as to say (*Rep.* v. 465 D) that the victor at the Olympic games enjoyed a blessed life (βίος μακαριστός).

Yet among the many judgments passed by the ancients on the athletes we can find scarcely any that are favourable. Allusion has been made to the strictures of Xenophanes and Euripides, who attack them for their uselessness to the state and for their want of cultivation. Even from the physical point of view their training appeared to thoughtful men of science utterly bad. Plato sees in the athletes a habit of body which is sleepy and very subject to disease, which is too highly and extravagantly trained, and which unfits them for social or political duties. They are without information, cultivation, or grace of manner; hard and brutal, all violence and fierceness (ib. 410, 411). Aristotle declares that the habit of body of athletes is not suitable for that vigorous physical condition which a citizen should have, nor for health and the procreation of children. It is too one-sided, and the discipline which developes it is too severe. Plutarch disapproves of the ἰσχὺς παλαιστική and of athletic training generally.

We must now hastily review the rise of athletic games at Rome. Exhibitions of gladiators, not of athletes, were the national sport. Cicero says to M. Marius of the athletic contests exhibited by Pompeius in B.C. 55, "Why should I think you regretted not having seen the athletes, when you have despised the gladiators?" A certain kind of athletics had indeed been indigenous in Italy from the earliest times (Liv. i. 35), and we hear of contests in wrestling and boxing at the Roman games; but the whole practice was utterly unsystematic (cf. Suet. *Aug.* 45), and so quite unlike the elaborate manner in which it was cultivated in Greece. It was from Greece that the scientific practice of athletics came. In B.C. 186 M. Fulvius Nobilior gave the first exhibition of professional Greek athletes at Rome (Liv. xxxix. 22). We do not, however, hear of a similar exhibition again till Sulla's time, but there were a few others during the last century of the Republic. Varro com-

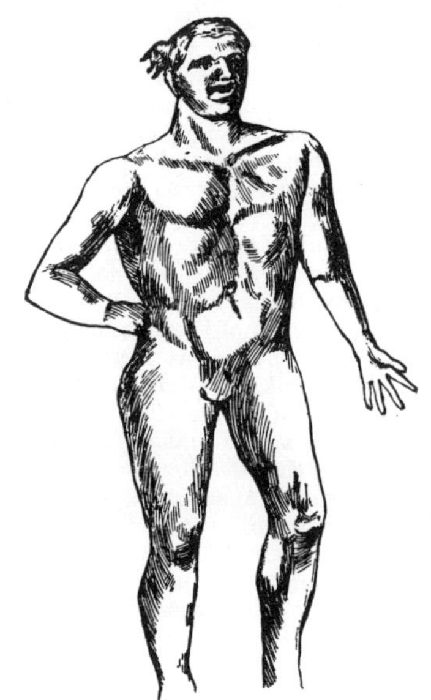

Roman Athlete. (Baumeister.)

plains, indeed, of there being a gymnasium at every villa (*R. R.* ii. 1, 1); but this was probably for medicinally prescribed exercises (*iatraliptice*), not regular athletics. But it was not till the Actian games were established by Augustus, and other periodic games (Dio Cass. li. 1) which comprised gymnastic contests in their programme, that athletics got a steady footing among the Romans. From that time these *certamina Graeca*, as they were called (Tac. *Ann.* xiv. 21), became more and more popular. Nero in A.D. 60 built a gymnasium and instituted a new set of games called Neronia, of which athletics formed a part, as they did also of the important Agon Capitolinus established by Domitian in A.D. 86, who further built a magnificent stadium for athletics in the Campus Martius, large enough to hold 30,000 spectators (Suet. *Dom.* 4, 5; Friedländer, p. 466). After this, athletics gradually attained increased prominence in the Roman games, till finally, in the fifth century, they supplanted the gladiatorial shows.

It is highly noticeable, however, that the names of the athletes which are preserved in inscriptions are almost all Greek; not more than four or five being Roman (Friedländer, p. 472). Everything connected with athletics, technical terms and all, are Greek (cf. Juv. iii. 68). The reason is that for a long time it was considered quite unbecoming the Roman dignity to be an athlete. The nakedness of the Greeks offended the Roman sense of propriety (Cic. *Tusc.* iv. 33, 70). The Romans saw the uselessness for war of the athletic training, for they themselves had been, as Polybius says (i. 6, 6), "the true athletes in the feats of war, trained in contests with the Samnites and Gauls."

Like all other classes in the community under the Roman Empire, the athletes crystallized into societies or guilds (σύνοδοι). They were well organized, had presidents called Xystarchi, and used to make provincial tours and give exhibitions (Friedländer, p. 475). The chief of these societies in the second century was that of the Herculanei (cf. *C. I. G.* 5906 foll.), who had their own special gymnasium, with its council-chamber (*curia*, Orelli, 2588), its records, its temple, and its president, who bore the title of ἀρχιερεύς, and who was also overseer of the imperial baths.

On athletics generally, the chief ancient work is Philostratus's Γυμναστικός (see Kayser's Teubner text, ii. 261–293). Modern writers are Krause, *Gymnastik und Agonistik der Hellenen*, passim; Hermann-Blümner, *Privataltertḥümer der Griechen*, §§ 36, 50; Becker-Göll, *Charikles*, ii. 213 foll.; Grasberger, *Erziehung und Unterricht im klassischen Alterthum*, vols. i., iii., passim; Guhl and Koner, *Das Leben der Griechen und Römer*, 52; and especially Friedländer, *Darstellungen aus der Sittengeschichte Roms*, ii. 459–491; M. Planck, in Pauly's *Real-Encyclopädie*; Bussemaker and Saglio, in *Dict. des Antiquités*; and Blümner, in Baumeister's *Denkmäler des klassischen Alterthums*, s. v. *Athletae*. See also the article GYMNASIUM.

Athlothĕtae (ἀθλοθέται). See AGONOTHETAE.

Athos (Ἄθως). The mountainous peninsula also called ACTÉ, which projects from Chalcidicé in Macedonia. At its extremity it rises to the height of 6349 feet; the voyage round it was so dreaded by mariners that Xerxes had a canal cut through the isthmus which connects the peninsula with the mainland to afford a passage to his fleet. The isthmus is about 1½ mile across, and there are distinct traces of the canal to be seen at the present day. The peninsula contained several flourishing cities in antiquity, and is now studded with numerous monasteries, cloisters, and chapels. In these monasteries some valuable MSS. of ancient authors have been discovered. See Riley, *Athos, or the Mountain of the Monks* (London, 1887).

Atia. The mother of Augustus Caesar. See AUGUSTUS.

Atia Lex. See LEX.

Atilia Lex. See LEX; TUTOR.

Atilius Fortunatiānus. A Latin grammarian of the fourth century A.D., who wrote a manual of prosody for schools (*Omnis Summa Metrorum*). See H. Keil, *Grammatici Latini*, vi. pp. 245–250.

Atilius Regŭlus. See REGULUS.

Atilla. The mother of the poet Lucan. See LUCANUS.

Atimia (ἀτιμία). The forfeiture, in Greece, of a man's civil rights. It was either total or partial. A man was totally deprived of his rights—both for himself and for his descendants—when he was convicted of murder, theft, false witness, partiality as arbiter, violence offered to a magistrate, and so forth. This highest degree of ἀτιμία excluded the person affected by it from the Agora, and from all public assemblies; from the public sacrifices, and from the law courts; or rendered him liable to immediate imprisonment if he was found in any of these places. It was either temporary or perpetual, and either accompanied or not with confiscation of property. Partial ἀτιμία involved only the forfeiture of some few rights, as, for instance, the right of pleading in court. Public debtors were suspended from their civic functions till they discharged their debt to the State. People who had once become altogether ἄτιμοι were very seldom restored to their lost privileges. The converse term to ἀτιμία was ἐπιτιμία. See Lelyveld, *De Infamia ex Iure Attico* (1835); Meier and Schömann, *Att. Process*, p. 563; Wachsmuth, *Hellen. Alterth.* (2d ed.), ii. 195 foll.; and the article INFAMIA.

Atinia Lex. See LEX.

Atlantes (Ἄτλαντες). An African people living near Mt. Atlas who daily cursed the sun at its rising and setting for its heat. (Herod. iv. 184).

Atlantes (ἄτλαντες) and **Telamōnes** (τελαμῶνες). Terms used in architecture, the former by the Greeks, the latter by the Romans, to designate those male figures which are sometimes fancifully used, like the female caryatides, in place of columns. Both words are derived from τλῆναι, and the former evidently refers to the fable of Atlas, who supported the vault of heaven; the latter perhaps to

Atlantes. (From Temple at **Agrigentum**: Prof. Cockerell.)

the strength of the Telamonian Aiax. A representation of such figures is given in the preceding illustration, from the temple of Zeus Olympius at Agrigentum. See CARYATIDES.

Atlantĭcum Mare. See OCEANUS.

Atlantĭdes (Ἀτλαντίδες). See HESPERIDES; PLEIADES.

Atlantis. See PLATO; TIMAEUS.

Atlas (Ἄτλας). "Bearer" or "Endurer." The son of the Titan Iapetus and Clymené (or, according to another account, Asia), brother of Menoetius, Prometheus, and Epimetheus. In Homer (*Od.* i. 52) he is called "the thinker of mischief," who knows the depths of the whole sea, and has under his care the pillars which hold heaven and earth asunder. In Hesiod he stands at the western end of the earth, near where the Hesperides dwell, holding the broad heaven on his head and unwearied hands. To this condition he is forced by Zeus, according to a later version, as a punishment for the part which he took in the battle with the Titans. By the ocean nymph Pleioné he is father of the Pleiades, and by Aethra of the Hyades. In Homer, the nymph Calypso is also his daughter, dwelling on the island Ogygia, the navel of the sea. Later authors make him the father of the Hesperides, by Hesperis. It is to him that Amphitrité flies when pursued by Poseidon. As their knowledge of the West extended, the Greeks transferred the abode of Atlas to the African mountain of the same name. Local stories of a mountain which supported the heaven would, no doubt, encourage the identification. In later times, Atlas was represented as a wealthy king, and owner of the garden of the Hesperides. Perseus, with the head of Medusa, turned him into a rocky mountain for his inhospitality. In works of art he is represented as carrying the heaven, or (after the earth was discovered to be spherical) the terrestrial globe.

Atlas. (From the Farnese collection now at Naples.)

Atlas Mons. The general name of the great mountain range which covers the surface of northern Africa between the Mediterranean and the Great Desert (Sahara) on the north and south, and the Atlantic and the Lesser Syrtis on the west and east.

Atossa (Ἄτοσσα). The daughter of Cyrus, and wife successively of her brother Cambyses, of Smerdis the Magian, and of Darius Hystaspes, by whom she became the mother of Xerxes.

Atramentum (μέλαν). A term applicable to any black liquid, but specifically used of three coloring substances. (1) *Atramentum sutorium*—blacking for leather. (2) *Atramentum tectorium* or *pictorium*—a black pigment used by painters. (3) *Atramentum librarium* (μέλαν γραφικόν)—ink, for which see WRITING AND WRITING MATERIALS.

Atrax (Ἄτραξ). (1) A town in Pelasgiotis in Thessaly, inhabited by the Perrhaebi, so called from the mythical Atrax, son of Peneus and Bura, and father of Caeneus and Hippodamia. Hence Caeneus is called Atracides, and Hippodamia, Atracis. (2) A river of Aetolia falling into the Ionian Sea.

Atrebătes. A people in Gallia Belgica, in the modern Artois, which is a corruption of their name. Their capital was Nemetocenna or Nemetacum, subsequently Atrebati, now Arras. Part of them crossed over to Britain, where they dwelt in the upper valley of the Thames, in what is now Oxfordshire and Berkshire.

Atreus (Ἀτρεύς). The son of Pelops and Hippodamia, grandson of Tantalus, and brother of Thyestes and Nicippé. He was first married to Cleola, by whom he became the father of Plisthenes; then to Aeropé, the widow of his son Plisthenes, who was the mother of Agamemnon, Menelaüs, and Anaxibia, either by Plisthenes or by Atreus; and lastly to Pelopia, the daughter of his brother Thyestes. The awful fate of the house of Pelops afforded materials to the tragic poets of Greece. In consequence of the murder of their half-brother Chrysippus, Atreus and Thyestes were obliged to take to flight. They were hospitably received at Mycenae; and, after the death of Eurystheus, Atreus became king of Mycenae. Thyestes seduced Aeropé, the wife of Atreus, and was in consequence banished by his brother. From his place of exile he sent Plisthenes, the son of Atreus, whom he had brought up as his own child, with orders to slay Atreus; but Plisthenes fell by the hands of Atreus, who did not know that he was his own son. In order to take revenge, Atreus, pretending to be reconciled to Thyestes, recalled him to Mycenae, killed his two sons, and placed their flesh before their father at a banquet, who unwittingly partook of the dreadful meal. Thyestes fled with horror, and the gods cursed Atreus and his house. The kingdom of Atreus was now visited by famine, and the oracle advised Atreus to call back Thyestes. Atreus, who went out in search of him, came to King Thesprotus, where he married his third wife, Pelopia, the daughter of Thyestes, whom Atreus believed to be a daughter of Thesprotus. Pelopia was at the time with child by her own father. This child, Aegisthus, afterwards slew Atreus, because the latter had commanded him to slay his own father, Thyestes. The oldest accounts of the Pelopidae do not mention the horrible stories that are generally connected with them. See AEGISTHUS; AGAMEMNON; PELOPIDAE.

Atrīdes (Ἀτρείδης). A son of Atreus. A name usually applied to Agamemnon and his brother Menelaüs.

Atriensis. A Roman house-slave belonging to the *familia urbana*, and having especial charge of the *atrium*. See Plaut. *Asin.* ii. 2 and 4.

Atrium. See DOMUS.

Atropatēné (Ἀτροπατηνή), or **Media Atropatia**, the northwestern part of Media, adjacent to Armenia, named after Atropates, a native of the country, who, having been made its governor by

Alexander, founded there a kingdom, which long remained independent.

Atrŏpos (Ἄτροπος, from ἀ priv. and τρέπω). "The Inflexible." The Fate who cuts the thread of life that is spun by Clotho, and measured off by Lachesis. See MOERAE; PARCAE.

Atta, T. QUINCTIUS or QUINTICIUS. A Roman dramatic poet, author of *togatae* (see COMOEDIA), who died B.C. 77, and was a contemporary of Afranius. He was celebrated for his power of drawing character, especially in conversational scenes in which women were introduced. Of his comedies only twelve titles remain, with a few insignificant fragments, which will be found in Ribbeck, *Scaenicae Romanorum Poesis Fragmenta*.

Attalīa (Ἀτταλεία). (1) A city of Lydia, formerly called Agroïra. (2) A city on the coast of Pamphylia, founded by Attalus II. Philadelphus, and subdued by the Romans under P. Servilius Isauricus.

Attălus. The name of several kings of Pergamus. (1) Son of Attalus, a brother of Philetaerus, succeeded his cousin Eumenes I., and reigned B.C. 241–197. He took part with the Romans in the struggle against Philip and the Achaeans. He was a wise and just prince, and was distinguished by his patronage of literature. (2) Surnamed PHILADELPHUS, second son of Attalus, succeeded his brother Eumenes II., and reigned B.C. 159–138. Like his father, he was an ally of the Romans, and also encouraged the arts and sciences. (3) Surnamed PHILOMĒTOR, son of Eumenes II. and Stratonicé, succeeded his uncle Attalus II., and reigned B.C. 138–133. In his will he made the Romans his heirs, but his kingdom was claimed by Aristonicus. See ARISTONICUS.

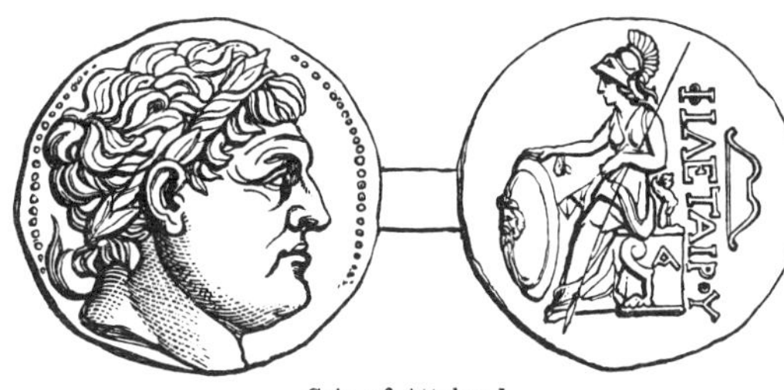

Coin of Attalus I.

Atthidogrăphi. See ATTHIS.

Atthis (Ἀτθίς). A chronicle of Attic history in which especial attention was paid to occurrences of political and religious significance. After the last half of the fourth century A.D., chronicles of this kind were composed by a number of writers (Atthidographi), among whom Androtion and Philochorus (q. v.) deserve special mention. These writings were much quoted by the grammarians.

Atthis or **Attis.** (Ἄτθις, Ἄττις). See ATTICA.

Attĭca (Ἀττική). A division of Greece, in the form of a triangle, two sides of which are washed by the Aegaean Sea, while the third is separated from Boeotia on the north by the mountains Cithaeron and Parnes. Megaris, which bounds it on the northwest, was formerly a part of Attica. In ancient times it was called Acté and Acticé, or the "coast-land" (ἀκτή), from which the later form, Attica, is said to have been derived. According to tradition, it derived its name from Atthis, the daughter of the mythical king Cranaüs; and old-fashioned etymologists found in it the root which appears in that of the goddess Athené. Attica is divided by many ancient writers into three districts. (1) The Highlands, the northeast of the country. (2) The Plain, the northwest of the country, including both the plain round Athens and the plain round Eleusis, and extending south to the promontory Zoster. (3) The Seacoast District, the south part of the country, terminating in the promontory Sunium. Besides these three divisions, we also read of (4) the Midland District, still called Mesogia, an undulating plain in the middle of the country. The soil of Attica is not very fertile. The greater part of it is not adapted for growing corn; but it produces olives, figs, and grapes, especially the two former, in great perfection. The country is dry; the chief river is the Cephissus, rising in Parnes and flowing through the Athenian plain. The abundance of wild flowers in the country made the honey of Mount Hymettus very celebrated in antiquity. Excellent marble was obtained from the quarries of Pentelicus, northeast of Athens, and a considerable supply of silver from the mines of Laurium near Sunium. The territory of Attica, including the island of Salamis, which belonged to it, contained between 700 and 800 square miles; and the population in its flourishing period was probably about 500,000, of which nearly four fifths were slaves.

Attica is said to have been originally inhabited by Pelasgians. Its most ancient political division was into twelve independent States, attributed to Cecrops, who, according to some legends, came from Egypt. Subsequently Ion, the grandson of Hellen, divided the people into four tribes, Geleontes, Hopletes, Argades, and Aegicores; and Theseus, who united the twelve independent States of Attica into one political body and made Athens the capital, again divided the nation into three classes, the Eupatridae, Geomori, and Demiurgi. Clisthenes (B.C. 510) abolished the old tribes and created ten new ones, according to a geographical division; these tribes were subdivided into demes or townships. See ATHENAE; CLISTHENES; DEMUS.

Attic Nights. See NOCTES ATTICAE; GELLIUS, AULUS.

Attic Style of Oratory. The name given to that style of ancient oratory that makes only a sparing use of verbal ornament, tropes, antitheses, and rhetorical devices, but is restrained, dignified, and severe. It is thus opposed to the so-called ASIATIC STYLE (q. v.). The best example of the severely Attic style is to be found in the orations of Demosthenes. See Cicero, *Brutus*, 95.

Attĭcus Herōdes, TIBERIUS CLAUDIUS. A Greek rhetorician, born about A.D. 104 at Marathon in Attica, who taught both at Athens and at Rome. Among his pupils were the future emperors, M. Aurelius and L. Verus. He was made consul by Antoninus Pius in A.D. 143, and died in 180, after having accumulated a large fortune, much of which he spent in embellishing Athens.

Attĭcus, T. POMPONIUS. A Roman of an old and wealthy equestrian family, born B.C. 109. He received a good education in boyhood and youth, and went in the year B.C. 88 to Athens, where he lived until 65, devoting himself entirely to study, and much respected by the citizens for his generosity and cultivated refinement. In 65, he returned to Rome, to take possession of the inheritance left him by his uncle and adoptive father, Q. Caecilius. He now became Q. Caecilius Pomponianus. From this time onward he lived on terms of intimacy with men like Cicero, Hortensius, and Cornelius Nepos (who wrote a life of him which we still possess). He avoided public life and the strife of parties. This fact, in addition to his general amiability and good nature, enabled him during the Civil Wars to keep on the best of terms with the leaders of the conflicting parties—Cicero, Brutus, and Antonius. He died after a painful illness, of voluntary starvation, in the year B.C. 32.

Atticus was the author of several works, the most considerable of which was a history (*Liber Annalis*) dedicated to Cicero. This gave a short epitome of the bare events of Roman history down to B.C. 54, arranged according to the series of consuls and other magistrates, with contemporaneous notices. But his most important contribution to Latin literature was his edition of the letters which he had received from Cicero. He also did great service by setting his numerous slaves to work copying the writings of his contemporaries. In philosophy, he was an Epicurean. The fragments of the *Liber Annalis* will be found in Peter, *Hist. Frag.* 214.

Attĭla (in German, Etzel). The son of Mundzuck, or, as he is less correctly called, Mandras, a Hun of royal descent, who succeeded his uncle Rugilas in A.D. 433, and shared the supreme authority with his brother Bleda. These two leaders of the barbarians who had settled in Scythia and Hungary threatened the Eastern Empire, and twice compelled Theodosius II. (q. v.) to purchase peace. Their power was feared by all the nations of Europe and Asia. The Huns themselves esteemed Attila their bravest warrior and most skilful general; while he gave out that he had found the sword of their tutelar god, the Scythian Mars, the possession of which was supposed to convey a title to the whole earth. He caused his brother Bleda to be murdered (A.D. 444); and when he announced that it had been done by the command of God, the murder was celebrated as a victory. Being now sole master of a warlike people, his unbounded ambition made him the terror of all nations; and he became, as he called himself, "the Scourge of God" for the chastisement of the human race. In a short time he extended his dominion over all the people of Germany and Scythia, and the Eastern and Western emperors paid him tribute. The Vandals, the Ostrogoths, the Gepidae, and a part of the Franks united under his banners, so that some historians assure us that his army amounted to 700,000 men. His portrait, as given by Jornandes, was that of a modern Calmuc, with a large head, swarthy complexion, flat nose, small sunken eyes, and a short square body. His looks were fierce, his gait proud, and his deportment stern and haughty; yet he was merciful to a suppliant foe, and ruled his own people with justice and lenity.

Having heard a rumour of the riches and power of Persia, he directed his march thither, but was defeated on the plains of Armenia, and fell back to satisfy his desire for plunder in the dominions of the Emperor of the East. He found a pretext for war, went over to Illyricum, and laid waste all the countries from the Euxine to the Adriatic. The emperor Theodosius collected an army to oppose his progress; but in three bloody battles Fortune declared herself for the barbarians, and Constantinople was indebted to the strength of its walls and to the ignorance of the enemy in the art of besieging, for its preservation. Theodosius was at the mercy of the victor, and was compelled to purchase peace. A scheme was laid in the court of Theodosius to assassinate Attila under the cover of a solemn embassy, which intention he discovered; and, without violating the laws of hospitality in the persons of the ambassadors, wisely preferred a heavy ransom for the principal agent in the plot, and a new treaty at the expense of fresh payments. On the accession of Marcian, Attila demanded tribute, which was refused; and, although much exasperated, he resolved first to turn his arms against the Western emperor Valentinian, whose licentious sister Honoria, in revenge for being banished for an intrigue with her chamberlain, sent an offer of herself to Attila. The Hun, perceiving the pretence this proposal supplied, preceded his irruptions into Gaul by demanding Honoria in marriage, with a share of the imperial patrimony. Being refused, he affected to be satisfied, and pretended he was only about to enter Gaul to make war upon Theodoric, king of the Ostrogoths. He accordingly crossed the Rhine, A.D. 450, with a prodigious host, and marked his way with pillage and desolation, until completely defeated by Theodoric and the famous Aëtius in the bloody battle of Châlons (451). He, however, recruited his forces, and passed the Alps the next year, invading Italy and spreading his ravages over all Lombardy. This visitation was the origin of the famous republic of Venice, which was founded by the fugitives who fled at the terror of his name. Valentinian, unable to avert the storm, repaired from Ravenna to Rome, whence he sent the prelate Leo with a solemn deputation to avert the wrath of Attila, who consented to leave Italy on receiving a vast sum as the dowry of Honoria and an annual tribute. He did not much longer survive these transactions; and his death was singular, he being found dead, in consequence of suffocation from a broken blood-vessel, on the night of his marriage with a beautiful young virgin named Hilda (453). His body was enclosed in three coffins—the first of gold, the second of silver, and the third of iron. The captives who had made the grave were strangled, in order that the place of interment might be kept concealed from his foes. See Thierry, *Histoire d'Attila* (4th ed. 1874); and HUNNI.

Attis (Ἄττις) or **Atys** (Ἄτυς). A mythological personage in the worship of the Phrygian goddess Cybelé-Agdistis. The son of this goddess, so ran the story, had been mutilated by the gods in terror at his gigantic strength, and from his blood sprang the almond-tree. After eating its fruit, Nana, daughter of the river Sangarius, brought forth a boy, whom she exposed. He was brought up first among the wild goats of the forests, and afterwards by some shepherds, and grew up so beautiful that Agdistis fell in love with him. Wishing to wed the daughter of the king of Pessinus in Phrygia, he was driven to madness by the goddess. He then fled to the mountains, and destroyed his manhood at the foot of a pine-tree, which received his spirit, while from his blood sprang violets to garland the tree. Agdistis besought Zeus that the body of her beloved one might know no corruption. Her prayer was heard; a tomb to Attis was raised on Mount Dindymus in the sanctuary of Cybelé, the priests of which had to undergo emasculation for Attis's sake. A festival of several days was held in honour of Attis and Cybelé in the beginning of spring. A pine-tree, felled in the forest, was covered with violets, and carried to the shrine of Cybelé as a symbol of the departed Attis. Then, amid tumultuous music and rites of wildest sorrow, they sought and mourned for Attis on the mountains. On the third day he was found again, the image of the goddess was purified from the contagion of death, and a feast of joy was celebrated, as wild as had been the days of sorrow. The poem of Catullus (q. v.) which deals with the story of Attis, in galliambic metre, is one of the weirdest and most powerful productions in all literature. With regard to it, see Ellis's Catullus (2d ed. 1889), and Grant Allen's *Attis* (1893).

Attius, Lucius. An early Roman poet of distinction, who forms a link between the ante-classical and classical periods of Latin literature; for Cicero, when a boy, had met him, and in after-life admired his verse. Attius was, like Horace, the son of a freedman, settled at Pisaurum. He began his career with a tragedy, the *Atreus*, and was the author of thirty-six more, besides *Annales* in hexameter verse, a history of Greek and Roman poetry (*Didascalia*), and two *praetextae*. His literary characteristics are dignity, vigour, and much rhetorical skill in the choice of words. Considerable fragments of his works remain to us, and can be found in Ribbeck's *Tragicorum Romanorum Fragmenta* (Leipzig, 1874); and L. Müller's *Lucilius* (1872). He is the author of the famous maxim of the tyrant, *Oderint dum metuant*, quoted by Cicero. He is said to have introduced some changes into the received forms of spelling, such as doubling the vowels when long, as in modern Dutch—thus *aara, vootum*. He died B.C. 94. See Boissier, *Le Poète Attius* (Paris, 1857).

Attius or **Attus Navius**. See Navius.

Atŭrus. The modern Adour; a river in Aquitania.

Auceps. A bird-catcher or fowler, whose occupation was called *aucupium* (*avis* + *capio*). The fowlers used for catching birds gins and snares (*laquei, pedicae*), rods tipped with bird-lime (*arundines, calami*), nets held by two parallel rods (*amites*), and traps (*transennae*).

Auctio signifies generally "an increasing, an enhancement," and hence the name is applied to a public sale of goods, at which persons bid against one another. As a species, *auctio* signifies a public sale of goods by the owner or his agent, or a sale of goods of a deceased person for the purpose of dividing the money among those entitled to it, which was called *auctio hereditaria*. The sale was sometimes conducted by an *argentarius*, or by a *magister auctionis*; and the time, place, and conditions of sale were announced either by a public notice (*tabula, album*), or by a crier (*praeco*).

The usual phrases to express the notification of a sale are *auctionem proscribere, praedicare*; and to determine on a sale, *auctionem constituere*. The purchasers (*emptores*), when assembled, were sometimes said *ad tabulam adesse*. The phrases signifying to bid are *liceri, licitari*, which was done either by word of mouth or by such significant hints as are known to all people who have attended an auction. The property was said to be knocked down (*addici*) to the purchaser. An entry was made in the books of the *argentarius* of the sale and the money due, and credit was given in the same books to the purchaser when he paid the money (*expensa pecunia lata, accepta relata*). Thus the book of the *argentarius* might be used as evidence for the purchaser, both of his having made a purchase and having paid for the thing purchased. If the money was not paid according to the conditions of sale, the *argentarius* could sue for it.

The *praeco* or crier seems to have acted the part of the modern auctioneer, so far as calling out the biddings and amusing the company. Slaves, when sold by auction, were placed on a stone or other elevated thing, and hence the phrase *homo de lapide emptus*. It was usual to put up a spear (*hasta*) in auctions—a symbol derived, it is said, from the ancient practice of selling under a spear the booty acquired in war. The term *asta publica* is used in Italy at the present time to signify an auction. By the auctio, the Quiritary ownership in the thing sold was transferred to the purchaser. See Bonorum Emptio; Sectio.

Auctor. (1) One who originates and proposes a *lex* or *senatus consultum*—in imperial times often used of the emperor. (2) In law, the owner and sometimes the vendor (*venditor*) of goods; also the maker of a will. (3) A person whose concurrence is necessary to give effect to a legal transaction. (4) A person under whose authority any legal act is done. See Tutor. (5) In criminal law, the instigator of a crime. (6) In jurisprudence, a jurist to whom the *ius respondendi* had been given by the emperor. See Iurisconsulti.

Auctorĭtas. The meanings of this word correlate with those of *auctor* (q. v.).

Auditorium. (1) A place where poets, orators, and critics were heard. (See Athenaeum.) (2) Under the Roman Empire, the enclosed courts about the Forum where magistrates heard civil causes. See Basilica.

Aufidia Lex. See Lex.

Aufĭdus. The principal river of Apulia, flowing with a rapid current into the Adriatic. Venusia, the birthplace of Horace, was on the Aufidus, now the Ofanto.

Augé (Αὐγή). Daughter of Aleus of Tegea, and mother of Telephus by Heracles (q. v.). See Telephus; Teuthras.

Augēas (Αὐγείας) or **Augĕas** (Αὐγέας). Son of Helios, or, according to another account, of Phorbas, and Hermioné. He was king of the Epeians in Elis, and one of the Argonauts. Besides his other possessions, for which Agamemnon and Trophonius built him a treasure-house, he was owner of an enormous flock of sheep and oxen, among which were twelve white bulls consecrated to the Sun. When Heracles, at the command of Eurystheus, came to cleanse his farm-yard, Augeas promised him the tenth part of his flock. But, the task completed, he refused the reward, on the ground that the work had been done in the service of Eurystheus. Heracles replied by sending an army against him, which was defeated in the passes of Elis by Eurytus and Cteatus, sons of Molioné; but Heracles appeared on the scene, and slew the Molionidae, and with them their uncle Augeas and his sons. See HERACLES; MOLIONIDAE.

Augītes (αὐγίτης). Probably the turquoise.

Augur. A diviner by means of birds. The derivation of the word is uncertain. Some ancient grammarians derived it from *avis* and *gero* (Festus, s. v. *augur;* Serv. *ad Verg. Aen.* v. 523), in support of which we may mention the analogy of *au-spex* and *au-ceps*, and the ancient forms *auger* and *augeratus* quoted by Priscian, i. 6, § 36; and this derivation is now accepted by Mommsen, Marquardt, Bouché-Leclercq, and others. Of modern suggestions may be mentioned that of Aufrecht and Kirchhoff, connecting the word with the Umbrian *uhtur* = *auctor* (cf. *ius est augurum cum auctoritate conjunctum*, Cic. *De Leg.* ii. 12, 31; and Nissen, *Das Templum*, p. 5); and that of Vaniček, from *avis* and the root *gar* (found in Sanskrit and in γηρύειν, *garrire*). Fick, and apparently Kuntze, connect it with *augeo, augustus* (cf. *augustum augurium* in Ennius), and take it to mean "assistant"; while Lange and Bréal see in the word the root *gush* (as in γεύω), and understand by it "an appreciator." By Greek writers on Roman affairs, the augurs are called αὔγουρες, οἰωνοπόλοι, οἰωνοσκόποι, οἰωνισταί, οἰωνομάντεις, οἱ ἐπ' οἰωνοῖς ἱερεῖς.

The augurs at Rome formed a priestly *collegium*, traditionally said to have been founded by Romulus, and in the most ancient times no transaction took place, either of a private or a public nature, without consulting the auspices, and hence we find the question asked in a well-known passage of Livy (vi. 41, 4), "Auspiciis hanc urbem conditam esse, auspiciis bello ac pace, domi militiaeque omnia geri, quis est, qui ignoret?" But the private augur seems to have fallen into contempt. Thus Cicero, while arguing in favour of divination in general, follows Ennius in classing the *Marsus augur* with other impostors (*de Div.* i. 58, 132).

The public augurs, on the other hand, are of great importance in Roman history. The collegium originally consisted of three patricians, of whom the king was one. During the regal period the number was doubled; in B.C. 300 it was raised to nine (four patricians and five plebeians); and in the last century of the Republic, under Sulla, to fifteen, and finally by Iulius Caesar to sixteen, a number which continued unaltered under the Empire. It can be shown that the college of augurs continued to exist until the end of the fourth century A.D. The office was, on account of its political importance, much sought after, and only filled by persons of high birth and distinguished merit. It was held for life, an augur not being precluded from holding other temporal or spiritual dignities. Vacancies in the collegium were originally filled up by co-optation; but after B.C. 104 the office was elective, the tribes choosing one of the candidates previously nominated. An *augurium* had to be taken before the augur entered upon his duties. In all probability the augurs ranked according to seniority, and the senior augur presided over the business of the collegium.

Augur with Lituus. (Bas-relief in Museum, Florence.)

The *insignia* of the office were the *trabea*, a state dress with a purple border, and the *lituus* (q. v.), a staff without knots and curved at the top.

The science of Roman augury was based chiefly on written tradition. This was contained partly in the *Libri Augurales*, the oldest manual of technical practice, and partly in the *Commentarii Augurales*, a collection of answers given in certain cases to the inquiries of the Senate. In ancient times the chief duty of the augurs was to observe, when commissioned by a magistrate to do so, the omens given by birds, and to mark out the *templum* or consecrated space within which the observation took place. The proceeding was as follows: immediately after midnight, or at the dawn of the day on which the official act was to take place, the augur, in the presence of the magistrate, selected an elevated spot with as wide a view as was obtainable. Taking his station here, he drew with his staff two straight lines cutting one another, the one from north to south, the other from east to west. Then to each of these straight lines he drew two parallel lines, thus forming a rectangular figure, which he consecrated according to a prescribed form of words. This space, as well as the space corresponding to it in the sky, was called a *templum*. (See TEMPLUM.) At the point of intersection in the centre of the rectangle was erected the *tabernaculum*. This was a square tent, with its entrance looking south. Here the augur sat down, asked the gods for a sign according to a prescribed formula, and waited for the answer. Complete quiet, a clear sky, and an absence of wind were necessary conditions of the observation. The least noise was sufficient to disturb it, unless indeed the noise was occasioned by omens of terror (*dirae*), supposing the augur to have observed them, or to intend doing so. As he looked south the augur had the east on his left, the west on his right. Accordingly, the Romans regarded signs on the left side as of prosperous omen, signs on the right side as unlucky—the east being deemed the region of light, the west that of darkness. The reverse was the case in ancient Greece, where the observer looked northwards. In his observation of birds the augur did not confine himself to noticing their flight. The birds were distinguished as *alites* and *oscines*. The *alites* included birds like eagles and vultures, which gave signs by their manner of flying. The *oscines* were birds which gave signs by their cry as well as their flight, such as ravens, owls, and crows. There were also birds which were held sacred to particular gods, and the mere appearance of which was an omen of good or evil. The augur's report was expressed in the words *aves admittunt*, "the birds allow it"; or *alio die*, "on another day," i. e. "the augury is postponed." The magistrate was bound by this report. The science of augury included other kinds of auspices besides the observation of birds, a cumbrous process which had dropped out of use in the Ciceronian age. These were: (1) Signs in the sky (*ex caelo*). The most important and decisive were thunder and lightning. Lightning was a favourable omen if it appeared to the left of the augur, and flashed to the right; unfavourable, if it flashed from right to left. In certain cases, as, for example, that of the assembling of the Comitia, a storm was taken as an absolute prohibition of the meeting. (2) Signs from the behaviour of chickens while eating. It was a good omen if the chicken rushed eagerly out of its cage at its food, and dropped a bit out of its beak; an unfavourable

Auspicia Pullaria. (Bas-relief, Rome.) (From Goega's *Bassi-rilievi*, I. tav. xvi.)

omen if it was unwilling, or refused altogether, to leave its cage, or flew away, or declined its food. This clear and simple method of getting omens was generally adopted by armies in the field, the chickens being taken about in charge of a special functionary (*pullarius*). (3) Signs given by the cries or motion of animals, as reptiles and quadrupeds, in their course over a given piece of ground (*signa pedestria* or *ex quadrupedibus*). (4) Signs given by phenomena of terror (*signa ex diris*). These might consist in disturbances of the act of *auspicatio*, such as the falling of an object, a noise, a stumble, a slip in the recitation of the formula; or a disturbance occurring in the course of public business, such as, for instance, an epileptic seizure taking place in the public assembly—an event which broke up the meeting.

The two last-mentioned classes of signs were generally not asked for, because the former were usually, the latter always, unlucky. If they made their appearance unasked, they could not be passed over, if the observer saw them or wished to see them. Every official was expected to take auspices on entering upon his office, and on every occasion of performing an official act. Thus the words *imperium* and *auspicium* were often virtually synonymous. The *auspicia* were further divided, according to the dignity of the magistrate, into *maxima* and *minora*. The greatest *auspicia* were those which were taken by the king, dictator, consuls, praetors, and censors; the lesser were taken by aediles and quaestors. If two magistrates, though *collegae* (colleagues), were of unequal dignity—assuming, for instance, that a consul and a praetor were in the same camp—the higher officer alone had the right of taking the auspices. If the *collegae* were equal, the auspices passed from one to the other at stated times. No public act, whether of peace or war (crossing a river, for instance, or fighting a battle), could be undertaken without auspices. They were especially necessary at the election of all officials, the entry upon all offices, at all Comitia, and at the departure of a general for war. They had, further, to be taken on the actual day and at the actual place of the given undertaking.

The augurs always continued in possession of important functions. In certain places in the city, for instance on the Arx, and at the meeting-place of the Comitia, there were permanent posts of observation for taking the regular auspices. These places were put under the care of the augurs. Their boundaries might not be altered, nor the view which they commanded interfered with. The augurs had authority to prevent the erection of buildings which would do this. They had also the power of consecrating priests, as well as of inaugurating a part of the localities intended for religious purposes, and the places where public business was carried on. They were always present at the Comitia, and were authorized, if the signs which they saw or which were reported to them justified the proceeding, to announce the fact and postpone the business. If the constitutional character of a public act was called in question, the college of augurs had the exclusive power of deciding whether there was a flaw (*vitium*), in it, or not. If there were, the act was necessarily annulled. The dress of the augur was usually the *praetexta* (q. v.), but sometimes (possibly on military expeditions) the *trabea*, as in the accompanying illustration.

Augur wearing the Trabea. (British Museum.)

By the end of the republican period the augurs, and the whole business of the auspices, had ceased to be regarded as deserving serious attention.

On the whole subject of augury among the Romans, see Mascov, *De Jure Auspicii apud Romanos* (Lips. 1721); Werther, *De Auguriis Romanis* (Lemgo, 1835); Creuzer, *Symbolik*, ii. p. 935, etc.; Müller, *Etrusker*, ii. p. 110, etc.; Hartung, *Die Religion der Römer*, i. p. 98, etc.; Göttling, *Geschichte der Röm. Staatsverf.* p. 198, etc.; Rubino, *Röm. Verfassung*, p. 34, etc.; Rein, art. *Augures* in Pauly's *Realencyclopädie*; Preller, *Römische Mythologie*, 109–111 (ed. 1858); Nissen, *Das Templum*, chap. i.; Mommsen, *Römisches Staatsrecht*, i. 73–114; Marquardt, *Römische Staatsverwaltung*, vi. 381-393; Lange, *Römische Alterthümer*, i. 286–298 (=i. 330–345); Walter, *Geschichte des römischen Rechts*, §§ 151, 152; Madvig, *Die Verfassung und Verwaltung des römischen Staates*, ii. 633–643; Mispoulet, *Les Institutions Politiques des Romains*, i. 73, ii. 416-423; Willems, *Le Droit Public Romain*, 239-242, 324-326; Kuntze, *Prolegomena zur Geschichte Roms*, 61–102; Bouché-Leclercq, art. *Augur* and *Auspicia* in Daremberg and Saglio's *Dict. des Antiquités*, and *Histoire de la Divination dans l'Antiquité* (1879–82).

Auguracŭlum. A place on the Arx, on the summit of the Capitoline Hill, consecrated for purposes of augury. See ARX; AUGUR; TEMPLUM.

Augusta. The name of several towns founded or colonized by Augustus. Of these, one of the most important was Augusta Praetoria (Aosta), a town of the Salassi in Upper Italy, at the foot of the Graian and Pennine Alps. The modern town still contains many Roman remains, the most important of which are the town gates and a triumphal arch. In all, seventy cities in different parts of the Roman Empire were named Augusta, among them London (Londinium), which was sometimes styled Augusta Trinobantia from the British tribe, the Trinobantes (Tac. *Ann.* xiv. 31). See LONDINIUM; SEBASTA; TREVIRI; VINDELICI.

Augustae Historiae Scriptōres. Six writers (Aelius Spartianus, Vulcatius Gallicanus, Trebellius Pollio, Flavius Vopiscus, Aelius Lampridius, and Iulius Capitolinus) who wrote the lives of the emperors from Hadrian to Numerianus (A.D. 117–284). These lives are all equally devoid of literary excellence, but appear to be written truthfully, and are valuable for the information which they give. The best text is that of H. Peter, 2 vols. (Leipzig, 1865). The only English translation is that of J. Bernard (London, 1740).

Augustāles, sc. *ludi;* or, **Augustalia**, sc. *certamina* (Σεβαστά, Αὐγουστάλια). Games celebrated in honour of Augustus Caesar at Rome and in other parts of the Empire. Two festivals were known under this name. (1) The 23d of September, the birthday of Augustus, celebrated after B.C. 13 by games held in the Circus (Dio Cass. liv. 26, 34). (2) The Augustalia proper held for ten days annually (Oct. 3–12), instituted in B.C. 19, when Augustus returned to Rome after settling the provinces (Dio Cass. liv. 34).

Augustāles, sc. *viri*. A religious association at Rome formed for the maintenance of the worship paid to the deified Caesars. See FLAMEN; MUNICIPIUM; SEVIRI; SODALITAS.

Augustīnus, AURELIUS. One of the most renowned Fathers of the Christian Church, was born at Tagasté, a city of Africa, November 13th, A.D. 354, during the reign of the emperor Constantius II. He has related his own life in the work to which he gave the title of *Confessiones*, and it is from this source, together with the *Retractationes*, some of his letters, and the *Vita Possidii* of the semi-Pelagian Gennadius, that we derive our principal information respecting him. His parents sent him to Carthage to complete his education, but he disappointed their expectations by his neglect of serious study and his devotion to pleasure, for in his sixteenth year he became very fond of women. For fifteen years he was connected with one, by whom he had a son. He left her only when he changed his whole course of life. A book of Cicero's, the *Hortensius*, which has not come down to our times, led him to the study of philosophy; and when he found that this did not satisfy his feelings, he went over to the sect of the Manichaeans. He was one of their disciples for nine years; but, after having obtained a correct knowledge of their doctrines, he left them, and departed from Africa to Rome, and thence to Milan, where he announced himself as a teacher of rhetoric. St. Ambrose was bishop of this city, and his discourses converted Augustine to the orthodox faith. The reading of St. Paul's epistles wrought an entire change in his life and character. The Catholic Church has a festival (May 3) in commemoration of this event. He retired into solitude, wrote there many books, and prepared himself for baptism, which he received in the thirty-third year of his age, together with his son Adeodatus, from the hands of Ambrose. He returned to Africa, sold his estate, and gave the proceeds to the poor, retaining only enough to support him in a moderate manner. As he was once present in the church at Hippo, the bishop, who was a very old man, signified a desire to consecrate a priest to assist and succeed him. At the desire of the people, Augustine entered upon the holy office, preached with extraordinary success, and, in the year 395, became bishop of Hippo. He entered into a warm controversy with Pelagius concerning the doctrines of free-will, of grace, and of predestination, and wrote a book concerning them. Augustine maintained that men were justified merely through grace, and not through good works. He died August 28th, A.D. 430, while Hippo was besieged by the Vandals.

There have been Fathers of the Church more learned—masters of a better language and a purer taste; but none have ever more powerfully touched the human heart and warmed it towards religion. Painters have therefore given him for a symbol a flaming heart. Augustine is one of the most voluminous of the Christian writers. His works, in Migne's *Patrologia Latina*, fill 16 volumes (xxxii.–xlvii.). The first of these contains the works which he wrote before he was a priest, and his *Retractationes* and *Confessiones;* the former a critical review of his own writings, and the latter a curious and interesting picture of his life. The remainder of these volumes consist of a treatise *On the City of God* (*De Civitate Dei*); commentaries on Scripture; epistles on a great variety of subjects, doctrinal, moral, and personal; sermons and homilies; treatises on various points of discipline; and elaborate arguments against heretics. With the exception of those of Aristotle, no writings contributed more than Augustine's to encourage the spirit of subtle disputation which distinguished the scholastic ages. They exhibit much facility of invention and strength of reasoning, with more argument than eloquence and more wit than learning. Erasmus calls Augustine a writer of obscure subtlety, who requires in the reader acute penetration, close attention, and quick recollection, and by no means repays him for the application of all these requisites. It was St. Augustine who finally established the vocabulary of ecclesiastical Latinity, setting the stamp of his authority upon the new coinages that fill the pages of Tertullian.

The best complete edition of his works is still that of the Benedictines, of which the last reprint was in 1836–40. There is an English translation of the whole in 15 vols. (Edinb. 1872–80). See Milman, *Latin Christianity*, 8 vols. (N. Y. and Lond. 1861–62); id. *Hist. of Christianity*, 3 vols., new ed. (N. Y. 1871); Cloth, *Der heil. Kirchenlehrer Augustin* (Aachen, 1840); Bindemann, *Der heilige Augustin* (Berlin, 1844–69); Dorner, *Augustin, sein theologisches System und seine religionsphilos. Anschauung*

(Berlin, 1873); Poujoulat, *Histoire de Saint Augustin*, 6th ed. (Tours, 1875); Böhringer, *Augustin* (Stuttgart, 1877–78); and Reuter, *Augustinische Studien* (Gotha, 1887). See also Regnier, *La Latinité des Sermons de Saint Augustin* (Paris, 1887). There is a new critical edition of the works of St. Augustine in the Vienna collection of the Latin Fathers (Corp. Vindobon. vol. xii.), edited by F. Weihrich (Vienna, 1877).

Augustŭlus, Romŭlus Momyllus. The last Roman emperor of the West, the son of Orestes, who commanded the Roman army in Gaul. Orestes caused his son to be crowned in A.D. 475, and during his reign the son was but a puppet in the hands of the father. In the following year, however, the young emperor was dethroned by Odoacer, king of the Heruli, who put Orestes to death, but treated Augustulus with consideration, allowing him to retire to Campania with an income of 6000 gold pieces for his support. The name Augustulus was given to this emperor in derision, but is nevertheless the appellation under which he is best known in history. See Odoacer.

Augustus. A title given to the Roman emperors, and equivalent to *sacrosanctus.* It is rendered into Greek by the term Σεβαστός (Dio Cass. liii. 16). The feminine form, Augusta, was often given to the women of the imperial family, like the modern titles "Royal Highness" and "Imperial Highness." Under Diocletian, the appellation, Augustus, was definitely applied to the two joint emperors, and the title, Caesar, to each of the heirs-presumptive. See Dominus.

Augustus Caesar. The first Roman emperor, was born on the 23d of September, B.C. 63, and was the son of C. Octavius, by Atia, a daughter of Iulia, the sister of C. Iulius Caesar. His original name was Gaius Octavius, and after his adoption by his great-uncle, C. Iulius Caesar Octavianus, Augustus being only a title given him by the Senate and the people in B.C. 27 to express their veneration for him. He was pursuing his studies at Apollonia when the news reached him of his uncle's murder at Rome, in March, 44. He forthwith set out for Italy, and upon landing was received with enthusiasm by the troops. He first joined the republican party in order to crush Antony, against whom he fought at Mutina in conjunction with the two consuls, C. Vibius Pansa and A. Hirtius. Antony was defeated, and obliged to retreat across the Alps; and the death of the two consuls gave Augustus the command of all their troops. He now returned to Rome, and compelled the Senate to elect him consul, and shortly afterwards he became reconciled to Antony. It was agreed that the Roman world should be divided between Augustus, Antony, and Lepidus, under the title of *triumviri rei publicae constituendae*, and that this arrangement should last for the next five years. They published a *proscriptio*, or list of all their enemies whose lives were to be sacrificed and their property confiscated; upwards of 2000 equites and 300 senators were thus put to death, among them Cicero. Soon afterwards, Augustus and Antony crossed over to Greece, and defeated Brutus and Cassius at the decisive battle of Philippi, in B.C. 42, by which the hopes of the republican party were ruined.

Augustus returned to Italy, where a new war awaited him (B.C. 41), excited by Fulvia, the wife of Antony. She was supported by L. Antonius, the consul and brother of the triumvir, who threw himself into the fortified town of Perusia, which Augustus succeeded in taking in 40. Antony now made preparations for war, but the death of Fulvia led to a reconciliation between the triumvirs, who concluded a peace at Brundusium. A new division of the provinces was again made: Augustus obtained all the parts of the Empire west of the town of Scodra in Illyricum, Antony the east provinces, and Lepidus Africa. Antony married Octavia, the sister of Augustus, in order to cement their alliance. In B.C. 36, Augustus conquered Sex. Pompey, who had held possession of Sicily for many years with a powerful fleet. Lepidus, who had landed in Sicily to support Augustus, was degraded by him, stripped of his power, and sent to Rome, where he resided for the remainder of his life, being allowed to retain the dignity of Pontifex Maximus. Meantime, Antony had repudiated Octavia, on account of his love for Cleopatra, and had alienated the minds of the Roman people by his arbitrary conduct. The Senate declared war against Cleopatra; and in September, B.C. 31, the fleet of Augustus gained a brilliant victory over Antony's near Actium in Acarnania. In the following year (30), Augustus sailed to Egypt. Antony and Cleopatra, who had escaped in safety from Actium, put an end to their lives. Augustus now became the undisputed master of the Roman world, but he declined all honours and distinctions which were likely to remind the Romans of kingly power. On the death of Lepidus, in B.C. 12, he became pontifex maximus. On those state matters which he did not choose to be discussed in public he consulted his personal friends, Maecenas, M. Agrippa, M. Valerius Messalla Corvinus, and Asinius Pollio. The wars of Augustus were chiefly undertaken to protect the frontiers of the Roman dominions. Most of them were carried on by his relations and friends, but several he conducted in person, as when, in 27, he attacked the warlike Cantabri and Astures in Spain. In 20, he went to Syria, where he received from Phraates, the Parthian monarch, the standards and prisoners which had been taken from Crassus and Antony. He died at Nola, on the 19th of August, A.D. 14, at the age of seventy-six. His last wife was Livia, who had been previously the wife of Tiberius Nero. He had no children by Livia, and only a daughter, Iulia, by his former wife Scribonia. Iulia had married Agrippa, and her two sons, Gaius and Lucius Caesar, were destined by Augustus as his successors. On the death of these two youths, Augustus was persuaded to adopt Tiberius, the son of Livia by her former husband, and to make him his colleague and successor. See Tiberius.

Augustus Caesar.

Augustus is described as having been something below the middle size, but extremely well proportioned (Suet. *Aug.* 79). His hair was inclined to curl, and of a yellowish-brown; his eyes were bright and lively; but the general expression of his countenance was remarkably calm and mild. His health was throughout his life delicate, yet the constant attention which he paid to it, and his strict temperance in eating and drinking, enabled him to reach the full age of man. As a seducer, adulterer, and sensualist, his character was like that of his uncle (Suet. *Aug.* 69, 71). In his literary qualifications, without at all rivalling the attainments of Iulius Caesar, he was on a level with most Romans of distinction of his time; and it is said that both in speaking and writing his style was eminent for its perfect plainness and propriety (Suet. *Aug.* 68 foll.). His speeches on any public occasion were composed beforehand, and recited from memory; in fact, so careful was he not to commit himself by any inconsiderate expression, that even when discussing any important subject with his own wife, he wrote down what he had to say, and read it before her. Like his uncle, he was somewhat tinged with superstition. He was deficient in military talent; but in every species of artful policy, in clearly seeing, and steadily and dispassionately following his own interest, and in turning to advantage all the weaknesses of others, his ability has been rarely equalled. His deliberate cruelty, his repeated treachery, and his sacrifice of every duty and every feeling to the purposes of his ambition, speak for themselves; and yet it would be unjust to ascribe to a politic premeditation all the popular actions of his reign. Good is in itself so much more delightful than evil that he was doubtless not insensible to the pleasure of kind and beneficent actions, and perhaps sincerely rejoiced that they were no longer incompatible with his interests.

Statue of Augustus. (Vatican.)

Among the various arts to which Augustus resorted to gain the good-will of his people, and perhaps to render them forgetful of their former freedom, one of the most remarkable was the encouragement which he extended to learning, and the patronage which he so liberally bestowed on all by whom it was cultivated. To this noble protection of literature he was prompted not less by taste and inclination than by sound policy; and in his patronage of the learned, his usual artifice had probably a smaller share than in those other parts of his conduct by which he acquired the favourable opinion of the world. Augustus was, in fact, himself an excellent judge of composition, and a true critic in poetry; so that his patronage was never misplaced, or lavished on those whose writings might have tended to corrupt the taste and learning of the age. The court of Augustus thus became a school of culture, where men of genius acquired that delicacy of taste, elevation of sentiment, and purity of expression which characterize the writers of the age. To Maecenas, the favourite minister of the emperor, the honour is due of having most successfully followed out the views of Augustus for promoting the interests of literature; but it is wrong to give Maecenas the credit, as some have done, of first having turned the attention of Augustus to the patronage of literature. On the contrary, he appears largely to have acted from the orders, or to have followed the example, of his imperial master.

Augustus was buried in a mausoleum, whose remains are still to be seen at Rome on the Via de' Pontefici. It was a pyramidal tower, 328 feet in height, covered with white marble, surmounted by a statue of the emperor, and divided into three stories by receding steps, each story being planted with cypress-trees. Before this structure was set the tablet of bronze containing the *index rerum a se gestarum*, which he had had prepared (Suet. *Aug.* 101). A copy of this important inscription was found in modern times on the inside of the *antae* of a temple at Ancyra (now Angora), in Galatia, and has been published in fac-simile by Prof. Mommsen, with a commentary. It is reproduced in the illustration on page 171.

For many interesting details regarding the personality of Augustus, see the life by Suetonius (ed. with Engl. notes by H. T. Peck, N. Y. 1889), and the following works: Ampère, *L'Empire Romain à Rome*, 3d ed. (Paris, 1867); Dezobry, *Rom in Jahrhunderte des Augustus* (Leipzig, 1837); Beulé, *Auguste, sa Famille, et ses Amis*, 4th ed. (Paris, 1868); Schiller, *Geschichte der röm. Kaiserzeit* (1883); and Gardthausen, *Augustus* (pt. i. 1891).

Aula (αὐλή). An open yard, or court. In the Homeric house the αὐλή served the purpose of a farm-yard, and was surrounded with farm-buildings and rooms for the men-servants of the house.

In the later Greek house it was a kind of quadrangle surrounded with a colonnade, into which the rooms of the house opened, and was used as a place for exercise and recreation (A. Winckler, *Die Wohnhäuser der Hellenen*). For further particulars, see DOMUS.

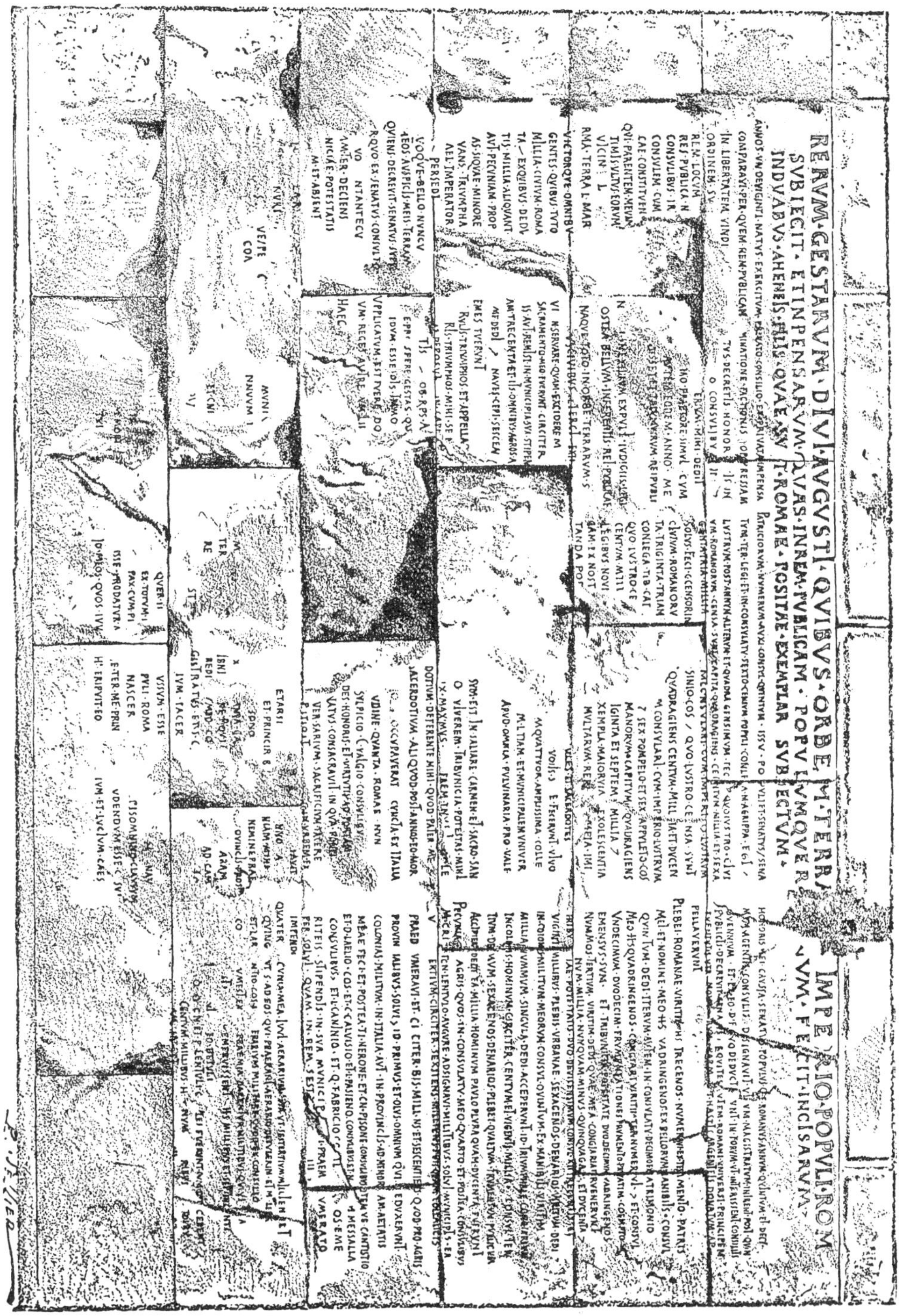

Aulaeum, usually in the plural, AULAEA (ἡ αὐλαία). A curtain, carpet, or hanging, mostly of the heavier and richer sort. Its uses were: (1) in temples to veil the statue of the god; (2) in houses, like the modern portière curtains; (3) to stretch over colonnades, and thus to form a tent; (4) as a

Wall of the Temple of Ancyra, bearing the Latin Text of the *Index Rerum Gestarum* of Augustus.

drop-curtain in the Roman theatres. This curtain disappeared under the stage instead of being rolled up. Hence *aulaea premuntur*, "the curtain is let down," when the play begins; and *aulaeum tollitur*, "the play is ended." See Wieseler, *Theatergebäude* (1851), and the articles SIPARIUM; TAPES; THEATRUM; VELUM.

Aulerci. A powerful Gallic race divided into three tribes: (1) AULERCI EBUROVĪCES, dwelling near the coast on the left bank of the Sequana (Seine) in what is now Normandy, and having as their chief town Mediolanum, afterwards Eburovices (Evreux). (2) AULERCI CENOMĀNI, dwelling southwest of the preceding tribe near the Liger (Loire), and having Subdinnum (Le Mans) as their capital. (3) AULERCI BRANNOVĪCES, dwelling east of the Cenomani near the Aedui (q. v.).

Aulis (Αὐλίς). A harbour in Boeotia on the Euripus, where the Greek forces assembled before sailing for Troy. See IPHIGENIA; TROJAN WAR.

Aulon (Αὐλών). (1) A district and town on the borders of Elis and Messenia with a temple of Asclepius. (2) A town in Chalcidicé in Macedonia. (3) A fertile, grape-producing valley in Italy near Tarentum.

Aulularia. One of the best of the comedies of Plautus (q. v.), but lacking the conclusion.

Aulus Gellius See GELLIUS, AULUS.

Aurea Domus. See DOMUS AUREA.

Aurelia Lex. See LEX.

Aureliāni. See GENABUM.

Aureliānus. (1) LUCIUS DOMITIUS. A Roman emperor (A.D. 270–275), distinguished for his military abilities and severity of character, was the son of a peasant, born about A.D. 212 in the territory of Sirmium in Illyria. His father occupied a small farm, the property of Aurelius, a rich senator. The son enlisted in the troops as a common soldier, successively rose to the rank of centurion, tribune, prefect of a legion, inspector of the camp, general, or, as it was then called, duke of a frontier; and at length, during the Gothic War, exercised the important office of commander-in-chief of the cavalry. In every station he distinguished himself by matchless valour, rigid discipline, and successful leadership. Theoclius affirms that in one day he killed forty-eight Sarmatians, and in several subsequent engagements nine hundred and fifty. This heroic valour was admired by the soldiers, and celebrated in their rude songs, the burden of which was "*Mille, mille, mille, mille, mille, mille, occidit.*" At length Valerian II. raised him to the consulship, and his good fortune was further favoured by a wealthy and noble marriage. His next elevation was to the throne, Claudius II., on his death-bed, having recommended Aurelian to the troops of Illyricum. The reign of this monarch lasted only four years and about nine months; but every instant of that short period was filled by some memorable achievement. He put an end to the Gothic War, chastised the Germans who invaded Italy, recovered Gaul, Spain, and Britain out of the hands of Tetricus, and destroyed the proud monarchy which Zenobia (q. v.) had erected in the East on the ruins of the afflicted Empire. Owing to the ungenerous excuse of the queen that she had waged war by the advice of her ministers, her secretary, the celebrated Longinus (q. v.), was put to death by the victor; but, after having graced his triumphal entry into Rome, Zenobia herself was presented with a villa near Tibur, and allowed to spend the remainder of her days as a Roman matron.

On his return to Rome, he surrounded the city with a new line of walls. He abandoned Dacia, which had been first conquered by Trajan, and made the southern bank of the Danube, as in the time of Augustus, the boundary of the Empire. He was killed by some of his officers while preparing to march against the Persians. (2) CAELIUS. A physician, a native of Numidia, who lived about the fourth or fifth century A.D. He left two books, one entitled, *Libri Quinque Tardarum sive Chronicarum Passionum*, and the other, *Libri Tres Celerum sive Acutarum Passionum*. Both are drawn from Greek authors,—from Themison, Thessalus, and, above all, Soranus. His work is particularly valuable, as preserving to us an account of many theories and views of practice which would otherwise have been lost; but even of itself it is deserving of much attention for the practical information which it contains. Caelius is remarkable for learning, understanding, and scrupulous accuracy; but his style is much loaded with technical terms, and by no means elegant. He has treated of the most important diseases which come under the care of a physician. He also wrote a compendium of the whole science of medicine in the form of a catechism (*Medicinales Responsiones*), of which considerable fragments remain. So far as known there are now no MSS. of Caelius Aurelianus in existence, the Lorsch codex used by Sichard in his *editio princeps* of the *Tardae Passiones* (Basle, 1529) having since that time been lost. The best edition of the two works together is that of Amman (Amsterdam, 1709), reprinted at Venice in 1757. See the treatise of Trilleri, *Notae in Cael. Aurel.* (Leipzig, 1817).

Aurelius, MARCUS. See ANTONINUS.

Aurelius Victor, SEXTUS. A Roman historian, born in Africa. He was probably governor of Pannonia under Julian in A.D. 361, and in 389 prefect of Rome. There is a history of the Caesars from Iulius to Constantius, written about A.D. 360, which bears his name. This appears, however, to be no more than a compilation from more comprehensive works, Suetonius being much employed. The same is the case with an *Epitome*, continued down to the death of Theodosius I. There is also a short but not altogether worthless book, entitled *De Viris Illustribus Urbis Romae*, which is attributed to Aurelius Victor. It begins with the Alban king Procas, and comes down to Cleopatra. It is not by Aurelius Victor, nor, again, is a little book which has been attributed to him, called *Origo Gentis Romanae*. This is full of forged quotations, and belongs to a much later period. Editions of all four of these works by Schröter (Leipzig, 1831), in 2 vols. There is also a good separate edition of the *De Viris Illustribus*, by Keil (Breslau, 1872), and of the *Origo*, by Sepp, new ed. (Eichstädt, 1885).

Aures. The earth-boards or mould-boards of the Roman plough. See ARATRUM.

Aureus of Augustus. (British Museum.)

Aureus. (1) The generic name for a Roman gold coin

(*aureus nummus*). (2) A gold coin which under the emperors was equal to about $5.10. It was first struck in the Second Punic War. See NUMISMATICS (Roman); NUMMUS; SOLIDUS.

Aurīga (ἡνίοχος). The driver of a chariot in the Circus. See CIRCUS; CURRUS.

Aurinia. A prophetess held in high repute among the ancient Germans (Tac. *Germ.* 8).

Auriscalpium (ὠτογλυφίς). A pick or probe for the ear (Mart. *Epist.* xiv. 23; Scribon, *Compos.* 230).

Aurōra. See EOS.

Aurum (χρυσός). Gold, from its malleability and the circumstance that it is found lying in lumps, was one of the earliest of metals used by man, and among the most primitive resources of civilization. This was suspected by the ancients, who make the earliest age of the world's history an age of gold. In the Heroic Age we find that gold was put to a great variety of uses. Homer speaks of the houses of Menelaüs and Alcinoüs as full of silver and gold; the armour of Glaucus was of gold (*Il.* vi. 236), so were the handmaids of Hephaestus (*Il.* xviii. 417), and the doves on Nestor's cup (*Il.* xi. 632). So in the decoration of the shield of Achilles, the chest of Cypselus, and other works of art, much gold was employed. And that this plenty of gold was not a mere figment of the poet we know from the best testimony, that of graves. At Mycenae, which is in Homer called πολύχρυσος, Dr. Schliemann has dug up a prodigious quantity of gold,—cups, and jugs, and masks, and ornaments of all sorts. The graves of the Crimea (though these are of later date) also yield abundance of gold, the corpses which are discovered in them being covered from head to foot with gold, beaten into the shape of animals, rosettes, and designs of all kinds. In the use of gold the wealthy Ionians of Asia Minor copied their neighbours, even binding their hair with it, in which custom the Athenians are said to have followed them (Thuc. i. 6). See CAELATURA.

There can be no question that to the smiths of early time gold must have been the metal which gave most scope for the artistic faculty. Its extreme softness and malleability enabled even workmen who had no more elaborate tools than a hammer and nails to work it into any given shape. All the vessels of Mycenae are thus hammered out and joined into shape by nails, and the earliest statues of the gods were produced by the same method, which was called by the ancients σφυρηλατεῖν. They did indeed sometimes, instead of welding two surfaces of gold together, unite them by a solder of borax (Schliemann's *Mycenae.* p. 231), but practically this process was unusual. Casting in hollow moulds belongs to a later period.

In the preparation of gold the ancients used only the simplest processes of melting and refining. When gold occurred mixed with silver they frequently did not separate the silver, but treated the mixed as a simple metal.

Asia was the source of gold, from the days when the Argonauts sailed to Colchis in search of the golden fleece, to the days when Alexander and his captains seized and dispersed the enormous hoards laid up during many generations by the Babylonian kings and their Persian successors. Arrian and Diodorus give us accounts which might well seem fabulous of the quantities of gold seized in the great cities of Asia. According to Diodorus (xvii. 71), in the city of Persepolis alone Alexander captured a treasure in gold and silver of 120,000 talents. The wealth in gold of Croesus is testified by his gift to Delphi (Herod. i. 50) of above 100 solid bricks of the metal. A private individual, Pythius, in the reign of Xerxes, possessed three millions of gold darics (Herod. vii. 27). The sources whence the gold of Asia was drawn were various—India was one of the chief. In Arabia, also, abundant gold was found and freely exported (Strabo, xvi. 3, 4). Lydia supplied great quantities of river-gold, both pure and mixed with silver. (See ELECTRUM.) But the richest source of all, in the opinion of the ancients, was the country of the Arimaspi (q. v.), where the gold was guarded by griffins, and with difficulty won from them by the hardy natives. Most modern writers suppose that the reality which gave rise to this fable was the gold mines of the Caucasus, whence gold penetrated through the country of the Scythians to Persia. A similar story was told or invented in regard to the Indian gold (Herod. iii. 102)—namely, that it was found in a country infested by huge ants (μύρμηκες), from whose pursuit men could only escape when riding on swift camels. The motive of these stories for deterring adventurers is very manifest.

The gold mines of Europe were also important. The Carthaginians, and after them the Romans, obtained their main supply from Spain, in the rivers of which country was a rich deposit of gold, notably in the Tagus. Both in Gaul and in Spain, at the time of the Roman conquests, whole districts were covered with rich auriferous deposits, yielding nuggets to the inhabitants on the application of the simplest systems of washing. In the provinces of Asturia and Lusitania, according to Pliny (*H. N.* xxxiii. 78), the workmen went through the laborious process of undermining whole hills by their excavations, and then turning on rivers to wash the fallen earth and separate the particles of metal. Gold was also found in the Italian Padus, in the Hebrus in Thrace, and other rivers. Polybius states (xxxiv. 10) that in his time great quantities of gold were found on the surface of the ground in Pannonia. In Greece proper, gold was found in small quantities in the islands of Siphnos and Thasos, and in larger quantities in the mountains of Thrace. These last, however, seem not to have yielded their full supply until they fell into the hands of Philip of Macedon, who procured from them, it is said, 1000 talents a year (Diod. xvi. 8).

Diodorus also informs us (iii. 12) that in Upper Egypt, on the confines of Aethiopia, were gold mines which were worked, from the time of the early kings of Egypt onwards, for the benefit of the state. But here the gold was not found as elsewhere, on the surface of the ground, but extracted from the heart of the mountains by a number of miserable slaves. Diodorus describes the process, which appears to be that of extracting gold from quartz. The stone, he says, which contained the metal was softened by fire, and then detached in masses by wedges of iron. These masses were brayed in stone mortars and ground to the fineness of sand. Finally, the gold was detached by washing, the workmen aiding the process with their hands and with fine sponges. The metal was purified by being placed, together with a certain quantity of lead, salt, tin, and bran, in jars hermetically sealed, and exposed for five days to the heat of a fire, after which time the foreign substances were found to have evaporated.

In his thirty-third book the elder Pliny traces the history of the use of gold in Rome from earliest times. He says (chap. v.) that when the Gauls sacked the city no more than 1000 pounds' weight of gold could be found in it for ransom. The stock of gold in the treasury had increased seven years before the Third Punic War to 17,410 pounds; and after the successful termination of that war the metal came into commoner use for decoration, as for covering ceilings and walls, as well as for vessels. The custom of wearing gold rings was so late in Rome that even Marius wore one of iron. (See ANULUS.) The great influx of the metal and its use for all purposes of luxury dated in Rome as in Greece from the time of Oriental conquest. For ancient testimonies as to gold mines, see Sabatier, *Production de l'Or, de l'Argent, et du Cuivre chez les Anciens;* and for the use of gold in coinage, see NUMISMATICS.

Aurum Coronarium. When a general in a Roman province had obtained a victory, it was the custom for the cities in his own provinces, and for those from the neighbouring states, to send golden crowns to him, which were carried before him in his triumph at Rome. In the time of Cicero it appears to have been usual for the cities of the provinces, instead of sending crowns on occasion of a victory, to pay money, which was called *aurum coronarium.* This offering, which was at first voluntary, came to be regarded as a regular tribute, and seems to have been sometimes exacted by the governors of the provinces even when no victory had been gained. By a law of Iulius Caesar, it was provided that the aurum coronarium should not be given unless a triumph was decreed; but under the emperors it was exacted on many other occasions, as, for instance, on the adoption of Antoninus Pius. It continued to be collected, apparently as a part of the revenue, in the time of Valentinian I. and Theodosius.

Aurum Lustrāle. A tax imposed by Constantine on all merchants and traders, and payable at every lustrum, or every five years. See Zosimus, ii. 38.

Aurunci. See ITALIA.

Ausci or **Auscii.** A people in Aquitania in Gaul.

Ausetāni. A Spanish people in what is now Catalonia. Their capital was Ausa (Vique).

Auson (Αὔσων). A son of Odysseus and Calypso, from whom the Ausones were said to be descended.

Ausŏnes (Αὔσονες); **Ausonia** (Αὐσονία). See ITALIA.

Ausonius, DECĬMUS MAGNUS. The most remarkable Latin poet of the fourth century A.D.; born about 310 at Burdigala (Bordeaux). He was son of the private physician of Valentinian I. and afterwards prefect of Illyria. Educated thoroughly in grammar, rhetoric, and law, he practised as an advocate in his native city, where he afterwards became professor of grammar and rhetoric. He was then invited by Valentinian to undertake the education of his son Gratian, who, after he had ascended the throne, conferred upon him the consulship and other distinctions. After the assassination of Gratian he retired to his estate near Burdigala, where he continued to reside, in full literary activity, till 390. He became a Christian, probably on accepting the office of tutor to the prince. Besides composing a turgid address of thanks to Gratian, delivered at Trèves, Ausonius wrote a series of poems, including verses in memory of deceased relatives (*Parentalia*), verses commemorating his colleagues (*Commemoratio Professorum Burdigalensium*), *Epitaphia, Eclogae, Epistulae, Epigrammata,* and a number of miscellaneous pieces, one of which (*Mosella*) is the narrative of a tour from Bingen on the Rhine to Berncastel (Tabernae) on the Moselle, and then up the Moselle past Neumagen (Noviomagum) to Trèves. Its subject has secured the poem some renown.

Ausonius is not a real poet, but he tries to make up for lack of genius by dexterity in metre, by the manipulation of words, and by ornaments of learning and rhetoric. The consequence is that his style is generally neither simple nor natural.

The *editio princeps* of Ausonius was published in Venice (1472 foll.). There are separate editions of the *Mosella* by Böcking, with notes (Berlin, 1828); a variorum (Bonn, 1842), this with a German translation; and by Schenkl (Berlin, 1883). There is an English translation by C. T. Brooks, in Waring's *Bride of the Rhine* (Boston, 1878). The other poems may be found in the editions by Schenkl (Berlin, 1883) and Peiper (Leipzig, 1886).

Auspex. See AUGUR; HARUSPEX.

Auspicium. See AUGUR; HARUSPEX.

Auster. Called Notus (Νότος) by the Greeks. The south wind, or, strictly, the southwest wind. It frequently brought with it fogs and rain; but at certain seasons of the year it was a dry, sultry wind, injurious both to man and to vegetation, the *sirocco* of the modern Italians. The name *auster* is from the root found in the Latin *uro,* "to burn."

Autariātae (Αὐταριᾶται). An Illyrian people living in the mountains of Dalmatia.

Authentĭcum. A private collection of the later imperial edicts, styled also *Liber Authenticorum,* made later than A.D. 560. See NOVELLAE.

Authepsa (αὐθέψης), which literally means "self-boiling" or "self-cooking," was the name of a vessel which was used for heating water, or for keeping it hot. Its form was not greatly different from that of our modern tea-urn, as shown by the annexed illustration.

Authepsa. (From the Naples Museum.)

Cicero speaks of authepsae among other costly Corinthian and Delian vessels. In later times they were made of silver.

Autochthŏnes (αὐτόχθονες). See ABORIGINES.

Autolўcus (Αὐτόλυκος). Son of Hermes and Chionê, or (according to another account) Philonis; father of Anticlea, the mother of Odysseus. In Greek mythology he figured as the prince of thieves. From his father he inherited the gift of making himself and all his stolen goods invisible, or changing them so as to preclude the possibility of recognition. He was an accomplished wrestler, and was said to have given Heracles instruction.

Automĕdon (Αὐτομέδων). Son of Diores; the comrade and charioteer of Achilles (q. v.), and afterwards of Pyrrhus, the son of Achilles.

Automolias Graphé (*αὐτομολίας γραφή*). An accusation brought against persons guilty of having deserted to the enemy. See ASTRATEIAS GRAPHÉ.

Autonoë (Αὐτονόη). A daughter of Cadmus and wife of Aristaeus, by whom she became the mother of Actaeon (q. v.). See Pausan. i. 44.

Autonŏmi (*αὐτόνομοι*). The Greek name for those States that were governed by their own laws and not subject to any foreign power.

Auxiliāres. See SOCII.

Auxo (Αὐξώ). See CHARITES.

Avernus. See LUCRINUS LACUS.

Avesta. See PERSIA; ZOROASTER.

Aviānus (or **Avianius**), FLAVIUS. A Latin fabulist, of whose works we have a collection of forty-two fables in elegiac verse, whose composition may conjecturally be assigned to the fourth century A.D. They are dedicated in prose to a certain Theodosius, by some identified with Theodosius Macrobius, the author of the *Saturnalia.* The book was used in the schools down through the Middle Ages, during which it was much imitated, as in the *Novus Avianus* of Alexander Neckam, composed in the thirteenth century. Good texts of Avianus are those of Lachmann (Berlin, 1845), Fröhner (Leipzig, 1862), and Robinson Ellis, with *apparatus criticus*, commentary, excursus, and index (London, 1887). The earliest *Novus Avianus* has been edited by Grosse (Königsberg, 1868); and the fragments of Neckam's work may be found in Fröhner, p. 65.

Aviēnus, RUFUS FESTUS. A Latin poet of the fourth century A.D. He wrote in hexameter verse a translation of the *Phaenomena* of Aratus (q. v.); a geography based upon Dionysius Periegetes (*Descriptio Orbis Terrarum*); and another geographical piece (*Ora Maritima*) in iambics, describing the coasts of the Mediterranean, Black, and Caspian seas. Of the last work only a part of the first book is extant. He is known to have written also, in iambics, a poetical version of Livy and a condensed paraphrase of the *Aeneid* of Vergil, of which poet he is, in style, an imitator. The *editio princeps* of the complete works was published in Venice (1488). A good edition is Holder's (Innsbruck, 1887).

Axamenta. The songs of the Salian priests. See CARMINA SALIARIA; SALII.

Axīné (ἀξίνη). See SECURIS.

Axis. See CURRUS.

Axius (Ἀξιός). The chief river of Macedonia, rising in Mount Scardus and flowing southeast into the Thermaicus Sinus.

Axŏnes (ἄξονες, κύρβεις). Wooden tablets painted white, and made to turn on an upright axis, on which were inscribed the laws of Solon (q. v.). See Hermann, *Staatsalterth.* § 107, 1.

Azōtus (Ἄζωτος). Ashdod or Ashdoud; a city of Palestine near the sea-coast. It was one of the five chief towns of the Philistines, and a seat of the worship of Dagon. See Herod. ii. 157.

B

B, as a symbol.

IN GREEK.—In late Greek inscriptions we sometimes find B (β) = βασιλικός, βοήθει, or βουλῆς; as Ψ. B. = ψηφίσματι βουλῆς, six times in all. B, β′ = 2; ͵β = 2000.

IN LATIN.—

B = Badius, beneficiarius, bonus, bos.

B = beteranus = veteranus (*C. I. L.* x. 719); also bixit = vixit.

B·B = bonis bene.

B·B·M·B = bonis bene, malis bene.

BB·VV = boni viri.

B·D = bona dea.

B·D·S·M = bene de se merenti; B·M·D·S = bene merenti de se.

B·F = bona fortuna, bonum factum.

B·M = bene merenti, bona mens, bonae memoriae, bos mas.

B·M·F = bene merenti fecit, bonae memoriae femina.

B·M·F·D·S = bene merenti fecerunt de suo.

B·M·M·P = bene merenti memoriam posuit.

B·M·P = bene merenti posuit, bonae memoriae puella.

B·M·P·C = bene merenti ponendum curavit.

B·M·R = bonae memoriae religiosa.

B·M·V = bonae memoriae vir.

B·P = bonus puer.

B·Q = bene quiescat.

B·R·P·N = bono rei publicae natus.

B·V = bene vale.

B·V·V = balnea, vina, Venus.

Baal. See BELUS.

Baalbek. See HELIOPOLIS.

Babel, TOWER OF. The tower mentioned in Genesis xi. as having been commenced by the descendants of Noah on the plain of Shinar (Sumir), in order to reach the heavens and thus escape from the danger of a second Deluge. Jehovah, however, confounded the language of the builders, so that they no longer understood one another, and thus became scattered. From this the tower, which remained unfinished, was called *Babel* or "confusion" (Heb. *balbel,* to confound). This etymology is, however, only a specimen of Old Testament paronomasia, in that *Babel* is in reality the Assyrian *bab-ili,* "the gate of God"—a Semitic rendering of the Sumirian name *Ca-dimíra.* Some fragments of a cuneiform text were discovered by Mr. George Smith containing a narrative closely parallel to the Biblical account. The story in Greek mythology of the attempt of the Giants to scale heaven is probably an echo of Babylonian tradition. See GIGANTES.

Nothing is known regarding the site of the Tower of Babel, beyond the fact that it was in or very near Babylon. It is generally held to be represented by the great pile Birs Nimroud, which stands in Borsippa, a suburb of Babylon, eight miles distant, and dedicated to the god Nebo. Sir Henry Rawlinson made the discovery that the pile consisted of seven stages of brickwork on an earthen platform, each stage being of a different colour. The temple was known as the Temple of the Seven Lights (planets), each stage being consecrated to a light or planet.

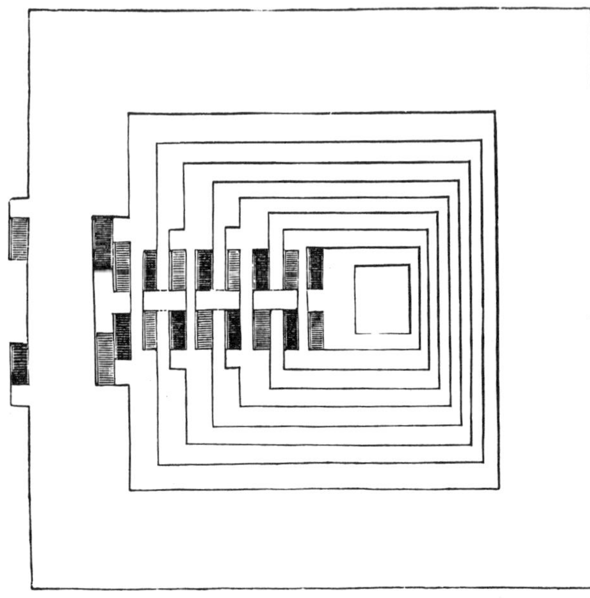

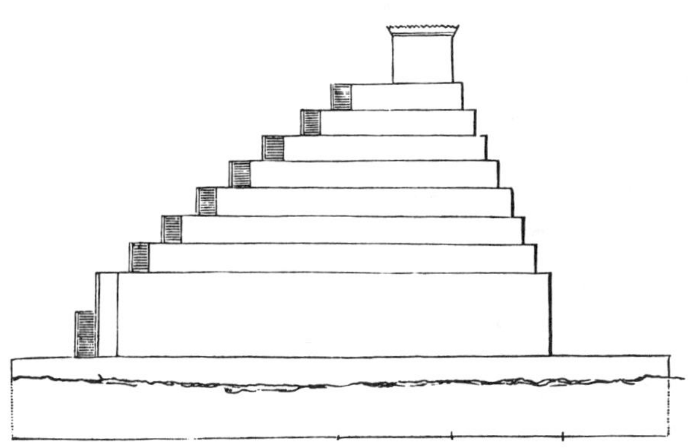

Plan and Elevation of the Temple at Borsippa. (From Oppert's measurement.)

Another proposed site is that of the ruins now called Bab-il, within the city of Babylon. Here the mound is 1100 yards in length and 800 in breadth. See Lenormant, *Les Origines de l'Histoire d'après la Bible*, vol. i. (1882); Smith, *Account of Genesis*, ed. by Sayce (1880); and Sayce, *Fresh Light from the Ancient Monuments* (3d ed. 1886).

Babrius (Βάβριος) or **Babrias** (Βαβρίας). The compiler of a comprehensive collection of Aesop's fables in choliambic metre. The book is probably to be assigned to the beginning of the first century B.C. Until 1842 nothing was known of Babrius but fragments and paraphrases, bearing the name of Aesopus. (See AESOPUS.) But in that year a Greek, Minoides Minas, discovered 123 of the original fables in the monastery on Mt. Athos. In 1857, he brought out 95 more, the genuineness of which was disputed by Cobet and other scholars. These were edited by Lewis in 1859, and are included in Bergk's *Anthologia Lyrica*, 4th ed. (1883). Babrius has been edited also by Lachmann (Berlin, 1845), and, with additions from the Bodleian and Vatican MSS., by Gitlbauer (Vienna, 1882). The style of Babrius is simple and pleasing, the tone fresh and lively. The fables of Phaedrus (q. v.) were imitated, with considerable closeness to the original, from the μῦθοι or μυθίαμβοι of Babrius. An excellent text, with dissertations, notes, and lexicon, is that of Rutherford (London, 1883).

Babȳlon (Βαβυλών). (1) The name of a fortress in Lower Egypt on the right bank of the Nile, opposite the pyramids of Ghizeh. It was said to have been founded by exiles from Babylonia, and under the Romans became a place of considerable importance. (2) A celebrated city, the capital of the Babylonian (Chaldaean) Empire, situated on the Euphrates. The ancient accounts of its origin and of the structure of the city are extremely confused. The god Belus (q. v.) is spoken of as its founder, and also Semiramis and Nitocris. According to Diodorus (ii. 7), Semiramis employed upon it two million workmen collected from all parts of her realm. It must be understood, however, that nearly all the ancient accounts of Babylon refer not to the primitive city, but to the later capital and residence of Nebuchadnezzar. Herodotus describes it in the first book of his history, as if from his personal observation.

The shape of the city of Babylon was that of a square, traversed each way by twenty-five principal streets, which, of course, intersected each other, dividing the city into 625 squares. These streets were terminated at each end by gates of brass of prodigious size and strength, with a smaller one opening towards the river. Respecting the height and thickness of the walls of Babylon, there are great variations among the ancient writers. Herodotus makes them 200 royal cubits (or 337 feet 8 inches) high and 50 royal cubits (or 84 feet 6 inches) broad, which seems incredible. A difficulty also presents itself with regard to the extent of the walls of Babylon. Herodotus makes them 120 stadia each side, or 480 in circumference. Pliny and Solinus give them the circuit at 60 Roman miles, which, reckoning eight stadia to a mile, agrees with the account of Herodotus. Strabo makes it 385 stadia. Diodorus, from Ctesias, assigns 360, but from Clitarchus, who accompanied Alexander, 365. Curtius gives 368. Taking the circumference of Babylon at 365 stadia, and these at 491 feet, each side of the square (which is equal to 91¼ stadia) will be 8.485 British miles, or nearly 8½. This gives an area of 72 miles and an inconsiderable fraction. It is to be remembered, however, that the walls, like those of most Oriental towns, enclosed rather populous districts than mere cities. That the area enclosed by the walls of Babylon was only partly built on is proved by the words of Quintus Curtius (v. 4), who says that "the buildings in Babylon are not contiguous to the walls, but some considerable space was left all around." Diodorus, moreover, describes a vast space taken up by the palaces and public buildings. The enclosure of one of the palaces was a square of 15 stadia, or near 1½ mile; the other of 5 stadia—here are more than 2½ square miles occupied by the palaces alone. Besides these, there were the Temple and Tower of Belus, of vast extent; and the Hanging Gardens. From all this, and much more that might be adduced, we may collect most clearly that much vacant space remained within the walls of Babylon; and this would seem to do away, in some degree, with the great difficulty respecting the magnitude of the city itself. Nor is it stated as the effect of the subsequent decline of Babylon, but as the actual state of it when Alexander first entered the place, for Curtius leaves us to understand that the system of cultivating a large proportion of the enclosed space originated with the foundation itself; and the history of its two sieges, by Cyrus and Darius Hystaspis, seems to show it (Rennell's *Geography of Herodotus*, i. 447). The walls of Babylon were built of brick baked in the sun, cemented with bitumen instead of mortar, and were encompassed by a broad and deep ditch, lined with the same materials, as were also the banks of the river in its course through the city, the inhabitants descending to the water by steps through the smaller brass gates already mentioned. Over the river was a bridge, connecting the two halves of the city, which stood, the one on its eastern, the other on its western bank; the river running nearly north and south. The bridge was five furlongs in length and thirty feet in breadth, and had a palace at each end, with, it is said, a subterranean passage beneath the river from one to the other, the work of Semiramis. Of this bridge no traces have yet been found.

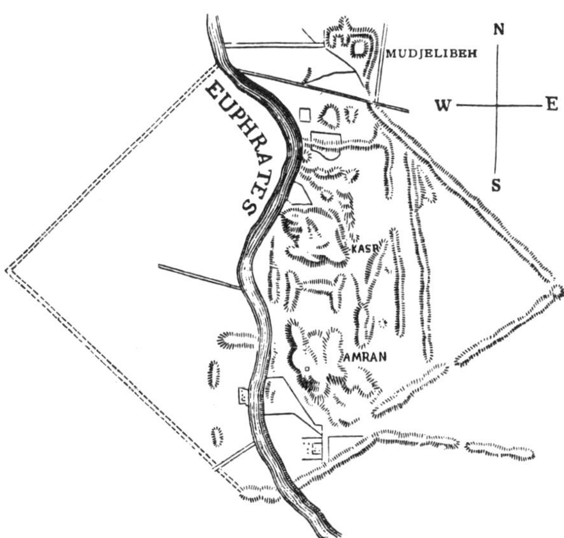

Plan of Babylon. (According to Rich.)

Within or near the city was the Temple of Belus, or Baal, which Herodotus describes as a square of two stadia; in the midst of this arose the celebrated tower, to which both the same writer and Strabo give an elevation of one stadium, and the same measure at its base. The whole was divided into eight separate towers, one above another, of decreasing dimensions to the summit, where stood a chapel, containing a couch, table, and other things of gold. Here the principal devotions were performed; and over this, on the highest platform of all, was the observatory, by the help of which the Babylonians are said to have attained to great skill in astronomy. A winding staircase on the outside formed the ascent to this stupendous edifice. The Old Palace, which stood on the east side of the bridge over the river, was 3¾ miles in extent. The New Palace, which stood on the west side of the river, opposite to the other, was 7½ miles in extent. It was surrounded with three walls, one within another, with considerable spaces between them. These walls, as also those of the other palace, were embellished with an infinite variety of sculptures, representing all kinds of animals to the life. Among the rest was a curious hunting-piece, in which Semiramis on horseback was throwing her javelin at a leopard, and her husband Ninus piercing a lion. In this last palace were the Hanging Gardens, so celebrated among the Greeks. They contained a square of 400 feet on every side, and were carried up in the manner of several large terraces, one above another, till the height equalled that of the walls of the city. The ascent was from terrace to terrace by stairs ten feet wide. The whole pile was sustained by vast arches raised upon other arches, one above another, and strengthened by a wall, surrounding it on every side, of twenty-two feet in thickness. On the top of the arches were first laid large flat stones, sixteen feet long and four broad; over these was a layer of reeds, mixed with a great quantity of bitumen, upon which were two rows of bricks closely cemented together. The whole was covered with thick sheets of lead, upon which lay the mould of the garden. And all this floorage was contrived to keep the moisture of the mould from running away through the arches. The earth laid thereon was so deep that large trees might take root in it; and with such the terraces were covered, as well as with all other plants and flowers that were proper to adorn a pleasure-garden. In the upper terrace there was an engine, or kind of pump, by which water was drawn up out of the river, and from thence the whole garden was watered. In the spaces between the several arches upon which this whole structure rested were large and magnificent apartments, that were very light, and had the advantage of a beautiful prospect. Amyitis, the wife of Nebuchadnezzar, having been bred in Media (for she was the daughter of Astyages, the king of that country), desired to have something in imitation of her native hills and forests; and the monarch, in order to gratify her, is said to have raised this prodigious structure. Near Babylon was the famous Birs Nimroud. See BABEL, TOWER OF.

Babylon was probably in the zenith of its glory and dominion just before the death of Nebuchad-

The Mudjelibeh or Kasr. (Rich.)

nezzar. The spoils of Nineveh, Jerusalem, and Egypt had enriched it; its armies had swept like a torrent over the finest countries of the East, and had at this time no longer an enemy to contend with; the arts and sciences, driven from Phœnicia and Egypt, were centred here; and hither the philosophers of the West came to imbibe instruction. The fall of Babylon, before the victorious arms of Cyrus, occurred B.C. 538. The height and strength of the walls had long baffled every effort of the invader. Having understood, at length, that on a certain day, then near approaching, a great annual festival was to be kept at Babylon, when it was customary for the Babylonians to spend the night in revelling and drunkenness, he thought this a fit opportunity for executing a scheme which he had planned. This was no other than to surprise the city by turning the course of the river—a mode of capture of which the Babylonians, who looked upon the river as one of their greatest protections, had not the smallest apprehension. Accordingly, on the night of the feast, he sent a party of his men to the head of the canal, which led to the great lake made by Nebuchadnezzar to receive the waters of the Euphrates while he was facing the banks of the river with walls of brick and bitumen. This party had directions, as soon as it was dark, to commence breaking down the great bank or dam which kept the waters of the river in their place, and separated them from the canal above mentioned; while Cyrus, in the meantime, dividing the rest of his army, stationed one part at the place where the river entered the city, and the other where it came out, with orders to enter the channel of the river as soon as they should find it fordable. This happened by midnight; for, by cutting down the bank leading to the great lake, and making, besides, openings into the trenches which, in the course of the two years' siege, had been dug around the city, the river was so drained of its water that it became nearly dry. When the army of Cyrus entered the channel from their respective stations on each side of the city, they rushed onward towards the centre of the place; and finding the gates leading towards the river left open in the drunkenness and negligence of the night, they entered them, and met by concert at the palace before any alarm had been given; here the guards, partaking, no doubt, in the negligence and disorder of the night, were surprised and killed. Soon after, the soldiers of Cyrus, having killed the guard, and meeting with no resistance, advanced towards the banqueting-hall, where they encountered Belshazzar, the ill-fated monarch, and slew him, with his armed followers. See, however, CYRUS, p. 460.

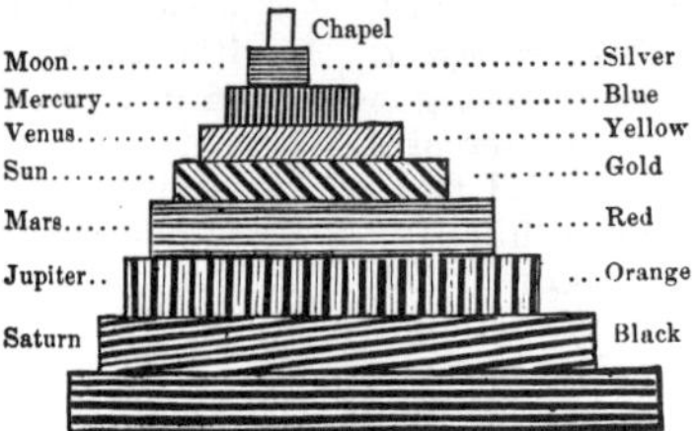

Section of Temple of the Seven Lights.

Under Cyrus, Babylon was reduced to the rank of a provincial city, and having revolted under Darius Hystaspis was severely punished, and by Xerxes plundered and despoiled, after which it steadily decayed. See BABYLONIA.

Babylonia (Βαβυλωνία; in the Assyrian inscriptions called *Babilu;* in the Persian, *Babirush*). A plain watered by the lower streams of the Tigris and Euphrates, and forming the modern province of Irak-Arabi. The boundaries of Babylonia varied considerably during the different periods of Babylonian and Assyrian power; but in general the northern boundary consisted partly of the Euphrates and its affluents, and partly of the frontier forts established by the monarchs of Assyria and Babylonia, these forts and their outposts forming in all probability the "Median Wall" of the classical writers. The Tigris River formed a natural eastern boundary-line, though the province of Namri (Kurdistan) lying east of that stream was sometimes included in the Chaldaean Empire. The Euphrates with the desert lying east of it was the western limit, while the territory terminated at the Persian Gulf on the south, this body of water in early times having extended further inland than at present. The country so bounded is spoken of in the Old Testament as Shinar, Babel, and "the land of the Chaldees," and has always been one of the richest and most fertile districts of Western Asia, so that Herodotus (i. 193) speaks of it as supplying one third of the grain produced by the whole Persian Empire—a fact to which the inscriptions bear witness. A magnificent system of artificial irrigation enhanced this natural productiveness, a network of canals having extended over the entire territory, some of them being still navigable, and the greatest of them—the Nar Malka, which connected the Tigris with the Euphrates—having been used as late as A.D. 700.

Babylonia was divided into several provinces of varying number and extent at different periods. The chief division was into the two large provinces of Sumir (Shinar) or South Babylonia, and Akkad or North Babylonia, which latter extended from the city of Babylon to the Assyrian frontier. Babylon was the capital of Sumir, and the double city Sippara-Akkad (Agade) on both banks of the Euphrates was the capital of North Babylonia. Minor divisions were Gan-Duniyas, Edina (Eden), Gambulu (Afadj) and Mat Kaldu, the land of the Chaldaeans on the Persian Gulf.

Ethnology and Civilization.—Babylonia was a land of mixed races, as is testified both by the sacred and profane writers of antiquity, and by the heterogeneous character of its linguistic and monumental remains. The first population was Ugro-Finnic in its racial affiliations, as is seen by the statues of this period, which exhibit features of a pure Tartar type, with doliocephalic skulls, high cheek-bones, and slanting eyes. This type is ethnically altered to the Proto-Medes and to the Elamites of Susiana. The name of Sumero-Akkadians has been applied to this people, who originally came from the mountains to the northeast, whence the name *Akkadai*, "mountaineers." At the time of their immigration into Babylonia they are believed to have brought with them the elements of civilization. Not long after them, the Semites entered Babylonia, their type also appearing in the glyptic remains; and later, other ethnic elements were added to the population by the natural operations of war and commerce. That the Semitic immigrants ultimately attained to a high degree of influence in the land is seen in the fact that as early as B.C. 3800 we find a Semitic line of kings, under Sargon of Akkad, ruling in North Babylonia.

The Babylonian people were possessed of a civilization whose greatness has only of late been properly appreciated; for the meagre notices in Herodotus and other ancient writers give little more than a faint suggestion of the truth. The recovery and decipherment in recent times of many thousands of inscribed tablets from the libraries of the oldest cities of Babylonia, give us a means of reconstructing a very accurate picture of the sociology of their ancient life, and one more clear in its details than that given us by the records of almost any other ancient people, except perhaps of Egypt.

The government was despotic, and of a typically Oriental type. The laws were administered by supreme judges under whom were ordinary judges, who sat in the gates of the temple and at the great gate of the city to hear causes, and gave judgment in strict conformity with precedent, the chief punishments being fines, loss of civic rights, imprisonment, and death. Appeals could be made to the king. The chief taxes were the "king's tax," or tax on all property; the "army tax"; and the tax levied, like the English "ship-money" of former

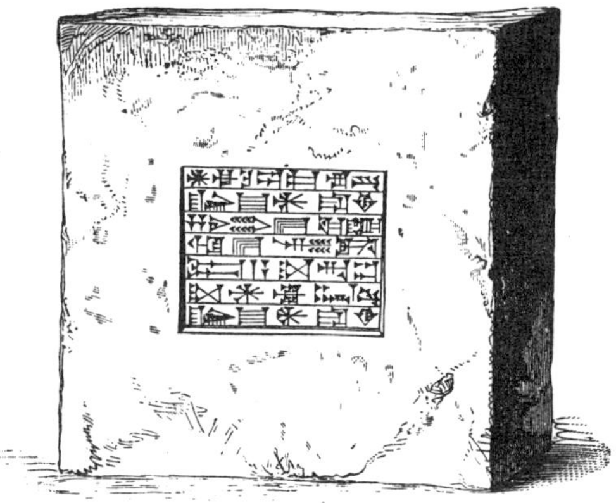

Babylonian Brick, with Cuneiform Inscription.

times, upon certain districts for ships. Local taxes were temple-tithes (*esritum*), the first-fruit tax, the sheep tax, and a tax for the maintenance of roads and canals. A silver currency was employed (talents, manehs, shekels, paras), coined money having been introduced in the reign of Darius. These early coins were perhaps the tetradrachma (q. v.) of the Athenian Greeks.

Women occupied a favourable position, especially after marriage, which was effected by both a religious and a civil ceremony. Offences against a mother were severely punished, sometimes even by mutilation. Women could own slaves and other property in their own right, and could even engage in business. All Chaldaeans of free birth were educated. Slaves were protected by law against harsh treatment from their masters; they could own property; and in fact were often taught trades and other self-supporting occupations by their owners.

Art, Literature, and Manufactures.—The recent explorations of Rassam at Sippara and of De Sarzec at Tel-lô have added immensely to our knowledge of Chaldaean art, which had hitherto been represented by a few engraved cylinders and gems. The statues discovered by these gentlemen have much artistic merit. The largest is nearly life-size, is accurate in its anatomy, and is carved in hard green diorite. Another even more remarkable piece of workmanship is a head cut in red porphyry, the execution making it evident that tools of rare excellence must have been used. Several bronze statuettes attest a knowledge of the art of casting metals. Many talismans and amulets have been found, the stones selected by the lapidaries being green and red jasper, haematite, chalcedony, crystal, carnelian, lapis-lazuli, sardonyx, and onyx. Music was cultivated, as the sculptors prove by their representations of the harp, cymbals, and other instruments.

Among the Sumero-Akkadian population, the scribe caste contained many members of high rank, and literature in consequence was highly esteemed. As has been already stated, every free Babylonian had a certain amount of education, including a knowledge of tablet writing. Libraries were common, and tablets have been found directing the student how to ask for such works as he needed from the libraries; whence it appears that a very careful system of cataloguing prevailed. Various schools of literature are noted as having existed, each influenced by local schools of thought. In the most ancient school of Eridhu, for example, magic was cultivated, with the result that many works on magic and its cognate subjects were written and compiled, among them the series of tablets known as the "books of spells relating to diseases of the head," and having a remarkable resemblance to the Atharvaveda or Black-Veda of the Aryans. The school of Erech produced the epic poem of Gizdhubar, consisting of twelve books arranged according to the twelve signs of the zodiac. An admirable specimen of Babylonian literature is a tablet, of which both Assyrian and Babylonian versions exist, describing the war in heaven between Merodach (Marduk) and the demon Tiamat. This tablet came from the library of the Temple of Nebo at Borsippa. Besides poetry and magic, the remains of these great libraries have yielded specimens of historical writing, legal, geographical, and religious composition, and treatises on astrology, divination, astronomy, and mythology, besides fables and proverbs. The greater part of the Chaldaean classics were copied by the Assyrians under Assur-bani-pal, and thus became a part also of the literature of the Northern Empire. See ASSYRIA.

The natural products of Babylonia were very numerous, comprising, besides corn and other cereals, many kinds of fruits, such as grapes and melons, and also vegetables—sesame, onions, garlic, cucumbers, etc. Trades were varied, and the tablets make especial mention of weaving, dyeing, pottery, building, and many other mechanical arts.

CHRONOLOGY AND HISTORY.—Hitherto students of Babylonia have been almost entirely dependent upon the fragmentary portions of the Canon of Kings, drawn up by the Graeco-Chaldaean priest Berosus (q.v.), about B.C. 268; but these lists are now confirmed and superseded by Babylonian Canon inscriptions dating from the sixth century before our era. The documents are: (1) a Canon of Kings by their dynasties, extending from B.C. 2200 until B.C. 647, partly mutilated, but capable of restoration; (2) the Tablet of Synchronous History of Assyria and Babylonia, which gives the names of the Babylonian kings from about B.C. 1800 to B.C. 732; (3) a Chronicle Tablet giving the chief events in Babylonia, the month and day being given in most cases, from B.C. 747 to B.C. 660; and (4) a collection of dated contract tablets extending from B.C. 680 to B.C. 150. This unequalled series of chronological documents gives an almost complete sequence to Babylonian history, and although there are still *lacunae*, the basis is now much more sure than when we were dependent solely upon the second-hand statements of Ctesias and Berosus.

It is now evident, from the monuments and inscriptions which have been obtained from the traditionally oldest cities of Chaldaea, that the civilization of the ancient people of Babylonia has an antiquity surpassing that of ancient Egypt. The earliest monument of which we can accurately fix the date is a stone whorl in the British Museum, brought from Sepharvaim by Mr. Rassam. It is an oval-shaped stone, inscribed in what is called *line* writing—that is, writing in which the characters are formed more by lines than by the ordinary wedges, a style that goes back to a time when the hieroglyphic or pictorial system of writing was beginning to be discontinued. The king's name inscribed is that of Sargon I., king of Akkad, who is now universally assigned to the remote antiquity of B.C. 3800, and other inscriptions of this distant period are to be found in other European museums. Older still, in all probability, are the very archaic records found by M. de Sarzec at Tel-lô, in the neighbourhood of Erech, which, written in the ancient agglutinative dialect of the Sumero-Akkadian inhabitants, must precede the Semitic inscriptions of the northern kingdom of Sargon and his successors. These early inscriptions are mostly of a very short character, containing little more than the names and titles of the kings who ruled the cities, but at the same time they afford us information as to the state of civilization existing in Chaldaea nearly 4000 years before the Christian era. The Empire had not become one consolidated whole, and polyarchy was the most prevalent form of government, each city being ruled by its local king. Thus, Sargon was king of Akkad, and especially styles himself king of "the city." Ur-bahu and Dungi were rulers of Ur, and others held sway in the cities of Eridhu, Larsa, and Babylon. Some of these early rulers claim the titles of king of Sumir (Shinar) and Akkad, a division which in after-time had the geographical signification of North and South Babylonia, but which in the earlier ages are certainly rather to be regarded as ethnic than local divisions of this early population. Babylon, though always one of the most important cities of the empire, was not the earliest capital, for the cradle of Chaldaean civilization was in the region of the south. Here all the ancient legends connected with Gizdhubar as Nimrod are located, and find their centre in the city of Uru-ki, the Erech of Genesis, the name of which means "the city of the land," or capital.

The next most important city in this southern region was Ur, the sacred city of the Moon-god, the ruins of which are marked by the mound of Mugheir, on the west bank of the Euphrates, the city from which Abram came. Larsa (Senkereh), the Ellasar of Gen. xiv.; Sergul or Kulunu, the Calneh of Genesis, now known as the site of Zerghul on the Shat-el-Hie; and Eridhu, the most sacred city of South Babylonia, called frequently the "Holy City," were all seats of local rulers.

The first ruler who succeeded in combining those various city kingdoms into one consolidated whole was Ur-bahu, whose reign must be placed about B.C. 2700. This ruler restored temples in nearly all the above-mentioned cities, and appointed "priest viceroys" to rule in them. He was succeeded by his son Dungi, who has left us a large number of inscriptions. Already Chaldaean civilization had made great progress and was far advanced, and the sciences, especially mathematics and astronomy, were studied; while the ships of Chaldaea navigated the Persian Gulf. The first really historical chronicle belongs to this period, and is found on a statue of Gudea, which shows the Babylonians already at war with Elam and the nations to the west. The wars with Elam form the chief features of the history of this period. In B.C. 2280 a powerful confederation of Elamites under Kudurnakhundi invaded South Chaldaea, and sacked the capital, Erech, carrying away the statue of the divine patroness Nana or Istar. This dynasty lasted until about B.C. 2120, and was very powerful, as shown by the numerous inscriptions of the kings found in various parts of Babylon. Of the kings of this period two are specially important—viz., Kudur-mabug, who appears to have been lord-paramount of the confederation of kings, and who claimed the title of "lord of the west," or Syria; and his son, Eri-aku, who was ruler of Larsa. This latter ruler is almost universally identified by Assyriologists with the Arioch, king of Ellasar, mentioned in Gen. xiv. This dynasty was overthrown by the powerful usurper, King Khammuragas, who appears not to have been of native Babylonian origin, but rather a Kassite or Cosscan who had settled in the land and availed himself of this period of depression to seize the throne. This Kassite dynasty is one of the most important periods in Babylonian history, as great political changes took place at this time. It was at this time that Babylon began to assume its position as the capital of the whole Empire. Khammuragas rebuilt the temples of Bel at Babylon, Nebo in Borsippa, and restored several of the sacred edifices in South Babylonia—at Ur, Erech, and Larsa—which had suffered at the hands of the Elamite invaders. His greatest public work, however, was the construction of a canal called the river of Khammuragas, "joy of men," which there is little doubt was the Nar Malka, or Royal River of the classics. This canal crossed North Babylonia, passing through Sippara, and is now represented by the Yusifieh Canal, one of the few ancient canals navigable at the present day. This dynasty lasted about 180 years, the founder himself ruling forty-five. The very numerous collection of inscriptions of this period in the British Museum shows that at this time Babylonia was occupied by a much mixed population, consisting of Sumero-Akkadians, Elamites, Kassites, and a large Semitic element. The Semites appear principally as traders and merchants.

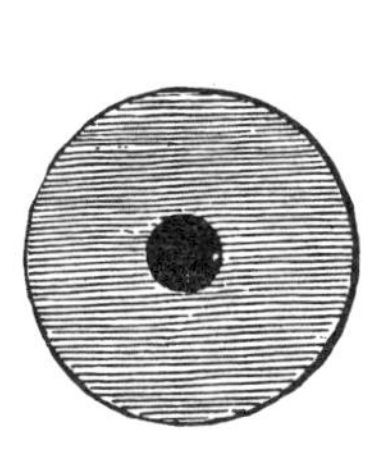

Babylonian Seal and its Impression. (British Museum.)

The three succeeding dynasties, extending over a period of about 600 years, consisted of a mixture of Semitic and non-Semitic princes, who ruled with Babylon as capital. The history of this period is chiefly to be derived from the Tablet of Synchronous History, and only a few Babylonian records of the period have been preserved. One of the most important is the memorial stone of Nebuchadnezzar I., B.C. 1150—a usurper who seized the throne and waged war against the rising Empire of Assyria. In this inscription the king records the result of a campaign against the Elamite chiefs in the region of Namri or Kurdistan, and on the banks of the Ulai River, on which the city of Shushan was afterwards built. The description of the campaign undertaken in the hot summer months is extremely graphic for so ancient a document: "In the month Tammuz he took the road; the rocks were burning and scorched like fire; from the gardens was burned all vegetation; there was no water in the springs, and cut off were the drinking-places; the strength of the great horses wearied, and to the warlike hero his courage returned." The writer then describes the battle, in which the Babylonians were undoubtedly worsted, and only saved from complete defeat by the aid of the governor of an adjacent city who refused to surrender to the Elamites. In return for this the city has a charter of freedom granted it, declaring it free from taxes and from the usual levy for men in time of war.

The history is, after this date, chiefly to be derived from Assyrian sources, and it is not until the time of Nabunazir, the Nabonassar of the Canon of Ptolemy, that we have any complete sequence of Babylonian history. Our information is now chiefly derived from the important, but unfortunately fragmentary, Chronicle Tablet already spoken of. Nabonassar, whose reign forms an important epoch in Babylonian history, ascended the throne in B.C. 747, and ruled for fourteen years. During his reign the country was twice invaded by the Assyrians, and, though they claim the victory, they do not seem to have shaken the king on his throne. Nadinu (the Nadinos of Ptolemy), who succeeded to his father's throne in B.C. 734, only ruled for two years, when one of the popular revolts unseated him and placed Ukinziru (the Chimzoros of Ptolemy) on the throne. In the third year the country was invaded by the armies of Tiglath-pileser III., king of Assyria, who drove the Babylonian king from his capital into the marshes of South Babylonia, where he found him and put him to death, ascending his throne under the Babylonian name of Pulu or Pul. This conquest of Babylonia, in B.C. 729, was a very important event in the history of the Kingdom, for it brought the two courts of the north and south kingdoms once more into close relationship. The death of Shalmaneser IV., king of Assyria, and the usurpation of the throne by Sargon the Tartan in B.C. 722, was the opportunity seized by the Babylonians for once more becoming independent, under the leadership of a prince of very ancient descent—Merodach-baladan II. This prince was one of the most popular rulers of the middle Babylonian Kingdom, and was supported by all classes of the people as well as by the Elamite court, who were the most powerful opponents of Assyria. For twelve years the wars in Syria and other parts of the Empire kept the Assyrians from despatching sufficiently strong forces to the south to crush this powerful prince. In B.C. 712, Sargon was purposing to march into Babylonia, when a counteraction was caused by the Babylonian prince sending an embassy to Hezekiah and the other princes of Syria, and raising a revolt which called the invaders away (2 Kings, xx. 6); but in B.C. 710 the storm broke, and Sargon captured Babylon, proclaiming himself king. On the assassination of Sargon in B.C. 705, Merodach-baladan returned, and after a reign of some nine months was driven from the land by Sennacherib, seeking refuge in the Elamite provinces on the east shore of the Persian Gulf. For some years Babylonia was now ruled by viceroys and princes appointed by the kings of Assyria, although several native princes attempted revolt. In B.C. 688, Sennacherib, after a very severe campaign, in which he defeated the allied Elamites and Babylonians, became sovereign of the two kingdoms. His son and successor, Esarhaddon, attempted to carry out a policy of a more conciliatory kind, and divided his time between the two courts; but the violent opposition of Egypt in Syria weakened his power, and the Elamites and Babylonians constantly harassed him. Shortly before his death he appointed his son Samas-sum-yukin (the Saosduchinos of Ptolemy) ruler, which appointment was confirmed by his son and successor Assur-bani-pal. This prince, tempted by the intrigue of the Babylonian priests, revolted against his brother, and was defeated after a terrible war, in which Babylon, Sippara, and Borsippa were besieged, and burned himself in his palace, B.C. 647. Kandalanu, who succeeded him, was little more than a viceroy, depending in every way upon the Ninevite court, although tablets are dated in his reign. On the disruption of the Assyrian Empire after the death of Assur-banipal, the throne of Babylon was seized by Nabu-abla-utzar, or Nabopolassar, the general of the Babylonian garrison, who had married a Median princess, and was himself, no doubt, of collateral descent from the royal line of Babylonian kings.

The general disruption of the states of Western Asia which took place in B.C. 625, subsequent upon the inroad of a large mass of Aryan and other invaders from the east, afforded the Babylonians an opportunity for throwing off the hated yoke of Assyria, and Nabopolassar was proclaimed king in B.C. 625. He was succeeded in B.C. 604 by his son Nebuchadnezzar, one of the greatest sovereigns who ever ruled over the ancient Empire. During a long reign of forty-three years the prince succeeded in recovering the long-lost provinces of the kingdom, and once more making Babylon queen of nations. He not only restored the Empire and rebuilt Babylon, but almost every temple and edifice throughout the land underwent restoration at his hands. It is an astonishing fact that not a single mound throughout Babylonia has as yet been opened by the explorers which has not been found to contain bricks, cylinders, or tablets inscribed with his name. In B.C. 599, he captured Jerusalem, and sent Jehoiakim captive to Babylon; and eleven years later, owing to the still disturbed state of the kingdom (B.C. 588), he destroyed the city, and removed most of the inhabitants to Chaldaea. Nebuchadnezzar was succeeded in B.C. 561 by his son Evil-merodach, who released Jehoiakim, but was murdered by his brother-in-law Nergal-Sharezer, who was the *rab makhu*, or "chief seer," of one of the temples. His reign lasted until B.C. 556, his son Labasi-Kudar (the Laborasoarchad of Ptolemy) only ruling a few months. The throne was in B.C. 556 usurped by a powerful and active prince, Nabu-naid or Nabonidus, the son of a "chief seer," whose reign is the most important, next to that of Nebuchadnezzar, in later Babylonian history. The inscriptions of this king are found in almost all temples, and some of them contain important historical facts. In a cylinder found at Sippara the king records his restoration of the temple at Kharran, which was destroyed by the Scythians, and in his sixth year, B.C. 549, he records the overthrow of Astyages, king of the Medes, and the capture of Ecbatana by Cyrus (q. v.). In the king's seventeenth year the whole land of Babylonia was in revolt against him for neglecting the duties of court and religion, leaving all to his son Belshazzar. During the summer of this year Cyrus invaded Babylonia, advancing from the neighbourhood of the modern Bagdad, and reaching Sippara on the fourteenth day of Tammuz (June), which the garrison yielded without fighting. Two days later, Tammuz 16, Babylon was taken in the same manner. Cyrus appointed Gobryas ruler. Three months later, Nabonidus, who was a prisoner, died, and after a week's mourning by the people was buried on the fourth day of Nisan, B.C. 538. Babylonia now became a Persian province, and under the rule of Cyrus (B.C. 538–529) and Cambyses (529–521) it appears to have been peaceful. On the accession to the throne of Darius, son of Hystaspes, the old rebellious spirit once more asserted itself, and for three years (521–519), the city held out against the Persians under Nadinta-Bel, who claimed to be Nebuchadnezzar, son of Nabonidus. Again, in B.C. 513, the city revolted under Arakha, an Armenian.

With the overthrow of the Persian monarchy Babylonia came under the short-lived dominion of Alexander the Great, who died in the capital (B.C. 323). Seleucus I., to whom it had been promised at the conference of Triparadisus, contested and won the possession of it from Antigonus (B.C. 312). About B.C. 140, it was taken from the Syrian monarchs by the Parthians. It came into the hands of the Romans only temporarily, first under Trajan (A.D. 114); under Septimius Severus (A.D. 199); and, again, under Julian (A.D. 363). When in 650 the successors of Mohammed put an end to the new Persian monarchy of the Sassanides, the province of Babylonia, where Bagdad was built (762–766), became the seat of the califs till 1258. Since 1638, when the Turks, for the second time, took it from the Persians, it has been under the dominion of Turkey, divided into the pachalics of Bagdad and Basra.

RELIGION.—During its long history many changes took place in the religion of Babylonia. The primitive Sumero-Akkadians had a sort of fetich-worship, regarding every object of nature as the abode of a spirit or living principle (Zi) which governed its relationship to man. The priests of this religion were a class of exorcists dealing only with the malevolent powers of nature—sickness, disease, and others hostile to the life of man. From the libraries of Nineveh the liturgies of these priests have been recovered in the form of magical formulas, incantations, and hymns, from which it appears that the first gods of the Sumero-Akkadian theogony are the Spirit of Heaven and the Spirit of Earth—the *Dingri*, or Creators—the parents of all the other gods. These other gods are very numerous, each locality having its own local pantheon, but in subordination to some one divine patron of the city.

One of the earliest seats of the Babylonian worship was Eridhu on the Persian Gulf, the seat of the worship of Ea, the "lord of the waves" as well as "lord of laws," and identified with the mysterious fish-divinity of Berosus (q. v.), who relates that he taught the early inhabitants of the land the elements of civilization. The wife of Ea was Dav-kina, the "lady of the earth." The pair had a son, Tammuz, "the only-begotten," whose worship is united to that of his sister, Istar, who is also his consort. Next in importance came, among the local deities, the god Mul-lil (Belus or Bel of the Semites), whose sacred city was Nipur (Niffer). He it was who, according to one version of the story of the Deluge, destroyed mankind. His name means "lord of ghost-land," and his wife, Ninkigat or Allat, is the "lady of ghost-land." Their child was Namtar, the demon of fever and goddess of fate, who controls the agencies of disease.

Coins with Effigies of the Tyrian Baal.

After the Semitic influence began to prevail, especially in the northern cities, Samas, the sun-god, assumes great importance. Many cities had their own local sun-god or solar hero; and in Sippara, where stood the Temple of E Bábara (The House of Lustre), this worship attained its highest development. The great Semitic prince Sargon I. (B.C. 3800) did much to advance the cult of the sun, which as it spread over Chaldaea brought about a gradual change in the religion of the country, resulting in an amalgamation of the Semitic and Akkadian systems. Thus grew up the worship of Bel-Merodach (Marduk) who gradually, from being only a local sun-god, became the great national deity, as Assur was of the Assyrians, so completely overshadowing all the other divinities that the later faith of Babylonia approaches a pure monotheism. His temple, which stood on the eastern side of Babylon, was one of the wonders of the world. (See BABYLON.) Other divinities of the later religion are Zirpanit, the wife of Merodach; Nebo (see ASSYRIA) with his spouse Tasmit; Ninep, the god of war; Nergal, the god of death; and Gibil, the fire-god.

BIBLIOGRAPHY.—See Layard, *Nineveh and Babylon* (1867); Lenormant, *Manuel d'Histoire Ancienne de l'Orient* (9th ed. 1882); id. *La Langue Primitive de la Chaldée* (1875); Oppert, *Histoire des Empires de Chaldée et d'Assyrie* (1865); Perrot and Chipiez, *History of Art in Chaldaea and Assyria* (Eng. trans. 1884); Rawlinson, *Cuneiform Inscriptions of Western Asia* (Brit. Mus. 1861–84); Sayce, *Ancient Empires of the East* (1884); id. *Fresh Light from the Ancient Monuments* (1885); Delitzsch, *Wo lag das Paradies?* (1881). The reader is also referred to the *Babylonian and Oriental Record*, begun in 1886; and, for a summary of very recent discoveries, to a paper by Prof. Sayce in the *Contemporary Review* for January, 1897.

Babylonĭcum (generally in the plural, BABYLONĬCA). A Babylonian shawl or coverlet placed on couches. Also a horse-blanket.

Bacca. (1) Properly a berry, and used of the olive. (2) A bead of glass, amethyst, etc., strung on a necklace or worn as the pendant in an earring. See INAURIS; MONILĖ.

Baccar or **Baccăris** (βάκχαρις). A plant as to whose identity there is considerable dispute, some assigning the name to the foxglove and others to the clary.

Bacchae (Βάκχαι). (1) The female followers of Bacchus or Dionysus (q. v.) in his wanderings through the East, and represented as crowned with vine-leaves, wearing fawn-skins, and carrying the thyrsus in their hands. They are also known as Maenades (from μαίνομαι, to rave) and Thyiades (from θύω, to sacrifice). (2) Priestesses of Bacchus or Dionysus. See BACCHANTES. (3) The title of a play by Euripides which treats of the arrival of Dionysus at Thebes and the death of Pentheus (q. v.).

Baccha. (Bas-relief from the Villa Borghese.)

Bacchanalia. Festivals held in Italy in honour of Bacchus. See DIONYSIA; LIBERALIA.

Bacchanalĭbus, SENĀTUS CONSULTUM DE. See DIONYSIA.

Bacchantes. Men and women who joined in the Dionysian festivals dressed in Asiatic robes and bonnets; and with their heads wreathed with vine and ivy leaves, with fawn-skins (νεβρίδες) flung over their shoulders, and thyrsi, or blunt spears twined with vine-leaves, in their hands, they ran through the country, shouting *Io Bacche! Euoi! Iacche!* Ἰὰ! Ἰή! swinging their thyrsi, beating on drums, and sounding various instruments. Indecent emblems were carried in procession, and the ceremonies often assumed a most immoral character and tendency. The women, who bore a chief part in these frantic revels, were called Bacchae, Maenades, Thyiades, Euades. See DIONYSIA.

Bacchiădae (Βακχιάδαι). A Corinthian clan descended from Bacchis, one of the early kings of Corinth. In their hands the royal power remained until overthrown by Cypselus (q. v.). See Pausan. ii. 4; Herod. v. 92.

Bacchĭdes. A comedy of Plautus (q. v.), and considered by critics as among his best. The original was possibly the Δὶς ἐξαπατῶν of Menander. The *Bacchides* was performed in B.C. 189. The first scenes were lost between the fourth and sixth centuries A.D.

Bacchius and **Bithus.** Two celebrated gladiators, of equal age and strength, who, after conquering many competitors, engaged with each other, and died of mutual wounds; whence the proverb to express equality, *Bithus contra Bacchium.* See Horace, *Epist.* i. 7, 20.

Bacchus (Βάκχος). See DIONYSUS; IACCHUS; LIBER.

Bacchylĭdes (Βακχυλίδης). A Greek lyric poet who flourished in the middle of the fifth century B.C. He was a native of Iulis in the island of Ceos, the nephew and pupil of Simonides, and a contemporary of Pindar. For a long time he lived with his uncle at the court of Hiero, tyrant of Syracuse. He also resided for a considerable time at Athens, where he won many victories in the dithyrambic contests. Later on his home was in the Peloponnesus. It would appear that he attempted to rival the many-sided talent of his uncle, but was inferior to him in sublimity and force. He attempted a great variety of styles: hymns, paeans, dithyrambs, drinking-songs, love-songs, and epigrams. Only fragments were known to exist until 1897, when the British Museum announced the discovery on an Egyptian papyrus of some 15 to 20 lyrics varying in length from 14 to 200 lines, but with serious *lacunae.*

Bacēnis Silva. A forest which separated the Suevi from the Cherusci. (Caes. *B. G.* vi. 10.)

Bactra (τὰ Βάκτρα) or **Zariaspa**. The modern Balkh. The capital of Bactria, at the northern foot of Mount Paropamisus (the Hindu Kush).

Bactria (Βακτρία) or **Bactriāna** (Βακτριανή). A province of the Persian Empire, bounded on the south by Mount Paropamisus, which separated it from Ariana; on the east by the northern branch of the same range, which divided it from the Sacae; on the northeast by the Oxus, which separated it from Sogdiana; and on the west by Margiana. It was included in the conquests of Alexander, and formed a part of the kingdom of the Seleucidae until B.C. 255, when Theodotus, its governor, revolted from Antiochus II., and founded the Greek kingdom of Bactria, which lasted till B.C. 134 or 125, when it was overthrown by the Parthians.

Bactrus (Βάκτρος). Now the Anderab; a river of Bactria emptying into the Oxus.

Bacŭlum (βακτηρία, ῥάβδος, σκῆπτρον, σκυτάλη). In Greece the practice of carrying a stick was as common as with us, as is seen by the testimony of Greek vases and sculptures, which show us walking-sticks of all forms and patterns. The Athenian dandies of the time of Aristophanes affected the straight cane with an ornamented head (Περσικὴ βακτηρία), while old men and rustics carried large canes with a crook (καμπύλη). In the ruder states of Greece, such as Sicyon and Sparta, huge club-like canes (σκυτάλαι) were common; and these at one time were the rage at Athens (Aristoph. *Av.* 1283).

It appears that the kings of Sparta carried a truncheon (βακτηρία) as the ensign of their authority. On the occasion of one of them lifting it up in a threatening attitude, Themistocles returned the celebrated answer, "Strike, but hear." In reference to this custom, the truncheon (*baculus*) was carried in the hand by actors on the Roman stage. The dicasts at Athens received, at the time of their appointment, a βακτηρία and σύμβολον as a mark of their authority.

Agamemnon with Staff. (From a Greek Vase.)

At Rome walking-sticks were unknown, except in the hands of the aged or infirm; but the staff was used upon the stage by actors who personated kings and princes (Suet. *Nero*, 24). See CADUCEUS; SCEPTRUM; SCYTALÉ.

Baebia Lex. See LEX.

Baecŭla. A town in Hispania Tarraconensis, west of Castulo, in the neighbourhood of silver mines.

Baeterrae. The modern Beziers; a town in Gallia Narbonensis, on the Obris, not far from Narbo.

Baetĭca. A division of Spain. See HISPANIA.

Baetis. The modern Guadalquivir (Wady el-Kiber); a river of southern Spain, formerly called Tartessus, rising in the territory of the Oretani and flowing southwest through Baetica, to which it gave the name, until it empties by two mouths into the Atlantic Ocean, north of Gades (Cadiz).

Bagistănus (Βαγίσταvος). A mountain of Media, southwest of Ecbatana, and sacred to Zeus. Here Semiramis (q. v.) formed a park or garden of twelve stadia in circumference, and cut her image on the face of the rock (Diod. Sic. ii. 13). Alexander is said to have visited the spot.

Bagōas (Βαγώας). An Egyptian eunuch, highly trusted and favoured by Artaxerxes III. Ochus, whom he poisoned, B.C. 338, giving his flesh to cats, because he had killed the sacred bull, Apis (q. v.). He was put to death by Darius III. Codomannus, whom he had attempted likewise to destroy, 336. The name Bagoas frequently occurs in Persian history, and is sometimes used by Latin writers as synonymous with *eunuchus*, which indeed seems to be the original meaning of the Persian word.

Bagrădas. A river of Northern Africa, falling into the Gulf of Carthage near Utica, near which Regulus was said to have slain the serpent 200 feet long (Plin. *H. N.* viii. 14).

Bähr, JOHANN CHRISTIAN FELIX, a classical scholar of distinction, was born at Darmstadt in 1798. He was educated at the University of Heidelberg, and won so much reputation as a classicist that at the early age of twenty-five he became Professor Ordinarius of Classical Philology in that ancient seat of learning (1823). He died November 27th, 1872. His greatest work is his *Geschichte der römischen Litteratur*, which first appeared in 1828, and reached its fourth edition in 1870. In it the subject is presented with a lucidity, taste, and accuracy that are rarely found combined in so unusual a degree. To this history he added three supplements, dealing respectively with the Christian poets and historians (1836), the Christian theology of the Latin Fathers (1837), and the later Roman literature of the Carlovingian period (1840). He also published an excellent edition of Herodotus, of which the second edition appeared in 1861.

Baiae. A city of Campania, on a small bay west of Neapolis, and opposite Puteoli. It was originally a village, but the numerous advantages of its situation soon rendered it much frequented and famous. Its foundation is ascribed in mythology to Baius, one of the companions of Odysseus. The cause of the rapid increase of Baiae lay in the fruitfulness of the surrounding country, in the beauty of its own situation, in the rich supply of shell and other fish which the adjacent waters afforded, and, above all, in the hot mineral springs which flowed from the neighbouring mountains and formed a chief source of attraction to invalids. Baiae was first called Aquae Cumanae. Numerous villas graced the surrounding country, and many were likewise built on artificial moles extending a great distance into the sea. It is now, owing to earthquakes and inundations of the sea, a mere waste compared with what it once was. The modern name is Baia. Many remains of the ancient villas may be seen beneath the water. The classics of the imperial age teem with allusions to the splendour, the luxury, and the frivolities of this famous ancient watering-place.

Baiŭlus (ἀχθοφόρος). A porter; any one employed to carry burdens, whether a slave or a freeman (Cic. *Par.* iii. 2). The bearers at funerals were called *vespillones*. See FUNUS.

Baiulus. (Rich.)

Bakers. See PISTOR.

Bala (Βάλας). An epithet of the Syrian king, Alexander (q. v.).

Balantion (βαλάντιον). A leathern bag slung around the neck, and used to carry the purse. See CRUMENA.

Balătro. A professional jester, buffoon, or parasite. In spite of the difference of quantity, *balatro* is probably connected with *balare* (to bleat like a sheep) and hence, to speak foolishly. It is doubtless also akin to *blatero*, a chatterer (Gell. i. 15). Balatrones were paid for their jests, and the tables of the wealthy were generally open to them for the sake of the amusement they afforded. See SCURRA; PARASITUS.

Balbīnus, DECĬMUS CAELIUS. A Roman who was proclaimed emperor by the Senate with Pupienus, on the death of the Gordians, A.D. 237. He was murdered by the soldiery after a year's reign.

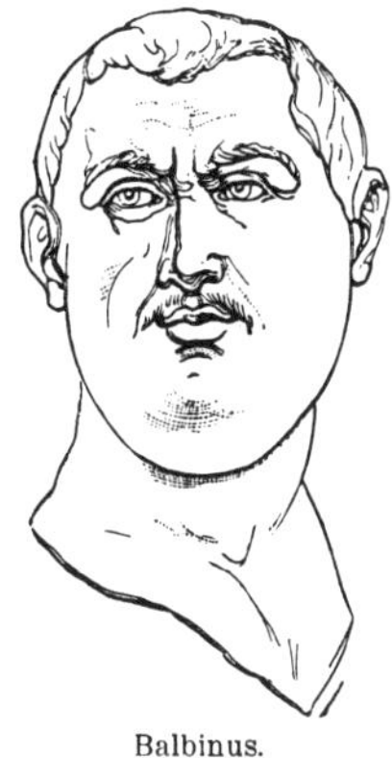
Balbinus.

Balbus, L. CORNELIUS, of Gades. A soldier who served under Pompey against Sertorius in Spain, and received from him the gift of Roman citizenship, and, returning with him to Rome, lived on intimate terms with Caesar as well as with Pompey. In B.C. 56, he was accused of having illegally assumed Roman citizenship; was defended by Cicero, whose speech has come down to us; and was acquitted. In the Civil War, Balbus had the management of Caesar's affairs at Rome. After the death of Caesar he gained the favour of Octavianus, who raised him to the consulship in B.C. 40.

Baleāres, also called **Gymnesiae** (Γυμνήσιοι) by the Greeks. Two islands in the Mediterranean, off the coast of Spain, distinguished by the epithets Maior and Minor, whence their modern names Majorca and Minorca. Their inhabitants, also called Baleares, were celebrated as slingers. They were subdued B.C. 123, by Q. Metellus, who assumed accordingly the surname Balearicus.

Ball, GAMES OF. See APORRHAXIS; CORYCOS; EPISCYRUS; FOLLIS; HARPASTUM; PILA; TRIGON; URANIA..

Ballētys (Βαλλητύς). See ELEUSINIA.

Ballista. See TORMENTUM.

Balneae, BALINEAE, BALNEUM, BALINEUM, THERMAE (ἀσάμινθος, βαλανεῖον, λοετρόν, λουτρόν).

GREEK BATHS.—Bathing was a practice familiar to the Greeks of both sexes from the earliest times, both in fresh water and salt. Thus, Nausicaa, daughter of Alcinoüs, king of Phaeacia, goes out with her attendants to wash her clothes; and after the task is done she bathes herself in the river (*Od.* vi. 58, 65). Odysseus, who is conducted to the same spot, strips and takes a bath, while Nausicaa and her servants stand aside. Warm springs were also resorted to for the purpose of bathing. The Ἡράκλεια λουτρά shown by Hephaestus or Athenė to Heracles are celebrated by the poets. Pindar speaks of the hot baths of the nymphs, and Homer (*Il.* xxii. 149) celebrates one of the streams of the Scamander for its warm temperature. Bathing in rivers or the sea (ψυχρολουτεῖν) was always common for the young. Not to know how to read and to swim were proverbial marks of the ignoramus. A plunge in the Eurotas always sufficed for the Lacedaemonians (Schol. on Thuc. ii. 36). There appears to have been a swimming-bath (κολυμβήθρα) at Athens in the time of Plato (*Rep.* 453 D).

The artificial warm bath was taken in a vessel called ἀσάμινθος by Homer, and ἔμβασις by Athenaeus. It was no doubt of wood or marble, as the epithet εὔξεστος is applied to it (*Od.* iv. 48), and in the case of Menelaus's Egyptian presents (*Od.* iv. 128) it was of silver. It would appear from the description of the bath administered to Odysseus in the palace of Circé, that this vessel did not contain water itself, but was only used for the bather to sit in while the warm water was poured over him, which was heated in a large caldron or tripod, under which the fire was placed, and when sufficiently warmed was taken out in other vessels and poured over the head and shoulders of the person who sat in the ἀσάμινθος. Where cleanliness merely was the object sought, cold bathing was adopted, which was considered as most bracing to the nerves; but after violent bodily exertion or fatigue warm water was made use of, in order to refresh the body and relax the over-tension of the muscles. Hesiod (*Op.* 754) protests against men elaborately cleaning (φαιδρύνεσθαι) their bodies with effeminate baths, i. e. those of high temperature, which shows that this luxury had begun in his day; and in Homer's time constant indulgence in the warm bath was considered as a mark of luxury and effeminacy (*Od.* viii. 249). The use of the warm bath was preceded by bathing in cold water (*Il.* x. 576). The later custom of plunging into cold water after the warm bath mentioned by Aristides (vol. i. Orat. 2, *Sacr. Serm.* p. 515), who wrote in the second century of our era, was no doubt borrowed from the Romans.

After bathing both sexes anointed themselves with oil, in order that the skin might not be left harsh and rough, especially after warm water. The use of precious unguents (μύρα) was unknown at that early period. In the heroic ages, as well as in later times, refreshments were usually taken after the bath (*Od.* vi. 97).

At Athens the frequent use of the public baths was regarded by strict moralists in the time of Socrates and Demosthenes as a mark of luxury and effeminacy; thus it is a sign of demoralization on the part of a ship's crew. Accordingly Phocion was said to have never bathed in a public bath, and Socrates to have made use of it very seldom. It was, however, only the warm baths to which objection was made, and which in ancient times were not allowed to be built within the city (Athen. i. 18 b); for the Greeks did not at all approve of people being dirty; only cleanliness, they thought, should be attained by the use of cold water.

The baths (βαλανεῖα) were either public (δημόσια, δημοσιεύοντα) or private (ἴδια, ἰδιωτικά). The former were the property of the state, but the latter were built by private individuals. Such private baths are mentioned by Plutarch (*Demetr.* 24). Baths of this kind were probably mostly intended for the exclusive use of the persons to whom they belonged (Xen. *Rep. Ath.* ii. 10.) There appears to have been a small, almost nominal, charge for the use of the public baths. Thus, in the inscription of Andania (i. 107), the price is fixed at two chalki = ½ obol.

We know very little of the baths of the Athenians during the republican period; for the account of Lucian in his *Hippias* relates to baths constructed after the Roman model. On ancient vases on which persons are represented bathing we seldom find anything corresponding to a modern bath in which persons can stand or sit; but there is always a round or oval basin (λουτήρ or λουτήριον), resting on a stand (ὑπόστατον), by the side of which those who are bathing are represented standing undressed and washing themselves, as is seen in the following illustration taken from Sir W. Hamilton's vases.

Public Basin for Men. (From a Greek Vase.)

But besides the λουτῆρες and λουτήρια there were also vessels for bathing, large enough for persons to sit in, which, as stated above, are called ἀσάμινθοι by Homer and πύελοι or μάκτραι by the later Greeks. The λουτήρ thus, as we shall see, corresponded to the Roman *labrum;* the πύελος to the *solium* or *alveus.*

In the baths there was also a kind of sudorific or vapour bath called πυρία or πυριατήριον, which is mentioned as early as the time of Herodotus (iv. 75). Among the chambers of the Greek bathing establishment was the ἀλειπτήριον, Lat. *unctorium.* Lucian (*Hipp.* p. 73) speaks of the ἀποδυτήριον with its ἱματιοφυλακοῦντες (*capsarii*); but as they seem to be unknown to Aristotle, they were probably introduced from Rome. Hence Aristotle tells us that those who stole clothes from the baths were punishable with death. As the baths most frequently adjoined the gymnasia and palaestra, one of the rooms of these latter buildings served the purpose of undressing-room (Xen. *Rep. Ath.* ii. 10). About these rooms the τριβαλλοί used to loaf, looking out for an invitation. We hear of wrestling and playing the cottabus, besides a great deal of conversation going on in the baths. To sing there was considered the part of a boor (Theophr. *Char.* 4).

Either the bath or simple anointing of the body generally formed part of the business of dressing for dinner. It was generally taken shortly before the δεῖπνον, or principal meal of the day. Epictetus (*Diss.* i. 1, 29) mentions noon as the hour, while voluptuaries bathed repeatedly. It was the practice to take first a warm or vapour, and afterwards a cold bath, though in the time of Homer the cold bath appears to have been taken first and the warm afterwards. The cold water was usually poured on the back or shoulders of the bathers by the βαλανεύς or his assistants, who are called παραχύται. The vessel from which the water was poured was called ὑδρία; there is mention also of the ἀρύταινα, which must have been much smaller. Bathing establishments for women existed among the Greeks, whether belonging to the state or maintained by private enterprise. We learn from Varro (*L. L.* ix. 68) that the earliest Greek *balneum* in Rome contained a department for women.

Roulez (*Choix de Vases peints du Musée de Leyde,* pl. xix. 1) gives us a vase painting of a bath in a palaestra, where two shower baths descend on men from spouts shaped like panthers' heads; and Panofka (*Bilder antiken Lebens,* pl. xviii. 9) shows us a bath for women similarly arranged, while an unpublished vase painting in the Louvre represents a κολυμβήθρα, or swimming-bath for women.

Shower Baths for Women. (From a Greek Vase.)

The persons who bathed probably brought with them strigils, oil, and towels, or had them carried by a slave. The strigil, which was called by the Greeks στλεγγίς or ξύστρα, was usually made of iron, but sometimes also of other materials. Pollux says (x. 181), "The cloth which is worn by women round their loins when taking the bath, or by the men who bathe them, is called ᾤα λουτρίς." The Greeks also used different materials for cleansing or washing themselves in the bath, to which the general name of ῥύμμα was given, and which were supplied by the βαλανεύς. This ῥύμμα usually consisted of a lye made of lime or wood-ashes (κονία), of nitrum, and of fuller's earth (γῆ κιμωλία, Aristoph. *Ran.* 710 and Schol.; Plat. *Rep.* iv. 430 A).

Among the Greeks a person was always bathed at birth, marriage, and after death; whence it is said of the Dardanians, an Illyrian people, that they bathe only thrice in their lives—at birth, marriage, and after death. The water in which the bride was bathed at Athens was taken from the fountain of Callirrhoë, which was called from the time of Pisistratus Ἐννεάκρουνος.

The natural warm springs (θερμὰ or Ἡράκλεια λουτρά) were not only esteemed as sacred to Heracles, but also considered highly medicinal. The hot springs of Aedepsus in Euboea were famed for their healing properties, as also was a cold spring which flowed for a time (Athen. iii. 73). In later times it became a great resort for pleasure as well as health, especially in the spring.

ROMAN BATHS.—The words *balneae, balineae, balneum, balineum, thermae*, are all commonly translated by our general term "bath" or "baths"; but in the writings of the earlier and better authors they are used with discrimination. *Balneum* or *balineum*, which is derived from the Greek βαλανεῖον, signifies, in its primary sense, a bath or bathing-vessel, such as most persons of any consequence among the Romans possessed in their own houses (Cic. *ad Att.* ii. 3), and hence the chamber which contained the bath, which is also the proper translation of the word *balnearium*. The diminutive *balneolum* is adopted by Seneca (*Ep.* 86, § 3) to designate the bath-room of Scipio, in the villa at Liternum, and is expressly used to characterize the modesty of republican manners as compared with the luxury of his own times. But when the baths of private individuals became more sumptuous, and comprised many rooms instead of the one small chamber described by Seneca, the plural *balnea* or *balinea* was adopted, which still, in correct language, had reference only to the baths of private persons. *Balneae* and *balineae*, which according to Varro (*L. L.* viii. 25, ix. 41) have no singular number,* were the public baths. But this accuracy of diction is neglected by many of the subsequent writers; and even in the time of the Republic, *balneum* was used for a public bath, but particularly by the poets, among whom *balnea* is not uncommonly used in the plural number to signify the public baths, since the word *balneae* could not be introduced in an hexameter verse. *Thermae* (θέρμαι, "hot springs") meant properly warm springs, or baths of warm water; but came to be applied to those magnificent edifices which grew up under the Empire, in place of the simple *balneae* of the Republic, and which comprised within their range of buildings all the appurtenances belonging to the Greek gymnasia, as well as a regular establishment appropriated for bathing (Juv. vii. 233). Writers, however, use these terms without distinction.

The Romans, in the earlier periods of their history, used the bath but seldom, and only for health and cleanliness, not as a luxury. Thus we learn from Seneca (*Ep.* 86, § 12) that the ancient Romans washed their legs and arms daily and bathed their whole body once a week. The room set apart for this purpose was called *lavatrina* or *latrina* (q. v.), and was placed near the kitchen, so that warm water might be easily procured.

It is not recorded at what precise period the use of the warm bath was first introduced among the Romans; but we learn from Seneca that Scipio had a warm bath in his villa at Liternum; which, however, was of the simplest kind, consisting of a single chamber, just sufficient for the necessary purposes, and without any pretensions to luxury. It was "small and dark," he says, "after the manner of the ancients." Seneca also describes the public baths of former times as *obscura et gregali tectorio inducta;* and while their arrangements were of the simplest kind, aediles of noble birth did not disdain to look after them personally. These were baths of warm *water;* but the practice of heating an apartment with warm air by a hollow underneath the floor, so as to produce a hot-air bath, is stated by Valerius Maximus (ix. 1, § 1) and by Pliny (*H. N.* ix. § 168) to have been invented by Sergius Orata, who lived in the age of L. Crassus, the orator, before the Marsic War.

In the time of Cicero, though young people used in summer to bathe in the Tiber, yet the use of baths, both public and private, of warm water and hot air, had become general; and we learn from one of his orations that there were already baths (*balneas Senias*) at Rome which were open to the public upon payment of a small sum (*pro Cael.* 25, 61). Besides public baths, others were built by private speculators, who either worked them themselves or leased them out. Sometimes even the State leased out the public baths under certain conditions, touching certain people to be admitted free, hours of opening and closing, height of water, etc. The lessee or worker of a bath (*balneator*) appears to have stood very low in social estimation (Juv. vii. 4).

Jordan has collected a vast number of the names of the baths from the Regionarii, and they appear to be nearly all called after the possessor, though we find one of Mercurius and one of Diana. There were baths, of course, in the country, and they professed to be quite up to city style—e.g. an inscription has *In praediis Aureliae Faustinianae balineus. Lavatur more urbico, et omnis humanitas praestatur* (Marini, *Atti de' Fratelli Arvali*, p. 532, where a similar profession of a *balneator* is to be found, *omnia commoda praestantur*). A sign-board, in Orelli 4326, of the Thermae of M. Crassus, offers salt and fresh water baths. These baths, which were worked by private individuals, appear to have been called *balnea meritoria.* Agrippa added 170 baths to those which existed already in Rome. In the time of Constantine there were no less than 856 in the city, and the Regionarii actually reckon 952 (Becker-Göll, *Gallus*, iii. 140).

In the earlier ages of Roman history a much greater delicacy was observed with respect to bathing, even among the men, than was usual among the Greeks; for, according to Valerius Maximus (ii. 1, § 7), it was deemed indecent for a father to bathe in company with his own son after he had attained the age of puberty, or a son-in-law with his father-in-law. But virtue passed away as wealth increased; and when the thermae came into use not only did the men bathe together in numbers, but even men and women stripped and bathed promiscuously in the same bath, as in certain Austrian cities to-day. It is true, however, that the public establishments generally contained separate baths for both sexes adjoining each other, as is seen to have been the case at the baths of Pompeii. Aulus Gellius (x. 3) relates a story of a consul's wife who took a whim to bathe at Teanum (Teano), a small provincial town of Campania, in the men's baths—probably because, in a small town, the female department, like that at Pompeii, was more confined and less convenient than that assigned to the men; and an order was consequently given to the quaestor, M. Marius, to turn the men out. In the Lex Metalli Vipascensis the women have the use of the bath from daybreak till the seventh hour, the men from the eighth hour till the second hour of the night. If at Rome there were separate establishments for the women, men at any rate appear to have been able to get into

* *Balnea* is, however, used in the singular to designate a private bath in an inscription quoted by Reinesius (*Inscr.* xi. 115).

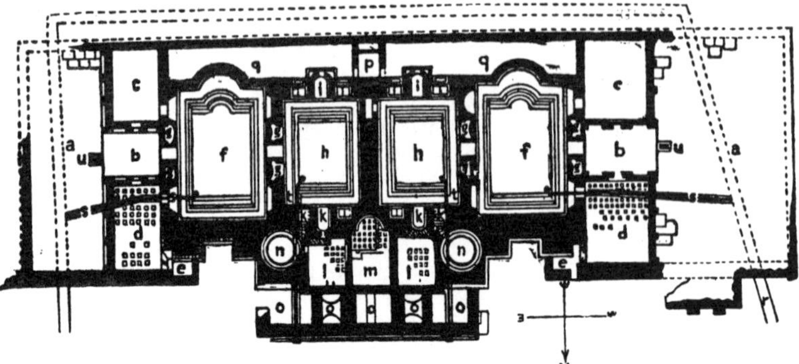

Plan of the Roman Baths at Badenweiler.

Women's Bath. *Men's Bath.*

EXPLANATION.

a. Fore court, *atrium*.
b. Central hall, *vestibulum*.
c. Undressing-room, *apodyterium*.
d. Anointing-room, *unctorium*.
e. Stoke-hole, *praefurnium*.
f. Cold bath, *frigidarium*.
g. Douche baths.
h. Warm bath, *tepidarium*.
i. Private baths, *solia*.
k. Passages for communication.
l. Hot baths, *caldaria*.
m. Hot-air bath, *laconicum*.
n. Reservoirs for cold and perhaps warm ablution.
o. Coal or wood store rooms.
p. Closets?
q. Attendants' rooms.
r. Underground exit drains
s. Leaden exit pipe.
t. Exit pipe.
u. Altar of Diana Abnoba.

them, and they were a possible place for assignations (Ov. *A. A.* iii. 639);—a passage which further shows that there were small private chambers with baths in them, such as we find in the Stabian baths at Pompeii. But whether the men and women were allowed to use each other's chambers indiscriminately, or some of the public establishments had only one common set of baths for both, the custom prevailed under the Empire of men and women bathing indiscriminately together (Plin. *H. N.* xxxiii. § 153). This custom was forbidden by Hadrian (Spart. *Hadr.* 18) and by M. Aurelius Antoninus (Capitolin. *Anton.* 23); and Alexander Severus prohibited any baths common to both sexes (*balnea mixta*), from being opened in Rome (Lamprid. *Alex. Sev.* 24). Although the practice was not adopted by women of respectability, yet this legislation was not permanently effective, and even the censures of the Fathers of the Christian Church and the canons of councils did not avail to suppress it. Justinian recognizes it as a ground of divorce, *si forte uxor ita luxuriosa est, ut commune lavacrum cum viris libidinis causa habere audeat.*

When the public baths (*balneae*) were first instituted, they were only for the lower orders, who alone bathed in public; the people of wealth, as well as those who formed the equestrian and senatorian orders, used private baths in their own houses. But as early even as the time of Iulius Caesar we find no less a personage than the mother of Augustus making use of the public establishments (Suet. *Aug.* 94); and in process of time, even the emperors themselves bathed in public with the meanest of the people.

The baths were opened at sunrise and closed at sunset. The many lamps found in the baths at Pompeii were used for lighting the rooms and the dark passages, according to Nissen, *Pomp. Stud.* 135, and do not necessarily imply night-bathing. But in the time of Alexander Severus it would appear that the baths were kept open after nightfall. The allusion in Juvenal (vi. 419) probably refers to private baths.

The price of a bath (*balneaticum*) was a quadrans, the smallest piece of coined money, from the age of Cicero downwards, which was paid to the keeper of the bath (*balneator*). Children below a certain age were admitted free (Juv. ii. 152).

The passage of Juvenal (vi. 447) which has been quoted to show that women paid no fee should be taken to imply that they paid a higher price than men. So by the Lex Metalli Vipascensis, which has been already referred to, the men pay half an *as*, the women an *as*. Faustus Sulla gave the people the use of the baths and oil on the day of his father's funeral, and Augustus on his return from Germany gave them baths and barbers for a day. Agrippa opened the baths gratuitously to both men and women for a year, and afterwards gave the people his Thermae. Such munificence was repeated by emperors and also by private individuals.

The baths were closed when any serious public misfortune happened, just as we should close our theatres; and Suetonius says that the emperor Caligula made it a capital offence to indulge in the luxury of bathing upon any religious holiday. They were originally placed under the superintendence of the aediles, whose business it was to keep them in repair, and to see that they were kept clean and of a proper temperature. In the provinces the same duty seems to have devolved upon the quaestor, as may be inferred from Aulus Gellius (x. 3).

The time usually assigned by the Romans for taking the bath was the eighth hour, or shortly afterwards (Mart. x. 48; xi. 52). Before that time none but invalids were allowed to bathe in public. Vitruvius reckons the hours best adapted for bathing to be from mid-day until about sunset. Spurinna took his bath at the ninth hour in summer and at the eighth in winter; and Martial speaks of taking a bath, when business had been pressing, at the tenth hour, and even later (iii. 36; x. 70).

When the water was ready and the baths prepared, notice was given by the sound of a bell—*aes thermarum* (Mart. xiv. 163). One of these bells, with the inscription *Firmi Balneatoris*, was found in the Thermae Diocletianae in the year 1548, and came into the possession of the learned Fulvius Ursinus (*Append. ad* Ciaccon. *De Triclin.*). A sundial was found in the new baths at Pompeii, and Lucian (*Hipp.* p. 8) places in the baths a sundial and a water-clock, with apparently some mechanism for striking the hours attached.

While the bath was used for health merely or cleanliness, a single one was considered sufficient at a time, and that only when requisite. But the luxuries of the Empire knew no such bounds, and the daily bath was sometimes repeated as many as seven and eight times in succession—the number which the emperor Commodus indulged himself with. Gordian bathed four or five times a day in summer and twice in winter; the emperor Gallienus six or seven times in summer and twice or thrice in winter. Commodus also took his meals in the bath—a custom which was not confined to a dissolute emperor alone.

It was the usual and constant habit of the Romans to take the bath after exercise, and previously to their principal meal (*cena*); but the debauchees of the Empire bathed after eating as well as before, in order to promote digestion, and so to acquire a new appetite for fresh delicacies. Nero is related to have indulged in this practice (Suet. *Nero*, p. 27; cf. Juv. i. 142). This practice of carrying off the effects of gluttony by artificial means of inducing perspiration, which had taken the place of the hard labour and exercise of sterner times, was severely condemned, and sometimes proved fatal. See CENA.

The Romans did not content themselves with a single bath of hot or cold water; but they went through a course of baths in succession, in which the agency of air as well as water was applied. It is difficult to ascertain the precise order in which the course was usually taken, if indeed there was any general practice beyond the whim of the individual. Under medical treatment the succession would, of course, be regulated by the nature of the disease for which a cure was sought, and would vary also according to the different practice of different physicians. It is certain, however, that it was a general custom to close the pores and brace the body after the excessive perspiration of the vapour bath either by anointing, or by pouring cold water over the head, or by plunging at once into the *piscina* or into a river (Auson. *Mosell.* 341). Musa, the physician of Augustus, is said to have introduced this practice (Plin. *H. N.* xxv. § 77; cf. Hor. *Epist.* i. 15, 4), which became quite the fashion, in consequence of the benefit which the emperor derived from it, though Dio Cass. (liii. 30) accuses Musa of having artfully caused the death of Marcellus by an improper application of the same treatment. In other cases it was considered conducive to health to pour warm water over the head before the vapour bath, and cold water immediately after it; and at other times warm, tepid, and cold water baths were taken in succession.

The two physicians Galen and Celsus differ in some respects as to the order in which the baths should be taken—the former recommending first the hot air of the *laconicum* (ἀέρι θερμῷ), next the bath of warm water (ὕδωρ θερμόν), afterwards the cold, and finally to be well rubbed (Galen. *de Methodo Medendi*, x. 10, pp. 708, 709, ed. Kühn); whilst the latter recommends his patients first to sweat for a short time in the tepid chamber (*tepidarium*), without undressing, then to proceed into the thermal chamber (*calidarium*), and after having gone through a regular course of perspiration there, not to descend into the warm bath (*solium*), but to pour a quantity of warm water over the head, then tepid, and finally cold, afterwards to be scraped with the strigil (*perfricari*), and finally rubbed dry and anointed (Cels. *de Med.* i. 4). Such, in all probability, was the usual habit of the Romans when the bath was resorted to as a daily source of pleasure, and not for any particular medical treatment; the more so as it resembles in many respects the system of bathing still practised among the Orientals, who, as Gell remarks, "succeeded by conquest to the luxuries of the enervated Greeks and Romans."

The principal ancient authorities on baths are: Vitruvius (v. 10); Lucian (Ἱππίας ἢ βαλανεῖον, a detailed description of a set of baths erected by an architect named Hippias); Pliny the Younger, in the two letters describing his villas; Statius, *Silv.* i. 5; Martial (vi. 42, and other epigrams); Seneca (*Epist.* 51, 56, 86), and Sidonius Apollinaris (*Epist.* ii. 2).

But it would be almost hopeless to attempt to arrange the information obtained from these writers were it not for the help afforded us by the extensive ruins of ancient baths—such as the Thermae of Titus, Caracalla, and Diocletian; the Thermae of Pompeii excavated in 1854–58; and numerous public and private baths throughout the whole extent of the Roman Empire, the most important of which are referred to in the list of authorities at the end of this article; but above all the public baths (*balneae*) of Pompeii, which were excavated in 1824–25. Before describing the details of the Roman public baths, attention may be called to the simpler baths used in private houses, although to a modern these seem extraordinarily elaborate in their arrangements.

The cut given on the preceding page is a ground-plan of the Roman baths at Badenweiler; and though less elaborate than the baths attached to some Pompeian private houses, it is interesting from its compactness and the arrangement of the women's and men's baths. A full account of them is given by Dr. Heinrich Leibnitz, *Die römischen Bäder bei Badenweiler* (Leipzig, 1860).

The so-called Old Baths, adjoining the Forum at Pompeii, afford an instance of a complete set of public baths so well preserved that in some of the chambers even the ceilings are intact. A ground-plan of these is given on the next page.

The whole building, which comprises a double set of baths, has six different entrances from the street, one of which, *b*, gives admission to the smaller set only, which are supposed to have been appropriated to the women, and five others to the male department, of which two, *c* and *c* 2, communicate directly with the furnaces, and the other three, *a* 3, *a* 2, *a*, with the bathing apartments, of which *a*, the nearest to the Forum, was the principal one; the other two, *a* 3 and *a* 2, being on different sides of the building, served for the convenience of those who lived on the north and east sides of the city. Passing through the principal entrance, *a*, which is removed from the street by a narrow footway surrounding the *insula* (the outer curb of which is marked upon the plan by the thin line drawn round it), and after descending three steps, the bather finds upon his left hand a small chamber, *x*, which contained a water-closet (*latrina*), and proceeds into a covered portico, *g g*, which ran round three sides of an open court—*atrium* (A)—which was 68 ft. long and 53 ft. broad; and these together formed the vestibule of the baths—*vestibulum balnearum* (Cic. *Pro Cael.* 26), in which the servants belonging to the establishment, as well as the attendants of the bathers, waited. There are seats for their accommodation placed underneath the portico (*g*, *g*). This *atrium* was the exercise ground for the young men, or perhaps served as a promenade for visitors to the baths. Within this court the keeper of the baths (*balneator*), who exacted

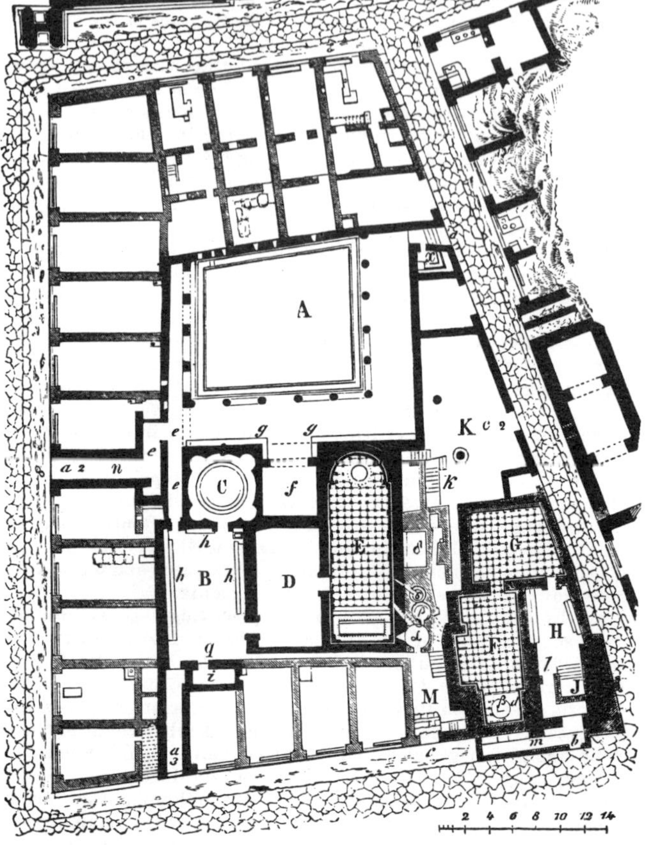

Plan of the Old Baths at Pompeii. (Overbeck.)

the *quadrans* paid by each visitor, was also stationed; and the box for holding the money was found in it. The room *f*, which runs back from the portico, might have been appropriated to him; but most probably it was an *oecus* or *exedra*, for the convenience of the better classes while awaiting the return of their acquaintances from the interior. In this court, likewise, as being the most public place, advertisements for the theatre, or other announcements of general interest, were posted up, one of which, announcing a gladiatorial show, still remains. At the two sides of the entrance to it were stone seats (*scholae*). *n* is the corridor which conducts from the entrance *a* 2 into the same vestibule; *o*, a small cell of similar use to the corresponding one in the opposite corridor, *d*; *e*, a passage of communication which leads into the chamber B, the *apodyterium*, a room for undressing; and which is also accessible from the street by the door *a* 3, through the corridor *p*, in which a small niche is observable, which probably served for the station of another *balneator*, who collected the money from those entering from the north street. In this room, which was 38 ft. long and 22 ft. broad, all the visitors must have met before entering the baths. The *apodyterium* probably belonged to the *frigidarium*, which in Pliny's villa it adjoined (Plin. *Epist.* v. 6, § 25); though in the great thermae at Rome the *frigidarium* and the *caldarium* had doubtless each a separate *apodyterium*. In the *apodyterium* the bathers removed their clothing, which was taken in charge by slaves known as *capsarii*, notorious in ancient times for their dishonesty (*Dig.* xlvii. 17).

The *apodyterium* was a spacious chamber, with stone seats along two sides of the wall (*h*, *h*). Holes are still visible on the walls, and probably mark the places where the pegs for the bathers' clothes were set. The chamber was lighted by a glass window, and had six doors. One of these doors led to the entrance *a* 2, one to the entrance *a* 3, one

Restoration of Apodyterium of Old Baths. (Overbeck.)

to the small room *i*, one to the furnaces, one to the *tepidarium* D, while the sixth opened upon the *frigidarium* C, with its cold plunge-bath (λουτρόν, *natatio, natatorium, piscina, baptisterium, puteus*).

The bath in this chamber is of white marble, and is 13 ft. 8 in. in diameter, and about 3 ft. 9 in. deep. It is approached by two marble steps, as shown in the following illustration.

From the *frigidarium* the bather who wished to go through the warm bath and sweating process entered the *tepidarium* D. This *tepidarium*, 33 ft. long by 18 ft. broad, did not contain water either at Pompeii or at the baths of Hippias, but was merely heated with warm air of an agreeable temperature,

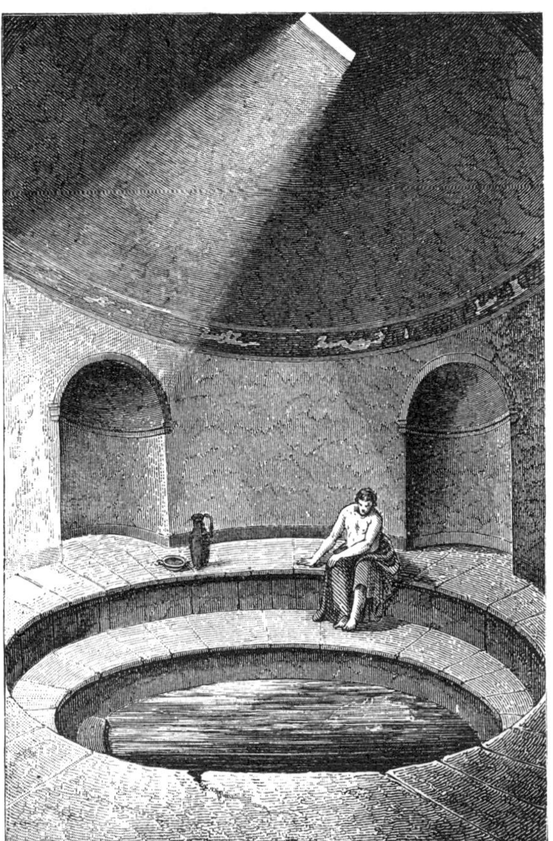

Frigidarium of the Old Baths at Pompeii. (Overbeck.)

in order to prepare the body for the great heat of the vapour and warm baths, and, upon returning, to obviate the danger of a too-sudden transition to the open air. In the baths at Pompeii this chamber served likewise as an *apodyterium* for those who took the warm bath; for which purpose the fittings-up are evidently adapted, the walls being divided into a number of separate compartments or recesses for receiving the garments when taken off by a series of figures of the kind called Atlantes (q. v.) or Telamones, which project from the walls and support a rich cornice above them. Three bronze benches were also found in the room, which was heated as well by its contiguity to the hypocaust of the adjoining chamber, as by a brazier of bronze (*foculus*), in which the charcoal ashes were still remaining when the excavation was made.

Brazier of the Old Baths at Pompeii.

Sitting and perspiring beside such a brazier was called *ad flammam sudare* (Suet. *Aug.* 82). A representation of it is given in the above illustration. Its whole length was 7 ft., and its breadth 2 ft. 6 in.

The *tepidarium* is generally the most highly ornamented room in baths. It was merely a room to sit in and be anointed in. In the Old Baths at Pompeii the floor is mosaic, the arched ceiling adorned with stucco and painting on a coloured ground, the walls red.

Anointing was performed by slaves called *unctores* and *aliptae* (q. v.). It sometimes took place before going to the hot bath, and sometimes after the cold bath, before putting on the clothes, in order to check the perspiration (Galen. x. 49). In some baths is a special room (*destrictarium* or *unctorium*) for this purpose. For an account of the various kinds of oils and scents used by the wealthy, see the fifteenth book of Athenaeus, the thirteenth book of the *Historia Naturalis* of Pliny, and cf. Suet. *Cal.* 37.

From the *tepidarium* a door opened into E, the *caldarium*, a chamber 53 ft. long and 17½ ft. wide. Its mosaic floor was directly above the furnace or hypocaust. Its walls also were hollow, forming a great flue filled with heated air. At one end was a round basin (*labrum*), and at the other a quadrangular bathing-place (πύελος, *alveus, solium, calida piscina*), approached from the platform (*schola*) by steps. The *alveus* was 16½ ft. long, 5½ ft. wide, and 2 ft. deep. The *labrum* was 7½ ft. in diameter and 8 in. deep, and was raised 3¼ ft. from the ground. It held cold water, for pouring upon the bather's head before he left the room. These basins are of marble in the Old Baths, but we hear of *alvei* of solid silver (Plin. *H. N.* xxxiii. § 152). Because of the great heat of the room, the *caldarium* was but slightly ornamented.

The Old Baths have no *laconicum*, which was a chamber still hotter than the *caldarium*, and used simply as a sweating-room, having no bath. It was said to have been introduced at Rome by Agrippa (Dio Cass. liii. 27), and was also called *sudatorium* and *assa*.

The *suspensurae*, or hanging-floors above the *hypocaustum*, are described in the following passage from Prof. Middleton's *Ancient Rome in 1885* (p. 334), from which the illustration on page 193 is taken:

"Vitruvius's description of the hypocausts, or hollow floors used for heating the hot rooms (*caldaria*), agrees closely with many existing examples. The lower floor was to be laid with 2 ft. tiles (*tegulae bipedales*) over a bed of concrete; on this, all over the area of the room, rows of short pillars (*pilae*) were built to support the upper or 'hanging floor' (*suspensura*). These *pilae* were to be 2 ft. high, made of *tegulae bessales*, or tiles 8 in. square, set, not in mortar, but with clay in the

Tepidarium. (Overbeck.)

joints. In existing examples these clay joints have been baked into brick by the action of the fire" (rather "hot air," for there was not a fire in the *hypocaustum*, but in the *hypocausis*). The passages from the furnace to the hypocaust and the flues in the walls appear to have been called *cuniculi* (Plin. *H. N.* ix. 134).

The *apodyterium* has a passage, *q*, communicating with the mouth of the furnace *r*, called *praefurnium* or *propigneum;* and, passing down that passage, we reach the chamber M, into which the *praefurnium* projects, and which is entered from the street at *c*. It was assigned to the *fornacatores*, or persons in charge of the fires. Of its two staircases, one leads to the roof of the baths, and one to the boilers containing the water. There were three boilers, one of which (*caldarium vas*) held the hot water; a second, the tepid (*tepidarium*); and the third, the cold (*frigidarium*). The warm water was turned into the warm bath by a pipe through the wall, marked on the plan. Underneath the hot chamber was set the circular furnace *d*, of more than 7 ft. in diameter, which heated the water and poured hot air into the hollow cells of the *hypocaustum*. It passed from the furnace under the first and last of the caldrons by two flues, which are marked upon the plan. The boiler containing hot water was placed immediately over the furnace; and, as the water was drawn out from thence, it was supplied from the next, the *tepidarium*, which was raised a little higher and stood a little way off from the furnace. It was already considerably heated from its contiguity to the furnace and the hypocaust below it, so that it supplied the deficiency of the former without materially diminishing its temperature; and the vacuum in this last was again filled up from the farthest removed, which contained the cold water received directly from the square reservoir seen behind them—a principle which has at length been introduced into the modern bathing establish-

Caldarium of the Old Baths. (Overbeck.)

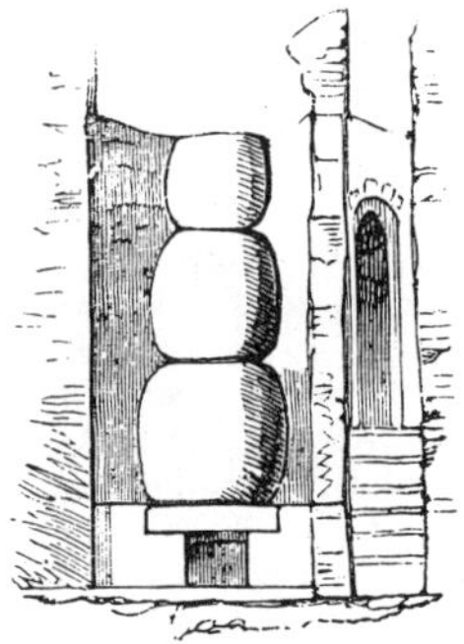
Boiler, *miliarium*. (From Pompeii.)

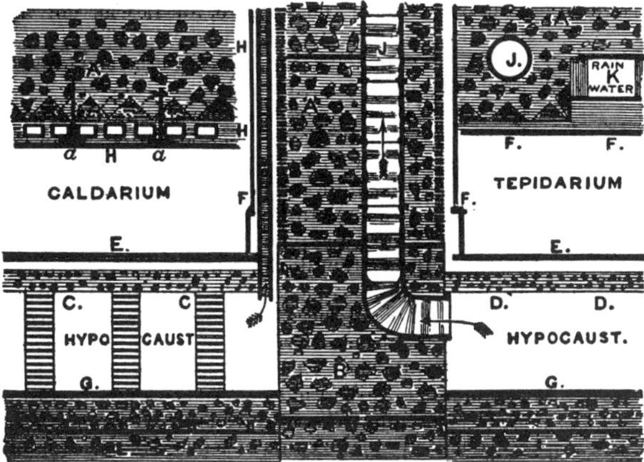

Method of Heating the Baths in the Thermae of Caracalla. (Middleton.)

AA. Concrete wall faced with brick.
B. Lower part of wall with no brick facing.
CC. Suspensura, or upper floor of hypocaust, supported by pillars.
DD. Another floor, with support only at the edges.
EE. Marble flooring.
FF. Marble plinth and wall lining.
GG. Under-floor of hypocaust, paved with large tiles.
HH. Horizontal and vertical sections of the flue tiles, which line the walls of the Caldarium.
aa. Iron holdfasts.
JJ. Socket-jointed flue-pipe of tepidarium.
K. Rain-water pipe.
LL. Vaults of crypt, made of pumice-stone concrete.

ments. The boilers themselves no longer remain, but the impressions which they have left in the mortar in which they were imbedded are clearly visible, and enable us to ascertain their respective positions and dimensions, the first of which, the *caldarium*, is represented on preceding page. Such coppers or boilers appear to have been called *miliaria*, from similarity of shape to a mile-stone (Pallad. i. 40; v. 8).

Behind the coppers there is another corridor leading into the court or *atrium* (K) appropriated to the servants of the bath, and which has also the convenience of an immediate communication with the street by the door at c 2.

We now proceed to the adjoining set of baths, which were assigned to the women. The entrance is by the door *b*, which conducts into a small vestibule, *m*, and thence into the *apodyterium* H, which, like the one in the men's bath, has a seat (*pulvinus, gradus*) on either side built up against the wall. This opens upon a cold bath, J, answering to the *natatio* of the other set, but of much smaller dimensions. There are four steps on the inside to descend into it. Opposite to the door of entrance into the *apodyterium* is another doorway which leads to the *tepidarium* H, which also communicates with the thermal chamber F, on one side of which is a warm bath in a square recess, and at the farther extremity the *labrum*. The floor of this chamber is suspended, and its walls perforated for flues, like the corresponding one in the men's baths. It is to be especially noticed that the *tepidarium* in the women's baths had no brazier, but had a hanging or suspended floor.

After having gone through the regular course of perspiration, the Romans made use of instruments called *strigiles* to scrape off the perspiration, much in the same way as we are accustomed to scrape the sweat off a horse with a piece of iron hoop, after he has run a heat, or comes in from violent exercise. The strigil was also used by the Greeks, who called it *στλεγγίς* or *ξύστρα*. These instruments, many of which have been discovered among the ruins of the various baths of antiquity, were made of bone, bronze, iron, and silver; all corresponding in form with the epithet of Martial, "*curvo distringere ferro*" (xiv. 51). The poorer classes were obliged to scrape themselves, but the more wealthy took their slaves to the baths for the purpose—a fact which is elucidated by a curious story related by Spartianus (*Hadr.* 17).

The strigil was by no means a blunt instrument, consequently its edge was softened by the application of oil that was dropped upon it from a small vessel called *guttus*, which had a narrow neck, so as to discharge its contents drop by drop, from whence the name is taken. A representation of a *guttus* is given on the following page. Augustus is related to have suffered from an over-violent use of the strigil (Suet. *Aug.* 80). Invalids and persons of a delicate habit made use of sponges, which Pliny says answered for towels as well as strigils, They were finally dried with towels (*lintea*) and anointed (Juv. iii. 262; Plin. *H. N.* xxxi. § 125 foll.).

The common people were supplied with these necessaries in the baths—*omnia commoda praestan-*

Women's Bath. (Pompeii.)

tur—as we saw above; but the more wealthy carried their own with them (Pers. v. 126).

After the operation of scraping and rubbing dry, they retired into, or remained in, the *tepidarium*

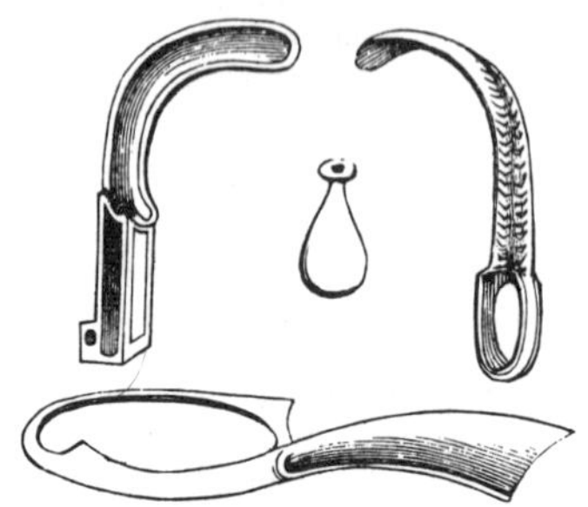

Strigils with Guttus. (Found in Roman Baths.)

until they thought it prudent to encounter the open air. But it does not appear to have been customary to bathe in the water, when there was any, either of the *tepidarium* or the *frigidarium;* the temperature only of the atmosphere in these two chambers being of consequence to break the sudden change from the extreme of heat to cold.

Notwithstanding the ample account which has been given of the plans and usages respecting baths in general, something yet remains to be said about that particular class known as *thermae,* of which establishments the baths, in fact, constituted the smallest part. The thermae, properly speaking, were a Roman adaptation of the Greek gymnasium, or *palaestra* (see PALAESTRA), as described by Vitruvius; both of which contained a system of baths in conjunction with conveniences for athletic games and youthful sports, *exedrae* in which the rhetoricians declaimed, poets recited, and philosophers lectured, as well as porticoes and vestibules for the idle, and libraries for the learned. They were decorated with the finest objects of art, both in painting and sculpture, covered with precious marbles, and adorned with fountains and shaded walks and plantations, like the groves of the Academy, and served at Rome all the purposes of a modern club. It may be said that they began and ended with the Empire, for it was not until the time of Augustus that these magnificent structures were commenced. M. Agrippa is the first who afforded these luxuries to his countrymen by bequeathing to them the thermae and gardens which he had erected in the Campus Martius. The Pantheon (q.v.), now existing at Rome, served originally as a vestibule to these baths; and, as it was considered too magnificent for the purpose, it is supposed that Agrippa added the portico and consecrated it as a temple, for which use it still serves. It appears from a passage in Sidonius Apollinaris that the whole of these buildings, together with the adjacent Thermae Neronianae, remained entire in the year A.D. 466. Little is now left beyond a few fragments of ruins and the Pantheon. The example set by Agrippa was followed by Nero, and afterwards by Titus, the ruins of whose thermae are still visible, covering a vast extent, partly underground and partly above the Esquiline Hill. Thermae were also erected by Trajan, Caracalla, and Diocletian, of the last two of which ample remains still exist; and even as late as Constantine, besides several which were constructed by private individuals, P. Victor enumerates sixteen.

Previously to the erection of these establishments for the use of the population, it was customary for those who sought the favour of the people to give them a day's bathing free of expense. Thus, according to Dio Cassius, Faustus, the son of Sulla, furnished warm baths and oil gratis to the people for one day; and Augustus, on one occasion, furnished warm baths and barbers to the people for the same period gratuitously, and at another time for a whole year to the women as well as the men. From thence it is fair to infer that the *quadrans* paid for admission into the *balneae* was not exacted at the thermae, which, as being the works of the emperors, would naturally be opened with imperial generosity to all, and without any charge, otherwise the whole city would have thronged to the establishment bequeathed to them by Agrippa; and in confirmation of this opinion it may be remarked that the old establishments, which were probably erected by private enterprise, were termed *meritoriae.* Most, if not all, of the other regulations previously de-

Chief Hall of the Thermae of Caracalla. (Restoration by Reber.)

tailed as relating to the economy of the baths apply equally to the *thermae;* but it is to these establishments especially that the dissolute conduct of the emperors, and other luxurious indulgences of the people in general, detailed in the compositions of the satirists and later writers, must be considered to refer.

The student is cautioned against an illustration found in all the older dictionaries. It is styled a "Representation of a Roman Bath," and is said to be from the Thermae of Titus at Rome. It is, in fact, a drawing made in 1553 by Giovanni Antonio Rasconi, an Italian architect, to illustrate a treatise by Johannes Antonius Siccus Cremensis, and was drawn after the description of the baths in Vitruvius. In that treatise it is styled simply "Figura Antiqui Balinei," but it was put forth by one P. A. Maffei in 1704 as a picture of the "Baths of Titus." Thence it got into many other works, and received, unfortunately, a general acceptance, though containing several important errors. See Marquardt, *Privatleben der Römer*, pp. 270, 271.

BIBLIOGRAPHY.—On the subject of the ancient baths the reader is referred to Baccius, *De Thermis Veterum* (Graevius, *Thes.* xii. 279–379); Ferrarius, *De Balneis* (Polneus, *Thes.* iii. 297–310); Montfaucon, *Antiq. Expl.* iii. 201–212; Palladio, *Le Terme dei Romani*, ed. Scamozzi; Cameron, *The Baths of the Romans;* Stieglitz, *Archäologie der Baukunst*, iii. 241–276; Hirt, *Geschichte der Baukunst*, iii. 233–236; Canina, *L'Architettura Antica* (2d ed. 1844); Bussemaker and Daremberg, *Œuvres d'Oribase*, ii. 865–875; Bechi in *Mus. Borbonico*, ii. 49–52; Gell, *Pompeiana*, chaps. vi., vii. (1837); Saglio, *Dict. des Antiquités*, i. 648–664; Guhl and Koner, *Das Leben der Griechen und Römer* (1876); Overbeck, *Pompeii* (4th ed. 1884); Nissen, *Pompeianische Studien*, chaps. v., vi., vii.; Becker's *Gallus*, ed. Göll, iii. 104–157; Marquardt, *Privatleben der Römer*, i. 262–288; Lanciani, *Ancient Rome in the Light of Recent Discoveries* (1888); Middleton, *Ancient Rome in 1885* (1885); and id. *Remains of Ancient Rome* (1892).

Balteus (in the plural, *baltea*). A belt (in Gk. *τελαμών*), and sometimes a woman's girdle. (1) A shoulder-belt, and oftenest a sword-belt. Among the Greeks, as the sword usually hung by the left hip, its belt was supported by the right shoulder, passing obliquely over the breast, as shown in the cameo here given from the Florentine Museum.

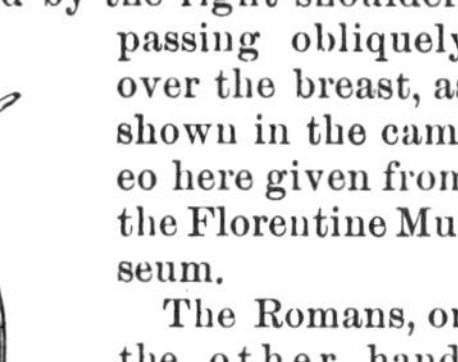

The Romans, on the other hand, usually wore the *balteus* over the left shoulder, though not always. (See Caes. *B. G.* v. 44.) Shield-belts among the Greeks were worn in the reverse order from the sword-belt, the two crossing over the breast.

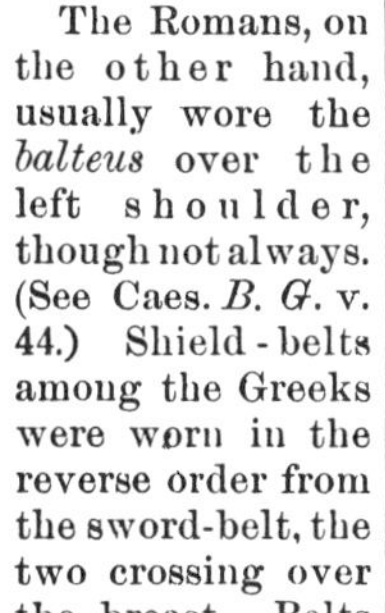

Balteus. (Florentine Museum.)

Belts were generally made of leather, sometimes ornamented with silver and gold. They were often employed also to support the quiver. The belts of the Roman emperors were so magnificent that a special officer (*baltearius*) had charge of them. See CINGULUM; PHARETRA.

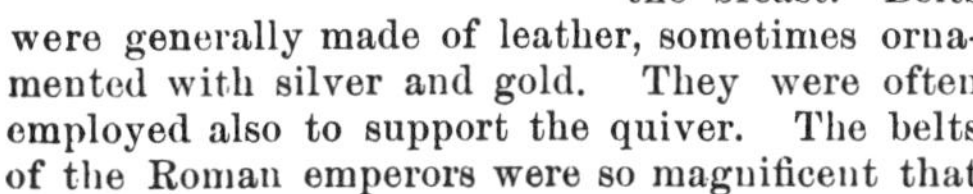

Belt of Homeric Warrior.

(2) A belt or collar passing round a horse's neck and breast, partly for protection, and partly for ornament. It was often decorated with embossed work, and sometimes carried bells. See PHALERA; TINTINNABULUM.

(3) The belt on the celestial globe representing the sun's course and bearing the signs of the zodiac (Manilius, i. 679).

(4) The *praecinctio* (*διάζωμα*) of the theatre. See THEATRUM.

(5) In architecture (Ionic), an ornamental band which encircles the *pulvinus*, or bolster of the capital (Vitruv. iii. 5, 7).

Bandusiae Fons. A fountain in Apulia some six miles from Venusia, and made famous by Horace in his ode (iii. 13) beginning

"O fons Bandusiae, splendidior vitro!"

Banishment. See DEPORTATIO; EXSILIUM; OSTRACISMUS; PHYGÉ; RELEGATIO.

Banks, Bankers, and Banking. See TRAPEZITAE.

Bantia. The modern Banzi; a town in Apulia near Venusia. Here was found the famous bronze tablet known as the TABULA BANTINA (q. v.), containing an important fragment of the Oscan language. See OSCI.

Baptae (*Βαπταί*). (1) A name given to the priests of Cotytto, the Greek goddess of lewdness, and derived by some from *βάπτω*, "to tinge" or "dye," from their painting their cheeks and blackening their eyelids. See COTYTTO. (2) A comedy of Eupolis (q. v.) in which he assailed the effeminacy and debauchery of his countrymen.

Baptisterium (*βαπτιστήριον*). A large basin into which bathers could plunge or even swim about (Plin. *Epist.* ii. 17, 11). It is more commonly called *natatorium* or *piscina.* See BALNEAE.

Baptisterium. (Pompeii.)

Barăthron (*βάραθρον*). A deep pit at Athens into which criminals and the dead bodies of executed criminals were cast. See Xen. *Hellen*, i. 7, 20; and the article CAEDES.

Barba. I. Greek (πώγων, γένειον, ὑπήνη).—Of these, γένειον, properly "chin," is the earliest word. Μύσταξ is the moustache; πάππος the hair on the nether lip; χνόος or ἴουλος the first down. Ὑπήνη is sometimes restricted to the hair about the upper and lower lips—that is, to the μύσταξ and the πάππος combined; γένειον to the beard proper, the hair on the chin. There is no special word for the whiskers.

Pericles, showing Greek Beard.

The Greeks regarded the beard as a badge of virility which it was a disgrace to be without; and in the Homeric time it had even a sanctity as among the Jews, so that a common form of entreaty was to touch the beard of the person addressed. It was only shaven as a sign of mourning, though in this case it was instead often left untrimmed. A smooth face was regarded as a sign of effeminacy (Athen. xiii. 565 a). The Spartans punished cowards by shaving off a portion of their beards. From the earliest times, however, the shaving of the upper lip was not uncommon.

In the time of Alexander the Great the custom of smooth shaving was introduced (Chrysippus *ap.* Athen. xiii. 565 a), and spread from the Macedonians, whose kings are represented on coins, etc.,

Coin of Alexander the Great.

with smooth faces, throughout the whole Greek world. Laws were passed against it, without effect, at Rhodes and Byzantium; and even Aristotle, we are told, conformed to the new custom (Diog. Laërt. v. 1), unlike the other philosophers, who retained the beard as a badge of their profession. A "man with a beard" (πωγωνοτρόφος) after the Macedonian period implies a philosopher (cf. Pers. iv. 1, *magister barbatus* of Socrates), and we have many allusions to this custom of the later philosophers in such proverbs as "the beard does not make the sage" (πωγωνοτροφία φιλόσοφον οὐ ποιεῖ, Plut. *De Is. et Osir.* 3).

II. Roman.—The Romans in early times wore the beard uncut, as we learn from the insult offered by the Gaul to M. Papirius (Liv. v. 41), and from Cicero (*Pro Cael.* 14); and, according to Varro and Pliny, the Roman beards were not shaven till B.C. 300, when P. Ticinius Menas brought over a barber from Sicily; and Pliny adds that the first Roman who was shaved (*rasus*) every day was Scipio Africanus. (Cf. Gell. iii. 4.) His custom, however, was soon followed, and shaving became a regular thing. The lower orders, then as now, were not always able to do the same, and hence the jeers of Martial (vii. 95; xii. 59). In the later times of the Republic there were many *iuvenes* who shaved the beard only partially, and trimmed it, so as to give it an ornamental form; to them the terms *bene barbati* and *barbatuli* are applied. We hear of young men oiling their chins to force a premature growth of beard (Petron. 75, 10).

In a general way, in Rome at this time, a long beard (*barba promissa*) was considered a mark of slovenliness and squalor. The censors L. Veturius and P. Licinius compelled M. Livius, who had been banished, on his restoration to the city to be shaved, and to lay aside his dirty appearance, and then, but not till then, to come into the Senate (Liv. xxvii. 34). The first time of shaving was regarded as the beginning of manhood, and the day on which this took place was celebrated as a festival (Juv. iii. 186). There was no particular time fixed for this to be done. Usually, however, it was when the young Roman assumed the *toga virilis.* Augustus did it in his twenty-fourth year, Caligula in his twentieth. The hair cut off on such occasions was consecrated to some god. Thus Nero put his into a golden box set with pearls, and dedicated it to Iupiter Capitolinus (Suet. *Ner.* 12).

Aureus of Augustus Caesar.

With the emperor Hadrian the beard began to revive. Plutarch says that this emperor wore it to hide some scars on his face. The practice afterwards became common, and till the time of Constantine the Great the emperors appear in busts and coins with beards; but Constantine and his successors to the end of the sixth century, with the exception of Julian, are represented as beardless. The contrast between the custom of the early emperors and those of Hadrian and his successors as to the beard is seen in the accompanying heads. The Romans, unlike the Greeks, let their beards grow in time of mourning; so did Augustus for the death of Iulius Caesar, and the time when he had it shaved off he made a season of festivity (Dio Cass. xlviii. 34). Other occasions of mourning on which the beard was allowed to grow were, appearance as a *reus,* condemnation, or some public calamity. For an account of barbers, see Tonsor.

Pertinax.

Barbări. Βάρβαροι was originally the Greek epithet for a people speaking any language but Greek. Its origin is onomatopoetic, since it is an attempt to imitate the confused sounds of a foreign language. It was not until after the Persian Wars that the name began to carry with it associations of hatred and contempt, and to imply vulgarity and want of cultivation. The national feeling of the Greeks had then risen to such intensity that they deemed themselves above all other peoples in gifts and culture, and looked down upon them with a sense of superiority.

The Romans were originally, like other non-Hellenic peoples, included by the Greeks under the name of *barbari*. But after the conquest of Greece, and the transference of Hellenic art and culture to Rome, the Romans took up the same position as the Greeks before them, and designated as barbarians all the nations who differed in language and manners from the Graeco-Roman world.

Barbarĭcus Sinus. A gulf on the eastern coast of Africa below the mouth of the Sinus Arabicus.

Barbers. See TONSOR.

Barbĭtos (*βάρβιτος*). See LYRA.

Barca (Βάρκη). Now Merjeh. The second city of Cyrenaica, in Northern Africa, 100 stadia from the sea. It appears to have been at first a settlement of a Libyan tribe, the Barraci, but about B.C. 560 was colonized by the Greek seceders from Cyrenē, and became so powerful as to make the western part of Cyrenaica virtually independent of the mother city. In B.C. 510 it was taken by the Persians, who removed most of its inhabitants to Bactria; and under the Ptolemies its ruin was completed by the erection of its port into a new city, which was named Ptolemaïs.

Barca or **Barcas** (Βάρκας). A Punic word meaning "lightning" or "gleaming," like the Hebrew *barak*, with which it is related. It is found as a sort of *agnomen* applied to the names of distinguished warriors. See HAMILCAR.

Barcĭno (Βαρκινών). Now Barcelona. A town of the Laletani in Hispania Tarraconensis, with an excellent harbour.

Bardi. A celebrated poetico-sacerdotal order among the ancient Gauls, who roused their countrymen to martial fury by their strains, and for this purpose were accustomed to follow the camp. From the language of Tacitus (*Germ.* 3), some have supposed that a similar order existed among the ancient Germans. The passage in question, however, involves a doubtful reading. They who adopt *barditus* as the true lection make it signify "a bard's song." The reading frequently adopted, however, is *barritus*, "a war-cry." Probability, nevertheless, is somewhat in favour of the Germans having also had their bards.

Bardocucullus. See CUCULLUS.

Barea. See SORANUS.

Bargusii. A people in the northeast of Spain, between the Pyrenees and the Iberus (Livy, xxi. 19).

Baris (*βᾶρις*). (1) A boat used on the Nile to transport merchandise, etc., across the river. It

Baris. (Rawlinson.)

is described in Herod. ii. 96. (2) In the Septuagint, the word denotes a tower or palace (Ps. xliv. 9).

Barium. A town of Apulia, on the Adriatic, noted for its fisheries, whence Horace calls it "fishy Barium" (*Sat.* i. 5, 97). It is now Bari.

Barsĭnē (Βαρσίνη). A daughter of Darius Codomannus, who married Alexander the Great, B.C. 324, and had by him a son named Heracles. She was secretly put to death by Cassander, along with her son, when the latter had reached his fourteenth year (Justin, xv. 2). According, however, to Diodorus Siculus (xx. 28), he was slain by Polysperchon, who had agreed with Cassander that he would commit the deed. Plutarch says that Polysperchon promised to slay him for 100 talents. We have followed Arrian (vii. 1) in making Barsinē the daughter of Darius. According to Plutarch (*Vit. Alex.*) she was the daughter of Artabazus; while another authority makes her father to have been named Pharnabazus. It is therefore said by some that two women of the same name are referred to—one a Greek and one a Persian, and both married to Alexander.

Basanistae (*βασανισταί*). See TORMENTUM.

Basănos (*βάσανος*). See TORMENTUM.

Bascania (*βασκανία*). See FASCINUM.

Bascauda. A word borrowed, like the English *basket*, from the ancient British language (Welsh, *basged*) and mentioned by Martial (xiv. 99) as imported from Britain. The original form of basket appears to have been imitated in silver (Juv. xii. 46).

Basilēia (*βασίλεια*). A festival with games, open to all Greeks, held at Lebadea in Boeotia, in honour of Zeus Basileus. See Diod. xv. 53.

Basĭleus (*βασιλεύς*). See ARCHON; MAGISTER BIBENDI; REX.

Basilia. (1) An island, famous for its amber, in the Northern Ocean. Modern writers have supposed that it is in reality to be identified with the southern extremity of Sweden, and mistaken by the ancients for an island. (2) A city on the Rhenus (Rhine), now Bâle, and in the Middle Ages known as Basula.

Basilĭca (*τὰ βασιλικά*). The Greek code of Roman law, commenced about A.D. 876 by the emperor Basil I., and finished by his son, Leo the Philosopher, who reigned A.D. 886–911. It comprised the Institutes, Pandects, Code, the Novellae, and the imperial Constitutions subsequent to the time of Justinian. It is in sixty books, subdivided into titles. The publication of this authorized body of law in Greek led to the gradual disuse of the original compilations of Justinian in the East; but by its means the Roman law was so firmly established in Eastern Europe and Western Asia as to maintain its hold there among the Greek populations to the present day. See Rudorff, *Röm. Rechtsgeschichte* (Leipzig, 1876), and the article IUSTINIANUS. The best modern edition of the *Basilica* is that of Heimbach, 6 vols. (Leipzig, 1833–70).

Basilĭca (*στοὰ βασιλική*; the pure Latin word being *regia*, sc. *aula*). A state building, used by the Romans as a hall of justice and a public meeting-place. The earliest basilica built at Rome was called the *Basilica Porcia*, after the famous M. Porcius Cato Censorius, who built it in B.C. 184, probably on the model of the *στοὰ βασίλειος* ("royal colonnade") at Athens. It stood in the Forum near the Curia. The later basilicas usually bore the name of the persons who built them. Buildings of the same kind were constantly erected in the provinces to serve as halls of exchange or courts of justice. The form of the basilica was oblong; the interior was a hall, either without any divisions or divided by rows of pillars, with a main nave, and two, or sometimes four, side-aisles. Galleries for spectators were often added above. If the basilica was used as a hall of justice, a space (usually in the form of a large semicircular niche, and containing a tribunal) was set up at the end of the nave for the accommodation of the court.

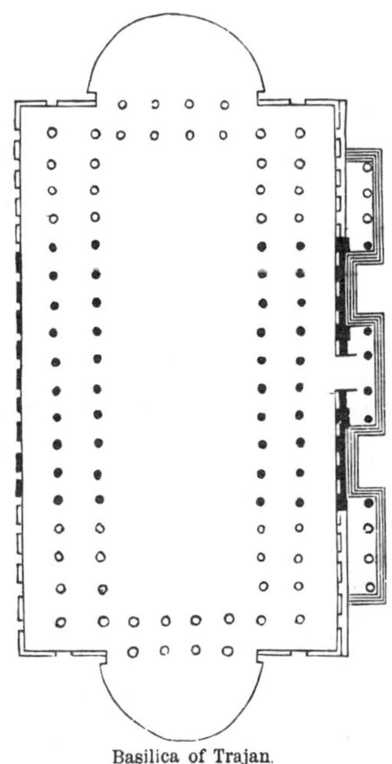

Basilica of Trajan.

After the time of Constantine the Great, of whose great basilica, with its nave and two aisles, magnificent ruins still remain, many basilicas were turned into Christian churches, and many churches were built upon the same plan.

Besides the *Basilica Porcia* already mentioned as having been the earliest Roman structure of the kind, there were at Rome fully twenty others erected at different periods, of which the following are most frequently mentioned by ancient authors: (1) *Basilica Sempronia*, constructed by Titus Sempronius, B.C. 171, and supposed to have been between the Vicus Tuscus and the Velabrum. (2) *Basilica Opimia*, which was above the Comitium. (3) *Basilica Pauli Aemilii*, or *Basilica Aemilia*, called also *Regia Pauli* by Statius. Cicero mentions two basilicas of this name, of which one was built, and the other only restored, by Paulus Aemilius. Both these edifices were in the Forum, and one was celebrated for its open peristyle of Phrygian columns, which Plutarch (*Vit. Caes.*) states was erected by L. Aemilius Paulus during his consulship, at an expense of 1500 talents, sent to him by Caesar from Gaul, as a bribe to gain him over from the aristocratical party. (4) *Basilica Pompeii*, called also *regia*, near the theatre of Pompey. (5) *Basilica Iulia*, erected by Iulius Caesar, in the Forum, and opposite to the Basilica Aemilia. It was from the roof of this building that Caligula scattered money among the people for several successive days. (6) *Basilica Flavia*, of the form on which the Christian churches were modelled. (7) *Basilica Ulpia* or *Traiani*, in the Forum of Trajan. (8) *Basilica Constantini*, erected by the emperor Constantine, supposed to be the ruin now remaining on the Via Sacra, near the Temple of Rome and Venus, and commonly called the Temple of Peace. Of all these magnificent edifices nothing now remains beyond the ground plan, and the bases and some portion of the columns and superstructure of several. The basilica at Pompeii is in better preservation; the external walls, ranges of columns, and tribunal of the judges being still tolerably perfect on the ground floor. See the illustration on page 199.

The Forum, or, where there was more than one, the one which was in the most frequented and central part of the city, was always selected for the site of a basilica; and hence it is that the classic writers not infrequently use the terms *forum* and *basilica* synonymously. See FORUM.

Basilīdes (Βασιλείδης). The father of Herodotus (q. v.).

Basilinda (*βασιλίνδα*). A children's game played by both Greeks and Romans, and practically identical with our game of "follow your leader." See Herod. i. 114; Suet. *Nero*, 35; Horace, *Epist.* i. 1. 59.

The Basilica at Trèves.

Basiliscus (*βασιλίσκος*). The basilisk, sometimes called *cockatrice*, from the vulgar belief in modern times that it is produced from the egg of a cock. Nicander describes it as having a small body, about three palms long, and of a shining colour. All the ancient authors speak with horror of the poison of the basilisk, which they affirm to be of so deadly a nature as to prove fatal, not only when introduced into a wound, but also when transmitted through another object. Avicenna relates the case of a soldier to whom, having transfixed a basilisk with a spear, its venom proved

Remains of the Basilica at Pompeii. (Overbeck.)

fatal, and also to his horse, whose lip was accidentally wounded by it. Linnaeus refers this creature, as mentioned by the ancients, to the *lacerta iguana*. Calmet supposes the Scriptural basilisk to be the same with the *cobra di capello*, but this is not found in Africa. The serpent which is described under the name of *buskah* answers very well in most respects to the ancient descriptions of the basilisk.

Basilīum (*βασίλειον*). A tall head-dress peculiar to the kings of Egypt and to the Egyptian goddess Isis (q. v.). See Plut. *De Is. et Osir.* 19.

Basilius (Βασίλειος). (1) A Christian writer, surnamed the Great, of Caesarea in Cappadocia. He was born of a noble family in A.D. 329, was educated in rhetoric at Constantinople and Athens by Libanius and Himerius, and subsequently took up the profession of advocate. But it was not long before he dedicated himself to the service of the Church. He distinguished himself especially by his resistance to Arianism and the measures he adopted for regulating the monastic system. He died, the bishop of his native city, in A.D. 379. He composed a revised liturgy still in use in the East, and known as the "Liturgy of the Holy Basil." Besides his writings on points of doctrine, we have an address by him to young men on the uses of Greek literature, the study of which he earnestly recommended, in opposition to the prej-

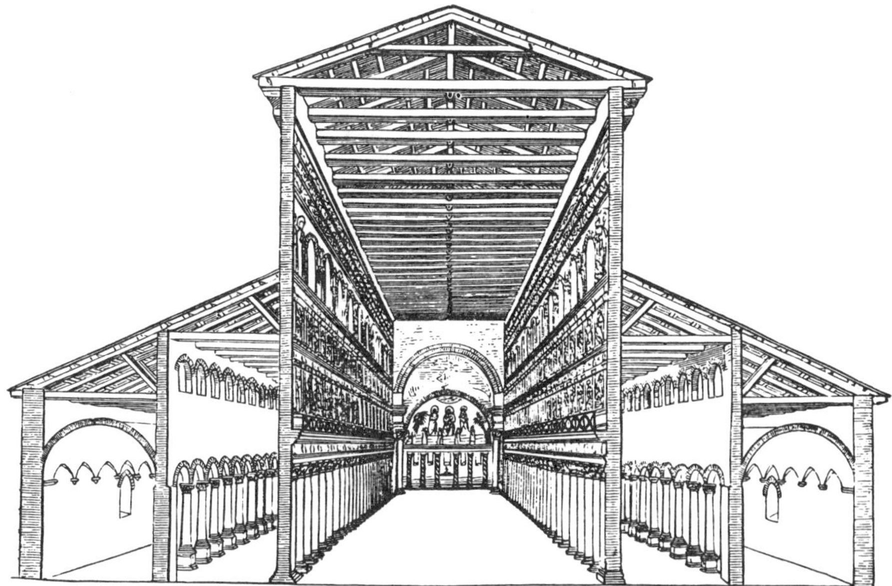

Basilica of St. Peter, erected in the time of Constantine.

udices of many Christians. He has also left a collection of four hundred letters, which are models in their way. Among them are those addressed to Libanius, his pagan instructor. A standard edition of his works is that of the Abbé Migne in 4 vols. (29–32) of his *Patrologia Graeco-Latina* (Paris, 1866). The Greek Church celebrates the day of his death (January 1st), the Roman Church that of his ordination (June 14th). (2) The name of several of the Byzantine emperors. See BYZANTINUM IMPERIUM.

Bassae. See PHIGALIA.

Bassăra, Bassăris (*βασσάρα, κασσάρα*). Originally a name given to the fox, and probably Egyptian in its origin, since in the hieroglyphs the fox is called *wasar* (Coptic *basor*); and Egyptian priests are found represented as wearing what appear to be fox-skins. (See Lepsius, *Denkmäler*, ii. 112, 128.) In Lydia and Thrace the word is applied to the dress of the Bacchanals (Bassarides), which is described as variegated and reaching to the feet. The Lydian Dionysus is hence styled Bassareus, but there is no genuine Hellenic conception of a fox in connection with Dionysus. See Roscher, *Ausführl. Lexikon der griech. und röm. Mythologie*, s. h. v.

Bassus, AUFIDIUS. A Roman historian of the time of Tiberius, who treated of the expiration of the Republic and the founding of the Empire. Quintilian (x. 1. 103) speaks of his *libri belli Germanici*, which may, however, have been a part of the other work. His narrative was continued by Pliny the Elder, and appears to have been used by Dio Cassius and Suetonius. Quotations from it are to be found in Seneca, *Suasoriae*, vi. 18 and 23. See H. Peter, *Hist. Fragm.* 308.

Bastarnae. A people who first inhabited that part of European Sarmatia which corresponds with a part of Poland and Prussia, and who afterwards established themselves in the south, to the left and right of the Tyras (Liv. xl. 58).

Basterna. A kind of litter or palanquin, used by Roman women, resembling the *lectica* (q. v.). The driver was called *basternarius*. See Ginzrot,

Basterna.

Die Wagen der Alten, from which the accompanying illustration is taken.

Batāvi. An old German nation, which inhabited a part of the present Holland, especially the island called Batavorum Insula (modern *Betuwe*), formed by that branch of the Rhine which empties into the sea near Lugdunum Batavorum (Leyden), together with the Vahalis (Waal) and Mosa (Maas). Their territories, however, extended much beyond the Waal. Tacitus commends their bravery. According to him they were originally the same as the Catti (q. v.), a German tribe, which had emigrated from their country on account of domestic troubles. This must have happened before the time of Caesar. When Germanicus was about to invade Germany from the sea he made their island the rendezvous of his fleet. Being subjugated by the Romans, they served them with such courage and fidelity as to obtain the title of friends and brethren. They were exempted from tributes and taxes, and permitted to choose their leaders among themselves. Their cavalry was particularly excellent. During the reign of Vespasian they revolted, under the command of Civilis, from the Romans, and extorted from them favourable terms of peace. Trajan and Hadrian subjugated them again. At the end of the third century the Salian Franks obtained possession of the Insula Batavorum. The capital of the nation was Lugdunum Batavorum, now Leyden (Tac. *Hist.* iv. 12; xix. 32).

Baths and Bathing. See BALNEAE.

Bathȳcles (Βαθυκλῆς). A celebrated artist, supposed to have been a native of Magnesia on the Maeander. The period when he flourished has given rise to much discussion. It was probably in the age of Croesus (Pausan. iii. 191).

Bathyllus (Βάθυλλος). (1) A young Samian, the favourite of Polycrates (q. v.), and alluded to by Anacreon. (2) An Alexandrian youth, the favourite of Maecenas, and noted for his graceful dancing in the pantomimes (Juv. vi. 63).

Batillum or **Vatillum.** An iron shovel with a short handle used for various purposes, especially as a fire-shovel, chafing-dish, and for burning incense. See Horace, *Sat.* i. 5. 36.

Batillum. (From an original in bronze found at Pompeii.)

Batrachomyomachia (Βατραχομυομαχία). The Battle of the Frogs and the Mice. The title of an epic poem, falsely bearing the name of Homer. It was a parody of the *Iliad*, and was probably written by Pigres (q. v.). (See HOMERUS.) It consists of 294 hexameters, and has been edited by Ernesti in his edition of Homer (Leipzig, 1759; reprinted at Glasgow, 1814); Matthiae (Leipzig, 1805); and Mitzschke (Berlin, 1874).

Battering-Ram. See ARIES.

Battiădae (Βαττίαδαι). Kings of Cyrené during eight generations. (1) BATTUS I., of Thera, led a colony to Africa at the command of the Delphic oracle, and founded Cyrené about B.C. 631. (2) ARCESILAÜS I., son of the preceding, reigned B.C. 599–583. (3) BATTUS II., surnamed "the Happy," son of the preceding, reigned 583–560 (?) (4) ARCESILAÜS II., son of the preceding, surnamed "the Oppressive," reigned about 560–550. His brothers withdrew from Cyrené, and founded Barca. (5) BATTUS III., or "the Lame," son of the preceding, reigned about 550–530, in which period Demonax, a Mantinean, with the aid of the people, gave a new constitution to the city, whereby the royal power was reduced within very narrow limits. (6) ARCESILAÜS III., son of the preceding, reigned about 530–514. (7) BATTUS IV., of whose life we have no accounts. (8) ARCESILAÜS IV., at whose death, about 450, a popular government was established. See CYRENÉ.

Battiădes (Βαττιάδης). A patronymic of Callimachus (q. v.) from his father Battus. The name is also applied to (1) the people of Cyrené, a place founded by Battus, and (2) to the kings of Cyrené. See CYRENÉ.

Battus (Βάττος). (1) A Lacedaemonian who, in

B.C. 631, built the town of Cyrené with a colony from the island of Thera. His proper name was Aristoteles, but he received the name of Battus from his having an impediment in his speech (βατταρίζω = to stutter), though Herodotus (iv. 155) says that βάττος is a derivative from a Libyan dialect, and means "king." He reigned over Cyrené for about thirty years, and was succeeded by his son Arcesilaüs. See BATTIADAE; CYRENÉ. (2) A shepherd of Pylos, who promised Hermes that he would not expose his theft of the flocks of Admetus, which were in charge of Apollo. Having broken his promise, he was turned into a stone (Ovid, *Met.* ii. 702).

Baucălis (βαύκαλις). A large wine-cooler, made usually of earthenware. See Athenaeus, xi. 784 c.

Baucĭdes (βαυκίδης). A kind of costly shoe of saffron colour worn by women (Poll. vii. 99.)

Baucis (Βαυκίς). See PHILEMON.

Bauli. A collection of villas between Misenum and Baiae in Campania.

Bavius. A dull poet who, with Mevius, attacked Vergil, Horace, and other Augustan writers. See Verg. *Ecl.* iii. 90; v. 36; Horace, *Epod.* x. 1; and the article VERGILIUS.

Baxeae or **Baxae.** Sandals made of leaves, twigs, or fibre, and worn by comic actors, while the *cothurnus* was peculiar to the tragic stage (Isidor. *Orig.* xix. 33). Philosophers also wore sandals of this description, at least in later times. Of the two *baxeae* shown in the accompanying illustration, the upper one was worn on the right foot. It has a loop on the right side for fastening the band which went across the instep. This band, together with the ligature connected with it,

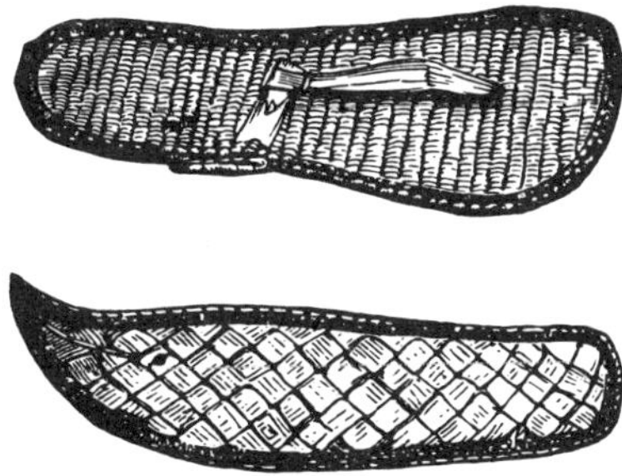

Baxeae. (British Museum.)

which was inserted between the great and the second toe, is made of the stem of the papyrus, undivided and unwrought. The lower figure shows a sandal in which the portions of the palm-leaf are interlaced with great neatness and regularity, the sewing and binding being effected by fibres of papyrus. The three holes may be observed for the passage of the band and the ligature already mentioned.

Beards. See BARBA.

Beast Fables. See NOVELS AND ROMANCES.

Bebaioseos Diké (βεβαιώσεως δίκη). An action to compel a vender to make a good title, or to perform the terms of a contract to sell. See Meier, *Att. Process*, p. 574.

Bebrȳces (Βέβρυκες). The original inhabitants of Bithynia (q. v.), which was also called Bebrycia, from Bebrycé, a daughter of Danaüs.

Becker, WILHELM ADOLF. A well-known writer on classical subjects, born at Dresden in 1796. Entering the University of Leipzig in 1816, he studied at first theology, and subsequently classical philology. In 1840, he travelled and studied in Italy, returning in 1842 to take the professorship of archæology at Leipzig, where his lectures were very largely attended. His lively imagination, prompted by his minute knowledge of antiquity, led him to write his two famous works, which have so successfully reproduced pictures of the ancient society of Greece and Rome, while giving in detail a vast amount of archæological information. These works are *Gallus* (Leipzig, 1838), a quasi-narrative of life at Rome under Augustus; and *Charikles* (Leipzig, 1840), a story of society in ancient Greece. These two works have been revised, re-edited, and translated by numerous scholars, and have been a storehouse of information to students in all lands. His formal treatise, *De Comicis Romanorum Fabulis* (Leipzig, 1837), is another valuable production, as is also his hand-book of Roman antiquities, carried on after his death by Marquardt. Becker died at Meissen, Sept. 29th, 1846.

Beda (VENERABĬLIS). The most distinguished scholar in the world at the time he lived, born at Durham (England) in or about the year A.D. 672. He remained for thirteen years in the monastery of St. Peter under the care of the abbot. He was ordained priest in his thirtieth year, and devoted his life to such literature as was possible in those days, gaining a knowledge of Greek, Latin, Hebrew, medicine, and astronomy. He was the author of numerous homilies, hymns, epigrams, biographies of saints, works on chronology and grammar, and commentaries on various books of the New Testament. His most valuable production is his *Historia Ecclesiastica Gentis Anglorum* in five books, to which we owe nearly all our information regarding the history of England to A.D. 731, and which King Alfred translated into Anglo-Saxon. A good English version is that of Giles (1843).

Bedriăcum or Bebriăcum. A hamlet in Cisalpine Gaul, between Verona and Cremona, where in the same year (A.D. 69) Otho was defeated by the troops of Vitellius, and Vitellius by those of Vespasian (Tac. *Hist.* i. 15). The modern name is Caneto.

Bed-clothing. See BABYLONICUM; LODIX; STRAGULUM.

Beds. See LECTUS.

Beer. See CERVESIA.

Beggars. See MENDICUS.

Bekker, IMMANUEL. A distinguished German philologist, who was born at Berlin in 1785. He took his degree at the University of Halle in 1807, being regarded as the most brilliant pupil of F. A. Wolf (q. v.). In 1811 he became Professor of Classical Philology at Berlin, where he died in 1871. Bekker's life-work lay in the line of manuscript recension, for which a long course of careful study in the libraries of France, Germany, England, and Italy well fitted him, and which he carried on independently of the printed editions. He did much valuable work upon the *Corpus Inscriptionum Graecarum;* and published *Anecdota Graeca*, 3 vols. (Berlin, 1814–21); besides important recensions of the texts of Plato, Aristotle, the Attic orators,

Aristophanes, Thucydides, Theognis, Sextus Empiricus, Livy, and Tacitus.

Belĕsys (Βέλεσυς). A Babylonian priest, who successfully conspired with Arbaces to overthrow Sardanapalus (q. v.), the king of Assyria.

Belgae. See GALLIA.

Belgĭca. See GALLIA.

Belgium. A division of Gallia Belgica. The name is often used of the whole country. See Caes. *B. G.* v. 24.

Belīdes. See BELUS.

Belĭdes. See BELUS.

Belisāna. A deity of the Gauls, identified by the Romans with Minerva.

Belisarius (Slavonic *Beli-Tsar*, "White Prince"). One of the greatest generals of his time, to whom the emperor Justinian chiefly owed the splendour of his reign. Sprung from an obscure family in Thrace, Belisarius first served in the body-guard of the emperor, but soon obtained the chief command of an army of 25,000 men, stationed on the Persian frontiers, and in A.D. 530 gained a complete victory over a Persian army not less than 40,000 strong. The next year, however, he lost a battle against the same enemy, who had forced their way into Syria—the only battle which he lost during his whole career. He was recalled from the army, and soon became, at home, the support of his master. In the year 532, civil commotions, proceeding from the rival factions of the circus, who called themselves the Green (*Prasini*) and the Blue (*Veneti*), and who caused great disorders in Constantinople, brought the life and reign of Justinian in the utmost peril; and Hypatius was already chosen emperor, when Belisarius, with a small body of faithful adherents, restored order. Justinian, with a view of conquering the dominions of Gelimer, king of the Vandals, sent Belisarius, with an army of 15,000 men, to Africa. After two victories, he secured the person and the treasures of the Vandal king. Gelimer was led in triumph through the streets of Constantinople, and Justinian ordered a medal to be struck, with the inscription *Belisarius Gloria Romanorum*, which has descended to our times. By the dissensions existing in the royal family of the Ostrogoths in Italy, Justinian was induced to attempt the reduction of Italy and Rome under his sceptre. Belisarius vanquished Vitiges, king of the Goths, made him prisoner at Ravenna (A.D. 540), and conducted him, together with many other Goths, to Constantinople. The war in Italy against the Goths continued; but Belisarius, not being sufficiently supplied with money and troops by the emperor, demanded his recall (A.D. 548). He afterwards commanded in the war against the Bulgarians, whom he conquered in the year 559. Upon his return to Constantinople he was accused of having taken part in a conspiracy; but Justinian was convinced of his innocence, and is said to have restored to him his property and dignities, of which he had been deprived. Belisarius died A.D. 565. His history has been much coloured by the poets, and particularly by Marmontel, in his politico-philosophical romance. According to his narrative, the emperor caused the eyes of the hero to be struck out, and Belisarius was compelled to beg his bread in the streets of Constantinople. Other writers say that Justinian had him thrown into a prison, which is still shown under the appellation of the Tower of Belisarius. From this tower he is reported to have let down a bag fastened to a rope, and to have addressed the passers by in these oft-quoted words: "Give an obolus to Belisarius (*Date obolum Belisario*), whom virtue exalted, and envy has oppressed." Of this, however, no contemporary writer makes any mention. Tzetzes (q. v.), a writer of the twelfth century, was the first who related this fable. Through too great indulgence towards his wife Antonia, Belisarius was impelled to many acts of injustice, and he evinced a servile submissiveness to the licentious Theodora, the wife of Justinian. See Mahon, *Life of Belisarius* (London, 1829).

Bellerŏphon (Βελλεροφῶν) or **Bellerophontes** (Βελλεροφόντης). Son of Glaucus of Corinth (or, according to another account, of Poseidon), and grandson of Sisyphus. His proper name is said to have been Hipponoüs; the name Bellerophontes implies that he was the slayer of some now unknown monster. In later times his name was wrongly explained as the slayer of a certain Corinthian, Bellerus, on account of which he was supposed to have fled to Proetus at Tiryns or Corinth. The wife of Proetus, Anteia (or Stheneboea), fell in love with the beautiful youth; he was deaf to her entreaties; she slandered him to her husband, who resolved on his destruction. He sent Bellerophon to Lycia, to his father-in-law Iobates, with a tablet in cipher, begging him to put the bearer to death. Iobates first commissioned Bellerophon to destroy the fire-breathing monster Chimaera, a task which he executed with the help of his winged horse Pegasus. (See PEGASUS.) Thereupon, after a fierce battle, he conquered the

Bellerophon, Pegasus, and Chimaera. (Tischbein, Hamilton Vases, vol. i. pl. 1.)

Solymi and the Amazons, on his return slew in ambush all the boldest among the Lycians, and Iobates now recognized his divine origin, kept him with him, and gave him half of his kingdom and his daughter to wife. The children of this marriage were Isander, Hippolochus, the father of Glaucus and Laodamia, and the mother of Sarpedon by Zeus. Afterwards Bellerophon was hated by all the gods, and wandered about alone, devouring his heart in sorrow. His son Isander was killed by Ares in battle against the Solymi, while Laodamia was sacrificed to the wrath of Artemis. This is the Homeric version; but, according to Pindar, Bellerophon's high fortune made him so overweening that he wished to mount to heaven on Pegasus. Zeus, however, drove the horse wild with a gadfly, and Bellerophon fell and came to a miserable end. He was honoured as a hero in Corinth, an enclosure being consecrated to him in the cypress grove of Craneion. See Morris, *Bellerophon in Argos*, etc.

Bellōna. (1) The Roman goddess of war, in early Latin called Duellona. An old Italian divinity, probably of Sabine origin. She was supposed to be the wife or sister of Mars, and was identified with the Greek Enyo (Ἐνυώ). Her temple, which was situated in the Campus Martius, outside the old Pomerium, was used for meetings of the Senate when it was dealing with the ambassadors of foreign nations, or Roman generals who claimed a triumph on their return from war, for it must be remembered that under such circumstances a general might not enter the city. The pillar of war (Columna Bellica) stood hard by. It was from this, as representing the boundary of the enemy's territory, that the Fetialis threw his lance on declaring war. See FETIALES.

(2) Quite a different goddess is the Bellona whom the Roman government brought from Comana in Cappadocia towards the beginning of the first century B.C., during the Mithridatic War. This Bellona was worshipped in a different locality, and with a service conducted by Cappadocian priests and priestesses. These Bellonarii moved through the city in procession at the festivals of the goddess, in black raiment, and shed their own blood at the sacrifice, wounding themselves for the purpose in the arms and loins with a two-edged axe, and prophesying amid a wild noise of drums and trumpets.

Bellovăci. A people of Gaul inhabiting the site of the modern Beauvais in the Isle de France. See Caes. *B. G.* ii. 4.

Bellows. See FOLLIS.

Bells. See TINTINNABULUM.

Belus (Βῆλος). (1) The son of Libya, granddaughter of Io and Poseidon, and father of Aegyptus, Danaüs, Cepheus, and Phineus, to each of whom the patronymic Belīdes is applied. The daughters of Danaüs are known as Belīdes. (2) A name given to several kings of the East, whose existence appears extremely doubtful. The most ancient is Belus, king of Assyria, father of Ninus, whose epoch it is impossible to determine. (3) A king of Lydia, father of Ninus (Herod. i. 7). The Belus of Assyria, or the remote East, is thought by some to be the same with the Great Bali of Hindu mythology, as well as the Baal who was the principal male deity of the Phœnician and Canaanitish nations. The Belus of Babylon and Assyria has no identity, however, with the Phœnician Baal, except that both bore the title of Bel-Ba'ab or "lord." See ASSYRIA; BABYLONIA. (4) A river in Syria where glass-making was invented (Plin. *H. N.* v. 19).

Bema (βῆμα). The platform from which the orators spoke in the Athenian assembly. See ECCLESIA; PNYX.

The Bema of the Pnyx at Athens.

Benācus Lacus. The modern Lago di Garda in the north of Italy, out of which the Mincius (Mincio) flows.

Bendideia (Βενδίδεια). A Thracian festival in honour of the goddess Bendis (q. v.), who is said to be identical with the Grecian Artemis, and with the Roman Diana. The festival was of a bacchanalian character. From Thrace it was brought to Athens, where it was celebrated in the Piraeus, in the month Thargelion. The temple of Bendis was called Βενδίδειόν.

Bendis (Βενδίς). A goddess of the moon among the Thracians. She was invested with power over heaven and earth, and identified by the Greeks with Artemis, Hecaté, and Persephoné. The worship of this goddess was introduced into Attica by Thracian aliens; and was so popular that in Plato's time it became a state ceremonial at Athens. A public festival was instituted called the Bendideia, at which there were torch-races and a solemn procession of Athenians and Thracians at the Piraeus. See ARTEMIS.

Beneficium, Beneficiarius. The word *beneficium* is of frequent occurrence in the Roman law, in the sense of some special privilege or favour granted by the praetor or the emperor to a class of persons on some special ground of equity; but the word was also used in other senses. In the time of Cicero it was usual for a general, or a governor of a province, to report to the treasury (*aerarium*) the names of those under his command who had done good service to the State; those whose names were entered in such report were said *in beneficiis ad aerarium deferri* (Cic. *Pro. Arch.* 5; *Ad Fam.* v. 20; and the note of Manutius). It was required by a Lex Iulia that the names should be given in within thirty days after the accounts of the general or governor. *In beneficiis* in these passages may mean that the persons so reported were considered as persons who had deserved well of the State, and so the word *beneficium* may have reference to the services of the individuals; but as the object for which their services were reported was the benefit of the individuals, it seems that the term had reference to the gratuity in the form of money or presents given for such services. The honours and offices of the Roman State in the republican period were called the *beneficia* of the Roman people.

Beneficium also signified any promotion conferred on or grant made to soldiers, who were thence called *beneficiarii;* this term was a common one, as we see from inscriptions in Gruter (li. 4; cxxx. 5), in some of which the word *beneficiarius* is represented by the two letters B. F. Beneficiarius is also used by Caesar (*De Bell. Civ.* i. 75) to express the person who had received a beneficium. It does not, however, appear from these passages what the beneficium actually was. It might be any kind of honour, or special exemption from service (Suet. *Tib.* 12).

Grants of land and other things made by the Roman emperors were called *beneficia*, and were entered in a book called Liber Beneficiorum. The secretary or clerk who kept this book was called *a commentariis beneficiorum*, as appears from an inscription in Gruter (clxxviii. 1).

It was the practice of the kings and leaders of the tribes which took possession of the western provinces of the Roman Empire to grant lands to their nobles to be held generally for life on condition of special personal service. Lands so granted were called *beneficia*. From about the end of the ninth century, when *beneficia* became hereditary, they were also called *feoda* or feuds, the two words being used indifferently to denote the same condition of landed property (Guizot, *Histoire de la Civilisation en France*, iii. p. 247). The beneficiarius is he who has a beneficium. Grants made for the purpose of endowing churches were called *beneficia*; hence the word "benefice" came to be applied to an ecclesiastical preferment.

Beneventum. The modern Benevento. A city of Samnium, about ten miles beyond Candium, on the Via Appia. Its name is said to have been originally Maleventum, and to have been changed because of the evil omen contained in it. (See EUPHEMISM.) The more auspicious name was given it in B.C. 271 (Livy, ix. 27). It remained in the possession of the Romans during the whole of the Second Punic War, and obtained the thanks of the Senate for its firm attachment to the Republic at that critical period (Livy, xxvii. 10). We subsequently hear of its being a second time colonized by the veteran soldiers of Augustus, and also a third time under Nero. Beneventum was situated near the junction of the Sabatus and Calor, now Sabbato and Calore. Its position was a very important one, since here the main roads intersected each other from Latium into southern Italy, and from Samnium into Campania. Under the Lombards, Beneventum became the capital of a powerful dukedom. It abounds in remains of ancient sculpture above any other town in Italy. The most beautiful relic of former days at this place is the Arch of Trajan, which forms one of the entrances into the city. Near Beneventum, Pyrrhus was defeated by Dentatus, B.C. 274.

Beneventum in Samnium.

Benfey, THEODOR. A distinguished philologist, who was born near Göttingen in 1809. He pursued the study of classical philology at the universities of Göttingen, Munich, Frankfort, and Heidelberg, and later won distinction by his *Lexicon of Greek Roots* (Berlin, 1839), and by his edition of the *Sâma Veda* (Leipzig, 1848)—a work which laid the foundation for the scientific study of the Vedas. He also published a Sanskrit grammar, with a chrestomathy and glossary (Leipzig, 1854), a shorter Sanskrit grammar (London, 1868), and a Sanskrit-English dictionary (London, 1866). In his magazine *Orient und Occident* he published, in 1863–64, a translation of the first *mandala* of the *Rig Veda*. To comparative mythology and folk-lore he contributed a translation of the *Panchatantra*, 2 vols. (Leipzig, 1859).

In 1862, Dr. Benfey was made Professor of Sanskrit and Comparative Philology at the University of Göttingen, a chair which he continued to fill until his death in 1881. He left unfinished a Vedic grammar, for which he had collected a large mass of material. His only work in classical literature was his earliest publication—a translation of Terence (Stuttgart, 1837).

No scholar did more than Benfey to enlarge the range of the study of Sanskrit, a work to which he brought the zeal of an enthusiast. As a comparative philologist he was in some respects a follower of Franz Bopp (q. v.), from whom, however, he deviated in deriving all Indo-European words from monosyllabic primitive verbs, a conception which depends upon his theory of the origin of stem suffixes. These he regarded as nearly all derived from a fundamental radical √ANT appearing in the present participle of verbs. In his defence of this singular thesis he is obliged to assume permutations of sound that violate the most elementary laws of the science of phonology. His view is to be found set forth both in his *Lexicon of Greek Roots*, in his Sanskrit grammar, and in numerous essays.

Benignĭtas. See AMBITUS.

Benna. A carriage; a word derived from the Keltic. As a wagon of basket-work is still called *benna* in Italian, *Benne* in South German, and *banne* in Belgium, it is conjectured that the vehicle from the Column of Antoninus shown here is a *benna*.

Benna. (From the Column of Antoninus.)

Bentley, RICHARD, perhaps the greatest among the classical scholars of England, was born at Oulton in Yorkshire, January 27th, 1662. After spending five years at the Wakefield Grammar School, he entered St. John's College, Cambridge, in 1676, taking the Bachelor's degree in 1679. No record has been kept of his career as an undergraduate, though he is known to have given evidence of a strong taste for classical study. In

1682, his college gave him the appointment of head-master to the Spalding Grammar School in Lincolnshire, an office which he shortly resigned to become tutor to the son of Dr. Stillingfleet, afterwards Bishop of Worcester. In 1689, he went to Oxford with his pupil, and gained such reputation by his erudition as to be twice appointed to deliver the Boyle Lectures on the "Evidences of Religion." In 1690 he took orders, and received from Bishop Stillingfleet various preferments, with the office of librarian to the Royal Library at St. James's. In 1700, he became Master of Trinity College, Cambridge, and in 1717, Regius Professor of Divinity. His arrogance, greed, and violence in his relations with his colleagues of the university made his subsequent career one of continual strife and controversy. In 1718, the University Senate voted to deprive him of his degrees; in 1734, his deposition as Master was pronounced; yet his ability and force of character were such that at the time of his death he still retained his offices as well as his degrees. He died July 14th, 1742.

As a philologist, Bentley may be truly said to have established the principles of historical criticism and opened a new era for classical scholarship, so that in Germany to-day his name is held in the highest honour as the greatest of England's philologists. His *Dissertation upon the Epistles of Phalaris* (1699) gave him an immediate reputation all over Europe. These *Epistles* purported to be the production of Phalaris (q. v.), and to date back to the sixth century B.C. This claim Bentley, in a paper published for Wotton, showed to be false, whereupon the Christchurch (Oxford) editor of the *Epistles*, the Hon. Charles Boyle (afterward Earl of Orrery) attacked Bentley in a dissertation which Dyce has characterized as "a tissue of superficial learning, dexterous malice, and happy raillery." To this Bentley, superior alike in scholarship and wit, made his immortal reply, to which no answer was ever given, and which is a marvellously brilliant effort, unique in being at once imposing in its learning and fascinating in its ingenious use of all the arts of controversy. The best edition is Wagner's (1874).

Other important works of Bentley are his *Letter to Mill*, on the chronicler John Malelas (1691); an edition of Horace (1711)—an epoch-making masterpiece, recently edited by Zangemeister (1869); an edition of Terence (1726); and an edition of *Paradise Lost* (1732), carried out on the same plan, and much less happily executed. A very remarkable proposal of Bentley's—remarkable considering the time at which it was put forth—was his plan, published in 1720, of printing an edition of the New Testament in which the received Greek text should be corrected by a careful comparison of the oldest existing Greek MSS., and with the Vulgate. This proposal, which was received with a storm of opposition, was not carried out; but the principles laid down by Bentley have been adopted, and have produced important results in the hands of Lachmann and other textual critics of later times. See Monk, *Life of Bentley*, 2 vols. (1833); and Jebb, *Bentley* (1882); with the article TEXTUAL CRITICISM.

Berecyntia (Βερεκυντία). A surname of Cybelé, from Mount Berecyntus in Phrygia, where she was particularly worshipped. See RHEA.

Berecyntii (Βερεκύντιοι) and **Berecyntae** (Βερεκύνται). A Phrygian tribe, celebrated by the poets in connection with Cybelé, so often styled *Berecyntia mater* (Verg. *Aen.* vi. 785).

Berecyntus (Βερέκυντος). A mountain in Phrygia Major, on the banks of the river Sangarius. It was sacred to Cybelé, who is hence styled *Berecyntia mater*. See RHEA.

Berenīcé (Βερενίκη). A name common to several women of antiquity. It is of Greek origin, and means "victory-bringing" or "bearer of victory," the initial B being written, according to Macedonian usage, for the letter Φ, or, in other words, Βερενίκη being put for Φερενίκη, just as the Macedonians said Βίλιππος for Φίλιππος. The most remarkable of this name were the following: (1) The granddaughter of Cassander, brother of Antipater. She married Philip, a Macedonian, probably one of the officers of Alexander, and became by him the mother of many children, among whom were Magas, king of Cyrené, and Antigoné, whom she married to Pyrrhus, king of Epirus. She followed into Egypt Eurydicé, daughter of Antipater, who returned to that country to rejoin her husband, Ptolemy I. Berenicé inspired this prince with so strong a passion that he put away Eurydicé, although he had children by her, and married the former. He also gave the preference, in the succession to the throne, to her son Ptolemy, notwithstanding the better claims of his offspring by Eurydicé. Berenicé was remarkable for her beauty, and her portrait often appears on the medals of Ptolemy I. along with that of the latter. (2) Daughter of Ptolemy Philadelphus and Arsinoé. She followed her mother into exile, and retired with her to the court of Magas, at Cyrené, who married Arsinoé and adopted Berenicé. This will serve to explain why Polybius and Justin make Berenicé to have been the daughter of Magas, while Callimachus gives Ptolemy Philadelphus and Arsinoé as her parents. After the death of Magas, Arsinoé engaged her daughter in marriage to Demetrius, son of Demetrius Poliorcetes; but, on the young prince's having come from Macedonia to Cyrené, she became attached to him herself. Demetrius, conducting himself insolently, was slain in a conspiracy, at the head of which was Berenicé. The latter thereupon married her brother Ptolemy (Euergetes) III. A short time after the nuptials Ptolemy was obliged to go on an expedition into Syria, and Berenicé made a vow that she would consecrate her beautiful head of hair to Aphrodité if her husband returned safe to Egypt. Upon his return she fulfilled her vow in the temple of Aphrodité Zephyrites. On the following day, however, the hair was not to be found. As both the monarch and his queen were greatly disquieted at the loss, Conon the Samaritan, an eminent astronomer of the day, in order to conciliate the royal favour, declared that the locks of Berenicé had been removed by divine interposition, and translated to the skies in the form of a constellation. Hence the cluster of stars near the tail of the Lion is called *Coma Berenices* (Berenicé's hair). Callimachus wrote a piece on this subject, now lost, but a translation of which into Latin verse by Catullus has reached our time (Catull. *Carm.* lxvi.). Berenicé was put to death B.C. 216, by the order of Ptolemy Philopator, her son. (3) A daughter of Ptolemy Philadelphus, given by him in marriage to Antiochus Theos, king of Syria, in order to cement a peace between the two countries. After the death of her father Antiochus put her aside, and recalled his former wife Laodicé. This last, having taken off Antiochus by poison, sought to destroy Berenicé also as well as her son. This son was surprised and carried off by an emissary of Laodicé's, and shortly after put to death; and Berenicé, in searching for him, was entrapped and slain, B.C. 246. (4) Called by some authors Cleopatra, was the only legitimate child of Ptolemy Lathyrus, and ascended the throne after the death of her father, B.C. 81. Sulla, who was at that time dictator, compelled her to marry, and share her throne with, her cousin, who took the name of Ptolemy Alexander. She was poisoned by the latter only nineteen days after the marriage. (5) Daughter of Ptolemy Auletes. The people of Alexandria having revolted against this prince in B.C. 58, drove him out, and placed upon the throne his two daughters, Trypheua and Berenicé. The former died soon after, and Berenicé was given in marriage to Seleucus, surnamed Cybiosactes. His personal deformity, however, and vicious character soon rendered him so odious to the queen that she caused him to be strangled. Berenicé then married Archelaüs; but Ptolemy Auletes having been restored by Gabinius, the Roman commander, she was put to death by her own father, B.C. 55. (6) A native of Chios, and one of the wives of Mithridates of Pontus. On the overthrow of this monarch's power by Lucullus, Berenicé, in obedience to an order from her husband, took poison along with his other wives, but this not proving effectual, she was strangled by the eunuch Bacchus, B.C. 71. (7) Daughter of Agrippa I., king of Iudaea, and born A.D. 28. She was at first affianced to Marcus, son of Alexander, but this young man having died, Agrippa gave her in marriage to his brother Herod, king of Chalcis, by whom she became the mother of two sons, Berenicianus and Hyrcanus. Having lost her husband when she was at the age of twenty, she went to live with her brother Agrippa, a circumstance which gave rise to reports injurious to her character. To put an end to these rumours, she made proposals to Polemo, king of Cilicia, and offered to become his wife if he would embrace Judaism. Polemo consented, but she soon left him, and returned, in all probability, to her brother, for she was with the latter when St. Paul was arrested at Jerusalem, A.D. 63. The commerce between the guilty pair became now so public that the rumour even reached Rome, and we find Juvenal alluding to the affair in one of his satires (vi. 155). She followed Agrippa when he went to join Vespasian, whom Nero had charged to reduce the Jews to obedience. A new scene now opened for her; she won the affections of Titus, and, at a subsequent period, when Vespasian was established on the throne, and Titus returned home after terminating the Jewish War, she accompanied him to Rome along with her brother Agrippa. At Rome she lived openly with Titus, and took up her abode in the imperial palace, as we learn from Dio Cassius, who states also that she was then in the flower of her age. Titus, it is said, intended even to acknowledge her as his wife; but he was compelled by the murmurs of his subjects to abandon this idea, and he sent her away from the city soon after his accession to the throne. Such, at least, is the account given by Suetonius (*Tit.* 7), who appears more entitled to belief than Dio Cassius, according to whom Titus sent Berenicé away before his accession to the throne, and refused to receive her again, when she had returned to Rome a short time after the commencement of his reign. There is a great difficulty attending the history of this Berenicé as regards her intimacy with Titus. She must, at least, have been forty-two years of age when she first became acquainted with the Roman prince, and fifty-one years old at the period of the celebrated scene which forms the subject of Racine's tragedy. Many are inclined to believe, therefore, that the Berenicé to whom Titus was attached was the daughter of Mariamné and Archelaüs, and, consequently, the niece of the Berenicé of whom we have been speaking; she would be twenty-five years old when Titus came into Iudaea. The story of Berenicé forms the subject of a play by Racine, *Bérénice.*

Berenīcé. (1) A city of Egypt on the coast of the Sinus Arabicus, from which a road was made across the intervening desert to Coptos on the Nile, by Ptolemy Philadelphus, 258 miles in length. From this harbour the vessels of Egypt took their departure for Arabia Felix and India. It was through the medium of Berenicé also, and the caravan route to Coptos, that the principal trade of the Romans with India was conducted. By this line of communication it is said that a sum not less than what would now be $2,000,000 was remitted by the Roman traders to their correspondents in the East, in payment of merchandise which ultimately sold for a hundred times as much. The ruins of the ancient Berenicé are found at the modern port of Habest. (2) A city of Cyrenaïca, called also Hesperis. In its vicinity the ancients placed the gardens of the Hesperides. It is now Bengazi, a poor and filthy town. Few traces of the ancient city remain above ground, although much might be brought to light by excavation.

Bergk, THEODOR. A distinguished classicist, who was born at Leipzig in 1812. Between the years 1842 and 1869 he held the chair of classical philology in three universities—Marburg, Freiburg, and Halle, retiring in 1869 from ill-health. His greatest completed work is his *Poetae Lyrici Graeci,* 3 vols. (Leipzig, 1843), of which the fourth edition appeared in 1878. After his retirement, he began his *Geschichte der griechischen Litteratur,* of which he finished only the first volume (Berlin, 1872), the second and third being edited by G. Hinrichs (Berlin, 1883–84). He died July 20th, 1881.

Bernays, JAKOB. A distinguished philologist, born of Jewish ancestry at Hamburg in 1824. He studied classical philology at Bonn, and became professor there in 1866. He was a prolific writer, but his *magnum opus* was his edition of Lucretius (1855). Other important publications were his life of Joseph Justus Scaliger (Berlin, 1855), *Lucian und die Cyniker* (1877), and a translation of the first three books of Aristotle's *Politics* (1872). His *Gesammelte Abhandlungen* were edited after his death by Prof. Usener of Bonn (1887). He died May 26th, 1881.

Bernhardy, GOTTFRIED. A well-known German classical scholar, was born near Frankfort in 1800. He pursued his studies at the University of Berlin, and in 1829 became director of the philological seminarium at Halle. His chief philological works are *Syntax der griechischen Sprache* (1829); *Paralipomena Syntaxis Graecae* (1854); and a critical edition of Suidas, 4 vols. (1834–53). His two works on Greek and Latin literature—*Griechische Literaturgeschichte* (1867–76) and the *Grundriss d. römischen Lit.* (5th ed. 1872)—are valuable contributions to historical literary study. He died May 14th, 1875.

Beroë (Βερόη). (1) An old woman of Epidaurus, nurse to Semelé. Heré assumed her shape when she persuaded Semelé not to receive the visits of Zeus if he did not appear in the majesty of a god (Ovid, *Met.* iii. 278). (2) The wife of Doryclus, whose form was assumed by Iris, at the instigation of Heré, when she advised the Trojan women to burn the fleet of Aeneas in Sicily (Verg. *Aen.* v.).

Beroea (Βέροια). (1) A large city of Macedonia, south of Edessa, and of great antiquity. Reference should be made to the Acts of the Apostles, xvii. 11. (2) A town of Syria, now Aleppo or Haleb, near Antioch, and enlarged by Seleucus Nicator, who named it Beroea after the town in Macedon. In the Old Testament it is called Chelbon.

Coin of Beroea, in Syria, with the Head of Trajan

Berōsus (Βηρωσός). A Greek writer, born in Bithynia, and a priest of Belus. He lived as early as the time of Alexander the Great, and about B.C. 280 wrote a work, dedicated to King Antiochus Soter, on Babylonian history, in three books (*Babylonica* or *Chaldaica*). The work must have been of great value, as it was founded on ancient priestly chronicles preserved in the Temple of Belus at Babylon. Its importance as an authority for the ancient history of Asia is fully attested by the fragments that remain, in spite of their scanty number and disordered arrangement. They are preserved for us chiefly in the works of Iosephus, Eusebius, and Syncellus, and have been edited by W. Richter (Leipzig, 1825), and by Müller in the second volume of the *Historicorum Graecorum Fragmenta* (of the "Collection Didot"), published at Paris in 1848. The work entitled *Antiquitatum Libri Quinque cum Commentariis Ioannis Annii* (Rome, 1498), published in Latin as a work of Berosus, was in reality written by the Dominican Giovanni Nanni of Viterbo.

Beryllus (βήρυλλος). The beryl; a precious stone of the emerald species, and much used by the Romans in the adornment of their cups. Pliny states that the Indian lapidaries were accustomed to colour rock-crystal in such a way as to counterfeit the beryl. The same writer speaks of six varieties of the beryl, or of what he considered such.

Berȳtus (Βηρυτός). Called in the Old Test. *Berotha* and *Berothai*. The modern Beirût; an ancient town of Phœnicia, about twenty-four miles south of Byblus, famous in the age of Justinian for the study of law, and styled by that emperor "the mother and nurse of the laws." The civil law was taught there in Greek, as it was at Rome in Latin. It had also the name of Colonia Felix Iulia, from Augustus Caesar, who made it a Roman colony, and named it in honour of his daughter (Plin. *H. N.* v. 20). The adjacent plain is renowned as the place where St. George, the patron saint of England, slew the dragon; in memory of which a small chapel was built upon the spot, dedicated at first to that Christian hero, but now changed to a mosque. It was frequently captured and recaptured during the Crusades.

Coin of Berytus.

Bes (*be-is* = *binae partes assis*). Two thirds of a unit. See As.

Besa or **Bessa** (βῆσα, βῆσσα, βησίον). An Alexandrian vessel used both as a drinking-cup and for holding perfumes, etc. The vessel was named from having upon it the features of the Egyptian god Bes, modelled in the clay. It was in the shape of a flask, broad at the bottom and narrowing towards the top. See Krause, *Angeiologie*, 379, 380, 407, 408.

Bessi (Βέσσοι). A people of Thrace dwelling in a district known as Bessica, between Mount Rhodopé and the northern part of the river Hebrus.

Bessus (Βῆσσος). A satrap of Bactria under Darius III., who, after the defeat of Darius by Alexander the Great at Arbela (B.C. 331), seized him with the intention of carrying him as a prisoner to his own satrapy. Being hotly pursued by the Macedonians, he murdered his royal captive and made his own escape. He was subsequently delivered into the hands of Alexander, and that monarch, according to one account (Justin, xii. 5), gave him up for punishment to the brother of Darius. Plutarch, however, states that Alexander himself punished the offender in the following manner: He caused two straight trees to be bent, and one of his legs to be made fast to each; then suffering the trees to return to their former posture, his body was torn asunder by the violence of the recoil (Plut. *Alex.*). Arrian makes Alexander to have caused his nostrils to be slit, the tips of his ears to be cut off, and the offender, after this, to have been sent to Ecbatana, and put to death in the sight of all the inhabitants of the capital of Media.

Bestiarii (θηριομάχοι). Persons who fought with wild beasts in the games of the Circus. They were either persons who fought for the sake of pay, and who were allowed to bear arms; or criminals, who were usually permitted to have no means of defence against the wild beasts. The *bestiarii* who fought with the beasts for the sake of pay, and of whom there were great numbers in the

Bestiarii. (Bas-relief, Palazzo Orsini, Rome.)

latter days of the Republic and under the Empire, are always spoken of as distinct from the gladiators, who fought with one another. It appears that there were schools in Rome in which persons were trained to fight with wild beasts (*scholae bestiarum* or *bestiariorum*). See GLADIATORES.

Betrothal. See MATRIMONIUM; SPONSALIA.

Betting. See ALEA; PIGNUS; SPONSIO.

Biaiōn Diké (βιαίων δίκη). An action brought in any case of brutal violence, and brought under the jurisdiction of the Forty. In practice, it was mainly restricted to (1) the illegal seizure by force of any kind of property, especially of slaves; and (2) the rape, or attempted rape, of a free person.

Biānor (Βιάνωρ). A son of the river-god Tiber, and of Manto, daughter of Tiresias. Servius makes him the founder of Mantua, and identical with Ocnus.

Bias (Βίας). (1) The son of Amythaon and Idomené, was king of Argos, and brother to the famous soothsayer Melampus (q. v.). (2) One of the Seven Wise Men of Greece. He was son of Teutamus, and was born at Priené, in Ionia, about B.C. 570. Bias was a practical philosopher, studied the laws of his country, and employed his knowledge in the service of his friends, defending them in the courts of justice, settling their disputes. He made a noble use of his wealth. His advice, that the Ionians should fly before the victorious Cyrus to Sardinia, was not followed, and the victory of the army of Cyrus confirmed the correctness of his opinion. The inhabitants of Priené, when besieged by Mazares, resolved to abandon the city with their property. On this occasion Bias replied to one of his fellow-citizens, who expressed astonishment that he made no preparations for his departure, "I carry everything with me." He remained in his native country, where he died at a very advanced age. His countrymen buried him with splendour, and honoured his memory. Some of his apophthegms are still preserved.

Bibacŭlus, M. FURIUS. A Latin poet, born at Cremona about B.C. 103. He appears to have composed a turgid poem entitled *Aethiopis*, on the legend, very probably, of the Aethiopian Memnon; and also another on the mouths of the Rhine. The latter is thought to have formed part of an epic poem on Caesar's wars in Gaul. Both works are lost, and we have only a couple of fragments remaining. Horace (*Sat.* ii. 5, 40) ridicules a laughable verse of his, in which Iupiter is represented as spitting snow upon the Alps: *Iupiter hibernas cana nive conspuet Alpes.* This line occurred in the beginning of a poem which he had composed on the Gallic War. Quintilian (x. 1, 96) enumerates Bibaculus among the Roman iambic poets, and in another part of his work (viii. 6, 18) gives this same line, citing it as an instance of harsh metaphor. To render his parody more severe, Horace substitutes Furius himself for the monarch of the skies, and, to prevent all mistake, applies to the former a laughable species of designation, drawn directly from his personal appearance, *pingui tentus omaso*, "distended with his fat paunch."

Bibăsis (βίβασις). A gymnastic dance practised among the Spartans by both men and women. See SALTATIO.

Bibliopōla (βιβλιοπώλης). A bookseller. See LIBER.

Bibliothēca (βιβλιοθήκη). A library. (1) GREEK. The large libraries of the Assyrian and Egyptian monarchs were unknown to the Greeks till the time of the Ptolemies. We do indeed hear of a library formed by Pisistratus (Aul. Gell. vii. 17), which Aulus Gellius calls "the first public library"; of another by Polycrates, the tyrant of Samos (Athen. i. 3); and among private collectors we hear of Nicocrates of Cyprus, Euclid the Archon, Euripides (Athen. i. 3), Euthydemus (Xen. *Memor.* iv. 2), and Aristotle (Strabo, xiii. 1). But it was the Macedonian rulers of Alexandria who first created a public library on a large scale. Ptolemy Philadelphus collected books from all parts of Greece and Asia, the larger number of which he deposited in the Museum (q. v.), a building in the Bruchium quarter of Alexandria, and the rest in the Serapeum. Zenodotus was the first librarian, after him Callimachus (who made a catalogue called the Πίνακες), then Eratosthenes, then Apollonius, and then Aristophanes. The number of volumes in the two libraries seems to have been between 500,000 and 600,000. Books in foreign languages were brought to Alexandria and translated for the purpose of being placed in the library, and the Septuagint version of the Old Testament is said to have been made in this way. Galen tells us that the autograph original copies of Aeschylus, Sophocles, and Euripides were procured for the library.

This priceless collection suffered considerably in the siege of Alexandria by Iulius Caesar, in the destruction of the Bruchium quarter by Aurelian (A.D. 273), and by the edict of Theodosius for the destruction of the Serapeum (A.D. 389). It is said to have been destroyed by the Arabs in A.D. 640 (Gibbon, ch. 51), but this tradition is now largely discredited.

A rival library to that at Alexandria was started by the kings of Pergamus, but was transported to Egypt by Antony, who made a present of its 200,000 volumes to Cleopatra. By the second or first century B.C. there seem to have been libraries in most Greek towns. (For bibliography, see below.)

(2) ROMAN. The first public library in Rome was that founded by Asinius Pollio (Plin. *H. N.* vii. 30), and was in the Atrium Libertatis on the Aventine. Iulius Caesar had projected a grand Greek and Latin library, and had commissioned Varro to take measures for the establishment of it; but the scheme was prevented by his death (Suet. *Iul.* 44). The library of Pollio was followed by that of Augustus in the Temple of Apollo on the Palatine Hill (Suet. *Aug.* 29), another, the Bibliotheca Octaviana (so called from Augustus's sister Octavia), forming part of the Porticus Octavia. There were also libraries on the Capitol, in the Temple of Peace founded by Vespasian, in the palace of Tiberius, besides the Ulpian Library (so called after its founder, Trajan), which was the most famous (Gell. xi. 17; Dio Cass. lxviii. 16). This library was attached by Diocletian, as an ornament, to his *thermae*.

Private collections of books were made at Rome soon after the Second Punic War, sometimes from the spoils of Grecian or Eastern conquest. Thus Aemilius Paulus brought to Rome the library of Perseus, king of Macedonia; Sulla, that of Apellicon of Teos; Lucullus, the extensive one of the kings of Pontus, to which he gave the public free access. The zeal of Cicero, Atticus, Varro, and others in increasing their libraries is well known. Serenus Sammonicus possessed a library of 62,000 books. Towards the end of the Republic it became, in fact, the fashion to have a room elegantly furnished as a library, and reserved for that purpose. However ignorant or unstudious a person might be, it was fashionable to appear learned by having a library, though he might never even read the titles of the books. Seneca (*De Tranq. An.* 9) condemns the rage for mere book-collecting, and rallies those who were more pleased with the outside than the inside. Lucian wrote a separate piece to expose this common folly.

We read of provincial libraries at Milan, Comum, Tibur, and Patrae.

A library generally had an eastern aspect (Vitruv. vi. 7). In Herculaneum a library, fully furnished, has been discovered. Round the walls, it had cases containing the books in rolls, and a rectangular case occupied the centre of the room: these cases were numbered. It was a very small room—so small that a person by stretching out his arms could touch both sides of it; yet it contained 1700 rolls. The cases were called either *armaria, loculamenta, foruli*, or *nidi*. Asinius Pollio had set the fashion in his public library of adorning the room with the portraits and busts of celebrated men, as well as statues of Minerva and the Muses. This example was soon followed in the private libraries of the rich. The *librarii a bibliotheca* or *bibliothecarii*, who had charge of the libraries, were usually slaves or freedmen. See LIBER.

On ancient libraries, see Ritschl, *Die alexandrinischen Bibliotheken;* Birt, *Das antike Buchwesen* (1882); Egger, *Callimaque et l'Origine de la Bibliographie;* Polybius, xii. 27; Lipsius, *De Bibliothecis Syntagma* in Opera, vol. iii.; Becker-Göll, *Gallus*, ii. 418–424; Séraud, *Les Livres dans l'Antiquité*, chap. x.; Taylor, *The Transmission of Ancient Books* (1875); Bernhardy, *Röm. Litter.* p. 65; Castellani, *Delle Biblioteche nell' Antichità* (Bologna, 1884); and the interesting chapter on the subject in Lanciani, *Ancient Rome in the Light of Recent Discoveries* (1888).

Bibracté. The modern Autun; a large town of the Aedui in Gaul, on the Arroux, one of the branches of the Liger (Loire). Its modern name is a corruption of Augustodunum, by which it was known in imperial times.

Bibrax. The modern Bièvre; a town of the Remi in Gallia Belgica, not far from the Aisne.

Bibŭlus, L. CALPURNIUS. A Roman statesman, one of the aristocratic party. He married Porcia, the daughter of Cato. He was Caesar's colleague in the consulship; but finding it impossible to thwart his designs, retired to his own house and took so little part in the conduct of affairs as to give rise to the epigram which Suetonius (*Iul.* 20.) has preserved:

> Non Bibulo quicquam nuper sed Caesare factumst;
> Nam Bibulo fieri consule nil memini.

Biclinium. A couch for two persons, used at meals (Plaut. *Bacch.* iv. 3, 84). The word is a hybrid, half Latin and half Greek. See TRICLINIUM.

Bicornĭger. An epithet of Bacchus.

Bicos (βῖκος). An earthen vessel with handles, used by the Greeks for holding wine, and sometimes for salted meat or fish.

Bidens. (1) See RASTRUM. (2) See BIDENTAL.

Bidental. An erection on a spot where lightning had fallen. The name is derived from the sacrifice of a young sheep (*bidens*) by the *haruspices* at the place. Sometimes, from the resemblance of the structure to the mouth of a well, it was called *puteal*, as in the case of the *puteal Libonis* or *Scribonianum* at the eastern end of the Forum Romanum, and another in the Comitium. (See PUTEAL.) When lightning had struck a spot, it was held necessary *condere fulgur*, either *publice* or *privatim*, according to the nature of the place. If a man had been killed by the lightning, it was not lawful to burn the corpse, but he was buried on the spot (Plin. *H. N.* ii. § 145). Everything which had been scorched or scattered by the lightning was solemnly collected by the pontiff (who was at a later date assisted by the *haruspices*) and piled up with a low muttered prayer. A *bidens* was offered, and a small enclosure, neither paved nor covered, was built around the heap, and was further surrounded by an exterior wall, bearing the legend *fulgur conditum.* Many inscriptions of this kind are still extant, and at Pompeii a bidental has been discovered, of which the outer protection is formed by eight Doric columns (Mazois, *Ruines de Pompéi*, t. iv., pl. ii. iii.). It was not lawful to tread this *locus religiosus*, or even to look into it (Ammian. xxiii. 5).

Remains of a Bidental. (Pompeii.)

From Horace (*A. P.* 471) it appears to have been believed that a person who was guilty of profaning a bidental would be punished by the gods with frenzy.

Bidiaei (βιδιαῖοι, βίδεοι or βίδυοι). Magistrates in Sparta whose business was to inspect the gymnastic exercises. Their house of meeting (ἀρχεῖον) was in the market-place (Pausan. iii. 11, § 2). They were either five or six in number, and had a president who is called in inscriptions πρέσβυς βιδέων (*C. I. G.* i. 611). See GYMNASIUM.

Bidis (Βῖδος). A small town in Sicily, west of Syracuse.

Bier. See FERETRUM; FUNUS.

Bifrons. An epithet of Ianus (q. v.) as being represented with two faces.

Ianus Bifrons. (From a coin.)

Biga or **Bigae.** The Latin name for a chariot and pair. See CURRUS.

Bigamia. See MATRIMONIUM.

Bigāti, sc. *nummi*. Roman coins (denarii), having the device of a two-horsed chariot (*biga*). See DENARIUS.

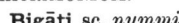

Bigati Nummi.

Bilbĭlis. The modern Baubola or Bambola, a town

of the Celtiberi in Hispania Tarraconensis, famous as being the native place of the poet Martial, who often refers to it with pleasure and affection. (See Mart. i. 49; x. 103, 104; xii. 18.) It stood on a rocky height in a barren, rugged country through which ran the river Salo. Bilbilis was noted for its manufacture of arms, and near it were the baths named from it Aquae Bilbitanae.

Bilix. See TELA.

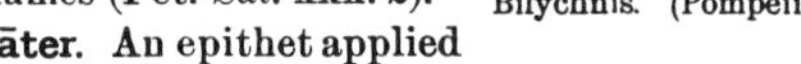
Bilychnis. (Pompeii.)

Bilychnis, sc. *lucerna.* A lamp furnished with two nozzles and wicks, so as to give out two separate flames (Pet. *Sat.* xxx. 2).

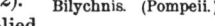

Bimāter. An epithet applied to Dionysus as having had, in a fashion, two mothers. See DIONYSUS.

Bingium. The modern Bingen; a town of Germania Prima, on the Rhine, west of Moguntiacum (Mayence). See Tac. *Hist.* iv. 70.

Bion (Βίων). (1) A Greek bucolic poet, who flourished in the second half of the second century B.C. He lived mostly in Sicily, where he is said to have died by poison. Besides a number of minor poems from his hand, we have a long descriptive epic called *The Dirge of Adonis.* His style is more remarkable for grace than for power or simplicity. (2) A native of Borysthenes, near the mouth of the Dnieper, who flourished about B.C. 250. Sold as a slave when a boy, he was freed by his master, who was a rhetorician. After studying at Athens, he lived for a considerable period at the court of Antigonus Gonatas in Macedonia. His sharp, incisive sayings were proverbial in antiquity, as in the passage of Horace (*Epist.* ii. 2, 60).

Bipalium. A double mattock. See PALA.

Bipennis. A two-edged axe. See SECURIS.

Birēmis (δίκωπος). See NAVIS.

Birrus or **Burrus** (βίρρος). A cloak or cape furnished with a hood; a heavy, coarse garment for use in bad weather. It was made of wool or beaver, with a long nap. The word is also used as synonymous with LACERNA, CUCULLUS, and SAGUM, all of which see.

Fisherman with Birrus. (From a Pompeian Statue.)

Bisaltes. A tribe dwelling in Macedonia.

Bisanthé (Βισάνθη). A Thracian town on the Propontis, subsequently known as Rhaedestum, whence its modern name Rodosto.

Bisellium. See SELLA.

Bissextum. See CALENDARIUM.

Bistŏnes (Βίστονες). A Thracian people who dwelt between Mount Rhodopé and the Aegean Sea, on Lake Bistonis, near Abdera. From the worship of Dionysus in Thrace, the female Bacchanals were called Bistonides. Pliny mentions one town as belonging to the Bistones, i. e. Tirida.

Bit. See FRENUM.

Bithynia (Βιθυνία). A district of Asia Minor, bounded on the west by Mysia, on the north by the Pontus Euxinus, on the east by Paphlagonia, and on the south by Phrygia Epictetus. It was possessed at an early period by Thracian tribes from the neighbourhood of the Strymon, called Thyni and Bithyni, of whom the former dwelt on the coast, the latter in the interior. The country was subdued by the Lydians, and afterwards became a part of the Persian Empire under Cyrus, and was governed by the satraps of Phrygia. During the decline of the Persian Empire, the northern part of the country became independent, under native princes, who resisted Alexander and his successors, and established a kingdom, which lasted till the death of Nicomedes III. (B.C. 74), who bequeathed it to the Romans. Under Augustus it was made a proconsular province. It was a fertile country, intersected with wooded mountains, the highest of which was the Mysian Olympus, on its southern border.

Coins of Bithynia, with the Heads of Roman Emperors.

The chief towns of Bithynia were Chalcedon, Prusa, Heraclea (Pontica), Nicaea, and Bithynium (Claudiopolis).

Biton (Βίτων) and **Cleŏbis** (Κλέοβις). The sons of Cydippé, a priestess of Heré at Argos. They were celebrated for their affection for their mother, whose chariot they once dragged during a festival to the Temple of Heré, a distance of forty-five stadia. The priestess prayed to the goddess to grant them what was best for mortals, and during the night they both died while asleep in the temple. (Herod. i. 31; Val. Max. v. 4; Cic. *Tusc. Disp.* i. 47).

Bitūmen. A word used by the Roman writers, especially Tacitus and Pliny, to indicate a species of mineral pitch or oil. The corresponding Greek word is ἄσφαλτος, the modern asphalt. It was brought chiefly from the Dead Sea (Asphaltites), and was used in building as a cement. In Syria it was quarried in solid blocks. In Zacynthus (Zante) there was and still is a pitch spring that has been at work for more than two thousand years. See Pliny, *H. N.* viii. 15; xxviii. 10.

Bituricum. The modern Bourges; known also in ancient times as AVARICUM; the chief town of the Bituriges, on the Avara (Evre), a branch of the Cher. The walls of the town are carefully described by Caesar (*B. G.* vii. 23), who besieged it and finally took it by assault in B.C. 52.

Bituriges. A numerous and powerful Keltic people in Gallia Aquitania, having in early times the supremacy over the other Kelts in Gaul. They were divided into two tribes: (1) BITURIGES CUBI, with Avaricum as their capital (Bourges); (2) BITURIGES VIVISCI or UBISCI—their capital was Burdigala (Bordeaux), on the left bank of the Garumna (Garonne).

Bivium. A road or street which branches into two forks (Plin. *H. N.* vi. 32; Verg. *Aen.* ix. 238); at the point of divergence between two such roads or streets in the town of Pompeii there is always found a fountain, as in the example here given, which represents a *bivium* in that city.

Bivium in Pompeii. (Rich.)

Bivouac. See CASTRA; EXCUBIAE.

Bizōné (Βιζώνη). A city of Thrace on the Pontus.

Bizya (Βιζύη). A Thracian city on the Euxine Sea, northwest of Byzantium. The poets declare it to have been shunned by swallows because of the fate of Tereus (q. v.). See Ovid, *Met.* vi. 424 foll.

Blabēs Diké (βλάβης δίκη). A general name for an action available in cases where one person had sustained a loss by the conduct of another, no matter whether the injury originated in a fault of omission or commission. The declaration of the plaintiff seems always to have begun with the words Ἔβλαψέ με, followed by the name of the defendant.

The proper Athenian court to take cognizance of the action was determined by the subject of litigation. Thus, a βλάβη in the market (cf. Aristoph. *Vesp.* 1407) would come before the Agoranomi; dangerous buildings, before the Astyonomi; commercial cases, before the Thesmothetae; and those relating to the law of inheritance, before the Archon Eponymus.

Blacksmiths. See FABER.

Blanket. See BABYLONICUM; STRAGULUM.

Blastophoenīces (Βλαστοφοίνικες). A people of Lusitania, of Phœnician origin. See Appian, *De Reb. Hisp.* vi. 56.

Blatta. A name given by Roman writers to an insect belonging to the orthoptera, of which the ancients knew several kinds. From their shunning the light, Vergil calls them *lucifugae*. The American cockroach (*blatta Americana*) is our species. See PURPURA.

Blemўes (Βλέμυες). A people of Aethiopia, presumably fabulous, as they are described as having no heads, but the eyes and mouth in their breasts. (See Pliny, *H. N.* v. 8; Amm. Marcell. xiv. 4). The name is also written Blemmyes (Βλέμμυες).

Boadicēa or **Boudicēa.** A queen of the Iceni in Britain, having been shamefully treated by the Romans, who even ravished her two daughters, excited an insurrection of the Britons against their oppressors during the absence of Suetonius Paulinus, the Roman governor, on an expedition to the island of Mona. She took the Roman colonies of Camalodunum, Londinium, and other places, and slew nearly 70,000 Romans and their allies. She was at length defeated with great loss by Suetonius Paulinus, and put an end to her own life, A.D. 61. See Tacitus, *Ann.* xiv. 31; and Tennyson's noble poem, *Boadicea*.

Boats. See NAVIS.

Bocchus. (1) A king of Mauretania, and father-in-law of Iugurtha (q. v.), with whom at first he made war against the Romans, but whom he afterwards delivered up to Sulla, the quaestor of Marius, B.C. 106. (2) The son of the preceding, who took part in the Civil Wars. He was confirmed in his kingdom by Augustus.

Bodotria or **Boderia Aestuarium.** The Firth of Forth; an estuary on the eastern coast of Scotland. See Tacitus, *Agric.* 23 and 25.

Boebēis (Βοιβηΐς). A lake in Thessaly near Mount Ossa (Herod. vii. 129).

Boeckh, PHILIPP AUGUST. An archæologist, born November 24th, 1785, at Karlsruhe. He entered the University of Halle in 1803, and was influenced by the remarkable prelections of F. A. Wolf (q. v.) to engage in the study of classical philology, of which he became professor at Heidelberg in 1809, leaving that chair to take the professorship of rhetoric and ancient literature at Berlin, where he lectured for some forty years with extraordinary success. His is one of the greatest names in the history of philology as a science, in that he conceived of it as an organically constituted whole; so that his lectures included grammar (formal and historical), exegesis, archæology proper, and the study of ancient literature, history, politics, religion, and society. In short, he aimed at an intellectual reproduction of antiquity on all its sides, as essential to a fruitful study of the classics. This view, which excited much opposition for a time, gave an undeniable impetus to profound and accurate scholarship. His great works are an edition of Pindar in 2 vols. (1811–22); his treatise *Die Staathaushaltung der Athener*, 2 vols. (1817; third ed., by Frankel, 1886)—a monument of subtle analysis, minute research, and vast learning; his *Metrologische Untersuchungen über Gewichte, Münzfusse und Masse des Alterthums* (1838); his *Urkunden über das Seewesen des attischen Staats* (1840); the *Corpus Inscriptionum Graecarum*, of which he began the publication at the cost of the Royal Academy of Berlin, and which has been continued by Franz, Kirchhoff, Curtius, Röhl, and others; editions of the *Antigone* of Sophocles (1843), and of the fragments ascribed to Philolaüs; besides a collection of lectures, essays, etc., with the title *Gesammelte kleine Schriften*, 7 vols. (1858–74). He died in Berlin, August 3d, 1867. See Von Leutsch, *Phil. Anz.* xvi. (1886).

Boëdromia (Βοηδρόμια). A festival celebrated at Athens on the seventh day of the month of Boëdromion, in honour of Apollo Boëdromios (Müller, *Dor.* ii. 8, § 5). The name Boëdromios, by which Apollo was called in Boeotia and other parts of Greece, seems to indicate that by this festival he was honoured as a martial god, who either by his actual presence or by his oracles afforded assistance in the dangers of war. The origin of the festival is, however, traced by different authors to different events in Grecian story. See Plutarch, *Theseus*, 27.

Boëdromion (Βοηδρομιών). The name of the third Attic month, answering to the latter half of September and the beginning of October. See CALENDARIUM.

Boeotarches (Βοιωτάρχης). The Boeotians in ancient times occupied Arné in Thessaly (Thuc. i. 12). Sixty years after the taking of Troy they were expelled by the Thessalians, and settled in the country then called Cadmeis, but afterwards Boeotia. The leader of the Boeotians was King Opheltas. It would seem that their kings ruled the whole country from Thebes. Later on, the country was divided into several States, containing each a principal city, with its allies and dependants. The number and names of these independent States are differently given by different writers on the subject; we know, however, for certain that they formed a confederacy called the Boeotian League, with Thebes at its head, and Freeman is of opinion that the political union grew out of an older Amphictyony. Common sanctuaries were the temple of the Itonian Athené near Coronea, where the Pamboeotia were celebrated, and the Temple of Poseidon in Onchestus. Thucydides (iv. 93) mentions seven independent States: Thebes, Haliartus, Coronea, Copae, Thespiae, Tanagra, and Orchomenus; and we learn from inscriptions that, at one time or other, the following belonged to the same class: Anthedon, Lebadea, Hyettus, Acraephia, Chorsia (or Korsia, Demosth. *F. L.* § 141, etc.), Thisbé, Chaeronea. O. Müller (*Orchom.* p. 403) supposes there were originally fourteen free States. Probably the number differed at different times.

Each of the principal towns of Boeotia seems to have had its δῆμος and βουλή. The βουλή was presided over by an archon, who probably had succeeded to the priestly functions of the old kings, but possessed little, if any, executive authority. The polemarchs, who, in treaties and agreements, are mentioned next to the archon, had some executive authority, but did not command forces—e. g. they could imprison, and they directed the levies of troops. But, besides the archon of each separate State, there was an archon of the confederacy —ἄρχων ἐν κοινῷ Βοιωτῶν—most probably always a Theban. His name was affixed to all alliances and compacts which concerned the whole confederacy, and he was president of what Thucydides calls the four councils, who directed the affairs of the league (ἅπαν τὸ κῦρος ἔχουσι). On important questions they seem to have been united; for the same author speaks of them as ἡ βουλή, and informs us that the determinations of the Boeotarchs required the ratification of this body before they were valid. We may now explain who these Boeotarchs were. They were properly the military heads of the confederacy, chosen by the different States; but we also find them discharging the functions of an executive in various matters. In fact, they are represented by Thucydides as forming an alliance with foreign States; as receiving ambassadors on their return home; as negotiating with envoys from other countries, and acting as the representatives of the whole league, though the βουλή refused to sanction the measures they had resolved on in the particular case to which we are now alluding. Another instance in which the Boeotarchs appear as executive is their interference with Agesilaüs, on his embarking from Aulis for Asia (B.C. 396), when they prevented him offering sacrifice as he wished. Still, the principal duty of the Boeotarchs was of a military nature: thus, they led into the field the troops of their respective States; and when at home they took whatever measures were requisite to forward the military operations of the league or of their own State. For example, we read of one of the Theban Boeotarchs ordering the Thebans to come in arms to the ecclesia for the purpose of being ready to attack Plataea. Each State of the confederacy elected one Boeotarch, the Thebans two, although on one occasion—i. e. after the return of the exiles with Pelopidas (B.C. 379)—we read of there being three at Thebes. The total number from the whole confederacy varied with the number of the independent States. Mention is made of the Boeotarchs by Thucydides, in connection with the battle of Delium (B.C. 424). There is, however, a difference of opinion with respect to his meaning: some understand him to speak of eleven, some of twelve, and others of thirteen Boeotarchs. Dr. Arnold is disposed to adopt the last number; and we think the context is in favour of the opinion that there were then thirteen Boeotarchs, so that the number of free States was twelve. At the time of the battle of Leuctra (B.C. 371), we find seven Boeotarchs mentioned; on another occasion, when Greece was invaded by the Gauls (B.C. 279), we read of four. Livy states that there were twelve, but before the time (B.C. 171) to which his statement refers Plataea had been reunited to the league. Still the number mentioned in any case is no test of the actual number, inasmuch as we are not sure that all the Boeotarchs were sent out by their respective states on every expedition or to every battle.

The Boeotarchs, when engaged in military service, formed a council of war, the decisions of which were determined on by a majority of votes, the president being one of the two Theban Boeotarchs who commanded alternately. Their period of service was a year, beginning about the winter solstice; and whoever continued in office longer than his time was punishable with death both at Thebes and in other cities. Epaminondas and Pelopidas did so on their invasion of Laconia (B.C. 369), but their eminent services saved them; in fact, the judges did not even come to a vote respecting the former (οὐδὲ ἀρχὴν περὶ αὐτοῦ θέσθαι τὴν ψῆφον). At the expiration of the year, a Boeotarch was eligible to office a second time, and Pelopidas was repeatedly chosen. From the case of Epaminondas and Pelopidas, who were brought before Theban judges (δικασταί) for transgression of the law which limited the time of office, we may conclude that each Boeotarch was responsible to his own State alone, and not to the general body of the four councils.

Mention is made by Livy of an election of Boeotarchs. He further informs us that the league (*concilium*) was broken up by the Romans B.C. 171. Still, it must have been partially revived, as we are told of a second breaking-up by the Romans after the destruction of Corinth, B.C. 146. See Freeman, *Hist. of Federal Government* (1893), and Ten Breujel, *De Foedere Boeotico* (Groningen, 1834).

Boeotia (Βοιωτία). A country of Greece proper, lying to the northwest of Attica, and shut in by the chains of Helicon, Cithaeron, Parnassus, and, towards the sea, Ptoüs; which mountains enclosed a large plain, constituting the chief part of the country. Numerous rivers, of which the Cephissus was the most important, descending from the heights, had probably stagnated for a long time, and formed lakes, of which the Copaïs was the largest. These same rivers appear to have formed the soil of Boeotia, which is among the most fruitful in Greece. Boeotia was also perhaps the most thickly settled part of Greece, for no other could show an equal number of important cities. This country, as we learn from the concurrent testimony of Strabo, Pausanias, and other ancient writers, was first occupied by several barbarous clans, under the various names of Aeones, Ectenes, Temmices, and Hyantes. To these succeeded, according to the common account, Cadmus and his followers, who, after expelling some of the indigenous tribes above mentioned, and conciliating others, founded a city, which became afterwards so celebrated under the name of Thebes, and to which he gave the name of Cadmea. The descendants of Cadmus were compelled, subsequently, to evacuate Boeotia, after the capture of Thebes by the Epigoni, and to seek refuge in the country of the Illyrian Encheleës (Herod. v. 61). They regained possession, however, of their former territory, but were once more expelled, as we learn from Strabo, by a numerous horde of Thracians and others. On this occasion, having withdrawn into Thessaly, they united themselves with the people of Arné, a district of that province, and for the first time assumed the name of Boeotians. After a lapse of some years, they were compelled to abandon Thessaly, when they once more succeeded in re-establishing themselves in their original abode, to which they now communicated the name of Boeotia. This event, according to Thucydides, occurred about sixty years after the capture of Troy; but, in order to reconcile this account with the statement of Homer, who distinctly names the Boeotians among the Grecian forces assembled at that memorable siege, the historian admits that a Boeotian division (ἀποδασμός) had already settled in this province prior to the migration of the great body of the nation (i. 12).

Boeotian Coin.

The government of Boeotia remained under the monarchical form till the death of Xanthus, who fell in single combat with Melanthus the Messenian, when it was determined to adopt a republican constitution. This, though imperfectly known to us, appears to have been a compound of aristocratic and democratic principles, the former being apparent in the appointment of thirteen annual magistrates named Boeotarchs (see BOEOTARCHES), who presided over the military as well as civil departments; the latter in the establishment of four councils, which were possessed, in fact, of the sovereign authority, since all measures of importance were to be submitted to their deliberation. The general assembly of the Boeotian Republic was held in the temple of the Itonian Athené. From the extent and population of their territory the Boeotians might have played the first part in Greece, if they had not been prevented by the bad government of the cities, by the jealousy of Thebes, and the consequent want of union. And yet the example of Epaminondas (q. v.) and Pelopidas (q. v.) afterwards showed that the genius of two men could outweigh all these defects. The Boeotians were regarded by their neighbours, the Athenians, as naturally a stupid race. Much of this, however, was wilful exaggeration, and must be ascribed to the national enmity which seems to have existed from the earliest times between these two nations. Moreover, this country produced, in fact, many illustrious men, such as Hesiod, Pindar, Plutarch, Epaminondas, and Pelopidas. In Boeotia, too, Mount Helicon was sacred to the Muses, to whom also many of the fountains and rivers of the country were consecrated. In Boeotia are several celebrated ancient battle-fields, the former glory of which has been increased by later events; namely, Plataea (now the village Kokla), where Pausanias and Aristides established the liberty of Greece by their victory over Mardonius; Leuctra, where Epaminondas triumphed over the Spartans; Coronea, where the Spartan Agesilaüs defeated the Thebans; and Chaeronea, where Philip founded Macedonian supremacy on the ruins of Grecian freedom. Near Tanagra, the birthplace of Corinna, the best wine was produced; here also cocks were bred, of remarkable size, beauty, and courage, with which the Grecian cities, passionately fond of cock-fighting, were supplied.

The best-known towns of Boeotia were Orchomenus, Tegyra, Haliartus, Coronea, and Chaeronea, near Lake Copaïs; Larymna, Phocae, Aulis, Delium, and Oropus, near the Euripus; Thisbé, Ascra, Thespiae, and Leuctra, near the Gulf of Corinth; Thebae, in the plain between Lake Hylica and Mount Teumessus; Potniae and Therapnae, south of Thebes; and Plataeae, Erethrae, Eleum, Tanagra, and Pherae, in the valley of the Asopus.

Boëthius (better **Boëtius**), ANICIUS MANLIUS TORQUĀTUS SEVERĪNUS. A Roman statesman and scholar, born in Rome about A.D. 475, and one of the distinguished family of the Anicii, who had for some time been Christians. Having been left an orphan in his childhood, he was taken in his tenth year to Athens, where he remained eighteen years, and acquired a stock of knowledge far beyond the average. After his return to Rome, he was held in high esteem among his contemporaries for his learning and eloquence. He attracted the attention of Theodoric, who in A.D. 510 made him consul, and, in spite of his patriotic and independent attitude, gave him a prominent share in the government. The trial of the consul Albinus, however, brought with it the ruin of Boëthius. Albinus was accused of maintaining a secret understanding with the Byzantine court, and Boëthius stood up boldly in his defence, declaring that if Albinus was guilty, so was he, and the whole Senate with him. Thus involved in the same charge, he was sentenced to death by the cowardly assembly whose cause he had represented. He was thrown into prison at Pavia, and executed in the year 525. While in prison he wrote his famous work, *De Consolatione Philosophiae*, in five books, a splendid testimony to his noble mind and to his scholarly attainments. The *editio princeps* was published at Nuremberg in 1473 by A. Coburger. An Anglo-Saxon version made by Alfred the Great exists, of which an edition by Fox appeared in London in 1864. A good edition of the Latin text is that of Peiper (Leipzig, 1871).

Besides writing the treatise *De Consolatione*, Boëthius also translated many works on philosophy, rhetoric, and mathematics from the Greek, most of which are extant. His translations from Aristotle gave him much influence in the development of scholasticism; and his manuals of geometry, arithmetic, and music were long used in the mediæval schools. He was the last Roman writer of any note to show a good knowledge of the Greek language and literature.

Bogud. See Bocchus.

Boiae (κλοιός). A collar of wood or iron put on the necks of slaves or criminals as a punishment. See the pun in Plaut. *Capt.* iv. 2, 109.

Boii. One of the most powerful of the Keltic people, said to have dwelt originally in Gallia Transalpina, but in what part of the country is uncertain. At an early time they migrated in two great swarms, one of which crossed the Alps and settled in the country between the Po and the Apennines; the other crossed the Rhine and settled in the part of Germany called Boihemum (Böhmen, Bohemia) after them, and between the Danube and the Tyrol. The Boii in Italy long carried on a fierce struggle with the Romans, but they were at length subdued by the consul P. Scipio in B.C. 191, and subsequently incorporated in the province of Gallia Cisalpina. The Boii in Germany maintained their power longer, but were at length subdued by the Marcomanni, and expelled from the country.

Bola, Bolae, or **Volae.** An ancient town of the Aequi, belonging to the Latin League.

Bolbé (Βόλβη). A lake in Macedonia, emptying itself by a short river into the Strymonic Gulf, near Bromiscus and Aulon.

Bolbitīné (Βολβιτίνη). Now Rosetta; a city of Lower Egypt, near the mouth of a branch of the Nile (the westernmost but one), which was called the Bolbitine mouth (τὸ Βολβίτινον στόμα).

Bolster. See Culcita; Pulvinus.

Bombycīnum (from βόμβυξ, "a silk-worm"). One of the names applied to silk, for which see Sericum.

Bombylius (βομβύλιος). A drinking-vessel with a very narrow mouth, whence it is called σύστομος or στενόστομος. The name is supposed to have been formed in imitation of the noise which water or any liquid makes in passing through a narrow opening.

Bombyx (βόμβυξ). The silk-worm. See Sericum.

Bomilcar. A Numidian, deep in the confidence of Iugurtha. When Iugurtha was at Rome, in B.C. 109, Bomilcar effected for him the assassination of Massiva. In B.C. 107, he plotted against Iugurtha. See Iugurtha.

Bomonīkes (βωμονίκης). Among the rigorous exercises to which the Spartan youths were subjected was a scourging before the altar of Artemis Orthia or Orthosia. He who held out longest under the scourging was styled Bomonikes—a great honour. See Plutarch, *Inst. Lac.* 239, 32.

Bomos (βωμός). An altar. See Ara.

Bona. In Roman law, the word *bona* is (1) sometimes used to express the whole of a man's property; and in the phrases *bonorum emptio, cessio, possessio*, the word *bona* has this meaning. It expresses all that concerns a man's proprietary position, whether as owner, possessor, creditor, or debtor. Thus the word *bona* is simply the property as an object; it does not express the nature of the relation between it and the person who has the ownership or enjoyment of it.

(2) In some places the word *bona* is used to signify a man's assets, i. e. his property after the deduction of that which he owes. It is also used for separate portions of a man's property.

The legal expression *in bonis*, as opposed to *dominium* or Quiritary ownership, means that property is held under a praetorian or equitable, and not under a civil or legal, title. The distinction is explained in the following passage of Gaius (ii. 40): "Among foreigners (*peregrini*) there is only one kind of ownership (*dominium*), so that a man is either the owner of a thing or he is not. And this was formerly the case among the Roman people; for a man was either owner *ex iure Quiritium*, or not owner at all. But afterwards the ownership was divided, so that now one man may be the owner of a thing according to strict law (*dominus ex iure Quiritium*), and at the same time another may be entitled to the beneficial ownership of it (*in bonis habere*). For instance, if I do not convey to you a *res mancipi*, either by the form of *mancipatio* or of *in iure cessio*, but simply deliver it to you, you acquire the praetorian title to the thing, but it will remain mine *ex iure Quiritium*, until possession gives you a civil title by usucaption. For when the usucaption is once complete, from that time it begins to be yours absolutely (*pleno iure*); that is, it is yours both *in bonis* and also yours *ex iure Quiritium*, just as if it had been mancipated to you, or transferred to you by *in iure cessio*."

Quiritary ownership originally and properly signified that ownership of a thing which was recognized by the law; it did not express a compound, but a simple notion, which was that of absolute ownership. But when it was once established that one man might have the Quiritary ownership, and another the sole right to the enjoyment of the same thing, the complete notion of Quiritary ownership became a notion compounded of the strict legal notion of ownership and that of the right to enjoy, as united in the same person. And as a man might have both the Quiritary ownership and the right to the enjoyment of a thing, so one might have the Quiritary ownership only, and another might have the enjoyment of it only. This bare ownership was sometimes expressed by the same terms (*ex iure Quiritium*) as that ownership which was complete, but sometimes it was appropriately called *nudum ius Quiritium* (Gaius, iii. 100). The historical origin of this double ownership is unknown. See Dominium; Ius; Mancipium.

Bona Cadūca. Caducum (from *cado*) signifies "that which falls," and in its general legal sense might be anything without an owner, or what the person entitled to neglected to take (Cic. *De Or.* iii. 31; *Phil.* x. 5); but the strict legal sense of *caducum* and *bona caduca* is that stated by Ulpian (*Fragm.* tit. xvii. *de caducis*), which is as follows:

If a thing is left by will to a person, so that he might take it by the *ius civile*, but from some cause does not take it, that thing is called *caducum*, as if it had fallen from him; for instance, if a legacy was left to an unmarried person, or a *Latinus Iunianus*, and the unmarried person did not within a hundred days obey the law (i. e. by marrying), or if within the same time the *Latinus* did not obtain the *ius Quiritium*, or if a *heres ex parte* or a legatee died or became a *peregrinus* before the opening of the will, the thing was *caducum*.

Caducum, or lapse of a devise, implies that a valid devise has been made, which the devisee is unable or unwilling to take.

Caducum further implies that the will of which the lapsed devise is a part has come into operation. Strictly speaking, a devise which failed in the testator's lifetime was not *caducum;* it was, however, treated like a *caducum*, and so said to be *in causa caduci* (*Cod.* vi. 51, 2).

Either a share of an inheritance or a particular *legatum* might become *caducum*. The law alluded to in the passage of Ulpian cited above is the Lex Iulia et Papia Poppaea. This law, which was passed in the time of Augustus (A.D. 9), had the double object of encouraging marriages and enriching the treasury—*aerarium* (Tac. *Ann.* iii. 25)—and contained with reference to these two objects a great number of provisions. Martial (v. 75) alludes to a person who married in order to comply with the law. For the *dos caduca*, see Dos.

Bona Dea ("The good goddess"). An Italian deity, supposed to preside over the earth and all the blessings which spring from it. She was also the patron goddess of chastity and fruitfulness in women. The names Fauna, Maia, and Ops were originally no more than varying appellations given by the priests to the Bona Dea. She is represented in works of art with a sceptre in her left hand, a wreath of vine leaves on her head, and a jar of wine at her side. Near her image was a consecrated serpent; indeed, a number of tame serpents were kept in her temple, which was situated in Rome on the slope of the Aventine. All kinds of healing plants were preserved in her sanctuary. She was regarded in Rome as an austere virgin goddess, whose temple men were forbidden to enter. She belonged, accordingly, to the circle of deities who were worshipped by the Vestal Virgins. The anniversary of the foundation of her temple was held on the 1st of May, when prayers were offered up to her for the averting of earthquakes. Besides this, a secret festival was held to her on behalf of the public welfare, in the house of the officiating consul or praetor of the city, by matrons and the Vestal Virgins, on the night of May 3–4. The mistress of the house presided. No man was allowed to be present at this celebration, or even to hear the name of the goddess. After offering a sacrifice of sucking pigs, the women performed a dance, accompanied by stringed and wind instruments. Under the Empire the festival degenerated into a mystic performance of extravagant and indecent character (Juv. vi. 313).

Bona Fides. A term frequently used by Roman writers, especially by the jurists, and is opposed in meaning to *mala fides* and *dolus malus*. It implies the absence of all fraud, insincerity, unfair dealing, and bad faith, and is hence a necessary ingredient in all binding contracts. *Bona fide possidere* is said of him who has acquired the possession of a thing under what he believes to be a good title.

In various actions arising out of mutual dealings, such as buying and selling, lending and hiring, partnership, and others, *bona fides* is equivalent to *aequum* and *iustum;* and such actions were sometimes called *bonae fidei actiones*. The formula of the praetor, which was the authority of the index, empowered him in such cases to inquire and determine *ex bona fide*, that is, according to the real merits of the case.

Bonam Copiam Iurāre. A phrase expressive of the act of taking an oath to one's solvency (Varro, *L. L.* vii. 105). The expression used by Cicero (*Ad Fam.* ix. 16), *bonam copiam eiurare*, is usually interpreted to mean the taking of an oath by a debtor to the fact of his insolvency. See Bonorum Cessio.

Bona Vacantia. The property left by a person at death not disposed of by will, and when there is no legal heir. See Heres.

Bonna. The modern Bonn. A town on the left bank of the Rhine, in Lower Germany, and in the territory of the Ubii; a strong fortress of the Romans, and the regular quarters of a Roman legion. See Germania.

Bononia. (1) See Felsina. (2) See Gesoriacum.

Bonōrum Cessio. As will be seen by reference to the article Bonam Copiam Iurare, the principle of relieving insolvent debtors, who fulfilled certain conditions, from liability to imprisonment was recognized to some extent under the Republic. Iulius Caesar, when consul, B.C. 48, as a temporary measure of relief in time of distress, owing to the Civil War, discharged debtors who made over their property to their creditors from their debts (Caes. *De Bell. Civ.* iii. 1; cf. Poste's *Gaius*, p. 347, 2d ed.).

Cessio bonorum was introduced by a Lex Iulia. This law allowed an insolvent debtor to make a voluntary assignment of his property to his creditors. By making such assignment, the debtor obtained three advantages: (1) He escaped imprisonment. (2) He did not become *infamis*. (3) In respect to property acquired subsequently to the assignment, he had the *beneficium competentiae* when sued by his old creditors—i. e. he could retain sufficient for his bare maintenance. He had not this right against creditors who had become so subsequent to the act of assignment. The property assigned by the debtor was sold by the process of *bonorum emptio* (q. v.), the proceeds being distributed among the creditors. It is to be noticed that the assignment did not operate as a discharge, after-acquired property being liable, subject to the limitation explained above.

Bonōrum Collatio. By the rules of the civil law, emancipated children had no rights to the inheritance of their father, since they had become strangers to his family. (See Emancipatio.) But in course of time the praetor granted to emancipated children the privilege of equal succession with those who remained in the power of the father at the time of his death. This favour was granted to emancipated children only on condition that they should bring into one common stock, to be distributed with their father's estate, whatever property they had at the time of the father's death, and which would have been acquired for the father in case they had still remained in his power. This was called *collatio bonorum*.

Bonōrum Emptio. The technical term in Roman jurisprudence for the seizure of goods. If a man sentenced to pay a certain sum did not perform his obligation within thirty days, the creditor obtained permission from the praetor to attach his goods. After a renewed respite of thirty days the sale followed by auction to the highest bidder, the intending purchaser bidding for the whole property, with its assets and liabilities. The former proprietor might intervene and promise payment at any time before the fall of the hammer. The property once knocked down to him, the buyer became the absolute owner. A person against whom these proceedings were taken incurred *infamia*. See MANUS INIECTIO.

Bonōrum Possessio. The technical term in Roman law for the succession which the praetor gave to the inheritance of a deceased person. See HERES.

Bonus Eventus. A Roman deity first worshipped by the rustics, and represented as holding in one hand a cup and in the other a spray

Bonus Eventus. (British Museum.)

of wheat or other grain (Varro, *R. R.* i.). He personified the favourable issue of events.

Books and the Book Trade. See BIBLIOTHECA; LIBER.

Boōnae (*βοῶναι*). Persons in Athens who purchased oxen for the public sacrifices and feasts. They are spoken of by Demosthenes in conjunction with the ἱεροποιοί and those who presided over the mysteries, and are ranked by Libanius (*Declam.* 8) with the σιτῶναι, generals, and ambassadors. They were elected by the Ecclesia. There is often found mention of them on inscriptions as paying into the treasury the money received for the hides of sacrificed animals (δερματικόν).

Boōtes. See ARCTOS.

Bopp, FRANZ. The founder of the science of comparative philology, and one of the pioneers of Sanskrit studies in Germany, born at Mayence, September 14th, 1791. His parents having removed to Aschaffenburg, the young Bopp there attended the gymnasium, and afterwards enjoyed the instruction of Windischmann. At the suggestion of Windischmann, he went to Paris in 1812 to continue his studies in Oriental languages, especially in Sanskrit, and after five years in Paris to London, where he remained until 1820. During his sojourn in Paris and London he received from the Bavarian Academy of Sciences an annual stipend of 1000 florins. In 1820 he was anxious to be made Professor of Sanskrit at Würzburg, but the authorities considered it entirely unnecessary to create a chair for that language. In the following year, however, the brothers Von Humboldt, after great exertions in his behalf, had him appointed *professor extraordinarius* for Oriental languages and the science of language at Berlin, where he was made a member of the Academy in 1822, and *professor ordinarius* in 1825—a position in which he was active until stricken with apoplexy in 1864. He died October 23d, 1867.

His principal works in the field of comparative philology are: *Ueber das Conjugationssystem der Sanskrit-Sprache in Vergleichung mit jenem der griechischen, lateinischen, persischen und germanischen Sprache* (Frankfort-on-the-Main, 1816), published in an English translation in 1819; *Vergleichende Grammatik des Sanskrit, Send, Armenischen, Griechischen, Lateinischen, Litauischen, Altslawischen, Gotischen und Deutschen* (Berlin, 1833–52; second edition 1856–61, third edition, posthumously, 1868–71); *Die keltischen Sprachen in ihrem Verhältnisse zum Sanskrit u. s. w.* (Berlin, 1839); *Ueber das Albanesische in seinen verwandtschaftlichen Beziehungen* (Berlin, 1855); *Vergleichendes Accentuationssystem* (Berlin, 1854). His Sanskrit publications include considerable extracts from the *Mahabhârata*, very valuable works on Sanskrit grammar, and the *Glossarium Sanscritum.*

Bopp was not, it is true, the first to remark upon the striking resemblance of Sanskrit to the classical and other European languages. That resemblance had been observed before 1588 by Filippo Sassetti, and subsequently by many others, noticeably by Père Cœurdoux in 1767, and by Sir William Jones in 1786; Jones claimed a common origin for Sanskrit, Persian, Greek, Latin, Gothic, and Keltic—an idea carried out in much greater detail by Friedrich von Schlegel (q. v.) in 1808. It was, however, reserved for Bopp to put this startling doctrine (for such, and even preposterous, it seemed to most classical scholars of that day) upon a scientific basis; and this he did, at the early age of twenty-five. His predecessors had noted chiefly the resemblances between individual words of Sanskrit and those other languages; Bopp turned his gaze upon the grammatical structure of all these tongues, and was convinced of its substantial identity in them all. The results of his investigations are embodied in the *Conjugationssystem.* The same method was thereafter applied successfully to the investigation of other families of speech. Bopp's object was, however, not merely the comparison of languages—this was with him only the means to an end—he sought to explain by this method the genesis of inflectional forms. His views on this point seem to have passed through three stages of development. (1) The first stage is represented by the *Conjugationssystem* of 1816. Friedr. von Schlegel (*Sprache und Weisheit der Indier*, 1808) had divided all languages into two groups, the *inflectional* and the *agglutinative;* inflection he called exclusively an *inner change* of the word, and denied to "suffixes" a derivation from originally independent words. Bopp adopted Schlegel's theory, but expanded it thus: a word may not only modify itself internally, but may absorb the "verbum substantivum," *esse*.

Bopp was clearly still under the influence of a doctrine commonly held at that time, that every sentence is necessarily a reflection of a logical judgment; as the result of this doctrine he declares that in strictness there can exist but one real verb, the verb *to be.* (2) Three years later, in the English edition of the *Conjugationssystem*, Bopp adopted the principle of *composition* to account for inflectional forms. The doctrine of roots had been advanced in Europe some forty years before, and Bopp, finding it not only substantiated by the structure of Sanskrit, but also expressed in detail by the ancient Hindû grammarians, made it his own task to account for the existing forms of language. A more important deviation from Schlegel's views is Bopp's derivation of the personal endings of the verb from the personal pronouns—an idea probably obtained indirectly from observation of the Semitic languages. "Of real inflections (in the Schlegelian sense) Bopp now recognizes only certain vowel-changes and the reduplication." (3) In his *Comparative Grammar* (1833), Bopp, breaking completely with Schlegel, commits himself to the "agglutinative" theory, according to which all words of Indo-European languages are derived from monosyllabic roots, which are either *verbal* or *pronominal;* the forms of inflection arise entirely from the combination of different roots, of which, in each combination, all but one have assumed a purely subordinate and modifying character. A curious *symbolic* principle is also advanced by him (e. g. the feminine forms are "fuller and rounder"), and a *mechanical* principle of balance, regulating the "weight" of syllables. Bopp speaks often of "physical laws" (which are nowadays called "phonetic laws"), and draws frequent metaphors from the natural sciences. Of great significance for his linguistic views are also his frequent personification of language, and the persistence with which he speaks only of its *decay*, of deterioration from an earlier stage of perfection, and not of its simultaneous *growth.*

Bopp's discoveries resulted less from any strictly scientific method of investigation instituted by him than from his remarkable genius, and it can therefore hardly be said that he founded a school. Though his discoveries needed much supplementing in detail (which they received in very great measure through the learning and genius of Pott); though his inclusion of the Malay-Polynesian languages in the Indo-European group has been entirely rejected by later scholars; and though his *Comparative Grammar* has been superseded by later works; yet the foundations of comparative philology are still in the main as he constructed them; and but for him linguistic students might still be building upon sand, as they built, and could not but build, ere his day.

The most recent and extensive work concerning Bopp is S. Lefmann's *Franz Bopp: sein Leben und seine Wissenschaft* (vol. i., Berlin, 1891), containing in a voluminous appendix Bopp's correspondence, never before published, with Windischmann, De Sacy, and other scholars of note. The best characterization of Bopp's scientific position is, however, still to be found in Delbrück's *Introduction to the Study of Language* (English translation by Miss Channing, Leipzig, 1884), from which the above sketch is largely taken. See also an article by A. Kuhn in *Unsere Zeit*, 1868; and one by Brugmann and Streitberg, forming an Introduction to vol. i. (1891-92) of their new periodical, *Indogermanische Forschungen.* The same volume also contains a notice of Lefmann's book.

Boots and Shoes. See CALCEUS; CALIGA; CREPIDA; SOLEA; SUTOR.

Borbetomăgus. The modern Worms, also called Vangiones, and at a later time Wormatia; a town of the Vangiones on the left bank of the Rhine in Upper Germany.

Boreas (Βορέας). In Greek mythology, the North Wind, son of Astraeus and Eos, brother of Zephyrus, Eurus, and Notus. His home was in the Thracian Salmydessus, on the Black Sea, whither he carried Orithyia from the games on the Ilissus, when her father, Erechtheus, king of Athens, had refused her to him in marriage. Their children were Calaïs and Zetes, the so-called Boreades, Cleopatra, the wife of Phineus, and Chioné, the beloved of Poseidon. (See EUMOLPUS.) It was this

Boreas. (Relief from the Tower of the Winds at Athens.)

relationship which was referred to in the oracle given to the Athenians, when the fleet of Xerxes was approaching, that "they should call upon their brother-in-law." Boreas answered their prayer and sacrifice by destroying a part of the enemy's fleet on the promontory of Sepias, whereupon they built him an altar on the banks of the Ilissus.

Boreasmi or Boreasmus (βορεασμοί or βορεασμός). A festival celebrated by the Athenians in honour of Boreas, which, as Herodotus (vii. 189) seems to think, was instituted during the Persian War, when the Athenians, being commanded by an oracle to invoke their γαμβρὸς ἐπίκουρος, prayed to Boreas. The fleet of Xerxes was soon afterwards almost entirely destroyed by a north wind, near Cape Sepias, and the grateful Athenians erected to his honour a temple on the banks of the Ilissus. Possibly, however, this merely revived an earlier celebration. A similar festival of Boreas was celebrated annually at Megalopolis, and by the Thurians. See Aelian, *V. H.* xii. 61.

Borsippa (τὰ Βόρσιππα). A suburb of Babylon, about eight miles distant from that city, and containing the pile Birs Nimroud, generally regarded as the remains of the Tower of Babel. See BABEL, TOWER OF.

Borysthĕnes (Βορυσθένης), afterwards DANAPRIS. The modern Dnieper, a river of European Sarmatia, flowing into the Euxine. Near its mouth, and at its junction with the Hypanis, lay the town of Borysthenes or Borysthenis (Kudak), also called Olbia, Olbiopolis, and Miletopolis, a colony of Miletus, and the most important Greek city on the north of the Euxine.

Bosius. See DUBOIS, SIMÉON.

Bospŏrus (Βόσπορος). A name applied to a strait of the sea. There were two straits known in antiquity by this appellation, namely, the Thracian and the Cimmerian Bosporus; the former now known by the name of the Straits or Channel of Constantinople, the latter the Straits of Caffa or

Theodosia, or, according to a later denomination, the Straits of Yenikalé. It connects the Palus Maeotis (Sea of Azov) with the Euxine. Various reasons have been assigned for the name. The best is that which makes the appellation refer to the early passage of agricultural knowledge from East to West (βοῦς, an ox, and πόρος, a passage). Nymphius tells us, on the authority of Accarion, that the Phrygians, desiring to pass the Thracian strait, built a vessel, on whose prow was the figure of an ox, calling the strait over which it carried them βοὸς πόρος, Bosporus, or the ox's passage (cf. Oxford in English). Dionysius of Halicarnassus, Valerius Flaccus and others of the ancient writers refer the name to the history of Io, who, when transformed into a cow (βοῦς) by Heré, swam across this strait to avoid her tormentor. Arrian says that the Phrygians were directed by an oracle to follow the route which an ox would point out to them, and that on one being roused by them for this purpose, it swam across the strait. (See Aesch. *Prom. Vinc.* 732; Long. i. 30.) The strait of the Thracian Bosporus properly extended from the Cyanean Rocks to the harbour of Byzantium or Constantinople. It is said to be sixteen miles in length, including the windings of its course, and its ordinary breadth about one and a half miles. In several places, however, it is very narrow; and the ancients relate that a person might hear birds sing on the opposite side, and that two persons might converse across it. Here Darius (q. v.) is said to have crossed on his expedition against the Scythians.

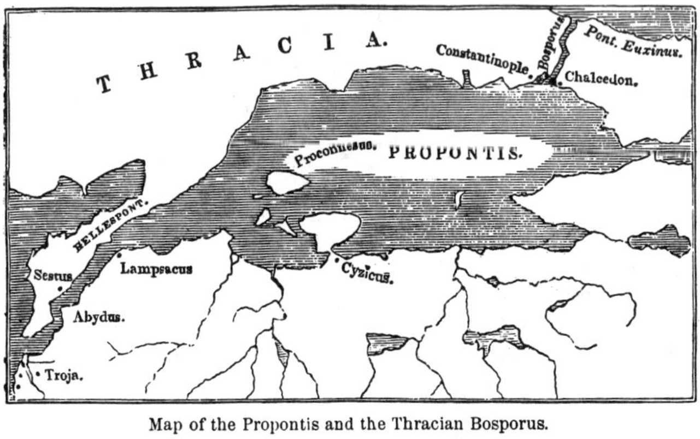

Map of the Propontis and the Thracian Bosporus.

Bostra (τὰ Βόστρα; O. T. Bozrah; Busrah). A city of Arabia, in an oasis of the Syrian Desert, south of Damascus.

Bottia (Βοττία) or **Bottiaea** (Βοττιαία). A district in Macedonia, on the right bank of the river Axius, extending in the time of Thucydides to Pieria on the west. The Bottiaei were a Thracian people, who, being driven out of the country by the Macedonians, settled in that part of the Macedonian Chalcidicé north of Olynthus which was called Botticé.

Botŭlus (ἀλλᾶς, φύσκη). A sausage; a favourite food of both Greeks and Romans, and sold in the streets and places of public resort by venders known as *botularii* (Mart. i. 42, 9). These sausages, like our own, were usually made of pork, cooked in a frying-pan, and eaten hot (Juv. x. 355; Petron. 31). Sausages were also made of the blood of animals, like the German *Blutwurst* (Tertull. *Apol.* 9). The name *tomaculum* is occasionally used for *botulus*, but rather means sausage-meat.

Bouae (βοῦαι). See AGELA.

Boukŏloi (βούκολοι). Members of a religious college at Pergamum during the Roman Empire, engaged in celebrating the mysteries of Dionysus καθηγήμων. There appear to have been colleges of a similar name throughout Ionia and Pontus. See Foucart, *Les Associations Religieuses chez les Grecs*, pp. 114–116.

Boulé (Βουλή). In the Homeric Age, a Boulé, or council of principal men, was probably a well-established and important feature in every Greek state. The Boulé of the Greek army before Troy consists of the kings or principal chieftains (βασιλῆες, γέροντες), who meet at the call of Agamemnon, commander-in-chief, for free and equal debate on questions of policy.

In historical times, a Boulé is found in very many Greek states, but it is only at Athens that the institution is intimately known to us. Here there were, strictly speaking, two bodies bearing this name—the Senate of the Areopagus (see AREOPAGUS) and the Senate of Five Hundred. It is the latter body which is always meant when the Boulé is spoken of without further designation, and it is this which is here described.

COMPOSITION, ORGANIZATION, ETC.—The membership of the Boulé, which under the Solonian constitution had been 400, 100 from each of the four old tribes, was raised by Clisthenes (B.C. 508–507) to 500, 50 from each of the ten new tribes. When, in 306, the tribes were increased to twelve, the Boulé was increased to 600, but in the time of Hadrian it was reduced to 500 again. The senators (βουλευταί) had to be at least thirty years of age. Their term of service was from the beginning to the end of an Attic year. They were selected by lot; the senators of one tribe not being taken indiscriminately from the entire tribe, but so that each deme of the tribe should have a fixed number of members. Possibly the demes nominated candidates by ballot, and the lot was used only to select the necessary number from among these nominees. Every senator, before entering into office, had to undergo an examination (δοκιμασία) by the retiring Senate. At the expiration of his term he had to render an account (εὔθυνα) of his official career.

In order to facilitate the despatch of business and to secure rotation of authority, the year was divided into ten periods (35 or 36 days each, in ordinary years), called *prytanies* (πρυτανεῖαι); and the senators of each tribe in turn assumed the leadership for one prytany, under the name of *prytanes* (πρυτάνεις). The prytanes had their headquarters in the *prytaneum* (πρυτανεῖον), or *tholos* (θόλος), a circular building near the Senate-house (βουλευτήριον). Matters of business could here be brought before them, with a view to prompt consideration by Senate and Ecclesia. Every day one of the prytanes was selected by lot as *epistates* (ἐπιστάτης τῶν πρυτανέων). He kept the public seal and the keys of the temples in which were deposited the public treasure and the public archives. In the fifth century this epistates also presided at the meeting of the Boulé held on his day, as well as at the meeting of the Ecclesia, if one was held. Early in the fourth century, perhaps in 378–377, a more complicated method of securing a chairman was introduced. The aforesaid epistates selected by lot nine *proëdri* (πρόεδροι), one from each of the non-prytanizing tribes, and out of the proëdri a second *epistates* (ἐπιστάτης τῶν προέδρων), to serve as chairman and carry forward, with the assistance of his fellow-proëdri, the legislative business of the day. No one could serve as ἐπιστάτης τῶν πρυτανέων or as ἐπιστάτης τῶν προέδρων for more than one day in the same year. The Boulé had also a secretary (γραμματεύς), who kept the records of both Boulé and Ecclesia. A session was held every day, except holidays; there would perhaps be 300 sessions in a year. The usual place of meeting was the βουλευτήριον, near the Agora. The pay for attendance was, in Aristotle's time, five obols per day.

FUNCTIONS: (1) *Legislative.*—According to the theory of the Athenian constitution, no subject could be acted upon in the Ecclesia until it had been considered in the Boulé and a bill (προβούλευμα) there drawn up. The Boulé, however, was a mere committee of the Ecclesia, not a co-ordinate legislative body. Its concurrence was not necessary to the passage of a measure.

(2) *Administrative.*—These were very numerous and extensive. For example: the Boulé decided on the claims of pauper cripples to receive the dole provided for by law; it determined who should belong to the cavalry (ἱππεῖς), and inspected the cavalry horses, condemning the unfit; it superintended the navy and the docks; above all, it had a general oversight of the public finance, presiding over the farming of taxes, the renting of mines, payments to the special financial officials, etc. These and other administrative duties doubtless constituted the bulk of the work of the Boulé.

(3) *Judicial.*—The Boulé, like other magistracies, could punish those who violated its authority. It could also, either of its own motion or on the denunciation (εἰσαγγελία) of a private citizen, pass sentence on officials, especially financial officials, for malfeasance in office. In the period of the developed democracy its power, in most cases, seems to have been limited to the imposition of a fine of 500 drachmas. The evidence, however, on this point is confusing. See J. W. Headlam, *Election by Lot at Athens*, chap. ii.

Bouleuseos Graphé (βουλεύσεως γραφή). An impeachment for conspiracy. In this case βουλεύσεως is the abbreviated form of ἐπιβουλεύσεως, and is the name for two very different actions at Attic law. (1) An action for conspiracy against life, and instituted (*a*) by the person attacked, if competent, or by his or her legal patron (κύριος); or (*b*) if the plot succeeded, by near kinsmen or the κύριος. (2) An action against the person who had wrongfully inscribed another as state debtor. See PSEUDENGRAPHÉS GRAPHÉ.

Bouleuterion (βουλευτήριον). See BOULÉ.

Boustrophēdon (βουστροφηδόν). The zigzag method of writing—i. e. alternately from right to left, and left to right. See ALPHABET.

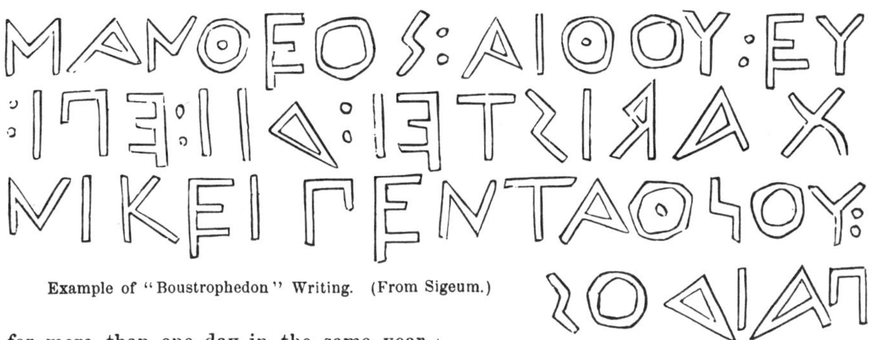

Example of "Boustrophedon" Writing. (From Sigeum.)

Bovillae. An ancient town in Latium at the foot of the Alban Mountains, on the Appian Way, about ten miles from Rome. Near it Clodius was killed by Milo (B.C. 52).

Bows and **Arrows.** See ARCUS; PHARETRA; SAGITTA.

Brabēum, Brabīum, or **Bravīum** (βραβεῖον). A prize given to the winner at the public games (Prudent. Περὶ Στεφ. v. 538). The cry *bravo*, as a sign of applause or approval, used to be derived from this word.

Bracae (ἀναξυρίδες, θύλακοι). Trousers; pantaloons. These were common to all the nations that encircled the Greek and Roman population, extending from the Indian to the Atlantic Ocean. Hence Aristagoras, king of Miletus, in his interview with Cleomenes, king of Sparta, described the attire of a large portion of them in these terms: "They carry bows and a short spear, and go to battle in trousers and with hats upon their heads." Hence, also, the phrase *bracati militis arcus*, implying that those who wore trousers were in general armed with the bow. In particular, we are informed of the use of trousers or pantaloons among the following nations: (1) The Medes and Persians (περὶ τὰ σκέλεα ἀναξυρίδας). (2) The Parthians and Armenians. (3) The Phrygians. (4) The Sacae. (5) The Sarmatae. (6) The Dacians and Getae. (7) The Teutones. (8) The Franks. (9) The Belgae. (10) The Britons (*veteres bracae Britonis pauperis*). (11) The Gauls (*Gallia Bracata*, now Provence; *sagatos bracatosque;* χρῶνται ἀναξυρίσι, ἃς ἐκεῖνοι βράκας προσαγορεύουσι).

The Gallic term "brakes," which Diodorus Siculus has preserved in the last-cited passage (lv. 30), also survives in the Scottish "breeks" and the English "breeches." Corresponding terms are used in all the Northern languages. (See Skeat,

Etymolog. Dict. s. v. "Breeches.") The Cossack and Persian trousers of the present day differ in no material respect from those which were anciently worn in the same countries.

In conformity with the preceding list of testimonies, the monuments of every kind which contain representations of the nations included in it, exhibit them in trousers, thus clearly distinguishing them from Greeks and Romans. An example is seen in the annexed group of Sarmatians, taken from the Column of Trajan.

Sarmatians wearing Bracae. (Column of Trajan.)

The proper bracae of the Eastern and Northern nations were loose (κεχαλασμέναι, *laxae*), and they are therefore very aptly, though ludicrously, described in Euripides as "variegated bags" (τοὺς θυλάκους τοὺς ποικίλους). To the Greeks they must have appeared highly ridiculous, although Ovid mentions the adoption of them by the descendants of some of the Greek colonists on the Euxine (*Trist.* v. 11, 34).

Bracae worn by Roman Soldier. (Column of Trajan.)

Trousers were principally woollen; but Agathias states that in Europe they were also made of linen and of leather; probably the Asiatics made them of cotton and of silk. Sometimes they were striped (*virgatae*), ornamented with a woof of various colours.

Roman soldiers fighting in the North were obliged to wear them, owing to the severity of the climate; and by the second century they were worn even at Rome. The emperor Alexander Severus wore white bracae; some of his predecessors, scarlet ones (*coccineae*).

Bracarius, meaning properly a breeches-maker (Lamprid. *Alex. Sever.* 24), came to be used of a tailor in general.

Bracāta Gallia. See GALLIA.

Bracchiālé (περιβραχιόνιον). A piece of defensive armour which covered the *bracchium*, or part of the arm between the wrist and the elbow. It is distinctly mentioned by Xenophon (*Cyrop.* vi. 4, 2) as part of the accoutrements worn by the Persians, and is sometimes seen on figures of Roman gladiators, though the Latin name does not occur in this sense, except, perhaps, in Trebell. *Claud.* 14.

Bracciolini, GIAN FRANCESCO POGGIO, one of the most noted names in the history of classical study, was born at Terranova, near Florence, in 1380. He studied Latin under John of Ravenna, and Greek under Manuel Chrysoloras, after which he became a copyist of manuscripts, in which pursuit his dexterity brought him the acquaintance of the chief scholars of Florence, by whose aid he was received into the service of the Roman curia (1403) as a secretary. In this office he showed himself an enthusiastic advocate of classical study, and took a most important part in the revival of learning, caring little or nothing for the exciting political and ecclesiastical movements of the period. Bracciolini (or Poggio, as he is usually called) is best known for his remarkable success in recovering the lost masterpieces of Latin literature by his researches in the libraries of monasteries and convents, where manuscripts of priceless value to the classicist were lying hitherto unknown. In one of his epistles he relates how he discovered at St. Gall, in Switzerland, Quintilian, Verrius Flaccus (in part), and the commentaries of Asconius Pedianus. To him, likewise, we owe manuscripts of Lucretius, Columella, Silius Italicus, Manilius, Vitruvius, Ammianus Marcellinus, Nonius Marcellus, Probus, Flavius Caper, and Eutyches. At Langres he unearthed Cicero's oration *Pro Caecina*, and at Monte Cassino a codex of Frontinus. No considerations of morality stood in Bracciolini's way when the question of securing a valuable manuscript was before him. If a codex could be gained only by fraud, he employed fraud, as when he actually bribed a monk at Hersfeld to abstract manuscripts of Livy and Ammianus from the convent library.

Bracciolini was an extensive traveller, and has left some lively pictures of the contemporary life and customs of different European countries, especially of England and Switzerland, as well as some curious notes on the remains of antique art in Rome. He likewise describes the trial of Jerome of Prague. To pure literature he was a voluminous contributor, writing orations, epistles, treatises on rhetoric, translations from the Greek, moral essays, and fabliaux, all in Latin, as well as a history of Florence, written in imitation of the style of Livy. His *Facetiae* are remarkable alike for their indecency and for their caustic satires on the secular clergy. Of this class, his most famous writings are his violent and often filthy diatribes against Valla and Filelfo, who retorted in kind, and thus established a bad precedent which was followed in the later controversies of the Scaligers (q. v.), Scioppius, Salmasius, and Milton.

Bracciolini, who remained a layman until his death, retired in 1452 to Florence, of which republic he became the chancellor and historian. There he died in 1459, and was buried in the Church of Santa Croce. A statue of him by Donatello commemorates his services to the humanities. His life has been written in English by Shepherd (Liverpool, 1802). See also J. A. Symonds, *The Renaissance in Italy* (1886).

Bracelets. See ARMILLA; CAELATURA.

Brachmānae or **Brachmānes** (Βραχμᾶνες). A name used by the ancient geographers, sometimes of a caste of priests in India (the Brahmins), sometimes, apparently, of all the people whose religion was Brahminism, and sometimes of a particular tribe. See INDIA.

Branchĭdae (Βραγχίδαι), afterwards DIDȲMA. A place on the sea-coast of Ionia, a little south of Miletus, and celebrated for its temple and oracle of Apollo, surnamed Didymeus. This oracle, which the Ionians held in the highest esteem, was said to have been founded by Branchus, son of Apollo by a Milesian woman. The reputed descendants of this Branchus, the Branchidae, were the hereditary ministers of this oracle (Herod. i. 157). The temple, called Didymaeum, which was destroyed by Xerxes, was afterwards rebuilt, and its ruins contain some beautiful specimens of the Ionic order of architecture.

Brasĭdas (Βρασίδας). The most distinguished Spartan in the first part of the Peloponnesian War (q. v.). In B.C. 424, at the head of a small force, having effected a dexterous march through the hostile country of Thessaly, he gained possession of many of the cities in Macedonia that were subject to Athens; his greatest acquisition was Amphipolis. In 422, with only a handful of helots and mercenary troops, he gained a brilliant victory over Cleon, who had been sent with a powerful Athenian force to recover Amphipolis. Brasidas was slain in the battle. He was buried within the city, and the inhabitants honoured him as a hero by yearly sacrifices and by games.

Thucydides praises alike the eloquence and the liberality and wisdom of Brasidas, and Plato compares him to Achilles.

Brasidēa (Βρασίδεια). A festival held annually at Sparta with orations and contests, in memory of Brasidas (q. v.), who, after his death, in B.C. 422, received the honours of a hero. See Pausan. iii. 14.

Brattea (not *bractea:* see Lachmann on Lucret. iv. 727). A finely-beaten-out plate of metal, especially of gold. Thicker plates were called *laminae.* The gold-beater is styled *brattearius* or *bratteator.* These plates were used for adorning statues, furniture, walls and ceilings, and garments which were then called *vestes auratae* or *sigillatae.* Pliny (*H. N.* xxxiii. § 61) says that from an ounce of gold, 750 plates, each four fingers square, could be beaten.

Brauron (Βραυρῶν). A deme of Attica on the eastern bank of the river Erasinus, with a celebrated temple of Artemis, who was in consequence called Brauronia.

Brauronia (τὰ Βραυρώνια). An Attic festival held every fifth year in the little town of Brauron, in honour of Artemis Brauronia. At Brauron, Orestes and Iphigenia (q. v.) on their return from Tauris were supposed to have landed and to have left the statue of the Tauric goddess. The festival was under the superintendence of ten ἱεροποιοί; and the chief solemnity consisted in the circumstance that Attic girls between the ages of five and ten years, dressed in crocus-coloured garments, went in solemn procession to the sanctuary, where they were consecrated to the goddess. During this act, the ἱεροποιοί sacrificed a goat, and the girls performed a propitiatory rite in which they imitated bears. This rite may have simply arisen from the fact that the bear was sacred to Artemis, especially in Arcadia; but a tradition preserved in Suidas relates its origin as follows: In the Attic town of Phanidae a bear was kept, which was so tame that it was allowed to go about quite freely, and received its food from and among men. One day a girl ventured to play with it, and, on treating the animal rather harshly, it turned round and tore her to pieces. Her brothers, enraged at this, went out and killed the bear. The Athenians thereupon were visited by a plague; and when they consulted the oracle, the answer was given that they would rid themselves of the evil which had befallen them if they would compel some of their citizens to make their daughters propitiate Artemis by a rite called ἀρκτεύειν, for the crime committed against the animal sacred to the goddess. The command was more than obeyed; for the Athenians decreed that from thenceforth all women, before they could marry, should have once taken part in this festival, and have been consecrated to the goddess. Hence the girls themselves were called ἄρκτοι, the consecration ἀρκτεία, the act of consecrating ἀρκτεύειν, and to celebrate the festival ἀρκτεύεσθαι.

There was also a quinquennial festival called Brauronia, which was celebrated by men and dissolute women, at Brauron, in honour of Dionysus.

Brennus. The Latinized form of the Keltic title *bran,* "a prince." (1) A general of the Galli Senones, who entered Italy, defeated the Romans at the river Allia, and entered their city without opposition. The Romans fled into the Capitol, and left the whole city in the possession of their enemies. The Gauls climbed the Tarpeian Rock in the night, and the Capitol would have been taken, had not the Romans been awakened by the noise of the sacred geese in the Temple of Iuno and immediately repelled the enemy. (See MANLIUS.) Camillus, who was in banishment, marched to the relief of his country, and totally defeated the Gauls, so that not one remained to carry home the news of their destruction.

The Brennus Shield. (Dodwell.)

The destruction of the Gauls by Camillus is the national account given by the Roman writers, and is replete with error and exaggeration. The domination of the Gauls in Italy was certainly of long continuance, and was not terminated in the dramatic manner of the legend. See CAMILLUS; CELTAE; Kuno, *Vorgeschichte Roms* (1878); and Mommsen, *Hist. of Rome*, vol. i. p. 427 foll.

(2) Another Gallic leader, who made an irruption into Greece at the head of an army of his countrymen consisting of 152,000 foot and 20,000

horse. After ravaging various parts of northern Greece, they marched against Delphi, and endeavoured to plunder the temple. But the army of the invaders, according to the Grecian account, were seized with a panic terror during the night, and being attacked at daybreak by the Delphians and others of the Greeks, retreated in the utmost confusion. Large numbers perished, the Greeks continually hanging on the skirts of the retreating foe; and Brennus, wounded, and dispirited by his overthrow, killed himself in a fit of intoxication, B.C. 278 (Pausan. x. 19).

Breviarium. (1) The title of the brief history of Rome by Eutropius (q. v.)—more fully *Breviarium ab Urbe Condita.* It is written in simple style, and was largely read both in the original Latin and in the Greek translation. The best text is that of W. Hartel (Berlin, 1872). (2) A similar work, written at about the same time by Sex. Rufus Festus (q. v.).

Breviarium Alariciānum, or simply **Breviārium.** Alaric the second, king of the Visigoths (A.D. 484–507), who reigned over part of Gaul and Spain, commissioned a body of jurists, no doubt Romans, to make a selection from Roman statute law and from the writings of Roman jurists, which should form a legal code for his Roman subjects. The code was completed in A.D. 506, and submitted to a council of bishops and nobles held at Aduris (Aire) in Gascony, and by them approved. The work was then promulgated by Gojaric, the count of the palace (*comes palatii*), a certified copy forwarded to each *comes,* and the use of any other law prohibited. In some of the MSS. it is called *Lex Theodosii,* and the name *Breviarium Alaricianum* does not appear until the sixteenth century. The Breviarium contains several sources of Roman law otherwise almost entirely unknown, especially Paulus and the first five books of the Codex Theodosianus. There exist besides the MSS. of the Breviarium the MSS. of epitomes made in the Middle Ages. The standard edition is that by Haenel (1849). See also Biedenweg, *Commentarii ad Formulas Visigoth. novissime repertas* (Berlin, 1856).

Briareus (Βριάρεως). See AEGAEON.

Bribery. See AMBITUS; CRIMEN REPETUNDARUM; DECASMUS.

Bricks. See FICTILE; LATER.

Bridges. See PONS.

Brigantes. The most powerful of the British tribes, inhabiting the whole of the north of the island from the Abus (Humber) to the Roman Wall, with the exception of the southeastern corner of Yorkshire, which was inhabited by the Parisii. The Brigantes consequently inhabited the greater part of Yorkshire, and the whole of Lancashire, Durham, Westmoreland, and Cumberland. Their capital was Eboracum, now York. They were conquered by Petilius Cerealis in the reign of Vespasian. There was also a tribe of Brigantes in the south of Ireland, between the rivers Birgus (Barrow) and Dabrona (Blackwater), in the counties of Waterford and Tipperary.

Brigantīnus Lacus. The modern Bodensee, or Lake Constance; also known to the ancients as Venetus and Acronius. The Rhenus (Rhine) flows through it.

Brilessus (Βριλησσός). A range of hills uniting Mount Pentelicus with Anchesmus.

Brisēis (Βρισηΐς). The daughter of Briseus of Lyrnessus, who fell into the hands of Achilles, but was seized by Agamemnon. Hence arose the dire feud between the two heroes. (See ACHILLES; AGAMEMNON; TROJAN WAR.) Her proper name was Hippodamia.

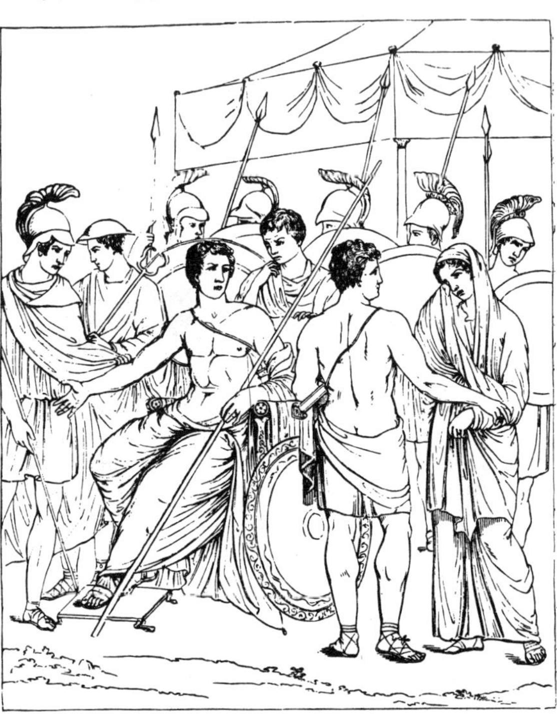

The Rape of Briseis. (Pompeian Painting.)

Britannia (Βρεττανία), called also ALBION. An island in the Atlantic Ocean, and the largest in Europe. The Phœnicians appear to have been early acquainted with it, and to have carried on there a traffic for tin. (See CASSITERIDES.) Commercial jealousy, however, induced them to keep their discoveries a profound secret. The Carthaginians succeeded to the Phœnicians, but were equally mysterious. Avienus (q. v.) in his poem entitled *Ora Maritima,* makes mention of the voyages of a certain Himilco, in this quarter, and professes to draw his information from the long-concealed Punic annals. Little was known of Britain until Caesar's time, who invaded and endeavoured, although ineffectually, to conquer the island. After a long interval, Ostorius, in the reign of Claudius, reduced the southern part of Britannia; and Agricola subsequently, in the reign of Domitian, extended the Roman dominion to the Frith of Forth and the Clyde. The whole force of the Empire, although exerted to the utmost under Septimius Severus, could not, however, reduce to subjection the hardy natives of the highlands. This emperor divided the country into two parts—Britannia Inferior or Southern

Britain, and Britannia Superior or Northern Britain—each under a special prefect. When the Empire was divided under Diocletian, Britain became a diocese of the *praefectura* of Gaul, and was governed by a *vicarius* residing at Eboracum (York). At this time it was marked out into five provinces, as follows: Britannia Prima (England south of the Thames), Britannia Secunda (Wales), Flavia Caesariensis (between the Thames, Severn, Mersey, and Humber), Maxima Caesariensis (all the rest of England up to the Wall of Hadrian), and Valentia (Scotland south of the Wall of Antoninus). Ptolemy enumerates fifty-six towns (*coloniae, municipia*) of Roman Britain, two of which (Eboracum and Verulamium) had the rights of Roman citizenship. Eboracum, Deva (Chester, *castra*), and Isca (Caerleon) were military centres, each being the station for a legion of Roman soldiers, chiefly, however, Gauls, Germans, and Iberians.

To what an extent the Romans succeeded in introducing the refinements of their civilization into Britain may be seen in the great number of their remains that have been found, including roads, houses, baths, painted walls, altars, ornaments, mosaics, sculpture, bronzes, coins, pottery, and various implements. Britain continued a Roman province until A.D. 426, when the troops, having been in a great measure withdrawn to assist Valentinian III. against the Huns, never returned. The Britons had become so enervated under the Roman yoke as to be unable to repel the incursions of the inhabitants of the north. They invoked, therefore, the aid of the Saxons (A.D. 407), by whom they were themselves subjugated and at length obliged to take refuge in the mountains of Wales.

Copper Coin of Antoninus Pius, about A.D. 138, showing figure of Britannia.

The name Britain was unknown to the Romans before the time of Caesar; though Aristotle as early as the fourth century B.C. speaks of the νῆσοι Βρεταννικαί. Some deduce the name of the Britons from the Gallic *Britti* (Cymric *brîth*), "painted," in allusion to the custom of a part of the inhabitants of painting their bodies; but Rhys rejects this etymology, without suggesting any that is more plausible. The other name, Albion, is etymologically connected with the Gaelic *alp*, "a high hill," or the Latin *albus*, "white." This was undoubtedly the Keltic name of the whole island.

Britain was famous for its Roman walls, of which traces remain to the present day. The first was built by Agricola, A.D. 79, nearly in the situation of the rampart of Hadrian and wall of Severus mentioned below. In A.D. 81, Agricola built a line of very strong forts from the Frith of Forth to the Frith of Clyde. This, however, was insufficient to check the barbarians after his departure. In A.D. 120, therefore, Hadrian erected a famous wall from Boulness on Solway Frith to a spot a little beyond Newcastle-upon-Tyne. It was sixty-eight English or seventy-four Roman miles long. Twenty years after this, Lollius Urbicus, under the emperor Antoninus, restored the second wall of Agricola, which is commonly called the Vallum Antonini. But the greatest of all was that of Severus, begun A.D. 209, and finished the next year, and which was only a few yards north of Hadrian's wall. It was garrisoned by ten thousand men. See Wright, *The Kelt, the Roman, and the Saxon* (1889); Coote, *The Romans of Britain* (1878); Scarth, *Roman Britain* (1883).

Britannĭcus. The agnomen of the son of the emperor Claudius by Messalina, and born in A.D. 42. Agrippina, the second wife of Claudius, induced the emperor to adopt her own son Nero, and to give him precedence in the succession. On the assumption of imperial power by Nero, Britannicus was put to death by poison (A.D. 55). His story is the subject of a play by Racine.

Britomartis (Βριτόμαρτις, "sweet maid"). A Cretan goddess, supposed to dispense happiness, and whose worship extended throughout the islands and along the coasts of the Mediterranean. Like Artemis, with whom she was sometimes identified, she was the patroness of hunters, fishermen, and sailors, and also goddess of birth and of health. Her sphere was Nature in its greatness and its freedom. As goddess of the sea she bore the name of Dictynna, the supposed derivation of which from the Greek δίκτυον, "a net," was explained by the following legend. She was the daughter of a huntress much beloved by Zeus and Artemis. Minos loved her, and followed her for nine months over valley and mountain, through forest and swamp, till he nearly overtook her, when she leaped from a high rock into the sea. She was saved by falling into some nets, and Artemis made her a goddess.

Brixellum. The modern Bregella or Brescella; a town on the right bank of the Padus (Po), in Gallia Cisalpina, where the emperor Otho (q. v.) committed suicide in A.D. 69.

Brixia. The modern Brescia; a town in Gallia Cisalpina. Through it flowed the river Mella.

Brizo (Βριζώ). A goddess localized in Delos, to whom women, in particular, paid worship as being the protectress of mariners. They set before her eatables of various kinds (fish being excluded) in little boats. She also presided over an oracle.

Bromius (Βρόμιος). From βρέμω, "to roar"; an epithet applied to Dionysus as the noisy god of the Bacchic revels.

Brontes (Βρόντης). See CYCLOPES.

Bronze. See AES.

Bruchīum (Βρυχεῖον). The Royal or Greek quarter of the city of Alexandria (q. v.) enclosed by its own walls. Here were the finest of the public buildings, and upon it the Ptolemies lavished every form of ornament—obelisks, sphinxes, flowers and gardens, and colonnades. Among the great structures that stood here were the famous Library and Museum with its hundreds of thousands of volumes, its corridors, theatre, menagerie, and lecture-halls; the Palace of the Ptolemies; the Caesarium or Temple of the Caesars; the Mausoleum of the Ptolemies (containing the body of Alexander the Great); and the Arsinoëum, a monument raised by Ptolemy Philadelphus to his sister Arsinoë. The name is also written PYRUCHIUM (Πυροχεῖον).

Bructĕri. A German people dwelling on each side of the Amisia (Ems), and as far south as Luppia (Lippe). They joined the Batavi (q. v.) in their revolt against the Romans in A.D. 69.

Brunck, RICHARD FRANÇOIS PHILIPPE. See article in the Appendix.

Brundisium. The modern Brindisi; a celebrated city on the coast of Apulia, in the territory of the Calabri. By the Greeks it was called Βρεντέσιον, a word which, in the Messapian language, signified a stag's head, from the resemblance which its different harbours and creeks bore to antlers.

Roman Pillar at Brundisium.

Herodotus speaks of it as a place generally well known (iv. 99). Brundisium soon became a formidable rival to Tarentum, which had hitherto engrossed all the commerce of this part of Italy. The Romans annexed it in B.C. 245 (Flor. i. 20). From this period the prosperity of this port continued to increase in proportion with the greatness of the Roman Empire. Large fleets were always stationed there for the conveyance of troops into Macedonia, Greece, or Asia; and from the convenience of its harbour, and its facility of access from every other part of Italy, it became a sort of Dover to the Calais of Dyrrhachium. At Brundisium the Appian Way ended.

Bruttiāni. Slaves whose duty it was to wait on Roman magistrates. The name is commonly explained as due to the fact that these slaves were originally taken from among the Bruttians, because this people remained steadfastly faithful to Hannibal (Aul. Gell. x. 3, § 19); but both Strabo (vi. 2, § 4) and Diodorus (xvi. 15) state that the word signifies in the Lucanian dialect "revolted slaves."

Bruttium, Bruttius, and **Bruttiōrum Ager,** more usually called **Bruttii,** after the inhabitants. The southern extremity of Italy, separated from Lucania by a line drawn from the mouth of the Laus to Thurii, and surrounded on the other three sides by the sea. It was the country called in ancient times Oenotria and Italia. The country is mountainous, as the Apennines run through it down to the Sicilian Straits; it contained excellent pasturage for cattle, and the valleys produced good corn, olives, and fruit. The earliest inhabitants of the country were Oenotrians. Subsequently some Lucanians, who had revolted from their countrymen in Lucania, took possession of the country, and were hence called Bruttii or Brettii, which word is said to mean "rebels" in the language of the Lucanians. This people, however, inhabited only the interior of the land; the coast was almost entirely in the possession of the Greek colonies. At the close of the Second Punic War, in which the Bruttii had been the allies of Hannibal, they lost their independence, and were treated by the Romans with great severity. They were declared to be public slaves, and were employed as lictors and servants of the magistrates.

Brutus. (1) L. IUNIUS BRUTUS. A celebrated Roman, the author, according to the Roman legends, of the great revolution which drove Tarquin the Proud from his throne, and which substituted the consular for the regal government. He was the son of Marcus Iunius and of Tarquinia, the second daughter of Tarquin. While yet young in years, he saw his father and brother slain by the order of Tarquin, and having no means of avenging them, and fearing the same fate to himself, he affected a stupid air, in order not to appear at all formidable in the eyes of a suspicious and cruel tyrant. This artifice proved successful, and he so far deceived Tarquin and the other members of the royal family that they gave him, in derision, the surname of Brutus, as indicative of his supposed mental imbecility. At length, when Lucretia had been outraged by Sextus Tarquinius, Brutus, amid the indignation that pervaded all orders, threw off the mask, and snatching the dagger from the bosom of the victim, swore upon it eternal exile to the family of Tarquin. Wearied out with the tyranny of this monarch, and exasperated by the spectacle of the funeral solemnities of Lucretia, the people abolished royalty, and confided the chief authority to the Senate and two magistrates, named at first praetors, but subsequently consuls. Brutus and the husband of Lucretia were first invested with this important office. They signalized their entrance upon its duties by making all the people take a solemn oath never again to have a king of Rome. Efforts, nevertheless, were soon made in favour of the Tarquins: an ambassador sent from Etruria, under the pretext of procuring a restoration of the property of Tarquin and his family, formed a secret plot for the overthrow of the new government; and the sons of Brutus be-

Lucius Iunius Brutus. (Vatican Museum.)

came connected with the conspiracy. A discovery having been made, the sons of the consul and their accomplices were tried, condemned, and executed by the orders of the father, although the people were willing that he should pardon them. From this time, Brutus sought only to die himself, and, some months after a battle between the Romans and the troops of Tarquin enabled him to gratify his wish. He encountered, in the fight, Aruns, the son of the exiled monarch; and with so much impetuosity did they rush to the attack that both fell dead on the spot, pierced to the heart each by the weapon of the other. The corpse of Brutus was carried to Rome in triumph.

Coin representing the Children of Brutus led to death by Lictors.

The consul Valerius pronounced a funeral eulogy over it, a statue of bronze was raised to the memory of the deceased in the Capitol, and the Roman women wore mourning for an entire year. (2) D. Iunius Brutus, master of the horse A.U.C. 418, and consul A.U.C. 429 (Liv. viii. 12, 29). (3) D. Iunius Brutus, consul A.U.C. 615, obtained a triumph for his successes in Spain. (4) M. Iunius Brutus, father of the Brutus who was concerned in the assassination of Caesar. He embraced the party of Marius, and was overcome by Pompey. After the death of Sulla, and the renewal of hostilities, he was besieged in Mutina by Pompey, who compelled him to surrender after a long resistance, and caused him to be put to death. He was brother-in-law to Cato by his wife Servilia. Brutus was an able lawyer, and wrote on the Civil Wars (Cic. *Brut.* 62; id. *Or.* ii. 32; id. *Pro Cluent.* 51). (5) Marcus Iunius Brutus, son of the preceding, was by the mother's side nephew of M. Cato (Uticensis). He accompanied his uncle to Cyprus, A.U.C. 695, where the latter was sent by Clodius to annex that island to the Roman Empire. It appears, however, that he did not copy the example of Cato's integrity; for, having become the creditor of the citizens of Salamis to a large amount, he employed one Scaptius, a man of infamous character, to enforce the payment of the debt, together with an interest four times exceeding the rate allowed by law (Cic. *Ad Att.* v. 21). When Cicero governed the province of Cilicia, to which Cyprus seems to have been annexed, Brutus wrote to him, and was supported by Atticus in his request, entreating him to give Scaptius a commission as an officer of the Roman government, and to allow him to employ a military force to exact from the Salaminians the usurious interest which he illegally demanded. Cicero was too upright a magistrate to comply with such requests, but they were so agreeable to the practice of the times that he continued to live on intimate terms with the man who could prefer them; and the literary tastes of Brutus were a recommendation which he could not resist; so that he appears soon to have forgotten the affair of Scaptius, and to have spoken and thought of Brutus with great regard. They both, indeed, were of the same party in politics, and Brutus actively exerted himself in the service of Pompey, although his own father had been put to death by the orders of that commander. Being taken prisoner in the battle of Pharsalia, he received his life from the conqueror. Before Caesar set out for Africa to carry on war against Scipio and Iuba, he conferred on Brutus the government of Cisalpine Gaul, and in that province Brutus accordingly remained, and was actually holding an office under Caesar while his uncle Cato was maintaining the contest in Africa and committed suicide rather than fall alive into the hands of the enemy. His character, however, seems to have been greatly improved since his treatment of the Salaminians, for he is said to have governed Cisalpine Gaul with great integrity and humanity. In the year B.C. 45 he returned to Rome, but afterwards set out to meet Caesar on his return from Spain, and, in an interview which he had with him at Nicaea, pleaded the cause of Deiotarus, tetrarch of Galatia, with such warmth and freedom that Caesar was struck by it, and was reminded of what he used frequently to say of Brutus—that what his inclinations might be made a very great difference; but that, whatever they were, they would be nothing lukewarm. It was about this time also that Brutus divorced his first wife, Appia, daughter of Appius Claudius, and married the famous Porcia, his cousin, the daughter of Cato. Soon after, he received another mark of Caesar's favour, in being appointed praetor urbanus, B.C. 44; and he was holding that office when he resolved to become the assassin of the man whose government he had twice acknowledged by consenting to act in a public station under it. He was led into the conspiracy, it is said, by Cassius, who sought at first by writing, and afterwards by means of his wife Iunia, the sister of Brutus, to obtain his consent to become an accomplice; and Plutarch informs us that when the attack was made on Caesar in the Senate-house, the latter resisted and endeavoured to escape, until he saw the dagger of

Marcus Iunius Brutus.

Brutus pointed against him, when he covered his head with his robe and resigned himself to his fate. See CAESAR.

After the assassination of Caesar, the conspirators endeavoured to stir up the feelings of the people in favour of liberty; but Antony, by reading the will of the dictator, excited against them so violent a storm of odium that they were compelled to flee from the city. Brutus retired to Athens, and used every exertion to raise a party there among the Roman nobility. Obtaining possession, at the same time, of a large sum of the public money, he was enabled to bring to his standard many of the old soldiers of Pompey who were scattered about Thessaly. His forces daily increasing, he soon saw himself surrounded by a considerable army, and Hortensius, the governor of Macedonia, aiding him, Brutus became master in this way of all Greece and Macedonia. He went now to Asia and joined Cassius, whose efforts had been equally successful. In Rome, on the other hand, the triumvirs were all-powerful; the conspirators had been condemned, and the people had taken up arms against them. Brutus and Cassius returned to Europe to oppose the triumvirs, and Octavius and Antony met them on the plains of Philippi. In this memorable conflict Brutus commanded the right wing of the republican army, and defeated the division of the enemy opposed to him, and would in all probability have gained the day if, instead of pursuing the fugitives, he had brought reinforcements to his left wing, commanded by Cassius, which was hard pressed and eventually beaten by Antony. Cassius, upon this, believing everything lost, slew himself in despair. Brutus bitterly deplored his fate, styling him, with tears of the sincerest sorrow, "the last of the Romans." On the following day, induced by the ardour of the soldiers, Brutus again drew up his forces in line of battle, but no action took place, and he then took possession of an advantageous post, where it was difficult for an attack to be made upon him. His true policy was to have remained in this state, without hazarding an engagement, for his opponents were distressed for provisions, and the fleet that was bringing them supplies had been totally defeated by the vessels of Brutus. The condition of things, however, was unknown to the latter, and, after an interval of twenty days, he hazarded a second battle. Where he himself fought in person, he was still successful; but the rest of his force was soon overcome, and the conflict ended in a total defeat of the republican army. Escaping with only a few friends, he passed the night in a cave, and, as he saw his cause irretrievably ruined, ordered Strato, one of his attendants, to kill him. Strato refused for a long time to perform the painful office; but, seeing Brutus resolved, he turned away his face, and held his sword while Brutus fell upon it. He died in the forty-third year of his age, B.C. 42.

A great deal of false glamour has been thrown around the character of Brutus. That he was a stern and consistent patriot throughout the whole of his career, the sketch which we have given of his movements prior to the assassination of Caesar most clearly disproves. Why hold office under one who was trampling upon the liberties of his country? Why require so much solicitation before engaging in the conspiracy? Was he not aware that Caesar was a usurper?—this would show a miserable want of penetration. Or if he preferred security to danger, where was the Roman patriot in this? The truth is that Brutus, notwithstanding all that has been said of him, was but a tardy patriot. His motives towards the close of his career were no doubt pure enough, but he ought to have had nothing to do with Caesar from the moment when that general began to act with treason towards his country. As a student and man of letters, the character of Brutus appears to more advantage than as a patriot. He was remarkable for literary application, usually rising with this view long before day, and it is said that on the evening previous to a battle, while his army was in a state of anxious suspense and alarm, he calmly occupied himself in his tent with writing an abridgment of the history of Polybius. One of the most singular circumstances in the life of Brutus is that of the so-called apparition which, it was said, appeared to him on one occasion in his tent at midnight. "Who art thou?" inquired Brutus. "Thy evil genius," replied the phantom; "we shall meet again at Philippi." And so it happened. The spirit reappeared on the eve of the second battle of Philippi—a story that reminds one of the Bodach Glas in *Waverley*. See Plutarch's life of Brutus.

Brygi (Βρύγοι) or **Bryges** (also BRUGI and BRUGES). A barbarous tribe in northern Macedonia, believed by the ancients to have been the ethnic source of the Phrygians; hence the name is sometimes use for Phryges. See PHRYGIA.

Bubassus (Βυβασσός). An ancient city of Caria, east of Cnidus, and giving its name to the bay, Bubassius Sinus.

Bubastis (Βούβαστις) or **Būbastus** (Βούβαστας). The capital of the Nomos Bubastites in Lower Egypt, which stood on the eastern bank of the Pelusiac branch of the Nile, and was the chief seat of the worship of the goddess Bubastis (Pasht), whom the Greeks identified with Artemis, and who was regarded as the daughter of Ra and bride of Ptah, symbolizing the sexual passion. More than 70,000 persons sometimes took part in her festivals at this place. Here also the cats sacred to Bubastis were buried. The modern name of the city is Tel Bast. Here in 1887 the French explorer, M. Naville, discovered the ruins of the great temple of Bubastis, and further excavations in 1888 showed the city to have been a very important place under the Hyksos. See AEGYPTUS.

Bubo. The horned owl.

Bucco (from *bucca*, the cheek). The name of a stock character continually introduced into the Atellan plays, and represented as a gabbling fool. Isidorus (*Orig.* x. 30) gives *bucco* = *garrulus*. See ATELLANAE FABULAE.

Buccŭla. See GALEA.

Bucephăla (Βουκέφαλα, also Βουκεφαλεία, Βουκεφαλία). A city on the Hydaspes in northern India, built by Alexander the Great after his battle with Porus, in memory of his favourite horse Bucephalus (q. v.), who died there.

Bucephălus (Βουκέφαλος). A horse belonging to Alexander the Great, so called either because his head resembled that of an ox (βοὸς κεφαλή); or because he had the mark of an ox's head impressed upon his flank; or, according to others, because, like an ox, he had a black mark upon his head, the rest of his body being white. Plutarch states that the horse had been offered for sale to Philip by a Thessalian, but had proved so unmanageable that the monarch refused to purchase, and ordered it to be taken away. Alexander thereupon expressing his regret that they were losing so fine a horse for want of skill and spirit to manage it, Philip agreed to pay the price of the steed if his son would ride it. The prince accepted the offer, and succeeded in the attempt. Bucephalus, after this, would allow no one but Alexander to mount him, and he accompanied the monarch in all his campaigns. In the battle with Porus, he received, according to the same authority, several wounds, of which he died not long after. An ancient writer, however, quoted by Plutarch, states that he died of age and fatigue, being thirty years old. See Arrian, *Anab.* v. 19.

Buchanan, GEORGE. A famous classical scholar, the most distinguished in the annals of Scottish classical philology. He was born of humble parentage at Killearn, in February, 1506. At the age of fourteen, his uncle sent him to the University of Paris, where he acquired a local reputation for his facility in writing Latin verse. In 1522, he returned to Scotland, and, after serving in a military expedition against the English, matriculated at the University of St. Andrews, from which at the end of one year he received the Bachelor's degree (1525). In 1526, he returned to France, where he soon took the Master's degree at the Scottish College of Paris, and after two years of great destitution succeeded in winning a professorship at the College of Sainte Barbe. In 1535, he once more visited Scotland, having been made tutor to the son of the Earl of Cassilis. Soon after he undertook the education of an illegitimate son of the king (James V.). Having written two satires against the Franciscan clergy (entitled *Somnium* and *Franciscanus*), he was imprisoned at the instigation of Cardinal Beaton, but escaping fled to France (1539), and was appointed to a professorship in the College of Bordeaux, by André de Gouvéa, its head. At the end of three years, an outbreak of the plague forced him to leave Bordeaux, whence he went to Paris, receiving a professorship in the college of the Cardinal le Moyne. By the influence of De Gouvéa he was called to the newly founded University of Coimbra in Portugal (1547). Here his heretical opinions led to his enforced seclusion in a monastery, where he began his celebrated version of the Psalms in Latin verse. Upon his release he visited England, subsequently returning to France to become tutor to the son of the Maréchal de Brissac (1555). In 1560, he returned to Scotland, which he now made his permanent home. In the struggles between Queen Mary and the Scottish peers, Buchanan bore a prominent part. He had been the classical tutor of the queen, to whom he dedicated his version of the Psalms, but after the death of Darnley, took sides with the faction of the nobles, joining at the same time the Reformed Church. In 1566, the regent, Murray, appointed him Principal of St. Leonard's College in the University of St. Andrews, and soon after Mary's imprisonment in Lochleven, Buchanan was made Moderator of the General Assembly. In 1568, he accompanied Murray to the famous Conference of York. While Lennox was regent, Buchanan assumed charge of the education of the young king, James VI., afterwards James I. of England, who in after-years always spoke of his learned tutor with respect and pride. From 1570 to 1578, Buchanan was Keeper of the Privy Seal, resigning it to devote his time to the preparation of a history of Scotland, which was published a month before his death. This event took place on September 28th, 1582, and was followed by his burial in the Greyfriars' Churchyard, Edinburgh.

As a classicist, Buchanan was best known for his skill in Latin verse, in which he easily ranked first among his contemporaries; and he is generally regarded as the most brilliant of all the British humanists of the sixteenth century. His range of subjects was wide, from versions of the Psalms, theological topics, and political pasquinades, to erotic verses whose indecency may be regarded as purely conventional, though grotesque enough as the production of a professed reformer of religion.

As a man, Buchanan was stern, strong-willed, and domineering, making many enemies, whom he attacked with a violence of invective that belonged to the customs of the age in which he lived. Besides the works mentioned above, he wrote a violent diatribe against the queen, *Detectio Mariae Reginae*, and a bold political tract *De Iure Regni*, in which he states the doctrine that kings exist only by the will of the people and for the people's good.

His writings were edited in the last century by the elder Burmann. See Irving, *Life of George Buchanan* (1817).

Bucĭna (βυκάνη). A kind of horn-trumpet, originally made out of a shell, in which case it is often, especially in poetry, denoted by *concha* (Gk. κόχλος), and was made not only from the *bucinum*, but from many other kinds of spiral shells. It is happily described by Ovid (*Metam.* i. 335).

The *bucina*, as seen in art, agrees closely with his description, and also with the shape of the shell *bucinum*, and, like it, might almost be described, in the language of conchologists, as spiral and gibbous. The two drawings in the annexed illustra-

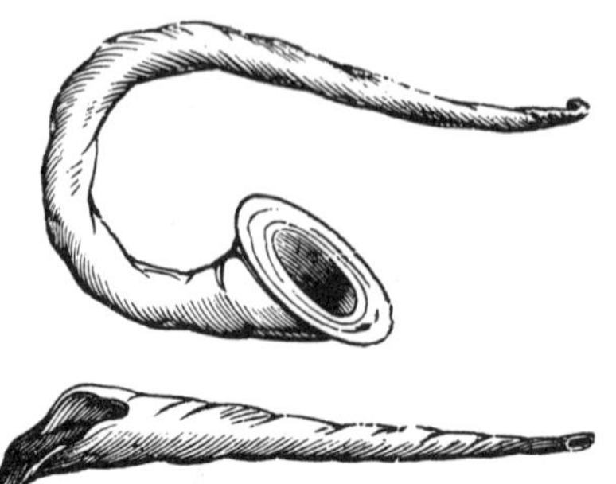

Bucinae. (From ancient frieze and sculpture.)

tion agree with this account. See CORNU; LITUUS; TUBA.

Bucolĭca (τὰ Βουκολικά). Ten poems of Vergil, written B.C. 41–39, in imitation and in part translations of Theocritus (q. v.). Many allusions to contemporary history are included. In the MSS. the individual poems are called *Eclogae*, and are to-day oftenest spoken of as "the Eclogues." A recent translation is that of S. Palmer (London, 1883). (See VERGILIUS.) Bucolica were also written in Greek by Bion and Moschus; and in Latin by Calpurnius Siculus (q. v.), under Nero; by Septimius Serenus (*Opuscula Ruralia*), of uncertain date; by Ausonius (q. v.); and by Boëthius (q. v.), whose *Carmen Bucolicum* has some merit. See Hunger, *De Poesi Romanorum Bucolica* (Halle, 1841); and W. Y. Sellar, *Roman Poets of the Augustan Age* (Oxford, 1883).

Bucolĭcum (τὸ Βουκολικὸν στόμα). One of the mouths of the Nile (Herod. vii. 134).

Bufo. The toad.

Bulgă (Keltic). A small leathern bag which was carried on the arm (Non. s. v. p. 78, ed. Mercer), in the same manner as the modern reticule, by travellers, who used it as a money bag (Lucil. *Sat.* vi. p. 20, 1 ed. Gerlach; Varro *ap.* Non. *l. c.*); and by farmers, as a pouch, containing the seed at sowing time (the πήρα σπερμοφόρος of the Greek Anthology), to which use the example here given was applied; it is borne by a figure furnished with various implements of husbandry on a beautiful silver *tazza* of the Neapolitan Museum (*Mus. Borb.* xii. 47).

Bulga. (Naples.)

Bulis (Βοῦλις). A town of Phocis on the shore of the Sinus Corinthiacus, southeast of Anticyra.

Bulla. A circular plate or boss of metal, so called from its resemblance in form to a bubble floating upon water. Bright studs of this description were used to adorn the sword-belt (*aurea bullis cingula; bullis asper balteus*). Another use of them was in doors the parts of which were fastened together by brass-headed, or even by gold-headed, nails. The magnificent bronze doors of the Pantheon at Rome are enriched with highly ornamented bosses.

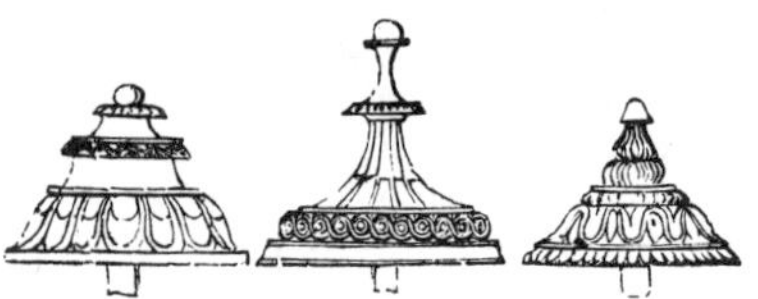

Bullae, or Bosses on Doors. (Pantheon, Rome.)

We most frequently read, however, of bullae as ornaments worn by children suspended from the neck, and especially by the sons of the noble and wealthy. Such a one is called *heres bullatus* by Juvenal. His bulla was made of thin plates of gold. Its usual form is shown in the annexed illustration, which represents a fine bulla preserved in the British Museum, and is of the size of the original.

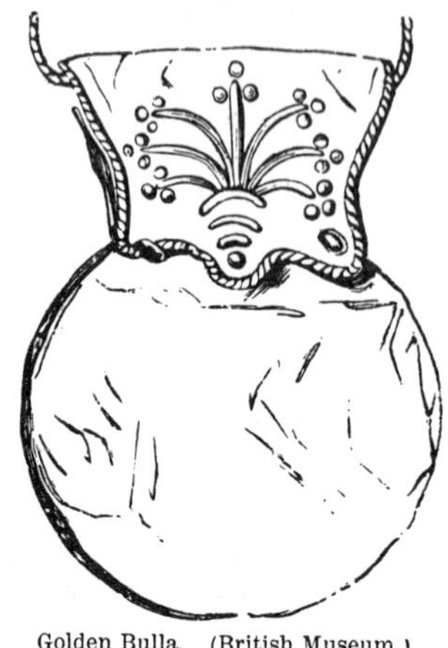

Golden Bulla. (British Museum.)

The bulla was worn by children of both sexes for ornament, as a token of paternal affection and a sign of high birth; and, as it was given to infants, it sometimes served, like other ornaments or playthings (*crepundia*), to recognize a lost child. Probably, also, it contained amulets. See AMULETUM.

Instead of the bulla of gold, boys of inferior rank, including the children of freedmen, wore only a piece of leather (*lorum*).

The use of the bulla, like that of the praetexta (q. v.), was derived from the Etruscans.

On arriving at adolescence, the bulla was laid aside, together with the praetexta, and it was often consecrated, on this occasion, to the Lares, or to some divinity. See FASCINUM.

Bullis (Βουλλίς). A town of Illyria, on the coast, south of Apollonia.

Bupălus (Βούπαλος). A sculptor and architect born in the island of Chios, and son of Anthermus, or rather Archennus. He encountered the animosity of the poet Hipponax (q. v.), the cause of which is said to have been the refusal of Bupalus to give his daughter in marriage to Hipponax, while others inform us that it was owing to a statue made in derision of the poet by Bupalus. The satire and invective of the bard were so severe that, according to one account, Bupalus hanged himself in despair (Horace, *Epod.* vi. 14). His brother's name was Athenis. In addition to the statue which Bupalus made in derision of Hipponax, other works are mentioned by Pliny as the joint productions of the two brothers. See Callim. *Frag.* 90, ed. Ernesti.

Buphonia (τὰ βουφόνια). A festival held in honour of Zeus at Athens. The legend connected with this festival is a singular one. Among the laws given by Triptolemus to the Athenians, three more especially remarkable were: "Reverence your elders—Honour the gods by offerings of the first fruits—Hurt not the labouring beast," i. e. the beast employed in agriculture. The first who offended against this last command was a person named Thaulon, who, at the feast of Ζεὺς Πολιεύς, observing a steer eating the sacred πόπανον on the altar, took up an axe and slew the trespasser. The expiation-feast (βουφόνια), instituted for the purpose of atoning for this involuntary offence, it was found afterwards expedient to continue. The ceremonies observed in it are not a little amusing. First was brought water by women appointed for the office, for the purpose of sharpening the axe and knife with which the slaughter was to be committed. One of these women having handed the axe to the proper functionary, the latter felled the beast and then took to flight. To slay the beast outright was the office of a third person. All present then partook of the flesh. The meal finished, the hide was stuffed, and the beast, apparently restored to life, was put to the plough. Now commenced the steer-trial. A judicial assembly was held in the Prytaneum, to which all were summoned who had been partakers in the above transaction. Each lays the blame upon the other. The water-bearers throw the guilt upon the sharpener of the axe and knife; the sharpener of the knife casts it upon the person delivering it to the feller of the beast; the feller of the beast upon the actual slaughterer, while this last ascribes the whole guilt to the knife itself. The knife, unable to speak, is found guilty and thrown into the sea.

Buprasium (Βουπράσιον). An ancient city of Elis mentioned by Homer (*Il.* ii. 615).

Bura (Βοῦρα). One of the twelve original cities of Achaea, formerly situated near the sea; but having been destroyed by an earthquake, it was rebuilt by the survivors about forty stadia from the shore, on the river Buraïcus (Herod. i. 145).

Buraïcus (Βουραϊκός). An epithet applied to Heracles, from his temple near Bura.

Burdigăla. The modern Bordeaux; the chief town of the Bituriges Vivisci, on the left bank of the Garumna (Garonne). Under the Empire it was a place of great commercial importance. Ausonius (q. v.), who was born there, describes it in his little poem entitled *Ordo Nobilium Urbium*. The only remaining Roman monument in the town is the amphitheatre locally known as the Arènes, or Palais Gallien. It is in a greatly damaged state.

Burdigalensē Itinerarium. See ITINERARIA.

Burgundiōnes or **Burgundii**. A powerful nation of Germany, dwelling originally between the Viadus (Oder) and the Vistula, and of the same race as the Vandals or Goths. They were driven out of their original abodes by the Gepidae, and the greater part of them settled in the country on the Maine. In the fifth century they settled in Gaul, where they founded the powerful kingdom of Burgundy. Their chief towns were Genava (Geneva) and Lugdunum (Lyons). See Dubois, *La Bourgogne*, vol. i. (Paris, 1867).

Burial Rites. See FUNUS.

Buris. The beam of the plough. See ARATRUM.

Burmann. The name of two celebrated Dutch classical scholars. (1) PIETER, known as "the elder," born at Utrecht, June 26th, 1668. He studied at the university of his native town, from which he received a degree in laws in 1688. He spent some time in travel, visiting the great seats of learning in Germany and Switzerland, and on his return practised law. In 1691, he was appointed receiver of taxes, and in 1696, Professor of Eloquence and History in his Alma Mater. To the duties of this chair he soon added those pertaining to the chair of Greek. In 1715, he was called to the University of Leyden to succeed the renowned Perizonius (q. v.) as Professor of Greek, Rhetoric, and History, where he remained until his death, which occurred March 31st, 1741. He was an indefatigable editor, producing commentaries on Phaedrus (1698), Horace (1699), Valerius Flaccus (1701), Petronius (1709), Velleius Paterculus (1719), Quintilian (1720), Ovid (1727), and Lucan (1740). He likewise edited the works of the Scottish scholar, George Buchanan (q. v.), and continued the *magnum opus* of Graevius, *Thesaurus Antiquitatum et Historiarum Italiae*, besides preparing a short manual of Roman Antiquities entitled *Antiquitatum Romanarum Brevis Descriptio* (1711). A number of his poems and orations in Latin were collected and published after his death. As a commentator, Burmann was diffuse, laborious, and pedantic, and his stately quartos are to-day but little consulted; yet they have furnished much material for succeeding editors who possessed the taste and discretion which he unfortunately lacked. As a controversialist, he possessed a most irascible temper, and was involved in many violent disputes with contemporary scholars, notably with Le Clerc and Bentley.

(2) PIETER, known as "the younger," the nephew of the preceding, was born at Amsterdam in 1714, and after studying at Utrecht, filled professorships at Franeker and at the Amsterdam Athenaeum, besides acting as the keeper of the public library at the latter place. His published works comprise editions of Aristophanes, Vergil, Claudian, and Propertius, besides a selection of the Latin Anthology (1759 and 1773). In 1777, he retired on a pension and died in the following year. The Anthology is his only work that is now regarded as important. See L. Müller, *Geschichte der class. Philologie in den Niederlanden* (Leipzig, 1869), and the article ANTHOLOGY.

Busīris (Βούσιρις). (1) A reputed king of Egypt, son of Poseidon and Lysianassa, daughter of Epaphus, or (as Plutarch states, from the Samian Agatho) of Poseidon and Anippé, daughter of the Nile. This king, in consequence of an oracle, offered up strangers on the altar of Zeus; for Egypt having been afflicted with a dearth for nine years, a native of Cyprus named Thrasius, a great soothsayer, came thither, and said that it would cease if they sacrificed a stranger every year to Zeus. Busiris sacrificed the prophet himself first of all, and then continued the practice. When Heracles, in the course of his wanderings, came into Egypt, he was seized and dragged to the altar; but he burst his bonds, and slew Busiris, his son Amphidamas, and his herald Chalbes. Historically, there is no such king as Busiris, and the myth is in all probability only a legend of the former sacrifice of human victims to Osiris (q. v.), of which name Busiris is only a corruption. (2) There were several cities named Busiris in ancient Egypt, the most celebrated being placed by Herodotus in the middle of the Delta. It possessed a noble temple of Isis. See Herod. ii. 59.

Bustirăpi. Persons suffering the extreme of poverty; and so called because they satisfied their cravings by snatching from the flames of the funeral pyre the bread and other eatables which the superstition of the living dedicated to the dead. See Catull. lix. 2.

Bustuaria. A prostitute who plied her vocation on the outskirts of the city among the *busta* and burial-places. See Mart. i. xxxv. 8.

Bustuarii. See FUNUS; GLADIATORES.

Bustum. A funeral pyre. See FUNUS.

Butes (Βούτης). (1) A Thracian, the son of Boreas. His brother Lycurgus, whose life he had attempted, banished him, and he settled on the island of Strongylé or Naxos. Finding here no wives for himself and his companions, he carried off some women from Thessaly, while they were celebrating a sacrifice to Dionysus. One of these, Coronis, whom he had forced to be his wife, prayed to Dionysus for vengeance. The god drove him mad, and he threw himself into a well. (2) An Athenian hero, son of the Athenian Pandion and Zeuxippé. A tiller of the soil, and a neat-herd, he was a priest of Atheué, the goddess of the stronghold, and of Poseidon Erechtheus, and thus ancestor of the priestly caste of the Butadae and Eteobutadae. He shared an altar in the Erechtheum with Poseidon and Hephaestus. The later story represented him as the son of Teleon and Zeuxippé, and as taking part in the expedition of the Argonauts. (3) A descendant of Amycus, king of the Bebryces. He was one of the Argonauts, and on passing the island of the Sirens leaped overboard in order to swim to it, but was caught up by Aphrodité, who conveyed him to Lilybaeum in Sicily. Here she became by him the mother of Eryx (q.v.). He was renowned as a boxer. (4) An armour-bearer of Anchises, and afterwards of Ascanius. Apollo assumed his form when he descended from heaven to encourage Ascanius in battle. Butes was killed by Turnus. See Verg. *Aen.* ix. 647 foll.

Buthrōtum (Βουθρωτόν). Now Butrinto; a town of Epirus, a flourishing seaport on a small peninsula, opposite Corcyra.

Būto (Βουτώ). (1) An Egyptian divinity, the nurse of Horus and Bubastis, the children of Osiris and Isis, whom she saved from the persecutions of Typhon by concealing them in the floating island of Chemnis. The Greeks identified her with Leto, and represented her as the goddess of night. See HORUS; ISIS; OSIRIS. (2) A city in Lower Egypt, stood near the Sebennytic branch of the Nile, on the lake of Buto. It was celebrated for its oracle of the goddess Buto, in honour of whom a festival was held at the city every year.

Buttmann, PHILIPP KARL. A distinguished classical scholar, who was born in Frankfort in 1764. He studied classical philology under Heyne, and in 1789 was made assistant in the Royal Library at Berlin, subsequently becoming the librarian (1811). From 1800 to 1808 he also held a professorship in the Joachimsthal Gymnasium in Berlin. His best-known works are his Greek grammar (1792), of which the twenty-second edition appeared in 1869; and his *Lexilogus*, 2 vols. (1818–25; 2d ed. 1860). It is a valuable study of the difficult words found in Homer and Hesiod. There is an English translation of it by Fishlake. Buttmann also published *Ausführliche griechische Sprachlehre*, 2 vols. (1819–27); *Demosthenes in Midiam* (1823); *Mythologus*, a collection of essays (1828–29); and continued Spalding's great edition of Quintilian. He also edited *Spener's Journal* from 1796 to 1808. He died June 21st, 1829.

Butȳrum (βούτυρον). Butter. The oldest mention of butter, though dubious and obscure, is in the account given of the Scythians by Herodotus (iv. 2). According to him they poured the milk of mares into wooden vessels, caused it to be violently stirred or shaken by their blind slaves, and thus separated the part that arose to the surface, which they considered more valuable and more delicious than that which was collected below it. Herodotus here evidently speaks of the richest part of the milk being separated from the rest by shaking; and that what he alludes to here was actually butter would plainly appear from comparing with what he says the much clearer account of his contemporary Hippocrates. "The Scythians," remarks this latter writer, "pour the milk of their mares into wooden vessels, and shake it violently; this causes it to foam, and the fat part, which is light, rising to the surface, becomes what is called butter (ὃ βούτυρον καλοῦσι)." Mention of butter occurs several times, in fact, in the writings of Hippocrates, and he prescribes it externally as a medicine; though he gives it another name, *pikerion* (πικέριον).

It would appear, however, that butter must have been very little known to the Greeks and Romans till the end of the second century. It appears, also, that when they had learned the art of making it, they employed it only as an ointment in their baths, and particularly in medicine. Pliny recommends it, mixed with honey, to be rubbed over children's gums, in order to ease the pain of teething, and also for ulcers in the mouth. The Romans, in general, seem to have used butter for anointing the bodies of their children to render them pliable; and we are told that the ancient Burgundians smeared their hair with it. Except in Dioscorides there is no indication that it was used by the Greeks or Romans in cookery or the preparation of food. No notice is taken of it by Apicius, nor is it mentioned by Galen for any other than medical purposes. This is easily accounted for by the ancients having entirely accustomed themselves to the use of oil; and, in like manner, butter at present is very little employed in Italy, Spain, Portugal, and the southern parts of France. One chief cause of this is the difficulty of preserving it for any length of time in warm countries, and it would seem that among the ancients in the south of Europe it was rather in an oily state and almost liquid.

Buxum (πύξος). The wood of the box-tree, employed largely in making tablets for writing (hence often called *cerata buxa*), for tops (Pers. iii. 51), and for combs (Juv. xiv. 194).

Buxentum. Originally Pyxus (Πυξοῦς); a town on the west coast of Lucania and on the river Buxentius, was founded by Micythus, tyrant of Messana, B.C. 471, and was afterwards a Roman colony.

Byblis (Βυβλίς). The daughter of Miletus and Idothea, who was in love with her brother Caunus, whom she pursued through various lands, till at length, worn out with sorrow, she was changed into a fountain. See Ovid, *Met.* ix. 446 foll.

Byblus (Βύβλος). (1) The modern Jebeïl; a very ancient city on the coast of Phœnicia, between Berytus and Tripolis, a little north of the river Adonis. It was the chief seat of the worship of Adonis. Here are the remains of a Roman theatre, of which the *cavea* or auditorium is nearly perfect. The name was anciently applied to the whole of Phœnicia. (2) A town of Egypt in the Delta, famous for its *papyrus* (q. v.).

Byrsa (Βύρσα, from the Punic BASRA, a fort). The citadel of Carthage. See CARTHAGO.

Byssus (βύσσος). A name derived from the Hebrew *bûtz*, and usually applied to linen, but sometimes to very fine cotton. In it the Egyptian mummies were wrapped. (See Herod. ii. 86; Plut. *Is. et Osir.* 39.) Strabo even applies the word to silk.

Byzacium (Βυζάκιον). The southern portion of the Roman province of Africa; now the southern part of Tunis. See AFRICA.

Byzantine Historians. See BYZANTINUM IMPERIUM, at the end.

Byzantīnum Imperium. The Byzantine or Eastern Roman Empire, comprehending at first, in Asia, the country on this side of the Euphrates, the coasts of the Black Sea, and Asia Minor; in Africa, Egypt; and in Europe, all the countries from the Hellespont to the Adriatic and Danube. This survived the Western Empire 1000 years, and was even increased by the addition of Italy and the coasts of the Mediterranean. It commenced in 395, when Theodosius divided the Roman Empire between his two sons, Arcadius and Honorius. The Eastern Empire fell to the elder, Arcadius, through whose weakness it suffered many misfortunes. During his minority Rufinus was his guardian and minister, between whom and Stilicho, the minister of the Western Empire, a fierce rivalry existed. The Goths laid waste Greece; Eutropius, the successor, and Gainas, the murderer of Rufinus, were ruined by their own crimes. The latter lost his life in a civil war excited by him (A.D. 400). Arcadius and his Empire were now ruled by his proud and covetous wife, Eudoxia, till her death (A.D. 404). The Isaurians and the Huns wasted the provinces of Asia and the country along the Danube. Theodosius the younger succeeded his father (A.D. 408), under the guardianship of his sister Pulcheria. Naturally of an inferior mind, his education had made him entirely imbecile, and unfit for self-command. Pulcheria, who bore the title of Augusta, administered the kingdom ably. Of the Western Empire, which had been ceded to Valentinian, Theodosius retained western Illyria. The Greeks fought with success against the king of the Persians, Varanes. The kingdom of Armenia, thrown into confusion by internal dissensions, and claimed at the same time by the Romans and the Persians, became now an apple of contention between the two nations (A.D. 440). Attila (q. v.) laid waste the dominions of Theodosius, and obliged him to pay tribute. After the death of her brother, Pulcheria was acknowledged empress (A.D. 450), being the first woman who attained this dignity. She gave her hand to the senator Marcian, and raised him to the throne. His wisdom and valour averted the attacks of the Huns from the frontiers, but he did not support the Western Empire in its wars against the Huns and Vandals with sufficient energy. He afforded shelter to a part of the Germans and Sarmatians, who were driven to the Roman frontiers by the incursions of the Huns. Pulcheria died before him, in 453. Leo I. (A.D. 457), a prince praised by contemporary authors, was chosen successor of Marcian. His expeditions against the Vandals (A.D. 467) were unsuccessful. His grandson Leo would have succeeded him, but died a minor shortly after him, having named his father, Zeno, his colleague (A.D. 474). The government of this weak emperor, who was hated by his subjects, was disturbed by rebellions and internal disorders of the Empire. The Goths depopulated their provinces till their king, Theodoric, turned his arms against Italy (A.D. 489). Ariadné, widow of Zeno, raised the minister Anastasius, whom she married, to the throne (A.D. 491). The nation, once excited to discontents and tumults, could not be entirely appeased by the alleviation of their burdens and by wise decrees. The forces of the Empire, being thus weakened, could not offer an effectual resistance to the Persians and the barbarians along the Danube. To prevent their incursions into the peninsula of Constantinople, Anastasius built the Long Wall, as it is called. After the death of Anastasius the soldiers proclaimed Justin emperor (A.D. 518). Notwithstanding his low birth, he maintained possession of the throne. Religious persecutions, which he undertook at the instigation of the clergy, and various crimes into which he was seduced by his nephew Justinian, disgrace his reign. After his early death, in 521, he was succeeded by the same Justinian, to whom, though he deserves not the name of the Great, many virtues of a ruler cannot be denied. He was renowned as a legislator, and his reign was distinguished by the victories of his general Belisarius; but how unable he was to revive the strength of his Empire was proved by its rapid decay after his death. Justin II., his successor (A.D. 565), was an avaricious, cruel, weak prince, governed by his wife. The Lombards tore from him part of Italy (A.D. 568). His war with Persia, for the possession of Armenia, was unsuccessful; the Avari plundered the provinces on the Danube, and the violence of his grief at these misfortunes deprived him of reason. Tiberius, his minister, a man of merit, was declared Caesar, and the general Justinian conducted the war against

Coin of Arcadius.

Coin of Honorius.

Coin of Theodosius II.

Persia with success. The Greeks now allied themselves, for the first time, with the Turks. Against his successor, Tiberius II. (A.D. 578), the empress Sophia and the general Justinian conspired in vain. From the Avari the emperor purchased peace; from the Persians it was extorted by his general Mauritius or Maurice (A.D. 582). This commander Tiberius declared Caesar in the same year. Mauritius, under other circumstances, would have made an excellent monarch, but for the times he wanted prudence and resolution. He was indebted for the tranquillity of the eastern frontiers to the gratitude of King Chosroës II., whom, in 591, he restored to the throne from which he had been deposed by his subjects. Nevertheless, the war against the Avari was unsuccessful, through the errors of Commentiolus. The army was discontented and irritated, now by untimely severity and parsimony and now by timid indulgence. It finally proclaimed Phocas, one of its officers, emperor. Mauritius was taken in his flight and put to death (A.D. 602). The vices of Phocas and his incapacity for government produced the greatest disorders in the Empire. Heraclius, son of the governor of Africa, took up arms, conquered Constantinople, and caused Phocas to be executed (A.D. 610). He distinguished himself only in the short period of the Persian War. During the first twelve years of his reign the Avari, and other nations of the Danube, plundered the European provinces, and the Persians conquered the coasts of Syria and Egypt. Having finally succeeded in pacifying the Avari, he marched against the Persians (A.D. 622), and defeated them; but during this time the Avari, who had renewed the war, made an unsuccessful attack on Constantinople in 626. Taking advantage of an insurrection of the subjects of Chosroës, he penetrated into the centre of Persia. By the peace concluded with Siroës (A.D. 628) he recovered the lost provinces and the Holy Cross. But the Arabs, who, meanwhile, had become powerful under Mohammed and the califs, conquered Phœnicia, the countries on the Euphrates, Iudaea, Syria, and all Egypt (A.D. 631–641). Among his descendants there was not one able prince. He was succeeded by his son Constantine III., probably in conjunction with his step-brother Heracleonas. The former soon died, and the latter lost his crown and was mutilated. After him, Constans, son of Constantine, obtained the throne (A.D. 642). His sanguinary spirit of persecution and the murder of his brother Theodosius made him odious to the nation. The Arabs, pursuing their conquests, took from him part of Africa, Cyprus, and Rhodes, and defeated him at sea (A.D. 653). Internal disturbances obliged him to make peace. After this he left Constantinople (A.D. 659), and in the following year carried on an unsuccessful war against the Lombards in Italy, in which he lost his life at Syracuse (A.D. 660). Constantine IV., Pogonatus, son of Constans, vanquished his Syracusan competitor Mezizius, and in the beginning of his reign shared the government with his brothers Tiberius and Heraclius. The Arabs inundated all Africa and Sicily, penetrated through Asia Minor into Thrace, and attacked Constantinople for several successive years by sea (A.D. 669). Nevertheless, he made peace with them on favourable terms. But, on the other hand, the Bulgarians obliged him to pay a tribute (A.D. 680). Justinian II., his son and successor, weakened the power of the Maronites, but fought without success against the Bulgarians and Arabs. Leonitius dethroned this cruel prince, had him mutilated, and sent to the Tauric Chersonese (A.D. 695). Leonitius was dethroned by Apsimar, or Tiberius III. (A.D. 698), who was himself dethroned by Trebelius, king of the Bulgarians, who restored Justinian to the throne (A.D. 705); but Philippicus Bardanes rebelled anew against him. With Justinian II. the race of Heraclius was extinguished. The only care of Philippicus was the spreading of Monotheism, while the Arabs wasted Asia Minor and Thrace. In opposition to this prince, who was universally hated, the different armies proclaimed their leaders emperors, among whom Leo III., the Isaurian, obtained the hegemony (A.D. 713–714). Leo repelled the Arabs from Constantinople, which

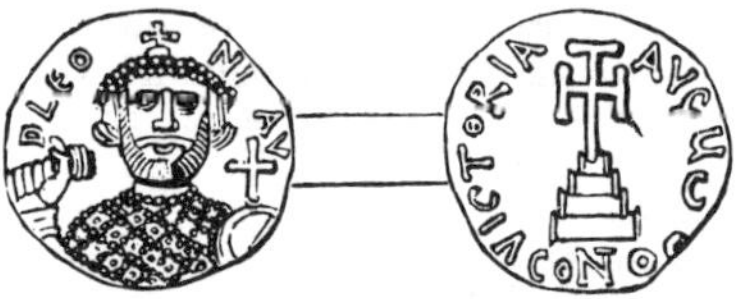

Gold Coin of Leo III. (British Museum.)

they had attacked for almost two years, and suppressed the rebellion excited by Basilius and the former emperor Anastasius. From 726 the abolition of the worship of images absorbed his attention, and the Italian provinces were allowed to become a prey to the Lombards, while the Arabs plundered the Eastern provinces. After his death (A.D. 741) his son Constantine V. ascended the throne, a courageous, active, and noble prince. He vanquished his rebellious brother-in-law Artabasdus, wrested from the Arabs part of Syria and Armenia, and overcame at last the Bulgarians, against whom he had been long unsuccessful. He died (A.D. 775), and was succeeded by his son Leo IV., who fought successfully against the Arabs; and this latter, by his son Constantine VI., whose imperious mother Irené, his guardian and associate in the government, raised a powerful party by the restoration of the worship of images. He endeavoured in vain to free himself from dependence on her and her favourite Stauratius, and died in 797, after having had his eyes put out.

Gold Coin of Irené. (British Museum.)

The war against the Arabs and Bulgarians was long continued; against the former it was unsuccessful. The design of the empress to marry Charlemagne excited the discontent of the patricians, who placed one of their own order, Nicephorus, upon the throne (A.D. 802). Irené died in a monastery. Nicephorus became tributary to the Arabs, and fell in the war against the Bulgarians (A.D. 811). Stauratius, his son, was deprived of the crown by Michael I., and he in turn by Leo V. (A.D. 813). Leo was dethroned and put to death by Michael II. (A.D. 820). During the reign of the latter the Arabs conquered Sicily, Lower Italy, Crete, and other countries. Michael prohibited the worship of images, as did also his son Theophilus. Theodora, guardian of his son Michael III., put a stop to the dispute about images (A.D. 841). During a cruel persecution of the Manichaeans, the Arabs devastated the Asiatic provinces. The dissolute and extravagant Michael confined his mother in a monastery. The government was administered in his name by Bardas, his uncle, and after the death of Bardâs by Basil, who was put to death by Michael (A.D. 867). Basil I., who came to the throne in 867, was

Gold Coin of Basil I. and his son Constantine. (British Museum.)

not altogether a contemptible monarch. He died A.D. 886. The reign of his learned son, Leo VI., was not very happy. He died A.D. 911. His son, Constantine VII., Porphyrogenitus, a minor when he succeeded his father, was placed under the guardianship of his colleague Alexander, and after Alexander's death, in 912, under that of his mother Zoë. Romanus Lacopenus, his general, obliged him, in 919, to share the throne with him and his children. Constantine subsequently took sole possession of it again, and reigned mildly but weakly. His son Romanus II. succeeded him in 959, and fought successfully against the Arabs. To him succeeded, in 963, his general Nicephorus, who was put to death by his own general, John Zimisces (A.D. 970), who carried on a successful war against the Russians. Basil II., son of Romanus, succeeded this able prince. He vanquished

Basil II. (From a Psalter at Paris.) (D'Agincourt, tav. 47.)

8*

the Bulgarians and the Arabs. His brother, Constantine IX. (A.D. 1025), was not equal to him. Romanus III. became emperor (A.D. 1028) by a marriage with Zoë, daughter of Constantine. This dissolute but able princess caused her husband to be executed, and successively raised to the throne Michael IV. (A.D. 1034), Michael V. (A.D. 1041), and Constantine X. (A.D. 1042). Russians and Arabs meanwhile devastated the Empire. Her sister Theodora succeeded her on the throne (A.D. 1053). Her successor, Michael VI. (A.D. 1056), was dethroned by Isaac Comnenus in 1057, who became a monk (A.D. 1059). His successor, Constantine XI., Ducas, fought successfully against the Uzes. Eudocia, his wife, guardian of his sons Michael, Andronicus, and Constantine, was intrusted with the administration (A.D. 1067), married Romanus IV., and brought him the crown. He carried on an unsuccessful war against the Turks, who kept him for some time prisoner. Michael VII., son of Constantine, deprived him of the throne (A.D. 1071). Michael was dethroned by Nicephorus III. (A.D. 1078), and the latter by Alexius I., Comnenus (A.D. 1081). Under his reign the crusades commenced. His son, John II., came to the throne in 1118, and fought with great success against the Turks and other barbarians. The reign of his son Manuel I., who succeeded him in 1143, was also not unfortunate. His son, Alexius II., succeeded (A.D. 1180), and was dethroned by his guardian Andronicus, as was the latter by Isaac (A.D. 1185). After a reign disturbed from without and within, Isaac was dethroned by his brother, Alexius III. (A.D. 1195). The crusaders restored him and his son Alexius IV., but the seditious Constantinopolitans proclaimed Alexius V., Ducas Murzuphlus, emperor, who put Alexius IV. to death. At the same time Isaac II. died. During the last reigns, the kings of Sicily had made many conquests on the coasts of the Adriatic. The Latins now forced their way to Constantinople (A.D. 1204), conquered the city, and retained it, together with most of the European territories of the Empire. Baldwin, count of Flanders, was made emperor; Boniface, marquis of Montferrat, obtained Thessalonica as a kingdom, and the Venetians acquired a large extent of territory. In Rhodes, Philadelphia, Corinth, and Epirus, independent sovereigns arose. Theodore Lascaris seized on the Asiatic provinces, bore the title of emperor at Nice, and was, at first, more powerful than Baldwin. A descendant of the Comneni, named Alexius, established a principality at Trebisond, in which his great-grandson John took the title of emperor. Neither Baldwin nor his successors were able to secure the tottering throne. He himself died in captivity among the Bulgarians (1206). To him succeeded Henry, his brother, with Peter, brother-in-law of Henry, and his son Robert (A.D. 1221). With the exception of Constantinople, all the remaining Byzantine territory, including Thessalonica, was conquered by John, emperor of Nice. Baldwin II., brother of Robert, under the guardianship of his colleague, John Brienne, king of Jerusalem, died in 1237. Michael Palaeologus, king of Nice, conquered Constantinople in 1261, and Baldwin died in the West a private person. The sovereigns of Nice, up to this period, were Theodore Lascaris (A.D. 1204); John Ducas Patatzes, a good monarch and successful warrior (A.D. 1222); Theodore II., his son (A.D. 1259), who was deprived of the crown by Michael Palaeologus (A.D. 1260). In 1261, Michael took Constantinople from the Latins. He laboured to unite himself with the Latin Church, but his son Andronicus renounced the connection. Internal disturbances and foreign wars, particularly with the Turks, threw the exhausted Empire into confusion. Andronicus III., his grandson, obliged him to divide the throne (A.D. 1322), and at length wrested it entirely from him. Andronicus died a monk (A.D. 1328). Andronicus IV., who ascended the throne in the same year, waged war unsuccessfully against the Turks, and died A.D. 1341. His son John was obliged to share the throne with his guardian, John Cantacuzenus, during ten years. The son of the latter, Matthew, was also made emperor, but John Cantacuzenus resigned the crown, and Matthew was compelled to abdicate (A.D. 1355). Under the reign of John, the Turks first obtained a firm footing in Europe, and conquered Gallipolis (A.D. 1357). The family of Palaeologus, from this time, were gradually deprived of their European territories, partly by revolt and partly by the Turks. The Sultan Amurath took Adrianople A.D. 1361. Bajazet conquered almost all the European provinces except Constantinople, and obliged John to pay him tribute. The latter was, some time after, driven out by his own son Manuel (A.D. 1391). Bajazet besieged Constantinople, defeated an army of Western warriors under Sigismund, near Nicopolis, and Manuel was obliged to place John, son of Andronicus, on his throne. Timour's invasion of the Turkish provinces saved Constantinople for this time (A.D. 1402). Manuel then recovered his throne, and regained some of the lost provinces from the contending sons of Bajazet. To him succeeded his son John (A.D. 1425), whom Amurath II. stripped of all his territories except Constantinople, and extorted from him a tribute (A.D. 1444). To the emperor John succeeded his brother Constantine. With the assistance of his general, the Genoese Justinian, he withstood the superior forces of the enemy with fruitless courage, and fell in the defence of Constantinople, by the conquest of which, May 29th, A.D. 1453, Mohammed II. put an end to the Greek or Byzantine Empire.

The events which have just been detailed are recorded by a series of Greek authors, known by the general name of Byzantine historians. Their works relate to the history of the lower Empire, from the fourth century to the conquest of Constantinople by the Turks, and to the Turkish history for some period later. They display in their writings the faults of a degenerate age, but are valuable for the information which they furnish, being the principal source from which we obtain the history of the decay of the Eastern Empire. The most valuable of the number are Zonaras, Nicetas, Nicephorus, and Chalcondylas. These four form a continued history of the Byzantine Empire to the year 1470. Of the remaining authors, who give us histories of detached portions of this same period, the following deserve particular mention, and are given in chronological order: (1) Procopius (q. v.); (2) Agathias; (3) Theophylactus; (4) Nicephorus, patriarch of Constantinople; (5) Johannes Scylitzes; (6) Anna Comnena; (7) Georgius Acropolita; (8) Georgius Pachymeres; (9) Johannes Cantacuzenus; (10) Georgius Codinus; (11) Constantinus Porphyrogenitus; (12) Ducas; (13) Anselmus Bandurius; (14) Petrus Gyllius; (15) Zosimus; (16) Georgius Phranza. Besides editions of individual works or of entire authors, we have the united works of these writers with a Latin translation in what is called the *Corpus Scriptorum Hist. Byzantiae*, 36 vols., by Labbé (Paris, 1654–1711); reprinted at Venice in 1729–33; and a similar collection in 48 vols. begun by Niebuhr, Bekker, Hase, and the Dindorfs (Bonn, 1828 foll.). See Krumbacher, *Geschichte der byzantinischen Litteratur* (Munich, 1891). For an account of the Eastern Empire, see Du Cange, *Hist. de l'Empire de Constantinople sous les Empereurs François* (1659); Gibbon, *Decline and Fall of the Roman Empire;* Hullmann, *Geschichte der byzantischen Handels* (1808); Heyne, *Antiquitates Byzantinae* (1808–11); Lebeau, *Hist. du Bas-Empire* (1824–36); Manast, *Esquisses Byzantines*, 2d ed. (1874); Finlay, *History of Greece*, 7 vols. (1856; 2d ed. 1877); Gasquet, *L'Empire Byzantin* (Paris, 1888); Mahaffy, *The Greek World under Roman Sway* (London, 1890); Bury, *History of the Later Roman Empire* (London, 1890); and Oman, *Story of the Byzantine Empire* (N. Y. 1892).

Byzantium (Βυζάντιον). A celebrated city of Thrace, on the shore of the Thracian Bosporus, called at a later period CONSTANTINOPOLIS, and made the capital of the Eastern Empire of the Romans. It was founded by a Dorian colony from Megara, or, rather, by a Megarian colony in conjunction with a Thracian prince. For Byzas, whom the city acknowledged, and celebrated in a festival as its founder, was, according to the legend, a son of Poseidon and Ceroëssa the daughter of Io, and ruled over all the adjacent country. The early commerce of Megara was directed principally to the shores of the Propontis, and this people had founded Chalcedon seventeen years before Byzantium, and Selymbria even prior to Chalcedon (Herod. iv. 144). When, however, their trade was extended still farther to the north, and had reached the shores of the Euxine, the harbour of Chalcedon sank in importance, and a commercial station was required on the opposite side of the strait. This station was Byzantium. The appellation of "blind men" given to the Chalcedonians by the Persian general Megabazus (Herod. iv. 144), for having overlooked the superior site where Byzantium was afterwards founded, does not therefore appear to

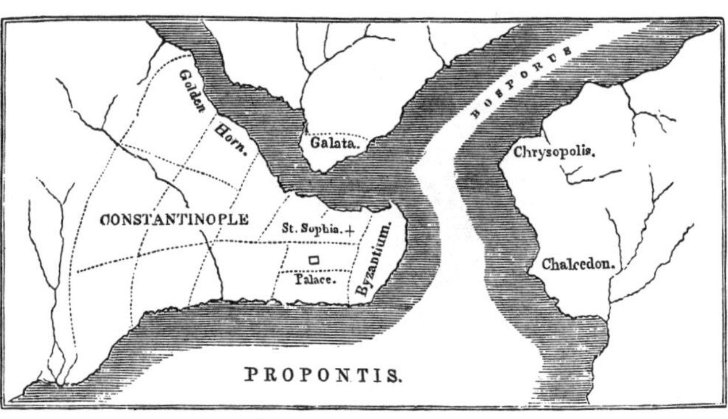

Map of Byzantium, or Constantinople.

have been well merited. As long as Chalcedon was the northernmost point reached by the commerce of Megara, its situation was preferable to any offered by the opposite side of the Bosporus, because the current on this latter side runs down from the north more strongly than it does on the side of Chalcedon, and the harbour of this city, therefore, is more accessible to vessels coming from the south. On the other hand, Byzantium was far superior to Chalcedon for the northern trade, since the current that set in strongly from the Euxine carried vessels directly into the harbour of Byzantium, but prevented their approach to Chalcedon in a straight course (Polyb. iv. 43). The harbour of Byzantium was peculiarly favoured by nature, being deep, capacious, and sheltered from every storm. From its shape, and the rich advantages thus connected with it, the harbour of Byzantium obtained the name of Chrysoceras, or "the Golden Horn," which was also applied to the promontory or neck of land that contributed to form it. And yet, notwithstanding all these advantages, Byzantium remained for a long time an inconsiderable town. The declining commerce of Megara, and the character which Byzantium still sustained of being a half-barbarian place, may serve to account for this.

At a subsequent period, the Milesians sent hither a strong colony, and so altered for the better the aspect of things that they are regarded by some ancient writers as the founders of the city itself. When, at a later day, the insurrection of the Asiatic Greeks had been crushed by Darius, and the Persian fleet was reducing to obedience the Greek cities along the Hellespont and the Propontis, the Byzantines, together with a body of Chalcedonians, would not wait for the coming of the Persians, but, leaving their habitations, and fleeing to the Euxine, built the city of Mesembria on the upper coast of Thrace (Herod. vi. 33). The Persians destroyed the empty city, and no Byzantium for some time thereafter existed. This will explain why Scylax, in his *Periplus*, passed by Byzantium in silence, while he mentions all the Grecian settlements in this quarter, and among them even Mesembria itself.

Byzantium reappeared after the overthrow of Xerxes, some of the old inhabitants having probably returned; and here Pausanias, the commander of the Grecian forces, took up his quarters (B.C. 479). He gave the city a code of laws, and a government modelled, in some degree, after the Spartan form, and hence he was regarded by some as the true founder of the city. The Athenians succeeding to the hegemony, Byzantium fell under their control, and received so many important additions from them that Ammianus Marcellinus, in a later age, calls it an Attic colony (xxii. 8). The city, however, was a Doric one, in language, customs, and laws, and remained so even after the Athenians had the control of it. The maintenance of this military post became of great importance to the Greeks during their warfare with the Persians in subsequent years, and this circumstance, together with the advantages of a lucrative and now continually increasing commerce, gave Byzantium a high rank among Grecian cities. After Athens and Sparta had weakened the power of each other by national rivalry, and neither could lay claim to the empire of the sea, Byzantium became an independent city, and turned its whole attention to commerce. Its strong situation enabled it, at a subsequent period, to resist successfully the arms of Philip of Macedon; nor did Alexander, in his eagerness to march into Asia, make any attempt upon the place. It preserved also a neutral character under his successors. The great evil to which the city of Byzantium was exposed came from the inland country, the Thracian tribes continually making incursions into the fertile territory around the place, and carrying off more or less of the products of the fields. The city suffered severely also from the Gauls, being compelled to pay a yearly tribute amounting at least to eighty talents.

After the departure of the Gauls it again became a flourishing place, but its most prosperous period was during the Roman sway. It had thrown itself into the arms of the Romans as early as the war against the younger Philip of Macedon, and enjoyed from that people not only complete protection, but also many valuable commercial privileges. It was allowed, moreover, to lay a toll on all vessels passing through the straits—a thing which had been attempted before without success—and this toll it shared with the Romans. But the day of misfortune at length came. In the contest for the Empire between Severus and Niger, Byzantium declared for the latter, and stood a siege in consequence which continued long after Niger's overthrow and death. After three years of almost incredible exertions the place surrendered to Severus. The few remaining inhabitants whom famine had spared were sold as slaves, the city was razed to the ground, its territory given to Perinthus, and a small village took the place of the great commercial emporium. Repenting soon after of what he had done, Severus rebuilt Byzantium, and adorned it with numerous and splendid buildings, which in a later age still bore his name; but it never recovered its former rank until the days of Constantine. Constantine had no great affection for Rome as a city, nor had the inhabitants any great regard for him. He felt the necessity, moreover, of having the capital of the Empire in some more central quarter, from which the movements of the German tribes on the one hand, and those of the Persians on the other, might be observed. He long sought for such a locality, and believed at one time that he had found it in the neighbourhood of the Sigaean promontory, on the coast of Troas. He had even commenced building here when the superior advantages of Byzantium as a centre of empire attracted his attention, and he finally resolved to make this the capital of the Roman world. For a monarchy possessing the western portion of Asia and the largest part of Europe, together with the whole coast of the Mediterranean Sea, nature herself seemed to have destined Byzantium as a capital.

Coin of Byzantium.

Constantine's plan was carried into rapid execution (A.D. 330). The ancient city had possessed a circuit of forty stadia, and covered merely two hills, one close to the water, on which the Seraglio at present stands, and another adjoining it, and extending towards the interior to what is now the *Besestan*, or great market. The new city, called Constantinopolis, or "City of Constantine," was three times as large, and covered four hills, together with part of a fifth, having a circuit of somewhat less than fourteen geographical miles. Every effort was made to embellish this new capital of the Roman world: the most splendid edifices were erected, including an imperial palace, numerous residences for the chief officers of the court, churches, baths, a hippodrome; and inhabitants were procured from every quarter. Its rapid increase called, from time to time, for a corresponding enlargement of the city, until, in the reign of Theodosius II., when the new walls were erected (the previous ones having been thrown down by an earthquake), Constantinople attained to the size which it at present has. Chalcondylas supposes the walls of the city to be 111 stadia in circumference; Gyllius, about 13 Italian miles; but, according to the best modern plans of Constantinople, it is not less than 19,700 yards. The number of gates is twenty-eight—fourteen on the side of the port, seven towards the land, and as many on the Propontis. The city is built on a triangular promontory, and the number of hills which it covers is seven. Besides the name of Constantinopolis (Κωνσταντίνου πόλις), this city had also the more imposing one of New Rome (Νέα Ῥώμη), which, however, gradually fell into disuse. According to some, the peasants in the neighbourhood, while they repair to Constantinople, say in corrupt Greek that they are going *es tam bolin* (i.e. ἐς τὰν πόλιν), "to the city," whence has arisen the Turkish name of the place, Stamboul. Constantinople was taken by the Turks under Mohammed II. on the 29th of May, A.D. 1453. See BYZANTINUM IMPERIUM; CONSTANTINUS.

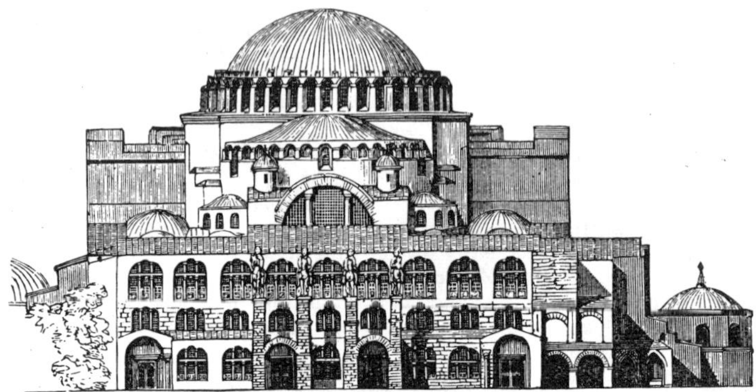

St. Sophia, at Constantinople.

Byzas (Βύζας). The legendary founder of Byzantium (q. v.). Cf. Diod. Sic. iv. 49.

K, C, X

K, as a symbol.

IN GREEK.—K = κάτθανε (on sepulchral inscriptions), Corinth, Crotona (on coins), Καῖσαρ, Κόϊντος, Καλανδῶν, καί (e. g. *C. I. G.* 111, 606, 1241, 1318, 2026, 2423). κ′ = 20; ͵κ = 20,000.

ϙ = *koppa*, a letter in the primitive Hellenic alphabet, originally placed between π and ρ, and answering to the Latin *q*, both in form and signification. As a numeral, it designates 90. The same letter is very frequently found on the coins of Corinth and her western colonies, particularly Crotona and Syracuse, as a symbol for the city. A koppa was also branded on Corinthian horses, as a kind of guarantee trade-mark, Corinth being famous for its stud. Hence κοππατίας (sc. ἵππος) in Arist. *Nub.* 23, 437; Fragm. Anagyrus, 41; or κοππάφορος in Lucian, *Adv. Indoctos*, § 5.

KΘ = καταχθονίοις θεοῖς (*C. I. G.* 1182, 5172 = Karbel, *Epigr.* 418).

KX = ? κοινοῖς χρήμασι (*C. I. G.* 5932).

IN LATIN.—K = Kaeso, Kalendae (very frequent before B.C. 180, thereafter generally displaced by KAL), kalendarium, candidatus, castellum, coniux, cardo, carissimus, casa.

ꓘ = castra (also K·K).

K·K = calumniae causae.

K·L = caput legis.

K·O = canophori Ostienses.

K·Q = kalendae Quinctiles.

K·S = carus suis.

C, as a symbol.

IN GREEK.—C (half of O) = half an obolus.

IN LATIN.—C = Caesar, Gaius, candidatus, castrum, cedit, centurio, censuerunt, cineres, circiter, circus, citra, civis, clarissimus, classiarius, Claudius, cohors, colonia, comitialis, compos, condemno (hence, *littera tristis* in Cic. *Mil.* 6. 15), coniux, consule, creatus, curavit, curia, etc.

Ɔ = Gaia, centurio, conductor, coronarum.

CC = Caesares (duo), Gai (duo). ƆƆ = Gaiae duae. ƆƆƆ = Gaiae tres.

·C·C = censuerunt cuncti, certa constans (legio), collegium centonariorum, colonia Claudia, coloni coloniae, constans Commoda (agens) curam carceris.

C·C·C· = coire convocari cogi, colonia copia Claudia, cum consilio collocutus, calumniae cavendae causa.

C·A = curam agens, custos armorum, colonia Augusta.

C·A·A·A = colonia Aelia Augusta Aeclanum.

C·A·D·A·I = colonis agrorum dandorum adsignandorum ius.

C·B = colonia Beneventana, coniugi bonae.

C·B·F (or M or M·F or M·P) = coniugi bonae fecit, merenti, merenti fecit, merenti posuit.

C·C·A·A·A = coloni coloniae Augustae Alexandrinae Abellinatium.

C·C·R = curator civium Romanorum.

C·D = compos dat, consulto decurionum.

C·D·D = creatus decreto decurionum.

C·E·B·Q = cineres eius bene quiescant.

C·F = clarissima femina, cl. filius, coniux fecit.

C·F·C = censores faciundum curarunt, coniux faciundum curavit.

C·F·C·C = collegium fabrum centonariorum Comensium.

C·F·F = carissimae filiae fecit.

C·I = colonia Iulia, clarissimus iuvenis.

C·K·F = coniugi karissimae fecit.

C·L = Gai libertus. Ɔ·L = mulieris libertus.

C·M = civitas Mathacorum, collegium mensorum.

C·M·F (P, V) = clarissimae memoriae femina, puer, vir.

C·P = Castor (et) Pollux, castra praetoria (peregrina), censoria potestati, comprobatum pondus, cui praeest.

C·P·F = Claudia pia fidelis (legio).

C·P·M·P = coniugi pientissimae memoriam posuit.

C·P·P = conductor publici portorii.

C·Q·V = cum quo (qua) vixit.

C·R·P = curator rei publicae.

C·S = carissimus sibi (suis), coniugi sanctissimae (suae), cum suis.

C·S·P·N·C = consularis senfascalis provinciae Numidiae Constantinae.

C·S·O = cum suis omnibus.

C·V = civitas Ulpia, clarissimus vir, colonia Viennensis.

C, as the symbol for 100, being the first letter of *centum*, is the youngest numerical symbol in Latin, for this letter originally represented the sound of G, which was introduced into the Roman alphabet at the beginning of the Second Punic War (according to Plut. *Quaest. Rom.* 277 D, by a freedman of Spurius Carvilius Ruga). (See ALPHABET.) The siglum for 100, in use before this time, was probably ⊗ = *θ*, the Etruscan designation for 100.

X (chi) as a symbol.

X = χιλίαρχος; X = 600.

XΜΓ = Χριστός, Μιχαήλ, Γαβριήλ (*Bull. de Corresp. Hellén.* ii. 30).

Cabalia (Καβαλία). A small district of Asia Minor, between Lycia and Pamphylia, with a town of the same name.

Cabeiri (*κάβειροι*). See CABEIRIA.

Cabeiria (*τὰ καβείρια*). The mysterious rites of the Pelasgic gods known as the Cabeiri, celebrated in the islands lying between Euboea and the Hellespont, in Lemnos, Imbros, and especially in Samothrace. This worship was also known on the adjacent coasts of Europe and Asia Minor, at Thebes and Andania in Greece, and, according to Strabo (iv. p. 198), in an island near Britannia. Like the Eleusinia, an almost complete secrecy had been maintained as to the ceremonies and teaching of these mysteries. Yet we know the names of the gods; and, from an examination of the various forms under which we find them, Lenormant has been able to discover what he calls a Cabeiric group. They are four in number, thus differing essentially from the Phœnician Kabirim, who, as their Semitic name shows, are also "great gods," but are eight in number, representing the planets and the universe formed from their union. The names of the Samothracian Cabeiri, as revealed by Mnaseas of Patara and Dionysodorus, two historians of the Alexandrian Age, are Axieros (= Demeter), Axiokersa (= Persephoné), Axiokersos (= Hades), Casmilos (= Hermes). (See the scholiast on Apoll. Rhod. i. 917.) Sometimes the two goddesses blend in one, viz. Earth (Varro, *L. L.* v. 58); sometimes as Aphrodité and Venus; but to most of the Romans they represent Iuno and Minerva (Serv. *ad* Verg. *Aen.* iii. 12). Axiokersos appears further as Zeus, Uranus, Iupiter, Apollo, Dionysus-Liber; and Casmilos as Mercurius or Eros. The group is a primal mother goddess, whose issue are two divinities, a male and a female, from whom again springs a fourth, Casmilos, the orderer of the universe. For a full discussion of the varied evidence on which this grouping is made, the reader is referred to Lenormant in Daremberg and Saglio, i. 757 foll.

Herodotus (ii. 51) is the first historian who mentions them. Though known while Athens was flourishing (Aristoph. *Pax*, 277), it was not till Alexandrian times that they really became famous. During this period Samothrace was a sort of sacred island, as it was under the Roman dominion, for the idea was prevalent that the Penates (Serv. *ad* Verg. *Aen.* ii. 325, iii. 12, viii. 619) were identical with the gods of Samothrace. Legend told how that Dardanus, Eetion, or Iasion, and Harmonia, wife of Cadmus, were children of Electra and Zeus; that Iasion was given the mysteries by Zeus, married Cybelé, and begat Corybas; and after Iasion was received among the gods, Dardanus, Cybelé, and Corybas brought the mysteries to Asia. The legends vary in details, but almost all agree in making Dardanus and Iasion sons of Zeus and Electra, and connecting the Samothracian mysteries with them. It is to be remarked, in passing, that, while legend brought the mysteries from Samothrace to Asia, there can be hardly any doubt that the passage was the other way (cf. Strabo, x. 472); for the whole tenor of the worship is Asiatic. We have many inscriptions of Romans who were initiated (*C. I. L.* iii. 713–721), and we hear besides of other Romans of high position who were initiated, among them probably Cicero (*Nat. Deor.* i. 42, 119). Throughout the Roman period the Cabeiric mysteries were held in high estimation, second only to the Eleusinian, and they were still in existence in the time of Libanius.

From the earliest times, the Pelasgi are said to have sacrificed a tenth of their produce to the Cabeiri in order to be preserved from famine. The chief priest was probably the *ἱεροφάντης* mentioned by Galen (iii. 576, ed. Kühn); and the purifying priest *κόης* or *κοίης*. The *βασιλεύς* of the inscriptions was the highest eponymous magistrate of Samothrace. As in all mysteries, the votary must be purified in body and mind before initiation; and thus we have some evidence of auricular confession. But, as far as we know, there was not any special preparatory intellectual training required. Women and children appear to have been admitted as well as men. Of the religious ceremonies themselves we may say we know nothing. They consisted of *δρώμενα καὶ λεγόμενα*. We hear of dances by the *pii Samothraces*, and the priests who executed these dances were called Saoi (?). The Romans, who traced their Penates to Samothrace, referred their Salii to these Saoi. There were two classes of votaries—the *μύσται* and the *μύσται εὐσεβεῖς*, *mystae pii*—the latter being apparently those initiated for the first time. In the Samothracian mysteries, *sacra accipere* (παραλαμβάνειν τὰ μυστήρια), which is the regular phrase for primary initiation, seems to be applied to the higher grades. But the whole matter is quite obscure and unsettled. See Hirschfeld in Conze, *Untersuchungen auf Samothrake*, pp. 37–39.

The scholiast on Apollonius Rhodius tells us that the initiated wore a purple band (ταινία) round their waist (which reminds us of the Brahminical thread); that Agamemnon quelled a mutiny of the Greeks by wearing one; and that Odysseus, who wore a fillet for the band, was miraculously saved in shipwreck. Preservation in times of peril, and especially in perils on the sea, was the chief service that the Cabeiri were supposed to render to those who called on them by name, and none knew their names except the initiated. It was the electric fires of the Cabeiri that, according to the legend, lighted on the heads of the Dioscuri during the Argonautic voyage. Diodorus further says, in the course of an important discussion on the Cabeiri (v. 47–49), that those who were initiated became more pious, more righteous, and in every respect better than they were before. On the basis of this, Lenormant thinks it probable that the doctrine of rewards and punishments in a future life was inculcated, though, with Lobeck, we may well suppose that no more is necessarily implied than the impulse to virtue, which is always united with religious emotion excited by impressive and gracious ceremonies. (Cf. Apoll. Rhod. i. 917.)

The initiations at Samothrace took place at any time from May to September (see inscriptions), in this differing from the Eleusinian and more resembling the Orphic Mysteries. There appears, however, to have been a specially great ceremony at the commencement of August (Plut. *Lucull.* 13).

From the manner in which Cicero speaks of the Samothracian mysteries in the passage already cited, it is probable that he was initiated. He says of their ceremonies, *quibus explicatis ad rationemque revocatis, rerum magis natura cognoscitur quam deorum.* And the Cabeiri themselves do appear to be symbols of the creation of the world. From the primeval mother emanate or differentiate themselves two elements — matter (earth) and force (especially fire, celestial and terrestrial). Indeed, the name Cabeiri appears to mean "the Burners," from καίειν (see Welcker, *Die Aeschyl. Trilogie*, pp. 161, 211), and by the action of the former on the latter the ordered world is generated. The etymological identity of the Pelasgian with the Phœnician Cabeiri is doubted by Lenormant; the name of the latter being from a Semitic root, which in Arabic appears as *kebir*, "great." Many hold that all the ceremonies of the Cabeiri, and those of the other mysteries, were pure inventions of the priests, nothing more than mere stories about gods. The reader, with regard to this phase of the subject, is referred to the article MYSTERIA.

For information on the Cabeiric mysteries, see Lobeck, *Aglaoph.* pp. 1202–1295; Schömann, *Griech. Alterth.* ii. 403–407; Preller, *Gr. Mythol.* i. 695–709; Welcker, *Gr. Götterlehre*, i. 328–333, iii. 173–189; and, above all, the article by Lenormant in Daremberg and Saglio, i. 757–774.

Cabillōnum. The modern Châlon-sur-Saône; a town of the Aedui on the Arar (Saône) in Gallia Lugdunensis.

Cabīra (τὰ Κάβειρα). A place in Pontus on the borders of Armenia; a frequent residence of Mithridates, who was defeated here by Lucullus, B.C. 71.

Cabīri. See CABEIRIA.

Caca. A sister of Cacus (q. v.), who, according to one version of the fable, became enamoured of Hercules, and showed the hero where her brother had concealed his oxen. For this she was deified. She presided over the excrements of the human body (cf. the verb *cacare*) and had a chapel (*sacellum*) at Rome, with a sacred fire continually burning in it, and virgins to perform her rites (Lactant. i. 20, p. 110, ed. Gall; Serv. *ad* Verg. *Aen.* viii. 190).

Caccăbus, less correctly CACABUS (κάκκαβος, κακκάβη). A cooking-pot. The statement of Varro, *L. L.* v. 127, *vas ubi coquebant cibum, ab eo caccabum appellarunt*, may be accepted in proof of the meaning of the word, however absurd as an etymology. The Greek forms κακκάβη and κάκκαβος both occur in the Comic Fragments, and the former is as old as Aristophanes.

Caccabus. (Pompeii.)

The different processes of boiling and frying are not always clearly distinguished in the ancient kitchen. (See SARTAGO.) It seems certain, however, that the caccabus was used for boiling meat, vegetables, etc.; and that it was placed immediately upon the fire, or upon a trivet (*tripus*) standing over it. It is thus distinguished from the *aenum*, which was suspended over the fire (Serv. *ad* Verg. *Aen.* i. 213); and from the *authepsa* (q. v.), which was probably not used for cooking at all. The material varied. Athenaeus mentions the κακκάβη as equivalent to the χύτρα—i. e. the earthen cooking-pot—and so usually in Latin (*fictilis*). But *caccabi* were sometimes of metal—*stanneus* (of tin), or *argenteus*. See Colum. *R. R.* xii. 42, 1.

Kakegorias Diké (κακηγορίας δίκη). An action for abusive language, brought in the Attic courts, and also known as κακηγορίου δίκη. Any person was liable who applied to another certain abusive epithets, such as "murderer" (ἀνδροφόνος), "parricide" (πατραλοίας), etc. (See APORRHETA.) By a law of Solon, it was equally forbidden to speak evil of the dead. If the person slandered was a public officer, the offender became liable, in addition to the usual penalty of 500 drachmas fine, to ἀτιμία, because in the person of the officer the State had also been insulted.

Kakologias Diké (κακολογίας δίκη). See KAKEGORIAS DIKÉ.

Kakōsis (κάκωσις). In the Attic law, κάκωσις signifies one of the following kinds of ill-treatment:

(1) The ill-treatment of parents by their children (κάκωσις γονέων), the term γονεῖς including also grandparents and great-grandparents. Refusal to supply the parents with means of support or to bury them with proper honours at death, equally with actual abuse or disobedience, formed instances of κάκωσις. An illegitimate child, however, was not liable to this action.

(2) Infidelity or ill-treatment of wives by their husbands (κάκωσις γυναικῶν), including also the neglect of the law of Solon by which the husband

was bound to visit his wife three times every month, at least, if she were an heiress (Plut. *Sol.* 30). In the comedy of Cratinus, called the *Wine Flask* (Πυτίνη), Comedy was represented as the wife of Cratinus, who brought an action against him because he neglected her and devoted all his attention to the wine-flask (Schol. *ad* Aristoph. *Equit.* 399).

(3) Injury committed against orphans or widows (*κάκωσις τῶν ὀρφανῶν καὶ χηρευουσῶν γυναικῶν*), who were all considered to be under the especial protection of the chief archon.

All cases of *κάκωσις* belonged to the jurisdiction of the chief archon in the case of citizens, or to the polemarch in the case of *metoeci* (Meier, *Att. Process*, p. 269; Perrot, *Essai sur le Droit Public*, p. 264). If a person wronged in any way orphans, heiresses, or widows, the archon could inflict a fine himself; or, if he considered the person deserving of greater punishment, could bring him before the Heliaea. Any private individual could also accuse parties guilty of *κάκωσις* by means of laying an information (*εἰσαγγελία*) before the chief archon, though sometimes the accuser proceeded by means of a regular indictment (*γραφή*), with an *ἀνάκρισις* before the archon. Those who accused persons guilty of *κάκωσις* incurred no danger, as was usually the case if the defendant was acquitted and they did not obtain the fifth part of the votes of the dicasts.

The punishment does not appear to have been fixed for the different cases of *κάκωσις*, but it was generally severe. Those found guilty of *κάκωσις γόνεων* lost their civil rights (*ἀτιμία*), but were allowed to retain their property; if the *κάκωσις* consisted in beating their parents, the hands of the offenders might even be cut off.

Kakotechniōn Diké (*κακοτεχνιῶν δίκη*). An action in the nature of one for the subornation of perjury, and might be brought against a party to a previous suit whose witnesses had been convicted of perjury in an action *ψευδομαρτυριῶν*. The details relating to this action are not known. See Meier, *Att. Process*, pp. 45, 386.

Cācus. In Italian mythology, a fire-spitting giant, the son of Vulcan, who lived near the place where Rome was afterwards built. When Hercules came into the neighbourhood with the cattle of Geryon, Cacus stole some of them while the hero was sleeping and dragged them backwards into his cave under a spur of the Aventine, so that their footprints gave no clue to the direction in which they had gone. He then closed the entrance to the cave with a rock, which ten pairs of oxen were unable to move. But the lowing of the cattle guided the hero, in his search, to the right track. He tore open the cave, and, after a fearful struggle, slew Cacus with his club (Ovid, *Fast.* i. 543 foll). Upon this he built an altar on the spot to Iupiter, under the title of Pater Inventor, "the discoverer," and sacrificed one of the cattle upon it. The inhabitants paid him every honour for freeing them of the monster; and Evander, who had been instructed by his mother, Carmentis, in the lore of prophecy, saluted him as a god. Hercules is then said to have established his own religious service, and to have instructed two noble families, the Potitii and the Pinarii, in the usages to be observed at the sacrifice (Livy, i. 7). This sacrifice was to be offered on the Ara Maxima, which he himself had built on the cattle-market (*Forum Boarium*) where the cattle had been pastured.

Cadāver. A corpse. See FUNUS.

Cadi (Κάδοι). A city of Phrygia Epictetus on the borders of Lydia.

Cadiscus (*καδίσκος*). A voting-urn. See PSEPHUS.

Cadmēa (Καδμεία). The citadel of Thebes. See THEBAE.

Cadmēis (Καδμηΐς). An ancient name of Boeotia (q. v.), and of Thebes (Hes. *Op.* 161). It is also applied to Semelé (q. v.).

Cadmus (Κάδμος). (1) The son of Agenor, king of Phœnicia, and of Telephassa. His sister Europa being carried off by Zeus, Cadmus, with his brothers Phoenix and Cilix, was sent out with the command to look for her, and not to return without her. In the course of his wanderings he came to Thrace. Here his mother, who had accompanied him so far, breathed her last; and Cadmus applied for counsel to the Delphic oracle. He was advised not to seek his sister any more, but to follow a cow which would meet him, and found a city on the spot where she should lie down. The cow met him in Phocis, and led him into Boeotia. He was intending to sacrifice the cow, and had sent his companions to a neighbouring spring to bring the necessary water, when they were all slain by a serpent, the offspring of Ares and the Erinys Tisiphoné, that guarded the spring. After a severe struggle, Cadmus destroyed the dragon, and at the command of Athené sowed its teeth over the neighbouring ground. A host of armed men sprang up, who immediately fought and slew each other, all except five. The survivors, who were called Spartoi, "sown," helped Cadmus to build the Cadmea, or the stronghold of what was afterwards Thebes, which bore his name. They were the ancestors of the Theban aristocracy; and one of them, Echion, "the serpent's son," became the husband of Cadmus's daughter, Agavé. Cadmus did atonement to Ares for eight years for the slaughter of the dragon. Then Zeus gave him to wife Harmonia, the daughter of Ares and Aphrodité, who bore him a son, Polydorus, and four daughters, Autonoé, Ino, Agavé, and Semelé. (See HARMONIA; SEMELÉ.) Crushed by the terrible doom which weighed upon his home, he afterwards sought retirement among the Enchelii in Illyria, a country which he named after his son Illyrius, who was born there. He resigned the kingdom to Illyrius; and then he and his wife Harmonia were changed into serpents, and carried by Zeus to Elysium.

The ancient tradition was that Cadmus brought sixteen letters from Phœnicia to Greece, to which Palamedes added subsequently four more, θ, ξ, φ, χ, and Simonides, at a still later period, four others, ζ, η, ψ, ω. The traditional alphabet of Cadmus is supposed to have been the following: A, B, Γ, Δ, E, F, I, K, Λ, M, N, O, Π, P, Σ, T, and the names were, Ἄλφα, Βῆτα, Γάμμα, Δέλτα, Εἶ, Faῦ, Ἰῶτα, Κάππα, Λάμβδα, Μῦ, Νῦ, Οῦ, Πῖ, Ῥῶ, Σίγμα, Ταῦ. The explanation which has just been given to the myth of Cadmus, and its connection with the Pelasgi, have an important bearing on the question relative to the existence of an early Pelasgic alphabet in Greece. See ALPHABET; PELASGI. (2) A native of Miletus, who flourished about B.C. 520. Pliny (*H. N.* vii. § 56) calls him the most ancient of the *logographi*. In another passage he makes him to have been the first prose-writer, though elsewhere he attributes this to Pherecydes. According to a remark of Isocrates (in his discourse Περὶ Ἀντιδόσεως), Cadmus was the first that bore the title of σοφιστής, by which appellation was then meant an eloquent man. He wrote on the antiquities of his native city. His work was abridged by Bion of Proconnesus. See LOGOGRAPHI.

Caducāriae Leges; **Cadūcum**. See BONA CADUCA.

Caduceus (κηρύκειον). The staff or mace carried by Greek ambassadors and heralds in time of war (Herod. ix. 100; Thuc. i. 53). The name is often given to the staff or wand with which Hermes, or Mercury, is conventionally represented.

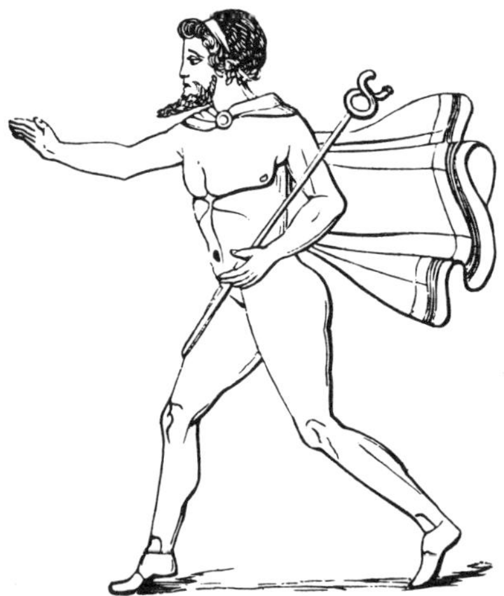

Hermes with Caduceus. (From an Ancient Vase.)

The caduceus was originally only an olive-branch with garlands, which were afterwards formed into snakes. About these snakes, later mythologists like Hyginus invented various stories—that Hermes once found two snakes fighting, and divided them with his wand; from which circumstance they were used as an emblem of peace.

From caduceus was formed the word *caduceator*, which signified a person sent to treat of peace. Thus Aulus Gellius tells us that Q. Fabius sent to the Carthaginians a spear and a caduceus as the emblems of war or peace (*hastam et caduceum, signa duo belli aut pacis*). The persons of the *caduceatores* were considered sacred.

It would appear, however, that the Roman ambassadors did not usually carry the caduceus, since Marcian informs us that they carried vervain (*sagmina*), so that no one might injure them, in the same manner as the Greek ambassadors carried the κηρύκεια. The illustration given above is from Millin's *Peintures de Vases Antiques*.

Cadurci. A people of Keltic Gaul, living between the two northern branches of the Garumna (Garonne). Their capital was Divona, afterwards Cadurci, and now Cahors.

Cadurcum. A kind of linen, of which the name is derived from the tribe which produced it, the Cadurci in Guienne. It was much used for bed-clothing, but also for garments, bandages, and tents. See Plin. *H. N.* xix. § 13.

Cadus (κάδος). A large earthenware vessel, most frequently used, like the *amphora* (q. v.), for holding wine after it had been drawn from the *dolium* (q. v.); and especially imported wine, as the Chian (Athen. xi. 473b). Other commodities were also stored in *cadi*—e. g. oil, figs, beans, honey, and salt fish. Its shape resembled that of the *amphora* (q. v.), except that its lower end was ovoid. The word sometimes denotes a well-bucket (γαυλός). Aristophanes twice (*Aves*, 1030, 1053) uses the word κάδος of the voting-urn, commonly styled καδίσκος. See CISTA; PSEPHUS.

Cadȳtis (Κάδυτις). A town of Syria, mentioned by Herodotus (ii. 159), supposed by some to be Gath, by others Jerusalem (El Kuds).

Caecias (καικίας). A northeast wind. See Aul. Gell. ii. 22.

Caecilia, GAIA, or **Tanaquil** See TANAQUIL.

Caecilia Lex. See LEX.

Caecilia Metella. See METELLA.

Caecilius Metellus. See METELLUS.

Caecilius Statius or **Statius Caecilius**. A writer of Latin comedy. He was a Gaul, of the race of the Insubrians, who were settled in Upper Italy, and was brought to Rome, probably about B.C. 194, as a prisoner of war. He was set free by one of the Caecilii, became very intimate with Ennius, and died not long after him, B.C. 166. It was long before he could obtain a footing on the stage; but, this once achieved, he won a considerable reputation, and was numbered among the masters of his craft. The influence of Ennius seems to have been apparent in the comparative care and regularity with which his pieces were constructed. Cicero, however, finds fault with his defective Latinity (Cic. *Ad Att.* vii. 3, 10); and we must therefore infer that, being of foreign extraction, he never succeeded in fully mastering the niceties of colloquial Latin. The titles of some forty of his plays have survived. The contents he mostly borrowed from Menander, and sixteen of his titles are those of plays of Menander. See Teuffel, *Caecilius Statius* (Tübingen, 1858).

Caecīna. The name of a family of the Etruscan city of Volaterrae, probably derived from the river Caecina, which flows by the town. (1) A. CAECINA, whom Cicero defended in a lawsuit, B.C. 69. (2) A. CAECINA, son of the preceding, who published a libellous work against Caesar, and was in consequence sent into exile after the battle of Pharsalia, B.C. 48. (3) A. CAECINA ALIĒNUS, quaestor in Baetica, in Spain, at Nero's death, and one of the foremost in joining the party of Galba. He served first under Galba, and afterwards under Vitellius; but, proving a traitor to the latter, he joined Vespasian, against whom also he conspired, and was slain by order of Titus.

Caecŭbus Ager. A marshy district in Latium, bordering on the Gulf of Amyclae, close to Fundi, celebrated for its wine (Caecubum) in the age of Horace. In the time of Pliny the reputation of this wine was entirely gone. See VINUM.

Caecŭlus. A son of Vulcan, conceived, as some say, by his mother as she was sitting by the fire, a spark having leaped forth into her bosom. After a life spent in plundering and rapine, he built

Praenesté; but, being unable to find inhabitants, he implored Vulcan to tell him whether he really was his father. Upon this a flame suddenly shone around a multitude who were assembled to see some spectacle, and they were immediately persuaded to become the subjects of Caeculus. Vergil says that he was found on the hearth, or, as some less correctly explain it, in the very fire itself, and hence was fabled to have been the son of Vulcan (Verg. *Aen.* vii. 680).

Caelatūra (τορευτική). Both the Greek and the Roman name come from the words denoting in the two languages "the graver's tool" (*caelum*, τορεύς); and in its general sense *caelatura* may be taken as meaning the arts employed in the production of ornamental works in metal, both in relief and in intaglio, including repoussé work, chasing, and engraving, but excluding statuary. See STATUARIA ARS.

The chief literary source of our information regarding the toreutic art is Pliny (*H. N.* xxxiii. §§ 154-157); and a complete list of the passages in the ancient writers, referring to this art, has been made by Overbeck in his *Antiken Schriftquellen*, s. v. "Toreutik." It is, however, from the artistic remains of antiquity that its history can best be studied—remains that are magnificently represented in the great museums of Europe.

The earliest specimens of ornamental metal-work discovered on Greek soil are those found by Dr. Schliemann at Hissarlik in the Troad, consisting of a large number of objects in gold, such as bracelets, ear-rings, and diadems. Among the specimens, of which a detailed description will be found in Schliemann's *Ilios* (London and N. Y., 1880), may be mentioned the following: bracelets, consisting of a thick gold plate piped with wire and adorned with spiral ornaments of gold wire soldered on the plate; a diadem, composed principally of hexagonal leaves of gold; hair-pins, consisting of a quadrangular plate ornamented with spirals of gold wires soldered on like the bracelets just mentioned; gold disks, of which one represents a flower of star form, in repoussé work. The appellation "Treasure of Priam" given by the discoverer to a large class of these objects is misleading, inasmuch as the art described in the Homeric poems is quite certainly of a more advanced character. The Hissarlik metal-work is, in fact, the product of a half-barbarous people, and its simple and unambitious character may be discerned in the preference for such ornamentation as the spiral (a form which is naturally suggested by the curling of gold wire) and in the infrequent representations of animal forms. An early though more advanced style is represented by the objects discovered by Schliemann at Mycenae, which may be approximately assigned to a date not later than B.C. 1000. The Mycenaean objects are, on the whole, the work of rude local artists, scarcely touched as yet by Oriental influence. The specimens in gold, which are extremely numerous, consist principally of plaques in repoussé work, bowls, diadems, and sepulchral masks rudely imitating the human countenance. Round bosses and other circular patterns, and especially combinations of spirals, are the basis of most of the patterns, but floral forms and imitations of insects and of marine life are also employed. Among the most instructive objects may be mentioned the following: (1) Gold diadems found on the heads of corpses. The diadems are generally piped with copper wire to give them greater solidity. (2) Lozenge-shaped buttons of wood plated with gold, ornamented with intaglio and repoussé work. (3) Perforated ornaments of gold with engravings in intaglio. (4) Gold cylinder adorned with rock crystal; a dragon of gold with scales of rock crystal. (5) Scabbards of

Gold Diadem from the so-called Treasure of Priam, as actually worn. (Schliemann, *Ilios*, p. 458.)

Brooches of Gold—actual size. (Schliemann, *Ilios*, p. 488.)

swords, representing a lion-hunt, winged monsters, fish, and plants. The manes of the lions are of red gold, the bodies of a paler tint in the same metal. A distinction of colour is also observed between the sea and the fish swimming in it, and further variety is obtained by the use of enamel in the background.

The next important epoch in the history of our subject has been denominated the Graeco-Phœnician, an epoch when the rude genius of the Greeks set itself to learn in the comparatively advanced artistic school of the Phœnicians. This is the period of art described, though with some poetic embellishment, in the Homeric poems, in which compositions the higher works of metallic art are spoken of as coming from a foreign and especially a Phœnician source. Thus it is from the king of Cyprus that Agamemnon receives the present of his cuirass (*Il.* xi. 19), and from Egypt that Menelaüs brings back tripods and the basket of Helen (*Od.* iv. 126 foll.). The crater destined by Menelaüs for Telemachus comes to him from the king of the Sidonians (*Od.* iv. 616; *Il.* xxiii. 741), and it is the Sidonians who made the silver crater given by Achilles as a prize at the Funeral Games. Even the elaborate Homeric description of the shield of Achilles may be shown to have had a tangible basis in works of Phœnician art. This Phœnician art, as revealed to us by the archæological discoveries of recent years, was not in itself original, but was formed by a curious blending of the art of the Egyptians and the Assyrians. It may best be studied in the numerous metal bowls that have been found in several localities, especially Cyprus and Italy, which had in early days relations with the Phœnician traders. The epoch generally assigned for the execution of these bowls is the seventh or eighth century B.C., though the manufacture of them according to traditional patterns may have continued to a later period. In the artistic designs of these vessels it is especially important to note the arrangement of the subjects in concentric zones, and the frequent mingling of Assyrian and Egyptian elements. See CYPRUS.

As specimens of early jewelry we may refer to the objects of gold (now in the Louvre and the British Museum) found by Salzmann at Camirus in Rhodes, which may be regarded as products of Phœnician art in the eighth century B.C. As an example of these we may take the pale gold plaques which belonged to a necklace and which are embossed with the alternate designs of a Centaur of primitive type with Egyptian head-dress, seizing a hind, and a winged female figure (the goddess Artemis or Anaïtis) holding a lion and a panther. Another plate is ornamented with a recumbent lion of Assyrian style: the mane is formed by massing together minute granules of gold, while the ears are marked out by lines formed of similar granules. On the same plaque is the head of an eagle, adorned, like the lion, with granulated designs. From the plaque itself are suspended pomegranates, chainlets, and heads of Egyptian style. Of early jewelry found in Greece proper we may notice the gold studs or ear-rings discovered in 1860 at Megara: they are decorated in repoussé, with human heads of Egyptian character, facing. Another interesting specimen of archaic jewelry, stated to have been found at Athens, and belonging probably to the first half of the sixth century B.C., is an ear-ring published in the *Journal of Hellenic Studies* (vol. ii. p. 324), on the oblong pendant of which is represented side by side a pair of female figures, beaten out in relief. The arms of both these figures are straightened closely to their sides, and their dress and attitude, though very archaic, present a resemblance to the Canephori of the Erechtheum.

Armlet found at Caeré.

Our knowledge of the jewelry of the fine period of Greek art is mainly derived from two great sources—the excavations in the tombs of southern Russia and in those of Etruria. Of the Etruscan jewelry, the Louvre, the Vatican, and the British Museum possess numerous and choice examples. The objects from southern Russia, which belong to a great extent to the fourth century B.C., are now in the Museum of the Hermitage, and may be studied in the elaborate *Comptes Rendus de la Commission Archéologique de St.-Pétersbourg*, and in the

Antiquités du Bosphore Cimmérien. The great European jewel-collections contain specimens, unrivalled in workmanship, of all the various objects of personal adornment—necklaces with pendants, ear-rings, bracelets, brooches, etc. The main effect in this jewelry is due to the combination of small figures and flowers in repoussé work, with fine filigree, granulated patterns, and vitreous inlays. Precious stones, such as garnets, are sometimes introduced, but in the best age the jeweller made comparatively little use of them. The ancient jeweller is distinguished by his delicate manipulation of the gold, his mastery of modelling, his extraordinary minuteness of work, and by the technical skill which produced the granulation (i.e. the soldering of extremely minute particles of gold on a leaf of gold) which is especially noticeable in the jewelry of Etruria. This Etruscan jewelry in its earlier period betrays an Oriental influence, but is in its later and finest stage so thoroughly Greek in character as to be a fair exponent of the capabilities of the Greek jewellers. For details as to the form of the various objects of personal ornament, the reader is referred to the separate articles in this dictionary; but, as furnishing a sample of the fertile invention and surpassing skill of the Greek workman, we may here refer to two classes of ear-rings, of which there are good specimens in the Gold-Ornament Room of the British Museum. The first class, which is the simpler and perhaps somewhat the earlier in date, consists of ear-rings formed of twisted wire and terminating at one end in the head of an animal, especially a lion. The second class consists of the specimens attached to the ear by a hook, which is covered by a round disk. The disk itself is generally adorned with some subject suitable for a medallion, such as a full face in relief, and beneath it are suspended one or more small figures. For these pendants Victories are often chosen, and an especial favourite is a tiny figure of Eros holding various objects, such as a scroll or a musical instrument. As exquisite specimens may be noticed a pair (*Comptes Rendus de la Comm. Arch. de St.-Pétersb.*, 1870–71, pl. vi., figs. 11, 12) composed of a rosette, from which hang three chains, the two outermost terminating in pendants: from the middle chain hangs a goose, inlaid about the feathers with granulated work. In the centre of the rosette is a garnet, from which radiate leaves in blue enamel, forming a star pattern.

The beautiful gold necklace shown in the illustration given below forms part of the Castellani Collection in the British Museum. It consists of a circlet of roses bearing alternate pendants of vases and female heads, all exquisitely modelled. The roses are each composed of three rosettes of diminishing sizes superimposed. Of the pendants, the centre head is simply that of a beautiful girl, while the two on each side of it have cows' horns and ears, and represent Io, who was changed by Zeus into a cow.

A very fine specimen of jewelry not intended for wear is the votive gold crown found at Armento, and now at Munich. It is composed of branches of oak intertwined with garlands of flowers, while winged figures are placed amid the foliage.

Another important branch of the toreutic art is constituted by the production of gold and silver vases, elaborately adorned—generally with reliefs in repoussé, or with ornaments separately made and soldered or riveted to the vessel. (See CRUSTA; EMBLEMA; and cf. Plin. *H. N.* xxxiii. § 139, etc.; Ovid, *Metam.* iii., v. 80; Juv. i. 76; Quintil. xi. 47.) With the increase of luxury under the successors of Alexander, this branch of art began to assume especial prominence. (Cf. Athenaeus, v. 29, 30; Plin. *H. N.* xxxiii. § 154, etc.) Among the more important vessels in the precious metals now extant should be mentioned the following: (1) The magnificent silver vase in the Hermitage Museum, which was found in the tomb of a Scythian king at Nicopolis. It has the form of an amphora, and on its upper part are friezes of Scythians and animals, in high-relief; leaves and flowers adorning the body of the vessel. The decoration is partly in repoussé, and partly consists in ornaments, like the lion-masks and the head of a winged horse, separately made and gilded and then soldered on. This vase has been assigned to the fourth century B.C. (2) Silver vase in the Antiquarium of Munich, ornamented externally with a circular frieze, in which are represented Trojan captives, in low relief. (3) The Corsini vase, on which see the memoir by Michaelis, *Das Corsinische Silbergefäss.* (4) Specimens in the Berlin Museum from the silver treasure found near Hildesheim (Hanover) in 1885, some of which go back to the time of Augustus or earlier. They have much executional merit, but present the Roman characteristics of exuberant ornament and exag-

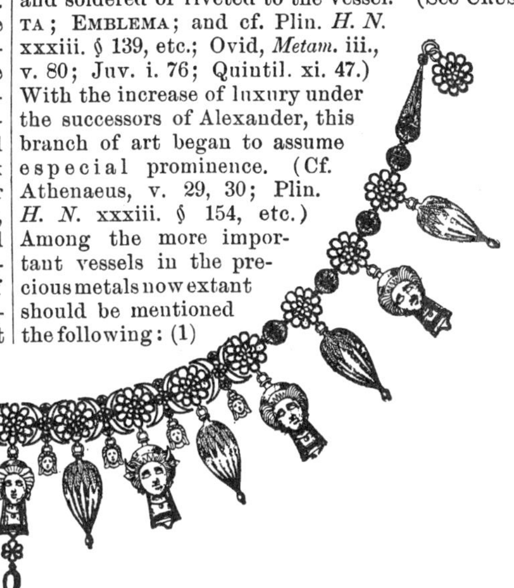

Etruscan Necklace from Tarentum (B.C. 600). (In the Castellani Collection, British Museum.)

Roman Mixing-bowl. (Found at Hildesheim; now in Berlin Museum.)

gerated relief. (5) Specimens in the Bibliothèque Nationale, Paris, from the treasure discovered at Bernay in France. The vases are of varying merit, and differ in date—one class being ornamented in very prominent repoussé, the other in lower relief with slight and delicate lines. (6) The gold patera of Rennes, into which are inserted gold coins ranging from Hadrian to Geta. The bottom of the vase is adorned with a large medallion executed in repoussé, and bordered by a wreath of laurel leaves in low-relief. (7) Silver vases found at Pompeii, and now in the Museum at Naples. This list may be concluded with a reference to the specimens in the celebrated silver treasure discovered at Rome in 1793, and now in the British Museum. It consists of caskets, vases, trappings, and ornaments of silver, and was probably executed for the most part about the end of the fifth century A.D. The figures and ornaments on most of the objects are generally embossed and chased, and gilding is applied to the salient parts. The figures, as might be expected at so late a period, are coarsely executed and of clumsy proportions.

To the examples of ornamental metal-work which have now been mentioned in this article, and which are principally in gold and silver, must be added certain specimens in bronze which are adorned (1) with engraved designs, (2) with figures in relief. A remarkable specimen of archaic Greek engraving is found on the bronze cuirass discovered in the bed of the Alpheus, and photographed in the *Bulletin de Corr. Hell.* (1883), p. 1, pl. i.–iii. Besides figures of animals, the design shows a group of six human figures. Engraved designs occur most frequently upon the circular metal disks used as mirrors by the ancients, the largest class of which comes from Etruria. Though on some of the Etruscan mirrors the drawings are of a masterly character, the greater number are executed loosely and without much regard to beauty of composition. See SPECULUM.

The covers of the mirrors of box-like form—mostly found in Greece proper—offer favourable specimens of reliefs executed in bronze. Several of them belong to a good period of Greek art; their subjects, as a rule, are borrowed from the cycles of Aphroditê and of Dionysus. Fine examples of Greek repoussé work in bronze are also to be seen in the plaques with figures in relief, which once served to ornament armour or other objects.

Engravings on mirrors of purely Greek work are rare. Among the most beautiful examples may be cited the mirror representing the Genius of the Cock Fights (Musée de Lyon), and the specimen with the hero Corinthus crowned by a woman who personifies the Corinthian colony of Leucas.

BIBLIOGRAPHY.—Schliemann, *Mycenae* (1878); Milchhöfer, *Die Anfänge der Kunst in Griechenland* (1883); Brunn, *Die Kunst bei Homer* (1859); Clermont-Ganneau, *L'Imagerie Phénicienne* (1880); Di Cesnola, *Cyprus* (1877); Calonna-Ceccaldi, *Monuments Ant. de Chypre* (1882); Dennis, *Cities and Cemeteries of Etruria* (1878); Castellani, *Dell' Oreficeria Italiana* (1872); Bucher, *Geschichte der technischen Künste* (1880); Newton, *Essays on Art and Archæology* (1883); De Linas, *Les Origines de l'Orfévrerie Cloisonnée* (1879); King, *Handbook of Engraved Gems* (1866); id. *Antique Gems and Rings* (1872); Martha, *L'Art Etrusque* (1888); Beulé, *L'Art Grec avant Périclés* (1870). See also a valuable paper on *Ancient Gold Work*, by Mr. Humphreys-Davenport, in *Harper's Magazine* for July, 1892; and the articles AES; ARGENTUM; AURUM; CRUSTA.

Caeles Vibenna. See VIBENNA.

Caelia Lex. See LEX.

Caelibātus. See AES UXORIUM; LEX IULIA ET PAPIA POPPAEA.

Caelius. (1) A young Roman of considerable talents and accomplishments, intrusted to the care of Cicero on his first introduction to the Forum. Having imprudently engaged in an intrigue with Clodia, the well-known sister of Clodius, and having afterwards deserted her, she accused him of an attempt to poison her, and of having borrowed money from her in order to procure the assassination of Dio, the Alexandrian ambassador. He was defended by Cicero in an oration which is still extant. (2) AURELIĀNUS, a medical writer. (See AURELIANUS.) (3) SABĪNUS, a writer in the age of Vespasian, who composed a treatise on the edicts of the curule aediles. (4) One of the seven hills on which Rome was built, but now deserted. Romulus surrounded it with a ditch and rampart, and it was enclosed by walls under the succeeding kings. It is supposed to have received its name from Caeles Vibenna. See ROMA.

Caelum (γλύφανον, τορεύς). The graver's tool. See CAELATURA.

Caementum (λατύπη, σκύρος). Rubble or small undressed stones used with mortar to form the concrete walls of Roman buildings. Vitruvius notes two kinds (ii. 8), the *opus reticulatum*, the more handsome but less durable kind of work; and the primitive *opus incertum*, less sightly but extremely strong, because of the way the stones were massed together.

Concrete was extensively used at Baiae in the Augustan Age, as a foundation for edifices built out into the sea (Tibull. 2, 3, 45; Hor. *Carm.* iii. 1. 33, 24. 3), the Romans having discovered that pozzolana and lime formed an hydraulic cement (Vitruvius, ii. 6, 1).

The most massive relic of Roman times in Great Britain, the great military wall which extended from the mouth of the Tyne to that of the Solway, is a structure of faced concrete, formed by erecting two faces of large stones and filling up the intervening space with alternate courses of rubble one foot deep, and mortar four inches deep.

Many of the great Roman achievements in building, especially in distant provinces, are to be attributed to this method of construction, which enabled them to raise, with comparatively unskilled hands, and from materials which are accessible in most regions or easily procured, structures which in a short time were united into solid homogeneous masses of great tenacity. See Middleton, *Ancient Rome in 1885*; id. *Remains of Ancient Rome* (1892); and the article DOMUS.

Caené (Καινή) or **Caenepŏlis** (Καινήπολις). (1) A town of Egypt, in the Panopolitan nome, supposed to be the present Gheuné. (2) A town near the promontory of Taenarus; its previous name was Taenarum. See TAENARUS.

Caeneus (Καινεύς). The son of Elatus and Hippia, one of the Lapithae of Gyrton in Thessaly. The story was that he was originally a girl named Caenis, whom her lover Poseidon changed, at her own request, into a man, and at the same time rendered her invulnerable. Caeneus took part in the Argonautic expedition and the Calydonian boar-hunt. At the marriage of Pirithoüs, the Centaurs, finding him invulnerable, crushed him to death with the trunks of trees, and he was afterwards changed into a bird. See PIRITHOÜS.

Caeni (Καινοί). A Thracian people, between the Black Sea and the Panysus.

Caenīna. A town of the Sabines, in Latium, whose king, Acron, is said to have carried on the first war against Rome. After their defeat, most of the inhabitants removed to Rome.

Caenis (Καινίς). See CAENEUS.

Caenys (Καῖνυς). A promontory of Italy north of Rhegium, facing the promontory of Pelorus in Sicily, and forming with it the narrowest part of the Fretum Siculum.

Caepio, CN. SERVILIUS. A Roman consul, B.C. 106, sent into Gallia Narbonensis to oppose the Cimbri, by whom, in 105, he was defeated, together with the consul, Cn. Mallius or Manlius. Eighty thousand soldiers and forty thousand camp-followers are said to have perished. Caepio survived the battle, but ten years afterwards (B.C. 95) he was brought to trial by the tribune C. Norbanus, on account of his misconduct in this war. He was condemned and cast into prison, where, according to one account, he died; but it was more generally stated that he escaped from prison and lived in exile at Smyrna.

Caeré (always called by the Greek writers Ἄγυλλα). One of the most considerable cities of Etruria, and universally acknowledged to have been founded by the Tyrrhenian Pelasgi (Dion. Hal. i. 20; iii. 60). It was situated near the coast, to the west of Veii. Ancient writers seem puzzled to account for the change of name which this city is allowed to have undergone, the Romans never calling it anything but Caeré, except Vergil (*Aen.* viii. 478). Strabo relates that the Tyrrheni, on arriving before this city, were hailed by the Pelasgi from the walls with the word Χαῖρε, according to the Greek mode of salutation; and that, when they had made themselves masters of the place, they changed its name to that form of greeting. Other variations of this story may be seen in Servius (*ad Aen.* viii. 597). According to one of them, given on the authority of Hyginus, the Romans, and not the Lydians, changed its name from Agylla to Caeré. All these explanations, however, are unsatisfactory. It has been supposed that Caeré might be the original name, or perhaps that which the Siculi, the ancient possessors, gave to the place before the Pelasgic invasion. According to Müller (*Die Etrusker*, vol. i. p. 87), the two names for the place point to two different stems or races of inhabitants. This same writer makes the genuine Etrurian name to have been Cisra.

The earliest record to be found of the history of Agylla is in Herodotus (i. 167). That writer informs us that the Phocaeans, having been driven from their native city on the shores of Ionia by the arms of Cyrus, formed establishments in Corsica, of which the Tyrrhenians and Carthaginians, jealous of their nautical skill and enterprising spirit, sought to dispossess them. A severe action accordingly took place in the Sea of Sardinia, between the Phocaeans and the combined fleet of the latter powers, in which the former gained the day; but it was such a victory as left them little room for exultation, they having lost several of their ships, and the rest being nearly all disabled. The Agylleans, who appear to have constituted the principal force of the Tyrrhenians, on their return home landed their prisoners and stoned them to death; for which act of cruelty they were soon visited by a strange calamity. It was observed that all the living creatures which approached the spot where the Phocaeans had been murdered were immediately seized with convulsive distortions and paralytic affections of the limbs. On consulting the oracle at Delphi, to learn how they might expiate their offence, the Agylleans were commanded to celebrate the obsequies of the dead and to hold games in their honour; which order, the historian informs us, was punctually attended to up to his time. We learn also from Strabo that the Agylleans always abstained from piracy, to which the other Tyrrhenian cities were much addicted. According to Dionysius, the Romans were first engaged in hostilities with Caeré under the reign of Tarquin the Elder, and subsequently under Servius Tullius, by whom a treaty was concluded between the two States (iii. 28). Long after, when Rome had been taken by the Gauls, the inhabitants of Caeré rendered the former city an important service by receiving their priests and Vestals, and defeating the Gauls on their return through the Sabine territory; on which occasion they recovered the gold with which Rome is said to have purchased its liberation. This is a curious fact, and not mentioned by any historian; but it agrees very well with the account which Polybius gives us of the retreat of the Gauls (i. 6). In return for this assistance, the Romans requited the Caerites by declaring them the public guests of Rome, and admitting them, though not in full, to the rights enjoyed by her citizens. They were made citizens, but without the right of voting; whence the phrases, *in Caeritum tabulas referre aliquem*, "to deprive one of his right of voting," and *Caerite cera digni*, "worthless persons," in reference to citizens of Rome, since what would be an honour to the people of Caeré would be a punishment to a native Roman citizen. See Hor. *Epist.* i. 6, 62, with the commentators.

Caerītum Tabŭlae. See CAERÉ

Caesar. A title of the Roman emperors, and originally a family name of the gens Iulia. It was assumed by Octavianus as the adopted son of the great dictator, C. Iulius Caesar, and was by him handed down to his adopted son Tiberius. It continued to be used by Caligula, Claudius, and Nero, as members either by adoption or female descent of Caesar's family; but though the family became extinct with Nero, succeeding emperors still retained the name as part of their titles, and it was the practice to prefix it to their own names, as, for instance, *Imperator Caesar Domitianus Augustus*. When Hadrian adopted Aelius Verus, he allowed the latter to take the title of Caesar (Spart. *Ael. Ver.* 1); and from this time, though the title of *Augustus* continued to be confined to the reigning emperor, that of *Caesar* was also granted the second person in the State and the heir-presumptive to the throne. See AUGUSTUS.

The name *Caesar* was variously derived by the ancients, some assigning it directly to *caedo*, to denote that the first bearer of the name was cut from his mother's uterus by the "Caesarian" operation (Plin. *H. N.* vii. 9, 7); and others explaining it from *caesaries*, because the first Caesar was born with a full head of hair (Fest. p. 44 Müll.). Doederlein (*Synon.* iii. 17) assigns it to *caesius*, as applied to the colour of the skin, or perhaps of the eyes.

Caesar, GAIUS IULIUS, or, as the name is written in English, JULIUS CAESAR, was born on the 12th of July, in B.C. 102 or 100. The latter date rests upon the statement of several ancient authorities, but Mommsen has shown that the earlier date is more probably correct. The Caesar family was of patrician stock. It belonged to the proud gens of the Iulii, who traced their ancestry back to the very beginning of Roman history. In the century between B.C. 160 and 60, several Caesars held public offices, at least four being honoured with the consulship.

Of the youth and education of Iulius Caesar little is known excepting that he was under the instruction of the distinguished teacher of grammar and rhetoric, M. Antonius Gnipho, who for a time taught in his home. Though allied by descent with the aristocracy, he was brought into relation with the popular party through the marriage of his aunt Iulia with the great leader Marius. In B.C. 83, he himself married Cornelia, the daughter of Marius's most ardent supporter, Cinna. This vexed Sulla, who, regaining the ascendency at Rome the following year, ordered Caesar to divorce her. Unlike Pompey and Piso, who put away their wives at Sulla's bidding, Caesar boldly refused. Sulla confiscated his property, and revoked the priesthood of Iupiter, which had been conferred upon him through the influence of Marius. As his life was now in danger, he went into hiding, hotly pursued from place to place by Sulla's emissaries. After a time his friends, aided by the Vestal Virgins, succeeded in securing pardon for him from Sulla, who is said to have granted it with the remark that Caesar would some time be the ruin of the aristocracy, for in him there was many a Marius. Soon afterwards, desirous of gaining the military experience considered necessary for a young Roman of rank, he joined the staff of M. Minucius Thermus, who was besieging Mytilené. Here he saved the life of a fellow-soldier, displaying so great bravery that he was honoured with a civic crown. After Mytilené fell he entered the service of P. Servilius in Cilicia; but immediately on hearing of the death of Sulla, in 78, he returned to Rome.

The following year Caesar introduced himself to public notice by bringing a charge of provincial extortion against Gnaeus Dolabella, who had been proconsul of Macedonia. Though unsuccessful, in 76 he was invited to accuse Gaius Antonius of similar misconduct in Greece. Antonius also was acquitted, but the young prosecutor gained great popularity and a considerable reputation for oratory by his pleas. He now started for Rhodes, to pursue the study of oratory under Molo. Near Miletus he was captured by pirates, and was detained on the island of Pharmacusa until he could get together a ransom of fifty talents (over $55,000). Having been set at liberty, he procured ships, captured the pirates, took them to Pergamus, and crucified them, thus carrying out a threat which he had jestingly pronounced when with them. He spent a short time at Rhodes, and then passed over to Asia, where he rendered gallant service against an army of Mithridates. In the winter of 74–73, he returned to Rome, having been chosen to fill a vacancy in the college of *pontifices*. He now threw himself into political life with an energy that yielded to no opposition and a reckless liberality that hesitated at no expenditure. He was affable to every one, and no applicant for aid went away empty-handed. He soon exhausted his inheritance, and became deeply involved in debt; but his popularity was unbounded. Having taken a stand in opposition to the Sullan constitution and the aristocracy, he received the offices in the gift of the people in regular succession. In 67, he was quaestor, serving under Antistius Vetus in Further Spain. In 65, he was curule aedile, with M. Bibulus as colleague. Extravagant expenditures upon games and buildings raised his popularity to the highest pitch. He increased the power and influence of the popular party in many ways, but by no single act did he kindle the enthusiasm of the populace more than by privately restoring the trophies of Marius, which had been destroyed by Sulla, and replacing them by night on the Capitol. Marius's veterans crowded around them with tears and shouting. The Senate, notwithstanding the formal denunciation of Marius as a public enemy, was obliged to yield to the popular feeling and leave them in the place of honour.

Caesar was charged with complicity in both the Catilinarian conspiracies, but evidence is wanting. In 62, he was praetor, carrying himself with great firmness and discretion amid scenes of violence. The following year he governed the province of Further Spain with distinction, both as a civil administrator and as a general. He subdued several tribes and captured the city of Brigantium, in the extreme northwestern part. At the expiration of his year of office he came back to Rome with ample means to satisfy his creditors. In 60, he was chosen consul for 59, the aristocracy making every effort to secure the election of Bibulus as his colleague to offset his influence. About this time he brought about a reconciliation between Pompey and Marcus Crassus, entering with them into the coalition known as the First Triumvirate. These ties were strengthened further by the marriage of his daughter Julia to Pompey. During his consulship he was influential in promoting the interests of Pompey and Crassus; at the same time he kept his standing with the people, and was especially serviceable to the important body of *equites*. Instead of the usual proconsular command for one year, he easily obtained the governorship of Cisalpine Gaul, Illyricum, and Transalpine Gaul, of which only the southeastern portion had been subdued, for five years, together with the control of four legions. During the next nine years (58–50), Caesar was engaged in the conquest of Transalpine Gaul. Summers were devoted to military operations; but when possible he spent a part of the winter in Cisalpine Gaul, in close communication with his friends at Rome. In 56, he again reconciled Pompey and Crassus, who met with him at Luca; in 55, his command was continued for five years longer. The conquest of Gaul was no easy matter, both from the advancement of its civilization and the character of the country (see GALLIA); but Caesar accomplished it, in a series of campaigns which, for variety and skill of tactics as well as unremitting energy of movement, are unsurpassed in the annals of warfare. He twice bridged the Rhine and invaded Germany; twice also he crossed over to Britain, reducing the tribes along the southeast coast to nominal subjection. By the year 50, Gaul was completely conquered, and well on the way towards complete organization as a Roman province.

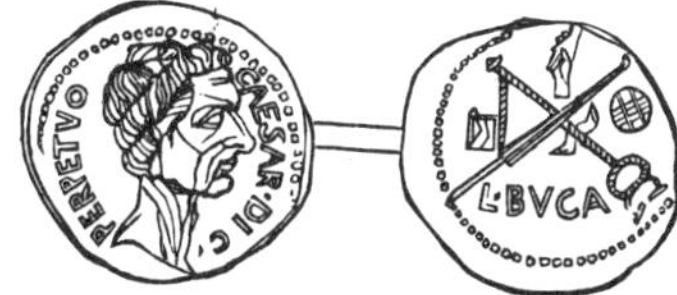

Coin of Iulius Caesar as Dictator.

The death of Iulia, Pompey's wife and Caesar's daughter, in 54, and that of Crassus a year later in the East, broke the common bond between the two great military leaders and put an end to the compact of the triumvirate. Pompey, viewing with jealousy and alarm the victorious career of his younger rival, entered into an alliance with the aristocratic party, and endeavoured to check the increasing power of Caesar by means of senatorial enactments. In his interest the Senate, early in B.C. 50, passed a decree that each of the commanders should give up a legion for the Parthian War. As Pompey had lent one of his to Caesar in 53, this was now demanded back. Although the intent of the whole matter was clearly to weaken Caesar, he gave up Pompey's legion and one of his own as directed; but the troops, instead of being despatched to the East, were placed in camp at Capua. It became clearer every day that Caesar's friends were powerless to obtain for him the recognition and privileges to which he was justly entitled; that the senatorial party and Pompey would scruple at nothing to gain the advantage over him. While his commission prevented him from entering Italy, and no dispensation from it was granted, Pompey was permitted to administer an important command in Spain through lieutenants, and at the same time remained at Rome. The climax was reached early in January, B.C. 49, when the Senate, amid great uproar, decreed that Caesar should disband his army by a certain date, under penalty of being considered a public enemy if he failed to do so; and that the magistrates should take measures to provide for the security of the State. The tribunes M. Antonius and Q. Cassius, who had in vain interposed their veto, were obliged to flee, and took refuge with Caesar, calling upon him to defend the inviolable sanctity of their office. War was now inevitable.

With the vigour and despatch characteristic of his previous military operations, Caesar at once crossed the river Rubicon, the southern boundary of his province. Within three months he was master of the whole of Italy, Pompey and the more zealous adherents of the aristocratic party having fled to Greece. He now set out for Spain, and soon dispersed the forces of Pompey there, meanwhile gaining possession of Sicily and Sardinia also, through his lieutenants Curio and Valerius. In Africa and Illyricum his officers were less successful; but on his way back from Spain he forced the surrender of Massilia, which in his absence had withstood a siege at the hands of Trebonius and Decimus Brutus. By this time Pompey had gathered a large army in Greece, and had also a powerful fleet at his service. Nothing daunted, Caesar crossed the Adriatic in January, 48, and with a far inferior force tried to blockade his opponent at Dyrrachium. Being unsuccessful, and also reduced to straits for supplies, he withdrew into Thessaly. Pompey followed, over-confident. The decisive battle was fought on the plain of Pharsalus, in Thessaly, August 9th, B.C. 48. Pompey had 47,000 infantry and 7000 cavalry, Caesar barely 22,000 infantry and 1000 cavalry. But superior generalship and discipline, and the courage of despair, won the day against greater numbers. Pompey fled to Egypt, where he was immediately murdered. When the news of the victory reached Rome, Caesar was appointed dictator for a year, and other offices also were conferred upon him, so that, under the forms of the old constitution, he possessed absolute authority.

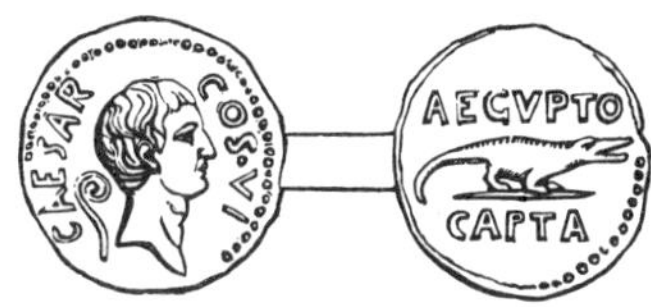

Coin of Iulius Caesar.

Having followed Pompey to Egypt, Caesar was there for a time in great danger on account of the disturbance known as the Alexandrine War, which arose from a dispute regarding the succession. He placed Cleopatra on the throne, and in the spring of 47 proceeded to Pontus, where he defeated Pharnaces, a son of Mithridates, near Zela, announcing the victory at Rome in the famous despatch, *Veni, vidi, vici*, "I came, I saw, I conquered." Early in 46, he crossed over to Africa, crushing the remnants of the senatorial forces there at the battle of Thapsus, April 6. Returning to Rome, where his supremacy was no longer disputed, he treated his former opponents with unlooked-for clemency, and inaugurated several salutary reforms, among which not the least important was the rearrangement of the calendar. The sons of Pompey gathered an army in Spain, which he defeated at the battle of Munda, March 17th, B.C. 45. During the ensuing months, Caesar's powers as a civil administrator had full scope. His projects, few of which were destined to be realized, were characterized by statesmanship of a high order, which has come to be the more admired the better it has been understood. But he was not beyond the reach of malice and envy. A conspiracy was formed against him; the leaders of it were Marcus Brutus and Cassius. The conspirators were actuated by different motives—some, no doubt, by personal jealousy and hatred; others by a patriotic desire to restore the old republican constitution; a few, perhaps, by ambitious designs upon the spoils of State. On the 15th of March, B.C. 44, as Caesar was entering the hall connected with Pompey's theatre to attend a meeting of the Senate, he was set upon, and fell pierced by twenty-three wounds.

Caesar holds a unique place in the history not merely of Rome, but of the world. In his time the government of Rome had been found wholly inadequate to meet the administrative demands of a great empire. More and more the military became paramount to the civil power in the State, and the old-time balance of political parties gave place to violent strifes between successful generals. The perpetuation of the Roman government demanded centralization of authority. Cherishing the ambition to become the great political leader of his generation, Caesar became supreme, not by usurpation, but by the natural exercise of extraordinary executive abilities under political conditions which admitted of no alternative between anarchy and absolutism. He appears to have had a truer insight into the needs of his country than any of his contemporaries. His genius was not, as often represented, merely destructive, but was constructive as well. After his death, Rome had no peace or prosperity till political authority was again concentrated in the hands of Augustus. But this many-sided man was great not merely as a statesman. As a general he is ranked in the same class with Alexander, Hannibal, and Napoleon; as an orator he was reckoned in his day second only to Cicero; and as a writer he has long since received a place among the world's greatest masters. Tall, with fair complexion and expressive black eyes, sensitive in regard to his appearance and neat to the verge of effeminacy, gracious in address and Epicurean in both tastes and beliefs, in external characteristics he might have passed for a man of the world, at home in the gay society of a luxurious capital. But in ambition, in energy, in the ability to form plans and to bring things to pass, he belied all appearances, and has probably made a deeper impression upon humanity than any other man that has ever lived.

Iulius Caesar. (Statue in the Palazzo dei Conservatori, Rome.)

With the exception of a few fragments, Caesar's speeches have perished. A like fate has befallen his poems, most of which were composed in early life, and his treatise on grammar, in two books. Among other writings that were published was a tract written in opposition to Cicero's panegyric on Cato, in two books (see ANTICATONES); a treatise on astronomy, and a collection of witticisms. Only his invaluable "Memoirs" are extant—"On the Gallic War" (*De Bello Gallico*), in seven books, and "On the Civil War" (*De Bello Civili*), in three books, the former published probably in B.C. 51. These works are written in a simple, concise, straightforward style, remarkably free from military technicalities of the sort to trouble the reader. They were no doubt designed to justify the author in the eyes of his countrymen, but their credibility on the whole is not thereby seriously impaired. An eighth book was added to the *Gallic War* by Aulus Hirtius; and unknown authors extended the *Civil War* by narratives concerning the Alexandrine, African, and Spanish wars.

BIBLIOGRAPHY.—The chief sources for the life of Caesar are his own writings and the works of Cicero (particularly the *Letters*), Sallust's *Catiline*, the biographies by Plutarch and Suetonius, and the treatises on Roman history by Velleius Paterculus, Appian, and Dio Cassius. The ancient authorities are examined with much painstaking by Drumann, in his *Geschichte Roms* (vol. iii.); worthy of mention, also, is the extended treatment of Caesar in Mommsen's *History of Rome* (vol. iv. of the English translation), in Duruy's *History of Rome* (vol. iii.), and in Merivale's *History of the Romans under the Empire* (vols. i., ii.). Special works are: Napoleon III., *Histoire de Jules César* (2 vols., with valuable atlas, Paris, 1865; English translation, New York, 1865); Delorme, *Cäsar und seine Zeitgenossen* (deutsch, bearbeitet von Doehler, Leipzig, 1873); Froude, *Caesar: a Sketch* (New York, 1884); and Fowler, *Julius Caesar and the Organization of the Roman Empire* (New York, 1892). For the history of Caesar's campaigns: Rüstow, *Heerwesen und Kriegführung Cäsars* (Nordhausen,

1862); F. de Saulcy, *Les Campagnes de Jules-César dans les Gaules* (Paris, 1865); A. von Göler, *Caesars gallischer Krieg und Theile seines Bürgerkrieges* (2d ed., Freiburg and Tübingen, 1880, reprinted 1884); Stoffel, *Histoire de Jules César: Guerre civile* (2 vols., with atlas of twenty-four plates, Paris, 1887); Judson, *Caesar's Army* (Boston, 1888); and Fröhlich, *Das Kriegswesen Cäsars* (Zürich, 1891). Useful, also, in this connection are: Rüstow, *Atlas zu Caesars gallischem Kriege* (Stuttgart, 1868); A. von Kampen, *XV. ad Caesaris de Bello Gallico Commentarios Tabulae* (Gotha, 1879); Jal, *La Flotte de César* (Paris, 1862); and especially Desjardins, *Géographie historique et administrative de la Gaule romaine* (4 vols., Paris, 1876–93). For Caesar's writings, see Fallue, *Analyse raisonnée des Commentaires de Jules César* (Paris, 1862); and Trollope, *The Commentaries of Caesar* (Philadelphia, 1880). For the extant portraits of him, see Bernoulli, *Römische Ikonographie* (vol. i., pp. 145–181).

The MSS. upon which the text of Caesar's Commentaries is based fall into two classes, known as *a* and *β*. The *a* group seems to be more faithful to the original form, but contains only the Gallic War; the best representatives are: a MS. of the ninth or tenth century at Amsterdam (A), three of the tenth century (B, C at Paris, R in the Vatican), and one of the eleventh century (M, also at Paris). The MSS. of the *β* class include also the Civil War with the continuations, the best being a Paris MS. of the eleventh or twelfth century (T), a Vatican MS. of the twelfth century (V), and one of the thirteenth century, at Vienna. Critical editions of Caesar's works are by Nipperdey (Leipzig, 1847) and Dübner (2 vols., Paris, 1867); convenient text-editions by Nipperdey (4th reprint, 1884); Dinter (3 parts, Leipzig, 1864–76; 2d ed. of *Gallic War*, 1884), and Hoffmann (2d ed., Vienna, 1888); critical editions of the *Gallic War* by Frigell (Upsala, 1861), Holder (with useful index, Freiburg, 1882), and Kübler (vol. i., Leipzig, 1893). Among the numerous annotated editions are those by Kraner (Berlin; *de Bel. Gal.*, 15te verbesserte Aufl., von W. Dittenberger, 1890; *de Bel. Civ.*, 10te umgearbeitete Aufl. von Fr. Hofmann, 1890), Doberenz (Leipzig, umgearbeitet von B. Dinter, *de Bel. Gal.*, 9te Aufl. 1890–92; *de Bel. Civ.*, 5te Aufl., 1884), Rheinhard (Stuttgart; *de Bel. Gal.*, 7te Aufl., herausg. von S. Herzog, 1892), Moberly (Oxford; *Gallic War*, 2d ed., 1878; *Civil War*, 1880), and Peskett (Cambridge; *Gallic War*, 5 vols., 1878–82; *Civil War*, Book I. 1890), Allen and Greenough (Boston; *Gallic War*, 1887), and Kelsey (Boston; *Gallic War*, 7th ed., 1894). Of the several lexicons to Caesar, Meusel's *Lexicon Caesarianum* (Berlin, 1887–93) and the *Lexicon Caesarianum* by Menge and Preuss (Leipzig, 1890) are the best. A brief bibliography of the more recent literature dealing with Caesar's works is given in Teuffel's *History of Roman Literature*, §§ 195, 196 (Eng. tr. by Warr, 1892).

Site and Ruins of Caesarea in Samaria.

Caesaraugusta or **Caesarēa Augusta**. The modern Saragossa; a town of Hispania Tarraconensis, named from its founder, Augustus Caesar. It was the birthplace of the poet Prudentius.

Caesarēa (Καισάρεια). (1) The principal city of Samaria, situated on the coast, and anciently called Turris Stratonis, "Strato's tower." Who this Strato was is not clearly ascertained. The first inhabitants were Syrians and Greeks (Joseph. *Ant. Iud.* xx. 6). It was subsequently made a magnificent city and port by Herod, who called it Caesarea, in honour of Augustus; and it now began to receive Jews among its inhabitants. Frequent contentious hence arose, in consequence of the diversity of faiths that prevailed within its walls. Here the Roman governor resided, and a Roman garrison was continually kept. Vespasian, after the Jewish War, settled a Roman colony in it, with the additional title of Colonia Prima Flavia. In later times it became the capital of Palaestina Prima. This city is frequently mentioned in the New Testament. Here King Agrippa was smitten, for neglecting to give God the praise when the people loaded him with flattery. Here Cornelius the centurion was baptized; and also Philip, the deacon, with his four daughters; and here Agabus the prophet foretold to Paul that he would be bound at Jerusalem (Acts, viii. 10). The modern name of the place is Kaisarieh. It was the birthplace of Eusebius. (2) The capital of Mauritania Caesariensis, and a place of some note in the time of the Roman emperors. It was originally called Iol, but was beautified at a subsequent period by Iuba, who made it his residence, and changed its name to Caesarea, in honour of Augustus. (3) CAESAREA AD ARGAEUM, the capital of Cappadocia, called by this name in the reign of Tiberius, previously Mazaca. It was situate at the foot of Mount Argaeus, as its name indicates, and was a place of great antiquity, its foundation having even been ascribed by some writers to Mesech, the son of Japhet (Ioseph. *Ant. Iud.* i. 6). The modern name is Kaisarieh. (4) CAESARĒA PHILIPPI, a town on the northern confines of Palestine, in the district of Trachonitis, at the foot of Mount Paneus, and near the springs of the Jordan. It was also called Leshem, Laish, Dan, and Paneas. The name Paneas is supposed to have been given it by the Phœnicians. The appellation of Dan was given to it by the tribe of that name, because the portion assigned to them was "too little for them," and they therefore "went up to fight against Leshem (or Laish, Judg. xviii. 29), and took it," calling it "Dan, after the name of Dan, their father" (Josh. xix. 47). Eusebius and Jerome distinguish Dan from Paneas as if they were different places, though near each other; but most writers consider them as one place, and even Jerome himself, on Ezek. xlviii., says that Dan or Leshem was afterwards called Paneas. Philip, the tetrarch, rebuilt it, or at least embellished and enlarged it, and named it Caesarea, in honour of the emperor Tiberius; and afterwards Agrippa, in compliment to Nero, called it Neronias. (5) CAESARĒA INSŬLA, now the island of Jersey.

Caesarion (Καισάριον). The son of Cleopatra, said to be hers by Iulius Caesar. Plutarch calls him the son of Caesar, but Dio Cassius and Suetonius doubt the assertion. He was put to death by Augustus Caesar. See Dio Cass. xlvii. 31; Suet. *Iul.* 52; *Aug.* 17.

Caesăris Arae. Mentioned by Ptolemy as near the Tanaïs, in what is now the country of the Don Cossacks. They are supposed to have been erected in honour of one of the Roman emperors by some neighbouring prince; perhaps by Polemo, in the reign of Tiberius. See Tac. *Ann.* xii. 15.

Caesarodūnum. The modern Tours; chief town of the Turones or Turoni, and subsequently called Turoni, on the Liger (Loire), in Gallia Lugdunensis.

Caesaromăgus. (1) The modern Beauvais; the capital of the Bellovaci in Gaul. (2) A city of the Trinobantes in Britain, answering, as is thought, to what is now Chelmsford.

Caesars, THE TWELVE. A collective name given to the first twelve rulers of imperial Rome: Iulius (B.C. 48–44); Augustus (B.C. 30–A.D. 14); Tiberius (14–37); Caligula (37–41); Claudius (41–54); Nero (54–69); Galba (69); Otho (69); Vitellius (69–70); Vĕspasian (70–79); Titus (79–81); Domitian (81–96). Their biographies were written by Suetonius in his *Vitae Duodecim Caesarum*, of which the standard text is that of Roth (Leipzig, 1858).

Caesius Bassus. A Latin poet, a friend of Persius the satirist, whose book he edited. He is said to have perished during the eruption of Vesuvius in A.D. 79. He had a high reputation in his day as a lyric poet, and is said to have composed a didactic poem on metre. There is a considerable fragment in prose on the same subject which bears the name of Caesius Bassus, but this is perhaps from a prose version of the poetical treatise, which we know to have been largely used by later writers, especially Iuba and Terentianus Maurus.

Caesonia, MILONIA. See CALIGULA.

Caestus (from *caedo;* and not to be confounded with *cestus*, from Greek κεστός). The thongs or bands of leather which were tied round the hands of boxers, in order to render their blows more powerful. These bands of leather were also frequently tied round the arm as high as the elbow, as is shown in the following statue of a boxer, the original of which is in the Louvre at Paris.

Statue of a Boxer with the Caestus. (From the Louvre.)

The caestus was used by boxers from the earliest times. The ordinary boxing-gloves were called in Greek ἱμάντες or ἱμάντες πυκτικοί. When Epeius and Euryalus in the *Iliad* (xxiii. 684) prepare themselves for boxing, they put on their hands thongs made of ox-hide. (Cf. Theocr. xxii. 81; Apoll. Rhod. ii. 53.) But it should be recollected that the caestus in heroic times appears to have consisted merely of thongs of leather, and differed materially from the frightful weapons loaded with lead and iron which were used in later times. The different kinds of caestus were called by the Greeks in later times μειλίχαι, σπεῖραι βόειαι, σφαῖραι, and μύρμηκες—of which the μειλίχαι gave the softest blows, and the μύρμηκες the most severe. The μειλίχαι, which were the most ancient, are described by Pausanias (viii. 40, § 3) as made of raw ox-hide cut into thin pieces, and joined in an ancient manner; they were tied under the hollow or palm of the hand, leaving the fingers uncovered. The athletae in the palaestrae at Olympia used the μειλίχαι only in practising for the public games.

The caestus used in later times in the public games was, as has been already remarked, a most formidable weapon. It was frequently covered with knots and nails, and loaded with lead and iron; whence Vergil, in speaking of it, says,

Ingentia septem,
Terga boum plumbo insuto ferroque rigebant.

Statius also speaks of *nigrantia plumbo tegmina*. Such weapons, in the hands of a trained boxer, must have frequently occasioned death. The μύρμηκες were, in fact, sometimes called γυιοτόροι, or "limb-breakers." Lucilius speaks of a boxer whose head had been so battered by the μύρμηκες as to resemble a sieve. See ATHLETAE; PUGIL.

Figures with the caestus frequently occur in ancient monuments. They appear to have been of various forms, as appears by the following specimens, taken from ancient monuments, of which drawings are given by Fabretti.

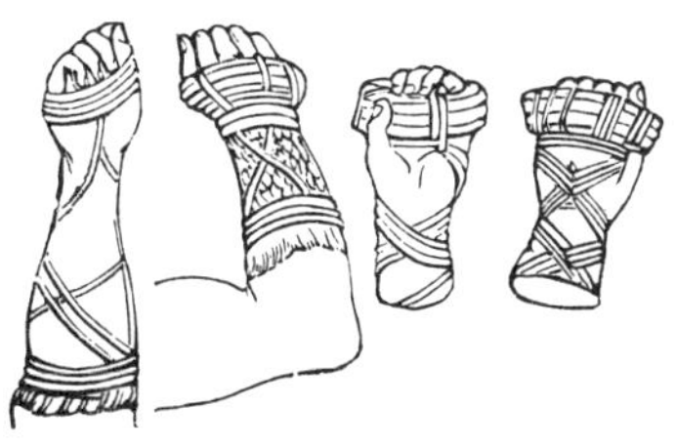

Caestus. (Fabretti.)

Caïcus (Καϊκός). A river of Mysia, rising in Mount Temnus and flowing past Pergamus into the Cumaean Gulf.

Caiēta. The modern Gaeta; a town in Latium on the borders of Campania, situated on a promontory of the same name, and on a bay of the sea called, after it, Sinus Caietanus. It possessed an excellent harbour, and was said to have derived its name from Caieta, the nurse of Aeneas.

Caius, Caia. See GAIUS, GAIA.

Cake. See PLACENTA; SCRIBLITA.

Calăber, QUINTUS, called SMYRNAEUS (Κόϊντος Σμυρναῖος). The author of a poem in fourteen books, intended as a continuation of the *Iliad* of Homer. He lived in the fourth century A.D. The poem was edited by Tychsen (Strasburg, 1807).

Calabria. The peninsula in the southeast of Italy extending from Tarentum to the Promontorium Iapygium, and forming part of Apulia (q. v.).

Calactē (Καλάκτα). Originally the name of part of the coast, and afterwards a town on the northern coast, of Sicily, founded by Ducetius.

Calagurris. The modern Calahorra; a town of the Vascones in Hispania Tarraconensis, near the Iberus (Ebro). It was the birthplace of Quintilian. The Calagurritani are said to have eaten their wives and children in the extremity of their hunger, rather than yield to Pompey in B.C. 71. See Val. Max. vii. 6.

Calăïs (Κάλαϊς) and **Zetes** (Ζήτης). The Boreadae, or sons of Boreas and Orithyia. They were both winged heroes, and took part in the Argonautic expedition. Coming in the course of the enterprise to Salmydessus, they set free Phineus (q. v.), the husband of their sister Cleopatra, from the Harpies, chasing them through the air on their wings. According to one story, they perished on this occasion; according to another, they were slain afterwards by Heracles on the island of Tenos, on their return from the funeral games of Pelias. (See ACASTUS.) This was in retribution for the counsel which they had given to the Argonauts on the coast of Mysia, to leave Heracles behind. Their graves and monuments were shown in Tenos. One of the pillars was said to move when the north wind blew. See ARGONAUTAE.

Calămis (Κάλαμις). A Greek artist, who flourished at Athens about B.C. 470. He worked in marble and metal, as well as gold and ivory, and was master of sculpture in all its branches, from the chiselling of small silver vessels to the execution of colossal statues in bronze. His Apollo, at Apollonia in Pontus, was 120 feet high. This statue was carried away to Rome by Lucullus and set up on the Capitol. We hear of statues of the gods and heroic women from his hand, as well as of men on horseback and four-horsed chariots. His horses are said to have been unsurpassed. His female figures, if we may believe the ancient critics, were characterized by antique harshness and severity, but relieved by a touch of grace and delicacy.

Calamistrum and **Calamister**. A curling-iron, so called from its resemblance to a reed (*calamus*), and used among the Romans as early as the time of Plautus (*Curc.* iv. 4, 21). It was sometimes employed by men, though such were considered effeminate. Figuratively, the word denotes an excess of literary ornament (Suet. *Iul.* 56).

Calămus (also HARUNDO; in Greek κάλαμος). A reed. Reeds were extensively used by the ancients for thatching; for making mats and other kinds of plaited work; and in the following uses:

(1) In music, to form the pandean pipes (σῦριγξ), which consisted of reeds of different lengths fastened by wax, as shown in the accompanying cut, taken from a terra-cotta relief in the British Museum. See SYRINX.

Calamus, Pan's Pipe. (From terra-cotta relief.)

(2) A light flute formed of a single reed.

(3) The shaft of an arrow.

(4) A reed pen (*calamus scriptorius*), sharpened like the modern quill pen with a knife, and cleft at the point. The best reeds for pen-making came from Egypt and Cnidus. These reed pens are still known in the East, and the Arabs use the word *kalam* to denote them. They were carried in a sort of writing-case called *theca calamaria* (καλαμίς). (Cf. Suet. *Claud.* 35.) See WRITING AND WRITING MATERIALS.

(5) A fishing-rod.

(6) The fowler's limed rod, which was sometimes composed of separate joints, so that it could be lengthened to suit the fowler's convenience. It was then called *harundo crescens* or *texta*, as well as *calamus* (Petron. *Sat.* 109).

(7) A light Egyptian boat made of reeds (*canna*, Juv. v. 89).

(8) A horizontal rod passed through the warp in weaving (*harundo*, Ovid, *Met.* vi. 55). See TELA.

Calantĭca; also **Calautica** (κρήδεμνον). A feminine head-dress of uncertain form, but thought by Rich to signify a sort of covering for the head with lappets hanging down to the shoulders on both sides, and when drawn together concealing the face. The word is sometimes used in the sense of *mitra* (q. v.).

Calānus (Κάλανος). A celebrated Indian philosopher, one of the gymnosophists. He followed Alexander from India, and, becoming ill when they had reached Persia, he desired to have his funeral pile erected. Having offered up his prayers, poured libations upon himself, and cut off part of his hair and thrown it into the fire, he ascended the pile, and did not move at the approach of the flames. Plutarch says that, in taking leave of the Macedonians, he desired them to spend the day in merriment and drinking with their king, "for I shall see him," said he, "in a little while at Babylon." Alexander died in Babylon three months after this. Calanus was in his eighty-third year when he burned himself on the funeral pile. See Cic. *De Div.* i. 23; Arrian, *Anab.* vii. 2, 4; Plut. *Vit. Alex.*; Aelian, *V. H.* ii. 41, 5, 6; Val. Max. i. 8.

Calăthus (κάλαθος, τάλαθος). A Greek word though found in Roman authors, the pure Latin word being *qualus* or *qualum*. The name *calathus* is applied to the following objects:

(1) A woman's work-basket, especially one that contained the materials for spinning. It was generally made of osiers or reeds, but sometimes of silver; and was narrow at the bottom and broad at the top, as in the annexed illustration taken from a painted vase (Millin).

Slave presenting her Mistress with a Calathus.

(2) A similar basket used for carrying fruits, flowers, grain, etc.

(3) A vessel shaped like a wicker *calathus* and used for holding milk; also a wine-cup of like shape (Verg. *Georg.* iii. 402).

(4) As a religious emblem, the *calathus* was carried in honour of Demeter and of Tellus as denoting abundance; and is found in connection with Athenê, the goddess of the art of weaving. Priestesses are also represented as wearing the calathus on their heads, and in imperial times the god Serapis (q. v.) is thus depicted.

Calatia. The modern Caiazzo; a town in Samnium, on the Appia Via, between Capua and Beneventum.

Calatīnus, A. ATILIUS. Consul B.C. 258, and dictator in 249, when he carried on the war in Sicily. He was the first dictator to command an army outside of Italy.

Calātor (from *calo*, to call; Gk. καλήτωρ, from καλέω). Originally a slave employed as a crier; later, the *nomenclator* (q. v.) who accompanied a candidate for political office on his canvass, and prompted him (Hor. *Epist.* i. 6, 50). (See AMBITUS.) The word is also applied to certain attendants on the members of the higher orders of priesthood.

Calaurēa (Καλαύρεια). The modern Poro; a small island in the Saronic Gulf off the coast of Argolis and opposite Troezen, possessing a celebrated Temple of Poseidon, which was regarded as an inviolable asylum. Hither Demosthenes fled to escape Antipater, and here he took poison, B.C. 322. His tomb was one of the sights of the island.

Calcar (μύωψ, ἐγκεντρίς). A spur, an implement not mentioned in Homer, who speaks only of the use of a goad (κέντρον). In Greek, it is in fact often doubtful whether the writer is referring to the spur or the goad. In works of art spurs are seldom represented, but bronze spurs have been found at Dodona.

The early adoption of this contrivance by the Romans appears from the mention of it in Plautus and Lucretius. It is afterwards often alluded to by Cicero, Ovid, Vergil, and subsequent Roman authors. On the other hand, we do not find that the Greeks used spurs, and this may account for the fact that they are seldom, if ever, seen on antique statues.

Calcaria, Bronze Spurs. (British Museum.)

The spurs of a cock are also called *calcaria*.

Calceus (ὑπόδημα κοῖλον). A shoe, part of the regular Roman dress, and usually worn in public. Each order, and every *gens*, had its particular kind of *calceus*. The patricians wore a *mulleus* or *calceus patricius*. This was a shoe of red leather with a high sole, like that of the *cothurnus*. The leather passed round the back of the heel, where it was furnished with small hooks, to which the straps were fastened. It was originally a part of the royal dress, and was afterwards worn by generals on the occasion of a triumph. In later times, with the rest of the triumphal costume, it became a part of the dress of the consuls. In the second rank came the *calceus senatorius*, or shoe worn by senators. This was black, and tied round the leg by four straps. In the case of patricians it was ornamented by a crescent-shaped clasp (*luna*). The *calceus* of the equites, and of ordinary citizens, was also black. The latter was called *pero*; it rose as high as the ankle, and was fastened with a simple tie.

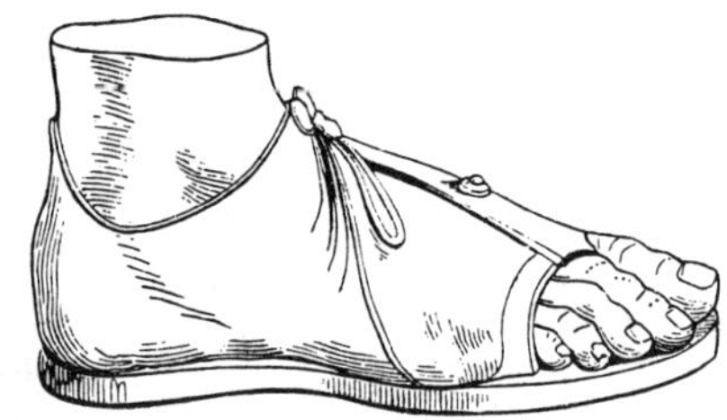

Ordinary Calceus. (From a Marble in the British Museum.)

Calchas (Κάλχας). A celebrated soothsayer, son of Thestor. He had received from Apollo the knowledge of future events; and the Greeks, accordingly, on their departure for the Trojan War, nominated him their high-priest and prophet. Among the interpretations of events imputed to him, it is said that he predicted that Troy could not be taken without the aid of Achilles; and that, having observed a serpent, during a solemn sacrifice, glide from under an altar, ascend a tree, and devour nine young birds with their mother, and afterwards become itself changed into stone, he inferred that the siege of Troy would last ten years. He also foretold that the Grecian fleet, which was at that same time detained by contrary winds in the harbour of Aulis, would not be able to sail until Agamemnon should have sacrificed his own daughter Iphigenia. Calchas likewise advised Agamemnon, during the pestilence by which Apollo desolated the Grecian camp, to restore Chryseïs to her father, as the only means of appeasing the god. (See Trojan War.) He was consulted, indeed, on every affair of importance, and appears to have often determined, with Agamemnon and Odysseus, the import of the oracles which he expounded. His death is said to have happened as follows. After the taking of Troy, he accompanied Amphilochus, son of Amphiaraüs, to Colophon in Ionia. It had been predicted that he should not die until he found a prophet more skilful than himself: this he experienced in the person of Mopsus. He was unable to tell how many figs were on the branches of a certain fig-tree; and when Mopsus mentioned the exact number Calchas retired to the wood of Claros, sacred to Apollo, where he expired of grief and mortification. Calchas had the patronymic, Thestorides.

Calculātor (λογιστής). In general, a keeper of accounts, but sometimes a teacher of arithmetic—an office of much repute among teachers. The name is derived from the *calculi* used in reckoning, for which see Abacus; Logistica.

Calculator. (Saglio.)

Calcŭli. See Abacus; Duodecim Scripta; Latrunculorum Ludus; Numeri.

Calda or **Calĭda** (sc. *aqua*). A hot drink of the Greeks and Romans, mentioned as early as Plato, who calls it θερμόν. It was probably nothing more than hot water, flavoured with spices and herbs; and though wine was often drunk with it, there is no good reason for considering *calda* a sort of punch or negus in which wine was already mixed. Hot water is occasionally mentioned as a drink (cf. Athenaeus, ii. 45 d; Lucian, *Asin.* p. 575; Mart. viii. 67), and the most that can be inferred from the passages usually cited is that wine was separately served while the guest had the choice of hot or cold water to mix with it, according to his taste. Shops or taverns called *thermopolia* served the same drink, and we read of decrees of the emperors closing them on the occasion of a death in the imperial family. (See Caupona.) The water was heated for this purpose in an *aënum* or *caccabus* (q. v.), and kept hot in the *authepsa* (q. v.), a vessel resembling our tea-urns.

Caldarium. (1) The hot chamber of Roman baths. (See Balneae.) (2) The boiler (χαλκεῖον) used in heating the water for the baths. (3) A portable cooking-stove. In this sense the word *caldarium* occurs only in late authors, though the thing itself is well known through numerous specimens found at Pompeii, and now in the Naples Museum. The classical term for it is probably *focus.* In Seneca's time, Roman epicurism brought these stoves into the dining-room (*cenatio*), that the dishes might be served to perfection.

The *caldarium* here figured has been described by Rich. The sides, which are hollow, contained water; and a small cock projects from one of them (seen in the engraving), by which it was drawn off. The four towers at the angles are provided with movable lids; the centre received the lighted charcoal, and cooking vessels might be placed on it or suspended over it. Another contrivance (see Authepsa) seems to combine the two purposes of supplying hot water and keeping dishes hot. It has the cylinder with a place in the centre for a charcoal fire, which is the characteristic of an *authepsa;* and it is also furnished with a shallow, oblong tray, into which the hot water from the cylinder was drawn by a cock, and on which dishes may have been placed.

Caldarium. (*Museo Borbonico*, xii. pl. 46.)

These *calduria* might be shaped like a mile-stone (as in a specimen figured *Mus. Borbon.* iv. pl. 59, also by Saglio) or in more eccentric designs (*dracones et miliaria et complures formas*, Sen. *Nat. Quaest.* iii. 24, § 2). The same passage describes boiler-tubes, not unlike those of the modern steam-engine. These contrivances show great skill in the economy of fuel and the conveniences of life.

Bronze Vessels for serving the Calda. (Pompeii.)

Calé. The modern Oporto; a port-town of the Callaeci in Hispania Tarraconensis, at the mouth of the Durius. From Porto Cale the modern name of the country, Portugal, is supposed to have come.

Caledonia. A country in the north of Britain, now called Scotland. The ancient Caledonia comprehended all those countries which lay to the north of the Forth and the Clyde. It was never completely subdued by the Romans, though Agricola penetrated to the Tay, and Severus into the very heart of the country. The name is probably the Latinized form of the native name, Calido, and first appears in Lucan (vi. 68). The root is found in the Welsh *celydd*, "a woody retreat." The Romans also called it Britannia Barbara.

See Tac. *Agric.* 11, 25, 26, 27; Ammian. Marcell. xxvii. 8; Plin. *H. N.* iv. 16; Ptolemy, ii. 3; Wilson, *Prehistoric Annals of Scotland;* Rhys, *Celtic Britain* (2d ed. 1884); and the article BRITANNIA.

Calendarium (more properly KALENDARIUM). Originally the account-book in which debts were entered. As these debts fell due on the Kalends, the name got its first signification from that fact; coming later to mean a register of the days, weeks, and months. The Greek terms are ἡμερολόγιον and ἐφημερίς.

(1) GREEK. The Greek year consisted of twelve months—some "full," i.e. of 30 days each; the others, "hollow" or incomplete, of 29 days each. This made up a lunar year of 354 days, 11 days short of the solar year. To maintain some correspondence between the lunar and the solar years, and to provide at least for the festivals of the seasons always occurring at the right time of year, the Athenians early resorted to the method of intercalation. A space of time was taken which included as many days as would exactly make up eight solar years, and could easily be distributed among the same number of lunar years. This space of time was called a "great year." Then in every third, sixth, and eighth year, a month of 29 or 30 days was inserted, so that the years in question consisted each of 383 or 384 days. This system was introduced at Athens by Solon. The period of eight years was sometimes called ἐνναετηρίς, or a period of nine years, because it began again with every ninth year; sometimes ὀκταετηρίς, or space of eight years. For this the astronomers, of whom Meton (q. v.) in the Periclean Age may be taken as a representative, substituted a more accurate system, which was afterwards adopted in Athens and other cities as a correction of the old calendar. This was the ἐννεακαιδεκαετηρίς of nineteen years. The alternate "full" and "hollow" months were divided into three decades, consisting of 10 or 9 days each, as the case might be. The days of the last decade were counted from more to less to correspond with the waning of the moon. Thus the 21st of the month was called the 10th of the waning moon, the 22d the 9th, the 23d the 8th, and so on. The reckoning of the year, with the order and names of the months, differed more or less in different States, the only common point being the names of the months, which were almost without exception taken from the chief festivals celebrated in them. The Athenians and the other Ionian peoples began their year with the first new moon after the summer solstice, the Dorians with the autumnal equinox, the Boeotians and other Aeolians with the winter solstice. The table given below shows the succession of the Attic months, the number of days they contained, and the corresponding months of our year.

1.	Hecatombaeon (Ἑκατομβαιών)	contained	30	days, and	corresponds	nearly to our	July.
2.	Metageitnion (Μεταγειτνιων)	"	29	"	"	"	August.
3.	Boedromion (Βοηδρομιών)	"	30	"	"	"	September.
4.	Pyanepsion (Πυανεψιών)	"	29	"	"	"	October.
5.	Maimacterion (Μαιμακτηριών)	"	30	"	"	"	November.
6.	Poseideon (Ποσειδεών)	"	29	"	"	"	December.
7.	Gamelion (Γαμηλιών)	"	30	"	"	"	January.
8.	Anthesterion (Ἀνθεστηριών)	"	29	"	"	"	February.
9.	Elaphebolion (Ἐλαφηβολιών)	"	30	"	"	"	March.
10.	Munychion (Μουνυχιών)	"	29	"	"	"	April.
11.	Thargelion (Θαργηλιών)	"	30	"	"	"	May.
12.	Scirophorion (Σκιροφοριών)	"	29	"	"	"	June.

At the time when the Julian Calendar was adopted by the Athenians, probably about the time of the emperor Hadrian, the lunar year appears to have been changed into the solar year; and it has further been conjectured that the beginning of the year was transferred from the summer solstice to the autumnal equinox. The intercalary month was a second Poseideon inserted in the middle of the year. The official system of numbering the years differed also very much in the various States. The years received their names from the magistrates, sometimes secular, sometimes spiritual. (See EPONYMUS.) Historical chronology was first computed according to Olympiads, or periods of four years, beginning B.C. 776, by the historian Timaeus in the third century B.C.

(2) ROMAN. The Roman year was supposed to have consisted, under Romulus, of 10 months—four "full" ones of 31 days (March, May, July, and October) and six "hollow" of 30 days (April, June, August, September, November, December). But, as a space of 304 days makes up neither a solar nor a lunar year, it is difficult to understand the so-called "year of Romulus." King Numa was popularly supposed to have introduced the year of 12 months by adding January and February at the end; for the Roman year, it must be remembered, began originally with March. By this system every month except February had an odd number of days: March 31, April 29, May 31, June 29, Quintilis 31, Sextilis 29, September 29, October 31, November 29, December 29, January 29, February 28. Numa is also credited with the attempt to square this lunar year of 355 days with the solar year of 365; but how he did it is not certainly known. The Decemviri in B.C. 450 probably introduced the system of adjustment afterwards in use. According to this, a cycle of four years was taken, in the second year of

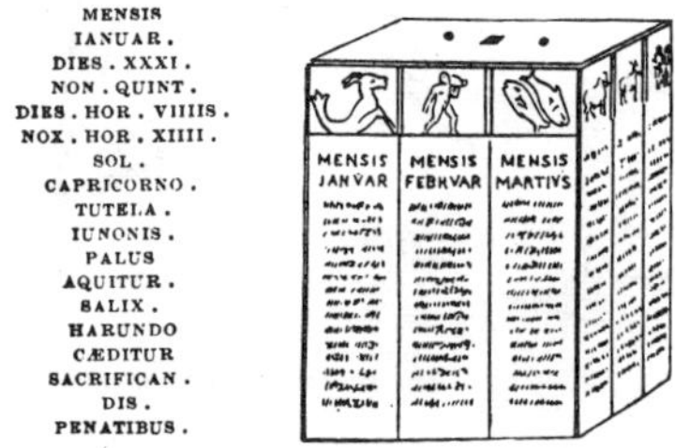

Roman Calendar, with Copy of Inscription for January. (Pompeii.)

which an intercalary month (*mensis mercedonius*) of 23 days was inserted between the 24th and 25th of February, and in the fourth year a month of 22 days between the 23d and 24th of February. Thus the period of four years amounted to 1465 days. But this gave the year an average of 366¼ days, or one day too many, so that a special rectification was necessary from time to time. This was probably carried out by the omission of an intercalary month. It was the business of the *pontifices* to keep the calendar in order by regular intercalation; but, partly from carelessness, partly from political motives, they made insertions and omissions so incorrectly as to bring the calendar into complete confusion, and destroy the correspondence between the months and the seasons. The mischief was finally remedied by Iulius Caesar, with the assistance of the mathematician Sosigenes. To bring the calendar into correspondence with the seasons, the year B.C. 46 was lengthened so as to consist of 15 months, or 415 days, and the calendar known as the Julian was introduced on the 1st of January, B.C. 45. This calendar is founded simply on the solar year, which is well known to be a discovery of the Egyptians. Caesar fixed this year at 365¼ days, which is correct within a few minutes. After this, the ordinary year consisted of 365 days, divided into 12 months, with the names still in use. Every fourth year had 366 days, a day being inserted at the end of February. The Julian Calendar maintained its ground till 1582, when Pope Gregory XIII. corrected the trifling error which still attached to it. The old names of the months were retained with two exceptions—that of Quintilis, which, in honour of Iulius Caesar, was called Iulius, and that of Sextilis, which in B.C. 8 was called Augustus, in honour of the emperor. The old divisions of the lunar month were also retained for convenience of dating. These were (*a*) the Kalendae, marking the first appearance of the new moon; (*b*) the Nonae, marking the first quarter; (*c*) the Idus, marking the full moon. Kalendae means properly the day of summoning, from *calare*, to summon. The pontifex was bound to observe the first phase, and to make his announcement to the Rex Sacrorum, who then summoned the people to the Capitol, in front of the Curia Calabra, so called from *calare*. Here he offered sacrifice, and announced that the first quarter would begin on the fifth or seventh day (inclusive) as the case might be. This day was called Nonae, as (according to Roman calculation) the ninth day before the full moon, and fell in March, May, July, and October on the 7th, in the other months on the 5th. The appearance of the full moon was called Idus (probably connected with the Etruscan word *iduare*, "to divide"), because it divided the month in the middle. The days of the month were counted backwards, in the first half of the month from the Nones and Ides, in the last half from the Kalends of the following month. The Romans also had a week called *internundinum*, or the interval between two *nundinae*. It consisted of eight days, and, like our weeks, could be divided between two months or two years. See FASTI.

After the establishment of the Republic the Romans named their years after the consuls, a custom which was maintained down to the reign of Justinian (A.D. 541). After the time of Augustus it became the practice in literature to date events from the foundation of Rome, which took place, according to Varro, in B.C. 753; according to Cato, in 751.

THE DAY.—The Greeks reckoned the civil day from sunset to sunset, the Romans (like ourselves) from midnight to midnight. The natural day was reckoned by both as lasting from sunrise to sunset. The divisions of the day were for a long time made on no common principle. It was for military purposes that the Romans first devised such a principle, dividing the night during service into four equal watches (*vigiliae*). Corresponding to this we find another division (probably calculated immediately for the courts of justice) into *mane* (sunrise to 9 or 10), forenoon (*ad meridiem*), afternoon (*de meridie*) until 3 or 4, and evening (*suprema*) from thence till sunset. After the introduction of sundials and water-clocks, the day and night were divided each into twelve hours; but the division was founded on the varying length of the day, so that each hour of the day was longer, and conversely each hour of the night shorter, in summer than in winter.

It should be observed that several of the Eastern nations, for the purpose of preventing confusion in their calculations with other nations, dropped the names of their months, and merely counted the months, as the first, second, third, etc., month. For extended information see Corsini, *Fast. Att.*, which, however, is very imperfect; Ideler, *Handbuch der mathem. u. technischen Chronol.* (Berlin, 1826); Clinton, *Fast. Hellen.* vol. ii. Append. xix.; and more especially K. F. Hermann, *Ueber griechische Monatskunde* (Göttingen, 1844); Th. Bergk, *Beiträge zur griechischen Monatskunde* (Giessen, 1845); A. Boeckh, *Ueber die vierjährigen Sonnenkreise der Alten* (Berlin, 1863); Mommsen, *Chronologie* (Leipzig, 1883); Ideler's work, *Lehrbuch der Chronologie*, 2 vols. (Berlin, 1826); Mommsen, *Die römische Chronologie* (Berlin, 1858); and Matzat, *Röm. Chronologie*, 2 vols. (Berlin, 1883). For further information connected with the ancient measurement of time see the articles ASTRONOMIA; DIES; HOROLOGIUM; LUSTRUM; NUNDINAE; SAECULUM; VIGILIAE.

Calēnus, Q. FUFIUS. A tribune of the plebs, B.C. 61, when he succeeded in saving P. Clodius (q. v.) from condemnation for his violation of the mysteries of the Bona Dea. In 59, he was praetor, and from this time appears as an active partisan of Caesar, in whose service he remained until Caesar's death (44). After this event Calenus joined M. Antonius, and subsequently had the command of Antony's legions in the north of Italy. He died in 41.

Cales. The modern Calvi; the chief town of the Caleni, an Ausonian people in Campania, on the Via Latina, said to have been founded by

Coin of Cales.

Calaïs, son of Boreas, and therefore called Threïcia by the poets. It was celebrated for its excellent wine. See VINUM.

Calĕtes or **Calĕti**. A people in Belgic Gaul near the mouth of the Sequana (Seine).

Calgăcus. See article in Appendix.

Calidarium. See CALDARIUM.

Caliendrum. A tall female head-dress, but whether a wig of false hair or an arrangement of draperies, it is not easy to determine. The Cruquian scholiast on the *locus classicus* of Horace (*Sat.* i. 8, 48) gives both explanations, without attempting to decide between them (*peplum capitis aut crinis suppositicius seu capillamentum aut galericulus capitisve ornamentum*). But *galericulus* may mean a wig (Suet. *Oth.* 12, with Casaubon's note); and the humour of the passage is decidedly in favour of this rendering: one of the two old women drops her false teeth in her flight, and the other her false hair.

Calĭga. A strong and heavy shoe, or rather sandal, worn by the Roman soldiers. Although the use of this species of *calceamentum* extended to the centurions, it was not worn by the superior officers. Hence the common soldiers, including centurions, were distinguished by the name of *caligati* (Suet. *Aug.* 25). Service in the ranks was also designated after this article of attire. Thus Marius was said to have risen to the consulship *a caliga*, i. e. from the ranks. The emperor Caligula (q. v.) received that cognomen when a boy, in consequence of wearing the *caliga*, which his father, Germanicus, put upon his son in order to please the soldiers (Tac. *Ann.* i. 41). The triumphal monuments of Rome show most distinctly the difference between the *caliga* of the common soldier and the *calceus* worn by men of higher rank. (See CALCEUS). The *caliga* exhibits a number of straps, through which the foot is partially seen; while the *calceus* (q. v.) is an ordinary closed shoe. The sole of the *caliga* was thickly studded with hobnails.

Caliga. (Arch of Trajan.)

The *caliga speculatoria* (Suet. *Calig.* 52), made for the use of couriers, was probably much lighter than the ordinary shoe worn by the soldiers. See SPECULATOR.

Caligŭla, GAIUS CAESAR AUGUSTUS GERMANĬCUS, son of Germanicus and Agrippina, was born A.D. 12, in the camp, probably in Germany, and was brought up among the legions (Suet. *Calig.* 8). Here he received from the soldiers the surname of Caligula, from his being arrayed, when quite young, like a common soldier, and wearing a pair of *caligae*, a kind of shoe or covering for the feet used chiefly by the common soldiers. This was done in order to secure towards him the goodwill of the troops. Caligula himself, however, disliked the appellation in after-days, and preferred that of Gaius Caesar, which is also his historical name. Upon his father's death he returned from Syria, and lived with his mother till her exile, when he removed to the residence of Livia Augusta, his great-grandmother, whose funeral oration he delivered in public, while he still wore the *praetexta*. He afterwards remained in the family of his grandmother, Antonia, until his twentieth year, when, being invited to Capreae by the emperor, he assumed the dress proper to manhood, but without the customary ceremonies.

In the court of his grandfather, his naturally mean and vicious temper appeared in a servile compliance with the caprices of those in power, in a wanton love of cruelty towards the unfortunate, and in the most abandoned and unprincipled debauchery; so that Tiberius observed that he was

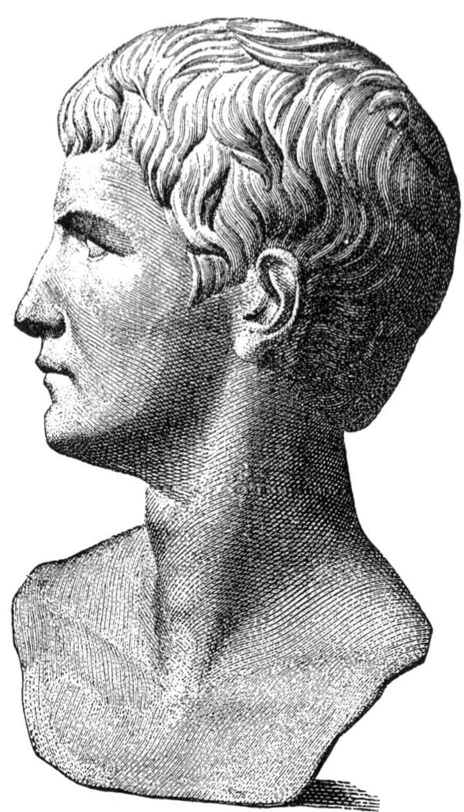

Caligula. (Bronze bust in Paris.)

breeding a second Phaëthon for the destruction of the world. Tiberius had, by his testament, appointed his two grandsons, Gaius Caesar and Tiberius Gemellus, the latter the son of Drusus, joint heirs of the Empire. The first act of Caligula, however, was to assemble the Senate for the purpose of declaring the invalidity of the will; and this being readily effected, and Tiberius Gemellus being declared too young to rule, Gaius Caesar Caligula was immediately proclaimed emperor. This appointment was received with the most unbounded joy both at Rome and in the provinces, and the conduct of the new prince seemed at first to promise one of the most auspicious of reigns. But this was all dissimulation on his part—a dissimulation which he had learned under his wily predecessor—for Caligula esteemed it prudent to assume the appearance of moderation, liberality, and justice, till he should be firmly seated on the throne, and freed from all apprehension lest the claims of the young Tiberius might be revived on any offence having been taken by the Senate. He interred, in the most honourable manner, the remains of his mother and of his brother Nero, set free all state prisoners, recalled the banished, and forbade all prosecutions for treason. He conferred on the magistrates free and independent power. Although the will of Tiberius had been declared, by the Senate, to be null and void, he fulfilled every article of it, with the exception only of that above mentioned. When he was chosen consul, he took his uncle Claudius as his colleague. Thus he distinguished the first eight months of his reign by many actions dictated perhaps by hypocrisy, but which appeared magnanimous and noble to the eyes of the world, when he fell, on a sudden, dangerously ill, in consequence, as has been imagined, of a love-potion given him by his mistress, Milonia Caesonia (whom he afterwards married), with a view to securing his inconstant affections. On recovering from this malady, whether weary by this time of the restraints of hypocrisy, or actually deranged in his intellect by the inflammatory effects of the potion which he had taken (Juv. vi. 614), the emperor threw off all appearance of virtue and moderation, as well as all prudential considerations, and acted on every occasion with the mischievous violence of unbridled passions and wanton power; so that the tyranny of Tiberius was forgotten in the enormities of Caligula. The most exquisite tortures served him for enjoyments. During his meals he caused criminals, and even innocent persons, to be stretched on the rack and beheaded; the most respectable citizens were daily executed. In the madness of his arrogance he even considered himself a god, and caused the honours to be paid to him which were paid to Apollo, to Mars, and even to Iupiter. He built a temple to his own divinity. At one time he wished that the whole Roman people had but one head, that he might be able to cut it off at a single blow. He frequently repeated the words of Attius, *Oderint dum metuant.* One of his greatest follies was the building of a bridge of vessels between Baiae and Puteoli, in imitation of that of Xerxes over the Hellespont. He himself consecrated this grand structure with great splendour; and, after he had passed the night following in a revel with his friends, in order to do something extraordinary before his departure he caused a crowd of persons, without distinction of age, rank, or character, to be seized and thrown into the sea. On his return he entered Rome in triumph, because, as he said, he had conquered nature herself. After this he made preparations for an expedition against the Germans; passed, with more than 200,000 men, over the Rhine; but returned after he had travelled a few miles, and that without having seen an enemy. Such was his terror that when he came to the river, and found the bridge obstructed by the crowd upon it, he caused himself to be passed over the heads of the soldiers. He then went to Gaul, which he plundered with unexampled rapacity. Not content with the considerable booty thus obtained, he sold all the property of his sisters Agrippina and Livilla, whom he banished. He also sold the furniture of the old court, the clothes of Augustus, Agrippina, etc. Before he left Gaul he declared his intention of going to Britain. He collected his army on the coast, embarked in a magnificent galley, but returned when he had hardly left the land, drew up his forces, ordered the signal of battle to be sounded, and commanded the soldiers to fill their helmets with shells, while he cried out, "This booty, ravished from the sea, is fit for my palace and the Capitol." When he returned to Rome he was desirous of a triumph on account of his achievements, but contented himself with an ovation. Discontented with the Senate, he resolved to destroy the greater part of the members and the most distinguished men of Rome, as was proved by two books which were found after his death, wherein the names of the proscribed were noted down, and of which one was entitled *Gladius* (Sword), and the other *Pugillus* (Dagger). He became reconciled to the Senate, however, when he found it worthy of him. He supported public brothels and gaming-houses in the palace, and received himself the entrance-money of the visitors. His horse, named Incitatus, was his favourite. This horse he made one of his priests, and, by way of insult to the Republic, declared it also consul. It was kept in an ivory stable and fed from a golden manger, and when it was invited to feast at the emperor's table gilded oats were served up in a golden basin of exquisite workmanship. He had even the intention of destroying the poems of Homer, and was on the point of removing the works and images of Vergil and Livy from all libraries—those of the former because, as he said, he was destitute of genius and learning; those of the latter because he was not to be depended upon as an historian. Caligula's morals were, from his youth upward, abominably corrupt, but after he had married and repudiated several wives, Caesonia retained a permanent hold on his affections. His extravagance equalled his cruelty, for in a single year he squandered the entire savings of Tiberius, some $28,000,000, a favourite amusement of his being to stand on a balcony and shovel gold-pieces into the street. At length, a number of conspirators, at the head of whom were Chaerea and Cornelius Sabinus, both tribunes of the praetorian cohorts, murdered him in the twenty-ninth year of his age, and the fourth of his reign, A.D. 41. His life was written by Suetonius. See Baring-Gould's *Tragedy of the Caesars* (London, 1893).

Coin of Caligula, with his head and that of Augustus (the latter crowned).

Calix (κύλιξ). (1) The drinking-cup, usually made of earthenware, round, with a broad top, feet, and horizontal handles. The usual capacity was three *cotylae*, or 1.3 pints. The *cantharus* (q. v.) differed from the *calix* in being larger and having vertical handles. Besides earthenware, other materials are mentioned as used in the making of *calices*—e. g. wood, brass, silver, terebinth (τέρμινθος), and possibly glass (Photius, s. h. v.). Certain places are mentioned by Athenaeus as noted for their manufacture of drinking-cups, among them Argos, Chios, Lacedaemon, Rhodes, and Teos; and Martial speaks of Surrentum and Saguntum.

Early Calix. (Birch.)

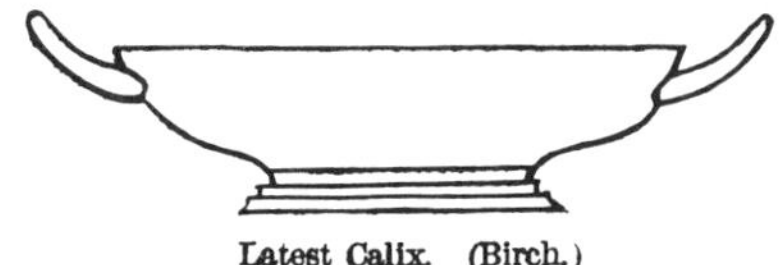
Latest Calix. (Birch.)

In Juvenal (v. 48) we read of *calices* called after a shoemaker of Beneventum, which had four nozzles. This was Vatinius (Mart. xiv. 96), who was afterwards a buffoon in the court of Nero (Tac.

Ann. xv. 34), and the cups were called *Vatinii* (Mart. x. 3, 4). See Birch, *Ancient Pottery* (1873).

(2) A tube regulating the supply of water, and attached to the end of each pipe where it entered the castellum of an aqueduct; it was probably of lead in the time of Vitruvius, such only being mentioned by him; but was made of bronze (*aēneus*) when Frontinus wrote, in order to check the roguery of the *aquarii*, who were able to increase or diminish the flow of water from the reservoir by compressing or extending the lead. As a further security, the *calix* was stamped with the owner's name as well as the capacity. There are two specimens of such *calices* in the Roman museums—one in the Vatican, another in the Museo Kircheriano. Pipes which had no *calix* were termed *solutae*.

Callaïci or **Callaeci**. A people of Spain, in the northwestern part of the country. They inhabited what was once Galicia (see Eutrop. iv. 19).

Callătis (Κάλλατις). A town of Moesia, on the Black Sea, originally a colony of Miletus, and afterwards of Heraclea.

Callé. See Calé.

Callias (Καλλίας) and **Hipponīcus** (Ἱππόνικος). A noble Athenian family, celebrated for their wealth. They enjoyed the hereditary dignity of torch-bearer at the Eleusinian Mysteries, and claimed descent from Triptolemus. The first member of this family of any note was the Callias who fought at the battle of Marathon, B.C. 490, and was afterwards ambassador from Athens to Artaxerxes, and, according to some accounts, negotiated a peace with Persia, B.C. 449, on terms most humiliating to the latter. On his return to Athens he was accused of having taken bribes, and was condemned to a fine of fifty talents. His son, Hipponicus, was killed at the battle of Delium in B.C. 424. It was his divorced wife, and not his widow, whom Pericles married. His daughter Hippareté was married to Alcibiades. Callias, son of this Hipponicus by the lady who married Pericles, dissipated all his ancestral wealth on sophists, flatterers, and women. The scene of Xenophon's *Banquet*, and also that of Plato's *Protagoras*, is laid at his house.

Callicolōné (Καλλικολώνη). A hill in the district of Troas, deriving its name (καλὴ κολώνη) from the pleasing regularity of its form, and the groves by which it seems for ages to have been adorned. It is mentioned by Homer in the *Iliad* (xx. 53, 151).

Callicrătes (Καλλικράτης). (1) An Athenian, who caused Dion (q. v.) to be assassinated. (2) An officer intrusted with the care of the treasures of Susa by Alexander. (3) An architect, who, in conjunction with Ictinus, built the Parthenon at Athens, and who undertook also to complete the Long Walls termed σκέλη (Plut. *Pericl.* c. 13). He appears to have flourished about B.C. 440. (4) A sculptor, distinguished principally by the minuteness of his performances. He is mentioned as a Lacedaemonian, and is associated with Myrmecides by Aelian (*V. H.* i. 17). In connection with this artist he is said to have made some chariots which could be covered with the wings of a fly, and to have inscribed on a grain of the plant *sesamum* some verses of Homer (Plin. vii. 21). Galen, therefore, well applies to him the epithet ματαιότεχνος. Athenaeus, however, relates that he engraved only large vases. The age in which he lived is uncertain.

Callicratĭdas (Καλλικρατίδας). A Spartan, who succeeded Lysander in the command of the fleet. He took Methymna, and routed the Athenian fleet under Conon. He was defeated and killed near the Arginusae, in a naval battle, B.C. 406. He was one of the last who preserved the true Spartan character, which had become greatly altered for the worse, during the Peloponnesian War, by the habit which the Lacedaemonians had contracted of fighting beyond the limits of their country.

Callidrŏmus (Καλλίδρομος). According to Livy (xxxvi. 15), the highest summit of Mount Oeta. It was occupied by Cato with a body of troops in the battle fought at the pass of Thermopylae between the Romans, under Acilius Glabrio, and the army of Antiochus; and, owing to this manœuvre, the latter was entirely routed.

Callimăchus (Καλλίμαχος). (1) A Greek artist, who flourished in the second half of the fifth century B.C. He was the inventor of the Corinthian order of pillar; and the art of boring marble is also attributed to him, though perhaps he did no more than bring it to perfection. The ancient critics represent him as unwearied in polishing and perfecting his work; indeed, they allege that his productions lost something through their excessive refinement and purity. One of his celebrated works was the golden chandelier in the Erechtheum at Athens.

(2) A Greek scholar and poet, the chief representative of the Alexandrian School. He was the son of Battus, and thus sprung from the noble family of the Battiadae. He at first gave his lectures in a suburb of Alexandria; but was afterwards summoned by Ptolemy Philadelphus to the Museum there, and in about B.C. 260 was made curator of the library. He held this office till his death, which took place about B.C. 240. He did a great service to literature by sifting and cataloguing the numerous books collected at Alexandria. The results of his labours were published in his great work, called Πίνακες, or "Tablets." This contained 120 books, and was a catalogue, arranged in chronological order, of the works contained in the library, with observations on their genuineness, an indication of the first and last word in each book, and a note of its bulk. This work laid the foundation of a critical study of Greek literature. Eight hundred works, partly in prose and partly in verse, were attributed altogether to Callimachus; but it is to be observed that he avoided, on principle, the composition of long poems, so as to be able to give more thought to the artistic elaboration of details. The essence of Callimachus's verse is art and learning, not poetic genius in the real sense. Indeed, some of his compositions had a directly learned object—the Αἴτια, or "Causes," for instance. This was a collection of elegiac poems in four books, treating, with great erudition, of the foundation of cities, the origin of religious ceremonies, and the like.

Through his writings, as well as through his oral instruction, Callimachus exercised an immense influence, not only on the course of learning, but on the poetical tendencies of the Alexandrian School (q. v.). Among his pupils were the most celebrated savants of the time, Eratosthenes, Aristophanes of Byzantium, Apollonius of Rhodes, and others. Of his writings only a very few have survived in a complete state. These are: six hymns, five of which are in epic and one in elegiac form, and sixty-four epigrams. The hymns, both in their language and their matter, attest the learned taste of their author. His elegy, entitled the *Coma Berenices*, or "Lock of Berenice," is imitated by Catullus in one of his remaining pieces. Ovid, in the twentieth of his *Heroides*, as well as in his *Ibis*, took poems of Callimachus for his models. Indeed, the Romans generally set a very high value on his elegies, and liked to imitate them. Of his other works in prose and poetry—among the latter may be mentioned a very popular epic called *Hecatê* — only fragments have survived. A good edition of the remains is that of Schneider, 2 vols. (1870–73); and of the Hymns and Epigrams those of Meineke (1861) and Wilamowitz (1882). See Couat, *La Poésie Alexandrine* (Paris, 1882).

Callīnus (Καλλῖνος). The creator of the Greek political elegy. He was a native of Ephesus, and flourished probably about B.C. 700, at the time when the kings of Lydia were harassing the Greek colonies of Asia Minor by constant wars. One elegy from his hand has survived, in which, in a simple and manly tone, he endeavours to arouse the degenerate youth of his fatherland.

Calliŏpé (Καλλιόπη). One of the Muses, daughter of Zeus and Mnemosynê. She presided over epic poetry and eloquence, and was represented holding a close-rolled parchment and sometimes a trumpet. She derived her name from her beautiful voice (ἀπὸ τῆς καλῆς ὀπός). Calliopé bore to Oeagrus a son named Linus, who was killed by his pupil Heracles (Apollod. i. 3, 2). She had also by the same sire the celebrated Orpheus. Others, however, made Apollo the sire of Linus and Orpheus. Hesiod (*Frag.* 97) says that Urania was the mother of Linus.

Calliopé, the Muse of Epic Poetry (Statue in the Vatican.)

Callipatīra (Καλλιπατείρα). The daughter of Diagoras, and wife of Callianax, an athlete. According to the common account, she went with her son, after the death of her husband, to the Olympic Games, having disguised herself in the attire of a teacher of gymnastics. When her son was declared victor, she discovered her sex in the joy of the moment, and was immediately arrested, as women were not allowed to appear on such occasions. The punishment to which she was liable was to be cast down from a precipitous and rocky height, but she was pardoned in consequence of the peculiar circumstances of her case. A law, however, was immediately passed, ordaining that the teachers of gymnastic exercises should appear naked at the games (Pausan. v. 6, 5).

Callĭphon (Καλλιφῶν). A painter, a native of Samos, who decorated with pictures the Temple of Artemis at Ephesus. The subjects of his pieces were taken from the *Iliad* (Pausan. v. 19).

Callipŏlis (Καλλίπολις). (1) A town on the east coast of Sicily not far from Aetna. (2) The modern Gallipoli, a town in the Thracian Chersonesus opposite Lampsacus. (3) A town in Aetolia.

Callirrhŏé (Καλλιρρόη) (1) afterwards called Enneacrunus (Ἐννεάκρουνος), or the "Nine Springs," because its water was distributed by nine pipes, was the most celebrated well in Athens, situated in the southeastern part of the city, and still retains its ancient name. (2) See ALCMAEON.

Callis. A narrow cow-path in the mountains (Isid. *Orig.* xv. 16, 20).

Callisté (Καλλίστη). An island of the Aegean; called also Thera (q. v.).

Callistēia (καλλιστεῖα). Beauty shows; festivals celebrated in different parts of Greece. See Athenaeus, xiii. 609.

Callisthĕnes (Καλλισθένης). A Greek historian, born at Olynthus about B.C. 360. He was a relation of Aristotle, from whom he received instruction at the same time as Alexander the Great. He accompanied Alexander on his Asiatic campaign, and offended him by refusing to pay him servile homage after the Persian fashion, and by other daring exhibitions of independence. The consequence was that the king threw his friend into prison on the pretext that he was concerned in a conspiracy against his life. Callisthenes died in captivity in B.C. 328, in consequence, probably, of maltreatment. Of his historical writings, particularly those dealing with the exploits of Alexander, only fragments remain; but he was always ranked among the most famous historians. Indeed, his reputation as the companion of Alexander and the historian of his achievements maintained itself so well that he was made responsible in literature for the romantic narrative of Alexander's life which grew up in the following centuries. This was translated into Latin towards the end of the third century A.D by Iulius Valerius (q. v.), and became the main authority for the mediæval adaptations of the myth of Alexander. See the work of Westermann, *De Callisthene* (Leipzig, 1838–42).

Callisto (Καλλιστώ) (called also HELĬCÉ). The daughter of Lycaon, king of Arcadia, and an attendant of Artemis. Zeus saw her, and, assuming the form of Artemis, accompanied the maiden to the chase and overcame her virtue. She long concealed her shame; but at length, as she was one day bathing with her divine mistress, the discovery was made, and Artemis, in her anger, turned her into a bear. While in this form she brought forth her son Arcas, who lived with her in the woods, until the herdsmen caught both her and him and brought them to Lycaon. (See ARCAS.) Some time afterwards she went into the temenus, or sacred enclosure of the Lycaean Zeus, which it was unlawful to enter. A number of Arcadians, among whom was her own son, followed to kill her, but Zeus snatched her out of their hands, and placed her as a constellation in the sky (Apollod. iii. 8; Hygin. *Fab.* 177). It was also fabled that at the request of Heré, Tethys forbade the constellation of the Bear to descend into her waves. This legend is related with great variety in the circumstances. According to one of these versions, Arcas, having been separated from his mother and reared among men, met her one day in the woods, and was on the point of slaying her, when Zeus transferred the mother and son to the skies.

Callistratia (Καλλιστρατία). A town in Paphlagonia on the coast of the Euxine.

Callistrătus (Καλλίστρατος). A Greek rhetorician, who probably flourished in the third century A.D. He was the author of descriptions of fourteen statues of celebrated artists—Scopas, for instance, Praxiteles, and Lysippus, written after the manner of Philostratus. His style is dry and affected, and he gives the reader no real insight into the qualities of the masterpieces which he attempts to describe.

Callium (Κάλλιον), called CALLIPŎLIS by Livy. A town in Aetolia in the valley of the Spercheus.

Callynteria (καλλυντήρια). See PLYNTERIA.

Calo. A common slave; often the slave of a soldier. The word is a contraction of *caclo*, akin to *cacula*. (See Fest. p. 146.) Even under the Republic the number of slaves following a Roman army was large; under the Empire it sometimes exceeded the number of the soldiers. Each legion was followed by its own *calones;* and to prevent confusion, in case of an attack, they were organized and subjected to military discipline. See LIXA; SERVUS.

Calor. A river in Samnium, flowing past Beneventum and falling into the Vulturnus.

Calpé (Κάλπη, Κάλπις). A lofty mountain in the most southern parts of Spain, opposite to Mount Abyla on the African coast. These two mountains were called the Pillars of Hercules. Calpé is now called Gibraltar, from the Arabic Gebel Tarik—i. e. "mountain of Tarik," Tarik being the Moorish general who first led the Moors into Spain, A.D. 710.

Calpis (κάλπις). An urn oftenest used for carrying water, but sometimes for holding unguents, wine, or as a cinerary urn. See HYDRIA.

Greek Women with Calpis.

Calpurnia. Daughter of L. Calpurnius Piso, consul B.C. 58, and last wife of Iulius Caesar, to whom she was married in B.C. 59. She survived her husband. See CAESAR, GAIUS IULIUS.

Calpurnia Gens. A plebeian gens which claimed to be descended from Calpus, a son of Numa. It was divided into the families of Bestia, Bibulus, and Piso.

Calpurnia Lex. See LEX.

Calpurnius. (1) A writer of mimes, not to be confounded with the pastoral poet of the same name. (2) A Christian in the time of Hadrian and Antoninus Pius, from whom we have fifty-one *Declamationes* remaining. (3) TITUS CALPURNIUS (called SICŬLUS), a Latin poet, a native of Sicily, lived during the first century of our era, under the emperor Nero. In the earliest editions of his works, and in all but one of the MSS., eleven eclogues pass under his name. Ugoletus, however, at a later period, guided by this single MS., showed that four of the eleven were the work of Nemesianus. The *Eclogues* of Calpurnius are not without merit, though greatly inferior in elegance and simplicity to Vergil's. They are dedicated to Nemesianus, his protector and patron, for he himself was very poor. In the time of Charlemagne these pieces were placed in the hands of young scholars. Besides these poems, which were written in imitation of Vergil's *Bucolica*, there exists a poetical panegyric, *De Laude Pisonis*, which is now generally attributed to Calpurnius. Editions of this are those of Held (Breslau, 1831), and Weber (Marburg, 1859); of the *Eclogues*, those by Glaeser (Göttingen, 1842); with Nemesianus by Schenkl (Prague, 1885); and with commentary, introduction, and appendix by Keene (London, 1887). A good translation of the *Eclogues* into English verse is that by E. J. L. Scott (London, 1891). See EINSIEDELN POEMS.

Calthŭla. A yellow garment. See CROCOTA.

Calumnia (in old Latin, *Kalumnia*). The Latin word for slander. It was technically applied to false accusations. The person falsely accused, if acquitted, had the right of accusing the prosecutor in his turn on the charge of *calumnia* before the same jury. In civil cases the penalty was a pecuniary fine; in criminal cases the *calumniator* lost his right to appear again as a prosecutor, and in early times was branded on the forehead with a K (Cic. *Pro Rosc. Am.* 20, 57).

Calvīnus, CN. DOMITIUS. Tribune of the plebs, B.C. 59, when he supported Bibulus against Caesar, praetor in B.C. 56, and consul in B.C. 53, through the influence of Pompey. He took an active part in the Civil War as one of Caesar's generals.

Calvus, GAIUS LICINIUS. A Roman, equally distinguished as an orator and a poet. In the former capacity he is mentioned with praise by Cicero (*Brut.* 81; *Ep. ad Fam.* vii. 24; xv. 51). He was also the friend of Catullus, and three odes (14, 50, 96) of that author's are addressed to him, in which he is commemorated as a most delightful companion, from whose society he could scarcely refrain. The fragments of his epigrams which remain do not enable us to judge for ourselves of his poetical merits. He is classed by Ovid among the licentious writers. He lived B.C. 82–47. See Teuffel, *Hist. of Rom. Lit.* § 213, 5–7.

Calycadnus (Καλύκαδνος). A considerable river of Cilicia Tracheia, navigable as far as Seleucia.

Calydnae (Κάλυδναι νῆσοι). (1) Two small islands off the coast of Troas. (2) A group of islands off the coast of Caria, belonging to the Sporades. The largest of them was called Calydna, and afterwards Calymna.

Calȳdon (Καλυδών). A city of Aetolia, below the river Evenus, and between that stream and the sea. It was famed in Grecian story on account of the boar-hunt in its neighbourhood (see MELEAGER), the theme of poetry from Homer to Statius. We are told by mythologists that Oeneus, the father of Meleager and Tydeus, reigned at

Calydon, while his brother Agrius settled in Pleuron. Frequent wars, however, arose between them on the subject of contiguous lands. Some time after the Peloponnesian War, we find Calydon in the possession of the Achaeans. It is probable that the Calydonians themselves invited over the Achaeans, to defend them against the Acarnanians (Pausan. iii. 10). Their city was, in consequence, occupied by an Achaean garrison, until Epaminondas, after the battle of Leuctra, compelled them to evacuate the place. It was still a town of importance during the Social War, and as late as the time of Caesar. Augustus accomplished its downfall by removing the inhabitants to Nicopolis.

Calymna (Κάλυμνα). See CALYDNAE.

Calypso (Καλυψώ). A daughter of Atlas, according to Homer (*Od.* ii. 52). Hesiod, however, makes her an ocean-nymph (*Theog.* 359), and Apollodorus a Nereid (i. 2). Like Circé, she was a goddess of human appearance, and dwelt in solitary state with her attendant nymphs on an island named Ogygia, in the midst of the ocean. Her isle presented such a scene of sylvan beauty as charmed even Hermes, one of the dwellers of Olympus (*Od.* v. 72). Calypso received and kindly entertained Odysseus, when, in the course of his wanderings, that hero was thrown upon her domains after his shipwreck. She detained him there for seven years, designing to make him immortal and to keep him with her forever; but Hermes arriving with a command from Zeus, she was obliged to consent to his departure. She gave the hero tools to build a raft or light vessel, supplied him with provisions, and reluctantly took a final leave of him. As regards her island, Homer seems to have conceived Ogygia to lie in the northwestern parts of the Western Sea, far remote from all other isles and coasts; and he thus brought his hero into all parts of that sea, and informed his auditors of all its wonders. Odysseus had two sons by Calypso, named Nausithoüs and Nausinoüs.

Calypso. (From a painted Vase.)

Calyptra (καλύπτρα). A veil worn by young women in Greece as well as in Italy, used to conceal the face from strangers. See Hom. *Od.* v. 232; Eurip. *Iph. T.* 372.

Camalodūnum. The modern Colchester; the capital of the Trinobantes in Britain, and the first Roman colony in the island. It was founded by the emperor Claudius, A.D. 43.

Camăra (καμάρα) or **Camĕra**. Any arched or vaulted covering, and anything with such a covering. It is chiefly used in the following senses:

(1) Of an arched roof which might be (*a*) an open trellis-work with creeping-plants, etc., trained over it; or (*b*) an arched or vaulted ceiling formed by semicircular bands or beams of wood, often gilded or fitted with plates of glass; or (*c*) a barrel-vault of solid stone-work, as that of the Tullianum prison at Rome. See CARCER.

(2) Small boats used in early times by the people who inhabited the shores of the Euxine and the Bosporus, and so called from their broad, arched deck, described by Tacitus (*Hist.* iii. 4).

Camarīna (Καμαρῖνα). A town on the southern coast of Sicily, at the mouth of the Hipparis, founded by Syracuse, B.C. 599. It was several times destroyed by Syracuse; and in the First Punic War was taken by the Romans, and most of the inhabitants sold as slaves.

Near the walls on the north was the Palus Camarina, which was a marshy pool formed by the stagnation of the Hipparis near its mouth. Its miasmatic vapours made the city unhealthy, for which reason the inhabitants were anxious to drain it, but were counselled by the Delphic Oracle not to do it (Μὴ κίνει Καμάριναν· ἀκίνητος γὰρ ἀμείνων). In spite of this advice, the marsh was drained, and in consequence the city was laid open to attack on that side, and was captured. The story is doubtless apocryphal, but the words of the oracle passed into a proverb among the Greeks. See Verg. *Aen.* iii. 700, 701 and Serv. *ad loc.*

Cambūnii Montes. The mountains which separate Macedonia and Thessaly. They were a continuation of the Ceraunian Mountains, terminating in Mount Olympus on the east.

Cambȳses (Καμβύσης). (1) An early monarch of the line of the Achaemenides, the successor of Teïspes, who was himself the successor of Achaemenes. He must not be confounded with Cambyses the son of Cyrus, who was, in fact, the second of the name in the line of Persian kings (Herod. vii. 11). (2) A Persian of good family, to whom Astyages, king of Media, gave his daughter Mandané in marriage. The issue of this union was Cyrus the Great (Herod. i. 46, 107). (3) The son and successor of Cyrus the Great, ascended the throne of Persia B.C. 530. Soon after the commencement of his reign, he undertook the conquest of Egypt, being incited to the step, according to the Persian account as given in Herodotus (iii. 1), by the conduct of Amasis, the king of that country. Cambyses, it seems, had demanded in marriage the daughter of Amasis; but the latter, knowing that the Persian monarch intended to make her, not his wife, but his concubine, endeavoured to deceive him by sending in her stead the daughter of his predecessor Apries. The historian gives another account; but it is more than probable that both are untrue, and that ambitious feelings alone on the part of Cambyses prompted him to the enterprise. Amasis died before Cambyses marched against Egypt, and his son Psammenitus succeeded to the throne. A bloody battle was fought near the Pelusiac mouth of the Nile, and the Egyptians were put to flight, after which Cambyses made himself master of the whole country, and received tokens of submission also from the Cyrenaeans and the people of Barca. The kingdom of Egypt was thus conquered by him in six months. See AEGYPTUS.

Cambyses now formed new projects. He wished to send a squadron and subjugate Carthage, to conquer Aethiopia, and to make himself master of the famous temple of Zeus Ammon. The first of these expeditions, however, did not take place, because the Phœnicians, who composed his naval force, would not attack one of their own colonies. The army that was sent against the Ammonians perished in the desert, and the troops at whose head he himself had set out against the Aethiopians were compelled by hunger to retreat. How far he advanced into Aethiopia can not be ascertained from anything that Herodotus says. Diodorus Siculus, however (i. 33), makes Cambyses to have penetrated as far as the spot where Meroë stood, which city, according to this same writer, he founded. (See MEROË.) After his return from Aethiopia, the Persian king gave himself up to the greatest acts of outrage and cruelty. On entering Memphis he found the inhabitants engaged in celebrating the festival of the reappearance of Apis, and, imagining that these rejoicings were made on account of his ill success, he caused the sacred bull to be brought before him, stabbed him with his dagger, of which wound the animal afterwards died. He also ordered the priests to be scourged.

Cambyses is said to have been subject to epilepsy from his earliest years; and the habit of drinking, in which he now indulged to excess, rendered him at times completely furious. No relation was held sacred by him when intoxicated. Having dreamed that his brother Smerdis was seated on the royal throne, he sent one of his principal confidants to Persia, with orders to put him to death, a mandate which was actually accomplished. His sister and wife Atossa, who lamented the death of Smerdis, he kicked so severely as to bring on an abortion. These and many other actions, alike indicative of almost complete insanity, aroused against him the feelings of his subjects. A member of the order called the Magi availed himself of this discontent, and, aided by the strong resemblance which he bore to the murdered Smerdis, as well as by the exertions of a brother who was also a Magian, seized upon the throne of Persia, and sent heralds in every direction, commanding all to obey, for the time to come, Smerdis, son of Cyrus, and not Cambyses. The news of this usurpation reached Cambyses at a place in Syria called Ecbatana, where he was at that time with his army. Resolving to return with all speed to Susa, the monarch was in the act of mounting his horse, when his sword fell from its sheath and inflicted a mortal wound in his thigh. An oracle, it is said, had been given him from Butus that he would end his life at Ecbatana, but he had always thought that the Median Ecbatana was meant by it. He died of his wound soon after, B.C. 522, leaving no children. Ctesias gives a different account. He makes Cambyses to have died at Babylon of a wound he had given himself on the femoral muscle, while shaving smooth a piece of wood with a small knife. According to Herodotus (iii. 66), Cambyses reigned seven years and five months. See PERSIA.

Camēnae. Prophetic nymphs, belonging to the religion of ancient Italy, although later traditions represent their worship as introduced into Italy from Arcadia, and some accounts identify them with the Muses. The most important of these goddesses was Carmenta or Carmentis, who had a temple at the foot of the Capitoline Hill, and altars near the Porta Carmentalis. The traditions which assigned a Greek origin to her worship state that her original name was Nicostraté, and that she was the mother of Evander, with whom she came to Italy. On the etymology of the word Camena, which is usually regarded as = *Casmena*, from the root of *carmen*, "the songstress" (Mommsen), see Nettleship, *Essays in Latin Literature*, pp. 47–50 (Oxford, 1885).

Camerarius, JOACHIM (Ger. KAMMERMEISTER), born at Bamberg, April 12th, 1500, was next to Melanchthon among the scholars who contributed to reviving the study of classical antiquities in Germany. His family, originally LIEBHARD, established itself towards the middle of the fifteenth century in Franconia, and assumed the name of Camerarius from the hereditary office of chamberlain to the Prince-Bishop of Bamberg. Joachim was first led to the study of the classics by George Helt, at the University of Leipzig. In 1518, he went to Erfurt and began to teach Greek, and in 1521 joined Melanchthon at Wittenberg. He published a translation of the First Olynthiac of Demosthenes in 1524, and, after worsting Erasmus at Bâle, was appointed in 1526 Professor of Greek at Nuremberg, and was sent in 1530 as delegate to Augsburg, where he took a large part in the preparation of the Confession. In 1535 he was called to Tübingen, where he founded the classical course, and after six years undertook with great success the reorganization of the University of Leipzig, where he remained for the rest of his life. He died in 1574. Camerarius was renowned not only as a great teacher, but especially as an industrious editor. He was among the first to revise texts with scientific care, and left nearly 150 works on varied subjects. Besides a number of biographies and books connected with the Reformation, his chief work is his *Commentarii Linguae Graecae et Latinae* (Bâle, 1551). He also edited the orations of Demosthenes, Sophocles (1556), Quintilian (1534), Cicero, 4 vols. (1540), Herodotus, Thucydides, Plautus (1552), Theocritus, the *Ethics* of Aristotle, Theophrastus, and wrote a numismatical work, *Historia Rei Nummariae*. See Bursian, *Geschichte der Class. Philologie* (Munich, 1883), pp. 185–190; and W. Pökel, *Philolog. Schriftstellerlexicon* (Leipzig, 1882).

Cameria. An ancient town of Latium, conquered by Tarquinius Priscus.

Camerīnum or **Camarīnum**, more anciently CAMERS. The modern Camerino; a town in Umbria on the borders of Picenum, and subsequently a Roman colony.

Camerīnus. A Roman poet, contemporary with Ovid, who wrote a poem on the capture of Troy by Hercules (Ovid, *Epist. ex Pont.* iv. 16, 18).

Camīcus (Καμικός). An ancient town of the Sicani on the southern coast of Sicily, and on a river of the same name, occupying the site of the citadel of Agrigentum.

Camilla. A queen of the Volsci, and daughter of Metabus and Casmilla. Her father, who reigned at Privernum, having by his tyranny rendered himself odious to his subjects, was by them expelled from his dominions, and forced to take refuge from their fury in the lonely woods. Here he bred up the infant Camilla, the sole companion of his flight; and, having dedicated her to the service of Diana, he instructed her in the use of the bow and arrow, and accustomed her to the practice of martial and sylvan exercises. She was so remarkable for her swiftness that she is described by the poets as flying over the corn without bending the stalks, and skimming over the surface of the water without wetting her feet. Attended by a train of warriors, she led the Volscians to battle against Aeneas. Many brave chiefs fell by her hand; but she was at length herself killed by a soldier of the name of Aruns, who, from a place of concealment, aimed a javelin at her. Diana, however, who had foreseen this fatal event, had commissioned Opis, one of her nymphs, to avenge the death of Camilla, and Aruns was slain in his flight from the combat by the arrows of the goddess (Verg. *Aen.* vii. 803 foll.; xi. 532 foll.).

Camilli, Camillae. Boys and girls employed in the sacrifices of the Flamen Dialis, the Flaminica Dialis, and in general in religious rites and ceremonies. They were required to be perfect in form and sound in health, free-born, and with both their parents alive; or, in other words, according to the expression of the Romans, *pueri seu puellae ingenui, felicissimi, patrimi matrimique.* The origin of these words gave rise to various opinions among the ancients. Dionysius supposed them to correspond to the κάδμιλοι among the Curetes and Corybantes; others connected them with Cadmilus or Casmilus, one of the Samothracian Cabeiri; but we know nothing certain on the matter. (See CABEIRIA.) Respecting the employment of the Camilli at Roman marriages, see MATRIMONIUM.

Camillus, M. FURIUS. A celebrated Roman, called the second Romulus, from his services to his country. After filling various important stations, and, among other achievements, taking the city of Veii, which had for the space of ten years resisted the Roman arms, he encountered at last the displeasure of his countrymen, and was accused of having embezzled some of the plunder of this place. Being well aware how the matter would terminate, Camillus went into voluntary exile, although his friends offered to pay the sum demanded of him. During this period of separation from his country, Rome, with the exception of the Capitol, was taken by the Gauls under Brennus (q. v.). Camillus, though an exile, was invited by the fugitive Romans at Veii to take command of them, but refused to act until the wishes of the Romans besieged in the Capitol were known. These unanimously revoked the sentence of banishment, and elected him dictator. The noble-minded Roman forgot their previous ingratitude, and marched to the relief of his country; which he delivered, after it had been for some time in the possession of the enemy. The Roman account says that Camillus, at the head of an army of forty thousand men, hastened to Rome, where he found the garrison of the Capitol on the point of purchasing peace from the invaders. "With iron, and not with gold," exclaimed Camillus, "Rome buys her freedom." An attack was instantly made upon the Gauls, a victory obtained, and the foe left their camp by night. On the morrow Camillus overtook them, and they met with a total overthrow. His triumphal entry into Rome was made amid the acclamations of thousands, who greeted him with the name of Romulus, Father of his Country, and Second Founder of the City. After performing another equally important service, in prevailing upon his countrymen to rebuild their city and not return to Veii, and after gaining victories over the Aequi, Volsci, Etrurians, and Latins, he died in the eighty-ninth year of his age, having been five times dictator, once censor, three times interrex, twice military tribune, and having obtained four triumphs (Plut. *Camill.;* Liv. v. 46 foll.; Flor. i. 13; Verg. *Aen.* vi. 825). We have touched on merely a few of the events connected with the history of Camillus, in consequence of the strong suspicion which attaches itself to the greater part of the narrative. In no instance, perhaps, have the family memorials of the Roman aristocracy more completely usurped the place of true history than in the case of Camillus. The part relative to the overthrow of the Gauls appears to be pure fiction. See Mommsen, *Hist. of Rome,* bk. ii. ch. 4.

Camīnus (κάμινος). A chimney. See DOMUS.

Camīrus (Κάμειρος). A Dorian town on the western coast of the island of Rhodes, and the principal town in the island before the foundation of Rhodes. Here Pisander was born.

Camisia. A linen shirt worn next to the skin, is first mentioned in the fourth century by St. Jerome (*Ep.* 64, n. 11), from whom we learn that the word was used in the popular language, and that in his time the camisia was worn by soldiers. It is also mentioned by Isidorus, and by Paulus (Fest. s. v. *supparus,* p. 311, M.), who gives it as the equivalent of the older word *subucula.* From the word *camisia* comes the French *chemise.*

Camp. See CASTRA; EXERCITUS.

Campăgus. A kind of boot worn by the Roman emperors and military officers under the later Empire (Trebell. Poll. *Gallien.* 16, with the note of Salmasius).

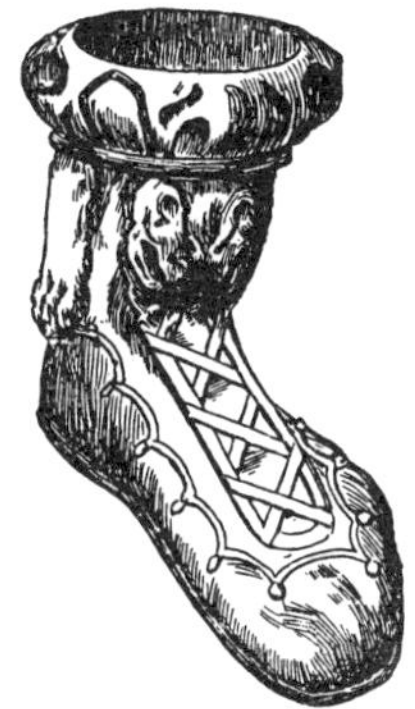

Campagus. (From Marble Statue of an Emperor found at Carthage.) (British Museum.)

Campana. A bell. See TINTINNABULUM.

Campāna Lex. See LEX.

Campania. A district of Italy, the name of which is probably derived from *campus,* "a plain." It was separated from Latium by the river Liris, and from Lucania at a later time by the river Silarus, though in the time of Augustus it did not extend farther south than the promontory of Minerva. In still earlier times, the "Ager Campanus" included only the country around Capua. Campania is a volcanic country, to which circumstance it mainly owed the extraordinary fertility for which it was celebrated in antiquity above all other lands. The fertility of the soil, allowing in parts three crops in a year, the beauty of the scenery, and the softness of the climate, the heat of which was tempered by the delicious breezes of the sea, procured for Campania the epithet Felix, a name which it justly deserved. It was the favourite retreat in summer of the Roman nobles, whose villas studded a considerable part of its coast, especially in the neighbourhood of Baiae (q. v.). The earliest inhabitants of the country were the Ausones and the Osci or Opici. These were subsequently conquered by the Etruscans, who became the masters of almost all the country. In the time of the Romans we find three distinct peoples, besides the Greek population of Cumae: (1) The CAMPĀNI, properly so called, a mixed race, consisting of Etruscans and the original inhabitants of the country, dwelling along the coast from Sinuessa to Paestum. They were the ruling race at Capua. (2) The SIDICĪNI, an Ausonian people, in the northwest of the country on the borders of Samnium. (3) The PICENTĪNI, in the southeastern part of the country.

Campaspé (Καμπάσπη). A mistress of Alexander the Great, immortalized by Apelles, to whom she sat as the model for his Aphrodité Anadyomené. See APELLES.

Campestré (sc. *subligar*). A kind of girdle or apron, which the Roman youths wore round their loins when they exercised naked in the Campus Martius. The campestré was sometimes worn in warm weather, in place of the tunic, under the toga (Hor. *Epist.* i. 11. 18).

Campidoctōres. Persons who, like the modern drill-sergeant, taught Roman soldiers their exercises. In the times of the Republic this duty was discharged by a centurion, or a veteran soldier of merit and distinction. See Plin. *Paneg.* 13.

Campi Raudii. A plain in the north of Italy, near Vercellae, where Marius and Catulus defeated the Cimbri in B.C. 101.

Campus Martius. The term *campus* (κάμπος) belongs to the language of Sicily, in which it signified a hippodrome or race-course; but among the Romans it was used to denote an open plain, covered with herbage, and set apart for the purpose of exercise or amusement. Eight of these plains are enumerated by P. Victor as appertaining to the city of Rome, among which the most celebrated was the Campus Martius, so called because it was consecrated to the god Mars. Some difference exists between Livy and Dionysius Halicarnassus respecting the period at which this consecration took place. The former states that upon the expulsion of the Tarquins the people took possession of their property (*ager Tarquiniorum*), situated between the city and the Tiber, and assigned it to the god of war, by whose name it was subsequently distinguished; whereas the latter says that the Ager Tarquiniorum had been usurped from that divinity, to whom it belonged of old, and appropriated by the Tarquins, so that it was only restored to its original service upon their expulsion, a statement which gains confirmation from a law of Numa, quoted by Festus, *secunda spolia in Martis aram in campo solitaurilia utra voluerit caedito.*

From the greater extent and importance of this plain beyond all the others, it was often spoken of as "the plain," κατ' ἐξοχήν, without any epithet to distinguish it; and, therefore, whenever the word is so used, it is the Campus Martius which is to be understood as always referred to.

The general designation, Campus Martius, comprised two plains, which, though generally spoken of collectively, are sometimes distinguished. The former of these was the so-called Ager Tarquiniorum, to which Juvenal refers, *inde Superbi Totum regis agrum;* the other was given to the Roman people by the vestal virgin Gaia Taratia or Suffetia, and is sometimes called Campus Tiberinus, and sometimes Campus Minor.

It is difficult to determine the precise limits of the Campus Martius, but in general terms it may be described as situated between the Via Lata and Via Flaminia on the north, the Via Recta on the south; as bounded by the Tiber on the west, and the Pantheon and gardens of Agrippa towards the east; and the Campus Minor, or Tiberinus, occupied the lower portion of the circuit towards the Via Recta, from the Pons Aelius to the Pons Ianiculensis. See PONS.

That the Campus Martius was originally without the city is apparent—first, from the passages of Livy and Dionysius above referred to; secondly, from the custom of holding the Comitia Centuriata there, which could not be held within the Pomoerium; hence the word *campus* is put for the comitia, which also explains the expression of Cicero, *fors domina campi*, and of Lucan, *venalis campus*, which means "the corrupt voters"; thirdly, because the generals who demanded a triumph, not being allowed to enter the city, remained with their armies in the Campus Martius; and, finally, because it was not lawful to bury within the city, whereas the monuments of the illustrious dead were among the most striking ornaments with which it was embellished. (See SEPULCRUM.) But it was included in the city by Aurelian when he enlarged the walls.

The principal edifices which adorned this famous plain are described by Strabo. It was covered with perpetual verdure, and was a favourite resort for air, exercise, or recreation when the labours of the day were over. Its ample area was crowded by the young, who there initiated themselves in all warlike and athletic exercises, and in the games usual to the palaestra; for which purpose the contiguous Tiber rendered it peculiarly appropriate in early times, before public baths were established. Hence *campus* is used as "a field" for any exercise, mental or bodily. Wooden horses were also kept in the Campus Martius—under porticos in winter, and in the open plain during summer—in order to give expertness in mounting and dismounting; a necessary practice when stirrups were not in use (Veget. i. 23). Horse-races (*equiria*) also took place here, except when the Campus was overflowed. The Campus Martius is the most densely populated portion of modern Rome. See ROMA.

Campus Scelerātus. A place within the walls of Rome, near the Porta Collina, where Vestal Virgins who had lost their chastity were buried alive (Liv. viii. 15). It was unlawful to bury the dead within the city, or to slay a vestal; but both these restrictions were evaded by a living entombment. See Festus, s. v. *probrum;* Suet. *Domit.* 8; Plin. *Epist.* iv. 11; Mayor on Juv. iv. 10; and the article VESTALES.

Camus. See CAPISTRUM.

Canăbus (κάναβος or κάνναβος). A wooden stock or framework used by potters and sculptors round which the clay was laid (Poll. vii. 164). In small statues (*sigilla*) and vessels it was of the simplest description, and mostly of the form of a cross, *crux* or *stipes* (Tertull. *Apol.* 12; *ad Nat.* i. 12). It is applied to very lean persons (Strattis *ap.* Pollux, x. 189; *Anth. P.* xi. 107), as we should say "a skeleton." It is the same word as the Latin *cannaba*, "a booth," both signifying a construction like a scaffold or framework. The word seems to have been also used for the outline figure which sculptors and painters used as a model (Suidas, s. h. v.).

Canăcé (Κανάκη). The daughter of Aeolus and Enareté, and mistress of Poseidon, by whom she had several children. She entertained an unnatural passion for her brother Macareus, and was punished by her father with death, or, according to another version, committed suicide with Macareus. See Apollod. i. 7, 3; Hyg. *Fab.* 238, 242; Ovid, *Heroid.* xi.

Canăchus (Κάναχος). A statuary of Sicyon, who studied his art under Polycletus (q. v.) at the beginning of the fifth century B.C. His chief work was a colossal Apollo in the Branchidae Sanctuary at Miletus, known to us by a bronze statuette in

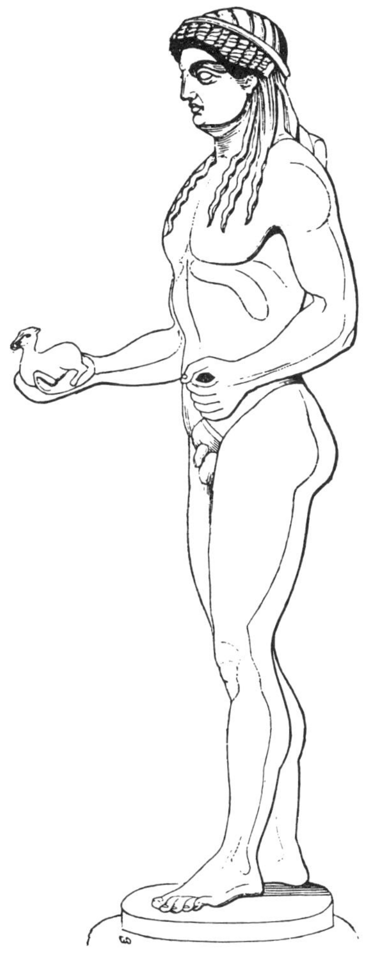

Apollo of Canachus. (British Museum.)

the British Museum. He also made the chryselephantine Aphroditê kept in Sicyon. His brother, Aristocles, was almost equally celebrated in the same department of art.

Canalicŭlus. Properly a small channel or canal, and also used in the following special senses: to denote (1) the channel or barrel of a catapult (Vitruv. x. 15); (2) a splint (Cels. viii. 2); (3) the grooves carved on the face of a triglyph between the three uprights (*femina*, *μηροί*), while those at each end where the outside *femina* sank to the level of the metope were called *semicanaliculi.* See CANALIS; COLUMNA.

Canālis (σωλήν). A channel or canal, is used, like its English derivatives, to signify a watercourse, whether open or closed, and next any other passage which resembles a watercourse.

The method of constructing conduits is described by Vitruvius (viii. 7), who distinguishes the canalis, which is lined with masonry (*structilis*), from the leaden *fistula* and the earthenware *tubulus.* A ruder kind of conduit was made of timber or earthenware to carry water from a spring or stream to cattle in a meadow. Again, *canalis* denotes a feeding-trough, which was in the case of domestic birds placed inside their house, and fed from the outside by pipes (Varro, *R. R.* iii. 7, 8; 11, 12).

Similarly *canalis* denotes the channel of a sewer, as, for instance, that in the Forum, which is at one spot exposed to view, and was a favourite station for loungers (Plaut. *Curc.* iv. 1, 15).

Canalis is also a trench or vein in a gold-mine (Plin. *H. N.* xxxiii. § 68); the barrel or channel for missiles (σῦριγξ) in a catapult (Vitruv. x. 13, 7); a reed-pipe (Calp. *Ecl.* iv. 76); in the medical writers, a splint (Cels. viii. 10, 65) or a canal of the human body (id. iv. 1, 38); and finally, in architecture, the "channel" or flat surface running between the *abacus* and the *echinus* inside the volute, as in the accompanying cut from one of the triglyphs of the temple of Segesta in Sicily. See COLUMNA.

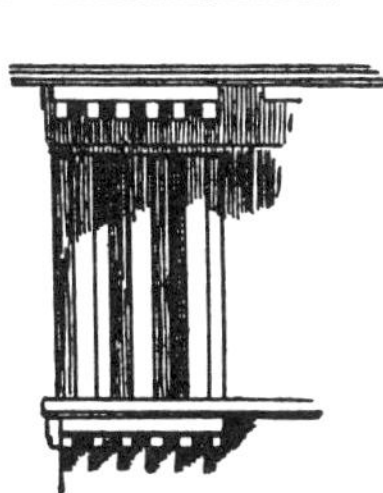

Canalis in Architecture.

Canaria (Καναρία). The largest of the cluster of islands called by the ancients Beatae and Fortunatae Insulae (q. v.), and now the Canary Islands. Pliny says that this island derived its name from the number of very large-sized dogs (*canes*) which it contained.

Canăthron (κάναρθον or κάνναθρον). A Laconian car made of wood, with an arched plaited covering (hence the derivation probably from κάννα, "a reed"), in which the Spartan ladies used to go to Amyclae for the celebration of the Hyacinthia. We may compare the Roman *pilentum* (q. v.). (See Polycrates in Athenaeus, xv. 4, 139 f.) The nature of its adornments was at times fantastic. Eustath. on *Il.* xxiv. 190 is in error in stating that κάνναθρον and πείρινς are the same. The latter is a basket put into the chariot, and used for holding the necessaries for a journey, and also for a seat (Buchholz, *Hom. Real.* ii. 1, 228).

Cancellarius. See CANCELLI.

Cancelli (κιγκλίδες, δρύφακτοι). A screen or lattice of open work, placed before a window, a doorway, the tribunal of a judge, or any other place. At Athens, in the Senate-house and law-courts δρύφακτοι were the inner partition, and κιγκλίδες the gates opening into it. Balconies projecting from the fronts of houses were also δρύφακτοι (*maeniana*). The material was originally wood, as the name δρύφακτος shows (L. and S. s. v.); and such were also the cancelli put up at Rome for temporary purposes, as when funeral games were given in the Forum (*cancelli fori*, Cic. *pro Sest.* 58, § 124; cf. Ov. *Am.* iii. 2, 64). But they might also be in metal, as in the cancelli before the Temple of Vesta, rebuilt by Severus, conjecturally restored by Lanciani from existing remains, or in marble. In the Basilica Iulia, low marble screens or cancelli shut in the otherwise open arches on the ground floor; and a great number of fragments of these screens are now scattered about the Forum.

Hence was derived the word *cancellarius*, which originally signified a porter who stood at the latticed or grated door of the emperor's palace. The cancellarius also signified a legal scribe or secretary who sat within the cancelli, or lattice-work, by which the crowd was kept off from the tribunals of the judges (Cassiod. *Var.* xi. 6). The chief scribe or secretary was called cancellarius κατ' ἐξοχήν, and was eventually invested with judicial power at Constantinople. From this word has come the modern "chancellor."

Candăcé (Κανδάκη). A name given to the queen-mothers in Meroë in Aethiopia. Some women of this name appear in history, but they seem to have been merely queen-regents, governing during the minority of their sons. Some ancient authors, however, state that it was customary for the Aethiopians to be governed by queens called each by the name of Candacé. Suidas speaks of a Candacé who was made prisoner by Alexander the Great, but this appears to be a mere fable. A Candacé, blind of one eye, made an irruption into Egypt during the reign of Augustus, B.C. 22. She took and pillaged several cities, but Petronius, the prefect of Egypt, pursued her and penetrated into her dominions, which he pillaged in turn, until she restored the booty which she had carried off from Egypt, and sued for peace (Dio Cass. lxiv. 5; Plin. *H. N.* vi. 29). Mention is also made in the sacred writings of a queen of Aethiopia named Candacé (Acts, viii. 27).

Candaules (Κανδαύλης). A monarch of Lydia, the last of the Heraclidae, dethroned by Gyges at the instigation of his own queen, whom he had insulted by showing her when naked to Gyges. (Consult Herod. i. 7 foll.) His true name appears to have been Myrsilus, and the appellation of Candaules to have been assumed by him as a title of honour, this latter being, in the Lydian language, equivalent to Heracles—i. e. the Sun.

Candavia (Κανδαουΐα), CANDAVII MONTES. The mountains separating Illyricum from Macedonia, across which the Via Egnatia ran.

Candēla. A candle, made either of wax (*cerea*) or tallow (*sebacea*), was used universally by the Romans before the invention of oil lamps (*lucernae*) (Varr. *L. L.* v. § 119). They had for a wick the pith of a kind of rush called *scirpus* (Plin. *H. N.* xvi. § 178). In Livy (xl. 29) *fasces candelis involuti* appear to be packets wrapped up in a kind of waxed cloth. In later times candelae were only used by the poorer classes; the houses of the more wealthy were always lighted by *lucernae* (Juv. iii. 287). See Becker-Göll, *Gallus*, ii. 390.

Candelābrum (λυχνεῖον, λυχνίον, λύχνιον, λυχνία). Originally a candlestick, but afterwards used to support lamps (λυχνοῦχος), in which signification the word most commonly occurs. The candelabra of this kind were usually made to stand upon the ground, and were of a considerable height. The most common sorts were made of wood (Cic. *ad Q. Fratr.* iii. 7); but those which have been found in Herculaneum and Pompeii are mostly of bronze. Sometimes they were made of the more precious metals, and even of jewels, as was the one which Antiochus intended to dedicate to Iupiter Capitolinus (Cic. *Verr.* iv. 28). In the temples of the gods and in palaces there were frequently large candelabra made of marble and fastened to the ground.

There is a great resemblance in the general plan and appearance of most of the candelabra which have been found. They usually consist of three parts: (1) the foot (βάσις); (2) the shaft or stem (καυλός); (3) the plinth or tray (δισκός), large enough for a lamp to stand on, or with a socket to receive a wax candle. The foot usually consists of three lions' or griffins' feet, ornamented with leaves; and the shaft, which is either plain or fluted, generally ends in a kind of capital on which the tray rests for supporting the lamp. Sometimes we find a figure between the capital and the tray, as is seen in the candelabrum on the right hand in the annexed illustration, which represents

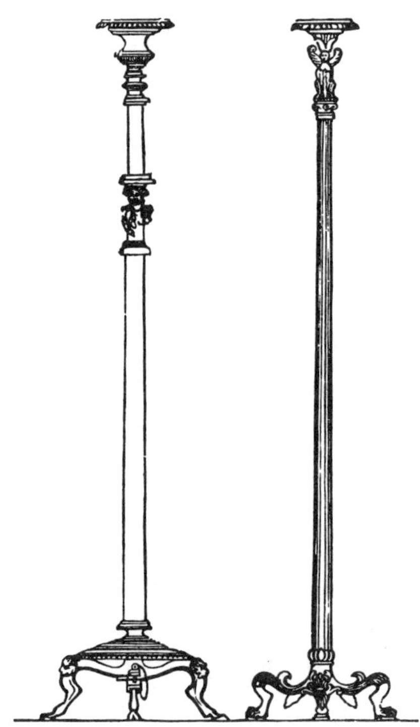

Pompeian Candelabra. (Naples.)

candelabra found in Pompeii, and now in the Museo Nazionale at Naples. The one on the left hand is also a representation of a candelabrum found in the same city, and is made with a sliding shaft, by which the light might be raised or lowered at pleasure.

The best candelabra were made at Aegina and Tarentum (Plin. *H. N.* xxxiv. 6).

There are also candelabra of various other forms, though those which have been given above are by far the most common. They sometimes consist of a figure supporting a lamp, or of a figure by the side of which the shaft is placed with two branches, each of which terminates in a flat disk, upon which a lamp was placed. A candelabrum of the

Pompeian Candelabrum. (Naples.)

latter kind is given in the preceding illustration. The stem is formed of a liliaceous plant; and at the base is a mass of bronze, on which a Silenus is seated, engaged in trying to pour wine from a skin which he holds in his left hand, into a cup in his right.

There was another kind of candelabrum, entirely different from those which have been described, which did not stand upon the ground, but was placed upon the table. These candelabra usually consist of pillars, from the capitals of which several lamps hang down, or of trees, from whose branches lamps also are suspended. The preceding illustration represents a very elegant candelabrum of this kind, found in Pompeii.

Pompeian Candelabrum. (Naples.)

The original, including the stand, is three feet high. The pillar is not placed in the centre, but at one end of the plinth, which is the case in almost every candelabrum of this description yet found. The plinth is inlaid in imitation of a vine, the leaves of which are of silver, the stem and fruit of bright bronze. On one side is an altar with wood and fire upon it, and on the other a Bacchus riding upon a tiger.

Candidātus. See Ambitus.

Candles. See Candela; Fax.

Candys (κάνδυς). A gown worn by the Medes and Persians over their trousers and other garments (Xen. *Anab.* i. 5, § 8). It had wide sleeves, and was made of woollen cloth, which was either purple or of some other splendid colour. In the Persepolitan sculptures, nearly all the principal personages are clothed in it.

Candys. (Persepolitan Sculpture.)

Canephoria (κανηφορία). The office of a *canephorus* (q. v.).

Canephŏrus (κανηφόρος). A basket-bearer. The κάνειον or κανοῦν, derived from κάννα, "a reed," was in the Homeric times a basket used for holding bread (*Il.* ix. 217) or other edibles for meals, or the sacred οὐλαί for sacrifice (*Od.* iii. 441). Some few golden utensils were used in state sacrifices, though the usual κανᾶ πομπικά were no doubt χαλκᾶ (Michaelis, *Parthenon*, p. 259). One of silver is referred to in the *C. I. G.* 2855, 19, and one of earthenware in Dion. H. ii. 23 (Grimm). At Athens the κανοῦν was used in religious service only. A particular part of the ceremony seems to have been called κανοῦν or κανᾶ, when the basket was carried round the altar (Eur. *H. F.* 926), laid down, and the οὐλαί taken therefrom. Κάναστρον signifies a bowl and also a dish made of cork or earthenware (Hom. *Epig.* xiv. 3). The Roman *canistrum* was used for just the same purposes as the Homeric κανοῦν—viz., for holding bread, necessaries for sacrifice, and remains of a feast (Hor. *Sat.* ii. 6, 105). Its epithets signify "flat"—e. g. *patulis*, *lata*, etc.

They were, then, flat baskets used, among other purposes, for carrying the requisites for religious ceremonies. At the Panathenaea they were carried by adult maidens of high birth, who were genuine native Athenians; but when a private individual sacrificed, his daughter or some maiden of his family acted as his *canephorus*.

Canephori. (British Museum.)

An antefixa in the British Museum (see illustration) represents two canephori approaching a candelabrum. Each of them elevates one arm to support the basket, while she slightly raises her tunic with the other.

Canes and Walking-sticks. See BACULUM.

Caniculāres Dies. Certain days in the summer, preceding and ensuing the heliacal rising of Canicula, or the dog-star, in the morning. The ancients believed that this star, rising with the sun, and joining his influence to the fire of that luminary, was the cause of the extraordinary heat which usually prevailed in that season; and accordingly they gave the name of *dog-days* to about six or eight weeks of the hottest part of summer. This idea originated with the Egyptians, and was borrowed from them by the Greeks. The Romans sacrificed a brown dog every year to Canicula, at its rising, to appease its rage. See SIRIUS.

Canidia. A Neapolitan courtesan, whose real name was perhaps Gratidia, beloved by Horace; but when she deserted him he revenged himself by holding her up to contempt as an old sorceress (*Epod.* v.; *Sat.* i. 8), though his famous palinode (*Carm.* i. 16), beginning *O matre pulchra filia pulchrior* is thought by some to have been intended as an apology to her.

Canis (*κύων*). (1) The dog; an animal domesticated among the ancients, and used for hunting, for guarding houses, and also kept as a pet. In Egypt it was even held in reverence, and at Cynopolis received divine honours in the person of the dog-headed (or jackal-headed) god Anubis (q. v.). Artemis was said to have given Procris a dog that was always sure of its prey, and from this dog tradition derived the mighty Molossian hounds and those of Sparta. The mastiff (*canis Anglicus*) was imported into Rome from Britain, and was carefully bred for the wild-beast fights (*venationes*) in the amphitheatre. Lap-dogs (*catuli*) were reared in Melita (Malta). House-dogs took the place of the modern domestic cat, a creature unknown to the Greeks and Romans. See FAELIS. (2) See SIRIUS.

Canistrum (*κάναστρον*). See CANEPHORUS.

Canna (*κάννα*). A cane or reed. See CALAMUS.

Cannae. A small village of Apulia, situated about five miles from Canusium, towards the sea, and at no great distance from the Aufidus. It was celebrated for the defeat of the Romans by Hannibal. Polybius tells us that, as a town, it was destroyed the year before the battle was fought, which took place on May 21st, B.C. 216. The citadel, however, was preserved, and the circumstance of its occupation by Hannibal seems to have been regarded by the Romans of sufficient importance to cause them considerable uneasiness and annoyance. It commanded, indeed, all the adjacent country, and was their principal southern depot of stores and provisions. The Greek writers, especially Polybius, generally use the name in the singular, *Κάννα*.

The decisive victory at Cannae was owing to three combined causes: the excellent arrangements of Hannibal, the superiority of the Numidian horse, and the skilful manœuvre of Hasdrubal in opposing only the light-armed cavalry against that of the Romans, while he employed the heavy horse, divided into small parties, in repeated attacks on different parts of the Roman rear. The Roman army contained 80,000 infantry and 6000 cavalry, the Carthaginians 40,000 infantry and 10,000 cavalry. Hannibal drew up his forces in the form of a convex crescent, having his centre thrown forward before the wings. He commanded the centre in person, and here he had purposely stationed his worst troops; the best were posted at the extremities of each wing, which would enable them to act with decisive advantage as bodies of reserve, they being, in fact, the rear of the other forces. Hasdrubal commanded the left wing, Hanno the right. On the Roman side, want of union between the two consuls, and want of spirit among the men, afforded a sure omen of the fortune of the day. Aemilius commanded the right, Varro the left wing; the proconsuls, Regulus and Servius, who had been consuls the preceding year, had command of the centre. What Hannibal foresaw took place. The charge of the Romans, and their immense superiority in numbers, at length broke his centre, which, giving way inward, his army now assumed the shape of a concave crescent. The Romans, in the ardour of pursuit, were carried so far as to be completely surrounded. Both flanks were assailed by the veterans of Hannibal, who were armed in the Roman manner; at the same time the cavalry of the Carthaginians attacked their rear, and the broken centre, rallying, attacked them in front. The consequence was that they were nearly all cut to pieces. The two proconsuls, together with Aemilius the consul, were slain. Varro escaped with seventy horse to Venusia. The Romans lost on the field of battle 70,000 men; and 10,000 who had not been present in the fight were made prisoners. The Carthaginian loss amounted to 5500 infantry and 200 cavalry. Such is the account of Polybius, whose statement of the fight is much clearer and more satisfactory than that of Livy. Hannibal has been censured for not marching immediately to Rome after the battle, in which city all was consternation. But an explanation of his conduct may be found under the article HANNIBAL. See also the account in Col. Dodge's valuable military study, *Hannibal* (N. Y. 1891).

Canoe. See CYMBA.

Canon (*κανών*). A word probably derived from *κάννα*, "a reed," and properly meaning a straight rod. Its special applications are as follows:

(1) In the Homeric shield, the *κανόνες* are the bars to which the shoulder-belt (*τελαμών*) was attached; or two parallel bars used as handles, through one of which the warrior placed his arm while he grasped the other. See the accompanying illustration.

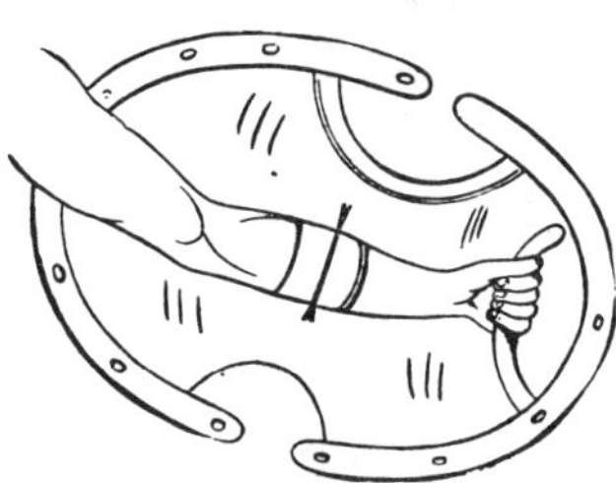

Canones on Homeric Shield.

(2) In weaving, a straight round rod to which the alternate threads of the warp were attached by means of strings having loops at each end, one loop fastening the string to the *κανών*, the other fastening it to the warp. This arrangement of strings and loops was called *μίτος* by the Greeks and *licia* by the Romans.

(3) A carpenter's rule, much like our own. See REGULA.

(4) The beam of a balance, more often called *ζυγόν* (*Anth. Pal.* xi. 334).

(5) Horizontal curtain-poles of silver-gilt (Chares *ap.* Athen. 538 d).

(6) In a figurative sense, *κανών* came to be used for whatever served as a rule, model, or norm. Thus, of grammatical rules (Auson. *Epigr.* 136), of the laws of style (Cic. *Ad Fam.* xvi. 17, 1), of logical tests of truth (Diog. Laërt. x. 27), and of the rules of sculpture (Galen. iv. 354–355 Kühn).

(7) In the fiscal affairs of the later Empire, *canon* was used of the regular payments of tribute, especially of corn sent to the capital (*Cod. Th.* xiv. 15, 3).

Canon Alexandrīnus. The so-called Alexandrian Canon, arranged by Aristophanes of Byzantium (q. v.) and his disciple Aristarchus (q. v.). The daily increasing multitude of books of every kind had become so great that there was no expression, however faulty, for which precedent might not be found; and as there were far more bad than good writers, the authority and weight of numbers were likely to prevail, and the language, consequently, to grow more and more corrupt. It was thought necessary, therefore, to draw a line between those classic writers to whose authority an appeal in matter of language might be made and the common herd of inferior authors. In the most cultivated modern tongues it seems to have been found expedient to erect some such barrier against the inroads of corruption; and to this preservative caution we are indebted for the vocabulary of the Academicians della Crusca, and the list of authors therein cited as affording *testi di lingua.* To this, also, we owe the great dictionaries of the Academies of France and Spain of their respective languages. But as for the example first set in this matter by the Alexandrian critics, its effects upon their own literature have been of a doubtful nature. In so far as the Canon has contributed to preserve to us some of the best authors included in it, we can not but rejoice. On the other hand, there is reason to believe that the comparative neglect into which those not received into it were sure to fall has been the occasion of the loss of a vast number of writers who would have been, if not for their language, yet for their matter, very precious; and who, perhaps, in many cases, were not easily to be distinguished, even on the score of style, from those that were preferred. The details of the Canon are as follows: (1) EPIC POETS. Homer, Hesiod, Pisander, Panyasis, Antimachus. (2) IAMBIC POETS. Archilochus, Simonides, Hipponax. (3) LYRIC POETS. Alcman, Alcaeus, Sappho, Stesichorus, Pindar, Bacchylides, Ibycus, Anacreon, Simonides. (4) ELEGIAC POETS. Callinus, Mimnermus, Philetas, Callimachus. (5) TRAGIC POETS. *First Class:* Aeschylus, Sophocles, Euripides, Ion, Achaeus, Agathon. *Second Class,* or *Tragic Pleiades:* Alexander the Aetolian, Philiscus of Corcyra, Sositheus, Homer the younger, Aeantides, Sosiphanes or Sosicles, Lycophron. (6) COMIC POETS. *Old Comedy:* Epicharmus, Cratinus, Eupolis, Aristophanes, Pherecrates, Plato. *Middle Comedy:* Antiphanes, Alexis. *New Comedy:* Menander, Philippides, Diphilus, Philemon, Apollodorus. (7) HISTORIANS. Herodotus, Thucydides, Xenophon, Theopompus, Ephorus, Philistus, Anaximenes, Callisthenes. (8) ORATORS. The ten Attic orators: Antiphon, Andocides, Lysias, Isocrates, Isaeus, Aeschines, Lycurgus, Demosthenes, Hyperides, Dinarchus. (9) PHILOSOPHERS. Plato, Xenophon, Aeschines, Aristotle, Theophrastus. (10) THE POETIC PLEIADES. Seven poets of the same epoch with one another: Apollonius the Rhodian, Aratus, Philiscus, Homer the younger, Lycophron, Nicander, Theocritus. See Couat, *La Poésie Alexandrine* (Paris, 1882); Susemihl, *Geschichte d. griech. Litteratur in der Alexand. Zeit,* 2 vols. (1892); and the article ALEXANDRIAN SCHOOL.

Canopĭcum (or **Canobĭcum**) **Ostĭum.** The westernmost mouth of the Nile, twelve miles from Alexandria. See NILUS.

Canōpus (Κάνωπος) or **Canōbus.** An important city on the coast of Lower Egypt, twelve geographical miles east of Alexandria. It was near the westernmost mouth of the Nile, which was hence called the Canopic mouth. It was celebrated for a great temple of Serapis, for its commerce, its luxury, and its debauchery. Here was prepared the dye known as henna, which the women of the East have always used to stain their finger-tips (Herod. ii. 113). Before the founding of Alexandria (q. v.) it was a most important place, but after B.C. 300, its greatness declined.

Cantăbri. A fierce and warlike people in the north of Spain, bounded on the east by the Astures, and on the west by the Autrigones. They were subdued by Augustus after a struggle of several years (B.C. 25–19).

Cantăbrum. A standard used in the time of the Roman Empire. Its form is unknown. See Tertull. *Apol.* 16.

Canthărus (*κάνθαρος*). (1) A kind of boat, of which little is known. See Aristoph. *Pax,* 143. (2) A drinking-cup, furnished with handles (*cantharus ansa*). It is said by some writers to have derived its name from one Cantharus, who first made cups of this form; according to others, from the resemblance to an inverted beetle (*κάνθαρος*). The cantharus was the cup sacred to Dionysus, who is frequently represented on ancient vases holding it in his hand, as in the following illustration, which is taken from a painting on an ancient vase, given by Millin (*Peintures Antiques,* pl. 53).

Dionysus with Cantharus. (From a Vase.)

Cantĭcum. A technical term of the Roman stage. In the narrower sense it denoted a melody or air composed in changing rhythms, the text to which was sung behind the stage to the accompaniment of a flute, while the actor expressed the meaning by pantomime. In Cicero's time, however, the *cantica* were sometimes performed by the actors. In a wider sense the word might mean any part in a play which was not simply recited, but sung or performed in melodrama with musical accompaniments. See DRAMA.

Cantium. A district of Britain, nearly the same as the modern Kent, but including Londinium (q. v.). The name is derived from the Keltic *kant*, an angle or curve.

Canulēia Lex. See LEX.

Canulēius, GAIUS. A Roman tribune of the people, who in B.C. 445 made a law permitting the marriage of patricians with plebeians, and also requiring that one of the two consuls should be chosen annually from among the plebeians. See Livy, iv. 3, etc.

Canusium (Κανύσιον). The modern Canosa. An important town in Apulia, on the Aufidus, founded, according to tradition, by Diomedes. It was, at all events, a Greek colony, and both Greek and Oscan were spoken there in the time of Horace. It was celebrated for its mules and its woollen manufactures, but had only a deficient supply of water. Many beautiful Greek vases have been discovered here, as well as coins and other remains. Livy states that the fugitives of the Roman army after the defeat at Cannae (q. v.) were generously received here, and treated with much kindness by Busa, a wealthy lady of the city. See Livy, xxii. 52.

Cap. See GALERUS; PILLEUS.

Capăneus (Καπανεύς). Son of Hipponoüs, and one of the seven heroes who marched against Thebes. He was struck by Zeus with lightning as he was scaling the walls of Thebes, because he had dared to defy the god. While his body was burning, his wife Evadné leaped into the flames and destroyed herself. See SEVEN AGAINST THEBES.

Capella. See CAPRA.

Capella. (1) MARTIĀNUS MINEUS FELIX. A poet, born, according to Cassiodorus, at Madaura in Africa; he calls himself, however, at the end of his work, "the foster-child of the city of Elissa"; whether it be that he was born at Carthage, or else received his education there, which latter is the more probable opinion of the two. The MSS., however, give him the title of "the Carthaginian." In process of time he attained to proconsular dignity, but whether he was a Christian or not is a matter of uncertainty. About the middle of the fifth century of our era he wrote at Rome a work bearing the appellation of *Satira* or *Satyricon*, divided into nine books. It is a species of encyclopædia, half prose and half verse, modelled after the Varronian satire. The first two books form a detached and separate work, entitled *De Nuptiis Philologiae et Mercurii*, and treating of the apotheosis of Philology and her marriage with Mercury. We find in it, among other things, a description of heaven, which shows that the mystic notions of the Platonists of that day approximated in a very singular manner to the truths of Christianity. In the seven following books Capella treats of the seven sciences which formed at that time the circle of human study—namely, grammar, logic, rhetoric, geometry, astrology (astronomy), arithmetic, and music, which comprehends poetry. (See LIBERALES ARTES.) This work, written in an exaggerated and pedantic style, was introduced into the schools in the Middle Ages; hence it was frequently copied, and the text has become extremely corrupt. The prosody shows that accent had begun to destroy the distinction of quantity, for we find, e. g., *lŏquax*, *flăgitaret*, *Canŏpus*, etc. On the text, see Dick, *De Martiano Capella Emendando* (Berne, 1885). The best edition of Capella is that of Eyssenhardt (Leipzig, 1866); the *editio princeps* was that of Bodianus (Vincent. 1499). The distinguished jurist, Grotius, edited the work when only fourteen years of age. (2) An elegiac poet, mentioned with commendation by Ovid (*Pont.* xvi. 36). We have no remains of his productions.

Capēna. (1) A gate of Rome, now the gate of St. Sebastian, in the southeast part of modern Rome. (2) A city of Etruria, southeast of Mount Soracté.

Caper, FLAVIUS. A Roman grammarian who flourished under Trajan. Of him we have two small treatises on orthography and doubtful words. Text in Keil's *Grammatici Latini*, vol. vii.

Capĕtus Silvius. See SILVIUS.

Caphāreus (Καφηρεύς). The modern Capo d' Oro; a rocky and dangerous promontory on the southeast coast of Euboea, where the Greek fleet is said to have been wrecked on its return from Troy (Eurip. *Troad.* 90).

Capis (also called CAPĒDO, CAPŬLA, and CAPEDUNCŬLA). A small earthen vessel or pitcher used in sacrifices. It had handles and is sometimes spoken of as a pitcher (*urceolus*), and sometimes as a cup (*poculum*). It is joined with the *lituus* among the sacred implements of the augurs, and both are often represented together on coins and medals.

Capistrum (φορβειά, κημός, φιμός). A word derived from *capio*, and denoting first of all a halter for animals, and apparently made of leather. It was used in holding the head of a quadruped which required any healing operation, in retaining animals at the stall, and in fastening them to the yoke. In representations of Bacchanalian processions, the tigers or panthers are attached to the yoke by capistra made of vine-branches.

Tigers with Capistra. (Vatican.)

In ploughing fields which were planted with vines or other trees, the halter had a small basket attached to it, enclosing the mouth, so as to prevent the ox from cropping the tender shoots (*fiscel-*

lis capistrari). Also, when goatherds wished to obtain milk for making cheese, they fastened a muzzle or capistrum, armed with iron points, about the mouth of the kid, to prevent it from sucking.

Capistrum. (From an Etruscan Vase.)

Bands of similar materials were used to tie vines to the poles (*pali*) or transverse rails (*iuga*) of a trellis.

The term φορβειά was also applied to a contrivance used by pipers (αὐληταί) and trumpeters to compress their mouths and cheeks, and thus to aid them in blowing. This was said to be the invention of Marsyas.

Capĭta aut Navia (NAVIM). "Heads or tails"; the name of a game derived from the fact that the early *as* had on one side a double-faced Ianus, and

Early As, showing Head and Prow of Ship.

on the other the prow of a ship. See AS. (Macrob. *Sat.* i. 7, 22; Fest. s. v. *navia*, p. 169 M.).

Capĭtal. A kerchief of woollen or linen cloth worn round the head by Roman women in early times, and, after it had gone out of general use, retained as part of the costume of certain priestesses (Varr. *L. L.* v. 180). Among these were the Vestals; a coin engraved by Saglio shows a kerchiefed female head and the letters V. V. —i. e. *Virgo Vestalis;* but not the Flaminica (Rich), whose coiffure was undoubtedly the *tutulus* (q. v.).

Capitālis. See CAPUT.

Capital Letters. See ALPHABET; MAIUSCULA.

Capĭte Censi. See CAPUT.

Capĭtis Deminutio. See DEMINUTIO CAPITIS.

Capitium. A portion of a woman's dress, said by Varro to be so called because it covers (*capit*) the breast (Varr. *L. L.* v. 131). The word itself might lead us to suppose that it was originally, like *capital*, a covering for the head; but there is express testimony that it was worn over the tunic, covering the breast and not the head.

Capĭto, ATĒIUS. See ATEIUS CAPITO.

Capĭto, C. FONTĒIUS. A friend of M. Antonius (q. v.), who accompanied Maecenas to Brundisium, B.C. 37, when the latter was sent to effect a reconciliation between Octavianus and Antony.

Capitoline Venus. See VENUS.

Capitoline Wolf. See ROMULUS.

Capitolīni Ludi. See LUDI.

Capitolīnus. (1) A surname of Iupiter, from his temple on the Mons Capitolinus. (2) A surname of M. Manlius (q. v.), who, for his ambition in aspiring to sovereign power, was thrown down from the Tarpeian Rock, which he had so nobly defended (Flor. i. 13 and 26). (3) MONS, one of the seven hills on which Rome was built, containing the citadel and fortress of the Capitol. (See CAPITOLIUM.) Three ascents led to its summit from below. (*a*) By the 100 steps of the Tarpeian Rock, which was probably on the steepest side, where it overhangs the Tiber. (*b*) The CLIVUS CAPITOLINUS, which began from the Arch of Tiberius and the Temple of Saturn, near the modern Hospital of the Consolazione, and led to the citadel by a winding path. (*c*) The CLIVUS ASȲLI, which, being less steep than the other two, was, on that account, the road by which the triumphant generals were borne in their cars to the Capitol. This ascent began at the Arch of Septimius Severus, and from thence, winding to the left, passed near the ruined pillars of the Temple of Concord, and from thence led to the Intermontium. The Capitoline Hill is said to have been previously called Saturnius, from the ancient city of Saturnia, of which it was the citadel. Afterwards it was known by the name of Mons Tarpeius, and finally it obtained the appellation first mentioned, from the circumstance of a human head (*caput*) being discovered on its summit, in making the foundations of the Temple of Iupiter. It was considered as forming two summits, which, though considerably depressed, are yet sufficiently apparent. That which looked to the south and the Tiber was the Tarpeian Rock or citadel, the other, which was properly the Capitol, faced the north and the Quirinal. The space which was left between these two elevations was known by the name of Intermontium. See ROMA.

Capitolīnus. (1) PETILIUS. A governor of the Capitol. (Compare the commentators on Horace, *Sat.* i. 4, 94.) It is also related that he was accused of having stolen, during his office, a golden crown, consecrated to Iupiter, and that, having pleaded his cause in person, he was acquitted by the judges, in order to gratify Augustus, with whom he was on friendly terms. (2) IULIUS, one of those later Roman historians whose works form what has been termed the Augustan History (Augusta Historia). He lived during the reigns of Diocletian and Constantine the Great, and we have from him the lives of Antoninus Pius, Marcus Aurelius, Verus, Pertinax, Albinus, Macrinus, the two Maximins, the three Gordians, Maximus, and Balbinus. He wrote other lives also which have not reached us. The greater part of his biographies are dedicated to Diocletian and Constantine. His works show carelessness and want of proper arrangement. See AUGUSTAE HISTORIAE SCRIPTORES.

Capitolium. A celebrated temple and citadel at Rome, on the Tarpeian Rock. The foundations were laid by Tarquinius Priscus, A.U.C. 139, B.C. 615. Its walls were raised by his successor Servius Tullius, and Tarquinius Superbus finished it,

A.U.C. 231, B.C. 533. It was not, however, consecrated until the third year after the expulsion of the kings. This ceremony was performed by the consul Horatius. It covered eight acres, was 200 feet broad, and about 215 long. It consisted of three parts, a nave sacred to Iupiter, and two wings or aisles, the right sacred to Minerva, and the left to Iuno. The ascent to it from the Forum was by a hundred steps. The magnificence and richness of this temple are almost incredible. All the consuls successively made donations to the Capitol, and Augustus bestowed upon it at one time 2000 pounds weight of gold. The gilding of the whole arch of the Temple of Iupiter, which was undertaken after the destruction of Carthage, cost, according to Plutarch, 21,000 talents, or $24,780,000. The gates of the temple were of brass, covered with large plates of gold. The interior was all of marble, and was adorned with vessels and shields of solid silver, with gilded chariots, etc. The Capitol was burned in the time of Sulla, A.U.C. 670, B.C. 83, through the negligence of those who kept it, and Sulla rebuilt it, but died before the dedication, which was performed by Q. Catulus in B.C. 69. It was again destroyed in the troubles under Vitellius, on the 19th of December, A.D. 69; and Vespasian, who endeavoured to repair it, saw it again in ruins at his death. Domitian raised it for the last time, and made it more grand and magnificent than had any of his predecessors, and spent 12,000 talents in gilding it. See ROMA.

Capitolium. (From a medal.)

Capitŭlum (*ἐπίκρανον, κιονόκρανον*). The capital of a column, which, in the infancy of building as an art, was nothing more than a simple abacus, or square tablet of wood, placed on the top of a wooden trunk, the original column, to form a broad bed for the architrave to rest upon. From this simple beginning, it became eventually the principal ornament of a column, and a prominent feature by which the different architectural orders are distinguished; being, like them, and strictly speaking, divided into three kinds, the Doric, Ionic, and Corinthian capitals, which, with the Roman alterations, make five varieties in use among the ancients; for the Tuscan is only a species of Doric; and the Composite is formed by a union of the Ionic and Corinthian, having the foliage of the latter surmounted by the volutes of the former — a bastard capital introduced in the Imperial Age, when the genius for invention was succeeded by a love for novelty and splendour, and first employed in the triumphal arches at Rome, where a specimen is still to be seen on the Arch of Titus. (See COLUMNA.)

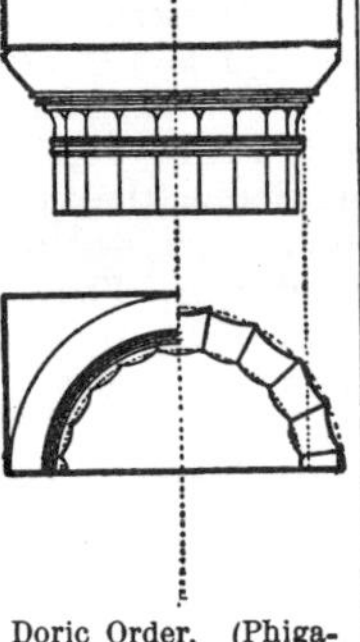
Doric Order. (Phigalea: Manch, pl. 11.)

(1) CAPITULUM DORĬCUM. (*a*) *Greek*. The Greek Doric capital, which is the simplest of all, being divided into no more than three principal parts: the large square abacus at the top, retaining in this order its primitive character to the last; the echinus, or quarter round, immediately below it; and the anuli, or anulets, just above the neck of the shaft.

(*b*) *Roman*. The Doric of the Romans is more complicated and varied in its parts. Instead of the simple abacus, they substituted a moulded cymatium and fillet; in place of the echinus, a novolo, often broken by carving, as in the example; instead of the anulets, either an astragal (*astragalus*), or a bead and fillet. The example is from a Roman temple near Albano.

Doric Order. (Albano: Manch, pl. 19.)

(2) CAPITULUM IONĬCUM. (*a*) *Greek*. The Greek Ionic capital consists of two leading features: the abacus, which is smaller and lower than in the Doric, but still square in its plan, though moulded on the exterior faces; and the volutes (*voluta*), or spiral mouldings on each side of the front, which are frequently connected by a pendent hem or fold, as in the example, and hang down much lower than the sculptural echinus between them.

Greek Ionic Capital. (Erechtheum, Athens: Fergusson.)

(*b*) *Roman*. The Roman Ionic does not differ very materially, nor in its essential parts, from the Greek specimens, excepting that it is often elaborately covered with carving; the volutes are in general smaller, and the tasteful hem which hangs down between them in the preceding engraving is never introduced; but that is not to be considered as a uniform characteristic of the Greek order; it does not occur in any existing edifices.

The annexed specimen of the Roman Composite is taken from the Arch of Titus.

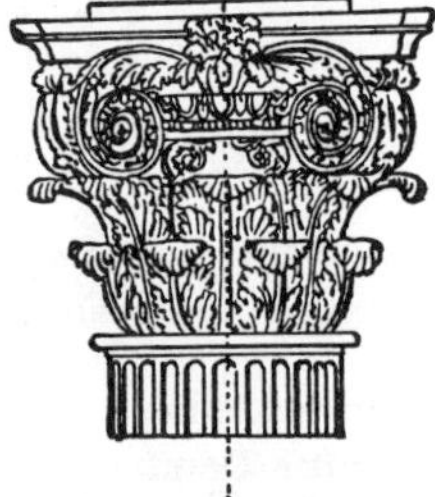
Roman Composite. (Arch of Titus.)

(3) CAPITULUM CORINTHIUM. The Corinthian capital is the richest of all the pure orders, and the specimens now remaining of it in Greece and Italy do not materially differ in any characteristic point. It consists of an abacus, not square, like that of the Doric and Ionic capitals, but hollowed on the sides, and having the angles cut off, and a rosette (*flos*) or other similar ornament in the middle. Under the aba-

cus are small volutes (*helices*, Vitruv. iv. 1, 12), bending downwards like stalks, two of which meet under each angle of the abacus, and two in the centre of each face of the capital, where they sometimes touch, and sometimes are interwoven with each other. The whole is surrounded by two circular rows of leaves (*folia*), each leaf of the upper row growing between and behind those of the lower one, in such a manner that a leaf of the upper row falls in the centre of each of the four faces of the capital. In the best examples these leaves are carved to imitate the acanthus or the olive-tree. See ARCHITECTURA.

Corinthian Capital. (From the Temple of Vesta at Tivoli.)

Cappadŏcia (Καππαδοκία). A district of Asia Minor, to which different boundaries were assigned at different times. Under the Persian Empire it included the whole country inhabited by a people of Syrian origin, who were called (from their complexion) White Syrians (Leucosyri), and also Cappadoces. Their country embraced the whole northeast part of Asia Minor, east of the river Halys and north of Mount Taurus, which was afterwards divided into Pontus and Cappadocia proper. (See PONTUS.) When this division took place is uncertain; but we find that under the Persian Empire the whole country was governed by a line of hereditary satraps, who eventually became independent kings. At a later period Cappadocia proper was governed by a line of independent monarchs. In A.D. 17, Archelaüs, the last king, died at Rome, and Tiberius made Cappadocia a Roman province. Cappadocia was a rough and mountainous region. Its fine pastures supported an abundance of good horses and mules.

Capra or **Capella** (Αἴξ). The brightest star in the constellation of the Auriga, or Charioteer, and said to have been originally the nymph or goat who nursed the infant Zeus in Crete. See AMALTHEA; ZEUS.

Capraria. (1) A small island off the coast of Etruria, inhabited only by wild goats, whence its name. (2) See AEGATES.

Capreae. The modern Capri; a small island, nine miles in circumference, off Campania, at the southern entrance of the Gulf of Puteoli. The scenery is beautiful, and the climate soft and genial. Here the emperor Tiberius (q. v.) lived the last ten years of his reign, indulging in secret debauchery, and accessible only to his favourites.

Capricornus. The Goat, a sign of the zodiac, between the Archer and the Waterman, and said to have fought with Iupiter against the Titans.

Caprĭpes. "Goat-footed." An adjective applied to Pan, to Faunus, and to the Satyrs, all of whom are represented in works of art as having goat's feet.

Caprōnae. Locks of hair falling over the forehead. The modern "bang" or "fringe" (Apul. *Flor.* i. 3. 3).

Caprotīna. See PHILOTIS.

Capsa (Κάψα). A strong and ancient city in the southwest of Byzacena, in Northern Africa, in a fertile oasis surrounded by a sandy desert, abounding in serpents. In the war with Iugurtha it was destroyed by Marius; but was afterwards rebuilt, and erected into a colony.

Capsa (dim. CAPSŬLA, CAPSELLA) or **Scrinium.** A box for holding books and papers among the Romans, usually made of beech-wood and of a cylindrical form. There is no doubt respecting their form, since they are often placed by the side of statues dressed in the toga. The accompanying illustration, which represents an open capsa with six rolls of books in it, is from a painting at Pompeii.

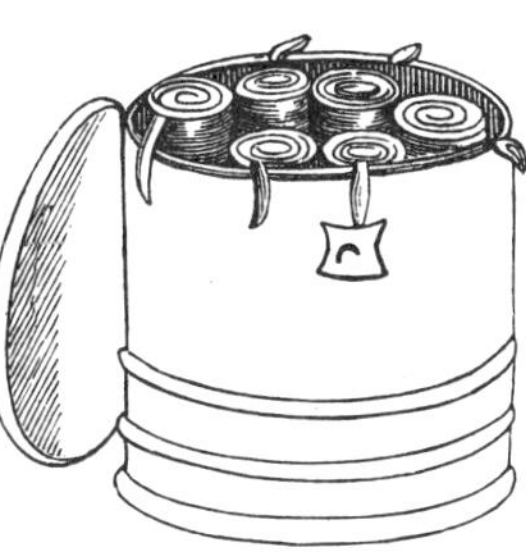

Capsa. (Pompeii.)

There does not appear to have been any difference between the capsa and the scrinium, except that the latter word was usually applied to those boxes which held a considerable number of rolls (Martial, i. 2. 4). Boxes used for preserving other things besides books were also called capsae, while in the scrinia nothing appears to have been kept but books, letters, and other writings.

The slaves who had the charge of these book-chests were called *capsarii*, and also *custodes scriniorum*; and the slaves who carried, in a capsa behind their young masters, the books, etc., of the sons of respectable Romans, when they went to school, were also called *capsarii*. We accordingly find them mentioned together with the *paedagogi*.

When the capsa contained books of importance, it was sealed or kept under lock and key; whence Horace says to his work, *Odisti claves et grata sigilla pudico* (*Epist.* i. 20, 3).

Capsarii. (1) A name applied to two classes of Roman slaves: (*a*) Those who took care of the clothes of persons bathing at the public bath-houses. (See BALNEAE.) (*b*) Those who had charge of the *capsae* in which books or letters were kept. (See CAPSA.) (2) Soldiers who guarded the chests containing the military papers and registers. (See *Dig.* l. 6, 7.)

Captīvi. "The Captives"; one of the most popular of the plays of Plautus, and styled rather extravagantly by Lessing "the best piece that has ever come upon the stage." It is unusually restrained in language and action (*fabula stataria*), and in the prologue Plautus takes credit for its freedom from indecency. It has no female characters and no love-intrigue. Good separate editions are those of Sonnenschein (London, 1880), Brix (Leipzig, 1884), and Hallidie (London, 1891).

Capua (Καπύη). A rich and flourishing city, the capital of Campania until ruined by the Romans. Its original name was Vulturnum, which was changed by the Tyrrheni, after they became masters of the place, to Capua. This latter name was mythically derived from that of their leader Capys, who, according to Festus, received this appellation from his feet being deformed and turned inward. The name is not of Latin, but probably of Oscan origin. The Latins, however, pretended, notwithstanding, to ascribe the foundation of the city to Romulus, who named it, as they stated, after one of his ancestors. Capua was the chief city of the southern Tyrrheni, and even after it fell under the Roman dominion continued to be a powerful and flourishing place. Capua deeply offended the Romans by opening its gates to Hannibal after the victory of Cannae (q. v.), though the luxury and debauchery of the place did much to impair the energy of his troops who wintered there. The vengeance inflicted by Rome upon the Capuans was, however, of a most fearful nature, when, five years after, the city again fell under its dominion. Most of the senators and principal inhabitants were put to death, the greater part of the remaining citizens were sold into slavery, and by a decree of the Senate the Capuani ceased to exist as a people. The city and territory, however, did not become thereupon deserted. A few inhabitants were allowed to remain in the former, and the latter was in a great measure sold by the Romans to the neighbouring communities. Iulius Caesar sent a powerful colony to Capua, and under the emperors it again flourished. But it suffered greatly from the barbarians in a later age; so much so, in fact, that the bishop Landulfus and the Lombard, Count Lando, transferred the inhabitants to Casilinum, on the Vulturnus, and this is the site of modern Capua.

Ruins at Capua.

Capŭlus (κώπη, λαβή). (1) The hilt of a sword, which was frequently much ornamented. (See Gladius.) The handles of knives were also elaborately carved; and of the beautiful workmanship sometimes bestowed on them, a judgment may be formed from the three specimens here introduced.

Capuli. (Montfaucon.)

(2) The handle of a plough (Ovid, *Pont.* i. 8, 57), of which the usual name was *stiva.* See Aratrum.

(3) A bier or coffin. See Funus.

Caput. A word which from the sense of "head," literal or metaphorical (including under the latter the meaning of "source," "beginning"), comes to signify: (1) A single person or thing as distinct from an aggregate (*Inst.* iii. 16, 6; *Dig.* 6, 1, 1, 3). Hence perhaps its use to express a "chapter" of a law (*Dig.* 9, 2, 2, pr.) and a territorial unit for the purpose of land taxation under the later Empire (*Cod.* 10, 2). (2) A human being (Caes. *B. G.* iv. 15), e. g. as a subject of the poll-tax (*Dig.* 50, 4, 18, 8); and in this sense even slaves may be included, as in the phrase *noxalis actio caput sequitur* (*Inst.* iv. 8, 5). But there is a tendency to restrict the term to citizens of some substance; thus the lowest century of Servius Tullius comprised the *proletarii* and *capite censi;* of whom the latter, having little or no property, were barely rated as so many *head* of citizens (Gell. xvi. 10; Cic. *de Rep.* ii. 22). (3) A human being regarded as capable of legal rights (= *persona*). (4) That capacity or those legal rights themselves.

Caput. The principal of a debt. See Fenus.

Caput Extōrum. The convex upper part of the liver of a victim, from which the haruspices chiefly drew their prognostications regarding coming events. Any disease or deficiency in this organ was regarded as of unfavorable import. It was divided into two parts—one called *familiaris,* from which the fate of friends was foretold; the other, *hostilis,* from which they predicted the fate of enemies. See Pliny, *H. N.* xi. §§ 189, 190;

Livy, viii. 9; Cic. *de Div.* ii. 12, 13, § 28 foll.; and the articles AUGUR; DIVINATIO; HARUSPEX.

Capys (Κάπυς). (1) Son of Assaracus, and father of Anchises. (2) A companion of Aeneas, from whom Capua was said to have derived its name.

Capys Silvius. See SILVIUS.

Carăbus (κάραβος, καράβιον). A coracle or boat made of wicker-work, and covered with rawhides. Caesar (*B. C.* i. 54) describes the carabus as used by him in Spain from having been seen by him in Britain. The subjoined illustration is taken from Valturius.

Carabus. (Valturius.)

Caracalla. A Gaulish outer garment resembling the Roman *lacerna* (q. v.), and first introduced at Rome by the emperor Aurelius Antoninus Bassianus, who compelled all plebeians who came to court to wear it, and hence received the name Caracalla, by which he is best known in history (Aurel. Vict. *Epit.* 21). In its longer form it came in later times to be worn by the clergy under the name of cassock (*sottana, soutane*). Like the *lacerna*, it was furnished with a cowl or hood (*cucullus*).

Caracalla, AURELIUS ANTONĪNUS BASSIĀNUS. The eldest son of Septimius Severus. His name Caracalla was derived from a species of Gallic cassock which he introduced at Rome; and that of Bassianus from his maternal grandfather. Caracalla was born at Lugdunum (Lyons), A.D. 188, and was appointed by his father to be his colleague in the government at the age of thirteen years; yet he is said, even at this early age, to have attempted his father's life. Severus died A.D. 211, and was succeeded by his two sons, Caracalla and Geta. These two brothers bore towards each other, even from infancy, the most inveterate hatred. After a campaign against the Caledonians, they concluded a disgraceful peace and then wished to divide the Empire between them; but their design was opposed by their mother, Iulia, and by the principal men of the State; so that Caracalla now resolved to get rid of his brother, by causing him to be assassinated. After many unsuccessful attempts, he pretended to desire a reconciliation, and requested his mother to procure him an interview with his brother in her own apartment. Geta appeared, and was stabbed in his mother's arms, A.D. 212, by several centurions, who had received orders to this effect. The praetorian guards were prevailed upon, by rich donations, to proclaim Caracalla sole emperor, and to declare Geta an enemy to the State; and the Senate confirmed the nomination of the soldiers. After this, the whole life of Caracalla was only one series of cruelties and acts of extravagant folly. All who had been in any way connected with Geta were put to death, not even their children being spared. The historian Dio Cassius makes the whole number of victims to have amounted to 20,000 (Dio Cass. lxxvii. 4). Among those who fell in this horrible butchery was the celebrated lawyer Papinianus. And yet, after this, by a singular act of contradiction, he not only put to death many of those who had been concerned in the murder of his brother, but even demanded of the Senate that he should be enrolled among the gods. His pattern was Sulla, whose tomb he restored and adorned. Like this dictator, he enriched his soldiers with the most extravagant largesses which extortion enabled him to furnish. The augmentation of pay received by them is said to have amounted to 280 millions of sesterces a year. As cruel as Caligula and Nero, but weaker than either, he regarded the Senate and people with equal hatred and contempt. From motives of avarice, he gave all the freemen of the Empire the right of citizenship, and was the first who received Egyptians into the Senate. Of all his follies, however, the greatest was his admiration of Alexander of Macedon. From his infancy he made this monarch his model, and copied him in everything which it was easy to imitate. He had even a Macedonian phalanx of sixteen thousand men, all born in Macedonia, and commanded by officers bearing the same names with those who had served under Alexander. Convinced, moreover, that Aristotle had participated in the conspiracy against the son of Philip, he caused the works of the philosopher to be burned. With equally foolish enthusiasm for Achilles, he made him the object of his deepest veneration. He went to Ilium to visit the grave of Homer's hero, and poisoned his favourite freedman, named Festus, to imitate Achilles in his grief for Patroclus. His conduct in his campaigns in Gaul, where he committed all sorts of cruelties, was still more degrading. He crossed over the Rhine into the countries of the Catti and Alemanni. The Catti defeated him, and permitted him to repass the river only on condition of paying them a large sum of money. He next marched through the land of the Alemanni as an ally, and built several fortifications. He then called together the young men of the tribe, as if he intended to take them into his service, and caused his own troops to surround them and cut them in pieces. For this barbarous exploit he assumed the surname of Alemannicus. In Dacia he gained some advantages over the Goths. He signed a treaty of peace at Antioch with Artabanus, the Parthian king, who submitted to all his demands. He invited Abdares, the king of Edessa, an ally of the Romans, to Antioch, loaded him with chains, and took possession of his estates. He exercised the same treachery towards Vologeses, king of Armenia; but the Armenians flew to arms and repulsed the Romans. After this, Caracalla went to Alexandria, to punish the people of that city for ridiculing him. While preparations were making for a great massacre, he offered hecatombs to Serapis, and visited the

Caracalla. (Vatican.)

Caricature of Caracalla as an Apple-seller. (Avignon.)

tomb of Alexander, on which he left his imperial ornaments by way of offering. He afterwards devoted the inhabitants for several days and nights to plunder and butchery, and seated himself, in order to have a view of the bloody spectacle, on the top of the Temple of Serapis, where he consecrated the dagger which he had drawn, some years before, against his own brother. His desire to triumph over the Parthians induced him to violate the peace, under the pretence that Artabanus had refused him his daughter in marriage. He found the country undefended, ravaged it, marched through Media, and approached the capital. The Parthians, who had retired beyond the Tigris to the mountains, were preparing to attack the Romans the following year with all their forces. Caracalla returned without delay to Mesopotamia, without having even seen the Parthians. When the Senate received from him information of the submission of the East, they decreed him a triumph and the surname Parthicus. Being informed of the warlike preparations of the Parthians, he prepared to renew the contest; but Macrinus, the praetorian prefect, whom he had offended, assassinated him at Edessa, A.D. 217, on his way to the Temple of Lunus. His reign had lasted more than six years. It is remarkable that this prince, although he did so much to degrade the throne of the Caesars, yet raised at Rome some of the most splendid structures that graced the capital. Magnificent thermae bore his name (see BALNEAE), and among other monuments of lavish expenditure was a triumphal arch, on which were represented the victories and achievements of his father, Severus, and of which an illustration is given on page 118. Notwithstanding his crimes, Caracalla was deified after death by a decree of the Senate.

Caractăcus. A king of the Silures in Britain, a people occupying what is now southern Wales. After withstanding, for the space of seven years (A.D. 43–50) the Roman arms, he was defeated in a pitched battle by Ostorius Scapula, and his forces put to the rout. Taking refuge, upon this, with Cartismandua, queen of the Brigantes, he was betrayed by her into the hands of the Romans, and led to Rome. Great importance was attached to his capture. Claudius, who was emperor at the time, augmented the territories of Cartismandua, and triumphal honours were decreed to Ostorius. This exploit was compared to the capture of Syphax by Scipio, and that of Perseus by Aemilius Paulus. The manly and independent bearing, however, of the British prince, when brought into the presence of the Roman emperor, excited so much admiration that his fetters were removed, and freedom was granted him, together with his wife and children, who had shared his captivity. There is no evidence that Caractacus ever returned to Britain, and he is believed to have been in Rome at the time of his death (Tac. *Ann.* xii. 33 foll.).

Tradition says that the Claudia mentioned by St. Paul (2 Tim. iv. 21) was his daughter and introduced Christianity into Britain, but there is no historical evidence to support this legend. Caractacus is believed to have died in A.D. 54.

Carălis or **Carăles.** The modern Cagliari; the chief town of Sardinia, with an excellent harbour.

Carambis (Κάραμβις). A promontory, with a city of the same name, on the coast of Paphlagonia.

Carānus (Κάρανος or Κάρηνος). A descendant of Heracles, and said to have settled at Edessa, in Macedonia, with an Argive colony, about B.C. 750, and to have become the founder of the dynasty of Macedonian kings.

Carausius. A native of Gaul, born among the Menapii. His naval abilities attracted the notice of Maximian, who gave him the command of a squadron against the pirates. He proved, however, unfaithful to his trust, and too much bent upon enriching himself. Maximian thereupon gave orders to put him to death; but Carausius, apprised of this in season, retired with his fleet to Britain. Here he succeeded in gaining over, or else intimidating, the only Roman legion that remained in the island, and finally proclaimed himself emperor. He forced the emperors Maximian and Diocletian to acknowledge his authority, which he maintained for the space of seven years (286–293). He was assassinated by Allectus.

Carbăsus (κάρπασος). Cotton; an Eastern product, originally called tree-wool (ἔρια ἀπὸ ξύλου), like the German *Baumwolle.* See Herod. iii. 106; and ib. 47. It was brought by the Phœnicians into Spain. The Greeks gained their first real knowledge of it at the time of the Indian expedition of Alexander the Great, after which its use became general. The finest cotton came from Egypt, where the priests wore cotton garments; and from Arabia. Caecilius Statius mentions cotton at Rome as early as B.C. 180, and later it was used not only for articles of clothing, but for tent-curtains, awnings, sails, etc. (See Plin. *H. N.* xii. § 39; xix. § 10; Cic. *Verr.* v. 12, § 30; Verg. *Aen.* iii. 357; Lucret. vi. 109.) There were manufactories of cotton goods in Malta, whence cotton clothing was called *vestis Melitensis* at Rome (Cic. *Verr.* ii. 72, § 176 *et al.*). Raw cotton was used for stuffing pillows in the East, and the Macedonians filled their saddles with it (Strabo, 693). Pliny speaks of cotton under the name *gossypium* (xii. § 39). The word *carbasus* is Indian, the Sanskrit form being *karpâsa*. On the use of cotton by the ancients, see Marquardt, *Privatleben*, pp. 470–474.

Carbatĭna (καρβατίνη). (1) A sort of rude shoe, made of untanned ox-hide, placed under the foot, and tied with several thongs in such a way as to cover the whole foot and part of the leg (Lucian, *Alex.* p. 246; Xen. *Anab.* iv. 5, 14). (2) A skin-covered structure used by besiegers. See TESTUDO.

Carbo. The name of a family of the gens Papiria. (1) C. PAPIRIUS CARBO, a distinguished orator, and a man of great talents but no principle. He was one of the three commissioners or triumvirs for carrying into effect the agrarian law of Tib. Gracchus. His tribuneship of the plebs, B.C. 131, was characterized by the most vehement opposition to the aristocracy; but after the death of C. Gracchus (121), he suddenly deserted the popular party, and in his consulship (120) undertook the defence of Opimius, who had murdered C. Gracchus. In 119, Carbo was accused by L. Licinius Crassus; and, as he foresaw his condemnation, he put an end to his own life. (2) CN. PAPIRIUS CARBO, one of the leaders of the Marian party. He was thrice consul—namely, in B.C. 85, 84, and 82. In 82, he carried on war against Sulla; but was at length obliged to fly to Sicily, where he was put to death by Pompey at Lilybaeum.

Carcăso. The modern Carcassonne; a town of the Tectosages, in Gallia Narbonensis.

Carcer (δεσμωτήριον). A prison.

(1) GREEK. Imprisonment was seldom used among the Greeks as a legal punishment for offences. Among the Athenians, with whom we are chiefly concerned, it was practically unknown in the sense of confinement for a definite period after conviction. They had neither the appliances in the shape of walls and bars, nor were they willing to incur the expense; and they preferred either banishment or the death penalty. Capital punishment was inflicted without hesitation for comparatively trifling offences, but by more humane methods than those of modern Europe until quite recent times.

Imprisonment before trial, on the other hand, was common enough, though bail was freely accepted in cases other than capital; the terror of exile was in general thought sufficient to keep a man to his bail (ἐγγύη). The farmers of the taxes and lessees of other revenues (τελῶναι, μισθούμενοι), as well as their sureties (οἱ ἐγγυώμενοι), were liable to imprisonment if the duties were not paid by a specified time; and in cases where default was to be feared, they might even be imprisoned at the discretion of the Senate or law-courts. This was the great safeguard to insure regularity of payment. Again, persons who had been mulcted in penalties might be confined till they paid them, not only in criminal cases, but in some civil actions instituted for damages as well. Certain of the ἄτιμοι also, if they exercised the rights of citizenship, were subject to the same consequences (Demosth. *c. Timocr.* p. 732, § 103). We read, moreover, of δεσμός as a public stigma put upon disgraceful offences, such as theft; but this was a προστίμημα or additional penalty, the infliction of which was at the option of the court; and the δεσμός itself was not so much an imprisonment as a public exposure in the ποδοκάκκη or stocks, for five days and nights—called also ἐν ξύλῳ δεδέσθαι (Demosth. *loc. cit.*, p. 700, § 2; pp. 732–733, §§ 103, 105; p. 736, §114). One more description of imprisonment remains to be noticed, that in the interval between condemnation and execution. In this last case, owing to the insecurity of the building, the prisoner was chained, and was under the special custody of the Eleven, who were also responsible for the execution itself. See HENDEKA.

There are several passages from which we might infer the existence at Athens of imprisonment as a punishment by itself—e. g. Plato, *Apol.* 37 C; *Laws*, ix. 864 E, 880 B, and especially x. 908. But such vague allusions prove nothing against the persistent silence of the historians and orators. "Of imprisonment as a punishment by itself," Schömann argues, "we have no certain example"; and this remark in his text is supported by a good note (*Antiq.* i. 489, Eng. trans.). The opposite and less probable opinion has, however, been maintained by K. F. Hermann (*Staatsalterth.* § 139) and Caillemer (*ap.* Daremberg and Saglio).

The prison at Athens is frequently mentioned in the orators, both by its usual name, δεσμωτήριον, and the euphemistic equivalent οἴκημα. But the plural δεσμωτήρια does not seem to occur in any Attic writer, though there are passages where, if a plurality of prisons existed at Athens, we should almost certainly find them mentioned. This argument seems almost decisive in favour of the opinion of J. H. Lipsius (*Att. Process*, p. 73 n.), that there was only one. The authority of Hesychius and the *Etymologicum Magnum* is insufficient to prove, in the face of probability, that there was an Athenian prison called Θησεῖον; and there is no proof that the other names for prisons recorded by the grammarians are to be referred to Athens. Among these local names was ἀναγκαῖον or ἀνάκαιον in Boeotia, κέραμος in Cyprus, κῶς at Corinth; and among the Ionians γοργύρη, as at Samos (Herod. iii. 145); βάλαικες or βαλαίκακες, βλέορον, ἴψον, σιρός, all mentioned by Hesychius. The appearance of the Latin *carcer* in the Sicilian Greek κάρκαρον, and conversely of the Greek λατομίαι in the Latin *lautumiae*, is noticed by Mommsen as a proof of the early intercourse between the Romans and Sicily (*R. H.* i. 167, Eng. trans.). Some of the above names may be slang or nicknames, such as are often applied to prisons in our own day: thus γοργύρα is explained to mean "a sewer"; ἴψον may be connected with ἶπος, "a mouse-trap." The gate through which criminals were led to execution was called χαρώνειον or θύρα χαρώνειος (Poll. viii. 102), a grim joke which can hardly have arisen at Athens, where executions were private.

The Attic expression for imprisonment was δεῖν, a word which by no means implies the use of chains or fetters. The phrase in the oath of the βουλευταί, or senators, οὐδὲ δήσω Ἀθηναίων οὐδένα, is explained by Demosthenes (*c. Timocr.* p. 746, § 147) as a security against arbitrary imprisonment by the executive government without trial. It was, in fact, the habeas corpus of the Athenian constitution. But he is careful to add (§ 151) that no such words occur in the oath of the Heliastae or dicasts; the law-courts had absolute power over men's lives, liberties, and fortunes. We have also the phrase ἄδεσμος φυλακή (as in Thuc. iii. 34), like the *libera custodia* of the Romans, signifying that a person was under strict surveillance and guard, though not confined within the walls of a prison.

(2) ROMAN. The oldest prison at Rome, traditionally the only one in early times (Juv. iii. 312), was called simply Carcer; and is still to be seen on the eastern slope of the Capitoline Hill, to the right of the ascent from the Forum. The name Mamertinus, usually applied to the Carcer, is mediæval and not classical. The Tullianum consists of a larger oblong upper and a smaller underground circular dungeon; the latter is that called the Tullianum, a name which has often been incorrectly explained. As the original erection of the

Section of the Tullianum at Rome.

Carcer was attributed to Ancus Marcius (Livy, i. 33), it was conjectured by the etymologists that the name Tullianum must have been derived from Servius Tullius, "evidently a double mistake, as the lower chamber would certainly not have been added after the upper one" (Middleton, *Anc. Rome*, p. 80). It is now agreed that it is from the *tullii*, or springs for whose waters it formed a reservoir; that it was built in the first instance simply to protect the water supply of the Capitol; and was only in later times used as a part of the prison when a captive, as in the well-known instance of Iugurtha, was doomed to be killed by cold and starvation (Festus and P. Diac. s. v. *tullii*, pp. 352–353, Müller; Plut. *Mar.* 12; Burn, *Rome and the Campagna*, p. 81). The name therefore originally meant "well-house." Thus Livy speaks of the infamous Pleminius as *deiectus in Tullianum* (xxix. 22), which in another passage is expressed by the words *in inferiorem demissus carcerem necatusque* (xxxiv. 44). It was here, too, that Lentulus and the other accomplices of Catiline were strangled by order of the *triumviri capitales;* and Sallust describes it as sunk twelve feet in the earth, strongly walled, and with a roof vaulted with stone arches (*Cat.* 55). In reality, as modern investigations have shown, the construction is so old that it points to a time when the arch was not used in Roman architecture, standing next among existing remains to the prehistoric walls on the Palatine; the roof being of stone slabs, each overlapping the one beneath it, an approximation to the true arch found also in the well-known treasury of Mycenae and other primitive buildings. The upper chamber is also of very early date, but later than the Tullianum; and it is not in its primitive condition. A projecting string-course on the outside records a restoration in the reign of Tiberius by the *consules suffecti* for the year A.D. 22. Another name for this part of the prison was Robur, in old Latin Robus. The Robur is spoken of as a place of execution in several passages (Livy, xxxviii. 59; Tac. *Ann.* iv. 29), and is spoken of by Middleton as "the scene of countless butcheries and slow torture such as the Romans delighted in." During each triumph, in his course up to the Capitol, the victorious general paused for a while near the Tullianum till word was brought him that some of his principal captives had been put to death in its gloomy vault. The Scalae Gemoniae (called by Pliny Gradus Gemitorii, "stair of sighs") led from the Forum to the door of the upper prison, and here the dead bodies of Sabinus, of Vitellius, of Seianus, and many other noted persons were exposed. (Cf. Tac. *Hist.* iii. 74, 85; Suet. *Tib.* 61; *Vitell.* 17; and the touching story in Pliny, *H. N.* viii. 145, of the faithful dog who there watched his master's body night and day and brought it food.)

The name Robur was given to the Tullianum from the oaken beams (*robora*) that lined it in early times. Plutarch (*Marius*, 12) calls the lower dungeon τὸ βάραθρον. A tradition of the Roman Church makes St. Peter and St. Paul to have been imprisoned here in the time of Nero, and declares the spring which still exists to have sprung up miraculously for the baptism of the jailers by St. Peter. The building has therefore been named S. Pietro in Carcere. See Middleton, *Remains of Ancient Rome*, i. pp. 151 foll., where a plan and section are given (London, 1892); and Mommsen, *Hist. of Rome*, i. 308 (American ed. 1888).

Sallust, in the passage already cited, gives an impressive picture of the lower vault in which Iugurtha and also Vercingetorix perished. "There is," he says, "in the prison a chamber named the Tullianum, about twelve feet below the surface of the earth. It is surrounded by walls, and covered by a vaulted roof of stone; but its appearance is repulsive and fearful, because of the neglect, the darkness, and the stench." Access to the lower dungeon was originally possible only through the hole in the ceiling. The exact proportions of the vault are 19 feet in length, 10 feet in width, and 6½ feet in height.

The name Mamertinus, often applied to this prison, was bestowed upon it in the early part of the Middle Ages from a statue of Mars (Mamers) which stood near it on the Clivus Argentarius. From the same statue is derived the modern name of the street, Via del Marforio.

This prison was obviously too small to contain any number of prisoners, and probably from the first was appropriated to those condemned to death. The earliest mention of another prison is in the days of the Decemvirate, B.C. 450. Appius Claudius is said to have built one for political purposes, to overawe the champions of plebeian liberties (Livy, iii. 57). It was into this prison that he was himself thrown, and committed suicide while awaiting his trial. At a later period we find an additional prison called Lautumiae, or stone-quarries, in the immediate neighbourhood of the original Carcer. It is not likely that there were ever any quarries on this spot, which was to the northwest of the Forum; but it may have been named after the Syracusan λατομίαι mentioned above, which were thus used. Varro (*L. L.* v. 151, Müll.) identified the Lautumiae with the Tullianum, and has been followed by some of the moderns; but they are distinguished by the best writers on Roman topography (Becker, *Röm. Alterth.* i. 262-268; Burn, p. 80).

With the growth of the city other prisons became necessary; but the words of Roman historians generally refer to these alone. Close to the Carcer, and between it and the Temple of Concord, were the Scalae Gemoniae (q. v.), where the bodies of criminals were exposed after execution.

Carcĕres. A row of small vaulted chambers, forming the starting-point of the races in the circus. See CIRCUS.

Carchēdon (Καρχηδών). The Greek name of Carthage. See CARTHAGO.

Carchesium (καρχήσιον). (1) A kind of cup, rather long, narrower in the middle than at either extremity, and with handles (ὦτα) stretching from the top to the bottom. Asclepiades (in Ath. 488 foll.)

Carchesium.

mentions *carchesia* among those vessels which have feet. It was a peculiarly Greek cup (Macrob. *Sat.* v. 21 *init.*), and generally of a splendid nature. (2) The same term designated the tops of a ship—i. e. the structure surmounting the mast immediately above the yards (*antennae*). See NAVIS.

Cardamȳlē (Καρδαμύλη). A town in Messenia; now Scardamoula.

Cardea. A Roman divinity, presiding over the hinges (*cardines*) of doors—that is, over family life (Tertull. *adv. Gnost.* 10).

Cardia (Καρδία). A town on the Thracian Chersonese, on the Gulf of Melas, the birthplace of Eumenes (q. v.). It was destroyed by Lysimachus, who built the town of Lysimachia in its immediate neighbourhood.

Cardo (θαιρός, στροφεύς, στρόφιγξ, γίγγλυμος). A hinge, a pivot.

The first figure in the annexed illustration is designed to show the general form of a door, as we find it with a pivot at the top and bottom (*a b*) in ancient remains of stone, marble, wood, and bronze. The second figure represents a bronze hinge in the Egyptian collection of the British Museum; its pivot (*b*) is exactly cylindrical. Under these is drawn the threshold of a temple, or other large edifice, with the plan of the folding-doors. The pivots move in holes fitted to receive them (*b b*), each of which is in an angle behind the antepagmentum. When Hector forces the gate of the Grecian camp, he does it by breaking both the

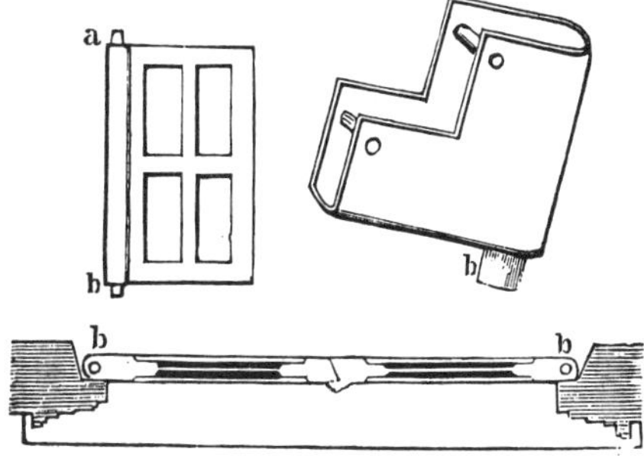

Door and Hinge.

hinges (ἀμφοτέρους θαιρούς)—i. e., as explained by the scholiasts, the pivots (στρόφιγγας) at the top and bottom. See CATARACTA.

According to the ancient lexicons, *cardo* denoted not only the pivot, but sometimes the socket (*foramen*) in which it turned. *Postis* appears to have meant the upright pillar (*a b*) in the frame of the door. The whole of this "post," including the pivots, appears to be called στροφεύς and *cardo* by Theophrastus and Pliny, who say that it was best made of elm, because elm does not warp, and because the whole door will preserve its proper form, if this part remains unaltered.

The Greeks and Romans also used hinges exactly like those now in common use. Four Roman hinges of bronze, preserved in the British Museum, are shown in the following illustration.

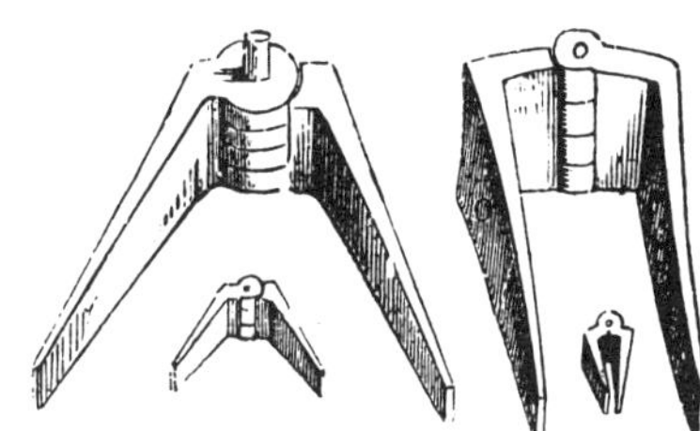

Cardines. (British Museum.)

The proper Greek name for this kind of hinge was γίγγλυμος: whence Aristotle applies it to the joint of a bivalve shell; and the anatomists call those joints of the human body *ginglymoid* which allow motion only in one plane, such as the elbow-joint.

The form of the door above delineated makes it manifest why the principal line laid down in surveying land was called *cardo* (see AGRIMENSORES); and it further explains the application of the same term to the North Pole, the supposed pivot on which the heavens revolved (Ovid, *Epist. ex Pont.* ii. 10, 45). The lower extremity of the universe was conceived to turn upon another pivot, corresponding to that at the bottom of the door; and the conception of these two principal points in geography and astronomy led to the application of the same term to the east and west also. Hence our "four points of the compass" are called by ancient writers *quatuor cardines orbis terrarum;* and the four principal winds, N., S., E., and W., are the *cardinales venti* (Serv. *ad* Verg. *Aen.* i. 85).

Cardūchi (Καρδοῦχοι). A powerful and warlike people, probably the Kurds of modern times, who dwelt in the mountains which divided Assyria from Armenia. See Xen. *Anab.* iii. 5, 15.

Caria (Καρία). A district of Asia Minor, in its southwestern corner. It is intersected by low mountain chains, running out far into the sea in long promontories, forming gulfs along the coast and inland valleys that were fertile and well-watered. The chief products of the country were corn, wine, oil, and figs. The coast was inhabited chiefly by Greek colonists. The inhabitants of the rest of the country were Carians, a people nearly allied to the Lydians and Mysians. The Greeks considered the people mean and stupid, even for slaves. The country was governed by a race of native princes, who fixed their abode at Halicarnassus. These princes were subject-allies of Lydia and Persia, and some of them rose to great distinction in war and peace. (See ARTEMISIA; MAUSOLUS.) Under the Romans, Caria formed a part of the province of Asia. As the Carians were often used as mercenaries, the proverb arose ἐν Καρὶ κινδυνεύειν, equivalent to the familiar Latin *experimentum facere in corpore vili.* Cf. the scholiast on Plato, *Laches*, 187 B; and Polyb. x. 32, 11.

The country was said to have got its name from Car (Κάρ), the brother of Mysus and Lydus (Herod. i. 171).

Caricature. See GRAFFITI.

Carīna. The keel of a ship. See NAVIS.

Carīnae. A street of Rome where Cicero, Pompey, and others of the principal Romans lived. From the epithet *lautae*, which Vergil applies to the Carinae, we may infer that the houses which stood in this quarter of ancient Rome were distinguished by an air of superior elegance and grandeur (*Aen.* viii. 361 foll.). The name Carinae is probably derived from the street's position in a hollow between the Coelian, Esquiline, and Palatine hills.

Carīnus, M. AURELIUS. The eldest son of the emperor Carus, who gave him the title of Caesar and the rank of Augustus, together with the government of Italy, Illyricum, Africa, and the West, when he himself was setting out, with his second son Numerianus, to make war against the Persians. Carus, knowing the evil qualities of Carinus, gave him this charge with great reluctance; but he had

Carinus.

no alternative, as Numerianus, though superior in every respect to his elder brother, was too young to hold so important a command. As soon as Carinus entered Gaul, which his father had particularly charged him to defend against the barbarians, who menaced an irruption, he gave himself up to the most degrading excesses, discharged the most competent men from public employment, and substituted the vile companions of his debaucheries. On hearing of the death of his father, he indulged in new excesses and new crimes. Still, however, his courage and his victories merit praise. He defeated the barbarians who had begun to attack the Empire, among others the Sarmatae, and he afterwards overthrew Sabinus Iulianus, who had assumed the purple in Venetia. He then marched against Diocletian, who had proclaimed himself emperor after the death of Numerian. The two armies met in Moesia, and several engagements took place, in which success seemed balanced. At last a decisive battle was fought near Margum, and Carinus was on the point of gaining a complete victory, when he was slain by a tribune of his own army, who had received an outrage at his hands. This event took place A.D. 285, so that the reign of Carinus, computing it from his father's death, was a little more than one year. His life was written by Vopiscus.

Caristia or **Charistia.** A Roman family celebration held on February 22 (viii. Kal. Mart.) following the Dies Parentales (February 13–21) and the Feralia (February 21), which days were sacred to the dead. The feast was a thanksgiving for the survivors. None but relatives were invited, and on this occasion quarrels and misunderstandings were ended; whence some derive the word Caristia from χαρίζομαι, but the better-approved spelling is against this view, and Ovid regards the word as connected with *carus* (Ovid, *Fast.* ii. 617).

Carmania (Καρμανία). A province of the ancient Persian Empire, bounded on the west by Persia proper, on the north by Parthia, on the east by Gedrosia, and on the south by the Indian Ocean. See PERSIA.

Carmēlus (Κάρμηλος). A range of mountains in Palestine, commencing on the northern border of Samaria, and running through the southwestern part of Galilee, till it terminates in the promontory of the same name (Cape Carmel).

Carmen. (1) DE FIGŪRIS. An anonymous didactic poem on rhetorical figures discovered in a MS. at Paris, and published by Quicherat, and later by Schneidewin (Göttingen, 1841). It consists of 185 or 186 hexameters, and treats of the figures of speech in such a way that each figure has three lines of the text. The peculiarities of its diction lead one to place its date during the later Empire. See Teuffel, *Hist. Roman Lit.*, Eng. trans., 451, 1. (2) DE PONDERĬBUS ET MENSŪRIS. A poem found in some of the MSS. of Priscian, but undoubtedly earlier than his time, and probably of the fourth or fifth century A.D. It has 208 hexameters, the best edition of which is that of F. Hultsch in his *Script. Metrolog. Rom.* (1866). (3) DE MORĬBUS. See CATO, DIONYSIUS. (4) DE PHILOMĒLA. See PHILOMELA.

Carmen Saeculāre. An ode written by Horace at the request of the emperor Augustus, to be sung at the celebration of the Ludi Saeculares, B.C. 17. (See LUDI.) It is composed in nineteen stanzas (seventy-six lines), in the Sapphic and Adonic

Remains of a Castellum at Carmel.

metre, which were divided between two choruses, one composed of boys and the other of girls, who sang now responsively and now in chorus. The arrangement of the stanzas between the two bands has been a subject of dispute among various editors; but all are agreed upon this much: that the first two stanzas were sung by the joint chorus, the second by the girls, the third by the boys, the ninth half by boys and half by girls, while the last stanza was again sung by the united bands.

Like most verses written to order, the *Carmen Saeculare* has little poetical merit, though rhetorically excellent. See HORATIUS.

Carmenta or **Carmentis**. An ancient Italian goddess of prophecy who protected women in childbirth. In Rome she had a priest attached to her, the *flamen Carmentalis*, and a shrine near the gate, under the Capitol, named after her Porta Carmentalis. On this spot the Roman matrons celebrated in her honour the festival of the Carmentalia, the flamen and pontifex assisting. Two Carmentae, called Porrima or Antevorta, and Postvorta, were worshipped as her sisters and attendants. These names were sometimes explained with reference to childbirth, sometimes as indicating the power of the goddess of fate to look into the past and future. In the legend of the foundation of Roma, Carmenta appears as the prophetic mother, or wife, of the Arcadian stranger Evander (q. v.). See CAMENAE.

Carmentalia. An old Roman festival held on the 11th and 15th of January in honour of Carmenta or Carmentis. See CARMENTA.

Carmentālis Porta. One of the gates of Rome in the neighbourhood of the Capitol. It was afterwards called Scelerata, because the Fabii passed through it in going to the fatal expedition where they perished (Verg. *Aen.* viii. 338).

Carmĭna Saliaria. The ritual songs (*axamenta*) of the Salii (q. v.), who sang them during the processions of Mars and Quirinus. These, by the middle of the first century B.C., had become unintelligible even to the priests themselves (Quint. i. 6, 40), and were consequently written down and henceforward repeated merely as a formula. L. Aelius Stilo wrote a commentary on them (Varro, *L. L.* vii. 2; Fest. 141, 146, 210, 239, Müll.). Only two or three connected bits of these hymns have come down to us, and these in a very corrupt state in the pages of the grammarians. (Cf. Terent. Maurus, p. 2261, Putsch.) They will be found collected and explained by Bergk (*Opusc.* i. 477) and Corssen (*Origines Poësis Rom.*, Berlin, 1846). See also Wordsworth, *Fragments and Specimens of Early Latin* (Oxford, 1874), and Allen, *Remnants of Early Latin*, p. 74 (Boston, 1884).

Carna. A Roman divinity, whose name is probably connected with *caro*, "flesh," for she was regarded as the protector of the physical well-being of man. Her festival was celebrated on June 1, and was believed to have been instituted by Brutus in the first year of the Republic. Ovid confounds this goddess with Cardea (q. v.). See Macrob. *Sat.* i. 12.

Carnac (KARNAK). See THEBAE (2).

Carnac. A village in France, twenty miles southeast of Lorient, remarkable for the number of its Gallo-Roman remains, found in a group of mounds known as "Caesar's Camp." These remains comprise pottery, glassware, coins, iron objects, bronzes, and statuary. See Miln, *Excavations at Carnac*, 2 vols. (1877–81).

Carnarium. (1) A larder. (2) A bar or beam furnished with meat-hooks or pegs for hanging hams, bacon, etc. (Plaut. *Capt.* iv. 4, 6). (3) A ditch or fosse into which the bodies of the poorest classes of the people were thrown. See the curious account of one on the Esquiline Hill, in Lanciani, *Ancient Rome in the Light of Recent Discoveries*, pp. 64–67.

Carnēa (τὰ Κάρνεια). A festival celebrated in honour of Apollo Carneus ("the protector of flocks") as early as the time of the immigration of the Dorians. In keeping up the celebration, the Dorians characteristically gave it a warlike colour, by transforming their original pastoral deity into the god of their fighting army. The Carnea lasted nine days, from the 7th to the 15th of the month Carneus (August-September). The proceedings symbolized the life of soldiers in camp. In every three *phratriae* or *obae* nine places were set apart, on which tents or booths were put up. In these tents nine men had their meals in common. All ordinary proceedings were carried on at the word of command, given out by a herald. One part of the festival recalled its originally rural character. This was a race, in which one of the runners, supposed to symbolize the blessings of harvest, started in advance, uttering prayers for the city. The others, called "vintage-runners," pursued him, and if they overtook him the occurrence was taken as a good omen; if they failed, as a bad one. After the twenty-sixth Olympiad (B.C. 676) a musical contest was added, at which the most celebrated artists in all Greece were accustomed to compete. The first artist who sang at this contest was Terpander (q. v.).

Carneădes (Καρνεάδης). A philosopher of Cyrené in Africa, founder of a sect called the Third or New Academy. The Athenians sent him with Diogenes the Stoic, and Critolaüs the Peripatetic, as ambassador to Rome, B.C. 155. Carneades excelled in the vehement and rapid, Critolaüs in the correct and elegant, and Diogenes in the simple and modest, kind of eloquence. Carneades, in particular, attracted the attention of his new auditory by the subtlety of his reasoning and the fluency of his language. Before Galba and Cato the Censor, he harangued with great variety of thought and copiousness of diction in praise of justice. The next day, to establish his doctrine of the uncertainty of human knowledge, he undertook to refute all his former arguments. Many were captivated by his eloquence; but Cato, apprehensive lest the Roman youth should lose their military character in the pursuit of Grecian learning, persuaded the Senate to send back these philosophers, without delay, to their own schools.

Carneades obtained such high reputation at home that other philosophers, when they had dismissed their scholars, frequently came to hear him. It was the doctrine of the New Academy that the senses, the understanding, and the imagination frequently deceive us, and therefore can not be infallible judges of truth; but that, from the impression which we perceive to be produced on the mind by means of the senses, we infer appearances of truth or probabilities. He maintained that these do not always correspond to the real nature of things, and that there is no infallible method of determining when they are true or false, and consequently that they afford no certain criterion of truth. Nevertheless, with respect to the conduct of life, Carneades held that probable appearances are a sufficient guide, because it is unreasonable that some degree of credit should not be allowed to those witnesses who commonly give a true report. He maintained that all the knowledge the human mind is capable of attaining is not science, but opinion. He died in B.C. 129. See NEW ACADEMY.

Carnēus. See CARNEA.

Carni. A Keltic people, dwelling north of the Veneti, in the Alpes Carnicae. See ALPES.

Carnuntum. An ancient Keltic town in Upper Pannonia, on the Danube, east of Vindobona (Vienna), and subsequently a Roman municipium or a colony.

Carnūtes. A powerful people in the centre of Gaul, between the Liger and the Sequana; their capital was Genabum (Orléans).

Carpătes (also called ALPES BASTARNĬCAE). The modern Carpathian Mountains; the mountains separating Dacia from Sarmatia.

Carpăthus (Κάρπαθος). The modern Scarpanto; an island between Crete and Rhodes, in the sea named after it. Its chief town was Posidium.

Carpenters. See FABER.

Carpentum. A cart; also a rectangular two-wheeled carriage, enclosed, and with an arched or sloping cover overhead.

The carpentum was used to convey the Roman matrons in the public festal processions; and, as this was a high distinction, the privilege of riding in a carpentum on such occasions was allowed to particular women by special grant of the Senate. This was done on behalf of Agrippina, who availed herself of the privilege so far as even to enter the Capitol in her carpentum (Tac. *Ann.* xii. 42). A medal was struck (see illustration) to commemorate this decree of the Senate in her favour. When Claudius celebrated his triumph at Rome, he was followed by his empress, Messalina, in her carpentum (Suet. *Claud.* 17).

Carpentum. (Medal of Caligula.)

This carriage contained seats for two, and sometimes for three persons, besides the coachman (Liv. i. 34). It was commonly drawn by a pair of mules (*carpentum mulare*), but more rarely by oxen or horses, and sometimes by four horses like a *quadriga*. For grand occasions it was very richly adorned. Agrippina's carriage, as above represented, shows painting or carving on the panels, and the head is supported by Caryatides (q. v.) at the four corners. The convenience and stateliness of the carpentum were also assumed by magistrates, and by men of luxurious habits, or those who had a passion for driving. When Caligula instituted games and other solemnities in honour of his deceased mother, Agrippina, her carpentum went in the procession (Suet. *Calig.* 15).

Carpenta, or covered carts, were much used by the Britons, and by the Gauls, the Cimbri, the Allobroges, and other Northern nations (Flor. i. 18 *et al.*). These, together with the carts of the more common form, including baggage-wagons, appear to have been comprehended under the term *carri* or *carra*, which is the Keltic name with a Latin termination. The Gauls and Helvetii took a great multitude of them on their military expeditions; and, when they were encamped, arranged them in close order, so as to form extensive lines of circumvallation (Caes. *B. G.* i. 24, 26).

The agricultural writers use *carpentum* to denote either a common cart or a cart-load—e. g. *xxiv stercoris carpenta* (Pallad. x. 1).

Carpessus. See CARTEA.

Carpetāni. A powerful people in Hispania Tarraconensis, with a fertile territory on the rivers Anas and Tagus. Their capital was Toletum (Toledo).

Carpi or **Carpiāni.** A German people dwelling between the Carpathian Mountains and the Danube.

Carpia. See CARTEA.

Carpophŏra (Καρποφόρα). See DEMETER.

Carpou Diké (καρποῦ δίκη). A civil action at Athens under the jurisdiction of the thesmothetae, instituted against a farmer for default in payment of rent (Meier, *Att. Proc.* p. 531). It was also adopted to enforce a judicial award when the unsuccessful litigant refused to surrender the land to his opponent, and might be used to determine the right to land, as the judgment would determine whether the plaintiff could claim rent of the defendant.

Carrae or **Carrhae** (Κάρραι). The Haran or Charran of the Scriptures; a city of Osrhoëné in Mesopotamia, where Crassus met his death after his defeat by the Parthians, B.C. 53. See CRASSUS.

Carrāgo. A kind of fortification, consisting of a great number of wagons placed round an army. It was employed by barbarous nations, as, for instance, the Scythians, Gauls, and Goths. See Veget. iii. 10.

Carriages. See BASTERNA; CARPENTUM; CARRUCA; CISIUM; CURRUS; ESSEDUM; REDA.

Carrūca. A carriage used in imperial times, and first mentioned by Pliny (*H. N.* xxxiii. § 140). Like the *reda* (q. v.), it was a travelling-carriage on four wheels. Nero is said to have travelled with 500 (Lamprid. *Heliog.* 31) or even 1000 carrucae (Suet. *Ner.* 30). These carriages were sometimes used in Rome by persons of distinction, like the carpentum (q. v.), in which case they appear to have been covered with plates of bronze, silver, and even gold, which were sometimes ornamented with embossed work. Martial speaks of an *aurea carruca* which cost the value of a farm; and Alexander Severus allowed senators at Rome to use carrucae and redae plated with silver (Lamprid. *Alex. Sev.* 43). These are the *carrucae argentatae*, the use of which within Rome spread in the course of the third century from the high officials to private persons. We have no representations of carriages in ancient works of art which can be safely said to be carrucae; but there are several illustrations of carriages ornamented with plates of metal. Carrucae were also used for carrying women, and were then, as well perhaps as in other cases, drawn by mules; whence Ulpian (*Dig.* 21. tit. 1, s. 38, § 8) speaks of *mulae carrucariae.*

Carrus. A two-wheeled cart like that shown in the annexed illustration. It was used in the Roman armies chiefly for the transportation of baggage and stores, and drawn by bullocks. See Caes. *B. G.* i. 3; Liv. x. 28.

Carrus. (Column of Trajan.)

Carseŏli. The modern Carsoli; a town of the Aequi, in Latium, colonized by the Romans.

Cart. See CARRUS; PLAUSTRUM.

Cartēa (also called CARTHAEA, CARPIA, CARPESSUS). More anciently Tartessus; a celebrated town and harbour in the south of Spain, at the head of the gulf of which Mount Calpé forms one side, founded by the Phœnicians, and colonized B.C. 170 by 4000 Roman soldiers.

Carthaea (Καρθαία). A town on the south side of the island of Ceos.

Carthāgo. A rich and powerful city on the northern coast of Africa, the capital of one of the greatest empires of antiquity. The Roman name Carthago and the Greek Καρχηδών are both corruptions of the native Punic Kirjath-Hadeshath, or "New Town," so called to distinguish it from Tyre, or possibly from the earlier settlement at Utica (q. v.)

Carthage was situated on the peninsula forming the northeast corner of modern Tunis, but topographers differ in their views of the exact locality. One school holds that the city occupied the north of the peninsula, while the other school places its site upon the southern portion. The most generally accepted view is the latter.

An important feature of the city was the hill with its citadel (Byrsa), surrounded by walls, and approached by a series of sixty steps. On the land side a triple wall, on which were mounted towers and casemates, surrounded the city, and afforded shelter for 300 elephants and some 4000 horses. Two artificial harbours—one rectangular, for merchant vessels, opening into the Bay of Tunis, and with a narrow passage that could be closed by chains, and a second circular harbour for ships of war—gave Carthage access to the sea. The second harbour (*Kothon*) contained in its centre an island with the official residence of the naval commander-in-chief. Although these harbours are now much diminished in size, their situation is still readily identified. Between the lagoon and the sea a strip of land, called by Roman writers the Taenia, is also plainly to be recognized to-day. Beyond the walls of the city was the beautiful suburb of Magalia or Megara (now Mara), and still farther a great necropolis of sepulchres strongly built and carefully preserved.

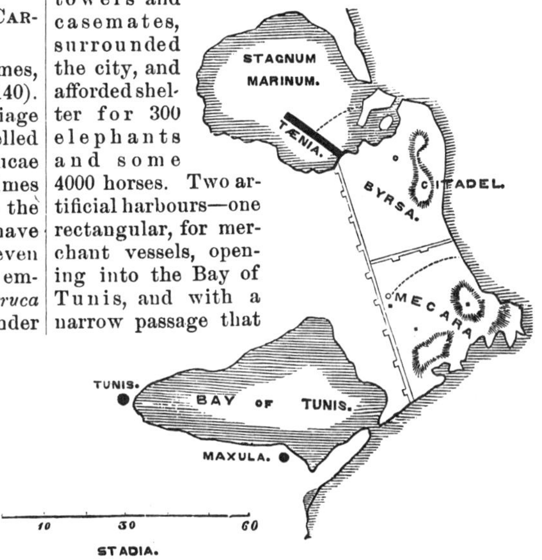

Plan of Tyrian Carthage.

The people of Carthage were members of the

great Semitic race, and belonged to the Phœnician branch, since Carthage was settled (probably about the middle of the ninth century B.C.) either by a colony directly sent from the Phœnician city of Tyre, or from the Tyrian offshoot, Utica. They were closely akin to the Canaanites who held Palestine before the Jewish invasion, and their language resembled the Hebrew. Because of their generally known Phœnician origin, the Romans called them Poeni or Punici, from Φοίνικες, signifying "the Red Men," or perhaps referring to the palms (φοίνικες), the symbol of the Syrian coast. The name *Sarranus*, given to Phœnician wares, serves also to connect the Poeni with their original Syrian home (Sil. Ital. ix. 319).

Carthage was the youngest of the Phœnician colonies in the northern territory of Africa, the earlier ones being Utica, Tunis, and Hadrumetum, in the district of Zeugitana, Hippo, and Leptis. Over all these, which were once independent of her, Carthage finally attained at once commercial and political supremacy. The history of this gradual rise to power is unknown, for no historical notices earlier than the sixth century B.C. are now available; and at that period Carthage was already the centre and the capital of a mighty empire, extending from the borders of Cyrenè to the Straits of Gibraltar, and holding as provinces the Balearic Islands, Malta, Sardinia, and some settlements on the coast of Spain and Gaul. An immense revenue flowed into the coffers of the State from the rich grain lands of Emporia and Byzacium southeast of the city, and commerce extending over the known world brought wealth to the citizens. South of the African coast, the power of Carthage extended as far as Lake Tritonis (q. v.), which was connected by a canal with the Lesser Syrtis. Besides the Carthaginians of pure Phœnician descent, the aristocracy of the Empire, three other classes of subjects are mentioned. These are: (*a*) the Libyo-Phœnicians, a mixed race, the offspring of intermarriages between the Libyans and the original Phœnician settlers; (*b*) the Libyans, an entirely different race from the Phœnicians, and to some extent ignorant even of the Punic language; and (*c*) the Nomads, who lived on the borders of the Empire towards the south, and professed an allegiance of a doubtful sort to the government of Carthage. The Libyo-Phœnicians formed the agricultural class, tilling the fields in Zeugitana; but were regarded with a certain suspicious dislike by the Carthaginians of pure blood, much as the Mexican gentry of unmixed Spanish lineage regard their fellow-countrymen of mixed descent. The Libyans, who were the original owners of the soil, and had been dispossessed by the Phœnician colonists, formed the bulk of the Carthaginian army; but the harsh treatment which they received, and perhaps the remembrance of their former ownership of the land, made them discontented, and, at times, mutinous. The Nomads furnished Carthage with a fierce and warlike irregular cavalry; yet their loyalty was always uncertain, and, in fact, it was by their aid that Rome finally subdued the Carthaginian people.

The commercial and maritime enterprise of the people of Carthage was remarkable in antiquity. They were great navigators and explorers. One of their admirals, Hanno (q. v.), as early as the sixth century B.C., sailed through the Straits of Gibraltar out into the Atlantic, passed down the western coast of Africa, entered the Senegal (Chretes?), and having reached a bay supposed to be on the southern borders of Sierra Leone, returned only when compelled to do so by the difficulty of provisioning his ship. A Greek MS. in the library of Heidelberg University professes to be the translation of the account which Hanno placed among the archives kept in the great Temple of Molech at Carthage. (See AFRICA.) A little later, a second Carthaginian, one Himilco, is believed to have visited the northern coasts of Europe.

Coin of Carthage, with Winged Horse.

RELIGION.—The religion of the Carthaginians, like that of the other Canaanitish peoples, was a form of fire-worship. As with all Semites, the rites and practice of religion formed a part of the daily life, and profoundly influenced the development of their civilization. Their chief god, Molech, represented the destructive influence of the sun, and in his temples human victims were immolated with fire. These victims were usually prisoners taken in war, but not always, for when Agathocles besieged the city, we are told that 200 noble children belonging to native families were offered up to secure the favour of the god. The moon-goddess Tanith or Tanist (Tanis) appears to have been identical with Ashtaroth, Melkart with Heracles, and a sea-god whom the Greeks identified with Poseidon was probably the same as the Philistine deity, Dagon. Rites in honour of deified heroes were celebrated, while animals—e. g. the lion, bull, serpent, etc.—and such of the Greek divinities as the Carthaginians had heard of in Sicily also received special worship. There is no evidence that the priests formed a separate caste, confined to certain families. On the contrary, sacrifices appear to have been offered by the magistrates and military leaders. The inscriptions and bas-reliefs thus far discovered and studied afford no confirmation of the charges made by the Greek and Roman writers, that the Carthaginians were guilty of obscene and unnatural practices in the conduct of their worship; and it is probable that the statements of the Christian Fathers refer to Roman and not to Phœnician Carthage. The morality of the Carthaginians, in fact, appears to have been originally of even an ascetic character, as befitted an industrious and largely agricultural people (Aristot. *Oecon.* i. 5). The Phœnician theory of cosmogony was given by a native author, Sanchoniathon, born either at Tyre or Berytus in the tenth century B.C., who wrote in Phœnician a history in nine books, containing an account of the theology and antiquities of Phœnicia, and of the neighbouring states. This work was translated into Greek under Hadrian by Philo of Byblus, and of it some fragments have been preserved in the history of Eusebius of Caesarea. An interesting summary of the substance of these fragments is given in Davis's *Carthage*, pp. 199–205 (N. Y. 1861).

GOVERNMENT.—The form of government at Carthage, which Aristotle praises for its stability and for its success in securing the general happiness and prosperity of the people, was aristocratic in its constitution (Aristot. *Polit.* ii. 8). The principal magistrates (*suffetes*, Heb. *sophetim*) have been compared to both the Roman consuls and the Spartan kings. Their number, however, is not definitely known, nor the extent of their term of office. They were eligible for re-election. A Senate, elected by popular vote, participated in the government with the *suffetes*, and was filled largely from the ranks of the wealthy. There appears to have been a sort of referendum to the people when the *suffetes* and the Senate disagreed upon any course of action. There existed also, side by side with the regular governmental organization, a power which, like that of the Spartan ephors, gradually gained the real control of the State. This was the highest aristocracy, which elected bodies of commissions (pentarchies) so constituted that the outgoing members preserved their power for another year, and thus impressed upon the institution a consistent and symmetrical policy. These pentarchies elected a council of 104 members, who at last usurped the authority of the State; though Hannibal succeeded in checking their power, and in restoring to the people some real share in the government.

HISTORY.—The history of Carthage falls naturally into four periods: (1) from the foundation of the city to the beginning of the wars with Syracuse, B.C. 410; (2) to the beginning of the war with Rome, B.C. 265; (3) to the destruction of the city by the Romans, B.C. 146; (4) from the restoration of the city to its final destruction by the Arabs, A.D. 698.

The foreign conquests of Carthage were undertaken with the object of securing her commerce. Justin tells us of a king, Malchus (the Latin form of the royal title), who, after successes in Africa and Sicily, was defeated in Sardinia, and turned his arms against his country. He must have lived between B.C. 600 and 550. A more historical personage is his successor Mago (between B.C. 550 and 500), said to be the founder of the military power of the Carthaginians. His sons were Hasdrubal and Hamilcar, his grandsons Hannibal, Hasdrubal, and Sappho, sons of Hasdrubal, and Himilco, Hanno, and Gisco, sons of Hamilcar. By the energy of this family the Carthaginian Empire was established over Sardinia, which was not lost till after the First Punic War, over the Balearic Islands and part of Sicily, and over portions of Liguria and Gaul. There are, however, few events of which the chronology is certain. The first is the sea-fight between the Etruscans and Carthaginians on the one hand and the Phocæans of Aleria in Corsica on the other, which occurred in B.C. 536. The Phocæans, driven from Asia Minor by Harpagus in 564, had settled at Aleria or Alalia in Corsica, but engaged in piracy, which demanded the interference of the commercial naval powers. The Phocæans won the battle, but with such loss that they abandoned Corsica, and settled at Velia in Italy. Polybius has preserved three treaties between Carthage and Rome, the first of which belongs to the year B.C. 509, the second probably to the period between B.C. 480 and 410. Their object is to restrict Roman commerce in Punic waters, and it is noticeable that the second treaty prescribes stricter limits than the first, and testifies to a considerable superiority of Carthage over Rome. To the period of about B.C. 500 belong the expeditions of Hanno and Himilco—the one to found colonies on the west coast of Africa, which was probably explored as far as the mouths of the Senegal and Gambia, the other to obtain a knowledge of the Atlantic, which resulted in the discovery of Britain. But the most important event of the first period was the battle of Himera, fought between Hamilcar and Gelo of Syracuse, about the year B.C. 480. Terillus, tyrant of Himera, on the north coast of Sicily, driven out by Thero of Agrigentum, implored and obtained help from the Carthaginians. Thero was assisted by Gelo of Syracuse. An account of this battle is given by Herodotus. The forces of Hamilcar consisted of 3000 ships and 300,000 men — Phœnicians, Libyans, Iberians, Ligurians, Helysci (perhaps Volscians), Sardinians, and Corsicans. He was defeated with great loss.

Carthaginian Warrior. (Cabinet de France.)

For seventy years the Carthaginians made no further effort for the subjugation of Sicily. This battle is one of the most important in ancient history. The expedition in which it terminated was undertaken in conjunction with that of the Persians against the Greeks of Attica. The nearly simultaneous defeats at Himera and Salamis decided the question whether Semitic or Aryan nations should hold the empire of the West. The only other events of any importance in this period of which we have an account are the more complete subjugation of the African dependencies by the family of Mago, and the settlement of the disputed boundary between Carthage and Cyrené.

The second period of 140 years (B.C. 410–269) is occupied with the attempts of Carthage to reduce Sicily to the condition of a subject province. At this time her settlements were confined to the western corner of the island, while on the eastern coast Syracuse undertook the defence of Grecian nationality, and waged the battle of Aryans against Semites, until both combatants fell before the supremacy of Rome. The repulse of the Athenians from Syracuse, and the same rivalry between Egesta and Selinus which had invited Athenian interference in the affairs of the island, induced the Carthaginians to renew an enterprise which had been interrupted for seventy years. Hannibal, son of Giso, stormed Selinus, and avenged at Himera the death of his grandfather. Overtures of peace were rejected, and preparations made for a more vigorous attack. In 406, Hannibal and Himilco destroyed the great city of Agrigentum, overthrew the mighty columns of her temples, and covered a flourishing site with a mass of ruins. Hannibal died before Agrigentum; Himilco proceeded to attack Gela. Syracuse was now governed by Dionysius, who from an obscure position had raised himself to the rank of despot. In 405, a treaty made by Carthage secured to her the possession of her conquests, and to Dionysius a firmer position on the throne. But he no sooner felt himself secure than he hastened to drive the enemy from the island. War broke out in 398, all Sicily fell before the Punic arms, and Dionysius, driven by Himilco to take refuge within the walls of Syracuse, was there besieged. Pestilence came to his assistance, and the Carthaginians were defeated; 150,000 Punic corpses lay unburied on Grecian soil; and Himilco, unable to bear the contempt of his fellow-citizens, starved himself to death. The Libyans rose in rebellion, and Carthage was threatened by an army of 200,000 men. The attempt of Mago, between 396 and 392, to procure a more favourable result had little effect. Ten years afterwards he led another expedition. The defeat of Cabala nearly lost the possession of the whole of Sicily, but the brilliant victory of Corsica restored the balance, and the Halycus was accepted as the boundary between the two peoples. Fourteen years of peace ensued. In 368, the misfortunes of Carthage encouraged Dionysius to a new but unsuccessful effort to complete the purpose of his life, but his death put an end to a renewal of the attempt, and his son and successor made peace with the Carthaginians. The weak government of Dionysius II. was favourable to the extension of Carthaginian Empire in Sicily; but they found an antagonist of different mettle in the Corinthian Timoleon, who, after liberating Syracuse from its tyrants, made war against Carthage for six years (B.C. 345–340). The defeat of the Crimissus (B.C. 340) was most crushing. The Holy Legion, composed of 2500 men of the best families of Carthage, was destroyed, and the host of mercenaries cut to pieces. Peace restrained the Carthaginians within their old boundary of the Halycus; the Greek cities were declared free; and Carthage promised never again to support a despot in Syracuse. The next thirty years contain little of note except traces of friendly intercourse between Carthage and Rome, and a record of assistance given to the Tyrians when besieged by Alexander the Great. She, however, sent ambassadors to Babylon to congratulate the conqueror on his return from Asia. Agathocles (q. v.) was the first to discover that the secular enemies of his countrymen were vulnerable in Africa. After becoming despot of Syracuse, and establishing his authority over the great towns in Sicily, he found that he had to reckon with the Carthaginians. Unsuccessful in the island, he transferred his forces to the mainland in 310, reduced Carthage to the last extremities, and would probably have obtained more signal success had not the revolt of Agrigentum called him home. Peace made in 306 continued till the death of Agathocles in 289. His loss encouraged the extension of Punic dominion, and at last obliged the Syracusans to call in the assistance of Pyrrhus, the chivalrous king of Epirus. He left Italy in 277, and in a short time drove the Carthaginians from the west and besieged them in the distant fortress of Lilybaeum. But his allies were untrue to him. Carthage and Rome were leagued against him. He left Sicily in 276, and his departure from Italy in the following year left the Carthaginians to stand in sharp antagonism to the Latin branch of the Aryan stock.

The third period of Carthaginian history extends from B.C. 264 to 146—from the outbreak of the first war with Rome to the final annihilation of the city by the conquerors. This is not the place for a detailed account of the Punic wars, which occupy a large space in every Roman history. We must content ourselves with a hasty summary. The first war, which lasted from B.C. 264 to 241, was a contest for the possession of Sicily. The Carthaginians in undertaking it felt secure of their mastery over the sea. Their ambassadors told the Romans that they could not even wash their hands in the sea without permission of the Carthaginians. Montesquieu considers it one of the chief causes of the rise of Roman greatness that they were careful to borrow from their enemies whatever was calculated to improve their own efficiency. The Romans not only built a fleet, but developed a novelty of tactics which precisely secured the object which they had in view. They were encouraged to further exertion by the victories of B.C. 260 and B.C. 256, and were schooled to caution by the defeat of the following year. The war was practically ended by the brilliant success of Catulus in B.C. 242, and Sicily was lost to the Carthaginians. The next three years and a half (241–237) were occupied by a civil war, which shows us on what insecure foundations the power of Carthage was based. The large army of mercenaries which had been employed against Rome was incautiously admitted into the city. Under pretence of demanding pay they rose against their employers, and were joined by the Libyans and Numidians, who cultivated the surrounding lands in unwilling subjection. The insurrection was quelled with difficulty, but a similar revolution in Sardinia was more successful—700 Carthaginians were barbarously murdered, and the possession of the island passed to the Romans. All we know of the twenty years which elapsed before the beginning of the second war with Rome is confined to the successes of Hamilcar and his family in Spain. In B.C. 218, Hannibal, who had sworn as a boy eternal enmity to the Romans, began the enterprise to which he devoted his life. His object was not so much to conquer Italian soil or Italian cities as to break up the confederacy upon which the greatness of Rome depended, and to undo the fabric of its empire stone by stone. He sought, therefore, on the one hand to rouse Greeks and Orientals to a joint attack upon the common foe, and on the other to sow dissension among the Latin, Sabellian, and Oscan tribes, and to urge them to reduce Rome to that position of comparative inferiority which she had occupied many centuries before. Both these plans failed. Hannibal was badly supported from home; he found that to combine in unity the shifting policy of the East was to weave a rope of sand; and he discovered, above all, that Roman supremacy was established on a basis of complete security. Far different, in fact, was her position, seated among kindred peoples bound to her by affinities of blood and language as well as interest, governed by the wise policy of a patriotic Senate, and restrained by the overpowering force of devoted legions, from that of the city of merchants, torn by factions, surrounded by alien and even hostile tribes, defended by mercenaries, and swayed by interest and passion. The defeat of Hasdrubal at the Metaurus in B.C. 207 crushed the last hope of the invader; Spain was recovered by the genius of Scipio; and in B.C. 203, Hannibal, not unwillingly, obeyed the order to embark from Italy to retard the ruin of his country which it was too late to save. The battle of Zama, in 202, put an end to the war in the following year. It was due to the magnanimity of Scipio and Hannibal that peace was concluded on such terms that, while Rome had no longer to fear Carthage as a rival, she was content to recognize her existence as a commercial community.

For the next six years, Hannibal governed the city which he had not been able to preserve. He reformed the constitution in a democratical sense, and paid with surprising facility the enormous indemnity demanded by Rome. He was engaged in planning a combination against Rome with Antiochus of Syria when he was driven from power, and forced to take refuge in the East, where shortly afterwards he fell a victim to Roman hatred.

The interval between B.C. 183 and 150 contains little besides the history of internal dissensions—struggles between the Roman party, the democratical party, and the party of Masinissa, which tore the city in sunder by their quarrels. The so-called Third Punic War (B.C. 149–146) is one of the saddest events in all history, and the greatest blot upon the reputation of the Romans. Jealousy of their old antagonists had been shown by constant acts of injustice, and at last the sight of the prosperity and riches of the city impressed upon the narrow mind of Cato the conviction that Carthage must be blotted out. A pretext for war was wantonly invented. The anxieties of the Carthaginians to secure peace at any sacrifice was made the instrument of their destruction. When they saw that their ruin was resolved upon, and that compromise was hopeless, they defended themselves with an energy which would have saved them at an earlier period. The sentence of the Roman Senate was ruthlessly carried out. The city burned for seventeen days, and concealed its very site under a heap of ashes. The plough was passed over it, and the ground was cursed forever. In the words of Mommsen, "where the industrious Phœnicians bustled and trafficked for five hundred years, Roman slaves henceforth pastured the herds of their distant masters."

The history of Roman Carthage, which constitutes the fourth period, can be given in a few words. In B.C. 122, Gaius Gracchus led 6000 colonists to Africa, and founded the city of Iunonia. The colony did not prosper. In B.C. 29, a second colony (Colonia Carthago) was sent out by Augustus in fulfilment of a design of Iulius Caesar. This became so prosperous that Herodian declares it to have disputed with Alexandria the second place in the Empire. In the middle of the fifth century, it became, under Genseric, the capital of the Vandal kingdom (439), and in A.D. 533 it was stormed by Belisarius. In A.D. 698, it was entirely destroyed by the general of the calif Abd-ul-Melek.

For centuries after this final destruction, the site of Carthage was a quarry for both the Africans and for the merchants of Europe. Genoese vessels, trading with Tunis in the Middle Ages, seldom returned without a cargo of Carthaginian marble. The cathedral of Pisa is even said to have been built out of the ruins of Carthage. Recent times, also, have aided in the work of devastation, since the marble blocks of the ancient walls have been within the last few years in part destroyed by the operations of the Tunisian railway. The aqueduct, over fifty miles in length, is the only remnant of the greatness of the city's past that still preserves a real impressiveness.

BIBLIOGRAPHY.—The reader is referred to the following works: Mer, *Mémoire sur le Périple d'Hannon* (Paris, 1888); Böttger, *Geschichte der Carthagen* (Berlin, 1827); Davis, *Carthage and her Remains* (N. Y. 1861); Hennebert, *Histoire d'Anibal* (Paris, 1870–78); Bosworth Smith, *Carthage and the Carthaginians* (London, 1879); Perrot and Chipiez, *History of Art in Phœnicia and her Dependencies* (Eng. trans. by Armstrong, 1885); Church, *Carthage, or the Empire of Africa* (London, 1886); and the sketch in Mommsen, *Hist. of Rome*, vol. ii. The famous novel of Gustave Flaubert, *Salammbô*, gives a vivid picture of ancient Carthage, and is both learned and brilliant. See also the articles DIDO; HANNIBAL; PUNIC WARS; and for a notice of the Carthaginian language, PHŒNICIA.

Carthāgo Nova (Καρχηδών, ἡ Νέα). The modern Carthagena; an important town on the east coast of Hispania Tarraconensis, founded by the Carthaginians under Hasdrubal, B.C. 243, and subsequently conquered and colonized by the Romans. It is situated on a promontory running out into the sea, and possesses one of the finest harbours in the world. At the entrance was a small island known as Scombraria, famous for the fish-sauce made from the *scombri* or mackerel caught here. See GARUM.

Cartibŭlum. A particular kind of table described by Varro (*L. L.* v. 125) as frequently seen in the *atria* of Roman houses during his boyhood

Cartibulum. (From Pompeii.)

(about B.C. 100). Both the name and the thing were apparently becoming obsolete in his time. It was an oblong slab of marble supported on a single bracket or console (*una columella*); it stood near the impluvium, and bronze vessels were placed upon it. Such a table has been discovered in more than one house at Pompeii, with a fountain behind it shaped like a cippus or square pillar, and flowing into the impluvium.

Carus, M. AURELIUS. A Roman emperor, who succeeded Probus. He was first appointed, by the latter, prætorian prefect, and after his death was chosen by the army to be his successor, A.D. 282. Carus created his two sons, Carinus and Numerianus, Caesars, as soon as he was elevated to the Empire, and, some time after, gave them each the title of Augustus. On the news of the death of Probus, the barbarians put themselves in motion, and Carus, sending his son Carinus into Gaul, departed with Numerianus for Illyricum, in order to oppose the Sarmatae, who threatened Thrace and Italy. He slew 16,000, and made 20,000 prisoners. Proceeding after this against the Persians, he made himself master of Mesopotamia, and of the cities of Seleucia and Ctesiphon, and took in consequence the surnames of Persicus and Parthicus. He died, however, in the midst of his successes, A.D. 283. (See APER.) His whole reign was one of not more than sixteen or seventeen months. Carus was deified after his death. According to Vopiscus, by whom his life was written, he held a middle rank between good and bad princes.

Carventum. A town of the Volsci, to which the Carventana Arx mentioned by Livy (iv. 53, 9) belonged, between Signia and the sources of the Trerus.

Carvilius Maxĭmus. (1) SPURIUS, twice consul, B.C. 293 and 273, both times with L. Papirius Cursor. In their first consulship they gained brilliant victories over the Samnites, and in their second they brought the Samnite War to a close. (2) SPURIUS, son of the preceding, twice consul, B.C. 234 and 228, is said to have been the first person at Rome who divorced his wife. See Valerius Maximus, ii. 1, 4; Aul. Gell. iv. 3; xvii. 21.

Caryae (Καρύαι). A town in Laconia near the borders of Arcadia, originally belonged to the territory of Tegea in Arcadia. Female figures in architecture that support burdens are said to have been called CARYATĬDES in token of the abject slavery to which the women of Caryae were reduced by the Greeks, as a punishment for joining the Persians at the invasion of Greece (Vitruv. i. 1, 5).

Caryatid. (From the Erechtheum, Athens.)

Caryanda (Καρύανδα). A city of Caria, on a little island, once probably united with the mainland. It was the birthplace of the geographer Scylax.

Caryatĭdes (καρυάτιδες). See CARYAE.

Carystus (Κάρυστος). A town on the southern coast of Euboea, founded by Dryopes, celebrated for its marble quarries and for the mineral known as *asbestos* (q. v.).

Casa. (1) A cottage. See DOMUS. (2) A bower or rustic arbour.

Casa Romŭli. The thatched cottage of Romulus on the Capitoline Hill at Rome, for which see the article DOMUS, p. 536.

Casaubon, ISAAC. A great classical scholar of the sixteenth century, born at Geneva, February 15th, 1559. When only twenty-four years of age, he was appointed professor of Greek at Geneva, from which town he was called in 1596 to a like chair at Montpellier. In 1598, he became royal librarian at Paris; but on the death of Henry IV. this position became insecure by reason of his Protestantism, and in 1610 he removed to England, where he was received with great favour by James I., who made him prebendary of Canterbury and Westminster. Casaubon was bitterly attacked by many as having sold his conscience for preferment, and thus becoming the hired advocate of James. In 1614, he wrote his *Exercitationes contra Baronium*, in criticism of the *Annales Ecclesiastici* of Cardinal Baronius.

Casaubon was a scholar of great application, retentiveness, and candour; indefatigable in research, and with an excellent faculty of illustration. He had by unwearied labour acquired a vast fund of information, and his diffuse and exhaustive commentaries show how richly stored a mind he possessed. He represents the non-Ciceronian school of sixteenth-century Latinity to which Scaliger and Lipsius also belonged, these three being known as the "Triumvirate" by their contemporaries. The works of Casaubon comprise the treatises *De Satirica Graeca Poësi et Romanorum Satira* (1605); *De Libertate Ecclesiastica* (1607); the *Exercitationes* already mentioned; and annotated editions of Strabo (1587); Dionysius Hal. (1588); Aristotle (1590); Pliny's Letters (1591); Theophrastus (1592); Diogenes Laërtius (1593); Suetonius (1595); Theocritus (1596); Athenaeus (1598–1600); the Hist. Augusta (1603); Persius (1605); Polybius (1609); and the *edit. prin.* of Polyaenus. Of these the most ambitious work is the commentary upon Athenaeus, in the preparation of which he spent ten years. Perhaps the most valuable is the Persius, which Scaliger enthusiastically styled "divine." Casaubon died in London, July 1st, 1614. His life has been written by Mark Pattison (Oxford, 1875), of which a second edition, edited by Prof. Nettleship, appeared in 1892.

Casca, P. SERVILIUS. A tribune of the plebs, B.C. 44, and one of Caesar's assassins.

Casci. See ABORIGINES.

Caseus (τυρός). Cheese, made by the Greeks and Romans of the milk of cows, sheep, and goats, and eaten either like cream cheese fresh, or dried and hardened. It was pressed into ornamental forms by moulds of boxwood. See Varro, *R. R.* ii. 11; Colum. vii. 8, 7; and especially Pliny, *H. N.* xi. § 97.

Casilīnum. A town in Campania on the Vulturnus, and on the same site as the modern Capua, celebrated for its heroic defence against Hannibal, B.C. 216.

Casĭna. A comedy of Plautus, which has come down to us in the form of an abridgment. It is based upon the Κληρούμενοι of Diphilus, with the addition of obscene and vulgar passages to suit the Roman taste. A good separate edition is that of Geppert (Berlin, 1866), and that of Schöll (Leipzig, 1890).

Casīnum. The modern S. Germano; a town in Latium on the river Casinus. Its citadel occupied the same site as the celebrated convent Monte Cassino.

Casiōtis. The district containing Casius (q. v.).

Casius. (1) The modern Ras Kasaroun; a mountain on the coast of Egypt, east of Pelusium, with a temple of Iupiter on its summit. Here also was the grave of Pompey. (2) Jebel Okrah; a mountain on the coast of Syria, south of Antioch and the Orontes.

Casmĕna (Κασμένη) or **Casmĕnae** (Κασμέναι). A town in Sicily, founded by Syracuse about B.C. 643.

Casperia or **Casperŭla.** A town of the Sabines on the river Himella.

Caspiae Portae or **Pylae** (Κάσπιαι Πύλαι). The Caspian Gates; a name given to several passes through the mountains round the Caspian. The principal of these was near the ancient Rhagae or Arsacia. Being a noted and central point, distances were reckoned from it (Polyb. v. 44, 5).

Caspii (Κάσπιοι). The name of certain Scythian tribes around the Caspian Sea.

Caspii Montes (τὸ Κάσπιον ὄρος). The modern Elburz Mountains; a name applied generally to the whole range of mountains which surround the Caspian Sea on the south and southwest, at the distance of from fifteen to thirty miles from its shore, and more especially to that part of this range south of the Caspian, in which was the pass called Caspiae Pylae (q. v.).

Caspīri (Κάσπειροι) or **Caspiraei** (Κασπιραῖοι). A people of India, whose exact position is doubtful; they are generally placed in Cashmere and Nepaul.

Caspium Mare (τὸ Κάσπιον πέλαγος). The modern Caspian Sea, also called HYRCANIUM, ALBĀNUM, and SCYTHĬCUM—names all derived from the people who lived on its shores; a great salt-water lake in Asia. Probably at some remote period the Caspian was united both with the Sea of Aral and with the Arctic Ocean. Both lakes have their surface considerably below that of the Euxine or Black Sea, the Caspian nearly 350 feet, and the Aral about 200 feet, and both are still sinking by evaporation. The whole of the neighbouring country indicates that this process has been going on for centuries past. Besides a number of smaller streams, two great rivers flow into the Caspian: the Rha (Volga) on the north, and the united Cyrus and Araxes (Kour) on the west; but it loses more by evaporation than it receives from these rivers.

Cassander (Κάσσανδρος). The son of Alexander's general, Antipater. His father, on his death-bed (B.C. 319), appointed Polysperchon regent, and conferred upon Cassander only the secondary dignity of chiliarch. Being dissatisfied with this arrangement, Cassander strengthened himself in various ways that he might carry on war with Polysperchon. First, he formed an alliance with Ptolemy and Antigonus, and next defeated Olympias and put her to death. Afterwards he joined Seleucus, Ptolemy, and Lysimachus in their war against Antigonus. This war was, on the whole, unfavourable to Cassander. In 306, Cassander took the title of king, when it was assumed by Antigonus, Lysimachus, and Ptolemy. But it was not until the year 301 that the decisive battle of Ipsus secured Cassander the possession of Macedonia and Greece. Cassander died of dropsy in 297, and was succeeded by his son Philip.

Cassandra (Κασσάνδρα). The daughter of Priam and Hecuba. She was beloved by Apollo, and promised to listen to his addresses, provided he would grant her the knowledge of futurity. This knowledge she obtained, but she was regardless of her promise; and Apollo, in revenge, determined that no credit should ever be attached to her predictions. Hence her warnings respecting the downfall of Troy, and the subsequent misfortunes of the

Cassandra.

race, were disregarded by her countrymen. When Troy was taken, she fled for shelter to the Temple of Athenè, but was exposed there to the brutality of Aiax, the son of Oïleus. In the division of the spoils she fell to the share of Agamemnon, and was assassinated with him on his return to Mycenae. (See AGAMEMNON.) Cassandra was called Priameïs from her father; and Alexandra, as the sister of Alexander or Paris.

Cassandrēa (Κασσάνδρεια). See POTIDAEA.

Cassia Lex. See LEX.

Cassiāni. See IURISPRUDENTIA.

Cassiodōrus or **Cassiodorius**, FL. MAGNUS AURELIUS. A distinguished statesman, and one of the few men of learning at the downfall of the Western Empire, was born about A.D. 480, and died about A.D. 575. He enjoyed the confidence of Theodoric the Great and his successors, and conducted for a long series of years the government of the Ostrogothic kingdom. Several of his works, besides fragments of his orations, are still extant: (1) a history of the world from Adam to A.D. 519 (*Chronica*), rather meagre in substance; (2) a history of the Goths (*Historia Gothica*) to 526, of which we have only the version of Iordanis (*De Origine Actibusque Getarum*), an abridgment; (3) a collection of official documents (*Variarum Libri* *xii.*); (4) a number of theological and semi-theological works, among which are the *Institutiones Divinarum et Saecularium Litterarum*, a verbose commentary on the Psalms; besides a treatise *De Anima;* and (5) grammatical works, of which only one, *De Orthographia*, deserves mention. Late in life, Cassiodorus entered the Benedictine Order, and in 540 retired to a monastery in Calabria which he had himself founded (A.D. 529). His teaching led the monks of that order to prize ancient literature, so that the Benedictines afterwards performed a priceless service to classical scholarship in preserving MSS. of authors who would in all probability have otherwise been lost to us. On this point, see the work of Olleris, *Cassiodore, Conservateur des Livres de l'Antiquité Latine* (Paris, 1841).

The *editio princeps* of all the extant works of Cassiodorus is that of Fornerius (Paris, 1579), reprinted in Migne's *Patrologia*. There is a good English translation of a part of the *Variarum*, by Hodgkin, *The Letters of Cassiodorus* (London, 1886), with an Introduction. See IORDANIS.

Cassiopēa (Κασσιέπεια) or **Cassiŏpé** (Κασσιόπη). The wife of Cepheus, in Aethiopia, and mother of Andromeda, whose beauty she extolled above that of the Nereids. (See ANDROMEDA.) She was afterwards placed among the stars.

Cassis. A helmet. See GALEA.

Cassiterīdes (Κασσιτερίδες). Islands in the Western Ocean, where tin was found, supposed to be the Scilly Islands of the moderns, together with a part of Cornwall. The term Cassiterides is derived from the Greek κασσίτερος, "tin." The tin was obtained by the islanders from the mainland, and afterwards sold to strangers. Solinus (ch. 22) mentions these islands under the name of Silurum Insulae, and Sulpicius Severus (ii. 51), under that of Sylina Insula.

Cassius. (1) SPURIUS CASSIUS VISCELLĪNUS. A Roman distinguished for having carried through the first agrarian law at Rome, by which he gained the enmity of his fellow-patricians, who accused him of seeking regal power and put him to death. He held the consulship in B.C. 502, 493, and 486. From his time, the Cassii are plebeians, having probably abandoned the patriciate. See AGRARIAE LEGES. (2) GAIUS CASSIUS LONGĪNUS, one of the conspirators against Iulius Caesar. Even when a boy he is said to have been remarkable for his pride and the violence of his temper, if we may believe the anecdotes recorded of him by Plutarch (*Brut.* 9) and Valerius Maximus (iii. 1). He accompanied Crassus into Parthia as his quaestor, and distinguished himself, after the death of his general, by conducting the wreck of the Roman army back to Syria in safety. At the beginning of the Civil War he was one of the tribunes of the people. We find him after this commanding the Syrian squadron in Pompey's fleet, and infesting the coasts of Sicily. A short time before the battle of Pharsalia he had burned the entire fleet of the enemy, amounting to thirty-five ships, in the harbour of Messana. The news of Pompey's defeat, however, deterred him from pursuing his advantages; and, resigning the contest, he submitted to Caesar in Asia Minor, when the latter was returning from Egypt into Italy. Cicero, however, asserts that at this very time Cassius had intended to assassinate the man whose clemency he was willing to solicit, had not an accident prevented the accomplishment of his purpose (*Philipp.* ii. 11). He was not only spared by Caesar, but was appointed by him one of his lieutenants, a favour bestowed by magistrates upon their friends, in order to invest them with a public character, and thus enable them to reside or to travel in the provinces with greater comfort and dignity. Even during the last campaign of Caesar in Spain, Cassius wrote to Cicero, saying that he was anxious that Caesar should be victorious, for that he preferred an old and merciful master to a new and cruel one (Cic. *Ep. ad Fam.* xv. 19). He also, together with Brutus, was appointed one of the praetors for the year 709, at a moment in which he was entirely discontented with Caesar's government; and he is said to have been the person by whose intrigues the first elements of the conspiracy were formed. Cassius had married Iunia, the sister of Brutus, and it was partly through her means that he made his approaches, when seeking to gain over her brother and induce him to join in the plot. After the assassination of Caesar, Cassius, together with Brutus, raised an army, and was met by Octavius and Antony at Philippi. The wing which Cassius commanded being defeated, he imagined that all was lost, and killed himself, B.C. 42. Brutus gave him an honourable burial, and called him, with tears, the last of the Romans. (3) PARMENSIS, so called from his having been born at Parma in Italy, was a Latin poet of considerable talent. He sided with Brutus and Cassius in the Civil War, and obtained the office of military tribune. After the defeat of the republican forces he retired to Athens, and was put to death by Q. Varius, who had been sent for that purpose by Octavianus. He must not be confounded with Cassius the Etrurian, who appears to have been a very rapid and poor writer. (4) HEMĪNA, an early annalist of Rome, who flourished about B.C. 145. (5) A Roman lawyer, who reduced to a scientific system the legal principles set forth by Ateius Capito. His school is called Cassiani. (6) A Roman orator, distinguished for his eloquence, and fond, at the same time, of indulging in satirical composition. He was exiled by Augustus to the island of Seriphus, where he ended his days in wretchedness. His full name was TITUS CASSIUS SEVERUS. (7) CASSIUS LONGĪNUS. See LONGINUS. (8) CASSIUS FELIX. A Greek physician, who lived in the reign of Tiberius and wrote a treatise with the title Ἰατρικαὶ Ἀπορίαι καὶ Προβλήματα Φυσικά. It is printed in Ideler's *Physici et Medici Graeci Minores* (Berlin, 1841). (9) DION. See DION.

Cassivelaunus. A British chief, ruled over the country north of the Tamesis (Thames), and was intrusted by the Britons with the supreme command on Caesar's second invasion of Britain, B.C. 54. He was defeated by Caesar, and was obliged to sue for peace. Cf. Caes. *B. G.* v. 11, 18.

Castalia (Κασταλία). A celebrated fountain on Mount Parnassus, in which the Pythia was accustomed to bathe; sacred to Apollo and the Muses, who were hence called Castalides.

Castellāni Cista. See CISTA CASTELLANIANA.

Castellum. The diminutive of *castrum*, and denoting (1) a small fortress, or (2) a small town containing a garrison (Curt. v. 3).

Castellum Aquae. A reservoir. See Aquae Ductus.

Casthanaea (Κασθαναία). A town of Thessaly, on the coast of Magnesia, northwest of the promontory Sepias. It is noticed by Herodotus in his account of the terrible storm experienced by the fleet of Xerxes off this coast (vii. 183).

Castor (Κάστωρ). Brother of Pollux. See Dioscuri.

Castra. (1) A Roman camp, fortified with a rampart and a ditch, outside of which a Roman army never spent a single night. It was marked out on a place selected for the purpose, generally upon the spur of a hill. The same plan was always observed, and the quarters were indicated by coloured flags and lances, so that the divisions of the army, as they came in, could find their places at once. In the middle of the second century B.C., according to the account of Polybius (vi. 27), the plan of a camp for a consular army of two legions, with the proper contingent of Italian allies and its auxiliary troops, was as follows (see plan): The camp was square, its front being on the side farthest from the enemy. It had two main streets through it. (*a*) The *via principalis*, 100 feet wide, which divided it into a front part amounting to about two-thirds of the whole, and a back part turned towards the enemy. This road ended at two gates: the *porta principalis dextra* and the *porta principalis sinistra*. (*b*) The *via praetoria*, which cut the *via principalis* at right angles, and divided the whole length of the camp into two parts. This road was 50 feet in width, and ended in two gates: the *porta decumana* in front and the *porta praetoria* on the side opening towards the enemy. In the front part were encamped the two legions, with their allied contingents. They lay in three double rows of tents on each side of the *via praetoria*, which made a right angle with the *via principalis*. Its whole length was divided by streets 50 feet in width, while across it, from one lateral rampart to the other, ran the *via quintana*. The front side of the rows of tents was turned towards the intervening streets. Starting from the *via praetoria*, the first two lines of tents on each side contained the cavalry and infantry of one legion each, while the third row, lying nearest to the rampart, contained the cavalry and infantry of the allied contingents. In the hinder part of the camp, directly upon the *via principalis*, and on both sides of the *via praetoria*, were the tents of the twelve military tribunes, opposite the four ranks of the legions. On both sides were the tents of the *praefecti* of the allied contingents, placed in the same way opposite those of the troops under their command. Then followed the headquarters, or *praetorium*, a space 200 feet square, intersected by the *via praetoria*. In this was the general's tent (*tabernaculum*); in front was the altar on which the general sacrificed, on the left the *augurale* for taking the auspices, and on the right the *tribunal*. This was a bank of earth covered with turf, on which the general took his stand when addressing the troops (see Adlocutio) or administering justice. On the right of the *praetorium* was the *quaestorium*, containing the quarters of the paymasters and the train of artillery. On the left was the *forum*, a meeting-place for the soldiers. Between these spaces and the lateral ramparts were the tents of the select troops who composed the body-guard of the general. Those of the cavalry had their front turned inwards, while those of the infantry were turned towards the wall. The tents of the picked allied troops occupied the hinder part of the camp, which was bounded by a cross-road 100 feet in breadth. The tents of the cavalry looked inwards, those of the infantry towards the rampart. The auxiliary troops were posted at the two angles of this space. The rampart was divided from the tents by an open space 200 feet in width. This was specially intended to facilitate the march of the troops at their entrance and exit.

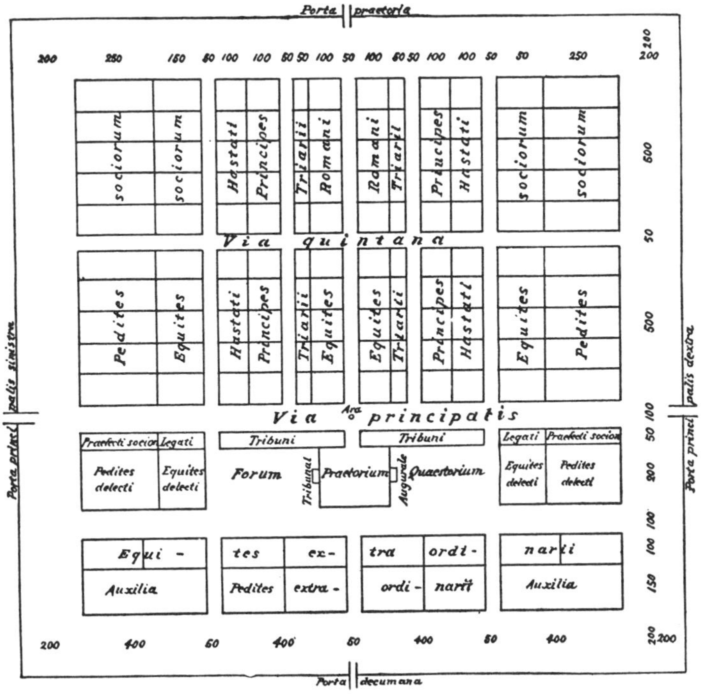

Plan of a Roman Camp. (After Polybius.)

The construction of the fortifications always began before the general's tent was pitched. The legionaries constructed the rampart and ditch in front and rear, while the allies did the same on either side. The stakes required for the formation of an *abattis* on the outer side of the wall were carried by the soldiers themselves on the march. The whole work was carried on under arms. The watches (*excubiae* and *vigiliae*) were kept with great strictness both by day and night. The *vigiliae*, or night-watches, were relieved four times, the trumpet sounding on each occasion. The posts of each night-watch were inspected by four Roman *equites*. The password for the night was given by the general. Each gate was guarded by outposts of infantry and cavalry, the light-armed troops (*velites*) being also distributed as sentries along the ramparts. When the camp was to break up, three signals were given; at the first, the tents were taken down and packed up; at the second, they were put upon beasts of burden and in wagons; and at the third, the army began its march.

After the time of Polybius the Roman military system underwent many changes, which involved alterations in the arrangements of the camp, but we have no trustworthy information on this subject in detail until the beginning of the second century A.D. The treatise of Hyginus (q. v.) on castrametation gives the following statements as to the practice of his time. The ordinary form of a camp was that of a rectangle, the length of which was about a third part greater than the breadth. In former times the legions were posted inside the camp; but now, being regarded as the most trustworthy troops, they were encamped along the whole line of ramparts, the width of which was now limited to 60 feet. They were separated from the interior of the camp by a road 30 feet wide (*via sagularis*), running parallel to the line of ramparts. The interior was now divided, not into two, but into three main sections. The midmost of these lay between the *via principalis*, which was 60, and the *via quintana*, which was 40 feet wide. It was occupied by the *praetorium* and the troops of the guard, and was called the wing of the *praetorium* (*latera praetorii*). The auxiliary troops were stationed in what was now the front part, or *praetentura*, between the *via principalis* and the *porta praetoria*, and the rear, or *retentura*, between the *via quintana* and the *porta decumana*. The *via praetoria*, which was also 60 feet wide, led only from the *praetorium* and the *forum* in front of it to the *porta praetoria*, as at this time the *quaestorium* was situated between the *porta decumana* and the *praetorium*. The general superintendence of the arrangements was, during the imperial period, in the hands of the *praefectus castrorum*. See PRAEFECTUS.

All the important literature on the subject of camps will be found in the work of Marquardt and Mommsen, v. 390–408.

(2) CASTRA PRAETORIĀNA. The permanent encampment on the outskirts of Rome where the Praetorian Guard was stationed (Suet. *Claud.* 21).

(3) CASTRA NAVALIA. A line of fortifications drawn up around a fleet to protect it from attack, when it was drawn up on the shore (Caes. *B. G.* v. 22). The term CASTRA NAUTĬCA is also used.

Castrenses. The *ministri* of the Roman emperor, whose residence in the early days of the Empire was often called *castra* or *praetorium*, in reference to his position as *imperator*. The whole of his servants formed the *familia castrensis*.

Castrum. See CASTELLUM.

Castrum. (1) INUI, a town of the Rutuli, on the coast of Latium, confounded by some writers with No. 2. (2) NOVUM (Torre di Chiaruccia), a town in Etruria, and a Roman colony on the coast. (3) NOVUM (Giulia Nova), a town in Picenum, probably at the mouth of the small river Batinum (Salinello).

Castŭla. A woman's petticoat. See TUNICA.

Castŭlo (Κασταλών). The modern Cazlona; a town of the Oretani in Hispania Tarraconensis, on the Baetis, and under the Romans an important place. In the mountains in the neighbourhood were silver and lead mines. The wife of Hannibal was a native of Castulo (Livy, xxiv. 41).

Cat. See FAELIS.

Catabathmus (Καταβαθμός) **Magnus** (i. e. great descent). A mountain and seaport at the inner curve of a deep bay on the north coast of Africa, considered to be the boundary between Egypt and Cyrenaïca.

Catacumbae (the name, not older than the third century A.D., is formed from κατὰ + κύμβη, "a hollow place"). A name given to subterranean burial-places, of which the most famous exist in Egypt, Rome, Naples, Syracuse, and Malta. The so-called Catacombs of Paris, as places of interment, are modern, dating from the close of the last century only.

The Catacombs of Egypt are vast in extent and extremely numerous, running through the range of mountains in the vicinity of Thebes. (See THEBAE.) Among them are especially to be noted the caverns in which the bodies of the Theban kings were originally interred. These were forty-seven in number, and, like the more elaborate of the other tombs, were covered with hieroglyphics and ornamented with pictures, mostly in fresco. The oldest of them now existing are not less than 4000 years of age, and have long since been plundered for the sake of the ornaments and other valuables contained in them. A most interesting collection of these frescoes can be found in the drawings and coloured plates of Wilkinson's *Manners and Customs of the Ancient Egyptians* (London, 1847).

The Roman Catacombs were originally quarries, of which some are of very great antiquity, antedating the traditional date of the founding of the city. These were subsequently extended so that at last all the seven hills of Rome were pierced by them. They are low dark corridors or vaulted halls excavated in the soft volcanic tufa and *puzzolana*, in the lateral walls of which apertures were made for the reception of corpses. In all there are some forty Catacombs, each forming a network of galleries, usually intersecting one another at right

Roman Catacombs. Gallery with Loculi. (From Northcote's *Roma Sotterranea*.)

angles, but occasionally radiating from a common centre. The passages are of an average height of eight feet and of an average width of from three to five feet. The apertures (*loculi*) used as graves run in tiers at the sides, and were covered in by marble slabs or tiles bearing either religious emblems or mortuary inscriptions. The whole length of the Roman Catacombs is from 500 to 550 miles, and they are estimated to have contained fully 6,000,000 bodies.

It must be remembered that while the Greeks and Romans finally adopted cremation as a means for disposing of their dead (see FUNUS), the Egyptians and Jews, and latterly the Christians, regarded interment as more in accordance with their views on the subject of a future life. Hence the Roman Christians used and greatly extended the subterranean excavations now called Catacombs, and only afterwards employed them for purposes of concealment during the various persecutions that harassed the Church at intervals from the time of Nero to that of Diocletian (A.D. 303). A popular error makes the Catacombs to have been originally the secret, anxiously concealed places of refuge of the primitive Christians; but they were rather, as Professor Springer says, "their legally recognized, publicly accessible places of burial. Reared in the midst of the customs of heathen Rome, the Christian community perceived no reason to depart from the artistic principles of antiquity. In the embellishment of the Catacombs they adhered to the decorative forms handed down by their ancestors; and in design, choice of colour, grouping of figures, and treatment of subject, they were entirely guided by the customary rules."

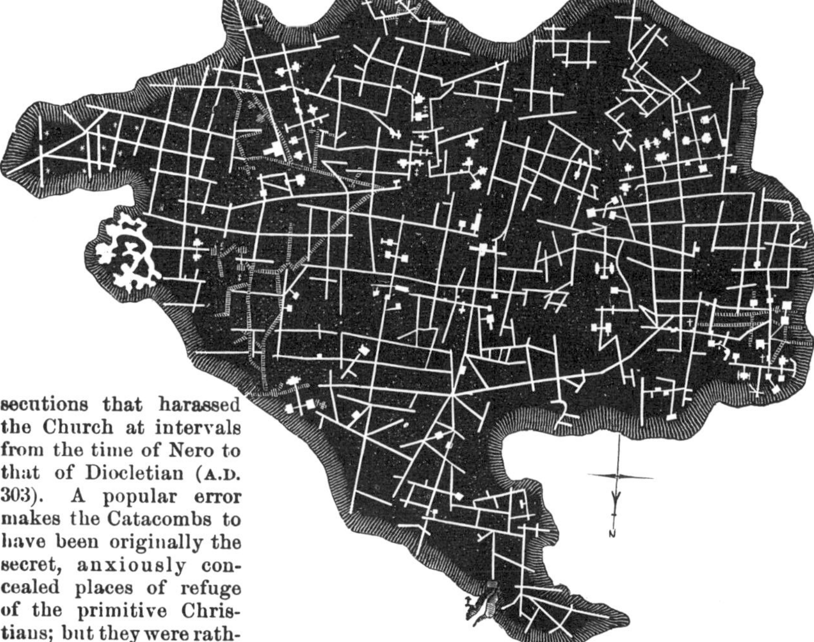

Ground Plan of Roman Catacombs.

The monotonous passages of the Catacombs are occasionally broken by the introduction of larger chambers used as *cubicula* or family burial-places. There are also chambers set apart for worship, but these are not earlier than the fourth century. The Christian excavations were made by a regular society of *fossores*. In most cases, the bodies to be interred were wrapped in cloth, and after the consecrated bread had been placed upon the breast, various other ornaments and memorials were added. Earthen lamps were frequently set by the slabs which closed the niches.

The decoration of the Catacombs is interesting as throwing light upon the development of early Christian art. Many of the paintings are frescoes of the first and second century, and in their subjects are chiefly symbolical of the hopes of Christianity, the Resurrection being a favourite theme. The Good Shepherd, the Miracles, Daniel in the den of lions, and the Hebrews in the fiery furnace, also occur with frequency. The fish, too, by a kind of acrostic, is likewise an important symbol, on which see ACROSTICHA. A great number of inscriptions, many of them of much interest, occur. There are no representations of scenes of martyrdom earlier than the fifth century.

The most important of the Catacombs and the only one that has been even yet quite thoroughly explored is that of St. Callistus on the Via Appia. The one farthest distant (six miles) is that of St. Alexander.

Interments in the Catacombs were discontinued in the fifth century, but the caverns were still visited as containing the tombs of the martyrs. As early as A.D. 370, Pope Damasus caused apertures for lighting to be made, and had the most important tombs furnished with inscriptions. In the year 537, during the siege of Rome by the Goths, the tombs were pillaged, and again by the Lombards in 755, for the sake of the ornaments of gold and silver contained in them. From the time of Pope Paschalis I. (817–824), the Catacombs gradually fell into oblivion, until under Pope Paul III. (in 1535) investigation of them was once more begun. The enthusiastic and learned priest, Father Bosio, spent thirty years in exploring the passages, and in making drawings of the most interesting objects, such as lamps, vases, and monuments, contained in them. His great work, *Roma Sotterranea*, was published (in Italian) in 1632, three years after his death, edited by Father Severani. It was translated into Latin by Father Aringhi, and is still the most important source of information on the subject. In 1720, appeared Boldetti's valuable folio, which was followed by the noble contribution of Seroux d'Agincourt, *Histoire de l'Art par les Monuments*, one of the most learned of all the works relating to the Catacombs. Other valuable books for the student are those of Perret, *Les Catacombes*

Interior of Corridor, Catacombs of St. Callistus.

de Rome (Paris, 1853); Northcote, *Roman Catacombs* (London, 1859); Dyer, *The City of Rome: its Vicissitudes and Monuments* (new ed. 1883); Roller, *Les Catacombes de Rome*, 2 vols. (Paris, 1881); De Rossi, *Roma Sotterranea* (Rome, 1864–77); and Boissier, *Promenades Archéologiques* (3d ed. Paris, 1887). Popular works are Hare's *Walks in Rome* (11th ed. London, 1883); Lagrèze, *Pompéi, les Catacombes, et l'Alhambra* (Paris, 1872); Rio, *Poetry of Christian Art* (Eng. trans. London, 1854); Forbes, *Rambles in Rome* (London, 1882); Farrar, *The Early Days of Christianity* (London, 1882); and Lanciani, *Rome Pagan and Christian* (Boston, 1893). The inscriptions to the number of some 10,000 are given by De Rossi in his *Inscriptiones Christianae* (1857–61).

Catadūpa (τὰ Κατάδουπα and οἱ Κατάδουποι). A name given to the cataracts of the Nile, and also to the parts of Aethiopia in their neighbourhood (Herod. ii. 17). The Latin word is used as a neuter plural. See NILUS.

Catagogia (καταγώγια). See ANAGOGIA.

Catagrăpha (καταγραφή). See PICTURA.

Catalauni. See CATELAUNI.

Catalepton (κατὰ λεπτόν). A collection of fourteen poems in elegiac and iambic verse on various subjects, and ascribed to Vergil, to whose age, at least, they certainly belong. They are often, but less correctly, called CATALECTA. See VERGILIUS.

Catalogue of Ships. A name popularly given to the second half of the second book of the *Iliad* (484–877), in which the poet enumerates the leaders and forces of the Greek host assembled against Troy.

Catalŏgus (κατάλογος). The list of those persons at Athens who were liable to military service. See ASTRATEIAS GRAPHÉ.

Catalysĕōs tou Demou Graphé (καταλύσεως τοῦ δήμου γραφή). An action brought against persons who altered, or tried to alter, the democratic form of government at Athens, and connected with the προδοσίας γραφή. See PRODOSIAS GRAPHÉ.

Catamītus. See GANYMEDES.

Catăna (Κατάνη). A city of Sicily, on the eastern coast, at the base of Aetna, and a short distance below the river Acis and the Cyclopum Scopuli. It was founded by a colony from Chalcis in Euboea, in B.C. 730, five years after the settlement of Syracuse. Catana, like all the other colonies of Grecian origin, soon became independent of any foreign control, and, in consequence of the fertility of the surrounding country, attained to a considerable degree of prosperity. It does not appear, however, to have been at any time a populous city; and hence Hiero of Syracuse was enabled without difficulty to transfer the inhabitants to Leontini. A new colony of Peloponnesians and Syracusans was established here by him, and the place called Aetna, from its proximity to the mountain.

After the death of Hiero, the new colonists were driven out by the Siculi, and the old inhabitants from Leontini then came, and, recovering possession of the place, changed its name again to Catana. We find Catana after this possessed for a short time by the Athenians, and subsequently falling into the hands of Dionysius of Syracuse. This tyrant, according to Diodorus Siculus (xiv. 15), sold the inhabitants as slaves, and gave the city to his mercenary troops, the Campani, to dwell in. It is probable, however, that he only sold those who were taken with arms in their hands, and that many of the old population remained, since Dionysius afterwards persuaded these same Campani to migrate to the city of Aetna. Catana fell into the power of the Romans during the First Punic War. The modern name is Catania, and the distance from it to the summit of Aetna is given as thirty miles.

Cataonia (Καταονία). A fertile district in the southeastern part of Cappadocia, to which it was first added under the Romans, with Melitené, which lies east of it. It had no important towns.

Cataphracti (κατάφρακτοι). (1) Mail-clad cavalry, found chiefly among the armies of the Eastern nations. They are first heard of in the army of the elder Cyrus, and later in the armies of Antiochus Epiphanes. From the time of Antoninus Pius they were common in the armies of Rome. The armour

Sarmatian Cataphract. (Column of Trajan.)

appears to have been a sort of scale-armour (φολιδωτός). (See Amm. Marcell. xvi. 10, 8; Tac. *Hist.* i. 79.) The word is probably Persian. See CRUPPELLARII. (2) The word *cataphractus* is sometimes applied to a ship with decks. See APHRACTUS; NAVIS.

Catapirātes (καταπειρατηρίη). A sounding-lead, consisting of a piece of lead fastened to a cord. The lead was greased, so that specimens of the kind of bottom might better attach themselves to it. See Lucilius, iii. 32 (p. 16 ed. Müll.).

Catapulta. See TORMENTUM.

Cataracta (καταρράκτης or βολίς). (1) A portcullis; so called because it fell with great force and a loud noise.

According to Vegetius, it was an additional defence, suspended by iron rings and ropes before the gates of a city, in such a manner that when the enemy had come up to the gates the portcullis might be let down so as to shut them in, and to enable the besieged to assail them from above. In the accompanying plan of the principal entrance to

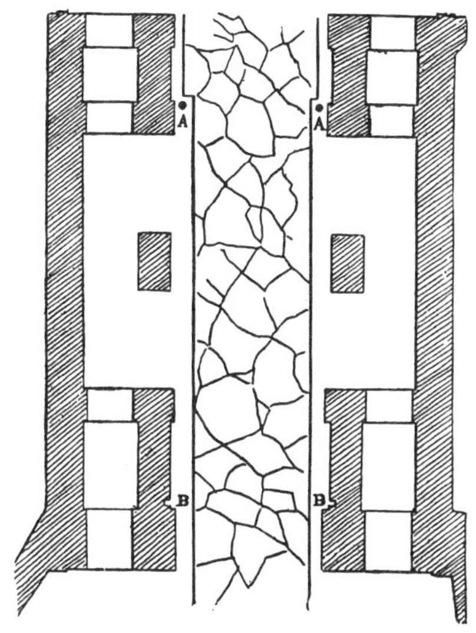

Plan of Gate at Pompeii.

Pompeii, there are two sideways for foot-passengers, and a road between them, fourteen feet wide, for carriages. The gates were placed at A A, turning on pivots (see CARDO), as is proved by the holes in the pavement, which still remain. This end of the road was nearest to the town; in the opposite direction, the road led into the country. The portcullis was at B B, and was made to slide in grooves cut in the walls. The sideways, secured with smaller gates, were roofed in, whereas the portion of the main road between the gates (A A) and the portcullis (B B) was open to the sky. When, therefore, an attack was made, the assailants were either excluded by the portcullis, or, if they forced their way into the barbican, and attempted to break down the gates, the citizens, surrounding and attacking them from above, had the greatest possible facilities for impeding and destroying them. Vegetius speaks of the *cataracta* as an *ancient* contrivance; and it appears to have been employed by the Jews at Jerusalem as early as the time of David. (See Jer. xxix.)

(2) A boarding bridge like the *corvus* of Duilius, so called because it descended like a portcullis. See CORVUS.

(3) A sluice, or perhaps a weir with sluices or hatches in it, for regulating the height of water in a running stream. See Plin. *Epist.* x. 69.

Catarrhactes (Καταρράκτης). (1) A river of Pamphylia, which descends from the mountains of Taurus in a great, broken waterfall (whence its name). (2) The term is also applied, first by Strabo, to the cataracts of the Nile, which are distinguished as Catarrhactes Maior and Catarrhactes Minor. See NILUS.

Catascŏpes Graphé (κατασκοπῆς γραφή). An action allowed by Attic law to be brought against spies, who if caught were put to the torture in order to extort from them information, and then executed. Only foreigners were liable to this action. Citizens guilty of the crime were accused of προδοσία. See PRODOSIAS GRAPHÉ.

Catascopium. A small vessel (*navis speculatoria*) used for reconnoitering (Aul. Gell. x. 25).

Catasta. A raised platform upon which slaves were exposed for sale, so that the intending purchasers might more readily examine their points (Tibull. ii. 3, 60; Pers. vi. 77). The platform was sometimes made to revolve, as appears from Statius (*Silv.* ii. 1, 72). When the platform was used in private sales it was called *catasta arcana* (Mart. ix. 60. 5). See SERVUS.

Cateia. A missile used in war by the Germans, Gauls, and some of the Italians, and ascribed by some writers to the Persians. It was supposed to resemble the *aclis*, which was a sort of dart studded with points, and about a foot and a half long. (See Aul. Gell. x. 25; Isid. *Orig.* xviii. 7; Serv. *ad Aen.* vii. 730.) The *cateia* was also known as *teutona*, from the name of the people.

Catelauni. The modern Châlons-sur-Marne; a town in Gaul, near which Attila (q. v.) was defeated by Aëtius and Theodoric, A.D. 451.

Catella. See CATENA.

Catēna, dim. CATELLA (ἅλυσις, dim. ἀλύσιον, ἀλυσίδιον). A chain.

Thucydides informs us that the Plataeans made use of "long iron chains" to suspend the beams which they let fall upon the battering-rams of their assailants. (See ARIES.) Under the Romans, prisoners were chained in the following manner: The soldier who was appointed to guard a particular captive had the chain fastened to the wrist of his left hand, the right remaining at liberty. The prisoner, on the contrary, had the chain fastened to the wrist of his right hand. Hence *dextras insertare catenis* means to submit to captivity: *leviorem in sinistra catenam.* The prisoner and the soldier who had the care of him (*custos*) were said to be *tied* to one another. Sometimes, for greater security, the prisoner was chained to two soldiers, one on each side of him. If he was found guiltless, they broke or cut asunder his chains. Instead of the common materials, iron or bronze, Antony, having got into his power Artavasdes, king of the Armenians, paid him the pretended compliment of having him bound with chains of gold (Vell. Paterc. ii. 82).

Chains which were of superior value, either on account of the material or the workmanship, are commonly called *catellae* (ἀλύσια), the diminutive expressing their fineness and delicacy as well as their minuteness. The specimens of ancient chains which we have in bronze lamps, in scales (see LIBRA), and in ornaments for the person, especially necklaces (see MONILÉ), show a great variety of elegant and ingenious patterns. Besides a plain circle or oval, the separate link is often shaped like the figure 8, or is a bar with a circle at each end, or assumes other forms, some of which are here shown. The links are also found so closely entwined that the chain resembles plaited wire or thread, like the gold chains now manufactured at Venice. This is represented in the lower figure of the illustration.

Catenae—Chain-links. (British Museum.)

These valuable chains were sometimes given as rewards to the soldiers; but they were commonly worn by ladies, either on the neck or around the waist; and were used to suspend pearls, or jewels set in gold, keys, lockets, and other trinkets.

Catenarius, sc. CANIS. A watch-dog chained up in the vestibulum of a Roman house, usually with the notice CAVE CANEM (Petron. 19, 72).

Dog in Mosaic. (Pompeii.)

Catervarii. See GLADIATORES.

Cathaea. A country of Asia, the precise situation of which is doubtful. Mannert places it northeast of the Malli, in the vicinity of the Hydraotes. The chief town was Sangala. Diodorus Siculus calls the people Catheri.

Cathaei (Καθαῖοι). A great and warlike people of India intra Gangem, upon whom Alexander made war; though modern Orientalists regard them as a warlike caste (*Kshatriyas*) rather than a separate tribe.

Catharmi. See LUSTRATIO.

Cathĕdra (καθέδρα). A seat. The word was more particularly applied to a seat with a back but no arms, whereas the *sella*, however splendid in its material or dignified in its associations, had neither. The back was usually curved or hollow, and low enough for the arm to rest upon it with ease, as in the preceding illustration, taken from Sir William Hamilton's work on Greek vases. On the cathedra is seated a bride, who is being fanned by a female slave with a fan made of peacock's feathers; under her feet is a footstool.

Cathedra. (From a Greek Vase.)

There was also the *cathedra longa*, or easy-chair; and, more luxurious still, the *cathedra supina*, resembling the modern steamer-chair. Then, as now, they were often made of wicker-work (*salices*).

The cathedra was more used by women than by men (hence *femineae*, Mart. iii. 63). It was a mark of effeminacy when a man was seen stretched out on a reclining-chair. To sit on cathedrae at table was, however, less luxurious than the ordinary reclining posture, and was considered proper for boys. (See CENA.) The seat was not stuffed, but a cushion was commonly placed upon it; and a cover might also be thrown over the back.

Professorial Chair. (Visconti.)

Another sort of cathedra was a sedan-chair, in which women were accustomed to be carried about, instead of in a lectica. The *nuda cathedra* of Juvenal (i. 65), in which the successful forger is carried *supinus*, is probably an uncurtained lectica; it is insolence rather than effeminacy which here provokes the rage of the satirist. See LECTICA.

Cathĕter (καθετήρ). A surgical instrument for drawing off water from the bladder. The pure Latin name is *fistula aenea*. See CHIRURGIA.

Catilīna, LUCIUS SERGIUS. A Roman of patrician rank, and the last of the gens Sergia. Of his father and grandfather little is known: the former would seem to have been in indigent circumstances, from the language of Quintus Cicero (*De Petitione Consulatus*, 2), who speaks of Catiline as having been born amidst the poverty of his father (*in patris egestate*). The great-grandfather, M. Sergius Silus or Silo, distinguished himself greatly in the Second Punic War, and was present at the battles of Ticinus, Trebia, Trasimenus, and Cannae. Pliny speaks of his exploits in a very animated strain.

The cruelty of Catiline's disposition, his undaunted resolution, and the depravity of his morals fitted him for acting a distinguished part in the turbulent and bloody scenes of the period in which he lived. He embraced the interest of Sulla, in whose army he held the office of quaestor. Many citizens of noble birth are said by Quintus Cicero to have fallen by his hand; and, according to Plutarch, he had assassinated his own brother during the Civil War; and now, to screen himself from prosecution, persuaded Sulla to put him down among the proscribed as a person still alive. He murdered too, with his own hands, his sister's husband, a Roman knight of peaceable character. One of the worst actions, however, of which he was guilty would seem to have been the killing of M. Marius Gratidianus, a near relative of the celebrated Marius. Sulla had put the name of this individual on the list of the proscribed, whereupon Catiline entered the dwelling of the unfortunate man, exhausted upon his person all the refinements of cruelty and insult, and, having at last put an end to his existence, carried his bloody head in triumph through the streets of Rome, and brought it to Sulla as he sat on his tribunal in the Forum. When this was done, the murderer washed his hands in the lustral water at the door of Apollo's temple, which stood in the immediate vicinity (Sen. *De Ira*, iii. 18).

Catiline was peculiarly dangerous and formidable, as his power of dissimulation enabled him to throw a veil over his vices. Equally well qualified to deceive the good, to intimidate the weak, and to inspire with his own boldness his depraved associates, he evaded two accusations brought against him by Clodius for criminal intercourse with a Vestal, and for monstrous extortions of which he had been guilty while proconsul in Africa (A.U.C. 687). He was charged also with having murdered his first wife and his son. A numerous group having been formed of young men of high birth and daring character, who saw no other means of extricating themselves from their enormous debts than by obtaining the highest offices of the State, Catiline was placed at their head. This eminence he owed chiefly to his connection with the old soldiers of Sulla, by means of whom he kept in awe the towns near Rome, and even Rome itself. At the same time, he numbered among his adherents not only the worst and lowest of the riotous populace, but also many of the patricians and men of consular rank. Everything favoured his audacious scheme. Pompey was pursuing the victories which Lucullus had prepared for him; and the latter was but a feeble supporter of the nobles in the Senate, who wished him, but in vain, to put himself at their head. Crassus, who had delivered Italy from the gladiators, was now striving with great eagerness after power and riches, and, instead of opposing, countenanced the growing influence of Catiline, as a means of his own aggrandizement. Caesar, who was labouring to revive the party of Marius, spared Catiline, and, perhaps, even encouraged him. Only two Romans remained determined to uphold their falling country: Cato and Cicero—the latter of whom alone possessed the qualifications necessary for the task. The conspirators were now planning the elevation of Catiline and one of his accomplices to the consulship. When this was effected, they hoped to obtain possession of the public treasures and the property of the citizens, under various pretexts, and especially by means of proscription. It is not probable, however, that Catiline had promised them the liberty of burning and plundering Rome. Cicero had the courage to stand as candidate for the consulship, in spite of the impending danger, of the extent of which he was perfectly aware. Neither insults nor threats, nor even riots and attempts to assassinate him, deterred him from his purpose; and, being supported by the richest citizens, he gained his election, B.C. 65. All that the party of Catiline could accomplish was the election of Gaius Antonius, one of their accomplices, as colleague of Cicero. This failure, however, did not deprive Catiline of the hope of gaining the consulship the following year. For this purpose he redoubled the measures of terror by means of which he had laid the foundation of his power. Meanwhile he had lost some of the most important members of his conspiracy. Antony had been prevailed upon, or compelled by Cicero, to remain neutral. Caesar and Crassus had resolved to do the same. Piso had been killed in Spain. Italy, however, was destitute of troops. The veterans of Sulla only waited the signal to take up arms. This signal was now given by Catiline. The centurion Manlius appeared among them, and formed a camp in Etruria. Cicero was on the watch, and a fortunate accident disclosed to him the counsels of the conspirators. One of them, Curius, was on intimate terms with a woman of doubtful reputation, Fulvia by name, and had acquainted her with their plans. Through this woman, Cicero learned that two knights had undertaken to assassinate him at his house. On the day which they had fixed for the execution of their plan they found his doors barred and guarded. Still Cicero delayed to make public the circumstances of a conspiracy the progress and resources of which he wished first to ascertain. He contented himself with warning his fellow-citizens, in general terms, of the impending danger. But when the insurrection of Manlius was made known, he procured the passage of the celebrated decree, "that the consuls should take care that the Republic received no detriment." By a decree of this kind, the consuls, or other magistrates named therein, were, in accordance with the custom of the State, armed with the supreme civil and military authority. It was exceedingly difficult to seize the person of one who had soldiers at his command, both in and out of Rome; still more difficult would it be to prove his guilt before those who were his accomplices with him, or, at least, were willing to make use of his plans to serve their own interests. Cicero had to choose between two evils—a revolution within the city, or a civil war; and he preferred the latter. Catiline had the boldness to take his seat in the Senate, known as he was to be the enemy of the Roman State. Cicero then rose and delivered that bold oration against him which was the means of saving Rome by driving Catiline from the city. The conspirators who remained—Lentulus, Cethegus, and other infamous senators—engaged to head the insurrection in Rome as soon as Catiline appeared at the gates. According to Cicero and Sallust, it was the intention of the conspirators to set the city on fire, and massacre the inhabitants. At any rate, these consequences might have easily followed from the circumstances of the case, without any previous resolution. Lentulus, Cethegus, and the other conspirators, in the meanwhile, were carrying on their criminal plots. They applied to the ambassadors of the Allobroges to transfer the war to the frontiers of Italy itself. These, however, revealed the plot, and their disclosures led to others still more important. The correspondence of the conspirators with their leader was intercepted. The Senate had now a notorious crime to punish. As the circumstances of the case did not allow a minute observance of form in the proceedings against the conspirators, the laws relating thereto were disregarded, as had been done in former instances of less pressing danger. Caesar spoke against immediate execution, but Cicero and Cato prevailed. Five of the conspirators were put to death. Gaius Antonius was then appointed to march against Catiline, but, on the eve of battle, under pretence of being disabled by the gout, he gave the command to his lieutenant Petreius. The battle was fought at Pistoria in

Etruria, and ended in the complete overthrow of the insurgents. Catiline, on finding that all was lost, resolved to die sword in hand, and his followers imitated his example (B.C. 62).

The history of Catiline's conspiracy has been written by Sallust in the extremely able monograph known as the *Bellum Catilinae*. See also the lives of Caesar and Cicero by Plutarch; Mommsen, *History of Rome*, iv. 203–209, 212–223; and the four orations of Cicero known as the *Orationes Catilinariae*, much read in schools. The story forms the subject of a tedious English play by Ben Jonson, entitled *Catiline's Conspiracy*, produced in 1611; and of a now-forgotten drama by Stephen Gosson. It is the basis of the historical novel by Herbert, *The Roman Traitor*.

Catillus or **Catīlus**. See TIBUR.

Catillus. See CATINUS.

Catīnus or **Catīnum**, dim. CATILLUS or CATILLUM. A dish or platter on which viands were served up. Other names for similar table utensils will here be noticed; but it must be admitted that the differences of shape, materials, or use are not always clearly indicated. Even the distinction, so essential to our notions, between dishes and plates does not seem to have been observed (Hor. *Sat.* i. 3, 92); there is, in fact, no Greek or Latin word for "a plate" in the modern sense. Varro describes the catinus as deep enough to hold the gravy of meat or vegetables (*L. L.* v. 120). They were mostly of earthenware, and were kept in various sizes; to have the catinus too small for its contents showed a want of style (Hor. *Ep.* ii. 4, 77). The historic turbot of Domitian required a dish made on purpose (Juv. iv. 131 foll.); Vitellius had gone a step beyond this, and built a special furnace in which to bake a gigantic *patina* (Plin. *H. N.* xxxv. § 163). The PATINA (dim. *patella*) was also commonly of earthenware; it was bowl-shaped, and occurs frequently in Horace in the sense of a dish; but it was likewise used for cooking, and then had a cover (Plaut. *Pseud.* iii. 2, 51). The actor Aesopus had a patina worth 100,000 sesterces; the material is not described. PAROPSIS (παροψίς) was in Greek applied either to the dish or its contents, as is proved by Athenaeus, with abundant quotations from the comic poets—though Atticists tried to restrict the word to the latter sense; in Roman writers it is always the former: originally a square or oblong side-dish for delicacies, it came to mean any dish. There was also an APSIS or *absis* (q. v.), either round or semicircular, like modern salad-plates; and GABATAE, said to have been of a deep shape. The LANX varied in form, but seems to have been always of metal; huge silver lances were among the most costly objects of Roman extravagance. We also find a paropsis in silver (*Dig.* xxxiv. 2, l. 19, § 9). The Greek πίναξ, a board and so a wooden trencher, might be of other materials—e. g. silver; but silver dishes were thought vulgar by the Greeks, at least in early times (Athen. vi. 430 a).

The *catillus* was a saucer for pickles or other condiments (Hor. *Sat.* ii. 4, 75).

Cato. A surname of the Porcian family, derived from the Sabine *catus*, cognate with *acutus*. (1) M. PORCIUS CATO, surnamed CENSORIUS, in allusion to the severity with which he discharged the office of a censor, and hence commonly styled, at the present day, "Cato the Censor." Other surnames were, PRISCUS, "the old," and MAIOR, "the elder," both alluding to his having preceded, in order of time, the younger Cato, who committed suicide at Utica. Cato the Censor was born in B.C. 234 at Tusculum, of plebeian parents. His family were in very moderate circumstances, and little, if anything, was known of it, until he himself made the name a conspicuous one. His father left him a small farm in the Sabine territory, and here the first years of his youth were spent. The state of public affairs, however, soon compelled him to take up arms for the defence of his country. The Second Punic War had broken out, and Hannibal had invaded Italy. Cato, therefore, served his first campaign, at the age of seventeen, under Fabius Maximus, when he besieged the city of Capua. Five years after this he fought under the same commander at the siege of Tarentum, and, after the capture of this place, became acquainted with the Pythagorean Nearchus, who initiated him into the principles of that system of philosophy, with which, in practice, he had already become familiar. The war being ended, Cato returned to his farm. Near this there stood a cottage belonging to Manius Curius Dentatus, who had repeatedly triumphed over the Sabines and Samnites, and had at length driven Pyrrhus from Italy. Cato was accustomed frequently to walk over to the humble abode of this renowned commander, where he was struck with admiration at the frugality of its owner, and the skilful management of the farm which was attached to it. Hence it became his great object to emulate his illustrious neighbour, and adopt him as his model. Having made an estimate of his house, lands, slaves, and expenses, he applied himself to husbandry with new ardour, and retrenched all superfluity. In the morning he went to the small towns in the vicinity to plead and defend the causes of those who applied to him for assistance. Thence he returned to his fields, where, with a plain cloak over his shoulders in winter, and almost naked in summer, he laboured with his servants till they had concluded their tasks, after which he sat down along with them at table, eating the same bread and drinking the same wine. Valerius Flaccus, a noble and powerful Roman, who occupied an estate in the neighbourhood of Cato's residence, persuaded the young Cato to remove to Rome, and promised to assist him by his influence and patronage. Cato came, accordingly, to the capital, with an obscure name, and with no other resources than his own talents and the aid of the generous Flaccus; but by the purity of his morals, the austere energy of his character, his knowledge of the laws, his fluency of elocution, and the great ability that marked his early forensic career, he soon won for himself a distinguished name. It was in the camp, however, rather than at the bar, that he strove to raise himself to eminence. At the age of thirty he went as military tribune to Sicily. The next year he was chosen quaestor, and was attached to the army which Scipio Africanus was to carry into Africa, at which period there commenced between him and that commander a rivalry and hatred which lasted until death. Cato, who had returned to Rome, accused Scipio of extravagance; and though he failed in supporting his charge, yet his zeal for the public good gained him great influence over the minds of the people. Five years subsequent to this, after having been already aedile, he was chosen praetor, and the province of Sardinia fell to him by lot. His integrity and justice, while discharging this office, brought him into direct and most favourable contrast with those who had preceded him. Here, too, it was that he became acquainted with the poet Ennius, who was then serving among the Calabrian levies attached to the army. From Ennius he acquired the Greek language, and, on his departure from the island, he took the bard along with him to Rome. He was finally elected consul, B.C. 193, and his colleague in office was Valerius Flaccus, his early friend. While consul he strenuously but fruitlessly opposed the abolition of the famous Oppian Law (see OPPIA LEX), and soon after this set out for Spain, which had attempted to shake off the Roman yoke. With newly raised troops, which he soon converted into an excellent army, he quickly reduced that province to submission, and obtained the honours of a triumph at Rome. Hardly had Cato descended from the triumphal chariot, when, laying aside the consular robe and assuming the garb of the lieutenant, he accompanied, as such, the Roman commander Sempronius into Thrace. He afterwards placed himself under the orders of Manius Acilius, the consul, to fight against Antiochus, and carry the war into Thessaly. By a bold march he seized upon Callidromus, one of the rockiest summits of Thermopylae, and thus decided the issue of the conflict. For this signal service, the consul, in the excess of his enthusiasm, embraced him in the presence of the whole army, and exclaimed that it was neither in his power, nor in that of the Roman people, to award him a recompense commensurate with his deserts (B.C. 191).

Seven years later he obtained the office of censor, notwithstanding the powerful opposition of a large part of the nobility, who dreaded to have so severe an inspector of public morals at a time when luxury, the result of their Asiatic conquests, had driven out many of the earlier virtues of the Roman people. He fulfilled this trust with inflexible rigour. Some of his acts, it is true, would seem to have proceeded from that pugnacious bitterness which must be contracted by a man engaged in constant strife and inflictions: thus, for example, he took away his horse from Lucius Scipio, and expelled Manilius from the Senate for kissing his wife in the presence of his children. Still, however, most of his proceedings when censor indicate a man who aimed, by every method, at keeping up the true spirit of earlier days. Hence, though his measures, while holding this office, caused him some obloquy and opposition, they met in the end with the highest applause; and when he resigned the censorship the people erected a statue to him in the Temple of Health, with an honourable inscription testifying his faithful discharge of the duties of his office. Cato's attachment to the old Roman morals was still more plainly seen in his opposition to Carneades (q. v.) and his colleagues, when he persuaded the Senate to send back these philosophers, without delay, to their own schools, through fear lest the Roman youth should lose their martial character in the pursuit of Grecian learning. The whole political career of Cato was one continued warfare. He was constantly accusing others, or made the subject of accusation himself. Livy, although full of admiration for his character, still does not seek to deny that Cato was suspected of having excited the accusation brought against Scipio Africanus, which compelled that illustrious man to leave the capital. He was also the means of the condemnation of Scipio Asiaticus, who would have been dragged to prison had not Tiberius Gracchus generously interfered. As for Cato himself, he was fifty times accused and as often acquitted. He was eighty-five years of age when he saw himself compelled to answer the last accusation brought against him, and the exordium of his speech on that occasion was marked by a peculiar and touching simplicity: "It is a hard thing, Romans, to give an account of one's conduct before the men of an age different from that in which one has himself lived."

The last act of Cato's public life was his embassy to Carthage, to settle the dispute between the Carthaginians and King Masinissa. This voyage of his is rendered famous in history, since to it has been attributed the destruction of Carthage. In fact, struck by the rapid recovery of this city from the loss it had sustained, Cato ever after ended every speech of his with the well-known words, *Praeterea censeo Carthaginem esse delendam* ("I am also of opinion that Carthage ought to be destroyed"). See CARTHAGO.

Cato died a year after his return from this embassy, in the eighty-fifth year of his age. Although frugal of the public revenues, he does not appear to have been indifferent to riches, nor to have neglected the ordinary means of acquiring them; and, if Plutarch speaks truly, some of the modes to which he had recourse for increasing his resources were anything but reputable. Towards the end of his life he was fond of indulging in a glass of wine, and of inviting daily some of his neighbours to sup with him at his villa; and the conversation on these occasions turned, not as one might have supposed, chiefly on rural affairs, but on the praises of great and excellent men among the Romans. He was twice married, and had a son by each of his wives. His conduct as husband and father was equally exemplary. In fact, Cato may be taken as a specimen of the Sabino-Samnite character, narrow, bigoted, and obstinate, yet inspired with a strong sense of duty and unimpeachable integrity.

Among the literary labours of Cato, the first that deserves mention is the treatise *De Re Rustica*, more properly styled *De Agri Cultura*, which appears to have come down to us in a mutilated state, since Pliny and other writers allude to subjects as treated of by Cato, and to opinions as delivered by him in this book, which are nowhere to be found in any part of the work now extant. In its present state, it is merely the loose, disconnected journal of a plain farmer, expressed with rude, sometimes with almost oracular, brevity; and it wants all those elegant topics of embellishment and illustration which the subject might have so naturally suggested. It consists solely of the dryest rules of agriculture, and some recipes for making various kinds of cakes and wine. Servius says it is addressed to the author's son, but there is no dedication now extant. It is divided into chapters, but the author, apparently, had never taken the trouble of reducing his precepts to any sort of method, or of following any general plan. The hundred and sixty-two chapters, of which this work consists, seem so many rules committed to writing, as the daily labours of the field suggested. He gives directions about the vineyard, then goes to his corn-fields, and returns again to the vineyard. His treatise, therefore, was evidently not intended as a regular and well-composed book, but merely as a journal of incidental observations. That this was its utmost pretension is further evinced by the brevity of the precepts, and the deficiency of all illustrations or embellishment. Of the style, he of course would be little careful, as his memoranda were intended for the use only of his family and his slaves. It is therefore always simple, and sometimes rude, but it is not ill-adapted to the subject, and suits our notions of the severe manners of its author and the character of the ancient Romans.

Besides this book on agriculture, Cato left behind him various works, which have almost entirely perished. He left a hundred and fifty orations (Cic. *Brutus*, 17), which were extant in the time of Cicero, though almost entirely neglected, and a book on military discipline (Veget. i. 8). Both Cicero and Livy have expressed themselves very fully on the subject of Cato's orations. The former admits that his "language is antiquated, and some of his phrases harsh and inelegant. But only change that," he continues, "which it was not in his power to change—add number and cadence—give an easier turn to his sentences, and regulate the structure and connection of his words, and you will find no one who can claim preference over Cato." Livy principally speaks of the facility, asperity, and freedom of his style.

Of the book on military discipline, a good deal has been incorporated into the work of Vegetius; and Cicero's orations may console us for the want of those of Cato. But the loss of the seven books *De Originibus*, which he commenced in his vigorous old age, and finished just before his death, must ever be deeply deplored by the historian and the antiquary. Cato is said to have begun an inquiry into the history, antiquities, and language of the Roman people, with a view to counteract the influence of the Greek taste introduced by the Scipios. The first book of the valuable work *De Originibus*, as we are informed by Cornelius Nepos, in his short life of Cato, contained the exploits of the kings of Rome. Cato was the first author who attempted to fix the era of the foundation of Rome, which he calculated in his *Origines*, and determined to have been in the first year of the 7th Olympiad, which is also the estimate followed by Dionysius of Halicarnassus. The second and third books treated of the origin of the different states of Italy, whence the whole work has received the name of *Origines*. The fourth and fifth books comprehended the history of the First and Second Punic Wars; and in the two remaining books the author discussed the other wars of the Romans till the time of Servius Galba, who overthrew the Lusitanians. The whole work exhibited great industry and learning, and, had it descended to us, would unquestionably have thrown much light upon the early periods of Roman history and the antiquities of the different states of Italy. Dionysius of Halicarnassus, himself a sedulous inquirer into antiquities, bears ample testimony to the research and accuracy of that part which treats of the origin of the ancient Italian cities. Cato was the first of his countrymen who wrote on the subject of medicine. This was done in a work entitled *Commentarius quo Medetur Filio, Servis, Familiaribus*. In this book of domestic medicine, duck, pigeons, and hare were the food he chiefly recommended to the sick. His remedies were principally extracted from herbs; and colewort or cabbage was his favourite cure (Plin. *H. N.* xx. § 9). The recipes, indeed, contained in his work on agriculture show that his medical knowledge did not exceed that which usually exists among a semi-barbarous race, and only extended to the most ordinary simples which nature affords. Aulus Gellius (vi. 10) mentions Cato's *Libri Quaestionum Epistolicarum*, and Cicero his *Apophthegmata* (*De Officiis*, i. 29)—the first example, probably, of that class of works which, under the appellation of *Ana*, were once so fashionable and prevalent in France.

On the life of Cato, see Plutarch and Cornelius Nepos; Cortese, *De M. Porc. Catonis Vita, Operibus, et Lingua* (Turin, 1883); and Weise, *Quaestionum Catonian. Capita V.* (Göttingen, 1887). The fragments of Cato's writings (except the work on agriculture) are collected by Jordan (Leipzig, 1860). The best text of the *Res Rustica* is that of Keil (Leipzig, 1884). See, on the language, the work of Cortese, *Grammatica Catoniana* (Turin, 1883).

(2) MARCUS, son of Cato the Censor by his first wife. He distinguished himself greatly in the battle of Pydna, against Perses, king of Macedonia, and received high eulogiums from Aemilius Paulus, the Roman commander on that occasion, whose daughter Tertia he afterwards married. He died while filling the office of praetor (Plut. *Cat. Mai.* 20, 24). (3) SALONIUS, or, as Plutarch calls him, SALONĪNUS (Σαλωνῖνος), son of Cato the Censor by his second wife. This second wife was the daughter of one Salonius, who had been Cato's secretary, and was, at the time of the marriage, a member of his retinue. Salonius, like his half-brother Marcus, died when praetor. He left, however, a son named Marcus, who attained to the consulship, and who was the father of Cato the younger, commonly called Uticensis (Plut. *Cat. Mai.* 27). (4) VALERIUS, a celebrated grammarian and poet in the time of Sulla. He was deprived of all his patrimony during the excesses of the Civil War, and then directed his attention to literary pursuits. To him has been ascribed the poem of 186 hexameters, entitled *Dirae in Battarum*, an imprecation against the person who had caused the loss of his estate, and a lament for his love, Lydia. Text by Putsche (Jena, 1828) and Ribbeck (Kiel, 1867). See the treatise on Cato by Naekius (Bonn, 1847), and Haupt's edition of Vergil, p. 576 (Leipzig, 1873); Suetonius mentions other works that have not come down to us —the *Diana* and the *Indignatio*—besides treatises on grammar and rhetoric. (5) MARCUS, called also MINOR, and UTICENSIS, from his death at Utica, was great-grandson to the censor of the same name, and was born B.C. 93. A short time after his birth he lost both his parents, and was brought up in the house of Livius Drusus, his uncle on the mother's side. Even in early life Cato displayed a maturity of judgment and an inflexible firmness of character far above his years; and Sarpedon, his instructor, being accustomed to take him frequently to the residence of Sulla, who had been his father's friend, the young Cato, then but fourteen years of age, struck with horror at the bloody scenes that were passing around him, asked his pre-

ceptor for a sword, that he might slay the tyrant. His affectionate disposition was clearly displayed in his strong attachment to Caepio, his brother by the mother's side, as may be seen by a reference to the pages of Plutarch. Being appointed to the priesthood of Apollo, he changed his residence, and took his share of his father's estate; but, though the fortune which he thus received was a considerable one, his manner of living was simpler and more frugal than ever. He formed a connection with Antipater of Tyre, the Stoic philosopher, made himself well acquainted with the tenets of that school, and ever after remained true to its principles, pushing them even to austerity. His first appearance in public was against the tribunes of the people, who wished to remove a column of the Porcian Basilica which incommoded their benches. This basilica had been erected by his great-grandfather, the censor, and the young Cato displayed on the occasion that powerful and commanding eloquence which afterwards rendered him so formidable to all his

Porcia and Cato Uticensis. (Vatican.)

opponents. His first campaign was in the war against Spartacus (q. v.), as a simple volunteer, his half-brother Caepio being a military tribune in the same army; and he distinguished himself so highly that Gellius, the praetor, wished to award him a prize of honour, which Cato, however, declined. He was then sent as military tribune to Macedonia. There he learned that Caepio was lying dangerously ill at Aenus in Thrace, and instantly embarked for that place in a small passage-boat, notwithstanding the roughness of the sea and the great peril which attended the attempt, but only arrived at Aenus just after Caepio had breathed his last. Stoicism was here of no avail, and the young Roman bitterly lamented the companion of his early years. According to Plutarch, there were some who condemned him for acting in a way so contradictory to his philosophical principles; but a more unfeeling charge was the one brought against him by Caesar, in his attack entitled *Anticatones* (q. v.). It was there stated that, after all the lavish expenditure in which Cato had indulged in performing the funeral obsequies of Caepio, and after having declined repayment from the daughter of the latter, he nevertheless passed Caepio's ashes through a sieve in search of the gold which might have melted down with them.

When the term of his service in Macedonia had expired, he travelled into Asia, and brought back with him the Stoic Athenodorus to Rome. He was next made quaestor, and discharged with so much impartiality the duties of this difficult office, and displayed so much integrity in its various details that, on the last day of his quaestorship, he was escorted to his house by the whole assembly of the people. So high, indeed, was the opinion entertained by his countrymen of the purity of his moral character that when, at the Floralia given by the aedile Messius, Cato happened to be a spectator, the people, out of respect for him, hesitated about ordering the prostitutes to strip themselves naked, according to long-established custom, nor would they allow this to be done until he had departed from the theatre (Val. Max. ii. 10, 8). When the conspiracy of Catiline was discovered, Cato supported by every means in his power the acts of Cicero, and was the first that gave him publicly the honourable title of Pater Patriae. Opposing after this the ambitious movements of the first triumvirate, they managed to have him removed to a distance, by sending him out as governor of the island of Cyprus. Having executed this trust with ability and success, and having deposited in the treasury nearly seven thousand talents of silver, he again took part in public affairs at Rome, and again continued his opposition to the triumvirate. When, however, the rupture took place between Pompey and Caesar, he sided with the former, and was left behind by him at Dyrrhachium to guard the military chest and magazine, while he pushed on after Caesar, who had been forced to retire from the siege of that city. Cato, therefore, was not present at the battle of Pharsalia. On receiving the news of this event, he sailed to Corcyra with the troops under his orders, and offered the command to Cicero, who declined it. He then proceeded to Africa, where he hoped to meet with Pompey; but on reaching Cyrenê he heard of his death, and was also informed that Pompey's father-in-law, Scipio, had gone to Iuba, king of Mauritania, where Varus had collected a considerable force. Cato immediately resolved to join them, and, in order to effect this, was compelled to make a long and painful march across a desert region, in which his troops suffered severely from hunger, thirst, and every hardship, but which privations his own example enabled them manfully to endure. After seven days of suffering his force reached Utica, where a junction between the two armies took place. The soldiers wished to have him for their general, but he yielded to what he conceived to be the superior claims of Scipio, who held the office of proconsul; and this fault on his part, of which he soon after had reason to repent, accelerated the ruin of the cause in which he had embarked. Scipio having wished, for Iuba's gratification, to put all the inhabitants of Utica to the sword, Cato strenuously opposed this cruel plan, and accepted the command of this important city, while Scipio and Labienus marched against Caesar. Cato had advised them to protract the war; but they hazarded an engagement at Thapsus, in which they were entirely defeated, and Africa submitted to the victor. After vainly endeavouring to prevail upon the fragments of the conquered army, as they came successively to Utica, to unite in defending that city against the conqueror, Cato furnished them with all the ships in the harbour to convey them wherever they wished to go. When the evening of that day came, he retired to his own apartments, and employed himself for some time in reading the *Phaedo* of Plato, a dialogue that turns upon the immortality of the soul. He endeavoured at the same time to lull the suspicions of his friends by seeming to take a lively interest in the fate of those who were escaping by sea from Utica, and by sending several times to the seaside to learn the state of the wind and weather. But towards morning, when all was quiet, he stabbed himself. He fell from his bed with the blow, and the noise of his fall brought his son and servants into the room, by whose assistance he was raised from the ground, and an attempt was made to bind up the wound. Their efforts to save him were in vain, for Cato had no sooner recovered his self-possession than he tore open the wound again in so effectual a manner that he instantly expired. He died at the age of forty-eight. When Caesar heard of his fate, he is said to have exclaimed, "I grudge thee thy death, Cato, since thou hast grudged me the saving of thy life." Such was the end of a man whom a better philosophy, by teaching him to struggle with his predominant faults instead of encouraging them, would have rendered truly amiable and admirable. He possessed the greatest integrity and firmness; and, from the beginning of his political career, was never swayed by fear or interest to desert that which he considered the cause of liberty and justice. During the Civil War he had the rare merit of uniting to the sincerest ardour in the cause of his party a steady regard for justice and humanity; he would not countenance cruelty or rapine because practised by his associates or coloured with a pretence of public advantages. But philosophical pride overshadowed the last scenes of his life, and led him to indulge his selfish feelings by suicide, rather than live for the happiness of his family and friends, and mitigate, as far as lay in his power, the distressed condition of his country. His character, however, was so pure, and, since Pompey's death, so superior to that of all the leaders engaged with him in the same cause, that his opponents could not refuse him their respect. (6) M. PORCIUS, son of the preceding, was spared by Caesar, but led a somewhat immoral life, until he effaced the stains upon his character by a glorious death at Philippi (Plut. *Cat. Min.* 73). (7) DIONYSIUS CATO. A name erroneously given to the author of a collection of moral maxims in four books, much used as a school-book in the Middle Ages, and translated into English before 1479 by Benedict Burgh, whose version was printed by Caxton. Each maxim consists of two hexameters, the whole number of maxims being 164. The style is fairly good, and shows the poem to date from about the third century A.D. The collection is preceded by fifty-six short proverbs in prose with a separate preface, by a different author, probably of later date. The hexameters are generally spoken of as *Disticha Catonis* (*Catonis Disticha de Moribus ad Filium*), and in a Paris MS. as *Liber Catonis Philosophi*, but the name Cato is probably used merely to designate the maxims as shrewd and wise. The addition of the name Dionysius is doubtless due to a confusion arising from the fact that one of the earlier MSS. of the *Disticha* contained also a translation of the *Periegesis* of Dionysius. A good text is that of Hauthal (Berlin, 1869).

Catreus. See CRETEUS.

Catti or **Chatti**. One of the most important nations of Germany, bounded by the Visurgis (Weser) on the east, the Agri Decumates on the south, and the Rhine on the west, in the modern Hesse and the adjacent countries. They were a branch of the Hermiones, and are first mentioned by Caesar under the erroneous name of Suevi. They were never completely subjugated by the Romans; and their power was greatly augmented on the decline of the Cherusci. Their capital was Mattium (Maden).

Catullus, GAIUS VALERIUS. A celebrated Roman poet, born in the territory of Verona, about B.C. 84. His praenomen, Gaius, is not given in any good MSS., which only mention his cognomen; but Gaius is accepted on the authority of Apuleius (*Apol.* 10). In consequence of an invitation from Manlius Torquatus, one of the noblest patricians of the State, he proceeded in early youth to Rome, where he appears to have kept but indifferent company, at least in point of moral character. He impaired his fortune so much by his extravagance that he complains he had no one

> Fractum qui veteris pedem grabati,
> In collo sibi collocare possit.

This, however, must have been written partly in jest, as his finances were always sufficient to allow him to keep up a delightful villa on the peninsula of Sirmio and an expensive residence at Tibur. With a view of improving his pecuniary circumstances, he adopted the usual Roman mode of reestablishing a diminished fortune, and accompanied Gaius Memmius, the celebrated friend of Lucretius, to Bithynia, where he was appointed praetor to that province. His situation, however, was but little ameliorated by this expedition, and, in the course of it, he lost a beloved brother who was along with him, and whose death he lamented in verse never surpassed in delicacy or pathos. He came back to Rome with a shattered constitution and a lacerated heart. From the period of his return to Italy to his decease, his time appears to have been chiefly occupied with the prosecution of amours in the capital or in the solitudes of Sirmio. He died B.C. 54.

The distracted and unhappy state of his country, and his disgust at the treatment which he had received from Memmius, were perhaps sufficient excuse for shunning political employments; but, when we consider his taste and genius, we cannot help regretting that he was merely an idler and a debauchee. He loved Clodia (supposed to have been the sister of the tribune Clodius), a beautiful but shameless woman, whom he has celebrated under the name of Lesbia. Among his friends he ranked not only most men of pleasure and fashion in Rome, but many of her eminent literary and political characters, such as Cornelius Nepos, Cicero, and Asinius Pollio. His enemies seem to have been as numerous as his loves or friendships, and competitions in poetry or rivalship in gallantry appear always to have been a sufficient cause for his dislike; and where an antipathy was once conceived, he was unable to put any restraint on the expression of his hostile feelings. His poems are chiefly employed in the indulgence and commemoration of these various passions. They have been divided into lyric, elegiac, and epigrammatic, an arrangement convenient from its generality, but to which all can not, with strictness, be reduced. He seems to have been the earliest lyric poet of Latium, notwithstanding the claim of Horace to the same honour. Much of his poetry appears to have been lost: the pieces that remain to us (116 in all) exhibit, in singular contrast, the sensual grossness which is imbibed from depraved habits and loose imaginations, together with exquisite touches of sentiment and taste, and the polish of intellectual cultivation. Those who turn with disgust from the coarse impurities that sully his pages may be inclined to wonder that praises of his delicacy should ever have been coupled with the name of Catullus. But to many of his effusions, distinguished both by fancy and feeling, this praise is justly due. Many of his amatory trifles are quite unrivalled in the elegance of their playfulness; and no author has excelled him in the purity and neatness of his style, the delightful ease and simplicity of his manner, and in graceful turns of thought and felicity of diction. Some of his pieces, which breathe the higher enthusiasm of the art, and are coloured with a singular picturesqueness of imagery, increase our regret at the manifest mutilation of his works. Among these, the most remarkable is, perhaps, the *Attis*, a poem in the galliambic metre, and unlike the work of any other Latin author in the strangeness of its subject and its weird imaginative power. No one of his poetical predecessors was more versed in Greek literature than Catullus, and his extensive knowledge of its beauties procured for him the appellation of *Doctus*.

Catullus translated many of the shorter and more delicate pieces of the Greeks, an attempt which hitherto had been thought impossible, though the broad humour of their comedies, the vehement pathos of their tragedies, and the romantic interest of the *Odyssey*, had stood the transformation. His stay in Bithynia, though little advantageous to his fortune, rendered him better acquainted than he might otherwise have been with the productions of Greece; and he was therefore, in a great degree, indebted to this expedition for those felicitous turns of expression, that grace, simplicity, and purity which are the characteristics of his poems, and of which hitherto Greece alone had afforded models. Indeed, in all his verses, whether elegiac or heroic, we perceive his imitation of the Greeks; and it must be admitted that he has drawn from them his choicest stores. His Hellenisms are frequent; his images, similes, metaphors, and addresses to himself are all Greek; and even in the versification of his odes we see visible traces of their origin. Nevertheless, he was the inventor of a new species of Latin poetry; and as he was the first who used such variety of measures, and perhaps invented some that were new, he was amply entitled to call the poetical volume which he presented to Cornelius Nepos *lepidus novus libellus*. The expressions, too, and idioms of the Greek language, which he has so carefully selected, are woven with such art into the texture of his composition, and so aptly paint the impassioned ideas of his muse, that they have all the fresh and untarnished hues of originality.

All the MSS. of Catullus are of recent date, and all are derived from a single codex (Codex Veronensis) of which Rather, bishop of Verona (A.D. 965) made some use, and which in the fourteenth century was again copied, as also a third time, and then finally lost. The earliest and best MS., copied directly from the Codex Veronensis, is one in Paris (Germanensis), nearly related to which is the Codex Oxoniensis, probably copied about the year 1400 (Bährens). In all, there are some seventy MSS. of Catullus, on which see R. Ellis's prolegomena.

Old editions of Catullus are those of Avancius (Aldus, Venice, 1502); of Muretus, with a commentary (Venice, 1554); of Scaliger (Paris, 1577); of Voss (London, 1684); and of Döring (Leipzig, 1788–92). Great editions are those of Lachmann (Berlin, 1829); of Schwabe (Berlin, 1886); of Bährens (Leipzig, 1885); and especially of Robinson Ellis, commentary (Oxford, 1876, 2d ed. 1889) and text (Oxford, 1866). Translations are: (French) by Rostand (Paris, 1880–82); (English) by Martin (1863), Cranstoun (1867), and Ellis (1871); and (German) by Riese (1884). Criticism of Catullus may be found in Ribbeck, *Catullus: eine literar-historische Skizze* (Kiel, 1863); Couat, *Étude sur Catulle* (Paris, 1875); Nettleship, *Essays in Latin Literature* (London, 1885); Vaccaro, *Catullo e la Poesia* (Palermo, 1885); Seitz, *De Catulli Carminibus in Tres Partes Distribuendis* (Rastatt, 1887). See also Munro, *Criticisms and Elucidations of Catullus* (1878); and Sellar, *Roman Poets of the Republic* (2d ed. 1881).

Catŭlus. (1) Q. LUTATIUS. A Roman naval commander, famous for his victory over the fleet of the Carthaginians, consisting of 400 sail, off the Aegates Insulae: forty of the Carthaginian vessels were sunk, seventy taken, and the remainder dispersed. This celebrated victory put an end to the First Punic War. (2) QUINTUS. A celebrated Roman, the colleague of Marius in the consulship, and one who jointly triumphed with him over the Cimbri. He was condemned to death by Marius, during the tyrannical sway of the latter, and suffocated himself in a newly plastered room by the steam caused by a large fire (Vell. Paterc. ii. 22).

Caturĭges. A Ligurian people in Gallia Narbonensis, near the Cottian Alps.

Caucasiae Pylae (Καυκάσιαι Πύλαι). See CAUCASUS.

Caucăsus, CAUCASII MONTES (Καύκασος, τὰ Καυκάσια ὄρη). The modern Caucasus; a great chain of mountains in Asia, extending from the east shore of the Pontus Euxinus (Black Sea) to the west shore of the Caspian. There are two chief passes over the chain, both of which were known to the ancients: one, near Derbent, was called Albaniae, and sometimes Caspiae Pylae; the other, nearly in the centre of the range, was called Caucasiae Pylae (Pass of Dariel). That the Greeks had some vague knowledge of the Caucasus in very early times is proved by the myths respecting Prometheus and the Argonauts, from which it seems that the Caucasus was regarded as at the extremity of the earth, on the border of the river Oceanus. When the soldiers of Alexander advanced to that great range of mountains which formed the northern boundary of Ariana, the Paropamisus, they applied to it the name of Caucasus; afterwards, for the sake of distinction, it was called Caucasus Indicus. See PAROPAMISUS.

Cauci. See CHAUCI.

Caucōnes (Καύκωνες). The name of peoples both in Greece and Asia, who had disappeared at later times. The Caucones in Asia Minor are mentioned by Homer as allies of the Trojans, and are placed in Bithynia and Paphlagonia by the geographers.

Caudex. See CODEX.

Caudium. A town in Samnium on the road from Capua to Beneventum. In the neighbourhood were the celebrated Furculae Caudinae, or Caudine Forks, narrow passes in the mountains, where a Roman army surrendered to the Samnites, and was sent under the yoke, B.C. 321. It is now called the valley of Arpaia.

Caulicŭli. In architecture, the eight smaller leaves or stalks in the Corinthian capital, springing out of the four principal ones by which the eight volutes of the capital are sustained. See CAPITULUM; COLUMNA.

Caulon or **Caulonia.** A town in Bruttium, northeast of Locri, originally called Aulon.

Caunus. See BYBLIS.

Caunus (Καῦνος). One of the chief cities of Caria, on its southern coast, in a very fertile but unhealthy situation. It was founded by the Cretans. Its dried figs (*Cauneae ficus*) were highly celebrated. The painter Protogenes was born here.

Caupo (κάπηλος, ξενοδόκος). An innkeeper who lodged travellers in his house, and was answerable for the safe custody of their property while they remained there (*Dig.* iv. 9, 1 pr.). See CAUPONA.

Caupōna. (1) An inn, where travellers obtained food and lodging; in which sense it answered to the Greek words πανδοκεῖον, καταγώγιον, and κατάλυσις. (2) A shop, where wine and ready-dressed meat were sold; in Greek, καπηλεῖον. The person who kept a *caupona* was called *caupo* or *copo;* a hostess is *copa*, rarely *caupona*.

I. GREEK INNS.—In the earliest ages of Greece, as in the East at all times and in newly settled colonies, there was no provision for the entertainment of travellers, and the duty of hospitality was universally acknowledged. (See HOSPITIUM.) The growth of traffic rendered inns necessary, and in later times they appear to have been very numerous. The great number of festivals which were celebrated in the different towns of Greece, besides the four great national games, to which persons flocked from all parts of the Hellenic world, must have required a considerable number of inns to accommodate strangers, not only in the places where the festivals were celebrated, but also on the roads leading to those places.

The accommodation provided was, however, far from luxurious, and the character both of the houses and of their landlords was very indifferent. Inns were regarded as little better than brothels: πανδοκεῦσαι καὶ πορνοβοσκῆσαι are joined together (Theophr. *Char.* 6); καπηλεία καὶ πορνεία (Poll. ix. 34). The orgies of Demetrius Poliorcetes in the Acropolis suggest to a comic poet that "he took it for an inn":

ὁ τὴν ἀκρόπολιν πανδοκεῖον ὑπολαβὼν
καὶ τὰς ἑταίρας εἰσαγαγὼν τῇ παρθένῳ

(Philippid. *fr.* 25 M. *ap.* Plut. *Demetr.* 26). Moreover, besides the charges of fraud and adulteration to which they were liable in common with other κάπηλοι or retail dealers, the hosts were often accused of more serious crimes. Two stories told by Cicero, but taken from Greek life, both turn on murders committed by innkeepers for the sake of gain (*De Inv.* ii. 4, § 14; *De Div.* i. 27, § 57). The higher classes used these πανδοκεῖα as little as possible; yet, in default of other accommodation, the public ambassadors of Athens were sometimes constrained to lodge and even to transact diplomatic business in them (Aesch. *De F. L.* § 97; Dem. *De F. L.* p. 390, § 158=175).

The word καπηλεῖον signified, as has been already remarked, a place where wine and ready-dressed provisions were sold. Κάπηλος signifies, in general, a retail trader who sold goods in small quantities. The term, however, is more particularly applied to a person who sold ready-dressed provisions, and especially wine on draught (Schol. Aristoph. *Plut.* p. 1156; Plat. *Gorg.* p. 518 B). When a retail dealer in other commodities is spoken of, the name of his trade is usually prefixed. These καπηλεῖα were not resorted to as clubs (λέσχαι, ἑταιρεῖαι), or for purposes of good-fellowship, but merely for sottish drinking; and hence were extremely disreputable. Isocrates tells us that in the "good old times" (i. e. the democracy of Solon and Cleisthenes) no respectable slave would have ventured to eat or drink in a καπηλεῖον: whereas in his own time young men of the greatest respectability, driven by an absurd prejudice from the schools of philosophy and rhetoric, spent their whole time in these and similar establishments, in drinking, gambling, and debauchery (Isocr. *Areop.* § 49; *Antid.* § 287). We are therefore not surprised to read of the low estimation in which innkeepers were held.

II. ROMAN INNS.—A Roman wayside inn for the reception of travellers was called not only *caupona*, but also *taberna*, *deversorium*, and *taberna deversoria* (the last in Plaut. *Men.* ii. 3, 81; Varr. *R. R.* i. 2, 23). Along all the great roads of Italy there were inns, as we see from the description which Horace gives of his journey from Rome to Brundusium (*Sat.* i. 5). They were built as a speculation by neighbouring proprietors, and either let to a landlord or managed by slaves. They usually included a *stabulum* for horses and mules; hence, in the Digest, *caupones* and *stabularii* are more than once mentioned together. Where the traffic was greatest, there might be several in the same place. To take the Appian Way alone, we find the station Tres Tabernae (Cic. *Ad Att.* ii. 12, 13), Forum Appii *differtum cauponibus* (Hor. l. c. 4), Tabernae Caediciae near Sinuessa (Fest. *Epit.* p. 45 M), *Caudi cauponas* (Hor. l. c. 51). From Plautus downward, these hostelries occur repeatedly in Latin literature. Ambassadors were usually received at the public expense in decent lodgings; but the Rhodian embassy of B.C. 167 was driven to a *sordidum deversorium* (Liv. xlv. 22). Cicero mentions a *copo de via Latina* suborned as a false witness (*Pro Cluent.* 59, § 163), and the discreditable tippling of Antonius in a *cauponula* a few miles from Rome on the Via Flaminia (*Phil.* ii. 31, § 77). Cynthia drove past a *taberna* on her way to Lanuvium, and the remarks of the tavern-brawlers disgusted her poet-lover (Propert. v. 8, 19). The sprightly Vergilian *Copa* (q. v.) shows us, in a very modern fashion, the competition between rival establishments and the advertiser's art in full operation. The accommodation at these places was generally of a poor kind, but extremely cheap. In Polybius's time in Cisalpine Gaul there were no items in the bill; the inclusive charge (inquired beforehand, it should be added) rarely exceeded half an *as* (Polyb. ii. 15). For the early imperial period we have the record of the well-known relief at Aesernia, representing a hostess reckoning with a parting guest. The dialogue between the two is given at length, and the charges are: bread and a pint of wine, 1 *as;* meat (*pulmentarium*), 2 *asses;* mule's provender, 2 *asses;* and another less decent item, for which we refer the curious to the inscription itself. (This relief is figured in the *Bullettino Napolitano*, vi. 1, and thence in Daremberg and Saglio; the inscription is in Mommsen, *Inscr. Regn. Neap.* 5078 = Orelli-Henzen, 7306).

At Rome there must have been many inns to accommodate strangers, but they are hardly ever spoken of. We, however, find frequent mention of houses where wine and ready-dressed provisions were sold, and which appear to have been numerous in all parts of the city. The houses where people were allowed to eat and drink were called, almost indiscriminately, *cauponae, popinae, thermopolia,* and *tabernae vinariae.* The specialty of the *thermopolia* is noticed under CALDA. These places were principally frequented by slaves and the lower classes, and are qualified by such epithets as *nigra, fumosa, immunda, uncta* (probably "greasy," though it has also been taken in a good sense). Among other discomforts, they were only furnished with stools to sit upon, instead of couches. This circumstance is illustrated by a painting found at Pompeii in a wine-shop, representing a drinking-scene in which there are four persons sitting on stools

A Wine-shop. (From a Painting at Pompeii.)

around a tripod table. The dress of two of the figures is remarkable for the hoods, which resemble those of the capotes worn by Italian sailors and fishermen at the present day. They use cups made of horn instead of glasses, and from their whole appearance evidently belong to the lower orders. Above them are different sorts of eatables hung upon a row of pegs.

From the moral point of view the Roman inns, whether lodging-houses or mere drink-shops, were no better than the Greek. Hence we find *salax taberna, fornix* joined with *uncta popina,* and the legal aspect in *Dig.* xxiii. 2, 43, § 9. Nor are other records wanting. Behind the wine-shop at Pompeii, where the painting described above was found, is the celebrated brothel, the contents of which are now carefully preserved in the Naples Museum. The Aesernian inscription already mentioned tells the same tale. Wine or eating shops used for immoral purposes were called *ganeae,* and are often classed with the *lustra.* Naturally, therefore, persons who kept houses of public entertainment of any kind were held in low estimation. The common opinion as to their honesty is expressed by the epithets *perfidus* and *malignus,* which Horace gives to them (I. *Sat.* i. 29; v. 4).

Under the emperors many attempts were made to regulate the *popinae,* but apparently with little success. Tiberius forbade all cooked provisions to be sold in these shops (Suet. *Tib.* 34); and Claudius commanded them to be shut up altogether. They appear, however, to have been soon opened again, if they were ever closed; for Nero restricted them to the sale of cooked vegetables, and prohibited meat (Suet. *Ner.* 16); and an edict to the same effect was also published by Vespasian. See Zell, *Die Wirthshäuser der Alten,* in his *Ferienschriften* (Freiburg, 1826); Becker-Göll, *Gallus,* iii. 27–45.

Caura. A town of Hispania Baetica.

Caurus or **Corus.** The Argestes of the Greeks; the northwest wind; and in Italy a stormy wind.

Causa Liberālis. See ASSERTOR.

Causia (καυσία). A felt hat with a broad brim, forming a part of the national costume of the Macedonians and neighbouring peoples. The name is derived from its keeping off the heat (καῦσις). A purple *causia* was worn by the Macedonian kings as part of the royal costume. See DIADEMA.

Hermes wearing the Causia. (From a Fictile Vase.)

Cauter (καυτήρ, καυτήριον). (1) A branding-iron or cautery, used either by surgeons or for branding cattle and slaves (Pallad. i. 43, 3). (2) An instrument employed in encaustic painting. See PICTURA.

Cautio, Cavēre. These words are of frequent occurrence in the Roman writers and jurists, and have a great variety of significations, according to the matter to which they refer. Their general meaning is that of security given by one person to another, or security which one person obtains by the advice or assistance of another. The general term (*cautio*) is distributed into its species according to the particular kind of the security, which may be by *satisdatio,* by a *fideiussio,* and in various other ways. The general sense of the word *cautio* is accordingly modified by its adjuncts, as *cautio fideiussoria, pigneraticia,* or *hypothecaria,* and so on. *Cautio* is used to express both the security which a *magistratus* or a *iudex* may require one party to give to another, which applies to cases where there is a matter in dispute of which a court has already cognizance; and also the security which is a matter of contract between parties not in litigation. The words *cautio* and *cavere* are more particularly used in the latter sense.

If a thing is made a security from one person to another, the *cautio* becomes a matter of *pignus* or of *hypotheca;* if the *cautio* is the engagement of a surety on behalf of a principal, it is a *cautio fideiussoria.*

The *cautio* was most frequently a writing, which expressed the object of the parties to it; accordingly, the word *cautio* came to signify both the instrument (*chirographum* or *instrumentum*) and the object which it was the purpose of the instrument to secure. The phrase *cavere aliquid alicui* expressed the fact of one person giving security to another as to some particular thing or act.

Cautiones which were a branch of *stipulationes* were such contracts as would be ground of actions.

In many cases a *heres* could not safely pay legacies, unless the legatee gave security (*cautio*) to refund in case the will under which he claimed should turn out to be bad. The *cautio Muciana* was the engagement by which the *heres* bound himself to fulfil the conditions of his testator's will, or to give up the inheritance. The *heres* was also, in some cases, bound to give security for the payment of legacies, or the legatee was entitled to the *bonorum possessio*. *Tutores* and *curatōres* were required to give security (*satisdare*) for the due administration of the property intrusted to them, unless the *tutor* was appointed by testament, or unless the *curator* was a *curator legitimus*. A *procurator* who sued in the name of an absent party might be required to give security that the absent party would consent to be concluded by the act of his *procurator;* this security was a species of *satisdatio*, included under the genus *cautio*. In the case of *damnum infectum*, the owner of the land or property threatened with the mischief might call for security on the person threatening the mischief.

If a vendor sold a thing, it was usual for him to declare that he had a good title to it, and that if any person recovered it from the purchaser by a better title, he would make it good to the purchaser; and in some cases the *cautio* was for double the value of the thing. This was, in fact, a warranty.

The word *cautio* was also applied to the release which a debtor obtained from his creditor on satisfying his demand; in this sense *cautio* is equivalent to a modern receipt; it is the debtor's security against the same demand being made a second time. Thus *cavere ab aliquo* signifies to obtain this kind of security. A person to whom the *usus fructus* of a thing was given might be required to give security that he would enjoy and use it properly, and not waste it.

Cavere is also applied to express the professional advice and assistance of a lawyer to his client for his conduct in any legal matter.

The word *cavere* and its derivatives are also used to express the provisions of a law by which anything is forbidden or ordered, as in the phrase *Cautum est lege*, etc. It is also used to express the words in a will by which a testator declares his wish that certain things should be done after his death. The preparation of the instruments of *cautio* was, of course, the business of a lawyer.

It is unnecessary to particularize further the species of *cautio*, as they belong to their several heads in the law.

Cavaedium. See DOMUS.

Cavalry. See EQUES; EXERCITUS.

Cavea. (1) The auditorium of a theatre. See THEATRUM. (2) A coop in which the sacred chickens were kept and carried to the place where the auguries were to be taken, by observing the manner in which they fed (Cic. *N. D.* ii. 3). See AUGUR.

Cavea with Sacred Chickens. (Rich.)

Cavēre. See CAUTIO.

Caÿster or **Caÿstrus** (Κάϋστρος). A celebrated river of Lydia and Ionia, flowing between the ranges of Tmolus and Messogis into the Aegaean, a little northwest of Ephesus. To this day it abounds in swans, as it did in Homer's time. The valley of the Caÿstrus is called by Homer "the Asian meadow," and is probably the district to which the name Asia was first applied.

Cea. See CEOS.

Ceădas (Κεάδας) or **Caeădas** (Καιάδας). A deep cavern or chasm, like the βάραθρον at Athens, into which the Spartans were accustomed to thrust persons condemned to death (Thuc. i. 134).

Cebenna or **Gebenna.** The modern Cevennes; a range of mountains in the south of Gaul, extending north as far as Lugdunum, and separating the Arverni from the Helvii.

Cebes (Κέβης). A Greek philosopher, and disciple of Socrates, and also one of the interlocutors whom Plato introduces in his dialogue entitled *Phaedo*. He was born at Thebes, and composed three dialogues, called *Hebdomé* (Ἑβδόμη), *Phrynichus* (Φρύνιχος), and *Pinax*, or the Picture (Πίναξ). The last is the only one which has come down to us. It is commonly cited by its Latin title *Cebetis Tabula* (i. e. *picta*), and is a moral sketch or picture of human life, written in a pleasing and simple style. Some critics have raised doubts as to the authenticity of this little work. It contains, indeed, a very pure vein of morality, but is not composed, as they think, in the true spirit of the Socratic school; and they are inclined, therefore, to regard it as the work of some Stoic who wished to show that happiness consisted in the practice of virtue. But it is expressly attributed to Cebes by Lucian (*De Mercede Conduct.* 42), and after him by Tertullian (*De Praescript. adv. Haeret.* 39), Diogenes Laërtius (ii. 125), Chalcidius, and Suidas. Wolff was the first among the moderns who ventured to call in question this testimony of the ancients. No work of antiquity has met with a wider circulation. In the Middle Ages it was extremely popular, and it has been translated into almost all the modern languages, including even the Arabic—this version, in fact (of the ninth century A.D.), being our only source for the close of the dialogue. The best editions of Cebes are that of Schweighäuser (Strassburg, 1806); that of Thieme (Berlin, 1810), with German notes of great merit; of Jerram (Oxford, 1877); and of Parsons (Boston, 1887).

Cebrēnis (Κεβρηνίς). Daughter of Cebren, a river god in the Troad, from whom the town of Cebrené, the river Cebren, and the surrounding district, Cebrenia, took their names.

Cecropia. See ATHENAE; ATTICA; CECROPS.

Cecrops (Κέκρωψ). A hero of the Pelasgic race, said to have been the first king of Attica. He was married to Agraulos, daughter of Actaeus, by whom he had a son, Erysichthon, who succeeded him as king of Athens, and three daughters, Agraulos, Hersé, and Pandrosos. In his reign Poseidon and Athené contended for the possession of Attica, but Cecrops decided in favour of the goddess. Cecrops is said to have founded Athens—the citadel of which was called Cecropia, after him—to have divided Attica into twelve communities, and to have introduced the first elements of civilized life. (See ATHENAE.) He instituted marriage, abolished bloody sacrifices, and taught his subjects how to worship the gods. The later Greek writers describe Cecrops as a native of Saïs in Egypt, who led a colony of Egyptians into Attica, and thus introduced from Egypt the arts of civilized life; but this account is rejected by some of the ancients themselves, and by the ablest modern critics.

Cedit Dies. See LEGATUM.

Cedrēnus, GEORGIUS. A Byzantine writer who wrote an historical work beginning with the creation of the world and continuing to the year A.D. 1057. Of his personality nothing is known. The history has been edited by Bekker (Bonn, 1839).

Celaenae (Κελαιναί). A great city in southern Phrygia, situated at the sources of the rivers Maeander and Marsyas. In the midst of it was a citadel, built by Xerxes, on a precipitous rock, at the foot of which the Marsyas took its rise; and near the river's source was a grotto celebrated by tradition as the scene of the flaying of Marsyas (q. v.) by Apollo. The Maeander took its rise in the very palace, and flowed through the park and the city, below which it received the Marsyas.

Celaeno (Κελαινώ). One of the Harpies. See HARPYIAE.

Celendĕris (Κελένδερις). A city on the coast of Cilicia Trachea, to the northeast of the Anemurian promontory. It was founded by the Phœnicians, and afterwards received a Samian colony.

Celer. (1) The joint architect with Severus of the famous Golden House (*Domus Aurea*) of Nero. See PALATIUM. (2) See EGNATII.

Celĕres. According to Livy (i. 15, 8), a bodyguard of 300 chosen by Romulus to attend him in peace and war. Livy leaves it uncertain whether they were cavalry or infantry. According to some accounts (cf. Dionys. ii. 13, 16, 29) they were infantry; while according to others (id. ii. 64) they included both, or were only cavalry. The last view is that which has been usually taken.

Celes (κέλης). (1) A horse for riding as distinguished from a draught or carriage horse. (2) A race-horse (Plin. *H. N.* xxxiv. § 10). (3) The same as CELOX (q. v.).

Celētrum. A town in Macedonia on a peninsula of the Lacus Castoris. It is probably to be identified with the later Diocletianopolis.

Celeus (Κελεός). King of Eleusis, husband of Metanira, and father of Demophon and Triptolemus. He received Demeter with hospitality at Eleusis, when she was wandering in search of her daughter. The goddess, in return, wished to make his son Demophon immortal, and placed him in the fire in order to destroy his mortal parts; but Metanira screamed aloud at the sight, and Demophon was destroyed by the flames. Demeter then bestowed great favours upon Triptolemus. (See TRIPTOLEMUS.) Celeus is described as the first priest, and his daughters as the first priestesses, of Demeter at Eleusis. See the Homeric hymn to Demeter, 146 foll.

Cella. (1) In its primary sense, *cella* means a store-room, of which the following were the principal descriptions: *cella penaria* or *penuaria*, where all kinds of provisions (*penus*) were stored, especially those of which a stock was laid in for a long time; *cella promptuaria, promptuarium,* or *promum,* the larder, where meat and other things required for immediate consumption were kept; *cella olearia*, the magazine of an olive-yard in which the oil was stored, and which, according to the treatises on farming, ought to be lighted from the south, that the oil might not be chilled in winter; while the *cella vinaria* should have a northern aspect, to avoid excessive heat and great changes of temperature. The *cella vinaria* described in the ancient authors is the store-room of a vineyard, in which the new wine was kept in *dolia* or *cupae*, while older wine was put into *amphorae* and matured in the *apotheca*. The *cella vinaria* was partly underground (Becker-Göll, *Gallus*, iii. 51, 422). The *cella vinaria* of a wine-merchant was discovered in 1789 under the walls of Rome. It was raised a little above the level of the ground, and divided into three compartments, the first ornamented with arabesques and a mosaic pavement, the second unpaved and containing a row of very large *dolia* two-thirds imbedded in sand, while the third was a narrow gallery, six feet high and eighteen feet long, with various earthenware vessels, also partially sunk in the sand and ranged in double rows against each wall. (See DOLIUM.) The slave to whom the charge of these stores was intrusted was called *cellarius, a rationibus cellae, promus, promus condus,* or *procurator peni;* under him was the *subpromus.* (2) Any number of small rooms clustered together. Thus the word was applied to the dormitories of slaves (Hor. *Sat.* i. 8. 8), to the bedrooms of an inn, and to the

Slave Cellae. (Rich.)

vaults of a brothel (Petron. 8, 4). A brothel is also called *cella inscripta*, because the price of each inmate was inscribed on the door (Mart. xi. 45, 1). The porter's lodge or janitor's office is called *cella ostiarii* (Petron. 29) or *cella ianitoris* (Suet. *Vitell.* 16). (3) In the baths the *cella caldaria, tepidaria,* and *frigidaria* are respectively those which contained the hot, tepid, and cold baths. See BALNEAE. (4) The interior of a temple was also called *cella.* See TEMPLUM.

Cellar. See APOTHECA; CELLA; DOMUS.

Cellarius. See CELLA.

Celox (κέλης, κελήτιον), from κέλλω, *cello,* "to urge on." A swift boat. This peculiar build of boat is said to have been invented by the Rhodians (Plin. *H. N.* vii. § 208). It was much used by pirates, but was more especially employed as attendant on the fleet, either for bringing news or negotiating with the enemy. Further, each State appears to have had such boats for various official purposes, just as we hear of δημοσίαι ἄκατοι at Athens (cf. Plaut. *Capt.* iv. 2. 93). Built for swiftness, they were necessarily narrow, and Appian calls one ὀξύ. They had no decks, and only one bench of oars (Polyb. v. 62, 3).

Celsus. (1) AULUS CORNELIUS. A celebrated physician. His native city is unknown; some writers contending for Rome, others for Verona. The time in which he lived has also been made a subject of controversy, but the most probable opinion is that he lived in the first half of the first century A.D., and wrote under Tiberius and Claudius. Celsus composed a large work, on the plan, in some measure, of an encyclopædia, in which he treated of philosophy, jurisprudence, warfare, agriculture, and medicine. It was entitled *De Artibus.* Unhappily, however, only the eight books (from the sixth to the fourteenth) which treat of medicine have come down to us.

Roman literature, otherwise so barren of good medical authorities, can boast of possessing in Celsus one who, for elegance, terseness, learning, good sense, and practical information, stands unrivalled. His preface contains an admirable exposition of the principles of the different schools which had risen up in medicine before his time; and in the remaining part of the first book there are many pertinent remarks on the best method of preserving the health. In the second, which treats of the general symptoms and phenomena of diseases in general, he has drawn freely from Hippocrates. The last part of this book is devoted to the subject of diet and regimen; and here his views will, with a few exceptions, be admitted by the unprejudiced to be wonderfully correct. In the third book he has treated of fevers; and here his distinctions, remarks upon critical days, and treatment will be found to be particularly deserving of attention. The other parts of his work it is unnecessary to go over minutely; but one may point out, as particularly valuable, his divisions and treatment of ulcers. It is remarkable that no ancient writer has treated of the diseases of the sexual organs with the same precision that he has done. The different shades of cutaneous diseases he has marked with a surprising degree of precision. But of the whole work the most interesting part, perhaps, is the seventh book, which treats of the operations of surgery according to the views of the Alexandrian School. His account of those performed upon the eye may be instanced as particularly excellent. The operation of lithotomy, as described by him, though not exactly the same as that now generally practised, has had, even in modern times, its admirers. Celsus has the merit of being the first author who makes mention of the application of the ligature to arteries for stopping hemorrhage. The best MSS. of Celsus are in the Vatican, the Laurentian Library, and in Paris—the oldest being of the tenth century. They all have a common origin. The best editions are those of Targa (Padua, 1769, and Verona, 1810); Milligan (Edinb. 1831); Ritter and Albers (Cologne, 1835); Renzi (Naples, 1851); and Daremberg (Leipzig, 1859). Milligan's edition has a good index, and that of Renzi a good lexicon. See Kissel, *Celsus, eine hist. Monog.* (Giessen, 1844), and on the Latinity, Brolen, *De Elocutione Celsi* (Upsala, 1872); also the articles CHIRURGIA and MEDICINA. (2) A Platonic, or perhaps Epicurean, philosopher who lived about A.D. 180. His name is famous as that of one of the bitterest enemies of Christianity. From a motive of curiosity, or, perhaps, in order to be better able to combat the new religion, Celsus caused himself to be initiated into the mysteries of Christianity, and to be received into that secret society which St. Clement of Rome is supposed to have founded. It appears, however, that the sincerity of the neophyte was distrusted, and that he was refused admittance into the higher ceremonies. The discontent to which this gave rise in the breast of Celsus inflamed his resentment against the Christians, and he wrote a work against them, entitled Ἀληθὴς Λόγος, "A true discourse," in which he employed all the resources of his intellect and eloquence to paint Christianity as a ridiculous and contemptible system, and its followers as a sect dangerous to the well-being of the State. There is no falsehood to which he has not recourse in order to represent in an untrue light the Christian scheme of morals, to parody and falsify the text of the Old and New Testaments, and to calumniate the character of Jesus Christ and his disciples. He styles Christianity a doctrine tending to pervert and corrupt the human race, and exhorts the government to extirpate the sect if it wishes to save the Empire. The discourse itself is lost; but Origen, who refuted it, in a work divided into eight books, has given us so complete an extract from it that by the aid of this we can follow all the principal reasoning of the author. Celsus wrote also a work against magicians and sorcerers (Κατὰ Μάγων), which is cited by Origen and Lucian. The latter, who was his friend, addressed to him his memoir on Alexander, the false prophet, in which he extols the wisdom of Celsus, his love for truth, and his amiable manners. See Keim, *Celsus' wahres Wort* (1873); Aubé, *La Polémique Païenne* (1878); and Pélagaud, *Étude sur Celse* (1878). (3) ALBINOVĀNUS, a friend of Horace, warned against plagiarism (*Epist.* i. 3, 15) and pleasantly ridiculed (*Epist.* i. 8) for his foibles.

Celtae (Κελταί). The ancients had no comprehensive name to denote generically the collective Keltic peoples. The Continental Kelts were called *Galli* or *Celtae* by the Romans, and Γαλάται or Κελταί by the Greeks, all these names being applied only to the Kelts of the Continent, with whom, in the popular view, the people of Britain had no ethnic relation. Caesar understood the racial identity of the Britanni with the Galli, Celtae, and Belgae, but the general usage of the words as stated above embodied the prevailing belief.

According to Prof. Rhys, it would appear probable that the west of Europe had in early times experienced two Keltic invasions, since the two distinct names in Greek and Latin are not used as synonymous, but as denoting two different ethnic divisions. Thus in the ecclesiastical writer Sulpicius Severus (fourth century A.D.), *Celticé* is differentiated from *Gallicé* (Migne, *Patrolog. Lat.* vol. xx. col. 201, *Dial.* i. 26); and Caesar, three centuries before, wrote that *one* of the three peoples of Gaul was called *Celtae* in its own tongue.

The two waves of migration may roughly be represented geographically as follows: (1) the Kelts of Gaul, Spain, the Isle of Man, Ireland, and Scotland; and (2) the Kelts dwelling near the Rhine, the Alps, and in England and Wales. Schleicher, in the *Rheinisches Museum* for 1859, expounded his theory of a Kelto-Italic period, according to which the people who afterwards separated into Greeks, Italians, and Kelts are regarded as having left the early home of the race together, the Greeks branching off first into Hellas. Then followed the Italo-Keltic period, during which the Italo-Kelts developed those linguistic forms which the Keltic and the Latin alone possess in common—e. g. the future in *-bo*, the passive formation in *-r*, the dative ending *-bus*, and the formative suffixes in *-tio* and *-tric*. See Peile, *Introduction to Greek and Latin Etymology*, pp. 21–27 (2d ed. 1872); and H. Ebel, *Keltische Studien*.

Historically, the Keltic and Latin races come into contact not earlier than the fifth century B.C., when the Gauls crossed the Alps and began first to press against the Etruscan communities in the north of Italy. Their leader, Bellovesus the Biturigan, directed the Insubrian migration into the valley of the Padus (Po), where the oldest Keltic settlement was established, to develop later into the important city of Mediolanum (Milan). A second invasion followed, and founded the towns of Brixia (Brescia) and Verona. Thenceforward, tribe after tribe poured into Italy, dislodging the Etruscans, and at last (B.C. 396) coming in contact with the Umbrians, and in 388 facing the Romans in successful battle. This was the year in which Brennus with 70,000 Gauls crossed the Tiber, won the bloody victory of the Allia (q. v.) on July 18, and three days later marched through the open gates of Rome. (On the date, see Mommsen, *Hist. of Rome*, i. 428, Amer. ed. 1888.) They often returned to Latium, but were less successful in following years. The Romans, who had at first despised them, now strained every nerve to avenge the defeat of the Allia. Camillus (q. v.) routed them at Alba (B.C. 367); Servilius Ahala repulsed them in front of the Porta Collina (B.C. 360); and the dictator Gaius Sulpicius Peticus won a decisive victory over them in 358. Yet in the year 350 they had again returned, and encamped for an entire winter on the Alban Mount, joining with the Greek pirates for plunder, till Lucius Furius Camillus, son of the great general, dislodged them. The increasing power of the Romans, and perhaps, as Mommsen suggests, changes beyond the Alps, put an end to the migrations from Gaul; and the Kelts began to settle down into a less predatory condition between the Alps and the Apennines as far south as the Abruzzi, the chief tribes being the Insubres, Boii, Lingones, and Senones, the territory of the last-named being on the coast of the Adriatic, from Ariminum to Ancona, the so-called Ager Gallicus. Here the Kelts, uniting with the Ligurians and Etrurians, gradually took on the character of a settled community, until at last they, with the rest of Italy, became subject to the all-embracing power of Rome.

Of the Kelts who first swept over Italy and destroyed Rome, the historians give a picturesque account. Brave, open, impetuous, they were swayed by every passing impression; "they devoted themselves chiefly to two things—fighting and *esprit*" (*rem militarem et argute loqui*, Cato, *Orig.* ii. frag. 2, ed. Jordan). Despising agriculture as disgraceful and unfit for freemen, they followed the profession of arms like soldiers of fortune. The Romans before the battle of the Allia had despised them as barbarians, and on the occasion of that memorable conflict had sent against them only an ill-organized and over-confident army. The legionaries were appalled when the onset of these fierce warriors smote the Roman phalanx. Stripped naked for battle, sword in hand, utterly heedless of death, the Keltic hosts of Brennus fell upon their enemies with an ardour and impetuosity that swept away an army in an instant. Yet, with all their bravery and brilliancy, the Kelts never made any lasting political impression upon the countries that they overran. They lacked the political, constructive instinct which the Latins and the Germans, too, possessed. They destroyed, but did not create, and in a few centuries had everywhere succumbed to the steadier valour and more enduring power of the Romans.

See Mommsen, *Hist. of Rome*, bk. ii. ch. iv.; Thierry, *Histoire des Gaulois* (Paris, 1828); Ebel, *Keltische Studien* (Eng. trans. London, 1863); Diefenbach, *Die Alten Völker* (Frankfurt, 1861); Belloguet, *Ethnogénie Gauloise* (Paris, 1858–61); Stark, *Keltische Forschungen* (Vienna, 1869); Reynaud, *De l'Esprit de la Gaule* (Paris, 1866); Scarth, *Roman Britain* (London, 1883); Rhys, *Celtic Heathendom* (1888); Wright, *The Celt, the Roman, and the Saxon* (4th ed. London, 1885); and also the article by Windisch, "Keltische Sprachen," in the *Allgemeine Encyklopädie der Wissenschaften und Künste;* Von Becker, *Versuch einer Lösung der Celtenfrage* (1883); Müllenhof, *Deutsche Alterthumskunde* (Berlin, 1887); Hübner, *Inscriptiones Britanniae Christianae;* Brambach, *Corpus Inscriptionum Rhenanarum;* vols. ii., iii., v., vii., and xii. of the *Corpus Inscriptionum Latinarum* of the Berlin Academy; and the articles BRITANNIA; DRUIDAE; GALLIA; HIBERNIA; HISPANIA; INDO-EUROPEAN LANGUAGES.

Celtibēri. A powerful people in Spain, consisting of Kelts, who crossed the Pyrenees at an early period, and became mingled with the Iberians, the original inhabitants of the country. They dwelt chiefly in the central part of Spain. Their country, called Celtiberia, was mountainous and unproductive. They were a brave and warlike people, and proved formidable enemies to the Romans. They submitted to Scipio Africanus in the Second Punic War, but the oppression of the Roman governors led them to rebel, and for many years they successfully defied the power of Rome. They were reduced to submission on the capture of Numantia by Scipio Africanus the Younger (B.C. 134), but they again took up arms under Sertorius, and it was not till his death (B.C. 72) that they began to adopt the Roman customs and language.

Celtĭci. (1) A people of Lusitania, whose territory lay below the mouth of the Tagus, and between that river and the Turdetani. They were of Keltic origin, as their name imports. Their chief town was Pax Iulia, now Beja. (2) A people in Gallaecia.

Cemeteries. See CATACUMBAE; SEPULCRUM.

Cena, less correctly COENA (δεῖπνον). The principal meal of the Greeks and Romans, corresponding to our dinner rather than supper. As the meals are not always clearly distinguished, it will be convenient to give a brief account of all of them under the present head.

I. GREEK. The materials for an account of the Greek meals, during the classical period of Athens and Sparta, are almost confined to incidental allusions of Plato and the comic writers. Several ancient authors, termed δειπνολόγοι, are mentioned by Athenaeus; but, unfortunately, their writings only survive in the fragments quoted by him. His great work, the *Deipnosophistae*, is an inexhaustible treasury of this kind of knowledge, though very ill-arranged. See ATHENAEUS.

The poems of Homer contain a real picture of early manners, in every way worthy of the antiquarian's attention. As they stand apart from all other writings, it will be convenient to exhibit in one view the state of things which they describe. It is not to be expected, however, that the Homeric meals should at all agree with the customs of a later period. Athenaeus (i. 8), who has entered fully into the subject, remarks on the simplicity of the Homeric banquets, in which kings and private men all partake of the same food. It was common enough for royal personages to prepare their own meals, and Odysseus (*Od.* xv. 322) declares himself no mean proficient in the culinary art.

Three names of meals occur in the *Iliad* and *Odyssey*—ἄριστον, δεῖπνον, δόρπον or δόρπος. The word ἄριστον uniformly means the early as δόρπον does the late meal; but δεῖπνον, though generally meaning the mid-day meal, is sometimes used where we should expect ἄριστον (*Od.* xv. 397) or even δόρπον (*Od.* xvii. 170). We should be careful, however, how we argue from the unsettled habits of a camp to the regular customs of ordinary life.

In the Homeric Age it was usual to sit at table; and this custom, we are told, was kept up in historical times by the Cretans. Each guest had generally his own table, and an equal share of food was placed before each (hence δαὶς ἐΐση), except when a specially distinguished guest was honoured by getting a larger portion (*Il.* vii. 321). What strikes us as peculiar in the Homeric dinners is their religious character. They partake more or less of the nature of a sacrifice, beginning with an offering of part of the meat to the gods, and both beginning and ending with a libation of wine; while the terms for slaughtering animals for a meal (ἱερεύειν, θύειν) and for the slaughtered animals (ἱερήϊα) are borrowed from the language of religious ceremony. The description of the dinner given by Eumaeus to Odysseus (*Od.* xiv. 420) gives a good picture of a dinner in the Homeric Age in humble society; and that given by Achilles to Odysseus (*Il.* ix. 219 foll.) may be taken as typical of the banquets of the great in the same period.

Beef, mutton, swine's and goat's flesh were the ordinary meats, generally eaten roasted, though sometimes boiled (*Il.* xxi. 363). Fish and fowls were almost unknown (Eustath. *ad* Hom. *Od.* xii. 330). Many sorts of wine are mentioned, notably the Maronean and the Pramnian. Nestor had wine eleven years old (*Od.* iii. 391). A small quantity was poured into each guest's cup to make a libation with (ἐπαρξάμενοι δεπάεσσιν), before the wine was regularly served out for drinking. The guests drank to each other (*Od.* iii. 40), and a second libation to the gods closed the repast (*Od.* iii. 332).

The Greeks of a later age usually partook of three meals, called ἀκράτισμα, ἄριστον, and δεῖπνον. The last, which corresponds to the δόρπον of the Homeric poems, was the evening meal or dinner; the ἄριστον was luncheon; and the ἀκράτισμα, which answers to the ἄριστον of Homer, was the early meal or breakfast.

The ἀκράτισμα was taken immediately after rising in the morning (Aristoph. *Aves*, 1286). It usually consisted of bread dipped in unmixed wine (ἄκρατος), whence it derived its name (Athen. i. 11).

Next followed the ἄριστον or luncheon. The time at which it was taken is uncertain, though we may conclude from many circumstances that it was about the middle of the day, and that the meal answered to the Roman *prandium*. The market time, at which provisions seem to have been bought for the ἄριστον, was from nine o'clock till noon. In Aristophanes (*Vesp.* 605–612) Philocleon describes the pleasure of returning home after attending the courts, and partaking of a good ἄριστον. It was usually a simple meal, but of course varied according to the habits of individuals (Xen. *Oecon.* xi. 18).

The principal meal, however, was the δεῖπνον. It was usually taken rather late in the day, frequently not before sunset (Lysias, *de Caed. Eratosth.* § 22).

The Athenians were a social people, and were very fond of dining in company. Entertainments were usually given, both in the Heroic Age and later times, when sacrifices were offered to the gods, either on public or private occasions; and also on the anniversary of the birthdays of members of the family, or of illustrious persons, whether living or dead. Plutarch (*Symp.* viii. 1, § 1) speaks of an entertainment being given on the anniversary of the birthdays of both Socrates and Plato.

Dining clubs were very common, the members of which contributed each a certain sum of money, called συμβολή, or brought their own provisions with them. When the first plan was adopted, they were said ἀπὸ συμβολῶν δειπνεῖν, and one individual was generally intrusted with the money to procure the provisions and make all the necessary preparations (Terence, *Eunuch.* iii. 4). When the second plan was adopted, they were said ἀπὸ σπυρίδος δειπνεῖν, because the provisions were brought in baskets. This kind of entertainment is spoken of by Xenophon (*Mem.* iii. 14, § 1). In Homer the word ἔρανος corresponds with the later ἀπὸ συμβολῶν δεῖπνον, while εἰλαπίνη denotes a public entertainment on a festival or some such occasion (Athen. viii. 362 e).

The most usual kind of entertainments, however, were those in which a person invited his friends to his own house. It was expected that they should come dressed with more than ordinary care, and also have bathed shortly before; hence, when Socrates was going to an entertainment at Agathon's, we are told that he both washed and put on his shoes—things which he seldom did (Plato, *Symp.* 174 A). As soon as the guests arrived at the house of their host, their shoes or sandals were taken off by the slaves, and their feet washed (ὑπολύειν and ἀπονίζειν). In ancient works of art we frequently see a slave or other person represented in the act of taking off the shoes of the guests, of which an example is given on the next page from a terra-cotta in the British Museum. After their feet had been washed, the guests reclined on the κλῖναι or couches.

Sitting at meals was, as has already been remarked, the practice of the Heroic Age, but in the classical period was confined to Crete. Women, however, when admitted to banquets on extraordinary occasions, such as a marriage (for they were generally excluded from table when guests were invited), took the sitting posture (Lucian, *Conv.* 13), and so did children (Xen. *Symp.* i. 8). A very common representation on funeral monuments is the family meal, with the husband reclining, and the wife and children sitting at his side. Where women are represented as reclining at a meal, they are meant for *hetaerae*.

It was usual for only two persons to recline on

each couch. In ancient works of art we usually see the guests represented in this way, but sometimes there is a larger number on one long κλίνη. The guests reclined with their left arms on striped pillows (ὑπαγκώνια), and having their right arms free. (Cf. Aristoph. *Vesp.* 1210.)

Slave taking off the Shoes of a Guest. (British Museum.)

After the guests had placed themselves on the κλῖναι, the slaves brought in water to wash their hands; and then the dinner was served up, the expression for which was τὰς τραπέζας εἰσφέρειν (Aristoph. *Vesp.* 1216). By τὰς τραπέζας εἰσφέρειν we are to understand not merely the dishes, but the tables themselves (Philoxen. *ap.* Athen. iv. 146 f). It appears that a table, with provisions upon it, was placed before each κλίνη: and thus we find in all ancient works of art which represent banquets or symposia, a small table or tripod placed before the κλίνη: and when there are more than two persons on the κλίνη, several such tables. These tables were evidently small enough to be moved with ease.

In eating, the Greeks had no knives or forks, but made use of their fingers only, except in eating soups or other liquids, which they partook of by means of a spoon (μύστρον), or a piece of bread scooped out in the shape of a spoon (μυστίλη) (Suidas, s. v. μυστίλη). After eating, they wiped their fingers on pieces of bread, called ἀπομαγδαλιαί, which were then thrown to the dogs (Aristoph. *Eq.* 415). Napkins (χειρόμακτρα) were not used till the Roman period.

It appears that the arrangement of the dinner was intrusted to certain slaves. The one who had the chief management of it was called τραπεζοποιός or τραπεζοκόμος (Athen. iv. 170 e; Pollux, iii. 41; vi. 13). The Greek word for a *menu* was γραμματίδιον (Athen. ii. 49 d).

It would exceed the limits of this work to give an account of the different dishes which were introduced at a Greek dinner, though their number is far below those which were usually partaken of at a Roman entertainment. The most common food among the Greeks was the μάζα, a kind of soft cake, which was prepared in different ways, as appears by the various names which were given to it (Pollux, vi. 76). The φυστὴ μάζα, of which Philocleon partakes on returning home from the courts (Aristoph. *Vesp.* 610), is said by the Scholiast to have been made of barley and wine. The μάζα continued to the latest times to be the common food of the lower classes. Wheaten or barley bread was the second most usual species of food; it was sometimes made at home, but more usually bought at the market. The vegetables ordinarily eaten were mallows (μαλάχη), lettuces (θρίδαξ), cabbages (ῥάφανοι), beans (κύαμοι), lentils (φακαῖ), etc. Pork was the favourite animal food, as was the case among the Romans. Sausages also were very commonly eaten. It is a curious fact, which Plato (*Rep.* iii. 13, 404) has remarked, that we never read in Homer of the heroes partaking of fish. In later times, however, fish was one of the favourite foods of the Greeks, insomuch so that the name of ὄψον was applied to it κατ' ἐξοχήν. A minute account of the fishes which the Greeks were accustomed to eat is given at the end of the seventh book of Athenaeus, arranged in alphabetical order.

The ordinary meal for the family was cooked by the mistress of the house, or by the female slaves under her direction; but for special occasions professional cooks (μάγειροι) were hired, of whom there appear to have been a great number (Diog. Laërt. ii. 72). They are frequently mentioned in the fragments of the comic poets, and those who were acquainted with all the refinements of their art were in great demand in other parts of Greece besides their own country. The Sicilian cooks, however, had the greatest reputation, and a Sicilian book on cookery by one Mithaecus is mentioned in the *Gorgias* of Plato (p. 518 B); but the most celebrated work on the subject was the Γαστρολογία of Archestratus (Athen. iii. 104 b).

A dinner given by an opulent Athenian usually consisted of two courses, called respectively πρῶται τράπεζαι and δεύτεραι τράπεζαι. Pollux (vi. 83), indeed, speaks of three courses, which was the number at a Roman dinner; and in the same way we find other writers under the Roman Empire speaking of three courses at Greek dinners; but before the Roman conquest of Greece and the introduction of Roman customs, we read of only two courses. The first course embraced the whole of what we consider the dinner—namely, fish, poultry, meat, etc. (ἐδέσματα); the second, which corresponded to our dessert and the Roman *bellaria*, consisted of different kinds of fruit, sweetmeats, confections, etc. (τρωγάλια). The Roman first course of salads, vegetables, etc., was unknown to the Greeks in the time of their independence.

When the first course was finished, the tables were taken away (αἴρειν, ἐκφέρειν, βαστάζειν τὰς τραπέζας), and water was given to the guests for the purpose of washing their hands. Crowns made of garlands of flowers were also then given to them, as well as various kinds of perfumes. Wine was not drunk till the first course was finished; but as soon as the guests had washed their hands, unmixed wine was produced in a large goblet, called μετάνιπτρον or μετανιπτρίς, of which each drank a little, after pouring out a small quantity as a libation. This libation was said to be made to the "good spirit" (ἀγαθοῦ δαίμονος), and was usually accompanied with the singing of the pæan and the playing of flutes. After this libation mixed wine was brought in, and with their first cup the guests drank to Ζεὺς Σωτήρ (Xen. *Symp.* ii. 1). With the σπονδαί the δεῖπνον closed; and at the introduction of the dessert (δεύτεραι τράπεζαι) the πότος, συμπόσιον, or κῶμος commenced, of which an account is given in the article SYMPOSIUM.

II. ROMAN. The Roman meals were *ientaculum* (ἀκράτισμα), *prandium* (ἄριστον), *merenda*, and *cena* (δεῖπνον).

Ientaculum, also called *silatum* (Fest. p. 346) because the wine used was sometimes perfumed with *seselis* or *silis*, was a slight morning meal taken at different times by early and late risers. Thus we find it taken by schoolboys at cock-crow (Mart. xiv. 233); but generally the Romans used to eat it about the third hour, certainly not later than the fourth (Mart. viii. 67, 9). The schoolboys had a kind of pancake (*adipata*); but usually the meal consisted of bread seasoned with salt or with honey, or dipped in wine, or of dates and olives. Alexander Severus used to have milk, eggs, and *mulsum* (Lamprid. *Alex. Sev.* 30). Bread and cheese (Apul. *Met.* i. 18), and even meat, appear to have been sometimes taken (Mart. xiii. 31); but to make the *ientaculum* a heavy meal was not in accordance with Roman manners.

As with our own fathers noon was the time for the principal meal of the day—viz., dinner—so with the primitive Romans this was the time for *cena* (Fest. 54; cf. p. 338, Müll.). It was only in later times that *prandium* became customary (Isid. *Orig.* xx. 2, 14). We may fairly translate this word "luncheon." When city life pushed the dinner-hour later and later, a mid-day meal became essential. It was taken about the sixth hour (*Anth. Pal.* x. 43, and scholiast), not so early as the fifth nor so late as the seventh. But if one took no *ientaculum*, he must needs take the *prandium* earlier, and this is the reason why we find Ausonius eating his *prandium* a little after the fourth hour (*Ephemeris* in *Corp. Poet. Lat.*, ed. Weber, p. 1217). *Prandium* seems to have been properly the name of the soldier's morning meal (Isid. *Orig.* xx. 2, 11). For the ordinary citizen, the meal varied from a piece of bread eaten in the hand (Sen. *Ep.* 83, 6) to an elaborate entertainment, with hot and cold fish, fowl, and meat, with vegetables and fruit. (Cf. Mayor on Plin. *Ep.* iii. 5, 11.) The meats were rather savoury dishes than solids—e. g. they were kernels of pork (*glandulae, glandia*, "sweetbreads"?). Often, as at our luncheons, the meat of the previous day's dinner was served cold or warmed up (Plaut. *Pers.* i. 3. 25). Wine (Tac. *Ann.* xiv. 2), hot wine and water (Mart. viii. 67, 7), and *mulsum* (Cic. *Cluent.* 60, 166) were drunk at it. This latter passage refers to a large wedding breakfast which is called *prandium*.

Merenda was in ancient times an afternoon meal, given to workmen, also called *antecenium* (Nonius, p. 59). If *prandium* was not taken at mid-day, *merenda* was a late *prandium* taken in the afternoon (Calp. *Ecl.* v. 60).

The principal meal of the day was *cena*, "dinner." The eighth hour in summer and the ninth in winter was sometimes the time for the bath (Plin. *Ep.* iii. 1, 8), and after that came dinner; but probably the bath was usually a little earlier. The ninth was considered the normal dinner-hour (Cic. *Fam.* ix. 26), though business must have often deferred it till after the tenth, and even later (Mart. iii. 36, 5). These were homely repasts; for the more fashionable banquets were, the earlier they began (Palmer on Hor. *Sat.* ii. 8, 3). Banquets which began earlier than the ninth hour were called *tempestiva convivia*, or *de die cenare* (Catull. 47, 5). The *cena* always lasted for what would seem to us a very long time. Even Pliny the Elder, who was so miserly of his time, used to spend three hours at his dinner (Plin. *Ep.* iii. 5, 13), while old Cato used to remain conversing over this meal until late at night (Cic. *Sen.* 14, 46). The business of the day was done, and the time for enjoyment had arrived; there was, accordingly, no necessity to break into the meal till bedtime, which was much earlier than with us, as the Romans got up at daybreak. Symposia, of course, lasted till midnight, and even morning. The ancient Romans, like the ancient Greeks, used to sit at dinner (Isid. *Orig.* xx. 11, 9), and Columella (xi. 1, 19) thinks the *vilicus* should not recline except on holidays; and Cato the Younger, in sign of mourning, always sat at meals after the battle of Pharsalia (Plut. *Cat. Min.* 56).

Symposium. (Millin.)

However, in the times with which we are best acquainted, the Romans dined in the *atrium* (Serv. on *Aen.* i. 730), in the circle of the family—the men reclining; the wife sitting on the *lectus* (Val. Max. ii. 1, 21); the children beside the couches (Suet. *Claud.* 32), or on a lower couch (Suet. *Aug.* 64), and with a separate and more frugal table (Tac. *Ann.* xiii. 16); the subordinate persons (Plaut. *Capt.* iii. 1, 11) and slaves on benches (*subsellia*). It was customary for the wife and children to dine with the men, except, apparently, in times of mourning (Suet. *Calig.* 24), though, of course, there were gentlemen's dinner-parties (Hor. *Sat.* ii. 8).

On the other hand, we find cases of women reclining where there was conceived to be nothing bold or indelicate in their posture. Thus, in the following illustration, taken from Montfaucon (*Ant. Exp. Suppl.* iii. 66), which seems intended to represent a scene of perfect matrimonial felicity, the husband and wife recline on a sofa of rich materials. A three-legged table is spread with viands before them, and their two sons are in front of the sofa, one of them sitting, in the manner above described, on a low stool, and playing with the dog. Several women and a boy are performing a piece of music for the entertainment of the married pair.

A Family Feast. (Montfaucon.)

The very wealthy Romans built separate dining-rooms, and to the article TRICLINIUM and those on LECTUS and PULVINUS the reader is referred for the arrangement of the couches and of the guests at table. For the tables, see MENSA.

During the later Republic and the Empire the number of guests at a private dinner-party was usually nine, and sometimes less (Gell. xiii. 11, 2), but to have more was considered unseemly (Cic. *Pis.* 27, 67). Generally uninvited guests (*umbrae*) were brought by one of the invited guests to make up the nine (*Epist.* i. 5. 28); or perhaps a client was asked, in order not to leave a place empty (Juv. v. 17). The guests used to dress for dinner—the dinner dress (*vestis cenatoria*) being generally a light, highly ornamented coloured tunic (*prasina synthesis*, Mart. x. 29. 4). It cannot be supposed that the changing of one's *synthesis* during dinner was other than vulgar ostentation (Mart. v. 79, 2), but it was sometimes required by religious ceremonials. Dress-sandals (*soleae*) were generally worn in the house of the host, but were taken off (*demere soleas*) before reclining for the meal. They were taken charge of by the guest's own slave whom he brought with him, for each guest had his own footman (*servus a pedibus*) to wait on him at table (Plaut. *Truc.* ii. 4, 16; Petron. 58 and 62). If the guest did not come in a litter, but walked, he often wore boots (*calcei*, Plin. *Ep.* ix. 47, 3). The regular expression for rising from table was *soleas poscere* (Hor. *Sat.* ii. 8. 77).

The places were pointed out to the guests by the *nomenclator* (Athen. ii. 47 e); and when they had taken up their reclining position (*accumbere, discumbere*) at table, water was brought round and poured over the hands of each guest (Plaut. *Pers.* v. 1. 17), and the hands wiped in a towel or napkin (*mantela, mappa*) provided by the host, though sometimes brought by the guest, in order to carry away the presents that the host frequently gave. (See APOPHORETA.) Later *mantele* was used for a table-cloth (Isid. *Orig.* xix. 26. 6). It was not till towards the end of the first century A.D. that table-cloths began to be used. Martial appears to be the first to allude to them (ix. 59, 7). Sometimes, apparently, grace was said (Quintil. *Declam.* 301, p. 583, ed. Burmann), and then the first of the three parts of the meal was proceeded with.

This was called *promulsis* or *gustatio, gustus;* also *frigida mensa*. The cold dishes of this part of the meal used in early times to occupy a place at the conclusion (Plut. *Quaest. Conviv.* viii. 9, 28). It consisted rarely of substantial meats, mostly of *hors d'œuvres* which whetted the appetite, and also served the purpose of the modern dinner-pill—e. g. shell-fish (Hor. *Sat.* ii. 4. 28), vegetables with savoury sauces (Mart. iii. 50, 4), olives (Hor. *Sat.* ii. 2, 46), mushrooms (Juv. v. 147), and also eggs; from which came the expression *ab ovo ad mala* (Hor. *Sat.* i. 3, 6), to signify from the beginning to the end of the meal. See further for the edibles which constituted the *gustus*, Apicius, 4, 5; Plin. *Ep.* i. 15; Macrob. *Sat.* l. c.; Celsus, ii. 29; Mart. x. 48, 7–12; v. 78, 3–5. The drink was *mulsum*, "mead"—a mixture of wine and honey; for plain wine was thought too strong (Hor. *Sat.* ii. 4, 26). Hence the term *promulsis*—i. e. the *mulsum* taken before the chief portion of the meal.

After this, followed the *cena* proper, which in early times, and even later in simple families, was the whole dinner (Mart. x. 48. 3). It is from Lucullus that Athenaeus dates the beginning of extravagance in dining. When this part of the meal consisted of several courses (*fercula, missus*)—we hear of six, Augustus never had môre (Suet. *Aug.* 74), and seven (Juv. i. 94), but the usual number was three (Mart. xi. 31)—the separate courses were called *prima, altera, tertia cena*, and appear to have followed in a regular order (Lucian, *De Merc. Cond.* 15). Each course was brought in on a tray (*repositorium*, Petron. 33), which was generally of wood, but sometimes of silver; and the arrangement of the viands on each dish and of the dishes on these trays was a branch of art (Juv. vii. 184), the artist being called *structor*. Indeed, the arranging of the whole dinner was so important a function that it required a special major-domo called *tricliniarcha* (Henzen, Index, p. 189), with his special *servi tricliniarii* (Henzen, 6367). It was probably only at the imperial court that there were tasters (*praegustatores*). Between the *promulsis* and the *cena*, as well as after each course of the *cena*, the *repositorium* was carried away and brought back with the following course, the table having been previously wiped down (Hor. *Sat.* ii. 8. 11), and the bits that had fallen having been gathered up by the *analecta* (Mart. vii. 20, 17). Occasionally the carver (*carptor, diribitor, scissor*), whose function the *structor* sometimes fulfilled (Mart. x. 48. 15), carved the meat (Petron. 36 and 40) at the open side of the table, and it was carried round by slaves (Petron. 33 and 40). Carving, too, was a branch of art and had its learned professors (Juv. xi. 137; cf. v. 120). Sometimes the course was put on the table and the guests themselves took what they desired, and in the way they did so it was easy to see what guests had the manners of good society (Lucian, *De Merc. Cond.* 15). There appear to have been *menus* (γραμματίδια, Athen. ii. 49 d). Between each course the guests washed their hands (Lamprid. *Heliog.* 25), for it must be remembered that the Romans used to eat with their fingers (Mart. v. 78, 6), except in the case of soup, eggs, and shell-fish, for which a *coclear* (q. v.) and a *ligula* (q. v.) were used.

The viands served up at luxurious dinner-parties are far too numerous to be described. Elaborate descriptions will be found in Hor. *Sat.* ii. 8; Macrob. *Saturn.* ii. 9, 12; Petron. 33 foll.; also in Becker-Göll, *Gallus*, chap. 8. They contained, as Philo says, "all the products of land and sea, rivers and air." Copious accounts of the different kinds of foods and drinks are given in *Gallus*, iii. 331–367, 412–442; Marquardt, *Privatleben*, 398–448; Daremberg and Saglio, s. v. *Cicaria*. To admit of the gluttony required to consume such dinners, vomiting was resorted to, rules for which were laid down by physicians (Cels. i. 3, 29, ed. Krause; Galen, vi. 391)—an indirect proof of the prevalence of over-eating among the wealthy. But such extravagance must have been confined to the upper classes, and can give us no idea of ordinary family meals. The bill of fare of a plain dinner is to be found in Martial (x. 48, 13 foll.). The main course consisted of kid, cutlets (*ofellae*), beans, early sprouts (*prototomi*), chicken, and cold ham. While eating, wine was usually drunk (Petron. 34), but in small quantities, for it was thought to blunt the taste (Hor. *Sat.* ii. 8, 38).

After the *cena* proper was taken away, and the tables were removed, the offerings to the gods (the *mola salsa*, etc.) were thrown into the hearth; and when a slave announced that the gods were propitious, silence for a short time was observed in respect for the gods (Serv. on *Aen.* i. 734). The gods were the Lares, and if they were not in the dining-room, they used to be carried in and placed on the table (Petron. 60), or a special table with a salt-cellar and some meat was placed before their shrine (Arnob. *adv. Gentes*, ii. 67).

Thereafter followed the dessert, *mensae secundae* (Hor. *Sat.* ii. 2, 122), also called *bellaria* (Gell. xiii. 11, 7), just as "second course" and "sweets" (in England) signify the same part of the meal. Other names were *impomenta*, *ἐπιδειπνίς*. It consisted of all sorts of pastry (see Becker-Göll, *Gallus*, iii. 363–367), fresh and dried fruits, apples, grapes, etc. The *mensae secundae* formed the transition to the *commissatio* (q. v.).

At distinguished dinner-parties the company was amused in various ways. These amusements were called *acroamata.* (See Reid on Cic. *Arch.* 9, 20.) Respectable and cultivated hosts used to afford readings by their *anagnostae* (Mayor on Juv. xi. 180), often of their own works, and we can well believe that this became an insufferable nuisance. It was no doubt a mark of culture to ask for some charming poetry (Pers. i. 30). The practice of reading during meals is still kept up in Roman Catholic colleges. Music, too, used to be introduced, sometimes choral and orchestral performances (*symphonia*, Cic. *Verr.* iii. 44, 105; and Wilkins on Hor. *Ars Poet.* 374). There used to be actors also (Plin. *Ep.* i. 15. 2), and story-tellers (*aretalogi*, Suet. *Aug.* 74). At "fast" entertainments there were introduced girls to play, sing, and dance (Liv. xxxix. 6; Hor. *Sat.* i. 2, 1; Mayor on Juv. xi. 162), gymnasts (*petauristae*), fools (*moriones*), "amusing vagabonds" (*scurrae*), etc. Formal speech-making was unknown. These amusements were produced during the *cena* and continued on into the *commissatio*, if such followed.

On Roman meals, see especially Marquardt, *Privatleben der Römer*, 257–260, 289–321; Becker-Göll, *Gallus*, iii. 311–370; Daremberg and Saglio, s. v. *Coena*, in which works all the literature on the subject is collected.

Cenacŭlum. See DOMUS.

Cenaeum (Κηναῖον ἄκρον). The northwestern promontory of Euboea, opposite Thermopylae, with a temple of Zeus Cenaeus.

Cenatoria Vestis. See CENA; SYNTHESIS.

Cenchreae (Κεγχρέαι). The eastern harbour of Corinth on the Saronic Gulf, important for its trade and commerce with the East.

Cenchrēis (Κεγχρηΐς). A small island off the Spiraeum Promontorium of Argolis.

Cenchrĭus (Κέγχριος). A river of Ionia near Ephesus and Mount Solmissus, where the Curetes, according to some, concealed and protected Leto after her delivery, when she was pursued by the power of Heré.

Cenomāni. A powerful Gallic people who crossed the Alps at an early period, and settled in the northwestern part of Italy, in the country of Brixia, Verona, and Mantua, and extended north as far as the confines of Rhaetia.

Cenotaphium (κενοτάφιον, κενὸς τάφος). A cenotaph—i. e. an empty, or honorary, tomb, erected sometimes as a memorial to a person buried elsewhere; oftener to one whose body could not be found for burial at all. See Verg. *Aen.* iii. 304; Xen. *Anab.* vi. 4, § 9; and the article FUNUS.

Censītor. A provincial census-taker. See CENSOR.

Censor (τιμητής). One of the officials whose duty it was (after B.C. 444) to take the place of the consuls in superintending the quinquennial census. The office was one of the higher magistracies, and could only be held once by the same person. It was at first confined to the patricians; but in B.C. 351 was thrown open to the plebeians, and after 339 one of the censors was obliged by law to be a plebeian. On the occasion of a census, the censors were elected soon after the accession to office of the new consuls, who presided over the assembly. They were usually chosen from the number of *consulares*, or persons who had been consuls. Accordingly the censorship was regarded, if not as the highest office of State, at least as the highest step in the ladder of promotion. The newly elected censors entered immediately, after due summons, upon their office. Its duration was fixed in B.C. 433 to eighteen months, but it could be extended for certain purposes. For the object of carrying out their proper duties—the census and the solemn purification (*lustrum*) that concluded it—they had the power of summoning the people to the Campus Martius, where, after B.C. 434, they had an official residence in the Villa Publica. The tribunes had no right of veto as against their proceedings in taking the census; indeed, so far as this part of their duties was concerned, they were irresponsible, being bound only in conscience by the oath which they took on entering upon and laying down their office. Having no executive powers, they had no lictors, but only messengers (*viatores*) and heralds (*praecones*). Their insignia were the *sella curulis* and a purple toga. The collegiate character of the office was so pronounced that, if one censor died the other abdicated. From the simple act of taking the census and putting up the new list of citizens, their functions were in course of time extended, so as to include a number of very important duties. Among these must be mentioned in particular a general superintendence of conduct (*regimen morum*). In virtue of this they had the power of setting a stigma upon any citizen, regardless of his position, for any conceivable offence for which there was no legal punishment. Such offences were neglect of one's property, celibacy, dissolution of marriage, bad training or bad treatment of children, undue severity to slaves and clients, irregular life, abuse of power in office, impiety, perjury, and the like. The offender might be punished with degradation—that is, the censors could expel a man from the Senate or the *ordo eques-*

ter; or they could transfer him from a country tribe into one of the less respectable city tribes, and thus curtail his right of voting; or, again, they could expel him from the tribes altogether, and thus completely deprive him of the right of voting. This last penalty might be accompanied by a fine in the shape of additional taxation. The censors had also the power of issuing edicts against practices which threatened the simplicity of ancient Roman manners—for instance, against luxury. These edicts had not the force of law, but their transgression might be punished by the next censors. The effect of the censorial stigma and punishment lasted until the next census. The consent of both censors was required to ratify it, and it directly affected men only, not women. The censors exercised a special superintendence over the *equites* and the Senate. They had the *lectio Senatus*, or power of ejecting unworthy members and of passing over new candidates for the senatorial rank—as, for instance, those who had held curule offices. The *equites* had to pass singly, each leading his horse, before the censors in the Forum, after the completion of the general census. (See TRAVECTIO.) An honourable dismissal was then given to the superannuated or the infirm; if an *eques* was now found, or had previously been found, unworthy of his order (as for neglecting to care for his horse), he was expelled from it. The vacant places were filled up from the number of such individuals as appeared from the general census to be suitable. (See EQUITES.) There were certain other duties attached to the censorship, for the due performance of which they were responsible to the people, and subject to the authority of the Senate and the veto of the tribunes. (1) The letting of the public domain lands and taxes to the highest bidder. (2) The acceptance of tenders from the lowest bidder for works to be paid for by the State. In both these cases the period was limited to five years. (3) Superintendence of the construction and maintenance of public buildings and grounds, temples, bridges, sewers, aqueducts, streets, monuments, and the like.

After B.C. 167, Roman citizens were freed from all taxation; and after the time of Marius, the liability to military service was made general. The censorship was now a superfluous office, for its original object, the census, was hardly necessary. Sulla disliked the censors for their power of meddling in matters of private conduct, and accordingly, in his constitution of B.C. 81, the office was, if not formally abolished, practically superseded. It was restored in B.C. 70, in the consulship of Pompey and Crassus, and continued to exist for a long time, until under the Empire it disappeared as a separate office. The emperor kept in his own hands the right of taking the census. He took over also the other functions of the censor, especially the supervision of morals, a proceeding in which he had Caesar's example to support him. The care of public buildings, however, he committed to a special body.

Censorīnus. (1) One of the ephemeral Roman emperors who appeared in so great numbers under the reign of Gallienus, and are known in later Roman history as "the Thirty Tyrants" (q.v.). Censorinus had been distinguished in camps and in the Senate: he had been twice consul, twice praetorian prefect, three times prefect of Rome, and four times proconsul. After having passed through this honourable career, he retired to the country, being now advanced in years, and lame from a wound he had received in the war against the Persians during the reign of Valerian. It was under these circumstances that he was proclaimed emperor at Bologna, A.D. 270, in spite, as it would appear, of his own wishes; and by a species of pleasantry he was nicknamed Claudius, in allusion to his lameness (*claudus*, "lame"). The strict discipline, however, which he wished to introduce gave offence, and he was slain by the very soldiers who had raised him to the throne. (2) A grammarian and philosopher, who flourished under Maximus and Gordianus, about A.D. 238. He wrote a small work entitled *De Die Natali,* which was so called because composed on occasion of the birthday of his wealthy friend Q. Cerellius (A.D. 238), and largely taken from the *Pratum* of Suetonius. It treats of the time of birth; of the influence of one's genius, as well as that of the stars, upon the birth-period of an individual; and embraces many other topics of a chronological, mathematical, and cosmographical character. The style of Censorinus is good, though not free from the blemishes natural to his time. We have also a fragment, *De Metris,* ascribed to the same writer. He composed also a work on accents, and another on geometry, but these last two have not reached us. The principal MSS. are the Codex Coloniensis (formerly Darmstadtiensis) of the seventh century, and one in the Vatican of the tenth century. The first critical edition of Censorinus was that of Jahn (Berlin, 1845). A later one is that of Hultsch (Leipzig, 1867). (3) C. MARCIUS. A Roman distinguished as having been the only one to be twice chosen censor (in B.C. 294 and again in 265).

Censuāles. Those who made the censor's lists.

Census (τίμημα). A register of persons and property, constituting a claim to the rights of citizenship at Athens and at Rome.

I. At ATHENS. The census at Athens seems to date from the constitution of Solon. This legislator made four classes (τιμήματα, τέλη). (*a*) *Pentacosiomedimni*, or those who received 500 measures, dry or liquid, from their lands. (*b*) *Knights* (ἱππεῖς), who had an income of 300 measures. (*c*) *Zeugitae* (ζευγῖται), whose income was 150 measures. (*d*) *Thetes* (θῆτες), or *capite censi.* The word τίμημα, as used in the orators, means the valuation of the property—i. e. not the capital itself, but the taxable capital. Now, if the valuation of the income was that given in the distribution of the classes just mentioned, it is not difficult to get at the valuation of the capital implied. Solon reckoned the dry measure, or *medimnus*, at a drachma. But it is probable that the income was reckoned at a twelfth part of the value of the land, on the same principle which originated the *unciarium foenus*, or $8\frac{1}{3}$ per cent., at Rome; and if so, the landed property of a *pentacosiomedimnus* was reckoned at a talent, or $12\times500=6000$ drachmas; that of a *knight* at $12\times300=3600$ drachmas; and that of a *zeugites* at $12\times150=1800$ drachmas. In the first class, the whole estate was considered as taxable capital; but in the second, only $\frac{5}{6}$, or 3000 drachmas; and in the third, $\frac{5}{9}$, or 1000 drachmas; to which Pollux alludes when he says, in his clumsy way, that the first class expended one talent on the public account; the second, 30 minas; the third, 10 minas; and the *thetes*, nothing.

In order to settle in what class a man should

be entered on the register (ἀπογραφή), he returned a valuation of his property, subject, perhaps, to the check of a counter-valuation (ὑποτίμησις). The valuation was made very frequently; in some states, every year; in others, every two or four years. The censors, who kept the register at Athens, were probably at first the *naucrari;* but afterwards the demarchs performed the office of censor. Although this institution of Solon's seems particularly calculated for the imposition of the property tax (εἰσφορά), Thucydides (i. 141), speaking of the year B.C. 428, says that it was then that the Athenians first raised a property tax of 200 talents. It seems, however, that the amount of the tax constituted its singularity; for certainly property-taxes were common not only in Athens, but in the rest of Greece, before the Peloponnesian War, and Antipho expressly says that he contributed to *many* of them. In the archonship of Nausinicus (Olym. 100, 3; B.C. 378) a new valuation of property took place, and classes (συμμορίαι) were introduced expressly for the property taxes. The nature of these classes, our knowledge of which principally depends on a note of Ulpian, is involved in considerable obscurity. Thus much, however, may be stated, that they consisted of 1200 individuals—120 from each of the ten tribes—who, by way of a sort of liturgy, advanced the money for others liable to the tax, and got it from them by the ordinary legal processes. In a similar manner classes were subsequently formed for the discharge of another and more serious liturgy, the trierarchy; and the *strategi*, who nominated the trierarchs, had also to form the *symmoriae* for the property taxes. (See LITURGIA.) What we have here said of the census at Athens renders it unnecessary to speak of the similar registrations in other states of Greece. When the constitution essentially depended on this distribution according to property, it was called a timocracy, or aristocracy of property (τιμοκρατία, ἀπὸ τιμημάτων πολιτεία).

(2) At ROME. After the establishment of the constitution of Servius Tullius, the number of Roman citizens was ascertained every five years (though not always with perfect regularity), to determine their legal liability to the payment of taxes and to military service. This process was called *census*. The census was originally taken by the kings; after the expulsion of the kings, by the consuls; and after B.C. 444, by special officers called *censores*. (See CENSOR.) The censors took the auspices on the night preceding the census; on the next day, their herald summoned the people to the Campus Martius, where they had an official residence in the Villa Publica. Each tribe appeared successively before them, and its citizens were summoned individually according to the existing register. Each had to state on oath his age, his own name, those of his father, his wife, his children, his abode, and the amount of his property. The facts were embodied in lists by the censors' assistants. The census of the provinces was sent in by the provincial governors. There was a special commission for numbering the armies outside the Italian frontier. The censors, in putting up the new lists, took into consideration not only a man's property, but his moral conduct. (See CENSOR.) The census was concluded with the solemn ceremony of reviewing the newly constituted army (*lustrum*). (See LUSTRUM.) The republican census continued to exist under the early Empire, but the last *lustrum* was held by Vespasian and Titus in A.D. 74. The provincial census, introduced by Augustus and maintained during the whole imperial period, had nothing to do with the Roman census, being only a means of ascertaining the taxable capacities of the provinces.

Centauri (Κένταυροι). A Thessalian race fabled to have been half men, half horses. The Centaurs and Lapithae are two mythical tribes, which are always mentioned together. The former are spoken of twice in the *Iliad* under the appellation of "wild-creatures" (Φῆρες), and once under their proper name. We also find the name Κένταυροι in the *Odyssey*. They seem to have been a rude mountain-tribe, dwelling on and about Mount Pelion. It is very doubtful whether Homer and Hesiod conceived them to be of a mingled form, as they were subsequently represented. In the fight of the Centaurs and Lapithae depicted on the shield of Heracles, the latter appear in panoply fighting with spears, while the former wield pine clubs. Pindar is the earliest

Centaur. (Rome, Capitoline Museum.)

poet extant who expressly describes them as semiferine. According to him (*Pyth.* ii. 78 foll.), the offspring of Ixion (q. v.) and the cloud, was a son named Centaurus, who, when grown up, wandered about the foot of Mount Pelion, where he united with the Magnesian mares, who brought forth the Centaurs—a race partaking of the form of both parents, their lower parts resembling their dams, and their upper parts their sire. The common account makes the Centaurs to have been the immediate offspring of Ixion and the cloud. By his wife Dia, Ixion had a son named Pirithoüs, who married Hippodamia, daughter of Adrastus, king of Argos. The chiefs of his own tribe, the Lapithae, were all invited to the wedding, as were also the Centaurs, who dwelt in the neighbourhood of Pelion. Theseus, Nestor, and other strangers were likewise present. At the feast, Eurytion, one of the Centaurs, becoming intoxicated with the wine, attempted to offer violence to the bride; the other Centaurs followed his example, and a dreadful conflict arose, in which several of them were slain. The Centaurs were finally driven from Pelion, and obliged to retire to other regions.

Centaur and Eros. (Louvre.)

According to the earliest version of this legend, Eurytion, the Centaur, being invited to the mansion of Pirithoüs, became intoxicated, and behaved so ill to the women that the heroes rose, and, dragging him to the door, cut off his ears and nose, which was the occasion of the "strife between the Centaurs and men" (*Od.* xxi. 295 foll.). When Heracles was on his way to hunt the Erymanthian boar, he was entertained by the Centaur Pholus; and this gave rise to a conflict between him and the other Centaurs, which terminated in the total discomfiture of the latter.

The most celebrated of the Centaurs was Chiron, the son of Cronus by the nymph Philyra. See CHIRON.

Centesĭma, sc. *pars*. Literally, "a hundredth part." A tax of one per cent. levied on all goods exposed for public sale throughout the Roman Empire. This tax was introduced after the civil wars, and the income resulting from it went to the military treasury (*aerarium militare*). It was also known as *vectigal rerum venalium* or *centesima rerum venalium*. See Tac. *Ann.* i. 78; Suet. *Calig.* 16; *Dig.* l. 16, 7.

Centesĭmae Usūrae. See FENUS.

Cento (κέντρων). Properly, a patchwork garment. In its secondary meaning the word was applied to a poem composed of verses or parts of verses by well-known poets, put together at pleasure so as to make a new meaning. Homer and Vergil were chiefly used for the purpose. The Christians were fond of making religious poems in this way, hoping thus to give a nobler colouring to the pagan poetry. For instance, we have an Homeric cento (*Homero-Centones*) of 2343 verses on the life of Christ, ascribed to Athenaïs, who, under the title of Eudocia was consort of the emperor Theodosius II. Another instance is a poem known as the *Christus Patiens*, or "the suffering Christ," consisting of 2610 verses from Euripides. Instances of Vergilian centos are the sacred history of Proba Faltonia (towards the end of the fourth century A.D.), and a tragedy entitled *Medea* by Hosidius Geta. See Delapierre, *Tableau de la Littérature du Centon* (Paris, 1875).

Centonarii. Makers of patchwork (*cento*) for clothes, and of the heavy cloths hung upon earthworks and other fortifications to protect them from fire or to break the force of missiles.

Centrītes (Κεντρίτης). A small river of Armenia, which it divided from the land of the Carduchi, north of Assyria.

Centum Cellae. The modern Civita Vecchia; a seaport town in Etruria, which first became a place of importance under Trajan, who built a villa here and constructed an excellent harbour.

Centumvĭri. Judges belonging to a court which was one of the two permanent courts of plebeian judges, instituted, probably, by Servius Tullius, and continuing until the fall of the Western Empire. The other collegium was that of the *decemviri* (q. v.). The actual number of centumviri varied at different periods. Festus (s. v. *centumviralia iudicia*) says that they were nominated by the praetor, three being taken from each of the thirty tribes. The ninety thus obtained would, with the presiding decemviri, make up the exact sum which the name denotes. When the number of tribes was increased in B.C. 241 to 35, there were 105 centumviri; but the old name was retained, according to Festus, for convenience, and under the Empire the number had risen to 180 (Plin. *Ep.* vi. 33). At this time it is improbable that they were any longer selected from the tribes, between whose number and their own there was no relation. From a passage of Dio Cassius, one might conjecture that they were taken by lot from the *decuriae iudicum* instituted by Augustus; and from Ovid (*Trist.* ii. 96), that no one could escape the duty if drawn. It would seem that under the Republic the court had no jurisdiction unless the whole number of members sat together, for it was only in the aggregate that they represented the people; but later (probably under Augustus) it was divided into four divisions or sub-courts, which sat and judged apart and independently of each other for the quicker despatch of business (Quint. *Inst.* xiii. 5, 6), though some causes were heard by two divisions sitting together (ib. v. 2, 1), and others even by the whole united body (ib. vi. 33), which then (Plin. *Ep.* v. 21), as under the Republic, was presided over by a praetor. The old custom was for the court to sit in the open Forum, but in Quintilian's time (xii. 5, 6) the four divisions sat on raised seats (*tribunalia*) in the Basilica Iulia.

The procedure before the centumviri was always that of the *legis actio* called *sacramentum*. Even when the *legis actiones* in the aggregate were swept away by the Lex Aebutia, about B.C. 240 (Voigt), the old process was expressly retained by that statute for *centumviralia iudicia* (Gaius, iv. 31; Gell. xvi. 10).

It seems to be the better opinion that the jurisdiction of the centumviri was limited to civil causes. The civil suits which fell under their cognizance especially were those known as real actions (Cic. *de Orat.* i. 38, 173), while the decemviri were more particularly concerned with questions of status (*libertas, civitas, familia*: Cic. *Pro Caec.* 33, 97; *Pro Domo*, 29, 78). The real actions comprise all suits claiming property or *iura in re aliena*, such as a right of way, a usufruct, etc., and those relating to inheritances; the scope of the centumviral jurisdiction is denoted by the planting of the *hasta* (the symbol of Quiritary ownership) in the ground where the court was sitting (Suet. *Octav.* 36), and by the use of the *festuca* in the sacramental procedure. See Schneider, *De Centumviralis Iudicii apud Romanos Origine*; Tigerström, *De Iudicibus apud Romanos.*

Centuncŭlus. A parti-coloured dress similar to that of the modern harlequin, worn by the actors of Roman pantomime. See CENTO; MIMUS; PANTOMIMUS.

Centuria. See COMITIA; EXERCITUS.

Centuriāta Comitia. See COMITIA.

Centurio (ἑκατοντάρχης). See EXERCITUS.

Centurĭpae (Κεντούριπαι). An ancient town of the Siculi, in Sicily, at the foot of Mount Aetna, and not far from the river Symaethus. Under the Romans it was one of the most flourishing cities on the island.

Centussis. A sum of 100 *asses*. See As.

Ceos (Κέως) or **Cea**. An island in the Aegean Sea, now Zea: one of the Cyclades (q. v.), between the Attic promontory Sunium and the island Cythnus, celebrated for its fertile soil and its genial climate. Its chief town was Iulis, the birthplace of Simonides, whence we read of the *Ceae munera neniae* (Hor. *Carm.* ii. 1. 38).

Cephălé (Κεφαλή). An Attic deme on the right bank of the Erasinus. It belonged to the tribe Acamantis.

Cephalĭon (Κεφαλίων). A Greek writer, whose native country is unknown. Cephalion is said to have lived during the reign of Hadrian, and to have been exiled to Sicily for some offence given to the emperor. He wrote an abridgment of universal history (Σύντομος Ἱστορικός) from Ninus to the death of Alexander. It was in the Ionic dialect, like the work of Herodotus, and, like this also, was divided into nine books, each named after one of the Muses. He composed also rhetorical declamations. His works are lost.

Cephallenia (Κεφαλληνία). The modern Cefalonia; called by Homer Samé (Σάμη) or Samos (Σάμος); the largest island in the Ionian Sea, separated from Ithaca by a narrow channel. It is very mountainous. Its chief towns were Samé, Palé, Cranii, and Proni. It never obtained political importance. It is now one of the seven Ionian islands ceded by Great Britain to Greece in 1864.

Cephaloedium (Κεφαλοίδιον). A town on the northern coast of Sicily in the territory of Himera.

Cephălon (Κεφάλων). A native of Gergitha in Troas, not to be confounded with Cephalion. Cephalon wrote an historical work entitled *Trojan Events* (Τρωϊκά). He appears to have been anterior to Alexander the Great, and is considered by Dionysius of Halicarnassus worthy of reliance as an historical writer. His work is lost.

Cephălus (Κέφαλος). (1) The son of Deïon, and a grandson of Aeolus, married to Procris, the eldest daughter of Erechtheus. They dwelt at Thoricos in Attica, and lived happily together till curiosity to try the fidelity of his wife entered the mind of Cephalus. Feigning a journey of eight years, he disguised himself and came to Procris with a splendid jewel, which he offered to her on dishonourable terms. After much hesitation she yielded, when her husband discovered himself and reproached her with her conduct. She fled from him in shame, but they were soon after reconciled. Cephalus went constantly to the chase; and Procris growing suspicious, as she had failed herself, fancied that he was attracted by the charms of some other fair one. She questioned the slave who used to accompany him; and he told her that his master used frequently to ascend the summit of a hill and cry out, "Come, Nephelé, come!" Procris went to the designated hill and concealed herself in a thicket; and on her husband's crying, "Come, Nephelé, come!" (which was nothing more than an invocation for some cloud, νεφέλη, to interpose itself between him and the scorching beams of the sun), she rushed forward towards her husband, who, in his astonishment, threw his dart and unwittingly killed her. (See Hyg. 189; cf. Ovid, *Met.* vii. 661 foll.) This legend is told with great variations. Cephalus, for his involuntary crime, was banished. He went to Thebes, which was at that time ravaged by a fox which nothing could overtake, and he joined Amphitryon in the chase of it. His dog Laelaps ran it down; but, just as he was catching it, Zeus turned them both to stone. Cephalus then aided Amphitryon against the Teleboans, and on their conquest he settled in the island named from him Cephallenia. (2) An Athenian orator, who flourished towards the end of the Peloponnesian War, and was one of those who contributed most to overthrow the rule of the Thirty Tyrants (q. v.). Although he lived during a very stormy period, and although no one ever proposed or caused to be passed more laws than he did, yet he never had any accusation brought against him—a remarkable fact in the history of Athens. We must not confound him with Cephalus, the father of Lysias, who came from Syracuse and settled at Athens. Suidas makes Cephalus to have been the first orator that made use of an exordium and peroration. (3) The father of Lysias the orator. He was a native of Syracuse, but settled at Athens as a resident sojourner, or one of the μέτοικοι.

Cephēis (Κηφηΐς). A name given to Andromeda as daughter of Cepheus (Ovid, *A. A.* i. 193).

Cephēnes (Κηφῆνες). (1) An ancient name of the Persians (Hdt. vii. 61). (See PERSIA.) (2) A name of the Aethiopians, from Cepheus, one of their kings.

Cepheus (Κηφεύς). (1) King of Aethiopia, son of Belus, husband of Cassiopea, and father of Andromeda (q. v.). He was placed among the stars after his death. (2) Son of Aleus, one of the Argonauts. He was king of Tegea in Arcadia, and perished with most of his sons in an expedition against Heracles.

Cephĭsia (Κηφισία). A deme of Attica, at the foot of Mount Brilessus, and near the source of the Cephissus. It was the favourite residence of Herodes Atticus, who had a beautiful villa here.

Cephisodŏtus (Κηφισόδοτος). A statuary of Athens, who flourished about B.C. 372. Two works of his are spoken of by the ancients—a Hermes nourishing Dionysus when an infant, and one of a public speaker in the act of delivering an oration.

There was another sculptor of the same name, usually called "the Younger," the son of Praxiteles, who flourished at Athens in B.C. 300.

Cephisŏphon (Κηφισοφῶν). A friend of Euripides, who is said to have both aided in the composition of his dramas and to have appeared as an actor in them on the stage.

Cephīsus (Κηφισός) and **Cephissus** (Κηφισσός). (1) A celebrated river of Greece, that rises at the foot of Parnassus, close to Lilaea, and, after traversing the plains of Phocis and part of the Boeotian territory, empties into the Copaic Lake in the latter country. (See COPAÏS.) Hesiod compares it to a serpent, from the many sinuosities of its course. The modern name is Mauro Potamo. According to the poets, the son of the river-god Cephissus introduced the worship of the Graces into Boeotia, and hence the peculiar attachment which they were said to have for the waters of this stream. (See GRATIAE.) (2) A river of Attica, generally distinguished by the name of Atticus, to prevent its being confounded with the Cephissus which flowed near Eleusis. (3) A river running near Eleusis. (4) A river of Argolis, flowing into the Inachus. (5) A river in the island of Salamis.

Cepotaphium (κηποτάφιον). A tomb placed in a garden (κῆπος). See SEPULCRUM.

Cer (Κήρ). See KERES.

Cera (κηρός). Wax. By metonymy the word is also used of the pages of a tablet, for which see TABULAE; TESTAMENTUM; WRITING AND WRITING MATERIALS. For its employment by athletes, see ATHLETAE; CEROMA. For its use in painting, see PICTURA.

Ceramīcus (Κεραμεικός). (1) Now Keramo; a bay of Caria, north of the peninsula of Doris, receiving its name from the city of Ceramus in its vicinity. (2) One of the most considerable and important parts of the city of Athens. Its name was derived from the hero Ceramus (Pausan. i. 3), or perhaps from some potteries which were formerly situated there (Herod. v. 88). It included probably the Agora, the Stoa Basileios, and the Poekilé, as well as various other temples and public buildings. Antiquaries are not decided as to the general extent and direction of this part of the ancient city, since scarcely any trace remains of its monuments and edifices; but we may certainly conclude, from their researches and observations, that it lay entirely on the south side of the Acropolis. See ATHENAE.

Cerămus (Κέραμος). A Dorian seaport town on the north side of the Cnidian Chersonesus, on the coast of Caria, from which the Ceramic Gulf took its name.

Cerăsus (Κερασοῦς). A flourishing colony of Sinopé on the coast of Pontus, at the mouth of a river of the same name; chiefly celebrated as the place from which Europe obtained both the cherry and its name (*cerasum*). Lucullus is said to have brought back plants of the cherry-tree (κέρασος) with him to Rome (Isid. *Orig.* xvii. 7, 16); but this refers probably only to some particular sorts, as the Romans seem to have had the tree much earlier. Cerasus fell into decay after the foundation of Pharnacia.

Ceraunii Montes (τὰ Κεραύνια ὄρη). The modern Khimara; a range of mountains extending from the frontier of Illyricum along the coast of Epirus, derived their name from the frequent thunder-storms which occurred among them (κεραυνός). These mountains made the coast of Epirus dangerous to ships. They were also called Acroceraunia, though this name was properly applied to the promontory separating the Adriatic and Ionian seas. The inhabitants of these mountains were called Ceraunii.

Cerbĕrus (Κέρβερος). The famous dog of Hades, the fruit of Echidna's union with Typhon. He was stationed at the entrance of hell, as a watchful keeper, to prevent the living from entering the infernal regions, and the dead from escaping from their confinement. Orpheus lulled him to sleep with his lyre; and Heracles dragged him from hell in the performance of his twelfth and last labour. (See HERACLES.) The poets differ in their descriptions of this fabled animal. Hesiod assigns him fifty heads, calling him κύων πεντηκοντακάρηνος. Sophocles (*Trach.* 1114) styles him Ἅιδου τρίκρανον σκύλακα, "the three-headed dog of Pluto," and in this last account the Latin poets generally coincide, describing him also as having serpents coiled about his neck. Horace, however, calls him *belua centiceps* (*Od.* ii. 13, 14), either by poetic amplification, or else in accordance with some Greek authority. Champollion traces a curious analogy between the Egyptian and the Grecian mythology as regards the dog of Hades.

Cerberus. (From a Bronze Statue.)

Cercasōrum (Κερκάσωρος πόλις). A city of Lower Egypt, on the west bank of the Nile, at the point where the river divided into its three principal branches.

Cercīna (Κερκίνα) and **Cercinītis** (Κερκινῖτις). Two low islands off the north coast of Africa, in the mouth of the Lesser Syrtis, united by a bridge, and possessing a fine harbour.

Cercĭtae (Κερκέται). A people of Asiatic Sarmatia, probably to be identified with the Circassians. They dwelt on the eastern coast of the Palus Maeotis, or Sea of Azov.

Cercōpes (Κέρκωπες). Droll and thievish gnomes who robbed Heracles in his sleep. Some place them at Thermopylae; others at Oechalia in Euboea, or in Lydia. (See Herod. vii. 216, and the article MELAMPYGUS.) A poem entitled Κέρκωπες was ascribed to Homer. (Cf. Müller, *Dorier*, ii. 12, § 10.)

Cercops (Κέρκωψ). (1) One of the oldest of the Orphic poets, the author of an epic on the descent of Orpheus into Hades. (See ORPHIC POETS.) (2) A Milesian poet, the rival of Hesiod. He is said to have written an epic called *Aegimius*, which is, by some, ascribed to Hesiod himself. See HESIODUS.

Cercūrus (κέρκουρος, κερκοῦρος). A light, swift, open vessel, first mentioned by Herodotus (vii. 97) as being used at the time of the Persian wars. It was propelled by oars, and was used both in commerce and in war (Liv. xxxiii. 19). Its invention was variously ascribed to the Corcyraeans and to the Cypriotes. See NAVIS.

Cercȳon (Κερκυών). Son of Poseidon or of Hephaestus. A cruel tyrant at Eleusis, who put to death his daughter Alopé and killed all strangers whom he overcame in wrestling. He was, in the end, conquered and slain by Theseus (q. v.).

Kerkȳra (Κέρκυρα). See CORCYRA.

Cerdo (κέρδων). A name given to the lowest class of workmen and derived from κέρδος, "gain." It is sometimes used with the addition of the name of the trade—e. g. *sutor cerdo*, "a cobbler"; *cerdo faber*, "a smith." The name is also generically used in a contemptuous sense like the English "snob," "cad," etc. See Juvenal, iv. 153, with Mayor's note.

Cerealia. See CERES.

Ceres (from the √ KR of *creare*). An old Italian goddess of agriculture. The Ceres who was worshipped at Rome is, however, the same as the Greek Demeter. Her cult was introduced under the Italian name at the same time as that of Dionysus and Persephoné, who in the same way

Ceres. (Pompeian Wall-painting.)

received the Italian names of Liber and Libera. (See Cic. *N. D.* ii. 24, 2.) It was in B.C. 496, on the occasion of a drought, that the Sibylline Books ordered the introduction of the worship of the three deities. This worship was so decidedly Greek that the temple dedicated on a spur of the Aventine in B.C. 490, over the entrance to the Circus, was built in Greek style and by Greek artists; and the service of the goddess, founded on the Greek myth of Demeter and Persephoné, was performed in the Greek tongue by Italian women of Greek extraction. The worshippers of the goddess were almost exclusively plebeian. Her temple was placed under the care of the plebeian aediles, who, as overseers of the corn market, had their official residence in or near it. The fines which they imposed went to the shrine of Ceres, as did the property of persons who had offended against them or against the tribunes of the plebs. Just as the patricians entertained each other with mutual hospitalities at the Megalesian Games (April 4–10), so did the plebeians at the Cerealia, or games introduced at the founding of the Temple of Ceres. Those held in later times were given by the aediles from the 12th to the 19th of April, and another festival to Ceres, held in August, was established before the Second Punic War. This was celebrated by women in honour of the reunion of Ceres and Proserpina. After fasting for nine days, the women, clothed in white, and adorned with crowns of ripe ears of corn, offered to the goddess the first-fruits of the harvest. After B.C. 191, a fast (*ieiunium Cereris*) was introduced by command of the Sibylline Books. This was originally observed every four years, but in later times was kept annually on the 4th of October. The native Italian worship of Ceres was probably maintained in its purest form in the country. Here the countrymen offered Ceres a sow (*porca praecidanea*) before the beginning of the harvest, and dedicated to her the first cuttings of the corn (*praemetium*). See DEMETER.

Kēres (Κῆρες). The personified necessity of death, described by Homer as formidable, dark, and hateful beings, because they carry off men to the joyless house of Hades. According to Hesiod, they are the daughters of Night (Nyx), and sisters of the Moerae (q. v.) and punish men for their crimes.

Cereus. A wax candle with a rush wick. See CANDELA.

Cerevisia. Ale or beer. See CERVESIA.

Cerilli. A town in Bruttium on the coast, a little south of the mouth of the Laüs.

Cerinthus (Κήρινθος). A town on the east coast of Euboea, on the river Budorus.

Cerné (Κέρνη). An island without the Pillars of Hercules, on the African coast, mentioned by Hanno (q. v.) in his *Periplus*, but not identified with any known to-day. Here he established a colony, and it was always the depot of the Carthaginians on the Atlantic coast of Africa. Hanno says that it was the same distance from the Columns of Hercules that Carthage was.

Cernĕre Hereditātem. See HERES; TESTAMENTUM.

Cernuus. See SALTATIO.

Cerōma (κήρωμα). A composition of wax, with different references: (1) A plaster, with wax as the principal ingredient (Hippocr. 397, 48); or, like κερίον, an ulcer exuding wax-like matter (Plin. Val. i. 25 fin.). (2) A mixture of oil, wax, and earth, with which athletes under the Roman Empire rubbed themselves before wrestling (Mart. iv. 19, vii. 32; Plin. *H. N.* xxxv. § 168; Plut. ii.

638 D). To keep the hair free from this compound, a cap was worn. (See Juv. iii. 68, with Mayor's note.) (3) The place where the *ceroma* was most used; hence, the wrestling-ring (Sen. *Brev. Vit.* xii. 3).

Cerretāni. An Iberian people in Hispania Tarraconensis, inhabited the modern Cerdagne in the Pyrenees; they were celebrated for their hams.

Cersus (Κέρσος). Now the Merkes; a river of Cilicia emptying into the Gulf of Issus on the east.

Certamīna. See ATHLETAE.

Certi, Incerti Actio. A name which has been given by some writers to those actions in which a determinate or indeterminate sum, as the case may be, is mentioned in the formula (*condemnatio certae pecuniae vel incertae*). See ACTIO.

Certonium (Κερτόνιον). A town in Mysia, mentioned only by Xenophon (*Anab.* vii. 8. 8).

Cerūchi (κεροῦχοι). The ropes which supported the yard of a ship, passing from it to the top of the mast. In some ancient monuments we see four, as in the following illustration, taken from

Vessel with Ceruchi. (From a Vatican MS. of Vergil.)

one of the pictures in the MS. of Vergil, which was given by Fulvius Ursinus to the Vatican Library.

Cerussa (ψιμύθιον). White-lead, or *plumbi subcarbonas.* The ancient ceruse was prepared by exposing lead to the vapours of vinegar, and the whole method is minutely described by Theophrastus (*De Lapid.* 101). Similar processes are described by Dioscorides and Vitruvius. Cerussa was in common use among women as a face enamel. See Plaut. *Most.* i. 3. 101.

Cervesia, Cervisia, or **Cerevisia** (ζῦθος). Ale or beer; a beverage scarcely ever drunk by the ancient Greeks and Romans, although it was very generally used by the surrounding nations, whose soil and climate were less favourable to the growth of vines (*in Gallia aliisque provinciis,* Plin. *H. N.* xxii. § 164; Tac. *Germ.* 23).

Herodotus's statement that the Egyptians drank "barley-wine" is supported by the inscriptions, in which it is called *hak, hank,* or *henk,* and by Strab. xvii. 1, 14, and Diod. i. 34, who describes it as a beverage almost as fragrant as wine, and calls it ζῦθος; while Columella (x. 114) tells us that the *radix Assyria* and lupine entered into its composition, the former doubtless to give it fragrance, the latter to serve the same purpose as the modern hop. But the methods of its preparation varied (Strab. ii. 5). A similar drink was made by the Ethiopians from millet and barley (ib. xvii. 2, 2).

The beer or barley-wine of Crete was known as κόρμα or κοῦρμι. A similar beverage passed under the name of βρῦτον in the north of Greece and Asia Minor, being made of barley by the Phrygians and Paeonians, of barley or of roots by the Thracians, while the Paeonians also made παραβίας or παραβίη from millet and fleabane (κόνυζα). Of the barley drink called πῖνον, Aristotle tells us that those inebriated by it fall on the back and on no other part of the body (Athen. x. 447). We are told by Xenophon that the Armenians, instead of drinking their ale or beer out of cups, placed it before them in a large bowl. This being full to the brim with the grains as well as the fermented liquor, the guests, when they pledged one another, drank together out of the same bowl by stooping down to it, although, when this token of friendship was not intended, they adopted the more refined method of sucking up the fluid through tubes of cane (Xen. *Anab.* v. 5, 26). Ζῦθος was the drink of Lusitania (Strab. iii. 3, 7); in Spain it was known as *caelia* or *cerea,* while *cervesia* was the name used in Gaul, where other drinks of the sort were common (Plin. l. c.). Thus Posidonius, in Athenaeus, says that while the richer classes in Gaul import wine from Italy and the district of Marseilles, the poor drink a beer made from wheat, with or without the addition of honey, which is called κόρμα. This Gallic use of beer is illustrated by a curious circular bottle found in Gaul and preserved in the Musée Carnavalet at Paris: it bears the legend, "Ospita reple lagona cervesa" (*Revue Archéologique,* 1868, xviii. 226).

The beverage of the Germans was made from barley or wheat (Tac. *Germ.* 23). The beer of Illyria and Pannonia was called *sabaia* or *sabaium* (Hieron. *Isai.* v. 19); and at the court of Attila in Pannonia a beverage called μέδος (mead?), or one of barley called κάμον, was used. The Greeks and Romans regarded this barbarian drink with contempt, as is seen by an epigram of the emperor Julian (*Anth. Pal.* ix. 365). See Bickerdyke, *Curiosities of Ale and Beer* (1886); and Mew and Astion, *The Drinks of the World* (1892).

Cervi, so called from their resemblance to the horns of a stag. Branches of trees interlaced with their points projecting, used in war, as palisading or *chevaux-de-frise,* in front of or upon earthworks or fortifications (Caes. *B. G.* vii. 72; Liv. xliv. 11, 4), and sometimes, where there were no fortifications, stuck simply into the level ground (Sil. Ital. x. 413, 414).

Cervīcal (προσκεφάλαιον, ποτίκρανον). A pillow or cushion, to support the head or shoulder, on a bed or dining-couch (Mart. xiv. 146; Suet. *Ner.* 6). The word is also used, like its Greek equivalents, in a less special sense to denote any cushion (Juv. vi. 353; Petron. 32, 1). See PULVINUS.

Bed with Cervical. (Pompeii.)

Kerycēum (Κηρύκειον). See CADUCEUS; PRAECO.

Keryx (κῆρυξ). A herald. See CADUCEUS; FETIALIS; PRAECO.

Cessio Bonōrum. See BONORUM CESSIO.

Cessio in Iure. See IN IURE CESSIO.

Cesticillus. A porter's knot, or pad for carrying burdens, known to us only through the gloss in Festus (s. v.). The Greek word is τύλη, or σπεῖρα, from its being twisted into a circular shape. See ARCULUM.

Cestius Pons. See PONS.

Cestrīné (Κεστρίνη). A district of Epirus, separated from Thesprotia by the river Thyamis. It was said to have taken its name from Cestrinus, the son of Helenus, having previously borne the appellation of Cammania.

Kestrosphendŏné (κεστροσφενδόνη). See FUNDA.

Cestrum (κέστρον). See PICTURA.

Cestus. See CAESTUS.

Cestus (κεστός). In Homer, an adjective applied to the girdle (ἱμάς) of Aphrodité, on which were embroidered all manner of enticements to love. It means "perforated"—i. e. with holes made by the needle—"embroidered," *acu pictus*—and is formed from the same base (viz. *kas* = *ferire*) as κεάζω, or κεντέω for κενστός. It is to be considered the same as the στρόφιον, ταινία, μίτρα, στηθοδεσμός, *fascia pectoralis*, *mammillare*, which is found on statues of Aphrodité worn next the skin (Mart. xiv. 206). (See Baumeister, *Denkmäler*, etc., p. 366, fig. 393.) It was accordingly made of some soft substance. In Mart. xiv. 66, *pellis* is probably what we should call kid. Its object was to support and sometimes to compress too full bosoms, like the modern corset, but it was not used, like the latter, to pinch in the figure. The Greeks and Romans were strangers to this injurious practice (Baumeister, l. c.), and, accordingly, every girl did not wear one. Winckelmann and Saglio consider that, owing to its splendour, the κεστός of Aphrodité was a belt worn outside the dress.

Cetēi (Κήτειοι). A people of Mysia, the old inhabitants of the country about Pergamus, and upon the Cetius, mentioned by Homer.

Cethēgus. (1) A Roman consul, in B.C. 332. He was obliged to lay down his office on account of some informality in his election. (2) M. CORNELIUS, a distinguished Roman orator. Being sent as praetor to Sicily, he quelled a sedition of the soldiers in that island. He was called to the censorship before he had been consul, a thing not in accordance with Roman usage, and obtained this latter office six years subsequently, B.C. 204. He carried on the war against the Carthaginians in Etruria, and defeated Mago, who was coming with support for Hannibal. In allusion to his persuasive eloquence, Ennius twice calls him *Suadae medulla*. Horace (*Epist.* ii. 2. 116; *A. P.* 50) cites him as an authority on the use of words. (3) C. CORNELIUS, proconsul in Spain in B.C. 200, defeated a numerous army of the Sedetani. Being elected consul B.C. 197, he gained a great victory over the Insubres, and on his return to Rome obtained the honours of a triumph. The people having afterwards chosen him censor, he assigned distinct places to the senators at the public games. (4) C. CORNELIUS, a Roman rendered powerful by his influence with Marius. He himself was wholly governed by a woman named Praecia, who obtained for Lucullus the government of Cilicia. (5) C. CORNELIUS, a Roman of the most corrupt and abandoned character, and one of the accomplices of Catiline. He was strangled in prison by order of the Senate. See CATILINA.

Cetīus (Κήτειος). A small river of Mysia, falling into the Caïcus close to Pergamus.

Ceto (Κητώ). A daughter of Pontus and Gaea, who married Phorcys, by whom she had the three Gorgons, the Graeae, Echidna, and the serpent that watched the golden apples in the Garden of the Hesperides.

Cetra or **Caetra** (καιτρέα, καίτρα). A small round shield made of ox-hide, and forming a part of the defensive armour of the Osci. (See ARMA.)

Soldiers with Cetrae. (From a MS. of Prudentius.)

It was also worn by the Spaniards and Mauretanians, and by the natives of Britain (Tac. *Agric.* 36).

It does not appear that the Romans ever wore the cetra. Livy compares it to the *pelta* of the Greeks and Macedonians, which was also a small light shield.

Cetus (κῆτος). Any large fish; sometimes the whale, but often the tunny-fish.

Ceȳx (Κήυξ). The husband of Halcyoné, and with her changed into a bird. See HALCYONÉ.

Chabōras. The same as the Aborrhas (q. v.).

Chabrias (Χαβρίας). A celebrated Athenian general. In B.C. 378, he was one of the commanders of the forces sent to the aid of Thebes against Agesilaüs, when he adopted for the first time that manœuvre for which he became so celebrated—ordering his men to await the attack with their spears pointed against the enemy and their shields resting on one knee. A statue was afterwards erected at Athens to Chabrias in this posture. In 376, he defeated the Lacedaemonians off Naxos, and in 361 commanded the ships of the Egyptian monarch Tachos, then in rebellion against Persia. At the siege of Chios (B.C. 357) he fell a victim to his excessive valour, refusing to abandon his ship after it was disabled.

Chaerĕa, C. CASSIUS. Tribune of the praetorian cohorts; formed the conspiracy by which the emperor Caligula (q. v.) was slain, A.D. 41. Chaerea was put to death by Claudius upon his accession.

Chaerēmon (Χαιρήμων). A Greek tragedian, who flourished at Athens about B.C. 380. His style was smooth and picturesque, but his plays were artificial, and better adapted for reading than for performance. A few fragments of them remain, which show some imaginative power (Arist. *Poet.* i. 9). Ed. by Bartsch (Mainz, 1843).

Chaeronēa (Χαιρώνεια). A town in Boeotia, on the Cephissus, near the frontier of Phocis, memorable for the defeat of the Athenians and the Boeotians by Philip of Macedon, which crushed the liberties of Greece, B.C. 338, and for Sulla's victory over the army of Mithridates, B.C. 86. Chaeronea was the birthplace of Plutarch. Several remains of the ancient city are to be seen at Capraena, more particularly a theatre excavated in the rock, an aqueduct, and the marble lion (broken in pieces) which adorned the sepulchre of the Boeotians who fell at the battle of Chaeronea.

Chairs. See CATHEDRA; SELLA.

Chalaeum (Χάλαιον). A port town of the Locri Ozolae on the Crissaean Gulf, on the frontiers of Phocis.

Chalastra (Χαλάστρα). A town in Mygdonia in Macedonia, at the mouth of the river Axius.

Chalcé (Χάλκη) or **Chalcia** (Χαλκία). An island of the Carpathian Sea, near Rhodes.

Chalcēdon (Χαλκηδών). A Greek city of Bithynia, on the coast of the Propontis, at the entrance of the Bosporus, nearly opposite to Byzantium, was founded by a colony from Megara in B.C. 685. After a long period of independence, it became subject to the kings of Bithynia, and most of its inhabitants were transferred to the new city of Nicomedia (B.C. 140). Under the Romans it regained much of its former importance. Here was held the fourth Ecumenical Council of the Church, in A.D. 451.

Chalcidĭcé (Χαλκιδίκη). (1) A district of Macedonia, between the Sinus Thermaicus and Strymonicus. The lower part of it formed three peninsulas—Phlegra or Pallené, Sithonia, and Athos. The small town of Chalcis gave name to this district. (2) Another in Syria, adjacent to the town of Chalcis.

Chalcidĭcum. An annex or addition to a basilica (q. v.), of a nature made clear by the so-called *fullonica* at Pompeii which bears this name in an inscription upon its front. This shows that the chalcidicum was an entrance-hall to a public building, designed for the shelter of persons waiting to be admitted, or who might transact their business under it; it was wholly or partially roofed, and might take the form either of a deep porch, or in some cases of a cloistered court. Such a vestibule is found in many Christian basilicas; the former type occurs in St. John Lateran and Sta. Maria Maggiore at Rome, the latter in St. Ambrogio at Milan. The foundations show that a chalcidicum of this kind once existed in front of the vast basilica of Constantine at Rome.

Chalcidius. A Platonic philosopher of the sixth century A.D., who translated the *Timaeus* of Plato into Latin with an elaborate commentary.

Chalcioecia (χαλκιοίκια). An annual feast, celebrated with sacrifices at Sparta, in honour of Athené surnamed Chalcioecus (q. v.), or Goddess of the Brazen House (Pausan. iii. 17, 3).

Chalcioecus (Χαλκίοικος). An epithet applied to Athené at Sparta, from her having a brazen temple (χαλκοῦς οἶκος). See Thuc. i. 34; Pausan. iii. 17, 3.

Chalcis (Χαλκίς). (1) The modern Egripo or Negroponte; the principal town of Euboea, situated on the narrowest part of the Euripus, and united with the mainland by a bridge. It was a very ancient town, originally inhabited by Abantes or Curetes, and colonized by Attic Ionians. Its flourishing condition at an early period is attested by the numerous colonies which it planted in various parts of the Mediterranean. It founded so many cities in the peninsula in Macedonia, between the Strymonic and Thermaic gulfs, that the whole peninsula was called Chalcidicé. In Italy it founded Cumae, and in Sicily, Naxos. Chalcis was usually subject to Athens during the greatness of the latter city. The orator Isaeus and the poet Lycophron were born at Chalcis, and Aristotle died there. (2) A town in Aetolia, at the mouth of the Evenus, situated at the foot of the mountain Chalcis, and hence also called Hypochalcis. (3) A city of Syria, in a fruitful plain, near the termination of the river Chalus; the chief city of the district of Chalcidicé, which lay to the east of the Orontes.

Chalcus (χαλκοῦς or χαλκίον). Under AES some account has been given of the use of bronze or copper for money, which began in most parts of the Greek world about B.C. 400. At Athens, the chalcus, or "copper" *par excellence*, is said by Pollux (ix. 65) to have been equivalent to the eighth of an obol; in some other places it was the sixth of an obol, and contained seven lepta.

Copper coins (χαλκία) were first issued at Athens in the archonship of Callias, B.C. 406. In the *Ecclesiazusae* (816) Aristophanes speaks of the demonetization of certain copper coins, and the reversion to a silver currency. It seems likely that the coins referred to in both these passages are the pieces still extant with the head of Athené on one side, and an owl with two bodies and one head on the other, which resemble the silver diobols of Athens. Coins of late period struck in Syria bear the inscription χαλκοῦς, which declares their value. Δίχαλκα and other multiples of the chalcus were also struck at Chios and other places. When, however, bronze coins do not bear inscriptions stating their value, the latter cannot with certainty be fixed. See NUMISMATICS.

Chaldaea (Χαλδαία). In the narrower sense, a province of Babylonia, about the lower course of the Euphrates, the border of the Arabian Desert, and the head of the Persian Gulf. It was intersected by numerous canals, and was extremely fertile. In a wider sense, the term is applied to the whole of Babylonia, and even to the Babylonian Empire, on account of the supremacy which the Chaldaeans acquired at Babylon. (See BABYLON.) Xenophon mentions Chaldaeans in the mountains north of Mesopotamia. Their original seat was most probably in the mountains of Armenia and Kurdistan, whence they descended into the plains of Mesopotamia and Babylonia. Respecting the Chaldaeans as the ruling class in the Babylonian monarchy, see BABYLONIA.

Chalk. See CRETA.

Chalkeia (τὰ χαλκεῖα). A very ancient festival celebrated at Athens, which at different times seems to have had a different character, for at first it was solemnized in honour of Athené, surnamed Ergané, and by the whole people of Athens, whence it was called Ἀθήναια or Πάνδημος. At a later period, however, it was celebrated only by artisans, especially smiths, and in honour of Hephaestus, whence its name was changed into χαλκεῖα. It was held on the thirtieth day of the month of Pyanepsion. Menander composed a comedy called Χαλκεῖα, a fragment of which is preserved in Athenaeus.

Chalus (Χάλος). A river of north Syria.

Chalўbes (Χάλυβες). A people of Pontus, in Asia Minor, who inhabited the whole coast from the Iasonium Promontorium to the vicinity of the river Thermodon, together with a portion of the inner country. They were celebrated in antiquity for the great iron mines and forges which existed in their country. See METALLUM.

Chalўbon (Χαλυβών; O. T., Helbon). A considerable city of northern Syria, probably the same as Beroea (q. v.).

Chalybs. A river of Hispania Tarraconensis, in the country of the Celtiberi, and one of the tributaries of the Iberus. Its waters were famed for hardening steel, so that the name χάλυψ was given to it from this circumstance. The modern name is the Queiles.

Chamāvi. A people in Germany, who first appear in the neighbourhood of the Rhine, but afterwards migrated east, defeated the Bructeri, and settled between the Weser and the Harz.

Chaŏnes (Χάονες). A Pelasgian people, one of the three peoples which inhabited Epirus, were at an earlier period in possession of the whole of the country, but subsequently dwelt along the coast from the river Thyamis to the Acroceraunian promontory, which district was therefore called Chaonia. By the poets, Chaonius is used as equivalent to Epiroticus (Ἠπειρωτικός).

Chaos (Χάος). According to Hesiod, the yawning, unfathomable abyss which was the first of all existing things. From Chaos arose Gaea (Earth), Tartarus (Hell), and Eros (Love). Chaos bore Erebus and Night; from their union sprang Aether and Hemera (Sky and Day). The conception of Chaos as the confused mass out of which, in the beginning, the separate forms of things arose is erroneous, and belongs to a later period.

Charadra (Χαράδρα). A town in Phocis, on the river Charadrus, situated on an eminence not far from Lilaea.

Charax (χάραξ, "a palisaded camp"). The name of several cities, which took their origin from military stations. The most remarkable of them stood at the mouth of the Tigris. See ALEXANDRIA (4).

Chares (Χάρης). (1) An Athenian general, who succeeded to the command after the condemnation and death of Leosthenes. He was sent by the Athenians against Alexander, tyrant of Pherae, but, instead of coming to action with the foe, he harassed the Athenian allies to such a degree by his extortions and oppression that the Social War was the result (B.C. 358). Some time after, he was sent to aid Byzantium against Philip of Macedon, but he only incurred the contempt of his foe, and excited the discontent of the allies, so that the Athenians finally recalled him, and put Phocion in his place. This, however, did not prevent them from choosing him for their general at the battle of Chaeronaea, where his ignorance and incapacity mainly contributed to the loss of the day. He was one of those whom Alexander ordered to be delivered up to him after the destruction of Thebes; but he succeeded in mollifying the conqueror, and was permitted to live at Athens.

(2) OF MITYLENÉ. A Greek historian, chamberlain of Alexander the Great. He was the author of a comprehensive work, containing at least ten books, upon the life—chiefly the domestic life—of this monarch. This history had the reputation of being trustworthy and interesting. Only a few fragments of it remain, ed. by Geier (Leipzig, 1844).

(3) OF LINDOS IN RHODES. A Greek artist, a pupil of Lysippus. In B.C. 280 he produced the largest statue known in antiquity—the colossal image of the Sun, 120 feet high, placed at the entrance of the harbour of Rhodes, and generally known as the Colossus of Rhodes. This was destroyed by an earthquake as early as B.C. 224. The thumbs were thicker than the average span of a man's hand, the fingers larger than many ordinary statues. See COLOSSUS; SEVEN WONDERS OF THE WORLD.

Charĭcles (Χαρικλῆς). (1) One of the Thirty Tyrants set over Athens by the Lacedaemonians, and possessing great influence among his colleagues (Xen. *Mem.* i. 2. 31). (2) A celebrated physician in the train of Tiberius. Towards the end of that emperor's life, Charicles, on taking leave of him, as if about to journey abroad, managed, in grasping the hand of Tiberius, to feel his pulse, and became instantly convinced that the latter had not more than two days to live, a secret which he divulged to Macro (Tac. *Ann.* vi. 50).

Charĭclo (Χαρικλώ). (1) A nymph, daughter of Apollo and wife of the centaur Chiron (q. v.). (2) A nymph, the mother of Tiresias (q. v.).

Charĭla (ἡ χαρίλα). One of the three festivals celebrated at Delphi every ninth year as a thanksgiving for having been delivered at one time from a famine.

Charilāus or **Charillus** (Χαρίλαος or Χάριλλος). A king of Sparta, son of Polydectes, who is said to have received his name from the general joy (χάρις) excited by the justice of his uncle Lycurgus, when he placed him, yet a new-born infant, on the royal seat, and bade the Spartans acknowledge him for their king.

Charīnus (Χαρῖνος). A comic dancer at Sparta; a stock character in the Doric comedy, like the Spanish Gracioso. See Müller, *Dorier*, iv. 7, § 3.

Charis (Χάρις). A name applied by Homer (*Il.* xviii. 382) to the wife of Hephaestus. In the *Odyssey*, on the other hand (viii. 267), Aphroditê is named as his spouse. It amounts to the same thing in the figurative explanation of the myth, since Grace and Beauty were both regarded as the characteristics of Hephaestus's labours. See CHARITES.

Charisĭa (Χαρίσια). A festival in honour of the Graces (Charites), with dances which continued all night. A cake was given to those who remained awake during the whole time.

Charisius, FLAVIUS SOSIPĂTER. A writer on Latin grammar, who flourished towards the end of the fourth century A.D. His *Ars Grammatica*, a work in five books, imperfectly preserved, is a compilation, made, without much intelligence, from the works of older scholars. Its value is derived from the numerous quotations it preserves from the older Latin literature. Our text is derived chiefly from the Codex Neopolitanus of the seventh or eighth century. The best critical text is that of H. Keil (in his *Grammatici Latini*), vol. i. (Leipzig, 1857).

Charistia. See CARISTIA.

Charĭtes (Χάριτες) or **Gratiae** (Graces). Goddesses of grace, and of everything which lends charm and beauty to nature and human life. According to Hesiod, they are the offspring of Zeus and the daughter of Oceanus and Eurynomê. Their names are Euphrosynê (Joy), Thalia (Bloom), and Aglaïa (Brilliance). Aglaïa is the youngest, and the wife of Hephaestus; for the inspiration of the Graces was deemed as necessary to the plastic arts as to music, poetry, science, eloquence, beauty, and enjoyment of life. Accordingly, the Graces are intimate with the Muses, with whom they live together on Olympus. They are associated, too, with Apollo, Athené, Hermes, and Peitho, but especially with Eros, Aphrodité, and Dionysus. Bright and blithe-hearted, they were also called the daughters of the Sun and of Aeglé (Gleam). They were worshipped in conjunction with Aphrodité and Dionysus at Orchomenus in Boeotia, where their shrine was accounted the oldest in the place, and where their most ancient images were found in the shape of stones said to have fallen from heaven. It was here that the feast of the Charitesia was held in their honour, with musical contests. At Sparta, as at Athens, two Charites only were worshipped, Cleta, or Sound, and Phaënna, or Light; at Athens their names were Auxo (Increase) and Hegemoné (Queen). It was by these goddesses, and by Agraulos daughter of Cecrops, that the Athenian youths, on receiving their spear and shield, swore faith to their country. The Charites were represented in the form of beautiful maidens, the three being generally linked hand in hand. In the older representations they are clothed; in the later, they are loosely clad or entirely undraped.

Charĭton (Χαρίτων). An erotic prose-writer of Aphrodisias in Caria, whose date is uncertain, but probably not earlier than the fifth century A.D. He was the author of a romance entitled *The Love Adventures of Chaereas and Callirrhoé* (τὰ περὶ Χαιρέαν καὶ Καλλιρροὴν ἐρωτικὰ διηγήματα), in seven books. Only one MS. of this is known to exist. A Latin version with notes was published by Reiske, 3 vols. (Amsterdam, 1750); a commentary by Beck (Leipzig, 1783); and a beautiful edition of the text in 1812 at Venice. A good French translation is that of Larcher in the *Bibliothèque des Romans Grecs* (Paris, 1797). It was rendered into English by Becket (London, 1764).

Charmandé (Χαρμάνδη). A great city of Mesopotamia, on the Euphrates.

Charmĭdes (Χαρμίδης). A son of Glaucon, cousin of Critias, and maternal uncle to Plato. He gives his name to one of the Platonic dialogues, in which he is represented as a youth at the opening of the Peloponnesian War.

Charmion (Χάρμιον). One of Cleopatra's female attendants, who killed herself after the example of her mistress.

Charmis (Χάρμις). A physician of Marseilles, in Nero's age, who revived the use of cold baths in Rome in cases of sickness, after the practice had been discontinued since the time of Antonius Musa (q. v.). He was very successful in his professional labours, and amassed great riches (Plin. *H. N.* xxix. 1).

Charon (Χάρων). (1) A deity of the lower world, son of Erebus and Nyx, who conducted the souls of the dead in a boat over the river Acheron to the infernal regions. The sum exacted for this service, from each of the shades ferried over by him, was never less than an obolus, nor could it exceed three. A piece of money, therefore, was generally placed by the ancients under the tongue of the deceased, in order to meet this necessary demand. Such as had not been honoured with a funeral were not permitted to enter Charon's boat without previously wandering on the shore for one hundred years. If any living person presented himself to cross the river of the dead, he could not be admitted into the bark before he showed Charon a golden bough, obtained from the Cumaean sibyl; and the ferryman was on one occasion imprisoned for an entire year because he had, though against his own will, conveyed Heracles across the stream without first receiving from him this necessary passport. The poets have represented Charon as a robust old man, of a severe though animated countenance, with eyes glowing like flame, a white and bushy head, vestments of a dingy colour, stained with the mire of the stream, and with a pole for the direction of his bark, which last is of a dark rusty hue.

Charon. (Stackelberg.)

The earliest mention of Charon in Grecian poetry seems to be in the ancient poem of the Minyas, quoted by Pausanias (x. 28). The fable itself is considered by some to be of Egyptian origin, and in support of this opinion they refer to the account of Diodorus Siculus relative to the statements made by the Egyptian priests. The latter asserted, it seems, that Orpheus and Homer had both learned wisdom on the banks of the Nile; and that the Erebus of Greece, and all its parts, personages, and usages, were but transcripts of the mode of burial in Egypt; and here the corpse was, on payment of an obolus, conveyed by a ferryman (named Charon in the language of Egypt) over the Acherusian Lake after it had received its sentence from the judges appointed for that purpose.

Charon, Hermes or Mercury, and Soul. (From a Roman lamp.)

(2) One of the earlier Greek historical writers, a native of Lampsacus, supposed to have flourished between the seventy-fifth and seventy-eighth Olympiads, about B.C. 464. Charon continued the researches of Hecataeus into Eastern ethnography. He wrote (as was the custom of the historians of his day) separate works upon Persia, Libya, Aethiopia, etc. He also subjoined the history of his own time, and he preceded Herodotus in narrating the events of the Persian War, although Herodotus nowhere mentions him. From

the fragments of his writings which remain, it is manifest that his relation to Herodotus was that of a dry chronicler to an historian, under whose hands everything acquires life and character. Charon wrote, besides, a chronicle of his own country, as several of the early historians did, who were thence called "Horographers" (ὧροι, corresponding to the Latin *annales*, ought not to be confounded with ὅροι, *termini, limites*). The fragments of Charon have been collected by Kreuzer, in his *Historicorum Graecorum Antiquissimorum Fragmenta*, p. 89 foll.; and by Müller, *Frag. Histor. Graec.* (Paris, 1841).

Charondas (Χαρώνδας). A celebrated legislator, born at Catana in Sicily, where he flourished about B.C. 650. We have very few details of his life. Aristotle merely informs us that he was of the bourgeois class of citizens, and that he framed laws for the people of Catana, as well as for other communities which, like them, were descended from Chalcis in Euboea. Aelian adds (*V. H.* iii. 17) that he was subsequently driven into exile from Catana, and took refuge in Rhegium, where he succeeded in introducing his laws. Some authors inform us that he compiled his laws for the Thurians; but he lived, in fact, a long time before the foundation of Thurium, since his laws were abrogated in part by Anaxilaüs, tyrant of Rhegium, who died B.C. 476. The laws of Charondas were, like those of many of the ancient legislators, in verse, and formed part of the instruction of the young. Their fame reached even to Athens, where they were sung or chanted at repasts. The preamble of these laws, as preserved to us by Stobaeus, is thought, so far, at least, as regards the form of expression, not to be genuine; and Heyne supposes it to have been taken from some Pythagorean treatise on the laws of Charondas.

The manner of this legislator's death is deserving of mention. He had made a law that no man should be allowed to come armed into the assembly of the people. The penalty for infringement was death. He became the victim of his own law; for, having returned from pursuing some robbers, he entered the city, and presented himself before the assembly of the people without reflecting that he carried a sword by his side. Some one thereupon remarked to him, "You are violating your own law." His reply was, "On the contrary, by Zeus, I will establish it"; and he slew himself on the spot.

Charta (χάρτη). Paper. See LIBER; PAPYRUS; WRITING AND WRITING MATERIALS.

Charybdis (Χάρυβδις). See SCYLLA.

Chasuāri, Chasuarii, or **Chattuarii**. A people of Germany, allies or dependants of the Cherusci. They dwelt north of the Chatti; and in later times they appear between the Rhine and the Mosa (Maas), as a part of the Franks.

Chatti. See CATTI.

Chauci or **Cauci**. A people in the northwestern part of Germany, between the Amisia (Ems) and the Albis (Elbe). They were never subdued by the Romans.

Cheironomia (χειρονομία). (1) The movement of the hands during dancing. (See SALTATIO.) (2) The gesticulation employed in pantomime. (See PANTOMIMUS.) (3) Sparring, for which the regular word is σκιαμαχία. See PUGILATUS.

Cheirotonia (χειροτονία). In the Athenian assemblies two modes of voting were practised—the one by ballot (see PSEPHUS), the other by a show of hands (χειροτονεῖν). The latter was the usual mode of conducting business. Secret voting, in general, was only used when the personal interests of individuals were concerned; as when the question was the condemnation or acquittal of a person put upon his trial, the remission of a punishment or of a pecuniary fine payable to the State, the conferring of citizenship on strangers, or finally the banishment of a citizen by ostracism. Open voting was employed on questions of public policy, such as war or peace, in voting upon laws, and in some special kinds of trials on matters which concerned the people, as upon προβολαί and εἰσαγγελία. In the elections of magistrates (ἀρχαιρεσίαι), some were chosen by lot (ἀρχὴ κληρωτή); others, and these of course the more important—e. g. the στρατηγοί—by show of hands (ἀρχὴ αἱρετή or χειροτονητή). The undoubted distinction between ψηφίζεσθαι and χειροτονεῖν is not always observed: we find the word ψηφίζεσθαι used where the voting was really by show of hands (Demos. *Olynth.* 1. § 2).

The χειροτονία was taken first on the affirmative, then on the negative, side of the question at issue: the number of hands was counted each time by the herald; and the president, upon the herald's report, declared whether the ayes or noes had the majority.

It is important to understand clearly the compounds of this word. A vote condemning an accused person is καταχειροτονία: one acquitting him, ἀποχειροτονία: ἐπιχειροτονεῖν is to confirm by a majority of votes: ἐπιχειροτονία τῶν νόμων was a revision of the laws, which took place at the beginning of the Attic year in the month of Hecatombaeon: ἐπιχειροτονία τῶν ἀρχῶν was a vote taken in the first assembly of each prytany on the conduct of the magistrates. In these cases, those who voted for the confirmation of the law, or the continuance in office of the magistrate, were said ἐπιχειροτονεῖν, those on the other side ἀποχειροτονεῖν: διαχειροτονία is a vote for one of two alternatives; ἀντιχειροτονεῖν to vote against a proposition; προχειροτονία is the show of hands on the previous question—i. e. whether the people desired further discussion or not. The compounds of ψηφίζεσθαι have similar meanings (Schömann, *Assemblies*, pp. 120, 125, 231, 251, 330).

Chelé (χηλή). A word formed from the base χα- "to gape," and used in various ways—of the cracks in a horse's hoof, for the hoof itself, and for many things that are hooked or forked—e. g. the claws of a crab, the talons of a bird, of a medical instrument (Hipp. 471, 54), of the notch of the arrow, of the two "fingers" of the "hand" (*manucla*) which in the *catapulta* (q. v.) grasped the back-drawn string, of a curved breakwater, and (in astronomy) of that part of the heavens next Virgo, embraced by the arms of the Scorpion (Verg. *Georg.* i. 33).

Chelidonia (χελιδόνια). In the island of Rhodes, when the swallows returned (i. e. in the month Boëdromion), boys, called χελιδονισταί, went from house to house asking gifts, professedly for the swallows, and singing a song that has been preserved in Athenaeus (viii. 360). The practice (χελιδόνια) was said to have been introduced by Cleobulus of Lindus at a time when the town was in great distress.

Chelidoniae Insŭlae (Χελιδόνιαι Νῆσοι, "Swallow Islands"). A group of five small islands, surrounded by dangerous shallows, off the promontory called Hiera or Chelidonia, on the south coast of Lycia.

Chelonātas (Χελωνάτας). A promontory, now Cape Tornese, in Elis, opposite Zacynthus; the most westerly point of the Peloponnesus.

Chelōné (Χελώνη). A nymph who was the only one of the deities that did not attend the nuptials of Zeus and Heré, and who even made the celebration a subject of ridicule. Hermes thereupon precipitated her into a river, on the banks of which her mansion was situated, and transformed her into a tortoise, under which shape she was doomed to perpetual silence, and to the necessity of always carrying her dwelling about with her. The Greek for a tortoise is χελώνη, and hence the fable arose.

Chelys (χέλυς). See LYRA.

Chemé (χήμη). (1) A cockle-shell. (2) A measure of capacity, which appears to have varied from 0.04 pint to 0.016 pint. The symbol for it is X. See F. Hultsch, *Metrologici Scriptores*, s. v. χήμη.

Chemmis (Χέμμις; later PANOPŎLIS, Πανόπολις). A great city of the Thebaïs, or Upper Egypt, on the east bank of the Nile, celebrated for its manufacture of linen, its stone quarries, and its temples of Pan and Perseus.

Cheniscus (χηνίσκος). An ornament resembling the head and neck of a goose (χήν), placed sometimes on the prow and sometimes on the stern of a ship. See NAVIS.

Chenisci. (From Paintings found at Herculaneum.)

Cheops (Χέοψ). The Greek form of the Egyptian Khufu, a king of Memphis in Egypt, of the Fourth Dynasty (cir. B.C. 3000), and famous as the builder of the largest of the pyramids by the forced labour of the people. He was succeeded by his brother Chephren (Khafra), who built the next largest pyramid. See Herod. ii. 124; and the article AEGYPTUS.

Chephren (Χεφρήν). A king of Egypt, the brother and successor of Cheops (q. v.), whose example of tyranny he followed, reigned fifty-six years, and built the second pyramid. The Egyptians so execrated the memory of the two brothers that they called the pyramids not by their names, but by the name of a poor shepherd, Philition, who lived near by. See PYRAMIS.

Chernĭbon or **Cheironiptron** (χέρνιβον, χειρόνιπτρον). A basin for holding the lustral water at a sacrifice, or, in general, for washing the hands. The water, whether sacrificial or not, was called χέρνιψ. The bowl was sometimes of silver and sometimes of gold. The shape was round, and both shallow and deep ones have been found. The pure Latin name is *malluvium*.

Chernips (χέρνιψ). See CHERNIBON.

Chersĭphron or **Ctesĭphon**. See EPHESUS.

Chersonēsus (Χερσόνησος; Attic, Χερρόνησος). A Greek geographical term, equivalent in meaning to the Latin *peninsula*. The earlier form is *Cherronesus*, the word being derived from χέρρος (later from χέρσος), "a continent" or "mainland," and νῆσος, "an island."

The most noted Chersonesi in ancient times were the following: (1) CHERSONESUS AUREA, or Golden Chersonesus, a peninsula of Farther India, corresponding, according to D'Anville, Rennell, Mannert, and others, to the modern Malacca. The positive knowledge of the ancient geographers can hardly be said to have extended much beyond this, their account of the regions farther to the east being principally derived from the natives of India. The name given to this region by the ancients has reference to the popular belief of its abounding in gold; and here, too, some inquirers into early geography have placed the Ophir of Solomon, an opinion maintained also by Iosephus. (2) CHERSONESUS CIMBRĬCA, a peninsula in the northern part of Germany, answering to the modern Jutland and Schleswig-Holstein. (3) CHERSONESUS TAURĬCA, a peninsula between the Pontus Euxinus and the Palus Maeotis, answering to the modern Crimea. The name was derived from the Tauri, a barbarous race who inhabited it. It was sometimes called Chersonesus Scythica and Chersonesus Magna. (4) CHERSONESUS THRACĬCA, often called simply "the Chersonesus," and the most important of all. It was a peninsula of Thrace, between the Sinus Melas and the Hellespont. The fertility of its soil, and its proximity to the coast of Asia Minor, early attracted an influx of Grecian settlers, and its shores soon became crowded with flourishing and populous cities. From this quarter the Athenians drew their chief supply of grain.

Cherusci. A people of Germany, between the Weser and the Elbe, southeast of the Chauci. Under the conduct of Arminius (q. v.) they defeated and slew three Roman legions commanded by Varus, A.D. 10, in the Saltus Teutobergiensis. They were afterwards defeated by Germanicus, and never recovered their former eminence.

Chiliarchus (χιλίαρχος). The commander of a thousand men. See EXERCITUS.

Chilo (Χείλων, Χίλων). A Spartan, ranked, on account of his wisdom and experience, among the Seven Sages of Greece. He directed his attention to public affairs, and became one of the *ephori*, B.C. 556 (Diog. Laërt. i. 68). Many of his maxims are quoted by the ancient writers, which justify the high reputation connected with his name. He died of joy at an advanced age, while embracing one of his sons who had gained a prize at the Olympic Games. Chilo appears to have travelled much abroad, and it is probable that he visited Sardis, the capital of Croesus, a monarch who had sought an alliance with Sparta (Herod. i. 69). It was at the court of the Lydian monarch, in all probability, that he saw Aesop, since Diogenes Laërtius speaks of a question put by the philosopher to the fabulist (Diog. Laërt. i. 68 foll.).

Chimaera (Χίμαιρα). A fire-breathing monster of Lycia, destroyed by Bellerophon (q. v.). According to Homer the Chimaera was of divine origin. In front it was a lion, behind it was a serpent, and in the middle a goat, and was brought up by King Amisodarus as a plague for men. Hesiod calls her the daughter of Typhon and Echidna, and by Orthos the mother of the Sphinx and the Nemean lion. He describes her as large, swift-footed, strong, with the heads of a lion, a goat, and a serpent. In numerous works of art, as in statues,

Bellerophon and the Chimaera. (From a Terra-cotta in the British Museum.)

and the coins of Corinth, Sicyon, and other cities, the Chimaera is generally represented as a lion, with a goat's head in the middle of its back, and tail ending in a snake's head. The bronze Chimaera of Arretium, now in Florence, is a very celebrated work of art. Even in antiquity the Chimaera was regarded as a symbol of the volcanic character of the Lycian soil.

Chimerium (Χειμέριον). A promontory on the coast of Epirus, opposite the island of Paxos.

Chion (Χίων). A native of Heraclea Pontica, and disciple of Plato. Animated by political zeal, he left Athens, where he had resided for the space of five years, attending the instructions of Plato, and returned home with the determination of freeing his native city from the yoke of tyranny. Clearchus, who ruled at Heraclea, was not, it is true, a good prince; but, in slaying him, Chion was the cause of this city's falling under a worse tyrant, Satyrus, the brother of Clearchus. Chion himself fell a victim to the latter's elevation to power (B.C. 353). We have seventeen letters said to have been written by Chion. They are principally addressed to his father, Matris; but their authenticity has been called in question, and the real author is supposed to have been a Platonist of the fourth century. The style is clear, simple, and animated. Edition by Orelli (Leipzig, 1816).

Chiŏné (Χιόνη). (1) Daughter of Boreas and Orithyia, mother of Eumolpus by Poseidon. (See EUMOLPUS.) (2) Daughter of Daedalion, mother of Philammon by Apollo, and of Autolycus by Hermes. She was slain by Artemis for venturing to compare her own beauty with that of the goddess.

Chionĭdes (Χιονίδης). Said to have been the earliest writer of the old Athenian comedy. (Cf. Aristot. *Poet.* iii. 5.) His representations date from B.C. 487. The names of three of his comedies are recorded, Ἥρωες, Πέρσαι ἢ Ἀσσύριοι, and Πτωχοί. To judge from these titles, we should conclude that his comedies had a political reference, and were full of personal satire; and from an allusion in Vitruvius (*Praef. in lib. vi.*) we may infer that they were gnomic, like those of Epicharmus. Ed. in Meineke, *Com. Frag.* vol. i.

Chios (Χῖος). The modern Scio. One of the largest and most famous islands of the Aegean, lay opposite to the peninsula of Clazomenae, on the coast of Ionia. It was colonized by the Ionians at the time of their great migration, and remained an independent and powerful maritime state till the defeat of the Ionian Greeks by the Persians, B.C. 494, after which the Chians were subjected to the Persians. The battle of Mycalé, 479, freed Chios from the Persian yoke, and it became a member of the Athenian League, in which it was for a long time the closest and most favoured ally of Athens; but an unsuccessful attempt to revolt, in 412, led to its conquest and devastation. Chios was celebrated for its wine and marble. Of all the States which aspired to the honour of being the birthplace of Homer, Chios was generally considered by the ancients to have the best claim; and it numbered among its natives the historian Theopompus, the poet Theocritus, and other eminent men. Its chief

Coin of Chios.

city, Chios (Khio), stood on the eastern side of the island.

Chiramaxium (χειράμαξα, χειραμάξιον). A sort of perambulator, or wheeled chair, drawn by hand. (See Petronius, 28.) In the accompanying illustration of a marble, the wheels are evidently ornamental.

Chiramaxium. (British Museum.)

Chiridōta. See TUNICA.

Chirisŏphus (Χειρίσοφος). A Lacedaemonian; was sent by the Spartans to aid Cyrus in his expedition against his brother Artaxerxes, B.C. 401. After the battle of Cunaxa, and the subsequent arrest of the Greek generals, Chirisophus was appointed one of the new generals, and, in conjunction with Xenophon (q. v.), had the chief conduct of the retreat. See ANABASIS; XENOPHON.

Chirogrăphum (χειρόγραφον). A word which meant first, as its derivation implies, a handwriting or autograph. In this, its simple sense, χείρ in Greek and *manus* in Latin are often substituted for it.

Like similar words in all languages, it acquired several technical senses. From its first meaning was easily derived that of a signature to a will or other instrument, especially a note of hand given by a debtor to his creditor. In this latter case it did not constitute the legal obligation (for the debt might be proved in some other way); it was only a proof of the obligation.

According to Asconius (*in Verr.* iii. 36), *chirographum*, in the sense of a promissory note, was distinguished from *syngrapha;* the former was always given for money actually lent, the latter might be a mere sham agreement to pay a debt which had never been actually incurred. The *chirographum* was kept by the creditor, and had only the debtor's signature; the *syngrapha*, on the contrary, was signed and kept by both parties. See CAUTIO; FALSUM.

In the Latin of the Middle Ages, *chirographum* was used to signify tribute collected under the sign-manual of a person in authority, similar to the briefs and benevolences of former times in Great Britain. It was also used, till comparatively recent times, in the English law for an indenture. Duplicates of deeds were written on one piece of parchment, with the word *chirographum* between them, which was cut in two in a straight or wavy line, and the parts given to the care of the persons concerned. By the canonists, as Blackstone remarks, the word *syngrapha* or *syngraphus* was employed in the same way, and hence gave its name to these kinds of writing.

Chirography. See PALAEOGRAPHY.

Chiron (Χείρων).) The most celebrated of the Centaurs, and son of Cronos and the nymph Philyra. Dreading the jealousy of his wife, Rhea, the god is said to have transformed Philyra into a mare, and himself into a steed; and the offspring of this union was Chiron, half man and half horse. This legend first appeared in the poem of the *Gigantomachia*, and it is also noticed by Pindar (*Pyth.* iii. 1, foll.). Probably the praise of Chiron by Homer (*Il.* xi. 832), for his love of justice, led to the view of him as the offspring of the god who ruled over the golden race of men. To Chiron was intrusted the rearing and educating of Iason and his son Medeus, Heracles, Aesculapius, and Achilles. Besides his knowledge of the musical art, which he imparted to his heroic pupils, he was also skilled in surgery, which he taught to the last two of this number. In the contest between Heracles and the Centaurs, Chiron was accidentally wounded in the knee by one of the arrows of the hero. Grieved at this unhappy event, Heracles ran up, drew out the arrow, and applied to the wound a remedy given by Chiron himself. But in vain; the venom of the hydra was not to be overcome. Chiron retired to his cave longing to die, but unable on account of his immortality, till, on his expressing his willingness to die for Prometheus, he was released by death from his misery. According to another account, he was, on his prayer to Zeus for relief, raised to the sky and made the constellation of Sagittarius. Chiron was the husband of Naïs or Chariclo, and their daughter Eudeïs was the mother of Peleus (Apollod. xiii. 12). In art, Chiron is represented as of a noble and intellectual cast of countenance; while the other Centaurs exhibit brutal and sensual traits. See Böttiger, *Vasengemälde*, iii. p. 144, etc., and the article CENTAURI.

Chiron. (Pompeian Painting.)

Chironomia (χειρονομία). The movement of the hands, which was an important part of Greek and Roman dancing, had the name of *χειρονομία.* Herodotus, in the story of Hippoclides standing on his head before the guests of Clisthenes, uses the curious expression τοῖσι σκέλεσι ἐχειρόνομησε (vi. 129). It was likewise a feature of any pantomimic performance. The word is also used in the sense of σκιαμαχία, or sparring (Pausan. vi. 10, § 3). See PANTOMIMUS; PUGILATUS; SALTATIO.

Chironŏmos (χειρονόμος). Generally, any person who employs the art of gesticulation to express his meaning without the aid of language; thence, also, a pantomimic actor on the stage (Juv. vi. 63); and one who performs any duty with regular, studied, or theatrical movements; whence the same term is applied by the satirists to the slave who carved up the dishes at great entertainments with a pompous flourish of his knife (Juv. v. 121; cf. Petron. xxxvi.).

Chiropĕdé (χειροπέδη). A handcuff (Diod. xx. 13). See MANICAE; PEDICAE.

Chiropodists. See TOILET.

Chirotonia (χειροτονία). See CHEIROTONIA; PSEPHUS.

Chirurgia (χειρουργία). Surgery; a word meaning literally "handiwork." The practice of surgery was at first considered by the ancients to be merely a part of a physician's duty; but, as in later times the two branches of the profession were to a great extent separated, it will perhaps be more convenient to treat of it under a separate head. Without touching upon the disputed question, which is the more ancient branch of the profession, or even trying to give such a definition of the word *chirurgia* as would be likely to satisfy both the physicians and the surgeons of the present day, it will be sufficient to determine the sense in which the word was used by the ancients; and then to give an account of this division of the science and art of medicine as practised among the Greeks and Romans, referring to the article MEDICINA for further particulars.

The word *chirurgia* is derived from χείρ, "the hand," and ἔργον, "a work," and is explained by Celsus (*De Med.* lib. vii. Praefat.) to mean that part of medicine *quae manu curat,* "which treats ailments by means of the hand"; in Diogenes Laërtius (iii. 85) it is said to cure διὰ τοῦ τέμνειν καὶ καίειν, "by cutting and burning." Omitting the fabulous and mythological personages, Apollo, Aesculapius, Chiron, etc., the only certain traditions respecting the state of surgery before the establishment of the republics of Greece, and even until the time of the Peloponnesian War, are to be found in the *Iliad* and *Odyssey.* There it appears that surgery was almost entirely confined to the treatment of wounds, and the imaginary power of enchantment was joined with the use of topical applications (*Il.* iii. 218). The Greeks received surgery, together with the other branches of medicine, from the Egyptians; and from some observations made by the archæologists who accompanied the French expedition to Egypt in 1798, and by subsequent investigators, it appears that there are documents fully proving that in very remote times this extraordinary people had reached a degree of proficiency of which few of the moderns have any conception. Upon the ceilings and walls of the temples at Karnac, Luxor, etc., bas-reliefs are seen, representing limbs that have been cut off with instruments very similar to those which are employed for amputations at the present day. The same instruments are again observed in the hieroglyphics, and vestiges of other surgical operations may be traced, which afford convincing proofs of the skill of the ancient Egyptians in this branch of medical science.

The earliest remaining surgical writings are those in the Hippocratic Collection, where there are ten treatises on this subject, of which, however, only one is considered undoubtedly genuine. Hippocrates (B.C. 460–357 ?) far surpassed all his predecessors in the boldness and success of his operations; and though the scanty knowledge of anatomy possessed in those times prevented his attaining any very great perfection, still one should rather admire his genius, which enabled him to do so much, than blame him because, with his imperfect information, he could not accomplish more. (See HIPPOCRATES.) The scientific skill in reducing fractures and luxations displayed in his works *De Fracturis, De Articulis,* excites the admiration of Haller (*Biblioth. Chirurg.*); and he was most probably the inventor of the *ambe,* an old surgical machine for dislocations of the shoulder, which, though now fallen into disuse, enjoyed for a long time a great reputation. In his work *De Capitis Vulneribus* he gives minute directions about the time and mode of using the trephine, and warns the operator against the probability of his being deceived by the sutures of the cranium, as he confesses happened to himself (*De Morb. Vulgar.* lib. v. tom. iii. p. 561, ed. Kühn). Amputation, in the modern sense of the word, is not described in the Hippocratic Collection; though mention is made of the removal of a limb at the joint, after the flesh has been completely destroyed by gangrene. The author of the "Oath" commonly attributed to Hippocrates binds his pupils not to perform the operation of lithotomy, but to leave it to persons specially accustomed to it (ἐργάτῃσι ἀνδράσι πρήξιος τῆσδε); from which it would appear as if certain persons confined themselves to particular operations.

The names of several persons are preserved who practised surgery as well as medicine in the times immediately succeeding those of Hippocrates; but, with the exception of some fragments, inserted in the writings of Galen, Oribasius, Aëtius, etc., all their writings have perished. Archagathus deserves to be mentioned, as he is said to have been the first foreign surgeon who settled at Rome, B.C. 219 (Plin. *H. N.* xxix. § 12). He was at first very well received, the *ius Quiritium* was conferred upon him, a shop was bought for him at the public expense, and he received the honourable title of Vulnerarius; which, however, on account of his frequent use of the knife and cautery, was soon changed by the Romans, who were unused to such a mode of practice, into that of Carnifex. Asclepiades, who lived at the beginning of the first century B.C., is said to have been the first person who proposed the operation of tracheotomy (Cael. Aurel. *De Morb. Acut.* i. 14, § 111; iii. 4, § 39). Ammonius of Alexandria, surnamed Λιθοτόμος, who is supposed to have lived rather later, is celebrated in the annals of surgery for having been the first to propose and to perform the operation of lithotrity, or breaking a calculus in the bladder when found to be too large for safe extraction. Celsus has minutely described his mode of operating (*De Med.* vii. 26, § 3, p. 436), which in some respects resembles that of Civiale and Heurteloup in the early part of the present century, and proves that, however much credit they may deserve for perfecting the operation and bringing it out of oblivion into public notice, the praise of having originally thought of it belongs to the ancients. "A hook or crotchet," says Celsus, "is fixed upon the stone in such a way as easily to hold it firm, even when shaken, so that it may not revolve backward; then an iron instrument is used, of moderate thickness, thin at the front end, but blunt, which, when applied to the stone and struck at the other end, cleaves it: great care must be taken that the instrument does not come into contact with the bladder itself, and that nothing fall upon it by the breaking of the stone." The next surgical writer after Hippocrates, whose works are still extant, is Celsus, who lived at the beginning of the first century A.D., and who has devoted the four last books of his work *De Medicina,* and especially the seventh and eighth, entirely to surgical matter. It plainly appears from reading Celsus that since the time of Hippocrates surgery had made very great progress, and had, indeed, reached a high degree of perfection. We find in him the earliest mention of the use of the ligature for the arrest of hemorrhage from wounded bloodvessels (v. 26, § 21, p. 262); and the Celsian mode of amputation was continued down to comparatively modern times (vii. 33, p. 451). He is the first author who gives directions for the operation of lithotomy (*De Med.* vii. 26, § 2, p. 432), and the method described by him (called the *apparatus minor,* or *Celsus's method*) continued to be practised till the commencement of the sixteenth century. It was performed at Paris, Bordeaux, and other places in France, upon patients of all ages, even as late as the latter part of the seventeenth century; and a modern author (Allan *On Lithotomy,* p. 12) recommends it always to be preferred for boys under fourteen. He describes (vii. 25, § 3, p. 428) the operation of *infibulatio*, which was so commonly performed by the ancients upon singers, etc., and is often alluded to in classical authors. (See Juv. vi. 73, 379; Seneca, in Lactant. *Divin. Instit.* i. 16; Mart. *Epigr.* vii. 82, 1, ix. 28, 12, xiv. 215, 1; Tertull. *De Corona Mil.* 11.) He also describes (vii. 25, § 1, p. 427) the operation of circumcision alluded to by St. Paul (1 Cor. vii. 18). Paulus Aegineta (*De Re Med.* vi. 53) transcribes from Antyllus a second method of performing the same operation.

The following description by Celsus of the necessary qualifications of a surgeon deserves to be quoted: "A surgeon," says he (lib. vii. Praefat.), "ought to be young, or, at any rate, not very old; his hand should be firm and steady, and never shake; he should be able to use his left hand as readily as his right; his eyesight should be clear, and his mind not easily startled; he should be so far subject to pity as to make him desirous of the recovery of his patient, but not so far as to suffer himself to be moved by his cries; he should neither hurry the operation more than the case requires, nor cut less than is necessary, but do everything just as if the other's screams made no impression upon him."

Omitting Scribonius Largus, Moschion, and Soranus, the next author of importance is Caelius Aurelianus, who is supposed to have lived about the beginning of the second century A.D., and in whose works there is much surgical matter, but nothing that can be called original. He rejected as absurd the operation of tracheotomy (*De Morb. Chron.* iii. 4, § 39). He mentions a case of ascites that was cured by tapping (ib. iii. 8, § 128), and also a person who recovered after being shot through the lungs by an arrow (ib. ii. 12, § 144).

Galen, the most voluminous and at the same time the most valuable medical writer of antiquity, is less celebrated as a surgeon than as an anatomist and physician. He appears to have practised surgery at Pergamus, but upon his removal to Rome (A.D. 165) he entirely confined himself to medicine (*De Meth. Med.* vi. *in fine*, tom. x. p. 455). His writings prove, however, that he did not entirely abandon surgery. His Commentaries on the treatise of Hippocrates *De Officina Medici*, and his treatise *De Fasciis*, show that he was well versed even in the minor details of the art. He appears also to have been a skilful operator, though no great surgical inventions are attributed to him.

Antyllus, who lived some time between Galen and Oribasius, is the earliest writer whose directions for performing tracheotomy are still extant, though the operation (as stated above) was proposed by Asclepiades about three hundred years before. Only a few fragments of the writings of Antyllus remain, and among them the following passage is preserved by Paulus Aegineta (*De Re Med.* vi. 33): "When we proceed to perform this operation, we must cut through some part of the windpipe, below the larynx, about the third or fourth ring; for to divide the whole would be dangerous. This place is commodious, because it is not covered with any flesh, and because it has no vessels situated near the divided part. Therefore, bending the head of the patient backward, so that the windpipe may come more forward to the view, we make a transverse section between two of the rings, so that in this case not the cartilage, but the membrane which unites the cartilages together, is divided. If the operator be a little timid, he may first stretch the skin with a hook and divide it; then, proceeding to the windpipe, and separating the vessels, if any are in the way, he may make the incision."

This operation appears to have been very seldom, if ever, performed by the ancients upon a human being. Avenzoar tried it upon a goat, and found it might be done without much danger or difficulty; but he says he should not like to be the first person to try it upon a man.

Oribasius, physician to the emperor Julian (A.D. 361), professes to be merely a compiler; and though there is in his great work, entitled Συναγωγαὶ Ἰατρικαί (*Collecta Medicinalia*), much surgical matter, there is nothing original. The same may be said of Aëtius and Alexander Trallianus, both of whom lived towards the end of the sixth century A.D. Paulus Aegineta has given up the fifth and sixth books of his work *De Re Medica* entirely to surgery, and has inserted much useful matter, derived in a great measure from his own observation and experience. Albucasis translated into Arabic great part of these two books as the basis of his work on surgery. Paulus was particularly celebrated for his skill in midwifery and female diseases, and was called on that account, by the Arabians, *Al-Kawábelí*, "the Accoucheur" (Abulfaraj, *Hist. Dynast.* p. 181, ed. Pococke). He probably lived towards the end of the seventh century A.D., and is the last of the ancient Greek and Latin medical writers whose surgical works remain. The names of several others are recorded, but they are not of sufficient eminence to require any notice here. For further information on the subject both of medicine and surgery, see MEDICINA; and for the legal qualifications, social rank, etc., both of physicians and surgeons, among the ancient Greeks and Romans, see MEDICUS.

The surgical instruments from which the accompanying engravings (Nos. 1 to 19) are made were found by a physician of St. Petersburg (Dr. Savenko) in 1819, at Pompeii, in the Via Consularis (Strada Consulare), in a house which is supposed to have belonged to a surgeon. They are now preserved in the museum at Portici. The engravings, with an account of them by Dr. Savenko, were originally published in the *Revue Médicale* for 1821, vol. iii. p. 427, etc. They were afterwards inserted in Froriep's *Notizen aus dem Gebiete der Natur- und Heilkunde* for 1822, vol. ii. n. 26, p. 57, etc. The accompanying figures are copied from the German work, in which some of them appear to be badly drawn. Their authenticity was at first doubted by Kühn (*De Instrumentis Chirurg. Veteribus Cognitis, et nuper Effossis*, Leipzig, 1823), who thought they were the same that had been described by Bayardi in his *Catal. Antiq. Monument. Herculani Effos.* (Nap. 1754, fol., n. 236–294). When, however, his dissertation was afterwards republished (*Opusc. Academ. Med. et Philol.*, Leipzig, 1827, ii. 309), he acknowledged himself to be completely satisfied on this point, and has given in the tract referred to a learned and ingenious description of the instruments and their supposed uses, from which the following account is chiefly abridged. It will, however, be seen at once that the form of most of them is so simple, and their uses so obvious, that very little explanation is necessary. Altogether they give a very high idea of both the science and the practice of surgery among the Romans.

1, 2. Two probes (*specillum*, μήλη) made of iron; the larger six inches long, the smaller four and a half. 3. A cautery (καυτήριον) made of iron, rather more than four inches long. 4, 5. Two lancets (*scalpellum*, σμίλη) made of copper; the former two inches and a half long, the other three inches. It seems doubtful whether they were used for blood-letting or for opening abscesses, etc. 6. A knife, apparently made of copper, the blade of which is two inches and a half long, and in the broadest part one inch in breadth; the back is straight and thick, and the edge much curved; the handle is so short that Savenko thinks it must have been broken. It is uncertain for what particular purpose it was used: Kühn conjectures that (if it be a surgical instrument at all) it may have been made with such a curved edge and such a straight thick back in order that it might be struck with a hammer, and so amputate fingers, toes, etc. 7. Another knife, apparently

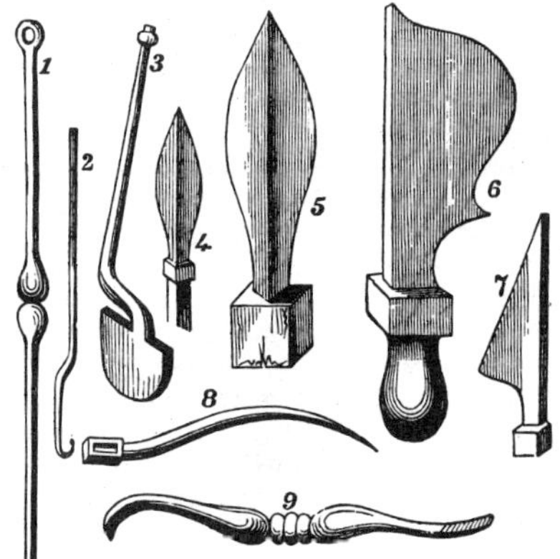

Surgical Instruments.

made of copper, the blade of which is of a triangular shape, two inches long, and in the broadest part eight lines in breadth; the back is straight and one line broad, and this breadth continues all the way to the point, which, therefore, is not sharp, but guarded by a sort of button. Kühn thinks it may have been used for enlarging wounds, etc., for which it would be particularly fitted by its blunt point and broad back. 8. A needle, about three inches long, made of iron. 9. An elevator (or instrument for raising depressed portions of the skull), made of iron, five inches long, and very much resembling those made use of at the present day. 10-14. Different kinds of forceps (*volsellae*). No. 10 has the two sides separated from each other, and is five inches long. No. 11 is also five inches long. No. 12 is three inches and a half long. The sides are narrow at the point of union, and become broader by degrees towards the other end, where, when closed, they would form a kind of arch. It should be noticed that it is furnished with a movable ring, exactly like the tenaculum forceps employed at the present day. No. 13 was used for pulling out hairs by the roots (τριχολαβίς). No. 14 is six inches long, and is bent in the middle. It was probably used for extracting foreign bodies that had stuck in the œsophagus, or gullet, or in the bottom of a wound. 15. A male catheter (*aenea fistula*), nine inches in length.

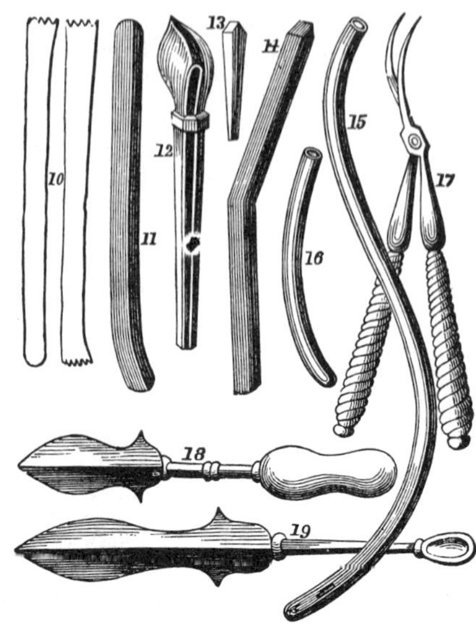

Surgical Instruments.

The shape is remarkable from its having the double curve like the letter S, which is the form that was re-invented in the last century by the celebrated French surgeon J. L. Petit. 16. Probably a female catheter, four inches in length. Celsus describes both male and female catheters (*De Med.* vii. 26, § 1, p. 429). 17. Supposed by Froriep to be an instrument for extracting teeth (ὀδοντάγρα, Pollux, iv. § 181); but Kühn, with much more probability, conjectures it to be an instrument used in amputating part of an enlarged uvula, and quotes Celsus (*De Med.* vii. 12, § 3, p. 404), who says that "no method of operating is more convenient than to

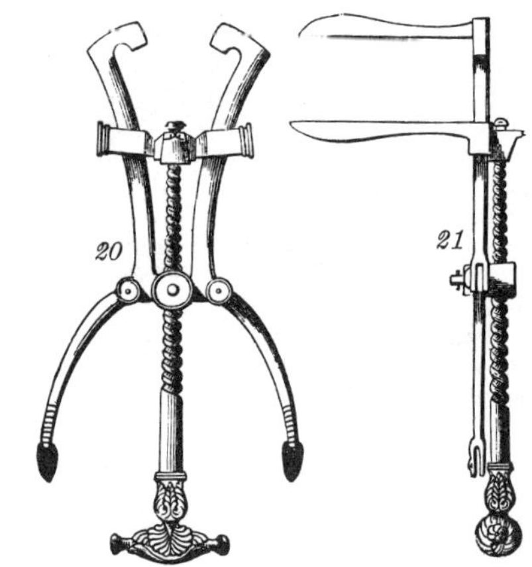

Surgical Instruments.

take hold of the uvula with the forceps, and then to cut off below it as much as is necessary." 18, 19. Probably two spatulae. Nos. 20–23 are perhaps the most interesting of all, as showing the means employed by the Romans in the exploration of some of the internal cavities of the body, for the discovery and treatment of disease. They are taken from Bened. Vulpi, *Illustraz. di tutti gli Strumenti Chirurgici*, etc. (Naples, 1847), Mem. 4, p. 39, etc., where there is a detailed and learned description of them. Nos. 20, 21 are two views of the same kind of instrument—viz., a dilator vaginae (διόπτρα, Paul. Aegin. vi. 73). No. 22 is a dilator ani (ἑδροδιαστολεύς, id. vi. 78); and No. 23, nippers for compressing veins or extracting splintered bones.

See Pliny, *Historia Naturalis*, bks. xx.–xxxii.; Rénouard, *Hist. of Medicine* (Eng. trans. Philadelphia, 1867); Ritter von Rittershain, *Die Heilkünstler des alten Roms* (Berlin, 1875); Coxe, *The Writings of Hippocrates and Galen Epitomized* (Phil. 1846); Watson, *The Medical Profession in Ancient Times* (N. Y. 1856); Dunglison, *Hist. of Medicine* (Phil. 1872); Daremberg, *Hist. des Sciences Médicales* (Paris, 1870–73); Garratt, *Myths in Medicine* (N. Y. 1884); and Müller, *Handbuch*, v. pp. 108 foll.

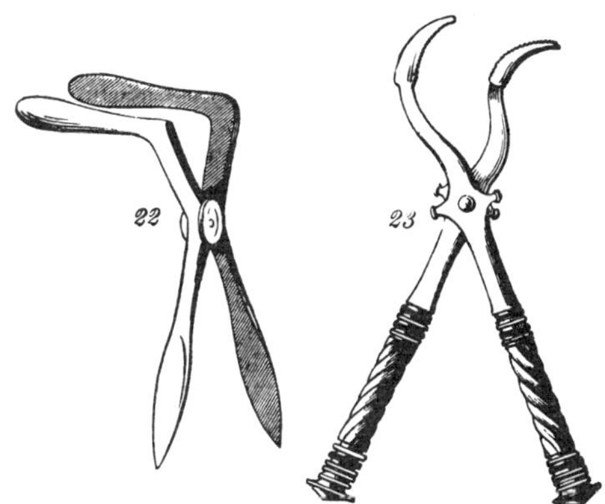

Surgical Instruments.

Chiton (χιτών). See EXOMIS; TUNICA.

Chitonia (Χιτώνια). A feast celebrated in the Attic village of Chitoné in honour of Artemis Chitonia, so called as wearing the loose tunic, or χιτών, of the huntress. A similar feast was held at Syracuse. See Athenaeus, xiv. p. 629.

Chlamys (χλαμύς). A short mantle forming a part of the outer raiment of the Greeks, and of the Romans in imperial times. Its material was usually woollen; and it differed from the ἱμάτιον, the usual *amictus* of the male sex, in these respects: that it was much smaller; also finer, thinner, more variegated in colour, and more susceptible of ornament. It moreover differed in being oblong instead of square, its length being generally about twice its breadth (Plut. *Alex.* 26).

The chlamys came originally from Macedonia and Thessaly, and was the dress of hunters, of travellers, especially on horseback, and of soldiers. It seems to have been part of the usual dress of a Spartan (Aristoph. *Lys.* 988) and was worn at Athens by the *ephebi* from about seventeen to twenty years of age (Philemon, p. 367, ed. Meineke).

The chlamys as worn by youths, by soldiers, and by hunters differed in colour and fineness, according to its purpose, and the age and rank of the wearer. The hunter commonly went out in a mantle of a dull, inconspicuous colour, as best adapted to escape the notice of wild animals (Poll. v. 18). The more ornamental mantles, being designed for women, were tastefully decorated with a border (*limbus*, Verg. *Aen.* iv. 137); and those worn by Phœnicians, Trojans, Phrygians, and other Asiatics were also embroidered, or interwoven with gold (Verg. *Aen.* iii. 483–484, xi. 775; Ovid, *Met.* v. 51). Actors had their chlamys ornamented with gold (Poll. iv. 116).

The usual mode of wearing the mantle was to pass one of its shorter sides round the neck, and to fasten it by means of a brooch (πόρπη, *fibula*), either over the breast, in which case it hung down the back, reaching to the calves of the legs; or over the right shoulder, so as to cover the left arm, as in the well-known example of the Belvedere Apollo. In other instances, it was made to depend gracefully from the left shoulder, of which the bronze Apollo in the British Museum (see right-hand figure) presents an example; or it was thrown lightly behind the back, and passed over either one arm or shoulder, or over both (as in left-hand figure); or, lastly, it was laid upon the throat, carried behind the neck, and crossed so as to hang

Chlamys. (The figure on the left from a painting on a vase; that on the right from the British Museum.)

down the back, and sometimes its extremities were again brought forward over the arms or shoulders. In short, the remains of ancient art of every description show in how high a degree the mantle contributed, by its endless diversity of arrangement, to the display of the human form in its greatest beauty. The aptitude of the mantle to be turned in every possible form around the body made it useful even for defence. The hunter used to wrap his chlamys about his left arm when pursuing wild animals, and preparing to fight with them (Poll. v. 18; Xen. *Cyneg.* vi. 17). Alcibiades died fighting with his mantle rolled round his left hand instead of a shield. The annexed illustration exhibits a figure of Poseidon armed with the trident in his right hand, and having a chlamys to protect the left. It is taken from a medal which was struck in commemoration of a naval victory obtained by Demetrius Poliorcetes, and was evidently designed to express his sense of Poseidon's succour in the conflict. When Artemis goes to the chase, as she does not require her mantle for pur-

Chlamys. (Poseidon from a medal, and Artemis from a statue in the Vatican.)

poses of defence, she draws it from behind over her shoulders, and twists it round her waist, so that the belt of her quiver passes across it, as shown in the statues of this goddess in the Vatican.

It appears from the bas-reliefs on marble vases that dancers took hold of one another by the chlamys, as the modern Greeks still do by their scarfs or handkerchiefs, instead of taking one another's hands.

Among the Romans the chlamys came more into use under the emperors. Caligula wore one enriched with gold (Suet. *Calig.* 19); and Alexander Severus, when in the country, one dyed with scarlet (Lamprid. *Al. Sev.* 40).

Chloé (Χλόη). "The blooming." An epithet of Demeter (q. v.).

Chloeia or **Chloia** (Χλόεια or Χλοιά). A festival celebrated at Athens in honour of Demeter Chloé, or simply Chloé, whose temple stood near the Acropolis (Hesych. s. v. Χλοιά). It was solemnized in spring, on the sixth of Thargelion, when the blossoms began to appear (hence the names Χλόη and Χλόεια), with the sacrifice of a goat and much mirth and rejoicing.

Chloris (Χλωρίς). (1) Daughter of the Theban Amphion and Niobé (q. v.). She and her brother Amyclas were the only children of Niobé not killed by Apollo and Artemis. She is often confounded with the following. (2) Daughter of Amphion of Orchomenos, wife of Neleus, king of Pylos, and mother of Nestor. (3) Wife of Zephyrus, and goddess of flowers, identical with the Roman Flora (q. v.).

Chlorus. See CONSTANTIUS.

Choaspes (Χωάσπης). (1) Now the Kerah or Kara-Su; a river of Susiana, falling into the Tigris. Its water was so pure that the Persian kings used to carry it with them in silver vessels when on foreign expeditions. (2) Now the Attock; a river in the Paropamisus, in India, falling into the Cophes (Cabul).

Chobus (Χῶβος). A river of Colchis falling into the Euxine, north of the mouth of the Phasis.

Choenix (χοῖνιξ). A Greek measure of capacity, the size of which is differently given; it was probably of different sizes in the several States. Pollux, Suidas, Cleopatra, and the fragments of Galen make it equal to three *cotylae* (=1.4866 pint English); another fragment of Galen and other authorities make it equal to four *cotylae* (=1.9821 pint English); Rhemnius Fannius and another fragment of Galen make it eight *cotylae* (=3.9641 pints English). The symbol for χοῖνιξ is $\overset{\iota}{\chi}$ or $\overset{\text{οι}}{\chi}$.

Choëphŏri (Χοηφόροι). "The Libation-bearers." The title of a play of Aeschylus (q. v.), the second in the Orestean trilogy, and named from the fact that the chorus is composed of captive Trojan women who are charged with the duty of bringing the libations to the tomb of Agamemnon. The subject of the play is the murder of Clytemnestra and Aegisthus by Orestes.

Choerĭlus (Χοιρίλος and Χοίριλλος). (1) An Athenian dramatist, one of the oldest Attic tragedians, who appeared as a writer as early as B.C. 520. He was a rival of Pratinas, Phrynichus, and Aeschylus. His favourite line seems to have been the satyric drama, in which he was long a popular writer.

(2) A Greek epic poet, born in Samos about B.C. 470, a friend of Herodotus and afterwards of the Spartan Lysander. He lived first at Athens and afterwards at the court of King Archelaüs of Macedonia, where he was treated with great consideration, and died about B.C. 400. He was the first epic poet who, feeling that the old mythology was exhausted, ventured to treat an historical subject of immediate interest, the Persian wars, in an epic entitled *Perseïs.* According to one account, the poem was read in the schools with Homer. The few fragments that remain show that it did not lack talent and merit; but little regard was paid to it by posterity. Ed. by Näke (Leipzig, 1817).

(3) Of Iasos in Caria. This Choerilus was also an epic poet, who accompanied Alexander the Great. Alexander promised him a gold-piece for every good verse he wrote in celebration of his achievements, but declared that he would rather be the Thersites of Homer than the Achilles of Choerilus. Cf. Hor. *A. P.* 357.

Choes (χόες). See DIONYSIA.

Chonia (Χωνία). The name in early times of a district in the south of Italy, inhabited by the Chones, an Oenotrian people. Chonia appears to have included the southeast of Lucania and the whole of the east of Bruttium as far as the promontory of Zephyrium.

Choragic Monument of Lysicrătes. See CHOREGUS.

Chorasmii (Χωράσμιοι). A people of Sogdiana, who inhabited the banks and islands of the lower course of the Oxus. They were a branch of the Sacae or Massagetae.

Choraules (χοραύλης). See CHORUS; TIBICEN.

Choregia (χορηγία). See CHOREGUS.

Chorēgus (χορηγός); in Latin, **Chorāgus.** The person who supplied a properly trained chorus.

(1) GREEK. The maintenance of a *choregia* (χορηγία) was one of the regularly recurring state burdens (ἐγκύκλιοι λειτουργίαι) at Athens. Originally the chorus consisted of all the inhabitants in the State. With the improvement of the arts of music and dancing, the distinction of spectators and performers arose; it became more a matter of art to sing and dance in the chorus; paid performers were employed; and at last the duties of this branch of worship devolved upon one person, selected by the State to be their representative, who defrayed all the expenses which were incurred on the different occasions. This person was the choregus. It was the duty of the managers of a tribe (ἐπιμεληταὶ φυλῆς) to which a *choregia* had come round, to provide a person to perform the duties of it; and the person appointed by them had to meet the expenses of the chorus in all plays, tragic or comic (τραγῳδοῖς, κωμῳδοῖς) and satirical; and of the lyric choruses of men and boys, the *pyrrhichistae*, cyclian dancers, and flute-players (χορηγεῖν ἀνδράσι, or ἀνδρικοῖς χοροῖς, παιδικοῖς χοροῖς, πυρριχισταῖς, κυκλίῳ χορῷ, αὐληταῖς ἀνδράσιν), etc. He had first to collect his chorus, and then to procure a teacher (χοροδιδάσκαλος), whom he paid for instructing the *choreutae.* The choregi drew lots for the first choice of teachers; for as their credit depended upon the success of their chorus in the dramatic or lyric contests, it was of great importance to them whose assistance they secured. When the chorus was composed of boys,

the choregus was occasionally allowed to press children for it, in case their parents were refractory. The chorus were generally maintained, during the period of their instruction, at the expense of the choregus, and he had also to provide such meat and drink as would contribute to strengthen the voice of the singers. The expenses of the different choruses are given by Lysias as follows: Chorus of men, 20 minae; with the tripod, 50 minae; pyrrhic chorus, 8 minae; pyrrhic chorus of boys, 7 minae; tragic chorus, 30 minae; comic, 16 minae; cyclian chorus, 300 minae. According to Demosthenes, the chorus of flute-players cost a great deal more than the tragic chorus. The choregus who exhibited the best musical or theatrical entertainment received as a prize a tripod, which he had the expense of consecrating, and sometimes he had also to build the monument on which it was placed. There was a whole street at Athens formed by the line of these tripod-temples, and called "The Street of the Tripods." A well-preserved specimen is the Choragic Monument of one Lysicrates, shown in the illustration. The laws of Solon prescribed forty as the proper age for the choregus, but this law was not long in force. See CHORUS.

Choragic Monument of Lysicrates.

(2) ROMAN. The choragus among the Romans (Plaut. *Trin.* iv. 2, 16) was a lender of costumes and properties, and to him the aediles used to give a contract for supplying the necessary accessories for a play. In Plautus (*Curc.* iv. 1), the choragus delivers a sort of parabasis. Under the Empire the *procurator summi choragii*, appointed probably by Domitian, was a regular imperial minister, with a great many subordinates, and had charge of the whole supply of decoration, machinery, and costume necessary for the performance of the various shows as well in the amphitheatre as in the theatre. A subdivision of this office was the *ratio ornamentorum*, which had special reference to the "make-up" of the actors. Under Gordian we find the name had vanished. Apuleius (*Apol.* i. 13) had spoken of the *choragium thymelicum;* but the functionary called *logista thymelae* now took the place of the *procurator summi choragii.* In the fourth century, at Rome the *praefectus urbi,* in the East the *praefectus praetorio,* and in Africa the *proconsul* looked after the games. In the fifth century, at Rome, Milan, and Carthage, we find this done by *tribuni voluptatum.*

Chorizontes (χωρίζοντες). "Separators." A name given to such of the ancient scholars and critics as held the belief that the *Iliad* and *Odyssey* of Homer were written by different authors. The names of only two of these critics—Xenon and Hellanicus—have come down to us. See HOMERUS.

Chorobătes (χωροβάτης). An instrument for determining the slope of an aqueduct and the levels of the country through which it was to pass. From the description given of it by Vitruvius, it appears to have differed but very slightly from a common carpenter's level, which consists of a straight rule supporting a perpendicular piece, against which hangs a plumb-line. The *chorobates* had two perpendiculars and plumb-lines, one at each end, instead of a single one in the middle (Vitruv. viii. 5, 1).

Chorus (χορός). The word χορός in GREEK meant a number of persons who performed songs and dances at religious festivals. When the drama at Athens was developed from the dithyrambic choruses, the chorus was retained as the chief element in the Dionysiac festival. With the old dramatists the choral songs and dances much preponderated over the action proper. As the form of the drama developed, the sphere of the chorus was gradually limited, so that it took the comparatively subordinate position which it occupies in the extant tragedies and comedies. The function of the chorus represented by its leader was to act as an ideal public, more or less connected with the *dramatis personae.* It might consist of old men and women or of maidens. It took an interest in the occurrences of the drama, watched the action with quiet sympathy, and sometimes interfered—if not to act, at least to advise, comfort, exhort, or give warning. At the critical points of the action, it performed long lyrical pieces with suitable action of dance and gesture. In the better times of the drama these songs stood in close connection with the action; but even in Euripides this connection is sometimes loose, and with the later tragedians, after the time of Agathon, the choral performance sank to a mere *intermezzo.* The style of the chorus was distinguished from that of the dialogue partly by its complex lyrical form, partly by its language, in which it adopted a mixture of Attic and Doric forms. The proper place of the chorus was on the orchestra, on different parts of which, after a solemn march, it remained until the end of the piece, drawn up, while standing, in a square. During the action it seldom left the orchestra to reappear, and it was quite exceptional for it to appear on the stage. As the performance went on, the chorus would change its place on the orchestra; as the piece required, it would divide into semi-choruses and perform a variety of artistic movements and dances. The name ἐμμέλεια was given to the tragic dance, which, though not lacking in animation, had a solemn and measured character. The comedy had its burlesque and often indecent performance called κόρδαξ; the satyric drama its Σίκιννις, representing the wanton movements of satyrs. The songs of the choruses, too, had their special names. The first ode performed by the entire body was called πάροδος; the pieces intervening between the parts of the play, στάσιμα; the songs of mourning, in which the chorus took part with the actors, κομμοί. The number of the members (χορευταί) was, in tragedies, originally twelve, and after Sophocles fifteen. This was probably the number allowed in the satyric drama; the chorus in the Old Comedy numbered twenty-four.

The business of getting the members of the chorus together, paying them, maintaining them during the time of practice, and generally equipping them for performance, was regarded as a λειτουργία, or public service, and devolved on a wealthy private citizen called a χορηγός, to whom it was a matter of considerable trouble and expense. We know from individual instances that the cost of a tragic chorus might run up to thirty minae (about $540), of a comic chorus to sixteen minae (about $265). If victorious, the *choregus* received a crown and a finely wrought tripod. This he either dedicated, with an inscription, to some deity as a memorial of his triumph, or set up on a marble structure built for the purpose in the form of a temple, in a street named the Street of Tripods, from the number of these monuments which were erected there. One of these memorials, put up by a certain Lysicrates in B.C. 335, still remains. (See CHOREGUS.) After the Peloponnesian War, the prosperity of Athens declined so much that it was often difficult to find a sufficient number of *choregi* to supply the festivals. The State, therefore, had to take the business upon itself. But many choruses came to an end altogether. This was the case with the comic chorus in the later years of Aristophanes; and the poets of the Middle and New Comedy accordingly dropped the chorus. This explains the fact that there is no proper chorus in the Roman comedy, which is an imitation of the New Comedy of the Greeks. In their tragedies, however, imitated from Greek originals, the Romans retained the chorus, which, as the Roman theatre had no orchestra, was placed on the stage, and as a rule performed between the acts, but sometimes during the performance as well. See DRAMA; THEATRUM.

The ROMAN chorus, in fact, belonged especially to the *crepidatae*—i. e. the tragedies modelled on and derived from the Greek ones; but it also appears in the national tragedy of the Romans, the *praetextatae*. Even though Diomedes declares that the Roman comedy had no chorus, yet this is only true generally, for there is an undoubted chorus of fishermen in the *Rudens* of Plautus. It was probably the whole company of actors (*caterva, grex*), not a chorus, which said the "Plaudite" with which comedies end. There appear to have been choruses in the *pantomimus* and in the *pyrrhica* of the Empire. There was no fixed number of *choreutae*. As that part of the theatre which was the Greek orchestra was given up to the spectators at Rome, the chorus had to occupy the stage (Vitruv. v. 6, 2). The Roman chorus took more part in the action of the drama than did the Greek chorus (Hor. *Ars Poet.* 193). It was led by a *magister chori*, who had his place in the middle of the chorus, and so was called *mesochorus* (Plin. *Epist.* ii. 14, 6). The musical accompaniment was played by a *choraules* on a double flute. Between the acts the chorus (probably in tragedy) and the tibicen (in comedy) used to sing or play (Donatus, *Arg. ad Andriam*); and Horace (*Ars Poet.* 194) especially urges that the subject of the songs should be pertinent to the action of the drama. The chorus was composed of men who were professionals (*artifices*), and who were for the most part slaves. As the chorus of the Romans sometimes represented women, they must have worn masks. They were probably dressed after the manner of the Greeks, and the dresses appear to have been very splendid, as was the whole production of plays at the end of the Republic and during imperial times —e. g. purple chlamydes were wanted for a chorus of soldiers, as is told in a well-known story of Lucullus (Hor. *Epist.* i. 6, 40).

The literature on the subject of the chorus is very extensive. The most important works are: B. Arnold, art. "Chor" in Baumeister's *Denkmäler des klassischen Alterthums*, pp. 383–391; Sommerbrodt, *Scaenica*; Muff, *Die chorische Technik des Sophokles*; R. Arnoldt, *Die chorische Technik des Euripides*; F. Castets in Daremberg and Saglio, art. "Chorus"; A. Müller, *Die griechischen Bühnenalterthümer*. In the two last works full reference is made to the numerous works on the subject. See also O. Ribbeck, *Die römische Tragödie im Zeitalter der Republik*, 607, 631 foll.; and the articles COMOEDIA; DITHYRAMBUS; DRAMA; THEATRUM; TRAGOEDIA.

Chronium Mare. A name applied by the ancients to the Frozen Ocean. The Cimbri, according to Pliny (iv. 13), called it Morimarusa—i. e. "the dead sea."

Chronogram. A device of the Romans of the later Empire, by which in an inscription the letters that form the numerals to denote its date were written larger than the rest. See Hilton, *Chronograms* (1882).

Chronologia (χρονολογία). See CALENDARIUM.

Chrysa (Χρύσα). A city on the coast of the Troad, near Thebes, with a temple of Apollo Smintheus; celebrated by Homer.

Chrysanthĭus (Χρυσάνθιος). An eclectic philosopher of Sardis; made high-priest of Lydia by the emperor Julian, and supposed to possess a power of conversing with the gods and of predicting future events.

Chrysāor (Χρυσάωρ). Son of Poseidon and Medusa, brother of Pegasus, and father of the three-headed giant Geryon and Echidna by the ocean-nymph Callirrhoë.

Chrysaŏreus (Χρυσαορεύς, "Of the Golden-Sword"). A surname of Zeus, from his temple at Stratonicé in Caria. There was a political union of certain Carian States, which held its meetings here, under the name of Chrysaorium. These States had votes in proportion to the number of towns they possessed.

Chrysēis (Χρυσηΐς). Daughter of Chryses, priest of Apollo at Chrysé, and taken prisoner by Achilles at the capture of Lyrnessus or the Hypoplacian Thebes. In the distribution of the booty she was given to Agamemnon. Her father Chryses came to the camp of the Greeks to solicit her ransom, but was repulsed by Agamemnon with harsh words. Thereupon Apollo sent a plague into the camp of the Greeks, and Agamemnon was obliged to restore her to her father to appease the anger of the god. Her proper name was Astynomé. See ACHILLES; TROJAN WAR.

Chryselephantīna (sc. ἀγάλματα). This term, though resting on no better authority than that of the Scholiast on Aristophanes (*Eq.* 1169), is now customarily used to denote those gold and ivory statues which were the highest attainments of Greek plastic art.

The use of these costly materials seems to have been originally a development of the early art of wood-carving. The first artists who produced chryselephantine statues were pupils of Dipoenus and Scyllis, the Cretan "Daedalids." Though we hear of no such works by these masters themselves, they used ivory in conjunction with ebony (Pausan. ii. 22, 5); by gilding the wood, a quite common proceeding, the transition would be made. The appropriateness of the two materials would then suggest the restriction of the ivory to nude parts, of gold to drapery, etc., a core of wood still underlying the whole. Such, probably, were the works of Doryclidas, Theocles, Dontas, and other artists of the earlier portion of the sixth century B.C. We do not hear of many chryselephantine works of importance during the late archaic or transitional period. The construction of colossal figures, such as the Olympian Zeus and the Athenè Parthenos of Phidias, or the Argive Herè of Polycletus, can have had little in common with mere wood-carving. For these, of course, a most elaborate internal framework was necessary. See COLOSSUS.

Chrysendĕta (χρυσένδετα). Metal dishes (*lances*) used by the Romans for serving up food at table. Martial mentions them several times (ii. 43; ii. 53; vi. 94; xi. 30; xiv. 97) as in use by the wealthy, and specially notices mullet as being served upon them. The derivation of the word and the epithet *flava* applied to them by Martial render it probable that these dishes were made of silver, and were adorned (probably on the rim) with ornaments in relief, wrought in gold and attached by means of soldering or riveting.

Chryses (Χρύσης). See CHRYSEIS.

Chrysippus (Χρύσιππος). (1) A son of Pelops, carried off by Laius (Apollod. iii. 5, 6). This circumstance became a theme with many ancient writers, and hence the story assumed different shapes, according to the fancy of those who handled it. The death of Chrysippus was also related in different ways. According to the common account, he was slain by Atreus, at the instigation of his step-mother, Hippodamia. (Consult Heyne *ad loc.*). (2) A Stoic philosopher of Soli in Cilicia Campestris. He fixed his residence at Athens, and became a disciple of Cleanthes, the successor of Zeno. He was equally distinguished for natural abilities and industry, seldom suffering a day to elapse without writing 500 lines. He wrote several hundred volumes, of which three hundred were on logical subjects, but in all he borrowed largely from others. He maintained, with the Stoics in general, that the world was God, or a universal effusion of his spirit, and that the superior part of this spirit, which consisted in mind and reason, was the common nature of things, containing the whole and every part. Sometimes he speaks of God as the power of fate and the necessary chain of events; sometimes he calls him fire; and sometimes he deifies the fluid parts of nature, as water and air; and again, the earth, sun, moon, and stars, and the universe in which these are comprehended, and even those men who have obtained immortality. He was very fond of the figure *sorites* in arguing, which is hence called by Persius "the heap of Chrysippus." His discourses abounded more in curious subtleties and nice distinctions than in solid arguments. In disputation, in which he spent the greatest part of his life, he discovered a degree of promptitude and confidence which approached towards audacity. He often said to his preceptor, "Give me doctrines, and I will find arguments to support them." It was a singular proof of his haughty spirit that when a certain person asked him what preceptor he would advise him to choose for his son, he said, "Me; for if I thought any philosopher excelled me, I would myself become his pupil." With so much contempt did he look down upon the distinctions of rank that he would never, as other philosophers did, pay his court to princes or great men, by dedicating to them any of his writings. The vehemence and arrogance with which he supported his tenets created him many adversaries, particularly in the Academic and Epicurean sects. Even his friends of the Stoic School complained that, in the warmth of dispute, while he was attempting to load his adversary with the reproach of obscurity and absurdity, his own ingenuity often failed him, and he adopted such unusual and illogical modes of reasoning as gave his opponents great advantages over him. It was also a common practice with Chrysippus, at different times, to take the opposite sides of the same question, and thus furnish his antagonists with weapons which might easily be turned, as occasion offered, against himself. Carneades, who was one of his most able and skilful adversaries, frequently availed himself of this circumstance, and refuted Chrysippus by convicting him of inconsistency. Of his writings (he is said to have published 700 works in all) nothing remains, except a few extracts which are preserved in the works of Cicero, Plutarch, Seneca, and Aulus Gellius. These fragments were collected and edited by Petersen in 1827. He died in the 143d Olympiad, B.C. 208, at the age of eighty-three. A statue was erected to his memory by Ptolemy. See the account in Zeller's *Stoics, Epicureans, and Sceptics* (Eng. trans. London, 1870).

Chrysoaspĭdes. See ARGYRASPIDES.

Chrysocĕras. "The Golden Horn"; originally the promontory upon which the city of Constantinople (Byzantium) was built. See BYZANTIUM.

Chrysogŏnus, L. CORNELIUS. A favourite freedman of Sulla, and a man of profligate character. He was the false accuser of Sex. Roscius, whom Cicero defended, B.C. 80.

Chrysolōras, MANUEL. A Greek scholar who is commonly regarded as having been the first to reintroduce Greek literature into Italy, in the fourteenth century. A native of Constantinople, he was sent by the Greek emperor John Palaeologus to Italy and England, in order to seek aid against the Turks. This mission, which was about the year 1390–91, made Chrysoloras known to many influential Italians; so that when, in 1397, he made his home in Florence as a teacher of Greek, he was received with much consideration. Poggio Bracciolini, Leonardo Bruno, Filelfo, Guarino Guarini, and many other scholars whose names are associated with the Renaissance, were pupils of Chrysoloras, who later engaged in the public service under the popes Gregory XII. and John XXIII. By order of the latter, he attended the Council of Constance, where he died, April 15th, 1415. Two of his works have been printed: the Ἐρωτήματα, for some time the only Greek grammar used in Western Europe; and *Epistolae III. de Comparatione Veteris et Novae*

Romae. A number of others, however, still exist in MS. His son, IOHANNES CHRYSOLORAS, was also noted as a teacher of Greek.

Chrysopŏlis (Χρυσόπολις). Now Scutari; a fortified place on the Bosporus, opposite to Byzantium, at the spot where the Bosporus was generally crossed. It was originally the port of Chalcedon.

Chrysostŏmus (Χρυσόστομος) (St. John). An eminent Father of the Church, born of a noble family at Antioch, A.D. 347. His father's name was Secundus, and the surname of Chrysostom, or "golden mouth," obtained by the son, was given to him on account of his eloquence. He was bred to the bar, but quitted it for an ascetic life: first, with a monk on a mountain near Antioch, and then in a cave by himself. He remained in this retirement six years, when he returned to Antioch, and, being ordained, became so celebrated for his talents as a preacher that, on the death of Nectarius, patriarch of Constantinople, he was chosen to supply his place. On obtaining this preferment, which he very unwillingly accepted, he acted with great vigour and austerity in the reform of abuses, and exhibited all the mistaken notions of the day in regard to celibacy and the monastic life. He also persecuted the pagans and heretics with great zeal, and sought to extend his episcopal power with such unremitting ardour that he involved himself in a quarrel with Theophilus, bishop of Alexandria, who enjoyed the patronage of the empress Eudoxia; which quarrel ended in his formal deposition by a synod held at Chalcedon, A.D. 403. He was, however, so popular in Constantinople that a formidable insurrection ensued, and the empress herself interfered for his return. Towards the end of the same year, owing to his zeal relative to a statue of Eudoxia, placed near the great church, and causing a disturbance of public worship, all his troubles were renewed. If true, that in one of his sermons the empress was compared by him to Herodias, who asked the head of John in a charger, the anger of Eudoxia was not altogether unjustifiable. The consequence of her resentment was the assembling of another synod, and in A.D. 404 the patriarch was again deposed and sent into exile. The place of his banishment was Cucusus, a lonely town among the ridges of Mount Taurus, on the confines of Cappadocia and Cilicia. He sustained himself with much fortitude; but having, by means of his great influence and many adherents, procured the intercession of the Western emperor, Honorius, with his brother Arcadius, he was ordered to be removed still farther from the capital, and died on the journey at Comana in Pontus, A.D. 407, at the age of sixty. Opinion was much divided in regard to his merits for some time after his death, but at length his partisans prevailed, and thirty years from his decease he was removed from his place of interment as a saint, and his remains were met in procession by the emperor Theodosius II., on their removal from the place of his original interment to Constantinople. The Roman Church celebrates St. Chrysostom on the 27th of January; the Greek Church, on the 13th of November.

Chrysostom was a voluminous writer, but more eloquent than either learned or acute. Although falling short of Attic purity, his style is free, copious, and unaffected, and his diction often glowing and elevated. The numerous treatises or sermons by which he chiefly gained his reputation are very curious for the information they contain on the customs and manners of the times, as elicited by his declamation against prevailing vices and follies. The first entire Greek edition of the works of Chrysostom was that of Sir Henry Saville, at Eton, in 8 vols. folio (1613); but that of Montfaucon, Paris, with annotations and his life, 11 vols. folio (1718–38, reprinted by the Abbé Migne, Paris, 1863), is by far the most complete. Some of the homilies will be found translated in the Oxford *Library of the Fathers.* The reader is referred, also, to the work of Neander, translated by Stapleton (1838), and to Newman's *Historical Sketches* (1873); Stephens, *St. Chrysostom: His Life and Times* (1872); Thierry, *Chrysostom et l'Impératrice Eudoxie* (2d ed. 1874); and Busk, *Life and Times of St. Chrysostom* (1885).

Chrysothĕmis (Χρυσόθεμις). (1) A daughter of Agamemnon and Clytaemnestra. (2) A Cretan, who first obtained the poetical prize at the Pythian games.

Chrysus (χρυσοῦς). See AURUM.

Chthonia (Χθονία). (1) Daughter of Erechtheus of Athens, who was sacrificed by her father to gain the victory over the men of Eleusis. (See ERECHTHEUS.) (2) An epithet of Demeter (q. v.).

Chthonia (χθόνια). A festival celebrated at Hermioné in honour of Demeter, surnamed Chthonia. A description of it is given by Pausanias (ii. 35, § 4, etc.), and it is also mentioned by Aelian.

Chthonian Gods (θεοὶ χθόνιοι, from χθών, "the earth"). The deities who rule under the earth, or who are connected with the lower world, as Hades, Pluto, Persephoné, Demeter, Dionysus, Hecaté, and Hermes.

Chytra (χύτρα). An earthen vessel for common use, especially for cooking. It was ordinarily left unpainted, and hence all unprofitable labour was described by the proverb χύτραν ποικίλλειν, "to paint a chytra." A very remarkable use of these vessels of earthenware among the Greeks was to put infants into them to be exposed (Aristoph. *Ran.* 1188). Hence the exposure of children was called ἐγχυτρίζειν, and the miserable women who practised it, ἐγχυτρίστριαι.

Chytri (Χύτροι, "Feast of Pots"). The third day of the Anthesteria. See DIONYSIA.

Chytrŏpus (χυτρόπους). A stand, on which was often placed the χύτρα to be heated. See CHYTRA. The name is also given to a χύτρα with legs.

Chytropus. (Panofka.)

Cibălae. A town of Lower Pannonia, situated on the Savus, about fifty miles from Sirmium, and about one hundred from the confluence of the Savus and the Danube. It was famous for the defeat of Licinius by Constantine, A.D. 314, and was also the birthplace of Gratian.

Ciborium (κιβώριον). Properly the shell of the Egyptian bean-plant (*colocasia*), the bean itself being called κύαμος. These shells, and indeed the leaves, too, were made into drinking-cups, and were, no doubt, of the same shape as the original shell—broad at the top and becoming narrow towards the bottom. They were smooth and large

(Hor. *Od.* ii. 7, 22), and often were wrought in a costly manner (Athen. xi. 477 e). No certain specimen of one can be given. In ecclesiastical Latin, *ciborium* means the vessel used to hold the Host, or consecrated wafer, during mass.

Cibōtus (Κιβωτός). See Apamea.

Cibўra (Κίβυρα). (1) Magna; a great city of Phrygia Magna, on the borders of Caria, said to have been founded by the Lydians, but afterwards peopled by the Pisidians. Under its native princes, the city ruled over a large district called Cibyratis. In B.C. 83, it was added to the Roman Empire. It was celebrated for its manufactures, especially of iron. (2) Parva; a city of Pamphylia, on the borders of Cilicia.

Cicāda (τέττιξ). A species of insect, frequently mentioned by the classical writers. It is originally a caterpillar, then a chrysalis, and is converted into a fly late in the spring. Its song is much louder and shriller than that of the grasshopper. The ancient writers, and especially the poets, praise the sweetness of their song; and Plutarch says they were sacred to the Muses. According to Aelian, only the male cicada sings, and that in the hottest weather. This is confirmed by the discoveries of modern naturalists. The cicada is extremely common in the south of Italy. It is found also in the United States, being called in some parts "the harvest-fly," and in others, very erroneously, "the locust."

Cicĕro. (1) Marcus Tullius. The greatest of the Roman orators. He was born at Arpinum, the native place of Marius, B.C. 106, the same year which gave birth to Pompey the Great. His family was ancient, and of equestrian rank, but had never taken part in public affairs at Rome, though both his father and grandfather were persons of consideration in the part of Italy in which they resided. His father, being a man of cultivated mind, determined to educate his two sons, Marcus and Quintus, on an enlarged and liberal plan, and to fit them for the prospect of those public employments which his own weak state of health incapacitated him from seeking. Marcus, the elder of the two, soon displayed indications of a superior mind, and we are told that his school-fellows carried home such accounts of his extraordinary parts that their parents often visited the school for the sake of seeing a boy who gave so much promise of future eminence. One of his earliest masters was the poet Archias, whom he defended afterwards in his consular year; and under his instruction he attained such proficiency as to compose a poem, though yet a boy, on the fable of Glaucus, which had formed the subject of one of the tragedies of Aeschylus. Soon after he assumed the *toga virilis*, he was placed under the care of Scaevola, the celebrated lawyer, whom he introduces so beautifully in several of his philosophical dialogues; and in no long time he gained a thorough knowledge of the laws and political institutions of his country. This was about the period of the Social War; and, according to the Roman custom, which made it a necessary part of education to learn military science by actual service, Cicero took the opportunity of serving a campaign under the consul Pompeius Strabo, father of Pompey the Great. Returning to pursuits more congenial to his natural tastes, he commenced the study of philosophy under Philo the Academic. But his chief attention was reserved for oratory, to which he applied himself with the assistance of Molo, the ablest rhetorician of the day; while Diodotus the Stoic exercised him in the argumentative subtleties for which the disciples of Zeno were so celebrated. At the same time he declaimed daily in Greek and Latin with certain young noblemen, who were competitors in the same race for honours with himself.

Cicero was the first Roman who found his way to the highest dignities of the State with no other recommendation than his powers of eloquence and his merits as a civil magistrate. The first case of importance which he undertook was the defence of Roscius Amerinus, in which he distinguished himself by his courageous defence of his client, who had been accused of parricide by Chrysogonus, a favourite of Sulla's. This obliging him, however, according to Plutarch, to leave Rome from prudential motives, the power of Sulla being at that time paramount, he employed his time in travelling for two years under pretence of his health, which he tells us was as yet unequal to the exertion of pleading. At Athens he met with T. Pomponius Atticus, whom he had formerly known at school, and there renewed with him a friendship which lasted through life, in spite of the change of interests and estrangement of affection so commonly attendant on turbulent times. Here, too, he attended the lectures of Antiochus, who, under the name of an Academic, taught the dogmatic doctrines of Plato and the Stoics. Though Cicero at first evinced considerable dislike for his philosophical views, he seems afterwards to have adopted the sentiments of the Old Academy, which they much resembled, and not until late in life to have relapsed into the sceptical tenets of his earlier instructor Philo. See Philosophia.

After visiting the principal philosophers and rhetoricians of Asia, he returned at the age of thirty to Rome, so strengthened and improved both in bodily and mental powers that he soon eclipsed in speaking all his competitors for public favour. Such brilliant gifts speedily gained him the suffrage of the people; and being sent to Sicily as quaestor, at a time when the metropolis itself was visited with a scarcity of corn, he acquitted himself in that delicate situation with so much success as to supply the clamorous wants of the Romans without oppressing the province from which the provisions were raised. Returning thence with greater honours than had ever before been decreed to a Roman governor, he gained for himself still further the esteem of the Sicilians by undertaking his celebrated prosecution of Verres (q. v.) for his misgovernment of Sicily. Verres, though defended by the influence of the Metelli and the eloquence of Hortensius (q. v.), was driven in despair into voluntary exile. Five years after his quaestorship Cicero was elected aedile. Though possessed of only a moderate fortune, he nevertheless, with the good sense and taste which mark his character, was enabled, while holding this expensive office, to preserve in his domestic arrangements the dignity of a literary and public man, without any of the ostentation of magnificence which often distinguished the candidate for popular applause. After the customary interval of two years, he was returned at the head of the list as praetor, and now made his first appearance on the Rostra in support of the Manilian law. (See Lex Manilia.) About the same time, also, he defended Cluentius. At the expiration of his praetorship, he refused to accept a foreign province, the usual reward of that magistracy; but, having the consulship in view, and relying on his interest with Caesar and Pompey, he allowed nothing to divert him from that career of glory for which he now believed himself to be destined. Having succeeded at length in attaining to the high office of which he was in quest, he signalized his consulship by crushing the conspiracy of Lucius Catiline; and the Romans hailed him, on the discovery and overthrow of this nefarious plot, as the Father and Deliverer of his country. His consulate was succeeded by the return of Pompey from the East, and the establishment of the First Triumvirate; which, disappointing his hopes of political greatness, induced him to resume his forensic and literary occupations. From these he was called away, after an interval of four years, by the threatening measures of P. Clodius (q. v.), who at length succeeded in driving him into exile. This event, which, considering the circumstances connected with it, was one of the most glorious of his life, filled him with the utmost distress and despondency. Its history is as follows: Clodius, Cicero's bitter enemy, had caused a law to be renewed, declaring every one guilty of treason who ordered the execution of a Roman citizen before the people had condemned him. The blow was aimed against Cicero, on account of the punishment he had caused to be inflicted, by the authority of the Senate, upon the accomplices of Catiline. The illustrious exconsul put on mourning, and appeared in public, accompanied by the equites and many young patricians, demanding the protection of the people. Clodius, however, at the head of his armed adherents, insulted them repeatedly, and ventured even to besiege the Senate-house. Cicero, upon this, went into voluntary exile. His conduct, however, in this reverse of fortune, showed anything but the firmness of a man of fortitude. He wandered about Greece, bewailing his miserable condition, refusing the consolations which his friends attempted to administer, and shunning the public honours with which the Greek cities were eager to load him. He ultimately took refuge in Thessalonica with Plancus. Clodius, in the meantime, procured new decrees, in consequence of which Cicero's country-seats were torn down, and a temple of Libertas built on the site of his house at Rome. His wife and children were also exposed to ill-usage from his embittered persecutors. A favourable change, however, soon took place in the minds of his countrymen. The insolence of Clodius became insupportable to all. Pompey encouraged Cicero's friends to get him recalled to Rome, and the Senate also declared that it would not attend to any business until the decree which ordered his banishment was revoked. Through the zeal of the consul Lentulus, and at the proposition of several tribunes, the decree of recall passed the assembly of the people in the following year, in spite of a bloody tumult, in which Cicero's brother Quintus was dangerously wounded; and the orator returning to his native country after an absence of ten months, was received with every mark of honour. The Senate met him at the city gates, and his entry resembled a triumphal procession. The attacks of Clodius, though they could now do little harm, were immediately renewed, until Cicero was freed from the insults of this turbulent demagogue by the hand of Milo, whom he afterwards, in a public trial for the deed, unsuccessfully defended. (See MILO.) Five years after his return from exile he received the government of Cilicia, in consequence of Pompey's law, which obliged those senators of consular or praetorian rank, who had never held any foreign command, to divide the vacant provinces among them. Cicero conducted a war, while

Cicero. (Capitoline Museum.)

in this office, with good success against the plundering tribes of the mountain districts of Cilicia, and was greeted by his soldiers with the title of Imperator. He resigned his command, and returned to Italy about the close of the year 50, intending to prefer his claim to a triumph; but the troubles which were just then commencing between Caesar and Pompey prevented him from obtaining one. His return home was followed by earnest endeavours to reconcile Pompey with Caesar, and by very spirited behaviour when Caesar required his presence in the Senate. But this independent temper was only transient; and at no period of his public life did he display such miserable vacillation as at the opening of the Civil War. His conduct, in this respect, had been faulty enough before, for he then vacillated between the several members of the First Triumvirate, defending Vatinius in order to please Caesar, and his bitter political enemy Gabinius to ingratiate himself with Pompey. Now, however, we find him first accepting a commission from the Republic; then courting Caesar; next, on Pompey's sailing for Greece, resolving to follow him thither; presently determining to stand neutral; then bent on retiring to the Pompeians in Sicily; and when finally he had joined their camp in Greece, exhibiting such timidity and discontent as to draw from Pompey the bitter remark, *Cupio ad hostes Cicero transeat, ut nos timeat* (Macrob. *Sat.* ii. 3).

After the battle of Pharsalia (B.C. 48) and the flight of Pompey, he refused to take the command of some troops then under the orders of Cato, but returned to Italy, which was governed by Antony, the representative of Caesar. His return was attended with several unpleasant circumstances, until the conqueror wrote to him, and soon after received him in the most friendly spirit. Cicero now devoted himself entirely to literature and philosophy. The state of his private affairs, however, involved him in great embarrassment. A large sum, which he had advanced to Pompey, had impoverished him, and he was forced to stand indebted to Atticus for present assistance. These difficulties led him to a step which it has been customary to regard with great severity—the divorce of his wife Terentia, though he was then in his sixty-second year, and his marriage with his rich ward Publilia, who was of an age disproportionate to his own. Yet, in reviewing this proceeding, we must not adopt the modern standard of propriety, forgetful of the character of an age which reconciled actions even of moral turpitude with a reputation for honour and virtue. Terentia was a woman of a most imperious and violent temper, and had, besides, in no slight degree contributed to his present embarrassment by her extravagance in the management of his private affairs. By her he had had two children—a son born the year before his consulship, and a daughter, whose loss he was now fated to experience. To Tullia he was tenderly attached, not only from the excellence of her disposition, but from her love of polite literature; and her death now took from him, as he so pathetically laments to Sulpicius, the only comfort which the course of public events had left him. His distress was increased by the unfeeling conduct of Publilia, whom he soon divorced for testifying joy at the death of her step-daughter. It was on this occasion that he wrote the treatise *De Consolatione*, with a view to mitigate the anguish of his sufferings. His friends were assiduous in their attentions; and Caesar, who had treated him with the utmost kindness on his return from Egypt, signified the respect he bore his character by sending a letter of condolence from Spain, where the remains of the Pompeian party still engaged him. But no attentions, however considerate, could soften Cicero's vexation at seeing the country he had formerly saved by his exertions now subjected to the dominion of a single master. His speeches, indeed, for Marcellus and Ligarius exhibit traces of inconsistency; but for the most part he retired from public business, and gave himself up to the composition of those works which, while they mitigated his political sorrows, have secured his literary fame.

The assassination of Caesar, which took place in the following year (B.C. 44), once more brought him on the stage of public affairs. He hoped to regain great political influence; but Antony took Caesar's place, and all that was left Cicero to do was to compose those vigorous orations against him which are known by the name of Philippics, and are equally distinguished for eloquence and patriotism. His enmity towards Antony induced him to favour the young Octavianus, although the pretended moderation of the latter by no means deceived him. With him originated all the energetic resolutions of the Senate in favour of the war which the consuls and the young Caesar were conducting against Antony in the name of the Republic; and for a time the prospect seemed to brighten. At last, however, Octavianus having possessed himself of the consulship, and having formed the alliance with Antony and Lepidus known as the Second Triumvirate, Cicero became convinced that liberty was at an end. At Tusculum, whither he had retired with his brother and his nephew, he learned that Octavianus had basely deserted him, and that his name, at Antony's demand, had been added to the list of the proscribed. He repaired, in a state of indecision, to the sea-coast and embarked. Contrary winds, however, drove him back to the shore. At the request of his slaves he embarked a second time, but soon returned again to await his fate at his country-seat near Formiae. "I will die," said he, "in that country which I have so often saved." Here, then, he was disposed to remain and to meet his death; but his slaves, who were warmly attached to him, could not bear to see him thus sacrificed; and when the party of soldiers sent to murder him was advancing towards the villa, they almost used force to make him enter his litter, and to allow them to carry him once more on board of the vessel, which was still lying at Caieta. But, as they were bearing the litter towards the sea, they were overtaken in the walks of his own grounds by the soldiers who were in search of him, and who were headed by one Herennius, a centurion, and by C. Popilius Laenas. Popilius was a native of Picenum, and had, on a former occasion, been successfully defended by Cicero, when brought to trial for some offence before the courts at Rome. As the assistance of advocates was given gratuitously, the connection between them and their clients was esteemed very differently from what it is among us; and it was therefore an instance of peculiar atrocity that Popilius offered his services to Antony to murder his patron, from no other motive than the hope of gaining his favour by showing such readiness to destroy his greatest enemy. The slaves of Cicero, undismayed at the appearance of the soldiers, prepared to defend their master; but he refused to allow any blood to be shed on his account, and commanded them to set down the litter and await the issue in silence. He was obeyed; and when the soldiers came up he stretched out his head with perfect calmness, and submitted his neck to the sword of Popilius. He died in his sixty-third year, B.C. 43. When the murder was accomplished the soldiers cut off his two hands also, as the instruments with which he had written his Philippic orations; and the head and hands were carried to Rome, and exposed together at the Rostra. Men crowded to see the mournful sight, and testified by their tears the compassion and affection which his unworthy death, and his pure and amiable character, had so justly deserved.

On the whole, antiquity may be challenged to produce an individual so upright and so amiable as Cicero. None interest us more in their lives; none excite more painful emotions in their deaths. Others may be found of loftier and more heroic character, who awe and subdue the mind by the grandeur of their views or the intensity of their exertions; but Cicero wins our affections by the integrity of his public conduct, the purity of his private life, the generosity, placability, and kindness of his heart, the playfulness of his temper, and the warmth of his domestic attachments. In this respect his letters are invaluable. Here we see the man without disguise or affectation, especially in his letters to Atticus, to whom he unbosomed every thought, and talked with the same frankness as to himself. It must, however, be confessed that the publication of this same correspondence has laid open the defects of his political character. Everything seemed to point out Cicero as the fittest person of the day to be a mediator between contending factions. And yet, after the eventful period of his consulship, we see him resigning the high station in the Republic which he himself might have filled, to the younger Cato, who, with only half his abilities, little foresight, and no address, possessed that first requisite for a statesman, firmness. Cicero, on the contrary, was irresolute, timid, and inconsistent. He talked, indeed, largely of preserving a middle course, but he was continually vacillating from one to the other extreme; always too confident or too dejected; incorrigibly vain of success, yet meanly panegyrizing the government of a usurper. His foresight, sagacity, practical good sense, and singular tact in directing men's measures, were lost for want of that strength of mind which points them steadily to one object. He was never decided, and never took an important step without afterwards repenting of it. Nor can we account for the firmness and resolution of his consulate, unless we discriminate between the ease of resisting a party and that of balancing contending interests.

We may now consider Cicero as a public speaker and writer. The ORATIONS that he is known to have composed amount in all to 107, of which seventy-seven, either entire or in part, have been preserved. All those pronounced by him during the five years intervening between his election to the quaestorship and the aedileship have perished, except that for M. Tullius, the *exordium* and *narratio* of which were brought to light by the discoveries of Mai in the Ambrosian Library at Milan. From the same quarter have been obtained many other proofs of the eloquence of Cicero, among the most important of which are a large fragment of the oration for Scaurus, and detached portions of that delivered against Clodius for his profanation of the mysteries of the Bona Dea. Of all the lost orations, the two most regretted are that in defence of Cornelius, and the speech delivered by him in the Temple of Bellona in quelling the disturbance excited by the law of Otho. (See ROSCIA LEX.) This last is said to have been one of the most signal victories of eloquence over the turbulence of human passions, while to the former Cicero himself frequently alludes as among the most finished of his compositions. The oration for Marcellus is maintained by many to be a spurious performance. It would seem, however, after weighing all the arguments adduced by modern critics, that a part is actually genuine, but that much has been subsequently interpolated by some rhetorician or declaimer.

Of the RHETORICAL WORKS of Cicero, the most admired and finished is the dialogue *De Oratore*, of which Cicero himself highly approved, and which his friends were accustomed to regard as one of the finest of his productions. In the *Oratoriae Partitiones*, the subject is the art of arranging and distributing the parts of an oration so as to adapt them in the best manner to their proper end—that of moving and persuading an audience. In the dialogue on famous orators, entitled *Brutus*, he gives a short description of all who had ever flourished in Greece or Rome, with any considerable reputation for eloquence, down to his own time. It was intended as a fourth and supplemental book to the treatise *De Oratore*. The *Orator*, addressed to Brutus, and written at his solicitation, was intended to complete the two works just mentioned. It enlarges on the favourite topic of Cicero, which had already been partially discussed in the treatise *De Oratore*—the character of the perfect orator; and seeks to confirm his favourite proposition—that perfection in oratory requires an extensive acquaintance with every art. It is on the merits of this work in particular that Cicero, in a letter to a friend, asserts his perfect willingness that his reputation should be staked. The *Topica* is a compendium of the *Topica* of Aristotle. The treatise *De Optimo Genere Oratorum* was originally intended as a preface to a translation of the celebrated orations of Demosthenes and Aeschines *De Corona*. The work *De Inventione* was a youthful performance; and that addressed to Herennius, according to the best authorities, never proceeded from his pen. In all Cicero's rhetorical works, except, perhaps, the *Orator*, he professes to have digested the principles of the Aristotelian and Isocratic schools into one finished system, selecting what was best in each, and, as occasion might offer, adding remarks and precepts of his own. The subject is considered in three distinct lights, with reference to (1) the case, (2) the speaker, and (3) the speech. The case, as respects its nature, is definite or indefinite; with reference to the hearer, it is judicial, deliberative, or descriptive; as regards the opponent, the division is fourfold—according as the fact, its nature, its quality, or its propriety is called in question. The art of the speaker is directed to five points: the sources of persuasion (whether ethical, pathetic, or argumentative), arrangement, diction, memory, delivery. And the speech itself consists of six parts: introduction (or exordium), statement of the case, division of the subject, proof, refutation, and conclusion or peroration. Cicero's laudatory orations are among his happiest efforts. Nothing can exceed the taste and beauty of those for the Manilian law, for Marcellus, for Ligarius, for Archias, and the Ninth Philippic, which is principally in praise of Servius Sulpicius. But it is in judicial eloquence, particularly on subjects of a lively cast, as in his speeches for Caelius and Muraena and against Caecilius, that his talents are displayed to the best advantage. To both kinds his urbane and pleasant cast of mind imparts inexpressible grace and delicacy; historical allusions, philosophical sentiments, descriptions full of life and nature, and polite raillery, succeed each other in the most agreeable manner, without appearance of artifice or effort. Of this nature are his pictures of the confusion of the Catilinarian conspirators on detection (*In Cat.* iii. 3); of the death of Metellus (*Pro Cael.* 10); of Sulpicius undertaking the embassy to Antony (*Philipp.* ix. 3); the character he draws of Catiline (*Pro Cael.* 6); and his fine sketch of old Appius frowning on his degenerate descendant Clodia (ib. 6). But, by the formation of a style which adapts itself with singular felicity to every class of subjects, whether lofty or familiar, philosophical or forensic, Cicero answers more exactly to his own definition of a perfect orator (*Orat.* 29) than by his plausibility, pathos, and vivacity. Among many excellences possessed by Cicero's oratorical diction, the greatest is its suitability to the genius of the Latin language; though the diffuseness thence necessarily resulting has exposed it, both in his own days and since his time, to the criticisms of those who have affected to condemn its Asiatic character, in comparison with the simplicity of Attic writers and the strength of Demosthenes. Greek, however, is celebrated for copiousness in its vocabulary and perspicuity in its phrases, and its consequent facility of expressing the most novel or abstruse ideas with precision and elegance. Hence the Attic style of eloquence was plain and simple, because simplicity and plainness were not incompatible with clearness, energy, and harmony. But it was a singular want of judgment, an ignorance of the very principles of composition, which induced Brutus, Calvus, Sallust, and others, to imitate this terse and severe beauty in their own defective language, and even to pronounce the opposite kind of diction deficient in taste and purity. In Greek, indeed, the words fall, as it were, naturally into a distinct and harmonious order; and, from the exuberant richness of the materials, less is left to the ingenuity of the artist. But the Latin language is comparatively weak, scanty, and unmusical, and requires considerable skill and management to render it expressive and graceful. Simplicity in Latin is scarcely separable from baldness; and justly as Terence is celebrated for chaste and unadorned diction, yet even he, compared with Attic writers, is flat and heavy. Again, the perfection of strength is clearness united to brevity; and to this combination Latin is usually unequal. From the vagueness and uncertainty of meaning which characterize its separate words, to be perspicuous it must be full. What Livy and, much more Tacitus, have gained in energy, they have lost in perspicuity and elegance. Latin, in short, is not a philosophical language; not a language in which a deep thinker is likely to express himself with purity or neatness. Now Cicero rather made a language than a style, yet not so much by the invention as by the combination of words. Some terms, indeed, his philosophical subjects compelled him to coin, and these are often admirable—e. g. *qualitas, quantitas*=ποιότης, ποσότης; but his great art lies in the application of existing materials, in converting the very disadvantages of the language into beauties, in enriching it with circumlocutions and metaphors, in pruning it of harsh and uncouth expressions, and in systematizing the structure of a sentence. This is that *copia dicendi* which gained Cicero the high testimony of Caesar to his inventive powers, and which makes him the greatest master of composition the world has ever seen.

We come next to Cicero's PHILOSOPHICAL WRITINGS, after a brief enumeration of which we shall offer a few remarks on the character of his philosophy itself. The treatise *De Legibus* has reached us in an imperfect state, only three books remaining, and these disfigured by numerous chasms that cannot be supplied. It traces the philosophic principles of jurisprudence to their remotest sources, sets forth a body of laws conformable to Cicero's idea of a well-regulated State, and is supposed to have treated in the books that are lost of the executive power of magistrates and the rights of Roman citizens. The treatise *De Finibus Bonorum et Malorum* is written after the manner of Aristotle, and discusses the chief good and the chief evil (*summum bonum et summum malum*); in it Cicero explains the several opinions entertained on this subject by the philosophers of antiquity. The *Academicae Quaestiones* relates to the Academic philosophy, whose tenets Cicero himself had embraced. It is an account and defence of the doctrines of the Academy. In the *Tusculanae Disputationes*, five books are devoted to as many different questions of philosophy, bearing the most strongly on the practice of life, and involving topics the most essential to human happiness. The *Paradoxa* contains a defence of six paradoxes of the Stoics. The work *De Natura Deorum*, in three books, embraces a full examination of the various theories of heathen antiquity on the nature of the gods, to which the treatise *De Divinatione* may be regarded as a supplement. The essay *De Officiis*, on moral duties, has, not unaptly, been styled the heathen Whole Duty of Man; nor have the dialogues *De Senectute* and *De Amicitia* been incorrectly regarded as among the most highly finished and pleasing performances of which any language can boast. We have to lament the loss of the treatises *De Consolatione, De Gloria*, and the one entitled *Hortensius*, in which last Cicero undertook the defence of learning and philosophy, and left to his illustrious competitor the task of arraigning them. It was this book which first led St. Augustine to the study of Christian philosophy and the doctrines of Christianity. The treatise *De Republica* has been in part rescued from the destroying hand of time by the labours of Mai. Except the works *De Inventione* and *De Oratore*, this was the earliest of Cicero's literary productions. It was given to the world in B.C. 53, just before its author set out for his proconsular government in Cilicia. He was then in his fifty-third year. The object and spirit of the work were highly patriotic. He wished to bring the constitution back to its first principles by an impression expositive of its theory; to inflame his contemporaries with the love of virtue by pourtraying the character of their ancestors in its primeval purity and beauty; and while he was raising a monument to all future ages of what Rome had been, to inculcate upon his own times what it ought still to be. We know it to have been his original purpose to make it a very voluminous work; for he expressly tells his brother that it was to be extended to nine books. Ernesti thinks that they were all given to the world, although Cicero, in a letter to Atticus, on which that learned and suggestive scholar makes this very remark, speaks of them as his *six* pledges or sureties for his good behaviour

Cicero, as a philosopher, belongs, upon the whole, to the New Academy. It has been disputed whether he was really attached to this system, or had merely resorted to it as being the best adapted for furnishing him with oratorical arguments suited to all occasions. At first its adoption was subsidiary to his other plans. But, towards the conclusion of his life, when he no longer maintained the place he was wont to hold in the Senate or the Forum, and when philosophy formed the occupation "with which," to quote his own words, "life was just tolerable, and without which it would have been intolerable," he doubtless became convinced that the principles of the New Academy, illustrated as they had been by Carneades (q. v.) and Philo, formed the soundest system which had descended to mankind from the schools of Athens. The attachment, however, of Cicero to the Academic philosophy was free from the exclusive spirit of sectarianism, and hence it did not prevent his extracting from other systems what he found in them conformable to virtue and reason. His ethical principles, in particular, appear eclectic, having been in a great measure formed from the opinions of the Stoics. Of most of the Greek sects he speaks with respect and esteem. For the Epicureans alone he seems, notwithstanding his friendship for Atticus, to have entertained a decided aversion and contempt. The general purpose of Cicero's philosophical works was rather to give a history of the ancient philosophy, than dogmatically to inculcate opinions of his own. It was his great aim to explain to his fellow-citizens, in their own language, whatever the sages of Greece had taught on the most important subjects, in order to enlarge their minds and reform their morals.

In theoretical investigation, in the development of abstract ideas, and in the analysis of qualities and perceptions, Cicero can not be regarded as in any degree an inventor or a profound original thinker, and can not be ranked with Plato and Aristotle. His peculiar merit as a philosophical writer lay in his luminous and popular exposition of the leading principles and disputes of the ancient schools, and no works transmitted from antiquity present so concise and comprehensive a view of the opinions of the Greek philosophers. The most obvious peculiarity of Cicero's philosophical writings is their form of dialogue. The idea was borrowed from Plato and Xenophon; but the nature of Cicero's dialogue is as different from that of the two Athenians as was his object in writing. With them, the Socratic mode of argument could hardly be displayed in any other shape; whereas Cicero's aim was to excite interest, and he availed himself of this mode of composition for the life and variety, the ease, perspicuity, and vigour which it gave to his discussions. The majesty and splendour of his introductions, the eloquence with which both sides of a question are successively displayed, the clearness and terseness of his statements on abstract points, his exquisite allusions to the scene or time of the supposed conversation, his digressions in praise of philosophy, and, lastly, the melody and richness of his style, unite to throw a charm around these productions which has been felt in every age.

Cicero's EPISTULAE, nearly one thousand (864) in all, are comprised in thirty-six books, sixteen of which are addressed to Atticus, three to his brother Quintus, one to Brutus, and sixteen to his different friends; and they form a history of his life from his fortieth year. Among those addressed to his friends (*Ad Familiares*) some occur written to him by Brutus, Metellus, Plancus, Caelius, and others. For the preservation of this most valuable department of Cicero's writings we are indebted to Tiro, the author's freedman, though we possess at the present day only a part of those originally published. The most interesting by far are the letters to Atticus, for they not only throw great light on the history of the times, but also give us a full insight into the private character of Cicero himself, who was accustomed at all times to unbosom his thoughts most freely to this friend of his. The authenticity of the correspondence with Brutus has been disputed by modern scholars, but the general opinion is favourable to the genuineness of all but two (xvi. and xvii.).

His POETICAL and HISTORICAL WORKS have suffered a hard fate. The latter class, consisting of his commentary on his consulship and his history of his own times, are altogether lost. Of the former, which comprised the heroic poems *Alcyone*, *Marius*, and on his own consulate, translations of parts of Homer, Aeschylus, Sophocles, and Aratus, epigrams, etc., but little remains except some fragments of the *Phaenomena* and *Diosemeia* of Aratus. It may, however, be questioned whether literature has suffered much by this loss. We should refrain from speaking contemptuously of the poetic powers of one who possessed so much fancy, so much taste, and so fine an ear; but his poems were principally composed in his youth; and afterwards, when his powers were more mature, his occupations did not allow even his active mind the time necessary for polishing a language then still more rugged in verse than it was in prose. Hence we find that his own contemporaries criticised unfavourably his attempts in verse, a fact to which he himself bears witness; and such specimens as remain show the ante-classical fondness for alliterative jingle; as, for instance, the famous line which he quotes in his *De Officiis* (i. 77):

"Cedant arma togae, concedat laurea laudi,"

and the absurdly egotistical hexameter sneered at by Juvenal in his Tenth Satire:

"O fortunatam natam me consule Romam!"

His contemporary history, on the other hand, can hardly have conveyed more explicit, and certainly would have contained less faithful, information than his private correspondence; while, with all the penetration he assuredly possessed, it may be doubted if his diffuse and graceful style of thought and composition was adapted for the depth of reflection and condensation of meaning which are the chief excellences of historical composition.

MANUSCRIPTS.—The MSS. of Cicero are so numerous and so scattered over Europe as to preclude an exhaustive enumeration of them here. The Laurentian Library alone contains 188 codices, of which the oldest dates back to the tenth century. The Bibliothèque Nationale at Paris possesses 231, collected prior to the Revolution of 1789. Six of these date from the ninth century; 138 are of the fifteenth. The oldest collection of the letters *ad familiares* is the Codex Vercellensis (now the Codex Mediceus) of the ninth century. Petrarch, in 1345, discovered at Verona the letters to Brutus, Q. Cicero, and Atticus. The MS. found by Petrarch has again been lost, so that only a copy of it remains. Other important Ciceronian MSS. are as follows: of the fourteen Philippics, the Vatican-Basilican MS. of the ninth century; of the orations against Verres, the Vatican palimpsest of the fourth (?) century, and two Wolfenbüttel MSS. dependent upon a Paris codex of the ninth century; of the Catilinarian orations, the Ambrosian Codex of the tenth century, and the Munich MSS. of the eleventh century; of the oration for Archias, the Codex Bruxellensis (Brussels) of the eleventh century; of the oration on the Manilian law, the Codex Erfurtensis of the twelfth century; of the oration for Milo, the Munich MS. (18,787) and a palimpsest at Turin; of the treatises *De Oratore*, *Brutus*, and *Orator*, the Codex Laudensis (Lodi), or rather three copies of that codex made after 1422; of the *Partitiones Oratoriae*, a Paris MS. of the eleventh century (No. 7231); of the *Topica*, a codex at Leyden and two at St. Gall; of the treatise *De Optimo Genere Oratorum*, a MS. at St. Gall; of the philosophical works, the Codices Leidenses (Vossiani, 84 saec. x., and 86 saec. xi.), the Codex Laurentianus S. Marci (257) of the tenth century, and the Codex Vindobonensis (Vienna) of the tenth century. A collection of 600 excerpts from Cicero's philosophical writings, made by a certain Hadoardus in the ninth century, is in the Vatican. For the treatise *De Legibus*, the best MSS. are the Leyden codices (Vossiani, 84 saec. x., and 86 saec. xi.); for the *Paradoxa*, the same; for the *De Finibus*, the Palatino-Vaticanus of the eleventh century; for the *Academica*, the Codices Leidenses already mentioned; for the *Tusculanae Disputationes*, a MS. at Paris dating from the tenth century, and one at Brussels of the twelfth century; for the *Timaeus*, the Codices Leidenses; for the *De Natura Deorum*, the same; for the *Cato Maior*, a Codex Leidensis (Voss. F. 12, saec. x.); for the *De Divinatione*, the Palatino-Vaticanus noted above; for the *De Fato*, a codex at Vienna (189); for the *Laelius*, a MS. at Munich of the tenth century; for the *De Officiis*, a MS. at Bern of the tenth century, and one of the same age at Paris (6601).

EDITIONS.—The *editio princeps* of the entire works of Cicero was that by P. Victorius (Venice, 1534–37). A famous old edition is that of Lambinus (Paris, 1566); and those of Graevius, unfinished (Amsterdam, 1684), Ernesti (Leipzig, 1737, last ed. 1820), Orelli (Zürich, 1826–30), revised with Baiter and Halm (1845–62), Nobbe (Leipzig, 1850), are very often cited. More recent are the editions by Klotz, 11 vols. (Leipzig, 1863–71); revised by C. F. W. Müller, not yet completed (Leipzig, 1878–), and Baiter and Kayser, 11 vols. (Leipzig, 1861–69), with index.

Among special editions may be mentioned that of the orations with English notes by Long, 4 vols. (London, 1855–62); of the oration on the Manilian law by Wilkins (London, 1885); of the Second Philippic by J. E. B. Mayor (London, 1878), and by Gantrelle (Paris, 1882); of the Catilinarian orations by Halm (latest ed. Berlin, 1886); of the oration for Archias by J. S. Reid (Cambridge, 1884); of the oration for Balbus by Reid (Cambridge, 1879); of the oration for Plancius by Holden (London, 1881); of the oration for Milo by Purton (Cambridge, 1877). Special editions of the rhetorical works are those of the *De Oratore*, 3 vols., by Wilkins (London, 1893); of the *Orator* by Sandys (London, 1885); of the *Brutus* by Kellogg (Boston, 1889); and of the *Partitiones Oratoriae* by Piderit (Leipzig, 1867). A critical revision of Cicero's philosophical works is that of Schiche (Prague, 1884); and special editions of individual treatises are that of the *De Legibus* by Vahlen (Berlin, 1883); of the *De Finibus* by Reid (in preparation), and Langen (Münster, 1888); of the *Academica* by Reid (London, 1885); of the *Tusculanae* by Heine (Leipzig, 1881); of the *De Natura Deorum* by J. B. Mayor, 3 vols. (Cambridge, 1885); of the *Cato Maior* by Reid (Cambridge, 1883), revised by Kelsey (Boston, 1884); of the *De Officiis* by Holden (Cambridge, 1884), and by Stickney (N. Y. 1888). An excellent edition of the correspondence of Cicero, with notes and an introduction, is that by Tyrrell and Purser (London, 1886, foll.). Recent collections of the fragments of Cicero's writings are those of Baiter and Kayser (1868), and C. F. W. Müller (1879).

SPECIAL WORKS.—Orelli, *Onomasticum et Indices*, 3 vols. (1838); Ernesti, *Clavis Ciceroniana* (Halle, 1831); Schütz, *Lexicon Ciceronianum*, 4 vols. (1817); Nizolius, *Lexicon Ciceronianum*, 3 vols. (last ed. 1820); Merguet, *Lexikon zu Cicero's Reden* (1877–84); Suringar, *Ciceronis Annales*, 2 vols. (1854); Hirtzel, *Untersuchungen z. Cicero's philosoph. Schriften* (1877); Levin, *Lectures on the Philosophy of Cicero* (Cambridge, 1871); Davidson, *Life of Cicero* (1894); Middleton, *Life of Cicero* (1741); Brückner, *Leben Cicero's* (1852); Forsyth, *Life of Cicero* (1864); A. Trollope, *Life of Cicero* (1880); Boissier, *Cicéron et ses Amis* (4th ed. 1888). See also Mommsen, *History of Rome*, vol. iv., and against his well-known view, the defence of Cicero by Gerlach (Basel, 1864).

(2) MARCUS, only son of the orator, and the person to whom the latter addressed his work *De Officiis*. He took part in the civil contest at an early age, and served under both Pompey and Brutus. After the battle of Philippi he retired to Sicily and joined the younger Pompey. Subsequently, however, he took advantage of the act of amnesty that was passed, and returned to Italy, where he lived for some time in a private capacity. Augustus, on attaining to sovereign power, made him his colleague in the consulship, and it was to Marcus Cicero, in his quality of consul, that he wrote an account of the victory at Actium and the conquest of Egypt. Marcus had the satisfaction of executing the decree which ordered all the statues and monuments that had been erected to Antony to be thrown down. After his consulship he was appointed governor of Syria, from which period history is silent respecting him. He died at an advanced age, and was notorious for dissipated and intemperate habits.

(3) QUINTUS, brother of the orator, and brother-in-law of Atticus. After having been praetor in B.C. 62, he obtained the government of Asia. He was subsequently a lieutenant of Caesar's in Britain, and only left that commander to accompany his brother, Marcus Tullius, as lieutenant, into Cilicia. After the battle of Pharsalia, in which he took part on the side of Pompey, he was proscribed by the triumvirate and put to death by the emissaries of Antony. He had a marked talent for poetry, and had planned a poem on the invasion of Britain by Caesar. He also composed several tragedies, imitated or else translated from the Greek, but which have not reached us. Eighteen lines of his are preserved in *Q. Ciceronis Reliquiae*, edited by Bücheler (Leipzig, 1869). He was perhaps the author of the piece *Commentariolum Petitionis*, usually printed along with Cicero's letters to him. It is addressed by Quintus to his brother when the latter was a candidate for the consulship, and gives advice with regard to the best means to acquire general popularity. There is an edition of this work by Eussner (Würzburg, 1872). On the authorship of the work see Hendrickson in the *Amer. Journal of Philology* for 1892, pp. 200–212.

Cicŏnes (Κίκονες). A Thracian people on the Hebrus, and near the coast of the Aegean.

Ciconia. (1) A word meaning literally "a stork," but also applied to a mimic gesture expressive of ridicule or contempt, produced by bending the forefinger into the form of a stork's neck, and pointing it towards the person ridiculed with a rapid motion of the two top joints up and down (Pers. i. 58, with the commentators; Hieron. *Epist.* 125, 18). (2) A contrivance employed by farmers to test a labourer's work in spade husbandry, and prove if all his trenches were dug to a uniform and proper width and depth. It consisted of an upright, with a cross-bar affixed to it, at right angles, like the letter T inverted, so that the long branch measured the depth, and the two shorter arms the width and evenness of the trench (Colum. iii. 13, 11).

Cicynna (Κίκυννα). A deme of Attica.

Cidăris (κίδαρις). See TIARA.

Cilicia (Κιλικία). A district in the southeast of Asia Minor, bounded by the Mediterranean on the south, Mount Amanus on the east, and Mount Taurus on the north. The western part of Cilicia is intersected by the offshoots of the Taurus, while in its eastern part the mountain chains inclose much larger tracts of level country; and hence arose the division of the country into Cilicia Aspera or Trachea, and Cilicia Campestris—the latter being also called Cilicia Propria. The first inhabitants of the country are supposed to have been of the Syrian race. The mythical story derived their name from Cilix, the son of Agenor, who started with his brothers, Cadmus and Phoenix, for Europe, but stopped short on the coast of Asia Minor, and peopled with his followers the plain of Cilicia. The country remained independent till the time of the Persian Empire, under which it formed a satrapy, but it appears to have been still governed by its native princes. Alexander subdued it on his march into Upper Asia, and after the division of his empire it formed a part of the kingdom of the Seleucidae. Its plains were settled by Greeks, and the old inhabitants were for the most part driven back into the mountains of Cilicia Aspera, where they remained virtually independent, practicing robbery by land and piracy by sea, till Pompey drove them from the sea in his war against the pirates; and, having rescued the level country from the power of Tigranes, who had overrun it, he erected it into a Roman province, B.C. 67–66. The mountain country was not made a province till the reign of Vespasian. The Cilicians bore a low character among the Greeks and Romans; so that the Carians (Κᾶρες), Cappadocians (Καππάδοκες), and Cilicians (Κίλικες) were called the "three bad K's" (τρία κάππα κάκιστα).

Ciliciae Pylae (αἱ Πύλαι τῆς Κιλικίας) or **Portae**. The chief pass between Cappadocia and Cilicia, through the Taurus, on the road from Tyana to Tarsus.

Cilicium (δέρρις). A haircloth. The material of which the Greeks and Romans almost universally made this kind of cloth was the hair of goats. The Asiatics made it of camel's-hair. Goats were bred for this purpose in Cilicia; and from this country the Latin name of the cloth was derived. Lycia, Phrygia, Spain, and Libya also produced the same article. The cloth obtained by spinning and weaving goat's-hair was nearly black, and was used for the coarse dress which sailors and fishermen wore, as it was the least likely to be destroyed by being wet; also for horse-cloths, tents, sacks, and bags to hold workmen's tools (*fabrilia vasa*), and for the purpose of covering military engines, and the walls and towers of besieged cities, so as to deaden the force of the ram (see ARIES), and to preserve the woodwork from being set on fire.

Among the Orientals, sackcloth, which was with them always haircloth, was worn to express mortification and grief. After the decline of the Roman power, it passed from its other uses to be so employed in Europe also. Monks and anchorites almost universally adopted the cilicium as fit to be worn for the sake of humiliation, and they supposed their end to be more completely attained if this part of their raiment was never washed.

Cilicium Maré (ἡ Κιλικία Θάλασσα). The northeastern portion of the Mediterranean, between Cilicia and Cyprus, as far as the Gulf of Issus.

Cilix (Κίλιξ). See CILICIA.

Cilla (Κίλλα). A small town in the Troad, celebrated for its temple of Apollo, surnamed Cillaeus.

Cillĭba (κιλλίβας, *cillibantium*). (1) In Greece, a trestle or stand for anything, especially for a shield (Aristoph. *Ach.* 1122). (2) In Rome, a dining-table, at first square (Varr. *L. L.* v. 118), and then round.

Cilnii. A powerful Etruscan family in Arretium, driven out of their native town in B.C. 301, but restored by the Romans. The Cilnii were nobles or Lucumones in their State, and some of them in ancient times may have held even the kingly dignity. The name has been rendered chiefly memorable by C. Cilnius Maecenas. See MAECENAS.

Cimber, L. TILLIUS. A friend of Caesar, receiving from him the province of Bithynia, but subsequently one of his murderers, B.C. 44.

Cimbri (Κίμβροι). A Keltic people, probably of the same race as the Cymry. (See CELTAE.) They appear to have inhabited the peninsula which was called after them Chersonesus Cimbrica (Jutland). In conjunction with the Teutones and Ambrones, they migrated south, with their wives and children, towards the close of the second century B.C.; and the whole host is said to have contained 300,000 fighting men. They defeated several Roman armies, and caused the greatest alarm at Rome. In B.C. 113, they routed the consul Papirius Carbo near Noreia, and then crossed over into Gaul, which they ravaged in all directions. In 109, they defeated the consul Iunius Silanus; and in 107, the consul Cassius Longinus, who fell in the battle; and in 105, they gained their most brilliant victory, near the Rhone, over the united armies of the consul Cn. Mallius and the proconsul Servilius Caepio. Instead of crossing the Alps, the Cimbri, fortunately for Rome, marched into Spain, where they remained two or three years. The Romans, meantime, had been making preparations to resist their formidable foes, and had placed their troops under the command of Marius. The barbarians returned to Gaul in 102. In that year the Teutones were defeated and cut to pieces by Marius near Aquae Sextiae (Aix) in Gaul; and next year (101) the Cimbri and their allies were likewise destroyed by Marius and Catulus, in the decisive battle of the Campi Raudii, near Verona, in the north of Italy. See Pullmann, *Die Cimbern* (1870).

Cimĭnus or **Ciminius Mons**. A range of mountains in Etruria, thickly covered with wood (Saltus Ciminius, Silva Ciminia), near a lake of the same name, northwest of Tarquinii.

Cimmerii (Κιμμέριοι). The name of a mythical and of a historical people. The mythical Cimmerii, mentioned by Homer, dwelt in the farthest West on the ocean, enveloped in constant mists and darkness. Later writers sought to localize them, and accordingly placed them either in Italy, near the lake Avernus, or in Spain, or in the Tauric Cherso-

nesus. The historical Cimmerii dwelt on the Palus Maeotis (Sea of Azov), in the Tauric Chersonesus, and in Asiatic Sarmatia. Driven from their abodes by the Scythians, they passed into Asia Minor on the northeast, and penetrated west as far as Aeolis and Ionia. They took Sardis, B.C. 635, in the reign of Ardys, king of Lydia; but they were expelled from Asia by Alyattes, the grandson of Ardys, about B.C. 600.

Cimmerius Bospŏrus (Κιμμέριος Βόσπορος). See BOSPORUS.

Cimōlus (Κίμωλος). An island in the Aegean Sea, one of the Cyclades, between Siphnos and Melos, celebrated for its fine white earth, used by fullers for cleaning cloths. See CRETA; FULLO.

Cimon (Κίμων). (1) The son of Miltiades and of Hegesipylé, the daughter of Olorus, a Thracian prince. His education, according to Plutarch, was very much neglected, and he himself indulged, at first, in every species of excess. At his father's death he seems to have succeeded to a very scanty fortune, and he would perhaps have found it very difficult to pay the fine of fifty talents which had been imposed upon his parent, and which the son was bound to pay to the public treasury, had not Callias, one of the wealthiest men of Athens, struck by the charms of his half-sister Elpinicé, undertaken to discharge the sum as the price of her hand. (See ELPINICÉ.) Cimon, however, had attracted notice and gained reputation by the spirit which he displayed on the occasion of leaving the city on the approach of the Persians, when he was the foremost to hang up a bridle in the Acropolis, as a sign that he placed all his hopes in the fleet; and also by the valour with which he fought at Salamis. Aristides, in particular, saw in him a fit coadjutor to himself and antagonist to Themistocles, and exerted himself in his favour; and the readiness with which the allied Greeks, when disgusted by the arrogance of Pausanias, united themselves with Athens, was owing in a great measure to Cimon's mild temper and to his frank and gentle manners. The popularity of Themistocles was already declining, while Cimon, by a series of successful enterprises, was rapidly rising in public favour. He defeated the Persians in Thrace, on the banks of the Strymon, took Eion, and made himself master of the whole country. He conquered the island of Scyros, the inhabitants of which were addicted to piracy; and brought thence to Athens what were deemed the bones of the national hero Theseus. He next subdued all the cities on the coast of Asia Minor, and went against the Persian fleet which lay at the mouth of the Eurymedon. The Persians, although superior in number, did not dare to abide an engagement, but sailed up the river to place themselves under the protection of their land forces. Cimon, however, provoked them to a battle, and, having defeated and sunk or taken two hundred ships, landed his men, flushed with victory, and completely routed the Persian army. Returning to Athens after these two victories thus achieved in a single day, he employed the perquisites of his command, and the resources which he had acquired from his successes over the barbarians, in the embellishment of his native city and in relieving the wants of the indigent. He laid a part of the foundations of the Long Walls with magnificent solidity at his own cost, and the southern wall of the citadel was built with the treasures which he brought from Asia into the coffers of the State. He also set the example of adorning the public places of the city with trees; and, by introducing a stream of water, converted the Academy, a spot about two miles north of the city, from an arid waste into a delightful grove. (See ACADEMIA.) He threw down the fences of his fields and orchards, that all who wished might enter and partake of their fruits. He not only gave the usual entertainments expected from the rich to the members of his own borough, but kept a table constantly open for them. He never appeared in public without a number of persons attending him in good apparel, who, when they met with any elderly citizen scantily clothed, would insist on exchanging their warm mantles for his threadbare covering. It was the office of the same persons respectfully to approach any of the poorer citizens of good character whom they might see standing in the market-place, and silently to put some small pieces of money into their hands. This latter kind of expenditure was certainly of a mischievous tendency; and was not the less that of a demagogue because Cimon sought popularity not merely for his own sake, but for that of his order and his party.

About B.C. 466, Cimon was sent to the Thracian Chersonesus, of which the Persians still kept possession, and having driven them out, next reduced the island of Thasus, and took possession of the Thasian gold mines on the neighbouring continent. Scarcely, however, had he returned to Attica, when an accusation was preferred against him of having been corrupted by the king of Macedonia, because he had refrained, not, according to the common account, from attacking the Macedonians then at peace with Athens, but from striking a blow at the Thracian tribes on the frontier of that kingdom, who had recently cut off the Athenian settlers on the banks of the Strymon. (See AMPHIPOLIS.) From this accusation Cimon had a very narrow escape. Having been sent, however, after this, with a body of troops to aid the Spartans before Ithomé, and the latter having, after some interval, sent back their Athenian allies, whom they suspected of not lending them any effectual assistance, the irritation produced by this national insult fell principally upon Cimon, who was known to be an admirer of the Spartan character and constitution, and he was accordingly driven into exile. Subsequent events, however, made the Athenians feel the want of this able commander, and he was recalled and sent on an expedition against Egypt and Cyprus; but was carried off by illness, or the consequences of a wound, in the harbour of Citium, which place he was besieging (B.C. 449). His spirit, however, still animated his countrymen; for the fleet, when sailing home with his remains, gained a naval victory over a large squadron of Phœnician and Cilician galleys near the Cyprian Salamis, and followed up this victory by another which they gained on shore, either over the troops which had landed from the enemy's ships, or over a land force by which they were supported.

Cimon was, beyond dispute, the ablest and most successful general of his day; and his victories shed a lustre on the arms of Athens which almost dimmed the glories of Marathon and Salamis.

(2) A famous painter, a native of Cleonae, who flourished about B.C. 460. He is said to have been the first to paint in perspective. See PICTURA.

Cinaethon (Κιναίθων). One of the most prolific of the Cyclic poets. See CYCLICI POETAE; HOMERUS.

Cinăra (Κινάρα). A small island in the Aegean Sea, east of Naxos, celebrated for its artichokes (κινάραι).

Cincia Lex. See LEX.

Cincinnātus, L. QUINCTIUS. A Roman patrician, whose name belongs to the earlier history of the Republic, and has a well-known and spirit-stirring legend connected with it. His son, Caeso Quinctius, had been banished on account of his violent language towards the tribunes, and the father had retired to his own patrimony, aloof from popular tumults. The successes of the Aequi and Volsci in B.C. 458 rendered the appointment of a dictator necessary, and Cincinnatus was chosen to that high office. The delegates who were sent to announce this to him found the Roman noble ploughing his own fields, and from the plough he was transferred to the highest magistracy of his native State. The dictator laid aside his rural habiliments, assumed the ensigns of absolute power, levied a new army, marched all night to bring the necessary succour to the consul Minucius, who was surrounded by the enemy and blockaded in his camp, and before morning surrounded the enemy's army, and reduced it to a condition exactly similar to that in which the Romans had been placed. The baffled Aequi were glad to submit to the victor's terms; and Cincinnatus, thereupon returning in triumph to Rome, laid down his dictatorial power, after having held it only fourteen days, and returned to his farm. At an advanced age he was again appointed dictator, to restrain the power of Spurius Maelius (q. v.), and again proved himself the deliverer of his country (Val. Max. iv. 4, 7; Liv. iii. 26).

Cincinnus (ἕλιξ). A ringlet of hair. See COMA.

Cincius Alimentus. See ALIMENTUS.

Cinctus (διάζωμα, περίζωμα). A sort of kilt reaching to the knees, worn by men, instead of the tunic, while working (Varr. *L. L.* v. 114).

Cinctus Gabīnus. See TOGA.

Cineas (Κινέας). A Thessalian, a minister and friend of Pyrrhus, and employed by the latter on many embassies. He had been a pupil of Demosthenes, and possessed considerable talent as an orator. Having been sent by Pyrrhus to Rome with proposals of peace, he compared the Senate, on his return, to an assembly of kings, and a war with the Romans to a contest with another Lernaean hydra. He died about B.C. 276. See PYRRHUS.

Cinerarium. A niche in a tomb, adapted for the reception of a large cinerary urn, or a sarcophagus, as contradistinguished from *columbarium* (q. v.), which was of smaller dimensions, and only formed to receive a pair of jars (*ollae*) (Inscript. *ap.* Grut. 850, 10). The illustration, which represents one side of a sepulchral chamber, as it appeared when first excavated, presents an arrangement similar to that set forth by the preceding inscription, with two *columbaria* at the bottom, over which are the same number of cinerary niches for urns, and a larger one in the centre (*cinerarium medianum*), with its sarcophagus. See SEPULCRUM.

Cinerarium. (Rich.)

Cinerarius. See CALAMISTRUM.

Cinĕres. See FUNUS; SEPULCRUM.

Cinesias (Κινησίας). A dithyrambic poet of Athens who was ridiculed by Aristophanes and other writers of comedy, in revenge for which he succeeded in securing the abolition of the *choregia* for comedy. See CHOREGUS.

Cinga. The modern Cinca; a river in Hispania Tarraconensis, falling with the Sicoris into the Iberus.

Cingetŏrix. A Gaul, one of the first men in the city of the Treviri (Trèves, Trier), who attached himself to the Romans, though son-in-law to Indutiomarus (q. v.), the head of the independent party.

Cingŭlum. See BALTEUS; ZONA.

Cingŭlum. A town in Picenum on a rock, built by Labienus shortly before the breaking out of the Civil War, B.C. 49. It is now Cingolo.

Cinĭflo. A slave who aided in dressing a lady's hair. The name is given from the *cinis* or powder employed for tinting the hair a light auburn (Serv. *ad* Verg. *Aen.* xii. 611). See COMA.

Cinna. (1) L. CORNELIUS. An adherent of Marius, who played a conspicuous part in the civil war between that leader and Sulla. Having attained to the consulship, after the proscription of Marius by his opponent, he began to exert himself for the recall of the former, and accused Sulla, who was just going as proconsul to Asia, of maladministration. That commander, however, took no notice of the complaint. After the departure of Sulla, he brought forward once more the law of Sulpicius, which admitted the Italians into all the thirty-five tribes without distinction. A savage riot ensued, numbers were slain, and Cinna, with his chief partisans, was driven from the city by his colleague Octavius. The Italian towns, regarding the cause of Cinna as their own, received him with the utmost cordiality. He collected thirty legions, called the proscribed to his support, and, with Marius, Sertorius, and Carbo, marched upon and took possession of Rome. A scene of bloodshed and lawless rapine now ensued, which has perhaps no parallel in ancient or modern times, and has deservedly procured for those who were the actors in it the unmitigated abhorrence of posterity. Cinna and Marius, by their own authority, now declared themselves consuls for the ensuing year; but Marius dying, after having held that office for only seventeen days, Cinna remained in effect the absolute master of Rome. During the space of three years after this victory of his, he continued to hold possession of the government at home, a period during which, as Cicero remarks, the Republic was without laws and without dignity. At length, however, Sulla, after terminating the war with Mithridates, prepared to march home with his army and punish his opponents. Cinna, with his colleague Carbo, resolved thereupon to cross the Adriatic, and anticipate Sulla by attacking him in Greece; but a mutiny of their troops ensued, in which Cinna was slain, B.C. 77. Haughty, violent, always eager for vengeance, addicted to debauchery, precipitate in his plans, but always displaying courage in their execution, Cinna attained to a power little less absolute than that afterwards held by Sulla or Caesar; and it is somewhat remarkable that he should be so little known that scarcely a single personal anecdote of him is to be found on record. (2) One of the conspirators against Caesar (Plut. *Caes.*). (3) GAIUS HELVIUS. A Roman poet, intimate with Caesar, and tribune of the people at the time when the latter was assassinated. According to Plutarch, he went to attend the obsequies of Caesar, but being mistaken by the populace for Cinna the conspirator, was torn to pieces by them. Helvius composed a poem entitled *Smyrna* (or *Zmyrna*), on which he was employed nine or ten years. Four fragments of it have reached us. It appears to have been characterized by considerable obscurity of meaning until the grammarian Crassicius wrote an able commentary upon it (Suet. *Gram.* 18). Some other fragments have also reached us of other productions of this poet. They may be found in L. Müller's edition of Catullus (1870).

Cinnămus, IOANNES (Ἰωάννης Κίνναμος). One of the best known of the Byzantine historians who flourished about A.D. 1150. He wrote the life of the emperor Manuel Comnenus and of his father in six books, still extant. Ed. by Meineke (Bonn, 1836).

Cinyps (Κίνυψ). The modern Wad-Khakan or Kinifo; a small river on the northern coast of Africa, between the Syrtes, and forming the eastern boundary of the proper territory of the African Tripolis. The district about it was called by the same name, and was famous for its fine-haired goats. The Roman poets use the adjective Cinyphius in the general sense of Libycus or Africus.

Cinўras (Κινύρας). Supposed, in the Greek mythology, to have been king of Cyprus, the oldest priest of Aphroditê in Paphos, the founder of that city, and the ancestor of the priestly family of the Cinyradae. His wealth and long life, bestowed upon him by Aphroditê, were proverbial; and from Apollo, who was said to be his father, he received the gift of song. He was accounted the founder of the ancient hymns sung at the services of the Paphian Aphroditê and of Adonis. Consequently he was reckoned among the oldest singers and musicians, his name, perhaps, being Phœnician, derived from *kinnor*, "a harp." The story added that he was the father of Adonis (q. v.) by his own daughter Myrrha, and that, when made aware of the sin, he took away his own life.

Cippus. (1) Originally the trunk of a tree with its branches lopped off, left standing in the ground as a stump, or else stuck in the ground. The cippus was sometimes sharpened to a point, and thus used in fortification as a sort of *chevaux-de-frise* (Caes. *B. G.* vii. 73). (2) A low column of stone, sometimes round, but oftener rectangular, and used (*a*) as a mark of the division of land by the *agrimensores* (q. v.); and (*b*) as a sepulchral monument, many of these having been exhumed. The illustration here given shows a cippus contained in the Townley collection in the British Museum, and erected to the memory of one Viria Primitiva.

On several cippi are found the letters S. T. T. L.; that is, *Sit tibi terra levis*, whence Persius says, *Non levior cippus nunc imprimit ossa* (*Sat.* i. 37).

It was also usual to place at one corner of the burying-ground a cippus, on which the extent of

Sepulchral Cippus. (British Museum.)

the burying-ground was marked, along the road (*in fronte*), and backward to the fields (*in agrum*) (Hor. *Sat.* i. 8, 12, 13). See SEPULCRUM.

Cippus or **Cipus**, GENUCIUS. A Roman praetor, on whose head horns suddenly sprouted as he was leaving the city. The haruspices declared this portent to indicate that if he re-entered Rome he would be made king, to avert which he imposed perpetual exile on himself (Ovid, *Met.* xv. 565; Val. Max. v. 6, 3).

Circé (Κίρκη). The sister of Aeëtes, king of Colchis, and daughter of the Sun and Persé, or Perseïs, one of the ocean-nymphs. Circé is celebrated for her skill in magic arts, and for her knowledge of subtle poisons. According to Homer (*Od.* x. 135 foll.), she dwelt in an island (Aeaea), attended by four nymphs, and all persons who approached her dwelling were first feasted, and then, on tasting the contents of her magic cup, converted into beasts. When Odysseus had been thrown on her shores, he deputed some of his companions to explore the country; these, incautiously partaking of the banquet set before them, were, by the effect of the enchanted potion, transformed into swine. When Odysseus himself, on hearing of their misfortune from Eurylochus, set out to release them or share their fate, he was met by Hermes, who gave him a plant named *moly* (μῶλυ), potent against her magic, and directed him how to act. Accordingly when she handed him the medicated cup, he drank of it freely; and Circé, thinking it had produced its usual effect, striking him with her wand, bade him go join his comrades in their sty. But Odysseus, drawing his sword, threatened to slay her; and the terrified goddess bound herself by a solemn oath to do him no injury. She afterwards, at his desire, restored his companions to their pristine form, and they all abode in her dwelling for an entire year. Circé is said to have had by Odysseus a son named Telegonus (q. v.), who afterwards unwittingly slew his own father in Ithaca, whither he had wandered in search of him. See ODYSSEUS.

Later writers took great liberties with the narratives of Homer and Hesiod. Thus, for example, Dionysius, the Cyclic poet, makes Circé the daughter of Aeëtes by Hecatê, the daughter of his brother Perses. He goes on to say that she was married to the king of the Sarmatians, whom she poisoned and seized his kingdom; but, governing tyrannically, she was expelled, and then fled to a desert isle of the ocean, or, as some said, to the headland named from her in Italy. (See CIRCEII.) The Latin writers thence took occasion to connect Circé with their own scanty mythology. See Cic. *N. D.* iii. 19, 48; and the article SCYLLA.

Circeii. An ancient town of Latium on the promontory Circeum (Κιρκεῖον), said by the Roman poets to have been the abode of Circé (q. v.). Its oysters were highly esteemed by the Romans (Juv. iv. 140).

Circesium (Κιρκήσιον). A city of Mesopotamia on the east bank of the Euphrates, at the mouth of the Aborrhas. It marked the extreme eastern limit of the Roman Empire.

Circīnus (καρκίνος, διαβήτης). A compass. The compass used by statuaries, architects, masons, and carpenters is often represented on the tombs of such artificers, together with the other instruments of their profession or trade. The annexed illustration exhibits two kinds of compasses, viz., the common kind used for drawing circles and

Circini. (Gruter, *Corp. Inscript.*)

measuring distances, and one with curved legs, probably intended to measure the thickness of columns, cylindrical pieces of wood, or similar objects. The common kind is described by the scholiast on Aristophanes, who compares its form with that of the letter A. The mythologists supposed this instrument to have been invented by Perdix, who was the nephew of Daedalus, and, through envy, thrown by him over the precipice of the Athenian Acropolis (Ovid, *Met.* viii. 251). Compasses of various forms were discovered in a statuary's house at Pompeii.

Circitōres, Circuitōres (περίπολοι). Horsemen who made the rounds in the Roman camp, and inspected the sentry posts. Four of these inspectors, who were selected for this duty every day, according to a regular cycle, received from the tribune written instructions as to the time when they were to visit each post, and the number of posts to be visited. After receiving their orders, they went and posted themselves by the first maniple of the *triarii*, the centurion of which was required to see that the hours of the watch were properly given by the sound of the trumpet; then, when the time came, the *circuitor* of the first watch proceeded on his rounds to all the posts; if he found the guards awake and on duty, he took their tablets; if he found them asleep, or any one absent from his post, he called upon the friends who accompanied him to witness the fact, and so passed on to the next post. The same was done by the *circuitores* of the other watches. The next morning, all the inspectors appeared before the tribunes, and presented the tablets they had received; any guard whose tablet was not produced was required to account for it. If the fault lay with the *circuitor*, he was liable to a stoning, which was generally fatal. See CASTRA.

Circius. A strong wind blowing in the southern part of Gaul from the northwest. See Aul. Gell. ii. 22.

Circulātor. The Roman name for any strolling juggler or mountebank who made his living by feats of magic or by the exhibition of trained animals (Petron. 68).

Circulator. (From a Terra-cotta Lamp.)

Circumlitio. See PICTURA.

Circumluvio. Alluvial land.

Circus (κίρκος). A building used by the Romans for chariot races and other amusements, the general form of which was borrowed from the ἱππόδρομος of the Greeks. (See HIPPODROMUS.) Its name is derived from the circuit made by the racing chariots (Varr. *L. L.* v. 153).

The Circus Maximus in Rome was for a long time the only building of the kind, and appears to have been the model from which all later *circi* were copied. Vitruvius does not mention the circus in his treatise on Roman architecture. According to the legend, Romulus held the Consualia, or games in honour of the Latin deity Consus (see CONSUALIA), in the Vallis Murcia, a long, narrow depression between the Palatine and Aventine hills. It was during the celebration of these games that the rape of the Sabine women is said to have taken place (Val. Max. ii. 4). The long, level bottom and sloping sides of the Vallis Murcia made it a naturally convenient place for races to be held and seen by a crowd of spectators, who probably stood or sat on the grassy slopes of the two hills long before any architectural structure was erected. See Ovid, *A. A.* i. 107.

Wooden seats (*fori*) for the people are said to have been first constructed by Tarquinius Priscus (Liv. i. 35), and these were frequently burnt and rebuilt in the same material: restorations in B.C. 327 and B.C. 174 are mentioned by Livy (viii. 20, and xli. 27). In the time of Iulius Caesar some of the seats were for the first time constructed of stone, but even then and many years later the upper tiers and galleries were still of wood. Very serious accidents are recorded to have happened under many of the emperors, owing to the failure of the wooden seats when crowded with people. No less than 1000 persons are said to have been killed in this way during the reign of Antoninus Pius. Dionysius (iii. 68), who describes the Circus Maximus as it was after Iulius Caesar's improvements, says that it then held 150,000 people. A destructive fire in B.C. 31 was followed by important restorations, and Augustus added a magnificent marble *pulvinar* or imperial box, and placed in the centre of the *spina* the Egyptian obelisk which now stands in the Piazza del Popolo (Suet. *Aug.* 43–45). In A.D. 36, another fire destroyed the upper tiers of seats on the Aventine side, and a great part of the Circus was soon restored and enlarged by Claudius, who rebuilt in white marble the *carceres*, which were then of tufa, and replaced the old wooden *metae* by new ones of gilt bronze (Suet. *Claud.* 21). After this restoration the Circus contained seats, partly of marble and partly of wood, for 250,000 spectators, showing that it had been much enlarged since the rebuilding of Iulius Caesar (Plin. *H. N.* xxxvi. § 102). In the reign of Domitian the marble seats were carried still higher, and thenceforth the danger of fire was much diminished, though wooden galleries (*maeniana*) appear to have existed at the top of the *cavea* for many years later.

Great additional splendour was given to the Circus Maximus by Trajan, as is recorded on the reverse of some of his first brasses; and from his time the building must have been among the most magnificent structures of the Roman world. The whole *cavea* with its tiers of seats, the *carceres*, the emperor's *pulvinar*, and the central *spina* were then of gleaming white marble, decorated with gold and colours, studded with jewel-like glass mosaics, and adorned with long lines of columns made of richly-tinted Oriental marbles and rows of large statues in marble and gilt bronze, together with costly metal screens and richly sculptured thrones for officials of rank (Plin. *Paneg.* 51). Still further accommodation was added by Constantine; and Constantius set on the *spina* a second obelisk, which his father had transported from Thebes (Aurel. Vict. *Caes.* 40), and which now stands in the piazza of the Lateran. After this final enlargement the Circus held, according to the *Notitia*, the almost incredible number of 385,000 people. The best MS. of the *Notitia* gives 485,000 as the number of possible spectators in the Circus, which probably includes the crowds of people outside the Circus on the upper slopes of the two hills, who would have a distinct though distant view of the whole arena. It is impossible to discover with absolute accuracy what the size of the Circus Maximus was when complete; it cannot, however, have been less than 2000 feet long, by more than 600 feet wide, measuring outside.

In spite of its enormous size very little now remains of the Circus Maximus; but the excavations of recent years have brought to light some very interesting portions of the substructures; and these, with the help of some drawings made in the sixteenth century, when a considerable portion of the Circus was still very complete, enable us to form a fairly accurate notion of its plan and general construction. Additional help is given by the well-preserved remains of the Circus of Maxentius, of which a plan is given on the following page. Though quite different in ground-plan, yet in the arrangement of the seats and in its external façade the Circus once closely resembled the Colosseum (q. v.), except that the general effect must have been much more splendid, since in the Circus nothing but marble and gilt bronze was visible. Part of the exterior façade of the Circus is fortunately shown in the great oil-painting in the museum at Mantua, giving a bird's-eye view of Rome as it was in the fifteenth century. A fac-simile of this is shown in De Rossi's *Piante di Roma anteriori al XVI*^mo^ *Secolo* (Rome, 1879). See also Middleton, *Anc. Rome in 1885*, p. 287, and fig. 10 on p. 83; id. *Remains of Anc. Rome* (London, 1892), vol. ii. pp. 40–60; and the article Roma. There is an interesting etching of the sixteenth century which shows a large portion (now destroyed) of the concrete vaults which supported the long line of the *cavea* seats. Excavations made a few years ago at the foot of the southwestern slope of the Palatine have exposed a long series of chambers, which formed part of the immense substructures of the Circus. These chambers were used for brothels (Juv. iii. 65), for refreshment stalls (Dionys. vii. 72), and other purposes. They open upon a road, paved with flint blocks, which appears to have run at the foot of the Palatine along the whole northeastern side of the Circus, and led from the Forum Boarium to the Porta Capena.

Circus Maximus. (Restoration by Benvenuti.)

Owing to their lofty positions, the palace of Augustus and the other imperial buildings on the Palatine must have commanded a very complete view of the races in the Circus; and some of the emperors built special additions to their palaces to enable them to see the games without leaving their residences (Suet. *Calig.* 18). See Palatium.

Arrangements of the Circus.—The drawing of the Circus of Maxentius given on the next page will serve to give an idea of the arrangements of the Circus Maximus, from which it was copied.

According to Livy, the Roman senators from a very early period had the privilege of special seats at the Circus. Augustus arranged a complete classification of the spectators. He reserved the *podium* for the Senate and persons of high rank, and allotted special seats to soldiers, married plebeians, boys and their *paedagogi*, women, etc. (See Suet. *Aug.* 44; *Nero*, 11; and the *Mon. Ancyranum*, ed. Mommsen, Berlin, 1883.) Until

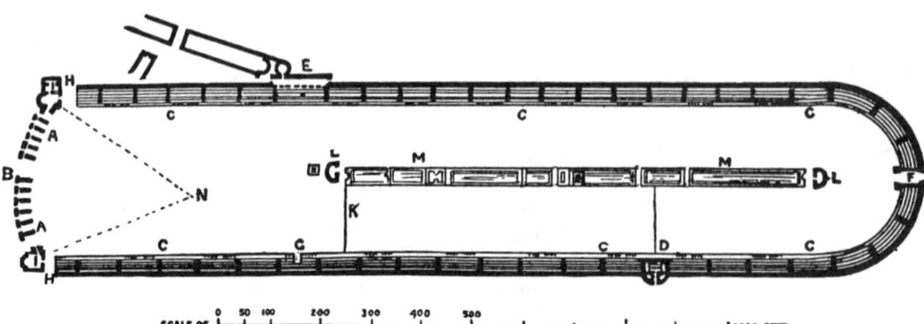

Plan of the Circus of Maxentius.

AA. Carceres.
B. Porta Pompae, entrance in centre of the carceres.
CC. Gradus, seats of the spectators.
D. Tribunal Iudicum.
E. Pulvinar, seat of the emperor.
F. Porta Triumphalis.
HH. Entrances between the carceres and gradus.
II. Towers.
K. Alba linea, starting line.
LL. Metae.
MM. Spinae.
N. (See p. 353.)

this classification, the fact that men and women sat together in the Circus had been one of its peculiarities as a place of amusement—a fact often alluded to by Ovid. Cushions (*pulvini*) were used, especially by ladies, on the hard marble seats, and footstools (*scabella*) were sometimes introduced, though each *gradus* was so low—only thirteen to fourteen inches high—that these can have been of but little use. See Ovid, *A. A.* i. 160–162.

A large number of interesting inscriptions have been found at different times, which throw much light on the way in which the seats were apportioned in the *circi* and amphitheatres of Rome. (See Lanciani, *Inscriz. d. Anfit. Flav.*, Rome, 1884.) The *cavea* was divided into bands called *maeniana* by the horizontal passages, *ambulacra* or *praecinctiones;* there were probably three of these divisions or *maeniana* in the Circus Maximus, without counting the gallery at the top. The lowest of these divisions was called *maenianum primum*, and the highest was called *summum;* each of these bands of seats was also divided by flights of steps into *cunei*, which were numbered; each line of seats (*gradus*) in each *cuneus* was also numbered; and as there were no divisions to separate one place from the next, each *gradus* was measured, and allotment was made to various classes of a fixed number of feet measured from one end. Thus, for example, the space allotted to a *collegium* of priests might be described as follows: "In the first *maenianum*, in the twelfth *cuneus*, nine feet of *gradi* 4 and 5."

In addition to the *cavea* proper and its *podium*, various state boxes were constructed of marble, with columns and arches to support the entablature and roof of each. One series of these (*cubicula* or *suggestus*) was over the *carceres*, and appears to have been occupied by the giver of the games (*editor spectaculorum*) and his friends. Another elevated box (the *tribunal iudicum*, D) was placed at one side for the umpires, who decided which chariot first crossed the line chalked on the arena in front of them. See Henzen, *Acta Fratrum Arval*, p. 37 (Berlin, 1874).

A separate *pulvinar* or state box (E) for the imperial family, of great size and magnificence, was erected on the Palatine side of the Circus Maximus (Suet. *Claud.* 4). An interesting relief of the third century A.D., found at Foligno, represents the presiding magistrate or *editor* of the games seated in his box over the *carceres;* he holds in his hand a bag of money, which he is about to give to the winning charioteer, who has driven up and is saluting him from below. A similar scene is represented on several of the ivory consular diptychs of the fourth and fifth centuries. (See Gori, *Thesaur. Vet. Dipt.*, Florence, 1759). The chief of these is the celebrated leaf of a fourth century diptych in the Museo Quiriniano at Brescia. On this the presiding consul sits in his *pulvinar;* in the arena below four *quadrigae* are racing round the *spina*, which, like that on the Lyons mosaic, is a long tank of water. The way in which the reins were looped round the body of the driver (*auriga*) is clearly shown; each holds in his hand what seems to be a combination of whip and goad; and they all wear *fasciae* round their legs and bodies. The horses' legs are also closely bound about with thongs. See Fröhner, *La Verrerie Antique* (Paris, 1879).

On the ivories the consul, or other president of the games, is usually represented in the *pulvinar*, magnificently robed in the *toga picta* and *pallium*, and in some cases holding in his hand the *mappa* or napkin with which he gave the signal for the start.

The starting end of the Circus was formed by a row of small vaulted chambers (*carceres*, A A), each large enough for one chariot and its horses. Of these *carceres* there were at the most twelve. Each had two doors—one behind, by which the chariot entered, and one in front, opening into the arena. This latter doorway was closed by folding doors, with open work (*cancelli*) in the panels. These doors were thrown open at the start by slaves (*tentores*), two to each doorway (as in the accompanying illustration), who flung them open simultaneously at the signal. In early times the races appear to have begun at the *carceres;* but later, the actual start took place at a line marked on the arena with white chalk or lime (*alba linea*), and hence sometimes called *creta* or *calx* (K). A similar white line for the finish was drawn opposite the judge's box (D), at a point unequally distant

Doors of Carceres opened by Slaves. (Museo Borgiano, Velletri.)

from the two *metae*. The starting-line was drawn opposite the *metae* that were nearest the *carceres*. The *carceres* received no light except what came

Doors of Carceres. (British Museum.)

through the grating. Their narrow openings are called *fauces*. The lofty state-boxes above the *carceres*, with their colonnades and arches, towered to an imposing height, and the whole structure was known as the *oppidum*, from its resemblance to the gate and towers of a city (Varr. *L. L.* v. 153).

A brass of Caracalla shows the external façade of the *oppidum*, and a sort of bird's-eye view beyond of the interior of the Circus, with its *spina*, central obelisk, and *aediculae*, and statues in *quadrigae* set at the top of the wall surrounding the *cavea*. It will be seen from the typical plan given above that the *carceres* (A A) are slightly curved on plan, and are constructed on a segmental line, the centre of which is struck from a point midway (N) between the line of the *spina* and the side of the *cavea*. This plan was adopted in order that the chariots in all the *carceres* might have as nearly as possible a position of equal advantage at the start. The special *carcer* occupied by each chariot was fixed on by drawing lots.

The *spina* (back-bone) was a long, low wall, or rather platform, of marble (M M), set in the middle of the arena to separate the going and returning course of the racers. The line of the *spina* is not parallel to that of the *cavea*, but is slightly inclined so as to leave a wider space at K than that near the semicircular end. The object of this seems to have been that the chariots might have more space where they were crowded together at the start than at other points where some would have begun to tail off.

Various mosaics and reliefs show the *spina* (M M) covered with a series of statues and ornamental structures, such as obelisks, small *aediculae* or shrines, columns surmounted by statues, altars, trophies, and fountains. In addition to these were two sets of seven marble eggs (*ova*) at each end of the *spina*—each set mounted on a small *aedicula*, to which access was given by a ladder. One of these eggs was removed after each lap (*curriculum*) was run (Varr. *Re Rust.* i. 2, 11), there being usually seven laps to each race (*missus*). According to Livy (xli. 27), these *ova* were first set on the *spina* by the censors in B.C. 174; but Dio Cassius attributes their introduction to Agrippa, in the reign of Augustus. He is, however, probably confusing them with another series of ornaments—seven dolphins, which were set on a similar *aedicula* and served a similar purpose (Juv. vi. 590). These dolphins must have been too heavy to take down, and were probably merely moved in some way to indicate the number of laps.

In some ancient representations, as in a mosaic found at Lyons and figured on page 355, the dolphins form fountains—water spouting from the mouth of each fish. This shows that they could not have been wholly removed. The eggs had some sacred connection with the Dioscuri, and the dolphins with Neptune (or Consus)—deities who were the patrons of horses and racing (Tertull. *De Spect.* 8). The Lyons mosaic, which no doubt represents the local circus, has what appears to have been a common form of *spina*, consisting of a long tank of water instead of the marble *podium*; statues and other ornaments stand on pedestals in the water. Two sarcophagi in the Sala della Biga in the Vatican have reliefs which represent a chariot-race of Cupids in the Circus Maximus, and show clearly the *spina* and its ornaments, among which are statues of Apollo Helios, Cybelé, Victory, a quadriga, and an obelisk, as well as the eggs and dolphins. The *metae* are shown at each end; a similar relief is given in the illustration above.

Metae. (Relief in the British Museum.)

The *metae* (L L), the goals, were three tall, conical objects (Ovid, *Met.* x. 106; Hor. *Carm.* i. 1, 5) set on a semicircular plinth, at a short distance from each end of the *spina*. From the time of Claudius, they were of gilt bronze decorated with bands in relief, as is shown in the above illustration from a relief in the British Museum. These formed the turning-points for the chariots. The *primae metae* are not, as might be expected, the ones nearest to the start, but those near the semicircular end of the Circus, round which the

Race in the Circus, showing the Spina, with the Dolphins, Obelisk, and Ova. (Ancient relief in the Vatican.)

chariots made their *first* turn. Tertullian (*De Spect.* v. 8) mentions that the ancient altar of Consus in the Circus Maximus was *ad primas metas;* it appears to have been in the *spina*, and was only exposed to view during the progress of the games.

Remains of the *spina*, stripped of all its rich marble decorations, exist in the Circus of Maxentius, at Vienne in France (*Bull. Inst.* 1861, p. 143), and in the circus of Carthage (Falbe, *L'Emplacement de Carthage*, p. 40).

The arena, or sandy floor of the Circus, like that of the Colosseum, was on some occasions strewn with glittering particles of mica, red lead, or perfumes, by the ostentatious extravagance of the emperors (Suet. *Cal.* 18). That part of the arena which formed the course for the chariots was known as the *spatium* (Juv. vi. 582). The space near the *carceres* was known as the *circus primus*, while that on each side of the *spina* was the *circus interior* (Varr. *L. L.* v. 154).

Before the construction of amphitheatres in Rome, the Circus Maximus was used for gladiatorial fights with wild beasts and other scenes of butchery. The Ancyraean inscription records that Augustus had no less than 3500 wild beasts slaughtered in the Circus, Forum, and amphitheatre, in twenty-six exhibitions.

In order to keep the beasts from reaching the spectators on the *cavea*, Iulius Caesar constructed a canal (*euripus*) ten feet wide and ten feet deep all round the arena; this was supplied by a stream which still runs through the site of the Circus, near the modern Via de' Cerchi (Suet. *Iul.* 39). After the erection of the amphitheatre of Statilius Taurus in the reign of Augustus, the Circus Maximus appears to have been no longer used for fights with beasts, and the *euripus* was therefore filled up by Nero (Plin. *H. N.* viii. § 21). It was, however, again introduced in later times (Lamprid. *Heliog.* 23).

OTHER CIRCI AT ROME.—Few remains of other *circi* exist to-day above ground at Rome. The important edifices of this sort were as follows:

(1) The Circus Flaminius which gave its name to the Campus Flaminius, an important part of the Campus Martius (q. v.). It was founded in honour of the censor C. Flaminius Nepos, killed at the battle of Lake Trasimenus, B.C. 217.

(2) The Circus of Caligula and Nero in the Horti Agrippinae, at the foot of the Vatican Hill (Suet. *Claud.* 21). No traces of this circus are visible at the present time.

(3) The Circus of Hadrian in the Campus Vaticanus, near the emperor's Mausoleum. No traces of it now remain.

(4) The Circus of Maxentius on the Via Appia, two miles from the walls of Rome, is sufficiently well preserved to show its original form, though it is completely stripped of its marble seats, columns, and other rich decorations. Till 1825 it was thought to be a circus built by Caracalla, but three inscriptions which were then found showed that it was dedicated in A.D. 311 to the memory of Romulus, who died in A.D. 309, by his father Maxentius. The plan of this circus is shown on page 352; the greater part of the external wall is still standing, but the concrete vaults which supported the seats have mostly fallen in.

(5) The Circus of Sallust, called after the historian.

THE CIRCUS GAMES.—The games in the circus (*Ludi Circenses*) opened with a grand procession (*pompa*), which gathered on the Capitoline Hill, passed down the Clivus Capitolinus into the Forum, along the Via Sacra, then branched off along the Vicus Tuscus, and so through the Velabrum into the Forum Boarium, where was the entrance into the Circus at the Porta Pompae. It then passed once round the *spina*, pausing to offer sacrifices and to salute the imperial *pulvinar*. The gorgeous procession which opens a modern bull-fight in Spain bears much resemblance to the Roman *pompa circensis:* it winds round the arena, and then pauses to salute the presiding official, who gives the signal to begin by throwing a key to the chief *espada*. The Roman procession was headed by the presiding magistrate, or in some cases by the emperor himself, in a *biga* or *quadriga*, wearing the dress and insignia of a triumphant general; probably a survival from the time when the *ludi circenses* were celebrated in honour of victorious generals. A gold wreath was held over his head by a slave (Liv. v. 14; Juv. x. 35–46; Dionys. vii. 72). Next came a crowd of noble citizens on foot and on horseback; then the chariots and horsemen who were to take part in the games, accompanied by musicians. Next in order were priests, grouped in their various *collegia;* bearers of holy water, incense, and sacrificial implements; and statues of deities in chariots (*tensae*) drawn by horses, mules, or elephants, or else borne in litters (*fercula*) on men's shoulders, and attended by noble Roman youths (Dionys. vii. 72). Statues in litters and in a car drawn by four elephants are shown in an ancient sarcophagus relief figured in the *Ann. Inst.* 1839, tav. o. The games mainly consisted of chariot-races; the cars (*currus*) being drawn by various numbers of horses, from two up to ten, and called *bigae*, *trigae*, *quadrigae*, *seiuges*, *septemiuges*, and so on according to the number attached to each car. In early times *bigae* and *quadrigae* were mostly used; but under the later Empire wonderful skill was displayed by some of the drivers in managing a large number of horses. In a *biga* both horses were under a yoke (*iugum*), and were called *equi iugales;* in chariots with four or more horses, only the two in the middle were yoked; those at the sides were merely attached by traces (*funes*), and were therefore called *equi funales*.

The chariots were light structures of wood bound with bronze, high in front and open behind. The Sala della Biga in the Vatican is so named from an ancient (restored) marble chariot, possibly a votive offering for victory in the Circus. See CURRUS.

Aurigae.—The drivers (*aurigae* or *agitatores*) were usually slaves or men of low class. They wore a short tunic laced round the body with leathern thongs (*fasciae*); other thongs bound their thighs. The accompanying illustration shows the statue of an *auriga*, no doubt some distinguished winner; it is now in the Vatican by the marble *biga;* the arms and legs have been restored, as well as the head. That shown in the cut does not belong to it. The *aurigae* wore a low, close-fitting cap—not a bronze helmet. Though belonging to a despised class, the favourite *aurigae* in the degraded times of the Empire were much honoured and fêted, and their society was sought after by the dissolute Roman youth. Very great skill, courage, and coolness were required to guide a chariot successfully round the sharp turns of the *metae*, among a jostling crowd of other horses and chariots, especially as each driver tried to upset his rivals. Constant accidents must have happened, for almost every ancient representation of a circus race shows one or more chariots overturned; and this was especially dangerous, as the *auriga* drove with the reins looped round his waist. That he might have a chance of cutting himself free in case of accident, he wore a curved knife (*falx*) stuck in his waist-bands; this is shown in the Vatican statue here given. No doubt one of the chief attractions of the Circus to the brutal Romans must have been the sight of the crushed limbs of an unfortunate driver among the struggling hoofs of his fallen horses, or under the wheels of a luckier rival. In spite of these dangers some drivers lived to win an enormous number of victories. The monument of the *auriga* Diocles (*circ.* A.D. 150) records that he defeated Scorpus, the winner of 2048 races; Pomp. Musclosus, the winner of 3559; and Pomp. Epaphroditus, who had won 1467 times. Diocles himself, when he retired from his profession at the age of forty-two, had won 3000 races of *bigae*, and 1462 with more than two horses. The victorious *auriga* received a prize of money; or in some cases, if a slave, he won his freedom. The prize was sometimes called the *brabeum* or *bravium* (βραβεῖον, Prud. *Peristeph.* v. 538; cf. St. Paul, 1 Cor. ix. 24), and the giver of the prize was known as the *brabeuta* (Suet. *Nero*, 53). The winners of important races, on which there was heavy betting, sometimes received enormous sums of money from patrons who had backed them (Juv. vii. 113, 243; Suet. *Claud.* 21; Capitol. *Ver.* 6). Martial (x. 74, 5) mentions one named Scorpus, who, in the reign of Domitian, won no less than fifty purses of gold in one hour's racing. M. Renan in November, 1878, read before the Société des Inscriptions in Paris a paper on an interesting inscription found in Rome, which recorded that a Moorish *auriga* named Crescens had during ten years (A.D. 115–124) won 1,556,346 sesterces with four horses called Circus, Acceptus, Delicatus, and Cotynus. Under the Empire, wealthy Roman citizens were not ashamed to act the part of *aurigae*, especially after Caligula and Nero had set the example.

Statue of an Auriga. (Vatican.)

Race-horses.—The horses used for racing purposes were mostly bred in Spain, Sicily, Mauritania, northern Greece, and, in late times, in Cappadocia. No expense or trouble was spared in their training, and the Romans were careful not to spoil the horse (in the way the modern English racer is ruined) by using it too soon. As a rule the Roman racer was not broken in till the age of three, nor allowed to run in a race till five. Consequently some of the horses won a surprising number of victories. A horse which had won 100 races was called *centenarius;* in the inscription of Diocles a horse called Tuscus is mentioned as the winner of 429 races; a horse belonging to Diocles himself was a *ducenarius.* Like the modern Romans, the ancients seem to have disfigured their horses by branding on the flank the initial or badge of the owner; which is shown on several mosaic pavements. Stallions were used, and apparently but few mares were trained for races. Almost all the names of race-horses which exist in mosaic pictures or in inscriptions are those of males. See Friedländer, *De Nominibus Equorum Circensium* (Königsberg, 1875).

The public training-stables of Rome consisted of six or more groups of buildings in Regio IX in the Campus Martius, and near the Circus Flaminius (see Jordan, *Topogr. der Stadt Rom*, ii. 554). In 1878, in the village of Oued-Atmenia in Algeria, some elaborate mosaic pavements were found in the villa of Pompeianus, proconsul of Africa under Honorius, who appears to have been a great breeder of Moorish horses for the Circus. Perspective views of the training-stables are represented on these mosaics, and other pictures show the racers in their stalls, carefully clothed from head to foot. The name of each horse is placed by it—e. g. Altus, Pullentianus, Delicatus, Polydoxus, etc., and an *auriga* named Cresconius is also depicted. Large coloured drawings of these by M. Martin were exhibited in Paris, in 1878, and afterwards published

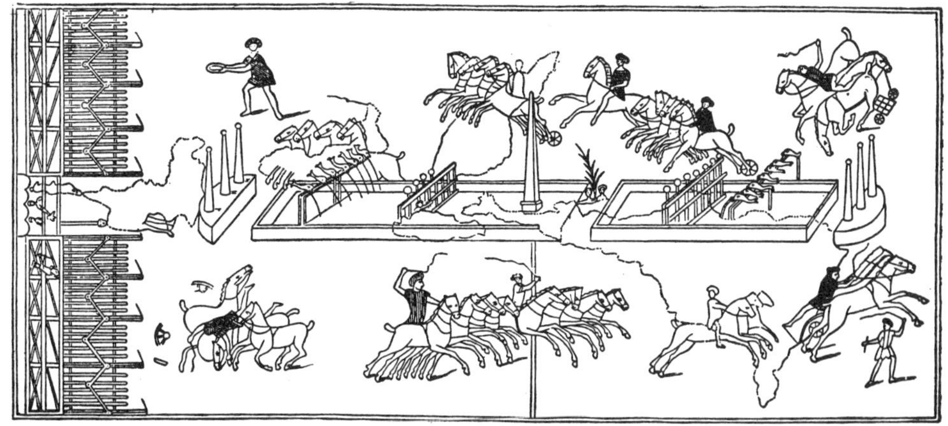

Circus Games. (Lyons Mosaic.)

by the Soc. Archéol. de Constantine, in 1879. The training-stables seem to have been centres of intrigue and villainy of all kinds: bribes were given, and horses were often "hocussed." Caligula, who spent much of his time in the stables of his favourite *factio*, is said to have poisoned the cleverest drivers of his rivals' horses. See Dio Cass. lix. 5 and 14.

Large sums of money were lost and won on the races (*sponsio*, "betting," Juv. xi. 202, with Mayor's note; Mart. *Ep.* xi. 1, 15). Race-cards (*libelli*) were sold with lists of the horses and names of the drivers; and these were also given in the advertisements of the games, which were painted in large letters on conspicuous walls: examples of these have been found at Pompeii. In addition to the chariots and their drivers, men on horseback appear to have galloped with the racers, exciting them with shouts; after the race these *iubilatores*, as they were called, seem to have called out the name of the winner. In some cases these attendants were on foot (*cursores*).

In early times only four chariots ran in each race (*missus*), one for each colour (see below); in later times eight or even ten chariots started together. The starting signal was given by the presiding magistrate, who waved a *mappa* (Liv. viii. 40, 2; xlv. 1, 6; Mart. xii. 29, 9); and hence Juvenal (xi. 193) calls the circus games *spectacula mappae*. Seven laps or circuits (*curricula*) of the *spina* appear to have been the usual length of each *missus*. (See Varro, quoted by Aul. Gell. iii. 10.) On one occasion Domitian reduced the number of laps to five, in order to get 100 *missus* into one day. In early times very few races were run in a day; even in the time of Iulius Caesar they did not usually exceed ten or twelve. Caligula increased the number to twenty, or on very grand occasions twenty-four; but in later times a long succession of races was run throughout the whole day from sunrise to sunset.

Intervals between sets of races were filled up by exhibitions of rope-dancing, tumbling, and feats of horsemanship, very like those of a modern circus. See DESULTOR.

In addition to these races and games, the young Romans sometimes held reviews and assaults of arms (*armaturae*) in the Circus Maximus; these were sometimes on foot (*armaturae pedestres*) and sometimes on horseback (*equestres*). One variety of this was called the *Ludus Troiae* (Tac. *Ann.* xi. 11; Suet. *Aug.* 43, and *Nero*, 7). Various other entertainments, such as feasts, were sometimes given in the Circus (Stat. *Silv.* i. 6, 28); or money was flung among a crowd in the arena. On one occasion Probus planted and stocked an artificial forest with wild animals and birds in the Circus Maximus, and finally let in the people to kill and carry off what they could (Vop. *Prob.* 19).

The *factiones* were companies or organizations of contractors who provided horses, drivers, and all other requisites for the games. The *factio* system was not developed till the time of the Empire; under the Republic a few citizens of knightly rank provided all the requisites. The giver of the entertainment (*editor spectaculorum*) only found the money, the whole business being managed by the *factiones*. Each *factio* was distinguished by a colour, which was worn by the *aurigae* and other performers in the *ludi*. At first there were only two *factiones*, distinguished by the colours red and white, *russata* and *albata;* next blue (*veneta*) was added, probably in the time of Augustus; and a fourth, green (*prasina*), came in soon after (Juv. xi. 196; and Tertull. *De Spect.* 9). Lastly, Domitian added purple and gold—*purpureus et auratus pannus* (Suet. *Dom.* 7). Under the later Empire each *factio* consisted of a sort of *collegium*, carefully organized and ranked in classes of every kind, such as the methodical and bureaucratic Romans delighted in. At the head of each was a *factionis dominus*, and under him were employés, slaves, and artisans of every sort required for the whole management of the *ludi*. The number and classes of a *familia quadrigaria* (a division of a *factio*) are given in an ancient inscription published by Gruter, 336–339. The *familia* consists of twenty-five *decuriones*—that is, at least 250 people, who are classified as follows: *aurigae, agitatores*, and *quadrigarii*, drivers of four-horse chariots; *conditores* and *succonditores*, grooms and helpers; *sellarii*, saddlers; *sutores*, cobblers; *sarcinatores*, tailors; *margaritarii*, pearl-embroiderers; *medici*, surgeons; *magistri* and *doctores*, perhaps trainers and instructors; *viatores*, messengers; *vilici*, farm-servants to supply fodder; *tentores*, probably the men who pulled the ropes to open the doors of the *carceres; sparsores*, water-men: these probably watered the dry arena to prevent clouds of dust from rising, and also brought water to refresh the men and horses.

The rivalry between the different colours of the factions and the heavy betting on the races often led to scenes of riot and bloodshed. (See FACTIO.) Even in Rome, faction fights frequently took place towards the declining period of the Empire, but it was not till after the transference of the Roman capital to Constantinople that these disturbances reached their highest pitch. In the sixth century, the great circus at Constantinople was frequently the scene of the most hideous slaughter, and on one occasion in the reign of Justinian the tumult was not suppressed till about 30,000 of the rioters had been killed (see Gibbon, *Decline and Fall*, cap. xl.). A great part of this circus is still well preserved, though stripped of all its rich marble linings and columns.

For the various festivals that were celebrated by circus games, see the separate articles on the CEREALIA, CONSUALIA, EQUIRIA, FLORALIA, and under LUDI.

For further information the reader should consult Tertullian, *De Spectaculis;* Panvinius, *De Ludis Circensibus* (Venice, 1600); Bulengerus, *De Circo Romano*, printed by Graevius, *Thesaur. Ant. Rom.* ix. (Lyons, 1694); Bianconi, *Descrizione dei Cerchi* (Rome, 1789); Bianchini, *Circi Max. Iconographia* (Rome, 1828); Canina, *Roma Antica*, vol. i. (Rome, 1830); Nibby, *Circo detto di Caracalla* (Rome, 1825); Magnin, *Origines du Théâtre* (Paris, 1838); Hodgkin, *Letters of Cassiodorus* (London, 1886); and articles in the *Ann. Inst. Arch. Rom.* for 1839, 1863, and 1870.

Ciris. A poem falsely ascribed to Vergil, and sometimes printed with his works. It consists of 541 hexameter lines, giving an account of the treacherous conduct of the Megarian princess Scylla towards her father, Nisus, and her transformation into the bird Ciris. It is dedicated to the son of Messalla, and draws largely upon Vergil's verse, eleven lines being copied outright, and eight with the change of only one word. Other portions suggest Catullus and occasionally Lucretius. The metrical treatment is less careful than Vergil's own, while the style is more lively. See Kreunen, *Prolegomena in Cirin* (Utrecht, 1882); Walz, *De Carmine Ciris* (Paris, 1881); Siecke, *De Niso et Scylla in Aves Mutatis* (Berlin, 1884); and R. Ellis in the *American Journal of Philology*, vol. viii. p. 399.

Cirrha (Κίρρα). See CRISSAEUS SINUS.

Cirrus. See COMA.

Cirta (Κίρτα), later CONSTANTĪNA. Now Constantine; a city of the Massylii in Numidia, fifty Roman miles from the sea; the capital of Syphax, and of Masinissa and his successors. Its position on a height, surrounded by the river Ampsagas, made it almost impregnable, as the Romans found in the Jugurthine, and the French in the Algerian wars. It was restored by Constantine the Great, in honour of whom it received its later name. A Roman bridge and the remains of a Roman aqueduct still interest the archæologist, and in 1858 a fine statuette of a Wingless Victory was discovered here.

Cisalpīna Gallia. See GALLIA.

Cisium. A light, open carriage with two wheels, like a gig, adapted for two persons. Its form is sculptured on the monumental column at Igel, near Treves (see illustration). It had a box or case, probably under the seat. The *cisia* were quickly drawn by mules *(cisia volantia)*. Cicero mentions the case of a messenger who travelled fifty-six miles in ten hours in such vehicles, which were kept for hire at the stations along the great roads—a proof that the ancients considered six Roman miles per hour as an extraordinary speed. The conductors of these hired gigs were called *cisiarii*, and were subject to penalties for careless or dangerous driving See Cic. *Pro Rosc. Amerin.* 7; Ulpian, xiii.

Cisium.

Cispadāna Gallia. See GALLIA.

Cisseus (Κισσεύς). A king in Thrace, and father of Theano, or, according to others (Eurip. *Hec.* 3), of Hecuba (q. v.), who is hence called Cisseïs (Κισσηΐς).

Cissia (Κισσία). A very fertile district of Susiana, on the Choaspes. The inhabitants, Cissii, were a wild, free people, resembling the Persians in their manners (Herod. iii. 91).

Cissus (Κισσός). A town of Macedonia, in the vicinity of Thessalonica, which contributed to the aggrandizement of that city.

Cissybium (κισσύβιον). A large rustic cup of wood with one or two handles and sometimes adorned with carving. (See Theocr. i. 27.) The name is derived from κισσός, and probably means "made of ivy-wood."

Cista, Cistella (κίστη, κιστίς). (1) Originally a wicker basket used for holding vegetables and other produce (Plin. *H. N.* xv. 60), and of either square or cylindrical shape. (2) A ballot-box, into which the voters cast their *tabellae*, and of which the form and general appearance are shown in the annexed illustration taken from a coin of the gens Cassia. It is to be carefully distinguished from the *sitella*, the urn from which the names of the tribes or centuries were drawn by lot. (See COMITIA.) (3) Any box or casket, usually of small size, and intended for almost any purpose—e. g. a book-box (= *capsa*), a jewel-case, a toilet-box. Of the last-named variety of *cista*, a great many very beautiful specimens have been found of basket-work. They appear to have been used largely for holding hair-pins, sponges, small mirrors, and scent-bottles. Most of them have been discovered in the southern part of Italy (Magna Graecia); fewer in Greece proper and in Etruria. The metal *cistae* (bronze or silver), on the other hand, come almost exclusively from Praenesté, where they were produced on a large scale. The most beautiful of these and the first to be discovered (about the year 1737) is the celebrated Ficoroni *cista*, now in the Museo Kircheriano at Rome. In 1866, Schoene described seventy *cistae* from Praenesté alone. In 1882, Fernique reported the number as having reached one hundred. (4) The name *cistae* was also given to the small boxes carried in the processions at the Greek festivals of Demeter and Dionysus, and containing the sacred things connected with the worship of the deities. (See Catull. lxiv. 259.) The shape was sometimes oblong; oftener cylindrical. To distinguish these from the common *cistae*, they are generally called *cistae mysticae*. See CISTOPHORUS; MYSTERIA.

Cista, voting-basket.

Cista, toilet-basket.

Cista Castellaniāna. An Etruscan casket discovered by Signor Castellani, a Roman jeweller, and now in the British Museum.

Cista Ficoroniāna. The most celebrated of the *cistae*, or jewel-caskets, found in Italy. It was discovered by an Italian scholar, Ficoroni, in 1745,

Cista Ficoroniana.

at Lugano, about five miles from Palestrina. An Englishman offered him a large sum for it, but he preferred to present it to the Museo Kircheriano of the Jesuit College in Rome, where it is still preserved. It is cylindrical in shape, about fifty centimetres high and forty-two in diameter, and bears upon its somewhat convex side representations of scenes from the story of the Argonauts. The finish of the drawing and the freshness and spirit of the composition make the work exceedingly attractive. An inscription upon it gives the name of the owner and the artist:

DINDIA . MACOLNIA . FILEAI . DEDIT
NOVIOS . PLAUTIOS . MED . ROMAI . FECID.

See O. Jahn, *Die Ficoronische Cista* (1852).

Cistellaria. A play of Plautus, of which only about one half has been preserved. The prologue contains an allusion to the Second Punic War as being still in progress. A good separate edition is that of Benoist (Lyons, 1863).

Cistellātrix. A lady's maid (Plaut. *Trin.* 253).

Cisterna. See PUTEUS.

Cisthēnē (Κισθήνη). (1) A mythical plain mentioned in the *Prometheus Vinctus* of Aeschylus (v. 799) as the abode of the Gorgons. (2) A town on the coast of Mysia. (3) A town on the coast of Lycia.

Cistophŏrus (κιστοφόρος). One who carried the *cista* in religious processions.

Cistophŏrus (κιστοφόρος). A term applied to certain silver coins issued in Asia Minor, in consequence of the type with which they were impressed—a Dionysiac *cista*, out of which a serpent glides. The other side of the coin bears the name or monogram of the city of issue. According to Dr. Imhoof, this coin originated in Ephesus shortly before B.C. 200, and its use rapidly extended throughout the dominions of Attalus I. of Pergamus. Henceforth the cistophorus became a sort of Pan-Asiatic coin, and was issued in vast quantities from many Asiatic mints. See *Numismatic Chronicle* (1883), p. 196.

Cistophorus. (Head.)

Citadel. See ACROPOLIS; ARX; CASTELLUM.

Cithaeron (Κιθαιρών). (1) A king of Plataea in Boeotia, remarkable for his wisdom. By his advice, Zeus pretended to be contracting a second marriage when Heré had quarrelled with and left him. The scheme succeeded, and the goddess became reconciled to her spouse (Pausan. ix. 3). This monarch is said to have given name to the well-known mountain-range in Boeotia. (2) A lofty range of mountains, separating Boeotia from Megaris and Attica. It was sacred to Dionysus and the Muses, and was celebrated for the death of Pentheus (q. v.) and Actaeon (q. v.). Here was celebrated the festival called Daedala (q. v.).

Cithăra (κιθάρα), **Citharista** (κιθαριστής). See LYRA.

Citharoeda. See LYRA.

Citharoedus (κιθαρῳδός). See LYRA.

Citium (Κίτιον). (1) A town in Cyprus, 200 stadia from Salamis, near the mouth of the Tetius; here Cimon, the celebrated Athenian, died, and Zeno, the founder of the Stoic school, was born. It is now Larnaca. (2) A town in Macedonia, northwest of Beroea.

City Editions of Homer. A name given by Homeric scholars to the "official" copies of the Homeric poems preserved by authority, and from which private copies were made. An edition means a single copy, and there were seven so-called "city" or "civic" editions—the Massaliotic, Sinopic, Chian, Cyprian, Argive, Cretan, and Lesbian (Aeolic). Of these the first four were Ionic, and the last three Aeolic. They are said by some to have been copied from the recension of the poems made by the commission of Pisistratus appointed to rearrange and edit them. See Mahaffy, *Hist. of Class. Greek Literature* (1880), vol. i. pp. 28, 29, and 35; and the article HOMERUS.

Cius (Κίος). An ancient city in Bithynia, on a bay of the Propontis called Cianus Sinus, was colonized by the Milesians. It was destroyed by Philip III., king of Macedonia; but was rebuilt by Prusias, king of Bithynia, from whom it was called Prusias (Polyb. xvi. 21).

Civic Editions of Homer. See CITY EDITIONS.

Civīlé Ius. See IUS CIVILÉ.

Civīlis, IULIUS. A powerful Batavian, who raised a sedition against the Roman State (A.D. 69–70) during the controversy for empire between Vitellius and Vespasian, but who was finally defeated by Petilius Cerealis. His end is not known. Tacitus, in his *Historiae* (bks. iv. and v.), has furnished us with interesting and copious details of this long-protracted conflict.

Civīlis Actio. See ACTIO.

Civis. A citizen. See CIVITAS.

Civĭtas. The technical Latin word for the right of citizenship. This was originally possessed, at Rome, by the patricians only. The plebeians were not admitted to share it at all until the time of Servius Tullius, and not to full civic rights until B.C. 337. In its fullest comprehension the *civitas* included: (1) the *ius suffragii*, or right of voting for magistrates; (2) the *ius honorum*, or right of being elected to a magistracy; (3) the *ius provocationis*, or right of appeal to the people, and in later times to the emperor, against the sentences passed by magistrates affecting life or property; (4) the *ius connubii*, or right to contract a legal marriage; (5) the *ius commercii*, or right to hold property in the Roman community. The *civitas* was obtained either by birth from Roman parents, or by manumission (see MANUMISSIO), or by presentation. The right of presentation belonged originally to the kings, afterwards to the popular assemblies, and particularly to the *comitia tributa*, and last of all to the emperors. The *civitas* could be lost by *deminutio capitis*. (See DEMINUTIO CAPITIS.) The *aerarii*, so called, had an imperfect *civitas*, without the *ius suffragii* and *ius honorum*. Outside the circle of the *civitas* stood the slaves and the foreigners, or *peregrini*. (See PEREGRINI.) The latter included: (1) strangers who stood in no international relations with Rome; (2) the allies, or *socii*, among whom the *Latini* (q. v.) held a privileged place; (3) the *dediticii*, or those who belonged to nations conquered in war. See IUS.

Though the Roman citizenship was conferred upon all the free inhabitants of the Empire in A.D.

212 by the emperor Caracalla, the grades of it were not all equalized, nor was it until the time of Justinian that *civitas* and *libertas* became convertible terms. See POLITEIA.

Clabulāris or **Clavulāris.** The *cursus clabularis* in the Theodosian Code and in Ammianus Marcellinus (xx. 4) denotes the system of military transport by means of carriages and vehicles. Iohannes Lydus derives the word from *clavus* (*De Mensibus*, i. 9). If we may trust the text of Cod. Theod. vi. 29, 2, § 2, *clabulare* is the name of a wagon, the word here also being used in connection with the transport service. Hence it has been derived from *clavulae* in the sense of rails.

Clabulare. (Pompeian Painting.)

Clampetia or **Lampetia.** A town in Bruttium, deserted in Pliny's time.

Clandestīna Possessio. See INTERDICTUM.

Clanis. (1) A river of Etruria, now the Chiano, forming two small lakes near Clusium, and flowing into the Tiber east of Vulsinii. (2) The more ancient name of the river Liris (q. v.).

Clanius. See LITERNUS.

Clarigatio. See FETIALES.

Clarus (Κλάρος). A small town on the Ionian coast, near Colophon, with a celebrated temple and oracle of Apollo, surnamed Clarius.

Clasp. See FIBULA.

Classes. See COMITIA.

Classiarii (ἐπιβάται). Marines. See EXERCITUS.

Classical Philology. See PHILOLOGY.

Classĭcum. The signal given by the *bucina* or horn for the meeting of the Comitia Centuriata at Rome, and for the meeting of the soldiers in camp, especially before they marched out to battle. See CORNU.

Classĭcus, IULIUS. A Trevirian prefect in the army of Vitellius (A.D. 69), who subsequently joined the Batavian Civilis in his resistance to the Romans. See CIVILIS.

Clastidium. A fortified town of the Ananes, in Gallia Cispadana, not far from the Padus (Po).

Clatri. A trellis or lattice-work used to protect and partially cover any aperture, as a window or door (Hor. *A. P.* 473).

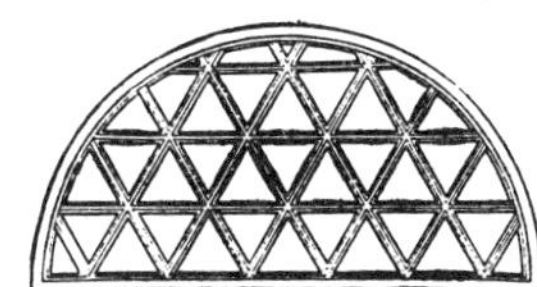

Clathri. (Circus of Caracalla.)

Claudia. See CLODIA.

Claudia Gens, both patrician and plebeian. The patrician Claudii were of Sabine origin, and came to Rome in B.C. 504, when they were received among the patricians. (See CLAUDIUS [1]). They were noted for their pride and haughtiness, their disdain for the laws, and their hatred of the plebeians. They bore various surnames, which are given under CLAUDIUS, with the exception of those with the cognomen Nero, who are better known under the latter name. The plebeian Claudii (Clodii) were divided into several families, of which the most celebrated was that of Marcellus.

Claudia Quinta. A Roman matron, and not a Vestal Virgin as is frequently stated. When the vessel conveying the image of Cybelé from Pessinus (B.C. 204) to Rome had stuck fast in a shallow at the mouth of the Tiber, the soothsayer announced that only a chaste woman could move it. Claudia, who had been accused of incontinency, took hold of the rope, and the vessel forthwith followed her. See Ovid, *Fast.* iv. 305–330.

Claudiānus, CLAUDIUS. A Latin poet, born at Alexandria in the second half of the fourth century A.D. In A.D. 395, he came to Rome. Here he won the favour of the powerful Vandal, Stilicho, and on the proposal of the Senate was honoured with a statue by the emperors Arcadius and Honorius. The inscription on this statue is still in existence (Mommsen, *Inscriptiones Regni Neapolitani*, No. 6794). His patron Stilicho fell in 408, and Claudian, apparently, did not survive him. We have express evidence that the poet was not a Christian. He was familiar with Greek and Latin literature, and had considerable poetical gifts, including a mastery of both language and metre. These gifts raise him far above the crowd of the later Latin poets, although the effect of his writing is marred by tasteless rhetorical ornament and exaggerated flattery of great men. His political poems, in spite of their laudatory colouring, have considerable historical value. Most of them are written in praise of Honorius and of Stilicho, for whom he had a veneration as sincere as was his hatred of Rufinus and Eutropius. Against the latter he launched a number of invectives. Besides the *Raptus Proserpinae*, or *Rape of Proserpine*, an unfinished epic in three books, in which his descriptive power is very brilliantly displayed, his most important poems are: (1) *De III. IV. VI. Consulatu Honorii;* (2) *De Nuptiis Honorii Fescennina;* (3) *Epithalamium de Nuptiis Honorii et Mariae;* (4) *De Bello Gildonico;* (5) *De Consulatu Stilichonis;* (6) *De Bello Pollentino;* (7) *Laus Serenae*, Serena being Stilicho's wife; (8) *Eidyllia*, seven in number; (9) *Epigrammata; Gigantomachia*, a fragment. He also wrote epistles in verse, a series of minor pieces, narrative and descriptive, and letters to Serena, and miscellaneous poems, including one on the magnet (*Magnes*).

The *Raptus Proserpinae* has come down in separate MSS., of which the best are two Codices Laurentiani, preserved in the Laurentine Library at Florence. These are of the twelfth and thirteenth centuries respectively. Others are at Leyden. Of the remaining poems there are excerpts (Excerpta Lucénsia) from a lost MS., now at Florence; and others (Excerpta Gyraldina) from the lost Codex Gyraldinus, now at Leyden. Good MSS. are also in the Vatican at Rome and in the Ambrosian Library at Milan. Editions of Claudianus have been published by Pulmann (Antwerp, 1571), J. Scaliger (Leyden, 1603), Heinsius (Leyden, 1650), Gesner, with good notes (Leipzig, 1759), Burmann (Amsterdam, 1760), König (Göttingen, 1808), and a critical ed. of the text by Jeep (Leipzig, 1876). See Hodgkin, *Claudianus, the Last of the Roman Poets* (Newcastle, 1875).

Claudiopŏlis (Κλαυδιόπολις). (1) A city of Bithynia, previously called Bithynium. It was situated above Tium, in a district named Saloné, celebrated for its excellent pastures and a cheese much esteemed at Rome. Under Theodosius it was made the capital of the province Honorias. Many years after, we learn from Anna Comnena (p. 967) and Leo Diaconus (iv. 9), who describe it as the most wealthy and flourishing city of Galatia, that it was almost totally destroyed by an earthquake, attended with vast loss of life. (2) A city of Cilicia Trachea, but assigned by Ammianus and Hierocles to Isauria. It was founded by Claudius, the Roman emperor, and was situated in a plain between two summits of Mount Taurus.

Claudius. See CLAUDIA GENS. (1) APPIUS CLAUDIUS SABĪNUS REGILLENSIS. A Sabine, a native of Regillum, and in his own country called Attus Clausus. He belonged to the pro-Roman party among his people, and when his advice was disregarded and war broke out between the two nations, he led a large number of seceders to Rome (B.C. 504), where he was enrolled among the patricians and received a large grant of land beyond the Anio. He was the founder of the great gens Claudia, one of the noblest in Roman history. He was a typical aristocrat, and his conduct towards the plebeians was marked by so much intolerance and severity during his consulship (B.C. 495) as to lead to the famous secession to the Mons Sacer in the following year. (2) APPIUS CLAUDIUS SABĪNUS REGILLENSIS. A son of the preceding, consul in B.C. 471. He was famed for the severity of his military discipline, which he pushed to such extremes that his soldiers deserted him. Having on this account been impeached by the tribunes, he committed suicide. (3) GAIUS CLAUDIUS SABĪNUS REGILLENSIS. A brother of the preceding, and one of the more moderate of the patricians. He defended his brother (?), the decemvir, when the latter was impeached. (4) APPIUS CLAUDIUS CRASSUS SABĪNUS REGILLENSIS, usually called the son of No. 2, but possibly the same person. He was consul in B.C. 451, and in the same year became one of the decemvirs appointed to revise the laws. (See DECEMVIRI.) In the following year he was reappointed, but his tyrannous conduct towards the plebeians, and especially his relation to the affair of Virginia, led to the downfall of the decemvirate. (See VIRGINIA.) Being impeached by Virginius, he either committed suicide or was killed in prison before his trial. (5) APPIUS CLAUDIUS CAECUS. A famous Roman, censor in B.C. 312. During his term of office he commenced the Via Appia and built the great Appian aqueduct. He retained the censorship for four years beyond the time allowed by law, and was twice consul (B.C. 307 and 296), and in the latter year carried on war against the Samnites and Etruscans. As an old man, Appius induced the Senate to reject the proposals for peace made by Cineas on behalf of Pyrrhus. (See PYRRHUS.) He was the first Roman writer of prose and verse of whom we have any record, being the author of a poem (subject unknown), and of a legal treatise *De Usurpationibus*. With Cn. Flavius, he published also a calendar of the religious festivals, and *legis actiones*. According to Quintilian (ii. 16, 7), he was the first to distinguish the two sounds R and S in writing. (See RHOTACISM.) Martianus Capella says that he set the fashion of omitting the use of the character Z. (See ALPHABET.) See Mommsen, *Hist. of Rome*, i. p. 432; id. *Römische Forschungen*, vol. i. (Berlin, 1864); and the treatise of Siebert (Cassel, 1863). In his old age he became blind, as the name Caecus implies. In Roman constitutional history, Appius is famous as having abolished the limitation of the full right of citizenship to land-owners. (6) APPIUS CLAUDIUS CAUDEX. A brother of the preceding, who was consul in B.C. 264, and took part in the First Punic War, conducting a campaign against the Carthaginians in Sicily. (7) PULCHER, a Roman consul in the First Punic War. When, previous to a naval engagement with the Carthaginians, the person who had charge of the sacred fowls told him that they would not eat, which was esteemed a bad omen, he ordered them to be thrown into the sea, exclaiming, "Then let them drink." After this, joining battle with the foe, he was defeated with the loss of his fleet. Having been recalled by the Senate, he gave another specimen of the haughty temper of the Claudian race, for, on being directed to nominate a dictator, he purposely named his own *viator*, an individual of the lowest rank (Cic. *N. D.* ii. 3). (8) NERO, a Roman consul in the Second Punic War, who, in conjunction with his colleague Livius Salinator, defeated Hasdrubal in Umbria, on the banks of the Metaurus (q. v.). (9) APPIUS CLAUDIUS PULCHER. A consul in B.C. 143, when he defeated the Salassi, an Alpine tribe. On his return, the Senate refused to give him a triumph, and when one of the tribunes tried to drag him from his chariot, he and his daughter Claudia, a Vestal, walked together to the Capitol. He was father-in-law to Tib. Gracchus, and acted as triumvir for the division of the public lands. He died soon after the death of Gracchus. (10) TIBERIUS NERO, father of the emperor Tiberius. He was distinguished for his naval skill in the Alexandrine War, under Iulius Caesar. At a subsequent period he incited a sedition in Campania by promising to restore the property of those who had suffered in the Civil Wars. This tumult, however, was soon quelled by the arrival of Octavianus; and Tiberius, together with his wife Livia, took refuge in Sicily and Achaia until the establishment of the Second Triumvirate made it safe for him to return to Rome. Livia having after this engaged the affections of Octavianus, Tiberius transferred to him the name and privileges of a husband (Tac. *Ann.* v. 1). (11) TIBERIUS NERO CAESAR GERMANĪCUS, the successor of Augustus, and son of the preceding. (See TIBERIUS.) (12) TIBERIUS CLAUDIUS DRUSUS NERO CAESAR GERMANĪCUS, more commonly known by his historical name of Claudius, succeeded to the Roman Empire on the death of Caligula. He was the second son of Drusus and Antonia, and consequently grand-nephew to Augustus. When the assassination of Caligula was made known, the first impulse of the court party and of the foreign guards was to massacre all who had participated in the murder. Several persons of distinction, who imprudently exposed themselves, became, in consequence, the victims of their fury. This violence subsided, however, upon their discovering Claudius, who had concealed himself in an obscure corner of the palace, and who, being dragged from his hiding-place, threw himself at their feet in the utmost terror and besought them to spare his life. The soldiers in the palace immediately saluted him emperor, and Claudius, in return, set the first example of paying the army for the imperial dignity by a largess from the public treasury. It is difficult to assign any other motive for the choice which the army made of Claudius than that which they themselves professed, "his relationship to the whole family of the Caesars." Claudius, who was now fifty years old, had never done anything to gain popularity, or to display those qualities which secure the attachment of the soldiery. He had been a rickety child, and the development of his faculties was retarded by his bodily infirmities; and although he outgrew his complaints, and became distinguished as a polite scholar and an eloquent writer, his spirits never recovered from the effects of disease and of severe treatment, and he retained much of the timidity and indolence of his childhood. During the reign of Tiberius he gave himself up to gross sensuality, and consoled himself under this degradation by the security which it brought with it. Under Caligula also he found

The Emperor Claudius. (Bust in the Vatican.)

his safety consist in maintaining his reputation for incapacity, and he suffered himself to become the butt of court parasites and the subject of their practical jokes. The excitement of novelty, on his first accession to the throne, produced efforts of sagacity and prudence of which none who had previously known him believed him capable; and during the whole of his reign, too, we find judicious and useful enactments occasionally made, which would seem to show that he was not in reality so foolish and incompetent as historians have generally represented him. It is most probable, therefore, that the fatuity which characterizes some parts of his conduct was the result, not of natural imbecility, but of the early and unlimited indulgence of sensuality.

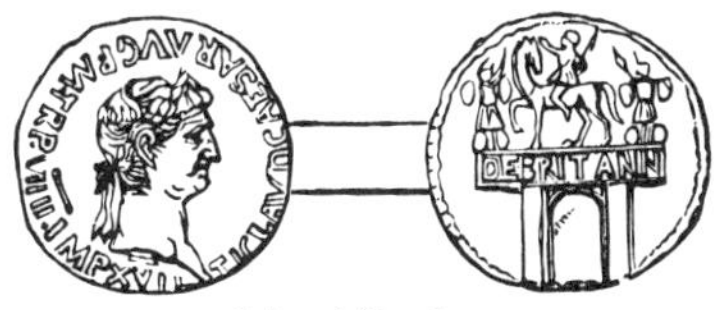

Coin of Claudius.

Claudius embellished Rome with many magnificent works; he made Mauritania a Roman province; his armies fought successfully against the Germans; and he himself triumphed magnificently in victories over the Britons, and obtained, together with his infant son, the surname of Britannicus. But in other respects he was wholly governed by worthless favourites, and especially by his empress, the profligate and abandoned Messalina (q. v.), whose cruelty and rapacity were as unbounded as her licentiousness. At her instigation it was but too common for the emperor to put to death, on false charges of conspiracy, some of the wealthiest of the nobles, and to confiscate their estates, with the money arising from which she openly pampered her numerous paramours. When the career of this guilty woman was terminated, Claudius was governed for a time by his freedman, Narcissus, and Pallas, another manumitted slave, until he took to wife his own niece, Agrippina, daughter of Germanicus, a woman of strong natural abilities, but of insatiable avarice, extreme ambition, and remorseless cruelty. Her influence over the feeble emperor was boundless. She prevailed on him at last to set aside his own son Britannicus, and to adopt her son, Domitius Ahenobarbus, by her former husband, giving him the name by which he is best known, Nero, and constituting him heir to the imperial throne. Claudius having afterwards shown a disposition to change the succession and restore it to Britannicus, fell a victim to the ambition of Agrippina, who caused him to be poisoned. A dish of mushrooms was prepared for the purpose, a kind of food of which the emperor was known to be especially fond, and the effects of the poison were hastened by the pretended remedies administered by Xenophon, the physician of the palace. It was given out that Claudius had suffered from indigestion, which his habitual gluttony rendered so frequent that it excited no surprise; and his death was concealed till Domitius Nero had secured the guards, and had quietly taken possession of the imperial authority. Claudius died in the sixty-fourth year of his age and the fourteenth of his reign, A.D. 54. His biography is to be found in the *Lives* of Suetonius. See Baring-Gould, *The Tragedy of the Caesars*, vol. i. (London, 1892). (13) Marcus Aurelius Claudius Gothĭcus. A Roman emperor, who reigned from A.D. 268 to 270. He was of an obscure Illyrian family, but won distinction by his brilliant military service under Decius, Valerian, and Gallienus, so that on the death of the last he succeeded to the imperial office. As emperor he won two great victories, defeating the Alemanni in the north of Italy, and in the next year (A.D. 269) the Goths in Dardania at Naïsus. He died at Sirmium in the year 270.

Claudius. See Clodius.

Claudius Quadrigarius. See Quadrigarius.

Claustrum. A fastening. See IANUA.

Clava (ῥόπαλον, κορύνη). A club or mace. The shape of the club is seen in works of art relating to Heracles, who is usually represented with a club, and therefore called *Claviger* (Ovid, *Met.* xv. 22, 284). Hence the expression *Herculi clavam subtrahere* of an impossible undertaking (Macrob. *Sat.* v. 3, § 16). The club was sometimes carried, instead of the walking-stick, by certain philosophers as a mark of affectation. In Homeric times the club, shod with iron or made of bronze, was used as a mace in fighting (*Il.* ix. 141); and in the army of Xerxes the Assyrians carried wooden clubs knotted with iron (Herod. vii. 63). Pisistratus had a body-guard of club-bearers (κορυνηφόροι), as less invidious in a free State than δορυφόροι, or men armed with spears (Herod. i. 59). Though the club or mace was not usual in the Greek army, it was used occasionally; and we thus read of Arcadian hoplites carrying clubs (Xen. *Hell.* vii. 5, § 20). On the Column of Trajan the club appears as the weapon of some auxiliary barbarians.

Heracles and the Nemean Lion. (From a Roman Lamp.)

Among the Romans the recruits were taught to fight with a club instead of a sword, against a dummy or stake (*palus*) set in the ground (Cic. *Sen.* 16 and 58).

Clavarium. See CLAVUS ad fin.

Clavātor. A sutler or soldier's servant. See CALO.

Clavĭger (1) (Κορυνήτης). "Club-bearing." An epithet of Heracles, who is represented with a club. (2) (Κλειδοῦχος). "Key-bearing." An epithet given by the Romans to Ianus as the god of doors; and by the Greeks to Eros (Cupid) as holding the key to hearts, and to Hecatē as the keeper of the keys of Hades.

Clavis (κλείς, dim. κλειδίον). A key. In Homer the κλείς is not a key in the modern meaning of the word, but rather a hook (having a leathern thong) which passed through the door from the outside and caught the bolts (ὀχῆες), so as to shoot them home or draw them back as required (*Od.* xxi. 6, 46–50). In some passages of Homer the word signifies simply a bolt (*Od.* i. 442; xxi. 241; L. and S. s. v.). In course of time locks and keys were made, much like those of modern times. Locks were used in Egypt at an early period, and were originally of wood, probably like those now used there, which are opened by a key furnished with several fixed pins, answering to a similar number that fall down into the movable tongue, into which the key is introduced, when they fasten or open the lock. At a later time we find iron keys in Egypt, consisting of a long straight shank, with three or more projecting teeth, like the one figured in preceding column. The earliest mention of a key, like our own, which could be taken out of the lock, is in the Book of Judges (iii. 23, 25).

Iron Egyptian Key. (Wilkinson.)

Schliemann found keys of copper and bronze in the remains of the cities in the Troad. The accompanying cut represents a copper key, found close by the so-called Treasury of Priam in the ruins at Hissarlik.

Copper Key found at Hissarlik. (Schliemann.)

The cut below represents a curious bronze key, with a ring for suspension, found in the ruins of Novum Ilium. "It has the shape of the so-called quadrangular images of Hermes, with an altar-like base forming one piece with the body, to which a quadrangular projection is fixed on the back, with a hole corresponding to the lock-bolt" (Schliemann, *Ilios*, pp. 620, 621).

Pliny (*H. N.* vii. § 198) ascribes the invention of keys to Theodorus of Samos; and the ancient writers speak of Carian, and especially of Laconian keys, because originally made by the Lacedaemonians. We learn from Aristophanes that the Laconian key had three teeth (τρεῖς γομφίους), probably like the Egyptian key figured above. Keys are mentioned by Aeschylus and Euripides; and Lysias, in his speech on the murder of Eratosthenes, speaks of the wife shutting the door and taking the key with her (τὴν κλεῖν ἐφέλκετια, c. 4), so that the husband was shut up in his chamber. In this case the door must have been locked from the outside.

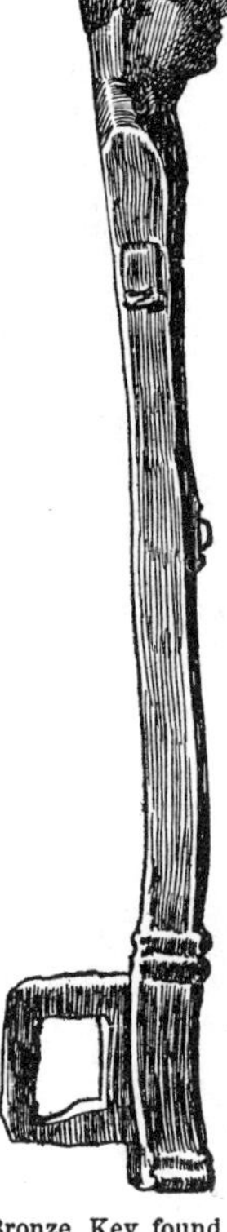

Bronze Key found at Novum Ilium. (Schliemann.)

Many Roman keys have been found much like our own, the larger ones usually of iron and the smaller of bronze; but there were also keys made of wood and gold in use in later times. Besides these there was the βαλανάγρα, a key or hook, which was passed through a hole in the door-post, and raised the βάλανοι or bolts of the lock, as in the Egyptian locks described above (Herod. iii. 155). It must have been a lock of this kind which the robber in Apuleius (*Met.* iv. 10) opens, by passing his hand through the hole, *qua clavi immittendae foramen patebat.* Roman keys, both of bronze and iron, have been found which were never intended to turn, the stems being square, and the webs, consisting of from one to five or six teeth, rising from a bar bent at an acute angle to the stem; which teeth would serve the purpose of elevating pegs, as in the Egyptian locks.

The street-door was usually fastened inside by bolts (*pessuli*) and a bar (*sera*), but it also had a key which the *ianitor* of the house kept. The cut given below represents a key found at Pompeii, and now in the Museum of Naples, the size of which indicates that it was used as a door-key. The tongue with an eye in it, which projects from the extremity of the handle, served to suspend it from the wrist of the *ianitor*. The rooms of the house were also opened inside with keys. The doors often had locks both inside and outside. This is evident from Plaut. *Most.* ii. 1, 57, where a Laconian key is mentioned for locking the door from the outside, compared with verse 78—

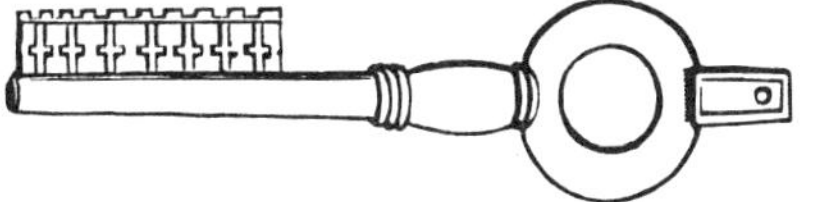

Door-key found at Pompeii.

> "Clavim cedo atque abi intro atque obclude ostium,
> Et ego hinc [i. e. foris] obcludam."

When a Roman woman first entered her husband's house, the keys of the store-rooms were handed to her. Hence the form of divorce, in the Twelve Tables, was that the husband took away the keys (*claves ademit, exegit,* Cic. *Phil.* ii. 28, 69); and the wife, when she separated from the husband, sent him back the keys (*claves remisit,* Ambros. *Ep.* 65). But the keys of the wine-cellar were not intrusted to the wife, and Fabius Pictor related a story of a married woman having been starved to death by her relatives because she picked the lock of the closet in which the keys of the wine-cellar were kept (Plin. *H. N.* xiv. § 89).

A skeleton key was known as *clavis adultera* (Sall. *Iug.* 12).

Clavis trochi (ἐλατήρ). A crooked stick used by Greek and Roman children in trundling hoops (Propert. iii. 14, 6). See TROCHUS.

Clavus (ἧλος, γόμφος). A nail. In the subterranean chamber at Mycenae (q. v.), supposed to be the treasury of Atreus, a view of which is given in Sir W. Gell's *Itinerary of Greece* (plate vi.), the stones of which the cylindrical dome is constructed are perforated by regular series of bronze nails, running in perpendicular rows, and at equal distances, from the top to the bottom of the vault. It is supposed that they served to attach thin plates of the same metal to the masonry, as a coating for the interior of the chamber; and hence it is that these subterranean works, which served for prisons as well as treasuries, like the one in which Danaë is said to have been confined, were called by the poets "brazen chambers." Two of these nails are represented in the annexed illustration, of two thirds the real size; they consist of 88 parts of copper to 12 of tin.

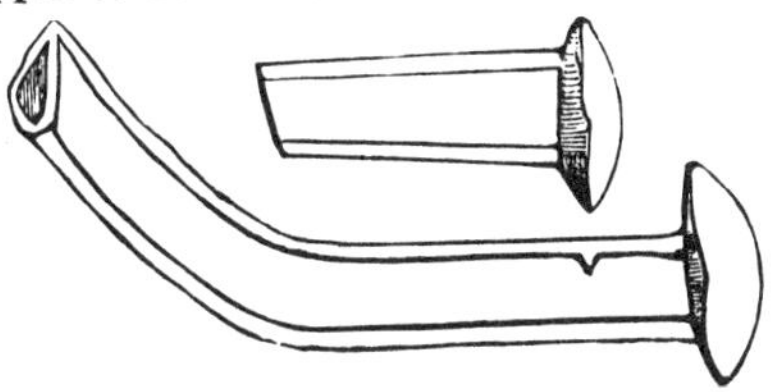

Bronze Nails (Greek).

Nails of this description were termed *trabales* and *tabulares* by the Romans, because they were used, in building, to join the larger beams (*trabes*) together. Hence Horace arms Necessitas with a nail of the same kind, or of adamant, wherewith to rivet, as it were, irrevocably the decrees of Fortune. Thus, too, Atropos is represented in the following illustration, taken from a cup found at Perugia, upon which the story of Meleager and Atalanta is embodied, with a hammer in her right hand, driving a nail which she holds against the wall with her left.

Atropos driving a Nail.

The next cut represents a nail of Roman workmanship, which is highly ornamented and very curious. Two of its faces are given, but the pattern varies on each of the four.

Ornamental Nails. (Roman.)

It is difficult to say to what use this nail was applied. The ornamented head shows that it was never intended to be driven by the hammer; nor would any part but the mere point, which alone is plain and round, have been inserted into any extraneous material. It might possibly have been used for the hair, in the manner represented in the illustration under ACUS.

Bronze nails were used in ship-building, and to ornament doors, as exhibited in those of the Pantheon at Rome; in which case the head of the nail was called *bulla,* and richly ornamented. See BULLA.

The soles of the shoes worn by the Roman soldier were also studded with nails, thence called *clavi caligarii.* (See CALIGA.) These do not appear to have been hobnails for the purpose of making the sole durable, but sharp-pointed ones, in order to give the wearer a firmer footing on the ground. The men received a donative for the purpose of providing themselves with these necessaries, which was thence called *claviarum.*

Clavus Annālis. At Volsinii, in Etruria, a nail was driven every year in the Temple of Nortia, the Fortuna of Etruscan mythology, in order to keep a reckoning of the years (Liv. vii. 3). This custom was introduced into Rome from Etruria, probably by the Tarquins, when they founded the Temple of Iupiter Optimus Maximus. An ancient law enacted that a nail should be driven each year by the chief magistrate on the Ides of September into the side of the *cella* of Iupiter on the Capitol. As the Romans thus kept a reckoning of their years, when letters were yet scarcely in use, this nail was called *clavus annalis.* (Liv. l. c.; Fest. p. 56, M.). This practice fell into disuse, but was afterwards revived, not for the purpose of marking the year, but from a superstitious feeling that any great calamity, such as a pestilence, would be averted if this ceremony was performed by the supreme magistrate. Hence we read of a dictator being appointed, more than once, for the sole purpose of driving in the nail (*clavi figendi causa*, Liv. l. c.).

Clavus Gubernacŭli. The handle or tiller of a rudder. See GUBERNACULUM; NAVIS.

Clavus Latus—Clavus Angustus. The *clavus* was a stripe of purple colour, worn by the Romans as a badge of distinction, and either sewn to the stuff or woven into it.

The LATUS CLAVUS (broad stripe) was, according to tradition, introduced by Tullus Hostilius from the Etruscans (Plin. *H. N.* ix. § 136). It was the distinctive badge of the senatorial order (Hor. *Sat.* i. 6, 28), and hence it is used to signify the senatorial dignity. In distinction to the *angustus clavus* it is called *purpura maior* (Juv. i. 106), and the garment it decorated, *tunica potens* (Stat. *Silv.* v. 2, 29). Pliny speaks of this distinctive use as late (*H. N.* xxxiii. § 29); yet its assumption by a *praeco*, the father of L. Aelius Stilo Praeconinus (whose official dress may have included the *angustus clavus*), was, as he admits, remarkable, as was also its use by Horace's praetor of Fundi (*Sat.* i. 5, 36). But there were relaxations of the restriction: thus Augustus wore the *tunica lati clavi* before he assumed the *toga virilis*, and it was afterward his custom to permit the sons of senators to wear it and attend the discussions of the Senate in order to train them in public affairs. If they were entering on a military career, he also made them military tribunes and prefects. These youths were called *laticlavii* (Suet. *Aug.* 38, 94); on the contrary, *tribunus angusticlavius* (Suet. *Otho*, 10). Wearing the *latus clavus* was also granted by the emperor as a favour to the sons of knights, as a preliminary step to their entering the Senate; if they relinquished or were disappointed in their hopes, they assumed the *angustus clavus* (Suet. *Vesp.* 2), but might again assume the *latus clavus*, like Priscus in Horace (*Sat.* ii. 7, 10). In the later Empire the *equites* appear to have encroached on the rights of the Senate in this respect, and Alexander Severus was only able to insist that knights should be distinguished from senators by the quality of the purple employed (Lamprid. *Alex. Sev.* 27). The Senate laid aside the *latus clavus* at times of mourning (Liv. ix. 7) and assumed the *angustus clavus* (Dio Cass. xxxviii. 14).

The ANGUSTUS CLAVUS (narrow stripe) was a badge of the equestrian order (Vell. Paterc. ii. 88, 2), but less distinctively so than the golden ring (Plin. *H. N.* xxxiii. § 29); for, as we shall see from the extant works of art, it was also worn by *camilli*, *lanistae*, and others not of equestrian rank, as a part of their ceremonial dress.

FORM.—It is agreed that the *clavi* were purple stripes woven in the fabric (Quint. viii. 5, 28) or sewn on it (*Dig.* 34, 2, 23, § 1); that they were employed to ornament the tunic, and no other garment; that the *angustus clavus* consisted of two narrow vertical stripes falling from each shoulder, down the front, and, as appears from frescoes, also down the back. But there has been great discussion concerning the form of the *latus clavus*, some contending that it was a single stripe running down the centre of the bosom of the *tunica*, some that there were two stripes, only differing from the *angustus clavus* in breadth, and, like it,

Angustus Clavus. (Niccolini, *Case e Monumenti di Pompeii.* III. Anfiteatro, tav. iii.)

running down the back (as Marquardt maintains). The latter view is now generally held, although it is impossible to conclude the discussion by appealing to any representation of a senator displaying this *ornamentum*, as it was not the custom of ancient sculptors to indicate a distinction of colour by a conventional system of lines.

It must be observed that *latus clavus*, *angustus clavus*, are often abbreviated expressions for *tunica lati* or *angusti clavi.* Thus Iulius Caesar is said to have worn a *latus clavus ad manus fimbriatus* (Suet. *Iul.* 45). That the *angustus clavus* consisted of two stripes is proved by Quintilian, xi. 3, 138: *Cui lati clavi ius non erit, ita cingatur, ut tunicae prioribus oris infra genua paulum, posterioribus ad medios poplites usque perveniant . . . ut purpuriae recte descendant, levis cura est.* Though we cannot point to the representation of an *eques* wearing this garb, we find it frequently shown in Pompeian paintings of persons of inferior rank who are in ceremonial dress, especially *camilli* and other attendants on religious rites, and of *lanistae.* In a wall-painting at Pompeii belonging to the worship of the goddess Epona, the two *camilli* and a man leading mules wear the *angustus clavus.* The latter may be a muleteer especially adorned for a festival of the goddess, or a person of higher rank performing

Angustus Clavus. (From figures in the Catacombs.)

some rite of her worship (*Annali dell' Inst. Arch.* 1872, pl. D).

The *angustus clavus* probably survives in the *clavi* on the dalmatic, which was recognized as an ecclesiastical garb in the earlier part of the fourth century (*Vita Sylvestri I.*, p. 266, Combéfis), though down to A.D. 640 the *clavi* are always represented as black, according to Marriott (*Vestiarium Christianum*, p. lv.).

Some writers maintain that the drawing below, representing Rome personified, clothed in a robe called *cyclas* (q. v.), shows the *latus clavus* falling in a broad purple stripe down the breast.

It is true that the singular (*latus clavus*) is generally used, but this is also true of the *angustus clavus*, which confessedly consisted of two stripes; while the employment of the plural, *latis clavis*, is striking in a passage of Varro, which also insists on the resemblance of the two garments, by using as an illustration of an analogy a tunic, in which of the two pieces (front and back) one has the *lati*, the other the *angusti*, *clavi*. (*Non, si quis tunicam in usu ita* [E. Schulze, *inusitate*] *consuit, ut altera plagula sit angustis clavis, altera latis, utraque pars in suo genere caret, analogia* [*L. L.* ix. 79]. Cf. for the use of the plural, Festus, p. 209 a, 23: *tunica autem palmata a latitudine clavorum dicebatur, quae nunc a genere picturae appellatur.*) Again, Augustus, among other affectations of simplicity, *usus est . . . clavo nec lato nec angusto* (Suet. *Aug.* 73), which is quite intelligible if the two ornaments differed only in breadth, but inexplicable on the other hypothesis; while Herodian (v. 5, 9) speaks of the

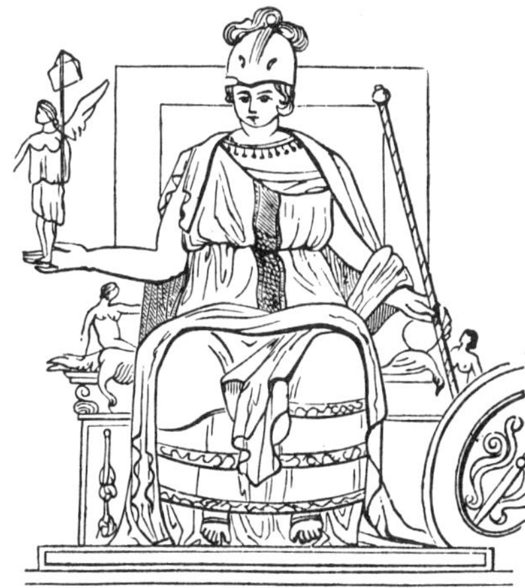

Supposed Latus Clavus. (From a painting of Rome personified.)

stripe down the centre of the tunic worn by the priests of the Sun, instituted by Elagabalus, as a Phœnician custom.

As the tunic was composed of a front piece and a back piece sewn together, the passage quoted above from Varro goes to show that the *lati clavi* were worn down the back as well as down the front. In support of this may be cited Varro, *Sat. Menipp.* 313, Bücheler: *quorum vitreae togae ostentant tunicae clavos*, which refers to togas made of such diaphanous material that the *clavi* could be seen through them at the back. With the same intent of displaying this mark of distinction, the wearer of the *tunica laticlavia* is to gird himself so that it may fall low (Quint. xi. 3, 139). Pliny observes that in his time it was becoming a fashion to weave the *tunica lati clavi* of a stuff resembling *gausapa* (*H. N.* viii. § 193). The false derivation quoted from Festus above for *palmata* as applied to *tunica* may possibly indicate that the breadth of the *latus clavus* was about a palm.

The equivalents used in the Greek writers are: *clavus*, σημεῖον: *tunica laticlavia*, ἡ πλατύσημος: *tunica angusticlavia*, ἡ στενόσημος: *tunica asema* (Lamprid. *Alex. Sev.* 33, 4), ἡ ἄσημος: *tunica clavata*, ἡ σημειωτός. See TUNICA.

The chief authorities for the subject are Ferrarius, *De Re Vestiaria* (Padua, 1654); Rubenius, *De Re Vestiaria Veterum Praecipue de Lato Clavo Libri Duo* (Antwerp, 1665); Ferrarius, *Analecta de Re Vestiaria* (Padua, 1690); Marquardt, *Röm. Privatleben* (1886), pp. 544 foll.; id. *Historia Equitum Rom.* pp. 77, 80; E. Schulze, in *Rhein. Mus.* (1875), pp. 120 foll. See also Hope, *The Costume of the Ancients* (2d ed. 1875); Racinet, *Le Costume Historique*, vol. ii. (1887).

Clay. See CRETA; FICTILÉ.

Clazomĕnae (Κλαζομεναί). An important city of Asia Minor, and one of the twelve Ionian cities, on the north coast of the Ionian peninsula, upon the Gulf of Smyrna. It was the birthplace of Anaxagoras, and was also celebrated for its temples of Apollo, Artemis, and Cybelé.

Cleander (Κλέανδρος). (1) A tyrant of Gela, who reigned B.C. 504–498 and was succeeded by his brother Hippocrates, whom Gelon deposed in B.C. 491. (2) A Phrygian slave, the favourite of the emperor Commodus (q. v.), and torn in pieces by the Roman mob during a bread-riot.

Cleanthes (Κλεάνθης). (1) A Greek philosopher, a native of Assos in Asia Minor. He was originally a boxer (Diog. Laërt. vii. 168), and while attending at Athens the lectures of Zeno, the founder of the Stoic philosophy, gained a livelihood at night by carrying water. He was Zeno's disciple for nineteen years, and in B.C. 263 succeeded him as head of the Stoic school. He died in his eighty-first year by voluntary starvation. A beautiful *Hymn to Zeus* is the only one of his writings that has come down to us, of which a good edition is that of Pearson (London, 1891). The titles of the others are given by Diogenes Laërtius (vii. 4). (2) A painter of Corinth.

Clearchus (Κλέαρχος). A Spartan, who distinguished himself in several important commands during the latter part of the Peloponnesian War, and at the close of it persuaded the Spartans to send him as a general to Thrace, to protect the Greeks in that quarter against the Thracians. But having been recalled by the ephors, and refusing to obey their orders, he was condemned to death. He thereupon crossed over to Cyrus, collected for him a large force of Greek mercenaries, and marched with him into Upper Asia, in B.C. 401, in order to dethrone his brother Artaxerxes, being the only Greek who was aware of the prince's real object. After the battle of Cunaxa and the death of Cyrus, Clearchus and the other Greek generals were made prisoners by the treachery of Tissaphernes, and were put to death. See Xenophon's *Anabasis*, bks. i. and ii.

Clemens (Κλήμης). (1) Called ROMĀNUS, to distinguish him from Clemens of Alexandria. One of the early Christians, said by Origen to have been the friend and fellow-traveller of St. Paul, and afterwards bishop of Rome, to which station he was chosen A.D. 67, or, according to some, A.D. 91. He was the author of an epistle to the church of Corinth. Of this work, the only manuscript extant was in the British Museum until 1875, when Bryennios published a complete MS. of 1056 found at Constantinople; and in 1876, Cambridge University got possession of a Syriac MS. of the year 1170. Archbishop Wake printed a translation in 1705. The best edition of the original is that of Lightfoot (1869; appendix 1877). See Cotterill, *Modern Criticism* (Edinb. 1884). Clemens is supposed to have died at Rome about the close of the first century, though a legend of the ninth century makes him to have been martyred in the Crimea in A.D. 102. Besides the epistle mentioned above, there have been ascribed to Clemens two Syriac epistles on Virginity, the so-called *Clementinae* ("Recognitions" and "Homilies"), and several letters; but these may all be regarded as spurious. (2) T. FLAVIUS, a Father of the Church, who flourished between A.D. 190 and 217, and is commonly called ALEXANDRĪNUS, to distinguish him from Clemens of Rome. He is supposed by some to have been a native of Athens, and by others of Alexandria, but of his real origin very little is known. He early devoted himself to study in the schools of the latter city, and had many preceptors. His Hebrew preceptor, whom he calls "the Sicilian bee," was unquestionably Pantaenus, a Jew by birth, but of Sicilian extraction, who united Grecian with sacred learning, and was attached to the Stoic philosophy. Clemens so far adopted the ideas of this preceptor as to espouse the moral doctrine of the Stoics. In other respects he followed the Eclectic method of philosophizing. While the pagan philosophers pillaged the Christian stores to enrich the Eclectic system, this Christian father, on the contrary, transferred the Platonic, Stoic, and Oriental dogmas to the Christian creed, as relics of ancient tradition originating in Divine revelation. His most distinguished follower was Origen.

In the hope of recommending Christianity to his catechumens, Clemens made a large collection of ancient wisdom, under the name of *Stromata* (Στρωματεῖς, "patchwork"), and intended to denote the miscellaneous nature of the philosophical and religious topics of which the work treats. He assigned as a reason for the undertaking, that much truth is mixed with the dogmas of philosophers, or, rather, covered and concealed in their writings, like the kernel within its shell. This work is of great value, as it contains many quotations and relates many facts not elsewhere preserved. Besides the *Stromata*, we have the following works of Clemens remaining: (*a*) *Protrepticon* (Λόγος Προτρεπτικός), or an exhortation to the Pagans; (*b*) *Paedagogus* (Παιδαγωγός), or the instructor; (*c*) the fragments of a treatise on the use of riches, entitled, "What rich man shall be saved?" The works of Clemens were first printed in Greek only, at Florence, in 1550. Of the various editions with Latin versions, the best is that of Archbishop Potter, 2 vols. (Oxford, 1715). A later edition is that of Klotz (Leipzig, 1834). A translation will be found in Clark's *Ante-Nicene Library* (1877–79). See Merk, *Clemens von Alexandria* (Leipzig, 1879); and Bigg, *Christian Platonists* (Bampton Lect. 1886).

Clementīnae. See CLEMENS (1).

Cleŏbis (Κλέοβις). See BITON.

Cleobūlus (Κλεόβουλος). One of the Seven Sages, of Lindus in Rhodes, son of Evagoras, lived about B.C. 580. He and his daughter, Cleobulinē or Cleobulē, were celebrated for their skill in riddles. To the latter is ascribed a well-known one on the subject of the year: "A father has twelve children, and each of these thirty daughters, on one side white, and on the other side black, and, though immortal, they all die." See AENIGMA; SEVEN SAGES.

Cleombrŏtus (Κλεόμβροτος). (1) A king of Sparta, who succeeded his brother Agesipolis I. He was defeated by Epaminondas in the battle of Leuctra, and lost his life on that occasion. (2) A son-in-law of Leonidas II., king of Sparta, who usurped the kingdom after the expulsion of that monarch, but was soon after expelled in turn and sent into banishment.

Cleomēdes (Κλεομήδης). A Greek writer, supposed to have been the author of the work which has reached us entitled Κυκλικῆς Θεωρίας Μετεώρων Βίβλια δύο, or Circular Theory of the Stars. He flourished in the second century A.D. Ed. by Schmidt (Leipzig, 1832).

Cleomĕnes (Κλεομένης). (1) King of Sparta, ascended the throne B.C. 519. At the beginning of his reign he undertook an expedition against the Argives, defeated them, and destroyed a large number who had taken refuge in a sacred grove. He afterwards drove out the Pisistratidae from Athens. This is the same Cleomenes whom Aristagoras endeavoured, but in vain, to involve in a war with the Persians. He afterwards managed, by undue influence, to procure an oracular response from Delphi, pronouncing his colleague Demaratus illegitimate, and thus obtained his deposition. Becoming alarmed, subsequently, lest the fraud should be discovered, Cleomenes fled secretly to Thessaly, and from thence passing into Arcadia, he began to stir up the people of this latter country against Sparta. The Lacedaemonians, fearing his intrigues, recalled him, but he died soon after his return, in a fit of insanity, by his own hand (Herod. v. 64; v. 49 foll.; v. 65, etc.). (2) Cleomenes II., succeeded his brother Agesipolis II. on the throne of Sparta, B.C. 371. The power of his country was then on the decline, and he possessed not the requisite talents to restore it to its former state. He reigned sixty years and ten months without having done anything worthy the notice of posterity (Pausan. iii. 6). (3) Cleomenes III., son of Leonidas II., ascended the Spartan throne B.C. 236. Dissatisfied at the prevailing manners of Sparta, he resolved to bring about a reform, and to restore the institutions of Lycurgus, after the example of Agis, who had lost his life in a similar attempt. Thinking that war would furnish the best opportunity for the execution of his design, he led his forces against the Achaeans, who were commanded by Aratus, and greatly distinguished himself. Returning after this to Sparta, with a portion of his army, he put to death the Ephori, made a new division of the lands, and introduced again the old Spartan system of education. He also took his brother Euclidas as his colleague on the throne, and thus for the first and only time the Spartans had two kings of the same family. After a long, and in many respects successful, series of operations against the Achaeans and Macedonians, the latter of whom had been called in by Aratus as allies, Cleomenes was defeated by Antigonus in the battle of Sellasia (B.C. 222), and immediately after fled to Ptolemy Euergetes in Egypt. This monarch treated him with some degree of generosity, but his successor, Ptolemy Philopator, a weak and suspicious prince, soon began to look upon him with an evil eye, and at last kept him in confinement. The Spartan monarch, in a fit of despair, and taking advantage of the temporary absence of Ptolemy from his capital, broke forth from the place where he had been kept in custody, along with thirteen of his friends, and endeavoured to arouse the inhabitants in the cause of freedom. But, finding their efforts fruitless, they fell by their own hands (B.C. 220). (4) An Athenian sculptor, who probably flourished in the Augustan Age. The celebrated Venus de' Medici, now at Florence, is perhaps his. He is described on the pedestal as son of Apollodorus. The "Germanicus" of the Louvre was the work of his son, who bore the same name.

Venus de' Medici of Cleomenes. (Uffizi Gallery, Florence.)

Cleon (Κλέων). An Athenian, the son of a tanner, and said himself to have exercised that trade. Of extraordinary impudence and little courage, slow in the field, but forward and noisy in the assembly, corrupt, but boastful of integrity, and supported by a coarse but ready eloquence, he gained such consideration by flattering the lower orders that he became the head of a party. By an extraordinary train of circumstances he came off victorious in the affair of Sphacteria (q. v.), the Athenian populace having chosen him one of their generals. Elated upon this with the idea that he possessed military talents, he caused himself to be appointed commander of an expedition into Thrace. He was slain in a battle at Amphipolis against Brasidas, the Spartan general, B.C. 422.

It is probably unfortunate in the interest of historical truth that the accounts we have of Cleon's personality exist only in the writings of Thucydides and a partisan play, *The Knights*, of Aristophanes, both of whom were violently prejudiced against Cleon, the former personally and the latter politically. For some remarks on this head, see the history of Grote.

Cleōnae (Κλεωναί). An ancient town in Argolis, on the road from Corinth to Argos, on a river of the same name flowing into the Corinthian Gulf. In its neighbourhood was Nemea, where Heracles killed the lion, which is accordingly called Cleonaeus Leo by the poets.

Cleopātra (Κλεοπάτρα and Κλειοπάτρα; the penult is scanned long in Juv. ii. 109; Luc. ix. 1071.) (1) A daughter of Idas and Marpessa, and the wife of Meleager (Hom. *Il.* ix. 557). (2) The wife of Philip of Macedon, whom that monarch married after he had repudiated Olympias. After the death of Philip, Olympias compelled her to destroy herself (Just. ix. 7). (3) A daughter of Philip and Olympias, and sister to Alexander the Great. She married Alexander of Epirus, who fell in Italy (Just. ix. 6, 1). After the death of Alexander of Macedon, her hand was sought by Perdiccas and others of his generals, but she was put to death by Antigonus. (4) A daughter of Mithridates, and the wife of Tigranes (Just. xxxviii. 3). (5) A daughter of Antiochus III. of Syria. She married Ptolemy V., king of Egypt, and was left guardian of her infant son Ptolemy VI., but she died soon after her husband, to the great regret of her subjects. (6) A daughter of Ptolemy Philometor, was the wife of three kings of Syria, and the mother of four—namely, of Antiochus Dionysius, by her first husband, Alexander Balas; of Seleucus V. and Antiochus VIII., by Demetrius Nicator; and, lastly, of Antiochus IX., surnamed Cyzicenus, by Antiochus Euergetes or Sidetes. She was compelled by her son, Antiochus VIII., to drink the poison which she had prepared for him, B.C. 120. (7) The most famous of the name was the daughter of Ptolemy Auletes, and remarkable for her beauty and personal accomplishments. According to the usage of the Alexandrian court, she married her young brother, Ptolemy XII., and began to reign with him in her seventeenth year. Both she and her husband, being minors, were placed by the will of their father under the guardianship of Rome, an office which the Senate assigned to Pompey. An insurrection breaking out in the Egyptian capital soon after the commencement of this reign, Cleopatra was compelled to yield to the tide of popular fury, and to flee into Syria, where she sought protection in temporary exile. The flight of this princess, though mainly arising from the tumult just mentioned, was unquestionably accelerated by the designs of the young king and his ambitious ministers. Their object became manifest when Cleopatra, after a few months' residence in Syria, returned towards her native country to resume her seat on the throne. Ptolemy prepared to oppose her by force of arms, and a civil war would inevitably have ensued, had not Caesar at that very juncture sailed to the coast of Egypt in pursuit of Pompey. A curious interview soon took place between Cleopatra and the Roman general. She placed herself on board a small skiff,

Cleopatra. (From a Composite Photograph of the Heads on four Egyptian Coins. Reproduced by permission from Gorringe's *Egyptian Obelisks*.)

under the protection of Apollodorus, a Sicilian Greek, set sail from the coast of Syria, reached the harbour of Alexandria in safety, and had herself conveyed naked into the chamber of the Roman commander in the form of a large package of goods. The stratagem proved completely successful. Cleopatra was now in her twentieth year, distinguished by extraordinary personal charms, and surrounded with all the graces which give to those charms their greatest power. Her voice was extremely sweet, and she spoke a variety of languages with propriety and ease. She could, it is said, assume all characters at will, which all alike became her, and the impression that was made by her beauty was confirmed by the fascinating brilliancy of her conversation. The day after this singular meeting, Caesar summoned before him the king, as well as the citizens of Alexandria, and made arrangements for the restoration of peace, procuring Cleopatra, at the same time, her share of the throne. Pothinus, however, one of Ptolemy's ministers, in whose intriguing spirit all the dissensions of the court had originated, soon stirred up a second revolt, upon which the Alexandrian War commenced, in which Ptolemy was defeated and lost his life by drowning. Caesar now proclaimed Cleopatra queen of Egypt; but she was compelled to take her brother, the younger Ptolemy, who was only eleven years old, as her husband and colleague on the throne. The Roman general continued for some time at her court, and she bore him a son, called, from the name of his putative father, Caesarion. During the six years which immediately followed these events, the reign of Cleopatra seems not to have been disturbed by insurrection, nor to have been assailed by foreign war. When her brother, at the age of fourteen, demanded his share in the government, Cleopatra poisoned him, and remained sole possessor of the regal authority. The dissensions among the rival leaders who divided the power of Caesar had no doubt nearly involved her in a contest with both parties; but the decisive issue of the battle of Philippi relieved her from the hesitation under which some of her measures appear to have been adopted, and determined her inclinations, as well as her interests, in favour of the conquerors. To afford her an opportunity of explaining her conduct, Antony summoned her to attend him in Cilicia, and the meeting which she gave him on the river Cydnus has employed the pen, not only of the historian, but of the prince of English dramatists.

The artifices of this fascinating princess, now in her twenty-seventh year, so far gained upon Antony as not only to divert his thoughts from his original purpose of subjecting her kingdom to the payment of tribute, but entirely to lull his ambition to sleep, and make him sacrifice his great stake as a candidate for the empire of the world. After a fruitless attack upon the territory of Palmyra, he hastened to forget his disgrace in the society of the Egyptian queen, passing several months at Alexandria in the wildest and most delirious dissipation. The death of his wife, and his subsequent marriage with Octavia, delayed for a time the crisis which his ungoverned passions were preparing for him. But, though he had thus extricated himself from the snares of Alexandria, his inclinations too soon returned to that unlucky city; for we find that when he left Rome to proceed against the Parthians, he despatched in advance his friend Fonteius Capito to conduct Cleopatra into Syria.

Cleopatra.

On his return from this disgraceful campaign, he incurred still deeper dishonour by once more willingly submitting to that bondage which had rendered him contemptible in the eyes of most of his followers.

Passing over events which have been alluded to in the article AUGUSTUS CAESAR, we come to the period that followed the battle of Actium, at which the desertion of Cleopatra with her galleys and the pursuit of her by the infatuated Antony changed the destiny of the Roman Empire (B.C. 30). When Octavianus advanced against Egypt, and Antony had been a second time defeated under the walls of Alexandria, Cleopatra shut herself up with a few attendants and the most valuable part of her treasures in a strong building which appears to have been intended for a royal sepulchre. To prevent intrusion by friend or enemy she caused a report to be circulated that she had retired into the monument to put herself to death. Antony resolved to follow her example, and threw himself upon his sword; but being informed, before he expired, that Cleopatra was still living, he caused himself to be carried into her presence, and breathed his last in her arms. Octavianus, after this, succeeded in getting Cleopatra into his power, and the queen at first hoped to subdue him by her attractions; but finding at last that her efforts were unavailing, and suspecting that her life was spared only that she might grace the conqueror's triumph, she ended her days, if the common account is to be credited, by the bite of an asp; though some ascribed her death to poison administered internally. A small puncture in the arm was the only mark of violence which could be detected on the body of Cleopatra, and it was therefore believed that she had procured death either by the bite of a venomous reptile or by the use of a poisoned bodkin. She died in her thirty-ninth year, having reigned twenty-two years from the death of her father. Octavianus, it is said, though deprived by this act of suicide of the greatest ornament of his approaching triumph, gave orders that she should have a magnificent funeral, and that her body, as she desired, should be laid by that of Antony. Her two children by Antony were reared by the neglected wife Octavia.

The name of Cleopatra has been linked by romance and poetry with those of the most fascinating women the world has seen—Helen of Troy, Mary Stuart, and Ninon de Lenclos—and has always exercised a powerful influence upon the imagination of men. In English literature the genius of Shakespeare and of Dryden has made her story the theme of dramas; while the resources of art have been exhausted to produce types that should satisfy the eye and the mind of the critic.

Cleopatris (Κλεοπατρίς). A city of Egypt, at the head of the Sinus Arabicus and in the immediate vicinity of Arsinoë. See ARSINOË.

Cleostrătus (Κλεόστρατος). An astronomer of Tenedos, who is said to have introduced the familiar Zodiac signs. He flourished about the year B.C. 500.

Clepsȳdra (κλεψύδρα). A water-clock. See HOROLOGIUM.

Clerk. See SCRIBA.

Clerūchi (κληροῦχοι). See CLERUCHIA.

Cleruchia (κληρουχία). A kind of Greek colony, which differed from the ordinary colonial settlement in the fact that the settlers remained in close connection with their mother-city. The Athenian *cleruchiae* are the only ones of which we have any detailed knowledge. A conquered territory was divided into lots of land, which were assigned to the poorer citizens as *cleruchi* or "holders of lots." The original inhabitants would be differently treated according to circumstances. In many cases they were compelled to emigrate; sometimes the men were killed and the women and children enslaved; but ordinarily the old inhabitants would have become the tenants of the settlers, and take, generally, a less privileged position. The settlers formed a separate community, elected their own officials, and managed their local affairs; but they continued to be Athenian citizens, with all the rights and duties of their position. They remained under the authority of Athens, and were obliged to repair to the Athenian courts for justice in all important matters. See COLONIA.

Clerus (κλῆρος). See HERES.

Cleta (Κλῆτα). See CHARITES.

Cletēres (κλητῆρες) or **Cletŏres** (κλήτορες). Summoners; persons who at Athens were witnesses to the prosecutor of a suit, that he had served the defendant with a notice of the action brought against him and of the day on which it would be necessary for him to appear for the first examination of the case. They were not, therefore, court officials, but only agents of the prosecutor, and their names were subscribed to his declaration. See Meier, *Att. Process*, pp. 212, 576.

Clibanarii. The same as *cataphracti* (q. v.).

Clibănus (κλίβανος). A covered vessel pierced round with small holes and used for baking bread, being enveloped in hot ashes whose warmth penetrated the holes (Petron. 35).

Clientēla. See CLIENTES.

Clientes. The name originally applied to such inhabitants of Rome as had lost or given up the citizenship of their own cities, and had settled in Roman territory. Here, having no legal rights, they were compelled, in order to secure their personal freedom, to seek the protection of some Roman citizen, a term which, in ancient times, could mean only a patrician. The relation thus set on foot was called *clientela*, and was inherited by the descendants of both parties. Accordingly the client entered into the family of his patron (*patronus*), took his gentile name, and was admitted to take part in the family sacrifices. The patron made over to him a piece of land as a means of support, protected him from violence, represented him at law, and buried him after his death. The client, on his part, accompanied his patron abroad and on military service, gave his advice in legal and domestic matters, and made a contribution from his property if his patron were endowing a daughter, or had to be ransomed in war or to pay a fine. The relation between patron and client is also illustrated by the fact that neither party could bring an action against the other in a court of law, or bear witness against him, or vote against him, or appear against him as advocate. A man's duty to his client was more binding than his duty to his blood relations, and any violation of it was regarded as a capital offence.

When Servius Tullius extended the rights of citizenship to the clients as well as to the plebeians, the bond between patron and client still continued in force, although it gradually relaxed with the course of time. At the end of the republican age the *status* of client, in the proper sense of the word, had ceased to exist. Under the Empire the *clientela* was a mere external relation between the rich and the poor, the great and the obscure. It involved no moral obligation on either side, but was based merely on the vanity of the one party and the necessity of the other. It was no unusual thing to find persons who had no settled means of subsistence trying, by flattery and servile behaviour, to win the favour of the great. Even philosophers and poets, like Statius and

Martial, are found in this position. The client performed certain services, called on his patron in the morning, accompanied him on public occasions, and was in turn invited to his table, received presents from him, and (if he could get it) a settled provision. Instead of inviting their numerous clients, the rich would often present them with a small sum of money called *sportula*. The relation was entirely a free one, and could be dissolved at pleasure by either party.

In the republican age whole communities, and even provinces, when they had submitted to the Roman yoke, would sometimes become clients of a single *patronus*. In this case the *patronus* would usually be the conquering general. Marcellus, for instance, the conqueror of Syracuse, and his descendants, were patrons of Sicily. The practical advantages which were secured to a foreign community by this permanent representation at Rome are obvious. Accordingly we find that, under the Empire, even cities which stood to Rome in no relation of dependence, such as colonies and *municipia*, sometimes selected a *patronus*. The *patronus* was, in such cases, always chosen from among the senators or *equites*. See Mommsen, *Abhandlung über das römische Gastrecht und die römische Clientel* (in *Römische Forschungen*) (Berlin, 1864–79); McLennan, *The Patriarchal Theory* (London, 1885); and Morey, *Outlines of Roman Law* (New York, 1889).

Clima (κλίμα). Literally "a slope" or "inclination"; a term used in the mathematical geography of the Greeks with reference to the inclination of various parts of the earth's surface to the plane of the equator. Before the globular figure of the earth was known, it was supposed that there was a general slope of its surface from south to north, and this was called κλίμα. But as the science of mathematical geography advanced, the word was applied to different belts of the earth's surface, which were determined by the different lengths of the longest day at their lines of demarcation. This division into climates was applied only to the northern hemisphere, as the geographers had no practical knowledge of the earth south of the equator. The term κλίμα was afterwards applied to the temperature of these belts; hence the meaning of the modern word *climate*.

Hipparchus (about B.C. 160) seems to have been the first who made use of this division; his system is explained at length by Strabo (ii. p. 132).

The word *clima* is found only in the later Latin, the pure Latin term being *inclinatio, declinatio*, or *devergentia*.

Climax (κλῖμαξ). (1) A ladder or staircase. (See DOMUS; SCALAE.) (2) An instrument of torture. See TORMENTUM.

Climax (Κλῖμαξ). The name applied to the western termination of the Taurus range, which extends along the western coast of the Pamphylian Gulf, north of Phaselis in Lycia. Alexander made a road between it and the sea.

Climberrum. The capital of the AUSCI (q. v.).

Clinias (Κλεινίας). (1) A Pythagorean philosopher and musician, 400 years before the Christian era. (2) An Athenian, said by Herodotus (viii. 17) to have been the bravest of his countrymen in the battle fought against the Persian fleet at Artemisium; and the Athenians are said by the same writer to have conducted themselves on that occasion with the greatest valour of any of the Greeks. This Clinias was the father of the celebrated Alcibiades (q. v.). He married Dinomaché, the daughter of Megacles, grandson to Agaristé, the daughter of Clisthenes, tyrant of Sicyon. He fell at the battle of Coronea.

Clinĭcus (κλινικός). (1) A visiting physician who attended his patient at the bedside (Mart. ix. 27). (See MEDICUS.) (2) An undertaker (Mart. i. 31). See VESPILLO.

Clinŏpus (κλινόπους). The foot of a bedstead. See LECTUS.

Clinton, HENRY FYNES. A remarkable English classical scholar, born at Gamston (Nottinghamshire) in 1781. Educated at Westminster School and at Christ Church, Oxford (1803), he showed an unusual aptitude for the study of classical literature and history, which he pursued with little interruption all his life, though he served as member of Parliament for Aldborough from 1806 to 1826.

His life-work was the elucidation of Greek and Roman chronology, and his two great productions stand upon a basis of such remarkably profound and enduring scholarship that they are unlikely ever to be superseded or disused. These are the *Fasti Hellenici: a Civil and Literary Chronology of Greece*, 4 vols. (1824–34), and the *Fasti Romani: a Civil and Literary Chronology of Rome and Constantinople from the Death of Augustus to the Death of Heraclius*, 2 vols. (1845–51). Of the former work, an epitome was published in 1850; and of the second, in 1854. Mr. Clinton died at Welwyn, October 24th, 1852. His literary remains were edited and published by Mr. C. F. J. Clinton in 1854.

Clīo (Κλειώ). The Muse who presided over history, and generally represented as holding a half-opened roll. The invention of the cithara was ascribed to her. Having drawn on herself the anger of Aphrodité, by taunting her with her passion for Adonis, Clio was inspired by the goddess with love for Pierus, the son of Magnes, and bore him a son named Hyacinthus (Apollod. i. 3, 2 foll.). Her name is derived from κλεῖος (Ionic for κλέος), "glory," "renown," etc., because she celebrates the glorious actions of the good and the brave.

Clio, the Muse of History. (From a Statue now in Sweden.)

Clipeus and **Clipeum** (ἀσπίς, σάκος). (1) The large shield used by the Greeks and the Romans, originally of circular shape, said to have been first used by Proetus and Acrisius of Argos (Pausan. ii. 25, § 6); and therefore called *clipeus Argolicus* According to other accounts, however, it was derived from the Egyptians (Herod. iv. 180).

One of the earliest extant representations of Greek shields is to be found in the engraving on a sword-blade found at Mycenae, representing a combat between men and lions (Helbig, *Homerische Epos*, p. 232). It will be seen that some of the men carry shields resembling a *scutum*, others shields which recall the shape of the Boeotian shield, and that each form covers about three quarters of the person, and is partly supported by a strap passing round the shoulders.

Early Representation of Greek Shields. (Helbig.)

The heroes of the *Iliad* carry a shield which is round (iii. 347) and large enough to cover the whole man (ἀμφιβρότη, ποδηνεκής). It is composed by sewing together circular pieces of untanned ox-hide, varying in number. These are strengthened on both sides by plates of bronze, the outer hides and plates being of smaller diameter, so that on the edge of the shield both hide and metal are thinnest (*Il.* xx. 275).

Sarpedon's shield is forged of plates of bronze, to which ox-hides are attached on the inside by golden rods or bolts (ῥάβδοι) running all round the circle. Ten circles of bronze run round Agamemnon's shield. Achilles' shield is composed entirely of metal in five plates—two of bronze, two of tin, and a central one of gold. The structure is bound together by a metal rim (ἄντυξ), which in Achilles' shield is triple. At the centre of the shield is a metal boss (ὀμφαλός). Agamemnon's shield is studded with twenty bosses of tin and a central one of *cyanus* (*Il.* xi. 34).

When not in use the shield was suspended by the τελαμών, which passed around the breast, the shield hanging at the back. (See BALTEUS.) The practice of decorating the shield had commenced in the Homeric Age (*Il.* xi. 36).

In later times the shields were smaller, usually covering the warrior from the neck to the knees only. Besides the circular or Argive shield, we frequently find mentioned one of an oval shape with a strong rim and apertures in the middle of each side (Eurip. *Phoeniss.* 1386). This is known as the Boeotian shield.

Greek Shield. (Tischbein.)

The shield was at last formed entirely of brass (πάγχαλκος), and a sort of apron, probably of leather or some thick material, was sometimes attached to it, especially when one did not wear greaves to protect his legs. The simplest arrangement to hold the shield consisted of two metal handles, one to pass the arm through and one to grasp with the hand; but the more elaborate arrangement is shown in the illustration from a terra-cotta vase published by Tischbein (iv. tab. 20). In it the broad band that runs across the shield like the diameter of a circle is of metal, the thong about the edge of the rim of leather (πόρπαξ).

At the close of a war it was customary for the Greeks to suspend their shields in the temples, when the πόρπακες were taken off, in order to render them unserviceable in case of any sudden or popular outbreak. Sometimes shields were kept in a case (σάγμα), (Aristoph. *Ach.* 574).

The ἀσπίς was the characteristic defensive weapon (ὅπλον) of the heavy-armed infantry (ὁπλῖται) during the historical times of Greece, and is opposed to the lighter πέλτη and γέρρον; hence we find the word ἀσπίς used to signify a body of ὁπλῖται (Xen. *Anab.* i. 7, § 10). It was distinctively a Greek shield, and thus none of the Eastern peoples who served under Xerxes (Herod. vii. 61 foll.) were armed with it.

The Roman *clipeus* is seen in the accompanying illustration from the Column of Trajan. According to Livy (i. 43), when the census was instituted by Servius Tullius, the first class only used the clipeus, and the second were armed with the *scutum* (q. v.); but after the Roman soldier received pay, the clipeus was discontinued altogether for the Sabine *scutum* (Liv. viii. 8; cf. ix. 19; Plut. *Rom.* 21; Diod. *Eclog.* xxiii. 3, who asserts that the original form of the Roman shield was square, and that it was subsequently changed for that of the Tyrrhenians, which was round).

Clipeus, Roman Shield. (Column of Trajan.)

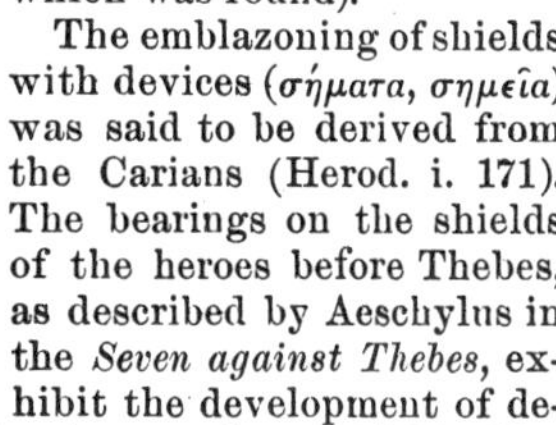

The emblazoning of shields with devices (σήματα, σημεῖα) was said to be derived from the Carians (Herod. i. 171). The bearings on the shields of the heroes before Thebes, as described by Aeschylus in the *Seven against Thebes*, exhibit the development of devices in post-Homeric times. Some shields, like Agamemnon's, bear subjects designed to strike terror; to that of Tydeus bronze bells are attached with the same object. Other subjects are purely mythological or indicate the owner's ancestry. This custom of emblazoning shields is illustrated on a very beautiful gem from the antique, in which the figure of Victory is represented inscribing upon a clipeus the name or merits of some deceased hero.

From the historians we find that while an individual sometimes attracted attention by an unusual device, cities made use of some common symbol for their shields which might be easily recognizable by their friends: thus the Lacedaemonians used Λ, the Sicyonians Σ, the Thebans Heracles's club—a practice of which the enemy sometimes took a treacherous advantage (Xen. *Hell.* iv. 4, 10; vii. 50; Pausan. iv. 58, 5).

Each Roman soldier also had his own name and a mark indicating his cohort inscribed upon his shield, in order that he might readily find his own when the order was given to unpile arms (Veget. ii. 17), and sometimes the name of the commander under whom he fought (Hirt. *Bell. Alex.* 58).

Victorious armies sometimes dedicated their own shields or an engraved shield of gold as an offering in a temple (Herod. i. 92). For decorative purposes, shields in metal or marble were often suspended from the roofs of porticoes or in the *atria* of private houses. See M. Albert in the *Revue Archéologique* (1881).

(2) CLIPEUS is also the name of a contrivance for regulating the temperature of the vapour-bath. See BALNEAE.

Clisthĕnes (Κλεισθένης). (1) A tyrant of Sicyon, who in B.C. 595 aided the Amphictyons in the Sacred War against Cirra, which ended in the destruction of that city. He was a resolute enemy of the Dorians, and in that spirit waged war on Argos. (See Herod. v. 67; vi. 125; Thuc. i. 18). (2) An Athenian, the son of Megacles and Agarista. He was the head of the Alcmaeonid family, and was opposed by Isagoras and the nobles; but by the support of the people reformed the constitution of the State upon a democratic basis. His changes were (1) the establishment of ten instead of four tribes, and the division into demes (see DEMUS); (2) the introduction of ostracism (see OSTRACISMUS); (3) the revival of election by lot; (4) the weakening of the power of the Heliastic court (see DICASTES). In spite of the interference of the Spartans under Cleomenes, these changes were finally established (B.C. 508). Of the later years of the life of Clisthenes, nothing definite is known. (Herod. v. 63–73; and vi. 131; Arist. 'Αθ. Πολ. 20, 21, 41.)

Clitarchus (Κλείταρχος). A Greek historian, son of the historian Dinon. He flourished about B.C. 300, and was the author of a great work, in at least twelve books, upon Alexander the Great. He was notoriously untrustworthy, and inclined to believe in the marvellous; his style was turgid and highly rhetorical; but his narrative was so interesting that he was the most popular of all the writers on Alexander. The Romans were very fond of his book, which was indeed the main authority for the narratives of Diodorus, Trogus Pompeius, and Q. Curtius. A number of fragments of it still survive.

Clitellae (κανθήλια). A pair of panniers, and therefore only used in the plural number. In Italy they were commonly used with mules or asses, but in other countries they were also applied to horses, of which an instance is given in the following illustration from the Column of Trajan; and Plautus figuratively describes a man upon whose shoulders a load of any kind, either moral or physical, is charged as *homo clitellarius*.

A particular spot in the city of Rome, and certain parts of the Via Flaminia, which, from their undulations in hill and valley, were thought to resemble the flowing line of a pair of panniers, were also termed Clitellae.

Clitellae. (Column of Trajan.)

Cliternum and **Cliternia.** A town of the Frentani in the territory of Larinum.

Clitomăchus (Κλειτόμαχος). A native of Carthage. In his early years he acquired a fondness for learning, which induced him to visit Greece for the purpose of attending the schools of the philosophers. From the time of his first arrival in Athens he attached himself to Carneades (q. v.), and continued his disciple until his death, when he became his successor in the academic chair. He studied with great industry and made himself master of the systems of the other schools, but professed the doctrine of suspension of assent, as it had been taught by his master. Cicero relates that he wrote four hundred books upon philosophical subjects. At an advanced age he was seized with a lethargy. Recovering in some measure the use of his faculties, he said, "The love of life shall deceive me no longer," and laid violent hands upon himself. He entered, as we have said, upon the office of preceptor in the Academy immediately after the death of Carneades, and held it thirty years. According to Cicero, he taught that there is no certain criterion by which to judge of the truth of those reports which we receive from the senses, and that, therefore, a wise man will either wholly suspend his assent, or decline giving a peremptory opinion; but that, nevertheless, men are strongly impelled by nature to follow probability. His moral doctrine established a natural alliance between pleasure and virtue. He was a professed enemy to rhetoric, and thought that no place should be allowed in society to so dangerous an art.

Clitor (Κλείτωρ) or **Clitorium.** A town in the north of Arcadia on a river of the same name, a tributary of the Aroanius. There was a fountain in the neighbourhood, the waters of which are said to have given to persons who drank of them a dislike for wine (Pausan. viii. 4, 21).

Clitumnus. A small river in Umbria, springing from a beautiful rock in a grove of cypress-trees where was a sanctuary of the god Clitumnus, and falling into the Tinia, a tributary of the Tiber.

Clitus (Κλεῖτος). A familiar friend and foster-brother of Alexander, who had saved the king's life in battle. Alexander killed him with a javelin in a fit of inebriety, because, at a feast, he preferred the actions of Philip to those of his son. See Plut. *Alex.* 16, 50–52.

Cloāca (ὑπόνομος). A sewer, or drain. Drains for the removal of a city's sewage are of very great antiquity, since at Nineveh excavations show a very complete system of sewers; while the same is true of Athens, where the remains of the ancient drains have been carefully described by Ziller (*Mittheil. des deutsch. Inst. in Athen* (1877), pp. 117–119).

The sewers of ancient Rome were much admired in ancient times, and were classed by Dionysius of Halicarnassus with the aqueducts and roads as the best proof of the greatness and magnificence of the Roman Empire (iii. 67) Many of the Roman cities in northern Italy and in Gaul still show remains of similar cloacae.

The chief of the ancient Roman sewers still existing is the famous Cloaca Maxima, running from the valley of the Subura at the foot of the Carinae, across the Forum under the south end of the Basilica Iulia, where it is exposed to view, and entering the river Tiber, near the Temple of Hercules in the Forum Boarium, by an arch of peperino shown in the illustration. The original dimensions of the arch were 12 ft. 4 in. in height, and 10 ft. 8 in. in width, but one-third of its height is now choked up by mud.

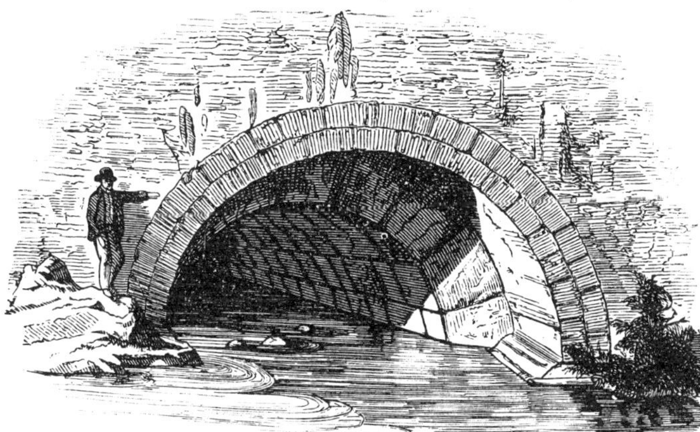

Present Condition of the Cloaca Maxima.

Another sewer, which like the Cloaca Maxima is still in use, enters the Tiber opposite to the Insula Tiberina. Its antiquity is very great, and it is constructed of large blocks of peperino uncemented. In the quay wall not far from the mouth of the Cloaca Maxima may be seen two smaller arched openings, one of which is now dry, the other discharges the waters of the Aqua Crabra.

M. Agrippa, during his aedileship, in B.C 36, showed great zeal in the supervision of the cloacae, traversing them in a boat and cleansing them at his own expense (Dio Cass. xlix. 43). He constructed a cloaca to drain the Campus Martius, which was connected with the Thermae of Agrippa and the Aqua Virgo. This was discovered under Urban VIII., and is at present in use under the name of the Chiavica della Rotonda.

The discoveries made at various times show that the network of smaller drains communicating with these main cloacae still exists, though in great part choked up. Brick is largely used in their construction; sometimes they are covered in with a barrel vault, sometimes by two tiles leaning against each other, sometimes by a single flagstone, but in some cases we find a primitive arrangement of projecting courses of stone which was observed in the drains of Athens.

The expense of cleansing and repairing these cloacae was, of course, very great, and was defrayed partly by the treasury and partly by an assessment called *cloacarium*. Under the Republic the administration of the sewers was intrusted to the censors and aediles; but under the Empire particular officers were appointed for that purpose, *cloacarum curatores*, mention of whom is found in inscriptions. Under the Empire condemned criminals were employed in cleansing the cloacae. (Plin. *Ep.* x. 44 [41].) Theodoric appointed an official to repair the drains, a striking instance of the esteem in which the barbarians held Roman civilization.

On the legal obligations relating to the cloacae at Rome, see Schmidt, *Interdicta de cloacis*, in *Zeitschrift f. gesch. Rechtswiss.* xv. 1, pp. 51 foll.; and for further details as to the Roman sewers, see Burn, *Rome and the Campagna*; Middleton, *Rome in 1885* (1885); id. *Remains of Ancient Rome* (London, 1892).

Cloacarium. See CLOACA

Cloacīna. A Roman divinity who presided over sewers (*cloacae*). More properly, however, the word should be written Cluacina (from *cluo* = *purgo*, Plin. xv. 29, 36), being so called because at the end of the war with the Sabines the Romans purified themselves in the vicinity of the statue of Venus with myrtle boughs (Pliny, l. c.). Later, the similarity of spelling caused a confusion with *cloaca, cloacina*. See Lactant i 20.

Cloak. See ABOLLA; AMICTUS; LACERNA; PAENULA; PALLIUM; SAGUM.

Cloanthus. One of the companions of Aeneas, from whom the family of the Cluentii at Rome claimed descent (Verg. *Aen.* v. 122).

Clocks. See HOROLOGIUM.

Clodia. (1) A sister of Clodius (q. v.) the tribune, and a woman of the most abandoned character. She married Q. Metellus Celer, and was suspected of having poisoned him. She is supposed to have been the Lesbia to whom Catullus wrote so many of his love poems. (See CATULLUS, and on the identity, the ingenious conjecture of Dr. A. Gudeman, on Plut. *Cicero*, 29, in the *Amer. Jour. of Philol.* vol. xi. no. 3.) (2) The younger sister of the preceding, and equally infamous in character. She married Lucullus, but was repudiated by him for her scandalous conduct.

Clodia Lex. See LEX.

Clodius Albīnus. See ALBINUS.

Clodius Pulcher, PUBLIUS. A noted Roman demagogue, the enemy of Cicero. He first appears in history as an officer of Lucullus in Asia (B.C. 70). In the following year he accused Catiline of extortion in Africa, but was bribed to abandon the prosecution. In B.C. 62, he was alleged to have had an intrigue with Pompeia, the wife of Iulius Caesar, to meet whom he profaned the rites of the Bona Dea by entering the house of Caesar where they were being held; but was detected by Caesar's mother, and subsequently tried for sacrilege, but escaped conviction by lavish bribery. It was because of this affair that Caesar divorced his wife, with the famous remark that those of his household must be above suspicion (Suet. *Iul.* 74). At the trial Clodius had attempted to prove an alibi, but Cicero's evidence showed that Clodius was with him in Rome only three hours before he pretended to have been at Interamna. In order to revenge himself upon Cicero, Clodius caused himself to be adopted into a plebeian family, that he might obtain the formidable power of a tribune of the plebs. As tribune in 58, supported by the triumvirs Caesar, Pompey, and Crassus, he drove Cicero into exile; but, notwithstanding all his efforts, he was unable to prevent the recall of Cicero in the following year. In 56, Clodius was aedile, and attempted to bring his enemy, T. Annius Milo, to trial. Each had gladiators in his pay, and frequent fights took place in the streets of Rome between the two parties. At the time when Clodius was a candidate for the praetorship and Milo for the consulship, on the 20th of January, B.C. 52, on the Via Appia, near Bovillae, an affray ensued between their followers, in which Clodius was killed. The mob was infuriated at the death of its favourite; and such tumults followed at the burial of Clodius that Pompey was appointed sole consul (*consul sine collega*), in order to restore order to the State. See CICERO; MILO; POMPEIUS.

Cloelia. A Roman virgin, given as a hostage to Porsenna. According to the old Roman legend, when Porsenna and the Romans made a peace after the affair of Mucius Scaevola (q. v.), the latter people gave hostages to the king—ten youths and ten maidens, children of noble parents—as a pledge that they would truly keep the peace which had been proclaimed. It happened, as the camp of the Etrurians was near the Tiber, that Cloelia, one of the maidens, escaped with her companions and fled to the brink of the river; and, as the Etrurians pursued them, they all rushed into the water and swam in safety across the stream. But the Romans, jealous of their reputation for good faith, sent them all back to the camp of Porsenna. Not to be outdone in generosity, the monarch gave her and her female companions their freedom, and permitted her to take with her half of the youths; whereupon, with the delicacy of a Roman maiden, she selected those only who were of tender years. The Romans raised an equestrian statue in her honour on the highest part of the Via Sacra (Liv. ii. 13). There is another story, that Tarquinius fell upon the hostages as they were conducted into the Etrurian camp, and with the exception of Valeria, who fled back to the city, massacred them all (Plin. xxxiv. 13).

Klopes Diké or **Klopes Graphé** (κλοπῆς δίκη or γραφή). The action for theft at Athens might be either private or public, and in the former case either before a diaetetes or a court, probably that of the thesmothetae (Meier, *Att. Process*, p. 66, with Lipsius's note 101). The various modes of procedure are enumerated by Demosthenes (*c. Androt.* p. 601, §§ 26, 27).

Closet. See CUBICULUM.

Clota Aestuarium. The modern Frith of Clyde on the western coast of Scotland.

Clothing. See for (1) Outer garments, ABOLLA, ALICULA, AMICTUS, BIRRUS, BRACAE, CALIPTRA, CASTULA, CENTO, CHLAMYS, COA VESTIS, CUCULLUS, CYCLAS, DIPLOIS, ENDROMIS, EXOMIS, FLAMMEUM, LACERNA, LACINIA, NEBRIS, PALLA, PALLIUM, PALUDAMENTUM, PEPLUM, RICA, SAGUM, SINUS, SUFFIBULUM, SYNTHESIS, TEGILLUM, TOGA, TRECHEDIPNUM, TUNICA, UMBO; (2) Under-garments, CHIRODOTA, CINGILLUM, COLOBIUM, DALMATICA, EXPAPILLATUS, INDUSIUM, INTERULA, PAENULA, RECTA, SUBUCULA, SUPPARUM, TUNICA; (3) Head-coverings, ALBOGALERUS, APEX, CALANTICA, CALIENDRUM, CAUSIA, CIDARIS, GALERUS, MITELLA, MITRA, OFFENDIX, PETASUS, PILLEUM, REDIMICULUM, THERISTRUM, TIARA, TUTULUS, VESICA; (4) Coverings for the Feet, BAXEAE, CALCEUS, CALIGA, COTHURNUS, CREPIDA, DIABATHRUM, ENDROMIS, FULMENTA, GALLICAE, LIGULA, MULLEUS, OBSTRAGULUM, PERO, PHAECASIUM, SANDALIUM, SOCCUS, SOLEA, TALARIA, ZANCHA; (5) Throat-covering, FOCALE; (6) Coverings for the Arms and Hands, DIGITALIA, MANICA.

Clotho (Κλωθώ). One of the Fates; the spinner of the thread of destiny. See MOERAE.

Clouds OF ARISTOPHANES. See NEPHELAE.

Clown. See BALATRO; SCURRA.

Club. See CLAVA.

Cluentius Habĭtus, AULUS. A Roman successfully defended by Cicero (B.C. 66) in an extant oration against a charge of poisoning. (Cf. Quint. ii. 17, 21).

Clupea (called by the Greek writers ASPIS). A town of Africa Propria, twenty-two miles east of Carthage. It was built upon a promontory which was shaped like a shield. Agathocles (q. v.) seized upon this place when he landed in Africa, fortified it, and gave it, from the shape of the promontory, the name of Aspis ("a shield" in Greek, same as *clupeus* in Latin).

Clusium. Now Chiusi; a town of Etruria, on the banks of the Clanis. Its more ancient name was Camers. The Gauls under Brennus besieged it, but marched to Rome without taking it. It was at Clusium that Porsenna held his court; and near this city he erected for himself the splendid mausoleum or labyrinth of which Pliny has transmitted to us a description on the authority of Varro. See LABYRINTHUS.

Clusius. A surname of Ianus, whose temple was closed (*clusum*) in peace.

Clymĕné (Κλυμένη). (1) A daughter of Oceanus and Tethys, who married Iapetus, by whom she had Atlas, Prometheus, Menoetius, and Epimetheus. (2) The mother of Phaëthon. (3) A female servant of Helen, who accompanied her in her flight with Paris.

Clymeneïdes. A patronymic given to Phaëthon's sisters, who were daughters of Clymené.

Clytaemnestra (Κλυταιμνήστρα). A daughter of Tyndarus, king of Sparta, by Leda. She was born, together with her brother Castor, from one of the eggs which her mother brought forth after her amour with Zeus under the form of a swan. She married Agamemnon, king of Mycenae, and when this monarch went to the Trojan War, he left his wife and family, and all his affairs, to the care of his relation Aegisthus. But the latter proved unfaithful to his trust, corrupted Clytaemnestra, and usurped the throne. Agamemnon, on his return home, was murdered by his guilty wife, who was herself afterwards slain, along with Aegisthus, by Orestes, son of the deceased monarch. For a more detailed account, see the articles AGAMEMNON and ORESTES.

Clytia (Κλυτία). In Greek mythology an ocean nymph, beloved by the Sun-god, who deserted her. She was changed into the heliotrope, a flower which is supposed always to turn its head in the direction of the sun's movement.

Cneph (Κνήφ) or **Cnuphis** (Κνοῦφις). An Egyptian deity regarded as the creator of the world, and represented in the form of a serpent.

Cnidus (Κνίδος). A town and promontory of Doris in Caria, at the extremity of a promontory called Triopium. The founder of the place is said to have been Triopas. From him it received at first the name of Triopium, which at a later period was confined merely to the promontory on which it stood (Herod. i. 174). Aphroditê was the chief deity of the place, and had three temples erected to her, under the several surnames of Doritis, Acraea, and Euploea. In the last of these stood a celebrated statue of the goddess, the work of Praxiteles (Pausan. i. 1; Plin. xxxvi. 5). Nicomedes of Bithynia wished to purchase this admirable production of the chisel, and actually offered to liquidate the debt of Cnidus, which was very considerable, if the citizens would cede it to him; but they refused to part with what they esteemed the glory of their city (Plin. l. c.). Off Cnidus took place in B.C. 394 a famous sea-fight between the Athenians, under Conon, and the Spartans, under Pisander, in which the former were victorious. The shores of Cnidus furnished in ancient times, as they do now, a great abundance of fish. The wines were famous, and Theophrastus speaks of the Cnidian onions as of a particular species, being very mild and not occasioning tears. Cnidus was the birthplace of the famous mathematician and astronomer Eudoxus; of Agatharchidas, Theopompus, and Ctesias. Excavations made at Cnidus in 1857–58 led to the discovery of many fine marbles, some of which may now be seen in the British Museum.

Cnōsus (Κνωσός, more correct than CNOSSUS, Κνωσσός, if we follow the language of coins; also GNŌSUS). The royal city of Crete, on the northern coast, at a small distance from the sea. Its earlier name was Caeratus, which appellation was given also to the inconsiderable stream that flowed beneath its walls. It was indebted to Minos for all its importance and splendour. That monarch is said to have divided the island into three portions, in each of which he founded a large city; and fixing his residence at Cnosus, it became the capital of the kingdom. It was here that Daedalus (q. v.) cultivated his art and planned the celebrated labyrinth.

Coa Vestis, also **Coa** (n. pl.). The Coan cloth or garments, mentioned by various authors, but most frequently by the Latin poets of the Augustan Age (e. g. Tibull. ii. 3, 53; 4, 29; Propert. i. 2, 2; ii. 1; v. (iv.) 2, 23; Hor. *Carm.* iv. 13, 13; *Sat.* i. 2, 101). From their expressions we learn that it had a great degree of transparency, that it was remarkably fine, that it was chiefly worn by women of loose reputation, and that it was sometimes dyed purple (Hor. *Carm.* l. c.) and enriched with stripes of gold. It has been supposed to have

Coa Vestis. (*Mus. Borbon.* viii. 5.)

been made of silk, because in Cos silk was spun and woven at an early period, so as to obtain a high celebrity. See SERICUM.

Coactor. A name applied to collectors of various sorts—e. g. to the servants of the publicani or farmers of the taxes, who collected the revenues for them (Cic. *Pro Rab. Post.* 11, § 30); also to those who collected the money from the purchasers of things sold at a public auction (id. *Pro Cluent.* 64, § 180). The father of Horace was a *coactor*, but there are no means of determining to which class he belonged (Hor. *Sat.* i. 6, 86; Suet. *Vit. Hor.*).

Cobet, CAREL GABRIEL, one of the most acute of modern text-critics and a Hellenist of great learning, was born at Paris, November 28th, 1813. He studied at The Hague and at the University of Leyden (1831–40), and showed so much ability as a philologist and student of classical antiquity that in 1840 the Dutch government sent him to Italy to pursue certain archæological investigations. In 1844 he was admitted to the doctorate at Leyden, and in 1846 became professor. He died October 26th, 1889. His publications are numerous and of great value, especially in the line of textual criticism, for which he showed great originality, sagacity, and insight. They are as follows: *Observationes Criticae in Platonis Comici Reliquias* (Amsterdam, 1840); *Oratio de Arte Interpretandi Grammatices et Critices*—his inaugural address—(1847); *Praefatio Lectionum de Historia Vetere* (1853); *Variae Lectiones quibus Continentur Observationes Criticae in Scriptores Graecos* (1854; 2d ed. 1873); an edition of Hyperides (1858); of Lysias (Amsterdam, 1863); of Xenophon's *Hellenica* (1862); of Diogenes Laërtius, in the Didot collection (Paris, 1850; 2d ed. 1862); *Miscellanea Philologica et Critica* (1873); *Miscellanea Critica* (1876); *Observationes Criticae in Dionysii Halicarnassensis Antiquitates Romanas* (1877); and *Collectanea Critica* (1878). He also edited for many years the philological journal *Mnemosyne* (Bibliotheca Philologica Batava), published at Leyden. See Hartmann, in the *Bibliogr. Jahrbuch*, xii. pp. 53 foll. (Berlin, 1889); id. *De Carolo Gabriele Cobet* (Berlin, 1890).

Cocălus (Κώκαλος). A mythical king of Sicily, who kindly received Daedalus (q. v.) on his flight from Crete, and with the assistance of his daughters put Minos to death, when the latter came in pursuit of Daedalus.

Cocceius Nerva. See NERVA.

Coccygius (τὸ Κοκκύγιον ὄρος). "Cuckoo-Mountain." A mountain of Argolis, between Halicé and Hermioné. Its previous name was Thornax, but it received the appellation of Coccygius from the circumstance that Zeus was metamorphosed there into the bird called Coccyx (Κόκκυξ) by the Greeks. On its summit was a temple sacred to that god, and another of Apollo at the base (Pausan. ii. 36).

Coché (Κωχή). A city on the Tigris, near Ctesiphon.

Cocintum Promontorium. A promontory of Bruttium in Lower Italy, below the Sinus Scylacius. The modern name is Cape Stilo. It marked the separation between the Ionian and Sicilian seas.

Cock-fighting. See GALLUS; VENATIONES.

Coclea or **Cochlea** (κοχλίας), which properly means a snail, was also used to signify other things of a spiral form.

(1) A screw, one of the mechanical powers, so named from its spiral form, which resembles the worming of a shell. The annexed illustration represents a clothes-press, from a painting on the wall of the Chalcidicum of Eumachia at Pompeii, which

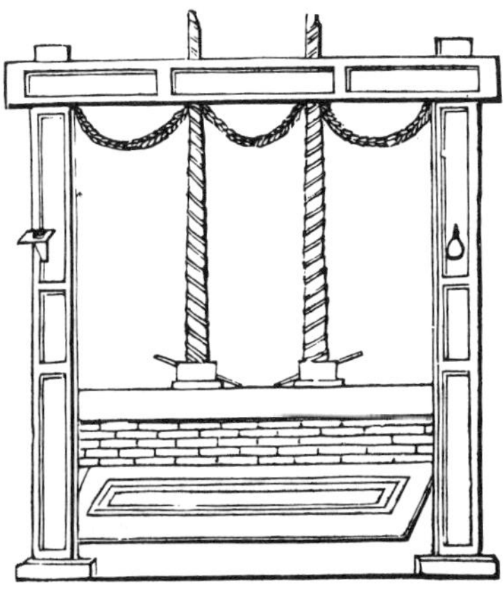

Coclea, or Clothes-press. (Pompeian Painting.)

is worked by two upright screws (*cocleae*) precisely in the same manner as our own linen-presses. A screw of the same description was also used in oil and wine presses. The thread of the screw, for which the Latin language has no appropriate term, is called περικόχλιον in Greek.

(2) A spiral pump for raising water, invented by Archimedes, from whom it has ever since been called the Archimedean screw. It is described at length by Vitruvius (x. 11). A pump of this kind was used for discharging the bilge-water in the ship of Hiero, which was built under the directions of Archimedes.

(3) A peculiar kind of door, through which the wild beasts passed from their dens into the arena of the amphitheatre. It consisted of a circular cage, open on one side like a lantern, which worked upon a pivot and within a shell, like the machines used in the convents and foundling hospitals of Italy, termed *rote*, so that any particular beast could be removed from its den into the arena merely by turning it round, and without the possibility of more than one escaping at the same time; and therefore it is recommended by Varro as peculiarly adapted for an aviary, so that a person could go in and out without affording the birds an opportunity of flying away. Schneider, however, maintains that the *coclea* in question was nothing more than a portcullis (*cataphracta*) raised by a screw, which interpretation does not appear so probable as the one given above. See Varro, *R. R.* iii. 5, 3.

Coclear (κοχλιάριον λίστριον). A kind of spoon which appears to have terminated with a point at one end, and at the other was broad and hollow like our own spoons. The pointed end was used for drawing snails (*cocleae*) out of their shells and eating them, whence it derived its name; and the broader part for eating eggs, etc. Martial mentions both these uses of the coclear (xiv. 121):

Sum cocleis habilis nec sum minus utilis ovis.

Coclearia, spoons. (*Museo Borbonico.*)

Coclear was also the name given to a small measure like our spoonful. According to Rhemnius Fannius, it was $\frac{1}{48}$ of the *cyathus*. See Isid. *Orig.* xvi. 26, 3; and the article LIGULA.

Coclearium and **Cochlearium**. A place where snails were fattened for the tables of Roman gourmands.

Cocles, PUBLIUS HORATIUS (given by Niebuhr as Marcus Horatius). A Roman who, at first with Sp. Lartius and Titus Herminius, and then alone, opposed the whole army of Porsenna at the head of the Sublician bridge, while his companions behind him were cutting off the communication with the other shore. When the bridge was destroyed, Cocles, after addressing a short prayer to the god of the Tiber, leaped into the stream, and swam across in safety with his arms. As a mark of gratitude, every inhabitant, while famine was raging within the city, brought him all the provisions he could stint himself of; and the State afterwards raised a statue to him and gave him as much land as he could plough round in a day (Liv. ii. 10). As Polybius relates the story, Horatius defended the bridge alone from the first and then perished in the river. Macaulay's spirited ballad on the subject is familiar to all.

Cocossātes. A people in Aquitania in Gaul, mentioned along with the Tarbelli.

Cocylium (Κοκύλιον). An Aeolian city in Mysia, whose inhabitants are mentioned by Xenophon.

Cocȳtus (Κωκυτός, "River of Wailing"). A river in Epirus, a tributary of the Acheron. Like the Acheron, the Cocytus was supposed to be connected with the lower world, and hence came to be described as a river in the lower world. See HADES.

Codānus Sinus. One of the ancient names of the Baltic. Mela (iii. 3, 6) represents it as full of large and small islands, the largest of which he calls Scandinavia; so also Pliny (iv. 13).

Codex, dim. **Codicillus** (the older form being *caudex:* Cato, *ap.* Front. *Epist. ad M. Anton.* i. 2). A word originally signifying the trunk or stem of a tree (Verg. *Georg.* ii. 30), and hence used to designate anything composed of pieces of wood.

(1) A log of wood, attached as a punishment to the feet of slaves, which they dragged with them, and on which they also sat sometimes (Plaut. *Poen.* v. 3, 39).

(2) Boats on the Tiber, which may originally have been like the Indian canoes, or were constructed of several roughly hewn planks nailed together in a rude and simple manner, were called *naves caudicariae*, or *codicariae*, or *caudiceae* (Fest. p. 46 M.; Varr., Sall. *ap.* Non. p. 535, 13; Sen. *Brev. Vit.* 13, 4). The surname of Caudex given to Appius Claudius must be traced to this signification. In later times the name was given to ships employed in transporting the corn from Ostia to Rome; and the sailors engaged in this traffic, called *caudicarii* or *codicarii*, formed a corporation.

(3) The name of *codex* was given to wooden tablets bound together and lined with a coat of wax, for the purpose of writing upon them; and when, at a later age, parchment or paper or other materials were substituted for wood, and put together in the shape of a book, the name of *codex* was often used as synonymous with *liber*, or book (Cic. *Verr.* i. 46, § 119). It was the name more particularly given to an account-book or ledger, *codex accepti et expensi* (q. v.). In the time of Cicero we find it also applied to the tablet on which a bill was written. At a still later period, during the time of the emperors, the word was used to express any collection of laws or constitutions of the emperors, whether made by private individuals or by public authority. See CODEX GREGORIANUS; CODEX IUSTINIANEUS; CODEX THEODOSIANUS.

The word *codex* is largely used by scholars of the MS. editions of the classics that are preserved in the libraries of Europe, and date some from the fifth to the tenth centuries A.D., but the greater number from the thirteenth to the fifteenth. They are of parchment (folio or quarto size), usually with marginal notes written by other hands than those of the original copyist of the codex. (See LIBER; PALÆOGRAPHY; TEXTUAL CRITICISM.) They are named (1) after persons who once owned them, as the Codex Petavinus of Ovid, named after one Petavius, and the Codex Vossianus of the same classic, after Voss; and (2) more commonly after the places where they are kept. Thus there are in ENGLAND, Codices Britannici or Londinenses (British Museum), Codices Cantabrigienses (Cambridge), and Codices Oxonienses (Oxford). These last are also often noted as Codices Bodleiani (from the Bodleian Library). In FRANCE, one finds Codices Parisini (Paris), Codices Bliaudifontani (Fontainebleau), Codices Sangermanenses (St. Germain), Codices Montepessulani (Montpellier), etc. In HOLLAND, there are Codices Amstelodamienses (Amsterdam) and Codices Leidenses (Leyden); in BELGIUM, Codices Bruxellenses (Brussels) and Codices Blandiniani (Blankenberg); in DENMARK, Codices Haunienses (Copenhagen); in SWITZERLAND, Codices Bernenses (Berne), Codices Basilienses (Bâle), Codices Einsidlenses (Einsiedeln), Codices Sangallenses (St. Gallen), and Turicenses (Zürich); in GERMANY, Codices Argentoratenses (Strassburg), Codices Berolinenses (Berlin), Codices Colonienses (Cologne), Codices Palatini (Heidelberg), Codices Fuldenses (Fulda), Codices Caroliruhenses (Carlsruhe), Codices Regiomontani (Königsberg), Codices Guelferbytani (Wolfenbüttel), Codices Monacenses (Munich), Codices Lipsienses (Leipzig), and Codices Vratislavienses (Breslau), etc.; in AUSTRIA, Codices Vindobonenses (Vienna) and Codices Budenses (Buda); in RUSSIA, Codices Petropolitani (St. Petersburg); in SPAIN, Codices Matritenses (Madrid) and Codices Toletani (Toledo). In ITALY, the terminology is varied. The great collections are at (1) Florence, in the Bibliotheca Laurentiana of the Church of San Lorenzo, comprising MSS. from the Public Library of San Marco founded by Cosimo de' Medici, and from the collection of Peter Leopold. Hence Florentine codices are styled variously, Florentini, Laurentiani, S. Marci, Medicei, and Leopoldini Laurentiani; (2) Milan, where the codices are called either Mediolanenses, from the name of the city, or Ambrosiani, from the Ambrosian Library; (3) Venice, where they are called Veneti, or (from the Library of St. Mark) Veneti Marciani, or simply Marciani; (4) Turin, Codices Taurinenses; (5) Verona, Codices Veronenses; (6) Rome, where the great storehouse is the Vatican Library (Bibliotheca Vaticana), enriched by MSS. from many sources—e. g. from Fulvius Orsini, from Heidelberg, from the Library of Urbino, etc. Hence the Codices Vaticani often receive names to specify more particularly their original sources, as Codices Ursiniani, Codices Palatini, Codices Urbinates, etc. (7) Naples, where the codices are called Neapolitani, or (from the old Bourbon Library) Borbonici. A complete list of Latin MSS. down to the seventh century is given by Prof. Hübner, in his *Grundriss z. Geschichte u. Encycl. der Klass. Philologie* (Berlin, 1876).

The diminutive *codicillus* was used in much the same way as *codex*. Respecting its meaning in connection with a person's will, see TESTAMENTUM.

Codex Accepti et Expensi. A book in which the memoranda of income and outgo hastily jotted down in the *adversaria*, or day-book, were carefully posted once a month. It undoubtedly consisted of a series of double pages (Plin. *H. N.* ii. § 22)—one debit (*acceptum*), the other credit (*expensum*); hence the book is sometimes called *codices*. The entries were made in a certain *ordo*, which is much insisted on as being of the essence of the codex, as opposed to the *adversaria* (Cic. *pro Rosc. Com.* ii. 6, 7). Now this *ordo* was no doubt chronological, the date by year and day being given, but if it was only this, it could be regarded as little else than a fair copy of the *adversaria*. So we must suppose that the codex was somewhat like the journal of modern book-keepers.

The codex was sufficient for the ordinary householder; but of course those who had extensive business transactions—such as the State, municipalities, companies, bankers—had to keep ledgers (*rationes, libri rationum*), each personal or nominal account being called *ratio*. Private individuals too, who had large property, had often to keep separate books for different heads of their business

—e. g. the *calendaria*, which were accounts of investments made and dividends received.

For other points, such as the relation of *transcripticia nomina* to the codex, and the importance of the latter in establishing a literal obligation, see LITTERARUM OBLIGATIO and the literature cited under that head.

Codex Gregoriānus. A collection of imperial Roman constitutions or enactments made by one Gregorianus, of whom nothing else is known; its date is not earlier than A.D. 295, as it contained an *exemplum edicti Diocletiani et Maximiani* of that year (*Coll. Leg. Mos. et Rom.* vi. 4). It comprised enactments of the emperors between Septimius Severus (A.D. 195–211) and Diocletian and Maximian (A.D. 285–305), and possibly even some as far back as Hadrian (A.D. 117–138). It was divided into at least thirty books — the books being subdivided into "titles" and "rubrics," the topics being arranged after the order of the Perpetual Edict of Salvius Iulianus.

Codex Iustinianēus. The motives by which the emperor Justinian was induced to codify the enactments of himself and earlier emperors were the scarcity of copies of the Code of Theodosius, and the consequent divergence between the law there laid down and that actually applied in the courts (*Cod.* i. 17, 2, 17). Accordingly, in February, A.D. 528, he appointed a commission of codification of ten persons, among them being Tribonianus, who played so important a part in the legislative work of the next few years, and who perhaps suggested to his master his whole scheme of legal reform. Their instructions were to compile a single code out of those of Gregorianus, Hermogenianus, and Theodosius II., and the imperial constitutions issued since the enactment of the last, whether by Justinian himself or his predecessors. They were authorized to omit all that was unnecessary or superfluous (e. g. preambles), to reconcile such enactments as were inconsistent with one another, and, where convenience required, to combine several into one, or to make any alterations in individual constitutions which they should deem necessary. The separate laws, whether technically *edicta, rescripta*, or *decreta*, were to be arranged in chronological order under generic titles; and each, so far as was possible, identified by date and the name of the prince to whom it owed its enactment. The work was completed in April, A.D. 529, and was published under the name Codex Iustinianeus, with force of law from the 16th of that month. The older codices and constitutions were at the same time deprived of all validity, and it was even forbidden to appeal to any *leges* cited in the writings of the jurists if they had been incorporated, even in a modified form, in the new code.

In the interval of four years and a half between this date and the completion of the Institutes (November, A.D. 533), Justinian had issued a large number of new constitutions of his own. This seemed to him to necessitate a revision of the Codex. Accordingly in the next year he appointed a new commission, consisting of Tribonianus, Dorotheus, professor at Berytus, and three others, for this purpose. Within a few months (November, A.D. 534) the original code and the constitutions issued after its enactment were deprived of all authority and withdrawn from circulation, their place being taken by the *Codex Repetitae Praelectionis*, or Codex which has come down to us. In this Justinian's own constitutions were incorporated, as well as many others which the earlier code had not contained. The *Codex Repetitae Praelectionis* consists of twelve books, each of which is divided into "titles" and "rubrics"; the single constitutions are arranged under their several titles in the order of time and with the names of the emperors by whom they were respectively made, and their dates.

The enactments in this code do not go further back than those of Hadrian, and those of his immediate successors are few in number. The arrangement corresponds tolerably closely with that of the Digest, the seven parts into which the fifty books of the latter are distributed answering to books i.–ix. of the code; but the matter of the last three books of the code is hardly treated of in the Digest. See INSTITUTIONES.

Codex Rescriptus. See PALIMPSEST.

Codex Theodosiānus. In A.D. 429, Theodosius II., whose capital was Constantinople, communicated to the Senate his resolution to form a compilation of the general constitutions issued from the time of Constantine (A.D. 306–337) to his own day, after the model of the Codices Gregorianus and Hermogenianus; and appointed a commission of a lawyer and eight State officials to execute the scheme. Nothing, however, was done for six years. In A.D. 435, a new commission was appointed, presided over, like the earlier one, by Antiochus, and the imperial instructions were repeated. The result of their labours, known as the Theodosian Code, was published in February, A.D. 438, with statutory force from January 1 in the following year.

The constitutions are arranged in chronological order, under "titles" and "rubrics," in sixteen books. The first five, which contain most of the enactments relating to private law, are in form modelled on the commentaries on the Edict. The sixth to the eighth books consist principally of administrative and constitutional ordinances; the ninth is criminal law; the tenth and eleventh relate to the financial system, and in part to procedure; the twelfth to the fifteenth, to the constitution and administration of towns and other corporations; and the sixteenth contains the constitutions which deal with the Church and the ecclesiastical system in general.

Our knowledge of this code is derived partly from incomplete MSS., partly from the code of Justinian, and partly from an epitome of its contents in the *Breviarium* (q. v.). The valuable edition of J. Gothofredus (6 vols. Leyden, 1665, re-edited by Ritter, Leipzig, 1736–45) contained the code in its complete form, except the first five books, for which it was necessary to use the epitome just referred to. This is also the case with the edition of this code contained in the *Ius Civile Anteiustinianeum* of Berlin (1815). But the discovery of a MS. of the *Breviarium* at Milan in 1820 by Clossius, and of a palimpsest of the Theodosian Code at Turin by Peyron, has contributed largely both to the critical knowledge of the other parts of this code, and has added numerous genuine constitutions to the first five books, especially Book i. Haenel's discoveries have added also to our knowledge of the later books, and his edition of the Theodosian Code (1842–44) is the latest and the best.

Codicarii. See CODEX.

Codicillus. See CODEX.

Codomannus. See DARIUS.

Codon (κώδον). A bell. See TINTINNABULUM.

Codrus (Κόδρος). The last king of Athens. He received the sceptre from his father Melanthus, and was far advanced in years when some of the Dorian States united their forces for the invasion of Attica. The Dorian army marched to Athens and lay encamped under its walls; and the oracle at Delphi had assured them of success, provided they spared the life of the Athenian king. A friendly Delphian, named Cleomantis, disclosed the answer of the oracle to the Athenians, and Codrus resolved to devote himself for his country in a manner not unlike that which immortalized among the Romans, at a later date, the name of the Decii. He went out at the gate disguised in a woodman's garb, and falling in with two Dorians, killed one with his bill, and was killed by the other. The Athenians thereupon sent a herald to claim the body of their king, and the Dorian chiefs, deeming the war hopeless, withdrew their forces from Attica. After the death of Codrus, the nobles, taking advantage, perhaps, of the opportunity afforded by a dispute between his sons, are said to have abolished the title of King, and to have substituted for it that of Archon. This new office was to be held for life, and then transmitted to the son of the deceased. The first of these hereditary archons was Medon, son of Codrus, from whom the thirteen following archons were called Medontidae, as being his lineal descendants. See ARCHON.

Coela (τὰ κοῖλα τῆς Εὐβοίας, "the Hollows of Euboea"). The western coast of Euboea, between the promontories Caphareus and Chersonesus, very dangerous to ships; here a part of the Persian fleet was wrecked B.C. 480 (Herod. viii. 113).

Coelé (Κοίλη). An Attic deme a little beyond the Militian Gate at Athens. Cimon and Thucydides were buried here.

Coelesyria (Κοίλη Συρία, "Hollow Syria"). The name given to the great valley between the two ranges of Mount Lebanon (Libanus and Anti-Libanus), in the south of Syria, bordering upon Phœnicia on the west and Palestine on the south. In the wars between the Ptolemies and the Seleucidae, the name was applied to the whole of the southern portion of Syria, which became subject for some time to the kings of Egypt.

Coelia Lex. See LEX.

Coelius. See CAELIUS.

Coelossa (Κοίλωσσα). A mountain in Sicyon near Phlius.

Coelus. In Roman mythology, the spouse of Terra. He is identified with the Greek Uranus (q. v.).

Coelus (Κοιλὸς λίμην). See CYNOSSEMA.

Coëmptio. Properly "a joint taking," so "a joint purchase." One of the three forms of marriage among the Romans. It was so called from the fiction of a purchase supposed to take place on the occasion. In the presence of five witnesses and a *libripens*, or holder of the balance, the bridegroom struck the balance with a bronze coin, which he handed to the father or guardian of the bride. At the same time he asked her whether she would be his wife, and she, in turn, asked him whether he would be her husband. See MATRIMONIUM.

Coena. See CENA.

Coenus (Κοῖνος). A son-in-law of Parmenio, and one of the ablest generals of Alexander the Great. He died on the Hyphasis, B.C. 327.

Coës (Κώης). An inhabitant of Mitylené who dissuaded Darius Hystaspis, in his Scythian expedition, from breaking up his bridge of boats over the Danube. Darius made him tyrant of Mitylené. On the outbreak of the Ionian revolt against the Persians (B.C. 501), he was stoned to death by the people of Mitylené. See DARIUS.

Coeus (Κοῖος). One of the Titans, son of Uranus and Gaea. (See TITANES.) He was the father of Leto by Phoebé.

Cognāti. See COGNATIO.

Cognatio. The Latin word for relationship. Cognatio included relationship on both the father's and mother's side, while *agnatio* implied relationship on the father's side only. (See FAMILIA.) *Agnatio* involved legal duties and rights, while cognatio, originally at least, brought with it only moral obligations. *Cognati* to the sixth degree had the right of kissing each other (*ius osculi*), and also the right of refusing to appear as witnesses against each other in a court of law. On the other hand, *cognati* were forbidden by custom, at least in the earlier times, to intermarry, or to appear in court against each other as accusers. When a man died, his *cognati* were expected to put on mourning for him. In course of time the *cognati* gradually acquired the rights proper to *agnati*. But natural relationship did not win full recognition until the time of Justinian, by whose legislation the rights of *agnati* were abolished.

Cognĭtor. One who appeared in the Roman courts of law to conduct an *actio* (q. v.) on behalf of another. He was also called *procurator*.

Cognōmen. See NOMEN.

Cohērēs. See HERES.

Cohors. A division of the Roman army. (See EXERCITUS). In the republican age the word was especially applied to the divisions contributed by the Italian allies. Down to B.C. 89, when the Italians obtained the Roman citizenship, they were bound to supply an infantry contingent to each of the two consular armies, which consisted of two legions apiece. This contingent numbered in all 10,000 infantry, divided into: (*a*) 20 *cohortes* of 420 men each, called *cohortes alares*, because in time of battle they formed the wings (*alae*) of the two combined legions; (*b*) four *cohortes extraordinariae*, or select cohorts of 400 men each.

From about the beginning of the first century B.C., the Roman legion, averaging 4000 men, was also divided into ten *cohortes*, each containing three *manipuli* or six *centuriae*. In the imperial times, the auxiliary troops assigned to the legions stationed in the provinces were also divided into cohorts (*cohortes auxiliariae*). These cohorts contained either 500 men (=5 *centuriae*), or 1000 men (=10 *centuriae*). They consisted either entirely of infantry, or partly of cavalry (380 infantry+120 cavalry; 760 infantry+240 cavalry). For the commanders of these cohorts, see PRAEFECTUS. The troops stationed in Rome were also numbered according to *cohorts*. (1) The *cohortes praetoriae*, originally nine, but afterwards ten in number, which formed the imperial body-guard. Each cohort consisted of 1000 men, including infantry and cavalry. (See PRAETORIANI.) The institution of a body-guard was due to Augustus, and was a development of the *cohors praetoria*, or body-guard of the republican generals. Its title shows that it was as old as the time when the consuls bore the name of *praetores*. This *cohors praetoria* was originally formed exclusively of cavalry, mainly of equestrian rank. But towards the end of the republican age, when every independent commander had his own *cohors praetoria*, it was made up partly of infantry, who were mainly veterans, partly of picked cavalry of the allies, and partly of Roman *equites*, who usually served their *tirocinium*, or first year, in this way. (2) Three, and in later times four, *cohortes urbanae*, consisting each of 1000 men, were placed under the command of the *praefectus urbi*. They had separate barracks, but ranked below the body-guard and above the legionaries. (3) Seven *cohortes vigilum*, of 1000 men each, were under the command of the *praefectus vigilum*. These formed the night police and fire brigade, and were distributed throughout the city, one to every two of the fourteen *regiones*. See VIGILES.

Coinage. See MONETA; NUMISMATICS.

Colacrĕtae (Κωλάκρεται). A financial board at Athens, whose duty it was to administer the fund accruing from the fines taken in the courts of justice. It was this fund from which the cost of the public meals in the Prytaneum and the salary of the Heliastae were defrayed. The name properly means "collectors of hams," and perhaps points to the fact that the hams of the victims sacrificed on certain occasions were given to the Colacretae as contributions to the meals in question.

Colăpis. A river of Pannonia.

Colchis (Κολχίς). A country of Asia, having Iberia on the east, the Euxine on the west, Caucasus on the north, and Armenia on the south. It is famous in poetic legends as having been the land to which the Argonautic expedition was directed in quest of the golden fleece. (See ARGONAUTAE.) It corresponds at the present day to what is called Mingrelia. The linen manufactured here was in high repute, and was made, according to Herodotus (ii. 105), after the manner of Egypt. This species of manufacture, together with the dark complexion and crisped locks of the natives, were so many arguments with the ancients to prove them of Egyptian origin, independently of other proofs drawn, according to Herodotus, from their language and mode of life (ii. 104).

Colias (Κωλίας). A promontory on the west coast of Attica, twenty stadia south of Phalerum, with a temple of Aphroditê, where some of the Persian ships were cast after the battle of Salamis.

Colisēum. See AMPHITHEATRUM.

Collārê (δέραιον, κλοιός). A band or chain attached to the neck (*collum*); a collar. Dogs with collars are frequently seen in ancient monuments, and a mosaic at Pompeii represents a watch-dog with his collar and chain attached. Varro says that farm-dogs should have collars with pointed nails attached to them, to protect them against the attacks of wolves and other beasts. Xenophon recommends that the collars (δέραια) of hunting-dogs should be soft and wide, so as not to rub the hair. Large wooden collars (κλοιοί) were sometimes put on mischievous dogs (Aristoph. *Vesp.* 897). Plates of bronze have been found, pierced with a hole to be suspended to the collar, containing the names of owners of dogs. See the illustration under CATENARIUS.

Iron or bronze collars were placed round the necks of slaves who had attempted to run away (Plaut. *Capt.* ii. 2, 107). Sometimes a plate was attached to the collar, containing the name and address of the master and offering a reward for the runaway slave. See SERVUS.

Collatia. A Sabine town in Latium, near the right bank of the Anio, taken by Tarquinius Priscus.

Collatīnus, L. TARQUINIUS. Grandson of Aruns, elder brother of Tarquinius Priscus. He derived his surname from Collatia, where he resided, and with the principality of which he was invested. Collatinus was the husband of the celebrated Lucretia (q. v.), and after the expulsion of the Tarquins, he and Brutus were elected the first consuls. His relationship, however, to the Tarquin family excited distrust, and when a law was passed banishing the whole Tarquinian house he was forced to lay down his office and depart from Rome. He ended his days at Lavinium (Liv. i. 60).

Collatio Bonōrum. See BONORUM COLLATIO.

Collectarii. See TRAPEZITAE.

Collegium. The general term in Latin for an association. The word was applied in a different sense to express the mutual relation of such magistrates as were *collegae*. Besides the *collegia* of the great priesthoods, and of the magistrates' attendants (see APPARITORES), there were numerous associations, which, although not united by any specifically religious objects, had a religious centre in the worship of some deity or other. Such were the numerous *collegia* of artisans (*opificum* or *artificum*), and the societies existing among the poor for providing funerals, which first appear under the Empire. The political clubs (*collegia sodalicia*) were associated in the worship of the Lares Compitales (q. v.), and were, indeed, properly speaking, *collegia compitalicia*, or "societies of the cross-ways." The religious societies were, in some instances, established by the State for the performance of certain public religious services; in other cases they were formed by private individuals, who made it their business to keep up the shrines of particular deities, often foreign, at their own expense. See SODALITAS; UNIVERSITAS.

Colliciae or **Colliquiae.** (1) Gutters made with concave tiles for carrying water from the roof (Vitruv. vi. 3). (2) Drains in the fields for draining water into the ditches (Colum. ii. 8 § 3).

Collīna Porta. (1) One of the gates of Rome, on the Mons Quirinalis. To this gate Hannibal rode up and threw a spear within the city (Ovid, *Fast.* iv. 871). (2) The name of one of the four *regiones* or wards into which Rome was divided by Servius Tullius. The other three were Palatina, Suburrana, and Esquilina (Liv. v. 41).

Collybistes (κολλυβιστής). See COLLYBUS.

Collȳbus (κόλλυβος). The smallest copper coin at Athens; the fourth of the *chalcus* (q. v.). Collybus seems to have been a common name for small money, since it signified generally "changing money," "the rate of exchange," and κολλυβιστής, "a money-changer." See TRAPEZITAE.

Collyrium (κολλύριον, diminutive of κολλύρα, "a roll"). (1) In medical language, a tent, pessary, or suppository, made of medicinal substances and inserted into the orifices of the body, such as the nostrils or the anus, or into an ulcer (Cels. v. 28). (2) A liquid eye-salve (Hor. *Sat.* i. 5, 30). Many instructions for the composition of these medicaments may be found in Marcell. Empir. 8.

Collȳtus (Κολλυτός). A deme of Attica belonging to the tribe Aegeis, and forming one of the districts into which the city of Athens was divided. It was the deme of Plato the philosopher.

Colobium. See TUNICA.

Colon (κῶλον). "A limb." A name given by the rhetoricians to the divisions or members of a composition. Much has been written by modern critics of the alleged "colometry," or arrangement into periods (κῶλα), of the orations of Demosthenes, in which they profess to see a rhythmical rule that produces an harmonious effect, as in the odes of Pindar; though the determination of each κῶλον is very arbitrary. See Blass in the *Rheinisches Museum* for 1869, p. 524, and his *Attische Beredsamkeit*, on Demosthenes, pp. 105 foll. Also Mahaffy's *Hist. of Class. Greek Lit.* vol. i. pp. 343–346 (1880).

Colōnae (Κολωναί). A small town in the Troad.

Colonia. (1) GREEK. In Greece, colonies were sometimes founded by vanquished peoples, who left their homes to escape subjection at the hand of a foreign enemy; sometimes as a sequel to civil disorders; sometimes to get rid of surplus population, and thereby to avoid internal convulsions. But in most cases the object was to establish and facilitate relations of trade with foreign countries. If a Greek city was sending out a colony, an oracle (before all others that of Delphi) was almost invariably consulted. Sometimes certain classes of citizens were called upon to take part in the enterprises; sometimes one son was chosen by lot from every house where there were several sons; and strangers expressing a desire to join were admitted. A person of distinction was selected to guide the emigrants and make the necessary arrangements. It was usual to honour these founders of colonies, after their death, as heroes. Some of the sacred fire was taken from the public hearth in the Prytaneum, and the fire on the public hearth of the new city was kindled thereat. And, just as each individual had his private shrines, so the new community maintained the worship of its chief domestic deities, the colony sending embassies and votive gifts to their principal festivals.

The relation between colony and mother-city was viewed as one of mutual affection. Any differences that arose were made up, if possible, by peaceful means, war being deemed excusable only in cases of extreme necessity. The charter of foundation contained general provisions for the arrangement of the affairs of the colony, and also some special enactments. The constitution of the mother-city was usually adopted by the colony, but the new city remained politically independent. If the colony sent out a fresh colony on its own account, the mother-city was generally consulted, or was at least requested to furnish a leader. The κληροῦχοι formed a special class of Greek colonists. (See CLERUCHIA.) The trade factories set up in foreign countries (in Egypt, for instance) were somewhat different from the ordinary colonies, the members retaining the right of domicile in their own fatherland.

(2) ROMAN. It was an old custom in Italy to send out colonies for the purpose of securing new conquests. The Romans, accordingly, having no standing army, used to plant bodies of their own citizens in conquered towns as a kind of garrison. These bodies would consist partly of Roman citizens, usually to the number of three hundred; partly of members of the Latin confederacy, in larger numbers. The third part of the conquered territory was handed over to the settlers. The *coloniae civium Romanorum* (colonies of Roman citizens) were specially intended to secure the two sea-coasts of Italy, and were hence called *coloniae maritimae.* The *coloniae Latinae*, of which there was a far greater number, served the same purpose for the mainland.

The duty of leading the colonists and founding the settlement was intrusted to a commission usually consisting of three members, and elected by the people. These men continued to stand in the relation of patrons (*patroni*) to the colony after its foundation. The colonists entered the conquered city in military array, preceded by banners, and the foundation was celebrated with special solemnities. The *coloniae* were free from taxes, and had their own constitution, a copy of the Roman, electing from their own body their Senate and other officers of State. To this constitution the original inhabitants had to submit. The *coloniae civium Romanorum* retained the Roman citizenship, and were free from military service, their position as outposts being regarded as an equivalent. The members of the *coloniae Latinae* served among the *socii*, and possessed the so-called *ius Latinum.* (See LATINITAS.) This secured to them the right of acquiring property (*commercium*) and settlement in Rome, and under certain conditions the power of becoming Roman citizens; though in course of time these rights underwent many limitations.

From the time of the Gracchi the colonies lost their military character. Colonization came to be regarded as a means of providing for the poorest class of the Roman populace. After the time of Sulla it was adopted as a way of granting land to veteran soldiers. The right of founding colonies was taken away from the people by Caesar, and passed into the hands of the emperors, who used it (mainly in the provinces) for the exclusive purpose of establishing military settlements, partly with the old idea of securing conquered territory. It was only in exceptional cases that the provincial colonies enjoyed the immunity from taxation which was granted to those in Italy.

See W. Roscher, *Kolonien, Kolonialpolitik, und Auswanderung* (1885); Grote, *Hist. of Greece*, chapters xxii.–xxvii.; the article "Colonia" by Caillemer in Daremberg and Saglio's *Dictionnaire des Antiquités;* Zumpt, *Ueber den Unterschied der Benennungen, Municipium, Colonia, Praefectura* (1840); Mommsen, *Die Stadtrechte von Malaca und Salpensa* (1855); Marquardt, *Handbuch*, vol. iv. (1873).

Colonia Agrippīna, or simply AGRIPPĪNA. The modern Cologne (Köln); a town on the left bank of the Rhine. There are medals of Colonia Agrippinensis, and the name is found in inscriptions. The place was originally called Oppidum Ubiorum (Tac. *Ann.* i. 36), and was the chief town of the Ubii; but afterwards Agrippina, the wife of Claudius and daughter of Germanicus, who was born at Oppidum Ubiorum while her father was in command there, prevailed on Claudius in A.D. 51 to send a colony of veterans thither. From that time the place was called after her name. Vitellius was at Cologne when the soldiers proclaimed him emperor (Suet. *Vitell.* 8).

Colonnade. See PORTICUS.

Colōnus (Κολωνός). A deme of Attica, ten stadia, or a little more than a mile, northwest of Athens, near the Academy; celebrated for a temple of Poseidon, a grove of the Eumenides, the shrine of Oedipus, and as the birthplace of Sophocles, who describes it in his *Oedipus Coloneus.*

Colŏphon (Κολοφών). A city of Ionia, northwest of Ephesus. It was founded by Andraemon, son of Codrus, and was situated about two miles from the coast, its harbour, called Notium, being connected with the city by means of long walls. Colophon was destroyed by Lysimachus, together with Lebedus, in order to swell the population of the new town he had founded at Ephesus (Pausan. i. 9). The Colophonians are stigmatized by several ancient writers as very effeminate and luxurious, and yet Strabo says that, at one period, this place possessed a flourishing navy, and that its cavalry was in such repute that victory followed wherever they were employed. Hence arose the proverb Κολοφῶνα ἐπιτίθεναι, "to add a Colophonian"—i. e. to put the finishing hand to an affair. The scholiast on Plato, however, gives another explanation of the saying, which appears somewhat more probable, though its authority is not so good. He states that the Colophonians had the right of a double vote in the general assembly of the Ionians, on account of the service they had rendered the confederacy by inducing the city of Smyrna to join it. Hence they were frequently enabled to decide points left undetermined from a parity of suffrages. It arose from this old saying that, in the early periods of the art of printing, the account which the printer gave of the place and date of the edition, being the last thing printed at the end of the book, was called the *colophon.* This city was one of the places which contended for the birth of Homer, and was unquestionably the native place of Mimnermus and Hermesianax.

Colōres. See PICTURA.

Colossae (Κολοσσαί). Once an important city of Great Phrygia, on the river Lycus, but so reduced subsequently that it might have been forgotten but for the epistle written to its inhabitants by the Apostle Paul.

Colossēum. See AMPHITHEATRUM.

Colossus (κολοσσός). A word of rare occurrence in the Attic writers, but used by both Greeks and Romans to signify a statue larger than life (Aesch. *Agam.* 406), and thence a person of extraordinary stature and beauty is termed *colosseros* by Suetonius (*Calig.* 35). In like manner the architectural ornaments in the upper stories of lofty buildings, which require to be of large dimensions in consequence of their remoteness, are termed *colossicotera* (κολοσσικώτερα, Vitruv. iii. 3).

Among the colossal statues of Greece the most celebrated, according to Pliny, was the bronze colossus at Rhodes by Chares (q. v.) of Lindus, a pupil of Lysippus, who gave twelve years (B.C. 292–280) to casting the statue. Its height is variously given as 90 and 120 feet. Fifty-six years after its erection it was thrown down by an earthquake and lay in ruins until A.D. 653, when the Arabs sold the pieces to a Jew of Edessa for old metal. In this one island there were more than 100 colossi. Pliny mentions another Greek colossus of Apollo, the work of Calamis, which cost 500 talents, and was thirty cubits high, in the city of Apollonia, whence it was transferred to the Capitol by M. Lucullus; and also those of Zeus and Heracles, at Tarentum, by Lysippus. To the list of Pliny must be added the more important colossal statues of Phidias, the most beautiful of which were his chryselephantine statues of Zeus, at Olympia (more than forty feet high, seated), and of Athené, in the Parthenon at Athens; the largest (more than seventy feet high, including the base) was his bronze statue commonly called Athené Promachos, on the Acropolis. See ATHENÉ; and the illustration in the article ATHENAE, p. 155.

Among the works of this description made expressly by or for the Romans, those most frequently alluded to are the following: (1) A statue of Iupiter upon the Capitol, made by order of Sp. Carvilius, from the armour of the Samnites, which was so large that it could be seen from the Alban Mount. (2) A bronze statue of Apollo at the Palatine Library, to which the bronze head now preserved in the Capitol probably belonged. (3) A bronze statue of Augustus in the Forum, which bore his name. (4) The colossus of Nero, which was executed by Zenodorus, and which is quoted by Pliny as a proof that the taste for bronze statues was lost, for this was adorned with gold and silver. Its height was 110 or 120 feet (Suet. *Nero,* 31). It was originally placed in the vestibule of the Domus Aurea, but was afterwards removed by Vespasian to the Via Sacra, and Hadrian again moved it to a position to the north of the Colosseum, where the basement upon which it stood is still to be seen; from it the contiguous amphitheatre is supposed to have gained the name of "Colosseum." Vespasian had converted it into a statue of the Sun. Twenty-four elephants were employed by Hadrian to remove it, when he was about to build the Temple of Venus at Rome (Spart. *Hadr.* 19). (5) An equestrian statue of Domitian, of bronze gilt, which was placed in the centre of the Forum (Stat. *Silv.* i. 1. 1). See Lesbazeilles, *Les Colosses Anciens et Modernes* (1876); Torr, *Rhodes in Ancient and Modern Times* (1887); and the articles CIRCUS, p. 351, and SEVEN WONDERS.

Colōtes (Κολώτης). (1) An Epicurean of Lampsacus, against whom Plutarch wrote two tracts. (2) A sculptor of Paros, who flourished about B.C. 444 and assisted Phidias in making the colossal figure of Zeus at Olympia.

Colours. See PICTURA.

Colum (ἠθμός, ἠθάνιον). A strainer or colander, used for straining wine, milk, olive-oil, drugs, perfumes, and other liquids. Such cola were made of hair, broom, or rushes (Verg. *Georg.* ii. 242, *Ecl.* x. 71; Colum. *R. R.* ix. 15, xii. 17, 19, 38). The cola employed for such domestic purposes, as straining wine, were sometimes made of linen, but frequently of some metal, such as bronze or silver. Such strainers are often represented in Greek vase-paintings; and several examples of elegant silver strainers of Greek workmanship have been found in the Crimea.

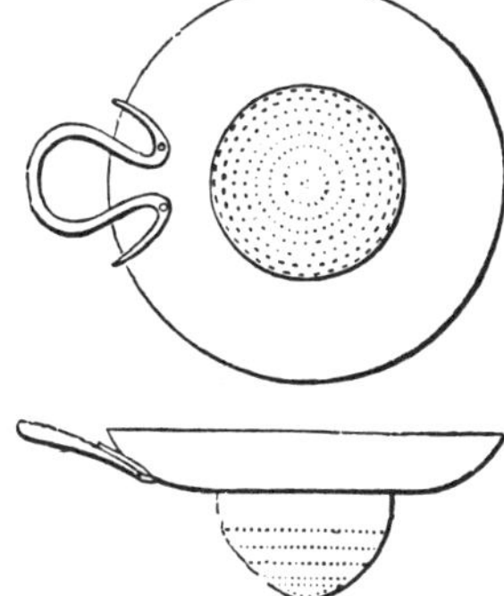
Colum, strainer. (*Museo Borbon.*)

The Romans filled the strainer with ice or snow (*colum nivarium*) in order to cool and dilute the wine at the same time that it was cleared. Several Etruscan vases have been discovered, in which the spout consists of a strainer, so that the liquid is clarified as it is poured out.

Ausonius (*Ep.* iv. 57) uses the word *colum* to denote the *nassa*, or weel for snaring fish. See NASSA.

Columbar. A kind of pillory, in which the head passed through a hole, like the holes in a pigeon-house, whence the name (Plaut. *Rud.* iii. 6. 49).

Columbarium (περιστερεών, περιστεροτροφεῖον). A dove-cote or pigeon-house.

The word is also used to denote the following objects, which derive their name from their resemblance to a dove-cote:

(1) A sepulchral chamber. The word was metaphorically applied to a subterranean vault provided with rows of small niches, lying one above the other, and intended for the reception of the urns containing the ashes of the dead. These large burial-places were built by rich people whose freedmen were too numerous to be interred in the family burial-place. They were also erected by the Caesars for their slaves and freedmen. Several of these still exist—for instance, that of Livia, the consort of Augustus, who built one for her freedmen on the Appian Way. Common burial-places, in which a niche could be bespoken beforehand, were sometimes constructed by private individuals on speculation for people who were too poor to have a grave of their own. Columbaria were usually built by religious or mercantile societies, or by burial clubs for their own members. In such cases the members contributed a single capital payment and yearly subscriptions, which gave them the right to a decent burial and a niche in the vault. The names of the dead were inscribed on marble tablets over each niche. See Lanciani, *Ancient Rome in the Light of Recent Discoveries*, pp. 129–133 (Boston, 1888).

Columbarium. (Villa Rufini.)

Each of the niches contained a pair of urns, with the names of the persons whose ashes they contained inscribed over them. The use of the word, and mode of occupation, is testified in the following inscription:

L. ABUCIUS HERMES IN HOC
ORDINE AB IMO AD SUMMUM
COLUMBARIA IX. OLLAE XVIII.
SIBI POSTERISQUE SUIS.

(2) A machine used to raise water for the purpose of irrigation. As described by Vitruvius, the vents through which the water was conveyed into the receiving trough were termed columbaria. (See ANTLIA.) The difference between that representation and the machine now under consideration consisted in the following points: The wheel of the latter is a solid one (*tympanum*) instead of radiated (*rota*), and was worked as a treadmill by men who stood upon platforms projecting from the flat sides instead of being turned by a stream Between the intervals of each platform a series of grooves or channels (*columbaria*) were formed in the sides of the tympanum, through which the water taken up by a number of scoops placed on the outer margin of the wheel, like the jars in the cut referred to, was conducted into a wooden trough below.

(3) The cavities into which the extreme ends of the beams upon which a roof is supported (*tignorum cubilia*), and which are represented by triglyphs in the Doric order, were termed columbaria by the Roman architects; that is, while they remained empty, and until filled up by the head of the beam.

(4) The apertures in the sides of a vessel, through which the oars passed (Fest. p. 169, Müll.).

Columella, L. IUNIUS MODERĀTUS. A Roman writer, born at Gades, in the reign of Augustus or Tiberius, and a contemporary, according to his own account, of Seneca and Celsus. The elder Pliny also frequently makes mention of him. His father, Marcus Columella, had possessions in the province of Baetica. The son betook himself at an early period to Rome, where he passed his life, with the exception of a few journeys to Syria and Cilicia. Two works of his remain: one, entitled *De Re Rustica*, in twelve books; the other, *De Arboribus*. This last made, very probably, part of a work on agriculture, in four books, which Columella had published as the first edition of that which we now have in twelve books. On this supposition, Cassiodorus was correct in saying that Columella had written a work in sixteen books on rural economy. This author appears to have been but little read. Among the ancients, Pliny, Servius, Cassiodorus, and Isidorus are the only ones who cite him. He fell into almost complete neglect after Palladius had made an abridgment of his work. (See PALLADIUS.) The style of Columella is pure and elegant; if any reproach can be made against him, it is that of being too studied in his language for the subject of which he treats.

The tenth book, which he originally intended to be the conclusion, is in verse (dactylic hexameters), and is a sort of supplement to the *Georgics* of Vergil, whose style Columella imitates with considerable success. It treats of gardening. The eleventh and twelfth books were subsequently added by the author, as not having exhausted his subject. The best MS. of Columella is the Codex Sangermanensis of the ninth century, now in St. Petersburg. The *Res Rustica* is contained in the collections of the *Scriptores Rei Rusticae*, and has been separately edited by Ress (Flensburg, 1795), and bk. x. in Wernsdorf's *Poetae Latini Minores*. (See Barberet, *De Columellae Vita et Scriptis* (Nancy, 1888).

Colŭmen (later CULMEN). The roof of a building, or more particularly the beam in the highest part of the slope of a roof.

Columna (κίων, στῦλος). A column, employed in architecture to support the entablature and roof of an edifice. It is composed of three principal parts: the capital (*capitulum*), the shaft (*scapus*), and the base (*spira*). The column was, moreover, constructed in three principal styles or orders, each possessing characteristic forms and proportions of its own, distinctive of the order, but by unprofessional persons most readily distinguished by the difference in the capitals. (1) DORĬCA, the Doric; the oldest, most substantial, and heaviest of all, which has no base, and a very simple capital. (See CAPITULUM.) (2) IONĬCA, the Ionic; the next in lightness, which is furnished with a base and has its capital decorated with volutes. (See CAPITULUM.) (3) CORINTHIA, the Corinthian; the lightest of all, which has a base and a plinth below it, and a deep capital ornamented with foliage. (See CAPITULUM.) To these are often added: (4) TUSCANĬCA, the Tuscan; only known from the account of Vitruvius, and which nearly resembled the Roman Doric; and (5) COMPOSĬTA, the Composite; a mixed order, formed by combining the volutes of the Ionic with the foliage of the Corinthian.

Figs. 1 and 2 give instances of the Doric style from the temple at Paestum and the Parthenon at Athens. The Doric column consists (A) of the shaft, which increases in diameter almost invisibly up to about one-quarter of its height, and diminishes slightly after that point. It has no base, but rests immediately on the stylobate. It is surrounded with semicircular flutings, meeting each other at a sharp angle. These were chiselled with a cedar-wood tool after the separate drums had been put together. (B) The capital. This consists of three parts—(*a*) the *hypotrachelion*, or neck of the column, a continuation of the shaft, but separated by an indentation from the other drums. It is wider at the top than at the bottom, and is generally ornamented with several parallel and horizontal rings. (*b*) The *echinus*, a circular moulding or cushion, which widens greatly towards the top. (*c*) The *abax* or *abacus*, a square slab supporting the architrave or epistylion. The height of the shaft is usually 5⅓ times, the distance between the columns 1⅓ times, the diameter of the base of the column. The architrave is a quadrangular beam of stone, reaching from pillar to pillar. On this again rests the frieze (*zophoros*), so called from the metopes which are adorned with sculptures in relief. These metopes are square spaces between the triglyphs; the triglyphs are surfaces cut into three concave grooves, two whole grooves in the centre, and two half grooves at the sides. One is placed over each pillar, and one between each pair of pillars. The entablature is completed by a projecting cornice, a slab crowned with a simple heading-course, the lower surface of which is ornamented with sloping corbels (σταγόνες, *mutuli*).

An instance is given in Fig. 3 from the temple on the Ilissus at Athens. These are loftier than the

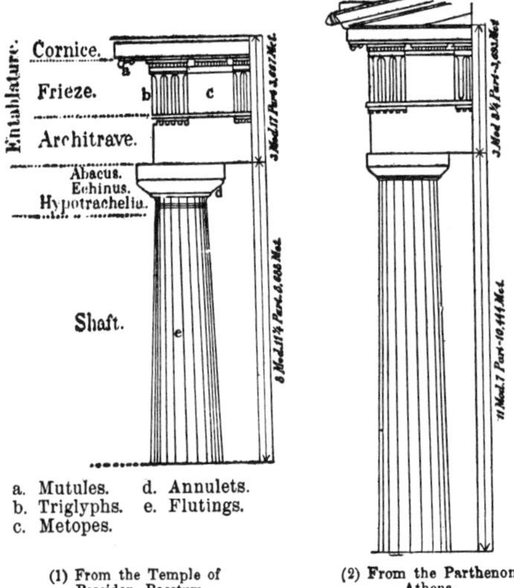

(1) From the Temple of Poseidon, Paestum. (2) From the Parthenon, Athens.

Doric Order.

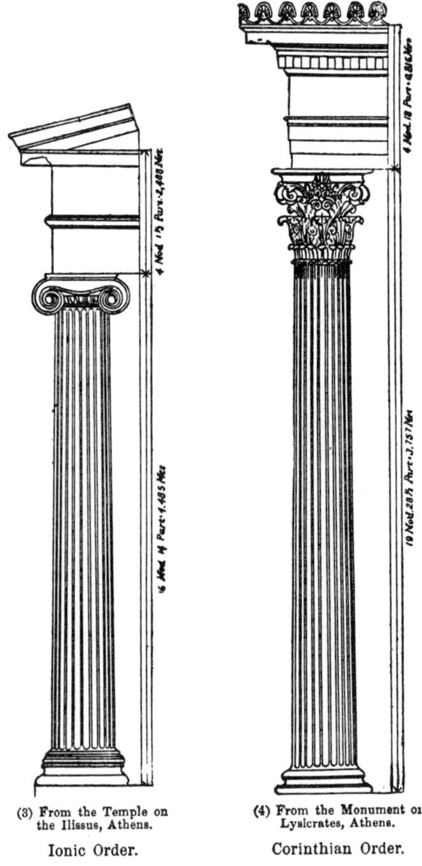

(3) From the Temple on the Ilissus, Athens.

Ionic Order.

(4) From the Monument of Lysicrates, Athens.

Corinthian Order.

Doric, their height being 8½–9½ times the diameter of the lower part. The enlargement of the lower part is also less than in the Doric columns, the distance between each column greater (2 diameters), the flutings (generally 24 in number) deeper, and separated by small flat surfaces. The Ionic column has a base, consisting of a square slab (πλίνθος), and several cushion-like supports separated by grooves. The capital, again, is more artistically developed. The neck, instead of flutings, has five leaves worked in relief. The echinus is very small and ornamented with an egg pattern. Over it, instead of the *abacus*, is a four-cornered cushion ending before and behind in spiral volutes, supporting a narrow square slab, which is also adorned with an egg pattern. The architrave is divided into three bands, projecting one above the other, and upon it rises, in an uninterrupted surface, the frieze, adorned with reliefs continuously along its whole length. Finally, the cornice is composed of different parts.

The CORINTHIAN column is shown in Fig. 4, from the monument of Lysicrates at Athens. The base and shaft are identical with the Ionic, but the capital takes the form of an open calix formed of acanthus leaves. Above this is another set of leaves, from between which grow stalks with small leaves, rounded into the form of volutes. On this rests a small abacus widening towards the top, and on this, again, the entablature, which is borrowed from the Ionic order. On the human figures employed instead of columns to support the entablature, see ATLAS; CANEPHORI; CARYAE.

The Romans adopted the Greek styles of column, but not always in their pure form. They were fondest of the Corinthian, which they laboured to enrich with new and often excessive ornamentation. For instance, they crowned the Corinthian capital with the Ionic, thus forming what is called the Roman or composite capital. The style known as TUSCAN is a degenerate form of the Doric. The Tuscan column has a smooth shaft, in height 7 diameters of the lower part, and tapering up to three-quarters of its lower dimensions. Its base consists of two parts—a circular plinth and a cushion of equal height. The capital is formed of three parts of equal height.

In other styles, too, the Romans sometimes adopted the smooth instead of the fluted shaft, as, for instance, in the Pantheon (q. v.).

This most beautiful of all architectural supports originated from the simplest beginnings. A few strong poles, or the straight trunks of trees, stuck into the ground, in order to support a cross-piece for a thatch of boughs or straw to rest upon, formed the first shaft (*scapus*) of a column. When a tile or slab of wood was placed under the bottom of the trunk to form a foundation and prevent the shaft from sinking too deeply into the ground, the first notion of a base (*spira*) was attained; and a similar one, placed on its top, to afford a broader surface for the cross-beam or architrave to rest upon, furnished the first capital. Thus these simple elements, elaborated by the genius and industry of succeeding ages, produced the several distinctive properties of the architectural orders.

One point, however, is to be constantly borne in mind—that the column of ancient architecture always implies a real, and not a fictitious, support; for neither the Greeks nor the Romans, until the arts had declined, ever made use of columns as the moderns do, in their buildings, as a superfluous ornament, or mere accessory to the edifice, but as a main and essentially constituent portion of the fabric, which would immediately fall to pieces if they were removed; and that the abusive application of coupled, clustered, incastrated, imbedded columns, etc., was never admitted in Greek architecture; for the chief beauty of the column consists in its isolation, by means of which it presents an endless variety of views and changes of scene, with every movement of the spectator, whether seen in rank or in file. See Mauch, *Die Architekt. Ordn. der Griech., Römer, und Neueren Meister* (5th ed. Berlin, 1862); Reber, *Geschichte der Baukunst im Alterthum* (Leipzig, 1866); Fergusson, *Hist. of Architecture*, vol. i. (2d ed. Boston, 1883); Lübke, *Hist. of Art*, 2 vols. (Eng. trans., N. Y. 1877).

Columna Cochlis. A column with a spiral staircase running through the centre so as to furnish a means of ascent to the top (Victor, *De Reg. Urb. Rom.* 8 and 9). These were usually *columnae triumphales*, surmounted by the statue of the person in whose honour the column was erected. Two still remain at Rome: (1) the Column of Trajan (shown in the illustration), erected by Apollodorus, A.D. 104; and (2) the Column of M. Aurelius Antoninus.

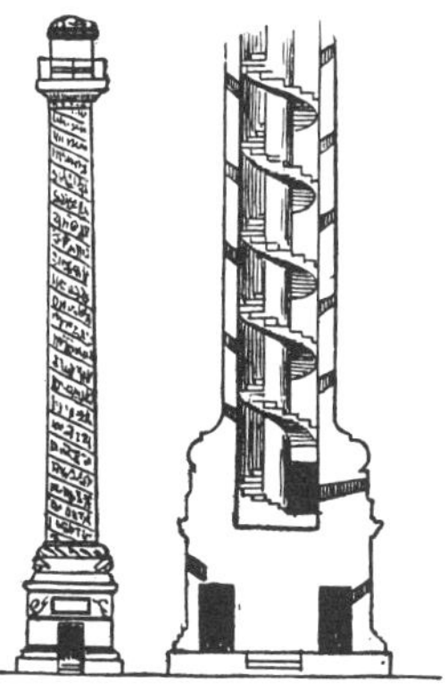

Columna Cochlis. (Column of Trajan.)

Columna Rostrāta. A column adorned with the beaks (*rostra*) of captured ships, originally set up in the Roman Forum to commemorate the naval victory of Duilius (q. v.) over the Carthaginians (B.C. 260). This monument was destroyed by lightning during the interval between the Second and Third Punic Wars. A new column was erected by the emperor Claudius and an inscription placed upon it. Mommsen (*Corp. Inscript. Lat.* i. 40) holds that either the original column had no inscription at all, or else a short and simple one. At any rate, the inscription on the column of Claudius, part of which was excavated in 1566 in the Forum, is not a copy of the first one, as many of the verbal forms contained in it are too antique, while others are too modern, for the age in which it professes to have been written. Thus, the form C is used for G; -ET for IT; ablatives in -D, elsewhere unknown (*dictatored, navaled*)—all of which are too archaic; while, on the other hand, S and M at the end of words are never omitted in it, and IN or EN is used for ENDO. A portion of the Columna Rostrata is now in the Palazzo dei Conservatori on the Capitol at Rome. See Wordsworth, *Fragments and Specimens of Early Latin*, pp. 170, 412–414; Ritschl, *Inscriptio quae fertur Columnae Rostratae Duilianae* (Berlin, 1852); Mommsen, *Corp. Inscript. Lat.* i. 195, pp. 37–40; and Allen, *Remnants of Early Latin*, pp. 67–68.

Columna Rostrata. (Restoration by Canina.)

Columna Triumphālis. Single columns were erected from the earliest times to commemorate persons or events. Early Roman examples are those in honour of C. Maenius and P. Minucius, mentioned by Pliny (*H. N.* xxxiv. § 21). Of a later date is the marble monolith to Iulius Caesar, set up in the Forum after his death (Suet. *Iul.* 85).

More important, as well on account of their imposing size as of their value to the archæologist, are the lofty and elaborate columns erected in imperial times. The finest of these monuments is that figured in the article COLUMNA COCHLIS, and which was voted by the Senate in honour of Trajan, and executed by Apollodorus in A.D. 104. The column itself is apparently of the Tuscan order, and is composed of huge drums of white marble, pierced within so as to form a spiral staircase, to which there is an entrance in the pedestal. A bas-relief of the chief episodes in the Dacian campaigns winds round the shaft. Including the bronze statue of the emperor, the total height was not less than 130 feet. It still stands in the Foro Traiano at Rome.

Column of M. Aurelius Antoninus.

The same mode of construction is found in the Antonine Column, erected in honour of Marcus Aurelius and illustrating his victories over the Marcomanni, still to be seen in the Piazza della Colonna. Much less admirable, artistically, was the column erected by Constantine in the Forum of Constantinople. It was erected on a pillar of white marble, 20 feet in height, and was composed of ten pieces of porphyry. On its summit, 120 feet from the earth, was a colossal bronze statue of Apollo, supposed to be the work of Phidias. A fragment of this structure survives at Constantinople under the name of "the Burnt Pillar." Of the time of the same emperor was the curious Serpentine Column of brass, formed of the twisted bodies of three brazen snakes, whose triple heads had once supported the golden tripod which the victors at Salamis had consecrated at Delphi in commemoration of the defeat of Xerxes. This pillar stood in the Hippodrome.

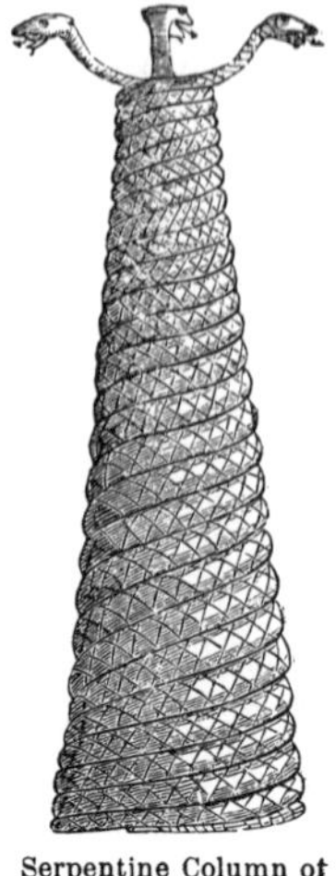

Serpentine Column of Constantine.

Latest of all was the Column of Theodosius II., figured below, whose base still exists at Constantinople.

Columnae Hercŭlis. "The Pillars of Hercules"; a name often given to Calpé and Abyla, or the heights on either side of the Straits of Gibraltar. The tradition was that the Mediterranean had no outlet in this quarter until Hercules broke through the mountain barrier, and thus formed the present straits. The rocky height on either side of the opening was fabled to have been placed there by him as a memorial of his achievement, and as marking the limits of his wanderings towards the west. See ABYLA; CALPÉ; MEDITERRANEUM MARE.

The name Columnae Herculis was also often applied to the two large pyramidal columns set up by the Phœnicians in their voyages as landmarks

Column of Theodosius II.

by which to recognize particular coasts on subsequent visits. These pillars were respectively dedicated to the Phœnician Hercules and to Astarté, as personifying the sun and the moon. (See Tac. *Germ.* 34.) The accompanying illustration is taken from a Tyrian coin.

Phœnician Pillars of Hercules.

Columnarium. A tax imposed in the time of Iulius Caesar upon the pillars (*columnae*) that supported a house. See Cic. *ad Att.* xiii. 6.

Colus. A distaff. See FUSUS.

Colūthus (Κόλουθος) and **Colluthus** (Κόλλουθος). A native of Lycopolis in Egypt, supposed to have lived about the beginning of the sixth century. He wrote a poem in six cantos, entitled *Calydonica* (Καλυδωνικά), as well as other pieces that are now lost. He is believed also, though without any great degree of certainty, to have been the author of a poem, in 392 verses, which bears the title of *The Rape of Helen* (Ἑλένης Ἁρπαγή). This poem commences with the nuptials of Peleus and Thetis, and the poet goes on to recount the judgment of Paris, the voyage of that prince to Sparta, and the abduction of Helen, which takes place after the first interview. This poem of Coluthus was discovered by Cardinal Bessarion along with that of Quintus Smyrnaeus, and can be found in the Didot collection edited by Lehrs and Dübner.

Coma (κόμη). The hair of the head. Besides this general term, there are various other words, both in Greek and Latin, signifying the hair, each of which acquires its distinctive meaning from some physical property of the hair itself or from some peculiarity in the mode of arranging it, the principal of which are as follows: (1) Ἔθειρα, a head of hair when carefully dressed. (2) Χαίτη, properly the mane of a horse or lion, is used to signify long, flowing hair. (3) Φόβη, when accurately used, implies the hair of the head in a state of disorder incident to a person under a sense of fear. (4) Πoκάς, from πείκω or πέκω, the hair when combed and dressed. (5) Θρίξ, a general term for hair, from the plural of which the Romans perhaps borrowed their word *tricae*—τρίχωσις and τρίχωμα are used in the same sense. (6) Κόρση (Att. κόρρη), from the old word κόρ, "the head," signifies properly the hair on the top of the head; and hence a particular fashion of arranging the

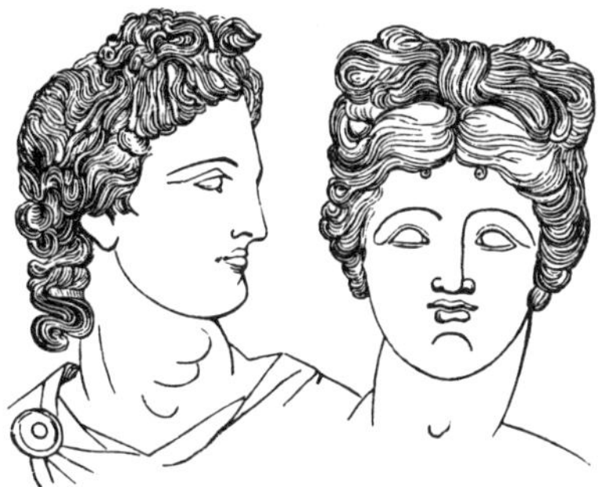

Apollo Belvedere. Artemis. (British Museum.)

hair among the Greek women was termed κόρυμβος; or, when worn in the same style by the men, it was designated by another derivative from the same word, κρώβυλος. To produce this effect the hair was drawn up all round the head from the front and back, and fastened in a bow on the top, as exemplified in the two preceding busts—one of the Apollo Belvedere, the other of Artemis—from the British Museum.

Instead of a band, the people of Athens fastened the bow with an ornamental clasp, fashioned like a grasshopper, to show that they were aborigines. Κρώβυλος is also used for a cap of network. (See CALANTICA.) (7) Μαλλός, which properly means wool, was also used for the short, round, curly hair, which resembles the fleece of a lamb, such as is seen in some of the early Greek sculptures, particularly in the heads of Heracles, one of which is subjoined from a specimen in the British Museum.

Heracles. (British Museum.)

(8) Κέρας was a Greek term used when the hair was combed up from the temples on each side, so as to give it the appearance of two horns, as is seen in the heads of fauns and satyrs, and in the bust of Zeus on the following page. (9) Κίκιννος, πλοχμός, χλιδαί, the hair which falls in ringlets, either natural or artificial, which was sometimes called βόστρυχος and πλόκαμος. All these terms, when strictly appropriated, seem to designate that singular style of coiffure which is observable in Etruscan and early Greek works, and common to both sexes, as is seen in the casts from the temple of Athené at Aegina in the British Museum.

Besides the generic *coma*, the Romans made use of the following terms, expressive of some peculiar qualities in the hair, or particular mode of arrangement: (1) *Capillus*, according to the old etymologists, *quasi capitis pilus*. (2) *Crinis*, the hair when carefully dressed. (3) *Caesaries*, which is said, though without much probability, to be connected with *caedo*, the hair of the male sex, because they wore it short, whereas the women did not. (4) *Cincinnus*, κίκιννος, the hair when platted and dressed in circles, like the head on page 17 (s.v. ACUS), as it is still worn by the women of Mola di Gaieta (Formiae). Martial terms these circles *anuli*, and Claudian *orbes*. (5) *Cirrus*, a lock of curly hair. The locks which fell over the forehead were termed *capronae* (προκόμιον), the modern "bang" or "fringe"; those which fell from the temples over the ears, *antiae*. Both the *antiae* and *capronae* are accurately traced in the figure of Cupid bending his bow, in the British Museum, from which the accompanying illustration is taken.

Cupid. (British Museum.)

All the Greek divinities are distinguished by a characteristic coiffure, modified in some respects as the arts progressed, but never altered in character from the original model; so that any person tolerably conversant with the works of Greek art may almost invariably recognize the deity represented from the disposition of the hair. We proceed to specify some of the principal ones.

Lion's Head. (British Museum.) Zeus. (Vatican.)

The head of the lion is the type upon which that of Zeus is formed, particularly in the disposition of the hair, which rises from the forehead and falls back in loose curls down the sides of the face, until it forms a junction with the beard. This is made clear by the two preceding illustrations, one of which is from a statue of Zeus in the Vatican, supposed to be a copy of the Phidian Zeus; and the other is a lion's head from the British Museum. The same disposition of the hair is likewise preserved in all the real or pretended descendants from Zeus, such as Aesculapius, Alexander, etc.

Serapis. (British Museum.)

Pluto or Serapis has the hair longer, straighter, and lower over the forehead, in order to give severity to the aspect, and with the modius on his head, as represented in the above drawing from the British Museum. The modius is decorated with an olive branch, for oil was used instead of wine in sacrifices to Pluto.

Poseidon. (British Museum.)

The hair of Poseidon is cut finer and sharper than that of Zeus. It rises from the forehead, and then falls down in flakes, as if wet, in the manner represented in the accompanying head from the British Museum.

Apollo is usually represented with the κρώβυλος; but when the hair is not tied up on the top of the head it is always long and flowing over the neck and shoulders, as represented in the annexed illustration from a very beautiful and early Greek sculpture in the British Museum. Hence he is called *intonsus* and ἀκερσεκόμης.

Apollo. (British Museum.)

Dionysus also wears his hair unshorn; for he, as well as Apollo, is typical of perpetual youth.

In the mature age of Greek art, Hermes has short curly hair, as represented by the head on the left hand in the illustration below, from a statue in the Vatican, which was for a long time falsely ascribed to Antinoüs; but in very early Greek works he is represented with braided hair, in the Etruscan style, and a sharp-pointed beard (see the right-hand illustration, from an altar in the Museum of the Capitol at Rome), whence he is termed *σφηνοπώγων*.

Hermes. (Vatican) Etruscan Hermes. (Cap. Mus.)

Hercules has short, crisp hair, like the curls between the horns of a bull, the head of which animal formed the model for his, as is exemplified in the subjoined drawings, one being the head of the Farnese Hercules, the other that of a bull, from a bas-relief at Rome, in which all the characteristics of Hercules, the small head, thick neck, and particular form of the hair, are strongly preserved.

Farnese Hercules. Head of Bull.

The hair of Heré or Iuno is parted in the front, and on the top of the head is a kind of diadem, called in Latin *corona*, and in Greek *σφενδόνη*, from its resemblance to a sling, the broad part of which is placed above the forehead, while the two lashes act as bands to confine the hair on the sides of the head and fasten it behind, in the manner represented in the annexed illustration from the British Museum.

Pallas is rarely seen without her helmet; but when portrayed with her head uncovered the hair is tied up in a knot at some distance from the head, and then falls from the band in long parallel curls.

Heré with *σφενδόνη*. (British Museum.)

Aphroditê and Artemis are sometimes adorned with the κόρυμβος; but both these divinities are more frequently represented with their hair dressed in the simple style of the young Greek girls, whose hair is parted in front, and conducted round to the back, so as to conceal the upper part of the ears. It is then tied in a plain knot at the nape of the neck, or, at other times, though less frequently, at the top of the head; both of which fashions are represented in the two illustrations subjoined; one, that on the right, Niobê, and the other from a bas-relief at Rome.

From a bas-relief at Rome. Niobê.

False hair, or wigs, φενάκη, πηνίκη, κόμαι προσθέται, τριχὲς προσθέται, *galerus*, *corymbium*, *caliendrum*, *capillamentum*, were also worn by the people of both countries (Mart. v. 68; xii. 23), and much esteemed by them.

Several passages of Latin literature show the fondness of the Roman women for blond hair, quantities of which were imported from Germany to be made up into wigs. (See Juv. vi. 120; Ovid. *A. A.* iii. 163.) Hence, in some of the statues, the hair was gilt, remains of which are discernible in the Venus dei Medici and in the Apollo of the Capitol; and both sexes dyed their hair when it grew gray (Plin. *H. N.* xxvi. § 164).

Ancient Wig. (Museum at Ghizeh.)

In very early times the Romans wore their hair long, as was represented in the oldest statues during the age of Varro, and hence the Romans of the Augustan Age designated their ancestors *intonsi* and *capillati*. But this fashion did not last after the year B.C. 300, as appears by the remaining works of art. The women, too, dressed their hair with simplicity, at least until the time of the emperors, and probably much in the same style as those of Greece; but at the Augustan period a variety of different head-dresses came into fashion, many of which are described by Ovid. Four specimens of different periods are given below. The first head on the left represents Octavia, the niece of Augustus, from the Museum in the Capitol at Rome; the next, Messalina, fifth wife of the emperor Claudius; the one below, on the left, Sabina, the wife of Hadrian; and the next, Plautilla, the wife of Caracalla, which last three are from the British Museum.

(1) Octavia. (Capitol. Mus.) (2) Messalina, wife of Claudius. (3) Sabina, wife of Hadrian. (4) Plautilla, wife of Caracalla. [The last three from the British Museum.]

Both countries had some peculiar customs connected with the growth of their hair and illustrative of their moral or physical conditions. The Spartans combed and dressed their heads with especial care when about to encounter any great danger, in which act Leonidas and his followers were discovered by the spies of Xerxes before the battle of Thermopylae. The sailors of both nations shaved off their hair after an escape from shipwreck or other heavy calamity and dedicated it to the gods. In the earlier ages, the Greeks of both sexes cut their hair close in mourning; but subsequently this practice was more exclusively confined to the women, the men leaving theirs long and neglected, as was the custom among the Romans.

In childhood—that is, up to the age of puberty—the hair of the males was suffered to grow long among both nations, when it was clipped and dedicated to some river or deity, from thence called κουροτρόφος by the poets, and therefore to cut off the hair means to take the *toga virilis*. At Athens this ceremony was performed on the third day of the festival Apaturia, which is therefore termed κουρεῶτις.

In both countries the slaves were shaved as a mark of servitude. On barbers, see TONSOR.

The Vestal Virgins also cut their hair short upon taking their vows; which rite still remains in the Roman Church, in which all women have their hair cut close upon taking the veil. The hair was fastened up with hair-pins (*acus crinales*) and combs (*pectines*), which we find made of boxwood, ivory, and tortoise-shell. The hair was also at times fastened with bands (*diademata*) of gold set with jewels, like the Greek *στεφάνη*. As to nets, the women used to wear *reticula*, sometimes made of gold threads. The *mitra* (Juv. iii. 66) has been explained elsewhere, and the *calautica*, or *calantica*, or *calvatica* was a cap with lappets covering the ears and with two strings for tying under the chin. Nonius says it was worn by women only. For other matters relating to the modes of dressing the hair, etc., see ACUS; DIADEMA; MITRA; PECTEN; RETICULUM.

Comāna (Κόμανα). (1) A city of Pontus, surnamed Pontica, to distinguish it from the Cappadocian city of the same name. It was situated to the north-east of Zela, and not far from the source of the Iris. This place was celebrated for the worship of the goddess Mâ, supposed to answer to the Bellona of the West. She was likewise revered with equal honours in the Cappadocian Comana. The priesthood attached to the temple was an office of the highest emolument and dignity, and was sought after by kings and princes. The city itself was large and populous. The festivals of the goddess, which were held twice a year, drew thither an immense concourse. There were no less than 6000 slaves attached to the service of the temple, and most of these were courtesans. Hence it was remarked that the citizens were generally addicted to pleasure, and the town itself was styled by some "Little Corinth." (2) A city of Cappadocia, celebrated for its temple of Artemis Taurica.

Comes. Originally a fellow-traveller; hence it is applied to the members of the retinue of a magistrate or high official sent into the provinces (cf. Cic. *Verr.* ii. 10, 27), and under the emperors the term is used especially of those accompanying the emperor or members of his family. From this it was a natural transition to apply the term to the courtiers generally, even when not on a journey; and in later Latin we find it used of the holders of the various State-offices. About the time of Constantine it became a regular honorary title, whence the modern *count* (French *comte*), including various grades, answering to the *comites ordinis primi, secundi, tertii.*

The names of the following officers explain themselves: Comes Orientis (of whom there seem to have been two, one the superior of the other), comes Aegypti, comes Britanniae, comes Africae, comes rei militaris, comes portuum, comes stabuli, comes domesticorum equitum, comes clibanarius, comes linteae vestis or vestiarii (master of the robes). In fact the emperor had as many *comites* as he had functions.

Comic Art. See GRAFFITI; PICTURA; SCULPTURA.

Comissatio (from *κῶμος* or *κωμάζω*, *comissari*). A drinking-bout following the *cena* (q. v.), and frequently prolonged into the night. Food was partaken of during the *comissatio*, but only as a relish for the wine. Cf. Plaut. *Most.* i. 4; Petron. 65; Suet. *Tit.* 7.

Combrēa (Κώμβρεια). A town in the Macedonian district of Crossaea.

Cominium. A town in Samnium, destroyed by the Romans in the Samnite wars (Livy, x. 44).

Comitia. The popular assemblies of the Romans, summoned and presided over by a *magistratus*. In the comitia the Roman people appeared as distributed into its political sections, for the purpose of deciding, in the exercise of its sovereign rights, upon the business brought before it by the presiding magistrate. The comitia must be distinguished from the *contiones*. The *contiones* were also summoned and presided over by a magistrate, but they did not assemble in their divisions, and they had nothing to do but to receive the communications of the magistrate. In all its assemblies at Rome the people remained standing. The original place of meeting was the Comitium, a part of the Forum. There were three kinds of comitia, viz.:

(1) THE COMITIA CURIĀTA. This was the assembly of the patricians in their thirty *curiae*, who, until the change of the constitution under Servius Tullius, constituted the whole *populus Romanus.* During the regal period they were summoned by the *rex* or *interrex*, who brought before them questions to be decided Aye or No. The voting was taken first in each curia by heads, and then according to curiae, in an order determined by lot. The business within the competence of this assembly was: (*a*) to elect a king proposed by the *interrex;* (*b*) to confer upon the king the *imperium*, by virtue of the *lex curiata de imperio;* (*c*) to decide on declarations of war, appeals, *arrogationes* (see ADOPTIO), and the reception of foreign families into the body of the patricians. The Servian constitution transferred the right of declaring aggressive war and the right of deciding appeals to the Comitia Centuriata, which, from this time onward, represented the people, now composed of both patricians and plebeians. After the establishment of the Republic, the Comitia Curiata retained the right (*a*) of conferring, on the proposal of the Senate, the imperium on the magistrates elected by the Comitia Centuriata, and on the dictator elected by the consuls; (*b*) of confirming, likewise on the proposal of the Senate, the alterations in the constitution decided upon by the Comitia Centuriata, and Tributa.

The extinction of the political difference between patricians and plebeians destroyed the political position of the Comitia Curiata, and the mere shadow of their rights survived. The assembly itself became an unreality, so much so that, in the end, the presence of the thirty *lictores curiati* and three augurs was sufficient to enable legal resolutions to be passed. (See LICTORS.) But the Comitia Curiata retained the powers affecting the reception of a non-patrician into the patrician order, and the powers affecting the proceeding of *arrogatio*, especially in cases where the transition of a patrician into a plebeian family was concerned. Evidence of the exercise of these functions on their part may be traced down to the imperial period.

(2) THE COMITIA CALĀTA were also an assembly of the patrician curiae. They were so called because publicly summoned (*calare*). The pontifices presided, and the functions of the assembly were: (*a*) to inaugurate the flamines, the rex sacrorum, and indeed the king himself during the regal period. (*b*) The *detestatio sacrorum*, previous to an act of *arrogatio*. This was the formal release of a person passing by adoption into another family from the *sacra* of his former family. (See ADOPTIO.) (*c*) The ratification of wills twice a year;

but this applies only to an early period. (*d*) The announcement of the calendar of festivals on the first day of every month.

(3) Comitia Centuriāta. The assembly of the whole people, patrician as well as plebeian, arranged according to the *centuriae* established by Servius Tullius. The original founder of the Comitia Centuriata transferred to them certain political rights which had previously been exercised by the Comitia Curiata. It was not, however, until the foundation of the Republic, when the sovereign power in the State was transferred to the body of citizens, that they attained their real political importance. They then became the assembly in which the people, collectively, expressed its will. The right of summoning the Comitia Centuriata originally belonged to the king. During the republican period it belonged, in its full extent, to the consuls and the dictator alone. The other magistrates possessed it only within certain limits. The *interrex*, for instance, could, in case of there being no consuls, summon the Comitia Centuriata to hold an election, but he could summon them for this purpose only. The censors could call them together only for the holding of the *census* and the *lustrum;* the praetors, it may be conjectured, only in the case of capital trials. In all other instances the consent of the consuls, or their authorization, was indispensable.

The duties of the Comitia Centuriata during the republican period were as follows: (*a*) To elect the higher magistrates: consuls, censors, and praetors. (*b*) To give judgment in all the capital trials in which appeal to the people was permitted from the sentence of the magistrate sitting in judgment. This popular jurisdiction was gradually limited to political trials, common offences being dealt with by the ordinary commissions. And in the later republican age the judicial assemblies of the Comitia Centuriata became, in general, rarer, especially after the formation of special standing commissions (*quaestiones perpetuae*) for the trial of a number of offences regarded as political. (*c*) To decide on declaring a war of aggression; this on the proposal of the consuls, with the approval of the Senate. (*d*) To pass laws proposed by the higher magistrates, with the approval of the Senate. This right lost much of its value after B.C. 287, when the legislative powers of the Comitia Tributa were made equal to those of the Comitia Centuriata. After this time the legislative activity of the latter assembly gradually diminished.

The Comitia Centuriata were originally a military assembly, and the citizens accordingly, in ancient times, attended them in arms. On the night before the meeting, the magistrate summoning the assembly took the auspices on the place of meeting, the Campus Martius. If the auspices were favourable, signals were given, before daybreak, from the walls and the citadel by the blowing of horns, summoning the citizens to a *contio.* The presiding magistrate offered a sacrifice and repeated a solemn prayer, and the assembly proceeded to consider the business which required its decision. Private individuals were not allowed to speak, except with the consent of the presiding magistrate. At his command the armed people divided themselves into their *centuriae,* and marched in this order to the Campus Martius, preceded by banners and headed by the cavalry. Arrived at the Campus, they proceeded to the voting, the president having again put the proposal to the people in the form of a question, *Velitis iubeatis Quirites?* ("Do you wish?" "Do you command?"). While the voting was going on, a red flag stood on the Ianiculum. The *equites,* who in ancient times used to begin the battles in war, opened the voting, and their 18 centuries were therefore called *praerogativae.* The result of their vote was immediately published, and, being taken as an omen for the voters who were to follow, was usually decisive. Then came the 175 centuries of the five *classes* of infantry in their order. Each century counted as casting one vote; this vote was decided by a previous voting within the century, which was at first open, but in later times was taken by ballot. If the 18 centuries of equites and the 80 centuries of the first class, with whom went the 2 centuries of mechanics (*centuriae fabrum*), were unanimous, the question was decided, as there would be a majority of 100 centuries to 93. If not, the voting went on until one side secured the votes of at least 97 centuries. The lower *classes* only voted in the rare cases where the votes of the higher *classes* were not united. The proceedings concluded with a formal announcement of the result on the part of the presiding magistrate, and the dismissal of the host. If no result was arrived at by sunset, or if unfavourable omens appeared during the proceedings, or while the voting was going on, the assembly was adjourned until the next convenient occasion.

This form of voting gave the wealthier citizens a decided advantage over the poorer, and lent an aristocratic character to the Comitia Centuriata. In the third century B.C. a change was introduced in the interest of the lower *classes.* Each of the thirty-five *tribus,* or districts, into which the Roman territory was divided, included two *centuriae* of *iuniores* and *seniores* respectively. (For the five *classes,* see Exercitus.) Thus each of the five *classes* included 70 centuries, making 350 centuries in all. To this number add the 18 centuries equitum, and the 5 centuries not included in the propertied classes — namely, 2 of *fabri* (mechanics), 2 of *tubicines* (musicians), and 1 of *proletarii* and *liberti* (the very poor and the freedmen), and the whole number of centuries amounts to 373. The centuries, it must be remembered, had by this time quite lost their military character. Under this arrangement the 88 votes of the *equites* and the first *classis* were confronted with the 285 votes of the rest. Besides this, the right of voting first was taken from the equites and given to the *centuria praerogativa* chosen by lot from the first *classis.* The voting, it is true, was still taken in the order of the *classes,* but the *classes* were seldom unanimous as in former times; for the interests of the tribus, which were represented in each *classis* by two centuries respectively, were generally divergent, and the centuries voted in the sense of their tribe. The consequence was that it was often necessary—indeed, perhaps that it became the rule, at least at elections—to take the votes of all the *classes.*

In early times the military arrangement was sufficient to secure the maintenance of order. But after its disappearance the *classes* were separated and the centuriae kept apart by wooden barriers (*saepta*), from which the centuries passed over bridges into an open inner space called *ovile* (sheepfold). On the position of the Comitia Centuriata during the imperial age, see below.

(4) Comitia Tribūta. This was the collective assembly of the people arranged according to the local distribution of tribes. (See Tribus.) When the tribuneship of the *plebs* was established (B.C. 494) the tribunes were allowed the right of summoning assemblies of the *plebs* in its tribes to consider questions affecting its interests. Out of these councils of the *plebs* (*concilia plebis*) were afterwards (B.C. 449) formed the Comitia Tributa, in which the patricians were represented as well as the plebeians; but the plebeians had the preponderance, as they were the more numerous, and as the voting qualification was exactly equal. By a law passed in B.C. 449, and finally ratified in 286, the *plebi scita*, or resolutions of the Comitia Tributa, were declared binding upon the whole *populus*. The consequence was that this assembly, side by side with the Comitia Centuriata, became the representative of the popular supremacy, and, indeed, its proper and constitutional organ. This was specially the case in regard to legislation, the more so as it was far simpler to summon the people by tribes than by centuries.

The right of summoning the Comitia Tributa lay chiefly, though not exclusively, with the *tribuni*. Their consent was regarded as an indispensable condition, if another magistrate wished to summon or preside over the Comitia Tributa. Until the latter years of the Republic, the assembly usually met upon the Capitol, and afterwards on the Campus Martius. The functions of the Comitia Tributa, gradually acquired, were as follows: (*a*) The election of all the lower magistrates, ordinary (as the *tribuni plebis*, *tribuni militum*, *aediles plebis*, *aediles curules*) and extraordinary, under the presidency partly of the tribunes, partly of the consuls or praetors. (*b*) The nomination of the *pontifex maximus*, and of the coöpted members of the religious *collegia* of the *pontifices*, *augures*, and *decemviri sacrorum*. This nomination was carried out by a committee of seventeen tribes chosen by lot. (*c*) To give judicial decisions in all suits instituted by the tribunes and aediles of the *plebs*, for offences against the *plebs* or its representatives. In later times these suits were mostly instituted on the ground of bad or illegal administration. The tribunes and aediles had, in these cases, the power of inflicting pecuniary fines ranging up to a large amount. (*d*) To pass resolutions on proposals made by the tribunes of the *plebs* and the higher magistrates on foreign and domestic affairs —on the conclusion of peace, for instance, or the making of treaties. Their power was almost unlimited, and the more important because, strictly speaking, it was only the higher magistrates who required the authorization of the Senate. Nor had the Senate more than the right of quashing a measure passed without due formalities.

The Comitia Tributa were summoned, at least seventeen days before the meeting, by the simple proclamation of a herald (*praeco*). As in the case of the Comitia Centuriata, business could neither be begun nor continued in the face of adverse auspices. Like the Comitia Centuriata, too, the tribal assembly met at daybreak and could not sit beyond sunset. If summoned by the tribunes, the Comitia Tributa could only meet in the city, or within the radius of a mile from it. The usual place of assembly was the Forum or the Comitium (q. v.). If summoned by other authorities, the assembly met outside the city, most commonly in the Campus Martius. The proceedings opened with a prayer, unaccompanied by sacrifice. The business in hand was then discussed in a *contio* (see above, p. 391 *a*); and the proposal having been read out, the meeting was requested to arrange itself according to its thirty-five tribes in the *saepta*, or wooden fences. Lots were drawn to decide which tribe should vote first. The tribe on which this duty fell was called *principium*. The result of this first vote was proclaimed, and the other tribes then proceeded to vote simultaneously, not successively. The votes given by each tribe were then announced in an order determined by lot. Finally, the general result of the voting was made known.

The proposer of a measure was bound to put his proposal into due form and publish it beforehand. When a measure came to the vote, it was accepted or rejected as a whole. It became law when the presiding magistrate announced that it had been accepted. The character of the comitia had begun to decline even in the later period of the Republic. Even the citizens of Rome took but little part in them, and this is still more true of the population of Italy, who had received the Roman citizenship in B.C. 89. The Comitia Tributa, in particular, sank gradually into a mere gathering of the city mob, strengthened on all sides by the influx of corrupt elements. The results of the voting came more and more to represent, not the public interest, but the effects of direct or indirect corruption. Under the Empire the Comitia Centuriata and Tributa continued to exist—in a shadowy form, it is true—down to the third century A.D. Iulius Caesar had deprived them of the right of deciding on war and peace. Under Augustus they lost the power of jurisdiction, and, practically, the power of legislation. The imperial measures were, indeed, laid before the Comitia Tributa for ratification, but this was all; and under the successors of Augustus even this proceeding became rarer. Since the time of Vespasian, the emperors, at their accession, received their legislative and other powers from the Comitia Tributa; but this, like the rest, was a mere formality. The power of election was that which, in appearance at least, survived longest. Augustus, like Iulius Caesar, allowed the Comitia Centuriata to confirm the nomination of two candidates for the consulship. He also left to the Comitia Centuriata and Tributa the power of free election to half the other magistracies— the other half being filled by nominees of his own. Tiberius transferred the last remnant of free elective power to the Senate, whose proposals, originating under imperial influence, were laid before the Comitia for ratification. The formalities, the auspices, prayer, sacrifice, and proclamation, were now the important things, and the measures proposed were carried, not by regular voting, but by acclamation. See Mommsen, *Römische Forschungen*, vol. i.; Becker and Marquardt, *Röm. Alterthümer*, vol. ii., pt. i., pp. 353–394, and pt. iii., pp. 1–196; Lange, *Röm. Alterthümer*, i. 341–355, 391–491; ii. 418–682; and the articles Tabellariae Leges; Lex; Pons.

Comitiālis Dies. See Dies.

Comitium. The name of a small space in Rome, bounded on the north by the Senate House (see Curia), and on the south by the Rostra (q. v.). Down to the second century B.C. it was used for the meetings of the assemblies and of the courts of law. After the removal of the rostra it became part of the Forum. See FORUM.

Commagēné (Κομμαγηνή). The northeasternmost district of Syria, lying between the Taurus and the Euphrates. It formed a part of the kingdom of Syria, after the fall of which it maintained its independence under a race of kings, the family of the Seleucidae, and was not united to the Roman Empire until the reign of Vespasian.

Commentarii. (1) Roman collections of historical documents, such as treaties, decrees, and short notices of important events. These became the sources from which many of the Roman historians drew their materials in treating of the early period. Of these collections may be noted (*a*) the COMMENTARII REGUM, professing to be the work of the kings themselves, and in reality containing very ancient records; (*b*) the COMMENTARII AUGŬRUM, kept by the college of augurs; (*c*) the COMMENTARII PONTIFĬCUM, also called ANNĀLES MAXĬMI, containing the names of the magistrates for each year and a record of all memorable events from the days of the kings down to the pontificate of P. Mucius Scaevola (B.C. 133); (*d*) the COMMENTARII MAGISTRATUUM (i.e. *consulum, quaestorum, censorum,* etc.), records of the transactions of individual magistrates. The greatest part of these records perished when Rome was destroyed by the Gauls (B.C. 388), though in some cases copies of them remained. See ANNALES; FASTI; LIBRI LINTEI. (2) The title of a number of historical and legal works by various Roman writers, the best known being those of Cicero (written in Greek with the title ὑπομνήματα), now lost, but largely used by Plutarch in his life of Cicero; the *Commentarii de Bello Gallico* and the *Commentarii de Bello Civili* of Iulius Caesar (q. v.); and the *Commentarii de Iure Civili* of the jurist Gaius (q. v.).

Commentarius, Commentarii (ὑπομνήματα). Properly notes or note-books. Hence the word acquires a variety of meanings, of which the most important are the following:

(1) *Commentarii domestici*, or family memorials, the records of events interesting to the members of particular families.

(2) The "memoirs" drawn up by public men as to events in which they had taken part. See above.

(3) Memoranda kept by different departments of the public service, the officials in charge of them being known as *a commentariis*.

(4) In towns a register kept of the official acts of the municipal authorities. We have interesting extracts from the *commentarii* of Caeré in an inscription in the Museum at Naples (Wilmanns, 2083).

(5) The unofficial record of recent events at Rome, sent by Caelius to Cicero in Cilicia, is called by him *commentarii rerum urbanarum* (Cic. *Ad Fam.* viii. 2, 2).

(6) The record of the daily occurrences at court kept in *commentarii diurni* (Suet. *Aug.* 64), a kind of private diary, which must be distinguished from the formal *acta* and also from

(7) *Commentarii principis*, the register of the emperor's official decisions (Plin. *Ep.* x. 106) and of accusations brought before him (Suet. *Calig.* 15).

(8) Tacitus once (*Ann.* xv. 74) speaks of *commentarii senatus*, by which he can hardly mean anything but the *acta senatus*. See ACTA.

Commentātor Cruquiānus. See CRUQUIUS.

Commerce. (1) GREEK. In the Homeric poems the Greeks are not represented as a people with a spontaneous inclination to commerce. Indeed, the position of the oldest Greek cities, far away from the sea, sufficiently shows that their founders can have had no idea of trade as a means of getting wealth. Greek navigation in ancient times was almost exclusively subservient to war and piracy, to which latter, for a long time, no stigma was attached in public opinion. And the trade carried on with Greece by the Asiatics, especially the Phœnicians, who then ruled the Greek seas, can hardly have been very active. The Greeks, having no agricultural or industrial produce to offer, could not have tempted many foreigners to deal with them. But in the centuries succeeding the Homeric Age the commerce of Greece was revolutionized.

The islands, especially Aegina and Euboea, were foremost in commercial undertakings; the only continental town which was at all successful in this way being Corinth, which was favoured by its incomparable position. It was the foundation of the Hellenic colonies in Asia Minor that first occasioned the free development of Greek trade. The exertions of the Ionians were mainly instrumental in creating two things indispensable to its success —namely, commercial activity, excited by contact with the ancient industries of the East, and a maritime power in the proper sense, which made it possible to oust the Phœnicians from the naval supremacy which they had so long maintained. This new commercial activity necessitated a larger use of the precious metals and the establishment of a gold and silver coinage, which the Ionians were the first among the Greeks to adopt. This proved a powerful stimulus to the development of commerce, or rather it was the very condition of its existence. Miletus took the first place among the trading colonies. The influence of these cities upon their mother country was so strong that even the Dorians gradually lost their national and characteristic dislike of trade and commerce, and threw themselves actively into their pursuit. Down to the sixth century B.C. Greek commerce had extended itself to the coasts of the Mediterranean and the inland seas connected with it, especially towards the East. It was not until a later time that Athens joined the circle of commercial cities. Even in Solon's time the Athenians had lived mainly by agriculture and cattle-breeding, and it was only with the growth of the democratic constitution that their commercial intercourse with the other cities became at all considerable. The Persian Wars, however, and her position as head of the naval confederacy, raised Athens to the position of the first maritime power in Greece. Under the administration of Pericles she became the centre of all Hellenic activity, not only in art and science, but in trade. It was only Corinth and Corcyra whose western trade enabled them to maintain a prominent position by the side of Athens. The Greeks of Asia Minor completely lost their commercial position after their conquest by the Persians. The naval supremacy of Athens, and with it its commerce, were completely annihilated by the Peloponnesian War. It was a long time before the Athenians succeeded in breaking down the maritime power of Sparta which that war had established. Having done so, they recovered, but only for a short time, a position of prominence not at all equal to their former supremacy by sea. The victory of the Macedonian power entirely destroyed the political and commercial importance of Athens, whose trade now fell behind that of other cities. The place of Athens, as the first maritime and commercial power, was taken by the city of Rhodes, founded in B.C. 408. By the second half of the fourth century B.C. the trade of Rhodes had extended itself over the whole known world, and its maritime law was universally observed until a much later period. After the destruction of Corinth, in the middle of the second century B.C., the island of Delos enjoyed a brief but brilliant period of prosperity. Among the commercial cities of the Graeco-Macedonian Empire, Alexandria in Egypt took the first place, and rose indeed to be the centre of European and Eastern trade. It was mainly through Alexandria that intercourse was kept up between Greece and the Eastern countries opened up by the campaigns of Alexander the Great.

One of the most important routes followed by Grecian traffic was that leading to the Black Sea, the coasts of which were fringed with Greek colonies. Besides Byzantium and Sinopé, the chief commercial centres in this region were Olbia, Panticapaeum, Phanagoria, and Phasis, from which trade-routes penetrated far into the barbarian countries of the interior. Other main routes led by Chios and Lesbos to the coasts of Asia Minor and by the Cyclades to that part of the Asiatic coast where lay the great cities of Samos, Ephesus, and Miletus. Hence they continued to Egypt and Cyrené, by Rhodes and Cyprus and the coast of Phœnicia. But in travelling to these parts from the Peloponnesus, men generally sailed by way of Crete, which had been long celebrated for its maritime enterprise. Round the promontory of Malea, the southernmost point of the Peloponnesus, and by Corcyra, they sailed northward to the coasts of the Adriatic, or westward to Italy and Sicily. Regular traffic beyond Sicily was rendered impossible by the jealousy of the Carthaginians and Etruscans, who were masters of the commerce in this region, and whose place was afterwards taken there by the Romans. A considerable land-traffic was carried on by the colonies with barbarians of the interior. But in Greece Proper the mountainous nature of the country and the absence of navigable rivers were unfavourable to communication by land, and the land-traffic accordingly was entirely thrown into the shade by the maritime trade. The only opportunity for commerce by land on a large scale was afforded by the great national festivals, which brought together great crowds of people from every part of Greece, and secured them a safe conduct. (See EKECHEIRIA.) In this way these festivals exactly corresponded to the trade fairs of modern Europe.

The exports of Greece consisted mainly of wine, oil, and manufactured goods, especially pottery and metal wares. The imports included the necessaries of life, of which Greece itself, with its dense population, artificially increased by slavery, did not produce a sufficient quantity. The staple was wheat, which was imported in large quantities from the coasts of the Black Sea, Egypt, and Sicily. Next came wood for houses and for ships, and raw materials of all kind for manufacture. The foreign manufactures imported were mostly objects of luxury. Finally we should mention the large number of imported slaves.

Comparing the circumstances of the ancient Greek maritime commerce with those of modern trade, we may observe that the ancients were much hampered by having no commission agencies and no system of exchange. The proprietor of the cargo sailed with it, or sent a representative with full powers. No transaction was carried on without payment in ready money, which was often rendered difficult by the existence of different systems of coinage. With uncivilized tribes, notably those on the Black Sea, a system of barter long maintained itself. As no goods could be bought without cash payments, and men of property generally preferred to lend out their capital to borrowers at high interest, a system of bottomry was extensively developed in Greek maritime trade. The creditor usually took care, in lending the capital necessary for loading the ship, to secure a lien on the ship or the cargo—or both. With this he undertook the risks of the business, charging interest at a very high rate, generally twenty to thirty per cent. The written contract contained other specifications as to the ship and the rate of interest, for the breach of which certain customary penalties were fixed. These had reference to the destination of the ship and, generally speaking, to the route and the time to be occupied; to the character and value of the wares, and to the repayment of the loan—the latter to determine whether it should be made on the ship's arriving at its destination or on its return home. In the first case the creditor would often sail with the ship, if he had no representative on the spot or at the port for which she was bound.

At Athens, and no doubt in other cities, the interests of the creditor were protected by a strict code of laws. Fraudulent appropriation of a deposit was punishable with death; dilatoriness in payment with imprisonment. The creditor was allowed to seize not only the security, but the whole property of the debtor. In other respects Athenian legislation secured several advantages to traders. Commercial cases came before the law courts in winter only, when navigation was impossible, and they had to be decided within a month. In ordinary cases of debt, the creditor could only seize on the debtor's property; but in commercial cases he was liable to be imprisoned if condemned to payment. In other matters aliens had to be represented in court by a citizen; in commercial cases they could appear in person. It was the duty of the Thesmothetae to see to the preparation of these cases. The trial was carried on and the verdict given by a special tribunal, the *ναυτοδίκαι* (q. v.). Merchants could easily obtain the considerable privilege of exemption from military service, though they were not legally entitled to it.

In general, it may be said that the Greek States, in consideration of the importance of trade, went very far in providing for its interests. They did their best to secure its safety and independence by force of arms, and concluded treaties with the same end in view. This is especially true of those agreements which regulated the legal relations of the citizens of any two States in their intercourse with each other, and prescribed the forms to be observed by the citizens of one State when bringing suits against those of another. The institution of πρόξενοι, corresponding to that of the modern consuls, was of immense benefit to the trading community. The Greek governments did a great deal in the way of constructing harbours, warehouses, and buildings for exchange in the neighbourhood of the harbours. The superintendence of the harbour traffic, like that of the market traffic, was intrusted to special government officials; in Athens, for instance, to the ten overseers of the Ἐμπόριον. (See AGORANOMI.) The Athenians had also a special board, called μετρονόμοι, to see that the weights and measures were correct. It was only in exceptional cases that the freedom of trade was interfered with by monopolies, nor was it usual to lay prohibitions upon imports. Prohibitions of exportation were, however, much commoner. In many States, as e. g. in Macedonia, it was forbidden to export building materials, especially wood for ship-building; and no grain might be exported from Attica. Again, no Athenian merchant was permitted to carry corn to any harbour but that of Athens; no citizen or resident alien could lend money on the security of ships carrying corn to any place but Athens. Even foreigners who came with corn into the harbour of Athens were compelled to deposit two-thirds of it for sale there. To prevent excessive profits being realized in the corn trade, it was made a capital offence for any private citizen to buy up more than fifty bushels at a time, or sell it at a profit of more than an obolus a bushel. The corn trade was under the superintendence of a board called σιτοφύλακες. In the prevailing activity of commerce, the tolls on exports and imports were a plentiful source of revenue to the government. See PORTORIUM.

In Greek society, petty trading was thought a vulgar and sordid pursuit, and was left to the poorer citizens and resident aliens (μέτοικοι). In Athens the class of resident aliens included a great number of the larger dealers; for the wealthier and more respectable citizens liked lending their capital to others engaged in trade better than engaging in trade themselves.

(2) ROMAN. In Italy an active commerce was early carried on at sea by the Etruscans, the other Italian peoples taking only a passive part in it. But Rome, from a very early time, became the commercial centre of Central Italy. It was situated on a river deep enough to admit large vessels, the upper course and tributaries of which were also navigable. Its position was much improved by the harbour at the colony of Ostia, said to have been constructed under Ancus Marcius. So long as the Etruscans and Carthaginians and (as in later times) the Greek cities of southern Italy and Sicily, like Tarentum and Syracuse, ruled the sea, the maritime power and commerce of Rome were restricted within very narrow limits. Even as late as the middle of the fourth century B.C. the traffic of Rome was confined to Sardinia, Sicily, and Africa. But with the extension of the Roman power, Roman commerce assumed wider dimensions. At the end of the republican period Roman ships were on every sea, and there was a flourishing interior trade in Italy and all the provinces. Wherever there was a navigable river it was used for communication, with the happiest results. After the Second Punic War, Rome gradually acquired the character of a great commercial city, where the products of the whole world, natural and industrial, found a market. The most considerable import was corn, and this at all periods of Roman history. (See ANNONA.) The chief exports of Italy were wine and oil, to which we must add, after the development of Italian industry, manufactured goods. The trading-harbour of Rome was Puteoli (Pozzuoli), on the Bay of Naples, while Ostia was used mainly by corn-ships. Petty dealing was regarded unfavourably by the Romans, as by the Greeks; but trade on a large scale was thought quite respectable, though in older times members of the Senate were not allowed to engage in it. Most of the larger undertakings at Rome were in the hands of joint-stock companies (see PUBLICANI), the existence of which made it possible for small capitalists to share in the profits and risks of commerce. It was indeed an old maxim of business men at Rome that it was better to have small shares in a number of speculations than to speculate independently. The corn trade, in particular, was in the hands of these companies. The government allowed them to transport corn from Sardinia, Sicily, Spain, Africa, and Egypt to Rome; whole fleets of vessels, constructed for the purpose, being appointed to this service. Foreign trade was subjected to a number of restrictions. The exportation of certain products was absolutely prohibited—for instance, iron, whether unwrought or manufactured, arms, coin, salt, and gold — and duties were levied on all imports. There were also numerous restrictions on trade in the interior, as each province formed a unit of taxation, in which toll had to be paid on entering or leaving it. Among the State monopolies, the most important was that of salt.

For more minute details regarding ancient commerce, see Reinaud, *Relations Politiques et Commercielles de l'Empire Romain avec l'Asie Orientale* (Paris, 1863); Lindsay, *A Hist. of Merchant Shipping and Ancient Commerce*, 4 vols. (2d ed. London, 1882); and Lanciani, *Ancient Rome in the Light of Recent Discoveries*, chap. ix. (Boston, 1888).

Commercium. A legal relation existing between two Italian States, according to which the citizens of each had the same right of acquiring property, especially landed property, in the territory of the other. Commercium also included the powers of inheriting legacies and contracting obligations. See CIVITAS.

Commissoria Lex. A term met with in the law of pledge and in the law of sale. In the former it meant the agreement between pledger and pledgee that the property pledged should be vested absolutely in the latter unless the debt which it secured was punctually discharged by the day fixed for payment. See PIGNUS.

In the law of sale, *lex commissoria* denotes an agreement between vendor and purchaser that the former shall be at liberty to rescind the contract if the latter does not perform his obligations under it in due manner and at the proper time (*Dig.* 18, 3, 1). This was not the same thing as a conditional sale; for in the latter, if the property were damaged or destroyed, the loss would fall on the vendor, whereas in our case, if the property was lost, damaged, or destroyed, the loss fell on the purchaser.

Commissum. One sense of this word is that of "forfeited," which is derived from the sense of the verb *committere*, "to attach legal effect to," "to make operative." Hence property forfeited by the coming into effect of a condition was said to be *commissum*, as when a *lex commissoria* (q. v.) was attached to a mortgage (*pignus*). *Commissa hereditas* is an inheritance forfeited as a penalty (Cic. *Verr*. i. 10, § 27).

Commius. A king of the Atrebates, who was advanced to that dignity by Caesar. He was sent by Caesar to Britain, but was cast into chains by the natives, and not released till they had been defeated by Caesar. In B.C. 52, he joined the other Gauls in their great revolt against the Romans, and continued in arms even after the capture of Alesia (Pseud. Caes. *B. G.* viii. 7-23).

Commixtio. See CONFUSIO.

Commodātum. A gratuitous loan in which the borrower (*commodatarius*) is bound to return the very thing lent, and not an equivalent. It thus differs from *mutuum* (q. v.).

Commodiānus. A Christian Latin poet, who flourished in the third century A.D., when he wrote two poems (*Instructiones* in acrostic and telestic verse, and the *Carmen Apologeticum*), showing a prosody based partly on accent and partly on syllabic quantity, and intended to be regarded as hexameters. Rhyme is also occasionally employed. Both poems are aimed against the heathen and the Jews. Edition by Dombart (Vienna, 1888).

Commŏdus, L. AURELIUS ANTONĪNUS. The son and successor of M. Aurelius Antoninus, who ascended the imperial throne A.D. 180. The reign of this prince is a scene of guilt and misery, which the historian is glad to dismiss with brevity. He appears, indeed, to have inherited all the vices of his mother, Faustina; and his father, in selecting him for his successor, allowed the feelings of the parent to triumph over the wisdom of the magistrate. He had accompanied his father on the expedition against the Marcomanni and the Quadi, but no sooner was Aurelius dead than his son became anxious to proceed to Rome, and soon concluded a hasty and disgraceful peace with the barbarians whom his father had been on the point of completely subjugating when he was cut off by disease. Notwithstanding the care which Aurelius had bestowed on his education, Commodus was ignorant to an extreme degree, having neither abilities nor inclination for profiting by the paternal example and instruction. On his return to Rome he speedily showed the bias of his natural disposition, giving himself up to unrestrained indulgence in the grossest vices. That he might do so without impediment, he intrusted all power to Perennis, praefect of the Praetorian Guard, a man of stern and cruel temper, who was at last slain by the soldiers for his severity.

A conspiracy against the life of Commodus having failed, it was followed by a long succession of judicial murders to gratify the vengeance of the cowardly and vindictive tyrant. He was next threatened by a new danger: disaffection had spread over the legions; and an attempt of Maternus, a private soldier, who headed a band of deserters and projected the assassination of Commodus during the celebration of the festival of Cybelé, was so ably conceived that it must have been successful but for the treachery of an accomplice. But neither duty nor danger could draw Commodus from the sports of gladiators or the pleasures of debauchery. Cleander, a Phrygian slave, soon succeeded to the place and influence of Perennis, and for three years the Empire groaned beneath his cruelty and rapacity. At length a new insurrection burst forth, which nothing could allay, the praetorian cavalry being defeated in the streets by the populace, until the unworthy favourite was, by the emperor's command, delivered to the insurgents. In the meantime, Commodus was indulging his base tastes and appetites, not only by gross sensuality, but by attempting to rival the gladiators. Being a very skilful archer and of great personal strength, he delighted in killing wild beasts in the amphitheatre, and thus pretending to rival the prowess of Hercules. In the gladiatorial contests, he publicly engaged so often that he was the conqueror in 735 combats. Though luxurious in his dress, frequently resorting to the baths eight times in the day, scattering gold dust in his hair, and, from the fear of admitting the approach of a razor in the hand of another, singeing off his beard, he was especially proud of exhibitions of personal strength, and frequently, in the garb of a priest, butchered victims with his own hands. Among the flatteries of the obsequious Senate none pleased him more than the vote which styled him the "Hercules of Rome," not even that which decreed to him the titles of Pius and Felix, or which offered to abolish the name of the Eternal City and substitute for it the title Colonia Commodiana. After thirteen years of unmitigated oppression, his favourite, Marcia, ultimately became the instrument by which the Roman world was delivered from its odious master. She discovered, from some private notes of Commodus, that herself, Laetus the praetorian praefect, and Eclectus the chamberlain, were on the list devoted to death. A conspiracy was immediately formed, Marcia administered poison to the emperor, and, lest the measure should not prove effectual, the deed was completed by suffocation, in A.D. 192. The life of Commodus has come down to us, written by Lampridius, in the *Historia Augusta*.

Commodus. (Bust in the Capitoline Museum, Rome.)

Comnēna, ANNA, daughter of the Byzantine emperor Alexius I. (Comnenus), and author of one of the most valuable of the Byzantine histories. She was born December 1st, 1083, and received a liberal education, showing at an early age a great fondness for literary pursuits, combined with an intriguing disposition, which found much to gratify it in the court of Constantinople. Failing to induce her father on his death-bed to leave the imperial crown to her, she set on foot a conspiracy to destroy the life of her brother Iohannes, the lawful heir (1118), but her husband, Nicephorus Bryennius, a nobleman of the court, refused his aid. Her brother spared her life and only temporarily deprived her of her property; but she retired from the court and, after spending some time in historical composition, entered a convent, where she died in 1148. Her life of her father, in eighteen books, is elaborately rhetorical and always eulogistic, yet it is of much value to the historian of the later Empire. Sir Walter Scott introduces her in a memorable chapter of his novel, *Count Robert of Paris.* The best edition of her history is that of Schopen and Reifferscheid, 2 vols. (1839–78). On her life and career, see Oster's work, *Anna Comnena*, 3 vols. (1868–71).

Comoedia (κωμῳδία). (1) GREEK. The Greek comedy, like the Greek tragedy and satyric drama, had its origin in the festivals of Dionysus. As its name, κωμῳδία, or the song of the κῶμος, implies, it arose from the unrestrained singing and jesting common in the κῶμος, or merry procession of Dionysus. According to the tradition, it was the Doric inhabitants of Megara, well known for their love of fun, who first worked up these jokes into a kind of farce. The inhabitants of Megara accordingly boasted that they were the founders of Greek comedy. From Megara, it was supposed, the popular farce found its way to the other Dorian communities, and one Susarion was said to have transplanted it to the Attic deme of Icaria about B.C. 580. No further information is in existence as to the nature of the Megarian or Dorian popular comedy. The local Doric farce was developed into literary form in Sicily by Epicharmus of Cos (about B.C. 540–450). This writer gave a comic treatment not only to mythology, but to subjects taken from real life. The contemporary of Epicharmus, Phormus or Phormis, and his pupil Dinolochus, may also be named as representatives of the Dorian comedy.

The beginnings of the Attic comedy, like those of the Attic tragedy, are associated with the deme of Icaria, known to have been the chief seat of the worship of Dionysus in Attica. Not only Thespis, the father of tragedy, but also Chionides and Magnes (about B.C. 550), who, if the story may be trusted, first gave a more artistic form to the Megarian comedy, introduced by Susarion, were natives of Icaria. Comedy did not become, in the proper sense, a part of literature until it had found welcome and consideration at Athens in the time of the Persian Wars; until its form had been moulded on the finished outlines of tragedy; and until, finally, it had received from the State the same recognition as tragedy. See TRAGOEDIA.

The OLD COMEDY, as it was called, had its origin in personal abuse. It was Crates who first gave it its peculiar political character, and his younger contemporary, Cratinus, who turned it mainly or exclusively in this direction. The masters of the Old Comedy are usually held to be Cratinus and his younger contemporaries, Eupolis and Aristophanes. It attained its youth in the time of Pericles and the Peloponnesian War—the period when the Athenian democracy had reached its highest development. These three masters had many rivals—who fell, however, on the whole beneath their level—among others Pherecrates, Hermippus, Teleclides, Phrynichus, Ameipsias, Plato, and Theopompus.

A good idea of the characteristics of the Old Comedy may be formed from the eleven surviving plays of Aristophanes (q. v.). The Greek tragedy has a meaning for all time; but the Old Comedy, the most brilliant and striking production of all Athenian literature, has its roots in Athenian life, and addressed the Athenian public only.

Dealing from the very first with the grotesque and absurd side of things, it was the scourge of all vice, folly, and weakness. The social life of Athens, so restless and yet so open, offered an inexhaustible store of material; and the comedian was always sure of a witty, laughter-loving public, on whom no allusion was lost. The first aim of the Athenian comedy was, no doubt, to make men laugh, but this was not all. Beneath it there lay a serious and patriotic motive. The poet, who was secured by the license of the stage, wished to bring to light and turn to ridicule the abuses and degeneracy of his time. The Attic comedians are all admirers of the good old times, and accordingly the declared enemies of the social innovations which were beginning to make their way—the signs in many cases, no doubt, of approaching decline. It was not, however, the actual phenomena of life which were sketched in the Old Comedy. The latter is really a grotesque and fantastic caricature; the colours are laid on thick, and propriety, as we moderns understand it, is thrown to the winds. These plays abound in coarseness and obscenity of the broadest kind, the natural survival of the rude license allowed at the Dionysiac festival. The choice and treatment of the subjects show the same tendency to the grotesque and fantastic. Fancy and caprice revel at their will, unchecked by any regard either for the laws of poetical probability or for adequacy of occasion. The action is generally quite simple, sketched out in a few broad strokes, and carried out in a motley series of loosely connected scenes. The language is always choice and fine, never leaving the forms of the purest Atticism. The metres admit a greater freedom and movement than those of the tragedy.

A comedy, like a tragedy, consisted of the dramatic dialogue, written mostly in iambic senarii, and the lyrical chorus. The division of the dialogue into πρόλογος, ἐπεισόδιον, and ἔξοδος, and of the chorus into πάροδος and στάσιμα, are the same as in tragedy. But, while the tragic chorus consisted of fifteen singers, there were twenty-four in the comic. A peculiarity of the comic chorus is the παράβασις, a series of lines entirely unconnected with the plot, in which the poet, through the mouth of the chorus, addresses the public directly about his own concerns or upon burning questions of the day. (See PARABASIS.) Like the tragedies, the comedies were performed at the great festivals of Dionysus, the Dionysia (q. v.) and the Lenaea (q. v.). On each occasion five poets competed for the prize, each with one play.

For a short time, but a short time only, a limitation had been put upon the absolute freedom with which the poets of the Old Comedy lashed the shortcomings of the government and its chief men. The downfall of the democracy, however, deprived them of this liberty. The disastrous issue of the Peloponnesian War had, moreover, ruined the Athenian finances, and made it necessary to give up the expensive chorus and with it the παράβασις. Thus deprived of the means of existence, the Old Comedy was doomed to extinction. In its place came what was called the MIDDLE COMEDY, from about B.C. 400 to 338. This was a modification of the Old Comedy, with a character corresponding to the altered circumstance of the time. The Middle Comedy was in no sense political; it avoided all open attack on individuals, and confined itself to treating the typical faults and weaknesses of mankind. Its main line was burlesque and parody, of which the objects were the tragedies and the mythology in general. It was also severe upon the lives of the philosophers. It dealt in typical characters, such as bullies, parasites, and courtesans. The writers of the Middle Comedy were very prolific, more than eight hundred of their plays having survived as late as the second century A.D. The most celebrated of them were Antiphanes of Athens and Alexis of Thurii; next to these came Eubulus, and Anaxandrides of Rhodes.

A new departure is signalized by the dramas of what is called the NEW COMEDY. In these, as in the modern society drama, life was represented in its minutest details. The New Comedy offered a play regularly constructed like that of tragedy, characterized by fine humour, and but seldom touching on public life. The language was that of ordinary society, and the plot was worked out in a connected form from the beginning to the dénouement. The chief art of the poets of the New Comedy lay in the development of the plot and the faithful portraiture of character. The stock subjects are illicit love affairs; for honest women lived in retirement, and stories of honourable love, therefore, were practically excluded from the stage. The ordinary characters are young men in love, fathers of the good-natured or the scolding type, cunning slaves, panders, parasites, and bragging officers. Besides the dialogue proper, we find traces of parts written in lyric metres for the higher style of singing. These were, in all probability, like the dialogue, performed by the actors.

The fate of the New resembles that of the Middle Comedy, only a few fragments of its numerous pieces having survived. Of some of them, however, we have Latin adaptations by Plautus and Terence. Its greatest master was Menander, besides whom should be mentioned Diphilus, Philemon, Philippides, Posidippus, and Apollodorus of Carystus. The New Comedy flourished from B.C. 330 till far into the third century A.D.

In about B.C. 300, the old Dorian farce was revived in a literary form in Southern Italy by Rhinthon, the creator of the *Hilarotragoedia* (Ἱλαροτραγῳδία). The *Hilarotragoedia* was for the most part a parody of the tragic stories. It is also called, from its creator, *fabula Rhinthonica*.

(2) ROMAN. Like the Greeks, the Italian people had their popular dramatic pieces—the *versus Fescennini*, for instance, which were at first introduced, in B.C. 390, from Etruria, in consequence of a plague, to appease the wrath of heaven. (See FESCENNINI VERSUS.) From this combination sprang the *satura*, a performance consisting of flute-playing, mimic dance, songs, and dialogue. The *Atellanae Fabulae* (q. v.) were a second species of popular Italian comedy, distinguished from others by having certain fixed or stock characters. The creator of the regular Italian comedy and tragedy was a Greek named Livius Andronicus, about B.C. 240. Like the Italian tragedy, the Italian comedy was, in form and contents, an imitation, executed with more or less freedom, of the Greek. It was the New Greek Comedy which the Romans took as their model. This comedy, which represents scenes from Greek life, was called *palliata*, after the Greek *pallium*, or cloak. The dramatic *satura* and the *Atellana*, which afterwards supplanted the *satura* as a concluding farce, continued to exist side by side. The Latin comedy was brought to perfection by Plautus and Terence, the only Roman dramatists from whose hands we still possess complete plays. We should also mention Naevius and Ennius (both of whom wrote tragedies as well as comedies), Caecilius, and Turpilius, with whom, towards the end of the third century B.C., this style of composition died out.

About the middle of the second century B.C., a new kind of comedy, the *fabula togata* (from *toga*), made its appearance. The form of it was still Greek, but the life and the characters Italian. The *togata* was represented by Titinius, Atta, and Afranius, who were accounted masters in this kind of writing. At the beginning of the first century B.C., the *Atellana* assumed an artistic form in the hands of Pomponius and Novius; and some fifty years later the *mimus*, also an old form of popular farce, was similarly handled by Laberius and Publilius Syrus. The *mimus* drove all the other varieties of comedy from the field, and held its ground until late in the imperial period. See FABULA; MIMUS; PANTOMIMUS; SATIRA.

The Roman comedy, like its model, the New Comedy of the Greeks, had no regular chorus, the intervals being filled up by performances on the flute. (See CHORUS.) The play consisted, like the Roman tragedy, partly of passages of spoken dialogue (*diverbia*) in iambic trimeters, partly of musical scenes called *cantica*. See CANTICUM.

For the details of comic acting and a bibliography, see DRAMA; THEATRUM.

Compensatio. A legal term corresponding to the English "set-off" or "counterclaim." See Gaius, iv. 64.

Comperendinatio. The technical term in Roman law for the postponement of a trial for a definite time by consent of both parties, each being bound to appear. It is to be distinguished from *ampliatio*, which seems to have meant an indefinite postponement, in consequence of uncertainty on the part of the jury.

Compes (πέδη). (1) A fetter or shackle for the ankles, and sometimes so constructed as to deprive the prisoner almost wholly of the power of walking. (2) An ornamental anklet worn by women. See PERISCELIS.

Competītor. See AMBITUS.

Compĭta. See COMPITALIA.

Compitalia, also called **Ludi Compitalicii**. A festival celebrated once a year in honour of the two Lares Compitales, to whom sacrifices were offered at the places where two or more ways met (*compita*). Dionysius (iv. 14) similarly ascribes its origin to Servius Tullius, and describes the festival as it was celebrated in his time. He relates that the sacrifices consisted of honey-cakes (πέλανοι), which were presented by the inhabitants of each house, and that the persons who assisted as ministering servants at the festival were not freemen, but slaves, because the Lares took pleasure in the service of slaves. He further adds that the Compitalia were celebrated a few days after the Saturnalia with great splendour, and that the slaves on this occasion had full liberty given them to do what they pleased. We are told by Macrobius (*Saturn.* i. 7, 34) that the celebration of the Compitalia was restored by Tarquinius Superbus, who sacrificed boys to Mania, the mother of the Lares; but this practice was changed after the expulsion of the Tarquins, and the heads of garlic and poppies were offered instead of human heads.

The persons who presided over the festival were the *magistri vicorum*. Public games were added at some time during the republican period to this festival, but were suppressed by command of the Senate in B.C. 64. Yet that the festival itself still continued to be observed, though the games were abolished, is evident from Cicero (*ad Att.* iii. 3). When Iulius Caesar dissolved most of the *collegia*, the Compitalia necessarily fell into disuse. Augustus restored the festival on an entirely new basis, not reviving the *collegia*, but assigning the charge of it to a newly constituted set of *magistri vicorum*. To the two Lares Compitales was now added the *genius Augusti* (Ovid, *Fast.* v. 145), and the festival was observed twice in the year, on May 1 and August 1. At an earlier time the Compitalia belonged to the *feriae conceptivae;* that is, festivals which were celebrated on days appointed annually by the magistrates or priests. The day on which this festival was celebrated appears to have been always in the winter.

Compluvium. See DOMUS, p. 544.

Compromissum. See IUDEX; ACTIO.

Compsa. A town of the Hirpini, in Samnium, near the sources of the Aufidus.

Comum. The modern Como; a town in Gallia Cisalpina, at the southern extremity of the west branch of the Lacus Larius (Lago di Como). It was originally a town of the Insubrian Gauls, and subsequently a Roman colony. It was the birthplace of the younger Pliny (Pliny, *Epist.* i. 3).

Comus (*κῶμος*). See CHORUS; COMOEDIA.

Comus (Κῶμος). The god of festive mirth and joy, represented as a winged youth, mentioned only in the later times of antiquity.

Concaedes. A barricade made of trees and placed across the road to hinder the approach of a hostile force (Tac. *Ann.* i. 50).

Concha (*κόγχη, κόγχος*). Literally, a sea-shell, and applied to a vessel made in the form of such a shell, and used for various purposes—e. g. as salt-cellars, for oils, perfumes, unguents, colours for painters, etc. A liquid measure was also called *concha*, and was of two capacities: one = .0412 pts. Eng.; the other, .1238 pts.

Conciliarii. See ASSESSOR.

Concilium. An assembly in general, sometimes used in a loose way to designate the comitia of the centuries (Liv. ii. 28), or any *contio*. For the *concilium plebis*, see COMITIA. The word also denotes the assemblies or meetings of confederate towns or nations, at which either their deputies alone, or any of the citizens who had time and inclination, met, and thus formed a representative assembly (Liv. i. 50). We find frequent traces of this, not only among the Italian nations, but also in the Greek States (*τὸ κοινόν*). (See ACHAEAN LEAGUE.) As the Romans conquered the neighbouring States of Italy, it was a regular part of their policy to break up the union of the vanquished tribes by forbidding the existence of such *concilia* (Liv. viii. 14, 10). But Augustus not merely allowed the *concilia* to continue where they had previously been held, but instituted them also in other provinces; and this representative character was recognized. In theory, they were associations formed for the worship of the imperial house. The president was the *ἀρχιερεύς*, or *sacerdos provinciae*, an official elected annually by the deputies (*legati*) from the most important towns. This dignitary was usually one of the most eminent and wealthy of the provincials, and had the immediate direction of the finances of the temple and its festivals; at a later time he had a certain power of control over all the priests of the province. After the concilium had taken part in the religious festival, it met again for the conduct of business. Its first duty was to pass the accounts of the expenditure connected with the provincial temple to Augustus, and to provide for the maintenance of the worship for the coming year; but then it was entitled to criticise the conduct of the governor, and either vote thanks to him or lay a complaint before the emperor (cf. the Inscription of Torigny, edited by Mommsen), which was frequently followed by his accusation (Plin. *Epist.* vii. 6). In this manner some control was exercised over the governor, and there was some approach to the creation of a representative body. See Marquardt, *Röm. Staatsverw.* i. 503–516, and his important essay in the *Ephem. Epigr.* (1872), pp. 200–214.

Concio. See CONTIO.

Conclāvĕ. A separate room in a house; or a suite of rooms that could be locked with the same key. See Fest. p. 38. 9, Müll.

Concordia. The Latin personification of concord or harmony, especially among Roman citizens. Shrines were repeatedly erected to Concordia during the republican period after the cessation of civil dissensions. The earliest was dedicated by Camillus in B.C. 367. The goddess Concordia was also invoked, together with Ianus, Salus, and Pax, at the family festival of the *Caristia*, on the 30th of March, and, with Venus and Fortuna, by married women on the 1st of April. (See MANES.) During the imperial period Concordia Augusta was worshipped as the protectress of harmony, especially of matrimonial agreement, in the emperor's household.

Concubīna (*παλλακή, παλλακίς*). A concubine. (1) GREEK. The *παλλακή* or *παλλακίς* occupied at Athens a kind of middle rank between the wife and the harlot (*ἑταίρα*). Demosthenes defines the position of each by saying that the harlot ministers to pleasure only, the concubine serves, while the wife is for the purpose of bearing children and acting as the faithful steward of her husband's goods (*c. Neaer.* § 122, p. 1386). Thus Antiphon speaks of the *παλλακή* of Philoneos as following him to the sacrifice, and also waiting upon him and his guest at table. If her person were violated by force, the same penalty was exigible from the ravisher as if the offence had been committed upon an Attic matron; and a man surprised by the quasi-husband in the act of criminal intercourse with his *παλλακή*, might be slain by him on the spot, as in the parallel case. (See ADULTERIUM.) It does not, however, appear very clearly from what political classes concubines were chiefly selected, as cohabitation with a foreign (*ξένη*) woman was strictly forbidden by law, and the provisions made by the State for virgins of Attic families must, in most cases, have prevented their sinking to this condition. Sometimes, certainly, where there were several destitute female orphans, this might take place, as the next of kin was not obliged to provide for more than one; and we may also conceive the same to have occurred with respect to the daughters of families so poor as to be unable to supply a dowry. The dowry, in fact, seems to have been a decisive criterion as to whether the connection between a male and a female Athenian, in a state of cohabitation, amounted to a marriage. If no dowry had been given, the child of such union would be illegitimate; if, on the contrary, a dowry had been given, or a proper instrument executed in acknowledgment of its receipt, the woman was fully entitled to all conjugal rights. It does not appear that the slave who was taken to her master's bed acquired any political rights in consequence; the concubine mentioned by Antiphon is treated as a slave by her master, and after his death undergoes a servile punishment.

(2) ROMAN. According to an old definition, an unmarried woman who cohabited with a man was originally called *pellex* or *paelex* (Gell. iv. 3), but afterwards by the more decent appellation of *concubina* (*Dig.* 50, 16, 144). *Concubinatus* is cohabitation other than marriage between free persons who were both unmarried, or between an unmarried free man and an *ancilla*. In the older times this was viewed as an offence deserving punishment (Liv. x. 31; xxv. 2); but when the possibility of a lasting affection between persons who had not *conubium* came to be recognized, the cohabitation of an unmarried man with his *liberta* or *ancilla* (Plaut. *Epid.* iii. 4, 29, 30) was regarded without censure. In Cicero's time (*De Orat.* i. 40, § 183) the name of *concubina* would have applied to a woman who cohabited with a man who had not divorced his wife; but this was not considered lawful concubinage in after-times. The Lex Iulia de Adulteriis of Augustus imposed severe penalties on *adulterium, incestus*, and *stuprum* (q. v.); but by the Lex Iulia and Papia Poppaea *concubinatus* was legalized and exempted from the penal provisions of the earlier statute (*Dig.* 25, 7, 3, 1), though an *honesta femina* who wished to become a *concubina* was not dispensed from them unless she made an express declaration of her intention or *testatio* (*Dig.* ib. 3, pr.). But a man who already had an *uxor* could not have a *concubina* at the same time (*Dig.* 50, 16, 144), nor apparently could a man have more than one *concubina* at a time; and widowers who already had children, and did not wish to contract another legal marriage, took a *concubina*, as we see in the case of Vespasian (Suet. *Vesp.* 3), Antoninus Pius, and M. Aurelius.

Concubinatus differed from lawful marriage in three especial respects. (1) In the relation of the parties, there being no *affectio maritalis* (Paul. *Sent. Rec.* ii. 20). (2) In the loss of reputation to the woman if *honesta*. Yet there is an inscription in Fabretti (p. 337) to the memory of Paullianus by Aemilia Prima, *concubina eius et heres*, which seems to show that the term *concubina* was not one that a woman need be ashamed of. (3) In its legal effects: it was not a marriage, and therefore the rules as to *dos, donatio propter nuptias, donatio inter virum et uxorem*, had no application; nor were the children in *patria potestas*, though their paternity was recognized; they could be legitimated, and under the emperors were entitled to maintenance, even from the legitimate children after the father's death (*Nov.* 89, 12, 6); also, they had some rights of succession on the father's dying intestate.

By later emperors *concubinatus* was discouraged, but it was not made generally unlawful until the ninth century, by Leo the Philosopher.

Cohabitation between two slaves was called *contubernium*, a name also applied to that between a slave and a free person (Paul. ii. 19, 6).

Condalium. A finger-ring worn on the first joint (κόνδυλος) of the forefinger (Fest. s. v. *condylus*; Plaut. *Trin.* iv. 3, 7, and 15).

Condemnatio. See ACTIO; IUDEX; JUDICIAL PROCEDURE.

Condictio. See ACTIO.

Conditorium. See FUNUS; SEPULCRUM.

Condrūsi. A German people in Gallia Belgica, the dependants of the Treviri, dwelling between the Eburones and the Treviri.

Conductio. See LOCATIO.

Condy (κόνδυ). An Asiatic drinking-vessel, sometimes used by the Greeks, made of silver or gold. According to some authorities it was of Persian (Athen. xi. 478 a), according to others of Cappadocian origin (Pollux, vi. 96).

Confarreatio. The form of marriage used by the patricians. See MATRIMONIUM.

Confectionery. See DULCIA.

Confiscatio. See PROSCRIPTIO.

Confluentes. The modern Coblentz; a town in Germany, at the confluence of the Mosella and the Rhenus. There was probably no Roman town here, however, but only a posting-station *ad confluentes* on the great Roman road; and the place was not made a *castrum* or fortress until the fifth century A.D. Of about that date are the remains of a Roman bridge of piles discovered in 1864, when the Moselle was unusually low.

Confusio. Properly the mixing of liquids, or the fusing of metals into one mass. If things of the same or of different kind were confused, either by the consent of both owners or by accident, the compound was the property of both. If the *confusio* was caused by one without the consent of the other, the compound was only joint property in case the things were of the same kind and perhaps of the same quality—as, for instance, wines of the same quality. If the things were different, so that the compound was a new thing, this was a case of what, by modern writers, is called *specificatio*, which the Roman writers expressed by the term *novam speciem facere*, as if a man made *mulsum* out of his own wine and his neighbour's honey. In such a case the person who caused the *confusio* became the owner of the compound, but he was bound to make good to the other the value of his property.

Commixtio applies to cases such as mixing together two heaps of corn; but this is not an instance in which either party acquires property by the *commixtio*. For if the mixture takes place, either accidentally or with mutual consent, or by the act of one alone, in all these cases the property of each person continues as before, for in all these cases it is capable of separation. A case of *commixtio* arises when a man's money is paid without his knowledge and consent, and the money, when paid, is so mixed with other money that it cannot be recognized; otherwise it remains the property of the person to whom it belonged.

Two things, the property of two persons, might become so united as not to be separable without injury to one or both; in this case, the owner of the principal thing became the owner of the accessory. Thus, in the case of a man building on another man's ground, the building belonged to the owner of the ground (*superficies solo cedit*); or in the case of a tree planted, or seed sown on another man's ground, the rule was the same. If a man wrote, even in letters of gold, on another man's parchment or paper, the whole belonged to the owner of the parchment or paper; in the case of a picture painted on another man's canvas, the canvas became the property of the owner of the picture.

But in all these cases the losing party was entitled to compensation, with some exceptions as to cases of *mala fides*.

Congiarium (sc. *vas;* from *congius*). (1) A vessel containing a *congius* (q. v.).

(2) In the early times of the Roman Republic, the *congius* was the usual measure of oil or wine which was, on certain occasions, distributed among the people; and thus *congiarium*, as Quintilian says, became a name for the gift as well as for the measure (*congiarium commune liberalitatis atque mensurae*, vi. 3, § 52). It does not follow that all the citizens or even heads of families received a *congius* apiece. The earliest mention of a distribution of oil is in B.C. 213, when two Cornelii Scipiones, afterwards called Africanus and Cethegus, in their aedileship gave a certain number of *congii* (the numeral has dropped out) to the inhabitants of each street (Livy, xxv. 2, with Madvig's note). Lucullus on returning from his Eastern victories distributed more than 100,000 casks of wine to the people (Plin. *H. N.* xiv. § 96). The name *congiarium* was also applied, less accurately, to presents of corn or other provisions.

Under the Empire the tranquillity of the capital was insured by a gigantic system of outdoor relief (see Frumentariae Leges), supplemented by frequent doles. The general term for these imperial presents is *largitio*, sometimes (especially on coins) *liberalitas*. Distributions to the soldiers were called *donativa*, to the people *congiaria;* but sometimes the former also are called *congiaria* (Cic. *Ad Att.* xvi. 8). The sums thus spent were enormous. Hadrian's congiarium was three *aurei* per head on his proclamation as emperor, and double that amount on his arrival in Rome; Commodus gave 725 *denarii* to each citizen. Marquardt has computed the imperial congiaria at an average of $450,000 a year from Iulius Caesar to Claudius, $1,500,000 a year from Nero to Septimius Severus; it must have been, however, a periodical emptying of the treasury rather than a continuous drain.

Congiarium was, moreover, used to designate presents or pensions given by men of rank to their friends, clients, or dependants. See Suet. *Iul.* 27; Sen. *De Brev. Vit.* 8. § 2.

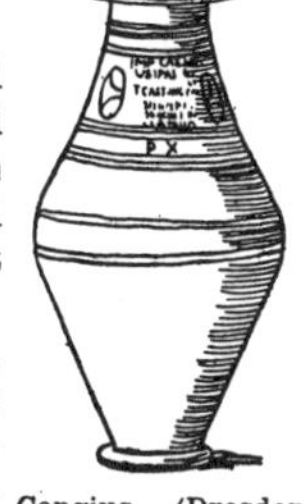
Congius. (Dresden Collection.)

Congius. A Roman liquid measure containing six sextarii (*Carm. de Pond.* 72), or the eighth part of the amphora. It was equal to the χοῦς of the Greeks, about 5.76 pints.

There is a congius in existence, known as the Farnese congius, but now at Dresden, bearing an inscription which states that it was made in the year A.D. 75, according to the standard measure in the Capitol, and that it contained, by weight, ten pounds. This congius is one of the means by which the attempt has been made to fix the weight of the Roman pound. See Libra.

Cato tells us that he was wont to give to each of his slaves a congius of wine at the Saturnalia and the Compitalia. Pliny relates, among other examples of hard drinking, that Novellius Torquatus of Mediolanum obtained a cognomen (*tricongius*, "a nine-bottle man") by drinking three congii of wine at one sitting (*H. N.* xiv. § 144).

Conimbrĭca. A town of Lusitania, near the sea-coast, on the river Munda, now Coimbra in Portugal.

Conisălus (Κονίσαλος). A deity worshipped at Athens with Priapus (q. v.)

Connubium. See Conubium.

Conon (Κόνων). (1) A distinguished Athenian commander, and one of the generals who succeeded Alcibiades in the command of the fleet during the Peloponnesian War. Having engaged Callicratidas, the Spartan admiral, he lost thirty vessels, and was compelled to take shelter in the harbour of Mytilênê, where he was blockaded by his opponent. The victory gained by the Athenians at the Arginusae released him at length from his situation. Being subsequently appointed, with five others, to the command of a powerful fleet, he proceeded to the Hellespont, where Lysander had charge of the Lacedaemonian squadron. The negligence of his fellow-commanders, the result of overweening confidence in their own strength, led to the fatal defeat at Aegos Potamos, and the whole Athenian fleet was taken, except nine vessels of Conon's division, with eight of which, thinking that the war was now desperate, he sailed to Salamis in the island of Cyprus. The ninth vessel was sent to Athens with the tidings of the defeat. In Cyprus, Conon remained at the court of Evagoras, watching for an opportunity to prove of service to his country. Such a state of affairs soon presented itself. The Lacedaemonians, having no more rivals in Greece, sent Agesilaüs with an army into Asia to make war upon the Persian king. Conon immediately repaired to Pharnabazus, the satrap of Lydia and Ionia, aided him with his counsels, and suggested to him the idea of exciting the Thebans and other Grecian communities against Sparta, so as to compel that State to recall Agesilaüs from the East. The plan was approved of by the king of Persia, and Conon, at the head of a Persian fleet, B.C. 394, attacked the Spartan admiral, Pisander, near Cnidus, and defeated him, with the loss of the greater part of his ships. Lacedaemon immediately lost the control of the sea, and her power in Asia Minor ceased. Conon thereupon, after ravaging the coasts of Laconia, returned to Attica, rebuilt the city walls as well as those of the Piraeus, with means which had been furnished by Pharnabazus, and gave on this occasion a public entertainment to all the Athenians. The Lacedaemonians, dispirited by the success of Conon, and alarmed at the re-establishment of the Athenian fortifications, sent Antalcidas to Tiribazus, one of the Persian generals, to negotiate a peace. The Athenians, on their part, deputed Conon and some others to oppose this attempt; but Tiribazus being favourably inclined towards Sparta, and in all probability jealous of

Pharnabazus, imprisoned Conon, under the pretext that he was endeavouring to excite an insurrection in Aeolis and Ionia. The Persian king, however, disapproved of the conduct of the satrap, and Conon was released. The latter thereupon returned to the island of Cyprus, where he fell sick and died, about B.C. 390. His remains were conveyed to Athens (Corn. Nep. *Conon;* Xen. *Hist. Gr.* i. 4, 10; id. ib. ii. 1, 21, etc.). (2) A native of Samos, distinguished as an astronomer and geometrician. None of his works have reached us; he is mentioned, however, by Archimedes, Vergil, Seneca, and others. Conon lived between about 300 and 260 years before our era. Apollonius, in the fourth book of his *Conic Sections,* thinks that many of Conon's demonstrations might be rendered more concise. He is mentioned as an astronomer by one of the commentators on Ptolemy, and Seneca (*Quaest. Nat.* vii. 3) informs us that he had made out a list of the eclipses of the sun that had been visible in Egypt. He is mentioned also by Vergil (*Eclog.* iii. 40), and by Catullus in his translation of the Greek poem of Callimachus, on the tresses of Berenicé. (3) A grammarian epitomized by Photius (q. v.).

Conopēum (κωνωπεῖον, from κώνωψ, "a mosquito"). A mosquito-curtain—i. e. a covering made to be expanded over beds and couches to keep away gnats and other flying insects. These curtains were much used in Egypt (Isid. *Orig.* xix. 5, 5), and by Roman ladies as early as Varro's time. (See Varro, *R. R.* ii. 10.) The *conopeum* (whence the English word "canopy") was also known in Latin as *cubiculare.*

Conquisitōres. Recruiting sergeants who were employed to go about the country, enlisting or impressing soldiers for the Roman army. See Liv. xxi. 11, 113; Cic. *Pro Mil.* 25, 67.

Consanguinei. See COGNATIO.

Conscripti. See SENATUS.

Consecratio. See APOTHEOSIS; INAUGURATIO.

Consensus. See OBLIGATIONES.

Consentes Dii. The name which the Romans gave to the twelve superior deities, or Dii Maiorum Gentium. The best derivation of the name is that which traces it to the participle of the obsolete verb *conso,* "to advise" or "counsel," the Dii Consentes (*quasi Consentientes*) being they who formed the council of the sky. Ennius has given their names in the two following lines:

> Iuno, Vesta, Ceres, Diana, Minerva, Venus, Mars,
> Mercurius, Iovi', Neptunus, Vulcanus, Apollo.

The conception is, however, originally Etruscan (Müller, *Etrusk.* ii. p. 81 foll.). The Romans also called them Dii Complices. See Arnob. iii. 123; and Corssen, *Nachricht.* 281.

Consentia. The chief town of the Bruttii, on the river Crathis; here Alaric died. It is now Cosenza.

Consentius, PUBLIUS. A Roman grammatical writer, who flourished in the fifth century A.D. and wrote two grammatical works: (1) *Ars Consentii de Duabus Partibus Orationis, Nomine et Verbo;* and (2) *Ars Consentii de Barbarismis et Metaplasmis.* Osann regards Consentius as a Gaul, from the internal evidence of these works. The only complete MS. of Consentius is one at Munich of the tenth century. The text is given by Keil in his *Grammatici Latini,* v. 386.

Considius Longus. See LONGUS.

Consilium. A council, or body of advisers. Such councils were called in, according to ancient Roman custom, by the presiding magistrate in civil and criminal cases. Even in the family tribunals, which decided cases affecting the members of the *gens,* a consilium of kinsfolk was thought necessary. The custom was that the presiding judge bound himself by the decision of his freely chosen *consilium,* but took the responsibility himself. The expression *consilium* was afterwards transferred to the regular juries of the courts which decided civil and criminal cases. (See CENTUMVIRI; IUDICES.) The emperors, too, made a practice of inviting a consilium of friends to assist them in their judicial decisions. After the time of Hadrian, the members of the imperial consilium or *consistorium* appear as regularly appointed and salaried officers, the Consiliarii Augusti. These were generally, though not exclusively, selected from the body of professional jurists. See CONSISTORIUM.

Consistorium. The Roman emperors, following an ancient practice of Roman magistrates, consulted their friends and followers (*amici, familiares, comites*) before giving judicial decisions in cases of importance. The *consilium principis,* or judicial council thus instituted, became a standing body in the time of Hadrian (Spart. *Hadr.* 8, 18).

The council was composed of persons of the greatest eminence; both senators of the highest rank and members of the order of *equites* sat in it.

The term *auditorium principis* is used as equivalent to *consilium.* It was not a general council for State affairs, and is not to be confused with the political council we find certain emperors convening. Its functions were generally confined to legal business. The emperor not only took its advice respecting his judgments, but also in all matters connected with legal administration. It was strictly consultative in character, the emperor not being bound in any way by its opinion. Changes were made in its constitution by Diocletian and his successors. The ordinary members of the reconstituted body, which is known as the *consistorium principis,* were called *comites consistoriani;* they were divided into the two classes of (1) *illustres,* (2) *spectabiles.* The *illustres* consisted of four great officers of the palace: viz., the *quaestor sacri palatii,* the *magister officiorum,* the *comes sacrarum largitionum,* and the *comes rei privatae.* The class of *spectabiles* was a larger one; its members are generally named simply *comites consistoriani.* Besides these two classes of ordinary and active members of the consistorium, there was a class of extraordinary members, called *vacantes.* There was also a class of purely honorary members. The functions of the consistorium seem to have been wider than those of the earlier *consilium,* since it acted as a council for advising the emperor in general matters of State.

Consolatio. The title of several works in Roman literature. (1) A treatise of Cicero, now lost, written after the death of his daughter Tullia (B.C. 45) and based upon Crantor's treatise περὶ πένθους. (See *Tusc. Disp.* i. 65; *ad Att.* xii. 14, 3.) The fragments of this work are to be found in Baiter and Kayser's text, xi. 71. See Schulz, *De Ciceronis Consolatione* (Greifswald, 1860). Cicero is supposed by some to have transcribed a portion at least of the

Consolatio in the first and third books of the *Tusculanae Disputationes*. (2) A probably spurious work called *Consolatio ad Liviam Augustam de Morte Drusi Neronis* and ascribed by Scaliger to Pedo Albinovanus, but by others to Ovid. There exists no early MS. of it, and it first appears in the *editio princeps* of Ovid, A.D. 1471. Hence it is believed to be the work of some Italian scholar of the fifteenth century. See Haupt, *Epicedion Drusi cum Commentariis* (Leipzig, 1849); and a paper by Nettleship in the *Transact. of the Oxford Phil. Soc.* (1885–86). (3) *Ad Marciam*, a treatise of the younger Seneca (q. v.), written by him to Marcia, the daughter of Cremutius Cordus, on the death of her son. See Schinnerer, *Seneca's Schrift an Marcia* (Hof. 1889). (4) A treatise written in prison by Boëthius (q. v.) about the year A.D. 524, and entitled *De Consolatione Philosophiae*. It is partly in the form of a dialogue, and is interspersed with metrical pieces after the fashion of a Menippean satire.

Constans. The youngest of the three sons of Constantine the Great and Fausta. After his father's death he received (A.D. 337) as his share of the Empire, Illyricum, Italy, and Africa. His territory was invaded by his brother Constantine, who was defeated and slain in the invasion (340). Constans became supreme over the whole Western Empire, but the weakness and profligacy of his character made him despised and disliked so that in 350 he was slain by the troops of the usurper Magnentius (q. v.).

Constantia. The name of several cities: (1) in Cyprus; (2) in Phœnicia; (3) in Palestine; (4) in Mesopotamia; (5) in Rhaetia, now Constanz.

Constantīna. (1) A Roman princess, daughter of Constantine the Great and wife of the emperor Gallus. (2) See CIRTA.

Constantinopŏlis (Κωνσταντίνου Πόλις). See BYZANTIUM.

Constantīnus. (1) GAIUS FLAVIUS VALERIUS AURELIUS CLAUDIUS, known as The Great, son of the emperor Constantius Chlorus and Helena (q. v.), was born A.D. 272, at Naïsus, a city of Dacia Mediterranea. When Constantine's father was associated in the government by Diocletian, the son was retained at court as a kind of hostage, but was treated with great kindness at first, and was allowed several opportunities of distinguishing himself. After the abdication of Diocletian, Constantius and Galerius were elevated to the rank of Augusti, while two new Caesars, Severus and Maximin, were appointed to second them. Constantine was not called to the succession. Diocletian, partial to Galerius, his son-in-law, had left the nomination of the two new Caesars to the latter; and the son of Constantius, whose popularity and talents had excited the jealousy of Galerius, and whose departure, although earnestly solicited by his father, was delayed from time to time under the most frivolous pretences, with difficulty at length obtained permission to join his parent in the West, and only escaped the machinations of the emperor by travelling with his utmost speed until he reached the western coast of Gaul. He came just in time to join the Roman legions, which were about to sail under his father's command to Britain, in order to make war upon the Caledonians. Having subdued the northern barbarians, Constantius returned to York (Eboracum), where he died in the month of July, in the year 306. Galerius, sure of the support of his two creatures, the Caesars, had waited impatiently for the death of his colleague, to unite the whole Roman Empire under his individual sway. But the moderation and justice of Constantius had rendered him the more dear to his soldiers from the contrast of these qualities with the ferocity of his rival. At the moment of his death, the legions stationed at York, as a tribute of gratitude and affection to his memory, and, according to some, at his dying request, saluted his son Constantine with the title of Caesar and decorated him with the purple. Whatever resentment Galerius felt at this, he soon perceived the danger of engaging in a civil war. As the eldest of the emperors, and the representative of Diocletian, he recognized the authority of the colleague imposed upon him by the legions. He assigned to him the administration of Gaul and Britain, but gave him only the fourth rank among the rulers of the Empire with the title of Caesar.

Under this official appellation Constantine administered the prefecture of Gaul for six years (A.D. 306–312), perhaps the most glorious, and certainly the most virtuous, period of his life. The title and rank of Augustus, which his soldiers had conferred upon Constantine, but which Galerius had not allowed him to retain, the latter gave to Severus, one of his own Caesars. This dignity had been expected by Maxentius, son of the abdicated emperor Maximian, the former colleague of Diocletian. Indignant at his disappointment, Maxentius caused himself to be proclaimed emperor by his army; and, to strengthen his usurpation, he induced his father to leave his retreat and resume the imperial title. A scene of contention followed, scarcely paralleled in the annals of Rome. Severus marched against the two usurpers; but was abandoned by his own troops, surrendered, and was slain. Galerius levied a great army, and marched into Italy against Maximian and Maxentius, who, dreading his power, retired to Gaul and endeavoured to procure the support of Constantine. This politic chief did not consider it expedient to provoke a war at that time and for no better cause; and, Galerius having withdrawn from Italy and returned to the East, Maximian and Maxentius returned to Rome. To aid him in the struggle, Galerius conferred the title of emperor on his friend Licinius; and thus there were at once six pretenders to the sovereignty of the Empire—namely, Galerius and Licinius; Maximian and his son Maxentius; Maximin, who had been nominated Caesar by Galerius; and Constantine, the son and successor of Constantius. Among these rivals Constantine possessed a decided superiority in prudence and abilities, both military and political. The harsh temper of Maximian soon led to a quarrel between him and his son Maxentius. Leaving Rome, he went to Gaul, to Constantine, who had become his son-in-law when he and his son were endeavouring to make head against Galerius. Here also Maximian found himself disappointed of that power which he so greatly longed to possess; and having plotted against Constantine, was detected and put to death. Galerius died not long after (311), leaving his power to be divided between his Caesars, Maximin and Licinius; so that there were now four competitors for the Empire: Constantine, Maxentius, Maximin, and Licinius. Maxentius speedily provoked open hostilities with Constantine, who marched at the head of a powerful army towards Rome.

It was while Constantine was proceeding on this momentous expedition that he made an open and public declaration in favour of Christianity. Before that time, the persecuting edicts of Diocletian had been much mitigated by the forbearance and leniency of Constantius; and Constantine not only followed his father's example in being merciful to the persecuted Christians, but even showed them some marks of positive favour. Very considerable numbers of them, in consequence, flocked to his standard and swelled the ranks of his army.

Constantine and Fausta.

Their peaceful, orderly, and faithful conduct, contrasting most favourably with the turbulent and dissolute behaviour of those who formed the mass of common armies, won his entire confidence. To what extent this led Constantine to form a favourable opinion of Christianity, or inclined him to view with esteem and respect the tenets which had produced such results, cannot be ascertained. How far, also, his avowed reception of Christianity was influenced by the prudence of the politician, how far by the conviction of the convert, it is impossible to determine. The accounts of his dream and his vision (see LABARUM), which united to enforce his trust in Christianity, bear too much the aspect of fiction, or of having been the illusive consequences of mental anxiety, brooding intensely on the possible results of a great religious revolution, to be woven into the narrative of sober history. The story goes, however, that on his march to Rome, either at Autun in Gaul, or near the Rhine, or at Verona in Italy, Constantine beheld in the sky a brilliant cross with the inscription Ἐν τούτῳ νίκα, "By this conquer!" and that on the night before his decisive battle with Maxentius a vision appeared to him in his sleep, bidding him inscribe the shields of his soldiers with the sacred monogram of the name of Christ. This, at least, is certain, that Constantine caused the Cross to be employed as the imperial standard, and advanced with it to promised victory. After the armies of Maxentius, led by his generals, had sustained two successive defeats, that emperor himself, awakening from his sensual and inactive life at Rome, advanced against his formidable assailant, and met him near the little river Cremera, about nine miles from the city. Maxentius lost the day, after a bloody conflict, and, in endeavouring to enter the city by the Milvian bridge, was precipitated into the Tiber, where he perished (October 27th, 312).

Constantine was received at Rome with acclamations; Africa acknowledged him, as well as Italy; and an edict of religious toleration, issued at Milan, extended the advantages, hitherto enjoyed by Gaul alone, to this prefecture also. After a brief stay at Rome, during which he restored to the Senate their authority, disbanded the Praetorian Guard, and destroyed their fortified camp, from which they had so long awed the city and given rulers to the Empire, Constantine proceeded to Illyricum to meet Licinius, with whom he had formed a secret league before marching against Maxentius. The two emperors met at Milan, where their alliance was ratified by the marriage of Licinius to Constantine's sister. During this calm interview, Constantine prevailed upon Licinius to repeal the persecuting edicts of Diocletian, and to issue a new one, by which Christianity was encouraged, its teachers were honoured, and its adherents advanced to places of trust and influence in the State. After the overthrow of Maximin by Licinius, and his death at Nicomedia, Constantine and his brother-in-law were now the only two that remained of the six competitors for the Empire; and the peace between them, which had seemed to be established on so firm a basis, was soon interrupted by a strife for sole supremacy. In the first war (A.D. 315) Constantine wrested Illyricum from his competitor. After an interval of eight years the contest was renewed. Licinius was beaten before Adrianople, the 3d of July, 323, and Constantine the Great was recognized as sole master of the Roman world.

The seat of empire was now transferred to Byzantium (q. v.), which took from him the name of Constantinople. Several edicts were issued for the suppression of idolatry; and the churches and property restored to the Christians, of which they had been deprived during the last persecution. A reconstruction of the Empire was effected upon a plan entirely new, and this renovated Empire was pervaded by the worship and the institutions of Christianity. That much of the policy of the statesman was mixed up with this patronage of the new religion can easily be imagined. But still, it would be wrong to make him, as some have done, a mere hypocrite and dissembler. The state of his religious knowledge, so far as we have any means of judging, was certainly very inadequate and imperfect; but he was well aware of the characters of the two conflicting religions, Christianity and Paganism, and the purity of the former could not but have made some impression upon his mind.

The private character of Constantine has suffered, in the eyes of posterity, from his stern treatment of Crispus, his son by his first wife, whom he had made the partner of his Empire and the commander of his armies. Crispus was at the head of the administration in Gaul, where he gained the hearts of the people. In the wars against Licinius he had displayed singular talents, and had secured victory to the arms of his father. But from that moment a strong and unnatural jealousy stifled every paternal feeling in the bosom of the monarch. He detained Crispus in his palace, surrounded him with spies and informers, and at length, in the month of July, 324, ordered him to be arrested in the midst of a grand festival, to be carried off to Pola in Istria, and there put to death. A cousin of Crispus, the son of Licinius and Constantine's sister, was at the same time sent, without trial, without even an accusation, to the block. His mother implored in vain, and died of grief. It is fair, however, to say that Niebuhr found evidence to support the view that Crispus aimed at supplanting his father. Fausta, the daughter of Maximian, the wife of Constantine, and the mother of the three princes who succeeded him, was shortly after stifled in the bath by order of her husband for infidelity.

In the following year the celebrated Council of Nicaea was held, at which he opposed the Arians, probably on political grounds only, as being the weaker party; for just before his death he received baptism from an Arian bishop, Eusebius of Nicomedia.

Constantine died at the age of sixty-three, at Nicomedia, July 22d, 337, after a reign of thirty-one years from the death of his father, and of fourteen from the conquest of the Empire. He left three sons, Constantine, Constans, and Constantius, among whom he divided his Empire. The first, who had Gaul, Spain, and Britain for his portion, was conquered by the armies of his brother Constans, and killed in the twenty-fifth year of his age, A.D. 340. Magnentius, the governor of the provinces of Rhaetia, murdered Constans in his bed, after a reign of thirteen years; and Constantius, the only surviving brother, now become the sole emperor, A.D. 353, punished his brother's murderer, and gave way to cruelty and oppression. He visited Rome, where he enjoyed a triumph, and died (361) in his march against Julian, who had been proclaimed emperor by his soldiers at Paris.

See the works of Eusebius (*De Vita Constantini*), Zosimus (Bk. II.), Eutropius, Aurelius Victor, and the *Panegyrici Veteres* (vi. 10); also Manso's *Leben Constantins des Grossen;* Burckhardt, *Die Zeit Constantins des Grossen;* and Broglie, *L'Église et l'Empire Romain.*

(2) The son of the preceding. See above. (3) A usurper who had himself proclaimed emperor in Britain during the reign of Honorius and Arcadius, in A.D. 407, reigning for four years and securing possession of Gaul and Spain, until defeated in 411 by Constantius, the able general of Honorius. By him Constantine was taken prisoner, carried to Ravenna, and there put to death. (4) The name of several emperors of the Eastern Empire. See BYZANTINUM IMPERIUM.

Constantius. (1) CHLORUS, son of Eutropius, and father of Constantine the Great, received at Paris the title of Caesar, which he obtained by his victories in Britain and Germany. He became the colleague of Galerius on the abdication of Diocletian; and, after bearing the character of a humane and benevolent prince, he died at York, and had his son for his successor, A.D. 306. (2) The third son of Constantine the Great. See CONSTANTINUS. (3) The father of Julian and Gallus, was son of Constantius by Theodora, and died A.D. 337. (4) A Roman general, who married Placidia, the sister of Honorius, and was proclaimed emperor, an honour he enjoyed only seven months. He died, universally regretted, A.D. 421, and was succeeded by his son Valentinian in the West.

Constitutiōnes. Enactments of the Roman emperors, in the exercise of their legislative authority, which had statutory force. They comprise the following varieties:

(1) *Orationes*, by which, in the earlier imperial period, the emperor submitted a "bill" to the Senate (*Inst.* ii. 17, 7). They were regarded as law apart from the senatus consulta, by which, in theory, they received the character of "acts," and are often cited as such in preference to the latter.

(2) *Edicta* or *edictales constitutiones*, general rules of law made by the emperor after the analogy of the edicts of the republican magistrates.

(3) *Mandata*, by which the emperor delegated his authority to other magistrates, such as *legati*, *praesides*, and *praefecti.*

(4) *Decreta* and *rescripta*, issued by the emperor in his capacity as praetor, judge, or supreme jurisconsult. Up to the time of Constantine they were by far the commonest kind of constitutio. *Decreta* were determinations of suits by the emperor either as sitting in a court of first instance or on appeal (Suet. *Aug.* 33); *rescripta* (Tac. *Ann.* vi. 9) were provisional decisions on the *legal* point at issue (as to which he had been consulted by a magistrate or a private individual), the facts being left to be inquired into, and a final judgment given, by another magistrate or *iudex*. Technically *rescripta* were of two kinds: *epistolae* and *subscriptiones* or *adnotationes*. The first are independent replies on consultation (*Dig.* 1, 4, 1, 1; *Inst.* iii. 20, 4), many issued by Hadrian, Severus, and Caracalla being extant in the Digest. The second are brief opinions on cases submitted to the emperor by petition, and written at the foot of the latter; this form being most commonly employed in answering private persons (*Dig.* 1, 4, 1, 1; *Cod.* 1, 23, 6).

In the Eastern Empire a peculiar kind of rescripts acquired the name of "pragmatic sanctions." They were drawn up in a peculiar and solemn form, and were more highly taxed than others. Zeno restricted their use to petitions preferred by corporations.

In framing constitutions of any kind the emperor was assisted by the council called *consistorium* (q. v.).

Constrātum. In general, any flooring made of planks. Thus *constratum navis*, "the deck of a ship" (Petron. 100); *constratum pontis*, "a bridgeway" (Livy, xxx. 10), etc.

Consualia. See CONSUS.

Consulāris. A term which, throughout the time of the Roman Republic, signifies a person who has been invested with the consulship; but under the Empire a mere title for the higher class of officers, who thereby obtained permission to have the insignia of a consul, without ever having actually been consuls. Hence the title was almost equivalent to that of an "honorary consul" (*consul honorarius;* Cod. Theod. vi. tit. 19, s. 1). The title was given especially to generals, as formerly persons after their consulship had usually undertaken the command of an army in the provinces. *Consularis* gradually became the established name for those intrusted with the administration of imperial provinces. During the second century A.D., the title *consularis* always denotes a governor who had actually held the office of consul or had received the title from the emperor; but by the fourth century it had become a mere title of a particular class of provincial governors. The emperor Hadrian divided Italy into four districts, and over each he placed an officer who likewise bore the title of *consularis*. At Constantinople the title was given to the superintendents of the aqueducts (*consulares aquarum*), who seem to have been analogous to the *curatores aquarum* of Rome.

Consŭles (originally PRAETŌRES, ὕπατοι). The Roman magistrates to whom the supreme authority was transferred from the kings, after the expulsion of the latter in B.C. 510. The consuls gave their name to the year. They were elected by the Comitia Centuriata, and down to B.C. 366 from the patricians only. The legal age at which a man might be elected was, in the time of Cicero, forty-three. The time of entering on the office varied in the early periods: in B.C. 222, it was fixed to March 15th; in 153, to the 1st of January. The accession of the new consuls was attended with the performance of certain ceremonies, among which may be mentioned a procession of the consuls to the Capitol, with the Senate, *equites*, and other citizens of position, as escort; an offering of white bulls to Iupiter, and the utterance of solemn vows.

The consuls were the representatives of the royal authority, and consequently all other magistrates were bound to obey them, with the exception of the tribunes of the *plebs* and the dictator. During a dictatorship their powers fell into abeyance. In the city their authority was limited by the right of appeal to the people and the veto of the tribunes. But in the army, and over their subordinates, they had full power of life and death. Some of their original functions passed from them in course of time. Thus in B.C. 444, the business of the census was made over to the censors; in 366, the civil jurisdiction within the city, so far as it included the right of performing the acts of adoption, emancipation, and liberation of slaves, was transferred to the praetors. In the field, however, having the criminal jurisdiction in their hands, they had also the right of deciding in civil cases affecting the soldiers. In the general administration of public business the consuls, although formally recognized as the supreme authority, gradually became, in practice, dependent upon the Senate and the Comitia, as they had only the power of preparing the resolutions proposed and carrying them out if accepted. Within the city their powers were virtually confined to summoning the Senate and the Comitia and presiding over their meetings. They also nominated the dictators, and conducted the elections and legislation in the Comitia and the levies of soldiers. After the office of dictator fell into abeyance, the power of the consuls was, in cases of great danger, increased to dictatorial authority by a special decree of the Senate. See COMITIA.

An essential characteristic of the consular office was that it was collegial, and therefore if one consul died another (called *consul suffectus*) was immediately elected. This *consul suffectus* had absolutely the same authority as his colleague, but he had to lay down his office with him at the end of the year for which the two had been originally elected.

The power of the two consuls being equal, the business was divided between them. In the administration of the city they changed duties every month, the senior taking the initiative. With regard to their insignia—namely, the *toga praetexta*, *sella curulis*, and twelve lictors—the original arrangement was that the lictors walked in front of the officiating consul, while the other was only attended by an *accensus*. In later times the custom was for the lictors to walk before the officiating consul and behind the other.

In the field each consul commanded two legions with their allied troops; if they were in the same locality, the command changed from day to day. The question of the administration of the provinces they either settled by consent, or left it to be decided by lot. With the extension of the Empire the consuls became unable to undertake the whole burden of warfare, and the praetors were called in to assist. The provinces were then divided into consular and praetorian; the business of assignment being left to the Senate, which, after the year 122, was bound to make it before the elections. In the first century B.C., a law of Sulla deprived the consuls of an essential element of their authority, the military *imperium;* for it enacted that the consuls should spend their year of office in Rome, and only repair to the provinces and assume the *imperium* after its conclusion.

In the Civil Wars the consular office completely lost its old position, and though it continued to exist under the Empire, it became, practically, no more than an empty title. The emperors, who often held the office themselves, like Caesar, for several years in succession, had the right of nominating the candidates, and therefore, in practice, had the election in their own hands. It became usual to nominate several pairs of consuls for one year, so as to confer the distinction on as many persons as possible. In such cases, the consuls who came in on January 1, after whom the year was named, were called *consules ordinarii*, the *consules suffecti* counting as *minores*. Until the middle of the first century A.D., it was a special distinction to hold the consulship for a whole year; but after that no cases of this tenure occur. In time the insignia (*ornamenta consularia*), or honorary distinctions of the office, were given, in certain degrees, even to men who had not been consuls at all. The chief duties of the consuls now were to preside in the Senate and to conduct the criminal trials in which it had to give judgment. But, besides this, certain functions of civil jurisdiction were in their hands, notably the liberation of slaves, the provision for the costly games which occurred during their term of office, the festal celebrations in honour of the emperor, and the like. After the seat of empire was transferred to Constantinople, the consulate was, towards the end of the fourth century, divided between the two capital cities. The consulate of the Western capital came to an end in A.D. 534, that of the Eastern in 541. From that time the emperor of the East bore the title of *consul perpetuus*.

Consus. A Roman deity, the god of counsel, as his name denotes. His altar was in the Circus Maximus, and was always covered, except on his festival-day, the 18th of August, called Consualia. Horse and chariot races were celebrated on this occasion; and the working-horses, mules, and asses were crowned with flowers and allowed to rest. Hence Consus has probably been confounded with Neptunus Equestris. It was at the Consualia that the Sabine maidens were carried off by the Romans. See CIRCUS.

Contaminatio. A technical term for the combination of the plots of several Greek plays in a single Roman drama. This was done with considerable ingenuity by both Plautus and Terence. Thus, the *Epidicus* of Plautus is undoubtedly a specimen of dramatic contamination (Ladewig, in the *Zeitschrift für die Alterthumswissenschaft* [1841]); and the *Andria* and *Eunuchus* of Terence are excellent examples—the former combining the plots of Menander's Ἀνδρία and Περινθία, and the latter the plots of the same poet's Εὐνοῦχος and Κόλαξ. See Ihne, *Quaestiones Terentianae* (Bonn, 1843); and Kampe, *Lustspiele d. Ter. und ihre Originale* (Halberstadt, 1884); also the prologue to the *Andria*. The only instance of a play made up of the plays of two different authors is found in the *Adelphoe* of Terence, which is based upon the Ἀδελφοί of Menander and the Συναποθνήσκοντες of Diphilus.

Contarii and **Contāti** (κοντόφοροι). Soldiers armed with the long pike called *contus* (Veget. *Mil.* iii. 6).

Contio (erroneously spelt CONCIO). A contraction for *conventio*; that is, a meeting, or *conventus*. In a loose mode of speaking it denotes any popular assembly, even among non-Romans, and any speech or harangue addressed to such an assembly; hence the common phrase *contionem habere* means indifferently "to hold a meeting" and "to make a speech." Written speeches are also sometimes called *contiones*. In the technical sense, however, a contio was an assembly of the Roman people convened regularly (*per praeconem*) by a magistrate or a *sacerdos publicus*. A general in the field by virtue of his *imperium* could summon his troops as often as he pleased to hear what he had to say to them (*adlocutio*), and what he said before the assembled army was *pro contione* (Sall. *Iug.* 8).

Military Contio. (Roman coin.)

Contorniāti. This Italian word (French and English *contorniates*) has been usually employed by numismatists to denote a particular class of circular metallic objects bearing various devices and legends, which were issued, though not for circulation as currency, under the Roman Empire. The ancient appellation of these objects is not known; their modern name has been derived from the circle (in Italian *contorno*) which marks both of their sides, in incuse. The metal of which contorniates are composed is copper, with a certain amount of alloy; in size they are, as a rule, somewhat larger than the "first brass" coins (*sestertii*) of the early Empire, but they are much thinner and are characterized by the circular depression already referred to. The greater number of them present on both sides a device in relief, which is generally obtained, not by striking from a die (as in the case of the medallions), but by process of casting from a mould.

The first issue of the contorniates, which are all of Western origin, is assigned by Eckhel to the time of Constantine (A.D. 306–337), and this date has been practically accepted by the most recent authorities on the subject. Their fabrication, according to Sabatier, ceased under Anthemius (A.D. 464–472).

The types or devices of the contorniates, though offering considerable varieties, may be considered to have reference to the public games and spectacles in the Circus, the Odeum, the Stadium, and the Amphitheatre. The legends are nearly always descriptive of the types. See Robert, *Étude sur les Médaillons Contorniates* (Brussels, 1882); and the article NUMISMATICS.

Contractus. See OBLIGATIONES.

Contrebia. One of the chief towns of the Celtiberi, in Hispania Tarraconensis, southeast of Saragossa.

Controversia. See IUDEX.

Controversiae. A series of compositions on legal subjects by the elder Seneca, originally in ten books. The questions treated are hypothetical cases, and are discussed by way of practice for actual cases. With the ten books of *controversiae* is one book of *suasoriae* (see DECLAMATIO), the whole collection bearing the title *Oratorum et Rhetorum Sententiae, Divisiones, Colores*. The work is a very valuable source of information regarding the history of rhetoric under the early Empire. Of the original ten books of the *controversiae*, only five (I., II., VII., IX., X.) have been preserved. The Gronovii published an edition, with notes in Latin (Amsterdam, 1672). Recent critical editions are those of Kiessling (Leipzig, 1872) and H. J. Müller (Prague, 1887). See RHETORICA.

Contubernāles (σύσκηνοι). Originally, men who served in the same army and lived in the same tent. It is derived from *taberna* (afterwards *tabernaculum*), "a military tent." Each tent was occupied by ten soldiers (*contubernales*), with a subordinate officer at their head, who was called *decanus*, and in later times *caput contubernii*.

Young Romans of illustrious families used to accompany a distinguished general on his expeditions or to his province, for the purpose of gaining under his superintendence a practical training in the art of war or in the administration of public affairs, and were, like soldiers living in the same tent, called his *contubernales* (Cic. *Pro Cael.* 30, 73).

In a still wider sense, the name *contubernales* was applied to persons connected by ties of intimate friendship and living under the same roof (Cic. *Ad Fam.* ix. 2); and hence when a free man and a slave, or two slaves, who were not allowed to contract a legal marriage, lived together as husband and wife, they were called *contubernales*, and their connection, as well as their place of residence, *contubernium* (Petron. 57, 6).

Contubernium (συσκηνία). See CONCUBINA; CONTUBERNALES.

Contumacia. The Latin term for disobedience to the commands of a magistrate or judge; especially, absence from a trial without sufficient excuse. If the accuser were absent, he was considered as dropping his charge (see TERGIVERSATIO), which he was not allowed to renew. The absence of the accused was taken as an admission of guilt. In a civil trial the consequence was immediate condemnation; and the like was the case in criminal trials if the accused failed to appear at the appointed time or on the last day of the trial. If the accused saw that his condemnation was certain, it was quite common for him to retire, and in capital cases to go into voluntary exile—a proceeding which in no way influenced the further course of the proceedings.

Contus (κοντός). (1) A pole with a pointed iron at the end, used as a punt-pole by boatmen. (2) A huge pike such as those carried by barbarian soldiers (Tac. *Hist.* i. 44).

Contus. (Mosaic at Praeneste.)

Conubium. The contracting of a *matrimonium iustum*, or valid marriage, with all its legal consequences. As such a marriage could only take place between persons of equal status, the patricians and the plebeians had each for a long time a separate *conubium*, until B.C. 445, when the two orders were equalized in this respect. See MATRIMONIUM.

Convĕnae. A people in Aquitania, near the Pyrenees, and on both sides of the Garumna; a mixed race, which had served under Sertorius, and were settled in Aquitania by Pompey. Near their chief town, Lugdunum, were the warm baths called Aquae Convenarum (Bagnères).

Conventiōnes. See OBLIGATIONES.

Conventus. See PROVINCIA.

Convivium (σύνδειπνον). See CENA; SYMPOSIUM.

Cooks and Cookery. See CENA; CULINA; DIAETETICA.

Coöptatio. The election of a new member by the members of a corporation (*collegium*) to supply a vacant place. Among corporations which long filled their vacancies in this way may be mentioned the college of pontifices and augurs. The election was preceded by the nomination of a proper candidate by one of the members, and followed by his inauguration. See COLLEGIUM.

Copa. A short poem of thirty-eight lines in elegiac verse, ascribed to Vergil by Charisius. In it the writer invites his friend to spend the heated hours of the day in a rustic arbour, where wine, fruit, and pleasant company await him under the care of mine hostess (*copa*), who is described as dancing to the castanets (*crotala*). The style resembles Vergil's, though the tone is much more sprightly. See Ilgen, *Animadversationes in Virgilii Copam* (Halle, 1820); Birt, *Historia Hexam. Lat.* (Bonn, 1876); Egli, *Pseudo-Vergil. Gedichte* (Leipzig, 1886); and Leo's edition (Berlin, 1891).

Copae (Κῶπαι). An ancient town in Boeotia, on the north side of the lake Copaïs, which derived its name from this place.

Copāïs (Κωπαῒς λίμνη). A lake in Boeotia, formed chiefly by the river Cephissus, whose waters were connected with the Euboean Sea by several subterranean channels, called by the modern Greeks *katavóthra*, which were not, however, sufficient to carry off the waters, especially in the spring when the Copaic plain was flooded by the rains. In the time of Alexander the Great an enormous tunnel was cut through the rock for the discharge of the water. (See EMISSARIUM.) This proved effective until it fell into ruins, when the district again became unwholesome and marshy. In 1886, however, it was once more properly drained by a French company. The modern name of the lake is Topolias; its Homeric name, Cephisis (Λίμνη Κηφισίς, *Il.* v. 709). Its eels were much prized in antiquity.

Cophen (Κωφήν) or **Cophes** (Κωφής). The modern Cabul; the only grand tributary river which flows into the Indus from the west. Its own principal tributary is the Choaspes.

Cophĭnus (κόφινος). A large wicker basket, made of willow branches. From Aristophanes (*Av.* 1310) it would seem that it was used by the Greeks as a basket or cage for birds. The Romans used it for agricultural purposes; and Columella, in describing a method of procuring early cucumbers, says that they should be sown in well-manured soil, kept in a cophinus, so that in this case we have to consider it as a kind of portable hot-bed. Juvenal (iii. 14), when speaking of the Jews, uses the expression *cophinus et foenum* (a truss of hay), figuratively to designate their high degree of poverty. See CORBIS.

Copia. (Naples.)

Copia. The goddess of plenty among the Romans, represented as bearing a horn filled with fruits, etc. See CORNU COPIAE.

Copis (κοπίς). (1) A sword or scimetar, curved like a sickle and used by the Thessalians and in the East (Eurip. *Electra*, 837; Xen. *Cyrop.* ii. 1). (2) A knife used in cutting the flesh of animals in sacrifices or in the kitchen (Plut. *Lyc.* 2).

Copper. See AES.

Coptos (Κοπτός). A city of the Thebaïs or Upper Egypt, lying a little to the east of the Nile, some distance below Thebes. Under the Ptolemies it occupied an important commercial position. In 1894 excavations conducted on its site by Mr. Petrie brought to light many valuable remains of the earliest Egyptian art.

Coquus. A cook. See CENA; CULINA.

Cora. An ancient town in Latium, in the Volscian Mountains, southeast of Velitrae. It is now called Cori, and contains an ancient temple and massive polygonal walls. See p. 409.

Coracesium (Κορακήσιον). A very strong city of Cilicia Aspera, on the borders of Pamphylia, standing upon a steep rock, and possessing a good harbour. It was the only place in Cilicia that offered a successful resistance to Alexander the Great.

Coralli. A savage people of Sarmatia Europea, who inhabited the shores of the Euxine, near the mouth of the Danube (Ovid, *Pont.* iv. 2, 37).

Corassiae (Κορασσίαι). A group of small islands in the Icarian Sea, southwest of Icaria. They must not be confounded, as they often are, with the islands Corseae or Corsiae, off the Ionian coast, and opposite the promontory Ampelos, in Samos (Pliny, *H. N.* iv. 12. 23).

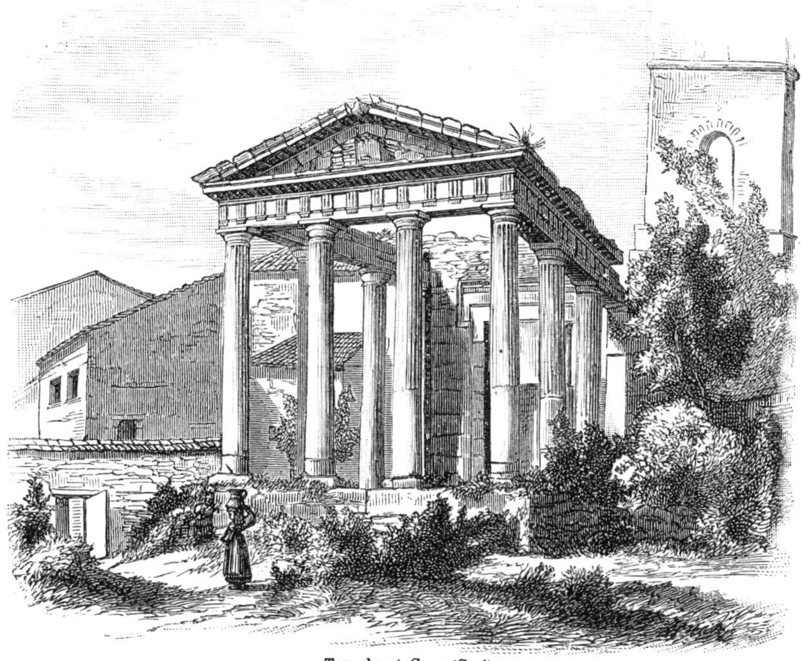

Temple at Cora (Cori).

Corax (Κόραξ). A Sicilian rhetorician, who flourished about B.C. 467, and wrote the earliest work on the art of rhetoric. It was entitled Τέχνη (Cic. *De Orat.* i. 20).

Corbis, Corbŭla, Corbicŭla. A basket of very peculiar form and common use among the Romans, both for agricultural and other purposes. It was made of osiers twisted together, and was of a conical or pyramidal shape (Varr. *L. L.* v. 139). A basket answering precisely to this description, both in form and material, is still to be seen in every-day use among the Campanian peasantry, which is called in the language of the country *la corbella*, a representation of which is introduced in the lower portion of the annexed illustration. The hook attached to it by a string

Corbis. (The upper specimen from a drawing at Herculaneum; the lower a basket used by Campanian peasantry.)

is for the purpose of suspending it to a branch of the tree into which the man climbs to pick his oranges, lemons, olives, or figs. The upper portion of the illustration (*Antichità di Ercolano*, tom. iii. tav. 29) represents a Roman farm, in which a farming man, in the shape of a dwarfish satyr, is seen with a pole (ἄσιλλα) across his shoulder, to each end of which is suspended a basket resembling in every respect the Campanian *corbella*. Like the *calathus*, which it somewhat resembles in shape, it is sometimes employed as a distinguishing emblem of Ceres.

Corbītae. Merchantmen of the larger class, so called because they hung out a *corbis* at the masthead for a sign (Festus; Nonius, s. v.). They were also termed *onerariae;* and hence Plautus, in order to designate the voracious appetites of some women, says *corbitam cibi comesse possunt* (*Cas.* iv. 1, 20). The modern *corvette* gets its name from the corbita.

Corbŭlo, Cn. Domitius. A general who distinguished himself by his campaigns against the Germans and the Parthians in the reigns of Claudius and Nero. To avoid the death destined for him by the orders of the jealous Nero, he committed suicide at Cenchreae, A.D. 67.

Corcȳra (Κέρκυρα, later Κόρκυρα). An island in the Ionian Sea, off the coast of Epirus, in which Homer is thought to have placed the fabled gardens of Alcinoüs. (See Scheria.) It is said to have been first known under the name of Drepané, perhaps from its similarity of shape to a scythe. To this name succeeded that of Scheria, always used by Homer, and by which it was possibly known in his time. From the *Odyssey* we learn that this island was then inhabited by Phaeacians, a people who, even at that early period, had acquired considerable skill in nautical affairs and possessed extensive commercial relations, since they traded with the Phœnicians, and also with Euboea and other countries (*Odyss.* vi. vii.).

Corcyra was in after-days the principal city of the island, and was situated precisely where the modern town of Corfu stands. Scylax speaks of three harbours, one of which is depicted as beautiful. In the Middle Ages, the citadel obtained the name of Κορυφώ, from its two conical hills or crests, which appellation was, in process of time, applied to the whole town and finally to the island itself. Hence the modern name of Corfu, which is but a corruption of the former. The following is a sketch of the history of this island. Its earlier periods are enveloped in the mist of uncertainty and conjecture. A colony of Colchians is said to have settled there about 1349 years before our era. In process of time, Corcyra, enriched and aggrandized by its maritime superiority, became one of the most powerful nations in Greece (Thuc. i. 1). The Corinthians, under Chersicrates, formed a settlement here in B.C. 753, and 415 years afterwards it was captured by Agathocles of Syracuse, who gave it to his daughter Lanessa upon her marriage with Pyrrhus of Epirus. It was occupied by the troops of the Illyrian queen Teuta, about fifty-eight years after its seizure by Agathocles, but was soon after taken from her by the Romans, under the consul Cn. Flavius; and, although it had the privileges of a free city, it remained under the Romans for many centuries. In the time of Strabo it was reduced to extreme misery. See Schmidt's treatise *Korkyräische Studien* (Leipzig, 1890). (2) An island in the Adriatic, on the coast of Illyricum, termed NIGRA, "Black" (in Greek Μέλαινα), to distinguish it from the more celebrated island of the same name. It is now Curzola. Apollonius accounts for the epithet just mentioned from the dark masses of wood with which it was crowned.

Cordax (κόρδαξ). An extremely indecent dance peculiar to the comic chorus. (See CHORUS; COMOEDIA.) The gestures, and, indeed, the costumes, of the choreutae were such that even the Athenians considered it justifiable only at the festival of Dionysus, when every one was allowed to be drunk in honour of the god; for if an Athenian citizen danced the cordax sober and unmasked, he was looked upon as the most shameless of men and forfeited altogether his character for respectability (Theophr. *Charact.* 6). Aristophanes himself, who did not much scruple at violating common decency, claims some merit for his omission of the cordax in the *Clouds*, and for the more modest attire of his chorus in that play. According to Athenaeus, the cordax was a sort of ὑπόρχημα, or imitative dance, in which the choreutae expressed the words of the song by comic gesticulations. Such a dance was the hyporcheme of the Spartan δεικελίκται—buffoons, whose peculiar mimic gestures seem to have formed the basis of the Dorian comedy, which prevailed in Megaris, and which probably was the parent stock, not only of the Attic, but also of the Sicilian and Italian comedy. The chief features of the cordax are probably preserved in the Neapolitan *tarantella*.

Cordŭba. The modern Cordova; one of the largest cities in Spain, and the capital of Baetica, on the right bank of the Baetis. It became a Roman colony B.C. 152, and was the birthplace of the two Senecas and of Lucan.

Corduēné. See GORDYENÉ.

Cordus, AULUS CREMUTIUS. A Roman writer of history who, under Tiberius, in A.D. 25, was accused of treason for having praised Brutus, the slayer of Caesar, and for styling Cassius "the last of the Romans" (Tac. *Ann.* iv. 34), though the real cause of his prosecution is to be found in some expressions that gave offence to Seianus, the emperor's powerful minister (Sen. *ad Marc.* xxii. 4). Besides his history he appears to have written a work on prodigies (*Admiranda*), and was favorably known as a pleader. See Held, *De Vita Scriptisque A. Cremutii Cordi* (Schweidnitz, 1841), and Rathlef, *De A. Cremutio Cordo* (Dorpat, 1860).

Koré (Κόρη). "The Maiden"; a name by which Persephoné is often called. See PERSEPHONÉ.

Coressus (Κόρεσσος). (1) A lofty mountain in Ionia, four miles from Ephesus, with a place of the same name at its foot. (2) A town in the island of Ceos.

Corfinium. The chief town of the Paeligni in Samnium, strongly fortified, and memorable as the place which the Italians in the Social War destined to be the new capital of Italy in place of Rome, on which account it was called Italica.

Coriarius (βυρσεύς, δερματομαλάκτης). A tanner. The tanners formed a guild at Rome distinct from the shoemakers. See Plut. *Numa*, 17.

Corinna (Κόριννα). A poetess of Thebes (fl. B.C. 490), or, according to others, of Tanagra, distinguished for her skill in lyric verse, and remarkable for her personal attractions. She was the rival of Pindar, while the latter was still a young man; and, according to Aelian, she gained the victory over him no less than five times. Pausanias, in his travels, saw at Tanagra a picture, in which Corinna was represented as binding her head with a fillet of victory, which she had gained in a contest with Pindar. He supposes that she was less indebted for this victory to the excellence of her poetry than to her Boeotian dialect, which was more familiar to the ears of the judges at the games, and also to her extraordinary beauty. Corinna afterwards assisted the young poet with her advice. It is related of her that she recommended him to ornament his poems with mythical narrations; but that when he had composed a hymn, in the first six verses of which (still extant) almost the whole of the Theban mythology was introduced, she smiled and said, "We should sow with the hand, not with the whole sack" (Pausan. ix. 22; Plut. *De Glor. Ath.*). She was surnamed "the Fly" (Μυῖα), as Erinna had been styled "the Bee." The poems of Corinna were all in the Boeotian or Aeolic dialect. Too little of her poetry, however, has been preserved to allow of our forming a safe judgment of her style of composition. The extant fragments refer mostly to mythological subjects, particularly to heroines of the Boeotian legends. These remains are given by Bergk in his *Poetae Lyrici Graeci* (4th ed. 1878).

Corinthiăcus Isthmus (Ἰσθμὸς Κορίνθου). An isthmus between the Saronicus Sinus and Corinthiacus Sinus, and uniting the Peloponnesus to the northern parts of Greece. Its breadth, in the narrowest part, was less than six miles (or not quite five miles). It has lately (1893) been cut by a canal. Ships were drawn, by means of machinery, from one sea to the other, near the town of Schoenus, over the narrowest part of the isthmus, which was called Δίολκος. This could only be accomplished, however, with the vessels usually employed in commerce, or with λέμβοι, which were light ships of war, chiefly used by the Illyrians and Macedonians. The tediousness and expense attending this process, and still more probably the difficulty of circumnavigating the Peloponnesus, led to frequent attempts, at various periods, for effecting a junction between the two seas; but all proved equally unsuccessful. Demetrius Poliorcetes abandoned the enterprise, because it was found that the two gulfs were not on the same level. We read of the attempt having been made before his time by Periander and Alexander, and, subsequently to Demetrius, by Iulius Caesar,. Caligula, Nero, and Herodes Atticus. Dio Cassius tells nearly the same story about digging through the isthmus as that which is related to travellers at this day. He says that blood issued from the ground; that groans and lamentations were heard, and terrible apparitions seen. In order to stimulate the perseverance of the people, Nero took a spade and dug himself (Dio Cass. lxiii. 16; and cf. Suet. *Ner.* 19). Lucian informs us, that Nero was said to have been deterred from proceeding, by a representation made to him, similar to that which Demetrius received respecting the unequal levels of the two seas (Plut. *De Cleom.*). The Isthmus of Corinth derived great celebrity from the games which were celebrated there every five years in honour of Palaemon or Melicerta, and subsequently of Poseidon (Pausan. i. 44). These continued in vogue when the other gymnastic exercises of Greece had fallen into neglect and disuse; and it was during their solemnization that the independence of Greece was proclaimed, after the victory of Cynoscephalae, by order of the Roman Senate and people (Polyb. xviii. 29; Liv. xxxiii. 32). After the destruction of Corinth, the superintendence of the Isthmian Games was committed to the Sicyonians by the Romans; on its restoration, however, by Iulius Caesar, the presidency of the games again reverted to the Corinthian settlers (Pausan. ii. 2). See ISTHMIA.

Corinthiăcus Sinus (Κορινθιακὸς κόλπος). The modern Gulf of Lepanto, an arm of the sea running in between the coast of Achaia and Sicyonia to the south, and that of Phocis, Locris, and Aetolia to the north. The gulf had the general appellation of Corinthian as far as the Isthmus, but it was divided into smaller bays, the names of which were sometimes poetically used for the entire gulf. Its different names were the Crissaean, Cirrhaean, Delphic, Calydonian, Rhian, and Halcyonian.

Corinthian Brass. See AES.

Corinthian Order of Architecture. See ARCHITECTURA; CAPITULUM; COLUMNA.

Corinthus (Κόρινθος). A famous city of Greece, situated on the isthmus of the same name. Commanding by its position the Ionian and the Aegean seas, and holding, as it were, the keys of the Peloponnesus, Corinth, from the pre-eminent advantages of its situation, was already the seat of opulence and the arts, while the rest of Greece was sunk in comparative obscurity and barbarism. Its origin is, of course, obscure; but we are assured that it already existed under the name of Ἐφύρη before the siege of Troy. According to the assertions of the Corinthians themselves, their city received its name from Corinthus, the son of Zeus; but Pausanias does not credit this popular tradition, and cites the poet Eumelus to show that the appellation was really derived from Corinthus, the son of Marathon (ii. 1). Homer certainly employs both names indiscriminately (*Il.* ii. 570; xiii. 663). Pausanias reports that the descendants of Sisyphus reigned at Corinth until the invasion of their territory by the Dorians and the Heraclidae, when Doridas and Hyanthidas, the last princes of this race, abdicated the crown in favour of Aletes, a descendant of Heracles, whose lineal successors remained in possession of the throne of Corinth during five generations, when the crown passed into the family of the Bacchiadae, so named from Bacchis, the son of Prumnis, who retained it for five other generations. After this the sovereign power was transferred to annual magistrates, still chosen, however, from the line of the Bacchiadae, with the title of πρυτάνεις.

The oligarchy so long established by this rich and powerful family was at length overthrown, about B.C. 629, by Cypselus, who banished many of the Corinthians, depriving others of their possessions, and putting others to death (Herod. v. 92). Among those who fled from his persecution was Demaratus, of the family of the Bacchiadae, who settled at Tarquinii in Etruria, and whose descendants became sovereigns of Rome. The reign of Cypselus was prosperous, and the system of colonization, which had previously succeeded so well in the settlements of Corcyra and Syracuse, was actively pursued by that prince, who added Ambracia, Anactorium, and Leucas to the maritime dependencies of the Corinthians.

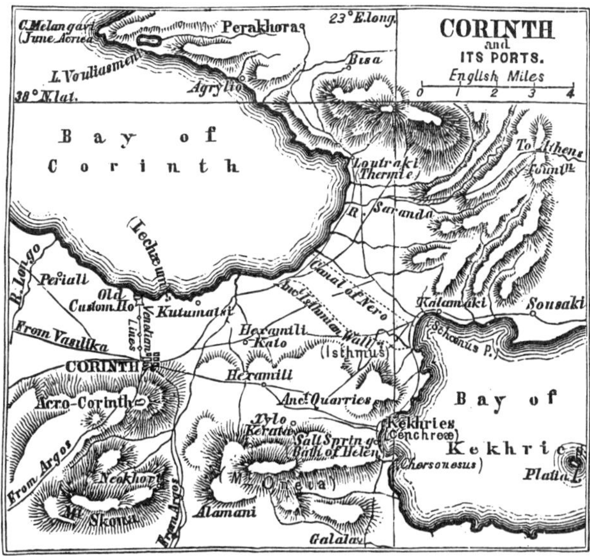

Corinth and its Ports.

Cypselus was succeeded by his son Periander. On the death of this latter (B.C. 585), after a reign of forty-four years, according to Aristotle, his nephew Psammetichus came to the throne, but lived only three years. At his decease Corinth regained its independence, when a moderate aristocracy was established, under which the Republic enjoyed a state of tranquillity and prosperity unequalled by any other city of Greece. We are told by Thucydides that the Corinthians were the first to build war-galleys or triremes; and the earliest naval engagement, according to the same historian, was fought by their fleet and that of the Corcyreans, who had been alienated from their mother-State by the cruelty and impolicy of Periander. The city is believed to have had at this time a population of 300,000 souls.

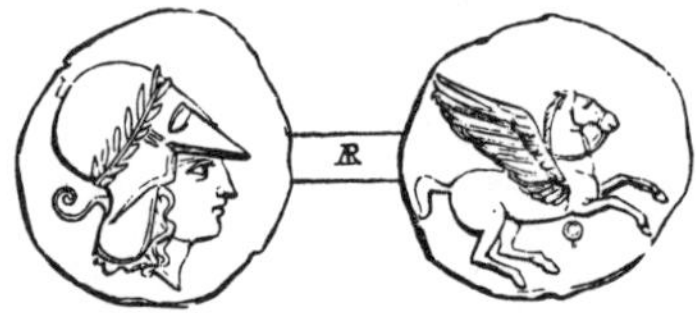

Coin of Corinth.

The arts of painting and sculpture, more especially that of casting in bronze, attained to the highest perfection at Corinth, and rendered this city the ornament of Greece, until it was stripped by the rapacity of a Roman general. Such was the beauty of its vases, that the tombs in which they had been deposited were ransacked by the Roman colonists whom Iulius Caesar had established there after the destruction of the city; and these, being transported to Rome, were purchased at enormous prices. See AES.

When the Achaean League (q.v.) became involved in a destructive war with the Romans, Corinth was the last hold of their tottering Republic; and had its citizens wisely submitted to the offers proposed by the victorious Metellus, it might have been preserved; but the deputation of that general having been treated with scorn and even insult, the city became exposed to all the vengeance of the Romans (Polyb. xl. 4. 1). L. Mummius, the consul, appeared before its walls with a numerous army, and after defeating the Achaeans in a general engagement, entered the town, now left without defence and deserted by the greater part of the inhabitants. It was then given up to plunder and finally set on fire; the walls also were razed to the ground, so that scarcely a vestige of this once great and noble city remained (B.C. 146). Polybius, who saw its destruction, affirmed that he had seen the finest paintings strewed on the ground, and the Roman soldiers using them as boards for dice or draughts. Pausanias reports (vii. 16) that all the men were put to the sword, the women and children sold, and the most valuable statues and paintings removed to Rome. (See MUMMIUS.) Strabo observes that the finest works of art which adorned that capital in his time had come from Corinth. He likewise states that Corinth remained for many years deserted and in ruins. Iulius Caesar, however, not long before his death, sent a numerous colony thither, by means of which Corinth was once more raised from its state of ruin, and renamed Colonia Iulia Corinthus. It was already a large and populous city and the capital of Achaia, when St. Paul preached the Gospel there for a year and six months (Acts, xviii. 11). It is also evident that when visited by Pausanias it was thickly adorned by public buildings and enriched with numerous works of art, and as late as the time of Hierocles we find it styled the metropolis of Greece. In a later age the Venetians received the place from a Greek emperor; Mohammed II. took it from them in 1458; the Venetians recovered it in 1699, and fortified the Acrocorinthus again; but the Turks took it anew in 1715, and retained it until driven from the Peloponnesus in 1822. In 1858, it was wholly destroyed by an earth-

Ancient Corinth. (Restoration.)

quake, since which time it has been rebuilt upon a site three miles to the northeast.

An important feature of the scenery around Corinth was the Acrocorinthus, a mention of which has been made in a previous article. (See ACROCORINTHUS.) On the summit of this hill was erected a temple of Aphroditê, to whom the whole of the Acrocorinthus, in fact, was sacred. In the times of Corinthian opulence and prosperity, it is said that the shrine of the goddess was attended by no less than one thousand female slaves, dedicated to her service as courtesans. These priestesses of Aphroditê contributed not a little to the wealth and luxury of the city, whence arose the well-known expression, οὐ παντὸς ἀνδρὸς εἰς Κόρινθον ἐστ' ὁ πλοῦς, or, as Horace expresses it (*Epist.* i. 17, 36), "*Non cuivis homini contingit adire Corinthum,*" in allusion to its expensive pleasures.

Corinth was famed for its three harbours—Lechaeum, on the Corinthian Gulf, and Cenchreae and Schoenus, on the Saronic. Near this last was the Δίολκος, where vessels were transported over the isthmus by machinery. The city was the birthplace of the painters Ardices, Cleophantus, and Cleanthes; of the statesmen Periander, Phidon, Philolaüs, and Timoleon; and of Arion, who invented the dithyramb.

See Wagner, *Rerum Corinthiacarum Specimen* (Darmstadt, 1824); Barth, *Corinthiorum Commercii et Mercaturae Historiae Particula* (Berlin, 1844); and E. Curtius, *Peloponnesos*, vol. ii. p. 514 foll.

Coriolānus, GAIUS MARCIUS. A distinguished Roman of patrician rank, whose story forms a brilliant legend in the early history of Rome. His name at first was Gaius Marcius, but having contributed, mainly by his great personal valour, to the capture of Corioli, and the defeat of a Volscian army, assembled for its aid, on the same day, he received for this gallant exploit the surname of Coriolanus. Not long after this, however, during a scarcity at Rome, he opposed the distribution of a supply of provisions, in part sent by Gelon of Sicily, and advised the patricians to make this a means of recovering the power which had been wrested from them by the commons. For this and other conduct of a similar nature, he was tried in the Comitia Tributa and condemned to perpetual banishment. To gratify his vindictive spirit, Coriolanus presented himself as a suppliant to Tullius Aufidius, the leading man among the Volsci; was well received by him and the whole nation; and, war being declared, was invested, along with Aufidius, with the command of the Volscian forces. By his military skill and renown Coriolanus at once defeated and appalled the Romans, till, having taken almost all their subject-cities, he advanced at the head of the Volscian army against Rome itself and encamped only five miles from it, at the Fossae Cluiliae. All was terror and confusion in the Roman capital. Embassy after embassy was sent to Coriolanus, to entreat him to spare his country, but he remained inexorable, and would grant peace only on condition that the Romans restored all the cities and lands which they had taken from the Volsci and gave to the latter the freedom of Rome, as had been done in the case of the Latins. After all other means of conciliation had failed, a number of Roman matrons, headed by the mother (Veturia) and the wife (Volumnia) of Coriolanus, proceeded to his tent, where their lofty remonstrances were more powerful than the arms of Rome had proved; and the son, after a brief struggle with his feelings, yielded to their request, exclaiming at the same time, "Oh, mother, thou hast saved Rome, but destroyed thy son!" The Volscian forces were then withdrawn, and Rome was thus saved, by feminine influence alone, from certain capture. On returning to the Volsci with his army, Coriolanus, according to one account, was summoned to trial for his conduct, and was slain in a tumult during the hearing of the cause, a faction having been excited against him by Tullius Aufidius, who was jealous of his renown (Dion. Hal. *Ant. Rom.* viii. 59). According to another statement, he lived to an advanced age among the Volscian people, often towards the close of his life exclaiming, "How miserable is the state of an old man in banishment!" (Plut. *Coriol.*; Liv. ii. 33 foll.). Niebuhr, who writes the name Gnaeus Marcius, on what he considers good authority, indulges in some acute speculations on the legend of Coriolanus. He thinks that poetical invention has here most thoroughly stifled the historical tradition. He regards the name Coriolanus as of the same kind merely with such appellations as Camerinus, Collatinus, Mugillanus, Vibulanus, etc., which, when taken from an independent town, were assumed by its πρόξενος, when from a dependent one, by its *patronus*. The capture of Corioli belongs merely, in his opinion, to an heroic poem. As for Coriolanus himself, he thinks that he merely attended the Volscian standard as leader of a band of Roman exiles. The story of Coriolanus has received a brilliant setting from the genius of Shakespeare.

Coriŏli. A town in Latium, capital of the Volsci, from the capture of which, in B.C. 492, Gaius Marcius obtained the surname of Coriolanus. See CORIOLANUS.

Corippus, FLAVIUS CRESCONIUS. An African scholar, who in the second half of the sixth century A.D. composed two historical epics—one in seven books (or eight), in celebration of the Libyan war of Iohannes Patricius (*Iohannis, sive de Bellis Libycis*); and the other on the exploits of Iustinus (A.D. 565–578), in four books (*De Laudibus Iustini*). The latter is in the worst manner of Byzantine flattery, but is written in a flowing style and in imitation of good models, such as Vergil and Claudian. His works have been edited by I. Bekker, with those of Merobaudes (q. v.), in the *Corp. Scriptorum Byzant.* (Bonn, 1836). The most recent text is that of Petschenig (Berlin, 1886). On the style of Corippus, see the monograph by Amann, *De Corippo Priorum Poetarum Lat. Imitatore* (Oldenb. 1885).

Cormăsa (Κόρμασα). An inland town of Pamphylia, or of Pisidia, taken by the consul Manlius.

Corn Laws. See FRUMENTARIAE LEGES.

Cornelia. (1) A daughter of Scipio Africanus Maior, and mother of Tiberius and Gaius Gracchus. Cornelia occupies a high rank for the purity and excellence of her private character, as well as for her masculine tone of mind. She was married to Sempronius Gracchus, and was left on his death with a family of twelve children, the care of whom devolved entirely upon herself. After the loss of her husband, her hand was sought by Ptolemy Philometor, king of Egypt, but the offer was declined. Plutarch speaks in high terms of her conduct during widowhood. Having lost all her children but three—one daughter, who was married to Scipio Africanus the younger, and two sons, Tiberius and Gaius—she devoted her whole time to the education of these. Valerius Maximus relates an anecdote of Cornelia, which has often been cited. A Campanian lady, who was at the time on a visit to her, having displayed to Cornelia some very beautiful ornaments which she possessed, desired the latter, in return, to exhibit her own. The Roman mother purposely detained her in conversation until her children returned from school, when, pointing to them, she exclaimed, "These are my ornaments!" (*Haec ornamenta mea sunt*, Val. Max. 4 init.). Plutarch informs us that some persons blamed Cornelia for the rash conduct of her sons in after-life, she having been accustomed to reproach them that she was still called the mother-in-law of Scipio, not the mother of the Gracchi (Plut. *T. Gracch.* 8). She bore the untimely death of her sons with great self-control, and a statue was afterwards erected in honour of her by the Roman people, bearing for an inscription the words "Cornelia, mother of the Gracchi" (Plut. *C. Gracch.* 4). (2) Daughter of Metellus Scipio, married to Pompey after the death of her first husband, Publius Crassus. She was remarkable for the variety of her accomplishments and the excellence of her private character. Plutarch makes her to have been versed, not only in the musical art, but in polite literature, in geometry, and in the precepts of philosophy (Plut. *Pomp.* 55). After the battle of Pharsalus, when Pompey joined her at Mitylené, Cornelia, with tears, ascribed all his misfortunes to her union with him, alluding at the same time to the unhappy end of her first husband, Crassus, in his expedition against the Parthians. (Cf. Lucan, viii. 88.) She was also a witness, from her galley, of the murder of her husband on the shores of Egypt (Plut. *Pomp.* 79). (3) A daughter of Cinna. She was Iulius Caesar's second wife, and mother of Iulia, the wife of Pompey. She died young. Plutarch says it had been the custom at Rome for the aged women to have funeral panegyrics, but not the young. Caesar first broke through this custom by pronouncing one upon Cornelia (Plut. *Caes.* 5).

Cornelia Gens. The most distinguished of all the Roman gentes. All its great families belonged to the patrician order. The names of its most distinguished patrician families are Cethegus, Cinna, Cossus, Dolabella, Lentulus, Scipio, and Sulla. The names of the plebeian families are Balbus and Gallus.

Cornelia Orestilla. See ORESTILLA.

Cornelius Nepos. See NEPOS.

Cornĭcen. A horn-blower in the Roman army who gave the signal for the attack, on an ox-horn mounted in silver. See CORNU.

Cornicŭlum. A town in Latium in the mountains north of Tibur, celebrated as the residence of the parents of Servius Tullius.

Cornificius. (1) QUINTUS, a contemporary of Cicero, distinguished for talents and literary acquirements, who attained to some of the highest offices in the State. Catullus and Ovid both speak of his poetic abilities, and he appears to have been the friend of both. Cornificius distinguished himself as propraetor in the Illyrian War, and also as governor of Syria and afterwards of Africa. In this latter province he espoused the cause of the Senate after Caesar's death, and received and gave protection to those who had been proscribed by the Second Triumvirate. He lost his life, however, while contending in that country against Sextius, who had been sent against him by Octavianus. Some scholars make this Cornificius to have been the author of the rhetorical treatise to Herennius commonly ascribed to Cicero. (See Quint. iii. 1. 21.) He is said also to have been an enemy of Vergil's, but this supposition violates chronology, since the poet only became eminent subsequent to the date when Cornificius died. (2) LUCIUS, a partisan of Octavianus, by whom he was appointed to accuse Brutus, before the public tribunal at Rome, of the assassination of Caesar (Plut. *Brut.* 27). He afterwards distinguished himself, as one of Octavianus's lieutenants, by a masterly retreat in Sicily during the war with Sextus Pompeius. He was consul, B.C. 35.

Cornĭger. "Horn-bearing." A surname of Bacchus (Ovid, *Fast.* iii. 481), and of Iupiter Ammon, who was worshipped in the form of a ram.

Cornū. A wind instrument, anciently made of horn, but afterwards of brass (Varr. *L. L.* v. 117). According to Athenaeus, it was an invention of the Etruscans. Like the *tuba*, it differed from the *tibia* in being a larger and more powerful instrument, and from the *tuba* itself in being curved nearly in the shape of a C, with a crosspiece to steady the instrument for the convenience of the performer. In Greek it is called στρογγύλη σάλπιγξ. It had no stopples or plugs to adjust the scale to any particular mode; the entire series of notes was produced without keys or holes, by the modification of the breath and of the lips at the mouthpiece. Probably, from the description given of it in the poets, it was, like our own horn, an octave lower than the trumpet. The *classicum*, which originally meant a signal, rather than the musical instrument which gave the signal, was usually sounded with the cornu.

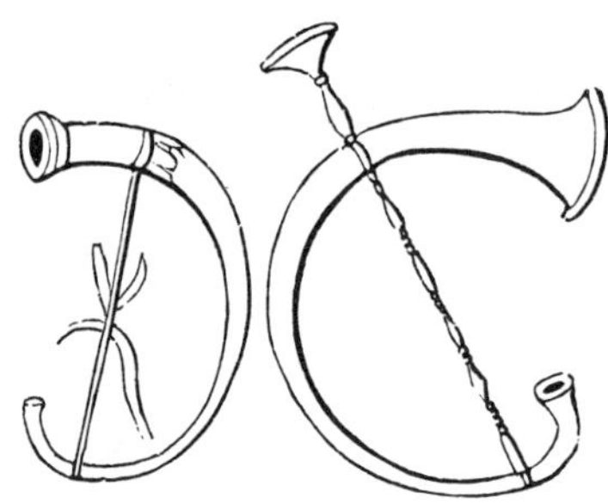

Cornua. (Bartholini.)

Cornu also signifies the end of the sailyards (see NAVIS), a part of the helmet in which the crest was fixed (see GALEA), the end of the stick on which books were rolled (see LIBER), a part of a bow, a part of the lyre, and the wing of an army. See EXERCITUS.

Cornu Copiae, or as one word, **Cornucopiae**, later **Cornucopia** (Ammian. Marcell. xxii. 9, § 1; xxv. 2, § 3). The horn of fruitfulness and abundance, used as the symbol of plenty. In mythology there are two different tales explaining the origin of this horn. One traces it to the horn of the goat Amalthea, which suckled Zeus. The horn was broken off and filled with fruits and flowers, and was afterwards placed by Zeus, together with the goat, among the stars. (See AMALTHEA.) Another legend relates that it was the horn of the river-god Acheloüs (q. v.), which was wrenched off by Heracles, and which became forthwith a horn of plenty. Later mythologists combined the two tales, and tried to explain how the horn of Amalthea became the horn of Acheloüs (Apollod. ii. 7, § 5). The origin of this symbol may perhaps be traced in the use of the horns of oxen or goats as drinking-cups; hence the ῥυτόν, or drinking-horn, which is frequently confounded with the horn of abundance (Athen. xi. 468 d, 497 c).

The cornucopia constantly appears in works of art, especially of the Roman period, as the symbol of abundance associated with various deities, as Fortuna, Ceres, etc. See COPIA.

Cornus (Κόρνος). A town in the western part of Sardinia (Livy, xxiii. 40, 41).

Cornūtus, L. ANNAEUS. A Greek philosopher, born at Leptis in Africa, who lived and taught at Rome during the reign of Nero. The appellation L. Annaeus appears to indicate a client or freedman of the Seneca family. His tenets were those of the Stoic sect, and his name was not without distinction in that school of philosophy. He excelled in criticism and poetry; but his principal studies were of a philosophical character. His merit as a teacher of the Stoic doctrine sufficiently appears from his having been the preceptor of the satirist Persius. Persius, dying before his master, left him his library, with a considerable sum of money; but Cornutus accepted only the books, and gave the money to the sisters of his pupil. The poet Lucan was also one of his students. Under Nero, Cornutus was driven into exile (A.D. 68) for his freedom of speech. The emperor having written several books in verse on the affairs of Rome, and his flatterers advising him to continue the poem, the honest Stoic had the courage to remark that he doubted whether so large a work would be read; and when it was urged that Chrysippus had written as much, he replied, "His writings were useful to mankind." After so unpardonable an offence against imperial vanity, the only wonder is that Cornutus escaped with his life. He composed some tragedies, and a large number of other works, the only one of which that has come down to us is the "Theory concerning the Nature of the Gods" (Θεωρία περὶ τῆς τῶν Θεῶν Φύσεως); or, as it is entitled in one of the MSS., "Concerning Allegories" (Περὶ Ἀλληγορίων). Cornutus, in fact, in this production seeks to explain the Greek mythology on allegorical and physical principles. It has been edited by Lang (Leipzig, 1881). See Jahn's prolegomena to his Persius, p. viii.

Coroebus (Κόροιβος). (1) A Phrygian, the son of Mygdon. He loved Cassandra, and for that reason fought on the side of the Trojans. (2) An Elean, who gained the victory in the stadium at the Olympic Games, B.C. 776, from which time the Olympiads begin to be reckoned. See CALENDARIUM.

Corolla. See CORONA.

Corollarium. A present consisting of a garland of gold or silver leaves, given to successful actors and performers in addition to other *honoraria*. It thus became a term for any free gift whatever.

Corōna (στέφανος). A crown; that is, a circular ornament of metal, leaves, or flowers, worn by the ancients round the head or neck, and used as a festive as well as funeral decoration, and as a reward of talent, military or naval prowess, and civic worth. It includes the synonyms, for which it is often used absolutely, στεφάνη, στέφος, στεφάνωμα, *corolla*, *sertum*, "a garland or wreath."

The use of crowns on public and private occasions was so general in antiquity that there was a special literature on the subject, of which we have remains in Theophrastus (*Hist. Pl.* vi. 6), Athenaeus (lib. xv.), Pliny (*H. N.* xxi. §§ 1–70, xxii. §§ 4–13), and Pollux (vi. 106–107). At Rome Claudius Saturninus wrote a book *De Coronis* (Tertull. *De Cor. Mil.* 7, 10, 12).

Crowns originally consisted of wool or the foliage of trees, especially myrtle-twigs or ivy, with which flowers of various kinds were subsequently interwoven. The makers and sellers of these garlands or crowns formed a distinct trade, and were called in Greece στεφανηπλόκοι or στεφανοποιοί, and in Rome *coronarii* (Plin. xxi. §§ 54, 177).

The flowers used in making crowns were called in Greek στεφανώματα, in Latin *coronamenta*.

The foliage and flowers were sometimes fastened together by the inner bark of the linden-tree, such garlands being known as *coronae sutiles*, also *nexae* and *sertae*. At Athens, the flower-market was called αἱ μυρρίναι, because myrtle (μύρτος) was the material most commonly used in making them. Many of the flower-girls were celebrated in antiquity, especially Glycera the mistress of Pausias (Plin. *H. N.* xxi. § 4; xxxv. § 125).

At Rome, the temple of the Lares, at the head of the Via Sacra, was most frequented by the venders of garlands. The crowns among the Romans were often made of the leaves of plants, especially ivy, myrtle, and parsley. At Athens, the violet was very popular, but both the Greeks and Romans preferred the rose to any other flower, calling it "the king of flowers" and "the rose of the loves." (See Achill. Tat. ii. 1; Anacr. 5.) They were especially used for convivial crowns; and garlands of them were in request at Rome even in the winter, so that they were grown under glass (Mart. iv. 22, 5; xiii. 127), and were also imported from Egypt (Mart. vi. 80). As luxury increased, the leaves of the *nardus* or spikenard were brought from India for crowns (Mart. xiii. 51; Plin. *H. N.* xxi. § 11). Garlands were also made of dried flowers, especially of amaranth, which, when moistened, had the appearance of fresh flowers, so that garlands of it were called *coronae hibernae*. The same name was given to crowns of artificial flowers (Plin. xxi. § 5). Sometimes they were made of a thin layer of metal covered with gold or silver, and called *corollae* or *corollaria inaurata* or *inargentata*.

The *corona Etrusca* was made of pure gold in the form of leaves, sometimes set with gems, and terminating in ribbons (*lemnisci*) of the same metal. It was held by a slave over the head of a general when he entered Rome in triumph (Plin. xxxiii. § 11).

Crowns adorned with such pendent ribbons were called *coronae lemniscatae* (Serv. *ad* Verg. *Aen.* v. 269, vi. 772). The lemnisci (λημνίσκοι) were first made of wool, adorned with ribbons (from λῆνος, "wool," Fest. p. 155, M.), afterwards of linden-bast, and subsequently of gold. Crowns so adorned were the highest rewards of victors, whence Cicero speaks of *palma lemniscata*, where *palma* means a victory or the highest reward (*Rosc. Am.* 35, 100).

Coronae longae resembled what we call festoons, and were employed to decorate the doors of houses, temples, amphitheatres, etc. (Ovid, *Fast.* iv. 738).

The *corona pactilis*, probably the same as the *corona plectilis* of Plautus (*Bacch.* i. 1, 37), *corona torta* (Propert. iii. 20, 18), *plexa* (Lucret. v. 1399), and as the στέφανοι πλεκτοί and κυλιστὸς στέφανος of the Greeks, was made of flowers, shrubs, grass, ivy, wool, or any flexible material twined or twisted together, and therefore opposed to the *corona sutilis* described above.

Corona Radiata.

Corona radiata was one assigned to the gods or to deified heroes, and hence was assumed by the later emperors in token of their divinity. They may be seen on many of the imperial coins.

Coronae tonsae were made of leaves only, closely cut, as for instance of the olive (Verg. *Aen.* v. 556).

Corona Triumphalis. (Medallion of Ventidius.)

Crowns were also among the Romans the highest distinction awarded for service in war. The most coveted were the *corona triumphalis* or laurel crown of a general in triumph; and the *corona obsidionalis*, presented to a general by the army which he had saved from a siege, or from a shameful capitulation. This was woven of grass growing on the spot, and called *corona graminea*. The *corona myrtea*, or *ovalis*, was the crown of bay worn by the general who celebrated the lesser triumph (*ovatio*).

Corona Obsidionalis.

The *corona civica* was of oak leaves, and was awarded for saving a citizen's life in battle. This secured for its possessor certain privileges, as freedom from taxes for himself, his father, and paternal grandfather. The golden ***corona muralis***, with embattled ornaments, was given for the storming of a wall; the *corona castrensis* or *vallaris*, also of gold, and ornamented in imitation of palisades, to the soldier who first climbed the wall of the enemy's camp; the *corona navalis*, with ornaments representing the beak of a ship, to the man who first boarded a ship. Under the Empire, the garland of bay was reserved exclusively for the emperor, and thus came to be regarded as a crown.

Corona Civica.

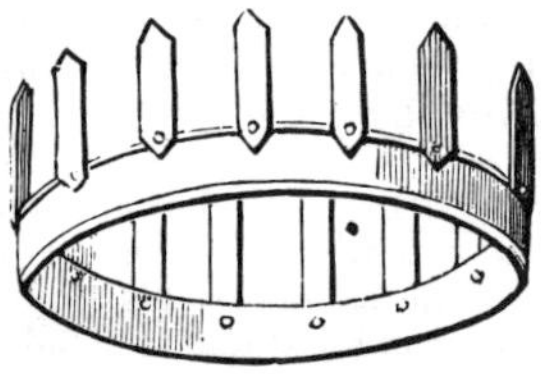

Corona Castrensis.

The rayed crown, the ***insigne*** of the deified emperors, was not worn by the emperors of the first and second century A.D. Golden crowns were originally the free offerings of provincials and allies to victorious generals for the celebration of their triumphs. But from this custom there arose, even in republican times, the habit of compelling a contribution of money (*aurum coronarium*) to the governor of the province. During the imperial age this contribution was on exceptional occasions offered as a present to the emperors, but it was often also made compulsory.

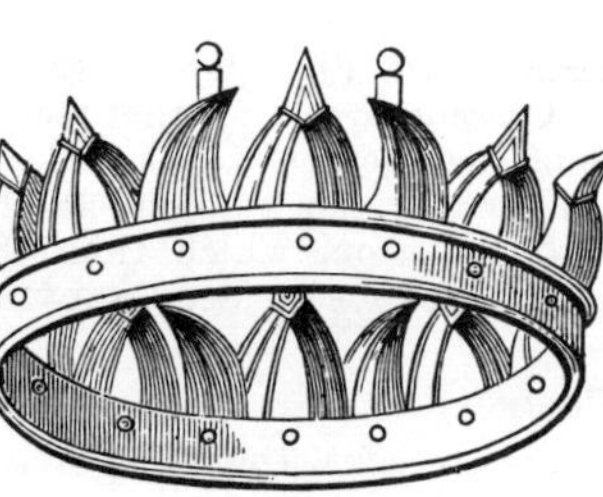

Corona Muralis.

Among the Greeks, a crown (στέφανος) was often an emblem of office. At Athens, for instance, a crown of bay was worn by the archons in office, the senators (βουλευταί), and the orators while speaking. It was also the emblem of victory at the games, and a token of distinction for citizens of merit. (See THEATRUM.) Such crowns of honour were made originally of olive branches, but later of gold. The honour of a crown could be conferred by the people or the Senate, or by corporations

Corona Navalis.

and foreign States. The latter would often present a crown to the whole commonwealth. If the people or Senate presented the crown, the presentation took place in the great assembly or in the Senate-house, but not in the theatre except by special decree. See Garcke, *De Horatii Corollis* (Altenburg, 1860); and Daremberg and Saglio, *Dictionnaire des Antiquités*, s. v. "Corona"; and on funeral crowns the article FUNUS.

Coronāti Quattuor. The name given to four Christian martyrs (Carpophorus, Severus, Severianus, Victorinus), killed, according to the tradition, by having crowns with sharp nails pressed down into their heads (A.D. 304). The Catholic Church commemorates their martyrdom on November 8. See Erbes, in the *Zeitschrift für Kirchengeschichte*, v. 466 (1882).

Corōné (Κορώνη). A town in Messenia on the west side of the Messenian Gulf, founded B.C. 371 by the Messenians, after their return to their native country, with the assistance of the Thebans.

Coronēa (Κορώνεια). A town in Boeotia, southwest of Lake Copaïs, and a member of the Boeotian League. (See BOEOTARCHES; BOEOTIA.) Here in B.C. 447, the Boeotians defeated the Athenians; and in B.C. 394, the allied Greeks were defeated by Agesilaüs (q. v.).

Corōnis (Κορωνίς). (1) Daughter of Phlegyas, and mother by Apollo of Aesculapius, who is hence called Coronides. See AESCULAPIUS. (2) Daughter of Phoroneus, king of Phocis, metamorphosed by Athené into a crow when pursued by Poseidon.

Corōnis (κορωνίς). The cornice of an entablature. The pure Latin word is *corona* or *coronix* (Vitruv. v. 2, 3).

Corpus Inscriptiōnum. See EPIGRAPHY.

Corpus Iuris Civīlis. The name given since the sixteenth century to the great collection of authorities on Roman law, made by the lawyer Tribonianus, of Sidé in Pamphylia, at the instance of the Eastern emperor Justinian (A.D. 527–565). To this collection we owe the preservation of the treasures of the ancient jurisprudence, which must certainly otherwise have been lost. The *Corpus Iuris* consists of four parts:

(1) CODEX IUSTINIANĒUS, called *repetitae praelectionis*, as being the revised edition of a code now lost, but which had appeared in 529. This was published in 534, and contains in twelve books the imperial law (*ius principale*), or the *constitutiones* of the emperors since Hadrian.

(2) PANDECTAE, or DIGESTA. The law of the jurists (*ius vetus*). These, published A.D. 533, are extracts from the works of thirty-nine ancient jurists, arranged in fifty books, according to subjects.

(3) INSTITUTIŌNES. A handbook of jurisprudence, founded mostly upon Gaius, and published in the same year.

(4) NOVELLAE (*constitutiones*), or supplementary ordinances of Justinian, mostly in Greek. These are preserved only in private collections of various compass, one of which, the *Authenticum* or *Liber Authenticorum*, was recognized as the authorized text, and gives the Greek rescripts in a Latin version. The best modern edition of the *Corpus Iuris Civilis* is that by Mommsen, Schöll, and Krüger (Berlin, 4th ed. 1886–88).

Correus. One indicted jointly with another person. See OBLIGATIONES; REUS.

Corrigia. (1) A shoe-string, sometimes made of dog-skin (Plin. *H. N.* xxx. § 35). (2) A whip-lash or rein (Edict. Dioclet. p. 26).

Corsi (Κύρνιοι). (1) The inhabitants of Corsica. (2) The inhabitants of part of northern Sardinia, who came originally from Corsica.

Corsĭca. An island of the Mediterranean, called by the Greeks Κύρνος. Its inhabitants were styled by the same people Κύρνιοι; by the Romans, Corsi. In later times the island took also the name of Corsis (ἡ Κορσίς). The inhabitants were a rude race of mountaineers, indebted for their subsistence more to the produce of their flocks than to the cultivation of the soil. Seneca, who was banished to this quarter in the reign of Claudius, draws a very unfavourable picture of the island and its inhabitants; describing the former as rocky, unproductive, and unhealthy, and the latter as the worst of barbarians (Sen. *De Consol. ad Helv.* c. 6, 8). His lines upon the character of the Corsicans are still remembered by them with resentment, and are as follows:

> Prima est ulcisci lex, altera vivere raptu,
> Tertia mentiri, quarta negare deos.

The Corsi appear to have derived their origin from Ligurian and Iberian (called by Seneca Spanish) tribes. Eustathius says that a Ligurian woman, named Corsa, having pursued in a small boat a bull which had taken to the water, accidentally discovered the island, which her countrymen named after her. The Romans took the island from Carthage in B.C. 231, and subsequently two colonies were sent to it—one by Marius, which founded Mariana, and another by Sulla, which settled on the site of Aleria. Mantinorum Oppidum, in the same island, is now Bastia; and Urcinium, Ajaccio. See Jacobi, *Histoire Générale de la Corse* (Paris, 1835); and Gregorovius, *Corsica* (Stuttgart, 1854; Eng. trans. Philadelphia, 1855).

Corslet. See ARMA; LORICA; THORAX.

Corsōté (Κορσωτή). A city of Mesopotamia on the Euphrates, which Xenophon found already deserted.

Corssen, WILHELM PAUL, a great classical philologist, was born at Bremen January 20th, 1820. From 1839 to 1843 he studied philology at Berlin, where he published (1844) *Origines Poesis Romanae.* He then taught for two years in Stettin, and in 1846 became an adjunct, and, later, full professor at Pforta. In 1866, he resigned the post and lived at Lichterfelde, near Berlin, devoting himself exclusively to his studies until his death in 1875. His chief works are: *Ueber Aussprache, Vokalismus, und Betonung der lateinischen Sprache*, 2 vols. (Leipzig, 1858–59; 2d ed. 1868–70); *Kritische Beiträge zur lateinischen Formenlehre* (Leipzig, 1863); *Kritische Nachträge zur lateinischen Formenlehre* (Leipzig, 1866); *Beiträge zur italischen Sprachkunde* (Leipzig, 1876); besides a number of treatises on old Italian dialects in Kuhn's *Zeitschrift für vergleichende Sprachforschung;* the treatise *De Volscorum Lingua* (Leipzig, 1858); and *Ueber die Sprache der Etrusker* (2 vols. Leipzig, 1874–75). Among the results of his stay at Pforta was *Alterthümer und Kunstdenkmäler des Cistercienser Klosters St. Marien und der Landesschule Pforta* (Halle, 1868).

Dr. Corssen's great work is his *Aussprache*, than which no more memorable publication in the field of Latin scholarship has ever appeared. Its massing of facts is a monument of scholarly research; while the acuteness of criticism, and the mastery of detail shown in the use to which the facts are put, rank Corssen with the greatest scholars of all time. Not equally successful was his attempt to solve the problems of Etruscan ethnology and language. So great was Dr. Corssen's authority on the dialects of Italy that when the first volume of his *Sprache der Etrusker* appeared, it was enthusiastically accepted as definitely clearing up the mystery that even Müller had failed to illuminate; and the author was hailed as "the Oedipus of the Etruscan Sphinx." But the sober second judgment of scholars did not confirm this verdict, and the second volume (which appeared soon after Corssen's death) was read in a far different spirit. In fact, though the work is laboriously learned, and bears everywhere the marks of immense research, its theories fail to commend themselves, and the volumes are now only historically interesting. See ETRURIA.

Cortex (φελλός). A cork used by fishermen to float their nets (Aesch. *Choëph.* 506).

Cortīna. (1) A caldron used for boiling. (2) The lid or covering over the Delphic tripod (see ORACULUM; TRIPUS), on which the priestess sat in giving responses (Verg. *Aen.* vi. 347). (3) An altar in the form of a tripod.

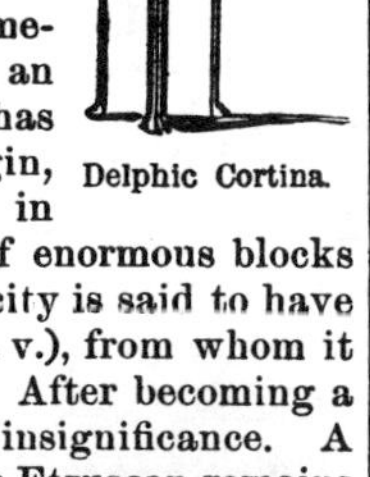
Delphic Cortina.

Cortōna. One of the twelve cities of Etruria, and very ancient. It lies northwest of Lake Trasimenus, over which it looks from an elevation of some 2000 feet. It has mighty walls of Pelasgic origin, among the most remarkable in Italy, one fragment composed of enormous blocks being 120 feet in length. The city is said to have been founded by the Umbri (q. v.), from whom it was wrested by the Etruscans. After becoming a Roman possession it sank into insignificance. A vast number of most interesting Etruscan remains have been found here, and are carefully preserved in the local museum. Roman tradition made Corythus, the father of Dardanus, the founder of the town, and Corythus is sometimes given as its early name.

Coruncanius, TIBERIUS. Consul B.C. 280, with P. Valerius Laevinus, and the first plebeian who was created Pontifex Maximus, as well as the first person at Rome who gave regular instruction in law. See Schrader, in the *Civilist. Magazin*, v. 187.

Corvīnus. (1) A name given to M. Valerius, from his having been assisted by a raven (*corvus*) while engaged in combat with a Gaul. (See VALERIUS.) (2) MESSĀLA, a distinguished Roman in the Augustan Age. See MESSALA.

Corvus (κόραξ). A sort of crane, used by Gaius Duilius (q. v.) against the Carthaginian fleet in the battle fought off Mylae in Sicily (B.C. 260). The Romans, we are told, being unused to the sea, saw that their only chance of victory was by bringing a sea-fight to resemble one on land. For this purpose they invented a machine, of which Polybius (i. 22) has left a minute description. In the fore part of the ship a round pole was fixed perpendicularly, twenty-four feet in height and about nine inches in diameter; at the top of this was a pivot, upon which a ladder was set, thirty-six feet in length and four in breadth. The ladder was guarded by crossbeams, fastened to the upright pole by a ring of wood, which turned with the pivot above. Along the ladder a rope was passed, one end of which took hold of the *corvus* by means of a ring. The *corvus* itself was a strong piece of iron, with a spike at the end, which was raised or lowered by drawing in or letting out the rope. When an enemy's ship drew near, the machine was turned outward, by means of the pivot, in the direction of the assailant. Another part of the machine, which Polybius has not clearly described, is a breastwork, let down (as it would seem) from the ladder, and serving as a bridge on which to board the enemy's vessel. By means of these cranes, the Carthaginian ships were either broken or closely locked with the Roman, and Duilius gained a complete victory. See Polyb. i. 22.

The word *corvus* is also applied to various kinds of grappling-hooks, such as the *corvus demolitor*, mentioned by Vitruvius for pulling down walls, or the terrible engine spoken of by Tacitus, which, being fixed on the walls of a fortified place, and suddenly let down, carried off one of the besieging party, and then, by a turn of the machine, put him down within the walls. The word is used by Celsus for a scalpel. It is hardly necessary to remark that all these meanings have their origin in the supposed resemblance of the various instruments to the beak of a raven.

Corybantes (Κορύβαντες). The ministers or priests of Rhea (q. v.), or Cybelé, the great mother of the gods, who was worshipped in Phrygia. In their solemn festivals they displayed the most extravagant fury in their dances in armour, as well as in the accompanying music of flutes, cymbals, and drums. Hence κορυβαντισμός was the name given to an imaginary disease, in which persons felt as if some great noise were rattling in their ears. The Corybantes are often identified with the Idaean Dactyli, and are thus said to have been

Corybantes and Cybelé, with Infant Zeus.

the nurses of Zeus when he was suckled by the goat Amalthea in Crete. See CURETES; DACTYLI; GALLI; ZEUS.

Corybantĭca (Κορυβαντικά). A festival and mysteries celebrated at Cnossus in Crete, in commemoration of one Corybas, who, in common with the Curetes (q. v.), brought up Zeus, and concealed him from his father Cronus (q.v.) in that island. Other accounts say that the Corybantes, nine in number, independent of the Curetes, saved and educated Zeus. A third legend states that Corybas was the father of the Cretan Apollo who disputed the sovereignty of the island with Zeus. But to which of these three traditions the festival of the Corybantica owed its origin is uncertain, although the first, which was current in Crete itself, seems to be best entitled to the honour. All that we know of the Corybantica is, that the person to be initiated was seated on a throne, and that those who initiated him formed a circle and danced around him. This part of the solemnity was called θρόνωσις or θρονισμός.

Corўbas (Κορύβας). The son of Iasion and Cybelé, who introduced the rites of the mother of the gods into Phrygia from the island of Samothrace. See CORYBANTICA; RHEA.

Corycia (Κωρυκία). A nymph, who became by Apollo the mother of Lycorus, or Lycoreus, and from whom the Corycian cave on Mount Parnassus was believed to have derived its name. (See Pausan. x. 6, 5.) The Muses are sometimes called by the poets Corycides Nymphae.

Corycĭdes. A name applied to the nymphs who were supposed to inhabit the Corycian cave on Mount Parnassus. They were the daughters of the river-god Plistus (Ovid, *Met.* i. 320; Apoll. Rh. ii. 711). The same name is also given to the Muses. See CORYCIA.

Corўcus (Κώρυκος). (1) A promontory of Ionia, southeast of the southern extremity of Chios. The high and rugged coast in this quarter harboured at one time a wild and daring population, greatly addicted to piracy; and who, by disguising themselves and frequenting the harbours in their vicinity, obtained private information of the course and freight of any merchant vessel, and concerted measures for the purpose of intercepting it. The secrecy with which their intelligence was procured gave rise to the proverb, Τοῦ δ' ἄρ' ὁ Κωρυκαῖος ἠκροάζετο, "This, then, the Corycean overheard," a saying that was used in cases where any carefully guarded secret had been discovered. The ancient appellation is still preserved in that of Kourko, which belongs to a bold headland forming the extreme point of the Erythrean peninsula towards Samos Pliny (*H.N.* v. § 31) calls it Coryceum Promontorium. (2) A small town of Cilicia Trachea, near the confines of Cilicia Campestris, on the sea-coast, and to the east of Seleucia Trachea. It appears to have been a fortress of great strength, and a mole of vast unhewn rocks is carried across the bay for about a hundred yards. It served at one time as the harbour of Seleucia, and was then a place of considerable importance. About twenty stadia inland was the Corycian cave (Κωρύκιον ἄντρον), celebrated in mythology as the fabled abode of the giant Typhoeus. In fact, many writers, as Strabo reports, placed Arima or Arimi, the scene of Typhoeus's torments, alluded to by Homer, in Cilicia, while others sought it in Lydia, and others in Campania. (3) A naval station on the coast of Lycia, about thirty stadia to the north of Olympus.

Corўcus (κώρυκος). A large leathern sack, filled with flour, fig-grains, or sand, hung up in the gymnasium, for the athletes to swing to and fro by striking it, whence the exercise is called κωρυκομαχία or κωρυκοβολία (Hesych. s. v.). The game is alluded to by Plautus (*Rud.* iii. 4, 16). From this game came the proverbial expression, πρὸς κώρυκον γυμνάζεσθαι (Diog. vii. 54), of labour in vain.

Corycus. (From the Cista Ficoroniana.)

Corymbus (κόρυμβος). A particular mode of wearing the hair among the Greek women, which is explained in the article COMA. The following illustration, taken from Millingen, represents a woman whose hair is dressed in this manner. The name literally means a bunch of ivy-berries, and was first applied to a form of garland.

Corymbus. (Millingen, *Peintures Antiques*, pl. 40.)

Coryphasium (Κορυφάσιον). A promontory in Messenia, enclosing the harbour of Pylos on the north, with a town of the same name upon it.

Corўthus (Κόρυθος). An Italian hero, son of Iupiter, husband of Electra, and father of Dardanus, is said to have founded Corythus, afterwards called Cortona (q. v.).

Corўtus (κωρυτός, γωρυτός). A bow-case. It was worn suspended by a belt over the right shoulder, and frequently held the arrows as well as the bow (Sil. Ital. xv. 773). On this account, it is often confounded with the *pharetra* or quiver.

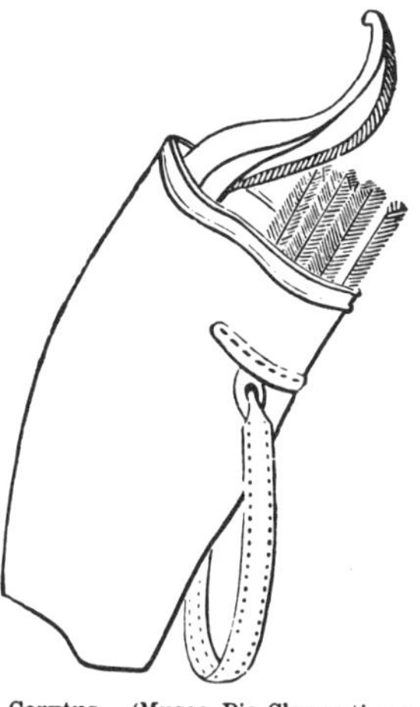

Corytus. (Museo Pio-Clementino.)

It is generally carried by the armed Persians who are represented on the Persepolitan bas-reliefs; and in this, as in many other respects, we observe the agreement between them and the European nations situated to the north of the Euxine Sea.

Cos (Κῶς). An island of the Aegean, one of the Sporades, west of the promontory of Doris. Its more ancient names were Cea, Staphylus, Nymphaea, and Meropis, of which the last was the most common. The colonizing of this island must have taken place at a very early date, since Homer makes mention of it as a populous settlement (*Il.* ii. 184). The inhabitants were of Dorian origin, and closely connected with the Doric colonies on the mainland. Its chief city was Cos, anciently called Astypalaea. Strabo remarks that the city of Cos was not large, but very populous, and seen to great advantage by those who came thither by sea. Without the walls was a celebrated temple of Aesculapius, enriched with many admirable works of art, and among others, two famous paintings of Apelles, the Antigonus and Aphrodité Anadyomené. The latter painting was so much admired that Augustus removed it to Rome and consecrated it to Iulius Caesar; and in consideration of the loss thus inflicted on the Coans, he is said to have remitted a tribute of one hundred talents which had been laid on them. Besides the great painter just mentioned, Cos could boast of ranking among her sons the first physician of antiquity, Hippocrates. The soil of the island was very productive, especially in wine, which vied with those of Chios and Lesbos. It was also celebrated for its purple dye, and for its manufacture of a species of transparent silk stuff. See COA VESTIS.

Coins of Cos.

Cos (ἀκόνη). A whetstone or grindstone, the latter being shown in the accompanying illustration from an engraved gem, representing Cupid sharpening his arrows.

Cos.

Cosa, Cossa, or **Cosae.** (1) Now Ansedonia; an ancient city of Etruria near the sea, with a good harbour, called Herculis Portus, and after the fall of Falerii one of the twelve Etruscan cities. The ancient towers and polygonal walls, 1600 yards in circumference, are still admirably preserved. (2) A town in Lucania near Thurii.

Cosmas (Κοσμᾶς). An Egyptian priest, often called Indopleustes (Ἰνδοπλευστής) from his voyages, who lived about A.D. 535. In his youth he was engaged in foreign trade and visited many countries, of which he wrote an account in twelve books, most of which are extant. The work was styled Τοπογραφία Χριστιανεκή. In it China is first undeniably mentioned, being styled *Tzinista*—the Persian *Chinistan*. Edition by Gallandi (1776).

Cosmētae (κοσμηταί). A class of slaves among the Romans, whose duty it was to dress and adorn ladies (Juv. vi. 476). Some writers on antiquities have supposed that the cosmetae were female slaves, but the passage of Juvenal is alone sufficient to refute this opinion; for it was not customary for female slaves to take off their tunics when a punishment was to be inflicted upon them. There was, indeed, a class of female slaves who were employed for the same purposes as the cosmetae; but they were called *cosmetriae*, a name which Naevius chose as the title for one of his comedies.

Cosmētes (κοσμητής). An officer in the Athenian gymnasia in the time of the Romans. See GYMNASIUM.

Cosmetics. See CERUSSA; FUCUS.

Cosmi (κόσμοι). The chief magistrates of Crete. See GERUSIA.

Cossaea (Κοσσαία). A district on the confines of Media and Persia, inhabited by a rude, warlike, predatory people, the Cossaei, whom the Persian kings never subdued. They were conquered by Alexander (B.C. 325–324), but after his death they soon regained their independence.

Cossus, AULUS CORNELIUS. A Roman consul (B.C. 428) who killed in single combat Lar Tolumnius, king of Veii, and dedicated his spoils to Iupiter Feretrius, this being the second of the three instances in which the *spolia opima* were won (Liv. iv. 19 and 20). See SPOLIA OPIMA.

Cossutius. A Roman architect who rebuilt, at the expense of Antiochus Epiphanes, the temple of the Olympian Zeus at Athens, about B.C. 168. See Reber, *Hist. of Ancient Art*, p. 249 (Eng. trans., N. Y. 1882).

Costume. See CLOTHING.

Cosȳra or **Cossyra.** Now Pantellaria; a small island in the Mediterranean near Malta.

Cothon (Κώθων). The artificial inner harbour of Carthage. See CARTHAGO.

Cothurnus, or more correctly COTURNUS (κόθορνος). The Greek name for a high shoe or buskin with several soles. It covered the whole foot, and rose as high as the middle of the leg. It was made so as to fit either foot, and was generally fastened in front with red straps. The cothurnus was properly a hunting-boot, but Aeschylus made it part of the costume of his tragic actors to give them a stature above the average. At the same time the hair was dressed high in order to maintain the proportion of the figure. The cothurnus was also used in the Roman tragedy. (See SOCCUS.) It must be remembered that though the name κόθορνος is Greek, the

Cothurni. (Daremberg and Saglio.)

Greeks do not use it of the tragic boot, which they call ὀκρίβας, or more usually ἐμβάτης.

Cotĭso. A king of the Dacians, who was conquered in the reign of Augustus by Lentulus.

Cotta, AURELIUS. (1) GAIUS, consul B.C. 75 with L. Octavius, was one of the most distinguished orators of his time, and is introduced by Cicero as one of the speakers in the treatises *De Oratore* and *De Natura Deorum*. (2) LUCIUS, praetor in B.C. 70, when he carried the celebrated law (*lex Aurelia iudiciaria*), which intrusted the *iudicia* to the senators, equites, and tribuni aerarii.

Cotta, L. AURUNCULEIUS. One of Caesar's legates in Gaul, who perished with Sabinus in the attack made upon them by Ambiorix, B.C. 54. See AMBIORIX.

Cottăbus (κότταβος). A Greek game very popular at drinking-bouts. The player lay on a couch, and in that position tried to throw a few drops of wine, in as high a curve as possible, at a mark, without spilling any of the wine. The mark was called κοτταβεῖον, and was a bronze goblet or saucer (πλάστιγξ) on the end of an upright rod (ῥάβδος); and it was a point to make a noise when hitting it. On the κοτταβεῖον was fastened a little image or a bust of Hermes, which was called μάνης, and which the player had to hit first with the wine. The wine was supposed to make a sound (λάταξ) both in hitting the figure and in falling afterwards into the saucer. This, of course, greatly increased the difficulty of the game.

Cottabus. (Vase from Corneto.)

There was another form of the game, in which the point was to make the wine hit the saucer while floating in a large vessel of water and sink it. The game was played in a chamber made for the purpose. The form of the room was circular, to give every player an equal chance of hitting the mark, which was placed in the centre. The victor generally received a prize agreed upon beforehand. The players also used the game to discover their chances of success in love. They uttered the name of their beloved while throwing the wine. A successful throw gave a good omen, an unsuccessful one a bad omen. A good player leaned upon his left elbow, remained quite quiet, and used only his right hand to throw with. The game came originally from Sicily, but became popular through the whole of Greece, and especially at Athens, where to play well was a mark of good breeding. It did not go out of fashion until the fourth century after Christ.

Vase-paintings representing the first form of the game exist in considerable numbers, one of them being reproduced in the preceding illustration. An apparatus for playing the cottabus was found some years ago in an Etruscan tomb at Perugia, where it is now preserved in the local museum. See Helbig, in the *Mittheil. des Kaiserl. Deutsch. Archäol. Inst., Römische Abth.*, for 1886, i. pp. 222 foll. and 234 foll. Also Becker-Göll, *Charikles*, ii. p. 366, and the *Annali dell' Inst.*, for 1868, pp. 217 foll.

Cottiae Alpes. The modern Mont St. Genèvre, generally, though erroneously, supposed to be the place where Hannibal crossed into Italy. (See ALPES.) They took their name from Cottius, a king of several Ligurian tribes in the Cottian Alps, which also derived their name from him. He submitted to Augustus, who granted him the sovereignty over twelve of these tribes, with the title of praefectus. Cottius thereupon made roads over the Alps, and erected (B.C. 8) at Segusio (Susa) a triumphal arch in honour of Augustus, extant at the present day. It is 44 feet in height and 39 in width, with projecting Corinthian columns at the corners and sacrificial scenes on the friezes.

Cottius. See COTTIAE ALPES.

Cotton. See CARBASUS; GOSSYPIUM.

Cottus. A giant with 100 hands, son of Uranus (Heaven) and Gaea (Earth). See GIGANTES.

Cotyaēum (Κοτυάειον). A town of Phrygia, south of Dorylaeum, on the Thymbris, a branch of the Sangarius. Suidas says that, according to some accounts, it was the birthplace of Aesop the fabulist. Alexander, a grammarian of great learning and a voluminous writer, was also a native of Cotyaeum. Late Byzantine writers term it the metropolis of Phrygia.

Cotȳla or **Cotȳlus** (κοτύλη, κότυλος). A kind of cup, with regard to whose shape and capacity little has been satisfactorily determined (Hom. *Od.* xv. 312).

Cotyōra (Κοτύωρα). A colony of Sinopé on the coast of Pontus Polemoniacus, celebrated as the place where the 10,000 Greeks embarked for Sinopé. See Xen. *Anab.* v. 5. 4.

Cotys (Κότυς). The name of several kings of Thrace. Ovid, during his exile at Tomi, addressed an epistle to one of them. (*Ex Pont.* ii. 9.)

Cotyttia or **Cottytes** (Κοτύττια, Κόττυτες). A festival which was originally celebrated by the Edonians of Thrace, in honour of a goddess called Cotys or Cotytto (Strab. x. 470). It was held at night, and, according to Strabo, resembled the festivals of the Cabeiri (q. v.) and the Phrygian Cybelé. But the worship of Cotys, together with the festival of the Cotyttia, was adopted by several Greek States, chiefly those which were induced by their commercial interest to maintain friendly relations with Thrace. The priests of the goddess were formerly supposed to have borne the name of *baptae;* but Buttmann has shown that this opinion is probably groundless. Her festivals were notorious among the ancients for the dissolute manner and the debaucheries with which they were celebrated (Suidas, s. v. Κότυς; Hor. *Epod.* xvii. 56; Theocr. vi. 40). Another festival of the same name was celebrated in Sicily (Plut. *Proverb.*), where boughs hung with cakes and fruit were carried about, which any person had a right to pluck off if he chose; but we have no mention that this festival was polluted with any of the licentious practices which disgraced those of Thrace and Greece, unless we refer the allusion made by Theocritus to the Cotyttia, to the Sicilian festival. Cf. Buttmann's essay, "Ueber die Kotyttia und die Baptae," in his *Mythologus*, vol. ii. p. 159.

Cotytto or **Cotys** (Κοτυττώ or Κότυς). A goddess worshipped by the Thracians, and apparently identical with the Phrygian Cybelé. Her worship was introduced at Athens and Corinth, where it was celebrated, in private, with great indecency and licentiousness. See Juv. ii. 92; and the article COTYTTIA.

Couch. See LECTUS.

Covinarii. See COVINUS.

Covīnus or **Covīnnus** (Keltic, *kowain*). A kind of car, the spokes of which were armed with long sickles, and which was used as a scythe-chariot chiefly by the ancient Belgians and Britons. The Romans designated by the name of *covinus* a kind of travelling-carriage, which seems to have been covered on all sides with the exception of the front. It had no seat for a driver, but was conducted by the traveller himself, who sat inside (Mart. xii. 24). There must have been a great similarity between the Belgian scythe-chariot and the Roman travelling-carriage, as the name of the one was transferred to the other; and we may reasonably conclude that the Belgian car was likewise covered on all sides except the front, and that it was occupied by one man, the *covinarius* only, who was, by the structure of his car, sufficiently protected. The *covinarii* (the word occurs only in Tacitus) seem to have constituted a regular and distinct part of a British army (Tac. *Agric.* 35, 36). See ESSEDUM.

Cradle. See CUNAE.

Cragus (Κράγος). A mountain consisting of eight summits, being a continuation of Taurus to the west, and forming at its extremity the southwestern promontory of Lycia. At its foot was a town of the same name on the sea-shore, between Pydna and Patara. Parallel to it, north of the river Glaucus, was the chain of Anticragus.

Cranaë (Κρανάη). The island to which Paris first carried Helen from Peloponnesus. Its locality is uncertain, but some identify it with Cythera.

Cranăus (Κραναός). King of Attica, the son-in-law and successor of Cecrops.

Cranii (Κράνιοι). A town of Cephallenia on the south coast.

Cranon (Κρανών) or **Crannon** (Κραννών). A city of Thessaly on the river Onchestus, southeast of Pharsalus. Near it was a fountain, the water of which was fabled to warm wine when mixed with it, so that the heat remained for two or three days.

Crantor (Κράντωρ). A philosopher of Soli, among the pupils of Xenocrates, B.C. 300. He was the first who wrote commentaries on the works of Plato. Crantor was highly celebrated for the purity of his moral doctrine, as may be inferred from the praises bestowed by the ancients upon him. From one of his works, Περὶ Πένθους, Cicero drew largely in writing the third book of the *Tusculanae*, and the lost treatise *De Consolatione* on the death of his daughter Tullia. Cf. Cic. *Acad.* ii. 44.

Crassĭpes, FURIUS. Cicero's son-in-law, husband to Tullia, from whom he was divorced shortly after their marriage in B.C. 56.

Crassus. (1) LUCIUS LICINIUS, a Roman orator and man of consular rank. In B.C. 119, being only twenty-one years of age, he made his debut in the Forum, in a prosecution against C. Carbo. Cicero says that he was remarkable, even at this early period, for his candour and his great love of justice. Crassus was but twenty-seven years old when his eloquence obtained the acquittal of his relation, the Vestal Licinia. Being elevated to the consulship in 95, he was the author of a law by which numbers of the allies, who passed for Roman citizens, were sent back to their respective cities. This law alienated from him the affections of the principal Italians, so that he was regarded by some as the primary cause of the Social War, which broke out three years after. Having Hither Gaul for his province, Crassus freed the country from the robbers that infested it, and for this service had the weakness to claim a triumph. The Senate were favourable to his application; but Scaevola, the other consul, opposed it, on the ground that he had not conquered foes worthy of the Roman people. Crassus conducted himself, in other respects, with great wisdom in his government, and not only did not remove from around him the son of Carbo, who had come as a spy on his conduct, but even placed him by his side on the tribunal, and did nothing of which the other was not a witness. Being appointed censor in 92, he caused the school of the Latin rhetoricians to be closed, regarding them as dangerous innovators for the young. Crassus left hardly any orations behind him, and he died while Cicero was yet in his boyhood; but still that author, having collected the opinions of those who had heard him, speaks with a minute and apparently perfect intelligence of his style of oratory. He was what may be called the most ornamental speaker that had hitherto appeared in the Forum. Though not without force, gravity, and dignity, these were happily blended with the most insinuating politeness, urbanity, ease, and gayety. He was master of the most pure and accurate language and of perfect elegance of expression, without any affectation or unpleasant appearance of previous study. Great clearness of language distinguished all his harangues; and, while descanting on topics of law or equity, he possessed an inexhaustible fund of argument and illustration. Some persons considered Crassus as only equal to Antonius, his great contemporary; others preferred him as the more perfect and accomplished orator. The most splendid of all the efforts of Crassus was the immediate cause of his death, which happened in B.C. 91, a short while before the commencement of the civil wars of Marius and Sulla, and a few days after the time in which he is supposed to have borne his part in the dialogue *De Oratore.* The consul Philippus had declared, in one of the assemblies of the people, that some other advice must be resorted to, since, with such a Senate as then existed, he could no longer direct the affairs of the government. A full Senate being immediately summoned, Crassus arraigned, in terms of the most glowing eloquence, the conduct of the consul, who, instead of acting as the political parent and guardian of the Senate, sought to deprive its members of their ancient inheritance of respect and dignity. Being further irritated by an attempt on the part of Philippus to force him into compliance with his designs, he exerted, on this occasion, the utmost effort of his genius and strength; but he returned home with a pleuritic fever, of which he died seven days after. This oration of Crassus, followed, as it was, by his almost immediate death, made a deep impression on his countrymen; who, long afterwards, were wont to repair to the Senate-house for the purpose of viewing the spot where he had last stood, and where he fell, as it may be said, in defence of the privileges of his order. (2) MARCUS, who was praetor B.C. 105. He was surnamed by his friends Agelastus (Ἀγέλαστος), because, according to Pliny (vii. 19), he never laughed during the whole course of his life; or because, according to Lucilius, he laughed but once (Cic. *De Fin.* v. 30). (3) MARCUS LICINIUS, called the Rich (*Dives*), the son of the preceding, and the most opulent Roman of his day, was of a patrician family, and the son of a man of consular rank. His father and brother perished in the proscriptions of Marius and Cinna while he was still quite young, and, to avoid a similar fate, he took refuge in Spain until the death of Cinna, when he returned to Italy and served under Sulla. Crassus proved very serviceable to this commander in the decisive battle (B.C. 83) that was fought near Rome; but afterwards, making the most unjust and rapacious use of Sulla's proscriptions, that leader, according to Plutarch, gave him up and never employed him again in any public affair. The glory which was then beginning to attend upon Pompey, though still young and only a simple member of the equestrian order, excited the jealousy of Crassus, and, despairing of rising to an equality with him in warlike operations, he betook himself to public affairs at home, and, by paying court to the people, defending the impeached, lending money, and aiding those who were candidates for office, he attained to an influence almost equal to that which Pompey had acquired by his military achievements. It was at the bar, in particular, that Crassus rendered himself extremely popular. He was not, it would seem, a very eloquent speaker, yet by care and application he eventually exceeded those whom nature had more highly favoured. When Pompey, or Caesar, or Cicero declined speaking in behalf of any individual, he often arose and advocated the cause of the accused. Besides this promptness to aid the unfortunate, his courteous and conciliating deportment acquired for him many friends, and made him very popular with the lower orders. There was not a Roman, however humble, whom he did not salute, or whose salutation he did not return by name.

The great defect, however, in the character of Crassus was his inordinate fondness for wealth; and, although he could not strictly be called an avaricious man, since he is said to have lent money to his friends without demanding interest, yet he allowed the love of riches to exercise a paramount sway over his actions, and it proved at last the cause of his unhappy end. Plutarch informs us that his estate at first did not exceed three hundred talents, but that afterwards it amounted to the enormous sum of seven thousand one hundred talents (nearly $8,500,000). The means by which he attained to this are enumerated by the same writer, and some of them are singular enough. Observing, says Plutarch, how liable the city was to fires, he made it his business to buy houses that were on fire and others that joined upon them; and he commonly got them at a low price, on account of the fear and distress of the owners about the result. A band of his slaves thereupon, regularly organized for the purpose, exerted themselves to extinguish the flames, and, after this was done, rebuilt what had been destroyed, and in this way Crassus gradually became the owner of a large portion of Rome. He gained large sums also by educating and then selling slaves. Plutarch, in fact, regards this as his principal source of revenue. With all this eager grasping after wealth, however, Crassus appears to have been no mean soldier, even though he displayed so few of the qualities of a commander in his Parthian campaign. Created praetor in B.C. 71, he was sent to terminate the war with Spartacus. He accordingly met, defeated him in several encounters, and at last, bringing him to a decisive action, ended the war by a single blow, Spartacus and forty thousand of his followers being left on the field. Not venturing to demand a triumph for a victory over gladiators and slaves, he contented himself with an ovation.

In 70, Crassus obtained the consulship, having Pompey for his colleague. At a subsequent period we find him implicated by an informer in the conspiracy of Catiline, but acquitted by acclamation the moment the charge was heard by the Senate. We now come to the closing scene in the career of Crassus. When Caesar, on returning from his government to solicit the consulship, found Pompey and Crassus at variance (which had been the case also during almost all the time that they were colleagues in the consular office), and perceived that, for the furtherance of his own ambitious views, the aid of these two individuals would be needed by him for opposing the influence of the Senate, as well as that of Cicero, Cato, and Catulus, he managed to reconcile them, and soon, in conjunction with both of them, formed the well-known league usually styled the First Triumvirate (B.C. 60), which proved so fatal to the liberties of the Roman people. By the terms of this compact Crassus obtained the government of Syria. In the law that was passed relative to this government of Crassus, no mention was indeed made of any war in its neighbourhood; still every one knew that he had connected with it an immediate invasion of Parthia (B.C. 55). Plutarch even states that he had fixed upon neither Syria nor Parthia as the limits of his expected good fortune, but intended to penetrate even to Bactria, India, and the shores of the Eastern Ocean. The only motive to this memorable and unfortunate undertaking was the rapacious love of wealth.

It was not, however, without considerable opposition from the people and the tribunes that Crassus was allowed to proceed on this expedition. All the influence of Pompey was necessary to prevent an expression of popular wrath, for no good was expected to result from hostilities against a people who had done the Romans no injury, and who were, in fact, their allies. When Crassus, moreover, had reached the gate of the city, the tribune Ateius attempted to stop him by force; but, failing in this, he immediately proceeded to perform a religious ceremony of the most appalling nature, by which he devoted the commander himself and all who should follow him on that service to the wrath of the infernal gods and a speedy destruction. Undismayed, however, by either denunciations or omens (Cic. *Div.* ii. 40), Crassus, embarking at Brundisium, proceeded into Asia by Macedonia and the Hellespont. As the enemy were not prepared for this unprovoked invasion, the Romans met with no resistance. At first Crassus overran the greater part of Mesopotamia; and, had he taken advantage of the consternation into which his sudden appearance had thrown the Parthians, he might, with the greatest ease, have extended his conquest to Babylonia itself. But, the season being far advanced, he did not think it expedient to proceed. On the contrary, having left in the different towns and strongholds a detachment of 7000 foot and 1000 horse, he returned into Syria and took up his winter quarters in that province. This retrograde movement was a fatal error. His occupations, too, during the winter were highly censurable, having more of the trader in them than the general. Instead of improving the discipline of the soldiers, and keeping them in proper exercise, he spent his time in making inquiry relative to the revenues of the cities, and in weighing the treasures which he found in the temple of Hierapolis. In the spring the Roman commander took the field, on the frontiers of Syria, with seven legions, four thousand horse, and an equal number of light or irregular troops. With this force he again passed the Euphrates, when he was joined by an Arabian chief, whom Plutarch calls Ariamnes, but who is elsewhere named Acbarus or Abgarus; and in this barbarian, owing to his knowledge of the country and his warm and frequent expressions of attachment to the Romans, Crassus unfortunately placed the utmost confidence. The result may easily be foreseen. Crassus intended to have followed the course of the Euphrates till he should reach the point where it approaches nearest to Seleucia and Ctesiphon, the capital of the Parthian Empire; but being dissuaded from this by his crafty guide, and directing his march across the plains, he was led at last into a sandy desert, where his army was attacked by the Parthian forces under Surenas. An unequal conflict ensued. The son of Crassus, sent with a detachment of Gallic horse to repel the Parthian cavalry, lost his life after the most heroic exertions; and his loss was first made known to his father by the barbarians carrying his head on a spear. Crassus himself, not long after, being compelled by his own troops to meet Surenas in a conference, was treacherously slain by the barbarians, and his head and right hand sent to the Parthian king, Orodes, who is said to have poured molten gold down the dead man's throat, saying, in allusion to his avarice, "Sate thyself now with that of which in life thou wert so greedy!" The whole loss of the Romans in this disastrous campaign was 20,000 killed and 10,000 taken prisoners. See Plut. *Crass.*; Dio Cass. xl. 13 foll.; and the article Parthia.

Crater (κρατήρ; Ionic κρητήρ; Lat. *crater* or *cratera*, from κεράννυμι, "to mix"). A vessel in which the wine, according to the custom of the ancients, who very seldom drank it undiluted, was mixed with water, and from which the cups were filled. In the Homeric Age the mixture was always made in the dining-room by heralds or young men (κοῦροι). The use of the vessel is sufficiently clear from the expressions so frequent in the poems of Homer: κρητῆρα κεράσασθαι—i. e. οἶνον καὶ ὕδωρ ἐν κρητῆρι μίσγειν: πίνειν κρητῆρα, "to empty the crater"; κρητῆρα στήσασθαι (*cratera statuere*), "to place the filled crater near the table"; κρητῆρας ἐπιστέφεσθαι ποτοῖο, "to fill the craters to the brim." The crater, in the Homeric Age, was generally of silver, sometimes with a gold edge, and sometimes all gold or gilt. It stood upon a tripod, and its ordinary place in the μέγαρον was in the most honourable part of the room, at the farthest end from the entrance, and near the seat of the most distinguished among the guests. The size of the crater seems to have varied according to the number of guests, for where their number is increased a larger crater is asked for. It would seem, at least at a later period (for in the Homeric poems we find no traces of the custom), that three craters were filled at every feast after the tables were removed. According to Suidas, the first was dedicated to Hermes, the second to Charisius, and the third to Zeus Soter; but others called them by different names; thus the first, or, according to others, the last, was also designated the κρατὴρ ἀγαθοῦ δαίμονος, "the crater of the good genius," κρατὴρ ὑγιείας and μετανιπτρίς or μετάνιπτρον, because it was the crater from which the cups were filled after the washing of the hands. There were special craters named from places, e. g. Lesbian, Laconian, Argive (Herod. iv. 152).

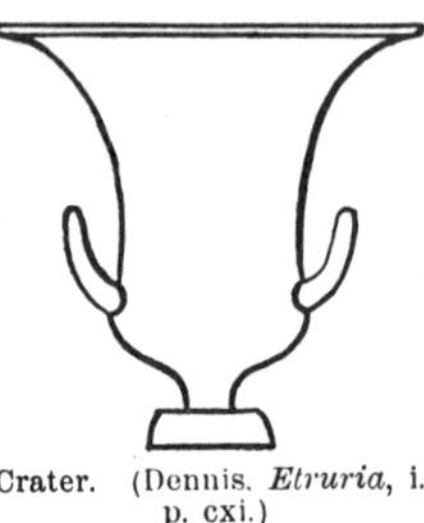

Crater. (Dennis, *Etruria*, i. p. cxi.)

Craters were among the first things on the embellishment of which the ancient artists exercised their skill. Homer mentions, among the prizes proposed by Achilles, a beautifully wrought silver crater, the work of the ingenious Sidonians, which, by the elegance of its workmanship, excelled all others on the whole earth. In the reign of Croesus, king of Lydia, the Lacedaemonians sent to that king a brazen crater, the border of which was all over ornamented with figures (ζώδια), and which was of such an enormous size that it contained 300 amphorae. Croesus himself dedicated to the Delphic god two huge craters, which the Delphians believed to be the work of Theodorus of Samos, and Herodotus was induced, by the beauty of their workmanship, to think the same. It was

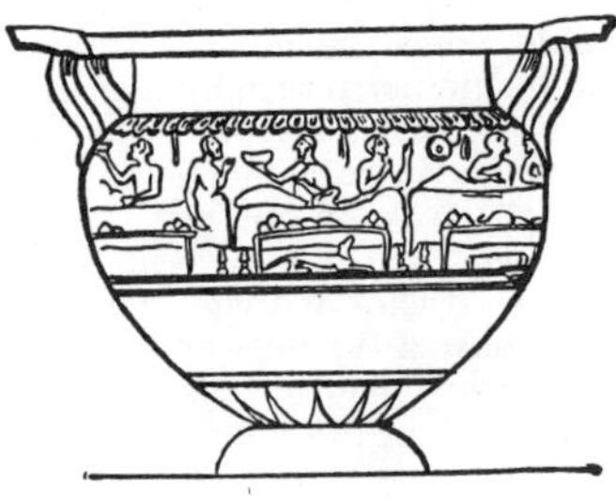

Crater. (Dennis, *Etruria*, i. p. cxii.)

about Ol. 35 that the Samians dedicated six talents (the tenth of the profits made by Colaeus on his voyage to Tartessus) to Heré, in the shape of an immense brazen crater, the border of which was adorned with projecting heads of griffins. This crater, which Herodotus calls Argive (from which we must infer that the Argive artists were celebrated for their craters), was supported by three colossal brazen statues, seven yards high, with their knees closed together.

The number of craters dedicated in temples seems everywhere to have been very great. Livius Andronicus, in his *Equus Troianus*, represented Agamemnon returning from Troy with no less than 3000 craters, and Cicero says that Verres carried away from Syracuse the most beautiful brazen craters, which most probably belonged to the various temples of that city. But craters were not only dedicated to the gods as *anathemata*, but were used on various solemn occasions in their service. In sacrifices the libation was always taken from a crater; and sailors, before they set out on their journey, used to take the libation with cups from a crater and pour it into the sea. The name crater was also sometimes used as synonymous with σιτλίον, *situla*, a pail in which water was carried.

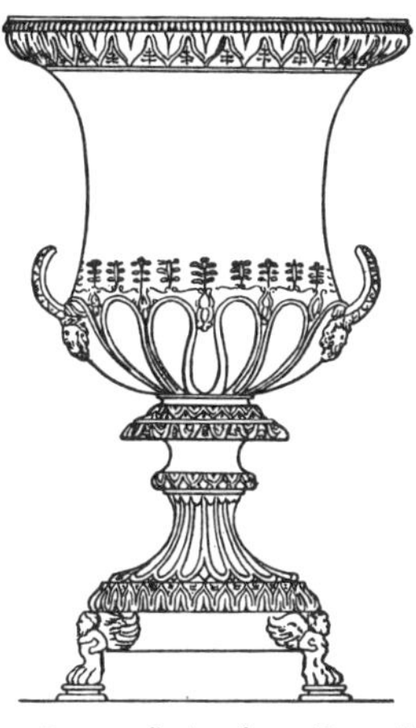
Bronze Crater from Pompeii. (Overbeck.)

The Romans used their *crater* or *cratera* for the same purposes for which it was used in Greece; but the most elegant specimens were, like most works of art, made by Greeks. See CAELATURA.

Cratĕrus (Κρατερός). (1) A distinguished general of Alexander the Great, on whose death (B.C. 323) he received, in common with Antipater, the government of Macedonia and Greece. He fell in a battle against Eumenes, in 321. (2) A Greek physician, who attended the family of Atticus.

Crates (Κράτης). (1) A celebrated Athenian poet of the Old Comedy, who began to flourish B.C. 449. (2) Of Thebes, a pupil of the Cynic Diogenes, and one of the most distinguished of the Cynic philosophers, flourished about B.C. 320. (See CYNICI.) (3) Of Mallus in Cilicia, a celebrated grammarian, who founded the school of grammar at Pergamus, and wrote a commentary on the Homeric poems (Διορθωτικά) in opposition to Aristarchus. In B.C. 157, he was sent by Attalus to Rome as an ambassador, where he was the first to introduce the study of grammar. Besides his Homeric studies, Crates wrote commentaries on Euripides and Aristophanes and a treatise on the Attic dialect (Περὶ Ἀττικῆς Διαλέκτου). See Wachsmuth, *De Cratete Mallota* (Leipzig, 1860); Susemihl, *Geschichte d. griech. Litt. in der Alexandr. Zeit*, ii. pp. 4–12 and 703; Conze, in the *Berl. Acad. Sitzungsber.* (1884); and Consbruch, in the *Comment. in Honorem Studemundi* (Strassburg, 1889). Also the articles GRAMMATICA; PHILOLOGY.

Crates (ταρσός, γέρρον). A hurdle, used by the ancients in many different ways—especially, as among ourselves, for agricultural purposes. Thus *textae crates* are the wattled hurdles of which sheep-folds are made (Hor. *Epod.* ii. 45); *vimineae crates* are bush-harrows (Verg. *Georg.* i. 95, 104). The name was also applied to any wooden frame composed of bars with interstices—our "crate," "grate"; and the interstices might be filled up with mats of straw, rushes, or fern (Colum. xii. 15). The following special senses may be noticed:

(1) *Crates* were used by the country people upon which to dry figs, grapes, etc., in the rays of the sun; or to screen growing fruit from the weather (Colum. xii. 16); or for spreading manure (Cat. *R. R.* 10). (2) A rack for provisions. (3) Among military terms we find *crates* used in forming the roadway of Caesar's bridge over the Rhine (Caes. *B. G.* iv. 17); for parapets or breastworks; as fascines for crossing ditches; and as mantlets or wooden screens for sheltering the advance of troops under cover (Ammian. Marcell. xxi. 12). From the *plutei*, which were employed in the same way, they differed only in being without the covering of raw hides. (4) By the besieged they were used joined together so as to form what Vegetius calls a *metella*, and filled with stones; these were then poised between two of the battlements, and as the storming-party approached upon the ladders, overturned on their heads (Veget. *Mil.* iv. 6). (5) In poetry, the wicker-work of shields is so called (Verg. *Aen.* vii. 633).

(6) A capital punishment was called by this name, whence the phrase *sub crate necari*. The criminal was either thrown into a pond or well and drowned under a hurdle (Tac. *Germ.* 12), or crushed by the weight of stones heaped upon it (Liv. iv. 50).

Crathis (Κρᾶθις). (1) A river in Achaia, falling into the sea near Aegae. (2) A river in Lower Italy, falling into the sea near Sybaris. Its waters were fabled to dye the hair blond (Eurip. *Troad.* 228).

Craticŭla (ταρρίον). A gridiron, several specimens of which have been found in Pompeii. In Petronius (31 and 70) the *craticula* is of silver and brought to the table by the slaves—an anticipation of the modern "silver grill."

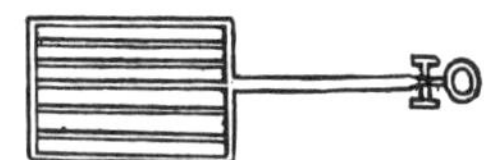
Bronze Craticula from Paestum (Handle restored).

Craticŭlum (κρατευτήριον). An andiron. See Poll. vi. 89.

Cratīnus (Κρατῖνος). (1) An Athenian comic poet, born in B.C. 519. It was not till late in life that he directed his attention to comic compositions. The first piece of his on record is the Ἀρχίλοχοι, which was represented about B.C. 448, at which time he was in his seventy-first year. In this play, according to Plutarch (*Cimon*), he makes mention of the celebrated Cimon, who had died the preceding year, B.C. 449; and from the language employed by the poet it may be inferred that he was on terms of close intimacy with the Athenian general. Soon after this, comedy became so licentious and virulent in its personalities that the magistracy were obliged to interfere. A decree was passed, B.C. 440, prohibiting the exhibitions of comedy; which law continued in force only during that year and the two following, being repealed in the archonship of Euthymenes. Three victories of Cratinus stand recorded after the recommencement of comic performances. With the Χειμαζόμενοι he was second, B.C. 425 (*Argum.*

Acharn.), when the Ἀχαρνεῖς of Aristophanes won the prize, and the third place was adjudged to the Νουμηνίαι of Eupolis. In the succeeding year he was again second with the Σάτυροι, and Aristophanes again first with the Ἱππεῖς (*Argum. Equit.*). In a parabasis of this play that young rival makes mention of Cratinus; where, having noticed his former successes, he insinuates, under the cloak of an equivocal piety, that the veteran was becoming doting and superannuated. The old man, now in his ninety-fifth year, indignant at this insidious attack, exerted his remaining vigour, and composed, against the contests of the approaching season, a comedy entitled Πυτίνη, or *The Flagon*, which turned upon the accusations brought against him by Aristophanes. The aged dramatist had a complete triumph (*Argum. Nub.*). He was first; while his humbled antagonist was vanquished also by Ameipsias with the Κόννος, though the play of Aristophanes was the favourite *Nubes*. Notwithstanding his notorious intemperance, Cratinus lived to an extreme old age, dying B.C. 422, in his ninety-seventh year. Aristophanes alludes to the excesses of Cratinus in a passage of the *Equites* (v. 526 foll.). In the *Pax*, he humorously ascribes the jovial old poet's death to a shock on seeing a cask of wine staved and lost. Cratinus himself made no scruple of acknowledging his failing (Schol. *in Pac.* 703). Horace, also, opens one of his Epistles (i. 19) with a maxim of the comedian's, in due accordance with his practice. The titles of thirty-eight of the comedies of Cratinus have been collected. His style was bold and animated (Pers. i. 123), and like his younger brethren, Eupolis and Aristophanes, he fearlessly and unsparingly directed his satire against the iniquitous public officer and the profligate of private life. The fragments of Cratinus may be found in Meineke, *Fragmenta Comicorum Graecorum* (Berlin, 1840). (2) There was also a younger Cratinus, a poet of the New Comedy and contemporary of Plato.

Cratippus (Κράτιππος). A Peripatetic philosopher of Mitylené, accompanied Pompey in his flight after the battle of Pharsalia, B.C. 48. He afterwards settled at Athens, where the young M. Cicero was his pupil in B.C. 44. By the elder Cicero's influence, Cratippus received the gift of Roman citizenship from Caesar.

Cratȳlus (Κρατύλος). A Greek philosopher, and disciple of Heraclitus. According to Aristotle (*Metaph.* i. 6), Plato attended his lectures in his youth. Cratylus is one of the interlocutors in the dialogue of Plato called after his name.

Cremĕra. A small river in Etruria, which falls into the Tiber a little above Rome; memorable for the death of the 300 Fabii in B.C. 477. Here also Constantine defeated Maxentius in A.D. 312. See FABII.

Cremna (Κρῆμνα). A strong place in the interior of Pisidia, lying, according to Ptolemy, on the declivity of Taurus, nearly six miles north of Selga. This fortress was considered by the Romans to be of so much consequence that they established a colony here.

Cremōna. A city of Cisalpine Gaul, northeast of Placentia and a little north of the Po. Cremona and Placentia were both settled by Roman colonies, B.C. 219 (Polyb. iii. 40). After the defeat on the Trebia, we find the consul P. Scipio retiring to Cremona (Liv. xxi. 56), and it appears that the Romans retained the place throughout the whole of the Second Punic War, though it suffered so much during its continuance, and afterwards from the attacks of the Gauls, that it was found necessary to recruit its population by a fresh supply of colonists. The colony, being thus renewed, continued to prosper for nearly a hundred and fifty years; when the Civil Wars, which ensued after the death of Caesar, materially affected its interests. Cremona, unfortunately, espoused the cause of Brutus, and thus incurred the vengeance of the victorious party. The loss of its territory, which was divided among the veteran soldiers of Augustus, is well known from the line of Vergil (*Eclog.* ix. 28), which is nearly repeated by Martial (viii. 55). The effect of this calamity would seem, however, to have been but temporary; and, in fact, we learn from Strabo that Cremona was accounted in his time one of the most considerable towns in the north of Italy. The civil wars which arose during the time of Otho and Vitellius were the source of much severer affliction to this city than any former evil, as the fate of the Empire was more than once decided between large contending armies in its immediate vicinity. After the defeat of Vitellius's party by the troops of Vespasian, it was entered by the latter (A.D. 69) and exposed to all the horrors that fire, the sword, and a licentious soldiery can inflict upon a city taken by storm. The conflagration of the place lasted four days. The indignation which this event excited throughout Italy seems to have been such that Vespasian, afraid of the odium it might attach to his party, used every effort to raise Cremona from its ruins by recalling the scattered inhabitants, reconstructing the public edifices, and granting the city fresh privileges.

Cremōnis Iugum. See ALPES.

Cremutius Cordus. See CORDUS.

Creon (Κρέων). (1) King of Corinth, and father of Creüsa or Glaucé, the wife of Iason. (See CREÜSA; MEDEA.) (2) The brother of Iocasté, mother and wife of Oedipus. (See OEDIPUS.) He ascended the throne of Thebes after Eteocles and Polynices had fallen in mutual combat, and gave orders that the body of the latter should be deprived of funeral rites, on which circumstance is founded the plot of the *Antigone* of Sophocles. See ANTIGONÉ; ETEOCLES; POLYNICES; SEVEN AGAINST THEBES.

Creophȳlus (Κρεώφυλος) of Chios. One of the earliest epic poets, and said to have been the friend or son-in-law of Homer (Plat. *Repub.* 600 C; Plut. *Lyc.*). An epic poem has been ascribed to him, entitled Οἰχαλίας ἅλωσις or Οἰχαλία, relating the contest of Heracles with Eurytus for the sake of Iolé, and the capture of Oechalia.

Crepĭda (κρηπίς), also called **Crepidŭla** (Plaut. *Pers.* iv. 2, 3). A kind of shoe of the nature of sandals, and to be considered as occupying a middle position between a closed boot and plain sandals. Originally it appears to have been worn by peasants, having a high and strong sole, often studded with nails (cf. Plin. *H. N.* xxxvi. § 127), sometimes fitted with leaden or brazen plates called Χῖαι κρηπῖδες (Hippocr. *ap.*

Crepida. (Foot of Hermes.)

Galen, xviii. A. p. 678, ed. Kuhn); and we are told that Hagnon, one of the followers of Alexander, had gold or silver nails in his *crepidae* (Athen. xii. 539 c). It sometimes had a low upper, with eyes (*ansae*) through which straps (*obstragula*, ἱμάντες), which were at times adorned with jewels or dyed with purple, were passed, fastening it over the instep; often it was closed at the back; but generally the upper consisted of a series of large loops (also called *ansae*), through which the fastening thong or thongs were passed. This kind of open network covering the instep explains the epithet πολυσχιδές (Lucian, *Rhet. Praecept.* 15). (See CALCEUS.) The name *crepida* is also given to a raised sidewalk or causeway for foot-passengers on the side of a street, as in the above illustration.

Crepida in Pompeian Street. (Rich.)

Crepitacŭlum. See SISTRUM.

Crepundia (τὰ σπάργανα). A generic term for children's playthings, such as rattles, dolls, toy hatchets, swords, etc. The name is also given to objects of a similar description tied about the necks of children, either as amulets or for purposes of identification (Plaut. *Mil. Glor.* v. 6; *Cist.* iv. 1, 13; *Rud.* iv. 4; Soph. *Oed. Tyr.* 1035). Specimens of these are represented as worn on the neck of a child in a statue of the Museo Pio-Clementino, copied in the accompanying engraving—viz., a half-moon (*lunula*) on the top of the right shoulder; then a double axe (*securicula ancipes*); next a bucket (*situla argenteola*); a sort of flower, not mentioned; a little sword (*ensiculus aureolus*); a little hand (*manicula*); then another half-moon; a dolphin (*delphin*), etc. See AMULETUM.

Child with Crepundia. (Museo Pio-Clementino.)

Cresphontes (Κρεσφόντης). A son of Aristomachus, who, with his brothers Temenus and Aristodemus, conquered the Peloponnesus. This was the famous conquest achieved by the Heraclidae. He and his two sons were subsequently slain by the Messenians. See ARISTODEMUS; HERACLIDAE.

Cressa. "The Cretan woman"; a term used by Ovid of Ariadné (*Am.* i. 7, 16) and of Aeropé (*A. A.* i. 327).

Crestonia (Κρηστωνία). A district in Macedonia between the Axius and the Strymon, near Mount Cerciné, inhabited by the Crestonaei, a Thracian people; their chief town was Creston or Crestoné, founded by the Pelasgians.

Creta (Κρήτη; in Italian, Candia; in Turkish, Kirit). One of the largest islands of the Mediterranean Sea, at the south of all the Cyclades. Its name is derived by some from the Curetes, who are said to have been its first inhabitants; by others, from the nymph Creté, daughter of Hesperus; and by others, from Cres, a son of Zeus and the nymph Idaea. It is also designated among the poets and mythological writers by the several appellations of Aeria, Doliché, Idaea, and Telchinia. According to Herodotus (bk. i.), this great island remained in the possession of various barbarous nations till the time of Minos (q. v.), son of Europa, who, having expelled his brother Sarpedon, became the sole sovereign of the country. These early inhabitants are generally supposed to be the Eteocretes of Homer (*Od.* xix. 172), who clearly distinguishes them from the Grecian colonists subsequently settled there.

Minos, according to the concurrent testimony of antiquity, first gave laws to the Cretans, and, having conquered the pirates who infested the Aegean Sea, established a powerful navy. In the Trojan War, Idomeneus, sovereign of Crete, led its forces to the war in eighty vessels, a number little inferior to that commanded by Agamemnon himself. According to the traditions which Vergil has followed, Idomeneus was afterwards driven from his throne by faction, and compelled to sail to Iapygia, where he founded the town of Salernum. At this period the island appears to have been inhabited by a mixed population of Greeks and barbarians. Homer enumerates the former under the names of Achaei, Dorians, surnamed Trichaïces, and Pelasgi. The latter, who were the most ancient, are said to have come from Thessaly, under the conduct of Teutamus, posterior to the great Pelasgic emigration into Italy. The Dorians are reported to have established themselves in Crete, under the command of Althemenes of Argos, after the death of Codrus and the foundation of Megara. In Crete was the famous labyrinth whose construction was ascribed to Daedalus, and about which so many legends cluster. See ARIADNÉ; DAEDALUS; ICARUS; LABYRINTHUS; MINOS; MINOTAURUS; PASIPHAÉ; THESEUS.

After the Trojan War and the expulsion of Idomeneus, the principal cities of Crete formed themselves into several republics, for the most part independent, while others were connected by federal ties. These, though not exempted from the dissensions which so universally distracted the Grecian States, maintained for a long time a considerable degree of prosperity, owing to the good system of laws and education which had been so early instituted throughout the island by the decrees of Minos. The Cretan code was supposed by many of the best-informed writers of antiquity to have furnished Lycurgus with the model of his most salutary regulations. It was founded, according to Ephorus, cited by Strabo, on the just basis of liberty and an equality of rights; and its great aim was to promote social harmony and peace by enforcing temperance and frugality. On this principle, the Cretan youths were divided into classes called Agelae, and all met at the Andreia, or public meals. Like the Spartans, they were early trained to the use of arms, and inured to sustain the extremes of heat and cold, and undergo the severest exercise; they were also compelled to learn their letters and certain pieces of music. The chief magistrates, called Cosmi (κόσμοι), were ten in number and elected annually. The Gerontes constituted the council of the nation, and were selected from those who were thought worthy of holding the office of Cosmus. There was also an equestrian order, who were bound to keep horses at their own expense. But though the Cretan laws resembled the Spartan institutions in so many important points, there were some striking features which distinguished the legislative enactments of the two countries. One of these was that the Lacedaemonians were subject to a strict agrarian law, whereas the Cretans were under no restraint as to the accumulation of moneyed or landed property; another, that the Cretan republics were for the most part democratic, whereas the Spartan was decidedly aristocratic. Herodotus informs us that the Cretans were deterred by the unfavourable response of the Pythian oracle from contributing forces to the Grecian armament assembled to resist the Persians (vii. 169). In the Peloponnesian War incidental mention is made of some Cretan cities as allied with Athens or Sparta, but the island does not appear to have espoused collectively the cause of either of the belligerent parties. The Cretan soldiers were held in great estimation as light troops and archers, and readily offered their services for hire to such States, whether Greek or barbarian, as needed them. In the time of Polybius the Cretans had much degenerated from their ancient character, for he charges them repeatedly with the grossest immorality and the most hateful vices. We know also with what severity they are reproved by St. Paul, in the words of one of their own poets, Epimenides (Ep. Tit. i. 12), *Κρῆτες ἀεὶ ψεῦσται, κακὰ θηρία, γαστέρες ἀργαί.*

The chief cities of Crete were Cnossus, Cydonia, Gortyna, and Lyctus, all of which see.

The Romans did not interfere with the affairs of Crete before the war with Antiochus, when Q. Fabius Labeo crossed over into the island from Asia Minor, under pretence of claiming certain Roman captives who were detained there. Several years after, the island was invaded by a Roman army commanded by M. Antonius, under the pretence that the Cretans had secretly favoured the cause of Mithridates; but Florus more candidly avows that the desire of conquest was the real motive which led to this attack. The enterprise, however, having failed, the subjugation of the island was not effected till some years later by Metellus, who, from his success, obtained the agnomen of Creticus. It was then (B.C. 67) annexed to the Roman Empire, and formed, together with Cyrenaïca, one of its numerous provinces, being governed by the same proconsul.

Crete forms an irregular parallelogram, of which the western side faces Sicily, while the eastern looks towards Cyprus; on the north it is washed by the Mare Creticum, and on the south by the Libyan Sea, which intervenes between the island and the opposite coast of Cyrené. Mount Ida, which surpasses all the other summits in elevation, rises in the centre of the island; its base occupies a circumference of nearly 600 stadia. To the west it is connected with another chain, called the White Mountains (Λευκὰ ὄρη), and to the east its prolongation forms the ridge anciently known by the name of Dicté. See Höck, *Kreta* (Göttingen, 1829); Pashley, *Travels in Crete* (London, 1837); Spratt, *Researches in Crete*, 2 vols. (London, 1865); Edwardes, *Letters from Crete* (London, 1887); and the article GORTYN.

Creta (sc. *terra*). Chalk or clay; so called from its abundance in the island of Crete (Creta), and so in Greek Κρητικὴ γῆ. The creta proper was simply chalk; *creta Eretria* was a species of earth found near Eretria in Euboea and used in medicine as an astringent; *creta Sarda* was fuller's earth, used in cleaning garments (see FULLO); *creta Cimolia* was a better kind of the same; and *creta Selinusia* (from Selinus in Sicily) furnished women with one of their numerous face-powders. (See CERUSSA; FUCUS.) Of some species of creta, vessels were made, on which see FICTILÉ. From the whiteness of chalk, it was spoken of tropically as denoting luck, contrasted with *carbo* (Pers. v. 108 with the commentators). The feet of slaves exposed for sale were chalked (Juv. i. 111), possibly to aid in tracking them if they escaped; hence *gypsati pedes* in Tibull. ii. 3, 60. The word *cretati* is sometimes applied to candidates for office, from the white robes they wore = *candidati*. See AMBITUS.

Creteus (Κρητεύς) or **Catreus** (Κατρεύς). The son of Minos by Pasiphaë or Creté, and father of Althemenes.

Cretheus (Κρηθεύς). Son of Aeolus and Enareté, husband of Tyro, and father of Aeson, Pheres, Amythaon, and Hippolyté. He was the founder of Iolcus.

Creüsa (Κρέουσα). (1) A daughter of Creon, king of Corinth, and wife of Iason. She received from Medea, as bridal presents, a diadem and a robe, both of which had been prepared with magic art and saturated with deadly poisons. On arraying herself in these, flames burst forth and destroyed her. Creon, the father of the princess, perished in a similar way, having thrown himself upon the body of his dying daughter, and being afterwards unable to extricate himself from the embrace of the corpse (Eurip. *Med.* 781 foll., 1156 foll.). According to the scholiast, she was also called Glaucé. (2) Daughter of Priam and Hecuba, and wife of Aeneas. When Troy was surprised by the Greeks, she fled in the night with her husband, but they were separated during the confusion, nor was her absence observed until the other fugitives arrived at the spot appointed for assembling. Aeneas a second time entered the burning city in quest of his wife; but while he was seeking for her through every quarter of Troy, Creüsa appeared to him as a deified personage, and appeased his alarm by informing him that she had been adopted by Cybelé among her own attendant nymphs; and she then urged him to pursue his course to Italy, with an intimation of the good fortune that awaited him in that land (Verg. *Aen.* ii. 562 foll.).

Cribrum (κόσκινον). A sieve; made of parchment perforated with holes, or of horse-hair, thread, papyrus, or rushes interwoven so as to leave interstices between each plat. The Romans sifted their flour through two kinds of sieves, called respectively *excussoria* and *pollinaria*, the latter of which gave the finest flour, termed *pollen*. Sieves of horse-hair were first made by the Gauls; those of linen by the Spaniards; and of papyrus and rushes by the Egyptians (Plin. *H. N.* xviii. 28; Cato, *R. R.* 76, 3; Pers. iii. 112). See p. 429.

Crimen. A legal term having two meanings in ordinary use: (*a*) a punishable offence; and (*b*) the accusation brought against the person by whom the offence is committed. In the first of these senses crimina were, in the oldest period of Roman history, regarded as wrongs against religion and the gods, and their punishment as an expiation offered to heaven (Serv. *ad* Verg. *Aen.* i. 632). In the Twelve Tables this implication of penal law

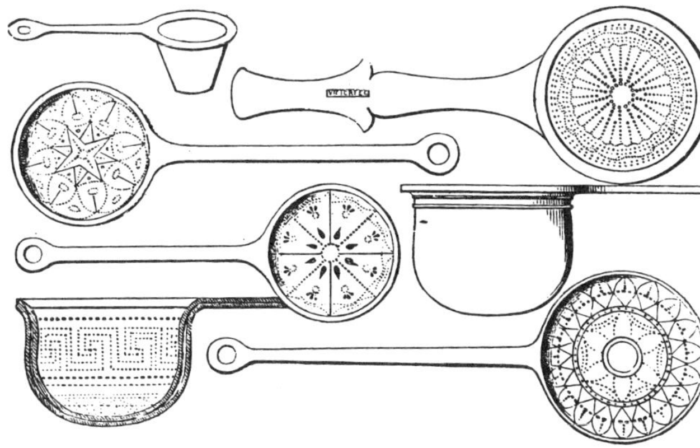

Bronze Cribra or Sieves from Pompeii. (Overbeck.)

with religion and religious sanctions has become less prominent, and we find a distinction between offences which are punished by a solemn legislative act of the State and offences atoned for by a fine paid to the injured person in satisfaction of his resentment, as to the amount of which the parties might come to terms (Fest. s. v. *talio*). From this distinction arose another, of more scientific value, between *delicta privata* and *crimina publica* (*Dig.* 21, 1, 17, 18), which is adhered to with tolerable consistency in the writings of the jurists and the later law. *Delicta privata*, or *delicta* simply, are civil offences, or what we call "torts"; *crimina publica* are what we call "crimes," offences against the State or community, the subject of prosecution before a criminal tribunal. But occasionally a delict is spoken of as a crimen (e. g. *extra furti crimen videri*, Gaius, iii. 197; *Inst.* iv. 1, 7), and in other passages (e. g. *Dig.* 48, 19, 1) a person who commits a crime is said *delinquere*. Crimes punishable by death, loss of *libertas*, by *interdictio aquae et ignis*, or *deportatio* were called *capitalia*.

Crimīsus (Κριμισός) or **Crimissus** (Κριμισσός). A river in the west of Sicily falling into the Hypsa; on its banks Timoleon defeated the Carthaginians, B.C. 339.

Crinagŏras (Κριναγόρας). A resident of Mitylené who flourished during the Augustan Age. He is the author of some fifty epigrams of the Greek Anthology. (Jacobs, *Anth. Graec.* pp. 876–878).

Crispus, FLAVIUS IULIUS. The eldest son of the emperor Constantine the Great, and named by him as Caesar in A.D. 317. He is thought to have aspired to the throne, for in 324 his father caused him to be put to death. See CONSTANTINUS, p. 404.

Crissaeus Sinus (Κρισσαῖος κόλπος). An arm of the Sinus Corinthiacus on the northern shore. It extends into the country of Phocis, and had at its head the town of CRISSA, whence it took its name. Its modern name is the Gulf of Salona, from the modern city of Salona, the ancient Amphissa, which was the chief town of the Locri Ozolae and lay to the northeast of Delphi.

Crista. See GALEA.

Critae (κριταί). Judges; a name applied by the Greeks to any person who did not judge of a thing as δικαστής—i. e. according to positive law—but rather according to his own personal sense of justice and equity (Herod. iii. 160). Specifically, the name was applied at Athens to a number of judges chosen by ballot from a body of selected candidates at the time of the Dionysia (q. v.). Their office was to judge of the merit of the different choruses and dramatic poems, and to award the prizes to the victors. It is supposed that there were in all ten κριταί—five for comedy and five for tragedy. See DRAMA.

Critheïs (Κριθηΐς). The reputed mother of Homer. See HOMERUS.

Critias (Κριτίας). An Athenian, a disciple of Socrates and Gorgias of Leontini. He was one of the most accomplished men of his time, and was distinguished as a poet and an orator. But he is best known as the chief of the Thirty Tyrants (q. v.), in defence of whose cause against the Liberators he fell in B.C. 403. He was the author of several tragedies. Some fragments of his poems have survived, the longest being from his political elegies. He seems to have had the gift of expression, but to have written in a harsh style.

Criton (Κρίτων). A rich citizen of Athens and a friend and disciple of Socrates. He made arrangements to enable Socrates to escape from prison just before his death, but the firmness of the philosopher, who refused to fly, foiled the plan. He was the author of seventeen philosophical dialogues, now lost; and a dialogue of Plato bears his name.

Crobȳlus (κρωβύλος). A fashion of wearing the hair drawn up into a knot (Thuc. i. 6), as shown in the accompanying illustration. See COMA.

Crobylus. (Rich.)

Crocodilopŏlis (Κροκοδείλων Πόλις). The name of several Egyptian cities, so named from the local worship of the crocodile. See Pliny, *H. N.* v. 9; and the second article ARSINOÉ.

Crocōta, dim. **Crocotŭla** (sc. *vestis*). A light, showy garment named from its saffron (*crocus*) colour. It was affected chiefly by women and by men of an effeminate character, and was probably worn between the under and upper garments.

Crocus (Κρόκος). A youth who, being unable to obtain the object of his affections, the nymph Smilax, pined away, and was changed into the crocus, or saffron. Smilax herself was metamorphosed into the smilax, or bindweed (Ovid, *Met.* iv. 283).

Croesus (Κροῖσος). The son of Alyattes, king of Lydia, and born about B.C. 590. He was the fifth and last of the Mermnadae, a family which began to reign with Gyges, who dethroned Candaules (q. v.). According to the account of Herodotus, Croesus was the son of Alyattes by a Carian mother, and had a half-brother, named Pantaleon, the offspring of an Ionian woman. An attempt was made by a private foe of Croesus to hinder his accession to the throne and to place the kingdom in the hands of Pantaleon; but the plot failed (Herod. i. 92), although Stobaeus informs us that Croesus, on coming to the throne, divided the kingdom with his brother. Plutarch states that the second wife of Alyattes, wishing to remove Croesus, gave one of the cooks in the royal household a dose of poison to put into the bread she made for Croesus. The woman informed Croesus, and gave the poisoned bread to the queen's children; and the prince, out of gratitude, consecrated at Delphi a golden image of this cook three cubits high. Croesus ascended the throne on the death of his father, B.C. 560, and immediately undertook the subjugation of the Greek communities of Asia Minor (the Aeolians, Ionians, and Dorians), whose disunited state and almost continual wars with one another rendered his task an easy one. He contented himself, however, after reducing them beneath his sway, with merely imposing an annual tribute, and left their forms of government unaltered. When this conquest was effected, he turned his thoughts to the construction of a fleet, intending to attack the islands, but was dissuaded from his purpose by Bias of Priené (Herod. i. 27). Turning his arms, upon this, against the nations of Asia Minor, he subjected all the country lying west of the river Halys, except Cilicia and Lycia; and then applied himself to the arts of peace, and to the patronage of the sciences and of literature. He became famed for his riches and munificence. Poets and philosophers were invited to his court, and, among others, Solon, the Athenian, is said to have visited his capital, Sardis. Herodotus relates the conversation which took place between the latter and Croesus on the subject of human felicity, in which the Athenian offended the Lydian monarch by the little value which he attached to riches as a means of happiness (Herod. i. 30), and by his saying that no man should be called happy until his death.

Not long after this, Croesus had the misfortune to lose his son Atys, who was accidentally killed by Adrastus (q. v.), leaving him with only a dumb child as his heir; but the deep affliction into which this loss plunged him was dispelled in some degree, after two years of mourning, by a feeling of disquiet relative to the movements of Cyrus and the increasing power of the Persians. Wishing to form an alliance with the Greeks of Europe against the danger which threatened him, a step which had been recommended by the oracle at Delphi (Herod. i. 53), he addressed himself, for this purpose, to the Lacedaemonians, at that time the most powerful of the Grecian communities; and having succeeded in his object, and made magnificent presents to the Delphic shrine, he resolved on open hostilities with the Persians. The art of the crafty priesthood who managed the machinery of the oracle at Delphi is nowhere more clearly shown than in the history of their royal dupe, the monarch of Lydia. He had lavished upon their temple the most splendid gifts—so splendid, in fact, that we should be tempted to suspect Herodotus of exaggeration if his account were not confirmed by other writers—and the recipients of this bounty, in their turn, put him off with an answer of the most studied ambiguity when he consulted their far-famed oracle on the subject of a war with the Persians. The response of Apollo was, that if Croesus made war upon this people "he would destroy a great Empire"; and the answer of Amphiaraüs (for his oracle, too, was consulted by the Lydian king) tended to the same effect (Herod. i. 53). The verse itself, containing the response of the oracle, is given by Diodorus (*Excerpt.* vii. § 28), and is as follows: Κροῖσος, Ἅλυν διαβὰς, μεγάλην ἀρχὴν καταλύσει, "Croesus, on having crossed the Halys, will destroy a great empire"—the river Halys being, as already remarked, the boundary of his dominions to the east. Croesus thought that the empire thus referred to was that of Cyrus; the issue, however, proved it to be his own.

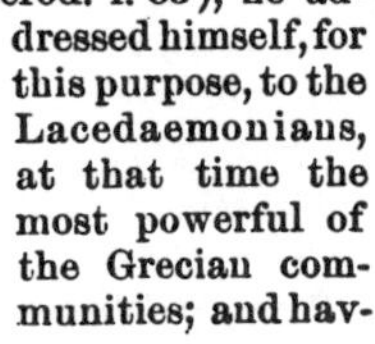

Croesus on the Pyre.

Having assembled a numerous army, the Lydian monarch crossed the Halys, invaded the territory of Cyrus, and a battle took place in the district of Pteria, but without any decisive result. Croesus, upon this, thinking his forces not sufficiently numerous, marched back to Sardis, disbanded his army, consisting entirely of mercenaries, and sent for succour to Amasis of Egypt and also to the Lacedaemonians, determining to attack the Persians again in the beginning of the next spring. But Cyrus did not allow him time to effect this. Having discovered that it was the intention of the Lydian king to break up his present army, he marched with all speed into Lydia, before a new mercenary force could be assembled, defeated Croesus (who had no force at his command but his Lydian cavalry) in the battle of Thymbra, shut him up in Sardis, and took the city itself after a siege of fourteen days and in the fourteenth year of the reign of the son of Alyattes.

With Croesus fell the Empire of the Lydians. Herodotus relates two stories connected with this event—one having reference to the dumb son of Croesus, who spoke for the first time when he saw a soldier in the act of killing his father, and, by the exclamation which he uttered, saved his parent's life, the soldier being ignorant of his rank; and the other being as follows: Croesus having been made prisoner, a pile was erected, on which he was placed in order to be burned alive. After keeping silence for a long time, the royal captive heaved a deep sigh, and with a groan thrice pronounced the name of Solon. Cyrus sent to know the reason of this exclamation, and Croesus, after considerable delay, acquainted him with the conversation between himself and Solon. The Persian king, relenting upon this, gave orders for Croesus to be released. But the flames had already begun to ascend on every side of the pile, and all human aid proved ineffectual. In this emergency Croesus prayed earnestly to Apollo, the god on whom he had lavished so many splendid offerings. That deity heard his prayer, and a sudden and heavy fall of rain extinguished the flames (Herod. i. 86 foll.). Croesus, after this, is said to have stood high in the favour of Cyrus, who profited by his advice on several important occasions; and Ctesias declares that the Persian monarch assigned him for his residence a city near Ecbatana, and that in his last moments he recommended Croesus to the care of his son and successor Cambyses; and entreated the Lydian, on the other hand, to be an adviser to his son. Croesus discharged this duty with so much fidelity as to give offence to the new monarch, who ordered him to be put to death. Happily for him, those who were charged with this order hesitated to carry it into execution; and Cambyses, soon after, having regretted his precipitation, Croesus was again brought into his presence and restored to his former favour. The rest of his history is unknown. As he was advanced in years, he could not have long survived Cambyses (Herod. iii. 36 foll.). The wealth of Croesus has passed into a proverb in all languages. See LYDIA.

Crommy̆on (Κρομμυών) or **Cromy̆on** (Κρομυών). A town in Megaris, on the Saronic Gulf, which afterwards belonged to Corinth. It is celebrated in mythology on account of its wild sow, which was slain by Theseus (q. v.).

Cronia (τὰ Κρόνια). A festival celebrated in Athens, and also at Rhodes, in honour of Cronus (q. v.). Greek writers apply the same name to the Roman Saturnalia (q. v.), which the Cronia seems to have resembled.

Cronius Mons (Κρόνιον ὄρος). A mountain in Elis near Olympia, with a temple of Cronus.

Cronus (Κρόνος). In Greek mythology, the youngest son of Uranus and Gaea, who mutilated and overthrew his father, and, with the assistance of the Titans, made himself sovereign of the world. He took his sister Rhea to wife, and became by her father of Hestia, Demeter, Heré, Hades, Poseidon, and Zeus. But his mother prophesied that one of his children would overthrow him. He accordingly swallowed them all except Zeus, whom Rhea saved by a stratagem. (See ZEUS.) Zeus, when grown up, obtained the assistance of the Ocean-nymph Thetis in making Cronus disgorge his children, and then, with the help of his kinsfolk, overpowered Cronus and the Titans. According to one version of the fable, Cronus was imprisoned in Tartarus with the Titans; according to another, he was reconciled with Zeus, and reigned with Rhadamanthus on the Islands of the Blessed. Cronus seems originally to have been a god of the harvest; whence it happens that in many parts of Greece the harvest month was called Cronion. His name being easily confused with that of Chronos (Χρόνος, "Time"), he was afterwards erroneously regarded as the god of time. In works of art he was represented as an old man, with a mantle drawn over the back of his head and holding a sickle in his hand. The Romans identified him with Saturnus, their god of sowing. See SATURNUS.

Cronus. (Pompeian Painting.)

Crophi (Κρῶφι). A mountain of Egypt, between Elephantiné and Syené. Between this mountain and another called Mophi were the sources of the Nile, according to a statement made to Herodotus by an Egyptian priest at Saïs (ii. 28).

Cropīa (Κρωπεία). An Attic deme belonging to the tribe Leontis.

Crotălum (κρόταλον). A kind of castanet or rattle used by dancers, and distinct from the *cymbalum* (q. v.) and the *sistrum* (q. v.). It was used by the Egyptians, and specimens of all these instruments have been found in the tombs or depicted on the monuments. The simplest form was a couple of shells or potsherds, pierced with holes and strung together; but brass and wood are also mentioned as materials (Eurip. *Cycl.* 204; Mart. xi. 16). Women who danced to the crotalum were called *crotalistriae* (Propert. v. 8, 39).

Crotalistria. (Spon.)

Crotōna or **Croton** (Κρότων). The modern Cotrone. A powerful city of Italy, in the Bruttiorum Ager, on the coast of the Sinus Tarentinus. Its foundation is ascribed to Myscellus, an Achaean leader, soon after Sybaris had been colonized by a party of the same nation, which was about B.C. 710. According to some traditions the origin of Crotona was much more ancient, and it is said to derive its name from the hero Croton. The residence of Pythagoras (q. v.) and his most distinguished followers in this city, together with the overthrow of Sybaris which it accomplished, and the exploits of Milo (q. v.) and of several other Crotonian victors in the Olympic Games, contributed in a high degree to raise its fame; and, in consequence, it was commonly said that the last athlete of Crotona was the first of the other Greeks. This city was also celebrated for its school of medicine, and was the birthplace of Democedes, who long enjoyed the reputation of being the first physician of Greece. About B.C. 510, Crotona sent an army of 100,000 men, commanded by the athlete Milo, against its powerful rival, Sybaris (q. v.), by which the latter city was destroyed. The removal of its rival, however, produced an enervating effect upon Crotona. As a proof of the remarkable change which took place in the warlike spirit of this people, it is said that, on their being subsequently engaged in hostilities with the Locrians, an army of 130,000 Crotoniatae were routed by 10,000 of the enemy on the banks of the Sagras. Such was, indeed, the loss they experienced in this battle that, according to Strabo, their city henceforth rapidly declined, and could no longer maintain the rank it had long held among the Italian republics. Dionysius the Elder, who was then aiming at the subversion of all the States of Magna Graecia, having surprised the citadel, gained possession of the town, which, however, he did not long retain. Crotona was finally able to assert its independence against his designs, as well as the attacks of the Bruttii; and when Pyrrhus invaded Italy it was still a considerable city. But the consequences of the war which ensued with that king proved so ruinous to its prosperity that above one half of its extent became deserted. Crotona was then occupied by the Bruttii, with the exception of the citadel, in which the chief inhabitants had taken refuge; these, being unable to defend the place against a Carthaginian force, soon after surrendered, and were allowed to withdraw to Locri. Crotona eventually fell into the hands of the Romans, in B.C. 193, and a colony was established there.

Crucifixion. See CRUX.

Crucis Inventio. See HELENA.

Crumēna (βαλάντιον or βαλλάντιον). A leathern bag slung round the neck and used as a purse. It usually hung down behind; hence we find a master walking *behind* the slave who carries the purse, so that he may keep an eye on it (Plaut. *Pseud.* i. 2, 37).

Cruppellarii (Keltic). A word used by the Gauls to designate a class of gladiators who fought in complete armour (Lamprid. *Alex. Sev.* 56). See CATAPHRACTI.

Cruquius (JACQUES DE CRUSQUE). A Flemish scholar, born at Messines, near Ypres, about the middle of the sixteenth century, and for many years professor of the classical languages at Bruges. He is best remembered by his elaborate commentary on Horace, which first appeared at Antwerp in 1578. A second and improved edition was issued in 1611. The value of this edition lies chiefly in the fact that it gives readings from four MSS., known as the Codices Blandinii, that were then preserved in the Benedictine monastery of Blankenberg (Mons Blandinius), and that were subsequently destroyed, possibly in the sack of the monastery by a mob in 1566 (Palmer). The importance of one of these MSS., known to Cruquius as *vetustissimus*, and now styled V, is very great, and the same thing is true of the marginal comments which it contained written by some unknown scholar, who is usually cited (from Cruquius) as the Commentator Cruquianus. Besides this edition of Horace, Cruquius published an edition of Cicero's *Oratio pro Milone* (Antwerp, 1582), an *Encomium Urbis Brugensis*, and some miscellaneous Latin verse. See André, *Bibliotheca Belgica*, s. v. "Cruquius"; Jordan, *De Commentatore Cruquiano* (Königsberg, 1883); and Palmer, *Satires of Horace* (Introduction), pp. xxix.–xxxi. (1883).

Crusta. A figure in low relief as distinguished from one in high relief, which was called *emblema* (Cic. *Verr.* ii. 4, 23). See CAELATURA; EMBLEMA.

Crustumerium or **Crustumium.** A town of the Sabines in the vicinity of Fidenae, and, like Fidenae, founded by a colony from Alba. Its great antiquity is attested by Vergil (*Aen.* vii. 629) and by Silius Italicus (viii. 367). From Pliny we learn that the Crustumini were vanquished by Romulus, and that a settlement was formed in their territory. Their city, however, was not finally conquered till the reign of the elder Tarquin (Liv. i. 38). The name of Crustumini Colles appears to have been given to the ridge of which the Mons Sacer formed a part. The tribe called Crustumina evidently derived its name from this ancient city (Liv. xlii. 34).

Crux (σταυρός, σκόλοψ). The cross; an instrument of capital punishment used from a very early period in the East.

The words σταυρόω and σκολοπίζω (more usually ἀνασταυρόω, ἀνασκολοπίζω) are applied to modes of execution which were certainly common among the Persians; and it is probable that impalement, as well as actual crucifixion, was thus denoted. It has been doubted whether the later or Roman method of crucifixion was practised by the Persians; but the case of Artayctes (Herod. ix. 120) seems to prove that nailing to a tree or plank was not unknown to them. It was the usual punishment of rebels—at least of those who headed revolt. Darius in the Behistun inscription boasts that he had "crucified" the leader of every rebellion that he had put down, giving their names (Rawlinson's *Herodotus*, vol. ii. Appendix); and it was inflicted on Inaros, the champion of Egyptian liberty (Thuc. i. 110). For the sake of ignominy, the bodies of those who had been otherwise executed were sometimes exposed on a cross after death, not always from humanity. Oroetes, after putting Polycrates to death in some horrible way which Herodotus refuses to describe, crucified the corpse (Herod. iii. 125). We find Xerxes thus treating the body of Leonidas, no doubt as a rebel (Herod. vii. 238); and at a later period Ptolemy Philopator does the same to Cleomenes after his suicide (Plut. *Cleom.* 38). According to a strange story in Pliny, Tarquinius Priscus adopted this form of posthumous disgrace to check the frequency of suicide among the citizens, driven to despair by the forced labour with which his gigantic building operations were carried on (*H. N.* xxxvi. § 107).

Among ancient nations, the Carthaginians were conspicuous for their cruelty, and crucifixion was horribly frequent among them; it was probably through their example that it was subsequently introduced into Sicily and Italy. It was the usual punishment of rebels, and, as is well known, was commonly inflicted on unsuccessful generals (Polyb. i. 11, 24, 79, etc.). In the war with their mercenaries and African subjects which followed immediately upon the conclusion of the First Punic War, the atrocities on both sides, ghastly enough in the narrative of Polybius, have been sensationally exaggerated in Flaubert's novel *Salammbô*.

The GREEKS were honourably distinguished in the ancient world for their aversion to torture and mutilation in every shape; indeed, it is only in quite recent times that Christian Europe has attained the same standard of refinement. In some ways they could be cruel enough, and the frequency of capital punishments showed a singular disregard of human life. The rage of faction led to massacres like that of Corcyra, on which Thucydides moralizes in a well-known passage (iii. 81 foll.). Prisoners of war were put to death in cold blood—the Plataeans by the Spartans (Thuc.

iii. 68); the Athenian prisoners after Aegospotami to the number of 3000 (Plut. *Alcib.* 37; *Lysand.* 13). The Athenians ordered a massacre of all the adult males in Mitylené, probably as many as 6000 (Thuc. iii. 36).

With all this, however, the Greeks habitually abstained from aggravating their executions, whether of criminals or prisoners of war, by insult and torture; and they especially abhorred outrages on women and children. This side of the Greek character is well brought out in Mahaffy's *Social Life in Greece;* see especially pp. 238, 262 foll., 3d ed. It was so from the earliest historical times. The tyrants of the seventh and sixth centuries are not charged with any atrocities like those of the Visconti and other mediæval despots in Italy; even the bull of Phalaris (q. v.) is now explained as an instrument of Phœnician Moloch-worship. A few isolated acts of vengeance are recorded of this period, only however in the outlying parts of the Grecian world, and therefore probably due to the contagion of barbarian example. During the struggles at Miletus between the wealthy citizens and the commonalty, the latter (who were called Γέργιθες) when victorious collected the children of the rich upon threshing-floors and had them trampled to death by oxen; the rich, having in turn gained the upper hand, burnt in pitch (κατεπίττωσαν: cf. the *tunica molesta* of Juvenal, viii. 235; Mart. x. 25) all whom they got into their power, along with their children (Heracl. Pont. *ap.* Ath. xii. 524 a). This story belongs probably to the "two generations" of civil strife at Miletus recorded by Herodotus; but no such horrors are mentioned in Greece proper, where even Helots and serfs ranked as Hellenes. Pisistratus and his sons governed according to the laws of Solon, and even the proceedings which arose out of the murder of Hipparchus fall short of the cruelties inflicted on regicides in quite recent times. There is, in fact, no evidence that crucifixion, impalement, and burning alive were regarded as Greek punishments, at least where, as in Hellas itself, there was no contact with less civilized races. It was the same with mutilations of all kinds, such as the blinding prescribed by the laws of Locri in Italy (Demosth. *c. Timocr.* p. 744, § 140) or the cutting off of hands and feet as practised by the Persians (Xen. *Anab.* i. 9, § 13). The cruelties alluded to in Aesch. *Eum.* 186–190, including impalement, are those not of Greeks, but of barbarians, and the distinction is pointedly drawn. The Greeks distinguished between reverence for the human body, for which they had a passionate admiration as shown in their athletic exercises and their works of art, and reverence for human life, which they held cheap enough. This feeling continued unimpaired as long as Greece retained her freedom.

In the Macedonian period Greece no longer enjoyed this happy immunity; as a mere province in a larger Hellenism, it was influenced by lower and less humane races. Alexander himself is not free from the stain of cruelty, as is shown by his treatment of real or supposed conspiracies against his person in the cases of Philotas and Hermolaüs. He is said to have either hanged or crucified 2000 Tyrians; he certainly crucified Musicanus, the Indian rajah who had rebelled after being reinstated in his dominions (Arrian, *Anab.* vi. 17). His successors improved upon his example: a year after his death Perdiccas and Eumenes crucified the aged Ariarathes of Cappadocia after other tortures (Diod. xviii. 16); Lysimachus threatened to crucify the Cyrenaic philosopher Theodorus, though an ambassador, but did not carry out his threat (Cic. *Tusc.* i. 43, § 102). Nicocreon of Cyprus, contemporary with Alexander, actually pounded the philosopher Anaxarchus to death in a mortar (Cic. *Tusc.* ii. 22, § 52). A similar story is told of an older philosopher, Zeno the Eleatic, and a tyrant of his native city (Cic. l. c.); but the accounts are contradictory. Nabis, the tyrant of Sparta, used as an engine of torture a figure studded with nails resembling the *Eiserne Jungfrau* of some German cities (Polyb. xiii. 7). It is not necessary to pursue the records of this period any further. The general aversion of the Greeks to degrading punishments was not understood by grammarians who lived under the law of the later Roman Empire, nor by scholars like Lipsius (*De Cruce*, 1592), in whose time even worse horrors were perpetrated.

The ROMANS were naturally a hard-hearted people, and Livy shows considerable audacity in saying that the dismembering of Mettius Fufetius was the only example in their history of a disregard of the laws of humanity; adding that they might boast that no nation had employed milder punishments (i. 28). From the language of Cicero (*Pro Rab. Perd.* 4, § 13) it has been inferred that crucifixion was in use in the regal period. But the words of the old law point rather to simple hanging (*infelici arbori reste suspendito*, Liv. i. 26), though the cross was no doubt called *arbor infelix* in later times. Cicero, who is arguing against the revival of the obsolete law of *perduellio* and the capital punishment of citizens in any shape, is speaking rhetorically throughout: he quotes the formula without the word *reste*, a misleading and doubtless intentional omission, and talks vaguely of the cross (§§ 10, 11, 16) and of the detested Tarquin (§ 13). No historical conclusions can be drawn from a speech so obviously designed to confuse the questions at issue. It is highly probable that the Romans derived this punishment from the Carthaginians; at least no mention of it appears to occur before the Second Punic War. First we find Hannibal crucifying a guide who had misled him (Liv. xxii. 13); then the Romans practise it on slaves and deserters (Liv. xxii. 33; xxx. 43, § 13; xxxiii. 36). This last passage describes a revolt among the slaves in Etruria, B.C. 196; the ringleaders are scourged and crucified, the rest given up to their masters to be dealt with at discretion. The enormous increase in the numbers of slaves under the later Republic heightened the dread of a rising among them, and the Roman system became more and more one of undisguised terrorism. Two desperate rebellions broke out in Sicily, and were only put down by regular armies—the first in B.C. 134–133, the second lasting four years, 102–99. After the pacification

Arbor Infelix. (Daremb. and Saglio.)

by the praetor M'. Aquillius in B.C. 99, a regulation was made, and strictly enforced by successive governors of the island, that no slave should be allowed to carry a weapon. A few years later, the praetor L. Domitius received a boar of remarkable size as a present; he inquired who had killed it, and finding that it was a slave employed as a shepherd, he summoned the man before him and asked him how he had contrived to destroy it. The shepherd, who expected a reward, replied that he had killed it with a boar-spear (*venabulo*); upon which Domitius at once ordered him to be crucified. Cicero tells this story with only faint disapproval, while he dwells complacently on the fact that there were no more revolts of the slaves in Sicily (Cic. *in Verr.* v. 3, 4, §§ 7, 8). When the servile war of Spartacus was at last put down by Crassus, the prisoners, to the number of 6000, were crucified all along the Appian Way, between Capua and Rome (App. *B. C.* i. 120). The power of masters over their slaves was at this period, and for some time later, absolute; even the good-natured Horace treats as a joke the possibility of their being crucified for slight offences (*Sat.* i. 3, 80 foll.). The first measure passed in their favour was the Lex Petronia (q. v.); Hadrian forbade them to be executed without the sentence of a magistrate; Antoninus Pius ordered that the murder of a slave by his master should be punished as homicide. Besides slaves, the provincials were liable to crucifixion for the greater crimes, such as murder, piracy (Suet. *Iul.* 4), brigandage, and especially for revolts and conspiracies. The obstinacy of the Jews was particularly exasperating to the Romans, and their repeated rebellions were followed by the wholesale infliction of this punishment; thus Varus (the same who perished in Germany) crucified 2000 at once (Joseph. *Ant.* xvii. 10, § 10); Gessius Florus several hundreds, including Roman citizens of Jewish birth (id. *B. I.* ii. 14, § 9); Titus so many that "room was wanting for the crosses, and crosses for the bodies" (id. ib. vi. 28); and Hadrian, after the final revolt, 500 a day for some time. Under the Empire the right of the *civis Romanus* was no longer respected; the first instance, probably, of the crucifixion of a citizen in Rome itself is that, under Galba, of a guardian who poisoned his ward (Suet. *Galb.* 9). Afterwards the odious distinction between the *honestiores* and *humiliores* was introduced, and this and other tortures were freely inflicted upon the latter, especially for *maiestas* or crimes against the State or the person of the emperor (Paul. *Sent.* v. 23, 1; *Dig.* 48, 19, tit. *de poenis*).

The mode of punishment is too well known to need much description. Scourging, as with Roman capital punishments in general, usually preceded it. Three kinds of crosses were in common use: the *crux commissa*, or T shape; the *crux immissa*, with a projection at the top, to which was affixed the *titulus*, setting forth the crime of the sufferer (this was the most common); and the *crux decussata*, in the shape of an X (St. Andrew's cross). The word *crux* is also applied to the single stake used in impalement; the latter process is alluded to by Seneca in two passages, but, as he is speaking of death by torture in general, it may be doubted, in the absence of direct evidence, whether this was a Roman custom (*Cons. ad Marciam*, 20, § 3, where crucifixion with the head downward is mentioned). The upright post is called *stipes*, the transverse beam *patibulum*; and it was this, rather than the entire instrument, which the criminal carried to the place of execution (Plaut. *Mostell.* i. 1, 53, and *ap.* Non. s. v. *patibulum*). It was impossible that the whole weight of the body should rest upon the nails; hence there was a piece of wood projecting from the *stipes* on which the sufferer sat, or rather rode (Tertull. *adv. Nat.* i. 12; cf. Iren. *adv. Haer.* i. 12). The expression *acuta si sedeam cruce*, in the famous lines of Maecenas *ap.* Sen. *Ep.* 101, probably refers to this support, and not, as Lipsius thought, to impalement. When it was wanting, the body was probably sustained by ropes; the combination of ropes with nails is mentioned by Pliny as charms (*H. N.* xxviii. § 46). See ECULEUS.

Patibulum. (Daremberg and Saglio.)

The martyrologies contain accounts of sufferers bound to the cross without the use of nails, and left to die of hunger and exhaustion; when it is added that in some instances they survived nine days, we must be allowed to disbelieve. The criminal was stripped of his clothes—the cloth around the loins, as to which the Christian tradition is constant, seems to have been exceptional—and usually hoisted on to the cross after it had been set up. Sometimes he was stretched upon it on the ground, and then lifted with it; but the former method was the commoner, and hence the phrases *cruci suffigere, in crucem agere* or *tollere*, occur oftener than *cruci affigere*. The well-known breaking of the legs to hasten death is alluded to by Plautus (*Poen.* iv. 2, 64) and Cicero (*Phil.* xiii. 12, § 27). The dead body was generally left hanging on the cross, to be devoured by birds and beasts; the feet were but little raised above the ground (not as in most pictures), and it was not out of the reach of the latter (Hor. *Ep.* i. 16, 48; Juv. xiv. 77). Sepulture was therefore forbidden, and a soldier set to watch the corpse (Petron. 111, 112). The place for these executions was always outside the walls of cities; at Rome it was the Campus Esquilinus, to the east of the city, part of which was afterwards occupied by the gardens of Maecenas.

With the establishment of Christianity the associations connected with the Cross led to its abolition, though not from humanity, as other cruel punishments were retained. Constantine at the beginning of his reign had sanctioned it in the case of slaves and freedmen, but later he abolished it.

See the article "Kreuz" in Kraus, *Realencyclopädie d. Christlichen Alterthums* (1886), where a list of the various forms of the cross is given; also Mortillet, *Le Signe de la Croix avant le Christianisme* (1866); Fulda, *Das Kreuz und die Kreuzigung* (Breslau, 1878); and Huschke, *Die Multa* (Leipzig, 1882).

Crypta (κρύπτη). Any long, narrow vault, either dark or dimly lighted. It is used in three specific senses: (1) A tunnel for draining purposes. (2) A dark vaulted passage in any building, as under the *cavea* in the amphitheatre or behind the *scena* of a theatre. (3) A covered corridor above ground, dimly lighted in summer for the sake of coolness, and very commonly attached to the sides of an open colonnade (*porticus*). This was probably the species of crypta known as *cryptoporticus*. See PORTICUS.

Cryptīa (κρυπτεία, κρυπτία, or κρυπτή). A system of secret police adopted by the Spartans in order to maintain their control over the Helots; perhaps, as Grote thinks, over the Perioeci also. As to the main features of this system there is no doubt. We learn that a number of active young Spartans were despatched every year by the Ephors, immediately upon their entry into office, to the different parts of the country. They were to post themselves as secretly as possible in convenient places from which to explore the neighbourhood and to make observations. If they found anything suspicious, they were either to report it or to suppress it themselves on the spot (Schömann, *Antiq.* i. 195, Eng. trans.). The institution served not merely to break up organization and to check the possibility of an outbreak among their oppressed subjects, but as a useful military training in habits of endurance suited to a dominant race. On the latter ground it is proposed by Plato for his ideal Cretan colony in the *Laws*, and his way of expressing himself shows that he is referring to a Spartan custom really existing (i. 633 B; vi. 763 B; cf. Grote, ii. 144 n.). The *cryptia* may thus be considered as to a certain extent a species of armed police force, and the young men who were ordered to undertake it appear also to have formed a special corps in the army; at least we read of a commander of the *cryptia* in the battle of Sellasia (Plut. *Cleom.* 28). To these undoubted facts later authors added some curious statements, which have been much criticised in recent times. According to Plutarch, who quotes Aristotle as his authority, the Ephors every year declared war formally against the Helots, in order that they might be killed without scruple; and they further, not every year as sometimes stated, but at intervals (διὰ χρόνου), sent young Spartans armed with daggers to assassinate such of the Helots as were thought formidable (Plut. *Lycurg.* 28). The language of Plutarch is somewhat loose. In one sentence he states that the young men went out into the roads by night and slew all whom they caught (τοὺς ἁλισκομένους), implying that the Helots lived under a sort of "curfew" law, which confined them to their houses at night to prevent conspiracies; in the next sentence that they often ranged over the fields, and despatched the strongest and bravest of them. The latter phrase, however, agrees with the account of Heraclides Ponticus that they killed ὅσους ἂν ἐπιτήδειον ᾖ (*Fragm.* ii. 4 *ap.* C. Müller, ii. 210). Otfried Müller, whose criticism habitually tends to soften the harsher features of the Spartan institutions, combats the notion that the Helots were annually hunted down and destroyed (*Dorians*, iii. 3, § 4); and Schömann calls it "an exaggeration which is really too absurd to deserve serious confutation" (*Antiq.* l. c.). Grote, no friend to Sparta, rejects the annual or periodical massacre of the Helots and the formal declaration of war against them, which, he justly observes, "would provoke the reaction of despair rather than enforce tranquillity"; and even suggests a doubt as to the fact of Aristotle's having really made the statement ascribed to him by Plutarch, on the ground that he does not mention the subject in his *Politics*, where he speaks at some length both of the Spartan constitution and of the Helots. See HELOTAE.

Cryptoportĭcus. See CRYPTA.

Ctesias (Κτησίας). A Greek historian, born in Cnidus in Caria, and a contemporary of Xenophon. He belonged to the family of the Asclepiadae at Cnidus. In B.C. 416, he went to the Persian court, and became private physician to King Artaxerxes Mnemon. In this capacity he accompanied the king on his expedition against his brother Cyrus, and cured him of the wound which he received in the battle of Cunaxa, B.C. 401. In 399, he returned to his native city, and worked up the valuable material which he had collected during his residence in Persia, partly from his own observation and partly from his study of the royal archives, into a History of Persia (Περσικά), in twenty-three books. The work was written in the Ionic dialect. The first six books treated the history of Assyria, the remaining ones that of Persia from the earliest times to events within his own experience. Ctesias's work was much used by the ancient historians, though he was censured as untrustworthy and indifferent to truth—a charge which may be due to the fact that he followed Persian authorities, and thus often differed, to the disadvantage of the Greeks, from the version of facts current among his countrymen. Only fragments and extracts of the book survive, and part of an abridgment in Photius (*Cod.* 72). The same is true of his Ἰνδικά, or notices of the researches which he had made in Persia on the geography and productions of India. See Blum, *Herodot und Ctesias* (Heidelberg, 1836); and Gilmore, *The Fragments of the Persica of Ctesias* (1888).

Ctesibĭca Machĭna. An hydraulic engine named after its inventor, Ctesibius (q. v.) of Alexandria. In the language of modern hydraulics it is a double-action forcing pump. Vitruvius, in his description (x. 10 [7]), speaks of it as designed to raise water, while Ctesibius's pupil, Hero (*Pneumat.* p. 180), describes, under the name of σίφων, a machine identical in principle, but of improved construction, and says that it was used as a fire-engine (εἰς τοὺς ἐμπρησμούς). Indeed, the same principle has been employed in modern fire-engines. The remains of such a σίφων were discovered at Castrum Novum, near Civitȧ Vecchia, in 1795, having probably served to supply the public baths with water.

The following cut illustrates the construction of Ctesibius's invention as described by Vitruvius. Two cylinders (*modioli*), B B, are connected by pipes with a receiver (*catinus*), A, which is closed by a cowl (*paenula*), D. In each cylinder a piston (*embolus masculus*), C, is worked by means of its rod (*regula*). In the bottom of each cylinder, and at the opening of each pipe into the receiver, is a movable lid or valve (*assis*), which only opens upwards. The bottoms of the cylinders are inserted into a reservoir, or connected with it by pipes. When one of the pistons is raised, a vacuum is produced in the cylinder, and the atmospheric pressure forces a stream

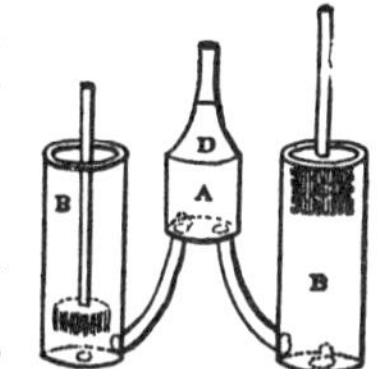

Ctesibica Machina. (Rich.)

of water past the raised valve into the cylinder. When this stream ceases, the valve falls; and if the piston is forced down, the water is driven out of the cylinder into the pipe, and past the valve into the receiver, and retained there by the closing of the valve. If the two pistons are worked alternately, so that one descends as the other rises, a continuous stream of water is forced out of the top of the *paenula.*

Ctesibĭus (Κτησίβιος). A native of Ascra and contemporary of Archimedes, who flourished during the reigns of Ptolemy II. and Ptolemy III., or between B.C. 260 and 240. He was the son of a barber, and for some time exercised at Alexandria the calling of his parent. His mechanical genius, however, soon caused him to emerge from obscurity, and he became known as the inventor of several very ingenious contrivances for raising water, etc. The invention of *clepsydrae,* or water clocks, is also ascribed to him. (Cf. Vitruvius, ix. 9.) He wrote a book on hydraulic machines, which is now lost. See CLEPSYDRA; CTESIBICA MACHINA; HOROLOGIUM.

Ctesĭphon (Κτησιφῶν). (1) A city of Assyria on the east bank of the Tigris, three Roman miles from Seleucia on the west bank. It first became an important place under the Parthians, whose kings used it for some time as a winter residence. (2) See AESCHINES; DEMOSTHENES.

Cuba, Cunīna, and **Rumīna.** Three Roman divinities worshipped as the protectors of children in the cradle (*cunae*). Libations of milk were made in their honour. See August. *De Civ. Dei,* iv. 10; Lactant. i. 20, 36.

Cubicularii. Slaves who had charge of the sleeping and dwelling rooms. They were commonly divided into watches (*stationes*) for day and night, and also into decuries (Orelli, 4663; Suet. *Domit.* 17). Under the later emperors the cubicularii of the palace were called *praepositi sacro cubiculo,* and were persons of high rank.

Cubicŭlum usually means a sleeping and dwelling room in a Roman house, but is also applied to the pavilion or box in which the Roman emperors were accustomed to witness the public games (Suet. *Ner.* 12; Plin. *Paneg.* 51). See CIRCUS.

Cubĭtus (πῆχυς). A measure of length used by the Greeks, Romans, and other nations, was originally the length of the human arm from the elbow to the wrist, or to the tip of the middle finger; the latter was its signification among the Greeks and Romans. It was equal to a foot and a half; and therefore the Roman cubit was a little less, and the Greek cubit a little more, than a foot and a half English—the respective lengths of the foot being, in millimetres, Greek 308.3, English 304.7, Roman 295.7. The Greek cubit was, millimetres 462.4, the Roman 443.6. The cubit was divided by the Greeks into 2 spans (σπιθαμαί), 6 handbreadths (παλαισταί), and 24 finger-breadths (δάκτυλοι); and by the Romans into $1\frac{1}{2}$ feet, 6 breadths (*palmi*), and 24 thumb-breadths (*pollices*). See Hultsch, *Metrol.* pp. 29, 62, and tables.

Cubus (κύβος). A die, cube. (See TESSERA.) A cubic foot of water was the *amphora* or *quadrantal,* the principal liquid measure. See QUADRANTAL.

Cucullus. (1) A funnel-shaped roll of paper used by the Roman shop-keepers to wrap powders, drugs, etc.—the English "screw" (Mart. iii. 2). Hence (2) a cowl, intended to be used in the open air, and to be drawn over the head to protect it from the injuries of the weather, instead of a hat or cap. It was worn by travellers, shepherds, husbandmen, and hunters; and by soldiers on service in cold climates, as is seen on Trajan's Column; and also in city life, even by persons of distinction who wished to go abroad without being recognized (Juv. vi. 330). The cowl was sometimes a separate garment (Mart. xiv. 132). Occasionally it formed part of the *lacerna* or *paenula* or other cloak, which was then said to be *cucullatus* (Isid. *Orig.* xix. 24, 17). This is shown in the figure annexed, from a relief representing a traveller leaving his inn (*Bullet. Napol.* 1848, 1). In either case the hood might be worn over the head or thrown back on the shoulder. The use of the cowl and also of the cape, which served the same purpose, was allowed to slaves by a law in the Codex Theodosianus. Cowls were imported into Italy from Saintonge in France (*Santonico cucullo,* Juv. viii. 145), and from the country of the Bardaei in Illyria. Those from the latter locality were probably of a peculiar fashion, which gave origin to the term *bardocucullus.*

Cucullus. (Figure from Aesernia.)

Cudo or **Cudon.** A helmet of very simple form, fitting close like a skull-cap, made of leather or the skins of wild animals (Sil. Ital. viii. 493). It is probably to be identified with the Homeric καταῖτυξ or helmet of Diomedes (*Il.* x. 258), described as ἄφαλον, "without knobs or projections," and ἄλοφον, "without plume or horse-hair crest"; known also by Greek representations of that hero, from one of which in bronze the annexed example is taken.

Cudo. (Rich.)

Cuirass. See LORICA; THORAX.

Cujacius (JACQUES DE CUJAS). A distinguished expounder of the Roman law. He was born at Toulouse in 1522, the son of a tanner, and after being educated in the law, lectured at Cahors in 1554, becoming in the following year professor in the University of Bourges. From this seat of learning he was called to Valence in 1557, returning to Bourges in 1576. He died October 4th, 1590. Cujacius won a remarkable reputation by his study of the MSS. of the Roman juristic writings, and by his brilliant emendations that served to remove much of the obscurity that had enveloped the nicer questions of Roman law. These emendations were published in part in the work entitled *Observationum et Emendationum Libri XVIII*—a treatise that contemporary writers styled *opus incomparabile.* He also published editions of the Institutes, Pandects, etc., of Justinian, a part of the Theodosian Code, a Greek version of the Justinian laws, besides commentaries on the *Consuetudines Feudorum,* and on several books of the Decretals. His *Observationes* included a wide range of classical reading and criticism, so that he is frequently cited by philologists and students of the ancient literatures as well as by jurists.

The first complete collection of the writings of Cujacius was the edition of Fabrot, 10 vols. (Paris, 1658), reprinted at Naples (1757); and at Venice and Modena in 11 vols. (1758–82). See Spangenberg, *Cujacius und seine Zeitgenossen* (Leipzig, 1822).

Culcĭta. See LECTUS.

Culex. "The Gnat." A poem often ascribed to Vergil, who is, in fact, known to have composed in his youth a poem with that title (Stat. *Silvae*, ii. 7, 73; Suet. *Vit. Lucani.* p. 50, Reiff.). The internal evidence is, however, against the view that the one now extant is the original, though some scholars (as Heyne and Hildebrandt) have supposed it to be the same with later interpolations. The *Culex* is a short epic of 414 hexameter lines, whose subject may be considered as partly pastoral and partly mock-heroic. A goatherd leads out his flocks to feed upon the pastures near Mount Cithaeron. Having fallen asleep, he is suddenly roused from his slumbers by the bite of a gnat; and, while awakening, he crushes to death the insect which had inflicted the wound. He then perceives a huge serpent approaching, which, if his sleep had not been broken, would inevitably have destroyed him. The shade of the gnat appears to the goatherd on the following night, and reproaches him with having occasioned its death at the moment when it had saved his life. The insect describes all that it had seen in the infernal regions during its wanderings, having as yet obtained no fixed habitation. Next day the goatherd prepares a tomb, in order to procure repose for the ghost of his benefactor, and celebrates in due form its obsequies. See Birt, *Hist. Hexam. Lat.* (Bonn, 1876); R. Ellis, in the *Jour. of Philology*, vol. xvi. p. 153; and Hildebrandt, *Studien auf d. Geb. d. röm. Poesie und Metrik* (Leipzig, 1887). The text is included in Ribbeck's edition of the works of Vergil, and edited by Leo (Berlin, 1891).

Culīna (ὀπτάνιον). A kitchen. The illustration represents a kitchen stove in the house of Pansa at Pompeii, with some cooking utensils upon it, as discovered when first excavated—viz., a strainer (*colum*), a kitchen knife (*culter coquinaris*), and an implement for dressing eggs (supposed *apalare*). See DOMUS, p. 546.

Kitchen Stove. (House of Pansa, Pompeii.)

Culpa. See article in the Appendix.

Culter, dim. CULTELLUS (μάχαιρα, κοπίς, σφαγίς). A knife with only one edge, which formed a straight line, the blade being pointed and its back curved. It was used chiefly for killing animals, either in hunting, in the slaughter-house, or at the altar. The *minister*, or attendant on the priest, is called *cultrarius*, since he and not the priest did the actual killing. The accompanying illustration is taken from Gruter (*Inscript.* vol. ii. p. 640, no. 11). The name *culter* was also applied to razors, pruning-knives, and kitchen knives. That in these cases the *culter* was different from those above represented, and most probably smaller, is certain; since, whenever it was

Cultri. (From Tombstone of a Cultrarius.)

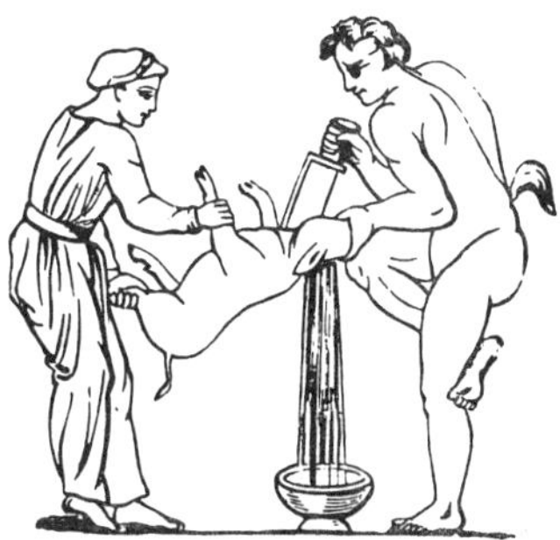
Cultrarius. (Bas-relief from Pompeii.)

Kitchen Utensils from Pompeii. (Overbeck.)

used for shaving or domestic purposes, it was always distinguished from the common culter by some epithet, as *culter tonsorius*, *culter coquinaris*.

Cultrarius. See CULTER.

Culullus. A *calix* or cup of earthenware used by the *pontifices* for sacrificial purposes.

Cumae. See article in the Appendix.

Cunae, Cunabŭla (λίκνον, σκάφη). A cradle. It has been thought that cradles were little used by the Greeks, at least in early times; since Plato, in a passage on the putting of infants to sleep, mentions only singing the lullaby and rocking in the arms (*Leg.* vii. 790 D). But various substitutes are mentioned.

Cradle. (Museum at Beaune.)

Heracles, according to tradition, was cradled in his father's shield (Theocr. xxiv. 4); Dionysus in a winnowing-fan (λίκνον, *vannus*), which accordingly was borne in his processions; other deities in the same manner. The ark or cradle in which children were exposed is *alveus*, σκάφη; but it is only in quite late authors that we find σκάφην διασείειν, "to rock the cradle" (Ael. *H. A.* xi. 14).

In the Roman period cradles were regularly used (Plaut. *Truc.* v. 13 and elsewhere), and were made to rock. We find a female slave called *cunaria* (Grut. *Inscript.* 311, 7); and a male slave, who perhaps in time became the child's *paedagogus* (*cunarum motor*, Mart. xi. 39, 1).

Cunaxa (Κούναξα). A small town in Babylonia, on the Euphrates, famous for the battle fought here between the younger Cyrus and his brother Artaxerxes Mnemon, in which the former was killed (B.C. 401). See ANABASIS; ARTAXERXES; CYRUS; XENOPHON.

Cunctātor. "The delayer." A nickname given to Q. Fabius Maximus (q. v.) because of his policy of delay in the Second Punic War.

Cuneiform. A name given to the form of writing whose characters resemble a wedge (*cuneus*). The French equivalent is *tête-à-clou*; the German, *keilformig*; and in English, the terms "cuneatic" and "arrow-headed" are sometimes used as synonyms. This species of writing was employed by the ancient Akkadians, Babylonians, Assyrians, Armenians, Elamites, and Persians, who have left us specimens of it upon clay, stone, metal, and glass, either moulded (as in the clay) or cut and chiselled (as upon the other substances). The use of the cuneiform characters dates from a period not later than B.C. 3800, and was continued until a century or so after the beginning of the Christian era. The oldest specimen now known to exist is an inscription upon a bit of porphyry assigned to the time of Sargon of Agadé. The latest example is preserved at Munich, and is as late as A.D. 80.

It is only in the present century that scholars have been able to decipher the cuneatic characters, and to interpret satisfactorily the inscriptions that contain them. It was, in fact, many years before any one conceived the notion that the curious arrow-headed marks on the vast ruins of Persepolis and other parts of Persia had anything to do with language at all. It was in 1618 that an inkling of the truth first entered the mind of Garcia de Silva Figuëroa, an ambassador of Philip III. of Spain. In that year he visited Persepolis, and, becoming imbued with a belief that the arrow-heads were some form of writing, had a portion of one inscription copied. This he carried back to Europe, where it attracted the attention of other savants. In 1674, the French traveller Chardin, after visiting Persepolis, published copies of three sets of inscriptions, with an account of the curious characters as observed by him, pronouncing them to be writing and not hieroglyphs, but expressing his conviction that no one would ever be able to decipher them. More than a century later (in 1782), a French botanist named Michaux sent to Paris a stone which he had found at Bagdad covered with cuneiforms. By this time the curiosity of the learned had become awakened, and the mystery surrounding these inscriptions excited the interest of the ablest scholars of Europe, who gradually accumulated a large number of specimens of the cuneiform, as other travellers brought back from the East valuable materials for study. It was long, however, before anything beyond mere conjecture was attained; and many varied and conflicting theories were put forward. The characters were said to be only fanciful designs of the Oriental architects and devoid of meaning. Again, they were explained (by Witte of Rostock) as due to the work of many generations of worms. Others explained them as the writing of the Guebres. Still others viewed them as charms, cabalistic signs, or astrological formulæ. Lichtenstein thought that he had found in them certain passages from the Korân written in Kufic. Kaempfer hesitated whether to explain them as Chinese or as modifications of the Hebrew. Other scholars pronounced them Runes, Oghams, Old Greek, or Samaritan.

The first light on this apparently insoluble problem was due to the acute researches of Karsten Niebuhr, who, without professing to read or interpret the inscriptions, proved the existence in them of three distinct varieties of cuneiform alphabet, instead of the single one that had been assumed before his time. The threefold inscriptions at Persepolis he then rightly explained as transcriptions of the same matter in the three alphabets. This brilliant discovery was developed by Tychsen of Rostock (1798) and Münter of Copenhagen (1800), whose labours cleared the way for the magnificent success of Georg Friedrich Grotefend (q. v.), who, on September 7th, 1802, presented to the Academy of Göttingen the first cuneiform alphabet with its phonetic equivalents. It may be observed that this date and meeting are doubly important in the history of language-study, for then was also presented the first reading of the Egyptian hieroglyphs by Heyne. Twenty years later, St. Martin demonstrated a part of the flexional system; and Burnouf, Lassen, Westergaard, Beer, Jacques, and finally Sir Henry Rawlinson followed, each with his contributions towards a more perfect understanding of the characters and of the language which they embodied. Rawlinson, it may be remarked, was the first to read and publish the 1000 or more lines of the great Behistun inscription. (See the *Journal of the Asiatic Society* for 1846.)

Inscriptions in the Persian cuneiform are usually in three parallel columns, being the same text translated into three languages and alphabets: Persian, Median (also called Scythic and New Susian), and Babylonian—these being the three great peoples under the dominion of the Achae-

Black Obelisk with Cuneiform Inscriptions. (British Museum.)

menian kings, who thus promulgated their decrees in three languages.

(1) Babylonian. This is the most ancient and most important of the three varieties of cuneiform. With it are inscribed tablets and cylinders, giving a vast amount of information on history, archæology, law, government, and mythology.

(2) Scythic. The Scythic cuneiform is never found alone (with one exception), and represents an alphabet of some 100 characters. The language which they embody is an Ugro-Finnic dialect, of which little as yet is known.

(3) Persian. The Persian cuneiform, which always stands first in the trilingual inscriptions, is the most recent of the three, and consists of some 44 characters. It is characterized by an oblique stroke which divides its words, and the wedges of which it is composed never cross one another. The language of the Persian cuneiform is cognate with the Avestan, and is the parent tongue of the modern Persian. This character was used in the period from B.C. 570–370. In it is written the great inscription of Darius Hystaspis at Behistun, containing a genealogical record, a description of the extent of his dominions, a list of the great events of his reign, with prayers to Ormuzd and the spirits. Most of these inscriptions have been found at Persepolis (q. v.), Behistun, Naksh-i-Rustam, and Hamadan.

Persian.

Scythic or New Susian.

Babylonian.

The Name Darius (Dâryavas) in Cuneiform Characters.

The cuneiform characters were originally pictures of the objects which they stood for (ideographs), like the Egyptian hieroglyphics and the earlier characters in Chinese; but as time went on the forms were modified and simplified so as to lose their pictorial character, though a few still suggest the primitive design.

At first they were drawn in outline on a vegetable substance (*likhusi*), but a little later on clay, to the difficulties of which are due the first modification in the original shapes of the letters. The subsequent use of stone and metal carried this modification still further. An archaic revival, however, set in during the age of Assur-bani-pal, when it became customary to use once more the most ancient characters. The signs, originally ideographic, became subsequently phonetic, denoting each a syllable. The cuneiform syllabary contains in all some 2000 signs—ideographic, syllabic, or purely phonetic—being sometimes used in one way and sometimes in another.

The characters were inscribed upon stone, glass, and metal with a chisel; and upon clay with a sharp-pointed stylus having three unequal faces—the largest for the outer and thickest wedges of the letters, the medium-sized for the medium strokes, and the smallest for the finer lines. The Babylonian clay tablets or "bricks" are in size from one inch upward, pillow-shaped, and covered with characters often so minute as to be difficult to read without a magnifying glass. (See illustration on page 179.) After the inscriptions had been made, the tablet was dried in the sun and then enclosed in a case on which the inscription was duplicated. These are styled "case-tablets." Tablets were also used by the Assyrians, especially by the literary classes; but the records of this people were very often carved upon the stone panels of their palaces and on colossal human-headed bulls. Cuneiforms have been found, likewise, on amethyst, jasper, and onyx.

Archaic Cuneiform Character for "Fish."

BIBLIOGRAPHY.—The bibliography of the subject is very extensive. The following standard works are selected out of a great number: Lassen and Westergaard, *Ueber die Keilinschriften* (1845); Hincks, *On the First and Second Kinds of Persepolitan Writing*, in the *Trans. of the Royal Iranian Society* (1846); Rawlinson, *Commentary on the Cuneiform Inscriptions of Babylon and Assyria* (1850); Grotefend, *Die Keilinschriften aus Behistun* (1854); Ménant, *Inscriptions Assyriennes* (1859); id. *Les Écritures Cunéiformes* (1864); Oppert, *La Grande Inscription de Khorsabad* (1866); De Gobineau, *Traité des Écritures Cunéiformes* (1864); Spiegel, *Die Altpersischen Keilinschriften* (2d ed. 1881); Ewald, *Geschichtliche Folge der semitischen Sprachen* (1871); Schrader, *Die Assyrisch-Babylonischen Keilinschriften* (1872); G. Smith, *Phonetic Values of Cuneiform Characters* (1871); Sayce, *Assyrian Grammar* (1872); Norris, *Assyrian Dictionary* (1871); Botta, *Mémoire sur l'Ecriture Cunéiforme Assyrienne* (1848); Oppert, *Les Inscriptions Assyriennes* (1862); Manant, *Recueil d'Alphabets* (1860); Delattre, *Les Inscriptions Historiques de Ninive et de Babylone* (1879); Taylor, *The Alphabet* (1883); Amiaud and Scheil, *Les Inscriptions de Salmanasar II.* (1890); Brunnon, *Classified List of Compound Cuneiform Ideographs* (1889); Bezold, *The Tell-el-Amarna Tables* (with autotype facsimiles) (1892); and the *Assyriologische Bibliothek*, edited by Delitzsch and Paul Haupt.

Cuneus (*σφήν*). A wedge. For its metaphorical uses, see EXERCITUS; THEATRUM.

Cunicŭlus (*ὑπόνομος, ὑπόρυγμα*). A mine or subterranean passage, so called from its resemblance to the burrowing of a rabbit.

The word is applied to natural passages underground; to sulphur mines; to the flues of furnaces; to sewers; and to the underground channels of aqueducts. But it is most commonly used as a military technical term, denoting either the "mines" of besiegers or the "countermines" of defenders. The earliest military writer, Aeneas Tacticus, gives full details as to the art of mining, including that of countermines; and most of the later writers have copied or abridged his account. Among the curious particulars given by him are the introduction of wasps, bees, and smoke into the mine, and the sounding for mines by laying the ear to the ground with a bronze shield between (*Poliorc.* 37). Another remarkable stratagem in countermining is described by Livy (xxxviii. 7) at the siege of Ambracia by the Romans, when the Ambraciots introduced into the besiegers' mine a "stink-pot" of burning feathers.

Cup. See CALATHUS; CALIX; CARCHESIUM; CULULLUS; CYATHUS; CYMBIUM; PATERA; PHIALA; POCULUM; SCAPHIUM; SCYPHUS.

Cupa. (1) A wooden cask, butt, or barrel, used like the largest earthen vessel, the *dolium*, to receive the fresh must from the wine-press (*torcular*) and to contain it during the process of fermentation. The cupa was always of wood; the *dolium*, like the *amphora*, always of earthenware. Hence of the derivatives, Fr. *cuve, cuvier*, Eng. *cooper*, follow the original meaning; while in It. *coppa*, Fr. *coupe*, Eng. *cup*, it is modified. The inferior wines were drawn for drinking from the cupa, without being bottled in *amphorae;* whence *vinum de cupa* is equivalent to our expression "from the wood." (2) Part of an olive-press. See TRAPETUM.

Cupēdo or **Cuppēdo.** A dainty, tid-bit, or delicacy of any kind. The Roman dealers in choice food were called *cupedinarii* and had their stalls in the Forum Cupedinis (Varr. *L. L.* v. 146).

Cupīdo. The god of love. See EROS.

Cura. The personification of care. See Hyginus, *Fab.* 220.

Cura, Curatēla, Curatio. See CURATOR; CURATORES.

Curātor. Curators were persons appointed either by law or by the magistrate to look after the property of certain classes of people, and to prevent its being squandered, because they were unfit or unable to properly take charge of it themselves. Those classes are mainly four: minors or *adulescentes* (i. e. persons who were *sui iuris* and between the age of puberty—twelve or fourteen [Gaius, i. 196; *Inst.* i. 22, pr.]—and twenty-five years); lunatics; interdicted prodigals; and a miscellaneous class, the *cura* of which was considerably later in origin.

The *cura* of minors is to be attributed to the fact that when a young person who was *sui iuris* reached puberty, and escaped from the supervision of his guardian (see TUTELA), he was regarded as having attained his full stature, intellectual no less than physical; he might marry and become a paterfamilias; he was liable to military service, entitled to vote in the comitia, and competent to hold public office; and he had the complete management of his own affairs. But it was felt to be a matter of necessity to give him some legal protection against designing and unscrupulous persons, for it became clear that his indiscretion and ignorance of business would frequently lead to his being overreached; and this was done, without interfering with the principle that full legal capacity was attained with puberty, by the Lex Plaetoria, passed certainly before B.C. 183, for it is mentioned by Plautus (*Pseud.* i. 3, 69), who died in that year. This statute (which appears to have first established the distinction between minority and full age) protected minors by subjecting any one who fraudulently overreached them to a *iudicium publicum* or prosecution (Cic. *de Off.* iii. 15, § 61), entailing a pecuniary fine and infamia on conviction; and after the introduction of *exceptiones* by the praetor, a minor who was fraudulently induced to enter into a contract could protect himself against action brought thereon by pleading the *exceptio legis Plaetoriae.* It being unlikely that in the face of this stringent procedure any one would have any dealings with minors whatever, the statute (Capitol. *Macr.* 10) apparently went on to provide that minors who wished to contract or deal with other persons, especially in the way of stipulation (Priscian, viii. 4; xviii. 9) and loan, should be compellable to receive a curator on their application, by whose assent to the transaction the penal consequences of the law should be avoided.

The principle of the Lex Plaetoria was carried still further by the praetor, who by means of *in integrum restitutio* protected minors generally against indiscretion causing them proprietary loss (*laesio*); he would set aside transactions into which they had entered, not only on the ground of fraud, but on a consideration of all the circumstances of the case, provided application were made to him within a year after the attainment of majority.

The Emperor Marcus Aurelius (Gaius, *Epit.* 1, 8) seems to have extended the scope of the *cura* of minors by providing that a minor might, on application to the proper magistrate, obtain a permanent curator to look generally after his property and aid him with advice. The principle was that he could not be compelled to have a general curator unless he pleased, except where he was involved in litigation; when a person who owed him money wished to discharge his debt and obtain a release (*Dig.* iv. 4, 7, 2); and possibly where he had disregarded the advice given to him by his guardian, on reaching puberty, to get one appointed for him. But apparently most minors were induced by the convenience of the system to have general curators to assist and advise them (Ulpian, *Reg.* 12, 4; Dio Cass. lii. 20).

The curators of minors were always appointed by the magistrate; a testamentary appointment in itself was void, though the magistrate would usually confirm it by nominating the same person (*Inst.* i. 23, 1; cf. Dio Cassius, xliv. 35); and, according to rule, the minor had to apply for a curator himself. The *munus* was a public one, and could not be declined except on specific grounds, carefully enumerated in the authorities (*Inst.* i. tit. 25); many curators had to give security that they would diligently look after the interests intrusted to them; and if suspected of malversation or negligence, they could be removed by the magistrate, and in cases of fraud were liable to the *suspecti crimen*, a quasi-criminal prosecution (*Inst.* i. tit. 26).

A minor was fully competent to perform legal acts, such as the conveyance of property or the making of contracts; but whether such legal acts had their full usual effect or not depended on whether they were sanctioned by the curator. Both alienations and contracts were *primâ facie* binding on him; but against both, if they were seriously prejudicial, or the curator's consensus had not been given, he could get himself *in integrum restitutus* by the magistrate (*Cod.* ii. 22, 3); and if the curator had not assented to a contract, he could not be compelled to disburse anything from the minor's property in discharge of it, or to pay costs or damages of actions brought in respect thereof by the other party. But a series of imperial enactments (*Cod.* v. 71, 16; v. 37, 22) placed him under very stringent regulations in respect of alienation of the ward's property, which as a general rule was not allowed without permission from a magistrate. If a minor wished to give himself in adrogation the curator's consent was necessary.

The cura of *furiosi* (lunatics and idiots) and interdicted prodigals or spendthrifts originated with the Twelve Tables, which placed *furiosi* under the cura of their nearest agnates, or, if there were no agnates, of their gentiles. Similarly the near relations of a *prodigus* might petition the magistrate for his interdiction from the management of his own affairs, and his subjection to the cura of his nearest agnates, though only if his property had come to him by the intestacy of his own father. In default of these *legitimi curatores*, one would be appointed for such persons by the magistrate (*Inst.* i. 23, 3).

In the time of Justinian other classes of persons were able to get a general curator by application to the magistrate, especially those suffering from weak health, impaired mental faculties, or bodily infirmity—e. g. the deaf and dumb (*Inst.* i. 23, 4). Similarly it would sometimes happen that an *impubes* would have a curator as well as a guardian —e. g. if there was litigation between himself and the latter (*Inst.* i. 21, 3), or if the latter was unfit or temporarily unable to discharge his duties (ib. 23, 5).

It will appear from what has been said that between a guardian and a curator an essential distinction lies in this, that the latter was especially intended to look after the ward's proprietary interests, whereas the former was *personae, non rei datus*.

The word *cura* has also other legal applications: (1) *cura bonorum*, as in the case of the goods of an insolvent debtor, which are secured for the benefit of his creditors; (2) *cura bonorum et ventris*, in the case of a woman being pregnant at the death of her husband; (3) *cura hereditatis*, where there is a dispute as to who is the *heres* of a person, and his supposed child is under puberty; (4) *cura hereditatis iacentis*, the charge of an inheritance of which the apparent heir has not yet declared his acceptance; (5) *cura bonorum absentis*, in the case of property of an absent person who had appointed no manager of it.

Curatōres. Public officers of various kinds under the Roman Empire, several of whom were first established by Augustus (Suet. *Aug.* 37). The most important of them were as follows:

(1) CURATŌRES ALVEI ET RIPĀRUM ET CLOACĀRUM, who had the charge of the navigation of the Tiber.

(2) CURATŌRES ANNŌNAE, who purchased corn and oil for the State, and sold it again at a small price among the poorer citizens. They were also called *curatores emendi frumenti et olei*, and σιτῶναι and ἐλαιῶναι. Their office belonged to the *personalia munera;* that is, it did not require any expenditure of a person's private property, but the curatores received from the State a sufficient sum of money to purchase the required amount (*Dig.* 50, tit. 8, s. 9, § 5).

(3) CURATŌRES AQUĀRUM. (See AQUAE DUCTUS.)

(4) CURATŌRES CALENDARII, who had the care in municipal towns of the *calendaria;* that is, the books which contained the names of the persons to whom public money, which was not wanted for the ordinary expenses of the town, was lent on interest. The office belonged to the *personalia munera.*

(5) CURATŌRES LUDŌRUM, who had the care of the public games as special commissioners. Persons of rank appear to have been usually appointed to this office (Tac. *Ann.* xi. 35; xiii. 22; Suet. *Calig.* 27).

(6) CURATŌRES OPĔRUM PUBLICŌRUM, who had the care of all public buildings, such as the theatres, baths, aqueducts, etc., and agreed with the contractors for all necessary repairs to them. Their duties under the Republic were discharged by the aediles and the censors.

(7) CURATŌRES REGIŌNUM, who had the care of the fourteen districts into which Rome was divided, and whose duty it was to prevent all disorder and extortion in their respective districts. This office was first instituted by Augustus (Suet. *Aug.* 30). There were usually two officers of this kind for each district. Alexander Severus, however, appears to have appointed only one for each; but these were persons of consular rank, who were to

have jurisdiction in conjunction with the *praefectus urbi* (Lamprid. *Alex. Sev.* 33).

(8) CURATŌRES REIPUBLĬCAE (with the name of the community added), also called *logistae*, who administered the landed property of municipia. These were appointed by the emperors. Ulpian wrote a separate work, *De Officio Curatoris Reipublicae.*

(9) CURATŌRES TABULĀRUM PUBLICĀRUM, three magistrates appointed by Tiberius in A.D. 16, to assist in keeping the public records.

(10) CURATŌRES VIĀRUM. See VIAE.

Curculio. "The Guzzler"; a comedy of Plautus with a slender plot, and written to ridicule the ways of parasites. It was composed later than B.C. 193. It is noticeable as having a sort of parabasis (q. v.) in the fourth act (sc. i.). An edition in Latin and German is that of Geppert (Berlin, 1845).

Cures. An ancient town of the Sabines, celebrated as the birthplace of T. Tatius and Numa Pompilius; from this town the Romans are said to have derived the name of Quirites (q. v.).

Curētes (Κουρῆτες). In Cretan mythology the Curetes were demigods armed with weapons of brass, to whom the new-born child Zeus was committed by his mother Rhea for protection against his father Cronus. They drowned the cries of the child by striking their spears against their shields. They gave their name to the priests of the Cretan goddess Rhea and of the Idaean Zeus, who performed noisy war-dances at the festivals of those deities. See CORYBANTES; RHEA; ZEUS.

Curētis. (1) A name given to Crete, as being the residence of the Curetes (Ovid, *Met.* viii. 136). See CURETES. (2) The earlier name of Aetolia.

Curia. A word which signifies both a division of the Roman people and the place of assembly for such a division.

(1) Each of the three ancient Romulian tribes, the Ramnes, Tities, and Luceres, was subdivided into ten curiae, so that the whole body of the populus was divided into thirty curiae (Liv. i. 13). It has commonly been asserted that the plebeians had no connection whatever with the curiae, and that the clients of the patricians were members of the curiae only in a passive sense. But Mommsen has adduced strong reasons for denying the purely patrician character of the curiae (*Röm. Forsch.* i. 140–150), and accepting the view of Dionysius (iv. 12, 20) that plebeians were admitted. In B.C. 209, we find a plebeian elected as Curio Maximus, and, according to all analogy, plebeians must have been admitted to the curiae long before one of them could be found holding the highest post of dignity. Plebeians also are represented as existing and voting side by side with patricians before the institution of any other than the Comitia Curiata. The extinction of the functions of the curiae is nowhere mentioned as a result of the decay of the patriciate. Again, the thirty lictors who represented the curiae, and therefore must have had the right of voting there, were plebeians. There is no reason whatever to believe that the right of making wills and adoptions before the curiae was limited to patricians, and we have one positive instance of a plebeian adopting before the curiae in the case of Clodius. Hence the common theory of the purely patrician character of the curiae must be abandoned. There is no historical evidence to show when the plebeians became members of them, but it is a reasonable conjecture that they were admitted at the time of the expulsion of the kings, when the Comitia Curiata lost their political power by the development of the Comitia Centuriata (Mommsen, *Hist.* i. 264). All the members of the different gentes belonging to one curia were called, in respect of one another, *curiales*. Each curia as a corporation had its peculiar *sacra* (Fest. pp. 174, 245), and besides the gods of the State they worshipped other divinities and with peculiar rites and ceremonies. For such religious purposes each curia had its own place of worship, called *curia*, which at first may have contained nothing but an altar, afterwards a *sacellum*, and finally a building in which the curiales assembled for the purpose of discussing political, financial, religious, and other matters (Paul. Diac. pp. 62, 64; Dionys. ii. 50). The religious affairs of each curia were taken care of by a priest, *curio*, who was assisted by another called Flamen Curialis. (See CURIO.) The thirty curiae had their own distinct names, which are said to have been derived from the names of the Sabine women who had been carried off by the Romans, though it is evident that some derived their names from certain districts or from ancient eponymous heroes. Few of these names only are known, such as curia Titia, Faucia, Calabra, Foriensis, Rapta, Veliensis, Tifata (Paul. Diac. pp. 49, 366; Fest. p. 174; Liv. i. 13). O. Gilbert has lately (*Gesch. und Topogr. der Stadt Rom im Alterthum*, 2 vols. 1883, 1885) advocated, with much ingenuity and learning, a theory that the curiae were based originally upon the gradual occupation of the seven hills of the Septimontium by tribes of different origin, and their ultimate federation.

(2) CURIA (βουλευτήριον) is also used to designate the place in which the Senate held its meetings. From this there gradually arose the custom of calling the Senate itself *curia* in the coloniae and municipia, but never the Senate of Rome. (See DECURIO). The official residence of the Salii, which was dedicated to Mars, was likewise styled *curia* (Cic. *De Div.* i. 17; Dionys. xiv. 5; Plut. *Camill.* 32).

The history and site of the Senate-house at Rome have been much discussed. Built by Tullus Hostilius (Varr. *L. L.* v. 155–156), the Curia Hostilia was burned at the funeral of Clodius (B.C. 52). Successive restorations by a son of Sulla and by Augustus are recorded in the names C. Cornelia and C. Iulia. Under Domitian the C. Iulia was again rebuilt. A still later building, ascribed to Diocletian, has been identified with the present church of S. Adriano on the northeast of the Forum. It is of brick, ornamented with stucco and marble. See Middleton, *Ancient Rome in 1888*; id. *Remains of Ancient Rome*, i. pp. 237, 385; ii. 139.

Curiāles. See CURIA.

Curiāta Comitia. See COMITIA.

Curiatii. A celebrated Alban family. Three brothers of this family fought with three Roman brothers, the Horatii, and were conquered by the latter. In consequence of their defeat Alba became subject to Rome. See HORATIUS, p. 843.

Curio. The person who stood at the head of a *curia* and had to manage its affairs, especially those of a religious nature. In their administration he was assisted by another priest, called Flamen Curialis. As there were thirty *curiae*, the number of curiones was likewise thirty, and they formed a college of priests, which was headed by one of them bearing the title of *curio maximus*. In later times he was elected by the people, but originally probably by co-optation.

Curio. (1) GAIUS, praetor B.C. 121, but did not attain to the consulship. Cicero speaks with praise of his oratory, an opinion founded, not on personal knowledge, but on the speeches he had left. (2) C. SCRIBONIUS, consul with Gnaeus Octavius, B.C. 76. On returning from the province of Macedonia, he triumphed over the Dardani, as proconsul, B.C. 72. Cicero often mentions him, and in his *Brutus* (cap. 49) enumerates him among the Roman orators, along with Cotta and others. (3) C. SCRIBONIUS, son of the preceding, a turbulent and unprincipled man, and an active partisan of Iulius Caesar's. Being deeply involved in debt when tribune of the plebs, Caesar gained him over by paying for him what he owed (Plut. *Pomp.* 58), and Curio immediately exerted himself with great vigour in his behalf. Caesar, it seems, was under obligations to him before this, since Curio is said to have saved his life when he was leaving the Senate-house after the debate about Catiline's accomplices, his personal safety being endangered by the young men who stood in arms around the building (Plut. *Caes.* 8). Plutarch ascribes Antony's early initiation into licentious habits to his acquaintance with Curio. On the breaking out of the Civil War, Caesar, after having possessed himself of Rome, sent Curio to take charge of Sicily. The latter subsequently crossed over from this island into Africa, with an armed force, against Iuba and the followers of Pompey, but was defeated and slain.

Curiosolītes. A people of Gaul, forming part of the Armoric tribes. Their territory lay to the northeast of the Veneti, and answers to what is now the territory of St. Malo, between Dinant and Lamballe, in the department Côtes-du-Nord.

Curītis. A name given to Iuno and said to be derived from the Sabine *curis*, "a spear" (Macrob. *Saturn.* i. 9). See QUIRITES.

Curium (Κούριον). A city of Cyprus, on the southern coast, or rather, according to the ancients, at the commencement of the western shore, at a small distance from which, to the southeast, there is a cape which bears the name of Curias. Curium is said to have been founded by an Argive colony, and it was one of the nine royal cities of Cyprus. See CYPRUS.

Curius Dentātus, MANIUS. A Roman, celebrated for his warlike achievements, and also for the primitive simplicity of his manners. In his first consulship (B.C. 290) he triumphed twice, once over the Samnites and then over the Sabines, and in this same year also he obtained an ovation for his successes against the Lucanians. He afterwards (B.C. 275), in his third consulship, triumphed over Pyrrhus and the Samnites. It was on this occasion that the Roman people first saw elephants led along in triumph (Flor. i. 18; Plin. *H. N.* viii. 6; Eutrop. ii. 14), and it was this victory that drove Pyrrhus from Italy. The simple manners of this distinguished man are often referred to by the Roman writers. When the ambassadors of the Samnites visited his cottage, they found him, according to one account, sitting on a bench by the fireside, and eating out of a wooden bowl (Val. Max. iv. 3, 5), and, according to Plutarch, boiling turnips. On their attempting to bribe him with a large sum of gold, he at once rejected their offer, exclaiming that a man who could be content to live as they saw him living had no need whatever of gold, and that he thought it more glorious to conquer the possessors of it than to possess it himself. His scanty farm and humble cottage, moreover, were in full accordance with the idea which Curius had formed of private wealth; for, after so many achievements and honours, he declared that citizen a pernicious one who did not find seven acres (*iugera*) sufficient for his subsistence (Plin. xviii. 3). According to Pliny, Dentatus was so named because born with teeth (*cum dentibus*) (*H. N.* vii. 15).

Curotrŏphos (κουροτρόφος). "Nurse of children." The title of several Greek goddesses—for instance, Gaea—who were regarded as protectresses of youth. Cf. Hesiod, *Theog.* 450; Macrob. *Saturn.* i. 10, 19, 20.

Currus, dim. **Curricŭlum** (ἅρμα). A chariot, a car. These terms appear to have denoted those two-wheeled vehicles for the carriage of persons which were open overhead, thus differing from the *carpentum* (q. v.), and closed in front, in which they differed from the *cisium* (q. v.). One of the most essential parts in the construction of the currus was the ἄντυξ, or rim; and it is accordingly seen in all the chariots which are represented in this article. Another indispensable part was the axle, made of oak (φήγινος ἄξων), and sometimes also of ilex, ash, or elm. The cars of Heré and Poseidon have metallic axles. One method of making a chariot less liable to be overturned was to lengthen its axle, and thus to widen the base on which it stood. The axle was firmly fixed under the body of the chariot, which, in reference to this circumstance, was called ὑπερτερία, and which was often made of wicker-work, enclosed by the ἄντυξ. Fat (λίπος) and pressed olives (*amurca*) were used to grease the axle.

The wheels (κύκλα, τροχοί, *rotae*) revolved upon the axle, as in modern carriages; and they were prevented from coming off by the insertion of pins (ἔμβολοι) into the extremities of the axle (ἀκραξονία). Pelops obtained his celebrated victory over Oenomaüs through the artifice of Hippodamia, who, wishing to marry Pelops, persuaded Myrtilus, the charioteer of his adversary, to omit inserting one of the linchpins in the axle of his car, or to insert one of wax. She thus caused the overthrow and death of her father, Oenomaüs, and then married the conqueror in the race.

Sir W. Gell describes, in the following terms, the wheels of three cars which were found at Pompeii: "The wheels light, and dished much like the modern, 4 feet 3 inches diameter, 10 spokes, a little thicker at each end." These cars were probably intended for the purposes of common life. From Xenophon we learn that the wheels were made stronger when they were intended for the field of battle. After each excursion the wheels were taken off the chariot, which was laid on a shelf or reared against a wall, and they were put on again whenever it was wanted for use.

The parts of the wheel were as follows:

(*a*) The nave or hub, called πλήμνη, χοινικίς, *modiolus*. The last two terms are founded on the resemblance of the nave to a modius or bushel.

The nave was strengthened by being bound with an iron ring, called πλημνόδετον.

(*b*) The spokes, κνῆμαι (literally, "the legs"), *radii*. We have seen that the spokes were sometimes ten in number. In other instances they were eight (κύκλα ὀκτάκνημα), six, or four. Instead of being of wood, the spokes of the chariot of the Sun, constructed by Hephaestus, were of silver (*radiorum argenteus ordo*).

(*c*) The felly, ἴτυς. This was commonly made of some flexible and elastic wood, such as poplar or the wild fig, which was also used for the rim of the chariot; heat was applied to assist in producing the requisite curvature. The felly was, however, composed of separate pieces, called arcs (ἀψῖδες). Hence the observation of Plutarch that, as a "wheel revolves, first one *apsis* is at the highest point, and then another." Hesiod evidently intended to recommend that a wheel should consist of four pieces.

(*d*) The tire, ἐπίσωτρον, *canthus*. Homer describes the chariot of Heré as having a tire of bronze upon a golden felly, thus placing the harder metal in a position to resist friction and to protect the softer. The tire was commonly of iron.

All the parts now enumerated are seen in an ancient chariot preserved in the Vatican, a representation of which is given in the following illustration.

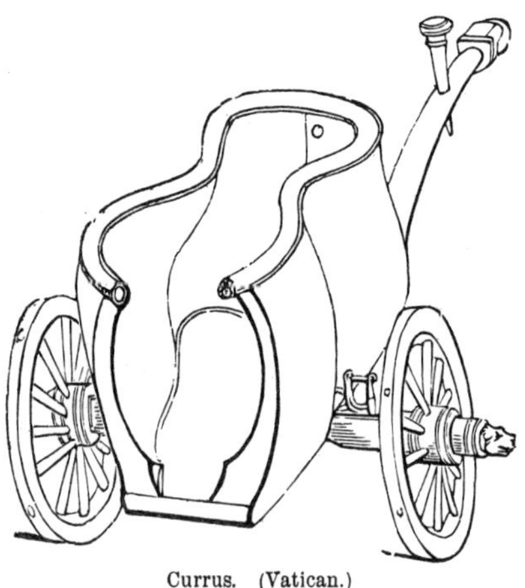

Currus. (Vatican.)

This chariot, which is in some parts restored, also shows the pole (ῥυμός, *temo*). It was firmly fixed at its lower extremity to the axle, whence the destruction of Phaëthon's chariot is represented by the circumstance of the pole and axle being torn asunder (*temone revulsus axis*). At the other end (ἀκρορρύμιον) the pole was attached to the yoke, either by a pin (ἔμβολος), as shown in the chariot above engraved, or by the use of ropes and bands. See IUGUM.

Carriages with two, or even three, poles were used by the Lydians. The Greeks and Romans, on the other hand, appear never to have used more than one pole and one yoke, and the currus thus constructed was commonly drawn by two horses, which were attached to it by their necks, and therefore called δίζυγες ἵπποι, συνωρίς, *gemini iugales, equi biiuges*.

If a third horse was added, as was not unfrequently the case, it was fastened by traces. It may have been intended to take the place of either of the yoke-horses (ζύγιοι ἵπποι) which might happen to be disabled. The horse so attached was called παρήορος. When Patroclus returned to battle in the chariot of Achilles, two immortal horses, Xanthus and Balius, were placed under the yoke; a third, called Pedasus, and mortal, was added on the right hand; and, having been slain, caused confusion, until the driver cut the harness by which this third horse was fastened to the chariot.

Currus with Three Horses. (Ginzrot.)

Ginzrot has published two drawings of chariots with three horses from Etruscan vases in the collection at Vienna. The ἵππος παρήορος is placed on the right of the two yoke-horses. We also observe traces passing between the two ἄντυγες, and proceeding from the front of the chariot on each side of the middle horse. These probably assisted in attaching the third or extra horse.

The Latin name for a chariot and pair was *biga*. (See BIGA.) When a third horse was added, it was called *triga;* and, by the same analogy, a chariot and four was called *quadriga;* in Greek, τετραορία or τέθριππος.

The horses were commonly harnessed in a quadriga after the manner already represented, the two strongest horses being placed under the yoke, and the two others fastened on each side by means of ropes. This is implied in the use of the epithets σειραῖος or σειραφόρος, and *funalis* or *funarius*, for a horse so attached. The two exterior horses were further distinguished from one another as the right and the left trace-horse. In a chariot-race described by Sophocles, the driver, aiming to pass the goal, which is on his left hand, restrains the nearest horse, and gives the reins to that which was farthest from it—viz., the horse in traces on the right hand (δεξιὸν δ' ἀνεὶς σειραῖον ἵππον). In the splendid triumph of Augustus after the battle of Actium, the trace-horses of his car were ridden by two of his young relations. Tiberius rode, as Suetonius relates, *sinisteriore funali equo*, and Marcellus *dexteriore funali equo*. As the works of ancient art, especially fictile vases, abound in representations of quadrigae, numerous instances may be observed in which the two middle horses (ὁ μέσος δεξιὸς καὶ ὁ μέσος ἀριστερός) are yoked together as in a biga; and, as the two lateral ones have collars (λέπαδνα) equally with the yoke-horses, we may presume that from the top of these proceeded the ropes which were tied to the rim of the car, and by which the trace-horses assisted to draw it. The first figure in the following illustration is the chariot of Aurora, as painted on a vase found at Canosa. The reins of the two middle horses pass through rings at the extremities of the yoke. All the particulars which have been mentioned are still more distinctly seen in the second figure, taken from a terra-cotta at Vienna. It represents a chariot overthrown in passing the goal at the circus.

The charioteer having fallen backwards, the pole and yoke are thrown upwards into the air; the two trace-horses have fallen on their knees, and the two yoke-horses are prancing on their hind-legs.

If we may rely on the evidence of numerous works of art, the currus was sometimes drawn by four horses without either yoke or pole; for we see two of them diverging to the right hand and two to the left, as in the beautiful cameo given below, which represents Apollo surrounded by the signs of the zodiac. If the ancients really drove the quadriga thus harnessed, we can only suppose the charioteer to have checked its speed by pulling up the horses and leaning with his whole body backwards, so as to make the bottom of the car at its hindermost border scrape the ground—an act and an attitude which seem not unfrequently to be intended in antique representations.

Currus with Four Horses.

The currus, like the *cisium*, was adapted to carry two persons, and on this account was called in Greek δίφρος. One of the two was, of course, the driver. He was called ἡνίοχος, because he held the reins, and his companion παραιβάτης, from going by his side or near him. Though in all respects superior, the παραιβάτης was often obliged to place himself *behind* the ἡνίοχος. He is so represented in the *biga* at page 92, and in the *Iliad* Achilles himself stands behind his charioteer Automedon.

Four-horse Chariots on Gems. (Berlin Museum.)

On the other hand, a personage of the highest rank may drive his own carriage, and then an inferior may be his παραιβάτης, as when Nestor conveys Machaon (πάρ' δὲ Μαχάων βαῖνε), and Heré, holding the reins and whip, conveys Athené, who is in full armour. In such cases a kindness, or even a compliment, was conferred by the driver upon him whom he conveyed, as when Dionysius, tyrant of Sicily, "himself holding the reins, made Plato his παραιβάτης." In the contest which has been already referred to, and which was so celebrated in Greek mythology, Oenomaüs intrusts the reins to the unfaithful Myrtilus, and assumes the place of his παραιβάτης, while Pelops himself drives with Hippodamia as his παραιβάτις, thus honouring her in return for the service she had bestowed.

The Persepolitan sculptures, and the innumerable paintings discovered in Egyptian tombs, concur with the historical writings of the Old Testament, and with the testimony of other ancient authors, in showing how commonly chariots were employed on the field of battle by the Egyptians, the Persians, and other Asiatic nations. The Greek poetry of the Heroic Ages proves with equal certainty the early prevalence of the same custom in Greece. The ἀριστῆες—i. e. the nobility, or men of rank —who wore complete suits of armour, all took their chariots with them, and in an engagement placed themselves in front. Such were the ἱππεῖς, or cavalry of the Homeric period—the precursors of those who, after some centuries, adopted the less expensive and ostentatious practice of riding on horseback, but who, nevertheless, in consideration of their wealth and station, still maintained their own horses, rather to aid and exhibit themselves individually on the field than to act as members of a compact body. In Homer's battles we find that the horseman — who, for the purpose of using his weapons and in consequence of the weight of his armour, is under the necessity of taking the place of παραιβάτης—often assails or challenges a distant foe from the chariot; but that, when he encounters his adversary in close combat, they both dismount, "springing from their chariots to the ground," and leaving them to the care of the ἡνίοχοι. So likewise Turnus is described by Vergil, *Desiluit Turnus biiugis; pedes apparat ire Comminus.* As soon as the hero had finished the trial of his strength with his opponent, he returned to his chariot, one of the chief uses of which was to rescue him from danger. When Automedon prepares to encounter both Hector and Aeneas, justly fearing the result, he directs his charioteer, Alcimedon, instead of driving the horses to any distance, to keep them "breathing on his back," and thus to enable him to effect his escape in case of need.

These chariots, as represented on bas-reliefs and fictile vases, were exceedingly light, the body often consisting of little besides a rim fastened to the bottom and to the axle. Unless such had been really their construction, it would be difficult to imagine how so great a multitude of chariots could have been transported across the Aegean Sea. The light and simple construction of war-chariots is also supposed by Vergil, when he represents them as suspended with all kinds of armour on the entrance to the temple of the Laurentian Picus.

We have already seen that it was not unusual in the Homeric battles to drive three horses, one being a παρήορος; in a single instance, that of Hector, four are driven together. In the games, the use of this number of horses was, perhaps, even more common than the use of two. The form of the chariot was the same, except that it was more elegantly decorated. But the highest style of ornament was reserved to be displayed in the quadrigae in which the Roman generals and emperors rode when they triumphed. The body of the triumphal car was cylindrical, as we often see it represented on medals. It was enriched with gold (*aureus currus*) and ivory. The utmost skill of the painter and the sculptor was employed to enhance its beauty and splendour. More particularly the extremities of the axle, of the pole, and of the yoke were highly wrought in the form of animals' heads. Wreaths of laurel were sometimes hung round it (*currus lauriger*), and were also fixed to the heads of the four snow-white horses. The car was elevated so that he who triumphed might be the most conspicuous person in the procession, and, for the same reason, he was obliged to stand erect (*in curru stantis eburno*). A friend, more especially a son, was sometimes carried in the same chariot by his side. When Germanicus celebrated his triumph, the car was "loaded" with five of his children in addition to himself. The triumphal car had, in general, no pole, the horses being led by men who were stationed at their heads.

The chariot was an attribute not only of the gods, but of various imaginary beings, such as Victory, often so represented on coins, vases, and sculptures; Night; and Aurora, whom Vergil represents as driving either two horses or four, in this agreeing with the figure in the illustrations on p. 445. In general, the poets are more specific as to the number of horses in the chariots of the deities, and it rarely exceeded two. Iupiter, as the father of the gods, drives four white horses when he goes armed with his thunderbolt to resist the giants; Pluto is drawn by four black horses.

The chariots of Iupiter and of the Sun are, moreover, painted on ancient vases with wings proceeding from the extremities of the axle (πτηνὸν ἅρμα; *volucrem currum*).

These supernatural chariots were drawn not only by horses, but by a great variety of brute or imaginary beings. Thus Medea received from the Sun a car with winged dragons. Iuno is drawn by peacocks, Diana by stags, Venus by doves or swans, Minerva by owls, Mercury by rams, and Apollo by griffins. To the car of Bacchus, and consequently of Ariadné, are yoked centaurs, tigers, and lynxes.

Chariots executed in terra-cotta (*quadrigae fictiles*), in bronze, or in marble, an example of which last is shown in the annexed illustration from an

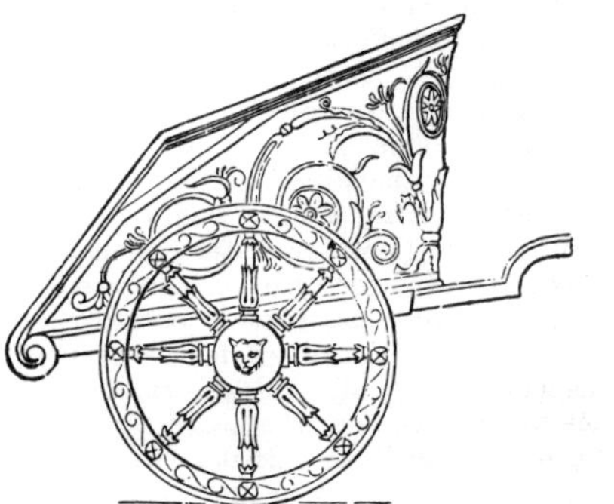

Biga. (Sala della Biga, Vatican.)

ancient chariot in the Vatican, were among the most beautiful ornaments of temples and other public edifices.

No pains were spared in their decoration, and Pliny informs us that some of the most eminent artists were employed upon them. In numerous instances they were designed to perpetuate the fame of those who had conquered in the chariot-race. As the emblem of victory, the *quadriga* was sometimes adopted by the Romans to grace the triumphal arch by being placed on its summit; and even in the private houses of great families, chariots were displayed as the indications of rank or the memorials of conquest and of triumph.

Cursive Writing. See ALPHABET; PALAEOGRAPHY.

Cursor, L. PAPIRIUS. See PAPIRIUS.

Cursōres. (1) Slaves whose duty it was to run before the carriages of their masters, for the same purpose as modern outriders. They were not used during the times of the Republic, but appear to have first come into fashion in the middle of the first century of the Christian era. The word *cursores* was also applied to all slaves whom their masters employed in carrying letters, messages, etc. (See CURSUS PUBLICUS.) (2) Runners in the foot-race, or competitors in the chariot race. See CURSUS.

Cursus (δρόμος, τρόχος). Foot-racing. In historic times, at the national festivals of Greece, several species of it had come into vogue. We may distinguish four sorts: (*a*) the στάδιον (or simply δρόμος); (*b*) the δίαυλος; (*c*) the ἐφίππιος or ἵππιος δρόμος; (*d*) the δολιχὸς δρόμος (or δόλιχος, proparox). A strange feature in these races was that they were not run on hard and firm ground (Lucian, *Anachars.* 27), but over a deeply sanded surface.

(*a*) The στάδιον was a race in which the runners (σταδιοδρόμοι) traversed the arena in a direct line (whence it was called εὐθύς, ἄκαμπτος) from one extremity to the other. This distance, as measured by the Olympic stadium, which became the general standard, was about 600 feet. The στάδιον corresponds to our "sprint," in which the runner does the whole run at his highest speed.

(*b*) The δίαυλος, or double course (properly = double pipe), required that the runners (διαυλοδρόμοι) should, after traversing the arena as in the στάδιον, turn round a post (καμπτήρ) and run back to their starting-point. Hence it was called δρόμος κάμπειος (from καμπή = *flexus*).

(*c*) The ἐφίππιος or ἵππιος did not, as might seem from its name, signify a horse-race, but a race of sufficient length to try the power of a horse. (See Hermann - Blümner, *Privatalt.* p. 346.) It was a test therefore of endurance as well as speed, being four stadia in length; that is, twice the δίαυλος.

(*d*) The true test of staying power, however, was the δόλιχος or long race, added to the Olympic Games (according to Philostratus, *Gymn.* 12) in Olymp. 15. The length of this race has been variously described as seven, twelve, twenty, or twenty-four stadia. We may suppose that it differed on different occasions.

Competition in foot-racing was open to runners of all ages, whether boys (παῖδες), striplings (ἀγένειοι), or grown men (ἄνδρες). Only those who belonged to the same class, as regards age (ἡλικιῶται), were permitted to compete with one another; seniors, of course, not being allowed to enter against their juniors. In Sparta even girls ran.

The competitors, being too numerous to contend all together, were entered in successive groups (τάξεις); those who should form each group, as well as the order in which the groups should run, being determined by lot (συνταχθῆναι ὑπὸ τοῦ κλήρου). When all the τάξεις in turn had run, the victors in each were formed into one group, which ran a final heat for the prize.

It is doubtless owing to their want of instruments for accurately measuring small portions of time that the Greeks have left us scarcely any means of computing the speed which foot-racers attained in the various kinds of running.

For some special forms of the foot-race, see LAMPADEDROMIA and STAPHYLODROMIA.

We have very meagre information regarding foot-racing as practised by the Romans. According to Dionysius of Halicarnassus (vii. 71, 73), it formed part of the Ludi Magni from the time of their institution. He, too, tells us that the runners wore the *subligaculum* round their loins. In the Capitoline Games (Dio Cass. lxvii. 8) young women, after the Spartan fashion, took part in the competition. Beyond these scanty notices and vague references to running for healthful exercise in the Campus Martius, very little has been handed down to us. This running in the Campus was not always competitive. That it was sometimes so, however, is plain from Martial, iv. 19. For chariot-racing, see CIRCUS and HIPPODROMUS.

Cursus Publĭcus. The postal-service of the Roman Empire.

Persia under Darius, son of Hystaspes, affords the earliest instance of a national postal-service. Mention is indeed made (*Liberat. Brev.* 23) of a class called *symmaci* as existing in the most ancient times among the Egyptians for the conveyance of letters by land, but we have no grounds for thinking that a postal-system was established in Egypt as a branch of the administration. In the Persian dominions, however, as we learn from Herodotus (iii. 28; vi. 105; viii. 98), horsemen, stationed at intervals and relieving one another, conveyed the imperial will in all directions from Susa, Ecbatana, or Babylon. The service was called ἀγγαρήϊον, and the couriers, ἄγγαροι. Messages of lesser urgency were carried by ἡμεροδρόμοι. In Greece there are no evidences of any such service, at least upon a similar scale, for the *hemerodromi* mentioned by Corn. Nepos (*Milt.* iv. 3) can scarcely have been a permanent institution. This was probably due to the geographical smallness of Greece; still more, however, to the utter absence of political unity among the Greeks, and the want of facilities for land traffic, in contrast with the easy communications by sea. But the vast extent of the Roman dominions, and the centralization of imperial functions in a single hand, again furnished the conditions of a postal-service, which accordingly arose and became a most important instrument of State administration. The practical wisdom of the Romans had from the beginning of their conquests taught them to make roads throughout the territories which they subdued, whence resulted a system of highways connecting the remotest parts of the Empire with Rome. These not only facilitated the marching of troops, but served the general purposes of transport and the conveyance of intelligence, forming, as they did, the material *condicio sine qua non* of the future *cursus publicus.* Within the last century of the Republic, also, certain practices had already been established, by which the development of the postal-service was largely conditioned. We now proceed to give some account of these.

Under the Republic, after the conquest of Italy, government officials despatched from Rome on public business were empowered to impose arbitrary requisitions on the subject Italians (*dediticii*) to supply them with necessaries for travelling. Among the Italian allies such functionaries usually obtained food, lodging, and means of transport from their guest-friends or from the principal personages in the friendly States which they visited. But when the Roman dominions included extra-Italian provinces, the fine distinction made in Italy between subjects and allies (*socii*) was in the provinces neglected, and the provincial allies were as summarily requisitioned by a *legatus* as were the provincial subjects. Senators or citizens employed on a public mission abroad received from the Senate a mandate (*diploma*) requiring subjects and allies alike to supply them with means of transport and other necessaries at all the successive stages of their journey. This in the natural course of things led to grave hardships, and complaints frequently arose. Restrictive enactments became necessary; and we read that Cato the Elder, when praetor in Sardinia, diminished or removed the expenses entailed upon the people of that island by the entertainment of the praetors officiating among them (Liv. xxxii. 27). It is doubtful, however, whether Cato issued a formal edict, or whether his good example alone operated towards the relief of the sufferers.

Among the various embassies which thus became grounds of hardship to the provincials there was one which deserves especial notice. This was called *libera legatio*, being a sort of mission from which all State employment was absent, granted as a favour sometimes to distinguished men, lasting for several years, and carrying with it all the previously mentioned liabilities on the part of the provincials. The *libera legatio*, owing to the indefiniteness of the privileges it conveyed, became a fearful cause of oppression. A law was carried in B.C. 63 by Cicero (Cic. *De Leg.* iii. 8, 18) restricting abuses of the *libera legatio* and limiting its duration to one year; but the reform thus effected was short-lived, for Iulius Caesar (Cic. *Ad Att.* xv. 11) again extended the term of a *libera legatio* to a possible five years.

During the last period of the Republic the Senate had frequent occasions for communicating in despatches with their generals or provincial governors, as well as with allied kings and States. For the conveyance of such despatches the authorities employed freedmen, slaves, or a certain class of couriers called *stratores* (*sternere*, "to saddle"). A class of messengers also existed called *tabellarii.* For pressing messages a general usually employed mounted men detached from his own staff. The *publicani*, as especially interested in transmitting and receiving intelligence to and from Rome, had a special class of *tabellarii*, whose services, however, were often borrowed by the magistrates, or by the *negotiatores*, speculators in corn or money, who were in constant relations with the provincial governors and with the *publicani.* The ships of the allies also were employed for the use of magistrates engaged abroad on public business. Thus for the purposes of transport and the conveyance of intelligence the dealings of the home government with the provincials were regulated mainly by the principle that the incidental labour and expenses should be borne as far as possible by the latter, while the interests to be served were those of the government alone.

It only remained for the Empire to organize and develop the system which had been established under the republican *régime.* The immense advantages of such an organization as a portion of the imperial administration were sufficiently obvious. Augustus accordingly appointed mounted couriers (*stratores* or *speculatores*) to be employed along the principal roads (Suet. *Aug.* 49). This implies the institution of stations (*mutationes*), at which they should relieve one another. But as this arrangement provided only for the conveyance of intelligence, it required to be supplemented by a transport system for the conveyance of money or other valuables of considerable weight. The necessity of constructing postal-stations ensued. The stations were called *mansiones,* which, being intended for lodgings, as their name indicates, were furnished not only with a supply for the immediate wants of man and beast, but also with the accommodation suitable for travellers. The *mansiones* were not so numerous along a road as the *mutationes,* or changing-stages. In accordance with republican precedent the expenses of the transport and postal system generally continued to fall upon the communities through whose territories the lines of stations lay. They accordingly had to provide conductors, guards, drivers, together with beasts of burden and rolling-stock, on receipt of the emperor's order (*diploma*), or that of the head of the postal system (a functionary designated in Trajan's time as *ab vehiculis*), who was generally a freedman of the emperor. Such warrants for the use of the post were issued occasionally by the consul, by the praefect of the praetorians, or by the governor of a province, but in all cases only with the emperor's special authority. While the document entitling to the use of the *cursus,* by virtue of being stamped with the emperor's seal, was called *diploma* (and other names which will hereafter be referred to), the right of issuing postal-warrants was, at least until a late period, called *evectio.* The expenses, moreover, of constructing stations and stocking them with necessaries had to be borne by the neighbouring communities. Along the line of one day's journey there were six or eight sets of stables, each of which had to maintain a total of forty beasts, including horses, mules, asses, etc. The communities also were bound to furnish and maintain the teams and to keep the stables in repair; they had further to secure the services of muleteers (*muliones*), mule-doctors (*mulomedici*), wheelwrights (*carpentarii*), grooms (*hippocomi*), and conductors or guards (*vehicularii*). From these heavy burdens Nerva relieved the people of Italy, and to commemorate his act a medal was struck bearing the inscription *vehiculatione Italiae remissa* (where *vehiculatio* = *cursus publicus*). Trajan, however, re-authorized (Plin. *Ep.* x. 121) the issue of postal-warrants in Italy, but restricted them to cases in which he had been personally consulted. We read (Spart. *Hadr.* 7) that Hadrian *statum cursum fiscalem instituit, ne magistratus hoc onere gravarentur.* According to Hirschfeld, in his note to these words, *cursus fiscalis* is in Spartianus equivalent to *cursus vehicularius,* and the emphasis lies upon the word *statum.* According to his view, therefore, the meaning of the whole sentence is that Hadrian made the postal-service throughout the Empire a department of the State administration, and appointed fixed stations, superintended by government officials, in order to relieve the *municipal* magistrates of all responsibility for them. Despite, however, these and other efforts in this direction, it was not until the time of Septimius Severus (Spart. *Sever.* 14) that the expenses of the post generally were made chargeable to the imperial treasury. But, even when this had been done, the subjects still continued to suffer, nor did any subsequent legislation materially alleviate the burden with which the *cursus* pressed upon them. Differences of opinion exist as to the exact nature of the reforms or changes attributed respectively to Nerva, Trajan, and the others above mentioned. Humbert says we must at least suppose, as Hudemann does, that Nerva entirely remitted, though only to Italy, the expenses of the service, so that the salaries of officials engaged in it, as well as the material cost, became alike chargeable to the treasury; that Trajan contented himself with merely checking the abuse of *evectio*; while Hadrian, besides extending the organization of the post through the whole Empire, must apparently have imposed the charges of it upon the *fiscus;* that Antoninus Pius again, like Trajan, making a step backwards, confined the contemplated reform to a mere restriction of expenses and of the right of issuing post-warrants; that Septimius Severus completely reorganized the *vehicularium munus,* and imposed the charges of it, in Italy and the rest of the Empire alike, upon the *fiscus* alone; but that the last and radical reform was incapable of maintaining itself, owing to the burdens it entailed upon the treasury. Diocletian, Constantine, and their successors all strove to perfect the organization of the post, and to define exactly what the liabilities of the cities in regard to it should be, together with determining the question who should have the *evectio,* or right of granting postal permits, and under what circumstances they might be justly granted.

In the later times of the Roman Empire the post became an ever-increasing burden to the cities; and as it injured them, in the same degree it prepared the way for its own ruin. Nevertheless a treaty ratified between Rome and Persia in A.D. 565 (Menander, *Prot.* p. 360, ed. Bonn) assured to the natives of the frontier provinces of the two empires the uses of the postal-service to and fro between them. See A. de Rothschild, *Hist. de la Poste aux Lettres depuis ses Origines* (Paris, 1873).

Curtius, Georg. One of the most distinguished classicists and philologists of the present century, born at Lübeck, April 16th, 1820. He pursued his studies at Bonn and Berlin, teaching for a time at the latter place and at Dresden. In 1849, he was made Professor Extraordinarius of Classical Philology at Prague, becoming in 1851 Professor Ordinarius. From Prague he was called in 1854 to a like chair at Kiel, and in 1862 to Leipzig. He died August 12th, 1885.

Curtius was the last and one of the greatest of the "old school" of classical philologists, and formulated in their final expression their etymological views. He was also profoundly learned in Greek, and in this department wrote a number of standard works: the *Griechische Schulgrammatik* (1852), which reached its fifteenth (German) edition in 1882, and has been translated into English in Dr. W. Smith's series in England, and forms the basis of Prof. Hadley's *Greek Grammar* in this country; also his *Erläuterungen* to the foregoing (1863, 3d ed. 1875) Eng. trans. (1870); the *Grundzüge der Griechischen Etymologie* (1858; 5th ed. in collaboration with Windisch, 1879), translated into English by Wilkins and England (1875–76); and *Das Verbum der Griechischen Sprache* (1873–76)—a very elaborate piece of work—translated by Wilkins and England (1880). Besides these important publications, he also put forth a treatise *De Nominum Graecorum Formatione* (1842); *Die Sprachvergleichung in ihrem Verhältniss zur klassischen Philologie* (1845); *Sprachvergleichende Beiträge zur griechischen und lateinischen Grammatik* (1846); *Philologie und Sprachwissenschaft* (1862); *Zur Chronologie der indo-germanischen Sprachforschung* (1867; 2d ed. 1873); *Zur Kritik der neuesten Sprachforschung* (1885); and in conjunction with Brugmann, G. Meyer, Fick, Windisch, and others, *Studien zur griech. und lat. Grammatik*, 10 vols. (1868–77). The ninth volume of this series contains Brugmann's famous paper on the nasal sonant, with which began the aggressive propaganda of the new school against the theories of Curtius and his predecessors. The new theories form the subject of a vigorous attack by Curtius himself in the *Kritik* mentioned above, in which he maintains the principle of "sporadic change" in addition to invariable phonetic law and the influence of analogy. (See PHILOLOGIA.) In 1878, Prof. Curtius founded with Lange, Ribbeck, and Lipsius the *Leipziger Studien zur klassischen Philologie*.

Curtius, METTUS. A Roman youth, who devoted himself, for his country, to the Manes, B.C. 362. According to the account given by Livy (vii. 6), the ground near the middle of the Forum, in consequence either of an earthquake or some other violent cause, sank down to an immense depth, forming a vast aperture; nor could the gulf be filled up by all the earth which could be thrown into it. At last the soothsayers declared that, if the Romans wished the commonwealth to be everlasting, they must devote to this chasm what constituted the principal strength of the Roman people. Curtius, on hearing the answer, demanded of his countrymen whether they possessed anything so valuable as their arms and courage. They yielded a silent assent to the question put them; whereupon, having arrayed himself in full armour and mounted his horse, Curtius plunged into the chasm, and the people threw after him their offerings and quantities of the fruits of the earth. Valerius Maximus (v. 6, 2) states that the earth closed immediately over him. Livy, however, speaks of a lake occupying the spot, called Lacus Curtius. In another part of his history (i. 13), he mentions this same lake as existing in the time of Romulus, and as having derived its name from Mettus Curtius, a Sabine in the army of Titus Tatius. In all probability it was of volcanic origin, since the early accounts speak of its great depth, and was not produced merely by the inundations of the Tiber. Tarquinius Priscus is said to have filled up this lake at the time that he drained the whole of this district and constructed the Cloaca Maxima. Possibly he may have been aided in this by a natural tunnel gradually formed through the basin of the lake itself.

Curtius Rufus, QUINTUS. A Roman historian who flourished in the first century of the Christian era. No particulars of his life are known, and no mention is to be found in the Roman writers that can be positively referred to him, though Suetonius mentions a Q. Curtius Rufus in his list of rhetoricians, and a Curtius Rufus is named by Tacitus (*Ann.* xi. 21) and by the younger Pliny (*Epist.* vii. 27). The ten books (*Historiarum Alexandri Magni Libri Decem*) that he wrote are believed to have been composed during the reign of Cláudius on the strength of a passage in the work itself (x. 9, 3–6), which seems to refer to the outbreak at Rome on the death of Caligula, to which the accession of Claudius put an end. (See Schultess, *De Senecae Quaestt. Nat.* [Bonn, 1872]; and Berger, *De Curtii Aetate* [Heidelberg, 1860]).

The history of Alexander the Great is treated in a rhetorical fashion with little historical insight, introducing a number of picturesque details which are grouped effectively; and the career of the great Macedonian is regarded as a series of brilliant and romantic adventures. There are a number of carefully finished speeches worked into the narrative and much sententious reflection. The style is evidently formed on that of Livy. The chief source of the *Historiae* is Clitarchus (q. v.). Of the original ten books, the first two are lost, and there are lacunae in the others. The work was read during the Middle Ages, and there are numerous MSS., the oldest being of the ninth century. The *Historiae* was edited by Erasmus (1518), and the first complete edition is that of Snakenburg (Delft, 1724). Later editions, with notes, are those of Schmieder (Göttingen, 1803), Mützell (Berlin, 1841), Zumpt (Brunswick, 1849), Vogel (3d ed. Leipzig, 1885), Schmidt (Prague, 1886), Dosson (Paris, 1887); bks. viii. and ix., with English notes, by Heitland and Raven (Cambridge, 1879). There is a lexicon to Curtius by Eichert (2d ed. Hanover, 1880). On the style, see the dissertations by Krah (Insterb. 1886), Eger (Giessen, 1885), Rauch (Meiningen, 1889); and for a general account, Dosson, *Étude sur Q. Curce, sa Vie, et son Œuvre* (Paris, 1887).

Curūlis Magistrātus. The name given to a class of magistracies which conferred the privilege of using the *sella curulis*, or chair of state. This was anciently made of ivory, or, at least, adorned with it. The magistrates who enjoyed this privilege were the dictator, consuls, praetor, censors, and curule aediles. They sat on this chair in their tribunals on all solemn occasions. Those commanders who triumphed had it with them in their chariots. Persons whose ancestors, or themselves, had borne any curule office, were called *nobiles* and had the *ius imaginum*. They who were the first of the family that had raised themselves to any curule office were called *homines novi*, "new men." As regards the origin of the term *curulis*, Festus deduces it from *currus*, "a chariot," and says that "curule magistrates" were so called because borne along in chariots; but see QUIRITES.

Custōdes, Custodiae. The soldiers who guarded the gates of a camp. See CASTRA; VIGILIAE.

Custodia. A watching, guard, or care of anything; hence the word comes to mean (1) custody, confinement, or restraint of a person; (2) persons set as a guard or watch; (3) the place where a guard is kept; (4) a prison, or place where a person is guarded; (5) persons in confinement or subject to any restraint.

Custodia rei is a technical term for the charge which a person undertakes of a thing intrusted to him by another, on account of which he is liable for any loss due to his *dolus* or *culpa*. See CULPA.

Customs Duties. See PORTORIUM.

Custos Urbis. See PRAEFECTUS URBIS.

Cutiliae Aquae. See AQUAE (1).

Cyănē (Κυανή). A Sicilian nymph and playmate of Persephonē, changed into a fountain through grief at the loss of the goddess.

Cyaneae (Κυάνεαι, sc. νῆσοι). Two small rugged islands at the entrance of the Euxine Sea, and forty stadia from the mouth of the Thracian Bosporus. According to Strabo, one was near the European the other near the Asiatic side, and the space between them was about twenty stadia. There was an ancient fable relative to these islands, that they floated about, and united to crush to pieces vessels which attempted to pass through the straits (Pomp. Mela, ii. 7). Pliny gives the same fable, but assigns, at the same time, the true cause of the legend. It arose from their appearing, like all other objects, to move towards or from each other when seen from a vessel in motion itself. The Argo, we are told by Apollonius Rhodius (ii. 601), had a narrow escape in passing through, and lost the extremity of her stern. Pindar says that they were alive and moved to and fro more swiftly than the blasts, until the expedition of the Argonauts brought death upon them (Pyth. iv. 371 foll.). On which passage the scholiast remarks in explanation that it was decreed by the Fates they should become "rooted to the deep" whenever a vessel succeeded in passing through them—a prediction accomplished by the Argo. Phineus had directed Iason and his companions to let fly a pigeon when they were near these islands, telling them that if the bird came safely through the Argo might venture to follow her. They obeyed the directions of the prophet-prince; the pigeon passed through safely with the loss of its tail; and then the Argonauts, watching the recession of the rocks and aided by Heré and Atheué, rowed vigorously on and passed through with the loss of a part of the rudder of their vessel. See ARGONAUTAE.

The term "Cyaneae" (Κυάνεαι), i. e. "dark blue" or "azure," is referred by the scholiasts on Euripides (*Med.* 2) to the colour of these rocks. In the description of Homer, however, as will be seen presently, a more poetic turn is given to the appellation. To the name Cyaneae is frequently joined that of "Symplegades" (Συμπληγάδες), i. e. "the Dashers," in allusion to their supposed collision when vessels attempted to pass through. Homer (*Od.* xii. 61) calls them Πλαγκταί, "Wanderers."

Cyanĕē (Κυανέη). Daughter of Maeander, mother of Caunus and of Byblis.

Cyănus (κύανος). A dark-blue substance supposed to be blue steel, mentioned by Homer and Hesiod as forming a part of works of metal—e. g. on Agamemnon's breastplate (*Il.* xi. 24) and on the shield of Heracles (*Sc. Her.* 143). The house of Alcinoüs had a cornice or frieze of κύανος (*Od.* vii. 87). In Theophrastus it is lapis lazuli (*Lapid.* 31). See Merriam's note on *Od.* vii. 87, in his *Phaeacians of Homer* (N. Y. 1880).

Cyăthus (κύαθος). A Greek and Roman liquid measure, containing one twelfth of the sextarius or .0825 of a pint English. It was, in later times at least, the measure of the common drinking-glass among the Romans, who borrowed it from the Greeks. The form of the cyathus used at banquets was that of a small ladle, by means of which the wine was conveyed into the drinking-cups from the large vessel (κρατήρ) in which it was mixed.

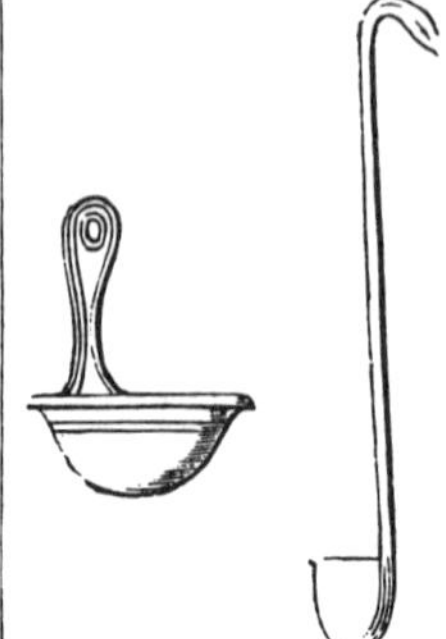

Cyathi. (*Museo Borbonico.*)

The cyathus was the *uncia*, considered with reference to the sextarius as the unit; hence we have *sextans* used for a vessel containing the sixth of the sextarius, or two cyathi, *quadrans* for one containing three cyathi, *triens* for four cyathi, *quincunx* for five cyathi, and so on.

Cyaxăres (Κυαξάρης). (1) A king of the Medes, grandson of Deioces, son of Phraortes, and father of Astyages. He was a prince of violent character, and this trait displayed itself in his treatment of the Scythians, a body of whom had taken refuge in his territories in consequence of a sedition. He received them kindly, allowed them settlements, and even went so far as to intrust some children to their care, in order to have them taught the Scythian language and a knowledge of archery. After some time had elapsed, the Scythians, accustomed to go forth to the chase, and to bring back to the king some of the game obtained by the hunt, returned one day with empty hands. Cyaxares gave vent to his temper by punishing them severely. The Scythians, indignant at this treatment, which they knew to be unmerited, resolved to slay one of the children confided to their care, and, after preparing the flesh like the game they had been accustomed to bring, to serve it up before Cyaxares, and betake themselves immediately to Alyattes at Sardis (Herod. i. 73, 74). This cruel revenge succeeded but too well. Cyaxares demanded the fugitives from King Alyattes, and on his refusal a war ensued. This war lasted for five years; in the sixth, an eclipse of the sun, which had been predicted by Thales, separated the contending armies (B.C. 610). Peace was soon restored through the mediation of Labynetus, king of Babylon, and Syennesis, king of Cilicia (Herod. i. 73 foll.). Herodotus also informs us (i. 103) that Cyaxares was the first who regularly trained the Asiatics to military service; dividing the troops, which had been imbodied promiscuously before his time, into distinct companies of lancers, archers, and cavalry. The historian then adds parenthetically, "this was he who waged war with the Lydians; when, during a battle, the day became night." This parenthetical remark evidently refers to the foregoing account of the eclipse. We are next informed that, having subdued all Asia above the river Halys, he marched with all that were under his command against Nineveh, resolving to avenge the death of his father by the destruction of that city. After he had defeated the Assyrians he laid siege to the city, but was forced to raise it by a sudden invasion of his territories. For a numerous army of Scythians, headed by Madyas, made an irruption into Media, defeated him in a pitched battle, and brought both him and all Upper Asia under subjection to them for eight-and-twenty years (Herod. i. 103 foll.). Then, in revenge for their galling impositions and exactions, he slew their chieftains, when intoxicated, at a banquet to which he had invited them; and, expelling the rest, recovered his former power and possessions. After this, the Medes took Nineveh and subdued the Assyrian provinces, all except the Babylonians, their confederates in the war. Cyaxares died after having reigned forty years (B.C. 634–594), including twenty-eight years of the Scythian dominion. (2) Son of Astyages, succeeding his father at the age of forty-nine years. Being naturally of an easy, indolent disposition and fond of his amusements, he left the burden of military affairs and the care of the government to Cyrus, his nephew and son-in-law, who married his only daughter, and was, therefore, doubly entitled to succeed him.

Cybaea. A merchant-ship or transport, mentioned only in Cicero's orations against Verres (iv. 8, § 17). It is properly an adjective, as Cicero speaks of *navis cybaea*, and describes it as most beautiful and richly adorned like a trireme (v. 17, § 44). The word perhaps comes from the Greek κύπη, a kind of ship mentioned by Hesychius.

Cybēbé (Κυβήβη). A name of Cybelé, used by the poets when a long penult is required. The form Cybellé is sometimes, though with less propriety, employed for a similar purpose. See RHEA.

Cybĕlé (Κυβέλη). See RHEA.

Cybistra (τὰ Κύβιστρα). An ancient city of Asia Minor, lying at the foot of Mount Taurus, in the part of Cappadocia bordering on Cilicia.

Cyclădes (Κυκλάδες). A name applied by the ancient Greeks to that cluster (κύκλος) of islands which encircled Delos. Strabo says that the Cyclades were at first only twelve in number, but were afterwards increased to fifteen. These, as we learn from Artemidorus, were Ceos, Cythnos, Seriphos, Melos, Siphnos, Cimolos, Prepesinthos, Olearos, Paros, Naxos, Syros, Myconos, Tenos, Andros, and Gyaros, which last, however, Strabo himself was desirous of excluding, from its being a mere rock, as also Prepesinthos and Olearos.

It appears from the Greek historians that the Cyclades were first inhabited by the Phœnicians, Carians, and Leleges, whose piratical habits rendered them formidable to the cities on the continent till they were conquered and finally extirpated by Minos (Thuc. i. 4; Herod. i. 171). These islands were subsequently occupied for a short time by Polycrates, tyrant of Samos, and the Persians; but after the battle of Mycalé (B.C. 479) they became dependent on the Athenians.

Cyclas (κυκλάς). A luxurious robe, of a circular form, worn by Roman women, to the bottom of which a border was affixed, inlaid with gold (Propert. iv. [v.] 7, 40). It was made of some thin material, perhaps muslin. Alexander Severus, in his various attempts to restrain the luxury of his age, enacted that women should possess only one cyclas each, and that it should not be adorned with more than six *unciae* of gold (Lamprid. *Alex. Sev.* 41). It continued to be a dress of ceremony in the fifth century, and was not used exclusively by women. It is related, among other instances of Caligula's effeminacy, that he sometimes appeared in public in a garment of this description (*cycladatus*, Suet. *Calig.* 52).

Cyclic Poets (CYCLĬCI POĒTAE). A name given by the ancient grammarians to a class of minor poets, who selected, for the subjects of their productions, events occurring as well during the Trojan War as before and after, and who, in treating of these subjects, confined themselves within a certain round or cycle (κύκλος, *circulus*) of fable. In order to understand the subject more fully, we must observe that there was both a Mythic and a Trojan cycle. The former of these embraced the whole series of fable, from the genealogies of the gods down to the time of the Trojan War; the latter comprised the fables that had reference to, or were in any way connected with, the Trojan War. Of the first class were Theogonies, Cosmogonies, Titanomachies, and the like; of the second, the poems of Arctinus, Lesches, Agias, Eugammon, Stasinus, and others. (See HOMERIC QUESTION.) At a later period the term *cyclic* was applied, as a mark of contempt, to two species of poems—one, where the poet confined himself to a trite and hackneyed *round* (κύκλος) of particulars (cf. Horace, *Ars Poet.* 132); the other, where, from an ignorance of the true nature of epic poetry, he indulged in an inordinate and tiresome amount of detail, going back to the remotest beginnings of a subject. The most celebrated of the Cyclic poems were the *Cypria* (q. v.), the *Aethiopis* (q. v.) of Arctinus, the *Little Iliad* (Ἰλιὰς Μικρά) of Pausanias, the *Nostoi* (q. v.) of Agias, the *Telegonia* of Eugammon, the *Batrachomyomachia* (q. v.), and the *Margites* (q. v.) of Pigres. See HOMERUS.

All that remains of the Cyclic poets is some sixty lines, which can be found in the appendix to Welcker's *Epischer Cyclus* (Bonn, 1835), and Düntzer, *Frag. d. Ep. Poësie* (Cologne, 1840). The chief ancient authority is the *Chrestomatheia* of Proclus (q. v.). See Mahaffy, *Hist. of Class. Gk. Lit.* vol. i. ch. vi. (1880), and the article EPOS in this Dictionary. On the meaning of the word κυκλικός, see D. B. Munro in the *Journal of Hellenic Studies* for 1883.

Cyclopean Walls. See CYCLOPES.

Cyclōpes (Κύκλωπες). A fabulous race, of gigantic size, having but one eye, large and round, placed in the centre of their forehead, whence, according to the common account, their name was derived—from κύκλος, "a circular opening," and ὤψ, "an eye." Homer makes Odysseus, after having left the country of the Lotus-eaters (Lotophagi), to have sailed on westward, and to have come to that of the Cyclopes, who are described by him as a rude and lawless race, who neither planted nor sowed, but whose land was so fertile as to produce of itself wheat, barley, and vines. They had no social institutions, neither assemblies nor laws, but dwelt separately, each in his cave, on the tops of lofty mountains, and each, without regard to others, governed his own wife and children. The adventure of Odysseus with Polyphemus, one of this race, will be found under the latter title. Nothing is said by Homer respecting the size of the Cyclopes in general, but every effort is made to give an exaggerated idea of that of Polyphemus. Hence some have imagined that, according to the Homeric idea, the Cyclopes were not in general of such huge dimensions or cannibal habits as the poet assigns to Polyphemus himself; for the latter does not appear to have been of the ordinary Cyclops-race, but the son of Poseidon and a sea-nymph; and he is also said to have been the

Section of the Treasury of Atreus at Mycenae.

strongest of the Cyclopes (*Od.* i. 70). Later poets, however, lost no time in supplying whatever the fable wanted in this respect, and hence Vergil describes the whole race as of gigantic stature and compares them to so many tall forest-trees (*Aen.* iii. 680). It is not a little remarkable that neither in the description of the Cyclopes in general, nor of Polyphemus in particular, is there any notice taken of their being one-eyed; yet in the account of the blinding of the latter, it seems to be assumed as a thing well known. We may hence, perhaps, infer that Homer followed the usual derivation.

Such is the Homeric account of the Cyclopes. In Hesiod, on the other hand (*Theog.* 139 foll.), we have what appears to be the earlier legend respecting these fabled beings, a circumstance which may tend to show that the *Odyssey* was composed by a poet later than Hesiod, and not by the author of the *Iliad.* In the *Theogony* of Hesiod the Cyclopes are only three in number—Brontes, Steropes, and Arges. They are the sons of Uranus and Gaea (Caelus and Terra), and their employment is to forge the thunderbolts for Zeus. They are said to be in every other respect like gods, excepting the one single eye in the middle of their foreheads, a circumstance from which Hesiod also, like Homer, deduces their general name (*Theog.* 144 foll.). In the individual names given by Hesiod we have evidently the germ of the whole fable. The Cyclopes are the energies of the sky—the thunder, the lightning, and the rapid march of the latter (Brontes, from *βροντή*, "thunder"; Steropes, from *στεροπή*, "the lightning"; Arges, from *ἀργής*, "rapid"). In accordance with this idea the term Κύκλωψ (*Cyclops*) itself may be regarded as a simple, not a compound term, of the same class with *μώλωψ*, Κέρκωψ, Κέκροψ, Πέλοψ; and the word *κύκλος* being the root, we may make the Cyclopes to be "the Whirlers," or, to designate them by a Latin name, *Volvuli.*

When the thunder, the lightning, and the flame had been converted by poetry into one-eyed giants, and localized in the neighbourhood of volcanoes, it was an easy process to convert them into smiths, the assistants of Hephaestus (Callim. *H. in Artem.* 46 foll.; Verg. *Georg.* iv. 173; *Aen.* viii. 416 foll.). As they were now artists in one line, it gave no surprise to find them engaged in a task adapted to their huge strength—namely, that of rearing the massive walls of Tiryns, for which purpose they were brought by Proetus from Lycia (Schol. *ad* Eurip. *Orest.* 955). Hence, too, the name "Cyclopean" is applied to this species of architecture, just as in Germany the remains of ancient Roman walls are popularly called "Riesenmauer" and "Teufelsmauer." One theory refers the name Cyclops to the circular buildings constructed by the Pelasgi, of which we have so remarkable a specimen in what is called the Treasury of Atreus, at Mycenae. From the form of these buildings, resembling within a hollow cone or beehive, and the round opening at the top, the individuals who constructed them are thought to have derived their appellation. (Cf. Gell's *Argolis*, p. 34.) Those who make them to have dwelt in Sicily blend an old tradition with one of more recent date. This last probably took its rise when Aetna and the Lipari Islands were assigned to Hephaestus, by the popular belief of the day, as his workshops; which could only have happened when Aetna had become better known, and Mount Moschylus, in the isle of Lemnos, had ceased to be volcanic.

A few remarks may fittingly be added here on the subject of the Cyclopean architecture. This style of building is frequently alluded to by the ancient writers. In fact, every architectural work of extraordinary magnitude, to the execution of which human labour appeared inadequate, was ascribed to the Cyclopes (Eurip. *Iph. in Aul.* 534; id. *Herc. Fur.* 15; id. *Troad.* 108; Strab. 373; Sen. *Herc. Fur.* 996; Stat. *Theb.* iv. 151; Pausan. ii. 25). The general character of the Cyclopean style is immense blocks of stone, without cement, placed

Cyclopean Pyramid at Cenchreae.

upon each other, sometimes irregularly and with smaller stones filling up the interstices, sometimes in regular and horizontal rows. The Cyclopean style is commonly divided into four eras. The first, or oldest, is that employed at Tiryns and Mycenae, consisting of blocks of various sizes, some of them very large, the interstices of which are, or were once, filled up with small stones. The second era is marked by polygonal stones, which nevertheless fit into each other with great nicety. Specimens exist at Delphi, Iulis, and at Cosa in Etruria. In this style there are no courses. The third era appears in the Phocian cities, and in some of Boeotia and Argolis. It is distinguished by the work being made in courses, and by the stones, though of unequal size, being of the same height. The fourth and youngest style presents horizontal courses of masonry, not always of the same height, but formed of stones which are all rectangular. This style is chiefly confined to Attica. The most reasonable opinion relative to the Cyclopean walls of antiquity is that which ascribes their erection to the ancient Pelasgi (q. v.). See Reber, *History of Ancient Art*, pp. 178–194 (Eng. trans. N. Y. 1882); and W. Gell, *Walls of Ancient Greece.*

Cyclops (Κύκλωψ). The title of a play of Euripides, which is remarkable as being the only undoubted specimen left to us of a Satyric drama (q. v.). The prologue is spoken by Silenus. He and his Satyrs are in search of Dionysus, who has been carried into the western seas by pirates. Odysseus appears, and his well-known adventure with the Cyclopes forms the rest of the plot, the story given in the *Odyssey* being closely followed. The play is little read, and has been seldom edited apart from the other works of Euripides, though there is a good recent edition with English notes by W. Long (Oxford, 1891). Shelley has rendered the *Cyclops* into English with a few omissions. There are no imitations. See Mahaffy, *Hist. of Class. Gk. Lit.* vol. i. pp. 377–379 (American ed.).

Cycnus (Κύκνος, "Swan"). (1) The son of Ares and Pelopia, who threw himself in the way of Heracles in Trachis, when the hero was on his way to Ceyx. According to another story, Heracles was sent against Cycnus by Apollo, because he lay in wait for the processions on their road to Delphi. In the contest between them, as described by Hesiod in his *Shield of Heracles*, Ares stood by the side of his son, while Heracles was supported by Athené and his faithful Iolaüs. Heracles slew Cycnus and even wounded Ares, when the latter attempted to avenge the fall of his son. Cycnus was buried with all due honours by his father-in-law Ceyx, but Apollo destroyed the tomb by an inundation of the river Anaurus. There was a son of Ares and Pyrené who bore the same name, and he too was said to have fallen in combat against Heracles. Ares attempted to avenge his son, when Zeus, by a flash of lightning, separated his angry children. After his death, so ran the story, Cycnus was changed by his father into a swan.

(2) The son of Poseidon and Calycé. He was exposed by his mother on the sea-shore and found by some fishermen, who named him Cycnus because they saw a swan flying round him. He was invulnerable and of gigantic strength and stature; his head (or, according to another account, his whole body) was as white as snow. He became king of Colonae in the Troad, and was twice married. A slanderous utterance of his second wife stung him to fury against the children of his first wife, so that he threw them into the sea in a chest. They were cast up alive on the island of Tenedos, where Tenes was king. At a later time Cycnus repented of his deed, sought for his son, and marched with him to the aid of the Trojans against the Greeks. They prevented the Greeks from landing; but both were at last slain by Achilles, who strangled the invulnerable Cycnus with his own helmet-strap. He was changed by Poseidon into a swan.

Cydias (Κυδίας). A painter, born in the island of Cythnus, one of the Cyclades, and who flourished B.C. 360. Hortensius, the orator, purchased his painting of the Argonauts for 144,000 sesterces (nearly $5800). This same work was afterwards transferred by Agrippa to the portico of Neptune (Plin. *H. N.* xxxv. 40).

Cydippé (Κυδίππη). The heroine of a very popular Greek love-story, which was treated by Callimachus in a poem now unfortunately lost. The later Greek prose romances were founded upon this version. Cydippé was the daughter of a well-born Athenian. It happened that she and Acontius, a youth from the island of Ceos, who was in love with her, had come at the same time to a festival of Artemis at Delos. Cydippé was sitting in the temple of Artemis when Acontius threw at her feet an apple on which was written, "I swear by the sanctuary of Artemis that I will wed Acontius." Cydippé took up the apple and read the words aloud, then threw it from her and took no notice of Acontius and his addresses. After this her father wished on several occasions to give her in marriage, but she always fell ill before the wedding. The father consulted the Delphic oracle, which revealed to him that the illness of his daughter was due to the wrath of Artemis, by whose shrine she had sworn and broken her oath. He accordingly gave her to Acontius in marriage.

Cydnus (Κύδνος). A river of Cilicia Campestris, rising in the Taurus and flowing through the midst of the city of Tarsus. It was celebrated for the coldness of its waters, in bathing in which Alexander the Great nearly lost his life (Plut. *Alex.* 19).

Cydonia (Κυδωνία). One of the chief cities of Crete, situated on the northwest coast, derived its name from the Cydones, a Cretan race, placed by Homer in the western part of the island. Cydonia was the place from which quinces (*Cydonia mala*) were first brought to Italy; and its inhabitants were among the best Cretan archers.

Cylindrus (κύλινδρος). (1) A roller for levelling the ground in agricultural and other operations (Verg. *Georg.* i. 178; Vitruv. x. 6). Unlike those of modern times, it did not revolve but was simply dragged upon the ground. (2) A precious stone cut or ground in a cylindrical form (Juv. ii. 61).

Cylindrus or Roller. (Rich.)

Cylix. See CALIX.

Cyllărus (Κύλλαρος). A beautiful Centaur, killed at the wedding-feast of Pirithoüs (q. v.). The horse of Castor was likewise called Cyllarus.

Cyllēné (Κυλλήνη). (1) The highest mountain in the Peloponnesus, on the frontiers of Arcadia and Achaia, sacred to Hermes, who had a temple on the summit, was said to have been born there, and was hence called Cyllenius. (2) A seaport town of Elis.

Cyllenius (Κυλλήνιος). An epithet applied to Hermes, from his having been born on Mount Cyllené.

Cylon (Κύλων). An Athenian of noble family who formed the plan of making himself tyrant of Athens (B.C. 612). At the time of the Olympic Games, he seized the Acropolis, where he was soon after closely besieged by the archons. Being at last destitute of food, he and his followers capitulated, after receiving a promise from the archon Megacles, one of the Alcmaeonidae, that their lives would be spared. In violation of this promise, however, they were all put to death, some being even murdered at the altar of the Eumenides. For this sacrilege, the Alcmaeonidae were tried by the nobles and banished (B.C. 596 or 595), at the instigation of Solon. The family retired to Phocis and remained exiles from Athens until the time of Lycurgus (B.C. 560). See ALCMAEONIDAE.

Cyma (κῦμα). In architecture, an *ogee*, a wave-shaped moulding, consisting of two curves, the one concave and the other convex. There were two forms—the *cyma recta*, which was concave above and convex below, and the *cyma reversa*, which was convex above and concave below. The diminutive *cymatium* or *cumatium* (κυμάτιον) is the more common name. The original form of the *cymatium* was, however, a simple hollow, the *cavetto*.

Cymba (κύμβη). Literally "a hollow," was a small boat, probably made originally from the hollow of a tree, used on rivers and lakes, etc., especially by fishermen. Pliny ascribes its invention to the Phœnicians (Plin. *H. N.* vii. 208). The poets give the name of *cymba* to Charon's boat (Verg. *Aen.* vi. 303). See CHARON.

Cymbălum (κύμβαλον). A musical instrument in the shape of two half globes, which were held one in each hand by the performer and played by being struck against each other. The word is originally Greek, being derived from κύμβος, "a hollow." In Greek it has several other significations, as the cone of a helmet; it is also used for ἀρδανία, the vessel of purification placed at the door of a house where there had been a death. Besides this, it is often employed metaphorically for an empty, noisy person, as Tiberius called Apion the grammarian *cymbalum mundi*. In the mediæval Latin it is used for a church or convent bell and sometimes for the dome of a church.

Cymbalistria. (Pompeii.)

The cymbal was usually made in the form of two half globes, either running off towards a point, so as to be grasped by the whole hand, or with a handle. It was commonly of bronze, but sometimes of baser material, to which Aristophanes alludes. As with the *crotalum*, the performers were usually women and were known as *cymbalistriae*. See CROTALUM; SISTRUM.

Cymbium (κυμβίον, κύμβος, κύμβη). A small cup, not round, but long and without handles. They were used as drinking-cups, and also as ladles for dipping out wine from the mixer. Various materials were employed in their construction, such as silver, clay, and chrysoprase. The name is derived from κύμβη, "a boat," with which compare our "butter-boat," "sauce-boat," etc.

Cymé (Κύμη). The largest of the Aeolian cities of Asia Minor, upon the coast of Aeolis, on a bay named after it Cumaeus (also Elaïticus) Sinus. It was the mother-city of Cumae in Campania.

Cymothoë (Κυμοθόη). One of the Nereides, represented by Vergil as assisting the Trojans, with Triton, after the storm with which Aeolus, at the request of Iuno, had afflicted the fleet (*Aen.* i. 148).

Cynaegīrus (Κυναίγειρος). An Athenian, celebrated for his courage. He was brother to the poet Aeschylus. After the battle of Marathon (B.C. 490) he pursued the flying Persians to their ships, and seized one of their vessels with his right hand, which was immediately severed by the enemy. Upon this he seized the vessel with his left hand, and when he had lost that also he still kept his hold with his teeth. Herodotus (vi. 114) merely relates that he seized one of the Persian vessels by the stern, and had his hand cut off with an axe. The more detailed account is given by Justin (ii. 9).

Cynaetha (Κύναιθα). A town of Arcadia, on the river Crathis, near the northern borders, and some distance to the northwest of Cyllené. It had been united to the Achaean League, but was betrayed to the Aetolians in the Social War. This was effected by some exiles, who, on their return to their native city, formed a plot for admitting the enemy within its walls. The Aetolians, accordingly, having crossed into Achaia with a considerable force, advanced to Cynaetha and easily scaled the walls; they then sacked the town and destroyed many of the inhabitants, not sparing even those to whose treachery they were indebted for their success. Polybius observes that the calamity which thus overwhelmed the Cynaethians was considered by many as a just punishment for their unusually depraved and immoral life.

Cynāné (Κυνάνη), **Cyna** (Κύνα), or **Cynna** (Κύννα). The half-sister of Alexander the Great, daughter of Philip by Audata, an Illyrian woman. She married her cousin, Amyntas, and on Alexander's death went to Asia, intending to marry her daughter Eurydicé to Arrhidaeus; but Perdiccas, who controlled Arrhidaeus, fearing this project, had her put to death (Diod. Sic. xix. 15).

Cynegetĭca. A poem on the chase, written in Latin by Grattius (q. v.) towards the end of the Augustan Age, and existing in an imperfect state. It traces the development of the chase from the earliest ages, and goes on to describe the chase itself, giving also an account of the different breeds of dogs and horses, with digressions on various themes. The technical details are carefully given, but the poem has no very great merit. The part of the poem still existing consists of 536 hexameter lines and five fragments of lines. The same title was chosen by the later poet Nemesianus (about A.D. 275), of which we have the first 425 lines (hexameters), partly in imitation of Calpurnius (q. v.). The poems of both Grattius and Nemesianus were edited together by Stern (Halle, 1832), by Haupt (Leipzig, 1838), and by Schenkl (Prague, 1885). See Birt, *Hist. Hexam. Lat.* p. 57. A treatise of Xenophon, in prose, on the chase is entitled Κυνηγετικός. See OPPIANUS.

Cynesii (Κυνήσιοι) or **Cynētes.** A people, according to Herodotus, dwelling in the extreme west of Europe, beyond the Kelts, apparently in Spain.

Cynĭci (Κυνικοί). A name given to the followers of Antisthenes who founded a distinct school of philosophy at Athens about B.C. 380. Antisthenes had been a pupil of Socrates, and, like that philosopher, he taught that speculative philosophy was unprofitable, and should be supplanted by the practical ethical teaching whose end is a moral and tranquil life. In this respect the Cynic School was like the Stoic, but differed in defining virtue to be extreme simplicity in living. This simplicity the followers of Antisthenes pushed so far as to violate the most elementary notions of cleanliness and even decency, and to plunge into the most frantic excesses of austerity, wearing filthy clothing, eating raw meat, and treating all who approached them with insulting rudeness. Hence the name Κυνικοί, "dog-like," was applied to them in its literal meaning, from their snarling insolence, though the name probably originated from the Gymnasium Cynosarges (q. v.), in which Antisthenes first taught. The most famous of the Cynics, Diogenes of Sinopé, accepted the name Κύων with a sort of pride, and was pleased to be styled "Diogenes the Dog," saying, however, that he did not, like other dogs, bite his enemies, but only his friends and for their own good. Besides Antisthenes and Diogenes, the best known Cynics were Crates of Thebes (Diog. Laërt. vi. 86), Hipparchia and her brother Metrocles, Monimus of Syracuse, Menippus of Sinopé, whom Lucian describes as "one of the ancient dogs who barks a great deal" (*Bis Accus.* 33); and at Rome, Demetrius, the friend of Seneca, Oenomaüs of Gadara, and Demonax of Cyprus. Cynicism became ultimately merged in Stoicism.

See Ueberweg, *Hist. of Philos.* vol. i. pp. 92–94 (Eng. trans. N. Y. 1872); Mullach, *Frag. Philosophorum Graecorum*, vol. ii. pp. 261–395; Diog. Laërt. vi.; and the articles ANTISTHENES; DEMONAX; DIOGENES; MENIPPUS.

Cynisca (Κυνίσκα). A daughter of Archidamus, king of Sparta, who was the first woman that ever turned her attention to the training of steeds, and the first that obtained a prize at the Olympic Games (Pausan. iii. 8).

Cyno (Κυνώ). The wife of a herdsman, and the one who nurtured and brought up Cyrus the Great, when exposed in infancy (Herod. i. 110). Her name in the Median language was Spaco, according to Herodotus, who makes Cyno the Greek translation of it, from κύων, "a dog," and adds that it signified in the Median tongue a female dog.

Cynocephăli (Κυνοκέφαλοι). A nation of India, who were said to have the heads of dogs, whence their name (Ctesias, *Ind.* 23; Aul. Gell. ix. 4). Diodorus Siculus speaks of them as resembling human beings of deformed visage and as sending forth human mutterings. It has been generally supposed that the Cynocephali of antiquity were nothing more than a species of large ape or baboon. Heeren, however (*Ideen*, i. 2, p. 689), thinks that Ctesias refers, in fact, to the Pariahs, or lowest caste of Hindoos; and that the appellation of Cynocephali is a figurative allusion to their degraded state. The name is also applied to the baboons revered by the ancient Egyptians. Thoth, the god of science, is often represented as dog-headed, and so Anubis (q. v.).

Cynosarges (Κυνόσαργες). A place in the suburbs of Athens, where the school of the Cynics was held. (See CYNICI.) It derived its name from a white dog (κύων ἀργός), which, when Diomus was sacrificing to Heracles, snatched away part of the victim. It was adorned with several temples. The most remarkable thing in it, however, was the Gymnasium, where all strangers, who had but one parent an Athenian, had to perform their exercises, because Heracles, to whom it was consecrated, had a mortal for his mother and was not properly one of the immortals. Cynosarges is supposed to have been situated at the foot of Mount Anchesmus.

Cynoscephălae (Κυνὸς Κεφαλαί, i. e. "Dogs' Heads)." Two hills near Scotussa in Thessaly, where the Thebans defeated the Pheraeans (B.C. 364) and where Flamininus gained his celebrated victory over Philip of Macedonia, B.C. 197.

Cynossēma (Κυνὸς Σῆμα, i. e. "Dog's Tomb"). A promontory in the Thracian Chersonesus near Madytus, so called because it was supposed to be the tomb of Hecuba, who had been previously changed into a dog. See HECUBA.

Cynosūra (Κυνοσουρά). (1) A nymph of Ida in Crete, one of the nurses of Zeus, and afterwards changed into a constellation. (2) A promontory of Attica, formed by the range of Pentelicus. (3) A promontory of Attica, facing the northeastern extremity of Salamis. It is mentioned in the oracle delivered to the Athenians prior to the battle of Salamis (Herod. viii. 76).

Cynthia (Κυνθία). A surname of Artemis, from Mount Cynthus, in the island of Delos, where she was born.

Cynthus (Κύνθος). A mountain of Delos, celebrated as the birthplace of Apollo and Artemis, who were hence called Cynthius and Cynthia respectively.

Cynuria (Κυνουρία). A district on the frontiers of Argolis and Laconia, for the possession of which the Argives and Spartans carried on frequent wars, and which the Spartans at length obtained about B.C. 550.

Cynus (Κῦνος). The chief seaport in the territory of the Locri Opuntii. According to some ancient traditions, it had long been the residence of Deucalion and Pyrrha; the latter was even said to have been interred here (Strab. ix. p. 425).

Cyparissia (Κυπαρισσία). A town in Messenia, on the western coast, on a promontory and bay of the same name.

Cyparissus (Κυπάρισσος). (1) Son of Telephus, who, having inadvertently killed his favorite stag, was seized with immoderate grief and metamorphosed into a cypress. (2) A small town in Phocis on Parnassus, near Delphi.

Cypria (Κυπρία). A poem in early days ascribed to Homer, but denied to him by Herodotus (ii. 117). Later, its author is variously given as Stasinus or Hegesias. It detailed the causes of the Trojan War, and served as a sort of introduction to the *Iliad*. See CYCLIC POETS; HOMERUS.

Cyprus (Κύπρος). A large island of the Mediterranean, south of Cilicia and west of Syria, identical, at least in part, with the Hebrew *Kittim*, which seems to be its oldest known name; but it appears to be sometimes included in the name Caphtor, a title that properly belongs to Crete with other islands and coast lands settled by the Caphtorim. Other ancient names of Cyprus, most of them poetical, are Aeria, Aerosa, Acamantis, Amathusia, Aphrodisia, Aphelia, Collinia, Cerastis, Cryptos, Meïnis, Ophiusa, Macaria, Paphos, Sphekeia. The derivation of the name is uncertain, but the principal authorities, ancient and modern, refer it to the Hebrew *kopher* or *gopher*, the name of a tree; sometimes, without adequate reason, connecting it with *cupressus*. Another derivation is from *cuprum*, "copper," formerly found in the island; but the χάλκος κύπριος or *aes cyprium* probably took its name from the island, not the island from the metal.

Cyprus is reckoned by Strabo (or Timaeus, whom he follows) to be the third in extent of the Mediterranean isles. Its shape was aptly compared by the ancients to the outspread skin of an ox, or to the fleece of a sheep. Its extreme length, from Cape Acamas (now Cape Arnaouti or Epiphanio) on the west to the promontory Dinaretum (now St. Andrea) on the east, is about 140 miles; its greatest breadth, from Crommyon (now Cormaciti) on the north to Cape Curias (now Cape Gatto), on the south, about 60; its width varying greatly, the long strip that ends at Dinaretum being very narrow and scarcely more than 10 miles across at any point. Off Dinaretum are several small islands called Kleides (Keys). The coast is provided with numerous bays; but the harbors are now mere roadsteads, though the remains of ancient artificial harbor moles are to be seen at several places (as New Paphos, Soli, etc.).

From Crommyon to Dinaretum, along and quite near the coast, extends a mountainous chain, of which the highest peaks are Buffavento (3240 ft.), Pentedactylon (2480 ft.), and Elias (2810 ft.). The principal ranges, however, are in the west and southwest, the highest point being Mount Olympus (Trodos or Troödos, 6590 ft.), nearly midway between Curium on the south coast and Soli on the north, from the top of which a view of the whole island can be obtained. Next in height is Mount Adelphi (Maschera, 5380 ft.), a few miles to the east; still farther east, a hill (4370 ft.) whose ancient name is unknown; and still farther east again, Mount Santa Croce (Stavros, 2300 ft.). The chain extends nearly to Famagousta (Ammochostos, Constantia-Salamis), with frequent spurs to the shore; and spurs also extend from Olympus radially to the north, west, and south. Between the two ranges is a vast plain, now called the Messouria, whose principal river is the Pidias (Pidaeas), emptying into the sea near Salamis. The Messouria to-day is one vast grain-field, interspersed with insignificant villages. The island formerly abounded in trees and timber, of which it is now mostly denuded, though the kharub, olive, fig, orange, date-palm, lemon, nectarines, apricots, etc., and others suited to the climate flourish. Wild grape-vines still grow to an immense size. Wine, of various sorts, is abundant; the best and most famous being the Commanderia wine, so named from its original producers, the Knights of St. John, at Colossi. Formerly Cyprus yielded to no region in fertility, producing an abundance of grain, wine, oil, and fruits. At the proper season the hills and uncultivated plains are carpeted with anemones, ranunculuses, crocuses, hyacinths, squills, and a great variety of other flowers, especially those with bulbous roots. One ancient epithet of Cyprus is εὐώδης. But agriculture, along with irrigation and drainage, is much neglected. Salt lakes, or "Salines," exist near Larnaca, the ancient Citium, furnishing now, as in the times of Pliny, vast supplies of salt for home consumption and exportation, the salt coating the surface as the summer heat evaporates the water. The climate is still that of the ancient *nimio calore*.

Copper Proconsular Coin of Cyprus.

Although the names of special historians have come down to us, we possess no ancient special treatise or history of the island, but are dependent for information anciently current upon the frequent mention in the Greek and Roman classics, with brief notices in the later historians. These are best collected in Engel's monograph *Kypros* (Berlin, 1841).

The earliest inhabitants have generally been supposed to be Phœnicians, and it is true that the Phœnician language retained its hold in certain parts of Cyprus as late as anywhere, contemporarily, of course, with the Greek, the Lycian (locally), and later with the Latin. The Cypriotes, however, spoke a language peculiar to themselves, as was long ago evident from the scattered glosses preserved by the grammarians and lexicographers, and as has lately been further and most conclusively shown by the recent discovery and decipherment of inscriptions in the peculiar Cypriote character. This language was essentially Greek; and the Greek of Cyprus to-day embraces many peculiarities of its own. The legendary hero of Cyprus was Cinyras, who is said to have come to the island at the time of the beginning of the Trojan War. Without going into the matter of the legend, it may be said that Greek inscriptions of the "Cinyradae" (the priestly caste of Old Paphos, etc.) have been found in the island within the last twenty years.

The chief religion of the island was notoriously the worship of Venus; but with few exceptions (as e. g. Zeus Labranios, introduced near Amathus from Caria) the religion and deities were introduced from Phœnicia, and thus indirectly from the farther East—with, however, some Greek modification. Aphroditê, Apollo, Hercules, and other deities usually called Greek or Roman were thus introduced, the Greek and Phœnician names of some of them appearing now and then on the same bilingual inscription. Aphroditê had her epithet of "Paphian" not only at Paphos, where her rites included all the extravagancies of Mylitta at Babylon, but at the other seats of her worship—Golgos, Dali, Cerynia, etc. Apollo Hylates, who had a temple at Curium, is called by that name and also by his Phœnician name of Resheph Mical on a bilingual inscription found at Dali. A temple to Eshmunmelqarth (=Aesculapius-Hercules), a Phœnician deity much like the Greek Palaemon and the Roman Portumnus, near the Salines at Larnaca, has furnished a number of Phœnician inscriptions of the fourth century B.C.; while a temple to Artemis Paralia, close at hand, has furnished a few Greek inscriptions and an immense number of valuable terra-cotta remains.

Colossal Male Head from Cyprus. (Di Cesnola.)

Aside from the mythical reign of Cinyras over the whole island, the territory, so far as we know, was broken up into a number of kingdoms, whose detailed history has well-nigh perished. A dynasty of Phœnician kings ruled over Citium, Idalium, and Tamassus in the fifth and fourth centuries B.C. Salamis, said to have been founded by Teucer, and by him named after his native city, had its own Greek kings at the same period. Paphos had its dynasty of the Cinyradae, who seem also to have extended their power over Amathus and certain other parts. Soli and Cythrea traced their origin to the Athenians; Lapethus and Cerynia to a Lacedaemonian colony under Praxander and an Achaean one under Cepheus; Curium to the Argives. A town Asiné, whose site is not known, is said to have been colonized by the Dryopians; Neo-Paphos by Agapenor. The promontory Acamas is said to have its name from the hero of the Trojan War. Old Paphos, Amathus, and Citium were founded by the Phœnicians; and of these, Citium (with Dali and Tamassus) seems to have retained its Phœnician character with less modification than the others. Carpassia seems also to have had a Phœnician origin. Articles of Phœnician manufacture—bronze, gold, silver, pottery, etc.—have been found in abundance all over the island.

Terra-cotta Vase from Citium, inscribed *Khthac.* (Di Cesnola.)

Aside from these scattered data, we know that Thothmes III. of Egypt (cir. B.C. 1500) conquered Cyprus; Belus of Tyre was at one time its master; ten kingdoms, including Soli, Chytri, Curium, Lapethus, Cerynia, Neo Paphos, Marium, Idalium, Citium, and Amathus, sent their submission to the Assyrian Esarhaddon (cir. B.C. 890); Sargon put the island to tribute (cir. B.C. 707); Apries (Pharaoh Hophra) of Egypt defeated some Cyprian monarchs near Citium, and returned home laden with their spoils; Amasis of Egypt overran the island and put it to tribute, but the Cyprian rulers joined Cambyses the Persian against the son of Amasis. The king of Amathus revolted from the Persians in the time of Darius, and the longest record extant in the Cypriote character commemorates one of the side issues of this struggle. In B.C. 477, the Athenians and Lacedaemonians conquered part of Cyprus from the Persians; and a war resulted in which the Greeks, with the Tyrians and Egyptians as allies, were on one side, and the Persians on the other. The power of Alexander the Great was both felt and helped in Cyprus, after which, under the Ptolemies, followed wars and doubtful sovereignty, till Demetrius Poliorcetes conquered the island (cir. B.C. 306). About B.C. 296, Ptolemy Soter took the island, after which it remained under Egypt till conquered by the Romans.

Literature and the arts flourished in Cyprus even from a very early period, as witness the "Cypria Carmina," by some attributed to Homer. Citium was the birthplace of Zeno. It is foreign to the present article to trace the history of the island during the Roman rule, the Arabs, the dukedoms of the Crusades, Richard of England, the Lusignans, the Turks, and the recent occupation by the English. Its geographical position made it the field for the exhibition of the arts, deeds, and cults of various nations; and its remains, as brought to light in the explorations of the last twenty-five

Vase, with Phœnician Inscription Burnt on the Clay.

years, have given a deeper insight into the ancient life and occupations and attainments of its successive peoples and masters than it had been thought possible hitherto to attain, and necessitated the rewriting of the principal chapters in the history of ancient art. From the time of Pococke, who, nearly three centuries ago, made his famous discoveries of Phœnician inscriptions (chiefly about Citium), down to the English occupation, scattered and partial explorations have been made. The discovery, in the first half of this century, of inscriptions in a character hitherto unknown, and their decipherment, from 1873 onward, has furnished most valuable clues to the history of religions in Cyprus and the transference of deities thither from the East, besides many minor historical matters and a vast addition to the knowledge of Greek dialects. The characters are syllabic, with peculiar laws of writing, and the language Greek. Some hundreds of these inscriptions are now known (the most of them found by Di Cesnola)—some bilingual (Phœnician and Cypriote) and some digraphic (Greek and Cypriote). The decipherment is a brilliant record—George Smith, of England, discovering the key in a bilingual inscription now in the British Museum; R. H. Lang simultaneously and independently proving the incorrectness of certain previous attempts by others; after which Samuel Birch made additional progress; and complete inscriptions were first read simultaneously and independently by Justus Siegismund and W. Deecke of Strassburg, M. Schmidt of Jena, and I. H. Hall of New York, since which time many writers have contributed lexicographic and dialectic additions.

The discoveries by exploration and excavation have been chiefly made (though the work of others is not inconsiderable) by L. P. di Cesnola, while U. S. Consul at Cyprus, from 1866 to 1877. His work covered nearly all parts of the island, discovering the sites of many ancient cities, and ruins of others whose ancient identity is not yet known, besides many temples, necropoles, ancient aqueducts, and other remains, including over 200 inscriptions, in Assyrian, Cypriote, Phœnician, Greek, and Latin. The greatest number (many thousands) and most important of the objects discovered are deposited in the Metropolitan Museum of Art in New York, though many found their way to European museums and private collections. The statuary, pottery, terra-cottas, glass, gold, silver, and gems are a unique and unrivalled collection, and their value for the study of Phœnician and Greek archæology, art, and history appears in their unceasing use in the learned publications of all countries. Since the occupation of Cyprus by the English, others have excavated and explored, but by no means on the same scale, the principal works accomplished being the further excavation of the site of the greater temple of Venus at Old Paphos, and some large operations near Salamis.

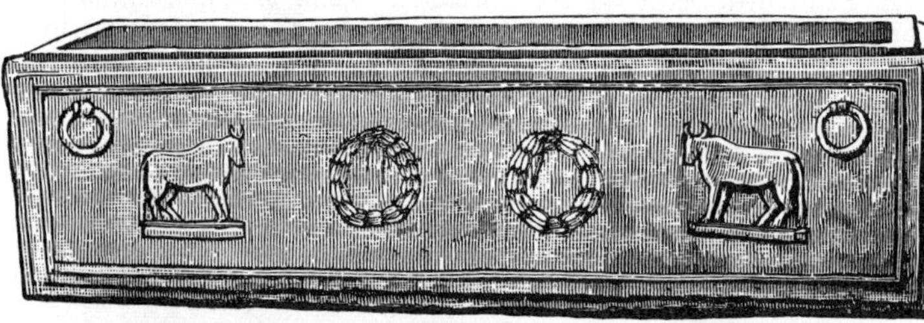
Cyprian Sarcophagus—Roman Period.

For authorities, among many, see Engel, *Kypros*, above referred to; Di Cesnola, *Cyprus* (New York and London, 1878); R. H. Lang, *Cyprus*, etc. (London, 1878). The literature in periodicals and minor volumes is very extensive.

Cypsĕla (τὰ Κύψελα). (1) A town in Arcadia on the frontiers of Laconia. (2) A town in Thrace on the Hebrus and the Egnatia Via.

Cypsĕlus (Κύψελος). A tyrant of Corinth, B.C. 655–625, so named because when a child he was concealed from the Bacchiadae (the Doric nobility of Corinth) by his mother in a chest (κυψέλη). He was succeeded in the tyranny by his son Periander.

Kyrbeis (κύρβεις). See AXONES.

Cyrenaïca (ἡ Κυρηναία). A country of Africa, east of the Syrtis Minor and west of Marmarica. It corresponds with the modern Barca. Cyrenaïca was considered by the Greeks as a sort of terrestrial paradise. This was partly owing to the force of contrast, as all the rest of the African coast along

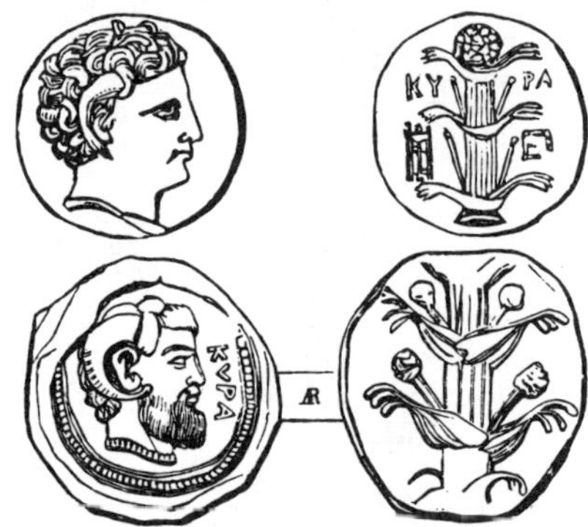

Coins of Cyrené, bearing the sacred Silphium Plant.

the Mediterranean, from Carthage to the Nile, was a barren, sandy waste, and partly to the actual fertility of Cyrenaïca itself. It was extremely well watered, and the inhabitants, according to Herodotus (iv. 199), employed eight months in collecting the productions of the land; the maritime places first yielded their fruits, then the second region, which they called the hills, and lastly those of the highest part inland. One of the chief natural productions of Cyrenaïca was an herb called *silphium*, a kind of laserpitium or assafœtida. It was fattening for cattle, rendering their flesh also tender, and was a useful aperient for man. From its juice, too, when kneaded with clay, a powerful antiseptic was obtained. The silphium formed a great article of trade, and at Rome the composition above mentioned sold for its weight in silver. It is for this reason that the silphium appeared always on the medals of Cyrené. Its culture was neglected, however, when the Romans became masters of the country, and pasturage was more attended to. Cyrenaïca was called Pentapolis from its having five cities of note in it—Cyrené, Arsinoë, Apollonia, Ptolemaïs, Berenicé, and Teuchira. All of these exist at the present day under the form of towns or villages. See CYRENÉ.

Cyrenaïci (Κυρηναϊκοί). A sect of philosophers who followed the doctrines of Aristippus (q. v.), and whose name was derived from their founder's having been a native of Cyrené, and from their school having been established in this place. Aristippus made the *summum bonum* and the τέλος of man to consist in enjoyment, accompanied by good taste and freedom of mind, τὸ κρατεῖν καὶ μὴ ἡττᾶσθαι ἡδόνων ἄριστον, οὐ τὸ μὴ χρῆσθαι (Diog. Laërt. ii. 75). Happiness, said the Cyrenaics, consists, not in tranquillity or indolence, but in a pleasing agitation of the mind or in active enjoyment. Pleasure (ἡδονή) is the ultimate object of human pursuit; it is only in subserviency to this that fame, friendship, and even virtue are to be desired. All crimes are venial, because never committed except through the immediate impulse of passion. Nothing is just or unjust by nature, but by custom and law. The business of philosophy is to regulate the senses in that manner which will render them most productive of pleasure. Since, then, pleasure is to be derived, not from the past or the future, but the present, a wise man will take care to enjoy the present hour, and will be indifferent to life or death. Such were the tenets of the Cyrenaic School. The short duration of this sect was owing, in part, to the remote distance of Cyrené from Greece, the chief seat of learning and philosophy; in part to the unbounded latitude which these philosophers allowed themselves in practice as well as opinion; and finally to the rise of the Epicurean School, which taught the doctrine of pleasure in a more philosophical form. The Cyrenaic teaching that pleasure is the only good was developed in a curious way by Hegesias (q. v.), who argued that as pleasure is the only good, and that as, by reason of the uncertainties of life, an existence of pure pleasure is impossible of attainment by man, the true philosopher will not seek to live, but will end his life by suicide. He therefore preached the doctrine of self-destruction. See Wendt, *De Philosophia Cyrenaica* (Göttingen, 1841); Von Stein, *De Philosophia Cyrenaica* (Göttingen, 1855); and Ueberweg, *Hist. of Philos.* vol. i. pp. 95–98 (Eng. trans. N. Y. 1872).

Cyrēné (Κυρήνη). (1) Daughter of Hypseus, mother of Aristaeus by Apollo, and carried by the god from Mount Pelion to Libya, where the city of Cyrené derived its name from her. (2) An important Greek city in the north of Africa, lying between Alexandria and Carthage. It was founded by Battus (B.C. 631), who led a colony from the island of Thera, and he and his descendants ruled over the city for eight generations. It stood eighty stadia (eight geographical miles) from the coast, on the edge of the upper of two terraces of table-land, at the height of 1800 feet above the sea, in one of the finest situations in the world. At a later time Cyrené became subject to the Egyptian Ptolemies, and was eventually formed, with the island of Crete, into a Roman province. The ruins of the city of Cyrené are very extensive. It was the birthplace of Carneades, Callimachus, Eratosthenes, and Aristippus. The territory of Cyrené, called Cyrenaïca, included also the Greek cities of Barca, Teuchira, Hesperides, and Apollonia, the port of Cyrené. Under the Ptolemies, Hesperides became Berenicé, Teuchira was called Arsinoë, and Barca was eclipsed by its port, which became a city called Ptolemaïs.

Cyreschăta. See CYROPOLIS.

Cyriacus of Ancona. See RENAISSANCE.

Cyrillus (Κύριλλος). (1) A bishop of Jerusalem, A.D. 351–386, and a firm opponent of the Arians, by whose influence he was banished three times from Jerusalem. His works are not numerous. The most important are lectures to catechumens, etc., and a letter to the emperor Constantius, giving an account of a luminous cross which appeared at Jerusalem in 351. The best editions are by Milles (Oxford, 1703), Touttée (Paris, 1720), and Reischl and Rupp (1845–60). There is an English translation of his works in the *Oxford Library of the Fathers*, vol. iii. (1838). See also the works by Gonnet (1876) and Marquardt (1882). (2) Bishop of Alexandria, A.D. 412–444, of which city he was a native. He was fond of power, and was of a remarkably polemical spirit. He persecuted the Jews, whom he expelled from Alexandria; and after a long protracted struggle he procured the deposition of Nestorius, bishop of Constantinople. He was the author of a large number of works, many of which are extant; but in a literary view they are almost worthless. The best edition is still that of Aubert, 6 vols. (Paris, 1638). See Newman's *Historical Sketches*, vol. ii.; Hefele's *History of the Councils*, vol. ii.; and Kopallik, *Cyril von Alexandria* (Mainz, 1881).

Kyrios (κύριος). A lord or guardian; a person charged with the protection of such members of a family as were regarded as incapable of protecting themselves. The early law of all countries takes notice of families only; in other words, it only takes notice of persons exercising *patria potestas*. Attic law, therefore, subordinates a woman to her blood-relations; though relieved from her parent's authority by his death, she continues subject through life to her nearest male relations as guardians (Maine, *Ancient Law*, p. 152 foll.). During marriage, of course, her husband was her κύριος; but when this relation was terminated by death or divorce, she acquired no more freedom than before, but returned to the guardianship of her own family. The term κύριος is applied to males only during minority; the κύριος of such was first, of course, the father, secondly the guardian appointed by his will, thirdly the nearest male relative. In cases of adoption, the natural father remained no longer the κύριος of the adoptee. See ADOPTIO; EPITROPOS; KAKOSIS.

Cyrnus (Κύρνος). The Greek name of the island of Corsica, from which is derived the adjective Cyrneus, used by the Latin poets.

Cyrnus. See THEOGNIS.

Cyropaedīa (Κύρου Παιδεία). A species of historical romance in eight books by Xenophon, professing to give an account of the early years of Cyrus the Great, but in reality setting forth an ideal system of kingly government. Some have considered the *Cyropaedia* as a criticism of the first two books of Plato's *Republic*, on which see Aulus Gellius, xiv. 3. It is the longest and most ambitious of all the works of Xenophon, and is interesting as containing in the form of an episode the earliest specimen of a love-romance—the story of the love of Abradatus and Panthea. The last chapter of the work is probably spurious. (See Mahaffy, *Hist. of Class. Gk. Lit.* ii. pp. 280–282.) Good editions are those of Breitenbach and Hertlein (1874); and Holden (1890).

Cyropŏlis (Κυρόπολις). A large city of Asia, on the banks of the Iaxartes, founded by Cyrus. It was also called Cyreschata. Alexander destroyed it, and built in its stead a city, called by the Roman geographers Alexandrea Ultima, by the Greeks, Ἀλεξανδρεία Ἐσχάτη, of which the Latin is a translation.

Cyrrhestĭcē (Κυρρηστική). The name given under the Seleucidae to a province of Syria, lying between Commagenē on the north and the plain of Antioch on the south.

Cyrrhus (Κύρρος). (1) A city of Macedonia in the vicinity of Pella. (2) A city of Syria, the capital of a district named after it, Cyrrhestica. It derived its name from the Macedonian Cyrrhus.

Cyrus (Κῦρος; in Persian, *Kurus*). (1) A celebrated conqueror, and the founder of the Persian Empire. He comes forth in a line of monarchs who ruled in Susiana. According to Herodotus, he was the son of Mandani, daughter of Astyages, king of the Medes. The father of Cyrus was the Persian Cambyses. It having been foretold that Mandani's son would become the lord of all Asia, Astyages attempted to destroy the infant, and delivered it to Harpagus, his attendant, to kill. Harpagus, however, fearing the anger of Mandani, gave the child to a herdsman, one Mitradates, who reared the young Cyrus as his own son, under the name of Agradates. When ten years of age, the true parentage of the boy was accidentally discovered by Astyages, who, after punishing Harpagus with great barbarity, sent Cyrus to his parents in Persia. When the young prince grew up, he headed a revolt against Astyages, who had become unpopular by his tyranny, and defeated him in battle (B.C. 559). The Medes then accepted Cyrus as their king.

He had not been long seated on the throne when his dominions were invaded by Croesus, king of Lydia, the issue of which contest was so fatal to the latter. (See CROESUS.) The conquest of Lydia established the Persian monarchy on a firm foundation, and Cyrus was now called away to the East by vast designs and by the threats of a distant and formidable enemy. Babylon still remained an independent city in the heart of his empire, and to reduce it was his first and most pressing care. On another side he was tempted by the wealth and weakness of Egypt, while his northern frontier was disturbed and endangered by the fierce barbarians who ranged over the plains that stretch from the skirts of the Indian Caucasus to the Caspian. Until these last should be subdued or humbled his Eastern provinces could never enjoy peace or safety. These objects demanded his own presence; the subjugation of the Asiatic Greeks, as a less urgent and less difficult enterprise, he committed to his lieutenants. While the latter, therefore, were executing his commands in the West, he was himself enlarging and strengthening his power in the East. After completing the subjugation of the nations west of the Euphrates, he marched upon Babylon (q. v.), which he took. The account of this conquest, as described by Herodotus, is given in the article BABYLON. Recent archæological discoveries, however, tend to discredit his narrative. A tablet-inscription found at Babylon states that Cyrus, "king of Elam," took Sippara and Babylon "without fighting." This took place in B.C. 538. See Sayce, *Fresh Light from the Ancient Monuments* (London, 1883); and his *Introduction to Ezra, Nehemiah, and Esther* (2d ed. London, 1887).

Cyrus enjoyed no long interval of repose. The protection which he afforded to the Jews was probably connected with his designs upon Egypt, but he never found leisure to carry them into effect. Soon after the fall of Babylon he undertook an expedition against one of the nations on the eastern side of the Caspian. According to Herodotus, it was the Massagetae, a nomadic horde which had driven the Scythians before them towards the West; and, after gaining a victory over them by stratagem, he was defeated in a great battle and slain. The event is the same in the narrative of Ctesias; but the people against whom Cyrus marched are called the Derbices, and their army is strengthened by troops and elephants furnished by Indian allies; while the death of Cyrus is speedily avenged by one of his vassals, Amorges, king of the Sacae, who gains a decisive victory over the Derbices, and annexes their land to the Persian Empire. Cyrus died in B.C. 529. His son and successor, Cambyses, had been made by him king of Babylon three years before. Cyrus was one of the greatest Asiatics who ever lived; and with the exception of Egypt, the greater part of the Old World was under his rule at the time of his death. His capitals were Ecbatana and Susa; and his tomb exists to-day at Murgab, near Pasargadae.

Cyrus. (Pasargadae.)

(2) Commonly called "the Younger," to distinguish him from the preceding, was the second of the four sons of Darius Nothus and Parysatis. According to the customs of the monarchy, his elder brother Artaxerxes was the legitimate heir-apparent; but Cyrus was the first son born to Darius after his accession to the throne, and he was also his mother's favourite. She had encouraged him to hope that, as Xerxes, through the influence of Atossa, had been preferred to his elder brother, who was born while their father was yet in a private station, so she should be able to persuade Darius to set aside Artaxerxes and declare Cyrus his successor. In the meanwhile he was invested with the government of the western provinces. This appointment he seems from the first to have considered as a step to the throne. He had, however, sagacity and courage enough to perceive that, should he be disappointed in his first expec-

tations, the co-operation of the Greeks might still enable him to force his way to the throne. It was with this view that he zealously embraced the side of Sparta in her struggle with Athens, both as the power which he found in the most prosperous condition and as that which was most capable of furthering his designs. According to Plutarch (*Artax.* 2), Cyrus went to attend his father's sick-bed with sanguine hopes that his mother had accomplished her purpose, and that he was sent for to receive the crown. On his arrival at court, however, he saw himself disappointed in his expectations, and found that he had only come to witness his father's death and his brother's accession to the throne. He accompanied Artaxerxes, whom the Greeks distinguished by the epithet of Mnemon, to Pasargadae, where the Persian kings went through certain mystic ceremonies of inauguration, and Tissaphernes took this opportunity of charging Cyrus with a design against his life. It would seem, from Plutarch's account, that one of the officiating priests was suborned to support the charge, though it is by no means certain that it was unfounded. Artaxerxes was convinced of its truth, and determined on putting his brother to death; and Cyrus was only saved by the passionate entreaties of Parysatis, in whose arms he had sought refuge from the executioner. On this occasion Artaxerxes suffered her to overpower both the suspicions suggested by Tissaphernes and the jealousy which the temper and situation of Cyrus might reasonably have excited. He not only pardoned his brother, but permitted him to return to his government. Cyrus felt himself not obliged, but humbled, by his rival's clemency; and the danger he had escaped only strengthened his resolution to make himself, as soon as possible, independent of the power to which he owed his life.

Immediately after his return to Sardis, he began to make preparations for the execution of his designs. The chief difficulty was to keep them concealed from Artaxerxes until they were fully matured; for though his mother, who was probably from the beginning acquainted with his purpose, was at court, always ready to put the most favourable construction on his conduct, yet Tissaphernes was at hand to watch it with malignant attention and to send the earliest information of any suspicious movement to the king. Cyrus, however, devised a variety of pretexts to blind Tissaphernes and the court, while he collected an army for the expedition which he was meditating. His main object was to raise as strong a body of Greek troops as he could, for it was only with such aid that he could hope to overpower an adversary who had the whole force of the Empire at his command; and he knew enough of the Greeks to believe that their superiority over his countrymen, in skill and courage, was sufficient to compensate for almost any inequality of numbers.

In the spring of B.C. 401, Cyrus began his march from Sardis. His whole Grecian force, a part of which joined him on the route, amounted to 11,000 heavy infantry and about 2000 targeteers. His barbarian troops were 100,000 strong. After directing his line of march through the whole extent of Asia Minor, he entered the Babylonian territory; and it was not until he reached the plain of Cunaxa, between sixty and seventy miles from Babylon, that he became certain of his brother's intention to hazard an engagement. Artaxerxes met him in this spot at the head of an army of 900,000 men. If we may believe Plutarch, the Persian monarch had continued to waver almost to the last between the alternatives of fighting and retreating, and was only diverted from adopting the latter course by the energetic remonstrances of Tiribazus. In the battle which ensued the Greeks soon routed the barbarians opposed to them, but committed an error in pursuing them too far; and Cyrus was compelled, in order to avoid being surrounded by the rest of the king's army, to make an attack upon the centre, where his brother led in person. He routed the royal body-guard, and being hurried away by the violence of his feelings the moment he espied the king, he engaged with him, but was himself wounded and slain by a common soldier. Had Clearchus acted in conformity with the directions of Cyrus, and led his division against the king's centre, instead of being drawn off into pursuit of the flying enemy, the victory must have belonged to Cyrus. According to the Persian custom of treating slain rebels, the head and right hand of Cyrus were cut off and brought to the king, who is said himself to have seized the head by the hair and to have held it up as a proof of his victory to the view of the surrounding crowd. Thus ended the expedition of Cyrus. The Greeks, after the battle, began to negotiate with the king through Tissaphernes, who offered to lead them home. He treacherously violated his word, however; and having, by an act of perfidy, obtained possession of the persons of the Greek commanders, he sent them up to the king at Babylon, where they were all put to death. The Greeks were not, however, discouraged, though at a great distance from their country and surrounded on every side by a powerful enemy. They immediately chose new commanders, in the number of whom was Xenophon, who has given an account of their celebrated retreat. See ANABASIS.

Cyrus (Κῦρος). A large river of Asia, rising in Iberia and falling into the Caspian; now the Kur. This river waters the great valley of Georgia, and is increased by the Aragui; the Iora, probably the Iberus of the ancients; and the Alasan, which is their Alazo.

Cyta (Κύτα). A city of Colchis, in the interior of the country, near the river Phasis, and northeast of Tyndaris. It was the birthplace of Medea. The inhabitants, like the Colchians generally, were famed for their acquaintance with poisonous herbs and magic rites. Scylax calls the place Malê (Μάλη). Medea was called Cytaeis from this her native city.

Cythēra (Κύθηρα). The modern Cerigo; an island off the southeast point of Laconia, with a town of the same name in the interior, the harbour of which was called Scandea. It was colonized at an early time by the Phœnicians, who introduced the worship of Aphroditê (q. v.) into the island, for which it was celebrated. This goddess was hence called Cytheraea, Cythereïs; and according to some traditions, it was in the neighbourhood of this island that she first rose from the foam of the sea.

Cythēris. A celebrated courtesan at Rome, the mistress of M. Antonius, and afterwards of the poet Gallus, the friend of Vergil, who in the Tenth Eclogue speaks of her as Lycoris.

Cythnus (Κύθνος). The modern Thermia; an island in the Aegean Sea, one of the Cyclades (q. v.).

Cytinium (Κυτίνιον). The most important of the four cities of Doris in Greece. According to Thucydides (iii. 95), it was situated to the west of Parnassus, and on the borders of the Locri Ozolae.

Cytōrum (Κύτωρον). A city of Paphlagonia, on the coast between the promontory Carambis and Amastris. It was a Greek town of great antiquity, since Homer alludes to it (*Il.* ii. 853), and it is thought to have been founded by a colony of Milesians. According to Strabo, it had been a port of the inhabitants of Sinopé. In its vicinity was a mountain, named Cytorus, which produced a beautifully veined species of box-tree (Catull. iv. 13; Verg. *Georg.* ii. 437). It is now Kidros.

Cyzicēnus Nummus. See CYZICUS; ELECTRUM.

Cyzicēnus Oecus. See DOMUS, p. 546.

Cyzĭcus (Κύζικος). (1) An island off the northern coast of Mysia, nearly triangular in shape, and about five hundred stadia in circuit. Its base was turned towards the Propontis, while the vertex advanced so closely to the continent that it was easy to connect it by a double bridge, which, as Pliny relates, was done by Alexander. Scylax, however, says that it was always a peninsula, and his authority is followed by Mannert, who is of opinion that the inhabitants may, after the time of Scylax, have separated it from the mainland by a canal or ditch, for purposes of security. It is certainly a peninsula at the present day, and there are no indications whatever of the bridges mentioned by Pliny and others. (2) A celebrated city of Mysia, on the island of the same name, situated partly in the plain which extended to the bridges connecting the island with the continent, and partly on the slope of Mount Arcton Oros. Its first foundation was ascribed to a colony of Pelasgi from Thessaly, under the conduct of Cyzicus, son of Apollo. In process of time the Pelasgi were expelled by the Tyrrheni, and these again made way for the Milesians, who are generally looked upon by the Greeks as the real settlers, to whom the foundation of Cyzicus is to be attributed. Cyzicus became, in process of time, a flourishing commercial city, and was at the height of its prosperity when, through the means of the kings of Pergamus, it secured the favour and protection of Rome. Florus speaks of its beauty and opulence. The Cyzicene commonwealth resembled those of Rhodes, Marseilles, and Carthage. The Romans, in acknowledgment of the bravery and fidelity displayed by the Cyzicenians when besieged by Mithridates (B.C. 75), granted to them their independence and greatly enlarged their territory. Under the emperors, Cyzicus continued to prosper, and in the time of the Byzantine sway it was the metropolis of the Hellespontine province. Cyzicus gave birth to several historians, philosophers, and other writers. The coins of this place, called Κυζικηνοὶ στατῆρες, were so beautiful as to be deemed a miracle of art. (See ELECTRUM.) Persephoné was worshipped as the chief deity of the place, and the inhabitants had a legend among them that their city was given by Zeus to this goddess as a portion of her dowry.

D

D, as a symbol.

IN GREEK.—Δ = a tribus of Elis (*Arch. Zeit.* 1880, p. 57), δέκεμος, δικαστής, δοῦλος (*C. I. G.* 3104), δῆμου (*C. I. G.* 2383, Ψ. Β. Δ. = ψηφίσματι βουλῆς, δήμου).

Δ = 10 in the old decimal system of Greek numeration, ΔΔ = 20, ΔΔΔ = 30; in the alphabetic system = 4; τὸ Δ (*C. I. G.* 2059) = τὸ τέταρτον.

IN LATIN.—D = Decimus, decurio, December, decessit, decimanus, decretum, dedit, defunctus, denarius, designatus, deus, Diana, dies, dignus, divus, dixit, dominus, donavit, duumvir, etc., etc.

D·D = dare debebit, dea Dia, dedit dedicavit, donum dedit, dis deae, domus divina.

DD = devoti.

D·D·D = datum decreto decurionum, deo donum dedit, dono dedit dedicavit.

D·D·D·D = datum de decreto decurionum, donum dat dicat dedicat.

D·A = defunctus annorum, discens aquiliferum.

D·B·S = diis bonis sacrum.

D·C = decreto conscriptorum, decurionum consulto, decurio civitatis.

D·C·S = de conscriptorum (consilii, collegii) sententia.

D·D·D·D·L·M = donum dat dicat dedicat libens merito.

DDD·NNN = domini nostri tres.

D·D·E = dare damnas esto.

D·D·L·D·D·D = dedit dedicavit loco dato decreto decurionum.

D·D·O = diis deabus omnibus.

D·D·P·P·P = decreto decurionum pecunia publica posuerunt.

D·D·V·L·L·M = dono dedit votum laetus libens merito.

D·F = dare facere, defunctus, dulcissimas filiae.

D·I·M = deus invictus Mithras.

D·L = dedit libens, deus Liber, die Lunae.

D·M = dea magna, deum mater, decurio municipii, devotae memoriae, diis Manibus, divino mandatu, dolus malus.

D·O = dari oportet.

D·O·M = deo optimo maximo.

D·P = de proprio deus patrius, diis parentibus, donum posuit.

D·P·E = devotus pietati eius.

D·P·P = dii Penates publici, de pecunia publica.

D·P·S = de pagi sententia, de pecunia sua, de proprio suo.

D·P·S·F·D = de pecunia sua factum dedit.

D·Q = decurio quaestor.

D·Q·A = de qua agitur.

D·Q·L·S·T·T·L = dic qui legis: sit tibi terra levis.

D·R·P = dignum re publica.

D·S = de suo, deus sanctus, deus Saturnus, discens signiferum.

D·S·F·C = de suo faciendum curavit.

D·S·P·D·D = de sua pecunia dono dedit.

D·S·R = de suo restituit.

D·S·S·F·C = de senatus sententia faciendum curavit.

D·S·V·L = de suo vivus libens.

D·T = dum taxat, de thesauro.

D·T·S = dis te servent.

D·V·V·A·S·P·P = duumvir viis aedibus sacris publicis procurandis.

D = 500, formed by halving ↀ, the Etruscan symbol for 1000.

Daae (Δάαι). See DAHAE.

Dacia (Δακία), as a Roman province, lay between the Danube and the Carpathian Mountains, and comprehended the modern Transylvania, Wallachia, Moldavia, and part of Hungary. The Daci were of the same race and spoke the same language as the Getae, and are therefore usually said to be of Thracian origin. They were a brave and warlike people. In the reign of Domitian they became so formidable under their king, Decebalus, that the Romans were obliged to purchase a peace of them by the payment of tribute. Trajan delivered the Empire from this disgrace. He crossed the Danube, and after a war of five years (A.D. 101–106) conquered the country, and made it a Roman province. At a later period Dacia was invaded by the Goths; and as Aurelian considered it more prudent to make the Danube the boundary of the Empire, he resigned Dacia to the barbarians, removed the Roman inhabitants to Moesia, and gave the name of Dacia (Aureliani) to that part of the province along the Danube where they were settled.

Dacĭcus. A surname of the emperor Trajan, from his conquest of Dacia. See TRAIANUS.

Dacier, ANNE LEFÈVRE, a famous French translator of the classics, was born at Saumur about 1654. She was the daughter of Tanneguy Lefèvre, a Huguenot scholar of some note. On her father's death, and when in her eighteenth year, she went to Paris, where she soon after published an edition of Callimachus, which secured for her a place among the editors of the Delphin Edition (q. v.) of the classics, for which she prepared notes on Florus, Dictys Cretensis, Aurelius Victor, and Eutropius. In 1681 appeared her prose version of Anacreon and Sappho, followed by similar translations of Terence, selected plays of Plautus and Aristophanes, the *Iliad* (1711), and the *Odyssey* (1716). It is by these translations that she will be longest remembered, as she brought to the work much spirit and enthusiasm, combined with a good share of literary insight, so that her renderings are still cited by modern scholars. In her versions of Homer especially, her direct, simple, and often homely language is admirably fitted to express the original. In defence of Homer against La Motte, she wrote a treatise *Des Causes de la Corruption de la Goût* (1714).

Mlle. Lefèvre married in 1683 M. André Dacier, who subsequently became secretary of the French Academy, and was himself a man of much erudition but little talent, so that he was wittily described as *un gros mulet chargé de tout le bagage de l'antiquité*. Both husband and wife received pensions from the king. Mme. Dacier died at the Louvre, where her husband was librarian, August 17, 1720. See Sainte-Beuve, *Causeries de Lundi*, and Burette's *Éloge sur Mme. Dacier*.

Dactўli (Δάκτυλοι). Fabulous beings, to whom the discovery of iron, and of the art of working it by means of fire, was ascribed. Mount Ida, in Phrygia, is said to have been the original seat of the Dactyli, whence they are usually called Idaean (Ἰδαῖοι) Dactyli. In Phrygia they were connected with the worship of Rhea, or Cybelé. They are sometimes confounded or identified with the Curetes, Corybantes, and Cabeiri (q. v.). See RHEA.

The name Δάκτυλοι ("Fingers") is variously explained from their number being five or ten, or because they dwelt at the foot (ἐν δακτύλοις) of Mount Ida. The original number seems to have been three—i. e. Kelmis (Κελμίς) the Smelter, Damnameneus (Δαμναμενεύς) the Hammer, and Acmon (Ἄκμων) the Anvil. This number was afterwards increased to five, then to ten, to fifty-two, and finally to one hundred. See Lobeck, *Aglaophamos*, 1166 foll.; Pollux, ii. 4; Diod. v. 64.

Dactyliothēca (δακτυλιοθήκη). A case or box where rings were kept. Such a ring-case has been recognized in a round ivory box found at Pompeii (*Mus. Borb.* ix. pl. xiv. 8). From the centre of the lid projects a vertical stick, on which the rings might be slid when the wearer took them off at his toilet. The same purpose may have been served by a bronze stand which was found at Talese. It consists of a rod resting on three feet. Down the rod may be slid a ring furnished with catches to hold it steady, to one of which is attached a vertical oval ring broken at the top so as to admit of rings or other articles of jewellery being slid upon it. The name was also applied to a cabinet or collection of jewels, as to which we learn from Pliny (*H. N.* xxxvii. § 11) that Scaurus, the stepson of Sulla, was the first person at Rome who had a collection of this kind, and that his was the only one till Pompey brought to Rome the collection of Mithridates, which he placed in the Capitol.

Dactyliotheca. (Pompeii.)

Dactўlus (δάκτυλος). A Greek measure, answering to the Roman *digitus*, each signifying "a finger-breadth" and being the sixteenth part of a foot. See PES.

Dadūchus (δᾳδοῦχος). A torch-bearer. A name applied to the person who, on the fifth day of the Eleusinian Mysteries, led the initiated, torch in hand, to the temple of Demeter, in memory of her wanderings with a lighted torch in search of Persephoné (q. v.). See ELEUSINIA; MYSTERIA.

Daedăla (τὰ Δαίδαλα). (1) A town of Caria, near the confines of Lycia and on the northern shore of the Glaucus Sinus. It was said to have derived its name from Daedalus, who, being stung by a snake on crossing the small river Ninus, died and was buried here. (2) A mountain, in the vicinity of the city of the same name and on the confines of Lycia.

Daedăla, Daedalēa (δαίδαλα, δαιδάλεια). (1) A term applied to the earliest iconic representations of the gods roughly hewn out of wood (ἄγαλμα ξύλου, Pausan. ix. 3, 2). From a very early period stones and trees received divine honours (Lucian, *Pseudom.* 30). Thus Artemis Sotera at Boiae was a myrtle (Pausan. iii. 22, 12); the Paphian Aphrodité, a conical stone. The effigy of the god, down to the latest times, was placed in a tree. The immediate predecessor, however, of the δαίδαλον was a squared beam or flat board, which, like the pillar, was probably draped and decorated. (See DAEDALUS.) (2) A peculiar festival held by the Boeotians in honour of Heré. The goddess had, according to the story, once quarrelled with Zeus and hidden herself on Mount Cithaeron. Her husband then spread the report that he was going to marry another wife, and had an image of oak-wood decked out in bridal attire and carried over Cithaeron on a chariot with a numerous train amid the singing of marriage hymns. Heré, in her jealousy, threw herself upon her supposed rival, but, on discovering the trick, reconciled herself, with laughter, to Zeus, took her seat on the chariot, and founded the festival in memory of the incident. The feast was celebrated every seven years by the Plataeans alone and called the Little Daedala. But every sixtieth year all the cities of the Boeotian federation kept it as the Great Daedala. At the Little Daedala, guided by the note of a bird, they fixed on a tree in a grove of oaks and cut a figure out of it, which they dressed in bridal attire and took, as in marriage procession, to the top of Cithaeron. Here they offered a goat to Zeus and a cow to Heré, and burned the image with the offering. At the Great Daedala the images made at the Little Daedala were distributed by lot among the cities of the Boeotian confederacy, and the same proceedings were then repeated (Pausan. ix. 3. 1, etc.).

Daedălus (Δαίδαλος, "cunning artificer"). The mythical Greek representative of all handiwork, especially of Attic and Cretan art. As such he was worshipped by the artists' guilds, especially in Attica. He is said to have been the son of the Athenian Metion, son of Eupalamus (the ready-handed), and grandson of Erechtheus. He was supposed to

Daedalus and Icarus. (Rome, Villa Albani.)

have been the first artist who represented the human figure with open eyes, and feet and arms in motion. Besides being an excellent architect, he was said to have invented many implements—the axe, for instance, the awl, and the bevel. His own nephew Talus (son of his sister Perdix) appeared likely to surpass him in readiness and originality. The invention of the saw, which he copied from the jawbone of a snake, of the potter's wheel, of the turning-lathe, of the axe, of the plumb-line, of glue, of the gimlet, and of other things of this kind, was attributed to him. Daedalus was so jealous of him that he threw him from the Acropolis; and, being detected in the act of burying the body, was condemned by the Areopagus, and fled to Crete to King Minos. Here, among other things, he made the labyrinth at Gnosus for the Minotaur. (See LABYRINTHUS.) He and his son Icarus were themselves confined in it, because he had given Ariadné (q. v.) the clue with which she guided Theseus through the maze. But the father and son succeeded in escaping, and fled over the sea upon wings of wax feathers made by Daedalus. Icarus, however, approached too near to the sun, so that the wax melted, and he fell into the sea and was drowned. The sea was called after him the Icarian, and the island on which his body was thrown up and buried by Heracles was called Icaria. Daedalus went to Camicus in Sicily, to King Cocalus, whose daughter loved him for his art, and slew Minos, who came in pursuit of him. He was supposed to have died in Sicily, where buildings attributed to him were shown in many places, as also in Sardinia, Egypt, and Italy, particularly at Cumae. In Greece a number of ancient wooden images were supposed to be his work—in particular a statue of Heracles at Thebes, which Daedalus was said to have made in gratitude for the burial of Icarus. Besides Icarus, Daedalus had a second son, Iapyx, said to be the founder of the Iapyges. See DAEDALA.

Daemon (δαίμων). Originally a term applied to deity in general, manifested in its active relation to human life, without special reference to any single divine personality. But as early as Hesiod the daemones appear as subordinates or servants of the higher gods. He gives the name especially to the spirits of the past age of gold, who are appointed to watch over men and guard them. In later times, too, the daemones were regarded as beings intermediate between the gods and mankind, forming, as it were, the retinue of the gods, representing their powers in activity, and intrusted with the fulfilment of their various functions. This was the relation, to take an instance, which the Satyrs and Sileni bore to Dionysus. But the popular belief varied in regard to these deities.

Another kind of daemones are those attached to individual men, attending them, like the Roman *genius* (q. v.), from birth to death. In later times two attendant daemones were assumed for every one; but this feeling was not universal, both good and evil being regarded as emanating at different times from the same daemon. The good spirit who gave rural prosperity and presided over vineyards (a sort of Hellenic brownie or Robin Goodfellow) was called Agathodaemon (ἀγαθοδαίμων).

On the famous daemon of Socrates, see the article SOCRATES.

Dagger. See PUGIO; SICA.

Dahae (Δάαι). A great Scythian people (Plin. *H. N.* vi. 19), who led a nomadic life over a great extent of country, on the east of the Caspian, in Hyrcania (which still bears the name of Daghestan), on the banks of the Margus, the Oxus, and even the Iaxartes. Some of them served as cavalry and as archers under Darius Codomannus and Alexander.

Dalmatia (Δαλματία) or **Delmatia**. A part of the country along the eastern coast of the Adriatic Sea, included under the general name of Illyricum, and separated from Liburnia on the north by the Titius (Kerka), and from Greek Illyria on the south by the Drilo (Drino), thus nearly corresponding to the modern Dalmatia. The capital was Dalminium or Delminium, from which the country derived its name. The next most important town was Salona, the residence of Diocletian. The Dalmatians were a brave and warlike people and gave much trouble to the Romans. In B.C. 119, their country was overrun by L. Metellus, who assumed, in consequence, the surname Dalmaticus, but they continued independent of the Romans. In B.C. 39, they were defeated by Asinius Pollio, of whose Dalmatic triumph Horace speaks; but it was not till the year 23 that they were finally subdued by Statilius Taurus. They took part in the great Pannonian revolt under their leader Bato; but after a three years' war were again reduced to subjection by Tiberius, in A.D. 9.

Dalmatĭca or **Delmatĭca** (δαλματική, δελματική). A tunic with long sleeves (Isid. *Orig.* xix. 22, 9), introduced at Rome in the second century A.D. It was made both with and without purple stripes, and was sometimes of wool and sometimes of silk. See CLAVUS LATUS; TUNICA.

Dalmatius. A nephew of Constantine the Great. He was invested by this emperor with the title of Caesar, and commanded against the Goths in Thrace, Macedonia, and Greece. Dalmatius fell in a tumult of his own soldiers, A.D. 337, brought about by the intrigues of Constantius, after the death of Constantine (Zosim. ii. 39 foll.).

Dalminium. See DALMATIA.

Damălis (Δάμαλις) or **Bous** (Βοῦς). A small place in Bithynia, on the shore of the Thracian Bosporus north of Chalcedon; celebrated by tradition as the landing-place of Io (q. v.) after her transformation into a heifer.

Damarātus. See DEMARATUS.

Damascēnus, NICOLĀÜS (Νικόλαος Δαμασκηνός). A Greek historical and philosophical writer who lived in the Augustan Age. His name is derived from that of his birthplace, Damascus. He was an intimate friend of Herod the Great, whom he survived. His chief work was a universal history in 144 books, of which only a few fragments remain. He also wrote an autobiography, a life of Augustus, a life of Herod, and some philosophical works. The standard edition of his fragments is that of Orelli (Leipzig, 1804; suppl. 1811).

Damascĭus (Δαμάσκιος). A philosopher, a native of Damascus. He commenced his studies under Ammonius at Alexandria, and completed them at Athens under Marinus, Isidorus, and Zenodotus. According to some, he was the successor of Isidorus. It is certain, however, that he was the last professor of Neo-Platonism at Athens. He appears to have been a man of excellent judgment, and to have had a strong attachment for the sciences, particularly mathematics. He wrote a work entitled Ἀπορίαι καὶ Λύσεις περὶ τῶν Πρώτων Ἀρχῶν, "Doubts and Solutions concerning the Origin of Things." Of this only two fragments remain—one preserved by Photius, which forms a biographical sketch of Isidorus of Gaza; the other treating Περὶ Γεννητοῦ, "Of what has been procreated." The remains of this work were edited, with a valuable preface, by J. Kopp (Frankfort, 1828). A Venetian MS. contains an unedited work of his, entitled Ἀπορίαι καὶ Λύσεις εἰς τὸν Πλάτωνος Παρμενίδην, "Doubts and Solutions relative to the Parmenides of Plato."

Damascus (Δαμασκός; in Hebrew, Dammesek; in Arabic, Dimeshk-es-Sham). One of the principal cities of Syria, in what was called Coelé-Syria, a few miles to the east of Antilibanus, where the chain begins to turn off to the southeast, under the name of Carmel. It is beautifully situated in an extensive and pleasant plain, and watered by a river called by the Greeks Bardiné or Chrysorrhoas, "the golden stream," now Barada. The Biblical name of this stream was Abana. Damascus is supposed to have been founded by Uz, the eldest son of Aram (Gen. x. 23). However this

South Wall of Damascus.

may be, it existed in the time of Abraham, and may be reckoned one of the most ancient cities of Syria. It was conquered by David (2 Sam. viii. 6), but freed itself from the Jewish yoke in the time of Solomon (1 Kings, xi. 23 foll.), and became the seat of a new principality, which often harassed the kingdoms of both Judah and Israel. It afterwards fell, in succession, under the power of the Assyrians and the Persians, and came from the latter into the hands of the Seleucidae. Damascus, however, did not flourish much under the Greek dynasty, as it had while held by the Persians. The Seleucidae neglected the place, and bestowed all their favour on the new cities erected by them in the northern parts of Syria; and here, no doubt, lies the reason why the later Greek and Roman writers say so little of the city itself, though they are all loud in their praises of the adjacent country. Damascus was seized by the Romans in the war of Pompey with Tigranes, B.C. 65, but still continued, as under the Greek dynasty, a comparatively unimportant place until the time of Diocletian. This emperor, feeling the necessity of a strongly fortified city in this quarter, as a dépôt for munitions of war and a military post against the frequent inroads of the Saracens, selected Damascus for the purpose. Everything was done, accordingly, to strengthen the place; extensive magazines were also established, and likewise numerous workshops for the preparation of weapons of war. It is not unlikely that the high reputation to which Damascus afterwards attained for its manufacture of sword-blades and other works in steel, may have had its first foundations laid by this arrangement on the part of Diocletian. The city continued from this time to be a flourishing place. In the seventh century it fell into the hands of the Saracens, and was for some time after this the seat of the califs. Its prosperity, too, remained unimpaired, since the route of the principal caravans to Mecca lay through it. It was sacked by Tamerlane, and finally became subject to the Turks.

Coin of Damascus.

The Great Mosque of Damascus still shows traces of the Graeco-Roman architecture. See Walch, *Antiquitates Damasc. Illustratae;* and Addison, *Damascus and Palmyra.*

Damasippus, LICINIUS. (1) A Roman praetor, B.C. 81, an adherent of Marius, and put to death by order of Sulla (Sall. *Cat.* 51, 32). (2) A contemporary of Cicero, who mentions him as a lover of statues, and speaks of purchasing a garden from Damasippus. He is probably the same person as the Damasippus ridiculed by Horace (*Sat.* ii. 3, 16, 64). It appears from Horace that Damasippus had become bankrupt, in consequence of which he intended to put an end to himself; but he was prevented by the Stoic Stertinius, and then turned Stoic himself, or at least affected to be one.

Damastes (Δαμάστης) of Sigeum. A Greek historian, and a contemporary of Herodotus and Hellanicus of Lesbos. His works are lost.

Damnonii. (1) Or DUMNONII or DUMNUNII, a powerful people in the southwest of Britain, inhabiting Cornwall, Devonshire, and the western part of Somersetshire, from whom was called the promontory Damnonium, also Ocrinum (C. Lizard), in Cornwall. (2) Or DAMNII, a people in North Britain, inhabiting parts of Perth, Argyle, Stirling, and Dumbarton shires.

Damnum. A Latin term which signifies loss or injury of any kind; but in its particular sense means loss or injury which a person has sustained in his property. Damnum in this particular sense may include loss of gain which a person is prevented from realizing (*lucrum cessans*), as well as loss of actually acquired property (*damnum emergens*). The causes of damnum are either chance, accident (*casus*), or acts or omissions of reasonable human beings for which they are held to be responsible. As a rule no liability arises out of loss or injury to property caused by accident. *Dolus malus* or *culpa*—i. e. wilful or negligent misconduct on the part of the person committing damnum—is, as a rule, necessary in order to constitute liability; but in exceptional cases a person may be liable, although neither *dolus malus* nor *culpa* can be imputed to him. A wrongful act by which damnum is caused may be either an independent delict, or the breach of some special duty to which a person has become subject as a breach of contract. The liability to make good a loss which another has suffered is *praestare damnum.* A person liable for damages is, as a rule, bound to put the injured party in the same position as he would have been in if the act by which the damage was done had not been committed. He may also be subject to a penalty.

Damnum Infectum. A term used in Roman law to denote damage not actually done, but apprehended on account of the dangerous condition of neighbouring property. If proceedings were not taken before damage had been done, the injured party had no action for damages subsequently; if, e. g. a ruinous house (*aedes ruinosae*) fell and damaged a neighbour before a *cautio* had been demanded, all the right that the damaged person had was to retain the materials that had fallen on his land (*Dig.* 39, 2, 6. 7, § 2. 8). Gaius states that a party who apprehended damage might have recourse to a *legis actio* in order to protect himself, but that the *stipulatio damni infecti* provided by the praetor in his edict for such cases was always sought as being the more convenient remedy (Gaius, iv. 31).

Damo (Δαμώ). A daughter of Pythagoras and Theano, to whom Pythagoras intrusted his writings, and forbade her to give them to any one. This command she strictly observed, although she was in extreme poverty and received many requests to sell them (Diog. Laërt. viii. 42).

Damŏcles (Δαμοκλῆς). A Syracusan, one of the companions and flatterers of the elder Dionysius. Damocles having extolled the great felicity of Dionysius on account of his wealth and power, the tyrant invited him to try what his happiness really was, and placed him at a magnificent banquet, in the midst of which Damocles saw a naked sword suspended over his head by a single horse-hair—a sight which quickly dispelled all his visions of happiness. The story is alluded to by Horace (*Carm.* iii. 1. 17) and by Persius (ii. 40).

Damon (Δάμων). (1) A Pythagorean philosopher of Syracuse, united by ties of the firmest friendship to Phintias (not Pythias, as the name is commonly given), another Pythagorean, of the same city. Dionysius, the tyrant, having condemned Phintias to death for conspiring against him, the latter begged that leave might be allowed him to go for a short period to a neighbouring place, in order to arrange some family affairs, and offered to leave one of his friends in the hands of Dionysius as a pledge for his return by an appointed time, and who would be willing, in case Phintias broke his word, to die in his stead. Dionysius, sceptical as to the existence of such friendship, and prompted by curiosity, assented to the arrangement, and Damon took the place of Phintias. The day appointed for the return of the latter arrived, and public expectation was highly excited as to the probable issue of this singular affair. The day drew to a close; no Phintias came; and Damon was in the act of being led to execution, when, of a sudden, the absent friend, who had been detained by unforeseen and unavoidable obstacles, presented himself to the eyes of the admiring crowd and saved the life of Damon. Dionysius was so much struck by this instance of true attachment that he pardoned Phintias, and entreated the two to allow him to share their friendship (Val. Max. iv. 7; Plut. *De Amic. Mult.*). (2) An Athenian sophist, the teacher of Pericles and perhaps of Socrates (Diog. Laërt. ii. 19).

Damophĭla (Δαμοφίλη). A poetess of Lesbos, intimate with Sappho. She composed a hymn on the worship of the Pergaean Artemis (Philostrat. *Vit. Apollon.* i. 20).

Damosia (δαμοσία). The escort or retinue of the Spartan kings in time of war (Xen. *Rep. Lac.* xiii. 1).

Damoxĕnus (Δαμόξενος). A boxer of Syracuse, excluded from the Nemean Games for killing his opponent in a pugilistic encounter. The name of the latter was Creugas; and the two competitors, after having consumed the entire day in boxing, agreed each to receive from the other a blow without flinching. Creugas first struck Damoxenus on the head, and then Damoxenus, with his fingers unfairly stretched out, struck Creugas on the side; and such, observes Pausanias, was the hardness of his nails and the violence of the blow that his hand pierced the side, seized on the bowels, and, drawing them outward, caused instant death to Creugas. A fine piece of sculpture has come down to us with this for its subject (Pausan. viii. 40).

Dana (Δάνα). A great city of Cappadocia, probably the same as the later Tyana (q. v.) (Xen. *Anab.* i. 2, 20).

Danaë (Δανάη). (1) The daughter of Acrisius, king of Argos, by Eurydicé, daughter of Lacedaemon. Acrisius inquired of the oracle about a son; and the god replied that he would himself have no male issue, but that his daughter would bear a son, whose hand would deprive him of life. Fearing the accomplishment of this prediction, he framed a brazen subterranean chamber, in which he shut up his daughter and her nurse, in order that she might never become a mother. (The Latin poets call the place of confinement a brazen tower.) But Zeus had seen and loved the maiden; and, under the form of a golden shower, he poured through the roof into her bosom. Danaë became, in consequence, the mother of a son, whom she and her nurse reared in secrecy until he had attained his fourth year. Acrisius then chanced to hear the voice of the child at play. He brought out his daughter and her nurse, and, putting the latter instantly to death, drew Danaë privately, with her child, to the altar of Hercean Zeus, where he made her answer on oath whose was her son. She replied that he was the offspring of Zeus. Her father gave no credit to her protestations. Enclosing her and the boy in a coffer, he cast them into the sea, at the mercy of the winds and waves, a circumstance which has afforded a subject for a beautiful lyric by the poet Simonides. The coffer was carried to the little island of Seriphus, where a person named Dictys drew it out in his nets (δίκτυα); and, freeing Danaë and Perseus from their confinement, treated them with the greatest kindness. Polydectes, the brother of Dictys, reigned over the island. He fell in love with Danaë; but her son Perseus, who was now grown up, was an invincible obstacle in his way. He had, therefore, recourse to artifice to deliver himself of his presence; and, feigning that he was about to become a suitor to Hippodamia, the daughter of Oenomaüs, he managed to send Perseus, who had bound himself by a rash promise, in quest of the head of the Gorgon Medusa, which he pretended that he wished for a bridal gift. When Perseus had succeeded, by the aid of Hermes, in slaying the Gorgon, he proceeded to Seriphus, where he found that his mother and Dictys had been obliged to fly to the protection of the altar from the violence of Polydectes. He immediately went to the royal residence; and when, at his desire, Polydectes had summoned thither all the people to see the head of the Gorgon, it was displayed, and each became a stone of the form and position which he exhibited at the moment of the transformation. Having established Dictys as king of Seriphus, Perseus returned with his mother to Argos; and, not finding Acrisius there, proceeded to Larissa in Thessaly, whither the latter had retired through fear of the fulfilment of the oracle. Here he inadvertently killed Acrisius. See ACRISIUS; PERSEUS.

There was a legend in Italy that Ardea, the capital of the Rutulians, had been founded by Danaë (Verg. *Aen.* vii. 372, 410). It was probably caused by the similarity of sound in Danaë and Daunia. Daunus is the father of Turnus.

Danaï (Δαναοί). A name originally belonging to the Argives, as being, according to the common opinion, the subjects of Danaüs (q. v.). In consequence, however, of the warlike character of the race, and the high renown acquired by them, Homer uses the name Danaï as a general appellation for the Greeks, when that of Hellenes was still confined to a narrower range. See DANAÜS.

Danaïdes (Δαναΐδες). The fifty daughters of Danaüs. See DANAÜS.

Danăla (τὰ Δάναλα). A city in the territory of the Troini, in the northeast of Galatia, notable in the history of the Mithridatic War as the place where Lucullus resigned the command to Pompey.

Danapĕris (also DANAPRIS). Another name for the Borysthenes, first mentioned in an anonymous

Periplus of the Euxine Sea. It is now the Dnieper. A little above its mouth the river widens into a kind of lake or marsh, called Liman, into which the Bog, the ancient Hypanis or Bogus, one of the principal tributaries of the Dnieper, discharges itself. See BORYSTHENES.

Danastris. See DANASTUS.

Danastus. Another name of the Tyras or Dniester. It is called Danastus by Ammianus Marcellinus (xxxi. 3), and Danastris by Constantine Porphyrogenitus. It rises from a lake amid the Carpathian Mountains in Galicia, and empties into the Black Sea after a course of about six hundred miles. The name Tyras (Τύρας) occurs in Ptolemy, Strabo, Stephanus of Byzantium, and Scymnus of Chios. Herodotus gives the Ionic form Τύρης (Herod. iv. 51).

Danaüs (Δαναός). A son of Belus and Anchinoë, and brother of Aegyptus. Belus assigned the country of Libya to Danaüs, while to Aegyptus he gave Arabia. Aegyptus conquered the country of the Melampodes and named it from himself. By many wives he became the father of fifty sons. Danaüs had by several wives an equal number of daughters. Dissension arising between him and the sons of Aegyptus, they aimed at depriving him of his kingdom; and, fearing their violence, he built, with the aid of Athenê, a fifty-oared vessel, the first that ever was made, in which he embarked with his daughters and fled over the sea. He first landed on the isle of Rhodes, where he set up a statue of the Lindian Athenê; but, not caring to remain in that island, he proceeded to Argos, where Gelanor, who at that time ruled over the country, cheerfully resigned the government to the stranger who had brought thither civilization and the arts. The people took the name of their new monarch, and were called Danaï (Δαναοί). The country of Argos being at this time extremely deficient in pure and wholesome water (see INACHUS), Danaüs sent forth his daughters in quest of some. As Amymonê, one of them, was engaged in the search, she was rescued by Poseidon from the intended violence of a satyr, and the god revealed to her a fountain called after her name and the most famous among the streams that contributed to form the Lernaean lake or marsh. The sons of Aegyptus came now to Argolis and entreated their uncle to bury past enmity in oblivion, and to give them their cousins in marriage. Danaüs, retaining a perfect recollection of the injuries they had done him and distrustful of their promises, consented to bestow upon them his daughters, whom he divided among them by lot; but on the wedding-day he armed the hands of the brides with daggers, and enjoined upon them to slay in the night their unsuspecting bridegrooms. All but Hypermnestra obeyed the cruel orders of their father; and cutting off the heads of their husbands, they flung them into Lerna, and buried their bodies with all due rites outside of the town. At the command of Zeus, Hermes and Athenê purified them from the guilt of their deed. Hypermnestra had spared Lynceus for the delicate regard which he had shown to her modesty. Her father, at first, in his anger at her disobedience, put her into close confinement. Relenting, however, after some time, he gave his consent to her union with Lynceus, and proclaimed gymnastic games, in which the victors were to receive his other daughters as the prizes. It was said, however, that the crime of the Danaïdes did not pass without due punshment in the lower world, where they were condemned to pour water forever into a perforated vessel.

Danaïdes. (Visconti, Museo Pio-Clementino.)

Dancing. See SALTATIO.

Danubius. See ISTER.

Daphnae (Δάφναι). A city of Egypt, about sixteen miles from Pelusium, on the route to Memphis. There was always a strong garrison in this place to keep in check the Arabians and the Syrians. Many Jews settled here after the destruction of Jerusalem.

Daphnê (Δάφνη). (1) The daughter of the river-god Peneus, in Thessaly, pursued by Apollo, who was charmed by her beauty; but as she was on the point of being overtaken by him, she prayed for aid, and was metamorphosed into a laurel-tree (δάφνη), which became in consequence the favourite tree of Apollo. (2) See MANTO.

Daphnê (Δάφνη). A beautiful spot, five miles south of Antioch in Syria, to which it formed a sort of park or pleasure garden. It was celebrated for the grove and temple dedicated to Apollo. Here was a sanctuary with the right of asylum which became famous, and to which pilgrims resorted in great numbers, making it a scene of perpetual vice. See the description in Gibbon's *Decline and Fall*, chap. xxiv. Hence *Daphnici mores* became proverbial.

Daphnephoria (δαφνηφορία). A festival celebrated every ninth year at Thebes in honour of Apollo, surnamed Ismenius or Galaxius. Its name was derived from the laurel branches (δάφναι) which were carried by those who took part in its celebration. A full account of the festival is given by Proclus (*Chrestomath.* p. 11). At one time all the Aeolians of Arnê and the adjacent districts, at the command of an oracle, laid siege to Thebes, which was at the same time attacked by the Pelasgians, and ravaged the neighbouring country. But when the day came on which both parties had to celebrate a festival of Apollo, a truce was concluded, and on the day of the festival they went with laurel-boughs to the temple of the god. But Polematas, the general of the Boeotians, had a vision in which he saw a young man who presented to him a complete suit of armour, and who made him vow to institute a festival, to be celebrated every ninth year, in honour of Apollo, at which the Thebans, with laurel-boughs in their hands, were to go to his temple. When, on the third day after this vision, both parties again were engaged in close combat, Polematas gained the victory. He now fulfilled his promise, and himself walked to the temple of Apollo in the manner prescribed by the being he had seen in his vision; and ever since that time, continues Proclus, this custom has been strictly observed.

Daphnis (Δάφνις). A Sicilian shepherd, son of Hermes by a nymph, and taught by Pan to play on the flute. He was regarded as the inventor of bucolic poetry. A Naiad, to whom he proved faithless, punished him with blindness, whereupon his father Hermes translated him to heaven. See the Fifth Eclogue of Vergil, 20–80.

Daphnus (Δαφνοῦς). A town of the Locri Opuntii, situated on the seacoast, at the mouth of a river of the same name, near the frontiers of the Epicnemidian Locri. Into the river Daphnus the body of Hesiod was thrown after his murder. See HESIODUS.

Darădus (Δάραδος) or **Daras** (Δάρας). A river of Africa, rising to the northwest of the Palus Nigrites, on Mount Mandras, and falling into the Atlantic to the north of the promontory Arsinarium. It is supposed to be the same with the Senegal.

Dardanarii. Monopolists at Rome who purchased and held grain in order to sell it at a high price. They were liable to severe punishment under the Empire. See Plin. *H. N.* xxx. § 9; *Dig.* 47, 11. 6.

Dardăni (Δάρδανοι). A people in Upper Moesia, occupying part of Illyricum.

Dardania (Δαρδανία). (1) A district of the Troad, lying along the Hellespont, southwest of Abydos, and adjacent to the territory of Ilium. Its people (Dardani) appear in the Trojan War, under Aeneas, in close alliance with the Trojans, with whose name their own is often interchanged, especially by the Roman poets. (2) A city in this district. See DARDANUS (2).

Dardănis or **Dardanium.** A promontory of Troas, south of Abydus, near which was situated the city of Dardanum. The Hellespont here begins to contract.

Dardănus (Δάρδανος). (1) The son of Zeus and Electra, the mythical ancestor of the Trojans, and through them of the Romans. The Greek traditions usually made him a king in Arcadia, from whence he emigrated first to Samothrace, and afterwards to Asia, where he received a tract of land from King Teucer, on which he built the town of Dardania. His grandson Tros removed to Troy the Palladium, which had belonged to his grandfather. According to the Italian traditions, Dardanus was the son of Corythus, an Etruscan prince of Corythus (Cortona); and, as in the Greek tradition, he afterwards emigrated to Phrygia. (2) Also DARDĂNUM (Δάρδανον), a Greek city in the Troad on the Hellespont, twelve Roman miles from Ilium, built by Aeolian colonists, at some distance from the site of the ancient city Dardania. From Dardanum arose the name of the Castles of the Dardanelles, after which the Hellespont is now called.

Dares (Δάρης). (1) A Trojan priest, mentioned by Homer (*Il.* v. 9). It is absurdly pretended, by some of the ancient writers, that he wrote an *Iliad*, or history of the Trojan War, in prose; and Aelian (*Var. Hist.* xi. 2) assures us that it still existed in his day, without telling us, however, whether he himself had read it or not. There can, of course, be no doubt that Aelian was deceived, and that the work which he took for the production of Dares was the composition of some sophist of a much later age. However this may be, the *Iliad* of which Aelian speaks no longer exists; but we have a Latin work remaining, written in prose, which was for some time regarded as a translation from the Greek original, and was ascribed to Cornelius Nepos, though abounding with absurdities and solecisms. It is entitled *Historia Excidii Troiae*, or *De Excidio Troiae*. It professes to be dedicated to the historian Sallust.

This work, together with that of Dictys Cretensis (q. v.) forms the original source of a famous romance of chivalry, which met with extraordinary success during the Middle Ages, and in the centuries immediately subsequent to the invention of printing. These works of Dares and Dictys having fallen into the hands of a Sicilian named Guido delle Colonne, a native of Messina, and a celebrated lawyer and poet of the thirteenth century, he conceived the idea of giving them that romantic air which would harmonize with the spirit of his age, when chivalry had acquired its greatest lustre. He consequently interpolated the narratives of the pretended poets of Phrygia and Crete with various adventures, suited to the taste of the time, such as tournaments, challenges, and single combats. His work having met with considerable success, he composed, in Latin prose, a romance of the war of Troy, into which he also introduced the war of the Seven against Thebes and the expedition of the Argonauts. He confounds together history and mythology, Greek and Oriental manners; his heroes are acquainted with alchemy and astronomy, and come into conflict with dragons, griffins, and other fabulous monsters. His romance was translated into almost every European language, and excited a general enthusiasm. Hence the desire which at that time seized the great families of Europe of claiming descent from one of the heroes of Trojan story; and hence the eagerness, on the part of the monks, to compose genealogies consisting of Greek and Roman names which had some analogy with the names of the sovereign princes of the Middle Ages. This same work of Dares Phrygius was the source whence Conrad of Würzburg, in the latter half of the thirteenth century, derived the materials of the poem which he composed in like manner on the war of Troy.

The oldest MS. of the *Historia de Excidio Troiae* is one at Paris, of the ninth century, and other MSS. are those of St. Gall, Bern, Bamberg, and Vienna. The work is at least as early as Isidorus, who mentions it (*Orig.* i. 41). The best edition is that by Meister (Leipzig, 1873). See Meister, *De Daretis Phryg.*, etc. (Breslau, 1871); Dunger's treatise in the Programme of the Vitzthum Gymnasium (Dresden, 1869); and Körting, *Dictys und Dares* (Halle, 1874). On the language, see the Index Latinitatis, in Meister's edition.

(2) One of the companions of Aeneas, celebrated as a pugilist, though conquered in the funeral games of Anchises by the aged Entellus (Verg. *Aen.* v. 369 foll.). This Dares, or a Trojan of the same name, was slain by Turnus in Italy (*Aen.* xii. 363).

Darīcus (στατὴρ δαρεικός) A daric; the gold coin which constituted for centuries, until the time of Alexander the Great, the main part of the coinage of Asia under Persian dominion. Gold darics are to be found in all great museums; their type is on the obverse a crowned archer kneeling, on the reverse a mere rude incuse; their weight is about 130 grains, and their intrinsic value about $5.40 of our money. In allusion to their type they were sometimes called τόξοται; whence the saying of Agesilaüs (Plut. *Ages.* 15) that he had been driven from Asia by 30,000 archers, when his recall was the result of Persian bribery at Athens and Thebes.

The Greeks connected the word δαρεικός with the name of Darius Hystaspis, to whom they attributed the first issue of these coins. This derivation, however, is certainly erroneous. Not only is there small likeness in sound between the name of the coin and that of the king in their Persian forms, but we learn from the Book of Ezra (ii. 69; viii. 27) that darics were in circulation in Palestine in the time of Cyrus; and M. Bertin has found the word *dariku* on a tablet of the reign of Nabonidus, which is still earlier (*Trans. Soc. Bibl. Arch.* 1883–1884, p. 87; cf. Head, *Historia Numorum*, p. 698). Of course in the cases just cited, though we have a complete proof of the great antiquity of the word *daric*, we cannot be sure whether a fixed weight of gold or a coin is intended. The probability is that the nations of the Euphrates valley did not coin money until they had conquered Lydia and Ionia in the time of Cyrus. Darius, Herodotus tells us, issued gold coin of great fineness (Herod. iv. 166); and this may have caused the Greeks to suppose that he issued the earliest Persian coins. The abundance of the darics in circulation in Asia Minor in the days of Xerxes is shown by the well-known story of Pythius the Lydian (Herod. vii. 28), who possessed four millions of them.

Gold Daric, actual size. (British Museum.)

Silver Daric, actual size. (British Museum.)

Besides the gold darics there circulated silver coins of the same shape and bearing the same device of the archer; these were commonly known as the σίγλος or shekel, but were sometimes termed silver darics (Plut. *Cimon*, 10). These were of the value of about $0.27.

Darius (Δαρεῖος; Pers. *Dâryavas*). (1) Surnamed HYSTASPIS (or son of Hystaspes), a satrap of Persia, born B.C. 548, and belonging to the royal line of the Achaemenides. His father Hystaspes had been governor of the province of Persia. Seven noblemen of the highest rank, among whom was Darius, conspired to dethrone the Magian Smerdis (q. v.), who had usurped the crown after the death of Cambyses, and, having accomplished their object (B.C. 521), resolved that one of their number should reign in his stead. According to Herodotus (iii. 84), they agreed to meet at early dawn in the suburbs of the capital, and that he of their number whose horse should first neigh at the rising of the sun should possess the kingdom. If we believe the historian, who gives two accounts of the matter, Darius obtained the crown through an artful contrivance on the part of his groom. It is more probable, however, that, in consequence of his relationship to the royal line, his election to the throne was the unanimous act of the other conspirators. It is certain, indeed, that they reserved for themselves privileges which tended at least to make them independent of the monarch, and even to keep him dependent upon them. One of their number is said to have formally stipulated for absolute exemption from the royal authority, as the condition on which he withdrew his claim to the crown; and the rest acquired the right of access to the king's person at all seasons, without asking his leave, and bound him to select his wives exclusively from their families. How far the power of Darius, though nominally despotic, was really limited by these privileges of his nobles, may be seen from an occurrence which took place in the early part of his reign, in the case of Intaphernes, who had been one of the partners in the conspiracy. He revenged himself, it is true, for an outrage committed by this individual, by putting him to death; but before he ventured to take this step, he thought it necessary to sound the other four, and to ascertain whether they would make common cause with the offender.

Nevertheless, Darius was the greatest and most powerful king that ever filled the throne of Persia. Cyrus and Cambyses had conquered nations; Darius was the true founder of the Persian State. The dominions of his predecessors were a mass of countries only united by their subjection to the will of a common ruler, which expressed itself by arbitrary and irregular exactions. Darius first organized them into an empire, of which every member felt its place and knew its functions. His realm stretched from the Aegean to the Indus, from the steppes of Scythia to the Cataracts of the Nile. He divided this vast tract into twenty satrapies or provinces, and prescribed the tribute which each was to pay to the royal treasury, and the proportion in which they were to supply provisions for the army and for the king's household. A highway, on which distances were regularly marked and spacious buildings placed to receive all who travelled in the king's name, connected the western coast with the seat of government; and along this road couriers trained to extraordinary speed transmitted the king's messages. See CURSUS PUBLICUS; PERSIA.

Darius, in the very beginning of his reign, meditated an expedition against the Scythians to check their incursions for all time to come by a salutary display of the power and resources of the Persian Empire. His march, however, was delayed by a rebellion which broke out at Babylon. The ancient capital of Assyria had been secretly preparing for revolt during the troubles that followed the fall of Smerdis, and for nearly two years it defied the power of Darius. At length the strategy of Zopyrus, a noble Persian, who sacrificed his person and his power to the interest of his master, is said to have opened its gates to him (circa B.C. 516). When he was freed from this care he set out for the Scythian war (B.C. 513 or 508).

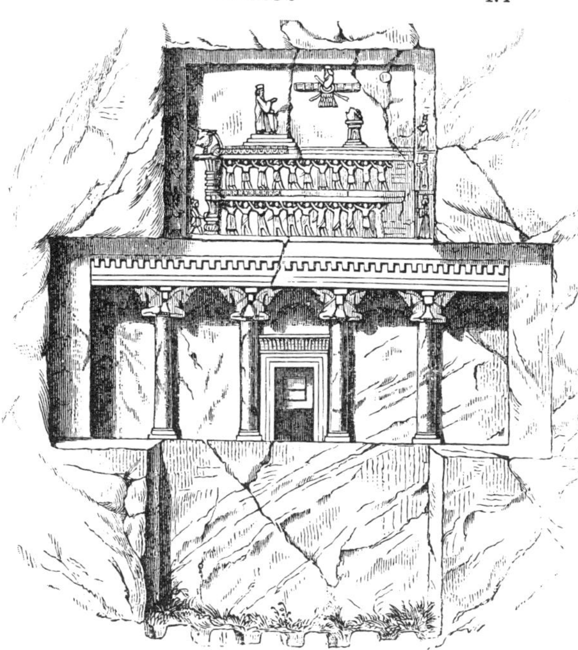

Rock-cut Tomb of Darius.

The whole military force of the Empire was put in motion, and the numbers of the army are rated at seven or eight hundred thousand men. This expedition of Darius into Scythia has given rise to considerable discussion. The first point involved is to ascertain how far the Persian monarch penetrated into the country. According to Herodotus (iv. 83), he crossed the Thracian Bosporus, marched through Thrace, passed the Danube on a bridge of boats, and then pursued a Scythian division as far as the Tanaïs. Having crossed this river, he traversed the territories of the Sauromatae as far as the Budini, whose city he burned. Beyond the Budini he entered upon a vast desert, and reached the river Oarus, where he remained some considerable time, erecting forts upon its banks. Finding that the Scythians had disappeared, he left these works only half finished, turned his course to the westward, and, advancing by rapid marches, entered Scythia, where he fell in with two of the divisions of the enemy. Pursuing these, he traversed the territories of the Melanchlaeni, Androphagi, and Neuri, without being able to bring them to an engagement. Provisions failing, he was eventually compelled to recross the Danube (see HISTIAEUS), glad to have saved a small portion of his once numerous army. According to other accounts (Strab. 305), Darius only came as far as the sandy tract between the Danube and the Tyras, in the present Bessarabia, where, in after-days, Antigonus was taken prisoner by the Scythians, with his whole army.

Another expedition undertaken by command of Darius was an invasion of India (Herod. iv. 44), the date, however, being doubtful. In this affair he was more successful, and conquered a part of the Punjab; not, however, the whole country, as some modern writers erroneously represent.

Some time after this, Miletus having revolted, and Aristagoras, its ruler, having solicited aid from the Athenians for the purpose of enabling it to maintain its independence, they sent twenty ships, to which the Eretrians added five more, in order to requite a kindness previously received from the Milesians. Aristagoras, upon the arrival of this fleet, resolved to make an expedition against Sardis, the residence of the Persian satrap. Accordingly, landing at Ephesus, the confederates marched inland, took Sardis, and drove the governor into the citadel. Most of the houses in Sardis were made of reeds, and even those that were built of brick were roofed with reeds. One of these was set on fire by a soldier, and immediately the flames spread from house to house and consumed the whole city. The light of the conflagration showing to the Greeks the great numbers of their opponents, who were beginning to rally, being constrained by necessity to defend themselves, as their retreat was cut off by the river Pactolus, the former retired through fear and regained their ships (B.C. 501). Upon the receipt of this entelligence, Darius, having called for a bow, put an arrow into it, and shot it into the air, with these words, "Grant, O God, that I may be able to revenge myself upon the Athenians." After he had thus spoken, he commanded one of his attendants thrice every time dinner was set before him, to exclaim, "Master! remember the Athenians." Mardonius, the king's son-in-law, was intrusted with the care of the war. After crossing the Hellespont, he marched down through Thrace, but, in endeavouring to double Mount Athos, he lost 300 vessels and, it is said, more than 20,000 men (B.C. 492). After this he was attacked in the night by the Brygi, who killed many of his men and wounded Mardonius himself. He succeeded, however, in defeating and reducing them to subjection, but his army was so weakened by these circumstances that he was compelled to return ingloriously to Asia. Darius, only animated by this loss, sent a more considerable force, under the command of Datis and Artaphernes, with orders to sack the cities of Athens and Eretria, and to send to him all the surviving inhabitants in fetters. The Persians took the isle of Naxos and the city of Eretria in Euboea, but were defeated with great slaughter by the Athenians and Plataeans under the celebrated Miltiades at Marathon (B.C. 490). Their fleet was also completely unsuccessful in an attempt to surprise Athens after the battle. (See MILTIADES; MARATHON.) The anger of Darius was doubly inflamed against Athens by the result at Marathon; and he resolved that the insolent people, who had invaded his territories, violated the persons of his messengers, and put his generals to a shameful flight, should feel the whole weight of his arm.

Cuneiform and Hieroglyphical Forms of "Darius."

The preparations he now set on foot were on a vast scale and demanded a longer time. For three years all Asia was kept in a continual stir; in the fourth, however, Darius was distracted by other causes—by a quarrel between his two sons respecting the succession to the throne, and by an insurrection in Egypt. In the following year, before he had ended his preparations against Egypt and Attica, he died, and Xerxes (q. v.) ascended the throne, in B.C. 485. Darius had reigned for thirty-six years. His memory was always held in veneration by the Persians and the other nations comprehended under his sway, whom he governed with much wisdom and moderation.

(2) The second of the name was styled Ὦχος. See OCHUS; CYRUS (2).

(3) The third of the name, and the last king of Persia, was son of Arsames, who had for his father Osthanes, one of the sons of Darius Ochus. His true name was Codomannus, and he had, before coming to the throne, acquired some reputation for personal courage, chiefly through an exploit which he had performed in one of the expeditions against the Cadusians, when he accepted a challenge from one of their stoutest warriors, and slew him in single combat. The eunuch Bagoas (q. v.) raised him to the throne, not so much, however, on this account, as because they had previously been friends, and because, perhaps, there was no other prince of the blood on whose gratitude he could safely rely. Codomannus, upon his accession (B.C. 336), which took place about the time when Philip of Macedon died, assumed the name of Darius. He soon discovered that Bagoas, who may have intended at length to seize the throne himself, designed that he should share the fate of his last two predecessors. A cup of poison had been prepared for him. But, having detected the plot, he called Bagoas into his presence and compelled him to drink the deadly draught.

The reign of Darius Codomannus was early disturbed by the invasion of Alexander. The Persian monarch, however, did not take the command of his forces until after the battle of the Granicus had been fought (334), and Alexander had advanced as far as Cilicia. He then proceeded to meet the invader, in all the pomp of royalty, but with an army ill fitted to contend against such an antagonist. Resolving to hazard an encounter, contrary to the advice of his Greek allies, Darius engaged in the battle of Issus, but was compelled to flee from the field with so much precipitation as to leave behind him his bow, shield, and royal mantle (333). His camp was plundered, and his mother, wife, and children fell into the hands of the conqueror. In vain, after this, did Darius supplicate for terms of peace. Alexander went on in his career of victory; and in a second pitched battle at Gaugamela, commonly called the battle of Arbela (q. v.), Darius again fought, and again was compelled to flee (331). His plan was now to advance into Media, lay waste the country through which he passed, and seek refuge finally on the other side of the Oxus, where he hoped that the conqueror would be content to leave him unmolested. Alexander allowed four months to elapse before he again set out in pursuit of Darius. He then advanced by forced marches in pursuit of him, and learned eventually that the monarch was a prisoner in the hands of Bessus (q. v.), one of his own satraps. A still more active pursuit now commenced, and the unhappy king, refusing to proceed any farther, was left mortally wounded in a chariot, while Bessus and his accomplices took to flight, accompanied by 600 horse. Darius expired before Alexander saw him (B.C. 330).

Alexander ordered his body to be buried in the sepulchre of his ancestors with royal magnificence, took charge of the education of his children, and married his daughter (Plut. *Alex.;* Arrian, *Exp. Al.*).

(4) The eldest son of Artaxerxes Mnemon, put to death for conspiring against his father (Plut. *Artax.*).

Dart. See HASTA; IACULUM; PILUM; TELUM; TRAGULA.

Dassaretii (Δασσαρήτιοι), **Dassarītae** (Δασσαρῖται), or **Dassarētae** (Δασσαρῆται). A people in Greek Illyria on the borders of Macedonia; their chief town was Lychnidus, on a hill, on the north side of the lake Lychnitis, which was so called after the town.

Datămes (Δατάμης). A distinguished Persian general, a Carian by birth, and satrap of Cilicia under Artaxerxes II. (Mnemon), but who revolted against the king. He defeated the generals who were sent against him, but was at length assassinated, B.C. 362. Cornelius Nepos, who has written his life, calls him the bravest and most able of all barbarian generals, after Hamilcar and Hannibal.

Datātim Ludĕre. See PILA.

Datētae (δατηταί). Distributors or liquidators, employed in the winding up of a partnership concern when a disagreement existed among the partners. The datetae were usually chosen by lot from among the public *diaetetae* (q. v.).

Datis (Δᾶτις). A Mede who commanded, along with Artaphernes, the Persian army that was defeated at Marathon, B.C. 490 (Herod. vi. 94).

Dator. The attendant who, during the game of ball, picked up the balls that fell, or supplied new balls to the players (Plaut. *Curc.* ii. 3, 15). See PILA.

Datum (Δάτον) or **Datus** (Δάτος). A Thracian town on the Strymonic Gulf, subject to Macedonia, with gold mines in Mount Pangaeus in the neighbourhood, whence came the proverb, a "Datum of good things" (Herod. ix. 75).

Daulis (Δαυλίς) or **Daulia** (Δαυλία). An ancient town in Phocis, situated on a lofty hill, celebrated in mythology as the residence of the Thracian king Tereus, and as the scene of the tragic story of Philomela and Procné. Hence DAULIAS is the name of both Procné and Philomela (q. v.).

Daunia. See APULIA.

Daunus (Δαῦνος). (1) Son of Lycaon and brother of Iapyx and Peucetius, with whom he settled in Apulia and divided it into three parts. (2) Son of Pilumnus and Danaë, husband of Venilia, and ancestor of Turnus (q. v.).

Days. See DIES.

Dea Dia. An early Roman goddess, probably identical with Acca Larentia and worshipped by the Fratres Arvales (q. v.). See ROMULUS.

Dead, BOOK OF THE. A famous funerary work of the ancient Egyptians, consisting of prayers and exorcisms intended for the benefit of the soul on its journey through Amenti (Hades). Such being its purpose, portions of it were placed with the mummy when entombed. Nearly one half of all the Egyptian papyri now in existence consist of copies of this work, and from them a good text of the whole has been constructed by Naville, in

Das Aegyptische Todtenbuch der XVIII bis XX Dynastie (Berlin, 1886). See, also, an interesting review of this work by Miss Edwards in the *Academy* (London) for September 10th, 1887.

Dealbatōres. Workmen mentioned in the Codex of Justinian (x. 64, 1), who appear to have been simply whitewashers, and not, as some have supposed, workmen employed to cover walls with a coating of white cement or stucco. *Dealbare* is to cover the walls with lime-wash (*calce ex aqua liquida dealbentur*, Vitruv. vii. 4, 3).

Death. See THANATOS.

Debĭtor. See OBLIGATIONES.

Decadarchia or **Decarchia** (δεκαδαρχία, δεκαρχία). A council or government of ten. (1) In Thessaly, established by Philip on his conquest of that country and the overthrow of its tyrants in B.C. 352, after a defeat in the previous year (Demosth. *Phil.* ii. p. 71, § 22). (2) Introduced by Lysander at the close of the Peloponnesian War, and established in many Greek cities by the Lacedaemonians, who intrusted to it the whole government of the State under the direction of a Spartan harmost. It always consisted of the leading members of the aristocratic party (Xen. *Hell.* vi. 3, § 8). The form δεκαδαρχία is used by Demosthenes of the Thessalian institution, and δεκαρχία by Xenophon and Isocrates of the Lacedaemonian.

Decadūchi (δεκαδοῦχοι). The members of a Council of Ten, who succeeded the Thirty Tyrants in the supreme power at Athens, B.C. 403. They were chosen from the ten tribes, one from each; two of the Thirty, if not more, were among them, and, like the Thirty, they relied on Spartan assistance against Thrasybulus and the exiles. They remained masters of Athens till the party of Thrasybulus obtained possession of the city and the democracy was restored; and, like the Thirty, were excepted from the amnesty, but allowed to retire into banishment. See THIRTY TYRANTS.

Decānus (Fr. *doyen*, Eng. dean). The head of ten men. The word does not seem to occur before the time of Constantine, and then, except in its ecclesiastical use, only in the Eastern Empire. It perhaps took the place of the classical *decurio* at a time when the latter word had acquired its special meaning in the colonies and municipia. We may distinguish three senses.

(1) A petty officer commanding a *contubernium* of ten men (Modestus, § 9).

(2) Officials at the court of Constantinople, but of no higher than menial rank (*Cod. Theod.* vi. 12). St. Chrysostom instances the ὕπαρχος (=*praefectus praetorio*) and δεκανός as at opposite ends of the social scale. Like other *officiales*, they were under the orders of the *magister officiorum*.

(3) The members of a guild or confraternity at Constantinople, charged with the burial of the dead (*Cod. Iust.* i. 2, 4 and 9). The institution appears to be a distinctly Christian one, and to have organized what had been previously a matter of casual charity—the decent burial of the poor.

Decapŏlis. See PALAESTINA.

Decaprōti (δεκάπρωτοι). In the Greek-speaking cities of the Roman Empire a committee of ten, or more rarely of twenty (εἰκοσάπρωτοι, *icosaproti*), was chosen from among the decuriones or provincial senators, and charged with the collection of the taxes, for which they were made responsible. These decaproti are to be distinguished from the *decem primi* (q. v.) in Rome and the Italian municipia, who were honorary representatives of their curia, but not magistrates.

Decasmus (δεκασμός) Bribery; strictly meaning a systematic bribery by division into sets of ten. There were two actions for bribery at Athens—one, called δεκασμοῦ γραφή, lay against the person who gave the bribe; and the other, called δώρων or δωροδοκίας γραφή, against the person who received it (Pollux, viii. 42). These actions applied to the bribery of citizens in the public assemblies of the people, of the Heliaea or any of the courts of justice, of the βουλή, and of the public advocates (συνήγοροι). Demosthenes, indeed, says that orators were forbidden by the law, not merely to abstain from receiving gifts for the injury of the State, but even to receive any present at all.

Actions for bribery were under the jurisdiction of the thesmothetae. The punishment on conviction was death (Isocr. *De Pace*, § 50) or payment of ten times the value of the gift received (Dinarch. *c. Demosth.* § 60). An additional punishment (προστίμημα) might be inflicted by the court; as in the case of Demosthenes, who was not only fined fifty talents, but thrown into prison (Plut. *Demosth.* 26).

Decastȳlos. See TEMPLUM.

Decătē (δεκάτη). See DECUMA.

Decebălus. A celebrated king of the Dacians, to whom Domitian paid an annual tribute. He was defeated by Trajan, and put an end to his own life, whereupon Dacia became a Roman province, A.D. 106 (Suet. *Dom.* 6). See DACIA.

Decelēa (Δεκέλεια). A deme of Attica, northwest of Athens, on the borders of Boeotia, near the sources of the Cephissus, seized and fortified by the Spartans in the Peloponnesian War.

Decempĕda. The standard Roman unit in measuring land. It was a pole ten feet in length used by the *agrimensores* (q. v.), who were thence called *decempedatores*. See Cic. *Phil.* xiii. 18, § 37.

Decem Primi. (1) The First Ten of the Roman Senate were originally the heads of the decuries into which the Senate of one hundred was divided. They took the office of interrex by turns, and are mentioned in that capacity at the first interregnum, on the death of Romulus (Liv. i. 17; cf. Dionys. ii. 57). When subsequently the representatives of the Tities and Luceres were admitted into the Senate, the Ramnes with their Decem Primi retained for some time their precedence over the other two tribes and gave their votes first (Plut. *Num.* 3; Dionys. ii. 58; iii. 1). The first in rank among them was the *princeps senatus*, who was appointed by the king, and was at the same time *custos urbis* (Dionys. ii. 12; I. Lydus, *De Mens.* i. 19). In the early republican period the Decem Primi seem to have been the consulars of the greater houses in order of seniority, then those of the lesser houses.

When the censors acquired the power of nominating the senators from among qualified persons, the Decem Primi were simply the first ten named by them; this choice was usually exercised according to merit, and a man who was generally acknowledged as the first Roman of his time was tolerably certain to become *princeps senatus* and to retain the dignity for life. Valerius Corvus, the two Fabii Maximi, Rullianus and Cunctator, L. Aemilius Paullus, and the two Africani, all seem to have enjoyed this honour. The censors were often partial and passionate in the exercise of their almost irresponsible authority; but even the memorable quarrel between Livius Salinator and Claudius Nero did not prevent their giving the first place in the Senate to Fabius Cunctator (Liv. xxix. 37, § 1).

(2) In municipal senates we constantly find a committee, generally of ten, sometimes of a greater or less number, chosen (apparently by the decurions themselves) out of the larger body. In Italy this institution can be traced very far back; we find it in Latium as early as the great Latin War of B.C. 340 (Liv. viii. 3, § 8).

(3) Wherever there was an *ordo*, Roman organization seems to have involved the appointment of ten, or sometimes six, primi. Below the senatorian rank we find them among *apparitores*, *lictores*, and *praecones;* in priestly colleges (*C. I. L.* vi. 2010); and among the *domestici* or body-guards of the later Empire (*Cod. Theod.* vi. 24).

Decemrēmis (δεκήρης). See Navis.

Decemvĭri. (1) Ten commissioners appointed (B.C. 451) to frame a code of laws for the Roman State at a time when the feuds between the patricians and plebeians were continuing with unabated animosity. Occasionally one of the consuls favoured the plebeians, and proposed some mitigation of the hardships under which they were labouring, or some increase of their privileges, but generally with little success. The Agrarian Law, brought forward by Spurius Cassius, continued to be the main demand of the commons and their supporters, but its passage was, on every occasion, either directly or indirectly prevented. At last the commons became convinced that they need hope for no complete redress of grievances until they should have previously secured the establishment of some constitutional principle, from which equal justice would, of necessity and from its very nature, emanate. Accordingly, Gaius Terentillus Harsa, one of the tribunes, proposed a law (B.C. 462) for a reform of the existing state of things. Its purport was that ten commissioners should be chosen, five by the patricians and five by the plebeians, to draw up a constitution, which should define all points of constitutional, civil, and criminal law; and should thus determine, on just and fixed principles, all the political, social, and civil relations of all orders of the Roman people. After much opposition on the part of the patricians, the law was passed, and three commissioners were at length sent to Greece, to collect from the Grecian States such notices of their laws and constitutions as might be serviceable to the Romans. After the absence of a year they returned; and the plebeians, finding it in vain to insist upon five of their own body forming part of the reviewers of the laws, yielded the point, and ten of the most distinguished of the patrician and senatorial body were chosen to form an entirely new and complete code of laws by which the State should be governed. They were named *Decemviri*, "the ten men" (*Decemviri Legibus Scribendis*), and during their office they were to supersede every other magistrate. Each in his turn was to administer the government for a day, or, according to others, for several days, till they should complete their legislative labours. After the careful deliberation of a few months, the result was laid before the people in the form of ten tables, fully written out, and exhibited in a conspicuous place where all might read them. Various amendments were proposed, and the ten tables again laid before the Senate, the curiae, and the centuries, and, having received the sanction of both orders of the State, were recognized as the very fountain of the laws, public and private. The Decemvirs had conducted matters so much to the satisfaction of the community that when, at the expiration of their year, they requested a renewal of their office, on the ground that they had still two more tables to form in order to complete their task, an election of new Decemvirs was ordered. (See Twelve Tables.) The patrician Appius Claudius, who took the leading part in the whole affair, was nominated to preside over this election. He acted in concert with the plebeians, by receiving votes for plebeian candidates, and for himself likewise, though it had been declared contrary to law that any functionary should be re-elected immediately after holding office. By dint of intrigue, however, Appius was re-elected, and along with him nine others, half of whom were patricians, half plebeians.

The new commission soon showed itself very different from the first. Each of the Decemvirs had twelve lictors, whereas the previous commission had the lictors only by turns, and a single *accensus* or officer preceded each of the rest. The lictors, too, now bore amid the fasces the formidable axe, the emblem of judgment on life and death, which the consuls, since the time of Valerius Publicola, had been obliged to lay aside during their continuance in the city. The Decemvirs seemed resolved to change the government of Rome into a complete oligarchy, consisting of ten, whose power should be absolute in everything. They assumed the right of superseding all other magistracies; and, at the conclusion of their second year, they showed no intention of resigning their offices or of appointing their successors. Matters had nearly reached a crisis when a war arose, the Sabines and the Aequi having united their forces and being desirous of availing themselves of the distracted state of Rome. The Decemvirs assembled the Senate, obtained its authority to raise an army, at the head of which they placed three of their number, and sent it against the Sabines. Another was raised and sent against the Aequi, while Appius Claudius remained at Rome to provide for the safety of the city and for the maintenance of the power of the Decemvirs. Both armies were defeated, and retired nearer to the city, dissatisfied rather than discomfited. Then occurred the affair of Virginia, and the decemviral power was at an end. See Claudius (4); Virginia; Liv. iii. 32 foll.; and Mommsen, *Hist. of Rome*, vol. i. pp. 345–371 (Eng. trans.).

(2) There were also military decemviri; and, on various emergencies, decemviri were created to manage and regulate certain affairs, after the same manner as boards of commissioners are now appointed. Thus there were decemviri for conducting colonies; decemviri who officiated as judges in litigated matters under the praetor; decemviri for dividing the lands among the veteran soldiers; decemviri to prepare and preside at feasts in honour

of the gods; decemviri to take care of the sacrifices (*Decemviri Sacris Faciundis*) and to guard the Sibylline Books. With regard to the last of these, however, it must be observed that the number, after having been originally two, and then increased to ten, was subsequently still further increased to fifteen and sixteen.

Decennalia or **Decennia**. A festival celebrated with games every ten years by the Roman emperors. This festival owed its origin to the fact that Augustus refused the supreme power when it was offered to him for life, and would only consent to accept it for ten years; and when these expired, for another period of ten years; and so on to the end of his life. The memory of this comedy, as Gibbon has called it, was preserved to the last ages of the Empire by the festival of the Decennalia, which was solemnized by subsequent emperors every tenth year of their reign, although they had received the *imperium* for life, and not for the limited period of ten years (Dio Cass. liii. 16; liv. 12; lviii. 24; lxxvi. 1).

Decetia. The modern Désize; a city of the Aedui, in Gallia Lugdunensis, on an island in the Liger (Loire). See Caes. *B. G.* vii. 33.

Decidius Saxa. See SAXA.

Decimatio. The selection, by lot, of every tenth man for capital punishment, when any number of soldiers in the Roman army had been guilty of certain military offences—usually cowardice, loss of standards in action, or mutiny. This punishment is not often mentioned in the early times of the Republic; but the case of the consul Appius Claudius and his mutinous army (B.C. 471) is recorded both by Livy (ii. 59) and Dionysius (ix. 50); the latter speaks of it as customary (πάτριος) for the offences named. Polybius notices it as usual when troops had given way to panic; the remainder were punished by having rations of barley instead of wheat served out to them, and by being made to lodge outside the camp (vi. 38). When, however, Crassus employed decimation in the servile war of Spartacus, he is described as having revived an ancient punishment which had long fallen into disuse (Plut. *Crass.* 10). In the Civil Wars it once more became common, and was retained under the Empire (Suet. *Galb.* 12). Sometimes only the twentieth man was punished (*vicesimatio*), or the hundredth (*centesimatio*) (Capitol. *Macr.* 12).

Decimātus. See QUINQUATRUS.

Decius. (1) PUBLIUS DECIUS MUS, a celebrated Roman consul, who, after many glorious exploits, devoted himself to the Manes for the safety of his country in a battle against the Latins, B.C. 337. His son, Decius, imitated his example, and devoted himself in like manner in his fourth consulship, when fighting against the Gauls and the Samnites at Sentinum, B.C. 296. His grandson is said to have done the same in the war against Pyrrhus and the Tarentines, B.C. 280 (Liv. vii. 21 foll.; id. viii. 10; Val. Max. v. 6). (2) GAIUS MESSIUS QUINTUS TRAIĀNUS. A native of Pannonia, sent by the emperor Philip to put down a sedition in Moesia. Instead of obeying his master's command, he assumed the imperial purple. His disaffected troops, it is said, forced him to this step. The emperor immediately marched against him, and a battle was fought near Verona, which terminated successfully for Decius, and Philip was either slain in the conflict or put to death after he fell into the conqueror's power. This took place A.D. 249, and from this period is dated the commencement of the reign of Decius. It was one of short duration, about two years. During this time, however, he proved a very cruel persecutor of the Christians. He greatly signalized himself against the Persians, but was slain in an action with the Goths, who had invaded his dominions. In advancing upon them he was, with the greater part of his troops, entangled in a morass, where, being surrounded by the enemy, he perished under a shower of darts, A.D. 251, aged fifty years. See Victor, *De Caes.* 29; Eutrop. ix. 4; Euseb. *Hist. Eccles.* vi. 39, etc.; Zonar. xii. 19, 20.

Declamatio. A term which came into use first in Cicero's time (*Brut.* 90, 310) for the rhetorical exercises employed in the training of orators. These were of two kinds: (*a*) *suasoriae;* (*b*) *controversiae.* The former were based upon some historical or legendary theme, and the pupil was required to treat some problem arising thence, as, for instance, whether Sulla should have resigned his dictatorship (Juv. i. 16) or Cato have committed suicide (Pers. iii. 45). These were regarded as suitable for beginners, as not requiring any wide or minute knowledge of law (Tac. *Dial.* 35). The latter dealt with legal questions, and took the form of the discussion of an imaginary case, such as might arise in the courts. Marcus Seneca (q. v.), the father of the philosopher, has left seven examples of *suasoriae,* thirty-five of *controversiae,* as well as ten books of *excerpta controversiarum,* which contain many interesting specimens of the kind of questions thus treated. The practice had at first a real value, and Cicero represents himself as continuing it for a great part of his life (*Tusc.* i. 4, 7), although in his later years he preferred philosophical topics. But, with the decline of free speech, the exercise sank into a mere occasion for display. The themes were hackneyed or extravagant, the language affected and full of strained antithesis and epigram (Quintil. viii. 3, 76; 5, 14, etc.); and what should have been a preparation for real life became an end in itself. The rage for declamation was at its height during the first century of the Empire. Quintilian's sober sense did much to check it; and though the practice did not wholly die out of the schools, it seems to have been confined within more reasonable limits. (Cf. Bernhardy, *Röm. Lit.* § 53; Petron. 1–3; and Mayor's notes on Juv. i. 16; vii. 150–170.)

Decoctor. A bankrupt; a term used in popular language to signify any spendthrift. The Romans were a frugal people, and spendthrifts were not only condemned by public opinion (Catull. xli. 4; Cic. *Cat.* ii. 3, 5) but punished by the censors with the *nota censoria,* which carried with it certain legal disabilities. By the Lex Roscia (B.C. 67) a certain place in the theatre was assigned to spendthrifts (Cic. *Phil.* ii. 18). According to Spartianus, Hadrian ordered that spendthrifts should be flogged ignominiously (*catomidiari*) in the amphitheatre and turned out (Spart. *Hadr.* 18). The Roman law against persons who would not pay borrowed money was very severe and is explained under NEXUM. Its severity, however, was mitigated by the *bonorum cessio* (q. v.). By a constitution of the emperors Valentinian, Theodosius, and Arcadius, any decurio who had dissipated the funds of the city (*decoctor pecuniae publicae*) was to be scourged.

Decrētum. A word meaning that which is determined in a particular case after examination or consideration. It is thus applied to a resolution of the Senate.

A decretum of the Senate would seem to differ from a *senatusconsultum*, in that it was limited to the special occasion and circumstances instead of being of general application. But this distinction in the use of the two words, as applied to an act of the Senate, is not consistently observed.

Cicero (*Ad Fam.* xiii. 56) opposes *edictum* to decretum, between which there is in this passage apparently the same analogy as between a *consultum* and a decretum of the Senate.

Decretum is the technical term for the decision and order which a magistrate gives in a particular case after an inquiry into its circumstances (*causae cognitio*). A *iudex* is said *condemnare* not *decernere;* the latter word being appropriate in judicial proceedings to a magistrate who has *iurisdictio.* A decretum, as one of the kinds of imperial constitutions, was a judicial decision in a case before the emperor in his capacity of supreme magistrate; cases were brought into the imperial court (*consistorium principis*) by *supplicationes* or *provocationes* of suitors.

The interpretations of law laid down by the emperor in his decreta were, as a rule, binding on all courts in subsequent cases.

Decŭma (sc. *pars*). "A tithe." This name was applied by the Romans to the tribute in kind, which Sicily, and at one time Asia Minor, had to pay out of the yearly production of wheat, wine, oil, and produce, instead of the *stipendium* usual in other provinces. It was a burden on the land called after it *ager decumanus*, and was exacted from the persons occupying at the time. Every year the number of cultivators, of acres under cultivation, and the produce of the harvest, were ascertained, and the right of exacting the *decuma* of the whole territory of a city sold to the highest bidder. In the case of Sicily this took place at Syracuse; in the case of Asia, in Rome. The purchaser of the decuma bound himself to deliver a certain quantity of corn in Rome; if the harvest were good, he found his advantage in the surplus. Such farmers of the decumae were called *decumani.* (See PUBLICANUS.) If the amount delivered were insufficient for the needs of the city, a second amount could be extracted by decree of the Senate or the people, which was paid for by the State. See ANNONA; FRUMENTARIAE LEGES.

Decumāna Porta. See CASTRA.

Decumāni. See DECUMA; PUBLICANI.

Decumātes Agri. See AGRI DECUMATES.

Decuncis. The *dextans*, or ten *unciae;* a division of the *as* (q. v.).

Decuria, from *decem*, "ten," and consequently a company of ten persons (Colum. i. 9, § 7).

(1) A division of the *curiae.* Each of the three ancient Roman tribes—the Ramnes, Tities, and Luceres—was divided into ten *curiae*, and each *curia* into ten decuriae, so that there were 300 decuriae, which, according to Niebuhr, were equivalent to the *gentes*, but this is doubtful (Dionys. ii. 7; Plut. *Rom.* 20; Cic. *de Rep.* ii. 8). The constitution of the *curiae* is discussed under CURIA. See also GENS.

(2) A corresponding division of the Senate. The original hundred members of the Senate were divided into ten decuriae, the heads of each decuria forming the Decem Primi in the Senate. (See DECEM PRIMI; SENATUS). In like manner in the municipal towns the Senate, usually called *curia*, was divided into decuriae. See DECURIONES.

(3) In the same way for military purposes each of the three Roman tribes was represented by 100 equites, called *centuriae.* The three *centuriae* were divided into ten *turmae*, each consisting of thirty men; every *turma* contained ten Ramnes, ten Tities, and ten Luceres, and each of these *decuriae* was commanded by a *decurio* (Liv. i. 13; Varr. *L. L.* v. 91). See EQUITES.

(4) The Iudices were divided into three decuriae, to which Augustus added a fourth, and Caligula a fifth decuria. See IUDEX.

(5) Collegia or corporations were divided into decuriae. Thus we read of decuriae of *scribae*, lictors, viatores, etc. The members of these decuriae were called *decuriales.*

(6) The tribes were divided into decuriae by electioneering agents for bribery and corruption (Cic. *Planc.* 18, 45; 19, 47). See AMBITUS.

Decuriālis. See DECURIA; DECURIONES.

Decurio. The head or representative of a *decuria.*

(1) The head of the *decuriae* into which the curiae and the Senate were divided. See DECURIA.

(2) The head or commander of the *decuriae* of the Equites. But *decurio* was in later times the name of an officer of a division of cavalry, though such division might contain any number of men (Veget. *Mil.* ii. 14).

(3) The head or representative of a *decuria* in corporations. In like manner we find a *decurio cubiculariorum*, a *decurio palatii*, a *decurio ostiariorum*, a *decurio Germanorum*, and there was even a decurio of slaves in the imperial household (Orelli, 2785).

(4) The most important decuriones were those in the municipal towns, who are the subject of the following article.

Decuriōnes, Curiāles. In the constitution of the Italian towns (*municipia, coloniae, praefecturae*), as regulated by the Lex Iulia Municipalis, B.C. 45, each municipality was governed by an assembly of the *populus*, which elected magistrates and made laws, and also by a senate, which was an administrative body. Subsequently, by a change corresponding to that which took place in Rome, the power of the popular assembly was transferred to the senate, which thus became the supreme municipal body for legislative and administrative purposes.

The municipal senate is sometimes called *senatus*, but the terms commonly used to denote it are *ordo decurionum*, or simply *ordo*, and in later times *curia.* Decuriones or curiales signify members of the senate, these words being used indifferently in the same sense.

As opposed to the decuriones, which formed a sort of patrician body, the rest of the people were styled *plebeii.* The number of the decuriones was fixed by the local senate, and vacancies were filled by co-optation. To be eligible as decurio, a person was required to be of a certain age; the limit was thirty (Tab. Heracl. 23), till reduced by Augustus to twenty-five for the municipal senate as well as for the Roman.

A property qualification, the amount of which depended on the constitution of each town, was attached to the acquisition of membership in a *curia*, but membership was not vacated by loss of property. We learn from Pliny (*Ep.* i. 19) that at Comum a person who had less than 100,000 sesterces could not become a decurio. Criminals, bankrupts, persons of infamous character, and persons who followed certain employments, as *praecones, designatores, libitinarii*, were incapable of holding this office (Tab. Heracl. 23 (25); cf. *Dig.* 50, 2, 12). Freedmen were likewise incapable.

The names of decuriones were inscribed on an album or register in a regular order, which was based partly on rank and partly on seniority. The album of Canusium, which was discovered in the last century and is now in the Museo Nazionale at Naples (Fabretti, *Inscr. C.* 9, p. 598; Orelli, No. 3721), shows the plan on which such an album was arranged.

Decursio, Decursus, Decurrere. (1) These words were used to signify the manœuvres of the Roman army, by which the soldiers were taught to make long marches in a given time, under arms and without quitting their ranks. They are frequently mentioned by Livy, and sometimes consisted of a sham fight between two divisions of the army (Liv. xl. 6, 5). With the standing armies under the Empire these manœuvres assumed a more regular form, and were constantly practised. Augustus and subsequently Hadrian ordered that the infantry and cavalry were to march out three times a month ten miles from the camp and ten miles back, fully armed and equipped. This is called by Vegetius *campicursio* (Veget. i. 27, iii. 4), and by Suetonius *campestris decursio* (Suet. *Galb.* 6).

(2) The same words were used to signify the military honours paid by soldiers at the funerals of distinguished generals or emperors. Such a decursio is first mentioned in connection with the funeral of Sempronius Gracchus, killed in the Second Punic War (Liv. xxv. 17, 4, 5). The soldiers marched three times around the funeral pyre (Verg. *Aen.* xi. 188; Tac. *Ann.* ii. 7; Suet. *Claud.* 1).

Decursio on Coin of Nero. (British Museum.)

(3) The decursio, which occurs on the coins of Nero, probably refers to the military manœuvres or sham fights in the circus. The above cut represents a horseman with a spear, and another carrying a standard. These games date from the time of the Republic and were continued under the Empire (Liv. xliv. 9, 3).

Decussis. Ten *asses;* as a Roman coin, a ten *as* piece, struck after the reduction of the weight of the as, but rarely found. (See As.) The name occurs in the Lex Aternia Tarpeia, B.C. 454.

Dedicatio. The Roman name for the consecration of a public sanctuary. The *pontifices* drew up the deed of foundation. When they had signified that they deemed the act permissible, and the consent of the people (in later times of the emperor) had been obtained, the rite was performed in the presence of the whole *collegium pontificum.* The Pontifex Maximus, whose head was veiled, and with him the representative of the people, took hold of the door-post with one hand, the former dictating, and the latter repeating after him, the formula of dedication. The people were represented usually by one of the two consuls, or a person or a commission (generally of two persons) elected by the people on the recommendation of the Senate. One of the persons forming the commission was generally the man who had vowed the dedication. The day on which the shrine was dedicated was regarded as the day of its foundation, and was inscribed in the calendar as a festival. See INAUGURATIO.

Deditícii. The lowest of the three classes of freedmen at Rome (Gaius, i. 26).

The Lex Aelia Sentia (A.D. 4) provided that, if a slave was put in bonds by his master as a punishment, or branded, or put to the torture on a criminal charge and convicted, or delivered to fight with men or beasts, or committed to a gladiatorial school (*ludus*) or a public prison, and was subsequently manumitted by the same or by another owner, he should acquire by manumission the status of a *peregrinus dediticius.* The *peregrini dediticii* were people who, in former times, having taken up arms and fought against the people of Rome, had surrendered themselves.

Gaius, from whom this account of the origin of *dediticii* is taken (*Inst.* i. 12–16), also informs us of the incapacities to which this class of freedmen were subject. Dediticii could never under any circumstances acquire Roman citizenship. They were not allowed to reside in Rome or within the hundredth mile-stone from it (cf. Liv. viii. 14, § 6); if they disobeyed this prohibition they forfeited their liberty and their goods and were made incapable of subsequent manumission. They did not participate in any of the rights of citizenship, but only had the status of *peregrini.* This class of persons had died out long before the time of Justinian; it was, however, formally abolished by that emperor (*Cod.* vii. 5).

The form of *deditio* occurs in Livy (i. 38).

Deditio. See DEDITICII.

Defensor Civitātis. The oppression of the lower orders of the people by the more powerful, which was prevalent throughout the Roman Empire in the fourth century, owing to the general weakness and corruption of local government, led to the institution of a new municipal officer, called *defensor civitatis, plebis, loci* (in Greek ἔκδικος), whose function it was to defend the rights of the inhabitants of a *civitas,* much as the citizens of the Scotch towns were protected in the Middle Ages by the Provost, of which relation Scott has given an interesting picture in his *Fair Maid of Perth,* i. 8, and ii. 3.

An edict of the emperor Valentinian I., issued in A.D. 364, established this office, but only for the province of Illyricum. By this edict the governor of the province was directed to choose a trustworthy person for each city of the dioceses subject to him, in order that the *plebs* of all Illyricum might be protected by means of public guardians (*patroni*) from injuries at the hands of the powerful (*Cod. Theod.* i. 29, 1).

In the next year, A.D. 365, Valentinian extended the office of defensor to all parts of his Empire, including Italy, but with some changes in its constitution. Each *civitas* acquired the right of choosing a defensor from its most eminent and independent citizens, who were bound to serve the office in a prescribed order.

The election of a defensor was made by the whole *civitas;* the choice of the township had to be confirmed by the emperor or his deputy. At first a defensor held office for five years, but the term was reduced by Justinian to two years. The protection of the inhabitants of his district from oppression of all kinds, and especially from that of the imperial governor and local authorities, was always considered to be the main object of a defensor civitatis. Moreover it was his business to prevent the taxes being made too burdensome. For the purpose of prosecuting oppressors, he had free access to the court of the governor, and, if necessary, he could bring his complaints against the governor or other officials before the emperor or ministers of the imperial government. The defensor acted as judge in civil cases of minor importance; his jurisdiction was first limited by Justinian to fifty *solidi,* and afterwards extended by that emperor to three hundred *solidi.* He had the right of appointing guardians and of registering many formal proceedings. In rank he had precedence of magistrates.

Deïanīra (Δηϊάνειρα or Δηάνειρα). The daughter of Althaea and Oeneus, and sister of Meleager. Acheloüs and Heracles both loved Deianira, and fought for the possession of her. Heracles was victorious, and she became his wife. She was the unwilling cause of her husband's death, by presenting him with the poisoned shirt which the Centaur Nessus (q. v.) gave her. In despair, she put an end to her own life. For details, see HERACLES.

Deïdamīa (Δηϊδάμεια). Daughter of Lycomedes, in the island of Scyros. When Achilles was concealed there in maiden's attire, she became by him the mother of Pyrrhus or Neoptolemus. See ACHILLES.

Deiecti Effusīvé Actio. At Rome, if any person threw or poured anything from the room of a house upon a place commonly frequented by people, and thereby caused damage, the praetor's edict gave the injured party an action against the occupant of the house or part of the house from which the thing had been thrown or poured. There was the same liability on account of a thing which had been suspended from a building, and which by its fall injured people, as for a thing which had been actually thrown.

Deigma (δεῖγμα). A particular place in the Piraeus, as well as in the harbours of other States, where merchants exposed samples of their goods for sale (Harpocrat. s. v. *Hesych.*; Pollux, ix. 34; Aristoph. *Eq.* 979). The samples themselves were also called *deigmata* (Plut. *Demosth.* 23).

Deilias Graphé (δειλίας γραφή). See ASTRATEIAS GRAPHÉ.

Deïŏces (Δηϊόκης). First king of Media, who after the Medes had thrown off the supremacy of the Assyrians, reigned B.C. 709–656. He built the city of Ecbatana, which he made the royal residence. He was succeeded by his son Phraortes (Herod. i. 16).

Deïonīdes (Δηϊονίδης). Miletus, son of Deïoné by Apollo.

Deïotărus (Δηϊόταρος). A tetrarch of Galatia, who adhered to the Romans in their wars against Mithridates, and was rewarded by the Senate with the title of king. In the Civil War he sided with Pompey, and was present at the battle of Pharsalia, B.C. 48. He is remembered as having been defended by Cicero before Caesar (B.C. 45), in the house of the latter at Rome, in the speech (*Pro Rege Deiotaro*) still extant. The charge against Deiotarus was of attempting to murder Caesar.

Deïphŏbé (Δηϊφόβη). The Sibyl at Cumae, daughter of Glaucus. See SIBYLLA.

Deïphŏbus (Δηΐφοβος). Son of Priam and Hecuba, who married Helen after the death of Paris (*Il.* xii. 94). On the capture of Troy by the Greeks he was slain and fearfully mangled by Menelaüs.

Deipnon (δεῖπνον). See CENA.

Delatio Nomĭnis. In Roman criminal procedure the first step was to apply to the praetor to allow the accusation to be made (*postulare*), the next formally to arraign the defendant (*nomen deferre*). The judge might himself take the initiative and declare his readiness to receive a *nominis delatio;* this, however, is mentioned among the oppressive proceedings of Verres (Cic. *in Verr.* ii. 38, § 94; iv. 19, § 40).

The *postulatio* and *nominis delatio* occur most frequently in prosecutions of magistrates and provincial governors for misconduct in office. See REPETUNDAE.

Delatōres. A term originally applied to those who gave notice to the officials of the treasury of moneys that had become due to the treasury. It subsequently received a wider application. A *delator* was not quite identical with our "informer"; the term covered two classes—one consisting of those who themselves acted as prosecutors, the other of those who simply gave information. The legislation of Augustus gave the first stimulus to the habit of delation by granting pecuniary rewards to those who secured the conviction of offenders against his laws relating to marriage (Tac. *Ann.* iii. 28). The Lex Iulia *de maiestate*, by rewarding the successful prosecutor with a fourth part of the estate of the condemned (Tac. *Ann.* iv. 20), gave a fatal encouragement to this class; and although Tiberius appears to have endeavoured at first to check the practice, it became during his reign a veritable scourge; and as his suspicious temper developed, he actually encouraged them. Caligula at the beginning of his reign *negavit se delatoribus aures habere* (Suet. *Calig.* 15), and Nero reduced the rewards of those who prosecuted offenders against the Papian law to the legal fourth part. Titus severely punished them; Domitian at first followed his example, but soon proved ready to use them as the tools of his tyrannous greed. They were again banished by Trajan (Plin. *Paneg.* 34), and denounced by a rescript of Constantine (*Cod.* x. 11, 5). But the need of this constant repression proves what a standing evil this class must have been to the State. See Mayor's notes on Juvenal, i. 33–36, iv. 48, x. 70; and the article MAIESTAS.

Delectus. See EXERCITUS.

Delia (τὰ Δήλια). The name of festivals and games celebrated at the great assemblage in the island of Delos (q. v.), the centre of an amphictyony, to which the Cyclades and the neighbouring Ionians on the coasts belonged (Hom. *Hymn. in Apoll.* 147, etc.) This amphictyony seems originally to have been instituted simply for the purpose of religious worship in the common sanctuary of Apollo, the θεὸς πατρῷος of the Ionians, who was believed to have been born at Delos. The Delia, as appears from the Hymn to Apollo, had existed from very early times, and were celebrated every fifth year (Pollux, viii. 104), and as Boeckh supposes, with great probability, on the sixth and seventh days of Thargelion, the birthdays of Apollo and Artemis. The members of the amphictyony assembled on these occasions (ἐθεώρουν) in Delos, in long garments, with their wives and children, to worship the god with gymnastic and musical contests, choruses, and dances. That the Athenians took part in these solemnities at a very early period is evident from the Deliastae (afterwards called θεωροί) mentioned in the laws of Solon (Athen. vi. p. 234). The sacred vessel (θεωρίς), moreover, which they sent to Delos every year, was said to be the same which Theseus had sent after his return from Crete. The Delians, during the celebration of these solemnities, performed the office of cooks for those who visited their island, whence they were called Ἐλεοδύται (Athen. iv. p. 173).

Delictum. See CRIMEN.

Delium (Δήλιον). A town on the coast of Boeotia, in the territory of Tanagra, near the Attic frontier, named after a temple of Apollo similar to that at Delos. Here the Athenians were defeated by the Boeotians, B.C. 424.

Delius (Δήλιος) and **Delia** (Δηλία). Surnames of Apollo and Artemis respectively, from the island of Delos (q. v.).

Dēlos (Δῆλος). An island of the Aegean, situated nearly in the centre of the Cyclades (q. v.). This island was called also Asteria, Pelasgia, Chlamydia, Lagia, Pyrpilis, Scythias, Mydia, and Ortygia. It was named Ortygia from ὄρτυξ, "a quail," and Lagia from λαγώς, "a hare," the island formerly abounding with both these creatures. On this account, according to Strabo, it was not allowed to have dogs at Delos, because they destroyed the quails and hares. The name Delos was commonly derived from δῆλος, "manifest," in allusion to the island having floated under the surface of the sea until made to appear and stand firm by order of Poseidon. This was done for the purpose of receiving Leto, who was on the eve of delivery, and could find no asylum on the earth, Heré having bound it by an oath not to receive her; but as Delos at the time was floating beneath the waters, it was freed from the obligation. Once fixed in its place, it continued, according to popular belief, to remain so firm as even to be unmoved by the shocks of an earthquake. This, however, is contradicted by Thucydides and Herodotus, who report that a shock was felt there before the Peloponnesian War (Thuc. ii. 8; Herod. vi. 98).

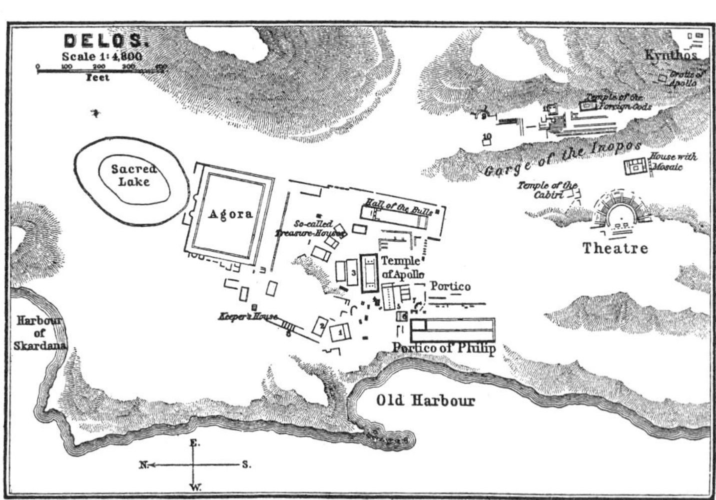

Plan of Delos, showing Excavations. (1890.)

Delos was celebrated as the natal island of Apollo and Artemis, and the solemnities with which the festivals of these deities were observed there never failed to attract large crowds from the neighbouring islands and the continent. Among the seven wonders of the world was an altar at Delos which was made of the horns of animals. Tradition reported that it was constructed by Apollo with the horns of deer killed in hunting by his sister Artemis. Plutarch says he saw it, and he speaks of the wonderful interlacing of the horns of which it was made, no cement nor bond of any kind being employed to hold it together. Portions of this altar are identified by archæologists in the scattered blocks of marble lately found in the so-called Hall of the Bulls, to the east of the great temple, and named from its "taurine" capitals representing recumbent bulls. The Athenians were commanded by an oracle, in the time of Pisistratus, to purify Delos, which they did by causing the dead bodies which had been buried there to be taken up and removed from all places within view of the temple. In the sixth year of the Peloponnesian War, they, by the advice of an oracle, purified it anew by carrying all the dead bodies to the neighbouring island of Rhenaea, where they were interred. After having done this, in order to prevent its being polluted in the time to come, they published an edict that for the future no person should be suffered to die, nor any woman to be brought to bed, in the island, but that, when death or parturition approached, they should be carried over into Rhenaea. In memory of this purification, it is said, the Athenians instituted a solemn quinquennial festival. See DELIA.

When the Persian armament, under Datis and Artaphernes, was making its way through the Grecian islands, the inhabitants of Delos left their rich temple, with its treasures, to the protection of its tutelary deities, and fled to Tenos. The fame of the sanctuary, however, saved it from spoliation. The Persians had heard that Delos was the birthplace of two deities who corresponded to those who held the foremost rank in their own religious system—the sun and moon. This comparison was probably suggested to them by some Greek who wished to save the temple. If we may credit the tradition which was current in the days of Herodotus, Delos received the highest honours from Datis. He would not suffer his ships to touch the sacred shore, but kept them at the island of Rhenaea. He also sent a herald to recall the Delians who had fled to Tenos, and offered sacrifice to the god, in which 300 talents of frankincense are said to have been consumed (Herod. vi. 97). After the Persian War, the Athenians established at Delos the treasury of the Greeks, and ordered that all meetings relative to the confederacy should be held there (Thuc. i. 96). In the tenth year of the Peloponnesian War, not being satisfied with the purifications which the island had hitherto undergone, they removed its entire population to Adramyttium, where they obtained a settlement from the Persian satrap Pharnaces (Thuc. v. 1). Here many of these unfortunate Delians were afterwards treacherously murdered by order of Arsaces, an officer of Tissaphernes (Thuc. viii. 108). Finally, however, the Athenians restored those that survived to their country after the battle of Amphipolis, as they considered that their ill success in the war proceeded from the anger of the god on account of their conduct towards this unfortunate people (Thuc. v. 32). Strabo says that Delos became a place of great commercial importance after the destruction of Corinth, as the merchants who had frequented that city then withdrew to this island, which afforded great facilities for carrying on trade on account of the convenience of its port, and its advantageous situation with respect to the coasts of Greece and Asia Minor, as well as from the great concourse of people who resorted thither at stated times. It was also very famous for its bronze. The Romans especially favoured the interests of the Delians, though they had conceded to the Athenians the sovereignty of the island and the administration of the temple (Polyb. xxx. 18). But on the occupation of Athens by the generals of Mithridates, they landed troops in Delos and committed the greatest devastations there in consequence of the inhabitants refusing to espouse their cause (B.C. 87). After this calamity it remained in an impoverished and deserted state. The town of Delos was situated at the foot of Mount Cynthus, in a plain watered by the little river Inopus, and by a lake called Trochoeides by Theognis and Herodotus. Remains of the great temple of Apollo, of the temple of Leto, a theatre, a private house, and of several porticoes are among the antiquities that are now visible. Since 1877, M. Homolle and others, on behalf of the French Archæological Institute, have prosecuted very extensive investigations on the site of the town. See Sallier, ***Hist. de l'Isle de Délos,*** in the ***Mém. de l'Académie des Inscriptions*** iii. 376; and Homolle, *Fouilles de Délos* (Paris, 1878).

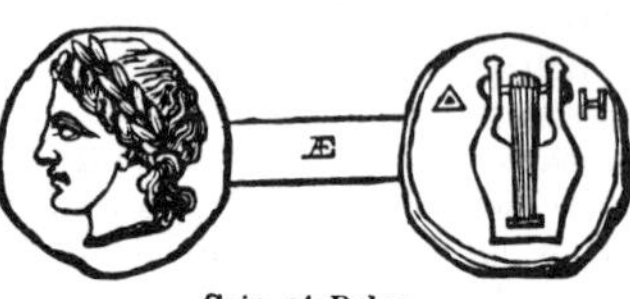

Coin of Delos.

Delos, Confederacy of. A league entered into by the Greek States under the hegemony of Athens in B.C. 478, with the primary object of defending Greece against the designs of Persia. The league obtained its name from the fact that the representatives of the States composing it met periodically at the island of Delos, in the temple of Apollo and Artemis. Each State contributed at its option either ships or money according to the assessment proposed by Aristides (q. v.), representing Athens, and ratified by the assembled delegates. The first assessment amounted to 460 talents, or about $550,000. The contributions were collected and administered by officers called Hellenotamiae (q. v.).

Delphi (Δελφοί). A small but important city of Phocis in Greece, situated on the southern side of Mount Parnassus and built in the form of an amphitheatre. Justin (xxiv. 6) says that it had no walls, but was defended by its precipices. Pausanias (x. 5) calls it πόλις, which seems to imply that it was walled like other cities. In earlier times it was, perhaps, like Olympia, defended by the sanctity of its oracle and the presence of its god. These being found insufficient to afford protection against the enterprises of the profane, it was probably fortified and became a regular city after the predatory incursions of the Phocians. The walls may, however, be coeval with the foundation of the city itself; their high antiquity is not disproved by the use of mortar in the construction, for some of the Egyptian pyramids are built in a similar manner.

The more ancient name of Delphi was Pytho, from the serpent Python, as is commonly supposed, which was said to have been slain by Apollo (Apollod. *Biblioth.* i. 4, 3). Whence the name Delphi itself was derived we are not informed. Some make the city to have received this name from Delphus, a son of Apollo. Others deduce the appellation from the Greek ἀδελφοί, "brethren," because Apollo and his brother Bacchus were both worshipped there, each having one of the summits of Parnassus sacred to him. The author of the Hymn to Apollo seems to pun on the word Delphi, in making Apollo transform himself into a dolphin (δελφίς—v. 494). Some supposed that the name was intended to designate Delphi as the centre or navel of the earth.

A short sketch of the history of this most celebrated oracle and temple will not be out of place. Though not so ancient as Dodona (q. v.), it is evident that the fame of the Delphic shrine had been established at a very early period, from the mention made of it by Homer and the accounts supplied by Pausanias and Strabo. The Homeric Hymn to Apollo informs us (391 foll.) that, when the Pythian god was establishing his oracle at Delphi, he beheld on the sea a merchant-ship from Crete; this he directed to Crissa, and appointed the foreigners the servants of his newly established sanctuary, near which they settled. When this story is stripped of the language of poetry, it can only mean that a Cretan colony founded the temple and oracle of Delphi. Strabo reports that it was at first consulted only by the neighbouring States; but that after its fame became more widely spread, foreign princes and nations eagerly sought responses from the sacred tripod, and loaded the altar of the god with rich presents and costly offerings (420). Pausanias states that the most ancient temple of Apollo at Delphi was formed, according to some, out of branches of bay, and that these branches were cut from the tree that was at Tempé. The form of this temple resembled that of a cottage. After mentioning a second and a third temple—the one raised, as the Delphians said, by bees from wax and wings, and sent by Apollo to the Hyperboreans, and the other built of brass—he adds that to this succeeded a fourth and more stately edifice of stone, erected by two architects named Trophonius and Agamedes (Pausan. x. 5). Here were deposited the sumptuous presents of Gyges and Midas, Alyattes and Croesus (Herod. i. 14, 51), as well as those of the Sybarites, Spinetae, and Siceliots, each prince and nation having their separate chapel or treasury for the reception of these offerings, with an inscription attesting the name of the donor and the cause of the gift. This temple having been accidentally destroyed by fire in B.C. 548, the Amphictyons undertook to build another for the sum of three hundred talents, of which the Delphians were to pay one fourth. The remainder of the amount is said to have been obtained by contributions from the different cities and nations. Amasis, king of Egypt, furnished a thousand talents of *electrum.* The Alcmaeonidae, a wealthy Athenian family, undertook the contract, and agreed to construct the edifice of Porine stone, but afterwards liberally substituted Parian marble for the front, a circumstance which is said to have added considerably to their influence at Delphi (Herod. ii. 180; v. 62). According to Strabo and Pausanias, the architect was Spintharus, a Corinthian. The vast riches accumulated in this temple led Xerxes, after having forced the pass of Thermopylae, to send a portion of his army into Phocis, with a view of securing Delphi and its treasures, which, as Herodotus affirms, were better known to him than the contents of his own palace. The enterprise, however, failed, owing, as it was reported by the Delphians, to the manifest interposition of the deity, who terrified the barbarians and hurled destruction on their scattered bands (Herod. viii. 37). Many years subsequent to this event, the temple fell into the hands of the Phocians, headed by Philomelus, who did not scruple to appropriate its riches to the payment of his troops in the war he was then waging against Thebes. The Phocians are said to have plundered the temple during this contest of gold and silver to the enormous amount of 10,000 talents, or about $11,000,000 (cf. Pausan. x. 2). At a still later period, Delphi became exposed to a formidable attack from a large body of Gauls, headed by their king, Brennus. These barbarians, having forced the defiles of Mount Oeta, possessed themselves of the temple and ransacked its treasures. The booty which they obtained on this occasion is stated to have been immense; and this they must have succeeded in removing to their own country, since we are told that, on the capture of Tolosa, a city of Gaul, by the Roman general Caepio, a great part of the Delphic spoils was found there. Pausanias, however, relates that the Gauls met with great disasters in their attempt on Delphi, and were totally discomfited through the miraculous intervention of the god (x. 23; cf. Polyb. i. 6, 5; ii. 20, 6). Sulla is also said to have robbed this temple as well as those of Olympia and Epidaurus. Strabo assures us that in his time the temple was greatly impoverished, all the offerings of any value having been successively removed. The emperor Nero carried off, according to Pausanias (x. 7), five hundred statues of bronze at one time. Constantine the Great, however, proved a more fatal enemy to Delphi than either Sulla or Nero. He removed the sacred tripods to adorn the Hippodrome of his new city, where, together with the Apollo, the statues of the Heliconian Muses, and a celebrated statue of Pan, they were extant when Sozomen wrote his history (Gibbon, *Decline and Fall,* ch. xvii.). Among these tripods was the famous one which the Greeks, after the battle of Plataea, found in the camp of Mardonius. The Brazen Column which supported this tripod is still to be seen at Constantinople. See the illustration on p. 386.

View of Delphi and Mount Parnassus.

The spot whence issued the prophetic vapour which inspired the priestess was said to be the central point (ὀμφαλός) of the earth, this having been proved by Zeus himself, who despatched two eagles from opposite quarters of the heavens, which there encountered each other (Pausan. x. 16). The Omphalos was marked by a stone in the shape of half an egg. Strabo reports that the golden tripod was placed over the mouth of the cave, whence proceeded the exhalation, and which was of great depth. On this sat the Pythia, who, having caught the inspiration, pronounced her oracles in extempore prose or verse; if the former, it was immediately versified by the poet always employed for that purpose. The oracle itself is said to have been discovered by accident. Some goats having strayed to the mouth of the cavern, were suddenly seized with convulsions; those likewise by whom they were found in this situation having been affected in a similar manner, the circumstance was deemed supernatural and the cave pronounced the seat of prophecy (Pausan. x. 5; Plut. *De Orac. Def.* p. 433). Earthquakes have long since obliterated the chasm. The priestess could only be consulted on certain days. The season of inquiry was the spring, dur-

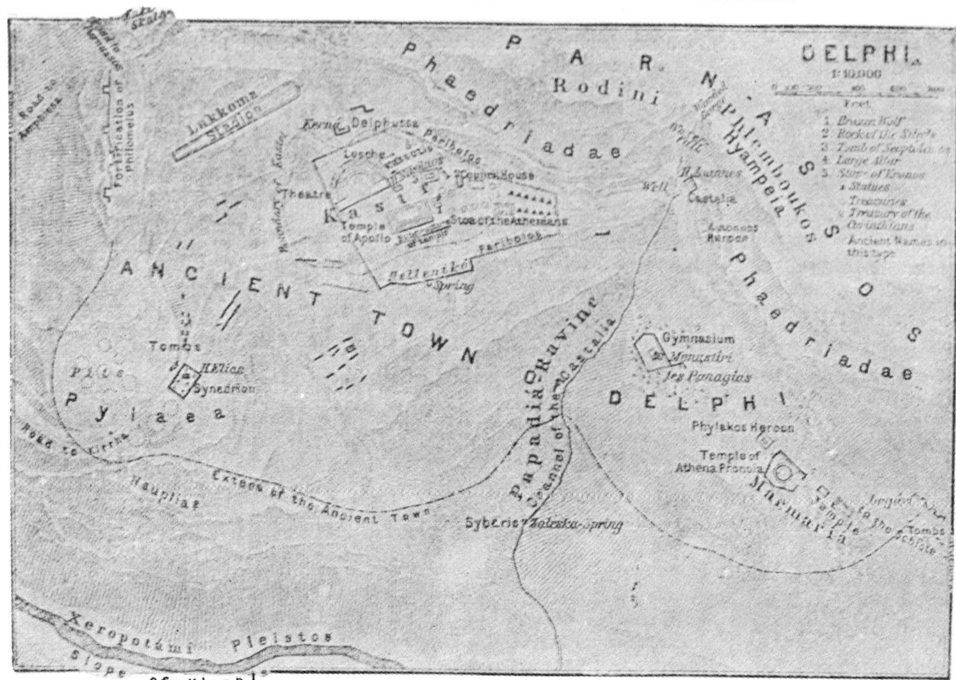

Plan of Delphi in 1890.

ing the month Busius (Plut. *Quaest. Graec.*). Sacrifices and other ceremonies were to be performed by those who sought an answer from the oracle before they could be admitted into the sanctuary.

The most remarkable of the Pythian responses are those which Herodotus records as having been delivered to the Athenians before the invasion of Xerxes (vii. 140); to Croesus (i. 47); to Lycurgus (i. 65); to Glaucus the Spartan (vi. 86). One relative to Agesilaüs is cited by Pausanias (iii. 8). There was, however, as it appears, no difficulty in bribing and otherwise influencing the Pythia herself, as history presents us with several instances of this imposture. Thus we are told that the Alcmaeonidae suggested on one occasion such answers as accorded with their political designs (Herod. v. 62, 90). Cleomenes, king of Sparta, also prevailed on the priestess to aver that his colleague Demaratus was illegitimate. On the discovery, however, of this machination, the Pythia was removed from her office (Herod. vi. 66). Delphi derived further celebrity from its being the place where the Amphictyonic Council held one of their assemblies, and also from the institution of the games which that body established after the successful termination of the Crissaean War. See AMPHICTYONES.

The site of Delphi is occupied by the modern hamlet of Kastri. There still exist at Delphi a part of the wall of the great temple of Apollo with columns and steps, a fragment of a curious marble sphinx, the "Column of the Naxians" with an inscription, a small part of the theatre, a carefully constructed tomb, remains of the Stoa of the Athenians, and some other remnants of the ancient buildings. For many interesting details regarding Delphi and the oracle, see A. Mommsen, *Delphika* (Leipzig, 1878), and Bouché-Leclerq, *Histoire de la Divination dans l'Antiquité*, vol. iii. (Paris, 1880); and on the temple, a valuable paper by Prof. Middleton in the *Journal of Hellenic Studies*, vol. ix. pp. 282–322. See also the article ORACULUM.

Delphĭca, sc. *mensa*. A table of bronze or marble, and made in imitation of the tripod. It was used at drinking-bouts and also for ornamental purposes (Mart. xii. 66).

Marble Delphica. (Rich.)

Delphic Oracle. See DELPHI; ORACULUM; PYTHIA.

Delphĭcus (Δελφικός). A surname of Apollo, from his sanctuary and worship at Delphi (q. v.).

Delphin Edition of the Latin classics. A name given to an edition of the classic authors, prepared by thirty-nine eminent scholars of the time for the use of the Dauphin (Delphinus) of France, the son of Louis XIV. The original editors of the whole were Bossuet and Huet, the Dauphin's tutors. The whole edition consists of sixty-four quarto volumes, and appeared at intervals from 1674 to 1730. The title-pages bear the words, "Ad Usum Serenissimi Delphini." The editors saw fit to expurgate all passages that appeared to them objectionable, and carried this process to absurd lengths, so that *ad usum Delphini* has passed into a phrase to denote that anything has been much Bowdlerized. For some curious details on this head see Larousse, *Dictionnaire du XIXᵉ Siècle*, s. v. "Ad Usum Delphini."

Delphini. (From a Bas-relief.)

Delphīni or **Delphīnes**. The dolphins, seven in number, placed on the *meta* of the circus. (See CIRCUS.) Their object was to give notice of the number of turns round the goals which had been run in each race. Seven courses round the *spina* constituted a single race; and, consequently, one of these dolphins was put up at one end of the course upon the completion of each circuit, and an egg (*ova curriculorum*) at the other, in order that there might be no mistake or dispute. The figure of a dolphin was selected in honour of Neptune; the egg, in honour of Castor and Pollux.

Delphinia (τὰ δελφίνια). A festival of the same expiatory character as the Apollonia, which was celebrated in various towns of Greece, in honour of Apollo, surnamed Delphinius, who was considered by the Ionians as their θεὸς πατρῷος. The name of the god, as well as that of his festival, must be derived from the belief of the ancients that in the beginning of the month of Munychion (probably identical with the Aeginetan Delphinius) Apollo came through the defile of Parnassus to Delphi and began the battle with Delphynê. As he thus assumed the character of a wrathful god, it was thought necessary to appease him, and the Delphinia accordingly were celebrated at Athens, as well as at other places where his worship had been adopted, on the sixth of Munychion. At Athens seven boys and seven girls carried olive-branches, bound with white wool (called the ἱκετηρία), into the Delphinium (Plut. *Thes.* 18).

Delphis (δελφίς). A mass of lead pointed with bronze or iron, perhaps in the shape of a dolphin, used for sinking an enemy's ship (Aristoph. *Eq.* 759; Thuc. vii. 41). In action, the delphis was hauled up from the deck to the point of a yard-arm, which was swung round by braces till over the hostile deck; the machine was then instantly let fall, after which it was again drawn up and deposited on board. The νῆες δελφινοφόροι were probably only of the transport class (ὁλκάδες), as swift (ταχεῖαι) triremes would have been impeded by the great weight.

Delphus (Δελφός). A son of Apollo and Celaeno, who, according to one account, was the founder of Delphi (Pausan. x. 6).

Delta. See AEGYPTUS.

Delūbrum. See TEMPLUM.

Demādes (Δημάδης). An Athenian orator, who belonged to the Macedonian party, and was a bitter enemy of Demosthenes. He was put to death by Antipater in B.C. 318. Demades was a man without principle, but a vigorous and brilliant orator, always speaking extemporaneously, and with such freshness and force as to rival Demosthenes himself. A long fragment of an oration (Περὶ Δωδεκαετίας) bears the name of Demades, but is probably spurious.

Demarātus (Δημάρατος). (1) The son and successor of Ariston on the throne of Sparta, B.C. 516. He was deposed, through the intrigues of Cleomenes, his colleague, on the ground of his being illegitimate. After his deposition he was chosen and held the office of magistrate; but being insultingly derided on one occasion by Leotychides, who had been appointed king in his stead, he crossed over into Asia to Darius, who received him honourably and presented him with lands and cities (Herod. vi. 65, 70). He enabled Xerxes subsequently to obtain the nomination to the empire, in preference to his elder brother Artabazarnes, by suggesting to him an argument, the justice of which was acknowledged by Darius (Herod. vii. 3). We find him after this, though an exile from his country, yet sending the first intelligence to Sparta of the designs of Xerxes against Greece. He accompanied that monarch on his expedition, frankly praised the discipline of the Greeks, and especially that of the Spartans; and before the battle of Thermopylae explained to him some of the warlike customs of the last-mentioned people. We learn also that he advised Xerxes to seize, with his fleet, the island of Cythera, off the coast of Laconia, from which he might continually ravage the shores of that country. The monarch did not adopt his suggestion, but still always regarded the exile Spartan as a friend, and treated him accordingly. (2) A rich citizen of Corinth, of the family of the Bacchiadae. When Cypselus had usurped the sovereign power of Corinth, Demaratus, with all his family, migrated to Italy, and settled at Tarquinii, 658 years before Christ. Commerce had not been deemed disreputable among the Corinthian nobility; and as a merchant, therefore, Demaratus had formed ties of friendship at this place. He brought great wealth with him. The sculptors Eucheir and Eugrammus, and Cleophantus the painter, were said to have accompanied him, and along with the fine arts of Greece he taught (so the popular account said) alphabetic writing to the Etrurians. His son called Lucumo went afterwards to Rome, and became king there under the name of Tarquinius Priscus (Liv. i. 34 foll.). (3) A Corinthian, in the time of Philip and his son Alexander. He had connections of hospitality with the royal family of Macedon, and, having paid a visit to Philip, succeeded in reconciling that monarch to his son. After Alexander had overthrown the Persian Empire, Demaratus, though advanced in years, made a voyage to the east in order to see the conqueror, and, when he beheld him, exclaimed, "What a pleasure have those Greeks missed, who died without seeing Alexander seated on the throne of Darius!" He died soon after, and was honoured with a magnificent funeral (Plut. *Alex.* 37, 56).

Demarchi (δήμαρχοι). The presidents of the demes (δῆμοι) in Attica, said to have been first appointed by Clisthenes when he abolished the ναύκραροι. (See NAUCRARIA.) They were probably elected by vote and not by lot. Their duties were various and important. Thus they convened meetings of the demotae, and took the votes upon all questions under consideration; they had the custody of the ληξιαρχικὸν γραμματεῖον, or book in which the members of the deme were enrolled (Demosth. *c. Eubul.* p. 1317, § 60); and they made and kept a register of the landed estates (χωρία) in their districts, whether belonging to individuals or the corporate property of the deme. See DEMUS.

Demens. See CURATOR.

Demensum. See SERVUS.

Dementia. See CURATOR.

Demētae (Δημῆται). A people of Britain, in the southwestern part of what is now Wales. Their chief town was Maridunum, now Caermarthen (Ptol. ii. 3, 23).

Demēter (Δημήτηρ). The daughter of Cronus and Rhea. Her name signifies Mother Earth, meaning that she was goddess of agriculture and of the civilization based upon it. Her children were: by Iasion, a son Plutus, the god of riches, and by her brother Zeus, a daughter Persephonê. Round Demeter and this daughter centre her worship and the fables respecting her. Hades carried off Persephonê, and Demeter roamed for nine days over the earth seeking her, till on the tenth day she learned the truth from the all-seeing Sun. She was angry with Zeus for permitting the act of violence; visited Olympus, and wandered about among men in the form of an old woman under the name of Deo, or the Seeker, till at length, at Eleusis, in Attica, she was kindly received at the house of King Celeus, and found comfort in tending his newly born son Demophoön. Surprised by his mother in the act of trying to make the

Demeter. (Mural Painting from Pompeii.)

child immortal by putting it into the fire, she revealed her deity, and caused a temple to be built to her, in which she gave herself up to her grief. In her wrath she made the earth barren, so that mankind were threatened with destruction by famine, as she did not allow the fruit of the earth to spring up again until her daughter was allowed to spend two thirds of the year with her. On her return to Olympus she left the gift of corn, of agriculture, and of her holy mysteries with her host, as a token of grateful recollection. She sent Triptolemus the Eleusinian round the world on her chariot, drawn by serpents, to diffuse the knowledge of agriculture and other blessings accompanying it—the settlement of fixed places of abode, civil order, and wedlock. Thus Demeter was worshipped as the goddess of agriculture and founder of law, order, and especially of marriage, in all places where Greeks dwelt, her daughter being usually associated with her. (See THESMOPHORIA.) The most ancient seats of her worship were Athens and Eleusis, where the Rharian plain was solemnly ploughed every year in memory of the first sowing of wheat. She was also much worshipped in Sicily, which from its fertility was accounted one of her favourite places of abode. (See ELEUSINIA.) As the goddess of fertility, Demeter was in many regions associated with Poseidon, the god of fertilizing water. This was particularly the case in Arcadia, where Poseidon was regarded as the father of Persephonê. She was also joined with Dionysus, the god of wine; and as mother of Persephonê and goddess of the earth, to which not only the seed, but the dead are committed, she is connected with the lower world under the name of Chthonia. In later times she was often confused with Gaea and Rhea or Cybelê. Besides fruit and honeycombs, the cow and the sow were offered to her, both as emblems of productivity. Her attributes are poppies and ears of corn (also a symbol of fruitfulness), a basket of fruit, and a little pig. Other emblems had a mystic significance—e. g. the torch, and the serpent, as living in the earth, and as symbolizing a renewal of life by shedding its skin. The Romans identified her with their own Ceres (q. v.).

Demetria (Δημητρία). An annual festival which the Athenians, in B.C. 307, instituted in honour of Demetrius Poliorcetes, who, together with his father Antigonus, was consecrated under the title of "saviour god." It was celebrated every year in the month of Munychion, the name of which, as well as that of the day on which the festival was held, was changed into Demetrion and Demetrias. A priest ministered at their altars, and conducted the solemn procession and the sacrifices and games with which the festival was celebrated (Diod. Sic. xx. 46; Plut. *Demetr.* 10, 46). To honour the new god still more, the Athenians at the same time changed the name of the festival of the Dionysia into that of Demetria, as the young prince was fond of hearing himself compared to Dionysus.

Demetrias (Δημητριάς). A town in Magnesia in Thessaly, on the innermost recesses of the Pagasaean Gulf, founded by Demetrius Poliorcetes, and peopled by the inhabitants of Iolcus and the surrounding towns. Its position was such that it was styled by the last Philip of Macedon one of the three fetters of Greece, the other two being Chalcis and Corinth (Liv. xxxii. 37).

Demetrius (Δημήτριος). (1) A son of Antigonus

and Stratonicé, surnamed Poliorcetes (Πολιορκητής), "besieger of cities," from his talents as an engineer and his peculiar skill in conducting sieges, especially by the aid of machines and engines either invented or improved by himself. At the age of twenty-two he was sent by his father against Ptolemy (B.C. 312), who had invaded Syria. He was defeated near Gaza, but soon repaired his loss by a victory over one of the generals of the enemy. He afterwards sailed with a fleet of 250 ships to Athens, and restored the Athenians to liberty, by freeing them from the power of Cassander and Ptolemy and expelling the garrison which was stationed there under Demetrius Phalereus. The gratitude of the Athenians to their deliverer passed all bounds, but Demetrius was soon summoned by his father to leave the flattery of their orators in order to resume the combined duties of an admiral and an engineer in the reduction of Cyprus. After a slight engagement with Menelaüs, the brother of Ptolemy, he laid siege to Salamis, the ancient capital of that island. The occurrences of this siege occupy a prominent place in history, not so much on account of the determined resistance opposed to the assailants and the great importance attached to its issue by the heads of the belligerent parties, as for a new species of warlike engine invented by Demetrius, and first employed by him against the city of Salamis. The instrument in question was called an ἑλέπολις, or "town-taker," and was an immense tower, consisting of nine stories, gradually diminishing as they rose in altitude, and affording accommodation for a large number of armed men, who thence discharged all sorts of missiles against the ramparts of the enemy. Ptolemy, dreading the fall of Salamis, which would pave the way, as he easily foresaw, for the entire conquest of Cyprus, had already made formidable preparations for compelling Demetrius to raise the siege. A memorable sea-fight ensued, in which the ruler of Egypt was completely defeated, with the loss of nearly all his fleet and 30,000 prisoners. An invasion of Egypt by Antigonus then took place, but ended disgracefully; and Demetrius was sent to reduce the Rhodians, who persisted in remaining allies of Ptolemy. The operations of Demetrius before Rhodes, and the resolute defence of the place by the inhabitants, present perhaps the most remarkable example of skill and heroism that is to be found in the annals of ancient warfare. The ἑλέπολις employed on this occasion greatly exceeded the one that was used in the siege of Salamis. Its towers were 150 feet high; it was supported on eight enormous wheels, and propelled by the labour of 3400 men. After a siege of a whole year, however, the enterprise was abandoned, a treaty was concluded with the Rhodians, and Demetrius, at the request of the Athenians, who were now again subjected to the Macedonians, proceeded to rescue Greece from the power of Cassander. In this he was so successful that he ultimately spread the terror of his arms over the whole of that country. The object of Antigonus and his son was now to effect the final subjugation of Macedonia, Egypt, and the East. The confederacy of Seleucus, Ptolemy, Lysimachus, and Cassander was therefore renewed, with the view of crushing these ambitious schemes, and in the battle of Ipsus they succeeded in effecting their object. Antigonus fell in the conflict, and Demetrius, after a precipitate flight of 200 miles, regained his fleet with only a small remnant of his once powerful host. Sailing soon after to Athens, he received information from the fickle inhabitants that they had resolved to admit no king within their city; upon which, finding that all Greece had now submitted to the influence of Cassander, he made a descent on the coast at Corinth for the mere purpose of plunder and revenge, and afterwards committed similar ravages along the whole coast of Thrace. Fortune, however, soon smiled again. Seleucus, jealous of the power of Lysimachus, whose territories now extended to the Syrian borders, resolved to strengthen his own dominions by forming an alliance with the family of Demetrius, which was still possessed of considerable claims and interests. He therefore made proposals for, and obtained in marriage, Stratonicé, the daughter of his former rival. The power of Demetrius again became formidable, an alliance with Ptolemy, who gave him his daughter Ptolemaïs in marriage, having also added to its increase. He compelled the Athenians to open their gates and receive a garrison; and having generously forgiven their previous fickleness, he turned his attention to Macedonia, and embracing an opportunity of interfering in the affairs of that country, which was afforded by dissensions between the two sons of Cassander, he cut off Alexander, one of the two princes, and made himself master of the throne. His restless ambition now projected new conquests in Europe and Asia. Turning his arms against Pyrrhus, he drove him from Thessaly, and then marched to Thebes, which he took by assault. About the same time also he built the city of Demetrias on the Pagasaean Gulf; and, in order to increase his naval power, formed a matrimonial union with the daughter of Agathocles, tyrant of Sicily. His fleet at length amounted to 500 galleys; while his land forces exceeded considerably 100,000 men, of which more than 12,000 were cavalry. This formidable power

Coin of Demetrius Poliorcetes.

excited the alarm of Lysimachus and Ptolemy; the latter advanced against Greece with his fleet, while the former, with Pyrrhus his ally, made a land attack on Macedon in two different points at once. Demetrius took the field with his usual alacrity, but when he approached the position of Pyrrhus the greater part of his troops deserted him and he was compelled to flee. Leaving Macedon a prey to Lysimachus and Pyrrhus, Demetrius passed over into Asia Minor with a body of his best troops, resolved to assail his adversary in the most vulnerable quarter. The enterprise was at first attended with the most brilliant success. In a short time, however, a check was imposed on his career by Agathocles, the son of Lysimachus, and Demetrius was compelled to apply for protection to his aged son-in-law Seleucus. The latter yielded to his solicitations only so far as to grant him permission to spend two months within his territory; and was subsequently induced by his courtiers to rid himself of so dangerous a guest, by sending him a prisoner to a strong fortress on the Syrian coast, about sixty miles south of Antioch. A sufficient revenue was allowed him for his support, and he was permitted to indulge in the chase and other exercises, always, however, under the eye of his keepers. At last, giving up all active pursuits, he died (B.C. 283) at the end of three years. The age of Demetrius at the time of his death was fifty-four. His posterity enjoyed the throne of Macedon in continued succession down to Perses, when the Roman conquest took place. See the life of Demetrius by Plutarch. (2) Son of Antigonus Gonatas, and grandson of Demetrius Poliorcetes, succeeded his father, B.C. 239. He made war on the Aetolians and the Achaeans, and was successful against both, especially the latter, whom he defeated, although under the command of Aratus. He had distinguished himself, before coming to the throne, by driving Alexander of Epirus out of Macedonia, and by stripping him of his own dominions. He reigned ten years, and was succeeded by Antigonus Doson. (3) Son of Philip III., of Macedonia, an excellent prince, greatly beloved by his countrymen, and sent by his father as a hostage to Rome, where he also made many friends. He was subsequently liberated, and not long after paid a second visit to the capital of Italy as an ambassador from Philip, on which occasion he obtained favourable terms for his father, when the latter was complained of to the Roman Senate by the cities of Greece. Returning home loaded with marks of distinction from the Romans, and honoured by the Macedonians themselves, who regarded him as the liberator of their country, he excited the jealousy of his own father and the envy and hatred of his brother Perses. The latter eventually accused him of aspiring to the crown, and of carrying on, for this purpose, a secret correspondence with the Romans. Philip, lending too credulous an ear to the charge, put his son Demetrius to death, and only discovered when too late the utter falsity of the accusation (Liv. xxxiii. 30; xxxix. 35 foll.; xl. 5, 24, 54 foll.). (4) A Syrian, called SOTER (Σωτήρ), or "the Preserver," the son of Seleucus Philopator, and sent by his father, at the age of twenty-three, as a hostage to Rome. He was living there in this condition when his father died of poison, B.C. 176. His uncle Antiochus Epiphanes thereupon usurped the throne, and was succeeded by Antiochus Eupator. Demetrius, meanwhile, having in vain endeavoured to interest the Senate in his behalf, secretly escaped from Rome, through the advice of Polybius the historian, and, finding a party in Syria ready to support his claims, defeated and put to death Eupator, and ascended the throne. He was subsequently acknowledged as king by the Romans. After this, he freed the Babylonians from the tyranny of Timarchus and Heraclides, and was honoured for this service with the title of Soter. At a subsequent period he sent his generals Nicanor and Bacchides into Iudaea, at the solicitation of Alcimus, the high-priest, who had usurped that office with the aid of Eupator. These two commanders ravaged the country, and Bacchides defeated and slew the celebrated Judas Maccabaeus. Demetrius at last became so hated by his own subjects, and an object of so much dislike, if not of fear, to the neighbouring princes, that they advocated the claims of Alexander Balas, and he fell in battle against this competitor for the crown after having reigned twelve years (from B.C. 162 to B.C. 150). His death was avenged, however, by his son and successor Demetrius Nicator (Just. xxxiv. 3, xxxv. 1). (5) Son of the preceding, and surnamed NICATOR (Νικάτωρ), or "the Conqueror." He drove out Alexander Balas, with the aid of Ptolemy Philometor, who had given him his daughter Cleopatra in marriage, though she was already the wife of Balas. He ascended the throne B.C. 146, but soon abandoned himself to a life of indolence and debauchery, leaving the reins of government in the hands of Lasthenes, his favourite, an unprincipled and violent man. The disgust to which his conduct gave rise induced Tryphon, who had been governor of Antioch under Balas, to revolt, and place upon the throne Antiochus Dionysius, son of Balas and Cleopatra, a child only four years of age. A battle ensued, in which Demetrius was defeated, and Antiochus, now receiving the surname of Theos, was conducted by the victors to Antioch and proclaimed king of Syria. He reigned, however, only in name. The actual monarch was Tryphon, who put him to death at the end of about two years and caused himself to be proclaimed in his stead. Demetrius, meanwhile, held his court at Seleucia. Thinking that the crimes of Tryphon would soon make him universally detested, he turned his arms in a different direction and marched against the Parthians, in the hope that, if he returned victorious, he would be enabled the more easily to rid himself of his Syrian antagonist. After some successes, however, he was entrapped and made prisoner by the Parthian monarch Mithridates, and his army was attacked and cut to pieces. His captivity among the Parthians was an honourable one, and Mithridates made him espouse his daughter Rhodoguna. The intelligence of this marriage so exasperated Cleopatra that she gave her hand to Antiochus Sidetes, her brother-in-law, who thereupon ascended the throne. Sidetes having been slain in a battle with the Parthians after a reign of several years, Demetrius escaped from the hands of Mithridates and resumed the throne. His subjects, however, unable any longer to endure his pride and cruelty, requested from Ptolemy Physcon a king of the race of the Seleucidae to govern them. Ptolemy sent Alexander Zubinas. Demetrius, driven out by the Syrians, came to Ptolemaïs, where Cleopatra, his first wife, then held sway, but the gates were shut against him. He then took refuge in Tyre, but was put to death by the governor (B.C. 125). Zubinas recompensed the Tyrians for this act by permitting them to live according to their own laws, and from this period commences what is called by chronologists the era of the independence of Tyre, which was still subsisting at the time of the Council of Chalcedon, 574 years after this event (Joseph. *Ant. Iud.* xiii. 9, 12, 17; Just. xxxvi. 1, xxxix. 1). (6) Surnamed EUKAERUS (Εὔκαιρος), "the Seasonable" or "Fortunate," was the fourth son of Antiochus Grypus. He was proclaimed king at Damascus, and, in conjunction with his brother Philip, to whom a part of Syria remained faithful, drove out Antiochus Eusebes from that country, compelling him to take refuge among the Parthians. The two brothers then divided Syria between them, Antioch being the capital of Philip and Damascus that of Demetrius. The latter afterwards marched to the aid of the Jews, who had revolted from their king, Alexander Ianneus. He was recalled, however, to his own dominions by the news of an invasion on the part of his own brother Philip. He took Antioch, and besieged Philip in Beroea; but the latter being assisted by the Parthians and the Arabians, Demetrius was besieged in his own camp and at length taken prisoner. He was brought to the king of Parthia, who treated him with great distinction and sent him into Upper Asia. He reigned a little over six years. (7) PEPAGOMĔNUS, a medical writer, who flourished during the reign of Michael VIII. (Palaeologus). By the order of this monarch, he wrote a work on the gout (Περὶ Ποδάγρας). We have two treatises under his name, but it is extremely doubtful whether he was indeed their author. The first is on the art of training falcons; the second, on the mode of breaking and training dogs. (8) PHALĒREUS (Φαληρεύς), a native of Phalerum in Attica, and the last of the more distinguished orators of Greece. He was the son of a person who had been slave to Timotheus and Conon. But, though born in this low condition, he soon made himself distinguished by his talents, and was already a conspicuous individual in the public assemblies when Antipater became master of Athens, for he was obliged to save himself by flight from the vengeance of the Macedonian party. He was compelled to quit the city a second time when Polysperchon took possession of it through his son. Subsequently named by Cassander as governor of Athens (B.C. 317), he so gained the affections of his countrymen that, during the six years in which he filled this office, they are said to have raised to him three hundred and sixty statues. Athenaeus, however, on the authority of Duris, a Samian writer, reproaches him with luxurious and expensive habits, while he prescribed, at the same time, frugality to his fellow-citizens and fixed limits for their expenditures. After the death of his protector, Demetrius was driven from Athens by Antigonus and Demetrius Poliorcetes (B.C. 306). The people of that city, always fickle, overthrew the numerous statues they had erected to him, although he had been their benefactor and idol, and even condemned him to death. Demetrius, upon this, retired to the court of Alexandria, where he lived upwards of twenty years. It is generally supposed that he was the individual who gave Ptolemy the advice to found the Museum and the famous Library. This prince consulted him also as to the choice of a successor. Demetrius was in favour of the monarch's eldest son, but the king eventually decided for the son whom he had by his second wife Berenicē. When Ptolemy II., therefore, came to the throne, he revenged himself on the unlucky counsellor by exiling him to a distant province in Upper Egypt, where Demetrius put an end to his own life by the bite of an asp (B.C. 282). Cicero describes Demetrius as a polished, sweet, and graceful speaker, but deficient in energy and power. Plutarch cites his treatise "On Socrates," which appears to have contained also a life of Aristides. The works of Demetrius are lost. There exists, it is true, under his name a treatise on elocution (Περὶ Ἑρμηνείας), a work full of ingenious observations; but critics agree in making it of later origin. Besides the treatise on elocution, there exists a small work on the apophthegms of the Seven Sages, which Stobaeus has inserted in his third discourse, as being the production of Demetrius Phalereus. (9) Of Sunium; a Cynic philosopher, who flourished at Corinth in the first century. During the reign of Caligula he taught philosophy at Rome, where he obtained the highest reputation for wisdom and virtue. He was banished from Rome in the time of Nero for his free censure of public manners. After the death of this emperor he returned to Rome, but the boldness of his language soon offended Vespasian and again subjected him to the punishment of exile. Apollonius, with whom he had formed a friendship, prevailed on Titus to recall him; but under Domitian he withdrew to Puteoli. Seneca, who was acquainted with him, speaks in the highest terms of his masculine eloquence, sound judgment, intrepid fortitude, and inflexible integrity (Sen. *De Vit. Beat.* 25).

Deminutio Capĭtis. Diminution of civil rights and legal capacity. A term by which the Romans denoted degradation to an inferior civil condition, through the loss of the rights of freedom, citizenship, or family. The extreme form of it, *deminutio capitis maxima*, was entailed by the loss of freedom, which involved the loss of all other rights. This would occur if a Roman citizen were taken prisoner in war, or given up to the enemy for having violated the sanctity of an ambassador or concluding a treaty not approved of by the people. Or again if he was sold into slavery, whether by the State for refusing military service, or for declining to state the amount of his property at the census, or by his creditors for debt. If a prisoner of war returned home, or if the enemy refused to accept him when given up to them, his former civil rights were restored. The intermediate stage, *deminutio capitis media* or *minor*, consisted in loss of civil rights consequent on becoming a citizen of another State, or on a decree of exile confirmed by the people, or (in imperial times) on deportation. Restoration of the civil status was possible if the foreign citizenship were given up, or if the decree of exile were cancelled. The lowest grade (*deminutio capitis minima*) was the loss of hitherto existing family rights by emancipation (which involved leaving the family), adoption, or (if a girl) by marriage. See CAPUT.

Demioprāta (δημιόπρατα). Property confiscated at Athens and sold by public auction. The confiscation of property was one of the most common sources of revenue in many Greek States; and Aristophanes (*Vesp.* 659; *Eq.* 103) mentions the δημιόπρατα as a separate branch of the public revenue at Athens. A chapter of Boeckh's *Public Economy* is devoted to this subject (book iii. ch. 14). These sales were under the direction of the *poletae* (q. v.), who presented their reports to the people in the first assembly of each prytany (Poll. viii. 95); they also set up lists of δημιόπρατα (probably after the sale) upon tablets of stone in the Acropolis, at Eleusis, and elsewhere. Several fragments of such lists are preserved in inscriptions; one of the most important, throwing light on the prices realized by the *poletae*, is discussed in Boeckh-Fränkel (ii. 129 foll.). On δημιόπρατα in general, see Boeckh-Fränkel, Index, s. v. "Güter."

Demiurgi (δημιουργοί). A general term among the Greeks for tradesmen, among whom they included artists and physicians. In old times they formed, at Athens, the third order, the other two being the Eupatridae and Geomori (see these names). In some States, Demiurgi was the name of the public officials: in the Achaean League, for instance, the ten Demiurgi were among the highest officers of the confederacy.

Demius (δήμιος). The public executioner at Athens, a slave, who was the servant of the Eleven. For references, see DEMOSII, HENDEKA, and TORMENTUM.

Democēdes (Δημοκήδης). A celebrated physician of Crotona (Herod. iii. 129). He practised medicine successively at Aegina, Athens, and Samos. He was taken prisoner by the Persians, in B.C. 522, and was sent to Susa to the court of Darius. Here he acquired great reputation by curing the king's foot and the breast of the queen Atossa. Notwithstanding his honours at the Persian court he was always desirous of returning to his native country, and in order to effect this, he procured by means of Atossa that he should be sent with some nobles to explore the coast of Greece and to ascertain in what parts it might be most successfully attacked. At Tarentum he escaped, and settled at Crotona, where he married the daughter of the famous wrestler Milo.

Demochăres (Δημοχάρης). An Athenian, the son of the sister of Demosthenes, and well known as an orator. Upon the restoration of the democracy by Demetrius Poliorcetes in B.C. 306, Demochares was at the head of the popular party for several years. He left orations and an elaborate history of his own times, only fragments of which remain. See the essay by Droysen in the *Zeitschrift für die Alterthumswissenschaft* (1836), xx. and xxi.

Democrătes (Δημοκράτης). A Pythagorean philosopher of whose life nothing is known, but who is remembered as the author of the so-called "Golden Maxims" (γνῶμαι χρυσαῖ), a number of moral sayings in the Ionic dialect. They are printed in Orelli's *Opusc. Graec. Vet. Sentent.* (Leipzig, 1819).

Democratia (δημοκρατία, "sovereignty of the people"). The Greek term for the form of constitution in which all citizens had the right of taking part in the government. This right was not always absolutely equal. Sometimes classes were formed on a property qualification and civil rights conferred accordingly (see TIMOCRATIA); but no class in this case was absolutely excluded from a share in the government, and it was possible to rise from one class to another. Sometimes provision was made by law to prevent any persons taking part in the administration but such as had proved their worth and capacity. In the absence of such limitations the democracy, as Plato in his *Republic* and Aristotle in his *Politics* observed, soon degenerated into a mob-government (ὀχλοκρατία) or developed into a despotism.

Democrĭtus (Δημόκριτος). A celebrated philosopher, born at Abdera, about B.C. 494 or 490, but according to some, B.C. 470 or 460. His father was a man of noble family and of great wealth, and contributed largely towards the entertainment of the army of Xerxes on his return to Asia. As a reward for this service the Persian monarch made him and the other Abderites rich presents and left among them several Chaldaean Magi. Democritus, according to Diogenes Laërtius, was instructed by these in astronomy and theology. After the death of his father he determined to travel in search of wisdom, and devoted to this purpose the portion which fell to him, amounting to one hundred talents. He is said to have visited Egypt and Ethiopia, the Persian Magi, and, according to some, even the Gymnosophists of India. Whether, in the course of his travels, he visited Athens or studied under Anaxagoras is uncertain. There can be little doubt, however, that during some part of his life he was instructed in the Pythagorean tenets, and particularly that he was a disciple of Leucippus (q. v.). After a long course of years thus spent in travelling, Democritus returned to Abdera, richly stored with the treasures of philosophy, but destitute even of the necessary means of subsistence. His brother Damosis, however, received him kindly and liberally supplied all his wants. According to the law of Abdera, whoever should waste his patrimony should be deprived of the rites of burial. Democritus, desiring to avoid this disgrace, gave public lectures to the people, chiefly from his larger Διάκοσμος, the most valuable of his writings; in return he received from his hearers many valuable presents and other testimonies of respect, which relieved him from all apprehension of suffering public censure as a spendthrift.

Democritus, by his learning and wisdom, and especially by his acquaintance with natural phenomena, acquired great fame and excited much admiration among the ignorant Abderites. By giving previous notices of unexpected changes in the weather, and by other artifices, he had the address to make them believe that he possessed a power of predicting future events; and they not only looked upon him as something more than mortal, but even proposed to invest him with the direction of their public affairs. From inclination and habit, however, he preferred a contemplative to an active life, and therefore declined these public honours and passed the remainder of his days in solitude. It is said that from this time he spent his days and nights in caverns and sepulchres; and some even relate that, in order to be more perfectly master of his intellectual faculties, he blinded himself by means of a burning-glass. The story, however, is utterly incredible, since the writers who mention it affirm that Democritus employed his leisure in writing books and in dissecting the bodies of animals, neither of which could well have been effected without eyes. Nor is greater credit due to the tale that Democritus spent his leisure hours in chemical researches after the philosopher's stone—the dream of a later age; or to the story of his conversation with Hippocrates, grounded upon letters which are said to have passed between the father of medicine and the people of Abdera on the supposed madness of Democritus, but which are evidently spurious. The only reasonable conclusion that can be drawn from these and other tales is that Democritus was a man of lofty genius and penetrating judgment, who, by a long course of study and observation, became an eminent master of speculative and physical science; the natural consequence of which was that, like Roger Bacon in a later period, he astonished and imposed upon his ignorant and credulous countrymen. Petronius relates that he was perfectly acquainted with the virtues of herbs, plants, and stones, and that he spent his life in making experiments upon natural bodies.

Democritus has been commonly known under the appellation of "The Laughing Philosopher,"

Democritus. (Naples Museum.)

and it is gravely related by Seneca (*De Ira*, ii. 10; *De Tranq.* 15) that he never appeared in public without expressing his contempt of the follies of mankind by laughter. Thus much, in fact, may be easily believed: that a man so superior to the generality of his contemporaries, and whose lot it was to live among a race of men who were stupid to a proverb, might frequently treat their follies with ridicule and contempt. Accordingly, we find that among his fellow-citizens he had the name of Γελασῖνος, or "the mocker" (cf. Juv. x. 33, 34).

Democritus appears to have been in his morals chaste and temperate, and his sobriety was repaid by a healthy old age. He lived and enjoyed the use of his faculties to the term of a hundred years, and at last died through mere decay.

Democritus expanded the atomic theory of his master Leucippus (q. v.), to support the truth of which he maintained the impossibility of division *ad infinitum;* and, from the difficulty of assigning a commencement of time, he argued the eternity of existing nature, of void space, and of motion. He supposed the atoms, originally similar, to be endowed with certain properties, such as impenetrability and a density proportionate to their volume. He referred every active and passive affection to motion, caused by impact, limited by the principle he assumed, that like can only act on like. He drew a distinction between primary motion and secondary; impulse and reaction; from a combination of which he produced rotary motion. Herein consists the law of necessity, by which all things in nature are ruled. From the endless multiplicity of falling atoms have resulted the worlds which we behold, with all the properties of immensity, resemblance, and dissimilitude which belong to them. The soul consists (such is his doctrine) of globular atoms of fire, which impart movement to the body. Maintaining his atomic theory throughout, Democritus introduced the hypothesis of images (εἴδωλα), a species of emanation from external objects, which make an impression on our senses, and from the influence of which he deduced sensation (αἴσθησις) and thought (νόησις). He distinguished between a rude, imperfect, and therefore false perception and a true one. In the same manner, consistently with his theory, he accounted for the popular notions of the Deity; partly through our incapacity to understand fully the phenomena of which we are witnesses, and partly from the impressions communicated by certain beings (εἴδωλα) of enormous stature and resembling the human figure which inhabit the air. To these he ascribed dreams and the causes of divination. He carried his theory into practical philosophy also, laying down that happiness consisted in an equability of temperament (εὐθυμία), whence he deduced his moral principles and prudential maxims. It was from Democritus that Epicurus (q. v.) borrowed the principal features of his philosophy. The fragments of Democritus have been collected and published by Mullach (Berlin, 1843), with notes. See Ueberweg, *History of Philosophy* (Eng. trans., N. Y 1872), vol. i. pp. 67–71; and the dissertation by E. Johnson, *Der Sensualismus des Demokrit* (Plauen, 1868).

Demodŏcus (Δημοδόκος). (1) A blind musician at the court of Alcinoüs, who sang in the presence of Odysseus (Hom. *Od.* viii. 44; Plut. *De Mus.*). (2) A Trojan chief, who came with Aeneas into Italy, where he was killed (Verg. *Aen.* x. 413).

Demoleon (Δημολέων). (1) A Centaur, killed by Theseus at the nuptials of Pirithoüs (Ovid, *Met.* xii. 356). (2) A son of Antenor, killed by Achilles (Hom. *Il.* xx. 395).

Demon. See DAEMON.

Demōnax (Δημώναξ). A philosopher of the second century B.C., who endeavoured to revive the philosophy of the Cynic School. Born in Cyprus, he went to Athens, where he became very popular, so that people vied with one another in presenting him with food, and even the young children gave him great quantities of fruit. Much less austere than Diogenes (q. v.), whom he took as his philosophic model, he nevertheless rebuked vice unsparingly, and was charged with neglecting the Eleusinian Mysteries, to which he replied: "If the mysteries are bad, no one should be initiated; and if they are good, they ought to be open to every one." He was a friend of Epictetus, who once rebuked him for not marrying, but was silenced by Demonax, who said, "Very well; give me one of your daughters for a wife"—Epictetus being himself a bachelor. Demonax lived to be nearly a hundred, and on his death was buried with great magnificence. See the *Demŏnax* of Lucian, in which the character of the philosopher is painted in glowing colours.

Demonēsi Insŭlae (Δημόνησοι). A group of islands in the Propontis (Sea of Marmora) belonging to Bithynia. The chief of these were Pityodes and Chalcitis, also called Demonesus.

Demophĭlus (Δημόφιλος). (1) An Athenian poet of the New Comedy, from whose Ὀναγός Plautus took his *Asinaria.* (2) A Pythagorean philosopher who wrote a work called Βίου Θεράπεια, of which a selection is extant under the name of Γνωμικὰ Ὁμοιώματα, which has been edited by Orelli (Leipzig, 1819). Of the life of Demophilus no particulars are known.

Demophoön (Δημοφόων) or **Demŏphon.** (1) See ELEUSINIA. (2) See PHYLLIS.

Demopoiētos (δημοποίητος). A newly made or naturalized citizen at Athens. See Demosth. *c. Steph.* i. p. 1125, § 78.

Demosii (δημόσιοι). Public slaves at Athens, bought by the State. The most numerous class were the τοξόται or Σκύθαι, a force of police, also called Σπευσίνιοι, from the first organizer of the service (Poll. viii. 131–132). Their duty was to preserve order in the assembly, courts, public places, and public works. They were at first encamped in tents in the Agora, and afterwards removed to the Areopagus. Certain of them were in personal attendance on officials. The corps dated from the year of Salamis, when 300 were bought; they were later increased to 1200 (Andoc. *De Pac.* 5, 7; Aesch. *De Fals. Leg.* § 173 f.).

Executioners, torturers, etc., whether police or not, were also slaves (Poll. viii. 71). Demosii were also employed in the treasury, in subordinate places in the assembly and courts, as checking-clerks (ἀντιγραφεῖς)—their amenability to torture making them especially serviceable for such duties. The State undertook their training.

In the mint were slave workmen, as also in the mines. Exceptionally, as at Arginusae, demosii rowed in the galleys. See SERVUS PUBLICUS.

Demosthĕnes (Δημοσθένης). (1) A celebrated Athenian orator, a native of the deme of Paeania, in the tribe Pandionis. His father, Demosthenes, was a citizen of rank and opulence, and the proprietor of a manufactory of arms; not a common blacksmith, as the language of Juvenal (x. 130) would lead us to believe. The son was born about B.C. 383, and lost his father at the early age of seven years, when he was left to the care of his mother, Cleobulé. The guardians to whom his father had intrusted the administration of a large property proving faithless to their charge and wasting a large portion of his patrimony, the orator's early studies were seriously hampered by the want of sufficient means, to say nothing of the delicate state of his own health. When Demosthenes was some sixteen years of age his curiosity was attracted by a trial in which Callistratus pleaded and won a cause of considerable importance. The eloquence which gained, and the applause which followed, his success so inflamed the ambition of the young Athenian that he determined to devote himself thenceforward to the assiduous study of oratory. He chose Isaeus as his master rather than Isocrates; from Plato, also, he imbibed much of the richness and the grandeur which characterize the writings of that philosopher. At the age of seventeen he appeared before the courts and pronounced against his faithless guardians, and against a debtor to his father's estate, five orations, which were crowned with complete success. These discourses, in all probability, had received the finishing touch from Isaeus, under whom Demosthenes continued to study for the space of four years after he had reached his majority.

An opening so successful emboldened the young orator to speak before the people in the assembly; but, when he made the attempt, his feeble and stammering voice, his interrupted respiration, his ungraceful gestures, and his ill-arranged periods, brought upon him general ridicule. Returning home in the utmost distress, he was encouraged by the kindness of the actor Satyrus, who, having requested Demosthenes to repeat some passage from a dramatic poet, pronounced the same extract after him with so much correctness of enunciation and in a manner so true to nature that it appeared to the young orator to be quite a different passage. Convinced, thereupon, how much grace and persuasive power a proper enunciation and manner add to the best oration, he resolved to correct the deficiencies of his youth, and accomplished this with a zeal and perseverance which have passed into a proverb. To free himself from stammering he spoke with pebbles in his mouth, a story resting on the authority of Demetrius Phalereus, his contemporary It also appears that he was unable to articulate clearly the letter R; but he vanquished that difficulty most perfectly, for Cicero says that he *exercitatione fecisse ut plenissime diceret.* He removed the distortion of features which accompanied his utterance by watching the movements of his countenance in a mirror; and a naked sword was suspended over his left shoulder while he was declaiming in private, to prevent its rising above the level of the right. That his enunciation might be loud and full of emphasis he frequently ran up the steepest and most uneven walks, an exercise by which his voice acquired both force and energy; and on the sea-shore, when the waves were violently agitated, he declaimed aloud, to accustom himself to the noise and tumult of a public assembly. He constructed a subterranean study, where he would often stay for two or three months together, shaving one side of his head, that in case he should wish to go abroad the shame of appearing in that condition might keep him within. In this solitary retreat, by the light of his lamp, he is said to have copied and recopied, ten times at least, the orations scattered throughout the history of Thucydides, for the purpose of moulding his own style after so pure a model.

Whatever may be the truth of these stories, Demosthenes got credit for the most indefatigable labour in the acquisition of his art. His enemies, at a subsequent period of his career, attempted to ridicule this extraordinary industry, by remarking that all his arguments "smelled of the lamp," and they eagerly embraced the opportunity of denying him the possession of natural talents. This criticism of Demosthenes seems to have rested chiefly on his known reluctance to speak without preparation. The fact is, that though he could exert the talent of extemporaneous speaking, he avoided rather than sought such occasions, partly from deference to his audience and partly from apprehending the possibility of a failure. Plutarch, however, who mentions this reluctance of the orator, speaks at the same time of the great merit of his extemporaneous effusions.

Demosthenes reappeared in public at the age of twenty-five years, and pronounced two orations against Leptines, the author of a law which imposed on every citizen of Athens, except the descendants of Harmodius and Aristogiton, the exercise of certain burdensome functions. The second of these discourses, entitled "Of Immunities," is regarded as one of his happiest efforts. After this, he became much engaged in the business of the bar, and these professional labours, added to the scanty portion of his patrimony which he had recovered from his guardians, appear to have formed his only means of support. But, whatever may have been the distinction and the advantages which Demosthenes acquired by his practice at the bar, his principal glory is derived from his political discourses. At the period when he engaged in public affairs the State was a mere wreck. Public spirit was at the lowest ebb; the laws had lost their authority; the austerity of early manners had yielded to the inroads of luxury, activity to indolence, and probity to venality. Of the virtues of their fathers there remained to the Athenians little save an attachment, carried almost to enthusiasm, for their native soil. On the slightest occasion this feeling of patriotism was sure to display itself; and, thanks to this sentiment, the people of Athens were still capable of making strenuous efforts for the preservation of their freedom. No one understood better than Demosthenes the art of exciting

Demosthenes. (Vatican Museum, Rome.)

and keeping alive this enthusiasm. His penetration enabled him easily to divine the ambitious plans of Philip of Macedon from the very outset of that monarch's operations, and he resolved to counteract them. His whole public career, indeed, had but one object in view, and that was war with Philip. For the space of fourteen years this monarch found the Athenian orator continually in his path, and every attempt proved unavailing to corrupt so formidable an adversary. These fourteen years, which immediately preceded the fall of Grecian freedom, constitute the brightest period in the history of Demosthenes. And yet his courage was political rather than military. At Chaeronea (B.C. 338) he fled from the field of battle, though in the Athenian assembly no private apprehensions could check his eloquence or influence his conduct. But, though overpowered in the contest with the enemy of Athenian independence, he received after his defeat the most honourable recompense which, in accordance with Grecian customs, a grateful country could bestow. Athens decreed him a crown of gold. The reward was opposed by Aeschines (q. v.). The combat of eloquence which arose between the two orators attracted to Athens an immense concourse of spectators. Demosthenes triumphed, and his antagonist, not having received the fifth part of the votes, was, in conformity with the existing law, compelled to retire into exile. A short time after this splendid victory Demosthenes was condemned for having suffered himself to be bribed by Harpalus, a Macedonian governor, who, dreading the anger of Alexander, had come to Athens to hide there the fruit of his extortion and rapine, and had bargained with the popular leaders of the day for the protection of the Republic. Demosthenes, having escaped from imprisonment, fled to Aegina (B.C. 324), whence he could behold the shores of his beloved country, and earnestly and constantly protested his innocence. After the death of Alexander he was restored, and his entry into Athens was marked by every demonstration of joy. A new league was formed among the Grecian cities against the Macedonians, and Demosthenes was the soul of it. But the confederacy was broken up by Antipater, and the death of the orator was decreed. He retired, thereupon, from Athens to the island of Calauria, off the coast of Argolis, and, being still pursued by the satellites of Antipater, terminated his life there by poison, in the temple of Poseidon, at the age of about sixty years, B.C. 322.

Before the time of Demosthenes there existed three distinct styles of eloquence: that of Lysias, mild and persuasive, which quietly engaged the attention and won the assent of an audience; that of Thucydides, bold and animated, which awakened the feelings and powerfully forced conviction on the mind; while that of Isocrates was, as it were, a combination of the two former. Demosthenes can scarcely be said to have adopted any individual as a model, although he bestowed so much untiring labour on the historian of the Peloponnesian War. He rather culled all that was valuable from the various styles of his great predecessors, working them up and blending them into one harmonious whole. In the general structure of many of his sentences he resembles Thucydides, but is simpler and more perspicuous and better calculated to be quickly comprehended by an audience. On the other hand, his clearness in narration and his elegance and purity of diction remind the reader of Lysias. But the argumentative parts of the speeches of Lysias are often deficient in vigour; whereas earnestness, power, zeal, rapidity, and passion, all exemplified in plain, unornamented language and a strain of close, business-like reasoning, are the distinctive characteristics of Demosthenes. The general tone of his oratory, indeed, was admirably adapted to an Athenian audience, constituted as it was of those whose habits of life were mechanical, and of those whom ambition or taste had led to the cultivation of literature. The former were captivated by strong good sense, urged with masculine force and inextinguishable spirit, and by the forcible application of plain truths; while there was enough of grace and variety to please more learned and fastidious auditors. Another very remarkable excellence of Demosthenes is the collocation of his words. The arrangement of sentences in such a manner that their cadences should be harmonious, and to a certain degree rhythmical, was a study much in vogue among the great masters of Grecian composition. See COLON.

The question has often been raised as to the secret of the success of Demosthenes. The universal approbation will appear the more extraordinary to a reader who for the first time peruses the orations. They do not exhibit any of that declamation on which loosely hangs the fame of so many aspirants to eloquence. There appears no deep reflection to indicate a more than ordinary penetration, or any philosophical remarks to prove the extent of his acquaintance with the great moral writers of his country. He affects no learning; he aims at no elegance; he seeks no glaring ornaments; he rarely touches the heart with a soft or melting appeal, and when he does, it is only with an effect in which a third-rate speaker would have surpassed him. He had no wit, no humour, no vivacity, in our acceptance of these terms. The secret of his power is simple, for it lies essentially in this, that his political principles were interwoven with his very spirit; they were not assumed to serve an interested purpose, to be laid aside when he descended from the bema and resumed when he sought to accomplish an object, but were deeply seated in his heart and emanated from its profoundest depths. The more his country was environed by dangers, the more steady was his resolution. Nothing ever impaired the truth and integrity of his feelings or weakened his generous conviction. It was his undeviating firmness, his disdain of all compromise, that made him the first of statesmen and orators; in this lay the substance of his power, the primary foundation of his superiority; the rest was merely secondary. The mystery of his influence, then, lay in his honesty; and it is this that gave warmth and tone to his feelings, energy to his language, and an impression to his manner before which every imputation of insincerity must have immediately vanished. We may thus perceive the meaning of Demosthenes himself, when, to one who asked him what was the first requisite in an orator, he merely replied, "Delivery" (*ὑπόκρισις*); and when asked what were the second and third requisites, gave the same answer as at first (Plut. *Vit. X. Orat.*). His meaning was this: a lifeless manner on the part of a public speaker shows that his own feelings are not enlisted in the cause which he is advocating, and it is idle for him, therefore, to seek to make converts of others when he has failed in making one of himself. On the other hand, when the tone of voice, the gesture, the look, the whole manner of the orator, display the powerful feelings that agitate him, his emotion is communicated to his hearers, and success is inevitable. Cf. Quintil. *Inst. Or.* xi. 3 init.

Of the orations we have sixty-one (half of them spurious), and fifty-six Introductions, or *προοίμια δημηγορικά*. In confining ourselves to the classification adopted by the ancient rhetoricians, we may arrange all these discourses under one of three heads. (I.) Deliberative discourses (*λόγοι συμβουλευτικοί*), treating of political topics, and delivered either before the Senate or the assembly of the people. (II.) Judicial speeches (*λόγοι δικάνικοι*), having for their object accusation or defence. (III.) Studied or set speeches (*λόγοι ἐπιδεικτικοί*), intended to censure or praise.

Seventeen of the orations of Demosthenes belong to the first of these classes, forty-two to the second, and two to the third.

Of the seventeen discourses which compose the first class, five treat of various subjects connected with the Republic, and twelve of the quarrels between the State and Philip. Our limits allow an examination of only a few of these that are most important in their character. Of the twelve harangues that turn upon the quarrels of the Republic with Philip, the first was pronounced in B.C. 351; the second, third, and fourth in B.C. 349; the fifth in B.C. 347; the sixth in B.C. 346; the seventh in B.C. 344; the eighth in B.C. 343; the ninth in B.C. 342; the tenth and eleventh in B.C. 341; and the twelfth in B.C. 340. The order here given is that of Dionysius of Halicarnassus, but no manuscript and no editions observe it. The manuscripts give the First, Second, Tenth, and Eleventh Philippics of Dionysius by name, and regard his fifth as forming the conclusion of the first. They give the title of Second, Third, and First Olynthiacs to his Second, Third, and Fourth. The remaining four (Sixth, Eighth, Ninth, Twelfth) have the following titles: "Of Peace," "Of Halonesus," "Of the Chersonesus," and "On the Letter of Philip." We shall now speak of them in chronological order. The (1 and 2) *Πρὸς Φιλίππον λόγος πρῶτος*, the First Philippic. Demosthenes here exhorts his fellow-citizens to prosecute the war with the greatest vigour against Philip. This monarch had, after the defeat of the Phocians, assumed a threatening attitude, as if wishing to establish himself in their country. The discourse we are now considering has been divided into two parts, which, according to Dionysius of Halicarnassus, were pronounced at different times; but this opinion is contradicted by most critics. (3, 4, 5) *Ὀλυνθιακός* Α, Β, Γ—The three Olynthiacs. Their object is to stimulate the Athenians to succour Olynthus and prevent its falling into the hands of Philip. (6) *Περὶ τῆς εἰρήνης*, "Of the Peace." Philip having obtained a seat in the council of the Amphictyons, Demosthenes advises his countrymen to preserve the peace with this prince. Libanius thinks that this discourse, though written by Demosthenes, was never delivered. Modern scholars are, however, of a different opinion. (7) *Κατὰ Φιλίππου λόγος* Β, the Second Philippic, pronounced after the return of Demosthenes from the Peloponnesus, where he had negotiated a peace between Sparta and Messenia. (8) *Περὶ τῆς Ἁλονήσου*, "Of Halonesus," or, rather, of a letter of Philip's, by which he makes a present to the Athenians of the island of Halonesus, which he had taken from the pirates, and demands of the Athenians to share with them the office of protecting the seas. Demosthenes strenuously opposes so insulting an offer; it is, however, far from certain whether he ever pronounced such a discourse as this. Libanius says that the ancient critics ascribed it to Hegesippus, the friend of Demosthenes. Suidas and the author of the *Etymologicum*

Magnum agree with him. (9) Περὶ τῶν ἐν Χερρονήσῳ πραγμάτων, ἢ ὁ περὶ Διοπείθεους, "Of the events in the Chersonesus, or of Diopithes." That general, sent at the head of a colony into the Chersonesus, had committed hostilities against the city of Cardia, the only one which Philip had reserved for himself in the conditions of peace. Diopithes had even made an inroad into Macedonia. Philip insisted on his being punished. Demosthenes undertakes in this oration to justify the conduct of the Athenian commander. (10) Κατὰ Φιλίππου λόγος Γ, the Third Philippic. The progress which Philip had made in Thrace, where he was preparing to lay siege to the cities of Perinthus and Byzantium, form the subject of this harangue. (11) Κατὰ Φιλίππου λόγος Δ, the Fourth Philippic, pronounced at the time when Philip had raised the siege of Perinthus, in order to fall upon Byzantium. Valckenaer (*Or. De Phil.* p. 250), Wolf (*Ad Lept. Proleg.* p. lx.), and Bekker do not acknowledge this as a production of Demosthenes. (12) Ὁ πρὸς τὴν ἐπιστολὴν Φιλίππου λόγος, "On the Letter of Philip." The letter of the king, to which this harangue refers, still exists. It contains many complaints, but no declaration of war. Taylor, Reiske, Valckenaer, and Bekker consider this letter to be spurious.

We come now to the second class of the orations of Demosthenes, namely, those of a judicial nature; and here a distinction must be made between those which refer to affairs connected with the State and those which relate to individual interests: in the former case, the procedure was called *κατηγορία*; in the second, *δίκη*—words which may be translated by "accusation" and "pleadings." Of the first species we have twelve harangues remaining, the most important one of which is that entitled Περὶ Στεφάνου, "On the Crown." Demosthenes had been twice crowned in the theatre during the Dionysiac festival: the first time after the expulsion of the Macedonian garrisons from the island of Euboea, and again after the alliance with the Thebans. In the year B.C. 338, Ctesiphon, who was then president of the Senate, had a decree passed by this body that, if the people approved, Demosthenes should be crowned at the approaching Dionysiac festival, in the public theatre, as a recompense for the disinterested manner in which he had filled various offices, and for the services which he had never for a moment ceased to render the State. This matter had to be confirmed by a *ψήφισμα*, or decree of the people; but, before it was brought before them, Aeschines presented himself as the accuser of Ctesiphon. He charged him with having violated the laws in proposing to crown a public functionary before the latter had given an account of the manner in which he had discharged his office; and to crown him, too, in the theatre, instead of the senate-house or the Pnyx, where this could alone be done; finally, in having alleged what was false, for the purpose of favouring Demosthenes. He concluded by demanding that a fine of fifty talents be imposed upon Ctesiphon. The matter remained for some time pending, in consequence of the troubles that followed the battle of Chaeronea. When, however, the influence of the Macedonian party had, through the exertions of Antipater, gained the ascendency in Athens, Aeschines believed it to be a favourable moment for the revival of his accusation. It was brought forward, therefore, again, in B.C. 330, or eight years after the proposition of Ctesiphon had been made. Aeschines thereupon pronounced his famous harangue, to which Demosthenes replied. This speech of Demosthenes is regarded, and justly so, not only as his masterpiece, but as the most perfect specimen that eloquence has ever produced. It is said that after this discourse Demosthenes no longer appeared as a public speaker. Ulpian, in his commentary on the oration *De Corona*, relates an anecdote which has been often cited. Demosthenes is endeavouring to fix the charge of bribery on Aeschines, whom he represents as corrupted by Philip and by Alexander, and consequently their hireling and not their friend or guest. Of this assertion he declares his willingness to submit the truth to the judgment of the assembly. "I call thee," says the orator, "the hireling, first of Philip and now of Alexander; and all these who are here present agree in opinion with me. If thou disbelievest it, ask them the question; but no, I will ask them myself. Athenians, does Aeschines appear to you in the light of a hireling or a friend of Alexander's?" In putting this question, Demosthenes purposely commits a fault of accentuation: he places the accent improperly on the antepenultima, instead of the last syllable, of *μισθωτός*—in the words of Ulpian, *ἑκὼν ἐβαρβάρισεν*—in order to draw the attention of the people from the question to the pronunciation. This had the desired effect: the accurate ears of the Athenians were struck with the mistake; to correct it, they called out *μισθωτός, μισθωτός*, "a hireling! a hireling!" from every part of the assembly. Pretending to receive the word as the expression of their sentiments on the guilt of Aeschines, he cried out, "Dost thou hear what they say?"

The simple pleadings (*δίκαι*) relative to matters of private interest, constitute the second class of judicial actions. Of these we have thirty remaining, which are as follows: (1) Discourses having relation to the proceedings instituted by Demosthenes against his guardians. They are five in number: of these, two are against Aphobus, and two against Onetor, his brother. (2) Λόγοι παραγράφικοι, or, as Cicero (*De Invent.* 1, 8) calls them, *constitutiones translativae.* We have seven discourses of this class from the pen of Demosthenes, viz.: against Zenothemis, against Apaturius, against Lacritus, against Phormion, against Pantaenetus, against Nausimachus, and Xenopithaea. (3) Discourses relative to the rights of succession and to questions of dower. These are four in number: against Macartatus, against Leochares, against Spudias, against Boeotus for his mother's dowry. (4) Discourses in matters of commerce and of debt. These are three in number: against Calippus, against Nicostratus, against Timotheus. (5) Actions for indemnity and for damages (*βλάβη, αἰκία*). The discourses under this head are five in number: against Boeotus, against Olympiodorus, against Conon, against Dionysiodorus, against Callicles. (6) Actions for perjury: two discourses against Stephanus, and one against Euergus and Mnesibulus. (7) Three discourses on the subject of the *ἀντίδοσις* (q. v.), or exchange of estates. The discourses under this head are the following: against Phoenippus, against Polycles, and respecting the crown of the trierarchia. It is unnecessary to speak of each of these thirty pleadings; a few remarks on some of them must suffice. The five discourses which Demosthenes pronounced against his guardians contain valuable details respecting his youth, his fortune, and the Athenian laws. Aphobus, one of the guardians, was condemned to pay Demosthenes the sum of ten talents. It does not appear whether he brought the two other guardians to trial or not. These discourses have some resemblance to those of Isaeus, his master. The παραγραφή for Phormio against Apollodorus has furnished occasion for a reproach to the memory of Demosthenes. We are told by Plutarch that Demosthenes "wrote an oration for Apollodorus, by which he carried his cause against the general Timotheus, in an action for debt to the public treasury; as also those others against Phormio and Stephanus, which formed a just exception against his character. For he composed likewise the oration which Phormio had pronounced against Apollodorus. This, therefore, was like furnishing the enemies with weapons out of the same shop."

The discourse against Macartatus, respecting the succession of Hagnias, is interesting from the circumstance of our having the defence of Macartatus by Isaeus, and from our being thus able to compare the pupil with his former master. It remains to speak of the third class of Demosthenes's orations, the λόγοι ἐπιδεικτικοί, "studied or set speeches." We have only two remaining, and these, very probably, are spurious. The one, ἐπιτάφιος λόγος, is a eulogy on the Athenians who had perished at Chaeronea; the other, ἐρωτικός λόγος, is written in praise of the beauty of the young Epicrates.

There are also six letters ascribed to Demosthenes; five of them are addressed to the people of Athens. All, however, are forgeries.

Good MANUSCRIPTS of Demosthenes are rare, but several of them are as old as the eleventh century, and most of them contain a very large portion, if not the whole, of the extant works. In all, there are some 170 MSS. They are divided by editors into three groups, of which the first is headed by a Codex Parisinus (S or Σ) of the tenth or eleventh century, distinguished by remarkable omissions in the text; the second is headed by a Marcianus Venetus (F) and another Codex Parisinus (γ), both of the eleventh century; the third by a Codex Monacensis (A), also of the eleventh century, distinguished by curious simplifications of hard passages. Editors are not entirely agreed as to the value of S or Σ, some maintaining that it gives the authentic text, others believing that it gives an edition by a clever scholar. The scholia on Demosthenes are inferior, the best being those in C. Müller (Paris, 1846–47) and *Scholia Graeca in Demosth.* (Oxford, 1851). On the MSS. see Vömel's *Prolegomena Critica* to his edition (Halle, 1856–57).

BIBLIOGRAPHY.—For the life of Demosthenes, the reader is referred to Schäfer's *Demosthenes und seine Zeit* (2d ed. Berlin, 1882); and for an exhaustive literary criticism, to Blass's *Attische Beredsamkeit* (1880). Butcher's *Introduction to the Study of Demosthenes* (London, 1881) and Brodribb's (1877) are useful. See also Croiset, *Des Idées Morales dans l'Eloquence Politique de Démosthène* (1871). The standard texts are those of Bekker (1866) and of L. Dindorf (Leip. 1878; rev. by Blass). For critical study of Demosthenes, the Apparatus Criticus of Schäfer in 5 vols. (London, 1824) is valuable, as are also the three volumes of *Annotationes Interpretum* of Dindorf (Oxford, 1849). The *editio princeps* of Demosthenes was that of Aldus (Venice, 1504). Good editions of the various orations with notes are as follows: *De Corona*, T. K. Arnold (London, 1860), Holmes (London, 1871), Drake (London, 1866), Simcox (Oxford, 1873), containing also the oration of Aeschines, D'Ooge (Chicago, 1875), Blass (Leipzig, 1890); *De Falsa Legatione*, Shilleto (London, 1874); *Contra Leptinem*, Beatson (London, 1864), King (London, 1880), and especially Sandys (Cambridge, 1890); *In Midiam*, Holmes (Buttmann), (London, 1868); of the *Olynthiacs*, Wilkins (London, 1860), T. K. Arnold (London, 1877); of the *Philippics*, Heslop (London, 1868), T. K. Arnold (London, 1868), Westermann (1825); of the First Philippic, Gwatkin (Rehdantz), (London, 1883); *Adv. Timocratem*, etc., Wayte (Camb. 1883); collections of *Select Private Orations*, Penrose (London, 1853), Sandys and Paley, in 2 pts., 9 orations (Camb. 1874–75), with French notes, Weil (Paris, 1877). See also Baiter and Sauppe's *Oratores Attici*, 8 vols. or one large quarto (1850); Bekker, 10 vols. with indices (Oxford, 1828); Dobson with variorum notes (London, 1828); and Jebb (London, 1882). Useful is Mitchell's *Index Graecitatis*, 3 vols. (London, 1828); and Westermann's *Geschichte d. Beredsamkeit* (1835) is to be commended for a general conspectus. The best translation into English is that of Kennedy in 5 vols. (London, 1852–63).

(2) An Athenian general, son of Alcisthenes, who obtained considerable reputation during a part of the Peloponnesian War. When the Spartan monarch Agis made an inroad into Attica, Demosthenes, on his part, harassed the coasts of the Peloponnesus, and seized upon and fortified the Messenian Pylos. This led to the affair of Sphacteria (q. v.), in which he had a conspicuous, or, rather, the principal share. He was afterwards sent with an armament to the relief of Nicias before Syracuse; but, by his precipitate measures there, brought defeat upon himself and the consequent ruin of the whole expedition. Demosthenes and Nicias were both put to death while in prison, notwithstanding the endeavours of the Spartan commander Gylippus to save their lives. Another account, alluded to by Plutarch, makes them to have been stoned to death (Thuc. iv. 3 foll.; Plut. *Nic.*).

(3) A Greek physician, a disciple of Alexander Philalethes, who obtained the same surname as his master—namely, Philalethes, or "Lover of Truth." He flourished about the commencement of our era, and turned his attention particularly to diseases of the eye. We have some fragments remaining of his writings on this subject, which appear to have formed part of a work often cited by Galen, Oribasius, and Aëtius.

Demotic Writing. A cursive form of the Egyptian hieroglyphic writing in use from the sixth century B.C. to the third century A.D. It was rarely used on the public monuments, though it is found on the Rosetta Stone (q. v.); but was

Demotic Writing. (Funerary Inscription.)

largely employed for documents, contracts, etc., and occasionally in religious formulas. See HIEROGLYPHICS.

Demus (δῆμος). A word which originally denoted a district or country. Then, because in the early days the lower classes lived in the country and the nobles in the city, it received the meaning of commons or common people. A third use, likewise derived from the original signification, is seen in its application to the local divisions, or townships as it were, of Attica.

A certain number of these δῆμοι, or demes, were included in each of the ten tribes established by Clisthenes to replace the four old Ionic tribes. Their exact number at that time is not positively known, though it is supposed by some, from a statement of Herodotus (v. 69), to have been one hundred. In the third century before Christ, at all events, they numbered one hundred and seventy-four (Strab. ix. 396). The names of one hundred and forty-five of these are known to us from inscriptions. If, however, we consider the division of some demes into καθύπερθεν and ὑπένερθεν, and of others between two different tribes, this sum is increased to one hundred and fifty-six (Milchhoefer, *Untersuchungen über die Demenordnung des Kleisthenes*, pp. 8–10; *C. I. A.* iii. index). The names were derived in part from places, as in the case of Acharnae, Rhamnus, etc., and in part from the founders of the demes, as in the case of Erchia and of Daedalidae (Aristot. *Athen. Polit.* 21). The largest deme, according to Thucydides, was Acharnae, which in the Peloponnesian War was able to furnish three thousand heavily armed troops (Thuc. ii. 19, 20).

At the time of his reforms Clisthenes admitted many resident aliens and even slaves to citizenship (Aristot. *Polit.* 3, 2), and to this fact is due that alteration in the official designation of citizens which he also introduced (Aristot. *Athen. Polit.* 21). They were no longer designated by the father's name only, but also by the name of the deme to which they belonged. The demes now became the centres of the local administrative power, and are said by Aristotle to have taken the place of the *naucraries* (*Athen. Polit.* 21). Each deme had its register of citizens, its own property, its own meetings and religious observances, and its own demarch. This officer made out the lists of the deme's property, kept in his possession the lexiarchic register, or register of qualified citizens, and convened the demesmen at will (Harpocration, s. v. Δήμαρχος). At these meetings the public business of the deme was transacted, such as the leasing of property, the election of officers, the revision of the lexiarchic register, and the enrolment of new members.

When a man was first admitted to citizenship he had the right to choose his own tribe and deme, but otherwise a man belonged to the same deme as his natural or adoptive father. The legitimate children of citizens could be enrolled on attaining their majority at the age of eighteen, and adopted children, whenever presented by their adoptive fathers. The enrolment took place in the presence of the assembled demesmen. If any member questioned the candidate's eligibility the matter was settled by a majority vote of those present (Demosth. *Eubul.* 1318). Illegal registration, however, was not uncommon, and certain demes, as Potamus for example, were notorious for this abuse (Harpocration, s. v. Ποταμός; Demosth. *Leoch.* 1091). To counteract this evil an official investigation of those inscribed in the register, called *diapsephisis* (Harpocration, s. v. Διαψήφισις), was held at various times by the deme. A similar examination was also held if, by any chance, the lexiarchic registers were lost or destroyed (Demosth. *Eubul.* 1306). If any one in the course of this inquiry was disfranchised by vote of the demesmen, he had the right of appeal to the courts. If the decision of the deme were sustained he was sold as a slave and his property was confiscated. But were he successful in his suit his name was restored to the register of the deme (Isaeus, 12; *Argum. ad Demosthenis Eubul.* 1298).

A man was not obliged to reside within the limits of the deme of which he was a member. But he could only hold property in another deme upon payment to the demarch of a tax, called ἐγκτητικόν. This tax, however, was sometimes remitted by the demes in the case of individuals to whom they desired to grant special privileges or honours (*C. I. A.* ii. 589).

Denarius. A Roman silver coin, so called because it originally contained 10 *asses*. In later times it = 16 *asses* = 4 *sestertii* = $\frac{1}{25}$ of an *aureus*. Its original weight was 4.55 gr. (= between $0.18 and $0.20); from B.C. 217 to Nero, 3.90 (about $0.14); after Nero's time 3.41 gr., the amount of pure silver being so reduced that it was worth only about $0.12. Its value subsequently sank more and

Denarii, actual size. (British Museum.)

more, until at the beginning of the third century A.D. it was worth only $0.06. When at the end of the third century Diocletian introduced a new silver coin of full value according to the Neronian standard (the so-called *argenteus*), the name *denarius* was transferred to a small copper coin. See NUMISMATICS.

Dendrophŏri. A Roman collegium or corporation of carpenters, frequently mentioned in inscriptions in imperial times. They formed originally a religious corporation, carrying the sacred tree in the worship of the Magna Mater (*collegium dendrophorum Matris magnae*), and were under the Quindecimviri. See inscriptions quoted by Marquardt, *Röm. Staatsverw.* iii. pp. 356, 380.

Denicāles Feriae. See FUNUS, p. 699.

Dens (ὀδούς). A tooth. (1) Artificial teeth were made and used by the ancients, as may be seen from several passages in the classic writers. Cicero (*De Legibus*, ii. 24) quotes a very old sumptuary law forbidding gold to be placed in the tomb with the body, but especially excepting the gold used in fastening the artificial teeth. Little is known of the degree of skill attained by ancient dentistry. Martial (i. 73) speaks of one Aeglé as provided with teeth "of purchased bones and ivory" (*dentata . . . emptis ossibus Indicoque cornu*).

(2) The word *dens* is also used of a number of pointed objects, such as the fluke of an anchor (Verg. *Aen.* vi. 3); the barb of a hunting-spear (Grat. *Cyneget.* 108); the prong of the implement called *ligo* (q. v.); of the ploughshare (Varr. *L. L.* v. 135); the tooth of a rake or harrow (*irpex, occa, rastrum*); the tooth of a saw (Ovid, *Met.* viii. 246); the wards of a key (Tibull. i. 2, 18); the hook of a clasp (Sidon. *Carm.* ii. 397); the cog of a wheel (Vitruv. x. 5); and poetically of a pruning-hook (*dens curvus Saturni*, Verg. *Georg.* ii. 406).

(3) DENS DENSUS is the name given to a fine-toothed comb (Tibull. i. 9. 68), a specimen of which,

Dens Densus, or Comb. (Rich.)

exactly like those in use to-day, is given in the above illustration of one found in a Roman tomb.

Denselētae or **Denthelētae** (Δενθηλῆται). A Thracian tribe living on the Haemus between the Strymon and Nessus (Plin. *H. N.* iv. 11).

Dentālé (ἔλυμα). The share-beam of a plough to which the share (*vomer*) was attached (Colum. ii. 2, 24). See ARATRUM.

Dentarpăga (ὀδοντάγρα). A forceps for drawing teeth (Varr. *ap.* Non. s. h. v.).

Dentātus, MANIUS CURIUS. See CURIUS DENTATUS.

Denticŭlus. A "dentil" in architecture (Vitruv. iii. 5, 11). Dentils are small square blocks

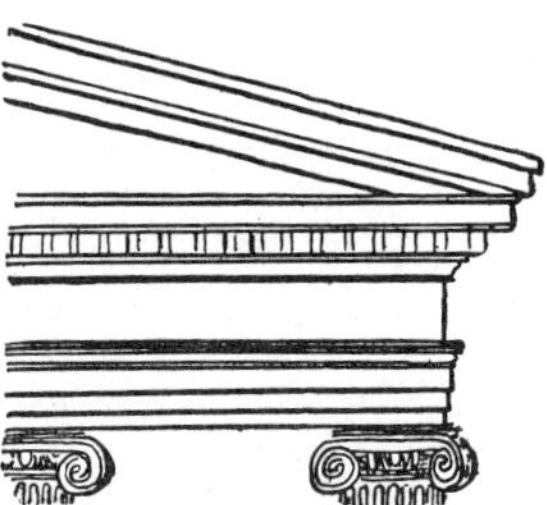

Denticuli. (Temple of Dionysus at Teos.)

with interstices between them, used in the entablature of columnar architecture.

Dentidūcum. A dentist's forceps (Cael. Aurel. *Tard.* ii. 4).

Dentifricium (ὀδοντότριμμα, ὀδοντόσμηγμα). Dentifrice or tooth-powder appears to have been skilfully prepared and generally used among the Romans. A variety of substances, such as the bones, hoofs, and horns of certain animals, crabs, egg-shells, and the shells of the oyster and the murex, constituted the basis of the preparation. Having been previously burned, and sometimes mixed with honey, they were reduced to a fine powder. Though fancy and superstition often directed the choice of these ingredients, the addition of astringents, such as myrrh, or of nitre and hartshorn ground in a raw state, indicates science which was the result of experience, the intention being not only to clean the teeth and to render them white, but also to fix them when loose, to strengthen the gums, and to assuage toothache (Plin. *H. N.* xxviii. §§ 178, 179; xxxi. § 117; xxxii. §§ 65, 79; Scrib. Larg. *Comp.* 59).

Dentists. See DENS; MEDICUS.

Deo (Δηώ). Another name for Demeter; hence her daughter Persephoné is called by the patronymic Deoïs and Deoïné (Callim. *Frag.* 48).

Deoïné (Δηωΐνη). See DEO.

Depas (δέπας). A cup with two handles, frequently mentioned by Homer. It seems to have been a generic term, like ποτήριον. It was used in libations, and was usually of gold (*Il.* xxiii. 196, xxiv. 285, etc.) but later of earthenware. The term is applied to the golden bowl or boat in which the sun floated back from west to east during the night (Stesich. *Fr.* 8 Bergk). As a specific term it was probably applied to cups of a bowl-like shape, and is therefore identified by Panofka and Dennis with the form given in the above illustration.

Depas. (Dennis, *Etruria.*)

The word is frequently used in Homer with the epithet ἀμφικύπελλον (*Il.* i. 584), which has given rise to much discussion. It was, however, probably a double-cup, with a bottom half-way up, like a dice-box. That this was the form of the cup is inferred from a passage of Aristotle (*Hist. An.* ix. 40), where he describes the cells of bees as having two openings divided by a floor, like the ἀμφικύπελλα. No specimen is known to exist.

Depontāni Senes. A name given at Rome to men sixty years of age, hence called *sexagenarii*, because they were freed from the obligation of voting in the Roman comitia; that is, of passing over the bridges (*pontes*) which led into the *saepta*, where the voting took place. (See COMITIA.) This is the most probable explanation of the word; and it is doubtful whether men of sixty years of age were absolutely deprived of the franchise, though this was the case if we accept literally the statement that they were thrust back from voting, *de ponte deiiciebantur* (Fest. pp. 75, 334 M.). Some ancient writers supposed that the name *depontani* had reference to a barbarous custom of antiquity, that men of sixty years of age were thrown down from the *pons sublicius* into the Tiber, but this interpretation was repudiated by Varro and Verrius (Fest. ll. cc.; Varr. *ap.* Non. p. 523; Cic. *Rosc. Am.* 35, 100; Ovid, *Fast.* v. 623; Macrob. i. 5; Plut. *Quaest. Rom.* 32).

Deportatio. Banishment to a specified locality, generally an island. This form of exile was devised under the early Roman emperors. It involved loss of civil rights, and generally also of property. See EXSILIUM.

Deposĭtum. A real contract which consists in one man intrusting a movable thing to another to keep until it is demanded back, and without any reward for the trouble of keeping it. The party who makes the *depositum* is called *deponens* or *depositor*, and he who receives the thing is called *depositarius*. The main object of a depositum is to benefit the *deponens* and not the *depositarius*. Accordingly the *depositarius* has, as a rule, no right to make use of the thing deposited, the contract by which one person lends a thing to another for his gratuitous use being *commodatum* and not depositum. The *deponens* is benefited by the depositum without being obliged to give anything in return. If money is promised to a person for taking care of a thing, the contract is *locatio conductio* and not depositum. If anything else except money is promised, the contract is one of the *innominati contractus*.

The *depositarius* is bound on demand to restore the thing deposited to the *deponens*, or to the person to whom the *deponens* has ordered it to be restored. If he cannot restore it, or cannot restore it uninjured, he is liable, should such loss or injury be due to his wilful misconduct (*dolus*), or to gross negligence (*culpa lata*), which is equivalent to wilful misconduct; but he is not liable on account of ordinary negligence (*culpa levis*), except under special circumstances, as that he has agreed to undertake such liability or has benefited in some way by the contract. The remedy by which the *deponens* could enforce these obligations is the *actio depositi directa*.

Roman law recognized an irregular kind of deposit, which consists in depositing "fungible" things, such as money, with another person, on the understanding that an equal quantity of things of the same kind shall be restored and not the identical things deposited, as in an ordinary deposit. In this case the *depositarius* has the use of the things deposited, the property in them passing to him; consequently he is subject to all risk of loss. This transaction is distinguished from a loan (*mutuum*) by the fact that it is entered into in the interest of the person who makes over the things, and not in that of the person who receives them.

Derbé (Δέρβη). A town in Lycaonia on the frontiers of Isauria (Pausan. iv. 15, § 4).

Derbĭces (Δέρβικες). A nation of Upper Asia, whom Ptolemy places in Margiana, where the Oxus, according to him, empties into the Caspian; but Strabo in Hyrcania, and others on the southern and western shores of the Caspian (Aelian, *V. H.* iv. 1).

Dercĕtis or **Dercĕto** (Δερκετίς or Δερκετώ), also called ATARGĀTIS. A Syrian goddess (Diod. Sic. ii. 4). She offended Aphrodité, who in consequence inspired her with love for a youth, to whom she bore a daughter, Semiramis; but ashamed of her frailty, she killed the youth, exposed her child in a desert, and threw herself into a lake near Ascalon. Her child was fed by doves, and she herself was changed into a fish. The Syrians thereupon worshipped her as a goddess. The upper part of the statue represented a beautiful woman, while the lower part terminated in the tail of a fish. She appears to be connected with the fish-god Dagon mentioned in the Old Testament as a deity of the Philistines.

Fish-god on Gems. (British Museum.)

Dercyllĭdas (Δερκυλλίδας). A Spartan who in B.C. 399 took command of the army levied for the defence of the Asiatic Greeks against Persia. He compelled Tissaphernes and Pharnabazus to sue for peace, but in 396 resigned the command to Agesilaüs (q. v.).

Dermatĭkon (δερματικόν, sc. ἀργύριον). "Hide-money"; that is, the money paid into the treasury at Athens from the sale of the hides of victims slain at the festivals (App. viii., vol. ii. pp. 100–102; *C. I. A.* ii. 741 A).

Dertōna (Δερτῶνα). The modern Tortona; an important town in Liguria on the road from Genua (Genoa) to Placentia (Ptol. iii. 1, 35).

Dertōsa (Δερτῶσα). Now Tortosa; a city of the Ilercaones in Spain, situated on the Iberus, a short distance above its mouth. Here was a bridge over the river, and along this route led the main military road to the southern parts of Spain and the colonies established there (Mela, ii. 6).

Desertor. In the military language of the Romans, a deserter. Those who deserted in time of peace were punished by reduction to the ranks (*gradus deiectio*), corporal chastisement, fines, or ignominious dismissal from the service (*missio ignominiosa*). Those who left the standards in time of war were usually punished with death. The *transfugae*, or deserters to the enemy, when taken, were sometimes deprived of their hands or feet (Liv. xxvi. 12), but generally were put to death. In imperial times they were exposed to wild beasts.

Designātor. See FUNUS; THEATRUM.

Designātus Consul. See CONSUL.

Desk. See SCRINIUM.

Desmoterion (δεσμωτήριον). See CARCER.

Despatches. See CURSUS PUBLICUS.

Despoena (Δέσποινα). "The mistress"; a title given to Aphrodité, to Demeter, and especially to Persephoné who was worshipped under this name in Arcadia (Plat. *De Leg.* 796 B).

Desponsionautae (δεσπονσιοναῦται). See HELOTAE.

Dessert. See CENA, pp. 311 and 314.

Desultor (ἀποβάτης, μεταβάτης). A word literally meaning "one who leaps off," and applied to a person who rode several horses or chariots, leaping from one to the other. As early as the Homeric times, we find the description of a man who keeps four horses abreast at full gallop, and leaps from one to another, amidst a crowd of admiring spectators (*Il.* xv. 679–684). In the games of the Roman circus this sport was also very popular. The Roman desultor generally rode only two horses at the same time, sitting on them without a saddle and vaulting upon either of them at his pleasure (Isid. *Orig.* xviii. 39). He wore a hat or cap made of felt. The taste for these exercises was carried to so great an extent that young men of the highest rank not only drove bigae and quadrigae in the circus, but

Desultor. (Bas-relief at Verona.)

exhibited these feats of horsemanship (Suet. *Iul.* 39). Among other nations this species of equestrian dexterity was applied to the purposes of war. Livy mentions a troop of horse in the Numidian army, in which each soldier was supplied with two horses, and, in the heat of battle and when clad in armour, would leap with the greatest ease and celerity from that which was wearied or disabled upon the back of the horse which was still sound and fresh (xxiii. 29).

The following illustration shows three figures of desultores—one from a bronze lamp, published

Desultores. (From an Ancient Lamp and Coins.)

by Bartoli (*Antiche Lucerne Sepolcrali*, i. 24), the others from coins.

Deucalion (Δευκαλίων). The son of Prometheus and Clymené, or of Prometheus and Pandora, and sometimes called the father (Thuc. i. 3), sometimes the brother of Hellen, the reputed founder of the Greek nation. His home was Thessaly, from which, according to general tradition, he was driven to Parnassus by a great deluge (Apollod. i. 7, 2), which, however, according to Aristotle (*Meteorol.* i. 14) occurred between Dodona and the Achelöus. The Greek legend respecting this memorable event is as follows: Deucalion was married to Pyrrha, the daughter of Epimetheus and Pandora. When Zeus designed to destroy the brazen race of men on account of their impiety, Deucalion, by the advice of his father, made himself an ark (λάρναξ), and, putting provisions into it, entered it with his wife Pyrrha. Zeus then poured rain from heaven and inundated the greater part of Greece, so that all the people, except a few who escaped to the lofty mountains, perished in the waves. At the same time, the mountains of Thessaly were burst through by the flood, and all Greece without the Isthmus, as well as all the Peloponnesus, were overflowed. Deucalion was carried along the sea in his ark for nine days and nights, until he reached Mount Parnassus. By this time the rain had ceased, and, leaving his ark, he sacrificed to Zeus the flight-giver (Φύξιος), who sent Hermes, desiring him to ask what he would. His request was to have the earth replenished with men. By the direction of Zeus, thereupon, he and his wife flung stones behind them, and those which Deucalion cast became men, and those thrown by Pyrrha women; from which circumstance the Greeks derived the name for "people" (λαός) from λᾶας, "a stone" (Apollod. i. 7, 2).

This narrative restricts the general deluge to Greece proper, perhaps originally to Thessaly; and it most incongruously represents others as having escaped as well as Deucalion; while at the same time, it intimates that he and his wife alone had been preserved in the catastrophe. The circumstance of the ark is thought by some to be borrowed from the Mosaic account, and to have been learned at Alexandria, for we elsewhere find the dove noticed. "The mythologists," says Plutarch, "inform us that a dove let fly out of the ark was to Deucalion a sign of bad weather if it came in again, of good weather if it flew away" (Plut. *De Sollert. An.*). The sacrifice and the appearance of Hermes likewise strongly remind us of Noah. (See, also, the article APAMEA.) The Latin writers take a different view of the deluge. According to them it overspread the whole earth, and all animal life perished except Deucalion and Pyrrha, whom Ovid, who gives a very poetical account of this great catastrophe, conveys in a small boat to the summit of Parnassus; while others make Aetna or Athos the mountain which yielded them a refuge (Ovid, *Met.* i. 253 foll.; Hyg. *Fab.* 153; Serv. *ad* Verg. *Eclog.* vi. 41). According to Ovid they consulted the ancient oracle of Themis respecting the restoration of mankind, and received the following response: "Depart from the fane, veil your heads, loosen your girded vestments, and cast behind you the great bones of your parent" (*Met.* i. 381 foll.). They were at first horror-struck at such an act of impiety, but at length Deucalion understood the words of the oracle as referring to the earth, the common mother of all. Rationalizing mythologists make the story an allegory in which Deucalion represents water (as if from δεύω), and Pyrrha, fire (πῦρ). The meaning of the legend will then be, that when the passage through which the Peneus carries off the waters that run into the vale of Thessaly, which is on all sides shut in by lofty mountains, had been closed by some accident, they overflowed the whole of its surface, till the action of subterranean fire opened a way for them. According to this view of the subject, then, the deluge of Deucalion was merely a local one; and it was not until the time of Ptolemy Philadelphus, when the Hebrew Scriptures became known to the Greeks, that some features borrowed from the universal deluge of Noah were incorporated into the story of the Thessalian flood. See Harcourt, *Doctrine of the Deluge* (London, 1838); Sayce, *Fresh Light from the Ancient Monuments* (London, 1886); Motais, *Le Déluge Biblique* (Paris, 1887).

Deunx. Eleven ounces, eleven twelfths of the *as* (q. v.), not represented by a coin; or eleven twelfths of anything (Varr. *L. L.* v. 172; Cic. *Caecin.* 6, 17).

Deva. (1) Now Chester; the principal town of the Cornii in Britain, on the Seteia (Dee). A number of Roman remains are to be seen at Chester, preserved in the Grosvenor Museum. (2) Now the Dee; an estuary in Scotland, on which stood the town Dovanna, near the modern Aberdeen.

Deverbium. See DIVERBIUM.

Deverra. One of the three goddesses worshipped by the Italians as protecting new-born children against the mischievous intrusion of the god Silvanus (q. v.). The two divinities who joined with Deverra in this function were Intercidona and Picumnus. See August. *De Civ. Dei*, vi. 9.

Deversorium. See CAUPONA.

Devotio. A Roman religious ceremony, by virtue of which a general whose army was in distress offered up as an atonement to the gods below, and a means of averting their wrath, the army, city, and land of the enemy; or some soldier in the Roman army; or even himself, as was the case with the Decii. (See DECIUS.) The general, standing on a spear and with veiled head, repeated a solemn formula dictated to him by the Pontifex. If the city and land of the enemy were offered, the gods were solemnly invited to burn the land or city. (See EVOCATIO.) The fate of the devoted person was left in the hands of the gods. If he survived, an image at least seven feet high was buried in the ground and a bloody sacrifice offered over it; he was meanwhile held incapable in future of performing any other religious rite, either on his own behalf or on that of the State.

Dexippus (Δέξιππος). (1) P. HERENNIUS, a Greek historian and rhetorician, born in Attica in the third century A.D. He held high office in Athens, and in the year 262, when the Goths invaded Greece, distinguished himself against them. He died about A.D. 280. Photius gives some account of three historical works by Dexippus—a history of Macedonia from the time of Alexander the Great; a general chronological history from the earliest times down to the year A.D. 268; and, finally, an account of the wars with the Goths in which Dexippus had himself fought. The fragments of these works, which are fairly numerous, are included in the collection of *Scriptores Historiae Byzantinae*. (2) A student of the philosopher Iamblichus, who wrote (about A.D. 350) a commentary on the Categories of Aristotle in the form of a dialogue, which is edited by Spengel (Munich, 1859).

Dextans. Ten ounces, ten twelfths of the *as* (q. v.), not represented by a coin; or ten twelfths of anything (Varr. *L. L.* v. 172; Suet. *Ner.* 32).

Dextrālé and **Dextrocherium** (from *dexter* and χείρ, "the hand"). Late Latin words, signifying a bracelet. See ARMILLA.

Dextralé. (From a Pompeian Painting.)

Dia (Δία). The daughter of Dioneus and wife of Ixion (q. v.), by whom (or, according to others, by Zeus) she became the mother of Pirithoüs (q. v.).

Dia (Δία). The ancient name of Naxos (q. v.).

Diabateria (διαβατήρια). A sacrifice offered to Zeus and Athené by the Spartan kings on passing the frontier of Laconia in command of an army (Xen. *Rep. Lac.* 13, § 2 foll.). If the victims were unfavourable they disbanded the army and returned home (Thuc. v. 54, 55, 116). We also find διαβατήρια offered by a Roman general in passing a swollen river (Plut. *Lucull.* 24).

Diabathron (διάβαθρον). A Greek slipper.

Diablintes. A branch of the Aulerci (q. v.).

Diacria (Διακρία). A mountainous district in the northeast of Attica, including the plain of Marathon. See ATTICA.

Diadēma (διάδημα). The white fillet round the brow which was the emblem of sovereignty from the time of Alexander the Great. Caesar refused it when offered him by Antonius, and it was not,

Diadema on Heads of Seleucus II., King of Syria (left-hand figure), and of Ptolemaeus II., King of Egypt (right-hand figure). (Coins in British Museum.)

in consequence, worn by the Roman emperors, except in a few cases. But when the seat of government was removed to Byzantium, Constantine adopted the Greek emblem of royalty (Aurel. Vict. 41).

Before the diadem was worn by the Roman emperors as a symbol of sovereignty, it was used as a head-dress by Roman women (Isid. *Orig.* xix. 31).

Diadŏchi. ("Successors," from διαδέχομαι.) A name given to the successors of Alexander the Great.

Diadŏseis (διαδόσεις). See DIANOMAE.

Diadumeniānus or **Diaduměnus**, M. OPELIUS. A son of the Roman emperor Macrinus, who bestowed upon him in A.D. 217 the titles of Caesar, Princeps Iuventutis, Imperator, and Augustus. After the victory of Elagabalus, he was sent to Artabanus, king of the Parthians, and was murdered at about the same date as that of his father's death. Diadumenianus is said by Lampridius to have been a most marvellously beautiful child, so that the biographer compares his face to a heavenly star; but if so, the coins on which his likeness appears do him a sad injustice.

Diaeta (δίαιτα). See DOMUS, p. 546.

Diaetētae (διαιτηταί). Public arbitrators at Athens, to whom the parties in a private suit might apply if they wished to avoid a trial before the Heliastae (q. v.). For this object a considerable number of citizens of advanced age were nominated. They received no salary, but a fee of a drachma from each party and as much from the complainant for every adjournment. In case of misconduct they could be called to account. The diaetetae were assigned to the parties by lot by the magistrate who (according to the character of the case) would have presided in the court of the Heliaea. To this magistrate (in case the parties did not appeal to the Heliaea against it), the diaetetes handed in the sentence he had delivered as the result of his investigation, to have it signed and published and thus made legal. The name of diaetetae was also given to private arbitrators named by agreement between the parties, on the understanding that their decision was to be accepted without appeal.

See Perrot, *Essai sur le Droit Public d'Athènes* (1869); and Thalheim, *Rechtsalterth.* pp. 98, 99 (1884).

Diaetetĭca (διαιτητική). One of the principal branches into which the ancients divided the art and science of medicine. The word is derived from δίαιτα, which meant much the same as our word diet. It is defined by Celsus (*De Medic.* Praef. lib. i.) to signify that part of medicine which cures diseases by means of regimen and diet. Taken strictly in this sense, it would correspond very nearly with the modern "dietetics," and this is the meaning which it always bears in the earlier medical writers.

In later times the comic poet Nicomachus (*Fr.* 1, 30 M. *ap.* Ath. vii. p. 291 c) introduces a cook who, among his other qualifications, implies that he is a physician; but no attention seems to have been paid to eating as a branch of medicine before the date of Hippocrates. Homer represents Machaon, who had been wounded in the shoulder by an arrow (*Il.* xi. 507) and forced to quit the field, as taking a draught composed of wine, goat's-milk cheese, and flour, which probably no surgeon in later times would have prescribed in such a case. Hippocrates seems to claim for himself the credit of being the first person who had studied this subject, and says that "the ancients had written nothing on it worth mentioning" (*De Rat. Vict. in Morb. Acut.* § 1, vol. ii. p. 26, ed. Kühn). Among the works forming the Hippocratic collection, there are four that bear upon this subject, of which, however, only one (viz. that just quoted) is considered to be undoubtedly genuine. It would be out of place here to attempt anything like a complete account of the opinions of the ancients on this point, so that in this article only such particulars are mentioned as may be supposed to have some interest for the classical reader.

In the works of Hippocrates and his successors almost all the articles of food used by the ancients are mentioned, and their real or supposed properties discussed, sometimes quite as fancifully as by Burton in his *Anatomy of Melancholy*. In some respects they appear to have been much less delicate than the moderns, as we find the flesh of the fox, the dog, the horse, and the ass spoken of as common articles of food. Beef and mutton were of course eaten, but the meat most generally esteemed was pork (see Oribas. *Coll. Med.* i. p. 585, Daremberg). A morbid taste for human flesh appears to have been secretly indulged in the time of Xenocrates (first century A.D.); so that the unnatural practice was forbidden by an imperial edict, which decree serves to illustrate the "strange and revolting anecdote," as Milman calls it, of the wild cry that, in a time of scarcity amounting to famine, assailed the ears of the emperor Attalus, "Fix the tariff for human flesh" (*pone pretium carni humanae*, Zosim. vi. 11).

With regard to the strength or quality of the wine drunk by the ancients, we may arrive at something like certainty from the fact that Coelius Aurelianus mentions it as something extraordinary that Asclepiades at Rome in the first century B.C. sometimes ordered his patients to double and treble the quantity of wine, till at last they drank half wine and half water (*De Morb. Chron.* ii. 7, p. 386). From this it appears that wine was commonly diluted with five or six times its quantity of water. Hippocrates also in particular cases recommends wine to be mixed with an equal quantity of water, and Galen approves of the proportion. According to Hippocrates, the proportions in which wine and water should be mixed together vary according to the season of the year; for instance, in summer the wine should be most diluted, in winter the least so. In one place the patient after great fatigue is recommended to get himself drunk once or twice, in which passage it has been doubted whether actual intoxication is meant or only the "drinking freely and to cheerfulness," in which sense the same word is used by St. John (ii. 10) and the Septuagint (Gen. xliii. 34; Cant. v. 1; and perhaps Gen. ix. 21).

Exercises of various kinds and bathing are also much insisted on by the writers on diet and regimen, but for further particulars on these subjects the articles BALNEAE and GYMNASIUM must be consulted. It may, however, be added that the bath could not have been very common, at least in private families, in the time of Hippocrates, as he says that "there are few houses in which the necessary conveniences are to be found" (*De Rat. Vict. in Morb. Acut.* § 18).

Another very favourite practice with the ancients, both as a preventive of sickness and as a remedy, was the taking of an emetic from time to time. In one of the treatises of the Hippocratic collection the unknown author recommends it two or three times a month. Celsus considers it more beneficial in the winter than in the summer (*De Medic.* i. 3, p. 28), and says that those who take an emetic twice a month had better do so on two successive days than once a fortnight. In the first century B.C. this practice was so commonly abused that Asclepiades rejected the use of emetics altogether. See Plin. *H. N.* xxvi. § 17.

It was the custom among the Romans to take an emetic immediately before their meals, in order to prepare themselves to eat more plentifully; and again soon after, so as to avoid any injury from repletion. Cicero, in his account of the day that Caesar spent with him at his house in the country (*Ad Att.* xiii. 52), says, "Accubuit, ἐμετικὴν agebat (*he was meditating an emetic*), itaque et edit et bibit ἀδεῶς et iucunde"; and this has by some persons been considered a sort of compliment paid by Caesar to his host, as it intimated a resolution to pass the day cheerfully and to eat and drink freely. He is represented as having done the same thing when he was entertained by King Deiotarus (Cic. *Pro Deiot.* 7, § 21). The glutton Vitellius is said to have preserved his own life by constant emetics, while he destroyed all his companions who did not use the same precaution; so that one of them, who was prevented by illness from dining with him for a few days, said, "I should certainly have been dead if I had not fallen sick" (Dio Cass. lxv. 2). It might truly be said, in the strong language of Seneca, *Vomunt, ut edant; edunt, ut vomant* (*Cons. ad Helv.* 9, § 10; cf. *De Provid.* 3, § 11; *Ep.* 95, § 21). By some, the practice was thought so effectual for strengthening the constitution that it was the constant regimen of all the *athletae*, or professed wrestlers, trained for the public shows, in order to make them more robust. Celsus, however, warns his readers against the too frequent use of emetics without necessity and merely for luxury and gluttony, and says that no one who has any regard for his health and wishes to live to old age ought to make it a daily practice. See Saalfeld, *Küche und Keller in Alt-Rom* (Berlin, 1883); and the articles ATHLETAE; CENA; MEDICINA; VICTUS; VINUM.

Diagŏras (Διαγόρας). (1) A native of the island of Melos and a follower of Democritus. Having been sold as a captive in his youth, he was redeemed by Democritus and trained up in the study of philosophy. He attached himself also to lyric poetry and was much distinguished for his success. His name, however, has been transmitted to posterity as that of an avowed advocate for the rejection of all religious belief. It is expressly asserted by ancient writers that when, in a particular instance, he saw a perjured person escape punishment, he publicly declared his disbelief of Divine Providence, and from that time spoke of the gods and all religious ceremonies with ridicule and contempt. He even attempted to lay open the sacred Mysteries, writing two books on the subject, called Φρύγιοι. A price at last was set upon his head, and he fled to Corinth, where he died. He lived about 416 years before Christ (Cic. *N. D.* i. 23; iii. 37; Val. Max. i. 1, § 7). (2) An athlete of Rhodes, who gained the prize in pugilism at the Olympic Games, B.C. 464. His victory was celebrated by Pindar in an ode which is still extant (Olymp. vii.), and which is said to have been inscribed in golden letters in the temple of the Lindian Athenė at Rhodes. According to Pindar, he twice obtained the victory in the games of Rhodes, four times at the Isthmian, and was successful also at the Nemean and other contests. Aulus Gellius (iii. 15) informs us that he saw his three sons crowned on the same day at the Olympic Games and expired through joy.

Diagrăpheis (διαγραφεῖς). See EISPHORA.

Dialects. A dialect, in the usual acceptance of the word, is a form of speech used by a limited number of people, or within a limited region, and differing from the language of the main branch of the race by reason of local usages due to separation and special conditions. The term also denotes any of the divisions of a linguistic family. It sometimes happens that those who use a particular dialect of a language come to be politically the most powerful branch, with greater wealth, refinement, and literary cultivation. Their dialect then ultimately becomes the standard form of the language, while the other variations of it sink to a subordinate position, and are then spoken of as *dialects*, and the first, which was originally of no more authority, is accepted as the normal form of speech. Thus, Latin became the great standard language of Italy, while its sister languages, Umbrian and Oscan, sank to the position of dialects. Thus, too, in England, the so-called Middle English, being spoken in that part of the country where the two great universities were situated, and being used by the early writers of the country, gradually became the tongue of the educated all over England and the literary form of speech, while the Northern English and the Southern English ceased to be heard except in the mouths of the uneducated. In Greek, the finest productions of literature were, on the whole, those of the Ionic Greeks, so that a form of the Ionic dialect (Attic) became the standard with which all others were compared, though the Doric and Aeolic, being used by many famous writers, never became, like Lowland Scotch or the Sussex speech in England, discredited and vulgar. Dialectic differences when perpetuated and intensified by continued separation and lack of intercourse between the peoples who use them at last develop into different languages. See INDO-EUROPEAN LANGUAGES.

I. GREEK DIALECTS.—The three main divisions of the dialects of Greece are usually said to be the Aeolic, Ionic, and Doric. The exact lines of division are, however, obscure, for one dialect often borrows from another when spoken by contiguous peoples. It must be remembered, also, that the racial divisions of the Greeks do not always coincide with the dialectic divisions; that there were hundreds of minor dialects of which no account can be taken here; and that these dialects shaded off one into the other by almost imperceptible gradations. Scholars differ most as to what dialects are to be called Aeolic, some restricting the name to the Lesbian and Asiatic. Brugmann classes Northwest Greek (of Phocis, Locris, Aetolia, Acarnania, Phthiotis, and Epirus), Elean, Arcadian-Cyprian, and Pamphylian as separate dialects (*Comp. Gram.* i. p. 6).

A. AEOLIC.—The Aeolic dialect was spoken in Macedonia, North Thessaly, Boeotia, Arcadia (?), Elis, Cyprus, and the northern part of Asiatic Hellas. Our knowledge of the *Lesbio-Aeolic* comes partly from inscriptions and partly from the fragments of Alcaeus and Sappho quoted by the grammarians and others, and from the statements of the grammarians themselves. Three of its inscriptions are of great importance—one found at Mitylenė recording the return of certain exiles in the time of Alexander the Great (*C. I. G.* 2166), one found at Pordoselena (*C. I. G.* 2166 *c.*), and a third found at Eresus (edited by Conze and Sauppe). The chief peculiarities of the Aeolic dialect are (1) a strong tendency to barytone pronunciation (e. g. σόφος, θῦμος, Ἀχίλλευς, for σοφός, θυμός, Ἀχιλλεύς); (2) the retention of the digamma (q. v.); (3) the loss of the dual; a second singular ending -σθα in verbs (e. g. ἔχεισθα); (4) a third plural ending in -ισι; (5) ζ appears as σδ; (6) the absence of the rough breathing. Its general character was lightness and rapidity of utterance; the Aeolic poets abound in anapaests and dactyls. The Athenians regarded the Lesbian language as somewhat barbaric (Plat. *Protag.* 341 C.). The *Thessalian-Aeolic*, which is known to us by a few inscriptions only, is a sort of bridge between the Lesbian and the Boeotian (Collitz), doubling the liquids, changing *a* to *o*, and using an infinitive in -μεν. The *Boeotian-Aeolic* is known from inscriptions and from the fragments of Corinna, though in these it is mixed with Ionic forms, as is also true of the Boeotian passages in the *Acharnians* of Aristophanes. The Boeotian-Aeolic differed from the Lesbian chiefly in the following particulars: (1) In not throwing back the accent; (2) in a fondness for aspiration; (3) in retaining τ or θ where the Lesbian changes it to σ; (4) in using δδ for σδ = ζ; (5) in allowing the uncontracted -αο and -αων to stand; (6) in using such genitives as ἐμοῦς, τεοῦς, for which the Lesbian has ἔμεθεν, σέθεν. (See Beerman in Curtius's *Studien*, ix. p. 85.) The *Elean-Aeolic* is known from several inscriptions, such as the bronze plate found at Olympia by Gell (*C. I. G.* 11) and the inscription of Damocrates (Kirchhoff in the *Archaeol. Zeit.* 1876). The *Arcadian-Aeolic* is nearer to the Doric than to the Lesbian in its forms. It has -αυ for the gen. sing. masc. of a-nouns, -οι as a dative (or locative) sing. of o-nouns, ἰν for εἰς and ἐν, and -τοι as a third sing. middle ending (e. g. γένητοι). (See Schrader in Curtius's *Studien*, x. pp. 273–280.) The *Cyprian* dialect is probably at the bottom Arcadian-Aeolic

(Herod. vii. 90; Pausan. viii. 5, 2)—a theory strengthened by the study of the Cypriote inscriptions by Birch, Deecke, Siegismund, Hall, Voigt, and others. See CYPRUS.

B. DORIC.—The Doric dialect was used in Doris, Argos, Laconia, Messenia, Crete, Sicily, Lower Italy (Magna Graecia), and the southern part of Asiatic Hellas. Ahrens recognizes two types—the severer Doric (spoken in Laconia, Crete, Cyrené, and Magna Graecia); and the milder Doric, influenced by Aeolic or Ionic usage (spoken in Argolis, Messenia, Megara, northern Greece, Asia Minor, and Sicily). It was used by the bucolic poets (Theocritus, Bion, Moschus), and by Pindar, Alcman, and others. Its principal features are (1) a tendency to use *ᾱ* for *η* and for *ω*; (2) the use of *-μες* (for *-μεν*) as a first plural verbal ending; (3) the use of *-ντι* as a third plural ending; (4) a strong tendency to oxytones (e. g. *ἐλέγον, ἀνθρώποι, παίδες*, for *ἔλεγον, ἄνθρωποι, παῖδες*); (5) the use of the digamma, which it retained longer than did any other Greek dialect; (6) peculiarities of contraction, such as *η* for *ει*, *ω* for *ου* (*ἦς* for *εἶς*, *ἦμεν* for *ἔσμεν*); (7) the shortening of long final syllables, usually when the length is due to a compensation for the loss of a consonant (e. g. *πός* for *πόδ-ς*, *λέγες* for *λέγεις*, *τίκτεν* for *τίκτειν*, etc.); (8) a free use of assimilation. There are many important inscriptions in Doric Greek. Chief among them are the famous Tables of Heraclea, found in the bed of the river Cavone in 1732 and 1735, and now partly in the Museo Nazionale at Naples and partly in the British Museum. Another (in the *Messenian-Doric*) was found at Andania, and though of late date (B.C. 95 ?) is valuable for its fulness and for some of the forms it exhibits. The *Megarian-Doric* is known from inscriptions at Byzantium; the *Corinthian* from inscriptions of Corcyra and Syracuse, both colonies of Corinth; the *Locrian* from the bronze tablet found at Oeanthia, and dating from the fourth century B.C.; the *Cretan* from treaty-tablets and others found in Crete (see GORTYN) and among the ruins of the Temple of Dionysus on the island of Teos. The general character of the Doric speech was slowness, deliberation, and fulness of sound, with the *πλατειασμός* which the Dorians shared with the Boeotians.

C. IONIC.—The character of the Ionic dialect, in its several subdivisions, gives striking evidence of its long-continued employment in literature. Its smoothness and harmony, its rich and full vowel-system, its variety and plasticity, all mark it out as eminently fitted for noble and expressive utterance in both prose and verse. It was used by the Greeks of Attica and Ionia and in most of the islands of the Aegean Sea. Under this head we may consider (1) the Old Ionic (Epic), (2) the New Ionic, (3) the Attic, and (4) the Common Dialect (New Attic).

The *Old Ionic* or *Epic* dialect is the Ionic of the poems of Homer. Strictly speaking it was not a genuine, popular form of speech in common use, but a mixed dialect, developed by the poets for artistic purposes. Its base is doubtless the spoken language of the district in which the *Iliad* and *Odyssey* were composed; but interwoven with this are forms and usages partly borrowed from other dialectic sources and partly modified by poetic license. Thus there is a strong Aeolic element in Homer, due perhaps in part to the Aeolic affinities of the Ionians of Smyrna, but cherished also because of the exigencies of the dactylic hexameter. Every page of the Homeric poetry shows a peculiar multiplicity of forms of the same word. Thus we find *ἵππου* and *ἵπποιο*, *μάχης* and *μάχησι*, *ἔπεσσι* and *ἔπεσι*, *ἥρωοι* and *ἡρώεσσι*: in the pronouns *ἐμοῦ, ἐμεῦ, ἔμεθεν*, and *ἐμεῖο, ἄμμες*, and *ἡμεῖς*. The augment is used or disused at pleasure, forms are contracted or not, diphthongs are shortened before succeeding vowels, the metrical value of vowels varies, both hiatus and elision are freely used—in a word, the widest license prevails and stamps the dialect as one established for the convenience of poets and not for the common use of men. "The polish of the style, the artistic perfection of the composition, and the elaborate nature of the syntax point back to a long series of years of development, during which poets and schools of poets composed and passed on by oral tradition many lays . . . which in course of time grew into more complete epic poems. Forms of speech had not then been fixed by the general use of writing; the poet willingly adopted any of the floating forms in common use around him, or caught and preserved for his purpose those older forms bequeathed by past generations: so that in this way we have an explanation of the remarkable fact that in Homeric Greek there are forms in use of such different ages—archaisms, as we might say, by the side of modernisms" (Merry). Some of the peculiarities of the Epic language, however, which were at one time ascribed to the license of the poet, are now properly recognized as the usage of the oldest Greek. The most interesting of these is the effect produced by the earlier existence of a spirant, no longer written, upon the quantity of a preceding syllable. This lost letter is sometimes *j* and sometimes *σ*—e. g. *θεὸς* (*j*)*ως*, *εἰς ἅλα* (*σ*)*αλτο*, *ἔτι γὰρ* (*σ*)*εχον*. The same is true of the digamma, to which, indeed, as late as the time of I. Bekker all such cases were ascribed. Real examples of the influence of the digamma in making position or in preventing elision are *φίλα Ϝείματα δύσω, οὕτω δὴ Ϝοῖκονδε, ἔπειτα Ϝάναξ*. See DIGAMMA.

This complex and conventional dialect founded upon an Ionic base was disseminated throughout all Greece by the rhapsodes, or public reciters, who chanted the epics at the great public assemblies and festivals. Its forms and expressions colour the compositions of authors of very different ages and various styles. It forms the basis of the lyric language of Stesichorus and Pindar; it pervades the prose of Herodotus; and it tinges the style of the early Attic dramatists with a distinctly epic hue. See EPOS.

The *New Ionic* dialect is found in the writings of the iambic elegiac poets Archilochus, Callinus, and Mimnermus, and in the prose of Herodotus and Hippocrates. This dialect has the following distinctive peculiarities: (1) the retention of the earlier *κ* for *π* in interrogative and relative words (e. g. *κοῖος, ὁκόσος*); (2) the interchange of *ει* and *ου* with the simple vowels (e. g. *εἴρομαι, ξεῖνος*, but *μέζων, δέξω*; and *μοῦνος, οὔνομα*, etc.); (3) the contraction of *οη* into *ω* (e. g. *βῶσαι, ἐννώσας*); (4) the use of *ηϊ* for *ει* (e. g. *βασιληΐη*); (5) crasis (e. g. *ὡνήρ, ὧλλοι*); (6) the disuse of the appended *ν*; (7) the use of *-αται, -ατο* for *-νται, -ντο* whenever these are added directly to the tense-stem (e. g. *ἀπίκαται, τιθέαται*); (8) the genitive plural in *-εων* for the Homeric *-άων* and Attic *-ῶν*.

The *Attic* dialect is probably a modification of the Ionic spoken before the founding of the Ionic colonies. It is to the student of literature the most important of all the forms of Greek, since it was used by Thucydides, Aeschylus, Xenophon, Plato, Sophocles, Euripides, Aristophanes, Lysias, Isocrates, Demosthenes, Aeschines, and many others of genius scarcely inferior to them. Attic occupies a middle ground between the harsher Doric and the softer Ionic, and was thus fitted to be the common speech of all cultivated Greeks, and is now used as the standard of comparison in the study of the Hellenic tongue. Literary Attic is divided into Old and New, the point of division being approximately the beginning of the Peloponnesian War (B.C. 431). The differences between the Old and the New are slight, and seem to point to a gradual adoption in literature of popular forms. The Old Ionic is seen in Thucydides and the tragedians; both the Old and the New are noticeable in Plato; while the comic writers and the orators show the usages of the New. It is in the New Attic that the Greek language reached the zenith of its grace, expressiveness, and symmetry, combining at once the σεμνότης of the Doric with the χάρις of the Ionic speech.

The general use of the Attic gradually led to its corruption, so that we find a modified form of it developed by the time of Alexander, which is known as the *Common* dialect (ἡ κοινὴ διάλεκτος). It was used by the Greek writers of later times, such as Aristotle, Polybius, Plutarch, Pausanias, Babrius, and Lucian—writers, however, who exhibit very different degrees of divergence from the Attic standard of purity.

The rise of the Alexandrian School (q.v.) of critics and grammarians did much to check the tendency to linguistic corruption in literature; but the popular speech, continually receiving additions from foreign sources and especially from the East, ultimately developed into a distinct idiom which is known as *Hellenistic Greek*, and which is the basis of the diction of the New Testament and also of the Septuagint. The variations from earlier standards exhibited in this form of speech are rather to be seen in the vocabulary than in the syntax; but the following come under the latter head: (1) a confusion in the use of moods (e. g. ἵνα with the present indicative, ὅταν with the past indicative); (2) a construction of cases unknown in Attic (e. g. γενέσθαι with the accusative, προσφωνεῖν with the dative); (3) a gradual disuse of the optative mood, for which the subjunctive is substituted.

The corruption of the spoken language went on continuously, much as in the case of the Latin. For centuries literature still struggled to preserve the usages of Attic or at least of the κοινὴ διάλεκτος, but at last this attempt ended, and the popular speech became also the language of literature, being first so used by Theodorus Ptochoprodromus, a monk of Constantinople, about A.D. 1160. From this date begins the history of modern Greek.

BIBLIOGRAPHY.—The first scientific treatment of the Greek dialects is found in the work of Ahrens, *De Graecae Linguae Dialectis*, 2 vols. (Berlin, 1839–1843). Many of his views require modification, however, owing to more recent investigations. Much valuable material will be found in Curtius's *Studien zur griechischen und lateinischen Grammatik*, 10 vols. (Leipzig, 1868–78); and Merzdorf's *Sprachwissensch. Abhandl.* (Leipzig, 1874). For the Homeric dialect see La Roche's edition of the *Iliad* (Berlin, 1870); D. B. Monro's *Grammar of the Homeric Dialect* (Oxford, 1882); and Seymour's *Introduction to the Homeric Language* (Boston, 1885). Examples are given by Cauer in his *Delectus* (Leipzig, 1883); Meister, *Die griechischen Dialekte* (Gött. 1882–89); and by Hoffmann, *Die griechischen Dialekte* (Gött. 1891). See also Boisacq, *Les Dialectes Doriens* (Paris, 1891); and Smyth, *Greek Dialects*, part i. Ionic (Oxford, 1894). For Hellenistic and vulgar Greek see Winer's *Grammar*, part ii. pp. 69–128, ed. Moulton; Mullach, *Grammatik der griechischen Vulgarsprache* (Berlin, 1856); and Sophocles, *Glossary of Later and Byzantine Greek* (Boston, 1870).

II. ITALIAN DIALECTS.—The dialects spoken in Italy in ancient times and surely traceable to an Aryan stock may be roughly divided into two main groups—the Umbro-Sabellian and the Latin-Faliscan. Their general relations and divisions are indicated in the diagram given under ITALIA, p. 892. Of the Umbro-Sabellian group, the principal dialects are the Umbrian and the Oscan. See OSCI; UMBRIA.

The Latin and the Faliscan are so closely allied that the Faliscan may be roughly regarded as only a rustic variation of the Latin. It was used by the people of Falerii, a city situated within Etrurian territory, and probably one of the twelve confederated cities of the Etruscan League. That the language of the Falisci was not Etruscan or cognate with Etruscan was noticed by the ancients (e. g. Strabo, v. p. 266; Dionys. Hal. i. 21; Cato *ap.* Pliny, *H. N.* iii. 5, § 1), and inscriptions found in the present century have confirmed its close affinity with Old Latin. Thus the Falisci used the Latin R instead of the Etruscan and Umbro-Sabellian character ꟼ, and possessed also the Old Latin Z. The principal phonetic peculiarity distinguishing the Faliscan from the Latin is the representation of an original *bh* medial by *f*, as in *lofertas* for *libertas*. See Deecke, *Die Falisker* (Strassburg, 1885); and Conway's *Italic Dialects* (announced in 1896).

Latin was originally spoken only in the plain of Latium (q. v.), and seems not to have developed any subordinate dialects. For its colloquial and rustic forms and usages, see SERMO PLEBEIUS. The best grammars of the language are those of Roby (2 vols., Oxford, 1881); Kühner, *Ausführliche Grammatik* (2 vols. Hanover, 1877–78); Stolz and Schmalz in Iwan Müller's *Handbuch der klassischen Alterthumswissenschaft*, vol. ii. (Nördlingen, 1885); and Gildersleeve, revised by Lodge (N. Y. 1894).

Besides the Latin-Faliscan and the Umbro-Sabellian, Greek was spoken in the Greek cities of southern Italy (Magna Graecia), Keltic by the Gaulish peoples in the north, Etruscan by the inhabitants of Etruria, and at one time in Campania and the plain of the Eridanus (Po); while at an early period, in the extreme southeast, inscriptions show the existence of a language whose affinities have not yet been wholly determined, but which is usually styled Messapian or Iapygian, and regarded as cognate with the language of the Veneti in the northeast of Italy. For these dialects, see the articles CELTAE; ETRURIA; MESSAPIA; VENETI.

Diālis Flamen. See FLAMEN.

Dialŏgus (διάλογος). A dialogue. As a form of literary composition, apart from its purely dramatic use, the dialogue plays an important part in the history of Greek and Roman letters. The vividness and pungency of rapid question and reply were fully appreciated by the earliest writers. The Homeric poems abound in passages whose great dramatic force is due to the use of this form. Herodotus continually employs it to give picturesqueness and life to his narrative; and this is true even of Thucydides, in whose history the so-called Melian dialogue at the close of the fifth book, the dialogue of Archidamus with the Plataeans (ii. 71–74), and of the Ambraciot herald and the Acarnanian soldiers of Demosthenes (iii. 113) are striking examples. The great popularity of the drama must have been a direct stimulus to the use of the dialogue in prose literature; so that it is not surprising to find Plato employing it in his philosophical writings, thus following the example of Alexamenus of Teos and Zeno of Elea (cf. Mahaffy, *Hist. of Class. Gk. Lit.* ii. pp. 170–174). In this way the philosophical argument is worked out in a most attractive form, the attack and defence excite a lively interest, and the reader is artfully made to accept the truth of the doctrine by witnessing, as it were, the utter overthrow of its assailants. The ἠθοποιΐα, or character-painting, of the dialogues of Plato has never been surpassed, even by the greatest dramatists. The subtlest touches are here given with wonderful deftness, and a whole gallery of portraits is presented to us as varied, as delicately drawn, and as life-like as those of Euripides, of Molière, or of Shakspeare. In some of them, however (e. g. the *Parmenides*, *Protagoras*, and *Symposium*), the artistic mistake has been made of reporting the conversation in the *oratio obliqua;* and in these the sustained indirectness of construction, the crowded infinitives, and the absurdity of supposing one man to repeat from memory the whole of an intricate dialogue, greatly diminish the pleasure of the reader.

The dialogues of Aristotle are very different from those of Plato, and are probably a reversion to the models of Alexamenus and Zeno. The form is still nominally that of a conversation, but in fact the *diverbium* appears only in the introductory parts, and after the argument is once under full headway it becomes an almost unbroken monologue. The conversational *prooemium* is, therefore, rather a device to secure the attention of the reader, than an essential part of the work as a whole; and the ἠθοποιΐα is conspicuously absent.

Such of the philosophical and rhetorical writings of Cicero as adopt the form of the dialogue are decidedly Aristotelian rather than Platonic in their arrangement and in their lack of dramatic ability. Such are the treatises *De Senectute*, *De Amicitia*, the *Brutus*, the *Tusculanae Disputationes*, the *De Oratore*, and the *De Republica*.

The so-called *Dialogi* of L. Annaeus Seneca (*Dialogorum Libri xii.*) get the name from the frequent introduction of a second speaker with the words *inquis*, *inquit*, *dicet aliquis*, etc., but they are in no true sense of the word dialogues at all.

In Latin literature the title DIALOGUS is given *par excellence* to a work of Tacitus (*Dialogus de Oratoribus*), a conversation between a number of literary celebrities of the time of Vespasian, who in it discuss the decay of oratory under the Empire. The style shows that the dialogue was composed at the time when the writer was in the Ciceronian period of his studies and was endeavouring to imitate the diction of that great master. Hence it differs in many respects from the later Tacitean compositions, so that some critics from the time of Lipsius have even suspected its authenticity; but in a letter of Pliny (ix. 10, 2) addressed to Tacitus is found an evident allusion to the *Dialogus*, even did not a careful study of the piece itself yield sufficient evidence of the authorship. See Weinkauff, *Untersuchungen über den Dialogus des Tacitus* (Cologne, 1880); and the elaborate work of Hirzel, *Der Dialog*, 2 vols. (1895). Editions are those of Ritter (Bonn, 1859), Michaelis (Leipzig, 1868), Peter (Jena, 1877), Andresen (Leipzig, 1879), Bährens (Leipzig, 1881), Peterson (Oxford, 1893), Bennett (Boston, 1894), and Gudeman (Boston, 1894).

Diamartyria (διαμαρτυρία). See ANACRISIS.

Diamastigōsis (διαμαστίγωσις). A solemnity performed at Sparta at the festival of Artemis Orthia (Pausan. iii. 16, § 6). The ceremony was this. Spartan youths (ἔφηβοι) were scourged on the occasion at the altar of Artemis, by persons appointed for the purpose, until their blood gushed forth and covered the altar. The scourging itself was preceded by a preparation by which those who intended to undergo the diamastigosis tried to harden themselves against its pains. Pausanias describes the origin of the worship of Artemis Orthia, and of the diamastigosis, in the following manner: A wooden statue of Artemis, which Orestes had brought from Tauris, was found in a bush by Astrabacus and Alopecus, the sons of Irbus. The two men were immediately struck mad at the sight of it. The Limnaeans and the inhabitants of other neighbouring places then offered sacrifices to the goddess; but a quarrel ensued among them, in which several individuals were killed at the altar of Artemis, who now demanded atonement for the pollution of her sanctuary. From henceforth, human victims were selected by lot and offered to Artemis, until Lycurgus introduced the scourging of young men at her altar as a substitute for human sacrifices.

The diamastigosis, according to this account, was a substitute for human sacrifice, and Lycurgus made it also serve his purposes of education, in so far as he made it a part of the system of hardening the Spartan youths against bodily sufferings (Plut. *Lyc.* 18).

Diāna (from the root of *dies*). An ancient Italian deity, whose name is the feminine counterpart of Ianus (originally Dianus). She was the goddess of the moon; of the open air and open country with its mountains, forests, springs, and brooks; of the chase; and of childbirth, since the moon was believed to foster growth (Cic. *N. D.* ii. 19). In the latter capacity she, like Iuno, bore the second title of Lucina. Thus her attributes were akin to those of the Greek Artemis, and in the course of time she was completely identified with her and with Hecaté, who resembled her. The most celebrated shrine of Diana was at Aricia (q. v.), in a grove (*nemus*), from which she was sometimes simply called Nemorensis (Plin. *H. N.* xix. 3, 33). This was on the banks of the modern lake of Nemi, which was styled the mirror of Diana. Here a male deity named Virbius (Ovid, *Fast.* vi. 756) was worshipped with her, a god of the forest and the chase. He was in later times identified with Hippolytus, the risen favourite of Artemis, and the oldest priest of the sanctuary (*Rex Nemorensis*, Suet. *Calig.* 35).

He was said to have originated the custom of giving the priest's office to a runaway slave, who broke off a branch from a particular tree in the precincts and slew his predecessor in office in single combat. In consequence of this murderous custom the Greeks compared Diana of Aricia with the Tauric Artemis, and a fable arose that Orestes had brought the image of that goddess into the grove. Diana was chiefly worshipped by women, who prayed to her for happiness in marriage or childbirth. The most important temple of Diana at Rome was on the Aventine, founded by Servius Tullius as the sanctuary of the Latin confederacy. On the day of its foundation (August 13) the slaves had a holiday. This Diana was completely identified with the sister of Apollo, and worshipped simply as Artemis at the Secular Games. (See LUDI.) A sign of the original difference, however, remained. Cows were offered to the Diana of the Aventine, and her temple adorned with cows', not with stags', horns, but it was the doe which was sacred to Artemis. See ARTEMIS.

Diana.

Dianium. The modern Denia; a town in Hispania Tarraconensis on a promontory of the same name (now Cape S. Martin) founded by the Massilians. Here stood a celebrated temple of Diana, from which the town derived its name (Plin. *H. N.* iii. 5, 11).

Dianŏmae (διανομαί) or **Diadŏseis** (διαδόσεις). Public doles to the Athenian people, resembling the Roman *congiarium*. To these belong the free distributions of corn (Aristoph. *Vesp.* 715 foll.), the *cleruchiae*, the revenues from the mines, and the theoric fund. See THEORICON.

Diapsephĭsis (διαψήφισις). A political institution at Athens, the object of which was to prevent aliens, or such as were the offspring of an unlawful marriage, from assuming the rights of citizens. As usurpations of this kind were not uncommon at Athens (Plut. *Pericl.* 37), various measures had been adopted against them; but, as none of them had the desired effect, a new method, the διαψήφισις, was devised, according to which the trial of spurious citizens was to be held by the demotae within whose deme intruders (παρέγγραπτοι) were suspected to exist; for if each deme separately was kept clear of intruders, the whole body of citizens would naturally feel the benefit. Every deme, therefore, obtained the right or duty at certain times to revise its lexiarchic registers, and to ascertain whether any had entered their names who had no claims to the rights of citizens. The assembly of the demotae, in which these investigations took place, was held under the presidency of the demarch or some senator belonging to the deme. When the demotae were assembled, an oath was administered to them, in which they promised to judge impartially. The president then read out the names of the demotae from the register, asking the opinion of the assembly (διαψηφίζεσθαι) respecting each individual, whether they thought him a true and legitimate citizen or not. Any one then had the right to say what he thought or knew of the person in question, and when any one was impeached a regular trial took place (Demosth. c. *Eubul.* p. 1301, § 9). If a person was found guilty of having usurped the rights of a citizen (ἀποψηφίζεσθαι), his name was struck from the lexiarchic register, and he himself was degraded to the rank of an alien. But if he did not acquiesce in the verdict, but appealed to the great courts of justice at Athens, a heavier punishment awaited him if he was found guilty there also; for he was then sold as a slave, and his property was confiscated by the State (Dion. Hal. *De Isaeo*, c. 16, and the fragment of the speech *pro Euphileto* there preserved).

If by any accident the lexiarchic registers had been lost or destroyed, a careful scrutiny of the same nature as that described above, and likewise called διαψήφισις, took place, in order to prevent any spurious citizen from having his name entered in the new registers. See DEMUS.

The oldest known διαψήφισις occurred in B.C. 445 (Plut. *Pericl.* 37; Schol. Aristoph *Vesp.* l. c.).

Diarium. A day's allowance for Roman slaves or soldiers. See SERVUS.

Diary. See COMMENTARIUS; EPHEMERIS.

Diasia (τὰ Διάσια). A great festival celebrated at Athens, without the walls of the city, in honour of Zeus, surnamed Μειλίχιος. The whole people took part in it, and the wealthier citizens offered victims (ἱερεῖα), while the poorer classes burned such incense as their country furnished (θύματα ἐπιχώρια). The Diasia took place in the latter half of the month of Anthesterion, with feasting, and was, like most other festivals, accompanied by a fair. The etymology of Διάσια given by most of the ancient grammarians (from Διός and ἄση) is false; the name is a mere derivative from Διός, as Ἀπολλώνια from Ἀπόλλων.

Diastȳlus (διάστυλος). See TEMPLUM.

Diatrēta (sc. *vasa*). Cups of glass mentioned by Martial (xii. 70, 9) of an egg-shape, and hence could not be put down, but must be emptied at a draught. See VITRUM.

Diaulos (δίαυλος). See CURSUS.

Diazōma (διάζωμα). See SUBLIGACULUM.

Diazomăta (διαζώματα). The broad passages in the Greek theatre, which horizontally divided the successive rows of seats into two or three flights. The Latin equivalent is *praecinctio* (q. v.). See THEATRUM.

Dicaea (Δικαία). A town in Thrace on Lake Bistonis (Herod. vii. 109).

Dicaearchia. See PUTEOLI.

Dicaearchus (Δικαίαρχος). (1) A native of Messana in Sicily. He was a scholar of Aristotle's, and is called a Peripatetic philosopher by Cicero (*De Off.* ii. 5); but, though he wrote some works on philosophical subjects, he seems to have devoted his attention principally to geography and statistics. His chief philosophical work was two dialogues on the soul, each divided into three books, one dialogue (Κορινθιακοί) being supposed to have been held at Corinth, the other at Mitylenè (Λεσβιακοί). In these he argued against the existence of the soul. The greatest performance, however, of Dicaearchus was a treatise on the geography, politics, and manners of Greece, which he called Βίος Ἑλλάδος, "The Life of Greece," a title imitated by Varro in his *Vita Populi Romani*. All the philosophical writings of Dicaearchus are lost. His geographical works have shared the same fate, except a few fragments. We have remaining one hundred and fifty verses of his Ἀναγραφὴ τῆς Ἑλλάδος, or "Description of Greece," written in iambic trimeters; and also two fragments of the Βίος Ἑλλάδος, one containing a description of Boeotia and Attica, and another an account of Mount Pelion. Dicaearchus's maps were extant in the time of Cicero (*Ep. ad Att.* vi. 2). Cicero was very fond of the writings of Dicaearchus, and speaks of him in terms of warm admiration (*Ad Att.* ii. 2). In one of the extant fragments Dicaearchus quotes Posidippus, and must therefore have been alive in B.C. 289. There is an edition of the fragments of Dicaearchus by Fuhr (Darmstadt, 1841).

Dicasterion (δικαστήριον). A word which indicates both the aggregate judges that sat in court and the place itself in which they held their sittings. For an account of the former, the reader is referred to the article DICASTES; with respect to the latter, our information is very imperfect. In the earlier ages there were five celebrated places at Athens set apart for the sittings of the judges who had cognizance of the graver causes in which the loss of human life was avenged or expiated—viz., the Areopagites and the Ephetae. These places were on the Areopagus; in the Palladium, a sacred place in the southeastern part of the city; in the Delphinium, a place sacred to the Delphian Apollo in the same district; in the Prytaneum, the ancient sacred hearth of the State, to the northeast of the Acropolis; and finally at Phreatto or Phreattys in the Piraeus, at the inlet of Zea (Schömann, *Antiq.* i. 465, Eng. trans.; and the great passage in Demosth. *c. Aristocr.* pp. 641–646). The antiquity of these last four is sufficiently vouched for by the archaic character of the division of the causes that were appropriated to each: in the first we are told that accidental deaths were discussed, in the second, homicides confessed, but justified; in the third there were quasi-trials of inanimate things, which, by falling and the like, had occasioned a loss of human life (see APSYCHON DIKÉ); in the fourth, homicides who had returned from exile and committed a fresh manslaughter were appointed to be tried. With respect to these ancient institutions, of which little more than the name remained when the historical age commenced, it will be sufficient to observe that in accordance with the ancient Greek feeling respecting homicide—viz. that it involved ceremonial pollution in all cases, irrespective of the degree of criminality—the presiding judge was invariably the king archon, the Athenian *rex sacrorum;* and that the places in which the trials were held were open to the sky, to avoid the contamination which the judges might incur by being under the same roof with a murderer (Antiph. *de Caed. Her.* § 11; cf. PHONOU DIKÉ).

The Heliaea properly so called, and probably, also, the majority of the Heliastic courts, were situated in the Agora; others in various parts of the city. The statement that there were not more than ten of these is probably erroneous. Besides the Heliaea, the first in numbers and importance, the following are named: the Parabyston (παράβυστον), in which the Eleven presided, and which is said to have received its name from its position in a remote quarter of the city; the Dicasterion of Metiochus, or Metichus, and that of Calleas (τὸ Κάλλειον), probably named after their builders; the Green Court (Βατραχιοῦν) and the Red Court (Φοινικιοῦν), the Middle Court (Μέσον), the Greater Court (Μεῖζον), the New Court (Καινόν), the Triangular Court (Τρίγωνον), and the Dicasterion at the holy place of Lycus (ἐπὶ Λύκῳ), probably near the Lyceum without the city. Dicasteries near the walls and in the street of the Hermoglyphi are mentioned with no further indication of their name. The Odeum, too, a building erected by Pericles and properly destined for musical performances, was used for the sittings of Heliastic courts; and so, probably, were other places of which no mention is found. The dicasts sat upon wooden benches, which were covered with rugs or matting (ψιαθία), and there were elevations or tribunes (βήματα), upon which the antagonist advocates stood during their address to the court. The space occupied by the persons engaged in the trial was protected by a railing (δρύφακτοι) from the intrusion of the bystanders; but in causes which bore upon the violation of the Mysteries, a further space of fifty feet all round was enclosed by a rope, and the security of this barrier guaranteed by the presence of the public slaves. See DEMOSII.

Dicastes (δικαστής). In its broadest acceptation a judge, but more particularly denoting the Athenian functionary of the democratic period, commonly rendered "juryman." Except, however, in the circumstance that they were sworn "well and truly" to discharge the duties intrusted to them, there was little resemblance between an Attic dicasterion and an English jury. As distinguished from the district judges (οἱ κατὰ δήμους δικασταί, better known by their later name of οἱ τετταράκοντα), and from the Nautodicae or judges in commercial cases, the dicastae are frequently styled Heliastae, and their courts the Heliastic courts. The name comes from ἡλιαία, a word which, like ἀγορά, denotes both the assembly and the place in which it was held; and the court of the Heliaea, as the most strongly manned and the first in dignity, being taken as a representative of the rest, both names were used indiscriminately. Their jurisdiction extended to matters of every kind without exception. In private causes it is highly probable that they acted originally as judges of the second instance—i. e. of appeal; but in public matters they acted as the primary and sole judicial authority. The Heliastae were instituted by Solon, but what was their original number and how they were nominated at first we do not know. At the time when democracy was fully developed, when the causes even of the subject allies were brought before the Athenian courts, there were 6000 dicasts or Heliasts, 600 for each tribe, chosen by lot. Previously the number cannot have been very small; and divisions of the whole body into sections, such as we find afterwards, may without hesitation be assumed to have existed in the earlier times also. The ballot (κληροῦν, ἐπικληροῦν τὰ δικαστήρια, Demosth. *c. Everg.* p. 1144, § 17; sometimes also πληροῦν, after the analogy of "manning" a ship, *c. Timocr.* p. 729, § 92) was conducted annually by the nine archons; according to some authorities their secretary (γραμματεύς) made the tenth.

The lots were drawn, and the persons chosen were sworn, in the earlier ages at a place called Ardettus, without the city, on the banks of the Ilissus; but in after-times at some other spot, of which we are not informed. The formula of the Heliastic oath, preserved in Demosthenes (*c. Timocr.* p. 746, §§ 149–151), passed until lately as genuine, and was accepted as such by Schömann in his early writings (*Att. Process*, etc.) as well as by other recent scholars. The first hint that, like most of the documents embodied in the Demosthenic speeches, it was the patchwork of a late grammarian, seems to have been given by Schömann in his *Antiquities* (1855); and the point was completely proved in a special dissertation by Westermann in 1859. The whole number of 6000 Heliasts was divided into ten sections of 500 each, so that 1000 remained over, in order, when necessary, to serve for the filling of vacancies in the sections. These sections, as well as the places of meeting, were called Dicasteria, and in each section members of all the tribes were mingled together. Each Heliast received, as a certificate of his appointment, a bronze tablet (πινάκιον, σύμβολον) with his name and the number or letter of the section to which he belonged (from A to K). Three of these σύμβολα have been found, inscribed as follows: B. ΑΝΤΙΧΑΡΜΟΣ ΛΑΜΠ[ΤΡΕΥΣ], Δ. ΔΙΟΔΩΡΟΣ ΦΡΕΑ[ΡΡΙΟΣ], E. ΔΕΙΝΙΑΣ ΑΛΑΙΕΥΣ: and bear besides representations of owls and Gorgon heads, and other devices symbolic of the Athenian people (Boeckh, *C. I. G.* nos. 207–209).

As often as courts were to be held the Heliastae assembled in the Agora, and the courts in which each section had to sit for the day were there assigned by the Thesmothetae by lot. But it did not happen always, or in every suit, that whole sections sat; on the contrary, sometimes cases were tried only by parts of a section, sometimes by several sections combined, according to the importance of the issues. Provision, however, was made that the number should be always an uneven one, in order to avoid an equality of the votes; and if we find the number of 200 or 2000 dicasts mentioned, we are to assume that the round numbers only are given instead of 201 or 2001. For examples of the actual figures, we have in Demosthenes a court of 1001 dicasts taken from two sections (δικαστηρίοιν δυοῖν εἰς ἕνα καὶ χιλίους ἐψηφισμένων, *c. Timocr.* p. 702, § 9); and one of 1501 from three sections in *Lex Seguer.* s. v. ἡλιαία. The usual number in the Heliaea appears to have been 501.

For the trial of certain classes of cases Heliastae of a peculiar qualification were required; as, for instance, in the case of profaners of the Mysteries, when the initiated only were allowed to judge; and in that of military offenders, who were left to the justice of those only whose comrades they were, or should have been at the time when the offence was alleged to have been committed. After this ballot on the day of the trial each member of the section received a staff with the colour and number of the court in which he had to sit; this might serve both as a ticket to procure admittance and also to distinguish him from any loiterer who might endeavour clandestinely to obtain a seat after business had begun. That the dicasts were not sworn afresh before every case seems certain—the oath originally taken at the annual election sufficed. The legal age of the Heliastae was at least thirty, and of course the full franchise (ἐπιτιμία) was another condition of eligibility. No perquisite was ever more jealously guarded. For an *atimos* to attempt to earn the dicast's fee was a capital offence, and a case is mentioned in which this law was actually carried out (Demosth. *c. Mid.* p. 573, § 182). It would appear that they were only balloted for from among those who voluntarily offered themselves; we have no information on this point, but after the custom of payment was introduced there would be no lack of candidates.

This payment (μισθὸς δικαστικός, more usually τὸ δικαστικόν) is said to have been first instituted by Pericles. It is generally supposed from Aristophanes (*Nub.* 863), who makes Strepsiades say that with the first obolus he ever received as a dicast he bought a toy for his son, that it was at first only one obolus. It increased rapidly under the influence of the demagogues (Aristot. *ap.* Schol. Aristoph. *Vesp.* 682; Schol. *Ran.* 140; Poll. viii. 113; Hesych. s. v. δικαστικόν; Suid. s. v. ἡλιασταί). Three oboli or the *triobolon* (τριώβολον) occurs as early as B.C. 425 in the comedies of Aristophanes, and is afterwards mentioned frequently (Aristoph. *Eq.* 51, 255; *Vesp.* 300, 663, 684). The payment was made at the end of the day's work by the Colacretae (q. v.), in exchange for the staff (βακτηρία) and ticket (σύμβολον) with which, as we have seen, each dicast was already provided on entering the court (Schol. *ad* Aristoph. *Plut.* 277; Suid. s. v. βακτηρία; Poll. viii. 16). No doubt the staves only were given up, to be redistributed on another trial; the bronze σύμβολα merely shown, and retained by the dicast, as they were inscribed with his name and had to serve him throughout the year; unless we are to suppose that two different kinds of σύμβολα were used.

Dicastĭcon (δικαστικόν). See DICASTES.

Dice. See ALA; TALUS; TESSERA.

Diké (Δίκη). The personification of Justice. In Greek mythology she is the daughter of Zeus and Themis, and sister of Eunomia (Order) and Eirené (Peace). She is represented as one of the Horae; as the attendant and adviser (πάρεδρος, ξύνεδρος) of her father; and as the avenger of wrong who smites the wicked with the sword forged for her by Aesa. In this last character she resembles the Erinnyes, though, unlike them, she not only punishes wrong but rewards virtue.

Diké (δίκη). A term of Attic law which signifies generally any proceedings at law by one party directly or mediately against others. The object of all such actions is to protect the body politic, or one or more of its individual members, from injury and aggression—a distinction which has in most countries suggested the division of all causes into two great classes, the public and the private, and assigned to each its peculiar form and treatment. At Athens the first of these was implied by the terms public δίκαι or ἀγῶνες, or still more peculiarly by γραφαί; causes of the other class were termed private δίκαι or ἀγῶνες, or simply δίκαι in its limited sense. There is a still further subdivision of γραφαί into δημόσιαι and ἴδιαι, of which the former is somewhat analogous to impeachments for offences directly against the State; the latter to criminal prosecutions, in which the State appears as a party mediately injured in the violence or other wrong done to individual citizens. It will be observed that cases frequently arise which, with reference to the wrong complained of, may with equal propriety be brought before a court in the form of the γραφή last mentioned, or in that of an ordinary δίκη; and under these circumstances the laws of Athens gave the prosecutor an ample choice of methods to vindicate his rights by private or public proceedings, much in the same way as a plaintiff in modern times may, for the same offence, prefer an indictment for assault or bring his civil action for trespass on the person. It will be necessary to mention some of the principal distinctions in the treatment of causes of the two great classes above mentioned before proceeding to discuss the forms and treatment of the private lawsuit.

In a δίκη, only the person whose rights were alleged to be affected, or the legal protector (κύριος) of such person, if a minor or otherwise incapable of appearing *suo iure*, was permitted to institute an action as plaintiff; in public causes, with the exception of some few in which the person injured or his family were peculiarly bound and interested to act, any free citizen, and sometimes, when the State was directly attacked, almost any alien, was empowered to do so. In all private causes, except those of ἐξούλης, βιαίων, and ἐξαιρέσεως, the penalty or other subject of contention was exclusively recovered by the plaintiff; while in most others the State alone, or jointly with the prosecutor, profited by the pecuniary punishment of the offender. The court fees, called πρυτανεῖα, were paid in private but not in public causes; and a public prosecutor who compromised the action with the defendant was in most cases punished by a fine of a thousand drachmas and a modified disfranchisement, while there was no legal impediment at any period of a private lawsuit to the reconciliation of the litigant parties (Meier, *Att. Process*, p. 163).

The proceedings in the δίκη were commenced by a summons to the defendant (πρόσκλησις) to appear on a certain day before the proper magistrate (εἰσαγωγεύς), and there answer the charges preferred against him (Aristoph. *Nub.* 1221). This summons was often served by the plaintiff in person, accompanied by one or two witnesses (see CLETERES), whose names were endorsed upon the declaration (λῆξις or ἔγκλημα). If there were an insufficient service of the summons, the lawsuit was styled ἀπρόσκλητος and dismissed by the magistrate (Hesych.). From the circumstance of the same officer who conducted the ἀνάκρισις being also necessarily present at the trial, and as there were besides *dies nefasti* (ἀποφράδες) and festivals during which none, or only some special causes could be commenced, the power of the plaintiff in selecting his time was, of course, in some degree limited; and of several causes, we know that the time for their institution was particularized by law (Aristoph. *Nub.* 1190). There were also occasions upon which a personal arrest of the party proceeded against took the place of, or at all events was simultaneous with, the service of the summons; as, for instance, when the plaintiff doubted whether such party would not leave the country to avoid answering the action; and accordingly we find that in such cases (Demosth. *c. Zenoth.* p. 890, § 29; *c. Aristog.* i. p. 788, § 60) an Athenian plaintiff might compel a foreigner to accompany him to the polemarch's office, and there produce bail for his appearance, or, failing to do so, submit to remain in custody till the trial. The word κατεγγυᾶν is peculiarly used of this proceeding. Between the service of the summons and appearance of the parties before the magistrate, it is very probable that the law prescribed the intervention of a period of five days (Meier, *Att. Process*, p. 580). If both parties appeared, the proceedings commenced by the plaintiff putting in his declaration, and at the same time depositing his share of the court fees (πρυτανεῖα), the non-payment of which was a fatal objection to the further progress of a cause (Matthiae, *de Iud. Ath.* p. 261). These were very trifling in amount. If the subject of litigation was rated at less than 100 drachmae, nothing was paid; if at more than 100 drachmae and less than 1000 drachmae, 3 drachmae was a sufficient deposit, and so on in proportion. The deposits being made, it became the duty of the magistrate, if no manifest objection appeared on the face of the declaration, to cause it to be written out on a tablet, and exposed for the inspection of the public on the wall or other place that served as the cause list of his court (Meier, *Att. Process*, p. 605).

The magistrate then appointed a day for the further proceedings of the anacrisis (q. v.), which was done by drawing lots for the priority in case there was a plurality of causes instituted at the same time; and to this proceeding the phrase λαγχάνειν δίκην, which generally denotes to bring an action, is to be primarily attributed. If the plaintiff failed to appear at the anacrisis, the suit, of course, fell to the ground; if the defendant made default, judgment passed against him (Meier, *Att. Process*, p. 623). Both parties, however, received an official summons before their non-appearance was made the ground of either result. An affidavit might at this, as well as at other periods of the action, be made in behalf of a person unable to attend upon the given day, and this would, if allowed, have the effect of postponing further proceedings (ὑπωμοσία); it might, however, be combated by a counter-affidavit to the effect that the alleged reason was unfounded or otherwise insufficient (ἀνθυπωμοσία); and a question would arise upon this point, the decision of which, when adverse to the defendant, would render him liable to the penalty of contumacy (Demosth. *c. Olymp.* p. 1174, § 25). The plaintiff was in this case said ἐρήμην ἑλεῖν; the defendant, ἐρήμην ὀφλεῖν, δίκην being the word omitted in both phrases. If the cause were primarily brought before an umpire (διαιτητής), the anacrisis was conducted by him; in cases of appeal it was dispensed with as unnecessary. The anacrisis began with the affidavit of the plaintiff (προωμοσία), then followed the answer of the defendant (ἀντωμοσία or ἀντιγραφή) (see ANTIGRAPHÉ), then the parties produced their respective witnesses, and reduced their evidence to writing, and put in originals, or authenticated copies, of all the records, deeds, and contracts that might be useful in establishing their case, as well as memoranda of offers and requisitions then made by either side (προκλήσεις). The whole of the documents were then, if the cause took a straightforward course (εὐθυδικία), enclosed on the last day of the anacrisis in a casket (ἐχῖνος), which was sealed and intrusted to the custody of the presiding magistrate till it was produced and opened at the trial. During the interval no alteration in its contents was permitted, and accordingly evidence that had been discovered after the anacrisis was not producible at the trial (Demosth. *c. Boeot.* i. p. 999, § 18). In some causes, the trial before the dicasts was by law appointed to come on within a given time; in such as were not provided for by such regulations, we may suppose that it would principally depend upon the leisure of the magistrate. The parties, however, might defer the day (κυρία) by mutual consent (Demosth. *c. Phaen.* p. 1042, § 12). Upon the court being assembled the magistrate called on the cause (Platner, *Process und Klagen*, i. 182), and the plaintiff opened his case. At the commencement of the speech the proper officer (ὁ ἐφ' ὕδωρ) filled the clepsydra with water. As long as the water flowed from this vessel the orator was permitted to speak; if, however, evidence was to be read by the officer of the court or a law recited the water was stopped till the speaker recommenced. The quantity of water, or, in other words, the length of the speeches, was not by any means the same in all causes: in the speech against Macartatus, and elsewhere, one amphora only was deemed sufficient; eleven are mentioned in the impeachment of Aeschines for misconduct in his embassy. In some few cases, as those of κάκωσις, according to Harpocration, no limit was prescribed. The speeches were sometimes interrupted by the cry κατάβα, "go down"—in effect, "cease speaking"—from the dicasts, which placed the advocate in a serious dilemma; for if after this he still persisted in his address, he could hardly fail to offend those who bade him stop; if he obeyed the order, it might be found, after the votes had been taken, that it had emanated from a minority of the dicasts (Aristoph. *Vesp.* 980). After the speeches of the advocates, which were in general two on each side, and the incidental reading of the documentary and other evidence, the dicasts proceeded to give their judgment by ballot. See PSEPHOS.

When the principal point at issue was decided in favour of the plaintiff, there followed, in the case of a δίκη τιμητή, a further discussion as to the amount of damages, or penalty, which the defendant should pay. (See TIMEMA.) If the penalty was already prescribed by law, the suit was described as ἀτίμητος, not requiring assessment (Demosth. *c. Mid.* p. 543, § 90). The method of voting upon this question seems to have varied, in that the dicasts used a small tablet instead of a ballot-ball, upon which those that approved of the heavier penalty drew a long line, the others a short one (Aristoph. *Vesp.* 167). Upon judgment being given in a private suit, the Athenian law left its execution very much in the hands of the successful party, who was empowered to seize the movables of his antagonist as a pledge for the payment of the money or institute an action of ejectment (ἐξούλης) against the refractory debtor. The judgment of a court of dicasts was in general decisive (δίκη αὐτοτελής); but upon certain occasions, as, for instance, when a gross case of perjury or conspiracy could be proved by the unsuccessful party to have operated to his disadvantage, the cause, upon the conviction of such conspirators or witnesses, might be commenced *de novo*. In addition to which, the party against whom judgment has passed by default had the power to revive the cause, upon proving that his non-appearance in court was unavoidable (Platner, *Process und Klagen*, i. 396); this, however, was to be exercised within two months after the original judgment. If the parties were willing to refer the matter to an umpire (διαιτητής), it was in the power of the magistrate to transfer the proceedings as they stood to that officer; and in the same way, if the diaetetes considered the matter in hand too high for him, he might refer it to the εἰσαγωγεύς, to be brought by him before an Heliastic court. The whole of the proceedings before the diaetetes were analogous to those before the dicasts, and bore equally the name of δίκη; but it seems that the phrase ἀντιλαχεῖν τὴν μὴ οὖσαν is peculiarly applied to the revival of a cause before the umpire in which judgment had passed by default.

The following are the principal actions, both public and private, which we read of in the Greek writers, and which are briefly defined in this Dictionary under their several heads:

Δίκη or Γραφή—Ἀγεωργίου: Ἀγραφίου: Ἀγράφου μετάλλου: Αἰκίας: Ἀλογίου: Ἀναγωγῆς: Ἀναυμαχίου: Ἀνδραποδισμοῦ: Ἀνδραπόδων: Ἀπατήσεως τοῦ δήμου: Ἀφορμῆς: Ἀπολείψεως: Ἀποπέμψεως: Ἀπορρήσεως: Ἀπροστασίου: Ἀργίας: Ἀργυρίου: Ἀσεβείας: Ἀστρατείας: Αὐτομολίας: Βεβαιώσεως: Βιαίων: Βλάβης: Βουλεύσεως: Κακηγορίας: Κακολογίας: Κακώσεως: Κακοτεχνιῶν: Κάρπου: Καταλύσεως τοῦ δήμου: Κατασκοπῆς: Κλοπῆς: Δεκασμοῦ: Δειλίας: Δώρων: Δωροξενίας: Ἐγγύης: Ἐνοικίου: Ἐπιτριηραρχήματος: Ἐπιτροπῆς: Ἐξαγωγῆς: Ἐξαιρέσεως: Ἐξούλης: Ἁρπαγῆς: Εἱργμοῦ: Ἑταιρήσεως: Ἱεροσυλίας: Ὑποβολῆς: Ὕβρεως: Λειπομαρτυρίου: Λειποναυτίου: Λειποστρατίου: Λειποταξίου: Μισθοῦ: Μισθώσεως οἴκου: Μοιχείας: Νομίσματος διαφθορᾶς: Οἰκίας: Παρακαταθήκης: Παρανοίας: Παρανόμων: Παραπρεσβείας: Παρεισγραφῆς: Φαρμάκων: Φόνου: Φωρᾶς ἀφανοῦς καὶ μεθημερίνης: Φθορᾶς τῶν ἐλευθέρων: Προαγωγίας: Προδοσίας: Προεισφορᾶς: Προικός: Ψευδεγγραφῆς: Ψευδοκλητείας: Ψευδομαρτυριῶν: Ῥητορική: Σκυρία: Σίτου: Συκοφαντίας: Συμβολαίων or Συνθηκῶν παραβάσεως: Τραύματος ἐκ προνοίας: Τυραννίδος. See DICASTES; JUDICIAL PROCEDURE; and for the Roman actions, ACTIO.

Dicrŏtus (δίκροτος). See NAVIS.

Dictaeus. See DICTÉ.

Dictamnum Promontorium. See DICTYNNAEUM PROMONTORIUM.

Dictātor. The Latin term for a magistrate appointed for special emergencies, after auspices duly taken by the consuls on the commission of the Senate. The dictator was never appointed for more than six months. The first instance of the appointment occurred in B.C. 501. The dictator was usually, though not always, chosen from the number of *consulares*, or men who had held the office of consul. No plebeian was elected before B.C. 356. He was always nominated for a particular or specified purpose, on the fulfilment of which he laid down his office. He combined the supreme judicial with the supreme military power, and there was, originally, no appeal against his proceedings, even the veto of the tribunes being powerless against him. He was free from responsibility for his acts, and could therefore not be called to account on the expiration of his term of office, the case of Camillus, who was so impeached, being very peculiar. (See Becker, *Röm. Alterth.* ii. pt. 2, p. 172.) That the dictator was free from subsequent attack is expressly stated by Dion. Hal. (v. 70, vii. 56), Appian (*B. C.* ii. 23), and others. His insignia were the *sella curulis* and the *toga praetexta*, and he was attended by twenty-four lictors, who represented the lictors of two consuls, and who even in the city bore axes in their bundles of rods, as a sign of unlimited power of life and death. His assistant was the *magister equitum* (master of the horse), who was bound absolutely to obey his commands, and whom he had to nominate immediately after his own election. The original function of the dictator was military; but after B.C. 363 a dictator was occasionally chosen, in the absence of the consuls, for other purposes than dealing with external danger or internal troubles—especially to hold the games or religious festivities. The office gradually passed out of use, though not legally abolished. The last military dictator was appointed in B.C. 206, the last absolutely in B.C. 202. The dictatorships of Sulla and Caesar who was named perpetual dictator not long before his death, were anti-republican and unconstitutional. After Caesar had been murdered, in B.C. 44, the office was abolished forever by a law of Marcus Antonius. See Mommsen, *Römische Staatsrecht*, ii. 133–172; Becker, *Röm. Alterth.* ii. pt. 2, p. 150 foll.

Dicté (Δίκτη). A mountain in the east of Crete, where Zeus is said to have been reared. Hence he bore the surname Dictaeus. The Roman poets frequently employ the adjective Dictaeus as synonymous with Creticus.

Dictionaries. See GLOSSARIUM; LEXICON.

Dictynna (*Δίκτυννα* or *Δίκτυνα*). A surname of both Britomartis and Artemis, two divinities who were subsequently identified. The name is connected with *δίκτυον*, "a hunting-net," and was borne by Britomartis and by Artemis as goddesses of the chase (Herod. iii. 59). See ARTEMIS; BRITOMARTIS.

Dictynnaeum or **Dictamnum Promontorium.** A promontory on the northern coast of Crete, towards the northwest. This promontory, answering to the Psacum Promontorium of Ptolemy, forms the termination of a chain called Tityrus by Strabo. On its summit was placed a celebrated temple of the nymph Britomartis or Dictynna (Diod. Sic. v. 76). See DICTYNNA.

Dictynnia (*τὰ Δικτύννια*). A festival with sacrifices, celebrated at Cydonia in Crete, in honour of Artemis, surnamed *Δίκτυννα*, from *δίκτυον*, "a hunter's net" (Diod. Sic. v. 76). Particulars respecting its celebration are not known. Artemis *Δίκτυννα* was also worshipped at Sparta (Pausan. iii. 12, § 7) and at Ambrysos in Phocis (Pausan. x. 36, § 3).

Dictys (*Δίκτυς*), called CRETENSIS. A Cretan, said to have accompanied Idomeneus to the Trojan War, and to have written a history of that contest. This work (*Ephemeris Belli Troiani*), according to the account that has come down to us, was discovered in the reign of Nero, in a tomb near Cnossus, which was laid open by an earthquake. It was asserted to have been written in Phœnician on bark, and translated into Greek by one Eupraxides or Eupraxis. We have a pretended Latin version by one C. Septimius, who probably lived in the time of the emperor Diocletian. The work of Septimius contains the first five books, with an abridgment of the remainder. This work is a part of the fictitious literature that sprang up in the first century of the Christian era, and, though worthless except as a literary curiosity, it was an important source of the romances of the Middle Ages. (See DARES). Good editions are those of Dederich (Bonn, 1832–37), and Meister (Leipzig, 1872). See Dunger, *Dictys-Septimius: über die ursprüngliche Abfassung und die Quellen der Ephemeris* (Dresden, 1878); and Gudeman in *Classical Studies in Honour of Henry Drisler* (N. Y. 1894).

Didascalia (*διδασκαλία*). (1) The performance of a drama. (2) The pieces brought forward for performance at a dramatic entertainment. (3) A board hung up in the theatre, with short notices as to the time and place of the contest, the competing poets, their plays and other successes, perhaps also the *choregi*, and the most celebrated actors. These documents, so important for the history of the drama, were first collected and arranged by Aristotle, whose example was followed by the Alexandrian scholars Callimachus, Aristophanes of Byzantium, and others. From these writings, also called *didascaliae*, but now unfortunately lost, come the scanty notices preserved by grammarians and scholiasts upon the particular tragedies and comedies. Following the example of the Greeks, the Romans provided the dramas of their own poets with *didascaliae*, as for instance those attached to the comedies of Terence and the *Stichus* of Plautus.

Didius Salvius Iuliānus. A Roman who bought the Roman Empire from the Praetorian Guards, when they put up the Empire for sale after the death of Pertinax, A.D. 193. The price paid was 25,000 sesterces ($1000) to each soldier. After reigning for two months (March 28 to June 1), he was murdered by the soldiers while Severus was marching against the city. See his life by Spartianus.

Dido (Διδώ), also called ELISSA, the reputed founder of Carthage. She was a daughter of a Tyrian king, Belus, Agenor, or Mutgo, and sister of Pygmalion, who succeeded to the crown after the death of his father. Dido was married to her wealthy uncle, Acerbas or Sichaeus, who was murdered by Pygmalion. Upon this, Dido secretly sailed from Tyre with his treasures, accompanied by some noble Tyrians, and passed over to Africa. Here she purchased as much land as might be enclosed with the hide of a bull, but she ordered the hide to be cut up into the thinnest possible strips, and with them she surrounded a spot on which she built a citadel called Byrsa (from *βύρσα*, "bull's-hide"). Around this fort the city of Carthage arose and soon became a powerful and flourishing place. The neighbouring king, Hiarbas, jealous of the prosperity of the new city, demanded the hand of Dido in marriage, threatening Carthage with war in case of refusal. Dido had vowed eternal fidelity to her late husband; but seeing that the Carthaginians expected her to comply with the demands of Hiarbas, she pretended to yield to their wishes, and under pretence of soothing the manes of Acerbas by expiatory sacrifices she erected a funeral pile, on which she stabbed herself in presence of her people. After her death she was worshipped by the Carthaginians as a divinity. Vergil has inserted in his *Aeneid* the legend of Dido, with various modifications. According to the common chronology, there was an interval of more than

300 years between the capture of Troy (B.C. 1184) and the foundation of Carthage (B.C. 853); but Vergil, nevertheless, makes Dido a contemporary of Aeneas, with whom she falls in love on his arrival in Africa. When Aeneas hastened to seek the new home which the gods had promised him, Dido, in despair, destroyed herself on a funeral pile. She was worshipped at Carthage and may be identified with Iuno Caelestis, the Roman representative of the Phœnician Astarté. See Verg. *Aen.* bks. i.–iv. and vi.; and the article AENEAS.

Didrachmon (*δίδραχμον*). See DRACHMA.

Didȳma (*τὰ Δίδυμα*). See BRANCHIDAE.

Didȳmus (*Δίδυμος*). A famous grammarian, the son of a seller of fish at Alexandria, who was born in the consulship of Antonius and Cicero, B.C. 63, and flourished in the reign of Augustus. Macrobius calls him the greatest grammarian of his own or any other time (*Saturn.* v. 18, 9). According to Athenaeus (iv. 139), he published 3500 volumes, and had written so much that he was called "the forgetter of books" (*βιβλιολάθας*), for he often himself forgot what he had written; and also "the man with brazen bowels" (*χαλκέντερος*), from his unwearied industry. He wrote, among other things, commentaries on Hesiod, Homer, Pindar, Bacchylides, Aeschylus, Sophocles, Euripides, Cratinus, Eupolis, Aristophanes, Menander, Antiphon, Isaeus, Hyperides, Aeschines, Demosthenes, and Thucydides; on Ion; and also on the plays of Phrynichus; several treatises against Iuba, king of Mauretania; a book on the corruption of style; and a great number of historical and antiquarian treatises. The most important production of Didymus was his very learned treatise on the edition of Homer by Aristarchus (q. v.), parts of which are preserved in the Venetian scholia on Homer. His lexical works, in fact, were the source of innumerable lexica, scholia, etc. The collection of proverbs extant under the name of Zenobius was partly taken from a previous collection made by Didymus. The fragments of Didymus may be found in the collection by M. Schmidt (Leipzig, 1854). See the account of Didymus in Wilamowitz, Eurip. *Heracles*, i. 157–168; and Susemihl, *Geschichte d. griech. Lit.* ii. 195–210, 688 foll. (1892). See DIDASCALIA; SCHOLIUM.

Diefenbach, LORENZ. A celebrated German philologist, born at Ostheim, in the Grand Duchy of Hesse, July 29th, 1806. He studied theology and philology at Giessen, and after travelling extensively, was settled as pastor and librarian at Solme-Laubach, and in 1848 at Frankfort-on-the-Main. Here, from 1865 until 1876, he was the second librarian to the city. A writer and scholar of much versatility, he produced a large number of works in general literature, including verse and prose fiction, besides the famous books on linguistic topics whereby he will be longest remembered. These are *Celtica*, 3 vols. (1840); *Vergleichendes Wörterbuch der Gothischen Sprache*, 2 vols. (1846–51); *Glossarium Latino-Germanicum Mediae et Infimae Aetatis* (1857), being a supplement to the great work of Ducange (q. v.); and *Origines Europae*, 2 vols. (1874), completed by Wülcker in 1885. Diefenbach died at Darmstadt, March 28, 1883.

Diengyēsis (*διεγγύησις*). See ENGYÉ.

Dies. The ancients distinguished (1) *dies civilis* (*νυχθήμερον*), the time in which the sun apparently completed a course around the earth, including thus both night and day; and (2) *dies naturalis* or the time between the rising and the setting of the sun. The civil day began with the Athenians at the setting of the sun; with the Romans (as with the Egyptians and Hipparchus) at midnight; with the Babylonians at the rising of the sun, and with the Umbrians at mid-day (Macrob. *Saturn.* i. 3; Gell. iii. 2).

At the time of the Homeric poems, the natural day was divided into three parts (*Il.* xxi. 111). The first, called *ἠώς*, began with sunrise and comprehended the whole space of time during which light seemed to be increasing—i. e. till mid-day (*Il.* viii. 66, ix. 84; *Od.* ix. 56). The second part was called *μέσον ἦμαρ* or mid-day, during which the sun was thought to stand still (Hermias, *ad* Plat. *Phaedr.* p. 342). The third part bore the name of *δείλη* or *δείελον ἦμαρ* (*Od.* xvii. 606; cf. Buttman's *Lexilog.* ii. n. 95), which derived its name from the increased warmth of the atmosphere. The last part of the *δείλη* was sometimes designated by the words *ποτὶ ἕσπερα* or *βουλυτός* (*Od.* xvii. 191; *Il.* xvi. 779).

The first and last of the divisions made at the time of Homer were afterwards subdivided into two parts. The earlier part of the morning was termed *πρωΐ* or *πρῴ τῆς ἡμέρας*; the later—i. e. from 9 or 10 till noon—*πληθούσης τῆς ἀγορᾶς* or *περὶ πλήθουσαν ἀγοράν*. The *μέσον ἦμαρ* of Homer was afterwards expressed by *μεσημβρία*, *μέσον ἡμέρας*, or *μέση ἡμέρα*, and comprehended, as before, the middle of the day, when the sun seemed neither to rise nor to decline. The two parts of the afternoon were called *δείλη πρωΐη* or *πρωΐα*, and *δείλη ὀψίη* or *ὀψία*. This division continued to be observed down to the latest period of Grecian history, though another more accurate division, and one more adapted to the purposes of common life, was introduced at an early period; for Anaximander, or according to others, Anaximenes, is said to have made the Greeks acquainted with the use of the Babylonian chronometer or sundial (called *πόλος* or *ὡρολόγιον*, sometimes with the epithet *σκιοθηρικόν* or *ἡλιαμάνδρον*), by means of which the natural day was divided into twelve equal spaces of time. These spaces were, of course, longer or shorter according to the various seasons of the year. The name hours (*ὧραι*), however, did not come into general use till a very late period, and the difference between natural and equinoctial hours was first observed by the Alexandrian astronomers. See Pollux, *Onom.* i. 68.

During the early ages of the history of Rome, the natural phenomena of increasing light and darkness formed with the Romans, as with the Greeks, the standard of division, as we see from the vague expressions in Censorinus (*De Die Nat.* 24). In the Twelve Tables only the rising and the setting of the sun and mid-day (*meridies*) were mentioned as the parts into which the day was then divided. Varro (*L. L.* vi. 4, 5) and Isidorus (*Orig.* v. 30 and 31) likewise distinguished three parts of the day—viz. *mane*, *meridies*, and *suprema*, sc. *tempestas*, after which no assembly could be held in the Forum.

But the division of the day most generally observed by the Romans was that into *tempus antemeridianum* and *pomeridianum*, the *meridies* itself being considered only as a point at which the one ended and the other commenced. As it was of importance that this moment should be known, an officer (see ACCENSI) of the consuls was directed to proclaim the time of mid-day, when from the Curia he saw the sun standing between the Rostra and the Graecostasis. The division of the day into twelve equal spaces, which, here as in Greece, were shorter in winter than in summer, was adopted at the time when artificial means of measuring time were introduced among the Romans from Greece. This was about the year B.C. 293, when L. Papirius Cursor, before the war with Pyrrhus, brought to Rome an instrument called *solarium horologium*, or simply *solarium* (Plaut. *ap. Gellium*, iii. 3, § 5; Plin. *H. N.* vii. § 212). In B.C. 263, M. Valerius Messala brought one which he had taken at the capture of Catina; and although this was incorrect, having been constructed for a place 4° farther south than Rome, it was in use for 99 years before the error was discovered. In B.C. 164, the censor Q. Marcius Philippus had a more exact sundial constructed; but the time was still unknown in cloudy weather. Scipio Nasica, therefore, erected in B.C. 159 a public clepsydra, which indicated the hours of the night as well as of the day (Censor. c. 23). Before the erection of a clepsydra it was customary for one of the subordinate officers of the praetor to proclaim the third, sixth, and ninth hours; which shows that the day was, like the night, divided into four parts, each consisting of three hours. In daily life numerous terms were in use to denote the different parts of the day, mostly of a general and somewhat vague character. (Cf. Varr. *L. L.* vi. 4–7; Servius on *Aen.* ii. 268; iii. 587; Isid. *Orig.* v. 31, 32.) See, also, the article HOROLOGIUM.

All the days of the year were, according to different points of view, divided by the Romans into different classes. For the purpose of the administration of justice and of holding assemblies of the people all the days were divided into *dies fasti*, *dies nefasti*, and *dies* partly *fasti*, partly *nefasti*.

1. *Dies fasti*, in the wider sense, were days on which legal and political business could be lawfully transacted. They were divided into:

(*a*) *Dies fasti*, in the narrower sense, marked with F in the calendars. On these legal business could be conducted (Ovid, *Fast.* i. 48, *fastus erit per quem lege licebit agi;* Varr. *L. L.* vi. 29, *dies fasti per quos praetoribus omnia verba sine piaculo licet fari*). The word is derived by the ancients from *fari;* but, although the root is undoubtedly the same, the more immediate connection is with *fas*.

(*b*) *Dies comitiales*, days on which meetings of the people could legally be held, and on which, if there was no meeting convened, courts could be opened (Macrob. *Saturn.* i. 16).

These days are marked C in the calendar.

2. *Dies nefasti* were days on which no legal or political business could be done (Varr. *L. L.* vi. 30). These are again divided into two quite distinct classes:

(*a*) *Dies nefasti* or *feriati*, on which no business could be done because the day was sacred to some festival. These are marked N̶P in the calendars. This sign was commonly interpreted *nefastus parte* or *nefastus principio*, and was explained to mean that the day was one during the earlier part of which no business could be done. But Mommsen (*Chronol.* p. 220; *C. I. L.* i. 366) showed that this view was quite untenable, and explains the sign to be, like M' when used as an abbreviation for Manius, a modification of the archaic M with five strokes (M̶V).

(*b*) *Dies religiosi* or *vitiosi*, sometimes called *atri*, marked in the calendars by R. These were unlucky days, which had been declared to be such by a decree of the Senate in consequence of some disaster which had taken place upon them. All the *dies postriduani* were included under this head —i. e. the days after the Kalends, the Nones, and the Ides—because these were believed to have been especially unfortunate (Ovid, *Fast.* i. 59, 60). On these days it was not only unlawful to transact any legal or political business, but it was also unlucky to begin any affair of importance. Cf. Gell. iv. 9, 5.

3. Days partly *fasti* and partly not, including:

(*a*) *Dies intercisi*, marked in the calendars by EN, for *endotercisi* (*endo* being an archaic form of *in*, as in *endoperator*). On these days a victim was sacrificed in the morning and the *exta* offered in the evening. Between the sacrifice and the offering the day was *fastus;* before the former and after the latter it was *nefastus* (Varr. *L. L.* vi. 31; Ovid, *Fast.* i. 49).

(*b*) *Dies fissi*, three in number. To two of these, March 24 and May 24, are prefixed the letters Q. R. C. F.—i. e. *quando rex* (*sacrorum*) *comitiavit, fas.* These days were, even in ancient times, confused with the *Regifugium*—i. e. February 24—and the letters were wrongly interpreted *quando rex comitio fugit.* To the third, June 15, is prefixed Q. ST. D. F.—i. e. *quando stercus delatum fas;* on this day the temple of Vesta was solemnly cleansed by the Vestals, and the filth carried away or thrown into the Tiber (Ovid, *Fast.* vi. 707), no other business being permitted on this day.

Mommsen (*C. I. L.* i. p. 373) calculates that the year contained 45 *dies fasti*, 194 *dies comitiales*, 48 *dies nefasti* or *feriati*, 57 *dies religiosi*, 8 *dies intercisi*, and 3 *dies fissi*.

Another division of the days of the year was of a purely religious character, with which naturally the former division to a certain extent coincided in a city so dominated by religious scruples as Rome:

1. *Dies festi*, on which the gods were honoured by (a) *sacrificia*, (b) *epulae*, (c) *ludi*, (d) *feriae*. See FERIAE.

2. *Dies profesti*, ordinary working-days.

3. *Dies intercisi*, of a mixed character.

For the NUNDINAE, see the article with that title.

Diespĭter. See IUPITER.

Diet. See DIAETETICA.

Diffareatio. See DIVORTIUM.

Digamma (δίγαμμα). A name given by grammarians of the first century to Vau, the sixth letter of the early Greek alphabet, but which in the classical had ceased to be used and was known only by inscriptions. The digamma ("double gamma") gets its name from its form Ϝ or Ϝ. Its sound was originally something like that of English *W*. Its form in the hieratic Egyptian was ƴ; in the ancient Phœnician, 𐤅; the square Hebrew, ו. It is found in Peloponnesian inscriptions as late as the sixth century B.C., but it had disappeared from the Ionic or Eastern Greek alphabet before the middle of the seventh century B.C., being retained only as a numeral = 6. From the Chalcidian or Western alphabet it was transmitted to Italy, retaining its position as the sixth letter, but acquiring the sound of *F*, a labio-dental fricative. See ALPHABET.

That its influence remained after it ceased to be written, is shown by the fact that in the Homeric poems it prevents elision where a final vowel stands before a word which originally had the digamma (e. g. φίλα ϝείματα δύσω). (See DIALECTS.) Too much was made of this fact at one time, and Mr. Payne Knight even published a text of Homer with the digamma restored, a part of this text being reprinted in this country by Dr. Charles Anthon in his edition of the *Iliad*. But more recent scholarship shows that many of the supposed instances are not those of words that originally were digammated, but which rather once had an initial spirant, *s* or *j*—e. g. εἰς ἅλα (σ) ἅλτο: ἔτι γὰρ (σ) ἔχον. See Hadley's *Essays*, pp. 56–80 (1873).

Words which finally lost the digamma in Greek still often show it in the cognate languages—e. g. οἶκος, Lat. *vicus; οἶνος*, Lat. *vinum; ὄϊς* (ὄϝις), Lat. *ovis; ῥήγνυμι*, Lat. *frango; ἔργον*, Eng. work. In Laconian it frequently became β—e. g. βάννας for ϝάναξ, βέργον for ϝέργον, etc.

The word δίγαμμα is not found earlier than the first century A.D., when it occurs in the grammarians. Dionysius of Halicarnassus describes it, but gives it no name (i. 20). Terentianus Maurus calls it δίγαμμος *littera* (163 K). Macrobius uses the word δίγαμμον (sc. στοιχεῖον) (*De Vero.* vi. 13). Quintilian (i. 7, 27) calls it *Aeolica littera* (cf. i. 4, 7), but it is not found in the later Lesbian inscriptions, and in Alcaeus and Sappho it is represented by β before ρ (e. g. βράκος for the Homeric ῥάκος = ϝράκος). See Monro, *Homeric Grammar* (1882); and King and Cookson, *Principles of Sound and Inflexion*, pp. 166–171 (Oxford, 1888).

Digentia. The modern Licenza; a small stream in Latium, beautifully cool and clear, flowing into the Anio, through the Sabine farm of Horace.

Digesta. See CORPUS IURIS CIVILIS; PANDECTAE.

Digitalia. See MANICA.

Digĭtus. See PES.

Diïpolĭa (τὰ Διϊπόλια, Διϊπόλεια, or Διπόλια). A festival celebrated in Athens on the 14th Scirophorion (June to July) to Zeus (Aristoph. *Pax*, 420) as the protector of the city. It was also called Buphonia, from the sacrifice of an ox connected with it. A labouring ox was led to the altar of Zeus in the Acropolis, which was strewn with wheat and barley. As soon as the ox touched the consecrated grain he was punished by a blow on the neck from an axe, delivered by a priest of a particular family, who instantly threw away the axe and took to flight. In his absence the axe was brought to judgment in the Prytaneum, and condemned, as a thing polluted by murder, to be thrown into the sea. To kill a labouring ox, the trusty helper of man, was rigidly forbidden by custom. In the exceptional sacrifice of one at this festival the ancient custom may be regarded as on the one hand excusing the slaughter, and on the other insisting that it was, nevertheless, equivalent to a murder.

Dikes. See MOLES.

Dilectus. The levying of soldiers for military service among the Romans. In the republican age all the citizens who were liable to service assembled in the Capitol on the day previously announced by the consuls in their *edictum*, or proclamation. The twenty-four *tribuni militum* were first divided among the four legions to be levied. Then one of the tribes was chosen by lot, and the presence of the citizens ascertained by calling the names according to the lists of the several tribes. The calling was always opened with names of good omen. (See OMEN.) If a man did not appear he would be punished, according to circumstances, by a fine, confiscation of property, corporal punishment, even by being sold into slavery. Four men of equal age and bodily capacity were ordered to come forward, and were distributed among the four legions; then another four, and so on, so that each legion got men of equal quality. As the proceeding was the same with the other tribes, each legion had a quarter of the levy for each tribe. No one man had exemption (*vacatio*) from service unless he was over forty-six years of age, or had served the number of campaigns prescribed by law—twenty in the infantry, ten in the cavalry—or held a city office or priesthood, or had a temporary or perpetual dispensation granted on account of special business of State. In ancient times the levy of the cavalry followed that of the infantry, in later times it preceded it. On the oath taken after the levy, see SACRAMENTUM.

About the year B.C. 100, Marius procured the admission of the *capite censi*, or classes without property, to military service. (See PROLETARII.) After this the legions were chiefly made up out of this class by enlistment; and though the liability to common military service still existed for all citizens, the wealthy citizens strove to relieve themselves of it, the more so as after Marius the time of service was extended from twenty campaigns to twenty years. In B.C. 89, Roman citizenship was extended to all the inhabitants of Italy, and all, therefore, became liable to service. The levies were, in consequence, not held exclusively in Rome, but in all Italy by *conquisitores*. These officials, though they continued to use the official lists of qualified persons, assumed more and more the character of recruiting officers. They were ready to grant the *vacatio*, or exemption, for money or favour, and anxious to get hold of volunteers by holding out promises. The legal liability to military service continued to exist in imperial times, but after the time of Augustus it was only enforced in regard to the garrison at Rome and on occasions of special necessity. The army had become a standing one, and even outside of Italy, except when a special levy of new legions was made, the vacancies caused by the departure of the soldiers who had served their time were filled up by volunteers. The levy was carried out by imperial commissioners (*dilectatores*), whose business it was to test the qualifications of the recruits. These were, Roman citizenship—for only citizens were allowed to serve, whether in the legions or in the guard and other garrison cohorts of Rome (*cohortes urbanae*)—physical capacity, and a certain height, the average of which was 5 feet 10 inches under the Empire. For the republican age we have no information on this point. See EXERCITUS.

Dimăchae (διμάχαι). Macedonian cavalry, who also fought on foot when ordered. See Pollux, i. 132.

Dimachaeri (διμάχαιροι). See GLADIATORES.

Diminutio Capĭtis. See DEMINUTIO CAPITIS.

Dinarchus (Δείναρχος). One of the ten Greek orators, for the explanation of whose orations Harpocration compiled his lexicon. (See CANON ALEXANDRINUS.) He was a Corinthian by birth, but settled at Athens and became intimate with Theophrastus and Demetrius Phalereus. Dionysius of Halicarnassus fixes his birth at B.C. 361. The time of his highest reputation was after the death of Alexander, when Demosthenes and other great orators were dead or banished. He seems to have made a living by writing speeches for those who were in need of them. Having always been a friend to the aristocratic party, he was involved in a charge of conspiracy against the democracy and withdrew to Chalcis in Euboea. He was allowed to return to Athens after an absence of fifteen years. On his arrival, Dinarchus lodged with one Proxenus, an Athenian, a friend of his, who, however, if the story be true, robbed the old man of his money. Dinarchus brought an action against him, and, for the first time in his life, made his appearance in a court of justice. The charge against Proxenus, which is drawn up with a kind of legal formality, is preserved by Dionysius of Halicarnassus. Of the numerous orations of Dinarchus, only three remain, and these are not entitled to any very high praise. One of them is against Demosthenes, touching the affair of Harpalus. The best MSS. of Dinarchus are the Codex Cripsianus and the Codex Oxoniensis. The extant orations of Dinarchus are found in the usual collections of the Attic orators, especially Baiter and Sauppe's *Oratores Attici;* and an edition by Thalheim (1887); elaborate commentary by Mätzner (1842).

Dindorf. (1) KARL WILHELM. A celebrated Hellenist, son of Gottlieb Immanuel Dindorf, and born January 2d, 1802, at Leipzig, where his father was Professor of Oriental Languages in the University. There the young Dindorf pursued his own studies in classical philology under Gottfried Hermann and C. D. Beck. In 1827, he received a call to the University of Berlin, which he declined, but in the following year accepted the title of Professor Extraordinarius at Leipzig. This he held until 1833, when he resigned it in order to devote himself entirely to research. For fifty years he continued to labour in the line of Greek and especially upon the dramatic poetry of Greece, and his contributions are of the very greatest value to modern scholarship. He died August 1st, 1883.

The most important works of Dindorf's long and productive labours are vols. vii.–xiii. of the great Invernizzi-Beck edition of Aristophanes (1820–34); a separate edition of Aristophanes, with notes and scholia (1835–39); of Aeschylus (1841–51); of Euripides (1834–63); an annotated edition of Sophocles (1832–36); a second volume of scholia to Sophocles, edited by Elmsley (1852); an edition of Demosthenes, with notes and scholia (1846–51); a work on the metres of Aeschylus, Sophocles, Euripides, and Aristophanes (1842); lexicons to Sophocles and Aeschylus (1873–76); a text of Homer (1855–56); the scholia to the *Odyssey* (1855), and to the *Iliad* (1875–77). In collaboration with Hase and his brother, Ludwig Dindorf, he edited the *Thesaurus Graecae Linguae* of Stephanus (1831–65). See Bursian, *Geschichte der class. Philologie* (Munich, 1883), pp. 861–870.

(2) LUDWIG AUGUST, brother of the preceding, born January 3d, 1805, was a classical scholar of some eminence. He collaborated with his brother and C. B. Hase upon the *Thesaurus Graecae Linguae* of Stephanus (9 vols. Paris, 1831–65); and published, independently, critical editions of Xenophon, Diodorus Siculus, Pausanias, Polybius, Dio Cassius, Zonaras, Hesiod, Euripides, and the *Historici Graeci Minores*, besides a work on the chronography of John Malelas, etc. He died September 6th, 1871.

Dindymēnē (Δινδυμηνή). See DINDYMUS.

Dindȳmus (Δίνδυμος) or **Dindȳma.** (1) A mountain in Phrygia on the frontiers of Galatia, near the town Pessinus, sacred to Cybelé, the mother of the gods, who is hence called Dindymené. (2) A mountain in Mysia, near Cyzicus, also sacred to Cybelé. See RHEA.

Dinia. A town of Gallia Narbonensis, and the capital of the Bodiontici. It is now Digne.

Dinocrătes (Δεινοκράτης). A very celebrated Macedonian architect, who offered to cut Mount Athos into a statue of Alexander. (See ATHOS.) That monarch took him to Egypt, and employed him in several works of art. Ptolemy Philadelphus directed him to construct a temple for his queen, Arsinoë, after her death; and the intention was to have the ceiling of lodestone and the statue of iron, in order that the latter might appear to be suspended in the air. The death of the artist himself frustrated the undertaking (Plin. *H. N.* xxxiv. 42). See EPHESUS, p. 599.

Dinostrătus (Δεινόστρατος). A famous mathematician of the Platonic school, the brother of Menechares, and a disciple of Plato. Pursuing the steps of his brother, who amplified the theory of conic sections, Dinostratus is said to have made many mathematical discoveries; but he is particularly distinguished as the inventor of the *quadratrix*, though there is some reason for ascribing the original invention of this curve to Hippias of Elea (Proclus, *Comment. in Eucl.* ii. 4).

Dio. See DION.

Diobŏlon (διώβολον). A small coin of two obols (see DRACHMA), which was given to each Athenian citizen during the festivals to pay for his seat in the theatre, whence the gift was called διωβελία (Xen. *Hell.* i. 7, § 2; Aristot. *Pol.* ii. 7, § 19). In Plautus the adjective *diobolaris* signifies anything very cheap or mean, like "tuppenny" in English.

Diocaesarēa (Διοκαισάρεια) (more anciently SEPPHŌRIS [Σεπφώρις]) in Galilaea was a small place until Herodes Antipas made it the capital of Galilaea, under the name of Diocaesarea.

Dioclĕa (Διοκλέα). A town of Dalmatia, the birthplace, according to some, of the emperor Diocletian (Aurel. Vict. *Epit.* 54).

Diocletian, EDICT OF. An edict published by the emperor Diocletian about A.D. 303, directing those engaged in the sale of provisions not to exceed certain fixed prices in times of scarcity. It is preserved in an inscription in Greek and Latin on the outer wall of the *cella* of a temple at Stratonicea (Eski-hissar) in Caria. It states the price of many varieties of provisions, and these inform us of their relative value at the time. The provisions specified include not only the ordinary food of the people, but also a number of articles of luxury. Thus mention is made of several kinds of honey, of hams, sausages, salt and fresh-water fish, asparagus and beans, and even *pernae Menapicae* (Westphalian hams). At the time when the edict was published the *denarius* was obviously much reduced in value, that coin appearing as the equivalent of a single oyster. The inscription was first copied by Sherard in 1709; it has been elaborately edited by M. Waddington, with new fragments and a commentary, 1864; and by Mommsen in the third volume of the *Corpus Inscriptionum Latinarum.* Portions of the Greek copy and the Latin preamble were found at Plataea in 1888–89 during the explorations of the American School of Classical Archæology. In 1890, during the excavations of the British School of Archæology, several hundred lines of the Greek version of the decree were discovered at Megalopolis, including a list of pigments with their prices.

Diocletianopŏlis (*Διοκλητιανούπολις*). A city of Thrace, so called in honour of Diocletian. Its site is not known. See CELETRUM.

Diocletiānus, GAIUS VALERIUS IOVIUS. A celebrated Roman emperor, born of an obscure family in Dalmatia at the town of Dioclea, from which he derived his first name, which was probably Docles, afterwards lengthened to the more harmonious Greek form of Diocles, and at length, after his accession to the Empire, to the Roman form of Diocletianus. He likewise, on this occasion, assumed the patrician name of Valerius. Some, however, make him to have been born at Salona. His birth-year is also differently given. The common account says A.D. 245, but other statements make him ten years older. He was first a common soldier, and by merit and success gradually rose to rank, serving in Gaul and in Moesia under Probus, and being present at the campaign against the Persians when Carus perished in so mysterious a manner. He commanded the household or imperial body-guard when young Numerianus, the son of Carus, was secretly put to death by Aper, his father-in-law, while travelling in a litter on account of illness, on the return of the army from Persia. The death of Numerianus being discovered, after several days, by the soldiers near Chalcedon, they arrested Aper and proclaimed Diocletian emperor, who, addressing the army from his tribunal in the camp, protested his innocence of the death of Numerianus, and then, upbraiding Aper for the crime, plunged his sword into his body. Diocletian made his solemn entry into Nicomedia in September, A.D. 284, and afterwards chose this town for his favourite residence. Carinus, the other son of Carus, having collected a force to oppose Diocletian, the two armies met at Margum in Moesia, where the soldiers of Carinus had the advantage at first, but Carinus himself having been slain by one of his own officers, both armies joined in acknowledging Diocletian emperor, A.D. 285. Diocletian was generous after his victory, and, contrary to the common practice, there were no executions, proscriptions, or confiscations of property. He even retained most of the officers of Carinus in their places. Diocletian, on assuming the imperial power, found the Empire assailed in various quarters, but his talents and energy soon succeeded in counteracting these evils. In the year 286, he chose his old friend Maximian, a brave, but rude and uncultivated soldier, as his colleague, and it is to the credit of both that the latter continued ever after faithful to Diocletian and willing to follow his advice. Maximian was stationed in Gaul, and on the German frontier, to repel invasion; Diocletian resided chiefly in the East, to watch the Persians, though he appears to have visited Rome in the early part of his reign. After the lapse of a few years Diocletian thought it necessary, in consequence of invasions and revolts in different parts of the Empire, to increase the number of his colleagues. On the 1st of March, 292, or, according to some, 291, he appointed Galerius a Caesar, and Maximian, at the same time, adopted, on his part,

Coin of Diocletian.

Constantius Chlorus. The two Caesars repudiated their respective wives; Galerius married Valeria, Diocletian's daughter, and Constantius married Theodora, daughter of Maximian. The two Caesars remained subordinate to the two Augusti, though each of the four was intrusted with the administration of a part of the Empire. Diocletian kept to himself Asia and Egypt; Maximian had Italy and Africa; Galerius, Thrace and Illyricum; and Constantius, Gaul and Spain. But it was rather an administrative than a political division. At the head of the edicts of each prince were put the names of all four, beginning with that of Diocletian. Diocletian resorted to this arrangement probably as much for reasons of internal as of external policy. By fixing upon three colleagues, one in each of the great divisions of the Empire, each having his army, and all mutually checking one another, Diocletian put a stop to military insolence and anarchy, though another danger remained—that of disputes and wars between the various sharers of the imperial power.

The new Caesars justified Diocletian's expectations. Successful wars were waged in different quarters of the Empire; and though Galerius at first met with a defeat from Narses, king of Persia, yet, in the following year, he gave the Persians a terrible overthrow. Narses sued for peace, which was granted by Diocletian, on condition of the Persians giving up all the territory on the right or western bank of the Tigris. This peace was concluded in 297, and lasted forty years. At the same time Diocletian marched into Egypt against Achillaeus, whom he besieged in Alexandria, which he took after a siege of eight months, when the usurper and his chief adherents were put to death. Diocletian is said to have behaved on this occasion with unusual sternness, several towns of Egypt, among others Busiris and Coptos, being destroyed. For several years after this the Empire enjoyed repose, and Diocletian and his colleagues were chiefly employed in framing laws and administrative regulations and in constructing forts on the frontiers. Diocletian kept a splendid court at Nicomedia, which town he embellished with numerous structures. He, or rather Maximian by his order, caused the magnificent Thermae at Rome to be built, the remains of which still bear Diocletian's name, and which contained, besides the baths, a library, a museum, and other establishments.

In February, 303, Diocletian issued an edict against the Christians, ordering their churches to be razed, their books to be burned, and all Christians to be dismissed from offices civil or military—with other penalties, exclusive, however, of death. Various causes have been assigned for this measure. It is known that Galerius had always been hostile to the Christians, while Diocletian had openly favoured them, and had employed them in his armies and about his person; and Eusebius speaks of the prosperity, security, and protection which they enjoyed under his reign. They had churches in most towns, and one at Nicomedia, in particular, under the very eye of the emperor. Just before the edict was issued, Galerius had repaired to Nicomedia to induce Diocletian to proscribe the Christians. He filled the emperor's mind with reports of conspiracies and seditions, and, aided by the artifices of the heathen priesthood, was at last successful. The barbarities that followed upon the issuing of the edict above referred to are beyond belief. Malicious ingenuity was racked to the utmost to devise tortures for the persecuted followers of Jesus. For the space of ten years did this persecution rage with scarcely mitigated horrors; and such multitudes were massacred in all parts of the Empire that at last the imperial murderers ventured to erect a triumphal column, bearing the barbarously boastful, yet false inscription, that they had extinguished the Christian name and superstition and restored the worship of the gods to its former purity and splendour. This was the last persecution under the Roman Empire.

In November, 303, Diocletian repaired to Rome, where he and Maximian enjoyed the honour of a triumph, followed by festive games. This was the last triumph that Rome saw. The populace of that city complained of the economy of Diocletian on that occasion, and so offended him by their gibes and sarcasms that he left Rome abruptly, in the month of December, in very cold weather. A long illness ensued, which confined him at Nicomedia; and soon after his recovery he was visited by Galerius, who persuaded and almost forced him to abdicate. According to others, however, Diocletian did so spontaneously. Setting off for Salona, in Dalmatia, he built himself, near this place, an extensive palace by the sea-shore, in which he lived for the rest of his life, respected by the other emperors, without cares and without regret. At the same time that Diocletian abdicated at Nicomedia, Maximian, according to an agreement between them, performed a similar ceremony at Milan. Maximian retired to his seat in Lucania; but, not being endowed with the firmness of Diocletian, he tried some time after to recover his former power, and wrote to his old colleague to induce him to do the same. "Were you but to come to Salona," answered Diocletian, "and see the vegetables which I raise in my garden with my own hands, you would no longer talk to me of empire." Diocletian died May 1, 313. See the studies by Preuss (1868) and Mason (1876).

Diodōrus (Διόδωρος). (1) An historian, surnamed SICŬLUS, because born at Agyrium in Sicily, and the contemporary of Iulius Caesar and Augustus. Our principal data for the events of his life are derived from his own work. In early life he travelled into Asia, Africa, and Europe, and on his return established himself at Rome, where he published a general history, in forty books, under the title of Βιβλιοθήκη Ἱστορική, or Historical Library. To this labour he devoted thirty years of his life. The history comprehended a period of 1138 years, besides the time preceding the Trojan War, and was carried down to the end of Caesar's Gallic war. His work was written after the death of Caesar. The first six books were devoted to the fabulous history anterior to the war of Troy, and of these the three former to the antiquities of barbarian States, the three latter to the archæology of the Greeks. But the historian, though treating of the fabulous history of the barbarians in the first three books, enters into an account of their manners and usages, and carries down the history of these nations to a point of time posterior to the Trojan War. Thus, in the first book he gives a sketch of Egyptian history from the reign of Menes to Amasis. In the eleven following books he details the different events which happened between the Trojan War and the death of Alexander the Great; while the remaining twenty-three books contain the history of the world down to the Gallic War and the conquest of Britain. We have only a small part remaining of this vast compilation—namely, the first five books; then from the eleventh to the twentieth, both inclusive; and, finally, fragments of the other books from the sixth to the tenth inclusive, and also of the last twenty. These rescued portions we owe to Eusebius; to John Malalas, Georgius Syncellus, and other writers of the Lower Empire, who have cited them in the course of their own works; but, above all, to the authors of the "Extracts respecting Embassies" and of the "Extracts respecting Virtues and Vices." We are indebted also for a part of them to the patriarch Photius, who has inserted in his *Myriobiblon* extracts from several of the books, from the thirty-first to the thirty-third, and from the thirty-sixth to the thirty-eighth and fortieth. Important additions have also been made from MSS. in the Vatican Library.

A great advantage possessed by Diodorus over most of the ancient historians is his indicating the order of time, though it must be acknowledged at the same time that his chronology offers occasional difficulties and often needs educing. Diodorus, who wrote at Rome, and at a period when the dominion of that city extended over the greater part of the civilized world, arranges his narrative in accordance with the Roman calendar and consular *fasti;* but he frequently adds the names of the Athenian archons who were contemporaneous.

With regard to the historical value of the work itself and the merits of the author, the most varying opinions have been entertained by modern writers. The principal fault of Diodorus seems to have been the too great extent of his work. It was not possible for any man living in the time of Augustus to write an unexceptionable universal history. It is not, then, a matter of surprise that Diodorus, who does not appear to have been a man of superior abilities, should have fallen into a number of particular errors and should have placed too much reliance on authorities sometimes far from trustworthy. Wherever he speaks from his own observation he may, perhaps, generally be relied upon; but when he is compiling from the writings of others he has shown little judgment in the selection. The literary style of Diodorus, though not very pure or elegant, is sufficiently perspicuous and presents but few difficulties, except where the MSS. are defective, as is frequently the case. The best editions of Diodorus are those of Wesseling (1746), L. Dindorf (1867–68), and Bekker (1853–54). (2) A native of Caria, and a disciple of the Megaric School. He was a great adept in that species of verbal combat which prevailed among the philosophers of his sect. It is said that a question was proposed to him in the presence of Ptolemy Soter by Stilpo, one of his fraternity, which he required *time* to answer, and on this account he was ridiculed by Ptolemy and denominated "Chronus" (Χρόνος). Mortified at this defeat, he wrote a book on the question, but nevertheless died of vexation. He is the reputed author of the famous sophism against motion: "If any body be moved, it is moved either in the place where it is or in a place where it is not, for nothing can act or suffer where it is not, and therefore there is no such thing as motion." Diodorus was rewarded for this discovery; for, having dislocated his shoulder, the surgeon who was sent for kept him for some time in torture, while he proved from the philosopher's own mode of reasoning that the bone could not have moved out of its place. (3) A Peripatetic philosopher, with whom the uninterrupted succession of the Peripatetic School terminated. He was a native of Tyre and a pupil of Critolaüs. Mention is often made of him in the selections of Stobaeus and also in the works of Cicero. The sovereign good, according to Diodorus, was to live in a becoming manner, free from toil and care, τὸ ἀμοχθήτως καὶ καλῶς ζῆν, or, *vacare omni molestia cum honestate*, as Cicero expresses it (*Acad.* ii. 42). (4) An orator and epigrammatic poet, a native of Sardis. He was surnamed Zonas (Ζωνᾶς). He fought in Asia and was contemporaneous with Mithridates the Great, against whom he was charged with conspiring. He defended himself successfully. Nine of his epigrams remain. (5) Another native of Sardis, who wrote historical works, odes, and epigrams. Strabo speaks of him as subsequent to the former and a contemporary and friend of his own. We have one of his epigrams remaining.

Diodŏtus (Διόδοτος). A Stoic philosopher, and teacher of Cicero, in whose house he died B.C. 59 (Cic. *Brut.* 90; *Ad Att.* ii. 20; *Tusc.* v. 39).

Diogĕnes (Διογένης). (1) A celebrated Cynic philosopher of Sinopé. His father, Icesias, a banker, was convicted of debasing the public coin, and was obliged to leave the country; or, according to another account, his father and himself were charged with this offence, and the former was thrown into prison, while the son escaped and went to Athens. Here he attached himself, as a disciple, to Antisthenes, who was at the head of the Cynics. Antisthenes at first refused to admit him into his house and even struck him with a stick. Diogenes calmly bore the rebuke and said, "Strike me, Antisthenes, but you will never find a stick sufficiently hard to remove me from your presence, while you speak anything worth hearing." The philosopher was so much pleased with this reply that he at once admitted him among his scholars. Diogenes fully adopted the principles and character of his master. Renouncing every other object of ambition, he determined to distinguish himself by his contempt of riches and honours and by his invectives against luxury. He wore a coarse cloak, carried a wallet and a staff, made the porticoes and other public places his habitation, and depended upon casual contributions for his daily bread. A friend whom he had desired to procure him a cell not executing his order so soon as was expected, he took up his abode in a πίθος, or large vessel, in the Metroum. It is probable, however, that this was only a temporary expression of indignation and contempt, and that he did not make it the settled place of his residence. This famous "tub" is indeed celebrated by Juvenal; it is also ridiculed by Lucian and mentioned by Seneca. But no notice is taken of so singular a circumstance by other ancient writers who have mentioned this philosopher. It cannot be doubted, however, that Diogenes practised the most hardy self-control and the most rigid abstinence—exposing himself to the utmost extremes of heat and cold and living upon the simplest diet, casually supplied by the hand of charity. In his old age, sailing to Aegina, he was taken by pirates and carried to Crete, where he was exposed to sale in the public market. When the auctioneer asked him what he could do, he said, "I can govern men; therefore sell me to one who wants a master." Xeniades, a wealthy Corinthian, happening at that instant to pass by, was struck with the singularity of his reply and purchased him. On their arrival at Corinth, Xeniades gave him his freedom and committed to him the education of his children and the direction of his domestic concerns. Diogenes executed this trust with so much judgment and fidelity that Xeniades used to say that the gods had sent a good genius to his house. During his residence at Corinth, the interview between him and Alexander is said to have taken place. Plutarch relates that Alexander, when at Corinth, receiving the congratulations of all ranks on being appointed to command the army of the Greeks against the Persians, missed Diogenes among the number, with whose character he was not unacquainted. Curious to see one who had given so signal an instance of his haughty independence of spirit, Alexander went in search of him and found him sitting in his tub in the sun. "I am Alexander the Great," said the monarch. "And I am Diogenes the Cynic," replied the philosopher. Alexander then requested that he would inform him what service he could render him. "Stand from between me and the sun," said the Cynic. Alexander, struck with the reply, said to his friends, who were ridiculing the whimsical singularity of the philosopher, "If I were not Alexander, I should wish to be Diogenes." This story is too good to be omitted, but there are several circumstances which in some degree diminish its credibility. It supposes Diogenes to have lived in his tub at Corinth, whereas it is certain that he lived there in the house of Xeniades, and that, if he had ever dwelt in a tub, he left it behind him at Athens. Alexander, moreover, was at this time scarcely twenty years old, and could not call himself Alexander the Great, for he did not receive this title till his Persian and Indian expedition, after which he never returned to Greece; yet the whole transaction represents him as elated with the pride of conquest. Diogenes probably was visited by

Alexander, when the latter held the general assembly of the Greeks at Corinth, and was received by him with rudeness and incivility, which may have given rise to the whole story. The philosopher at this time would have been about seventy years of age.

Various accounts are given concerning the manner and time of his death. It seems most probable that he died at Corinth, of mere decay, in the ninetieth year of his age and in the 114th Olympiad. A column of Parian marble, terminating in the figure of a dog, was raised over his tomb. His fellow-townsmen of Sinopé also erected brazen statues in memory of the philosopher. Diogenes left behind him no system of philosophy. After the example of his school, he was more attentive to practical than to theoretical wisdom. See Hermann, *Zur Geschichte und Kritik des Diogenes* (Heilbronn, 1860); and the article CYNICI.

Diogenes in his πίθος or "Tub." (From a fragment of a Lamp in the British Museum.)

(2) A native of Apollonia in Crete, who was a pupil of Anaximenes and contemporary with Anaxagoras. Schleiermacher, however, affirms, from the internal evidence of the fragments of the two philosophers, that Diogenes preceded Anaxagoras. But Diogenes might have written before Anaxagoras and yet have been his junior, as we know was the case with Empedocles. Diogenes followed Anaximenes in making air the primal element of all things; but he carried his views further, and regarded the universe as issuing from an intelligent principle, by which it was at once vivified and ordered, a rational as well as sensitive soul, but still without recognizing any distinction between matter and mind. Diogenes wrote several books on Cosmology (Περὶ Φύσεως).

(3) LAËRTIUS, so called from his native city, Laërté in Cilicia. He wrote the lives of the philosophers (Φιλόσοφοι Βίοι), in ten books, which are still extant. The period when he lived is not exactly known, but it is supposed to have been during the reigns of Septimius Severus and Caracalla. Diogenes is thought to have belonged to the Epicurean School. He divides all the Greek philosophers into two classes: those of the Ionic and those of the Italic school. He derives the first from Anaximander, the second from Pythagoras. After Socrates, he divides the Ionian philosophers into three branches: (*a*) Plato and the Academics, down to Clitomachus; (*b*) the Cynics, down to Chrysippus; (*c*) Aristotle and Theophrastus. The series of Italic philosophers consists, after Pythagoras, of the following: Telanges, Xenophanes, Parmenides, Zeno of Elea, Leucippus, Democritus, and others down to Epicurus. The first seven books are devoted to the Ionic philosophers; the last three treat of the Italic school.

The work of Diogenes is a crude contribution towards the history of philosophy. It contains a brief account of the lives, doctrines, and sayings of most persons who have been called philosophers; and though the author is evidently a most unfit person for the task which he imposed upon himself, and has shown very little judgment and discrimination in the execution of it, yet the book is extremely useful as a collection of facts, which we could not have learned from any other quarter, and is entertaining as a sort of *pot-pourri* on the subject. The article on Epicurus is valuable, as containing some original letters of that philosopher, which comprise a fairly satisfactory epitome of the Epicurean doctrines and are very useful to the readers of Lucretius. The best editions of Diogenes are those of Hübner (Leipzig, 1828–31) and Cobet (Paris, 1850).

Diogeniānus (Διογενειανός). A Greek grammarian of Heraclea. About the middle of the second century A.D. he made extracts, in five books, from the great collection of glosses compiled about a century before by Pamphilus. These extracts form the foundation of the lexicon of Hesychius (q. v.). A collection of proverbs made by him is preserved in an abridged form. See LEXICON.

Diomedēae Insŭlae (Διομήδειαι νῆσοι). Five small islands in the Adriatic Sea, north of the promontory Garganum in Apulia, named after Diomedes. (See DIOMEDES.) The largest of these, called Diomedea Insula or Trimerus (Tremiti), was the place whither Iulia, the daughter of Augustus, was exiled (Tac. *Ann.* iv. 71).

Diomēdes (Διομήδης). (1) The son of Tydeus and Deïpylé. He was king of Aetolia, and one of the bravest of the Grecian chiefs in the Trojan War, ranking next to Achilles and Aiax. Homer represents him as one of the favourites of Athené. Among his exploits, it is recorded of him that he engaged in single combat with Hector and Aeneas; that he wounded Ares, Aeneas, and Aphrodité; and that, in concert with Odysseus, he carried off the horses of Rhesus and the palladium, and secured the arrows of Philoctetes. Diomedes was deprived of the affection of his wife Aegialé through the wrath and vengeance of Aphrodité, by whose influence, during his absence at the war, she had become attached to Cyllabarus, the son of Sthenelus. Diomedes was so afflicted at the estrangement of Aegialé that he abandoned Greece and settled at the head of a colony in Magna Graecia, where he founded a city, to which he gave the name of Argyripa, and married a daughter of Daunus, prince of the country. In the progress of his voyage to Italy, Diomedes was shipwrecked on that part of the Libyan coast which was under the sway of Lycus, who seized and confined him. He was, however, liberated by Callirrhoé, the tyrant's daughter, who became so fond of him that upon his quitting the African shores she put herself to death. Diomedes, according to one account, died in Italy at a very advanced age; while another legend makes him to have been slain by his father-in-law Daunus. His companions were so much afflicted by his death that they were changed into birds. Vergil, however, makes this transformation earlier in date, and to have taken place during the lifetime of Diomedes (*Aen.* xi. 272). He seems to have followed the tradition recorded by Ovid (*Met.* xiv 457), that Agnon, one of Diomedes's companions in his voyage from Troy, insulted Aphrodité with contemptuous language, and that the goddess, in revenge, transformed not only Agnon, but many others of Diomedes's followers into birds. (See DIOMEDEAE INSULAE.) (2) A king of the Bistones, in Thrace, son of Ares and Cyrené. His mares fed on human flesh. Heracles sailed to this quarter, having been ordered, as his eighth labour, to bring these mares to Mycenae. The hero overcame the grooms of Diomedes and led the mares to the sea. The Bistones pursued with arms. Heracles, leaving the mares in charge of Abderus, one of his companions, went to engage the foe. Meantime the mares tore their keeper to pieces; and the hero, having defeated the Bistones and slain Diomedes, built a city by the tomb of Abderus, which he called Abdera after him. Heracles brought the mares to Eurystheus, who turned them loose, and they strayed to Mount Olympus, where they were destroyed by the wild beasts (Apollod. ii. 5, 8). Another account makes Heracles to have given Diomedes to be devoured by his own mares, and Eurystheus to have consecrated them to Heré (Diod. Sic. iv. 15). (3) A Roman grammarian of the fourth century A.D., whose work, entitled *Ars Grammatica*, has come down to us in three books. It is taken from the same sources as the contemporary work by Charisius (q. v.), and is chiefly valuable for the notices on literary history contained in the third book and taken from the *De Poetis* of Suetonius. The best text of Diomedes is that in Keil, *Grammatici Latini* (i. 298). On his Latinity see the treatise of Paucker (Berlin, 1883).

Diomosia (διωμοσία). See ANTOMOSIA.

Dion (Δίων). (1) An inhabitant of Syracuse, who became a disciple of Plato, invited to the court of Syracuse by the elder Dionysius. He was nearly connected with Dionysius by having married his daughter, and because his sister was one of his wives; and he was also much esteemed by him, so as to be employed on several embassies. At the accession of the younger Dionysius, Plato was again, at Dion's request, invited to Syracuse. (See PLATO.) In order, however, to counteract his influence, the courtiers obtained the recall of Philistus, a man notorious for his adherence to arbitrary principles. This faction determined to supplant Dion, and availed themselves of a real or supposititious letter to fix on him the charge of treason. Dion, precluded from defence, was transported to Italy, and from thence proceeded to Greece, where he was received with great honour. Dionysius became jealous of his popularity in Greece, especially at Athens, stopped his remittances, confiscated his estates, and compelled his wife, who had been left at Syracuse as an hostage, to marry another person. Dion, incensed at this treatment, determined to expel the tyrant. Plato resisted his intentions; but, encouraged by other friends, he assembled a body of troops, and with a small force sailed to Sicily, took advantage of the absence of Dionysius in Italy, and freed the people from his control. Dionysius returned; but, after some conflicts, was compelled to escape to Italy. The austere and philosophic manners of Dion, however, soon lost him the favour of his countrymen, and he was supplanted by Heraclides, a Syracusan exile, and obliged to make his retreat to Leontini. He afterwards regained the ascendency and caused Heraclides to be assassinated, which robbed him ever after of his peace of mind. An Athenian, an intimate friend, formed a conspiracy against his life, and Dion was assassinated in the fifty-fifth year of his age, B.C. 354 (Diod. Sic. xvi. 6 foll.; Plut. *Dion.*; Corn. Nep. *Dion*).

(2) DIO CASSIUS COCCEIĀNUS, son of Cassius Apronianus, a Roman senator, born A.D. 155, at Nicaea, in Bithynia. His true name was Cassius, but he assumed the other two names, as being descended on the mother's side from Dion Chrysostom. Thus, though he was on his mother's side of Greek descent, and though, in his writings, he adopted the prevailing language—Greek—of his native province, he must be considered as a Roman. Dio Cassius passed the greater part of his life in public employments. He was a senator under Commodus and governor of Smyrna after the death of Septimius Severus; and afterwards consul, as also proconsul in Africa and Pannonia. Alexander Severus entertained the highest esteem for him, and made him consul for the second time, with himself, though the Praetorian Guards, irritated against him on account of his severity, had demanded his life. When advanced in years (about A.D. 229), he returned to his native country. Dio published a Roman history, in eighty books, the fruit of his researches and labours for the space of twenty-two years. It embraced a period of 983 years, extending from the arrival of Aeneas in Italy, and the subsequent founding of Rome, to A.D. 229. Down to the time of Iulius Caesar, he only gives a summary of events; after this, he enters somewhat more into details; and from the time of Commodus he is very circumstantial in relating what passed under his own eyes. We have fragments remaining of the first thirty-six books: but there is a considerable portion of the thirty-fifth book, on the war of Lucullus against Mithridates, and of the thirty-sixth, on the war with the pirates and the expedition of Pompey against the king of Pontus. The books that follow, to the fifty-fourth inclusive, are nearly all entire: they comprehend a period from B.C. 65 to B.C. 12, or from the eastern campaign of Pompey and the death of Mithridates to the death of Agrippa. The fifty-fifth book has a considerable gap in it. The fifty-sixth to the sixtieth, both included, which comprehend the period from A.D. 9 to A.D. 54, are complete, and contain the events from the defeat of Varus in Germany to the death of Claudius. Of the following twenty books we have only fragments and the meagre abridgment of Xiphilinus. The eightieth or last book comprehends the period from A.D. 222 to A.D. 229, in the reign of Alexander Severus. The abridgment of Xiphilinus, as now extant, commences with the thirty-fifth and continues to the end of the eightieth book. It is a very indifferent performance, and was made by order of the emperor Michael VII., Parapinaces. The abbreviator, Xiphilinus, was a monk of the eleventh century.

The fragments of the first thirty-six books, as now collected, are of four kinds: (*a*) FRAGMENTA VALESIĀNA, such as were dispersed throughout various writers, scholiasts, grammarians, lexicographers, etc., and were collected by Henri de Valois. (*b*) FRAGMENTA PEIRESCIĀNA, comprising large extracts, found in the section entitled "Of Virtues and Vices," in the great collection or portative library compiled by order of Constantine VII., Porphyrogenitus. The manuscript of this belonged to Peiresc. (*c*) The fragments of the first thirty-four books, preserved in the second section of the same work of Constantine's, entitled "Of Embassies." These are known under the name of FRAGMENTA URSINIĀNA, because the manuscript containing them was found in Sicily by Fulvio Orsini. (*d*) EXCERPTA VATICĀNA, by Mai, which contain fragments of books i.–xxxv. and lxi.–lxxx. To these are added the fragments of an unknown continuator of Dio, which go down to the time of Constantine. Other fragments from Dio belonging chiefly to the first thirty-five books were found by Mai in two Vatican MSS., which contain a collection made by Maximus Planudes. The annals of Zonaras also contain numerous extracts from Dion.

Dio has taken Thucydides for his model; but the imitator is comparable with his original neither in arrangement and the distribution of materials nor in soundness of view and just and accurate reasoning. His style is generally clear, where there appears to be no corruption of the text, though full of Latinisms. His diligence is unquestionable, and, from his opportunities, he was well acquainted with the circumstances of the Empire during the period for which he is a contemporary authority; and, indeed, we may assign a high value to his history of the whole period from the time of Augustus to his own age. Nor is his work without value for the earlier periods of Roman history, in which, though he has fallen into errors, like all the Greek and Roman writers who have handled the same obscure subject, he still enables us to correct some erroneous statements of Livy and Dionysius. The best editions are those of Fabricius, completed by Reimar, 2 vols. (Hamb. 1751); of Sturz, 8 vols. (Leipzig, 1824–25); of Bekker (1849); and especially of L. Dindorf (revised by Melber, 1890 foll.). The small Tauchnitz edition, 4 vols. 16mo, contains all the fragments.

(3) Surnamed CHRYSOSTŎMUS, or the Golden-mouthed, on account of the beauty of his style, was a native of Prusa in Bithynia, born about A.D. 50. He was a sophist and Stoic. Being in Egypt when Vespasian, who had been proclaimed emperor by his own army, came there, he was consulted by that prince on the proper course to be adopted under the circumstances. Dion had the candour to advise him to restore the Republic. Afterwards he resided for years at Rome, till, one of his friends having engaged in a conspiracy against Domitian, Dion, fearing for himself, fled to what is now Moldavia, where he remained till the tyrant's death, labouring for his subsistence with his own hands. Domitian having been assassinated, the legions quartered on the Danube were about to revolt, when Dion got upon an altar and harangued them so effectually that they submitted to the decision of the Senate. Dion was in high favour with Nerva and Trajan, and when the latter triumphed after his Dacian victories the orator sat in the emperor's car in the procession. He returned to Bithynia, where he spent the remainder of his life. Accusations of peculation and treason were brought against him, but rejected as frivolous. He died at an advanced age, but it is not known in what year. We have eighty orations attributed to him, which are very neatly written in pure Attic Greek, but are not of much intrinsic value. The best editions are those of Reiske, 2 vols. (Leipzig, 1784); Emper (1844); and L. Dindorf (1857).

Dionaea (*Διώναια*). See DIONÉ.

Diōné (*Διώνη*). A female Titan, loved by Zeus, by whom she became the mother of Aphrodité, who is hence called Dionaea and sometimes even Dioné. Hence Caesar is called Dionaeus Caesar, because he claimed descent from Venus (Aphrodité).

Dionysia (*τὰ Διονύσια*). A celebration in honour of Dionysus (q. v.), which was held in Athens in a special series of festivals, namely:

(1) The OSCHOPHORIA, supposed to have been instituted by Theseus on his return from Crete. This was celebrated in the month of Pyanepsion (October to November), when the grapes were ripe. It was so called from the shoots of vine (*ὄσχοι*) with grapes on them, which were borne in a race from the temple of Dionysus in Limnae, a southern suburb of Athens, to the sanctuary of Athené Sciras, in the harbour town of Phalerum. The bearers and runners were twenty youths (*ἔφηβοι*) of noble descent whose parents were still living, two being chosen from each of the ten tribes. The victor received a goblet containing a drink made of wine, cheese, meal, and honey, and an honorary place in the procession which followed the race. This procession, in which a chorus of singers was preceded by two youths in woman's clothing, marched from the temple of Athené to that of Dionysus. The festival was concluded by a sacrifice and a banquet.

(2) The SMALLER (*τὰ μικρά*), or RUSTIC DIONYSIA. This feast was held in the month of Poseideon (December to January), at the first tasting of the new wine. It was celebrated, with much rude merriment, throughout the various country districts. The members of the different tribes first went in solemn processions to the altar of the god, on which a goat was offered in sacrifice. The sacrifice was followed by feasting and revelry, with abundance of jesting and mockery and dramatic improvisations. Out of these were developed the elements of the regular drama (see DRAMA), for in the more prosperous villages, pieces—in most cases the same as had been played at the urban Dionysia—were performed by itinerant troupes of actors. The festival lasted some days, one of its chief features being the Ascoliasmus, or bag-dance. The point of this was to dance on one leg, without falling, upon oiled bags of inflated leather. (See ASCŎLIA.) The Ἀλῷα, Harvest-home (or Feast of Threshing-floors), was celebrated at Athens and in the country in the same month to Demeter and Persephoné in common.

(3) The LENAEA (*Λήναια*), or Feast of Vats. This was held at Athens in the month of Gamelion (January to February), at the Lenaeum, the oldest and most venerable sanctuary of Dionysus in the city. After a great banquet, for which the meat was provided at the public expense, the citizens went in procession through the city, with the usual jesting and mockery, to attend the representation of the tragedies and comedies at the theatre.

(4) The ANTHESTERIA. Celebrated for three days in Anthesterion (February to March). On the first day (*Πιθοιγία*, or opening of casks) the casks were first opened, and masters and servants alike tasted the new wine. On the second (*Χόες*, or Feast of Beakers), a public banquet was held, at which a beaker of new wine was set by each guest. This was drunk with enthusiasm, to the sound of trumpets. The most important ceremony, however, was the marriage of the Basilissa, or wife of the Archon Basileus, with Dionysus, the Basilissa being re-

garded as representing the country. The ceremony took place in the older of the two temples in the Lenaeum, which was never opened except on this occasion. The last day was called Χύτροι, or the Feast of Pots, because on this day they made offerings of cooked pulse in pots to Hermes, as guide of the dead, and to the souls of the departed, especially those who had perished in the flood of Deucalion.

(5) The GREAT URBAN DIONYSIA (τὰ μέγαλα). This festival was held at Athens for six days in the month of Elaphebolion (March to April) with great splendour, and attended by multitudes from the surrounding country and other parts of Greece. A solemn procession was formed, representing a train of Dionysiac revellers. Choruses of boys sang dithyrambs, and an old wooden statue of Dionysus, worshipped as the liberator of the land from the bondage of winter, was borne from the Lenaeum to a small temple in the neighbourhood of the Acropolis and back again. The glory of this festival was the performance of the new tragedies, comedies, and satyric dramas, which took place, with lavish expenditure, on three consecutive days. In consequence of the immense number of citizens and strangers assembled, it was found convenient to take one of these six days for conferring public distinctions on meritorious persons, as in the case of the presentation of the golden crown to Demosthenes.

The Dionysia were celebrated at Rome under the name of BACCHANALIA. The circumstances of their introduction are given in detail by Livy, (xxxix. 8–19). According to his account, a Greek priest brought into Etruria the secret nightly celebration of this worship. It was not only accompanied by all manner of licentious excesses, but was also made the occasion for planning the most revolting crimes—perjury, forgery, false accusations, poisoning, and assassination. From Etruria the contagion spread to Rome. According to Livy, at first the rites were comparatively innocent. Women only were initiated, and that by day, three times in the year, and the priesthood was held by matrons in turn. It is quite possible that in this statement Livy has in view the worship of Stimula or Simila, an early Italian deity, afterwards identified with Semelé, whence Ovid (*Fast.* vi. 503–515) regards her rites as of a Bacchanalian character. Possibly Vergil is thinking of the same when (*Aen.* vii. 385) he speaks of the Bacchic rites as existing in Italy in the time of Aeneas. In any case it is hardly conceivable that the corrupt Etruscan cult should have so much changed its character in passing into Rome as Livy's account would require us to believe. He goes on to tell how a certain Pacullia Annia, a Campanian priestess, claiming to be acting under the inspiration of the gods, changed the whole character of the worship. She was the first to admit men, by initiating her own sons; she altered the time of celebration from the day to the night, and held initiations five times every month instead of three times a year. The promiscuous admission of men and women and the license of night opened the way to all manner of debauchery and crime. The most horrible immoralities were practised, the wildest frenzy indulged in. Men flung themselves about as if possessed, and uttered frantic prophecies; women dressed as Bacchanals, with dishevelled locks, ran down to the Tiber and plunged into the water torches which, composed of a mixture of sulphur and lime, were not extinguished in the waves. The initiated were a vast number, including many of high birth, both men and women. To secure the complete subjugation of the votaries a rule was made that none should be admitted who were not under twenty years of age, a time at which the judgment is weak and the passions strong. For some time, although the existence of these rites was generally known, not only by report, but also by the clanging of cymbals and the howlings of the devotees by night, their real nature was not suspected. But in B.C. 186, the lewd and criminal character of the meetings was brought to the knowledge of the consuls. P. Aebutius, the orphan of a Roman knight, had been left by the death of his guardians to the charge of his mother Duronia and his stepfather Sempronius Rutilus. The latter had embezzled his property, and in order to escape punishment desired either to make away with the youth or to get him wholly into his power. Duronia, who was entirely devoted to her husband, determined to avail herself of the Bacchanalia for the corruption or destruction of her son. She informed him that at a time when he was ill she had vowed that he should be initiated into the Bacchic rites if he recovered, and that now was the time to discharge the vow. Aebutius, taking the matter lightly, mentioned it to a freedwoman, Hispala Fecenia, with whom he had a *liaison;* but she, in the utmost terror and distress, warned him of the dangers that he was incurring—she, when still a slave, had accompanied her mistress to the orgies, and had seen the vile practices of the votaries. Aebutius, returning to his mother, refused to be initiated, without disclosing his reasons. She, in a fury, drove him from the house. He took refuge with his father's sister, and at her advice laid the whole facts of the case before the consuls. Hispala was induced by them to confess all that she knew. The Senate was consulted and full powers given to the consuls to investigate the matter. Prompt measures were taken to secure evidence and to prevent the escape of the guilty. The inquiry led to the belief that more than 7000 men and women were implicated in the affair. Those who were merely initiated, and had taken the oath binding them to every kind of crime and lewdness, were punished with imprisonment; those against whom actual guilt was found—and these, we are told, were the majority—received capital punishment. The women for the most part were handed over to their relations, or to those who were responsible for them, for private execution; the rest were put to death in public.

One of the most ancient and precious records of the old Latin language preserved to us is the bronze tablet, commonly called the SENĀTUS CONSULTUM DE BACCHANALĬBUS, containing the letter in which the consuls communicated to the magistrates *in agro Teurano* (Tirioli, in the country of the Bruttii) part (as Mommsen thinks) of the decree of the Senate passed on this occasion (cf. Mommsen, *C. I. L.* i. 196; Ritschl, *P. L. M. E.* tab. xviii.; Allen's *Early Latin*, pp. 28–31 [Boston, 1880]; and Cortese, *Latini Sermonis Vetustioris Exempla*, p. 9 [Turin, 1892]). Doubtless it is only a specimen of many which *mutatis mutandis* were sent throughout Italy. The Bacchanalia are rigidly prohibited: if any one, Roman, Latin, or ally, considers himself under a religious obligation *bacanal habere*, he can only do so by obtaining permission from the *praetor urbanus*, confirmed by a vote of the Senate in which not less than one hundred have taken part. No priest, president, or common purse is allowed, nor any kind of common vow. Not more than two men or three women (five in all) may celebrate the rites, except by special permission. These regulations were carried out with unflinching rigour, apparently not without the use of military force (Cic. *De Leg.* ii. 15, 37); but it was some years before the Bacchanalian rites were completely extinguished in southern Italy (Liv. xxxix. 41, xl. 19). The Liberalia (q. v.) were of an entirely different character. The bronze tablet mentioned above is now preserved at Vienna.

Dionysiăca (Διονυσιακά). An epic poem, in forty-eight books, by the Christian Greek poet Nonnus, of Panopolis in Egypt, during the fifth century A.D. See NONNUS.

Dionysius (Διονύσιος). (1) THE ELDER, a celebrated tyrant of Syracuse, raised to that high rank from the station of a simple citizen, was born in that city, B.C. 430. He was son-in-law to Hermocrates, who, having been banished by an adverse party, attempted to return by force of arms and was killed in the action. Dionysius was dangerously wounded, but he recovered and was afterwards recalled. In time he caused himself to be nominated one of the generals, and, under pretence of raising a force sufficient to resist the Carthaginians, obtained a decree for recalling all the exiles, to whom he gave arms. Being sent to the relief of Gela, then besieged by the Carthaginians, he effected nothing against the enemy, pretending that he was not seconded by the other commanders; and his friends suggested that, in order to save the State, the supreme power ought to be confided to one man, reminding the people of the times of Gelon, who had defeated the Carthaginians. The General Assembly therefore proclaimed Dionysius supreme chief of the Republic about B.C. 405, when he was twenty-five years of age. He increased the pay of the soldiers, enlisted new ones, and, under pretence of a conspiracy against his person, formed a guard of mercenaries. He then proceeded to the relief of Gela, but failed in the attack on the Carthaginian camp; he, however, penetrated into the town, the inhabitants of which he advised to leave it quietly in the night under the escort of his troops. On his retreat he persuaded those of Camarina to do the same. This raised suspicion among his troops, and a party of horsemen, riding on before the rest, raised, on their arrival at Syracuse, an insurrection against Dionysius, plundered his house, and treated his wife so cruelly that she died in consequence. Dionysius, with a chosen body, followed close after, set fire to the gate of Acradina, forced his way into the city, put to death the leaders of the revolt, and remained undisputed possessor of the supreme power. The Carthaginians, being afflicted by a pestilence, made proposals of peace, which were accepted by Dionysius, and he then applied himself to fortifying Syracuse, and especially the island of Ortygia, which he made his stronghold, and which he peopled entirely with his trusty partisans and mercenaries, by the aid of whom he put down several revolts. After reducing the towns of Leontini, Catana, and Naxus, he engaged in a new war with Carthage, in which he met with the most brilliant success, making himself master of numerous towns in Sicily, and becoming eventually feared both in Italy and Sicily. In order to raise money, he allied himself with the Illyrians, and proposed to them the joint plunder of the temple of Delphi; the enterprise, however, failed. He then plundered several temples, such as that of Persephonē at Locri; and as he sailed back with the plunder, with a fair wind, he, being a humourist in his way, observed to his friends, "You see how the immortal gods favour sacrilege." Having carried off a golden mantle from a statue of Zeus, consecrated by Gelon out of the spoils of the Carthaginians, he replaced it by a woollen garment, saying that this was better suited to the vicissitudes of the seasons. He also took away a golden beard from Aesculapius, observing that it was not becoming for the son of a beardless father (Apollo) to make a display of his own beard. He likewise appropriated to himself the silver tables and golden vases and crowns in the temples, saying that he would make use of the bounty of the gods (Cic. *N. D.* iii. 34). He made a descent with a fleet on the coast of Etruria, and plundered the temple at Caerē or Agylla of 1000 talents. With these resources he was preparing himself for a new expedition to Italy, when a fresh Carthaginian armament landed in Sicily, B.C. 383, and defeated Dionysius, whose brother Leptines fell in the battle. A peace followed, of which Carthage dictated the conditions.

This peace lasted fourteen years, during which Dionysius remained the undisturbed ruler of Syracuse and one half of Sicily, with part of southern Italy. He sent colonies to the coasts of the Adriatic, and his fleets navigated both seas. Twice he sent assistance to his old ally, Sparta: once against the Athenians, B.C. 374, and again in 369 after the battle of Leuctra, when the Spartans were hard pressed by Epaminondas. Meantime the court of Dionysius was frequented by many distinguished men, philosophers and poets. Plato is said to have been among the former, being invited by Dion (q. v.), the brother-in-law of Dionysius; but the philosopher's declamations against tyranny led to his being sent away from Syracuse. The poets fared little better, as Dionysius himself aspired to poetical fame, for which, however, he was not so well qualified as for political success. Those who did not praise his verses were in danger of being led to prison. Dionysius twice sent some of his poems to be recited at the Olympic Games, but they were hissed by the assembly. He was more successful at Athens. A tragedy of his obtained the prize, and the news of his success almost turned his brain. He had just concluded a fresh truce with the Carthaginians, after having made an unsuccessful attack on Lilybaeum, at the expiration of the fourteen years' peace; and he now gave himself up to rejoicings and feastings for his poetical triumph. In a debauch with his friends he ate and drank so intemperately that he fell senseless, and soon after died, B.C. 367, in the sixty-third year of his age, having been tyrant of Syracuse for thirty-eight years. Dionysius, his elder son by Doris, succeeded him in the sovereignty.

Dionysius was a clever statesman and generally successful in his undertakings. He did much to strengthen and extend the power of Syracuse, and it was probably owing to him that all Sicily did not fall into the hands of the Carthaginians. He was unscrupulous, rapacious, and vindictive; but several of the stories related of his cruelty and suspicious temper appear improbable, or at least exaggerated. An account of the famous prison, or "Ear of Dionysius," will be found under the title LAUTUMIAE.

(2) The second of the name, styled THE YOUNGER, was son of Dionysius I. by Doris. His father, whom he succeeded, had left the State in a prosperous condition, but young Dionysius had neither his abilities nor his prudence and experience. He followed at first the advice of Dion, who, although a republican in principle, had remained faithful to his father, and who now endeavoured to direct the inexperienced son for the good of his country. For this purpose Dion invited his friend Plato to Syracuse, about B.C. 364. Dionysius received the philosopher with great respect, and, in deference to his advice, reformed for a while his loose habits and the manners of his court. But a faction, headed by Philistus, who had always been a supporter of the tyranny of the elder Dionysius, succeeded in prejudicing the son against both Dion and Plato. Dion was exiled, under pretence that he had written privately to the Senate of Carthage for the purpose of concluding a peace. Plato urgently demanded of Dionysius the recall of Dion, and not being able to obtain it, he left Syracuse, after which Dionysius gave himself up to debauchery without restraint. Dion, meanwhile, was travelling through Greece, where his character gained him numerous friends. Dionysius, moved by jealousy, confiscated his property and obliged his wife to marry another. Upon this, Dion collected a small force at Zacynthus, with which he sailed for Sicily and entered Syracuse without resistance. Dionysius retired to the citadel in Ortygia, and after some resistance, in which Philistus, his best supporter, was taken prisoner and put to death, he quitted Syracuse by sea and retired to Locri, the country of his mother, where he had connections and friends. Dion having been treacherously murdered, several tyrants succeeded each other in Syracuse, until Dionysius himself came and retook it about B.C. 346. Instead, however, of profiting by his ten years' exile, he had grown worse. Having, during the interval of his absence from Syracuse, usurped the supreme power in Locri, he had committed many atrocities, had put to death several citizens and abused their wives and daughters. Upon his return to Syracuse, his cruelty and profligacy drove away a great number of people, who emigrated to various parts of Italy and Greece, while others joined Hicetas, tyrant of Leontini and a former friend of Dion. The latter sent messengers to Corinth to request assistance against Dionysius. The Corinthians appointed Timoleon leader of the expedition. This commander landed in Sicily, B.C. 344, entered Syracuse, and soon after obliged Dionysius to surrender. Dionysius was sent to Corinth, where he spent the remainder of his life in the company of actors and low women. Some say that at one time he kept a school. Several repartees are related of him, in answer to those who taunted him upon his altered fortunes, which are not destitute of wit or wisdom (Plut. *Dion;* Diod. Sic. xvi. 5 foll.).

(3) DIONYSIUS THRAX, a celebrated Greek grammarian, a native of Byzantium, or perhaps of Alexandria (Suidas). Coming to Rome about B.C. 80, he engaged in teaching rhetoric and grammar. Of numerous manuals, commentaries, etc., that he published, one entitled Τέχνη Γραμματική has come down to us, and is of very great importance, as it became the basis for all subsequent grammars, and for many centuries was a standard text-book, either in the original or in Latin translations. From it, through the Latin equivalents, came the technical terms of modern grammar, such as "case" (*casus*, πτῶσις), "plural" (*pluralis*, πληθυντικός), "singular" (*singularis*, ἑνικός), "nominative" (*nominativus*, ὀνομαστική), etc. In the fourth century the book was translated into Armenian, and this version, which contains five more chapters than the Greek MSS., has given a definitive text of the whole. It is to be found in Bekker's *Anecdota Graeca* (Berlin, 1821), but especially in the recent edition by Uhlig (Leipzig, 1884). A French translation is given in Cirbied, *Mémoires et Dissertations sur les Antiquités Nationales et Étrangères* (Paris, 1824). On Dionysius see Gräfenhan, *Geschichte d. Class. Phil.* i. p. 402 foll. (Bonn, 1850); Lersch, *Sprachphilosophie der Alten*, i. p. 64 foll. (Leipzig, 1841); Steinthal, *Geschichte der Sprachwissenschaft*, 2d ed. (Berlin, 1891); Sayce, *Science of Language*, Introduction; Hübschmann, *Casuslehre*, pp. 15 foll.; Suidas, s. v. Διονύσιος; and the article GRAMMATICA.

(4) HALICARNASSENSIS or HALICARNASSEUS, an historian and critic, born at Halicarnassus in the first century B.C. We know nothing of his history beyond what he has told us himself. He states that he came to Italy at the termination of the civil war between Augustus and Antony (B.C. 29), and that he spent the following two-and-twenty years at Rome in learning the Latin language and in collecting materials for his history. He died at Rome, B.C. 7. The principal work of Dionysius is his work on Roman antiquities (Ῥωμαϊκὴ Ἀρχαιολογία), which commenced with the early history of the people of Italy and terminated with the beginning of the First Punic War, B.C. 265. It originally consisted of twenty books, of which the first ten remain entire. The eleventh breaks off in the year B.C. 312, but several fragments of the latter half of the history are preserved in the collection of Constantine Porphyrogenitus, and to these a valuable addition was made in 1816, by Mai, from an old MS. Besides, the first three books of Appian were founded entirely upon Dionysius, and Plutarch's biography of Camillus must also be considered as a compilation mostly taken from the *Antiquitates Romanae*, so that perhaps, upon the whole, we have not lost much of his work. The intention of the author in writing his history was to give the Greeks a more accurate and favourable idea than they had hitherto entertained of the Roman people and its civilization, for it had always fretted the Easterns to have been conquered by a race of mere "barbarians." The work is founded upon a very careful and thorough study of authorities, and is one of our chief sources of information upon ancient Roman history in its internal and external development. Good editions of the *Antiquitates* are those of Reiske, 6 vols. (Leipzig, 1774–76), Schwartz (Leipzig, 1877), and Jacoby 2 vols. (1885–88). The first edition in the original Greek was that of R. Stephanus (Paris, 1546).

Dionysius also wrote a treatise on rhetoric (Τέχνη Ῥητορική); criticisms (Τῶν Ἀρχαίων Κρίσις) on the style of Thucydides, Lysias, Isocrates, Isaeus, Dinarchus, Plato, and Demosthenes; a treatise on the arrangement of words (Περὶ Συνθέσεως Ὀνομάτων); and some other short essays. The first complete edition of the entire works of Dionysius was that of Sylburg (Frankfort, 1586; reprinted at Leipzig, 1691). More recent editors of the rhetorical works are Gros (Paris, 1826) and Westermann.

(5) The author of a Greek poem in 1186 hexameters, entitled Τῆς Γῆς Οἰκουμένης Περιήγησις, "A Description of the Habitable World." It is not clearly ascertained where he was born. The probability is, however, that he was a native of Charax in Susiana. It is uncertain, also, when he flourished; he belonged, however, according to the general opinion, to the latter part of the third or the beginning of the fourth century A.D. He derived from his poem the surname of Periegetes. This production of his has little merit as a work of imagination and but feeble interest for the geographer. The commentary, however, of Eustathius upon it possesses some value from the miscellaneous information which is scattered throughout. There are two Latin translations of the poem—one by Rufus Festus Avienus (q. v.) and the other by Priscianus (q. v.). The last and best edition of the *Periegesis* is that of Bernhardy (Leipzig, 1828), in the first volume of his *Geographi Graeci Minores*.

(6) A Christian writer, called AREOPAGĪTA, from his having been a member of the court of Areopagus at Athens. He was converted to Christianity by St. Paul's preaching (Acts, xvii. 34). He is reported to have been the first bishop of Athens, being appointed to that office by the apostle Paul, and to have suffered martyrdom under Domitian. His fundamental thought is the absolute transcendence of God. During the Middle Ages a great number of writings were circulated under his name, and were collected together and printed at Cologne in 1536, and subsequently at Antwerp in 1634 and at Paris in 1646. They have now, for a long time, been deemed spurious, although scholars differ in respect to the times and authors of the fabrication. The most probable reasoning, however, fixes them at the end of the fourth century. The standard text is that of Corderius, reprinted by the Abbé Migne. Trans. by Parker (1894). See Harnack's *Dogmengeschichte*, vol. ii., and the studies by Niemeyer (1869) and Schneider (1884).

(7) Surnamed EXIGUUS, or "the Little," on account of the smallness of his stature, a Scythian monk of the sixth century, who became an abbot at Rome. Cassiodorus, who was his intimate friend, speaks highly of his learning and character. At the request of Stephen, bishop of Salona, he drew up a body of canons entitled *Collectio sive Codex Canonum Ecclesiasticorum*, etc., translated from the Greek, containing the first fifty apostolical canons, as they are called, with those of the councils of Nice, Constantinople, Chalcedon, Sardis, and including 138 canons of certain African councils. He afterwards drew up a collection of the decretals. To him some ascribe the mode of computing the time of Easter, and of dating from the birth of Christ.

(8) Of Colophon, an artist, contemporary with Polygnotus, whom he imitated. Aristotle describes him as a realist in the treatment of his subjects.

(9) DIONYSIUS CATO. See CATO, p. 302.

Dionȳsus (Διώνυσος or Διόνυσος). The god of luxuriant fertility, especially as displayed by the vine; and therefore the god of wine. His native place, according to the usual tradition, was Thebes, where he was born to Zeus by Semelé (q. v.), the daughter of Cadmus. Semelé was destroyed by the lightning of her lover, and the child was born after six months. Zeus accordingly sewed it up in his thigh till ripe for birth, and then gave it over to Ino, the sister of Semelé. (See ATHAMAS.) After her death Hermes took the boy to the nymphs of Mount Nysa, or according to another version, to the Hyades of Dodona, who brought him up and hid him in a cave away from the anger of Heré. It cannot be ascertained where Mount Nysa was originally supposed to be. In later times the name was transferred to many places where the vine was cultivated, not only in Greece, but in Asia, India, and Africa. When grown up, Dionysus is represented as planting the vine, and wandering through the wide world to spread his worship among men, with his wine-flushed train (θίασος)—his nurses and other nymphs, Satyrs, Sileni, and similar woodland deities. Whoever welcomed him kindly, like Icarius in Attica and Oeneus in Aetolia, received the gift of wine; but those who resisted him were terribly punished. A whole series of fables is apparently based upon the tradition that in many places, where a serious religious ritual existed, the dissolute worship of Dionysus met with a vigorous resistance. See LYCURGUS; MINYADAE; PENTHEUS; PROETUS.

This worship soon passed from the mainland of Greece to the wine-growing islands, and flourished pre-eminently at Naxos. Here it was, according to the story, that the god wedded Ariadné (q. v.). In the islands a fable was current that he fell in with some Tyrrhenian pirates, who took him to their ship and put him in chains. But his fetters fell off, the sails and the mast were wreathed with vine and ivy, the god was changed into a lion, while the seamen threw themselves madly into the sea and were turned into dolphins. In forms akin to this the worship of Dionysus passed into Egypt and far into Asia. Hence arose a fable, founded on the story of Alexander's campaigns, that the god passed victoriously through Egypt, Syria, and India as far as the Ganges, with his army of Sileni, Satyrs, and inspired women, the Maenades or Bacchantes, carrying their wands (θύρσοι) crowned with vines and ivy. Having thus constrained all the world to the recognition of his deity, and having with Heracles, assisted the gods, in the form of a lion, to victory in their war with the Giants, he was taken to Olympus, where, in Homer, he does not appear. From Olympus he descends to the lower world, whence he brings his mother, who is worshipped with him under the name of Thyoné ("the wild one"), as Leto was with Apollo and Artemis. From his mother he is called Thyoneus, a name which, with others of similar meaning, such as Bacchus, Bromios, Euios, and Iacchos, points to a worship founded upon a different conception of his nature.

In the myth with which we have been hitherto concerned, the god appears mainly in the character and surroundings of joy and triumph. But, as the god of the earth, Dionysus belongs, like Persephoné, to the world below as well as to the world above. The death of vegetation in winter was represented as the flight of the god into hiding from the sentence of his enemies, or even as his extinction; but he returned again from obscurity, or rose from the dead, to new life and activity. In this connection he was called Zagreus ("torn in pieces") and represented as a son of Zeus and his daughter Persephoné, or sometimes of Zeus and Demeter. In his childhood he was torn to pieces

Dionysus and Lion. (Choragic Monument of Lysicrates.)

by the Titans, at the command of the jealous Heré. But every third year, after spending the interval in the lower world, he is born anew. According to the Orphic story, Athené brought her son's heart to Zeus, who gave it to Semelé or swallowed it himself, whereupon the Theban or younger Dionysus was born. The grave of Dionysus was shown at Delphi in the inmost shrine of the Temple of Apollo. Secret offerings were brought thither, while the women who were celebrating the feast awakened Licnites; in other words, invoked the new-born god cradled in a winnowing-fan on the neighbouring mountain of Parnassus. Festivals of this kind, in celebration of the extinction and resurrection of the deity, were held by women and girls only, amid the mountains at night, every third year, about the time of the shortest day. The rites, intended to express the excess of grief and joy at the death and reappearance of the god, were wild even to savagery, and the women who performed them were hence known by the expressive names of Bacchae, Maenads, and Thyiades. They wandered through woods and mountains, their flying locks crowned with ivy or snakes, brandishing wands and torches, to the hollow sounds of the drum and the shrill notes of the flute, with wild dances and insane cries and jubilation. The victims of the sacrifice—oxen, goats, even fawns and roes from the forest—were killed, torn in pieces, and eaten raw, in imitation of the treatment of Zagreus by the Titans. Thrace and Macedonia and Asiatic Greece were the scene of the wildest orgies; indeed, Thrace seems to be the country of their birth. In Asiatic Greece, it should be added, the worship of Dionysus-Zagreus came to be associated with the equally wild rites of Rhea (Cybelé) and Atys and Sabus or Sabazius (q. v.). In Greece proper the chief seats of these were Parnassus, with Delphi and its neighbourhood, Boeotia, Argos, and Laconia, and in Boeotia and Laconia especially the mountains Cithaeron and Taÿgetus. They were also known in Naxos, Crete, and other islands. They seem to have been unknown in Attica, though Dionysus was worshipped at the Eleusinian Mysteries, with Persephoné and Demeter, under the name of Iacchos, as brother or bridegroom of Persephoné. (See MYSTERIA.) But the Attic cycle of national festivals in honour of Dionysus represents the idea of the ancient and simple Hellenic worship, with its merry usages. Here Dionysus is the god who gives increase and luxuriance to vineyard and tree. For he is a kindly and gentle power, terrible only to his enemies, and born for joy and blessing to mankind. His gifts bring strength and healing to the body, gladness and forgetfulness of care to the mind, whence he was called Lyaeus, or the loosener of care. They are ennobling in their effects, for they require tending, and thus keep men employed in diligent labour; they bring them together in merry meetings, and inspire them to music and poetry. Thus it is to the worship of Dionysus that the dithyramb and the drama owe their origin and development. In this way Dionysus is closely related, not only to Demeter, Aphrodité, Eros, the Graces, and the Muses, but to Apollo, because he inspires men to prophesy.

The most ancient representation of Dionysus consists of wooden images with the φαλλός (*membrum virile*) as the symbol of generative power. In works of art he is sometimes represented as the ancient Indian Dionysus, the conqueror of the East. In this character he appears, as in the Vatican statue incorrectly called Sardanapalus, of high stature, with a luxuriant wealth of hair on head and chin. Sometimes again, as in numerous statues which have survived, he is a youth of soft and feminine shape, with a dreamy expression, his long, clustering hair confined by a fillet or crown of ivy, generally naked, or with a fawn or panther skin thrown lightly over him. He is either reposing or leaning idly back with the θύρσος, grapes, or a cup in his hand. Often, too, he is surrounded by the Fauns of his retinue, Maenads, Satyrs, Sileni, Centaurs, etc., or by Nymphs, Muses, Cupids—indeed, in the greatest possible number and variety of situations. Besides the vine, ivy, and rose, the panther, lion, lynx, ox, goat, and dolphin were sacred to him. His usual sacrifices were the ox and the goat.

On the Italian god Liber, afterwards identified by the Romans with Dionysus, see LIBER.

Diophantus (Διόφαντος). A mathematician of Alexandria, who, according to the most received opinion, was contemporary with the emperor Julian. This opinion is founded upon a passage of Abulfaraj, an Arabian author of the thirteenth century. He names, among the contemporaries of the emperor Julian, Diophantes (for Diophantus) as the author of a celebrated work on algebra and arithmetic; and he is thought to have derived his information from an Arabic commentator on Diophantus, Muhammed al Buziani, who flourished about the end of the eleventh century. The reputation of Diophantus was so great among the ancients that they ranked him with Pythagoras and Euclid. From his epitaph in the Anthology the following particulars of his life have been collected: that he was married when thirty-three years old, and had a son five years after; that the son died at the age of forty-two, and that Diophantes did not survive him above four years; whence it appears that Diophantus was eighty-four years old when he died. Diophantus wrote a work entitled Ἀριθμητικά, in thirteen books, of which only six remain. It would seem that in the fifteenth, and even at the beginning of the seventeenth, century all the thirteen books still existed. The arithmetic of Diophantus is not merely important for the study of the history of mathematics, but is interesting also to the mathematician himself from its furnishing him with luminous methods for the resolution of analytical problems. We find in it, moreover, the first trace of that branch of the exact sciences called algebra. There exists also a second work of Diophantus, on *Polygon Numbers* (Περὶ Πολυγόνων Ἀριθμῶν). He himself cites a third, under the title of Πορίσματα, or *Corollaries*. A good edition of Diophantus is still that of Fermat (Toulouse, 1670). It is based upon that of Meziriac (Paris, 1621), with additions. A valuable translation of the *Arithmetica* into German was published by Otto Schulz (Berlin, 1822). The latest edition of the text is by Tannery (Leipzig, 1893).

On the so-called Diophantine Analysis, see Euler's *Algebra*, pt. ii. The reader is referred to Heath's *Diophantos of Alexandria* (1885).

Diopīthes (Διοπείθης). (1) An absurd character at Athens, half fanatic and half impostor, who traded in oracles and was the butt of the comic poets (Aristoph. *Vesp.* 380; *Aves*, 988, schol.). (2) An Athenian general, father of the poet Menander, sent out to the Thracian Chersonesus, about B.C. 344, at the head of a body of Athenian colonists (κληροῦχοι). Becoming involved in disputes with the Cardians, who had the support of Philip of Macedon, the latter sent a letter of remonstrance to Athens. Diopithes was impeached by the Macedonian party among the Athenians, but was ably defended by Demosthenes in the oration, still extant, "On the Chersonesus" (B.C. 341), so that he was permitted to retain his command. Subsequently he engaged in a military expedition against Philip, with much spirit and success (Diod. xvi. 75; Aristot. *Rhet.* ii. 8, 11).

Dioscorĭdes (Διοσκορίδης). A Greek physician and man of science. He flourished about the middle of the first century A.D., and was the author of a work *De Materia Medica* (Περὶ Ὕλης Ἰατρικῆς) in five books. For nearly 1700 years this book was the chief authority for students of botany and the science of healing. Two short essays on specifics against vegetable and animal poisons (*Alexipharmaca* and *Theriaca*) are appended to it as the sixth and seventh books; but these are probably from the hand of a later Dioscorides of Alexandria. A work on family medicine is also attributed to him, but is not genuine. The *Materia Medica* has been edited by Sprengel (1829–30).

Dioscorĭdis Insula (Διοσκορίδους νῆσος, Ptol.), or **Dioscorĭda** (Διοσκορίδα). An island situated at the south of the entrance of the Arabian Gulf and now called Socotra (Ptol. viii. 22).

Dioscūri (Διόσκουροι—i. e. sons of Zeus). The horse-tamer Castor (Κάστορ) and Polydeuces (Πολυδεύκης, Pollux), the master of the art of boxing. In Homer they are represented as the sons of Leda and Tyndareos, and called in consequence Tyndaridae; as dying in the time between the rape of Helen and the Trojan War, and as buried in Lacedaemon. But even under the earth they were alive. Honoured by Zeus, they lived and died on alternate days and enjoyed the prerogatives of godhead. In the later story sometimes both, sometimes only Polydeuces is the descendant of Zeus. (See LEDA.) They undertook an expedition to Attica, where they set free their sister Helen whom Theseus had carried off. They took part in the expedition of the Argonauts. (See AMYCUS; ARGONAUTAE.) Castor, who had been born mortal, fell in a contest with Idas and Lynceus, the sons of their paternal uncle Aphareus. The fight arose, according to one version, in a quarrel over some cattle which they had carried off; according to another, it was about the rape of two daughters of another uncle Leucippus, Phoebé and Hilaïra, who were betrothed to the sons of Aphareus. On his brother's death, Polydeuces, the immortal son of Zeus, prayed his father to let him die, too. Zeus permitted him to spend alternately one day among the gods his peers, the other in the lower world with his beloved brother. According to another story, Zeus, in reward for their brotherly love, set them in the sky as the constellation Gemini, or the morning and evening star. They are the ideal types of bravery and dexterity in fight. Thus they are the tutelary gods of warlike youth, often sharing in their contests, and honoured as the inventors of military dances and melodies. The ancient symbol of the twin gods at Lacedaemon was two parallel beams (δόκανα), joined by cross-pieces, which the Spartans took with them to war. They were worshipped at Sparta and Olympia with Heracles and other heroes. At Athens, too, they were honoured as gods under the name of Ἄνακες. At sea, as in war, they lend their aid to men. The storm-tossed mariner sees the sign of their beneficent presence in the flame at the mast-head (Hor. *Carm.* i. 3). He prays and vows to them the sacrifice of a white lamb, and the storm soon ceases. (See HELENA.) The rites of hospitality are also under their protection. They are generally represented with their horses Xanthus and Cyllarus, as in the celebrated colossal group of the Campidoglio in Rome. Their characteristic emblem is an oval helmet crowned with a star.

Dioscuri (Castor and Pollux). (From a Coin in the British Museum.)

The worship of Castor and Pollux was from early times current among the tribes of Italy. They enjoyed especial honours in Tusculum and Rome. In the latter city a considerable temple was built to them near the Forum (B.C. 484) in gratitude for their appearance and assistance at the battle of the Lake Regillus twelve years before. In this building, generally called simply the Temple of Castor, the Senate often held its sittings. It was in their honour, too, that (after B.C. 305) the solemn review of the Roman *equites* was held on the 15th of July. The names of Castor and Pollux, like that of Hercules, were often in use as familiar expletives, but the name of Castor was invoked by women only (Aul. Gell. xi. 6), since man had caused his death. Both were worshipped as gods of the sea, particularly in Ostia, the harbour town of Rome. Their image is to be seen stamped on the reverse of the oldest Roman silver coins. See NUMISMATICS.

Dioscuria (Διοσκούρια or Διοσκούρεια, *C. I. G.* 1444). Festivals celebrated in various parts of Greece in honour of the Dioscuri, the heroes

Castor and Polydeuces (Pollux). The Spartan Dioscuria, mentioned by Pausanias (iv. 27, § 1), were celebrated with sacrifices, rejoicings, and drinking. At Cyrené the Dioscuri were likewise honoured with a great festival (Schol. *ad* Pind. *Pyth.* v. 629). The Athenian festival of the Dioscuri has been mentioned under ANAKEIA, where they were worshipped under the name of Ἄνακες. Their worship was very generally adopted in Greece, especially in the Doric and Achaean States (Pausan. x. 33, 3; 38, 3), as we conclude from the great number of temples dedicated to them; but scarcely anything is known respecting the manner in which their festivals were celebrated.

The festival of the Dioscuri was celebrated at Rome with great splendour on the Ides of Quinctilis, the 15th of July, the day on which they were believed to have assisted the Romans against the Latins in the battle of the Lake Regillus. On this occasion the *equites*, who regarded the Dioscuri as their patrons, went in a magnificent procession, crowned with olive chaplets and wearing their state dress, the trabea, from the Temple of Mars outside the city, through the main streets, across the Forum, and by the ancient temple of the Dioscuri (Dionys. vi. 13). See EQUITES.

Dioscurĭas (Διοσκουριάς). A maritime town of Colchis at the mouth of the small river Charus. It was afterwards called Sebastopolis, and was, in the earliest ages, the port most frequented in Colchis by distant as well as neighbouring nations speaking different languages—a circumstance that still distinguishes Iskuriah, which name is only a corruption of the ancient one.

Diospŏlis (Διόσπολις). (1) MAGNA, a famous city of Egypt. (See THEBAE.) (2) PARVA, a city of Egypt, west of Tentyra, and on the western side of the Nile. It was the capital of the nome Diospolites.

Diōta (δίωτος). A vessel with two "ears" (ὦτα) or handles, and often used as synonymous with amphora, though equally applicable to any vessel with two handles. See AMPHORA.

Diota. (Naples Mus.)

Diovis. See IUPITER.

Diphĭlus (Δίφιλος). A poet of the new Attic comedy, a native of Sinopé, and contemporary of Menander. He is supposed to have written some one hundred pieces, of which we have the titles and fragments of about fifty. The *Casina* and *Rudens* of Plautus are modelled on two plays of Diphilus; and Terence has adopted some scenes from one of them (the Συναποθνήσκοντες) in his *Adelphoe*. Diphilus took his subjects both from common life and from mythology. Most of the passages that have been preserved relate to matters of cookery, the longest being one of forty-one lines. Both the judgments passed on him in antiquity and his remaining fragments justify us in recognizing him as one of the most gifted poets of his age. These fragments are collected in Meineke, i. pp. 445–457; iv. pp. 375–430.

Diphros (δίφρος). See CURRUS; SELLA.

Diphthĕra (διφθέρα). A leathern cloak worn in Greece by workmen and rustics. See Aristoph. *Nubes*, 72.

Diplax (δίπλαξ). A double cloak. See PALLIUM.

Diploïs (διπλοΐς). See PALLIUM.

Diplōma (δίπλωμα). (1) A sort of passport, consisting of two leaves (whence the name originated), which was given to a messenger or other person travelling upon public business, in order that he might readily obtain everything necessary on his journey, without delay or hindrance (Cic. *Fam.* vi. 12; Plin. *Ep.* x. 31; Capitol. *Pert.* 1). See CURSUS PUBLICUS. (2) A document drawn up by a chief-magistrate, which conferred some particular privilege upon the person to whom it was given (Suet. *Nero*, 12).

Diplomatics. See PALAEOGRAPHY.

Dipoenus (Δίποινος). A Greek sculptor, born in Crete, who flourished in Argos and Sicyon about B.C. 560. In conjunction with his countryman Scyllis he founded an influential school of sculpture in the Peloponnesus of the Daedalian style. See DAEDALA; STATUARIA ARS.

Dipolia. See DIIPOLIA.

Diptĕros (δίπτερος). An architectural term used of a temple with a double row of columns. See TEMPLUM.

Diptȳcha (δίπτυχα). Two writing-tablets fastened at the back by wires upon which, as upon hinges, they opened and shut. They were also known as *pugillares*. When three or more tablets are joined they are called *triptycha* or *polyptycha*. For further details see TABULA.

Diptychon. (Herculaneum.)

The DIPTȲCHA CONSULARIA, frequently mentioned in the later times of the Empire, were made of ivory, and were presented by the consuls to the emperor and to their friends on the day on which they entered upon their office. Other magistrates, such as the quaestors, also distributed diptycha on the same occasion (Symmach. *Ep.* ii. 81). These diptycha contained the portraits and names of the consuls, with other representations in bas-relief. Several of these diptycha are still extant—sixty-one in all, according to Marquardt—the earliest bearing the date of A.D. 406 and the latest of 541.

Dirae. (1) A name of the Furiae. See ERINYES; FURIAE. (2) See CATO, VALERIUS.

Dircé (Δίρκη). The wife of Lycus, who married her after divorcing his former wife Antiopé. Dircé treated Antiopé with great cruelty; and accordingly, when Amphion and Zethus, the sons of Antiopé by Zeus, obtained possession of Thebes, they took a signal vengeance upon Dircé. They tied her to a wild bull, which dragged her about till she perished. They then threw her body into a fountain near Thebes, which was henceforth called the fountain of Dircé. (See ANTIOPÉ.) The adjective Dircaeus is frequently used as equivalent to Boeoticus.

Diré or **Deré** (Δειρή, called by Ptolemy Δηρή). A promontory of Africa over against the coast of Arabia, and at the narrowest part of the Sinus Arabicus or Red Sea. From its appearance as it stretched along the coast, it received the appellation of Diré (Δειρή) or "the neck." The modern name is Bab-el-Mandeb.

Diribitōres. Officers who, at the Roman elections, divided the votes when taken out of the *cistae*, so as to determine which had the majority. See Cic. *In Pis.* 15.

Discordia. The Roman goddess of strife. See ERIS.

Discus (δίσκος). (1) A circular plate or quoit of stone, iron, or bronze made for throwing to a distance as a feat of strength or skill. Of this game (δισκοβολία) it is sufficient to say that it was identical with our "putting the shot." See *Odyssey*, viii. 186–200. A very celebrated representation in art is the Discobolus of the sculptor Myron, whose powerful portrayal of the initial attitude of the thrower has been praised by critics from the time of Quintilian. (Cf. Quintil. ii. 13, § 10.) Many of the copies of the original vary the pose so as to represent the athlete's head as not turned aside, and this is the case with the famous statue in the Vatican. The most correct reproduction is that now in possession of Prince Lancelotti, and kept in his private bed-chamber in the Palazzo Lancelotti, Rome. (2) A dish or plate.

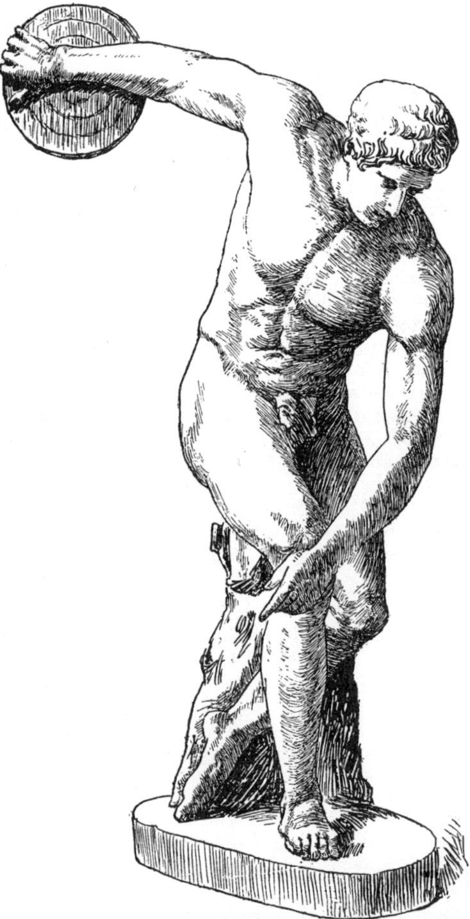

Discus Thrower. (Vatican.)

Dish. See LANX; PATINA.

Dis Pater (*Dives Pater*, "Father Dives" or The Rich). The ruler of the world below, worshipped by the Romans as the god who corresponded to the Greek Pluto (q. v.). His worship, like that of Proserpina, was first introduced in the early days of the Republic, at the command of the Sibylline Books. Dis Pater had a chapel near the altar of Saturnus, and a subterranean altar on the Campus Martius in common with Proserpina. This was only opened when, as at the Secular Games, sacrifices were offered to both. The victims offered thus were black animals.

Dispensātor. A steward in the Roman city household, who had the charge of the accounts and made the payments (Cic. *Att.* xi. 1; Juv. i. 91; Mart. v. 42). The dispensator was usually, perhaps always, a slave. If there was a procurator in the house, the dispensator was under him and acted simply as cashier. Thus we read in Petronius (30) that the procurator received the rents, while the dispensator paid out the money in the atrium. If there was a dispensator on the country estate, he was nearly the same as the *villicus* (*Dig.* l. 16, 166). The imperial procuratores discharged important duties, not only at the court but in Rome and the provinces (Plin. *H. N.* vii. § 129). How valuable was the appointment may be seen from the fact that Otho extorted a million sesterces from a slave whom he had recommended to Galba for the office of dispensator (Suet. *Oth.* 5).

Dissen, GEORG LUDOLF, a German classical scholar, was born near Göttingen, December 17th, 1784. He studied philology and philosophy at the university of his native city (1804–1808), and not long after receiving his degree was made Professor Extraordinarius at the University of Marburg, soon returning, however, to take the same office at Göttingen, where in 1817 he became Professor Ordinarius. Besides two valuable treatises—*De Temporibus et Modis Verbi Graeci* (Gött. 1809) and *De Philosophia in Xenophontis de Socrate Commentariis Tradita* (Marburg, 1812)—he published valuable editions of Pindar (1830), Tibullus (1831), and of the *Oration on the Crown* of Demosthenes (1837). His minor writings (*Kleine lat. und deutsche Schriften*) appeared in 1839 after his death, which occurred September 21st, 1837.

Distaff. See COLUS; FUSUS.

Dithyrambus (διθύραμβος). A hymn sung at the festivals of Dionysus to the accompaniment of a flute and a dance round the altar. (See DIONYSIA.) The hymn celebrated the sufferings and actions of the god in a style corresponding to the passionate character of his worship. In the course of time it developed into a distinct kind of Greek lyric poetry. It was in Corinth that it first received anything like a definite artistic form, and this at the hands of Arion, who was therefore credited by the ancients with its actual invention. The truth probably is that he was the first who divided the festal song of the chorus into strophe and antistrophe, an arrangement from which tragedy took its rise. (See TRAGOEDIA.) Dithyrambs were sung at Athens twice in the year—at the Great Dionysia in the spring and at the Lenaea in the beginning of winter. The chorus consisted of fifty persons, who stood in a circle round the altar. The dithyramb was further developed by Lasus of Hermionê, the lyric poet and musician who lived about B.C. 520 at the court of the Pisistratidae. By several innovations in music and rhythm, especially by a stronger and more complete instrumentation, this artist gave it greater variety and a more secular character. He also introduced the prize contests for the best dithyramb, and apparently abolished the antistrophical division; at least this is not found in the dithyrambs of his pupil Pindar. With Lasus and Pindar, Simonides and Bacchylides may be named as among the foremost dithyrambic poets of their time. At the dithyrambic contests the poets of the different tribes contended for the prize. Each had its chorus, brilliantly fitted out at great expense by the richer citizens. Besides the honour of the victory the poet received a tripod; the chorus, and the people which it represented, an ox for the sacrificial feast. These performances were very popular for a long time; but, as the new tendency developed itself, voices of authority made themselves heard, condemning them as involving a serious degeneracy in art. There is, in fact, no doubt that in the form which it assumed after the time of the Peloponnesian War the dithyramb did violence to the older taste. More and more it lost the inner unity and beautiful proportion which that feeling required. A continuous and rapid change of rhythm and mode was accompanied by an extraordinary boldness of diction, in keeping with the wild character of the composition. In the hands of inferior poets this often passed into turgidity and bombast, if not into mere nonsense. Solo pieces were inserted to relieve the choruses, the text was gradually subordinated to the music, and the dithyramb was thus gradually transformed into a kind of opera. Though the subjects of the poems had long ceased to be taken exclusively from the cycle of Dionysiac myths, they were never, of course, entirely out of harmony with the lyrical spirit of the dithyramb.

There was a very considerable number of dithyrambic poets. The best known are Melanippides (q. v.) of Melos (about B.C. 415), who is generally held responsible for the degeneracy of the dithyramb and the excess of instrumental music; his disciple Philoxenus of Cythera, who died in 380; Timotheus of Miletus, who died in 357, and his contemporaries Polyidus and Telestes. Of the whole literature we possess nothing but fragments. See CHORUS; MUSICA.

Dittography. The name given to a clerical error frequently found in MSS. It consists in writing twice what should properly be written only once. Thus in the best MS. (Σ) of the *Fals. Leg.* of Demosthenes, we find Ἀριστοφῶν καὶ ὁ Ἀριστόδημος for Κτήσιφων καὶ ὁ Ἀριστόδημος. One of the scholiasts on Horace *Carm.* i. 27, 19 doubles two syllables, writing *laboraborabas* for *laborabas.* A very extraordinary instance is found in the Codex Puteolanus of Livy, which in xxvii. 11, 11, has *dedissent et ius liberum eosdem dedissent et ius liberum eosdem dedissent et ius liberum eosdem dedissent* — a proof of how mechanically the scribes performed their work. See TEXTUAL CRITICISM.

Dium (Δῖον). (1) An important town in Macedonia on the Thermaic Gulf (Thuc. iv. 28). (2) A promontory on the northern coast of Crete where the island has its greatest breadth (Ptol. iii. 17, 7).

Dius Fidius. See SANCUS.

Diverbium. Dialogue. See DIALOGUS.

Diversorium. A wayside inn. See CAUPONA.

Divĭco. The leader of the Helvetians in the war against L. Cassius in B.C. 107. He was at the head of the embassy sent to Iulius Caesar, nearly fifty years later, B.C. 58, when he was preparing to attack the Helvetians (Caes. *B. G.* i. 13).

Divinatio (prevision of the future). (1) In general the word is applied to all prophecy or foretelling in the simplest sense of the word. Among the Romans, prophecy was based, not on inspiration, as with the Greeks, but on the observation of definite signs, such as the *omen* (or voice), the prodigies and the auspices taken note of by the augurs. (See AUGUR.) The science of the *haruspices* (or the foretelling of events from the inspection of the carcases of sacrificial victims) was a later importation from Etruria. The ancient Romans were not familiar with the divinatio from *sortes* or lots, which was common in many parts of Italy. The Sibylline Books threw no light on future events. (See SIBYLLA.) Towards the end of the republican period the sciences of the augurs and haruspices lost their significance, and the Greek oracles, in the various forms of their craft, with the Chaldaean astrology, came into vogue, and carried the fashion in the society of the Empire. On divination among the Greeks see MANTIKÉ.

(2) In the language of Roman law, *divinatio* meant the legal inquiry for deciding who, among many advocates proposing themselves, was the fittest to undertake a prosecution, and also the speeches by which the various advocates tried to make good their competency for the task. Thus Cicero's oration called *Divinatio in Caecilium* was pronounced by him against Q. Caecilius Niger, a sham accuser of Verres, who claimed the right to prosecute, but who would have played into the hands of the accused.

Divīsor. See AMBITUS.

Divitiăcus. An Aeduan noble and brother of Dumnorix (q. v.). He was a warm adherent of the Romans and of Caesar, who, in consideration of his entreaties, pardoned the treason of Dumnorix in B.C. 58 (Caes. *B. G.* i. 3, 16–20). He is mentioned by Cicero (*De Div.* i. 41) as a Druid.

Divodūrum (Διουόδουρον). The modern Metz; subsequently Mediomatrici, and still later Metis or Mettis, the capital of the Mediomatrici in Gallia Belgica (Ptol. ii. 9, 12).

Divŏna. See CADURCI.

Divortium. Divorce. (1) GREEK. The term for this act was ἀπόλειψις or ἀπόπεμψις, the former denoting the act of a wife leaving her husband, and the latter that of a husband dismissing his wife (Demosth. *c. Onet.* i. p. 865, § 4; *c. Neaer.* p. 1362, § 52, 1365, § 59). The only Greek States respecting whose laws of divorce we have any knowledge are Athens and Sparta. In both States the law permitted either husband or wife to call for and effect a divorce, though it was much easier for a husband to get rid of his wife than for a wife to escape from her husband. At Sparta, it seems, a man might dismiss his wife if she bore him no issue; the recorded instances, however, are those of kings, and private inclination was sacrificed to State policy (Herod. v. 39; vi. 61). The law at Athens allowed a man to divorce his wife without ceremony, simply by his act of sending her out of his house (ἐκπέμπειν, ἀποπέμπειν), upon which she returned to the guardianship of her nearest male relation. (See KYRIOS.) The husband was then bound to return the dowry which she had brought him, or to pay her interest at the rate of nine obols per mina per month—18 per cent. per annum; and in addition to this to provide alimony (σῖτος). A husband thus dismissing his wife usually did so, as might be expected, in the presence of witnesses (Lys. *c. Alcib.* i. § 28). What became of the children in such a case is not mentioned, but it is probable that they remained with the father. Adultery on the part of the wife compelled her husband to divorce her, or himself incur the penalty of atimia (Lex *ap.* Demosth. *c. Neaer.* p. 1374, § 87). When, on the other hand, a wife wished to leave her husband, if both parties agreed upon a divorce no further proceedings were required: mutual consent was sufficient to dissolve a marriage. If the husband objected, she was obliged to appear in person before the archon, and state in writing the grounds of her application (Plut. *Alcib.* 12). She had to conduct her case quite alone, for, as she was in her husband's power until judgment was given, no one had a right to come forward as her advocate. It has been maintained that she could be represented by her κύριος, but the notorious case of Alcibiades and his ill-used wife Hipparetê, in the passage just cited, leaves little doubt that she could not. The action thus brought by a woman was called ἀπολείψεως δίκη. Her right to a separation would depend on the treatment she had received (see KAKOSIS); but of the nature of the archon's jurisdiction we know but little. The husband's loss of freedom (i. e. by becoming a prisoner of war and being sold into slavery) is mentioned as affording an absolute claim to a divorce.

(2) ROMAN. The word *divortium* signified generally a separation; and, in a special sense, a divorce or dissolution of marriage. Several authorities (Gell. iv. 3; Dionys. ii. 25) state that divorce was unknown at Rome in early times, and that the first instance of divorce occurred in B.C. 233, when Sp. Carvilius Ruga put away his wife on the ground of barrenness. It is said that the act of Carvilius was generally disapproved of (Val. Max. ii. 1–4). It is probable that divorce on account of the misconduct of the wife was in use from a very early period; but the case of Carvilius Ruga may have been the beginning of the lax system of divorce which prevailed towards the end of the free Republic and under the Empire.

The marriage by which the husband acquired *manus* over his wife, as well as the later free marriage, was dissoluble; but the marriage of a *flamen,* which was solemnized by *confarreatio,* could never under any circumstances be severed. See MATRIMONIUM.

A corresponding form to that by which a marriage had been created was used for dissolving it: thus a marriage entered into by *confarreatio* was put an end to by a similar ceremony, called *diffarreatio* (Festus, s. v. *diffarr.*). If a wife had passed into the *manus* of her husband by *coemptio,* she could only be released by a *remancipatio,* which, according to Gaius, the husband could be compelled to execute (i. 137). These formal restrictions on the right of divorce disappeared under the free form of marriage, which did not bring the wife *in manum viri.* The theory on which Roman marriage was based admitted the utmost facility of divorce: the consent and conjugal affection of the parties were regarded as the essential part of a marriage, and this *affectio maritalis* was necessary for the continuance as well as for the creation of a marriage. Accordingly, either party might declare his or her consent to dissolve the connection. No judicial decree and no interference of any public authority was necessary to dissolve the marriage. A divorce which was brought about by one party renouncing the marriage and not by mutual consent was called a *repudium.* It was customary for one who renounced a marriage to send a distinct notice or declaration of intention to the other party, and it was doubted in the time of Cicero whether the simple fact of either party marrying again without any such notice having been given was sufficient to constitute a divorce (Cic. *Orat.* i. 40). The ceremony of breaking the *nuptiales tabulae,* or of taking the keys of the house from the woman and turning her out of doors, was probably considered to be an act of itself significant enough; but the general practice was apparently to deliver a written notice, and perhaps to assign a reason. By the Lex Iulia *de adulteriis* it was required that a *repudium* should be executed in the presence of seven witnesses, Roman citizens of the age of puberty (*Dig.* xxiv. 2, 9). This prevented an adulteress from setting up the pretence of a *repudium* as an excuse for her conduct. See ADULTERIUM.

Not only the wife herself, but also her father, if she was under his power, might dissolve the marriage. This right of a paterfamilias was made practically ineffectual by a decree of the emperor Marcus. Towards the latter part of the Republic and under the Empire, divorces became very common. Cn. Pompeius divorced his wife Mucia for alleged adultery, and his conduct was approved (Cic. *Ad Att.* i. 12, 18); and Cicero speaks (*Ad Fam.* viii. 7) of Paulla Valeria as being ready to serve her husband on his return from his province with notice of divorce. Cicero himself divorced his wife Terentia after living with her for thirty years, and married a young woman whom he also divorced. Cato the Younger divorced his wife Marcia, that his friend Hortensius might marry her and have children by her; for this is the true meaning of the story (Plut. *Cat. Min.* 25). Maecenas put away his wife Terentia so often that the Roman wits said that he had been a hundred times married, and always to the same woman; Sempronius Sophus divorced his wife because she had once been to the public games without his knowledge. Seneca declared that there were women at Rome who reckoned the years by their husbands rather than by the consuls. Juvenal mentions one who had had eight husbands in five years; and Tertullian sums up the prevailing practices epigrammatically in the sentence, "The fruit of marriage is divorce" (*Apol.* 6). By the Lex Papia Poppaea a freedwoman who had married her patron was prevented from divorcing herself (*Dig.* xxiv. 2, 11) so as to be capable of marrying any one else. From an early time penalties were imposed on those who divorced without good cause, and also on those who by their conduct made a divorce necessary.

A man was punished by *nota censoria,* a woman by loss of *dos* (q. v.). There was the *retentio dotis propter mores* when the divorce was caused by the fault of the wife, and also the *retentio propter liberos* which was the right of the husband to deduct an additional amount of *dos* in case there were children of the marriage. The free right of divorce was not taken away by the early Christian emperors, but its exercise except on grounds defined by statute was severely punished. Justinian went further than his predecessors in limiting the legal grounds of divorce. He even punished divorce by mutual consent unless the object of the parties was to live a life of chastity (*Dig.* 34, 2; *Cod. Theod.* iii. 16; *Cod.* v. 17). See Lecky, *Hist. of European Morals*, ii. pp. 304–308; Wächter, *Ueber Ehescheidungen bei den Römern;* Bader, *La Femme Romaine* (Paris, 1877); Friedländer, *Sittengeschichte Roms*, ch. v. (6th ed. Leipzig, 1888); Baecker, *Le Droit de la Femme dans l'Antiquité* (1880).

Diyllus (Δίυλλος). An Athenian, the author of a history of Greece and Sicily, in twenty-six or twenty-seven books; and also of a work on drinking-bouts (Συμποσιακά). His date is uncertain, but he probably flourished in the first century B.C. (Diod. xvi. 14, 78, etc.).

Dobērus (Δόβηρος). A town in Paeonia in Macedonia, east of the river Echedorus (Thuc. ii. 98).

Dobree, Peter Paul, an English scholar of eminence, born in the island of Guernsey of French ancestry, in 1782. He studied under Porson at the University of Cambridge, and on the death of that distinguished Hellenist undertook to edit his unpublished papers, which had come into the possession of Trinity College. In 1820, appeared the *Plutus* of Aristophanes with Porson's notes; and in 1822, the Lexicon of Photius. In the same year, Dobree was made Regius Professor of Greek. On his death in 1825, he left an edition of Demosthenes in MS., which was edited and published by his successor.

Dokăna (τὰ δόκανα, from δοκός, "a beam"). An ancient symbolical representation of the Dioscuri (Castor and Polydeuces) at Sparta. It consisted of two upright beams with others laid across them transversely (Plut. *De Amor. Fratr.*). This rude symbol of fraternal unity evidently points to a very remote age, in which scarcely any attempts in sculpture can have been made. At a later time, when works of art were introduced into all the spheres of ordinary life, this rude and ancient object of worship, like many others of its kind, was not superseded by a more appropriate symbol. The Dioscuri were worshipped as gods of war, and we know that their images accompanied the Spartan kings whenever they took the field against an enemy. But when in the year B.C. 504 the two kings, during their invasion of Attica, failed in their undertaking on account of their secret enmity towards each other, it was decreed at Sparta that in future only one king should command the army, and in consequence should be accompanied by only one of the images of the Dioscuri (Herod. v. 75). It is not improbable that these images, accompanying the kings into the field, were the ancient δόκανα, which were now disjointed, so that one half of the symbol remained at Sparta, while the other was taken into the field by one of the kings. See Daedala; Dioscuri.

Dokimasia (δοκιμασία). The name used at Athens to denote the process of ascertaining the capacity of the citizens for the exercise of public rights and duties. If, for instance, a young citizen was to be admitted among the Ephebi (q. v.), he was examined in an assembly of his district to find out whether he was descended on both sides from Athenian citizens, and whether he possessed the physical capacity for military service. All officials, too—even the members of the Senate—had to submit to an examination before entering upon their office. The purpose of this was to ascertain, not their actual capacity for the post, which was presupposed in all candidates, but their descent from Athenian citizens, their life and character, and (in the case of some offices which involved the administration of large sums) even the amount of their property. The examination was carried on in public by the archons in the presence of the Senate, and any one present had the right to raise objections. If such objections were held to be valid the candidate was rejected; but he had the right to appeal to the decision of a court, which would take cognizance of the matter in judicial form. On the other hand, if he were accepted, any one who thought his claims insufficient had the right of instituting judicial proceedings against him. If the decision was adverse he would lose his office, and was further liable to punishment varying according to the offence charged against him—which might be, for instance, that of unlawfully assuming the rights of a citizen. A speaker in a public assembly might thus be brought before a court by any citizen, for no one not possessed of the full right of citizenship could legally address the people. The question might thus be raised whether the orator were not actually *atimos*, or guilty of an offence which involved *atimia* (q. v.).

Docimia (Δοκιμία) and **Docimēum** (Δοκίμειον). A town of Phrygia near Synnada and famed for the marble quarries in its vicinity.

Doctors. See Chirurgia; Medicina; Medicus.

Doctus. A title given by the Roman writers to various poets, especially to Pacuvius (Hor. *Epist.* ii. 1, 56) and Catullus (Ovid, *Amor.* iii. 9, 62; Mart. viii. 73, 8). It is to be understood in the sense of "accomplished," "polished." Cf. Hor. *Odes*, i. 1, 29, where it is applied to poets in general, as being taught by the Muses.

Döderlein, Ludwig, a great classical scholar and teacher, was born at Jena, December 19th, 1791. He began his higher studies at Pforta when sixteen years of age, continuing them under Thiersch at Munich, under Kreuzer and Voss at Heidelberg, and under Boeckh, Buttmann, and Wolf at Berlin. He reached the doctorate at Erlangen in 1813, and in 1815 was called to the chair of philosophy at Bern, transferring himself in 1819 to Erlangen, with the titles of Professor of Philosophy and Director of the Philological Seminary in the University, and Rector of the Gymnasium. At Erlangen he remained until his death, November 9th, 1863. His publications comprise editions of Tacitus (Halle, 1847); Horace (*Epistles*, Leipzig, 1856–58; *Satires*, 1860); and the *Iliad* (Leipzig, 1863–64); besides the following works, some of them of enduring value: *Latein. Synonyme und Etymologien*, 6 vols. (Leipzig, 1826–38); *Lat. Wortbildung* (Leipzig, 1838); *Handbuch d. lat. Synonymik* (Leipzig, 1839–49); *Handbuch d. lat. Etymologie* (Leipzig, 1841); *Reden und Aussätze* (Frankfort, 1860); *Homerisches Glossarium*, 3 vols. (Erlangen, 1850–58); and a German Anthology—*Deutsche Mustersammlung* (1840).

Döderlein was fully as remarkable as a teacher as for his scholarship, and appears to have made upon his hearers a profound and ineffaceable impression. To great acuteness and unfailing tact he added an enthusiasm, energy, and vigour that carried at once himself and his hearers away. Thoroughly imbued with the very genius of antiquity, the great masters of classical literature were to him not subjects of study but, as he himself called them, "intimate and cherished friends," and into all who listened to him he inspired much of his own passionate zeal. An untiring worker, rising every morning soon after midnight to pursue his researches, he left behind him both in his works and in the memories of his pupils the figure of a great and impressive personality.

Dodōna (Δωδώνη). (1) A celebrated city and oracle of Epirus, whose exact position has only of late been ascertained. We are not assisted here by any accurate ancient traveller like Pausanias, nor have we any itineraries or faithful measurements of distances to guide us; all is vague and indefinite. Dionysius of Halicarnassus placed it four days' journey from Buthrotum and two from Ambracia (*Antiq. Rom.* i. 5). It is universally allowed that the temple of Dodona owed its origin to the Pelasgi at a period much anterior to the Trojan War; since many writers represent it as existing in the time of Deucalion, and even of Inachus (Aesch. *Prom. Vinct.* 679). Herodotus distinctly states that it was the most ancient oracle of Greece, and represents the Pelasgi as consulting it on various occasions (ii. 52). Hence the title of "Pelasgic" assigned to Zeus, to whom the temple was dedicated (*Iliad*, xvi. 233). Of the existence, however, of another oracle in Thessaly of the same name no doubt can be entertained; and to this the prayer of Achilles, in Homer, probably had reference. Setting aside the fables which Herodotus has transmitted to us, and to which he evidently attached no belief, his report of the affinity which existed between the service of this temple and that of Thebes in Egypt is deserving of attention. It appears from this author that in his time the service of the temple was performed by women; and he has recorded the names of the three priestesses who officiated when he visited Dodona (ii. 55). Strabo, however, asserts that these duties were originally allotted to men, from the circumstance of Homer's mention of the Selli as being attendant upon the gods. The term Selli was considered by many ancient writers to refer to a people of Pelasgic origin (Soph. *Trach.* v. 1160 foll.; Aristot. *Meteorol.* 1, 14).

The responses of the oracle were originally delivered from the sacred oak or beech (φηγός) (Soph. *Trach.* v. 173). The god revealed his message in the rustling of the leaves, and the priests interpreted its meaning. Its reputation was at first confined to the inhabitants of Epirus, Acarnania, Aetolia, and the western parts of Greece (Pausan. vii. 21), but its fame was afterwards extended over the whole of that country, and even to Asia, as we know that on one occasion the oracle was consulted by Croesus (Herod. i. 46). The Boeotians were the only people who received the prophetic answers from the mouth of men; to all other nations they were always communicated by the priestesses of the temple. The reason of this exception is stated at length by Strabo (401), on the authority of Ephorus. Dodona was the first station in Greece to which the offerings of the Hyperboreans were despatched, according to Herodotus; they arrived there from the Adriatic, and were thence passed on to the Maliac Gulf (iv. 33). Among the several offerings presented to the temple by various nations, one dedicated by the Corcyreans is particularly noticed. It was a brazen figure placed over a caldron of the same metal; this statue held in its hand a whip, the lash of which consisted of three chains, each having an astragalus fastened to the end of it; these, when agitated by the wind, struck the caldron and produced so continued a sound that 400 vibrations could be counted before it ceased. Hence arose the various proverbs of the Dodonean caldron and the Corcyrean lash. Menander, in one of his plays, compared an old nurse's chatter to the endless sound of this kettle (*Menand. Reliq. ed.* Meineke, p. 27). See ORACULA.

We hear of the oracle of Dodona at the time of the Persian invasion (Herod. ix. 93); and again in the reign of Agesilaüs, who consulted it previously to his expedition into Asia. It is stated by Diodorus Siculus (xiv. 13) that Lysander was accused openly of having offered to bribe the priestess. The oracle which warned the Molossian Alexander of his fate is well known from Livy (viii. 24). From Demosthenes we learn that the answers delivered from time to time to the Athenians were laid up in the public archives, and he himself appeals to their testimony on more than one occasion. At length, during the Social War, Dodona was, according to Polybius (iv. 67), almost entirely destroyed in an irruption of the Aetolians, under their leader Dorimachus, then at war with Epirus. It is probable that the temple of Dodona never recovered from this disaster, as in Strabo's time there was scarcely any trace left of the oracle, but the town must still have existed, as it is mentioned by Hierocles among the cities of Epirus in the seventh century, and we hear of a bishop of Dodona in the council of Ephesus. All accounts seem to agree that Dodona stood either on the declivity or at the foot of an elevated mountain called Tomarus or Tamarus. Hence the term Tomuri, supposed to be a contraction for Tomaruri (Τομαροῦροι), or guardians of Tomarus, which was given to the priests of the temple. The site of Dodona was at one time supposed to be near Janina in Epirus, but recent explorations in the valley of Dramisius at the foot of Mount Olytzika have brought to light many dedicatory inscriptions to Zeus Naïos and Dioné, with other evidences that make this the probable site of the oracle. See Leake, *Northern Greece*, vols. i. and iv.; the *Revue Archéologique* for 1877, pp. 329, 397; and Carapanos, *Dodone et ses Ruines* (1878). (2) A city and oracle of Thessaly. It has given rise to much controversy whether Homer (*Il.* ii. 750) refers to this or the city of Epirus, and the scholiasts and commentators are divided in their opinions.

Dodonaeus (Δωδωναῖος). A surname of Zeus from Dodona. See Homer, *Il.* xvi. 233.

Dodonĭdes (Δωδωνίδες). The priestesses who gave oracles in the temple of Zeus in Dodona. See DODONA.

Dodrans. Nine twelfths or three fourths of a Roman *as;* three fourths. Hence the phrase *heres ex dodrante* was used of an heir to three fourths of an estate. See As.

Dodwell Vase. A small Greek vase covered with a lid and found at Corinth. The lid shows the representation of a boar-hunt and is inscribed with names. The body of the vase is ornamented with figures of animals. Its pattern shows traces of Phœnician influence. The Dodwell vase is now in the Old Pinacothek at Munich. See Zahn, *Beschreibung der Galerie bemalter Vasen der königlichen bayerischen Sammlung* (Munich, 1854); Lau and Krell, *Die griechischen Vasen*, etc. (Leipzig, 1877); and the article VAS.

Dodwell Vase. (Munich.)

Dog-days. See CANICULARES DIES.

Dogmatĭci (δογματικοί). See MEDICINA.

Dogs. See CANIS.

Dolabella. The name of a celebrated patrician family of the Cornelia gens. Those most deserving of notice are: (1) CN. CORNELIUS DOLABELLA, consul B.C. 81, whom the young Iulius Caesar accused in the year 77 of extortion in his province. (2) CN. CORNELIUS DOLABELLA, praetor urbanus B.C. 81. With Verres as his legate he plundered his province in Cilicia, and upon his return was accused, betrayed by Verres, and condemned. (3) P. CORNELIUS DOLABELLA, the son-in-law of Cicero, whose daughter Tullia he married in B.C. 51. He was one of the most profligate men of his age, and his conduct caused Cicero great uneasiness. On the breaking out of the Civil War he joined Caesar, and fought on his side at the battle of Pharsalia (B.C. 48), and was raised by him to the consulship in 44. He afterwards received from Antony the province of Syria. On his way to his province he plundered the cities of Greece and Asia Minor, in consequence of which the Senate sent against him Cassius, who took Caesarea, in which Dolabella had taken refuge. That he might not fall into the hands of his enemies he committed suicide, B.C. 43.

Dolābra, dim. DOLABELLA (σμίλη, σμιλίον). A tool consisting of a long handle and a double head, which terminated on one side in a sharp blade, the edge of which ran parallel to the handle (while the

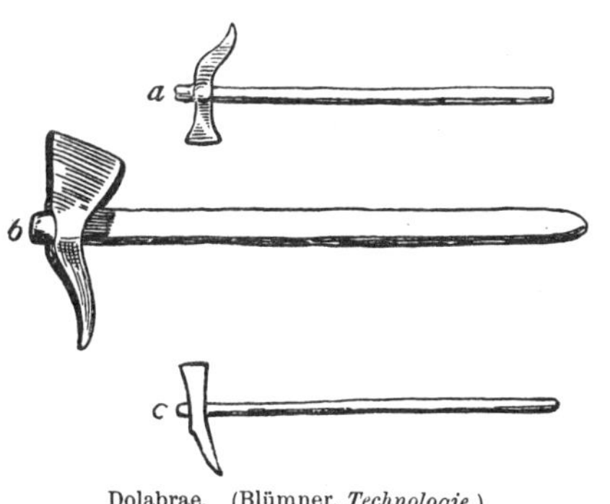

Dolabrae. (Blümner, *Technologie.*)

blade of the *ascia* was at right angles to the handle), and on the other side in a pick, which was usually curved (*falx*). In this form it was used for hewing wood, for pruning where the pruning-hook was not strong enough, for making stockades, and for breaking down ramparts and walls. It was consequently a tool familiar to the Roman soldier, as may be seen in the accompanying illustration (fig. *b*) from Trajan's Column. For the purpose, however, of excavating or breaking up the earth (Pallad. ii. 1 and 3; iii. 21), a dolabra with a straighter pick appears to have been used, as is shown in fig. *a*, from a relief on a tomb. Of a similar form is fig. *c*, which represents the dolabra used by masons (Isid. *Orig.* xix. 19, 11). The hatchet used at sacrifices and by butchers was also called *dolabra*.

Dolĭché (Δολίχη). (1) A town of Thessaly in the Perrhaebian district, to the southeast of Azorus. Here the Roman consul Q. Marcius Philippus received a deputation from the Achaean League, at the head of which was Polybius, who accompanied the Roman army in their singular and perilous march through the defiles of Olympus into Pieria (Liv. xlii. 53; id. xliv. 2). (2) A town of Syria, situated in the district Euphratensis and northwest of Zeugma.

Dolĭchos (δόλιχος). See CURSUS; STADIUM.

Dolium (πίθος). A large jar of earthenware into which new wine was placed to ferment. Many of them were large enough to hold a man, and were shaped like a huge caldron with globular bodies and wide mouths. Diogenes (q. v.) the Cynic took up his abode in a dolium (not in a tub, as popularly said), and in some ancient works of art he is depicted as lolling in one of these vessels during his celebrated interview with Alexander the Great. See Diog. Laërt. vi. 23; Sen. *Ep.* 90, 14.

DOLIA CURTA were urinals placed in the narrow streets between the houses for the convenience of those who passed by (Lucret. iv. 1026; Macrob. iii. 16, § 15; Suet. *Vesp.* 23).

Dolia were also used as coffins. In the Crimea, near Sebastopol, sixteen πίθοι were discovered, four feet four inches high, and two feet two inches in diameter.

Makers of dolia were known as *doliarii*.

Dolius (Δόλιος). A slave of Penelopé who, with his six sons, welcomed Odysseus home and joined him against the suitors (*Odys.* xxiv. 498).

Dolls. See PUPA.

Dolo (δόλων). (1) A weapon consisting of a long staff with a short iron point (Verg. *Aen.* vii. 664). (2) A secret poniard or dagger inserted in a walking-stick (Plut. *Tib. Gracch.* 10; Suet. *Claud.* 13, *Domit.* 17) or a whip (*Dig.* 9, 2, 52). (3) A small topsail of a ship.

Dolonci (Δόλογκοι). A people of Thrace (Herod. vi. 34).

Dolŏpes (Δόλοπες). A powerful people in Thessaly, who dwelt on the Enipeus and fought before Troy. At a later time they dwelt at the foot of Mount Pindus; and their country, called Dolopia, was reckoned part of Epirus (Herod. vii. 132).

Dolus Malus. See CULPA.

Domestĭci. See PRAETORIANI.

Domicilium. A term of Roman law, signifying a man's permanent home. The following is the well-known definition of *domicilium* given in the *Corpus Iuris* (*Cod.* x. 40, 7): "In eo loco singulos habere domicilium non ambigitur, ubi quis larem rerumque ac fortunarum suarum summam constituit, unde rursus non sit discessurus, si nihil avocet, unde cum profectus est peregrinari videtur, quo si rediit peregrinari iam destitit." In a passage of the *Digest* a man's home is thus defined (*Dig.* l. 16, 203): "Sed de ea re constitutum esse (respondit) eam domum unicuique nostrum debere existimari, ubi quisque sedes et tabulas haberet suarumque rerum constitutionem fecisset." A man acquired domicilium by making a place his residence and intending to remain in it permanently (*animus manendi*). Domicilium was lost by abandonment, and the question of the existence of domicile was treated as one of fact to be determined by the circumstances of each case.

The conception of domicile has far more important consequences in modern systems of law than in ancient; it is the foundation of a branch of what is sometimes called private international law, but more correctly the conflict of laws.

Dominium. *Dominium* or *rerum dominium* signifies ownership of property, and *dominus* is the owner. *Proprietas* is frequently used as an equivalent to *dominium;* and when ownership is distinguished from *usus fructus*, the word *proprietas* is preferred to *dominium* as an expression for ownership. The term *dominium* or *dominium legitimum* is, strictly speaking, confined to ownership *ex iure Quiritium*—i. e. to civil ownership—and does not include ownership *in bonis*—i. e. praetorian ownership.

Ownership is not defined by Roman legal writers, but the general notion implied in the term is clear. It is a right which, subject to certain legal limitations, entitles a person to exercise full control over a corporeal thing to the exclusion of all other persons. Ownership cannot, however, be defined by enumerating all the powers which may be incidental to it, as the *ius utendi, fruendi, possidendi, disponendi,* since ownership may exist notwithstanding that one or more of these powers is detached from it. A thing may be considered to belong to a person whose powers over it are very much curtailed; hence arises the difficulty of defining ownership. The limitations to which ownership in Roman law is subject are either general or special. The former are imposed for the purpose of enforcing the precept *sic utere tuo ut alienum non laedas:* they prevent owners from so using their powers as to injure adjoining owners or the public generally. Special limitations on ownership arise by persons acquiring rights over property owned by some one else. For instance, the owner may be bound to allow to another person a certain use or enjoyment of the thing of which he is *dominus*, or to abstain from doing certain acts on or to his property and for the benefit of some other person. The only rights of this kind recognized by Roman law are *servitus, emphyteusis, superficies, pignus:* such rights are called *iura in re aliena;* they are protected, like *dominium*, by actions *in rem:* their nature is more fully explained under the head of SERVITŪS. Ownership is in its nature single and entire; consequently the same thing cannot belong to several separate owners, but several persons may be joint *domini* or owners of one thing.

Domĭnus. A master, owner. The word was applied as a title of respect to a superior in rank or station. Thus the head of a family was sometimes called *dominus* by the free members of his family as well as by his slaves. The title of *dominus* came to be ascribed to the emperor. The history of this use of the word, which corresponds with changes in the character of the emperor, is briefly as follows: Augustus refused to be called *dominus* (Suet. *Aug.* 53, with Peck's note), as did also Tiberius (Suet. *Tib.* 27); and Caligula was the first emperor who allowed himself to be addressed by the title (Victor. *Caes.* 3). Domitian claimed the titles of *Deus et Dominus* (Dio Cass. lxii. 13). Trajan only wished to be called *princeps* (Plin. *Paneg.* §§ 2, 63, 88). Pliny in his letters always addresses Trajan as *dominus*, but in doing so he does not intend to make use of an official title. *Dominus* first appears on imperial monuments in the reign of Septimius Severus. Aurelian first adopted the title *Deus et Dominus* on his coins. Diocletian allowed himself to be publicly addressed as *dominus*. From the fourth century the emperors freely ascribe the title to themselves. The reason why the earlier emperors objected to being styled *dominus* is to be found in the fact that they still kept up a pretence of republican equality. Now the word *dominus* to a Roman, like δεσπότης to a Greek, means a master in relation to slaves, or (politically) a tyrant, the possessor of arbitrary power (Sall. *Iug.* 85). Later, when the imperial power had become hedged about by precedent and tradition, the emperor willingly accepted the title as his due.

The word *dominus*, besides retaining its full force as a term of great dignity, underwent a further development as a social title. In Suet. *Claud.* 21, it is applied by the emperor to his plebeian guests as an ordinary title of courtesy. In Mart. vi. 88, it is equivalent to "Mister." It is used by Ovid (*Am.* iii. 7. 11) as a term of affection. In the modern languages it has developed through the Low Latin forms *domnus, domna, donnus, dominicella* into the Portuguese *dom*, Span. *don, doña*, Fr. *dame, madame (mea domna), demoiselle*, and Old English *dan*. See Peck's note to Suet. *Aug.* 53.

Domitia. (1) LEPĬDA, aunt of Nero, accused of magic and put to death (A.D. 54) through the intrigues of Agrippina, who was jealous of her influence over Nero (Tac. *Ann.* xii. 64 foll.). (2) DOMITILLA, wife of Vespasian, who had by her Titus and Domitian and a daughter named Domitilla. She had been the mistress of a Roman knight and passed for a freedwoman; but she was declared of free birth on having been acknowledged by her father Flavius Liberalis, who held the situation of scribe to one of the quaestors. She died before Vespasian came to the throne (Suet. *Vesp.* 3). (3) LONGĪNA, daughter of the famous Corbulo, the general of Nero. She married Aelius Lamia, but was seduced by Domitian and, after the birth of a daughter, publicly raised to the throne. Hardly, however, had the emperor elevated her to the station of Augusta, when his jealousy was alarmed by certain familiarities to which she admitted the pantomime Paris, so that he drove her from the palace. The ascendency which she had acquired, however, over the vicious emperor was too strong to be thus suddenly dissolved, and she was recalled to her former station. Domitia was concerned, it is thought, in the conspiracy by which the emperor lost his life. She died during the reign of Trajan (Suet. *Dom.* 3).

Domitiānus, TITUS FLAVIUS. The second son of Vespasian, born at Rome A.D. 51. Vespasian, well aware of his natural disposition, reposed no confidence in him during his whole reign. Domitian, however, accompanied his father and his brother Titus in their triumph at the close of the Jewish War. Upon the death of Vespasian he endeavoured to foment troubles in the Empire and share the succession with Titus. The latter, however, forgave him, treated him with great kindness, and made him his colleague in the consulship, always declaring to him that he intended him for his successor. Domitian is accused of hastening the death of Titus by poison—a charge, however, not warranted by the circumstances of Titus's death. The beginning of his reign was marked by moderation and a display of justice bordering upon severity. His affected great zeal for the reformation of public morals, and punished with death several persons guilty of adultery as well as some vestals who had broken their vows. He completed several splendid buildings begun by Titus—among others an *odeum*, or theatre for musical performances. The most important event of his reign was the conquest of Britain by Agricola, but Domitian grew jealous of that great commander's reputation and recalled him to Rome. His suspicious temper and his pusillanimity made him afraid of every man who was distinguished either by birth and connections or by merit and popularity, and he mercilessly sacrificed many to his fears, while his avarice led him to put to death a number of wealthy persons for the sake of their property. The usual pretext for these murders was the charge of conspiracy or treason, and thus a numerous race of informers was created and maintained by this system of spoliation. His cruelty was united to a deep dissimulation, and in this particular he resembled Tiberius rather than Caligula or Nero. He either put to death or drove away from Rome the philosophers and men of letters; Epictetus was one of the exiled. He found, however, some flatterers among the poets, such as Martial, Silius Italicus, and Statius. The latter dedicated to him his *Thebaïs* and *Achilleïs* and commemorated the events of his reign in his *Silvae*. But, in reality, the reign of Domitian was other than favourable to the Roman arms, except in Britain. In Moesia and Dacia, in Germany and Pannonia, his armies were defeated and whole provinces lost (Tac. *Agric.* 41). Domitian himself went twice into Moesia to oppose the Dacians, but, after several defeats, concluded a disgraceful peace with their king Decebalus, whom he acknowledged as sovereign, and to whom he agreed to pay tribute, which was afterwards discontinued by Trajan. Yet Domitian made a pompous report of his victories to the Senate and assumed the honours of a triumph. In the same manner he triumphed over the Cotti and the Sarmatians, which made Pliny the Younger say that the triumphs of Domitian were always evidence of some advantages gained by the enemies of Rome. In A.D. 95, Domitian assumed the consulship for the seventeenth time, together with Flavius Clemens, who had married Domitilla, a relative of the emperor. In that year a persecution of the Christians is recorded in the history of the Church, but it seems that it was not directed particularly against them, but against the Jews, with whom the Christians were often confounded by the Romans. Flavius Clemens and his wife were among the victims. In the following year, A.D. 96, a conspiracy was formed against Domitian among the officers of his guards and several of his intimate friends, and his wife, the infamous Domitilla, herself is said to have participated in it. The immediate cause of it was his increasing suspicion, which threatened the life of every one around him, and which is said to have been stimulated by the predictions of astrologers and soothsayers, whom he was very ready to consult. He was killed in his apartments by several of the conspirators, after struggling with them for some time, in his forty-fifth year and in the fifteenth of his reign. On the news of his death the Senate assembled and elected M. Cocceius Nerva emperor.

Domitian. (Cameo in Paris.)

The character of Domitian is represented by all ancient historians in the darkest colours, as being a compound of timidity and cruelty, of dissimulation and arrogance, of self-indulgence and stern severity towards others. He gave himself up to every excess and plunged into the most degrading vices. Conceiving at last the idea of arrogating divine honours to himself, he assumed the titles of Lord and God and claimed to be a son of Minerva. Soon after he had succeeded to the government he indulged in that love of solitude which pride and fear combined to render in a very short time the most confirmed of all his habits. In the beginning of his reign, says his biographer, he accustomed himself to spend several hours every day in the strictest privacy, employed frequently in nothing else than in catching flies and piercing them with a sharp instrument. Hence the well-known remark made by Vibius Crispus, who, when asked whether there was any one with the emperor, replied, "No, not even a fly." Domitian took a delight in inspiring others with terror, and Dio Cassius tells of a singular banquet, to which he invited the principal members of the Senate and equestrian order, where everything wore the appearance of an intended execution. He once even convened the Senate to determine in what way a large turbot should be cooked, whether whole or divided (Juv. iv.). The Senate, after his death, issued a decree that his name should be struck out of the Roman annals and obliterated from every public monument. His career is sketched in detail by Imhoff (1857).

Domitia Gens. A celebrated plebeian family, divided into two branches—that of the Calvini and that of the Ahenobarbi. The Calvini attained to the consular office B.C. 331, and the Ahenobarbi in B.C. 191. The latter, at length, in the person of Nero, became invested with imperial power; but with this emperor perished the male line of the Domitii. Domitian belonged to this family only through his mother Domitia.

Domitia Lex. See LEX.

Domitilla. See DOMITIA.

Domitius Afer. See AFER.

Domitius Ahenobarbus. See AHENOBARBUS.

Domitius Calvīnus. See CALVINUS.

Domitius Corbŭlo. See CORBULO.

Domitius Marsus. See MARSUS.

Domitius Ulpiānus. See ULPIANUS.

Domna, IULIA PIA. A native of Emesa, of low birth, but married to the Roman emperor Septimius Severus (A.D. 175), by whom she had Caracalla and Geta. She was a woman of much intellectual power and both political and literary ability, having great influence over her husband, after whose death she was intrusted by Caracalla with the conduct of state business of the first importance. When Caracalla was put to death by Macrinus (A.D. 217) she was at first treated with much consideration; but having excited the suspicion of Macrinus, she was banished from Antioch, and soon after ended her own life by voluntary starvation

Iulia Pia Domna. (Vatican Museum.)

(A.D. 217). She is described as a woman of much beauty but of loose morals; and is accused by Spartianus, Aurelius Victor, Eutropius, and Orosius of having maintained an incestuous intercourse with Caracalla, so that she was popularly known at Alexandria as "Iocasta." Dio Cassius, however, her contemporary, does not mention this scandalous story. Iulia was the great-aunt of Elagabalus and of Alexander Severus.

Domus (*οἰκία, οἴκησις, οἰκητήριον*, a dwelling-house; *οἶκος*, generally a room; in Homer and the tragedians, *δόμος*, but more usually in the plural as a dwelling-house). A house.

I. PRE-HISTORIC.—One special form of hut appears to have been commonly used by many different races of men at an early stage of their development. This was a small circular structure made of branches of trees stuck into the ground in a circle, and then bent inwards till their ends met and were tied together at the top. This rude frame-work was then filled in by wattled work woven in and out, and the whole was daubed over with tempered mud or clay. The hut of Achilles, thatched with rushes (*Il.* xxiv. 450), was probably a dwelling of this sort.

In historic times a survival of this ancient circular form of house existed in the form of the Prytaneum in Athens and elsewhere, and also in the Athenian Θόλος, which was built in the newer part of Athens as an adjunct, in a more convenient position for the use of the Prytanes. The Tholus was a round building with a conical roof, and must have had some resemblance to the Roman Temple of Vesta, to which the same name was frequently applied. The original Temple of Vesta was a round hut formed with wattle-work of osiers (Ovid, *Fast.* vi. 261 foll.; Fest. p. 250 M.).

Even during the imperial period in Rome one or more wattled huts were preserved in memory of the primitive dwellings of its founders. One of these, which stood at the western angle of the Palatine Hill, was known as the *Casa Romuli* (Dionys. i. 79); it was twice burned and repaired during the reign of Augustus (Dio Cass. xlviii. 43, and liv. 29). The Tugurium Faustuli is probably another name for the same thing. Another hut, also called after Romulus, appears to have been preserved on the Capitoline Hill (Vitruv. ii. 1; Sen. *Contr.* i. 6).

Casa Romuli.

A careful representation of this early form of house, as used by the prehistoric Latin race, exists in the small sepulchral "house-urns," which are found in considerable numbers in the early cemeteries of central Italy and elsewhere. These curious pieces of archaic pottery have small movable doors fixed with a wooden peg. See Virchow, *Die italienischen und deutschen Haus-Urnen* (Berlin, 1884).

During the many centuries which elapsed before the commencement of the historic period of Greece, a state of society existed very different from that with which Greek literature has made us familiar. Instead of large cities, a number of small, highly fortified towns or villages were ruled in an autocratic way by some chieftain of semi-Oriental habits, who lived in a style of much luxury and splendour, surrounded by a group of followers, very much like those of a mediæval feudal lord. At this early period wealth and splendour, which in historic times were devoted to the more public uses of the agora, the council chamber, and the temples of the gods, were lavished on the palace of the chief. It is this period that is celebrated in the Homeric poems which, there is every reason to believe, give us a faithful, if highly coloured, picture of the magnificence which adorned the dwellings of wealthy chiefs, such as Alcinoüs and, in a lesser degree, Odysseus. The recent discoveries made by Dr. Schliemann and Dr. Dörpfeld, within the massive walls of Tiryns (the *Τίρυνς τειχιόεσσα* of Homer), have for the first time shown us that the stately and richly decorated palaces of the *Odyssey* were not wholly the offspring of a poet's fancy. See TIRYNS.

II. THE HOMERIC PALACE OF ODYSSEUS.—The palace of Odysseus, as depicted in the *Odyssey*, may be taken as representing the Homeric house. It has been most clearly described by Prof. Gardner, of whose valuable paper in the *Quarterly Review* (January, 1886) what follows under this head is practically a summary.

The Homeric house consisted of three parts:

αὐλή, the fore-court; *δῶμα* or *μέγαρον*, the hall of the men; and *θάλαμος*, called in later times *γυναικωνῖτις*, the apartments of the women. The house was entered by massive folding-doors (*θύραι δικλίδες*), and on either side were stone seats (*ἕδραι*). The doors led into the *αὐλή*, or open court-yard, which was used as a kind of farm-yard. On either side and behind were chambers (*θάλαμοι*) used for various purposes, such as grinding the corn (*Od.* xx. 105), and sometimes for sleeping in (*Od.* xix. 48). In one corner of the court was the *θόλος*, a circular building. In the midst of the court was the altar of *Ζεὺς ἑρκεῖος*. In the court were two colonnades or porticoes, each called *αἴθουσα*, one on either side right and left of the court-yard (*αἴθουσα αὐλῆς*), and the other opposite the entrance to the court-yard and along the front of the *δῶμα* or *μέγαρον*. The latter is often considered as part of the *πρόδομος*, so that *αἴθουσα* and *πρόδομος* are often used as synonymous terms. Crossing the *αἴθουσα*, the visitor passed into the *μέγαρον* or *δῶμα*, where the chiefs lived. At either end of the *μέγαρον* was a door, one leading into the court-yard through the *αἴθουσα*, and the other into the women's apartments, the *θάλαμος*, properly so called. In front of either door was a threshold (*οὐδός*), probably raised. The threshold in front of the door into the *μέγαρον* was made of ash-wood, and the threshold in front of the door into the women's apartments was of stone, *λάϊνος οὐδός* (*Od.* xx. 258), a distinction which is most important for understanding the combat between Odysseus and the suitors. By the ashen threshold was the *δουροδόκη*, or spear-stand, close to one of the pillars (*Od.* i. 128). The *μέγαρον* was of great size. In the palace of Odysseus the three hundred suitors of Penelopé feasted in it. Its height was that of the house itself, and its roof was supported by lofty pillars (*κίονες*). In the upper part of the *μέγαρον* was the *ἐσχάρα*, or hearth, where the food was cooked (*Od.* xx. 123), and the smoke escaped through a hole in the roof, as in the old Roman *atrium*. Besides the two principal doors of the *μέγαρον* already mentioned, there was a third, or postern-door, called *ὀρσοθύρη*, the position of which has given rise to much dispute. It should, however, probably be placed, for the reasons given by Gardner and Jebb, on the side of the *μέγαρον*, as shown in the plan (Plan, 6), leading into the *λαύρη* (*Od.* xxii. 128, 137), or narrow passage which gave access to the women's apartments from the outer court-yard, thus avoiding the necessity of passing through the *μέγαρον* (Plan, 8).

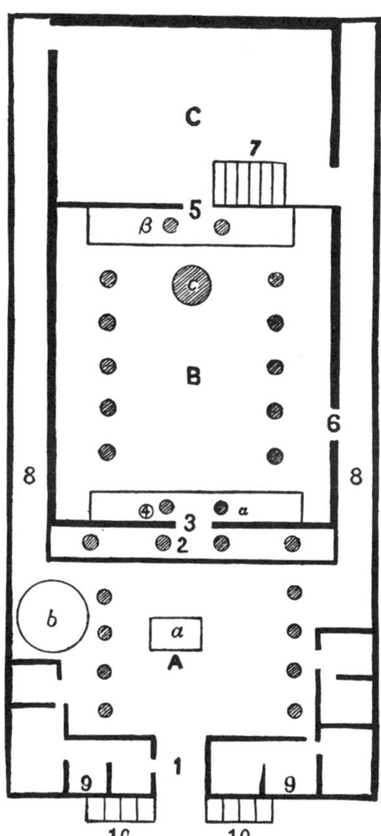

Palace of Odysseus. Ground-plan. (Gardner.)

A. *αὐλή*, fore-court.
a. Altar of *Ζεὺς ἑρκεῖος*.
b. *θόλος*.
B. *δῶμα* or *μέγαρον*, men's hall.
c. *ἐσχάρα*.
C. *θάλαμος*, women's hall.
1. *θύραι δικλίδες*.
2. *αἴθουσα*, *πρόδομος*.
3. *θύρα*.
4. *δουροδόκη*.
α. *μέλινος οὐδός*.
β. *λάϊνος οὐδός*.
5. *θύρα*.
6. *ὀρσοθύρη*.
7. *κλίμαξ*.
8. *λαύρη*.
9, 9. *θάλαμοι*.
10, 10. *ἕδραι*.

The women's rooms, or *θάλαμος*, properly so called, also styled *μέγαρα γυναικῶν* (*Od.* xxii. 151), were immediately behind the *μέγαρον* on the ground-floor, directly communicating with the latter by a door. This is clear from the whole narrative in the *Odyssey* of the combat between Odysseus and the suitors. The passages proving this have been critically examined by Prof. Jebb in the essay quoted below. (Cf. *Od.* xvii. 506, xx. 389, etc.; see also iv. 718.) Here the women sat engaged in weaving and domestic occupations. Here was the nuptial chamber, with the marriage-bed made by Odysseus with his own hands (*Od.* xxiii. 192, 295). The ordinary sleeping and other rooms of the women were in the upper story (*ὑπερῷϊον*), which was reached by a ladder, *κλίμαξ* (*Od.* xxi. 5; cf. *Od.* ii. 358, iv. 760; *Il.* ii. 514, xvi. 184; Eustath. *ad Od.* i. 328, p. 1420, 53). Hence we find Penelopé, after sleeping with Odysseus in the nuptial chamber, ascending with her handmaids into the upper chamber (*Od.* xxiii. 364). It is therefore a mistake on the part of some modern writers to describe the women's rooms as situated only in the upper story. In the women's rooms was the armory (*θάλαμος ὅπλων*, cf. *Od.* xxii. 140, 151–156), and the treasury at the further extremity (*θάλαμος ἔσχατος*), with a high roof (*Od.* xxi. 8). In the women's part of the house there was also an open court, in which grew an olive-tree in the palace of Odysseus (*Od.* xxiii. 190).

For further details regarding the Homeric house, reference may be made to Gardner, *Journ. of Hellenic Studies*, iii. p. 264 foll.; Jebb, ib. vii. p. 170 foll.; Dörpfeld, in Schliemann's *Tiryns* (London, 1866); Winckler, *Die Wohnhäuser der Hellenen* (Berlin, 1868); Protodikos, *De Aedibus Homericis* (Leipzig, 1877); Rumpf, *De Aedibus Homericis* (Giessen, 1884). Valuable accounts of the architecture and other arts of the Homeric period are given by Helbig, *Das homerische Epos* (1876), and by Buchholz, *Die homerischen Realien* (Leipzig, 1883–85).

III. The later Greek House.—The discoveries of recent years have shown that bricks made of unbaked clay were very extensively used down to quite late times for the private houses of the Greeks, and this is one reason why examples of Hellenic domestic architecture are so very rare. Burnt bricks were first introduced by the Romans (Blümner, *Technol. u. Terminol.*, etc., ii. p. 11). Till quite recently very few remains of Greek houses were known to exist. The excavations, however, made in the Greek city of Naukratis in the Egyptian Delta during 1884–86 by Messrs. Flinders Petrie and Ernest Gardner have brought to light remains of a large number of Greek streets and houses, all built of sundried brick, coated with painted stucco. The accompanying figure shows part of Mr. Petrie's discoveries: A is a single house forming a complete *insula*, as the Romans would call it; it consists of six rooms, with what was probably a small central open court. B B appear to be shops. C C are narrow streets. In this Greek city the streets seem all to be very narrow, and the *insulae* are mostly very small—in many cases, like the figured example, consisting of one house only. Though but very scanty remains were found of the unbaked-brick walls, yet in a few places patches of painted stucco on the exterior were found *in situ*. Though walls of this sort would last very well so long as they were roofed over and protected by their coating of hard stucco, yet when once they had fallen into a ruined state the process of decay would be rapid and complete, even in Egypt, and of course much more so in a more rainy climate.

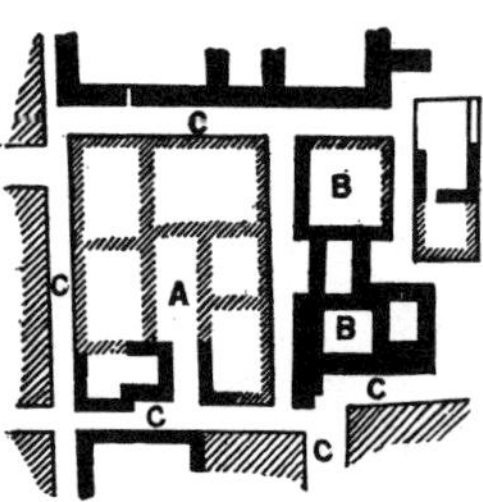

Plan of a Greek House at Naukratis in Egypt.

The other more important examples of Greek domestic architecture which have yet been discovered are some houses in the Piraeus, the foundations of which were exposed in 1884 during the laying out of a new street by the municipality. (See Dr. Dörpfeld, in *Mittheil. d. deutsch. archäol. Inst. in Athen*, vol. ix. no. 3, 1884.) The figure shows a reduction made from Dr. Dörpfeld's plan.

On the southeast and southwest sides the block faces upon streets; it appears to be a double house, though this is not quite certain, owing to the impossibility of ascertaining the positions of all the doors. On the northwest side remains were found of a large open peristyle, apparently derived from the αὐλή of the earlier Hellenic plan; under the covered porticus of this cloister an altar was found, probably dedicated to Zeus Herkeios. On the southeast side the house was entered through a long shallow porch, with two columns, in which stood another altar, probably that of Apollo Agyieus. This porch led into a small open court, surrounded on three sides by a covered walk (στοά or *porticus*). The pavement of this was laid so as to drain into an open gully, through which the rainwater escaped into a drain. In one corner of the court was a well, and on the other side a stone cistern for storing water; a second cistern stood in the room adjoining the open court on the northwest. Some remains of paving were found, as is indicated on the plan. In one room it consists of stone flags; in another of a sort of rude mosaic, formed of pebbles set in concrete. On the southwest side are some rooms which were entered directly from the street; these may have been shops or public offices. Traces of a staircase leading to an upper floor were found at one end of the room with the flagging pavement. This block measures, without counting the large peristyle, about 140 feet by 75 feet. The clear open space of the peristyle was about 68 feet wide; its other dimension was not discovered. It is possible that this block may have been all part of the same house—one portion being the ἀνδρωνῖτις, or men's part, and the rest the γυναικωνῖτις, or women's part.

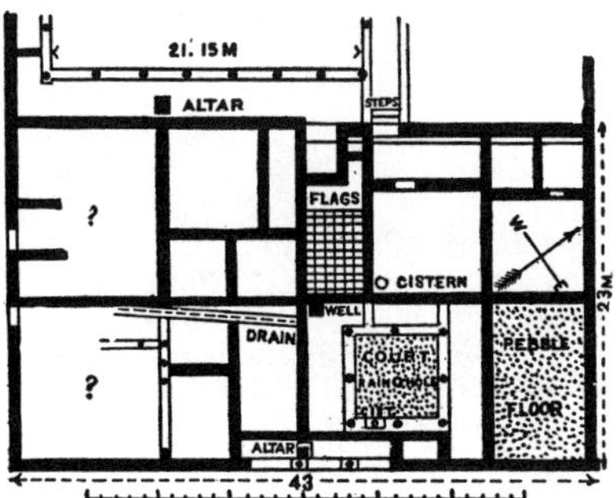

Plan of a Greek House discovered in the Piraeus.

During the most flourishing period of Greece the private houses appear to have been small and simple in design; splendour of materials and ornament were reserved for the temples of the gods and the public buildings, such as the Agora and the great στοαί, which in Athens especially contributed so largely to the architectural magnificence of the city. The front of the house towards the street was not large, as the apartments extended rather in the direction of its depth than of its width. In towns the houses were often built side by side, with party walls between (ὁμότοιχοι οἰκίαι). The exterior wall was plain and often covered with plaster or stucco. Sometimes, as in Tanagra, the exterior was adorned with what was probably terra-cotta (Dicaearch. p. 245, Fuhr). Plutarch says that Phocion's house was ornamented with plates of bronze (Plut. *Phoc.* 18). Unbaked clay, as we have already shown, was used for the walls; thus it was easy for the Plataeans to break through the party walls of their houses, so as to communicate with each other. For the same reason the burglar was called τοιχωρύχος, because he found it easier to obtain an entrance into houses by breaking through the soft walls than by the door or windows (Plat. *De Leg.* 831 E).

Foreigners were specially struck by the mean appearance of the private houses of Athens in the time of Pericles, as strongly contrasting with the splendour of the public buildings (Thuc. ii. 14, 65). "A stranger," says Dicaearchus, "might doubt upon a sudden view whether this were really the city of Athens," so mean were the houses and crooked and narrow the streets. It was not till the time of Demosthenes that good houses began to be built in Athens.

In all cases the country houses must have been

much finer buildings than those in the old cities, where streets were narrow and sites often very cramped (Isocr. *Areop.* § 20). Thucydides (ii. 14) speaks of the preference of the Athenians for houses in the country. See VILLA.

The plan and whole arrangement of town and country houses would naturally be absolutely different, and it is unreasonable to suppose that one fixed type of house was used by the Greeks. Existing remains show us that the Roman houses had as many varieties of plan as we have now, and yet many archæologists have written as if there was one stereotyped plan of house used in classical times. The somewhat pedantic language of Vitruvius (vi. 7, 10) on the subject has tended to support the belief in the existence of one fixed type of Greek house, but at his date, in the reign of Augustus, archæology was practically an unknown science, and it may reasonably be suggested that the so-called Greek plan of Vitruvius does not represent the domestic architecture of the bygone days when the Greeks were an independent race, but rather Vitruvius's private notion, as a practising architect, of a house to be built for some wealthy Roman in the revived pseudo-Hellenic style which began to be popular in the reigns of the early emperors of Rome.

Nevertheless, many of Vitruvius's statements may be of great use in illustrating difficult passages in older Greek writers, which treat of some details in the Hellenic house, especially when the description is compared with some of the existing Roman dwellings, which are evidently designed to some extent after a real or supposed Greek model.

Greek houses had three principal features in common. First, there were one or two open courts, surrounded by the various rooms. Secondly, in a Greek family the women lived in private apartments allotted to their respective use. Hence the house was always divided into two distinct portions, already mentioned—the Andronitis (ἀνδρωνῖτις), or men's apartments, and the Gynaeconitis (γυναικωνῖτις), or women's apartments. Thirdly, the Gynaeconitis was, as a general rule, in larger houses behind the Andronitis, and on the same floor as the latter Much difficulty has been occasioned in the arrangement of a Greek house by the statement of Vitruvius (vi. 7 [10]) that the principal entrance led at once into the Gynaeconitis, and that the Andronitis therefore was behind the women's rooms, or rather, if we construe his words strictly, by their side. But such an arrangement is alike inconsistent with the careful state of seclusion in which the Greek women were kept, and also with the positive statements of the writers of the period. It is very likely that Vitruvius misunderstood to some extent the descriptions given by his Greek authorities, and has assigned to the Gynaeconitis the arrangement of the Andronitis.

The plan below of the ground-floor of a Greek house of the larger size, with two courts or peristyles, is taken, with slight alterations, from Guhl and Koner. It is of course conjectural, but it will serve for the *probable* arrangements (for further we cannot go) of the Greek house at the period we are speaking of. Other plans, differing very much from this, have been given by several modern writers; but this appears on the whole the most consistent with the ancient authorities. In smaller

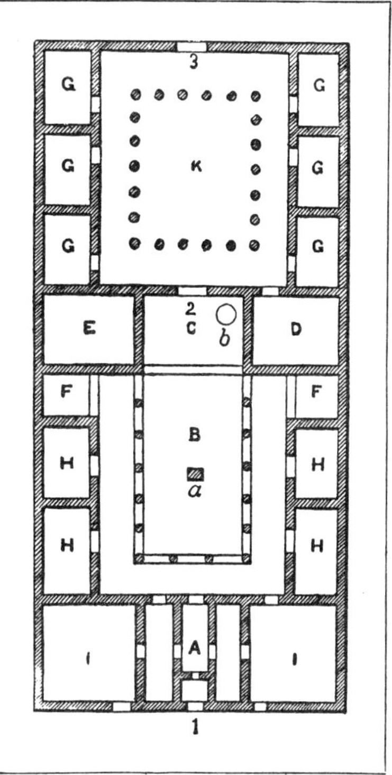

Plan of a Greek House. (Guhl and Koner.)

A. Entrance-hall.
B. Peristyle of the Andronitis.
  a. Altar of Ζεὺς ἑρκεῖος.
C. Andron, or dining-hall.
  b. ἑστία.
K. Peristyle of the Gynaeconitis.
H. Rooms of the Andronitis.
F. Perhaps sanctuaries of the θεοὶ κτήσιοι and θεοὶ πατρῷοι.
D. Thalamos.
E. Amphithalamos.
G. Rooms of the Gynaeconitis, for working in wool and other purposes.
I. Rooms of the Andronitis, and in some houses perhaps shops opening to the street.
1. Πρόδομος, and farther back, street-door, αὔλειος θύρα.
2. Door between the men's and women's rooms, μέσαυλος or μέταυλος θύρα.
3. Garden-door, κηπαία θύρα.

houses the Gynaeconitis was much more limited, having no open court, and in some cases was restricted to the upper story.

Some other matters connected with a Greek house require notice.

(1) *Upper Stories.*—When there was an upper story (ὑπερῷον, διῆρες), it seldom extended over the whole space occupied by the lower story. The principal use of the upper story was for the sleeping apartments, both of the family and of the slaves. Houses rarely had more than two stories; but in later times we find in the larger towns mention of houses with three stories (τριστέγη, Artemid. iv. 46; Acts, xx. 8, 9). The access to the upper floor seems to have been sometimes by stairs (ἀναβαθμοί) on the outside of the house, leading up from the street, as was the case at Rome (Aristot. *Oec.* ii. 5, p. 1347, 5). The upper story was sometimes let, or used for lodging guests (Antiph. *De Venef.* § 14). But in some large houses there were rooms set apart for the reception of guests (ξενῶνες) on the ground-floor.

Portions of the upper story sometimes projected beyond the walls of the lower part, forming balconies or verandas (προβολαί, γεισιποδίσματα, Pollux, i. 81), like the Roman *maeniana*.

(2) *Roofs.*—The roofs were generally flat, and it was customary to walk about upon them, as on the *solaria* at Rome (Lys. *adv. Simon.* § 11; Aristoph. *Lysistr.* 389), or to pass from one house to another (Demosth. *c. Androt.* p. 609, § 53). But high-pitched roofs were also used, covered with tiles (κέραμος, Pollux, i. 81).

(3) *Doors.*—For particulars, see IANUA and CLAVIS. In the interior of the house the place of doors was sometimes supplied by curtains (παραπετάσματα, παρακαλύμματα), which also hung between the pillars of the peristyle. They were either plain, dyed, or embroidered (Pollux, x. 32; Theophr. 5).

and that the smoke escaped through an opening in the roof; but it is not easy to understand how this could be the case when there was an upper story. The καπνοδόκη mentioned by Herodotus (viii. 137) was not really a chimney, but only an opening in the roof. But the κάπνη of Aristophanes (*Vesp.* 143) seems to have been really a chimney, as it is described by the Scholiast on the passage as pipe-shaped (σωληνοειδής). In any case, the chimney seems to have been used only in the kitchen (ὀπτάνιον, Alexis *ap.* Athen. ix. p. 386 b).

(7) *Decoration.*—The decorations of the interior were very plain at the period to which our description refers. The floors were mere plaster. At a late period coloured stones were used (Plin. *H. N.* xxxvi. § 184). Mosaics are first mentioned as introduced under the kings of Pergamus. The

Aula of Greek House. (Von Falke.)

(4) *Windows.*—The principal openings for the admission of light and air were in the uncovered peristyle and perhaps in the roofed part of the peristyle; but it is incorrect to suppose that the houses had no windows (θυρίδες), or at least none overlooking the street. They appear to have been chiefly in the upper story, and in ancient works of art women are represented looking out of them (Aristoph. *Thesm.* 797, *Eccles.* 961).

(5) *Privies.*—These were called ἀπόπατοι, ἄφοδοι, or κοπρῶνες. Their position is nowhere expressly indicated, but they were probably, as in Roman houses (see below), in proximity to the kitchen.

(6) *Heating.*—Artificial warmth was procured by little portable stoves (ἐσχάρια, ἐσχαρίδες) or chafing-dishes (ἀνθράκια). (See FOCUS.) It is often supposed that the chimney was altogether unknown, walls, up to the fourth century B.C., seem to have been only whitewashed. The first instance of painting them is that of Alcibiades (Andoc. *In Alcib.* § 17)—an innovation that met with considerable opposition (Xen. *Mem.* iii. 8, § 10; *Oecon.* ix. 2). Plato mentions the painting of the walls of houses as a mark of a τρυφῶσα πόλις (*Repub.* ii. 373 A). These allusions prove that the practice was not uncommon in the time of Plato and Xenophon. We have also mention of painted ceilings at the same period, and at a later period this mode of decoration became general.

(8) *Letting and Price of Houses.*—There was a great deal of speculation in the building and letting of houses at Athens (Xen. *Oecon.* iii. 1). A distinction was made at Athens between the οἰκία, which was a dwelling-house for a single family, and the συνοικία, which was adapted to hold sev-

eral families—like the Roman *insula*. The lodging-houses were let mostly to foreigners who came to Athens on business, and especially to the μέτοικοι, whom the law did not allow to acquire real property, and who therefore could not purchase houses of their own. Pasion, the banker, had a lodging-house valued at 100 minas (Demosth. *c. Steph.* i. p. 1110, § 28). Two counting-houses are mentioned by Isaeus (*De Hagn. Her.* § 42) as yielding a return of rather more than 8½ per cent. interest on the purchase-money. But this probably was much below the average. The summer season was the most profitable for the letting of houses, when merchants and other visitors flocked to Athens. The rent was commonly paid by the month. Lodging-houses were frequently taken on speculation by persons called ναύκληροι or σταθμοῦχοι (Ammon., Harpocrat.), who made a profit by underletting them, and sometimes for not very reputable purposes (Isaeus, *De Philoct. Her.* § 19). Boeckh has given an account from the ancient writers of the prices of houses at Athens, which seem to have been very small. They varied from 3 minas ($54) to 120 minas ($2160), according to their size, situation, and condition, from 30 to 50 minas ($540 to $900) being an ordinary price (Boeckh, *Publ. Econ. of Athens*, pp. 65, 141; *Staatshaush.* i. p. 84).

For further details regarding the Greek house, see the commentators on Vitruvius; Schneider, *Epim. ad Xen. Mem.*; Hirt, *Die Lehre der Gebäude*, pp. 287–289; Stieglitz, *Archäol. d. Baukunst*, vol. ii. pt. 2, pp. 150–159; Krause, *Deinokrates*, p. 488 foll.; Winckler, *Die Wohnhäuser der Hellenen* (Berlin, 1868); Becker-Göll, *Charikles*, ii. p. 105 foll.; Hermann-Blümner, *Griech. Privatalt.* p. 143 foll.; Guhl and Koner, *Leben d. Griech. u. Röm.* p. 95 foll., 5th ed.); Laloux, *L'Architecture Grecque* (1888).

IV. The Roman House.—The earliest dwellings of the Latins on the Palatine Hill were probably mere huts of mud-daubed osiers, like the hut of Romulus, which was preserved as a sacred relic for many centuries. After the burning of Rome by the Gauls, the city was rebuilt in haste, with very narrow streets and on no regular plan (Liv. v. 55). Even the houses of the richest citizens were small and of inexpensive materials, such as unburnt brick or soft brown tufa. No examples of fired bricks are known in Roman buildings till the time of Iulius Caesar; and the remarks of Vitruvius seem to refer wholly to crude or sun-dried bricks, of which no examples in Rome have survived to modern times. Down to the beginning of the last century of the Republic, Romans of rank continued to live in small houses. In B.C. 125, the censors censured Lepidus, the augur, because he paid 6000 sesterces (about $250) for his house rent (Vell. Paterc. ii. 10); and Sulla, when a young man, paid only 3000 sesterces for his rooms on the ground-floor, while a freedman in the upper part of the same house paid only 2000 sesterces, or $80 (Plut. *Sull.* c. 1).

The earliest regulation we find respecting houses is a law of the Twelve Tables that each building should be separated from another by a space of 2½ feet called *ambitus* (Fest. pp. 5, 11, M.). But this enactment was disregarded, and was again enforced by Nero when he rebuilt the city (Tac. *Ann.* xv. 43; see below). As Rome increased in population, the houses were raised in height. The *insula*, in which the lower and middle classes lived, was a building of several stories, let out in flats or separate rooms to different families or persons. The *domus* or *aedes privatae*, on the contrary, was a separate house, in later times a palace, usually with only one story above the ground-floor, the abode of the rich and great, and inhabited for the most part by a single family; though, as in the case of the palazzi in modern Rome, parts of them, especially at the back or top of the *domus*, were sometimes rented (Plaut. *Trin.* i. 2, 157; Suet. *Ner.* 44, *Vitell.* 7). In the general description of a Roman house our remarks apply only to the *domus*, properly so called, as the *insula* was built on an entirely different plan.

The insula is defined by Festus (p. 111, M.) to be a building not joined by common walls with neighbouring houses, but surrounded by a street, so that it stood like an island surrounded by rivers or the sea. It was thus, as has been said, very much like one of the large hotels in modern cities, with one or more courts, and bounded on all sides by streets, like the Louvre Hotel at Paris. The ground-floor was usually rented for shops (*tabernae*), and the upper stories in flats or separate rooms, as in continental and American cities at the present day. Such an *insula*, containing various tenements and shops, is the house of Pansa at Pompeii, described below. The number of *insulae* at Rome naturally exceeded that of the *domus*; and accordingly we find in the *Notitia*, which was compiled between A.D. 334 and 357, that there were at Rome 44,171 *insulae* and 1782 *domus* (Marquardt, *Staatsverw.* ii. p. 120). To the same effect Suetonius, in describing the fire at Rome under Nero, speaks of the "immense number" of *insulae* that were burned, in addition to the palaces (*domus*) of the nobles (Suet. *Ner.* 38). Becker and some other writers erroneously suppose that a single floor or a separate room in such a house was also called *insula*, but the proper name for such a separate lodging was *cenaculum* (Becker-Göll, *Gallus*, ii. p. 221).

It was apparently usual for an *insula* to have been built on speculation, and let by the proprietor to different occupants (Plut. *Crass.* 2; Mart. iv. 37). Hence the stories or separate rooms were called *cenacula meritoria* (Suet. *Vitell.* 7; Juv. iii. 234) or *conducta*. Cicero had some shops, which he let (Cic. *Ad Att.* xiv. 9). The rent (*pensio*) at Rome was considerable, even for a miserable garret (Juv. iii. 166, 225). Poor persons in the time of Iulius Caesar appear to have paid 2000 sesterces ($80 or $85) as the usual rent (Suet. *Caes.* 38). Caelius was said to have paid 30,000 sesterces (about $1200) for the rent of a third floor in the *insula* of P. Clodius, though Cicero says the real rent was only one third of this sum (*Cael.* 7, 17). The *insularii* were not the occupants of the *insulae*, but the agents who had charge of the *insulae* and collected the rents. They were also called *procuratores insularum*. The *insula* appears to have been named after the person to whom it belonged. Thus we find in inscriptions the *insula Arriana Polliana*, the *insula Sertoriana*, etc. (Orelli, 4324).

The upper stories and the separate rooms of the *insula* were, as we have already said, called *cenacula*. This word properly signifies rooms to dine in; but after it became the fashion to dine in the upper part of the house, all the rooms above the ground-floor were called *cenacula* (Varr. *L. L.* v. 162). There were different flights of stairs connecting the upper stories with the lower part of the house, as we find to be the case in houses at

Pompeii. Sometimes the stairs had no connection with the lower part of the house, but ascended at once from the street (Liv. xxxix. 14, 2; xxi. 62, 3). As the different stories could not all be lighted from openings in the roof, as in the *domus*, they had windows looking out into the street (Liv. i. 41, xxiv. 21). They also had sometimes balconies, supported by brackets, projecting into the street, from which an occupant could shake hands with his next-door or opposite neighbour (Mart. i. 86). These balconies were called *maeniana*, and the same name was also given to the stories which projected over those below, as we see in some old houses in England (Fest. p. 134, 22, M.; Isid. xv. 3, 11; Vitruv. v. 1, 2). Projecting stories were forbidden in A.D. 368 to be erected in Rome (Ammian. Marcell. xxvii. 9, 8) on account of the narrowness of the streets, and were again forbidden by the emperors Honorius and Theodosius unless there was an open space, in some cases of ten, in others of fifteen feet, clear of any adjacent building (*Cod. Iust.* viii. 10, 11). Such a projecting story is seen in some of the Pompeian houses.

Maenianum, or Projecting Story. (Overbeck, *Pompeii.*)

We find mention of a house three stories high in B.C. 218 (Liv. xxi. 62, 3); and Martial considered the third story, where he lived, as very high. If we were to estimate the height of the Roman houses by the way in which they are spoken of by the ancient writers, we should probably assign to them too many stories; for the houses, as Friedländer observes, very likely appeared higher than they really were in consequence of the narrowness of the streets. We have no express mention of any houses more than four stories high; but from various circumstances we may infer that some of the houses at Rome had a larger number of stories than are expressly mentioned. Thus Augustus limited the height of houses to seventy feet, which implies that they had been built still higher, and Cicero describes the houses as hoisted up and suspended in the air (*Leg. Agr.* ii. 35, 96). See Friedländer, *Sittengesch. Roms*, i. p. 5 foll.

The houses let for hire were in Rome, as in modern cities at the present day, badly built by speculators. The upper stories were of wood (*tabulata, contignationes*) and frequently fell down, while their material made them more liable to fires, which were very frequent in Rome. Catullus speaks ironically of the advantages of a beggar, who had nothing to fear from fire or the fall of houses. The returns from house property in Rome were large, but people feared to invest in it on account of fires (Gell. xv. 1). The inundations of the Tiber also caused the fall of houses. For further details, see Friedländer, i. p. 26 foll.

It was not, however, till the reign of Nero that a complete reform was effected in the arrangement and construction of the houses and streets of Rome. Nero had a new and elaborate Building Act drawn up, which required fire-proof materials, such as *peperino*, a hard volcanic stone, to be used for the external walls of houses. He also enacted that each building should have separate walls and a space (*ambitus*) left open all round it. As a means of escape and assistance in the case of fire he also caused arcades or colonnades to be built at his own expense in front of the *insulae*. In Trajan's reign the limit of height for street houses was fixed at sixty feet (Aurel. Vict. *Epit.* 13). The emperors Antoninus and Verus again made an ordinance about the space to be left round the *insulae* (*Dig.* viii. 2, 14).

We now turn to the history and construction of the DOMUS, or mansion of the great and wealthy. It was not till the last century of the Republic, when wealth had been acquired by conquests in the East, that houses of any splendour began to be built; but it then became the fashion not only to build houses of an immense size, but to adorn them with marble columns, paintings, statues, and costly works of art. They covered a large space, most of the rooms being on the ground-floor. The spacious *atria* and *peristylia*, being open to the sky, did not permit an upper story, which, if it existed, must have been confined to the sides of the building, and could not have been very high, as otherwise it would have darkened the *atria* and *peristylia*. These splendid mansions were erected for the most part on the hills and along the slopes of the Palatine, on the side near the Forum, which was the favourite quarter for the Roman nobles. In later times the various palaces of the emperors swallowed up almost the whole of this site.

The house of the orator L. Crassus on the Palatine, built about B.C. 92, was the first which had marble columns. For this, Crassus was severely blamed, and the stern republican M. Brutus nicknamed him the "Palatine Venus." This house was valued at 6,000,000 sesterces (about $240,000); but Pliny says that it yielded in magnificence to the house of Q. Catulus on the same hill, and was much inferior to that of C. Aquilius on the Viminal. The house of Catulus had a fine colonnade (*porticus*), adorned with the spoils of the Cimbric War. It was near the house of Cicero, as a portion of the colonnade was destroyed when Clodius razed the house of Cicero (Val. Max. vi. 3, § 1).

In B.C. 78, M. Lepidus, for the first time in Rome, used the rich Numidian marble not only for columns, but even for the thresholds of his doors; yet the fashion of building magnificent houses increased so rapidly that the house of Lepidus, which in his consulship was the first in

Rome, was thirty-five years later eclipsed by a hundred others. Lucullus was especially celebrated for the magnificence of his houses. The Romans were exceedingly fond of marble for the decoration of their abodes. An advance in costly magnificence was made by the ædile M. Aemilius Scaurus in the middle of the first century B.C. He purchased the house of L. Crassus and greatly enlarged it. He introduced, as the supports of his atrium, columns of the black "Lucullean" marble no less than thirty-eight feet in height, and of which the weight was so great that he had to provide security for an indemnity in case of injury that might be done to the main sewers while these immense blocks of marble were being carted through the streets (Plin. *H. N.* xxxvi. § 5 foll.). This house was sold to Clodius for nearly 15,000,000 sesterces (about $600,000)—a price, says Pliny, worthy of the madness of kings. This is the highest price recorded in the time of the Republic for a house. The consul Messalla bought the house of Autronius for 3,400,000 sesterces (about $140,000), and Cicero the house of Crassus (not L. Crassus, the orator) for 3,500,000 sesterces (about $140,000) (Cic. *Ad Att.* i. 13, 6, with Tyrrell's note; *Ad Fam.* v. 6). Cicero's house was on the lower slope of the Palatine towards the *Regia*, the official residence of Iulius Caesar as Pontifex Maximus, whom Cicero calls his neighbour (*Ad Fam.* v. 6, *Ad Att.* xiii. 45). These houses will serve as samples of the value of the mansions of the nobles during the Republic. Sallust speaks of them as like cities in size (*Cat.* 12), and Seneca describes them in the same terms under the Empire (*Ep.* 90, 43), when the imperial palaces became still more magnificent. Many of them, like the houses of Sallust and Maecenas, described below, were surrounded by gardens. The rich noble, we are told, was not content unless he had a *rus in urbe* (Mart. xii. 57, 21), and the extensive pleasure-grounds are alluded to in other passages.

According to Vitruvius, the principal parts of a Roman house were: (1) *Vestibulum*, (2) *Ostium*, (3) *Atrium*, (4) *Alae*, (5) *Tablinum*, (6) *Fauces*, (7) *Peristylium*. The parts of a house which were considered of less importance, and of which the arrangement differed in different houses, were: (1) *Cubicula*, (2) *Triclinia*, (3) *Oeci*, (4) *Exedrae*, (5) *Pinacotheca*, (6) *Bibliotheca*, (7) *Balineum*, (8) *Culina*, (9) *Cenacula*, (10) *Lararium* or *Sacrarium*, (11) *Diaetae*, (12) *Solaria*, (13) *Cellae*. We shall speak of each in order.

(1) *Vestibulum.*—There has been much dispute respecting the exact signification of this word, which has arisen from the different meanings attached to it at different periods of history and in different kinds of houses. In the palaces of the nobles the *vestibulum* was a vacant space before the house, forming a court-yard or entrance-court, surrounded on three sides by the house, and open on the fourth to the street. The two wings ran out beyond the façade of the building, and the door was in the third side opposite the street. In some houses the projecting sides were occupied by shops opening into the street. In the *vestibulum* the clients assembled, till the door was opened, to pay their respects (*salutatio*) to the master of the house, so that they might not be left standing either in the street or within the house (Gell. xvi. 5, §§ 3, 8; *vestibulum, quod est ante domum*, Varr. *L. L.* vii. 81; Macrob. vi. 8, § 15). Hence in the smaller houses in Rome and the municipal towns, there was either no *vestibulum*, so that the door opened straight upon the street, or the *vestibulum* was simply indicated by the door standing back a few feet from the street, as in many of the houses at Pompeii. Sometimes there were steps from the street leading up to the *vestibulum* (Sen. *Ep.* 84). In the houses of the nobility the *vestibulum* was adorned with statues, arms, and other trophies (Plin. *H. N.* xxxv. § 7). Public buildings also had *vestibula*, as the curia or senate-house (Liv. i. 48, ii. 48), and various temples (Liv. *Ep.* 86).

(2) *Ostium.*—The *ostium* was the entrance to the house, and is constantly used as synonymous with *ianua* and *fores*, "the door." But *ostium* properly signified the small vacant space before the *ianua*, whence Plautus (*Pers.* v. 1, 6) says *ante ostium et ianuam*. Here stood the *antae* (q. v.), two posts or pillars flanking the doorway. On the threshold the word *Salve* was frequently wrought in mosaic, as we see in the Pompeian houses; and over the threshold there sometimes hung a cage containing a magpie or a parrot, taught to greet those who entered (Petron. 28; Mart. vii. 87, 6; xiv. 76). Over the door a few words of good omen were sometimes written, such as *nihil intret mali* (Orelli-Henz. *Inscr.* 7287), or *deprecatio incendiorum* (Plin. *H. N.* xxviii. § 20). Sometimes the house was indicated by a sign over the door, as in mediæval times. Thus we are told that Augustus was born *ad Capita Bubula* (Suet. *Aug.* 5), and Domitian, *ad Malum Punicum* (Suet. *Dom.* 1). The street-door itself is fully described under IANUA.

Whether the street-door opened into a hall or directly into the *atrium* has been a subject of dispute. Vitruvius mentions no entrance-hall in a Roman house; but there are reasons for believing there must have been an entrance-hall in the palaces of the nobility, as behind the door there was a small room (*cella*) for the house-porter (*ostiarius* or *ianitor*), and it is difficult to suppose that this was in the *atrium* (Petron. 28), especially as a dog was kept by his side, chained to the wall, with a written warning *Cave Canem* (Plaut. *Most.* iii. 2, 169). Sometimes a dog was painted on the wall (Petron. 29) or wrought in mosaic on the pavement, as we find in the House of the Tragic Poet at Pompeii. (See illust. p. 296.) At the end of the hall, which seems to have been called *ostium*, there was no inner door, as Becker describes, but the entrance to the *atrium* was closed by a curtain (*velum*), which was drawn aside by the usher when he admitted strangers to an interview (Lamprid. *Alex. Sev.* 5, *Heliog.* 14; Sen. *Ep.* 20). The entrance-hall was small, so that a person in the *atrium* could look through it at those walking in the street (Suet. *Calig.* 41).

(3) *Atrium.*—The first point to be determined in connection with the *atrium*, upon which the whole disposition of a Roman house depends, is whether the *atrium* and the *cavum aedium* or *cavaedium* denote two separate courts or one and the same. Some modern writers maintain that they were distinct courts, and accordingly place three courts in a Roman house—first the *atrium*, then the *cavum aedium* in the centre, and lastly the *peristylium* in the rear. But this view cannot be maintained; it is rejected by the best modern authorities; it is in direct opposition to the statements of Varro (*L. L.* v. 161) and Vitruvius (vi. 3 and 8), who call

Restoration of the Interior of Roman House. (Overbeck, *Pompeii.*)

sometimes the chief room of the house *atrium* and sometimes *cavum aedium;* and it is contradicted by the fact that no houses in Pompeii have yet been discovered containing more than two courts —namely, the *atrium* and the *peristylium.* We may therefore conclude that the *atrium* and the *cavum aedium* denote the same room, the only difference perhaps being that *cavum aedium* indicated originally the open part, and *atrium* the entire area; but in general the two words are used as synonymous. The *atrium* or *cavum aedium* was a large room or court roofed over, with the exception of an opening in the centre, called *compluvium,* towards which the roof sloped so as to throw the rain-water into a cistern in the floor, termed *impluvium* (Varr. l. c.; Fest. p. 108, M.; Liv. xliii. 13, 6; Plaut. *Amph.* v. 1, 56). The water from the *impluvium* flowed into a well (*puteus*) under ground; for before the construction of the aqueducts the Romans were dependent upon wells for their supply of water. The word *impluvium,* however, is sometimes employed in a wider sense to denote the whole uncovered space in the *atrium,* and therefore the opening in the top as well as the cistern at the bottom (Cic. *Act. in Verr.* i. 23, 61, with the note of Pseudo-Ascon. p. 177, Or.). *Compluvium* in like manner is sometimes used in the same wide signification as equivalent to *impluvium* (Suet. *Aug.* 92). The *compluvium* was sometimes covered with hangings, as a protection against the sun (Ovid, *Met.* x. 595). The breadth of the *impluvium,* according to Vitruvius, was not less than a quarter nor greater than a third of the breadth of the *atrium;* its length was in the same proportion according to the length of the *atrium.*

Vitruvius (vi. 3) distinguishes five kinds of *atria* or *cava aedium,* which were called by the following names:

(*a*) *Tuscanicum.* In this the roof was supported by four beams, crossing each other at right angles, the included space forming the *compluvium.* This kind of *atrium* was the most ancient of all.

(*b*) *Tetrastylum.* This was of the same form as the preceding, except that the main beams of the roof were supported by pillars, placed at the four angles of the *impluvium.*

(*c*) *Corinthium* was on the same principle as the tetrastyle, only that there were a greater number of pillars around the *impluvium,* on which the beams of the roof rested.

(*d*) *Displuviatum* had its roof sloping the contrary way to the *compluvium,* so that the water fell outside the house instead of being carried into the *impluvium,* and was carried off by gutters.

(*e*) *Testudinatum* was constructed in the same way as the *displuviatum,* but it was roofed all over and had no *compluvium.* We are not informed, however, how light was admitted into an *atrium* of this kind.

The *atrium,* as we have already seen, was originally the only room of the house, serving as sitting-room, bedroom, and kitchen, which it probably continued to do among the lower classes even in later times (Serv. *ad* Verg. *Aen.* i. 726, ix. 648). Here was the *focus,* or hearth, which served not only for cooking, but from its sacred character was used also for the receptacle of the Lares or Penates that were sometimes kept in little cupboards near the hearth (Plaut. *Aul.* ii. 18, 15; Tibull. i. 10, 20; Juv. viii. 110; Petron. 29). The Lar, or tutelary god of the house, stood close to the entrance behind the door leading into the *atrium* (Ovid, *Fast.* i. 136 foll.); and we find him so placed in some of the Pompeian houses. Near the sacred flame the members of the family took the common meal, and the same custom continued in the country even in the time of Augustus (Hor. *Sat.* ii. 6, 65 foll.). In the *atrium* the master of the house kept his *arca* (q. v.), or money-chest, which was fastened to the floor. Here stood the nuptial bed (*lectus genialis*) against the back wall, opposite the entrance to the *atrium,* whence it was also called *lectus adversus* (Gell. xvi. 9). Here sat the mistress of the house, spinning and weaving with her maids (Liv. i. 57, 9). Here all visits were paid and here the patron received his clients (Hor. *Ep.* i. 5, 31). Here the corpse was placed before it was carried out to burial. (See FUNUS.) Here, in the *alae,* were placed the waxen *imagines* (q. v.) of the ancestors of the house.

But as wealth increased, and numerous clients came to wait upon their patron, new rooms were built, and the *atrium* ceased to be the only room for the family. A kitchen (*culina*) was made for cooking; the Lares were placed in a special *lararium;* the meals were taken in the upper story, hence called *cenaculum;* the master and mistress slept in a separate *cubiculum.* As the *atrium* now became the reception-room, it was fitted up among the wealthy with much splendour and magnificence for the reception of their clients. The opening in the roof was enlarged for the admission of more light, and was supported by pillars frequently made of costly marble. Between the pillars and along the walls, statues and other works of art were placed (Cic. *Verr.* i. 23, 61). In the middle of the *impluvium* was a marble fountain, with jets of water, frequently adorned with reliefs, of which many beautiful specimens have been found at Pompeii. Near the fountain, where the hearth formerly stood, was a marble table, called *cartibulum* (q.v.). The *atrium,* however, still continued, as in ancient times, to be the chief room of the house, and it was not only the room for the reception of guests, but its primitive character was preserved by its retaining the symbolical nuptial couch (Hor. *Ep.* i. 1, 87), the *imagines* of the ancestors, and the instruments for weaving and spinning.

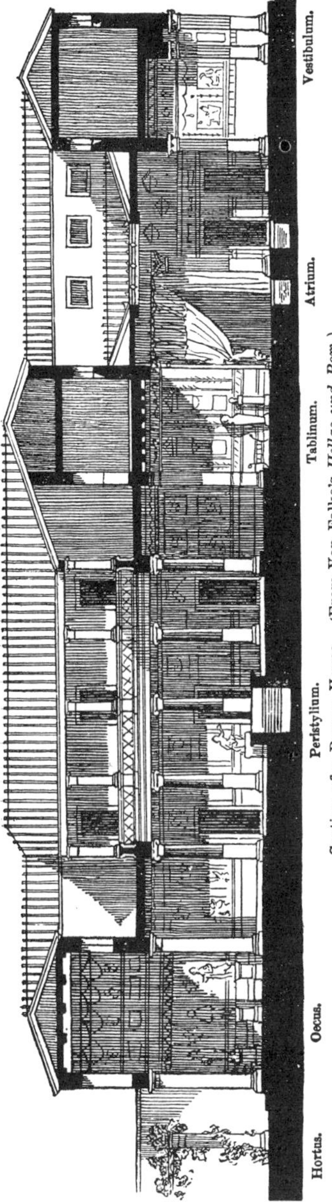

Section of a Roman House. (From Von Falke's *Hellas und Rom.*)

The rooms which opened out of the *atrium* were lighted only through the *compluvium,* as there were no windows, as a general rule, upon the ground-floor.

(4) *Alae,* wings, were two small quadrangular apartments or recesses on the left and right sides of the *atrium* (Vitruv. vi. 4), but at its farther end and open to the *atrium,* as we see in the Pompeian houses. Here the *imagines* were kept in the houses of the nobles. But as the *alae* were really a part of the *atrium,* the *imagines* were frequently described as standing in the *atrium* (Juv. viii. 19 foll.; Plin. *H. N.* xxxv. § 6; Ovid, *Fast.* i. 591; Marquardt, *Privatl.* p. 235).

(5) *Tablinum* was in all probability a recess or room at the farther end of the *atrium* opposite the door leading into the hall, and was regarded as part of the *atrium.* It contained the family records and archives (Vitruv. vi. 4 and 8). It appears, from the houses of Pompeii, to have been separated not by a door, but simply by a curtain or *velum,* while it had a door at the back leading into the *peristylium.* Marquardt supposes that the *tablinum* was originally an alcove made of wood (whence its name) built at the back of the *atrium,* in which meals were taken during the summer, and was afterwards joined to the *atrium* by breaking through the walls of the latter.

With the *tablinum* the Roman house appears to have originally ceased, the sleeping-rooms being arranged on the upper floor. But when the *atrium* and its surrounding rooms were used for the reception of clients and other public visitors, it became necessary to increase the size of the house, and the following rooms were accordingly added:

(6) *Fauces* was a passage by the side of the *tablinum,* which passed from the *atrium* to the *peristylium,* or open court, as we see in the Pompeian houses. We must not suppose, however, that the plural indicates two passages (Vitruv. vi. 4).

(7) *Peristylium* was in its general form like the *atrium,* but it was one third greater in breadth, measured transversely, than in length (Vitruv. vi. 4); but we do not find these proportions preserved in the Pompeian houses. It was a court open to the sky in the middle; the open part, which was surrounded by columns, had a fountain in the centre, and was planted with flowers, shrubs, and trees forming a *viridarium.* The *atrium* and *peristylium* were the two important parts of a Roman house.

The arrangement of the rooms leading out of the *peristylium,* which are next to be noticed, varied, as has been remarked, according to the taste and circumstances of the owner. It is therefore impossible to assign to them any regular place in the house.

(*a*) *Cubicula,* bed-chambers, appear to have been usually small. There were separate *cubicula* for the day and night (*cubicula diurna et nocturna,* Plin. *Ep.* i. 3); the latter were also called *dormitoria,* and were mostly on the upper floor (*id.* v. 6, 21). Vitruvius (vi. 7) recommends that they should face the east for the benefit of the rising sun. They sometimes had a small ante-room, which was called by the Greek name of προκοιτών, in which the *cubicularius,* or valet, probably slept (Plin. *Ep.* ii. 17, 23). In some of the Pompeian houses we find a recess in which the bed was placed. This recess was called *zotheca* or *zothecula.*

(*b*) *Triclinia,* dining-rooms, are treated of in a separate article. See TRICLINIUM.

(*c*) *Oeci,* from the Greek οἶκος, were spacious halls or saloons borrowed from the Greeks, and were frequently used as *triclinia.* (Cf. Plin. *H. N.* xxxvi. § 184.) They were to have the same proportions as *triclinia,* but were to be more spacious on account of having columns, which *triclinia* had not (Vitruv. vi. 5). Vitruvius mentions four kinds of *oeci:*

(*a*) The *Tetrastyle,* which needs no further description. Four columns supported the roof.

(*β*) The *Corinthian,* which possessed only one

row of columns, supporting the architrave (*epistylium*), cornice (*corona*), and a vaulted roof.

(*c*) The *Egyptian*, which was more splendid and more like a basilica than a Corinthian *triclinium.* In the Egyptian *oecus*, the pillars supported a gallery with paved floor, which formed a walk round the apartment; and upon these pillars others were placed, a fourth part less in height than the lower, which surrounded the roof. Between the upper columns windows were inserted.

(*d*) The *Cyzicene* (Κυζικηνός) appears in the time of Vitruvius to have been seldom used in Italy. These were meant for summer use, looking to the north, and if possible facing gardens, to which they opened by folding-doors. Pliny had *oeci* of this kind in his villa.

(*e*) *Exedrae*, which appear to have been in form much the same as the *oeci*, for Vitruvius (vi. 5) speaks of the *exedrae* in connection with *oeci quadrati*, were rooms for conversation and the other purposes of society (Cic. *De Nat. Deor.* i. 6, 15). They served the same purpose as the *exedrae* in the Thermae and Gymnasia, which were semicircular rooms with seats for philosophers and others to converse in. See BALNEAE.

(*f, g, h*) *Pinacotheca*, *Bibliotheca*, and *Balineum* (see BALNEAE), are treated of in separate articles.

(8) *Culina*, the kitchen.—The food was originally cooked in the *atrium*, as has been already stated, but the progress of refinement afterwards led to the use of another part of the house for this purpose. In the kitchen of Pansa's house, of which a restoration is given below, a stove for stews and similar preparations was found, very much like the charcoal stoves used in the present day. Before it lie a knife, a strainer, and a kind of frying-pan with four spherical cavities, as if it were meant to cook eggs.

Culina, or Kitchen, in Pansa's House.

In this kitchen, as well as in many others at Pompeii, there are paintings of the Lares and Penates, to whom the hearth in the *atrium* was sacred, and under whose care the kitchen was also placed (Arnob. ii. 67). In the country the meals were taken in the kitchen, as they were in ancient times in the *atrium* (Colum. i. 6). The kitchen was in the back part of the house, and in connection with it was the *pistrinum*, or bake-house, where bread was baked at home (Varr. *ap.* Non. p. 55, 18); but after B.C. 171 there were public bake-houses in Rome. (See PISTOR.) In Pompeii have been found sinks of kitchens, called *confluvia* (Varr. *ap.* Non. p. 544, 20) or *coquinae fusoria* (Pallad. *R. R.* i. 37).

In close and inconvenient proximity to the kitchen was the *latrina*, or privy, in order that a common drain might carry off the contents of both to the *cloaca* or public sewer (Varr. l. c.; Colum. x. 85; cf. Plaut. *Curc.* iv. 4, 24; Suet. *Tib.* 58; Apul. *Met.* i. c. 17, p. 15). In many of the Pompeian houses we find the *latrina* contiguous to the kitchen, as is shown in the annexed cut from the house

Culina and Latrina in the House of Sallust. (Gell, *Pompeiana*, p. 107.)

of Sallust. On the right are two small arches, which are the kitchen stove. On the left is an arched recess, which is the *latrina*. At the bottom is the mouth of a pipe supplying it with water.

(9) *Cenacula*, or rooms in the upper stories, have been already explained.

(10) *Lararium* or *Sacrarium.*—The Lares or Penates were originally placed near the hearth of the house in the *atrium*, but when the latter became only a reception-room they were removed to a special chapel, called *Lararium* (Lamprid. *Alex. Sev.* 29, 31) or *Sacrarium* (Cic. *ad Fam.* xiii. 2), in which statues of other divinities were also placed. Such a chapel is found in the *peristylium* of many of the Pompeian houses.

(11) *Diaeta* does not denote any particular kind of room, but is a word borrowed from the Greek (δίαιτα) to signify a room used for any of the purposes of life (Plin. *Ep.* ii. 17, 12). Thus it denotes a bed-chamber (Plin. *Ep.* vi. 16, 14), a dining-room (Sidon. Apoll. *Ep.* ii. 2), a summer-house or a room in a garden (Plin. *Ep.* ii. 17, 20; *Dig.* 7, 1, 66, § 1; Orelli, *Inscr.* 4373, etc.). It is also the collective name of a set of chambers. Thus Pliny speaks (*H. N.* v. 6, 31) of two *diaetae*, in one of which were four bed-chambers and in another three.

(12) *Solarium*, literally a place for basking in the sun, denotes a terrace on the flat roof of a house, frequently used by the Romans, as is still the case in Italy and the East (Isid. xv. 3, 12; Plaut. *Mil. Glor.* ii. 3, 69; ii. 4, 25; Suet. *Claud.* 10). In the time of the emperors these *solaria* on the tops of houses were turned into gardens, which contained even fruit-trees and fish-ponds (Sen. *Ep.* 122). Somewhat similar were the *solaria* built by Nero on the colonnades in front of the *insulae* and *domus* (Suet. *Ner.* 16). Sometimes the *solaria* were covered by a roof (Orelli, *Inscr.* 2417).

(13) *Cellae servorum, familiares* or *familiaricae*, the small bedrooms of the slaves, were usually situated in the upper story, as in the house of Pansa at Pompeii, or in the back of the house, with the exception of the *cella* of the house-porter, which naturally was close to the front door (Colum. i. 6; Cic. *Phil.* ii. 27, 67; Hor. *Sat.* i. 8, 8).

Cella also denoted the store-room, of which there

were several, bearing various names, according to their contents. Of these an account is given under CELLA.

Cellars underground and vaulted are rarely mentioned (*hypogea concamerationesque*, Vitruv. vi. [8] 11), though several have been found at Pompeii.

V. SOME EXISTING REMAINS OF ROMAN HOUSES. —The oldest remains of a house in Rome are those of the Regia, which was the residence of the Pontifex Maximus and built on the site of the house occupied by Numa. It stood at the southeast limits of the Forum, adjoining the House of the Vestal Virgins. (See Dio Cass. xliii. 42, xliv. 17; Gell. iv. 6.) Another house which is also of interest from its early date is that known as "the House of Livia" or "of Germanicus," which is built in a hollow in the northwestern part of the Palatine Hill. That it is probably not later in date than the time of Augustus is shown by the construction of its walls, which are formed of concrete faced with very neat *opus reticulatum* of tufa, no brick being used. The figure below shows its plan, which, owing to the irregularity of the site, is at two different levels, the small rooms grouped round the staircase F being at a much higher level than the larger rooms by the *atrium:* the stairs D lead from the *atrium* up to the higher floor behind. The main entrance is at B, approached down a short flight of steps. C C are pedestals for a statue and an altar; E E are bedrooms; G is a narrow *crypto-porticus*, which branches out of H, another dark passage, forming hidden communications with different buildings on this part of the Palatine. A is a third vaulted passage which leads to Caligula's palace; this is possibly the path by which Caligula's murderers escaped when they hid themselves in the house of Germanicus (Joseph. *Ant. Iud.* xix. 1, 2; Suet. *Calig.* 58).

The paintings in the principal rooms of this house are among the finest examples of Roman wall decoration that still exist. See Renier, *Les Peintures du Palatin.*

The floors are formed of marble mosaic in simple geometrical patterns, very neatly fitted together, with much smaller *tesserae* than were used under the later Empire.

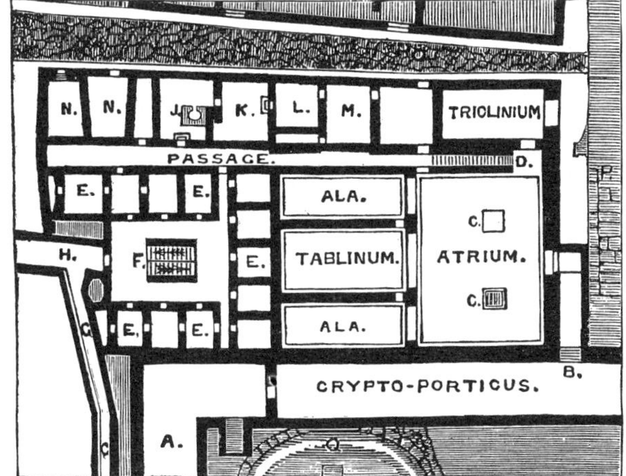

Plan of the so-called House of Livia.

A. Passage.
B. Stairs.
C C. Pedestals for statues.
D. Stairs.
E E. Bedrooms.
F. Stairs.
G. Crypto-Porticus.
H. Crypto-Porticus.
Q. Piscina.
J K L M. Bath-rooms.
N N. Shops.
O O. Street.
P. Early Building.

On the upper floor a long passage, approached by the staircase D, divides the house into two parts. J K L M seem to be small bath-rooms. N N are shops with no communication with the house, facing a public street, O O. At P are remains of a very ancient tufa building. Q is a *piscina*, which seems partly to have supplied the house with water. A number of inscribed lead pipes were found, but these were of later date than the house itself; water was laid on to the upper as well as to the ground floors.

In 1874, remains of a very interesting house of the time of Augustus were found on the Esquiline Hill, not far from the Basilica of S. Maria Maggiore. From its position on the line of the Servian wall and *agger*, it has been called "the House of Maecenas," who lived in that quarter, where he converted the public burial-ground into a large park (Hor. *Sat.* i. 8, 14). One fine room of this house, still well preserved, is of especial interest. It appears to have been a sort of greenhouse for plants and flowers, and is a large vaulted chamber, with a semicircular apse at one end. All round the walls are tiers of high steps once lined with marble, intended to form stands for rows of flower-pots—arranged exactly as in a modern conservatory. Prof. Mohr (*Bull. Inst. Arch.* for 1875) has pointed out that the cultivation of shrubs and flowers in this way was largely practised by the Romans. On each side of the hall are six recesses, decorated with paintings of garden scenes, with fountains among the flowers, treated in a skilfully deceptive way, so as to look as if each recess were a window opening upon a real garden. The light was admitted only through openings in the barrel-vault of the hall, on which were paintings of similar floral subjects—a remarkable example of the theatrical scene-painter's style of decoration which was popular among the Romans.

The House of Sallust, the historian, was one of the finest houses in Rome. It had, like the House of Maecenas, extensive gardens, whence the residence was frequently called Horti Sallustiani. So large were the gardens that the emperor Aurelian, who preferred living there to the Palatine, erected in them a colonnade 1000 paces long, in which he took horse exercise. Part of this house still exists in the narrow valley between the Pincian and Quirinal Hills, near the Porta Collina in the Servian wall. The following figure shows the plan of the existing remains, which will be soon destroyed by the filling up of the valley where the building stands to make new boulevards—a most serious loss. The circular part A is a lofty domed hall; B B is a balcony-like gallery, supported on corbels, which runs round the outside of the main building, at a height of about forty feet above the ground; C is a fine vaulted room, with two stories over it; D D is a retaining wall, built against the scarped face of the cliff to keep the crumbling tufa rock from decay; E E are rooms in four or five

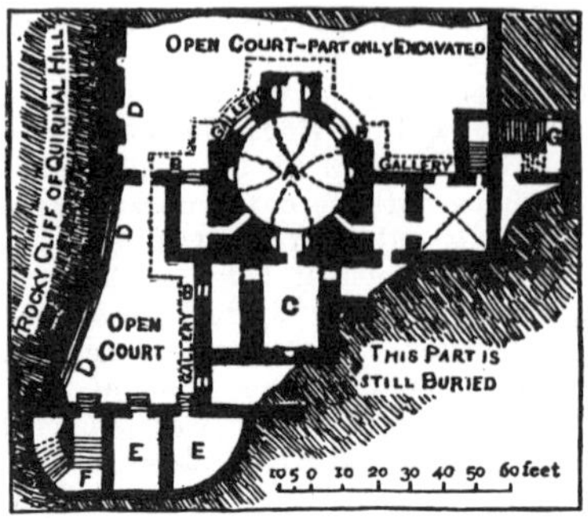

House of Sallust in Rome.

stories, some with concrete and others with wooden floors; F are winding marble-lined stairs, with mosaic landings, which led to the top of the house and the rooms on the higher level of the hill. This part is still about seventy feet high. G is another marble-lined staircase. A great part of the house is still unexcavated. The date of the existing portion is of the first century A.D., and is evidently part of additions made by the early emperors. In the sixteenth century an immense quantity of valuable marbles, including magnificent columns of Oriental alabaster and Numidian stone, were found in the ruins of Sallust's house and used to decorate several of the churches of Rome.

VI. Pompeian Houses.—Though of course less magnificent than the palaces of Rome, the houses of Pompeii, from their exceptionally perfect state of preservation, are of especial value as examples of Roman domestic architecture, and have the advantage of being in most cases of known date. Few are older than the Christian era, and none of course are later than A.D. 79, when the city was overwhelmed by the eruption of Vesuvius. The existing remains show us, as a rule, only the ground-floor of each house; and it should be remembered that a number of the best rooms—especially, there is reason to believe, the bedrooms and the women's apartments—were on the upper floors. The presence of stairs in apparently all the houses proves that one-storied buildings were practically unknown in Pompeii; the few fragments of the upper story which have been found standing show that, in some cases at least, the upper part of the house was partly constructed of wood, and was arranged so as to project beyond the line of the lower story, very like the half-timbered houses of England and France in the fifteenth and sixteenth centuries.

In one respect the Pompeian arrangement resembled that of mediæval and modern Italy; that is, the street-front on the ground-floor, even of large and handsome houses, was usually occupied by a row of shops. In some cases these shops have no doorway or passage communicating with the main house, and were probably rented by the owner to independent tradesmen; in others the shops could be entered from the house, and in these cases we may suppose that the shops were managed by the slaves or clients of the house-owner.

The accompanying plan shows a small shop, to which is joined the residence of its owner, forming a small block independent of the adjoining larger house. (1) An open archway, in which a wooden shop-front was fitted; the threshold of this opening is rebated to receive the wooden partition, part of which was hinged so as to form a narrow door; the upper part would be closed at night by flap-shutters hinged at the top, an arrangement very like that of a modern Oriental bazaar. This method of constructing shop-fronts was very common, not only in Pompeii, but in Rome and elsewhere. The presence of a shop appears always to be indicated by this long grooved sill, with marks of the hinged door on one side. A large number of examples still exist in Rome. The L-shaped counter (2) is formed of concrete and brick stuccoed; in it are inserted a row of *amphorae*, apparently for the reception of hot food or drink of some kind. At one end is a charcoal stove (3); 5, 5 are the dining-room and store-room of the shopkeeper; 4 is the staircase leading to the sleeping apartments. The whole forms a complete house of the smallest type.

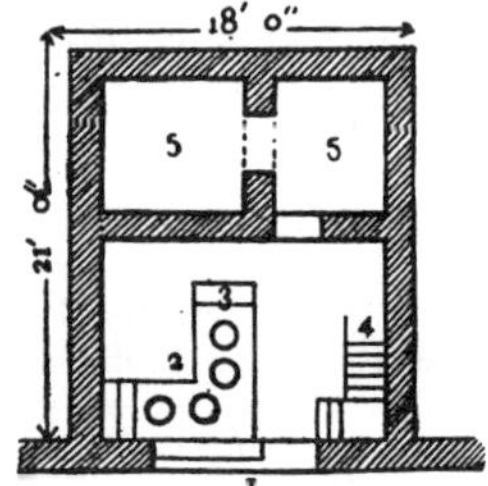

Plan of House with Shop.

The two illustrations annexed represent two *atria* of houses at Pompeii. The first is the *atrium*

Atrium of the House of the Quaestor. (Pompeii.)

of what is usually called the "House of the Quaestor." The view is taken near the entrance-hall facing the *tablinum*, through which the columns of the peristyle and the garden are seen. This *atrium*, which is a specimen of what Vitruvius calls the Corinthian, is surrounded by various rooms, and is beautifully painted with arabesque designs upon red and yellow grounds.

The next illustration represents the *atrium* of what is usually called the "House of Ceres." In

Atrium of the House of Ceres. (Restoration.)

the centre is the *impluvium;* and, as there are no pillars around the *impluvium*, this *atrium* must belong to the kind called by Vitruvius the "Tuscan."

The three following plans are good typical examples of the best class of houses in Pompeii. The first is popularly known as "the House of the Tragic Poet."

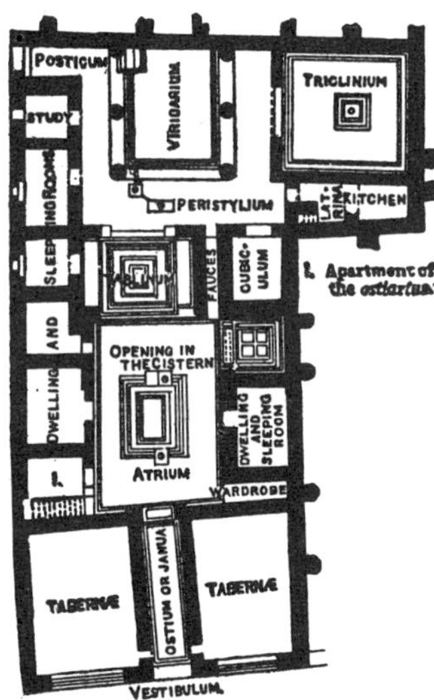

House of the Tragic Poet.

Like most of the other houses at Pompeii, it had no *vestibulum* according to the meaning which we have attached to the word. The *ostium*, or entrance-hall, which is six feet wide, is nearly thirty long—a length occasioned by the shops on each side. Near the street-door there is a figure of a large fierce dog worked in mosaic on the pavement, and beneath it is written *Cave Canem*, as here shown. The two large rooms on each side of the vestibule appear from the large openings in front of them to have been shops; they communicate with the entrance-hall, and were therefore probably occupied by the master of the house. The *atrium* is about twenty-eight feet in length and twenty in breadth; its *impluvium* is near the centre of the room, and its floor is paved with white *tesserae*, spotted with black. On the left-hand corner of the *atrium* is a small room (marked 1 in plan), perhaps the *cella* of the *ostiarius*, with a staircase leading to the upper rooms. On each side of the *atrium* are chambers for the use of the family or intended for the reception of guests, who were entitled to claim hospitality. When a house did not possess a *hospitium* (q. v.), or rooms expressly for the reception of guests, they appear to have been lodged in rooms attached to the *atrium*. At the farther end of the *atrium* is the *tablinum*, with the *fauces*, or passage, at the side, leading into the *peristylium*, with Doric columns and garden (*viridarium*). The large room on the right of the peristyle is the *triclinium;* beside it is the kitchen, with a *latrina*.

Pompeian Mosaic. (Overbeck.)

The second illustration contains the ground-plan of an *insula* surrounded by shops, which belonged to the owner and were let by him. The house itself, which is usually called the "House of Pansa," evidently belonged to one of the principal men of Pompeii. Including the garden, which

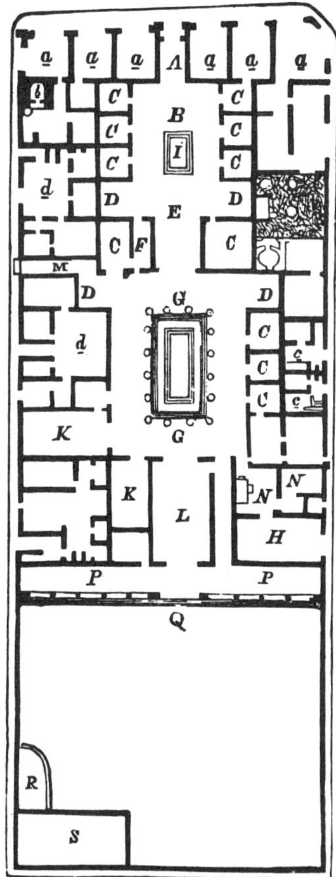

Ground-plan of an Insula, known as the House of Pansa.

is a third of the whole length, it is about 300 feet long and 100 wide.

A. *Ostium*, or entrance-hall, paved with mosaic. B. Tuscan *atrium*. I. *Impluvium*. C. Chambers on each side of the *atrium*, probably for the reception of guests. D. *Ala*. E. *Tablinum*, which is open to the *peristylium*, so that the whole length of the house could be seen at once; but as there is a passage (*fauces*), F, beside it, the *tablinum* might probably be closed at the pleasure of the owner. C. Chambers by the *fauces* and *tablinum*, of which the use is uncertain. G. *Peristylium*. D. Recesses in the *peristylium*. C. *Cubicula* by the side of the *peristylium*. K. *Triclinium*. L. *Oecus*, and by its side there is a passage leading from the *peristylium* to the garden. M. Back door (*posticum ostium*) to the street. N. *Culina*. H. Servants' hall, with a back door to the street. P. Portico of two stories, which proves that the house had an upper floor. The site of the staircase, however, is unknown, though it is thought there is some indication of one in the passage M. Q. The garden. R. Reservoir for supplying a tank, S.

The preceding rooms belonged exclusively to Pansa's house; but there were a good many apartments besides in the *insula*, which were not in his occupation: *a*. Six shops let out to tenants. Those on the right and left hand corners were bakers' shops, which contained mills, ovens, etc., at *b*. The one on the right appears to have been a large establishment, as it contains many rooms. *c*. Two houses of a very mean class, having formerly an upper story. On the other side are two houses much larger, *d*.

VII. General Details of Roman Houses.—(1) *Walls*.—The wall (*paries*) in earlier times was made of some easily worked stone, such as tufa or peperino in large square blocks; or for the best houses unburnt brick was used. In the time of Augustus concrete began to be the chief building material, and later kiln-dried bricks. The inner walls were originally whitewashed (see Dealbatores), and later were covered with stucco (*opus albarium*). The plain surface of the walls was broken by quadrangular panels, called *abaci* (Plin. *H. N.* xxxiii. § 159; xxxv. §§ 3, 32). (See, also, Abacus.) In the second century B.C., the practice was introduced from Greece of painting these panels with an endless variety of figures, landscapes, buildings, gardens, etc., of which we have numerous examples in the existing remains of houses in Rome and Pompeii. See Pictura.

In addition to painting, other methods of decoration were used: in Rome especially the chief way of ornamenting the rooms of the best houses was by lining the walls with slabs of sawn marble, moulded into a skirting below and a cornice above. Great magnificence of effect was produced by the skilful admixture of marbles of different rich colours, the moulded part being usually of a deeper tint than the flat surfaces. In the most careful work these marble linings were fastened to the walls by bronze clamps, but more often the slabs were simply attached by a thick bedding of cement behind them (Sen. *Ep.* 86, § 4).

Another very rich method of decoration was the application of stucco reliefs enriched with gold and colours. A third system, applied also to vaults, was to encrust the walls with mosaics, chiefly made of glass *tesserae* of the most brilliant jewel-like colours. See Musivum Opus.

Specimen of Decorative Wall-painting at Pompeii. (Reber.)

In fact, splendour of effect and a brilliant *ensemble* were the characteristics of Roman house-decoration from the Augustan era down to later times.

(2) *Roofs*.—The roofs (*tecta*) of Roman houses were in the oldest times covered with straw. Next came the use of shingles for the roofing of houses, which continued down to the time of the war with Pyrrhus (Plin. *H. N.* xvi. § 36). Subsequently clay tiles, called *tegulae* and *imbrices*, superseded the shingles. The roofs of houses were sometimes flat, but they were also gabled (*pectenata*) like modern houses. These were of two kinds, the *tecta pectenata*, sloping two ways, and the *tecta testudinata*, sloping four ways (Fest. p. 213, M). Both kinds of roofs were *displuviata*—that is, sloping towards the street—and the houses had around

Roof in Peristyle of the House of C. Vibius. (Overbeck.)

them an *ambitus*, or vacant space of $2\frac{1}{2}$ feet, to receive the rain-water running off the roofs. The projecting eaves of roofs were called *suggrundae*. The gabled roofs rose to a point called *fastigium* (q. v.). For the most magnificent buildings, such as some of the imperial palaces, the roofs were covered with tiles made of white marble, or even with bronze tiles plated with gold. For further details, see TEGULA.

(3) *Floors.*—The floor (*solum*) of a room was seldom boarded (*strata solo tabulata*, Stat. *Silv.* i. 5, 57), except in the upper stories. The floor on the ground-floor was usually of stone, and, in the case of common houses, consisted of small pieces of stone, brick, tiles, etc. (*ruderatio, opus ruderatum*), beaten down (*pavita*) with a rammer (*fistuca*), whence the word *pavimentum* became the general name for a floor (Plin. *H. N.* xxxvi. § 185 foll.). Sometimes the floors were paved with thin slabs of richly-coloured marbles, brought from Northern Africa, Arabia, or Greece (Tibull. iii. 3, 16; Sen. *Ep.* 86, 6; Pallad. i. 9), and still more frequently with mosaics (*opus musivum*). See PAVIMENTUM and MUSIVUM OPUS.

In Rome and other parts of Italy, owing to the wonderful strength of the *pozzolana*, the upper floors of houses were very frequently made of concrete cast in one great slab on temporary boarding, fixed at the required level. This set into one compact mass, like a piece of solid stone. On this, mosaic and other paving was laid, as on the ground-floors.

(4) *Ceilings.* — Ceilings were very commonly semicircular or "barrel" vaults (*camarae*), decorated with stucco reliefs, mosaics, or painting. (See CAMARA.) The *extrados* of the vault was filled in level with concrete to form the floor above. Wooden ceilings and flat concrete ceilings were decorated in the same way. One common method of ceiling decoration, applied both to brick and concrete or to wooden ceilings, was to divide the whole area into a number of deeply sunk panels, like pits or lakes (*lacus, lacunae*), whence they were called *lacunaria* or *laquearia*. These were richly ornamented, either by stucco reliefs gilt and coloured, or, in the case of wooden ceilings, by inlaid work of ivory, ebony, or other precious materials as well as by paintings. In a few cases the "coffers" were covered with enriched bronze plates, thickly gilt.

(5) *Windows.* — The Roman houses had few windows (*fenestrae*). The *atrium* and *peristylium* were lighted, as we have seen, from above, and the smaller rooms leading out of them generally derived their light from them and not from windows looking into the street. The rooms only on the upper stories (*cenacula*) seem to have been usually lighted by windows, and looked out upon the street as well as the inner courts. Hence they are frequently mentioned by the ancient writers (Livy, i. 41, xxiv. 21; Hor. *Carm.* i. 25; Propert. iv. [v.], 7, 16; Juv. iii. 270). In Pompeii, in like manner, the ground-floor rooms were mostly lighted from the inner courts, so that few lower windows opened on the street. There is an exception to this in the "House of the Tragic Poet," which has six windows on the ground-floor. Even in this case, however, the windows are not near the ground, as in a modern house, but are six feet six inches above the foot-pavement, which is raised one foot seven inches above the centre of the street. The windows are small, being hardly three feet by two; and at the side there is a wooden frame, in which the window or shutter might be moved backwards or forwards. The lower part of the wall is occu-

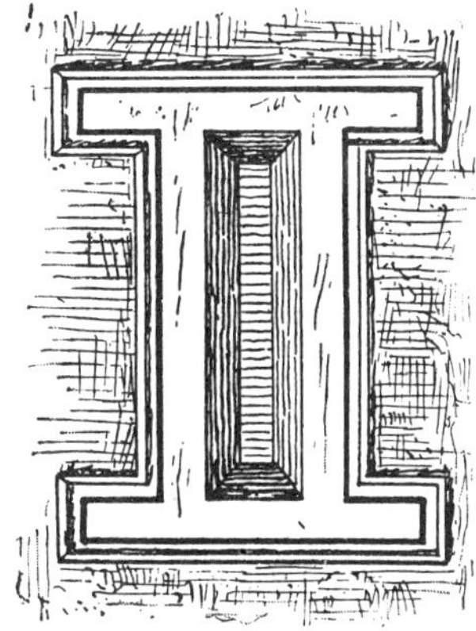

Pompeian Fenestra or Window. (Overbeck.)

pied by a row of red panels four feet and a half high. The following illustration represents part of the wall, with the apertures for windows above it, as it appears from the street. The tiling upon the wall is modern, and is only placed there to preserve it from the weather.

Wall with Apertures for the Windows in a House at Pompeii.

There has been much discussion whether glass windows were known to the ancients; but in the excavations at Pompeii many fragments of flat glass have been discovered, and in the *tepidarium* of the public baths a bronze lattice was found with some of the panes still inserted in the frame (Gell, *Pompeiana*, i. p. 99). (See VITRUM.) Besides glass, other transparent substances were also used, such as talc, the *lapis specularis* of Pliny. Windows made of this were called *specularia* (Sen. *Ep.* 90, 25).

(6) *Doors.*—The subject of doors, with their locks and keys, is discussed under IANUA and CLAVIS. It is only necessary to mention here that many of the rooms in Roman houses had no doors, but only curtains, *vela, aulaea, centones* (Sen. *Ep.* 80; Plin. *Ep.* ii. 17; Petron. 7; Lamprid. *Alex. Sev.* 4, *Heliog.* 14). Sometimes, when there were doors, curtains were also drawn across them. See VELUM.

(7) *The Heating of Houses.*—The rooms were heated in winter in different ways. The *cubicula, triclinia,* and other rooms which were intended for winter use, were built in that part of the house upon which the sun shone most; and in the mild climate of Italy this frequently enabled them to dispense with any artificial mode of warming the rooms. Rooms exposed to the sun in this way were sometimes called *heliocamini* (Plin. *Ep.* ii. 17, 20; *Dig.* 8, 2, 17). The rooms were occasionally heated by hot air, which was introduced by means of pipes from a furnace below (Plin. *Ep.* ii. 17, v. 6, 24; Sen. *Ep.* 90), but more frequently in earlier times by portable furnaces or braziers (*foculi*), in which charcoal was burned. (See FOCUS.) The *caminus*, however, was a fixed stove, in which wood appears to have been usually burned (Suet. *Vitell.* 8; Hor. *Sat.* i. 5, 81; *Ep.* i. 11, 19; Cic. *Ad Fam.* vii. 10; Sidon. Apoll. *Ep.* ii. 2). It has been a subject of much dispute among modern writers whether the Romans had chimneys for carrying off the smoke, except in the baths and kitchens. From many passages in ancient writers it certainly appears that rooms usually had no chimneys, but that the smoke escaped through the windows, doors, and openings in the roof (Vitruv. vii. 3, 4); but chimneys do not appear to have been entirely unknown to the ancients, as some have been found in the ruins of ancient buildings, and it is impossible to believe that among a luxurious people like the Romans in imperial times, they were unacquainted with the use of chimneys.

Bronze Braziers from Pompeii. (Overbeck.)

(8) *The water supply* of a good Roman house was very complete; in towns the main usually ran under the pavement in the middle of the street, and from it "rising mains" branched off to the houses right and left, and often were carried to the upper stories, where a cistern supplied the fountain-jets (*salientes*) and other purposes below. For further details on the water-supply, see AQUAE DUCTUS.

VIII. BIBLIOGRAPHY.—Becker-Göll, *Gallus*, ii. pp. 213 foll.; Marquardt, *Privatl.* pp. 208 foll.; Guhl and Koner, pp. 462 foll., 5th ed.; Hirt, *Gesch. d. Baukunst*, iii. pp. 267 foll.; Fergusson, *Hist. of Arch.* i. pp. 363 foll.; Burn, *Rome*, pp. lxvii. foll.; Friedländer, *Sittengesch.* i. pp. i. foll., pp. 26 foll.; Ménard, *La Vie Privée des Anciens* (Paris, 1880–83); Zumpt, *Ueber die bauliche Einrichtung des röm. Wohnhauses* (Berlin, 1844); Mazois, *Le Palais de Scaurus* (Paris, 1859). Although a large number of well-illustrated works on Pompeii have been recently published, they have by no means superseded the earlier ones, which describe a great deal that is now lost; this is specially the case with Sir William Gell's valuable *Pompeiana* (London, 1824); and second part (London, 1832). The objects discovered are well illustrated by Pistolesi, *Real Museo Borbonico* (1824–67). Dyer's *Ruins of Pompeii* (London, 1867) is a convenient hand-book. Niccolini and others, *Le Case di Pompeii* (Naples, 1854–84), is a valuable work, which gives recent discoveries. A very splendidly illustrated work is the *Recueil des Peintures, etc., de Pompéi* (Paris, 1870–77). See also Zahn, *Die schönsten Ornamente aus Pompeji* (Berlin, 1827–59); Mazois and Gau, *Les Ruines de Pompéi* (Paris, 1824–38); Ternite, *Wandgemälde aus Pompeji* (Berlin, no date); Presuhn, *Les Décorations de Pompéi* (Leipzig, 1878); Mau's edition of Overbeck's *Pompeji* (Leipzig, 1884); and Nissen, *Pompejanische Studien* (Leipzig, 1877). Reference may be made to the extensive bibliography at the end of the article POMPEII in this Dictionary. Middleton, in his *Ancient Rome in 1888*, and *Remains of Ancient Rome* (London, 1892), gives some account of existing houses in Rome.

Domus Aurea. See PALATIUM.

Donatio Inter Virum et Uxōrem. By the Roman law, during marriage, neither husband nor wife could, as a general rule, make a gift of anything to one another. This rule would, however, only apply where there was no *conventio in manum;* for in such a case the rule of law would be unnecessary, because a gift between husband and wife would be legally impossible. The reason for this rule was said to be the preservation of the marriage relation in its purity, as a contract subsisting by affection, and not maintained by purchase or by gift from one party to the other. The reason seems a singular one, but it is that which is given by the Roman writers. It has apparently a tacit reference to the power of divorce, and appears like an implied recommendation of it when the conjugal affection ceases. Donationes of this kind were, however, valid when there were certain considerations, as *mortis causa, divortii causa, servi manumittendi gratia.* By certain imperial constitutions, a woman could make gifts to her husband in order to qualify him for certain honours. It must be remembered that when there was no *conventio in manum*, a wife retained all her rights of property which she did not surrender on her marriage (see Dos), and she might, during the marriage, hold property quite distinct from her husband. It was a consequence of this rule as to gifts between husband and wife that every legal form by which the gift was affected to be transferred, as *mancipatio*, *cessio*, and *traditio*, conveyed no ownership; stipulations were not binding, and *acceptilationes* were no release. See MATRIMONIUM.

Donatio Mortis Causa. There were in Roman law three kinds of *donatio mortis causa:* (1) When a man, under no present apprehension of danger, but moved solely by a consideration of human mortality, makes a gift to another. (2) When a man, being in immediate danger, makes a gift to another in such a manner that the thing immediately becomes the property of the donee. (3) When a man, under the like circumstances, gives a thing in such a manner that it shall become the property of the donee in case the giver dies. Every person could receive such a gift who was capable of receiving a legacy.

It appears, then, that there were several forms of gift called *donatio mortis causa;* but the third seems the only proper one, and that of which mention is chiefly made, for it was a rule of law that a donation of this kind was not perfected unless death followed, and it was revocable by the donor. A thing given absolutely could hardly be a *donatio mortis causa*, for this *donatio* had a condition attached to it—namely, the death of the donor and the survivorship of the donee. The thing might be a thing capable of *traditio*, or delivery, or it might be a promise of a sum of money to be paid after the death of the testator. It would appear as if the law about such donations was not free from difficulty. They were finally assimilated to legacies in all respects by Justinian, though this had been done in some particulars before his time. Still they differed in some respects from legacies, for such a donation could take effect though there was no *heres;* and a filius familias, who could not make a will, might, with his father's consent, make a *donatio mortis causa*.

Donatio Propter Nuptias signifies in Roman law that which is given by a husband or by any other person to a woman on the occasion of her marriage, whether it be by way of security for her dowry or for her support during the marriage or widowhood. Justinian required this *donatio* whenever the wife brought a dowry; and it was enacted that it should be equal in amount to the dowry, and should be increased when the dowry was increased. Such a gift was the property of the wife, but it was managed by the husband, and he was bound to apply it to its proper purposes; but he could not alienate it, even with the consent of the wife (*Cod.* v. 3). See MATRIMONIUM.

Donatīvum. A present of money made to Roman soldiers. In the republican age donatives were distributed on the occasion of a triumph, the expense being defrayed out of the money raised by selling the spoil. Under the Empire it was usual for the emperor to grant a *donativum* on his accession. Tiberius on this occasion made a present of some $3,750,000 to the army; and the sum increased in later reigns. After the time of Claudius it became the fashion for the emperor to purchase the favour of the praetorians by a special largess. See CONGIARIUM; PRAETORIANI.

Donātus. (1) AELIUS. A celebrated grammarian, born in the fourth century of our era, about A.D. 333. He was preceptor to St. Jerome, who speaks with great approbation of his talents and of the manner in which he explained the comedies of Terence. Independently of his commentaries on Vergil and Terence, Donatus composed a treatise (*Ars Donati Grammatici Urbis Romae*) in two parts. In one (*Ars Minor*) he treats of the eight parts of speech only, and in the other (*Ars Maior*), deals with grammar more elaborately. This work was highly esteemed and so much used in the Middle Ages that the word *donat* (Chaucer) became the generic term for a grammar. The commentary on Vergil appears to have been worthy neither of the author commented on nor of the reputation of the grammarian to whom it is ascribed, if we may judge from the contemptuous allusions made to it by Servius; but of it only the preface and the introduction (*enarrationes*) are now extant, besides quotations given in Servius. The commentary on Terence, however, is extremely valuable, though we have it in a form different from that which it originally possessed. The chief MS. of the commentaries of Donatus is one at Paris of the eleventh century. The *editio princeps* appeared at Rome in 1472. The text of the *Ars* is contained in Keil's *Grammatici Latini*, vol. iv. (Leipzig, 1856–1880). See Gräfenhan, *Geschichte d. class. Philologie*, iv. 107; J. Becker, *De Donati in Terentium Commentario* (Mayence, 1870); and Rosenstock, *De Donato*, etc. (Königsberg, 1886). (2) Not to be confounded with the preceding is TIBERIUS CLAUDIUS DONATUS, who wrote *Interpretationes* on the *Aeneid*, probably in the fourth century. Of the author, nothing is known. The work, which is preceded by a short epistle, was first published at Naples in 1535, and is included in the editions of Vergil by Fabricius (Basle, 1561), and Lucius (Basle, 1613). See Ribbeck's Prolegomena to Vergil, 185; and Burkas, *De Ti. Claud. Donati in Aen. Commentario* (Jena, 1889). (3) A bishop of Numidia, in the fourth century. According to some writers he was the founder of the sect of Donatists, which grew out of a schism produced by the election of a bishop of Carthage. He was deposed and excommunicated in councils held at Rome and at Arles in the years A.D. 313 and 314, but was for some time after supported by a party at home. His end is unknown.

Donūsa (*Δόνυσα*) or **Donusia** (*Δονουσία*). One of the smaller Sporades in the Aegaean Sea near Naxos. It produced green marble, whence Vergil calls the island *viridis*. Under the Roman emperors it was used as a place of banishment.

Doors. See IANUA.

Dora (*τὰ Δῶρα*), **Dorus, Dorum**, called DOR in the Old Testament. The most southerly town of Phœnicia on the coast, on a kind of peninsula at the foot of Mount Carmel.

Dorian Hexapolis. See DORIS, p. 554.

Doric Dialect. See DIALECTS.

Doris (*Δωρίς*). (1) Daughter of Oceanus and Thetis, wife of her brother Nereus, and mother of the Nereides. The Latin poets sometimes use the name of this divinity for the sea itself. (2) One of the Nereides, daughter of the preceding.

Doris (Δῶρις). (1) A small and mountainous country in Greece, formerly called Dryopis, bounded by Thessaly on the north, by Aetolia on the west, by Locris on the south, and by Phocis on the east. It contained four towns —Boum, Citinium, Erineus, and Pindus—which formed the Dorian tetrapolis. These towns never attained any consequence; but the country is of importance as the home of the Dorians (Δωριεῖς), one of the great Hellenic races, who conquered Peloponnesus. It was related that Aegimius, king of the Dorians, had been driven from his dominions by the Lapithae, but was reinstated by Heracles; that the children of Heracles hence took refuge in this land when they had been expelled from the Peloponnesus; and that it was to restore them to their rights that the Dorians invaded the Peloponnesus. Accordingly, the conquest of Peloponnesus by the Dorians is usually called the Return of the Heraclidae. (See HERACLIDAE.) The Dorians were divided into three tribes: the Hylleis, Pamphyli, and Dymanes. They were the ruling class throughout the Peloponnesus; the old inhabitants were reduced to slavery, or became subjects of the Dorians under the name of Perioeci (Περίοικοι). (2) A district in Asia Minor consisting of the Dorian settlements on the coast of Caria and the neighbouring islands. Six of these towns formed a league, called the "Dorian Hexapolis," consisting of Lindus, Ialysus, and Camirus in the island of Rhodes, the island of Cos, and Cnidus and Halicarnassus on the mainland.

Doriscus (Δορίσκος). A town in Thrace at the mouth of the Hebrus, in the midst of an extensive plain of the same name, where Xerxes reviewed his vast forces (Herod. vii. 25, etc.).

Dorium (Δώριον). A town of Messenia, where Thamyris the musician challenged the Muses to a trial of skill. Pausanias (iv. 33) notices this ancient town, of which he saw the ruins near a fountain named Achaia.

Dormitorium (δωμάτιον). A bed-chamber, usually small and sparely furnished (Plin. *H. N.* xxx. 17). See DOMUS.

Dormitorium. (From the Vatican Vergil.)

Doron (δῶρον). A hand-breadth. See PES.

Dorpon (δόρπον). See CENA, p. 310.

Dorso, C. FABIUS. A Roman, who, according to the old legend, when Rome was in the possession of the Gauls, issued from the Capitol, which was then besieged, to go and offer on the Mons Quirinalis a stated sacrifice enjoined on the Fabian house. In the Gabian cincture, and bearing the sacred vessels in his hands, he descended from the Capitol and passed through the enemy without betraying the least signs of fear. When he had finished his sacrifice, he returned to the Capitol unmolested by the foe, who were astonished at his boldness and did not obstruct his passage or molest his sacrifice (Liv. v. 46).

Dorus (Δῶρος). A son of Hellen, and the mythical ancestor of the Dorians (Diod. iv. 60).

Dory (δόρυ). A spear. See HASTA.

Dorylaeum (Δορύλαιον). A town in Phrygia Epictetus, on the river Thymbris, with warm baths, which are used at the present day.

Doryphŏri (δορυφόροι). See MERCENARII.

Dos. A dowry. See MATRIMONIUM.

Dositheus (Δωσίθεος). A grammarian who flourished towards the end of the fourth century A.D. He wrote a Latin grammar for Greek boys, with a literal Greek translation, which was not fully completed. With this was bound up (whether by Dositheus himself is uncertain) a miscellany of very various contents by another author. This comprises (1) anecdotes of the emperor Hadrian; (2) fables of Aesop; (3) an important chapter on jurisprudence; (4) mythological stories from Hyginus; (5) an abridgment of the Iliad; (6) an interesting collection of words and phrases from ordinary conversation, styled Ἑρμηνεύματα. The Latin grammar has the Greek translation inserted in the Latin text, thus: *Ars τέχνη grammatica γραμματική est ἐστίν scientia γνῶσις*. The Latin is the text of a grammar now lost, Dositheus making only the Greek translation. A separate edition of the grammar is that of Keil (Halle, 1869–71). Other parts of the work are edited by Böcking (Bonn, 1832), and Keil, *Grammatici Latini*, vii. 424. See Hagen, *De Dosithei Magistri quae Feruntur Glossis* (Berne, 1877); and Schönemann, *De Lexicographis Antiquis* (Bonn, 1886).

Dōson. A surname of Antigonus III., because he promised and never performed; δώσων, "about to give"; i. e. always promising. See ANTIGONUS.

Dossennus, FABIUS. A Roman comic poet and writer of Atellan fables, who enjoyed some reputation as a popular dramatist. Seneca makes mention of the inscription on his tomb, which ran as follows: *Hospes resiste, et sophiam Dossenni lege* (Sen. *Ep.* lxxxix. 6).

Dossennus. One of the stock characters of the Atellanae Fabulae, and representing the typical sharper, *dottore*. See Vel. Longus in the *Grammatici Latini* (ed. Keil), vii. 79, 4; and Mommsen, *Unterital. Dial.* 118.

Dossuarius or **Dorsuarius**. A name given to any animal carrying burdens on its back (Varr. *R. R.* ii. 6 and 10). It carried its load either by means of panniers (*clitellae*) or the pack-saddles (*sagmae*),

Dossuarii. (Column of Theodosius.)

whence we read of *equus sagmarius*. Hence came the German *Saum*-pferd and the English *sumpter*-horse.

Doulos (δοῦλος). A slave. See SERVUS.

Drabescus (Δραβῆσκος). A town in the district Edonis in Macedonia, on the Strymon.

Dracănum (Δράκανον). A town and promontory in the island Icaria.

Drachma (δραχμή). The name of a weight and of a denomination of coin among the Greeks. As weight and as coin it was the hundredth part of the *mina*, and was divided into six lesser units called ὀβολοί. The ancients (*Etym. Mag.* s. v. ὀβελίσκος) connected the word with δράσσομαι, "I grasp," and δράγμα, "a handful," and supposed that a drachm was originally the value in silver of a handful of six ὀβολοί, or wedge-shaped pieces of metal, which circulated as money. It is, however, very doubtful if this derivation is not a mere fancy; it is far more probable that δραχμή, like δαρεικός, is connected with the Persian word *darag*, "a part," since the weight of the drachma seems to be derived by division of the *mina*, rather than the weight of the mina to be produced by multiplication of the drachma.

The ordinary denominations of Greek coins were: for gold, the didrachma (double drachma), drachma, hemi-drachma, and smaller divisions; for silver, the same, with the addition of the tetra-drachma, and occasionally of the decadrachma. The weight of the drachma varied according to the standard to which it belonged; the heaviest drachma was the Aeginetan of 96 grains, worth in silver rather more

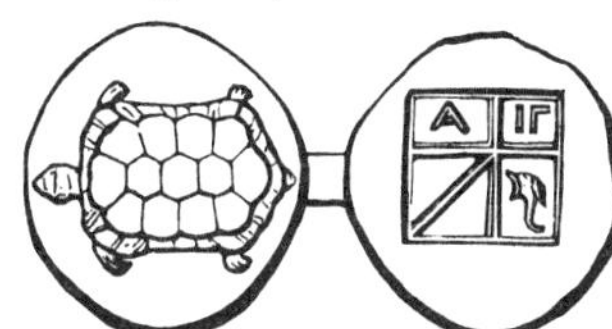

Aeginetan Drachma, actual size. (British Museum.)

than twenty-five cents of our money; it was called at Athens παχεῖα δραχμή (Pollux, ix. 76). The Athenian drachma weighed but 67.5 grains, and the Co-

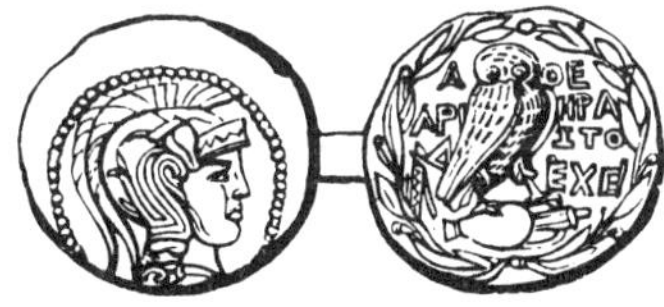

Attic Drachma: late, actual size. (British Museum.)

rinthian only 45 grains, value about twelve cents. The sign for drachma in Attic inscriptions is ⊢. As the Romans reckoned in sesterces, so the Greeks generally reckoned by drachmae; and when a sum is mentioned in the Attic writers, without any specification of the unit, drachmae are usually meant. See NUMISMATICS; PONDERA.

Draco. See CALDARIUM; SIGNA MILITARIA.

Draco (Δράκων). A very celebrated Athenian legislator, who flourished about B.C. 621. Suidas tells us that he brought forward his code of laws (θεσμοί) in this year, and that he was then an old man. Aristotle (*Pol.* ii. *fin.*) says that Draco adapted his laws to the existing constitution, and that they contained nothing particular beyond the severity of their penalties. The slightest theft was punished capitally, as well as the most atrocious murder; and Demades remarked of his laws that they were written with blood, and not with ink (Plut. *Solon*, 17). Draco, however, deserves credit as the first who introduced written laws at Athens; and it is probable that he improved the criminal courts by his transfer of cases of bloodshed from the archon to the ephetae, since before his time the archons had a right of settling all cases arbitrarily and without appeal—a right which they enjoyed in other cases until Solon's time. It appears that there were some offences which he did not punish with death; for instance, loss of civil rights was the punishment of attempting to alter one of his laws (Demosth. *c. Aristocr.* p. 714, Bekker). Draco was an archon (Pausan. ix. 36, 8), and, consequently, an Eupatrid; it is not, therefore, to be supposed that his object was to favour the lower orders, though his code seems to have tended to abridge the power of the nobles. The Athenians, it is said, could not endure the rigour of his laws, and the legislator himself was obliged to withdraw to the island of Aegina. Here he is said by Suidas to have been suffocated in the theatre beneath the number of cloaks and garments which the people of the island, according to the usual mode of expressing approbation among the Greeks, showered upon him. He was buried in the theatre.

Dracontius, BLOSSIUS AEMILIUS. A Latin poet who lived and practised as an advocate at Carthage towards the end of the fifth century A.D. He was a man of real poetic gifts and considerable reading, but his style is spoiled by rhetorical exaggeration and false taste. His surviving works are: (1) A number of short epics upon subjects taken from the old mythology and school-room rhetoric (e. g. Hylas, Raptus Helenae, *Deliberativa Achillis*, etc.). (2) An apologetic poem (*Satisfactio*) addressed in the form of an elegy to Gunthamund, king of the Vandals (A.D. 484–496), whose wrath he had excited by writing a panegyric on a foreign prince. (3) A Christian didactic poem (*De Laudibus Dei* or *Hexaëmeron*) in three books. This is a fairly poetical treatment of the story of the Creation. (4) Two *epithalamia* in hexameters. composed in early youth. (5) Several distichs *De Origine Rosarum* and *De Mensibus*. He is probably the author, also, of 971 hexameters, entitled *Orestis Tragoedia*, attributed during the Middle Ages to Horace or Lucan. The *editio princeps* of the complete works of Dracontius is that of Arevalo (Rome, 1791). Earlier editions give only the *Satisfactio* and the *Hexaëmeron*. The minor poems of Dracontius have been edited by Duhn (Leipzig, 1873). Editions of the *Orestis Tragoedia* are those of Mähly (Leipzig, 1866) and Schenkl (Prague, 1867). See, also, Rossberg, *De Dracontio* (Göttingen, 1880).

Drakenborch, ARNOLD, a distinguished Dutch classical scholar, was born at Utrecht, January 1st, 1684. He studied at both Utrecht and Leyden, receiving the degree in law in 1706. His attention, however, had been very strongly attracted to the study of archæology and history, and in 1704 he had already won much commendation by his treatise *De Praefectis Urbis*, dealing with the city government of Rome. In 1716, he became Professor of History and Eloquence at the university of his native town, succeeding Burmann, who had accepted a call to Leyden. This post he held until his death, which occurred on January 16th, 1748. Besides the treatise *De Praefectis*, mentioned above, of which a third edition appeared at Bayreuth in 1787, Drakenborch published a dissertation on the advantages to be derived from classical study (1715), an edition of Silius Italicus (Utrecht, 1717), and his *magnum opus*, an edition of Livy in seven volumes (Amsterdam, 1738–46). This work is still often cited and contains much valuable material, though marred by a lack of definite method, so that Scipio Maffei even said of it that "the only thing that gave it value was the high price at which it was sold." A portrait of Drakenborch is given at the commencement of the first volume of his Livy.

Drama (δρᾶμα). IN ATHENS the production of plays was a State affair, not a private undertaking. It formed a great part of the religious festival of the Dionysia, in which the drama took its rise (see DIONYSIA); and it was only at the Greater Dionysia that pieces could be performed during the author's lifetime. The performances lasted three days and took the form of musical contests, the competitors being three tragic poets, with their tetralogies, and five comic poets, with one piece each. The authority who superintended the whole was the archon, to whom the poets had to bring their plays for reading and apply for a chorus. If the pieces were accepted and the chorus granted, the citizens who were liable for the *choregia* undertook at their own cost to practise and furnish for them one chorus each. (See LITURGIA.) The poets whose plays were accepted received a reward from the State. The State also supplied the regular number of actors, and made provision for the maintenance of order during the performances. At the end of the performance a certain number of persons (usually five) were chosen by lot from a committee (ἀγωνοθέται) nominated by the Senate to award the prizes, and bound by solemn oath to give their judgment on the plays, the *choregi*, and the actors. The poet who won the first prize was presented with a crown in the presence of the assembled multitude—the highest distinction that could be conferred on a dramatic author at Athens. The victorious *choregus* also received a crown, with the permission to dedicate a votive offering to Dionysus. This was generally a tripod, which was set up either in the theatre or in the temple of the deity or in the Street of Tripods, so named from this custom, an inscription being put on it recording the event, as in that of Panofka, *Musée Blacas*, pl. I. (British Museum): Ακαμαντὶς ἐνίκα φυλή: Γλαύκων καλός. The actors in the successful play received prizes of money, besides the usual *honoraria*.

From the time of Sophocles the actors in a play were three in number. They had to represent all the parts, those of women included. This involved changing their costume several times during the performance. The three actors were distinguished as *protagonistes, deuteragonistes*, and *tritagonistes*, according to the importance of their parts. If the piece required a fourth actor, which was seldom the case, the *choregus* had to provide one. The *choregus* had also to see to the position and equipment of the mute actors.

In earlier times it is possible that the persons engaged in the representation did not make a business of their art, but performed gratuitously, as the poets down to the time of Sophocles appeared upon the stage. But the dramatic art gradually became a profession requiring careful preparation, and winning general respect for its members as artists. The chief requirements for the profession were distinctness and correctness of pronunciation, especially in declamatory passages, and an unusual power of memory, as there was no prompter in a Greek theatre. An actor had also to be thoroughly trained in singing, melodramatic action, dancing, and play of gesture. The latter was especially necessary, as the use of masks precluded any facial expression. The actors were according to strict rule assigned to the poets by lot; yet a poet generally had his special protagonist, on whose peculiar gifts he kept his eye in writing the dramatic pieces.

The Athenian tragedies began to be known all over the Hellenic world as early as the time of Aeschylus. The first city outside of Attica that had a theatre was Syracuse, where Aeschylus brought out some of his own plays. Scenic contests soon began to form part of the religious festivals in various Greek cities, and were celebrated in honour of other deities besides Dionysus. It was a habit of Alexander the Great to celebrate almost every considerable event with dramatic exhibitions, and after him this became the regular custom. A considerable increase in the number of actors was one consequence of the new demand. The actors called themselves artists of Dionysus, and in the larger cities they formed permanent societies (σύνοδοι) with special privileges, including exemption from military service and security in person and property. These companies had a regular organization, presided over by a priest of their patron-god Dionysus, annually elected from among their members. A treasurer and officers completed the staff. At the time of the festivals the societies sent out their members in groups of three actors, with a manager and a flute-player, to the different cities. This business was especially lively in Ionia and on the Euxine, the societies of Teos being the most distinguished. The same arrangement was adopted in Italy, and continued to exist under the Roman Empire.

The universal employment of masks was a remarkable peculiarity of costume. (See PERSONA.) It naturally excluded all play of feature, but the masks corresponded to the general types of character, as well as to the special types indicated by the requirements of the play. Certain conven-

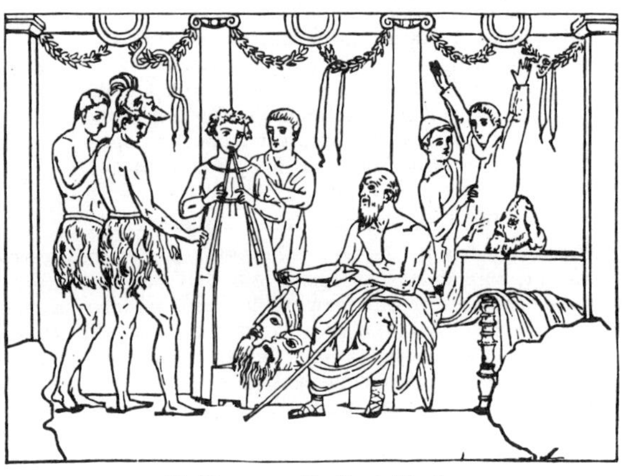

Masking-room of a Greek Theatre.

tionalities were observed in the colour of the hair. Goddesses and young persons had light hair; gods and persons of riper age, dark brown; aged persons, white; and the deities of the lower world, black. The height of the masks and top-knots varied with the age of the actors and the parts they took. Lucian ridicules the "chest-paddings and stomach-paddings" of the tragic actors (*De Salt.* 27). Their stature was considerably heightened in tragedies by the high boot (see COTHURNUS), and the defects in proportion corrected by padding and the use of a kind of gloves. The conventionalities of costume, probably as fixed by

(1) Mask of Perseus with Cap of Darkness. (2) Pompeian Mask.

Aeschylus, maintained themselves as long as Greek tragedies were performed at all. Men and women of high rank wore on the stage a variegated or richly embroidered long-sleeved χιτών, reaching to the feet, and fastened with a girdle as high as the breast. The upper garment, whether ἱμάτιον or χλαμύς, was long and splendid, and often embroidered with gold. Kings and queens had a purple train and a white ἱμάτιον with a purple border; soothsayers, a netted upper garment reaching to the feet. Persons in misfortune, especially fugitives, appeared in soiled garments of gray, green, or blue; black was the symbol of mourning. Soothsayers always wore a woollen garment of network; shepherds, a short leathern tunic; while each of the gods had some distinguishing mark, as the bow for Apollo, the caduceus for Hermes, the aegis for Athené. So with the well-known heroes: Heracles bore a club; Perseus, the cap of darkness. Kings wore a crown, and carried a sceptre. Warriors appeared in complete armour. Old men bore a staff with a curved handle, introduced by Sophocles. Messengers who brought good news were crowned with olive or laurel. Myrtle crowns denoted festivity. Foreigners wore some one special badge, as a Persian turban for Darius (Aesch. *Pers.* 661). From the time of Euripides, heroes in misfortune (e. g. Telephus and Philoctetes) were sometimes dressed in rags.

In the Satyric Drama the costumes of the heroic characters resembled in all essentials what they wore in the tragedies, although, to suit the greater liveliness of the action, the χιτών was shorter and the boot lower. In the Old Comedy the costumes were taken as nearly as possible from actual life, but in the Middle and New Comedy they were conventional. The men wore a white coat; youths, a purple one; slaves, a motley, with mantle to match; cooks, an unbleached double mantle; peasants, a fur or shaggy coat, with wallet and staff; panders, a coloured coat and motley overgarment. Old women appeared in sky-blue or dark yellow; priestesses and maidens, in white; courtesans, in motley colours, and so on. Red hair marked a roguish slave; beards were not given to youths or old men. The eyebrows were strongly marked and highly characteristic. When drawn up, they denoted pride or impudence. A touchy old man had one eyebrow drawn up and one down. The members of the chorus were masked and dressed in a costume corresponding to the part assigned them by the poet. (On their dress in the Satyric Drama, see SATYRIC DRAMA.) The chorus of the comedy caricatured the ordinary dress of the tragic

Comedy Scene. (Painting from Pompeii.)

chorus. Sometimes they represented animals, as in the *Frogs* and *Birds* of Aristophanes. In the *Frogs* they wore tight dresses of frog-colour, and masks with a mouth wide open; in the *Birds*, large beaks, bunches of feathers, combs, and so on, to imitate particular birds.

(2) ROMAN. Dramatic performances in Rome, as in Greece, formed a part of the usual public festivals, whether exceptional or ordinary, and were set on foot by the aediles and praetors. (See LUDI.) A private individual, however, if he were giving a festival or celebrating a funeral, would have theatrical representations on his own account. The giver of the festival hired a troupe of players (*grex*), the director of which (*dominus gregis*) bought a play from a poet at his own risk. If the piece was a failure the manager received no compensation. But after its performance the piece became his property, to be used at future representations for his own profit. In the time of Cicero, when it was fashionable to revive the works of older masters, the selection of suitable pieces was generally left to the director. The Romans did not, like the Greeks, limit the number of actors to three, but varied it according to the requirements of the play. Women's parts were originally played by men, as in Greece. Women first appeared in mimes, and not till very late times in comedies. The actors were usually freedmen or slaves, whom their masters sent out to be educated, and then hired them out to the directors of the theatres. The profession was technically branded with *infamia*, nor was its legal position ever essentially altered. The social standing of actors was, however, improved through the influence of Greek education; and gifted artists like the comedian Roscius, and Aesopus, the tragedian, in Cicero's time, enjoyed the friendship of the best men in Rome. The instance of these two men may show what profits could be made by a good actor. Roscius received, for every day that he played, $175, and made an annual income of some $21,000. Aesopus, in spite of his great extravagance, left $852,500 at his death. Besides the regular *honoraria*, actors, if thought to deserve it, received other and voluntary presents from the giver of the performance. These often took the form of finely wrought crowns of silver or gold work. Masks were not worn until Roscius made their use general. Before his time actors had recourse to false hair of different colours and paint for the face. Young men wore black wigs; slaves, red ones; old men, white ones. The costume in general was modelled on that of actual life, Greek or Roman, but parasites were conventionally represented in black or gray (Pollux, iv. 148). As early as the later years of the Republic, a great increase took place in the splendour of the costumes and the general magnificence of the performance. In tragedy, particularly, a new effect was attained by massing the actors in great numbers on the stage.

BIBLIOGRAPHY.—For the historical development of the drama, see CHORUS; COMOEDIA; MIMUS; SATIRA; THESPIS; TRAGOEDIA. For the theatre and the setting of plays, see THEATRUM. For the actors, see HISTRIO. For theatrical costumes, see CHLAMYS; HIMATION; PERSONA; TUNICA. For the great dramatic writers of Greece, see AESCHYLUS; ARISTOPHANES; CRATINUS; EUPOLIS; EURIPIDES; SOPHOCLES. For the great Roman writers, see ENNIUS; LIVIUS (ANDRONICUS); PLAUTUS; SENECA; TERENTIUS. Valuable works on the subject of the ancient drama are the following: Witzschell, *The Athenian Stage* (Eng. tr. London, 1850); Walford, *Handbook of the Greek Drama* (London, 1856); Donaldson, *The Theatre of the Greeks* (8th ed. London, 1875); Bergk, *Griech. Literaturgeschichte*, vol. iii. (Berlin, 1884); Bernhardy, *Grundriss d. griech. Litteratur*, vol. ii. pt. ii. (Halle, 1880); Schneider, *Das Attische Theaterwesen* (Weimar, 1835); Klein, *Geschichte des Dramas*, vols. i.–iii. (Leipzig, 1866); Haigh, *The Attic Theatre* (Oxford, 1889).

Drancae. See ZARANGAEI.

Drangiāna (Δραγγιανή). A part of Ariana, bounded by Gedrosia, Carmania, Arachosia, and Aria. It sometimes formed a separate satrapy, but was more usually united to the satrapies either of Arachosia or of Gedrosia or of Aria. In the north of the country dwelt the Drangae, a warlike people, from whom the province derived its name. The Ariaspae inhabited the southern part of the province, which was known for its production of tin.

Dravus. The modern Drave; a tributary of the Danube, flowing through Noricum and Pannonia, and after receiving the Murius (Muhr) falling into the Danube east of Mursa (Esseck).

Drepănum (Δρέπανον). A sickle. (1) Also DREPĂNA (τὰ Δρέπανα), more rarely DREPĂNĒ (Trapani), a seaport town in the northwest corner of Sicily, founded by the Carthaginians. It was here that Anchises died, according to Vergil. (2) Also DREPANĒ, a town in Bithynia, the birthplace of Helena (q. v.), mother of Constantine the Great, in whose honour it was called Helenopolis and made an important place. (3) The ancient name of Corcyra.

Dress. See CLOTHING.

Druentia. The modern Durance; a large and rapid river in Gallia Narbonensis, rising in the Alps, and flowing into the Rhone near Avenio (Avignon). See Auson. *Mosella*, 479.

Drugs. See MEDICINA.

Druĭdae and **Druĭdes.** The priests of religion among the ancient Gauls and Britons. Britain, according to Caesar (*B. G.* vi. 13 and 14), was the great school of the Druids, and their chief settlement was in the island called Mona by Tacitus, now Anglesey. To this island the natives of Gaul and Germany, who wished to be thoroughly versed in the mysteries of Druidism, resorted to complete their studies.

Caesar's account of the Druids is as follows: "They attend to divine worship, perform public and private sacrifices, and expound matters of religion. A great number of youths are gathered round them for the sake of education, and they enjoy the highest honour in the nation; for nearly all public and private quarrels come under their jurisdiction; and when any crime has been committed, when a murder has been perpetrated, when a controversy arises about a legacy or about landmarks, they are the judges too. They fix rewards and punishments; and should any one, whether a private individual or a public man, disobey their decrees, then they exclude him from the sacrifices. This is with them the severest punishment. The persons who are thus laid under interdict are regarded as impious and wicked; everybody recoils from them, and shuns their society and conversation, lest he should be injured by associating with them. They cannot obtain legal redress when they ask for it, nor are they admitted to any honourable office. All these Druids have one chief, who enjoys the supreme authority amongst them. When he dies, he is succeeded by that member of the order who is most prominent amongst the others, if there be any such single individual; if, however, there are several men equally distinguished, the successor is elected by the Druids. Sometimes they even go to war about this supremacy. At a certain time of the year, the Druids assemble on the territory of the Carnutes, which is believed to be the centre of all Gaul, in a sacred place. To that spot are gathered from everywhere all persons that have quarrels, and these abide by their judgments and decrees. It is believed that this institution was founded in Britain, and thence transplanted into Gaul. Even nowadays, those who wish to become more intimately acquainted with the institution generally go to Britain for instruction.

"The Druids take no part in warfare; nor do they pay taxes like the rest of the people; they are exempt from military service, and from all public burdens. Attracted by such rewards, many come to be instructed of their own choice, while others are sent by their parents. They are reported to learn in the school a great number of verses, so that some remain there twenty years. They think it an unlawful thing to commit their lore to writing, though in the other public and private affairs of life they frequently make use of the Greek alphabet.

"Beyond all things they are desirous to inspire a belief that men's souls do not perish, but transmigrate after death from one individual to another; and they hold that people are thereby most strongly incited to bravery, as the fear of death is thus destroyed. Besides, they hold a great many discourses about the stars and their motion, about the size of the world and of various countries, about the nature of things, about the power and might of the immortal gods; and they instruct the youths in these subjects."

Some further details are given by Pliny the Elder in his *Historia Naturalis* (xxix. 62, 1; xxiv. 12, 1; xxx. 4, 1). Besides their priestly character, the Druids appear to have practised magic, and to have been thoroughly versed in botany and in other sciences. The oak was especially sacred among them, and in oak-groves they performed their rites. The mistletoe was particularly reverenced, and Pliny tells us that it was removed from the tree by a Druid clothed in white, who cut it with a golden knife and gave it to a second Druid also in white, who, standing on the ground, received it. Pliny further speaks of a distinguishing badge, "the serpent's egg," worn by the Druids, and formed by the poisonous spittle of a great number of serpents twined together and gathered by moonlight. It was worn in the bosom and was regarded as a powerful talisman. The account of Pliny refers to the Druids of Gaul, but there is no reason for supposing that there existed any essential difference between the Druidism of Gaul and that of Britain as described by Caesar. Mr. Whitley Stokes asserts that the Druids of Ireland were of less importance, forming not a priestly class, but simply a species of wizards and soothsayers.

The Druids, by reason of their great influence with the people, were a cause of continual trouble to the Roman conquerors, keeping alive the national aspirations and encouraging rebellion. Hence, the emperor Claudius formally refused the privilege of practising Druidical rites, and when Suetonius Paulinus defeated the Britons on the island of Mona (Anglesey) the sacred groves were destroyed. Yet on the Continent, Druidism continued to have followers down to the final overthrow of paganism.

Scholars at the present day are extremely conservative in making any general statements regarding the Druids, and nearly all the elaborate theories that were formerly held are now regarded as unsafe. Even the view that the huge structures of stone found in Keltic countries were Druidical altars, or mark the seats of Druidical worship, is no longer accepted. The so-called Druidical temples at Avebury and Stonehenge in England, and at Carnac in France, were very possibly not Druidical at all; since similar structures have been found in Scandinavia and other parts of Europe where Druidism never existed. Regarding the etymology of the name *Druid* nothing certain can be alleged. Among the tentative and traditional explanations are the following: from the Keltic *deru*, "an oak"; the Old German *druthin*, "a master"; the Saxon *dry*, "a magician"; the Irish *drui*, "a sacred person, or priest"; and in the Keltic compare *derouyd*, "a prophet" (De Chiniac). The old etymology from δρῦς is absurd. The feminine form of the Latinized *Druida* is *Druias* (Lamprid. *Alex. Sev.* 60) or *Druis* (Vop. *Aurel.* 41). The Greek masculine form is Δρυΐδης (Aristoph. *Fr.* 30).

See Pelloutier, *Histoire des Celtes* (Paris, 1771); Davis, *Mythology and Rites of the British Druids* (London, 1809); Pictet, *Du Culte des Cabires chez les Anciens Irlandais* (Geneva, 1824); Higgins, *Celtic Druids* (London, 1829); Thierry, *Histoire des Gaulois* (Paris, 1828); Reynaud, *De l'Esprit de la Gaule* (Paris, 1866); Barth, *Ueber die Druiden der Kelten* (Erlangen, 1828); Scarth, *Roman Britain* (London, 1883); Rhys, *Celtic Heathendom* (London, 1888). Besides Caesar and Pliny, scattering notices of the Druids are found in Cicero (*De Divinatione*), Diodorus Siculus, Strabo, Pomponius Mela, Tacitus, Lucan, Lampridius, Vopiscus, Ausonius (*Professores*), Ammianus Marcellinus, Origen, and Clemens Alexandrinus.

Drum. See TYMPANUM.

Drusilla. (1) LIVIA. The wife of Augustus Caesar. See LIVIA. (2) LIVIA, a daughter of Germanicus and Agrippina, born at Augusta Trevirorum (Trèves) A.D. 15. She was far from inheriting the excellent qualities of her mother. Her own brother Caligula seduced her, and then gave her in marriage, at the age of seventeen, to Lucius Cassius Longinus, a man of consular rank. Subsequently, however, he took her away from her husband and lived with her as his own wife. This connection lasted until the death of Drusilla, A.D. 38, and at her decease Caligula abandoned himself to the most extravagant sorrow. Divine honours were rendered to her memory, and medals were struck in her honour with the title of Augusta. She was twenty-three years of age at the time of her death (Suet. *Calig.* 24). Dio Cassius calls the name of her husband Marcus Lepidus, differing in this from Suetonius. He may possibly refer to a second husband, who may have been given her, for form's sake, a short time before her death (Dio Cass. lix. 3). (3) A daughter of Agrippa, king of Iudaea, remarkable for her beauty. She was at first affianced to Epiphanes, son of Antiochus, king of Commagené. But, on his declining to submit to the rite of circumcision and become a Jew, the marriage was broken off. She was then given to Azizus, king of Emesa. Not long after, however, Drusilla renounced the religion of her fathers, abandoned her husband, and espoused Antonius Felix, a freedman of the emperor Claudius, and brother to Pallas, the freedman of Nero. This is the Felix who was governor of Iudaea and is mentioned in the Acts of the Apostles. Drusilla was with Felix at Caesarea when St. Paul appeared before the latter. She had a son by her second husband, named Agrippa, who perished in the eruption of Vesuvius which took place during the reign of Titus (Joseph. *Ant. Iud.* xix. 9).

Drusus. (1) CLAUDIUS NERO, son of Tiberius Claudius Nero and of Livia, was born B.C. 38. He served early in the army, and was sent, in B.C. 17, with his brother Tiberius, against the Rhaeti and the Vindelici, who had made an irruption into Italy. He defeated the invaders, pursued them across the Alps, and reduced their country. Horace has celebrated this victory in one of his finest odes (iv. 4). Drusus married Antonia Minor, daughter of Antony and Octavia, by whom he had Germanicus and Claudius, afterwards emperor, and Livia or Livilla. In B.C. 14, being sent to quell an insurrection in Gaul, he succeeded by his conciliatory address. In the following year he attacked the Germans, and, carrying the war beyond the Rhine, he obtained a series of victories over the Sicambri, Cherusci, Catti, and Tencteri, and advanced as far as the Visurgis (Weser), for which the Senate bestowed on him and his posterity the surname of Germanicus. In B.C. 9, Drusus was made consul. He was soon after sent by Augustus against the Germans, crossed the Visurgis, and advanced as far as the Albis (Elbe). He imposed a moderate tribute on the Frisians, which, being afterwards aggravated by his successors, caused a revolt in the reign of Tiberius (Tac. *Ann.* iv. 72). He caused a canal to be cut, for the purpose of uniting the Rhine to the Yssel, which was known long after by the name of Fossa Drusi. Drusus did not cross the Albis, but retired towards the Rhine. Before he reached that river, he died, at the age of thirty, in consequence, as it was reported, of his horse falling upon him and fracturing his leg (Livy, *Epit.* 142). Tiberius, who was sent for in haste, and found his brother expiring, accompanied his body to Rome, where his funeral was performed with the greatest solemnity. Both Augustus and Tiberius delivered orations in his praise. Drusus was much regretted by both the army and the Romans in general, who had formed great expectations from his manly and generous character. (2) The son of the emperor Tiberius by Vipsania, daughter of Agrippa. He served with distinction in Pannonia and Illyricum, and was consul with his father, A.D. 21. In a quarrel with the imperial favourite Seianus, he gave the latter a blow in the face. Seianus, in revenge, seduced his wife Livia or Livilla, daughter of Drusus the elder and of Antonia; and the guilty pair destroyed Drusus by poison, which was administered by the eunuch Lygdus. The crime remained a secret for eight years, when it was discovered after the death of Seianus, and Livia was put to death (Tac. *Ann.* i. 24, etc.; iv. 3 foll.). (3) Caesar, son of Germanicus and Agrippina, and brother of Nero Caesar and Caligula. He married Aemilia Lepida, who was induced by Seianus to betray her husband. Deluded himself by the arts of that evil minister, he conspired against the life of his brother, Nero Caesar, and was starved to death by order of Tiberius (Tac. *Ann.* iv. 60). (4) M. LIVIUS. See LIVIAE LEGES.

Statue of Drusus from Pompeii. (Overbeck.)

Dryădes (Δρυάδες). Wood-nymphs. See NYMPHAE.

Dryas (Δρύας). Father of the Thracian king Lycurgus (q. v.), who is hence called Dryantides.

Drymaea (Δρυμαία) or **Drymus** (Δρύμος). A town in Phocis, a little south of the Cephissus.

Drymus. (1) See DRYMAEA. (2) A strong place in Attica, on the frontiers of Boeotia.

Drymussa (Δρυμοῦσσα). An island off the coast of Ionia, opposite Clazomenae (Thuc. viii. 31).

Dryŏpé (Δρυόπη). The daughter of King Dryops and beloved by Apollo, who, in order to get possession of her, changed himself into a tortoise. Dryopé took the creature into her lap, whereupon it became a serpent. This sudden transformation frightened away the companions of Dryopé, thus leaving her alone with the god, who then accomplished his purpose. Soon after she married Andraemon, but became by Apollo the mother of Amphissus, who founded the town of Oeta and built there a shrine to his father. Dryopé was at last carried off by the wood-nymphs and became one of them. See Ovid, *Met.* ix. 331.

Dryŏpes (Δρύοπες). A Pelasgic people, who dwelt first in Thessaly, from the Spercheus to Parnassus, and afterwards in Doris, which was called from them Dryopis. Driven out of Doris by the Dorians, they migrated to other countries, and settled in Peloponnesus, Euboea, and Asia Minor. See Herod. viii. 31.

Dryops (Δρύοψ). The son of the river-god Spercheus. He was the father of Dryopé (q. v.) and the reputed ancestor of the Dryopes (q. v.).

Dryos Cephălae (Δρυὸς Κεφαλαί). A narrow pass of Mount Cithaeron in Boeotia, between Athens and Plataeae.

Dubis. The modern Doubs, a river in Gaul, rising in Mons Iurassus (Jura), flowing past Vesontio

(Besançon), and falling into the Arar (Saône) near Cabillonum (Châlons). Caesar (*B. G.* i. 38) calls it Aldnasdubis according to many MSS.

Dubris Portus. The modern Dover; a seaport town of the Cantii in Britain; here was a fortress erected by the Romans against the Saxon pirates. It is mentioned in both the *Itinerarium* and the *Notitia.*

Du Cange, CHARLES DUFRESNE, SIEUR. One of the most famous of French scholars, born at Amiens, December 18th, 1610. He adopted the profession of a parliamentary advocate in Paris, but passed the greater part of his life in study, having a remarkably versatile and retentive mind. He is well known by his works on Byzantine history, and pre-eminently by his great *Glossarium ad Scriptores Mediae et Infimae Latinitatis*—a treasure-house of valuable information regarding mediæval Latin. It first appeared in three folio volumes at Paris in 1678, and was subsequently greatly enlarged by the Benedictines of St. Maur to six volumes (Paris, 1733-36), to which four more volumes were added by the Benedictine Charpentier (1766). A new edition appeared in seven volumes by G. A. Henschel (Paris, 1840-46), to which Diefenbach added supplements (Frankfort, 1857 and 1867). Still another edition was begun in 1883 to consist of ten volumes. Besides this invaluable lexicon, Du Cange put forth a *Glossarium ad Scriptores Mediae et Infimae Graecitatis* (Paris, 1688); *Historia Byzantina* (Paris, 1680); the *Annals* of Zonaras, with notes (Paris, 1686); and *Chronicon Paschale* (Paris, 1689). See Feugère, *Essai sur la Vie et les Ouvrages de Ducange* (Paris, 1852).

Ducas, MICHAEL (Μιχαὴλ ὁ Δοῦκας). A Byzantine historian who held office under the last of the Greek emperors, Constantine XIII. On the capture of Constantinople by the Turks (A.D. 1453), he escaped to Lesbos, where he wrote a history of the period from the time of John VI., Palaeologus (A.D. 1355), to the capture of Lesbos by the Turks (1462). Though written in barbarous Greek, the history is clear and impartial and of considerable value. The best edition is that of Bekker (Bonn, 1834), which has appended to it an early Italian translation.

Ducenarii. The name of various officers and magistrates in the imperial period, of whom the principal were as follows:

(1) The imperial *procuratores,* who received a salary of 200 sestertia (Dio Cass. liii. 15). We read of *centenarii,* etc., as well as of ducenarii. (See Capitol. *Pert.* 2; Orelli, *Inscript.* No. 946.)

(2) A class or decuria of iudices, first established by Augustus. They were so called because their property, as valued in the census, only amounted to 200 sestertia, and they tried causes of small importance (Suet. *Aug.* 32).

(3) Officers who commanded two centuries, and who held the same rank as the *primi hastati* in the ancient legion (Veget. ii. 8).

(4) The imperial household troops, who were under the authority of the *magister officiorum* (*Cod.* i. tit. 31; xii. tit. 20).

In the third century A.D. and later, the title is often applied in inscriptions to *protectores Augusti* and to many officials of equestrian rank, as *praefecti legionum, praefecti vehiculorum, imperatori a consiliis.* In these cases it appears to denote the rank as well as the salary of the official, and is seldom used without the addition of another title (Th. Mommsen in *Ephem. Epigraphica,* v. 121-127). The office of a ducenarius is *ducenaria* or *ducena.*

Ducetius (Δουκέτιος). A Sicilian chief who carried on a war with the Greeks of that island in the middle of the fifth century B.C. Defeated by the Syracusans, he surrendered and was exiled to Corinth. Subsequently returning to Sicily, he founded there the city of Calacté, and died B.C. 440 (Diod. xi. and xii.).

Duella. See UNCIA.

Duēnos Inscription. The name commonly given to a very interesting inscription found at Rome near the Quirinal in 1880. It is inscribed upon three small earthen pots connected together, and is written from right to left. It reads as follows: IOVEI SAT DEIVOS QOI MED MITAT NEI TED ENDO COSMIS VIRCO SIED ASTED NOISI OPE TOITESIAI PACARI VOIS. DVENOS MED FECED EN MANOM EINOM DZENOINE MED MAAO STATOD. This, rendered into classical forms, is probably to be read thus: *Iovi, Saturno divis qui* (=*si quis*) *me mittet, ne te endo* (=*in te*) *comis virgo sit ast nisi Opi Tutesiae pacari vis. Duenus me fecit in Manum: enim die noni me Mano stato*—i. e. "If any one brings me to the gods Iupiter and Saturn, let not any maiden be kind to thee, unless thou shalt offer a sacrifice to Ops Tutesia. Duenus made me for an offering to the Dead (Manus); therefore, on the ninth day, set me for the offering to the Dead."

Important peculiarities of this inscription, which seems to be at least as early as B.C. 300, are the use of *q* before *o*, the *ei* for *ĕ*, and the *dz* used to represent the sound of *dy*=*j*. See Dressel, in the *Annali dell' Instituto,* lii. 158; Bücheler, in the *Rhein. Museum,* xxxvi. 235 foll.; Schneider, *Dialectorum Italicarum Exempla,* i. 19 (Leipzig, 1886); Jordan in *Hermes,* xvi. 225-60; Cortese, *Latini Sermonis Vetustioris Exempla* (Turin, 1892); and for a fac-simile, the article EPIGRAPHY in this Dictionary. Notes on the text are given by Schneider. See also Maarenbrecher in the *Rheinisches Museum* for 1896.

Duilia Lex. See LEX.

Duilian Column. See COLUMNA ROSTRATA.

Duilius Nepos, GAIUS. A Roman consul, the first who obtained a victory over the naval power of Carthage, B.C. 260. After his colleague, Cn. Corn. Scipio, had been taken at sea by the Carthaginians in the First Punic War, Duilius proceeded, with a newly built Roman fleet, to Sicily, in quest of the enemy, whom he met near the Lipari Islands; and, by means of grappling-irons, so connected the ships of the Carthaginians with his own that the contest became a sort of land-fight. By this unexpected manœuvre he took eighty and destroyed thirteen of the Carthaginian fleet and obtained a naval triumph, the first ever enjoyed at Rome. There were some medals struck in commemoration of this victory, and a column was erected on the occasion. This column (called Columna Rostrata, because adorned with beaks of ships) was, as Livy informs us, struck down by lightning during the interval between the second and third Punic wars. See COLUMNA ROSTRATA.

Dulcia. Confectionery, sweetmeats, "candy." A general name applied to sweets made with honey, as distinguished from pastry, or sweet dishes made with meal, fruit, milk, etc. See Lamprid. *Elagab.* 27 and 32; and the articles DIAETETICA; PISTOR.

Dulciarii. See PISTOR.

Dulgibīni. A people in Germany, dwelling on the right bank of the Weser (Ptol. ii. 11, 17).

Dulichium (Δουλίχιον). See ECHINADES.

Dumnŏrix. A chieftain of the Aedui, and brother of Divitiacus. He was an enemy of the Romans, and was put to death by Caesar's order, B.C. 54 (Caes. *B. G.* i. 3).

Dungeon. See CARCER.

Dunium. See DUROTRIGES.

Duodĕcim Scripta (κύβοι, διαγραμμισμός: in late Greek τάβλα). A game of mixed chance and skill, which must have been substantially the same as our backgammon. The following points of identity may be regarded as established: The game was played on a board of twelve double lines with fifteen white and fifteen black men; the throws were counted as we count them; "blots" (ἄζυγες) might be captured; the pieces (whether they started from home or not) had to be brought home; and the winner was he who first cleared off his men. On the other hand, there were three dice instead of two (see TESSERA), and it is impossible to say where the men started or how blots taken up re-entered. In the initial position the pieces may have stood in three rows of five or five rows of three, and either in the player's own table with a view to the double journey or in the opponent's table with a view to the journey home. With the three dice the pieces would soon be scattered, and thus a less artificial arrangement than our own may be thought probable. The phrase ὀπισθιδίη ὁδὸς in Agathias may seem to favour the notion that they were played out and home. The board was ἄβαξ (see ABACUS), more generally *tabula*, or from its raised rim *alveus, alveolus;* the men ψῆφοι, *calculi;* the situation at any point of the game, θέσις; to move, τιθέναι, *dare;* to retract a move, ἀνατιθέναι, *reducere.* In a fragment of Cicero (*ap.* Non. p. 170, s. v. *Scripta*) we find: *Itaque tibi concedo, quod in duodecim scriptis solemus, ut calculum reducas, si te alicuius dati poenitet.* This privilege is more likely to have been of the nature of odds granted by a superior player than a regular rule of the game.

The classical Greek writers mostly use κύβοι, κυβεύειν, of games into which skill entered as well as of mere dicing. That κυβεία was a game of skill as well as chance is clear from Plato (*Rep.* x. 604 C, *Phaedr.* 274 D) and from a story told by Plutarch (*Artax.* 17); cf. Ter. *Adelph.* iv. 7, 21. Ovid alludes to the Duodecim Scripta (*A. A.* iii. 363–364) among games which lovers are to play together; others are *latrunculi* (357–358, 361–362), and "go-bang" (365–366). Martial includes among his modest wants *tabulamque calculosque* (ii. 48). The celebrated jurisconsult P. Mucius Scaevola was famed for his skill at Duodecim Scripta (Cic. *de Or.* i. 50, § 217). Quintilian (xi. 2) further tells the story that Scaevola, after losing a game, accurately recalled all the throws and the way that each had been played; pointing out the move where he had made a mistake, and verifying his own recollections by those of his opponent. This is cited as an example of memory and logical sequence (*ordo*).

None of the above passages shed much light on the details of the game. Our knowledge of them is mostly gained from an epigram of Agathias (*Anth. Pal.* ix. 482; also in Brunck, *Anal.* iii. 60) on a case of special ill-luck which befell the emperor Zeno (A.D. 474–491). This epigram has been discussed by many scholars, but until lately was never rendered intelligible. The problem has been solved independently by M. Becq de Fouquières, in his *Jeux des Anciens*, and Dr. H. Jackson, in the English *Journal of Philology;* on the few points where they differed, Dr. Jackson has since given in his adherence to M. Becq de Fouquières's conclusions.

More than a hundred ancient boards, serving for six different games, had been found in Rome alone down to 1877 (Marquardt, *Privatl.* 838); but only a single example shows the twelve lines. This is of marble, bears a Christian inscription, and is of very rude workmanship and illiterate spelling. It has been engraved by Gruter (*Mon. Chr.* p. 1091), Becq de Fouquières (p. 364), and in a simplified form, omitting the inscription, by Rich. This is to all intents and purposes a backgammon board, exhibiting the four half tables of six lines each.

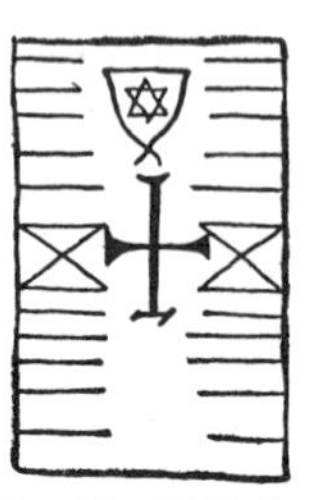

Board for Duodecim Scripta. (Rich.)

Mention is made of boards and men of costly materials or of peculiar construction. In Petronius (33) Trimalchio plays on a board of terebinth-wood, with dice of crystal, and with gold and silver denarii for black and white men. Pliny (*H. N.* xxxvii. § 13) has an absurdly rhetorical account of the splendours of an *alveus lusorius*, in gold and jewels, borne in Pompey's third triumph, B.C. 61; in the centre of it was a golden moon of thirty pounds' weight. The emperor Claudius had his carriage fitted with a board which could not upset, in order to play when travelling (Suet. *Claud.* 33). The *tabula lusoria* described by Martial (xiv. 17) was also specially adapted for two different games, probably on opposite sides. The first line refers to the Duodecim Scripta; the second, modelled on a couplet of Ovid (*Trist.* ii. 477–478), to the game of draughts (*latrunculi*), in which the player left with but one man is bound to lose to his opponent who has two. See Becq de Fouquières, *Jeux des Anciens*, 2d ed. (1873), pp. 357–383; H. Jackson, in *Journ. of Philol.* vii. 236–243; Marquardt, *Privatl.* 834–838; and Falkener, *Games Ancient and Oriental* (1892).

Duodĕcim Tabulārum Lex. See DECEMVIRI; TWELVE TABLES.

Duo Viri. "The two men"; a name applied to various magistrates and commissioners at Rome and in the *coloniae* and *municipii.* The form *duumvir*, "one of the two men," is used in the singular (Liv. ii. 42, 5, etc.); it is doubtful whether *duumviri* should ever be used in the plural. Some editors print it so, but in the MSS. and inscriptions we generally find only *iiviri;* in *C. I. L.* i. 1196 we have *duo viri*, and also *duo vir* (cf. *C. I. L.* vi. 3732); but there seems to be no epigraphic authority for *duumviri.* That Cicero knew only *tres viri*, not *triumviri*, is shown by *Ep. Fam.* viii. 13, 2. The most important of these "commissions of two" were the following:

(1) DUO VIRI IURI DICUNDO, the highest magistrates in the municipal towns.

(2) DUO VIRI SACRORUM, to whom was at first intrusted the charge of the Sibylline Books (q. v.) (cf. Liv. iii. 10, 7). The commission was afterwards made to consist of ten (Liv. vi. 37, 12; 42, 2), and subsequently, probably by Sulla, of fifteen.

(3) DUO VIRI NAVALES, an extraordinary commission appointed for the purpose of equipping or repairing a fleet (Mommsen, *Röm. Staatsr.* ii. 565).

(4) DUO VIRI AEDI DEDICANDAE, elected by the people for the purpose of dedicating a temple. The duty was always performed by one of the two only, and the election of a second seems to have been due solely to the desire of the Romans to have two colleagues in each magistracy (Liv. vii. 28, xxii. 33, xxxv. 41). The *duo viri aedi locandae*, who gave out the contract for the erection of a temple, were not necessarily the same as those who dedicated it (cf. Liv. xxii. 33 with xxiii. 21, 7), although they frequently were.

(5) DUO VIRI VIIS EXTRA URBEM PURGANDIS were officers under the aediles, first mentioned in the Lex Iulia Municipalis, and possibly therefore instituted by Caesar. They were abolished by Augustus when the *curatores viarum* were instituted (Dio, liv. 26).

(6) DUO VIRI PERDUELLIŌNIS. (See PERDUELLIO.)

(7) DUO VIRI QUINQUENNĀLES, the censors in the municipia.

Duplarii or **Duplicarii**. Soldiers who received, on account of their good conduct, double allowance (*duplicia cibaria*), and perhaps in some cases double pay likewise (Varr. *L. L.* v. 90; Liv. ii. 59, xxiv. 47; Orelli, *Inscript.* No. 3535). The forms are *duplicarius* (Or. 3533), *dupliciarius* (ib. 3534), *duplaris* (Veget. ii. 7), *duplarius* (Or. 3531).

Dupondius or **Dupondium**. A coin of two asses, struck after the reduction of the weight of the *as*. (See As.) It was in use under the Empire, when it was the weight of half an ounce (Marquardt, *Röm. Staatsverw.* ii. pp. 8, 11). As the Romans applied the uncial division of the *as* to the foot, *dupondium* also signified two feet (Colum. iii. 15, § 2).

Dura (τὰ Δοῦρα). (1) A town in Mesopotamia on the Euphrates, founded by the Macedonians. It was also styled NICANŎRIS and EURŌPUS (Ammian. Marc. xxiii. 5). (2) A fortified place in Assyria on the Tigris (Polyb. v. 52). It is still called Dúr.

Duranius. A river in Aquitania, near the Dordagne (Auson. *Mosella*, 464). It enters the Garumna (Garonne) on the right bank near Bordeaux.

Duria (Δουρίας). The name of two small rivers in Italy, now the Dora Baltia and the Dora Riparia, both rising in the Alps and emptying into the Padus (Po) (Plin. *H. N.* iii. 16).

Duris (Δοῦρις). A Samian writer of history who flourished about B.C. 350. He was a descendant of Alcibiades, and at one time was tyrant of Samos. Only fragments now remain of his historical writings, which were as follows: (1) A history of Greece (Ἡ τῶν Ἑλληνικῶν Ἱστορία), from B.C. 370 to B.C. 281; (2) Περὶ Ἀγαθοκλέα Ἱστορίαι; (3) Σαμίων Ὧροι; (4) Περὶ Εὐριπίδου καὶ Σοφοκλέους; (5) Περὶ Νόμων; (6) Περὶ Ἀγώνων; (7) Περὶ Ζωγραφίας; (8) Περὶ Τορευτικῆς; (9) Λιβυκά. The fragments were collected by Hulleman (Utrecht, 1841).

Durius (Δούριος). The modern Douro; one of the chief rivers of Spain, near Numantia, and flowing into the Atlantic.

Durobrivae. (1) A town of the Cantii in Britain, now Rochester. (2) A British town north of the Thames, by some identified with Godmanchester.

Durocasses (called also DROCAE and FANUM DRUĬDUM). A city of the Eburovices, in Gallia Lugdunensis, southwest of Lutetia (Paris). In its vicinity was the principal residence of the Druids in Gaul (Caes. *B. G.* vi. 13). The modern name is Dreux.

Durocortōrum. The modern Rheims; the capital of the Remi in Gallia Belgica, subsequently called Remi (Caes. *B. G.* vi. 44).

Duronia. A town in Samnium, in Italy, west of the Caudine passes (Liv. x. 39).

Durotrĭges. A people in Britain, in Dorsetshire and the west of Somersetshire; their chief town was Dunium (Dorchester).

Durovernum or **Darvernum**. The modern Canterbury; a town of the Cantii in Britain, afterwards called Cantuaria.

Duumvir. See DUO VIRI.

Dux. See PROVINCIA.

Dyardănes or **Oedănes** (Οἰδάνης). A great river of India (Q. Curt. viii. 9), possibly to be identified with the Brahmaputra.

Dymas (Δύμας). Father of Hecuba (*Iliad*, xvi. 718), who is hence called Dymantis.

Dymé (Δύμη) or **Dymae** (Δῦμαι). A town in the west of Achaia, near the coast; one of the twelve Achaean towns (Herod. i. 145).

Dyras (Δύρας). A river of Thessaly, twenty stadia beyond the Sperchius, said to have sprung from the ground in order to assist Heracles when burning on Oeta (Herod. vii. 199).

Dyrrhachium (Δυρράχιον). The modern Durazzo, formerly called EPIDAMNUS (Ἐπίδαμνος); a town in Greek Illyria, on a peninsula in the Adriatic Sea. It was founded by the Corcyreans and received the name of Epidamnus; but since the Romans regarded this name as one of bad omen, reminding them of *damnum*, they changed it into Dyrrhachium. It was the usual place of landing for persons who crossed over from Brundisium, and was to that town what Calais is to Dover. Here commenced the great Via Egnatia. The place was one of much commerce, so that Catullus (xxxvi. 15) calls it *taberna Hadriae*, "the shop of the Adriatic." During the Civil Wars it was the headquarters of Pompey, who kept his military stores here. In A.D. 345 it was destroyed by an earthquake.

Dysōrum (Δύσωρον). A gold-producing mountain in Macedonia between Chalcidicé and Odomanticé (Herod. v. 17).

Dyspontium (Δυσπόντιον). A town of Pisatis in Elis, of great antiquity, north of the Alpheus. It was destroyed by the Eleans in their war with the Pisatae. See Pausan. vi. 22.

E

E, as a symbol.

IN GREEK.—E·Θ = ἐπικουρίοις θεοῖς (*C. I. G.* 158, 213).

EE = εὐχὴν ἐποίησεν.

E = 5, τὸ Ē = τὸ πέμπτον (*C. I. G.* 2572).

H = ἡμέρας (ἡμερῶν).

IN LATIN.—E = eius, (h)eres, est, evocatus, exsculpsit.

E·A·E = eques alae eiusdem.

E·M = ex monitu.

E·M·V = egregiae memoriae vir.

E·O·B·Q = ei ossa bene quiescant.

E·R·P = e re publica.

E·S·C·R·C = e senatus consulto reficiendum curavit.

E·S·F·S·F·L = ei sine fraude sua facere liceto.

E·T·F = ex testamento fecit.

E·V·S = ex voto suscepto.

Ear-rings. See INAURIS.

Ebĕnus (ἔβενος) and **Hebĕnus** (ἔβενος). Ebony; spoken of by Vergil as produced only in India, but by Herodotus mentioned as one of the articles of tribute paid by the Ethiopians to the king of Persia (Verg. *Georg.* ii. 117; Herod. iii. 97). By the ancients it was frequently inlaid with ivory because of the contrast of the colours.

Eblāna. A place in Hibernia mentioned by Ptolemy and identified with the site of Dublin.

Eborācum or **Eburācum** (Ἐβόρακον). The modern York; a town of the Brigantes in Britain, which, having been made a Roman station by Agricola, became the chief Roman settlement in the island. It was both a municipium and a colony, and was the residence of the Roman emperors when they visited Britain. Here the emperors Septimius Severus and Constantius Chlorus died. Many Roman remains still exist at York, and in its vicinity are portions of Roman walls. A number of important inscriptions have also been found here, besides articles of glass, metal, and stone. The name Eboracum is the Latinized form of the British Caer-Evrauc. See Eutrop. viii. 19; *Inscript. Orell.* 190; Spart. *Sever.* 19; Aurel. Vict. *De Caes.* 20; and Raine, *York* (1893).

Ebūdae or **Hebūdae.** The modern Hebrides; islands in the Western Ocean off Britain (Pliny, *H. N.* iv. 30; Solin. 23). Five are named by Ptolemy, two being called Ebudae, and the others Maleus, Epidium, and Ricina.

Ebur. Ivory. See ELEPHAS.

Eburōnes. A German people, who crossed the Rhine and settled in Gallia Belgica, between the Rhine and the Mosa (Maas). See Caes. *B. G.* ii. 4.

Eburovīces. See AULERCI.

Ebŭsus. The modern Iviza; the largest of the Pityusae Insulae, off the east coast of Spain.

Ecbatăna (τὰ Ἐκβάτανα; Heb. *Acmetha*). (1) The capital of Media, situated, according to Diodorus (ii. 13), about twelve stadia from Mount Orontes. The genuine orthography of the word appears to be Agbatana (Ἀγβάτανα), a form employed by Ctesias. Ecbatana, being in a high and mountainous country, was a favourite residence of the Persian kings during summer, when the heat of Susa was almost insupportable. The Parthian kings also, at a later period, retired to it in the summer to avoid the excessive heat of Ctesiphon. According to Herodotus (i. 98), Ecbatana was built near the close of the eighth century B.C. by Deïoces, the founder of the Median monarchy. The Book of Judith (i. 2) assigns the building of this city, or, rather, the erection of its citadel, to Arphaxad, in the twelfth year of the reign of Nebuchadnezzar, king of Assyria. Some writers make Arphaxad the same with Deïoces, while others identify him with Phraortes, the son of the latter, who might have repaired the city or else made some additions to it.

Herodotus furnishes us with no hint whence we may infer the relative position of Ecbatana on the map of Media. His description of the fortress or citadel, however, is particular. "The Medes," he remarks, "in obedience to their king's command, built those spacious and massive fortifications now called Ecbatana, circle within circle, according to the following plan: each inner circle overtops its outer neighbour by the height of the battlements alone. This was effected partly by the nature of the ground, a conical hill, and partly by the building itself. The number of the circles was seven; within the innermost were built the palace and the treasury. The circumference of the outermost wall and of the city of Athens may be regarded as nearly equal. The battlements of the first circle are white; of the second, black; of the third, scarlet; of the fourth, azure; of the fifth, orange. All these are brilliantly coloured with different paints. But the battlements of the sixth circle are silvered over, while those of the seventh are gilt. Deïoces constructed these walls around his palace for his own personal safety; but he ordered the people to erect their houses in a circle around the outer wall" (i. 98 foll.). The Orientals, however, according to Diodorus Siculus, claimed a far more ancient origin for Ecbatana. Ctesias not only describes it as the capital of the first Median monarchy, founded by Arbaces, but as existing prior to the era of the famed and fabulous Semiramis, who is said to have visited Ecbatana in the course of her royal journeys and to have built there a magnificent palace. She also, with immense labour and expense, introduced abundance of excellent water into the city by perforating the adjacent Mount Orontes, and forming a tunnel, fifteen feet broad and forty feet high, through which she conveyed a lake-stream (Diod. Sic. ii. 13). The palace stood below the citadel. Its tiles were of silver and its capitals, entablatures, and wainscotings of gold and silver. This metal the Seleucidae coined into money, amounting to the sum of 4000 talents, or $4,730,000.

Ecbatana was taken by Cyrus in B.C. 549, and remained a splendid city under the Persian sway, the great king spending at this place the two hottest months of the year. The Macedonian conquest did not prove destructive to Ecbatana, as it had to the royal palace at Persepolis. Alexander deposited in Ecbatana the treasures taken from Persepolis and Pasargada, and one of the last acts of his life was a royal visit to the Median capital. Although not equally favoured by the Seleucidae, it still retained the traces of its former grandeur; and Polybius has left on record a description of its state under Antiochus the Great, which shows that Ecbatana was still a splendid city, though it had been despoiled of many of its more costly decorations (Polyb. x. frag. 4). When the Seleucidae were driven from Upper Asia, Ecbatana became the favourite summer residence of the Arsacidae, and at the close of the first century it still continued to be the Parthian capital (Tac. *Ann.* xv. 31). When the Persians, under the house of Sassan, A.D. 226, recovered the dominion of Upper Asia, Ecbatana continued to be a favourite and secure place of residence. The natural bulwarks of Mount Zagros were never forced by the Roman legions. Consequently, as we learn from Ammianus Marcellinus, near the close of the fourth century Ecbatana continued to be a strongly fortified city. See G. Rawlinson's *Herodotus*, vol. i. p. 226 (1875); and on the site, Sir Henry Rawlinson in the *Journal of the Royal Geog. Society* for 1841.

(2) A town of Syria, in Galilaea Inferior, at the foot of Mount Carmel. Here Cambyses (q. v.) gave himself a mortal wound as he was mounting his horse, and thus fulfilled the oracle which had warned him to beware of Ecbatana (Herod. iii. 64).

Ecclesia (ἐκκλησία). The assembly of the people, which in Greek cities had the power of final decision in public affairs.

(1) At ATHENS every citizen in possession of full civic rights was entitled to take part in it from his twentieth year upwards. In early times one ecclesia met regularly once a year in each of the ten prytanies of the Senate (see BOULÉ); in later times four, making forty annually. Special assemblies might also be called on occasion. The place of meeting was in early times the market-place, in later times a special locality, called the Pnyx; but generally the theatre, after a permanent theatre had been erected. To summon the assembly was the duty of the Prytanes, who did so by publishing the notice of proceedings. There was a special authority, a board of six Lexiarchi (ληξίαρχοι) with thirty assistants, whose business it was to keep unauthorized persons out of the assembly. The members on their appearance were each presented with a ticket, on exhibiting which, after the conclusion of the meeting, they received a payment of an *obolus* (about three cents), in later times of three obols. After a solemn prayer and sacrifice the president (ἐπιστάτης) communicated to the meeting the subjects of discussion. If there were a previous resolution of the Senate for discussion, he put the question whether the people would adopt it or proceed to discuss it. In the debates every citizen had the right of addressing the meeting, but no one could speak more than once. Before doing so he put a crown of myrtle on his head. The president (but no one else) had the right of interrupting a speaker. If his behaviour were unseemly, the president could cut short his harangue, expel him from the rostrum and from the meeting, and inflict upon him a fine not exceeding 500 drachmae ($83). Cases of graver misconduct had to be referred to the Senate or Assembly for punishment. Any citizen could move an amendment or counter-proposal, which he handed in writing to the presiding πρυτανεία. The president had to decide whether it should be put to vote. This could be prevented, not only by the mere declaration of the president that it was illegal, but by any one present who bound himself on oath to prosecute the proposer for illegality. The speaker might also retract his proposal. The votes were taken by show of hands. (See CHIROTONIA.) The voting was never secret, unless the question affected some one's personal interest, as in the case of ostracism. In such cases a majority of at least 6000 votes was necessary. The resolution (ψήφισμα) was announced by the president, and a record of it taken, which was deposited in the archives, and often publicly exhibited on tables of stone or bronze. After the conclusion of business, the president, through his herald, dismissed the people. If no final result was arrived at, or if the business was interrupted by a sign from heaven, such as a storm or a shower of rain, the meeting was adjourned. Certain classes of business were assigned to the ordinary assemblies.

The functions of the ecclesia were:

(*a*) To take part in legislation. At the first regular assembly in the year the president asked the question whether the people thought any alteration necessary in the existing laws. If the answer were in the affirmative, the proposals for alteration were brought forward, and in the third regular assembly a legislative commission was appointed from among the members of the Heliaea or jury for the current year. (See HELIAEA.) The members of this commission were called νομοθέται. The question between the old laws and the new proposals was then decided by a quasi-judicial process under the presidency of the θεσμοθέται, the proposers of the new law appearing as prosecutors, and advocates, appointed by the people, coming forward to defend the old one. If the verdict were in favour of the new law, the latter had the same authority as a resolution of the ecclesia. The whole proceeding was called "voting (ἐπιχειροτονία) upon the laws." In the decadence of the democracy the custom grew up of bringing legislative proposals before the people, and having them decided at any time that pleased the proposer.

(*b*) Election of officials. (See PROBOLÉ.) This only affected, of course, the officials who were elected by show of hands, as the strategi and ministers of finance, not those chosen by lot. In the first ecclesia of every prytany the archon asked the question whether the existing ministers were to be allowed to remain in office or not, and those who failed to commend themselves were deposed.

(*c*) The banishment of citizens by ostracism. See OSTRACISMUS.

(*d*) Judicial functions in certain exceptional cases only. (See EISANGELIA.) Sometimes, if offences came to its knowledge, the people would appoint a special commission of inquiry, or put the inquiry into the hands of the Areopagus or the Senate. Offences committed against officials or against private individuals were also at times brought before the assembly, to obtain from it a declaration that it did, or did not, think the case one which called for a judicial process. Such a declaration, though not binding on the judge, always carried with it a certain influence.

(*e*) In legal co-operation with the Senate the ecclesia had the final decision in all matters affecting the supreme interests of the State, as war, peace, alliances, treaties, the regulation of the army and navy, finance, loans, tributes, duties, prohibition of exports or imports, the introduction of new religious rites and festivals, the awarding of honours and rewards, and the conferring of the citizenship.

(2) At SPARTA all the Spartiatae, or citizens in possession of full civic rights, were entitled to take part in the deliberations of the Assembly from their thirtieth year onwards. The Assembly was convoked once a month at the full moon by the kings, and later by the ephors as well. After B.C. 600 it met in a special building in the market-place at Sparta, the Scias, the members standing, not sitting, as in the Athenian ecclesia. Its business was to accept or reject proposals made by the γερουσία or Senate. (See GERUSIA.) It made its will known by acclamation, or, in doubtful cases, by separation of the parties into different places. The right of bringing forward proposals and speaking in the debates belonged only to the kings, the members of the Gerusia, and the ephors; in all other cases special consent was required. The functions of the Assembly were the election of the officials and senators to decide (in doubtful cases) on the regal succession, on war and peace, treaties, legislation, and other matters affecting the State.

Ecclesiazūsae (Ἐκκλησιάζουσαι). "The Women in Council." A comedy of Aristophanes (q. v.), in which the Athenian women are represented as getting into the Ecclesia in the guise of men and altering the Constitution. This play contains the longest word in the Greek language, an extraordinary compound of 169 letters and 77 syllables, covering six verses of the play (1169–1174).

Ecclēti (ἔκκλητοι). The name of an assembly in Sparta of which little is known. It is mentioned only by Xenophon (*Hell.* ii. 4, § 38 *et al.*).

Ecdĭcus (ἔκδικος). The name of an officer in many of the towns of Asia Minor under the Roman dominion. The word is translated in the ancient glossaries by *cognitor*, "agent" or "attorney." The ecdicus was the agent of a city in its foreign business and its relations with the central government, and especially in prosecuting its claims against debtors. In Cicero's time the office seems to have been occasional and something like that of an ambassador. Under the Empire it was placed on a permanent footing (Plin. *Ep.* x. 111). The Defensor Civitatis (q. v.) of the later Empire was also called ἔκδικος in Greek.

Ekdŏsis (ἔκδοσις). See FENUS.

Ekecheiria (ἐκεχειρία). The "truce of God" (literally, "holding of hands"), observed in Greece at the great festivals which were visited by strangers—e. g. the national games and the Eleusinia in Attica. This peace was proclaimed by heralds throughout Greece, to secure the visitors to the games freedom in passing backwards and forwards and security during the festival. In the case of the Eleusinia the truce lasted one and a half month and ten days. See Gell. i. 25, 8; and the article ELEUSINIA.

Echelĭdae (Ἐχελίδαι). A deme of Attica, east of Munychia, named after a hero Echelus.

Echĕmus (Ἔχεμος). A king of Arcadia, who slew, in single combat, Hyllus, the son of Heracles, during the Dorian invasion of the Peloponnesus. As a result of the combat, the Heraclidae (q. v.) were obliged to promise not to repeat their attempt on the Peloponnesus for fifty years (Herod. ix. 26). See HYLLUS.

Echĕtus (Ἔχετος). A king of Epirus whose daughter Metopé or Amphissa yielded to the solicitations of her lover Aechmodicus. As a punishment, Echetus blinded her and caused Aechmodicus to be castrated (*Odyss.* xviii. 85; xxi. 308).

Echidna (Ἔχιδνα). A monster and robber in Greek legends, half maiden, half snake, the daughter of Chrysaor and Callirrhoé, or, according to another story, of Tartarus and Gaea. Her home was the country of the Arimi in Cilicia, where she brought forth to Typhoeus a number of monsters, Cerberus, the Chimaera, Sphinx, Scylla, the serpent of Lerna, the Nemean lion, the vulture that devoured the liver of Prometheus, etc. (See TYPHOEUS.) She was surprised in her sleep and slain by Argus. See Herod. iv. 8–10, and the article ARGUS.

Echinădes (Ἐχινάδες νῆσοι). A group of small islands at the mouth of the Acheloüs belonging to Acarnania, said to have been formed by the alluvial deposits of the Acheloüs. They appear to have derived their name from their resemblance to the *echinus*, or sea-urchin. The largest of these islands was named Dulichium, and belonged to the kingdom of Odysseus, who is hence called Dulichius. See Herod. ii. 10.

Echīnus (ἐχῖνος). The hedgehog or sea-urchin, and hence a name for things having a similar shape. (1) A pot, pitcher, or saltcellar (Hor. *Sat.* i. 6, 117). (2) The casket, probably of a cylindrical shape, in which documents were sealed up between the ἀνάκρισις and the trial. (3) In Doric architecture, the ovolo or convex part of the capital immediately beneath the abacus (Vitruv. iv. 3 and 7).

Echīnus (Ἐχῖνος). A town in Thessaly on the Maliac Gulf, said to have derived its name from Echion, who sprang from the dragon's teeth. See ECHION.

Echinussa. See CIMOLUS.

Echīon (Ἐχίων). (1) One of the heroes who sprang from the dragon's teeth sown by Cadmus. (See SPARTI.) He was the husband of Agavé and father of Pentheus, who is hence called Echionides. (2) Son of Hermes and Antianira; took part in the Calydonian hunt and in the expedition of the Argonauts. (3) A distinguished Greek painter who flourished about B.C. 352. One of his pictures, representing Semiramis passing from the state of a handmaid to that of a queen, is supposed by many to be the original of the picture known as the Aldobrandini Marriage discovered at Rome in 1606 and now in the Vatican. See Woltmann and Woermann, *Hist. of Painting*, i. p. 115 (1880).

Echionius. An epithet applied to the city of Thebes as founded by the aid of Echion (Ovid, *Met.* iii. 311).

Echo (Ἠχώ). A daughter of Aër and Gaea, who chiefly resided in the vicinity of the Cephissus. She was once one of Heré's attendants; but, having offended that goddess by her deception, she was deprived, in a great measure, by her of the power of speech. Heré declared that in future she should have but little use of her tongue, and immediately she lost all power of doing any more than to repeat the sounds which she heard. Echo happening to see the beautiful youth Narcissus, became deeply enamoured of him. But, her love being slighted, she pined away till nothing remained of her but her voice and bones. The former still exists, the latter were converted into stone (Ovid, *Met.* iii. 341 foll.).

Echoĭci Versus, also called **Serpentīni**. A name given to verses in which the first words of the hexameter are repeated as the second half of the following pentameter. The name is also given to palindromes, in which the line reads the same both backwards and forwards. These trifles were composed by both the Greeks and the Romans. Martial speaks slightingly of them (*carmen supinum*, ii. 86). The following will serve as illustrations:

ἤδη μοι Διος ἄρ' ἀπάτα παρὰ σοι Διομήδη.
(Kaibel, *Epigr. Gr.* 1124.)

Roma tibi subito motibus ibit amor.
(Sidon. *Epist.* ix. 14.)

Nemo te cedis, murorum si decet omen.
(*Anthol. Lat.* 325.)

In the following, the distich read backwards, word by word, gives a second distich:

Praecipiti modo quod decurrit tramite flumen
Tempore consumptum iam cito deficiat.
(Sidon. *Epist.* ix. 14.)

These verses were also styled *analytici versus* and *reciproci versus*. Further examples will be found in Apoll. Sid. (*Epist.* viii. 11), Venantius Fortunatus, Sedulius, and among the *Poetae Latini Minores* (iv. 260–267). See Friedländer on Martial ii. 86; and for other metrical whims, the articles ABECEDARII VERSUS; ACROSTICHA; CENTO; HYMNUS; LEONINI VERSUS; SOTADICI VERSUS.

Eclectĭci (ἐκλεκτικοί). A name given to those ancient students of philosophy who, from the existing philosophical beliefs, tried to select (ἐκλέγειν) the doctrines that seemed to them most reasonable, and out of these constructed a new system. (Cf. Diog. Laërt. prooem. 21.) The name was first generally used in the first century B.C. Stoicism and Epicureanism had made the search for pure truth subordinate to the attainment of practical virtue and happiness; Skepticism had denied that pure truth was possible to discover; Eclecticism sought to reach by selection the highest possible degree of probability, in the despair of attaining to what is absolutely true. In Greek philosophy, the best known Eclectics were the Stoics Panaetius (B.C. 150) and Posidonius (B.C. 75); the New Academic, Carneades (B.C. 155), and Philo of Larissa (B.C. 75). Among the Romans, Cicero, whose cast of mind made him always doubtful and uncertain of his own attitude, was thoroughly eclectic, uniting the Peripatetic, Stoic, and New Academic doctrines, and seeking the probable (*illud probabile*). The same general line was followed by Varro, and in the next century the Stoic Seneca propounded a philosophical system largely based upon eclecticism.

In the latest Greek philosophy appears an eclectic system consisting of a compromise between the Neo-Pythagoreans and the various Platonic sects. Still another school is that of Philo Iudaeus (q. v.), who at Alexandria, in the first century A.D., interpreted the Old Testament allegorically, and endeavoured to harmonize it with selected doctrines of Greek philosophy. Neo-Platonism (q. v.), the last product of Greek speculation, was also a fusion of Greek philosophy with Oriental religion. Its chief representatives were Plotinus (A.D. 230), Porphyrius (A.D. 275), Iamblichus (A.D. 300), and Proclus (A.D. 450). The desire of this school was to attain right relations between God and man; it was therefore religious.

See Ueberweg, *Hist. of Philosophy*, vol. i. pp. 217–221 (Eng. trans. N. Y. 1872); Mayor, *A Sketch of Ancient Philosophy*, pp. 212 foll. (Cambridge, 1881); Ritter, *Hist. of Ancient Philosophy*, vol. iv., first part (Eng. trans. Oxford, 1838–46); Zeller, *Hist. of Eclecticism in Gk. Philosophy* (Eng. tr. London, 1882); Levin, *Lectures on the Philosophy of Cicero* (London, 1871); Hirtzel, *Untersuchungen z. Cicero's philosoph. Schriften* (1877–83); and the article PHILOSOPHIA. Cicero's *Academica* should be read, as also his *Tusculanae* (bk. iv.) and his *De Natura Deorum*.

Eclogue (*ecloga*, ἐκλογή). A selected piece of writing. Properly a poem taken out of a larger collection, and so applied, at the time of the Roman Empire, to a short poem, as an idyl or satire. The term was especially applied to the pastoral poems of Vergil and Calpurnius Siculus. See BUCOLICA.

Ekmartyria (ἐκμαρτυρία). The deposition of a witness, who, by reason of absence abroad or illness, was unable to attend in court. His statement was taken down in writing, in the presence of persons expressly appointed to receive it, and afterwards, upon their swearing to its identity, was read as evidence in the cause. They were said μαρτυρεῖν τὴν ἐκμαρτυρίαν: the absent witness, ἐκμαρτυρεῖν: the party who procured the evidence, ἐκμαρτυρίαν ποιεῖσθαι. It was considered as the testimony of the deponent himself, not that of the certifying witnesses, and therefore did not come within the description of hearsay evidence, which (except the declaration of a deceased person) was not admissible at Athens. (See AKOEN MARTYREIN.) The deponent (like any other witness) was liable to an action for false testimony if the contents of the deposition were untrue, unless he could show that it was incorrectly taken down or forged, in which case the certifying witnesses would be liable. An ἐκμαρτυρία was allowed to a witness about to start on a journey, if he could not conveniently wait (Isaeus, *Or.* 3 [*Pyrrhus*], § 20). The form of ἐκμαρτυρία, or what purports to be such, occurs in Demosth. *c. Lacrit.* p. 929, § 20; 934, § 34.

Ecphŏra (ἐκφορά). See FUNUS.

Ectēnes (Ἔκτηνες). A people who, according to Pausanias, first inhabited the territory of Thebes, in Boeotia. Ogyges (q. v.) is said to have been their first king. They were exterminated by a plague, and succeeded by the Hyantes. See Pausan. ix. 5.

Ectȳpus (ἔκτυπος), properly an adjective, "formed in a mould" (τύπος, *forma*), or "wrought in high relief," thus distinguished from ἀνάγλυφος, "in low relief." Hence (1) the noun ECTȲPUM, a cast in plaster or terra-cotta, which presents the objects in relief (Plin. *H. N.* xxxv. § 152). The accompanying examples, on the following page, are from a terra-cotta and mould in the British Museum. (2) ECTYPA GEMMA (Sen. *Ben.* iii. 26) or *scalptura* (Plin. *H. N.* xxxvii. § 173), an engraved stone cut in relief, now called a cameo. See CAELATURA; GEMMA.

Eculeus, or, less correctly, **Equuleus**. An in-

Ectypum. (British Museum.)

strument of torture commonly used at Rome in extracting evidence from slaves. It was a wooden horse, as the name implies, on which the sufferer was mounted and then stretched or racked with weights or pulleys (Sen. *Ep.* 67, § 3). Rich (s. v.) thinks that the infliction consisted in being seated on a sharp point, as in impalement—a form of cruelty not unknown in recent times, of which he gives a specimen. Very little is really known about this and the other engines of torture among the Greeks and Romans. Cicero says that slaves accused of murder might expect the eculeus at the trial, the *crux* on conviction (*Pro Mil.* 21, § 57; 22, § 60). Seneca mentions as the usual modes of torture, *fidiculae, talaria, eculeus*, and *ignis* (*De Ira*, iii. 19, § 1). Rich supposes the criminal to have been made to sit upon a sharp point with weights attached to his arms and legs, as shown in the illustration here given, representing an instrument of torture formerly used at Mirandola in Italy and, curiously enough, called "the colt" (*il cavaletto*). See CRUX; FIDICULA; FLAGELLUM; TORMENTUM.

Supposed form of Eculeus. (Rich.)

Edessa (῎Εδεσσα). (1) Also called Antiochia Callirrhoë (Old Test. UR), a very ancient city in the north of Mesopotamia, the capital of Osroëné, and the seat of an independent kingdom from B.C. 137 to A.D. 216. (See ABGARUS.) Here Caracalla was murdered, A.D. 217. In Christian times, Edessa was celebrated for its schools of theology. (2) A city of Macedonia, once the capital and the burial-place of the kings (Plut. *Pyrrh.* 26).

Edetāni or **Sedetāni**. A people in Hispania Tarraconensis, east of the Celtiberi (Liv. xxiv. 20). They possessed the celebrated cities of Caesaraugusta (Saragossa), Saguntum (Murviedro), and Valentia (Valencia).

Edfou (Edfu); in Egyptian, *Teb;* in Coptic, *Atbô;* called also APOLLINOPŌLIS MAGNA. A town of Upper Egypt on the left bank of the Nile. It was founded by Ptolemy IV. (Philopator) in the third century before Christ, and is famous for the remains of two temples, the larger of which is the best preserved of any in Egypt. An illustration of it is given on page 26. Its length is 451 feet, and the breadth of its façade, 250 feet. It is entered by a gateway 50 feet in height between two immense truncated pylons 115 feet high, the whole surface being covered with sculptures and inscriptions in bas-relief. See Mariette, *Monuments of Upper Egypt* (1877); Lepsius, *Denkmäler aus Aegypten und Aethiopen* (1849–60); and Brugsch, *Reiseberichte*.

Edictum. The Roman term for any written announcement made by a magistrate to the people. An *edictum* was sometimes temporary only—as, e. g., the announcements of the public assemblies or games; sometimes it contained permanent enactments—as, for instance, the *edicta* of the censors against luxury. The name was especially applied to the proclamations issued by judicial functionaries on assuming office, and stating the principles or rules which they intended to follow in the exercise of their authority. The *edicta* of the ædiles relative to the markets belong to this class. One kind of *edictum* was specially important in its bearing upon Roman law, the *edictum* of the praetor. In his *edictum* the praetor laid down the rules which he would observe in arranging the proceedings of the regular courts and of his voluntary jurisdiction, and in deciding cases which did not appear to be covered by the written enactments of the Twelve Tables or later legislation. These *edicta*, written on wood, stone, or bronze, were in early times published only as occasion required, but in later times the praetors regularly promulgated them on entering upon their office. They prevented the fossilization of the law, and allowed the enactments of the Twelve Tables to adapt themselves in natural development to the changing circumstances of civic life and intercourse. It is true that the *edicta* had no force beyond the praetor's year of office, but, as every new praetor observed what was found in the *edicta* of his predecessors, a permanent nucleus of constantly repeated rules, called *edictum perpetuum* ("continuous edict"), was formed in course of time. This became, for the later period, a recognized source of customary law, side by side with the *leges* proper. At length, under Hadrian, the mass of *edicta* was reduced to system by Salvius Iulianus, and received the force of law at the imperial command. This body of law included the accepted *edicta* of the *praetor urbanus* and the other praetors administering law in the provinces, of the proconsuls, propraetors, and ædiles. It was called *edictum perpetuum, ius praetorium*, or *ius honorarium*—the latter because its authors had held public offices (*honores*). On this collection the *Corpus Iuris* of Justinian is in great part founded. The emperor and imperial officials, as *praefectus urbi* and *praefectus praetorio*, had also the right of issuing *edicta*. See CORPUS IURIS.

Edictum Theodorīci. The first collection of law that was made after the downfall of the Roman power in Italy. It was promulgated by Theodoric, king of the Ostrogoths, probably on his visit to Rome in A.D. 500, though some authorities fix the date after 506. It consists of 154 chapters (besides a prologue and epilogue), parts of which may be traced to the Code and Novellae of Theodosius II., to the Codices Gregorianus and Hermogenianus, and to the *Sententiae* of Paulus; and, though it was doubtless drawn up by Roman writers, the original sources are more disfigured and altered than in any other compilation. Though the Ostrogothic kingdom was in point of fact quite independent of the Eastern Roman Empire, in constitutional theory it was considered part of it, the king representing the Caesar, and his army being reckoned a portion of the emperor's forces; consequently the Roman law was still held binding in Italy, for the barbarian invaders no less than for the old inhabitants. Hence the Edict of Theodoric, so far as it went, was intended as law for both nationalities; but where it had made no change in the Gothic rules, the latter were still applied to the barbarians, while the Roman law was to prevail for the Romans in those cases to which the Edict was not applicable. After Narses had again united Italy to the empire of Justinian, the latter's legislation was established in Italy (A.D. 554), and the Edict of Theodoric had no longer any authority.

This edict was first printed in the edition of Cassiodorus by Nivellius (Paris, 1579), and there is an edition by G. F. Rhon (Halle, 1816). Cf. also Von Glöden, *Das römische Recht im ostgothischen Reich* (1843); Hänel, *Lex Rom. Visig.* (1847); and Rudorff, *Röm. Rechtsgeschichte*, i. 288, 303. Hodgkin, *Italy and her Invaders*, iii. p. 342, gives the prologue and epilogue and an analysis of the contents of the Edict.

Editio Princeps. A name given to the first printed edition of any classical author. The *editio princeps* often has a special value to text-critics in that its text is sometimes derived from a MS. that has since been lost. The oldest printed edition of any classic is that of the *De Officiis* of Cicero, which appeared at Mainz in 1465. Soon after the invention of printing (about 1440), the great publishing houses of Aldus Manutius (son and grandson, 1449–1597) in Venice, of Giunta in Florence, and others in Switzerland, Germany, France, and the Low Countries, sent out printed copies of the ancient texts with commentaries and grammars, as well as Latin translations of Greek authors, thus aiding in the revival of letters known as the Renaissance. Many of the *editiones principes* are not dated; sometimes the date is given in a chronogram (see CHRONOGRAM) in the preface. (See Hilson, *Chronograms* [London, 1882], and id. *Chronograms Continued* [London, 1885]). The place of publication is usually in its ancient or mediæval Latin form, but sometimes in Greek (as Enetiai for Venice), and rarely in Slavonic (as Bnezieh, Mnezik, or Mletka, for the same place). For the benefit of the student, the following list is given, comprising the names oftenest found on the title-pages of early editions: ARGENTORĀTUM (Strassburg); AUGUSTA or AUGUSTA VINDELICŌRUM (Augsburg); BASILĒA (Basel, Bâle); BIPONTUM (Deux Ponts, Zweibrücken); BONONIA (Bologna); CADOMUM (Caen); CAESARAUGUSTA (Saragossa); CANTABRĬGA (Cambridge); CORŌNA (Cronstadt); DORTRĂCHUM (Dort, Dordrecht); EBORĂCUM (York); ELEUTHEROPŎLIS or FRANCAVILLA (Freystadt); GRATIANOPŎLIS (Grenoble); HAFNIA or HAUNIA (Copenhagen); HALA (Halle); HERBIPŎLIS (Würzburg); HOLMIA (Stockholm); INSŬLA or INSULAE (Lille); ISPALIS (Seville); LEODĬCUM (Liège); LIPSIA (Leipzig); LUGDŪNUM (Lyons); LUGDUNUM BATAVORUM (Leyden); LUTETIA (Paris); MASSILIA (Marseilles); MATISCO (Macon); MEDIOLĀNUM (Milan); MOGUNTIĂCUM (Mainz, Mayence); MONS REGĀLIS (Mondovi); MUSSĬPONS or PONTIMUSSUM (Pont-à-Musson); NEAPŎLIS (Naples); NEAPŎLIS CASIMIRIĀNI (Neustadt); OENĬPONS (Innsbruck); OLISĬPO, ULYSSĬPO, or ULYSSIPŎLIS (Lisbon); OXONIA (Oxford); PETROPŎLIS (St. Petersburg); PROBATŎPOLIS (Schaffhausen); REGIOMONTIUM (Königsberg); ROTOMĂGUS (Rouen); SARUM (Salisbury); TARVISIUM (Treviso); TOURNĂCUM (Tournai); TRAIECTUM, TRAIECTUM RHENI, or ULTRAIECTUM (Utrecht); TRECAE or CIVĬTAS TRICASSŌNA (Troyes); TRIDENTUM (Trent); TURŎNI or CAESARODŪNUM (Tours); VENETIA or ENETIAI (Venice). See Deschamps, *Dictionnaire de Géographie à l'Usage du Libraire* (Paris, 1870).

Greek type (very imperfect) was first used in the edition of the *De Officiis* mentioned above. The first edition of a work in Greek minuscules was an edition of the grammar of Lascaris by Paravinus (Milan, 1476). In 1494 the *Anthologia Graeca* of Lascaris appeared at Florence, printed wholly in Greek capitals. The first edition of a classical Greek author is that of the *Idyls* of Theocritus (i.–xviii.), with the *Works and Days* of Hesiod, which was published in 1481.

The following list of the most famous of the *editiones principes* is taken from Gudeman's valuable *Outlines of the History of Classical Philology* (Boston, 1894):

GREEK.

1481. Theocritus (bks. i.–xviii.), together with Hesiod, *Works and Days*.
1488. Homer (ed. Chalcondylas). (Valla's Latin transl. of the *Iliad* was printed as early as 1474.)
1495. Hesiod, Opera omnia (Aldus).
1495–98. Aristotle (Aldus).
1496. Euripides, *Medea*, *Hippolytus*, *Alcestis*, *Andromaché* (I. Lascaris); Apollonius (Lascaris); Lucian (Florence).
1498. Aristophanes (except *Lysistrata* and *Thesmophoriazusae*), Opera omnia (Basle, 1532).
1499. Aratus (in *Astronomi Vett. ap.* Aldum).
1500. Callimachus, *Hymns* (Lascaris).
1502. Herodotus, Thucydides, Sophocles (Aldi).
1503. Euripides, Opera (except *Electra*, edit. by Victorius [1545], from Cod. Laurent. xxxii. 2).
1513. Plato, Oratt. Att. [Hyperides, papyrus discovered 1847]; Pindar (together with Callim., Dionys. Perieg., Lycophron) (Aldus).
1514. Athenaeus (Aldus).
1516. Xenophon (except *Agesilaüs*, *Apologia*, Πόροι [Iunta]); Opera omnia, 1525, ap. Aldum; Strabo (transl. printed in Rome, 1470); Pausanias.
1518. Aeschylus (Aldus).
1530. Polybius (by Vincent. Opsopocus, i. e. Koch). Latin transl. by Nic. Perrotto (bks. i.–v.), printed 1473.
1533. Diogenes Laërtius (Froben, Basle).
1539. Diodorus (bks. xvi.–xx.). Latin transl. (bks. i.–v.) by Poggio, 1472.
1544. Josephus (Basle).
1548. Dio Cassius (R. Stephanus).
1551. Appian.
1572. Plutarch (H. Stephanus). Latin transl. by Campanus (1471).

LATIN.

1465. Cicero, *De Officiis* (Mainz); Lactantius (Rome).
1469. Caesar, Vergil, Livy, Lucan, Apuleius, Gellius (Rome).
1470. Persius, Juvenal, Livy, Martial, Quintilian (Rome); Tacitus, Juvenal, Sallust, Horace (Venice); Terence (Strassburg).
1471. Ovid (Rome and Bonn); Nepos (Venice).

1472. Plautus (G. Merula), Catullus, Tibullus, Propertius, Statius (Venice).
1473. Lucretius (Brescia).
1474. Valerius Flaccus (Bonn).
1475. Seneca's Prose Works.
1484. Seneca's Tragedies (Ferrara).
1485. Pliny the Younger (Venice).
1498. Ciceronis Opera omnia.
1520. Velleius Paterculus (Basle).

BIBLIOGRAPHY.—See Saxe, *Onomasticon* (1775–1790); Schweiger, *Handbuch d. class. Bibliographie* (1830–34); Hain, *Repertorium Bibliographicum*, 4 vols. (1838); Hoffman, *Lexicon Bibliographicum*, for Greek authors only, 3 vols. (1832); Brunet, *Manuel du Libraire* (1880); Egger, *Histoire du Livre* (Paris, no date); Bouchot, *The Printed Book* (1887); Sotheby, *Principia Typographica* (1858); Berjean, *Early Printers' Marks* (1866); Silvestre, *Marques Typographiques* (1867); Brunet, *Connaissances Nécessaires à un Bibliophile* (1872); Legrand, *Bibliographie Hellénique* (1885); Hawkins, *First Books and Printers of the Fifteenth Century* (N.Y. 1884); Humphreys, *Hist. of the Art of Printing* (1867); the valuable monograph, s. v. "Typography," in the *Encyclopædia Britannica*, by J. H. Hessels, vol. xxiii. pp. 681–697; and the articles LEXICON; LIBER; MANUTIUS; STEPHANUS, in this Dictionary.

Edoni (Ἤδωνοι) or **Edōnes** (Ἤδωνες). A Thracian people, between the Nestus and the Strymon, celebrated for their orgiastic worship of Bacchus; whence Edonis in the Latin poets signifies a female Bacchanal, and Edonus is used as equivalent to Thracicus.

Education. (1) GREEK. The Dorians of Crete and Sparta followed a peculiar line in the matter of education. Throughout Greece generally the State left it to private effort, but in Sparta and Crete it came under the direct supervision of the community. At Sparta, as soon as a child was born, a commission of the elders of its tribe had to decide whether it should be reared or exposed. If it was weakly or deformed it was exposed in a defile of Mount Taÿgetus. Till his seventh year a boy was left to the care of his parents. After this the *παιδονόμος*, or officer presiding over the whole department of education, assigned him to a division of children of the same age called a *βούα*. Several of such *βοῦαι* together formed a troop or *ἴλη* (Dor. *ἴλα*). Each *βούα* was superintended by a *βουαγός*, each *ἴλη* by an *ἰλάρχης*. Both these officers were elected from among the most promising of the grown-up youths, and were bound to instruct the children in their exercises. The exercises were calculated to suit the various ages of the children, and consisted in running, leaping, wrestling, throwing the spear and the discus, as well as in a number of dances, particularly the war dance or *πυρρίχη* (q. v.). The dancing was under the constant superintendence of the *παιδονόμος* and five *βιδιαῖοι* under him. The discipline was generally directed to strengthening or hardening the body. The boys went barefoot and bareheaded, with hair cut short, and in light clothing. From their twelfth year they wore nothing but an upper garment, which had to last the whole year. They slept in a common room without a roof, on a litter of hay or straw, and from their fifteenth year on rushes or reeds. Their food was extremely simple, and not sufficient to satisfy hunger. A boy who did not want to be hungry had to steal; if he did this cleverly he was praised, and punished if detected. Every year the boys had to undergo a flogging at the altar of Artemis Orthia, as a test of their power to endure bodily pain. They were whipped till the blood flowed, and deemed it a disgrace to show any sign of suffering. (See BOMONIKES; DIAMASTIGOSIS.) Reading and writing were left to private instructors; but music, and choral singing in particular, formed a part of the regular discipline. The understanding was assumed to be formed by daily life in public and the conversation of the men, to which the boys were admitted. Every Spartan boy looked up to his seniors as his instructors and superiors, the consequence being that in Sparta the young behaved to their elders with more modesty and respect than in any other Greek city. Besides this, every man chose a boy or youth as his favourite. He was bound to set the boy an example of all manly excellence, and was regarded as responsible and punishable for his delinquencies. This public education and the performance of the regular exercises, under the superintendence of the *βιδιαῖοι*, lasted till the thirtieth year. In the eighteenth year the boy passed into the class of youths. From the twentieth year, when military service proper began, to the thirtieth, the youth was called an *εἴρην* or *ἰρήν*. He was not regarded as a man or allowed to attend the public assembly till his thirtieth year.

The girls had an education in music and gymnastic exercises similar to that of the boys, and at the public games and contests each sex was witness of the performances of the other. The girls' dress was extremely simple, consisting of a sleeveless tunic reaching not quite down to the knees and open at the sides. In this, however, there was nothing which interfered with modesty and propriety of behaviour.

In Crete the system of education was generally similar to that of Sparta. But the public training did not begin till the seventeenth year, when the boys of the same age joined themselves freely into divisions called *ἀγέλαι*, each led by some noble youth, whose father was called *ἀγελάτας* and undertook the supervision of the games and exercises. It is probable that the young men remained in this organization till their twenty-seventh year, when the law compelled them to marry.

At Athens, as in Greece generally, the father decided whether the child should be reared or exposed. The latter alternative seems to have been not seldom adopted, especially when the child was a girl. If the education of a child was once fairly commenced the parents had no power to put it out of the way. At the birth of a boy the door of the house was adorned with a branch of olive; at the birth of a girl, with wool. On the fifth or seventh day after birth the child underwent a religious dedication at the festival of the Amphidromia ("running round"). It was touched with instruments of purification, and carried several times round the burning hearth. On the tenth day came the festival of naming the child, with sacrifice and entertainment, when the father acknowledged it as legitimate. To the end of the sixth year the boys and girls were brought up together under female supervision, but after this the sexes were educated apart. The girl's life was almost entirely confined to her home: she was brought up under the superintendence of women and with hardly anything which can be called profitable instruction. The boy was handed over to a slave older than himself called παιδαγωγός. It was the slave's duty to watch the boy's outward behaviour, and to attend him, until his boyhood was over, whenever he went out, especially to the school and the gymnasium. The laws made some provision for the proper education of boys. They obliged every citizen to have his son instructed in music, gymnastics, and the elements of letters (γράμματα) —i. e. writing, reading, and arithmetic. They further obliged the parents to teach their boys some profitable trade, in case they were unable to leave them a property sufficient to maintain them independent. If they failed in this, they forfeited all claim to support from the children in old age. But with schools and their arrangements the State did not concern itself. The schools were entirely in private hands, though they were under the eye of the police. The elementary instruction was given by the γραμματισταί, or teachers of letters, the teacher writing and the scholars copying. The text-books for reading were mostly poems, especially such as were calculated to have an influence on the formation of character. The Homeric poems were the favourite reading-book, but Hesiod, Theognis, and others were also admitted. Collections of suitable passages from the poets were early made for the boys to copy, learn by heart, and repeat aloud. The higher instruction given by the γραμματικός was also of this literary character.

Mathematics were introduced into the school curriculum as early as the fifth century, drawing not till the middle of the fourth century B.C. Instruction in music proper began about the thirteenth year. The profound moral influence attributed to music in Greek antiquity made this art an essential part of education. It brought with it, naturally, an acquaintance with the masterpieces of Greek poetry. The instrument most practised was the lyre, from its suitableness as an accompaniment to song. The flute was held in less esteem. See MUSICA.

The aim of education was supposed to be the harmonious development of mind and body alike. Instruction in gymnastics was consequently regarded as no less essential than in music, and began at about the same age. It was carried on in the παλαίστρα under the παιδοτρίβαι, who were, like the γραμματικοί, private, not public, instructors. The boys began their gymnastics in the palaestra, and completed them in the gymnasia under the superintendence of the γυμνασταί. The ἔφηβοι, in particular, or boys between sixteen and nineteen, practised their exercises in the gymnasia, till, in their twentieth year, they were considered capable of bearing arms and employed on frontier service. At this point they became liable to enlistment for foreign service, and obtained the right of attending the meeting of the public assembly. Towards the end of the fifth century B.C. the class of σοφισταί, or professors of practical education, arose. These gave the young men an opportunity of extending their education by attending lectures in rhetoric and philosophy, but the high fees charged by the sophists had the effect of restricting this instruction to the sons of the wealthy.

(2) ROMAN. Among the Romans the father was free, when the new-born child was laid before him, either to expose it, or to take it up as a sign that he meant to rear it. He had also the right of selling his children or putting them to death. It was not till the beginning of the third century A.D. that the exposure of children was legally accounted murder, nor did the evil practice cease even then. If the child was to be reared, it was named, if a boy, on the ninth day after birth, if a girl, on the eighth. The day was called *dies lustricus*, or day of purification. A sacrifice in the house, accompanied with a feast, gave to the child's life a religious dedication. A box with an amulet was hung round the child's neck as a protection against magic. (See AMULETUM; BULLA.) Official lists of births were not published until the second century after Christ. In earlier times, in the case of boys, the name was not formally confirmed until the assumption of the *toga virilis*. The child's physical and moral education was, in old times, regularly given at home under the superintendence of the parents, chiefly the mother. The training was strict, and aimed at making the children strong and healthy, religious, obedient to the laws, temperate, modest in speech and action, strictly submissive to their superiors, well-behaved, virtuous, intelligent, and self-reliant. The girls were taught by their mothers to spin and weave. The boys were instructed by their fathers in ploughing, sowing, reaping, riding, swimming, boxing, and fencing; in the knowledge necessary for household management; in reading, writing, and counting; and in the laws of the country. The Romans did not, like the Greeks, lay stress on gymnastics, but only carried physical exercises to the point necessary for military service. The contests and exercises took place in the Campus Martius, which, down to the time of the Empire, was the favourite arena of the youths. The State took as little care of mental as of physical education. If a man could not educate his children himself, he sent them to a master. From an early time there were elementary teachers (*litteratores*) at Rome, corresponding to the Greek γραμματισταί. These were sometimes slaves, who taught in their masters' houses for their benefit. Sometimes they were freedmen, who gave instruction either in families or in schools (*schola* or *ludus*) of their own. They received their salary monthly, but only for eight months in the year — no instruction being given between June and November. Boys and girls were taught together. The elementary instruction included reading, writing, and arithmetic; arithmetic being, as among the Greeks, practised by counting on the fingers. In later times grown-up boys learned arithmetic with a special master (*calculator*), who was paid at a higher rate than the *litterator*. With the duodecimal system in use arithmetic was regarded as very difficult. (See MATHEMATICA.) The reading-lessons included learning the Twelve Tables by heart.

After the Second Punic War it became usual, at first in single families, and afterwards more and more generally, to employ a *litterator*, or *grammaticus*, to teach Greek. The chief element in this instruction was the explanation of Greek poets, above all of Homer, whose writings became a school-book among the Romans as among the Greeks. At the same time higher instruction was given in Latin as well, the text-books being the Latin *Odyssey* of Livius Andronicus, the works of Terence, and in later times of Vergil, Horace, and others. The exposition of these authors gave an opportunity of communicating a variety of information. Girls were educated on the same lines. The highest point in Roman education was attained by the schools of the rhetoricians, which came into existence before the end of the republican age. In these schools, as in those of the *grammatici*, Greek was at first the only language taught. Since the time when Greek literature became the highest educational standard, boys, and sometimes girls, were taught Greek from their earliest years. They were put into the hands of a Greek *paedagogus* or a Greek female slave, and learned the first rudiments from Greek schoolmasters. As the range of subjects widened so as to include, among other things, music and geometry, more importance came to be attached to scholastic education. This tendency was strengthened by the increased demand for Greek culture which manifested itself under the Empire throughout the length and breadth of the Western provinces. Education was carried out on stricter lines as the old system of home-training disappeared, mainly owing to the diffusion of an effeminate refinement and the parents' habit of putting their children into the hands of Greek slaves.

The ordinary educational course generally concluded with a boy's sixteenth or seventeenth year, though rhetorical instruction was sometimes continued far beyond this limit; and towards the end of the republican age young men of intellectual ambition would often go to Greece to enlarge their sphere of culture.

On the 17th of March, the festival of the Liberalia, boys who had reached the age of puberty, or their fifteenth year, took off, in the presence of the Lares, their *bulla* and *toga praetexta*, or purple-edged toga, and put on the unadorned *toga virilis*. They were then, after a sacrifice at home, taken by their fathers or guardians, accompanied by friends and relations, to the Forum and enrolled in the lists of citizens. The boys were from this time, in the eyes of the law, capable of marriage, bound to military service, and, in fact, had now entered upon their *tirocinium*, which was regarded as the last stage of education. See TIROCINIUM.

After the time of Vespasian the higher public instruction began to be a matter of imperial concern. Vespasian paid away the sum of $4250 annually to the Latin and Greek rhetoricians in Rome. Hadrian founded the Athenaeum, the first known public institution for the higher education, with salaried teachers. (See ATHENAEUM.) After his time philosophers, rhetoricians, and grammarians were publicly appointed to lecture in all the larger cities of the Empire. They were maintained partly at the expense of the respective communities, partly by the emperors, and enjoyed in all cases certain immunities conferred by the State.

(3) THE HIGHER EDUCATION.—In the days of the Roman Empire there existed at Athens and some of the other Greek cities what closely corresponded to the universities of modern times. Athens had always been what Pericles called "the school of Greece;" and in the early centuries of the Christian era it contained an organized faculty (χορός, συνουσία, ἀγέλη) of accomplished professors, who lectured to a body of students drawn from every quarter of the civilized world. The university at Athens was gradually formed as the result of two previously existing institutions—the Ephebi (ἔφηβοι) and the schools of the philosophers and sophists. The Ephebi, or free Athenian youths, were in early times enrolled as a body primarily intended for the defence of the State. They were educated both physically and mentally, and they formed the nucleus of what afterwards became the student body of the university. Two changes in the constitution of the Ephebi prepared the way for their transformation from a quasi-military body into a university. These changes were (1) the neglect of the principle of compulsory enrollment, and (2) the fact that membership ceased to be confined to Athenians or even to Greeks alone.

These changes left a body of young men, organized and regularly enrolled, free to follow such a course of training as best suited their inclinations and capacities, and ready to be turned to any line of study that had the advocacy of brilliant, energetic, and popular men. The schools of the philosophers supplied the influence necessary for completing the change from a military college to a great university.

Four schools of philosophy had, since the time of the Macedonian wars, been flourishing at Athens. These were the Academic or Platonic School, the Peripatetic or Aristotelian School, the Stoic School, and the Epicurean. Each of these schools from the time of its foundation had received an endowment sufficient to maintain and perpetuate it. Plato (q. v.) had purchased a small garden near the Eleusinian Way, in the grove of Academé, for 3000 drachmas. His philosophic successors, Xenocrates and Polemon, continued to teach in the same spot; their wealthy pupils and other friends of learning added to the grounds, and bequeathed sufficient funds for the support of the philosopher, and thus practically endowed an academic chair (θρόνος). Later we find that the endowment of this chair had so increased that its annual income was 7000 *aurei*. In like manner Aristotle (q. v.) left to his successor, Theophrastus, the valuable property near the Ilissus; and Theophrastus, in the will whose text has come down to us in Diogenes Laërtius (v. 2, 14), completed the permanent endowment of the Peripatetic chair. So Epicurus left his property in the Ceramicus to be the nucleus of an endowment for his school (Diog. Laërt. xx. 10), and the Stoics were probably in like manner made independent. Around these four schools of philosophy which, being endowed, taught gratuitously, a multitude of teachers of rhetoric, grammar, literature, logic, physics, and mathematics clustered, and many chairs were endowed by the Roman emperors. The world soon learned to think of Athens as a great seat of learning and culture, brilliant and renowned. Students flocked to her from every quarter of the world. It appears to have been necessary to become enrolled among the Ephebi, but the scholars selected for themselves their own instructors, and attended such lectures as they chose. The number of these students became enormous. Theophrastus alone lectured to as many as two thousand men. The records show the names of many foreign students, some of them being of the Semitic race. The most noted writers of Rome had studied at this university, of whom Cicero, Ovid, and Horace are perhaps the most brilliant names. The customs of the university may be gathered from a perusal of the works of Aulus Gellius, Libanius (A.D. 314), and Philostratus, author of the Βίοι Σοφιστῶν (A.D. 250). From these sources we learn that matriculation took place early in the year; that the students wore a gown (τρίβων) like that of the undergraduates at the English universities; that they pursued athletic sports with much ardour; that at the theatre a special gallery was reserved for them; that certificates of attendance at the courses of lectures were required; that they were under the general direction of a president (κοσμητής); that fees were exacted in the shape of an annual contribution to the university library; that breaches of discipline were punished, as at Oxford, by fines; that the relation between student and professor was very close, so that for a student to cease to take a course was very cutting; and that the students themselves "touted" for the professors. "Most of the young enthusiasts for learning," says Gregory Nanzianzen, "become mere partisans of their professors. They are all anxiety to get their audiences larger and their fees increased. This they carry to portentous lengths. They post themselves over the city at the beginning of the year; as each new comer disembarks he falls into their hands; they carry him off at once to the house of some countryman or friend who is best at trumpeting the praises of his own professor" (Libanius, i. 13).

Private tutors (φύλακες) were often employed. They looked over the students' notes, "coached" them on the subjects in which they were most interested, and helped them at their exercises. At the end of the year there seems to have been an examination (δοκιμασία).

Freshmen appear to have been subject to a sort of hazing (τελεταί). Gregory, in a funeral address over his friend Basil, recalls some of the memories of their sport with freshmen. We find one of the professors, Proaeresius, asking his class not to haze a new student, Eunapius, because of his feeble health. Sometimes the inferior officers of the university were subjected to similar annoyances, and Libanius tells of one of the tutors who was tossed in a blanket, an exercise known to the Romans as *sagatio*.

Many of the coincidences between ancient and modern university life are interesting. The following is a quotation from Libanius, who gives an account of how his classes conducted themselves:

"I send my proctor to summon the students to my lecture, but they are in no mood to hurry, though they ought to be. They stay outside to sing songs which we have all heard till we are tired, or else amuse themselves with foolish merriment and jesting. This they do until the lecture has actually begun. Then they come in and keep whispering to one another, to the annoyance of the real students, about the races, or actresses, or opera-dancers; or about some contest either past or future." And he adds, very naïvely, "I had a very different class of students once. Perhaps some one may say that the fault is mine, and that my lectures are not as good as they used to be; but some of my best students now do not think so; they declare solemnly that I now quite surpass myself; and that while my lectures were always admirable, there is more in them now than there ever was before" (i. 199).

Schools of philosophy and letters similar to those at Athens sprang up at other great cities in the later Roman Empire—at Constantinople, at Rhodes, at Scepsis in the Troad, Massilia (Marseilles), Tarsus, and especially at Alexandria, which last city was definitely designed by the Ptolemies to be a centre of scientific research and investigation, to which end they gave it a magnificent library (see BIBLIOTHECA), handsome buildings, and ample endowments.

BIBLIOGRAPHY.—See Compayré, *History of Paedagogy* (Eng. trans. Boston, 1886); Grasberger, *Erziehung und Unterricht im klassischen Alterthum* (Würzburg, 1864–80); Eckstein, *Lateinischer und griechischer Unterricht* (Leipzig, 1887); K. Schmidt, *Geschichte der Pädagogik*, vol. i. 3d ed. (Cöthen, 1873); W. A. Schmidt, *Geschichte der Denk- und Glaubensfreiheit*, pp. 404–448 (Berlin, 1847); Mahaffy, *Old Greek Education* (London, 1882); Capes, *University Life in Ancient Athens* (London, 1874); Dittenberger, *De Ephebis Atticis* (Göttingen, 1863); Dumont, *Essai sur l'Ephébie Attique* (Paris, 1876); Portelette, *L'Ephébie en Grèce* in *L'Instruction Publique* for December, 1878; Becker-Göll, *Charicles*, ii. pp. 19 foll.; Göll's excursus on Becker's *Gallus*, ii. pp. 61–114; Marquardt, *Privatleben*, pp. 80 foll.; Saalfeld, *Der Hellenismus in Latium* (Wolfenbüttel, 1883); Davidson's *Aristotle*, in the "Great Educators' Series" (N. Y. 1892); Baumeister, *Denkmäler des klassischen Alterthums*, vol. iii., s. v. "Schulen"; and in this Dictionary the articles ALEXANDRIAN SCHOOL; ATHENAEUM; GEOGRAPHICA; GRAMMATICA; GYMNASIUM; LIBERALES ARTES; LOGISTICA; LUDUS LITTERARIUS; PHILOSOPHICA; RHETORICA; SCHOLA; SOPHISTES.

Eedna (τὰ ἔεδνα). See MATRIMONIUM.

Eëtion (Ἠετίων). King of the Hypoplacian Thebé, in Cilicia, and father of Andromaché, the wife of Hector. See ANDROMACHÉ.

Effigies. See IMAGINES.

Effractor (τοιχωρύχος, *effractarius*). A burglar. As the name τοιχωρύχος implies, the Greek burglar sought to effect an entrance through the wall of a house, rather than through the doors or windows. (See DOMUS, p. 538.) In Attic law he was reckoned among the κακοῦργοι whose crimes were capital (Demosth. *c. Lacrit.* p. 940, § 47); the summary processes called ἀπαγωγή and ἐφήγησις were available against him; he is often coupled with the λωποδύτης (e. g. Aristoph. *Plut.* 165), both offences being hedged in with special penalties because they were so easy to commit. The midnight terrors of a rich miser behind his flimsy walls are amusingly depicted by Lucian (*Gall.* p. 748, Reitz). See KLOPES DIKÉ.

The Romans did not shrink from capital punishments, at least under the Empire; and yet the crime of *effractio* was not visited with death, as among the Greeks. Their houses were better built than those of the Greeks, and thus they did not legislate under the influence of panic. The penalty was hard labour for life (*opus perpetuum*), and for burglary by night, in the mines (*poena metalli*). The trial was before the *praefectus vigilum*, or chief of police (Sidon. Apollin. *Ep.* ix. 7; *Dig.* 1, 15, 1).

Egeria. A Roman goddess of fountains, who was also a goddess of birth, and possessed the gift of prophecy. It was from her fountain, in the sacred enclosure of the Camenae, before the Porta Capena in Rome, that the Vestal Virgins brought the water necessary for the baths and purifications of their office. There was another fountain of Egeria in the precincts of Diana at Aricia. In Roman legend, Egeria was the consort and counsellor of King Numa, who used to meet her in a grotto in the precincts of the Camenae. After the death of her lover she fled to the shrine of the Arician Diana, by whom, as her wailings disturbed the worship, she was changed into the fountain which bore her name. Married women worshipped her at Rome as a goddess of childbirth.

Egesta. See SEGESTA.

Egnatia. A town in Apulia on the coast of Italy. It was celebrated for its miraculous stone or altar, which of itself set on fire frankincense and wood—a prodigy which afforded amusement to Horace and his friends, who looked upon it as a mere trick (*Sat.* I. v. 98). Egnatia was situated on the high-road from Rome to Brundisium, which from Egnatia to Brundisium bore the name of the Via Egnatia. The continuation of this road on the other side of the Adriatic from Dyrrhachium to Byzantium also bore the name of Via Egnatia. It was the great military road between Italy and the East. Commencing at Dyrrhachium, it passed by Lychnidus, Heraclea, Lyncestis, Edessa, Thessalonica, Amphipolis, Philippi, and traversing the whole of Thrace, finally reached Byzantium. Egnatia is called Gnatia in Horace by a popular contraction like that which gives us "Frisco" for San Francisco.

Egnatii. A Roman family of Samnitic origin. (1) GELLIUS EGNATIUS. A leader of the Samnites in the Third Samnite War. He fell in battle against the Romans in B.C. 295. (2) MARIUS EGNATIUS. A general of the Italian allies in the Social War, who was killed in battle, B.C. 89. (3) M. EGNATIUS RUFUS. A Roman of some note who was aedile in B.C. 20, and praetor in the following year. Having conspired against Augustus, he was put to death in B.C. 18. (4) P. EGNATIUS CELER. A Stoic philosopher, the teacher of Barea Soranus (q. v.), who was the chief witness against his upright pupil when accused of treason under Nero. See Juv. iii. 116, with Mayor's note.

Egypt. See AEGYPTUS.

Eicosté (εἰκοστή). A customs duty of one-twentieth (five per cent.) upon all commodities exported or imported by sea in the States of the allies subject to Athens. This tax was first imposed in B.C. 413–412, in the place of the direct tribute (φόρος) which had up to this time been paid by the subject allies; and the change was made with the hope of raising a greater revenue (Thuc. vii. 28). This tax, like so many others, was farmed, and the farmers of it were called εἰκοστολόγοι.

Eidothea (Εἰδοθέα). A sea-goddess, daughter of Proteus (q. v.), the old man of the sea (Hom. *Od.* iv. 366).

Eidyllia. See IDYLLIUM.

Einsiedeln Poems. A name given to the extensive fragments of two bucolic poems in Latin of unknown authorship, contained in a MS. of the tenth century found at Einsiedeln. One has forty-nine hexameters and the other thirty-nine. The first is a poetical contest and the second a dialogue. The last line of the second poem is that of Verg. *Ecl.* iv. 10. Both poems praise Nero in a fulsome vein. For criticism see Bücheler in the *Rhein. Museum*, xxvi. 235; and Peiper in the preface to his *Senecae Trag.* suppl. (Breslau, 1870). The style resembles that of Calpurnius (q. v.).

Eïon (Ἠϊών). A town in Thrace, at the mouth of the Strymon, twenty-five stadia from Amphipolis, of which it was the harbour (Thuc. iv. 102).

Eiren or **Iren** (εἴρην, ἴρην). The third class of Spartan youth with regard to age, the series being: παῖδες (aged 7–18), μελλίρανες (18–20), ἴρανες (20–30). The last were distinguished again as πρωτίρανες or σφαιρεῖς, according as they were near the lower or upper limit (Plut. *Lyc.* 17). The boys and youths forming a βούα or ἴλα chose as their leader (βουαγός) the wisest and bravest of the ἴρανες (Plut. ib.; Xen. *Rep. Lac.* ii. 11). These leaders excepted, the ἴρανες partook with their elders of the common meal (ἀνδρεῖα). See Müller, *Dorians*, ii. 315; Gilbert, *Staatsalterth.* i. pp. 68, 71; and the article EDUCATION; on the form of the word, see Kuhn's *Zeitschr.* viii. 53; *Philol.* x. 431; and Curt. *Stud.* iv. 1, 116.

Eirēné (Εἰρήνη). See IRENÉ.

Eiresiōné (εἰρεσιώνη). See PYANEPSIA.

Eisagōgeis (εἰσαγωγεῖς). In Attic law, a term which denotes (1) the name of any ordinary magistrates to whom application was made for the purpose of bringing a case (εἰσάγειν) into the proper court; and (2) particular magistrates, probably ten in number, chosen by lot to try (εἰσάγειν) some sorts of ἔμμηνοι δίκαι. See EMMENOI DIKAI; and the *Corp. Inscript. Gr.* i. 37, 38.

Eisangelia (εἰσαγγελία). Properly, an announcement made in presence of a legal authority. In Attic jurisprudence it was a special form of public prosecution, instituted especially for offences which appeared to inflict injury, directly or indirectly, upon the State, but which it was impracticable to prosecute under the regular and customary procedure. The accusation was put into writing and handed in to the Senate; if the Senate received it the accused was arrested, or had to get three persons to stand surety for him. But if the charge were one of treason or an attack upon the constitution this was not allowed. If the voting on the guilt or innocence of the accused were unfavourable, the Senate itself fixed the penalty, supposing it fell short of the amount which lay within its competence (500 drachmae, or $83). If not, the Senate referred the case at once to one of the courts of the Heliaea, or even to the ἐκκλησία, or Assembly, to which the prosecutor might, indeed, have applied from the first. If the *ecclesia* decided to take up the case, the first thing it did was to fix the penalty in case there were no legal provisions on this point. It then either entered on the investigation and decided the case or handed it over to a court of law. The name εἰσαγγελία was also given to the prosecution of judges in office for neglect of their duties, and to certain charges lodged before the archons—namely, charges against children for ill-treatment of parents, against husbands for ill-treatment of heiresses, and against guardians for ill-treatment of their wards. See ARCHON.

Eisiteria (εἰσιτήρια, sc. ἱερά). Sacrifices offered at Athens, upon entrance into office; according to Suidas (s. v.) upon the first day of the new year, which in consequence was kept as a holiday. Besides the higher magistrates, the Senate offered εἰσιτήρια through one of its members chosen for the purpose (Demosth. *c. Mid.* p. 552, § 114). When an embassy set out, at least on the most important occasions, the Senate and principal magistrates offered εἰσιτήρια for its success and dined together. The ἐξιτήρια on going out of office (Hesych.) are less well attested (Schömann, *Assemblies*, p. 306).

Eisphŏra (εἰσφορά). An income-tax, levied only

in extraordinary cases. It was based on the Solonian division of classes into *Pentacosiomedimni*, *Hippeis*, *Zeugitae*, and *Thetes*, the last of whom were not taxed at all. The taxable capital was estimated at twelve times a man's net income as estimated by himself. In the case of the *Pentacosiomedimni*, with a minimum income of 500 drachmae and minimum capital of 6000 drachmae (=1 talent, or $1080), the whole property was treated as taxable capital (τίμημα). In the case of the *Hippeis* (300–3600 drachmae), five sixths in that of the *Zeugitae* (150–1800 drachmae), five ninths, or 1000 drachmae. The first instance of the levy of an *eisphora* occurred in B.C. 428. In B.C. 378 another method of levying it was introduced under the archon Nausinicus. According to this, the taxable capital of the highest class was fixed at one fifth of the whole property. The resident aliens (μέτοικοι), as well as the citizens, were liable to pay the *eisphora*. On the method of collecting it, see SYMMORIAE.

Elaea (Ἐλαία). An ancient city on the coast of Aeolis in Asia Minor, which at one time served as the harbour of Pergamus. The gulf on which it stood was named after it Sinus Elaïticus.

Elaeothesium (ἐλαιοθέσιον). The oiling-room in a set of baths, where the oils and unguents were kept, and to which the bather retired to be rubbed and anointed. In large establishments a separate chamber was appropriated for this purpose, adjoining the *frigidarium*, or cold chamber (Vitruv. v. 11, 2). See BALNEAE.

Elaeus or **Eleus** (Ἐλαιοῦς or Ἐλεοῦς). A town on the southeast point of the Thracian Chersonesus, with a harbour and an *heroum* of Protesilaüs. See Herod. vi. 140.

Elagabălus. (1) ELAGABAL, a deity among the Phœnicians. This deity, according to Capitolinus (*Macr.* 9) and Aurelius Victor, was the Sun. Lampridius, however, fluctuates between the Sun and Iupiter, while Spartianus (*Caracall.* 11) leaves it uncertain. The orthography of the name is also disputed, some writing it Elagabal, others Eleagabal and Alagabal. Herodian gives us an accurate description of the form under which this deity was worshipped (v. 3, 10 foll.); he also informs us that by this appellation the Sun was meant, and that the deity in question was revered not only by the Syrians, but that the native satraps and barbarian kings were accustomed to send splendid presents to his shrine. According to Herodian, the god Elagabalus was worshipped under the form of a large black stone, round below and terminating above in a point—in other words, of a conical shape. This description is confirmed by the medals of Emesa, the principal seat of his worship, on which the conical stone is represented. So also, on the medals of Antoninus Pius, struck in this same city, an eagle appears perched on a cone. The same thing appears on medals of Caracalla, and on one an eagle with expanded wings stands before a conical stone in the middle of a hexastyle temple. (2) M. AURELIUS ANTONĪNUS, a Roman emperor. He was the grandson of Maesa, sister to the empress Iulia, the wife of Septimius Severus. Maesa had two daughters, Soaemias or Semiamira, the mother of the subject of this article, and Mammaea, mother of Alexander Severus. The true name of Elagabalus was Varius Avitus Bassianus, and he was reported to have been the illegitimate son of Caracalla. He was born at Antioch, A.D. 204. Maesa took care of his infancy, and placed him, when five years of age, in the temple of the Sun at Emesa, to be educated as a priest; and through her influence he was made, while yet a boy, high-priest of the Sun. That divinity was called in Syria Elagabal, whence the young Varius assumed the name of Elagabalus. After the death of Caracalla and the elevation of Macrinus, the latter having incurred by his severity the dislike of the soldiers, Maesa availed herself of this feeling to induce the officers to rise in favour of her grandson, whom she presented to them as the son of the murdered Caracalla. Elagabalus, who was then in his fifteenth year, was proclaimed emperor by the legion stationed at Emesa. Having put himself at their head, he was attacked by Macrinus, who at first had the advantage; but he and his mother Soaemias, with great spirit, brought the soldiers again to the charge and defeated Macrinus, who was overtaken in his flight and put to death, A.D. 218. Elagabalus, having entered Antioch, wrote a letter to the Senate, professing to take for his model Marcus Aurelius Antoninus, a name revered at Rome; and he also assumed that emperor's name. The Senate acknowledged him, and he set out for Rome, but delayed for several months on his way amid festivities and amusements, and at last stopped at Nicomedia for the winter. In the following year he arrived at Rome and began a career of debauchery, extravagance, and cruelty which lasted the remaining three years of his reign, and the disgusting details of which are given by Lampridius, Herodian, and Dio Cassius. He surrounded himself with gladiators, actors, and other base favourites, who made an unworthy use of their influence. He married several wives, among others a Ves-

Elagabalus. (Bust in the Capitol, Rome.)

tal. The imperial palace became a scene of debauch and open prostitution. Elagabalus, being attached to the superstitions of the East, raised a temple on the Palatine Hill to the Syrian god whose name he bore, and plundered the temples of the Roman gods to enrich his own. He put to death many senators, and established a senate of women, under the presidency of his mother, Soaemias, which body decided all questions relative to women's dresses, and to visits, precedence, and amusements. He wore his pontifical vest as high-priest of the Sun, with a rich tiara on his head. His grandmother Maesa, seeing his folly, thought of conciliating the Romans by associating with him, as Caesar, his younger cousin, Alexander Severus, who soon became a favourite with the people. Elagabalus, who had consented to the association, became afterwards jealous of his cousin and wished to deprive him of his honours, but he could not obtain the consent of the Senate. His next measure was to spread the report of Alexander's death, which produced an insurrection among the praetorians; and Elagabalus, having repaired to the camp to quell the mutiny, was murdered, together with his mother and his favourites, and his body was thrown into the Tiber, A.D. 222. He was succeeded by Alexander Severus. Elagabalus was eighteen years of age at the time of his death, and had reigned three years, nine months, and four days (Lamprid. *Elagab.*; Herodian, v. 3 foll.; Dio Cass. lxxviii. 31 foll.; lxxix. 1 foll.).

Elaphebolia (ἐλαφηβόλια). The greatest festival in the town of Hyampolis in Phocis, and celebrated in honour of Artemis, in commemoration, it is said, of a victory which its inhabitants had gained over the Thessalians, who had ravaged the country and reduced the Phocians in the neighbourhood of the town nearly to the last extremity (Plut. *De Mul. Virt.* p. 244 B; Pausan. x. 35, § 4). The only particular which we know of its celebration is, that a peculiar kind of cake (ἔλαφος) was made on the occasion (Athen. xv. p. 646 e). These cakes were, as their name indicates, probably made in the shape of a stag or a deer and offered to the goddess.

Elaphebolion (Ἐλαφηβολιών). The ninth month of the Attic year, answering to the last of March and the early part of April. See CALENDARIUM.

Elăra (Ἐλάρα). The daughter of Orchomenus or Minyus, and mother by Zeus of the giant Tityus. Through fear of Herè, Zeus concealed her under the earth (Apollod. i. 4, 1).

Elatēa (Ἐλάτεια). (1) A town in Phocis (Pausan. x. 34, § 1), situated near the Cephissus in a fertile valley, which was an important pass from Thessaly to Boeotia. (2) A town in Pelasgiotis in Thessaly, near Gonni. (3) Or ELATRĒA, a town in Epirus, near the sources of the Cocytus.

Elătus (Ἔλατος). One of the Lapithae, and father of Polyphemus and of Caeneus, who is hence called Elateius.

Elāver. The modern Allier; a river in Aquitania, a tributary of the Liger (Loire).

Elea. See VELIA.

Eleatic School. See PHILOSOPHIA.

Electra (Ἠλέκτρα). (1) One of the Oceanides, wife of Atlas, and mother of Dardanus by Zeus (Ovid, *Fast.* iv. 31). (2) A daughter of Atlas and Pleionè, and one of the Pleiades. (See PLEIADES.) (3) One of the daughters of Agamemnon (q. v.). Upon the murder of her father, after his return from Troy, Electra rescued her brother Orestes, then quite young, from the fury of Aegisthus, by despatching him to the court of her uncle Strophius, king of Phocis. There Orestes formed the well-known attachment for his cousin Pylades, which, in the end, led to the marriage of Electra with that prince. According to one account, Electra had previously been compelled, by Aegisthus, to become the wife of a Mycenean rustic, who, having regarded her merely as a sacred trust confided to him by the gods, restored her to Orestes on the return of that prince to Mycenae and on his accession to the throne of his ancestors. Electra became, by Pylades, the mother of two sons, Strophius and Medon. Her story has formed the basis of three extant plays, the *Choëphori* of Aeschylus, and the *Electra* of Sophocles and Euripides. See ORESTES.

Electra.

Electrĭdes Insŭlae. See ERIDANUS.

Electrum (ἤλεκτρος or ἤλεκτρον). Lepsius has maintained (*Ueber die Metalle in den ägypt. Inschriften*, Appendix) that the early Greek usage was to employ the masculine form when the mixture of gold and silver was intended; the neuter form when the mineral which we call amber was meant. It is likely that the Greeks were acquainted in very early times with the use of amber, trade in this mineral having taken place in pre-historic days between North and South Europe. They must also have been early acquainted with the compounded metal, since gold alike in Asia and Europe is commonly found mixed with silver. Which of the two substances, therefore, was first called electrum is a matter quite open to dispute. They will be spoken of in turn.

(1) AMBER. Beads of amber were found in the royal tombs at Mycenae, and chemical analysis (Schliemann, *Tiryns*, p. 370) has proved that this amber came from the Baltic and not from elsewhere. Similar beads have also been found in the very early tombs at Ialysus in Rhodes. At a later period amber is mentioned in the *Odyssey* (xv. 460, xviii. 295) as a material of necklaces. In one of these passages the necklace is spoken of as an import from Phœnicia. It is also stated (iv. 73) that the walls of the palace of Menelaüs were adorned with amber, as well as with gold, silver, and ivory. The author of the *Shield of Heracles*, ascribed to Hesiod, speaks of that shield (141) as adorned with electrum, in which case, however, the metal may be meant. In South Italy amber was used in the archaic period as a material for statuettes and reliefs; many specimens of this kind of work are in the British Museum. It is probable that the amber of early Greece was imported by the Phœnicians who sailed round the coast to the north of Europe, especially in view of the fact that after the Homeric Age amber disappeared from Greek tombs, and does not again figure until Roman times, when a regular trade with the Baltic coast had sprung up.

(2) MIXED GOLD AND SILVER. The earliest certain mention of this mixed metal as electrum (rather ἤλεκτρος) is in Sophocles's *Antigone*, 1037,

where the substance is said to come from Sardis; for Sardis by the Pactolus was noted in antiquity as the place whence came the river-gold, mixed when found with a considerable percentage of silver. Herodotus, however, speaking of this same Sardian metal in connection with the donaria of Croesus to Delphi (i. 50), calls it white gold, λευκὸς χρυσός. Pliny remarks (*H. N.* xxxiii. § 80) that gold is invariably found mixed with silver (which is true), and that when the proportion of silver reaches a fifth the metal is called electrum. He adds that electrum was made by art as well as found.

This white gold or electrum is used on the sword-blades found at Mycenae for purposes of inlaying. In later times it was used, as being a harder material than gold, for objects in which hardness was desirable. By far the most important use to which it was put was as a material for coins.

In the seventh century B.C., or possibly late in the eighth, the kings of Lydia began to issue stamped money of electrum, using probably the metal in its natural state, and the maritime cities of the Asiatic coast and of Euboea adopted the idea. (See PONDERA.) For some time, until silver

Early Electrum Stater, probably struck at Miletus before B.C. 623. (British Museum.)

was first minted at Aegina, all the coinage of the world consisted of stamped pellets of electrum, though no doubt unstamped bars of gold and silver circulated with them. It is observed by Mr. Head (*Numismatic Chronicle*, 1875, p. 254), in his account of early electrum coins, that the mixed metal had two advantages over pure gold in circulation: (1) it was more durable; (2) the proportionate value of gold to silver being 13⅓ to 1 (Herodotus says 13), and electrum being of three-fourths the value of gold, each coin of electrum would pass as the equivalent of ten silver bars of equal weight.

Croesus is believed to have first introduced into Asia coined money of gold and silver in place of electrum. See NUMISMATICS.

Electrўon (Ἠλεκτρύων). Son of Perseus and Andromeda, and father of Alcmené, the wife of Amphitryon. See AMPHITRYON.

Electryōné (Ἠλεκτρυώνη). A patronymic given to Alcmené, daughter of Electryon.

Elegīa (ἐλεγεῖον, a distich consisting of an hexameter line followed by a pentameter; then in the plural, a collection of such distichs, and hence ἐλεγεία). The general term in Greek for any poem written in the elegiac metre, a combination of the dactylic hexameter and pentameter in a couplet. The word ἔλεγος is probably not Greek, but borrowed from the Lydians, and means a plaintive melody accompanied by the flute. How it happened that the word was applied to elegiac poetry, the earliest representatives of which by no means confined it to mournful subjects, is doubtful. It may be that the term was chosen only in reference to the musical setting, the elegy having originally been accompanied by the flute. Like the epic, the elegy was a production of the Ionians of Asia Minor. (See EPOS.) Its dialect was the same as that of the epos, and its metre only a variation of the epic metre, the pentameter being no more than an abbreviation of the hexameter. The elegy marks the first transition from the epic to lyric proper. The earliest representatives of the elegy, Callinus of Ephesus (about B.C. 700) and Tyrtaeus of Aphidnae in Attica (about B.C. 600), gave it a decidedly warlike and political direction, and so did Solon (B.C. 640–559) in his earlier poems, though his later elegies have mostly a contemplative character. The elegies of Theognis of Megara (about B.C. 540), though gnomic and erotic, are essentially political. The first typical representative of the erotic elegy was Mimnermus of Colophon, an elder contemporary of Solon. The elegy of mourning or sorrow was brought to perfection by Simonides (q. v.) of Ceos (died B.C. 469). After him the emotional element predominated. Antimachus of Colophon (about B.C. 400) gave the elegy a learned tinge, and was thus the prototype of the elegiac poets of Alexandria, Phanocles, Philetas of Cos, Hermesianax of Colophon, and Callimachus (q. v.) of Cyrené, the master of them all. The subject of the Alexandrian elegy is sometimes the passion of love, with its pains and pleasures, treated through the medium of images and similes taken from mythology; sometimes learned narrative of fable and history, from which personal emotion is absent.

This type of elegy, with its learned and obscure manner, was taken up and imitated at Rome towards the end of the Republic. The Romans soon easily surpassed their Greek masters both in warmth and sincerity of feeling and in finish of style. The elegies of Catullus are among their earliest attempts; but in the Augustan Age, in the hands of Cornelius Gallus, Propertius, Tibullus, and Ovid, the elegiac style was entirely appropriated by Latin literature. Ovid, in his *Fasti*, showed how a learned subject could be treated in this metre. From his time onward the elegiac metre was constantly employed, and was used even in schools for practice in style. In the later literature it was applied, like the epic metre, to every possible subject, as, for instance, by Rutilius Namatianus in the description of his return from Rome to Gaul (A.D. 416). In the sixth century A.D. the poet Maximianus, born in Etruria at the beginning of that century, is a late instance of a genuine elegiac poet.

On the elegy, see an article by O. Crusius in the *Wochenschrift für klass. Phil.* for 1885; Eichner, *De Poetarum Lat. Distichis* (Breslau, 1866); Prien, *Symmetrie und Responsion der röm. Elegie* (Lübeck, 1867); Madvig in his *Adversaria*, ii. 110; and Gruppe, *Die röm. Elegie*, ed. by Schulze (Berlin, 1884).

Elenchus. A large drop ear-ring consisting of a single pearl; also often worn as a bangle (Plin. *H. N.* ix. 56; Juv. vi. 459). See INAURIS.

Eleos (Ἔλεος). An Athenian deity personifying pity (Pausan. i. 17, § 1).

Elephantīné (Ἐλεφαντίνη νῆσος). An island in the Nile, with a city of the same name, opposite to Syené, and seven stadia below the Little Cataract. It was the frontier station of Egypt towards Ethiopia, and was strongly garrisoned under the Persians and the Romans (Ptol. iv. 5, § 70). The original name of the island was Ebo—Eb being in the language of hieroglyphics symbolical of the elephant and of ivory. Here was a temple of Cnuphis and here also a Nilometer. Many important inscriptions have been found here; and until 1822 (when they were destroyed by the governor) there existed the ruins of the temple and of a granite gateway of the time of Alexander III. See Mariette, *Monuments of Upper Egypt* (1877); A. B. Edwards, *A Thousand Miles up the Nile* (1877).

Elephantis (Ἐλεφαντίς). The author of erotic and indecent books, generally supposed to have been a woman, but of whose personality nothing is known. See Mart. xii. 43, 4; Suet. *Tib.* 43.

Elĕphas (ἐλέφας, *ebur; elephantus*, poet., Verg. *Georg.* iii. 26; *Aen.* iii. 464, vi. 896). African ivory was known to the ancients, through Phœnician trade, long before the elephant. Accordingly, early writers—Homer, Hesiod, Pindar—speak of the material only. Herodotus, indeed, was aware of its origin (iv. 191; Plin. *H. N.* viii. § 7), but the Greeks generally only became acquainted with the animal from the Macedonian expeditions into Asia, the Romans from the arrival of Pyrrhus in Italy. Both words—ἐλέφας, *ebur*—possibly contain the Egyptian *âb*, "ivory, elephant" (Schrader, *Linguist. histor. Forsch. zur Handelsgesch.* i. 71).

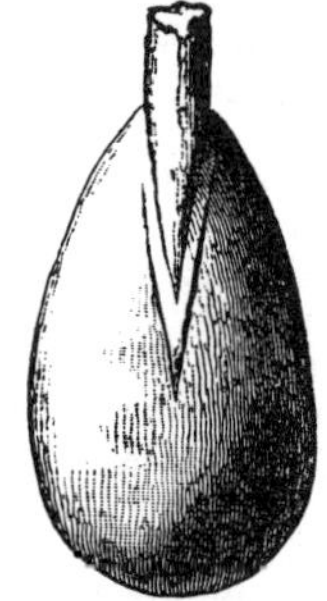
Ivory Spoon. (Schliemann.)

The use of ivory in the manufacture of small objects of use or ornament, and for purposes of decoration, is earliest in Egypt and Assyria. There have been found, for instance, castanets, stick-handles, hilts and hefts, combs, flutes, sceptres, caskets, statuettes, made of the tusk, and many different articles of furniture inlaid with it. In Homer, besides its employment when carved in mass, it is referred to in connection with walls, doors, harness, etc., and was then probably attached in plates by nails to a metal or wooden ground. In later times true inlaying was resorted to, and almost every kind of furniture, as beds, sofas, thrones, carriages even, enriched with the precious material.

Among objects not enumerated above may be mentioned masks and writing-tablets. The latter (δέλτοι, *libri elephantini*), with two, three, or more leaves (*diptycha, triptycha, pentaptycha*, etc.), were either entirely, or had their covers only, of ivory. Those extant are chiefly of the later Roman age. They are of two classes, *consularia* and *ecclesiastica*, distinguished by the subjects of the carvings on their covers, the former being figures of consuls at the *pompa circensis, missiones*, etc., while the latter are of a Biblical nature (Müller, *Arch. d. Kunst*, § 312, n. 3). They were presented to officers and dignitaries to commemorate their appointment. See DIPTYCHA.

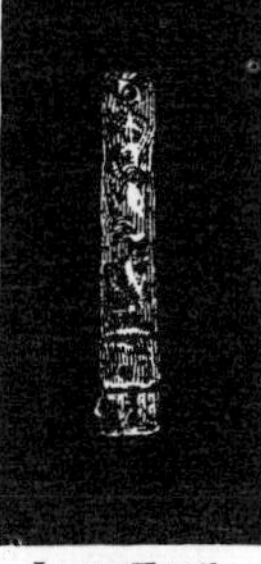
Ivory Handle. (Schliemann.)

For further information see H. Blümner, *Technol. u. Terminol. d. Gewerbe*, etc., ii. 361–375, where there is a full bibliography; and cf. the article CHRYSELEPHANTINA.

Elephēnor (Ἐλεφήνωρ). The son of Chalcodon and Melanippê, and prince of the Abantes. He was one of the suitors of Helen, and led a force against Troy, before which city he was slain by Agenor.

Eleusinia (τὰ Ἐλευσίνια). A title chiefly applied to a festival held by the Athenians in the autumn, in honour of Demeter, Persephonê, and Iacchus, consisting of sacrifices, processions, and certain mystical ceremonies. It was one of the most important festivals of Greece.

The mythical origin of the Eleusinia is contained in the Homeric hymn to Demeter, which tells how Persephonê, while gathering flowers, was, with the connivance of Zeus, carried off by the god of the lower world, Hades or Polydegmon (the great receiver); and how her mother Demeter, daughter of Rhea, searching distractedly for her child, is advised by Hecatê to consult Helios, who sees all things; and how Helios in pity tells her that Zeus has granted to Hades to carry off her daughter to be his wife. Forthwith Demeter changes herself into an old woman; and as she wanders forth disconsolate through the world she comes to Eleusis, and sits down on the cheerless stone by a well. The daughters of Celeus, the king of Eleusis, come to the well to draw water. They bring her to their home, where Metanira, wife of Celeus, gives her the latest born child, Demophoön, to nurse. But Demeter is still bowed down with grief; she sits dignified but silent in her room, till the jests and raillery of Iambê, the servant-maid, at last make her smile. She consents to take food and drink, but will have no wine, only a mixture (κυκεών) of water with barley-meal and mint. Days go on, and the child Demophoön thrives beyond what mortal child was wont, for a goddess was his nurse; she used to anoint him daily with ambrosia and place him in the fire by night. But a little more time and the child would have been immortal, when one night Metanira saw the nurse place him in the fire and cried aloud with terror. Then the anger of Demeter blazed forth, and the aged nurse transformed herself into the goddess, told who she was, what she had intended to do, and how that the little faith of the mother had robbed the child of immortality, and finally bade the people of Eleusis to erect a temple for her on the hill above the fountain, when she herself would prescribe the services they must perform in order to gain her favour. They did so, and Demeter dwelt there, shunning all association with the other gods who had been parties to the carrying off of her daughter. For a year Demeter dwelt there—a year of want, for nothing grew; and the human race would have perished, had not Zeus agreed that Persephonê should return. Gladly did Persephonê obey the summons of Hermes; but Hades persuaded her to eat a pomegranate seed before she left, and that prevented her staying away from him for a whole year. So Persephonê returns, and great is the joy of mother and daughter, in which the faithful Hecatê sympathizes. Rhea is then sent down by Zeus to her daughter and effects the reconciliation. The corn comes up in abundance in the Rarian plain; Demeter returns to Olympus to dwell with the gods, and prescribes to Celeus and to his sons Triptolemus, Diocles, and Eumolpus the solemnities and divine services that were in future time to be paid her; and hence the famous Eleusinian Mysteries were a direct appointment of the great goddess Demeter herself.

Such was the story of the origin of the mysteries; but how the mysteries came to be Athenian depends on another story, which concerns the union of Eleusis with Athens. Erechtheus warred with the Eleusinians (Pausan. i. 38, 3), who were helped by one Eumolpus, a Thracian, son of Poseidon (Apollod. iii. 14, 4) and founder of the mysteries (Lucian, *Demon.* 34). The difficulties connected with the exact birthplace and genealogical position of Eumolpus (see Roscher, *Lexikon der Mythol.* s. v. *Eumolpus*) we may pass over, remembering that he is, according to this legend, a foreigner (Plut. *De Exsilio*, p. 607, 10). Eleusis was conquered, and to the Athenians fell the political headship, but to the family of Eumolpus and the daughters of the Eleusinian king Celeus was assigned the high-priesthood (ἱεροφαντία) of the Eleusinian worship. The other family which held a priesthood in the mysteries, the Kerykes, were said to have been descended from Keryx, the son of Eumolpus; though the family itself considered its ancestors to have been Hermes and Aglauros, daughter of Erechtheus, and so genuine Athenians (Pausan. i. 38, 3).

Mysteries were celebrated in honour of Demeter, Persephoné, and Dionysus in Asia Minor (e. g. at Cyzicus); in Egypt on Lake Mareotis (Strab. xvii. p. 800); in Sicily at Gela and elsewhere (Herod. vii. 153; Diod. Sic. v. 77); in Boeotia at Plataea (Herod. ix. 62, 65, 101); in many parts of Arcadia (Pausan. ii. 14, 1; viii. 15, 1); and in Messenia at Andania (Pausan. iv. 1, 5). But the most splendid and important of all the Eleusinia were those of Attica, which may be regarded as having consisted of two parts: (1) the Lesser Mysteries at Agrae, and (2) the Greater Mysteries at Eleusis.

(1) THE LESSER MYSTERIES AT AGRAE (τὰ ἐν Ἄγραις). These were held in the spring at Agrae, a place on the Ilissus, southeast of the Acropolis. There is no doubt that they were held in the month Anthesterion, when there were the first signs of returning vegetation just after field-work began (*C. I. G.* 103, l. 20). The exact date cannot be fixed, but Mommsen's suggestion is most probable, that the chief day was the 20th, the same day of the month as the Greater Mysteries were held on in Boedromion, to which the Lesser Mysteries had many points of similarity, even in matters connected with the calendar — e. g. the same length of the mystery truce (*C. I. G.* 71). Mommsen supposes that the 19th was a day of preparation, and the 20th and 21st the special mystery days. These Lesser Mysteries were considered as a prelude to the Greater (Schol. on Aristoph. *Plut.* 845), being on a much smaller scale; but initiation in the Lesser was generally required before the candidate could present himself for initiation into the Greater (Plat. *Gorg.* 497 C). The mysteries at Agrae consisted probably to a large extent of purifications, for which the water of the Ilissus was much used (Polyaen. v. 17). They were held more especially in honour of Persephoné, called Pherrephatta here, than of Demeter (Schol. on Aristoph. *Plut.* 845). It appears that the carrying off of Persephoné was the most important representation in these mysteries. Again we hear that at Agrae the fate of Dionysus was pourtrayed (μίμημα τῶν περὶ τὸν Διόνυσον, Steph. Byzant. s. v. Ἄγραι). The death of Dionysus-Zagreus took place on the 13th of Anthesterion, the day on which the festival of the Chytri was held (see DIONYSIA); so perhaps on the ninth day after, the 21st (for funeral rites on the ninth day after death, the ἔνατα, see Aesch. *Ctesiph.* § 225), the funeral ceremony may have been held and his violent death related in a drama. A great many, especially strangers, were initiated into these mysteries who did not proceed to initiation into the regular Eleusinia; the legend, too, said it was for the purpose of initiat-

Initiation of Heracles. (Vase from Panticapaeum.)

ing Heracles, who was a stranger and according to the primitive regulations could not be initiated into the Eleusinia, that these Lesser Mysteries were established (Schol. on Aristoph. *Plut.* 845, 1013).

(2) The Greater Mysteries at Eleusis. Two days are fixed by definite evidence—viz. the 16th Boëdromion for the Ἅλαδε μύσται (Polyaen. iii. 11, 11; *De Glor. Ath.* 349 fin.), and the 20th for the Iacchus day (Plut. *Cam.* 19, *Phoc.* 28). The fixing of other days depends on conjecture, but can be determined with a considerable degree of certainty. A month before the middle of Boëdromion—i. e. the middle of Metageitnion—the σπονδοφόροι used to announce the mystery truce to the neighbouring States (Aesch. *Fals. Leg.* § 133), so as to give the strangers time to make all arrangements necessary for a visit to Athens. During the latter portion of this month the votary who intended to be initiated used to betake himself to some private man who had gone through all the grades of initiation, was examined by him as to his freedom from sin, received instruction as to what purifications and offerings were necessary to gain the favour of the goddesses, and submitted the actual offerings for his inspection and approval. This instructor was the μυσταγωγός. He certified to the Hierophant the fitness of the applicant and introduced him, this proceeding being apparently called σύστασις. Sincere devotees appear to have fasted for nine days (cf. Hom. *Hymn. Dem.* 47), from the 13th to the 21st—i. e. ate nothing during the day, taking whatever food they did take between sunset and sunrise, like the Mahomedans during Ramadan; and votaries generally appear to have abstained from domestic birds, fish, pomegranates, apples, and beans (Porphyr. *Abst.* iv. 16). On the 15th of Boëdromion the formal assemblage (ἀγυρμός, Hesych. s. v.) was held of those citizens and strangers who intended to take part in the mysteries—though this assemblage does not appear to have been absolutely essential, at least in late times (*C. I. G.* 523). At the beginning of the 16th, in the evening (the day is reckoned from sunset to sunset), Chabrias's distribution of wine to the people in honour of his victory at Naxos used to take place (Plut. *Phoc.* 6); and the next morning began the first formal act of the festival—viz. the πρόρρησις or Ἅλαδε μύσται. A proclamation was made by the Archon Basileus (Poll. viii. 90) and by the Hierophant and Daduchus in the Stoa Poecilé (Schol. on Aristoph. *Ran.* 369), for the departure of all strangers and all murderers; and then the order for purification given, "Ye mystae, to the sea!" The "sea" was sometimes the Piraeus (Plut. *Phoc.* 28), though probably only in time of Attica being occupied by enemies; but generally the Ῥειτοί, two salt streams on the Sacred Road, one dedicated to Demeter, the other to Coré, which contained fish that the priests alone were allowed to eat (Pausan. i. 38, 1; Hesych. s. v.). The next day, the 17th, sacrifices (ἱερεῖα) were offered for the safety of the State by the Archon Basileus and the ἐπιμεληταί in the Eleusinium at Athens; and at all these sacrifices the θεωροί of foreign States seem to have taken part (Eurip. *Suppl.* 173). The night of the 18th may have been spent by the very devout in sleeping in the Temple of Aesculapius, southwest of the Acropolis, or in the Iaccheum (Boeckh on *C. I. G.* 481), also called the Temple of Demeter. It was just where the road from the Piraeus entered Athens (Pausan. i. 2, 4). The early morning of that day till about 9 A.M. was devoted to ordinary business, as we find decrees issued bearing that date (Mommsen, pp. 95, 225, 226). After this hour the Epidauria was celebrated in the Temple of Demeter or Iacchus and in the Temple of Aesculapius. It was, as has been seen, a supplementary sacrifice for those who came late, and legend said it was instituted for the sake of Aesculapius, who himself came late for the mysteries. Doubtless, however, the thought really lay in this, that Aesculapius was supposed by his wondrous skill to have raised again Iacchus from the dead, and the festival probably was incorporated in the Eleusinia when the worship of Epidaurus became connected with that of Athens (Herod. v. 82). Meanwhile there were being brought from Eleusis certain religious objects—playthings, it was said, of the child Iacchus—bone (ἀστράγαλος), top (στρόβιλος), ball (σφαῖρα), apples (μῆλα), tambourine (ῥόμβος), looking-glass (ἔσοπτρον), fleece (πόκος), fan (λίκνον), and such like, as is learned from Clement of Alexandria (*Protrept.* p. 15, ed. Potter; cf. Lobeck, *Aglaoph.* 701, 702). Phalli were perhaps also carried among these mystical objects (see Phallus); but we must remember that the statue of Iacchus, as we shall see, which was carried in procession to Eleusis on the 19th, was not kept at Eleusis during the year, but at Athens, having been brought back some day shortly after the conclusion of the mysteries; for there was no Iaccheum at Eleusis (Mommsen, p. 253). The Athenian Ephebi met this convoy at the Temple of Echo (evidence from inscriptions in Mommsen, p. 252), and conveyed it to Athens by nightfall. In the early morning of the 19th, there were occasionally decrees passed. In the forenoon the Iacchus procession started from the Eleusinium and proceeded to the Iaccheum, where they got the statue of Iacchus; perhaps then definitely organized the procession in the building assigned for that purpose (Pausan. i. 2, 4); and then passing through the Ceramicus (Schol. on Aristoph. *Ran.* 399) left Athens by the Sacred Gate (Plut. *Sull.* 14), priests and people crowned with myrtle and ivy, the rich ladies till the time of the orator Lycurgus riding in carriages (Schol. on Aristoph. *Plut.* 1014). The statue of Iacchus was probably that of a fair child crowned with myrtle and holding a torch, hence called φωσφόρος ἀστὴρ in Aristophanes (*Ran.* 342). There were many ceremonies to be performed as the procession passed along the Sacred Way to Eleusis—ceremonies which had to be given up during the Peloponnesian War, while Attica was invaded by the Peloponnesians (Plut. *Alcib.* 34). One section of the procession repaired to the Cephissus and took baths therein, another to the bath by Anemocritus's statue near the tomb of Scirus the soothsayer, who came from Dodona to Eleusis to assist the Eleusinians in the war against Erechtheus and was slain. The Phytalidae sacrificed to Phytalus in Laciadae, where lay a temple to the Mourning (Ἀχέα) Demeter, and to Coré, with whose worship that of Athené and Poseidon was joined (Pausan. i. 37, 2). At the palace of Crocon, the Croconidae perhaps bound small bands of saffron thread round the right wrist and right foot of each mystes (cf. Phot. s. v. κροκοῦν), which was considered as a protection from the evil eye.

Occasionally during the procession the majority of those who took part in it indulged in flouts and gibes at one another, a proceeding called γεφυρισ-

μός, the origin of which title is unknown, but is generally associated with the bridge over the Cephissus (Strab. ix. 400). Chants in honour of Iacchus were sung constantly during the procession, which swelled louder as when, near midnight, Iacchus arrived at Eleusis amid the blaze of torches (Soph. *Oed. Col.* 1045). That the procession did not arrive till late at night is plain from the splendid chorus in the *Ion* (1076 foll.), which sings of the torches and of the moon and stars dancing in heaven at the sight. The journey from Athens to Eleusis is really only four hours long, but the various ceremonies performed during the course of the procession extended it to three or four times its normal length. On the next morning certain sacrifices were performed, consisting probably in part of swine, to Demeter (Schol. on Aristoph. *Pax*, 374). An inscription in Mommsen, p. 257, orders sacrifices to be made by the *ἱεροποιοί* to Hermes Enagonius, the Graces, Artemis, and certain heroes, Telesidromus and Triptolemus. It is not known what these sacrifices were at Eleusis; at Andania they were, besides others, a sheep to Persephoné and a sow to Demeter. In later times the Ephebi made supplementary sacrifices of cattle. The bulls were brought unbound to the altar, and the Ephebi struggled with them to hold them as they were being sacrificed.

The 22d and 23d were the *μυστηριώτιδες ἡμέραι*, and the ceremonies celebrated thereon were *παννυχίδες*. During the evening of the 22d was probably what was called *λαμπάδων ἡμέρα*, which consisted of a symbol of search after Coré with torches (Lactant. *Inst.* i. 21), performed principally by and for the less highly initiated, who conducted the search crowned with myrtle, wearing a fawn-skin, and holding a wand, the mystagogues of the several initiates taking part in the search—the whole proceeding being perhaps an interlude in the story of Demeter and Coré, which appears to have been represented in the temple on this night. After it, came with much ceremonial the partaking of the *κυκεών*, a mixture of mint, barley-meal, and water. This was a cardinal feature in the ceremony, being, if we may so say, a participation in the Eleusinian sacrament. It was in remembrance of Demeter being refreshed after her long wandering and fruitless search. Thereafter followed what was called the *παράδοσις τῶν ἱερῶν* (Suidas, s. v.): certain relics and amulets were given to the votary to touch or kiss or even taste, the votary repeating, as the priest tendered him the objects with a regular question (Arnob. *Adv. Gentes*, v. 26), a formula (*σύνθημα*), given by Clement of Alexandria (*Protrept.* p. 18). It appears that some kind of memento of this ceremony was given by the priest to the votaries, which a sincere believer used to keep in a linen cloth (Apul. *Apol.* p. 140). The actual *ἱερὰ* themselves were kept in a chest (*τελέτης ἐγκύμονα μυστίδα κίστην*, Nonnus, *Dionys.* ix. 127) bound with purple ribbons, and consisted among others of sesame cakes of particular shapes, pomegranates, salt, ferules, ivy, poppy-seeds, quinces, etc. (Clem. Alex. *Protrept.* p. 19): the uninitiated were not allowed to see these "even from the housetop" (Callim. *Hymn to Ceres*, 4).

Not very different appear to have been the ceremonies of the 23d. There were many wand-bearers but few bacchants, as the superintendents of the mysteries used to say (Plato, *Phaed.* 69 C), and it was for these latter, the more highly initiated mystae of at least a year's standing, generally called *ἐπόπται*, that the ceremonies of the 23d were held, and they were the highest and greatest. Here, too, was probably a *παράδοσις τῶν ἱερῶν*, the sacramental words used in receiving which being *ἐκ τυμπάνου ἔφαγον, ἐκ κυμβάλου ἔπιον, ἐκερνοφόρησα, ὑπὸ τὸν παστὸν ὑπέδυον*. All this undoubtedly points to the Phrygian worship of Sabazius, which was introduced by the Orphics into the Eleusinian mysteries. On the afternoon of the 23d was held that portion of the feast which was called *πλημοχόαι* (Athen. x. p. 496) or *πλημοχόη* (Poll. x. 74), a sacrifice to the dead. The *πλημοχόη* was a broad-bottomed earthen jar, and two such were used in the ceremony, one filled with wine and the other with water, the contents of the one thrown to the east and of the other to the west, while mystic words (*ὗε κύε*) were spoken. This sacrifice formed a fitting conclusion to the mysteries in the special sense, the *μυστηριώτιδες ἡμέραι*. It ended with a *χαίρετε* to the dead, which conclusion was called *προχαιρητήρια* (Harpocr. 161, 9).

The next morning, the 24th, occurred perhaps the *βαλλητύς*, also called *τύπται*, a sort of sham fight, enjoined, it seems, in the Homeric hymn (267 foll.). There was a similar contest, called *λιθοβολία*, at the festival of Damia and Auxesia at Troezen (cf. Pausan. ii. 32, 2). On this same morning and afternoon were the *ἀγῶνες σταδιακοί*. They were called Eleusinia or Demetria, and the prize was some barley grown on the Rarian Plain (Schol. on Pind. *Ol.* ix. 150, 166). There is no reason to suppose that these games were not annual (see Hermann, *Gottesd. Alterth.* § 55, 39). In early times these games probably lasted two days; but in later times, on the 25th, the theatrical representations of the *Διονύσου τεχνῖται* were held, and we have some inscriptions referring to the sacrifices offered by this guild. As time went on, the 26th and 27th appear to have been devoted to such theatrical exhibitions (Rangabé, 813, 6), held perhaps for the purpose of keeping the visitors in the country. The people do not appear to have returned to Athens in a regular procession, though Lenormant thinks they did, and that the *γεφυρισμός* and the *πλημοχόη* were incidents in that return journey. The mystery truce lasted till the middle of Pyanepsion (*C. I. G.* 71).

(3) The Priests and Priestesses. (*a*) The most important priest was the *Hierophant* (*Ἱεροφάντης*). In lists of the Eleusinian priests he is put first (*C. I. G.* 184, 190). He was nominated for life (Pausan. ii. 14, 1) from the Eleusinian family of the Eumolpidae, and was generally an elderly man and bound to a life of strict chastity. There was only one Hierophant at a time, and his name was never mentioned (Lucian, *Lexiph.* 10), though in late inscriptions we find the Roman gentile name but not the praenomen or the cognomen given (*C. I. G.* 187). His principal duty was, clothed in an Oriental style, with a long robe and a turban (*στρόφιον*), as his name indicates, to show and explain the sacred symbols and figures—perhaps in a kind of chant or recitative, as he was required to have a good voice (cf. Plut. *Alcib.* 22; Epictet. iii. 21, § 16). (*b*) The *Daduchus* (*δᾳδοῦχος*) or torch-bearer was inferior to the Hierophant, and of the same rank with the Keryx (*C. I. G.* 185, compared with 188). Originally he was descended from the Eleusinian Triptolemus (Xen. *Hell.* vi. 3, 6); but about B.C. 380 this family

died out, and the Lycomidae, the family to which Themistocles belonged, which celebrated a local worship of Demeter at Phlyae full of Orphic doctrines and ceremonies, succeeded to the daduchia (see Boeckh on *C. I. G.* i. p. 441 f.). It is uncertain whether the name of the Daduchus was sacred. His head-dress was Oriental, as we may infer from a Persian soldier mistaking a Daduchus for a king (Plut. *Arist.* 5). His main duty was to hold the torch at the sacrifices, as his name indicates; but he shared with the Hierophant several functions, reciting portions of the ritual, taking part in certain purifications in the πρόρρησις, and even in the exhibition of the mysteries (Suid. s. v. δᾳδουχεῖ). For these two priests, the Hierophant and the Daduchus, who had to be men of tried sanctity, there was a regular consecration on their entering office. It was the τέλος τῆς ἐποπτείας, and was called ἀνάδεσις καὶ στεμμάτων ἐπίθεσις, because the sign of it consisted in placing on the head of the new priest the diadem of purple and the wreath of myrtle which they wore permanently. (*c*) The *Keryx* or *Hierokeryx* (Κῆρυξ, Ἱεροκῆρυξ). According to Eleusinian tradition, the Kerykes traced their origin back to Keryx, a younger son of Eumolpus; but they themselves considered their ancestors to be Hermes and one of the daughters of Cecrops—Aglauros according to Pausanias (i. 38, 3), Pandrosos according to Pollux (viii. 103). His duties were chiefly to proclaim silence at the sacrifices (Poll. iv. 91). (*d*) The *Epibomios* (ὁ ἐπὶ βωμῷ). In early times he was certainly a priest (*C. I. G.* 71 a, 39); he is generally mentioned in connection with the other three priests, but not always. No family laid especial claim to this priesthood. His name, as well as that of the Keryx, was probably not sacred. The four Eleusinian priests were among those who were maintained in the Prytaneum—were ἀείσιτοι, as they were called (*C. I. G.* 183 foll.). (*e*) The *Hierophantis* (Ἱερόφαντις). There was originally only one at a time; she belonged to Demeter (*C. I. G.* 434, 2), and her name was sacred; but a new one was added when Hadrian's wife Sabina was deified as the younger Demeter (ib. 435, 1073). Perhaps at this time or afterwards the priestesses came to be multiplied. (See the Schol. on Soph. *Oed. Col.* 683). They lived a life of perfect chastity during their tenure of office, though they might have been married previously. It is uncertain to what family the original Hierophantis of Demeter belonged; that of the younger belonged to a branch of the Lycomidae. The duties of the Hierophantis corresponded to those of the Hierophant. Pollux (i. 14) appears to call these priestesses προφάντιδες, and perhaps they were also called μέλισσαι (Hesych. s. v.). (*f*) *Female torch-bearer*, Δᾳδουχήσασα (*C. I. G.* 1535). (*g*) *Priestess* (Ἱέρεια). She was not hieronymous, but eponymous. These priestesses belonged to the family of the Phillidae.

Eleusinian Priest. (Vase from Kertch; Gerhard, *Ges. Abh.*, taf. 77.)

Their duties corresponded in all probability with those of the Epibomius. (*h*) The *Spondophori* (Σπονδοφόροι) were sent out to the adjoining country a month before the ceremony to announce the truce for the mysteries (Aesch. *Fals. Leg.* § 133). They belonged to the families of the Eudanemi and Kerykes. (*i*) *Minor offices:* (1) φαιδρύντης τοῖν θεοῖν (Inscr. in Mommsen, p. 227), perhaps belonging to the Eleusinium of the city. (2) ὑδρανός, whom Hesychius describes as ἁγνίστης τῶν Ἐλευσινίων. He probably superintended the ἅλαδε μύσται. (3) ἰακχαγωγός and κουροτρόφος, female nurses attending on the child Iacchus (Poll. i. 35). (4) Perhaps the same may be said of the δαειρῖτις, but it is very uncertain. It is known that Persephoné was originally called Daeira in the Eleusinian worship. (5) ἱεραύλης (ib. 184, c. 18) was probably the head of the ὑμνῳδοί and ὑμνητρίδες (Poll. i. 35), a sort of choir. (6) Who the παναγεῖς and the πυρφόροι were, beyond what can be inferred from their names, cannot be determined. Lenormant says the παναγεῖς were intermediate between the ministers and the initiates. Though not strictly a priest, yet as exercising an important function in the mysteries, (*j*) the *mystagogi* (μυσταγωγοί) may be mentioned here. They had to be men who had passed through all the grades of initiation. They were probably under the cognizance of the State, in a manner licensed. Prior to presenting himself for initiation, each votary had to place himself under the guidance of one of these mystagogues, and get instruction from him as to the various purifications and ceremonies he was to perform. It was only by the carelessness of mystagogues that unworthy applicants ever got admission to the mysteries. After due examination, if the mystagogue was satisfied, he presented the applicant or returned his name to the Archon Basileus or his assistants. This was called σύστασις. If a mystagogue could not say what purificatory sacrifices were required for a special candidate, recourse was had to (*k*) an *Exegetes* (Ἐξηγήτης), who appears to have been elected by the people from the Eumolpidae or Kerykes, and whose business it was to decide such difficult cases and generally to give *responsa* on Eleusinian ecclesiastical law. There were many books of the mysteries (cf. Lenormant, *Contemp. Rev.* xxxvii. 871) which were intended to have been strictly kept from the uninitiated, and which appear to have contained not only what ritual was to be performed in various cases, but also, perhaps, the allegorical and symbolical interpretations of some of the myths. Cf. Galen, viii. 181, ed. Kuhn; Lobeck, *Aglaoph.* 194.

The priests of the mysteries, especially the Eumolpidae, appear to have had a special ecclesiastical court (ἱερὰ γερουσία) for trying offences of impiety, in connection with the festival, which court they conducted according to unwritten laws of immemorial antiquity (Lys. *in Andoc.* § 10). To prosecute before this court was called δικάζεσθαι πρὸς Εὐμολπίδας. Their punishments, according to Caillemer (D. and S., s. v. *Asebeia*), were strictly religious—exclusion from the mysteries, deprivation of title of initiate, and such like. The curse and excommunication were most solemn—priests and priestesses, turning to the west, uttered the words of imprecation and shook their garments ([Lys.] *in Andoc.* § 51). It may be that this court was the only tribunal for cases of what we may call heterodoxy, impiety consisting in the performance of rites contrary to the traditional one and to that held by the priests; while other kinds of procedure, superadded to the religious investigation and condemnation, were adopted in accordance with ordinary criminal law in cases of impiety, which consisted of disorder and vulgar profanity. These charges were brought before the Senate of Five Hundred sitting in the Eleusinium of the city on the day after the mysteries (Andoc. *De Myst.* § 111). The penalty was death (Thuc. vi. 61 fin.) or banishment (Andoc. § 15), with confiscation of goods (*C. I. A.* i. 277), for profanation of the mysteries. The accuser, if he did not get the fifth part of the votes, suffered a kind of ἀτιμία (Andoc. § 33)—i. e. was deprived of the right to enter the temples and fined the usual 1000 drachmas. Many shrank from themselves bringing the accusation, and used to inform the Archon Basileus of the profanation they had observed, and if he thought it serious he made the accusation officially.

(4) Civil Functionaries connected with the Festival. The chief civil superintendence of the festival was intrusted to the Archon Basileus, who was assisted by four ἐπιμεληταί, elected by the people, two from the people generally and one each from the families of the Eumolpidae and Kerykes (Aristot. *ap.* Harpocr. p. 118). The Archon generally appears to have appointed an assistant (πάρεδρος). The duties of the Archon and his assistant were to sacrifice and pray for the prosperity of the people, both at Athens and Eleusis, and to have general police supervision over the whole solemnity (Lys. *c. Andoc.* § 4). The ἐπιμεληταί had also such duties as looking after the sacrifices, testing the offerings of the votaries, classifying and marshalling the different grades of initiates, managing certain moneys, etc., as may be inferred from the similar duties attaching to the officials of this name at Andania. As to the finances of the festival generally, according to *C. I. G.* 71 a, 29, three ἱεροποιοί had the administration of them.

(5) The Initiates. Originally only Athenians were admitted; legend said that Heracles and the Dioscuri (Plut. *Thes.* 33) had to be adopted prior to initiation; but later all Greek-speaking people who were not murderers were admissible to be initiated (Isocr. *Paneg.* § 42). Barbarians were excluded (Lucian, *Scyth.* 8); but it was not at all necessary to be an Athenian citizen. Women (Aristid. *Eleus.* vol. i. p. 257, Jebb), and even perhaps slaves (Theophilus, *Fr.* i., vol. ii. p. 473, Kock), were admissible. Children were admitted to the first grade only; but among the children brought to Eleusis one was picked out for special initiation, and "to appease the divinity by a more exact performance" of the ceremonies required (Porphyr. *Abst.* iv. 5). The boy or girl had to be an Athenian of high birth (Bekk. *Anecd.* 204), perhaps of the special family of the Lycomidae, Eumolpidae, or the like; and was probably initiated standing on the steps of the altar, while the rest stood afar off. The parents of the child had to make extensive offerings and pay a large fee. Originally admission was free for all initiates; but by virtue of a law passed by the orator Aristogiton, each initiate paid a fee to the public treasury (Lenormant, *Contemp. Review*, xxxviii. p. 123).

The ordinary proceeding was for the initiate to receive his first introduction as a child and afterwards the higher grades as a man. The whole cycle of the mysteries was a *trieteris*, and could be gone through in two years; even the Homeric hymn extends the whole legend beyond a year; and when the Orphic theology blended Iacchus-Zagreus into the story, the regular course of two years came to be adopted. There is a high probability that the first-year votaries at Eleusis viewed a drama representing the usual story of Demeter and Coré, while the second-year votaries were shown the whole legend of Zagreus; and as to the whole course of the actual mysteries, there is a possibility that the following arrangement was that adopted, though it must be remembered that it is little more than conjecture and given for what it is worth:

(*a*) First Spring at Agrae—the votaries mourn for Coré ravished by Hades.

(*b*) First Autumn at Eleusis—mourning with Demeter for the loss of her daughter, and exhibition of the ordinary legend.

(*c*) Second Spring at Agrae—the murder of Zagreus and his heart being given to Coré (who here seems to take the place of Semelé), and conception of Iacchus.

(*d*) Second Autumn at Eleusis—rebirth of Iacchus, who is carried in procession to Demeter at Eleusis, and there the votaries sympathize in the joy of the earth-goddess, who once more has her child and grandchild about her.

That there were different grades of initiates hardly needs proof: the μύσται were those who had received any degree of initiation, the ἐπόπται or ἔφοροι the second-year votaries. Suidas (s. v. ἐπόπται) says so explicitly. (Cf. Harpocr. s. v. ἐπωπτευκότων, and Plut. *Demetr.* 26.) There were mystic ceremonies for both these classes of initiates, one on each of the two days, 22d and 23d. While any one introduced by a mystagogue could get admission to the ceremonies of the first year, the μύησις, the ἐπόπτεια or ἐποψία could only be seen by those who got a ticket from the δᾳδοῦχος. A ticket of that kind has been discovered marked ΔΑΔ and ΕΠΟΨ, with the symbols of an ear of corn and a poppy. What those ceremonies were is the most important and interesting point in our subject, but the seal of silence which was laid on the votaries has not been broken. This secrecy was most strenuously enjoined and most rigorously enforced, as we have seen. The prosecution of Alcibiades for holding a travesty of the mysteries in his own house and Andocides's speech on the subject are well known. Aeschylus is said to have divulged the mysteries in styling Artemis a daughter of Demeter (Herod. ii. 156; Pausan. viii. 37, 6) and in other matters (Aristot. *Nic. Eth.* iii. 1, 17), and to have only barely escaped death. Diagoras of Melos (Diod. xiii. 6) was banished from Athens and a price set on his head for having divulged the mysteries. It was the prevailing belief of antiquity that he who was guilty of divulging the mysteries was sure to bring down divine vengeance on himself and those associated with him (Hor. *Carm.* iii. 2, 26).

(6) The Ceremonies in the Temple. They were performed in the temple of the two goddesses at Eleusis, a building reckoned one of the greatest masterpieces of the Periclean Age. Ictinus superintended the whole. Coroebus built the lower story, with four rows of columns which divided the interior space. On his death Metagenes took up the work and added an upper story, and Xenocles built a cupola roof with an opening (ὄπαιον)

in the middle for the light (Plut. *Pericl.* 13; Vitruv. vii. Pref. §§ 16, 17). The dimensions of the whole building were 223 feet by 179, the measurement of the cella being 175 feet by 179. The temple had no pillars in the façade till the architect Philon, in the time of Demetrius of Phalerum, built a pronaos with twelve pillars. The temple stood inside a large enclosure, which was approached by a propylaeum, there being yet another propylaeum leading to the temple. Inside this enclosure Lenormant has fixed the position of the ἀγέλαστος πέτρα, where Demeter was said to have rested in her wanderings, as the rock where the great statue of Demeter Achea, now at Cambridge, stood—i. e. on the axis of the first propylaeum close to a well, which he also identifies as Callichorum. (See the Πρακτικὰ τῆς Ἀρχαιολογικῆς Ἑταιρίας for 1883, and M. Blavette in *Bulletin de Correspondance Hellénique*, viii. [1884], pp. 254 foll.). The temple of Ictinus, though built on the site of an older and smaller one, must be distinguished from the most ancient temple which stood more to the north, occupying a platform which overlooked the well Callichorum and the ἀγέλαστος πέτρα, exactly on the spot where the Homeric hymn (273) orders it to be built. The great temple of Ictinus was called by the ancients μυστικὸς σηκός (Strab. ix. 395), and the inner portion τελεστήριον or ἀνάκτορον or μέγαρον (cf. Lobeck, *Aglaoph.* 59).

The ceremony was doubtless dramatic. "Deo and Coré," says Clement of Alexandria (*Protrept.* p. 12), "have become a mystic drama. Eleusis illustrates by the light of the torches of the Daduchus the carrying off of Coré, the wandering journeys and grief of Deo." The ceremony, then, was dramatic. Aelius Aristides (*Eleus.* i. 256) asks, "Where else do the recitals of the narratives chant forth greater marvels, or does the ceremonial (τὰ δρώμενα) involve a greater affrightment (ἔκπληξιν), or does the spectacle match more fully what the ear hears?" The drama consisted of δρώμενα and λεγόμενα, the former being much the more important, for the ancient religious worship addressed itself more to the eye than to the ear. There were hymns and chants (Pausan. ix. 27, 2), speeches and exhortations (ῥήσεις, παραγγέλματα), recitals of myths (μύθων φῆμαι), and wailings for the loss of Persephoné (Proclus on Plat. *Polit.* p. 384). There were kinds of dancing or rhythmical movements by those performing the ceremony (Lucian, *De Salt.* 15), clashing of cymbals (Vell. i. 4, 1), sudden changes from light to darkness (Dio Chrys. xii. 387), "toilsome wanderings and dangerous passages through the gloom, but the end is not yet, and then before the end all kinds of terror, shivering and quaking, sweating and amazement, when suddenly a wondrous light flashes forth to the worshipper, and pure regions and meadows receive him: there are chants, voices, and dances, solemn words and holy images; and amongst these the votary now perfected is freed at last and is released, he wanders to and fro with a crown on his head, joining in the worship and in the company of pure and holy men; and he sees the uninitiated and unpurified crowd of the living in the thick mire and mist, trampling one another down, and huddled together, abiding ever in evils through fear of death and disbelief in the good things yonder" (Themist. in Stob. *Serm.* cxx. 26). Lucian (*Catapl.* 22) represents a man having entered Hades and got into the dark asking his companion if what was represented at Eleusis was not like this. Claudian's description (*De Rapt. Proserp.* init.) is sufficiently terrible; and amidst that rhetoric Lenormant fancies he can infer that the votaries, waiting anxiously outside the building, saw the glimmer of the lighted interior through the ὀπαῖον: then was heard the noise of the preparations for the play, the doors were thrown open, and the Daduchus appeared with torches in his hands, and the statue of Demeter was seen in gorgeous vestments and brilliantly lighted up. It is more probable that the whole performance took place inside the temple. But that figures of the gods were introduced is certain, which flitted noiselessly (ἀψοφητί, Themist. *Or.* xvi. 224, ed. Dind.) across the stage; but the images were incomplete, not simple but overcharged with strange attributes.

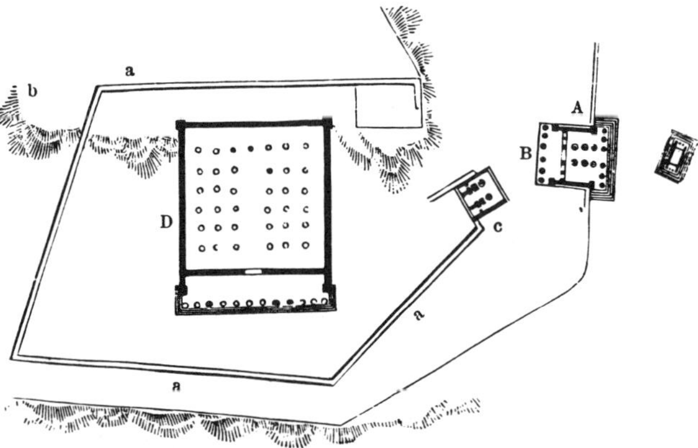

Plan of the Temple Enclosure at Eleusis.

A, outer *peribolos*; a a, inner *peribolos*; B, greater *propylaea*; C, lesser *propylaea*; D, Great Temple of the Mysteries, with portico of Philon (183 ft. × 37½ ft.), and *Telesterion*, or interior of the temple (178 ft. × 170 ft.), with eight rows of seats, partly hewn out of the rock.

they were ever in motion and represented in a dim and murky light. To be more precise, the mystic drama of Demeter and Coré was unfolded to the mystae, the first-year initiates; but the epoptae were shown a representation of what Clement calls "the mysteries of the dragon," which is the story of Zeus uniting himself with Persephoné (called Brimo: cf. *Philosophumena*, viii. p. 115, ed. Miller) in the form of a serpent, and the whole tale of Iacchus-Zagreus was probably told (Clem. Alex. *Protrept.* pp. 13–15; Tatian, *Or. ad Graecos*, 13 [9 ed. Migne]; and Lenormant, p. 426). There was shown to the epoptae a representation, symbolical probably of creation, in which we hear (Euseb. *Praep. Evang.* iii. 12) that the Hierophant used to assume the part of the Creator, the Daduchus that of the sun, the altar-priest that of the moon, and the Hierokeryx that of Hermes. Again, "the last, the most solemn, and the most wonderful act of the ἐποψία" was shown—the ear of corn cut in perfect stillness; the blade of corn symbolized, we are told, the great and perfect ray of light issuing from the Inexpressible One, whatever that means, or rather, perhaps, it was the symbol of life, the cutting down being death.

This may lead us to what is to be said in conclusion on the moral and religious import of the mysteries. If we choose to regard them in a cold, un-religious way, we can say that they were a somewhat melodramatic performance, splendid no doubt, full of what Lobeck calls fireworks (*pyrotechnia*), but a mere theatrical display. That there were connections between the mysteries and the theatre (the Hierophants are said to have borrowed costume from the dramas of Aeschylus, Athen. i. p. 22, if the reverse is not rather the case) need not surprise us; and that modern archæologists profess to find in the temple of Eleusis evidences of machinery by which the spectacle was worked (Preller in Pauly, iii. 89; Lenormant, p. 415) is only natural; for there undoubtedly was a spectacle, a religious spectacle. But anything moral or religious may be made ridiculous if one chooses to regard it from the lower plane of the intellect alone, and does not take into account the subjective condition of the moral worker or the religious worshipper. The universal voice of the great names of pagan antiquity, from the Homeric hymn down to the writers of the late Roman Empire, attest to the wonderfully soothing effect the mysteries had on the religious emotions, and what glad hopes they inspired of good fortune in the world to come. *Neque solum,* says Cicero (*De Leg.* ii. 14, 36), *cum laetitia vivendi rationem accepimus, sed etiam cum spe meliore moriendi.* For the object aimed at was rather, not that the initiate should be taught anything that would appeal merely to his intellect, but should be moved and have his higher impulses stirred. "The light of the sun is bright for the initiated alone," sing the chorus of mystae in the *Ranae* (454). Not but that there were many scenes and symbols of a somewhat coarse nature—phallic rites, ἱεροὶ γάμοι, such as those represented by the Hierophant and Hierophantis, which portrayed perhaps the unions of Zeus and Demeter, Zeus and Persephoné, and which entered into the higher worship, but which are probably grossly exaggerated by the Christian writers, who did not take into consideration their symbolical meaning. The truths, however, which these and other symbolical performances contained were known only to the Hierophant, and explained by him to those whom he thought fit to hear them. Even the ἐπόπται only knew part of the mystic secrets, γνῶναί τι τῶν ἀπορρήτων (Sopatros, *Distinct. Quaest.* p. 121). The multitude of worshippers took it all on faith, but, as Mahaffy finely remarks, "even the coarsest features were hallowed and ennobled by the spirit of the celebrants, whose reverence blinded their eyes while it lifted up their hearts."

The Eleusinian Mysteries lasted for more than five centuries after Greece became a Roman province. As late as the time of the emperor Julian they still enjoyed a considerable portion of their primeval sanctity, and were held in the highest esteem by the Neo-Platonic philosophers. The edict of Valentinian and Valens against secret worships did not extend to the Eleusinia, the prefect of Achaea, Pretextatus, having represented that the life of the Greeks would be barren and comfortless without the mysteries. The Hierophant who initiated Maximus and Eunapius in the fourth century was the last Eumolpid. Subsequently Mithraic worship was blended with the Eleusinian; but the mysteries did not finally perish till the destruction of Eleusis by Alaric in his invasion of Greece, A.D. 396.

For further discussion on the mysteries, see CABEIRIA; MYSTERIA; ORPHICA. The principal works to consult on the Eleusinia are: St. Croix, *Récherches sur les Mystères;* Creuzer, *Symbolik,* iv. 33 foll.; Lobeck, *Aglaophamus,* especially pp. 3–228; K. O. Müller, *Kleine Schriften,* ii. 242–311 (a reprint of his article "Eleusinia" in Ersch and Grüber); Petersen in Ersch and Grüber, xxviii. 219 foll., especially 252–269, in the second volume of the article "Griechenland"; id. *Der Geheime Gottesdienst;* Guigniaut, *Mémoires sur les Mystères de Ceres et de Proserpine* in the *Mémoires de l'Académie des Inscr.* xxi.; Preller in Pauly, art. "Eleusinia," and "Griechische Mythologie," i. 643–653; id. *Mythologie* (1873–75); Hermann, *Gottesdienstliche Alterthümer,* §§ 35, 55; Maury, *Religions de la Grèce,* ii. pp. 297–381; Schömann, *Griechische Alterthümer,* ii. 380–402; August Mommsen, *Heortologie der Athener,* 62–75, 222–269; Baumeister, *Denkmäler,* s. vv. "Eleusinia" and "Eleusis"; Lenormant, *Monographie de la Voie Sacrée Éleusinienne* (1864), and "The Eleusinian Mysteries" in the *Contemporary Review,* xxxvii. and xxxviii. (May, July, and September, 1880); and Sauppe, *Die Mysterieninschrift von Andania.*

Eleusis or **Eleusin** (Ἐλευσίς, Ἐλευσίν). (1) An ancient city of Boeotia, which stood, according to tradition, near Copae and the Lake Copaïs, and was, together with another ancient city, named Athenae, inundated by the waters of that lake. Stephanus of Byzantium reports that when Crates drained the waters which had overspread the plains the city of Athenae became visible (s. v. Ἀθῆναι). (2) A city of Attica, equidistant from Megara and the Piraeus, and famed for the celebration of the mysteries of Demeter. According to some writers it derived its name from a hero, whom some affirmed to be the son of Hermes but others of Ogyges (Pausan. i. 38). Its origin is certainly of the highest antiquity, as it appears to have already existed in the time of Cecrops, but we are not informed by whom, or at what period, the worship of Demeter was introduced there. Eusebius places the building of the first temple in the reign of Pandion; but, according to other authors, it is more ancient. Celeus is said to have been king of Eleusis when Demeter first arrived there. See ELEUSINIA.

At one period Eleusis was powerful enough to contend with Athens for the sovereignty of Attica. This was in the time of Eumolpus. The controversy was ended by a treaty, wherein it was stipulated that Eleusis should yield to the control of Athens, but that the sacred rites of Demeter should be celebrated at the former city. Demeter and Triptolemus were both worshipped here with peculiar solemnity, and here also was shown the Rarius Campus, where Demeter was said to have first sown corn (Pausan. i. 38). The temple of Eleusis was burned by the Persian army in the invasion of Attica (Herod. ix. 65), but was rebuilt, under the administration of Pericles, by Ictinus, the architect of the Parthenon (Plut. *Pericles*). This magnificent structure was entirely destroyed by Alaric in the year A.D. 396. Eleusis, though so considerable and important a place, was classed among the Attic demes and belonged to the tribe Hippothoöntis. The colossal statue of the Eleusinian Demeter, the work of Phidias, after having suffered many mutilations, was taken to England by Dr. Clarke and Mr. Cripps in 1801, and now stands in the vestibule of the University Library at Cambridge. The temple itself was cleared by Sir William Gell, and important excavations have been made by the Greek Archaeological Society since 1887.

Eleutheria (τὰ ἐλευθέρια). The feast of liberty; a festival which the Greeks, after the battle of Plataea (B.C. 479), instituted in honour of Zeus Eleutherius (the deliverer). It was intended not merely to be a token of their gratitude to the god, but also as a bond of union among themselves; for, in an assembly of all the Greeks, Aristides carried a decree that delegates from all the Greek States should assemble every year at Plataea for the celebration of the Eleutheria. The town itself was at the same time declared sacred and inviolable, as long as its citizens offered the annual sacrifices which were then instituted on behalf of Greece. Every fifth year these solemnities were celebrated with contests (ἀγὼν τῶν Ἐλευθερίων) in which the victors were rewarded with chaplets. The annual solemnity at Plataea, which continued to be observed down to the time of Plutarch (*Arist.* 19 and 21), was as follows: On the sixteenth of the month of Maemacterion, a procession, led by a trumpeter, who blew the signal for battle, marched at daybreak through the middle of the town. It was followed by wagons loaded with myrtle-boughs and chaplets, by a black bull, and by free youths who carried the vessels containing the libations for the dead. No slave was permitted to minister on this occasion. At the end of this procession followed the archon of Plataea, who was not allowed at any other time during his office to touch a weapon or to wear any other but white garments, now wearing a purple tunic and with a sword in his hand, and also bearing an urn, kept for this solemnity in the public archives (γραμματοφυλάκιον). When the procession came to the place where the Greeks who had fallen at Plataea were buried, the archon first washed and anointed the tombstones, and then led the bull to a pyre and sacrificed it, praying to Zeus and Hermes Chthonius, and inviting the brave men who had fallen in the defence of their country to take part in the banquet prepared for them. See Thuc. iii. 58.

Eleutheria was also the name of a festival celebrated in Samos, in honour of Eros.

Eleutherius (Ἐλευθέριος). "The Deliverer." An epithet applied to Zeus. See ELEUTHERIA.

Eleutherna (Ἐλευθέρνα). An important city of Crete on the northwestern slope of Mount Ida, and traditionally founded by the Curetes. Dio Cassius (xxxvi. 1) tells a story of how a breach was made in its towers by the use of vinegar, at the time when the city was taken by Q. Metellus Creticus. In sixteenth century MSS. the ancient ruins of the place are spoken of as enormous, but of them few vestiges now remain.

Eleuthĕro-Cilĭces. A name given to those of the Cilicians who had fled to the mountains when the Greek settlers established themselves in that country. The appellation, which means "Free Cilicians," has reference to their independent mode of life. The Greeks, however, connected a fable with this. According to them, when Myrina, queen of the Amazons, was extending her conquests over Asia Minor, the Cilicians were the only people that voluntarily surrendered to her, and hence they were allowed to retain their freedom (Diod. Sic. iii. 55). Cicero came in contact with them during his government in Cilicia and partially brought them under the Roman sway, but they soon after became as free and independent as ever (*Ad Fam.* xv. 4; *Ad Att.* v. 20).

Eleuthĕro-Lacōnes. A title conferred by Augustus on a considerable part of the Laconian nation, consisting of several maritime towns, for the zeal which the inhabitants had early testified in favour of the Romans. Enfranchisement and other privileges accompanied the title (Pausan. iii. 21).

Eleuteropŏlis (Ἐλευθερόπολις). A city of Palestine, sixteen Roman miles northeast from Ascalon, and twenty miles southwest from Jerusalem. Its earlier name was Bethogabris (Βαιτογαβρά). In the days of Eusebius and Jerome, however, it was an important and flourishing city. In modern Latin, Eleutheropolis is the name given to Freistadtl in Hungary, and to Freibourg and Freiburg.

Eleuthĕrus (Ἐλεύθερος). A river forming the boundary between Syria and Phœnicia.

Eleutho (Ἐλεύθω). A surname of Ilithyia, from her *coming* (ἐλθεῖν), when invoked, to the aid of women in labour (Pind. *Ol.* vi. 72).

Eleven, THE. See HENDEKA.

Elgin Marbles. A collection of ancient sculptures brought from Greece to England by the Earl of Elgin, in 1812, while he was British ambassador to the Porte. On the strength of a firman from the Sultan authorizing Lord Elgin to examine, measure, and remove certain stones and inscriptions from the Athenian acropolis, his agents took possession of these marbles, which are said to have cost the ambassador nearly £75,000. In 1816, they were acquired by the British Museum for £35,000, and are now the property of the British nation, though a bitter controversy has from that time to this been waged sporadically, both as to the artistic value of the statues and as to the propriety of their removal from Greece. The chief marbles formed a part of the Parthenon, and were probably designed by Phidias and executed under his direction. They are mainly statues from the pediments and metopes, together with a large portion of the frieze of the *cella.* In addition, there are also figures from the Erechtheum and from the Temple of Niké Apteros. See Ellis, *Elgin Marbles* (London, 1847); Newton, in the *Contents of the British Museum, Elgin Room* (London, 1881–82); Michaelis, *Ancient Marbles in Great Britain* (Eng. trans. by Fennell, Cambridge, 1882); and the article ATHENAE. On the Phidian theory of their origin, see an article by W W. Story in *Blackwood's Magazine* for December, 1873.

Eliăci (Ἠλειακοί). A name given to the school of philosophy established by Phaedo of Elis (Diog. Laërt. ii. 106). It was instituted after the Socratic model by Phaedo of Elis, and was continued by Plistanus, an Elian, and afterwards by Menedemus of Eretria.

Elicius. A surname of Iupiter at Rome, because he was invoked to send down lightning (Ovid, *Fast.* iii. 328; and cf. Livy, i. 20).

Elimberrum or **Climberrum.** A town of the Ausci in Aquitania (Mela, iii. 2).

Elimēa (Ἐλίμεια) or **Elimiōtis** (Ἐλιμιῶτις). A

district of Macedonia, on the frontiers of Epirus and Thessaly, originally belonging to Illyria. Its inhabitants, the Elimaei, were Epirots (Arrian, *Anab.* i. 7, § 5).

Elis (Ἦλις; Doric, Ἆλις). A district of the Peloponnesus, lying west of Arcadia. At the period of the Peloponnesian War the name of Elis was applied to the whole of that northwestern portion of the peninsula situated between the rivers Larissus and Neda which served to separate it from Achaea and Messenia. But in earlier times this tract of country was divided into several districts or principalities, each occupied by a separate clan or people, of whom the Caucones were probably the most ancient, so that Strabo affirms that, according to some authors, the whole of Elis once bore the name of Cauconia. Before the siege of Troy, the Epei, an Elean tribe, are said to have been greatly reduced by their wars with Heracles, who conquered Augeas their king, and the Pylians commanded by Nestor. They subsequently, however, acquired a great accession of strength by the influx of a large colony from Aetolia, under the conduct of Oxylus, and their numbers were further increased by a considerable detachment of the Dorians and Heraclidae. Iphitus, descended from Oxylus, and a contemporary of Lycurgus, re-established the Olympic Games, which, though instituted, as it was said, by Heracles, had been interrupted for several years (Pausan. v. 4). The Pisatae, having remained masters of Olympia from the first celebration of the festival, long disputed its possession with the Eleans, but they were finally conquered, when the temple and the presidency of the games fell into the hands of their rivals. The preponderance obtained by the latter is chiefly attributable to the assistance they derived from Sparta, in return for the aid afforded to that State in the Messenian War. From this period we may date the ascendency of Elis over all the other surrounding districts hitherto independent. It now comprised not only the country of the Epei and Caucones, which might be termed Elis Proper, but the territories of Pisa and Olympia, forming the ancient kingdom of Pelops, and the whole of Triphylia.

The troops of Elis were present in all the engagements fought against the Persians, and in the Peloponnesian War zealously adhered to the Spartan confederacy, until the conclusion of the treaty after the battle of Amphipolis, when an open rupture took place between this people and the Lacedaemonians, in consequence of protection and countenance afforded by the latter to the inhabitants of Lepraeum, who had revolted from them (Thuc. v. 31). Such was the resentment of the Eleans on this occasion that they imposed a heavy fine on the Lacedaemonians, and prohibited their taking part in the Olympic Games. They also made war upon Sparta, in conjunction with the Mantineans, Argives, and Athenians; and it was not till after the unsuccessful battle of Mantinea that this confederacy was dissolved (Thuc. v. 81). The Lacedaemonians, on the other hand, avenged those injuries by frequent incursions into the territory of Elis, the fertility of which presented an alluring prospect of booty to an invading army. They were beaten, however, at Olympia under the command of Agis (Pausan. v. 4); and again repulsed before the city of Elis, whither they had advanced under Pausanias (Diod. Sic. xiv. 17). At length the Eleans, wearied with the continual incursions to which their country was exposed, since it furnished entire subsistence to the army of the enemy, gladly sued for peace. Not long after, however, we find them again in arms, together with the Boeotians and Argives, against Sparta (Xen. *Hist. Gr.* vii. 2). At the battle of Mantinea they once more fought under the Spartan banners, jealousy of the rising ascendency obtained by the Thebans having led them to abandon their interests (id. vii. 5, 1). Pausanias writes that when Philip acquired the dominion of Greece the Eleans, who had suffered much from civil dissensions, joined the Macedonian alliance, but refused to fight against the Athenians and Thebans at Chaeronea, and on the death of Alexander they united their arms with those of the other confederates, who carried on the war of Lamia against Antipater and the other commanders of the Macedonian forces. Some years after, Aristotimus, son of Damaretus, through the assistance of Antigonus Gonatas, usurped the sovereignty of Elis; but a conspiracy having been formed against him he was slain at the altar of Zeus Soter, whither he had fled for refuge (Pausan. v. 4, 5). During the Social War the Eleans were the firmest allies of the Aetolians in the Peloponnesus; and though they were on more than one occasion basely deserted by that people, and sustained heavy losses in the field as well as from

Coins of Elis with Effigies of Zeus.

the devastation of their territory and the capture of their towns, they could not be induced to desert their cause and join the Achaean League. These events, described by Polybius, are the last in which the Eleans are mentioned as an independent people; for, though they do not appear to have taken any part in the Achaean War, they were included with the rest of the Peloponnesus in the general decree by which the whole of Greece was annexed to the Roman Empire. Elis was by far the most fertile and populous district of the Peloponnesus, and its inhabitants are described as fond of agriculture and rural pursuits (Polyb. iv. 73).

Elis was divided into three districts—Elis Proper, or "Hollow Elis" (ἡ Κοίλη Ἦλις), Pisatis, and Triphylia. The first of these occupied the northern section of the country and has already been alluded to; the second, or Pisatis, was that part of the Elean territory through which flowed the Alpheus after its junction with the Erymanthus. It derived its name from the city of Pisa; the third, or Triphylia, formed the southern division.

(2) The capital of Elis, situated on the Peneus, at the distance of 120 stadia from the sea. It was, like many other towns of Greece, at first composed of several detached villages, which, being united after the Persian War, formed one considerable city. It always, however, remained without walls, as it was deemed sacred and under the immediate protection of the god whose festival was there solemnized. Hence, in early times, according to Ephorus, those troops which were obliged to traverse this country delivered up their arms on entering it and received them again upon quitting the frontier. But this primitive state of things was not of long duration, for we subsequently find the Elean territory as little respected as any other Grecian State by the powers at war with that republic. Still the peace and tranquillity thus enjoyed for a time by the Eleans, together with the vast concourse of persons attracted by the Olympic Games, greatly contributed to the prosperity and opulence of their city. See OLYMPIA.

Elīso. See ALISO.

Elissa. See DIDO.

Ellopia (Ἐλλοπία). (1) A district in the north of Euboea, near the promontory Cenaeum, with a town of the same name. The whole island of Euboea is sometimes called Ellopia. (2) An ancient name of the district about Dodona in Epirus.

Ellotia or **Hellotia** (τὰ ἑλλώτια or ἐλλώτια). A festival with a torch-race celebrated at Corinth in honour of Athené as a goddess of fire (Athen. xv. p. 678 a, b).

A festival of the same name was celebrated in Crete in honour of Europa. The ἐλλωτίς, from which the festival derived its name, was, according to Seleucus (*ap.* Athen. l. c.), a myrtle garland twenty cubits in circumference, which was carried about in the procession at the festival of the Ellotia.

Ellychnium (ἐλλύχνιον). See LUCERNA.

Elmsley, PETER. An English classical scholar, born in 1773. He was educated at Westminster School and at Merton College, Oxford, receiving his Bachelor's degree in 1794. He took orders in 1798, but inheriting a fortune from an uncle, he decided to devote himself to literary studies and to Greek literature in particular. During a prolonged residence in Edinburgh he contributed many papers on classical topics to the *Edinburgh Review*. In 1816 he visited Italy in search of classical MSS., and spent the winter of 1818 in researches at the Laurentian Library at Florence. In the following year he did good work in deciphering some of the papyri found in Herculaneum, assisting Sir Humphry Davy. In 1823 he was made Principal of St. Alban's Hall and Camden Professor of Ancient History in the University of Oxford. He died at Oxford, March 8th, 1825.

Elmsley is best known by his critical editions of the *Alcestis*, *Andromeda*, *Bacchae*, *Electra*, *Heraclidae*, and *Medea* of Euripides; of the *Oedipus Tyrannus* and *Oedipus Coloneus* of Sophocles; and of the *Acharnians* of Aristophanes (1809). He also edited Thucydides. See *Elmsleiana Critica* (1833).

Elogium. An inscription on tombs, doors, images of ancestors, votive tablets, etc. Many of these elogia (ἐλεγεῖα) are preserved to us from the pedestals of the statues with which Augustus adorned the colonnades of the temple of Mars in the Forum (Hor. *Carm.* iv. 8, 13) and from the *hermae* in libraries. They are of some historical value, though not always representing original sources of information. For specimens, see the *Corp. Inscript. Lat.* i. pp. 277, 281, and Wilmanns pp. 622 foll.; also the *Poetae Lat. Minores* (ed. Bährens), v. 396. For the etymology of the word *elogium* see Curtius's *Kleine Schriften*, ii. 230 (Leipzig, 1880); and for discussion, Hildesheimer, *De Libro de Viris Illustribus Urbis Romae* (Berlin, 1880).

Elōné (Ἠλώνη). A town of the Perrhaebi, in Thessaly, afterwards called Limoné.

Elpēnor (Ἐλπήνωρ). One of the companions of Odysseus, who were metamorphosed by Circé into swine and afterwards back into men. Intoxicated with wine, Elpenor one day, while asleep on Circé's roof, fell and broke his neck (*Od.* x. 552).

Elpinīcé (Ἐλπινίκη). A daughter of Miltiades, married to Callias (Plut. *Per.* 10). See CIMON.

Elusātes. A people in Aquitania in the interior of the country (Caes. *B. G.* iii. 27). Their chief town was Elusa, now Euse.

Elymaei. See ELYMAÏS.

Elymāïs (Ἐλυμαΐς). A district of Susiana, which derived its name from the Elymaei or Elymi, a warlike and predatory people (Ptol. vi. 3, § 3). They were also found in the mountains of Great Media, and were probably among the most ancient inhabitants of the country north of the head of the Persian Gulf. In the Old Testament, Susiana is called Elam.

Elymi. See ELYMUS.

Elȳmus (Ἔλυμος). A natural son of Anchises and brother of Eryx; one of the Trojans who fled from Troy to Sicily. With the aid of Aeneas they built the towns of Aegesta and Elymé. The Trojans who settled in that part of Sicily called themselves Elymi, after Elymus.

Elysii Campi (ELYSIUM, Ἠλύσιον πέδιον). The abode of the blessed in another world, where they enjoyed all manner of the purest pleasures. In the Homeric mythology the Elysian Fields lay on the western margin of the earth, by the stream of Oceanus, and to them the mortal relatives of the king of the gods were transported, without tasting of death, to enjoy an immortality of bliss (*Od.* iv. 563 foll.). In the time of Hesiod, the Elysian Plains had become the Isles of the Blessed (μακάρων νῆσοι) in the Western Ocean (*Op. et D.* 171). Pindar, who has left a glowing description of Elysium, appears to reduce the number of these happy islands to one (*Ol.* ii. 129). At a later day a change of religious ideas ensued, brought about by the increase of geographical knowledge, and Elysium was moved down to the lower world as the place of reward for the good. The Vergilian conception respecting Elysium made it a region blessed with perpetual spring, clothed with continual verdure, beautiful with flowers, shaded by pleasant groves, and refreshed by never-failing fountains. Here the righteous lived in perfect felicity, communing with each other, bathed in a flood of light proceeding from their own sun, and with the sky at eve lighted up by their own constellations: *solemque suum, sua sidera norunt* (Verg. *Aen.* vi. 541). Their employments below resembled those on earth, and whatever had greatly engaged their attention in the upper world continued to be a source of innocent enjoyment in the world below (Verg. *Aen.* vi. 653). See HADES.

Elysium. See ELYSII CAMPI.

Emancipatio. The formal liberation of a son from the control (*manus*) of his father. If the son were sold three times over all the rights of his father came to an end. If then a father wished to make a son his own master (*sui iuris*), he made him over three times by *mancipatio* or a fictitious sale to a third person. The third person emancipated him the first and second time, so that he came again into the control of his father. After purchasing him a third time he either emancipated him himself, and thus became his *patronus*, or he sold him back to the father, to whom he now stood, not in the relation of a son, but *in mancipio*, so that the father could liberate him without more ado. In this case the father remained *patronus* of the son. The emancipated son did not, as in the case of adoption (see ADOPTIO), pass into the *patria potestas* of another, and therefore retained his father's family name; but he lost his right to inherit in default of a will. See MANUS.

Emansor. A soldier who exceeds his furlough.

Emathia (Ἠμαθία). A district of Macedonia, between the Haliacmon and the Axius. The poets frequently give the name of Emathia to the whole of Macedonia, and sometimes even to the neighbouring Thessaly.

Emathĭdes (Ἠμαθίδες). The nine daughters of Pierus, king of Emathia. See PIERIDES.

Emathion (Ἠμαθίων). Son of Eos and Tithonus, brother of Memnon, from whom he seized the government of the Ethiopians. He was slain by Heracles when travelling in search of the golden apples of the Hesperides. See Hes. *Theog.* 985.

Embas (ἐμβάς). This is sometimes used as a generic term for a closed boot, so called because one's foot "got into" (ἐμβαίνειν) it, and it was not merely fastened to the foot like a sandal. But at Athens ἐμβάς had a special signification; it was a cheap sort of boot first manufactured in Thrace, and in kind like low κόθορνοι (Poll. vii. 85), closed-in boots with rectangular soles, often wooden. These ἐμβάδες were worn by men (Aristoph. *Eccl.* 47) and by the poorer classes (id. *Vesp.* 1157).

Embatēa (ἐμβατεία). In Attic law this word (like the corresponding English one, *entry*) was used to denote a formal taking possession of real property. Thus, when a son entered upon the land left him by his father, he was said ἐμβατεύειν, or βαδίζειν εἰς τὰ πατρῷα, and thereupon he became *seised*, or possessed of his inheritance. If any one disturbed him in the enjoyment of this property, with an intention to dispute the title, he might maintain an action of ejectment, ἐξούλης δίκη. Before entry he could not maintain such action. Ἐξούλη is from ἐξίλλειν, an old word signifying to eject. The supposed ejectment, for which the action was brought, was a mere formality. The defendant, after the plaintiff's entry, came and turned him off, ἐξῆγεν ἐκ τῆς γῆς. This proceeding (called ἐξαγωγή) took place quietly and in the presence of witnesses; the defendant then became a wrong-doer, and the plaintiff was in a condition to try the right. See EXOULES DIKÉ.

Emblēma (ἔμβλημα), **Emblemăta**. (1) Emblemata were metal ornaments, such as masks, busts, medallions, figures of men and animals, wrought in relief and artificially attached by soldering or riveting to the interior or exterior of metal bowls, vases, cups, etc. (Cic. *in Verr.* iv. 22). Such ornaments were sometimes made of gold and silver, and had an artistic and pecuniary value even when detached from the objects to which they belonged. Thus, the plunderer Verres took especial care to wrench off emblemata from vases and cups. Emblemata must be distinguished from metal ornaments in relief (such as those produced in repoussé), which formed an integral part of the vase itself: the essence of the emblema was that it could be detached, if necessary, from the vase which it ornamented. Many of the metal masks, figures, dishes, etc., in modern museums are doubtless emblemata which have been broken off from vases.

Crustae were metal vase-ornaments similar to emblemata. The *crustae* were made by artisans called *crustarii*.

(2) The word *emblema* is also used to signify inlaid work (Cic. *Brut.* 79). This usage is, however, rare; and as a general rule when the words *emblema, emblemata* occur in the ancient authors and in modern archæological treatises, the metal ornaments described above are designated. See CAELATURA.

Embolĭma (Ἐμβόλιμα). A city of the Paropamisadae in Northern India, near the fortress of Aornos (Q. Curt. viii. 12, § 1).

Embolium (ἐμβόλιον). An interlude recited or sang between the acts of a play by an actress, hence styled *emboliaria* (Plin. *H. N.* vii. 49).

Embŏlum (ἔμβολον). The beak of a ship. See NAVIS; ROSTRUM.

Emerĭta Augusta. A town of Lusitania, below Norba Caesarea, on the northern bank of the Anas (Guadiana). It is now Merida.

Emerĭti. Roman soldiers who were discharged from military duty (Val. Max. vi. 1, 10; Ovid, *Trist.* iv. 8, 21), having served the full time required by law—viz., twenty years for the legionaries and sixteen for the praetorians (Tac. *Ann.* i. 78; Dio. Cass. lv. 23).

Emĕsa or **Emissa** (Ἔμισσα). A city of Syria on the east bank of the Orontes, the native city of Iulia Domna, Elagabalus (q. v.), and of Alexander Severus. It was the scene of the decisive battle between Aurelian and Zenobia (A.D. 273).

Emetics. See DIAETETICA.

Emissarium (ὑπόνομος). The name given to an artificial channel by which an outlet is formed to carry off any stagnant body of water (Cic. *Ad Fam.* xvi. 18). In Greece, in the early times of the Minyae of Orchomenus, we find the natural channels (*katavóthra*, as they are now called) which carry off the waters of the Boeotian Cephissus through Lake Copais to the sea supplemented by two artificial emissaria or tunnels. The longer of the two, connecting the lake with the lower course of the Cephissus, is nearly four miles in length, according to Forchhammer, and with about twenty perpendicular shafts sunk into it, some of which are from 100 to 150 feet in depth. The second tunnel, much shorter, unites the lakes Copaïs and Hylica, running under the Acraephian Plain at no great depth, and is likewise provided with shafts. Both tunnels and shafts are now choked up, but can still be traced. The natural *katavóthra* being insufficient to carry off the waters of the Cephissus, much of what was once fertile alluvial land is now turned to a swamp and awaits the efforts of modern enterprise. An abortive attempt to clear out these tunnels was made by an engineer named Crates under the orders of Alexander the Great (Strab. ix. p. 407), and it was announced in 1888 that the reclamation of Lake Copaïs was again to be attempted.

Herodotus describes with marked interest the tunnel of Eupalinus at Samos, by which a supply of fresh water was introduced into the city, and gives it the first place among the "three greatest works of the Greeks," the others being the mole in the harbour of Samos and the Heraeum or temple of Herê (iii. 60). These works unquestionably date from the tyranny of Polycrates, the most flourishing period of Samos, which ended about B.C. 522.

In Italy the Etruscans were the first great masters in the art of tunnelling, and the Romans learned it from them. The Cloaca Maxima itself is quite as much an emissary as a sewer, draining the Forum and the Velabrum, which previously were swamps. (See CLOACA.) But the greatest Roman emissarium is that of Lake Fucinus. Iulius Caesar is said to have first conceived the idea of this stupendous undertaking (Suet. *Iul.* 44), which was carried into effect by the emperor Claudius (Tac. *Ann.* xii. 57). The length of the emissary, which lies nearly in a direct line from the lake to the river Liris (Garigliano), is 15,600 English feet, or three miles all but 80 yards. The number of workmen employed was 30,000, and the time occupied in the work eleven years (Suet. *Claud.* 20). For more than a mile the tunnel is carried under a mountain, of which the highest part is 1000 feet above the level of the lake, and through a stratum of rocky formation so hard that every inch required to be worked by the chisel. The remaining portion runs through a softer soil, not much below the level of the earth, and is vaulted with brick. Perpendicular shafts (*putei*) are sunk at various distances into the tunnel, and a number of lateral openings (*cuniculi*), some of which separate themselves into two branches, one above the other, are likewise directed into it, the lowest at an elevation of five feet from the bottom. Through these the materials excavated were carried out.

Emissarium.

The immediate mouth of the tunnel was at some distance from the margin of the lake. The upper end of the tunnel itself consists of a splendid archway of the Doric order, nineteen feet high and nine wide, formed out of large blocks of stone, resembling in construction the works of the Claudian aqueduct. The mouth through which the waters discharged themselves into the Liris was more simple and is represented in the preceding illustration.

The modern work of Prince Torlonia (1862–75) is an extension and enlargement of the tunnel of Claudius.

Emmelīa (ἐμμέλεια). The serious and majestic dance of the chorus in the Greek tragedy. See CHORUS; TRAGOEDIA.

Emmenĭdae (Ἐμμενίδαι). A noble family of Agrigentum claiming descent from Polynices (q. v.). Of this family was Aenesidamus, whose sons, Theron and Xenocrates, are celebrated by Pindar as victors in the games.

Emmēnoi Dikai (ἔμμηνοι δίκαι). A name given in Attic law to those suits that were not allowed to be pending for more than a month. Most of these were suits respecting commerce or mines, in which delay would be especially injurious.

Emōdi Montes (τὰ Ἠμωδὰ ὄρη). Part of a chain of mountains in Asia. That part of the chain which Alexander crossed in order to invade Bactriana was called Paropamisus; the more easterly continuation of the range was termed Emodi Montes; and its still farther continuation, even to the Eastern Ocean, was styled Imaüs. See IMAÜS.

Empedŏcles (Ἐμπεδοκλῆς). A native of Agrigentum in Sicily, who flourished about B.C. 450. He was distinguished not only as a philosopher, but also for his knowledge of natural history and medicine, and as a poet and statesman. After the death of his father Meto, who was a wealthy citizen of Agrigentum, he acquired great weight among his fellow-citizens by espousing the popular party and favouring democratic measures.

His consequence in the State became at length so great that he ventured to assume several of the distinctions of royalty, particularly a purple robe, a golden girdle, a Delphic crown, and a train of attendants. The skill which he possessed in medicine and natural philosophy enabled him to perform many wonders, which he passed upon the superstitious and credulous multitude for miracles. He pretended to drive away noxious winds from his country and thereby put a stop to epidemic diseases. He is said to have checked, by the power of music, the madness of a young man who was threatening his enemy with instant death; to have restored a woman to life who had lain breathless thirty days; and to have done many other things, equally astonishing, after the manner of Pythagoras. On account of all this he was an object of universal admiration. Besides medical skill Empedocles possessed poetical talents. The fragments of his verses are scattered throughout the ancient writers; and Fabricius is of opinion that he was the real author of those ancient fragments which bear the name of the "Golden Verses of Pythagoras," and may be found printed at the end of Göttling's edition of Hesiod. His principal works were a didactic poem on Nature (Περὶ Φύσεως), and another entitled Καθαρμοί, which seems to have recommended virtuous conduct as a means of averting disease. Gorgias of Leontini, the well-known orator, known as "the Nihilist," was his pupil, whence it may seem reasonable to infer that Empedocles was no inconsiderable master of the art of eloquence. According to the common account he threw himself into the burning crater of Aetna, in order that the manner of his death might not be known, and that he might afterwards pass for a god; but the secret was discovered by means of one of his brazen sandals, which was thrown out from the mountain in a subsequent eruption of the volcano. This story is rejected, however, as fictitious by Strabo and other writers. According to Aristotle he died at sixty years of age.

His views in philosophy are variously given. By some he is called a Pythagorean, in consequence of a resemblance of doctrine in a few unessential points. But the principles of his theory evidently show that he belongs to the Eleatic School. Empedocles taught that originally All was one, a God eternal and at rest; a sphere and a mixture (σφαῖρος, μίγμα), without a vacuum, in which the elements of things were held together in undistinguishable confusion by love (φιλία), the primal force which unites the like to like. In a portion of this whole, however, or, as he expresses it, in the members of the Deity, strife (νεῖκος), the force which binds like to unlike, prevailed, and gave the elements a tendency to separate themselves, whereby the first became perceptible as such, although the separation was not so complete but that each contained portions of the others. Hence arose the multiplicity of things. By the vivifying counteraction of love, organic life was produced, not, however, so perfect and so full of design as it now appears; but, at first, single limbs, then irregular combinations, till ultimately they received their present adjustments and perfection. But, as the forces of love and hate are constantly acting upon each other for generation or destruction, the present condition of things cannot persist forever, and the world which, properly, is not the All, but only the ordered part of it, will again be reduced to a chaotic unity, out of which a new system will be formed, and so on forever. There is no real destruction of anything, but only a change of combinations.

Of the elements (which he seems to have been the first to describe as four distinct species of matter), fire, as the rarest and most powerful, he held to be the chief, and, consequently, the soul of all sentient and intellectual beings which issue from the central fire, or soul of the world. The soul migrates through animal and vegetable bodies in atonement for some guilt committed in its unembodied state when it is a daemon, of which he supposed that an infinite number existed. The seat of a daemon, when in a human body, is the blood. Closely connected with this view of the objects of knowledge was his theory of human knowledge. In the impure separation of the elements it is only the predominant one that the senses can apprehend; and, consequently, though man can know all the elements of the whole singly, he is unable to see them in their perfect unity, wherein consists their truth. Empedocles therefore rejects the testimony of the senses, and maintains that pure intellect alone can arrive at a knowledge of the truth. This is the attribute of the Deity, for man cannot overlook the work of love in all its extent; and the true unity is open only to itself. Hence he was led to distinguish between the world as presented to our senses (*κόσμος αἰσθητός*) and its type, the intellectual world (*κόσμος νοητός*). Lucretius, who praises Empedocles highly even while criticising his philosophy, appears to have taken him as a model. (Cf. Lucret. i. 716 foll.) The fragments of Empedocles have been published, with a commentary, by Sturz (1805); by Peyron (1810); Karsten (1838); Stein (1852); and Bergk (2d ed. Leipzig, 1866). Good monographs are those by Lommatsch (1830); Reynaud (1848); Hollenberg, *Empedoclea* (Berlin, 1853); Gladisch, *Empedocles und die Aegypter* (Leipzig, 1858); and Winnefeld, *Die Philosophie des Empedocles* (Rastatt, 1862).

Emperor. See Imperator.

Emphrūri (*ἔμφρουροι*). From *φρουρά*, the name given to the body of Spartan citizens and Perioeci during the period in which they were liable to military service (Xen. *Rep. Lac.* 5, § 7). This period lasted to the fortieth year from manhood (*ἀφ' ἥβης*)—that is to say, to the sixtieth year from birth; and during this time a man could not go out of the country without permission from the authorities.

The only exemption was for the father of three sons, who became *ἄφρουρος* (Aelian, *V. H.* vi. 6). The word *φρουρά*, as Schömann observes, is characteristic of Spartan modes of thought; all Laconia was a camp, the Spartiatae a garrison.

Emphyteusis (*ἐμφύτευσις*, lit. "an implanting"). A perpetual and "real" right in agricultural land which belongs to another person, entitling the *emphyteuta* to cultivate it practically as though it were his own, on condition of paying a fixed rent (*pensio, canon*) to the *dominus*, or owner, somewhat after the nature of the English "fee-farm" rent ("feodifirma," *Magna Carta*, c. 37).

The origin of emphyteusis is traceable to the *agri vectigales*, first distinctly mentioned about the time of Hadrian—large tracts of grazing land in

Italy, belonging to the State, religious corporations (e. g. the Vestal Virgins), or the smaller *civitates* and *municipia*, but held and enjoyed by private persons subject to the payment of a perpetual rent (*vectigal*), or let out upon very long leases. The rights of such occupiers, at first purely contractual, acquired a "real" character, analogous to that of genuine ownership, from the praetor, who protected their possession (*Dig.* 2, 8, 15, 1) by interdicts and by a *utilis actio in rem* (*actio vectigalis*), availing even against the lessor when non-payment of rent was not alleged (*Dig.* vi. 3, 1, 2). An addition had thus been made to the *iura in re aliena* of Roman law: the right was alienable both *inter vivos* and by will, and descended to the tenant's heirs on his intestacy, though at that time it had not acquired a specific name.

Empirĭci. See MEDICINA.

Emplecton (ἔμπλεκτον). See MURUS.

Emporiae (Ἐμπορίαι) or **Emporĭum** (Ἐμπόριον, Ἐμπορεῖον). The modern Ampurias; a town of the Indigetes in Hispania Tarraconensis, near the Pyrenees, situated on the river Clodianus, founded by the Phocaeans from Massilia (Livy, xxi. 60).

Emporium (τὸ ἐμπόριον). A place for wholesale trade in commodities carried by sea. The name is sometimes applied to a seaport town, but it properly signifies only a particular place in such a town. The word is derived from ἔμπορος, which signifies in Homer a person who sails as a passenger in a ship belonging to another person (*Od.* ii. 319, xxiv. 300); but in later writers it denotes the merchant who carries on commerce with foreign countries, and differs from κάπηλος, the retail dealer, who purchases his goods from the ἔμπορος and retails them in the market-place (Plat. *Protag.* 313 C). The emporium at Athens was under the inspection of certain officers, who were elected annually (ἐπιμεληταὶ τοῦ ἐμπορίου). See EPIMELETAE.

Empti et Vendĭti Actio. The Roman seller had an *actio venditi*, and the buyer an *actio empti*, to recover damages for breach of the duties imposed by the contract of sale upon the other party. Both are *actiones directae*, and belong to the class of remedies known as *bonae fidei iudicia* (Gaius, iv. 62; *Inst.* iv. 6, 28).

Emptio. See BONORUM EMPTIO.

Emptio et Venditio. In Roman law the contract of buying and selling consists in the buyer agreeing to give a certain sum of money to the seller, and the seller agreeing to give to the buyer some certain thing for his money. After the agreement is made the buyer is bound to pay his money, even if the thing which is the object of purchase should be accidentally destroyed before it is delivered; and the seller must deliver the thing with all its intermediate increase. The seller must also guarantee a good title to the purchase (see EVICTIO), and he must also guarantee that the thing has no concealed defects, and that it has all the good qualities which he (the seller) attributes to it. It was with a view to check frauds in sales, and especially in the sales of slaves, that the seller was obliged, by the edict of the curule aediles (see EDICTUM), to inform the buyer of the defects of any slave offered for sale: *Qui mancipia vendunt, certiores faciant emtores quod morbi vitiique,* etc. In reference to this part of the law, in addition to the usual action arising from the contract, the buyer had against the seller, according to the circumstances, an *actio ex stipulatu, redhibitoria,* and *quanti minoris.* Horace, in the beginning of the second epistle of the second book, alludes to the precautions to be taken by the buyer and the seller of a slave.

Empūsa (Ἔμπουσα). A monstrous spectre, which was believed by the Greeks to devour human beings. It was said to be sent by Hecaté and to assume various shapes, being sometimes known as Ὀνοκώλη, Ὀνοσκελίς, "Donkey-footed." (See Aristoph. *Ran.* 293; *Eccl.* 1056). By some it was identified with Hecaté herself. See LAMIAE; MORMOLYCEA.

Enarephŏrus (Ἐναρήφορος). Son of Hippocoön. He was a passionate admirer of Helen when she was still very young, so that Tyndareus intrusted her to the care of Theseus. See HELENA.

Encarpa (ἔγκαρπα). Festoons of fruit and flowers, employed as a decorative ornament in sculpture or painting (Vitruv. iv. 1, 7), as shown by the example, from a Roman sepulchral monument.

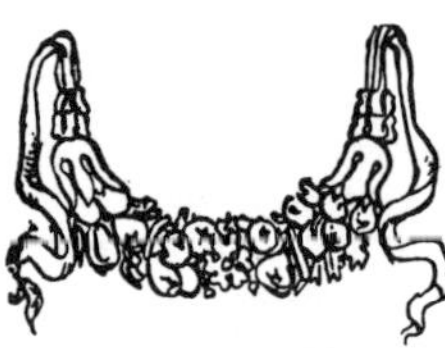

Encarpa. (Rich.)

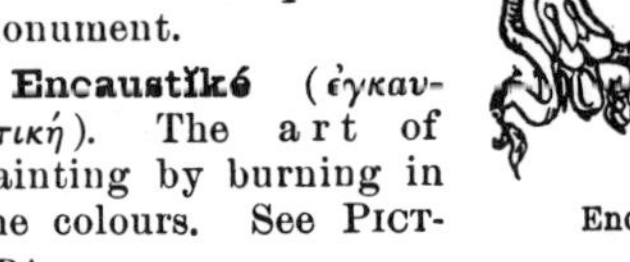

Encaustĭké (ἐγκαυστική). The art of painting by burning in the colours. See PICTURA.

Encelădus (Ἐγκέλαδος). Son of Tartarus and Gaea, and one of the hundred-armed giants who made war upon the gods. He was killed by Zeus, who buried him under Mount Aetna. See GIGANTES.

Encombōma (ἐγκόμβωμα). An article of Greek attire—viz. a sort of apron tied round the body in a knot (whence the name arose), and worn by slaves to keep the tunic clean (Longus, ii. 33), by young girls (Varr. *ap.* Non. s. v. p. 542), and also on the comic stage (Iul. Pollux, iv. 18). Both of these latter uses are exemplified by the annexed figure of a young woman playing on the double pipes, from a marble bas-relief representing a scene from some play.

Encomboma. (Rich.)

Encomion (ἐγκώμιον). Originally the song sung by the chorus at the κῶμος, or festal procession, held at the great national games in honour of the victor, either on the day of his victory or on its anniversary. The word came afterwards to denote any song written in celebration of distinguished persons, and in later times any spoken or written panegyric whatever.

Endeïs (Ἐνδηΐς). Daughter of Chiron and the Naiad Chariclo, wife of Aeacus, mother of Peleus and Telamon (Pind. *Nem.* v. 21).

Endeixis (ἔνδειξις). A term in Athenian jurisprudence, denoting a prosecution in notorious cases—as, for instance, against the Prytanes, if they refused to put a question to the vote in the great assembly. It was especially employed against persons who, although lying under *atimia*, presumed to claim a share in civic rights, as (particularly) by instituting prosecutions, or appearing, speaking, and voting in the assembly. See APAGOGÉ.

Endoeus (Ἔνδοιος). An Athenian sculptor who flourished about the year B.C. 560, though tradition made him the student of Daedalus and to have fled with him from Crete. A statue of Athené by him was removed by Augustus Caesar from Tegea to Rome (Pausan. i. 26, § 5).

Endrŏmis (ἐνδρομίς). (1) A boot of leather or felt, rising as far as the calf or above it and fitting close to the foot. In front it was open and fastened with straps. It was specially adapted for journeys or hunting, and consequently appears often in representations of Artemis and of the Erinyes. Runners in races, too, often wore it (Sidon. Apollin. *Carm.* ii. 400). (2) In Roman times *endromis* was used for a thick woollen rug (Tertull. *Pall.* 4), sometimes in the palaestra thrown over the body after violent exercise (Juv. vi. 246), but also used by the humbler classes as a protection against cold and rain (Mart. iv. 19, xiv. 126; cf. Juv. iii. 102).

Roman Endromis. (Rich.)

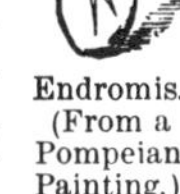
Endromis. (From a Pompeian Painting.)

Endymion (Ἐνδυμίων). In Greek mythology, the beautiful son of Aëthlius (or, according to another story, of Zeus) and Calycé, daughter of Aeolus, king of Elis, father of Epeus, Aetolus, and Paeon, the first of whom won the government of the country by conquering in a race which his father had set on foot. He was loved by Selené, the moon-goddess, by whom he had fifty daughters. They were supposed to symbolize the fifty lunar months which intervened between the Olympic Games. His grave was at Olympia. Another story made him a shepherd or hunter on Mount Latmos in Caria. Zeus bestowed on him eternal youth and eternal life in the form of unbroken slumber. Selené descended every night from heaven to visit and embrace the beautiful sleeper in his grotto. The usual story, however, makes Selené to have thrown him into a sleep so that she might kiss and caress him without his knowledge. A beautiful statue in the British Museum represents Endymion, and the legend inspired Keats to write one of the most exquisite poems in English literature.

Enechȳra (ἐνέχυρα). A word denoting the goods, usually movables, handed over to a creditor as security—as, for example, bronze, slaves, horses, etc. It was forbidden to pledge weapons and agricultural implements (Aristoph. *Plut.* 450; Diod. i.79), or slaves already mortgaged to a creditor. If the money advanced was not paid back by the time specified, the security passed into the possession of the creditor (Demosth. *c. Aphob.* ii. p. 841, § 18).

The right of taking property in pledge is stipulated in some inscriptions for breach of contract (*C. I. A.* ii. Nos. 565, 11; 600, 36). No seizure of this sort could take place during several of the religious festivals of the Athenians, such as the Dionysia, the Lenaea, the Thargelia, etc. (*Att. Process*, ed. Lipsius, p. 338, n. 393).

Engȳé (ἐγγύη). See PRAES.

Engyēsis (ἐγγύησις). See MATRIMONIUM.

Engȳum (Ἔγγυον). A town in the interior of Sicily, possessing a celebrated temple of the great mother of the gods (Diod. Sic. iv. 79; Cic. *Verr.* iv. 44; v. 72).

Enīpeus (Ἐνιπεύς). (1) A river in Thessaly, rising in Mount Othrys, receiving the Apidanus, near Pharsalus, and flowing into the Peneus (Ovid, *Met.* i. 579). Poseidon assumed the form of the god of this river in order to obtain possession of Tyro, who was in love with Enipeus. She became by Poseidon the mother of Pelias and Neleus. (2) A small river in Pisatis (Elis) flowing into the Alpheus.

Enna (Ἔννα) or **Henna**. An ancient town of the Siculi in Sicily, on the road from Catana to Agrigentum, said to be the centre of the island (ὀμφαλὸς Σικελίας). It was surrounded by fertile plains, which bore large crops of wheat; it was one of the chief seats of the worship of Demeter; and, according to later tradition, it was in a flowery meadow near this place that Pluto carried off Persephoné.

Ennaetēris (ἐνναετηρίς). See CALENDARIUM.

Ennăta (ἔννατα). See FUNUS.

Ennea Hodoi (Ἐννέα Ὁδοί). A spot in Thrace, near which the city of Amphipolis was founded. It appears to have derived its name, which means "the Nine Ways," from the number of roads which met here from different parts of Thrace and Macedon. It was here, according to Herodotus (vii. 114), that Xerxes and his army crossed the Strymon on bridges, after having offered a sacrifice of white horses to that river and buried alive nine youths and nine maidens.

Ennius. (1) QUINTUS, the "father of Roman poetry," was born at Rudiae in Calabria, B.C. 239. He served in the Second Punic War and held the post of centurion in Sardinia, whence he was brought to Rome by Cato, B.C. 204. We have no ground for attributing to Cato any appreciation of Ennius's poetical gifts; he was no doubt attracted by his vigour and practical capacity. Established at Rome, Ennius gained a livelihood by giving instruction in the Greek language and by translating Greek plays for the Roman stage. His talents soon brought him recognition. Among those who honoured him with their friendship was the great Africanus, beside whose tomb the poet's bust is said to have been placed. In B.C. 189, he accompanied the consul M. Fulvius Nobilior into his province of Aetolia, expressly to record his exploits. In grateful recollection of this service the son of Fulvius in B.C. 184, with the approval of the people, assigned him a lot among the *triumviri coloniae deducendae*, thus constituting him a Roman citizen. To this he alludes in the last book of his *Annales* with justifiable pride, *Nos sumu' Romani, qui fuimus ante Rudini.* His honours did not, however, bring him wealth. Cicero relates that his old age was passed in poverty, but he did not allow this to cloud his genial temper. He is said to have keenly enjoyed the pleasures of convivial

Supposed Bust of Ennius. (Tomb of the Scipios.)

intercourse, and died of an attack of the gout at the age of seventy (B.C. 169).

Ennius was a remarkably prolific writer, and left untouched few departments of poetical composition. He probably did not commence his literary career till middle life, and he certainly continued it till the time of his death (Cic. *Brut.* 78). In the absence of certain data for determining the chronological order of his writings, it will be best to enumerate them in the order of their importance. His chief work was the *Annales*, an epic chronicle of Roman history and legend from the time of Aeneas to his own day, in eighteen books, written in hexameter verse. The first twelve books formed a connected poem, and may have been published together B.C. 172 (cf. Aul. Gell. xvii. 21, 43), though Teuffel thinks the whole work was issued in successive parts of three books each. Of this renowned work, so justly celebrated in antiquity, which gained for its author the title of "the Roman Homer," sufficient fragments still remain to enable us to appreciate the qualities of his genius, and to deplore the loss of historical and literary material which it contained. The first book seems to have been the most poetical, and is naturally the most often quoted. The longest passages we possess are the Dream of Hia and the Auspices of Romulus and Remus, about ten lines each. The second and third books continued the regal period to its close, but are almost entirely lost to us. In all these the poet made a free use of supernatural machinery. The fourth, fifth, and sixth books began the *Annales* proper and carried the history of the Republic down to the conquest of Italy and the war with Pyrrhus; of these we possess a few short but striking fragments. In the third triad the Punic Wars were described—the first briefly, as having been already treated by Naevius (for whose rude Saturnian verse Ennius shows much contempt); the second, in which he himself had been an actor, at greater length and not without mythological embellishment. The thirteenth book began with a fresh exordium, as also did the sixteenth, which headed the closing series and brought the history down to B.C. 181 at least, if not somewhat later. The poem gained immediate popularity. It is recorded that large crowds attended its public recitation, and Vergil is said to have "introduced many lines into the *Aeneid* with the view of pleasing a people devoted to Ennius" (*populus Ennianus*). Its high estimation continued far into the times of the Empire, as we know from abundant evidence. It is not until Macrobius that we find it falling into neglect.

Next in importance to the *Annales* come the tragedies. These were free imitations of Greek dramas, generally those of Euripides, though a few recall by their titles the works of Aeschylus and Sophocles. The list is thus given by Ribbeck: *Achilles*, *Achilles* (from Aristarchus), *Aiax*, *Alcumena*, *Alexander*, *Andromaché Aechmalotis*, *Andromeda*, *Athamas*, *Cresphontes*, *Erechtheus*, *Eumenides*, *Hectoris Lutra* (or *Lustra*), *Hecuba*, *Iphigenia*, *Medea Atheniensis*, *Medea Exul*, *Menalippa*, *Nemea*, *Phoenix*, *Telamo*, *Telephus*, *Thyestes*. Their composition extended over the whole period of his literary life, B.C. 204–169, in which latter year the *Thyestes* was written. It has been doubted whether Ennius used the chorus. If not, such a play as the *Eumenides*, where the chorus is the chief character, would have had to be entirely recast; and, besides, the criticisms of the *Ars Poetica* presuppose a Roman tragic chorus. The reservation of the orchestra for the senators' seats would, of course, make choral evolutions impossible; but with this exception the plays of Ennius were closely modelled on their Greek originals. The magniloquence of their style and their moral grandeur made them special favourites with the public. Cicero gives them high praise, and it is to him that we are indebted for the greater part of the scanty fragments that remain. A *praetexta*, entitled *Sabinae* (Rape of the Sabine Women), has been attributed to Ennius by Vahlen from a passage of Iulius Victor, and there is some ground for conjecturing that the *Ambracia* was a drama of the same class, celebrating the deeds of Fulvius.

There also remain, besides the titles, some insignificant traces of two comedies by him—*Cupuncula* and *Pancratiastes*. But his bent of mind was unsuited for comedy, and he is mentioned by Volcacius Sedigitus only *antiquitatis causa!*

Ennius was addicted to philosophical speculations. His convictions oscillated between the mystic doctrines of Pythagoras and the scepticism of Euhemerus. Both found expression in his works. In the *Annales* he mentioned that the soul of Homer migrated into his own. In the *Epicharmus*, a distant precursor of the *De Rerum Natura*, written in trochaic tetrameters, he explained the tenets of Pythagoreanism. In the *Euhemerus* (erroneously supposed by some to have been a prose work) he adopted the mythologic theory of that superficial writer. It is probable that both these works formed part of the four (or six) books of *Saturae*—i. e. miscellaneous poems in various metres. To these, also, belonged the *Sota*, mentioned by Varro; the *Protrepticus*, or "Art of Life"; the *Hedyphagetica*, a treatise on gastronomics, based on that of Archestratus of Gela; and a few epigrams, the most celebrated of which were the epitaphs on Africanus and on himself.

Ennius was filled with a proud and noble self-consciousness. He entered Rome (1) as a missionary of culture and free-thought; and (2) as a consecrator of ancient tradition. He gave to Latin literature an impulse it never quite lost. In nearly every field he led the van. To him, more than to any one, it owes its predominant tone of sober directness and moral strength. In him Greek culture, grafted on an Oscan or Messapian stock, combined with Roman patriotism to form for the first time that special intellectual type, enthusiastic but disciplined, imitative yet independent, Hellenic in source but in development intensely national, which we can trace all through the subsequent course of Roman letters, and most conspicuously in their best and most illustrious representatives. In formal polish he was no doubt deficient; yet he is often imitated by later writers, and by none with happier effect than Vergil.

BIBLIOGRAPHY.—The earliest edition of his fragments was in the *Fragm. Poët. Vet. Lat. a Rob. Stephano Congesta*, etc. (Henr. Stephanus, Paris, 1564). Far more complete was the edition of Hieronymus Columna (Naples, 1590), reprinted with the emendations and commentaries of M. A. Debrius and G. I. Voss by F. Hesselius of Rotterdam (Amsterdam, 1707).

The best modern edition of the whole of Ennius is that of J. Vahlen (Leipzig, 1854). He is also included in Wordsworth's *Fragments and Specimens of Early Latin* (Oxford, 1874), and in L. Müller's

Enn. Carm. Reliquiae, accedunt Cn. Naevi Belli Poenici quae supersunt (St. Petersburg, 1885).

In the year 1595, Paulus Merula published at Leyden an edition of the *Annales*, which, among other alterations, included additional fragments said to come from a MS. treatise *De Continentia Vett. Poetarum ad Traianum Principem*, by L. Calpurnius Piso. This MS. has never appeared, and its very existence is suspected. Merula's edition was reprinted with revisions by E. Spangenberg (Leipzig, 1825). Cf. Hoch, *De Enn. Ann. Fr. a Paulo Merula Auctis* (Bonn, 1839), and J. Lawicki, *De Fraude P. Merulae* (Bonn, 1852). Books VII.-IX. (Punic Wars) have been treated by T. Hug, *Dissertatio Inaug.* (Bonn, 1852); Book I. by H. Ilberg (Bonn, 1852).

The tragic fragments by M. A. Debrius, in his *Syntagma Tragoediae Latinae I.* (Antwerp, 1593), reprinted at Paris in 1607 and 1619; also in the *Collectanea Vett. Tragg.* of P. Scriverius (Leyden, 1620). The fragment of the *Medea*, including additions to those given by Hessel and Merula, with a dissertation on Roman tragedy, by H. Planck (Göttingen, 1807). Also in *Analecta Crit. Poesis Rom. Sen. Relig. Illustrantia*, by F. Osann (Berlin, 1816). A critical edition of his dramatic fragments, published by F. H. Bothe, in *Poet. Scen. Lat.* (Halberstadt, 1821–1823; Leipzig, 1840). Also in Ribbeck's *Scaenicae Rom. Poësis Fragmenta*, 2 vols. (Leipzig, 1852–55).

Other Ennian fragments are given in *Enn. Carm.* ed. P. Burmann; in the *Anthol. Vett. Lat. Epigr. et Poem.* (Amsterdam, 1759). Of this an enlarged edition was published by H. Meyer (Leipzig, 1835). The *Hedyphagetica* fragments were collected by J. C. Wernsdorf in the *Poetae Lat. Minores*, vols. i.–v. part i. (Altenburg, 1780–88); vol. v. 2, 3–5 (Helmstadt, 1791–99). The ancient authorities for the poet's life and writings are given by Hessel, Spangenberg, and Teuffel (*Rom. Lit.* vol. i.; Eng. edit. London, 1891). Special discussions in Vahlen, *Die Annalen des Ennius* (Berlin, 1886); H. Jordan, *Quaest. Enn.* (Königsberg, 1885). For general criticisms of his style and genius, see Patin, *Études sur la Poésie Latine*, vol. ii. (Paris, 1869); Sellar, *R. Poets of Republic*, vol. i. (Oxford, 1881).

(2) A grammarian of whose personality nothing is known, but who is mentioned by Suetonius as being probably the author of a work on letters, syllables, and metres, usually ascribed to the poet Ennius (Suet. *Gram.* 1). To him is perhaps to be credited the introduction of shorthand writing at Rome. See W. Deecke in the *Rhein. Museum*, xxxvi. 577; and the article NOTAE.

Ennodius, MAGNUS FELIX. A Latin rhetorician and poet. He was born about A.D. 473 in the south of Gaul, and died in 521 as bishop of Pavia. Among other works, he wrote between 504 and 508 an extremely fulsome panegyric on Theodoric the Great and a biography of Epiphanius, his predecessor in the see. Both these writings have a value for the historian. Besides these we have a collection of twenty-eight model speeches (*Dictiones*), some of which were really delivered; nine books of letters (297 in number) and two of poems, sacred and secular. The first book of poems contains longer, the second shorter and occasional pieces. Both show a certain command of form, and treat of journeys, marriages, etc. The panegyric on Theodoric has been translated into German by Fertig in his work *Ennodius und seine Zeit* (vols. i. and ii. Passau, 1855; vol. iii. Landshut, 1858). A good edition of Ennodius is that of Vogel (Berlin, 1885), after Hartel (Vienna, 1882).

Enoikiou Diké (ἐνοικίου δίκη). An action brought to recover the rents withheld from the owner during the period of his being kept out of possession. If the property recovered were not a house, but land (in the more confined sense of the word), the action for the rents and profits was called καρποῦ δίκη.

Enomotia (ἐνωμοτία). A subordinate division of the λόχος in the Spartan army. See LOCHOS; MORA.

Ensigns. See SIGNUM; VEXILLUM.

Ensis. See GLADIUS.

Entablature. See INTABULAMENTUM.

Entăsis (ἔντασις), called by Vitruvius *adiectio*. An architectural term applied to the swelling in a column from the lower end to a certain point, after which a diminution takes place to the *hypotrachelium*, which forms part of the capital. In some ancient columns, as at Assos, the entasis is much exaggerated; in others, as at Corinth, it is entirely absent.

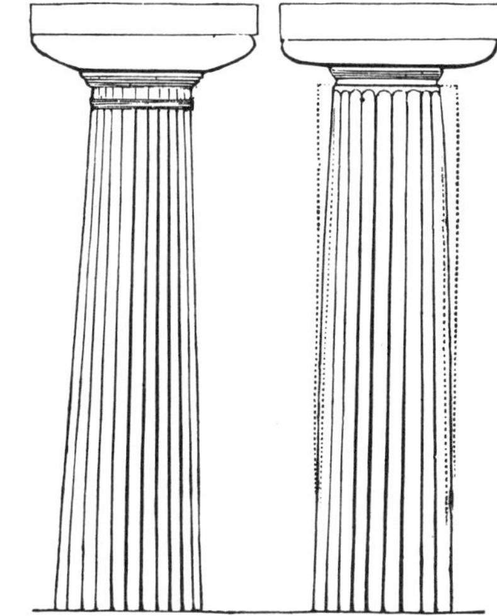

Entasis. (From Doric Columns at Paestum.)

Examples of the absence and presence of entasis are represented in the illustration: from the great temple at Paestum (to left), from a later building in the same city (to right).

Entella (Ἔντελλα). A town of the Sicani in the interior of the island of Sicily, on the west side, said to have been founded by Entellus, one of the companions of the Trojan Acestes.

Entellus. A Sicilian who, though advanced in years, entered the lists against the Trojan Dares and conquered him in a pugilistic encounter (Verg. *Aen.* v. 387 foll.).

Enyalius (Ἐνυάλιος), "The Warlike," frequently occurs in the *Iliad* (never in the *Odyssey*) as an epithet of Ares. At a later time Enyalius and Ares were distinguished as two different gods of war. The name is evidently derived from Enyo (q. v.).

Enȳo (Ἐνυώ). The daughter of Phorcys and Ceto, according to Hesiod (*Theog.* 273). She was a war-goddess and one of the companions of Ares, and answers to the Bellona of the Romans. Some mythologists make her the sister, others the wife, of Ares. See BELLONA.

Eōra. See AEORA.

Eordaea (Ἐορδαία and Ἐορδία). A district and town in Northwestern Macedonia, peopled by the Eordaei (Thuc. ii. 99).

Eos (Ἠώς). The Greek name of Aurora (q. v.), the goddess of morning, whence the epithet *Eous* is applied to all the eastern parts of the world (Ovid, *Fast.* iii. 406). She was the daughter of Hyperion and Thia or Euryphassa. At the close of each night she arose from the couch of her consort Tithonus and, drawn on a chariot by the steeds Lampus and Phaëton, ascended to heaven from the river Oceanus to announce the coming of the sun to gods and mortals. In Homer she accompanies the sun on his course, and in the tragic poets is identified with Hemera or the Day. For her relations with Cephalus, Orion, and Tithonus, see the respective articles. By the last named she had Memnon; and by Astraeus, she had Zephyrus, Boreas, Notus, and Hesperus.

Epaminondas (Ἐπαμεινώνδας). A Theban statesman and soldier, son of Polymnis, and in whose praise, for both talents and rectitude, there is a remarkable concurrence of ancient writers. Nepos observes that before Epaminondas was born and after his death Thebes was always in subjection to some other power; while he directed her councils she was at the head of Greece. His public life extends from the restoration of democracy by Pelopidas and the other exiles, B.C. 379, to the battle of Mantinea, B.C. 362. In the conspiracy by which that revolution was effected he took no part, but thenceforward he became the prime mover of the Theban State. His policy was first directed to assert the right and to secure the power to Thebes of controlling the other cities of Boeotia, several of which claimed to be independent. In this cause he ventured to engage his country, single-handed, in war with the Spartans, who marched into Boeotia, B.C. 371, with a force superior to any which could be brought against them. The Theban generals were divided in opinion whether a battle should be risked, for to encounter the Lacedaemonians with inferior numbers was universally esteemed hopeless. Epaminondas prevailed upon his colleagues to venture it, and devised on this occasion a new method of attack. Instead of joining battle along the whole line he concentrated an overwhelming force on one point, directing the weaker part of his line to keep back. The Spartan right being broken and their king slain, the rest of the army found it necessary to abandon the field. This memorable battle was fought at Leuctra (B.C. 371). The moral effect of it was much more important than the mere loss inflicted upon Sparta, for it overthrew the prescriptive superiority in arms claimed by that State ever since its reformation by Lycurgus.

This brilliant success led Epaminondas to the second object of his policy, the overthrow of the supremacy of Sparta and the substitution of Thebes as the leader of Greece in the democratic interest. In this hope a Theban army, under his command, marched into the Peloponnesus early in the winter, B.C. 369, and, in conjunction with the Eleans, Arcadians, and Argives, invaded and laid waste a large part of Laconia. Numbers of the Helots took that opportunity to shake off a most oppressive slavery; and Epaminondas struck a deadly blow at the power of Sparta by establishing these descendants of the old Messenians on Mount Ithomé in Messenia, as an independent State, and inviting their countrymen, scattered through Italy and Sicily, to return to their ancient patrimony. Numbers obeyed the call. This memorable event is known in history as the return of the Messenians, and two hundred years had elapsed since their expulsion. In B.C. 368, Epaminondas again led an army into the Peloponnesus; but, not fulfilling the expectations of the people, he was disgraced and, according to Diodorus (xv. 71), was ordered to serve in the ranks. In that capacity he is said to have saved the army in Thessaly when entangled in dangers which threatened it with destruction, being required by the general voice to assume the command. He is not again heard of in a public capacity till B.C. 366, when he was sent to support the democratic interest in Achaia, and by his moderation and judgment brought that whole confederation over to the Theban alliance without bloodshed or banishment. It soon became plain, however, that a mere change of masters—Thebes instead of Sparta—would be of no service to the Grecian States. Achaia first, then Elis, then Mantinea and a great part of Arcadia, returned to the Lacedaemonian alliance. To check this defection, Epaminondas led an army into the Peloponnesus for the fourth time, in B.C. 362. Joined by the Argives, Messenians, and part of the Arcadians, he entered Laconia and endeavoured to take Sparta by surprise; but the vigilance of Agesilaüs just frustrated his scheme. Epaminondas then marched against Mantinea, near which was fought the celebrated battle in which he fell. The disposition of his troops on this occasion was an improvement on that by which he had gained the battle of Leuctra, and would have had the same decisive success, but that, in the critical moment, when the Lacedaemonian line was just broken, he received a mortal wound, said to have been inflicted by Gryllus, the son of Xenophon. The Theban army was paralyzed by this misfortune; nothing was done to profit by a victory which might have been made certain; and this battle, on which the expectation of all Greece waited, led to no important result.

Whether Epaminondas could much longer have upheld Thebes in the rank to which he had raised her is very doubtful; without him she fell at once to her former obscurity. His character is certainly one of the noblest recorded in Greek history. His private life was moral and refined, his public conduct uninfluenced by personal ambition or by personal hatred. He was a sincere lover of his country; and if, in his schemes for her advancement, he was indifferent to the injury done to other members of the Grecian family, this is a fault from which, perhaps, no Greek statesman except Aristides was free. His life was written in Latin by Cornelius Nepos; and in recent times in German by Bauch (1834) and Pomtow (1870). See also Sankey, *Spartan and Theban Supremacies* (London, 1877).

Epangelia (ἐπαγγελία). If a citizen of Athens had incurred ἀτιμία, the privilege of taking part or speaking in the public assembly was forfeited. (See ATIMIA.) But as it sometimes might happen that a person, though not formally declared ἄτιμος, had committed such crimes as would, on accusation, draw upon him this punishment, it was, of course, desirable that such individuals, like real ἄτιμοι, should be excluded from the exercise of the rights of citizens. Whenever, therefore, such a person ventured to speak in the assembly, any Athenian citizen had the right to come forward in the assembly itself and demand of him to establish his right to speak by a trial or examination of his conduct (δοκιμασία τοῦ βίου), and this demand, denouncement, or threat was called ἐπαγγελία or ἐπαγγελία δοκιμασίας. The impeached individual was then compelled to desist from speaking, and to submit to a scrutiny into his conduct and if he was convicted a formal declaration of ἀτιμία followed.

Epaphrodītus (Ἐπαφρόδιτος). (1) A freedman and favourite of the emperor Nero, whom he assisted in committing suicide. He was himself put to death by Domitian. The philosopher Epictetus (q. v.) was his freedman. (2) M. METTIUS. A Greek grammarian of Chaeronea, the slave and subsequently the freedman of Modestus, Roman prefect of Egypt. He resided at Rome under Nero, and died there about A.D. 95. He was the author of several commentaries and grammatical works.

Epăphus (Ἔπαφος). A son of Zeus and Io. This mythological personage is the instrument by which Grecian myth derived the rulers of more ancient countries from its own gods and princes. Epaphus, according to the legend, was born in Egypt, and married Memphis, the daughter of the Nile, by whom he had a daughter named Libya. The same fable made him the founder of the city of Memphis (Aesch. *Prom. Vinct.* 850 foll.; Herod. ii. 153). Libya bore to Poseidon Agenor, the father of Cadmus and Europa, and also Belus, who had by another daughter of the Nile, named Anchinoë, two sons, Danaüs and Aegyptus (Apollod. ii. 1, 4). See IO.

Eparĭti (ἐπάριτοι). A corps of picked troops in Arcadia, which was formed to preserve the independence of the Arcadian towns, when they became united as one State after the defeat of the Spartans at Leuctra. They were 5000 in number, and were paid by the State. Cf. Hesych. s. v. ἐπαρόητοι: Thirlwall, v. 90.

Epaulia (ἐπαύλια). See MATRIMONIUM.

Epēi (Ἐπειοί). A people of Elis. See ELIS.

Epetium (Ἐπέτιον). A town of the Lissii in Dalmatia with a good harbour (Plin. *H. N.* iii. 25).

Epeunacti or **Epeunactae** (ἐπεύνακτοι, ἐπευνακταί). A class of citizens at Sparta who are said to have been the offspring of slaves and the widows of Spartan citizens. Theopompus tells us (Athen. vi. p. 271 c) that in the Messenian War, in consequence of the great losses which the Spartans sustained, they married the widows of those who were slain to Helots, and that these Helots were admitted to the citizenship under the name of ἐπεύνακτοι. See PARTHENIAE.

Epēus (Ἐπειός). (1) Son of Panopeus and builder of the Trojan horse. See *Iliad*, xxiii. 665. (2) Son of Endymion, king of Elis. From him the Epei derived their name.

Ephebēum (ἐφηβεῖον). A spacious apartment in the Greek gymnasium, where the youths performed their exercises in the presence of their masters (Vitruv. v. 11; Strab. v. 4, 7). See EPHEBI; GYMNASIUM.

Ephēbi (ἔφηβοι). The Athenian name for youths over the age of eighteen. The completion of a boy's eighteenth year was the occasion of a festival, at which the ἔφηβος made a drink-offering to Heracles and entertained his friends with wine. His hair, hitherto worn long, was cut, and the locks dedicated to Apollo. For the two following years the ephebi were mainly employed in gymnastic exercises, and after that time the proper civic ἐφηβεία commenced. After an examination (δοκιμασία) to test the genuineness of their civic descent and their physical capacity, the ephebi were entered on the list of their tribe, presented to the people assembled in the theatre, armed with spear and shield, and taken to the sanctuary of Agraulos at the foot of the citadel, where they bound themselves by a solemn oath to the service and defence of their country. For the next two years they served as guards on the frontier. After the completion of their twentieth year they were admitted to the meetings of the assembly and employed in foreign service. Their dress was the χλαμύς and the πέτασος. See Dittenberger, *De Ephebis Atticis* (Gött. 1863); Dumont, *Essai sur l'Ephébie Attique* (Paris, 1876); Portelette, *L'Ephébie en Grèce* in *L'Instruction Publique* for December, 1878; and the article EDUCATION, p. 570.

Ephegēsis (ἐφήγησις). See APAGOGÉ.

Ephemĕris (ἐφημερίς). An account book; also a diary. See COMMENTARIUS.

Ephesia (τὰ Ἐφέσια). A great gathering of Ionians at Ephesus, the ancient capital of the Ionians in Asia. It was held every year, and had, like all *panegyreis*, a twofold character—that of a bond of political union among the Greeks of the Ionian race, and that of a common worship of the Ephesian Artemis. Thucydides compares it (iii. 104) to the ancient Delia (q. v.). Respecting the particulars of its celebration, we only know that it took place at night and was accompanied with much mirth and feasting, and that mystical sacrifices were offered to the Ephesian goddess (Thuc. l. c.; Dion. Hal. *Antiq. Rom.* iv. 25). That games and contests formed likewise a chief part of the solemnities is clear from Hesychius (s. v.), who calls the Ephesia an ἀγὼν ἐπιφανής. The drunken revelry described in the love-tale of Achilles Tatius (books vi.–viii.) is not mentioned by these authors. See EPHESUS.

From the manner in which Thucydides and Strabo speak of the Ephesia, it seems that it was only a panegyris of a part of the Ionians, perhaps of those who lived in Ephesus itself and its vicinity.

Ephesiae Littĕrae (Ἐφέσια γράμματα). Mystic words engraved on the crown, the girdle, and the feet of the Ephesian Artemis (Eustath. *ad* Hom. *Od.* p. 1864). When pronounced, they were regarded as a charm (Menand. *ap.* Suid. s. v. ἀλεξιφάρμακα = *fr.* 360 M.). Written copies, apparently on strips of parchment like the Jewish phylacteries, were worn as amulets (Athen. xii. 548 c. = *fr.* 15 M.). They cured diseases, charmed away evil spirits, and gave victory in contests of various kinds. They are among the περίεργα, or "curious arts," of Acts, xix. 19, where see the commentators, and cf. Conybeare and Howson, *St. Paul*, ii. 13 (first edition, London, 1852). The charms and amulets of Alexander of Tralles (q. v.), a physician of the sixth century, seem to have been a survival of the

Ἐφέσια γράμματα, though he was almost certainly a Christian and employs Hebrew as well as Greek mystical expressions. See AMULETUM.

Ephesian Tales. See NOVELS AND ROMANCES.

Ephĕsis (ἔφεσις). An appeal to the Athenian assembly from the decision of the public arbitrators (διαιτηταὶ κληρωτοί) of the δημόται, or of the magistrates. See Pollux, viii. 62, 63.

Ephĕsus (Ἔφεσος). A city of Ionia, near the mouth of the river Caÿster, called by Pliny (*H. N.* v. 29) *alterum lumen Asiae.* Mythology assigns, as its founders, Ephesus, the son of the river Caÿster, and Cresus (Κρῆσος), a native of the soil (Pausan. vii. 2). Another account makes it to have been settled by Ephesus, one of the Amazons (Steph. Byzant. s. v.; *Etymol. Mag.* s. v.). According to a third tradition, the place owed its origin to the Amazons. If we follow the better authority of Strabo, we will find a settlement to have been first made in this quarter by the Carians and Leleges. Androclus, the son of Codrus, came subsequently with a body of Ionian colonists (Pausan. vii. 2). He protected the natives who had settled from devotion about the Temple of Artemis and incorporated them with his followers, but expelled those who inhabited the town above, which the Carians and Leleges had built on Mount Prion (Pausan. l. c.). Pliny enumerates other names for the city, such as Alopé, Morges, Ortygia, Ptelea, Samornia, Smyrna, Trachea, etc.

Bronze Coin of Ephesus.

Lysimachus, wishing to protect Ephesus from the inundations to which it was yearly exposed by the overflowings of the Caÿster, built a city upon the mountain and surrounded it with walls. The inhabitants were unwilling to remove into this, but a heavy rain falling, and Lysimachus stopping the drains and flooding their houses, they were glad to exchange. The port of Ephesus had originally a wide mouth, but foul with the mud lodging in it from the Caÿster. Attalus Philadelphus and his architect were of opinion that if the entrance were contracted, it would become deeper and in time be capable of receiving ships of burden. But the slime, which had before been moved by the flux and reflux of the tide and carried off, being stopped, the whole basin, quite to the mouth, was rendered shallow. The situation, however, was so advantageous as to overbalance the inconveniences attending the port. The town increased daily, and under the Romans was considered the chief emporium of Asia this side of Taurus. In the arrangement of the provinces under the Eastern emperors it became the capital of the province of Asia. Towards the end of the eleventh century Ephesus experienced the same fate as Smyrna (q. v.). A Turkish pirate, named Tangripanes, settled here; but the Greek admiral, Ioannes Ducas, defeated him in a bloody battle and pursued the flying Turks up the Maeander to Polybotum. In 1306, it was among the places which suffered from the exactions of the Grand Duke Roger; and two years after it surrendered to the sultan Saysan, who, to prevent future insurrections, removed most of the inhabitants to Tyriaeum, where they were massacred. In the conflicts which desolated Asia Minor at a subsequent period, Ephesus was again a sufferer, and the city became at length reduced to a heap of ruins.

Ephesus was famed for its splendid temple of Artemis or Diana. The statue of the goddess was regarded with peculiar veneration and was believed by the people to have fallen from the skies. It was never changed, though the temple had been more than once restored. This rude object of primeval worship was a block of wood, said by some to be of beech or elm, by others cedar, ebony, or vine, and attesting its very great antiquity by the fashion in which it had been formed. It was carved into the similitude of Artemis, not as the graceful huntress, but an allegorical figure which we may call the goddess of nature, with many breasts, and the lower parts formed into an Hermaean statue, grotesquely ornamented, and discovering the feet beneath. (See illustration on p. 137). It was gorgeously apparelled, the vest embroidered with emblems and symbolical devices, and to prevent its tottering a bar of metal was placed under each hand. A veil or curtain, which was drawn up from the floor to the ceiling, hid it from view, except while service was in progress in the temple. This image was preserved till the later ages in a shrine, on the embellishment of which mines of wealth were consumed. The priests of Artemis suffered emasculation, and virgins were devoted to inviolable chastity. They were eligible only from the superior ranks, and enjoyed a great revenue with privileges, the eventual abuse of which induced Augustus to restrict them.

The reputation and the riches of their goddess had made the Ephesians desirous of providing for her a magnificent temple. The fortunate discovery of marble in Mount Prion gave them new vigour. The cities of Asia contributed largely, and Croesus defrayed the expense of many of the columns. The spot chosen for it was a marsh, as most likely to preserve the structure free from gaps and uninjured by earthquakes. The foundation was made with charcoal rammed down and with fleeces. The base consumed immense quantities of marble. The edifice was erected on a basement with ten steps. The architects were Chersiphron of Crete and his son Metagenes (B.C. 541); and their plan was continued by Demetrius, a priest of Artemis; but the whole was completed by Daphnis of Miletus and a citizen of Ephesus, the building having occupied 220 years. It was the first specimen of the Ionic style in which the fluted column and capital with volutes were introduced. The whole length of the temple was 425 feet, and the breadth 220; with 127 columns of the Ionic order and of Parian marble, each of a single shaft and sixty feet high. These were donations from kings, according to Pliny (*H. N.* xxxvi. 14), but there is reason to doubt the correctness of the text where this assertion is made. Of these columns thirty-six were carved; and one of them, perhaps as a model, by Scopas. The temple had a double row of columns, fifteen on either side; but Vitruvius has not determined if it had a roof, probably over the cell only. The folding-doors or gates had been continued four years in glue, and were made of cypress wood, which had been treasured up for four generations, highly polished. These were found by Mutianus as fresh and as beautiful 400 years after as when new. The ceiling was of cedar; and the steps for ascending the roof were of the single stem of a vine.

The dimensions of this great temple excite ideas of uncommon grandeur from their massiveness; but the notices of its internal ornament increase one's admiration. It was the repository in which the great artists of antiquity dedicated their most perfect works to posterity. Praxiteles and his son Cephisodorus adorned the shrine; Scopas contributed a statue of Hecaté; Timareté, the daughter of Micon, the first recorded female artist, finished a picture of the goddess, the most ancient in Ephesus; and Parrhasius and Apelles employed their skill to embellish the walls. The excellence of these performances may be supposed to have been proportionate to their price; and a picture of Alexander grasping a thunderbolt, by the latter, was added to the superb collection at the expense of twenty talents of gold. This description, however, applies chiefly to the temple as it was rebuilt, after the earlier temple had been partially burned (perhaps the roof of timber only), by Herostratus, who chose that method to ensure to himself an immortal name, on the very night that Alexander the Great was born. Twenty years after, that magnificent prince, during his expedition against Persia, offered to appropriate his spoils to the restoration of it if the Ephesians would consent to allow him the sole honour and would place his name on the temple. They declined the proposal, however, with the flattering remark that it was not right for one deity to erect a temple to another; national vanity was, however, the real ground of their refusal. The architect who superintended the erection of the new edifice was Dinocrates, of whose aid Alexander afterwards availed himself in building Alexandria (Vitruv. ii. praef.; Plut. *Alex.* 72; Plin. *H. N.* vii. 37; Solin. 40). The extreme sanctity of the temple inspired universal awe and reverence; and it was for many ages a repository of foreign and domestic treasure. There property, whether public or private, was secure amid all revolutions. The conduct of Xerxes was an example to subsequent conquerors, and the impiety of sacrilege was not suffered by the Ephesian goddess; but Nero deviated from this rule in removing many costly offerings and images and an immense quantity of silver and gold. It was again plundered by the Goths from beyond the Danube in the time of Gallienus — a party under Raspa crossing the Hellespont and ravaging the country until compelled to retreat, when they carried off a prodigious booty.

The destruction of so illustrious an edifice deserved to have been carefully recorded by contemporary historians. We may conjecture that it followed the triumph of Christianity. The Ephesian reformers, when authorized by the imperial edicts, rejoiced in the opportunity of insulting Artemis, and deemed it piety to demolish the very ruin of her habitation. When, under the auspices of Constantine and Theodosius, churches were erected, the pagan temples were despoiled of their ornaments or accommodated to other worship. The immense dome of Saint Sophia now rises from the columns of green jasper which were originally placed in the Temple of Artemis, and were taken down and brought to Constantinople by order of Justinian. Two pillars in the great church at Pisa were also transported thence. The very site of this stupendous and celebrated edifice was long undetermined, but in 1869 was discovered by Mr. J. T. Wood—an Englishman who found a clue to its situation in two letters from Antoninus Pius to the Ephesians (A.D. 145–150); in another letter from Hadrian, dated September 27th, A.D. 120; and in an inscription which prescribed the order of the processions to the temple. Excavations continued until 1874 have greatly added to our knowledge of the temple. See Falkner, *Ephesus and the Temple of Diana* (1862); Wood, *Discoveries at Ephesus* (1877); and Fergusson, *The Temple of Diana at Ephesus* (1883).

Ephĕsus, SEVEN SLEEPERS OF. See SEVEN SLEEPERS OF EPHESUS.

Ephĕtae (ἐφέται). A judicial court of high antiquity at Athens, consisting of fifty-one judges elected from the noblest Athenian families. It gave decisions in cases of murder at five different places, differing according to the character of the case. If the crime had a religious character, the Archon Basileus presided. (See ARCHON.) Solon did not abolish this court, but handed over to the newly organized Areopagus (q. v.) its most important functions—the power of deciding cases of intentional murder, poisoning, malicious wounding, arson, and the like. The nearest relations of the murdered person were bound by religious sanction to avenge his blood. At the funeral, and after that in the market-place, they uttered a solemn denunciation, which bade the murderer keep away from all public places, assemblies, and sanctuaries, and to appear before the court. The Archon Basileus, after the charge had been announced and received, repeated this denunciation. The preliminary investigation, and determination of the place where the court was to be held, followed at three appointed times in three successive months. The case was not finally dealt with till the fourth month. On the first two days of the final trial the two parties, after solemnly taking an oath, conducted their case in person. On the third day judgment was given, in case the accused had not gone into voluntary exile. If he had, his property was confiscated, but he was pursued no further. Intentional murder was punished with death, malicious wounding with exile; the man's property was confiscated in both cases. In the court of Areopagus if the votes of the judges were equal the accused was acquitted. If the homicide were legally allowed (as, for instance, that of an adulterer) or legally innocent (as in self-defence), the case was investigated in the Delphinium, a sanctuary of the Delphic Apollo; and only a religious purification was exacted. Cases of unintentional homicide, murder of an alien, and instigation to murder, were taken at the Palladium, a sanctuary of Pallas. Instigation to murder was punished with banishment and confiscation of property, the murder of an alien with banishment, unintentional murder with banishment until the kinsmen of the murdered person gave permission to the slayer to return. In the time of Demosthenes it would seem that the cases which used to be heard at the Delphinium and Palladium were handed over to the Heliastae. Thus the Ephetae had only two courts left them—that in Phreatto, a place in the Piraeus, near the sea, and the Prytaneum. The former had only to judge in the rare event of a person banished for unintentional homicide being charged with intentional murder. As he might not set foot on land, he was heard standing in a ship, and if found guilty was punished with banishment for life. At the Prytaneum a regular court was held on inanimate objects and animals which had been the cause of death to a human being. See APSYCHON DIKÉ; and the works by Lange, *Die Epheten und der Areopag vor Solon*; and Philippi, *Der Areopag und die Epheten.*

Ephialtes (Ἐφιάλτης). (1) One of the Aloadae (*Il.* v. 385). See ALOEUS. (2) A Malian, who in B.C. 480, when Leonidas was defending the pass of Thermopylae, guided a body of Persians over the mountain path, and thus enabled them to fall on the rear of the Greeks. (3) An Athenian statesman, a friend and partisan of Pericles, whom he assisted in carrying his political measures. He was instrumental in abridging the powers of the Areopagus — a measure assailed by Aeschylus in his *Eumenides*. Ephialtes thus made himself so obnoxious to the aristocratic party that his enemies had him assassinated, probably in the year B.C. 456.

Ephippĭum (ἐφίππιον or ἐφίππειον). A saddle-cloth or pad. The saddle with a "tree" was unknown till the fourth century, although the pack-saddle seems to be of much earlier occurrence.

In the absence of stirrups (later *staffae, stapides,* etc.), which are not mentioned till the emperor Mauricius (A.D. 602), there were several ways of mounting—as jumping with or without the aid of a lance-shaft, with the assistance of others (ἀναβολεῖς), or from steps (ἀνάβαθρα). The last were set up, according to Plutarch, along the main roads by C. Gracchus. Or, the horse was taught to kneel at the word of command (Sil. Ital. x. 465).

In more ancient art the horse is represented ridden bare-backed. Later, saddle-cloths, often double or with pads beneath, and fastened with one to three girths, appear with increasing frequency. The most elaborate trappings of this kind are seen on Scythian antiquities of the fourth century B.C.

The use of trappings was originally regarded as effeminate by the Romans (Varro on Cato, *De Lib. Educ.*), but they were used in pomps. Their development may be seen by a comparison of the examples appearing on the columns of Trajan, Antoninus, and Theodosius. On the first and second, and in the equestrian statue of M. Aurelius, are to be seen cloths alone, and pads filling up the hollow of the horse's back with and without cloths. It is only on the Theodosian Column that the true saddle, with a bow behind and before, appears for the first time. The new name *sella* now emphasizes the new fashion.

Ephippium. (Coin of Labienus.)

Ephŏri (ἔφοροι, "overseers"). A board of five members at Sparta, elected annually from all the citizens. It is said to have been established by Lycurgus or King Theopompus (B.C. 770). The original intention was that it should give decisions in private matters, and represent the absent kings in certain of their duties, especially in the superintendence of the officials and of public discipline. But their circle of authority gradually widened, till it came to mean a superintendence over the whole commonwealth, including the kings. The ephors had the right of raising objections against their actions, calling them, like other officials, to account for their conduct, punishing them with fines and reprimands, and even prosecuting them before the Senate, and threatening them with deposition and death. They were the only citizens who were not obliged to rise in the kings' presence, a fact which gives a good idea of the relative position of the two parties. Besides the duty of opposing everything which they thought adverse to the laws and interests of Sparta, they had from early times the right of summoning the deliberative and legislative assemblies, the Γερουσία and Ἐκκλησία, to make proposals to them, and take the lead in proceedings left to their management. Two of them regularly accompanied the kings on their campaigns. It is probable also that they had the superintendence of the public treasure. In their capacity of protectors of the public discipline their authority extended itself to the minutest details of private life. In regard to the Helots and Perioeci it was still more absolute. Even on a *perioecus* they could pass sentence of death without trial. (See PERIOECI.) On important occasions a majority of their votes was required. At the end of their annual office, on which they entered at the beginning of the Spartan year or at the time of the autumnal equinox, they were liable to be called to account by their successors. The year was dated by the name of the first ephor on the board.

Ephŏrus (Ἔφορος). Of Cymae in Aeolis, a celebrated Greek historian, a contemporary of Philip and Alexander, flourished about B.C. 340. He wrote a universal history (Ἱστορίαι), in thirty books, the first that was attempted in Greece. It covers a period of 750 years, from the return of the Heraclidae to B.C. 341. Of this history Diodorus Siculus made an extensive use. The work, however, has perished, with the exception of a few fragments, which may be found in Müller's *Historicorum Graecorum Fragmenta* (Paris, 1841–73).

Ephȳra (Ἐφύρα). (1) The ancient name of Corinth; whence Ephyreius is used as equivalent to Corinthian. See CORINTHUS. (2) A town in Thessaly, afterwards called Cranon. (3) A town in Epirus, afterwards called Cichyrus.

Epibătae (ἐπιβάται). Marines appointed to defend the vessels in the Athenian navy, and entirely distinct from the rowers as well as from the land soldiers, such as hoplitae, peltasts, and cavalry (Xen. *Hell.* i. 2, § 7; v. 1, § 11). It appears that the ordinary number of epibatae on board a trireme was ten, though in Thucydides vi. 42 we find 700 epibatae for a fleet of 100 ships, sixty of which were equipped in the ordinary way and forty had troops on board. In consequence of the number of heavy-armed men ἐκ τοῦ καταλόγου on the expedition, the Athenians appear to have reduced the number of regular epibatae from ten to seven.

The epibatae were usually taken from the Thetes, or fourth class of Athenian citizens (Thuc. vi. 42); but on one occasion, in a season of extraordinary danger, the citizens of the higher classes were compelled to serve as epibatae (Thuc. viii. 24).

The term is sometimes also applied by the Roman writers to the marines (Hirt. *Bell. Alex.* 11;

Bell. Afric. 63); though these are more usually called *classiarii milites.*

Epiblēma (ἐπίβλημα). See Pallium; Tunica.

Epibŏlé (ἐπιβολή). A fine imposed by a magistrate on any official, or official body, for a misdemeanor. The various magistrates at Athens had, each in his own department, a summary penal jurisdiction—i. e. for certain offences they might inflict a pecuniary mulct or fine, not exceeding a fixed amount; if the offender deserved further punishment, it was their duty to bring him before a judicial tribunal, the magistrate proposing the penalty. Thus, in case of injury done to orphans and heiresses, or of misconduct at the great Dionysia, the archon might fine the parties; the generals could fine a phylarch for disobedience; the same power belonged to the τειχοποιοί (Aesch. *c. Ctes.* § 27). If the person fined would not submit to it, the magistrate had to lay the case before a court (Lys. *pro Milit.* § 11): that was always required when a demarch imposed a fine (*C. I. A.* ii. 573 b). The amount of the fine (τέλος) which the individual magistrate might inflict, we do not know; the Senate of Five Hundred was competent to fine to the extent of 500 drachmas.

These ἐπιβολαί are to be distinguished from the penalties awarded by a jury or court of law (τιμήματα) upon a formal prosecution, and from the fine of a thousand drachmas, which the accuser in a public action incurred when he dropped his accusation or failed to obtain a fifth part of the votes, or when a citizen refused to obey the summons to appear as a witness in court: in all these cases the magistrates had no discretionary power.

Epicasté (Ἐπικάστη). Commonly called Iocasté (q. v.). See *Odyss.* xi. **271.**

Epicephesia (Ἐπικεφησία). A deme of Attica belonging to the tribe Oeneïs.

Epicharmus (Ἐπίχαρμος). The first Greek comic writer of whom we have any definite account. He was a Syracusan, either by birth or emigration (Theocr. *Epig.* 17). Some writers make him a native of the island of Cos, but all agree that he passed his life at Syracuse. It was about B.C. 500, thirty-five years after Thespis began to exhibit, eleven years after the commencement of Phrynichus, and just before the appearance of Aeschylus as a tragedian, that Epicharmus produced the first comedy properly so called. Before him, this department of the drama was little more than a series of licentious songs and sarcastic episodes, without plot, connection, or consistency. (See Comoedia; Drama.) He gave to each exhibition continuity, and converted the loose interlocutions into regular dialogue (Aristot. *Poet.* v. 5). The subjects of his Doric comedies, as we may infer from the extant titles of thirty-five of them, were partly parodies of mythological subjects, and, as such, not very different from the dialogue of the satyric drama, and partly political, and in this respect may have furnished a model for the dialogue of the Athenian comedy. (See Rhinthonica Fabula.) Tragedy had, some years before the era of Epicharmus, begun to assume its dignified character. The woes of heroes and the majesty of the gods had, under Phrynicus, become its favourite themes. The Sicilian poet seems to have been struck with the idea of exciting the mirth of his audience by the exhibition of some ludicrous matter dressed up in all the grave solemnity of the newly invented art. Discarding, therefore, the low drolleries and scurrilous invectives of the ancient κωμῳδία, he opened a novel and less objectionable source of amusement by composing a set of burlesque dramas upon the usual tragic subjects. They succeeded, and the turn thus given to comedy long continued; so that when it once more returned to personality and satire, as it afterwards did, tragedy and tragic poets were the constant objects of its parody and ridicule. The great changes thus effected by Epicharmus justly entitled him to be called the Inventor of Comedy (Theocr. *Epig.* 17), though it is probable that Phormis or Phormus preceded him by a few Olympiads (Aristot. *Poet.* iii. 5). But his merits do not rest here: he was distinguished for elegance of composition as well as originality of conception. Demetrius Phalereus says that Epicharmus excelled in the choice and collocation of epithets, on which account the name of Ἐπιχάρμιος was given to his kind of style, making it proverbial for elegance and beauty. So many were his dramatic excellences that Plato terms him the king of comic writers, and in a later age and foreign country Plautus chose him as his model (Hor. *Epist.* ii. 1. 58) and is thought to have borrowed from him the plot of the *Menaechmi.* The parasite who figures so greatly in the plays of the New Comedy and in those of Plautus was first brought upon the stage by Epicharmus.

The plays of Epicharmus, to judge from the fragments still left us, abounded in apophthegms, little consistent with the ideas we might otherwise have entertained of their nature from our knowledge of the buffooneries whence his comedy sprang and of the writings of Aristophanes, his partially extant successor. Epicharmus, however, was a philosopher and a Pythagorean (Diog. Laert. viii. 78). We find Epicharmus still composing comedies B.C. 485 (Suidas, s. v. Ἐπίχ.), and again during the reign of Hiero, B.C. 477. He died at the age of ninety or ninety-seven years. Epicharmus is said by some authorities to have added the letters ξ, η, ψ, ω to the Greek alphabet, but inscriptions show that these characters were in use at Miletus half a century before his reputed birth. See Clermont-Ganneau, *Origine des Caractères Complémentaires de l'Alphabet Grec* in the *Mélanges Graux* (Paris, 1884). See also Lorenz, *Leben und Schriften des Epicharmus* (1864); Klein, *Griechisches u. römisches Drama* (1865); and Donaldson's *Theatre of the Greeks*, pp. 187–88 (8th ed. 1875).

Epicheirotonia (ἐπιχειροτονία). See Ecclesia.

Epichȳsis (ἐπίχυσις). A wine-jug with a narrow neck and small lip and with a handle (Menand. *Fr.* 490 M.); usually of metal—i. e. silver among the luxurious, bronze where simplicity was studied. Among the Romans it took the place of the earlier *guttus*, a narrow-necked cruet without a handle (Varr. *L. L.* v. 124); and glass became the favourite material. It was not unlike a modern claret-jug.

Epichysis. (Rich.)

Epiclērus (ἐπίκληρος, also ἐπικληρῖτις and ἔγκληρος). The name given to the daughter or daughters of an Athenian citizen who had no son, or whose sons had died leaving no male issue. The ἐπίκληρος was not, in our sense of the word, an "heiress," but rather a person who went with the estate. The heir was either the person to whom her father had devised the property on condition of marrying her, or her son or sons. It was deemed an object of importance at Athens to preserve the οἶκος. This was effected, where a man had no child, by adoption (εἰσποίησις); if he had no sons or grandsons, but a daughter, he might bequeath his property to any person, but the devisee was obliged to marry her; on the other hand, if he died intestate, her nearest relative might claim her in marriage, and the inheritance was transmitted through her to a grandson, who was, when of full age, adopted into the maternal grandfather's family (Isae. *Pyrrh.* § 73). Such an epiclerus might be claimed in marriage by her father's brothers, or in default of such by their sons or by the sons of her father's sisters, or by her father's uncles. If the daughter was poor (θῆσσα), the nearest of kin was bound by law either to marry her himself or to portion her, the law fixing a sliding scale for the different classes of the census—e. g. 500 drachmas, if he be of the highest class, etc. If there were several in the same degree of consanguinity, each of them had to contribute their share (πρὸς μέρος). Upon the nearest relative making his claim before the archon, public notice was given of the claim; it was written on the σανίς, and read out in the following assembly (Poll. viii. 95), and at a later day the herald put the question εἴ τις ἀμφισβητεῖν ἢ παρακαταβάλλειν βούλεται. If no one appeared to dispute the claim, the archon adjudged the heiress to him; if other claimants appeared, the archon instituted an anakrisis, and a court was held for the decision of the right, which was determined according to the Athenian law of consanguinity.

Even when a woman was already married, her husband was obliged to give her up to a man with a better title; and men sometimes put away their former wives in order to marry heiresses (Isae. *Pyrrh.* § 64). Even after the decision of the court had been given in favour of one claimant, any other person who could show a better title might bring an action against the husband and claim the heiress ([Demosth.] *c. Macart.* p. 1054, § 16). The limit of time for making such a claim is not known.

The estate never passed into the possession of the husband of the heiress (Isae. *Ciron.* § 31); their son when of full age was adopted into his maternal grandfather's family (Isae. *Pyrrh.* § 73) and took possession of the estate. He then became his mother's legal protector (κύριος), and was bound to find her maintenance. If there were more sons, they shared the property equally. There were epicleri at Mitylenè and Phocis. With the Lycians daughters only could inherit.

Epicnemidii Locri. See LOCRIS.

Epic Poetry. See EPOS.

Epicrătes (Ἐπικράτης). (1) An Athenian who helped to expel the Thirty Tyrants (q. v.). Later, being sent on a mission to King Artaxerxes of Persia, he was accused of receiving a bribe from that monarch. Though acquitted of this charge, he was afterwards convicted of a similar offence and escaped death by flight. He is ridiculed by the comic poets for his large beard, whence he received the nickname σακεσφόρος (Plat. Com. *Presb.* 4 Meineke). (2) Of Ambracia; an Athenian writer of the Middle Comedy (Aelian, *N. A.* xii. 10).

Epictētus (Ἐπίκτητος). An eminent Stoic philosopher, born in a servile condition at Hierapolis in Phrygia, about A.D. 50. The names of his parents are unknown; neither do we know how he came to be brought to Rome. But in that city he was for some time a slave to Epaphroditus, a freedman of Nero, who had been one of his body-guard An anecdote related by Origen, which illustrates the fortitude of Epictetus, would also show, if it were true, that Epaphroditus was a most cruel master. Epictetus, when his master was twisting his leg one day, smiled and quietly said, "You will break it"; and when he did break it, only observed, "Did I not tell you that you would do so?" It is not known how or when Epictetus managed to effect his freedom, but he could not have been still a slave when he left Rome in consequence of an edict against philosophers. This event, the only one in his life the date of which can be assigned, took place, as has been said, in the year A.D. 89, being the eighth year of Domitian's reign. Epictetus then retired to Nicopolis in Epirus, and it is a question whether he ever returned to Rome. The chief ground for believing that he did is a statement of Spartianus (*Hadr.* 16), that Epictetus lived on terms of intimacy with the emperor Hadrian; while it is agreed, on the other hand, that there is no good evidence of any of his discourses having been delivered at Rome, but that they contain frequent mention of Nicopolis. This argument, however, is hardly sufficient to overthrow the express testimony of Spartianus. It is not known when he died. Suidas says that he lived till the reign of Marcus Aurelius, yet the authority of Aulus Gellius is strong on the other side. He, writing during the reign of the first Antonine, speaks of Epictetus, in two places, as being dead (*Noct. Att.* ii. 18; xvii. 19).

Epictetus led a life of exemplary contentment, simplicity, and virtue, practising in all particulars the morality which he taught. He lived for a long while in a small hut, with no other furniture than a bed and a lamp, and without an attendant; until he benevolently adopted a child whom a friend had been compelled by poverty to expose, and hired a nurse for its sake. A teacher of the Stoic philosophy, he was the chief of those who lived during the period of the Roman Empire. His lessons were principally, if not solely, directed to practical morality. His favourite maxim, and that into which he resolved all practical morality, was "bear and forbear," ἀνέχου καὶ ἀπέχου. He appears to have differed from the Stoics on the subject of suicide. We are told by Arrian, in his Preface to the *Discourses*, that he was a powerful and inspiring lecturer; and, according to Origen (*c. Cels.* 7, *ad init.*), his style was superior to that of Plato. It is a proof of the estimation in which Epictetus was held, that, on his death, his lamp was purchased by some aspirant after philosophy more eager than wise for 3000 drachmas, or over $500. Though it is said by Suidas that Epictetus wrote much, there is good reason to believe that he himself wrote nothing. His Διατριβαί were taken down by his pupil Arrian, and published after his death in eight books, of which four remain. The same Arrian compiled the *Enchiridion* or "manual," an abstract of the teaching of his master, and wrote a life of Epictetus, which is lost. Some fragments have been preserved, however, by Stobaeus. Simplicius has also left a commentary on his doctrine in the Eclectic manner. The best edition of the remains of Epictetus is still that of Schweighäuser, 5 vols. (Leipzig, 1800). The text and a Latin translation by Dübner (1840) may be recommended. The best English translations are those of Higginson, with a sketch of Epictetus (Boston, 1865); Long (London, 1877); and Rolleston (1881). See the popular work of Canon Farrar, *Seekers after God* (1863).

Epicūrus (Ἐπίκουρος). A celebrated philosopher, born in the year B.C. 341, in the island of Samos, whither his father had gone from Athens, in the year B.C. 352, among 2000 colonists then sent out by the Athenians. Yet he was an Athenian by right, belonging to the deme Gargettus and to the tribe Aegeïs. His father Neocles is said to have been a school-master, and his mother Chaeristrata to have practised arts of magic, in which it was afterwards made a charge against Epicurus that, when he was young, he assisted her (Diog. Laërt. x. 4). Having passed his early years in Samos and Teos, he went to Athens at the age of eighteen. He had begun to study philosophy when only fourteen, from a desire, which the teachers to whom he had applied had failed to satisfy, of understanding Hesiod's description of chaos. In Samos he is said to have received lessons from Pamphilus, a follower of Plato (Cic. *N. D.* i. 26). On the occasion of this his first visit to Athens, Epicurus stayed there for a very short time. He left it in consequence of the measures taken by Perdiccas after the death of Alexander the Great, and went to Colophon to join his father. In B.C. 310, he went to Mitylené, where he set up a school. Staying only one year at this latter place, he next proceeded to Lampsacus, where he taught for four years. He returned to Athens in the year B.C. 306, and now founded the school which ever after was named from him the Epicurean. He purchased a garden (Κῆποι Ἐπικούρου) for eighty minae (about $1450), wherein he might live with his disciples and deliver his lectures, and henceforth remained in Athens, with the exception only of two or three visits to his friends in Asia Minor, until his death, from stone in the bladder, B.C 270. He was in his seventy-second year when he died, and he had then been settled in Athens as a teacher for thirty-six years.

Epicurus is said by Diogenes Laërtius (x. 9) to have had so many pupils that even whole cities could not contain them. Hearers came to him from distant places; and while men often deserted other schools to join that of Epicurus, there were only two instances, at most, of Epicurus being deserted for any other teacher. Epicurus and his pupils lived together in the garden of which we have spoken, in a state of friendship, which, as it is usually represented, could not be surpassed—abstaining from putting their property together and enjoying it in common for the quaint yet significant reason that such a plan implied mutual distrust. The friendship subsisting between Epicurus and his pupils is commemorated by Cicero (*De Fin.* i. 20). In this garden, too, they lived in the most frugal and decorous manner, though it was the delight of the enemies of Epicurus to represent it differently, and though Timocrates, who had once been his pupil and had abandoned him, spread such gossip as that Epicurus used to vomit twice a day after a surfeit and that harlots were inmates of the garden. (See LEONTIUM.) An inscription over the gate of the garden told him who might be disposed to enter that barley-cakes and water would be the fare provided for him (Sen. *Ep.* 31); and such was the chastity of Epicurus that one of his principal opponents, Chrysippus, endeavoured to account for it, so as to deny him any merit, by saying that he was without passions (Stob. *Serm.* 117). Epicurus remained unmarried, in order that he might be able to prosecute philosophy without interruption. His most attached friends and pupils were Hermachus of Mitylené, whom he appointed by will to succeed him as master of the school; Metrodorus, who wrote several books in defence of his system; and Polyaenus. Epicurus's three brothers, Neocles, Chaeredemus, and Aristobulus, also followed his philosophy, as also one of his servants, Mys, whom at his death he made free. Besides the garden in Athens, from which the followers of Epicurus, in succeeding time, came to be named "the philosophers of the garden" (Juv. *Sat.* xiii. 122; xiv. 319), Epicurus possessed a house in Melité, a village near Athens, to which he used often to retire with his friends. On his death he left this house, together with the garden, to Hermachus, as head of the school, to be left by him again to whosoever might be his successor. See EDUCATION.

In physics Epicurus trod pretty closely in the footsteps of Democritus; so much so, indeed, that he was accused of taking his atomic cosmology from that philosopher without acknowledgment. He made very few, and these unimportant, alterations. According to Epicurus, as also to Democritus and Leucippus before him, the universe consists of two parts, matter (*σῶμα*) and space, or vacuum (*τὸ κενόν*), in which matter exists and moves; and all matter, of every kind and form, is reducible to certain indivisible particles or atoms (*ἄτομοι*), which are eternal. These atoms, moving, according to a natural tendency, straight downward, and also obliquely, have thereby come to form the different bodies which are found in the world, and which differ in kind and shape, according as the atoms are differently placed in respect to one another. It is clear that, in this system, a creator is dispensed with; and indeed Epicurus, here again following Democritus, set about to prove, in an *a priori* way, that this creator could not exist, inasmuch as nothing could arise out of nothing, any more than it could utterly perish and becoming nothing. The atoms have existed always, and always will exist; and all the various physical phenomena are brought about, from time to time, by their various motions. The soul itself is made of a finer and more subtle kind of atoms, which, when the body dies and decays, separate and are dissipated. The various processes of sense are explained on the principles of materialism. From the surfaces of all objects continually flow thin, filmy images of things (*εἴδωλα*), which, by impact on the organism, cause the phenomena of vision, hearing, etc.

It remains to speak of the Epicurean system of ethics. Setting out with the two facts that man is susceptible of pleasure and pain and that he seeks the one and avoids the other, Epicurus declared that it is a man's duty to endeavour to increase to the utmost his pleasures and diminish to the utmost his pains—choosing that which tends to pleasure rather than that which tends to pain, and that which tends to a greater pleasure or to a lesser pain rather than that which tends respectively to a lesser pleasure or a greater pain. He used the terms pleasure and pain in the most comprehensive way, as including pleasure and pain of both mind and body; and esteemed the pleasures and pains of the mind as incomparably greater than those of the body. The highest pleasure, then, is peace of mind (ἀταραξία, ἀπονία), and this comes from φρόνησις or the ability to decide what line of conduct will best secure true happiness. Death, he says, is not to be feared, for "where we are, death is not; and where death is, we are not."

Epicurus. (Baumeister.)

The period at which Epicurus opened his school was peculiarly favourable. In place of the simplicity of the Socratic doctrine, nothing now remained but the subtlety and affectation of Stoicism, the unnatural severity of the Cynics, or the debasing doctrine of indulgence taught and practised by the followers of Aristippus. The luxurious refinement which now prevailed in Athens, while it rendered every rigid scheme of philosophy, as well as all grossness of manners, unpopular, inclined the younger citizens to listen to a preceptor who smoothed the stern and wrinkled brow of philosophy, and, under the notion of conducting his followers to enjoyment in the bower of tranquillity, led them unawares into the path of moderation and virtue. Hence the popularity of his school. It cannot be denied, however, that from the time when this philosopher appeared to the present day, an uninterrupted course of censure has fallen upon his memory; so that the name of his sect has almost become a proverbial expression for everything corrupt in principle and infamous in character. The charges brought against Epicurus are that he superseded all religious principles by dismissing the gods from the care of the world; that if he acknowledged their existence, it was only in conformity to popular prejudice, since, according to his system, nothing exists in nature but material atoms; that he showed great insolence and vanity in the disrespect with which he treated the memory of former philosophers and the characters and persons of his contemporaries; and that both he and his disciples were addicted to the grossest sensuality.

With respect to the first charge, it certainly admits of no refutation. The doctrine of Epicurus concerning nature militated directly against the agency of a Supreme Being in the formation and government of the world, and his misconceptions with respect to mechanical motion and the nature of divine happiness led him to divest the Deity of some of his primary attributes. It is not true, however, that he entirely denied the existence of superior powers. Cicero charges him with inconsistency in having written books concerning piety and the reverence due to the gods, and in maintaining that the gods ought to be worshipped, while he asserted that they had no concern in human affairs. That there was an inconsistency in this is obvious. But Epicurus professed that the universal prevalence of the ideas of gods was sufficient to prove that they existed; and, thinking it necessary to derive these ideas, like all other ideas, from sensations, he imagined that the gods were beings of human form and made known to men by the customary emanations. He believed that these gods were eternal and supremely happy, living in the intermundane spaces (μετακόσμια) in a state of quiet, and meddling not with the affairs of the world. He contended that they were to be worshipped on account of the excellence of their nature, and not because they could do men either good or harm (Cic. *N. D.* i. 41; Sen. *Ben.* iv. 19).

The Epicurean school was carried on, after Hermachus, by Polystratus and many others, concerning whom nothing is known; and the doctrines which Epicurus had taught underwent few modifications. When introduced among the Romans, these doctrines, though very much opposed at first, were yet adopted by many distinguished men, as Lucretius, Atticus, and Horace. Under the emperors, Pliny the Younger and Lucian of Samosata were noted Epicureans. See LUCRETIUS.

Our chief sources of information respecting the doctrines of Epicurus are the tenth book of Diogenes Laërtius and the poem of Lucretius, *De Rerum Natura*. Information is also furnished by the writings of Cicero, especially the *De Finibus* and the *De Natura Deorum;* by those of Seneca, and by the treatise of Plutarch, "Against Colotes." Epicurus, according to Diogenes Laërtius, was a more voluminous writer than any other philosopher, having written as many as 300 volumes, in all of which he is said to have studiously avoided making quotations. All that now remains of his works are the letters contained in the tenth book of Diogenes Laërtius and parts of two books of his treatise on Nature (Περὶ Φύσεως), which were discovered at Herculaneum. The last were published at Leipzig in 1818, being edited by Orelli; further fragments will be found in the sixth volume of the *Hercul. Voll. Collectio Altera*, of which the first part appeared at Naples in 1866. A critical edition of the first two letters was given by Schneider (Leipzig, 1813). See Lange's *Geschichte des Materialismus* (Iserlohn, 1866); Trezza, *Epicuro e l'Epicureismo* (Florence, 1877); Zeller, *Philosophy of the Stoics, Epicureans, and Skeptics* (Eng. trans. 1880); Wallace, *Epicureanism* (1880); monographs by Gizycki (Halle, 1879) and Kreibig (Vienna, 1885); Susemihl, i. 87 foll., and the article PHILOSOPHIA.

Epicȳdes (Ἐπικύδης). A Carthaginian of Sicilian origin who served with his brother Hippocrates, under Hannibal, with much distinction. He was the leader of the Punic party in Syracuse after the murder of the tyrant Hieronymus, and defended that city against the Roman general Marcellus.

Epidamnus (Ἐπίδαμνος). See DYRRHACHIUM.

Epidauria (τὰ Ἐπιδαύρια). A festival at Athens in honour of Aesculapius (q. v.). See MYSTERIA.

Epidaurus (Ἐπίδαυρος). (1) A town in Argolis on the Saronic Gulf, forming, with its territory Epidauria, a district independent of Argos, and was not included in Argolis till the time of the Romans. It was the chief seat of the worship of Aesculapius, whose temple was situated about five miles from the town. On the inscriptions lately found there, see Gardner, *New Chapters in Greek History*, ch. xii. (1892). (2) Styled LIMĒRA, a town in Laconia, on the east coast, said to have been founded by Epidaurus in Argolis.

Epideipnis (ἐπιδειπνίς). A second course at dinner. See CENA.

Epidelium (Ἐπιδήλιον). A town on the southeastern coast of Laconia with a temple of Apollo which contained an image of the god, said to have been cast into the sea at Delos and to have drifted ashore at Epidelium. See Curtius, *Pelop.* ii. 298 (1852).

Epidĭcus (ἐπίδικος). An heiress. See EPICLERUS.

Epidĭcus. A play of Plautus (q. v.) written after B.C. 195, with a somewhat complex plot and rather dull. Editions by Jacob (Lübeck, 1835), Geppert (Berlin, 1865), and Gray (Cambridge, 1893).

Epidium. (1) One of the Ebudae Insulae, supposed to be the same with the modern Ila. (2) A promontory of Caledonia, corresponding to the southern extremity of the peninsula of Cantire.

Epidŏseis (ἐπιδόσεις). Voluntary contributions, either in money, arms, or ships, which were made by the Athenian citizens in order to meet the extraordinary demands of the State. When the expenses of the State were greater than its revenue, it was usual for the prytanes to summon an assembly of the people, and after explaining the necessities of the State, to call upon the citizens to contribute according to their means. Those who were willing to contribute then rose and mentioned what they would give, while those who were unwilling to give anything remained silent or retired privately from the assembly. The names of those who had promised to contribute, together with the amount of their contributions, were written on tablets, which were placed before the statues of the Eponymi, where they remained till paid.

These ἐπιδόσεις, or voluntary contributions, were frequently very large. Sometimes the more wealthy citizens voluntarily undertook a trierarchy, or the expenses of equipping a trireme (Demosth. *c. Mid.* p. 566, § 161). We read that Pasion furnished 1000 shields, together with five triremes, which he equipped at his own expense (Demosth. *c. Steph.* i. p. 1127, § 85). The liberality of Demosthenes himself was especially noteworthy; and his acts of munificence were recorded in the decree by which a crown was voted to him.

Epigamia (ἐπιγαμία). The right of contracting a valid marriage, with all its legal consequences. It was possessed only by citizens of the same State: aliens could acquire it only by special legal authorization—i. e. a decree of the popular assembly. At Athens even the *metoeci*, or resident aliens, were excluded from it. Cf. the article CONUBIUM.

Epigĕnes (Ἐπιγένης). (1) Of Sicyon, said to have been the oldest writer of tragedy, and to have preceded even Thespis. (2) An Athenian poet of the Middle Comedy who flourished about B.C. 380.

Epigŏni (Ἐπίγονοι, "descendants"). The sons of the Grecian heroes who were killed in the First Theban War. (See POLYNICES.) The War of the Epigoni is famous in ancient history. It was undertaken ten years after the first. The sons of those who had perished in the first war resolved to avenge the death of their fathers. The god, when consulted, promised them victory if led by Alcmaeon, the son of Amphiaraüs. Alcmaeon accordingly took the command. Another account, however, given by Pausanias (ix. 9, 2), makes Thersander, son of Polynices, to have been at the head of the expedition. The other leaders were Amphilochus, brother of Alcmaeon; Aegialeus, son of Adrastus; Diomedes, of Tydeus; Promachus, of Parthenopaeus; Sthenelus, of Capaneus; and Eurypylus, of Mecisteus. The Argives were assisted by the Messenians, Arcadians, Corinthians, and Megarians. The Thebans obtained aid from the neighbouring States. The invaders ravaged the villages about Thebes. A battle ensued, in which Laodamas, the son of Eteocles, slew Aegialeus, and fell himself by the spear of Alcmaeon. The Thebans then fled; and, by the advice of Tiresias, they secretly left their city, which was entered and plundered by the Argives, and Thersander was placed on the throne.

With the exception of the events of the Trojan War and the return of the Greeks, nothing was so closely connected with the *Iliad* and *Odyssey* as the War of the Argives against Thebes, since many of the principal heroes of Greece, particularly Diomedes and Sthenelus, were themselves among the conquerors of Thebes, and their fathers before them, a bolder and wilder race, had fought on the same spot, in a contest which, although unattended with victory, was still far from inglorious. Hence, also, reputed Homeric poems on the subject of this war were extant, which perhaps really bore a great affinity to the Homeric time and school. The second part of the *Thebaïs*, which related to the exploits of the Epigoni, was, according to Pausanias (ix. 9, 2), ascribed by some to Homer himself. The *Epigoni* was still commonly ascribed to Homer in the time of Herodotus (iv. 32). See HOMERUS.

Epigramma (ἐπίγραμμα). Properly an inscription, such as was often written upon a tomb, a votive offering, a present, a work of art, and the like, to describe its character. Inscriptions of this sort were from early times put into metrical form, and the writer generally tried to combine good sense and spirit in them. They were generally, though not always, written in the elegiac metre.

The greatest master of Greek epigram was Simonides of Ceos, the author of several of the sepulchral inscriptions on the warriors who fell in the Persian Wars. His lines are remarkable for repose, clearness, and force, both of thought and expression. Fictitious inscriptions were often written, contain ing brief criticisms on celebrated men—as poets, philosophers, artists—and their productions. The form of the epigram was also used to embody in concise and pointed language the clever ideas or the passing moods of the writer, often with a tinge of wit or satire. The occasional epigram was a very favourite form of composition with the Alexandrian poets, and remained so down to the latest times. Some writers, indeed, devoted themselves entirely to it. Many of the choicest gems of Greek literature are to be found in the epigrams. The epigrammatists used other metres besides the elegiac, especially the iambic. In later times more complex and almost lyrical measures were employed. The Greek Anthology has preserved some 4500 epigrams, of the greatest variety in contents, and from the hand of more than 300 poets. (See ANTHOLOGY.) Among these are found some of the most celebrated names of ancient and of later times. A great number of epigrams are also found in inscriptions.

Of all the Greek varieties of lyric poetry, the epigram was earliest welcomed at Rome. It lived on in an uninterrupted existence from Ennius till the latest times, being employed sometimes for inscriptions, sometimes for other and miscellaneous purposes. In the first application, the epigram was used after Ennius on sepulchral monuments, utensils, works of art, etc. In the first century B.C. epigrams were written by Pompilius, Q. Lutatius Catulus, Varro Atacinus, Licinius Calvus, and by others to whom erotic verses are ascribed. Many of the short poems of Catullus are truly epigrammatic, and in the second half of the first century A.D. Martial handled the epigram in various forms and with the power of a master. Augustus Caesar, Pedo, Cornificia, Sulpicia, and Gaetulius also wrote epigrams. Ausonius has several examples. We also have a collection of epigrams by Luxorius in the sixth century A.D. Many such poems are preserved in inscriptions, besides a great number in manuscript, which in modern times have been collected into a Latin Anthology. In its last form of development, the epigram figures largely in the writings of modern Latinists—the most successful of whom in this department were Bembo, Scaliger, Buchanan, More, Stroza, Sannazarius, Melanchthon, Porson, and Landor. Scaliger, in the third book of his *Poetics*, classifies the epigram according to its possession of *mel* (adulatory epigram), *fel* (vindictive epigram), *sal* (witty epigram), and *acetum*—with a fifth class combining two or more of these components. An excellent epigrammatic definition of the epigram is the following of unknown authorship:

> "Omne epigramma sit instar apis: sit aculeus illi;
> Sint sua mella; sit et corporis exigui."

This has been cleverly paraphrased in English as follows:

> "The qualities rare in a bee that we meet,
> In an epigram never should fail:
> The body should always be little and sweet,
> And a sting should be left in its tail."

A French writer, Lebrun, has left the following epigrammatic comparison of the merits of Catullus and Martial:

> "Par ses traits fins Martial nous surprit,
> Mais la finesse a sa monotonie.
> De l'épigramme il n'avait que l'esprit;
> Catulle seul en eut tout le genie."

BIBLIOGRAPHY.—A collection of Greek epigrams of the earlier sort can be made from the works mentioned under EPIGRAPHY; and the various editions of the Anthologies should be consulted—e. g. that of Boissonade, Jacobs, and Dübner in Didot's *Bibliotheca Scriptorum Graecorum;* and the *Anthologia Latina* of Riese (Teubner series) and Bährens (1883). See also Corraeus, *De Toto Eo Poematis Genere Quod Epigramma Dicitur* (1590); Cottunius, *De Conficiendo Epigrammate* (1632); V. Gallus, *De Epigrammate* (1641); Vavassor, *De Epigrammate Liber* (1669); Heumann, *Anthologia Latina* (1721); Fayolle, *Dictionnaire d'Epigrammes* (1817); Booth, *Epigrams, Ancient and Modern* (1863); and Dodd, *Epigrammatists of Mediæval and Modern Times*, 2d ed. (1875), which last contains a bibliography of the subject. A number of metrical verses in English of the best Greek epigrams is published by Bell (London, 1880), and a very good selection, with introduction, Greek text, translation, and notes, is that of Mackail (London, 1892). See Butler, *Amaranth and Asphodel* (1881).

Epigrăpheis (ἐπιγραφεῖς). See EISPHORA.

Epigraphy. From ἐπιγράφειν = *inscribere.* A word conventionally used to describe the scientific study of inscriptions. In its widest sense it has reference to all inscriptions, including words engraved on rings, or stamped on coins, lamps, jars, vases, and other articles of use or ornament; but more strictly it relates to the historical inscriptions carved upon slabs of stone (i. e. lapidary inscriptions), or upon plates of bronze and other metal. Classical philology and archæology owe an inestimable debt to the study of the inscriptions that have been preserved to us from the Greek and Roman world, and to the inscriptions of these two great centres of civilization this short sketch must be confined. (For other epigraphic remains, see the articles ASSYRIA; BABYLONIA; CUNEIFORM INSCRIPTIONS; HIEROGLYPHICS; PERSIA. For inscriptions on coins, see the article NUMISMATICS.)

I. GREEK.—The inscriptions of ancient Greece are more valuable than those of Rome, for the twofold reason that they date much further back in point of time, and because, being usually carved on marble, they have more generally survived the ravages of time than the bronze plates employed by the Romans, which were either melted by various conflagrations that consumed the buildings where they were stored, or else were carried off by invading armies to be made over into coins. There are, however, some inscribed Greek tablets of bronze still surviving, as well as thin plates of lead marked with inscriptions. (See the *Archäolog. Zeitung* for 1877, p. 196; and id. for 1878, p. 71; Franz, *Elementa Epigr. Graecae*, p. 168; and Roberts, *Greek Epigraphy*, pp. 234–242.) One of the Greek bronze plates is represented on the next page. It contains part of a treaty between Oeanthea and Chaleion.

Immense numbers of inscriptions were set up in ancient times, in all public buildings, in temples and theatres, and by the side of the great roads. Delphi and Olympia abounded in them; while the Parthenon and Acropolis at Athens, the Heraeum at Samos, the Artemisium at Ephesus, and, in fact, all the important sanctuaries, were great storehouses of inscriptions recording laws, decrees, treaties, gifts, arbitrations, and other memorable events of political and religious life. In all, some 30,000 ancient Greek inscriptions are known to scholars.

A brief account of the Greek alphabet is given

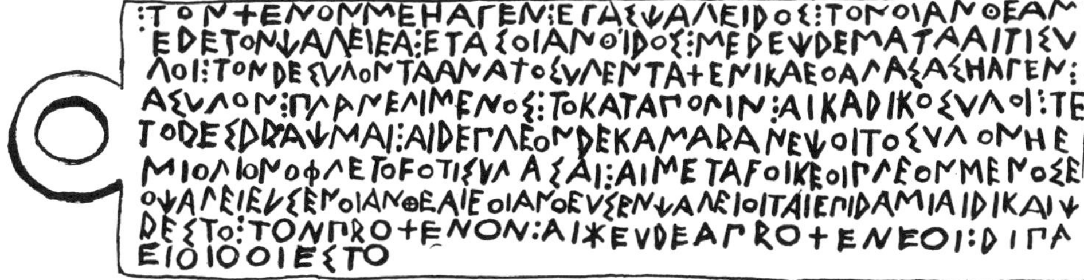

Bronze Treaty Tablet found at Oeanthea. (Woodhouse Collection.)

under the title ALPHABET, to which reference may be made. The alphabet itself is found in inscriptions in the so-called "abecedaria," of which one of the most interesting is the "Formello Alphabet," found at Formello near Veii, in Italy, in 1882 by Prince Chigi, and of which a representation is given below. It is the only abecedarium in existence which contains the archaic Greek forms of every one of the twenty-two Phœnician letters arranged precisely in the accepted Semitic order. (Cf. Roberts, *Greek Epigraphy*, p. 20.) It also enables us to determine the alphabetic position and the form of the Greek letter which represents the *san* (*shin*)—i. e. ⊞. (See Kirchhoff, *Studien zur Geschichte des griechischen Alphabets*, pp. 134 foll.). Other abecedaria are the "Alphabet of Caeré," on a black vase found in 1836 by Galassi at Cervetri (Kirchhoff, pp. 134 foll.); the "Alphabet of Colle," found painted on a tomb near Sienna in 1698; the "Cepolla Alphabet," found near Basta in Calabria by Luigi Cepolla in 1805 (Kirchhoff, p. 157); the "Corinthian Alphabet" (incomplete), on a piece of pottery from Corinth (Kirchhoff, p. 103); and the "Ionic Alphabet," from a fragment of a marble stelé found by Newton at Calymna (Roberts, p. 19).

The Formello Alphabet.

The usual form for the Greek inscribed marbles was the στήλη, a slab from three to five feet high and from three to four inches in thickness, slightly tapering to the top, which was plain or ornamented with a slight moulding. Another form of marble was the βωμός, or altar, square or circular. There are also pillars (κίονες), sarcophagi, statue-bases, and even the walls of the *cellae* of temples (*C. I. G.* 2905). Letters cut on walls and στῆλαι were picked out in blue or red pigment.

The oldest Greek inscriptions yet discovered are from the island of Thera (Santorin) in the Aegean, which are mortuary records, and are by some scholars dated as far back as the tenth century B.C. The oldest, however, to which a definite date can be assigned are found cut on the knee of a colossal statue at Abu Simbel in Egypt by Greek mercenaries in the service of Psammetichus, king of Egypt, and hence dating from the end of the seventh or the beginning of the sixth century B.C. Next in order come the inscriptions upon the bases of the statues set along the Sacred Way leading to the Temple of Apollo at Branchidae near Miletus, and assigned to the sixth century B.C. An inscription found by Newton at Halicarnassus, and known as the "Lygdamis Inscription," is of the time of Herodotus (B.C. 453), and is important as exhibiting the Ionic alphabet in almost exactly the form in which it was legally adopted at Athens, fifty years later. A fac-simile of this is given by Roberts in his *Greek Epigraphy*, p. 175. (See, also, Newton and Pullan, *Historical Discoveries at Halicarnassus*, etc., pp. 23 foll.). A very interesting Greek inscription is that upon the trophy set up at Delphi by the Greeks to commemorate the Persian defeat at Plataea, and now in the Hippodrome at Constantinople, whither it was brought by Constantine. See COLUMNA.

Inscription from a Block of Stone found at Thera. Ἐπάγατος ἐποίει.

Greek inscriptions may be conveniently grouped under the following heads: (1) Historical and Political (ψηφίσματα, νόμοι, treaties, records of awards and arbitrations between rival cities, letters from kings and other rulers, public accounts, lists of treasures, and laudatory inscriptions in honour of individuals); (2) Religious (rituals, laws relating to priests, calendars of sacrifices, rules of augury, etc.; prayers and imprecations, leases of sacred lands, oracles, etc.); (3) Private (dedications and honourary inscriptions, epitaphs, sepulchral inscriptions, boundary stones of mortgaged lands, inscriptions on statues, etc.). The finest collections of Greek inscribed marbles are those at Athens, London (British Museum), Paris (Louvre), Smyrna, Constantinople, and Oxford.

II. ROMAN.—The oldest Latin inscriptions do not date from an earlier period than the beginning of the sixth century B.C. The oldest of all is probably the so-called "Fibula Praenestina," a gold clasp found at Praenesté in 1886, with a short inscription written from right to left. Next in point of time comes the celebrated "Duenos Inscription" (q. v.), written (also from right to left) on three earthen pots, figured on p. 608, and called the "Vascula Dresseliana," from the archaeologist, Dr. Dressel.

Other Latin inscriptions of great historical and linguistic interest are those on the tombs of the Scipios, now in the Vatican Library, and other *tituli sepulcrales*, the Carmen Arvale (see FRATRES ARVALES), the Senatus Consultum de Bacchanalibus (see DIONYSIA, p. 521), and a number of *leges*, such as the Lex Acilia Repetundarum (*C. I. L.* 198); Lex Luci Lucerini on a stone found at Luceria (*C. I. L.* ix. 782), the Lex Luci Spoletini found at Spoletum in 1876 (Cortese, *Latini Sermonis Vetust. Exempla*, p. 11), the Lex Antonia Rubrica (*C. I. L.* 204), the Lex Salpensana and the

Lex Malacitana from Spain (*C. I. L.* ii. 1963, 1964), etc.

Vascula Dresseliana, showing the Duenos Inscription.

Roman inscriptions are, as a rule, of a much more formal character than the Greek, and are expressed in regular conventional formulae, with abbreviated designations of status for freemen, slaves, children, freedmen, and all the dignities and functions of official, military, and sacerdotal life. Formulaic, also, are the legal inscriptions of all kinds—the *sortes*, prayers, dedicatory sentences, and execrations—thus exemplifying the methodical and orderly character of the Roman mind. The most important of the epigraphic abbreviations are given in this Dictionary under the different letters of the alphabet. Informal inscriptions, especially the *graffiti* scratched upon the walls and elsewhere, are likewise numerous and valuable, and have a literature of their own. See GRAFFITI. The finest collections of Roman inscriptions are at Rome (Vatican, Capitoline Museum, etc.), Naples (Museo Nazionale), London (British Museum), Paris (Louvre), Vienna, and Munich.

Besides the Latin inscriptions proper, of which some 70,000 are now known, there are dialectic inscriptions in Oscan and Umbrian, and some 6000 in Etruscan. See ETRURIA; OSCI; TABULA BANTINA; TABULAE IGUVINAE; UMBRIA.

III. HISTORY OF EPIGRAPHY.—The ancients themselves fully recognized the historical value of inscriptions, so that both orators and historians continually cite them as evidence. (See Demosth. *De Falsa Legat.* 428; Aeschin. *In Ctes.* 75; Herod. iv. 88; v. 58; vii. 228; ix. 81; Thucyd. v. 18; and cf. Eurip. *Suppl.* 1202 foll.). Regular collections of Greek inscriptions were made by Philochorus (B.C. 300), Polemo (hence called στηλοκόπας), Aristodemus, and others. Cicero, Livy, Pliny the Elder, and Suetonius often cite important inscriptions. As soon as the revival of learning began after the downfall of the Roman Empire, the study of epigraphy commenced—first of the Latin remains by scholars like Poggio Bracciolini and Signorili in the fourteenth century, and then of both Greek and Latin by Cyriacus of Ancona, who copied great numbers of monumental inscriptions, in which he was followed by Marcanova, Felice Feliciano, Ferrarino, Marino Sanudo, and others in the fifteenth century. The first printed collections were published by Spreti (Ravenna, 1489), Peutinger (Augsburg, 1509), Huttich (Mayence, 1520), and Albertini (Rome, 1521). Early *corpora inscriptionum* are those of Apianus (Ingolstadt, 1534), Gruter (1603; re-edited by Graevius, 1707), Gudius (ed. by Hessel, 1731), Reinesius (1682), Fabretti (1699), Muratori (1739), Maffei (1749), and Donati (1765–75). Among these collections, however, were many inaccurately copied inscriptions and many actual forgeries and falsifications, so that only after critical study and acute investigation could they be used with safety. The sifting of the inscriptions by Maffei, Marini, and others with a view to the detection of falsehood and to scientific research, laid the foundations of critical epigraphy. In 1828, Orelli (q. v.) published two volumes of Roman inscriptions embodying the researches of Marini and others, and in the same year August Boeckh published the first volume of the *Corpus Inscriptionum Graecarum*, subsequently augmented by other volumes and by the labours of Franz and Kirchhoff. The publication of these works fixed the methods of epigraphy; and from this time on, numerous epigraphists have devoted themselves to the study of inscriptions and to the working up in monographs of the results obtained in their investigations. The great *Corpus Inscriptionum Latinarum* was projected as early as 1732 by Maffei, but was not actually begun until the work had been taken up by the Royal Academy of Sciences of Berlin. The first volume (*Inscriptiones Antiquissimae ad C. Caesaris Mortem*) appeared in 1863, containing also the *Fasti Consulares* and indices. Up to 1895, fifteen volumes had appeared under the editorship of Mommsen, Henzen, De Rossi, Hübner, Ritschl, Zangemeister, Wilmanns, Hirschfeld, Dessau, and others. The arrangement adopted is the geographical.

Of late, great attention to the study of inscriptions has been given by students of the dialects, especially the dialects of Greece, as the information which the epigraphic remains afford is much more reliable than that derived from literature with its conventional and frequently artificial language. See DIALECTS.

IV. BIBLIOGRAPHY.—Standard works on Greek epigraphy are the following: Franz, *Elementa Epigraphices Graecae* (1840); Keil, *Analecta Epigraphica* (1842); Reinach, *Traité d'Epigraphie Grecque* (Paris, 1885); Hicks, *Manual of Greek Historical Inscriptions* (Oxford, 1882); Roberts, *Introduction to Greek Epigraphy* (Cambridge, 1887). Important collections of Greek Inscriptions are the *Corpus Inscriptionum Graecarum*, 4 vols. (1828–1877); the *Corpus Inscriptionum Atticarum*, 3 vols. (1873–83); Lebas, *Voyage Archéologique en Grèce et en Asie Mineure*, 6 vols. (Paris, 1847); Keil, *Sylloge Inscriptionum Boeoticarum* (Leipzig, 1847); Kaibel, *Epigrammata Graeca ex Lapidibus Conlecta* (Berlin, 1878); Rangabé, *Antiquités Helléniques*, 2 vols. (Athens, 1842–55); Rose, *Inscriptiones Graecae Vetustessimae* (Cambridge, 1825); Roehl, *Imagines Inscriptionum Graec. Antiquissimarum* (Berlin, 1883); Hicks and Newton, *Collection of Anc. Gk. Inscript. in the British Museum*, 3 parts (Oxford, 1874–86); Cumanudes, Ἀττικῆς Ἐπιγραφαὶ Ἐπιτύμβιοι (Athens, 1871); Dittenberger, *Sylloge Inscriptionum Graecarum* (Leipzig, 1883); and with especial reference to the dialects, Cauer, *Delectus Inscriptionum Graecarum*, etc. (Leipzig, 1883); Collitz, *Sammlung der griechischen Dialekt-Inschriften*, 3 vols. (Göttingen, 1884–86); Larfeld, *Sylloge Inscriptionum Boeoticarum Popularem Dialectum Exhibentium* (Berlin, 1883); Roehl, *Inscript. Graec. Antiquiss. praeter Atticas in Attica Repert.* (Berlin, 1882); Hoffman, *Die griechischen Dialekte* (Göttingen, 1891). On the language of the Greek inscriptions see especially Meisterhans, *Grammatik der attischen Inschriften* (Berlin, 1885); Meister, *Die griechischen Dialekte* (Göttingen, 1882–89); and the bibliography given in the article DIALECTS. Other valuable supplementary reading will be found in the following: Hinrichs, the article "Griechische Epigraphik" in I. Müller's *Handbuch;* Newton, *Essays on Art and Archaeology* (London, 1880); Newton and Pullan, *History of Discoveries at Halicarnassus*, etc., 2 vols. (London, 1862); the article by Egger, *Des Collections des Inscriptions Grecques*, in the *Journal des Savants* for 1871; and Westermann in Pauly's *Real-Encyclopädie*, s. v. "Inscriptions."

Standard works on Roman epigraphy are the following: Cagnat, *Cours d'Épigraphie Latine* (2d ed. Paris, 1890); Egbert, *Introd. to Study of Lat. Inscriptions* (N. Y. 1895); Bone, *Anleitung zum Lesen, Ergänzen, und Datiren römischer Inschriften* (Trèves, 1881); Blanchère, *Hist. de l'Épigraphie Romaine* (Paris, 1887); the article "Römische Epigraphik" in I. Müller's *Handbuch;* and that by E. Hübner in the *Encyclopaedia Britannica*, s. v. "Inscriptions," vol. xiii. pp. 124–133. Valuable collections of Latin inscriptions are the *Corpus Inscriptionum Latinarum*, 15 vols. (Berlin, 1863 foll.); Morcelli, *Lexicon Epigraphicum* (Padua, 1819); Zell, *Handbuch der römischen Epigraphik*, 2 vols. (Heidelberg, 1850–52); Ritschl, *Priscae Latinitatis Monumenta Epigraphica*, with 5 supplements (Berlin, 1862); Hübner, *Exempla Scripturae Epigraphicae Latinae* (Berlin, 1885); and for general and convenient use, the two following: Wilmanns, *Exempla Inscriptionum Latinarum*, 2 vols. (Berlin, 1873); and Dessau, *Inscriptiones Latinae Selectae*, vol. i. (Berlin, 1892). A good selection of Latin inscriptions, with an introduction and commentary, is that of Wordsworth, *Fragments and Specimens of Early Latin* (Oxford, 1874), containing also literary remains. Elementary is the work of F. D. Allen, *Remnants of Early Latin* (Boston, 1884). A short and convenient collection, showing the forms of the letters, is that of Cortese, *Latini Sermonis Vetustioris Exempla Selecta* (Turin, 1892). For very early and dialectic Latin, see Schneider, *Dialectorum Italicarum Aevi Vetustioris Exempla Selecta* (Leipzig, 1886); and for Etruscan, Oscan, and Umbrian, Mommsen, *Die Unteritalische Dialekte* (Leipzig, 1850); Fabretti, *Corpus Inscrip. Italicarum Antiquitoris Aevi*, and its supplements (Turin, 1867, 1872–77); and the bibliography given in the articles ETRURIA; OSCI; UMBRIA. Christian inscriptions are collected by De Rossi (see CATACUMBAE); by Le Blant, *Inscriptions Chrétiennes de la Gaule*, 2 vols. (Paris, 1857–65); and by Hübner, *Inscriptiones Britanniae Christianae* (Berlin, 1876), and id. *Inscript. Hispaniae Christ.* (Berlin, 1871). See, also, Le Blant, *L'Épigraphie Chrétienne en Gaule et dans l'Afrique* (Paris, 1890). General supplementary reading will be found in Curtius's *Studien* (Leipzig, 1868–78); in Hübner's *Grundriss zu Vorlesungen über die lateinische Grammatik* (2d ed. Berlin, 1880); and the *Dizionario Epigrafico di Antichità Romane* (Rome, 1886 foll.).

Epimelētae (*ἐπιμεληταί*, "overseers"). The name given at Athens to commissioners nominated as occasion might require for the superintendence of departments. Some of these commissioners were regularly elected every year—as e. g. the ten *epimeletae* of the wharves, who were responsible for the care of the ships of war and equipments stored in the docks; and the ten commissioners of the Emporium, whose duty it was to enforce the laws relative to duties and commerce. For the commissioners of the revenue, see TAMIAS.

Epimenĭdes (Ἐπιμενίδης). A Cretan, contemporary with Solon, and born perhaps in B.C. 659, at Phaestus, in the island of Crete, according to some accounts, or at Cnosus according to others. Many marvellous tales are related of him. It is said that, going by his father's order in search of a sheep, he laid himself down in a cave, where he fell asleep and slept for fifty years, on which legend Goethe has written a poem. He then made his appearance among his fellow-citizens with long hair and a flowing beard, and with a knowledge of medicine and natural history which then appeared more than human. Another story told of this Cretan was that he had the power of sending his soul out of his body and recalling it at pleasure; that he had familiar intercourse with the gods, and possessed the power of prophecy. The event of his life by which he is best known was his visit to Athens at the request of the inhabitants, in order to pave the way for the legislation of Solon by purifications and propitiatory sacrifices. These rites were intended, according to the spirit of the age, to allay the feuds and party dissensions which prevailed there; and, although what he enjoined was mostly of a religious nature (for instance, the sacrifice of a human victim, the consecration of a temple to the Eumenides, and of two altars to Hybris and Anaidea, the two evil powers which were exerting their influence on the Athenians), there can be little doubt that his object was political, and that Solon's constitution would hardly have been accepted had it not been recommended and sanctioned by some person who, like Epimenides, claimed from men little less than the veneration due to a superior being. The Athenians wished to reward Epimenides with wealth and public honours, but he refused to accept any remuneration, and demanded only a branch of the sacred olive-tree and a decree of perpetual friendship between Athens and his native city. Epimenides is said to have lived, after his return to Crete, to the age of 157 years. Other accounts give his age as nearly 230 years. Divine honours were paid him by the Cretans after his death.

Epimenides composed a theogony and other poems concerning religious mysteries. He wrote also a poem on the Argonautic Expedition, and other works, which are entirely lost. His treatise on oracles and responses, mentioned by St. Jerome, is said to have been the work from which St. Paul quotes in the epistle to Titus (i. 12). See Diog. Laërt. i. 109; Val. Max. viii. 13. See the monograph by Schultess, *De Epimenide Crete* (Vienna, 1877).

Epimētheus (Ἐπιμηθεύς). "Afterthought." Brother of Prometheus and husband of Pandora. See PANDORA; PROMETHEUS.

Epimēthis. A patronymic of Pyrrha, the daughter of Epimetheus (Ovid, *Met.* i. 390).

Epinikion (*ἐπινίκιον*). A prize hymn, such as the odes of Pindar (q. v.), sung by the chorus in honour of the victors at the great national games.

Epiphanēa (Ἐπιφάνεια). (1) A town of Cilicia Campestris, southeast of Anazarbus, and situated on the small river Carsus, near the range of Mount Amanus (Plin. *H. N.* v. 27). (2) A city of Syria, on the Orontes, below Apamea. Its Oriental and true name was Hamath, and it was reckoned by the people of the East one of the most magnificent cities in the world, having been founded, as they imagined, by Hamath, one of the sons of Canaan. Allusion is frequently made to Hamath in the Old Testament. (Cf. Gen. x. 18; 2 Sam. viii. 9; 2 Kings, xlviii. 34.) Its name was changed to Epiphanea, in honour of Antiochus Epiphanes.

Epiphănes (Ἐπιφανής). A surname of Antiochus IV. and Antiochus XI., kings of Syria.

Epiphanius (Ἐπιφάνιος). A bishop of Salamis in Cyprus, in the fourth century. He was born of Jewish parents, near Eleutheropolis, in Palestine, about A.D. 320, and appears to have been educated in Egypt, where he imbibed the principles of the Gnostics. At length he left them, and, becoming an ascetic, returned to Palestine and adopted the discipline of St. Hilarion, the founder of monachism in that country. Epiphanius erected a monastery near the place of his birth, over which he presided till he was made bishop of Salamis in 367. Here he remained about thirty-six years, and composed most of his writings. In 391 he commenced a controversy with John, bishop of Jerusalem, relative to the Platonic doctrines of the learned and laborious Origen, against which he wrote and preached with implacable bitterness. John favoured Origen's views, but Epiphanius found in Theophilus, the violent bishop of Alexandria, a worthy coadjutor, who, in 399, convened a council and condemned all the works of Origen. Epiphanius himself then called a council in Cyprus, A.D. 401, and reiterated this condemnation. Afterwards, he embroiled himself with the empress Eudoxia; for on the occasion of her asking him to pray for the young Theodosius, who was dangerously ill, he replied that her son should live provided she would disavow the defenders of Origen. To this presumptuous message the empress indignantly answered that her son's life was not in the power of Epiphanius, whose prayers were unable to save that of his own archdeacon who had recently died. After thus vainly endeavouring to gratify his sectarian animosity, he resolved to return to Cyprus; but he died at sea on the passage, A.D. 403. The principal works of Epiphanius are: (1) Πανάριον, or a Treatise on Heresies—that is, peculiar sects (*αἱρέσεις*). This is the most important of his writings and treats of eighty sects, from the time of Adam to the latter part of the fourth century. (2) Ἀνακεφαλαίωσις, or an Epitome of the Panarion. (3) Ἀγκυρωτόν, or a Discourse on the Faith, explaining the doctrine of the Trinity, Resurrection, etc. (4) A treatise on the ancient weights, measures, and coins of the Jews. St. Jerome admires Epiphanius for his skill in the Hebrew, Syriac, Egyptian, Greek, and Latin languages, and styles him "Pentaglottus" (Πεντάγλωττος), or the Five-tongued. His writings are of great value, as containing numerous citations from curious works which are no longer extant. See the monograph by Lipsius (Vienna, 1865).

Epipŏlae (Ἐπιπολαί). See SYRACUSAE.

Epirredium. See REDA.

Epīrus (Ἤπειρος). A country to the west of Thessaly, lying along the Adriatic. The Greek term, which answers to the English word *mainland*, appears to have been applied at a very early period to that northwestern portion of Greece which is situated between the chain of Pindus and the Ionian Gulf and between the Ceraunian Mountains and the river Acheloüs—this name being probably used to distinguish it from the large, populous, and wealthy island of Corcyra, which lay opposite to the coast. It appears that, in very ancient times, Acarnania was also included in the term, and in that case the name must have been used in opposition to all the islands lying along the coast (Hom. *Od.* xiv. 100).

The inhabitants of Epirus were scarcely considered Hellenic. The population in early times had been Pelasgic. The oracle at Dodona was always called Pelasgic, and many names of places in Epirus were also borne by the Pelasgic cities of the opposite coast of Italy. But irruptions of Illyrians had barbarized the whole nation; and though Herodotus speaks of Thesprotia as a part of Hellas, he refers rather to its old condition, when it was a celebrated seat of the Pelasgians, than to its state at the time when he wrote his history. In their mode of cutting the hair, in their costume, and in their language, the Epirotes resembled the Macedonians, who were an Illyrian race. Theopompus, cited by Strabo, divided the inhabitants of Epirus into fourteen different tribes, of which the most renowned were the Chaonians, Thesprotians, and Molossians. The Molossians claimed descent from Molossus, son of Neoptolemus and Andromaché. Tradition reported that the son of Achilles, Neoptolemus or Pyrrhus, as he is also called, having crossed from Thessaly into Epirus on his return from the siege of Troy, was induced, by the advice of an oracle, to settle in the latter country, where, having subjugated a considerable extent of territory, he transmitted his newly formed kingdom to Molossus, his son by Andromaché, from whom his subjects derived the name of Molossi.

The history of Molossia is involved in great obscurity until the period of the Persian invasion, when the name of Admetus, king of the Molossi, occurs from the circumstance of his having generously afforded shelter to Themistocles when in exile and pursued by his enemies, although the influence of that celebrated statesman had previously been exerted against him in some negotiations which he had carried on at Athens (Thuc. i. 136). Admetus was succeeded by his son Tharybas or Tharymbas, who appears to have been a minor towards the beginning of the Peloponnesian War, when we find his subjects assisting the Ambraciots in their invasion of Acarnania. Tharybas is represented by Plutarch (*Pyrrh.*) as a wise and able monarch, and as encouraging science and literature. His successor is not known; but some years after, we hear of a prince called Alcetas, who was dethroned by his subjects but restored by Dionysius of Syracuse (Pausan. i. 11). Neoptolemus, his son, reigned but for a short time and left the crown to his brother Arybas, together with the care of his children. Alexander, the eldest of these, succeeded his uncle, and was the first sovereign of Epirus who raised the character and fame of that country among foreign nations by his talents and valour. His sister Olympias had been married to Philip of Macedon before his accession to the throne of Epirus, and the friendship thus cemented between the two monarchs was still further strengthened by the union of Alexander with Cleopatra, the daughter of Philip. It was during the celebration of their nuptials at Edessa that the king of Macedon was assassinated. Alexander of Epirus seems to have been an ambitious prince, desirous of conquest and renown. There is good reason for believing that he united the Chaonians, Thesprotians, and other Epirotic clans, together with the Molossians, under his sway, as we find the title of king of Epirus first assumed by him (Diod. Sic. xvi. 72). Having been applied to by the Tarentines to aid them against the attacks of the Lucani and Bruttii, he eagerly seized this opportunity of adding to his fame and enlarging his dominions. He therefore crossed over into Italy with a considerable force, and, had he been properly seconded by the Tarentines and the other colonies of Magna Graecia, the barbarians, after being defeated in several engagements, must have been conquered. But Alexander, being left to his own resources and exertions, was at length surrounded by the enemy and slain (B.C. 326) near Pandosia in the Bruttian territory (Livy, viii. 24). On the death of Alexander the crown devolved on his cousin Aeacides, the son of Arybas, the former king, of whom little is known, except that, having raised an army to assist Olympias against Cassander, his soldiers mutinied and deposed him; not long after, however, he appears to have been reinstated. His brother Alcetas, who succeeded him, was engaged in a war with Cassander, which proved disastrous; for, being defeated, his dominions were overrun by the forces of his victorious enemy, and he himself was put to death by his rebellious subjects. The name of Pyrrhus, who now ascended the throne, gives to the history of Epirus an importance it never would otherwise have possessed. (See PYRRHUS.) Alexander, the eldest son of Pyrrhus, succeeded his father, whom he sought to emulate by attempting afresh the conquest of Macedon. On this occasion Antigonus Gonatas was again vanquished and driven from his dominions. But Demetrius, his son, having raised another army, attacked Alexander and presently compelled him to evacuate the Macedonian territory (Just. xxvi. 3). At the expiration of two other insignificant reigns, the royal line of the Aeacidae becoming extinct, the Epirots determined to adopt a republican form of government, which prevailed until the subjugation of Macedon by the Romans. Having been accused of favouring Perseus in the last Macedonian War, they became the objects of the bitterest vengeance of the Romans, who treated them with unusual severity. Aemilius Paullus destroyed seventy of their towns and sold 150,000 of the inhabitants into slavery. Epirus, having lost its independence, was then annexed as a province to the Roman Empire. See Merleker, *Darstellung des Landes und der Berwohner von Epeiros* (Königsberg, 1841); and Bowen, *Athos, Thessaly, and Epirus* (London, 1852).

Epīrus Nova. See ILLYRICUM.

Episcepsis (ἐπίσκηψις). See MARTYRIA.

Episcŏpi (ἐπίσκοποι). Inspectors or commissioners, who were sometimes sent by the Athenians to interfere in the affairs of subject States (*C. I. A.* i. 9, 10). The episcopi exercised civil authority, and perhaps judged on the spot small causes where Athenians were concerned. The episcopus in Aristophanes carries two ballot-boxes (κάδω, *Av.* 1032, 1053). From the same source we learn that these episcopi received a salary at the cost of the State to which they were sent, and that they were appointed by lot.

Epistătes (ἐπιστάτης). See BOULÉ.

Epistŏla (ἐπιστολή). A letter, written upon paper for transmission to an absent person, as distinguished from one written upon waxed tablets (Cic.; Caes.; Tac.; Mart. *Ep.* xiv. 11, *chartae epistolares.*) The annexed illustration represents a letter

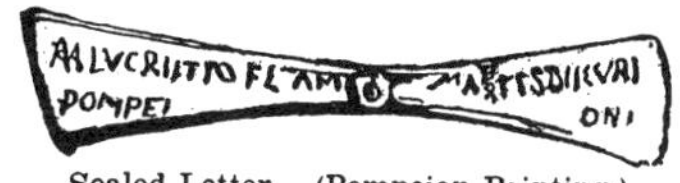

Sealed Letter. (Pompeian Painting.)

folded and sealed, with its direction, as represented by a painting on the walls of a house at Pompeii, in which it is accompanied by various implements employed for writing, both on paper and wax. It is engraved in the *Mus. Borb.* xiv. tav. A and B, 1852, where the address upon it is thus deciphered: MARCO LUCRETIO FLAMINI MARTIS DECURIONI POMPEI.—"To Marcus Lucretius, Priest of Mars, Decurion, Pompeii." (See WRITING AND WRITING MATERIALS.) Letters usually had prefixed to them the name of the sender and the person addressed, and were not signed at the end. The following are some of the usual forms: CICERO VARRONI (Cicero to Varro); CICERO DOLABELLAE S. (Cicero to Dolabella, greeting); CICERO PLANCO S. D. (Cicero to Plancus gives greeting); CICERO IMP. PLANCO (Cicero, the commander, to Plancus); CICERO D. BRUTO S. P. D. (Cicero to Decimus Brutus gives a hearty greeting); CICERO TERENTIAE SUAE (Cicero to his Terentia). S. stands for *salutem;* S. D. *salutem dicit;* and S. P. D. for *salutem plurimam dicit.* Formulas of courtesy that often begin letters are the following: S. V. B. E. (*si vales, bene est*); S. V. B. E. E. V. (*si vales bene est; ego valeo*); S. V. E. Q. V. B. E. E. Q. V. (*si vos exercitusque valetis bene est; ego quoque valeo*), etc. Phrases of courtesy or affection at the end of a letter are the following: *Vale.—Cura ut valeas.—Da operam ut valeas.—Fac ut diligentissime te ipsum custodias.—Cura ut valeas et me, ut amas, ama.—Cura ut valeas et nos ames et tibi persuadeas te a me fraterne amari.—Vale et nos dilige.—Bene vale et me dilige.—Fac valeas meque ames.—Tu, ut instituisti, me diligas rogo, proprieque tuum esse tibi persuadeas.—Fac valeas meque mutuo diligas.—Etiam atque etiam vale.*

The date and place, if written at all, are given at the end of the letter. Thus: *Data pr. Kal. Mai. Brundisii.—Hoc ex Nicia*, etc.

The epistle plays an important part in ancient as in modern literature, though in classical Greek literature the number of genuine letters is small. The collection attributed to Plato, though highly interesting and regarded by Grote as authentic, is rejected by recent scholarship; and so the letters ascribed to Demosthenes, to Aeschines, and to Xenophon. The nine that bear the name of Isocrates are universally accepted as his. (See ISOCRATES.) Three letters of Epicurus are preserved by Diogenes Laërtius. Specimens of the official epistle are to be seen in the oration of Demosthenes on the Crown. Much valuable information on the history of the times is gathered from the later Greek letters of Gregory Nanzianzenus, Basil, Chrysostom, and other ecclesiastical writers.

Letter writing was from an early period cultivated among the Romans, and both official and personal letters of eminent men soon began to be collected, such as the letters of the elder Cato to his son, and of Cornelia to C. Gracchus. At a later period, those of Caesar, Brutus, and especially of Cicero, were preserved. Most of the Roman letters remaining to us are not the genuine private correspondence of their authors, but were from the first written with an eye to publication, like the priggish and self-conscious epistles of the younger Pliny. The most valuable correspondence ever preserved is that of Cicero, whose letters to the number of nearly one thousand were published by his amanuensis, Tiro (q. v.). These are the familiar effusions of the orator, written with no view to publication, and are invaluable for the light they throw upon the personality of the writer and the history of his times. See CICERO.

Examples of letters in historical works are those in Antipater, Quadrigarius, and especially in Sallust. The epistolary form was also used by the jurists for their *responsa* on questions of law; by scholars for their learned discussions (e. g. Verrius Flaccus, Lactantius, etc.); by physicians for medical expositions (e. g. Marcellus Empiricus and Oribasius); and by the rhetoricians of the imperial age as a form of stylistic exercise. (See Teuffel, *Hist. of Rom. Lit.*, Eng. trans., i. pp. 73–76). Next to the letters of Cicero, those of Pliny the Younger are most read. Other important letter-writers are Seneca, Fronto, Symmachus, Sidonius, and still later Salvianus, Ruricius, Ennodius, Lactantius, Ambrose, Jerome, Augustine, and Cassiodorus. Specimens of Vergil's correspondence are given by Macrobius (i. 24, 11).

The poetical epistle was cultivated as early as B.C. 146 by Sp. Mummius, who, when in camp before Corinth, addressed satirical letters in verse to friends at Rome (Cic. *Ad Att.* xiii. 6, 4). Several of the satires of Lucilius were composed in the form of letters, and the poem of Catullus to Manlius (68 A) is in the epistolary form. The most successful in this department of literature were Horace in his two books of *Epistolae* and Ovid in the imaginary love-letters (*Heroides*) and in his own genuine lamentations from exile (*Tristia* and the *Epistolae ex Ponto*). Statius, Ausonius, and Claudianus are later examples of the poetical epistolographer.

Forged letters are frequently found in Latin literature. Instances are the *Epistulae Medicinales* professedly from Hippocrates to Maecenas, and the celebrated fourteen letters which form the alleged correspondence between Seneca and St. Paul, which were, however, accepted as genuine by St. Jerome (*De Vir. Illust.* 12), and by St. Augustine (*Epist.* 153). On these see Fleury, *St. Paul et Sénèque* (Paris, 1853); Lightfoot, *St. Paul's Epist. to the Philippians*, p. 260 (London, 1868); and Aubertin, *Sénèque et St. Paul* (Paris, 1869).

BIBLIOGRAPHY. — See Roberts, *Hist. of Letter Writing* (1843); Grote, *Plato and the other Companions of Socrates*, ii. pp. 220 foll.; Czwalina, *De Epistularum Actorumque, etc. Fide et Auctoritate* (Bonn, 1871); Nisard, *Notes sur les Lettres de Cicéron* (Paris, 1882); and Tyrrell's introduction to his edition of the Correspondence of Cicero (1893). The Greek epistolographers are collected by Hercher in his *Epistolographi Graeci* (Paris, 1873); and on the Latin rhetorical letter writers see Halm's *Rhetores Latini*, pp. 447 foll. and 589. On the epistle in fiction, see NOVELS AND ROMANCES.

Epistŏla. See CONSTITUTIONES.

Epistŏleus (ἐπιστολεύς). The vice-admiral of the Spartan fleet who took command in case of the disability of the admiral (ναύαρχος). See Xen. *Hellen.* i. 1, 23; Pollux, i. 96.

Epistomium (ἐπιστόμιον). The cock of a water-pipe, or of any vessel containing liquids to be drawn off in small quantities when required (Vitruv. ix. 8, 11). The illustration represents an original bronze water-cock found at Pompeii.

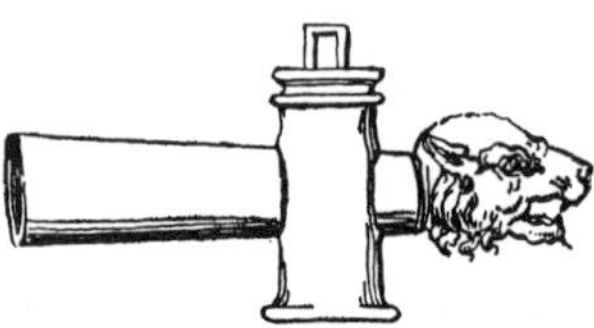

Epistomium of Bronze. (Pompeii.)

Epistylium (ἐπιστύλιον). The architrave, or lower member of an entablature, consisting of one or several beams (in the Parthenon, three), resting upon the capitals. Its function is to bind the columns of the peripteros into a whole, and to distribute the weight of the superstructure (Plut. *Pericl.* 13). The name is sometimes given to the whole entablature.

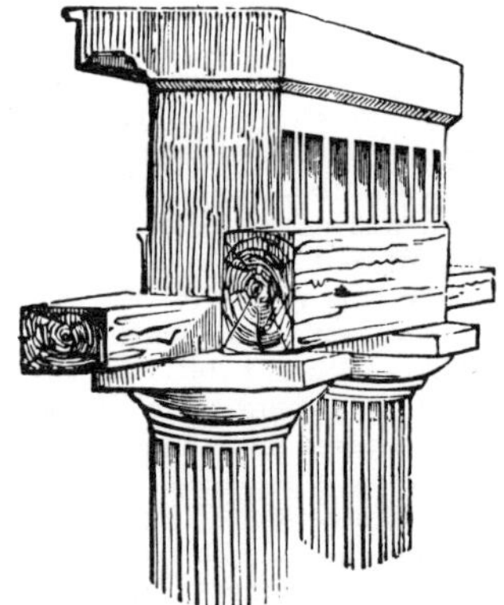

Epistylium. (Doric Portico at Pompeii.)

Epitaphium (ἐπιτάφιον) or **Epitaphius** (ἐπιτάφιος λόγος). A funeral oration. See FUNUS.

Epitaphs. See TITULUS.

Epithalamium (τὸ ἐπιθαλάμιον μέλος). A nuptial song. (See MATRIMONIUM.) In Greek, Sappho, Anacreon, Stesichorus, and Pindar composed poems of this kind, of which, however, only fragments remain. We have three epithalamia of Catullus, of which that on the marriage of Peleus and Thetis is one of the most splendid in all literature. In the imperial age, Statius, Ausonius, Claudianus, Paulinus of Nola, Sidonius Apollinaris, Dracontius, Ennodius, Luxorius, Venantius Fortunatus wrote poems of the same class that have survived. Those of Ausonius and Luxorius are Vergilian centos. (See CENTO.) A collection of Latin epithalamia may be found in Wernsdorf's *Poetae Latini Minores*, iv. pt. ii. 462.

Epitimia (ἐπιτιμία). The full possession of civic privileges, the opposite of *atimia* (q. v.)

Epitŏmé. The name given to several abridgments by various Roman authors. The most important are (1) An abridgment of Livy's history commonly called *Periochae* (*T. Livi Periochae Omnium Librorum*). (See LIVIUS.) (2) A short history of the Roman emperors down to Theodosius I. and ascribed to Aurelius Victor (q. v.). (3) The *Epitome Iliadis*, a school-book of 1070 hexameters, which contains a summary of the story of the *Iliad*. This work, whose author was unknown, was much read during the Middle Ages, being sometimes styled Homerus and sometimes (by a curious error) Pindarus Thebanus. Bergk (*Philologus*, xiv. p. 184) conjectures that the writer was the Atticus mentioned by Persius (i. 50). The text will be found in Wernsdorf's *Poetae Lat. Minores*, iv. pp. 617–752; and has been edited by Weytingh (Leyden and Amsterdam, 1809) and Plessis (Paris, 1885). The poem is now ascribed to Silius Italicus (q. v.). See Verres, *De Silii Punicorum et Italici Iliadis Lat. Quaestiones Grammaticae et Metricae* (Münster, 1888). (4) The *Epitome Iuliani*, a collection of imperial *constitutiones*, made between A.D. 535 and 555.

Epitrierarchemătos Diké (ἐπιτριηραρχήματος δίκη). See TRIERARCHIA.

Epitrŏpes Graphé (ἐπιτροπῆς γραφή). A suit brought against a guardian for neglect or abuse of his ward. See EPITROPUS; KAKOSEOS DIKÉ.

Epitrŏpus (ἐπίτροπος). Literally, a person to whose charge anything is intrusted (Herod. iii. 63); but more specifically a term of Attic law denoting the guardian of orphan children. There were two kinds of ἐπίτροποι: (1) those appointed by the will of the deceased father, usually relatives of the children; and (2) in the absence of a will the next of kin, corresponding to the Roman *tutores legitimi*, the archon deciding who were best entitled to the charge, and giving them the authority to act as guardians (Poll. viii. 89; Lys. *De Aristoph. Bon.* § 9). If there were no relatives to undertake the office, the archon selected guardians from the whole body of the citizens. The legal number of guardians is not known. The duties of an ἐπίτροπος included the maintenance (τροφή), education (παιδεία), and protection of the ward, the assertion of his rights, the management of his property, and provision for the widow of the deceased if she remained in the house of her late husband. The guardianship expired when the ward reached his eighteenth year.

Epōdon (ἐπῳδόν) or **Epōdos** (ἐπῳδός). A name applied by grammarians to any poem in which a long and a short line are combined, especially an iambic trimeter and dimeter. The so-called *Epodes* of Horace were by him styled simply *Iambi* (*Epod.* xiv. 7). See Beck, *De Vera Epodon Horat. Indole* (Troppau, 1873); and the article HORATIUS.

Epōmis (ἐπωμίς). See TUNICA.

Epŏna. From *epus* = *ecus* or *equus*. A Roman goddess presiding over horses. Paintings and statues of her were frequently placed in stables.

Eponia (ἐπώνια). See TELOS.

Eponȳmus (ἐπώνυμος). Properly the person after whom anything is named. This was in various Greek States the unofficial title of the magistrates after whom (in default of a generally received standard of chronology) the year was designated. In Athens this would be the first archon, in Sparta the first ephor, in Argos the priestess of Heré. When the *ephebi*, at Athens, were enrolled in the list of the citizens who could be called out for military service, the name of the first archon of the year was attached. And when the citizens of various ages were summoned to military service, a reference was made to the Archon Eponymus, under whom they had been originally enrolled. The ancient heroes, who gave their name to the ten tribes of Clisthenes, and the heroes worshipped by the demes, were also called *eponymi*. The statues of the former were in the market-place, and it was near them that official notices were put up. See CALENDARIUM.

Epōpeus (Ἐπωπεύς). Son of Poseidon and Canacé, the daughter of Aeolus, brother of Aloeus. He migrated from Thessaly to Sicyon, where he became king. He was killed by Lycus for the sake of Antiopé, who, it was alleged, was by him mother of Zethus.

Epoptae (ἐπόπται). See ELEUSINIA.

Eporedia. The modern Ivrea, a town in Gallia Cisalpina, on the Duria, in the territory of the Salassi, colonized by the Romans, B.C. 100, to serve as a bulwark against the neighbouring Alpine tribes.

Epos (ἔπος). (1) GREEK.—Many indications point to the fact that the oldest poetry of the Greeks was connected with the worship of the gods, and that religious poetry of a mystical kind was composed by the priests of the Thracians, a musical and poetical people, and diffused in old times through Northern Greece. The worship of the Muses was thus derived from the Thracians, who in later times had disappeared from Greece Proper; and accordingly the oldest bards whose names are known to the Greeks—Orpheus, Musaeus, Eumolpus, Thamyris—are supposed to have been Thracians also. The current ideas of the nature and action of the gods tended more and more to take the form of poetical myths respecting their birth, actions, and sufferings. Hence, these compositions, of which an idea may be derived from some of the so-called Homeric Hymns, gradually assumed an epic character. In course of time the epic writers threw off their connection with religion, and struck out on independent lines. Confining themselves no longer to the myths about the gods, they celebrated the heroic deeds both of mythical antiquity and of the immediate past. Thus, in the Homeric descriptions of the epic age, while the bards Phemius and Demodocus appear as favourites of the gods, to whom they are indebted for the gift of song, they are not attached to any particular worship. The subjects of their song are not only stories about the gods, such as the loves of Ares and Aphrodité, but the events of recent times, the conquest of Troy by means of the wooden horse, and the tragic return of the Achaeans from Troy. Singers like these, appearing at public festivals, and at the tables of princes, to entertain the guests with their lays, must have existed early in Greece Proper. It was, however, the Ionian Greeks of Asia Minor who first fully developed the capacities of epic poetry. By long practice, extending probably through centuries, a gradual progress was probably effected from short lays to long epic narratives; and at the same time a tradition delivered from master to scholar handed on and perfected the outer form of style and metre. Thus, about B.C. 900, epic poetry was brought to its highest perfection by the genius of Homer, the reputed author of the *Iliad* and *Odyssey*. After Homer it sank, never to rise again, from the height to which he had raised it. See HOMERUS.

It is true that in the following centuries a series of epics, more or less comprehensive, were composed by poets of the Ionic school in close imitation of the style and metre of Homer. But not one of them succeeded in coming even within measurable distance of their great master. The favourite topics of these writers were such fables as served either to introduce, or to extend and continue, the *Iliad* and *Odyssey*. They were called Cyclic Poets perhaps because the most important of their works were afterwards put together with the *Iliad* and *Odyssey* in an epic cycle, or circle of lays. The Cyprian poems (τὰ Κύπρια), of Stasinus of Salamis in Cyprus (B.C. 776), formed the introduction to the *Iliad*. These embraced the history of the period between the marriage of Peleus and the opening of the *Iliad*. At about the same time Arctinus of Miletus composed his *Aethiopis* in five books. This poem started from the conclusion of the *Iliad*, and described the death of Achilles, and of the Ethiopian prince Memnon, the contest for the arms of Achilles, and the suicide of Aias. The *Destruction of Ilium*, by the same author, was in two books. By way of supplement to the Homeric *Iliad*, Lesches of Mitylené, either about B.C. 708 or 664, wrote a *Little Iliad*, in four books. This embraced the contest for the arms of Achilles, the appearance of Neoptolemus and Philoctetes, and the capture of the city. The transition from the *Iliad* to the *Odyssey* was formed by the five books of Νόστοι (*The Return of the Heroes*), written by Agias of Troezen. The *Telegonia*, by Eugammon of Cyrené (about 570), continued the *Odyssey*. This was in two books, embracing the history of Odysseus from the burial of the suitors until his death at the hands of his son Telegonus. These poems and those of the other cyclics were, after Homer, the sources from which the later lyric and dramatic poets drew most of their information. But only fragments of them remain. See CYCLIC POETS.

A new direction was given to epic poetry in Greece Proper by the didactic and genealogical poems of Hesiod of Ascra, about a hundred years after Homer. Hesiod was the founder of a school, the productions of which were often attributed to him as those of the Ionic school were to Homer. One of these disciples of Hesiod was Eumelus of Corinth (about B.C. 750), of the noble family of the Bacchiadae. But his poems, like those of the rest, are lost. See HESIODUS.

The most notable representatives of mythical epic poetry in the following centuries are Pisander of Camirus (about B.C. 640), and Panyasis of Halicarnassus (during the first half of the fifth century). In the second half of the fifth century Choerilus of Samos wrote a *Perseïs* on the Persian Wars, the first attempt in Greece at an historical epic. His younger contemporary, Antimachus of Colophon, also struck out a new line in his learned *Thebaïs*, the precursor and model of the later epic of Alexandria. The Alexandrians laid great stress on learning and artistic execution in detail, but usually confined themselves to poems of less magnitude. The chief representatives of the Alexandrian school are Callimachus (about B.C. 250), Rhianus, Euphorion, and Apollonius of Rhodes. The last made a futile attempt to return to the simplicity of Homer. His *Argonautica* is, with the exception of the Homeric poems, the only Greek epic which has survived from the ante-Christian era. In the 200 years between the fourth and sixth centuries A.D., the mythical epic is represented by Quintus Smyrnaeus, Nonnus, Colluthus, Tryphiodorus, Musaeus, and the apocryphal Orpheus. Nonnus, Colluthus, and Tryphiodorus were Egyptians. Nonnus and Musaeus, alone among these writers, have any claim to distinction. The talent of Nonnus is genuine, but undisciplined; Musaeus knows how to throw a charm into his treatment of a narrow subject. The whole series is closed by the *Iliaca* of Joannes Tzetzes, a learned but tasteless scholar of the twelfth century A.D. See TZETZES.

As Homer was the master of the mythical, so Hesiod was the master of the didactic epic. After him this department of poetry was best represented by Xenophanes of Colophon, Parmenides of Elea, and Empedocles of Agrigentium, in the sixth and fifth centuries B.C. In the Alexandrian period, didactic poetry was much taken up, and employed upon the greatest possible variety of subjects. But none of its representatives succeeded in writing more than poetic prose, or in handling their intractable material with the mastery which Vergil shows in his Georgics. The period produced the astronomical epic of Aratus of Sicyon (about B.C. 275), and two medical poems by Nicander of Colophon (about 150). Under the Roman Empire more didactic poetry was produced by the Greek writers. Maximus and the so-called Manetho wrote on astrology. Dionysius Periegetes on geography, Oppian on angling, and an imitator of Oppian on hunting. The Alexandrian period also produced didactic poems in iambic senarii, as, e.g., several on geography bearing the names of Dicaearchus and Scymnus, which still survive.

(2) ROMAN. — The Romans possibly had songs of an epic character from the earliest times; but these were soon forgotten. They had, however, a certain influence on the later and comparatively artificial literature, for both Livius Andronicus in his translation of the *Odyssey*, and Naevius in his *Punic War*, wrote in the traditional Italian metre, the *versus Saturnius*. Naevius was, it is true, a national poet, and so was his successor Ennius, but the latter employed the Greek hexameter metre, instead of the rude Saturnian. To follow the example of Ennius, and celebrate the achievements of their countrymen in the form of the Greek epic, was the ambition of several poets before the fall of the Republic. A succession of poets, as Hostius, the tragedian Attius, and Furius were the authors of poetical annals. Here it is proper also to mention Cicero's epics on Marius and on his own consulship, besides the poem of Terentius Varro of Atax (Atacinus) on Caesar's war with the Sequani (*Bellum Sequanicum*). Latin epics on Greek mythical subjects seem to have been rare in the republican age. At least we know of only a few translations, as that of the *Iliad* by Mattius and Ninnius Crassus, and of the *Cypria* by Laevinus. Toward the end of the republican age it was a favourite form of literary activity to write in free imitation of the learned Alexandrians. Varro of Atax, for example, followed Apollonius of Rhodes in his *Argonautica*; others, like Helvius Cinna and the orator Licinius Calvus, preferred the shorter epics so much in favour with the Alexandrians. Only one example in this style is completely preserved, the quasi epithalamium (lxiv.) of Catullus. This is the only ex-

ample we possess of the narrative epic of the Republic.

But in the Augustan Age both kinds of epic, the mythic and the historical, are represented by a number of poets. Varius Rufus, Rabirius, Cornelius Severus, and Pedo Albinovanus treated contemporary history in the epic style; Domitius Marsus and Macer turned their attention to the mythology. The *Aeneid* of Vergil, the noblest monument of Roman epic poetry, combines both characters. Of all the epic productions of this age, the only ones which are preserved intact are the *Aeneid*, a panegyric on Messala, which found its way into the poems of Tibullus, and perhaps two poems, the *Culex* and *Ciris*, both often attributed to Vergil. See VERGILIUS.

In the first century A.D. we have several examples of the historical epic: the *Pharsalia* of Lucan, the *Punica* of Silius Italicus, a *Bellum Civile* in the satirical romance of Petronius, and an anonymous panegyric on Calpurnius Piso, who was executed for conspiracy under Nero, A.D. 65. The heroic style is represented by the *Argonautica* of Valerius Flaccus, and the *Thebaïs* and *Achilleïs* of Statius, to which we may add the metrical epitome of the *Iliad* by the so-called Pindarus Thebanus. The politico-historical poems of the succeeding centuries, by Publius Porfirius Optatianus in the fourth century, Claudianus, Merobaudes, Sidonius Apollinaris in the fifth, Priscian, Corippus, and Venantius Fortunatus in the sixth, are entirely panegyric in character, and intended to do homage to the emperor or men of influence. Of all these poets, Claudianus is the most important. He and Dracontius (towards the end of the fifth century) are among the last who take their subjects from mythology.

Didactic poetry, which suited the serious character of the Romans, was early represented at Rome. In this the Romans were in many ways superior to the Greeks. Appius Claudius Caecus and the elder Cato were authors of gnomic poetry. Ennius, the tragedian Attius, and several of his contemporaries wrote didactic pieces; the satires of Lucilius and Varro were also in part didactic. It was, however, not till the end of the republican period that the influence of Greek literature gave predominance to the Greek epic form. It was then adopted by Varro of Atax, by M. Cicero, and above all by Lucretius, whose philosophical poem *De Rerum Natura* is the only didactic poem of this period that has been preserved intact, as it is one of the most splendid monuments of Roman genius. In the Augustan Age many writers were active in this field. Valgius Rufus and Aemilius Macer followed closely in the steps of the Alexandrians. Grattius wrote a poem on hunting, a part of which still survives; Manilius, an astronomical poem which survives entire. But the *Georgics* of Vergil throw all similar work, Greek or Latin, into the shade. Ovid employs the epic metre in his *Metamorphoses* and *Halieutica*, the elegiac in his *Fasti*.

In the first century A.D. Germanicus translated Aratus. Columella wrote a poem on gardening; an unknown author (often called Lucilius), the *Aetna*. The third century produced the medical poem of Sammonicus Serenus, and that of Nemesianus on hunting. In the fourth we have Ausonius, much of whose work is didactic; Palladius on agriculture; an adaptation of Aratus and of Dionysius Periegetes by Avienus, with a description of the sea-coasts of the known world in iambics; in the fifth, besides some of Claudianus's pieces, a description by Rutilius Namatianus in elegiacs of his return home. The book of Dionysius Periegetes was adapted by Priscian in the sixth century. A collection of proverbs, bearing the name of Cato, belongs to the fourth century. In most of these compositions the metrical form is a mere set off; and in the school verses of the grammarians, as in those by Terentianus Maurus on metres, and in those by an anonymous author on rhetorical figures, and on weights and measures, there is no pretence of poetry at all.

See Lang, *Homer and the Epic* (London, 1893); Haube, *De Carminibus Epicis Saeculi Augusti* (Breslau, 1870); id. *Die Epen des silb. Zeitalters*, etc. (Fraustadt, 1886); and an article by Winckelmann in Jahn's *Archiv*, ii. 558. On the language of Roman epic poetry, see Köne, *Sprachgebrauch d. röm. Epiker* (Münster, 1840).

Epulōnes (Masters of the Feast). The office of *epulo* at Rome was created B.C. 196 to relieve the Pontifices. It was, from the first, open to plebeians, and could be held with the great offices of State. The first duty of the epulones was to provide the banquets (*epulum*) of the Capitoline deities. (See LECTISTERNIUM.) In later times they had also to provide for and superintend the public entertainment (*epulae*) of the people, when the Senate dined on the Capitol. Such entertainments

Epulo on Roman Coin.

were always provided at the games given by private individuals, or by the State, on occasions of religious festivals, dedications of temples, assumptions of office, triumphs, funerals, birthdays in the imperial household, and the like. The Collegium Epulonum consisted originally of three members (*tres viri epulones*) and afterwards of seven (*septem viri epulones*), a name which it retained even after Caesar had raised the number to ten. Its existence can be traced down to the end of the fourth century. In the illustration given above from a Roman denarius, an epulo is shown engaged in preparing the couch for the *epulum Iovis*.

Epŭlum. See EPULONES; LECTISTERNIUM.

Epytĭdes. A patronymic given to Periphas, the son of Epytus and the companion of Ascanius (Verg. *Aen.* v. 547).

Equarius. A horse-doctor (Val. Max. ix. 15, 2). The illustration from a Roman bas-relief discovered in southern France shows a veterinary surgeon bleeding a horse.

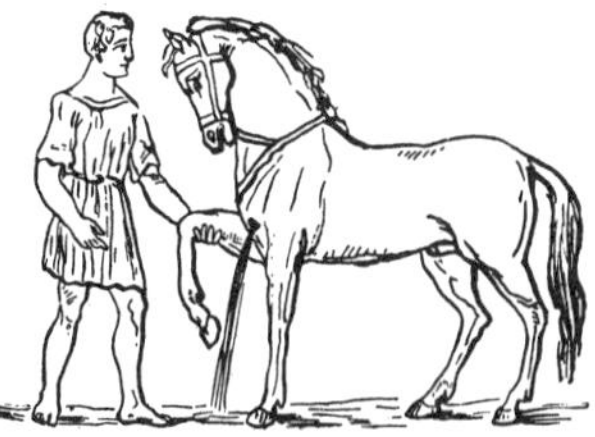
Equarius. (Rich.)

Equester (Ἵππιος). A title given to several deities, but especially to Poseidon and Neptune, who first created the horse, and in whose honour, therefore, horse-races were held (Pausan. v. 15, 4; Livy, i. 9).

Equestrian Ring. See Ius Anuli Aurei.

Equiria or **Equirria.** A festival established at Rome by Romulus in honour of Mars, when horse-races and games were exhibited in the Campus Martius. It took place on the 27th of February (Varr. *L. L.* v. 3; Ovid, *Fast.* ii. 859).

Equĭtes (horsemen or knights). The *equites* were originally a real division of the Roman army. At the beginning of the kingly period they were called Celeres, and their number is said to have been 300, chosen in equal parts from the three tribes of the Ramnes, Tities, and Luceres. (See Tribus.) A hundred formed a *centuria*, each *centuria* being named after the tribe from which it was taken. Thirty made a *turma*, and ten were under the command of a *decurio* (q. v.), while the whole corps was commanded by the *tribunus celerum.* During the course of the kingly period the body of equites was increased to sixteen *centuriae*, and the constitution of Servius Tullius finally raised it to eighteen. When the twelve new centuries were formed, consisting of the richest persons in the State, whose income exceeded that of the first class in the census, the corps of equites lost the exclusively patrician character which had hitherto distinguished it. At the same time its military importance was diminished, as it no longer formed the first rank, but took up a position on the wings of the phalanx. (See Exercitus.) The equites, however, retained both in the State and in the army their personal prestige. In the Comitia they voted first, and in *centuriae* of their own. They were the most distinguished troops in the army. No other soldiers were in a position to keep two horses and a groom apiece, a costly luxury, although they received an allowance for the purchase and keep of their horse. After the introduction of the pay system they received three times as much as the ordinary troops; on occasion of a triumph three times the ordinary share of booty; and at the foundation of a colony a much larger allotment than the ordinary colonist. The 1800 *equites equo publico*, or equites whose horses were purchased and kept by the State, were chosen every five years, at the census. The election was carried out in the republican period originally by the consuls, but in later times by the censors. After the general census was completed, the censors proceeded to review the equites (*recognitio*). They were arranged according to their tribes, and each of them, leading his horse by the hand, passed before the tribunal of the censors in the Forum. All who had served their time, and who were physically incapacitated, received their discharge. If an eques were judged unworthy of his position, he was dismissed with the words, "Sell your horse" (*Vende equum*). If there were nothing against him, he was passed on with the words *Traduc equum* ("Lead your horse past"). The vacancies were then filled up with suitable candidates, and the new list (*album equitum*) read aloud. In later times, the eques whose name was first read out was called *princeps iuventutis.* See Princeps.

During their time of service (between the ages of 17 and 46) the equites were bound to serve in a number of campaigns not exceeding ten. When their service expired, they passed into the first censorial class. The senators alone among the equites were, in earlier times, allowed to keep their *equus publicus*, their name on the roll, and their rights as equites unimpaired. But of this privilege the senators were deprived in the time of the Gracchi. The

Representation of the Ceremony of Transvectio on Roman Censorial Coins. (Spanheim.)

number of the *equites equo publico* remained the same, as no addition was made to the sum expended by the State on the horses. Young men of property sometimes served on their own horses (*equo privato*) without any share in the political privileges of the equites. After the Second Punic War the body of equites gradually lost its military position, and finally ceased to exist as a special troop. In the first century B.C. the members of the equestrian *centuriae* only served in the *cohors praetoria* of the general, or in the capacity of military tribunes and *praefecti* of cohorts.

The wealthy class, who were in possession of the large capital which enabled them to undertake the farming of the public revenues, and who consequently had the opportunity of enriching themselves still further, had long enjoyed a very influential position. In B.C. 123 the *lex iudiciaria* of Gaius Gracchus transferred to the possessors of the equestrian census (400,000 sestertii, or about $17,000) the right to sit on juries, which had previously belonged exclusively to members of the Senate. Thus an *ordo equester*, or third order, standing between the Senate and the people, was formed, which began to play an important part in politics. Its members were called equites even if they were not enrolled in the *centuriae equitum.* The contests between the Senate and the equites for the exclusive right to sit on the juries continued with varying fortunes until the end of the Republic. Augustus allowed the *ordo equester* to continue in existence as a class in possession of a certain income; but the old fiscal and judicial system came to an end, and the *ordo* accordingly lost all its former importance. On the other hand, the equites proper rose into a position of great consideration. They were divided into six *turmae*, headed by an imperial prince as *princeps iuventutis.* True, they had no further standing as a corporation; but the emperor employed them in a variety of confidential posts. The title *eques equo publico* was necessary for the attainment of the office of military tribune, and for a number of the most important military posts. The power of conferring or withdrawing the title came at length to rest with the emperor alone. The review of the equites, which used to take place every five years, now became a mere ceremony, and was united by Augustus with the ancient annual parade (*transvectio*) of the 15th of July. The equites, in full uniform, rode through the Forum to the Capitol, past the Temple of Mars or Honos.

After the transference of the seat of government to Constantinople, the *turmae equitum* sank into the position of a city corporation, standing between the Senate and the guilds, and in possession of special privileges. The insignia of the equites were a gold ring and a narrow purple border on the tunic. (See CLAVUS ANGUSTUS; IUS ANULI AUREI; TUNICA.) At the *transvectio* they wore the *trabea*, a mantle adorned with purple stripes, and crowns of olive. After B.C. 67 the first fourteen rows in the theatre were assigned to them.

See Zumpt, *Ueber die römischen Ritter*, etc. (Berlin, 1840); Marquardt, *Historiae Equitum Romanorum* (Berlin, 1840); Mommsen, *Röm. Staatsrecht*, iii. 476–569; and the paragraph on the *cursus honorum* under HONORES.

Equuleus. See ECULEUS.

Equus Octōber. See PALILIA.

Equus Tutĭcus. A town of Samnium, on the Appian Way, distant, according to the itineraries, twenty-two Roman miles from Cluvia, which is itself ten miles northeast of Beneventum. The term Tuticus is Oscan, equivalent to the Latin *magnus*. Much discussion has arisen among geographers as to the precise situation of this place. The branch of the Appian Way on which Equus Tuticus stood runs nearly parallel with that which Horace seems to have followed in his well-known journey to Brundisium. Horace, in speaking (according to the scholiasts) of Equus Tuticus, alludes to the unmanageable nature of the name in verse, *Mansuri oppidulo, quod versu dicere non est* (*Sat.* i. 5, 87). Modern scholars do not think Equus Tuticus to have been the town in question, but it was certainly on the road from Rome to Brundisium (Cic. *Ad Att.* vi. 1. 1), and no more likely place has been suggested as the one that Horace had in mind. See Palmer *ad loc.*

Erae (Ἐραί). A small but strong seaport town on the coast of Ionia north of Teos (Thuc. viii. 19).

Erăna (Ἔρανα). (1) A town on Mount Amanus, the chief seat of the Eleutherocilices in the time of Cicero (*Ad Fam.* xv. 4). (2) A town of Messenia.

Erănos (ἔρανος, Lat. *cena collaticia*). The Greek term for an organized club or society, for the purposes of feasting and amusement, whose members were called ἐρανισταί. Sometimes it would be formed in connection with the worship of particular deities. Sometimes, again, the object of an ἔρανος would be mutual assistance by advances of money. The government encouraged these clubs, because their corporate character made it easier to settle with expedition any legal proceedings arising out of their affairs. Trials of this kind, for refusal to pay subscriptions, or to repay loans, had to be settled within a month. See Becker-Göll, *Charikles*, ii. pp. 296 foll.

Erasīnus (Ἐρασῖνος). The chief river in Argolis, rising in Lake Stymphalus, and, after disappearing under the earth, flowing through the Lernaean Marsh into the Argolic Gulf.

Erasistrătus (Ἐρασίστρατος). A physician of Iulis, in the island of Ceos, and grandson of Aristotle by a daughter of this philosopher. After having frequented the schools of Chrysippus, Metrodorus, and Theophrastus, he passed some time at the court of Seleucus Nicator, where he gained great reputation by discovering the secret malady which preyed upon the young Antiochus, the son of the king, who was in love with his stepmother, Queen Stratonicé (Appian. *Bell. Syr.* 59). It was at Alexandria, however, that he principally practised. At last he refused altogether to visit the sick, and devoted himself entirely to the study of anatomy. The branches of this study which are indebted to him for new discoveries are, among others, the doctrine of the functions of the brain and that of the nervous system. He immortalized himself by the discovery of the *viae lacteae;* and he would seem to have come very near to that of the circulation of the blood. Comparative anatomy furnished him with the means of describing the brain much better than had ever been done before him. He also distinguished and gave names to the auricles of the heart (Galen, *De Dogm. Hipp. et Plat.* vii.; *De Usu Part.* viii.; *De Administr. Anat.* vii.; *An Sanguis*, etc.). A singular doctrine of Erasistratus is that of the πνεῦμα, or the spiritual substance which, according to him, fills the arteries, which we inhale in respiration, which from the lungs makes its way into the arteries, and then becomes the vital principle of the human system. As long as this spirit moves about in the arteries, and the blood in the veins, man enjoys health; but when, from some cause or other, the veins become contracted, the blood then spreads into the arteries and becomes the source of maladies; it produces fever when it enters into some noble part or into the great artery, and inflammations when it is found in the less noble parts or in the extremities of the arteries. Erasistratus rejected entirely blood-letting, as well as cathartics; he supplied their place with dieting, tepid bathing, vomiting, and exercise. In general, he was attached to simple remedies; he recognized what was subsequently termed *idiosyncrasy*, or the peculiar constitution of different individuals, which makes the same remedy act differently on different persons. A few fragments of the writings of Erasistratus have been preserved by Galen.

Erasmus, DESIDERIUS (the pseudo-classical form of GEERT GEERT'S), was born at Rotterdam, October 27, 1466 or 1467, of illegitimate birth. His father is the hero of Charles Reade's remarkable historical novel, *The Cloister and the Hearth*. Erasmus as a child studied at Gouda, Utrecht, and finally under Alexander Hegius at Deventer. When older he lived successively at Bois-le-Duc, the Augustinian College at Delft, and at the Collège Montaigu in Paris, of which latter residence he says in his *Colloquia*, "From it I carried away nothing but a body infected by disease and a plentiful supply of vermin." About 1487 he was ordained priest by the Bishop of Utrecht. Being in great need of money he took pupils, and with one of these, Lord Mountjoy, he visited England in 1497, spending some time at Oxford and making the acquaintance of such distinguished Englishmen as Colet, Grocyn, Latimer, and Linacre, and afterwards of Warham and Sir Thomas More. From 1499 to 1506 he travelled extensively, visiting Paris, Orléans, St. Omer's, Louvain, and Brussels, where in 1504 he delivered a Latin oration before the Archduke Philip. In 1506 he again visited England, where he entered himself at Cambridge for the B.D. and D.D. degrees, the first of which he soon received. In the same year he travelled in Italy and received a papal dispensation allowing him to lay aside the priestly dress. In Venice he met the great scholars Mersurus, Alexander, Baptista Egnatius, and the others whose works were then issuing from the presses of Aldus. In Padua he became tutor to the natural son of James IV. of Scotland. Erasmus remained in Italy until 1509, received everywhere with marks of great distinction, having by this time won a reputation for brilliant scholarship, and in April of that year revisited England, where he became the guest of More at London, and by the influence of Bishop Fisher of Rochester was appointed Lady Margaret Professor of Divinity and Regius Reader of Greek in the University of Cambridge, at which seat of learning the study of Greek was then of recent introduction.

Erasmus had now, by his writings, his orations, and by the force of a most attractive personality, attained to a great reputation among the accomplished and learned men of Europe. Presents flowed in upon him, and from this time to the end of his life he lived in ease and opulence. Archbishop Warham sent him large sums of money and secured him a pension of a hundred crowns. A like pension was granted him by Lord Mountjoy. Offers of church preferment were made to him in many countries; the Duke of Bavaria offered him a chair in the new University of Ingolstadt with no duties attached; Louvain offered him a professorship with the degree of D.D.; the Austrian archduke Ferdinand promised him a pension of 400 florins if he would only take up his residence in Vienna; Pope Clement VII. sent him 200 florins; Pope Adrian VI. wished to give him a deanery; and King Francis I. joined with the Bishop of Bayeux in a vain effort to secure Erasmus for France. Presents of wine from his numerous admirers and of sweetmeats from the nuns of Cologne reached him continually.

In 1513 Erasmus left England, and being possessed of a restless disposition, aggravated by a nervous disorder, he travelled from place to place upon the Continent; and after several years of almost incessant journeying back and forth he made his home at Basle, to which he had first been attracted by the fame of its press and of the distinguished men whom he met there, among them Zwingli the reformer, Hans Holbein the artist, and the circle of admiring students who clustered about Erasmus, such as Beatus Rhenanus, his biographer, Sapidus, Oecolampadius, Beer, Myconius, and Glareanus.

In 1520 he settled permanently in Basle, and there became the general editor of Froben's press, which, during the eight years of Erasmus's association with it, took the lead of all the presses in Europe, both in the value of the works which issued from it and in the excellence of its typographical execution. In these works Erasmus had an important share as translator and editor, but his part can not be readily differentiated from those of his numerous associates. The prefaces and dedications were always of his composition. Besides the great labour of these duties he found time to write a large number of pamphlets, often polemic, and to carry on a correspondence that sometimes compelled him to write forty letters in a single day. "I receive daily," he says, "letters from remote parts, from kings, princes, prelates, and learned men, and even from persons of whose existence I was ignorant."

The religious disturbances in Switzerland, and the death of Froben, led him in 1529 to remove to Freiburg, where he resided for six years, returning in 1535 to Basle. The new pope, Paul III., nominated him to a deanery with an income of 1500 ducats and hinted at a cardinal's hat for him. An attack of dysentery, however, carried him off July 12, 1536, in his sixty-ninth year.

Erasmus was a man of a singularly refined and amiable character—witty, judicious, and of great erudition, coupled with a gift of literary expression rare even in so elegant a scholar. Alone among the learned men of his time he exhibits a "sweet reasonableness" and a freedom from bigotry, either theological or philological, that is perhaps his most striking characteristic. While criticising, often with inimitable wit and satire, the theological warriors of his own Church, he exhibits little sympathy with the Protestant champions. The coarseness and vulgarity of Luther's controversial writings were especially offensive to him; and he disliked the unfavourable influence of religious polemics upon the development of literature. He stands, in fact, as "the supreme type of cultivated common-sense applied to human affairs, and no man of letters has ever attained to anything approaching the influence wielded by Erasmus during his own century. . . . He owed his position to the wonderful range of his activity, to his astonishing productiveness, to the breadth and sanity of his views, and to the delightful qualities of wit, humour, and unfailing vivacity which distinguish all his work" (Hume Brown). As a classicist, he stands between the strict humanists of the Latin Renaissance on the one hand and the Graecizing scholars who follow him. As Pattison puts it, he is a mean between Politian and Joseph Scaliger. He was, in fact, rather a great man of letters than a great scholar. He knew little or nothing of the true principles of text criticism, he was not scrupulously accurate, and his Greek learning was very imperfect. Judged by a comparison with the classic models, his Latin even is at times almost barbarous. But this is only a narrow view. The Latinity of Erasmus had qualities above those of mere correctness and purity. It was with him a living and a spoken tongue, rich, plastic, natural, and full of virile force, and not like the Latin of Bembo and Sadoleto—a mere echo, a cold and lifeless imitation.

The personal appearance of Erasmus is thus described by his disciple, Beatus Rhenanus: "In stature not tall, but not noticeably short; in figure well built and graceful; of an extremely delicate constitution, sensitive to the slightest change of climate, food, or drink. . . . His complexion was fair; light blue eyes and yellowish hair. Though his voice was weak, his enunciation was distinct; the expression of his face was cheerful; his manner and conversation were polished, affable, and even charming."

Of his numerous works, the following are of especial importance to the classical student: the *Adagia* or *Adagiorum Chiliades*, a manual of the wit and wisdom of the ancient world with a finely executed commentary (1st ed. Paris, 1500; enlarged eds. 1515 and 1536); an edition of the Greek Testament with a new Latin version and notes, the text of which became the starting-point of modern exegetical science (Basle, 1516; later editions in 1519, 1522, 1527, 1535); *Ciceronianus*, a satire on the pedantic imitations of Cicero by the Italian school of Latinists; and the *Colloquia*, his most famous work, of which the first edition appeared in 1519 and was afterwards greatly enlarged. It consists of a series of familiar dialogues in Latin on a great variety of topics—social, religious, and political—and marked by wit, fancy, and a brilliant audacity of treatment.

The first complete edition of the works of Erasmus appeared in 9 vols. at Basle in 1540; the standard edition is that of Le Clerc in 10 vols. (Lyons, 1703–06). To the Basle edition is prefixed a memoir of Erasmus by Beatus Rhenanus, and his life has been written at length by Knight (Cambridge, 1726); Jortin, 2 vols. (London, 1748); Burigny (Paris, 1752); Müller (Hamburg, 1828); Stichart (Leipzig, 1870); Drummond, 2 vols. (London, 1873); Feugère (Paris, 1874); Pennington (London, 1875); and Froude (London, 1894). See also Nisard in his *Études sur la Renaissance* (Paris, 1855); Seebohm, *Oxford Reformers* (2d ed. London, 1869); Milman, *Essays* (London, 1870); and Pökel, *Philolog. Schriftstellerlexicon* (Leipzig, 1882).

Erăto (Ἐρατώ). One of the Muses, who presided over lyric, tender, and amorous poetry. She is said to have invented also hymns to the gods, and to have presided likewise over pantomimic dancing. She is represented as crowned with roses and myrtle, and holding a lyre in her hand. See MUSAE.

Erato.

Eratosthĕnes (Ἐρατοσθένης). A distinguished contemporary of Archimedes, born at Cyrené, B.C. 276. He possessed a variety of talents seldom united in the same individual. His mathematical, astronomical, and geographical labours are those which have rescued his name from oblivion, though he was, besides, famous for his athletic prowess. The Alexandrian school of sciences, which flourished under the first Ptolemies, had already produced Timochares and Aristyllus; and Eratosthenes had not only the advantages arising from the instruments and observations of his predecessors, but the great Alexandrian library, which probably contained all the Phœnician, Chaldaic, Egyptian, and Greek learning of the time, was intrusted to his superintendence by the third Ptolemy (Euergetes), who had invited him to Alexandria.

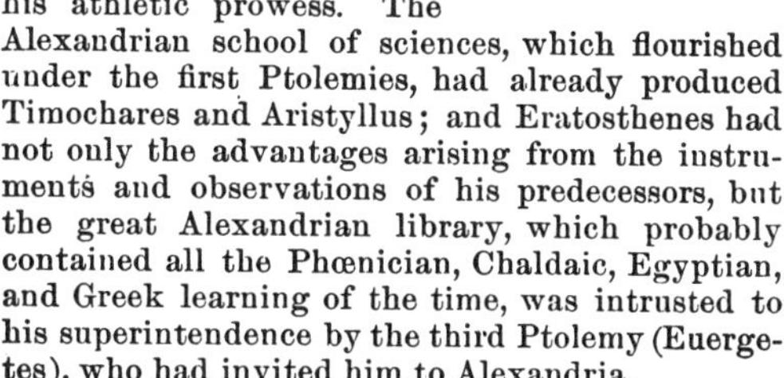

The only work attributed to Eratosthenes which has come down to us entire is entitled Καταστερισμοί, and is merely a catalogue of the names of forty-four constellations, and the situations in each constellation of the principal stars, of which he enumerates nearly five hundred, but without one reference to astronomical measurement. We find Hipparchus quoted in it, and mention made of the motion of the pole, that of the polar star having been recognized by Pytheas. These circumstances, taken in conjunction with the vagueness of the descriptions, render its genuineness extremely doubtful.

If Eratosthenes be really the author of the Καταστερισμοί, it must have been composed merely as a *vade mecum*, for we find him engaged in astronomical researches far more exact and more worthy of his genius. By his observations he determined that the distance between the tropics, that is, twice the obliquity of the ecliptic, was $\frac{11}{83}$ of an entire circumference, or 47° 42′ 39″, which makes the obliquity to be 23° 51′ 19.5″, nearly the same as that supposed by Hipparchus and Ptolemy. As the means of observation were at that time very imperfect, the instruments divided only to intervals of 10′, and as corrections for the greater refraction at the winter solstice, for the diameter of the solar disc, etc., were then unknown, we must regard this conclusion as highly creditable to Eratosthenes. His next achievement was to measure the circumference of the earth. He knew that at Syené the sun was vertical at noon in the summer solstice; while at Alexandria, at the same moment, it was below the zenith by the fiftieth part of a circumference: the two places are nearly on the same meridian (error 2°). Neglecting the solar parallax, he concluded that the distance from Alexandria to Syené is the fiftieth part of the circumference of the earth; this distance he estimated at five thousand stadia, which gives two hundred and fifty thousand stadia for the circumference. Thus Eratosthenes has the merit of pointing out a method for finding the circumference of the earth. But his data were not sufficiently exact, nor had he the means of measuring the distance from Alexandria to Syené with sufficient precision.

Eratosthenes has been called a poet, and Scaliger, in his commentary on Manilius, gives some fragments of a poem attributed to him, entitled Ἑρμῆς, one of which is a description of the terrestrial zones. It is not improbable that these are authentic.

That Eratosthenes was an excellent geometrician we can not doubt, from his still extant solution of the problem of two mean proportionals, preserved by Theon, and a lost treatise quoted by Pappus, *De Locis ad Medietates*.

Eratosthenes appears to have been one of the first who attempted to form a system of geography. His work on this subject, entitled Γεωγραφικά (*Geographica*), was divided into three books. The first contained a history of geography, a critical notice of the authorities used by him, and the elements of physical geography. The second book treated of mathematical geography. The third contained the political or historical geography of the then known world. The whole work was accompanied with a map.

Eratosthenes also busied himself with chronology, and suggested the Julian calendar, in which every fourth year has 366 days. Some remarks on his Greek chronology will be found in Clinton's *Fasti Hellenici* (vol. i. pp. 3, 408); and on his list of Theban kings, in Rask's work on the ancient Egyptian chronology (Altona, 1830).

The properties of numbers attracted the attention of philosophers from the earliest period, and Eratosthenes also distinguished himself in this branch. He wrote a work on the duplication of the cube—Κύβου Διπλασιασμός—which we only know by a sketch that Eudoxus has given of it, in his treatise on the Sphere and Cylinder of Archimedes. Eratosthenes composed, also, another work in this department, entitled Κόσκινον, or "the Sieve," the object of which was to separate prime from composite numbers. Eratosthenes arrived at the age of eighty years, and then, becoming weary of life, died by voluntary starvation (B.C. 196). The best editions of the Καταστερισμοί are that of Schaubach, with notes by Heyne (Göttingen, 1795), and that of Matthiae, in his Aratus (Frankfurt, 1817). The fragments of Eratosthenes have been collected by Bernhardy in his work *Eratosthenica* (Berlin, 1822), and the poetical remains separately by Hiller (Leipzig, 1872). See, also, Berger, *Die geographischen Fragmente des Eratosthenes* (Leipzig, 1880).

Erbessus (Ἐρβησσός). A strongly fortified town of Sicily, northeast of Agrigentum, which the Romans made their principal place of arms in the siege of the last-mentioned city. It was soon after destroyed (Polyb. i. 18).

Erchīa (Ἐρχεία). One of the demes of Attica, and belonging to the tribe Aegeïs. Its position has not been positively ascertained. This was the native demus of Xenophon and Isocrates. See Young, *Erchia: a Deme of Attica* (N. Y. 1891).

Ercta or **Ercté** (Εἱρκτή, Ἑρκτή). A remarkable isolated mountain on the northwestern coast of Sicily near Panormus. Its height is 1950 feet. Its chief celebrity was gained in the First Punic War, towards the close of which Hamilcar Barca (q. v.) shut himself with his army into this natural fortress, and maintained himself there against all the efforts of the Romans to dislodge him, for nearly three years. See Polyb. i. 56, 57; Diod. Sic. xxiii. 20.

Mount Ercta.

Erĕbus (Ἔρεβος). (1) A deity of the lower world, sprung from Chaos. From him and his sister Nyx (Night) came Aether and the Day (Hesiod, *Theog.* 123 foll.). (2) A dark and gloomy region in the lower world, where all is dreary and cheerless. According to the Homeric notion, Erebus lay between the earth and Hades, beneath the latter of which was Tartarus. It was therefore not an abode of the departed, but merely a passage from the upper to the lower world. Oriental scholars derive the name Erebus from the Hebrew *'ereb*, evening.

Erechthēïs (Ἐρεχθηΐς). The well of salt water in the Acropolis at Athens (Apollod. iii. 14. 1). See ERECHTHEUM.

Erechthēum (Ἐρέχθειον). The original sanctuary of the tutelary deities of Athens, Athené Polias (the goddess of the city), Poseidon, and Erechtheus. It was situated on the Acropolis. The old temple, said to have been built by Erechtheus, was burned by the Persians in B.C. 480. The restoration was perhaps begun as far back as the time of Pericles, but, according to the testimony of an inscription preserved in the British Museum was still unfinished in 409. The new temple was, even in antiquity, admired as one of the most beautiful and perfect works of the Attic-Ionic style. It was sixty-five feet long and nearly thirty-six broad, and was divided into two main parts. Entering through the eastern portico of six Ionic pillars, one came into the *cella* of Athené Polias, with an image of the goddess, and a lamp that was always kept burning. To the solid wall at the back was attached the Erechtheum proper. Here were three altars, one common to Poseidon and Erechtheus, the other to Hephaestus and the hero Butes. Connected with this, by three doors, was a small front chamber, with seven half-columns adorning the western wall, and three windows between them. This chamber was approached through a hall attached to the north side of the temple, adorned with seven Ionic columns in front, and one on each side. Under this was a cleft in the rock, said to have been made by the stroke of Poseidon's trident during his contest

Restoration of the Erechtheum from the Northeast. (Reber.)

with Athené for the possession of the Acropolis. Corresponding to this on the south side was a small hall, supported not by pillars, but by caryatides. This was called the Hall of Coré, and it probably contained the tomb of Cecrops. From it a step led down to a court, once walled round, in which were the Pandroseum (see PANDROSOS), the sacred olive-tree of Athené, and the altar of Zeus Herkeios. On the east side, in front of the temple of Athené Polias, stood the altar on which the great hecatomb was offered at the Panathenaea. See plan under ACROPOLIS.

Erechtheus (Ἐρεχθεύς). A mythical king of Athens. According to Homer (*Il.* ii. 547, etc.; *Odyss.* vii. 81), he was the son of Earth by Hephaestus, and was reared by Athené. Like that of Cecrops, half of his form was that of a snake—a sign that he was one of the aborigines. Athené put the child in a chest, which she gave to the daughters of Cecrops—Agraulos, Hersé, and Pandrosos—to take care of, forbidding them at the same time to open it (Hygin. *Poet. Astr.* ii. 13). The first two disobeyed, and in terror at the serpent-shaped child (or, according to another version, the snake that surrounded the child), they went mad, and threw themselves from the rocks of the Acropolis. Another account made the serpent kill them. Erechtheus drove out Amphictyon, and got possession of the kingdom. He then established the worship of Athené, and built to her, as goddess of the city (Πολιάς), a temple, named after him the Erechtheum. Here he was afterwards himself worshipped with Athené and Poseidon. He was also the founder of the Panathenaic festival. He was said to have invented the four-wheeled chariot, and to have been taken up to heaven for this by Zeus, and set in the sky as the constellation of the Charioteer. His daughters were Orithyia and Procris. (See BOREAS; CEPHALUS.) Originally identified with ERICHTHONIUS, he was in later times distinguished from him, and was regarded as his grandson, and as son of Pandion and Zeuxippé. His twin-brother was Butes, his sisters Procné and Philomela. The priestly office fell to Butes, while Erechtheus assumed the functions of royalty. By Praxithea, the daughter of Cephissus, he was father of the second Cecrops (see PANDION, 2), of Metion (see DAEDALUS), of Creüsa (see ION), as well as of Protogenia, Pandora, and Chthonia. When Athens was hard pressed by the Eleusinians under Eumolpus, the oracle promised him the victory if he would sacrifice one of his daughters. He chose the youngest, Chthonia; but Protogenia and Pandora, who had made a vow with their sister to die with her, voluntarily shared her fate. Erechtheus conquered his enemies and slew Eumolpus, but was afterwards destroyed by the trident of his enemy's father, Poseidon. The myth of Erechtheus has suggested the subject for Swinburne's tragedy *Erechtheus* (London, 1876).

Erechthīdes. A name given to the Athenians from their king Erechtheus (Ovid, *Met.* vii. 430).

Eressus or **Erĕsus** (on coins the name is always written Ἔρεσος). A city of Lesbos, situated on a hill at a distance of twenty-eight stadia from Cape Sigrium. It derives celebrity from having given birth to Theophrastus. Phanias, another disciple of the great Stagirite, was likewise a native of this place. According to Archestratus, quoted by Athenaeus, Eressus was famous for the excellence of its wheaten flour.

Eretria (Ἐρέτρια). (1) A town of the island of Euboea, situated on the coast of the Euripus southeast of Chalcis. It was said by some to have been founded by a colony from Triphylia in Peloponnesus; by others its origin was ascribed to a party of Athenians belonging to the deme of Eretria. The latter opinion is far more probable, as this city was doubtless of Ionic origin (Herod. viii. 46). We learn from Strabo that Eretria was formerly called Melaneïs and Arotria, and that at an early period it had attained to a considerable degree of prosperity and power. The Eretrians conquered the islands of Ceos, Teos, Tenos, and others; and in their festival of Artemis, which was celebrated with great splendour, three thousand soldiers on foot, with six hundred cavalry and sixty chariots, were often employed to attend the procession (cf. Livy, xxxv. 38). Eretria, at this period, was frequently engaged in war with Chalcis, and Thucydides reports (i. 15) that on one occasion most of the Grecian States took part in the contest. The assistance which Eretria then received from the Milesians induced that city to coöperate with the Athenians in sending a fleet and troops to the support of the Ionians, who had revolted from Persia at the instigation of Aristagoras (Herod. v. 99), by which measure it became exposed, in conjunction with Athens, to the vengeance of Darius. That monarch accordingly gave orders to his commanders, Datis and Artaphernes, to subdue both Eretria and Athens and bring the inhabitants captive before him. Eretria was taken after six days' siege, and the captive inhabitants brought to Asia. Darius treated the prisoners kindly, and settled them in the district of Cissia (Herod. vi. 119). Eretria recovered from the effects of this disaster and was rebuilt soon after. We find it mentioned by Thucydides, towards the close of his history (viii. 94), as revolting from Athens on the approach of a Spartan fleet under Hegesandridas, and mainly contributing to the success obtained by that commander. After the death of Alexander, this city surrendered to Ptolemy, a general in the service of Antigonus; and in the Macedonian War, to the combined fleets of the Romans, the Rhodians, and Attalus (Livy, xxxii. 16). It was subsequently declared free by order of the Roman Senate (Polyb. xviii. 28 foll.). This place, as we learn from Athenaeus, was noted for the excellence of its flour and bread. At one time it possessed a distinguished school of philosophy and dialectics. The ruins of Eretria are still to be observed close to a headland which lies opposite to the mouth of the Asopus in Boeotia. (2) A deme of Attica. (3) A town of Thessaly, near Pharsalus, and between that city and Pherae.

Erētum. A town of the Sabines, north of Nomentum and northeast of Fidenae, and at no great distance from the Tiber. Its name frequently occurs in the Roman historians. The antiquity of the place is attested by Vergil (vii. 711). It was subsequently the scene of many a contest between the Romans and Sabines, leagued with the Etruscans (Livy, iii. 29).

Ergastŭlum. A prison and place of correction attached to the farms and country-villas of the Romans, in which those of the slave *familia* who were kept in fetters (*compediti, nexi, vincti*) were lodged and made to work in irons; whereas the rest, who were not chained, were provided with separate accommodation (*cellae, contubernia*) in other parts of the establishment (Columell. i. 6. 3; cf. 8. 16; Apul. *Apol.* p. 482; Brut. in Cic. *Fam.* xi. 13).

Erichthonius (Ἐρεχθόνιος). (1) Son of Dardanus (see DARDANUS) and Batea. He was the father of Tros. (2) The same as Erechtheus (q. v.).

Ericius. "A hedgehog"—i. e. a military engine full of sharp spikes, which was placed by the gate of the camp to prevent the approach of the enemy (Caes. *B. C.* iii. 67).

Ericussa (Ἐρικοῦσσα). One of the Lipari Islands, now Varcusa. See AEOLIAE INSULAE.

Eridănus (Ἠρίδανος). A river-god, on the banks of whose river amber was found (Hesiod, *Theog.* 338). In later times the Eridanus was supposed to be the same as the Padus (Po), because amber was found at its mouth. Hence the Electrides Insulae, or "Amber Islands," are placed at the mouth of the Po, and here Phaëthon was supposed to have fallen when struck by the lightning of Zeus.

Erigŏné (Ἠριγόνη). (1) The daughter of Icarius. Her father having been taught by Bacchus the culture of the grape, and having made wine, gave of it to some shepherds, who, thinking themselves poisoned by the draught, killed him. When they came to their senses, they buried him; and his daughter Erigoné, being guided to the spot by her father's faithful hound Maera, hanged herself through grief (Apollod. iii. 14. 7; Hyg. *Fab.* 130). Zeus translated the father and daughter, along with the faithful Maera, to the skies; Icarius became *Boötes*, and Erigoné, *Virgo;* while the hound was changed, according to Hyginus, into *Procyon;* but, according to the scholiast on Germanicus, into the *Canis Maior*, which is therefore styled by Ovid (*Fast.* iv. 939) *Canis Icarius.* (2) The daughter of Aegisthus and Clytaemnestra, and mother of Penthilus by Orestes (Pausan. ii. 18, 5).

Erinna (Ἤριννα). (1) A poetess, and the friend of Sappho. She flourished about the year B.C. 610. All that is known of her is contained in the following words of Eustathius (*ad Il.* ii. p. 327): "Erinna was born in Lesbos, or in Rhodes, or in Teos, or in Telos, the little island near Cnidus. She was a poetess, and wrote a poem called 'the Distaff' (Ἠλακάτη) in the Aeolic and Doric dialect; it consisted of 300 hexameter lines. She was the friend of Sappho, and died unmarried. It was thought that her verses rivalled those of Homer. She was only nineteen years of age when she died." Chained by her mother to the spinning-wheel, Erinna had as yet known the charm of existence in imagination alone. She probably expressed in her poem the restless and aspiring thoughts which crowded on her youthful mind as she pursued her monotonous work. We possess at the present day only four lines by Erinna; for though three epigrams ascribed to her are given by Schneidewin in his *Delectus Poësis Graecae Elegiacae* (Göttingen, 1839), two at least are not genuine. (2) A poetess mentioned by Eusebius under the year B.C. 354. This appears to be the same person who is spoken of by Pliny (*H. N.* xxxiv. § 8), as having celebrated Myro in her poems. No fragments of her poetry remain, and her very existence has been questioned.

Erinÿes (Ἐρινύες). See EUMENIDES.

Eriphȳlé (Ἐριφύλη). In Greek mythology, sister of Adrastus and wife of Amphiaraüs (q. v.). Bribed with a necklace by Polynices, she prevailed on her husband to take part in the war of the Seven against Thebes, in which he met his death. In revenge for this she was slain by her son Alcmaeon (q. v.). See SEVEN AGAINST THEBES.

Eris (Ἔρις). The Greek name for the goddess of Discord, sister of Ares. See PARIS; TROJAN WAR.

Ernesti. (1) JOHANN AUGUST. A distinguished philologist and theologian of the last century, born at Tennstädt, in Germany, August 4th, 1707. He studied at Pforta, Wittenberg, and Leipzig, and in 1731 became co-rector with Gesner of the Thomas School in Leipzig, succeeding Gesner as rector in 1734. In 1742 he was called to the University of Leipzig as Professor Extraordinarius of Classical Literature, and became Professor Ordinarius of Rhetoric in 1756. He died September 11th, 1781.

Ernesti and his colleague Gesner (q. v.) are regarded as the founders of the modern German school of ancient literature. By their breadth of view, sound discipline, and contagious enthusiasm, they stimulated their pupils to those labours that resulted in transferring to Germany the supremacy in letters long held by the universities of Holland.

Ernesti's principal works (besides a multitude of pamphlets, programmata, etc.) are the following: *Initia Doctrinae Solidioris* (1736); *Initia Rhetorica* (1730); editions of Xenophon's *Memorabilia* (1737); Suetonius (1748); Tacitus (1752); the *Clouds* of Aristophanes (1754); Homer (1759–64); Callimachus (1761); Polybius (1764); of the *Quaestura* of Corradus; the Greek lexicon of Hedericus; the *Bibliotheca Latina* of Fabricius (unfinished); also *Archaeologia Litteraria* (1768); and *Horatius Tursellinus de Particulis* (1769). His best work, however, is the edition of Cicero, in 5 vols. (1737–39), to which is added the valuable *Clavis Ciceroniana* (6th ed. Halle, 1831). His Latin orations, which won for him the name of "the German Cicero," are collected under the title *Opuscula Oratoria* (2d ed. 1767; suppl. vol. 1791). His philological treatises were published as *Opuscula Philologica et Critica* (1764; 2d ed. 1776). See Bursian, *Geschichte d. Class. Philol.* pp. 400–404 (Munich, 1883).

(2) JOHANN CHRISTIAN GOTTLIEB, a nephew of the preceding, was born at Arnstadt in 1756; and studied at Leyden, where he became Professor of Philosophy in 1782, and of Rhetoric in 1802. He died in the last-named year (June 5th). He edited the fables of Aesop in Greek (1781); Hesychius (1785); Suidas (1786); the *Punica* of Sil. Italicus (1791–92); and also put forth a *Lexicon Technologiae Graecorum Rhetoricae* (1795); a *Lexicon Technologiae Romanorum Rhetoricae* (1797); and *Cicero's Geist und Kunst* (1799–1802).

Eroantheia (τὰ ἠροάνθεια). A festival of women, celebrated in the Peloponnesus in the spring season (Phot. *Lex.* p. 95; Hesych. s. v.).

Erogatio. The technical term for the distribution of water from the aqueducts at Rome. See AQUAEDUCTUS.

Eros (Ἔρως). The god of love among the Greeks. His name does not occur in Homer; but in Hesiod (*Theog.* 120 foll.) he is the fairest of the deities, who subdues the hearts of both gods and men. He is born from Chaos at the same time as the Earth and Tartarus, and is the comrade of

Aphroditê from the moment of her birth. Hesiod conceives Eros not merely as the god of sensual love, but as a power which forms the world by inner union of the separated elements—an idea very prevalent in antiquity, especially among the philosophers. According to the later and commoner notion, Eros was the youngest of the gods, generally the son of Aphroditê by Ares or Hermes, always a child, thoughtless and capricious. He is as irresistible as fair, and has no pity even for his own mother. Zeus, the father of gods and men, arms him with golden wings, and with bow and unerring arrows, or burning torches. Anteros, the god of mutual love, is his brother, and his companions are Pothos and Himeros, the personifications of longing and desire, with Peitho (Persuasion), the Muses, and the Graces. In later times he is surrounded by a crowd of similar beings, Erotes or Loves. (For the later legend of Eros and Psychê, see PSYCHÊ.)

One of the chief and oldest seats of his worship was Thespiae in Boeotia. Here was his most ancient image, a rough, unhewn stone. His festival, the Erotia or Erotidia, continued till the time of the Roman Empire to be celebrated every fifth year with much ceremony, accompanied by gymnastic and musical contests. Besides this he received special honour and worship in the gymnasia, where his statue generally stood near those of

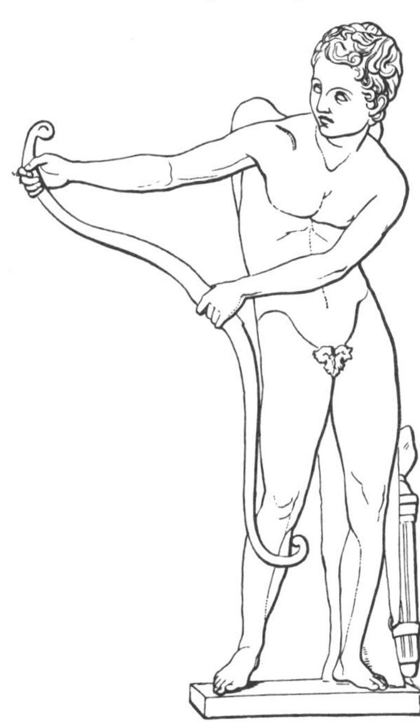

Eros. (Rome, Capitoline Museum.)

Hermes and Heracles. In the gymnasia, Eros was the personification of devoted friendship and love between youths and men; the friendship which proved itself active and helpful in battle and bold adventure. This was the reason why the Spartans and Cretans sacrificed to Eros before a battle, and the sacred band of youths at Thebes was dedicated to him; why a festival of freedom (Ἐλευθέρια) was held at Samos in his honour, as the god who bound men and youths together in the struggle for honour and freedom; and why at Athens he was worshipped as the liberator of the city, in memory of Harmodius and Aristogiton (q. v.).

In works of art Eros was usually represented as a beautiful boy, close upon the age of youth. In later times he also appears as a child with the attributes of a bow and arrows, or burning torches, and in a great variety of situations. The most celebrated statues of this god were by Lysippus, Scopas, and Praxiteles whose Eros at Thespiae was regarded as a masterpiece, and unsurpassable. The famous torso in the Vatican, in which the god wears a dreamy, lovelorn air, is popularly, but probably erroneously, traced to an original by Praxiteles. The Eros trying his bow, in the Capitoline Museum at Rome, is supposed to be the copy of a work by Lysippus (see illustration). The Roman god Amor or Cupido was a mere adaptation of the Greek Eros, and was never held in great esteem. ANTĔROS was the brother of Eros and punished those who did not requite the love of others (Ovid, *Met.* xiii. 750).

Erotia or **Erotidia** (Ἐρώτια or Ἐρωτίδια). The most solemn of all the festivals celebrated in the Boeotian town of Thespiae. It took place every fifth year, and in honour of Eros, the principal divinity of the Thespians. Respecting the particulars nothing is known, except that it was solemnized with contests in music and gymnastics (Plut. *Amat.* 1; Pausan. ix. 31, § 3; Athen. xiii. p. 561). At this festival married couples made up any quarrels they might have. The worship of Eros seems to have been early established at Thespiae, where the ancient symbolic representation of the god—a rude stone—was long looked upon with reverence (Pausan. ix. 27, § 1). See EROS.

Erotic Literature. See ELEGIA; NOVELS AND ROMANCES; PRIAPEIA.

Errhephoria or **Ersephoria** (ἐρρηφόρια or ἐρσηφόρια). See ARRHEPHORIA.

Ersê or **Hersê**. See CECROPS; ERECHTHEUS.

Erycīna (Ἐρυκίνη). A surname of Aphroditê, from Mount Eryx in Sicily, where she had a temple. The Erycinian Aphroditê appears to have been the same with the Phœnician Astartê, whose worship was brought over by the latter people, and a temple erected to her on Mount Eryx. In confirmation of this, we learn from Diodorus Siculus that the Carthaginians revered the Erycinian Aphroditê equally as much as did the natives themselves (Diod. Sic. iv. 83).

Erymanthian Boar. See HERACLES.

Erymanthus (Ἐρύμανθος). (1) A mountain-chain in the northwest angle of Arcadia, celebrated in fable as the haunt of the savage boar destroyed by Heracles (Apollod. ii. 5. 3; Pausan. viii. 24; Homer, *Od.* vi. 103). Apollonius places the Erymanthian monster in the wilds of Mount Lampea; but this mountain was that part of the chain where the river Erymanthus took its rise. (2) A river of Arcadia, descending from the mountain of the same name, and flowing near the town of Psophis. After receiving another small stream, called the Aroanius, it joins the Alpheus on the borders of Elis. The modern name of the Erymanthus is the Dogana.

Erysichthon (Ἐρυσίχθων). "Render of the earth." The son of the Thessalian king Triopas, who cut down trees in a grove sacred to Demeter, for which he was punished by the goddess with a fearful hunger, that caused him to devour his own flesh (Ovid, *Met.* viii. 738; Callim. *Hymn. in Dem.* 34 foll.).

Erythīa (Ἐρύθεια). (1) One of the Hesperides (q. v.). (2) The daughter of Geryon (q. v.), who got her name from the island near the coast of Hispania, where her father lived (Hesiod, *Theog.* 290; Pausan. x. 17. 5).

Erȳthrae (Ἐρυθραί). One of the twelve cities of Ionia, situated near the coast opposite Chios (Herod. i. 142). Its founder was said to have been Erythrus, the son of Rhadamanthus, who established himself here with a body of Cretans, Carians, and Lycians. At a later period came Cnopus, son of Codrus, with an Ionian colony, whence the city is sometimes called CNOPOPŎLIS (Κνωπούπολις). The city did not lie exactly on the coast, but some little distance inland, and had a harbour on the coast named Cissus (Livy, xxxvi. 43). Erythrae was famous as the residence of one of the Sibyls at an early period, and in the time of Alexander we find another making her appearance here, with similar claims to inspiration. See SIBYLLA.

Erythraeum Maré (ἡ ἐρυθρὰ θάλασσα). A name applied to the whole ocean by the Greeks, extending from the coast of Ethiopia to the island of Taprobana, when their geographical knowledge of India was in its infancy. They believed the name to be derived from that of Erythras, an ancient monarch who reigned along these coasts, and asserted that his grave was to be found in one of the adjacent islands (Curtius, viii. 9, 14). Afterwards, when the Greeks learned the existence of an Indian Ocean, the term was applied merely to the sea below Arabia, and to the Arabian and Persian Gulfs. In this latter sense Strabo uses the name. Herodotus follows the old acceptation of the word, according to the opinion prevalent in his age. The appellation was probably derived from Edom (Esau), whose descendants were called Idumaeans, and inhabited the northern parts of Arabia. They navigated upon the Red Sea and Persian Gulf, and also upon the Indian Ocean; and the Oriental name Edom signifying *red*, the sea of the Idumaeans was called the Red Sea and the Erythraean Sea (Ἐρυθρὰ θάλασσα), of which the Latin *Mare Rubrum* is a translation.

Eryx (Ἔρυξ). A son of Butes and Aphroditê, who, relying upon his strength, challenged all strangers to fight with him in the combat of the caestus. Heracles accepted his challenge after many had yielded to his superior dexterity, and Eryx was killed in the combat, and buried on the mountain where he had built a temple to Aphroditê (Verg. *Aen.* v. 402).

Eryx (Ἔρυξ). A mountain of Sicily, at the western extremity of the island, and near the city of Drepanum. It was fabled to have received its name from Eryx, who was buried there. On its summit stood a famous temple of Aphroditê Erycina, and on the western declivity was situated the town of Eryx, the approach to which from the plain was rocky and difficult. At the distance of thirty stadia stood the harbour of the same name (Polyb. i. 55; Diod. xxiv. 1; Cic. *in Ver.* ii. 8). The Phœnicians were most probably the founders of the place and also of the temple, and the Erycinian Aphroditê appears to be identified with the Astartê of the latter people. The native inhabitants in this quarter were called Elymi, and Eryx is said by some to have been their king. Vergil makes Aeneas to have founded the temple. The town was destroyed by the Carthaginians in the time of Pyrrhus, who a short time previous had taken it by storm, and the inhabitants were removed to Drepanum (Diod. xxii. 14, xxiii. 9). It soon, however, revived, owing to the celebrity of the adjacent temple. In the First Punic War it fell into the hands of the Romans, but was surprised by Barcas, the Carthaginian commander, and the inhabitants who escaped the slaughter were again removed to Drepanum (Diod. xxiv. 2). The place never recovered from this blow; the sanctity of the temple drew, indeed, new inhabitants around, but the city was never rebuilt. No traces of the temple remain at the present day.

Eschăra (ἐσχάρα). A hearth. See FOCUS.

Esquilīnus Mons. See ROMA.

Essedarii. See ESSEDUM.

Essedŏnes. A people of Sarmatia Asiatica, to the east of the Palus Maeotis.

Essĕdum, rarely **Essĕda,** said to be a Keltic word. The name of a chariot used, especially in war, by the Britons, Gauls, and Belgae, perhaps also by the Germans (Verg. *Georg.* iii. 204; Serv. *ad loc.*).

According to the account given by Caesar (*B. G.* iv. 35) the method of using the essedum in the ancient British army was very similar to the practice of the Greeks in the heroic ages, as described in the article CURRUS. The principal difference seems to have been that the essedum was stronger and more solid than the δίφρος—that it was open before instead of behind; hence the driver was able to run along the pole (*de temone Britanno excidet*, Juv. iv. 125) and then to retreat with the greatest speed into the body of the car, which he drove with extraordinary swiftness and skill. From the extremity of the pole he threw his missiles, especially the *cateia* (Val. Flacc. *Argon.* vi. 83). It appears also that these cars were purposely made as noisy as possible, probably by the creaking and clanging of the wheels (Tac. *Agric.* 35; Claud. *Epigr.* 4); and that this was done in order to strike dismay into the enemy. The drivers of these chariots were called in Latin *essedarii* (Caes. *B. G.* iv. 24). Tacitus (*Agric.* 12) observes that the driver of the car ranked above his fighting companion, which was the reverse of the Greek usage.

The essedum was adopted for purposes of convenience and luxury among the Romans (Propert. ii. 1, 76; Cic. *Ad Att.* vi. 1; Ovid, *Am.* ii. 16, 49). Cicero (*Phil.* ii. 24, § 58) mentions the use of it by Antonius as a piece of effeminacy disgraceful to a tribune of the people; but in the time of Seneca it seems to have become common (*Fr.* 48, Hase). As used by the Romans the essedum had no seat for the driver; the traveller drove himself (Ovid, l. c.), and always, it would seem, with a pair of horses, whereas with the *cisium* the number varied. The essedum, like the *cisium*, appears to have been kept for hire at the post-houses or stations (Mart. x. 104). See MANSIO.

Essui. A people in Gaul, west of the Sequana (Caes. *B. G.* v. 24).

Eteŏcles (Ἐτεοκλῆς). A son of Oedipus and Iocasta. After his father's flight it was agreed between him and his brother Polynices that they should both share the kingdom and reign alternately, each a year. Eteocles, by right of seniority, first ascended the throne; but after the first year of his reign had expired he refused to give up the crown to his brother according to their mutual agreement. Polynices, resolving to punish so gross a violation of a solemn engagement, fled to the court of Adrastus, king of Argos, where he married Argia, the daughter of that monarch; and having prevailed upon Adrastus to espouse his cause, the latter undertook what was denominated the First Theban War, twenty-seven years, as is said, before the Trojan one. Adrastus marched against Thebes with an army, of which he took the command, having with him seven celebrated chiefs, Tydeus, Amphiaraus, Capanaeus, Parthenopaeus, Hippomedon, Eteoclus, son of Iphis, and Polynices. The Thebans who espoused the cause of Eteocles were Melanippus and Ismarus, sons of Astacus, Polyphontes, Megareus, Lasthenes, and Hyperbius. All the Argive leaders, with the exception of Adrastus, fell before Thebes, Eteocles also being slain in single combat with Polynices. Ten years after the conclusion of this war arose that of the Epigoni, or the sons of the slain chieftains of Argos, who took up arms to avenge the death of their sires. (See EPIGONI.) Lists of the seven Argive commanders are given by Aeschylus in his *Seven against Thebes*, by Euripides in his *Phoenissae* and *Supplices;* and by Sophocles in his *Oedipus Coloneus.* They all agree, except that in the *Phoenissae* the name of Adrastus is substituted for that of Eteoclus. See SEVEN AGAINST THEBES.

Eteŏclus (Ἐτέοκλος). One of the seven chiefs of the army of Adrastus, in his expedition against Thebes. He was killed by Megareus, the son of Creon, under the walls of Thebes (Apollod. iii. 6). See SEVEN AGAINST THEBES.

Etesiae (Ἐτησίαι ἄνεμοι, Herod. vi. 140). The Etesian Winds, derived from ἔτος, "year," signified any periodical winds, but more particularly the northerly winds which blew in the Aegean for forty days from the rising of the dog-star.

Etruria or **Tuscia** (Τυρρηνία, Τυρσηνία). A country of Italy once inhabited by the people known as the Etruscans (Tusci). It lay west of the river Tiber and the Apennines, extending to the sea, and including the valley of the Arno. When authentic history begins, the Etruscans, in addition to this territory, held also the valley of the Padus (Etruria Circumpadana) and a further strip south of the Tiber (Etruria Campaniana). From the former territory they were crowded southward by the Gauls (see CELTAE), and from the latter the Romans subsequently drove them. Etruria Proper was a confederation of twelve States or cities (*duodecim populi Etruriae*), of which no complete list has reached us, though it is fairly certain that the following towns were eleven of the twelve: Veii, Caeré, Tarquinii, Clusium, Cortona, Perusia, Volsinii, Vulci, Vetulonia, Volaterrae, and Arretium. The twelfth was in all probability either Falerii, Populonia, or Rusellae. Of the northern league, the following were important towns: Felsina (Bononia), Mantua, Ravenna, Chiavenna, and Hatria or Hadria, which gives its name to the Hadriaticum Mare. In the south, Capua and Nola were rich and powerful cities. Like Etruria Proper, the northern league was one of twelve States.

ETHNOLOGY.—The earliest traditions to which we now have access make the Etrurians a Lydian people (Herod. i. 94, 166, 171). But this theory, which was carefully considered by Dionysius of Halicarnassus in his work on the origins of Rome, appears to rest upon no convincing evidence. Dionysius notes that it is not mentioned by Xanthus, the historian of Lydia, and sums up the results of his own investigations by saying that "the Etruscans do not resemble any other people either in language or in manners." This conclusion is interesting, for Dionysius had given much thought and time to the consideration of the question, and is said to have written a work on the Etruscans in twenty books, during the reign of Augustus, when there was a sort of Etrurian revival, in which everything Etruscan was the fashion. The identification of the Etruscans with the Lydians was very likely due to a confusion of the Lydian Τορρηβοί with the name Τυρσηνοί or Τυρρηνοί, applied to the Etruscans by the Greeks. (Cf. Hesiod, *Theog.* 1015; Ovid, *Met.* iii. 577 foll.; Plin. *H. N.* iii. 19; Tac. *Ann.* iv. 24; and see Mommsen, *Hist. of Rome*, bk. i. ch. ix.) The confusion was easier because of the maritime prowess of both peoples and their piratical practices (Herod. vi. 22; Strab. 219).

Modern investigators have not been deterred by the ill success of Dionysius from attempting to solve the problem of the ethnological affinities of the Etruscans; but no definite and generally accepted conclusions have yet been reached. For purposes of investigation there have been collected some 6000 or more Etruscan inscriptions, the characters resembling Pelasgian or early Greek. There are also vast collections of their pottery,

Map of Ancient Etruria.

bronzes, jewels, and other works of Tuscan art. Fifteen bilingual inscriptions give some further aid on the side of the language, but less than one might suppose, for they consist only of proper names. The longest inscription yet discovered is that found at Perugia in 1822, consisting of forty-six lines, in red, upon two sides of a block of stone (the "Cippus Perusinus"). These records are in the main mortuary records taken from tombs, walls, or the labels and seals of mortuary niches, or still oftener painted upon urns or cut into sarcophagi. They usually give the name, parentage, age, and rank of the deceased, with a list of the offices that he held. The most noted investigations of the origins and affinities of the Etruscans have been those of K. O. Müller, whose dissertation on the subject in two volumes (Breslau, 1828; 2d ed. Stuttgart, 1877) received a prize from the Academy of Sciences at Berlin, and Wilhelm Corssen (q. v.), who also published two elaborate volumes (Leipzig, 1874–75). Later works are those of Deecke and Pauli.

By these scholars some progress has been made towards a knowledge of the peculiarities of the Etruscan language. Besides proper names, some 200 other words have been deciphered, among them a number of numerals, including the first six digits, the common words denoting relationships, and several verbal forms. As a matter of general interest, the following list of Etruscan words may be given from Pauli:

clan	son.	thu	five.
puia	wife.	huth	six.
sekh	daughter.	suthinese	urn-niches.
lautni	a freedman.	tular	pillar (*cippus*).
cvil (cver)	gift, dedication.	amce	fuit.
mach	one.	ma	est.
ci	two.	ture	dat.
zal	three.	turce	dedit.
sa	four.	arce	habuit.

Relationship is expressed by separate words (as above), or (more commonly) by suffixes: thus, *Aulesa*, "wife of Aulé," *Theprisa*, "wife of Thepri," etc. Other linguistic facts that have been satisfactorily established regarding the Etruscan tongue are these: the existence of gender, the use of enclitics, the genitive singular in *-s*, the dative in *-si* or *-thi*, the absence of distinction between the nominative and accusative in nouns, and the formation of a plural in *-r* or *-l*.

The Egyptian monuments speak of a people called Tursha as taking part with the Sardinians, Teucri, and other people from the coasts of "the North" in an invasion of Egypt about B.C. 1200; but the Tursha can not be definitely identified with the Tyrrhenians any more than can the Tyrrhenians with the Etruscans. Support is given to the Lydian hypothesis by the discovery made in 1886 by two French scholars, who found in the island of Lemnos a sepulchral monument with two Etruscan inscriptions, though of a dialectic character. Now, Thucydides states that Lemnos was inhabited by Tyrrheni, so that in the finding of these inscriptions Pauli sees evidence of the identity of the two peoples. See Bréal in the *Bulletin de Correspondance Hellénique*, vol. x. (1886); and Pauli, *Eine vorgriechische Inschrift von Lemnos* (Leipzig, 1886).

An interesting discovery was made in 1891 by Prof. Krall of Vienna. About 1850, a mummy was deposited in the Museum of Agram by an Austrian traveller who had brought it from Egypt. When unrolled, it was found that the linen cloths in which it had been wrapped were covered with written characters. These, when examined in 1867 by Brugsch Pasha, were pronounced by him to be Ethiopic. In 1877 Sir Richard Burton explained them as Nabathean. It remained for Prof. Krall to prove that the characters are Etruscan, and that the words which they embody are found in the existing inscriptions of Etruria. They form, in fact, a book, of which the text originally consisted of twelve columns. More than two hundred lines are intact, including the last paragraph of the book. The mummy around which the linen bands were wrapped is that of a woman, and the gilding on the face and shoulders proves it to belong to the Greek or Roman period. Now, as Etruscan was still spoken and read in the first century A.D., it is easy to see how an Etruscan book could have found its way to Egypt, when both Etruria and Egypt were parts of the same Empire. The few words of the book that had been identified in 1893 make it probable that it is one of the semi-religious, semi-magical works for which the Etruscans were celebrated. With the material for study and comparison afforded by the continuous text of this book, the problem of the Etruscan language seems likely to be brought at least measurably near to a satisfactory solution. The transcription and photographs of the text, with an account of Prof. Krall's discovery, were published by the Imperial Academy of Vienna in 1892 (*Die Etruskischen Mumienbinden des Agramer National-Museums*). See, also, an article by Prof. Sayce in the *Fortnightly Review* for February, 1893.

Until lately philologists were in the main divided into two great camps on the question of the racial and linguistic affinities of the Etruscans—one set of scholars holding to the theory of a Semitic origin and the other to that of an Aryan. (See INDO-EUROPEAN LANGUAGES.) But the actual failure of Dr. Corssen to establish the Aryan hypothesis has to some extent simplified the problem, and the controversy is now carried on over the Semitic theory and the Ugro-Altaic, this last having been very ingeniously, though not convincingly, set forth by Dr. Isaac Taylor in his *Etruscan Researches* (London, 1874). There are many coincidences that make the Semitic hypothesis seem plausible. There are Semitic peculiarities traceable in the language—e. g. the reduplication of consonants, the omission of short vowels, and the retrograde writing. The religion of the Etruscans was a species of mysticism like that of the Semites of Carthage; their ruling class was a priesthood and their theology a system of casuistry, as with the Jews; while their rites were gloomy and horrible, like those of the Phœnicians. Again, their art possesses the peculiar rigidity, the conventionality, and the lack of expression that mark the art and architecture of the Asiatic Semites. Finally, their physical characteristics were Semitic in that the Etruscans depicted themselves upon their monuments as short, thickset, with large heads and clumsy limbs (cf. Verg. *Georg.* ii. 193), and the aquiline nose that is one of the most noticeable peculiarities of the Semitic peoples. But while these coincidences are striking, they are not conclusive, and perhaps the most reasonable view is that of Müller, who regards the Etruscans as an Asiatic non-Aryan people intermingled with Aryan elements derived from the tribes which they gradually conquered and subdued. Their earliest home in Italy was on the Padus, and as late as Livy's time the people of the Rhaetian Alps spoke a dialect of Etruscan (Livy, v. 33; Plin. *H. N.* iii. 20; Justin. xx. 5; and Oberziner, *I Reti* [1883]). The theory of a blending of two races, or rather of the grafting of an Aryan branch upon a non-Aryan stock, would account for the two main features that present themselves in the Etruscan problem — the fact that, in the main, the Etruscans have nothing in common with their neighbours of Italy, and the additional fact that their language does seem to show some slight traces of Aryan influence — about as much, for instance, as that of the British Kelts left upon the dialect of their Teutonic conquerors. This hypothesis is at least reasonable, unless we are willing to accept the conclusion of the scholars who disparagingly regard the Etruscan people and the Etruscan language as *sui generis*, representing a race and a speech that have become extinct.

Conestabile and others hold that the Etrurian people contained two distinct elements—the one native and servile, the other foreign and occupying the relation of lordship. Caeré and Cortona are said to have been Pelasgic cities before they were possessed by the Etruscans; and certain inscriptions once classed as Etruscan are now ascribed to the more ancient Pelasgi (q. v.). Livy states that the dialect of the Etrurians who inhabited the towns differed from that of the Etrurians of the country districts. Again, as Dr. Taylor points out, the rapid destruction of the Etrurian power in Campania and in the valley of the Padus makes it probable that it was a dominion of conquest rather than of colonization, and that the *Rasena*, or Etruscans proper, were a ruling aristocracy, of high culture and great ability, but few in number. All this is, in the main, corroborative of Müller's view.

GOVERNMENT AND CIVILIZATION.—The Etrurian government was a federal league of the twelve cities already mentioned, each ruled by magistrates annually elected from a class of priestly nobles of hereditary rank. These magistrates bore the titles Lauchmé (Lucμmo), Purtsvana (Porsena), and Marunuch, roughly corresponding to the Roman officers of Consul, Imperator, and Dictator. The official insignia afterwards used in Rome — the purple robe, the praetexta, the lictors and fasces, the *sella curulis*, and the *apparitores*—were derived from Etruria. The representatives of the twelve towns met at the temple of Voltumna at a place not now known (cf. Livy, iv. 23). Books of laws existed in accordance with which the internal affairs of the State were managed (*Libri Disciplinae*), as well as the religious rites and the division of the people. (See Festus, s. v. *Rituales*).

Etruscans. (Painting from Caeré.)

That the civilization of the Etruscans was a highly developed one is shown by the little that we know of their social laws as well as by the evidences of their wealth, luxury, and power. The position of women was a high one; the wife was the social equal of the husband, as is shown by the sepulchral honours paid her, and by the pictures of domestic life pourtrayed on the sarcophagi and the vases. For a long time the Etruscans ranked as one of the three great naval powers of the Mediterranean. They are known, also, to have been familiar with the sciences, to have been skilled in mining, metallurgy, astronomy, and medicine, while their knowledge of engineering was conspicuous in the massive walls of their cities, built of huge blocks, perfectly fitted without cement, and in their roads, tunnels, and chambered tombs.

In art and art-manufactures, the Etruscans stand very high. Their jewellery, which is in patterns formed by soldering on minute grains of gold, excites admiration, while their bronze-work, coinage, and mirrors are of very fine workmanship. Vast numbers of painted vases, found chiefly in tombs, possess both an historical and an artistic value. See FICTILE; VAS.

The religion of the Etruscans played a most important part in their lives, since they were proverbially devoted to the exercises of their faith, and we have, in fact, already noted that their very form of government was largely a system of sacerdotalism. Hence Livy describes the nation as *gens ante omnes alias dedita religionibus* (v. 1; see also i. 56 and v. 15); the early Fathers of the Christian Church denounced Etruria as *genetrix et mater superstitionis;* and Dionysius even went so

Etruscan Canal in the Valley of the Marta. (Reber.)

far as to derive the name *Tuscus* from θυοσκόος = *thurifer*. Their sepulchral monuments show them to have entertained a belief in a future life; while Varro, Cicero, and Martianus Capella all speak of the important part which divination played in their daily life—their affairs of State, even, being regulated by haruspices and augurs. The deities of Greece and Rome appear in their mythology [e. g. Ani (Ianus), Maris (Mars), Nethuns (Neptunus), Uni (Iuno), Artumes (Artemis), Velch (Vulcanus)], besides whom there are a number of native gods, such as Fufluns, Tinia, Turms, Thesan, answering roughly to Bacchus, Iupiter, Mercury, and Aurora. The Sun and Moon figure as Usil and Lala. Other gods, some of whom are occasionally mentioned by the Roman writers, are Manius and Mania, king and queen of the lower world, Nortia (Fortuna), into the door of whose temple at Volsinii nails (*clavi annales*) were driven to mark the successive years, Summanus, the god of night, Vertumnus, the god of Autumn, and the Novensiles, a collective name of all the gods who hurled thunderbolts.

HISTORY.—Varro records a tradition that the Etruscan State was founded in the year B.C. 1044, and the Roman legends represent the Etruscans as a powerful and wealthy people at the time when Rome was founded. Later, but still during the early years of Rome, Etruria figures in history as a great naval power, allied with Carthage against the Greeks, and having kings of its own race dominant over the Romans, as the Roman historians themselves admit in recording the legend of the migration of the Tarquins from Tarquinii to Rome, and the sway of the Tarquinian dynasty. An Etruscan cemetery has been discovered on the Esquiline at Rome; the Caelian Hill bears the name of an Etruscan chief, Caeles Vibenna, while one of the oldest quarters of the city near the Palatine bore the name Vicus Tuscus. (See Mommsen, i. 4, p. 80; id. 9, p. 174 of the American ed.; cf. also Varr. *L. L.* v. 46). That the period of Etruscan domination at Rome was one of much prosperity to the city is seen by the stories that have been transmitted to us of the magnificence of the Tarquins, and more forcibly by the vastness of the engineering works constructed at that time, such as the Cloaca Maxima, the Capitoline temple, and the Servian Wall. See CLOACA.

Even after the expulsion of the kings from Rome, Etruria was still the greatest military power in Italy, and for a century the young Republic of Rome taxed all its energies in resisting the single Tuscan State of Veii, whose people in B.C. 476 actually succeeded in capturing the Ianiculum. During the period from B.C. 540 to 474, the Etruscans divided with the Greeks and Carthaginians the control of the Mediterranean, expelling the Greek colonists from Corsica (B.C. 538), an island which they still held in 453. In B.C. 525 they attacked the Greeks in Cumae, but in 474, Hiero of Syracuse, in a great naval battle fought off the Campanian coast, broke their naval power, and won a victory which is celebrated by Pindar in an extant ode (*Pyth.* i. 72). In 414, however, a contingent of their Etruscan ships was sent to aid the Athenians in their ill-fated expedition against Sicily. From this time the power of Etruria rapidly declined. In Campania, the Greeks of Cumae, aided by the Samnites, routed the Etruscan forces, and the Samnites carried Capua by storm; while in the north of Italy the Gauls swept down from the Alps, and, after overwhelming city after city, crossed the Apennines and made their way into the heart of Etruria. The rich Etruscan city of Melpum fell in B.C. 396, and not many years later, attacked by the Romans on the south, the

Remains of the Servian Wall upon the Aventine, Rome.

southern province submitted to the Latin arms (B.C. 351). In 311, the Romans crossed the boundary formed by the Ciminian Forest, in spite of several successive defeats sustained by them at the hands of the Etruscans, and won a decisive victory in the year 283 at the Vadimonian Lake. Tarquinii almost immediately fell; and in 280 Volaterrae, the great northern fortress of the Etruscans, having succumbed, the long struggle ended with the complete triumph of the Roman arms.

Though conquered, the Etruscan cities appear to have been treated with mildness and consideration, and to have sustained towards Rome the position of allies rather than subjects. In the Second Punic War they furnished supplies to the Roman fleet, and later they were actually admitted to the Roman franchise (B.C. 89). Some of the greatest names in the later history of the Roman State are the names of men of Etruscan lineage. Pompeius Magnus (Pompu), Maecenas, and the family of Caecina were among these; and under the emperors many other distinguished men show in their lineage kinship with the noble families of Etruria. In fact, as stated above, during the Augustan age an Etruscan fad generally prevailed at Rome, like our Anglomania of to-day or the Gallomania of 1856–70; and Etruscan ancestry was a thing to be proud of.

The debt of Rome to her Etruscan neighbours has been variously regarded. In the Latin language, apart from a comparatively few terms of religion, augury, and warfare, there are no real traces of Etrurian influence. To the Romans, the Etruscans were always an alien race (Cic. *N. D.* ii. 4; Plaut. *Curc.* 150), with whom, indeed, they traded and fought, and whose divination they employed; yet they never owned kinship with them, but rather let them hold the same relation towards Rome as did the Carthaginians, with whom the Latins also fought and traded. Yet the sway of the Etruscan kings at Rome did add much to the Roman ceremonial and the usages of Roman life. To Etruria are due the insignia of office, the fasces, the curule chair; and to the same source Rome owed the circus, the gladiatorial shows, the races, the triumph, the early monetary system, the rudiments of military science, the knowledge of augury, the *tibicines*, the *lituus*, and the art of building substantial houses, aqueducts, and sewers.

BIBLIOGRAPHY.—See K. O. Müller, *Die Etrusker*, 2d ed. (Stuttgart, 1877); Lepsius, *Inscriptiones Umbricae et Oscae* (Leipzig, 1841); Corssen, *Ueber die Sprache der Etrusker* (Leipzig, 1874–75); Deecke, *Corssen und die Sprache der Etrusker* (Stuttgart, 1875); id. *Etruskische Forschungen* (1875–76); Isaac Taylor, *Etruscan Researches* (London, 1874); Mommsen, *Unteritalische Dialekte* (Leipzig, 1840); id. *Hist. of Rome*, bk. i. ch. 9; Pauli, *Etruskische Studien;* id. *Inschriften Nordetruskischen Alphabets* (Leipzig, 1885); Dennis, *Cities and Cemeteries of Etruria* (London, 1878); Rochette, *Lectures on Ancient Art*, ch. iv. (London, 1854); Gray, *History of Etruria* (London, 1843); the Earl of Crawford, *Etruscan Inscriptions* (London, 1872); Oberziner, *I Reti* (Rome, 1883); Ellis, *The Asiatic Affinities of the Old Italians* (London, 1870); id. *Etruscan Numerals* (London, 1872); id. *Sources of the Etruscan and Basque Languages* (London, 1886); and Bugge, *Der Ursprung der Etrusker* (Christiania, 1886). For the Etruscan inscriptions see Fabretti's *Corpus Inscr. Ital.* and Pauli's *Corp. Inscr. Etrusc.* (now appearing).

Etymologĭcum Magnum. The oldest Greek lexicon in existence, dating probably from the tenth century A.D., and by an unknown author. It professes to give the roots of the words contained in it. The proposed etymologies are often mere guesses, but the work is historically valuable as embodying a great number of traditions and notices of the meanings of unusual words. There are modern editions by Schäfer (Leipzig, 1816), Sturz (*Etymologicum Gudianum*) (Leipzig, 1818), and Gaisford (Oxford, 1849). See LEXICON.

Etymology. See PHILOLOGY.

Euandros (Εὔανδρος). See EVANDER.

Euboea (Εὔβοια). Now Negropont; the largest island of the Aegaean Sea, lying along the coasts of Attica, Boeotia, and the southern part of Thessaly, from which countries it is separated by the Euboean Sea, called the Euripus in its narrowest part. Its early name was MACRIS. Euboea is about ninety miles in length; its extreme breadth is thirty miles, but in the narrowest part it is only four miles across. Throughout the length of the island runs a lofty range of mountains, which rise in one part as high as 7266 feet above the sea. It contains, nevertheless, many fertile plains, and was celebrated in antiquity for the excellence of its pasturage and corn-fields. According to the ancients it was once united to Boeotia, from which it was separated by an earthquake. In Homer (*Il.* ii. 536) the inhabitants are called Abantes, and are represented as taking part in the expedition against Troy. In the northern part of Euboea dwelt the Histiaei, from whom that part of the island was called Histiaea; below these were the Ellopii, who gave the name of Ellopia to the district, extending as far as Aegae and Cerinthus; and in the south were the Dryopes. The centre of the island was inhabited chiefly by Ionians. It was in this part of Euboea that the Athenians planted the colonies of Chalcis and Eretria, which were the two most important cities in the island. After the Persian Wars Euboea became subject to the Athenians, who attached much importance to its possession; and consequently Pericles made great exertions to subdue it, when it revolted in B.C. 445. Under the Romans Euboea formed part of the province of Achaea. See Bursian, *Topogr. von Euboia* (1859).

Euboĭcus, "belonging to Euboea." An epithet applied to Cumae, because that city was built by a colony from Chalcis, a town of Euboea (Ovid, *Fast.* iv. 257; Verg. *Aen.* vi. 2, ix. 710).

Eubulĭdes (Εὐβουλίδης). A native of Miletus and successor of Euclid in the Megaric school. He was a strong opponent of Aristotle, and seized every opportunity of censuring his writings and calumniating his character. He introduced new subtleties into the art of disputation, several of which, though often mentioned as proof of great ingenuity, deserve only to be remembered as examples of egregious trifling. Of these sophistical modes of reasoning, called by Aristotle "Eristic syllogisms," a few examples may suffice. (1) *The Lying.* If, when you speak the truth, you say, you lie, you lie: but you say you lie when you speak the truth; therefore, in speaking the truth, you lie. (2) *The Occult.* Do you know your father? Yes. Do you know this man who is veiled? No. Then you do not know your father, for it is your father who is veiled. (3) *Electra.* Electra, the daughter of Agamemnon, knew her brother and did not know him; she knew Orestes to be her brother, but she did not know that person to be her brother who was conversing with her. (4) *Sorites.* Is one grain a heap? No. Two grains? No. Three grains? No. Go on, adding one by one; and if one grain be not a heap, it will be impossible to say what number of grains make a heap. (5) *The Horned.* You have what you have not lost: you have not lost horns; therefore you have horns. In such high repute were these quibbles that Chrysippus wrote six books on the first of them; and Philetas of Cos died of consumption which he contracted in the close study which he bestowed upon them (Diog. Laërt. i. 111).

Eubūlus (Εὔβουλος). (1) A formidable opponent of Demosthenes at Athens. (2) A comic poet of Athens, born in the deme of Atarnea. He exhibited about B.C. 375. Eubulus stood on the debatable ground between the Old and Middle Comedy; and to judge from the fragments in Athenaeus, who quotes more than fifty of his comedies by name, he must have written plays of both sorts. He composed, in all, 104 comedies. The remains will be found in Meineke's *Fragmenta Com. Graec.* i. pp. 355–367 and iii. pp. 203–272.

Eucheir (Εὔχειρ). (1) A painter related, as was said, to Daedalus, and who, according to Theophrastus (*ap.* Pliny, *H. N.* vii. 56), introduced painting into Greece. The name, in truth, however, is merely a figurative one for a skilful artist generally (εὔχειρ, "skilful," "dexterous"). (2) A modeller, styled also EUCHĪRUS (Pausan. vi. 4. 2), and one of the most ancient. He and Eugrammus are said to have accompanied Demaratus in his flight from Corinth to Etruria. Here again both names are figurative. (3) An Athenian sculptor. He made a statue of Hermes, which was placed at Phenea (Pausan. viii. 14. 7). Pliny ranks him among those artists who excelled in forming brazen statues of combatants at the public games, armed men, huntsmen, etc.

Eucleia (εὔκλεια). A festival celebrated at Corinth in honour of Artemis. It is mentioned only by Xenophon (*Hell.* iv. 4, § 2), and no particulars are known about it.

Euclīdes (Εὐκλείδης). (1) A native of Megara, founder of the Megaric, or Eristic sect. Endowed by nature with a subtle and penetrating genius, he early applied himself to the study of philosophy. The writings of Parmenides first taught him the art of disputation. Hearing of the fame of Socrates, Euclid determined to attend upon his instructions, and for this purpose removed from Megara to Athens. Here he long remained a constant hearer and zealous disciple of the moral philosopher; and when, in consequence of the enmity which subsisted between the Athenians and Megareans, a decree was passed by the former that any inhabitant of Megara who should be seen in Athens should forfeit his life, he frequently came to Athens by night, from the distance of about twenty miles, concealed in a long female cloak and veil, to visit his master (Aul. Gell. vii. 10). Not finding his propensity to disputation sufficiently gratified in the tranquil method of philosophizing adopted by Socrates, he frequently engaged in the business and the disputes of the civil courts. Socrates, who despised forensic contests, expressed some dissatisfaction with his pupil for indulging a fondness for controversy (Diog. Laërt. ii. 30). This circumstance probably proved the occasion of a separation between Euclid and his master; for we find him, after this time, at the head of a school in Megara (Diog. Laërt. iii. 6), in which his chief employment was to teach the art of disputation. Debates were conducted with so much vehemence among his pupils that Timon said of Euclid that he had carried the madness of contention from Athens to Megara. That he was, however, capable of commanding his temper appears from his reply to his brother, who, in a quarrel, had said, "Let me perish if I be not revenged on you." "And let *me* perish," returned Euclid, "if I do not subdue your resentment by forbearance and make you love me as much as ever."

In argument Euclid was averse to the analogical method of reasoning, and judged that legitimate argument consists in deducing fair conclusions from acknowledged premises. He held that there is one supreme good, which he called by the different names of Intelligence, Providence, God; and that evil, considered as an opposite principle to the sovereign good, has no existence. The supreme good, according to Cicero, he defined to be that which is always the same. In this doctrine, in which he followed the subtlety of Parmenides rather than the simplicity of Socrates, he seems to have considered good abstractly as residing in the Deity, and to have maintained that all things which exist are good by their participation of the first good, and, consequently, that there is, in the nature of things, no real evil. It is said that when Euclid was asked his opinion concerning the gods, he replied, "I know nothing more of them than this: that they hate inquisitive persons."

(2) A celebrated mathematician of Alexandria, considered by some to have been a native of that city, though the more received opinion makes the place of his birth to have been unknown. He flourished B.C. 280, in the reign of Ptolemy Lagus, and was professor of mathematics in the capital of Egypt. His scholars were numerous, and among them was Ptolemy himself. It is related that the monarch having inquired of Euclid if there was not some mode of learning mathematics less barbarous and requiring less attention than the ordinary one, Euclid, though otherwise of an affable disposition, dryly answered that there was "no royal road to geometry" (μὴ εἶναι βασιλικὴν ἀτραπὸν πρὸς γεωμετρίαν). Euclid was the first person who established a mathematical school at Alexandria, and it existed and maintained its reputation till the Mohammedan conquest of Egypt. Many of the fundamental principles of the pure mathematics had been discovered by Thales, Pythagoras, and other predecessors of Euclid; but to him is due the merit of having given a systematic form to the science, especially to that part of it which relates to geometry. He likewise studied the cognate sciences of Astronomy and Optics; and, according to Proclus, he was the author of "Elements" (Στοιχεῖα), "Data" (Δεδομένα), "An Introduction to Harmony" (Εἰσαγωγὴ Ἁρμονική), "Phaenomena" (Φαινόμενα), "Optics" (Ὀπτικά), "Catoptrics" (Κατοπτρικά), "On the Division of the Scale" (Κατατομὴ Κανόνος), and other works now lost. His most valuable work, "The Elements of Geometry," in thirteen books, with two additional books by Hypsicles, has been repeatedly published—the first edition at Venice (1482) in a Latin trans-

lation from the Arabic. The first Greek text appeared at Basle in 1533. The edition of Peyrard is among the best. It appeared at Paris in 1814-16-18, in 3 vols. This edition is accompanied with a double translation—one in Latin and the other in French. M. Peyrard consulted a manuscript of the latter part of the ninth century, which had belonged to the Vatican library, and was at that time in the French capital. By the aid of this he was enabled to fill various *lacunae*, and to re-establish various passages which had been altered in all the other manuscripts and in all the editions anterior to his own. The best recent edition is that of Heiberg, 5 vols. (1883-88). The only English edition of all the works ascribed to Euclid is that of Gregory (Oxford, 1703). See Dodgson, *Euclid and his Modern Rivals* (1879); Allman, *Greek Geometry from Thales to Euclid* (1889); and Ball, *Short Hist. of Mathematics*, pp. 48-57 (1888).

Euctēmon (Εὐκτήμων). (1) A Greek astronomer. (See METON.) (2) A rhetorician mentioned by the elder Seneca, who has preserved some quotations from his works (*Controv.* iii. 19, 20; iv. 25; v. 30, 34).

Eudēmus (Εὔδημος). A native of Rhodes and noted as a peripatetic philosopher and disciple of Aristotle, many of whose works he edited. One of these bears the name of Eudemus (Ἠθικὰ Εὐδήμεια), in seven books, probably a recension of all Aristotle's ethical lectures arranged by Eudemus. See Gell. xiii. 5, and the article ARISTOTELES.

Eudocia (Εὐδοκία). (1) A Roman empress, wife to Theodosius the Younger. Her original name was Athenaïs, and she was the daughter of Leontius, an Athenian philosopher; but on her marriage she embraced Christianity, and received the baptismal name of Eudocia. She was a woman of beauty and talent. She versified several books of the Old Testament, and wrote several paraphrases on some of the Jewish prophets; but became suspected by her husband of conjugal infidelity, and, being degraded, she was allowed to seek a refuge in the Holy Land. Here she devoted herself to religious studies, but the jealousy of her suspicious husband still pursued her; and having learned that two priests, whom she had chosen as the companions of her exile, were accustomed to pay her frequent visits and were loaded by her with presents, Theodosius sent Saturninus, one of the officers of his court, to Jerusalem, who put to death the two priests without even the formality of a trial. Irritated at this new insult, Eudocia caused Saturninus to be slain—a deed more likely to darken than avenge her innocence. The emperor contented himself with depriving her of all the badges of her rank, and reducing her to the conditions of a private individual. She lived twenty years after this event, in the bitterest penitence, and died at the age of sixty-seven years, in A.D. 460.

The principal work ascribed by some to Eudocia is *Homerocentra* (Ὁμηρόκεντρα), or a life of the Saviour, in 2443 hexameters, formed from verses and hemistichs selected from the poems of Homer. (See CENTO.) Others, however, make Pelagius, surnamed Patricius, who lived in the fifth century, its author. Eudocia left, also, a poem on the martyrdom of Cyprian. The best edition of the *Homerocentra* is that of Teucher (Leipzig, 1798). (2) The Younger, daughter of the preceding and of Theodosius II., married Valentinian III. After the assassination of her husband by Petronius Maximus, she was obliged to marry the usurper. Eudocia, out of indignation and revenge, called in Genseric, king of the Vandals, who came to Italy, plundered Rome, and carried Eudocia with him to Africa. Some years afterwards she was sent back to Constantinople, where she died, A.D. 462. (3) The widow of Constantine Ducas, married to Romanus Diogenes, an officer of distinction, A.D. 1068, and associated him with her upon the throne. Three years after, Michael, her son, by means of a revolt, was proclaimed emperor, and caused his mother to be shut up in a convent, where she spent the rest of her life. She left a treatise on the genealogies of the gods and heroes, which displays an extensive acquaintance with the subject. It is printed in Villoison's *Anecdota Graeca* (Venice, 1781).

Eudoxus (Εὔδοξος). A celebrated astronomer and geometrician of Cnidus, who flourished B.C. 366. He studied at Athens and in Egypt, but probably spent some of his time at his native place, where he had an observatory. He is said to have been the first who taught in Greece the motions of the planets. His works are lost (Sen. *Quaest. Nat.* vii. 3; Vitruv. ix. 9; Plin. *H. N.* ii. 47).

Euergĕtae (Εὐεργέται). A people of Upper Asia, whose true name was Ariaspae. The Greeks called them Euergetae, or benefactors, translating the Persian appellation which was added to their name. This title they are said to have received in return for succour afforded to the army of Cyrus, when it was suffering, in these regions, from cold and hunger (Curt. vii. 3).

Euergĕtes (Εὐεργέτης). A surname, signifying benefactor, given to Ptolemy III. and IV. of Egypt, as also to some kings of Syria, Pontus, etc.

Eugamon (Εὐγάμων) or **Eugammon.** One of the Cyclic poets, a native of Cyrené, who flourished about B.C. 568. He wrote a continuation of the *Odyssey*, in two books, with the title *Telegonia* (Τηλεγονία), and giving an account of the events from the fight with the suitors to the death of Odysseus. The substance of the poem is preserved in the *Chrestomathia* of Proclus. See CYCLIC POETS.

Euganei. A people who formerly inhabited Venetia, on the Adriatic Sea, and were driven towards the Alps and the Lacus Benacus by the Heneti or Veneti (Livy, i. 1).

Eugenius (Εὐγένιος). (1) A general who opposed Diocletian in A.D. 290, but was slain the very same day at the gates of Antioch, while attempting to make himself master of that city. (2) A usurper in the reign of Theodosius the Great, of Gallic extraction, A.D. 392. He was defeated, taken prisoner, and put to death, after having held power for two years (Zosim. iv. 54 foll.).

Eùgubine Tables. See TABULAE IGUVINAE.

Euhemĕrus (Εὐήμερος). A native of Messena, as is generally supposed, though perhaps of Messana. Being sent on a voyage of discovery by Cassander, king of Macedon, about B.C. 316, he came, as he himself asserted, to an island called Panchaea, in the capital of which, Panara, he found a temple of the Triphylian Zeus, where stood a column inscribed with a register of the births and deaths of many of the gods. Among these he specified Uranus, his sons Pan and Cronos, and his daughters Rhea and Demeter; as also Zeus, Heré, and Poseidon, who were the offspring of Cronos. Accordingly, the design of Euhemerus was to show, by investigating their actions and recording the places of their births and burials, that the mythological deities were mere mortal men, raised to the rank of gods on account of the benefits which they had conferred upon mankind. Ennius translated this celebrated work of Euhemerus, which was entitled Ἱερὰ Ἀναγραφή. The translation, as well as the original work, excepting some fragments, is lost; but many particulars concerning Euhemerus and the object of his history are mentioned in a fragment of Diodorus Siculus, preserved by Eusebius. Some quotations have also been saved by St. Augustine, and others have been made by Lactantius in his treatise *De Falsa Religione* (i. 11). This work was undoubtedly a covert attack on the established religion of the Greeks.

Euius (Εὔιος). A surname of Bacchus, given him, according to the poets, by Zeus, whom he was aiding in the contest with the giants. Zeus was so delighted with his valour that he called out to him, Εὖ υἱέ, "Well done, O son!" Others suppose it to have originated from a cry of the Bacchantes, Εὐοῖ. Cf. Lachm. on Lucret. v. 743.

Eulaeus (Εὔλαιος, O. T. ULAI). A river in Susiana, rising in Great Media, passing east of Susa, and falling into the head of the Persian Gulf.

Eumaeus (Εὔμαιος). The faithful swineherd of Odysseus, who gave his master a friendly welcome on his return home in the guise of a beggar, and aided him in the slaughter of the suitors (*Odyss.* xv. 402, etc.). See ODYSSEUS.

Eumēlus (Εὔμηλος). (1) A son of Admetus, king of Pherae in Thessaly, by Alcestis, daughter of Pelias, and who married Iphthimé, the sister of Penelopé. He went to the Trojan War, and had the fleetest horses in the Grecian army. He distinguished himself in the funeral games of Patroclus (*Il.* ii. 714, 763 foll.). (2) Son of Amphilytus and one of the Corinthian line termed Bacchiadae. He was the author of a history of Corinth in heroic verse (Pausan. ii. 1). Eumelus joined Archias when the latter went to found Syracuse.

Eumĕnes (Εὐμένης). (1) Of Cardia, served as private secretary to Philip and Alexander; and on the death of the latter (B.C. 323) obtained the government of Cappadocia, Paphlagonia, and Pontus. Eumenes allied himself with Perdiccas, and carried on war for him in Asia Minor against Antipater and Craterus. On the death of Perdiccas in Egypt, Antigonus employed the whole force of the Macedonian army to crush Eumenes. Notwithstanding the numerical inferiority of his forces, Eumenes maintained his ground against his enemies for some years, till he was surrendered by the soldiery to Antigonus, by whom he was put to death, 316. He was a great general and statesman, and had he been a native Macedonian would probably have occupied a more important position among the successors of Alexander. (2) I., king of Pergamum, who reigned B.C. 263–241, and was the successor of his uncle Philetaerus. (3) II., king of Pergamum, who reigned B.C. 197–159, and was the son and successor of Attalus I. He inherited from his predecessor the friendship and alliance of the Romans, which he took the utmost pains to cultivate. Pergamum became under his rule a great and flourishing city, in which he founded that celebrated library that rose to be a rival even to that of Alexandria. See PERGAMUM.

Eumenīa (Εὐμένεια). A city of Phrygia, north of Peltae, which probably derived its name from Eumenes, king of Pergamus. Steph. Byz. s. v. Εὐμένεια.

Eumenĭdes (Εὐμενίδες), also called ERINŸES (Ἐρινύες), and by the Romans Furiae or Dirae. Originally a personification of curses pronounced upon a guilty criminal. The name Erinys, which is the more ancient one, was derived by the Greeks from the verb ἐρίνω or ἐρευνάω, "I hunt down," or "persecute," or from the Arcadian word ἐρινύω, "I am angry"; so that the Erinyes were either the angry goddesses, or the goddesses who hunt or search for the criminal. The name Eumenides, which signifies "the well-meaning," or "soothed goddesses," is a mere euphemism, because people dreaded to call these fearful goddesses by their real name, and it was said to have been first given them after the acquittal of Orestes by the court of the Areopagus, when the anger of the Erinyes had become soothed. It was by a similar euphemism that at Athens the Erinyes were called σεμναὶ θεαί, or the Revered Goddesses.

In the sense of "curse" or "curses," the word Erinys or Erinyes is often used in the Homeric poems, and Aeschylus calls the Eumenides Ἀραί, that is, curses. According to the Homeric notion, the Erinyes, whom the poet conceives as distinct beings, are reckoned among those who inhabit Erebus, where they rest until some curse pronounced upon a criminal calls them to life and activity. The crimes which they punish are disobedience towards parents, violation of the respect due to old age, perjury, murder, violation of the laws of hospitality, and improper conduct towards suppliants. The notion which is the foundation of the belief in the Eumenides seems to be that a parent's curse takes from him upon whom it is pronounced all peace of mind, destroys the happiness of his family, and prevents his being blessed with children. As the Eumenides not only punished crimes after death, but during life on earth, they were regarded also as goddesses of fate, who, together with Zeus and the Moerae or Parcae, led such men as were doomed to suffer into misery and misfortunes. In the same capacity they also prevented man from obtaining too much knowledge of the future. Homer does not mention any particular names for the Erinyes, nor does he seem to know of any definite number. Hesiod, who is likewise silent upon these points, calls the Erinyes the daughters of Gaea, who conceived them in the drops of blood that fell upon her from the body of Uranus. Epimenides called them the daughters of Cronos and Euonymé, and sisters of the Moerae; Aeschylus calls them the daughters of Night; and Sophocles, of Scotos (Darkness) and Gaea. In the Greek tragedians, with whom (e. g. in the *Eumenides* of Aeschylus) the number of these goddesses is not limited to a few, no particular name of any one Erinys is yet mentioned, but they appear in the same capacity, and as the avengers of the same crimes, as before. They are sometimes identified with the Poenae, though their sphere of action is wider than that of the Poenae. From their hunting down and persecuting the accursed criminal, Aeschylus calls them κύνες or κυνηγέτιδες. No prayer, no sacrifice, and no tears can move them, or protect the object of their persecution; and when they fear lest the criminal should escape them, they call in the assistance of Diké, with whom they are closely connected, the maintenance of strict justice being their only object. The Erinyes were more ancient divinities than the Olympian gods, and were therefore not under the rule of Zeus, though they honoured and esteemed him; and they dwelt in the deep darkness of Tartarus, dreaded by gods and men. Their appearance is described by Aeschylus as Gorgo-like, their bodies covered with black, serpents twined in their hair, and blood dripping from their eyes; Euripides and other later poets describe them as winged beings. The appearance they have in Aeschylus was more or less retained by the poets of later times; but they gradually assumed the character of goddesses who punished crimes after death, and seldom appeared on earth. On the stage, however, and in works of art, their fearful appearance was greatly softened down, for they were represented as maidens of a grave and solemn mien, in the richly adorned attire of huntresses, with a band of serpents around their heads, and serpents or torches in their hands. With later writers, though not always, the number of Eumenides is limited to three, and their names are TISIPHŎNÉ, ALECTO, and MEGAERA. At Athens there were statues of only two. The sacrifices which were offered to them consisted of black sheep and νηφάλια—i. e. a drink of honey mixed with water. Among the objects sacred to them we hear of white turtle-doves and the narcissus. They were worshipped at Athens, where they had a sanctuary and a grotto near the Areopagus; their statues, however, had nothing formidable, and a festival, Eumenidia, was there celebrated in their honour. Another sanctuary, with a grove which no one was allowed to enter, existed at Colonus. Under the name of Μανίαι, they were worshipped at Megalopolis.

Eumenides. (From a Painted Vase.)

Eumenĭdes (Εὐμενίδες). A play of Aeschylus (q. v.), the third of the great Orestean trilogy. It represents Orestes pursued by the Furies to Athens, where he is tried by the Areopagus for the murder of his mother. Clytaemnestra, and acquitted by the casting vote of Athené, so that in his person the family curse comes to an end. For a critical discussion of the play see K. O. Müller's *Eumenides*, Eng. trans. (Cambridge, 1835). Separate editions, with English verse translation and notes by Drake (London, 1853); and Paley (London, 1880). See also Rose, *Greek Dramas*, vol. ii. (London, 1872); and on the story of the play, the articles ORESTES; PELOPIDAE.

Eumenidīa (Εὐμενίδεια). A festival in honour of the Eumenides. It was observed once a year with sacrifices and libations. At Athens none but free-born citizens were allowed to participate in the solemnity, and of these none but such as were of known virtue and integrity. See EUMENIDES.

Eumenius. A Roman rhetorician of Augustodunum (Autun) in Gaul who flourished about A.D. 290. Four orations of his are preserved—one on the restoration of the school at Autun by Constantius Chlorus, delivered in A.D. 296 or 297, and three panegyrics. Text by Bährens (Leipzig, 1874). See Seeck in Jahn's *Jahrbücher*, cxxxvii. 713; Kilian, *Der Panegyrist Eumenius* (Münnerstadt, 1869); Sachs, *De Quattuor Panegyricis*, etc. (Halle, 1885); and the article PANEGYRICUS.

Eumolpĭdae (Εὐμολπίδαι). The most distinguished and venerable among the priestly families in Attica, believed to be the descendants of the Thracian bard Eumolpus, the introducer of the Eleusinian mysteries into Attica (Diod. Sic. i. 29; Apollod. iii. 15, § 4.) The ἱεροφάντης was always a member of the family of the Eumolpidae, as Eumolpus himself was believed to have been the first hierophant (Hesych. s. v. Εὐμολπίδαι; Tac. *Hist.* iv. 83). For the judicial powers of the Eumolpidae, see the article ELEUSINIA, p. 582.

Eumolpus (Εὔμολπος). In Greek mythology, the son of Poseidon and Chioné, the daughter of Boreas and Orithyia. After his birth he was thrown by his mother into the sea, but his father rescued him and brought him to Aethiopia, to his daughter Benthesicymé. When he was grown up, Endius, the husband of Benthesicymé, gave him one of his daughters in marriage, but he desired the other as well, and was accordingly banished, and came with his son Ismarus or Immaradus to the Thracian king Tegyrius in Boeotia. As successor to this king he marched to the assistance of his friends the Eleusinians against the Athenian Erechtheus, but was slain with his son. (See ERECHTHEUS.) According to another story, Immaradus and Erechtheus both fell, and the contending parties agreed that the Eleusinians should submit to the Athenians, but should retain the exclusive superintendence of the mysteries of Eleusis, of which Eumolpus was accounted the founder (Thucyd. ii. 15; Isocrat. *Panath.* 78). He was also spoken of as a writer of consecrational hymns, and as having discovered the art of cultivating the vines and trees in general. The Eumolpidae, his descendants, were the hereditary priests of the Eleusinian ritual. See ELEUSINIA.

Eunapius (Εὐνάπιος). A Greek rhetorician, born at Sardis in A.D. 347. In 405 he wrote biographies of twenty-three older and contemporary philosophers and sophists. In spite of its bad style and its superficiality, this book is our chief authority for the history of the Neo-Platonism of that age. There is an edition by Boissonade (Amst. 1822). We have also several fragments of his continuation of the chronicle of Herennius Dexippus. This continuation, in fourteen books, covered the period from A.D. 268 to 404, and was much used by Zosimus. See DEXIPPUS.

Eunēus (Εὔνηος). A son of Iason and Hypsipylé See HYPSIPYLÉ; IASON.

Eunomia (Εὐνομία). See HORAE.

Eunomius (Εὐνόμιος). The leader of an extreme sect of Arians (Eunomians) in the fourth century A.D. He was born at Dacora in Cappadocia, and was well known as the pupil and associate of Aëtius (q. v.) at Alexandria. By the support of Eudoxius, he became Bishop of Cyzicus (A.D. 360), but soon after resigned the episcopal office to become the leader of a party. The confession of faith which in 383 he sent to Theodosius the Great was rejected and he spent a number of years as an exile in Mauretania, Illyricum, Moesia, and elsewhere, until at last he was permitted to return to his native place to spend the remainder of his life. He died at Dacora about the year 394. Most of his works have been lost, owing to the fact that their destruction was ordered by various imperial edicts. We still possess, however, his Exposition of Faith and his Ἀπολογητικός, written in defence of his doctrines.

The teachings of Eunomius were by his followers set even above the Scriptures. They represent an extreme type of Arianism, in denying not only the equality of the Son with the Father, but even any similarity (ὁμοιότης). See Klose, *Geschichte und Lehre des Eunomius* (Kiel, 1833).

Eunūchus (εὐνοῦχος). A eunuch. See SERVUS.

Eunūchus. A play of Terence based upon the Εὐνοῦχος of Menander and the Κόλαξ of the same writer. It is one of the liveliest of the Terentian comedies, and obtained an exceptional success during the poet's lifetime. It was first produced in B.C. 161, the same year as the *Phormio*. The *Eunuchus* has been imitated in modern times in the *Bellamira* of Sir Charles Sedley, in *Le Muet* of Brueys, and in *L'Eunuque* of Fontaine. It is edited (with the *Andria*) by Papillon (London, 1877).

Eunus (Εὔνους). A Sicilian juggler and slave, a native of Apamea in Syria. He was the leader of the Sicilian slaves in the Servile War (B.C. 134–132) (Livy, *Epit.* xlv.). He was defeated by the consul P. Rupilius, and died in prison at Morgantia (Florus, iii. 20; Plut. *Sull.* 36).

Eupalium (Εὐπάλιον) or **Eupolium** (Εὐπόλιον). A town of the Locri Ozolae, north of Naupactus.

Eupatorium or **Eupatoria** (Εὐπατόριον or Εὐπατορία). (1) A town of Pontus, at the confluence of the Lycus and Iris. It was begun by Mithridates under the name Eupatoria, and received from Pompey, who finished it, the title of Magnopolis. (2) A town in the northwestern part of the Tauric Chersonesus, on the Sinus Carcinites. It was founded by one of the generals of Mithridates.

Eupatrĭdae (Εὐπατρίδαι). The members of the ancient noble families of Attica. After the abolition of royal power they found themselves in exclusive possession of political rights, and distinguished from the Γηωμόροι or agriculturists, and the Δημιουργοί or mechanics. The constitution of Solon deprived them of this privilege. But their landed property and the priestly dignities which they had possessed of old assured them a certain influence for a considerable time. See SOLONIAN CONSTITUTION.

Euphaes (Εὐφάης). A prince who succeeded Androcles on the throne of Messenia, and in his reign the first Messenian war began. He died B.C. 730 (Pausan. iv. 5, 6).

Euphemism and **Antiphrăsis**. See PHILOLOGY.

Euphēmus (Εὔφημος). Son of Poseidon and Europa, daughter of Tityus, husband of Laonomé, the sister of Heracles. His father conferred on him the gift of moving so swiftly over the sea that his feet remained dry. He was originally one of the Minyae of Panopeus in Phocis, but afterwards settled on the promontory of Taenarum in Laconia, and took part in the Calydonian hunt and the expedition of the Argonauts. When the Argonauts came to the lake of Triton, Triton gave Eumolpus a clod of earth, and Medea prophesied that if he threw this into the entrance of the lower world at Taenarum, his descendants of the tenth generation would be masters of Libya. The clod, however, was lost in the island of Thera, and his descendants were compelled to hold possession of this island, from which at length, in the seventeenth generation, Battus came forth and founded Cyrené in Libya. See Apollon. Rhod. ii. 562; Hygin. *Fab.* 14; Herod. iv. 150.

Euphorbus (Εὔφορβος). A Trojan, son of Panthoüs, renowned for his valour. He wounded Patroclus, and was killed by Menelaüs (*Il.* xvii. 60). Pausanias relates (ii. 17) that in the temple of Heré, near Mycenae, a votive shield was shown, said to be that of Euphorbus, suspended there by Menelaüs. Pythagoras, who maintained the transmigration of souls, declared that, in the time of the Trojan War, his soul had animated the body of Euphorbus; and as a proof of the truth of his assertion, he is said to have gone into the temple where the shield was hanging, and to have recognized and taken it down (Hor. *Carm.* i. 28. 11).

Euphorion (Εὐφορίων). (1) A tragic poet of Athens, son of Aeschylus. He conquered four times with posthumous tragedies of his father's composition, and also wrote several dramas himself. One of his victories is commemorated in the argument to the *Medea* of Euripides, where we are told that Euphorion was first, Sophocles second, and Euripides third with the *Medea*, B.C. 431. (2) An epic and epigrammatic poet, born at Chalcis in Euboea, B.C. 276, and who became librarian to Antiochus the Great. He wrote various poems, entitled *Hesiod*, *Alexander*, *Arius*, *Apollodorus*, etc. His *Mopsopia* or *Miscellanies* (Μοψοπία ἤ ἄτακτα) was a collection, in five books, of fables and histories relative to Attica, a very learned work, but rivalling in obscurity the *Cassandra* of Lycophron. The fifth book bore the title of *Chiliad* (Χιλιάς), either because it consisted of a thousand verses, or because it contained the ancient oracles that referred to a period of a thousand years. Perhaps, however, each of the five books contained a thousand verses, for the passage of Suidas respecting this writer is somewhat obscure and defective, and Eudocia, in the "Garden of Violets," speaks of a fifth Chiliad, entitled Περὶ Χρησμῶν, "Of Oracles." Quintilian recommends the reading of this poet, and Vergil is said to have esteemed his productions very highly. A passage in the tenth eclogue (v. 50 foll.) and a remark made by Servius (*Ad Eclog.* vi. 72) have led Heyne to suppose that C. Cornelius Gallus, the friend of Vergil, had translated Euphorion into Latin verse. This poet was one of the favourite authors of the emperor Tiberius, one of those whom he imitated, and whose busts he placed in his library. The fragments of Euphorion were collected and published by Meineke in his work *De Euphorionis Chalc. Vita et Scriptis* (1823), and in his *Analecta Alexandrina* (Berlin, 1843). See also Kock, *Frag. Com. Graec.* (1880). The amours of Euphorion with Nicia or Nicaea, the wife of King Alexandria of Euboea, are often alluded to in the poems of the Greek Anthology. See Brunck, *Anal.* vol. ii. pp. 3, 43.

Euphrānor (Εὐφράνωρ). A distinguished statuary and painter. He was a native of Corinth, but practised his art at Athens about B.C. 336 (Quint. xii. 10. 6; Plin. *H. N.* xxxv. 8). Of one of his works, a beautiful sitting Paris, we have probably a copy in the Museo Pio-Clementino. His best paintings were preserved in a porch in the Ceramicus.

Euphrātes (Εὐφράτης). (1) A native of Oreus in Euboea and a disciple of Plato. He quitted Athens for the court of Perdiccas, king of Macedonia, with whom he became a favourite. After the death of this monarch he returned to his country, and headed a party against Philip, the successor of Perdiccas and father of Alexander. Being shut up, however, within the walls of Oreus, he put an end to his own life. According to some, he was killed by order of Parmenio. (2) A Stoic philosopher and native of Alexandria, who flourished in the second century. He was a friend of the philosopher Apollonius of Tyana, who introduced him to Vespasian. Pliny the Younger (*Epist.* i. 10) speaks highly of his character. When he found his strength worn out by disease and old age, he voluntarily put a period to his life by drinking hemlock, having first, for some unknown reason, obtained permission from the emperor Hadrian.

Euphrātes (Εὐφράτης). One of the largest and best-known rivers of Asia. The Euphrates rises near Arzé, the modern Erzeroum. Its source is among mountains, which Strabo makes to be a part of the most northern branch of Taurus. At first it is a very inconsiderable stream, and flows to the west, until, encountering the mountains of Cappadocia, it turns to the south, and, after flowing a short distance, receives its southern arm, a large river coming from the east and rising in the southern declivity of the range of Mount Ararat. This southern arm of the Euphrates is the Arsanias, according to Mannert, and is the river which the 10,000 crossed in their retreat (*Anab.* iv. 5), and of which mention is made by Pliny in reference to the campaigns of Corbulo. The Euphrates, by this accession of waters, becoming a very large stream, descends rapidly in a bending course, nearly west-southwest to the vicinity of Samosata. The range of Amanus here preventing its farther progress in this direction, it turns off to the southeast, a course which it next pursues, with some variation, until it reaches Circesium. To the south of this place it enters the immense plains of Sennar, but is forced to run again to the southeast and approach the Tigris. The union of these rivers finally takes place near Coma. The river formed by their junction is called Shat-al-Arab, or River of Arabia. It has three principal mouths, besides a small outlet. The whole length of the Euphrates, including the Shat-al-Arab, is 1700 miles. Its name is the Greek form of the original appellation Phrat, which signifies fruitful or fertilizing. The Oriental name is sometimes also written Perath, as in Gen. ii. 14, 15, 18, and Josh. i. 4. The Persian form is *Ufratu;* Syriac, *Ephrat;* Arabic, *Furat.* On the condition and topography of the Euphrates, see Ainsworth, *The Euphrates Expedition* (1888).

Euphrosȳnē (Εὐφροσύνη). One of the Charites or Graces. See CHARITES.

Eupŏlis (Εὔπολις). A writer of the Old Comedy, who was born at Athens about the year B.C. 446. He was therefore a contemporary of Aristophanes, who, in all probability, was born a year or two after. Eupolis is supposed to have exhibited plays for the first time in B.C. 429. In B.C. 425 he was third with his Νουμηνίαι, when Cratinus was second and Aristophanes first. In B.C. 421 he brought out his Μαρικᾶς and his Κόλακες, and his Αὐτόλυκος and Ἀστρατευτοί the following year (Schol. on Aristoph. *Nub.* 552, 592; Schol. on Aristoph. *Pac.* 803). The titles of more than twenty of his comedies have been collected. A few fragments remain. Eupolis was a bold and severe satirist on the vices of his day and city. Persius (i. 124) terms him *iratus* (cf. Hor. *Sat.* i. 4. 1 foll.). In the Μαρικᾶς he attacked Hyperbolus (Aristoph. *Nub.* 551); in the Αὐτόλυκος he ridiculed the handsome pancratiast of that name; in the Ἀστράτευτοι he lashed the useless and cowardly citizens of Athens, and denounced Melanthus as an epicure. In the Βάπται he inveighed against the effeminacy of his countrymen. In his Λακεδαίμονες he assailed Cimon, accusing him, among other charges, of an unpatriotic bias towards everything Spartan. (See Plut. *Cim.* 16, who says that this play had a great influence on the public feeling.) Aristophanes seems to have been on bad terms with Eupolis, whom he charges with having pillaged the materials for his Μαρικᾶς from the Ἱππῆς (*Nubes*, 551 foll.), and with making scurrilous jokes on his premature baldness (Schol. *Ad Nub.* 532). Eupolis appears to have been a warm admirer of Pericles as a statesman and a man, as it was reasonable that such a comedian should be, if it be true that he owed his unrestrained license of speech to the patronage of that celebrated statesman. His death was generally ascribed to the vengeance of Alcibiades, whom he had lampooned, probably in the Βάπται (Cic. *Ad Att.* vi. 1). By his orders, according to the common account, Eupolis was thrown overboard during the passage of the Athenian armament to Sicily (B.C. 415). Cicero, however, calls this story a popular error; since Eratosthenes, the Alexandrian librarian, had shown that several comedies were composed by Eupolis some time after the date assigned to this pseudo-assassination. His tomb, too, according to Pausanias, was erected on the banks of the Asopus by the Sicyonians, which makes it most probable that this was the place of his death. The fragments of Eupolis will be found in Meineke's *Fragmenta Com. Graec.* i. pp. 104–146; and ii. pp. 426–579 (Berlin, 1839–47); and are separately edited by Runkel (Leipzig, 1829). A Latin translation of them will be found in Bothe, *Frag. Com. Graec.* (Paris, 1855).

Eupompus (Εὔπομπος). A Greek painter, a native of Sicyon, who flourished about B.C. 400. He was the founder of the Sicyonian school of painting, which laid great emphasis on professional knowledge (Plin. *H. N.* xxxv. 75).

Eurīpĭdes (Εὐριπίδης). (1) A celebrated Athenian tragic poet, son of Mnesarchus and Clito. He was born B.C. 480, in Salamis, on the very day of the Grecian victory near that island. His mother, Clito, had been sent over to Salamis, with the other Athenian women, when Attica was given up to the invading army of Xerxes; and the name of the poet, which is formed like a patronymic from the Euripus, the scene of the first successful resistance to the Persian navy, shows that the minds of his parents were full of the stirring events of that momentous crisis. Aristophanes repeatedly imputes meanness of extraction, by the mother's side, to Euripides (*Thesmoph.* 386, 455; *Acharn.* 478; *Equit.* 17; *Ranae*, 840). He asserts that she was an herb-seller; and, according to Aulus Gellius (xv. 20), Theophrastus confirms the comedian's insinuations. Whatever one or both of his parents might originally have been, the costly education which the young Euripides received implies a certain degree of wealth and consequence as then at least possessed by his family. The pupil of Anaxagoras, Protagoras, and Prodicus (an instructor famous for the extravagant terms which he demanded for his lessons), could not have been the son of persons at that time very mean or poor. It is most probable, therefore, that his father was a man of

Euripides. (Naples Museum.)

property, and made a *mésalliance.* In early life we are told that his father made Euripides direct his attention chiefly to gymnastic exercises, and that, in his seventeenth year, he was crowned in the Eleusinian and Thesean contests (Aul. Gell. xv. 20). Even at this early age he is said to have attempted dramatic composition. He seems also to have cultivated a natural taste for painting, and some of his pictures were long afterwards preserved at Megara. At length, quitting the gymnasium, he applied himself to philosophy and literature. Under the celebrated rhetorician Prodicus, one of the instructors of Pericles, he acquired that oratorical skill for which his dramas are so remarkably distinguished. Quintilian, in comparing Sophocles with Euripides, strongly recommends the latter to the young pleader as an excellent model. Cicero, too, was a great admirer of Euripides. From Anaxagoras, Euripides imbibed those philosophical notions which are occasionally brought forward in his works, and for which reference may be made to the monograph of Parmentier, *Euripide et Anaxagore* (Paris, 1893). Here, too, Pericles was his fellow-disciple. With Socrates, who had studied under the same master, Euripides was on terms of the closest intimacy, and from him he derived those maxims so frequently interwoven into his dramas that Socrates was suspected of largely assisting the tragedian in their composition.

Euripides began his public career as a dramatic writer in B.C. 455, the twenty-fifth year of his age. On this occasion he was the third with a play called the *Pleiades.* In B.C. 441, he won the prize. In B.C. 431, he was third with the *Medea*, the *Philoctetes*, the *Dictys*, and the *Theristae*, a satyric drama. His competitors were Euphorion and Sophocles. He was first with the *Hippolytus*, B.C. 428, the year of his master's (Anaxagoras's) death; second, B.C. 415, with the *Alexander* (or *Paris*), the *Palamedes*, the *Troades*, and the *Sisyphus*, a satyric drama. It was in this contest that Xenocles was first (Aelian. *V. H.* ii. 8). Two years after this the Athenians sustained the total loss of their armament before Syracuse. In his narration of this disaster, Plutarch gives an anecdote (*Nicias*) which, if true, bears a splendid testimony to the high reputation which Euripides then enjoyed. Those among the captives, he tells us, who could repeat any portion of that poet's works were treated with kindness, and even set at liberty. The same author also informs us that Euripides honoured the soldiers who had fallen in that siege with a funeral poem, two lines of which he has preserved. The *Andromeda* was exhibited B.C. 412; the *Orestes*, B.C. 408.

Soon after this time the poet retired into Magnesia, and from thence into Macedonia, to the court of Archelaüs. As in the case of Aeschylus, the motives for this self-exile are obscure and uncertain. We know, indeed, that Athens was by no means the most favourable residence for distinguished literary merit. Report, too, pronounced Euripides unhappy in his own family. His first wife, Melito, he divorced for adultery; and in his second, Choerilé, he was not more fortunate. To the poet's unhappiness in his matrimonial connections Aristophanes refers in his *Ranae* (1045 foll.). Envy and enmity among his fellow-citizens, infidelity and domestic vexations at home, would prove powerful inducements to the poet to accept the invitations of Archelaüs. Perhaps, too, a prosecution in which he became involved, on a charge of impiety, grounded upon a line in the Hippolytus (Aristot. *Rhet.* iii. 15), might have had some share in producing this determination to quit Athens; nor ought we to omit that, in all likelihood, his political sentiments may have exposed him to continual danger. In Macedonia he is said to have written a play in honour of Archelaüs, and to have inscribed it with his patron's name, who was so much pleased with the manners and ability of his guest as to appoint him one of his ministers. He composed in this same country also some other dramatic pieces, in one of which (the *Bacchae*) he seems to have been inspired by the wild scenery of the land to which he had come. No further particulars are recorded of Euripides, except a few apocryphal anecdotes and apophthegms. His death is said to have been, like that of Aeschylus, of an extraordinary kind. Either from chance or malice the aged dramatist was exposed, according to the common account, to the attack of some ferocious hounds, and was by them so dreadfully mangled as to expire soon afterwards, in his seventy-fifth year. This story, however, is clearly a fabrication, for Aristophanes, in the *Ranae*, would certainly have alluded to the manner of his death had there been anything remarkable in it. He died B.C. 406 (Clinton, *Fast. Hellen.* i. 81). The Athenians entreated Archelaüs to send the body to the poet's native city for interment. The request was refused, and, with every demonstration of grief and respect, Euripides was buried at Pella. A cenotaph, however, was erected to his memory at Athens.

We have some cutting sayings of Sophocles concerning Euripides, although the former was so void of all the jealousy of an artist that he mourned over the death of his rival; and, in a piece which he shortly after brought upon the stage, did not allow his actors the ornament of a garland. The jeering attacks of Aristophanes are well known, but have not always been properly estimated and understood. Aristotle, too, brings forward many important causes for blame; and when he calls Euripides "the most tragic of poets" (*Poet.* xiii. 10), he by no means ascribes to him the greatest perfection in the tragic art generally; but he alludes, by this phrase, to the effect which is produced by his dramatic catastrophes. In Euripides we no longer find the essence of ancient tragedy pure and unmixed; its characteristic features are already partly effaced. These consisted principally in the idea of destiny which reigns in them, in ideal representation, and the importance of the chorus. The idea of destiny had, indeed, come down to him from his predecessors as his inheritance, and a belief in it is inculcated by him, according to the custom of the tragedians; but still, in Euripides, destiny is seldom considered as the invisible spirit of all poetry, the fundamental thought of the tragic world. On the other hand, he derived it from the regions of infinity, and, in his writings, inevitable necessity often degenerates into the caprice of chance. Hence he can no longer direct it to its proper aim—namely, that of elevating, by its contrast, the moral free-will of man. Very few of his dramas depend on a constant combat against the dictates of destiny, or an equally heroic subjection to them. His men, in general, suffer, because they must, and not because they are willing. The contrasted subordination of idea, loftiness of character and passion, which in Sophocles, as well as in the graphic art of the Greeks, we find observed in this order, are in him exactly reversed. In his plays passion is the most powerful; his secondary care is for character; and if these endeavours leave him sufficient room, he seeks now and then to bring in greatness and dignity, but more frequently amiability. Euripides has, according to the doctrine of Aristotle (*Poet.* xv. 7, xxvi. 31), frequently represented his personages as bad without any necessity—for example, Menelaüs in the *Orestes*. More especially, it is by no means his object to represent the race of heroes as pre-eminent above the present race by their mighty stature, but he rather takes pains to fill up the chasm between his contemporaries and the olden time, and reveal the gods and heroes of the other side in their undress. This is what Sophocles meant when he said that he himself represented men as they should be, Euripides as they were. It seems to be a design of Euripides always to remind his spectators, "See, these beings were men; they had just such weaknesses, and acted from exactly the same motives as yourselves, and as the meanest among you does." In other words, Euripides is the first of the realists among the Greeks.

In his dramas the chorus is generally an unessential ornament, its songs are often altogether episodical, without reference to the action. The ancient comic writers enjoyed the privilege of sometimes making the chorus address the audience in their own name, this being called a Parabasis. Although it by no means belongs to tragedy, yet Euripides, according to the testimony of Iulius Pollux, often employed it, and so far forgot himself in it that in the *Danaïdes* he made the chorus, consisting of women, use grammatical forms which belonged to the masculine gender alone. In the music of the accompaniments he adopted all the innovations of which Timotheus (q. v.) was the author, and selected those measures which are most suitable to the sensuous nature of his poetry. He acted in a similar way as regarded prosody; the construction of his verses is rather florid, and approaches irregularity. He strives after effect in a degree which can not be conceded even to a dramatic poet. Thus, for example, he seldom lets any opportunity escape of having his personages seized with sudden and groundless terror; his old men always complain of the infirmities of old age, and are particularly given to mount, with tottering knees, the ascent from the orchestra to the stage, which frequently represented the declivity of a mountain, while they lament their wretchedness. His object throughout is emotion, for the sake of which he not only offends against ancient decorum, but sacrifices the symmetry of his plays. He likes to reduce his heroes to a state of beggary; makes them suffer hunger and want; and brings them on the stage with all the external signs of indigence, covered with rags, as Aristophanes so humourously throws in his teeth in the *Acharnians* (410–448).

Euripides, as already stated, had studied philosophy, and prided himself upon his familiarity with philosophical doctrine. Hence, as contrasted with his two dramatic predecessors, Aeschylus and Sophocles, his rationalistic method of treatment seemed to his audiences startling and almost impious. His allegorical interpretations must often have had a flavour of sacrilege about them, and the whole spirit and temper of his plays were an embodiment of the "higher criticism" of the day. The Athenians were prone to identify the sentiments of his characters with those of the author himself. It is related of him that he made Bellerophon come on the stage with a panegyric on riches, in which he preferred them before every domestic joy; and said, at last, "If Aphroditê (who had the epithet of 'golden') shone like gold, she would indeed deserve the love of men" (Sen. *Epist.* 115). The audience, enraged at this, raised a great tumult, and were proceeding to stone the orator as well as the poet. Euripides, on this, rushed forward and exclaimed, "Wait patiently till the end; he will fare accordingly." Thus, also, he is said to have excused himself against the accusation that his Ixion spoke too abominably and blasphemously, by replying that, in return, he had not concluded the piece without making him revolve on the wheel. He has also great command of that sophistry of the passions which gives things only one appearance. The following verse (*Hippol.* 608) is notorious for its expression of what casuists call mental reservation:

"My tongue took an oath, but my mind is unsworn."

In the connection in which this verse is spoken, it may indeed be justified, as far as regards the reason for which Aristophanes ridicules it in so many ways; but still the formula is pernicious on account of the turn which may be given it. Another sentiment of Euripides (*Phoeniss.* 534), "It is worth while committing injustice for the sake of empire; in other things it is proper to be just," was continually in the mouth of Caesar, in order to make a wrong application of it (Suet. *Iul.* 30). Seductive enticements to the enjoyment of sensual love were another article of accusation against Euripides among the ancients. Thus, for example, Hecuba, in order to incite Agamemnon to punish Polymnestor, reminds him of the joys Cassandra had afforded him; who, having been taken in war, was his slave, according to the law of the heroic ages: she is willing to purchase revenge for a murdered son by consenting to and ratifying the degradation of a daughter who is still alive. This poet was the first to take for the principal subject of a drama the wild passion of a Medea or the unnatural love of a Phaedra, as, otherwise, it may be easily understood, from the manners of the ancients, why love, which among them was far less ennobled by delicate feelings, played merely a subordinate part in their earlier tragedies. Notwithstanding the importance imparted to female characters, he brings out a multitude of sayings concerning the weaknesses of the female sex and the superiority of men, as well as a great deal drawn from his own experience in domestic relations. A cutting saying, as well as an epigram, of Sophocles have been handed down to us by Athenaeus, in which he explains the pretended hatred of Euripides for women by supposing that he had the opportunity of learning their frailty through his own unhallowed desires.

That independent freedom in the method of treating the story, which was one of the privileges of the tragic art, frequently, in Euripides, became caprice. It is well known that the fables of Hyginus, which differ so much from the relations of other writers, are partly extracted from his plays. As he often overturned what had hitherto been well known and generally received, he was obliged to use prologues, in which he announces the situation of affairs according to his acceptation, and makes known the course of events. (Compare the amusing scene in Aristophanes, *Ranae*, 1177 foll., and Porson's explanation of the employment of such prologues by Euripides, *Praelect. in Eurip.* p. 8 foll.). These prologues make the beginnings of the plays of Euripides monotonous, and produce the appearance of deficiency of art.

The style of Euripides is, on the whole, not sufficiently compressed, and it has neither the dignity and energy of Aeschylus nor the chaste grace of Sophocles. In his expressions he frequently aims at the extraordinary and strange, and, on the other hand, loses himself in commonplace. For these reasons, as well as on account of his almost ludicrous delineation of many characteristic peculiarities (such as the clumsy deportment of Pentheus in a female garb, when befooled by Bacchus [*Bacchae*, 782 foll.], or the greediness of Heracles [*Alcestis*, 764 foll.], and his boisterous demands on the hospitality of Admetus), Euripides was a forerunner of the New Comedy. Menander, in fact, expressed admiration for him, and declared himself to be his scholar; and there is a fragment of Philemon, full of extravagant admiration of him. "If the dead," he says, or makes one of his personages say, "really possessed sensation, as some suppose, I would hang myself in order to see Euripides."

Of the 120 dramas which Euripides is said to have composed, we have remaining in their complete form only eighteen tragedies and one satyric piece. The following are the titles and subjects: (1) Ἑκάβη, *Hecuba.* The sacrifice of Polyxena, whom the Greeks immolate to the shade of Achilles, and the vengeance which Hecuba, doubly unfortunate in having been reduced to captivity and deprived of her children, takes upon Polymnestor, the murderer of her son Polydorus, form the subject of this tragedy. The scene is laid in the Grecian camp in the Thracian Chersonesus. The shade of Polydorus, whose body remains without the rites of sepulture, has the prologue assigned it. Ennius and L. Attius, and in modern times Erasmus, have translated this play into Latin verse. (2) Ὀρέστης, *Orestes.* The scene of this play is laid at Argos, the seventh day after the murder of Clytaemnestra. It is on this day that the people, in full assembly, are to sit in judgment upon Orestes and Electra. The only hope of the accused is in Menelaüs, who has just arrived; but this chief, who secretly aims at the succession, stirs up the people in private to pronounce sentence of condemnation against the parricides. The sentence is accordingly pronounced, but the execution of it is left to the culprits themselves. They meditate taking vengeance by slaying Helen; but this princess is saved by the intervention of Apollo, who brings about a double marriage by uniting Orestes with Hermioné, the daughter of Helen, and Electra with Pylades. Some commentators think that they recognize the portrait of Socrates in that of the simple and virtuous citizen who, in the assembly of the people, undertakes the defence of Orestes. This play is ascribed by some to Euripides the Younger, nephew of the former. (3) Φοινίσσαι, *Phoenissae.* The subject of this piece is the death of Eteocles and Polynices. The chorus is composed of young Phœnician women, sent, according to the custom established by Agenor, to the city of Thebes, in order to be consecrated to the service of the temple at Delphi. The prologue is assigned to Iocasta. The subject of the *Phoenissae* is that also of the *Thebaïs* of Seneca. Statius has likewise imitated it in his epic poem. (4) Μήδεια, *Medea.* The vengeance taken by Medea on the ungrateful Iason, to whom she has sacrificed all, and who, on his arrival at Corinth, abandons her for a royal bride, forms the subject of this tragedy. What constitutes the principal charm of the play is the simplicity and clearness of the action, and the force and natural cast of the characters. The exposition of the plot is made in a monologue by the nurse: the chorus is composed of Corinthian women. It is asserted that Euripides gave to the world two editions of this tragedy, and that, in the first, the children of Medea were put to death by the Corinthians, while in the second, which has come down to us, it is their mother herself who slays them. According to this hypothesis, the

1378th verse and those immediately following, in which Medea says that she will impose on Corinth, contemptuously styled by her the land of Sisyphus, an expiatory festival for this crime, have been retained by mistake in the revision in which they should have disappeared. Medea has no expiation to demand of the Corinthians, if they are not guilty of the murder of her sons. Aelian informs us (*V. H.* v. 21) that the Corinthians prevailed upon Euripides to alter the tradition in question. According to others, they purchased this compliance for the sum of five talents. (5) Ἱππόλυτος στεφανοφόρος, *Hippolytus Coronifer*, "Hippolytus Crowned." The subject of this tragedy is the same with that which Racine has taken for the basis of his *Phèdre*, a subject eminently tragical. It presents to our view a weak woman, the victim of the resentment of Aphroditê, who has inspired her with a criminal passion. An object of horror to him whom she loves, and not daring to reveal her own shame, she dies, after having compelled Theseus, by her misrepresentations, to become the destroyer of his own son. The title of this tragedy is probably derived from the crown which Hippolytus offers to Artemis. Euripides at first gave it the name of Ἱππόλυτος καλυπτόμενος. He afterwards retouched it, and, changing the catastrophe and the title, reproduced it in the year that Pericles died. It gained the prize over the pieces of Iophon and Ion, which had competed with it in the contest. It is sometimes cited under the title of the *Phaedra*, and the celebrated chef-d'œuvre of Racine is an imitation of it, as is also the tragedy of Seneca. (6) Ἄλκηστις, *Alcestis*. The subject of this tragedy is moral and affecting. It is a wife who dies for the sake of prolonging her husband's existence. Its object is to show that conjugal affection and an observance of the rites of hospitality are not suffered to go without their reward. Heracles, whom Admetus had kindly received while unfortunate, having learned that Alcestis, the wife of the monarch, had consummated her mournful sacrifice, seeks her in the shades, and restores her to her husband. The play, by reason of its happy ending, is hardly to be considered a tragedy, but more of a tragi-comedy. The story of Alcestis has inspired a number of fine poems in English literature, notably *Balaustion's Adventure*, by Robert Browning. Others who have treated the same theme are William Morris, W. S. Landor, Palgrave, Mrs. Hemans, and W. M. W. Call. (7) Ἀνδρομάχη, *Andromachê*. The death of the son of Achilles, whom Orestes slays, after having carried off from him Hermionê, forms the subject of the piece. The scene is laid in Thetidium, a city of Thessaly, near Pharsalus. Some have asserted that the aim of Euripides in writing this tragedy was to render odious the law of the Athenians which permitted bigamy. (8) Ἱκέτιδες, *Supplices*, "The Suppliants." The scene of this tragedy is laid in front of the temple of Demeter at Eleusis, whither the Argive women, whose husbands have perished before Thebes, have followed their king Adrastus, in the hope of persuading Theseus to take up arms in their behalf, and obtain the rites of sepulture for their dead, whose bodies were withheld by the Thebans. Theseus yields to their request and promises his assistance. In exhibiting this play in the fourteenth year of the Peloponnesian War, Euripides wished, it is said, to detach the Argives from the Spartan cause. His attempt, however, failed, and the treaty was signed by which Mantinea was sacrificed to the ambition of Lacedaemon. (9) Ἰφιγένεια ἡ ἐν Αὐλίδι, *Iphigenia in Aulide*, "Iphigenia at Aulis." The subject of this tragedy is the intended sacrifice of Iphigenia, and her rescue by Artemis, who substitutes another victim. It is the only one of the plays of Euripides that has no prologue, for it is well known that the *Rhesus*, which also lacks it, had one formerly. (10) Ἰφιγένεια ἡ ἐν Ταύροις, *Iphigenia in Tauris*, "Iphigenia among the Tauri." The daughter of Agamemnon, rescued by Artemis from the knife of the sacrificer, and transported to Tauris, there serves the goddess as a priestess in her temple. Orestes has been cast on the inhospitable shores of this country, along with his friend Pylades, and by the laws of the Tauri they must be sacrificed to Artemis. Recognized by his sister at the fatal moment, Orestes conducts her back to their common country. A monologue by Iphigenia occupies the place of a prologue and exposition. The scene where Iphigenia and her brother became known to each other is of a deep and touching interest, and has been imitated by Guimond de la Touche and Goethe. (11) Τρῳάδες, *Troades*, "The Trojan women." The action of this piece is prior to that of the *Hecuba*. The scene is laid in the Grecian camp, under the walls of Troy, which has fallen into the hands of the foe. A body of female captives have been distributed by lot among the victors. Agamemnon has reserved Cassandra for himself; Polyxena has been immolated to the manes of Achilles; Andromachê has fallen to Neoptolemus, Hecuba to Odysseus. The object of the poet is to show us in Hecuba a mother bowed down by misfortune. The Greeks destroy Astyanax, and his mangled body is brought in to the mother of Hector, his own parent being by this time carried away in the train of Neoptolemus. Ilium is then given as a prey to the flames. This succession of horrors passes in mournful review before the eyes of the spectator; yet there is no unity of action to constitute a subject for the piece, and consequently the play has no dénouement. Poseidon appears in the prologue. Seneca and M. de Chateaubrun have imitated this tragedy. (12) Βάκχαι, *Bacchae*, "The female Bacchanalians," sometimes quoted as the *Pentheus*, for Euripides seldom names his plays after the chorus. The arrival of Bacchus at Thebes and the death of Pentheus, who is torn in pieces by his mother and sister form the subject of this drama, in which Bacchus opens the scene and makes himself known to the spectators. The *Bacchae* is regarded by Jebb as "in its own kind, by far the most splendid work of Euripides that we possess." It is a succession of rich paintings, of tragic situations, of brilliant verses, unique among existing Greek plays in picturesque splendour. The spectacle which this tragedy presented must have been at once imposing and well calculated to keep alive curiosity. Some have held that the play is a recantation by the poet of his former irreligious sentiments; but on this see Tyrrell in the introduction to his edition of the *Bacchae* (1892). It is related that the *Bacchae* was performed before Orodes and his court, when the actor sustaining the part of Agavê gave a hideous reality to the action by holding up the bloody head of the Roman general Crassus, just slain in battle by the Parthian warriors of the king (Mommsen, *Hist. of Rome*, iv. p. 436). (13) Ἡρακλεῖδαι, *Heraclidae*. The descendants of Heracles, persecuted by Eurystheus, flee for refuge to Athens, and implore the protection of that city. The Athenians lend aid, and Eurystheus becomes the victim of the vengeance he was about bringing upon them. Iolaüs, an old companion of Heracles, explains the subject to the spectators. The poet manages to impart an air of great interest to the piece. (14) Ἑλένη, *Helena.* The scene is laid in Egypt, where Menelaüs, after the destruction of Troy, finds Helen, who had been detained there by Proteus, king of that country, when Paris wished to convey her to Ilium. The action passes at the isle of Pharos, where Theoclymenus, the son and successor of Proteus, keeps Helen in custody with the view of espousing her. She employs a stratagem in order to escape from his power. The dénouement of this piece resembles that of the *Iphigenia in Tauris.* (15) Ἴων, *Ion.* Ion, son of Apollo and Creüsa, daughter of Erechtheus, king of Athens, has been brought up among the priests at Delphi. The design of Apollo is to make him pass for the son of Xuthus, who has married Creüsa. The interest of the play consists in the double danger which Creüsa and Ion run, the former of being slain by Ion and the latter of perishing by the poison prepared for him by a mother who is ignorant of his being her son. The play, however, is somewhat complicated, and has need of a long exposition, which is assigned to Hermes. The scene is laid at the entrance of Apollo's temple in Delphi, a place expressly chosen in order to give to the spectacle an air of pomp and solemnity. A religious tone, full of gravity and softness, pervades the whole piece. There is much resemblance between this tragedy and the *Athalie* of Racine. (16) Ἡρακλῆς μαινόμενος, *Hercules furens.* After having killed, in his frenzy, his wife and children, Heracles proceeds to submit himself to certain expiatory ceremonies, and to seek repose at Athens. Amphitryon appears in the prologue: the scene is laid at Thebes. (17) Ἠλέκτρα, *Electra.* The subject of this play has been treated also by Aeschylus and Sophocles, but by each in his peculiar way. Euripides transfers the scene from the palace of Aegisthus to the country near Argos: the exposition of the play is made by a cultivator, to whom Electra has been compelled to give her hand, but who has taken no advantage of this, but has respected in her the daughter of a royal line. (18) Ῥῆσος, *Rhesus.* A subject derived from the tenth book of the *Iliad.* Some able critics have tried to prove that this piece was never written by Euripides.—Φαέθων, *Phaëthon.* Of this play we have about eighty verses remaining. Clymené, the mother of Phaëthon, is the wife of Merops, king of the Ethiopians, and Phaëthon passes for the son of this prince. The young man, having conceived some doubts respecting his origin, addresses himself to the Sun. The catastrophe, which cost him his life, is well known. In the tragedy of Euripides, the body of her son is brought to Clymené, at the very moment when Merops is occupied with the task of procuring for him a bride.—Δανάη, *Danaë.* Of this play we have the commencement alone, unless the sixty-five verses, which commonly pass for a part of the prologue, are to be considered as the production of some imitator,

A production deserving especial mention is the satyric drama entitled *Cyclops* (Κύκλωψ). The story is drawn from the *Odyssey.* The subject is Odysseus depriving Polyphemus of his eye, after having intoxicated him with wine. In order to connect with the story a chorus of satyrs, the poet supposes that Silenus, and his sons, the satyrs, in seeking over every sea for Bacchus, whom pirates have carried away, have been shipwrecked on the coast of Sicily, where they have fallen into the hands of Polyphemus. The Cyclops has made slaves of them, and has compelled them to tend his sheep. Odysseus, having been cast on the same coast, and having been, in like manner, made captive by Polyphemus, finds in these satyrs a willing band of accomplices. They league with him against their master, but their excessive cowardice renders them very useless auxiliaries. They profit, however, by his victory, and embark with him. See CYCLOPS; SATYRIC DRAMA.

Of the numerous incomplete remains of Euripides that have reached us, some notice must be taken. In 1890, papyri discovered by Mr. Petrie at Tel Gurob in Egypt were found to contain fragments of a lost play of Euripides—the *Antiopé.* These fragments are reproduced and edited by Mahaffy in *The Flinders Petrie Papyri* (Dublin, 1891).

The ancient writers cite also a poem of Euripides, Ἐπικήδειον, "Funeral Hymn," on the death of Nicias and Demosthenes, as well as of the other Athenians who perished in the disastrous expedition against Syracuse. We possess also two epigrams of Euripides, each consisting of four verses, one of which has been preserved in the Anthology and the other in Athenaeus. There have, besides, come down to us five letters, ascribed to Euripides, and written with admirable purity and simplicity of style. There are also many fragments from the lost plays of Euripides scattered among the writings of antiquity. Of these fragments Nauck collected 1117, some, however, being of doubtful authenticity. The best known of the lost plays are the *Andromeda, Bellerophon, Cresphontes, Erechtheus, Oedipus,* and *Telephus.*

The popularity of Euripides was very great in antiquity, as in modern times, as is shown by the number of ancient scholars who wrote commentaries on his works—among them being Dicaearchus, Callimachus, Aristophanes of Byzantium, Callistratus, and especially Didymus. An inscription at Tegea shows that his plays were represented as late as the second century B.C., winning victories at Athens, Delphi, and Dodona (*Bulletin de Correspondance Hellénique,* January-April, 1893). At Rome, Euripides was translated and adapted by Ennius and by Pacuvius. In the fourth century A.D. a curious cento, the Χριστὸς Πάσχων (*Christus Patiens*), of 2610 verses, was made from the plays of Euripides. (See CENTO.) Later, Dante, who mentions neither Aeschylus nor Sophocles, praises Euripides; and from the sixteenth century to the present time he has been a popular favourite, giving inspiration to many imitators in French, English, and German.

BIBLIOGRAPHY.—Few classical authors are so fully represented by MSS. as is Euripides. Nearly every European library of importance and of any age contains at least one, though no single MS. contains all the plays. The three plays oftenest found are the *Hecuba, Orestes,* and *Phoenissae,* owing to the fact that these three were much read in the schools under the Eastern Empire. The nine plays, *Hecuba, Orestes, Phoenissae, Hippolytus, Medea, Alcestis, Andromaché, Troades,* and *Rhesus,* are known in two "families"—one represented by the Codices Vaticanus, Hauniensis, Parisinus, and two Marciani Veneti, and the second (an inferior family) by later MSS. of the thirteenth and fourteenth centuries. The MSS. of the first family mentioned are the oldest that we have, but are not earlier than the twelfth century. The great majority of the copies are very poor. The only MSS. containing all the nine plays mentioned above are the Codex Vaticanus and the Codex Hauniensis; but of the former some pages are missing, while of the latter the text is in places so corrupt as to be of little use. The remaining ten plays are found in only two MSS.—the Palatinus (in the Vatican) and Florentinus II.—both of the fourteenth century. Three plays (the *Helena*, *Hercules Furens*, and *Electra*) are found only in the Codex Florentinus II. A palimpsest of the fifth or sixth century contains a part of the *Phaëthon*, and of this play an interesting "reconstruction" made by Goethe will be found in vol. xxxiii. pp. 22–43 of the 1840 edition of his works. The extant scholia on Euripides are from the nine select plays only. The best complete edition of the scholia is that of W. Dindorf, in four vols. (1863).

The *editio princeps* of Euripides is that of J. Lascaris (Florence, 1496), but contains only the *Medea*, *Hippolytus*, *Alcestis*, and *Andromaché*. The Aldine edition by Musurus (Venice, 1503) contains all the plays except the *Electra*, which was first published by P. Victorius (1545). The first edition of any critical value is that by Valckenaer in his *Phoenissae* (1755), and in his *Diatribe in Euripidis Perditorum Dramatum Reliquias* (1767), attacking the authenticity of the *Rhesus*. The best criticism of the text has been done by Porson (1797), Elmsley (1813), G. Hermann (1838), Badham (1851), and Nauck (1885). Recent complete editions are those of W. Dindorf (in his *Poetae Scenici*, 5th ed. 1870), Kirchhoff (1867), and Paley (2d ed. 1872), with commentary. Of separate plays, the following editions deserve special mention: of the *Bacchae* by R. Y. Tyrrell (1892), by Paley (1877), and by Sandys (1880); of the *Alcestis* by Earle (1894), Jerram, (1884); of the *Hecuba* by Paley (1877); of the *Hercules Furens* by Hutchinson and Gray (1878), and by Paley (1883); of the *Troades* by Tyrrell (1882); of the *Hippolytus* by Arnold after Witzschel (1853), Mahaffy and Bury (1881), and by Berthold (1880); of the *Medea* by Verrall (1881); of the *Orestes* by Paley (1879); of the *Andromaché* by Pflugk and Klotz, with Latin notes (1858); of the *Phoenissae* by Paley (1879); of the *Ion* by Badham (1879), Verrall (1890); of the *Iphigenia in Aulide* by Pflugk and Klotz (1860); of the *Iphigenia in Tauris* by Jerram (1884) and England (1886); of the *Heraclidae* by Beck (1881); and of the *Helena* by Jerram (1881). Prose translation by Coleridge (London, 1885). See Mahaffy, *Introduction to the Study of Euripides* (London, 1879).

(2) A nephew of the preceding (Suid. s. v.; Böckh, *De Trag. Graec.* xiv. and xviii.), commonly styled Euripides Junior. He was a dramatic poet, like his uncle, and exhibited, besides his own compositions, several plays of the latter, then dead; one of these gained the prize. Böckh and others suspect that he reproduced the *Iphigenia in Aulis*, and perhaps the *Palamedes*. To this Euripides is ascribed, by Suidas, an edition of Homer.

Eurīpus (Εὔριπος). (1) Any part of the sea where the ebb and flow of the tide were remarkably violent, is the name especially of the narrow strait which separates Euboea from Boeotia. At Chalcis there was a bridge over the Euripus uniting Euboea with the mainland. (2) See AMPHITHEATRUM.

Eurōpa (Εὐρώπη). A daughter of Agenor (called by some Phoenix), king of Phœnicia. Zeus, becoming enamoured of her, according to the old legend, changed himself into a beautiful white bull, and approached her, "breathing saffron from his mouth," as she was gathering flowers with her companions in a mead near the seashore. Europa, delighted with the tameness and beauty of the animal, caressed him, crowned him with flowers, and at length ventured to mount on his back. The disguised god immediately made off with his burden, plunged into the sea, and swam with Europa to the island of Crete, landing not far from Gortyna. Here he resumed his own form, and beneath a plane-tree soothed and caressed the trembling maiden. The offspring of their union were Minos, Rhadamanthus, and Sarpedon. Asterius, king of Crete, subsequently married Europa, and reared her sons (Apollod. iii. 1; Hes. and Bacchyl. *ap. Schol. ad Il.* xii. 292; Ovid, *Met.* ii. 833 foll.; *Fast.* v. 605).

Eurōpa (Εὐρώπη). One of the three main divisions of the ancient world. With the northern parts of it the ancients were very slightly acquainted — viz., what are now Prussia, Sweden, Denmark, Norway, and Russia. They applied to this quarter the general name of Scandinavia, and thought it consisted of a number of islands. From the Portuguese Cape to the Ural Mountains, the length of modern Europe may be reckoned at about 3300 miles, and from Cape Nord to Cape Matapan, about 2350.

The etymologies given for the name Europa are numerous: (1) from the maiden Europa (q. v.); (2) from Eurus, the southeast wind; (3) from εὐρύς and ὤψ, applied to the continent as distinguished from the islands, and hence = "Broad Land," an explanation favoured by Hermann; and (4) from the Semitic *erebh*, "darkness," i. e. "the land of the setting sun," or "land of the West."

As regards the progress of geographical discovery, it may be remarked that the earliest notices of Europe are in the writings of the Greeks, who inhabited the southeastern corner of the continent. From this country the geographical knowledge of Europe extended by degrees to the west and north. Homer was acquainted with the countries round the Aegean Sea. He had also a fairly accurate general notion respecting those which lie on the south coast of the Black Sea; but what he says about the countries west of Greece, on the shores of the Mediterranean, is a mixture of fable and truth, in which the fabulous part prevails. It would seem that, in his age, these seas were not yet visited by his countrymen, and that he obtained his knowledge from the Phœnicians, who had probably for some time sailed to these regions, but who, according to the common policy of trading nations, spread abroad false accounts of these unknown countries, in order to deter other nations from following their track, and participating in the advantages of this distant commerce. It is probable, also, that the Phœnicians long excluded the Greeks from the navigation of the Mediterranean; for when the latter began to form settlements beyond their native country, they first occupied the shores of the Aegean, and afterwards those of the Black Sea. As the European shores of this last-mentioned sea were not very well adapted for agriculture, their early settlements were mostly on the Asiatic coasts, and, consequently, little addition was made by these colonies to the geographical knowledge of Europe. But the navigation of the Phœnicians was checked in the middle of the sixth century before Christ, apparently because of their subjugation by the Persians. About this time, also, the Greeks began to form settlements in the southern parts of Italy and on the island of Sicily, and to navigate the Mediterranean Sea to its full extent. Accordingly, we find that in the time of Herodotus (B.C. 450) not only the countries on each side of the Mediterranean, and the northern shores of the Black Sea, were known to the Greeks, but that, following the track of the Phœnicians, they ventured to pass the Pillars of Hercules, and to sail as far as the Cassiterides, or Tin Islands, by which name the Scilly Isles and a part of Cornwall must be understood. It is even reported that some of their navigators sailed through the English Channel and entered the North Sea, and perhaps even the Baltic. (See Antichan, *Les Grands Voyages de Découvertes des Anciens* [Paris, 1891]). Thus a considerable part of the coasts of Europe was discovered, while the interior remained almost unknown. When the Romans began their conquests, this deficiency was partly supplied. The conquest of Italy was followed by that of Spain and the southern parts of Gaul, and, not long afterwards, Sicily, Greece, and Macedonia were added. Caesar conquered Gaul and the countries west of the Rhine, together with the districts lying between the different arms by which that river enters the sea. His two expeditions into Britain made known also, in some measure, the nature of that island and the character of its inhabitants. (See BRITANNIA.) Thus, in the course of little more than two hundred years, the interior of all those countries was explored, the shores of which had been previously known. In the meantime, nothing was added to the knowledge of the coasts, the Greeks having lost their spirit of discovery by sea, and the Romans not being inclined to naval enterprise. After the establishment of imperial power at Rome, the conquests of the Romans went on at a much slower rate, and the boundaries of the Empire soon became stationary. This circumstance must be attributed chiefly to the nature of the countries which were contiguous to those boundaries. The regions north of the Danube are mostly plains, and at that time were inhabited only by wandering tribes, who could not be subjected to a regular government. Such, at least, are the countries extending between the Carpathian Mountains and the Black Sea, and therefore the conquest of Dacia by Trajan was of short continuance and speedily abandoned. The countries between the Alps and the Danube were soon added to the Empire; but as the nations who inhabited the tracts north of that river had not given up a nomadic life, they were enabled to elude the Roman yoke. (See GERMANIA.) The most important addition to the Empire and to geographical knowledge was the conquest of Britain during the first century after Christ, to which, in the following century, the south of Scotland was added. Nothing seems to have been gained afterwards. The geography of Ptolemy contains a considerable number of names of nations, places, and rivers in those countries which were not subjected to the Romans. Probably they were obtained from natives and from Roman traders who had ventured to penetrate beyond the boundaries of the Empire. But these brief notices are very vague, and in most cases it is very difficult to determine what places and persons are indicated. See GEOGRAPHIA.

Eurōpus (Εὐρωπός). See RHAGAE; TITARESIUS.

Eurōtas (Εὐρώτας). The chief river in Laconia, on which Sparta stood, rises in Mount Boreum, in Arcadia, and flows into the Laconian Gulf (Thuc. ii. 139).

Eurus (Εὖρος). The east wind, properly the east-southeast (Hom. *Il.* ii. 145).

Euryălus (Εὐρύαλος). (1) One of the Argonauts and also of the Epigoni (q. v.). (2) A Trojan, son of Opheltius, and one of the followers of Aeneas. Vergil has immortalized the inseparable friendship between him and Nisus. See NISUS.

Eurybătes (Εὐρυβάτης). The herald of Odysseus, whom he followed to Troy (Hom. *Il.* i. 319, etc.).

Eurybătus (Εὐρύβατος). An Ephesian, whom Croesus sent with a large sum of money to the Peloponnesus to hire mercenaries for him in his war with Cyrus. He, however, deserted to Cyrus, and betrayed the whole matter to him. In consequence of this treachery his name passed into a proverb among the Greeks (Aesch. *in Ctes.* 43).

Eurybia (Εὐρυβία). Daughter of Pontus and Gaea, and mother of Astraeus, Pallas, and Perses (Hesiod. *Theog.* 375).

Eurybiădes (Εὐρυβιάδης). A Spartan, commander of the combined Grecian fleet at the battles of Artemisium and Salamis. Although Sparta sent only ten ships, he was appointed to this office, by the desire of the allies, who refused to obey an Athenian (Herod. viii. 3). See THEMISTOCLES.

Euryclēa (Εὐρύκλεια). The daughter of Ops, and purchased by Laërtes of Ithaca. She reared Telemachus, and when Odysseus returned home, recognized him in his beggar's disguise by a scar (*Odyss.* xix. 385, etc.). See ODYSSEUS.

Eurydĭcé (Εὐρυδίκη). (1) The wife of Orpheus, who, while fleeing before Aristaeus, was bitten by a serpent in the grass and died of the wound. Her disconsolate husband determined to descend to the lower world, to endeavour to procure her restoration to life. Pluto and Persephoné listened to his prayer; and Eurydicé was allowed to return, on the express condition that Orpheus should not look back upon her till they had arrived in the regions of day. Fearing that she might not be following him, the anxious husband looked back and thereby lost her. (See ORPHEUS.) (2) The wife of Amyntas, king of Macedonia (Justin, vii. 4, 5). She had, by her husband Alexander, Perdiccas and Philip, and one daughter called Euryoné, who was married to Ptolemy Alorites. A criminal infatuation for her daughter's husband, to whom she offered her hand and the kingdom, made her conspire against Amyntas, who must have fallen a victim to her infidelity, had not Euryoné discovered it. Amyntas forgave her. Alexander ascended the throne after his father's death, and perished by the ambition

Hermes, Eurydicé, and Orpheus. (Villa Albani.)

of his mother. Perdiccas, who succeeded him, shared his fate; but Philip, who was the next in succession, secured himself against all attempts from his mother, and ascended the throne with peace and universal satisfaction. Eurydicé fled to Iphicrates, the Athenian general, for protection. The manner of her death is unknown. (3) A daughter of Antipater, and the wife of Ptolemy I. of Egypt, by whom she had several children. After the death of Alexander the Great she proceeded to Alexandria for the purpose of rejoining her husband, and brought with her Berenicé, her niece, who proved the source of all her misfortunes; for Berenicé inspired Ptolemy with so strong a passion that he took her as his second wife, and allowed himself to be controlled by her influence (Plut. *Pyrr.* 4). Eurydicé and her children retired to the court of Seleucus, king of Syria. One of her daughters subsequently married Agathocles, son of Lysimachus; and another, Demetrius Poliorcetes. Ptolemy Ceraunus, the eldest of her sons, seized upon the kingdom of Macedonia. Eurydicé followed him to that country, and contributed to conciliate the minds of the Macedonians towards him, through the respect which they entertained for the memory of her father Antipater. Ptolemy Ceraunus having been slain, B.C. 280, in a battle against the Gauls, Macedonia was delivered up to the ravages of these barbarians, and Eurydicé fled for protection to the city of Cassandrea. In order to attach the inhabitants more strongly to her interests, she gave them their freedom; and they, through gratitude, established a festival called after her, Eurydicea. The rest of her history is not known. (4) A daughter of Amyntas and Cynané. Her previous name was Adea, afterwards changed to Eurydicé. She married Arrhidaeus, the half-brother of Alexander, and for some time, through the aid of Cassander, defended Macedonia against Polysperchon and Olympias. Having been forsaken, at length, by her own troops, she fell into the hands of Olympias, together with her husband. Both were put to death by that queen (Justin, xiv. 5).

Eurylŏchus (Εὐρύλοχος). A companion of Odysseus, and the only one that escaped from the house of Circé when his friends were metamorphosed into swine (Hom. *Od.* x. 203, xi. 23, etc.).

Eurymĕdon (Εὐρυμέδων). Son of Thucles, an Athenian general in the Peloponnesian War (Thuc. iii. 80, 81, 85).

Eurymĕdon (Εὐρυμέδων). A small river in Pamphylia, celebrated for the victory which Cimon gained over the Persians on its banks (B.C. 469).

Eurymĕnae (Εὐρυμεναί). A town of Magnesia in Thessaly, east of Ossa (Livy, xxxix. 25).

Eurȳmus (Εὐρυμός). Father of the seer Telemus, who is hence called Eurymides (*Odyss.* ix. 509).

Eurynŏmé (Εὐρυνόμη). Daughter of Oceanus, and mother of Leucothoë (Apollod. i. 2. 2). By Zeus she became the mother of the Charites or of Aropus (Hes. *Theog.* 908). Eurynomé is also a surname of Artemis at Phigalea in Arcadia, where she was represented as a mermaid.

Eurȳphon (Εὐρυφῶν). A Cnidian physician, a contemporary of Hippocrates, but probably older in years, since he is deemed the author of the Cnidian aphorisms (Κνίδιαι Γνῶμαι) which are quoted by Hippocrates.

Eurȳpon (Εὐρυπῶν), otherwise called **Eurytion** (Εὐρυτίων). Grandson of Procles. He was the third king of that house at Sparta, and thenceforward gave it the name of Eurypontidae.

Eurypȳlus (Εὐρύπυλος). (1) Son of Euaemon, and leader of a body of troops before Troy. (2) Son of Poseidon and Astypalaea, king of Cos, killed by Heracles. (3) Son of Poseidon and Astypalaea, king of the Meropes of Cos. He was slain by Heracles, who had been driven on to the coast on his return from Troy. The struggle was a hard one, but Heracles was assisted by Zeus. The daughter of Eurypylus, Chalciopé, became mother of Thessalus by Heracles. (4) Son of Telephus and Astyoché. Astyoché, bribed by her brother Priam with the present of a golden vine, persuaded Eurypylus to bring the last succour to the Trojans shortly before the fall of the city. After performing deeds of bravery, he fell by the hand of Neoptolemus. (5) Son of Euaemon, king of Ormenium in Thessaly, one of the suitors of Helen. He was among the bravest of the Greek heroes who fought before Troy, and of his own accord offered to engage Hector in single combat. In the later story he appears in connection with the worship of Dionysus. At the division of the Trojan spoil he received an image of Dionysus, made by Hephaestus and presented to Dardanus. This had been kept in a chest as a Palladium. When Eurypylus opened the chest and beheld the image he fell into a madness. The Delphic oracle promised that he should be healed if he dedicated the image in a spot where men offered barbaric sacrifices. Accordingly he dedicated it at Aroë in Achaea, where an offering of the finest youth and fairest virgin was made annually to Artemis. The bloody act was abolished, and the milder service of Dionysus introduced in its place.

Eurysăces (Εὐρυσάκης). The son of the Telamonian Aias and Tecmessa. An Athenian tradition made him and his brother Philaeus to have given up to Athens the island of Salamis in return for the rights of Athenian citizenship (Pausan. i. 35, § 2).

Eurysthĕnes (Εὐρυσθένης). A son of Aristodemus, who reigned conjointly with his twin-brother Procles at Sparta. It was not known which of the two was born first; the mother, who wished to see both her sons raised on the throne, refused to declare it; and they were both appointed kings of Sparta by order of the oracle of Delphi, B.C. 1102. After the death of the two brothers, the Lacedaemonians, who knew not to what family the right of seniority and succession belonged, permitted two kings to sit on the throne, one of each family. The descendants of Eurysthenes were called Eurysthenidae, and those of Procles, Proclidae. It was inconsistent with the laws of Sparta for two kings of the same family to ascend the throne together, yet that law was sometimes violated by oppression and tyranny. Eurysthenes had a son called Agis, who succeeded him. His descendants were called Agidae. There sat on the throne of Sparta thirty-one kings of the family of Eurysthenes, and only twenty-four of the Proclidae. The former were the more illustrious (Herod. iv. 147, vi. 52; Pausan. iii. 1).

Eurystheus (Εὐρυσθεύς). Son of Sthenelus and Nicippé. (See PERSEUS.) He was king of Mycenae, and through the cunning of Heré got power over Heracles, and imposed upon him the celebrated twelve labours. In pursuing the children of Heracles, and attempting to bring about by force their expulsion from Attica, he was defeated and slain in his flight by Hyllus. See HYLLUS.

Eurȳtis. A patronymic of Iolé, daughter of Eurytus (Ovid, *Met.* ix. 395).

Eurȳtus (Εὔρυτος). A skilled archer who was king of Oechalia, and father of Iolé. See HERACLES, p. 792.

Eusebius (Εὐσέβιος). (1) PAMPHĬLI. One of the most distinguished of the earlier Christian writers, the friend of Constantine, born in Palestine, probably at Caesarea, about A.D. 264. He pursued his studies at Antioch, and is believed to have received holy orders from Agapius, bishop of Caesarea. After having been ordained presbyter, he set up a school in his native city, and formed an intimate acquaintance with Pamphilus, bishop of Caesarea, who suffered martyrdom under Galerius, A.D. 309, and in memory of whose friendship he added to his name the term *Pamphili*—i. e. (the friend) of Pamphilus. After the martyrdom of his friend he removed to Tyre, and thence to Egypt, where he himself was imprisoned. On his return from Egypt, he succeeded Agapius in the see of Caesarea, A.D. 315. In common with many other bishops of Palestine, he at first espoused the cause of Arius; but at the Council of Nice, in 325, where the emperor Constantine assigned to Eusebius the office of opening the session of the assembly, the opinions of the heresiarch were condemned. He is said, however, to have raised some objections to the words "consubstantial with the Father," as applied to the Son in the Nicene creed. His intimacy with his namesake Eusebius, bishop of Nicomedia, who openly espoused the cause of Arius, led him also to favour the same, and to use his influence with the emperor for the purpose of reinstating Arius in the Church, in defiance of the opposition of Athanasius. The party to which he attached himself were called Eusebians, from their leader Eusebius of Nicomedia, and they seem to have acted in a great degree through hostility towards Athanasius and his supporters, as they did not, as yet, openly advocate the objectionable tenets of Arius, who had himself apparently submitted to the decrees of the Council of Nice. Eusebius was deputed by the Council of Tyre to defend before Constantine the judgment which it had passed against Athanasius. The part which he took in this controversy caused him to be stigmatized as an Arian, though it appears that he fully admitted the divinity of Christ. He was, however, unwilling to believe him συναΐδιος or "co-eternal" with the Father. He was much in favour with Constantine, with whom he maintained a correspondence. He died soon after his imperial patron, in 339 or 340.

Eusebius was one of the most learned men of his time. He had read all sorts of Greek authors, whether philosophers, historians, or divines, of Egypt, Phœnicia, Asia, Europe, and Africa. All his studies were directed towards the religion which he professed, and if he cultivated chronology, it was with the view of establishing on a solid basis the confidence to which the historical books of the Old Testament present a claim. He exhibited the fruits of his researches in a Chronicle, or Universal History (Παντοδαπὴ Ἱστορία), divided into two books. In the first of these, to which he gave the name of "Chronography" (Χρονογραφία), he relates the origin and the history of all nations and empires, from the creation of the world down to A.D. 325. In this first portion of the work, Eusebius introduced extracts from various historical writers whose productions are now lost, such as Alexander Polyhistor, Berosus, Amydenus, Manetho, etc. The second part, entitled "Chronical Canon" (Χρονικὸς Κανών), consisted of synchronistic tables, giving, by periods of ten years each, the names of sovereigns, and the principal events which had taken place, from the call of Abraham (B.C. 2017). In compiling this part of his labours Eusebius availed himself of the Chronography of Sextus Iulius Africanus, which he inserted almost entire in his Canon, completing it by the aid of Manetho, Iosephus, and other historians. This he continued also to his own times. We possess a Latin translation of this chronicle, made by St. Jerome; it is not, however, a simple version, since this father continued the dates down to the year 378, and made several changes also in the first part of the work. The Greek text itself is lost; and though Georgius Syncellus has inserted many fragments of it in his Chronicle, and Eusebius himself has done the same in his *Praeparatio Evangelica*, the remembrance of this original text was so far lost, that doubts began to be entertained whether that of the first book had ever existed, some critics being persuaded that Eusebius had written no other chronological work besides his *Canon*. Joseph Scaliger, however, undertook to reconstruct the first book of the work, by uniting all the fragments scattered throughout the writings of the various authors to whom allusion has been made. The whole subject has at length been cleared up in later times, and all uncertainty on this point has been put completely to rest since 1792, when an Armenian of Constantinople, named Georgius Iohannis, discovered an Armenian translation of the entire work. The first book of the Chronicle of Eusebius, with which we are made acquainted through the medium of this translation, is preceded by a preface, in which the author gives an account of the plan and difficulty of his undertaking. It is divided into forty-eight chapters, of which the first twenty-two embrace the chronology of the Chaldaeans, Assyrians, Medes, Lydians, Persians, Hebrews, and Egyptians, comprehending under the latter head the dynasty of the Ptolemies. The remaining chapters, from the twenty-third to the forty-eighth, are devoted to the chronology of the Greeks and Romans, down to the time of Iulius Caesar.

Eusebius was also the author of an Ecclesiastical History (Ἐκκλησιαστικὴ Ἱστορία), in ten books, from the origin of Christianity down to A.D. 324, a year which immediately preceded the triumph of the Catholic church over Arianism. This history was translated into Latin by Rufinus, a priest of Aquilea, in the fourth century, who made, however, retrenchments as well as additions, and added a supplement in two books, which extends to the death of Theodosius the Great.

The other works of Eusebius which have relation to the department of ecclesiastical history are the following: (1) Περὶ τῶν ἐν Παλαιστίνῃ Μαρτυρησάντων, "Of those who suffered martyrdom in Palestine." The period referred to is the persecution of Dioclesian and Maximin, from 303 to 309. (2) Λόγος Τριακονταετηρικός, "Thirty-year Discourse," i. e. an eloge on Constantine, pronounced in the thirtieth year of his reign, A.D. 335. (3) Περὶ τοῦ κατὰ Θεὸν Βίου τοῦ Μακαρίου Κωνσταντίνου τοῦ Βασιλέως. A life of Constantine, in four books. (4) Τῶν Ἀρχαίων Μαρτύρων Συναγωγή, "A Collection of Ancient Martyrs." This work is lost, but many fragments have been preserved by the legendary writers of subsequent ages. (5) A life of Pamphilus, of which there remains a solitary fragment. (6) Περὶ τῶν κατὰ Διαφόρους Καιροὺς ἐν Διαφόροις Πόλεσιν Ἀθλησάντων Ἁγίων Μαρτύρων, "Of the holy martyrs that have contended for the faith at various times and in various places." Another work of Eusebius forms the principal one of his theological writings. This is his (7) Εὐαγγελικῆς Ἀποδείξεως Προπαρασκευή, or *Praeparatio Evangelica.* This work, though its subject is one entirely sacred in its nature, yet contains a great number of valuable notices respecting the mythology of the pagan nations, and the philosophy of the Greeks in particular. We find in it, also, numerous passages taken from more than four hundred profane writers, and in this list are many whose productions are now lost. The *Praeparatio Evangelica* is addressed to Theodotus, bishop of Laodicea, and is divided into fifteen books. To prepare his readers for a demonstration of evangelical truths by reasons purely philosophical, and, by collecting together a mass of citations drawn from profane authors, to show how far superior Christianity is to all the systems of the pagan world—such is the object of Eusebius in the work under consideration. In the first six books he proves the futility of the heathen doctrines; the nine following ones develop the motives which have induced the followers of Christianity to prefer to them the Jewish system of theology as contained in the Old Testament. One must not omit another work of Eusebius, entitled (8) Περὶ τῶν Τοπικῶν Ὀνομάτων ἐν τῇ Θείᾳ Γραφῇ, "Of the places mentioned in the sacred writings." It was in two books. The second book, which treats of Palestine, has alone reached us; we have it in Greek, and also in a Latin version by St. Jerome. Still another work of Eusebius, (9) Θεοφάνεια, in four books, was discovered in 1839 by Tattam in an Italian monastery. Editions of the work on chronology are that of Scaliger (Leyden, 1659), and that of Mai and Zohrab (Milan, 1818). The best editions of the Ecclesiastical History are that of H. Stephens (Paris, 1544), reprinted with the Latin version of Christophorson, at Geneva, 1612; that of Heinichen (Leipzig, 1827); Burton (Oxford, 1838; reprinted with an introduction by W. Bright, 1872); and that of Migne in the *Patrologia Graeco-Latina,* vols. xix.–xxiv. (1857–66). The life of Constantine accompanies the first of these. The last edition of the entire work of Eusebius is that of Dindorf, in 4 vols. (Leipzig, 1867–71), unfinished. There is a translation of Eusebius in Clark's *Theological Library.* See Schaff, *Church History* (ii. 872–9). (2) A native of Emesa, surnamed PITTĂCUS, slain in 554 by order of the emperor Gallus, and to whom Ammianus Marcellinus (xiv. 7) gives the title of *concitatus orator.* (3) A native of Myndus, in Caria, a contemporary of the preceding. Eunapius makes mention of him in the life of Maximus; and, according to Wyttenbach, he is the same with a third Eusebius, of whom Stobaeus has left us two fragments.

Eustathius (Εὐστάθιος). (1) An archbishop of Thessalonica, who flourished in the twelfth century under the emperors Manuel, Alexius, and Andronicus Comnenus. He is celebrated for his erudition as a grammarian, and is especially known as a commentator on Homer and Dionysius the geographer. It is evident, however, that in the former of these commentaries (Παρεκβολαί) he is largely indebted to the *Deipnosophistae* of Athenaeus. The commentary of Eustathius was united to the edition of Homer which appeared at Rome (1542–50) in 3 vols., and was reprinted at Basle (1560), also in 3 vols. The best edition is the Leipzig one of 1825–30, 6 vols., by G. Stallbaum; for that of Politus, undertaken in 1730, with a Latin version, was never finished. The three volumes of it which appeared at Florence (1730–35) extend only to the end of the fifth book of the *Iliad.* Müller and Baumgarten-Crusius have performed a valuable service for the student, in publishing extracts from Eustathius along with the text of the *Iliad* and *Odyssey.* The commentary on Dionysius is less valuable, from the scanty nature, most probably, of the materials employed. A commentary on Pindar is lost, with the exception of the *Prooemium,* which has been edited by Schneidewin (Göttingen, 1837). Some letters of the archbishop are to be found in the public libraries of Europe, of which a part was edited by Tafel in 1832. Eustathius died about the year 1194. (2) A native of Egypt, called by some EUMATHIUS, and styled in one manuscript Πρωτονοβιλίσσιμος καὶ μέγας χαρτοφύλαξ, "Protonobilissimus and great archivist." He was the author of a romance, entitled, Τὸ καθ' Ὑσμίνην καὶ Ὑσμινίαν Δρᾶμα, "Hysminé and Hysminias." It is a lifeless performance. The work has been twice published—first at Paris (1618), with the version, and under the care, of Gaulmin, and again by Teucher (Leipzig, 1792). This last contains merely the text and the version of Gaulmin, without either preface or notes. (3) An ancient jurist, called EUSTATHIUS ROMĀNUS, who wrote a work called Ὑπόμνημα and another (Περὶ Ὑποβόλου). The so-called *Practica* is not his.

Eustratius (Εὐστράτιος). A late commentator on Aristotle. He lived about the beginning of the twelfth century, as metropolitan of Nicaea under the emperor Alexis Comnenus. Two of his works are now extant in a fragmentary condition—(1) a commentary on the second book of the *Analytica;* and (2) a commentary on the *Ethica Nicomachea*—this last being in part the work of other scholars. In the Middle Ages these commentaries were much read in the Latin version of Robert of Lincoln.

Eustȳlos (εὔστυλος). See TEMPLUM.

Euterpé (Εὐτέρπη). One of the Muses. She presided over music, and is generally represented as holding two flutes. To her was ascribed by the poets the invention of the tragic chorus. The name means "the well-delighting one," from εὖ, "well," and τέρπω, "to delight." See MUSAE.

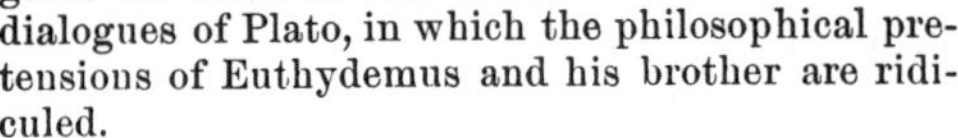

Euterpé, the Muse of Lyric Poetry. (From a statue in the Vatican.)

Euthycrătes (Εὐθυκράτης). A sculptor of Sicyon, son and pupil of Lysippus, flourished about B.C. 300. He was peculiarly happy in the proportions of his statues. Those of Heracles and Alexander were in general esteem, and particularly one of Medea, which was borne on a chariot by four horses (Plin. *H. N.* xxxiv. 8).

Euthydēmus (Εὐθύδημος). A sophist of Chios, who, with his brother Dionysodorus, migrated to Thurii in Italy. He gives its name to one of the dialogues of Plato, in which the philosophical pretensions of Euthydemus and his brother are ridiculed.

Euthȳna (εὔθυνα) and (in late Greek only) **Euthȳné** (εὔθυνη). A settlement of account. At Athens all officials were bound to give an account of their administration at the end of their term of office. This account was rendered to the λογισταί, assisted by ten εὔθυνοι, or special auditors. (See LOGISTAE.) Within a period of thirty days after the term of office had come to an end, these functionaries issued, to all whom it might concern, a public notice to lay before them any complaints they might have to make against the retiring officials. In case such complaints were made, the matter was brought to an issue by legal procedure. No official was allowed to leave the country, or take any measure affecting his property, or take another office, before his account was given. See the law cited in Andoc. x. 39; Boeckh, *Public Econ.* i. pp. 254 foll.

Eutocius (Εὐτόκιος). A native of Ascalon of about A.D. 560. He is known for his commentaries on Apollonius of Perga, the geometrician, and Archimedes, four of which have been preserved.

Eutrapĕlus (Εὐτράπελος). "Ready-witted." The nickname of a Roman knight, PUBLIUS VOLUMNIUS, who was the boon companion of Antony in his debauches. His mistress, Cytheris, called after him Volumnia, was given by him to Antony (Cic. *Ad Att.* xv. 8. 1; Hor. *Epist.* i. 18. 31).

Eutrēsis (Εὔτρησις). A small town in Boeotia between Thespiae and Plataea with a temple and oracle of Apollo, who had therein the name Eutresites. It was said to have once been the home of Zethus and Amphion (Hom. *Il.* ii. 502).

Eutropius. (1) A Latin historian of the fourth century. He bore arms under Julian in his expedition against the Parthians, as he himself informs us (x. 16), and is thought to have risen to senatorial rank. Suidas makes him of Italian origin, while some modern writers, on the other hand, advance the hypothesis that he was a native of Gaul, and was perhaps identical with the Eutropius to whom some of the letters of Symmachus are addressed. The manuscripts give him the title of Vir Cl., which may stand for either Vir Clarissimus or Vir Consularis, but which in either sense indicates an advancement to some of the highest offices in the State. He wrote several works, of which the only one remaining is an abridgment of Roman history (*Breviarium ab Urbe Condita*), in ten books. It is a brief and dry outline, without either elegance or ornament, yet containing certain facts which are nowhere else mentioned. The work commences with the foundation of the city, and is carried on to the death of Jovian, A.D. 364. At the close of this work Eutropius announces his intention of continuing the narrative in a more elevated style, inasmuch as he will have to treat of great personages still living. It does not appear that he ever carried this plan into execution. The best editions are those of Grosse (Halle, 1813), Hartel (Berlin, 1872), and of Droysen (Berlin, 1878). There is a lexicon to Eutropius by Eichert (Breslau, 1850). On his style see Sorn, *Die Sprachgebrauch des Eutropius*, pt. i. (Halle in Austria, 1888), pt. ii. (Laibach, 1889). The *Breviarium* was translated into Greek by one Paeanius, whose version is still in great part extant, and is edited in Droysen's edition of Eutropius. See Duncker, *De Paeanio Eutropii Interprete* (Greiffenberg, 1880). See, also, HISTORIA MISCELLA. (2) A eunuch and minister of the emperor Arcadius, who rose by infamous practices from the lowest condition to the highest pitch of opulence and power. He was probably a native of Asia, was made chamberlain to the emperor in the year A.D. 395, and, after the fall of Rufinus, succeeded that minister in the confidence of his master, and rose to unlimited authority. He was even created consul, a disgrace to Rome never before equalled. An insult offered to the empress was the cause of his overthrow; and he was sent into perpetual exile at Cyprus. He was soon afterwards, however, brought back on another charge; and after being condemned, was beheaded in 399 (Zosim. v. 10, 18, etc.).

Eutychĭdes (Εὐτυχίδης). A sculptor of Sicyon, a pupil of Lysippus. He flourished in B.C. 300.

Euxīnus Pontus. See PONTUS EUXINUS.

Evadné (Εὐάδνη). A daughter of Iphis or Iphicles of Argos, who slighted the addresses of Apollo, and married Capaneus (q. v.), one of the seven chiefs who went against Thebes. When her husband had been struck with thunder by Zeus for his blasphemies and impiety, and his ashes had been separated from those of the rest of the Argives, she threw herself on his burning pile and perished in the flames (Verg. *Aen.* vi. 447; Stat. *Theb.* xii. 800).

Evagŏras (Εὐαγόρας). King of Salamis, in Cyprus, from about B.C. 410 to 374. He was assisted by the Athenians in his wars against the Persians (Xen. *Hell.* ii. 1, § 29). There is extant an oration of Isocrates in praise of Evagoras and addressed to his son Nicocles, who succeeded him.

Evander (Εὔανδρος, "the good man"). A figure in Latin mythology. He was said to be the son of Hermes and an Arcadian nymph (Pausan. viii. 43, § 2; Plut. *Quaest. Rom.* 53). Sixty years before the Trojan War he led a Pelasgian colony to Latium from Pallantium in Arcadia, and founded a city, Pallantium, near the Tiber, on the hill which was afterwards named after it the Palatine. Further it was said that he taught the rude inhabitants of the country writing, music, and other arts; and introduced from Arcadia the worship of certain gods, in particular of Pan, whom the Italians called Faunus, with the festival of the Lupercalia (q. v.), which was held in his honour. Evander was worshipped at Rome among the heroes of the country (see INDIGETES), and had an altar on the Aventine Hill. But the whole story is evidently an invention of Greek scholars, who derived the Lupercalia from the Arcadian Lycaea. The name Εὔανδρος is perhaps a translation of the Italian Faunus, while Carmenta, his mother, is an ancient Italian goddess; but on this, see Nettleship, *Lectures and Essays*, pp. 50 foll.

Pallas, the son of Evander, is in like manner a creation of the poets. In Vergil he marches, at the command of his father, to assist Aeneas, and falls in single combat with Turnus. (See Verg. *Aen.* viii. 575.) Evander had also two daughters, Romé and Dyna.

Evarchus (Εὔαρχος). A river of Asia Minor, flowing into the Euxine, to the southeast of Sinopé. It formed the ancient boundary between Paphlagonia and Cappadocia.

Eventus. See BONUS EVENTUS.

Evēnus (Εὔηνος). (1) A river of Aetolia, rising in Mount Oeta, and flowing into the sea, 120 stadia west of Antirrhium. It derived its name from Evenus, the father of Marpessa, who was carried off by Idas, the son of Aphareus; and Evenus, being unable to overtake the latter, threw himself into the river, which was henceforth called after him. (2) A river of Mysia, falling into the Sinus Elaïticus near Pitané.

Everricŭlum. A fishing-net which, as appears from the annexed illustration, did not differ from our own. See Varr. *R. R.* iii. 17. 7.

Everriculum. (Fresco in the Palace of Titus, Rome.)

Evictio. In Roman law *evincere* means generally to deprive a person of a thing or right, of which he is in the enjoyment, by legal process; but the commonest case of *evictio* is that of the contract of sale. (See EMPTIO ET VENDITIO.) The vendor not being bound to make the purchaser owner of the thing sold (*Dig.* xix. 1. 11. 2), things were often bought and sold which did not belong to the vendor; and as the latter could give no better title than he had himself, the purchaser was liable to be deprived of the *res vendita* (i. e. "evicted") by the lawful owner. Originally there seems to have been no obligation on the vendor to compensate on such eviction, except in sales by mancipation, when the vendor was bound to return double the price to the purchaser, in such an event (Paul. *Sent.* rec. 2. 17. 3); but in ordinary sales it seems to have become usual for the purchaser to stipulate from the vendor for a penal sum of twice the amount of the purchase-money (*stipulatio duplae*), if deprived of the property by any one with a better title. Eventually it became a general rule of law that if the purchaser was "evicted" by legal process, the vendor must indemnify him (*Dig.* xxi. 2. 1).

Evius. See DIONYSUS; EUIUS.

Evocāti (those who are summoned or called out). The term applied in the Roman army to soldiers who had served their time and obtained their dismissal, but who, upon the general summoning them by name, returned to the service on condition of receiving certain privileges. These were, exemption from all service except in battle, a rank and pay equal to those of the centurions, and prospect of advancement. The enlistment of *evocati* was especially common in the civil wars. Sometimes they were distributed in the legion, sometimes they formed a special and select troop, divided into *centuriae.* We sometimes find them, in isolated instances, under the early Empire. On the difference between them and the *veterani*, see VETERANI. They are represented on sepulchral monuments with the vine-rod (*vitis*) in one hand, a sword on the left side (*parazonium*), and a roll of paper, indicating, perhaps, their carte of discharge, in the other; as shown by the above illustration, from a sepulchral marble, which also bears the inscription AUR. IULIANUS. EVOK. See Cic. *Fam.* iii. 6; Caes. *B. G.* vii. 65; *B. C.* i. 17.

Evocatus. (Rich.)

Evocatio (calling out). The term for the solemn summons given to the tutelary gods of a besieged city to leave it, and to migrate to Rome. (See Macrob. *Sat.* iii. 9.). The Romans always vowed, at the same time, to build them a temple at Rome. An example of a deity "evoked" in this way was Iuno Regina, who was originally worshipped at Veii, but afterwards had a temple in Rome on the Aventine.

Exagia or **Hexagia** (ἐξάγια). See PONDERA.

Exagōgé (ἐξαγωγή). An ejectment to test the right to property. See EXOULES DIKÉ.

Exagōges Graphé (ἐξαγωγῆς γραφή). An action which, it is claimed, might be instituted against one who, acting as κύριος of an Athenian woman, married her to a foreigner in a foreign land (*Att. Process*, ed. Lipsius, p. 443 foll.). Our information concerning this suit is very scanty.

Exairesĕos Diké (ἐξαιρέσεως δίκη, also ἀφαιρέσεως δίκη). An action brought at Athens to recover damages for the attempt to deprive the plaintiff of his slave; not when the defendant claimed property in the slave, but when he asserted him to be a freeman. As the condition of slavery at Athens incapacitated a man from taking any legal step in his own person, if a reputed slave wished to recover his rights as a freeman, he could only do it by the assistance of one who was himself a freeman, and who was said ἐξαιρεῖσθαι or ἀφαιρεῖσθαι αὐτὸν εἰς ἐλευθερίαν (Lys. *c. Pancl.* § 10), *in libertatem vindicare.*

Exāmen. See LIBRA.

Exampaeus (Ἐξαμπαῖος). A fountain which, according to Herodotus (iv. 52), flows into the Hypanis, where the river is four days' journey from the sea, and renders bitter its waters that before were sweet.

Exauctoratio. See EXERCITUS; MISSIO.

Exauguratio. The act of taking away from a place or thing the sacred character which it had received by *inauguratio, consecratio,* or *dedicatio.* That such an act was performed by the augurs, and never without consulting the pleasure of the gods by *augurium,* is implied in the name itself (Liv. i. 55; Dionys. Hal. *Antiq. Rom.* iii. p. 162). Temples, chapels, and other consecrated places, as well as priests, were considered as belonging to the gods. No consecrated place whatever could be employed for any profane purpose, or dedicated to any other divinity than that to which it originally belonged, without being previously exaugurated; and priests could not give up their sacred functions, nor could a vestal virgin, after the expiration of her thirty years of service, enter into matrimony, without first undergoing the process of exauguratio (Gellius, vi. (vii.) 7. 4).

Exceptio. See ACTIO.

Excubiae. See CASTRA.

Excubitōres. A word which properly means watchmen or sentinels of any kind (Caes. *B. G.* vii. 69), but is more particularly given to the soldiers of the cohort who guarded the palace of the Roman emperor (Suet. *Ner.* 8; *Oth.* 6). Their commanding officer was called *tribunus excubitor* (Suet. *Claud.* 42). When the emperor went to an entertainment at the house of another person, the excubitores appear to have accompanied him, and to have kept guard as in his own palace (Suet. *Oth.* 4).

Excubitorium. A watch-house, station-house, or barracks for Roman soldiers or police (P. Vict. *Sub Reg. Urb. Rom.* ad fin.), as to which see the articles CASTRA; EXCUBITORES; VIGILES. A very interesting excubitorium—that of the seventh battalion of city police—was discovered at Rome in 1868, near the church of S. Crisogono. It was originally a private house, rented for the use of a body of police, and so occupied for many years. The archaeological and historical interest of this building lies in the fact that the policemen, when off duty, had amused themselves by writing on the walls, thus leaving us a very vivid picture of the daily routine of an ancient policeman's life, and also of his sentiments, expressed in language that is always direct and plain, and frequently profane. See the essay by Henzen in the *Annali dell' Instituto* for 1869; Prof. Lanciani's *Ancient Rome in the Light of Recent Discoveries,* ch. viii. (Boston, 1888); Nocella, *Le Inscrizione nell' Escubitorio della VII[ma] Coorte de' Vigili* (Rome, 1887); Middleton, *Remains of Ancient Rome,* ii. pp. 257–260 (London, 1892); and the article GRAFFITI.

Execution. See BONORUM EMPTIO.

Exĕdra (ἐξέδρα). An alcove, or semi-circular extension of the colonnade in a Greek gymnasium. It was furnished with seats on which the philosophers usually sat to talk with their disciples (Cic. *N. D.* i. 6). In private houses the *exedra* was a room intended for conversation, fitted with a bench running around the wall. See GYMNASIUM.

Exegētes (ἐξηγητής). An expounder, interpreter, is used both in an ordinary and an official sense. A local guide or *cicerone* is so styled (Pausan. i. 41, § 2); Aeschines, ridiculing Demosthenes for his conduct on the embassy, calls him the ἐξηγητής of the absurd stories with which he regaled his colleagues (Aesch. *De Fals. Leg.* § 40). More usually, however, the word was applied to any interpreter of laws, whether sacred or secular, but especially the former (*Etym. Mag.* s. v.), as the Eupatridae (q. v.). Among the Eupatrids, again, the Eumolpidae (q. v.) were ἐξηγηταί of a special class of sacred laws, those, namely, relating to the Eleusinian mysteries; these laws were unwritten, and of immemorial antiquity ([Lys.] *c. Andoc.* § 10). But with regard to the written and civil laws of Athens in democratic times, the notion of several grammarians that there was a class of ἐξηγηταί or expounders of them, answering to the Roman jurisconsults, is untenable, and indeed no longer held; the silence of the orators is sufficient proof that no such persons existed (Ruhnken on Timaeus, *Lex. Plat.* s. v.). In Athenian courts, both the dicasts and the presiding judges acted without the guidance of trained lawyers, and required the laws which they administered to be intelligible to plain men. At the same time, the conservatism of ancient religion involved a frequent appeal to experts in purely ceremonial matters. Thus, the guilt of a homicide and the punishment of it were to be determined by the law-courts; but if the homicide were proved accidental or justifiable, the ceremonial expiation, the reconciliation with the relatives of the deceased, and the disposal of the corpse remained as the province of ἐξηγηταί.

In an official sense, the exegetae were a board of three persons, to whom application might be made in matters relating to sacred law; they were all to be Eupatrids, and one of them necessarily a member of the family of the Eumolpidae. The mode of their appointment is not known; and the question whether they took cognizance of all appeals from private persons like those mentioned above, or only of public matters, is open to some doubt. They attended in the assembly of the people, and interpreted the διοσημίαι, or signs from heaven; they had thus the power of stopping the business in hand, corresponding to the *obnuntiatio* of the Roman augurs. But we may be sure that the democratic Athenians would not allow an absolute or irresponsible veto to these or any other officials; their action, like that of an Epistates who refused to put the question to the vote, was no doubt liable to impeachment; in practice it is probable that only a shower or other unmistakable phenomenon was allowed to break up the meeting, so that their duty would be purely a formal one (Poll. viii. 124, 188; *Etym. Mag.* s. v.; Ruhnken on Timaeus; Müller on Aesch. *Eumen.* pp. 162 foll.; Schömann, *Antiq.* i. 429, E. T.; Gilbert, *Staatsalterth.* i. 360).

Exercĭtus (στρατός, στράτευμα). A body of men organized and armed for the defence of the State; an army.

I. GREEK. The most military people among the Greeks were the Spartans, whose whole life was spent in the practice of martial exercises, so that even the meals shared in common by all free Spartan citizens (συσσιτία) were arranged with reference to military service. (See SYSSITIA.) With them the duty of actual service began with the twentieth year, and did not end until their capacity for that service ceased to exist. After their sixtieth year, however, all Spartan soldiers were exempt from foreign duty. In the Lacedaemonian army, the heavy-armed troops (ὁπλῖται) were originally all citizens, but as early as the Persian Wars, the perioechi served side by side with the native Spartans, though in separate divisions (λόχοι). The Helots who accompanied the troops served as attendants (ὑπασπισταί) to the hoplites, and as light-armed troops in battle. (See HELOTAE; HYPASPISTAE.) A picked body of men (ἱππεῖς) was formed from among the hoplites, and served as a special body-guard to the kings. They were 300 in number, and were all active, powerful young men under thirty years of age, selected and commanded by three officers, known as ἱππαγρέται. The ἱππεῖς, as the name implies, must have been originally horsemen, but were no longer so in the time of the Persian Wars (Herod. viii. 124). A corps of light infantry was formed in the district of Sciritis, and was hence called Sciritae, the especial duty assigned to them being the outpost service of the camp, reconnoitring on the march, and in battle the support of the left wing. From the end of the fifth century B.C., the Spartan army was divided into six *morae* (μόραι), each commanded by a πολέμαρχος (Xen. *Lac.* 11. 4). As the number of Spartan citizens decreased, these ultimately composed merely the *cadre* of the *mora*, which were brought up to their full complement by the addition of perioechi; though the officers were always Spartans, as were the members of the royal staff. Each *mora* was divided into four (or five) companies (λόχοι). The cavalry played only an unimportant part in the Spartan army. (See HIPPEIS.) In time of war the ephors (see EPHORI) commanded the veteran troops. In early times the kings divided the supreme command between them, but after B.C. 512, only one commanded, unless more than one general was needed from the circumstances of the case. The Spartans maintained a fleet in which Helots served as marines and oarsmen. In cases of great necessity these were sometimes transferred to the army to serve as hoplites, in which case they received their freedom, and were then known as νεοδαμώδεις. The fleet was commanded by ναύαρχοι, or admirals.

At Athens every freeborn man was liable to military service, the only exceptions being the holders of public offices, and, in early times, the very lowest class of citizens. Every youth on reaching his eighteenth year (ἔφηβος) served for ten years, most frequently on the frontier, during which time his military education was completed, though he was then liable to serve at any time up to his sixtieth year. In time of war the Assembly fixed the number of men required for duty: in extreme cases a *levée en masse* (πανστρατιά) was resorted to. Ten generals (στρατηγοί) were elected by the people annually, and it was their duty to levy the troops and organize them in such a way that the men of each tribe (φυλή) were commanded by the same officer (φύλαρχοι). These phylarchs, as well as the taxiarchs (ταξίαρχοι), or captains of companies, were elected by the people. This levy served as hoplites, while the men of the lowest class (θῆτες) were sometimes used as light-armed troops (πελτάσται), and sometimes with the fleet. As the age of military service extended from the eighteenth to the sixtieth year, there were thus forty-two classes of age, and every man was mustered in a list (κατάλογος) under the name of the Archon Eponymus under whom he first reached the military age (Schömann, *Antiq. Greece,* Eng. trans. p. 423; but cf. Aristotle, *Polit. Ath.* § 53, with Kenyon's note). The men of the first two classes who served on the frontier were called περίπολοι. After the twentieth year they could be sent on foreign service. The army contained ten battalions (τάξεις), sometimes called φυλαί, of which the subdivisions were called λόχοι. The troops were sometimes equipped with the aid of the resident aliens (μέτοιχοι) of Attica, and in earlier times by the contingents contributed by the allies. From the time of Pericles on, the cavalry received pay amounting to some four obols, or about $0.12 a day, with an allowance for the horseman's attendant. On the cavalry, see HIPPEIS.

Early Greek Soldier. (Stelé of Aristion.)

In most of the other Greek States the hoplites, consisting of wealthy citizens, formed the main strength of the army, and generally helped to turn the scale in engagements in which the light-armed troops and the cavalry played a subordinate part. They fought in the φάλαγξ (q. v.), in closely serried lines eight deep. The flower of the troops were stationed on the right wing as the post of honour, to advance to meet the foe amid the singing of the paean. When at a distance of about 200 yards, at the signal of a trumpet, they raised the battle-cry (ἀλαλά) and charged either at a run or at quick step. It was only the Spartans who slowly advanced at an even pace and to the sound of flutes. A request for permission to bury the dead was the formal admission of defeat. The enduring token of victory was a trophy composed of the armour captured from the defeated side. It was usual to join battle on ground which was suitable for the phalanx. The Peloponnesian War was the means of introducing many innovations, including the formation of a regular force of light infantry, called πελτασταί (q. v.). Still more decisive in the transformation of the general system of Greek warfare was the famous retreat of the Ten Thousand, the first important mercenary army among the Greeks which tried to make the phalanx of hoplites suit the ground better, and to utilize at the same time the light infantry, or peltasts, and the γυμνῆτες (spearmen, bowmen, and slingers). Iphicrates, the first distinguished general of mercenary troops, introduced a lighter equipment by substituting a small πέλτη for the heavy shield, adopting a longer sword and spear, lighter shoes, and a linen corslet.

In the course of the fourth century B.C. the army composed of civilians gave way more and more to the mercenary army, which, by its intimate knowledge of the use of its weapons, gained an immense advantage in actual war. An important novelty was the oblique battle-order, the discovery of Epaminondas (q. v.). In this the great mass and strength of the hoplites was drawn up in considerable depth on one of the two wings, without any expansion of the front. The hoplites could thus make a vigorous attack on the centre of the enemy's wing, while the true centre and the other wing of the assailants were held in reserve, with a view to advancing later to crush the enemy.

The Macedonian method of warfare, invented by King Philip II. and his son Alexander the Great, was based upon the Greek military organization adapted to Macedonian requirements. For this purpose, that organization was duly developed, and the different parts of the army, the infantry and cavalry, light and heavy-armed troops, military levies, allies and mercenary troops, were blended together into a far freer and more effective system than the Greeks ever attained in their art of war. In point of numbers the strongest component part of the Macedonian army, as elsewhere, was the heavy and light infantry. The former consisted of the πεζέταιροι, a body of Macedonians of free but not noble origin, corresponding to the Greek hoplites, though not so heavily armed. Like the hoplites, they fought in a phalanx, but this was generally deeper than theirs, being eight and afterwards sixteen men deep. They formed six τάξεις, corresponding to the number of the districts of Macedonia, each of which was represented by one τάξις. (See further under PHALANX.) The ὑπασπισταί were the equivalent of the Hellenic peltasts, and were a standing corps of 3000 men. Besides these there were strong contingents of other kinds of light infantry, especially spearmen and archers. While in the Greek armies the number of the cavalry had always been small, they formed nearly one-sixth of the whole army which Alexander took with him on his Asiatic expedition, and consisted of an equal number of light and heavy cavalry. (See further under HIPPEIS.) The central point in the great battles of Alexander was the phalanx; on the right of this were placed the ὑπασπισταί, the heavy and light Macedonian cavalry, the spearmen, and archers; on the left, the Thracian peltasts, the Hellenic contingent of cavalry, with the Thessalian cavalry, and light troops, horsemen, and archers. The two wings were reckoned from the centre of the phalanx, the right being usually reserved for the attack, and led by the king. The light troops began the attack, which was supported by the heavy Macedonian cavalry, followed by the ὑπασπισταί. The heavy infantry came up in detachments to keep the line unbroken, and formed an oblique battle-array. Thus the main attack was made by the heavy cavalry, and no longer, as with the other Greeks, by the phalanx. On the contrary, the phalanx formed the solid centre of the whole army—a centre which it was impossible for the enemy to break, and which was itself irresistible in attack. Under the successors of Alexander, the phalanx was, however, regarded as strengthening the whole army and lengthening the formation, rather than as a factor of offensive operations. The battle was decided by the wings, which were composed of cavalry—one wing being destined for the attack while the other remained on the defensive. The light infantry and the elephants which were now brought into use were brought to bear as occasion demanded, but were chiefly used in masking the preparatory movements of the attacking wing, very much, in fact, as cavalry is used in the modern German tactics.

During the third century B.C., the cavalry declined in importance and hence in numbers, while the heavy-armed infantry, with the formidable σάρισσα, twenty-four feet long, became more and more effective. The phalanx was now used in attacking, and its onset usually decided the battle. In that century, mercenary armies became very common, and at last Greek military science yielded to that of the Romans mainly because the tactics of the phalanx were ill-suited to a hand-to-hand engagement. See LOCHUS; MORA; PHALANX.

II. ROMAN.—Down to the year B.C. 104, when the people, alarmed by the advance of the formidable Cimbri, kept C. Marius in the consulate for five years in disregard of the Constitution, the Roman army had been nothing more than a militia of citizens, the body of the free burgesses in arms, as established by Servius Tullius. (See COMITIA CENTURIATA.) The whole population was divided into five classes. The first class was divided between cavalry (*equites*) and infantry (*pedites*), and all five classes into *iuniores* and *seniores*, the former being employed for active service in the field, and the latter for the defence of the city. Every citizen from his seventeenth to his forty-fifth or fiftieth year was liable to service unless he belonged to the lowest class (*proletarii*), or had already served in twenty campaigns on foot or in ten campaigns as a cavalryman. The military levy was by tribes, and was made in a general assembly of citizens at the Capitol or on the Campus Martius, an equal number of men being taken from each tribe. (See DILECTUS.) The regular levy was 8500 *seniores* and 17,000 *iuniores*, a total of 25,500 men. These were formed into four legions of 4250 or 4500 men each, and a body of 1800 cavalry. The rest of the recruits formed a reserve to supply the losses sustained by the legions. There were generally two consular armies, each of two legions, besides contingents of the allies of equal infantry and double cavalry strength, as the native Roman cavalry was inferior, and preferred always to fight dismounted. A legion was made up as follows: 1200 *velites* (light-armed skirmishers, also called *accensi*, *rorarii*, and *ferentarii*), 1200 *hastati*, 1200 *principes*, 600 *triarii*, and 300 *equites*. The *hastati*, *principes*, and *triarii* were each divided into ten *manipuli*, or companies, and an equal number of *velites* were attached to each. The *hastati* and *principes* formed respectively the first and second line, and were armed with spears (*hastae*); the *triarii* were the reserve, and carried the *pilum*, a short and very heavy spear, which they hurled into the ranks of the enemy immediately before closing with them in a hand-to-hand struggle with the sword (*gladius*).

Roman Soldiers. (Column of Trajan.)

Each *manipulus* was commanded by a centurion (*centurio*), having a second centurion for his lieutenant. The first centurion of the first *manipulus* of the *triarii*, who was known as *primus pilus*, in the absence of a superior officer, took command of the whole legion. The chief command of the legion was held in turn by the six military tribunes (*tribuni militum*), each of whom commanded for two months at a time; but after the first civil wars, a single officer (*legatus*) permanently directed each legion, having the military tribunes as his staff.

The protracted wars with Pyrrhus and Carthage led to the first important change in the constitution of the army. From this time, the practice of giving the soldiers regular pay was established, and paved the way for the establishment of a regular army, which took place, as noted above, in the consulship of Marius, from which time the enlisted man was a professional soldier, serving continuously in the army for twenty years. The legion now consisted of 6000 troops, divided into ten cohorts of 600 men each, uniformly armed with the *pilum*. The place of the *velites* was supplied by foreign mercenaries, bowmen (*sagittarii*) from Crete, javelin-men (*iaculatores*) from Mauretania, and slingers (*funditores*) from the Baleares. The cavalry was also chiefly foreign, with a few Roman *equites* in special posts of honour. The general had a body-guard (*praetoriani*) of some 5000 men, with high pay and special privileges. At this time the silver eagle was adopted as the standard (see SIGNUM; VEXILLUM), and was carried by the first century of the first cohort. There were also auxiliary troops of varying number divided into *cohortes*, and consisting of both infantry and cavalry.

Under Caesar the legion consisted nominally of about 5000 men, though actually of less. According to Rüstow it was divided into ten cohorts of 300 or 360 men each; each cohort into three maniples of 100 to 120 men each; and each maniple into two centuries of 50 to 60 men each. In battle the ten cohorts were regularly drawn up as in the following figure, which represents the *acies triplex* of Caesar:

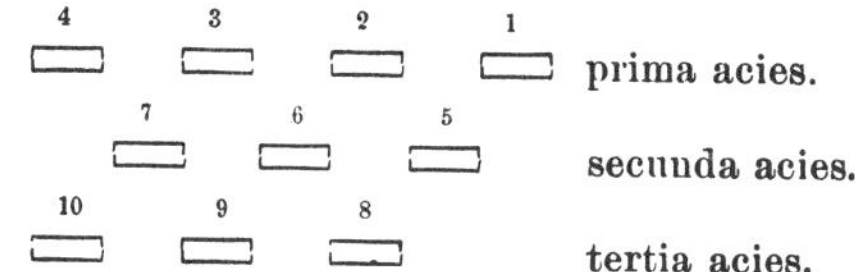

The cavalry, divided into *turmae*, or squadrons, and commanded by a *decurio*, was usually stationed on both wings; but at Pharsalus on only one; while at Bibracté it was held in the rear. The defensive order of battle was the hollow square (*orbis*), which corresponds with the formation on the march called *agmen quadratum*. The general term for the army on the march is *agmen*; in battle order, *acies*. When the signal for the march was given, the *extraordinarii* (q. v.) with the allies of the right wing moved first, then the legions, and last the allies of the left wing with part of the cavalry who were said *claudere agmen* or *cogere agmen*. An army marching in close order was called *agmen iustum* or *agmen pilatum*. The van is *primum agmen*; the centre, *medium agmen*; the rear, *extremum* or *novissimum agmen*. The formation called *agmen quadratum*, shown below, was adopted when a sudden attack was expected. The baggage was then placed within the lines.

The commander-in-chief was called *dux* or *imperator*; the commanders of the legions, *legati*; the staff of the legions were the *tribuni militum*; the orderlies and aides, *contubernales* or *comites praetori*; the paymaster and quartermaster-general, *quaestor*. In case there were not sufficient legates, the quaestor also commanded the legion.

Under Augustus the completion of the Roman standing army was carried out, and twenty-five

Agmen Quadratum. (Antonine Column.)

legions were maintained throughout the Empire, besides the Praetorian Guard. Under Trajan there were thirty legions; under Septimius Severus, thirty-three. At this time the name *legatus* was changed to *praefectus*, the first cohort was doubled in strength (*cohors milliaria*), and the minimum strength of the legion was fixed at 6100 infantry and 726 cavalry. See LEGIO.

Under the Republic and the early Empire, the military drill was very severe, comprising running, jumping, wrestling, swimming (both naked and in full armour), besides drill, the use of intrenching tools, and long marches at the rate of four miles per hour, with a load of from 35 to 60 lbs. This was required not only from recruits but from veterans as well. The equipment of the soldier was very heavy. The wagons transported the general baggage (*impedimenta*) and the tents; yet each soldier, besides his shield, helmet, breastplate, *pilum*, and sword, was obliged to carry corn for seventeen days, stakes for the palisade of the camp, and intrenching tools (Veget. i. 19).

In the time of Polybius the regular pay of a soldier of the legion was about $0.07 per diem (⅓ of a *denarius*), that of a centurion, $0.14; and that of a cavalryman, $0.20. Caesar fixed the pay of a soldier at 225 *denarii* (about $45) per annum. Under Domitian it was raised to 300 denarii ($60). Out of this the soldier paid for his clothes and accoutrements (Tac. *Ann.* i. 17). The only superior officer's pay that is known is that of the *tribunus legionis*, in the third century A.D., when it was 25,000 sesterces ($1000). On the pay and other service conditions of the Praetorian Guard, see PRAETORIANI.

The regular food of the Roman soldier was wheat made into a kind of porridge (*puls*) or bread (*panis*), and occasionally meat and vegetables (*legumina*). Vinegar was allowed the soldiers for the drink called *posca* (q. v.). Provisions were also often gathered by foraging, in which case they naturally depended on the soldier's luck. For the rewards of military service, see the articles CORONA; OVATIO; TRIUMPHUS.

Military punishments were of various sorts, comprising (*a*) whipping (*castigatio*); (*b*) a fine (*pecuniaria multa*); (*c*) loss of rank (*militiae mutatio*); (*d*) drumming out of camp (*ignominiosa missio;* cf. the pseud. Caes. *Bell. Afr.* 54, 4); (*e*) the substitution of barley for wheat in their rations; (*f*) decimation (see DECIMATIO); (*g*) death, which could be inflicted only by the consul under the Republic, and by the emperor or *legatus* under the Empire.

On his honourable discharge (*honesta missio*), the soldier received either land or a present of money, ranging from 3000 denarii ($600) to 5000 denarii ($1000). A discharge for physical disability or sickness was called *causaria missio*.

BIBLIOGRAPHY.—An extensive bibliography on the Greek army will be found in the article "Die griechischen Kriegsalterthümer" in Iwan Müller's *Handbuch der klassischen Alterthumswissenschaft*, iv. pp. 226–231 (1887). Good special works are Rüstow and Köchly, *Geschichte des griechischen Kriegswesens* (1852); Köpke, *Kriegswesen der Griechen in heroischen Zeitalter;* and Droysen, *Untersuchungen über Alexander des Grossens Heerwesen und Kriegsführung* (1885).

On the military organization of Rome, a vast bibliography is collected by Schiller in Iwan Müller's *Handbuch*, vol. ii. The following works will be found useful: Lange, *Historia Mutationum Rei Militaris Romanorum* (1846); Rüstow, *Heerwesen und Kriegsführung Cäsars*, 2d ed. (1862); Judson, *Caesar's Army* (1888); Lindenschmidt, *Die Tracht und Bewaffnung des römischen Heeres während der Kaiserzeit* (1882); Von Göler, *Cäsars gallischer Krieg* (1880); Hartung, *Römische Auxiliartruppen* (1870–75); and Bouché-Leclercq, *Institutions Romaines*, pt. iv. (1884).

On the arms, equipment, etc., of the soldiers, see ARMA; CALIGA; CLIPEUS; FUNDA; GALEA; GLADIUS; HASTA; LORICA; OCREA; PILUM; SCUTUM. On the different branches of the service, see EQUITES; FUNDITORES; IACULATORES; MERCENARII; PRAETORIANI; SAGITTARII; VELITES. On the system of encampment, see CASTRA. On the functions of the general, see IMPERATOR.

Exetastae (ἐξετασταί). Special commissioners sent out by the Athenian people to investigate any matters that might claim attention. Thus we find mention of exetastae being appointed to ascertain whether there were as many mercenaries as the generals reported. It appears to have been no uncommon plan for the commanders, like the French officials of the Second Empire, who received pay for troops, to report a greater number than they possessed, in order to receive the pay themselves; in which case they were said "to draw pay for empty places in the mercenary force" (Aesch. *c. Ctes.* § 146). The commissioners, however, who were sent to make inquiries into the matter, often allowed themselves to be bribed (Aesch. *c. Timarch.* § 113; *De F. L.* § 177).

Another kind of exetastae is shown by inscriptions to have existed at Athens for a short time in the early part of the third century B.C. They were auditors of accounts, and are mentioned as checking the expenses of psephismata (i. e. of recording them) and of the erection of statues (*C. I. A.* i. 297, 298, 300). In this sense of auditors of public accounts the name occurred in some other Greek States.

Exhēres. See HERES.

Exhibendum, Actio ad. A praetorian action *in personam* (*Inst.* iv. 6, 31), usually of a preliminary character, by which a plaintiff who was unable to pursue his right by legal process without the production of a thing, could enforce such production upon any person who was able to make it (*Dig.* x. 4, 2); and it was immaterial whether that person was owner, or had civil or merely natural possession, of the thing in question (*Dig.* ib. 3, 15), or had fraudulently parted with the possession of it (*Dig.* ib. 5, 2); but it was essential that the plaintiff should have a pecuniary or proprietary interest in the production, or else the action would not lie (*Dig.* ib. 13).

Exilium. See EXSILIUM.

Exiteria or **Epexodia** (ἐξιτήρια, ἐπεξόδια). Sacrifices offered by generals before they set out on an expedition (Xen. *Anab.* vi. 5, § 2). The principal object was to discover from the accompanying signs the favourable or unfavourable issue of the undertaking on which they were about to enter.

Exodia (ἐξόδια, from ἐξ and ὁδός). Amusing interludes in verse, inserted by the Romans in other plays, but chiefly in the Atellanae (Livy, vii. 2). It is difficult to ascertain the real character of the exodia; but from the words of Livy we must infer that, although distinct from the Atellanae, they were closely connected with them, and never performed alone. Hence Juvenal speaks of the *exodium Atellanae* (*Sat.* vi. 71), and Suetonius (*Tib.* 45) *exodium Atellanicum*. They were, like the Atellanae themselves, played by young and well-born Romans, and not by the professional actors. The exodia have generally been considered as short comedies or farces which were performed after the Atellanae—an opinion founded upon the vague and incorrect statement of the Scholiast on Juvenal (*Sat.* iii. 174). But the words of Livy, *exodia conserta fabellis*, seem rather to indicate interludes, which, however, must not be understood as if they had been played between the acts of the Atellanae, which would suggest a false idea of the Atellanae themselves; but as several Atellanae were performed on the same day, it is probable that the exodia were played between them. This supposition is also supported by the etymology of the word itself, which signifies something ἐξ ὁδοῦ, *extra viam*, or something not belonging to the main subject, and thus is synonymous with ἐπεισόδιον. The play, as well as its name of exodium, seems to have been introduced among the Romans from Italian Greece; but after its introduction it appears to have become very popular among the Romans, and continued to be played down to a very late period (Suet. *Domit.* 10).

Exōmis (ἐξωμίς). (1) A particular kind of Greek tunic, afterwards adopted by the Romans, without sleeves, very short (*substricta*), and entirely open down the right side, so that, when put on, the right shoulder (ὦμος), as well as the arm and breast, were left exposed (Aul. Gell. vii. 12. 1). Hence, the person wearing it was styled *expapillatus*. It was the usual dress of persons employed in active and laborious occupations, such as slaves, rustics, artisans, and huntsmen; hence, in works of art, it is frequently worn by Vulcan, Charon, Daedalus, and Amazons, all of whom pursued a life of toil or industry. (2) The same name was given to the *pallium* (q. v.), when worn so as to present the same appearance (Poll. vii. 48).

Exomis. (Rich.)

Exostra (ἐξώστρα). (1) One of the many machines used in the theatres of the ancients. Its introduction was ascribed to Aeschylus. In order to represent a scene in an interior, a movable chamber corresponding to the size of any of the three doors was devised, which was wheeled out (ἐκκύκλημα) or pushed out (ἐξώστρα) (Poll. iv. 128; Schol. *ad* Aristoph. *Acharn.* 375). Donaldson thinks the ἐξώστρα was used to exhibit the interior of an upper chamber; this would find support in the late meaning of the word, "balcony." A special use of both machines was to exhibit to the eyes of the spectators the results or consequences of such acts, as murder or suicide, as could not be permitted to take place in the *proscenium*, and were therefore described as having occurred behind the *scena*. See Donaldson, *Theatre of the Greeks*, ed. 7, p. 238 foll.; C. O. Müller, *Eumen.* p. 103, *Kleine Schriften*, i. p. 524; and Alb. Müller, *Bühnenalterth.* pp. 142–148, where there is a full discussion of the passages where the contrivance is mentioned.

(2) The name *exostra* was also applied to a peculiar kind of bridge, which was thrown from a tower of the besiegers upon the walls of a besieged town, and across which the assailants marched to attack those of the besieged who were stationed on the ramparts to defend the town (Polyb. ii. 6, 8).

Exoules Diké (ἐξούλης δίκη). An action under the Attic law, for ejectment, resorted to by a plaintiff when his title to the property in question was so much better than the defendant's as to be indisputable. Thus a son or other male descendant (also a son adopted during the testator's lifetime) might enter (see EMBATEIA), and become possessed of the estate immediately after the owner's death (Isae. *Pyrrh.* § 61). Such an heir made a formal entry upon the land, and thereby became "seised" or possessed of it; then the adverse claimant came and turned him off (Demosth. *c. Leoch.* p. 1090, § 32). This proceeding took place quietly and in the presence of witnesses (Isae. *Pyrrh.* § 22); and then the heir might bring against him an action for ejectment.

These proceedings by entry, ouster, etc., were a relic of ancient times, when, before regular processes were invented, parties adopted a ruder method and took the law into their own hands. There was then an actual ouster, accompanied often with violence and breach of the peace, for which the person in the wrong was not only responsible to the party injured, but was also punishable as a public offender. Afterwards, in the course of civilization, violent remedies became useless and were discontinued; yet the ceremony of ejection was still kept up as a form of law, being deemed by lawyers a necessary foundation of the subsequent legal process. Thus at Rome, in the earlier times, one party used to summon the other by the words *ex iure te manum consertum voco*, to go with him to the land in dispute, and (in the presence of the praetor and others) turn him out by force. Afterwards this was changed into the symbolical act of breaking a clod of earth upon the land, by which the person who broke intimated that he claimed a right to deal with the land as he pleased.

Expedīti. A name given to light-armed troops as opposed to *impediti;* or to any "flying column" organized for rapid marching. See EXERCITUS.

Exploratōres. Scouts. See EXERCITUS.

Exsequiae. See FUNUS.

Exsilium (φυγή). (1) GREEK. Among the Greeks, exile was the legal punishment for homicide (see EPHETAE), and for sundry other offences, such as wounding with intent to kill, the murder of a non-citizen for impiety (ἀσέβεια); and was often voluntary on the part of those who wished to avoid some other form of punishment. It was also, at times, a political measure, adopted especially in times of civil disturbance, and might carry with it ἀτιμία and loss of property, except in the case of ostracism. (See OSTRACISMUS.)

(2) ROMAN. Among the Romans there was, originally, no such thing as a direct expulsion from the city (Cic. *Pro Caec.* 34); but a man might be cut off from fire and water, the symbol of civic communion, which of course practically forced him to leave the country. This *interdictio aquae et ignis* was originally inflicted by the Comitia Centuriata, and later by the permanent judicial commissions appointed to try certain serious offences, as, for instance, treason, arson, and

poisoning. In case of the capital charge the accused was always free to anticipate an unfavourable verdict, or the *interdictio aquae et ignis*, by withdrawing into voluntary exile; for exile was originally conceived not as a punishment, but as a means of escaping punishment (Cic. *Pro Dom.* 34), and we hear of the *ius exsulandi* (cf. Schwegler, *Römische Geschichte*, i. p. 438). Voluntary exile, as being a confession of guilt, was regularly confirmed by a plebiscitum; and when the exile was recalled, the decree was also annulled by legislative act. *Interdictio* seems to have been primarily regarded as clearing the State from any guilt that might have been incurred in the eyes of the gods by letting the criminal go unpunished. The exsilium involved in the lesser *deminutio capitis* (q. v.), or loss of citizenship, if the banished person became citizen of another State; or if the people declared the banishment to be deserved; or if the *interdictio aquae et ignis* was pronounced after he had gone into exile. It was only in very serious cases that a man's property was also confiscated. Real banishment was first inflicted under the Empire. See DEPORTATIO; INTERDICTIO; RELEGATIO.

Exsuperantius, IULIUS. A Roman historian of the fourth or fifth century A.D., who wrote a monograph *De Marii, Lepidi, ac Sertorii Bellis Civilibus*, preserved in a MS. of Sallust at Paris and dating from the eleventh century. The treatise is largely drawn from the *Iugurtha* and *Historiae*, and contains a number of absurd historical errors, such as confounding the elder with the younger Marius. It was last edited by Bursian (Zürich, 1868).

Extispex (ἡπατοσκόπος, σπλαγχνοσκόπος). A diviner who professed to interpret the will of the

Extispex. (Villa Borghese.)

gods, and to predict the future, by inspecting the entrails of victims slain at the altar (Cic. *Div.* ii. 18). See AUGUR; DIVINATIO; HARUSPEX.

Extraordinarii (ἐπίλεκτοι). Picked soldiers set about the person of the consul in the Roman army (Polyb. vi. 28). From them a special bodyguard, known as the *ablecti*, were taken. The extraordinarii consisted of about a third of the cavalry and a fifth of the infantry of the allies—i. e. for a legion of 4500 men, there were but 1040 extraordinarii. (See EXERCITUS.) The number of the *ablecti* is not known.

F

F, as a symbol.

F = fabri, faciunt (fecit, fecerunt, faciundum, factus), fastus, feliciter, feriae, fidelis, filius (the most frequent), fines, flamen, Flavius, Fortuna, functus.

F·C = faciendum curavit.

F·C·P = fulgur conditum publice.

F·D·F = filiae dulcissimae fecerunt.

F·D·S = fecerunt de suo.

F·D·S·S·C = faciundum de senatus sententia curaverunt.

F·F = felix fidelis, filius fecit, fiscus frumentarius Flavia felix (firma, fidelis), sc. legio.

F·K·F = filio karissimo fecit.

F·I = fieri iussit.

F·M·F = filio mater fecit, filius matri fecit.

F·P = filio prissimo, filio posuit, flamen perpetuus, Fortuna Praenestina, frumentum publicum, funus publicum.

F·P·M·F = filii patri merenti fecerunt.

F·P·P = frater pius posuit.

F·S = filio suo, fecit sibi, Fortunae sacrum.

F·S·ET·S·L·L·P·Q·E = fecit sibi et suis libertis libertatus posterisque eorum.

F·S·S = fiunt supra scripti (ae, a).

F·V·L = familia villae Lucullanae.

F·V·P = filiae vivus posuit.

Fabăris or **Farfărus**. A small river in Italy, in the Sabine territory, between Reaté and Cures.

Fabatarium. A vessel in which a kind of bean soup (*puls fabacea*, Macrob. i. 12 med.) was probably served (Lamprid. *Heliog.* 20).

Fabātus, CALPURNIUS. The grandfather of Calpurnia, wife of Pliny the Younger, who addressed to him a number of letters. In A.D. 64 he was accused of complicity in the adultery and magic of Lepida, wife of C. Cassius, but escaped by an appeal to Nero (Tac. *Ann.* xvi. 8).

Fabātus, L. ROSCIUS. A lieutenant of Caesar, who went over to Pompey in the Civil Wars, and was killed at the battle of Mutina (B.C. 43).

Faber (τέκτων). The name given indiscriminately to any artisan or mechanic who works in hard materials, such as wood, stone, metal, etc., in contradistinction to one who moulds or models in soft substances, like wax or clay, who received the appellation of *plastes*. It is, consequently, accompanied in most cases by a descriptive epithet which determines the calling of the workman alluded to; as *faber tignarius*, a carpenter; *faber ferrarius*, a blacksmith; *faber aeris* or *aerarius*, *marmoris*, *eboris*, a worker in bronze, marble, and ivory; and so on. The Greek term has not quite so extensive a meaning as the Latin one, being rarely applied to a worker in metal, who was expressly called χαλκεύς or σιδηρεύς, though some passages occur where it is so used. The accompanying illustration represents a carpenter's shop,

Carpenter's Shop. (From a painting found at Herculaneum.)

from a painting found at Herculaneum, in which the workmen are represented under the form of genii, according to the conventional treatment of the ancient schools, for subjects of this nature, in which scenes of ordinary life are depicted. The fabri attached to the army were under the command of a special officer (*praefectus fabrorum*) (Caes. *B. C.* i. 24).

Fabia. A vestal virgin, sister to Terentia, Cicero's wife. She was accused of criminal intercourse with Catiline, and brought to trial in consequence, but was defended by Cicero and acquitted.

Fabia Gens. A numerous and powerful patrician house of ancient Rome, which became subdivided into several families or branches, distinguished by their respective cognomina, such as Fabii Maximi, Fabii Ambusti, Fabii Vibulani, etc. Pliny (*H. N.* xviii. § 3) says that the name of this house arose from the circumstance of its founders having excelled in the culture of the bean (*faba*), the early Romans having been remarkable for their attachment to agricultural pursuits. The Fabii are said, by the ordinary authorities, to have been of Sabine origin, and to have settled on the Quirinal from the time of the earliest Roman kings. After the expulsion of the Tarquinii, the Fabian, as one of the older houses, exercised considerable influence in the Senate. Caeso Fabius, being quaestor with L. Valerius, impeached Spurius Cassius in B.C. 486, and had him executed. It has been noted as a remarkable fact, that, for seven consecutive years from that time, one of the two annual consulships was filled by three brothers Fabii in rotation. One of the three brothers, Q. Fabius Vibulanus, fell in battle against the Veientes in the year B.C. 479. In the following year, under the consulship of Caeso Fabius and Titus Virginius, the whole house of the Fabii proposed to leave Rome, and settle on the borders of the territory of Veii, in order to take the war against the Veientes entirely into their own hands. After performing solemn sacrifices, they left Rome in a body, mustering three hundred and six patricians, besides their families, clients, and freedmen, and encamped on the banks of the Cremera in sight of Veii. There they fortified themselves, and maintained for nearly two years a harassing warfare against the Veientes and other people of Etruria. At last, in one of their predatory incursions (B.C. 477), they fell into an ambuscade, and, fighting desperately, were all exterminated (Livy, ii. 48 foll.). Dionysius of Halicarnassus (ix. 19) gives also another account of this disaster, which he considers less credible. According to this latter form of the legend, the three hundred and six Fabii set off for Rome, in order to offer up a sacrifice in the chapel of their house. As they went to perform a pious ceremony, they proceeded without arms or warlike array. The Etrurians, however, knowing their road, placed troops in ambush, and, falling on the Fabii, cut them to pieces. It is said that one only of the Fabii escaped this massacre, having been left quite young at Rome (Livy, ii. 50; Dion. Hal. ix. 22). His name was Q. Fabius Vibulanus, and he became the ancestor of all the subsequent Fabii. He was repeatedly consul, and was afterwards one of the Decemviri with Appius Claudius for two consecutive years, in which office he disgraced himself by his connivance at the oppressions of his colleague, which caused the fall of the decemvirate. See DECEMVIRI; FABII.

Fabius. (1) M. AMBUSTUS, consul in B.C. 360, and again several times after. He fought against the Hernici and the Tarquinians, and left several sons. (2) Q. MAXIMUS RULLIĀNUS, son of the preceding, attacked and defeated the Samnites, B.C. 324, in the absence and against the orders of his commanding officer, the Dictator Papirius, who would have brought him to punishment for disobedience, but was prevented by the intercession of the soldiers and the people. This Fabius was five times consul, and dictator twice. He triumphed over the Samnites, Marsi, Gauls, and Etrurians. His son, Q. Fabius Gurges, was thrice consul, and was grandfather of Q. Fabius Maximus Verrucosus, one of the most celebrated generals of Rome. (3) Q. MAXĬMUS VERRUCŌSUS, the celebrated opponent of Hannibal. He is said to have been called Verrucosus from a wart on his lip, *verruca* being the Latin name for "a wart." In his first consulship he triumphed over the Ligurians. After the victory of Hannibal at Lake Trasimenus (B.C. 217), he was named prodictator by the unanimous voice of the people, and was intrusted with the preservation of the Republic. The system which he adopted to check the advance of Hannibal is well known. By a succession of skilful movements, marches, and countermarches, always choosing good defensive positions, he harassed his antagonist, who could never draw him into places favourable for his attack, while Fabius watched every opportunity of availing himself of any error or neglect on the part of the Carthaginians. This mode of warfare, which was new to the Romans, acquired for Fabius the name of CUNCTĀTOR or "delayer," and was censured by the young, the rash, and the ignorant; but it was probably the means of saving Rome from ruin. Minucius, who shared with Fabius the command of the army, having imprudently engaged Hannibal, was saved from total destruction by the timely assistance of the dictator. In the following year, however, B.C. 216, Fabius being recalled to Rome, the command of the army was intrusted to the consul Terentius Varro, who rushed imprudently to battle, and the defeat at Cannae made manifest the wisdom of the dictator's previous caution. Fabius was chosen consul the next year, and was again employed in keeping Hannibal in check. In B.C. 210, being consul for the fifth time, he retook Tarentum by stratagem, after which he narrowly escaped being caught himself in a snare by Hannibal near Metapontum (Livy, xxvii. 15 foll.). When, some years after, the question was discussed in the Senate, of sending Scipio with an army into Africa, Fabius opposed it, saying that Italy ought first to be rid of Hannibal. Fabius died some time after at a very advanced age.

(4) His son, called likewise QUINTUS FABIUS MAXĬMUS, who had also been consul, died before him. (5) His grandson QUINTUS FABIUS MAXĬMUS SERVILIĀNUS, being proconsul, fought against Viriathus in Spain, and concluded with him an honourable peace (Livy, *Epit.* 54). He was afterwards consul repeatedly, and also censor. He wrote annals, which are quoted by Macrobius (*Sat.* i. 16). (6) His brother by adoption, QUINTUS FABIUS MAXĬMUS AEMILIĀNUS, the son of Aemilius Paulus (Livy, xlv. 41), was consul B.C. 144, and was the father of Fabius, called (7) ALLOBROGĬCUS, who subdued not

only the Allobroges, but also the people of southern Gaul, which he reduced to a Roman province, called from that time Provincia. QUINTUS FABIUS MAXĬMUS, a grandson of Fabius Maximus Servilianus, served in Spain under Iulius Caesar, and was made consul B.C. 44. Two of his sons or nephews were consuls in succession under Augustus. There was also a Fabius consul under Tiberius. Panvinius and others have reckoned that during a period of about five centuries, from the time of the first Fabius who is mentioned as consul to the reign of Tiberius, forty-eight consulships, seven dictatorships, eight censorships, seven augurships, besides the offices of master of the horse and military tribune with consular power, were filled by individuals of the Fabian house. It could also boast of thirteen triumphs and two ovations. (4) PICTOR, born about B.C. 254, the first Roman who wrote an historical account of his country in Greek. This historian, called by Livy *scriptorum antiquissimus*, appears to have been ill qualified for the labour he had undertaken, either in point of judgment, fidelity, or research; and to his carelessness, more than even to the loss of monuments, may be attributed much of the uncertainty which to this day hangs over the early ages of Roman history. Fabius lived in the time of the Second Punic War. His family received its cognomen from Gaius Fabius, who, having resided in Etruria and there acquired some knowledge of the fine arts, painted with figures the temple of Salus, in the year B.C. 303. The historian was grandson of the painter. He served in the Second Punic War, and was present at the battle of Trasimenus. After the defeat at Cannae he was sent by the Senate to inquire from the oracle at Delphi what would be the issue of the war, and to learn by what supplications the wrath of the gods might be appeased. His annals commenced with the age of Aeneas, and brought down the relation of Roman affairs to the author's own time—that is, to the end of the Second Punic War. We are informed by Dionysius of Halicarnassus that, for the great proportion of the events which preceded his own age, Fabius Pictor had no better authority than tradition. He probably thought that if he had confined himself to what was certain in those early times, his history would have become dry, insipid, and incomplete. This may have induced him to adopt the myths which the Greek historians had invented concerning the origin of Rome, and to insert whatever he found in family traditions, however contradictory or uncertain. Dionysius has also given many examples of Pictor's improbable narratives, his inconsistencies, his negligence in investigating the truth of what he relates as facts, and his inaccuracy in chronology. In particular, as we are told by Plutarch in his life of Romulus, Fabius followed an obscure Greek author, Diocles, in his account of the foundation of Rome, and from this source have flowed all the stories concerning Mars, the Vestal, the Wolf, Romulus and Remus, etc. Polybius, who flourished shortly after those times, and was at pains to inform himself accurately concerning all the events of the Second Punic War, apologizes on one occasion for quoting Fabius as an authority. Livy quotes him eight times. The fragments are given by H. Peter in his *Hist. Relliquiae*, i. 5, 109. See also Schwegler, *Römische Geschichte*, i. 412; Mommsen, *Römische Forschungen*, ii. 279; H. Nissen in the *Rheinisches Museum*, xxii. 565; Harless, *De Fabiis et Aufidiis Rerum Rom. Scriptoribus* (Bonn, 1853); C. Peter, *Zur Kritik d. Quellen d. ält. röm. Geschichte* (Halle, 1879); Heydenreich, *Fabius Pictor und Livius* (Freiburg, 1878); and the article LIVIUS.

Fables. See NOVELS AND ROMANCES.

Fabrateria. The modern Falvaterra; a Volscian town in Latium, on the right bank of the Trerus, subsequently colonized by the Romans.

Fabretti, RAFFAELE. A distinguished Italian archaeologist, born at Urbino in Umbria in 1618. He studied law at Cagli and in his native city, where he took the doctor's degree at the age of eighteen. He soon after attracted the notice of Cardinal Lorenzo Imperiali, by whose influence he was employed in important political negotiations in Spain, where he acted as treasurer and later as auditor to the Papal legation at Madrid, remaining there for thirteen years. Returning to Rome, he became a judge, and then an auditor of legation at Urbino. Having always had a strong predilection for antiquarian studies, he now, by the invitation of Cardinal Carpegna, found an opportunity of prosecuting them at his leisure. Taking up his residence in Rome, he began the archaeological investigations that have made his name memorable, by a most minute study of the topography and ruins of the Campagna, spending day after day in solitary expeditions on his horse Marco Polo, of which he has written pleasantly as being an animal with a keen scent for buried monuments.

In 1680, Fabretti published his first important work, entitled *De Aquis et Aquae Ductibus Veteris Romae*—a treatise which cleared up many obscure points in the topography of Latium, and which is printed in the *Thesaurus* of Graevius (iv. 1677). Other treatises of his are that *De Columna Traiani Syntagma* (Rome, 1683); and the *Inscriptionum Antiquarum Explicatio* (Rome, 1699). The former contains an explanation also of the famous Iliac Table, a bas-relief now in the Capitol, and representing scenes in the Trojan War. Both these works throw much light on Roman archaeology, and are especially important for their recognition of the comparative method of studying epigraphic remains. Fabretti became involved in a controversy with Gronovius (q. v.) regarding the interpretation by the former of a passage in Livy, and the two scholars assailed each other in the abusive vocabulary of contemporary scholarship, Fabretti styling Gronovius *Grunnovius* or "grunter," and Gronovius retorting by calling Fabretti *faber rusticus*.

Fabretti died in January, 1700, having been for a number of years keeper of the archives of the Castello S. Angelo, under Innocent XII.—an office of great responsibility.

Fabri. The mechanics, carpenters, smiths, etc., in the Roman army. After the end of the republican age they formed an independent corps in every army, and were employed especially in the restoration of bridges, siege and defence works, artillery, etc. They were under the command of the *praefectus fabrûm*, or chief engineer, who was chosen by the general-in-chief, and was immediately responsible to him.

Fabrĭca, sc. *officina*. A general name for the workshop of a mechanic, especially of a carpenter (Lucret. iv. 513) or cabinet-maker.

Fabricius. (1) GAIUS, surnamed LUSCĪNUS. A Roman, consul for the first time in the year B.C. 283, when he triumphed over the Boii and Etrurians. After the defeat of the Romans, under the consul Laevinus, by Pyrrhus (B.C. 281), Fabricius was sent by the Senate as legate to the king, to treat for the ransom of the prisoners, or, according to others, to propose terms of peace. Pyrrhus is said to have endeavoured to bribe him by large offers, which Fabricius, poor as he was, rejected with scorn, to the great admiration of the king. Fabricius being again consul, B.C. 279, was sent against Pyrrhus, who was then encamped near Tarentum. The physician of the king is said to have come secretly to the Roman camp, and to have promised Fabricius to poison his master for a bribe. The consul, indignant at this, had him put in fetters and sent back to Pyrrhus, on whom this instance of Roman integrity made a strong impression. Pyrrhus soon after sailed for Sicily, whither he was called by the Syracusans, then hard pressed by the Carthaginians. Fabricius, having defeated the Samnites, Lucanians, and Bruttii, who had joined Pyrrhus against Rome, triumphed over these nations. Pyrrhus, afterwards returning to Italy, was finally defeated and driven away by M'. Curius Dentatus, B.C. 276. Two years after, Fabricius being consul for the third time, with Claudius Cinna for his colleague, ambassadors came from King Ptolemy of Egypt to contract an alliance with Rome. Several instances are related of the extreme frugality and simplicity which marked the manners of Fabricius. When censor, he dismissed from the Senate P. Cornelius Rufinus, who had been twice consul, and had also held the dictatorship, because he had in his possession ten pounds' weight of silver plate. Fabricius died poor, and the Senate was obliged to make provision for his daughters (Plut. *Pyrrh.*), and in order to show the greatest possible respect for his memory he was interred within the Pomoerium, though the law forbade such burials. (2) LUCIUS. A *curator viarum*, B.C. 62, who built the Pons Fabricius between the city and the Insula Tiberina (q. v.).

Fabricius, IOANNES ALBERTUS (JOHANN ALBERT FABER). A celebrated bibliographer, born at Leipzig, November 11, 1668. He studied at Leipzig and Quedlinburg, taking the degrees in philosophy, and afterwards pursuing medicine and theology. At Quedlinburg, two books that he found in the library of Samuel Schmidt (Barthuiss's *Adversaria* and Morhoff's *Polyhistor*) gave him the suggestions that led to the preparation of his two great works, the *Bibliotheca Latina* and the still more important *Bibliotheca Graeca.* The first appeared at Hamburg in 1697, and was revised and emended by Ernesti in three volumes (Leipzig, 1773). Its secondary title explains its scope: *Notitia Auctorum Veterum Latinorum Quorumcumque Scripta ad Nos Venerunt.* The divisions adopted in this compilation are, (1) The writers preceding the age of Tiberius; (2) The writers from Tiberius to the Antonines; (3) The writers from the Antonines to the decay of the language; (4) The fragments from old authors, with chapters on the early Christian literature. The *Bibliotheca Graeca* is further styled *Notitia Scriptorum Veterum Graecorum Quorumcumque Monumenta Integra aut Fragmenta Edita Extant, tum Plerorumque e Manuscript. ac Deperditis.* This work, which has been styled *maximus antiquae eruditionis thesaurus*, is in fourteen quarto volumes, appearing at Hamburg at intervals from 1705 to 1728, and subsequently revised by Harles (Hamburg, 1790). Its divisions are marked off by Homer, Plato, Christ, Constantine, and by the capture of Constantinople in 1453, with a sixth section devoted to canon law, medicine, and jurisprudence. Besides these two great compilations, Fabricius, who was a most voluminous writer, put forth 126 other works, some of them, however, being books that he edited only, and none of them of any especial interest to the classical student.

Fabricius held at different times the posts of librarian and Professor of Rhetoric and Ethics (1699), and Rector of the School of St. John at Hamburg. He declined chairs at Greifswald (1701) and Wittenberg. He died at Hamburg, April 30, 1736. The details of his life are given by his son-in-law, Reimar, in his work *De Vita et Scriptis J. A. Fabricii Commentarius* (Hamburg, 1757).

Fabrilia. Mechanics' tools of every description (Hor. *Epist.* ii. 1. 116).

Fabŭla Milesia. See NOVELS AND ROMANCES.

Fabŭla Palliāta, Togāta, etc. See COMOEDIA.

Fabŭla Rhinthonĭca. See RHINTHON.

Fabŭlae Perottiānae. See PHAEDRUS.

Facciolati, JACOPO. A famous Italian lexicographer and stylist, born at Toriggia in 1682. He studied at Padua, and in the university of that city was made Professor of Logic and Regent of the Schools, continuing this connection for forty-five years. After putting forth several new editions of existing books, such as the *Thesaurus Ciceronianus* of Nizolius, and the polyglot vocabulary in seven languages of Calepino, he began his magnificent work, the *Totius Latinitatis Lexicon*, the first volume of which appeared at Padua in 1771. Of this splendid production it has been said that the whole body of Latinity, if lost, might be restored from this great lexicon. It is, in fact, the source of all the Latin lexicons now in use, and is an imperishable monument to the learning, industry, and judgment of its chief author. In its preparation, Facciolati was ably assisted by his pupil, Egidio Forcellini (q. v.), who had also aided in the Calepine vocabulary, and to whom is said to be due the suggestion of the new lexicon itself. The fourth and last volume appeared in 1771, after the death of both the editors. Subsequent editions are the English one in two vols. (London, 1826), and that of De Vit (1858–87). Facciolati was a writer of extremely elegant Latin, and a number of his letters have been published. His reputation in his own lifetime was very great, so that he received most flattering offers from the other universities of Europe, all of which he declined. He died at Padua in 1769. His life has been written by Ferrari (1799) and Gennari (1818). See the article LEXICON.

Facetiae. See JESTS.

Factiōnes Aurigārum. See CIRCUS, p. 356.

Factor. The player who threw the ball on receiving it from the *dator* in the game of ball spoken of as *datatim ludere*. See PILA.

Factorium. An oil-press, so called from the *factor*, who pressed the olives (Cat. *R. R.* 64, 1; 66, 1). The name *factum* was given to the oil pressed out at one making (Varr. *R. R.* i. 24, 3).

Faelis (*αἴλουρος* or *αἰέλουρος*, "wag-tail"). The

cat, an animal domesticated by the Egyptians as early as the thirteenth century B.C., and by them regarded as a sacred animal, so that it was a capi-

Ancient Egyptian Cats. (Painting from the Monuments.)

tal offence to kill one (Diod. Sic. i. 83). The cat typified to them the lunar goddess Pasht, and was frequently embalmed and sent to Bubastis for burial. (See BUBASTIS.) The early Greeks and Romans do not appear to have domesticated the cat as we have done, but instead employed a species of weasel (γαλῆ, *mustela*), or the white-breasted marten (*faelis foina*). See Hehn, *Kulturpflanzen und Hausthiere* (last ed. rev. by Schrader, 1894); and Houghton's *Natural History of the Ancients*, pp. 40–50. Cats first appear in literature as house animals about the fourth century A.D., but even as late as the Middle Ages they were comparatively rare and costly.

Faesŭlae. The modern Fiesole; a city of Etruria, situated on a hill three miles northeast of Florence. It was the headquarters of Catiline's army (Cic. *Cat.* iii. 6).

Fala or **Phala.** (1) A wooden structure, of considerable height, used in sieges, from which missiles were thrown (Fest. p. 88, 12; Ennius *ap.* Non. p. 114, 7). (2) Phalae are mentioned by Juvenal (vi. 590) with the *columnae delphinorum* in the circus. Hence they are supposed by some writers to be columns on the *spina* of the circus, supporting the *ova*, as similar columns supported the dolphins. (See CIRCUS.) But Servius (*ad* Verg. *Aen.* ix. 705) says they were towers on which fights took place, erected between the *euripus* and the *metae;* and they were probably movable towers used in the sham fights of the circus.

Falacrīné or **Falacrīnum.** A Sabine town between Asculum and Reaté. It was the birthplace of the emperor Vespasian.

Falarīca. (1) A peculiar kind of spear intended to be discharged as a missile from the hand, and employed in warfare as well as the chase (Verg. *Aen.* ix. 705; Livy, xxxiv. 14; Grat. *Cyneg.* 342). It is described as a missile of the largest dimensions (Non. s. v.), with an immense iron head and strong wooden shaft, weighted near the top by a circular mass of lead (Isidor. *Orig.* xviii. 7, 8), exactly as represented by the annexed figure, from an ancient monument published by Alstorp (*De Hastis Veterum*, p. 158).

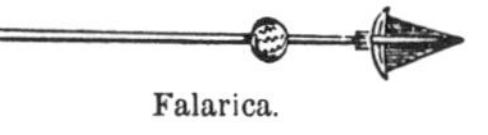

Falarica.

Another specimen of very similar character is exhibited on a sepulchral marble discovered at Aquileia, published by Bertoli. (2) A missile invented by the people of Saguntum, similar in many respects to the preceding, but of a still more formidable description (Livy, xxi. 8). It was chiefly employed in sieges, and discharged with prodigious violence, by the assistance of machinery (Lucan, vi. 198), from a lofty wooden tower.

Falconia, PROBA. See PROBA.

Falcŭla. See FALX.

Faleria. A town of Picenum, southwest of Firmum, now Falleroni (Pliny, *H. N.* iii. 13).

Falerii or **Falerium.** A town in Etruria, situated on a height near Mount Soracté, originally a Pelasgic town, but afterwards one of the twelve Etruscan cities. Its inhabitants were called Falisci, and were regarded by many as of the same race as the Aequi, whence we find them often called Aequi Falisci. After a long struggle with Rome, the Faliscans revolted again at the close of the First Punic War (B.C. 241), when the Romans destroyed their city. A new town was built on the plain. The white cows of Falerii were valued

Gate of Falerii.

at Rome for sacrifices. There still remain ruins of a theatre, forum, *piscina*, gate, etc., of Roman construction, and a number of tombs.

Falernus Ager. A district in the north of Campania, extending from the Massic hills to the river Vulturnus. It produced some of the finest wine in Italy, which was reckoned only second to the wine of Setia. See VINUM.

Falisci. See DIALECTS; FALERII.

Faliscus. See GRATTIUS.

Falsarius. See FALSUM.

Falsum. The crime of falsum is not defined by Roman legal writers, but it consisted of acts of fraud which were injurious to *fides publica*, such as forgery, counterfeiting money, and perverting the course of justice by fraud and perjury. The oldest legislative provisions at Rome against any acts of this description are those of the Twelve Tables, to the effect that a person who gave false testimony should be thrown from the Tarpeian

Rock (Gell. xxi. 53), and that a judge who took a bribe should be liable to capital punishment (Gell. xxi. 7); but there were trials for false testimony before the enactment of the Twelve Tables (Livy, iii. 24, 25, 29; iv. 21). The next legislation in falsum, so far as is known, was contained in one of the Leges Corneliae passed in the time of the dictator Sulla, which was divided, according to Cicero, into two heads, the Lex Testamentaria and the Lex Numaria (*Verr.* ii. 1, 42), with reference to the two species of the crime the statute was directed against. Paulus, who gives its provisions, entitles it Lex Cornelia Testamentaria; it is also known by the more general title Lex Cornelia de Falsis.

The Lex Cornelia appears to have included only two specific kinds of falsum: (1) forgery and suppression of wills, and (2) adulteration of the coinage.

An offence against either branch of this law was a *crimen publicum*, and was under the cognizance of a standing *quaestio*. The punishment of falsum under the law (at least when Paulus wrote) was *deportatio in insulam* (see DEPORTATIO) for the "honestiores," and the mines, crucifixion, or other degrading punishment for the "humiliores." In place of *deportatio in insulam* the punishment, according to the statute itself, was probably the old form of banishment, known as *ignis et aquae interdictiō* (q. v.). The property of a convicted person was confiscated.

The penalty of the Lex Cornelia was extended by piecemeal legislation to cases not comprised in the lex, but all of a similar kind. This supplementary law is sometimes referred in legal treatises to the Lex Cornelia, as if it had been an original part of that law. The instrument fabricated or falsified might be either public or private, as e. g. a rescript or edict of the emperor, an account book, or an instrument of sale.

Persons guilty of falsifying documents are called *falsarii*. As a precaution against such persons, it was enacted in the time of Nero that *tabulae* or written contracts should be pierced with holes and a triple thread passed through the holes, in addition to the signature (Suet. *Ner.* c. 17; Paul. v. 25, 6). In the time of Nero it was also provided that the first two parts (*cerae*) of a will should have only the testator's signature, and the remaining one those of the witnesses. Likewise, in order to prevent fraud, it was enacted under the emperor Claudius that a person who was employed by a testator to write a will should be liable to the penalty of the Lex Cornelia if he inscribed a legacy to himself, although he did so at the dictation of the testator (Cod. ix. 23, 3; Suetonius, *Ner.* 17, attributes this law to Nero). The Lex de Falsis was further extended to fraudulent assumptions of names and rank, and to false pretences, as in the case of a contract to sell a thing to a person, when the vendor had already contracted to sell the same thing to some one else. The *crimen falsi* was also made to include perjury, the corruption of judges, and other kindred offences. By a senatusconsultum in the fourteenth year of Tiberius, the penalties of the law were extended to those who for money undertook to maintain causes, or to procure testimony; and by a senatusconsultum passed somewhat earlier, conspiracies for the ruin of innocent persons were comprised within the limits of the law.

According to Paulus (v. 25, 1), the refusal to accept in payment genuine coin stamped with the head of the princeps was on the same footing as the adulteration of the coinage, though in this case the element of fraud seems wanting. The use of false measures and weights was punished as falsum. It appears from numerous passages in the Roman writers that the crime of falsum in its different forms was very common, and especially in the case of wills. See Rein, *Das Criminalrecht der Römer*, p. 774, etc.

Faltonia, PROBA. See PROBA.

Falx, dim. **Falcŭla** (ἅρπη, δρέπανον, dim. δρεπάνιον). A sickle; a scythe; a pruning-knife or pruning-hook; a bill; a falchion; a halbert.

As *culter* denoted a knife with one straight edge, "falx" signified any similar instrument, the single edge of which was curved (δρέπανον εὐκαμπές; γαμψὰς δρεπάνας; *curvae falces; curvamine falcis ahenae; adunca falce*). By additional epithets the various uses of the falx were indicated, and its corresponding varieties in form and size. Thus the sickle, because it was used by reapers, was called *falx messoria;* the scythe, which was employed in mowing hay, was called *falx foenaria;* the pruning-knife and the bill, on account of their use in dressing vines, as well as in hedging and in cutting off the shoots and branches of trees, were distinguished by the appellation of *falx putatoria, vinitoria, arboraria,* or *silvatica,* or by the diminutive *falcula.*

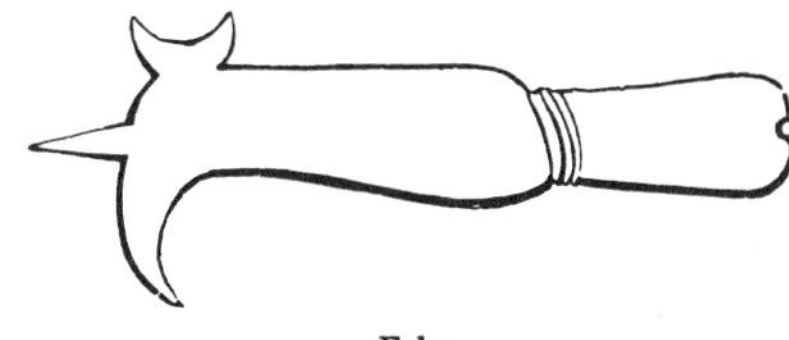

Falx.

The illustration is taken from a MS. of Columella, and explains his description of the various parts of the *falx vinitoria.* (See CULTER.) After the removal of a branch by the pruning-hook, it was often smoothed, as in modern gardening, by the chisel. (See DOLABRA.) The edge of the falx was often toothed or serrated (ἅρπην καρχαρόδοντα; *denticulata*). The indispensable process of sharpening these instruments (ἅρπην χαρασσέμεναι, ἅρπην εὐκαμπῆ νεοθηγέα) was effected by whetstones, which the Romans obtained from Crete and other distant places, with the addition of oil or water, which the mower (*foenisex*) carried in a horn upon his thigh.

Numerous as were the uses to which the falx was applied in agriculture and horticulture, its employment in battle was almost equally varied, though not so frequent. The Geloni were noted for its use. It was the weapon with which Zeus wounded Typhon; with which Heracles slew the Lernaean Hydra; and with which Hermes cut off the head of Argus (*falcato ense; harpen Cyllenida*). Perseus, having received the same weapon from Hermes, or, according to other authorities, from Hephaestus, used it to decapitate Medusa and to slay the sea-monster. Hence, it may be concluded that the falchion was a weapon of the most remote antiquity; that it was girt like a dagger upon the waist; that it was held in the hand by a short hilt; and that, as it was, in fact, a dagger or sharp-pointed blade, with a proper falx projecting from one side, it was thrust into the flesh up to this lateral curvature.

The weapon which has just been described, when attached to the end of a pole, would assume the form and be applicable to all the purposes of the mediæval halberd. Such must have been the *asseres falcati* used by the Romans at the siege of Ambracia. Sometimes the iron head was so large as to be fastened, instead of the ram's head, to a wooden beam, and worked by men under a *testudo* (q. v.).

Lastly, the Assyrians, the Persians, the Medes, and the Syrians in Asia, and the Gauls and Britons in Europe (see COVINUS), made themselves formidable on the field of battle by the use of chariots with scythes fixed at right angles (εἰς πλάγιον) to the axle and turned downward, or inserted parallel to the axle into the felly of the wheel, so as to revolve, when the chariot was put in motion, with more than thrice the velocity of the chariot itself; and sometimes also projecting from the extremities of the axle. See CURRUS.

Familia. The Latin name for a household community, consisting of the master of the house (*pater familias*), his wife (*mater familias*), his sons and unmarried daughters (*filii* and *filiae familias*), the wives, sons, and unmarried daughters of the sons, and the slaves. All the other members of the family were subject to the authority of the *pater familias*. (For the power of the husband over his wife, see MANUS.) In virtue of his paternal authority (*patria potestas*), the *pater familias* had absolute authority over his children. He might, if he liked, expose them, sell them, or kill them. These rights, as manners were gradually softened, were more and more rarely enforced; but they legally came to an end only when the father died, lost his citizenship, or of his own will freed his son from his authority. (See EMANCIPATIO.) They could, however, be transferred to another person if the son were adopted, or the daughter married. A son, if of full age, was not in any way interfered with by the *patria potestas* in the exercise of his civil rights. But in the exercise of his legal rights as an individual, he was dependent always on his father. He could, for instance, own no property; but all that he acquired was, in the eye of the law, at the exclusive disposal of his father. The *pater familias* alone had the right of making dispositions of the family property by mortgage, sale, or will. See McLennan, *The Patriarchal Theory* (1885).

Family Names. See NOMEN.

Famōsi Libelli. See LIBELLUS.

Fanatĭci. See FANUM.

Fannia. A Minturnian woman who entertained Marius when he came to Minturnae in his flight (B.C. 88), because though formerly he had pronounced her guilty of adultery, he had compelled her husband Tatinius to restore her dowry (Val. Max. viii. 2, § 3).

Fannius Caepio. A Roman who conspired with Murena against Augustus (B.C. 22), and was put to death.

Fannius Quadrātus. See QUADRATUS.

Fannius Strabo, C. A son-in-law of C. Laelius Sapiens (q. v.), introduced by Cicero as a speaker in his *De Republica* and his *Laelius* (*De Amicitia*).

Fanum. Any locality consecrated by the pontiffs—a word derived by the ancients from *fari*, because the *pontifices in sacrando fati sunt finem* (Varr. *L. L.* vi. 54; Fest. pp. 88, 93). It was a consecrated spot, whether a building was erected upon it or not. The consecrated places in the Forum, where the couches of the gods were placed in the *lectisternium* (q. v.), were also called fana, in reference to which the phrase *fana sistere* was used (Fest. p. 351). Even a tree struck by lightning was deemed a *fanum* (Fest. p. 92). Everything not consecrated—that is, not a fanum—was considered *profanum*; and a *res fanatica* might, in accordance with the pontifical law, be again made into a *res profana* by certain ceremonies (Macrob. *Sat.* iii. 3, 4).

Fanatici, properly speaking persons belonging to a fanum, were more specifically priests of the goddess of Comana in Cappadocia, whose worship was introduced into Rome under the name of Bellona. They performed the worship with wild and frantic rites, whence the word *fanaticus* obtained its secondary meaning, and has passed into modern languages. They were also called *Bellonarii* (Acro *ad* Hor. *Sat.* ii. 3, 223). In celebrating the festival of the goddess they marched through the city in dark clothes, with wild cries, blowing trumpets, beating cymbals and drums, and in the temple inflicting wounds upon themselves, the blood from which they poured out as an offering to the goddess (Tibull. i. 6, 43 foll.; Hor. *Sat.* ii. 3, 223; Juv. vi. 511; Mart. xi. 84, 3, xii. 57, 11; Lucan, i. 565; Lamprid. *Commod.* 9). *Fanatici* was also the name given to the priests of Isis (*C. I. L.* vi. n. 2234) and Cybelé (Juv. ii. 122; Prudent. *Perist.* x. 1061).

Fanum Fortūnae. The modern Fano; a town in Umbria at the mouth of the Metaurus, with a celebrated temple of Fortuna, whence the town derived its name.

Farce. See COMOEDIA; RHINTHON; SATIRA.

Farfărus. See FABARIS.

Farmers of Public Taxes. See PUBLICANI; TELONAE.

Farming. See AGRICULTURA.

Farnese Bull. A remarkable monolithic group of statuary by the Rhodian sculptors Apollonius and Tauriscus, representing the sons of Antiopé binding Dircé to a wild bull. (For the story see ANTIOPÉ; DIRCÉ.) This group was found at Rome in the Thermae of Caracalla in a badly mutilated condition, and was restored under the supervision of Michael Angelo and, later, by the Milanese sculptor Bianchi. The boldness and life of the group originally carved from a single block of marble are unrivalled by any similar work. It is represented in the illustration on page 86. The parts restored are the head of the bull, the whole of Antiopé (except the feet), the upper parts of Dircé, and all of Zetheus and Amphion except one torso and one leg. The group is now in the Museo Nazionale at Naples.

Farnese Hercules. A colossal statue executed by Glycon of Athens, and representing Hercules clothed in a lion's skin and resting on his huge club, while in his right hand he holds the three golden apples of the Hesperides. The statue, which is now in the Museo Nazionale at Naples, was found at Rome in the Thermae of Caracalla in 1540. It then lacked the legs and the left hand, which were restored by Della Porta after a model in terra cotta by Michael Angelo. Twenty years later the original legs were found in a well three miles from the place whence the statue itself was taken. The work is evidently of a comparatively late period, and shows a tendency to exaggeration in the overstrained effort to express muscular strength, which led Thackeray to characterize it as a "clumsy, caricatured porter." It is reproduced in the illustration on page 793.

Farreum. See MATRIMONIUM.

Fas. See FASTI; IUS.

Fasces. The Latin name for a bundle of rods, tied together by a red strap, and enclosing an axe, with its head outside. The fasces were originally the emblem of the king's absolute authority over life and limb, and as such passed over to the high magistrates of the Republic. In the city, however, the latter had to remove the axe and to lower the rods in the presence of the popular assembly as the sovereign power. The lowering of the fasces was also the form in which the lower officials saluted the higher. The king was preceded by lictors bearing twelve fasces, and so were the consuls and proconsuls. The proconsuls, however, were, since the time of Augustus, only allowed this number if they had actually been consuls previously. The dictator had twenty-four fasces, as representing the two consuls, and his *magister equitum* had six. Six was also the number allotted to the proconsuls and propraetors outside the city, and in the imperial age to those proconsuls who had provinces in virtue of their having held the praetorship. The praetors of the city had two, the imperial legates administering particular provinces had five fasces. One was allotted to the *flamen Dialis* and (from or after B.C. 42) to the Vestal Virgins. Fasces crowned with bay were, in the republican age, the *insignia* of an officer who was saluted as Imperator. During the imperial age, this title was conferred on the emperor at his accession, and soon confined exclusively to him. The emperor was accordingly preceded by twelve *fasces laureati*. The lictors held their fasces over the left shoulder; but at funerals, the fasces of a deceased magistrate, and his arms, were carried reversed behind the bier.

Lictor with Fasces. (From a bas-relief in the Museum of Verona.)

The fasces appear to have been in later times made of birch (*betulla*, Pliny, *H. N.* xvi. § 75), but earlier of the twigs of the elm (Plaut. *Asin.* ii. 3, 74; iii. 2, 29). They are said to have been derived from Vetulonia, a city of Etruria (Sil. Ital. viii. 485; cf. Livy, i. 8); but for this there is no real authority (cf. Schwegler, *Röm. Gesch.* i. 278, 581, 671).

The next illustration, taken from the consular coins of C. Norbanus, contains, in addition to the fasces, the one a *spica* and *caduceus*, and the other a *prora*, *caduceus*, and *spica*.

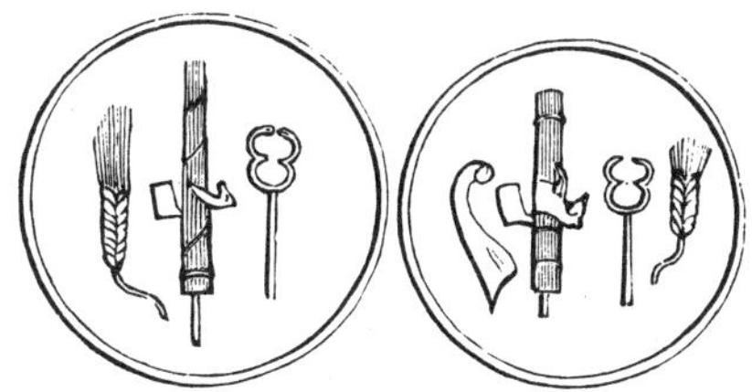

Fasces on Consular Coins.

Fascia, dim. **Fasciŏla** (ταινία, ἀπόδεσμος). Any long, narrow strip of cloth employed as a bandage. (1) A band worn round the head as an ensign of royalty (Suet. *Iul.* 79). (2) A band worn by women round the chest for the improvement of the figure (Terent. *Eun.* ii. 3, 23; Propert. v. 9, 49; Ovid, *A. A.* iii. 276, 622). See STROPHIUM. (3) A band worn round the legs and shins, a kind of stocking; hence called *fasciae crurales* (*Dig.* xxxiv. 2, 25) and *tibiales* (Suet. *Aug.* 82). That such bandages also covered the feet is clear from the epithet of *fasciae pedules* (*Dig.* xxxiv. 2, 26). Cicero reproached Clodius with effeminate habits for wearing purple fasciae upon his feet, and the *calantica*, a woman's ornament, upon his head (*De Har. Resp.* 21, § 44; *Fragm. Or. in Clod. et Cur.*; cf. Non. p. 537). Afterwards *fasciae crurales* became common even with the male sex (Hor. *Sat.* ii. 3, 255; Val. Max. vi. 2, § 7). White fasciae, worn by men (Val. Max. l. c.), were a sign of extraordinary refinement in dress; the mode of cleaning them was by rubbing them with a white, tenacious earth, resembling our pipe-clay (Cic. *Ad Att.* ii. 3). (4) The sacking of the bed on which the mattress rested (Mart. v. 62, xiv. 159). (5) Fasciae were also the swaddling-clothes in which infants were wrapped (Plaut. *Truc.* v. 13). (6) In architecture, any long, flat surface of wood, stone, or marble, such as the band which divides the architrave from the frieze in the Doric order, and the surfaces into which the architrave itself is divided in the Ionic and Corinthian orders (Vitruv. iii. 5, 10). See EPISTYLIUM.

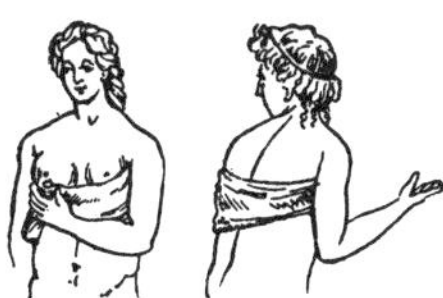

Fascia Worn by Women. (Rich.)

Fascia, Swaddling-clothes. (Pompeian Painting.)

Fascia. (From the Temple of Bacchus at Teos.)

Fascĭnum. Enchantment by the evil eye, words, or cries, exercised on persons (especially children), animals, and things, as, for instance, on a piece of ground. The word was also applied to the counter-charm, by which it was supposed that the enchantment could be averted, or even turned against the enchanter. Amulets of various kinds were employed as counter-charms. They were supposed either to procure the protection of a particular deity, or to send the enchanter mad by means of terrible, ridiculous, or obscene objects. The name fascinum was thus specially applied to the *phallus* (q. v.), or effigy of the male organ of generation, which was the favourite counter-charm of the Romans. An image of this fascinum was contained in the bulla worn as an amulet by children, and was also put under the chariot of a general at his triumph, as a protection against envy. See AMULETUM; and MALUS OCULUS in Appendix.

Fascĭnus. An early Latin divinity identical with Mutunus or Tutunus (q. v.). He was worshipped as the author of sorcery and evil spirits, and his symbol was the *fascinum.* See AMULETUM; FASCINUM; PHALLUS; PRIAPUS.

Fasēlus (φάσηλος). A light boat or skiff, made of wicker-work, papyrus, or even of baked earth (*fictilis*, Juv. xv. 127), and said to have received its name from the *faselus* or kidney-bean, because of a resemblance in shape. It was of various sizes, and used with or without sails (Cic. *Ad Att.* i. 13; Serv. *ad* Verg. *Georg.* iv. 289).

Fasti, sc. *dies.* Properly speaking, the Roman court-days, on which the praetor was allowed to give his judgments in the solemn formula *Do Dico Addico*, and generally to act in his judicial capacity. The name was further applied to the days on which it was lawful (*fas*) to summon the assembly and the Senate (*dies comitiales*); for these days might be used as court-days in case the assembly did not meet; while on *dies fasti* proper no meeting of the *comitia* could take place. The opposite of *dies fasti* were the *dies nefasti*, or days on which on account of purifications, holidays, *feriae*, and on other religious grounds, the courts could not sit, nor the Comitia assemble. (See FERIAE.) The *dies religiosi* were also counted as *nefasti.* Besides the 38–45 *dies fasti* proper, the 188–194 *dies comitiales*, the 48–50 *dies nefasti*, and 53–59 *dies religiosi*, there were 8 *dies intercisi*, which were *nefasti* in the morning and evening because of certain sacrifices which took place then, but fasti for the remaining hours. There were also 3 *dies fissi* (split days), which were *nefasti* until the conclusion of a particular proceeding—e. g. the removal of the sweepings from the Temple of Vesta on June 15th, but *fasti* afterwards.

The division of days into *fasti* and *profesti*, or holidays and workdays, only affected private life, though many *dies nefasti*, as *feriae*, would be identical with *dies fasti.*

The list of the *dies fasti* was of immense importance as affecting legal proceedings, and indeed all public life. For a long time it was in the hands of the *pontifices*, and was thus only accessible to the patricians; but at last (B.C. 304) Gnaeus Flavius published it and made it generally accessible. This list, called simply *Fasti*, was the origin of the Roman calendar, which bore the same name. In this calendar the days of the year are divided into weeks of eight days each, indicated by the letters A to H. Each day has marks indicating its number in the month, its legal significance (F = *fastus*, N = *nefastus*, C = *comitialis*, EN = *intercisus*). The festivals, sacrifices, and games occurring on it are also added, as well as notices of historical occurrences, the rising and setting of the stars, and other matters. No trace remains of any calendar previous to Caesar; but several calendars composed after Caesar's reform have been preserved. Ovid's *Fasti* is a poetical explanation of the Roman festivals of the first six months. We have also many fragments of calendars, painted or engraved on stone, belonging to Rome and other Italian cities; for it was common to put up calendars of this kind in public places, temples, and private houses. There are two complete calendars in existence—one an official list written by Furius Dionysius Philocalus in A.D. 354, the other a Christian version of the official calendar, made by Polemius Silvius in A.D. 448. See CALENDARIUM; DIES.

The word fasti was further applied to the annual lists of the triumphs, high officials, consuls, dictators, censors, and priests. These lists were originally, like the other fasti, made out by the *pontifices.* Some fragments of them have survived, among which may be mentioned the Fasti Capitolini, so called from the Roman Capitol, where they are now preserved. They were originally, in B.C. 36–30, engraved on the marble wall of the Regia, or official residence of the Pontifex Maximus, and afterwards continued first to B.C. 12, and afterwards to A.D. 13.

Fasti Hellenĭci and **Fasti Romāni.** See CLINTON, HENRY FYNES.

Fastigium (ἀετός, ἀέτωμα). Literally, a slope; in architecture, a pediment. The triangle which surmounts each end of a rectangular building, and which, in fact, represents the gable end of the roof. (See ANTAE.) It is composed of the cornice of the entablature which forms its base, the two converging cornices at the sides, and the *tympanum* or flat surface enclosed by them, so called from its resemblance to a three-cornered tambourine (Vitruv. iii. 3, iv. 6; Cic. *de Orat.* iii. 46, § 180; Livy, xl. 2). This flat surface was generally ornamented with sculpture; originally, in the early temples of Zeus, with a simple eagle as a symbol of the god, an instance of which is afforded by the coin represented in the above illustration (Beger, *Spicil. Antiq.* p. 6), whence the Greek name ἀετός, which was at first applied to the *tympanum* and afterwards to the whole pediment, and in after-times with elaborate sculptures in high relief. See ANTEFIXA; TEMPLUM.

Fastigium. (From a coin.)

The dwelling-houses of the Romans might have sloping roofs, but ornamental gables were not allowed; hence, when the word is applied to them, it is not in its strictly technical sense, but designates the roof simply, and is to be understood of one which rises to a ridge as distinguished from a flat one (Cic. *ad. Q. Fr.* iii. 1, 4, § 14; Verg. *Aen.* viii. 491). Among other divine honours, the Romans decreed to Caesar the liberty of erecting a fastigium to his house (Plut. *Caes.* 81; see ACROTERIUM)—that is, a portico and pediment towards the street like that of a temple. See DOMUS.

Fatum. See FORTUNA; MOERAE; NEMESIS; TYCHÉ.

Fatuus, Fatua. See FAUNUS, FAUNA.

Fauces. See DOMUS.

Fauna, Faula, or **Fatua.** A goddess of the Latins. According to the old Roman legends, by which all the Italian deities were originally mortals, she was the daughter of Picus, and the sister and wife of Faunus. One account makes her to have never left her bower, or let herself be seen of men; and to have been deified for this reason, becoming identical with the Bona Dea, and no man being allowed to enter her temple (Macrob. i. 12). According to another tradition, she was not only remarkable for her modesty, but also for her extensive and varied knowledge. Having, however, on one occasion, made free with the contents of a jar of wine, she was beaten to death by her husband with myrtle-twigs. Repenting, however, soon after of the deed, he bestowed on her divine honours. Hence, in the celebration of her sacred rites, myrtle-boughs were carefully excluded; nor was any wine allowed to be brought, under that name, into her temple; but it was called "honey," and the vessel containing it also was termed *mellarium*, "honey-jar" (cf. Macrob. i. 12). Fauna is said to have given oracles from her temple after death, which circumstance, according to some, affords an etymology for the name Fatua or Fatuella, which was often borne by her (from *fari*, "to declare"). There can be little doubt that Fauna is identical not only with the Bona Dea, but with Terra, Tellus, and Ops—in other words, with the Earth personified (Macrob. l. c.). See FAUNUS.

Faunalia. Festivals at Rome in honour of Faunus. They were celebrated on the 13th of February, or the Ides of the month. On this same day occurred the slaughter of the Fabii (Ovid, *Fast.* ii. 193 foll.). There was another festival of the same name, which was celebrated on the Nones of December (Hor. *Carm.* iii. 18).

Faunus or **Fatuus.** "The well-wisher" (from *favere*), or perhaps "the speaker" (from *fari*). (On the etymology of the word see Nettleship, *Lectures and Essays*, pp. 50–54). One of the oldest and most popular Roman deities, who was identified with the Greek Pan on account of the similarity of their attributes. (See PAN.) As a good spirit of the forest, plains, and fields, he gave fruitfulness to the cattle, and was hence called Inuus. With all this he was also a god of prophecy, called by the name of Fatuus, with oracles in the sacred groves of Tibur, around the well Albunea, and on the Aventine. The responses were said to have been given in Saturnian verse. (Cf. Varro, *L. L.* vii. 36.) Faunus revealed the future in dreams and strange voices, communicated to his votaries while sleeping in his precincts upon the fleeces of sacrificed lambs. A goddess of like attributes, called Fauna and Fatua, was associated in his worship. She was regarded sometimes as his wife, sometimes as his sister. (See BONA DEA.) Just as Pan was accompanied by the Πανίσκοι, or little Pans, so the existence of many Fauni was assumed besides the chief Faunus. They were imagined as merry, capricious beings, and in particular as mischievous goblins who caused nightmares. In fable Faunus appears as an old king of Latium, son of Picus, and grandson of Saturnus, father of Latinus by the nymph Marica. After his death he is raised to the position of a tutelary deity of the land, for his many services to agriculture and cattle-breeding. Two festivals, called Faunalia, were celebrated in his honour—one on the 13th of February, in the temple on the island in the Tiber, the other on the 5th of December, when the peasants brought him rustic offerings and amused themselves with dancing.

Faunus. (Gori, *Gem. Ant. Flor.* vol. i. pl. 94.)

Fausta. (1) CORNELIA, daughter of Sulla, and married to Milo, the partisan of Cicero. She disgraced herself by a criminal affair with the historian Sallust (Hor. *Sat.* i. 2, 41; Schol. Cruq. *et* Acr. *ad loc.*). (2) FLAVIA, the daughter of Maximian, and wife of Constantine the Great. When her father wished her to join him in a plot for assassinating her husband, she disclosed the whole affair to the latter. After exercising the most complete ascendency over the mind of her husband, she was eventually put to death by him, on his discovering the falsity of a charge which she had made against Crispus, the son of Constantine by a previous marriage (Eutrop. x. 2, 4; Victor. *Epit.* 40, 41). See CONSTANTINUS.

Faustīna. (1) ANNIA GALERIA, daughter of Annius Verus, prefect of Rome. She married Antoninus Pius before his adoption by Hadrian, and died in the third year of her husband's reign, thirty-six years of age (A.D. 141). She was notorious for her licentiousness, yet her husband appeared blind to her frailties, and after her death even accorded unto her divine honours. Her effigy appears on a large number of medals (Dio Cass. xvii. 30; Capitol. *Anton. P.* 3). (2) ANNIA, or the Younger, daughter of the preceding, married her cousin Marcus Aurelius, and died A.D. 176, in a village of Cappadocia, at the foot of Mount Taurus, on her husband's return from Syria. She is represented by Dio Cassius and Capitolinus as even more profligate in her conduct than her mother; and yet Marcus, in his *Meditations* (i. 17), extols her obedience, simplicity, and affection. Her daughter Lucilla married

Faustina as Mater Castrorum.

Lucius Verus, whom Marcus Aurelius associated with him in the Empire, and her son Commodus succeeded his father as emperor (Capitol. *M. Aurel.* 6, 19, 26).

Faustĭtas. A goddess among the Romans, supposed to preside over cattle and the productions of the seasons generally. Faustitas is probably equivalent to the *Felicitas Temporum* of the Roman medals (Hor. *Carm.* iv. 5, 18).

Faustŭlus. The name of the shepherd who, in the old Roman legend, found Romulus and Remus being suckled by the she-wolf, and who took both the children to his home and brought them up. See ROMULUS.

Faventia. Now Faenza; a town in Gallia Cisalpina, on the river Anemo and the Via Aemilia. It was celebrated for its manufacture of linens (Pliny, *H. N.* xix. 1).

Favonius. See ZEPHYRUS.

Favonius, MARCUS. An imitator of Cato Uticensis, whose character and conduct he copied so closely as to receive the nickname of "Cato's ape." He seems to have had some ability as an orator, but no specimens of his speeches have descended to us. He was put to death by Octavianus after the battle of Philippi in B.C. 42. See Val. Max. vi. 2, § 7; Plut. *Cat. Min.* 32, 46; id. *Pomp.* 60, 67; id. *Brut.* 12, 34; id. *Caes.* 41.

Favorīnus (Φαβωρῖνος). A native of Arelaté in Gaul, who lived at Rome during the reigns of Trajan and Hadrian, and enjoyed a high degree of consideration. He is said to have been born an hermaphrodite or a eunuch, yet was once charged with adultery by a Roman of rank; so that he afterwards used to boast of three things—that being a eunuch, he had been accused of adultery; that though a Gaul, he both wrote and spoke Greek; and that though he had given offence to the emperor, he still lived. He wrote numerous works, but no part of them has reached us except a few fragments in Stobaeus. Aulus Gellius, however, has preserved for us some of his dissertations in a Latin dress (*Noct. Att.* xii. 1; xiv. 1, 2; xvii. 10). Gellius, in fact, regarded him with great admiration, and in his *Noctes Atticae* plays Boswell in a mild way to Favorinus's Johnson. Favorinus loved to write on topics out of the common path, and more or less whimsical; he composed, for example, a eulogy on Thersites, another on quartan fever, etc. Having had the misfortune to offend the emperor Hadrian, his statues, which the Athenians had raised to him, were thrown down by that same people. He bequeathed his library and mansion at Rome to Herodes Atticus. Favorinus was a friend of Plutarch, who dedicated a work to him. For further particulars relating to this individual, consult Philostratus (*Vit. Sophist.* i. 8, 1), and Lucian (*Eunuch.* 7; *Demon.* 12 foll.), and Prof. Nettleship's paper on Aulus Gellius in his *Lectures and Essays*, etc. (1885).

Fax (φανός). A torch. The descriptions of poets and mythologists, and the works of ancient art, represent the torch as carried by Diana, Ceres, Bellona, Hymen, Phosphorus, by women in bacchanalian processions, and, in an inverted position, by Sleep and Death. In ancient marbles the torch appears to be formed of wooden staves or twigs, either bound by a rope drawn round them in a spiral form, or surrounded by circular bands at equal distances. The inside of the torch may be supposed to have been filled with flax, tow, or other vegetable fibres, the whole being abundantly impregnated with pitch, rosin, wax, oil, and other inflammable substances. As the principal use of torches was to give light to those who went abroad after sunset, the portion of the Roman day immediately succeeding sunset was called *fax* or *prima fax* (Gell. iii. 2, § 11; Macrob. *Sat.* i. 3, § 8). The torch was one of the necessary accompaniments and symbols of marriage. See MATRIMONIUM.

Fax. (Column of Antoninus.)

Feast Days. See DIES; FERIAE.

Feather-beds. See LECTUS.

Febris. The goddess, or rather the averter, of fever (Val. Max. ii. 5, 6; Cic. *N. D.* iii. 25). She had three sanctuaries at Rome.

Februalia. A feast at Rome of purification and atonement, in the month of February; it continued for twelve days. The month of February, which, together with January, was added by Numa to the ten months constituting the year of Romulus, derived its name from this general expiatory festival, the people being then purified (*februati*) from the sins of the whole year (Ovid, *Fast.* ii. 19).

February. See CALENDARIUM.

Februum. See LUPERCALIA.

Februus. An ancient Italian divinity, to whom the month of February was sacred. The name is connected with *februare* (to purify). See FEBRUALIA.

Feciāles. See FETIALES.

Felicĭtas. The personification of good fortune among the Romans. She was worshipped in various sanctuaries in Rome, her attributes being the cornucopia and the herald's staff. See FAUSTITAS.

Felis. See FAELIS.

Felix, ANTONIUS. Procurator of Judaea, in the reigns of Claudius and Nero. He induced Drusilla, wife of Azizus, king of Emesa, to leave her husband; and she was still living with Felix in A.D. 60, when St. Paul preached before him "of righteousness, temperance, and judgment to come." He was recalled in A.D. 62.

Felix, MINUCIUS. See MINUCIUS FELIX.

Felsĭna. The ancient capital of Northern Etruria, afterwards known as Bononia (Bologna), a name given to it by the Romans after they had conquered the Boii (B.C. 191), the Boii having taken the place from the Etruscans (Livy, xxxiii. 37, etc.). Here Octavianus, Antony, and Lepidus arranged the terms of the Second Triumvirate (Suet. *Aug.* 96). See Burton, *Etruscan Bologna* (1876). Under the Empire the city was sometimes the chosen residence of the emperors. In the Middle Ages it became a place of great importance.

Feminalia. A garment worn in winter by Augustus Caesar, who was very susceptible to cold (Suet. *Aug.* 82). Casaubon supposes them to have been bands or fillets (see FASCIA) wound about the thighs; they are more probably to be identified with the *bracae*, and may be best translated "drawers." These are mentioned under the name περιμηρίδια as worn by the Roman horsemen (Arrian, *Tact.* p. 14, ed. Blancard).

Fenestella. A scholarly Roman historian, who lived in the time of Augustus. The elder Pliny places his death in the reign of Tiberius. Fenestella wrote an historical work entitled *Annales*, from which Asconius Pedianus has derived many materials in his commentaries on Cicero's Orations. Of this work only fragments remain. Another production, *De Sacerdotiis et Magistratibus Romanorum*, is sometimes attributed to him, but incorrectly, since it is from the pen of Fiocchi (Floccus), a native of Florence, and was written at the commencement of the fourteenth century. Fenestella was seventy years old at the time of his death. The fragments of Fenestella's *Annales* are collected by H. Peter, *Hist. Frag.* 272. See the treatises by Mercklin, *De Fenestella Historico et Poeta* (Dorpat, 1844), and Poeth, *De Fenestella Historiarum Scriptore*, etc. (Bonn, 1849).

Fenestra. (1) A window. (See DOMUS, pp. 540, 551.) (2) A loophole in a tower from which arrows

Windows in the House of the Tragic Poet. (Pompeii.)

and other missiles were discharged (Caes. *B. C.* ii. 9). (3) A hole pierced in the lobe of the ear for holding ornaments (Juv. i. 104). See INAURIS.

Fenni. A savage people, reckoned by Tacitus (*Germ.* 46) as distinct from the natives of Germania. They probably dwelt in the eastern part of what is now Prussia, and were the same as the modern Finns. Ptolemy calls them Φίννοι.

Fenus (τόκος). Interest on money. (1) GREEK. In Greece the rate of interest on invested capital was not restricted by law, but was left entirely to arrangement between the parties concerned (Lys. *c. Theomn.* i. 18). The average rate, compared with that usually given at the present day, was very high, far higher than the rent either of houses or land. This is partly explained by the proportionately greater scarcity of ready money, and by the fact that it was difficult to accumulate a large amount of capital.

In the time of Demosthenes, 12 per cent. was regarded as a rather low rate of interest, and higher rates, up to 18 per cent., were quite common. In bottomry (τὸ ναυτικὸν δάνεισμα) the ordinary rate of interest at Athens was 20 per cent. In the event of failure in the payment of interest due, compound interest was charged. In the computation of interest two different methods were employed. It was usual to specify either the sum to be paid by the month on every mina (equal in intrinsic value of silver to about $16.50), or the fraction of the principal which was annually paid as interest. Capital therefore was said to be invested at a drachma, if for every mina (100 drachmae) there was paid interest at the rate of one drachma —i. e. 1 per cent. monthly, and consequently 12 per cent. per annum. Or again, if 12½ per cent. yearly interest was to be paid, the capital was said to be invested at "one eighth." In most cases the interest appears to have been paid monthly, and on the last day of the month; but payment by the year was not unknown. In bottomry the interest was according to the terms of the contract.

(2) ROMAN. At Rome, as at Athens, the rate of interest was originally unrestricted, and it was not until after hard struggles that, by the laws of the Twelve Tables, a regular yearly rate of interest at one twelfth of the capital, or 8⅓ per cent., was established. But this and subsequent legal limitations were all the less effectual for putting down usury, because they were valid in the case of Roman citizens only, and not in that of foreigners. Usury was accordingly practised under the name of foreigners up to the end of the second century B.C., when the laws against it were extended so as to include aliens. Through intercourse with Asia and Greece, a change in the payment of interest was gradually introduced, which in the first half of the first century B.C. was generally adopted. Capital was no longer lent by the year, but by the month, and monthly interest was paid on the first day of each month; notice of intention to call in the loan was given on the Ides (the 13th or 15th day of the month), and reimbursement took place on the first day (Kalends) of the following month. The regular rate of interest with this reckoning was 1 per cent. monthly, or 12 per cent. per annum. The accumulation of large fortunes in Rome at the end of the Republic considerably lessened the rate of interest on safe investments. The chief field for usury was then the provinces, whose inhabitants were compelled by the exorbitant imposts to be continually raising loans at any price. The custom, long permitted, of adding the year's unpaid interest to the principal was first forbidden by the later Roman law. Justinian permanently fixed the rate of interest in ordinary investments at 6 per cent., in commercial enterprises at 8 per cent., and in bottomry, in which it had previously been unlimited on account of the risk incurred by the stock on long voyages, at 12 per cent.

Feralia. The last day of the Roman festival called the Parentalia. See MANES; PARENTALIA.

Fercŭlum (from *fero*). A term applied to any kind of tray or platform used for carrying anything. Thus it is used to signify the tray or frame

Roman soldiers carrying on a *ferculum* the Golden Candlestick. (Arch of Titus.)

on which several dishes were brought in at once at dinner (Petron. 35); and hence *fercula* came to mean the number of courses at dinner, and even the dishes themselves (Suet. *Aug.* 74; Serv. *ad* Verg. *Aen.* i. 637; Juv. i. 94, with Mayor's note, and the article CENA, p. 313).

The ferculum was also used for carrying the images of the gods in the procession of the circus (Suet. *Iul.* 76), the ashes of the dead in a funeral (Suet. *Calig.* 15), and the spoils in a triumph (Suet. *Iul.* 37; Livy, i. 10); in all which cases it appears to have been carried on the shoulders or in the hands of men. This is shown in the illustration from the Arch of Titus, where Roman soldiers are carrying on a ferculum the Golden Candlestick. The most illustrious captives were sometimes placed on a ferculum in a triumph, in order that they might be better seen (Sen. *Herc. Oet.* 110).

Ferentarii. See EXERCITUS, p. 650.

Ferentīnum. (1) A town of Etruria, south of Volsinii, birthplace of the emperor Otho. (2) An ancient town of the Hernici in Latium, southwest of Anagnia, colonized by the Romans in the Second Punic War.

Ferentum. See FORENTUM.

Feretrius. A surname of Iupiter, derived from *ferire*, "to strike"; for persons who took an oath called upon Iupiter to strike them if they swore falsely as they struck the victim which they sacrificed. Others derived it from *ferre*, because people dedicated (*ferebant*) to him the *spolia opima*. See Fest. s. h. v.; Livy, i. 10; Propert. iv. 10, 46.

Feretrum (φέρετρον). A bier. See FUNUS.

Feriae. Holidays at Rome, dedicated to the worship of some deity. A distinction was drawn between *feriae privatae*, or holidays observed by *gentes*, families, and individuals, and *feriae publicae*, or public holidays. Public holidays were either fixed or movable, or occasional. The fixed holidays (*feriae stativae*) were forty-five in number, and were celebrated every year on a definite day and registered accordingly in the calendar. The movable holidays (*feriae conceptivae*) were also annual, but were held on changing days, and had therefore to be announced beforehand by the consuls, or in their absence by the praetor. The occasional holidays (*imperativae*) were commanded on special occasions by the authorities with the consent of the pontifices. Such were, for instance, the *supplicationes*, a solemn service to the gods to celebrate a victory or the like. One of the principal movable festivals was the FERIAE LATĪNAE. This was originally a celebration by the Latin race held on the Alban Mount in honour of Iupiter Latiaris. It was subsequently transformed by Tarquinius Superbus into a festival of the Latin League. Its most notable ceremony consisted in the sacrifice of white bulls, a portion of whose flesh was distributed to each of the cities of the League represented at the sacrifice. If any city did not receive its portion, or if any other point in the ceremonial was omitted, the whole sacrifice had to be repeated. Originally it lasted one day, but afterwards was extended to four. It was then celebrated in part on the Alban Mount by the Roman consuls, in presence of all the magistrates; and in part on the Roman Capitol, a race being included in the performance. It was announced by the consuls immediately after their assumption of office, nor did they leave Rome for their provinces until they had celebrated it. The date therefore depended on that of the assumption of office by the higher magistrates.

The FERIAE SEMENTĪVAE or SEMENTĪNA DIES, were kept at Rome in the time of the sowing of the fields, for the purpose of praying to Tellus and Ceres for a good crop. It was fixed by the pontifices, and lasted for only one day (Varr. *L. L.* vi. 26).

The FERIAE VINDEMIĀLES (Aug. 22–Oct. 15) were the vintage festival.

The FERIAE AESTĪVAE or FERIAE MESSIS (June 24–Aug. 1) were the "summer vacation" when fashionable Romans went out of town (Gell. ix. 15).

FERIAE PRAECIDANEAE were probably only days of preparation for the regular feriae (Gell. iv. 6).

Feriae Latīnae. See FERIAE.

Feronia. An old Italian goddess, of Sabine origin, but also much worshipped in Etruria. She seems originally to have been regarded in the same light as Flora, Libera, and Venus. The Greeks called her a goddess of flowers; on coins she is represented as a girl in the bloom of youth, with flowers in her hair. She was also worshipped as the goddess of emancipation from slavery. She had a very celebrated shrine at the foot of Mount Soracté in Etruria, where the whole neighbourhood used to bring her rich votive offerings and the firstfruits of the field. The annual festivals served as fairs, such was the crowd of people who flocked to them. The mythical king Herulus or Erulus of Praenesté was regarded as her son. He had three lives, and had to be slain three times by Evander in consequence (Verg. *Aen.* viii. 564).

Ferrum. Iron. See METALLUM.

Fescennīna, sc. *carmina*. One of the earliest kinds of Italian poetry, which consisted of rude and jocose verses, or rather dialogues in extempore verses (Livy, vii. 2), in which the merry country folks assailed and ridiculed one another (Hor. *Epist.* ii. 1, 145). This amusement seems originally to have been peculiar to country people, but it was also introduced into the towns of Italy and at Rome, where it is found mentioned as one of those in which young people indulged at weddings (Serv. *ad Aen.* vii. 695; Seneca, *Controv.* 21, *Med.* 113; Plin. *H. N.* xv. 22). There are rather feeble specimens of these in the four poems by Claudian *De Nuptiis Honorii Augusti et Mariae.* The Fescennina were one of the popular amusements at various festivals, and on many other occasions, but especially after the harvest was over.

After their introduction into the towns they seem to have lost much of their original rustic character, and perhaps were modified by the influence of Greek refinement (see Verg. *Georg.* ii. 385, etc.; Tibull. ii. 1, 55; Catull. lxi. 127); they remained, however, in so far the same as to be at all times irregular and mostly extempore doggerel verses, usually in the Saturnian metre, though the specimens which are preserved are in trochaics, and the cretic is called *pes Fescenninus* by Diomedes, p. 479 (Keil). Sometimes, however, *versus Fescennini* were also written as satires upon persons (Macrob. *Sat.* ii. 4, 21). That these railleries had no malicious character, and were not intended to hurt or injure, may be inferred from the circumstance that one person often called upon another to answer and retort in a similar strain. The

Fescennina are asserted by Festus (s. h. v.) to have been introduced among the Romans from Etruria, and to have derived their name from Fescennia, a town of that country. But, in the first place, Fescennia was not an Etruscan, but a Faliscan town, and, in the second, this kind of amusement was at all times so popular in Italy that it can scarcely be considered as peculiar to any particular place. The derivation of a name of this kind from that of some particular place was formerly a favourite custom, as may be seen in the derivation of *caerimonia* from Caeré. Festus gives an alternative derivation from *fascinum*, either because they were thought to be a protection against sorcerers and witches, or because fascinum (*phallus*), the symbol of fertility, had in early times, or in rural districts, been connected with the amusements of the fescennina. This etymology is far more probable. Teuffel (*Rom. Lit.* § 5) attempts to combine the two, suggesting that fescennia may have derived its name from *fascinum*. Nettleship (*Journ. Phil.* xi. 190) plausibly assumes a substantive *fescennus*, "a charmer," from *fas*, "saying"; hence *fescennini* would be "the verses used by charmers." See Müller, *Die Etrusker*, ii. 296; Zell, *Ferienschriften*, ii. 121; Broman, *De Versibus Fescenninis* (Upsala, 1852); Corssen, *Origines Poësis*, etc., 124; Rossbach, *Die römische Ehe* (1853); Nettleship, *Lectures and Essays*, pp. 60 foll. (Oxford, 1885); and the articles MATRIMONIUM; SATURA.

Fescennium or **Fescennia**. A town of the Falisci in Etruria, and consequently, like Falerii, of Pelasgic origin. (See FALERII). From this town the Romans are said to have derived the Fescennina carmina (q. v.).

Festi Dies. See DIES; FERIAE.

Festivals. See DIES; FERIAE.

Festūca. Properly any stem, stalk, or straw of grain, or blade of grass (Varr. *L. L.* v. 31, § 38). In two passages it is generally explained as a synonym of the praetor's rod (*vindicta*) laid upon the slave's head in *manumissio* (Plaut. *Mil. Glor.* iv. 1, 15; Pers. v. 175). But Conington on the latter passage has pointed out that the ordinary use of *festuca* would suit these two places equally well; so that, after all, the traditional rendering may be a mistake. Plutarch says that one of the lictors threw stubble (κάρφος) on the manumitted slave (*De Ser. Num. Vind.* p. 550 B); and the words *lictor iactat* seem to imply something of this kind rather than touching with a staff. Possibly both ceremonies accompanied the act of manumission, the praetor applying the *vindicta* with his own hand, the lictor throwing the stubble. See MANUMISSIO.

Festus. (1) SEXTUS POMPĒIUS. A grammarian, supposed to have lived before the third century A.D. He made an abridgment, in alphabetical order, of the large work of Verrius Flaccus (q. v.), on the signification of words (*De Verborum Significatu*)—a rich storehouse of most important information on Roman antiquities and early Latin. This abridgment has been divided by editors into twenty books, each of which contains a letter. Festus has passed over in silence those words which Verrius had declared obsolete, and he intended, it would seem, to have treated of them in a separate work. Sometimes he does not coincide in the opinions of Verrius (e. g. on *monstrum*), and on these occasions he gives his own views of the subject matter. The abridgment of Festus is one of the most useful books that we possess; it has experienced, however, in some respects, an unhappy fate. It existed entire down to the eighth century, when one Paul Warnefrid (commonly quoted as Paulus Diaconus) conceived the idea of making a small and meagre extract from it. This compilation, dedicated to Charlemagne, henceforward supplanted the original work in the libraries of the day, and the latter was so far lost to modern times that but a single manuscript copy (Codex Farnesinus, now in Naples) of it was found, and this an imperfect one, commencing with the letter M. It was brought from Illyria, and was first copied as a whole by Politian in 1485. The first edition of the epitome of Paulus was printed by Zarotus (Milan, 1471). Paulus and Festus were printed together at Milan (1510), and at Venice by Aldus Manutius (1513). More valuable is the edition by Agostino (Venice, 1559–60), with its collation of the Farnese MS. The edition of Joseph Scaliger (1565) contains many acute emendations, as does that of Fulvius Ursinus (Rome, 1581). The best editions are those of Dacier (Paris, 1681); Egger (Paris, 1838); K. O. Müller (Leipzig, 1839; 2d ed. 1880); Thewrewk de Ponor (Pesth, 1891). See the excellent paper on Verrius Flaccus by Nettleship, *Lectures and Essays* (Oxford, 1885); also Hoffmann, *De Festi 'De Verborum Significatu' Quaestiones* (Königsberg, 1886); Bugge, *Altlatein bei Festus u. Paulus* in the *Neue Jahrb. für Philol. u. Pädagogik*, 105. 91; and the article LEXICON. (2) PORCIUS, governor of Iudaea after Felix, whom the Jews solicited to condemn St. Paul or to order him up to Jerusalem. The apostle's appeal to Caesar (the emperor Nero) frustrated the intentions of both Festus and the Jews (*Acts*, xxv. 1 foll.). (3) RUFIUS, or RUFUS. The author of an abridgment of Roman history (*Breviarium Rerum Gestarum Populi Romani*) based upon Eutropius and Florus, and written about A.D. 369. It is dedicated to the emperor Valens. Editions are those by Forster (Vienna, 1874), and Wagener (Prague, 1886). See also Jacobi, *De Festi Breviarii Fontibus* (Bonn, 1874), and Mommsen, *C.I.L.* vi. 537.

Fetiāles. A collegium (Livy, xxxvi. 3) of Roman priests who acted as the guardians of the public faith. It was their province, when any dispute arose with a foreign State, to demand satisfaction, to determine the circumstances under which hostilities might be commenced, to perform the various rites attendant on the solemn declaration of war, and to preside at the formal ratification of peace. These functions are briefly but comprehensively defined by Varro (*L. L.* v. 86, ed. Müller), to which may be added the old law quoted by Cicero (*De Leg.* ii. 9, 21): FOEDERVM, PACIS, BELLI, INDVTIARVM ORATORES FETIALES IVDICESQVE SVNTO (IVS NOSCVNTO, *Madvig*); BELLA DISCEPTANTO. Dionysius (ii. 72) and Livy (i. 32) detail at considerable length the ceremonies observed by the Romans in the earlier ages, when they felt themselves aggrieved by a neighbouring people. It appears that when an injury had been sustained, four fetiales (Varr. *ap.* Non.) were deputed to seek redress, who again elected one of their number to act as their representative. This individual was styled the *pater patratus populi Romani*. They were dressed in the garb of priests, and a wreath of sacred herbs gathered within the enclosure of the

Capitoline Hill (*verbenae, sagmina*), was borne befor them by one of their number, who was hence called Verbenarius (Pliny, *H. N.* xxii. § 5). Thus equipped, at least two of their number proceeded to the confines of the offending tribe, where they halted and the Pater Patratus addressed a prayer to Iupiter, calling the god to witness, with heavy imprecations, that his complaints were well founded and his demands reasonable. He then crossed the border, and the same form was repeated in nearly the same words to the first native of the soil whom he might chance to meet; again a third time to the sentinel or any citizen whom he encountered at the gate of the chief town; and a fourth time to the magistrates in the Forum in presence of the people. If a satisfactory answer was not returned within thirty days, after publicly delivering a solemn renunciation—in which the gods celestial, terrestrial, and infernal were invoked—of what might be expected to follow, he returned to Rome, and, accompanied by the rest of the fetiales, made a report of his mission to the Senate. If the people (Livy, x. 45), as well as the Senate, decided for war, the Pater Patratus again set forth to the border of the hostile territory, and launched a spear tipped with iron, or charred at the extremity and smeared with blood (emblematic doubtless of fire and slaughter) across the boundary, pronouncing at the same time a solemn declaration of war. The demand for redress and the proclamation of hostilities were alike termed *clarigatio*, which word the Romans in later times explained by *clare repetere* (Pliny, l. c.; Serv. *ad* Verg. *Aen.* ix. 53, x. 14; cf. Livy, viii. 14, 5). When the Romans had to carry on wars beyond the sea, this proceeding was inconvenient. Hence a characteristic device was adopted. They transferred a piece of land in the Circus Flaminius to a prisoner taken from the enemy, and set up on this before the Temple of Bellona a column, which was accounted as standing on hostile territory (Serv. l. c.).

Fetialis. (Rich.)

Several of the formulae employed on these occasions have been preserved by Livy (i. 24, 32) and Aulus Gellius (xvi. 4), forming a portion of the Ius Fetiale by which the college was regulated. The services of the fetiales were considered absolutely essential in concluding a treaty (Livy, ix. 5); and we read that at the termination of the Second Punic War fetiales were sent over to Africa, who carried with them their own *verbenae* and their own flint stones for smiting the victim. Here also the chief was termed Pater Patratus (Livy, xxx. 43).

The institution of these priests was ascribed by tradition, in common with other matters connected with religion, to Numa (Dionys. ii. 71); and although Livy (i. 32) speaks as if he attributed their introduction to Ancus Martius, yet in an earlier chapter (i. 24) he supposes them to have existed in the reign of Hostilius. Little mention is made of the fetiales after the time of the Second Punic War, though the *collegium* is known to have existed as late as the second century A.D.

The number of the fetiales cannot be ascertained with certainty, but Varro quoted by Nonius (xii. 43) states that it amounted to twenty; of whom Niebuhr supposes ten were elected from the Ramnes and ten from the Titienses. They were originally selected from the most noble families; their office lasted for life (Dionys. ii. 72); and it seems probable that vacancies were filled up by the college (*coöptatione*) until the passing of the Lex Domitia, when in common with most other priests they would be nominated in the Comitia Tributa. This, however, is nowhere expressly stated.

The etymology of *fetialis* is uncertain. Varro (*L. L.* v. 86) would connect it with *fidus* and *foedus;* Festus with *ferio* or *facio;* but it is more probably connected with *fateri* and the Oscan *fatium*, so that *fetiales* would = *oratores*, "speakers." The spelling *feciales* is incorrect.

The explanation given by Livy (i. 24) of the origin of the title Pater Patratus is satisfactory: *Pater Patratus ad jusjurandum patrandum, id est, sanciendum fit foedus.*

Fever, GODDESS OF. See FEBRIS.

Fibrēnus. A small stream of Latium, running into the Liris, and forming before its junction a small island. This island belonged to Cicero, and was his birthplace.

Fibŭla (περόνη). A clasp for fastening garments, resembling our brooches or safety-pins

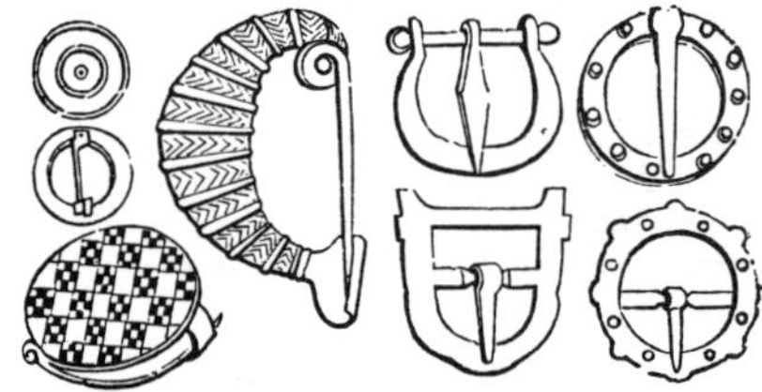
Fibulae. (British Museum.)

(Livy, xxvii. 19). It consisted of a hoop and a needle, sometimes elastic, sometimes fixed by a joint. Some fibulae were in the shape of buckles.

Fibŭla Praenestīna. See PRAENESTINE BROOCH.

Fictĭlĕ (πλαστική, κέραμον). A word applied to anything made of earth or clay; pottery. In Greek the special word for moulding in soft materials, πλάσσω, with its derivatives πλάσμα, πλάστης, πλαστική, was gradually applied only to clay, in which sense the words *plastes* and *plasticé* passed into Latin. Then, as clay played an important part in the preparation of works in bronze, the use of these words was extended to metal, and still further to statuary in stone and marble. The Latin equivalent of πλάσσω is *fingo*, which originally was applied only to the moulding of soft stuffs, but later was used for statuary of all kinds as opposed to *pingo;* in this extended sense we have also *fictor* and *figmentum*, but the usual application of *fictor* is confined to modelling in clay, just as *fictor, figlinus, figulus* refer only to work in clay. The original term for clay is κέραμος, whence the forms κεραμεύς, κεραμεύω, etc., applied not merely to the potter, but broadly to any worker in clay. From πηλός (applied to the clay of the bricklayer, and also to that of the potter) we have πηλουργός, πηλοπλάθος, corresponding to

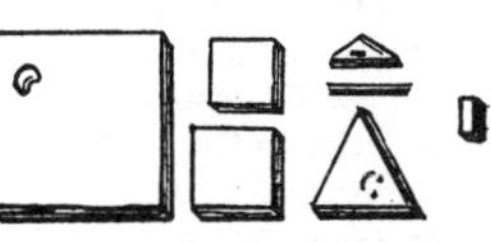
Brick Forms. (Rich.)

the poetical use of *lutum;* whereas, however, *argilla* = modelling clay, ἄργιλος = clay without reference to its plastic uses, γῆ κεραμίς = *terra* or *creta figularis;* hence also *ars cretaria.*

The simplest, and at the same time one of the oldest, branches of the primeval art of working in clay is the manufacture of bricks (*lateres*, πλίνθοι) and tiles (*tegulae*, κέραμοι), the invention of which (at Athens) was ascribed by the Greeks to the mythical personages Euryalus and Hyperbius (Plin. *H. N.* vii. 194), and to Talus, the nephew of Daedalus. So far as bricks were used at all, their use was generally confined to private buildings; and Greeks and Romans for ages employed only unbaked or sun-dried bricks. Bricks baked in the kiln came into use at a later date. The first to employ them extensively were the Romans, probably at the period when the population of the city rendered it necessary to build houses of several stories, which demanded a more solid material. In imperial times such bricks were the common material for private and public buildings. The walls were built of them, and then overlaid with stucco or marble. Building with baked bricks extended from Rome into Greece, and, generally speaking, wherever the Romans carried their arms they introduced their exceptional aptitude for making excellent bricks. Bricks which presented flat surfaces, to be used for walls or pavements, were made of the most varied dimensions, but were for the most part thinner than ours. Besides these, there were also rounded bricks for building dwarf columns, and for the construction of circular walls. For the Assyrian and Babylonian bricks, see the articles ASSYRIA; BABYLONIA; CUNEIFORM.

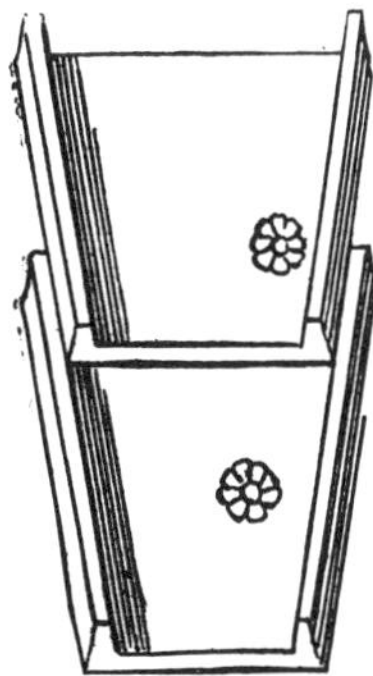

Tegulae of Baked Clay with maker's stamp. (Rich.)

All that we know of the Greek method of brick-making is that the earthy clay (πῆλος) was carved out with trowels (ἀμαί) and laid in mould; it was moistened with water and kneaded with the feet, but it is uncertain whether the bricks were modelled by hand or pressed into a mould. The Romans were careful in the selection of clay; they rejected sandy or stony clay, both on account of the weight and liability to damp; a whitish clay was preferred (*terra albida, cretosa*), or else a reddish clay (*rubrica*), or the softer kind of sandy loam (*sabulo masculus*). The special times for brick-making were spring or autumn; after baking it was usual to leave the bricks for some time to dry. Vitruvius recommends the use of those which are two years old and thoroughly dry; and quotes a law of Utica, ordaining that bricks for walls must be five years old. The clay was carefully purified, damped, and mixed with chopped straw; it was then either formed by the hand or pressed in a mould, and set to dry in the sun. In some parts of Spain and Asia Minor bricks are said to have been made so light that they would not sink in water.

The usual size of bricks in Greece was 5 palms square (πεντάδωρα) for public, and 4 palms square (τετράδωρα) for private buildings; in Rome the size usually adopted was the γένος Λύδιον, 1½ Roman foot long by 1 foot broad (*sesquipedales*). Palladius recommends bricks of 2 Roman feet long (*bipedales*) by 1 foot broad and 4 inches high. In later times there seems to have been no definite rule as to size.

For roofs, flat tiles were chiefly used, which were provided with a raised rim on both of their longer sides, and were so formed that the upper fitted into the lower. Concave tiles also were used (*imbrex*, καλυπτήρ) of the form of a half-cylinder, which covered the adjoining edges of the flat tiles. The lowest row was commonly finished off with ornamental moulding. From the same material as bricks were also made pipes for conveying water for sewers, and for warm air; the section in the first two cases was round, in the last square. See BALNEAE; HYPOCAUSTUM.

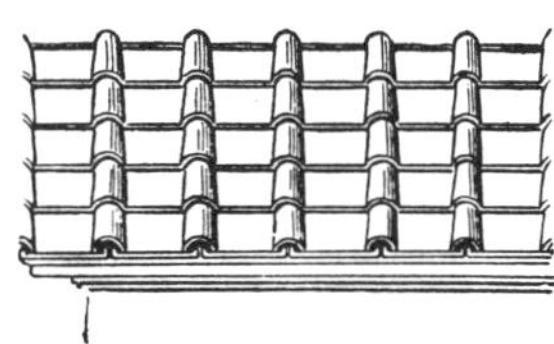

Tiled Roof. (Portico of Octavia, Rome.)

Pottery in its proper sense, the manufacture of utensils, is very old. The potter's wheel was known even before Homer's time (*Il.* xviii. 600), and was probably derived by the Greeks from Egypt. (See AEGYPTUS, p. 26.) Corinth and Athens, where the neighbouring promontory of Colias furnished an inexhaustible supply of fine potter's clay, were, in fact, the headquarters of the manufacture of Greek pottery. Next came Aegina, Samos, Lacedaemon, and other places in Greece itself, which always remained the principal seat of this manufacture, especially in the form of vases of painted clay. These were exported in large numbers to the countries on the Mediterranean and Black Seas. The high estimation in which Greek, and especially Attic, pottery was held is proved by the numerous vases which have been discovered in tombs, chiefly in Italy. Moreover, they represent almost every period. The excellence of the workmanship lies in the material, which is very fine, and prepared with the utmost care; also in the execution and in the baking. Its thinness as well as the hardness of its sides, even in vessels of large dimensions, astonishes experts in such matters. The shapes are mostly produced by the potter's wheel, but also by hand in the case of vessels too large to be conveniently placed on the wheel; for example, the largest wine-jars. The prehistoric pottery from Mycenae, the Troad, and other Hellenic sites, was also made by hand. Whereas small vessels were made of a single piece, in the case of large ones, the body, han-

Clay Quarry. (From a tablet at Berlin.)

Tile Stamp. (Birch.)

dles, feet, and neck were fashioned separately, and then united. They were first dried in the sun, then twice baked, before and after the painting. The colours are no less admirable than the workmanship. The clay shows a beautiful bright reddish yellow, which is produced by the addition of colouring matter, and is also further intensified by a thin coating of glaze. The black colour, which often verges upon green and is of a brilliant lustre, is then applied. Either (1) the design stands out black against the bright background, or (2) the figures appear in red on a black ground, the former being the earlier method. Other colours, especially white or dark-red, were applied after the black glaze had been burned into the clay by the second baking, and served as a less lasting adornment. In later times yellow, green, blue, brown, and gold were also used.

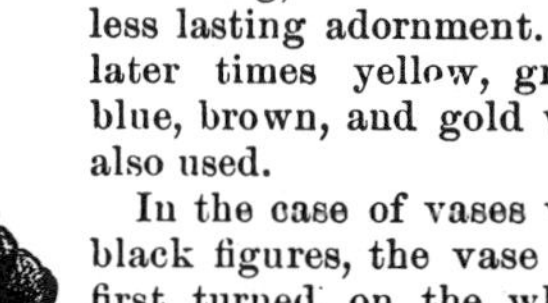

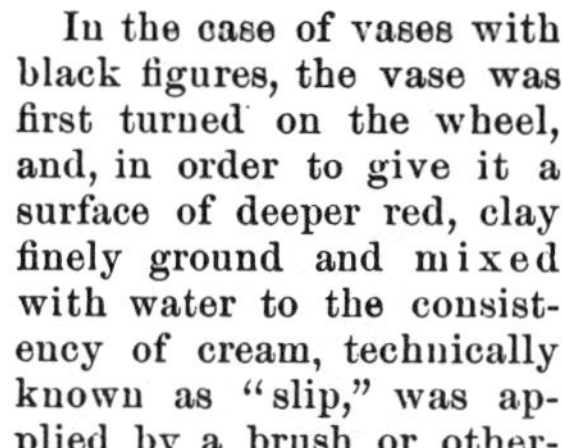

Archaic Vase with Owl Head and Characteristics of a Woman. (Schliemann, *Troja.*)

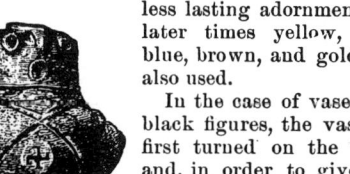

In the case of vases with black figures, the vase was first turned on the wheel, and, in order to give it a surface of deeper red, clay finely ground and mixed with water to the consistency of cream, technically known as "slip," was applied by a brush or otherwise while it was still revolving. The outline of the design was next roughly sketched, either with a point or in light-red ochre with a brush. The vase was then dried in the sun, and again put on the wheel, and the glaze, finely powdered and mixed with water, was applied to it with a brush as it revolved. The vase was then, in some cases, fired for the first time in the kiln in order to provide a smooth, almost non-absorbent surface for the use of the painter. The painter then put on the black-enamel figures and ornaments with a brush. After the firing of the enamel, the details were drawn in by incised lines, cutting through the enamel down to the clay body of the vase.

Archaic Greek Vases. (Birch.)

In vases with red figures, instead of the figures being painted in black, the ground was covered with black enamel and the figures left, showing the glazed red "slip" which covers the whole vase. This method produced a great artistic advance in the beauty of the figures, the details and inner lines of which could be executed with freedom and ease by brush-marked lines, instead of by the laborious process of cutting incised lines through the very hard black enamel.

Lastly, the form deserves great praise. The vases of the best period present the most tasteful elegance of form, that is at once fine and strong, and the most delicate proportion of the various parts to each other and to the whole, without interfering with their practical utility. It was not until the times when taste had begun to degenerate that the fashion was introduced of giving to

Corinthian Vase. (Height, 8½ inches; greatest diameter, 11¼ inches. Vulci.)

clay ware, by means of moulds, all kinds of grotesque forms of men and beasts, and of furnishing them with plastic, as well as painted, ornamentation.

The technique of ancient pottery is illustrated by the following figures. The first represents a potter seated in front of an oven, from which he takes with a stick a small vase which has been newly glazed, while two other vessels are standing to dry on an oven, the door of which is closed. The remaining figures, from a tablet at Berlin, explain themselves.

Greek Potter at Work. (Edwards.)

Among the votive tablets in the Louvre there are two from Corinth. The first of these represents an early Greek type of kiln, which is domed over, and has a space for the fuel on one side and a door in the side of the upper chamber, through which the pottery could be put in and withdrawn. The second shows a potter applying painted bands while the vessel revolves on the wheel.

The ovens (*κάμινοι, fornaces*) for baking vases seem to have differed very little from those of the present day. The remains of such ovens, dating from a late Roman period, have been found in Germany, France, England, and Italy. The most perfect, perhaps, was that found in 1881, at the little Roman colonia situated between the villages of

Potter at Work. (Berlin tablet.)

Heddernheim and Praunheim near Frankfort; it has now been destroyed by the owner of the property on which it was found, but an excellent set of plans were drawn up before its destruction, by Donner, and published in the *Annali dell' Inst.* 1882 (Tav. U 3–6).

The following illustrations are from paintings on a number of *πίνακες*, or small clay tablets, found at Penteskaphia near Corinth in 1879, and now in the Museum at Berlin. They date from the sixth century B.C.

In the preceding cut, the potter is seated beside his wheel, which he turns with one hand, while with the other he applies ornament either with

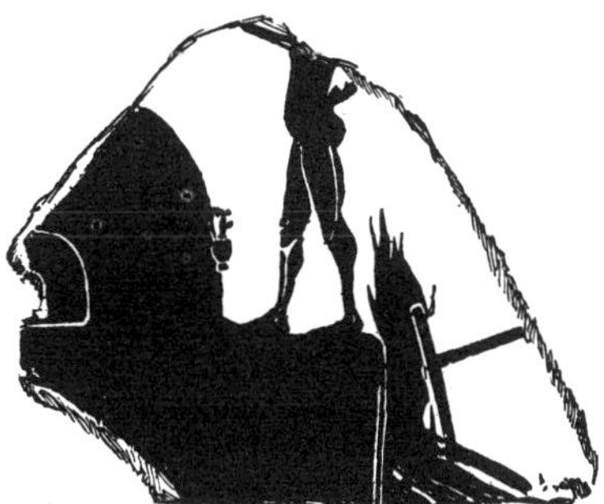

Exterior of Furnace. (Berlin tablet.)

a brush or stick; if the ornament was engraved alone, this would have to be done while the clay was still moist; if painted, the vase would be first dried in the air.

The Romans, with whom, as early as the time of the second king, Numa, a guild (*collegium*) of potters existed, neither had vessels of painted clay amongst their household goods, nor did they employ it for the ornamentation of their graves. In earlier times at least, they used only coarse and entirely unornamented ware. They imported artistically executed vases from their neighbours, the Etruscans. In the last hundred years of the Republic, as well as in the first hundred years after Christ, the chief place for the manufacture of the red crockery generally used in households was Arretium (Pliny, *H. N.* xxxv. 160; Mart. i. 54, 6, xiv. 98; Dennis, *Etruria*, ii. 335). The ware of this place was distinguished by a coral-red colour, and was generally furnished with glaze and delicate reliefs; in fact, ornamentation in relief was widely employed in later Roman pottery. Very much valued was the domestic ware, called *vasa Samia*, which was an imitation of the earlier pottery brought from the island of Samos. It was formed of fine, red-coloured clay, baked very hard, of thin make, and very delicate workmanship. It was glazed and generally adorned with reliefs, and served especially for the table use of respectable people who could not afford silver.

Interior of Furnace. (Berlin tablet.)

While this fine ware was made by hand, the manufacture of ordinary pottery, as well as of bricks and pipes, especially under the Empire, formed an important industry among capitalists,

Drinking-bowl and Dish of Clay. (Pompeii.)

who, on finding good clay on their estates, built potteries and tile-works, and either worked them on their own account through slaves, or had them carried on by lessees. The emperor himself, after the time of Tiberius, and the members of the imperial family, especially the women, pursued a similar trade, as is shown by the trade-mark which, according to Roman custom, was borne by clay manufactures.

The production of large statues of clay, apart from the purpose of modelling, belongs amongst the Greeks to the early times. It continued much longer amongst the Italians, especially amongst the Etruscans, who furnished the temples at Rome with clay images of the gods before the victorious campaigns in the East brought marble and bronze productions of Greek art to Rome. On the other hand, throughout the whole of antiquity, the manufacture of small clay figures of very various kinds, for the decoration of dwellings and graves, and for playthings for children, etc., was most extensively practised. They were generally made in moulds, and after baking were decorated with a coating of colour. The excellence which Greek art attained in this department, as in others, is shown by the "figurines" discovered at Tanagra in and after 1874. Very important, too, was the manufacture of clay reliefs, partly with figured repre-

Etruscan Sarcophagus of Terra-Cotta from Caeré. (Louvre.)

sentation and partly with arabesque patterns, for the embellishment of columns, windows, cornices, and also of tombstones and sarcophagi.

The reader is referred for further details and illustrations to the article VAS, and to the following works: Krause, *Angeiologie* (1854); Blümner, *Technologie und Terminologie*, etc., vol. ii.; Birch, *History of Ancient Pottery* (2d ed. 1873); Jacquemart, *History of the Ceramic Art* (Eng. trans. 1873); Kekulé, *Thonfiguren aus Tanagra* (1878); Jännicke, *Grundriss der Keramik* (1879); Henzen, *Catalogue des Figurines Antiques de Terre Cuite du Musée du Louvre* (1883); Kekulé, *Die Antiken Terracotten* (1880); id. *Die Terracotten von Sicilien* (1884); Dumont and Chaplain, *Céramiques* (1888); Pottier, *Les Statuettes de Terre Cuites dans l'Antiquité* (1890); and Robert, *La Céramique* (1892).

Fiction. See NOVELS AND ROMANCES.

Ficulea or **Fĭculnea.** An ancient town of the Sabines, east of Fidenae (Livy, i. 38).

Fideiussor. A surety. See INTERCESSIO.

Fidēnae. Sometimes FIDĒNA (Castel Giubileo), an ancient town in the land of the Sabines, five miles northeast of Rome, situated on a steep hill between the Tiber and the Anio. It is said to have been conquered and colonized by Romulus; but it was probably colonized by the Etruscan Veii, with which city it is found in close alliance. It frequently revolted, and was as frequently taken by the Romans. Its last revolt was in B.C. 438, and in the following year it was destroyed by the Romans, but was afterwards rebuilt.

Fidentia. A town in Cisalpine Gaul, on the Via Aemilia, between Parma and Placentia. Here Sulla's generals defeated Carbo, B.C. 82.

Fidepromissor. See INTERCESSIO.

Fides. The string of a lyre or harp. See LYRA.

Fides. The Roman personification of honour in the keeping of word or oath. As Fides Publica, or Honour of the People, this goddess had a temple on the Capitol, founded by King Numa, to which the Flamines Dialis, Martialis, and Quirinalis rode in a covered chariot on the first of October. At the sacrifice they had their right hands wrapped up to the fingers with white bands. The meaning of the covered chariot was that honour could not be too carefully protected; of the covered right hand, that the right hand, the seat of honour, should be kept pure and holy. The goddess was represented with outstretched right hand and a white veil. Her attributes were ears of corn and fruits, joined hands, and a turtle-dove.

Fidicŭla, or plural **Fidicŭlae.** An instrument of torture, consisting of a number of strings (Suet. *Tib.* 62, *Calig.* 33). Like the *eculeus* and the modern rack, it stretched the limbs until the joints were dislocated (Marquardt, *Privatl.* 180). See CRUX; ECULEUS; TORMENTUM.

Fidius. See SANCUS.

Fiducia. If a person transferred his property to another on condition that it should be restored to him, this contract was called *fiducia*, and the person to whom the property was so transferred was said *fiduciam accipere.* A man might transfer his property to another for the sake of greater security in time of danger, or for other sufficient reason. The contract of fiducia or pactum fiduciae also existed in the case of pignus, and in the case of mancipation. (See EMANCIPATIO.) The *hereditas* itself might be an object of fiducia. The trustee was bound to discharge his trust by restoring the thing; if he did not, he was liable to an *actio fiduciae* or *fiduciaria*, which was an *actio bonae fidei.* If the trustee was condemned in the action, the consequence was *infamia.*

Fiduciaria Actio. See FIDUCIA.

Fife. See TIBIA.

Figlīna Ars. See FICTILÉ.

Figŭlus. See FICTILÉ.

Figŭlus, P. NIGIDIUS. A Pythagorean philosopher of high reputation, who flourished about sixty years B.C. He was so celebrated on account of his knowledge that Gellius does not hesitate to pronounce him, next to Varro, the most learned of the Romans. Mathematical and physical investigations appear to have occupied a large share of his attention; and such was his fame as an astrologer that it was generally believed, in later times at least, that he had predicted in the most unambiguous terms the future greatness of Octavianus on hearing the announcement of his birth. In the Eusebian Chronicle he is styled "Pythagoricus et Magus." He, moreover, possessed considerable influence in political affairs during the last struggles of the Republic; was one of the senators selected by Cicero to take down the depositions and examinations of the witnesses who gave evidence with regard to Catiline's conspiracy, B.C. 63; was praetor in B.C. 59; took an active part in the civil war on the side of Pompey; was compelled in consequence by Caesar to live abroad, and died in exile B.C. 44. A letter of consolation addressed to him by Cicero (*Ad Fam.* iv. 13) is extant.

Aulus Gellius, who entertained the strongest admiration for the talents and acquirements of Figulus, says that his works were little studied, and were of no practical value, in consequence of the subtlety and obscurity by which they were characterized; but the quotations adduced by him (xix. 14) as specimens scarcely bear out the charge, when we consider the nature of the subject. The names of the following pieces have been preserved: *De Sphaera Barbarica et Graecanica*, *De Animalibus*, *De Extis*, *De Auguriis*, *De Ventis*, and *Commentarii Grammatici* in at least twenty-four books. The fragments which have survived have been carefully collected and illustrated by Rutgersius in his *Variae Lectiones*, iii. 16 (Leyden, 1618). See Hertz, *De Nigidii Studiis atque Operibus* (Berlin, 1845); Klein, *De Vita Nigidii* (Bonn, 1861); Breysig, *De Nigidii Figuli Fragmentis* (Berlin, 1854); and Röhrig, *De Nigid. Figulo* (Coburg, 1887).

Figūris, CARMEN DE. See CARMEN.

Filelfo, FRANCESCO. See PHILELPHUS.

Filiusfamilias. See FAMILIA.

Fimbria, C. FLAVIUS. (1) A jurist and an orator, consul B.C. 104 (Cic. *pro Planc.* 5; 21; *Brut.* 34; 45). (2) Son of the preceding, and one of the most violent partisans of Marius and Cinna during the civil war with Sulla. In B.C. 86 he was sent into Asia as legate of Valerius Flaccus, whom he induced the soldiers to put to death. He then carried on war against Mithridates; but in 84 he was attacked by Sulla, and being deserted by his troops, put an end to his life (Livy, *Epit.* 32).

Fimbriae (θύσανοι; in grammarians also κροσσοί). Tassels; a fringe. When the weaver had finished any garment on the loom (see TELA), the thrums, i.e. the extremities of the threads of the warp, hung in a row at the bottom. In this state they were frequently left, being considered ornamental. Often also, to prevent them from ravelling, and to give a still more artificial and ornamental appearance, they were separated into bundles, each of which was twisted, and tied in one or more knots. The thrums were thus, by a very simple process, transformed into a row of tassels. The linen shirts found in Egyptian tombs sometimes show this ornament along their lower edge, and illustrate, in a very interesting manner, the description of these garments by Herodotus (ii. 81). Among the Greeks and Romans fringes were seldom worn except by women (Pollux, vii. 64). We find, however, a long-sleeved tunic with *fimbriae* at the wrists, worn by Iulius Caesar (Suet. *Iul.* 45; cf. CLAVUS LATUS). Of the manner of displaying them the best idea may be formed by an inspection of the annexed illustration, taken from a small bronze, representing a Roman lady who wears an inner and an outer tunic, the latter being fringed, and over these a large shawl or pallium.

Fimbriae. (From an ancient bronze.)

Among barbarous nations the upper garment was often worn with a fringe by men.

Finance. See AERARIUM; FISCUS; MONETA; PORTORIUM; PUBLICANI; TELONAE.

Finitōres. See AGRIMENSORES.

Fire, GOD OF. See HEPHAESTUS; VULCANUS.

Fire-Brigade. See VIGILES.

Fire-Engines. See SIPHO.

Firmiānus Symphosius, CAELIUS. The author of a collection of a hundred riddles, each consisting of three hexameters, intended for use during the Saturnalia. The diction and prosody are correct, though the work is probably as late as the fifth century A.D. The title of the book is *Aenigmata*. The text is to be found in Wernsdorf's *Poetae Latini Minores*, vol. vi., and there is a commentary in the edition by Heumann (Hanover, 1722). See Paul, *De Symposii Aenigmatis* (Berlin, 1854); and the translation into French by Corpet (Paris, 1868).

Firmĭcus Maternus. (1) IULIUS. A Sicilian, the author of an astrological work in eight books (*Matheseos Libri*), finished A.D. 354. It is a complete system and defence of astrology, conceived in the Neo-Platonic spirit, and hostile to Christianity. It contains the earliest known mention of alchemy (iii. 15). The work is monotonous in diction, and hazy in its reasoning. The *editio princeps* appeared at Venice in 1499. A critical edition by K. Sittl was in 1892 announced as in preparation. See M. Bonner in the *Revue de Philologie*, viii. 187; and Dombart in the *Jahrb. für Philol.* 125, 590. (2) A Christian writer of about the same period as the preceding, who wrote *De Errore Profanarum Religionum* in 346 or 347 A.D. Nothing is known of the personality of the author, whose diction is rhetorical but plebeian. Good editions are those of Bursian (Leipzig, 1856) and Halm (with Minucius) (Vienna, 1867).

Firmum. A town in Picenum, three miles from the coast, where there was a strongly fortified harbour (Castellum Firmanum). (Mela, ii. 4.)

Firmus or **Firmius.** One of those ephemeral Roman emperors known in history by the name of tyrants, because they were usurpers of power under legitimate sovereigns. He was born in Seleucia in Syria, and owned extensive possessions in Egypt. Urged on by the impetuosity and love of change peculiar to the Egyptian Greeks, he seized upon Alexandria, and assumed the title of Augustus, one of his objects being to aid the cause of Zenobia (q. v.) who had already been conquered by Aurelian, but whose power was still not completely overthrown. Aurelian marched against Firmus with his usual rapidity, defeated him, took him prisoner, and inflicted on him the punishment of the cross (A.D. 273). Firmus is described as having been of extraordinary stature and strength of body. His aspect was so forbidding that he obtained in derision the surname of Cyclops. His life was written by Vopiscus.

Fiscāles. See GLADIATORES.

Fiscellus. That part of the chain of the Apennines which separates the Sabines from Picenum (Plin. *H. N.* vi. 12). Mount Fiscellus was reported by Varro to be the only spot in Italy in which wild goats were to be found (Varro, *R. R.* ii. 1).

Fiscus. The emperor's private purse, as distinguished from the public treasury (*aerarium*). It was instituted by Augustus, and was under the exclusive control of the emperor. The chief sources from which it was replenished were the entire revenues of the imperial provinces, the produce of unclaimed estates, and of confiscations. The main items of fiscal expenditure were the army, the fleet, and war material, the salaries of officials, the provision of corn for Rome, postal communication, and the public buildings. For the officials who administered the fiscus, see PROCURATOR; see also AERARIUM.

Fissi Dies. See DIES, p. 512.

Fish. See DIAETETICA; VICTUS.

Fistūca. An instrument used for ramming down pavements and threshing-floors and the foundations of buildings (Cato, *R. R.* 18, 28), and also for driving piles (Caes. *B. G.* iv. 17).

Fistŭla. Properly a reed, a Pan's-pipe (σύριγξ); then a water-pipe (σωλήν), usually made of lead, but in the villa of Antoninus Pius of pure silver (cf. Stat. *Silv.* i. 5, 48).

Flabellum (ῥιπίς, ῥιπίδιον). A fan (Terent. *Eun.* iii. 5, 50). The fans of the Greek and Roman ladies were made with the leaves of the lotus plant, of peacock's feathers (Prop. ii. 24, 11), or some expensive material, painted in brilliant colours (Mart. iii. 82). They were not constructed to open and shut, like ours, but were stiff, and had a long handle, the most convenient form for the manner in which they were used—viz., for one person to fan another, a slave always being employed for the purpose, known as *flabelliger* (Plaut. *Trin.* ii. 129). The left-hand figure in the illustration represents a fan of lotus leaf, from a Pompeian painting; the right-hand one, of peacock's feathers, from a painting discovered at Stabia. See Uzanne, *Les Ornements de la Femme* (Paris, 1892).

Flabella.

Flaccus, A. PERSIUS. See PERSIUS.

Flaccus, FULVIUS. The name of two distinguished families in the Fulvia and Valeria gentes. Many of the members of both families held the highest offices in the State; but the best known are: (1) M. FULVIUS FLACCUS, the friend of the Gracchi, consul in B.C. 125, and one of the triumvirs for carrying into execution the agrarian law of Tib. Gracchus. He was slain, together with C. Gracchus, in B.C. 121. (See GRACCHUS.) (2) L. VALERIUS FLACCUS, consul in B.C. 100 with Marius, when he took an active part in putting down the insurrection of Saturninus. In B.C. 86 he was chosen consul in place of Marius, but was put to death by his soldiers at the instigation of Fimbria. (3) CALPURNIUS, a rhetorician of the time of the emperor Hadrian. He is the author of fifty-one *declamationes*, usually printed with those of Quintilian. (See QUINTILIANUS.) (4) C. VALERIUS FLACCUS, a native of Padua, who lived in the time of Vespasian, and wrote the *Argonautica*, an unfinished heroic poem, in eight books, on the Argonautic expedition, which is extant, and of which the best editions are those of Wagner (Göttingen, 1805), Thilo (Halle, 1863), Schenkl (Berlin, 1871), and Bährens (Leipzig, 1875). The poem is a free imitation of Apollonius Rhodius, and is in style animated, rhetorical, and rich. (5) GRANIUS. See PAPIRIUS.

Flaccus, M. VERRIUS. See VERRIUS FLACCUS.

Flaccus, Q. HORATIUS. See HORATIUS.

Flaccus, SICŬLUS. A professional *agrimensor* of the time of Nero, the author of a treatise *De Condicionibus Agrorum*, part of which has been preserved. See AGRIMENSORES.

Flagrum, dim. **Flagellum** (μάστιξ). A "cat" or scourge, made with a great number of knotted and twisted tails, like the numerous feelers of the polypus, which are consequently designated by the same name (Ovid, *Met.* iv. 367). It was chiefly employed for the punishment of slaves (Juv. vi. 478; Hor. *Sat.* i. 2, 41), but also as a driving whip, in threshing grain, for self-punishment by the priests of Cybelé, and in the contests of gladiators, as in the illustration below. It is characterized

Flagellum.

by the epithet *horribile*, in some cases even produced death, and the nature of the wound caused by it is always specified by words which are descriptive of cutting, such as *caedere, secare, scindere*, etc. The flagrum was frequently knotted with bones or heavy bits of bronze (ἀστραγαλωτή), or even furnished with hooks, in which case it was called *scorpio*. A whip with a single lash was known as *scutica*. A scourged slave was styled *flagrio*. During the Saturnalia (q. v.) the scourge was put away under the seal of the master. See SERVUS.

Flags. See SIGNUM; VEXILLUM.

Flamen (from *flare*, one who blows or kindles the sacrificial fire; or from the root of *flagro*, to burn). The special priest of a special deity among the Romans (Cic. *De Leg.* ii. 8). There were fifteen flamines—three higher ones (*flamines maiores*) of patrician rank: these were the *flamen Dialis* (of Iupiter), *Martialis* (of Mars), and *Quirinalis* (of Quirinus). The remaining twelve were *flamines minores*, plebeians, and attached to less important deities, as Vulcanus, Flora, Pomona, and Carmenta. Their office was for life, and they could be deprived of it only in certain cases. The emblem of their dignity was a white conical hat (*apex*) made out of the hide of a sacrificed animal, and having an olive branch and woollen thread at the top. This the flamines were obliged to wear always out of doors—indeed, the *flamen Dialis* had originally to wear it indoors as well. They were exempted from all the duties of civic life, and excluded at the same time from all participation in politics. In course of time they were allowed to hold urban offices, but even then they were forbidden to go out of Italy.

The flamen Dialis was originally not allowed to spend a night away from home; in later times,

Coin of a Flamen Martialis. (Spanheim)

under the Empire, the pontifex could allow him to sleep out for two nights in the year. Indeed, the flamen Dialis, whose superior position among the flamens conferred upon him certain privileges, as the *toga praetexta*, the *sella curulis*, a seat in the Senate, and the services of a lictor, was in proportion obliged to submit to more restrictions than the rest. He, his wife, their children, and his house on the Palatine were dedicated to this god. He must be born of a marriage celebrated by *confarreatio*, and live himself in indissoluble marriage. If his wife died, he resigned his office. In the performance of his sacred functions he was assisted by his children as *camilli*. (See CAMILLUS.) Every day was for him a holy day, so that he never appeared without the insignia of his office, the conical hat, the thick woollen *toga praetexta* woven by his wife, the sacrificial knife, and a rod to keep the people away from him. He was preceded by his lictor, and by heralds who called on the people to stop their work, as the flamen was not permitted to look upon any labour. He was not allowed to set eyes on an armed host; to mount, or even to touch, a horse; to touch a corpse, or grave, or a goat, or a dog, or raw meat, or anything unclean. He must not have near him or behold anything in the shape of a chain; consequently there must be no knots, but only clasps, on his raiment; the ring on his finger was broken, and any one who came into his house with chains must instantly be loosened. If he were guilty of any carelessness in the sacrifices, or if his hat fell from his head, he had to resign. His wife, the *flaminica*, was priestess of Iuno. She had, in like manner, to appear always in her insignia of office—a long woollen robe, with her hair woven with a purple fillet (*tutulum*) and arranged in pyramidal form, her head covered with a veil and a kerchief, and carrying a sacrificial knife. On certain days she was forbidden to comb her hair. The chief business of the flamines consisted in daily sacrifices; on certain special occasions they acted with the pontifices and the Vestal Virgins. The three superior flamines offered a sacrifice to Fides Publica at the Capitol on the Kalends of October, driving there in a two-horse chariot. During the imperial period flamines of the deified emperors were added to the others. See the illustration under APEX.

Flaminia Via. See VIAE.

Flaminĭca. See FLAMEN.

Flaminīnus. (1) TITUS QUINCTIUS. A distinguished Roman general, made consul B.C. 198, before he was thirty years of age, and had the province of Macedonia assigned to him, with the charge of continuing the war against Philip, which had then lasted for two years, without any definite success on the part of the Romans. In his first campaign he drove Philip from the banks of the Aoüs, and, among other important movements, succeeded in detaching the Achaeans from the Macedonian alliance. In the following year Flamininus, being confirmed by the Senate in his command as proconsul, before commencing hostilities afresh, held a conference with Philip on the coast of the Maliac Gulf, and allowed him to send ambassadors to Rome to negotiate a peace. These negotiations, however, proving fruitless, Flamininus marched into Thessaly, where Philip had taken up a position, and totally defeated him in the battle of Cynoscephalae, in a spot broken by small hills, between Pherae and Larissa. The Macedonians lost 8000 killed and 5000 prisoners. After granting peace to the Macedonian monarch on severe and humiliating terms, Flamininus was continued in his command for another year, B.C. 196, to see these conditions executed. In that year, at the meeting of the Isthmian Games, where multitudes had assembled from every part of Greece, Flamininus caused a crier to proclaim, "that the Senate and people of Rome, and their commander Titus Quinctius, having subdued Philip and the Macedonians, now restored the Corinthians, Phocians, Locrians, Euboeans, Thessalians, Achaeans, etc., to their freedom and independence, and to the enjoyment of their own laws." Bursts of applause followed this announcement, and the crowd pressed forward to express their gratitude to Flamininus, whose conduct throughout these memorable transactions was marked by a wisdom, moderation, and liberality seldom found united in a victorious Roman general. He was thus the means of prolonging the independence of the Greek States for half a century more. In the following year, B.C. 195, Flamininus was intrusted with the war against Nabis, tyrant of Lacedaemon, who had treacherously seized upon the city of Argos. The Roman commander marched into Laconia, and laid siege to Sparta, but met with a brave resistance, and at last agreed to grant peace to Nabis on condition that he should give up Argos and all the other places which he had usurped, and restore their lands to the descendants of the Messenians. His motives for granting peace to Nabis were, he said, partly to prevent the destruction of one of the most illustrious of the Greek cities, and partly the great preparations which Antiochus, king of Syria, was then making on the coast of Asia. Livy suggests, as another probable reason, that Flamininus wished to terminate the war himself, and not to give time to a new consul to supersede him and reap the honours of the victory. The Senate confirmed the peace with Nabis, and in the following year, B.C. 194, Flamininus, having settled the affairs of Greece, prepared to return to Italy. Having repaired to Corinth, where deputations from all the Grecian cities had assembled, he took a friendly leave of them, withdrew his garrisons from all their cities, and left them to the enjoyment of their own freedom. On returning to Italy, both he and his soldiers were received with great demonstrations of joy, and the Senate decreed him a triumph for three days. Before the chariot of Flamininus, in the celebration of this triumph, appeared, among the hostages, Demetrius, son of Philip, and Armenes, son of Nabis; and in the rear followed the Roman prisoners, who had been sold as slaves to the Greeks by Hannibal during the Second Punic War, and whose liberation Flamininus had obtained from the gratitude of the Grecian States. The Achaeans alone are said to have liberated 1200, for whom they paid 100 talents (about $110,000) as compensation-money to their masters. In the year B.C. 183, Flamininus was sent to Prusias, king of Bithynia, upon the ungracious mission of demanding the person of Hannibal, then in his old age, and a refugee at the court of Prusias. The monarch was prevailed upon to violate the claims of hospitality, but the Carthaginian prevented this treachery by destroying himself with poison. In the year B.C. 168, Flamininus was made augur, in the room of C. Claudius deceased (Livy, xlv. 44), after which he is no longer mentioned in history (Plut. *Flamin.*).

(2) LUCIUS, brother of the preceding, commanded the Roman fleet during the first campaign of Quinctius, and scoured the coasts of Euboea, Corinth, and other districts at that time allied or subject to the king of Macedonia. He was afterwards expelled from the Senate by Cato, when censor, for having put to death a Gallic prisoner to gratify a favourite of his (Plut. *Flamin.*).

Flaminius. (1) GAIUS, consul for the first time in B.C. 223, when he gained a victory over the Insubrian Gauls; and censor in 220, when he executed two great works which bore his name—viz., the Circus Flaminius and the Via Flaminia. In his second consulship (217) he was defeated and slain by Hannibal, at the battle of the Lake Trasimenus (Livy, xxi. 57; 63; id. xxii., etc.; Polyb. ii. 32, etc.). (2) GAIUS, a son of the preceding, was curule aedile in B.C. 196, when he distributed great quantities of grain among the people at a nominal price, this grain having been given him by the Sicilians as a memorial of gratitude to his father, who had governed them with much integrity. He was praetor in 193 and consul in 185, when he defeated the Ligurians.

Flammearii. Makers of *flammea.* See FLAMMEUM.

Flammeŏlum. See FLAMMEUM.

Flammeum, dim. **Flammeŏlum.** The marriage veil, worn by a Roman bride on her wedding-day. It was of a brilliant yellow colour (Plin. *H. N.* xxi. 22), like a flame, from which circumstance the name arose; and of large dimensions, sufficient to cover the whole person from head to foot. During the ceremony it was worn over the head, to shield the downcast looks of virgin modesty (Lucan. ii. 361), as exhibited in the annexed figure, from a Roman marble, representing a bride (*nupta*) at her wedding; and was so retained until she arrived at her new home, when she was unveiled by her husband; as is exemplified by the fellowing figure, also from a Roman marble, in which the bride is seen sitting unveiled upon a couch, but with the flammeum still on her shoulders, and exhibiting a very natural gesture of feminine modesty, or regret for the loss of her old friends and companions. See MATRIMONIUM.

Flammeum. (Rich.)

Flammeum. (Rich.)

Flanatĭcus Sinus. A gulf lying between Istria and Liburnia, in the Adriatic. It was also called Polaticus Sinus, from the town of Pola in its vicinity. The name Flanaticus was derived from the adjacent town of Flanona. The modern name is the Gulf of Quarnaro (Plin. *H. N.* iii. 19).

Flavia Domitilla. See DOMITILLA.

Flavia Gens. Celebrated as the house to which the emperor Vespasian belonged. During the later period of the Roman Empire the name Flavius descended from one emperor to another, Constantius, the father of Constantine the Great, being the first in the series.

Flavian Emperors. A name applied specifically to three Roman emperors—Vespasian, Titus, and Domitian—as belonging to the *gens Flavia* (Suet. *Vesp.* 1).

Flaviānum Ius. See IURISPRUDENTIA.

Flavius, GNAEUS. The secretary to the censor Appius Claudius Caecus, and memorable for having made public certain technicalities of legal procedure that had previously been known to the patricians alone. These were the *actiones legis*, the rules of the Calendar, the *formulae*, etc. He was made a senator by Claudius, and was curule aedile in B.C. 303, a choice which so disgusted the patricians that the greater part of the nobles laid aside their insignia—the gold rings and *phalerae.* Flavius met their contemptuous treatment with great coolness and hauteur, and a number of anecdotes are preserved of this rivalry. See Pliny, *H. N.* xxxiii. 1; Cic. *Pro Mur.* 11; Livy, ix. 46; Gell. vii. 9.

Flavius. A brother of the German patriot Arminius (q. v.) and a distinguished officer in the Roman army (Tac. *Ann.* ii. 9).

Flavius Fimbria. See FIMBRIA.

Flavius Iosēphus. See IOSEPHUS.

Flavius Vopiscus. See VOPISCUS.

Flavus. (1) L. CAESETIUS, a tribune of the people, deposed from his office in B.C. 44 by Julius Caesar for having removed the crowns from Caesar's statues and for imprisoning a person who had saluted Caesar by the title of *rex*. At the next election for consul, Flavus received many votes, and for his defiant bearing towards the dictator enjoyed a considerable popularity (Suet. *Caes.* 79, 80; Plut. *Caes.* 61; *Ant.* 12). (2) SUBRIUS, an officer in the Praetorian Guards who took an active part in Piso's conspiracy against Nero in A.D. 66 (Dio Cass. lxii. 24).

Flax. See LINUM.

Fleet. See CLASSIS; NAVIS.

Flesh. See DIAETETICA; VICTUS.

Flevum, Flevo. See RHENUS.

Flora. The goddess of flowers, and a very ancient Italian deity, being one of those said to have been worshipped by Tatius. Her festival was termed Floralia, and was celebrated at the end of April and beginning of May. It greatly degenerated, however, in the course of time, and became so offensive to purity as not to bear the presence of virtuous characters. The story of Cato the Censor in relation to this festival is well known (Val. Max. ii. 10). The Romans, who in general displayed great crudity in the legends which they invented for their deities, said that Flora had been a courtesan, who, having acquired immense wealth at Rome in the early days of the Republic, left it to the Roman people, on condition of their always celebrating her birthday with feasts (Plut. *Quaest. Rom.* 35; Lactant. 1, 24). Flora being an ancient Latin deity, was addressed by the title of *Mater* (Cic. *in Verr.* v. 14; Lucret. v. 738). In later times, Flora was identified with the Greek Chloris. See HORAE.

Flora. (From an ancient statue.)

Floralia or **Florāles Ludi.** A festival which was celebrated at Rome in honour of Flora or Chloris. It was said to have been instituted in B.C. 238, on the occasion of the dedication of a temple to Flora by the aediles L. and M. Publicius in the Circus Maximus (*C. I. L.* i. 392), at the command of an oracle in the Sibylline Books, for the purpose of obtaining from the goddess her protection of the blossoms (Plin. *H. N.* xviii. § 286). In the consulship of L. Postumius Albinus and M. Popilius Laenas (B.C. 173), it was made an annual festival, at the command of the Senate, by the aedile C. Servilius (Mommsen, *Röm. Münzw.* p. 645), as the blossoms in that year had severely suffered from winds, hail, and rain. By degrees it was extended to six days (April 28–May 3).

The celebration was, as usual, conducted by the aediles, and was carried on with excessive merriment, drinking, and lascivious games (Mart. i. 3; Sen. *Epist.* 96). From Valerius Maximus we learn that theatrical and mimic representations formed a principal part of the various amusements, and that it was customary for the assembled people on this occasion to require the actresses to appear naked on the stage, and to amuse the multitude with indecent gestures and dances. The last day was devoted to a beast-hunt in the Circus, but there were no races. Similar festivals, chiefly in spring and autumn, are in Southern countries seasons for rejoicing, and, as it were, called forth by the season of the year itself, without any distinct connection with any particular divinity; they are to this day very popular in Italy, and in ancient times we find them celebrated from the southern to the northern extremity of Italy. (See ANTHESPHORIA, and Justin, xliii. 4.) The Floralia were originally festivals of the country people (Preller, *Röm. Myth.* 379), which were afterwards, in Italy as in Greece, introduced into the towns, where they naturally assumed a more dissolute and licentious character, while the country people continued to celebrate them in their old and merry but innocent manner; and it is highly probable that such festivals did not become connected with the worship of any particular deity until a comparatively late period. This would account for the late introduction of the Floralia at Rome, as well as for the manner in which we find them celebrated there.

Florentia. The modern Firenze, or Florence; a town in Etruria, sprung from the ancient Fiesolé, and subsequently a Roman colony, situated on the Arnus (Arno). The Florentini are mentioned by Tacitus (*Ann.* i. 79) as sending a deputation to Rome in A.D. 16. Its greatness as a city dates from the Middle Ages. See Perrens, *Histoire de Florence* (1877–80); Yriarte, *Florence* (1882).

Flōrus. (1) L. ANNAEUS (in one MS. called IULIUS), a Latin historian, who was born, according to the common opinion, in Spain, but, as others maintain, in Gaul, and who wrote in the reign of Trajan. He was still living in the time of Hadrian, and is perhaps the same individual to whom, according to Spartianus, this emperor addressed some sportive verses. Florus has left an abridgment of Roman History, entitled *Epitome de Gestis Romanorum,* divided into two (in some MSS. four) books. It commences with the origin of Rome, and extends to A.U.C. 725, when Augustus closed the Temple of Ianus, a ceremony which had not taken place for 206 years previous. This work is based not merely upon Livy, but upon many earlier historians, no part of whose works any longer remains. It is less a history than a eulogy of the Roman people, written with elegance, but at the same time, in an oratorical style, and not without affectation. Oftentimes facts are merely hinted at, and events are passed over with a flourish of rhetoric; while the declamatory tone which everywhere prevails, and the concise and sententious phrases in which Florus is fond of indulging, impart an air of formality to his writings, and render them monotonous, and sometimes obscure. Florus likewise commits many errors of a geographical nature, and on many occasions is defective in point of chronology. His text has reached us in a very corrupt state, and abounds with interpolations. The epitome was very popular in the Middle Ages. The best edition of Florus is that of Jahn (1852), revised by Halm (Leipzig, 1854). See Heyn, *De Floro Historico* (Bonn, 1866); Bizos, *Flori Hist.*

etc. *de Vero Nomine, Aetate, Scriptis* (Paris, 1876); and on the style, Egen, *De Floro Hist. Elocutionis Tacit. Imitatore* (Münster, 1882), and Thomé, *De Flori Elocutione* (Frankenstein, 1881). Florus is possibly identical with the author of a school theme on Vergil, of which the introduction has been preserved, and is printed in Halm's edition of the epitome, and with the poet on whom Hadrian cracked the joke preserved by Spartianus (*Hadr*. 16). This Florus, however, is called PUBLIUS in one MS. See E. Müller, *De P. Annio Floro Poeta* (Berlin, 1855), and Eyssenhardt, *Hadrian und Florus* (Berlin, 1882). (2) IULIUS, a poet of the time of Horace (*Epist*. i. 3; ii. 2). (3) GESSIUS or CESTIUS, a procurator of Iudaea, A.D. 64–65, whose oppression was the chief cause of the Jewish revolt in 66 (Tacit. *Hist*. v. 10).

Flowers. See HORTUS.

Flowers, GODDESS OF See CHLORIS; FLORA.

Flute. See TIBIA.

Focālé. A covering for the throat (*fauces*), sometimes drawn also over the ears (Mart. iv. 41). It was made of wool and worn by infirm and delicate persons. Its use by others was regarded as effeminate (Hor. *Sat*. ii. 3, 255).

Focus, dim. **Focŭlus** (ἑστία: ἐσχάρα, ἐσχάρις, dim. ἐσχάριον). A fireplace; a hearth; a brazier. The fireplace, while serving all the requirements of ordinary life, possessed a sacred character both among the Greeks and Romans. In the primitive Greek house the ἐσχάρα stood against, or near, the back wall of the μέγαρον, the kitchen and living-room of the family; in the more spacious dwellings of a later age it was transferred, with other objects of domestic worship, to a small private chapel, vaulted so as to resemble the Tholos, the dome-shaped ἑστία of the State. The well-known use of the hearth as a sanctuary for suppliants occurs as early as Homer (*Od*. vii. 153–169). See DOMUS.

Among the Romans the fireplace was dedicated to the Lares of each family (Plaut. *Aul*. ii. 8, 16); a consecration which did not interfere with its homely uses. On festivals the housewife decorated the hearth with garlands (Ovid, *Trist*. v. 5, 10); a woollen fillet was sometimes added, nor were animal sacrifices unknown (Propert. v. 6, 1–6). The phrase *pro aris et focis* expressed attachment to all that was most dear and venerable (Cic. *N. D*. iii. 40, § 94). At Rome, too, the progress of wealth and refinement led to the removal of the focus and Penates to an inner apartment (Marquardt, *Privatl*. 234). In the Pompeian houses we see the *atrium*, now become a reception-room, adorned with a fountain and a marble table (*cartibulum*), but no longer with a hearth. See LARARIUM.

The focus was usually a fixture, constructed of stone or brick, and elevated a few inches above the ground. It was also frequently made of bronze, variously ornamented, and could then be carried from room to room.

Focus from Caeré. (British Museum.)

The small portable brazier or chafing-dish, called *foculus* or ἐσχάριον, was especially used in sacrifices; and the same name was applied to the hollow or fire-pan at the top of an altar (Livy, ii. 12; Cic. *Pro Domo*, 47, § 123; see ARA). The movable focus or foculus was also employed in the kitchen (Plaut. *Capt*. iv. 2, 68; Juv. iii. 262), and for

Bronze Foci from Pompeii. (Overbeck.)

keeping things hot was brought into the dining-room (Sen. *Ep*. 78, § 23). See CALDARIUM, and the illustration under AUTHEPSA.

Fodīna. See METALLUM.

Foederātae Civitātes, Foederāti, Socii. In extending her influence and dominions beyond the seven hills, Rome followed two alternative courses. One was to conclude a treaty of alliance with a community between which and herself there had previously been no relation; the other was to reduce such community to complete subjection by conquest or enforced surrender (Livy, xxxiv. 17; iv. 30; viii. 2). Where there was a treaty of alliance (*foedus*), the allied community was described by the terms prefixed to this article. At first, of course, such allies were exclusively Italian; in particular the Socii and Latini, who forced on the Social War, B.C. 90, though no town which had obtained the Roman civitas, or which was a Roman or Latin colony (see COLONIA), was said to be foederata. But even long before that war Rome had attached allies to herself by treaty outside Italy, both states governed on the republican principle and foreign princes (e. g. Ptolemaeus Philadelphus, B.C. 273, Dio Cass. 147; and Hiero of Syracuse, a year later, Polyb. i. 16). After the extension of the Roman imperium into the provinces, two kinds of foederati populi or civitates have to be distinguished: those whose territory lay within the bounds of a Roman province, and those which were genuinely foreign. The latter, however, after the subjection of the kings of Macedon and Syria, were constantly becoming mere tribute-payers to Rome (Livy, xlii. 6; xlv. 13, 44), and as a general rule had to be content with concealing their practical vassalage (Sall. *Iug*. 14) under the thin disguise of "friends and allies of the Roman people" (Caes. *B. G*. i. 3, 35, 43; iv. 12; vii. 31; Cic. *Pro Lege Manilia*, 5, 12).

The foedera were of three kinds, stipulating merely for friendship between the contracting parties, or for reciprocal hospitality, or for military subvention. Those of the first kind (Polyb. iii. 22; Livy, xxxviii. 38) provided that the two States should not engage in war with one another without first making every attempt at an amicable settlement (e. g. the treaty with Alba, Dionys. iii. 3), and contained regulations as to the sojourn of the citizens of each on the territory of the other, and the measure of legal protection they should enjoy (e. g. Carthage, Polyb. iii. 22–24). Other terms in such treaties, especially when concluded after a war, are exemplified by those with Carthage after the Sicilian and Second Punic Wars, with Philip of Macedon, and with Antiochus. Treaties of the second kind, which bargained for greater intimacy between the two States, are exemplified by that with the Aedui (Caes. *B. G.* i. 31). Those providing for military assistance varied with the power and eminence of the allied State; sometimes they placed the parties on an absolute equality (Livy, xxxiv. 57)—e. g. those with Camerinum and Heraclea, with the Aetolians, the Jews (Iosephus, *Ant. Iud.* xii. 10, 6), and Rhodians; in other cases the *socius* was subordinated to Rome, being required to "respect her majesty" (Cic. *Pro Balb.* 16, 35; *Dig.* xlix. 15, 7, 1); it remained free, but practically was at Rome's orders, as a client at those of his patron, though the Romans admitted their obligation to afford full protection (Livy, xxx. 42), and included the *socius* in their own treaties with neighbouring peoples (Polyb. iii. 22 foll., xv. 18; Livy, xxx. 37, xxxviii. 11, 38).

The condition of the socii and foederati was originally one of tolerable independence, subject to the obligation of furnishing a contingent to the Roman army; but it was continuously depressed by the increasing power of Rome, and the resulting discontent culminated in the Social War, at the termination of which the Leges Iulia and Plautia Papiria brought the Roman civitas within the reach of all who were domiciled in Italy (see CIVITAS), from whose territories this class of community now disappeared. Civitates foederatae seem, however, to have acquired the benefits of these statutes only on condition of becoming *fundus* (see below).

There were also foederatae civitates in most of the provinces, their treaty of course being anterior to the formation of the province itself; thus there were three in both Sicily and Baetica, and others in Asia Minor; Athens, Rhodes, and Tyre were also federate towns, and Cicero (*Pro Scauro*, 44) regards it as a dishonour to Sardinia that in all that island there was no town which "was free and united by friendship with the Roman people." These federate towns in the provinces enjoyed certain privileges not shared by the ordinary provincial town. Their citizens were exempted from payment of the land impost (*vectigal*), and perhaps from some of the other ordinary taxes of the State; and they possessed αὐτονομία, the independent control of their own affairs, with some measure of legislative and judicial power, excluding the authority of the provincial governor; but this perhaps was more theoretical than practical, especially when a Roman army came their way (Plut. *Pomp.* 10). It is hardly necessary to say that the foederatae civitates were forbidden to embark on any independent foreign policy. They were free to adopt the civil law of Rome in whole or part. Thus even before the Social War it was not unusual for the Socii and Latini to adopt Roman laws into their own system. In such cases the State which adopted a Roman statute was said *in eam legem fundus fieri;* but of course it did not thereby obtain for its citizens any privileges with respect to the Roman State.

Foedus. See FOEDERATAE CIVITATES.

Foenŭs. See FENUS.

Follis, dim. **Follicŭlus.** (1) An inflated ball of leather, no doubt originally the skin of a quadruped filled with air. The Roman games of ball, of which Marquardt reckons five, are described under PILA. The follis was the largest as well as the lightest and softest ball in use, as the *pila* was the hardest, the *paganica* being intermediate between the two (Mart. xiv. 45; cf. vii. 32). According to Marquardt, the follis might be either filled with air (κενή), or lightly stuffed with feathers; but this is perhaps a wrong inference, as the *plumea pondera follis* (Mart. iv. 19) may simply mean "light as a feather"; and it is only the *paganica* and *pila* which are expressly stated to have been so stuffed. It was not the same, however, as the tightly-blown modern football; it was much more like a child's ball, so soft that it could hurt no one, and hence is recommended as a gentle exercise, fit for small boys and old men, but to which *iuvenes* would not condescend (Mart. xiv. 47). The *folliculus* (τὸ φούλλικλον καλούμενον) is said to have been invented by one Atticus of Naples, a teacher of gymnastics (παιδοτρίβης), for the benefit of Pompeius Magnus (Athen. i. p. 14 foll.). Augustus, who was rather delicate in health, took to it comparatively early in life, soon after the Civil Wars (Suet. *Aug.* 83). For the *follis pugilatorius* of Plautus (*Rud.* iii. 4, 16), see CORYCUS. (Becker-Göll, *Gallus*, iii. 171 foll.).

Folles. (From a Coin of Gordianus III.)

(2) An air-cushion or mattress (Lamprid. *Elagab.* 25).

(3) A pair of bellows (φῦσα), consisting of two boards, with an air-valve (*parma*), united by a skin of ox or cow hide, so as to form a machine similar to what we now use, as shown in the annexed figure, from a terra-cotta lamp (Cic. *N. D.* i. 20; Pers. v. 11). Bellows, also made of goat's skin (*folles hircini*), are mentioned by Horace (*Sat.* i. 4, 19).

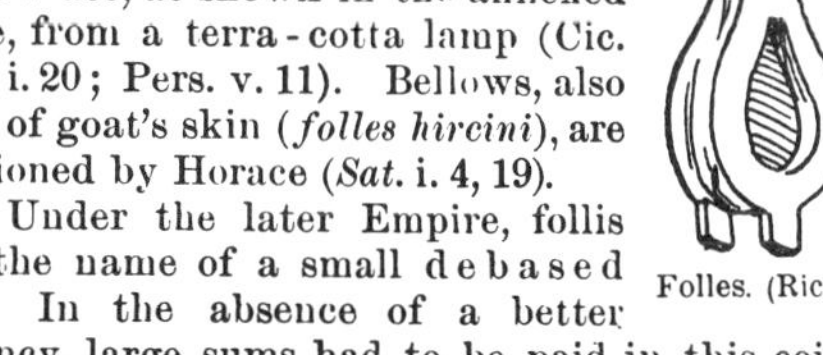
Folles. (Rich.)

(4) Under the later Empire, follis was the name of a small debased coin. In the absence of a better currency, large sums had to be paid in this coinage, which for the purpose was done up in bags, also called *folles*, analogous to the "purses of piastres" still used in reckoning in the East. The number of coins that went to a bag was probably 500, and its worth $\frac{1}{12}$ of a *solidus*, or about $0.25. From this the follis became, under Constantine and his successors, a "money of account," which was used in reckoning gold and silver as well as copper (Euseb. *H. E.* x. 6, § 1; Cod. Theod. vi. 2, 8).

Fons. (1) A spring. (2) A fountain. Ornamental edifices were erected by both the Greeks and Romans over natural springs, such as the temple of Erechtheus at Athens and of Poseidon at Mantinea (both over salt springs), that of Salmacis at Halicarnassus (Vitruv. ii. 8, § 12), and that of the so-called Grotto of Egeria near Rome. (Cf. Vitruv. viii. 3, § 7; Plin. *H. N.* xxxvi. § 154.)

At Rome, also, a good proportion of the water brought into the city by the aqueducts was devoted to the public fountains. Of these there were two classes, the *lacus* (ponds or reservoirs) and the *salientes* or *jets d'eau*. Agrippa alone is said to have constructed 700 *lacus* and 500 *salientes*. Fountains

Street Fountain. (Pompeii.)

were also used in the *atria* of houses (see DOMUS), and the basins exhibited a great variety of ornament, sculptural and otherwise. On the Monte Cavallo at Rome is a fountain representing the colossal figure of a river-god, perhaps the Rhine, which pours a stream into a basin of granite

Statues at a Fountain. (Pompeii.)

twenty-seven feet in diameter. There are other excellent examples in the Capitoline Museum, and the celebrated group of the Farnese Bull (q. v.) probably once adorned a fountain. Some of the fountain-statuettes are of the finest artistic workmanship. See Stieglitz, *Archäol. d. Baukunst*, ii. pt. 2, pp. 76, 79; Middleton, *Remains of Ancient Rome*, ii. pp. 329, 349, 350, 351 (London, 1892).

Fontēius, CAPĬTO. See CAPITO.

Fonteius, MARCUS. Propraetor in Narbonese Gaul, between B.C. 76 and 73, accused in 69 of extortion in his province, and defended by Cicero in an oration, part of which is extant.

Fontus. The Roman god of springs, son of Ianus and Iuturna. He had an altar in Rome on the Ianiculum. A special festival, the Fontinalia, was held in his honour on the 13th October, at which garlands were thrown into the springs, and laid round the wells (Varr. *L. L.* vi. 22).

Food and Drink. See CENA; DIAETETICA.

Fools. See MORIO.

Fools, FEAST OF. See FORNACALIA.

Forcellini, EGIDIO. A distinguished Italian lexicographer, born near Padua, August 26th, 1688. Being of humble parentage, he had few opportunities for early training, so that he was of mature age when he began a course of advanced study in the philological seminary of Padua under Facciolati (q. v.). His great ability, zeal, and industry, however, soon gave him an honourable rank, so that he was appointed an assistant to his teacher, with whom his name is inseparably associated in their joint work, the great Latin lexicon (*Totius Latinitatis Lexicon*) whose completion was in great part due to the untiring labour of Forcellini. Notebook in hand, he read through not only the entire body of Latin literature, but also the whole collection of inscriptions, including those on coins and medals, and thus compiled the most comprehensive and valuable vocabulary of the language that had ever been made, with both the Greek and the Italian equivalent of every word. The lexicon appeared in 1771 in 4 vols., three years after Forcellini's death, which occurred April 4th, 1768. Besides this *magnum opus*, Forcellini had assisted his master in the preparation of the so-called Calepine Vocabulary, and from 1724 to 1731 was Professor of Rhetoric in the seminary at Ceneda. See LEXICON.

Forceps. Tongs, pincers, nippers, or pliers, used in antiquity for various purposes. (1) A pair of tongs (*πυράγρα, θερμαστρίς*) for taking heated metal out of the fire, or holding it upon the anvil; used by smiths, and therefore attributed to Vulcan and the Cyclopes. (See INCUS.) (2) As a surgical instrument, a forceps (*λαβίς*, Hippocr.). Several specimens found at Pompeii are figured under CHIRURGIA. (3) In military language, a tenaille; in which sense, however, *forfex* is more used (Amm. Marc. xvi. 11, § 3). See FORFEX.

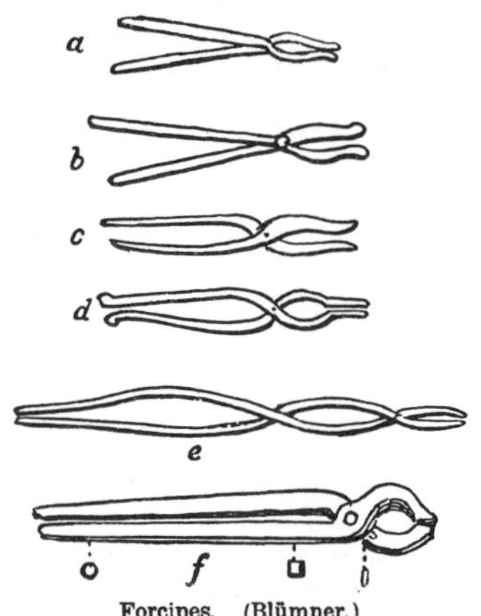

Forcipes. (Blümner.)

a, *b*, and *e*, from vase-paintings; *c*, from the altar of Vulcan at Veii; *d*, from a bas-relief; *f*, from an original now in the Zürich Museum.

Fordicidia or **Hordicidia.** A festival celebrated in Rome in honour of Tellus, goddess of the earth, on 15th April. See TELLUS.

Forentum or **Ferentum.** A town in Apulia, surrounded by fertile fields and in a low situation, according to Horace (*Carm.* iii. 4, 16).

Fores. See IANUA.

Forfex, dim. **Forfĭcŭla** (ψαλίς, dim. ψαλίδιον). Shears (Serv. *in* Verg. *Aen.* viii. 453), used (1) in shearing sheep, as represented in the annexed illustration, which is taken from a carnelian in the Stosch collection of antique gems at Berlin; (2) in cutting hair (Schol. *in* Eurip. *Orest.* 954); (3) in clipping hedges, myrtles, and other shrubs (ψαλιστοὶ μυρρινῶνες, Hierocles, *ap.* Stob. *Serm.* 65, p. 415).

Forfex, shears. (From a gem.)

In military manœuvres the forfex was a body of troops arranged in the form of a V, so as to receive and overcome the opposite body, called a *cuneus* (Gell. x. 9).

In architecture the term ψαλίς denoted a construction which was probably the origin of the arch, consisting of two stones leaning against each other so as to form an acute angle overhead, as is seen in the ruins of Tiryns. See p. 117.

Fori. Gangways. See CIRCUS; NAVIS.

Forĭca (θάκος), generally in the plural **Forĭcae.** A set of public water-closets, like the *cabinets d'aisance* of French cities, and put at the disposal of the passers-by for a small fee. They were farmed out by contractors, as we learn from Juvenal (iii. 38). See the anecdote in Theophrast. *Char.* 14. The *foricae* are not to be confounded with the public urinals (*dolia*) set at the street corners, and whose contents were sold to the laundries for bleaching clothes. See FULLO.

Fork. See FURCA.

Forma, dim. **Formŭla, Formella** (τύπος). A pattern, a mould; any contrivance adapted to convey its own shape to some plastic or flexible material, including moulds for making pottery, pastry, cheese, bricks, and coins. Several moulds for use in cookery are among the kitchen utensils

Forma, Mould for Coins.

found at Pompeii. The moulds for coins were made of a kind of stone which was indestructible by heat (Pliny, *H. N.* xxxvi. § 168). The mode of pouring into them the molten metal for casting the coins will be best understood from the preceding illustration, which represents one side of a mould, engraved by Seroux d'Agincourt. For the moulds used in casting terra-cottas, see ECTYPUS. The shoemaker's last was also called *forma, formula,* and *tentipellium,* and in Greek καλόπους (Plat. *Symp.* 191 A). The spouts and channels of aqueducts were likewise styled *formae.*

Formello Alphabet. See EPIGRAPHY, p. 607.

Formiae (Mola di Gaëta). A very ancient town in Latium, on the Via Appia, in the innermost corner of the beautiful Sinus Caietanus (Gulf of Gaeta). It was founded by the Pelasgic Tyrrhenians, and was the fabled abode of Lamus and the Laestrygones (Hom. *Od.* x. 81). Near this place were numerous villas of the Roman nobles; of these the best known is the Formianum of Cicero, in the neighbourhood of which he was killed, and whose remains are still visible at the Villa Marsana. The hills of Formiae produced good wine (Hor. *Carm.* i. 20, 11).

Formiānum. A villa of Cicero near Formiae, and in whose vicinity he was murdered by order of Antony.

Formŭla. See ACTIO in the Appendix.

Fornacalia. A Roman festival held in February in honour of Fornax, the goddess of ovens. It was said to have been founded by Numa, and may be described as a thanksgiving for the earliest enjoyment of the newly-gathered corn. It was held in the Forum by the Curiae, or ancient unions of kinsmen, under the superintendence of the Curio Maximus, or president of the masters of the curiae. Corn was baked in ovens in the ancient fashion. All who missed the festival were called fools (*stulti*), as being supposed not to know which was their curia, and had to make an offering at the so-called Feast of Fools (*stultorum feriae*) on the 17th February, the day of the Quirinalia. See Pliny, *H. N.* xviii. 8; Ovid, *Fasti,* ii. 513–532; Varro, *L. L.* vi. 13; Festus, s. v. *Stultorum Feriae.*

Fornax (κάμινος), dim. **Fornacŭla.** (1) An oven or kiln for baking pottery. (See FICTILÉ.) (2) A smelting-furnace (*fornax aeraria*). (3) A lime-kiln (*fornax calcaria*). (4) The furnace of a bath (*fornax balinei*). See BALNEAE.

Fornax. A Roman goddess, who presided over baking the corn in the oven (*fornax*), and who was worshipped at the festival of the Fornacalia (Ovid, *Fasti,* ii. 525).

Fornix. A vaulted arch or vaulted chamber, such as were common at Rome below the level of the sidewalks, and were so frequently used by prostitutes that the name *fornicaria* = *meretrix* (Tertull. *De Anima,* 35). See MERETRIX.

Forpex. A pair of curling irons; the word is sometimes treated as a mere corruption of *forceps.* But the derivation from *pecto* is obviously appropriate; and it seems to have been an old word (Cat. *R. R.* x. 3) revived, like many others, by late authors (Sidon. Apoll. *Epith.* xv. 184). See CALAMISTRUM.

Fortūna (Τύχη). The goddess of good luck, worshipped from remote antiquity in Italy. Her cultus was supposed to have been introduced into Rome by King Servius Tullius, popularly believed to be her favourite and confidant. He was said to have founded her oldest sanctuaries, as, for instance, that of Fors Fortuna, or lucky chance, on the right bank of the Tiber below Rome. To this a pilgrimage was made down the river by land and water on the anniversary of its foundation (June 26). As time went on, the worship of Fortuna became one of the most popular in Italy. She was worshipped at a great number of shrines under various titles given according to the various circumstances of life in which her influence was supposed to have effect. These titles were *Fortuna Primigenia*, who determines the destiny of the child at its birth; *Fortuna Publica* or *Populi Romani*, the tutelary goddess of the State; *Fortuna Caesaris* or *Augusta*, the protectress of the emperor; *Fortuna Privata*, or of family life; *Fortuna Patricia, Plebeia, Equestris*, of the different orders, classes, and families of the population; *Fortuna Liberûm*, of children; *Virginalis*, of maidens; *Muliebris*, of women. *Fortuna Virilis* was the goddess of woman's happiness in married life, of boys and of youths, who dedicated to her the first cuttings of their beards, calling her from this *Fortuna Barbata.* Other epithets of Fortuna were *Victrix*, or giver of victory; *Conservatrix*, or preserver; *Dux* or *Comes*, the leader or attendant; *Redux*, who brings safe home; *Tranquilla*, the giver of prosperous voyages. This Fortuna was worshipped with Portunus in the harbour of Rome. There were also *Fortuna Bona* and *Mala*, good and evil Fortune; *Blanda* or flattering, *Obsequens* or yielding, *Dubia* or doubtful, *Viscata* or enticing, *Brevis* or fickle, and *Manens* or constant. Trajan at last founded a special temple in her honour as the all-pervading power of the world. Here an annual sacrifice was offered to her on New Year's Day. In works of art she was represented with the same attributes as the Greek Τύχη (see TYCHÉ). Fortuna, in her general character as a goddess of Nature and of Fate, had an ancient and celebrated temple, in which oracles were delivered, at Praenesté and Antium. See PRAENESTÉ.

Goddesses of Fortune. (*Fortunae Antiates*, coin of the *gens Rustia*, from Gerhard, *Ant. Bildw.* taf. iv. 3, 4.)

Fortunātae Insŭlae or **Fortunatōrum Insŭlae** (αἱ τῶν μακάρων νῆσοι). "The Islands of the Blessed." The early Greeks, as we learn from Homer, placed the Elysian Fields, into which favoured heroes passed without dying, at the extremity of the earth, near the river Oceanus. (See GEOGRAPHIA). In poems later than Homer, an island is spoken of as their abode; and though its position was of course indefinite, the poets, and the geographers who followed them, placed it beyond the pillars of Hercules. Hence, when the Canary and Madeira Islands were discovered in the ocean, off the west coast of Africa, the name of Fortunatae Insulae was applied to them. See ELYSII CAMPI.

Fortunatiānus. (1) ATILIUS, the author of a manual on metres (*Ars Atilii Fortunatiani*) dedicated to a young Roman who had asked for a work on the metres of Horace, which this manual specifically treats near the end. It is drawn from Caesius Bassus, Iuba, and probably from some Greek source. It has been edited by Keil in his *Grammatici Latini*, vi. 278, and separately (Halle, 1885). (2) C. CHIRIUS, author of a text-book on rhetoric in the form of a catechism. The chief sources are Quintilian and Cicero. The text of this work, which is in three books, can be found in Halm's *Rhetorici Latini Minores*, pp. 79 foll.

Forŭli. A small town of the Sabines, near the junction of the Himella with the Tiber.

Forŭlus. A small book-case, differing from the *armarium* (q. v.) in not being stationary, but easily portable (Suet. *Aug.* 31).

Forum. A word which first signified an open space (*area*) before any building, especially before a sepulchre (Fest. s. v.). It is no doubt connected with *foris*, and so means any place "out of doors." The characteristic features of a Roman forum were, that it was a levelled space of ground of an oblong form, and surrounded by buildings, houses, temples, basilicas or porticoes (Vitruv. v. 1, 2). The forum at Pompeii, now completely excavated and showing very handsome architectural surroundings, affords a good general notion of the usual appearance of these places and the way they were laid out. A forum was originally used as a place where justice was administered, and where goods were exhibited for sale (Varro, *L. L.* v. 145). One must accordingly distinguish between two kinds of fora, of which some were real market-places, while others were places of meeting for the popular assembly and for the courts of justice. Mercantile business, however, was not altogether excluded from the latter, and it was especially the bankers and usurers who kept their shops in the buildings and porticoes by which they were surrounded. The latter kinds of fora were sometimes called *fora iudicialia*, to distinguish them from the mere market-places.

Among the *fora iudicialia* the most important was the FORUM ROMĀNUM, which was simply called *Forum*, as long as it was the only one of its kind which existed at Rome. At a late period of the Republic, and during the Empire when other *fora iudicialia* were built, the Forum Romanum was distinguished from them by the epithets *vetus* or *magnum*. It was situated between the Palatine, the Capitoline, and the Quirinal Hills, and its extent was seven *iugera* (Varro, *R. R.* i. 2). It was originally a swamp or marsh, but was said to have been filled up by Romulus and Tatius, and to have been set apart as a place for the administration of justice, for the assemblies of the people, and for other kinds of public business. It was drained by the construction of the Cloaca Maxima in the time of the last kings. (See CLOACA; EMISSARIUM.) In the larger sense, as applied to the whole valley surrounded by the three hills just named, the Forum included the Comitium, or the open place of assembly for the curiae (Varro, *L. L.* v. 155) in the centre of the Forum proper. Ancient rostra were an elevated platform (*suggestum*), from which the orators addressed the people, and which derived their name from the circumstance that, after the subjugation of Latium, the sides of the platform were adorned with the beaks (*rostra*) of the ships of the Antiates (Livy, viii. 14). In subsequent times, when the curiae had lost their importance, the accurate distinction between Comitium and Forum likewise ceased, and the Comitia Tributa were sometimes held in the Circus Flaminius; but towards the end of the Republic the Forum seems to have been chiefly used for judicial proceedings, and as a sort of Exchange. The orators, when addressing the people from the rostra, and even the tribunes of the people in the early times of the Republic, used to front the Comitium and the Curia; but C. Gracchus, or perhaps C. Licinius, introduced the custom of facing the Forum, thereby acknowledging the sovereignty of the people. In B.C. 308 the Romans adorned the Forum, or rather the bankers' shops (*argentariae*) around, with the gilded shields which they had taken from the Samnites: and this custom of adorning the Forum with these shields and other ornaments was subsequently always observed during the time of the Ludi Romani, when the aediles rode in their chariots (*tensae*) in solemn procession around the Forum (Livy, ix. 40). After the victory of C. Duilius over the Carthaginians the Forum was adorned with the celebrated Columna Rostrata (q. v.). In the upper part of the Forum, or the Comitium, the laws of the Twelve Tables were exhibited for public inspection, and it was probably in the same part that in B.C. 304 Cn. Flavius exhibited the Fasti, written on white tables (*in albo*), that every citizen might be able to know the days on which the law allowed the administration of justice. (See DIES.) Besides the ordinary business which was carried on in the Forum, we read that gladiatorial games were held in it (Vitruv. v. 1, 2), and that prisoners of war and faithless colonists or legionaries were put to death there (Livy, vii. 19; ix. 24; xxviii. 28). Down to the latest times of the Republic, the Forum was the usual place where funeral games were given; on these occasions it was temporarily enclosed with wooden railings (Cic. *Pro Sest.* 58, 124). See CANCELLI.

The ancient structures in the Forum were restored by Theodoric in the sixth century A.D., and down to the eighth century the original level was unchanged; but during the Middle Ages the magnificent edifices of ancient Rome were used as a quarry from which churches and secular buildings drew their building-stones, marbles, columns, and even their lime, which was derived from burning the ancient marble in kilns. Still more eagerly were the bronzes appropriated, so that it is not surprising that so few works of art, comparatively, have survived. In the eleventh century, the Forum was covered with the towers and fortress-walls of the mediaeval nobles, and the ultimate demolition of these covered the ground with a layer of rubbish to which fresh deposits were continuously made, especially when new buildings were reared and new streets constructed. The result is that the original level is now in some places fully forty feet below the surface. From the Middle Ages down to the present century, the site of the Forum was called Campo Vaccino. Its desolate area was given up to the buffaloes and oxen of the peasantry, to the scattered workshops of the meaner artisans, and to the few ruined columns that protruded from the rubbish as a melancholy reminiscence of its former glories. Such investigations and excavations as were first made under Raphael (especially in 1546–47) were undertaken solely in the search for works of art, and the trenches were soon refilled; but in the present century, more scientific research began. In 1803 the Arch of

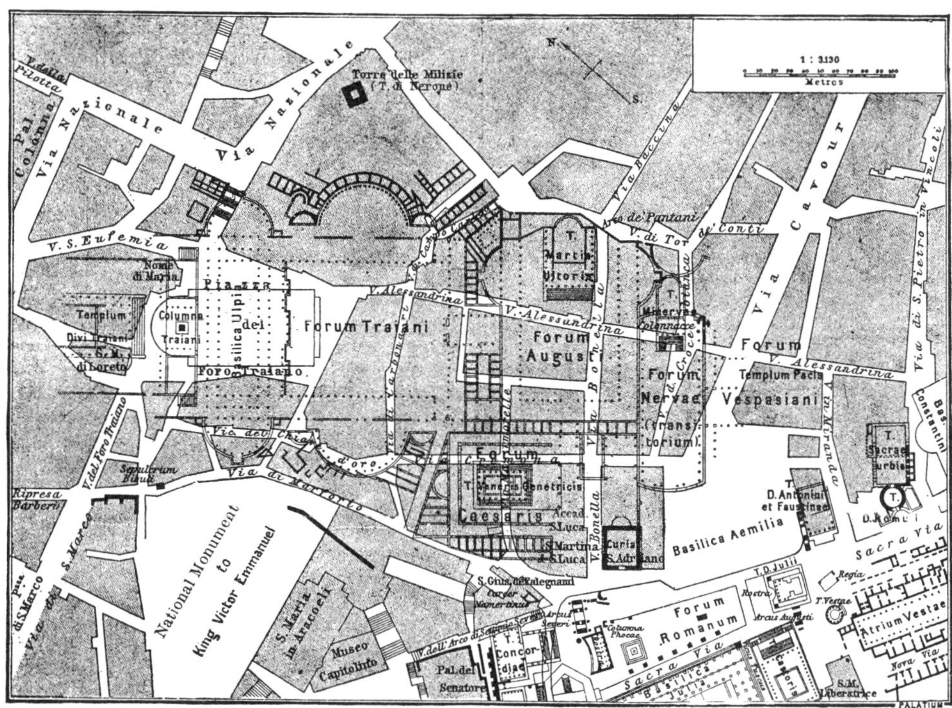

Plan of the Imperial Fora (1893).

Septimius Severus (see page 118), in 1813 the Column of Phocas, and in 1816–19 the Capitoline Hill with its temples were disinterred by Carlo Fea. Subsequently to 1835, the Basilica Iulia was in part recovered by Canina, and since 1871, when the Italian government occupied Rome as the capital of Italy, the work of excavation has been pushed with vigour. The Temples of Castor, Caesar, Faustina, Vespasian, etc., the Atrium Vestae, and the rest of the Basilica have been exhumed, besides a good part of the adjacent streets.

In the period between Iulius Caesar and Trajan the five imperial fora were erected.

(1) The first of these, and the second *forum iudiciarium*, was built by the dictator Caesar out of the spoils of the Gallic War, and was called FORUM CAESĂRIS or IULII. The site chosen was exceptionally crowded and valuable, immediately to the northeast of the Forum Romanum, and a hundred million sesterces ($4,000,000) were paid for it. The levelling of the ground cost large additional sums; in the centre stood the magnificent temple of Venus Genetrix, the tutelary goddess of Caesar's family, which he had vowed at the battle of Pharsalia (Suet. *Iul.* 26). Nothing now remains of this Forum but five half-buried arches.

(2) The FORUM AUGUSTI, the next in date, stood back from the Forum Iulii in the same direction. The central area was occupied by the temple of Mars Ultor, commemorating the battle of Philippi, though it was not finished until forty years later, and dedicated in B.C. 2 (Vell. Pat. ii. 109, § 2). Augustus further adorned his Forum with statues of the most distinguished men of the Republic, and issued a decree that only the *iudicia publica* and the *sortitiones iudicum* should take place in it (Suet. *Aug.* 29 and 31). After the Forum Augusti had severely suffered by fire, it was restored by Hadrian (Spart. *Hadr.* 19).

(3) The FORUM PACIS was built to enclose the Temple of Peace, dedicated by Vespasian A.D. 75. It commemorated the close of the civil wars which had filled the short reigns of Galba, Otho, and Vitellius, the undisputed authority of the emperor, and the taking of Jerusalem (Suet. *Vesp.* 9; Dio Cass. lxvi. 15). According to Pliny (*H. N.* xxxvi. § 102) the three most magnificent buildings in Rome were the Basilica of Paullus, the Forum of Augustus, and Vespasian's Temple of Peace. The site was to the southeast of the Forum of Augustus, but did not quite join it, a wide street from the Subura to the Forum Romanum being left between. This narrow strip afterwards became the Forum Transitorium of Nerva. There are no remains of the Temple of Peace.

(4) The situation of the FORUM OF NERVA has been already indicated. It was called TRANSITORIUM, on account of the highway which ran through it; or PALLADIUM, from containing a Temple of Minerva. The two Corinthian columns, buried to about half their height, and now called Colonnacce, belonged to this temple; part of the outer wall of the Forum is also extant.

(5) The FORUM TRAIĀNI was probably the most magnificent of all. It occupied a large space between the Capitoline and Quirinal Hills, the latter of which was cut back to a height of 100 Roman feet, as shown by the inscription on the Column of Trajan. The entrance was at the lower or southern end, where a triumphal arch, surmounted by a statue of Trajan in a six-horse chariot, divided it from the Forum of Augustus. The open space was surrounded by a double row of porticos, and enlarged by four enormous apses or semicircular extensions, one of which can still be traced in the slope of the Quirinal. In the centre stood the Basilica Ulpia, which fills the greater part of the modern Foro Traiano; beyond it was a cloistered court (*atrium*) surrounding the celebrated column which bears Trajan's name, and flanked by two libraries—one for Greek, the other for Latin MSS. At the upper end it was closed by the Temple of Trajan, dedicated by his successor. The splendour of the Forum Traiani greatly impressed the later Romans. Ammianus Marcellinus, in an account of a visit made to Rome by the emperor Constantius, describes a guest of that prince, a Persian, as amazed by this great work, "so exquisite," says the historian, "that the gods themselves would find it hard to refuse their admiration" (xvi. 14).

Different from these fora were the numerous markets at Rome, some of them reaching back to a very high antiquity. The most important was the FORUM BOARIUM, or cattle market, occupying a large space between the Velabrum and the Tiber; the notion that it derived its name from the statue of an ox, whencesoever imported (Ovid, *Fast.* vi. 477), can hardly be right, as it was almost certainly so named long before statues were introduced at Rome. Others which took their names from the goods sold in them were the FORUM OLITORIUM and PISCATORIUM, for vegetables and fish, SUARIUM for pigs, CUPEDĬNIS or CUPEDINARIUM for dainties.

Of the Forum Romanum the bearings and dimensions form one of the most disputed points of Roman topography. The excavations at Pompeii, however, have opened the Forum of that city, the remains of which are sufficiently preserved to enable us to trace the ground-plans of the various edifices surrounding it, and to assign some probable use to each of them; and will thus

Roman Forum Restored.

afford a general notion of the usual appearance of these places, and of the manner in which they were laid out. The central area is paved with large square flags, on which the bases for many statues still remain, and surrounded by a Doric colonnade of two stories, backed by a range of spacious and lofty buildings all round. The principal entrance is through an archway (*fornix*) (A), on the lower end of the annexed plan, and by the side of a temple of the Corinthian order (B), supposed to have been dedicated to Iupiter. On the opposite flank of this temple is another entrance into the Forum, and by its side the public prison (*carcer*) (C), in which the bones of two men with fetters on their legs were found. Adjacent to this is a long shallow building (D), with several entrances from the colonnade, surmised by the Italian archaeologists to have been a public granary (*horreum*). The next building is another temple of the Corinthian order

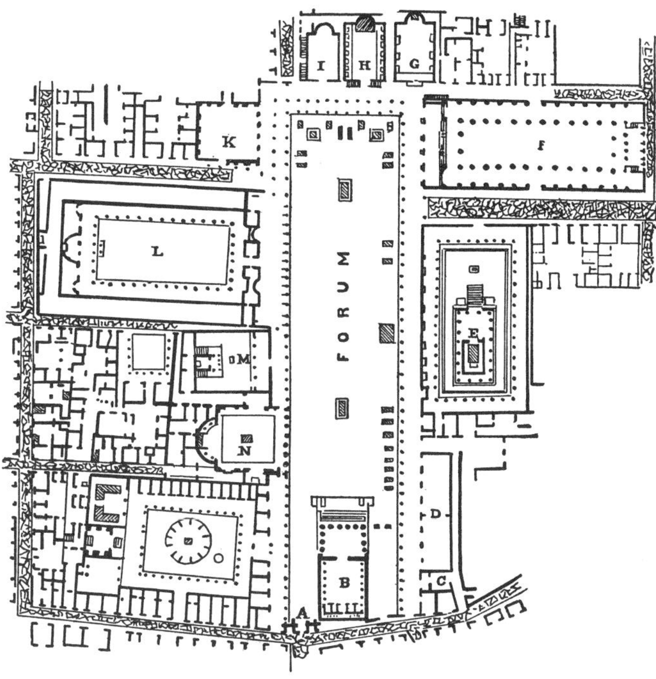

Plan of the Forum at Pompeii. (Rich.)

(E), dedicated to Apollo, as is learned from an inscription found on the spot. It stands in an area enclosed by a blank wall and peristyle, to which the principal entrance is in a side street, abutting on the Forum, and flanking the basilica (F), beyond which there are three private houses out of the precincts of the Forum. The farther or southern side of the square is occupied by three public edifices (G, H, I), nearly similar to one another in their plans and dimensions. All these were decorated with columns and statues, fragments of which were found upon the floor; but there are no sufficient grounds for deciding the uses for which they were destined. The first is merely conjectured to have been a council chamber (*curia*); the second, the treasury (*aerarium*); and the last, another curia. Beyond these is another street, opening on the Forum; and, turning the angle, are the remains of a square building (K), for which no satisfactory use can be suggested. The space behind is occupied by the sites of three private houses. The next object is a large plot of ground (L), surrounded by a colonnade (*porticus*) and a cloister (*crypta*), and decor-

Restoration of the North Side of the Forum at Pompeii. (Overbeck.)

ated in front, where it faces the Forum, by a spacious entrance porch or vestibule (*chalcidicum*), all of which were constructed at the expense of a woman named Eumachia. Beyond this is a small temple (M) upon a raised basement, attributed by some to Mercury, by others to Quirinus; and adjoining it, an edifice (N), with a large semicircular tribune or absis at its farther extremity, supposed to have been a meeting-hall for the Augustales, or a town-hall (*senaculum*) for the Pompeian Senate. The rear of both these structures is covered by the premises belonging to a fuller's establishment (*fullonica*). The last structure (O) is a magnificent building, with various appurtenances behind it, commonly called the Pantheon, from twelve pedestals placed in a circle round an altar in their centre, supposed to have supported the statues of the Dii Magni, or twelve principal divinities.

On the whole subject see Marucchi, *Descrizione del Foro Romano* (Rome, 1883); Lanciani, *Ancient Rome in the Light of Recent Discoveries* (Boston, 1888); Nichols, *The Roman Forum* (London, 1877); Jordan, *Capitol, Forum, und Via Sacra* (Rome, 1884); Ziegler, *Das Alte Rom* (Stuttgart, 1882); Middleton, *Ancient Rome in 1885*, chaps. v. vi. viii.; id. *Remains of Ancient Rome*, vol. i. chaps. vi. vii. and vol. ii. chap. i. (London, 1892); and the article ROMA.

Forum. The name of several towns, originally simply markets or places for the administration of justice. (1) APPII, in Latium, on the Appia Via, in the midst of the Pomptine marshes, forty-three miles southeast of Rome, founded by the censor Appius Claudius when he made the Appia Via. Here the Christians from Rome met the apostle Paul. (2) GALLŌRUM, now Castel Franco, between Mutina and Bononia, memorable for the two battles fought there between M. Antonius and the consuls Pansa and Hirtius. (3) IULII or IULIUM (Fréjus), a Roman colony founded by Iulius Caesar, B.C. 44, in Gallia Narbonensis, on the coast; the birthplace of Agricola. (4) IULIUM. (See ILLITURGIS.) (5) POPILII, in Lucania, east of Paestum. (6) SEGUSIANŌRUM, now Feurs, in Gallia Lugdunensis, on the Liger (Loire). (7) VOCONTII, now Vidauban, east of Canet, in Gallia Narbonensis.

Fosi. A people of Germany, the neighbours and allies of the Cherusci, in whose fate they shared (Tac. *Germ.* 36). See CHERUSCI.

Fossa. See CASTRA.

Fossa or **Fossae.** A canal. (1) CLUILIA or CLUILIAE, a trench about five miles from Rome, said to have been the ditch with which the Alban king Cluilius protected his camp when he marched against Rome in the reign of Tullus Hostilius. (2) CORBULŌNIS, a canal cut in the reign of Claudius, by Corbulo, between the Rhine and the Meuse (Tac. *Ann.* xi. 20). (3) DRUSIĀNAE or DRUSĪNAE, a canal which Drusus caused his soldiers to dig in B.C. 11, uniting the Rhine with the Yssel. (4) MARIĀNA or MARIĀNAE, a canal dug by command of Marius during his war with the Cimbri, in order to connect the Rhone with the Mediterranean. (5) XERXIS. See ATHOS.

Framea. See HASTA.

France. See GALLIA.

Franci. A confederation of Germanic tribes, which first appeared on the stage of history in the last quarter of the second century of our era. It was formed in place of the earlier league of the Cherusci (q. v.), and comprised the Sigambri, the Chamavi, Ampsivarii, Bructeri, Chatti, Salii, etc., along the Middle and Lower Rhine. As the Franks are first mentioned during the reign of Antoninus (A.D. 240), Mannert concludes that their confederation was not the result of aggression from Rome, but of internal wars; and these wars he conceives to have been chiefly of self-defence against the Saxon confederation, which, occupying the north of Germany, sought to extend itself westward to the Rhine. The Germans lying between the Saxons and that river found it necessary to unite in order to resist their northern invaders, and did so successfully under their new name of Franks. Various etymologies have been assigned to this appellation; but it probably comes from the German term *frank*, meaning "free," and indicating a race of freemen; and is the source of the name France, which first came into use in the ninth century A.D. The Franks soon became powerful enough to act on the offensive, and, crossing the Rhine to meet other foes, they spread their devastations from the banks of that river to the foot of the Pyrenees; nor were they stopped by these mountains. Spain, in turn, was overrun; and when the exhausted country no longer supplied a variety of plunder, the Franks seized on some vessels and transported themselves into Mauritania. They were afterwards driven out of Gaul by the Roman arms, and from the reign of Probus (A.D. 277) to that of Honorius seem to have contented themselves with occasional irruptions. They obtained a permanent footing in Gaul during the last years of the reign of Honorius. About the year 496, Clovis, or Chlodowig (his proper Teutonic name), by reducing the several Frankish principalities under his own sceptre and conquering the last remnant of the Western Roman Empire in Gaul, is held to have founded the French monarchy (481–511). His Frankish kingdom was, nevertheless, by no means commensurate with modern France, consisting merely of the northern German provinces on probably both banks of the Rhine, of the present kingdom of the Netherlands, and of so much of France as lies north of the Loire, with the exception of Brittany, where large bodies of Britons, expelled from their insular home by the Saxons, had established themselves and long maintained their independence. Of the southern half of France, the larger part, situated to the west of the Rhone, was included in the Visigothic kingdom of Spain; while the provinces to the east of that river were held, together with Savoy and Switzerland, by the Burgundians. Chlodowig attacked both. Against the Burgundians he effected little or nothing, but he was more successful against their western neighbours. Assisted by the hatred which the Catholic natives entertained towards their Arian master, he, before his death, reduced the Visigothic dominions in Gaul to the single province of Languedoc, incorporating all the rest in his Frankish realm. His sons and grandsons, in time, not only subdued Burgundy, but brought many German nations, as the Thuringians, Allemanni, and Bavarians, into complete feudal subjection. There were two great divisions of the Franks—the Salian Franks and the Ripuarian Franks—with separate laws, afterwards collected into two codes, the Lex Salica and the Lex Ripuariorum. See GALLIA.

Fratres Arvāles. The Arval Brethren; a Roman *collegium* or company of priests, twelve in number, and so called, according to Varro (*L. L.* v. 85), from offering public sacrifices for the fertility of the fields (*arva*). Their extreme antiquity is proved by the legend which refers their institution to Romulus, of whom it is said that when his nurse Acca Larentia lost one of her twelve sons, he allowed himself to be adopted by her in his place, and called himself and the remaining eleven "Fratres Arvales" (Gell. vi. 7).

The office of the Fratres Arvales was for life, and was not taken away even from an exile or captive. They wore, as a badge of office, a chaplet of ears of corn (*spicea corona*) fastened on their heads with a white band (*infula*) (Plin. *H. N.* xviii. § 6). These passages, with a single reference in Minucius Felix (*Oct.* 25), comprise all the extant notices of the Fratres Arvales in the ancient writers. But the discovery of a large number of inscriptions has placed the locality of their sanctuary beyond a doubt, and has thrown a flood of light on their constitution and ceremonial as well as on that of other Roman priesthoods. In the Vigna Ceccarelli, at a place called Affoga l'Asino, on the Via Portuensis, inscriptions upon stone tablets have been found at intervals from 1570 to the present time, which sufficiently identify that spot as the grove of the Dea Dia where the chief festival of the Arvales was held. By the end of the last century, sixty-seven documents had been recovered, and these were published with a valuable commentary by Marini (Rome, 1795). In 1867 more systematic excavations were undertaken with the aid of funds supplied by the King and Queen of Prussia, and the results were given to the world by Henzen in the works mentioned at the end of this article. We have now the *acta* of ninety-six annual meetings of the college, ranging in date from A.D. 14, the last year of Augustus, to 241, in the reign of Gordian; besides a number of fragments found at various times in Rome itself. From these we are able to form a clear idea of the officers of the college, the ceremonies they performed, and the mode of filling up vacancies in their body. Some of these minutes of proceedings, as they may be called, are much fuller than others, the most important being that of 218, the first year of Elagabalus, which includes the celebrated Hymn. The passage in Varro being the only mention of the Arvales that dates from republican times, it is a highly probable conjecture that this may have been one of the obsolete or half-forgotten cults, several of which, we know, were revived by Augustus. The *sacrificium Deae Diae in luco* is named in the law of Constantius and Constans, about 346, which, in the interest of the public amusement, provided for the maintenance of such temples as had games connected with them. In 382, by a decree of Gratian, the disestablishment of all pagan worships was completed, and their remaining endowments confiscated.

The regular number of brethren was twelve; the attendance at the annual meetings, as shown by the inscriptions, varied between three and nine. An exception occurs early in the reign of Nero; in the year 57 twelve Fratres met, exclusive of the emperor, who was also a member according to the invariable practice, and in this instance, it would appear, a supernumerary. From the time of Augustus it had become usual to appoint princes of the imperial family as extra members of the most dignified priestly colleges (Dio Cass. li. 20). Vacancies as they occurred were filled up by co-optation, originally free, but under the empire usually controlled by an imperial rescript indicating the person to be elected, like the *congé d'elire* of modern times. For the purpose of an election the brethren met on the summons of the *magister* in the Regia, the temple of Iupiter Stator, that of Divus Iulius, or latterly in the temple of Concord; and the votes were given in writing (*per tabellas*). The newly elected member was solemnly admitted by the *magister*, for which the phrase used is *ad sacra vocat.*

Like most Roman *collegia*, the Arvales had their presiding officer, called *magister*, elected annually in the grove of the Dea Dia on the second or great day of the May festival, but not coming into office until the 17th of December following: *a Saturnalibus primis ad Saturnalia secunda* is the oft-recurring formula. The *promagister*, who acted in the absence of the *magister*, appears to have been nominated by him for an indefinite period, and was not a regularly elected officer of the college. Next in importance to the *magister* was the *flamen*, elected annually upon the same occasion to assist in the sacrifices; he could also be represented by a *proflamen*, or by a member without that title *qui vice flaminis fungebatur*. Either of these dignities was often conferred by way of compliment on the emperor, who usually discharged its duties by deputy, and either might be re-elected in consecutive years or after an interval. There were, besides, four *pueri ingenui patrimi et matrimi, senatorum filii* (called also *Camilli*), who waited on the brethren during the sacrificial feast, and shared it themselves sitting on *cathedrae*, while their elders reclined. The college had also its staff of servants; some *servi publici*, assigned to its use by the emperor and reckoned as belonging to his *familia*, an *aedituus* in charge of the sacred precinct, and lastly the *calatores*.

The principal duty of the Arvales was to celebrate a three days' festival in honour of the Dea Dia, supposed by Marini to be Ceres, but now identified with Ops. This festival was sometimes held on the XVI., XIV., and XIII., sometimes on the VI., IV., and III. Kal. Iun.—i. e. on the 17th, 19th, and 20th, or the 27th, 29th, and 30th of May; in either instance, it will be seen, with a bye-day between the first and second feast days, while the third immediately followed the second. The precise time was fixed in the January of each year, and solemnly proclaimed by the *magister* or his deputy from the temple of Concord on the Clivus Capitolinus. The festival undoubtedly belonged to the order of *feriae conceptivae*, or those fixed by proclamation. On the first and last of the three days the college met in Rome, usually at the house of the *magister*, but sometimes also *in Palatio in templo Divorum*; offered fruits, incense, and wine at sunrise to the Dea Dia; anointed her statue; bathed, and changed the *praetexta* in which they had sacrificed for a white dinner-dress (*album cenatorium*; cf. SYNTHESIS). Between dinner and dessert (*mensa prima* and *mensa secunda bellariorum*) they rose from table, reclined on more magnificent couches than those of the *triclinium* (*toralibus segmentatis*), repeated the offerings of wine, incense, and first-fruits (*fruges libatae*); then divided the *bellaria*, and received each man a *sportula* or perquisite for attendance. This, in the period from Trajan to the Antonines amounted to 100 denarii, the boys receiving 25; in the impoverished times of the third century it was reduced to 25 denarii for members of the college.

On the second day of the feast, which was the most important of the three, the Arvales assembled in the grove of Dea Dia already described. The grove included a circus for games and several temples, among which the Caesareum or *aedicula* of deified emperors and the Tetrastylum are mentioned. The sacrifices were begun early in the day by the *magister* or his deputy, acting alone; he first offered two young pigs in order to expiate the unavoidable desecration of the sacred grove by the use of the axe in pruning and felling it, then a white heifer (*vacca honoraria*) as a victim to the Dea Dia herself. In the forenoon he was joined by his colleagues, who breakfasted on the offerings already made, and then proceeded to fresh ceremonies. They sacrificed a fat lamb; made an offering, not further described, with earthenware pots placed on a table; sent out two of their number to collect grains of corn, probably from the crowd collected at the temple doors, passed them on to one another, receiving them in the left hand and giving with the right, and finally handing them to the attendants; placed the *ollae* on the altar, and then threw them away that they might not be used again (this is the probable explanation of the obscure phrase *ollas precati sunt et ostiis apertis per clivum iactaverunt*); and shared *panes laureati*, followed by turnips and another vegetable mysteriously described (*lumemulia cum rapinis*). The images were now anointed (the plural *deas* is used here only, and seems to refer to Acca Larentia and the Dea Dia as separate divinities); the temple was cleared of all but the priests, and the doors shut. Then with their tunics girded up for the dance, taking written copies of the formula from their attendants, and dividing right and left into two bodies, they proceeded to recite the hymn which had made the name of Fratres Arvales so interesting (*ibi sacerdotes clusi succincti, libellis acceptis, carmen descindentes tripodaverunt in verba haec*).

The text here given is that of Mommsen (*Hist.* i. 231, Eng. trans.), with which those of Preller (*Röm. Myth.* p. 428) and Marquardt, after Bücheler (*Index Schol. Bonnens. Aest.* 1876), agree in the main. A rude Saturnian metre is discernible in the hymn:

Enos, Lases, iuvate,
Neve lue rue, Marmar, sins incurrere in pleores.
Satur fu, fere Mars! limen sali! sta! berber!
Semunis alternei advocapit conctos.
Enos Marmar iuvato.
Triumpe.

In Mommsen's rendering:

To the gods—
Nos, Lares, iuvate,
(*Aid us, ye Lares*),
Neve luem ruem (=ruinam) sinas incurrere in plures.
(*Nor suffer pestilence and destruction to come upon the people*).
Satur esto, fere Mars.
(*Be thou satiate, fierce Mars*).

To the individual brethren—
In limen insili! sta! verbera!
(*Leap o'er the threshold! Halt! Beat* [the ground]).

To all the brethren—
Semones alterni advocate cunctos.
(*Call alternately the heroes all*).

To the god—
Nos, Mamers, iuvato!
(*Aid us, Mars*).

To the individual brethren—
Triumpe.
(*Hurrah!*)

Each of the first five lines was repeated thrice, *triumpe* five times in the inscription, but probably six were intended. There are other indications of mistakes on the part of the stonecutter. Comments on the text, etc., will be found in Marini, *Atti e Monumenti dei Fratelli Arvali* (Rome, 1795); Henzen, *Scavi vel Bosco Sacro dei Fratelli Arvali* (Rome, 1868); id. *Acta Fratrum Arvalium* (Berlin, 1874); the *Corp. Inscript. Lat.* vi. 2021–2119; Wordsworth, *Fragments and Specimens of Early Latin* (London, 1874); Mommsen, *Hist. of Rome*, i. pp. 175 foll.; Marquardt, vi. 428–443; Allen, *Remnants of Early Latin* (Boston, 1880).

After the recitation the doors were thrown open and the service-books handed back to the attendants; and the brethren now proceeded to the election of a Magister and a Flamen for the ensuing year, followed by the distribution of the *sportula* and of roses. Next came races in the circus of the grove, in which *bigae, quadrigae,* and *desultores* are mentioned: the Magister or his deputy presided at the games, habited in the *ricinium* (see RICINIUM), and gave away the prizes. The brethren then returned to Rome and dined together, usually in the house of the Magister.

Of the other functions of the Fratres Arvales a short account will be sufficient. Whenever iron was brought into the grove, as for cutting the inscriptions for the *acta*, or the lopping and felling of the trees (already mentioned), there were sacrifices *ob ferrum illatum*, and, when the work was done, *ob ferrum elatum*. When the trees fell from decay or, worse still, were struck by lightning, and when replanting was undertaken, still more solemn sacrifices (*suovetaurilia maiora*) were offered on the spot. The Arvales also met for the *nuncupatio* or solemn pronouncing of vows for important events in the imperial family—the birthday, marriage, illness or recovery of the emperor, his setting out for or returning from serious undertakings, the confinement of an empress, etc. The Ambarvalia (q. v.), according to the most probable opinion, were entirely separate from the functions of the Fratres Arvales.

Freedmen. See LIBERTI.

Fregellae. The modern Ceprano; a town of the Volsci on the Liris in Latium, conquered by the Romans, and colonized in B.C. 328.

Fregēnae, sometimes called FREGELLAE. A town of Etruria, on the coast between Alsium and the Tiber, colonized by the Romans, B.C. 245.

Frentāni. A Samnite people dwelling on the coast of the Adriatic, from the river Sagrus on the north (and subsequently almost as far north as from the Aternus) to the river Frento on the south, from which they derived their name. They submitted to the Romans in B.C. 304.

Frento. The modern Fortore; a river in Italy, forming the boundary between the Frentani and Apulia, and falling into the Adriatic Sea.

Frenum (χαλινός). A horse's bridle, comprising, as with us, the bit (στόμιον) and reins as well as the head-stall. Xenophon, in his treatise *De Re Eq.* (vi. § 7), describes the curb-bit as having sharp prickles. See illustration on opposite page.

Frieze. See ZOPHORUS.

Frigidarium. See BALNEAE.

Frisii. A people in Germany inhabiting the

Ancient Bronze Bridle. (British Museum.)

coast from the east mouth of the Rhine to the Amisia (Ems), and coterminous on the south with the Bructeri. They were allies of the Romans before A.D. 28, when the oppression of the governor Olennius led to their revolt, and they were never again subject to Rome (Dio Cass. liv. 32; Tac. *Ann.* xiii. 54). In the fifth century they joined the Saxons and Angli (q. v.) in their invasion of Britain.

Fritillus (φιμός). A dice-box. See TESSERA.

Frogs OF ARISTOPHANES. See BATRACHAE in the Appendix.

Frontālē. See AMPYX.

Frontīnus, SEXTUS IULIUS. A Roman writer and soldier, born about A.D. 40, and governor of Britain A.D. 75–78, where he distinguished himself by the conquest of the Silures. He was the author of two treatises that are still extant—one on the art of war and another on the Roman aqueducts. He was nominated Curator Aquarum, or Superintendent of the Aqueducts, in 97, and died in 106. His military treatise is in three books (*Strategematon Libri Tres*), and was published as a supplement to another work now lost, which related to the theory of war. To these three books a fourth book has been added by some unknown writer, on which see the dissertation by Fritze (Halle, 1889). The treatise on aqueducts (*De Aquis Urbis Romae*) is in two books, and contains many valuable historical notices. Fragments of a treatise on gromatics (see GROMATICI) have also descended to us. The first complete edition of Frontinus was that of Keuchen (Amsterdam, 1661). A good text is that of Dederich (Leipzig, 1855). The principal edition of the *Strategemata* (with notes) is still that of Oudendorp (2d ed. Leipzig, 1779), lately re-edited by Gundermann (Leipzig, 1888); of the *De Aquis*, that by Dederich (with notes and a German version). See Lanciani, *Topografia di Roma Antica*, etc. (Rome, 1881).

Fronto, M. CORNELIUS. (1) A Latin writer, born at Cirta, in Africa, of an Italian family, about A.D. 100. After studying in his own country, he came to Rome in the reign of Hadrian, and acquired great reputation as a rhetorician and grammarian. Antoninus Pius appointed him preceptor to his two adopted sons, Marcus Aurelius and Lucius Verus, whose confidence and affection he gained, as is proved by their letters. After being consul (A.D. 143), Fronto was appointed to a government in Asia, which his bad health prevented him from filling. His learning and conversation are mentioned with praise by Aulus Gellius, the historian Appian, and others of his contemporaries. He died in the reign of Marcus Aurelius, at an advanced age. Until this century we had nothing of Fronto's works, except fragments of his treatise *De Differentia Verborum*, being a vocabulary of the so-called synonyms; but in 1815, Angelo Mai, having discovered in the Ambrosian Library at Milan a palimpsest MS., on which had been originally written some letters of Fronto to his two pupils, deciphered the text wherever the writing was not entirely obliterated, and published it with notes. It happened, by singular good fortune, that Mai, being some years after appointed librarian of the Vatican, discovered in another palimpsest volume another part of Fronto's letters, with the answers of Marcus Aurelius and Verus. Both the volumes came originally from the monastery of St. Columbanus, at Bobbio, the monks having written them over with the Acts of the First Council of Chalcedon, and it had happened that one of the volumes was transferred to Milan and the other to Rome. Mai published the whole in a new edition (Rome, 1823 and 1846). The MSS. have been subsequently collated by Du Rieu (revision by Naber, Leipzig, 1867). These letters are very valuable, as throwing additional light on the age of the Antonines, confirming what we know of the excellent character of Marcus Aurelius, and also showing his colleague Verus in a more favourable light than he had been viewed before. Two or three short epistles of Antoninus Pius are also interesting. There are, besides, many letters of Fronto to various friends, some of which are in Greek. Fronto's style is excessively mannered, monotonous, and pedantic; he mixes Latin and Greek in a macaronic fashion; and shows himself to be a conceited prig. He was, however, an admirer of the early Roman literature and a man of upright and independent character. See Droz, *De M. Corn. Frontonis Institutione Oratoria* (Besançon, 1885); and on the diction, the treatise of Priebe (Stettin, 1885). (2) A native of Emesa, a rhetorician, who lived at Rome in the time of Alexander Severus. He taught eloquence also at Athens, and was the rival of the first Philostratus. The critic Longinus was his nephew. He has left two epigrams on points of grammar (Jacobs, *Anth. Graec.* iii. 56; xiii. 398).

Fructus. See USUSFRUCTUS.

Fruit, GODS OF. See HORAE; POMONA; VERTUMNUS.

Frumentariae Leges. From the earliest times the supply of corn at Rome was considered one of the duties of the government. Not only was it expected that the government should take care that the corn-market (*annona*) was properly supplied, but likewise that in all seasons of scarcity it should purchase corn in the surrounding countries and sell it to the people at a moderate price (Livy, ii. 9, 34; iv. 12, 52; x. 11, etc.; xxvi. 40). This price, which is spoken of as *annona vetus*, could not rise much without exciting formidable discontent; and the administration was in all such cases considered to have neglected one of its most important duties. The superintendence of the corn-market belonged in ordinary times to the aediles; but when great scarcity prevailed, an extraordinary officer was appointed for the purpose, under the title of Praefectus Annonae (Livy, ii. 27, 5; iv. 12, 8).

With the decay of agriculture in Italy, the government had to pay still further attention to the supply of corn for the city. In addition to this, an indigent population gradually increased in Rome, which could not purchase corn even at the moderate price at which it was usually sold, and who demanded to be fed at the expense of the State. Even in early times it had been usual for the State on certain occasions, and for wealthy individuals who wished to obtain popularity and influence, to make occasional donations of corn to the people (Mommsen, *Rom. Hist.* ii. 372). But such donations were only casual; and it was not till the year B.C. 123 that the first legal provision was made for supplying the poor at Rome with corn at a price much below its market value. In that year, C. Sempronius Gracchus brought forward the first *lex frumentaria*, by which each citizen was entitled to receive every month a certain quantity of wheat (*triticum*) at the price of 6⅓ asses (about $0.06) for the modius, which was equal to nearly 1 peck English (cf. Mommsen, *Die römischen Tribus*, p. 179, n. 4, and p. 182, n. 18; Livy, *Epit.* 60; Appian, *B. C.* i. 21)—only a trifle more than half the market price. It must not be supposed that each person was allowed to receive as much as he pleased every month; the quantity must of course have been fixed, and was probably five modii monthly, as in later times. This quantity was given only to fathers of families; but it was not confined to the poor, for every citizen had a right to it, whether he were rich or poor (*viritim*, Cic. *Tusc. Disp.* iii. 20, 48); and even Piso, who had been consul, applied for his share at the distribution (Cic. l. c.). It appears, however, from the anecdote which Cicero relates about Piso, that each citizen had to apply in person, a regulation which would of itself deter most of the rich. The example that had been set by Gracchus was too tempting not to be followed, although it emptied the treasury and at the same time taught the poor to become State-paupers instead of depending upon their own exertions for obtaining a living. It thus crowded the city with an idle population.

The demagogue Apuleius Saturninus went still further. In B.C. 100 he brought forward his Lex Apuleia, by which the State was to sell corn at ⅚ of an *as* for the modius. The city quaestor Q. Caepio pointed out that the treasury could not bear such an expense (cf. Mommsen, *Gesch. d. röm. Münzwesen*, p. 560), and the most violent opposition was offered to the measure. It is doubtful whether it ever passed into a law; and it is at all events certain that it was never carried into execution. The Lex Livia, which was proposed by the tribune M. Livius Drusus in B.C. 91, was likewise never carried into effect, as it was annulled by the Senate, together with all his other laws, as passed in opposition to the auspices. Of the provisions of this Lex Frumentaria we have no account (Livy, *Epit.* lxxi.). About the same time, either shortly before or shortly after the Lex Livia, the tribune M. Octavius, supported by the aristocracy, brought forward the Lex Octavia, which modified the law of Gracchus to some extent, so that the public treasury did not suffer so much. He probably either raised the price of the corn, or diminished the number of modii which each citizen was entitled to receive (Cic. *Brut.* 62, 222). Sulla went still further, and by his Lex Cornelia, B.C. 82, did away altogether with these distributions of corn (Sall. *Hist. Fragm.* i. 45, 11, Kritz). But the Senate soon found it inexpedient to deprive the people of their customary largesses, as the popular party began to increase in power; and it was accordingly at the desire of the Senate that the consuls in B.C. 73 brought forward the Lex Terentia Cassia, which was probably only a renewal of the Lex Sempronia, with one or two additions respecting the manner in which the State was to obtain the corn. The law enacted that each Roman citizen should receive 5 modii a month at the price of 6⅓ asses for each modius. Occasionally extraordinary distributions of corn were made in virtue of decrees of the Senate.

All the *leges frumentariae* that have been hitherto mentioned had sold corn to the people, although at a price much below what the State had paid for it; but as the great party-leaders towards the close of the Republic were ready to purchase the support of the people at any sacrifice to the State, the distribution of corn became at length quite gratuitous. Caesar, in his consulship, B.C. 59, had threatened to make it so (Cic. *Ad Att.* ii. 19); and this threat was carried into execution in the following year, B.C. 58, by the Lex Clodia of the tribune Clodius. The corn was thus in future distributed without any payment; and the abolition of the payment cost the State a fifth part of its revenues (Cic. *Pro Sest.* 25, 55, with Schol. Bob. p. 301, ed. Orelli). In B.C. 57, Pompey received by the Lex Cornelia Caecilia the superintendence of the corn-market (*cura annonae*) for a period of five years; but no alteration was made in the distribution of corn by virtue of this measure. At this time the distribution of corn must have cost the State nearly $3,500,000 a year.

The consequences of such a system did not escape the penetration of Caesar; and accordingly, when master of the Roman world, he resolved to remedy the evils attending it, as far as he was able. He did not venture to abolish altogether these distributions of corn, but he did the next best thing in his power, which was the reduction of the number of recipients. During the Civil Wars numbers of persons who had no claim to the Roman franchise had settled at Rome, in order to obtain a share in the distributions of corn. The first thing, therefore, that Caesar did was to have an accurate list made out of all the corn-receivers, and to exclude from this privilege every person who could not prove that he was a Roman citizen. By this measure the 320,000 persons who had previously received the corn were at once reduced to 150,000. Having thus lessened the number of corn-receivers, he enacted that this number should not be exceeded for the future, and that vacancies which occurred by death should be filled up every year by lot by the praetor urbanus (Suet. *Caes.* 55; Dio Cass. xliii. 21). It is further exceedingly probable that, as a general rule, the corn was not *given* even to these 150,000, but sold at a low price, as had been the case at an earlier period; and that it was only to the utterly destitute that the corn was supplied gratuitously; the latter class of persons were furnished with tickets, called *tesserae nummariae* or *frumentariae* (Suet. *Octav.* 41).

The useful regulations of Caesar fell into neglect after his death, and the number of corn-receivers was soon increased beyond the limits of 150,000, which had been fixed by the dictator. This we learn from the Monumentum Ancyranum, in which Augustus (§ 15) enumerates the number of persons to whom he had given congiaria at different times; and there can be no doubt that the receivers of the congiaria and of the public corn were the same. Thus, in B.C. 44, and on the three following occasions, he distributed the congiaria to 250,000 persons; and in B.C. 5 the number of recipients had amounted to 320,000. At length, in B.C. 2, Augustus reduced the number of recipients to 200,000, and renewed many of Caesar's regulations (Suet. *Octav.* 40; Dio Cass. lv. 10). The chief regulations of Augustus seem to have been: (1) That every citizen should receive monthly a certain quantity of corn (probably 5 modii) on the payment of a certain small sum. As the number of recipients was fixed by Augustus at 200,000, there were consequently 12,000,000 modii distributed every year. Occasionally, in seasons of scarcity, or in order to confer a particular favour, Augustus made these distributions wholly gratuitous; they then became congiaria. (2) That those who were completely indigent should receive the corn gratuitously, as Iulius Caesar had determined, and should be furnished for the purpose with *tesserae nummariae* or *frumentariae,* which entitled them to the corn without payment (Suet. *Octav.* 41).

The system which had been established by Augustus was followed by his successors; but as it was always one of the first maxims of the State policy of the Roman emperors to prevent any disturbance in the capital, they frequently lowered the price of the public corn, and frequently distributed it gratuitously as a congiarium. Hence the cry of the populace, *panem et circenses.* No emperor ventured to abolish the public distributions of corn; the most that he dared do was to raise the price at which it was sold. When, therefore, we find it stated in Dio Cassius (lxii. 18) that Nero did away with the distributions of corn after the burning of Rome, we cannot understand this literally, but must suppose that he either raised the price of the commodity, or, what is more probable, obliged those poor to pay for it who had previously rereceived it gratuitously. The care which the emperors took to keep Rome well supplied with corn is frequently referred to in their coins by the legends, *Annona, Ubertas, Abundantia, Liberalitas,* etc. We find in a coin of Nerva the legend *plebei urbanae frumento constituto* (Eckhel, vol. vi. p. 406).

In course of time, the sale of the corn by the State seems to have ceased altogether, and the distribution became altogether gratuitous. Every corn-receiver was therefore now provided with a *tessera,* or ticket, and this tessera, when once granted to him, became his property. Hence it came to pass that he was not only allowed to keep the tessera for life, but even to dispose of it by sale, and bequeath it by will (*Dig.* v. 1, 52; xxxix. 1, 49; xxxix. 1, 87). Every citizen living in Rome, even freedmen and criminals (Sen. *De Benef.* iv. 28, 2), was competent to hold a tessera, with the exception of senators.

Another change was also introduced at a later period, which rendered the bounty still more acceptable to the people. Instead of distributing the corn every month, wheaten bread, called *annona civica,* was given to the people. It is uncertain at what time this change was introduced, but it seems to have been the custom before the reign of Aurelian (A.D. 270–275), as it is related of this emperor that on his return from his eastern expedition he distributed among the people a larger quantity of bread, and of a different form from that which had been usually given (Vopisc. *Aurel.* 35; Zosim. i. 61). The bread was baked by the *pistores,* who delivered it to the various depots in the city, from which it was carried away on certain days by the holders of the tesserae (Orelli, *Inscript.* no. 3358). These depots had steps (*gradus*) leading to them, whence the bread was called *panis gradilis;* and there were the strictest regulations that the bread should only be distributed from these steps, and should never be obtained at the baker's (Cod. Theod. xiv. 17, 3, 4). When Constantine transferred the seat of government to Constantinople, the system of gratuitous distribution of bread was also transferred to that city; and in order to encourage the building of houses, all householders were entitled to a share of the imperial bounty (Zosim. iii. 32). The distribution of bread at Rome was, however, still continued.

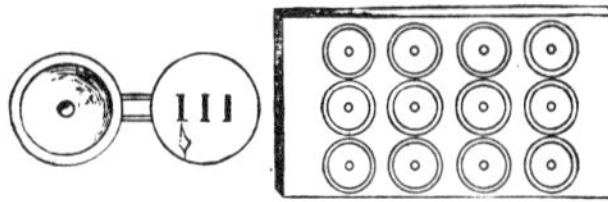

Tesserae Frumentariae. (Rich.)

Frumentarii, sc. *negotiatores.* Corn-dealers or corn-merchants (Cic. *De Off.* iii. 13, § 57; Livy, iv. 12). The latter passage shows their unpopularity in times of scarcity; they were liable to the same charges of "forestalling and regrating" as the Athenian σιτοπῶλαι, and as the corn-dealers of modern times until the present century. On the frumentarii of the legions, see LEGIO.

Frumentatio. See FRUMENTARIAE LEGES.

Frusĭno. Now Frosinone; a town of the Hernici in Latium, and subsequently a Roman colony. It was celebrated for its prodigies and portents.

Fucentis, Fucentia. See ALBA (1).

Fucĭnus Lacus. Now the Lago di Celano or Capistrano. A large lake in the centre of Italy and in the country of the Marsi, about thirty miles in circumference, into which all the mountain streams of the Apennines flow. As the waters of this lake frequently inundated the surrounding country, the emperor Claudius constructed an *emissarium* or artificial channel for carrying off the waters of the lake into the river Liris. This emissarium, which is nearly perfect, is almost three miles in length. See EMISSARIUM.

Fucus (φῦκος). A general term to signify the cosmetic which the Greek and Roman ladies employed in painting their cheeks, eyebrows, and other parts of their faces. The practice of painting the face was very general among the Greek ladies, and probably came into fashion in consequence of their sedentary mode of life, which robbed their complexions of their natural freshness, and induced them to have recourse to artificial means for restoring the red and white of nature (Xen. *Oecon.* 10, § 10). The practice was of great antiquity, and was probably first introduced among the Asiatic Ionians from the East, where the custom has prevailed from the earliest times. The resemblance between the Hebrew *pūch*, "paint," and φῦκος, is probably not accidental; the connection is accepted by Muss-Arnolt, the original meaning of both words being sea-weed, from which an alkaline dye was prepared.

The ladies at Athens did not always paint their faces when at home, but only when they went abroad, or wished to appear beautiful or captivating. Of this we have an example in the speech of Lysias on the murder of Eratosthenes, in which it is related (§ 17) that the wife, on leaving her husband to visit her paramour, painted herself (cf. Aristoph. *Lys.* 149, *Eccl.* 878, *Plut.* 1064; Plut. *Alcib.* 39). In order to produce a fair complexion, white lead (ψιμύθιον, *cerussa*) was employed (Alexis, fr. 96, 17 M). In order to give a blooming tinge to the cheeks, "rouge" was prepared from vegetable reds (Aristoph. *Lys.* 48). Ancient cosmetics were not always free from noxious drugs; and besides ψιμύθιον, already mentioned, red lead (μιλτός, *minium*) and mineral alkali (νίτρον, Att. λίτρον) were employed. The usual word for applying paint is ἐντρίβεσθαι, "to rub in," whence the dyes themselves are called ἐντρίμματα (Plut. *Crass.* 24). The eye-brows and eyelids were stained black with στίμμα or στίμμις, *stibium*, a sulphuret of antimony, which is still employed by the Turkish ladies for the same purpose. The eye-brows were likewise stained with ἄσβολος, a preparation of soot (cf. Juv. ii. 93 foll.). Ladies who used paint were occasionally betrayed by perspiration, tears, etc., of which a humorous picture is given by Xenophon (*Oecon.* 10, § 8; cf. Plaut. *Most.* i. 3, 119).

Woman Painting her Face (Tischbein).

Among the Romans the art of painting the complexion was carried to a still greater extent than among the Greeks; and even Ovid did not disdain to write a poem on the subject (*A .A.* iii. 206), though the genuineness of the fragment of the *Medicamina Faciei*, ascribed to this poet, is doubtful. The Roman ladies even went so far as to paint with blue the veins on the temple, as has been inferred from Propertius (iii. 11, 9, L. Müller). The favourite rouge was from a kind of moss; another was *purpurissum*, a mixed composition (Plaut. *Most.* i. 3, 104). The ridiculous use of patches (*splenia*), which was common among the English ladies in the reign of Queen Anne and the early Georges, was not unknown to the Roman ladies (Mart. ii. 29, 9; viii. 33, 22; x. 22). The more effeminate of the male sex at Rome also employed paint. Cicero speaks (*In Pison.* 11, § 25) of the *cerussatae buccae* of his enemy, the consul Piso.

On a Greek vase (Tischbein, *Engravings*, ii. 58) we see the figure of a woman engaged in putting the paint upon her face with a small brush (cf. Böttiger, *Sabina*, i. 24 foll., 51 foll.; Becker-Göll, *Charikles*, i. 261 foll.; *Gallus*, iii. 164 foll.).

Fufia Caninia Lex. See Lex.

Fugitivarius. See Servus.

Fugitīvus. See Servus.

Fulcra. The ends of the framework on which the pillows of a couch or the cushions of a chair were placed, resembling the head of a modern sofa. They are invariably ornamented with inlaid bronze, sometimes of the richest kind, and are surmounted by bronze ornaments often representing the head and shoulders of a mule or ass, turning sideways and backwards, with ears put down and a vicious expression. For the head of the ass is sometimes substituted that of a boy, or the head and neck of a goose. The lower part is decorated with a round boss from which springs a bust of a *genius* in full relief, or of some youthful divinity, such as Bacchus or Hercules. The framework to which these ornaments are attached is described in Juvenal (xi. 93–98). The *genius fulcri* is mentioned ib. vi. 22 and elsewhere. See W. C. F. Anderson in the *Classical Review* for 1889, p. 322; and the article Lectus.

Fulgentius, Fabius Planciădes. A Latin grammarian, a native of Carthage, who wrote towards the end of the fifth century A.D. His works include, among other things, an allegorical interpretation of the ancient mythology in three books (*Mythologiae*), the form of which reminds one of Martianus Capella (q. v.); an allegorical exposition of the *Aeneid* (*Vergiliana Continentia*); an explanation of strange and antiquated words illustrated by forged citations (*Expositio Sermonis Antiqui*); and a sort of universal history (*De Aetatibus Mundi*), of which fourteen books are extant. The plan of this last work is the absurd one called λειπογράμματος — that is, in the respective books, one letter of the alphabet in succession remains unemployed, a fact which is duly announced at the beginning and close of each book. Of the first three works, the text is printed in the edition of the *Mythographi Latini* by Staveren (Leyden, 1742). The *De Aetatibus* has been edited by Reifferscheid (Breslau, 1883–84). See Zink, *Der Mytholog Fulgentius* (Würzburg, 1867).

Fullo (γναφεύς or κναφεύς). A fuller or laundryman. The fuller's trade was one of the most important and most widely extended in Greek and Roman antiquity. It embraced all the processes, now distributed among different trades, necessary for converting the rough web into smooth cloth, the chief material used by the ancients for clothing. It was also usual to send clothes to the fuller for cleaning and working up. Clothes when sent to be cleaned were stamped with the feet

Mural Painting from the Fullonica, Pompeii. (Overbeck.)

in pits or troughs filled with warm water and substances which separated the fat from them, as urine, nitre, and fuller's earth. Soap was not known before the time of Pliny, who speaks of *sapo* (q. v.) as a Gallic invention (*H. N.* xxviii. § 191). If the object was to felt the web and make it thicker and stronger, the same process was gone through, and the cloth was then beaten with rods, washed out in clean water, dried, carded with a kind of thistle or with the skin of a hedgehog, fumigated with sulphur, rubbed in with fuller's earth to make it whiter and stronger, and finally dressed by brushing, shearing, and pressing. The fuller's earth, when well rubbed in, prevented the clothes from becoming soiled too soon, and freshened up the colours which the sulphur had destroyed. Some frescoes preserved on the walls of an ancient fuller's shop at Pompeii give a clear notion of the different processes. The *fullones* at Rome formed one of the oldest guilds. Like all mechanics, they worshipped Minerva as their tutelary goddess, and took a prominent part in her chief festival, the Quinquatrus. See Schöttgen, *Antiquitates Triturae et Fulloniae;* Beckmann, *Hist. of Inventions*, vol. ii. pp. 92 foll. (ed. Bohn); Blümner, *Technol. und Terminol.* i. pp. 157 foll.

Fullo. (From a Pompeian Painting.)

Fullonĭca. A fuller's shop. See FULLO.

Fulmenta (κάσσυμα). An extra thick sole for the shoe or sandal frequently used to increase the height of the wearer. They were made of cork (Pliny, *H. N.* xvi. 13).

Fulvia Gens. An illustrious family at Rome, the branches of which were those of Curvus, Nobilior, Flaccus, Paetinus, Maximus, Centumalus, etc.

Fulvia. (1) A woman of good family, but loose character. She disclosed to Cicero the details of the conspiracy of Catiline, which she had learned from Quintus Curius, whose mistress she was (Sall. *Cat.* 23). (2) A bold, ambitious woman, at first the wife of Clodius Pulcher (q. v.), the demagogue, and, after his death, of Marcus Antonius the triumvir. She first came into notice on the assassination of Clodius, when, having caused the corpse to be brought into the vestibule of her dwelling and having assembled the populace, she caused, by her tears and language, a violent outbreak. Some years after this, on having become the wife of Antony, she took an active part in the proscriptions of her husband, and is said to have even sacrificed to her own vengeance several individuals who had given her offence. After the head of Cicero was brought to Antony, she took it on her knees, broke forth into insults to the character of the dead orator, and then, with fiendish malice, pierced the tongue with a golden needle. Having been left at Rome by Antony during the war against Brutus and Cassius, she became all-powerful in that city, named the praetors at her own pleasure, sold the government of the provinces, and even decreed a triumph to Lucius, the brother of Antony, who had no claim whatever to one. When, after the battle of Philippi, Antony visited the East to regulate affairs in that quarter, Fulvia, irritated by his intercourse with Cleopatra, tried to induce Octavianus to take up arms against him. Not succeeding in this, she took them up against Octavianus himself, in conjunction with her brother-in-law Lucius, who now professed open opposition to the illegal power of the Triumvirate. After very bold and spirited efforts, however, on her part, she was besieged with her brother-in-law at Perusia and compelled to surrender to the power of Octavianus. Fulvia, after this, retired to Greece, and rejoined her husband, but was coldly received by him. She died at Sicyon, in B.C. 40, through chagrin and wounded pride, as was believed, at her husband's attachment to Cleopatra (Vell. Paterc. ii. 74; Plut. *Ant.;* id. *Cic.*).

Fulvius. (1) L. CURVUS. Consul in the year B.C. 322, and, six years after, master of the horse to the dictator L. Aemilius (Livy, viii. 38; ix. 21). (2) M. CURVUS PAETĪNUS. Consul in place of T. Minucius, B.C. 305. He took the city of Bovianum, in the country of the Samnites (Livy, ix. 44). (3) CN. PAETĪNUS. Consul B.C. 300. He gained a memorable victory over the Samnites near Bovianum, and enjoyed a triumph. Three years after he carried on successful operations in Etruria as propraetor (Livy, ix. 44; xv. 91). (4) SER. PAETĪNUS NOBILIOR. Consul in B.C. 255, along with Aemilius Paulus Lepidus. These two commanders sailed for Africa after the overthrow of Regulus by the Carthaginians, gained a naval victory, compelled the foe to raise the siege of Clypea, and carried off an immense booty from the Carthaginian territories. They were shipwrecked, however, on their return to Italy, and of 200 vessels only eighty were saved. (5) Q. FLACCUS. Consul in B.C. 237, 224, 212, and 209. He defeated Hanno near Bovianum, and laid siege to Capua, which surrendered to him after the lapse of a year. The conquered were treated with great cruelty. (See CAPUA.) Some time subsequent to this, he marched against the Hirpini, Lucanians, and other nations of Italy, who, alarmed at the severities inflicted on Capua, surrendered to him the garrisons which had been placed in their cities by Hannibal (Livy, xxiii. 21; xxiv. 29; xxv. 2). (6) M. NOBILIOR. Praetor in Spain B.C. 193. He carried the Roman arms to the Tagus, making himself master also of Toletum (Toledo), up to that period deemed impregnable. Having obtained the consulship, in B.C. 189, he was intrusted with the war in Greece, during which he took Ambracia, traversed Epirus as conqueror, and reduced to submission the island of Cephallenia. Two years after this he was accused before the Senate of having maltreated the allies of the Roman people, but was acquitted of the charge, and received the honour of a triumph. In the year 179 he was elected censor along with Aemilius Lepidus, his bitter foe. Apprehending injury to the State from their known enmity, the leaders of the Senate adjured both individuals to lay aside their differences for the good of their country. A reconciliation accordingly took place, and nothing occurred to disturb these friendly feelings during the rest of their joint magistracy. Fulvius raised many public structures, a basilica, a forum, etc. He also constructed a port at the mouth of the Tiber (Livy, xxxiii. 42; xxxv. 7; xx. 22, etc.). His friendship with the poet Ennius and other literary men is well known, and caused Cato the Censor to criticise him severely. (7) Q. FLACCUS. Praetor B.C. 182. He took, in this capacity, the city of Urbicua in farther Spain, and defeated the

Celtiberi in the battle of Ebura, killing in this and in another encounter 35,000 men. On his return to Rome he received a triumph, and in the same year (179) the consulship. In B.C. 174 he was elected censor along with Posthumius Albinus. These two censors were the first that paved the streets of Rome, B.C. 174. The next year he built a temple to Fortune, and, to adorn it, carried off a large portion of the marble tiles from the Temple of the Lacinian Juno in Lower Italy. The Senate compelled him to restore these. The popular account made him to have been deprived of reason for this act of sacrilege, as he committed suicide soon after (Livy, xxxix. 56, 40; xl. 16; Vell. Paterc. i. 10). (8) M. FLACCUS. Consul B.C. 125. He seconded the projects of Tiberius Gracchus to obtain for the States of Italy the rights of citizenship. Being afterwards sent against the Gauls, he defeated them, and obtained a triumph. Four years subsequently he became involved in the extreme measures of the Gracchi relative to the agrarian law, and perished in an affray which arose. See GRACCHUS.

Fumarium. See VINUM.

Funālis. A taper, used in the same manner as a torch (see FAX), but made of papyrus and other fibrous plants, twisted like a rope and smeared with pitch and wax. It was, indeed, as Antipater describes it, "a light coated with wax" (*Anth. Pal.* vi. 249). At the Saturnalia, funales were presented by clients to their patrons, and were lighted in honour of Saturn, sometimes on other occasions (Cic. *De Off.* iii. 20). The neuter, *funale*, denotes a sort of chandelier for holding torches (Ovid, *Met.* xii. 247).

Funālis Equus (παράσειρος, σειράφορος). An outrigger to a chariot drawn by horses abreast of each other (Stat. *Theb.* vi. 462). When the chariot

Funalis Equus. (Ginzrot.)

had four horses attached, two outriggers were added, one on each side of the yoke-horses (*iugales*), and called respectively *dexter* and *sinister* (Suet. *Tib.* 6). The name *funarius* is also used. See Isidor. *Orig.* xviii. 35.

Funambŭlus (σχοινοβάτης). A rope-dancer. The art of dancing on the tight rope was carried to as great perfection among the Romans as it is with us (Terence, *Hecyr. prol.* 4; Hor. *Epist.* ii. 1, 210; Juv. iii. 77; xiv. 265, 272, with Mayor's note). If we may judge from a series of paintings discovered in the excavations at Herculaneum the performers placed themselves in an endless variety of graceful and sportive attitudes. The emperor M. Aurelius, in consequence of the fall of a boy, caused feather-beds (*culcitrae*) to be laid under the rope to obviate the danger of such accidents (Capitol. *M. Ant. Phil.* 12). One of the most difficult exploits was running down the rope (Suet. *Nero*, 11) at the conclusion of the performance. Germanicus and the emperor Galba attempted to exhibit elephants walking on the rope (Plin. *H. N.* viii. § 5; Suet. *Galba*, 6). See SALTATIO.

Rope-dancers. (From a painting at Herculaneum.)

Funarius Equus. See FUNALIS EQUUS.

Funda (σφενδόνη). (1) A sling for discharging stones, or leaden plummets (*glandes*)—a weapon commonly used in warfare by the Spaniards, Persians, Egyptians, and other foreign nations; and also occasionally by the Romans, as is shown by the annexed illustration, representing a Roman soldier in the army of Trajan, from the column erected in honour of that emperor (Plin. *H. N.* vii. 37; Verg. *Georg.* i. 309). (2) (ἀμφίβληστρον). A casting-net; employed, like our own, for taking fish in rivers (Verg. *Georg.* i. 141; Serv. ad l.; Isidor. *Orig.* xix. 5, 2); but apparently cast from behind, and over the right shoulder, instead of being discharged from the left shoulder and in front of the person throwing it, as is now the practice. (3) A bag or pack slung over the shoulders, for the convenience of carrying money, or any other small articles (Macrob. *Sat.* ii. 4); probably so called because, with the straps which fastened it, it had the appearance of a sling, as shown by the annexed illustration, from the device on a bronze lamp. (4) (σφενδόνη, πυελίς). The bezel of a ring—that is, the rim in which the gem is set and which holds it as a sling does its stone; more especially so called when the setting is transparent (Plin. *H. N.* xxxvii. 37, 42).

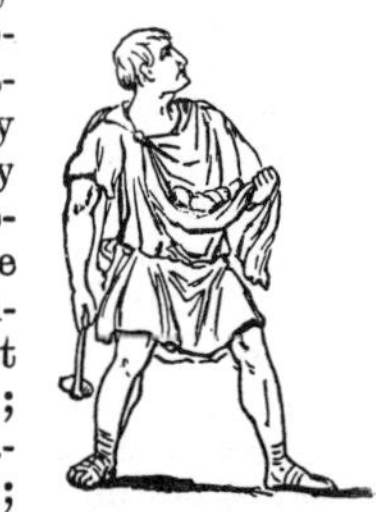

Funditor.

Funda (bag).

Funda. (Rich.)

Fundānus. A lake near Fundi in Italy, which discharges itself into the Mediterranean. According to Pliny (*H. N.* xiv. 6), the Lacus Fundanus was originally called Amyclanus, from the city of Amyclae in its vicinity.

Fundi. The modern Fondi; an ancient town in Latium on the Appia Via, at the head of a narrow bay of the sea running a considerable way into the land, called the Lacus Fundanus. The surrounding country produced good wine (Mart. xiii. 113).

Funditōres (*funda*, "a sling"). The light-armed slingers in the Roman army. They were usually raised by recruiting, or contributed by the allies. See EXERCITUS; FUNDA.

Fundŭla. A *cul-de-sac*, or blind-alley (Varro, *L. L.* v. 145).

Funus. A funeral, so termed because, in ancient times, the Romans were buried by torch light, twisted ropes (*funalia*) smeared with pitch being carried by the mourners for the purpose (Isidor. *Orig.* xi. 2, 34; Donat. *ad* Terent. *Andr.* i. 1, 81). Under this title, it is here intended to give an account of the burial rites of the Greeks and Romans. The tombs will be explained in the article SEPULCRUM.

(1) GREEK. The Greeks attached great importance to the burial of the dead. They believed that souls could not enter the Elysian Fields till their bodies had been buried; and accordingly we find the shade of Elpenor in the *Odyssey* (xi. 66, etc.) earnestly imploring Odysseus to bury his body. So strong was this feeling among the Greeks that it was considered a religious duty to throw earth upon a dead body which a person might happen to find unburied (Hor. *Carm.* i. 28, 36); and among the Athenians, those children who were released from all other obligations to unworthy parents were nevertheless bound to bury them (Aesch. *c. Timarch.* § 14). The neglect of burying one's relatives is frequently mentioned by the orators as a grave charge against the moral character of a man, since the burial of the body by the relations of the dead was considered a religious duty by the universal law of the Greeks. The common expressions for the funeral rites, *τὰ δίκαια, νόμιμα* or *νομιζόμενα, προσήκοντα*, show that the dead had, as it were, a legal and moral claim to burial.

At the moment of death the eyes and mouth were closed by one of those present (Plat. *Phaed.* 118). According to Lucian, the obolus to serve as Charon's fare was at once placed in the mouth of the corpse. This coin was also called *δανάκη* (Hesych. s. v.). The custom is first mentioned by Aristophanes (*Frogs*, 139), and does not appear to have been in use at a very early date. Confirmation of the practice is given by actual discoveries, for coins are frequently found in Greek tombs, and in some between the teeth of the skeleton. The body was then washed (Eurip. *Phoen.* 1319, 1667), anointed with perfumes, and clothed in rich garments, generally white in colour. These were buried or burned with the body, but the number of them was limited by a law of Solon (Plut. *Sol.* 21). A wreath of flowers was placed upon the head (Eurip. *Phoen.* 1632). Golden wreaths, in imitation of laurel or other foliage, were sometimes used, and have been found in graves.

The corpse, thus prepared, was laid out (*πρόθεσις, προτίθεσθαι*) on a bed (*κλίνη*), which appears to have been of the ordinary kind, with a pillow (*προσκεφάλαιον*) for supporting the head and back (Lys. *c. Eratosth.* § 18). By a law of Solon it was ordered that the *πρόθεσις* should take place inside the house (Lex *ap.* Demosth. *c. Macart.* p. 1071, § 62). As among the Romans, the feet were turned towards the door (Hom. *Il.* xix. 212). Vases of a special kind (*λήκυθοι*), probably containing perfumes, were placed beside the body (Ar. *Eccl.* 1032, 538). These vases were also buried with the coffin, and a large number of them have been found in graves in Attica. A few of them are in the ordinary black and red figured styles, but the greater number are of a special ware of great beauty, manufactured for funeral purposes. In this ware the ground is white, and scenes are painted upon it in bright colours, in a freer and less rigid style than in the vases with red or black figures. See E. Pottier, *Étude sur les Lécythes Blancs Attiques, à Représentations Funéraires* (Paris, 1883); Benndorf, *Griechische und sicilische Vasenbilder* (Berlin, 1869); and the article VAS. A honey-cake (*μελιτοῦττα*), intended as a sop for Cerberus, was also placed by the side of the corpse (Aristoph. *Lys.* 601). Before the door, a vessel of water was placed (*ἀρδάνιον*), in order that persons who had been in the house might purify themselves from the pollution of death by sprinkling water on their persons (Eurip. *Alc.* 98).

The near relatives of the deceased assembled round the bed on which he was laid, and uttered loud lamentations. Although more violent signs of grief were forbidden by Solon (Plut. *Sol.* 21), we find that Lucian (*De Luctu*, 12) mentions as accompaniments of the *πρόθεσις*, not only groaning and wailing, but also beating of breasts, tearing of hair, laceration of cheeks, rending of garments, and sprinkling of ashes upon the head. It was perhaps with the object of limiting the time for these excesses of grief that Solon ordained that the burial should take place on the day after the *πρόθεσις*, before sunrise, and that Plato (*Leges*, xii. 959 A) declared that the *πρόθεσις* should not last longer than was necessary to show that death had really taken place. It appears that singers were hired to lead the mourning chant at the *πρόθεσις* (Lucian, *De Luctu*, 20).

The accompanying illustration, representing the *πρόθεσις*, is taken from Pottier. The corpse lies

The *πρόθεσις*. (From a Greek vase.)

upon a couch, and is covered with a rich garment. The head alone is unveiled, and is surrounded with a fillet (*ταινία*). Two female figures stand beside the couch, with gestures of grief. One of them carries a tray or basket, across which two fillets are laid. Other fillets are placed across the couch. In the background is a mirror, or fan, perhaps intended for the keeping away of flies (cf. Dio Cass. lxxiv. 4, 2).

The ἐκφορά. (From a stamped terra-cotta plaque found at the Piraeus.)

The funeral (ἐκφορά, ἐκφέρειν) took place legally, as has been already remarked, on the day following the πρόθεσις. It might, however, be put off several days to allow of the arrival of distant friends (Plut. *Timol.* 39). The early morning was the usual time (Plat. *Leges*, xii. 960 A). The bier was borne either by hired bearers (νεκροφόροι, Poll. vii. 195), or, in cases where it was decided to honour the dead, by specially selected citizens (Plut. *Timol.* 39). The men walked before the corpse and the women behind, and it appears that musicians were hired to play mournful tunes on the flute and sing dirges (θρῆνοι) at the ἐκφορά as well as at the πρόθεσις. Those who accompanied the funeral wore mourning garments of a black or dark colour (Eurip. *Alc.* 427). The head was also shaved or the hair cut as a sign of grief (Hom. *Od.* iv. 197; *Il.* xxiii. 46, 135, 141, 146; Bion. *Idyll.* i. 81).

Representations of the ἐκφορά are rare. The foregoing illustration represents a stamped terra-cotta plaque found at the Piraeus (in the collection of M. Rayet, *Convoi Funèbre*, No. 75). The corpse lies upon a couch. The head is bare; the rest of the body covered. The couch is placed upon a car drawn by two horses, though mules were oftener used. Mourners accompany it with gestures of grief. A female attendant carries upon her head a vessel, probably to serve for libations. Another attendant plays upon the double flute.

It was the custom, at Athens at any rate, to hold public funerals for those who had fallen in war. Thucydides (ii. 34) describes with some minuteness the proceedings usual on such occasions. The πρόθεσις of the bones took place on a platform (or perhaps in a booth or tent) erected for the purpose in some public place. On the day of the funerals, coffins of cypress wood, one for each tribe, were carried upon wagons. Each coffin contained the bones of the members of the tribe to which it was assigned. An empty couch, adorned as for a funeral, was borne in the procession to represent those whose bodies had not been found. The procession was accompanied by any citizens and aliens who wished to attend, and by women who were related to those who had fallen. In Greece, funeral orations were pronounced only at public funerals of the kind described, not, as at Rome, over individuals, even though they were specially distinguished (Dion. Hal. v. 17). This custom seems to have arisen about the time of the Persian Wars. In other respects the procedure at a public funeral does not seem to have differed from that in use at private burials.

In spite of the statement of Lucian (*De Luctu*, 21) that the Greeks burned their dead and the Persians buried them, it is certain, both from literary evidence and also from the excavation of tombs, that burning and burying were both practised by the Greeks. The word θάπτειν is used of the burial of the ashes after cremation, but κατορύττειν refers only to the burial of an unburned body. We hear of burial also among the Spartans (Plut. *Lyc.* 27; Thuc. i. 134). In Homer there is no mention of any burial without burning; but in graves at Mycenae, skeletons have been found which showed no traces of fire. Evidence both of burning and burying has been found in graves of a later date in many parts of the Greek world. See Hermann-Blümner, *Privatalterth.* p. 375.

Funeral Pyre.

The pile of wood (πυρά) upon which the body was burned was sometimes erected over the grave in which the ashes were to be buried. There is a full description of cremation in the Homeric period in *Iliad* (xxiii. 161 foll.), where Achilles celebrates the funeral of Patroclus. The pyre was made a hundred feet in length and breadth, and the bodies of sheep, oxen, horses, dogs, and twelve Trojan captives were placed upon it. Honey and perfumes were also poured upon it before it was lighted. When the pyre had burned down, the remains of the fire were quenched with wine, and the relatives and friends collected the bones or ashes (*Il.* xxiv. 791). The remains thus collected were placed in a receptacle sometimes of gold, but generally of a less precious material, and buried. A description of these receptacles, of the other articles placed in the tomb, and of the tomb itself will be found in the article SEPULCRUM.

When bodies were buried without previous cremation, they were generally placed in coffins, which were called by various names, as σοροί, πύελοι, ληνοί, λάρνακες, δροῖται, though some of these names were also applied to the urns in which the bones were collected. For further information upon this point, see the article SEPULCRUM.

Immediately after the funeral was over, the relatives partook of a feast which was called περίδειπνον or νεκρόδειπνον (Lucian, *De Luctu*, 24). It was the custom that this feast should be given at the house of the nearest relative (Demosth. *De Cor.* p. 321, § 355).

Funeral Banquet. (From a bas-relief; *Marmora Oxon.*)

Other ceremonies were performed on the third, the ninth, and the thirtieth days after the funeral, and were called respectively τρίτα, ἔνατα, and τριακάς or τριακάδες (Poll. viii. 146). The rites on the thirtieth day (Poll. i. 66, iii. 102) included a repetition of the funeral feast.

It was also the custom to bring offerings to the tomb on certain days in each year (Plato, *De Leg.* iv. 717 E). Herodotus mentions that these annual sacrifices to the dead were called γενέσια (iv. 26), from which it is inferred that they were offered on the birthday of the deceased (cf. Diog. Laërt. x. 18). The name νεκύσια was also used in the same sense. The ceremonies which were performed at these stated intervals might be used at any other time, if for some reason it was necessary to appease the departed spirit. The word ἐναγίζειν was used for the act of offering, ἐναγίσματα for the things offered on these occasions. These consisted of libations (χοαί) of wine, oil, milk, honey mixed with water or milk (Aesch. *Pers.* 609 foll.), which were poured upon the ground (γάποτοι, Aesch. *Pers.* 621). Elaborate banquets were sometimes prepared, burned in honour of the dead, and buried in a trench (Lucian, *Char.* 22). Wreaths were also placed upon the grave-stones, and they were anointed with perfumes.

The period of mourning varied in length at different places. At Athens the τριακάς seems to have ended it on the thirtieth day after the funeral (Lysias, *De Caede Erat.* § 14). At Sparta it lasted only eleven days (Plut. *Lyc.* 27).

Certain special rites were used in particular cases. A spear was carried in front of the body of any person who had died a violent death, as a symbol of the revenge which was to follow the murderer (Eurip. *Troad.* 1148). In the case of those who had committed suicide, the hand which had done the deed was cut off and buried separately (Aeschin. *in Ctes.* § 244). Certain criminals, who were put to death by the State, were also deprived of burial, which was considered to be an additional punishment (Plut. *Them.* 22; Thuc. i. 134). The bodies of those persons who had been struck by lightning were regarded as sacred (ἱεροὶ νεκροί); they were not buried with others (Eurip. *Suppl.* 935), but usually on the spot where they had been struck (Artemid. *Oneirocr.* ii. 9, p. 146).

It has been already mentioned that in the public funerals of those killed in war, an empty couch was carried in the procession to represent those whose bodies had not been found. In other cases, where a person was supposed to be dead, though his body was not found, funeral rites were performed for him (Eurip. *Hel.* 1241 foll.). If such a person was afterwards found to be alive, he was considered impure, and was not allowed to enter temples till certain rites had been performed. These rites consisted in a symbolism of birth and the ceremonies connected with it. The δευτερόποτμος or ὑστερόποτμος was washed, wrapped in swaddling clothes, and fed with milk. Having been thus born again into life, he was freed from his impurity (Plut. *Q. R.* 5).

(2) ROMAN.—Among the Romans also the burial of the dead was a most solemn duty. It was incumbent upon any one who found an unburied body at least to cast earth upon it three times (Hor. *Od.* i. 28). If no funeral rites had been performed, the soul of the dead man could not be received among the shades, but wandered homeless upon the earth (Tertull. *De Anim.* 56).

A near relative of the dying person caught the last breath in his mouth (Verg. *Aen.* iv. 684). As soon as he was dead his eyes were closed by one of those present (Lucan. *Phars.* iii. 740). Then followed the *conclamatio*, variously explained as (1) a cry *in articulo mortis*, which seems probable from Propertius (v. 7, 23; cf. Ovid, *Trist.* iii. 3, 43);

The *Conclamatio*, or lamentation for the dead. (From a Roman relief.)

(2) the recall of the dead by uttering his or her name three times, in order to ascertain the fact of death if there was no answer—a custom still in use at the death-bed of a Pope; (3) as commonly understood, the lamentation for the dead when there was no longer any possibility of doubt. The mourners called repeatedly the name of the deceased, with loud cries, and exclamations such as *vale* (Lucan, *Phars.* ii. 22; Catullus, ci.; Ovid, *Met.* x. 62, *Fasti*, iv, 852).

The body was then washed with warm water and anointed with perfumes and spices (Pers. iii. 103). That this took place after the *conclamatio* is learned from Ammianus Marcellinus (xxx. 10). The corpse was then clothed either in the toga (Juv. iii. 173 with Mayor's note), or in the state robes of any office which had been held by the deceased (Livy, xxxiv. 7; Polyb. vi. 53). The garments in which the corpse was clothed were sometimes splendid and costly (*vestes purpureae*, Verg. *Aen.* vi. 221; *pretiosae*, Val. Max. v. 5, 4). Precious ornaments were often added. Rings, for example, are often found in graves, and we learn from Propertius (iv. 7, 9) that they were sometimes burned with the body. Flowers were also used for the adornment of the couch on which the corpse was laid; and a censer (*acerra*) was placed beside it (Fest. *Epit.* p. 18). The following illustration from a Roman relief in the Lateran Museum (Baumeister, p. 239) represents the *lectus funebris*, on which the corpse of a woman lies dressed. Two women mourners (*praeficae*) stand behind, and by their side a man in the act of putting a garland on the head of the corpse. On each side of the *lectus funebris* is a torch. On the left side is a woman blowing the flute, and above another with folded hands; on the right side sit three women, wearing the *pilleus* (probably manumitted slaves); below is the family of the deceased. Among the Romans, as among the Greeks, it was customary to place a small coin in the mouth of the deceased, for the purpose of paying Charon's passage-money.

The Lectus Funebris. (Lateran Museum, Rome.)

This is alluded to by Juvenal (iii. 267) and Propertius (iv. 11, 7), but not by earlier writers. Coins, however, have been found in graves of an earlier date than the Second Punic War (*C. I. L.* i. p. 27); and in graves at Praenesté, dating from the third century B.C., coins were actually found in the mouths of the skeletons (*C. I. L.* i. 28). In imperial times the practice was common.

The preparations necessary for the due laying out of the body were performed by the *pollinctores* (Plaut. *Asin.* v. 2, 60), who probably took the cast of the dead man's face, from which the wax *imago* was made, to be kept in the *atrium* of the house by his descendants, and used in funeral processions in a way shortly to be described. The *pollinctor* was furnished by the *libitinarius* or undertaker, who entered into a contract for conducting the whole funeral. The latter got his name from the fact that he exercised his business at the temple or grove of Libitina, the goddess of corpses and funerals (Plut. *Num.* 12, § 1; *Quaest. Rom.* 23). Deaths were also registered at this temple (Suet. *Ner.* 39), and the offering called *lucar Libitinae* was made. See LUCAR.

When the body had been thus prepared and adorned, it was laid upon a couch of state, generally in the *atrium* of the house, with the feet towards the door (Pers. iii. 105). Outside the door of the house were placed branches of cypress or pine (Serv. *ad Aen.* iii. 64), for the purpose of warning those who might be polluted by entering a house in which was a corpse. The cypress was apparently only used by those of good position. We are told by Servius (*ad Aen.* v. 64) that the corpse lay in state for seven days before burial. This can only have been the case in exceptional circumstances, when some form of embalming was used.

Funerals were conducted by the family of the deceased (*funus privatum*), except in cases where a public funeral (*funus publicum*) was voted, either by the Senate (Cic. *Phil.* ix. 7) or in provincial towns by the *decuriones*, as a mark of honour or respect to the deceased. This honour was paid in the case of foreign kings who died in Italy (Val. Max. v. 1, 1); and men who had fallen in the service of their country (Val. Max. v. 2, 10).

A public invitation was given to all important funerals by a herald (*praeco*). Hence the phrases *funus indicere, funus indictivum* (Suet. *Iul.* 84; Cic. *De Leg.* ii. 24, 61). The formula of invitation has been preserved: "OLLUS QUIRIS LETO DATUS. EXSEQUIAS, QUIBUS EST COMMODUM, IRE IAM TEMPUS EST. OLLUS EX AEDIBUS EFFERTUR." (Fest. p. 254 d, 34.) *Translaticium funus* is used for an unceremonious burial (Suet. *Ner.* 33).

In ancient times all funerals took place by night (Serv. *ad Aen.* xi. 143); in later times only those of children (Serv. l. c.), and poor people whose means did not admit of sufficient display for the day-time (Mart. viii. 75). The torches with which funerals were always accompanied were probably a relic of burial by night, though no doubt they also served for lighting the pyre.

An opportunity for the display of splendour was given by the funeral procession, and was so largely used by families of wealth and position that sumptuary laws to regulate such expenses are found among the Tables of the Decemviri (Cic. *De Leg.* ii. 23, 59) and the enactments of Sulla (Plut. *Sull.* 35). The order of the funeral procession was regulated by the *designator* or *dissignator*, whose attendants were dressed in black. The order in which the various parts of the procession came is uncertain, but it is generally supposed that at the head of it were the musicians (*siticines*), who made use of *tubae*, *tibiae*, and *cornua*. The number of *tibicines* was by the Twelve Tables limited to ten (Cic. *De Leg.* ii. 23, 59). Then followed (at any rate in earlier times) the mourning women, called *praeficae*, who sang the *nenia* or *lessus*, a mournful song in praise of the dead man (Cic. *De Leg.* ii. 24, 62). Then followed in some cases dancers and *mimi* (Suet. *Iul.* 84), who were allowed, as at a triumph, free license of jesting. We learn from Suetonius (*Vesp.* 19) that it was the custom for the *archimimus* to wear a mask in the likeness of the deceased, to imitate his speech and manners, and even to make jests at his expense.

The most striking part of the procession was probably formed by the *imagines*. It is said by Polybius (vi. 53) that the *imagines*, or wax masks representing distinguished ancestors of the deceased, were brought out from their resting-place in the *atrium*, and each was worn by a man chosen to resemble as nearly as possible the person whom he was supposed to represent and clothed in the dress of the office which the prototype of the mask had held. Each rode upon a chariot, and was accompanied with due pomp of lictors and other insignia of his office. Thus all the distinguished ancestors of the dead man were present in effigy at his funeral. If he was of good birth, many families to which he was related were represented by their *imagines* (Tac. *Ann.* iii. 76), and the actual number was sometimes very great. At the funeral of Marcellus there are said to have been 600 (Serv. *ad Aen.* vi. 802). Sometimes, as a special honour, spoils, crowns, and other records of victories and triumphs were carried before the bier. The procession was also swelled by the slaves who were liberated by the will of the deceased, all with shorn heads, wearing the *pilleus* (Livy, xxxviii. 55). The bier itself was sometimes carried by these liberated slaves (Pers. iii. 106); or in the case of emperors, by magistrates and senators (Suet. *Aug.* 100). The body was placed uncovered on a bier or couch (*feretrum*, *torus*), which in great funerals was elaborately decorated (Suet. *Iul.* 84). In some cases, probably when decay had begun to disfigure the features, the body was placed in a coffin (*capulus*), and a waxen representation (*effigies*) was exposed to view instead (Tac. *Ann.* iii. 5).

In the burial of the poor and of slaves of course this pomp was absent. Hired bearers (*vespillones*), six (Mart. vi. 77, 10) or four (id. viii. 75, 9) in number, carried the body in a simple wooden coffin or bier, which was not buried with the body (*sandapila*, Mart. ii. 81).

The relatives of the deceased followed behind the bier, dressed in mourning. The sons of the deceased had their heads veiled, while the daughters went uncovered and with dishevelled hair (Plut. *Quaest. Rom.* 11). Mourning was shown by very much the same signs as in modern times—viz., by the absence of adornment and the wearing of black garments (Juv. x. 245; Prop. v. 7, 28; Tac. *Ann.* iii. 2; *pullus*, Juv. iii. 213). Under the emperors white seems to have been substituted for black as the mourning colour for women (Plut. *Quaest. Rom.* 26; Stat. *Silv.* iii. 3, 3). The women were also in the habit of crying aloud, tearing their hair and lacerating their cheeks in the funeral procession itself (Prop. iii. 13, 27).

In this order the funeral train proceeded to the Forum. There it halted before the Rostra, the wearers of the *imagines* took their seats upon curule chairs, and the *laudatio funebris* was pronounced, generally by a near relative of the deceased (Polyb. vi. 53), though in the case of a *funus publicum* this function might be assigned by a *senatusconsultum* to one of the magistrates (Quint. *Instit.* iii. 7, 2).

From the Forum the procession moved on to the place of burning or burial, which, according to a law of the Twelve Tables, was obliged to be outside the city, though special exceptions were sometimes made (Cic. *De Leg.* ii. 23, 58). Both burning and burial were in use among the Romans. Cicero (*De Leg.* ii. 22, 56) and Pliny (*H. N.* vii. § 187) both hold the view that burial was the more ancient custom. Pliny further says that burning was introduced because it was found that the bodies of those killed in distant countries and buried there were dug up and scattered by the enemy. It is conjectured, however, that the change was partly brought about by motives of health and convenience. In certain families the practice of burial was kept up, after burning had become general. Sulla was the first of the Cornelii to be burned. The reason, according to Cicero and Pliny, of the departure from the custom of his family was, that he feared lest his own bones should receive the same treatment as he had given to those of Marius. In later times burning became far more common than burial, though the latter was always used in the case of children who died before they had cut their teeth (Plin. *H. N.* vii. 72; Juv. xv. 140), and in the case of those who had been struck by lightning. It seems also that persons of the poorest classes were always buried. After the introduction of Christianity burial again came into use instead of burning. The view that burial was older than cremation is confirmed by some Roman customs. According to pontifical law, the essential part of the funeral ceremony was the casting of earth upon the face of the corpse (Cic. *De Leg.* ii. 22, 57). Again, when a body was to be burned, it was the custom to cut off some portion of it, called *os resectum*, which was subsequently buried (Fest. *Epit.* p. 148). By this means the newer and more convenient method was adopted, while the ancient regulation which prescribed burial was still carried out.

The remaining rites varied, according as the body was to be buried or burned. In the case of burial the body was placed in the grave either on the bier on which it had been carried, or in a sarcophagus. Numerous objects were also placed in the grave. (See SEPULCRUM.) The ceremonies which followed had the double object of making the grave a *locus religiosus*, and of purifying the family and house which had been defiled by the presence of a corpse. Earth was thrown upon the face of the dead (Cic. *De Leg.* ii. 22, 57), a pig was sacrificed, and an offering was made to the Lares. The day on which these sacrifices took place was called *feriae denicales* (Fest. *Epit.* p. 70). A funeral feast called *silicernium* was also held, apparently on the day of the funeral, and by the grave (Varr. *ap.* Non. p. 48, 8). The period of mourning lasted nine days (*novendiale*), though it is uncertain whether this period was reckoned from the day of death or the day of burial (Serv. *ad Aen.* v. 64). At the end of this period a *sacrificium novendiale* was offered to the dead, and a *cena novendialis* was held (Tac. *Ann.* vi. 5).

The burning of a body sometimes took place at the spot where the ashes were to be interred. In this case the funeral pile (*rogus, pyra*) was erected over the trench which was subsequently to be the grave (*bustum*). The body, however, was often burned at a place near the monument, specially destined for this purpose, *ustrinum, ustrina* (Fest. *Epit.* p. 32). The pyre was built of wood, in the form of an altar (Verg. *Aen.* vi. 177). A law of the Twelve Tables ordered that it should not be smoothed with an axe (Cic. *De Leg.* ii. 23, 59). Pyres were sometimes painted (Plin. *H. N.* xxxv. § 49), and cypress-trees were placed in front (Ovid, *Trist.* iii. 13, 21). On the top of the pile the corpse was placed, with the couch on which it had been carried. Many things were placed on the pyre by the relations and mourners, such as clothes, arms, ornaments, hunting nets and apparatus, horses, dogs, birds (Plin. *Epist.* iv. 2). It was also sprinkled with perfumes, gums, and spices.

The pyre was lighted by one of the relatives, with face turned away (Verg. *Aen.* vi. 224). When it was burned down, the glowing ashes were extinguished with water or wine (Verg. *Aen.* vi. 226). Those who had taken part in the funeral uttered a last farewell (Verg. *Aen.* ii. 644) and departed, while the nearest relatives remained to collect the bones and ashes when they were dry. This was probably done as a rule on the day of the funeral. The bones were sprinkled with wine (though it is not certain that this sprinkling is to be separated from that mentioned above), dried with a linen cloth, and placed in an urn or box with perfumes and spices. The urn was then placed in the sepulchre.

It has already been mentioned that if the body was burned, the *os resectum* was buried separately. The ceremonies of the *feriae denicales* were used, as in the case of the burial, including the throwing of earth upon the remains of the dead (Cic. *De Leg.* ii. 22, 57). It does not appear at what moment this was done; but the object of it was to consecrate the place of burial, to make it a *locus religiosus*. After the bones and ashes of the deceased had been placed in the urn, the persons present were thrice sprinkled by a priest with pure water from a branch of olive or laurel, for the purpose of purification (Verg. *Aen.* vi. 229); after which they were dismissed by the *praefica* or some other person, by the solemn word *Ilicet*, that is, *ire licet.* In the case of burning, the practices connected with the *silicernium* and the *novendiale* seem to have been the same as in the case of burial (see above). When those who had accompanied the funeral returned home, they underwent a purification called *suffitio*, which consisted in being sprinkled with water and stepping over a fire (Fest. p. 3). It was then also, perhaps, that the house was swept with a special kind of broom (Fest. p. 58, s. v. *Everriator*).

In the case of important funerals, scenic or gladiatorial exhibitions were often given. (See GLADIATORES.) Scenic exhibitions were less common; but the Didascalia to the *Adelphoe* of Terence states that that play was performed at the *ludi funebres* of Aemilius Paullus (B.C. 160), and we are informed by Livy that *ludi scenici* as well as gladiatorial combats were exhibited at the death of T. Flamininus (B.C. 174). There were also distributions of food (*visceratione*s) and public banquets (Suet. *Iul.* 26).

It remains to give some account of the annual rites performed at the tombs in honour of the Manes. Certain days in February (13th–21st) were set apart as *dies parentales*, or *parentalia.* The last of these days was specially known as *feralia* (Ovid, *Fasti*, ii. 569). The ceremonies performed at this time are described by Ovid (*Fasti*, ii. 533 foll.). Offerings to the Manes (*inferiae*) were brought to the tomb. These consisted of wine and milk, honey and oil, the blood of victims, especially of black sheep, pigs, and cattle (Arnob. vii. 20), various fruits, bread, salt, and eggs (Juv. v. 84). The tomb was adorned with wreaths and flowers, especially roses and violets (Ovid, l. c.). A meal was also eaten at the grave. A *triclinium funebre*, intended apparently for this purpose, was found at Pompeii and is represented in the accompanying illustration. During the *dies parentales* temples were

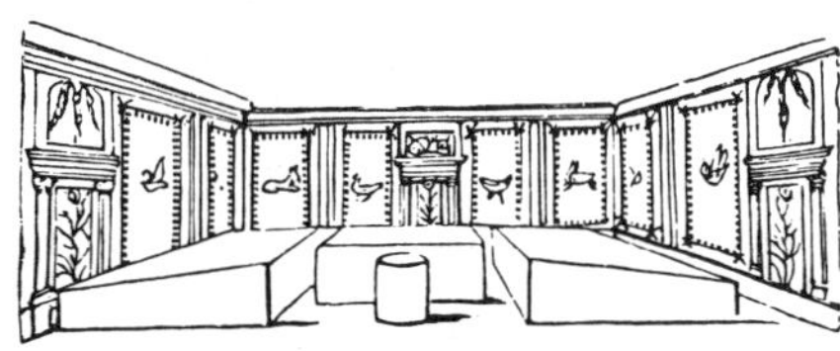

Funereal Triclinium. (Pompeii.)

shut and marriages forbidden (Ovid, *Fasti*, ii. 557 foll.), and the magistrates laid aside the insignia of their office (Lydus, *De Mens.* iv. 24). The terms *parentare, parentatio*, were also applied to similar rites performed on other days of the year, such as the day of birth, death, or burial of the person to be honoured. Special days were also appropriated to roses and violets (*rosatio, rosaria, rosalia, violatio;* Plin. *H. N.* xxi. § 11).

BIBLIOGRAPHY.—References may be made to Feydeau, *Histoire des Usages Funèbres*, etc. (Paris, 1856). For the Greek usages, see Becker-Göll, *Charikles*, iii. 114–167; Hermann-Blümner, *Privatalterth.* pp. 361 foll.; and Graves, *Burial Customs of the Ancient Greeks* (Brooklyn, 1891). For the Roman usages, see Becker-Göll, *Gallus*, iii. 481–547; and Marquardt, *Privatleben*, pp. 340–385.

Fur (φώρ). A thief; humorously called "a man of three letters" (*homo trium litterarum*, Plaut. *Aul.* ii. 4, 46). See FURTUM.

Furca (δίκρανον). (1) A two-pronged fork, a hay-fork, pitchfork, etc. (Verg. *Georg.* i. 264). The name is also given to a flesh-fork (Petron. 95), and to any forked prop or stay—e. g. for vines (Verg. *Georg.* ii. 259); for planks (Livy, i. 35); for fishing-nets (Pliny, *H. N.* lx. § 9). Table-forks were not used by the ancients, who took their food from the plate with their fingers, except in the case of shell-fish and eggs, for which they had a sort of combination fork and spoon. (See CENA, p. 313, and COCLEAR.) The diminutive FURCILLA denotes a smaller fork, but still a large one according to our notions. (2) As an instrument of punishment, *furca* means a contrivance something like a yoke passing around the back of the neck and down each arm. This the criminal or slave wore while being whipped through the streets—whence FURCIFER is an expression equivalent to our "gallows-bird" (Plaut. *Amphit.* i. 1, 132, and often). (3) The word is also used of the gibbet or gallows (Paul. *Dig.* 33). (4) (στῆριγξ, στήριγμα). The part of a carriage-pole which fastens into the axle.

Furcŭlae Caudīnae. See CAUDIUM.

Furiae. See EUMENIDES.

Furii. A family which migrated from Medullia in Latium, and came to settle at Rome under Romulus, and was admitted among the patricians. Camillus (q. v.) was of this family, and it was he who first raised it to distinction.

Furīna. An early Latin goddess, whose name, in the time of Varro, was known to very few (Varr. *L. L.* v. 3). There was a sacred grove of this goddess beyond the Tiber (in which Gaius Gracchus was slain), and this, with the similitude of the name, led Cicero and others to identify Furian with the Furies (Cic. *N. D.* iii. 18). The Furinalia were celebrated on the 25th of July.

Furius Bibacŭlus. See BIBACULUS.

Furnus (ἰπνός). (1) An oven, usually a baker's oven (Plaut. *Cas.* ii. 5, 1). (See PISTOR.) (2) A baker's shop (Hor. *Sat.* i. 4, 37). (See PISTOR.) (3) A hot-air, or vapour-bath, as distinguished from *balneum*, which is a warm water bath. See BALNEAE.

Furtum. Theft; the robbery of movable things, though furtum could be committed without actually carrying off the object, as in the case of a thing deposited (*depositum*), the unlawful use of which was furtum. Furtum was either *manifestum* or not, the former when the thief was caught in the act. It was called *furtum conceptum* when a stolen object was found in a person's possession; and if a person gave to a third person stolen goods, the third person could bring an *actio furti oblati* against the giver. The punishment for *furtum manifestum* was *capitalis*—i. e. affecting one's *caput* (q. v.). A thief killed while committing robbery at night was held by the Twelve Tables to be lawfully killed; but in the daytime he could be killed only when he resisted with a deadly weapon (*telum*). See KLOPES DIKÉ.

Fuscĭna (τρίαινα). A trident, i. e. a large fork with several branches (usually three) employed by fishermen in spearing fish. It was the symbol of Neptune as the god of the ocean. By the class of gladiators known as *retiarii* it was used as a weapon. See GLADIATORES.

Fustibălus. A kind of sling. See FUNDA.

Fustuarium (ξυλοκοπία). A punishment inflicted upon soldiers for desertion or other serious offences, in which the offender was beaten to death with heavy sticks (*fustes*) laid on by his comrades (Livy, v. 6).

Fusus (ἄτρακτος). A spindle; usually made of a stick about twelve inches in length, and used with the distaff (*colus*), for twisting or spinning the fibres of wool or flax into thread (Pliny, *H. N.* xi. 27; Ovid, *Met.* vi. 22). Golden spindles were sent to ladies of rank (Herod. iv. 162). In the rural districts of Italy, women were forbidden to spin when they were travelling on foot, the act being considered of evil omen (Pliny, *H. N.* xxviii. 5). The distaff and spindle, with the wool and thread upon them, were carried in bridal processions; and without the wool and thread, they were often suspended by women as offerings of religious gratitude, especially in old age, or on relinquishing the constant use of them. They were most frequently dedicated to Minerva, the patroness of spinning, and of the arts connected with it. The spindle was kept in the *calathus* (q. v.).

Woman with Distaff and Spindle. (Frieze of the Forum Palladium, Rome.)

G

G, as a symbol.

IN GREEK.—Γ = Γαῖος, γερουσίας (Ψ·Γ).

Γ = 5 |ᐃ| = 50 |Χ| = 5000 |Μ| = 50,000 (decimal system).

γ′ = 3 ‚γ = 3000. See ABACUS.

IN LATIN.—G = Galeria, Galli, Gallica, gener, Genius, gens (in Africa), centuria (*C. I. L.* xiv. 2278).

G = Gaius (instead of the usual C — rare), cf. Orelli, *Inscript.* 467, 1660, 4680. See GAIUS; GAIA.

G·D·N = Genius domini nostri.

G·F = garum factum, Gemina felix (legio).

G·H·L = genius huius loci.

G·M = genius municipii.

G·P·R·F = genio populi Romani feliciter.

G·R = Germani Raeti.

G·S = Germania superior.

Gabae (Γάβαι). (1) A city of Persia, in the province of Persis, placed by Ptolemy southeast of Pasargada, on the confines of Carmania. (2) A city of Sogdiana, southwest of Cyreschata. Gabae was one of the first places to which the exploits of Alexander gave celebrity in that country. It is the same with the Gabaza of Curtius (Quint. Curt. viii. 4, 1).

Gabăli (Γαβάλεις). A people in Gallia Aquitanica, whose chief town was Anderitum (Antérieux or Javoux) (Caes. *B. G.* vii. 75).

Gabălus. A word said to be formed from the Hebrew language, and equivalent to the Latin *crux* (q. v.): a cross or stake upon which criminals were impaled (Varr. *ap.* Non. s. v. p. 117); whence the same word is also used to designate a worthless fellow, or one who deserved impalement (Capitol. *Macrin.* 11).

Gabăta. A particular kind of dish for table service, in fashion at Rome during the time of Martial; but respecting its characteristics nothing is known (Mart. vii. 48; xi. 31).

Gabiāna (Γαβιανή) or **Gabiēné** (Γαβιηνή). A district of the Persian province of Susiana (q. v.), west of Mount Zagros.

Gabii (Γάβιοι). A town in Latium, on the Lacus Gabinus between Rome and Praenesté, a colony from Alba Longa; and the place, according to tradition, where Romulus and Remus were brought up. It was taken by Tarquinius Superbus by stratagem (Livy, i. 53, 54), and was in ruins in the time of Augustus. In its neighbourhood are the stone quarries from which a part of Rome was built. The modern name is Castiglione.

Gabīna. The name of Iuno, worshipped at Gabii (Verg. *Aen.* vii. 682).

Gabinia Lex. See LEX.

Gabinius, AULUS. A tribune of the plebs in B.C. 66, when he carried a law conferring upon Pompey the command of the war against the pirates; and consul in 58, when he took part in the banishment of Cicero. In the year 57 he went to Syria as proconsul, and restored Ptolemy Auletes to the throne of Egypt, in opposition to a decree of the Senate. On his return to Rome in 54 he was accused both of *maiestas* and the *crimen repetundarum*, for the illegal receipt of 10,000 talents from Ptolemy, and was defended by Cicero. He was condemned on the latter charge, and went into exile. In the civil war he fought on the side of Caesar. He died about B.C. 47.

Gabīnus Cinctus. See TOGA.

Gadăra (*τὰ Γάδαρα*). A large fortified city of Palestine, situated on an eastern tributary of the Jordan. Vespasian, in his first campaign in Galilee, took it, slaughtered the inhabitants, and burned the city (Ioseph. *B. I.* iii. 7 § 1).

Gades (Semitic *gadir*, "a hedge," "stockade"; *τὰ Γάδειρα*). The modern Cadiz; a very ancient town in Hispania Baetica, founded by the Phœnicians, and one of the chief seats of their commerce in the west of Europe, situated on a small island of the same name (Isla de Leon), separated from the mainland by a narrow channel. Herodotus says (iv. 8) that the island of Erythia was close to Gadeira; whence most later writers supposed the island of Gades to be the same as the mythical island of Erythia, from which Hercules carried off the oxen of Geryon. Its inhabitants received the Roman franchise from Iulius Caesar, and Strabo mentions as a striking proof of its wealth and importance that, in the census taken under Augustus, Gades was the residence of some 500 equites—a number greater than in any town of Italy except Patavium (Padua). Gades was allied with Rome in the Second Punic War (Livy, xxxii. 2). The city was rich, luxurious, and immoral. Its dancing girls with their lascivious dances are often spoken of in Roman literature. See SALTATIO.

Gadfly. See OESTRUS.

Gaditānum Fretum. Now the Strait of Gibraltar. See ABYLA; CALPÉ.

Gaditānus Sinus. Now the Bay of Cadiz.

Gaea (*Γαῖα*). The Greek goddess of the earth. According to Hesiod she came into being after Chaos, and brought forth of herself the Sky (*Οὐρανός*), the mountains, and the Sea (*Πόντος*). By Uranus she was mother of the Titans, Cyclopes, and Hecatoncheires. From the blood of her mutilated husband sprang the Erinyes, Giants, and Melian nymphs; to Pontus she bore Nereus, Thaumas, Phorcys, Ceto, and Eurybia. Other terrible beings, such as the giants Typhon, Antaeus, and Tityus, were her offspring, as also the *autochthones* or aborigines, such as Erechtheus and Cecrops. In Homer she is invoked with Zeus, the Sun, Heaven, and Hell as a witness to oaths, and was worshipped with the sacrifice of a black lamb; but she was especially honoured as the mother of all, who nourishes her creatures and pours rich blessings upon them. In Athens, in particular, she was worshipped as *κουροτρόφος*, or the nourisher of children, and at the same time as the goddess of death, who summons all her creatures back to her and hides them in her bosom. She was honoured also as the primeval prophetess, especially in Delphi, the oracle of which was at first in her possession as the power who sent forth the vapours which inspired the seer. The corresponding Roman goddess was Tellus (q. v.).

Gaesum (*γαῖσον*). A very strong and weighty javelin, which appears to have been made, both head and stock, of solid iron (Poll. vii. 156), and to have been employed as a missile rather than as a spear, each warrior carrying two as his complement (Varr. *ap.* Non. s. v. p. 555). The weapon was of Gallic origin (Verg. *Aen.* viii. 662); though it was sometimes used by the Romans, the Iberians, the Carthaginians (Livy, xxvi. 6), and the Greeks. See HASTA.

Gaetulia (*Γαιτουλία*). The interior of Northern Africa, south of Mauretania, Numidia, and the region bordering on the Syrtes, reaching to the Atlantic Ocean on the west, and of very indefinite extent towards the east and south. The pure Gaetuli were not an Aethiopic (i. e. Negro), but a Libyan race, and were most probably the ancestors of the Berbers (Ritter, *Erdkunde*, i. pp. 1034 foll.). Cossus Lentulus brought the Gaetulians under Roman rule, receiving for this a triumph and the surname Gaetulicus.

Gagae (*Γάγαι*). A town on the coast of Lycia, whence came quantities of jet (*γαγάτης λίθος*, *Gagates lapis*) still called in German *gagat* (Plin. *H. N.* xxxvi. 19 § 34).

Gagātes lapis. See GAGAE.

Gainas. A Goth, the minister of the emperor Arcadius from 399 to 401. He succeeded the eunuch Eutropius, whose death he had contrived, and soon after revolted against the imperial authority, uniting his forces with those of his countryman Tribigild. He then received from the weak Arcadius the title of Commanding General of the Roman Armies, and practically became emperor, but was slain in a conflict with the Huns (A.D. 401).

Gaisford, THOMAS. A distinguished classical scholar, born at Ilford, England, in 1779. He studied at Christ Church College, Oxford, where he took his degree in 1804. After publishing an elaborate edition of the *Enchiridion* of Hephaestion, he was made Public Examiner (1810), and in 1811 Regius Professor of Greek. From 1819 to 1847 he was rector of the parish of Westwell, and from 1831 was Dean of Christ Church. He died in 1855. Among the most valuable of his classical publications are an edition of the *Poetae Graeci Minores* (1814–20), Suidas, 3 vols. (1834), of the *Etymologicum Magnum* (1848), of the *Scriptores Latini Rei Metricae* (1837), of the *Paroemiographi Graeci* (1836), of Stobaeus (1822), of Herodotus (1824), of Sophocles (1826), and of Eusebius (1852).

Gaius, Gaia. A praenomen very common at Rome to both sexes. (On the name see F. D. Allen in *Harvard Studies in Class. Philology*, iii. pp. 71–87 [1891]). C (the old form of G), in its natural position, denoted the name of the male, and when reversed, that of the female; thus, C was equivalent to Gaius; but Ↄ to Gaia. Female praenomina, which were marked with an inverted capital, were, however, early disused among the Romans. The custom after this was, in case there was only one daughter, to name her after the *gens*. If there were two, to distinguish them by *maior* and *minor* added to their names; if there were more than two, they were distinguished by their number, Prima, Secunda, etc. Thus we have, in the first case, Tullia, the daughter of Cicero; Iulia, the daughter of Caesar; and in the second, Cornelia Maior, Cornelia Minor, etc. (See NOMEN.) Gaius and Gaia are the typical names of husband and wife in Roman usage; and at weddings the bridegroom and bride were called respectively Gaius and Gaia (cf. Festus, s. v. *Gaia;* and the marriage formula pronounced by the bride, *Ubi tu Gaius, ego Gaia*).

Gaius. One of the most accomplished professors of Roman law and writers on that subject. He was a native of the Asiatic provinces, and spent his days in Rome under Hadrian, Antoninus Pius, and Marcus Aurelius (about A.D. 110–180). His writings were numerous; but we possess in a tolerably complete form nothing but his *Institutiones*, or introduction to the private law of the Romans. This was discovered by Niebuhr in 1816 on a palimpsest of the fifth century at Verona, having before been known in quotations only. The work is in four books, the first of which treats of the family, the second and third of property, and the fourth of legal procedure. Popular and intelligible without being superficial, it was a favourite hand-book of law, and served as a foundation for the *Institutiones* of Justinian. As a jurist Gaius belongs to the conservative school of the Sabiniani. (See ATEIUS CAPITO.) The first edition of Gaius was that of Göschen and Hollweg (Berlin, 1820), the third edition being revised by Lachmann (Berlin, 1842). The best text is now that of Huschke in the Teubner series; while translations into English with commentaries have been made by Abdy and Walker (Cambridge, 1870), E. Poste (Oxford, 1875), Muirhead (Edinburgh, 1880), and Mears (London, 1882).

Gaius Caesar. See CALIGULA.

Galaesus (Γαλαῖσος) and **Galēsus.** A river in the south of Italy, now the Galeso, flowing into the Gulf of Tarentum through the meadows where the sheep grazed, whose wool was so celebrated in antiquity (Livy, xxv. 11).

Galanthis. See GALINTHIAS.

Galatēa (Γαλάτεια, "the milk-white"). A sea-nymph, daughter of Nereus and Doris. According to a Sicilian story, which the poets Philoxenus and Theocritus have made famous, she was pursued by the uncouth monster Polyphemus (q. v.), being herself in love with the beautiful Acis. The jealous giant crushed Acis with a rock, and the nymph changed her beloved into the Sicilian river which bears his name. The legend of Acis and Galatea has been a favourite theme in English literature. Adaptations of it are to be found in Gay's *Acis and Galatea*, J. S. Blackie's *Galatea*, Proctor's *Death of Acis*, R. Buchanan's *Polypheme's Passion*, and Austin Dobson's *Tale of Polypheme.*

Galatea. (Naples Museum.)

Galatia (Γαλατία). A country of Asia Minor, composed of parts of Phrygia and Cappadocia, and bounded on the west, south, and southeast by those countries, and on the northeast, north, and northwest by Pontus, Paphlagonia, and Bithynia. It derived its name from its inhabitants, who were Gauls that had invaded and settled in Asia Minor at various periods during the third century B.C. They speedily overran all Asia Minor within the Taurus, and exacted tribute from its various princes; but Attalus I. gained a complete victory over them (B.C. 230), and compelled them to settle down within the limits of the country thenceforth called Galatia, and also, on account of the mixture of Greeks with the Celtic inhabitants which speedily took place, Graeco-Galatia and Gallograecia. The people of Galatia adopted to a great extent Greek habits and manners and religious observances, but preserved their own language, so that even in the fourth century A.D. Jerome says that the speech of the Galatians resembles the local dialect of the Treviri in Gaul. They retained also their political divisions and forms of government. They consisted of three great tribes—the Tolistobogi, the Trocmi, and the Tectosages—each subdivided into four parts,

Coin of Galatia, with the head of Roman emperor.

called by the Greeks τετραρχίαι. At the head of each of these twelve tetrarchies was a chief or tetrarch. At length one of the tetrarchs, Deiotarus, was rewarded for his services to the Romans in the Mithridatic war by the title of king, together with a grant of Pontus and Armenia Minor; and after the death of his successor,

Amyntas, Galatia was made by Augustus a Roman province (B.C. 25). Its only important cities were: in the southwest, Pessinus, the capital of the Tolistobogi; in the centre, Ancyra, the capital of the Tectosages; and in the northeast, Tavium, the capital of the Trocmi. From the Epistle of St. Paul to the Galatians, we learn that the Christian churches in Galatia consisted in great part of Jewish converts. See Thierry, *Hist. des Gaulois.*

Galaxius (Γαλάξιος). A small river in Boeotia, near which stood the temple of Apollo Galaxius. The name is derived from the fact that its waters were of the colour of milk (*γάλα*), due to the chalky nature of the soil.

Galba. (1) SERGIUS, an orator anterior to Cicero. While holding the government of Spain, he treacherously murdered 30,000 Lusitanians. Having been accused for this by Cato the Censor, he was about to be condemned, when he wrought upon the feelings of the people by embracing before them his two sons, still quite young, an act which saved him (Cic. *Orat.* i. 53). In the year B. C. 144 he was consul. (2) GAIUS SULPICIUS, a Roman lawyer, father of the emperor. He was consul in A.D. 22. (3) SERVIUS SULPICIUS, born in the reign of Augustus, of a patrician family. He served with distinction in Germany, and was afterwards proconsul, first in Africa, and subsequently in Hispania Tarraconensis, in which office he gained a reputation for justice and moderation. He was still in Spain when Iulius Vindex, the proconsul of Upper Gaul, rose against Nero. Galba joined Vindex, and Otho, governor of Lusitania, followed his example. The assembled multitudes saluted Galba as emperor and Augustus; but he declared that he was acting only as the lieutenant of the Senate and people of Rome, in order to put an end to the disgraceful tyranny of Nero. The Praetorian Guards soon after, having revolted against Nero, proclaimed Galba, and the Senate acknowledged him as emperor. Galba hastened from Spain to Rome, where he began by calling to account those favourites of Nero who had enriched themselves by proscriptions and confiscations and by the extraordinary prodigality of that emperor; but it was found that most of them had already dissipated their ill-gotten wealth. Galba, or, rather, the intimates who governed him, then proceeded against the purchasers of their property, and confiscations became again the order of the day. The new emperor, at the same time, exercised great parsimony in his administration, and endeavoured to enforce strict discipline among the soldiers, who had been used to the prodigality and license of the previous reign. Being past seventy years of age, Galba, on this and other accounts, soon became the object of popular dislike and ridicule, and revolts against him broke out in various quarters, several of which were put down and punished severely. Galba thought of strengthening himself by adopting Piso Licinianus, a young patrician of considerable personal merit, as Caesar and his successor; upon which Otho, who had expected to be the object of his choice, formed a conspiracy among the Guards, who proclaimed him emperor. Galba, unable to walk, caused himself to be carried in a litter, hoping to suppress the mutiny; but, at the appearance of Otho's armed partisans, his followers left him, and even the litter-bearers threw the old man down and ran away. Some of the legionaries came up and put Galba to death, after a reign of only seven months, counting from the time of Nero's death, A.D. 68. Galba was seventy-two years old when he was taken off. He was succeeded by Otho (Suet. *Galba;* Tac. *Hist.* i. 4 foll.; Dio Cass. lxiii. 29, lxiv. 1 foll.).

Coin of the Emperor Galba.

Galé (γαλῆ). Probably a species of weasel. See FAELIS.

Galea (κράνος, poet. κόρυς, πήληξ). A helmet, casque. The helmet was originally made of skin or leather, whence is supposed to have arisen its appellation, *κυνέη*, meaning properly a helmet of dogskin, but applied to caps or helmets made of the hide of other animals, not necessarily worn as armour (*ταυρείη*, *κτιδέη*, Hom. *Il.* x. 258, 335; *αἰγείη*, *Od.* xxiv. 230; Herod. vii. 77; *galea lupina*, Propert. iv. 11, 19), and even to those which were entirely of bronze or iron (*Od.* xviii. 377). The leathern basis of the helmet was also very commonly strengthened and adorned by the addition of either bronze or gold (*Il.* xi. 352). Helmets which had a metallic basis were in Latin properly called *cassides* (Tac. *Germ.* 6), although the terms *galea* and *cassis* are often confounded. A casque (*cassis*) found at Pompeii is preserved in the collection at Goodrich Court in England. The perforations for

Helmets. (From the collection at Goodrich Court.)

the lining and exterior border are visible along its edge. Among the materials used for the lining of helmets were felt (*πῖλος*, *Il.* x. 265) and sponge (Aristot. *H. A.* v. 16).

The helmet, especially that of skin or leather, was sometimes a mere cap conformed to the shape of the head, without either crest or any other ornament. In this state it was probably used in hunting (*galea venatoria*, C. Nep. *Dat.* iii. 2), and was called *καταῖτυξ*, in Latin *cudo*. The preceding illustration shows an example of it as worn by Diomede in a small Greek bronze, which is also in the collection at Goodrich Court. The additions by which the external appearance of the helmet was varied, and which served both for ornament and protection, were the following: (1) The *φάλος*, which was either single, double (*ἀμφίφαλος*, *δίφαλος*), or quadruple (*τετράφαλος*). It has been held that the *φάλος* was the projecting peak of the helmet. According to this view, τετράφαλος is admittedly unintelligible, and it is certain that the φάλος was a ridge of metal, afterwards called κῶνος (Buttmann), which served as a support for the crest. Instances occur where there are two or more such ridges. In the illustration below, from a gem with the head of Atheně Parthenos, the φάλοι are represented by

Helmets. (From gems.)

a Sphinx and two Pegasi. (2) The helmet thus adorned was very commonly surmounted by the crest (*crista*, λόφος), which was often of horse-hair (ἵππουρις, ἱπποδάσεια, *hirsuta iuba*, Propert. iv. 11, 19), and made so as to look imposing and terrible. The helmet often had two or even three crests (cf. the illustration above with the head of Athené, having a helmet with a triple crest). In the Roman army of later times the crest served not only for ornament, but also to distinguish the centurions (Veget. ii. 13). The annexed illustration from a part of a centurion's tomb, from Petronell, shows the transverse crest. (3) The two cheek-pieces (*bucculae*, παραγναθίδες), which were usually attached to the helmet by hinges, so as to be lifted up and down. They had buttons or ties at their extremities for fastening the helmet on the head. A strap passed under the wearer's chin, in the case of the Homeric helmet (*Il.* iii. 371), but apparently cheek-pieces were not movable. (4) The beaver, or visor, a peculiar form of which is supposed to have been the αὐλῶπις τρυφάλεια—i. e. the perforated beaver (Hom. *Il.* xi. 353). The gladiators wore helmets somewhat of this kind (Juv. viii. 203), and specimens of them, not unlike those worn in the Middle Ages, have been found at Pompeii. See the illustration to GLADIATORES.

Helmet. (Baumeister.)

Galēnus, CLAUDIUS (Κλαύδιος Γαληνός). A celebrated Greek physician, born at Pergamus about A.D. 131. His father gave him a liberal education. His anatomical and medical studies were commenced under Satyrus, a celebrated anatomist; Stratonicus, a disciple of the Hippocratic School; and Aeschrion, a follower of the Empirics. After the death of his father he travelled to Alexandria, at that time the most famous school of medicine in the world. His studies were so successfully pursued that he was publicly invited to return to his native country. At the age of thirty-four he settled at Rome, where his celebrity became so great from the success of his practice, and more especially from his great knowledge of anatomy, that he quickly drew upon himself the jealousy of all the Roman physicians. He became physician to the emperor Marcus Aurelius, and at the solicitation of many philosophers and men of rank, he commenced a course of lectures on anatomy; but the jealousy of his rivals quickly compelled him to discontinue them, and eventually to leave Rome altogether, being in daily fear of assassination. Many particulars of his life may be gathered from his own writings; nothing is known, however, about the period of his return home as well as that of his death. All that can be learned is merely that he was still living in the reign of Septimius Severus.

Galen was a most prolific writer. Though several of his works were destroyed in the conflagration of his dwelling, and others by the lapse of time, still the following productions of his now exist in print: (1) Eighty-three treatises, the genuineness of which is now well established. (2) Nineteen of rather doubtful origin. (3) Forty-five that are certainly spurious. (4) Nineteen fragments, more or less extensive in size. (5) Fifteen commentaries on the works of Hippocrates.

Among the productions of Galen that are of a philosophical character may be enumerated the following: A treatise against Favorinus; a dissertation on the opinions of Hippocrates and Plato; a commentary on the Timaeus of Plato, and several discourses on Dialectics. See Diels, *De Galeni Historia Philosopha* (Bonn, 1870).

Operative surgery is the department of his profession which is least indebted to him; and yet even here he has left some monuments of his boldness and ingenuity. He has described minutely an operation performed by him upon the chest of a young man, by which he perforated the breast-bone and laid bare the heart, in order to give vent to a collection of matter seated in the thorax. The subject of ulcers is handled by him very scientifically in his book *De Methodo Medendi* (Θεραπευτικὴ Μέθοδος). His commentaries on Hippocrates show his acquaintance with fractures and dislocations. The subject of hygiene (Ὑγιεινά) he treated at great length in a work consisting of six books. His treatise *De Facultate Alimentorum* (Περὶ Τροφῶν Δυνάμεως) contains very important observations on the nature of foods, and furnishes an exposition of his opinion on the subject of dietetics. Materia Medica and Pharmacy appear to have been the objects of his particular study, and both are handled by him in several of his works. His treatise *De Compositione Medicamentorum Secundum Locos* (Περὶ Συνθέσεως Φαρμάκων τῶν κατὰ Τόπους) contains a copious list of pharmaceutical preparations. Of all his works, none was long so much studied and commented upon as the one entitled *Ars Medica* (Τέχνη Ἰατρική), a general outline of medicine. In several works he gives an elaborate system of the arterial pulses, which, as usual with his doctrines, was taken up by all subsequent writers; and abridged expositions of it may be found in Philaretus, Paulus Aegineta, Actuarius, Rhazes, and Avicenna. The best edition of Galen is that of Kühn, 20 vols. (Leipzig, 1821–1833). See Daremberg, *Des Connaissances de Galien* (Paris, 1841); the epitome in English by Coxe (Philadelphia, 1846); Berdoe, *Origin and Growth of the Healing Art* (London, 1893); and the articles CHIRURGIA; MEDICINA.

Galeomyomachia (Γαλεομυομαχία). "The Battle of the Cats and Mice;" a poem written in the mock-heroic vein by a Greek monk, Theodorus Prodromus (q. v.), who lived in the twelfth century A.D. It is in the main imitated from the pseudo-Homeric Batrachomyomachia (q. v.). An edition of it was published by Ilgen (Halle, 1796).

Galeōtae. See GALEUS.

Galepsus (Γαληψός). (1) A town in Macedonia, on the Toronaic Gulf (Herod. vii. 122). (2) A colony of Thasos, on the coast of Thrace (Thuc. iv. 107).

Galericŭlum. See GALERUS.

Galerius Maximiānus. See MAXIMIANUS.

Galerius Trachălus. See TRACHALUS.

Galērus or **Galērum,** dim. **Galericŭlum** (probably connected with *galea,* and so with γαλέη). Originally a cap of skin or fur, fitting close to the head, worn by rustics (Verg. *Moret.* 122), hunters (Grat. *Cyneg.* 340, where it is of badger-skin), gymnasts in the palaestra to keep the hair clean (Mart. xiv. 50), and by the old inhabitants of Latium instead of a helmet (Verg. *Aen.* vii. 688; cf. CUDO). For the galerus worn by various priests—e. g. the Pontifices Salii and Flamines and the *albogalerus* or *albus galerus* of the Dialis—see APEX. The word is also applied to a wig, the *empti capilli* of Ovid (*A. A.* iii. 165; cf. CALIENDRUM; COMA); worn not only from vanity or to conceal baldness (Suet. *Oth.* 12), but for the sake of disguise by profligates of both sexes in their nocturnal rambles (Juv. vi. 120, with the schol.); and on the stage as part of the make-up (Guhl and Koner, 5th ed. p. 762).

Galerus (Du Choul, *Castramet.* p. 100).

Galēsus. See GALAESUS.

Galeus (Γάλεος). That is "the lizard," son of Apollo and Themisto, from whom the GALEŌTAE, a family of Sicilian soothsayers, derived their origin. Their principal seat was Hybia.

Galgăcus. See CALGACUS in Appendix.

Galilaea (Γαλιλαία, from the Hebrew *galil,* "a circle" or "circuit"). A celebrated country of Palestine, forming the northern division. Iosephus (*Bell. Iud.* iii. 3) divides it into Upper and Lower, and he states that the limits of Galilee were, on the south, Samaris and Scythopolis to the flood of Jordan. It contained four tribes—Issachar, Zebulon, Naphthali, and Asher—a part also of Dan, and part of Peraea, or the country beyond Jordan. Upper Galilee was mountainous, and was called Galilee of the Gentiles from the heathen nations established there who were enabled, by the mountainous nature of the country, to maintain themselves against all invaders. Strabo enumerates among its inhabitants, Egyptians, Arabians, and Phœnicians. Lower Galilee, which contained the tribes of Zebulon and Asher, was adjacent to the Sea of Tiberias or Lake of Gennesareth. Galilee, according to Iosephus, was very populous, contained 204 cities and towns, and paid 200 talents in tribute. Its principal city was Caesarea Philippi. The inhabitants of Galilaea were very industrious, and, being bold and intrepid soldiers, they bravely resisted the nations around them. The Jews of Iudaea regarded them with much contempt. Their language was a corrupt and unpolished dialect of Syriac, with a mixture of other languages. It was probably this corrupt dialect that led to the detection of Peter as one of Christ's disciples (Mark, xiv. 70). The Saviour was called a Galilean (Matt. xxvi. 69), because he was brought up at Nazareth, a city of Galilaea; and as his apostles were mostly, if not all, natives of this province, they also are called Galileans and "men of Galilee" (Acts, i. 11). See Merrill, *Galilee in the Time of Christ* (2d ed. 1885).

Galinthias (Γαλινθιάς), or, in Latin, **Galanthis.** Daughter of Proetus of Thebes, and a friend of Alcmenė. When Alcmenė was on the point of giving birth to Heracles, and the Moerae and Ilithyae, at the request of Herė, were endeavouring to delay the birth, Galinthias suddenly rushed in with the false report that Alcmenė had given birth to a son. The hostile goddesses were so surprised by this information that they dropped their arms. Thus the charm was broken and Alcmenė was enabled to give birth to Heracles. The deluded goddesses avenged the deception practised upon them by metamorphosing Galinthias into a weasel (γαλῆ). Hecatė, however, took pity upon her and made her her attendant, and Heracles afterwards erected a sanctuary to her (Ovid, *Met.* ix. 306).

Galla. (1) The wife of Constantius, son of Constantius Chlorus. She was the mother of Gallus Caesar. (2) The second wife of Theodosius the Great. (3) PLACIDIA, daughter of the preceding by Theodosius. When Alaric took Rome in A.D. 410, she fell into his hands, and four years later was married by Ataulphus, king of the Goths. Upon his death she was returned to her country, and in 417 married Constantius III., by whom she had the emperor Valentinian III. During the minority of her son she was regent of the Western Empire, dying about the year 450. See Gibbon, *Decline and Fall,* chapters xxxi., xxxiii., xxxv.

Gallaecia (Καλλαικία). The country of the Gallaeci or Callaeci in the north of Spain, between the Astures and the Durius (Dio Cass. xxxvii. 53). Its inhabitants were some of the most uncivilized in Spain. They were defeated with great slaughter by D. Brutus, consul B.C. 138, who obtained in consequence the surname of Gallaecus.

Gallery. See CAVEA; PORTICUS.

Galley. See NAVIS.

Galli. See CELTAE; GALLIA.

Galli (Γάλλοι, in post-classical authors only). The eunuch priests of Cybelė or the Great Mother, whose worship, so far as it can be traced historically, had its original seat in Phrygia (Marmor Parium, *ap.* C. Müller, *Fragm.* i. 544, where it is placed under the reign of Erichthonius, king of Attica, B.C. 1506; Strabo, x. pp. 469, 472, xii. p. 567, where the names Κυβέλη, Δινδυμήνη, etc., are said to be derived from Phrygian localities; Κυβέλην ἀπὸ τοῦ τόπου, Diod. iii. 58). The Phrygian language was Indo-European, as appears from the extant inscriptions (Rawlinson's *Herod.* vol. i. App. 666); and the worship of Cybelė has been thought to be also Indo-European; Avestan names have been traced in it—Berecyntus = *Berezat;* Corybantes = *Gereuantô* (Labatut in *Rev. Numism. Belge,* 1868, p. 286). Other names, however, are of distinctly Semitic affinities; Rhea perhaps = the Babylonian Ri (Mulita or Mylitta), and Nana more certainly = the Babylonian *Nana,* modern Syrian *Nani.*

The origin of the name of Galli is not absolutely certain, but it was doubtless a native Phrygian word; of course it has nothing to do with the Galatae or Gauls, whose first appearance in these countries dates only from B.C. 278. There is no reason to reject the tradition which derives it from a river in Phrygia; there were two small rivers called Gallus, both tributaries of the Sangarius, and the one which flows by Pessinus must be meant, whose water was fabled to cause this particular form of religious madness (Ovid, *Fast.* iv. 363; Plin. *H. N.* v. § 147, xi. § 261, xxxi. § 9). A form *gallantes*, as if from *gallare*, "to rave like a priest of Cybelé," is cited from Varro (*ap.* Non. p. 119, 5). In their wild, enthusiastic, and boisterous rites the Galli recalled the legends of the Corybantes (q. v.). According to an ancient custom, they were always castrated (*spadones, semimares, semiviri, nec viri nec feminae*), and it would seem that, impelled by religious enthusiasm, they performed this operation on themselves (Ovid, *Fast.* iv. 237; Plin. *H. N.* xi. § 261, xxxv. § 165; Martial, iii. 81, xi. 74; Juv. vi. 512 foll.; Catull. *Attis*). See RHEA.

Gallia. An extensive and populous country of Europe, bounded on the west by the Atlantic, on the north by the Insula Batavorum and part of the Rhenus (Rhine), on the east by the Rhenus and the Alps, and on the south by the Pyrenees. The greatest breadth was 600 English miles, but much diminished towards each extremity. Its length was from 480 to 620 miles. It was therefore more extensive than modern France before the Revolution, though inferior to the Empire under Napoleon I. Gaul was originally divided among the three great peoples—the Belgae, the Celtae, and the Aquitani. The Romans called the inhabitants of this country by one general name, Galli, while the Greeks styled them Κελταί. (See CELTAE.) The Greeks called the country itself Galatia (Γαλατία) and Celtica (Κελτική). Of the three great nations of Gaul, the Celtae were the most extensive and the Belgae the bravest. The Belgae and Celtae were of like blood, though differing in temperament, the Belgae being more staid and less impulsive and vivacious, while the Celtae showed the mercurial disposition of the modern French. The Aquitani, on the south, were of a different (Iberian) stock, unlike the rest of the Gauls both physically and temperamentally, being dark of complexion, less sociable, and somewhat less intelligent, but more tenacious of purpose and enduring—traits which still mark the inhabitants of the Basque provinces to-day. The Celtae extended from the Sequana (Seine) in the north to the Garumna (Garonne) in the south. Above the Celtae lay the Belgae, between the Seine and the Lower Rhine. They were intermixed with Germanic tribes. The Aquitani lay between the Garonne and the Pyrenees, and were intermingled with Spanish tribes. These three great divisions, however, were subsequently altered by Augustus (B.C. 27), who extended AQUITANIA into Celtica as far as the Liger or Loire; the remainder of Gallia Celtica above the Liger was called GALLIA LUGDUNENSIS, from the colony of Lugdunum (Lyons); while the territory towards the Rhine was added to the Belgae under the title of GALLIA BELGĬCA. Lastly, the south of Gaul, which, from having been the first provinces possessed by the Romans, had been styled Gallia Provincia, was distinguished by the name of NARBONENSIS, from the city of Narbo (Narbonne). This province was also anciently called Gallia Bracata, from the *bracae* or trousers worn by the inhabitants; while Gallia Celtica was styled Comata, from the long hair (*coma*) worn by the natives. These four great provinces, in later ages, were called the four Gauls, and subdivided into seventeen others.

As far back as one can penetrate into the history of the West, we find the race of the Gauls occupying that part of the continent comprehended between the Rhine, the Alps, the Mediterranean, the Pyrenees, and the Ocean, as well as the two great islands situated to the northwest, opposite the mouths of the Rhine and Seine. Of these two islands, the one nearer the continent was called *Alb-in*, "White Island" (cf. the remark of Pliny, *H. N.* xiv. 16, *Albion insula, sic dicta ab albis rupibus quas mare alluit*"). The other island bore the name of *Er-in*, "Isle of the West" (from *Eir* or *Iar*, "the west"). The continental territory received the special appellation of *Galltachd*, "Land of the Gauls." From this word the Greeks formed Γαλατία, and from this latter the generic name of Γαλάται. The Romans proceeded by an inverse method, and from the generic term Galli deduced the geographical denomination Gallia.

The population of Gaul was divided into families or tribes, forming among themselves many distinct communities or nations. Oftentimes they united together, in their turn, and formed confederations or leagues. Such were the confederations of the Celtae, Aedui, Armorici, Arverni, etc.

The Gaul was robust and of tall stature. His complexion was fair, his eyes blue, his hair of a blond or chestnut colour, to which he endeavoured to give a red or flaming hue by certain applications (Pliny, *H. N.* xxviii. 12; Mart. viii. 33). The hair itself was worn long (Diod. Sic. v. 28). The beard was allowed to grow by the people at large; the nobles, on the other hand, removed it from the face, excepting the upper lip, where they wore thick moustaches. The attire common to all the tribes consisted of trousers or *bracae* (Armoric). These were of striped materials. They wore also a short cloak, having sleeves, likewise formed of striped materials, and descending to the middle of the thigh. Over this was thrown a short cloak or *sagum* (*sae*, Armoric; cf. Isidor. *Orig.* xix. 24), striped like the shirt, or else adorned with flowers and other ornamental work, and, among the rich, superbly embroidered with silver and gold (Verg. *Aen.* viii. 660; Sil. Ital. iv. 152; Diod. Sic. v. 28). It covered the back and shoulders, and was secured under the chin by a clasp of metal. The lower classes, however, wore in place of it the skin of some animal, or else a thick and coarse woollen covering. The offensive arms of the nation were, at first, hatchets and knives of stone; arrows pointed with flint or shells; clubs; spears hardened in the fire, and named *gaïs* (in Latin *gaesum*, in Greek γαισόν and γαισός); and others called *cateïa*, which they hurled while on fire against the enemy. Foreign traffic, however, made them acquainted, in process of time, with arms of iron, as well as with the art of manufacturing them for themselves from the copper and iron of their own mines. Among the arms of metal which thenceforward came into use may be mentioned the long sabre of iron or copper and a pike resembling the halberd, the wound in-

Head of Gaul. (Villa Amendola.)

flicted by which was considered mortal. For a long time the Transalpine as well as the Cisalpine warriors of the Gallic race had rejected the use of defensive armour as inconsistent with true courage, and a point of honour had induced them even to strip off their vestments and engage naked with the foe. This prejudice, however, was almost entirely effaced in the second century when the military costume of Rome and Greece formed a singular combination with the ancient array of the Gaul. To a helmet of metal, of greater or less value according to the fortune of the warrior, were attached the horns of an elk, buffalo, or stag; while for the rich there was a headpiece representing some bird or savage beast, the whole being surmounted by a bunch of feathers, which gave to the warrior a gigantic appearance (Diod. Sic. v. 28). Similar figures were attached to their bucklers, which were long, quadrangular, and painted with the brightest colours. A buckler and casque after this model, a cuirass of wrought metal, after the Greek and Roman fashion, or a coat of mail formed of iron rings, after the manner of Gaul (Varr. *L. L.* iv. 20); an enormous sabre hanging on the right thigh, and suspended by chains of iron or brass from a belt glittering with gold and silver, and adorned with coral; a collar, bracelets, rings of gold around the arm and on the middle finger (Pliny, xxxiii. 1); trousers; a *sagum* hanging from the shoulder; and long red moustaches — such was the Gallic warrior.

Hardy, daring, impetuous, born, as it were, for martial achievements, the Gallic race possessed, at the same time, an ingenious and active turn of mind. They were not slow in equalling their Phœnician and Grecian instructors in the art of mining. The same superiority to which the Spaniards had attained in tempering steel, the Gauls acquired in the preparation of brass. Antiquity assigns to them the honour of various useful inventions, which had hitherto escaped the earlier civilization of the East and of Italy. The process of tinning was discovered by the Bituriges; that of veneering by the Aedui (Pliny, *H. N.* xxxiv. 17). The dyes, too, of Gaul were not without reputation (Pliny, viii. 48). In agriculture, the wheel-plough and boulter were Gallic discoveries (Pliny, *H. N.* xviii. 18; xviii. 11). With the Gauls, too, originated the employment of marl for enriching the soil (Pliny, xviii. 6 foll.). The cheeses of Mount Lozère, among the Gabali; those of Nemausus; and two kinds made among the Alps, became, in time, much sought after by the inhabitants of Italy (Pliny, xi. 49). The Gauls also prepared various kinds of fermented drinks, such as barley-beer, called *cervisia* (Pliny, xxii. 15); and likewise another kind of beer, made from corn, and in which honey, cumin, and other ingredients were mingled. (See CERVISIA.) The froth of beer was employed as a means for leavening bread: it was used also as a cosmetic, and the Gallic women frequently applied it to the face, under the belief that it imparted a freshness to the complexion (Pliny, xxii. 25). It was from the Greeks of Massilia that they learned the process of making wine, as well as the culture of the grape.

The dwellings of the Gauls, spacious and of a round form, were constructed of posts and hurdles, and covered with clay both within and without; a large roof, composed of oak-shingles and stubble, or of straw cut and kneaded with clay, covered the whole (Vitruv. i. 1). Gaul contained both open villages and cities: the latter, surrounded by walls, were defended by a system of fortification, of which we find no example elsewhere. Caesar gives a description of these ramparts (*B. G.* vii. 23). To the

Restoration of Wall of Mursceints. (Duruy.)

north and east, among the more savage tribes, there were no cities properly so called; the inhabitants resided for the most part in large enclosures, formed of trunks of trees.

It was, as has been already remarked, in war, and in the arts applicable to war, that the genius of the Gauls displayed itself to most advantage. This people made war a regular profession, while the management of arms became their favourite employment. To have a fine martial mien, to retain for a long period strength and agility of body, was not only a point of honour for individuals, but a duty to the State. At regular intervals, the young men went to measure their size by a girdle deposited with the chief of the village, and those whose corpulence exceeded the official standard were severely reprimanded as idle and intemperate persons, and were, besides, punished with a heavy fine. In preparing for foreign expeditions, a chieftain of acknowledged valour generally formed a small army around him, consisting, for the most part, of adventurers and volunteers who had flocked to his standard; these were to share with him whatever booty might be obtained. In internal wars, however, or defensive ones of any importance, levies of men were forcibly made; and severe punishments were inflicted on the refractory, such as the loss of noses, ears, an eye, or some one of the limbs (Caes. *B. G.* vi. 4). If any dangerous crisis arrived, the supreme chief convened an armed council (Caes. *B. G.* v. 66). All persons able to bear arms were compelled to assemble at the place and day indicated, for the purpose of deliberating on the situation of the country, of electing a chief, and of discussing the plan of campaign. It was expressly provided by law that the individual who came last to the place of rendezvous should be cruelly tortured in the presence of the assembled multitude (Caes. *B. G.* v. 66). This form of assembly was, however, of rare occurrence, and was only resorted to in the last extremity. Neither infirmities nor age freed the Gallic noble from the necessity of accepting or seeking military commands. Oftentimes were seen, at the head of the forces, chieftains hoary and almost enfeebled by age, who could even scarcely retain their seats on the horse which supported them (Hirt. *B. G.* viii. 12). This people would have believed that they dishonoured their aged warriors by making them die elsewhere than on the field of battle.

To the ferocity of the attack and to the violence of the first shock were reduced nearly all the military tactics of the Gauls on level ground and in pitched battle. In the mountainous regions, on the other hand, and especially in the vast and thick forests of the North, war had a close resemblance to the chase: it was prosecuted in small parties, by ambuscades and all sorts of stratagems; and dogs, trained up to pursue men, tracked out and aided in conquering the foe (Silius Ital. x. 77; Ovid, *Met.* i. 533; Mart. iii. 47). A Gallic army generally carried along with it a multitude of chariots for the baggage, which embarrassed its march (Hirt. *B. G.* viii. 14; Caes. *B. G.* i. 51). Each warrior bore a bundle of straw, put up like a sack, on which he was accustomed to sit in the encampment, or even in the line of battle while waiting the signal to engage (Hirt. *B. G.* viii. 15).

The Gauls, like other nations, for a long period were in the habit of killing their prisoners of war, either by crucifixion, or by tying them to trees as a mark for their weapons, or by consigning them to the flames amid cruel rites. Long prior, however, to the second century of our era, these barbarous practices were laid aside, and the captives of transalpine nations had nothing to fear but servitude. Another custom, not less savage, that of cutting off the heads of their slain enemies on the field of battle, was not slower in disappearing. It was long a settled rule in all wars that the victorious army should possess itself of such trophies as these; the common soldiers fixed them on the points of their spears, the horsemen wore them suspended by the hair from their horses; and in this way the conquerors returned to their homes, making the air resound with their triumphal shouts. Each one then hastened to nail up these hideous testimonials of his valour to the gate of his dwelling; and, as the same thing was done with the trophies of the chase, a Gallic village bore a strong resemblance to a charnel-house. Carefully embalmed and saturated with oil of cedar, the heads of hostile chieftains and of famous

Tomb of Gallic Chief. (Musée de Cluny, Paris.)

warriors were deposited in large coffers, and arranged by their possessor according to the date of acquisition. Sometimes the skull, cleansed and set in gold or silver, served as a cup in the temples, or circulated in the festivities of the banquet, and the guests drank out of it to the glory of the victor and the triumphs of their country. These fierce and brutal manners prevailed for a long period over the whole of Gaul. Civilization, in its onward march, abolished them by degrees, until, at the commencement of the second century, they were confined to the savage tribes of the North and West. It was there that Posidonius found them still existing in all their vigour, when the sight of so many human heads, disfigured by outrages and blackened by the air and the rain, roused in him mingled emotions of horror and disgust.

The Gauls affected, as more manly in its character, a strong and rough tone of voice (Diod. Sic. v. 31). They conversed but little, and by means of short and concise phrases, which the constant use of metaphors and hyperboles rendered obscure and almost unintelligible to strangers. But, when once animated by dispute, or incited by something that was calculated to interest or arouse, at the head of armies or in political assemblies, they expressed themselves with copiousness and fluency.

The Gauls, in general, were accused of drinking to excess—a habit which took its rise both in the grossness of their manners and in the wants of a cold and humid climate. The Massilian and Italian traders were not slow in furnishing the necessary means for the indulgence of this vice. Cargoes of wine found their way, by means of the navigable rivers, into the very heart of the country. Drink was also conveyed over land in wagons (Diod. Sic. v. 26). About the first century, however, of our era, drunkenness began gradually to disappear from among the higher classes, and to be confined to the lower orders, at least with the nations of the South and East.

Milk and the flesh of animals, especially that of swine, formed the principal food of the Gauls. A curious account of their repasts is given by Posidonius (*ap.* Athen. iv. p. 13). After an excessive indulgence in the pleasures of the banquet, they loved to seize their arms and defy each other to the combat. At first it was only a sportive encounter; but, if either party chanced to be wounded, passion got so far the better of them that, unless separated by their friends, they continued to engage till one or the other of them was slain. So far, indeed, did they carry their contempt of death and their ostentatious display of courage, that they might be seen agreeing, for a certain sum of money or for so many measures of wine, to let themselves be slain by others; mounted on some elevated place, they distributed the liquor or gold among their most intimate friends, and then reclining on their bucklers, presented their throats to the sword (Posidon. l. c.). Others made it a point of honour not to retire from their dwellings when falling in upon them, nor from the flames, nor from the tides of ocean and the inundations of rivers; and it is to this foolish daring that the Gauls owed their fabulous renown of being an impious race, who lived in open war with nature.

The working of mines, and certain monopolies enjoyed by the heads of tribes, had placed in the hands of some individuals enormous capital; hence the reputation for opulence which Gaul enjoyed at the period of the Roman invasion, and even still later. It was the Peru of the ancient world. The riches of Gaul even passed into a proverb (Ioseph. ii. 28; Plut. *Caes.*; Suet. *Caes.*, etc.). Posidonius makes mention of a certain Luern or Luer (Λουέρνιος, Posidon. *ap.* Athen. iv. p. 13; Λουέριος, Strab. 191), king of the Arverni, who caused a shower of gold and silver to descend upon the crowd as often as he appeared in public. He also gave entertainments in a rude style of barbarian magnificence; a large space of ground was enclosed for the purpose, and cisterns were dug in it, which were filled with wine, mead, and beer.

Properly speaking, there was no domestic union

or family intercourse among the Gallic nations; the women were held in dependence and servitude. The husband had the power of life and death over his wife as well as over his offspring. When a person of high rank suddenly died, and the cause of his death was not clearly ascertained, his wife or wives (for polygamy was practised among the rich) were seized and put to the torture; if the least suspicion was excited of their having been privy to his death, the victims perished in the midst of the flames, after the most frightful punishments (Caes. *B. G.* vi. 19). One custom, however, shows that even then the condition of women had undergone some degree of melioration: this was the community of goods between husband and wife. The children remained under the care of their mother until the age of puberty (Caes. *B. G.* vi. 18).

Among some nations of Belgic Gaul, where the Rhine was an object of superstitious adoration, a curious custom prevailed; the river was made the means of testing the fidelity of the wives. When a husband had doubts respecting its paternity, he took the new-born infant, placed it on a board, and exposed it to the current of the stream. If the plank and its helpless burden floated safely upon the waters, the result was deemed favourable, and all the father's suspicions were dissipated. If, on the contrary, the plank began to sink, the infant perished, and the parent's suspicions were confirmed.

Government and Religion.—Two privileged orders ruled in Gaul over the rest of the population—the priests and the nobles. The people at large were divided into two classes—the inhabitants of the country and the residents of cities. The former of these constituted the tribes or clients appertaining to noble families. The client cultivated his patron's domains, followed his standard in war, and was bound to defend him with his life. To abandon his patron in the hour of peril was regarded as the blackest of crimes. The residents of cities, on the other hand, found themselves beyond the control of this system of clientship, and, consequently, enjoyed greater freedom. Below the mass of the people were the slaves, who do not appear, however, to have been at any time very numerous.

When we examine attentively the character of the facts relative to the religious belief of Gaul, we are led to recognize the existence of two classes of ideas, two systems of symbols and superstitions entirely distinct from each other; in a word, two religions—one, altogether reasonable in its character, based on the personification of natural phenomena and recalling by its forms much of the polytheism of Greece; the other, founded on a material, metaphysical, mysterious, and sacerdotal pantheism, presenting at least a superficial conformity with the religions of the East. This latter has received the name of Druidism, from the Druids, who were its first founders and priests; the other system has been called the Gallic Polytheism. (See Druidae.) Druidism was said to have been established in Gaul by Heus or Hesus, a warrior and law-giver who was subsequently deified. The polytheistic system which prevailed, more especially in Southern Gaul, was fundamentally like that of the Greeks and Romans themselves. In its list of deities were Tarann, the god of thunder, the Gallic Zeus, though in parts of Gaul Hesus held this supremacy; Pennin, the god of the mountains (Livy, xxi. 38); Bel or Belew, the sun-god, the Gallic Apollo (Auson. *Carm.* 2); Teutates, the Gallic Hermes, presiding over the useful arts and commerce (Minuc. Fel. 30; Lactant. *Div. Inst.* i. 21); Ogmius, represented as leading a train of captives by chains of gold and amber proceeding from his mouth, typifying the power of eloquence; and Arduenna, the goddess of the forests. These deities, as was natural, were identified by Caesar with the gods of the Roman system (Caes. *B. G.* vi. 7).

The God Tarann. (Gadoz, *Relig. Gaul.* pl. i.)

This resemblance between the two systems of religion changed into identity when Gaul, subjected to the dominion of Rome, had felt for some years the influence of Roman ideas. It was then that the Gallic polytheism, honoured and favoured by the emperors, ended its career by becoming totally merged in the polytheism of Italy; while, on the other hand, Druidism, its mysteries, its doctrine, and its priesthood, were utterly proscribed. See Druidae.

General History.—The history of Gaul divides itself naturally into four periods. The first of these comprises the movements of the Gallic tribes while yet in their nomadic state. None of the races of the West ever passed through a more agitated or brilliant career. Their course embraced Europe, Asia, and Africa; their name is recorded with terror in the annals of almost every nation. They burned Rome; they wrested Macedonia from the veteran legions of Alexander; they forced Thermopylae and pillaged Delphi; they then proceeded to pitch their tents on the plains of the Troad, in the broad parks of Miletus, on the borders of the Sangarius, and those of the Nile. They besieged Carthage, menaced Memphis, and numbered among their tributaries the most powerful monarchs of the East; they founded in Upper Italy a powerful empire, and in the bosom of Phrygia they reared another—Galatia, which for a long time exercised its sway over the whole of Lower Asia. See GALATIA.

During the Second Period—that of their sedentary state—we see the gradual development of social, religious, and political institutions, conformable to their peculiar character as a people; institutions original in their nature, and a civilization full of movement and of life, of which Transalpine Gaul offers the purest and most complete model. One might say, in following the animated scenes of this picture, that the theocracy of India, the feudal system of the Middle Ages, and the Athenian democracy had met on the same soil for the purpose of contending with each other and reigning by turns. Soon this civilization undergoes a change; foreign elements are introduced, brought in by commerce, by the relations of neighbourhood, by reaction from subjugated nations. Hence arose and multiplied a variety of social combinations. In Italy it is the Roman influence that exerts itself on the manners and institutions of the Gauls; in the south of Gaul it is that of the Massiliots; while in Phrygia one finds a most singular compound of Gallic, Grecian, and Phrygian civilization. To this succeeds the Third Period in the history of the Gallic race—that of national struggles and subjugation. By a singular coincidence, it is always by the Roman sword that the power of the Gallic tribes is destined to fall; in proportion as the Roman dominion extends, that of the Gauls recedes and declines. It would seem, indeed, that the victors and the vanquished, in the battle on the banks of the Allia, followed each other over the whole earth to decide the ancient quarrel of the Capitol. In Italy, the Cisalpine Gauls were reduced, but only after two centuries of obstinate resistance. When the rest of Asia had submitted to the yoke, the Galatae still defended against Rome the independence of the East. Gaul eventually fell, but through complete exhaustion, after a century of partial conflicts and nine years of general war under Caesar. Finally, the names of Caractacus and Galgacus shed a splendour on the last and ineffectual efforts of Keltic freedom. It is everywhere an unequal conflict between ardent and undisciplined valour on the one hand, and cool and steady perseverance on the other. The Fourth Period comprehends the organization of Gaul into a Roman province, and the gradual assimilation of transalpine manners to the customs and institutions of Italy—a work commenced by Augustus and completed by Claudius. See Thierry, *Histoire des Gaulois* (1827, last ed. 1872); the *Recueil des Historiens des Gaules et de la France*, edited by Bouquet and others, 26 vols. (1738–1885); Marin de Tyr, *La France avant César* (Paris, 1865); De la Forte Maison, *Les Francs* (Paris, 1868); Godwin, *Hist. of France*, vol. i. (New York, 1860), the best account of ancient Gaul in the English language; Martin, *Histoire de France* (4th ed. 1865); Fauriel, *Histoire de la Gaule Méridionale* (Paris, 1836); Coulanges, *Histoire des Institutiones Politiques de l'Ancienne France* (Paris, 1877); and the authors cited in the articles CELTAE and DRUIDAE (q. v.).

Gallia Bracāta. See GALLIA.

Gallia Cisalpīna. "Gaul this side of the Alps," with reference to Rome, a name given to the northern part of Italy, as occupied by the Gallic tribes which had poured over the Alps into this extensive tract of country. It is also called GALLIA CITERIOR. Livy assigns to these migrations of the Gauls as early a date as B.C. 600. Having securely established themselves in their new possessions, they proceeded to make further inroads into various parts of Italy, and thus came into contact with the forces of Rome. More than two hundred years had elapsed from the time of their first invasion, when they totally defeated the Roman army on the banks of the Allia, and became masters of Rome itself. The defence of the Capitol and the exploits of Camillus (Livy, v. 47 foll.), or, rather, if Polybius be correct (ii. 18), the gold of the vanquished and the dangers which threatened the Gauls at home, preserved the State. From that time, the Gauls, though they continued by frequent incursions to threaten and even to ravage the territory of Rome, could make no impression on that power. Though leagued with the Samnites and Etruscans, they were almost always unsuccessful. Defeated at Sentinum in Umbria, near the Lake Vadimonis in Etruria, and in a still more decisive action near the port of Telamo in the same province (Polyb. ii. 19 foll.), they soon found themselves forced to contend, not for conquest, but for existence. The same ill success, however, attended their efforts in their own territory. The progress of the Roman arms was irresistible; the Gauls were beaten back from the Adriatic to the Po, from the Po to the Alps, and soon beheld Roman colonies established and flourishing in many of the towns which had so lately been theirs. Notwithstanding these successive disasters, their spirit, though curbed, was still unsubdued; and when the enterprise of Hannibal afforded them an opportunity of retrieving their losses and wreaking their vengeance on the foe, they eagerly embraced it. It is to their zealous co-operation that Polybius ascribes in a great degree the primary success of that expedition. By the efficient aid which they afforded Hannibal, he was enabled to commence operations immediately after he had set foot in Italy, and to follow up his early success with promptitude and vigour (Polyb. iii. 66). As long as this great commander maintained his ground and gave employment to all the forces of the enemy, the Gauls remained unmolested, and enjoyed their former freedom, without being much burdened by a war which was waged at a considerable distance from their borders; but when the tide of success had again changed in favour of Rome and the defeat of Hasdrubal, together with other disasters, had paralyzed the efforts of Carthage, they once more saw their frontiers menaced; Gaul still offered some resistance, even after Carthage itself had been obliged to sue for peace; but it was weak and unavailing; and about twelve years after the termination of the Second Punic War, it was brought under entire subjection and became a Roman province. Under this condition it continued to receive various accessions of territory as the Romans extended their dominions towards the Alps, till it comprised the whole of that portion of Italy which lies between those mountains and the rivers Magra and Rubicon. It was sometimes known by the name of Gallia Togata (Mela, ii. 4; Plin. iii. 14), to distinguish it from Transalpine Gaul, to which the name of Gallia Comata was applied (Cic. *Phil.* viii. 9). The epithet Togata alludes to the rights of citizenship conferred on the natives of the country. The towns of Cisalpine Gaul obtained the privileges of Latin cities, and, consequently, the right of wearing the Roman toga, by a law of Pompeius Strabo (Ascon. *Com. in Or. in Pison.* p. 490), about B.C. 88.

According to Polybius, Cisalpine Gaul was included in the figure of a triangle, which had the Alps and Apennines for two of its sides, and the Adriatic, as far as the city of Sena Gallica, for the base. This is, however, but a rough sketch. (See ITALIA.) Polybius describes the country as abounding in wine, corn, and every kind of grain, and in fine wool. Herds of swine, both for public and private supply, were bred in its forests; and such was the abundance of provisions of every kind that travellers when at an inn did not find it necessary to agree on the price of any article which they required, but paid so much for the whole amount of what was furnished them; and this charge, at the highest, did not exceed half a Roman *as* (Polyb. ii. 15).

Gallia Comāta. See GALLIA.

Gallia Togāta. See GALLIA CISALPINA.

Gallia Transalpīna. A name given to Gaul Proper, to distinguish it from Gallia Cisalpina.

Gallĭcae. Gallic shoes, the French *galoches*, English *goloshes*. They were low shoes, not reaching quite so high as the ankle, had one or more thick soles, and small upper leather, which was entirely open over the front of the instep, like the modern golosh and the right-hand figure in the illustration; or laced in front, and fastened by a ligature round the top, as in the left-hand example; whence they are classed among the *soleae* by the Latin writers, to distinguish them from the regular *calcei*, which were close-fitting high-lows that completely enveloped the foot and ankle. They were partially adopted at Rome before the age of Cicero, and were worn with the *lacerna;* but such a style of dress was regarded as indecorous and anti-national (Cic. *Phil.* ii. 30; Gell. xiii. 21). Under the Empire they came into more common use, and were made for all classes.

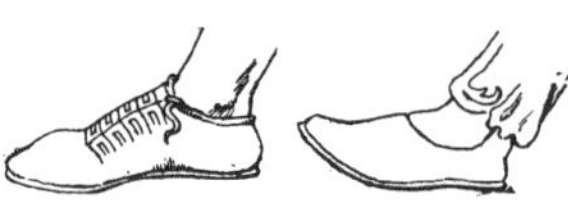

Gallicae. (From a sarcophagus, Villa Amendola, Rome.)

Galliēnus, PUBLIUS LICINIUS VALERIANUS EGNATIUS. A son of the emperor Valerian, made Caesar and colleague to his father in A.D. 253. He defeated, in a great battle near Mediolanum (Milan), the Alemanni and other northern tribes which had made an irruption into Upper Italy, and gave evidence on that occasion of his personal bravery and abilities. He was also well-informed in literature, and was both an orator and a poet, winning some distinction by an epithalamium. When Valerian was taken prisoner by the Persians, A.D. 260, Gallienus took the reins of government, and was acknowledged as Augustus. He appears to have then given himself up to debauchery and the company of profligate persons, neglecting the interests of the Empire, and taking no pains to effect the release of his father from the hard captivity in which he died. The barbarians attacked the Empire on every side, revolts broke out in various provinces, where several commanders assumed the title of emperor, while Gallienus was loitering at Rome with his favourites. Yet now and then he seemed to awaken from his torpor at the news of the advance of the invaders; and, putting himself at the head of the legions, he defeated Ingenuus, who had usurped the imperial title in Illyricum. Gallienus disgraced his victory by horrible cruelties. Meantime Probus, Aurelianus, and other able commanders were strenuously supporting the honour of the Roman arms in the East, where Odenatus of Palmyra acted as a useful ally to the Romans against the Persians. Usurpers arose in Egypt, in the Gauls, in Thrace, in almost every province of the Empire, from which circumstance this period has been styled the Reign of the Thirty Tyrants. At last Aureolus, a man of obscure birth, some say a Dacian shepherd originally, but a brave soldier, was proclaimed emperor by the troops in Illyricum, entered Italy, took possession of Mediolanum, and even marched against Rome while Gallienus was absent. Gallienus returned quickly, repulsed Aureolus, and defeated him in a great battle, near the Addua, after which the usurper shut himself up in Mediolanum. Here he was besieged by Gallienus; but, during the siege (A.D. 268), the emperor was murdered by conspirators (Aurel. Vict. 33; Eutrop. ix. 8; Trebell. Poll. *Gallien.*, Zonaras, xii. 24 foll.). The reign of Gallienus is memorable for the plague that swept over the Empire. During its height, it is said that there were 5000 deaths daily in the city of Rome; while the population of Alexandria was diminished nearly two thirds. The plague was followed by a general famine.

Gallienus.

Gallīna. A fowl; a chicken. Of the different species of domestic fowls, the most important were *gallinae*, which were divided into three classes: (*a*) *gallinae villaticae*, the common chicken; (*b*) *gallinae Africanae* or *Numidicae*, the same probably with the μελεαγρίδες of the Greeks; and (*c*) *gallinae rusticae*. The last were found in great abundance in the Insula Gallinaria, but it is so difficult to determine from the descriptions transmitted to us what they really were, that it is uncertain whether they ought to be regarded as pheasants, as red-legged partridges, as wood-grouse, or as some species of game different from any of these. The *Africanae*, always scarce and dear, were treated almost exactly in the same manner as peacocks, and never became of importance to the farmer. The *rusticae* are little spoken of except as objects of curiosity, and Columella declares that they would not breed in confinement.

Among the breeds celebrated for fighting were the Tanagrian, the Rhodian, and the Chalcidian; but these were not the most profitable for the market. The points of a good barn-yard fowl are minutely described by Varro, Columella, and Palladius. Some were permitted to roam about (*vagae*) during the day, and pick up what they could, but the greater number were constantly shut up (*clausae*) in a poultry-yard (*gallinarium, ὀρνιθοβοσκεῖον*), which was an enclosed court (*saeptum*) with a warm aspect, strewed with sand or ashes wherein they might burrow, and covered over with a net. It contained hen-houses (*caveae*), to which they retired at night and roosted upon poles stretched across (*perticae*) for their convenience, nests (*cubilia*) for the laying hens being constructed along the walls. The whole establishment was under the control of a poultryman (*aviarius custos* or *curator gallinarius*).

Chickens, when fattened for sale, were shut up in dark, narrow cribs, light and motion being unfavourable to the process; or each bird was swung separately in a basket, with a small hole at each end, one for the head, the other for the rump, and bedded upon the softest hay or chaff, but so cramped in space that it could not turn round. In this state it was crammed with wheat, linseed, barley-meal kneaded with water into small lumps (*turundae*), and other farinaceous food, the operation requiring from twenty to twenty-five days (Varr. iii. 9; Colum. viii. 2, etc., 12; Plin. *H. N.* x. § 46 foll.; Pallad. i. 27, 29).

Gallinaria. (1) An island off the coast of Liguria, celebrated for the number of its hens, whence its name (Varro, *R. R.* iii. 9, 17). (2) SILVA, a forest of pine-trees near Cumae in Campania (Cic. *Ad Fam.* ix. 23).

Gallinarium (ὀρνιθοβοσκεῖον). A poultry-yard. See GALLINA.

Gallio, IUNIUS. (1) A Roman rhetorician, the friend of the elder Seneca, whose son he adopted. He was put to death by Nero. (2) The son of the elder Seneca, adopted by the preceding.

Gallius, QUINTUS. A Roman who stood for the praetorship in B.C. 64. As a result of the election, he was accused of bribery by M. Calidius, and defended by Cicero in an oration of which only fragments remain. He was praetor in B.C. 63, and presided at the trial of C. Cornelius. His son, Q. Gallius, was praetor in B.C. 43, and was put to death by the Second Triumvirate.

Gallograecia. See GALATIA.

Gallows. See CRUX.

Gallus (Γάλλος). A river in Galatia, falling into the Sangarius, near Pessinus. From it the priests of Cybelé are said to have obtained their name of Galli. See GALLI; RHEA.

Gallus, SULPICIUS. (1) A distinguished orator, was praetor B.C. 169, and consul 166, when he fought against the Ligurians. In 168 he served as tribune of the soldiers under Aemilius Paulus in Macedonia, and during this campaign predicted an eclipse of the moon. (2) C. CORNELIUS, was born at Forum Iulii (Fréjus) in Gaul, of poor parents, about B.C. 66. He went to Italy at an early age, and began his career as a poet when he was about twenty years of age. He had already attained considerable distinction at the time of Caesar's death, 44; and upon the arrival of Octavianus in Italy after that event, Gallus embraced his party, and soon acquired great influence with him. In 41 he was one of the triumvirs appointed by Octavianus to distribute lands in the north of Italy among his veterans, and on that occasion he afforded protection to the inhabitants of Mantua and to Vergil. He afterwards accompanied Octavianus to the battle of Actium, 31, and commanded a detachment of the army. After the battle, Gallus was sent with the army to Egypt, in pursuit of Antony; and when Egypt was made a Roman province, Octavianus appointed Gallus the first prefect of the province. He remained in Egypt for nearly four years; but he incurred at length the enmity of Octavianus, though the exact nature of his offence is uncertain. According to some accounts he spoke of the emperor in an offensive and insulting manner; he erected numerous statues of himself in Egypt, and had his own exploits inscribed on the pyramids. The Senate deprived him of his estates, and sent him into exile; whereupon he put an end to his life by falling upon his own sword, B.C. 27. The intimate friendship existing between Gallus and the most eminent men of the time, as Asinius Pollio, Vergil, Varus, and Ovid, and the high praise they bestow upon him, prove that he was a man of great intellectual powers and acquirements. Ovid (*Trist.* iv. 10. 5) assigns to him the first place among the Roman elegiac poets; and we know that he wrote a collection of elegies in four books, the principal subject of which was his love of Lycoris. (See Vergil's Tenth Eclogue.) But all his productions have perished; for the four epigrams in the Latin Anthology attributed to Gallus could not have been written by a contemporary of Augustus. Gallus translated into Latin the poems of Euphorion of Chalcis, but this translation is also lost. Some critics attributed to him the poem *Ciris*, usually printed among the works of Vergil. See Völker, *De C. Galli Vita et Scriptis*, pt. i. (Bonn, 1840), pt. ii. (Elberfeld, 1844); A. Nicolas, *De la Vie et des Ouvrages de C. Gallus* (Paris, 1851). His story is made the basis of the well-known work of W. Becker on Roman antiquities. See BECKER. (3) TREBONIĀNUS. A Roman emperor, who reigned A.D. 251–254. His full name was C. VIBIUS TREBONIĀNUS GALLUS. He served under Decius in the campaign against the Goths, 251, and is said to have contributed by his treachery to the disastrous issue of the battle, which proved fatal to Decius and his son Herennius. Gallus was thereupon elected emperor, and Hostilianus, the surviving son of Decius, was nominated as his colleague. He purchased a peace of the Goths by allowing them to retain their plunder, and promising them a fixed annual tribute. In 253, the Goths again invaded the Roman Empire, but they were driven back by Aemilianus, whose troops proclaimed him emperor in Moesia. Aemilianus thereupon marched into Italy; and Gallus was put to death by his own soldiers, together with his son Volusianus, before any collision had taken place between the opposing armies. The name of Gallus is associated with nothing but cowardice and dishonour. In addition to the misery produced by the inroads of the barbarians during this reign, a deadly pestilence broke out in 252, and continued its ravages over every part of the Empire for fifteen years.

Gallus (ἀλέκτωρ, ἀλεκτρυών). The cock; a bird not mentioned in the earlier Greek writers, but found figured on the silver coins of Samothrace and Himera in the sixth century B.C. Athenaeus says that it was introduced into Greece from Persia. The cock was used by the Greeks in divination (see ALECTRYOMANTIA), and was carefully bred by both the Greeks and Romans for fighting. (See ALECTRYOMACHIA; VENATIONES.) The finest game-cocks were bred at Rhodes and Tanagra. The cock was sacred to Mars and to Aesculapius, Nox, and the Lares.

Gambling. See ALEA.

Gamelia (γαμηλία). A feast accompanied by offerings given by the father of a bridegroom or by the bridegroom himself to the members of his phratry, or rather to the οἰκεῖοι among the phratores, on which occasion the bride was introduced to and enrolled among the phratores (Harpocr. s. v. ἡ εἰς τοὺς φράτορας εἰσαγωγὴ τῶν γυναικῶν. Cf. *Etym. Mag.* p. 220, 50 foll.). Thus she became a sharer in her husband's *sacra*. This ceremony probably took place in the month of Gamelion (Mommsen, *Heortol.* p. 344). In Mommsen's opinion there is no difference in meaning between ἡ γαμηλία and τὰ γαμήλια.

Gamelion (Γαμηλιών). The seventh month of the Attic year, answering to the last half of January and the first half of February. Its earlier name was Ληναιών. See CALENDARIUM.

Games. See LUDI.

Gamŏri (γάμοροι). See GEOMORI.

Gamos (γάμος). See MATRIMONIUM.

Gandarĭdae (Γανδαρίδαι), **Gandarītae** (Γανδαρῖται), or **Gandărae** (Γανδάραι, Skt. Gandháras). An Indian people, in the middle of the Punjâb, between the rivers Acesines (Chenab) and Hydraotes (Ravee), whose king, at the time of Alexander's invasion, was a cousin and namesake of the celebrated Porus. From them the Afghan city of Kandahar gets its name.

Ganea. A low eating-house, generally used at Rome for immoral purposes. See CAUPONA.

Gangarĭdae (Γαγγαρίδαι). A people near the mouths of the Ganges. Ptolemy assigns them a capital, called Ganga Regia, on the western side of the Ganges. The Gangaridae were allies of the Prasii, who lay nearer the Indus towards the northwest. The united forces of these two nations awaited the army of Alexander on the other side of the Hyphasis; but report made them so formidable in numbers and valour that the wearied and alarmed Macedonians refused to cross the stream, in spite of all the efforts and remonstrances of their king (Justin, xii. 8; Q. Curt. ix. 2; Verg. *Georg.* iii. 27).

Ganges (Γάγγης, Ind. *Gangâ*). A famous river of India, which, in the language of Hindustan, is called P a d d a, and is also named B u r r a G a n g â, or the Great River, and Gangâ, or the river, by way of eminence; and hence the European name of the stream is derived. The Sanskrit name of the Ganges (Padda) signifies "foot," because the Brahmins, in the *Vishnu-Purana*, make the river to flow from the great toe of the left foot of Vishnu, the preserving deity. This mighty stream, together with the Brahmaputra, whose twin-sister it has been denominated, has its source in the vast mountains of Thibet. This river was unknown to Herodotus, as he does not mention it, though it became famous a century afterwards. Its source was for a long period involved in obscurity. A survey, however, was made by the Anglo-Indian government, and it was found to issue in a small stream, under the name of Bhagirathi, from under a mass of perpetual snow, accumulated on the southern side of the Himalayah Mountains. It is computed to be 1557 miles in length, and at five hundred miles from its mouth is, during the rainy season, four miles broad and sixty feet deep. Its principal tributaries are the Jumna, the Jahnavi, and the Brahmaputra. The whole number of streams which flow into it is eleven.

The name is also applied by the ancient writers to a large city on the Ganges at its great bend towards the east, perhaps the same as Allahabad. See INDIA.

Gangetĭcus Sinus (Κόλπος Γαγγητικός). Now the Bay of Bengal, into which the Ganges falls (Ptol. i. 13, § 4).

Gangra (Γάγγρα). A city of Paphlagonia, near the borders of Galatia. In the time of King Deiotarus (q. v.) it was a royal residence, and under the Empire, the capital of Paphlagonia.

Ganymēda (Γανυμήδα). See HEBÉ.

Ganymēdes (Γανυμήδης). The son of Tros, king of Dardania, brother of Ilus and Assaracus. According to Homer he was carried away by the gods for his beauty, to be the cup-bearer of Zeus, and one of the immortals. In the later legend he is carried away by Zeus himself in the shape of an eagle, or by the eagle of Zeus. To make amends to his father, Zeus presented him with four immortal horses for his chariot. Ganymedes was after-

Ganymedes and the Eagle. (Thorwaldsen.)

wards regarded as the genius of the sources of the Nile, and the astronomers made him into the constellation Aquarius. The rape of Ganymede was represented in a group by the sculptor Leochares (q. v.).

Gaol. See CARCER.

Garăma (Γαράμη). See GARAMANTES.

Garamantes (Γαράμαντες). The southernmost people known to the ancients in North Africa, dwelt far south of the Great Syrtis in the region called Phazania (Fezzan), where they had a capital city, Garama. They are mentioned by Herodotus as a great people (iv. 183). He tells a number of curious things about them and their country—that the land is fertilized with salt, that their oxen have horns bending so far forward as to compel them to walk backward as they feed, etc. For other notices, see Plin. *H. N.* v. 5, § 8; Mela, i. 8.

Gardens. See HORTUS.

Gargānus Mons (τὸ Γάργανον). The modern Monte Gargano; a mountain and promontory in Apulia, on which were oak forests (Hor. *Carm.* ii. 9, 7).

Gargaphia (Γαργαφία). A valley near Plataea, with a fountain of the same name, where Actaeon was torn to pieces by his dogs (Ovid, *Met.* iii. 156). The fountain of Gargaphia was situated about a mile and a half distant from Plataea, on Mount Cithaeron, towards the Athenian frontier (Herod. ix. 25).

Gargăra (τὰ Γάργαρα). The southern summit of Mount Ida, in the Troad, with a city of the same name at its foot (Hom. *Il.* viii. 48).

Gargettus (Γαργηττός). A deme of Attica, on the northwest slope of Mount Hymettus; the birthplace of the philosopher Epicurus. See the monograph by Young, *Gargettus, an Attic Deme*, in the *Classical Studies in Honour of Henry Drisler* (N. Y. 1894).

Gargilius Martiālis. A Roman writer, who flourished in the third century A.D., and was the author of a great work, based upon Greek and Latin sources, on agriculture and veterinary science. Considerable fragments remain, dealing with the treatment of cattle (*De Cura Boum*) and the medical uses of herbs and fruit (*Medicina ex Holeribus et Pomis*). These fragments are found chiefly in the fourth book of the so-called Plinius Valerianus (q. v.). The chief sources of Martialis were Dioscorides, Galen, Hippocrates, Aristotle, and Celsus. The fragments of the treatise *De Cura Boum* were edited by Schuch (Donaueschingen, 1857); see also Rose, *Anecdota Graeca et Graecolatina* (Berlin, 1870).

Garītes. A people in Aquitania, neighbours of the Ausci (Caes. *B. G.* iii. 27).

Garlands. See CORONA.

Garmantis or **Garamantis.** A nymph, mother of Iarbas by Iupiter. See Verg. *Aen.* iv. 198.

Garments. See CLOTHING.

Garret. See DOMUS, p. 545.

Garum (γάρον). A sauce made of the blood and entrails of fish salted, and resembling caviare (Plin. *H. N.* xxxi. § 43; and Hor. *Sat.* ii. 8. 46).

Garumna. Now the Garonne, a river of Gaul, which rises in the valley of Arran, to the south of Bertrand, among the Pyrenees, and falls into the Oceanus Cantabricus, or Bay of Biscay. The general course of this river, which extends to about 250 miles, is northwest. It unites with the Duranius (Dordogne), below Burdigala (Bourdeaux). According to Iulius Caesar's division of Gallia, the Garumna was the boundary of Aquitania, and separated that district from Gallia Celtica. This river is navigable to Tolosa (Toulouse) (Mela, iii. 2).

Garumni. A Gallic people in Aquitania, on the Garumna.

Gates. See IANUA; PORTA.

Gatheae (Γαθεαί). A town in Arcadia on the river Gatheatas. (Pausan. viii. 34.)

Gaugamēla (τὰ Γαυγάμηλα). A village of Assyria, in the district of Aturia, and about 500 stadia from Arbela (Arrian, vi. 1). The decisive battle between Alexander and Darius took place near this spot in B.C. 331; but, as Arbela was a considerable town, the Greeks chose to distinguish the conflict by the name of the latter. Gaugamela signified, in Persian, "the house of the camel," and is said to have been so called because Darius, the son of Hystaspes, having escaped upon his camel across the deserts of Scythia, when retreating from the latter country, placed the animal here, and devoted the revenue of certain villages for its maintenance (Plut. *Alex.* 31).

Gaulus (γαυλός). A large full-bodied vessel used either as a goblet (Plaut. *Rud.* v. 2, 32), a milk-pail (Hom. *Od.* ix. 223), a water-bucket (Herod. vi. 119), etc.

Gaulus (Γαῦλος). (1) A small island adjacent to Melité or Malta, now called Gozo (Plin. *H. N.* iii. 8). (2) Another below the south shore of Crete, now called Gozo of Candia, for distinction's sake from Gozo of Malta.

Gaurus Mons or **Gaurānus Mons.** A volcanic range of mountains in Campania, between Cumae and Neapolis, in the neighbourhood of Puteoli, producing good wine, and memorable for the defeat of the Samnites by M. Valerius Corvus, B.C. 340 (Livy, vii. 32, 33).

Gausăpa, Gausăpé, and **Gausăpum** (γαύσαπης). A woollen cloth with a long nap on one side, but smoother on the other, used by both sexes for clothing, as well as for table-cloths, napkins, bed-covers, etc. (Plin. *H. N.* viii. 73; Ovid, *A. A.* ii. 300; Mart. xiv. 152). The name is also used of wigs of light flaxen hair—a colour much admired by the Roman ladies. See CALIENDRUM; COMA.

Gauze. See COA VESTIS.

Gaza (Γάζα). (1) One of the five Philistine principalities, situated towards the southern extremity of Canaan, about sixteen miles south of Ascalon, and a small distance from the Mediterranean. Its port was called Gazaeorum Portus. As the name of the city of Gaza appears in the first book of Moses (x. 18), Mela must of course be mistaken, who says it is of Persian origin, and states that Cambyses made this place his chief magazine in the expedition against Egypt (Mela, i. 11). It was, however, an important and strongly-fortified place, as being situated so near the borders of that country. Alexander took and pillaged it, after it had made a powerful resistance for the space of three months (Arrian, ii. 27; Quintus Curtius, iv. 6). Antiochus the Great sacked it, and it was several times taken from the Syrians by the Maccabees (Iosephus, *Ant. Iud.* xiii. 21). It was afterwards subjected to new losses, so that St. Luke states (*Acts*, viii. 26) that it was, in his time, a desert place. The town was subsequently called Constantia. It is now termed by the Arabs, Ghuzzeh. The ancient name in Hebrew signifies "strong." (2) A city in the Persian province of Sogdiana. It was one of the seven cities that rebelled against Alexander the Great in B.C. 328.

Gazette. See ACTA.

Gé (Γῆ). See GAEA.

Gebenna Mons. See CEBENNA.

Gedrosia (Γεδρωσία). The farthest province of the Persian Empire on the southeast, and one of the subdivisions of Ariana, bounded on the west by Carmania, on the north by Drangiana and Arachosia, on the east by India, or, as the country about the lower course of the Indus was called, Indo-Scythia, and on the south by the Mare Erythraeum, or Indian Ocean. It is known in history chiefly through the distress suffered for want of water by the army of Alexander in passing through it (Arrian, *Anab.* vi. 24).

Gela (Γέλα or Γέλη). A city on the south coast of Sicily, on a river of the same name, founded by Rhodians from Lindus, and by Cretans, B.C. 690. It soon obtained great power and wealth; and, in 582, it founded Agrigentum. Gelon transported half of its inhabitants to Syracuse: the place gradually fell into decay, and in the time of Augustus was not inhabited. The poet Aeschylus died here. See GELON.

Gelānor (Γελάνωρ). A descendant of Inachus, king of Argos. When Danaüs, likewise a descendant of Inachus, came to Argos, and laid claim to the sovereign power, the citizens were doubtful in whose favour they should decide. While they were hesitating, a wolf fell upon the cattle which were feeding before the city, and killed the bull who was defending them. The citizens regarded this as a sign from heaven, and, interpreting the wolf as meaning Danaüs, they compelled Gelanor to retire in his favour. (See DANAÜS.) In the *Supplices* of Aeschylus, Pelasgus is king of Argos. He gives Danaüs a friendly welcome, and defends him against the sons of Aegyptus. But he is vanquished by them, retires from the sovereignty spontaneously in favour of the stranger, and leaves the country.

Geldŭba. The modern Gelb, below Colonia Agrippina (Cologne), a fortified place of the Ubii, on the Rhine, in Lower Germany (Tac. *Hist.* iv. 26, etc.).

Gellia Gens. A plebeian gens at Rome of Samnitic origin. To it belonged the generals Gellius Statius and Gellius Egnatius. (See EGNATII.) The chief branch of the Gellii at Rome bore the name Publicola.

Gellius. (1) CN. An early Roman historian, a contemporary of the Gracchi. His history of Rome, though lost, is frequently quoted by the later writers. (2) AULUS. A Latin grammarian, born at Rome in the early part of the second century, and who died at the beginning of the reign of Marcus Aurelius. We have but few particulars of his life, though it is known that he studied rhetoric under Antonius Iulianus and Sulpicius Apollinaris at Rome, and philosophy under Favorinus at Athens, and that, on his return to Rome, while still at an early age, he was made one of the centumviri or judges in civil causes (*Noct. Att.* xiv. 2). Gellius has left behind him one work, entitled *Noctes Atticae*, "Attic Nights." It was written, as he informs us in the preface, during the winter evenings in Attica, to amuse his children in their hours of relaxation. It appears from his own account that he had been accustomed to keep a commonplace book, in which he entered whatever he heard in conversation, or met with in his private reading, that appeared worthy of remembrance. In composing his *Noctes Atticae*, he seems merely to have copied the contents of his commonplace book, with a little alteration in the language, but without any attempt at classification or arrangement. It is, in fact, a huge scrap-book containing anecdotes and arguments, bits of history and pieces of poetry, and dissertations on various points in philosophy, geometry, and grammar. Amid much that is trifling and puerile, it gives information on many subjects relating to antiquity of which we must otherwise have been ignorant. It is divided into twenty books, which are still extant, excepting the eighth and the first part of the preface to the whole. Of the eighth book, the table of contents has come down. He mentions, in the conclusion of his preface, his intention of continuing the work, which purpose he probably, however, never carried into effect. The style of Aulus Gellius is in general unfit for imitation. In his fondness for archaisms, he is often carried too far, and introduces too many forms of expression from the earlier comic poets, whom he seems most anxious to take for his models in this respect. That he invented, however, any new terms himself seems hardly probable. His language, in fact, belongs to the so-called African style of Latinity, with a mingling of archaic forms and those that are characteristic of the plebeian speech. (See AFRICAN PERIOD OF LATINITY; SERMO PLEBEIUS.) The standard editions of Aulus Gellius are those of Carrio (Paris, 1585); Gronovius (Leyden, 1706; revised by Conradi, 1762); Lion (Göttingen, 1824); and M. Hertz (Berlin, 1883; smaller ed. Leipzig, 1886). The *Noctes Atticae* has been translated into English by Beloe (London, 1800); into French by De Chaumont, Flambart, and Buisson (Paris, 1862); and into German by Weiss (Leipzig, 1875). For a valuable analysis of the *Noctes Atticae*, and a critical estimate of Gellius, see Prof. Nettleship's *Essays in Latin Literature* (Oxford, 1885). On the language, see Gorges, *De Quibusdam Sermonis Gell. Proprietatibus* (Halle, 1883); and Cooper, *Sermo Plebeius* (N. Y. 1895).

Gelon (Γέλων). (1) A native of Gela in Sicily, who rose from the station of a private citizen to be supreme ruler of Gela and Syracuse. He was descended from an ancient family, which originally came from Telos, an island off the coast of Caria, and settled at Gela, when it was first colonized by the Rhodians. During the time that Hippocrates reigned at Gela (B.C. 498–491), Gelon was appointed commander of the cavalry, and greatly distinguished himself in the various wars which Hippocrates carried on against the Grecian cities in Sicily. On the death of Hippocrates, who fell in battle against the Siculi, Gelon seized the supreme power (B.C. 491). Soon afterwards a more splendid prize fell in his way. The nobles and landholders (γάμοροι) of Syracuse, who had been driven from the city by an insurrection of their slaves, supported by the rest of the people, applied to Gelon for assistance. This crafty leader, gladly availing himself of the opportunity of extending his dominions, marched to Syracuse, into which he was admitted by the popular party (B.C. 485), who had not the means of resisting so formidable an opponent (Herod. vii. 154 foll.). Having thus become master of Syracuse, he appointed his brother Hiero governor of Gela, and exerted all his endeavours to promote the prosperity of his new acquisition. In order to increase the population of Syracuse, he destroyed Camarina, and removed all its inhabitants, together with a great number of the citizens of Gela, to his favourite city. By his various conquests and his great abilities, he became a very powerful monarch; and therefore, when the Greeks expected the invasion of Xerxes, ambassadors were sent by them to Syracuse, to secure, if possible, his assistance in the war. Gelon promised to send to their aid two hundred triremes, twenty thousand heavy-armed troops, two thousand cavalry, and six thousand light-armed troops, provided the supreme command were given to him. This offer being indignantly rejected by the Lacedaemonian and Athenian ambassadors, Gelon sent, according to Herodotus, an individual named Cadmus to Delphi, with great treasures, and with orders to present them to Xerxes if he proved victorious in the coming war (Herod. vii. 157–164). This statement, however, was denied by the Syracusans, who said that Gelon would have assisted the Greeks, if he had not been prevented by an invasion of the Carthaginians, with a force amounting to three hundred thousand men, under the command of Hamilcar. This great army was entirely defeated near Himera by Gelon and Theron, monarch of Agrigentum, on the same day, according to Herodotus, on which the battle of Salamis was fought (Herod. vii. 165 foll.). An account of this expedition is also given by Diodorus Siculus (xi. 21), who states that the battle between Gelon and the Carthaginians was fought on the same day as that at Thermopylae. There seems, indeed, to have been a regular understanding between Xerxes and the Carthaginians, in accordance with which the latter were to attack the Greeks in Sicily, while the Persian monarch was to move down upon Attica and the Peloponnesus.

Gelon appears to have used with moderation the power which he had acquired by violence, and to have endeared himself to the Syracusans by his just government, and by the encouragement he gave to commerce and the fine arts. Plutarch states that the Syracusans would not allow his statues to be destroyed together with those of the other tyrants, when Timoleon became master of the city (Plut. *Timol.*). He died B.C. 478, and was succeeded by his brother Hiero (Aristot. *Polit.* v. 12).

(2) The son of Hiero II., king of Syracuse, who died before his father.

Gelōni (Γελωνοί). A Scythian people, dwelling in Sarmatia Asiatica, to the east of the river Tanaïs (Don) (Herod. iv. 108). Their chief city was called Gelonus.

Gemīnus (Γεμῖνος). A Rhodian astronomer who flourished about B.C. 77, and wrote an extant work (Εἰσαγωγὴ εἰς τὰ Φαινόμενα), a descriptive treatment of elementary astronomy. The text is given in Halma's edition of Ptolemy (Paris, 1819).

Gelotopoei (γελωτοποιοί). See PARASITI.

Gemma (λίθος). A precious stone. The art of cutting gems was learned by the Greeks, at an early period, from the Egyptians, who had practised it from remote antiquity. The Aethiopians used engraved stones as coins (λίθοι ἐγγεγλυμένοι), and engraved seals may have been used for money in Greece prior to the invention of coinage. (See NUMISMATICS.) At first the cutting was only concave, the gems being set in rings and used as seals. The subjects are usually human or animal forms, especially lions, bulls, and horses. The oldest Greek gems, numbers of which have been found at Mycenae and Ialysus, are bean-shaped ("lenticular") or pebble-shaped ("glandular"), differing thus from the cylinders and scarabs of Assyria and Egypt. Cameos or stones carved in relief first came into use, it would seem, in the time of Alexander the Great, and were used as ornaments. For cameos precious stones of various colours were used, especially the onyx. The layers of the stone were so treated that the figures stood out vividly on a dark ground. Mnesarchus of Samos, the father of the philosopher Pythagoras (about B.C. 600) is the oldest Greek jeweller whose name has come down to us. In the fourth centu-

Phœnician Gem. (King Collection.)

Athenê, by Aspasios. (Red jasper, in Vienna Cabinet.)

The Strozzi Medusa, by Solon. (Chalcedony, in British Museum Cabinet.)

Artemis.

Perseus.

Gems from Pompeii. (Naples Museum.)

ry B.C. the most celebrated master was Pyrgoteles, the only artist whom Alexander the Great would allow to cut his likeness. In the age of Augustus we hear of Dioscorides, who cut the emperor's likeness on a stone which was used as a seal by the succeeding Caesars. The Etruscans and Romans took up the art very early, but never attained the same perfection as the Greeks, importing gems largely from both Greece and Egypt. The scarab or beetle-shaped gems, so little valued by the Greeks, were intensely admired by the Etruscans, whose art in so many respects exhibits Egyptian characteristics.

Dancing Satyr.

Satyr with infant Dionysus.

Cameos. (Naples Museum.)

The fashion of making collections of beautiful gems arose as early as the first century B.C. The intaglios, or cut stones, have come down to us in greater numbers than any of the monuments of ancient art. Those which belonged to the advanced periods of style present examples of the most beautiful workmanship, the most original composition, and the most interesting subjects, the latter being mainly taken from mythology. Among the remaining Greek cameos an important place, both for size and beauty, must be given to the Gonzaga Cameo in St. Petersburg. This, it has been conjectured, represents the bust of Ptolemy Philadelphus and Arsinoé, his sister and wife; though it more probably commemorates Nero and Agrippina. The largest and most splendid of the cameos which have come down from the Roman period are those at Vienna and Paris, representing, in groups and figures, the family of Augustus. Gems engraved with humorous designs were called *grylli*. (See ANTIPHILUS.) These usually combined half a dozen incongruous forms arranged into the semblance of some well-known object, and occasionally with a hidden meaning. Thus, the accompanying example from a gem in the King Collection is made up of a wolf, a boar, and a lizard so blended as to form a helmet, the emblems respectively of Mars, Minerva, and Mercury.

Gryllus. (King Collection.)

Whole vessels were sometimes made of single stones, and adorned with reliefs. An instance is the Mantuan Vase now at Brunswick, 6⅛ inches high, 2⅛ inches thick, consisting of a single onyx. The lid, handle, and base are of gold. Two parallel lines of gold divide the surface into three parts, the middle one of which has twelve figures, representing the festival of the Thesmophoria, in three groups; while the highest and lowest are adorned with leaves, flowers, ears of corn, fruits, bulls' heads, and other objects connected with the worship of Demeter. Works of this kind were sometimes made of coloured glass. The most celebrated instance of this sort is the Portland Vase, found filled with ashes in the tomb of Alexander Severus, and now in the British Museum. Its height is about 10 inches. The material is a dark blue transparent glass, with beautiful reliefs in white opaque enamel.

Herodotus (vii. 69) speaks of a sharp stone as being used in engraving gems. Many of the ancient gems, especially those used as coins, were engraved with obsidian, of which knives were made. A minute metal disk with a sharp edge and worked by a drill was used in cutting the deeper parts of the pattern. (Cf. Pliny, *H. N.* xxvii. 76; and Murray, *Handbook of Greek Archaeology*, pp. 147–148). A sort of emery-powder (*smyris*) was employed to charge the tools. The *crustae* of diamonds and fragments of *ostracitis* were used as diamond-points.

For some account of the extraordinary profusion of precious stones in the East and among the successors of Alexander, see Diod. Sic. xviii. 26; Athen. xi. p. 781; Strab. xv. p. 718, and other passages quoted by Krause, *Pyrgoteles*, p. 113. The extravagant luxury of the Romans of the Empire rivalled that of the Diadochi.

The Gonzaga Cameo, Nero and Agrippina (?). (Sardonyx, Russian Imperial Cabinet.)

Pearls and emeralds were the favourite stones of the Romans. Iulius Caesar gave Servilia, the mother of Brutus, a pearl worth 6,000,000 sesterces ($240,000). The famous pearl which Cleopatra dissolved and drank was one of a pair set in ear-rings, and worth 10,000,000 sesterces ($400,000). Claudius Aesopus, son of the great actor, in imitation of this feat, did the same thing, snatching, however, the gem from the ear of Caecilia Metella, a beauty of the day. Caligula wore pearls on his shoes; Nero had them sprinkled over his bed-coverings. Pliny tells how, at a wedding party—a rather quiet affair—Lollia Paulina, the wife of Caligula, was covered with pearls and emeralds which shone in alternate rows on her head, neck, and fingers, and of which the cost was 40,000,000 sesterces ($1,600,000), as she proved by showing to him the receipted bills for them. "Pearls," he says in another place, "are the quintessence of extravagance." Claudius used an emerald as an eye-glass with

The Gemma Augustea, at Vienna.

Augustus and Livia receiving Drusus and Tiberius on their return from their Vindelic and Rhaetian campaigns. (Sardonyx, Vienna Cabinet.)

which to watch the circus games. The opal was also much admired, and Pliny tells how one Nonius was proscribed by Antony the triumvir so that he might be robbed of a magnificent opal in his possession. Pliny also speaks of the ruby (*carbunculus*) and the amethyst as much esteemed. (See AMETHYSTUS.) The ancients perhaps knew of the diamond, but could not have properly valued it, since the art of polishing and cutting it was not learned until it was discovered in modern times by Berquier of Bruges in the fifteenth century. (See ADAMAS.) Besides being worn in rings, gems were set in *armillae* or bracelets in many forms, including spirals and bangles; in *monilia* or necklaces of consecutive rows, one found at Pompeii having seventy-one pendants; and in ear-rings. (See INAURIS.) Jewels also profusely adorned the drinking-cups used at banquets, and the dainty little boxes of gold and silver used by the ladies in the mysteries of their toilets.

As might be expected, there was a large traffic in imitations of the precious stones, executed in both paste and glass, and with much fidelity. Pliny (*H. N.* xxxvii. 197) speaks of "glass jewels in cheap rings" for the lower classes; and there exist to-day at Rome collections of these imitations which cannot be distinguished from the genuine stones by the eye. (See VITRUM.) The stone most successfully copied was the emerald, but we hear of counterfeits of the amethyst, ruby, and sapphire.

Eros.
Peleus. Thetis. Poseidon.

The Portland Vase. (British Museum.)

This passion on the part of the wealthy for precious stones was naturally favourable to the growth of mineralogical knowledge. Pliny quotes a large number of writers who had treated of gems between Theophrastus and himself. Some of these writers seem to have had a personal knowledge of India. Pliny devotes the final book of his *Historia Naturalis* to gems, regarding them as the most perfect works of nature. The book consists of an historical introduction (§§ 1–5); of an account of the most important gems, arranged by colours (§§ 6–54); and an account of minor gems in alphabetical order. The book concludes with a few general instructions for detecting fraud. This book, which is the best representative of ancient science in this branch of mineralogy, shows us that the ancients were remarkably close observers of gems, availing themselves of all methods, short of chemical analysis and other instruments of modern physical research. Moreover, in the case of precious stones, minuteness of observation was stimulated by the desire of guarding against or of committing a fraud (*H. N.* xxxvii. § 197 foll.). Besides a minute study of colours of gems, frequently illustrated by Pliny's felicitous comparisons, the tests enumerated involve a study of weight, consistency (*corpus*), hardness, conductivity, transparency, diffractive power, friction, taste, and smell.

There are no traces in Theophrastus of magical properties attributed to gems. In Pliny, the doctrines of the Magi are frequently quoted, but usually with ridicule. Some of the medicinal virtues of gems apparently accepted by Pliny may appear little better than the doctrines of the Magi. But while Pliny is not in a position to criticise the alleged virtues of gems applied as medicine, he consistently rejects their supernatural powers under other conditions. The magical system is seen fully developed in the *Lithica* of Orpheus. (See AMULETUM.) This poem claims to be a statement of the magic properties of gems made by the seer Theodamas to the poet Orpheus. The work is generally assigned to a time subsequent to the edict of Constantius against magic, in A.D. 357, and not long after Valens, although Krause (*Pyrgoteles*, p. 6) ascribes it to the fifth century B.C.; and King dates it "at least as early as the second century B.C." The latter scholar gives an English verse translation (*Precious Stones*, p. 375).

Intaglio, with head of Africa. (King Collection.)

Much confusion and uncertainty exist as to the true nomenclature of gems. Both in ancient and modern times there has been considerable looseness of usage as to the meaning of names. In many instances where the ancient word exists in modern language, it denotes a stone entirely different from that originally signified. For example, σάπφειρος is certainly the *lapis lazuli*, and has no connection with the sapphire, which was called *hyacinthus*.

See Krause, *Pyrgoteles, oder die edlen Steine der Alten* (Halle, 1856); Lenz, *Mineralogie der alten Griechen und Römer* (Gotha, 1861); C. W. King, *Natural History of Precious Stones and Gems, and of Precious Metals* (London, 1870); id. *Hand-book of Engraved Gems* (London, 1866); id. *Antique Gems and Rings* (London, 1873); Middleton, *The Engraved Gems of Classical Times* (London, 1891); Blümner, *Technologie*, iii. 227 (Leipzig, 1875–87); Murray, *Hand-book of Greek Archaeology*, pp. 40–50, 146–173 (London, 1892); and an article in *Harper's Magazine* for 1879, vol. lix. pp. 532–541. On the use of gems in rings, see ANULUS; on the art of gem engraving, see SCALPTURA.

Gemoniae (sc. *scalae*) or **Gemonii** (sc. *gradus*). A flight of steps cut out of the Aventine, down which the bodies of criminals strangled in the prison were dragged, and afterwards thrown into the Tiber (Val. Max. vi. 3, 3). See CARCER, p. 278.

Genăbum or **Cenăbum**. The modern Orléans; a town in Gallia Lugdunensis, on the north bank of the Ligeris (Loire), the chief town of the Carnutes, subsequently called Civitas Aurelianorum, or Aurelianensis Urbs, whence its modern name.

Genauni. A people in Vindelicia, the inhabitants of the Alpine valley now called Valle di Non, subdued by Drusus (Hor. *Carm.* iv. 14, 10).

Genesia. See FUNUS, p. 697.

Genesius, IOSĒPHUS. A Byzantine historian who wrote (about A.D. 940) a history of the emperors from A.D. 813 to 886. Edition by Lachmann (Bonn, 1834).

Genĕtrix. "The mother," a name used by Ovid, as a title of Cybelé, in the place of *mater*, or *magna mater;* but it is better known as a surname of Venus (Lucret. i. 1), to whom Caesar dedicated a temple at Rome, as the mother of the Julian gens.

Genetyllis (Γενετυλλίς). A name applied to Aphrodité as protecting births, and also to her companions (Γενετυλλίδες).

Genēva or **Genāva**. The modern Geneva; the last town of the Allobroges, on the frontiers of the Helvetii, situated on the south bank of the Rhone, at the spot where the river flows out of the Lacus Lemannus. There was a bridge here over the Rhone. (Caes. *B. G.* i. 6.)

Genius ("creator, begetter," from *gigno*). The Italian peoples regarded the Genius as a higher power which creates and maintains life, assists at the begetting and birth of every individual man, determines his character, tries to influence his destiny for good, accompanies him through life as his tutelary spirit, and lives on in the Lares after his death. (See LARES.) As a creative principle, the Genius is attached, strictly speaking, to the male sex only. In the case of women his place is taken by Iuno, the personification of woman's life. Thus, in a house inhabited by a man and his wife, a Genius and a Iuno are worshipped together. But in common parlance, it was usual to speak of the Genius of a house, and to this Genius the marriage bed (*lectus genialis*) was sacred. A man's birthday was naturally the holiday of his attendant Genius, to whom he offered incense, wine, garlands, cakes, everything, in short, but bloody sacrifices, and in whose honour he gave himself up to pleasure and enjoyment; for the Genius wishes a man to have pleasure in the life that he has given him. Hence

Genius of Wine. (Pompeian Mosaic.)

the Romans spoke of enjoying one's self as indulging one's Genius, and of renunciation as spiting him (Hor. *Carm.* iii. 17, 14; Pers. iv. 27). Men swore by their Genius as by their higher self, and by the Genius of persons whom they loved and honoured. The philosophers originated the idea of a man having two Genii, a good and a bad one; but in the popular belief the notion of the Genius was that of a good and beneficent being. Families, societies, cities, and peoples had their Genius as well as individuals. The Genius of the Roman people (*Genius Publicus* or *Genius Populi Romani*) stood in the Forum, represented in the form of a bearded

Harpocrates, and Snake as Genius Loci. (*Pitture d'Ercolano*, i. 207.)

man crowned with a diadem, a cornucopia in his right hand, and a sceptre in his left. An annual sacrifice was offered to him on the 9th of October. Under the Empire the Genius of Augustus, the founder of the Empire, and of the reigning emperor, were publicly worshipped at the same time. Localities also, such as open spaces, streets, baths, and theatres, had their own Genii (Inscr. Orell. 343, 1697). These were usually represented under the form of snakes; and hence the common habit of keeping tame snakes. See ANGUIS.

The Greeks also had a similar belief in Genii, calling them δαίμονες, or daemons, of whom Hesiod mentions the number as 30,000, who are appointed to be the ministers of Zeus and the guardians of men. He regards them as the souls of the righteous. Pindar speaks of a γενέθλιος δαίμων, which seems to be exactly the equivalent of the Roman Genius. See DAEMON.

Gennadius. A presbyter of Marseilles, who in the fifth century A.D. continued St. Jerome's list of ecclesiastical writers (*viri illustres*). See HIERONYMUS.

Gennētae (*οἱ γεννῆται*). The Athenian term for the members of the 360 ancient families (*γένναι*), thirty of which made up one of the twelve *φρατρίαι* of the four old Ionic tribes. These families consisted of some thirty houses, who referred their origin and name to a common ancestor, and observed a common worship, with special priests to superintend it. The objects of this worship were Zeus Herkeios (the god of house and home), Apollo Patroös (the god of the family), the heroes of the family, and other tutelary deities. In case a family worship rose to the dignity of a state ceremonial, the priestly office remained hereditary in the family (*γέννα*). If there were no nearer relations, the members of the *γέννα* had a law of inheritance which they observed among themselves. Maintained by these religious and legal ties, the *γένναι* and the *φρατρίαι* survived the old Ionic tribes, after the abolition of the latter by Clisthenes. The president of the *γέννα* superintended the enrolment of new members into it at the feast of the Apaturia, the occasion on which the new members of the *φρατρίαι* were also enrolled. (See APATURIA.) A citizen who did not belong to a *γέννα* could only become a member of one by adoption, and under certain conditions. See PHRATRIA.

Gens (from the root GEN of *geno = gigno*). A Roman family in the widest sense of the word, descended on the male line from a common ancestor, and therefore bearing a common name. So long as the patricians were the only citizens with full rights, there could of course be no gentes not patrician. The oldest gentes belonged to the tribes of the Latin Ramnes and the Sabine Tities. Besides these there were the gentes belonging to the Alban families, brought to Rome by King Tullus Hostilius; and embodied by the other gentes in the community as a third tribe, the Luceres. These, the most ancient, were called *gentes maiores* as distinguished from the *gentes minores*, which included the plebeians whom Tarquinius Priscus raised to the rank of patricians. There were in later times instances of plebeian gentes being raised to patrician rank; but these became rarer and rarer, so that the number of patrician gentes was finally much reduced. During the last years of the Republic we hear of only fourteen still in existence, including thirty *familiae* (or families in the narrower sense). Many large gentes were divided into houses (*stirpes*) who had a common cognomen in addition to the name of their gens; thus the gens Cornelia included the Cornelii Maluginenses, Cornelii Cossi, Cornelii Scipiones, Cornelii Rufini, Cornelii Lentuli, Cornelii Dolabellae, Cornelii Cethegi, Cornelii Cinnae, Cornelii Sullae. Among the plebeians, as among the patricians, the *familia* naturally developed into a larger circle of relationship; but gentes in the old sense were not formed by the process. Though the plebeian had his gentile name, and afterwards his *cognomen*, he had not the real *ius gentilicium*. See IUS.

All *gentiles*, or members of a gens, had a right to its common property, which included a common burial-place. They also had a testamentary law of their own which lasted on into the imperial period. When a member of a gens died without heirs of his body, the next to inherit (as in the case of the plebeians) were the *agnati*, or *gentiles* on the male side, who could prove their relationship: failing these, the *gentiles* divided the inheritance. The existence of this law rendered it, in old times, necessary to obtain the *consensus* of the whole gens in cases of adoption and testamentary bequest. Another consequence of it was, that it was the duty of the *gentiles* to provide a *curator* for insane persons and spendthrifts, and a guardian for minors. See CURATOR.

Every gens had its meetings, at which resolutions were passed binding its individual members in matters affecting the gens. It was a decree of the gens Manlia, for instance, which forbade any one of its members to bear the praenomen Marcus. As every *familia*, whether patrician or plebeian, had certain sacrifices which it was bound to perform, so had every gens, as a larger or extended *familia*. All members of the gens were entitled, and indeed bound, to take part in the *sacra gentilicia*, or common worship of the gens. These *sacra* ceased to exist with the extinction of a gens; and if a member of a gens left it, this right and duty also came to an end. It should be added that certain public religious services were assigned to particular gentes, that of Hercules, for instance, to the gens Pinaria. See Mommsen, *Römisches Staatsrecht*, iii. i. pp. 15–22; Becker, *Handbuch*, ii. 1.

Gensĕric (more correctly **Gaiserich**). A king of the Vandals, was the illegitimate son of Godigiselus, succeeding his brother Gonderic in A.D. 429. In the same year he left Spain, which had been partly conquered by the Vandals, and crossed over into Africa, at the solicitation of Boniface, governor of that province, who had been induced, by the arts of his rival Aetius, to rebel against Valentinian III., emperor of the West. Boniface soon repented of the step he had taken, and advanced to meet the invader. But his repentance came too late. The Moors joined the standard of Genseric, and the powerful sect of the Donatists, who had been bitterly attacked by the Catholics, assisted him against their adversaries. Boniface was defeated, and obliged to retire into Hippo Regius, where he remained till he obtained a fresh supply of troops. Having ventured upon a second battle, and being again defeated, he abandoned the province to the barbarians, and sailed away to Italy. Hippo Regius fell after a siege of thirteen months, and was sacked with an almost infernal fury, which laid waste indiscriminately churches, fields, and houses, and earned for the name of Vandal the enduring infamy which a proverb can confer. A peace was concluded between Genseric and the Emperor of the West, by which all Africa to the west of Carthage was ceded to the Vandals. This peace, however, did not long continue, and the city of Carthage was taken by the Vandals, by surprise, A.D. 439. The Emperors of the West and East made great preparations for the recovery of the province, but an alliance which Genseric made with Attila, king of the Huns, effectually secured him against their attempts. Genseric's next object was the formation of a naval power. An immense number of ships were built, and his fleets ravaged the shores of Sicily and Italy. (See ATTILA.) Invited by the empress Eudoxia, he sailed up the Tiber, A.D. 455, and permitted his soldiers, for the space of fourteen days, to pillage Rome. In A.D. 460 he destroyed the fleet which the emperor Majorian had collected for the invasion of Africa; and, as his power increased, his ravages became more extensive. The island of Sardinia was conquered, and Spain, Italy, Sicily, Greece, Egypt, and Asia Minor were plundered every year by the Vandal pirates. Leo, the emperor of the East, at last resolved to make a vigorous effort for the recovery of Africa. A great army was assembled, and the command was given to Basilicus. He landed at Bona, and at first met with considerable success, but was at length obliged to retire from the province. After this victory Genseric met with no further opposition, but remained undisturbed master of the sea till his death, which happened A.D. 477. He was succeeded by his son Hunneric. Genseric was an Arian, and is said to have persecuted the Catholics with great cruelty (Procopius, *De Bell. Vand.*; Gibbon, *Decline and Fall*, chaps. xxxiii.–xxxvi.). See VANDALI.

Gentīles. Persons belonging to the same *gens*. See GENS.

Gentilicium Nomen. See NOMEN.

Gentius. A king of the Illyrians, allied with Perseus, King of Macedonia, and conquered by the Romans under Anicius Gallus, B.C. 167.

Genua. The modern Genoa, a thriving commercial town in Liguria, situated at the extremity of the Ligurian Gulf (Gulf of Genoa), and subsequently a Roman municipium. For some time during the Second Punic War it was held by Mago, the Carthaginian. The place had no political importance before the Middle Ages, when it was called Janua.

Genucia Gens. A patrician gens at Rome, of which the chief families bore the names Aventinensis and Augurinus.

Genucia Lex. See LEX.

Genūsus. A river in Greek Illyria, north of the Apsus (Livy, xliv. 30).

Geographia (γεωγραφία). The world, as conceived of in the *Iliad*, is a round plain encircled by a great river, Oceanus—not the Atlantic, of which Homer seems to have no knowledge at all, but a purely mythical stream. The sky is a great concave roof propped up by pillars which the mighty Atlas (q. v.) upholds. On the large, flat disc of the earth is a sort of belt or zone, of which Homer appears to have a definite notion. It includes Greece, for which, however, he has no collective name, since with him Hellas denotes only a district of Thessaly (*Iliad*, ii. 683). Acarnania and Epirus are not mentioned by name. On the north of the Aegean, the Thracians are known, including the Paeonians along the Axius (ii. 850). In Asia Minor, the topography of the Troad is familiar to the poet; Lydia is mentioned as Maeonia; while his references to the interior of Asia Minor—Phrygia, Pamphylia, etc.—are vaguely indefinite. Of the Aegean islands, Crete, Rhodes, Tenedos, Imbros, Samothrace (Samos), Lesbos, and Lemnos are specifically mentioned. Beyond this belt, Homer knows little or nothing of the world. In the North, the milk-fed nomads are noted (xiii. 5); in the South, the Aethiopes, "remotest of men," are indicated. Near the banks of Oceanus dwell the Pygmies. The Egyptian Thebes (ix. 381) and Sidon (vi. 289) occur, and the word "Phœnician" appears once (xxiii. 744).

The *Odyssey* represents a more extended geographical knowledge. Chios is mentioned; and so are Delos, the Dorians, Ithaca, and Sicily. The Phœnicians are now well known; the Aethiopes

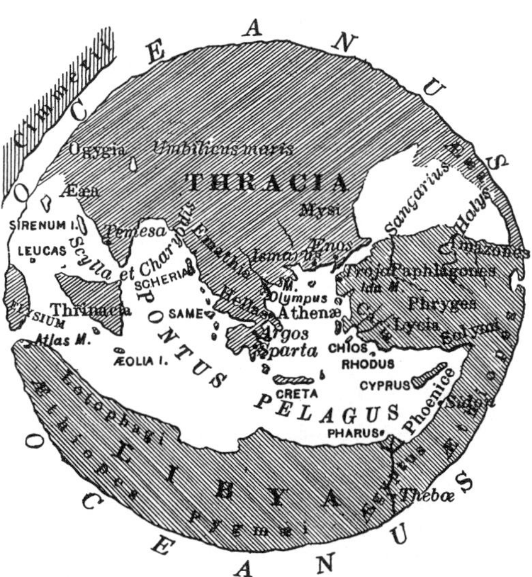

The World according to Homer.

are now clearly defined and divided into two sections, the eastern and the western. Scylla and Charybdis, the Lotus-eaters, and the Phaeacians are new. All this, however, is hazy and obscure. (See Jebb, *Homer*, ch. ii. [Glasgow, 1887].)

The Phœnicians and their kinsmen, the Carthaginians, by their commercial enterprise, did much to secure a knowledge of the coast of Africa, and sailed westward as far as the Canaries. Herodotus speaks of them as circumnavigating Africa. A famous voyage was that of Hanno (q. v.), the Carthaginian, who seems to have gone beyond what is now Sierra Leone. But geographical study and geographical literature took their rise, like historical literature, among the Ionian Greeks of Asia Minor. Their extensive commerce and their activity in founding colonies enlarged their geographical horizon. The necessity was thus felt of utilizing and recording the knowledge already

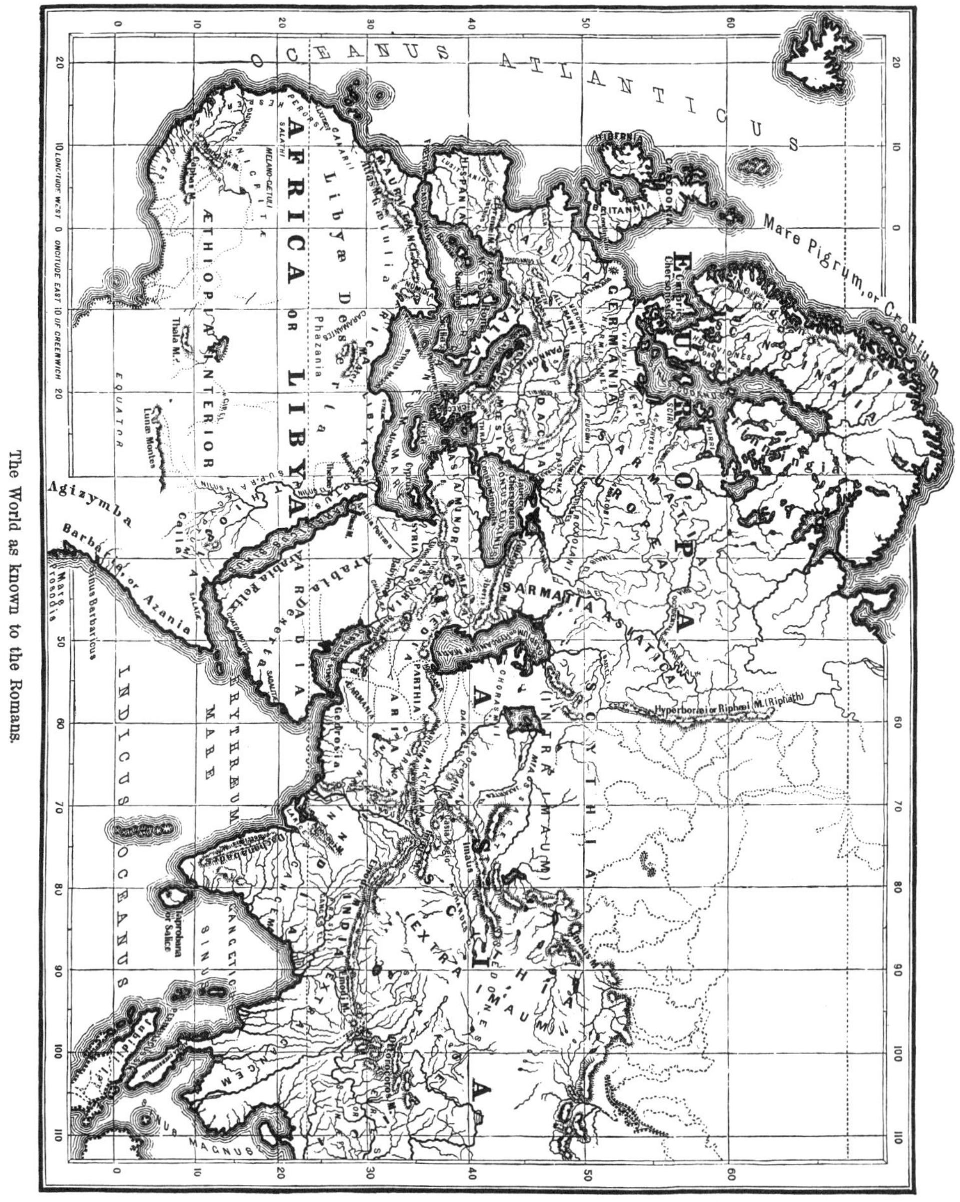

The World as known to the Romans.

acquired for the purpose of discovering the form and constitution of the earth. The first attempt at outlining a map of the world was made by Aristagoras of Miletus about B.C. 550. His kinsman Hecataeus, one of the writers called λογογράφοι, who flourished about fifty years later, corrected and enlarged this map and added a commentary. (See LOGOGRAPHI.) This commentary, of which only fragments are preserved in quotations, is the oldest piece of purely geographical writing in Greek. The geographical chapters in the history of Herodotus (about B.C. 450) compensate us to a certain extent for the loss of this work, and of the other works of the λογογράφοι on history and geography; but they treat only the eastern half of the then known world. It became, indeed, in the absence of a regular tradition of geographical science, a usual thing for historians to insert geographical disquisitions into their works. The writings of Thucydides, Xenophon, Ctesias, Ephorus, Theopompus, Timaeus, and others down to the time of Polybius, afford examples of this.

The first purely geographical work which has come down to us in a complete state is the *Periplus* (Περίπλους), bearing the name of Scylax, written in the first part of the fourth century B.C. It is a description of the coast of the Mediterranean Sea. About the same time the astronomer Eudoxus of Cnidus made a great advance in the theory of physical geography. It was he who first adduced mathematical proof of the spherical shape of the earth, which had been asserted before his time by Pythagoras. The division of the globe into five zones (two frigid, two temperate, and one torrid) is also due to him. About B.C. 330, Pytheas of Massilia (Marseilles) explored towards the northwest as far as the northern end of the British Islands and the coasts of the German Ocean. About the same time, the campaigns of Alexander the Great opened up Asia as far as India to Greek research. Nearchus made a report of exceptional value on his coast voyage from the Indus to the Euphrates. All these discoveries were embodied, about B.C. 320, in a new map by Dicaearchus of Messana, a disciple of Aristotle. He was the first scholar who treated physical geography in a scientific manner. He assumed the existence of a southern hemisphere, and made an estimate of the earth's circumference, to which he gave the exaggerated measurement of 40,000 miles. His map remained for a long time the standard work of the kind. The southern and eastern parts of India were still further opened out under Alexander's successors, in consequence of the campaigns of the Seleucidae, and several journeys were undertaken by ambassadors, among which that of Megasthenes should be mentioned. The commercial expeditions of the Ptolemies resulted in fresh knowledge of the coasts of Arabia and East Africa.

The first person to arrange the mass of geographical material, hitherto collected, into a really scientific system, was Eratosthenes (q. v.) of Cyrené (about B.C. 276–175). He found his materials in the rich collections of the Alexandrian Library, Alexandria being then the central point of the commerce of the world. He was fully equipped for his task by his acquirements both in physical science and mathematics, and in history and philology. He endeavoured for the first time to estimate the earth's circumference by a measurement of degrees carried out over a space of fifteen degrees of latitude, though the imperfection of his method brought out too large a quantity. The name of Hipparchus of Nicaea (about B.C. 140) marks a considerable advance. He may be called the founder of mathematical geography, as he applied geographical length and breadth to determine the position of places on the earth's surface. He also superseded the rectangular and equidistant projection of parallels and meridians, hitherto used in maps, by a projection which, with few modifications, is identical with the one now in use. The parallels were represented by segments of a circle, the meridians by straight lines or curves, corresponding with the portion of surface to be represented, drawn at distances corresponding to the actual distances on the surface of the globe. The estimate of the earth's circumference, which was accepted as correct down to the tenth century A.D., was that of Posidonius of Apamea (about B.C. 90). Taking as his basis the measurement of the shortest distance from Alexandria to Rhodes, he brought out the result as 4500 geographical miles, or too little by nearly one-sixth.

Only fragments remain of the writings of these geographers, and others contemporary with them; but we possess the great work of Strabo of Amasia, finished about A.D. 20, the most important monument of descriptive geography and ethnology which has come down from Greek antiquity. Thanks to the Roman conquest, he was in a position to give a more accurate description of the West than his predecessors. Up to this time all that the Romans had done for geographical research was to open up Western Europe and Northern Africa to the Greek scientists. An immense service was rendered to science by Agrippa, under the direction of Augustus. He measured and indicated on a map the distance between the stations on the great military roads and along the coasts of the Roman Empire, thus contributing enormously to our knowledge of ancient topography, and laying a foundation for our maps. These data formed the basis of a new map of the world, which was first set up in Rome. Numerous copies were probably taken for the larger cities of the Empire, and smaller portable ones distributed among the military and the administrative officers. It is probably upon copies of this kind that the *Itineraria* and the *Tabula Peutingeriana* are based. See ITINERARIA.

In the first century A.D. much was added to geographical knowledge by the expeditions of the Romans into the interior of North Africa and the North of Europe. About A.D. 50 Apollonius of Antioch explored India, going beyond the Punjab and possibly as far as the Ganges. The most important literary works of the Romans on geography belong to this period. These are (1) the compendium of Pomponius Mela; (2) the geographical books of Pliny the Elder's great encyclopaedia (*Historia Naturalis*), an uncritical compilation, but the only representative we have of a number of lost works; and (3) the *Germania* of Tacitus, an essay mainly of an ethnographic character. The last great contribution made to geographical science in antiquity is the work of the Alexandrian astronomer Ptolemy (about A.D. 150). This consists mainly of lists of the places marked on the current maps which he makes his authorities, with their latitude and longitude. After Ptolemy, the geographical literature of the Greeks and Romans alike has nothing to show but compilations and extracts. Towards the end of the sixth century, Stephanus of Byzantium compiled a dictionary of geography, which is valuable for the quantity of in-

The World according to Ptolemy.

formation taken from the older and lost writings which it embodies. The book of Pausanias (about A.D. 175) is valuable as bearing on the special topography of Greece. Cosmus, called Indicopleustes, wrote in the reign of Justinian a work called *Topographia Christiana*, giving an account of India. In it occurs the first mention by name of China. See Bunbury, *History of Ancient Geography*, 2 vols. (1883); St. Martin, *Histoire de Géographie;* Riese, *Geographica* (1881); Schmidt, *Zur Geschichte der geographischen Litteratur bei Griechen und Römern* (1887); Berger, *Geschichte der wissenschaftl. Erdkunde bei den Griechen* (1891); and Antichan, *Les Grands Voyages de Découvertes des Anciens* (1891). The remains of the *Geographici Graeci Minores* are edited by C. Müller, 2 vols. (Paris, 1882); the *Geographi Latini* by Riese (Frankfort, 1878).

Geomŏri (*γεωμόροι*). In many Doric States, particularly in Syracuse, a term denoting the territorial aristocracy; but in Athens it was applied to the landed commonalty, distinguished from the *Εὐπατρίδαι*, or nobles, on the one side, and the *Δημιουργοί*, on the other. See SOLONIAN CONSTITUTION.

Geoponĭci (*γεωπονικοί*). The ancient writers on agriculture; for instance (among the Greeks), the philosopher Democritus, and in later times, Xenophon, in his *Oeconomicus*. No other Greek works of the kind have come down to us, except the collection called *Geoponica*. This consists of twenty books, and contains extracts from writers of the most widely distant periods. The compiler was a Bithynian, Cassianus Bassus, who lived about the middle of the tenth century A.D., and undertook the work at the suggestion of the emperor Constantine VII. He based it upon a collection of extracts made by a certain Vindanius Anatolius. Agriculture was held in high esteem by the Romans, and the subject was in consequence a favourite one with their men of letters. A number of their works on it have come down to us: the *Res Rustica* of the elder Cato, a similar work by the encyclopaedic scholar, Marcus Terentius Varro, the *Georgica* of Vergil; and after Christ the writings of Columella, Gargilius Martialis, and Palladius. The *Georgica* of Vergil are in verse; as is one book of Columella. See Beckh, *De Geoponicorum Codicibus Manuscriptis* (1886); and the work by Gemoll (1887). See SCRIPTORES REI RUSTICAE.

Temple at Gerasa.

Georgĭca (*γεωργικά*). The title of Vergil's poem on husbandry. See VERGILIUS.

Gephyraei (*Γεφυραῖοι*). An Athenian family to which Harmodius and Aristogiton belonged.

Gepĭdae. A Gothic people who fought under Attila, and afterwards settled in Dacia, on the banks of the Danube. They were conquered by the Langobardi or Lombards.

Geraerae (*γεραιραί*). The fountain priestesses who took part in the Anthesteria. See DIONYSIA.

Geraestus (*Γεραιστός*). A promontory and harbour at the southern extremity of Euboea, with a celebrated temple of Poseidon (Thuc. iii. 3).

Geranēa (*Γεράνεια*). A range of mountains running along the western coast of Megaris, terminating in the promontory Olmiae in the Corinthian territory (Thuc. i. 105).

Gerănos (*γέρανος*). A dance. See HYPORCHEMA.

Gerăsa (*Γέρασα*). A city of Coele-Syria (Ptol. v. 15), about thirty-five miles east of the Jordan. The historical notices of this place are very scanty, yet the extent and magnificence of the existing ruins show it to have been once a great and wealthy city. Its site is now called Djerash, and there are remains of two theatres, two large temples and five or six smaller ones, a forum, two fine baths, a triumphal arch, a large reservoir, and two bridges. See Thomson, *The Land and the Book*, vol. iii. (N.Y. 1886).

Gergis (Γέργις) or **Gergĭthă** (τὰ Γέργιθα). A city of Dardania in Troas, a settlement of the ancient Teucri, and, consequently, a town of very great antiquity (Herod. iv. 122). Gergis, according to Xenophon, was a place of much strength. It had a temple sacred to Apollo Gergithius, and was said to have given birth to the Sibyl, who is sometimes called Erythraea, from Erythrae, a small place on Mount Ida (Dion. Hal. i. 55), and at others Gergithia.

Gergovia. A fortified town of the Arverni in Gaul, situated on a high and inaccessible hill, west or southwest of the Elaver (Allier), probably in the neighbourhood of the modern Clermont.

Germāni. See GERMANIA.

Germania (Γερμανία). The Roman name for the territory bounded on the west by the river Rhenus (Rhine); on the east by the river Vistula and the Carpates (Carpathian) Mountains; on the south by the river Hister or Danubius (Danube); and on the north by the German Ocean. The northern and northeastern parts of Gallia Belgica were also called GERMANIA PRIMA and GERMANIA SECUNDA under the Empire, in contrast to which Germany Proper was styled GERMANIA MAGNA, GERMANIA BARBĂRA, and GERMANIA TRANSRHENĀNA.

The Roman writers describe it as a dreary waste, covered for the most part with dense forests and morasses, and subject to heavy frosts and almost continuous cold, so that it is probable that the clearing of the soil and the draining of the swamps have, since the days of the Roman Empire, considerably modified the climate of the country. The wooded mountains of Southern Germany were usually called Silvae by the Romans, the most famous being the Hercynia Silva or Hercynius Saltus, including the modern Schwarzwald or Black Forest, the Odenwald, the Thüringerwald, the Erzgebirge, the Harz, and the Riesengebirge (cf. Caes. *B. G.* vi. 24). The chief rivers of Germany were the Rhenus, Danubius, Vistula, Amisia (Ems), Visurgis (Weser), Albis (Elbe), and Viadus (Oder).

The people whom the Romans called Germani were a branch of the Teutonic race, and are first mentioned in history in the fourth century B.C. The name is of uncertain etymology, being by some derived from a Keltic root, meaning "the shouters" (i. e. βοὴν ἀγαθοί), by others from a second Keltic root meaning "neighbours," and by others from the German *ger*, *gwer*—i. e. *Heer*, = "the warriors." Tacitus says (*Germania*, 2) that the name Germani was applied to the Tungri, the first German people to cross the Rhine, and appears to have been extended in its use by the Gauls to the whole race. The name Teutones was not the generic name for them in the time of the Romans, but is the base of the modern appellation *Deutsch;* the same with the Gothic *Thiuda*, "the people." The modern French name for the Germans, *Allemands*, is derived from the name of the tribes, who formed a league on the upper Rhine under the appellation Alemanni or Alamanni (*alle Männer*).

The Germans, though having no common name, regarded themselves as having a common descent from Mannus, the first man, son of the god Tuisco.

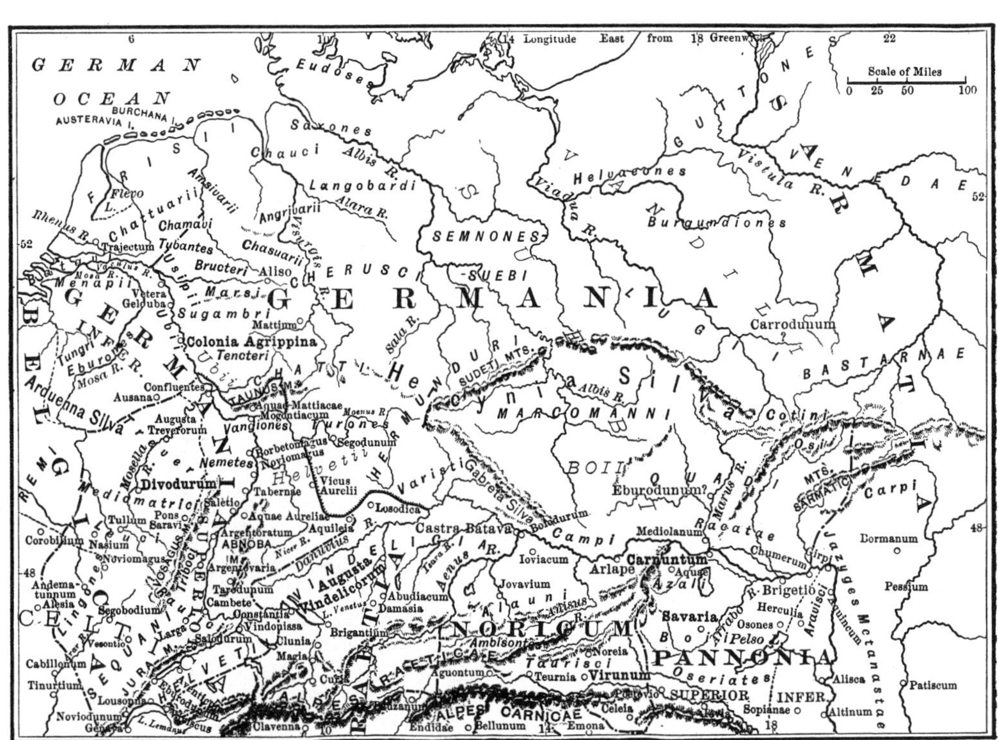

Mannus was fabled to have had three sons, from whom sprang the three great German peoples—the Istaevones, Ingaevones, and the Herminones. The first of these are the people with whom the Romans were oftenest brought into contact, since they held both banks of the Rhine. Subdivisions of this race were the Ubii (near Cologne); the Usipetes, Tencteri, Sicambri, and Bructeri (from the Lippe to the Ruhr); the Chatti or Catti (Hesse), and the Batavi (q. v.). Famous groups of the Ingaevones were the Frisii, the Chauci, and the Cherusci, along the North Sea and the banks of the Weser and the Ems. The most numerous of the three great divisions were the Herminones in Central Germany, extending to the east as far as the Vistula and the Carpathians. They included the powerful Suevi (to whom belonged the Marcomanni of Bohemia and the Semnones of Brandenburg), the Hermunduri of the Thüringerwald, the Lombardi or Langobardi at the mouth of the Elbe, the Vandali along the upper banks of the same river, the Heruli west of the Vistula, and the Quadi in what is now Moravia. See Böttger, *Wohnsitze der Deutschen in dem von Tacitus beschriebenem Lande* (Stuttgart, 1877); and the accompanying map.

The Germani were a stalwart, vigorous, and warlike race, with long, blond hair, fresh complexions, and blue eyes, living in wooden huts, which they often shared with their cattle, and engaging in the chase and in the fierce joys of warfare. Though violent and often cruel, they were not given to treachery, but were, as a rule, kindly and hospitable. Chastity was highly esteemed in women and was rarely lacking among them. The wife was wholly subject to the husband, but was treated with great consideration by him and consulted in the important affairs of life. The children were bred up to be hardy and enduring, the boys being taught at an early age the use of weapons. The majority of the people were free (*ingenui*), though there was a second class, described by Tacitus as *liberti* (*leti*, A. S. *laet*), who had no political rights, and a third class composed of slaves (*servi*) who were either prisoners taken in war or those persons who had been sold for debt. Some tribes had kings, and there was a small body of nobles (*nobiles*). All freemen, however, were equal in respect to their political equality, the only difference between them being in the amount of the blood-money (A. S. *wergild*) imposed as a fine for the killing of a king, a noble, or an ordinary *ingenuus*. The special privilege of the famous warriors of the tribe was to gather around them bands of young men emulous of the fame of their chieftains (*principes*). Such bands are called by Tacitus *comitatus*, and contain the germ of the later feudal system. The central governing body was the general assembly of the freemen in arms, they constituting the *civitas* or nation. The king was elected from the nobles, and did not succeed by inheritance. The divisions of the people were hardly territorial, but corresponded to the divisions of the armed host. The *pagus* and *vicus*, of which the Roman historians speak, were in reality divisions of the people. At the time when Caesar wrote, the Germans were in a state of transition, passing from the nomadic to an agricultural, settled condition. In Tacitus, they have entirely ceased to be nomadic, but have become attached to a definite territory.

As to the religion of the Germans, the notices that have reached us are scanty. The chief deity

Head of Ancient German. (Baumeister.)

was Wotan, the same as the Scandinavian Odin, the god of the sky and the air, delighting in warfare and the chase, and represented as riding upon a white horse. Donar, the Scandinavian Thor, the god of thunder, was identified by the Romans with Hercules and afterwards with Iupiter. A third deity was Tyr or Ziu, the god of war, regarded by Tacitus as Mars. A goddess, Nerthus, was worshipped by the tribes along the Baltic, presiding over marriage, the household, the children, and the realm of the dead. She is the same as the Saxon Fria or Frigg, and the Frankish Holda. There were also three fatal sisters—two fair and beneficent, one dark and malign; besides giants, elves, and dwarfs. After death, the brave were believed to enter Walhalla. The priests were very influential among the Germans, offering sacrifices, and predicting the future from the neighing of horses and the flight of birds.

History.—The Germans first appear in history in the campaigns of the Cimbri and Teutones (B.C. 113), the latter of whom were undoubtedly a Germanic people. About fifty years afterwards, Ariovistus, a German chief, crossed the Rhine with a vast host of Germans and subdued a great part of Gaul; but he was defeated by Caesar with great slaughter in B.C. 58 and driven beyond the Rhine. Caesar twice crossed this river (in 55 and 53), but made no permanent conquest on the eastern bank.

In the reign of Augustus, his step-son Drusus carried on war in Germany with great success for four years (B.C. 12–9), and penetrated as far as the Elbe. In the course of his operations he cut a canal between the Yssel and the Rhine, and built no less than fifty forts along the latter river. On his death (B.C. 9), his brother Tiberius succeeded to the command; and under him the country between the Rhine and the Visurgis (Weser) was entirely subjugated, and seemed likely to become a Roman province. But in A.D. 9, the impolitic and tyrannical conduct of the Roman governor Quinctilius Varus provoked a general insurrection of the various German tribes, headed by Arminius (q. v.), the Cheruscan, who had himself been a soldier of Rome, and for his bravery had been made a knight. Varus and his legions were enticed into the Teutoburg Forest, where, in the narrow defiles, the Germans fell upon them with impetuous fury, so that they were defeated and destroyed,

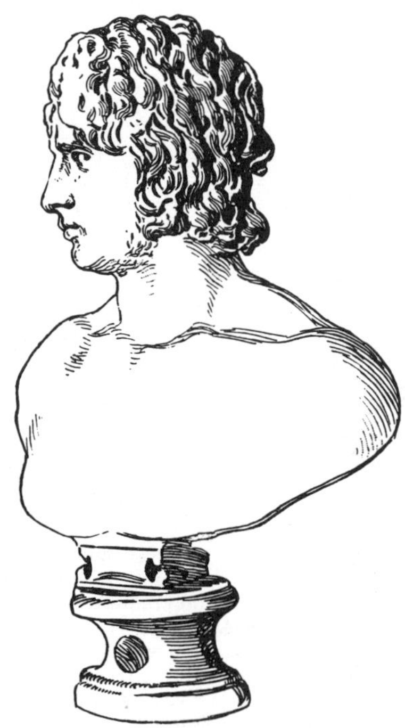

Supposed Bust of Arminius. (Capitoline Museum.)

and the Romans lost all their conquests east of the Rhine. (See VARUS.) The defeat of Varus was avenged by the successful campaigns of Germanicus (q. v.), who would probably have recovered the Roman dominions east of the river, had not the jealousy of Tiberius recalled him to Rome in A.D. 16. (See Knoke, *Die Kriegszüge des Germanicus in Deutschland* [Berlin, 1887].) From this time the Romans abandoned all further attempts to conquer Germany; but in consequence of the civil dissensions which broke out there soon after the departure of Tiberius, they were enabled to obtain peaceable possession of a large portion of South-western Germany between the Rhine and the Danube, to which they gave the name of the Agri Decumates (q. v.). On the death of Nero, several of the tribes in Western Germany joined the Batavi in their insurrection against the Romans (A.D. 69–71). Domitian and Trajan were forced to repel the attacks of various German clans; but in the reign of Antoninus Pius, the Marcomanni, joined by other tribes, made a more formidable attack upon the Roman dominions, and even threatened the Empire with destruction. For thirteen years Marcus Aurelius with difficulty held in check the vast hordes of barbarians, who were striving to overwhelm the Roman lines of defence, which comprised powerful fortresses and a great wall, remains of which are still to be seen in Southern Germany. Around these forts sprang up towns, such as Vindobona (Vienna) and Iuvavum (Salzburg) in the east, and Moguntiacum (Mayence), Colonia Agrippina (Cologne), Argentoratum (Strassburg) and Bonna (Bonn) in the west. From this time the Romans were often called upon to defend the left bank of the Rhine against their dangerous neighbours, especially against the two powerful confederacies of the Alemanni and Franci; and in the fourth and fifth centuries the Germans obtained possession of some of the fairest provinces of the Empire.

The influence of the Germans upon the Romans was great and continued to increase as time went on. Large numbers of the northern warriors enlisted in the legions even as early as the time of Iulius and Augustus Caesar, and gradually the whole army became permeated with German customs. Brunner even regards the history of the later Empire as the history of a continual conflict between the Germans and the Western Iberian elements; and has massed a great number of curious and striking facts to support his view. See his *Deutsche Rechtsgeschichte*, I. pp. 32–39 (Leipzig, 1887).

The Goths founded a great Germanic kingdom in the fourth century; the Burgundians conquered the whole of the valley of the Rhone; and the Vandals swept over Spain. (See GOTHI; VANDALI.) The West Goths crossed the Danube, penetrated into Italy, and under Alaric captured Rome itself. In the fifth century they conquered Southern Gaul and nearly the whole of Spain. In the invasion of the Huns under Attila, the Goths fought against him with the Romans, routing him at Châlons (A.D. 451), and soon after, Odoacer, chief of the Heruli, became master of Italy in 476. See ODOACER.

BIBLIOGRAPHY.—The sixth book of Caesar, *De Bello Gallico*, and the *Germania* of Tacitus give the earliest accounts of the Germans. These are admirably summarized and discussed by Stubbs in his *Constitutional History of England*, i. pp. 12–57 (Oxford, 1875). Standard treatises are the following: Leo, *Vorlesungen über die Geschichte des deutschen Volks*; Suzenheim, *Geschichte des deutschen Volks*, 3 vols. (1866–69); Lewis, *History of Germany* (1874), based on the work of D. Müller; Arnold, *Ansiedelungen und Wanderungen deutscher Stämme* (1875); Penke, *Die Herkunft der Deutschen* (1884); Ozanam, *Les Germains avant le Christianisme* (1872); Waitz, *Deutsche Verfassungsgeschichte*, vol. i. 3d ed. (1880); Babsch, *Die alten Germanen* (1880); Geoffroy, *Rome et les Barbares*, 2d ed. (1874); Lehmann, *D. Volk d. Sueben von Cäsar bis Tacitus* (1883); Müller, *Geschichte des deutschen Volks*, 11th ed. (1884). See also C. Kingsley, *Roman and Teuton*, 2d ed. (1887).

Germania. A valuable monograph by Tacitus, descriptive of ancient Germany and the Germans. See GERMANIA; TACITUS.

Germanĭcus Caesar. The son of Nero Claudius Drusus, adopted son of his uncle Tiberius, and

Germanicus. (Louvre.)

grandson of Livia, the wife of Augustus, born B.C. 15. In A.D. 7 he became quaestor, five years before the legal age; and in the same year served with distinction in the war against the Pannonians and Dalmatians. In the year 11 he accompanied Tiberius in his campaigns against the Germans, who were flushed with the pride of their recent exploit in annihilating the Roman legions of Varus; but after a few desultory incursions he returned to Rome. In A.D. 14, however, he was put in command of eight legions stationed on the Rhine. He was first called upon to quell a formidable revolt of the Roman troops, who on the death of Augustus mutinied for increased pay and a shorter term of service. Tact and firmness, united to great affability of demeanor, on the part of Germanicus, made him successful in his task, and he became the idol of the army, though for a long time the disaffection smouldered and at times broke out into open rebellion. At last, however, a campaign against the enemy was begun. Germanicus crossed the Rhine and fell upon the hostile Marsi, laying waste their territory for fifty miles and sparing neither age nor sex. On his return he routed the formidable tribes of the Bructeri, the Tubantes, and the Usipetes, who tried to block his way. In A.D. 15 he attacked the Catti, took their chief town (Mattium), and treated the foe with the same unsparing severity. Soon afterwards, he took prisoner Thusnelda, the patriotic wife of the German hero Arminius. She was pregnant at the time, and her husband, infuriated at her capture, roused up not only his own people, the Cherusci, but all the neighbouring tribes, and hurled his forces upon the Romans. Near the Teutoburg Forest, where bleached the bones of Varus and his legions, Germanicus again met the Germans. The conflict was long and doubtful. The Romans finally prevailed over the undisciplined valour of the barbarian hosts; yet so uncertain was the result that the victors decided to retire to the Rhine, which was done amid continuous fighting. In the next year, with a flotilla of 1000 vessels, he undertook another campaign on the lower Rhine. A great battle was fought on the plain of Idistavisus (near Hausberg), in which Arminius and his warriors were utterly routed. Arminius himself only escaped by disguising his person. It was on the occasion of this battle that eight eagles were seen hovering over the forest. "Come!" cried Germanicus to his troops, "Follow the birds of Rome, your own divinities!"—an exhortation that excited the courage of the legions to the highest pitch. Later, he once more devastated the country of the Marsi and the Catti.

In A.D. 16, Tiberius, who was jealous of his growing fame, recalled him to Rome. The whole population poured out to meet him, and on the 26th of May he celebrated his triumph with great splendour, Thusnelda being led along the Via Sacra among the captives. Soon afterwards, Germanicus was placed over the Eastern Provinces with the highest *imperium;* but Tiberius set Cn. Piso in command of Syria, probably with secret instructions to thwart and embarrass Germanicus in every possible way. Piso's wife Plancina, also, a haughty and imperious woman, was incited by the ex-empress Livia, mother of Tiberius, to annoy, in innumerable petty ways, the noble wife of Germanicus, Agrippina, who had been his companion in all his campaigns, and whose influence had on one occasion even quelled a revolt of the soldiery (Tac. *Ann.* i. 41). As was to be expected, a bitter quarrel soon arose between Germanicus and Piso, and when Germanicus fell ill in A.D. 19, rumours that Piso had poisoned him were rife; though Germanicus himself attributed his illness to sorcery. His death took place on October 9th of the same year.

Agrippina, wife of Germanicus. (Capitoline Museum, Rome.)

Tacitus says that his body bore no marks of poison (*Ann.* ii. 73). Never had Rome more deeply lamented the death of an illustrious son. His liberal views, unostentatious demeanour, and kind heart, combined with courage and military genius, made the whole people his admirers. Unusual honours were granted to him on his death—a public tomb, a triumphal arch, and the insertion of his name in the Salian Hymns. He left six children, among whom were Gaius (Caligula), and Agrippina, the mother of Nero.

Distinguished as much for culture as for military accomplishments, he was an orator and author as well as a general. Ovid, who dedicated to him the second edition of his *Fasti*, praises his poetry. His paraphrase of the *Phaenomena* of Aratus in 725 lines, and three fragments (246 lines) of a paraphrase of the same writer's *Prognostica*, still survive. They are remarkable for learning, command of metre, and a pleasing style. The *Phaenomena* is dedicated to Tiberius, and described by the author himself as the work of a beginner. These poems used erroneously to be attributed to Domitian, who did not, however, take the title of Germanicus until he was emperor. Three collections of scholia upon them, by no means without value, have also survived. The best edition of the *Aratea* of Germanicus, with the scholia, is that of Breysig (Berlin, 1867). See Beaufort, *Hist. de César Germanicus* (Leyden, 1741); Beulé, *Tibère et l' Héritage d' Auguste* (1870); and Höfer, *Feldzug des Germanicus im Jahr* 16 (1885).

Geronthrae (Γερόνθραι). A town of Laconia, to the north of Helos, founded by the Achaeans long before the invasion of the Dorians and the Heraclidae, and subsequently colonized by the latter. When Pausanias visited Laconia, he found Geronthrae in possession of the Eleuthero-Lacones. It contained a temple and grove of Ares, and another temple of Apollo (Pausan. iii. 22).

Gerra (τὰ Γέρρα). One of the chief cities of Arabia, and a great emporium for the trade of Arabia and India, on the northeast coast of Arabia Felix. The inhabitants, called Gerraei, were said to have been originally Chaldaeans who were driven out of Babylon.

Gerrae (γέρρον). Anything made of wickerwork; hence trifles, trash (Plaut. *Epid.* ii. 2. 45).

Gerrhi (Γέρροι). A people of Scythia, in whose country the Borysthenes rises. The kings of Scythia were buried in their territories (Herod. iv. 71).

Gerrhus (Γέρρος). A river of Scythia, which flowed towards the sea and fell into the Hypacris (Herod. iv. 56).

Gerŭlus. A porter. See Baiulus.

Gerusia (γερουσία; a council of old men, γέροντες). The supreme deliberative authority among the Spartans, according to the constitution of Lycurgus. It consisted of twenty-eight men of at least sixty years of age, called γέροντες (*senatores*), elected by the public assembly for life. The meetings of the Gerusia were presided over by the two kings, who had the right of voting. The number of the council therefore amounted to thirty. It was their duty to deliberate beforehand on all important affairs of State, and to prepare preliminary resolutions upon them, to be voted upon by the public assembly. They had also jurisdiction in the case of all offences which were punishable by death or loss of civil rights. They sat in judgment, if necessary, even on the kings, in later times associating the ephors with them in this function. Their authority, like that of the kings, suffered considerable restriction at the hands of the ephors. They had a similar position in the Cretan constitution, according to which only the members of the highest magistracy, called the κόσμοι, or regulators, could enter the council, and that only after a blameless term of administration. See Busolt, *Griechische Geschichte*, i. 94–135; Grote, *Hist. of Greece*, ii. pt. ii. ch. vi.; Arnold, *Thucydides*, i. App. ii. in later edition.

Gerȳon (Γηρυών) or **Gerȳŏnes** (Γηρυόνης). A giant with three bodies and powerful wings, the son of Chrysaor and Callirrhoë. He dwelt in the island of Erythia, lying in the ocean, in the extreme west; and was the possessor of a herd of red cattle, watched by the shepherd Eurytion, and a two-headed dog called Orthrus. It was one of the twelve labours of Heracles (q. v.) to carry off these cattle, and after a violent contest to slay the pursuing Geryon with his arrows.

Gesner, Johann Matthias. A German classical scholar, born at Roth, April 9th, 1691. He studied philology at the University of Jena, and after receiving his degree became librarian at Weimar (1715), afterwards filling the offices of Rector of the Gymnasium at Ansbach (1729), and Rector of the Thomas School at Leipzig (1730). At the Thomas School he had for his colleagues Ernesti and Johann Sebastian Bach. When the University of Göttingen was founded, he was called to the chair of Rhetoric in that institution, acting also as librarian. He died at Göttingen, August 3d, 1761.

His published works include an edition of the *Philopatris* ascribed to Lucian (1714), of the *Scriptores Rei Rusticae* (2d ed. 1773), of Quintilian (1738), of Claudian (1759), of the younger Pliny (2d ed. 1770), of Horace (2d ed. 1772), and of the Orphic Hymns; besides a *Novus Linguae et Eruditionis Romanae Thesaurus*. See Ernesti, *Opuscula Oratoria* (1762); and *Göttinger Professoren* (1872).

Gesoriăcum. The modern Boulogne; a port of the Morini in Gallia Belgica, at which persons usually embarked to cross over to Britain (Mela, iii. 2). It was subsequently called Bononia, whence its modern name.

Gesta Romanōrum. See Novels and Romances.

Gestatio. A part of an ornamental garden or pleasure-ground, divided into shady walks and vistas of sufficient extent for the proprietor and his guests to be carried about them for exercise in a palanquin (*lectica*). See Pliny, *Epist.* v. 6, 17; ii. 17, 13.

Gesticularia. A pantomimic actress, who expressed the character she had to personate by dancing and mimetic action of the hands and feet (Gell. i. 5, 2).

Geta, Septimius. The brother of Caracalla, by whom he was assassinated, A.D. 212. See Caracalla.

Getae (Γέται). A Thracian people, called Daci by the Romans. Herodotus (iv. 95) and Thucydides place them south of the Ister (Danube), near its mouths; but in the time of Alexander the Great they dwelt beyond this river and north of the Triballi.

Ghosts. See UMBRA.

Gibbet. See CRUX.

Gig. See CISIUM.

Gigantes (Γίγαντες). In Homer the Gigantes are a wild and gigantic race of aborigines, kinsmen of the gods, as are the Cyclopes and Phaeacians. With their king Eurymedon, they are destroyed for their wickedness. Hesiod makes them the sons of Gaea, sprung from the blood of the mutilated Uranus. Neither Hesiod nor Homer knew anything of their struggle with the gods (*Gigantomachia*), the story of which seems to be a reflection of the myth of the Titans and their contest with the gods, and to be associated with local legends. The two are often confused by later poets. The place of the contest was Phlegra, or the place of burning; and Phlegra was always localized in volcanic regions. In the earlier stories it is on the Macedonian peninsula of Pallenê; and in later times on the Phlegraean plains in Campania between Cumae and Capua, or again at Tartessus in Spain. Led on by Alcyoneus and Porphyrion, they hurled rocks and burning trunks of trees against heaven. But the gods called Heracles to their assistance, a prophecy having warned them that they would be unable to destroy the giants without the aid of a mortal. Heracles slew not only Alcyoneus, but gave the others, whom the gods had struck down, their death-blow with his arrows. As Enceladus was flying, Athenê threw the island of Sicily upon him. Polybotes was buried by Poseidon under the island of Nisyros, a piece of the island of Cos, which Poseidon had broken off with his trident, with all the giants who had fled there. Besides these, the following names are given among others: Agrius, Ephialtes, Pallas, Clytius, Eurytus, Hippolytus, Thoön.

In the oldest works of art the Giants are represented in human form and equipped with armour and spears; but in course of time their attributes became terrific — awful faces, long hanging hair and beard, the skins of wild animals for garments, trunks of trees and clubs for weapons. In the latest representations, but not before, their bodies end in two scaly snakes instead of feet, as in the

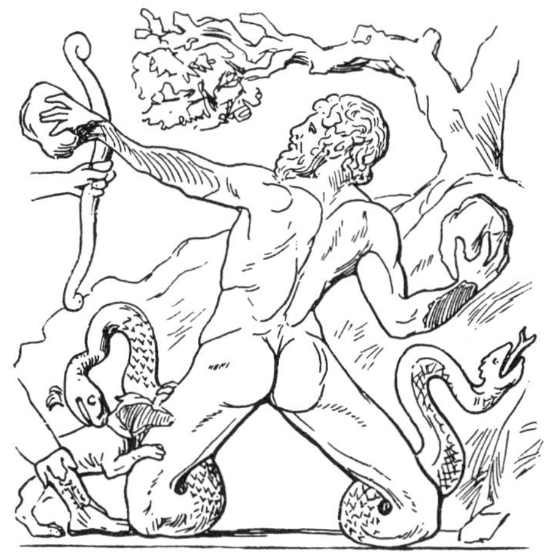

Giant in Conflict with Artemis. (Roman relief in Vatican Museum.)

illustration. In the Gigantomachia of Pergamus, the grandest representation of the subject in antiquity, we find a great variety of forms; some quite human, others with snakes' feet and powerful wings, others with still bolder combinations of shape; some are naked, some clothed with skins, some fully armed, and others slinging stones. See Mayer, *Die Giganten und Titanen* (Leipzig, 1887); and the articles PERGAMENE SCULPTURES; TITANES.

Gigantomachia. See GIGANTES.

Gigōnus (Γίγωνος). A town and promontory of Macedonia on the Thermaic Gulf.

Gildo. A Moorish chief who governed Africa for several years under the Western Empire, but in A.D. 397 became a subject of the Eastern Empire, of which Arcadius was then the head. He was taken prisoner by Stilicho, acting for the emperor Honorius, and hanged himself in despair in A.D. 398. The Latin poet Claudianus has made this war the subject of a poem (*De Bello Gildonico*). See CLAUDIANUS.

Gimlet. See TEREBRA.

Ginglȳmus (γίγγλυμος). Literally, a joint which moves in a socket, like the elbow; thence a hinge (Xen. *Eq.* xii. 6), the action of which resembles that of a joint in the human frame. The

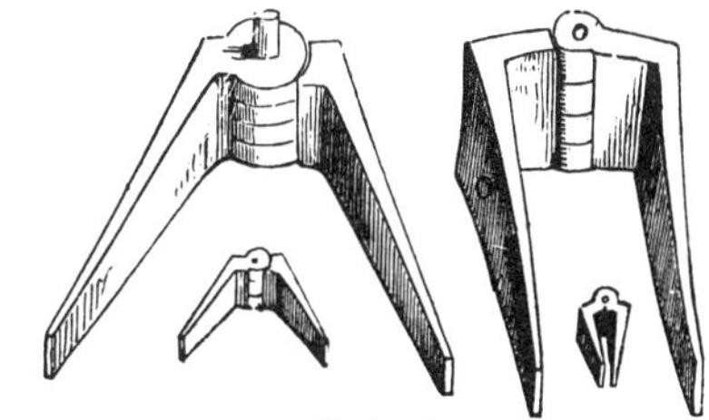

Ginglymi.

cabinets of antiquities contain numerous specimens of these contrivances, framed in the different patterns in use at this day, and of all sizes. Of the two examples here given, the first is from Pompeii, the other is preserved in the British Museum. The Latin name is not met with in any Roman writer, and consequently requires authority; but the Greek one is undoubted.

Gingras (γίγγρας). A fife or flute. See TIBIA.

Girgillus. The roller turned by a windlass, in order to raise water from a well by means of a rope and bucket; a contrivance precisely similar to those used in many country places at the present day, as shown by the annexed example from a marble sarcophagus of the Vatican Cemetery (Isidor. *Orig.* xx 15).

Girgillus. (Rich.)

Gisco or **Gisgo** (Γίσκων, Γέσκων). (1) The son of Hamilcar, defeated and killed in the battle of Himera (B.C. 480). (2) The son of Hanno, who unsuccessfully opposed Timoleon after the latter had routed the Carthaginians at the Crimissus in B.C. 339. (3) A commander of the Carthaginian garrison at Lilybaeum at the close of the First Punic War. In B.C. 241 he was seized and murdered by the mutinous mercenary troops with whom the Carthaginian government had sent him to treat. See CARTHAGE.

Gitiădas (Γιτιάδας). The last Spartan artist of any distinction, flourishing about B.C. 516. He completed the so-called Brazen House of Athené at Sparta. He won some distinction as a poet.

Glabrio, Manius Acilius. (1) Consul, B.C. 191, when he defeated Antiochus at Thermopylae. (2) Praetor urbanus in 70, when he presided at the impeachment of Verres; and consul in 67, and subsequently the successor of L. Lucullus in the command of the war against Mithridates, in which, however, he was superseded by Cn. Pompey. (3) The son of the preceding. He was one of Caesar's lieutenants in the Civil Wars. He was twice defended by Cicero on capital charges, and acquitted.

Gladiatōres (μονομάχοι). Persons who fought with swords (*gladii*) in the circus, the forum, or in later times in the amphitheatre, for the amusement of the Roman people (Quintil. *Declam.* 302). They are said to have been first exhibited by the Etruscans, and to have had their origin from the custom of killing slaves and captives at the funeral pyres of the deceased (Tertull. *De Spectac.* 12; Serv. *ad* Verg. *Aen.* x. 519). A show of gladiators was called *munus*, and the person who exhibited it, the *editor*, *munerator*, or *dominus*, who was honoured during the day of exhibition, if a private person, with the insignia of a magistrate (Flor. iii. 20).

Bustuarius. (From an Engraved Gem.)

Gladiators were first exhibited at Rome in B.C. 264, in the Forum Boarium, by Marcus and Decimus Brutus, at the funeral of their father (Val. Max. ii. 4, 17). They were at first confined to public funerals (*bustuarius*), but afterwards fought at the funerals of most persons of consequence, and even at those of women (Suet. *Iul.* 26). Private persons sometimes left a sum of money in their will to pay the expenses of such an exhibition at their funerals (Hor. *Sat.* ii. 3, 84). Combats of gladiators were also exhibited at entertainments by the degraded nobles of Campania (Sil. Ital. xi. 51), though not at Rome, and especially at public festivals by the aediles and other magistrates, who sometimes exhibited immense numbers with the view of pleasing the people. (See Aediles.) Under the Empire the passion of the Romans for this amusement rose to its greatest height, and the number of gladiators who fought on some occasions appears almost incredible. After Trajan's triumph over the Dacians, there were more than 10,000 exhibited (Dio Cass. lxviii. 15).

Gladiators consisted either of captives, slaves, and condemned malefactors, or of freeborn citizens who fought voluntarily. Of those who were condemned, some were said to be condemned *ad gladium*, in which case they were obliged to be killed at least within a year; and others *ad ludum*, who might obtain their discharge at the end of three years. Freemen who became gladiators for hire were called *auctorati*, and their hire *auctoramentum* or *gladiatorium* (Suet. *Tib.* 7). They also took an oath on entering upon the service, similar to that which is preserved by Petronius (117): *In verba Eumolpi sacramentum iuravimus, uri, vinciri, verberari, ferroque necari, et quicquid aliud Eumolpus iussisset, tamquam legitimi gladiatores, domino corpora animasque religiosissime addicimus.* Even under the Republic, freeborn citizens fought as gladiators (Livy, xxviii. 21), but they appear to have belonged only to the lower orders, and the profession was considered degrading (cf. Mommsen, *C. I. L.* i. 1418), though to some it had many attractions. Under the Empire, however, both knights and senators fought in the arena (Suet. *Iul.* 39; *Aug.* 43; *Ner.* 12), and even women (Suet. *Dom.* 4); a practice which was at length forbidden in the time of Severus (Dio Cass. lxxv. 16).

Gladiators were kept in schools (*ludi*), where they were trained by persons called *lanistae*. The whole body of gladiators under one *lanista* was frequently called *familia*. They sometimes were the property of the *lanistae*, who let them out to persons who wished to exhibit a show of gladiators; but at other times belonged to citizens, who kept them for the purpose of exhibition, and engaged *lanistae* to instruct them. Thus Spartacus (q. v.) belonged to the school of Lentulus at Capua (Flor. iii. 8), and Caesar had one at the same place. Domitian built four *ludi* at Rome, and there were several others in Italy and the provinces. The number of gladiators which any citizen might keep was limited by the Senate in B.C. 68 (Suet. *Iul.* 10), but Caligula did away with the restriction (Dio Cass. lix. 14). The superintendence of the *ludi*, which belonged to the emperors, was intrusted to a person of high rank, called *curator* or *procurator*. The arrangements of a *ludus gladiatorius* are now known to us from one excavated at Pompeii. See illustration on next page.

The gladiators fought in these schools with wooden swords, called *rudes* (Suet. *Cal.* xxxii. 54). Great attention was paid to their diet, in order to increase the strength of their bodies, and they were fed with nourishing food, called *gladiatoria sagina*.

Gladiators were sometimes exhibited at the funeral pyre, and sometimes in the forum, but more

Gladiators. (Overbeck.)

frequently in the amphitheatre. (See AMPHITHEATRUM.) The person who was to exhibit a show of gladiators published some days before the exhibition bills (*libelli*), containing the number and sometimes the names of those who were to fight; e. g. at Pompeii we have (*C. I. L.* iv. 1189): A. SUETTII CERTI AEDILIS FAMILIA GLADIATORIA PUGNABIT POMPEIIS PRID. KAL. IUN. VENATIO ET VELA ERUNT; and similar notices. When the day came, they were led along the arena in procession, and matched by pairs; and their swords were examined by the *editor* to see if they were sufficiently sharp (Suet. *Tit.* 9). At first there was a kind of sham battle, called *praelusio*, in which they fought with wooden swords, or the like (Sen. *Epist.* 117), and afterwards at the sound of the trumpet the real battle began. When a gladiator was wounded, the people called out "Habet!" or "Hoc habet!" and the one who was vanquished lowered his arms in token of submission. His fate, however, depended upon the people, who turned up their thumbs if they wished him to be killed (Hor. *Ep.* i. 18, 66; Juv. iii. 36), and ordered him to receive the sword (*ferrum recipere*), which gladiators usually did with the greatest firmness. A relief has been discovered at Cacillargues, showing a combat between a Samnite and a *retiarius*, with four spectators, one of whom, a woman, is holding up her thumbs. There is no clear evidence that the wish that mercy should be shown was expressed by pressing down the thumbs (Pliny, *H. N.* xxviii. § 25 is barely to the point); this was indicated rather by waving handkerchiefs (Mart. xii. 29, 7). If the life of a vanquished gladiator was spared, he obtained his discharge for that day, which was called *missio* (Mart. xii. 29, 7); and hence in an exhibition of gladiators *sine missione*, the lives of the conquered were never spared. This kind of exhibition, however, was forbidden by Augustus (Suet. *Aug.* 45).

Pompeian Barracks for Gladiators. (Overbeck.)

Palms were usually given to the victorious gladiators, and hence a gladiator who had frequently conquered is called *plurimarum palmarum gladiator* (Cic. *Pro Rosc. Amer.* vi. 17); money also was sometimes given (Suet. *Claud.* 21). Old gladiators, and sometimes those who had only fought for a short time, were discharged from the service by the *editor* at the request of the people, who presented each of them with a rudis or wooden sword; whence those who were discharged were called *rudiarii* (Cic. *Phil.* ii. 29, 74; Hor. *Ep.* i. 1, 2). If a person was free before he entered the ludus, he became on his discharge free again; and if he had been a slave, he returned to the same condition again, unless he received the cap of freedom (*pilleus*). A man, however, who had been a gladiator, was always considered to have disgraced himself, and consequently it appears that he could not obtain the equestrian rank even if he afterwards acquired sufficient property to entitle him to it; and a slave who had been sent into a *ludus* and there manumitted, merely acquired the status of a *peregrinus dediticius*. See DEDITICII.

Shows of gladiators were abolished by Constantine, but appear notwithstanding to have been generally exhibited till the time of Honorius, by whom they were finally suppressed.

Gladiators were divided into different classes, according to their arms and different mode of fighting, or other circumstances. The names of the most important of these classes are given in alphabetical order:

Andabatae (Cic. *Ad Fam.* vii. 10) wore helmets without any aperture for the eyes, so that they were obliged to fight blindfold, and thus excited the mirth of the spectators. They are generally believed to have fought on horseback, but this is denied by Orelli (*Inscr.* 2577) and Friedländer; the name cannot be derived from ἀναβάτης. It is perhaps Keltic, with the meaning "blind-fighter" (Whitley Stokes, in *Academy*, Feb. 9, 1889).

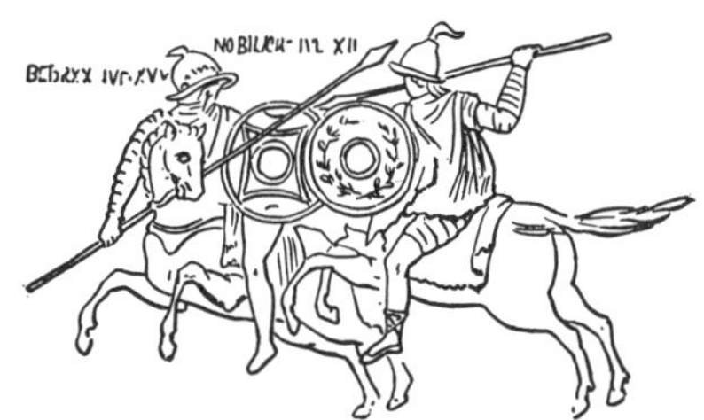

Andabatae. (From the Amphitheatre, Pompeii.)

Bustuarii were those who fought on the funeral pyre. See illustration, p. 732.

Catervarii was the name given to gladiators when they did not fight in pairs, but when several fought together (Suet. *Aug.* 45).

Dimachaeri appear to have been so called, because they fought with two swords (Artemid. ii. 32; Orelli, *Inscr.* 2584).

Equites were those who fought on horseback (Orelli, *Inscr.* 2569, 2577).

Essedarii fought from chariots (*esseda*), like the Gauls and Britons. They are frequently mentioned in inscriptions (Orelli, 2566, 2584, etc.; cf. Petron. 45).

Fiscales were those under the Empire who were trained and supported from the *fiscus* (Capitol. *Gord.* 33).

Hoplomachi appear to have been those who fought in a complete suit of armour (Suet. *Cal.* 35; Mart. viii. 74).

Laquearii were those who used a noose (*laqueus*) to catch their adversaries (Isid. xviii. 56).

Meridiani were those who fought in the middle of the day, after combats with wild beasts had taken place in the morning. These gladiators were very lightly armed (Suet. *Claud.* 34).

Myrmillones are said to have been so called from their having the image of a fish (*mormyr*, μορμύρος) on their helmets (Fest. s. v. *Retiarii*). Their arms were like those of the Gauls, and they did not differ much from the kind called Galli. They were usually matched with the *retiarii* or Thracians (Cic. *Phil.* iii. 12, 31; vii. 6, 17; Juv. viii. 200; Suet. *Cal.* 32, *Dom.* 10).

Ordinarii was the name applied to all the regular gladiators who fought in pairs in the ordinary way (Suet. *Aug.* 45, *Cal.* 26).

Postulaticii were such as were demanded by the people from the *editor*, in addition to those who were exhibited (Sen. *Epist.* 7).

Provocatores fought with the Samnites (Cic. *Pro Sest.* 64. 134), but we do not know anything respecting them except their name.

Retiarii carried only a three-pointed lance, called *tridens* or *fuscina*, a dagger (Val. Max. i. 7, 8), and a net (*rete*), which they endeavoured to throw over their adversaries, and then to attack them with the fuscina while they were entangled. The *retiarius* was dressed in a short tunic, and wore nothing on his head. If he missed his aim in throwing the net, he betook himself to flight, and endeavoured to prepare his net for a second cast, while his adversary followed him round the arena in order to kill him before he could make a second attempt. His adversary was usually a *secutor* or a *myrmillo* (Suet. *Cal.* 30, *Claud.* 34; Orelli, 2578). In the following illustration a combat is represented between a *retiarius* and a *myrmillo;* the former

Myrmillo and Retiarius. (Mosaic in the Library at Madrid.)

has thrown his net over the head of the latter, and is proceeding to attack him with the *fuscina.* The *lanista* stands behind the *retiarius.*

Samnites were so called because they were armed in the same way as that people, with a helmet with a high crest (Juv. vi. 256), and were particularly distinguished by the oblong *scutum.*

Secutores are supposed by most writers to be so called because the *secutor* in his combat with the *retiarius* pursued the latter when he failed in securing him by his net. Other writers think that they were the same as the *suppositicii*, mentioned by Martial (v. 24), who were gladiators substituted in the place of those who were wearied or were killed (Suet. *Cal.* 30; Juv. vi. 108, with the Schol. viii. 210). If the old reading in a letter of Cicero's (*Ad Att.* vii. 14) is correct, Iulius Caesar had no less than 600 *secutores* in his *ludus* at Capua; but we probably ought to read *scutorum* instead of *secutorum.*

Suppositicii. See *Secutores.*

Thraces or *Thraeces* were armed, like the Thracians, with a round shield or buckler (Fest. s. v. *Thraeces*), and a short curved sword or dagger (*sica*, Suet. *Cal.* 32), which is called *falx supina* by Juvenal (viii. 201), and wore greaves on both legs. They were usually matched, as already stated, with the *myrmillones.*

Velites had light spears (Ovid, *Ib.* 45).

Paintings of gladiatorial combats, as well as of the other sports of the amphitheatre, were favourite subjects with the Roman artists (Pliny, *H. N.* xxxv. § 52). Several statues of gladiators have come down to us, which are highly admired as works of

Borghese Gladiator (?) of Agasias. (Louvre.)

art; of these, the most celebrated is the athlete by Agasias of the Borghese Collection, now in the Museum of the Louvre, and the Dying Gladiator, in the Capitoline Museum. The latter, which inspired the famous stanza in *Childe Harold*, is now, however, regarded as a wounded Gaul. Gladiatorial combats are represented in the bas-reliefs on the tomb of Scaurus at Pompeii, and illustrate in many particulars the brief account which has been given in this article of the several classes of gladiators. These bas-reliefs are represented in the following illustrations from Mazois (*Pomp.* i. pl. 32; and Overbeck, *Pompeii*, p. 165). The figures are made of stucco, and appear to have been moulded separately, and attached to the plaster by pegs of bronze or iron. In various parts of the frieze are written the name of the person to whom the gladiators belonged, and also the names of the gladiators themselves, and the number of their victories. The first pair of gladiators on the left hand represents an equestrian combat. Both wear helmets with visors, which cover the whole face, and are armed with spears and round bucklers. In the second pair the gladiator on the left has been wounded; he has let fall his shield, and is imploring the mercy of the people by raising his hands towards them. His antagonist stands behind him waiting the signal of the people. Like all the other gladiators represented on the frieze, they wear the *subligaculum* or short apron tied above the hips. The one on the left appears to be a *myrmillo*, and the one on the right, with an oblong shield (*scutum*), a Samnite. The third pair consists of a Thracian and a *myrmillo*, or Samnite, the latter of whom is defeated. The fourth group consists of four figures; two are *secutores* and two *retiarii*. The *secutor* on his knee appears to have been defeated by the *retiarius* behind him; but as the *fuscina* is not adapted for producing certain death, the other *secutor* is called upon to do it. The *retiarius* in the distance is probably destined to fight in his turn with the surviving *secutor*. The last group consists of a *myrmillo* and a Samnite; the latter is defeated.

In the second illustration two combats are represented. In the first a Samnite has been conquered by a *myrmillo;* the former is holding up his hand to the people to implore mercy, while the latter apparently wishes to become his enemy's executioner before receiving the signal from the people; but the *lanista* holds him back. In the other combat a *myrmillo* is mortally wounded by a Samnite. It will be observed that the right arm of every figure is protected by rings of armour, which the left does not require on account of the shield. See Lipsius, *Saturnalia* (1675) and *De Amphitheatro* in Graev. *Thesaur*. vol. ix.; Friedländer, *Sittengeschichte*, vol. ii.; Wallon, *Histoire de l'Esclavage* (Paris, 1879); and the article VENATIO.

Gladiators.

Gladiatorium. The pay given to a freeman who trained and served as a gladiator. See Livy, xliv. 31, and the article GLADIATORES.

Gladius (ξίφος; poet. ἄορ, φάσγανον). A sword, by the Latin poets called *ensis*. The ancient sword had generally a straight, two-edged blade (ἄμφηκες), rather broad, and of nearly equal width from hilt to point. Gladiators, however, used a sword which was curved like a scimitar. In times of the remotest antiquity swords were made of bronze, but afterwards of iron. The Greeks and Romans wore them on the left side, so as to draw them out of the sheath (κόλεος, *vagina*) by passing the right hand in front of the body to take hold of the hilt with the thumb next to the blade. Hence Aeschy

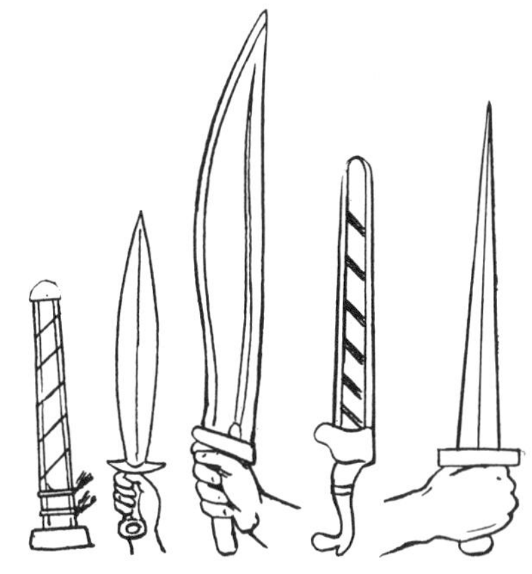

Greek Swords and Scabbards. (Guhl and Koner.)

lus distinguishes the army of Xerxes by the denomination of μαχαιροφόρον ἔθνος, alluding to the obvious difference in their appearance in consequence of the use of the *acinaces* instead of the sword. See ACINACES.

The early Greeks used a very short sword. Iphicrates, who made various improvements in armour about B.C. 400, doubled its length, so that an iron sword found in a tomb at Athens, and represented by Dodwell, was two feet five inches long, including the handle, which was also of iron. The Roman sword, as was the case also with their other offensive weapons, was larger, heavier, and more formidable than the Greek. Its length gave occasion to the joke of Lentulus upon his son-in-law, who was of very low stature, "Who tied my son-in-law to his sword?" To this Roman sword the Greeks applied the term σπάθη, which was the name of a piece of wood of the same form used in weaving. (See TELA.) The ancient British sword was still larger than the Roman. The principal ornamentation of the sword was bestowed upon the hilt. See CAPULUS.

1 

2 

1. Monument of an Illyrian Soldier, found at Bingen. 2. Scabbard. (Mayence, Germany.)

Gladius is sometimes used in a wide sense, so as to include *pugio* (q. v.). In the republican period of Rome, the gladius was worn by magistrates only when exercising military command. Under the Empire it was one of the insignia of the emperor and of those nominated by him. The *ius gladii* is the right of criminal jurisdiction conferred by the emperor on provincial governors. See ARMA; MACHAERA; MUCRO.

Glans (μολυβδίς). A large leaden slug or plummet, cast in a mould, and used instead of a stone to be discharged from a sling (Livy, xxxviii. 20, 21, 29). The illustration represents an original found at the ancient Labicum; the letters FIR are for *firmiter*, "Throw steadily," or *Feri Roma* (Inscript. Orelli, 4932), "Strike, O Rome!" Others have been found in Greece, inscribed with the figure of a thunderbolt, or ΔΕΞΑΙ, "Take this."

Glans.

Glaphȳra (Γλαφύρα). A mistress of Marcus Antonius who placed her son Archelaüs on the throne of Cappadocia as a favour to her. (Dio Cass. xlix. 32.)

Glass. See VITRUM.

Glaucé (Γλαύκη). (1) One of the Nereides, the name Glaucé being only a personification of the color of the sea (γλαυκός). (2) Daughter of Creon of Corinth, also called Creüsa. See CREON.

Glaucias (Γλαυκίας). (1) An Illyrian king who fought against Alexander the Great in B.C. 335. In 316 he offered a refuge to Pyrrhus, then an infant, and refused to give him up to Cassander. Nine years later he invaded Epirus and placed Pyrrhus on the throne of that country. See PYRRHUS. (2) An Aeginetan statuary who flourished in B.C. 488. He made a bronze chariot and statue of Gelon (q. v.).

Glaucon (Γλαύκων). The brother of Plato, who makes him one of the speakers in his dialogue *De Republica.*

Glaucus (Γλαῦκος). (1) A sea deity, probably only another form of Poseidon, whose son he is, according to some accounts. Like the marine gods in general, he had the gift of prophecy; and we find him appearing to the Argonauts (Apoll. Rh. i. 1310 foll.), and to Menelaüs (Eurip. *Orest.* 356 foll.), and telling them what had happened, or what was to happen. In later times sailors were continually making reports of his soothsaying (Pausan. ix. 22). Some said that he dwelt with the Nereides at Delos, where he gave responses to all who sought them. According to others, he visited each year all the isles and coasts, with a train of monsters of the deep (κήτεα), and, unseen, foretold in the Aeolic dialect all kinds of evil. The fishermen watched for his approach, and endeavoured by fastings, prayer, and fumigations to avert the ruin with which his prophecy menaced the fruits and cattle. At times he was seen among the waves, and his body appeared covered with mussels, seaweed, and stones. He was heard evermore to lament his fate in not being able to die (Plat. *Rep.* x. 611). This last circumstance refers to the common legendary history of Glaucus. He was a fisherman, it is said (Pausan. l. c.; Ovid, *Met.* xiii. 904 foll.), of Anthedon, in Boeotia. Observing one day the fish which he had caught and thrown on the grass to bite it, and then to jump into the sea, his curiosity incited him to taste it also. Immediately on his doing so he followed their example, and thus became a sea-god. Another account made him to have obtained his immortality by tasting the grass, which had revived a hare he had run down in Aetolia. He was also said to have built and steered the Argo, and to have been made a god of the sea by Zeus during the voyage. An account of the story of his love for Scylla will be found under SCYLLA. See Gädecken, *Glaukos, der Meeresgott* (Göttingen, 1860).

(2) A son of Sisyphus, king of Corinth, by Meropé, the daughter of Atlas, born at Potniae, a village of Boeotia. According to one account, he restrained his mares from having intercourse with the stallions; upon which Aphrodité inspired the former with such fury that they tore his body to pieces as he returned from the games which Adrastus had celebrated in honour of his father. Another

version of the story makes them to have run mad after eating a certain plant at Potniae (*Etymol. Mag.* s. v. Ποτνιάδες; Hyg. *Fab.* 250; Verg. *Georg.* iii. 268).

(3) A son of Minos and Pasiphaë, who, when a child, pursuing a mouse, fell into a vessel of honey and was smothered. His father, ignorant of his fate, consulted the oracle to know where he was, and received for answer that there was a three-coloured cow in his herd, and that he who could best tell what she was like could restore his son to life. The soothsayers were all assembled, and Polyidus, the son of Coiranus, said that her colour was that of the berry of the briar, green, red, and, lastly, black. Minos thereupon desired him to find his son; and Polyidus, by his skill in divination, discovered where he was. Minos then ordered him to restore him to life; and, on his declaring his incapacity so to do, shut him up in a chamber with the body of his child. While here, the soothsayer saw a serpent approach the body, and he struck and killed it. Another immediately appeared, and seeing the first one dead, retired, and came back soon after with a plant in its mouth, and laid it on the dead one, which instantly came to life. Polyidus, by employing the same herb, recovered the child. Minos, before he let him depart, insisted on his communicating his art to Glaucus. He did so, but as he was taking leave he desired his pupil to spit into his mouth. Glaucus obeyed, and lost the recollection of all he had learned (Apollod. iii. 3. 1). Hyginus makes him to have been restored to life by Aesculapius (*Poet. Astron.* ii. 14).

(4) The grandson of Bellerophontes, and son of Hippolochus, prince of the Lycians. With his kinsman Sarpedon, he was leader of the Lycian auxiliaries of Priam, and met Diomedes in the *mêlée*. The two chieftains recognized each other as friends and guests of their grandfather Bellerophontes and Oeneus, and exchanged armour, Glaucus parting with his golden suit for the brazen arms of Diomedes. When the Greek intrenchments were stormed, Glaucus had reached the top of the wall when he was put to flight by an arrow shot by Teucer. He protected Hector when wounded by Achilles; with Apollo's aid he avenged Sarpedon, and took a prominent part in the struggle for the body of Patroclus. He finally met his death at the hand of Aias.

Glaucus Sinus. A gulf of Lycia, at the head of which stood the city of Telmissus or Macri, whence in ancient times the gulf was sometimes also called Sinus Telmissius.

Glossa (γλῶσσα) and **Glossēma** (γλώσσημα). In the language of text-criticism, a "gloss." The word underwent a gradual development of meaning, which may be described with brevity. By the earliest Greek commentators and editors of texts, γλῶσσα denoted any word in an author that required definition or explanation. Such were (*a*) archaisms; (*b*) ἅπαξ λεγόμενα and newly-coined words; (*c*) provincialisms; (*d*) barbarisms; and (*e*) technical terms (cf. Arist. *Poet.* 21, § 4–6; *Rhet.* iii. 3, 2; Quint. i. 8). In editing or transcribing a text it was usual for the editor or transcriber to define the γλῶσσα by writing opposite to it in the margin the more familiar synonym (ὄνομα κύριον). The term γλῶσσα soon came to be applied to the pair of words—the word in the text and the definition in the margin—the two being regarded as constituting a single whole. Finally, the explanation alone was called a γλῶσσα. With these glosses begins the history of lexicography; for collections of them began to be made, and published separately as *glossaria* or glossaries. Such was the compilation of the elegiac poet Philetas of Cos, whose collection was the first attempt at an Homeric glossary (cf. Susemihl, *Geschichte d. griech. Lit. in d. alexandr. Zeit*, i. p. 174 foll.). We know of glosses as early as the fifth century B.C., for Democritus of Abdera is said to have written a treatise Περὶ Ὁμήρου ἢ Ὀρθοεπέιης καὶ Γλωσσάων. (See LEXICON.) Glosses soon ceased to be purely lexical, and from definitions became commentary—geographical, historical, philosophical, or philological—according to the taste or purpose of the glossographer. When these explanatory glosses are fairly brief, they are usually styled *scholia* (σχόλια); when long, they constitute ὑπομνήματα or regular commentaries, such as the Alexandrians wrote. See ALEXANDRIAN SCHOOL.

The principal glossographers among the Greeks were Philetas (about B.C. 290), Zenodotus of Ephesus (about B.C. 280), compiler of Γλῶσσαι Ὁμηρικαί; Aristophanes of Byzantium (B.C. 200), whose glosses are partly preserved by Pollux; Diodorus, Artemidorus, Nicander of Colophon, Aristarchus of Samothrace, Crates of Mallos, Zenodotus of Mallos, Didymus Chalcenteros, Apollonius Sophista (about B.C. 20), Neoptolemus, known distinctively as ὁ γλωσσογράφος; Apion (at Rome under Claudius), Erotion, Pamphilus, Aelius Herodianus, Pollux, Phrynichus in the second century A.D., Ammonius of Alexandria in the fourth century, the famous Hesychius (q. v.), Photius, Suidas, Zonaras, and the author of the *Etymologicum Magnum* (q. v.). Of the Romans, Aurelius Opilius, Aelius Stilo, Varro, Verrius Flaccus, and Festus deserve especial mention. Of technical glosses, those on the legal compilations of Justinian are very important. Of these, two famous compilers were Cyrillus and Philoxenus.

See Matthaei, *Glossaria Graeca* (1774–75); Vater, *Litteratur der Grammatiken, Lexica, und Wörtersammlungen*, etc. (2d ed. by Jülg, Berlin, 1847); Hübner, *Encyclopädie*, pp. 37–40; Löwe, *Prodromos Corporis Glossariorum Latinorum* (1876); id. *Glossae Nominum* (1884); and (now in preparation) the *Corpus Glossariorum* (by the Royal Saxon Soc. of Letters). On the legal glosses, see Biener, *Geschichte der Novellen*, pp. 225 foll.; and for Biblical glosses, the article "Gloss" in McClintock and Strong's *Cyclopaedia of Biblical Literature*, vol. iii. See also in this Dictionary, the articles LEXICON; SCHOLIUM; TEXTUAL CRITICISM.

Glossarium. See GLOSSA; LEXICON.

Glota or **Clota.** A river of Britain, now the Clyde, falling into the Glota Aestuarium, or Frith of Clyde.

Glycĕra, also dim. **Glycerium.** "Sweet one," a favourite name of Greek and Roman courtesans.

Glycerius. Head of the Western Empire for one year (A.D. 473–74), but dethroned by the Eastern Court in favour of Iulius Nepos. Glycerius later became Bishop of Salona in Dalmatia.

Glycon (Γλύκων). An Athenian artist, who probably flourished in the first century B.C. He executed the famous colossal statue of the Farnese Hercules, now at Naples. See HERACLES.

Gnatia. See EGNATIA.

Gnidus. See CNIDUS.

Gnipho, M. ANTONIUS. A Roman rhetorician of Gallic birth (B.C. 114), whose school at Rome was attended by Cicero (Suet. *Gramm.* 7).

Gnomic Poets. See EPOS.

Gnomon (*γνώμων*). The index or pin on a sundial which marks the hour by the shadow it casts (Pliny, *H. N.* ii. § 74; Vitruv. i. 6, 6). See HOROLOGIUM.

Gnomon. (From a cup found at Antium.)

Gnostĭci (Γνοστικοί). A religious sect which flourished in the first century of the Christian era. In the New Testament, *γνῶσις* denotes the profound appreciation of Christian truth; with the Gnostics it means a sort of transcendental and mystic understanding, which saw and knew the allegories and subtleties which they professed to find in the sacred writings. They claimed a kinship between all the religions of the world, and asserted their possession of special traditions from certain of Christ's disciples, and the gift of prophecy. The sources of Gnosticism were three—Greek idealism, Oriental pantheism, and Christian revelation, and it was always a heresy of the learned rather than of the masses whom its subtleties repelled. The four points upon which nearly all the Gnostics agreed were as follows: (1) God is incomprehensible; (2) Matter is eternal and antagonistic to God in that it conditions and limits the divine efficiency; (3) Creation is the work of a Demiurgus, either subordinate to God or perhaps actually opposed to him; (4) The human nature of Christ was only a deception. See AEON.

Gnosticism reached its highest point A.D. 150, after which it rapidly declined. Its importance is to be found in the fact that its arbitrary treatment of the Scriptures forced the Church to a more thorough study of the historical tradition, and to establish the principle that nothing is to be regarded as true Christianity which is not shown to be derived from Christ and his apostles. See Matter, *Histoire Critique du Gnosticisme* (2d ed. 1883); King, *The Gnostics and their Remains* (1873); and Mansel, *The Gnostic Heresies*, edited by Lightfoot (1875).

Gnosus, Gnossus. See CNOSSUS.

Gobrȳas (Γωβρύας). A Persian, one of the seven noblemen who conspired against the usurper Smerdis. See DARIUS.

Gold. See AURUM; NUMISMATICS.

Gold and Ivory See CHRYSELEPHANTINA.

Golden Ass. See APULEIUS; LUCIANUS; NOVELS AND ROMANCES.

Golden Verses (*ἔπη χρυσᾶ*). A name given to a number of gnomic sayings that have come down, traditionally, from the Pythagorean philosophers, often expressed obscurely, and containing much that is of later date than that of their professed origin. They contain the condensed morals of the older epics (see EPOS), and embody the teachings of practical virtue. They are printed at the end of Göttling's edition of Hesiod (2d ed. Gotha, 1843). See DEMOCRATES; PYTHAGORAS.

Golgi (Γολγοί). A town in Cyprus, of uncertain site, a Sicyonian colony, and one of the chief seats of the worship of Aphroditê.

Gomphi (Γόμφοι). A town in Hestiaeotis in Thessaly, a strong fortress on the confines of Epirus, commanding the chief pass between Thessaly and Epirus.

Gomphus (*γόμφος*). Properly a Greek word, which signifies a large wedge-shaped pin (Schol. Aristoph. *Ep.* 463; Tertull. *Apol.* 12) driven between two objects, to increase the firmness or tightness of contiguous members, whence the same term was adopted by the Romans to designate the large, round-headed, and wedge-shaped stones

Gomphi. (Pompeii.)

which they used to place at intervals between the ordinary curb-stones bounding the foot-path or *trottoir*.

Gonātas (Γονατᾶς). One of the Antigoni. See ANTIGONUS.

Gonni (Γόννοι) or **Gonnus** (Γόννος). A strongly fortified town of the Perrhaebi in Thessaly, on the river Peneus and at the entrance of the vale of Tempé (Herod. vii. 128).

Gordiaei or **Gordyaei** (Γορδυαῖοι). Mountains in Armenia, where the Tigris rises.

Gordian Knot. See GORDIUS.

Gordiānus. (1) MARCUS ANTONĪNUS AFRICĀNUS. A Roman, born during the reign of the first Antonine, of one of the most illustrious and wealthy families of Rome, and who made himself very popular during his quaestorship by his munificence, and the large sums which he spent in providing games and other amusements for the people. He also cultivated literature, and wrote several poems, among others one in which he celebrated the virtues of the two Antonines. Being intrusted with the government of several provinces, he conducted himself in such a manner as to gain universal approbation. He was proconsul of Africa in A.D. 237. When an insurrection broke out in that province against Maximinus, on account of his exactions, and the insurgents saluted Gordianus as emperor, he prayed earnestly to be excused, on account of his age, being then past eighty, and to be allowed to die in peace; but, the insur-

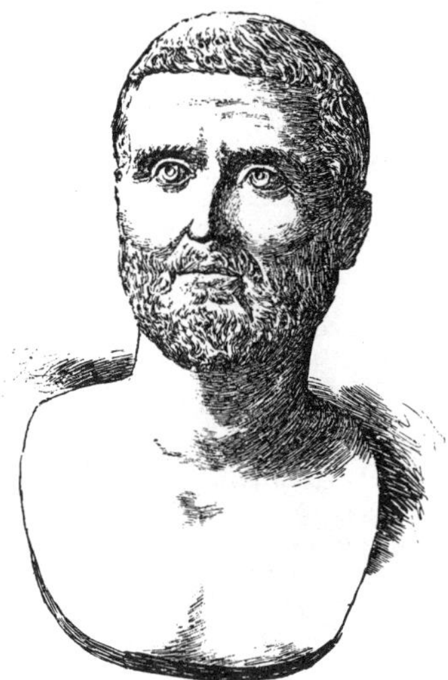

The Elder Gordianus. (Capitoline Museum.)

gents threatening to kill him if he refused, he accepted the perilous dignity, naming his son Gordianus as his colleague, and both made their solemn entry into Carthage amid universal applause. The Senate cheerfully confirmed the election, proclaiming the two Gordiani as emperors, and declaring Maximinus and his son to be the enemies of their country. Meantime, however, Capellianus, governor of Mauritania, collected troops in favour of Maximinus, and marched against Carthage. The younger Gordianus came out to oppose him, but was defeated and killed, and his aged father, on learning the sad tidings, strangled himself. Their reign had not lasted two months altogether, yet they were greatly regretted, on account of their personal qualities. (2) M. ANTONIUS AFRICĀNUS, son of Gordianus, was instructed by Serenus Samonicus, who left him his library, which consisted of 62,000 volumes. He was well informed, and wrote several works, but was rather too fond of pleasure, which latter circumstance seems to have recommended him to the favour of the emperor Elagabalus. Alexander Severus advanced him subsequently to the consulship. He afterwards passed into Africa as lieutenant to his father, and, when the latter was elevated to the throne, shared that dignity with him. But, after a reign of not quite two months, he fell in battle, at the age of forty-six, against Capellianus, a partisan of Maximinus. (See GORDIANUS, 1.) (3) MARCUS ANTONĪNUS PIUS, grandson, on the mother's side, of the elder Gordianus, and nephew of Gordianus the younger, was twelve years of age when he was proclaimed Caesar by general acclamation of the people of Rome, after the news had arrived of the death of the two Gordiani in Africa. The Senate named him colleague of the two new emperors Maximus and Balbinus, but in the following year (A.D. 238) a mutiny of the Praetorians took place at Rome, Balbinus and Maximus were murdered, and the boy Gordianus was proclaimed emperor. His disposition was kind and amiable, but at the beginning of his reign he trusted to the insinuations of a certain Maurus and other freedmen of the palace, who abused his confidence, and committed many acts of injustice. In the second year of his reign a revolt broke out in Africa, where a certain Sabinianus was proclaimed emperor, but the insurrection was soon put down by the governor of Mauritania. In the following year Gordianus, being consul with Claudius Pompeianus, married Furia Sabina Tranquillina, daughter of Misitheus, a man of the greatest personal merit. Misitheus disclosed to Gordianus the disgraceful conduct of Maurus and his friends, who were immediately deprived of their offices and driven away from court. From that moment Gordianus placed implicit trust in his father-in-law, on whom the Senate conferred the title of "Guardian of the Republic." In the next year, news came to Rome that the Persians under Sapor had invaded Mesopotamia, had occupied Nisibis and Carrhae, entered Syria, and, according to Capitolinus, had taken Antioch. Gordianus opened the temple of Ianus, according to an ancient custom which had been long disused, and, setting out from Rome at the head of a fine army, marched through Illyricum and Moesia, where he defeated the Goths and Sarmatians, and drove them beyond the Danube. Gordianus presently crossed the Hellespont, and proceeded into Syria, delivered Antioch, defeated the Persians in several battles, retook Nisibis and Carrhae, and drove Sapor back to his own dominions. The Senate voted him a triumph. In the year after, A.D. 244, Gordianus advanced into Persian territory, and defeated Sapor on the banks of the Chaboras; but while he was preparing to pursue him, Philippus, an officer in the Guards, who had contrived to spread discontent among the soldiers by attributing their privations to the inexperience of a boyish emperor, was proclaimed by the army his colleague in the Empire. Gordianus consented, but soon after was murdered by Philippus. Gordianus was about twenty years old when he died. His body, according to Eutropius, was carried to Rome, and he was numbered among the gods (Herodian, vii. 10 foll.; viii. 6 foll.; Eutrop. ix. 2).

Gordium (Γόρδιον, also Γορδίειον). The ancient capital of Phrygia, situated on the Sangarius; the royal residence of the kings of the dynasty of Gordius, and the scene of Alexander's celebrated exploit of cutting the Gordian knot. See GORDIUS.

Gordius (Γόρδιος). An ancient king of Phrygia, and father of Midas, but originally a poor peasant. Internal disturbances having broken out in Phrygia, an oracle informed the inhabitants that a wagon would bring them a king, who would put an end to their troubles. Shortly afterwards Gordius suddenly appeared riding in his wagon in the assembly of the people, who at once acknowledged him as king. Gordius, out of gratitude, dedicated his chariot to Zeus, in the acropolis of Gordium. The pole was fastened to the yoke by a knot of bark; and an oracle declared that whosoever should untie the knot should reign over all Asia. Alexander, on his arrival at Gordium, cut the knot with his sword, and applied the oracle to himself (Plut. *Alex.* 18).

Gordyēné (Γορδυηνή) or **Corduēné**. A mountainous district in the south of Armenia Major, between the Arissa Palus (Lake Van) and the Gordyaei Montes (Mountains of Kurdistan). Its warlike inhabitants, called Gordyaei, or Cordueni, were no doubt the same people as the Carduchi of the earlier Greek geographers, and the modern Kurds. The Gordyaei Montes separate the valley of the Tigris from the great table-land of Iran.

Gorgé (Γόργη). Daughter of Oeneus (q. v.) and sister of Deianira, both of whom retained their original forms when their other sisters were metamorphosed by Artemis into birds.

Gorgias (Γοργίας). (1) A Greek sophist and rhetorician, known as "the Nihilist," a native of Leontini in Sicily. In B.C. 427, when already advanced in years, he came to Athens on an embassy from his native city, to implore aid against the Syracusans. The finished style of his speaking excited general admiration. He was successful in the object of his mission, and immediately returned home; but he soon came back to Athens, which he made his headquarters, travelling through Greece, like the other sophists, and winning much popularity and profit from a large number of disciples. He survived Socrates, who died in 399, and ended his days at Larissa in Thessaly in his hundred and fifth year.

His philosophy was a nihilistic system, which is summed up in three propositions: (*a*) Nothing exists; (*b*) If anything existed, it could not be known; (*c*) If anything did exist, and could be known, it could not be communicated. He declined to assume the name of sophist, preferring that of rhetorician. He professed not to teach virtue, but the art of persuasion; in other words, to give his disciples such absolute readiness in speaking, that they should be able to convince their hearers independently of any knowledge of the subject. He did not found his instruction on any definite rhetorical system, but gave his pupils standard passages of literature to learn by heart and imitate, practising them in the application of rhetorical figures. He appeared in person, on various occasions, at Delphi, Olympia, and Athens, with model speeches which he afterwards published. It must be remembered that it was Gorgias who transplanted rhetoric to Greece, and who helped to diffuse the Attic dialect as the literary language of prose. There remain two works ascribed to him, but not genuine—the so-called *Apology of Palamedes*, and the *Encomium on Helen*. See the article by Baumstark in the *Rheinisches Museum* for 1860, pp. 624–626; and Blass, *Attische Beredsamkeit*, pp. 44–72.

Rondanini Medusa. (Glyptothek, Munich.)

(2) A Greek rhetorician of the second half of the first century B.C. He was tutor to the younger Cicero, and was the author of a treatise on the figures of speech, which is in part preserved in a Latin paraphrase by Rutilius Lupus. See RUTILIUS LUPUS.

Gorgo (Γοργώ). The wife of Leonidas, king of Sparta. A fine repartee of hers is given by Plutarch. When a woman, a stranger, observed to her, "You Spartan women are the only ones that rule men," she replied, "True, for we are the only ones that give birth to men" (Plut. *Lacon. Apophth.*).

Gorgo (Γοργώ). The capital of the Chorasmii in Bactriana. It is supposed to correspond to the modern Urghenz.

Gorgo (Γοργώ). Homer makes mention of the terrible head of the Gorgon, a formidable monster (*Odyss.* xi. 633). This head is a terror in Hades, and in the aegis of Zeus. Hesiod speaks of three Gorgons: Stheno (Valeria, the mighty), Euryalé (Lativolva, the wide-wandering), and Medusa (Guberna, the ruler). They are the daughters of the aged sea-god Phorcys and Ceto, and sisters of the Graiae. (See GRAIAE.) They dwell on the farthest shore of Ocean, in the neighbourhood of Night and of the Hesperides. They are awful beings, with hair and girdles of snakes, whose look turns the beholder to stone. They are also often represented with golden wings, brazen claws, and enormous teeth. Medusa is mortal, but the other two immortal. When Perseus cut off Medusa's head, Chrysaor and the winged horse Pegasus, with whom she was with child by Poseidon, sprang forth from the streaming blood. The head was given by Perseus to Athené, who set it in her shield. Heracles received a lock of the hair from Athené as a present. When endeavouring to persuade Cephalus of Tegea to take part in his expedition against Hippocoön of Sparta, the king represented that he feared an attack from his enemies the Argives in Heracles's absence. Heracles accordingly gave to Steropé, the daughter of Cephalus, the lock of Medusa's hair in a brazen urn, bidding her, in case the enemy approached, to avert her head and hold it three times over the walls, for the mere aspect of it would turn the enemy to flight.

In consequence of the belief in this power of the Gorgon's head, or Gorgoneion, to paralyze and terrify an enemy, the Greeks carved images of it in its most terrifying forms, not only on armour of all sorts, especially shields and breastplates, but also on walls and gates. Thus, on the south wall of the Athenian Acropolis, a large gilded Gorgoneion was set on an aegis (Pausan. i. 21, § 4). In the popular belief the Gorgon's head was also a means of protection against all enchantment, whether of word or act, and we thus find it throughout Greek history employed as a powerful amulet, and often carved with graceful settings on decorative furniture and costly ornaments. But the Greek artists, with their innate sense of beauty, knew, even in the case of the Gorgon, how to give adequate expression to the idea which lay at the root of the story. The story said that Medusa had been a fair maiden, whose luxuriant hair had been turned by Athené into snakes in revenge for the desecration of her sanctuary. Accordingly the head of Medusa is represented in works of art with a countenance of touching beauty, and a wealth of hair wreathed with snakes. The face was imagined as itself in the stillness of death, and thus bearing the power to turn the living to stone. The most beautiful surviving instance of this conception is the Rondanini Medusa now at Munich. The story of Medusa has suggested several fine bits of English verse, among them D. G. Rossetti's *Aspecta Medusa* and Hake's sonnet, *The Infant Medusa*.

Gortyn (Γορτύν) or **Gortȳna** (Γόρτυνα). An ancient city in Crete on the southern shore of the island, and situated on the banks of the river Lethaeus. By its two harbours, Metallum and Lebena, it communicated with the sea. Here were temples to Zeus, Apollo, and Artemis; and near the fountain of Saurus was a spring overhung by a palm-tree, a spot which tradition declared to be the scene of the loves of Zeus and Europa (q. v.). Next to Cnossus, Gortyn was the most powerful town of Crete, and between these two cities there existed an almost continuous feud. Under the

Romans, Gortyn became the capital of the island. In 1884, an archaic inscription was found on the site of Gortyn, by Halbherr, in the bed of a mill-stream. Two fragments of the same inscription had been previously found, the new discovery making a practically complete record of a collection of laws regulating the private relations of the people of the city, with regard to such subjects as inheritance, adoption, heiresses, marriage, and divorce. The inscription is regarded as a little earlier than the year B.C. 400. See Merriam, *The Law Code of the Cretan Gortyna* (1886) (text, translation, and commentary); and Simon, *Zur Inschrift von Gortyn* (Vienna, 1886).

Gossypium. The cotton-tree. See CARBASUS.

Gothi, Gotthi, or **Gothōnes** (in their own language GUTANS or GUTÔS). A powerful northern nation, who acted an important part in the overthrow of the Roman Empire. The name Gothi, or Goths, appears first in history in the third century, and it was then used by the Roman writers as synonymous with the more ancient one of Getae, a people who lived on the banks of the lower Danube, near the shores of the Euxine; but the identity of the two races, though maintained by Jakob Grimm, is now generally rejected. The old Scandinavian tradition in the Eddas makes their chief, Odin or Woden, to have come from the banks of the Dniester to the shores of the Baltic many centuries before the Christian era.

About the middle of the third century of our era, the Goths are recorded to have crossed the Dniester, and to have devastated Dacia and Thrace. The emperor Decius lost his life in opposing them in Moesia (A.D. 251), after which his successor Gallus induced them by money to withdraw again to their old dwellings on the Dniester. They then seem to have spread eastward, and to have occupied the country about the Cimmerian Bosporus, whence they sailed across the Euxine, occupied Trebizond, and ravaged Bithynia. In the year 269 they landed in Macedonia, but were defeated by the emperor Claudius II., hence styled Gothicus. Three years after, Aurelian gave up Dacia to a tribe of Goths, who are believed to have been the Visigoths or Western Goths, while those who ravaged Asia Minor were the Ostrogoths or Eastern Goths. This distinction of the race into two grand divisions appears about this time. Under Constantine I. the Goths from Dacia invaded Illyricum, but were repelled. Constantine II. afterwards allowed a part of them to settle in Moesia, who seem to have soon after embraced Christianity, as it was for them that Ulphilas (Wulfila) translated the Scriptures, about the middle of the fourth century, into the dialect called Moeso-Gothic. About the year 375, the Huns, coming from the East, fell upon the Ostrogoths, and drove them upon the Visigoths, who were living north of the Danube. The latter, being hard pressed, implored permission of the Roman commander to be allowed to cross that river, and take shelter in the territory of the Empire. The emperor Valens consented, and a vast multitude of them were allowed to settle in Moesia, where soon afterwards they quarrelled with the Roman authorities, invaded Thrace, and defeated and killed Valens, who came to oppose them (A.D. 378). From that time they exercised great influence over the Byzantine court, either as allies and mercenaries, or as formidable enemies. Towards the end of the fourth century, Alaric, being chosen king of the Visigoths, invaded Northern Italy, but was defeated by Stilicho near Verona (A.D. 402). He came again, however, about six years after, and plundered Rome (A.D. 410). His successor Ataulphus (Atawulf) made peace with the Empire, and repaired to the south of Gaul, where the Visigoths founded the kingdom of Toulouse, from which they afterwards passed into Spain, where a Visigothic dynasty reigned for more than two centuries, till it was conquered by the Moors.

Meanwhile the Ostrogoths or Eastern Goths, who had settled in Pannonia, after the destruction of the kingdom of the Huns, extended their dominion over Noricum, Rhaetia, and Illyricum, and about the year 489 they invaded Italy, under their king, Theodoric, and defeated Odoacer, king of the Heruli, who had assumed the title of King of Italy, a title which Theodoric then took for himself, with the consent of the Eastern emperor. Theodoric was an able prince: his reign was a period of rest for Italy, and his wise administration did much towards healing the wounds of that country. But his successors degenerated, and the Gothic dominion over Italy lasted only till 553, when it was overthrown by Narses, the general of Justinian.

From this time the Goths figure no longer as a power in the history of Western Europe, except in Spain. Their name, however, is found perpetuated long after in Scandinavia, where a kingdom of Gotha existed until the twelfth century, distinct from Sweden Proper, until both crowns were united on the head of Charles Swerkerson (A.D. 1161), who assumed the title of King of the Swedes and the Goths. It is probable, however, that the Gothland of Sweden is etymologically not "the land of the Goths," but "the land of the Gauts," a distinct though kindred people. An Ostrogothic people also settled the Crimea in the fourth century, so that the peninsula was officially styled Gothia by the Greek Church down to the eighteenth century. In 1750, the Jesuit Mondorf learned from a native of the Crimea that his countrymen spoke a dialect bearing some likeness to German. The Gothic language is now classed with the Scandinavian in the "East Germánic group." See INDO-EUROPEAN LANGUAGES.

On the early history of the Goths, consult Iordanis, *De Getarum sive Gothorum Origine et Rebus Gestis;* Isidorus, *Chronicon Gothorum;* and Procopius, *De Bello Gothico.* The first two, however, are not to be trusted implicitly when they treat of the remote genealogy and origin of the Gothic race. See H. Bradley, *The Goths* (1888).

Gothīni. A Celtic people in the southeast of Germany, subject to the Quadi (Tac. *Germ.* 43).

Gothōnes. See GOTHI.

Gown. See PALLA; STOLA; TOGA.

Grabātus (κράβατος or κράββατος, the French *grabat*). A small low couch or bed of the commonest description (Cic. *Div.* ii. 63; Verg. *Moret.* 5), such as was used by poor people, having a mere network of cords stretched over the frame (Lucil. *Sat.* vi. 13; Gerlach. Petron. 97. 4), to support the mattress, precisely as represented by the annexed illustration from a terra-cotta lamp.

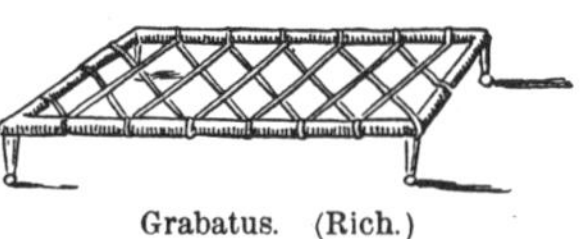
Grabatus. (Rich.)

Gracchus. (1) TIBERIUS SEMPRONIUS, the father of the Gracchi, married Cornelia, daughter of Scipio Africanus the Elder. He died while his sons were young, having twice filled the office of consul, and, according to Plutarch, obtained two triumphs. He was censor in B.C. 169. As a soldier he carried on war with distinction against the Celtiberi in Spain (B.C. 181) and the Sardinians (177). He had twelve children by Cornelia. After the death of her husband, Cornelia refused all offers of marriage, and devoted herself to the charge and education of her children, who, as Plutarch tells us, were less the inheritors of manly virtue by being sprung from the noblest blood in Rome than they were its possessors from the careful nurture of their mother Cornelia (Plut. *Gracch.*). (2) TIBERIUS, elder son of the preceding, was born B.C. 163. Tiberius served his first campaign in Africa under his uncle Scipio, and having obtained the office of consul's quaestor, we find him next under Mancinus, the unfortunate commander in the Numantine War. His name, which the Numantines respected from remembering his father's virtues, is said to have procured the terms under which Mancinus obtained safety for his army; but the Senate, on his return, was so much displeased at the unfavourable nature of these conditions that it resolved on giving up all the principal officers to the Numantines. By the good-will, however, of the popular assembly, influenced, as it would seem, by the soldiers and their connections in the lower classes, it was decided to send Mancinus as the real criminal, and to spare the other officers for the sake of Gracchus. Treatment of this nature was likely to rouse Gracchus against the Senate, and make him the friend of the poor; and accordingly, in three years afterwards, we find him beginning his short career as a political agitator. He was elected tribune of the people B.C. 128, and immediately began to attempt the revival of the Licinian Rogations. (See AGRARIAE LEGES; ROGATIONES LICINIAE.) In so doing he appears to have had in view the two grand principles which that law involved—namely, the employment of freemen in preference to slaves in cultivating the soil, and especially the more generally recognized principle of the equitable division of the public land. Three commissioners were appointed to superintend the working of the new law which Gracchus had proposed, if Plutarch may be trusted, with the approval of some of the most eminent persons of the times, among whom were Mucius Scaevola and Crassus the orator. Such general interest was excited by the question, that crowds arrived from all parts of the country to support either side; and there appeared no doubt which way the matter would go when left to the tribes. The aristocracy, however, secured the veto of M. Octavius, one of the tribunes, and thereby quashed the proceedings whenever the law was brought on, which violent mode of opposition led Gracchus to exercise his veto on other questions, stop the supplies, and throw the government into the most complete helplessness.

Thus far the contest had been constitutional; but now, Gracchus, irritated by continual opposition, invited Octavius to propose his [Gracchus's] ejection from the office of tribune; and on his refusal, pleading the utter uselessness of two men so different in sentiment holding the same office, he put the question to the tribes that Octavius be ejected. When the first seventeen out of the thirty-five tribes had voted for it, Gracchus again implored him to resign; and, on his entreaty proving unsuccessful, polled another tribe, constituting a majority, and sent his officers to drag Octavius from the tribune's chair. The Agrarian Law was forthwith passed; and Gracchus himself, his brother Caius, and his father-in-law Appius Claudius, were appointed the commissioners. But the Senate, to show their opinion of the whole proceeding, withheld from him the usual allowance for a public officer. While things were in this state, Attalus, king of Pergamus, bequeathed his kingdom and treasures to the Roman people; and, to enhance his own popularity, Gracchus proposed to divide the treasure among the recipients of land under the new law, to enable them to stock their farms, and to commit the management of the kingdom of Pergamus to the popular assembly. This brought matters to a greater pitch of distrust than ever. Gracchus was accused by one senator of aspiring to tyranny, and by another of having violated the sanctity of the tribunitian office in deposing Octavius. On this point Gracchus strove to justify himself before the people, but his opponent seemed to have gained an advantage so great as to induce him to postpone the assembly. When at last he did make his defence, it rested, if Plutarch is correct, on false analogies, and on avoiding the question of the inviolability of a public officer. At this juncture Gracchus seems to have trembled for that popularity which alone preserved him from impeachment; and, lest it should fail, endeavoured to secure his own reëlection to the office of tribune. The other party had demurred as to his eligibility to the office two years in succession, and on the day of election this point occupied the assembly till nightfall. Next morning, accompanied by a crowd of partisans, he went to the Capitol; and, on hearing that the Senate had determined to oppose him by force, armed his followers with staves, and prepared to clear the Capitol. At this juncture, Publius Scipio Nasica, having in vain called on the consul to take measures for the safety of the State, issued from the Temple of Faith, where the Senate had assembled, followed by the whole nobility of Rome. He put the mob to flight, seized their weapons, and attacked all who fell in his way. About three hundred perished, and among the slain was Gracchus, who was killed by repeated blows on the head, B.C. 133 (Plut. *Tib. Gracch.*). See Mommsen, *Hist. of Rome*, vol. ii. pp. 92–126 (American ed. 1888). (3) GAIUS, was nine years younger than his brother Tiberius, and at his death was left with Appius Claudius as commissioner for carrying out the Agrarian Law. By the death of Appius, and of Tiberius's successor, Licinius Crassus, the agrarian commission consisted of Fulvius Flaccus, Papirius Carbo, and himself; but he refrained from taking any part in public affairs for more than ten years after the death of Tiberius. During this time the provisions of his brother's law were carried out by Carbo and Flaccus; but Gaius does not seem to have begun his career as an independent political leader until the year B.C. 123, when, on his return from Sardinia, where he had been for two years, he was elected tribune of the people. His first act was to propose two laws, one of which, directed against the degraded tribune Octavius, disqualified all who had been thus degraded from holding any magistracy; and the other, having in view Pompilius, a prominent opponent of the popular party, denounced the banishment of a Roman citizen without trial as a violation of the Roman laws. The first was never carried through; to the latter was added a third, by which Pompilius was banished from Italy, or, according to technical phraseology, interdicted from fire and water. These measures were followed by others, by which he aimed at establishing his own popularity. One of them was a poor-law, by which a monthly distribution of corn was made to the people at an almost nominal price. (See FRUMENTARIAE LEGES.) The effect of this law was to make the population of Rome paupers, and to attract all Italy to partake of the bounty. Next came organic changes, as they would now be called; and of these the most important was the transference of the judicial power from the senators, wholly or in part, to the equestrian order. This measure, according to Cicero, worked well; but, in weighing his opinion, we must remember his partiality for the *equites*, and add to this the fact that his eulogies occur in an advocate's speech (*In Verr. Act.* i.).

Gracchus now possessed unlimited power with the populace; and, at the end of the year, not more than ten candidates for the office of tribune having appeared, he was again elected. His second tribuneship was mostly employed in passing laws respecting the colonies, in which matter the aristocratic agent, Livius Drusus, outdid him; and, having won the confidence of the people by his apparent disinterestedness, ventured (being himself a tribune) to interpose his veto to one of Gracchus's measures. The appointment of Gracchus, soon after, to the office of commissioner for planting a colony near Carthage removed him from the scenes of his popularity; and, soon after his return, a proposal was made to repeal the very law which he had been engaged in carrying out, relative to the colony in Africa. This law was not his own measure, but that of one Rubrius, another of the tribunes, and was one of those enactments which had alienated from Gracchus the favour of the people, it having been represented by his opponents as an impious act to build again the walls of Carthage, which Scipio had solemnly devoted to perpetual desolation. Gracchus was now a private person, his second tribuneship having expired; but yet, as such, he opposed the proposition to repeal, and, unfortunately for himself, united with M. Fulvius Flaccus, one of the commissioners of the Agrarian Law, and a man whose character was respected by no party in the Republic. The reputation of Gracchus had already suffered from his connection with Fulvius; and now he took part with him in designs which could be considered as nothing less than treasonable. Charging the Senate with spreading false reports, in order to alarm the religious scruples of the people, the two popular leaders assembled a numerous body of their partisans armed with daggers, and, being thus prepared for violence, they proceeded to the Capitol, where the people were to meet in order to decide on the repeal of the law of Rubrius. Here, before the business of the day was yet begun, a private citizen, who happened to be engaged in offering a sacrifice, was murdered by the partisans of Fulvius and Gracchus for some words or gestures which they regarded as insulting. This outrage excited a general alarm; the assembly broke up in consternation; and the popular leaders, after trying in vain to gain a hearing from the people, while they disclaimed the violence committed by their followers, had no other course left than to withdraw to their own homes. There they concerted plans of resistance, which were considered by the people as an open rebellion against the government of the country. The consul Opimius, exaggerating, perhaps, the alarm which he felt from the late outrage, hastily summoned the Senate together; the body of the murdered man was exposed to the view of the people, and the Capitol was secured at break of day with an armed force. The Senate, being informed by Opimius of the state of affairs, proceeded to invest him with absolute power to act in defence of the commonwealth, in the usual form of a resolution, "that the consul should provide for the safety of the Republic." At the same time Gracchus and Fulvius were summoned to appear before the Senate to answer for the murder laid to their charge. Instead of obeying, they occupied the Aventine Hill with a body of their partisans in arms, and invited the slaves to join them, promising them their freedom. Opimius, followed by the senators and the members of the equestrian order, who, with their dependants, had armed themselves by his directions, and accompanied by a body of regular soldiers, advanced against the rebels, who had made two fruitless attempts at negotiation, by sending to the consul the son of Fulvius. In the meantime the conduct of Gaius Gracchus was that of a man irresolute in the course which he pursued, and with too much regard for his country to engage heartily in the criminal attempt into which he had suffered himself to be drawn. He had left his house, it is said, in his ordinary dress; he had already urged upon Fulvius to propose the terms of a compromise to the Senate; and now, when the Aventine was attacked, he took personally no part in the action. The contest, indeed, was soon over. The rebels were presently dispersed. Fulvius was dragged from the place to which he had fled for refuge, and was put to death; while Gracchus, finding himself closely pursued, fled across the Tiber, and, taking shelter in a grove sacred to the goddess Furrina, was killed, at his own desire, by a servant who had accompanied his flight. His head, together with that of Fulvius, was cut off and carried to the consul, in order to obtain the price which had been set upon both by a proclamation issued at the beginning of the conflict; and the bodies, as well as those of all who had perished on the same side, were thrown into the Tiber. In addition to this, the houses of Gracchus and Fulvius were given up to plunder, their property was confiscated, and even the wife of Gracchus was deprived of her dowry. It is said that in this sedition there perished altogether of the partisans of the popular leaders about 3000, partly in the action and partly by summary executions afterwards, under the consul's orders.

There is little doubt that Gracchus aimed at monarchical power, but many writers, among them Mommsen, justify his purpose on the plea that an absolute monarchy is a less evil than an absolute oligarchy such as that which existed at Rome in the second century B.C. See Mommsen, *Hist. of Rome*, vol. ii. pp. 127–160 (American ed. 1888).

(4) SEMPRONIUS, a Roman nobleman, banished

to Cercina, an island off the coast of Africa, for his adulterous intercourse with Iulia, the daughter of Augustus. After an exile of fourteen years, he was put to death by a party of soldiers sent for that purpose by Tiberius (Tac. *Ann.* i. 53).

Graces. See CHARITES; GRATIAE.

Gradīvus. An epithet of Mars (q. v.) and usually derived from *gradior*, as though "the strider." Prof. Minton Warren suggests an alternative derivation from *grand-is*, *grand-ire*, with reference to growth (*American Journal of Philology*, iv. 71).

Gradus. (1) A set of bed-steps, consisting of several stairs (Varro, *L. L.* v. 168), which were

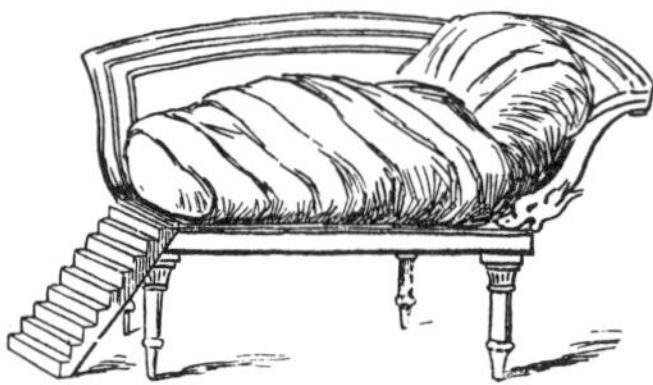

Gradus. (From the Vatican Vergil.)

requisite for ascending the highest couches. See LECTUS.

(2) A flight of steps leading to the *pronaos* of a temple (Cic. *Ad Att.* iv. 1). In Greek temples there were usually but three steps, but Roman architects added a dozen or more, dividing them into several flights. The number of steps, however, was always uneven, so that a person ascending, and commencing with the right foot (*pes dexter*), might place the same one on the topmost step when he entered the porch, to enter with the left foot being ill-omened (Vitruv. iii. 4. 4; Petron. 30).

(3) The seats on which the spectators sat in a theatre, amphitheatre, or circus. See AMPHITHEATRUM.

(4) The parallel ridges, like steps, on the inside of a dice-box (*fritillus*), for the purpose of mixing the dice when shaken, and giving them a disposition to rotate when cast from it (Auson. *Profess.* i. 28).

Gradus in a dice-box. (Rich.)

(5) A studied and feminine arrangement of the hair, when artificially disposed in parallel waves or gradations rising one over the other, like steps (Quint. xii. 10. 47), the same as now termed "crimping." Nero is said to have had his head always dressed in this manner (Suet. *Nero*, 51); and a statue representing that emperor in the character of Apollo Citharœdus (given under NERO) has the hair parted in the centre, and regularly crimped on both sides, like a girl's. (6) As a measure of length (βῆμα), the *gradus* was half a pace (*passus*), and contained 2½ feet, Greek and Roman respectively. The Greek βῆμα, therefore, was rather more and the Roman *gradus* rather less than 2½ feet English.

Gradus Cognatiōnis. See COGNATIO.

Graeae (Γραῖαι). "The old women," daughters of Phorcys and Ceto, and three in number—Pephredo, Enyo, and Dino, also called Phorcydes. They had gray hair from their birth, and only one tooth and one eye in common, which they borrowed from each other when they needed them. See Hesiod, *Theog.* 270.

Graecia. The Roman name of Hellas or Greece. See HELLAS.

Graecia Magna or **Graecia Maior.** A name given to the districts in the south of Italy inhabited by the Greeks. This name was never used simply to indicate the south of Italy; it was always confined to the Greek cities and their territories, and did not include the surrounding districts inhabited by the Italian tribes. It appears to have been applied chiefly to the cities on the Tarentine Gulf—Tarentum, Sybaris, Croton, Caulonia, Siris (Heraclea), Metapontum, Locri, and Rhegium; but it also included the Greek cities on the west coast, such as Cumae and Neapolis. Strabo extends the appellation even to the Greek cities of Sicily. See Lenormant, *La Grande-Grèce*, 3 vols. (Paris, 1881); and the article ITALIA.

Graecostăsis (Γραικόστασις). Professor Middleton defines the Graecostasis as a platform in the Forum, on which foreign ambassadors stood to hear the speeches from the Rostra or Comitium, like the Diplomatic Gallery in the American Senate and House. The Graecostasis got its name from the fact that the first envoys thus honoured were Greeks from Massilia (Marseilles), as stated by Iustinus (xliii. 5, § 10). Cicero speaks of it as being a place from which disorderly persons often interrupted the debates. It appears to have occupied a different place before and after the reconstruction of the Forum by Iulius Caesar. It is mentioned by Varro (*L. L.* v. § 155) as of stone, and standing to the right of the Curia—this statement referring to the older structure. Archaeologists formerly regarded the term as denoting the foreign embassy at Rome. See Burn, *Rome and the Campagna*, pp. 84, 107, 123; Mommsen, *History of Rome*, i. p. 577 (American ed. 1888); Middleton, *Remains of Ancient Rome*, i. pp. 237, 256 (London, 1892), and cf. the article FORUM.

Graevius (GRAEFE), JOHANN GEORG. A German classical scholar who was born at Naumburg, January 29, 1632. He studied law for a time at Leipzig, but by the influence of Gronovius was led to remove to Deventer, where he turned his attention to literature, attending lectures, also, at Amsterdam, on history. In 1658 he became the successor of Gronovius at Deventer, and in 1661 was called to the University of Utrecht as Professor of Eloquence, to which chair in 1667 was attached the duty of lecturing on political history. He refused calls to the Universities of Heidelberg, Leyden, and Padua; but accepted a pension from Louis XIV. of France. He died January 11, 1703. He edited the works of Cicero (1684, foll.), and also published editions of Hesiod, Callimachus, Iustinus (1668), Catullus, Tibullus, Propertius, Suetonius (1674), and Florus (1680). He is best known, however, by his *Thesaurus Antiquitatum Romanarum*, in twelve vols. (1699). See L. Müller, *Geschichte der class. Philologie in den Niederlanden*, pp. 44 foll. (Leipzig, 1869).

Graffiti (plural of the Italian *graffito*, "a scratching"). A name used of the inscriptions, drawings, and scrawls found upon the walls, doorposts, pillars, and tombs of Rome, Pompeii, and other ancient cities. They are the work of idlers—schoolboys, slaves, loungers, etc.—and are valuable as giving an insight into the daily life, habits, and thoughts of the common people, as well as furnishing, at times, valuable hints as to the nature of the popular language. (See SERMO PLEBEIUS.) They are usually scratched with some sharp instrument—for instance, a *stilus*, or written with charcoal or red chalk—and are of the most varied character, as might be expected, comprising quotations from the poets, doggerel verses, insulting, coarse, and often obscene words and figures, caricatures, popular catchwords, and amatory effusions, in each of the three languages common in southern Italy—Greek, Latin, and Oscan. They are often of a more serious character, intended as handbills. Of this class, we find advertisements of plays, election notices, public announcements, and admonitions to servants. The following is an example of the political *graffito:* A. VETTIVM FIRMVM AED. O.V.F.D.R.P.V.O.V. F. PILICREPI FACITE (*Aulum Vettium Firmum aedilem, oro vos faciatis, dignum re publica virum oro vos. facite pilicrepi, facite!*), an appeal to the *pilicrepi* or ball-players of the city to rally round a kindred spirit and friend of sport. Many quotations from the poets appear, Ovid and Propertius being great favourites, but only one complete line from Vergil is found among the *graffiti* collected by Garrucci. Of the poetic quotations from the *Aeneid*, the following (i. 1) is interesting as throwing light on the vulgar pronunciation of the letter R: ALMA VILVMQVE CANO TLO—. Occasionally a line from some poet is altered to suit the purposes of the writer, as the following: CANDIDA ME DOCVIT NIGRAS ODISSE PUELLAS, evidently a variation of the Propertian line: *Cynthia me docuit castas odisse puellas*, and intended to flatter some blonde. A love-quarrel between Virgula and her lover Tertius is indicated by the following: VIRGVLA TERTIO SVO: INDECENS ES. There are many allusions to athletic and gladiatorial games. One Epaphras, whose name often appears, is told that he "doesn't know how to play ball" (EPAPHRA PILICREPVS NON ES), and some friend of Epaphras has drawn a line through the last three words. School-boys have scratched their lessons by way of practice on the walls, since there are long lists of nouns, verbs, etc., and alphabets repeated again and again.

Supposed Caricature of the Crucifixion.

An interesting *graffito* is that represented in the preceding illustration. It was first published by Father Garrucci in 1857, and is now in the Kircherian Museum of the Jesuit College at Rome. Apparently it belongs to the third century A.D., and is in ridicule of a person, one Alexamenos, who is represented as worshipping a crucified figure depicted with the head of an ass. Beneath is scrawled in Greek the sentence ΑΛΕΞΑΜΕΝΟΣ ΣΕΒΕΤΕ [ΣΕΒΕΤΑΙ] ΘΕΟΝ, "Alexamenos worships (his) God." It was found in one of the subterranean chambers of the Palatine in 1856. Scholars are not wholly agreed as to the subject of this caricature, some believing it to be a blasphemous representation of Christ, while others think it refers to Anubis, the jackal-headed god of Egypt. Prof. Lanciani in his *Ancient Rome in the Light of Recent Discoveries* (Boston, 1888) mentions an interesting collection of *graffiti* discovered in 1868 on the walls of an *excubitorium*, or station-house, and made by the Roman policemen when off duty. These can be seen in the *Annali dell' Instituto* for 1869, edited by Henzen.

Graffito from the Palatine, Rome.

Another well-executed drawing from the Palatine walls is that given above. It represents an ass turning a mill with the inscription, LABORA ASELLE QVOMODO EGO LABORAVI ET PRODERIT TIBI ("Toil on, little ass, as I have done, and much good may it do you!"), possibly written by a slave who had been made to do a turn at the mill (*pistrinum*) as a punishment (cf. Ter. *Andr.* i. 2. 28). The subjoined *graffito*, which resembles the attempt of a modern school-boy, is from the barracks at Pompeii, and was executed on the barrack-wall with a piece of red chalk by a Roman soldier. It caricatures one Nonius Maximus, whose name appears elsewhere on the same walls coupled with insulting words, and who was probably a centurion whose strictness had made him unpopular.

Graffito in Chalk from Pompeii.

Another Pompeian wall-caricature refers to a fierce town-and-country fight in the amphitheatre between the Pompeians and Nucerians, as the result of which Nero forbade the Pompeians to open the amphitheatre for a period of ten years. The *graffito* represents an armed man descending into the arena bearing the palm of victory, while on the other side a prisoner is being dragged away in bonds. The legend in the corner gives a clue to the meaning of the caricature. It reads: CAMPANI VICTORIA VNA CVM NV-

Caricature from the Outer Wall of a Private House. (Pompeii.)

CERINIS PERISTIS ("Campanians, you suffered in the victory as well as the Nucerians!")

The first notice of this class of inscriptions appeared in the *Journal de Fouilles* for October 18th, 1765; and in 1792 the German archaeologist Murr published at Nuremberg a collection of *graffiti* that had been transcribed for him by a friend. A supplement to this appeared in 1793.

The first good collection published was that of Bishop C. Wordsworth in 1837, consisting wholly of *graffiti* from Pompeii, and reprinted in his *Miscellanies* in 1879. A large number of them in Latin are given in the *Corpus Inscriptionum Latinarum*, vol. iv. (ed. Zangemeister), under the title *Inscriptiones Parietariae Pompeianae, Herculanenses, et Stabianae*, and in the supplementary volume. Inscriptions in Oscan will be found in Fiorelli's *Inscriptionum Oscarum Apographa* (1854). See, also, Garrucci, *Graffiti de Pompéi* (Paris, 1856); Parton, *Caricature* (N. Y. 1878); and the article POMPEII.

Graffito from Pompeii, representing the Labyrinth. (*Mus. Borb.* xiv. *tav. a*, 1852.)

Grain, PUBLIC DISTRIBUTION OF. See FRUMENTARIAE LEGES.

Grallae. A pair of stilts used by actors in personating Pan or the satyrs on the Roman stage (Fest. s. v. *grallatores*).

Grammar. See GRAMMATICA.

Grammăteus (*γραμματεύς*). The Greek word for a writer, secretary, or clerk. At Athens the officials had numerous clerks attached to them, who were paid by the State and belonged to the poorer class of citizens. But there were several higher officials who bore the title of grammateus. The Boulé, or Senate, for instance, chose one of its members by show of hands to be its clerk or secretary for one year. His duty was to keep the archives of the Senate. So, too, a secretary was chosen by lot from the whole number of senators for each prytany to draft all resolutions of the Senate. (See PRYTANIS.) His name is therefore generally given in the decrees next to that of the president and the proposer of the decree. The name of the grammateus of the first prytany was also given with that of the archon, as a means of marking the year with more accuracy. At the meetings of the Ecclesia, a clerk, elected by the people, had to read out the necessary documents. The office of the *ἀντιγραφεῖς*, or checking clerks, was of still greater importance. The *ἀντιγραφεύς* of the Senate, elected at first by show of hands, but afterwards by lot, had to take account of all business affecting the financial administration. The *ἀντιγραφεύς* of the administration had to make out, and lay before the public, a general statement of income and expenditure, and exercised a certain amount of control over all financial officials. In the Aetolian and Achaean leagues the grammateus was the highest officer of the league after the *strategi* and *hipparchi*.

Grammatĭca (*γραμματική*, *litteratura*). (1) IN GREECE.—The term *γραμματική*, in the scientific sense, included, in antiquity, all the main philological branches, grammar proper, lexicography, prosody, the lower and higher criticism, antiquities—everything, in short, necessary to the understanding and explanation of *γράμματα*, or the treasures of literature, whether their form or their matter be in question. It was first developed into a special science during the Alexandrian Age, in Alexandria and Pergamum, where the great libraries gave ample opportunity for philological studies on the scale above indicated. It was the restoration of the text of the Homeric poems and the explanation of their words and contents that primarily exercised the minds of the scholars. (See ALEXANDRIAN SCHOOL.) Hesiod, the lyric poets, the dramatists, and certain prose writers next engaged their attention. The progress and development of philology is marked by the names of Zenodotus (about B.C. 280), Aristophanes of Byzantium (260–183), and Aristarchus (about 170), the three chief representatives of the Alexandrian School. To these must be added Crates (about 160), the head of the school of Pergamum, and the opponent of the Alexandrians. The name of Aristarchus (q. v.) represents the highest point of philological learning and criticism in antiquity. He was the founder of the celebrated school of Aristarcheans, which continued to exist and to maintain an uninterrupted tradition down to the first century of the imperial age. His disciple, Dionysius Thrax, wrote the oldest manual of grammar that we possess, and his work compiled for the use of his students at Rome (Τέχνη Γραμματική) became the basis of all subsequent grammars and was used for centuries either in the original or in Latin translations. From it, through the Latin equivalents, came most of the technical terms of modern grammar. (See DIONYSIUS THRAX, p. 523.) He did not, however, originate these terms. Some of them are as old as the time of Plato, who recognizes two parts of speech, the noun (ὄνομα) and the verb (ῥῆμα). Aristotle names four—noun, verb, article (ἄρθρον), and conjunction (συνδεσμός). The Stoic grammarians give six—noun, verb, article, conjunction, proper noun (προσηγορία), and adverb. Aristarchus raised the number to eight—noun, verb, article, conjunction, pronoun (ἀντωνομία), adverb (ἐπίρρημα), participle (μετοχή), and preposition (πρόθεσις). The Greeks, who were accustomed to see in Homer all possible wisdom, claimed that he knew of the eight parts of speech, citing in proof of it two lines (*Iliad*, i. 185; xxii. 59), each of which contains them all. By far the most celebrated of the later Aristarcheans was Didymus Chalcenterus, born about B.C. 63. His writings are the chief foundation of the Byzantine collections of *scholia*. The science of γραμματική gradually narrowed its scope till it confined itself to grammar in the restricted sense of the word—namely, accidence and syntax, combined with lexical researches into the dialects, and into the usages of special periods of literature and special groups of authors. The most eminent scholars of the Empire are Apollonius Dyscolus (about A.D. 150), the founder of scientific syntax, who endeavoured to reduce the whole of empirical grammar to a system, and his son, Aelius Herodianus, a still more important personage. The writings of the latter form one of the chief authorities of the later grammarians, such as Arcadius. The lexical writings of the earlier scholars were often very comprehensive, and have only survived in fragments or in later extracts, such as that of Hesychius. They had consisted mainly of collections of glosses (γλῶσσαι) or strange and antiquated expressions. (See GLOSSA.) But in the second century A.D. the influence of the reviving sophistic literature and education turned the attention of lexicographers to the usage of the Attic writers. (See LEXICON.) This tendency is represented in the surviving works of Pollux, Harpocration, and others. To the same period belongs Hephaestion's manual of prosody, which is the only complete treatise on this subject. Athenaeus, at the beginning of the third century, wrote a work (the *Deipnosophistae*) of inestimable value to the student of antiquities. Longinus, who died A.D. 273, may be regarded as the last considerable scholar of the ancient world. The later grammarians restricted themselves to compiling extracts from the works of earlier ages.

(2) AT ROME.—After the middle of the second century B.C. a lively interest in the history of literature and the study of language arose in Rome. It had been excited by the lectures on Greek authors given by Crates of Mallos during his sojourn in Rome as ambassador (B.C. 159). Not only writers of repute, such as Attius and Lucilius, but men like Aelius Stilo, a member of the equestrian order, who was actively engaged in public life, took up these studies with eagerness. What was afterwards known of the primitive Latin language we owe mainly to Aelius Stilo. He was the master of the great encyclopaedist, Marcus Terentius Varro, Cicero's contemporary. This great scholar left his mark on every department of philological research, and his writings were the storehouse from which the following generations mainly drew their information. Besides Varro, other men of note occupied themselves with grammatical study in the Ciceronian age, notably Nigidius Figulus. Iulius Caesar was the author of a treatise on accidence. There were numerous scholars in the Augustan Age, among whom Verrius Flaccus and Hyginus deserve especial notice. In the first century A.D. we have Remmius Palaemon, Asconius Pedianus, Valerius Probus, and the elder Pliny. It was Remmius Palaemon who is mainly responsible for having made Vergil the centre of scholastic instruction for the Latin world, as Homer was for the Greek. During the second century A.D., under Hadrian and the Antonines, we notice a revived interest in the older literature. This period is distinguished by the names of Suetonius, Terentius Scaurus, and Aulus Gellius. Suetonius aspired to the many-sided learning of Varro, and, like Varro, was much quoted by later writers.

After this time, the grammarians tended more and more to confine their studies to points of language, to abandon independent research, and to depend on the labours of their predecessors. The chief value of their writings consists in the fact that they have preserved many fragments of ancient learning. Their extracts are usually made for school purposes, and put together in *artes*, or manuals of accidence, orthography, prosody, and metre. Such are the books of Marius Victorinus, Donatus, Servius, Charisius, Diomedes, who are all to be assigned to the fourth century A.D. Nonius Marcellus belongs to the same period. He is the author of a work (*De Compendiosa Doctrina*) which, though dreary and uncritical, is invaluable for the stores of old Latin which it has preserved. The sixth century is marked by the name of Priscian, whose work in eighteen books (*Institutiones Grammaticae*) is the most important grammatical treatise that has come down to us from the Romans. It was the standard book on the subject through the Middle Ages, and more than 1000 MSS. of it have been preserved. We may further notice Terentianus Maurus, the author of a versified treatise on metre in the third century; Macrobius, who in the fifth century composed a miscellany of antiquities called *Saturnalia;* and Isidorus, bishop of Seville, in the seventh century, whose *Origines* is the last work founded on a real study of ancient authorities.

See Egger, *Essai sur l'Histoire des Théories Grammaticales dans l'Antiquité* (Paris, 1854); Classen, *De Grammaticae Graecae Primordiis* (Bonn, 1829); Lersch, *Sprachphilosophie der Alten* (Bonn, 1841); Steinthal, *Geschichte der Sprachwissenschaft bei den Griechen und Römern* (2d ed. Berlin, 1891); Rumpel, *Casuslehre* (Halle, 1845); R. Schmidt, *Stoicorum Grammatica* (Halle, 1839); Blau, *De Aristarchi Discipulis* (Jena, 1883); Hörschelmann, *De Dionysii Thracis Interpretibus Veteribus* (Leipzig, 1874); Uhlig's prolegomena to his edition of Dionysius Thrax (Leipzig, 1884); Lange, *Das System der Syntax des Apollonius Dyscolus* (Göttingen, 1852); Schlitte, *De C. Iulio Caesare Grammatico* (Halle, 1865); Wilmanns, *De M. T. Varronis Libris Grammaticis* (Berlin, 1864); Steub, *De Probis Grammaticis* (Jena, 1871); the monograph in I. Müller's *Handbuch*, vol. i.; and the articles LIBERALES ARTES; PHILOLOGIA; RHETORICA.

Grammatĭcus (γραμματικός). See EDUCATION.

Grammatistes (γραμματιστής). See EDUCATION.

Grammatophylacium (γραμματοφυλάκιον). See TABLINUM.

Grampius Mons. A mountain of Caledonia, forming one of a large range of mountains extending from east to west through almost the whole breadth of modern Scotland, from Loch Lomond to Stonehaven. The range is now called the Grampian Hills, and the name is derived from the Mons Grampius, which is mentioned by Tacitus as the spot where Galgacus waited the approach of Agricola (*Agric.* 29). Some scholars defend GRAUPIUS as the proper form.

Granīcus (Γράνικος). A small river of Mysia, rising in Mount Ida, and falling into the Propontis (Sea of Marmora) east of Priapus; memorable as the scene of the victory of Alexander the Great over the Persians (B.C. 334) (Arrian, *Exp. Alex.* i. 13), and, in a less degree, for a victory of Lucullus over Mithridates, B.C. 73.

Granius Liciniānus. A Roman historian, who probably flourished in the second century A.D. He was the author of a work of some forty books, compiled in the style of *annales*, ending with the death of Caesar. Some considerable fragments have been found in modern times of books xxviii.–xxxvi., covering the history of the years B.C. 163–178. Licinianus was first edited from a codex in the British Museum by Pertz (Berlin, 1857). See Madvig, *Kleine philol. Schriften* (Leipzig, 1875).

Granūa (Γρανούα). A tributary of the Danube in Southeastern Germany.

Graphé (γραφή). See DIKÉ; JUDICIAL PROCEDURE.

Graphiarium (also **Graphiaria Theca**). A sheath or case for holding the *graphium* (q. v.) or *stilus*, used for writing on tablets (Mart. xiv. 20; Suet. *Claud.* 35). See WRITING AND WRITING MATERIALS.

Graphis (γραφίς). See PICTURA.

Graphium (γραφίον). A sharp-pointed instrument made of iron or bronze, used for writing on modern tablets covered with wax. The accompanying illustration shows the graphium shut (the top figure) and opened (the bottom figure) (Suet. *Caes.* 82; *Calig.* 28). It is some eight inches in length. See STILUS.

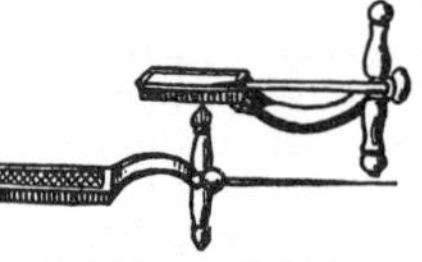

Graphium. (Rich.)

Grassatōres. See LATROCINIUM.

Gratiae. The Latin name for the Graces. See CHARITES.

Gratiānus. (1) The eldest son of Valentinian I., succeeding, after his father's death, A.D. 375, to a share of the Western Empire, having for his portion Gaul, Spain, and Britain. His brother, Valentinian II., then an infant under five years of age, had Italy, Illyricum, and Africa, under the guardianship, however, of Gratianus, who was therefore, in reality, ruler of all the West. His uncle Valens had the Empire of the East. Gratianus began his reign by punishing severely various prefects and other officers who had committed acts of oppression and cruelty during his father's reign. At the same time, through some insidious charges, Count Theodosius, father of Theodosius the Great, and one of the most illustrious men of his age, was beheaded at Carthage. In the year 378, Valens perished in the battle of Adrianople against the Goths, and Gratianus, who was hastening to his assistance, was hardly able to save Constantinople from falling into the hands of the enemy. In consequence of the death of his uncle, Gratianus, finding himself ruler of the whole Roman Empire during the minority of his brother Valentinian, called to him young Theodosius, who had distinguished himself in the Roman armies. Gratianus appointed him his colleague, a choice equally creditable to both and fortunate for the Empire, and gave him the provinces of the East. Gratianus now returned to Italy, but was obliged soon after to hasten to Illyricum to the assistance of Theodosius, and repelled the Goths, who were threatening Thrace. Thence he was forced to march to the banks of the Rhine, to fight the Alemanni and other barbarians. Having returned to Mediolanum in the year 381, he had to defend the frontiers of Italy from other tribes, who were advancing on the side of Rhaetia. Gratianus showed himself stern and unyielding towards the remains of the heathen worship. At Rome he overthrew the altar of Victory and confiscated the property attached to it, as well as all that which belonged to the other priests and the vestals. He also refused to assume the title and insignia of Pontifex Maximus, a dignity till then considered as annexed to that of emperor. These measures gave a final blow to the old worship of the Empire; and although the senators, who, for the most part, were still attached to it, sent him a deputation, at the head of which was Symmachus, they could not obtain any mitigation of his decrees. In the year 383, a certain Maximus revolted in Britain, and was proclaimed emperor by the soldiers, to whom he promised to re-establish the temples and the old religion of the Empire. He invaded Gaul, where he found numerous partisans. Gratianus advanced to meet him, but was forsaken by most of his troops, and obliged to hasten towards Italy. He was seized at Lugdunum, and put to death by the partisans of Maximus. He was little more than twenty-four years of age, and had reigned about eight years. (2) A usurper who assumed the imperial purple in Britain (A.D. 407), but was murdered by his troops in a few months. He was succeeded by Constantine. See CONSTANTINUS (3), p. 405.

Grattius. A contemporary of Ovid (cf. Ovid, *ex Pont.* iv. 16, 34) and the author of an extant poem on the chase (*Cynegetica*), of which 536 hexameters are extant and five fragments. From an allusion in the fortieth line, Grattius is without good reason regarded by some as a native of Falerii, and hence is often styled FALISCUS. The poem has been edited with a commentary by Stern (Halle, 1832), and revised by Haupt (Leipzig, 1838). The best text is that of Bährens (Leipzig, 1879). See CYNEGETICA.

Graviscae. An ancient city of Etruria, subject to Tarquinii, and colonized by the Romans B.C. 183. It was situated in the Maremma, and its air was unhealthful, whence Vergil calls it *intempestae Graviscae* (*Aen.* x. 184).

Greece. See HELLAS.

Greek, Pronunciation of. Three different methods of pronouncing Greek have been followed in the schools of America and England. They may be called, respectively, the English method; the Reuchlinian or modern Greek method; and the Erasmian method.

I. THE ENGLISH METHOD gives the letters their ordinary English sounds, but follows the Latin rules of accent (accenting the penult if it is long in quantity, but otherwise the antepenult). This method is still current in England, but has almost disappeared in the United States.

II. THE REUCHLINIAN METHOD, called after Reuchlin (q. v.), a great scholar of the fifteenth century, who was one of its earliest advocates, aims to follow the pronunciation of the modern Greeks. Of the vowels, η, υ, ει, οι, and υι, all have the sound of *i* in *machine;* αι is pronounced much like *a* in *fate*. In the diphthongs αυ, ευ, ηυ, and ωυ, υ is pronounced like *v* when the diphthong stands before a vowel, or β, γ, δ, ζ, λ, μ, ν, ρ; otherwise like *f*. π, κ, τ, after nasals, are pronounced like *b, g, d*. χ has the two sounds of German *ch*. δ is pronounced like *th* in *then*, β like *v*, γ like *ch* in German *ach*, ζ like English *z*. It has been argued that scholars ought to agree to pronounce Greek as the Greeks of to-day pronounce it, but many changes and corruptions have crept in during the centuries since the classical period; so that the pronunciation which prevails in Athens at present differs widely from that of ancient times. This method has therefore found few adherents in England or America, though it has been strongly advocated by a number of eminent men.

III. THE ERASMIAN METHOD, first proposed by Erasmus in a humorous dialogue published at Basle in 1528 (see below), is the one which is now prevalent in the United States and on the continent of Europe, though with various modifications. In the United States the ordinary pronunciation is as follows: α like *a* in *father;* η like *a* in *fate;* ε like *e* in *met;* ι like *i* in *machine;* ω like *o* in *note;* ο the same sound, but shorter; υ as French *u* or German *ü;* αι like *ai* in *aisle;* ει like *ei* in *freight* (or more often like *ei* in *height*); οι like *oi* in *boil;* υι like *ui* in *quit;* αυ like *ou* in *out;* ευ like *eu* in *feud;* ου like *ou* in *soup;* ᾳ, ῃ, ῳ like α, η, ω. The consonants are pronounced as in English, except that γ is always hard; before a palatal it is pronounced like *n* in *anxious;* ζ like *dz;* θ like *th* in *thin* (not like *th* in *this*); σ never like *z;* τ never aspirated; χ like German *ch* in *ach*. The written accent is followed in pronunciation.

We have so far been describing the methods of pronunciation generally followed by modern scholars. How the ancient Greeks pronounced is very difficult to determine, but on many points a tolerable degree of certainty can be arrived at. When the comic poets transcribed the cry of a sheep with βῆ, βῆ, it is plain that β was not pronounced like *v*, or η like *i* in *machine*, as in modern Greek. So, too, υ cannot have been pronounced like *i* in *machine*, as is seen from the description of the two sounds in Dion. Hal. (*Comp.* xiv. 96), and from the existence of the diphthong υι. It is probable that υ originally received the sound of *oo* in *boot*, later that of French *u* (German *ü*), and not until the ninth or tenth century of our era the sound of *i* in *machine*. αι and οι were true diphthongal sounds until a late period (αι = *ah-ee* = *i* in *pine;* οι = *o-ee* = *oi* in *boil*, nearly). ει was at first a true diphthong (ἕ-εε = *e* in *ere*, nearly); about B.C. 400 it came to be the simple sound of *ei* in *rein;* and not till much later was it sounded like *ei* in *seize*. αυ and ευ were true diphthongs (*ah-oo* and *ĕ-oo*). ου was originally a diphthongal sound, but later assumed the sound of *ou* in *youth*. υι was probably like French *ui* in *lui*. In the so-called improper diphthongs, ᾳ, ῃ, ῳ, the ι was probably pronounced until about the second century B.C., when it became silent, and was often omitted, even in writing. Of the consonants β, which in modern Greek has the sound of *v*, was reckoned a mute by the ancient Greeks, and hence must have been sounded as in English. The same argument proves that γ and δ received their English, rather than their modern Greek, sounds. But γ before palatals had the sound of *n* in *anxious*. σ was pronounced like *s* in *sink*, except before middle mutes and liquids, when it was pronounced like *s* in *as*. ζ had the sound of *sd* or *zd*, as is seen from such compounds as Ἀθήναζε (for Ἀθήνασ-δε), and from the fact that the preposition συν loses ν before ζ, just as before στ, σπ, etc. The aspirates φ, χ, θ were pronounced as two sounds (*p-h, k-h, τ-h*), as in English *uphill, block-house, hothouse*. This conclusion is drawn from the fact that these consonants were classed as mutes and not as spirants. The ancient consonant called *digamma* or *vau* (Ϝ) was probably pronounced like English *w* rather than *v*, as the strong *v*-sound would not have disappeared so quickly or completely as the digamma did.

The accent in ancient Greek consisted in a raising of the pitch, and not in the stress or duration of the sound. But the latter element was added at the period of the decay of the language, and the Greeks of to-day make all accented vowels long and all unaccented vowels short. When this change took place can be determined only approximately, but it must have been during the Alexandrian period and before the beginning of our era, as may be gathered from some of the rules of prosody observed by such poets as Babrius and Nonnus. The difference between high pitch and low pitch, according to Dionysius of Halicarnassus, amounted to almost a fifth (Dion. Hal. *Comp.* 58).

BIBLIOGRAPHY.—Erasmus, *De Recta Latini Graecique Sermonis Pronunciatione* (Basle, 1528); Seyffarth, *De Sonis Litterarum Gr.* (Leipzig, 1824); A. Kirchhoff, *Studien zur Geschichte des griech. Alphabets* (Berlin, 1877); K. Zacher, *Die Aussprache des Griech.* (Leipzig, 1888). More valuable than any of these is F. Blass, *The Pronunciation of Ancient Greek*, translated by Purton (Cambridge, 1890). Material for this article has been freely drawn from the latter.

Green Faction. See CIRCUS, p. 356.

Gregŏras, NICEPHŎRUS. One of the most important Byzantine historians, born about A.D. 1295, and died about 1359. His principal work is entitled *Historia Byzantina*, in thirty-eight books. It begins with the capture of Constantinople by the Latins in 1204, and extends to 1359. It has been edited in part by Schopen (Bonn, 1830).

Gregoriānus Codex. See CODEX GREGORIANUS.

Gregorius (Γρηγόριος). (1) Surnamed NAZIANZĒNUS, and usually called GREGORY NAZIANZEN. He was born in a village near Nazianzus in Cappadocia about A.D. 329, and prosecuted his studies at Athens, where he earned a great reputation for his knowledge of rhetoric, philosophy, and mathematics. Among his fellow students was Julian, the future emperor, and Basil, with the latter of whom he formed a most intimate friendship. Gregory remained at Athens about six years (350–356), and then returned home. Having received ordination, he continued to reside at Nazianzus, where he discharged his duties as a presbyter, and assisted his father, who was bishop of the town. In A.D. 372 he was associated with his father in the bishopric; but after the death of the latter in 374, he refused to continue Bishop of Nazianzus, as he was averse to public life and fond of solitary meditation. After living some years in retirement, he was summoned to Constantinople in 379, in order to defend the orthodox faith against the Arians and other heretics. In 380 he was made Bishop of Constantinople by the emperor Theodosius; but he resigned the office in the following year (381), and withdrew altogether from public life. He lived in solitude at his paternal estate at Nazianzus, and died there in 389 or 390. His extant works are about 45 orations or sermons, 243 letters, and 407 poems of a very varied description, comprising hymns, prayers, epitaphs, epigrams, etc. His discourses, though sometimes really eloquent, are generally little more than favourable specimens of the rhetoric of the schools, more earnest than Chrysostom, but less attractive. The Benedictine edition was published at Paris (1778–1842). See the monographs by Ullmann (Eng. trans. 1851); and by A. Benoît (Paris, 1876). (2) NYSSĒNUS, bishop of Nyssa in Cappadocia, was the younger brother of Basil, and was born at Caesarea in Cappadocia, about A.D. 331. He was made bishop of Nyssa about 372, and, like his brother Basil and their friend Gregory Nazienzen, was one of the pillars of orthodoxy. He died soon after A.D. 394. Like his brother, he was an eminent rhetorician, though his oratory often offends by its extravagance. His works are printed in Migne's *Patrologia*, vols. xliv.–xlvi. (3) Styled THAUMATURGUS, from his miracles, was born at Neocaesarea in Cappadocia, of heathen parents. He was converted to Christianity by Origen about A.D. 234, and subsequently became the bishop of his native town. He died about the year 265. His celebrated Ἔκθεσις, or confession of faith, is a summary of the theology of Origen. It is said to have been divined by him through a revelation from the Virgin Mary and the Apostle John. Other treatises of doubtful authenticity are attributed to him. His works are printed in vol. x. of the Patristic collection of the Abbé Migne. See Ryssel, *Gregorius Thaumaturgus: sein Leben und seine Schriften* (Leipzig, 1880); and Harnack, *Dogmengeschichte*, vol. i. (Freiburg im Breisg. 1888). (4) OF TOURS, called "the Father of Frankish History," was born at Arverna (Clermont), about A.D. 540, his baptismal name being Georgius Florentius. He became Bishop of Tours in 573, and after the death of Chilperic, whom Gregory calls "the Nero and the Herod of our times," and by whom he was much harassed, he enjoyed general esteem and consideration down to the end of his life in 594. He is best known by his *Historiae sive Annalium Francorum Libri X.*, which is the chief authority for the history of Gaul in the sixth century, beginning with an epitome of universal history, and developing the narrative with greater fulness as he proceeds. In it the author shows himself unskilled in literary composition, and his Latinity is especially interesting as a specimen of the gradual blending of the classic Latin into the rustic Latin from which the Romance languages emerged. His works are printed in vol. lxxi. of the Abbé Migne's collection. There is a French translation by Bordier, 2 vols. (1859–61), and Jacobs, 2 vols. (1861). See Löbell, *Gregor von Tours und seine Zeit* (2d ed. 1869); Pattison, *Essays*, vol. i. (1889); and on his language, Bonnet, *Le Latin de Grégoire de Tours* (1891).

Gridiron. See CRATICULA.

Grimm's Law. The peculiar type or character of the Teutonic languages, distinguishing them as a class from the other Indo-European languages, is prominently determined by a general change in the pronunciation of those consonants commonly known as mutes or explosives. The other consonants remain in general unchanged, thus: *n* in Eng. *new*, Lat. *novus*; *m* in Eng. *name*, Lat. *nōmen*; *r* in Eng. *acre*, Lat. *ager*; *l* in Eng. *light*, Lat. *lux*; *w* in Eng. *will*, Lat. *velle*; *y* in Eng. *yoke*, Lat. *jugum*; *s* in Eng. *seven*, Lat. *septem*; but the explosives (*k, t, p, g, d, b, gh, dh, bh*) occupied so prominent a place in the mechanism of the parent speech, one or more of them appearing in almost every word, that the changes which they underwent in passing into the Teutonic form could not fail to impress upon the Teutonic languages a distinct mark of individuality. The credit of first discovering the uniformity of these changes is largely due to a Danish scholar, Rasmus Kristian Rask (1787–1832), but the formulation of them in the shape of a general law and the exhibition of the parallelism contained in the second or High German shifting are the work of Jakob Grimm (1785–1863), first made public in the second edition of the first volume of his *Deutsche Grammatik* (1822).

I. THE GENERAL TEUTONIC or first shifting. The most essential facts are the following:

(1) Indo-European	*gh*	*dh*	*bh*	become
Teutonic	ʒ (*g*)	*đ* (*d*)	*ƀ* (*b*)	
(2) Indo-European	*g*	*d*	*b*	become
Teutonic	*k*	*t*	*p*	
(3) Indo-European	*k*	*t*	*p*	become
Teutonic	*h*	*þ*	*f*	

(1) The Indo-European voiced aspirates (*gh, dh, bh*) represent an explosion of voiced breath followed by an after-puff; the pronunciation of *dh*, e. g. may be crudely illustrated by the sound of *d-h* in *sandhill.* These sounds passed readily and very early into the *affricatae* *g*ʒ, *dđ* (cf. *dž* in the pronunciation of Eng. *j*), *bƀ*, which double sounds were then unified into the pure spirants ʒ, *đ*, *ƀ*. The first of these (ʒ) is the voiced form of German *ch*, and equivalent to the Modern Greek medial gamma, and may be produced by driving voiced breath over the tongue set nearly in the position for English *y*. The sound *đ* lies between English *th* in *then* and *z* (*ž*) in *azure.* Finally, *ƀ* may be produced by pronouncing English *v* with the two lips instead of with the under lip and upper teeth. These three spirants, ʒ, *đ*, *ƀ*, became quite generally changed to voiced explosives or mediae (*g*, *d*, *b*) in the West Germanic dialects (i. e. all except Scandinavian and Gothic), though the spirants ʒ and *ƀ* (*v*) remained medially in all but the High German dialects; contrast Eng. *lay*, *day* with Germ. *legen*, *tag*, and Eng. *raven*, *have* with Germ. *rabe*, *haben.* With the understanding, therefore, that *g*, *d*, *b* represent sometimes spirants and sometimes explosives we may set the formula, Indo-European *gh*, *dh*, *bh* > Teutonic *g*, *d*, *b*. The regular correspondences in the cognate languages are as follows:

I.-E.	Sanskrit.	Gr.	Lat. Initial.	Lat. Medial.	Teuton.
gh	*h*	χ	*h*	*h* (*g*)	*g* (ȝ)
dh	*dh*	θ	*f*	*d*	*d* (*đ*)
bh	*bh*	φ	*f*	*b*	*b* (*ƀ*)

Examples:

Sanskrit.	Greek.	Latin.	Teutonic. Goth.	Teutonic. Eng.
haṅsá-, goose	χήν	(*h*)*anser*	*gans*	*goose*
váhati, convey	ὄχος, wagon	*veho*	*wigs*	*way*
dhā-, set, make	ἔθηκα, set	*fēcī*	*gadēþs*	*deed*
vidhávā, widow	ἠίθεος, bachelor	*vidua*	*widuwō*	*widow*
bhárati, bears	φέρω	*fero*	*baíran*	*bear*
lúbhyati, desires		*lubet*	*liubs*	*lief* / *love*

(2) The Indo-European voiced explosives (*mediae*) become voiceless (*tenues*). The labial *b* was evidently a rare sound in Indo-European, and as an initial sound it seems not to have existed at all. The following are the regular correspondences:

Indo-Europ.	Sanskrit.	Greek.	Latin.	Teutonic.
g	*j*	γ	*g*	*k*
d	*d*	δ	*d*	*t*
b	*b*	β	*b*	*p*

Examples:

Sanskrit.	Greek.	Latin.	Teutonic. Goth.	Teutonic. Eng.
jánas-, race	γένος	*genus*	*kuni*	*kin*
jắnu-, knee	γόνυ	*genu*	*kniu*	*knee*
ájra-, pasture	ἀγρός	*ager*	*akrs*	*acre*
dáça, ten	δέκα	*decem*	*taíhun*	*ten*
vḗda, I know	οἶδα	*video*	*wait*	*wot*
Lithuan. *dubùs*, deep			*diups*	*deep*

(3) The Indo-European voiceless explosives (*tenues*) become voiceless spirants:

Indo-Europ.	Sanskrit.	Greek.	Latin.	Teutonic.
k	*ç*	κ	*c*	*h*
t	*t*	τ	*t*	*þ* (*th*)
p	*p*	π	*p*	*f*

Examples:

Sanskrit.	Greek.	Latin.	Teutonic. Goth.	Teutonic. Eng.
çvan-, dog	κύων	*canis*	*hunds*	*hound*
aṣṭáu, eight	ὀκτώ	*octō*	*ahtáu*	*eight*
tráyas, three	τρεῖς	*trēs*	*þreis*	*three*
bhrắtar-, brother	φράτωρ	*frāter*	*brōþar*	*brother*
pād-, foot	πούς	*pēs*	*fōtus*	*foot*
nápāt-, grandson	(νέποδες)	*nepōs*	Germ. *neffe*	*nephew*

In the interest of simplification we have thus far omitted all mention of another Indo-European series of gutturals, included in the group known as velars or back-gutturals, and which show in Greek, Latin, Keltic, and Teutonic a labial development. The most characteristic correspondences are the following:

Indo-Europ.	Sanskrit.	Greek.	Latin.	Teutonic.
q	*k* (*c*)	π, τ, κ	*qu*, *c*	*hw*
g	*g* (*j*)	β, δ, γ	*gu* (*v*), *g*	*kw*
gh	*gh* (*jh*)	φ, θ, χ	*gu* (*v*), *f*	*gw*

In Sanskrit the palatals *c*, *j*, *jh* appear before vowels which *were* in Indo-European *e*, *i*, *ə*. In Greek, π, β, φ appeared before *o*-vowels, and I.-E. *m*, *n*, *r*, *l*; τ, δ, θ appeared before *e*-vowels (τ also before *i*-vowels). In Latin, *qu*, *gu* (*v*) appear in general before vowels (except *u*); *f* (< I.-E. *gh*) before *r*. Examples:

Sanskrit.	Greek.	Latin.	Teutonic. Goth.	Teutonic. Eng.
ka-, who	πόθεν, whence	*quod*	*hvas*	*who*
sácatē, follows	ἕπομαι	*sequor*	*saíhvan*	*see*
gámati, comes	βαίνω	*veniō*	*qiman*	*come*
jīvá-, alive	(βίος)	*vīvus*	*qius*	*quick*
gharmá-, warmth	θερμός	*formus*	*warmjan*	*warm*
Lithuan. *snẽgas*, snow	νίφα (acc.)	*nivis* (gen.)	*snáiws*	*snow*

The apparent exceptions to the laws stated may be chiefly summarized under the following heads:

1. Dissimilation of Indo-European aspirates in Sanskrit and Greek. In Greek it took place after the voiced aspirates had become voiceless, thus: I.-E. *dh-dh* > Sanskr. *d-dh*, Gr. τ-θ, Teuton. *d-d*; cf.:

Indo-Europ.	Sanskrit.	Greek.	Teutonic. (Gothic.)
dhədhēmi	*dádhāmi*	τίθημι	
bheudh-	*bódhati*	πεύθομαι	*anabiudan*
bheidh-		πείθω	*bidjan*
bhendh-	*bándhu-*	πενθερός	*bindan*
dhigh-	*dih-*	τεῖχος	*deigan*
bhāghú-	*bāhú-*	πῆχυς	OHG. *buog*

cf. Grassman, *Kuhn's Zeitschr.* xii. 81 foll.

2. Shifting of *k*, *t*, *p* checked by preceding spirant in the combinations I.-E. *sk*, *st*, *sp* and Teuton. *ht* (< I.-E. *kt*), *ft* (< I.-E. *pt*); cf. Lat. *piscis*, Goth. *fisks*; Lat. *stāre*, Goth. *standan*; Lat. *rectus*, Goth. *raíhts*; Gr. ἔστι, Goth. *ist*; Lat. *spuere*, Goth. *speiwan*; Lat. *noctis* (genit.), Goth. *nahts*; Gr. κλέπτης, Goth. *hliftus*; Lat. *captus*, Goth. *hafts*. See Brugmann, *Compar. Gramm.* i. § 528.

3. Interchange of mediae and tenues and of mediae and aspirates in Indo-European, especially at the end of roots. This dualism was probably due originally to the character of the following consonant. So are to be explained, e. g. Gr. πυθμήν, O.Eng. *botm*; Gr. ἀστεμφής, O.H.G. *stampfōn*; Goth. *táikns*, *teihan*, etc.

4. The phenomena discussed under article VERNER'S LAW (q. v.).

II. THE HIGH GERMAN or second shifting. This affects only a portion of the West Germanic dialects. It began in the fifth century A.D. in the extreme south, affecting most powerfully the dialects of the Lombards, Allemans, Bavarians, and Southern Franks, but losing its force as it spread towards the north (cf. Braune, *Paul-Braune's Beitr.* i. 1 foll.). The frontier between the present High German and Low German dialects is formed without any reference to the older dialectal divisions by the final halt in the shifting of the *tenues*. The dialects which change initial *t* to *ts* (*z*), medial and final *t* to *s*, medial *p*, *k* to *f*, *ch* are High German, the others Low German. This frontier crosses Germany from west to east. Its course is approximately indicated by a line drawn from Aix-la-Chapelle through Düsseldorf, Siegen, Cassel, Magdeburg, Lübben, Fürstenberg (south of Frankfurt-on-the-Oder) to the Slavic language-frontier at Birnbaum on the Warthe. The most prominent features of this second shifting may be exhibited by a comparison of the sounds concerned as they at present stand in English and modern German. The English retains these sounds approximately in their original West Germanic values. The modern German as a normalized standard language occu pies in its adoption of the results of shifting a middle position between the south German dialects which shifted most and the northern which shifted least. The second shifting affected the dentals most radically.

	Tenues.			Mediae.			Spirants.		
English	*k*	*t*	*p*	*g* (*y*)	*d*	*b* (*v*)	*h*	*th* (*þ*)	*f*
Germ. Initial and after conson.	*k*	*ts* (=*z*)	*pf*	*g*	*t*	*b*	*h*	*d*	*f*
Germ. After vow.	*ch*	*ss*	*f*						

Examples: (1) Eng. *cold*, Germ. *kalt;* Eng. *yoke*, Germ. *joch;* Eng. *break*, Germ. *brechen.* (2) Eng. *ten*, Germ. *zehn;* Eng. *token*, Germ. *zeichen;* Eng. *heart*, Germ. *herz;* Eng. *bite*, Germ. *beissen;* Eng. *goat*, Germ. *geiss.* (3) Eng. *path*, Germ. *pfad;* Eng. *sleep*, Germ. *schlafen.* (4) Eng. *gird*, Germ. *gürten;* Eng. *ghost*, Germ. *geist;* Eng. *day*, Germ. *tag;* Eng. *honey*, Germ. *honig.* (5) Eng. *dead*, Germ. *tot;* Eng. *drink*, Germ. *trinken;* Eng. *deed*, Germ. *that;* Eng. *bread*, Germ. *brot.* (6) Eng. *blood*, Germ. *blut;* Eng. *love*, Germ. *lieben.* (7) Eng. *home*, Germ. *heim;* Eng. *heath*, Germ. *heide;* Eng. *laugh*, Germ. *lachen;* Eng. *might*, Germ. *macht.* (8) Eng. *that*, Germ. *das;* Eng. *thorn*, Germ. *dorn;* Eng. *wether*, Germ. *widder;* Eng. *earth*, Germ. *erde.* (9) Eng. *ford*, Germ. *furt;* Eng. *floor*, Germ. *flur.*

For treatment of the West Germ. double consonants, *gg, dd, bb, kk, tt, pp*, etc., cf. Wilmanns, *Deutsche Grammatik*, §§ 47, 48, 76, 84; Brugmann, *Compar. Grammar*, i. §§ 532, 535, 540.

Reference may be made to Brugmann, *Elements of the Comparative Grammar of the Indo-Germanic Languages*, i. §§ 342–344, 374–376, 393–395, 439–444, 527–541 (Eng. transl. N. Y. 1887); Wilmanns, *Deutsche Grammatik*, §§ 17 foll.; Kluge, *Paul's Grundriss der germ. Philol.* i. pp. 324 foll.; Behaghel, *Paul's Grundriss*, i. pp. 584 foll.; Brandt, *German Grammar*, §§ 407 foll., and *Amer. Journ. Philol.* i. 146 foll.; Skeat, *Principles of English Etymology*, first series, chs. vii, viii.

Griphus (γρῖφος). Literally "a net;" then any intricate, puzzling, or "catch" question. A riddle, enigma (Gell. i. 4, 4). See AENIGMA.

Grōma. The measuring instrument used by land-surveyors, who were from it called *gromatici*. See AGRIMENSORES.

The groma is represented on the gravestone of a *gromaticus* found some years ago at Ivrea (Rossi, *Groma e Squadro*, 1877, p. 43). The design is not in perspective, but, if allowances be made for the inexperience of the artist, it explains fairly well the nature of the instrument. Two small planks crossing one another at right angles are supported on a column or post (*ferramentum*). Plummets (probably four, though there are only two in the monument) are suspended from the planks to guide the operator in securing a vertical position of the column, and a horizontal for the cross-pieces. The small circles at the point of section in the drawing may represent a hole in the continuation of the column for the operator to look through, or a large hole in the cross-pieces to allow of their being tipped up to a certain angle if necessary. The latter is the more likely, for in that case the continuation of the column would serve as a support to prevent the cross from falling. In any case it obstructs the view along the planks.

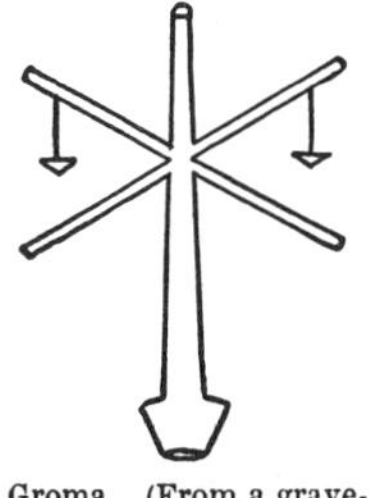

Groma. (From a gravestone at Ivrea.)

The use of the instrument is obvious. It is intended to guide a surveyor in drawing real or imaginary lines at right angles to one another, more especially in fixing the *cardo* (or north and south line) and *decumanus* (or east and west line) essential to the orientation of any *templum* or to the laying out of a Roman camp. See CASTRA.

Gromatĭci. Land-measurers. See AGRIMENSORES.

Gronovius (GRONOV). The name of three distinguished Dutch classical scholars.

(1) JOHANN FRIEDRICH, born at Hamburg, September 20th, 1613. He studied at Bremen and at the Universities of Leipzig, Jena, and Altdorf, after which he spent some time in travel in both France and Italy. In 1643 he became Professor of Rhetoric and History at Deventer in the Netherlands, and in 1658 succeeded Daniel Heinsius, at Leyden, as Professor of Greek. He died at Leyden, December 28th, 1671.

He edited, with commentaries, Statius (1653), Plautus (1664), Livy (1645), Pliny the Elder (1669), Tacitus (1672), the tragedies of Seneca (1661), and published separately various notes upon Phaedrus, Seneca, and other authors, these being subsequently incorporated with the works of his more distinguished son. A valuable contribution to the study of numismatics is the treatise *De Sestertiis*, in four books, which appeared in 1643.

(2) JAKOB, son of the preceding, born at Deventer, October 20th, 1645. He early distinguished himself at Leyden, and in 1668 visited England, where he became intimate with Casaubon, Pocock, and Pearson. While in England he spent several months in collating a number of rare MSS. at the Universities of Oxford and Cambridge. Soon after he declined a professorship at Deventer, and in 1671 visited France, where he made the acquaintance of some of the greatest scholars of that country. In the following year he travelled in Spain and Italy, accepting in the latter country a chair in the University of Pisa offered him by the Grand Duke of Tuscany. Resigning this at the end of two years, he returned to Leyden, where he soon after accepted the professorship, which he held to the end of his life, declining several calls from foreign universities, and passing his time in congenial work, though often embroiled in literary quarrels, in which he sustained his part with extreme violence of temper and a remarkable power of vituperative scurrility. He died October 21st, 1716.

His most important work is his *Thesaurus Antiquitatum Graecarum*, in thirteen vols. folio (Leyden, 1698–1702), reprinted at Venice (1732–37)—a work modelled on the great *Thesaurus Antiquitatum Romanarum* of Graevius (q. v.). He also brought out new editions of the authors edited by his father, and himself edited and annotated Macrobius (1670), Polybius (1670), Tacitus (1721), Cicero (1691), Ammianus Marcellinus (1709), Minucius Felix (1707), Gellius (1706), Herodotus (1715), Cebes (1689), the poems ascribed to Manetho, the *Dactylotheca* of Gorlaeus, the *Lexicon* of Harpocration, besides publishing a great number of pamphlets, theses, discourses, etc.

(3) ABRAHAM, son of the preceding, was born at Leyden in 1694, and died there in 1775. He was for a long time librarian to the University, and is known by his editions of Iustinus (1719), Tacitus (with his father, 1721), and Mela (1722).

Grote, GEORGE, the distinguished historian of Greece, was born at Clay Hill in Kent, England, November 17th, 1794. Educated at the Charterhouse, he did not enter one of the universities, but connected himself with a banking-house, in which he remained for thirty-two years, devoting his leisure to literary and political pursuits. In 1823 he began the special studies necessary for an exact and critical knowledge of Greek history, and in 1846 put forth the first two volumes of the great *History of Greece*, the twelfth and last volume of which appeared in 1856 (4th ed. London, 1872). It begins with the earliest period and carries on the narrative to the end of the generation contemporaneous with Alexander the Great. It is notable for its accurate geographical details, for the spirit and vigour of its passages descriptive of martial exploits, and, above all, for its obvious purpose of showing the elevating and inspiring influence of freedom upon human activity. In this last respect the history of Grote has been called a Liberal history of Greece, as that of Bishop Thirlwall is undeniably a Tory history. Each chapter is, in a way, a monograph in itself, and the work as a whole is one of the greatest masterpieces of historical research that have ever been put forth. It was followed by *Plato and the Other Companions of Socrates*, 3 vols. (London, 1865); and *Aristotle*, edited by Bain and Robertson, 2 vols. (London, 1872), forming a sort of supplement to the *History*.

In 1862 Grote was elected Vice-Chancellor of the University of London, and in 1868 President of the Council of University College. In 1869 a peerage was offered him by Mr. Gladstone, but was declined. Grote died June 18th, 1871, and was buried near Gibbon in Westminster Abbey. His life was written by his wife (1873); and a good critical review of his work as an historian by Professor Bain in the remarks prefixed to the edition of Grote's minor works (1873).

Grotefend. The name of several archaeologists of distinction. (1) GEORG FRIEDRICH, born at Münden in Hanover, June 9th, 1775. He was educated at Münden, Ilfeld, and the University of Göttingen. In 1797 he became master in the Göttingen Gymnasium, and soon after wrote his treatise *De Pasigraphia* (1799), which led to his being made Pro-rector of the Gymnasium at Frankfort-on-the-Main, and soon after Co-rector. In 1821 he was called to the rectorship of the Gymnasium at Hanover, which he held until 1849. He died December 15th, 1853.

In 1823-24 Grotefend revised Wenck's Latin grammar, and followed this publication with a smaller grammar for the use of schools (1826). His *Rudimenta Linguae Umbricae*, eight parts (1835-38), is an attempt to explain the remains of the Umbrian dialect (see UMBRIA); and soon after he put forth a similar work relating to the Oscan, *Rudimenta Linguae Oscae* (1839). In 1840-42 appeared, in five parts, his work *Zur Geographie und Geschichte von Altitalien*. He will, however, be longest remembered by his brilliant work in discovering a clue to the decipherment of the Persian cuneiform inscriptions that had so long defied all attempts at elucidation. Grotefend communicated his discovery to the Royal Society of Göttingen in 1800. The points that he was the first to establish were (*a*) that the Persian inscriptions contain three different varieties of cuneiform, so that the decipherment of one would give a clue to the decipherment of the others; (*b*) that the characters of the Persian cuneiform are alphabetic and not syllabic; (*c*) that they must be read from left to right; (*d*) that the alphabet consists of forty letters, including the signs for long and short vowels. These discoveries laid a solid basis for the work of those who followed and who finally solved the remaining problems. The details of the methods that led to his discoveries are given by Grotefend in his *Neue Beiträge zur Erläuterung der persepolitanischen Keilinschrift* (1837); and *Neue Beiträge zur Erläuterung der babylonischen Keilinschrift* (1840). See CUNEIFORM.

(2) KARL LUDWIG, son of the preceding, was born at Frankfort, December 22d, 1809. He studied at Göttingen, and held a post in the Royal Archives of Hanover from 1853. He died October 27th, 1874. His chief work was done in numismatics, epigraphy, and history. He published *Die Münzen der griechischen, parthischen, und indoskythischen Könige von Baktrien* (1839); *Imperium Romanum Tributim Descriptum* (1863); *Chronologische Anordnung der athenischen Silbermünzen* (1872); and a number of historical papers in the *Zeitschrift des historischen Vereins für Niedersachsen* (1850-74).

Grotius, HUGO (HUIG VAN GROOT). A Dutch scholar and jurist of great distinction, born at Delft, April 10th, 1583. As a boy he was extraordinarily precocious, entering the University of Leyden in his eleventh year, having already become well known for his skill in Latin versification. At Leyden he studied under Joseph Justus Scaliger, and when only fifteen years of age edited the very difficult, and, in fact, encyclopædic, work of Martianus Capella (Leyden, 1599). After a year spent in travel, he was admitted to the doctorate in law, and entered upon regular practice as an advocate. Though unusually successful in his chosen profession, he still reverted to letters, and in 1600 edited the remains of Aratus with the versions of Cicero, Germanicus, and Avienus. He also wrote much excellent Latin verse, and three dramas in Latin, one of which (*Adamus Exul*) is thought to have furnished a number of suggestions to Milton for his *Paradise Lost*. In 1614 he edited the *Pharsalia* of Lucan, of which edition a recension was published by Usener at Greifswald in 1862. Later, he put forth an edition of Silius Italicus, and a celebrated translation of the *Anthologia Graeca Planudea*. In 1657 he composed *Annales et Historiae de Rebus Belgicis*, an historical work of much value, and recalling by its terse and pointed style the Latinity of Tacitus. He is best known to the world at large, however, by his remarkable treatise *De Iure Pacis et Belli* (1625)—a work of profound and searching scholarship, which long remained the standard authority on international law. To describe his stormy career as a theologian and statesman would be beyond the scope of the present work. He died at Rostock, August 29th, 1645.

Few men have shown so great an aptitude for so many fields of intellectual labour. He was profoundly learned as a classical scholar, uniting elegance to accuracy. As a theologian he was probably the most soundly critical exegete of his age.

An able and acute historian, a philosopher of depth and ingenuity, an influential and original statesman and diplomat, a poet of much distinction, and a jurist who will always rank among the greatest in the history of jurisprudence—no wonder that an amazed contemporary styled him "a monster of learning."

The fullest biography of Grotius, with a complete list of his works, is that of Lehmann (Delft, 1727). There is also a good life of him in English by C. Butler (London, 1826). See L. Müller, *Gesch. d. class. Philol. in den Niederlanden*, p. 38 (Leipzig, 1869); and Pökel, *Philolog. Schriftstellerlexikon*, s. v. "Grotius" (Leipzig, 1882).

Grove. See LUCUS.

Grudii. A people in Gallia Belgica, subject to the Nervii, north of the Scheldt.

Grumentum. A town in the interior of Lucania, on the road from Beneventum to Heraclea.

Grylli. See ANTIPHILUS; GEMMA.

Gryllus (Γρύλλος). The elder son of Xenophon, who fell at the battle of Mantinea, B.C. 362, after he had, according to some accounts, given Epaminondas his mortal wound (Pausan. x. 8, 11).

Grynēum (Γρύνειον) or **Grynēa** (Γρύνεια). One of the twelve cities of Aeolis, situated on the coast of Lydia, near the northern confines, and northwest of Cymé. It was celebrated for the worship of Apollo, who thence derived the surname of Gryneus (Verg. *Eclog.* vi. 72; *Aen.* iv. 345). The temple of the god was remarkable for its size, and for the beauty of its white marble.

Gryps (γρύψ) or **Gryphus.** A griffin; a fabulous animal, with the body of a lion and the head and wings of an eagle, dwelling in the Rhipaean Mountains, between the Hyperboreans and the one-eyed Arimaspi (q. v.), and guarding the gold of the north. The Arimaspi mounted on horseback, and attempted to steal the gold, and hence arose the hostility between the horse and the griffin. The belief in griffins came from the East, where they are mentioned among the fabulous animals which guarded the gold of India (Herod. iii. 116; iv. 13). See AURUM.

Guard. See CASTRA; PRAETORIANI; VIGILES.

Gubernăculum (πηδάλιον). A rudder; originally nothing more than a large oar with a broad blade, either fastened by braces (*funes*, ζεύγλαι) outside the quarters of the vessel or passed through an aperture in the bulwarks. Later, it was furnished with a cross-bar, which served as a tiller, like the left-hand figure, from a Pompeian painting. Its different parts were distinguished by the following names: *ansa*, the handle, *a*; *clavus*, the shaft, *b*; *pinna*, the blade, *c*. The word is frequently used in the plural; because the ancient vessels were commonly furnished with two rudders, one on each quarter, each of which had its own helmsman, if the vessel was a large one; but were both managed by a single steersman when it was small enough. See GUBERNATOR; NAVIS.

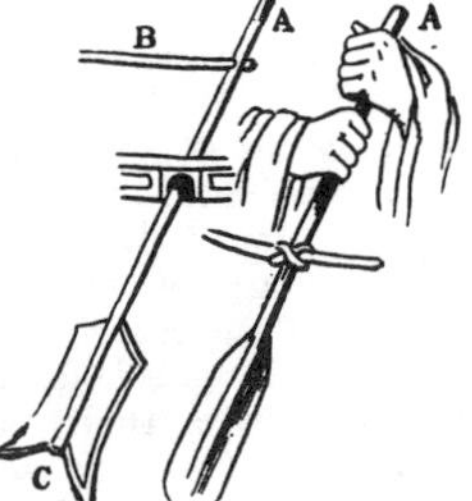

Gubernacula. (Pompeii.)

Gubernātor (κυβερνήτης). A helmsman or pilot, who sat at the stern to steer the vessel (Cic. *De Sen.* 9), gave orders to the rowers, and directed the management of the sails (Verg. *Aen.* x. 218; Lucan. viii. 193). He was next in command to the *magister* and immediately above the *proreta*.

Gubernator. (From a bas-relief found at Puteoli.)

Gugerni or **Guberni.** A people of Germany, who crossed the Rhine and settled on its left bank, between the Ubii and Batavi.

Guild. See COLLEGIUM.

Gulussa. A Numidian, second son of Masinissa, and brother to Micipsa and Mastanabal. He left a son, named Massiva. See IUGURTHA.

Gustatio. Any kind of delicacy taken as a relish or stimulant to the appetite before a meal (Petron. 21, 31). See CENA, p. 313.

Gustatorium. The tray upon which a *gustatio* (q. v.) was served up; often made of valuable materials, and lined with tortoise-shell (Petron. *Sat.* xxxiv. 1; Plin. *Ep.* v. 6, 37; cf. Mart. xiv. 88).

Guttae. Drops, in architecture, used principally under the triglyphs of the Doric order, in the architrave, and under the taenia (Vitruv. iv. 3, 4), as in the above example; but sometimes also applied under the mutules of the order (Vitruv. iv. 3, 6). They are shaped like the frustra of cones, and represent the drops of water which distil from above, and hang in pendent drops below.

Guttae. (Rich.)

Guttōnes. See GOTHI.

Gutturnium (πρόχοος). A water-jug or ewer; employed especially for pouring water over the hands before and after meals (Fest. s. v.).

Gutturnium. (Pompeii.)

Guttus (λήκυθος). A vessel with a narrow mouth or neck, from which liquids were poured in drops (*guttae*); hence its name (Varr. *L. L.* v. 124 M). Varro goes on to say that for pouring out wine at the banquet it had been superseded by the *epichysis* and *cyathus*; but retained its place in sacrificial libations, especially of the domestic sort (Hor. *Sat.* i. 6, 118, with Orelli's note). The guttus was of the plainest shape and materials; it differed from the *capis* (also used in sacrifices), *epichysis*, and *urceus* in being without a handle; and was usually

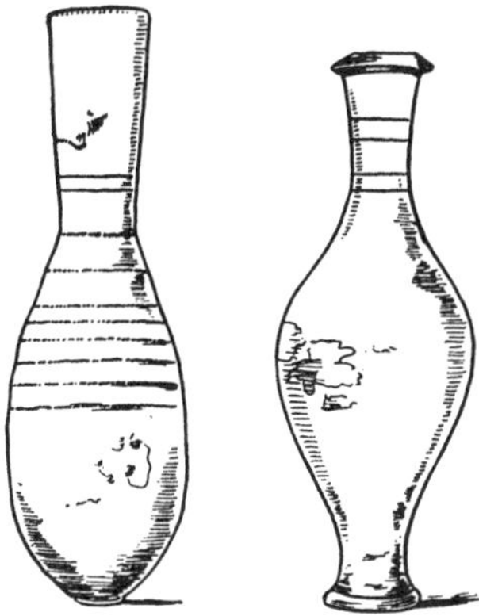

Gutti. (British Museum.)

of coarse pottery. It was in common use as an oil-cruet, whether at table (Gell. xvii. 8, § 5), or at the bath (Juv. iii. 263).

Gyărus (Γύαρος). A small island of the Archipelago, classed by Stephanus of Byzantium among the Sporades, but belonging rather to the Cyclades. It lay southwest of Andros, off the coast of Attica. So wretched and poor was this barren rock, being inhabited only by a few fishermen, that they deputed one of their number to wait upon Augustus, then at Corinth, after the battle of Actium, to petition that their taxes, which amounted to 150 drachmae (about $25), might be diminished, as they were unable to raise more than 100. This island became subsequently notorious, as the spot to which criminals or suspected persons were banished by order of the Roman emperors (Juv. i. 73; x. 70). The modern name is Chioura.

Gyes (Γύης). See GYGES.

Gygaeus Lacus (Γυγαία Λίμνη). A small lake in Lydia, north of Sardis (Herod. i. 93).

Gȳges (Γύγης), more correctly **Gyes** (Γύης). A son of Uranus and Gaea, represented as having a hundred hands. He, with his brothers, made war against the gods, and was afterwards punished in Tartarus. See COTTUS; GIGANTES; TITANES.

Gyges (Γύγης). A Lydian, to whom Candaules, king of the country, showed his wife with her person exposed. The latter, having discovered this, was so incensed, although she concealed her anger at the time, that, calling Gyges afterwards into her presence, she gave him his choice either to submit to instant death, or to slay her husband. Gyges chose the latter alternative, married the queen, and ascended the vacant throne, about 680 years before the Christian era. He was the first of the Mermnadae who ruled in Lydia. He reigned thirty-eight years, and distinguished himself by the presents which he made to the oracle of Delphi (Herod. i. 8 foll.). The wife of Candaules above mentioned was called Nyssia, according to Hephaestion. The story of Rosamund, queen of the Lombards, as related by Gibbon, bears an exact resemblance to this of Candaules (cf. Schlosser, *Weltgeschichte*, vol. ii. pt. 1, p. 82). Plato relates a curious legend respecting this Gyges, which differs essentially from the account given by Herodotus. He makes him to have been originally one of the shepherds of Candaules, and to have descended into a chasm, formed by heavy rains and an earthquake in the quarter where he was pasturing his flocks. In this chasm he discovered many wonderful things, and particularly a brazen horse having doors in it, through which he looked, and saw within a corpse of more than mortal size, having a golden ring on its finger. This ring he took off and reascended with it to the surface of the earth. Attending, after this, a meeting of his fellow-shepherds, who used to assemble once a month for the purpose of transmitting an account of their flocks to the king, he accidentally discovered that, when he turned the bezel of the ring inward towards himself, he became invisible, and when he turned it outward, again visible. Upon this, having caused himself to be chosen in the number of those who were sent on this occasion to the king, he murdered the monarch, with the aid of the queen, whom he previously corrupted, and ascended the throne of Lydia (Plat. *De Rep.* ii.; cf. Cic. *De Off.* iii. 9).

Gylippus (Γύλιππος). A Lacedaemonian, sent, B.C. 414, by his countrymen to assist Syracuse against the Athenians, which he effected by the overthrow of Nicias and Demosthenes. He afterwards joined Lysander off Athens, and aided him by his advice in the capture of that city. Lysander sent him to Lacedaemon with the money and spoils which had been taken, the former amounting to 1500 talents (B.C. 404). But Gylippus, unable to resist the temptation, unsewed the bottom of the bags, thus leaving the seals untouched at the top, and abstracted 300 talents. His theft, however, was discovered by means of the memorandum contained in each bag, and to avoid punishment he went into voluntary exile (Plut. *Nicias;* Diod. Sic. xiii. 106).

Gymnasiarches (γυμνασιάρχης). See GYMNASIUM.

Gymnasiarchia (γυμνασιαρχία). See LITURGIA.

Gymnasium (γυμνάσιον). Gymnastics were thought by the ancients a matter of such importance that this part of education alone occupied as much time and attention as all the others put together; and while the latter necessarily ceased at a certain period of life, gymnastics continued to be cultivated by persons of all ages. The word "gymnastics" is derived from γυμνός (naked), because the persons who performed their exercises in public or private gymnasia were either entirely naked, or merely covered by the short χιτών.

The great partiality of the Greeks for gymnastic exercises was productive of infinite good. It gave to the body that healthy and beautiful development by which the Greeks excelled all other nations, and which at the same time imparted to their minds power and elasticity. The plastic art also must have found its first and chief nourishment in the gymnastic and athletic performances. Respecting the advantages of gymnastics in a medical point of view, see ATHLETAE; MEDICINA.

Gymnastics, in the widest sense of the word, comprehended also the agonistic and athletic arts (ἀγωνιστική and ἀθλητική)—that is, the art of those who contended for the prizes at the great public games in Greece, and of those who made gymnastic performances their profession. In a narrower sense, however, the gymnasia had, with very few exceptions, nothing to do with the public contests, but were places of exercise for the purpose of strengthening and improving the body, or, in other words, places for physical education and training; and it is chiefly in this point of view that they will be considered in this article.

Gymnastic exercises among the Greeks seem to have been as old as the Greek nation itself, as may be inferred from the fact that gymnastic contests are mentioned in many of the earliest legends of Grecian story; but they were, as might be supposed, of a rude and mostly of a warlike character. They were generally held in the open air, and in plains near a river, which afforded an opportunity for swimming and bathing. The Attic legends, indeed, referred the regulation of gymnastics to Theseus (Pausan. i. 39, § 3), but according to Galen it seems to have been about the time of Clisthenes that gymnastics were reduced to a regular and complete system. Great progress, however, must have been made as early as the time of Solon, as appears from some of his laws which are mentioned below. It was about the same period that the Greek towns began to build their regular gymnasia as places of exercise for the young, with baths, and other conveniences for philosophers and all persons who sought intellectual amusements. There was probably no Greek town of any importance which did not possess its gymnasium. In many places, such as Ephesus, Hierapolis, and Alexandria in Troas, the remains of the ancient gymnasia have been discovered in modern times. The oldest remains are those of the gymnasium at Olympia, which can not be earlier than the end of the fourth century B.C. (Bötticher, *Olympia*, p. 363 foll.).

Athens possessed three great gymnasia—the Lyceum (Λύκειον), Cynosarges (Κυνόσαργες), and the Academia (Ἀκαδημία), to which, in later times, several smaller ones were added. All places of this kind were, on the whole, built on the same plan, though, from the remains, as well as from the descriptions still extant, it is evident that there were many differences in their detail. We have no detailed account of a gymnasium of the best period. The most complete description of a gymnasium

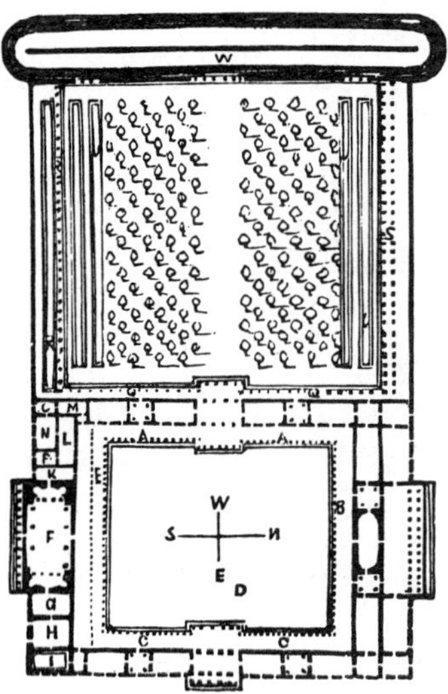

Plan of Gymnasium.

which we possess is that given by Vitruvius (v. 11), which, however, is very obscure, and at the same time defective, in so far as many parts which seem to have been essential to a gymnasium are not mentioned in it. Of the numerous plans which have been drawn, that of W. Newton, in his translation of Vitruvius, may here be given with a few alterations, although some of the details are open to criticism.

The peristylium (D) in a gymnasium, which Vitruvius incorrectly calls palaestra, is in the form of a square or oblong, and is two stadia (1200 feet) in circumference. It consists of four porticoes. In three of them (A B C) spacious exedrae with seats were erected, in which philosophers, rhetoricians, and others, who delighted in intellectual conversation, might assemble. A fourth portico (E), towards the south, was double, so that the interior walk was not exposed to bad weather. The double portico contained the following apartments: The Ephebeum (F), a spacious hall with seats in the middle, and one-third longer than broad, destined for the exercises of youths. On the right is the Coryceum (G), used for exercises with the sack (κώρυκος), perhaps the same room which in other cases was called Apodyterium; then came the Conisterium (H) adjoining, where the body was sprinkled with dust; and next to the Conisterium, in the returns of the portico, is the cold bath, λουτρόν (I). On the left of the Ephebeum is the Elaeothesium, where persons were anointed by the aliptae (K). Adjoining the Elaeothesium is the Frigidarium (L), or more probably the Tepidarium, where there was a lukewarm bath. From thence is the entrance to the Propnigeum (M), on the returns of the portico; near which, but more inward, behind the place of the Frigidarium, is the vaulted sudatory (N), in length twice its breadth, which has on the returns the Laconicum (O) on one side, and opposite the Laconicum the hot bath (P). These are the more essential and primitive parts of a gymnasium. But in the time of Vitruvius important additions were made to it. On the outside three porticoes are built: one (Q), in passing out from the peristyle, and, on the right and left, the two stadial porticoes (R, S), of which the one (S) that faces the north is made double and of great breadth, the other (R) is single, and so designed that in the parts which encircle the walls, and which adjoin the columns, there may be margins for paths not less than ten feet; and the middle is so excavated that there may be two steps, a foot and a half in descent, to go from the margin to the plane (R), which plane should not be less in breadth than twelve feet; by this means those who walked about the margins in their apparel would not be annoyed by those who were exercising themselves. This portico is called by the Greeks ξυστός, because in the winter season the athletae exercised themselves in these covered stadia. The ξυστός had groves or plantations between the two porticoes, and walks between the trees, with seats of signine work. Adjoining the ξυστός (R) and double portico (S) are the uncovered walks (U), which in Greek are called περιδρομίδες, to which the athletae, in fair weather, went from the winter-xystus to exercise. Beyond the xystus is the stadium (W), so large that a multitude of people might have sufficient room to behold the contests of the athletae. In this description of Vitruvius, two important parts of other Greek gymnasia (the Apodyterium and the Sphaeristerium) are not mentioned.

The Greeks bestowed great care upon the outward and inward splendour of their gymnasia, and adorned them with the statues of gods, heroes, victors in the public games, and of eminent men of every class. Hermes was the tutelary deity of the gymnasia, and his statue was consequently seen in most of them.

The earliest regulations which we possess concerning the gymnasia are contained in the laws of Solon. One of these laws forbade all adults to enter a gymnasium during the time that boys were taking their exercises, and at the festival of the Hermaea. The gymnasia were, according to the same law, not allowed to be opened before sunrise, and were to be shut at sunset (Lex *ap.* Aeschin. *c. Timarch.* § 12). Another law of Solon excluded slaves from gymnastic exercises (Aeschin. *c. Timarch.* § 138; Plut. *Solon*, 1). Boys who were children of an Athenian citizen and a foreign mother (*νόθοι*) were not admitted to any other gymnasium but the Cynosarges (Plut. *Them.* 1). Some of the laws of Solon, relating to the management and the superintendence of the gymnasia, show that he was aware of the evil consequences which these institutions might produce, unless they were regulated by the strictest rules. As we, however, find that adults also frequented the gymnasia, we must suppose that, at least as long as the laws of Solon were in force, the gymnasia were divided into different parts for persons of different ages, or that persons of different ages took their exercise at different times of the day. In the time of Plato the salutary regulations of Solon appear to have been no longer observed, and we find persons of all ages visiting the gymnasia (Plat. *De Rep.* v. p. 452; Xen. *Sympos.* 2, § 18). Athens now possessed a number of smaller gymnasia, which are sometimes called palaestrae, in which persons of all ages used to assemble, and in which even the Hermaea were celebrated by the boys, while formerly this solemnity had been kept only in the great gymnasia, and to the exclusion of all adults (Plat. *Lys.* p. 206). These changes, and the laxity in the superintendence of these public places, caused the gymnasia to differ very little from the schools of the athletae; and it is perhaps partly owing to this circumstance that writers of this and subsequent times use the words gymnasium and palaestra indiscriminately. But K. F. Hermann (*Privatalt.* § 36) seems to have proved that the gymnasium was never used for a place of training.

Married as well as unmarried women were, at Athens and in all the Ionian States, excluded from the gymnasia; but at Sparta, and in some other Doric States, maidens, dressed in the short *χιτών*, were not only admitted as spectators, but also took part in the exercises of the youths. Married women, however, did not frequent the gymnasia.

Respecting the superintendence and administration of the gymnasia at Athens, we know that Solon in his legislation thought them worthy of great attention; and the transgression of some of his laws relating to the gymnasia was punished with death. His laws mention a magistrate, called the Gymnasiarch (*γυμνασίαρχος* or *γυμνασιάρχης*), who was intrusted with the whole management of the gymnasia, and with everything connected therewith. His office was one of the regular liturgies, like the choregia and trierarchy, and was attended with considerable expense. He had to maintain and pay the persons who were preparing themselves for the games and contests in the public festivals, to provide them with oil, and perhaps with the wrestlers' dust. It also devolved upon him to adorn the gymnasium or the place where the contests took place (Xen. *De Rep. Athen.* 1, § 13). The Gymnasiarch was a real magistrate, and invested with a kind of jurisdiction over all those who frequented or were connected with the gymnasia; and his power seems even to have extended beyond the gymnasia, for Plutarch (*Amator.* c. 9, etc.) states that he watched and controlled the conduct of the ephebi in general. He had also the power to remove from the gymnasia teachers, philosophers, and sophists, whenever he conceived that they exercised an injurious influence upon the young. Another part of his duties was to conduct the solemn games at certain great festivals, especially the torch-race (*λαμπαδηφορία*), for which he selected the most distinguished among the ephebi of the gymnasia. The number of Gymnasiarchs was, according to Libanius on Demosthenes (*c. Mid.* p. 510) ten, one from every tribe. They seem to have undertaken their official duties in turns, but in what manner is unknown. Among the external distinctions of a Gymnasiarch were a purple cloak and white shoes (Plut. *Anton.* 33). In early times the office of Gymnasiarch lasted for a year, but under the Roman emperors we find that sometimes they held it only for a month, so that there were twelve or thirteen Gymnasiarchs in one year. This office seems to have been considered so great an honour that even Roman generals and emperors were ambitious to hold it. Other Greek towns, like Athens, had their own Gymnasiarchs, but we do not know whether, or to what extent, their duties differed from the Athenian Gymnasiarchs. In Cyrenė the office was sometimes held by women.

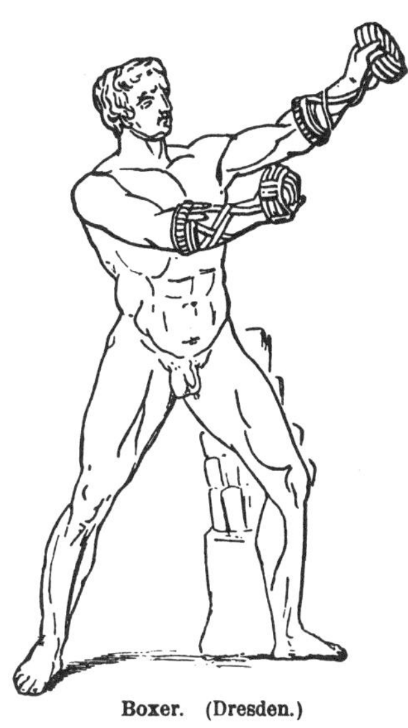

Boxer. (Dresden.)

An office which is not mentioned before the time of the Roman emperors, but was nevertheless decidedly connected with the gymnasia, is that of Cosmetes. He had to arrange certain games, to register the names and keep the lists of the ephebi, and to maintain order and discipline among them. He was assisted by an Anticosmetes and two Hypocosmetae. This officer appears only after the reorganization of the gymnasia in the second century B.C., when they served also as places for intellectual instruction. See EDUCATION, p. 572.

An office of very great importance, in an educational point of view, was that of the Sophronistae (*σωφρονισταί*). Their province was to inspire the youth with a love of *σωφροσύνη*, and to protect this virtue against all injurious influences. In early times their number at Athens was ten, one from every tribe, with a salary of one drachma per day (*Etym. Mag.* s. h. v.). Their duty not only required them to be present at all the games of the ephebi, but to watch and correct their conduct wherever they might meet them, both within and without the gymnasium.

The Wrestlers. (Uffizi Gallery, Florence.)

The instructions in the palaestrae, sometimes attached to gymnasia, were given by the Gymnastae (*γυμνασταί*) and the Paedotribae (*παιδοτρίβαι*); at a later period Hypopaedotribae were added. The Paedotribes was required to possess a knowledge of all the various exercises which were performed by the gymnasia; the Gymnastes was the superior teacher, and was expected to know the physiological effects and influences on the constitution of the youths, and therefore assigned to each of them those exercises which he thought most suitable.

The anointing of the bodies of the youths, and strewing them with dust, before they commenced their exercises, as well as the regulation of their diet, was the duty of the Aliptae. (See ALIPTAE.) These men sometimes also acted as surgeons or teachers. Galen mentions among the gymnastic teachers a *σφαιριστικός*, or teacher of the various games at ball; and it is not improbable that in some cases particular games may have been taught by separate persons.

The games and exercises which were performed in the gymnasia seem, on the whole, to have been the same throughout Greece. Among the Dorians, however, they were regarded chiefly as institutions for hardening the body and for military training; among the Ionians, and especially the Athenians, they had an additional and higher object, namely, to give to the body and its movements grace and beauty, and to make it the basis of a healthy and sound mind.

Among the games we may mention: (1) The ball (*σφαίρισις, σφαιρομαχία*, etc.), which was in universal favour, and was here, in Greece, as at Rome, played in a variety of ways, as appears from the words *ἀπόρραξις, ἐπίσκυρος, φαινίνδα*, or *ἁρπαστόν*, etc. Every gymnasium contained one large room for the purpose of playing at ball in it (*σφαιριστήριον*). (2) *Παίζειν ἑλκυστίνδα, διελκυστίνδα*, or *διὰ γραμμῆς*, was a game in which one boy, holding one end of a rope, tried to pull the boy who held its other end across a line marked between them on the ground. (3) The top (*βέμβηξ, βέμβιξ, ῥόμβος, στρόβιλος*), which was as common an amusement with Greek boys as in our own days. (4) The *πεντάλιθος*, which was a game with five stones, which were thrown up from the upper part of the hand and caught in the palm. (5) *Σκαπέρδα*, which was a game in which a rope was drawn through the upper part of a tree or a post. Two boys, one on each side of the post, turning their backs towards one another, took hold of the ends of the rope and tried to pull each other up. This sport was also one of the amusements at the Attic Dionysia. These few games will suffice to show the character of the gymnastic sports.

The more important games, such as running (*δρόμος*), throwing of the *δίσκος* and the *ἄκων*, jumping and leaping (*ἅλμα*, with and without *ἁλτῆρες*), wrestling (*πάλη*), boxing (*πυγμή*), the pancratium (*παγκράτιον, πένταθλον, λαμπαδηφορία*), dancing (*ὄρχησις*), etc., are described in separate articles.

A gymnasium was, as Vitruvius observes, not a Roman institution, and Dionysius of Halicarnassus (*Ant. Rom.* vii. 70–72) expressly states that the whole *ἀγωνιστική* of the Romans, though it was practised at an early period in the Ludi Maximi, was introduced among the Romans from Greece. Their attention, however, to developing and strengthening the body by exercises was considerable, though only for military purposes. The regular training of boys in the Greek gymnastics was foreign to Roman manners, and even held in contempt (Plut. *Quaest. Rom.* 40). Towards the end of the Republic many wealthy Romans, who had acquired a taste for Greek manners, used to attach to their villas small places for bodily exercise, sometimes called gymnasia, sometimes palaestrae, and to adorn them with beautiful works of art. The emperor Nero was the first who built a public gymnasium at Rome (Suet. *Ner.* 12); another was erected by Commodus (Herodian, i. 12, 4). But although these institutions were intended to introduce Greek gymnastics among the Romans, yet they never gained any great importance, as the magnificent thermae, amphitheatres, and other colossal buildings had always greater charms for the Romans than the gymnasia.

See Burette, *Histoire des Athlètes*, in the *Mém. de l'Acad. des Inscript.* i. 3; G. Löbker, *Die Gymnastik der Hellenen* (Münster, 1835); Wachsmuth, *Hellen. Alterth.* vol. ii. p. 344, etc., 2d ed.; Müller, *Dorier*, iv. 5, § 4, etc.; Becker-Göll, *Charikles*, ii. 213–251; *Gallus*, iii. 168–188; and especially J. H. Krause, *Die Gymnastik u. Agonistik der Hellenen* (Leipzig, 1841); and Dittenberger, *De Ephebis Atticis* (ib. 1863). The histories of education among the ancients, especially that of Grasberger, likewise contain much useful information on the subject. See ATHLETAE; EDUCATION.

Gymnastes (*γυμναστής*). See GYMNASIUM.

Gymnastics. See ATHLETAE; GYMNASIUM.

Gymnesiae (Γυμνησίαι νῆσοι). See BALEARES.

Gymnesii or **Gymnētes** (*γυμνήσιοι* or *γυμνῆτες*). A class of bond-slaves at Argos, who may be compared with the Helots at Sparta (Steph. Byz. s. v. Χίος; Pollux, iii. 83). Their name shows that they attended their masters on military service in the capacity of light-armed troops, but no particulars are known about them.

Gymnētae (*γυμνῆται*). A name for the different sorts of sharp-shooters employed in the Greek armies since the Persian Wars, in place of the light-armed slaves. It was only after the expedition of the Ten Thousand that they came to form an essential part of a Greek army. They were generally recruited from the barbarous nations who were specially distinguished in the use of particular missiles. The archers (*τοξόται*), for instance, were generally Cretans, the slingers (*σφενδονῆται*) Rhodians and Thessalians, while the javelin men (*ἀκοντισταί*) were taken from the semi-Hellenic populations in the west of Greece, notably the Aetolians and Acarnanians. The common characteristic of all these troops was the absence of all defensive weapons. It was among the Lacedaemonians that they were introduced latest. Alexander the Great had a corps of 2000 of them, with which he opened his campaign against the Persians. Half of these were spearmen and the other half archers. See EXERCITUS.

Gymnopaedia (*γυμνοπαιδία*). A great festival held at Sparta from about the 6th to the 10th of July in honour of Apollo, Artemis, and Leto (Pausan. iii. 11, § 7). It was an exhibition of all kinds of accomplishments in gymnastics, music, and dancing, given by boys, youths, and men for the benefit of the citizens and of the numerous strangers who flocked to Sparta for the occasion, and were hospitably entertained there. Old bachelors were excluded from the festivities (Schömann, *Antiq.* i. 264, Eng. transl.).

Gymnosophistae (Γυμνοσοφισταί). "Naked Sages." A name given by the Greek writers to a certain class of Indian ascetics belonging to the caste of the Brahmins, and who, in accordance with the prevalent belief, thought that, by subjecting the body to sufferings and privations, and by withdrawing from all intercourse with mankind, they could effect a reunion of the spiritual nature of man with the divine essence. Most of these ascetics dispensed almost entirely with the use of clothes, and many of them went entirely naked. Hence the name applied to them by the Greeks. Many of these hermits appear in former times to have studied the abstract sciences with great success, and they have always been considered by the orthodox Hindus as the wisest and holiest of mankind. The Gymnosophists often burned themselves alive, as Calanus did in the presence of Alexander (Arrian, *Anab.* vii. 18; Plut. *Alex.* 65 foll.; Diod. Sic. xvii. 107).

Gynaeconītis (*γυναικωνῖτις*). See DOMUS, p. 539.

Gynaeconŏmi (*γυναικονόμοι*). Magistrates in many Greek States, who exercised a censorship over the conduct of women and to some extent of men also, especially the young. At Sparta there were *παιδονόμοι*, but not *γυναικονόμοι*. The far-reaching Spartan discipline brought both sexes alike under the control of the authorities, and such special officers may not have been required. Aristotle mentions them as a well-known institution in two passages of the *Politica* (iv. 12 [15], § 9; vi. 5 [8], § 13), and each time observes that they were characteristic of aristocracies rather than of oligarchies or democracies — a remark which alone is almost sufficient to prove that they did not exist at Athens in his time. We find them at Chaeronea, Syracuse, Andania, and at Gambreion near Pergamum.

They were associated with the Areopagus in the maintenance of public decency and the enforcement of sumptuary laws. They superintended even the meetings of friends in their private houses — e. g. at weddings, and on other festive occasions. Meetings of this kind were not allowed to consist of more than thirty persons, and the *γυναικονόμοι* had the right of entering any house and sending away all the guests above that number. They also controlled the eccentricities of female attire; women who went unsuitably dressed in public were liable to a fine of 1000 drachmas, and these fines were recorded on a tablet suspended to a plane-tree in the Ceramicus (Harpocrat. s. v. *ὅτι χιλιάς*; Hesychius, s. v. *πλάτανος*). The number of these officers and the mode of their appointment are alike unknown.

Gyndes (Γύνδης). A river of Assyria, rising in the country of the Matieni (in the mountains of Kurdistan) and flowing into the Tigris, celebrated through the story that Cyrus the Great drew off its waters by 360 channels. See Herod. i. 189.

Gypsoplastes. One who takes casts in plaster of Paris (*gypsum*). See Cassiod. *Var. Ep.* vii. 5.

Gyrton or **Gyrtona** (Γυρτών, Γυρτώνη). An ancient town in Pelasgiotis in Thessaly, on the Peneus.

Gythĭum (Γύθιον, Γυθεῖον). An ancient seaport town of Laconia, situated near the head of the Laconian Gulf, southwest of the mouth of the river Eurotas. In the Second Persian War, the Spartan fleet was stationed here, and here the Athenians under Tolmides burned the Spartan arsenal in B.C. 455 (Thuc. i. 102).

H

H, as a symbol.

In Greek.—H = ἡμέρας, ἡμερῶν, υἱός (*C. I. G.* 5762) ὥρας (ib. 3013).

In Latin.—H = habet (habens), hic (and its forms), heres, homo, hora. H H = heredes.

H·A = Herculaneus Augustalis.

H·B = homo bonus.

H·C = hic conditus, Hispania Citerior, honoris causa, honore contentus, horrearius cohortis.

H·F = heres fecit, honestissima femina, honore functus.

H·I = Hercules invictus.

H·L = haec lex, hic locus.

H·M = hoc monumentum (very frequent), honesta missione.

H·P = heres posuit, hic positus.

H·V = Hercules victor, honore usus.

H·B·F = homini bono fecit.

H·B·Q = hic bene quiescat.

H·D·S = heres de suo.

H·E·F = heres eius fecit.

H·E·P = hic est positus.

H·E·T = heredes ex testamento.

H·L·O = (uti) hac lege oportebit.

H·L·R = (ante) hanc legem rogatam.

H·M·V = honestae memoriae vir.

H·N·C = Hispania Nova Citerior.

H·P·C = heres ponendum curavit.

H·P·R = hostes populi Romani.

H·A·I·R = honore accepto impensam reliquit.

H·B·M·F = heres bene merenti fecit.

H·E·N·S = heredem exterum non sequetur.

H·M·I·A = huic monumento itus actus.

H·S·B·Q = hic situs bene quiescat.

H·S·O·B = hic situs; ossa bene.

H·V·V·S = Herculi victori votum solvit.

H·A·S·F·C = heres a se faciundum curavit.

H·C·E·C·E·B·Q = hic conditus est; cineres ei bene quiescant.

H·C·S·P·P = honore contentus sua pecunia posuit.

H·L·D·M·A = huic loco dolus malus abesto.

H·L·S·H·N·S = hic locus sepulturae heredem non sequetur.

H·L·T·C·S = hunc locum tessellavit cum suis.

H·M·A·H·N·P = hoc monumentum ad heredes non pertinebit.

H·M·D·M·A·B·M·M·C = huic monumento dolus malus abesto, bene merenti memoriae causa.

H·M·S·S·H·N·S = hoc monumentum, sive sepulcrum, heredem non sequetur.

H·O·T·B·Q = hic ossa tibi bene quiescant.

H·S·E·S·T·T·L = hic situs est, sit tibi terra levis.

H·S·E·T·F·I·H·F·C = hic situs est, titulum fieri iussit, heres faciundum curavit.

H·S·H·A·N·L = hoc sepulcrum heredibus abalienare non licet.

H·V·O·B·Q = hic volo ossa bene quiescant.

H·V·S·R·L·D·D·D = honore usus sumptus remisit, loco dato decreto decurionum.

Habēna. (1) (ἡνίαι). Mostly in the plural. Reins for driving; hence ἡνίοχος, a charioteer or driver. (2) (ῥυταγωγεύς). A halter-rope (Ammian. xix. 8, 7). (3) The sheets of a sail—i. e. the ropes by which the lower ends of the sail are braced or slacked (Val. Flacc. iv. 679). (4) The word is also used in general of any strap or thong, as the strap of a spear (see Amentum), the thong of a sandal (Gell. xiii. 21, 2), of a helmet (Val. Flacc. vi. 365), the thong of a whip (Ovid, *Her.* ix. 81), and in medicine, a bandage (Suet. *Aug.* 80).

Hades (ᾍδης). According to the belief current among the Greeks, the world of the dead, or the abode of Hades, with its wide doors, was in the depths of the earth. In the *Odyssey*, its entrance and outer court were on the western side of the river Oceanus, in the ground sacred to Persephoné, with its grove of barren willows and poplars. Here was the home of the Cimmerians, veiled in darkness and cloud, where the sun never shines. This court, and indeed the lower world in general, is a meadow of asphodel, an unattractive weed of dreary aspect usually planted on graves. The actual abode of the subterranean powers is Erebus (Ἔρεβος), or the impenetrable darkness. In later times entrances to the lower world were imagined in other places where there were cavernous hollows which looked as if they led into the bowels of the earth. Such places were Hermioné and the promontory of Taenarum in the Peloponnesus, Heraclea on the Euxine, and Cumae in Italy, where the mythical Cimmerii were also localized. The lower world of Homer is intersected by great rivers—the Styx, Acheron ("river of woe"), Cocytus ("river of wailing"), a branch of the Styx, Phlegethon and Pyriphlegethon ("rivers of fire"). The last two unite and join the waters of the Acheron. In the post-Homeric legend, these rivers are represented as surrounding the infernal regions, and another river appears with them, that of Lethé, or oblivion. In the waters of Lethé the souls of the dead drank forgetfulness of their earthly existence. The lower world once conceived as separated from the upper by these rivers, the idea of a ferryman arose. This was Charon (q. v.), the son of Erebus and of Nyx, a gloomy, sullen old man, who took the souls in his boat across Acheron into the realm of shadows. The souls were brought down from the upper world by Hermes, and paid the ferryman an obolus, which was put for this purpose into the mouths of the dead. Charon had the right to refuse a passage to souls whose bodies had not been duly buried. (See Funus, p. 697.) In Homer it is the spirits themselves who refuse to receive any one to whom funeral honours have not been paid. At the gate lies the dog Cerberus, son of Typhaon and Echidna. He is a terrible monster with three heads, and mane and tail of snakes. He is friendly to the spirits who enter, but if any one tries to escape he seizes him and holds him fast.

The ghosts of the dead were in ancient times conceived as incorporeal images of their former selves, without mind or consciousness. In the *Odyssey* the seer Tiresias is the only one who has retained his consciousness and judgment, and this as an exceptional gift of Persephoné. But they have the power of drinking the blood of animals, and having done so they recover their consciousness and power of speech. The soul, therefore, is not conceived as entirely annihilated. The ghosts retain the outer form of their body, and follow, but instinctively only, what was their favourite pursuit in life. Orion in Homer is still a hunter, Minos sits in judgment, as when alive. Perhaps the punishments inflicted in Homer on Tityus, Tantalus, and Sisyphus (Ixion, the Danaides, Pirithoüs, and others belong to a later story) should be regarded in this light. The penalties inflicted on them in the upper world may be merely transferred by Homer to their ghostly existence; for the idea of a sensible punishment is not consistent with that of an unconscious continuance in being. It must be remembered, at the same time, that Homer several times mentions that the Erinyes punish perjurers after death. It must be concluded, then, that the ancient belief is, in this instance, found side by side with the later and generally received idea that the dead, even without drinking blood, preserved their consciousness and power of speech. Connected with it is the notion that they have the power of influencing men's life on earth in various ways. The most ancient belief knows nothing of future rewards of the righteous, or, indeed, of any complete separation between the just and the unjust, or of a judgment to make the necessary awards. The judges of the dead are in the later legend Minos, Rhadamanthys, Aeacus, and Triptolemus. It was a later age, too, which transferred Elysium and Tartarus to the lower world—Elysium as the abode of the blessed, and Tartarus as that of the damned. In the earlier belief these regions had nothing to do with the realm of Hades. The name Tartarus (Τάρταρος) was in later times often applied to the whole of the lower world. The spirits of those who had lived a life of average merit were imagined as wandering on the asphodel meadow. See in English literature the *Epic of Hades*, by Lewis Morris, and *Ades, King of Hell*, by Buchanan.

In general it must be said that the ancient ideas of a future life were always subject to considerable changes, owing to the influence of the doctrines taught in the mysteries, and the representations of poets, philosophers, sculptors, and painters. (See POLYGNOTUS.) The general tendency was to multiply the terrors of Hades, especially at the gates and in Tartarus. (For the deities of the lower world, see EUMENIDES; HADES; PERSEPHONÉ.) The Greek beliefs on the subject found their way to Rome through the instrumentality of the poets, especially Vergil; but they did not entirely supplant the national traditions. See Alger, *Critical History of the Doctrine of a Future Life*, with an exhaustive bibliography of the subject (10th ed. Boston, 1880); Ettig, *Acheruntica* (Leipzig, 1891); and the articles LARES; LARVAE; MANES; MANIA; ORCUS.

Hades (Ἀΐδης; Attic, Ἅιδης or ᾅδης [ἀϊδής]). In Greek mythology, the son of Cronus and Rhea, who received the dominion of the lower world at the division of the universe after the fall of Cronus, his brothers, Zeus and Poseidon, being made lords respectively of the sky and sea. With his queen Persephoné he held sway over the other powers of the infernal regions, and over the ghosts of the dead. The symbol of his invisible empire was the helmet that made men invisible. This was given to him by the Cyclopes to aid him in the battle of the gods with the Giants. Originally he was, to all appearance, conceived as bringing down the dead himself to the lower world in his chariot, or as driving them down with his staff; but in the later belief the office of conductor of souls belonged to Hermes. Hades is the enemy of all life, heartless and inexorable, and hated, accordingly, by gods and men. Sacrifice and prayer are of no avail with him, and he is therefore only worshipped on exceptional occasions. But, like Persephoné, he was sometimes represented in a milder light, being called Pluto (Πλούτων, Πλοῦτος), or the giver of wealth. This because it is from the depths of the earth that corn and its attendant blessings are produced. As old as Hesiod is the advice to the plougher to call upon Zeus of the lower world, as well as upon Demeter. He is also styled Polydectes and Polydegmon, as receiving at last all men in his realms.

Hades. (Palazzo Chigi, Rome.)

The most celebrated of the myths referring to Hades is that of the rape of Persephoné. In works of art he is represented as resembling his brothers Zeus and Poseidon, but with gloomy features and hair falling over his brow, the key of the infernal world in his hand, and the dog Cerberus at his side. Sometimes he appears as a god of agriculture, with a cornucopia, or a two-pronged pickaxe. The plants sacred to him were the cypress and the narcissus; black sheep were offered to him in sacrifice. When mortals invoked him, they struck the earth with the hand.

By the Romans Hades was identified partly with Orcus, partly with Dis.

Hadrānum (Ἄδρανον). A town of Sicily, near Mount Aetna, having in its vicinity a river of the name of Hadranus. It was founded by Dionysius (Diod. Sic. xiv. 38).

Hadria. See HADRIATICUM MARE.

Hadrianopŏlis (Ἁδριανόπολις). The modern Adrianople. A town in Thrace, on the right bank of the Hebrus, situated in an extensive plain, founded by the emperor Hadrian. In the Middle Ages it ranked second to Constantinople alone.

Hadriānus, PUBLIUS AELIUS. (1) A Roman emperor, born at Rome A.D. 76. He lost his father when ten years of age, and had for his guardians Trajan, who was his relation, and Cornelius Tatianus, a Roman knight. His father's name was Aelius Hadrianus Afer. It is conjectured that the surname of Afer was given the latter because he had been governor of Africa, and that he is the same Hadrianus who put the martyr Leontius to death at Tripolis in the reign of Vespasian. Hadrian's father was Trajan's first cousin; for he was the son of Ulpia, the sister of Marcus Ulpius Trajanus, the emperor Trajan's father. Hadrian began very early to serve in the army, and was tri-

Coin of Hadrian.

bune of a legion before Domitian's death. The forces in Lower Moesia chose him to congratulate Trajan upon his being adopted by Nerva, and it was he that acquainted Trajan with the first news of Nerva's death. He regained the emperor's favour, which he had almost entirely lost by his extravagant expenses and the debts which he had in consequence incurred, and finally married Trajan's grandniece, Sabina, chiefly through the aid of Plotina the empress. His subsequent rise was rapid, and he was the companion of Trajan in most of his expeditions. He particularly distinguished himself in the war against the Dacians, and was successively appointed praetor, governor of Pannonia, and consul. The orations he composed for Trajan increased his fame (Spart. *Hadr.*). After the siege of Atra, in Arabia, Trajan left him in command of his army, and when he found his death approaching, adopted him, although the reality of this adoption is disputed by some authorities, who attribute his elevation to the intrigues of Plotina.

On the death of Trajan he assumed the reins of government (A.D. 117), with the concurrence of the Syrian army. The Senate readily ratified the act. The first care of Hadrian was to make a peace with the Persians, and to restore all the provinces just taken from them, making the Euphrates the boundary of the Roman Empire. He had then to turn his attention to certain revolts and insurrections in Egypt, Libya, and Palestine; and, after quickly concluding a peace with the Parthians, returned to Rome, A.D. 118. The Senate decreed him a triumph, and honoured him with the title of Pater Patriae; but he refused both, and required that Trajan's image should triumph. He sought popularity by a repeal of fifteen years accumulation of arrears of public debt, by a vast reduction of taxation generally and by immense largesses to the people. He was less generous to certain senators accused of a plot against him, four of whom, although of consular rank and intimates of Trajan, he caused to be put to death.

A year after his return to Rome, Hadrian marched against the Alani, the Sarmatians, and the Dacians, but showed a greater desire to make peace with the barbarians than to extend the prowess of the Roman arms. This policy has been attributed to envy of the fame of his warlike predecessor; but a due consideration of the subsequent history of the Empire will amply justify him against the imputation; for it had reached an extent which rendered all increase to its limits a source of weakness rather than of strength. Hadrian was an active and incessant traveller, visiting every province in the Empire, not simply to indulge his curiosity, but to inspect the administration of government, repress abuses, erect and repair public edifices, and exercise all the vigilance of personal examination. (See Dürr, *Die Reisen des Kaisers Hadrian* [Vienna, 1881]). In A.D. 120, he passed over from Gaul to Britain, where he caused a wall to be built from the mouth of the Tyne to Solway Frith, in order to secure the Roman provinces from the incursions of the Caledonians.

Like Trajan, he lived familiarly with his friends, but was much more suspicious, and would not repose in them the same confidence. When at Rome he cultivated all kinds of literature, conversing with learned men, and giving and receiving information in their society. Hadrian had once again to visit the East to repress the Parthians, who paid little regard to treaties. On his return he passed the winter at Athens, and was initiated in the Eleusinian Mysteries. He published no edict against the Christians, yet they nevertheless suffered considerable persecution, until, upon the remonstrance of Quadratus, bishop of Athens, and Aristides, an eminent Christian, he ordered the persecution to cease; but no credit is due to the unauthorized assertion of Lampridius that he thought of building a temple to the Saviour. His treatment of the Jews, on the other hand, was extremely severe, though ample provocation had been given by that turbulent people, for they had raised disturbances towards the end of Trajan's reign, which were not completely quelled until the second year of Hadrian. But now a more formidable insurrection broke out under Barcochebas ("Son of a Star"), who, though a robber by profession, had given himself out as the Messiah. It required a war of three years to reduce the revolted Jews to complete subjection, and after this was accom-

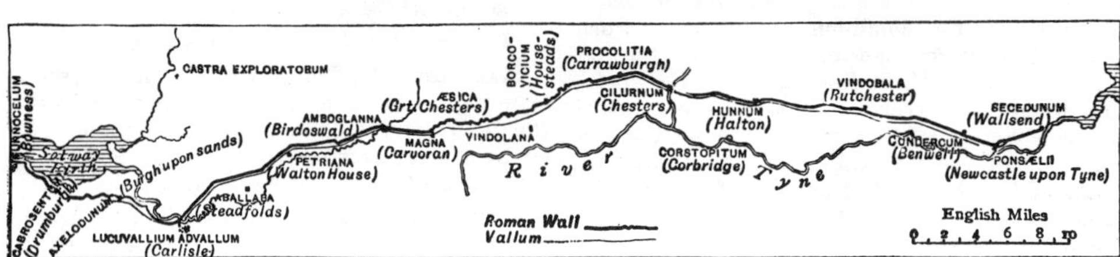

Map of Hadrian's Wall, with the chief Stations. (After Collingwood Bruce.)

plished, there was scarcely any indignity that was not inflicted on the conquered nation. Jerusalem was rebuilt under the new title of Aelia Capitolina, uniting the family name of the emperor with

Hadrian. (British Museum.)

the Roman surname of Iupiter; and in the execution of his plan Hadrian studiously profaned all the places which had been most revered by both Jews and Christians, whom he seems to have confounded together. He built a temple in honour of Iupiter Capitolinus upon the mountain where had stood that of the true God; placed a marble hog upon that gate of the city which looked towards Bethlehem; erected in the place where Jesus was crucified a statue of Venus; and in that where he rose from the dead, an image of Iupiter. In the grotto of Bethlehem, where the Saviour was born, he established the worship of Adonis. The Jews were also forbidden the very sight of Jerusalem, which they were not permitted to enter save on one day in the year—the anniversary of the destruction of the city. After the conclusion of the Jewish War Hadrian returned to Italy, where a lingering illness put a stop to his unsettled mode of life, and eventually terminated his existence. Having no children of his own, Hadrian first adopted for his successor L. Ceionius Commodus, more generally known by the name of Verus, to which last he prefixed that of Aelius after his adoption by the emperor. Verus, however, who was remarkable for nothing but his excessive effeminacy and debauched mode of life, died soon after, and Hadrian made a very excellent selection in the person of Antoninus. (See ANTONINUS PIUS.) Hadrian died not long after at Baiae, A.D. 138, in the sixty-third year of his age and the twenty-second of his reign. His disorder was the dropsy, from which disease his sufferings were so great as apparently to affect his reason.

Hadrian was, in general, a just and able ruler, yet there were times when he showed himself revengeful, suspicious, and cruel. His treatment of his wife Sabina does no honour to his memory, his passion for Antinoüs (q. v.) taints it; while his excessive superstition, to which even that favourite fell a victim, entitles him to a large measure of contempt. He was, in fact, a peculiar character, full of paradoxes—witty, pedantic, droll, dull, impulsive, sociable, suspicious, morbidly self-conscious, and persevering in nothing. The greater portion of the Romans appear to have formed a just estimate of his character long before his death, and it was with difficulty that Antoninus could obtain from the Senate the usual compliment of having him ranked among the gods. Their dread of the soldiery, by whom Hadrian was greatly beloved, appears to have conquered their reluctance.

Hadrian did much towards restoring and improving the city of Rome. He also erected a splendid temple to Trajan, a temple to Venus and Roma, and the great Mausoleum in the district beyond the Tiber, now known as the Castle of St. Angelo. In this, he and a number of his successors were buried. For an illustration of it see the article MAUSOLEUM.

Hadrian wrote several works. He was fond of entering the lists against the poets, philosophers, and orators of the day, and Photius mentions several declamations of the emperor's, written for such occasions, as still existing in his time, and not devoid of elegance. Hadrian composed a history of his own times, which he published under the name of his freedman Phlegon; and Doritheus the grammarian made at a subsequent period a collection of his decisions and rescripts. All that we have of his productions at the present day are some speeches, decrees, and (Greek) epigrams, and an epigrammatic address to his soul, written a

Ruins of the Temple of Venus and Roma, built by Hadrian.

short time before his death, and remarkable for its beauty. It suggested to Pope his "Vital spark of heavenly flame," and runs as follows:

"Animula, vagula, blandula,
Hospes comesque corporis,
Quae nunc abibis in loca.
Pallidula, rigida, nudula,
Nec, ut soles, dabis jocos?"

(Spart. *Hadr.* 25.) See Gregorovius, *Geschichte des Kaisers Hadrianus* (1851).

(2) A philosopher of Tyre, who studied under Herodes, and taught rhetoric after him at Athens. He was also secretary to the emperor Commodus (ἀντιγραφεὺς τῶν ἐπιστολῶν). He died at Rome after having attained the age of eighty years. There are only fragments remaining of the works of this writer.

Hadriatĭcum Mare. The Adriatic Sea (ὁ Ἀδρίας), properly called by the Romans MARE SUPĔRUM or Upper Sea, as opposed to the Mare Inferum or Tyrrhenian Sea. The Romans also, in imitation of the Greeks, used the feminine form HADRIA or ADRIA. The Adriatic separated Italy from Illyricum, Dalmatia, and Epirus, and is connected at its southern extremity with the Ionian Sea. It was first explored by the Phocaeans of the Greeks (Herod. i. 163). The ancient writers frequently speak of it as dreaded by sailors for its sudden storms (Hor. *Carm.* i. 3, 15; iii. 9, 23, etc.). The name is derived from the Etruscan city Hatria, at the mouth of the Padus (Po).

Hadrumētum or **Adrumētum** (Ἀδρούμητον). A flourishing city founded by the Phœnicians in North Africa, and the capital of Bycazena under the Romans.

Haemon (Αἵμων). (1) The son of Pelasgus and father of Thessalus, from whom the ancient name of Thessaly, Haemonia or Aemonia, was believed to be derived. The Roman poets frequently use the adjective Haemonius as equivalent to Thessalicus. (2) Son of Creon of Thebes, and in love with Antigoné. He killed himself on hearing that she had been condemned by his father to be entombed alive.

Haemonia (Αἱμονία). See HAEMON.

Haemus (Αἶμος). The modern Balkans. A lofty range of mountains separating Thrace and Moesia. The pass over them most used in antiquity was in the western part of the range, called Succi or Succorum Angustiae, also Porta Traiani (Sulu Derbend), between Philippopolis and Serdica. The fabulous origin of the range is that Haemus and his wife Rhodopé were changed into mountains for daring to call themselves Zeus and Heré (Ovid, *Met.* vi. 87).

Haeres. See HERES.

Hagnus (Ἁγνοῦς). A deme of Attica, west of Paeania, and belonging to the tribe Acamantis.

Hair. See COMA.

Hairdressers. See TONSOR.

Hairpins. See ACUS.

Halae (Ἁλαί). (1) HALAE ARAPHENĬDES (Ἀραφηνίδες). A deme of Attica belonging to the tribe Aegeïs. It served as the harbour of Brauron and possessed a temple of Artemis. (2) HALAE AEXONĬDES (Αἰξωνίδες). A deme of Attica belonging to the tribe Cecropis. It was situated on the western coast. (3) A town on the Opuntian Gulf.

Halcyŏné or **Alcyŏné** (Ἀλκυόνη). (1) A Pleiad, daughter of Atlas and Pleioné, and beloved by Poseidon. (2) Daughter of Aeolus and Enareté or Aegialé, and wife of Ceÿx. They lived so happily that they were presumptuous enough to call each other Zeus and Heré, for which Zeus metamorphosed them into birds. Others relate that Ceÿx perished in a shipwreck; that Alcyoné, for grief, threw herself into the sea; and that the gods, out of compassion, changed the two into birds. It was fabled that during the seven days before, and as many after, the shortest day of the year, while the female bird was breeding, there always prevailed calms at sea—hence our expression "halcyon days." For the use of this myth in English literature, see F. Tennyson's *Halcyone;* E. W. Gosse, *Alcyone* (a sonnet in dialogue); and Mrs. Preston's *Alcyone.*

Hales (Ἄλης). (1) A river of Ionia, near Colophon, famous for the coldness of its water. (2) A river in the island of Cos.

Halēsa or **Alaesa** (Ἄλαισα). A town on the northern coast of Sicily, on the river Halesus, founded by the Greek mercenaries of Archonides, a chief of the Siculi, and originally called ARCHONIDION.

Halēsus. A chief of the Auruncans and Oscans, the son of a soothsayer, and an ally of Turnus, slain by Evander. He came to Italy from Argos in Greece, whence he is called Agamemnonius, Atrides, or Argolicus. He is said to have founded Falerii (Serv. *ad.* Verg. *Aen.* vii. 723).

Half-uncials. See PALAEOGRAPHY.

Halia (ἁλία). The Spartan Assembly.

Halia. See HELIOS, p. 780.

Haliacmon (Ἁλιάκμων). The modern Vistriza. An important river in Macedonia, rising in the Tymphaean mountains, forming the boundary between Eordaea and Pieria, and falling into the Thermaic Gulf. Caesar incorrectly makes it the boundary between Macedonia and Thessaly.

Haliartus (Ἁλίαρτος). An ancient town in Boeotia, south of the lake Copaïs, destroyed by Xerxes in his invasion of Greece (B.C. 480), but afterwards rebuilt. Under its walls Lysander lost his life (395).

Halias (Ἁλίας). A district on the coast of Argolis between Asiné and Hermioné, so called because fishing was the chief occupation of its inhabitants. Their town was called Haliae or Halies.

Halicarnassus (Ἁλικαρνασσός). The modern Budrum. A celebrated city of Asia Minor, stood in the southwestern part of Caria, opposite to the island of Cos. It was founded by Dorians from Troezen. With the rest of the coast of Asia Minor it fell under the dominion of the Persians, at an early period of whose rule Lygdamis made himself tyrant of the city, and founded a dynasty which lasted for some generations. His daughter Artemisia assisted Xerxes in his expedition against Greece. Halicarnassus was celebrated for the Mausoleum, a magnificent edifice which Artemisia II. built as a tomb for her husband Mausolus (B.C. 352), and which was adorned with the works of the most eminent Greek sculptors of the age. (See ARCHITECTURA.) Fragments of these sculptures, which were discovered built into the walls of the citadel of Budrum, are now in the British Museum. Halicarnassus was the birthplace of the historians Herodotus and Dionysius. See Newton, *Discoveries at Halicarnassus* (1862–63).

Halicȳae (Ἁλικύαι). A town in the northwest of Sicily, between Entella and Lilybaeum, long in the possession of the Carthaginians.

Halĭmus (Ἁλιμοῦς). A deme of Attica, a little south of Athens, and belonging to the tribe Leontis.

Halipĕdon (Ἁλίπεδον). A plain near the Piraeus in Attica.

Halirrhothius (Ἁλιρρόθιος). The son of Poseidon and Euryté, who attempted to violate Alcippé, daughter of Ares and Agraulos, but was slain by Ares. Ares was brought to trial by Poseidon for this murder, on the hill at Athens, which was hence called Areopagus, or Hill of Ares.

Haliūsa (Ἁλιοῦσα). Now Karavi; an island in the Argolic Gulf.

Halizōnes (Ἁλιζῶνες). A people of Bithynia, with a capital city Alybé (*Il.* ii. 856).

Halm, Karl. A distinguished classical scholar, born at Munich in 1809. He was educated at the University of Munich, and from 1839 to 1849 taught in Speier and Hadamar. In 1849 he was made Rector of the Maximilians Gymnasium at Munich, and in 1856 Professor of Classical Philology in the University of Munich and Director of the Royal Library. He died at Munich, October 10th, 1882. His principal works are critical editions of Cicero (1845–56), Quintilian (1868–69), Cornelius Nepos (1871); Cicero's Orations, with a commentary (1845-1848), and selected orations (1854–66); the fables of Aesop in the Teubner series (1852); Florus (1854); and Tacitus (4th ed. 1883). Among his shorter treatises are the *Lectiones Stobenses* (1841–42); a catalogue of the Fathers of the Latin Church (1865); and a most valuable catalogue of the Library at Munich (1876–81).

Halma (ἅλμα). See Pentathlon.

Halmydessus. See Salmydessus.

Halmȳris (Ἁλμυρίς, sc. λίμην). A bay of Moesia formed by the southern mouth of the Danube. Upon it was situated a town of the same name.

Halonnēsus (Ἁλόννησος), and **Halonēsus** (Ἁλόνησος). An island of the Aegaean Sea, off the coast of Thessaly, and east of Sciathos and Peparethos, with a town of the same name upon it. The possession of this island occasioned great disputes between Philip and the Athenians: there is a speech on this subject among the extant orations of Demosthenes, but probably written by Hegesippus. See Philippus.

Halosydné (Ἁλοσύδνη). "Sea-born." An epithet applied to Thetis and to Aphrodité.

Athlete with Halteres. (Tassie.)

Haltēres (ἁλτῆρες). Heavy weights of stone or lead, like our dumb bells, intended to increase the muscular exertion of gymnastic exercises, being held in each hand while leaping, running, dancing, etc. (Mart. vii. 67; xiv. 49).

Haluntium. See Aluntium.

Halus. See Alus.

Halȳcus (Ἅλυκος). A river in the south of Sicily, flowing into the sea near Heraclea Minoa.

Halys (Ἅλυς). The modern Kizil-Irmak, i. e. "Red River;" the greatest river of Asia Minor, rising in the Anti-Taurus range of mountains, on the borders of Armenia Minor and Pontus, and after flowing through Cappadocia and Galatia, and dividing Paphlagonia from Pontus, falling into the Euxine Sea between Sinopé and Amisus. In early times it divided the Indo-European races which peopled the western part of Asia Minor from the Semitic (Syro-Arabian) races of the rest of southwest Asia; and it separated the Lydian Empire from the Medo-Persian (Herod. i. 6).

Hamadryădes (Ἁμαδρυάδες). See Nymphae.

Hamaxa (ἅμαξα). See Currus.

Hamaxĭtus (Ἁμαξιτός). A small town on the coast of the Troad. See Smintheus.

Hamaxobii (Ἁμαξόβιοι). A people in European Sarmatia, in the neighbourhood of the Palus Maeotis, were a nomad race, as their name, "dwellers in chariots," signifies.

Hamilcar (Ἀμίλκας). (1) A Carthaginian general, son of Mago, or, according to others, of Hanno, conquered by Gelon, in Sicily, the same day that Xerxes was defeated at Salamis. Herodotus (vii. 165) states that he was never seen either living or dead after the battle in which his army was defeated. According to Polyaenus, however (i. 27, 2), Gelon destroyed him by a stratagem while sacrificing. (2) Surnamed Rhodănus, a Carthaginian general of considerable talent. Perceiving his fellow-citizens to be greatly disquieted at the projects of Alexander of Macedon (B.C. 332), he betook himself to that prince, in order, if possible, to penetrate his designs, and give his countrymen timely notice of them. After the death of Alexander he returned to Carthage, where he was put to death, on false accusations of treason, as the recompense of his devotion to his country (Just. xxi. 5). (3) A Carthaginian general, in the time of Agathocles, tyrant of Sicily. He came to the succour of Syracuse when besieged by that usurper. Being gained over, however, by the gold of Agathocles, he prevailed on the Syracusans to make peace, and favoured by his inaction the schemes of the tyrant. The Carthaginian Senate condemned him to lose his head, but he died at Syracuse, B.C. 311, before the sentence could be made public (Just. xxii. 2). (4) The son of Giscon; a Carthaginian general, sent into Sicily about B.C. 311, to oppose the progress of Agathocles. On his arrival he gained a victory, which opened to him the gates of several large cities. In attempting to make himself master of Syracuse, during the absence of Agathocles in Africa, he was taken prisoner and put to death, B.C. 309. (5) Surnamed Barca, the leader of the popular party at Carthage, appointed in the eighteenth year of the First Punic War (B.C. 247) to the command of the Carthaginian armies. No particulars have been preserved respecting his early life or the time of his birth; but it is learned from Nepos (*Hamil.* 1) that he was very young when he obtained the command. He ravaged with his fleet the coast of the Bruttii and the Epizephyrian Locrians, and afterwards seized upon a strong fortress in Sicily, which was situated between Eryx and Panormus. In this place he continued for some years, with very little support from the Carthaginian government; and, although the Romans were masters of almost the whole of the island, they were unable to dislodge him. He frequently ravaged the southern coasts of Italy as far as Cumae, and defeated the Roman troops in Sicily. On one occasion he took Eryx, which he held till the conclusion of the war. The Romans at length fitted out a fleet to cut off all communication between Hamilcar and Carthage; the Carthaginian fleet sent to his assistance was defeated by the Roman consul Lutatius Catulus (B.C. 241), and the Carthaginians were obliged to sue for peace. This was granted by the Romans; and Hamilcar led his troops from Eryx to Lilybaeum, whence they were conveyed to Africa. But a new danger awaited Carthage. The Carthaginian treasury was exhausted; and it was proposed to the troops that they should relinquish a part of the pay which was due to them. The soldiers rejected the proposal, appointed two of their number, Spendius and Matho, commanders, and proceeded to enforce their demands. Being joined by many of the native tribes of Africa, they defeated Hanno, the Carthaginian general sent against them, and brought Carthage to the brink of ruin. In these desperate circumstances Hamilcar was appointed to the command, and at length succeeded in subduing them after the war had lasted three years and four months. After the end of this war Hamilcar was sent into Spain (B.C. 238). He remained in Spain nearly nine years, during which time he extended the dominion of Carthage over the southern and eastern parts of that country. He fell in a battle against the natives (B.C. 229), leaving three sons, Hasdrubal, Mago, and Hannibal.

The abilities of Hamilcar were of the highest order; and he directed all the energies of his mind to diminish the power of Rome. Polybius states his belief (Bk. iii.) that his administration would soon have produced another war with the Romans, if he had not been prevented by the disorders in which his country was involved through the war of the mercenaries. Hamilcar was succeeded in his command in Spain by his son-in-law Hasdrubal, who must not be confounded with Hasdrubal, the brother of Hannibal. See Polyb. i., ii.; Corn. Nep. *Hamil.* 3, and the striking picture given in Flaubert's novel, *Salammbô.* (6) A Carthaginian general, son of Bomilcar, conquered by the Scipios (B.C. 215) when besieging Ilitingis, in Hispania Baetica, along with Hasdrubal and Mago. He is supposed by some to be the same with the Hamilcar who, fifteen years after, at the head of a body of Gauls, took and sacked Placentia, and was defeated and slain before Cremona. Others affirm that he was taken prisoner three years later in a battle fought near the Mincius, and served to grace the victory of the conqueror (Livy, xxiii. 49; xxxi. 10; xxxii. 23; Pliny, *H. N.* iii. 1).

Hammer. See MALLEUS.

Hamper. See CORBIS.

Hamus (*ἄγκιστρον*). A fish-hook, made by the ancients in shapes precisely like our own.

Hand, FERDINAND GOTTHELF. A German classical scholar born at Plauen in Saxony, 1786. He was Professor of Classical Philology at the Gymnasium of Weimar (1810–17), and in 1817 was transferred to the University of Jena as Professor of Greek Literature. In the same year he was made Aulic Counsellor, and Con-rector of the philological seminary. He died at Jena in 1851. He is best remembered by his treatise, in four vols., *De Particulis Latinis Commentarii* (Leipzig, 1829–45).

Hanging Gardens. See HORTUS.

Hannĭbal (Ἀννίβας, equivalent in Punic to *gratia Baalis;* cf. the Biblical *Hanniel*). (1) The son of Gisco who in B.C. 409 aided the Segestans against the Selinuntines. He took Selinus and Himera, but died in 406 while besieging Agrigentum. (2) Son of Gisco, the commander of Lilybaeum at the close of the First Punic War. He was besieged in Agrigentum by the Romans in B.C. 262, but broke through the lines and escaped. He ravaged the coast of Italy, was defeated by Duilius (260), and failed in the defence of Sardinia (259), being soon after slain by his mutinous soldiers. (3) Son of Hamilcar Barca (see HAMILCAR), and born in B.C. 247. At the age of nine he went to Spain with his father, who, previous to his departure, took his son to the altar, and, placing his hand on the sacrifice, made him swear that he would never be a friend to the Romans. It does not appear how long Hannibal remained in Spain, but he was at a very early age associated with Hasdrubal, who succeeded his father in the command of the Carthaginian army in that country.

On the death of Hasdrubal, B.C. 221, he obtained the undivided command of the army, and quickly conquered the Olcades, Vaccaeans, Carpesians and the other Spanish tribes that had not been subdued by Hasdrubal. The inhabitants of Saguntum, alarmed at his success, sent messengers to Rome to inform the Romans of their danger. A Roman embassy was accordingly sent to Hannibal, who was passing the winter at Carthago Nova, to announce to him that the independence of Saguntum was guaranteed by a treaty between the Carthaginians and Romans (concluded B.C. 226), and that they should consider any injury done to the Saguntines as a declaration of war against themselves. Hannibal, however, paid no regard to this remonstrance. More than twenty years had elapsed since the termination of the First Punic War, during which period the Carthaginians had recovered their strength, and had obtained possession of the greater part of Spain; and now a favourable opportunity had arrived for renewing the war with the Romans. In B.C. 219, Hannibal took Saguntum (q. v.) after a siege of eight months, and employed the winter in making preparations for the invasion of Italy. He first provided for the security of Africa and Spain by leaving an army of about 16,000 men in each country. The army in Africa consisted principally of Spanish troops, and that in Spain of Africans, under the command of his brother Hasdrubal. He had already received promises of support from the Gauls who inhabited the north of Italy, and who were anxious to deliver themselves from Roman domination. Having thus made every necessary preparation, he set out from Carthago Nova, late in the spring of B.C. 218, with an army of 80,000 foot and 12,000 horse. In his march from the Iberus to the Pyrenees he was opposed by a great number of the native tribes, but these were quickly defeated, though with loss. Before crossing the Pyrenees, he left

Hanno to secure his recent conquests with a detachment from his own army of 11,000 men. He sent back the same number of Spanish troops to their own cities, and with an army now reduced to 50,000 foot and 9000 horse he advanced to the Rhone.

Meanwhile, two Roman armies had been levied: one, commanded by the consul P. Cornelius Scipio, was intended to oppose Hannibal in Spain; and a second, under the consul T. Sempronius, was designed for the invasion of Africa. The departure of Scipio was delayed by a revolt of the Boian and Insubrian Gauls, against whom was sent the army which had been intended for the invasion of Spain, under the command of one of the praetors. Scipio was therefore obliged to remain in Rome until a new army could be raised. When the forces were ready, he sailed with them to the Rhone, and anchored at the eastern mouth of the river, being persuaded that Hannibal must still be at a considerable distance from him, as the country through which he had to march was difficult, and inhabited by many warlike tribes. Hannibal, however, quickly surmounted all these obstacles, crossed the Rhone, though not without some opposition from the Gauls, and continued his march up the left bank of the river. Scipio did not arrive at the place where the Carthaginians had crossed the river till three days afterwards; and, despairing of overtaking them, he sailed back to Italy with the intention of meeting Hannibal when he should descend from the Alps. Scipio sent his brother Gnaeus into Spain, with the greater part of the troops, to oppose Hasdrubal. Hannibal continued his march up the Rhone till he came to the Isara. Marching along that river, he crossed the Alps, descended into the valley of the Dora Baltea, and followed the course of the river till he arrived in the territories of the Insubrian Gauls. See Troger, *Hannibal's Zug* (Innsbruck, 1878); Buchheister, *Hannibal's Zug über die Alpen* (Hamburg, 1887).

Hannibal. (Von Falke.)

Hannibal completed his march from Carthago Nova to Italy in five months, during which time he lost a great number of men, especially in his passage over the Alps. According to a statement engraved by his order on a column at Lacinium, in the country of the Brutii, which Polybius saw, his army was reduced to 12,000 Africans, 8000 Spaniards, and 6000 cavalry when he arrived in the territories of the Insubrian Gauls. After remaining some time in the neighborhood of the Insubrians to recruit his army, he marched southward, and encountered P. Cornelius Scipio on the right bank of the river Ticinus. In the battle which ensued the Romans were defeated, and Scipio, with the remainder of the army, retreating along the left bank of the Po, crossed the river before Hannibal could overtake him and encamped near Placentia. He afterwards retreated more to the south, and intrenched himself strongly on the right bank of the Trebia, where he waited for the arrival of the army under the other consul, T. Sempronius. Sempronius had already crossed over into Sicily with the intention of sailing to Africa, when he was recalled to join his colleague. After the union of the two armies, Sempronius determined, against the advice of Scipio, to risk another battle. The skill and fortune of Hannibal again prevailed; the Romans were entirely defeated, and the troops who survived took refuge in the fortified cities. In consequence of these victories, the whole of Cisalpine Gaul fell into the hands of Hannibal; and the Gauls, who, on his first arrival, were prevented from joining him by the presence of Scipio's army in their country, now eagerly assisted him with both men and supplies.

In the following year, B.C. 217, the Romans made great preparations to oppose their formidable enemy. Two new armies were levied. One was posted at Arretium, under the command of the consul Flaminius, and the other at Ariminum, under the consul Servilius. Hannibal determined to attack Flaminius first. In his march southward through the swamps of the basin of the Arnus, his army suffered greatly, and he himself lost the sight of one eye. After resting his troops for a short time in the neighbourhood of Faesulae, he marched past Arretium, ravaging the country as he went, with the view of drawing on Flaminius to a battle. Flaminius, who appears to have been a rash, headstrong man, hastily followed Hannibal; and, being attacked in the basin of Lake Trasimenus, was completely defeated by the Carthaginians, who were posted on the mountains which encircle the valley. Three or four days afterwards, Hannibal cut off a detachment of Roman cavalry, amounting to 4000 men, which had been sent by Servilius to assist his colleague. Hannible appears to have entertained hopes of overthrowing the Roman dominion, and to have expected that the other States of Italy would take up arms against Rome, in order to recover their independence. To win over the affections of the Italians, he dismissed without ransom all the prisoners whom he took in battle; and, to give them an opportunity of joining his army, he marched slowly along the eastern side of the peninsula, through Umbria and Picenum, into Apulia; but he did not meet with that co-operation which he appears to have expected. After the defeat of Flaminius, Q. Fabius Maximus was appointed dictator, and a defensive system of warfare was adopted by the Romans for the rest of the year.

In the following year, B.C. 216, the Romans resolved upon another battle. An army of 80,000 foot and 6000 horse was raised, which was commanded by the consuls L. Aemilius Paulus and C. Terentius Varro. The Carthaginian army now amounted to 40,000 foot and 10,000 horse. Both armies were encamped in the neighbourhood of Cannae in Apulia. In the battle which was fought near this place, the Romans were defeated with dreadful carnage, and with a loss which, as stated by Polybius, is quite incredible; the whole of the infantry engaged in battle, amounting to 70,000, was destroyed, with the exception of 3000 men, who escaped to the neighbouring cities, and also all the cavalry, with the exception of 300 belonging to the allies and 70 that escaped with Varro. A detachment of 10,000 foot, which had been sent to surprise the Carthaginian camp, was obliged to surrender as prisoners. The consul L. Aemilius and the two consuls of the former year, Servilius and Attilius, were also among the slain. Hannibal lost only 4000 Gauls, 1500 Africans and Spaniards, and 200 horse. This victory placed the whole of Lower Italy in the power of Hannibal, but it was not followed by such important results as might have been expected. Capua and most of the cities of Campania espoused his cause, but the majority of the Italian States continued true to Rome. The defensive system was now strictly adopted by the Romans, and Hannibal was unable to make any active exertions for the further conquest of Italy till he received a re-enforcement of troops. He was in hopes of obtaining support from Philip of Macedon and from the Syracusans, with both of whom he formed an alliance; but the Romans found means to keep Philip employed in Greece, and Syracuse was besieged and taken by Marcellus, B.C. 214–12. In addition to this, Capua was taken by the Romans, B.C. 211. Hannibal was therefore obliged to depend upon the Carthaginians for help, and Hasdrubal was accordingly ordered to march from Spain to his assistance. Gnaeus Scipio, as already observed, had been left in Spain to oppose Hasdrubal. He was afterwards joined by P. Cornelius Scipio, and the war was carried on with various success for many years, till at length the Roman army was entirely defeated by Hasdrubal, B.C. 212. Both the Scipios fell in the battle. Hasdrubal was now preparing to join his brother, but was prevented by the arrival of the young P. Cornelius Scipio in Spain, B.C. 210, who quickly recovered what the Romans had lost. In B.C. 210 he took Carthago Nova; and it was not till B.C. 207, when the Carthaginians had lost almost all their dominions in Spain, that Hasdrubal set out to join his brother in Italy. He crossed the Alps without meeting with any opposition from the Gauls, and arrived at Placentia before the Romans were aware that he had entered Italy. After besieging this town without success, he continued his march southward; but, before he could effect a junction with Hannibal, he was attacked by the consuls C. Claudius Nero and M. Livius, on the banks of the Metaurus in Umbria; his army was cut to pieces, and he himself fell in the battle. This misfortune obliged Hannibal to act on the defensive; and from this time till his departure from Italy in B.C. 203, he was confined to Bruttium; but, by his superior military skill, he maintained his army in a hostile country without any assistance from his government at home. After effecting the conquest of Spain, Scipio passed over into Africa to carry the war into the enemy's country, B.C. 204. With the assistance of Masinissa, a Numidian prince, he gained two victories over the Carthaginians, who hastily recalled their great commander from Italy to defend his native State. Hannibal landed at Septis, and advanced upon Zama, five days' journey from Carthage towards the west. Here he was entirely defeated by Scipio, B.C. 202; 20,000 Carthaginians fell in the battle, and an equal number were taken prisoners. The Carthaginians were obliged to sue for peace, and thus ended the Second Punic War, B.C. 201. See ZAMA.

After the conclusion of the war, Hannibal vigorously applied himself to correct the abuses which existed in the Carthaginian government. He reduced the power of the perpetual judges (as Livy, xxiii. 46, calls them), and provided for the proper collection of the public revenue, which had been embezzled. He was supported by the people in these reforms; but he incurred the enmity of many powerful men, who represented to the Romans that he was endeavouring to persuade his countrymen to join Antiochus, king of Syria, in a war against them. A Roman embassy was consequently sent to Carthage to demand the punishment of Hannibal as a disturber of the public peace; and Hannibal, aware that he should not be able to resist his enemies supported by the Roman power, escaped from the city and sailed to Tyre. From Tyre he went to Ephesus to join Antiochus, B.C. 196, and contributed to fix him in his determination to make war against the Romans. If Hannibal's advice as to the conduct of the war had been followed, the result of the contest might have been different; but he was only employed in a subordinate command, and had no opportunity for the exertion of his great military talents. At the conclusion of this war Hannibal was obliged to seek refuge at the court of Prusias, king of Bithynia, where he remained about five years, and on one occasion obtained a victory over Eumenes, king of Pergamus. But the Romans appear to have been uneasy so long as their once formidable enemy was alive. An embassy was sent to demand him of Prusias, who, being afraid of offending the Romans, agreed to give him up. To avoid falling into the hands of his ungenerous enemies, Hannibal destroyed himself by poison at Nicomedia in Bithynia, B.C. 183, in the sixty-fifth year of his age.

The personal character of Hannibal is known to us only from the events of his public life, and even these have not been recorded by any historian of his own country; yet we cannot read the history of these campaigns, even in the narrative of his enemies, without admiring his great abilities and courage. Polybius remarks: "How wonderful is it that in the course of sixteen years, during which he maintained the war in Italy, he should never once dismiss his army from the field, and yet be able, like a good governor, to keep in subjection so great a multitude, and to confine them within the bounds of their duty, so that they never mutinied against him nor quarrelled among themselves. Though his army was composed of people of various countries—of Africans, Spaniards, Gauls, Carthaginians, Italians, and Greeks—men who had different laws, different customs, and different languages, and, in a word, nothing among them that was common—yet, so dexterous was his management that, notwithstanding this great diversity, he forced all of them to acknowledge one authority, and to yield obedience to one command. And this, too, he accomplished in the midst of very varied fortune. How high as well as just an opinion must these things convey to us of his ability in war! It may be affirmed with confidence that if he had first tried his strength in the other parts of the world and had come last to attack the Romans, he could scarcely have failed in any part of his design" (Polyb. iii.; vii. 8, 9; xiv. 16; Livy, xxi. 39; Nepos, *Hannibal*).

See Hennebert, *Histoire d'Annibal* (Paris, 1870–78); Church, *Carthage* (London, 1886); Krumbholz, *D. Alpenübergang d. Hannibal* (Dresden, 1872); Maissiat, *Annibal en Gaule* (Paris, 1874); De Vaudancourt, *Hist. des Campagnes d'Annibal en Italie*, 3 vols. (Milan, 1812); Perrin, *La Marche d'Annibal des Pyrénées au Pô*, with map (Paris, 1887); Dodge, *Hannibal* (New York, 1891); Mommsen, *Hist. of Rome*, vol. ii.; and the articles CANNAE; CARTHAGO; PUNIC WARS; SCIPIO.

Hannibaliānus. The son of Constantius Chlorus and Theodora, and hence half-brother to Constantine the Great, by whom he was put to death in A.D. 337 with the other members of the Flavian house whose existence was supposed to menace the interests of the new Augusti. See CONSTANTINUS.

Hanno (Ἄννων, meaning in Punic "merciful" or "mild"). (1) A commander sent by the Carthaginians on a voyage of colonization and discovery along the Atlantic coast of Africa. This expedition is generally supposed to have taken place about B.C. 570. Gail, however, places it between B.C. 633 and 530. On his return to Carthage, Hanno deposited an account of his voyage in the temple of Moloch (Cronus). A translation of this account from the Punic into the Greek tongue has come down to us. The title of the Greek work is as follows: Ἄννωνος, Καρχηδονίων Βασιλέως, Περίπλους τῶν ὑπὲρ τὰς Ἡρακλέους Στήλας Λιβυκῶν τῆς Γῆς Μερῶν, ὃν καὶ Ἀνέθηκεν ἐν τῷ τοῦ Κρόνου Τεμένει. "The Voyage of Hanno, commander of the Carthaginians, round the parts of Libya beyond the Pillars of Heracles, which he deposited in the temple of Cronus." With regard to the extent of coast actually explored by this expedition, some remarks have been made in another article. (See AFRICA.) The *Periplus* was translated into English by Falconer (1797). See Mer, *Mémoire sur le Périple d'Hannon* (Paris, 1888); and Antichan, *Les Grands Voyages de Découvertes des Anciens* (Paris, 1891). (2) A Carthaginian commander, who aspired to the sovereignty of his native city. His design was discovered, and he thereupon retired to a fortress, with 20,000 armed slaves, but was taken and put to death with his son and all his relations (Just. xxi. 4). (3) A commander of the Carthaginian forces in Sicily along with Bomilcar (B.C. 310). He was defeated by Agathocles, although he had 45,000 men under his orders, and his opponent only about 14,000 (Just. xxii. 6). (4) A Carthaginian commander, defeated by the Romans near the Aegades Insulae (B.C. 242). On his return home he was put to death. (5) A leader of the faction at Carthage opposed to the Barca family. He voted for surrendering Hannibal to the foe, after the ruin of Saguntum, and also for refusing assistance to that commander after the battle of Cannae (Livy, xxi. 3, xxiii. 12). (6) A Carthaginian, who, wishing to pass for a god, trained up some birds, who were taught by him to repeat the words, "Hanno is a god" (Aelian, *Var. Hist.* xv. 32).

Haplography, also called **Lipography**. A common error found in classical MSS. by which a letter, syllable, or word which should be written twice is written only once. Thus *decus* often appears where the copyist intended to write *dedecus*, *dicit* where he meant *didicit*, etc. It is the opposite of Dittography (q. v.). See TEXTUAL CRITICISM.

Har. See HORUS.

Harēna. See ARENA.

Harlot. See MERETRIX.

Harma (Ἅρμα). A small place in Boeotia, near Tanagra (*Il.* ii. 499). It got its name traditionally from the chariot (ἅρμα) of Adrastus, which broke down at this place; or, according to others, from the fact that the chariot of Amphiaräus (q. v.) was here swallowed up by the earth (Pausan. ix. 19, § 4).

Harma (ἅρμα). See CURRUS.

Harmamaxa (ἁρμάμαξα). See CURRUS.

Harmătus (Ἁρματοῦς). A city and promontory on the coast of Aeolus in Asia Minor, on the north side of the Sinus Elaïticus.

Harmodius (Ἁρμόδιος). An Athenian who, together with ARISTOGĪTON (Ἀριστογείτων), became the cause of the overthrow of the Pisistratidae. The names of Harmodius and Aristogiton were immortalized by the gratitude of the Athenians. Aristogiton was a citizen of the middle class; Harmodius a youth distinguished by the comeliness of his person. They were both perhaps remotely allied to one another by blood, and were united by ties of the closest intimacy. The youth had received an outrage from Hipparchus, which roused both the resentment and the fears of his friend, lest Hipparchus should abuse his power to repeat the insult. But Hipparchus, whose pride had been wounded by the conduct of Harmodius, contented himself with an affront aimed at the honour of his family. By his orders, the sister of Harmodius was invited to take part in a procession, as bearer of one of the sacred vessels. When, however, she presented herself in her festal dress, she was publicly rejected, and dismissed as unworthy of the honour. This insult stung Harmodius to the quick, and kindled the indignation of Aristogiton. They resolved to engage in the desperate enterprise of overthrowing the ruling dynasty. They communicated their plan to a few friends, who promised their assistance; but they hoped that, as soon as the first blow should be struck, they would be joined by numbers, who would joyfully seize the opportunity of recovering their freedom. The conspirators fixed on the festival of the Panathenaea as the most convenient season for effecting their purpose. This festival was celebrated with a procession, in which the citizens marched armed with spears and shields, and was the only occasion on which, in time of peace, they could assemble under arms without exciting suspicion. It was agreed that Harmodius and Aristogiton should give the signal by stabbing Hippias, while their friends kept off his guards, and that they should trust to the general disposition in favour of liberty for the further success of their undertaking. When the day came, the conspirators armed themselves with daggers,

Harmodius and Aristogiton. (Copies in the Naples Museum.)

which they concealed in the myrtle-boughs that were carried on this occasion. But while Hippias, surrounded by his guards, was in the Ceramicus, directing the order of the procession, one of the conspirators was observed to go up to him, for he was easy of access to all, and to enter into familiar conversation with him. The two friends, on seeing this, concluded that they were betrayed, and that they had no hope left but of revenge. They instantly rushed into the city, and, meeting Hipparchus, killed him before his guards could come up to his assistance. These, however, arrived in time to avenge his death on Harmodius. Aristogiton escaped for the moment through the crowd, but was afterwards taken. When the news was brought to Hippias, instead of proceeding to the scene of his brother's murder, he advanced with a composed countenance towards the armed procession, which was yet ignorant of the event, and, as if he had some grave discourse to address to them, desired them to lay aside their weapons, and meet him at an appointed place. He then ordered his guards to seize the arms, and to search every one for those which he might have concealed upon his person. All who were found with daggers were arrested, together with those whom, on any other grounds, he suspected of disaffection. Aristogiton was put to death, according to some authors, after torture had been applied to wring from him the names of his accomplices. It is said that he avenged himself by accusing the truest friends of Hippias. The mistress of Aristogiton, one Leaena (q. v.), whose only crime was to have been the object of his affection, underwent the like treatment. She was afterwards celebrated for the constancy with which she endured the most cruel torments (Herod. v. 55; vii. 123; Thuc. i. 20; vi. 54 foll.). These events took place in B.C. 514.

After the expulsion of Hippias the tyrannicides received almost heroic honours. Statues were erected to them at the public expense, and their names never ceased to be repeated with affectionate admiration in the popular songs of Athens, which assigned them a place in the Islands of the Blessed, by the side of Achilles and Tydides; and when an orator wished to suggest the idea of the highest merit and of the noblest services to the cause of liberty, he never failed to remind his hearers of Harmodius and Aristogiton. No slave was ever called by their names. Plutarch has preserved a reply of Antipho, the orator, to Dionysius the elder, of Syracuse. The latter had asked the question, which was the finest kind of bronze? "That," replied Antipho, "of which the statues of Harmodius and Aristogiton were made." He lost his life in consequence. Their statues, made by Antenor and set up in the Agora, were carried away by Xerxes when he took Athens in B.C. 480, but were restored by Alexander the Great.

Harmonia (Ἁρμονία). The daughter of Ares and Aphroditê, and wife of Cadmus. (See CADMUS.) At her marriage all the gods were present on the Acropolis of Thebes, and offered her their wedding-gifts. Cadmus gave her a costly garment and a necklace, the workmanship of Hephaestus, which he had received from Aphroditê, or (according to another account) from Europa. These gifts, so the story runs, had everywhere the fatal property of stirring up strife and bloodshed. It was with them that Polynices corrupted Eriphylê, who drove her husband Amphiaraüs to his destruction in the Theban War, and was murdered in revenge by her son Alcmaeon. It was for their sake that Alcmaeon and Phegeus and his sons were slain. (See ALCMAEON; PHEGEUS.) The jewels were at length deposited by the sons of Alcmaeon in the sanctuary of Delphi. According to a later story, Phaÿllus, a leader of the Phocians in the war against Philip of Macedon, carried off, among other treasures, the necklace of Harmonia, and gave it to his mistress, the wife of Ariston of Oeta; but her youngest son set fire to the house in a fit of madness, and the mother, with the necklace, was consumed.

Harmostae (ἁρμοσταί, "regulators"). A board consisting of twenty members, at Sparta; probably a kind of higher police, whose duty it was to maintain a supervision over the districts inhabited by the Perioeci. After the Peloponnesian War the name was given to the officials who were sent into the conquered cities to command the garrisons, and to see that the oligarchical constitution was maintained.

Harpa. A harp, with a curved back in the form of a sickle (ἅρπη, *falx*), like the annexed example, from an Egyptian painting. (See Venant. *Carm.* vii. 8. 63, in which passage it is expressly distinguished from the lyre, and as an instrument used by foreigners.)

Harpa. (Egyptian.)

Harpagīa (τὰ Ἁρπαγεῖα), or **Harpagĭum** (Ἁρπάγιον). A small town in Mysia, between Cyzicus and Priapus, the scene of the rape of Ganymedes, according to some legends.

Harpăgo and **Harpăga** (ἁρπάγη). A hook or grappling-iron used in domestic economy for taking meats from the caldron, drawing up pails from wells, etc. In war, hooks of huge size (*ferreae manus*) were used by the Romans in grappling with hostile ships (Florus, ii. 2), and were said to have been invented by Pericles (Plin. *H. N.* vii. § 57).

Bronze Harpago or Flesh-hook. (British Museum.)

Harpăgus (Ἅρπαγος). (1) A noble Median, who is said to have preserved the infant Cyrus. He was afterwards one of the generals of Cyrus, and conquered the Greek cities of Asia Minor. See CYRUS. (2) A Persian general of Darius I. who made Histiaeus prisoner. See HISTIAEUS.

Harpălus (Ἅρπαλος). (1) A Macedonian, appointed by Alexander the Great superintendent of the royal treasury, with the administration of the satrapy of Babylon. Having embezzled large sums of money, he crossed over to Greece in B.C. 324, and employed his treasures in gaining over the leading men at Athens to support him against Alexander and his vicegerent, Antipater. He is said to have corrupted Demosthenes himself (Arr. *An.* iii. 6, 19), as well as Demades and Charicles, the son-in-law of Phocion. He failed, however, in his general object, for Antipater, having demanded his surrender from the Athenians, it was resolved to place him in confinement until the Macedonians should send for him. He succeeded in making his escape from prison, and fled to Crete, where he was assassinated soon after his arrival by Thimbron, one of his own officers. (2) A Greek astronomer, who introduced some improvements into the cycle of Cleostratus. Harpalus lived before Meton (q. v.).

Harpalȳcé (Ἁρπαλύκη). (1) Daughter of Harpalycus, king in Thrace, brought up by her father as a warrior, on the milk of cows and mares. After his death she became a robber in the forest, being able to outrun horses. She was at last snared and killed by shepherds (Hyg. *Fab.* 193). (2) The daughter of Clymenus and Epicasté. She was seduced by her own father, upon whom she afterwards revenged herself by killing her younger brother and serving him up as food on the father's table. By the gods she was changed into a bird.

Harpăsa (Ἅρπασα). A city of Caria on the river Harpasus.

Harpastum (ἁρπαστόν). A ball. See PILA.

Harpăsus (Ἅρπασος). (1) A river of Caria, flowing north into the Maeander. (2) A river of Armenia Maior, flowing south into the Araxes.

Harpīna (Ἅρπινα) or **Harpinna** (Ἅρπιννα). A town in Pisatis (Elis) near Olympia, named after a daughter of Asopus.

Harpocrătes (Ἁρποκράτης). See HORUS.

Harpocration (Ἁρποκρατίων), VALERIUS. A Greek scholar of Alexandria, who lived probably in the second century A.D. He was the author of a lexicon to the ten great Attic orators (Περὶ τῶν Λέξεων τῶν Δέκα Ῥητόρων, or briefly Λεξικὸν τῶν Δέκα Ῥητόρων), which has survived, though in a very fragmentary form. It contains, in alphabetical order, notes on the matters and persons mentioned by the orators, with explanations of the technical expressions; thus forming a rich store of valuable information on matters of history, literature, and the constitution and judicial system of Athens. Suidas and the author of the *Etymologicum Magnum*, borrowed largely from Harpocration. Modern editions are those of Bekker (Berlin, 1833), and Dindorf (Oxford, 1853). See Boysen, *De Harpocrat. Fontibus* (Kiel, 1876).

Harpȳiae (Ἅρπυιαι). The Harpies were originally the goddesses of the devastating storm, symbolizing the sudden and total disappearance of men. Homer only names one of them (*Il.* xvi. 150), Podargé, or "the swift-footed," who, in the shape of a mare, bore to Zephyrus the horses of Achilles. In Hesiod (*Theog.* 267) the Harpies appear as winged goddesses with beautiful hair, daughters of Thaumas and Electra, sisters of Iris, with the names of Aëllo and Ocypeté. In the later story their number increased, their names being Aëllo-

Harpy. (Painted Vase from Tel-Defenneh of B.C. 650.)

pus, Ocythoë, Nicothoë, and Celaeno. They are there represented as half-birds, half-maidens, and as spirits of mischief. In the story of the Argonauts, for instance, they torment Phineus by carrying off and polluting his food till they are driven off by Calaïs and Zetes, and either killed or banished to the island of the Strophades, where they are bound by an oath to remain. See Verg. *Aen.* iii. 211–244.

Harpy Monument. A remarkable work of Lycian art discovered in 1838 on the acropolis of Xanthus in Lycia by Sir C. Fellowes, and now deposited in the British Museum. It dates from about B.C. 500, and is a rectangular tower made of a single block of limestone with a flat roof directly

Harpy. (From the Harpy Monument.)

under which is a frieze of white marble, twenty-one feet from the ground, representing (probably) the Harpies carrying off the daughters of Pandareus (Hom. *Od.* xx. 78 foll.). For a fuller description and criticism, see Conze in the *Archäolog. Zeitung* for 1869, p. 80, and Perry, *Greek and Roman Sculpture* (1882), pp. 111–117.

Harrow. See CRATES; IRPEX.

Harūdes or **Charūdes.** A people in the army of Ariovistus (q. v.) at the time of his defeat by Caesar (B.C. 58). They are believed to have come from the Cimbric Chersonese (Jutland).

Harundo. See CALAMUS.

Harūspex. An Etruscan soothsayer, whose function it was to interpret the divine will from the entrails of sacrificial victims, to propitiate the anger of the gods as indicated by lightning or other marvels, and to interpret their significance according to Etruscan formulae. This art had long been practised in Etruria, and was referred to a divine origin. In the course of the republican era it found a home in the private and public life of the Romans, winning its way as the native priesthoods, intrusted with similar functions, lost in repute. From the time of the kings to the end of the Republic, haruspices were expressly summoned from Etruria by decrees of the Senate on the occurrence of prodigies which were not provided for in the Pontifical and Sibylline Books. Their business was to interpret the signs, to ascertain what deity demanded an expiation, and to indicate the nature of the necessary offering.

It then lay with the priests of the Roman people to carry out their instructions. Their knowledge of the signs given by lightning was only applied in republican Rome for the purpose of averting the omen portended by the flash. (See PUTEAL.) But under the Empire it was also used for consulting the lightning, either keeping it off or drawing it down. From about the time of the Punic Wars, haruspices began to settle in Rome, and were employed both by private individuals and state officials to ascertain the divine will by examination of the liver, gall, heart, lungs, and caul of sacrificial victims. They were especially consulted by generals when going to war. Their science was generally held in high esteem, but the class of haruspices who took pay for their services did not enjoy so good a reputation. Claudius seems to have been the first emperor who instituted a regular *collegium* of Roman haruspices, consisting of sixty members of equestrian rank, and presided over by a *haruspex maximus*, for the regular service of the State. This *collegium* continued to exist till the beginning of the fifth century A.D. See Fraudsen, *Haruspices* (Berlin, 1823); Bouché-Leclercq, *Histoire de la Divination dans l'Antiquité*, four vols. (Paris, 1879–82); and the articles AUGUR; DIVINATIO.

Hasdrŭbal (Ἀσδρούβας, meaning in Punic "(whose) help (is) Baal"). (1) A Carthaginian general, son of Mago, who succeeded to the titles and glory of his father. It was under his conduct that the Carthaginians carried the war into Sardinia. He received in that island a wound which caused his death, B.C. 420 (Just. xix. 1). (2) Son of the preceding, made war upon the Numidians, and freed Carthage from the tribute she had been compelled to pay for being permitted to establish herself on the coast of Africa (Just. xix. 2). (3) A son of Hanno, sent into Sicily at the head of a powerful army to oppose the Romans. He was defeated by Metellus, the Roman proconsul, B.C. 251. Hasdrubal fled to Lilybaeum, but was condemned to death by his countrymen at home. (4) Son-in-law of Hamilcar, distinguished himself under the orders of that general in the war with Numidia. On the death of his father-in-law he was appointed commander, and carried on military operations in Spain during eight years. He reduced the greater part of that country, and governed it with wisdom and prudence. He founded Carthago Nova (Carthagena). The Romans, wishing to put a stop to his successes, made a treaty with Carthage, by which the latter bound herself not to carry her arms beyond the Iberus. Hasdrubal faithfully observed the terms of this compact. He was slain, B.C. 220, by a slave whose master he had put to death (Livy, xxi. 2; Polyb. ii. 1, 13, iii. 12, x. 10). (5) Son of Hamilcar, brought from Spain large reinforcements for his brother Hannibal. He crossed the barrier of the Alps, and arrived in Italy, but the consuls Livius Salinator and Claudius Nero, having intercepted the letters which he had written to Hannibal, informing him of his arrival, attacked him near the river Metaurus, and gave him a complete defeat, B.C. 208. Hasdrubal fell in the battle, with 56,000 of his troops. The Romans lost about 8000 men, and made 5400 prisoners. The head of Hasdrubal was severed from his body, and was thrown a few days afterwards into the camp of Hannibal. Before attempting to enter Italy by land, Hasdrubal attempted to cross the sea from Spain, but was defeated by the Roman governor of Sardinia (Livy, xxi. 23; Polyb. xi. 1). (6) A Carthaginian commander, son of Giscon, who commanded the forces of his country in Spain during the time of Hannibal. Being seconded by Syphax, he afterwards carried on the war against the Romans in Africa, but was defeated by Scipio. He died B.C. 206 (Livy, xxiv. 41, xxix. 35, xxx. 5). (7) A Carthaginian, surnamed "the Kid" (*haedus*), an opponent of the Barca faction. He advised his countrymen to make peace with the Romans, and censured the ironical laugh of Hannibal in the Carthaginian Senate, after the peace was concluded. (8) A Carthaginian general, who, during the siege of Carthage by the Romans, commanded an army of 20,000 men without the walls, with which he kept constantly harassing the besiegers. Being compelled at last to take refuge with his forces within the city, he took command of the place, and for a long time bravely withstood the attacks of the Romans. After the capture of the city, he retired with the Roman deserters, who had no quarter to expect, into the temple of Aesculapius in the citadel, resolved to bury himself under its ruins, taking with him, at the same time, his wife and two young sons. At length, however, having secretly left the temple, he threw himself at the feet of Scipio, and supplicated for life. Scipio granted his request, and showed him as a suppliant to the deserters in the temple. These desperate men, after venting against him a torrent of reproaches, set fire to the temple, and perished amid the flames. His wife, when the fire was kindling, displayed herself on the walls of the building in the richest attire she could procure, and, having upbraided her husband for his cowardice, slew her two sons, and threw herself, with them, into the burning pile (Appian, *Bell. Pun.* 131).

Hasta (ἔγκος, παλτόν). The lance. In the earlier history of the Roman army the first four classes under the Servian constitution, and in later times, the *triarii*, or hindmost rank, were armed with this weapon. (See LEGIO.) At length, however, the *pilum* was introduced for the whole infantry of the legion. (See PILUM.) To deprive a soldier of his *hasta* was equivalent to degrading him to the rank of the *velites*, who were armed with javelins. A blunt hasta with a button at the end (*hasta pura*) continued to be used in later times as a military decoration. The spear frequently had a leathern thong tied to the middle of the shaft, which was called ἀγκύλη by the Greeks, and *amentum* or *ammentum* by the Romans, and which was of assistance in throwing the spear. The javelin to which the ἀγκύλη was attached was called μεσάγκυλον (Poll. i. 136; Xen. *Anab.* iv. 2, § 28; Verg. *Aen.* ix. 665). The preceding figure, taken from Sir W. Hamilton's *Etruscan Vases* (iii. pl. 33), represents the *amentum* attached to the spear at the centre of gravity, a little above the middle. The *amentum* added to the effect of throwing the lance by giving it rotation, and hence a greater degree of steadiness and directness in its course.

Spear with Amentum. (From an Etruscan Vase.)

The hasta was employed in many symbolical ceremonies. The *fetialis* (q. v.), for instance, hurled a blood-stained hasta into the enemy's territory as a token of declaration of war, and if a general devoted his life for his army he stood on a hasta while repeating the necessary formula.

Greek Warrior with Spears. (Hope.)

The hasta was also set up as a symbol of legal ownership when the censor farmed out the taxes, when state property—booty, for instance—was sold; at private auctions (hence called *subhastationes*), where it was the ancient equivalent of our red flag, and at the sittings of the court of the *centumviri*, which had to decide questions of property.

Hastāti. See EXERCITUS.

Hat. See CAUSIA; PETASUS; PILLEUS.

Hatchet. See ASCIA; SECURIS.

Hatria (Ἀτρία) and **Adria** (Ἀδρία). (1) A city of Cisalpine Gaul between the mouths of the Padus and the Athesis, and still called Adria. It was of Greek or Etruscan origin. (2) A city in Picenum about five miles from the Adriatic Sea. It is now called Atri. It was one of the eighteen Latin colonies which remained faithful to Rome at the time of Hannibal's invasion (Polyb. iii. 88).

Haupt, MORITZ. A German classical scholar,

born at Zittau in Saxony in 1808, and educated at the University of Leipzig under G. Hermann. Later he lectured as a *privat-docent* at Leipzig, being made extraordinary professor in 1841 and ordinary professor in 1843. In 1848 he was dismissed from his chair as having shared in the revolutionary movements of that year, but in 1853 he was called to Berlin to succeed his friend Lachmann. He died in 1874.

Besides a number of works on Germanic literature and philology, Haupt published *Quaestiones Catullianae* (1837); a monograph on the *Epicedion Drusi* (1849); an edition of the *Halieuticon* and *Cynegetica* of Grattius and Nemesianus (1838); additions to Lachmann's observations on the *Iliad* (1847); a recension of Hermann's Bion and Moschus (1849), and of his Aeschylus (1852); an edition of Horace (1851); a school edition of the *Metamorphoses* of Ovid (1853); a monograph on Calpurnius and Nemesianus (1854); a small text of Catullus, Tibullus, and Propertius (1853); an edition of the *Germania* of Tacitus (1855); of Vergil (1858). His *Opuscula* were collected and edited by Wilamowitz-Möllendorff (1876). See an appreciative paper by Prof. Nettleship in his *Lectures and Essays* (Oxford, 1885).

Hauton Timorumĕnos. See TERENTIUS.

Head-dress. See COMA; INFULA; MITRA; REDIMICULUM; VITTA.

Hearse. See FUNUS; PLAUSTRUM.

Hearth. See FOCUS; VESTA.

Heating Arrangements. See DOMUS; FOCUS.

Hebé (Ἥβη). Daughter of Zeus and Heré, and goddess of eternal youth. She was represented as the handmaiden of the gods, for whom she pours out their nectar, and the consort of Heracles after his apotheosis. She was worshipped with Heracles in Sicyon and Phlius, especially under the name Ganymedé or Dia. She was represented as freeing men from chains and bonds, and her rites were celebrated with unrestrained merriment. The Romans identified Hebé with Iuventas, the personification of youthful manhood. As representing the eternal youth of the Roman State, Iuventas had a chapel on the Capitol in the front court of the Temple of Minerva, and in later times a temple of her own in the city (Livy, v. 54). It was to Iupiter and Iuventas that boys offered prayer on the Capitol when they put on the *toga virilis*, putting a piece of money into their treasury. Two fine poems in English are suggested by the myth of Hebé—one the *Fall of Hebé*, by Thomas Moore, and the other, *Hebé*, by James Russell Lowell.

Hebraei. See IUDAEI.

Hebron (Χεβρών and Ἐβρών). A city in the south of Iudaea, the first capital of the kingdom of David, who reigned there for seven and a half years as king of Judah only.

Hebrus (Ἕβρος). The modern Maritza; the principal river in Thrace, rising in the mountains of Scomius and Rhodopé, and falling into the Aegaean Sea near Aenos, after forming by another branch an estuary called Stentoris Lacus. The Hebrus was celebrated in Greek legends. On its banks Orpheus was torn to pieces by the Thracian women; and it is frequently mentioned in connection with the worship of Dionysus.

Hebūdae. See EBUDAE.

Hecaërgé (Ἑκαέργη). (1) A Hyperborean maiden, daughter of Boreas. She was one of those who introduced the worship of Artemis into Delos. (2) An epithet often applied to Artemis as being one who effects her works from a distance, which is the meaning of the word. The masculine form (ἑκάεργος) is in like manner applied to Apollo.

Hecălé (Ἑκάλη). A poor old woman who hospitably received Theseus when he had gone out to hunt the Marathonian bull, and offered to Zeus a sacrifice for the safe return of the hero. As she died before his return, Theseus decreed that the people of the Attic tetrapolis should offer a sacrifice to her and to Zeus Hecalesius. See THESEUS.

Hecalesia (Ἑκαλήσιον ἱερόν). A festival at Athens in honour of Zeus Hecalesius. It was instituted by Theseus, in commemoration of the kindness of Hecalé towards him when he was going on his adventure against the Marathonian bull.

Hecataeus (Ἑκαταῖος). (1) A Greek chronicler, born of a noble family at Miletus, about B.C. 550. In his youth he travelled widely in Europe and Asia, as well as in Egypt. At the time of the Ionian revolt he was in his native city, and gave his countrymen the wisest counsels, but in vain. After the suppression of the rising, he succeeded by his tact and management in obtaining some alleviation of the hard measures adopted by the Persians. He died about 476. The ancient critics assigned him a high place among the Greek historians who preceded Herodotus, though pronouncing him inferior to the latter. His two works, of which only fragments remain, were: (*a*) A description of the earth (Περίοδος Γῆς or Περιήγησις), which was much consulted by Herodotus, and was apparently used to correct the chart of Anaximander. It was in two parts, one relating to Europe and the other to Asia, Egypt, and Libya. (*b*) A treatise on Greek fables, entitled Γενεαλογίαι, or *Genealogies*, and also Ἱστορίαι, in four books, on the poetical traditions of the Greeks. The fragments of Hecataeus have been edited by Klausen (Berlin, 1831) and C. and Th. Müller (Paris, 1841). See Schäffer, *Hecataeus* (1885); and the article LOGOGRAPHI. (2) An Abderite, a contemporary of Alexander the Great. He was a philosopher, critic, and grammarian, and probably was the author of a history of the Jews cited often by Iosephus.

Hecăté (Ἑκάτη). A Greek goddess, though perhaps of non-Hellenic origin. She was unknown to Homer, but in Hesiod she was the only daughter of the Titan Perses and of Asteria, the sister of Leto. She stood high in the regard of Zeus, from whom she had received a share in the heaven, earth, and ocean. She was invoked at all sacrifices, for she could give or withhold her blessing in daily life, in war, in contests on the sea, in the hunting-field, in the education of children, and in the tending of cattle. Thus she appeared as a personification of the divine power, and was the instrument through which the gods effected their will, though themselves far away. In later times she was confused with Persephoné, the queen of the lower world, or associated with her. Sometimes she was regarded as the goddess of the moon (Selené) or as Artemis, sometimes she was identified with foreign deities of the same kind. Being conceived of as a goddess of night and of the lower world, she was, as time went on, transformed into a deity of ghosts and magic. She was represented as haunting crossways and graves, accompanied by the dogs of the Styx, with the spirits of the dead and troops of spectral forms in her train. She lent powerful

Hecaté. (Causei, *Museum Romanum*, vol. i. tav. 21.)

aid to all magical incantations and witches' work. All enchanters and enchantresses were her disciples and *protégés;* Medea, in particular, was regarded as her votary. She was worshipped in private and in public in many places—for instance, in Samothrace, Thessaly, Lemnos, Athens, and Aegina—and had a celebrated temple near Stratonicea in Caria. Her images were set up in the front of houses and by the road-side, with altars in front of them and a roof above them. On the last day of the month, which was sacred to her, offerings were made to her in the crossways of eggs, fish, and onions. The victims sacrificed to her were young dogs, black ewes, and honey.

In works of art she is usually portrayed in three forms, represented by three statues standing back to back. Each form has its special attributes—torches, keys, daggers, snakes, and dogs. In the Gigantomachia of Pergamum she appears with a different weapon in her three right hands—a torch, a sword, and a lance.

Hecatombaea (Ἑκατόμβαια). (1) A festival celebrated in honour of Heré by the Argives and people of Aegina. It received its name from ἑκατόν and βοῦς, being a sacrifice of a hundred oxen, which were always offered to the goddess, and the flesh distributed among the poorest citizens. There were also public games, first instituted by Archinus, a king of Argos, in which the prize was a shield of brass with a crown of myrtle. (2) An anniversary sacrifice called by this name in Laconia, and offered for the preservation of the hundred towns which once flourished in that country.

Hecatombaeon (Ἑκατομβαιών). The first month in the Attic year, corresponding with the last half of July and the first of August. The Spartans called it Ἑκατομβεύς (Arist. *H. A.* v. 11, 2.) See CALENDARIUM.

Hecatombé (ἑκατόμβη). A word whose original meaning was a sacrifice of a hundred oxen; but in early times it was applied generally to any great sacrifice, without any idea either of oxen or definite number. Mr. A. Platt in the (Eng.) *Journal of Philology* for 1893, makes ἑκατόμβη to mean originally one ox in each hundred. See SACRIFICIUM.

Hecatomnos (Ἑκατόμνως). A king of Caria, the father of Mausolus and Artemisia. See ARTEMISIA; MAUSOLUS.

Hecatompĕdon. See PES; TEMPLUM.

Hecatomphonia (τὰ ἑκατομφόνια, from ἑκατόν, "a hundred," and φονεύω, "to kill"). A solemn sacrifice offered by the Messenians to Zeus, when any of them had killed a hundred enemies. Aristomenes is said to have offered up this sacrifice three times in the course of the Messenian wars against Sparta (Pausan. iv. 19).

Hecatompŏlis (Ἑκατόμπολις). An epithet given to Crete, from the hundred cities which it once contained (Hom. *Il.* ii. 649). The same epithet was also applied to Laconia. The greater part of these, however, were probably, like the demes of Attica, not larger than villages.

Hecatompȳlos (ἑκατόμπυλος, "Hundred-gated"). (1) An epithet often applied to Thebes in Egypt. See THEBAE. (2) A city of Parthia near the centre of the country and once the capital.

Hecăton (Ἑκάτων). A Stoic philosopher of Rhodes who studied under Panaetius and wrote numerous works now lost.

Hecatoncheires (Ἑκατόγχειρες, "the hundred-handed ones"). In Hesiod these are three giants, each with fifty arms and a hundred hands, sons of Uranus and Gaea. Their names are Briareōs, Cottus, and Gyes. Owing to their hostile attitude to him, their father kept them imprisoned in the bowels of the earth; but on the advice of Gaea, the gods of Olympus summoned them from their prison to lend assistance against the Titans, and, after their victory, set them to watch the Titans, who had been thrown into Tartarus. Homer mentions Briareōs, called by men Aegaeon, as the son of Poseidon, and mightier than his father (*Il.* i.).

Hecatonnēsi (Ἑκατόννησοι). The Hundred Islands; the name of a group of small islands between Lesbos and the coast of Aeolis (Herod. i. 151).

Hector (Ἕκτωρ). The son of Priam and Hecuba and the most valiant of all the Trojan chiefs that fought against the Greeks. He married Andromaché, daughter of Eëtion, by whom he became the father of Astyanax. Hector was appointed commander of all the Trojan forces, and for a long period proved the bulwark of his native city. He was not only the bravest and most powerful, but also the most amiable, of his countrymen, and particularly distinguished himself in his conflicts with Aiax, Diomedes, and many other of the most formidable leaders. The fates had decreed that Troy should never be destroyed as long as Hector lived. The Greeks, therefore, after the death of Patroclus, who had fallen by Hector's hand, made a powerful effort under the command of Achilles; and, by the intervention of Athené, who assumed the form of Deïphobus, and urged Hector to encounter the Grecian chief, contrary to the remonstrances of Priam and Hecuba, their effort was crowned with success. Hector fell, and his death accomplished the overthrow of his father's kingdom. The dead body of the Trojan warrior was attached to the chariot of Achilles, and insultingly dragged away to the Grecian fleet; and thrice every day, for the space of twelve days, was it also dragged by the victor around the tomb of Patroclus (*Il.* xxii. 399 foll.; xxiv. 14 foll.). During all this time the corpse of Hector was shielded from dogs and birds, and preserved from corruption, by the united care of Aphrodité and Apollo. The body was at last ransomed by Priam, who went in person for this purpose to the tent of Achilles. Splendid obsequies were rendered to the deceased, and with these the action of the *Iliad* terminates. Vergil makes Achilles to have dragged the corpse of Hector thrice round the walls of Troy (*Aen.* i. 483). Homer, however, is silent on this point. According to the latter, Hector fled thrice round the city-walls before engaging with Achilles; and, after he was slain, his body was immediately attached to the car of the victor, and dragged away as stated above. The incident, therefore, alluded to by Vergil must have been borrowed from one of the Cyclic poets, or perhaps some tragic writer.

Hecŭba (Ἑκάβη). The daughter of Dymas, a Phrygian prince (or, according to others, of Cisseus, a Thracian king, while others, again, made her the daughter of the river-god Sangarius and Metopé). She was the second wife of Priam, king of Troy (Apollod. iii. 12, 6), and bore him nineteen children (*Il.* xxiv. 496), of whom the chief were Hector, Paris, Deïphobus, Helenus, Troïlus, Polites, Polydorus, Cassandra, Creüsa, and Polyxena. When she was pregnant with Paris (q. v.), she dreamed that she brought into the world a burning torch, which reduced her husband's palace and all Troy to ashes. On her telling this dream to Priam, he sent for his son Aesacus, by a former wife Arisbé, the daughter of Merops, who had been reared and taught to interpret dreams by his grandfather. Aesacus declared that the child would be the ruin of his country, and recommended him to expose it. As soon as born, the babe was given to a servant to be left on Ida to perish; but the attempt proved a fruitless one, and the prediction of the soothsayer was fulfilled. After the ruin of Troy and the death of Priam, Hecuba fell to the lot of Odysseus, and embarked with the conquerors for Greece. The fleet, however, was detained off the coast of the Thracian Chersonese by the appearance of the spectre of Achilles on the summit of his tomb, demanding to be honoured with a new offering. Polyxena was, in consequence, torn from Hecuba and immolated by Neoptolemus on the grave of his father. The grief of the mother was increased by the sight of the dead body of her son Polydorus, washed upon the shore, who had been cruelly slain by Polymestor, king of Thrace, to whose care Priam had consigned him. Bent on revenge, Hecuba managed, by artifice, to get Polymestor and his two children in her power, and, by the aid of her fellow-captives, she effected the murder of his sons, and then put out the eyes of the father. This act drew upon her the vengeance of the Thracians: they assailed her with darts and showers of stones; and, in the act of biting a stone with impotent rage, she was suddenly metamorphosed into a dog (Ovid, *Met.* xiii. 429 foll.). Hyginus says that she threw herself into the sea (*Fab.* 111), while Servius states that she was changed into a dog when on the point of casting herself into the waters (*Ad Aen.* iii. 6). The story of Hecuba forms the subject of a play by Euripides (q. v.).

Hecȳra (Ἑκυρά). "The Mother-in-Law." A comedy of Terence, based upon a Greek original of authorship now unknown. It has little or no plot, and seems to be an attempt at a new style of dramatic writing. Hence it was unpopular with Roman audiences, and did not get a successful hearing until B.C. 160, on its third production, five years after it was first put on the stage. Separate editions by Spengel (Berlin, 1879), Sloman (London, 1886), and Benoist and Psichari, 2d ed. (Paris, 1887). See TERENTIUS.

Hedna (ἕδνα). See MATRIMONIUM.

Hegēmon (Ἡγήμων). A native of Thasos and author of satyric dramas in the age of Alcibiades who was his friend, and managed to get him freed from an accusation that had been brought against him. A parody by this poet, entitled Γιγαντομαχία, was being presented when the news arrived of the defeat of Nicias in Sicily. This Hegemon was called Phacé (φακῆ, "lentil"), conferred on him as a nickname. He wrote also a comedy entitled Φίλιννα.

Hegemŏné (Ἡγεμόνη). See CHARITES.

Hegemonia (ἡγεμονία, "leadership"). A Greek name for the supremacy of States, and with it the direction, more or less absolute, of the business of the confederacy. In the language of Athenian law ἡγεμονία meant the presidency in the courts, which belonged in different cases to different officials. Their business was to receive the charge, make the arrangements for the trial, and preside while it was going on.

Hegesiănax (Ἡγησιάναξ). A Greek writer, a native of Alexandria-Troas, and contemporary with Antiochus the Great, by whom he was patronized. He was the author of an historical work and indulged also in poetic composition, having written a poem entitled τὰ Τρωϊκά, "Trojan Affairs." Some ascribed to him the Cyprian Epic. He was likewise a writer of tragedies; and, according to Athenaeus, from whom these particulars are obtained, was also a tragic actor, having improved and strengthened his voice, which was naturally weak, by abstaining for eighteen years from eating figs.

Hegesias (Ἡγησίας). (1) A Greek orator, born in Magnesia on Mount Sipylus in the first half of the third century B.C. He was the founder of what was termed the Asiatic style of oratory. See RHETORICA. (2) A famous Cyrenaic philosopher who flourished about B.C. 340, and known as Πεισιθάνατος from his arguments in favor of suicide. See CYRENAICI. (3) A statuary who is thought to have wrought the figures of the Dioscuri on the Capitol at Rome. He is probably the same as Hegias, supposed by some to be another person.

Hegesīnus (Ἡγησίνους) of Pergamum. The successor of Evander and the immediate predecessor of Carneades in the chair of the Academy, flourished about B.C. 185.

Hegesippus (Ἡγήσιππος). An Athenian orator and a contemporary of Demosthenes, to whose political party he belonged. The grammarians ascribe to him the oration on Halonesus, which has come down to us under the name of Demosthenes.

Hegetoria. See PLYNTERIA.

Hegias. See HEGESIAS.

Heinsius. (1) DANIEL (DANIEL HEINS), a distinguished scholar of the so-called "Dutch Renaissance." He was born at Ghent, June 9th, 1580. In 1594 he entered the University of Francken to perfect himself in Greek, having already won notice by his scholarship. Soon after he settled at Leyden, where he spent the remainder of his life, associated with such men as Joseph Scaliger, Douza, and Paulus Merula. In 1602 he was made Professor of Latin at the University, in 1605 Professor of Greek, and in 1607 University Librarian. He died at the Hague, February 25th, 1655.

His works include editions of Silius Italicus (1600), Hesiod (1603), Theocritus, Bion, and Moschus (1604), Horace (1610), Aristotle and Seneca (1611), Terence (1618), Livy (1620), Ovid (1629), and the *Epistolae* of Joseph Scaliger (1627). He also published three volumes of original Latin poems —*Iambi* (1602), *Elegiae* (1603), *Poemata* (1605)—and poems in Dutch and Latin (1604). See L. Müller, *Geschichte d. class. Philologie in den Niederlanden*, pp. 38 foll. (Leipzig, 1869).

(2) His son NIKOLAES was also a scholar of much distinction (born 1620, died 1681). He spent the greater part of his life in travel for the purpose of studying and collating classical MSS. He published editions of Ovid (1652; 3d ed. 1661), Paterculus (1678), and Valerius Flaccus (1680).

Heir. See HERES.

Helciarius. One who tows a vessel against the stream by a tow-line (*helcium*) (Mart. iv. 64, 22), as shown by the annexed illustration, which represents a vessel laden with corn and oil towed by two grotesque figures.

Helciarii. (From a Mosaic found at Lerida, Spain.)

Helĕna (Ἑλένη). (1) The beautiful daughter of Zeus and Leda, the wife of Tyndareos of Sparta. She was sister of the Dioscuri and of Clytaemnestra. The post-Homeric story represented her as carried off, while still a maiden, by Theseus, to the Attic fortress of Aphidnae, where she bore him a daughter, Iphigenia. She was afterwards set free by her brothers, who took her back to Sparta. She was wooed by a number of suitors, and at length gave her hand to Menelaüs, by whom she became the mother of one child, Hermioné. In the absence of her husband she was seduced and carried away to Troy by Paris, the son of Priam, taking with her great treasures. This was the origin of the Trojan War. The Trojans, in spite of the calamity she had brought upon them, loved her for her beauty, and refused to restore her to her husband. She, however, lamented the folly of her youth, and yearned for her home, her husband, and her daughter. After the death of Paris she was wedded to Deïphobus, assisted the Greeks at the taking of Troy, and betrayed Deïphobus into Menelaüs's hands. With Menelaüs she finally returned to

Helen and Paris. (Naples Museum.)

Sparta after eight years' wandering, and lived thenceforth with him in happiness and concord.

According to another story, mainly current after the time of Stesichorus, Paris carried off to Troy not the real Helen, but a phantom of her created by Heré. The real Helen was wafted through the air by Hermes, and brought to King Proteus in Egypt, whence, after the destruction of Troy, she was taken home by Menelaüs. (See Herod. ii. 112–120.) After the death of Menelaüs she was, according to one story, driven from Sparta by her step-sons, and fled thereupon to Rhodes to her friend Polyxo, who hanged her on a tree. Another tradition represented her as living after death in wedlock with Achilles on the island of Leucé. She was worshipped as the goddess of beauty in a special sanctuary at Therapné in Laconia, where a festival was held in her honour. She was also invoked, like her brothers the Dioscuri, as a tutelary deity of sailors. (See DIOSCURI.)

In the *Iliad*, Helen is apparently regarded as one who is not responsible for the ruin that she works, two passages seeming to imply that she was carried off by force (ii. 356 and 390). In the *Odyssey* she is also excused by the fact that she sins because a god has so willed it. (Cf. *Odyss.* xxiii. 222). Mr. Gladstone in his Homeric studies even regards her as not only a type of womanly loveliness, but of almost Christian penitence as well! The story of Helen has received a splendid setting in the genius of poets of every age. She is the most famous woman of all antiquity. In Goethe's *Faust* (pt. ii.) she is allegorically introduced as typifying the classical spirit of beauty. In English, see the *Hellenics* of Walter Savage Landor, Tennyson's *Dream of Fair Women*, and Andrew Lang's poem *Helen of Troy*, with the appended essay.

(2) FLAVIA IULIA, commonly known in ecclesiastical history by the name of St. Helena, the first wife of Constantius Chlorus. She was born of obscure

parents, in a village called Drepanum, in Bithynia, which was afterwards raised by her son Constantine to the rank of a city, under the name of Helenopolis. Her husband Constantius, on being made Caesar by Diocletian and Maximian (A.D. 292), repudiated Helena, and married Theodora, daughter of Maximian. Helena withdrew into retirement until her son Constantine, having become emperor, called his mother to court, and gave her the title of Augusta. He also supplied her with large sums of money, which she employed in building and endowing churches, and in relieving the poor. About A.D. 325 she set out on a pilgrimage to Palestine, and, having explored the site of Jerusalem, she thought that she had discovered the sepulchre of Jesus, and also the cross on which he died. With it she is said to have found the crosses of the two thieves, and to have learned which was the true one by the miracle it wrought in restoring to health a sick person to whose bedside it was carried. She built a church on the spot supposed to be that of the Holy Sepulchre, which has continued to be venerated by that name to the present day. She also built a church at Bethlehem, in honour of the nativity of the Saviour. From Palestine she rejoined her son at Nicomedia, in Bithynia, where she expired, in the year 327, at a very advanced age. She is numbered by the Roman Church among the saints, and her festival is August 18th.

Helĕna (Ἑλένη). A deserted and rugged island in the Aegean, opposite to Thoricus, and extending from that parallel to Sunium. It received its name from the circumstance of Paris having landed on it, as was said, in company with Helen, when they were fleeing from Sparta (Pliny, *H. N.* iv. 12; Mela, ii. 7). Strabo, who follows Artemidorus, conceived it to be the Cranaë of Homer (*Il.* iii. 444). Pliny calls it Macris. The modern name is Macronisi.

Helĕnus (Ἕλενος). A famous soothsayer, son of Priam and Hecuba, and the only one of their sons who survived the siege of Troy. He was so chagrined, according to some, at having failed to obtain Helen in marriage after the death of Paris that he retired to Mount Ida, and was there, by the advice of Calchas, surprised and carried away to the Grecian camp by Odysseus. Among other predictions, Helenus declared that Troy could not be taken unless Philoctetes (q. v.) could be prevailed to quit his retreat and repair to the siege. After the destruction of Troy, he, together with Andromaché, fell to the share of Pyrrhus, whose favour he conciliated by deterring him from sailing with the rest of the Greeks, who (as he foretold) would be exposed to a severe tempest on leaving the Trojan shore. Pyrrhus not only manifested his gratitude by giving him Andromaché in marriage, but nominated him as his successor in the kingdom of Epirus, to the exclusion of his own son Molossus, who did not ascend the throne until after the death of Helenus. A son named Cestrinus was the offspring of the union of Helenus with Andromaché (Verg. *Aen.* iii. 294 foll.).

Helepŏlis (ἑλέπολις). Literally, "destroyer of cities;" the name given to an engine invented by Demetrius Poliorcetes (q. v.) for besieging fortified places, consisting of a square tower placed upon wheels, and run up to the height of nine stories, each of which was furnished with machines for battering and discharging projectiles of enormous size and weight (Diod. Sic. xx. 48, 91; Vitruv. x. 22; Ammian. xxiii. 4, 10). See DEMETRIUS, p. 485.

Heliădes (Ἡλιάδες) and **Heliădae** (Ἡλιάδαι). (1) The daughters of Helios (the Sun) and Clymené. They were three in number—Lampetié, Phaëthusa, and Phoebé; or seven, according to Hyginus—Meropé, Helié, Aeglé, Lampetié, Phoebé, Aethria, and Dioxippé. They were so afflicted at the death of their brother Phaëthon (see PHAËTHON) that they were changed by the gods into poplars, and their tears into amber, on the banks of the river Po (Ovid, *Met.* ii. 340; Hyg. *Fab.* 154). (2) Children of Helios and the nymph Rhodus. They were seven in number, and were fabled to have been the first inhabitants of the island of Rhodes. See RHODUS.

Heliaea. See DICASTERION; DICASTES.

Heliastae (Ἡλιασταί). See DICASTES.

Helĭcé (Ἑλίκη). (1) Another name for the Ursa Maior, or "Greater Bear." (See ARCTOS.) (2) One of the chief cities of Achaia, situated on the shore of the Sinus Corinthiacus, near Bura (Herod. i. 146). It was celebrated for the temple and worship of Poseidon, thence called Heliconius. Here, also, the general meeting of the Ionians was convened, while yet in the possession of Aegialus, and the festival which then took place is supposed to have resembled that of the Panionia, which they instituted afterwards in Asia Minor (Pausan. vii. 24). A tremendous influx of the sea, caused by a violent earthquake, overwhelmed and completely destroyed Helicé two years before the battle of Leuctra, B.C. 373. The details of this catastrophe will be found in Pausanias (vii. 24) and Aelian (*Hist. Anim.* xi. 19). Eratosthenes, as Strabo reports, beheld the site of this ancient city, and he was assured by sailors that the bronze statue of Poseidon was still visible beneath the waters, holding an hippocampus, or sea-horse, in his hand, and that it formed a dangerous shoal for their vessels. Two thousand workmen were afterwards sent by the Achaeans to recover the dead bodies, but without success.

Helĭcon (Ἑλικών). (1) A famous mountain in Boeotia, near the Gulf of Corinth. It was sacred to Apollo and the Muses, who were thence called Heliconiades. This mountain was famed for the purity of its air, the abundance of its water, its fertile valleys, the density of its shades, and the beauty of the venerable trees which clothed its sides. On the summit was the grove of the Muses, where these divinities had their statues, and where also were statues of Apollo and Hermes, of Bacchus by Lysippus, of Orpheus, and of famous poets and musicians (Pausan. ix. 30). A little below the grove was the fountain of Aganippé. The source Hippocrené (q. v.) was about twenty stadia above the grove. It is said to have burst forth when the horse Pegasus struck his hoof into the ground (Pausan. ix. 31), whence its name, ἵππου κρήνη. These two springs supplied two small rivers named Olmius and Permessus, which, after uniting their waters, flowed into the lake Copaïs, near Haliartus. The modern name of Helicon is Palaeovouni, and of Hippocrené, Kryopēgadi, or "cold spring." (2) A river of Macedonia, near Dium, the same, according to Pausanias (ix. 30), with the Baphyrus.

Heliconiădes. A name given to the Muses, from

their fabled residence on Mount Helicon, which was sacred to them (Lucret. iii. 1050).

Heliocamīnus. See Domus, p. 552.

Heliodōrus (Ἡλιόδωρος). (1) A Greek poet, from whom sixteen hexameters are cited by Stobaeus (*Serm.* 98), containing a description of that part of Campania situated between the Lucrine Lake and Puteoli, and where Cicero had a country residence. Some suppose him to have been the same with the rhetorician Heliodorus mentioned by Horace (*Sat.* i. 5. 2), as one of the companions of his journey to Brundisium. (2) An Athenian physician, of whom Galen makes mention, and who also wrote a didactic poem, under the title of Ἀπολυτικά, "Justification," of which Galen cites seven hexameters. (3) A native of Larissa, who left a treatise on optics, under the title of Κεφάλαια τῶν Ὀπτικῶν, which is scarcely anything more than an abridgment of the optical work ascribed to Euclid. He cites the optics of Ptolemy. The time when he flourished is uncertain; from the manner, however, in which he speaks of Tiberius, it is probable that he lived a long time after that emperor. Oribasius has preserved for us a fragment of another work of Heliodorus, which treats of the κοχλίας, a machine furnished with a screw for drawing water. (4) A Greek romance-writer, who was born at Emesa in Phœnicia, and flourished under the emperors Theodosius and Arcadius at the close of the fourth century. He was raised to the dignity of a bishop of Tricca in Thessaly. Heliodorus is best known as the author of a Greek romance, entitled Αἰθιοπικά, being the history of Theagenes and Chariclea, the latter a daughter of a king of Aethiopia. It is in ten books. This work was unknown in the West until a soldier of Anspach, under the Margrave Casimir of Brandenburg, assisting at the pillage of the library of Matthias Corvinus, at Buda, in 1526, being attracted by the rich binding of a manuscript, carried it off. He sold the prize afterwards to Vincent Obsopaeus, who published it at Basle in 1534. This was the celebrated romance of Heliodorus. Poetry, battles, piracies, and recognitions fill up the piece; there is no picture of the mind, no attempt at character-drawing carried on with the development of the action. The incidents point to no particular era of society, although one may perceive, from the tone of sentiment throughout, that the struggle had commenced between the spirit of Christianity and the grossness of pagan idolatry. Egypt is neither ancient Egypt, nor the Egypt of the Ptolemies, nor the Egypt of the Romans. Athens is neither Athens free nor Athens conquered—in short, there is no individuality either in the places or persons; and the vague pictures of the French romances of the seventeenth century give scarcely a caricatured idea of the model from which they were drawn. Various editions have been published of the romance of Heliodorus. The best are those of Bekker (1855) and Hirschig, in his *Erotici Scriptores* (1856). There is an English translation by Smith (London, 1856). See, also, Dunlop, *History of Fiction*, pp. 18–24 (3d ed. 1845), where an analysis of the novel is given; Chauvin, *Les Romanciers Grecs et Latins*, ch. viii. (1862); Rohde, *Der griechische Roman* (1876); and the article Novels and Romances.

Heliogabălus. See Elagabalus.

Heliopŏlis (Ἡλιούπολις). (1) A famous city of Egypt, situated a little to the east of the apex of the Delta, not far from modern Cairo. In Hebrew it is styled On or Aun. In the Septuagint it is called Heliopolis, or City of the Sun; in Jeremiah (xliii. 13), Beth Shemim—i. e. *domus solis.* Herodotus also mentions it by this name, and speaks of its inhabitants as being the wisest and most ingenious of all the Egyptians (ii. 3). According to Berosus, this was the city of Moses. It was also a place of resort for all the Greeks who visited Egypt for instruction. Hither came Herodotus, Plato, Eudoxus, and others, and secured much of the learning which they afterwards disseminated among their own countrymen. Plato, in particular, resided here three years. Manetho (q. v.), the historian, was also here as a priest. The city was built, according to Strabo, on a long, artificial mound of earth, so as to be out of reach of the inundations of the Nile. It had an oracle of Apollo and a famous Temple of the Sun. In this temple was fed and adored the sacred ox Mnevis, as Apis was at Memphis. This city was laid waste with fire and sword by Cambyses, and its chapter of priests all slaughtered. Strabo saw it in a deserted state and shorn of all its splendour. Heliopolis was famed also for its fountain of excellent water, which still remains, and gave rise to the subsequent Arabic name of the place, Ain Shems, or the Fountain of the Sun. The modern name is Matareieh, or cool water. A solitary obelisk of red granite is all that remains at the present day of this once celebrated place; and the two obelisks known as "Cleopatra's Needles" were originally brought from Heliopolis to Alexandria. (See Alexandria.) (2) A celebrated city of Syria, thirty-five miles northwest of Damascus, and southwest of Emesa, on the opposite side of the Orontes. Its Grecian name, Heliopolis (Ἡλιούπολις), "City of the Sun," is merely a translation of the native term Baalbek, which appellation the ruins at the present day retain. [See illustration on the following page.] Heliopolis was famed for its Temple of the Sun (Baal), erected by Antoninus Pius, though by the natives now ascribed to Solomon; and the ruins of this celebrated pile still attest its former magnificence. Of these the most notable are the Great Temple, a rectangular building 200 feet by 162, with a peristyle of 54 Corinthian columns; a smaller temple called the Temple of Iupiter; and a circular building of fine proportions long used as a Greek Church. Heliopolis was made a Roman colony by Iulius Caesar, and was garrisoned under Augustus. Later it was pillaged by the Arabs and by Timur (A.D. 1400), and since that time has gradually decayed. It is now only a wretched hamlet of a few hundred inhabitants. See Wood and Dawkins, *Ruins of Baalbec* (1757); Cassas, *Voyage Pittoresque de la Syrie* (1799); and Renan, *Mission de Phénicie* (1864).

Helios (Ἥλιος). In Greek mythology, the Sun-god, son of the Titan Hyperion (whose name he bears in Homer) and the Titaness Thea; brother of Selenē (the Moon) and Eos (Dawn). The poets apply the name Titan to him in particular, as the offspring of Titans. He is represented as a strong and beautiful god, in the bloom of youth, with gleaming eyes and waving locks, and a crown of rays upon his head. In the morning he rises from a lovely bay of the Ocean in the farthest East, where the Æthiopians dwell. To give light to gods and men he climbs the vault of heaven in a chariot drawn by four snow-white horses, breathing light and fire; their names are Eoös, Aethiops, Brouté, and Steropé. In the evening he sinks with his chariot into the Ocean, and while he sleeps is carried round along the northern border of the earth to the East again in a golden boat, shaped like a bowl, the work of Hephaestus. He is called Phaëthon, from the brilliant light that he diffuses; he is the All-seer (Panoptes), because his rays penetrate everywhere. He is revealer of all that is done on earth; it is he who told Hephaestus of the intrigue of Ares and Aphroditê, and showed Demeter who had carried off her daughter. He was accordingly invoked as a witness to oaths and solemn protestations.

Temple at Heliopolis.

On the island of Trinacria (Sicily) he had seven flocks of sheep and seven herds of cattle, fifty in each. It was his pleasure, on his daily journey, to look down upon them. Their numbers were not to be increased or diminished; for if this was done, his wrath was terrible. (See ODYSSEUS.) In the 700 sheep and oxen the ancients recognized the 700 days and nights of the lunar year. The flocks were tended by Phaëthusa (the goddess of light) and Lampetié (the goddess of shining), his daughter by Neaera. By the ocean Nymph Persé or Perseïs he was father of Aeëtes, Circé, and Pasiphaë, by Clymené the father of Phaëthon, and Augeas was also accounted his son. His children had the gleaming eyes of their father.

After the time of Euripides, or thereabouts, the all-seeing Sun-god was identified with Apollo, the god of prophecy. Helios was worshipped in many places, among which may be mentioned Corinth and Elis. The island of Rhodes was entirely consecrated to him. Here an annual festival (Ἅλια) was held during the summer in his honour, with chariot-racing and contests of music and gymnastics; and four consecrated horses were thrown into the sea as a sacrifice to him. In B.C. 278 a colossal bronze statue by Chares of Lindus was erected to him at the entrance of the harbour of Rhodes. (See COLOSSUS.) Herds of red and white cattle were, in many places, kept in his honour. White animals, and especially white horses, were sacred to him; among the birds the cock, and among trees the white poplar. See, in English literature, the poem by Keats, *Hyperion*, and the first book of W. S. Landor's *Gebir*.

The Latin poets identified Helios with the Sabine deity Sol, who had an ancient place of worship on the Quirinal at Rome, and a public sacrifice on the 8th of August; but it was the introduction of the ritual of Mithras which first brought the worship of the sun into prominence in Rome. See MITHRAS.

Hell. See HADES.

Hellanīcus (Ἑλλανικός). One of the Greek logographi or chroniclers, born at Mitylené in Lesbos about B.C. 490. He is said to have lived till the age of eighty-five, and to have gone on writing until after B.C. 406. In the course of his long life he composed a series of works on genealogy, chorography, and chronology, of which the fragments are collected by C. and Th. Müller (Paris, 1841).

He was the first writer who attempted to introduce a systematic chronological arrangement into the traditional periods of Greek, and especially Athenian, history and mythology. His theories of the ancient Attic chronology were accepted down to the time of Eratosthenes (q. v.). See LOGOGRAPHI.

Hellanodĭcae (Ἑλλανοδίκαι). Judges in the Olympian and Nemean Games. See NEMEA; OLYMPIA.

Hellas (Ἑλλάς). A name originally given to a district and city of Thessaly in the division Phthiotis (Hom. *Il.* ii. 684), then further extended to the whole of Thessaly, and finally adopted as a general appellation for all Greece. Hellas is a peninsula, the easternmost of the three that project from the south of Europe into the Mediterranean Sea. Its western coast is rough and mountainous, while its eastern shores abound in gulfs, bays, and harbours. From this geographical cause Greece for a long time knew little or nothing of Italy and the West, but sustained very close relations, political and commercial, with the countries of Asia Minor—a fact of immense importance in her historical development. Because of her long line of coast, she first received, in great measure, the quickening which comes from immigration and the contact with new ideas that inevitably follows; so that Greece, largely by reason of her physical conformation and position, most readily responded to the influences of oriental culture, and thus became the cradle of European civilization.

Hellas is divided into two parts by the Gulf of Corinth, which would have completely severed them were it not for the narrow Isthmus of Corinth. This, until it was cut by the modern canal (August, 1893), united the southern division (Peloponnesus) with the northern (Hellas Proper). Hellas as a whole is marked off from the rest of Europe by a mountain chain, an extension of the Balkans, known in ancient times as the Haemus. From this range ran the chains from north-northwest to south-southeast, which form the skeleton of Greece. What may be called the backbone of the country is the range that first separates Illyria from Macedonia and Epirus from Thessaly, and then continues down through the whole peninsula. The most important single chain is Pindus (7111 feet), with its branch Othrys. Various single peaks are Olympus in Thessaly (9750 feet), Ossa, Pelion, Tymphrestus (7606 feet), Parnassus (8036 feet), and Helicon, all in Hellas Proper; with Cyllenê, Aroania, and Erymanthus in the Peloponnesus, whose two important spurs are the Taÿgetus and Parnon. The Ionian Isles, Corcyra, Cephallenia, Leucas, and Zacynthus, off the western coast, follow the same direction as the mountain chains of the Peloponnesus and the mainland.

The rivers of Greece are small streams, little more than brooks, flowing usually south or west. In Hellas Proper there are four principal rivers, all having their source on Mount Lacmon of the Pindus range. The Aoüs flows into the Adriatic, the Peneus and Haliacmon into the Thermaic Gulf, and the Acheloüs into the Gulf of Patrae. In the Peloponnesus, the important streams rise near the north of Taÿgetus, the Eurotas flowing south and the Alpheus west.

The Hellenes were a branch of the family to which most of the European peoples belong, and which is variously described as Aryan, Indo-Germanic, and Indo-European, whose original home is uncertain, being by some placed in Asia and by others in Europe. (See INDO-EUROPEAN LANGUAGES.) It is generally held, however, that the original inhabitants of Greece entered it from the north at a very remote period, probably during the Stone Age; that they were in the nomadic stage of development; and that they came on in successive waves of immigration, each of which pushed farther south the people who had already preceded it. Even after the whole of Hellas had been covered by these early tribes, succeeding waves followed, overspreading the territory occupied by others. Such a wave of later immigration was that which is known to the legendary historians as "the return of the Heraclidae." (See HERACLIDAE.) This pressure from behind had the effect of driving out many who had settled in the mainland into the adjacent islands, and ultimately to far distant lands, such as the coasts of Asia Minor, Sicily, the shore of the Euxine, and the north of Africa. Hellas in its wider sense is, therefore, to be understood of the united settlements of Hellenes in all parts of the then known world, and it was in this sense that the Hellenes themselves understood it, since to them the word always had an ethnic rather than a territorial significance. The name Ἕλληνες in Homer refers only to the Thessalian people mentioned above; and in fact the Homeric poems have no general designation for the Greeks as a whole. They are called Danaï (Δαναοί), Argivi (Ἀργεῖοι), and Achaei (Ἀχαιοί), and it was not much before the time of Herodotus, Thucydides, and Scylax that the terms Ἑλλάς and Ἕλληνες received their full extension of meaning. The Orientals spoke of the Greeks as "Ionians"; the Italians called them Graeci, from one of the ancient tribes of Epirus, the Γραικοί—a word older than Ἕλληνες, but disused and then revived by Sophocles, according to Eustathius (*ad* Hom. *Il.* p. 890, 14; cf. Hesych. i. p. 854; Steph. Byz. s. h. v.; and Tzetzes, schol. to Lycophron's *Alexandra*).

On the Greek language, see DIALECTS; on the art, see ARCHITECTURA; CAELATURA; PICTURA; STATUARIA ARS; on the religion, see MYSTERIA; MYTHOLOGIA; RELIGIO. A brief description of each of the divisions of Greece will be found under their respective titles.

The time which elapsed from the appearance of the Hellenes in Thessaly to the siege of Troy is usually known by the name of the Heroic Age. Thucydides informs us (i. 4) that the commencement of Grecian civilization is to be dated from the reign of Minos of Crete, who acquired a naval power and cleared the Aegean Sea of pirates. Among the most celebrated heroes of this period were Bellerophon and Perseus, whose adventures were laid in the East; Theseus, the king of Athens; and Heracles. Tradition also preserved the account of expeditions undertaken by several chiefs united together, such as that of the Argonauts, of the Seven against Thebes, and of the siege of Troy. See TROJAN WAR.

It is learned from Thucydides (i. 12) that the population of Greece was in a very unsettled state for some time after the Trojan War. Of the various migrations which appear to have taken place, the most important in their consequences were those of the Boeotians from Thessaly into the country afterwards called Boeotia, and of the Dorians into Peloponnesus. At about the same period the western coast of Asia Minor was colonized by the Greeks. The ancient inhabitants of Boeotia, who had been driven out of their homes by the invasion of the Boeotians, together with some Aeolians (whence it has acquired the name of the Aeolian migration) left Boeotia and settled in Lesbos and the northwestern corner of Asia Minor. They were not long afterwards followed by the Ionians, who, having been driven from their abode on the Corinthian Gulf, had taken refuge in Attica, whence they emigrated to Asia Minor and settled on the Lydian coast. The southwestern part of the coast of Asia Minor was also colonized at about the same period by Dorians. The number of Greek colonies, considering the extent of the mother country, was very great; and the readiness with which the Greeks left their homes to settle in foreign lands forms a remarkable feature of their national character. In the seventh century before Christ the Greek colonies took another direction: Cyrené, in Africa, was founded by the inhabitants of Thera, and the coasts of Sicily and the southern part of Italy became studded with so many Greek cities that it acquired the name of the Great, or Greater, Greece (Magna Graecia). (On the settlement of the Greek cities in Southern Italy, see Lenormant, *La Grande Grèce*, 3 vols. [Paris, 1881].)

The two States of Greece which attained the greatest historical celebrity were Sparta and Athens. The power of Athens was of later growth; but Sparta had, from the time of the Dorian conquest, taken the lead among the Peloponnesian States, a position which she maintained by the conquest of the fertile country of Messenia, B.C. 688. Her superiority was probably owing to the nature of her political institutions, which are said to have been fixed on a firm basis by her celebrated lawgiver Lycurgus, B.C. 884. At the head of the nation were two hereditary kings, but their power was greatly limited by a jealous aristocracy. Her territories were also increased by the conquest of Tegea in Arcadia. Athens rose to importance only in the century preceding the Persian Wars; but even in this period her power was

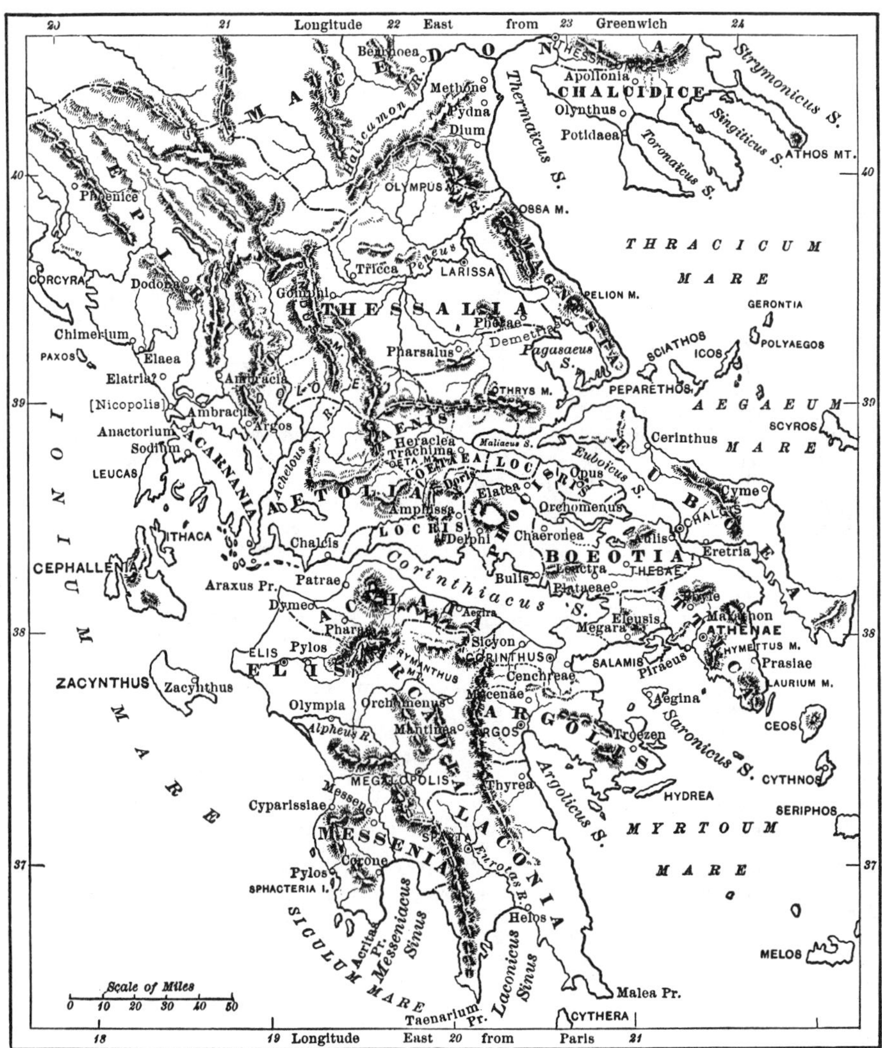

Map of Ancient Greece.

not more than a match for the little States of Megaris and Aegina. The city was long harassed by internal commotions till the time of Solon, B.C. 594, who was chosen by his fellow-citizens to frame a new constitution and a new code of laws, to which much of the future greatness of Athens must be ascribed. We have already seen that the kingly form of government was prevalent in the Heroic Age. But, during the period that elapsed between the Trojan War and the Persian invasion, hereditary political power was abolished in almost all the Greek States, with the exception of Sparta, and a republican form of government established in its stead. In studying the history of the Greeks, one must bear in mind that almost every city formed an independent State, and that, with the exception of Athens and Sparta, which exacted obedience from the other towns of Attica and Laconia respectively, there was hardly any State which possessed more than a few miles of territory. Frequent wars between themselves were the almost unavoidable consequence of the existence of so many small States nearly equal in power. The evils which arose from this condition of things were partly remedied by the influence of the Amphictyonic Council and by the religious games and festivals which were held at fixed periods in different parts of Greece, and during the celebration of which no wars were carried on. In the sixth century before the Christian era, Greece rapidly advanced in knowledge and civilization. Literature and the fine arts were already cultivated in Athens under the auspices of Pisistratus and his sons; and the products of remote countries were introduced into Greece by the merchants of Corinth and Aegina. See COMMERCE.

This was the most splendid period of Grecian history. The Greeks, in their resistance to the Persians, and the part they took in the burning of Sardis, B.C. 499, drew upon them the vengeance of Darius. After the reduction of the Asiatic Greeks, a Persian army was sent into Attica, but was entirely defeated at Marathon, B.C. 490, by the Athenians under Miltiades. Ten years afterwards the whole power of the Persian Empire was directed against Greece; an immense army, led in person by Xerxes, advanced as far as Attica, and received the submission of almost all the Grecian States, with the exception of Athens and Sparta. But this expedition also failed; the Persian fleet was destroyed in the battles of Artemisium and Salamis; and the land forces were entirely defeated in the following year, B.C. 479, at Plataea in Boeotia. Sparta had, previous to the Persian invasion, been regarded by the other Greeks as the first power in Greece, and accordingly she obtained the supreme command of the army and fleet in the Persian War. But, during the course of this war, the Athenians had made greater sacrifices and had shown a greater degree of courage and patriotism, so that after the battle of Plataea a confederacy was formed by the Grecian States for carrying on the war against the Persians. Sparta was at first placed at the head of it; but the allies, disgusted with the tyranny of Pausanias (q. v.), the Spartan commander, gave the supremacy to Athens. The allies, who consisted of the inhabitants of the islands and coasts of the Aegean Sea, were to furnish contributions in money and ships, and the delicate task of assessing the amount which each State was to pay was assigned to Aristides. The yearly contribution was settled at 460 talents (about $542,800), and Delos was chosen as the common treasury. The Athenians, under the command of Cimon, carried on the war vigorously, defeated the Persian fleets, and plundered the maritime provinces of the Persian Empire.

During this period the power of Athens rapidly increased; she possessed a succession of distinguished statesmen—Themistocles, Aristides, Cimon, and Pericles — who all contributed to the advancement of her power, though differing in their political views. Her maritime greatness was founded by Themistocles, her revenues were increased by Pericles, and her general prosperity, in connection with other causes, tended to produce a greater degree of culture than existed in any other part of Greece. Literature was cultivated, and the arts of architecture and sculpture, which were employed to ornament the city, were carried to a degree of excellence that has never since been surpassed. See ATHENAE.

While Athens was advancing in power, Sparta had to maintain a war against the Messenians, who again revolted, and were joined by a great number of the Spartan slaves (B.C. 461–455). But, though Sparta made no efforts during this period to restrain the Athenian power, it was not because she wanted the will, but the means. These, however, were soon furnished by the Athenians themselves, who began to treat the allied States with great tyranny, and to regard them as subjects, and not as independent States in alliance. The tribute was raised from 460 to 600 talents, the treasury was removed from Delos to Athens, and the decision of all important suits was referred to the Athenian courts. When any State withdrew from the alliance, its citizens were considered by the Athenians as rebels, and immediately reduced to subjection. The dependent States, anxious to throw off the Athenian dominion, entreated the assistance of Sparta, and thus, in conjunction with other causes, arose the war between Sparta and Athens, which lasted for twenty-seven years (B.C. 431–404), and is usually known as the Peloponnesian War (q. v.). It terminated by again placing Sparta at the head of all Greece. Soon after the conclusion of this war, Sparta engaged in a contest with the Persian Empire, which lasted from B.C. 400 to 394. The splendid successes which Agesilaüs, the Spartan king, obtained over the Persian troops in Asia Minor, and the manifest weakness of the Persian Empire, which had been already shown by the successful retreat of only ten thousand Greeks from the very heart of the Persian Empire (see XENOPHON), appear to have induced Agesilaüs to entertain the design of overthrowing the Persian monarchy; but he was obliged to return to his native country to defend it against a powerful confederacy, which had been formed by the Corinthians, Thebans, Argives, Athenians, and Thessalians, for the purpose of throwing off the Spartan dominion. The confederates were not, however, successful in their attempt; and the Spartan supremacy was again secured for a brief period by a general peace, made B.C. 387, usually known by the name of the peace of Antalcidas. Ten years afterwards, the rupture between Thebes and Sparta began, which led to a general war in Greece, and for a short time gave Thebes the hegemony of Hellas. The greatness of Thebes was principally owing to the wisdom and valour of two of her sons—Pelopidas and Epaminondas. After the death of Epaminondas at the battle of Mantinea, B.C. 362, Thebes again sank to its former obscurity. The Spartan supremacy was, however, wholly destroyed, and her power still further humbled by the restoration of Messenia to independence, B.C. 369. From the conclusion of this war to the reign of Philip of Macedon, Greece remained without any ruling power. It is only necessary here to mention the part which Philip took in the Sacred War (q. v.), which lasted ten years (B.C. 356–346), in which he appeared as the defender of the Amphictyonic Council, and which terminated by the conquest of the Phocians. The Athenians, urged on by Demosthenes, made an alliance with the Thebans for the purpose of resisting Philip; but their defeat at Chaeronea, B.C. 388, secured for the Macedonian king the supremacy of Greece. In the same year a congress of Grecian States was held at Corinth, in which Philip was chosen general-in-chief of the Greeks in a projected war against the Persian Empire; but his assassination in B.C. 336 caused this enterprise to devolve on his son Alexander. See ALEXANDER; MACEDONIA.

The conquests of Alexander extended the Grecian influence over the greater part of Asia west of the Indus. After his death the dominion of the East was contested by his generals, and two powerful empires were permanently established—that of the Ptolemies in Egypt and the Seleucidae in Syria. The dominions of the early Syrian kings embraced the greater part of Western Asia; but their Empire was soon divided into various independent kingdoms, such as that of Bactria and Pergamus, in all of which the Greek language was spoken, not merely at court, but to a considerable extent in the cities. From the death of Alexander to the Roman conquest, Macedon remained the ruling power in Greece. The Aetolian and Achaean leagues were formed, the former B.C. 284, the latter B.C. 281, for the purpose of resisting the Macedonian kings. Macedonia was conquered by the Romans B.C. 197, and the Greek States declared independent. This, however, was merely nominal; for they only exchanged the rule of the Macedonian kings for that of the Roman people; and in B.C. 146, Greece was reduced to the form of a Roman province, called Achaea, though certain cities, such as Athens, Delphi, and others, were allowed to have the rank of free towns. The history of Greece, from this period, forms part of that of the Roman Empire. See ROMA.

Greece was overrun by the Goths in A.D. 267, and again in A.D. 398, under Alaric; and, after being occupied by the Crusaders and Venetians, at last fell into the hands of the Turks, on the conquest of Constantinople; from whom it was again liberated in 1828. See the articles ATHENAE; BYZANTINUM IMPERIUM; SPARTA; MACEDONIA; and the following works of reference. —GEOGRAPHY: Wordsworth, *Greece Pictorial, Historical, and Descriptive* (1882); Tozer, *Lectures on the Geography of Greece* (1874); Bursian, *Geographie des Griechenland*, 3 vols. (1862–73); Mahaffy, *Rambles and Studies in Greece* (1878); E. Curtius, *Peloponnesos*, 2 vols. (1852); Clark, *Peloponnesus* (1858); Lacroix, *Les Isles de la Grèce* (1881). HISTORY: Thirlwall, *Hist. of Greece*, 8 vols. (2d ed. 1855); Grote, *Hist. of Greece* (to B.C. 300), 12 vols. (1870); E. Curtius, *Hist. of Greece* (Eng. trans. by Ward, 5 vols. 1868–72); Cox, *Hist. of Greece* (to the death of Alexander the Great); id. *The Athenian Empire* (1877); id. *Greeks and Persians* (1876); Droysen, *Geschichte des Hellenismus*, 6 vols. (1877–1878); Curteis, *Rise of the Macedonian Empire* (1878); Lloyd, *Age of Pericles* (1875); Hertzberg,

Country about Athens. (From the painting by A. de Curzon.)

Griechenland u. d. Herrschaft der Römer, 3 vols. (1875); Mahaffy, *The Greek World under Roman Sway* (1890); Freeman, *History of Federal Government in Greece* (2d ed. 1893); Duncker, *Hist. of Greece* (Eng. trans. by Aleyne, 1883; last German edition, 1885). CHRONOLOGY: Clinton, *Fasti Hellenici*, 3 vols. (1834–51); Peter, *Zeittafeln d. griechischen Geschichte* (1877). IN GENERAL: Paparrigopoulo, *Histoire de la Civilisation Hellénique* (Paris, 1878); Döring, *Hellas* (Frankfort, 1876); Felton, *Greece, Ancient and Modern* (Boston, 1880); Gilbert, *Greek Constitutional Antiquities* (Eng. trans. 1895); Göll, *Kulturbilder aus Hellas und Rom*, 2 vols. (1878); Guhl and Koner, *The Life of the Greeks and Romans*, fully illustrated (Eng. trans. 1877; last German ed. 1893); Von Falke, *Hellas und Rom*, richly illustrated (Eng. trans. 1882); Schömann, *Antiquities of Greece* (Eng. trans. 1880); Overbeck, *Geschichte der griechischen Plastik*, 2 vols. (1880–82); Perry, *Greek and Roman Sculpture* (1882); Blümner, *Technologie und Terminologie der Gewerbe und Künste bei Griechen und Römern*, 4 vols. (1875–86); Mahaffy, *Social Life in Greece* (last ed. 1887). On recent archaeological discoveries, see P. Gardner, *New Chapters in Greek History* (N. Y. and London, 1892).

Hellé (Ἕλλη). See PHRIXUS.

Hellen (Ἕλλην). The mythical ancestor of the Hellenes. He was the son of Zeus and Dorippé, husband of Orseïs, and father of Aeolus, Dorus, and Xunthus. From his two sons, Aeolus and Dorus, the Aeolians and Dorians claimed descent; and from the two sons of Xanthus (Achaeus and Ion) tradition derives the Achaeans and Ionians. Hellen is described as reigning over Phthia in Thessaly. See HELLAS.

Hellēnes. See HELLAS.

Hellenĭca (Ἑλληνικά). An historical treatise by Xenophon (q. v.), dealing with the period of forty-eight years preceding the battle of Mantinea (B.C. 362). As it begins where the history of Thucydides (q. v.) ends, the first part is sometimes called the "Paralipomena of Thucydides." The *Hellenica* is in seven books, and is written in a dry, somewhat uninteresting style. Separate editions with notes are those of Hailstone (bks. i. and ii., 1867); Breitenbach (1863); Büchsenschütz (1876); and Dowdall (bk. i. 1890); of bks. i.–iv. by Manatt (Boston, 1886), and v.–vii. by Bennett (Boston, 1892). A fine English version is that of Dakyns in his translation of Xenophon (1893). See XENOPHON.

Hellenotamiae (Ἑλληνοταμίαι). The name of a board of ten members, elected annually by lot as controllers of the fund contributed by the members of the Athenian confederacy. The treasure was originally deposited at Delos, but after B.C. 461 was transferred to Athens. The yearly contributions of the cities owning the Athenian supremacy amounted at first to 460 talents (some $542,800); during the Peloponnesian War they were increased to nearly 1300 talents ($1,534,000). See DELOS, CONFEDERACY OF.

Hellespontus (Ἑλλήσποντος). (1) Now the Dardanelles, the long narrow strait which joins the Propontis (Sea of Marmora) with the Aegean Sea. Its length is some fifty miles, and its width varies from six at the upper end to one or less. The narrowest part is between the ancient cities of Sestus and Abydus, where Leander is said to have swum across to visit Hero. (See LEANDER.) Here, also, Xerxes (q. v.) crossed on his bridge of boats. The name Ἑλλήσποντος (Sea of Hellé) was derived from the myth of Hellé; on which see the article PHRIXUS. (2) Under the Roman Empire, the name Hellespontus was given to a province in the northern part of Mysia, with Cyzicus for its capital.

Hellomĕnum (Ἑλλόμενον). A seaport town of the Acarnanians on the island of Leucas.

Hellopia. See ELLOPIA.

Helm. See GUBERNACULUM.

Helmet. See ARMA; GALEA.

Helōrus (Ἕλωρος) and **Helōrum.** A town on the eastern coast of Sicily, south of Syracuse, at the mouth of the river Helorus.

Helos (τὸ Ἕλος). (1) A town in Laconia, on the coast, in a marshy situation, whence its name (ἕλος = marsh). It was commonly said that the Spartan slaves called Helotes (Εἵλωτες), were originally the Achaean inhabitants of this town who were reduced by the Dorian conquerors to slavery. (2) A town or district of Elis on the Alpheus.

Helōtae (Εἱλῶται), and **Helōtes** (Εἵλωτες). The Helots or bondsmen of the Spartans. The common account of the origin of this class is, that the inhabitants of the maritime town of Helos were reduced by Sparta to this state of degradation, after an insurrection against the Dorians already established in power. This explanation, however, rests merely on an etymology, and that by no means probable. The word Εἵλως is probably a derivative from ἑλεῖν in a passive sense, and consequently means "a prisoner"—a derivation known in ancient times. It seems likely that they were an aboriginal race, which was subdued at a very early period, and which immediately passed over as slaves to the Doric conquerors. In speaking of the condition of the Helots, their political rights and their personal treatment will be considered under different heads, though in fact the two subjects are very nearly connected.

The first were doubtless exactly defined by law and custom, though the expressions made use of by ancient authors are frequently vague and ambiguous. "They were," says Ephorus, "in a certain point of view public slaves. Their possessor could neither liberate them nor sell them beyond the borders." From this it is evident that they were considered as belonging properly to the State, which to a certain degree permitted them to be possessed by individuals, reserving to itself the power of enfranchising them. But to sell them out of the country was not in the power even of the State; and such an event seems never to have occurred. It is, upon the whole, most probable that individuals had no power to sell them at all, as they belonged chiefly to the landed property, and this was inalienable. On these lands they had certain fixed dwellings of their own, and particular services and payments were prescribed to them. They paid as rent a fixed measure of corn; not, however, like the Perioeci, to the State, but to their masters. As this quantity had been definitely settled at a very early period, the Helots were the persons who profited by a good, and lost by a bad, harvest, which must have been to them an encouragement to industry and good husbandry, as would not have been the case if the profit and loss had merely affected the landlords. In fact, by this means, as is proved by the accounts respecting the Spartan agriculture, a careful cultivation of the soil was kept up. By means of the rich produce of the lands, and in part by plunder obtained in war, they collected a considerable property, to the attainment of which almost every access was closed to the Spartans. The cultivation of the land, however, was not the only duty of the Helots; they also, at the public meals, attended upon their masters, who, according to the Lacedaemonian principle of a community of property, mutually lent them to one another (Xen. *Rep. Lac.* vi. 3; Aristot. *Pol.* ii. 2, 5). A large number of them was also employed by the State in public works. In the field the Helots never served as hoplites, except in extraordinary cases; and then it was the general practice afterwards to give them their liberty. This seems first to have occurred under Brasidas in B.C. 424. (Cf. Thuc. iv. 80, vii. 19.) On other occasions they attended the regular army as light-armed troops (ψιλοί); and that their numbers were very considerable may be seen from the battle of Plataea, in which 5000 Spartans were attended by 35,000 Helots. Although they did not share the honour of the heavy-armed soldiers, they were in turn exposed to a less degree of danger; for, while the former, in close rank, received the onset of the enemy with spear and shield, the Helots, armed only with their slings and javelins, were in a moment either before or behind the ranks, as Tyrtaeus accurately describes the relative duties of the light-armed soldier (γυμνής) and the hoplite. Sparta, in her better days, is never recorded to have unnecessarily sacrificed the lives of her Helots. A certain number of them were allotted to each Spartan (Herod. ix. 28; Thuc. iii. 8). At the battle of Plataea this number was seven. Those who were assigned to a single master were probably called ἀμπίτταρες. Of these, however, one in particular was the servant (θεράπων) of his master, as in the story of the blind Spartan, who was conducted by his Helot into the thickest of the battle of Thermopylae, and, while the latter fled, fell with the other heroes (Herod. vii. 229). It appears that the other Helots were in the field placed more immediately under the command of the king than the rest of the army (Herod. vi. 80, 81). In the fleet they composed the large mass of the sailors (Xen. *Hist. Gr.* vii. 1, 12), in which service at Athens the inferior citizens and slaves were employed. It is a matter of much greater difficulty to form a clear notion of the treatment of the Helots, and of their manner of life; for the rhetorical spirit with which later historians have embellished their views has been productive of much confusion and misconception. Myron of Prienê, in his account of the Messenian War, drew a very dark picture of Sparta, and endeavoured at the end to rouse the feelings of his readers by a description of the fate which the conquered underwent. "The Helots," says he, "perform for the Spartans every ignominious service. They are compelled to wear a cap of dog's skin (κυνῆ), to have a covering of sheep's skin (διφθέρα), and are severely beaten every year without having committed any fault, in order that they may never forget they are slaves. In addition to this, those among them who, either by their stature or their beauty, raise themselves above the condition of a slave, are condemned to death, and the masters who do not destroy the most manly of them are liable to punishment." Myron's statements, however, are to be received with considerable caution.

Plutarch relates (*Lycurg.* 28) that the Helots were compelled to intoxicate themselves, and to perform indecent dances, as a warning to the Spartan youth. Yet Helot women discharged the office of nurse in the royal palaces, and doubtless obtained the affection with which the attendants of early youth were honoured in ancient times. It is, however, certain that the Doric laws did not bind servants to strict temperance; and hence examples of drunkenness among them might well have served as a means of recommending sobriety. It was also an established regulation that the national songs and dances of Sparta were forbidden to the Helots, who, on the other hand, had some extravagant and lascivious dances peculiar to themselves, which may have given rise to the above report.

It was the curse of this bondage, which Plato terms the hardest in Greece, that the slaves abandoned their masters when they stood in greatest need of their assistance; and hence the Spartans were even compelled to stipulate in treaties for aid against their own subjects (Thuc. i. 118, v. 14; cf. Aristot. *Pol.* ii. 6, 2). A more favourable side of the Spartan system of bondage is seen in the fact that a legal way to liberty and citizenship stood open to the Helots. The many intermediate steps seem to prove the existence of a regular mode of transition from the one rank to the other. The Helots who were esteemed worthy of an especial confidence were called ἀργεῖοι; the ἀφέται were probably released from all service. The δεσποσιοναῦται, who served in the fleets, resembled probably the freedmen of Attica, who were called "the out-dwellers" (οἱ χωρὶς οἰκοῦντες). When they received their liberty, they also obtained permission to dwell where they wished (Thuc. iv. 80, v. 34), and probably, at the same time, a portion of land was granted them without the lot of their former masters. After they had been in possession of liberty for some time, they appear to have been called νεοδαμώδεις (Thuc. vii. 58), the number of whom soon came near to that of the citizens (Plut. *Ages.* 6). The μόθωνες or μόθακες were Helots, who, being brought up together with the young Spartans, obtained freedom without the rights of citizenship.

The number of the Helots has been estimated by K. O. Müller and Schömann as having been some 225,000 at the time of the battle of Plataea, as against an estimated total population of 380,000 or 400,000 (Müller, *Dorians*, vol. ii. p. 30 foll., Eng. trans.). See Thirlwall, *Hist. of Greece*, i. 309–313; Gilbert, *Staatsalterth.* i. 31–36; and the article CRYPTEIA.

Helvecōnae. A people in Germany, between the Viadus and the Vistula, south of the Rugii and north of the Burgundiones, reckoned by Tacitus among the Ligii (*Germ.* 43).

Helvetia. See HELVETII.

Helvetii. (Ἑλουήττιοι). A nation of Gaul, conquered by Caesar. Their country is generally supposed to have answered to modern Switzerland; but ancient Helvetia was of less extent than modern Switzerland, being bounded on the north by the Rhenus and Lacus Brigantinus, or Lake of Constance; on the south by the Rhodanus and the Lacus Lemannus, or Lake of Geneva; and on the west by Mons Iurassus (Jura) (Caes. *B. G.* i. etc.; Tac. *Hist.* i. 67, 69). The chief town of the Helvetii was Aventicum, now Avenches. They were divided into four *pagi* or cantons, of which the names of only two are known—the Pagus Tigurinus (the most important pagus) and the Pagus (Vicus) Verbigenus (Urbigenus). It must be noted that the name Helvetia is a purely modern one—the country being spoken of in ancient times simply as Ager Helvetiorum.

The Helvetii first appear in history during the war between the Romans and the Cimbri. In B.C. 107 the people of the Pagus Tigurinus defeated the Roman consul Cassius Longinus, while others of the race invaded Gaul and Italy, sharing in the defeat inflicted on the Cimbri by Marius and Catulus in B.C. 101. In the year 58, they attempted, on the advice of Orgetorix, an Helvetic chief, to migrate to Gaul, but were defeated and driven back by Caesar; after which the Romans planted colonies in these territories, with three fortresses at Aventicum, Vindonissa (Königsfelden), and Noviodunum (Nion). Under the later emperors, the country of the Helvetii, with that of the Sequani and Rauraci, formed the province known as Maxima Sequanorum. See Mommsen, *Die Schweiz in röm. Zeit* (Zürich, 1854).

Helvia. Mother of the philosopher Seneca (q. v.).

Helvidius Priscus. See PRISCUS.

Helvii. A people in Gaul, between the Rhone and Mount Cebenna, which separated them from the Arverni. They were for a long time subject to Massilia, but afterwards belonged to the province of Gallia Narbonensis. Their country produced good wine.

Helvius Cinna. See CINNA.

Helvius Pertĭnax. See PERTINAX.

Hemĕra (ἡμέρα). See DIES.

Hemerodrŏmi (ἡμεροδρόμοι). Trained runners employed as couriers in the Greek States, and used to carry the official tidings of important events. They were capable of performing remarkably long distances in a very short space of time; on which see Herod. vi. 105; Plut. *Arist.* 20. They are also called ἡμεροσκόποι (Herod. vii. 183).

Hemeroscŏpi. See HEMERODROMI.

Hemichrȳsus. See STATER.

Hemicongius. Half a *congius*. See CONGIUS.

Hemicyclium (ἡμικύκλιον). (1) A semicircular alcove, sufficiently large to admit of several persons sitting in it at the same time, for the enjoyment of mutual converse. The ancients constructed such places in their own pleasure-grounds (Cic. *De Am.* 1; Sidon. *Ep.* i. 1), and also as public seats in different parts of a town for the accommodation of the inhabitants (Suet. *Gramm.* 17). (2) A sundial of simple construction invented by Berosus. See HOROLOGIUM.

Hemīna (ἡμίνα). A measure of capacity, containing half a sextarius (Festus, s. v. Rhemn. Fann. *De Pond.* 67); whence, also, a vessel made to contain that exact quantity (Pers. i. 129).

Hemīna, CASSIUS. See CASSIUS.

Hemiobŏlus, Hemiobolion. See OBOLUS.

Hemiolia (ἡμιολία). A particular kind of ship (Gell. x. 25), used chiefly by the Greek pirates (Arrian, *Anab.* iii. 2, 5); constructed in such a manner that half of its side was left free from rowers, in order to form a deck for fighting purposes.

Hemiolia. (Rich.)

Hemipodion. See PES.

Hemistāter. See STATER.

Hemsterhuys, TIBERIUS, often spoken of under the Latinized form HEMSTERHUSIUS. A Dutch classical scholar born at Groningen, January 9th, 1685. He was educated at the Universities of Groningen and Leyden, entering the former at the age of fifteen, and being appointed Professor of Mathematics and Philosophy in Amsterdam at the age of nineteen. In 1706 he brought out an edition of the *Onomasticon* of Pollux which had been begun by Lederlin, but was so mortified by the criticism made upon it by Richard Bentley (q. v.) as to refuse to open a Greek book for months. In 1717 he was called to the chair of Greek at the University of Franeker, and from 1738 discharged the duties of a professor of history, being transferred to Leyden in 1740. He died April 7th, 1766.

His chief works are editions of the *Colloquia* and *Timon* of Lucian (1708); of the *Plutus* of Aristophanes (1744); annotations on Xenophon of Ephesus (last ed. 1784); ed. Pollux (1706); a Latin trans. of the *Birds* of Aristophanes in Kuster's edition; besides notes contributed to Ernesti's Callimachus and to Burmann's Propertius. See the *Eulogium* of Ruhnken (1789), the *Supplementa Annotationis ad Eulogium* (Leyden, 1874), and L. Müller, *Geschichte d. class. Philologie in den Niederlanden*, pp. 74–82 (Leipzig, 1869).

Hen. See GALLINA.

Hendĕka (οἱ Ἕνδεκα, "The Eleven"). A term applied at Athens to a band consisting of ten members, chosen by lot, and their secretary. Their duty was to superintend the prisons, receive arrested prisoners, and carry out the sentences of the law. The capital sentence was executed by their subordinates. They also had penal jurisdiction in the case of delinquents discovered in the act of committing offences punishable with death or imprisonment. If they pleaded guilty, the Eleven inflicted the punishment at once; if not, they instituted a judicial inquiry and presided at the decision of the case. They had the same power in the case of embezzlement of confiscated property, of which they had lists in their possession. Under Demetrius Phalereus they received the name of νομοφύλακες. See Hermann, *Staatsalterth.* § 138.

Henĕti (Ἐνετοί). An ancient people in Paphlagonia, dwelling on the river Parthenius, fought on the side of Priam against the Greeks, but had disappeared before the historical times. They were regarded by many ancient writers as the ancestors of the Veneti in Italy. See VENETI.

Heniŏchi (Ἡνίοχοι). A people in Colchis, north of the Phasis, notorious as pirates.

Henna. See ENNA.

Hephaestĭa (Ἡφαιστία). (1) One of the two principal towns in the island of Lemnos, the other being Myrina (Herod. vii. 140). (2) A deme of Attica belonging to the tribe Acamantis.

Hephaestīa (Ἡφαίστεια). A festival at Athens, celebrated annually, in honour of Hephaestus. See LAMPADEPHORIA.

Hephaestiădes Insŭlae. See AEOLIAE INSULAE.

Hephaestion (Ἡφαιστίων). (1) A Macedonian, celebrated as the friend of Alexander the Great, with whom he had been brought up. He died at Ecbatana, B.C. 325, to the great grief of Alexander, who ordered mourning for him throughout the whole Empire. (2) A Greek scholar, a native of Alexandria, who flourished about the middle of the second century A.D., and was tutor to the emperor Verus before his accession. He wrote a work on prosody, in forty-eight books, which he at first abridged into eleven books, then into three, and finally into one. The final abridgment, called a manual on metres (Ἐγχειρίδιον περὶ Μέτρων), has come down to us. It gives no more than a bare sketch of prosody, without any attempt at theoretical explanation of the facts; but it is, nevertheless, of immense value, since it is the only complete treatise on Greek prosody which has survived from antiquity, and quotes verses from the lost poets. Attached to it is a treatise on the different forms of poetry and composition, in two incomplete versions. The manual has a preface by Longinus, and two collections of scholia. It has been edited by Gaisford, with notes (last ed. 1856); and by Westphal (1866).

Hephaestium (Ἡφαίστιον). A name given to a region in the extremity of Lycia, near Phaselis, from which fire issued when a burning torch was applied to the surface. This was owing to the naphtha with which the soil was impregnated (Sen. *Epist.* 79).

Hephaestus (Ἥφαιστος). In Greek mythology, the god of fire, and of the arts which need fire in the execution. Roscher proposes various derivations of the name—from ἁφή (ἅπτω), "a lighting," or from the root of φαίνω, "to shine." He was said to be the son of Zeus and Heré, or, according to Hesiod, of the latter only. Being ugly, and lame in both feet, his mother was ashamed of him, and threw him from Olympus into the ocean, where he was taken up by Eurynomé and Thetis and concealed in a subterranean cavern. Here he remained for nine years, and fashioned a number of exquisite works of art, among them a golden throne with invisible chains, which he sent to his mother by way of revenge. She sat down in it, and was chained to the seat so fast that no one could release her. On this it was resolved to call Hephaestus back to Olympus. Ares wished to force him back, but was frightened off by his brother with firebrands. Dionysus at length succeeded in making him drunk and bringing him back in this condition to Olympus. But he was destined to meet with his former luck a second time. There came a quarrel between Zeus and Heré, and Hephaestus took his mother's part; whereupon Zeus seized him by the leg and hurled him down from Olympus. He fell upon the island of Lemnos, where the Sintians, who then inhabited the island, took care of him and finally revived him. From this time Lemnos was his favourite abode. His lameness was, in the later story, attributed to this fall (Hom. *Il.* i. 590 foll.).

The whole story—the sojourn of Hephaestus in the cavern under the sea and his fondness for Lemnos—is, in all probability, based upon volcanic phenomena—the submarine activity of volcanic fires and the natural features of the island of Lemnos. Here there was a volcano called Mosychlus, which was in activity down to the time of Alexander the Great. The friendship existing between Dionysus and Hephaestus may be explained by the fact that the best and finest wines are grown in the volcanic regions of the South.

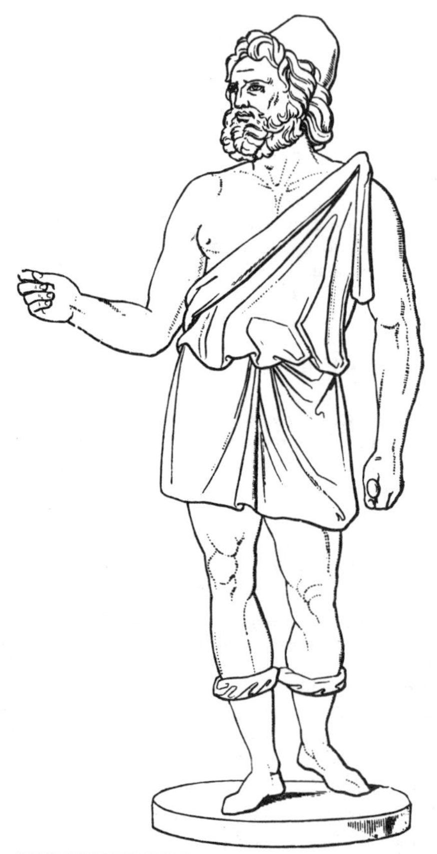

Hephaestus. (Bronze Statue in British Museum.)

As a master in the production of beautiful and fascinating works of art, Hephaestus is in the *Iliad* the husband of a Charis, and in the *Odyssey* of Aphrodité, and in Hesiod of Aglaea. (See CHARITES.) The story of his marriage with Aphrodité was not, apparently, widely known in early antiquity. Through his artistic genius he appears, and most especially in the Athenian story, as the intimate friend of Athené. In Homer he lives and works on Olympus, where he makes palaces of brass for himself and the other deities; but he has a forge also on Mount Mosychlus in Lemnos; the later story gives him one under Aetna in Sicily, and on the sacred island, or island of Hephaestus, in the Lipari Islands, where he is heard at work with his companions the Cyclopes. All the masterpieces of metal which appear in the stories of gods and heroes—the aegis of Zeus, the arms of Achilles, the sceptre of Agamemnon, the fatal necklace of Harmonia, the fire-breathing bulls of Aeëtes, the golden torchbearers in the palace of Alcinoüs, and others —were attributed to the art of Hephaestus. To help his lameness he made, according to Homer, two golden maidens, with the power of motion, to lean upon when he walked. He was much worshipped in Lemnos, where there was an annual festival in his honour. All fires were put out for nine days, during which rites of atonement and purification were performed. Then fresh fire was brought on a sacred ship from Delos, the fires were kindled again, and a new life, as the saying went, began. At Athens he was worshipped in the Academy, in connection with Athenê and Prometheus (q. v.). In October the smiths and smelters celebrated the Χαλκεῖα, a feast of metal-workers, in his honour and that of Athenê; at the Ἀπατούρια sacrifices were offered to him, among other gods, as the giver of fire, and torches were kindled and hymns were sung; at the Ἡφαίστεια, finally, there was a torch-race in his honour. The Greeks frequently set small dwarf-like images of Hephaestus near their fireplaces. In works of art he is represented as a vigorous man with a beard, equipped, like a smith, with hammer and tongs; his left leg is shortened, to show his lameness. The Romans identified him with their Vulcanus (q. v.).

Heptanŏmis (Ἑπτανομίς). Middle Egypt, one of the three divisions of the country.

Heptapȳlos (ἑπτάπυλος). "Seven-gated." A name of Thebes in Boeotia, distinguishing it from the Egyptian Thebes, which is called "hundred-gated" (ἑκατόμπυλοι).

Hera. See HERÊ.

Heraclēa (Ἡράκλεια). A name given to more than forty towns in Europe, Asia, Africa, and the islands of the Mediterranean. They are supposed to have derived this name from Heracles, and to have either been built in honour of him or placed under his protection. The most famous of these places were:

IN GREECE.—(1) A city of Elis, near the centre of the province, to the southeast of Pisa, near the confluence of the Cytherus and Alpheus. (2) A city of Acarnania, on the shore of the Ionian Sea, and opposite the island of Carnus. (3) A city of Epirus, on the confines of Athamania and Molossis, and near the sources of the Aras. (4) LYNCESTIS, a town of Macedonia, at the foot of the Candavian Mountains, on the confines of Illyria. Its ruins still retain the name of Erekli. Mention is made of this town in Caesar (*B. C.* iii. 79). (5) SINTĬCA, the principal town of the Sinti in Thrace. We are informed by Livy (xl. 24) that Demetrius, the son of Philip, was here imprisoned and murdered. Mannert thinks it the same with the Heraclea built by Amyntas, the brother of Philip. (6) TRACHINIA, a town of Thessaly, founded by the Lacedaemonians, and a colony from Trachis, about B.C. 426, in the sixth year of the Peloponnesian War (Thuc. iii. 92). It was distant about sixty stadia from Thermopylae and twenty from the sea. Iason, tyrant of Pherae, took possession of this city at one period, and caused the walls to be pulled down (Xen. *Hist. Gr.* vi. 4, 27). Heraclea, however, again arose from its ruins, and became a flourishing city under the Aetolians, who sometimes held their general council within its walls (Livy, xxv. 5). It was taken by the Roman consul, Acilius Glabrio, after a long and obstinate siege (Livy, xxxvii. 24; Polyb. x. 42).

IN ITALY, GAUL, etc.—(7) A city of Lucania in Italy, and situated between the Aciris and Siris. It was founded by the Tarentini after the destruction of the ancient city of Siris, which stood at the mouth of the latter river (B.C. 428). This city is rendered remarkable in history, as having been the seat of the general council of the Greek states (8) A city of Campania, more commonly known by the name of Herculaneum. (9) CACCABARIA, a city on the confines of Italy and Gaul, in Narbonensis Secunda. It was situated on the coast, to the south of Forum Iulii. (10) MINŌA, a city of Sicily on the southern coast, northeast of Agrigentum, at the mouth of the river Camicus. It was founded by Minos when he pursued Daedalus hither, and was subsequently called Heraclea from Heracles, after his victory over Eryx—so, at least, said the fables of the day. Some authorities make the original name to have been Macara, and Minos to have been not the founder but the conqueror of the place (Mela, ii. 7; Livy, xxxiv. 35).

IN ASIA, AFRICA, etc.—(11) PONTĬCA (Ἡράκλεια Πόντου). A city on the coast of Bithynia, about twelve stadia from the river Lycus. It was founded by a colony of Megareans, strengthened by some Tanagreans from Boeotia; the numbers of the former, however, so predominated that the city was in general considered as Doric. This place was famed for its naval power and its consequence among the Asiatic States. Memnon composed a history of the tyrants who reigned at Heraclea during a space of eighty-four years; but we have only now the abridgment of Photius, which is confirmed by incidental notices contained in Aristotle (*Polit.* vi. 5). (12) A city of Aeolis, at the entrance of the Gulf of Adramyttium, opposite Mitylenê. (13) A city in southern Aeolis, on the seacoast, near Cumae. (14) A city of Caria, on the seacoast, near the mouth of the river Latmus, between Miletus and Prienê (Ptol. v. 10). It was called, for distinction's sake from other places of the same name, HERACLĒA LATMI. (15) A city of Syria, in the district of Cyrrhestica, northwest of Hierapolis and northeast of Beroea, near the confines of Comagenê. (16) A city of Lower Egypt, situated in the Delta, to the northeast of the Canopic mouth of the Nile. (17) HERACLEOPŎLIS MAGNA, a city of Egypt, in the Heracleotic nome, of which it was the capital. The ichneumon was worshipped here. (18) HERACLEOPŎLIS PARVA, a city of Egypt, southwest of Pelusium, within the Delta.

Heracleopŏlis (Ἡρακλεοὐπολις). (1) PARVA (ἡ μικρά), called SETHRON, a city of Lower Egypt. (2) MAGNA (ἡ μεγάλη), the capital of the Nomos Heracleopolites in Middle Egypt identical with Heraclea. See above.

Herăcles (Ἡρακλῆς: Latin, HERCŬLES). Heracles is not only one of the oldest heroes in the Greek mythology, but the most famous of all. Indeed, the traditions of similar heroes in other Greek tribes, and in other nations, especially in the East, were transferred to Heracles; so that the scene of his achievements, which is, in the Homeric poems, confined on the whole to Greece, became almost coextensive with the known world;

and the story of Heracles was the richest and most comprehensive of all the heroic myths.

Heracles was born in Thebes, and was the son of Zeus by Alcmené, the wife of Amphitryon, whose form the god assumed while he was absent in the war against the Teleboi. On the day which he should have been born, Zeus announced to the gods that a descendant of Perseus was about to see the light, who would hold sway over all the Perseïdae. Heré cunningly induced her consort to confirm his words with an oath. She hated the unborn son as the son of her rival, and hence in her capacity as the goddess of childbirth caused the queen of Sthenelus of Mycenae, a descendant of Perseus, to give birth prematurely to Eurystheus, while she postponed the birth of Heracles for seven days. Hence it was that Heracles, with his gigantic strength, came into the service of the weaker Eurystheus. Heré pursued him with her hatred during the whole of his natural life. He and his twin brother Iphicles, the son of Amphitryon, were hardly born, when the goddess sent two serpents to their cradle to destroy them. Heracles seized them and strangled them. The child grew up to be a strong youth, and was taught by Amphitryon to drive a chariot, by Autolycus to wrestle, by Eurytus to shoot with the bow, and by Castor to use the weapons of war. Chiron instructed him in the sciences, Rhadamanthus in virtue and wisdom, Eumolpus (or according to another account, Linus) in music. When Linus attempted to chastise him, Heracles struck him dead with his lute. Amphitryon, accordingly, alarmed at his untamable temper, sent him to tend his flocks on Mount Cithaeron.

It was at this time, according to the Sophist Prodicus, that the event occurred which occasioned the fable of the "Choice of Heracles" (Xen. *Mem.* ii. 2). Heracles was meditating in solitude as to the path of life which he should choose, when two tall women appeared before him—the one called Pleasure, the other called Virtue. Pleasure promised him a life of enjoyment, Virtue a life of toil crowned by glory. He decided for Virtue. After destroying the savage lion of Cithaeron, he returned, in his eighteenth year, to Thebes, and freed the city from the tribute which it had been forced to pay to Erginus of Orchomenus, whose heralds he deprived of their ears and noses. Creon, king of Thebes, gave him, in gratitude, his daughter Megara as wife. But it was not long before the Delphic oracle commanded him to enter the service of Eurystheus, king of Mycenae and Tiryns, and perform twelve tasks which he should impose upon him. This was the humiliation which Heré had in store for him. The oracle promised him, at the same time, that he should win eternal glory, and indeed immortality, and change his present name Alcaeus (from his paternal grandfather) or Alcides (from ἀλκή, "strength") for Heracles ("renowned through Heré"). Nevertheless, he fell into a fit of madness, in which he shot down the three children whom Megara had borne him. When healed of his insanity, he entered into the service of Eurystheus.

The older story says nothing of the exact number (twelve) of the labours (ἆθλοι) of Heracles. The number was apparently invented by the poet Pisander of Rhodes, who may have had in his eye the contests of the Phœnician god Melkart with the twelve hostile beasts of the Zodiac. It was also Pisander who first armed the hero with the club, and the skin taken from the lion of Cithaeron or Nemea. Heracles was previously represented as carrying bow and arrows, and the weapons of a Homeric hero.

THE TWELVE LABOURS OF HERACLES were as follows: (1) The contest with the invulnerable lion of Nemea, the offspring of Typhon and Echidna. Heracles drove it into its cavern and strangled it in his arms. With the impenetrable hide, on which nothing could make any impression but the beast's own claws, he clothed himself, the jaws covering his head. (2) The hydra or water-snake of Lerna, also a child of Typhon and Echidna. This monster lived in the marsh of Lerna, near Argos, and was so poisonous that its very breath was fatal. It had nine heads, one of which was immortal. Heracles scared it out of its lair with burning arrows, and cut off its head; but for every head cut off two new ones arose. At length Iolaüs, the charioteer of Heracles and son of his brother Iphicles, seared the wounds with burning brands. Upon the immortal head he laid a heavy mass of rock. He anointed his arrows with the monster's gall, so that henceforth the wounds they inflicted were incurable. Eurystheus refused to accept this as a genuine victory, alleging the assistance offered by Iolaüs. (3) The boar of Erymanthus, which infested Arcadia. Heracles had been commanded to bring it alive to Mycenae, so he chased it into an expanse of snow, tired it out, and caught it in a noose. The mere sight of the beast threw Eurystheus into such a panic that he slunk away

Heracles and the Nemean Lion. (Pompeian painting. Overbeck.)

into a tub underground and bid the hero, in future, to show the proof of his achievements outside the city gates. (On the contest with the Centaurs which Heracles had to undergo on his way to the chase, see PHOLUS and CHIRON.) (4) The hind of Mount Cerynea, between Arcadia and Achaia. Another account localizes the event on Mount Maenalus, and speaks of the Maenalian hind. Its horns were of gold and its hoofs of brass, and it had been dedicated to Artemis by the Pleiad Taÿgeté. Heracles was to take the hind alive. He followed her for a whole year up to the source of the Ister in the country of the Hyperboreans. At length she returned to Arcadia, where he wounded her with an arrow on the banks of the Ladon, and so caught her. (5) The birds that infested the lake of Stymphalus, in Arcadia. These were man-eating monsters, with claws, wings, and beaks of brass, and feathers that they shot out like arrows. Heracles scared them with a brazen rattle, and succeeded in killing part, and driving away the rest, which settled on the island of Aretias in the Black Sea, to be frightened away, after a hard fight, by the Argonauts. (6) Heracles was commanded to bring home for Admeté, the daughter of Eurystheus, the girdle of Hippolyté, queen of the Amazons. After many adventures he landed at Themiscyra, and found the queen ready to give up the girdle of her own accord. But Heré spread a rumour among the Amazons that their queen was in danger, and a fierce battle took place, in which Heracles slew Hippolyté and many of her followers. On his return he slew, in the neighbourhood of Troy, a sea-monster, to whose fury King Laomedon had offered up his daughter Hesione. Laomedon refused to give Heracles the reward he had promised, whereupon the latter, who was hastening to return to Mycenae, threatened him with future vengeance. (See LAOMEDON.) (7) The farm-yard of Augeas, king of Elis, in which lay the dung of three thousand cattle, was to be cleared in a day. Heracles completed the task by turning the rivers Alpheus and Peneus into the yard. Augeas now contended that Heracles was only acting on the commission of Eurystheus, and on this pretext refused him his promised reward. Heracles slew him afterwards with all his sons, and thereupon founded the Olympian Games. (See AUGEAS). (8) A mad bull had been sent up from the sea by Poseidon to ravage the island of Creté, in revenge for the disobedience of Minos. (See MINOS.) Heracles was to bring him to Mycenae alive. He caught the bull, crossed the sea on his back, threw him over his neck and carried him to Mycenae, where he let him go. The animal wandered all through the Peloponnesus and ended by infesting the neighbourhood of Marathon, where he was at length slain by Theseus. (9) Diomedes, a son of Ares, and king of the Bistones in Thrace, had some mares which he used to feed on the flesh of the strangers landing in the country. After a severe struggle, Heracles overcame the king, threw his body to the mares, and took them off to Mycenae, where Eurystheus let them go. (10) The oxen of Geryones, the son of Chrysaor and the ocean nymph Callirrhoé. Geryones was a giant with three bodies and mighty wings, who dwelt on the island of Erythea, in the farthest West, on the borders of the Ocean stream. He had a herd of red cattle, which were watched by the shepherd Eurytion and his two-headed dog Orthrus, the offspring of Typhon

Heracles and Bull. (From a bas-relief in the Vatican.)

and Echidna. In quest of these cattle, Heracles, with many adventures, passed through Europe and Libya. On the boundary of both continents he set up, in memory of his arrival, the two pillars which bear his name, and at length reached the Ocean stream. Oppressed by the rays of the neighbouring sun, he aimed his bow at the Sun-god, who marvelled at his courage, and gave him his golden bowl to cross the Ocean in. Arrived at Erythea, Heracles slew the shepherd and his dog, and drove off the cattle. Menoetius, who tended the herds of Hades in the neigbourhood, brought news to Geryones of what had happened. Geryones hurried in pursuit, but after a fierce contest fell before the arrows of Heracles. The hero returned with the cattle through Iberia, Gaul, Liguria, Italy, and Sicily, meeting everywhere with new adventures, and leaving behind him tokens of his presence. At the mouth of the Rhone he had a dreadful struggle with the Ligyes; his arrows were exhausted, and he had sunk in weariness upon his knee, when Zeus rained a shower of innumerable stones from heaven, with which he prevailed over his enemies. The place was ever after a stony desert plain, and was identified with the Campus Lapidosus near Massilia (Marseilles). (See, further, CACUS; ERYX.) Heracles had made the circuit of the Adriatic and was just nearing Greece, when Heré sent a gadfly and scattered the herd. With much toil he wandered through the mountains of Thrace as far as the Hellespont, but then only succeeded in getting together a part of the cattle. After a dangerous adventure with the giant Alcyoneus, he succeeded at length in returning to Mycenae, where Eurystheus offered up the cattle to Here (Apollod. i. 6, 1). (11) The golden apples of the Hesperides. (See HESPERIDES.) Heracles was ignorant where the gardens of the Hesperides were to be found in which the apples grew. He accordingly repaired to the nymphs who dwelt by the Eridanus, on whose counsel he surprised Nereus, the omniscient god of the sea, and compelled him to give an answer. On this he journeyed through Libya, Egypt, and Ethiopia, where he slew Antaeus, Busiris, and Emathion. (See under these titles.) He then crossed to Asia, passed through the Caucasus, where he set Prometheus free, and on through the land of the Hyperboreans till he found Atlas. Following the counsel of Prometheus, he sent Atlas to bring the apples, and in his absence bore the heavens for him on his shoulders. Atlas returned with them, but declined to take his burden upon his shoulders again, promising to carry the apples to Eurystheus himself. Heracles consented, and asked Atlas to take the burden only a moment, while he adjusted a cushion for his head; he then hurried off with his prize. Another account represents Heracles as slaying the serpent Ladon, who guarded the tree, and plucking the apples himself. Eurystheus presented him with the apples; he dedicated them to Athené, who restored them to their place. (12) Last he brought the dog Cerberus up from the lower world. This was the heaviest task of all. Conducted by Hermes and Athené, he descended into Hades at the promontory of Taenarum. In Hades he set Theseus free, and induced the prince of the infernal regions to let him take the dog to the realms of day, if only he could do so without using his weapons. Heracles bound the beast by the mere strength of arm, and carried him to Eurystheus, and took him back again into Hades. While in the upper world the dog, in his disgust, spat upon the ground, causing the poisonous herb aconite to spring up.

His tasks were now ended, and he returned to Thebes. His first wife, Megara, he wedded to his faithful friend Iolaüs, and then journeyed into Oechalia to King Eurytus, whose daughter Iolé he meant to woo. The king's son Iphitus favoured his suit, but Eurytus rejected it with contempt. Soon after this Autolycus stole some of Eurytus's cattle, and he accused Heracles of the robbery. Meanwhile, Heracles had rescued Alcestis, the wife of Admetus (q. v.), from death. Iphitus met Heracles, begged him to help him in looking for the stolen cattle, and accompanied him to Tiryns. Here, after hospitably entertaining him, Heracles threw him, in a fit of madness, from the battlements of his stronghold. A heavy sickness was sent on him for this murder, and Heracles prayed to the god of Delphi to heal him. Apollo rejected him, whereupon Heracles attempted to carry away the tripod. A conflict ensued, when Zeus parted the combatants with his lightning. The oracle bade Heracles to hire himself out for three years for three talents, and pay the money to Eurytus. Hermes put him into the service of Omphalé, queen of Lydia, daughter of Iardanus, and widow of Tmolus. Heracles was degraded to female drudgery, was clothed in soft raiment and set to spin wool, while the queen assumed the lion skin and the club. The time of service over, he undertook an expedition of vengeance against Laomedon of Troy. He landed on the coast of the Troad with eighteen ships, manned by the boldest of heroes, such as Telamon, Peleus, and Oïcles. Laomedon succeeded in surprising the guard by the ships and in slaying Oïcles. But the city was stormed, Telamon being the first to climb the wall, and Laomedon, with all his sons except Podarces, was slain by the arrows of Heracles. (See PRIAMUS.) On his return Heré sent a tempest upon him. On the island of Cos he had a hard conflict to undergo with Eurytion, the son of Poseidon, and his sons. Heracles was at first wounded and forced to fly, but prevailed at length with the help of Zeus.

After this Athené summoned the hero to the battle of the gods with the giants, who were not to be vanquished without his aid. (See GIGANTES.) Then Heracles returned to the Peloponnesus, and took vengeance on Augeas and on Neleus of Pylos, who had refused to purify him for the murder of Iphitus. (See AUGEAS; MOLIONIDAE; NELEUS; PERIDYMENUS.) In the battle with the Pylians he went so far as to wound Hades, who had come up to their assistance. Hippocoön of Sparta and his numerous sons he slew in revenge for their murder of Oeonus, a son of his maternal uncle Licymnius. In this contest his ally was King Cepheus of Tegea, by whose sister Augé he was father of Telephus. Cepheus with his twenty sons were left dead on the field.

Heracles now won as his wife Deïanira, the daughter of Oeneus of Calydon. (See ACHELOÜS.) He remained a long time with his father-in-law, and at length, with his wife and his son Hyllus, he passed on into Trachis to the hospitality of his friend Ceyx. At the ford of the river Evenus he encountered the Centaur Nessus, who had the right of carrying travellers across. Nessus remained behind and attempted to do violence to Deïanira, upon which Heracles shot him through with his poisoned arrows. The dying Centaur gave some of his infected blood to Deïanira, telling her that, should her husband be unfaithful, it would be a means of restoring him. Heracles had a stubborn contest with Theodamas, the king of the Dryopes, killed him, and took his son Hylas away. He then reached Trachis, and was received with the friendliest welcome by King Ceyx. Next he started to fight with Cycnus (q. v.), who had challenged him to single combat; and afterwards, at the request of Aegimius, prince of the Dorians, undertook a war against the Lapithae, and an expedition of revenge against Eurytus of Oechalia. He stormed the fortress, slew Eurytus with his sons, and carried off Iolé, who had formerly been denied him, as his prisoner. He was about to offer a sacrifice to his father Zeus on Mount Cenaeum, when Deïanira, jealous of Iolé, sent him a robe stained with the blood of Nessus. It had hardly grown warm upon his body when the dreadful poison began to devour his flesh. Wild with anguish, he hurled Lichas, who brought him the robe, into the sea, where he was changed into a tall cliff. In the attempt to tear off the robe, he only tore off pieces of his flesh. Apollo bade him be carried to the top of Oeta, where he had a great funeral pyre built up for him. This he ascended; then he gave Iolé to his son Hyllus to be his wife, and bade Poeas, the father of Philoctetes, to kindle the pyre. According to another story, it was Philoctetes himself, whom Heracles presented with his bow and poisoned arrows, who performed this office. The flames had hardly started up, when a cloud descended from the sky with thunder and lightning, and carried the son of Zeus up to heaven, where he was welcomed as one of the immortals. Heré was reconciled to him, and he was wedded to her daughter Hebé, the goddess of eternal youth. Their children were Alexiares ("Averter of the Curse") and Anicetus ("the Invincible"), the names merely personifying two of the main qualities for which the hero was worshipped.

About the end of Heracles nothing is said in the *Iliad* but that he, the best-loved of Zeus's sons, did not escape death, but was overcome by fate, and by the heavy wrath of Heré. In the *Odyssey* his ghost, in form like black night, walks in the lower world with his bow bent and his arrows ready, while the hero himself dwells among the immortals, the husband of Hebé. For the lives of his children, and the end of Eurystheus, see HYLLUS.

Heracles was worshipped partly as a hero, to whom men brought the ordinary libations and offerings, and partly as an Olympian deity, an immortal among the immortals. Immediately after his apotheosis his friends offered sacrifice to him at the place of burning, and his worship spread from thence through all the tribes of Hellas. Diomus the son of Colyttus, an Athenian, is said to have been the first who paid him the honours of an immortal. It was he who founded the gymnasium called Cynosarges, near the city. This gymnasium, the sanctuary at Marathon, and the temple at Athens were the three most venerable shrines of Heracles in Attica. Diomus gave his name to the Diomeia, a merry festival held in Athens in honour of Heracles. Feasts to Heracles (Ἡράκλεια), with athletic contests, were celebrated in many places. He was the hero of labour and struggle, and the patron deity of the gymnasium and the palaestra. From early times he was regarded as having instituted the Olympic Games; as the founder of the Olympic sanctuaries and the Olympic truce, the planter of the shady groves, and the first competitor and victor in the contests. During his earthly life he had been a helper of gods and men, and had set the earth free from monsters and rascals. Accordingly he was invoked in all the perils of life as the saviour (σωτήρ) and the averter of evil (ἀλεξίκακος). Men prayed for his protection against locusts, flies, and noxious serpents. He was a wanderer, and had travelled over the whole world; therefore he was called on as the guide on marches and journeys (ἡγεμόνιος). In another character he was the glorious conqueror (καλλίνικος) who, after his toils are over, enjoys his rest with wine, feasting, and music. Indeed, the fable represents him as having, in his hours of repose, given as striking proofs of inexhaustible bodily power as in his struggles and contests. Men liked to think of him as an enormous eater, capable of devouring a whole ox; as a lusty boon companion, fond of delighting himself and others by playing the lyre. In Rome, as Hercules, he was coupled with the Muses, and, like Apollo elsewhere, was worshipped as Μουσαγέτης (Hercules Musarum), or master of the Muses. (On the connection between Heracles and the Muses, see Klügmann in the *Commentationes in Honorem Th. Mommseni*, p. 262 [1877], and Lobeck, *Phryn.* 430). Under Augustus, Marcius Philippus built a temple to him at Rome as Hercules Musarum (Suet. *Aug.* 29, with Peck's note). After his labours he was supposed to have been fond of hot baths (θέρμαι) which were accordingly deemed sacred to him. Among trees, the wild olive and white poplar were consecrated to him; the poplar he was believed to have brought from distant countries to Olympia.

Owing to the influence of the Greek colonies in Italy, the worship of Heracles was widely diffused among the Italian tribes. It attached itself to local legends and religion; the conqueror of Cacus, for instance, was originally not Heracles, but a powerful shepherd called Garanos. Again, Heracles came to be identified with the ancient Italian deity Sancus or Dius Fidius, and was regarded as the god of happiness in home and field, industry and war, as well as of truth and honour. His altar was the Ara Maxima in the cattle-market (Forum Boarium), which he was believed to have erected himself. (See CACUS.) Here they dedicated to him a tithe of their gains in war and peace, ratified solemn treaties, and invoked his name to witness their oaths. He had many shrines and sacrifices in Rome, corresponding to his various titles, *Victor* (Conqueror), *Invictus* (Unconquered), *Custos* (Guardian), *Defensor* (Defender), and others. His rites were always performed in Greek fashion, with the head covered. It was in his temple that soldiers and gladiators were accustomed to hang up their arms when their service was over. In the stone-quarries the labourers had their Hercules Saxarius (Hercules of the Stone). He was called the father of Latinus, the ancestor of the Latins, and to him the Roman gens of the Fabii traced their origin. The ancient family of the Potitii were said to have been commissioned by the god in person to provide, with the assistance of the Pinarii, for his sacrifices at the Ara Maxima (Livy, i. 7). In B.C. 310 the Potitii gave the service into the hands of the *servi publici*. Before a year had passed

Farnese Hercules. (Naples Museum.)

the flourishing family had become completely extinct.

In works of art Heracles is represented as the ideal of manly strength, with full, well knit, and muscular limbs, serious expression, a curling beard, short neck, and a head small in proportion to the limbs. His equipment is generally the club and the lion's skin. The type appears to have been mainly fixed by Lysippus. The Farnese Hercules, by the Athenian Glycon, is probably a copy of one by Lysippus. Heracles is portrayed in repose, leaning on his club, which is covered with the lion's skin. (See FARNESE HERCULES.) The Heracles of the Athenian Apollonius (q. v.), now only a torso, is equally celebrated. See Vogel, *Hercules secundum Graecorum Poetas*, etc. (Halle, 1830); and Roscher, *Ausführliches Lexikon d. griech. und röm. Mythologie*, s. h. v.

Heraclīānus (Ἡρακλιανός). An officer of the emperor Honorius who put Stilicho to death in A.D. 408, and got the government of Africa as his reward. After serving against Alaric and the usurper Attalus, whom Alaric had made emperor, Heraclianus revolted and invaded Italy. The attempt was unsuccessful, and on his return to Carthage he was there put to death by order of Honorius, in A.D. 413. See STILICHO.

Heraclīdae (Ἡρακλεῖδαι). A name given in ancient legend to a powerful Achaean race or family, the fabled descendants of Heracles. According to the account of the ancient writers, the children of Heracles, after the death of that hero, being persecuted by Eurystheus, took refuge in Attica, and there defeated and slew the tyrant at the Scironian Rock, near the Saronic Gulf. When their enemy had fallen, they resumed possession of their birthright in the Peloponnesus; but they had not long enjoyed the fruits of their victory before a pestilence, in which they recognized the finger of heaven, drove them again into exile. Attica again afforded them a retreat. When their hopes had revived, an ambiguous oracle encouraged them to believe that, after they had reaped their third harvest, they should find a prosperous passage through the Isthmus into the land of their fathers. But, at the entrance of the Peloponnesus, they were met by the united forces of the Achaeans, Ionians, and Arcadians. Their leader Hyllus, the eldest son of Heracles, proposed to decide the quarrel by single combat; and Echemus, king of Tegea, was selected by the Peloponnesian confederates as their champion. Hyllus fell; and the Heraclidae were bound by the terms of the agreement to abandon their enterprise for a hundred, or, according to some accounts, for fifty, years. Yet both Cleodaeus, son of Hyllus, and his grandson Aristomachus, renewed the attempt with no better fortune. After Aristomachus had fallen in battle, the ambiguous oracle was explained to his sons Aristodemus, Temenus, and Cresphontes; and they were assured that the time, the third generation, had now come, when they should accomplish their return; not, however, as they had expected, over the guarded Isthmus, but across the mouth of the western gulf from Naupactus, where the opposite shores are parted by a channel only a few furlongs broad. Thus encouraged, with the aid of the Dorians, Aetolians, and Locrians, they crossed the strait, vanquished Tisamenus, son of Orestes, and divided the fairest portion of the Peloponnesus among them. (See DORIS.) For the historical significance of this legend, see HELLAS. For the play of Euripides on the subject of the Heraclidae, see EURIPIDES, p. 639.

Heraclīdes (Ἡρακλείδης). (1) Surnamed PONTĬCUS. A Greek philosopher, born at Heraclea in Pontus about B.C. 380. He came early to Athens, where he became a disciple of Plato and Aristotle, and had made a reputation by about B.C. 340. He was the author of some sixty works on a great variety of subjects—philosophy, mathematics, music, grammar, poetry, political and literary history, and geography. He was a learned and interesting writer, but somewhat deficient in critical power. There are a few fragments of his works remaining, besides an extract from a book on constitutions which bears his name, edited by Köler (Halle, 1804), Coraës (Paris, 1805), and Müller. See Deswert, *De Heraclide Pontico* (Louvain, 1830), and F. W. Schmidt, *De Heraclidae Pontici etc. Dialogis Deperditis* (Breslau, 1867). (2) A Syracusan, the son of Lysimachus, and one of the generals when Syracuse was attacked by the Athenians in B.C. 415. (3) A commander of the mercenary troops under the younger Dionysius at Syracuse. He subsequently joined Dion in expelling Dionysius, and was himself assassinated in B.C. 354. (4) A physician of Tarentum who flourished in the second century B.C. and wrote on Materia Medica.

Heraclītus (Ἡράκλειτος). (1) A Greek philosopher of Ephesus, who lived about B.C. 535–475, during the time of the first Persian domination over his native city. As one of the last of the family of Androclus, the descendant of Codrus, who had founded the colony of Ephesus, Heraclitus had certain honorary regal privileges, which he renounced in favour of his brother. He likewise declined an invitation of King Darius to visit his court. He was an adherent of the aristocracy, and when, after the defeat of the Persians, the democratic party came into power, he withdrew in ill-humour to a secluded estate in the country, and gave himself up entirely to his studies. In his later years he wrote a philosophical treatise, which he deposited in the temple of Artemis, making it a condition that it should not be published till after his death. He was buried in the market-place of Ephesus, and for several centuries later the Ephesians continued to engrave his image on their coins.

Heraclitus was one of the subtlest of all the metaphysicians of Greece, and his importance as a philosopher lies in the fact that he was the founder of an independent metaphysical system which sought to obviate the difficulty of overcoming the contradictions between the one and the phenomenal many. His great work "On Nature" (Περὶ Φύσεως), in three books, was written in the Ionian dialect, and is the oldest monument of Greek prose. Considerable fragments of it have come down to us. The language is bold, harsh, and figurative; the style is so careless that the syntactical relations of the words are often hard to perceive; and the thoughts are profound. All this made Heraclitus so difficult a writer that he went in antiquity by the name "the Obscure" (ὁ σκοτεινός), and Lucretius attacks him on this ground (i. 638–644). From his gloomy view of life he is often called "the Weeping Philosopher," as Democritus is known as "the Laughing Philosopher." Cf. Juv. x. 28 foll.

Knowledge, according to Heraclitus, is based upon perception by the senses. Perfect knowledge is only given to the gods, but a progress in knowledge is possible to men. Wisdom consists in the recognition of the intelligence which, by means of the world-soul, guides the universe. Everything is in an eternal flux (πάντα ῥεῖ); nothing therefore, not even the world in its momentary form, nor the gods themselves, can escape final destruction. The ultimate principle into which all existence is resolvable is fire. As fire changes continually into water and then into earth, so earth changes back to water and water again to fire. The world, therefore, arose from fire, and in alternating periods is resolved again into fire, to form itself anew out of this element. The division of unity, or of the divine original fire, into the multiplicity of opposing phenomena, is "the way downwards," and the consequence of a war and a strife. Harmony and peace lead back to unity by "the way upwards." Nature is constantly dividing and uniting herself, so that the multiplicity of opposites does not destroy the unity of the whole. The existence of these opposites depends only on the difference of the motion on "the way upwards" from that on "the way downwards"; all things, therefore, are at once identical and not identical. The principle of the universe is "becoming," which implies that everything is and, at the same time, is not, so far as the same relation is concerned.

The letters ascribed to Heraclitus are spurious. See Bernays, *Heraclitea* (Bonn, 1848); id. *Die heraklitischen Briefe* (Berlin, 1859); Lassalle, *Die Philosophie Herakleitos' des Dunkeln*, 2 vols. (Berlin, 1858) — the most exhaustive monograph on the philosophy of Heraclitus; and Schuster, *Heraklit von Ephesus* (Leipzig, 1872). The fragments of Heraclitus were edited and published in England in 1877 by Bywater. See PHILOSOPHIA.

(2) An Academic philosopher of Tyre, whose treatise Περὶ Ἀπίστων still exists and has been edited by Westermann (Brunswick, 1843).

Heraea (Ἡραία). A town in Arcadia, on the right bank of the Alpheus, near the borders of Elis.

Heraea (τὰ Ἡραῖα). A festival held at Argos every five years in honour of Heré, the goddess of the country. The priestess of Heré drove in a car drawn by white oxen to the Heraeum, or temple of the goddess, situated between Argos and Mycenae. Meantime the people marched out in procession, the fighting men in their arms. There was a great sacrifice of oxen (ἑκατόμβη), followed by a general sacrificial banquet and games of all sorts. A special feature of these was a contest in throwing the javelin, while running at full speed, at a shield set up at the end of the course. The victor received a crown and a shield, which he carried in the final procession. Like feasts were held at Aegina, Samos, Elis, Cos, Athens, and other places (Hermann, *Gottesd. Alterth.* § 51, n. 28).

Heraei Montes (τὰ Ἥραια ὄρη). A range of mountains in Sicily, running from the centre of the island southeast, and ending in the promontory Pachynum.

Heraeum (Ἡραῖον). The name given to any temple of Heré, that at Argos being the most famous.

Heralds. See PRAECO.

Herald's Staff. See CADUCEUS.

Herbĭta (Ἕρβιτα). A town in Sicily, north of Agyrium, in the mountains, the residence of the tyrant Archonides.

Herculaneum Ἡράκλειον). (1) A town in Samnium. (2) A city of Campania, on the coast, and not far from Neapolis (Naples). The form HERCULĀNUM is modern. Nothing is known respecting the origin of Herculaneum, except that fabulous accounts ascribed its foundation to Hercules on his return from Spain (Dion. Hal. i. 44). It may be inferred, however, from a passage in Strabo, that the town was of great antiquity. It may be reasonably conjectured, too, that Herculaneum was a Greek city, but that its name was altered to suit the Latin or Oscan pronunciation. At first it was only a fortress, which was successively occupied by the Osci, Tyrrheni, Pelasgi, Samnites, and lastly by the Romans. Being situated close to the sea, on elevated ground, it was exposed to the southwest wind, and from that circumstance was reckoned particularly healthful. We learn from Velleius Paterculus that Herculaneum suffered considerably during the civil wars (cf. Florus, i. 16). This place is mentioned also by Mela (ii. 4). Ovid likewise notices it under the name of Urbs Herculea (*Met.* xv. 711). Herculaneum, according to the common account, was overwhelmed by an eruption of Vesuvius in the first year of the reign of Titus, A.D. 79. Pompeii and Stabiae, which stood near, shared the same fate. It is possible, however, that the subversion of Herculaneum was not sudden, but progressive, since Seneca mentions a partial demolition which it sustained from an earthquake (*Nat. Quaest.* vi. 1). After being buried for more than sixteen hundred years, these cities were accidentally discovered—Herculaneum in 1719, by labourers in deepening a well; and Pompeii some years after. It appears that Herculaneum is in no part less than forty feet, and in some parts one hundred and twelve feet below the surface of the ground. Little was done to exhume the city until 1738, when some regular excavations were made. Above the city stand the two modern villages of Portici and Resina in the suburbs of Naples; and to the fear of undermining their buildings is due the fact that so much of the ancient city is still beneath the earth. The chief edifice of Herculaneum that has been disinterred is a fine theatre, built only a short time before the eruption and capable of accommodating 8000 persons. Part of the Forum, a colonnade, two small temples, and a villa have also been recovered, besides ruins of baths. Many other valuable remains of antiquity, such as busts, manuscripts, etc., have been found in the ruins of this ancient city, and are deposited in the Museo Nazionale at Naples. See Barré, *Herculaneum et Pompéi*, 8 vols., with 800 plates (Paris, 1837–40); Comparetti and De Petra, *La Villa Ercolanese dei Pisoni* (Turin, 1883); the works mentioned in Furchheim's *Bibliography of Pompeii, Herculaneum, and Stabiae* (Naples, 1891); and the articles PAPYRUS; POMPEII.

Hercŭles. (1) See HERACLES. (2) A son of Alexander the Great by Barsiné, the widow of the Rhodian Memnon, and murdered by Polysperchon, B.C. 310.

Hercŭles Musārum. See HERACLES, p. 793.

Herculeum. (1) PROMONTORIUM, a promontory in the Bruttiorum Ager, forming the most southern angle of Italy to the east, now Capo Spartivento. (2) FRETUM, the strait which forms the communication between the Atlantic and Mediterranean. See ABILA; CALPÉ; COLUMNAE HERCULIS.

Hercŭlis Columnae. See COLUMNAE HERCULIS.

Hercŭlis Monoeci Portus. See MONOECUS.

Hercŭlis Portus. See COSA.

Hercynia Silva, Hercynius Saltus, Hercynium Iugum. An extensive range of mountains in Germany, covered with forests, described by Caesar (*B. G.* vi. 24, 25) as nine days' journey in breadth, and more than sixty days' journey in length, extending east from the territories of the Helvetii, Nemetes, and Rauraci, parallel to the Danube, to the frontiers of the Dacians. Under this general name Caesar appears to have included all the mountains and forests in the south and centre of Germany. The name is still preserved in the modern Harz and Erz. See GERMANIA.

Herdonia. A town in Apulia, destroyed by Hannibal.

Heré (Ionic, Ἥρη, and in Attic, Ἥρα: the name is often connected with the Latin *hĕra;* but on this, see Curtius, p. 119). In Greek mythology, the queen of heaven, eldest daughter of Cronus and Rhea, sister and lawful consort of Zeus. According to Homer, she was brought up in her youth by Oceanus and Tethys. But every place in which her worship was localized asserted that she was born there, and brought up by the Nymphs of the district. She is said to have long lived in secret intimacy with Zeus before he publicly acknowledged her as his lawful consort. Her worshippers celebrated her marriage (ἱερὸς γάμος) in the spring time. In the oldest version of the story it took place in the Islands of the Blessed, on the shore of the Ocean stream, where the golden apple-tree of the Hesperides sprang up to celebrate it. But this honour, too, was claimed by every place where Heré was worshipped. According to one local story, Zeus obtained the love of Heré by stealth, in the form of a cuckoo.

Heré seems originally to have symbolized the feminine aspects of the natural forces of which Zeus is the masculine representative. Hence she is at once his wife and his sister, shares his power and his honours, and, like him, has authority over the phenomena of the atmosphere. It is she who sends clouds and storms, and is mistress of the thunder and lightning. Her handmaids are the Horae or goddesses of the season, and Iris, the goddess of the rainbow. Like Zeus, men worship her on mountains, and pray to her for rain. The union of sun and rain, which wakes the earth to renewed fertility, is symbolized as the loving union of Zeus and Heré. In the same way a conflict of the winds is represented as the consequence of a matrimonial quarrel, usually attributed to the jealousy of Heré, who was regarded as the stern protectress of honourable marriage. Hence arose stories of Zeus ill-treating his wife. It was said that he scourged her, and hurled Hephaestus from heaven to earth when hurrying to his mother's assistance; that in anger for her persecution of his son Heracles, he hung her out in the air with golden chains to her arms and an anvil on each foot (*Il.* viii. 400). There were also old legends which spoke of Heré allying herself with Athené and Poseidon to bind Zeus in chains. Zeus was only rescued by the giant Aegaeon, whom Thetis called to his assistance. The birth of Athené was said to have enraged Heré to such a pitch that she became the mother of Typhon by the dark powers of the infernal regions. In fact, this constant resistance to the will of Zeus, and her jealousy and hatred of her consort's paramours and their children, especially Heracles, become in the poets a standing trait in her character.

In spite of all this, Homer represents her as the most majestic of all the goddesses. The other Olympians pay her royal honours, and Zeus treats her with all respect and confides all his designs to her, though not always yielding to her demands. She is the spotless and uncorruptible wife of the king of Heaven; the mother of Hephaestus, Ares, Hebé, and Ilithyia, and indeed may be called the only lawful wife in the Olympian court. She is, accordingly, before all other deities the goddess of marriage and the protectress of purity in married life. She is represented as of exalted but severe beauty, and appears before Paris as competing with Aphrodité and Athené for the prize of loveliness. In Homer she is described as of lofty stature, large eyes (βοῶπις), white arms (λευκώλενος), and beautiful hair. On women she confers bloom and strength; she helps them, too, in the dangerous hour of childbirth. Her daughters Hebé and Ilithyia personify both these attributes.

In earlier times Heré was not everywhere recognized as the consort of Zeus; at the primitive oracle of Dodona, for instance, Dioné occupies this position. The Peloponnesus may be regarded as

Head of Heré. (Naples. Supposed to be from a Statue by Polyclitus.)

the earliest seat of her worship, and in the Peloponnesus, during the Homeric period, Argos, Mycenae, and Sparta are her favourite seats. Of these, according to the poet, she is the passionate champion in the Trojan War. In later times the worship of Heré was strongly localized in Argos and Mycenae. At Argos she took the same commanding position as Athené at Athens, and the year was dated by the names of her priestesses. Between these cities, at the foot of Mount Euboea, was situated the Heraeum (Ἡραῖον), a temple held in great honour. (See HERAEA.) At Corinth she was the goddess of the acropolis. At Elis a garment was offered her every five years by sixteen ladies chosen for the purpose, and maidens held a race in her honour on the race-course at Olympia. Boeotia had its feast of the *Daedala* (q. v.); Samos its large and splendid temple, built by Polycrates. The cuckoo was sacred to her as the messenger of spring, the season in which she was wedded to Zeus; so were the peacock and the crow, and among fruits the pomegranate, the symbol of wedded love and fruitfulness. Hecatombs were offered to her in sacrifice, as to Zeus.

In works of art she is represented as seated on a throne in a full robe, covering the whole figure. On her head is a sort of diadem, often with a veil; the expression of the face is severe and majestic, the eyes large and wide open, as in the Homeric description. The ideal type of Heré was found in the statue by Polyclitus in the temple at Argos. This was a colossal image, in gold and ivory, representing the goddess on her throne, her crown adorned with figures of the Graces and the Seasons, a pomegranate in one hand, and in the other a sceptre with the cuckoo on the top. The Farnese Heré at Naples, and the Ludovisi Iuno in Rome, are copies of this work. The Romans identified Heré with their own Iuno (q. v.).

Hereditas. See HERES.

Herennia Gens. A plebeian house at Rome originally Samnite. The Herennii were the patrons of the Marii (Livy, ix. 3).

Herennius. (1) SENECIO, a native of Spain, and a senator and quaestor at Rome under Domitian. His contempt for public honours, his upright character, and his admiration of Helvidius Priscus, whose life he wrote, made him hateful to the emperor, and caused him to be accused of high treason. He was condemned to death, and his work burned by the public executioner (Tac. *Agric.* 3; Pliny, *Ep.* iii. 33). (2) The father of Pontius the Samnite commander, who advised his son either to give freedom to the Romans ensnared at the Caudine Pass, or to exterminate them all (Livy, ix. 1 foll.). (3) GAIUS, a Roman, to whom a treatise on rhetoric in four books, ascribed by some to Cicero, is addressed. The treatise in question is generally regarded as not having been written by the Roman orator, but either by Antonius Gnipho or Q. Cornificius, usually cited simply as the "Auctor ad Herennium." See W. W. Fowler in the *Jour. of Philology*, x. 197; Krönhert, *De Rhet. ad Herennium* (Königsberg, 1873); the edition by F. Marx; and the article CORNIFICIUS. (4) See MODESTINUS.

Heres. An heir. (1) GREEK. At Athens, if a person died intestate, leaving sons, all of equal birthright, and none of them disinherited, the sons inherited the property in equal parts (ἰσόμοιροι), the eldest probably receiving the same share as the rest. If there were daughters, they were provided for by dowries given by the brothers, which, in case they were divorced or childless after marriage, went back to the remaining heirs. Girls so dowered were called ἐπίπροικοι. This was a matter of usage and not of formal law. If a man had no sons of his own, he usually adopted a son to continue the family and the religious worship connected with it. (See ADOPTIO.) If he had daughters, he would marry one of them to the adopted son; in this case the chief share of the inheritance would fall to this married daughter and her husband, the rest receiving dowries. If there were only daughters surviving, the succession passed to them. In such a case the next of kin had a legal right to one of the heiresses (ἐπίκληρος), and could demand to marry her, even if she had married some one else before receiving the inheritance; and poor heiresses (θῆσσαι), on the other hand, had a legal claim on their nearest of kin, either for marriage or for a provision suitable to their circumstances. (See EPICLERUS.) If a man had married an heiress, he was bound by custom and tradition, if he had sons, to name one as heir to the property which had come with his wife, and thus to restore the house of the maternal grandfather. Children born out of wedlock were illegitimate, and had no claim on the father's estate. If a man died intestate, leaving no heirs either of his body or adopted, his nearest relations in the male line inherited, and in default of these, those in the female line as far as the children of first cousins. Any one thinking he had a legal claim to the inheritance made an application to the archon to hand it over to him. The application was posted up in public, and read out in the following Ecclesia (Assembly). The question was then asked whether any one disputed the claim, or raised a counter-claim. If not, the archon assigned the inheritance to the claimant; otherwise the matter was decided by a lawsuit. Even after the assignment of an inheritance, it might be disputed in the lifetime of the holder, and for five years after his death. The claim of the nearest relation to an heiress was in the same way lodged with the archon and ratified before the Assembly.

(2) ROMAN. If a Roman died intestate, leaving a wife and children of his body or adopted, they were his heirs (*sui heredes*). But this did not apply to married daughters who had passed into the *manus* of their husbands, or the children who had been freed by emancipation from the *potestas* of their father. If the man left no wife or children, the *agnati*, or relations in the male line, inherited, according to the degree of their kinship. If there were no *agnati*, and the man was a patrician, the property went to his gens. The *cognati*, or relations in the female line, were originally not entitled to inherit by the civil law. But, as time went on, their claim was gradually recognized more and more to the exclusion of the *agnati*, until at last Justinian entirely abolished the privilege of the latter, and substituted the principle of blood-relationships for that of the civil law. Vestal Virgins were regarded as entirely cut off from the family union, and therefore could not inherit from an intestate, nor, in case of their dying intestate, did the property go to their family, but to the State. On the other hand, unlike other women, they had unlimited right of testamentary disposition. If a freedman died intestate and childless, the *patronus* and his wife had the first claim to inherit, then their children, then their *agnati*, and (if the *patronus* was a patrician) then his gens. In later times, even if a freedman, dying childless, left a will, the *patronus* and his sons had claim to half the property. Augustus made a number of provisions in the matter of freedmen's inheritance. The civil law made it compulsory on a man's *sui heredes* to accept an inheritance (*hereditatem adire*)

whether left by will or not. But as the debts were taken over with the property, the *edictum* of the praetor allowed the heirs to decline it. *A fortiori*, no other persons named in the will could be compelled to accept the legacy. See TESTAMENTUM.

Heres necessarius was a slave of the testator, who made him heir and *liber* at the same time. He was thus heir by necessity, becoming so without any action of his own, by the mere operation of the law. If a testator knew himself to be insolvent, he sometimes made a slave his heir to avoid the ignominy attached to a person whose property was sold to pay his debts (Gaius, ii. 154, etc.). The property of such an heir, acquired after his manumission, was not liable for the debts of the deceased. An insolvent inheritance was called *damnosa hereditas*.

Heres ex asse was the phrase used to describe one who was sole heir. So *heres ex dodrante*, an heir to three-quarters of an estate (Suet. *Iul.* 83); *heres ex parte sexta*, to the sixth; *ex parte dimidia*, to the half, etc.

See Hunger, *Das Erbrecht;* and Gans, *Das Erbrecht in weltgeschichtlicher Entwickelung*, 4 vols. (Berlin, 1823–35).

Herillus (Ἥριλλος). A native of Carthage, a Stoic philosopher, the disciple of Zeno of Citium, though differing from him in various points of doctrine. He held that the chief good is knowledge (ἐπιστήμη), a notion attacked by Cicero. (See Diog. Laërt. vii. 165 foll.; Cic. *Academ.* ii. 42; *De Fin.* ii. 11, 13 and often).

Hermae (Ἑρμαῖ), and dim. **Hermŭli** (ἑρμίδια). Pillars which terminated generally with a head of Hermes. In the earliest times Hermes (in whose worship the number 4 played a great part) was worshipped, especially in Arcadia (Pausan. viii. 4, § 4), under the form of a simple quadrangular pillar of marble or wood, with the significant mark of the male sex. As art advanced, the pillar was surmounted, first with a bearded head, and afterwards with a youthful head of the god. Hermes being the god

Hermes-pillar. (Pompeii.)

of traffic, roads, and boundaries, such pillars were erected to him in the streets and squares of towns; in Attica they were also erected along the country roads as mile-stones. Sometimes they were inscribed with apothegms and riddles; sometimes also with inscriptions in honour of those who had fought bravely for their country (Demosth. *Lept.* 112; Aeschin. *Or.* 3, § 183). In Athens there was an especially large number of them; in the market-place to the northwest of the Acropolis, the Hermae, erected partly by private individuals and partly by corporations, formed a long colonnade extending between the Hall of Paintings (στοὰ ποικίλη) and the Royal Hall (στοὰ βασίλειος). Accordingly, the latter was sometimes called the Hall of the Hermae. When the heads of other divinities (such as Athenê, Heracles, Eros) were placed on such a pillar, it was then called Hermathena, Hermeracles, or Hermeros. At Rome the Hermae were used in the decoration of houses and villas, and also as posts for the ornamental railings of gardens. Great numbers have been preserved, and are now to be seen in the European museums.

Hermaea (Ἕρμαια). A festival celebrated at Cydonia, in the island of Crete, at which the slaves enjoyed complete freedom, and were waited upon by their masters, the usage suggesting the Roman Saturnalia (q. v.). Other feasts in honour of Hermes were held at Athens in the gymnasia, at Pheneos, Tanagra, Pellenê, etc.

Hermaeum or **Mercurii Promontorium** (Ἑρμαία ἄκρα). (1) On the southern shore of Crete. (2) A promontory of Sardinia, on the western shore, a little to the north of Bosa, now Capo della Cacca. (3) A promontory of Africa, in the district Zeugitana, now Cape Bon. It lay opposite Lilybaeum in Sicily (Polyb. i. 29).

Hermagŏras (Ἑρμαγόρας). (1) Of Temnos, a distinguished Greek rhetorician of the time of Cicero, belonging to the Rhodian school of oratory (Quint. iii. 1, § 16). (2) A Greek rhetorician, surnamed CARION, who taught rhetoric at Rome in the time of Augustus (Quint. iii. 1, § 18).

Hermann. See ARMINIUS; GERMANIA.

Hermann. (1) JOHANN GOTTFRIED JAKOB. A distinguished German classical philologist, born at Leipzig, November 28, 1772. He studied law and literature at Leipzig and Jena, and after acting as *privat-docent* at Leipzig for four years, he became Professor Extraordinarius of Philosophy in that university, occupying subsequently the chair of Eloquence (1803), and of Poetry (1809). From 1834 he conducted the philological seminary. He died December 31, 1848.

Hermann was a scholar of great originality in research, and his presentation of the results arrived at was remarkable for vigour and directness. He is especially noted for the new principles developed by him in the study of classical prosody and Greek grammar, with regard to the former of which he endeavoured to establish a philosophical theory based upon the categories of Kant. His metrical views will be found in his dissertations *De Metris Graecorum et Romanorum Poetarum* (Leipzig, 1796); *Handbuch der Metrik* (1798); *Elementa Doctrinae Metricae* (1816); *Epitome Doctrinae Metricae* (1818, 4th ed. 1869); and *De Metris Pindari* in Heyne's edition of Pindar (1817). His grammatical theories are set forth in his treatise *De Emendanda Ratione Graecae Grammaticae* (1801), and in his annotations on Vigier's *De Graecae Dictionis Idiotismis* (1802; 4th ed. 1834), and *Libri IV. de Particula ἄν* (1831). He also edited the *Hecuba, Hercules Furens, Bacchae, Supplices, Alcestis*, and *Ion* of Euripides; Aeschylus (1859); Sophocles (completing the edition begun by Erfurdt), the *Clouds* of Aristophanes, the *Trinummus* of Plautus, the *Poetica* of Aristotle, the Homeric Hymns, the Lexicon of Photius, and Bion and Moschus. On the significance of mythology he wrote a treatise, *De Mythologia Graecorum Antiquissima* (1807) and the *Briefe über Homer und Hesiodus*, the latter in collaboration with Creuzer (Heidelberg, 1818). In his *Opuscula* (8 vols. 1827–1876) he treats of a wide range of topics, with breadth, force, and originality. See the memoirs by Jahn in the *Biogr. Aufsätze* (Leipzig, 1849), Köchly (1874), and Bursian, *Geschichte der class. Philologie*, etc., pp. 575 foll., 666–686 (Munich, 1883).

(2) Karl Friedrich. A classical scholar born at Frankfort, August 4, 1804. He was educated at Heidelberg and Leipzig, and after spending some time in Italy (1825), was appointed Professor of Classical Philology at the University of Marburg in 1832. In 1840 he accepted a call to Göttingen, where he died, January 8, 1856. His principal works are his *Lehrbuch der griechischen Antiquitäten* (1841; 6th ed. 1892); *Geschichte und System der platonischen Philosophie* (1839); and *Culturgeschichte der Griechen und Römer* (1857).

Hermanūbis (Ἑρμανοῦβις). The son of Osiris and Nephthis, represented as a human being with a jackal-head. (Cf. Anubis). He symbolizes the Egyptian priesthood (Diod. i. 18, 87).

Hermaphrodītus (Ἑρμαφρόδιτος). In Greek mythology, the son of Hermes and Aphroditê, born on Mount Ida, and endowed with the beauty of both deities. When a grown youth, he was bathing in the Carian fountain of Salmacis, and the nymph of the fountain, whose love he rejected, prayed the gods that she might be indissolubly united with him. The prayer was answered, and a being sprang into existence which united the qualities of male and female. The fable probably arose from the inclination, prevalent in the Eastern religions, towards confusing the attributes of both sexes. In Cyprus, for instance, a masculine Aphroditus, clad in female attire, was worshipped by the side of the goddess Aphroditê. Figures of hermaphrodites are common in art, one of the finest being the Sleeping Hermaphrodite in the Museo delle Terme at Rome. Less modest representations are given by Clarac (pl. 666 foll.). See Müller, *Archäol. der Kunst*, §§ 128 n. 2, 392 n. 2.

Hermarchus (Ἕρμαρχος). A rhetorician of Mitylenê who became a disciple of Epicurus, and finally succeeded him as head of the school about B.C. 270. A letter of Epicurus to him is preserved by Cicero (*De Fin.* ii. 30). His philosophical works are lost. See Diog. Laërt. x. 17, 24.

Hermas (Ἑρμᾶς). The author of a famous treatise entitled Ποιμήν, or "The Shepherd," once of great repute, so that it was read in the churches. The work is divided into three books—I. *Visiones;* II. *Mandata;* III. *Similitudines.* Its object is to rebuke the worldliness of professed Christians and to exhort sinners to repentance. By some, Hermas has been identified with the Hermas of St. Paul's *Epistle to the Romans*, xvi. 14; but the present belief places him in the second century. It was preserved only in a Latin translation entitled *Pastor* until 1847, when D'Abbadie discovered an Ethiopic version. Since then a great part of the Greek text has been recovered from various sources, and in 1890 a codex containing the whole. The earlier Greek text, compiled from the Codex Sinaiticus and an Athos MS., has been edited by Hilgenfeld (1888), who also edited the Latin version (1877). There is a good edition of the Greek and Latin texts together by Gebhardt and Harnack (1877). See Zahn, *Der Hirt des Hermas* (1868); Salmon, *Introduction to the New Testament* (4th ed. 1889); and the *Johns Hopkins University Circular*, iii. 75 and iv. 23.

Hermathēna. A sort of statue, raised on a square pedestal, in which the attributes of Hermes and Athenê were blended. See Hermae.

Hermeneutics. The same as exegesis, a term technically used of the interpretation of a text from the study of critical materials such as manuscripts, editions, and quotations. The word is from the Greek ἑρμηνεύω, "to interpret." See Textual Criticism.

Hermes (Ἑρμῆς; Dor. Ἑρμᾶς). The son of Zeus and of the Naiad Maia, daughter of Atlas. Immediately after his birth upon the Arcadian mountain of Cyllenê, he gave proof of his chief characteristics—inventiveness and versatility, united with fascination, trickery, and cunning. Born in the morning, by mid-day he had invented the lyre; in the evening he stole fifty head of cattle from his brother Apollo, which he hid so skilfully in a cave that they could not be found. After these exploits he lay down quietly in his cradle. Apollo, by means of his prophetic power, discovered the thief and took the offender to Zeus, who ordered the cattle to be given up. Hermes, however, so delighted his brother by his playing on the lyre that, in exchange for it, he allowed him to keep the cattle, resigned to him the golden staff of fortune and of riches, with the gift of prophecy in its humbler forms, and from that time forth became his best friend. Zeus made his son herald to the gods and the guide of the dead in Hades. In this myth are contained allusions to several attributes of the god.

In many districts of Greece, and especially in Arcadia, the old seat of his worship, Hermes was regarded as a god who bestowed the blessing of fertility on the pastures and herds, and who was happiest when spending his time among shepherds and dallying with Nymphs, by whom he had numberless children, including Pan and Daphnis. In many places he was considered the god of crops, and also as the god of mining and of digging for buried treasure. His kindliness to man is also shown in his being the god of roads. At cross-roads in particular, there were raised in his honour, and called by his name, not only heaps of stones, to which every passer-by added a stone, but also the quadrangular pillars known as Hermae (q. v.). At Athens these last were set up in the streets and open spaces, and also before the doors. Every unexpected find on the road was called a gift of Hermes (ἕρμαιον). Together with Athenê, he escorted and protected heroes in perilous enterprises, and gave them prudent counsels. He took special delight in men's dealings with one another, in exchange and barter, in buying and selling; and in all that is won by craft or by theft. Thus he was the patron of tradespeople and thieves, and was himself the father of Autolycus (q. v.), the greatest of all thieves. He, too, it was who endowed Pandora, the first woman, with the faculty of lying, and with flattering discourse and a crafty spirit. On account of his nimbleness and activity he was the messenger of Zeus, and knew how to carry out his father's commands with adroitness and cunning, as in the slaying of Argos (the guard of Io), from which he derived his epithet of Argos-slayer (Ἀργειφόντης). Again, as Hermes was the sacrificial herald of the gods, it was an important part of the duty of heralds to assist at sacrifices. It was on this account that the priestly race of the Κήρυκες claimed him as the head of their family. (See ELEUSINIA.) Strength of voice and excel-

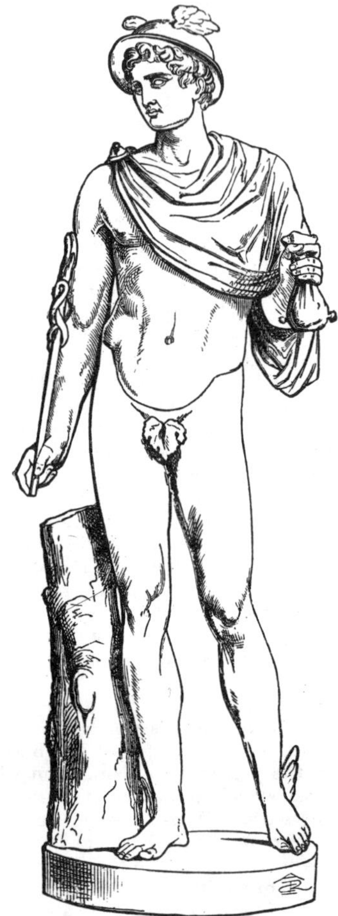

Statue of Hermes. (Capitoline Museum, Rome.)

lence of memory were supposed to be derived from him in his capacity of herald. Owing to his vigour, dexterity, and personal charm, he was deemed the god of gymnastic skill, which makes men strong and handsome, and the especial patron of boxing, running, and throwing the discus; in this capacity the palaestrae and gymnasia were sacred to him, and particular feasts called Hermaea were dedicated to him. He was the discoverer of music (for besides the lyre he invented the shepherd's pipe), and he was also the god of wise and clever discourse. A later age made him even the inventor of letters, figures, mathematics, and astronomy. He was, besides, the god of sleep and of dreams; with one touch of his staff he could close or open the eyes of mortals; hence the custom, before going to sleep, of offering him the last libation. As he was the guide of the living on their way, so he was also the conductor of the souls of the dead in the nether-world (ψυχοπομπός), and was as much loved by the gods of those regions as by those above. For this reason sacrifices were offered to him in the event of deaths, Hermae were placed on the graves, and, at oracles and incantations of the dead, he was honoured as belonging to the lower world; in general, he was accounted the intermediary between the upper and lower worlds. His worship early spread throughout the whole of Greece. As he was born in the fourth month, the number four was sacred to him. In Argos the fourth month was named after him, and in Athens he was honoured with sacrifices on the fourth of every month. His altars and images (mostly simple Hermae) were in all the streets, thoroughfares, and open spaces, and also at the entrance of the palaestra.

In art he is represented in the widely varying characters which he assumed, as a shepherd with a single animal from his flock, as a mischievous little thief, as the god of gain with a purse in his hand (see illustration), with a strigil as patron of the gymnasia, at other times with a lyre, but oftenest of all as the messenger of the gods. He was portrayed by the greatest sculptors, such as Phidias, Polyclitus, Scopas, and Praxiteles, whose Hermes with the infant Dionysus was discovered in 1877, in the temple of Heré, at Olympia. It is mentioned by Pausanias (vi. 19, 1), and is described by Treu in his *Hermes mit dem Dionysosknaben* (Berlin, 1878). In the older works of art he appears as a bearded man (see illustration, p. 240); in the later ones, he is found in a graceful and charming attitude, as a slim youth with tranquil features, indicative of intellect and good-will. His usual attributes are wings on his golden sandals (πέδιλα), and a flat, broad-brimmed hat (see PETASUS), which in later times was ornamented with wings, as was also his staff. This last (ῥάβδος, κηρύκειον, *caduceus*) was originally an enchanter's wand, a symbol of power that produces wealth and prosperity, and also an emblem of influence over the living and the dead (see CADUCEUS), yet even in early times it was regarded as a herald's staff and an emblem of peaceful intercourse. It consisted of three shoots, one of which formed the handle, the other two being intertwined at the top in a knot. The place of the latter was afterwards taken by serpents; and thus arose our ordinary type of herald's staff. By the Romans, Hermes was identified with Mercurius (q. v.). For examples of the myths of Hermes in English literature, see Shelley's *Homeric Hymn to Mercury*, and Keats's *Ode to Maia*, with some fine passages in the *Prometheus Bound* of the former poet.

Hermes Trismegistus (Ἑρμῆς Τρισμέγιστος). The Greek name for the Egyptian god Thoth, regarded as the author of civilization, the inventor of writing, of art, science, and religion. The sacred canon of the Egyptians, in forty-two books divided into six sections, constituting an encyclopaedia of general learning, was ascribed to him under the name of the "Hermetic Books." They treat of religion, and of the arts and sciences, hieroglyphics, astronomy, medicine, mathematics, cosmography, etc. The date of the composition of this canon is not known, but it is evidently late, as the influence of Hellenic culture and the Neo-Platonic philosophy is clearly traceable. The Greek and Latin texts of these books exist only in fragments gathered from Stobaeus, Cyril, Lactantius, Suidas, and others. The Ebers Papyrus (1877) is regarded as one of the medical books of the series. See Ménard, *Hermès Trismégiste* (1866); and Pietschmann, *Hermes Trismegistos* (Leipzig, 1876).

Hermesiănax (Ἑρμησιάναξ). A Greek elegiac poet of Colophon in Ionia, who lived in the time of Alexander the Great, about B.C. 330, and was a scholar and friend of Philetas. He composed erotic elegies in the style of those by his compatriot, Antimachus. The three books containing his compositions he entitled *Leontium* (Λεόντιον), after his mistress. A fragment of ninety-eight lines of the third book has been preserved, in which love-stories of poets and wise men from Orpheus down to Philetas are treated in a rather disconnected manner, but not without spirit. There are editions by Hermann (*Opuscula Academica*, iv. p. 239), by Bach (Halle, 1829), and by Bailey (London, 1839). See Bergk, *De Hermesianactis Elegia* (Marburg, 1845).

Hermetic Books. See HERMES TRISMEGISTUS.

Hermĭas (Ἑρμίας or Ἑρμείας). (1) A Mysian eunuch, tyrant of Assos, and the friend and patron of Aristotle, who married his adopted daughter Pythias. In B.C. 344 Hermias was seized by Mentor, the Greek general of the king of Persia, and by him sent to the Persian court, where he was put to death. (See Diog. Laërt. v. 3; Diod. xvi. 52.) (2) A Christian writer towards the close of the second century, a native of Galatia, who has left a short discourse in ridicule of the pagan philosophers, entitled Διασυρμὸς τῶν ἔξω Φιλοσόφων. It appears to be an imitation of a discourse of Tatian's, but it is an imitation by a man of ability. He ridicules the want of harmony that prevails among the systems of the Greek philosophers, which is the cause of all their speculations being crowned with no positive result.

Herminia Gens. An ancient patrician family at Rome, one of whose members, T. Herminius, kept the bridge with Horatius Cocles against the army of Porsena. See HORATIUS.

Herminius Mons. The modern Sierra de la Estrella; the chief mountain in Lusitania, south of the Durius. It is some 7000 feet in height.

Hermiŏnē (Ἑρμιόνη). A town on the eastern coast of Argolis on a bay deriving its name (Hermionicus Sinus) from the town. It was originally founded by the Dryopes, and was long a flourishing city, famous for its temple of Demeter Cthonia. It belonged to the Achaean League.

Hermiŏnē (Ἑρμιόνη). The only child of Menelaüs and Helen, and married to Neoptolemus, the son of Achilles, immediately on her father's return from Troy, in fulfilment of a promise he had made there. According to a post-Homeric tradition, she had been previously promised to Orestes (q. v.), who claimed her on the ground of his prior right; and on his claim being refused by Neoptolemus, killed his rival with his own hands, or at any rate caused his death, at Delphi. Orestes took Hermionē to his home, and had by her a son, Tisamenus.

Hermiŏnes. A division of the people of Germania, which included the Suevi, Hermunduri, Chatti, and Cherusci. See GERMANIA.

Hermionĭcus Sinus. A bay on the coast of Argolis, near Hermionē. It is now the Gulf of Castri.

Hermippus (Ἕρμιππος). (1) A Greek poet of the Old Comedy, an elder contemporary of Aristophanes and a bitter opponent of Pericles (Plut. *Pericl.* 32, 33), whose mistress, Aspasia, he prosecuted on a charge of atheism. Only a few fragments of his dramas, as also of his libellous iambic poems, after Archilochus's manner, have been preserved. They are remarkable for the cleverness of their style. They are collected by Meineke, *Frag. Com. Graec.* i. pp. 90–99; ii. 380–417. (2) Of Smyrna, a distinguished philosopher, the author of a great biographical work (Βίοι) frequently quoted by later writers. He flourished about the year B.C. 200.

Hermocrătes (Ἑρμοκράτης). One of the Syracusan generals, when the Athenians attacked Syracuse, B.C. 414. He was banished by the Syracusans (410), and having endeavoured to effect his restoration by force of arms and with the aid of the Persian satrap Pharnabazus, was slain in 407. See PELOPONNESIAN WAR.

Hermodōrus (Ἑρμόδωρος). A philosopher of Ephesus, who is said to have assisted, as interpreter, the Roman decemvirs in the composition of the first ten tables of laws which had been collected in Greece (B.C. 451) (Cic. *Tusc.* v. 36). "An ancient tradition mentions," says Niebuhr, "as an auxiliary to the Decemviri, in this code, Hermodorus, an Ephesian, the friend of the sage Heraclitus, whom his fellow-citizens had banished because he filled them with shame, and they desired to be all on an equality in profligacy of conduct. It cannot, indeed, be well explained how this story could have been invented, for which nothing but a celebrated name could have given occasion, while that of Hermodorus appears to have been known to the Greeks themselves only by the saying of his friend. On this ground, the naming of the statue, which was inscribed as his at Rome, may pass for genuine." See TWELVE TABLES. (2) A native of Salamis, the architect of the Temple of Mars in the Flaminian Circus at Rome.

Hermogĕnes (Ἑρμογένης). (1) A Greek rhetorician of Tarsus in Cilicia, who flourished in the middle of the second century A.D. He came to Rome as a rhetorician as early as his fifteenth year, and excited universal admiration, especially on the part of the emperor Marcus Aurelius. In his twenty-fourth year he lost his memory, and never recovered it, though he lived to a great age. After his death his heart is said to have been found to be covered with hair. His work on rhetoric, which still exists, enjoyed a remarkable popularity, and was for a long time the principal text-book of rhetoric; it was also epitomized, and was the subject of numerous commentaries. The work itself consists of five sections: (i.) On points at issue in legal causes; (ii.) On the art of discovering arguments; (iii.) On the various forms of oratorical style; (iv.) On political orations in particular, and on the art of eloquent and effective speaking; (v.) The last section consists of rhetorical exercises (Προγυμνάσματα), which were cast into a fresh form by Aphthonius, and translated into Latin by Priscian, with the title *Praeexercitamenta*. It is printed in Halm's *Rhetores Latini*, p. 551. See Hoppichler, *De Hermogene Progymnasmatum Scriptore* (1884). (2) HERMOGĔNES TIGELLIUS. (See TIGELLIUS.) (3) An architect of Alabanda, who is said to have devised the so-called pseudo-dipterus form of temple. See TEMPLUM.

Hermogeniānus. The latest Roman jurist of whom the Digest contains any citation, and who flourished about A.D. 300.

Hermolāus (Ἑρμόλαος). A Macedonian youth, a page of Alexander the Great. He formed a conspiracy against the king's life in B.C. 327, but the plot was discovered, and Hermolaüs and his accomplices were stoned to death by the Macedonians. The reason for his plot was a desire to avenge himself on Alexander, who had ordered him to be whipped for slaying a wild boar in a hunting expedition without waiting to give the king the honour of the first blow (Q. Curt. viii. 6–8).

Hermonthis (Ἕρμωνθις). The chief town of the Nomos Hermonthitis on the western bank of the Nile in Upper Egypt, near Thebes.

Hermopŏlis (Ἑρμόπολις). "City of Hermes." (1) PARVA (ἡ μικρά), a city of Lower Egypt, stood upon the canal which connected the Canopic branch of the Nile with Lake Mareotis. (2) MAGNA (ἡ μεγάλη), an ancient city in Middle Egypt, standing on the west bank of the Nile, a little below the confines of Upper Egypt. This place was famous for its worship of Anubis (q. v.) or Hermanubis; and was the sacred burial-place of the ibis.

Hermotīmus (Ἑρμότιμος). A native of Clazomenae; a philosopher of the Ionian school, of whom many marvels were told. Tradition represented him as a person gifted with a power by which his soul could leave his body, and so bring him tidings of distant events with wonderful speed. At last, his enemies burned his body in the absence of his soul, thus putting an end to him and to his wanderings (Pliny, *H. N.* vii. 42).

Hermundūri. One of the most powerful nations of Germany, belonging to the Suevic race, and dwelling between the Main and the Danube. Though long the allies of the Romans, they at length joined the Marcomanni against them in the reign of Marcus Aurelius.

Hermus. (1) (Ἕρμος). A large river in Asia Minor, rising in Mount Dindymené, and after flowing through the plain of Sardis, falling into the Gulf of Smyrna, between Smyrna and Phocaea. It formed the boundary between Aeolia and Ionia. (2) (τὸ Ἕρμος). A deme of Attica, belonging to the tribe Acamantis, on the road from Athens to Eleusis.

Hernĭci. A people in Latium, belonging to the Sabine race, who inhabited the mountains of the Apennines between the lake Fucinus and the river Trerus, and were bounded on the north by the Marsi and Aequi, and on the south by the Volsci. Their chief town was Anagnia. They were a brave and warlike people, and long offered a formidable resistance to the Romans, who finally formed a league with them on equal terms in the third consulship of Sp. Cassius, B.C. 486. They were finally subdued by the Romans, B.C. 306.

Hero (Ἡρώ). See LEANDER.

Hero (Ἥρων). (1) A native of Alexandria and disciple of Ctesibius, who flourished about B.C. 125. He placed engineering and land-surveying on a scientific basis, and was celebrated as a mechanician, and invented the hydraulic clock, the machine called "the fountain of Hero," and a forcing-pump used as a fire-engine. (See CTESIBICA MACHINA.) He enjoyed a high reputation, and is mentioned by Gregory Nazianzen with Euclid and Ptolemy. He is now, however, principally known by some remains of his writings on mechanics. His extant writings are: (*a*) "On the Machine Called the Chiroballistra" (Χειροβαλλίστρας κατασκευὴ καὶ συμμετρία); (*b*) "Barulcus" (Βαροῦλκος), a treatise on the raising of heavy weights, which is mentioned by Pappus, and was found by Golius in Arabic; (*c*) "Belopoeica" (Βελοποιϊκά), a treatise on the manufacture of darts; (*d*) "On Pneumatic Machines" (Πνευματικά). In this work is the first and only notice among the ancient writers of the application of steam as a moving power. There is an English translation by Greenwood (London, 1851). (*e*) "On the Construction of Automata" (Περὶ Αὐτοματοποιητικῶν), contained in the *Math. Veteres;* it describes a number of small machines and mechanical toys. (*f*) "On Dioptrics," from which Heliodorus, a mathematician who flourished after the commencement of the Christian era, has left an extract. (*g*) Μετρικά, consisting of geometrical and trigonometrical problems and solutions. Other works of Hero, now lost, are mentioned by Pappus, Eutocius, Heliodorus, etc. Hero describes the theodolite, the cyclometer, and the steam-engine; and discusses the centre of gravity. His works have been edited by F. Hultsch (Berlin, 1864). See the treatise on Hero by T. H. Martin (Paris, 1854); and the account in Ball's *Short History of Mathematics* (London, 1888). (2) Of Constantinople, commonly called the Younger, who is supposed to have flourished about A.D. 900. In a work attributed to him (on Geodesy), he states that the precession of the equinoxes had produced seven degrees of effect since the time of Ptolemy, so that he must have been about 500 years later than Ptolemy. The writings of Hero the Younger relate to warlike machines, tactics, and practical geometry. (3) A mathematician, who flourished about the middle of the fifth century.

Herōdas. See HERONDAS.

Herōdes (Ἡρώδης). (1) Surnamed THE GREAT and ASCALONĪTA, second son of Antipater the Idumaean, was born B.C. 71, at Ascalon, in Iudaea. At the age of twenty-five he was made by his father governor of Galilee, and distinguished himself by the suppression of a band of robbers and the execution of their leader. He was summoned before the Sanhedrim for having done this by his own authority, and having put these men to death without a trial; but, through the strength of his party and the zeal of his friends, he escaped censure. He at first embraced the party of Brutus and Cassius; but, after their death, reconciled himself to Antony, who appointed him and Phasael tetrarchs of Iudaea. In B.C. 40 the Parthians invaded Iudaea, and placed Antigonus on the throne, making Hyrcanus and Phasael prisoners. Herod escaped to Rome, where, by the influence of Antony, he was appointed king of the Jews. But the Roman generals in Syria assisted him very feebly, and it was not till the end of the year B.C. 38 that Jerusalem was taken by Sossius. The commencement of Herod's reign dates from the following year. In the year 38 he had married Mariamné, the granddaughter of Hyrcanus, hoping to strengthen his power by this match with the Asmonaean family, which was very popular in Iudaea. On ascending the throne Herod appointed Ananel of Babylon high-priest, to the exclusion of Aristobulus, the brother of Mariamné. But he soon found himself compelled, by the entreaties

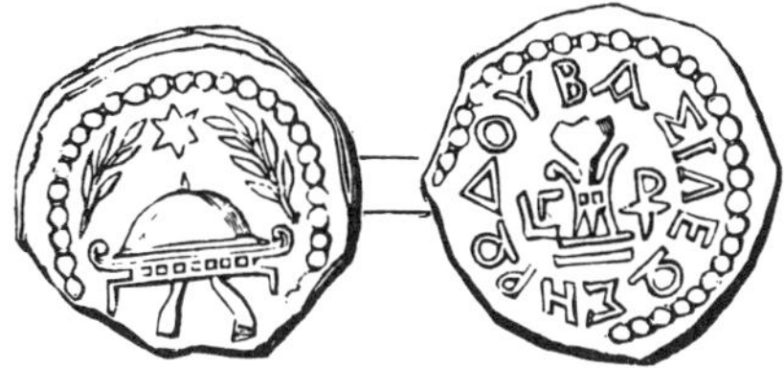

Coin of Herod the Great.

of Mariamné and the artifices of her mother Alexandra, to depose Ananel and appoint Aristobulus in his place. Not long after, however, Aristobulus was secretly put to death by the command of Herod. Alexandra having informed Cleopatra of the murder, Herod was summoned to answer the accusation before Antony, whom he pacified by liberal bribes. When setting out to meet Antony, he had commanded his brother Joseph to put Mariamné to death in case he should be condemned, that she might not fall into Antony's power. Finding, on his return, that his brother had revealed this order to Mariamné, Herod put him to death. In the civil war between Octavius and Antony, Herod joined the latter, and undertook, at his command, a campaign against the Arabians, whom he defeated. After the battle of Actium, he went to meet Octavius at Rhodes, having first put to death Hyrcanus, who had been released by the Parthians, and had placed himself under Herod's protection some years before. He also imprisoned Mariamné and Alexandra, commanding their keepers to kill them upon receiving intelligence of his death. Octavius, however, received him kindly, and reinstated him in his kingdom. On his return, Mariamné reproached him with his intentions towards her, which she had again discovered. This led to an estrangement between Herod and his queen, which was artfully increased by his sister Salomé, till, on one occasion, enraged at a new affront he had received from Mariamné, Herod assembled some of his friends and accused her of adultery. She was condemned and executed. After her death Herod suffered the deepest remorse, and shut himself up in Samaria, where he was seized with an illness which nearly proved fatal. In the year B.C. 26 he put to death the sons of Babas, the last princes of the Asmonaean family.

He now openly disregarded the Jewish law, and introduced Roman customs. He particularly shocked the people by erecting a stately theatre and an amphitheatre in Jerusalem, in the latter of which he celebrated games in honour of Augustus. Ten men conspired against his life, but were detected and executed with the greatest cruelty. To secure himself against rebellion, he fortified Samaria, which he named Sebasté (equivalent to the Latin Augusta), and he built Caesarea and other cities and fortresses. In the year B.C. 17 he began to rebuild the temple at Jerusalem. The work was completed in eight years, but the decorations were not finished for many years after (John, ii. 20). Herod's power and territories continued to increase, but the latter part of his reign was disturbed by the most violent dissensions in his family, of which a minute account is given by Iosephus. He died in March, B.C. 4, in the thirty-fourth year of his reign and the seventieth of his age. Iosephus relates that, shortly before his death, he shut up many of the principal men of the Jewish nation in the Hippodrome, commanding his sister Salomé to put them to death as soon as he expired, that he might not want mourners. They were released, however, by Salomé upon Herod's death.

The birth of Christ took place in the last year of Herod's reign, four years earlier than the era from which the common system of chronology dates the years A.D. (Ioseph. *Ant. Iud.* xiv. 17 foll., xv. 1 foll., xvi. 1 foll.; *Bell. Iud.* i. 17, etc.). It was Herod of whom Augustus said, after he had heard of the former's having put to death his own sons, Alexander and Aristobulus, that he would rather be Herod's hog (ὗν) than his son (υἱόν), punning upon the similarity of the two terms, and alluding at the same time to the aversion with which the hog was regarded by the Jews (Macrob. *Sat.* ii. 4). It was this king who ordered the massacre of the children at Bethlehem.

(2) **Archelaus.** A son of Herod the Great, who succeeded his father and was made ethnarch of Iudaea, Samaria, and Idumaea by Augustus Caesar (B.C. 3). In A.D. 7, however, for his misgovernment, he was removed from his office and banished to Nienna in Gaul, where he died.

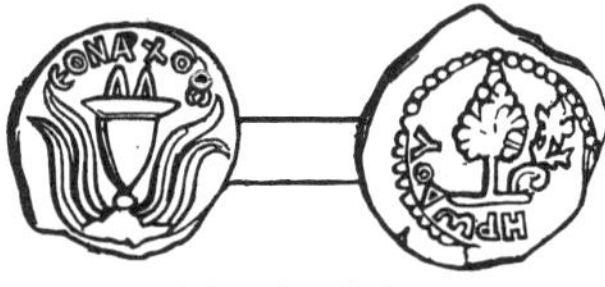

Coin of Archelaus.

(3) **Antĭpas**, a son of Herod the Great, whom his father, in his first will, declared his successor in the kingdom, but to whom he afterwards gave merely the office of tetrarch over Galilee and Peraea, while he appointed his other son Archelaüs king of Iudaea. Antipas, after being confirmed in these territories by Augustus, married the daughter of Aretas, king of Arabia. He divorced her, however, A.D. 33, that he might marry his sister-in-law Herodias, the wife of his brother Philip, who was still living. John the Baptist, exclaiming against this union, was seized, and subsequently beheaded. Afterwards, A.D. 39, Herodias, being jealous of the prosperity of her brother Agrippa, who, from a private person, had become king of Iudaea, persuaded her husband Herod Antipas to visit Rome, and to desire the same dignity from Tiberius. Agrippa, being apprised of his design, wrote to the emperor, accusing Antipas of being implicated in the affair of Seianus, upon which he was banished to Lugdunum, in Gaul. This is the Antipas who, being at Jerusalem at the time of the Saviour's suffering, ridiculed Jesus, whom Pilate had sent to him, dressed him in mock attire, and sent him back to the Roman governor as a king whose ambition gave him no umbrage. The year of his death is unknown, though it is certain that he and Herodias ended their days in exile, according to Iosephus, in Spain. (4) **Agrippa I.**, son of Aristobulus and Berenicé, and grandson of Herod

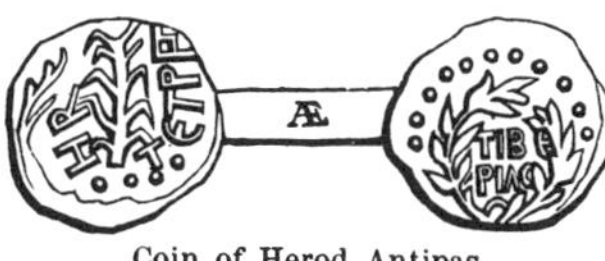

Coin of Herod Antipas.

the Great. He was educated at Rome with the future emperor Claudius, and Drusus the son of Tiberius. Having given offence to Tiberius, he was thrown into prison; but Caligula, on his accession (A.D. 37), set him at liberty, and gave him the tetrarchies of Abilené, Batanaea, Trachonitis, and Auranitis. On the death of Caligula in 41, Agrippa, who was at the time in Rome, assisted Claudius in gaining possession of the Empire. As a reward for his services, Iudaea and Samaria were annexed to his dominions. His government was mild, and he was exceedingly popular among the Jews. It was probably to increase this popularity that he caused the apostle James to be beheaded and Peter to be cast into prison (A.D. 44). The manner of his death, which took place at Caesarea in the same year, is related in Acts, xii. By his wife Cypros he had a son Agrippa and three daughters—Berenicé,

Coin of Herod Agrippa.

Mariamné, and Drusilla. (5) Son of Agrippa I., was educated at the court of Claudius, and at the time of his father's death was seventeen years old. Claudius kept him at Rome, and sent Cuspius Fadus as procurator of the kingdom, which thus again became a Roman province. On the death of Herodes, king of Chalcis (48), his little principality was given to Agrippa, who subsequently received an accession of territory. Before the outbreak of the war with the Romans, Agrippa attempted in vain to dissuade the Jews from rebelling. He sided with the Romans in the war, and after the capture of Jerusalem he went with his sister Berenicé to Rome, and died in the seventieth year of his age, A.D. 100. It was before this Agrippa that the apostle Paul made his defence, A.D. 60 (Acts, xxv., xxvi.). (6) ATTĬCUS (in full, TIBERIUS CLAUDIUS ATTĬCUS HERŌDES). See ATTICUS, HERODES.

Herodiānus (Ἡρωδιανός). (1) The author of an extant history, in the Greek language, of the Roman Empire, in eight books, from the death of Marcus Aurelius to the commencement of the reign of Gordianus III. (A.D. 180–238). He states that the events described by him occurred during the period of his own life, which serves to fix his date, but of the details of his career nothing is known. He seems to have made Thucydides his model, and his narrative is characterized by sobriety, impartiality, and in general by accuracy. His style is good in spite of numerous Latinisms. There are editions by Bekker (1855) and Mendelssohn (1883). See Kreuzer, *De Herodiani Vita*, etc. (1881); and on the language and style, the treatise of P. Schmidt, *Die Syntax des Historikers Herodian*, pt. i. (1891); pt. ii. (1893). (2) AELIUS. A celebrated grammarian, son of Apollonius Dyscolus, and a native of Alexandria, from which place he went to Rome, where he secured the favour of the emperor Marcus Aurelius, to whom he dedicated his work on prosody (Καθολικὴ Προσῳδία), in twenty-one books. His reputation in antiquity was very great, so that Priscian styles him *maximus auctor artis grammaticae*. Of his numerous works, only fragmentary selections now exist, largely in citations in other grammarians. These are enumerated by Fabricius (*Bibl. Graec.* vi. pp. 278 foll.), and edited by Lentz, with indexes, in 2 vols. (Leipzig, 1870). See Lehrs, *Herodiani Scripta Tria* (Königsberg, 1848); Hiller, *Quaestiones Herodianae* (Bonn, 1866); Hilgard, *Excerpta ex Libris Herodiani* (Leipzig, 1887); and Stephan, *De Herodiani Technici Dialectologia* (Strassburg, 1889).

Herodĭcus (Ἡρόδικος). (1) A Babylonian grammarian, a follower of Crates of Mallos, and a violent opponent of the school of Aristarchus, against whose followers he wrote an epigram that is preserved in the Greek Anthology (Jacobs, *Anth. Graec.* ii. p. 64). He wrote a work on Comedy, entitled Κωμῳδούμενα, and various miscellanies. (2) A Thracian physician, who was one of the preceptors of Hippocrates. He seems to have been among the first to insist upon the great importance of systematic exercise in preserving the health. See Plato, *Protag.* § 20.

Herodŏtus (Ἡρόδοτος). (1) A celebrated Greek historian, born at Halicarnassus in Caria, B.C. 484 (Clinton, *Fasti Hellenici*, vol. i. p. 29, 2d ed.). He was of Dorian extraction, and of a distinguished family. His father was named Lyxes, his mother Rhoeo or Dryo. Panyasis, an eminent epic poet, whom some ranked next to Homer, was his uncle either by the mother's or father's side. The facts of his life are few and doubtful, except so far as we can gather them from his own works. Not liking the government of Lygdamis, the grandson of Queen Artemisia, who was tyrant of Halicarnassus, Herodotus retired for a season to the island of Samos, where he is said to have cultivated the Ionic dialect of the Greek, which was the language there prevalent. Before he was thirty years of age he joined a number of his fellow-exiles in an attempt, which proved successful, to expel Lygdamis. But the banishment of the tyrant did not give tranquillity to Halicarnassus, and Herodotus, who himself had become an object of dislike, again left his native country and visited Athens, where he made the acquaintance of many of the brilliant writers of the time. Of these, Sophocles became his intimate friend, and wrote a poem in his honour in B.C. 440, a fragment of which is preserved by Plutarch. (See Hanna, *Sophokles' Beziehungen zu Herodot* [1875]). Eusebius states that he received at Athens many public marks of distinction. As Athenian citizenship was not open to him, he joined, as it is said, a colony which the Athenians sent to Thurii in Southern Italy, about B.C. 443. He is said to have died in Thurii, and to have been buried in the market-place.

Herodotus is regarded by many as the father of profane history, and Cicero (*De Leg.* i. 1) calls him *historiae patrem;* by which, however, nothing more must be meant than that he is the first profane historian whose work is distinguished for its finished form, and has come down to us entire. Thus Cicero himself, on another occasion, speaks of him as the one *qui princeps genus hoc (scribendi) ornavit* (*De Orat.* ii. 13); while Dionysius of Halicarnassus has given us a list of many historical writers who preceded him.

Herodotus presents himself to our consideration in two points: as a traveller and observer, and as an historian. The extent of his travels may be ascertained pretty clearly from his history; but the order in which he visited each place, and the time of his visit, cannot be determined. The story of his reading his work at the Olympic Games, on which occasion he is said to have received universal applause, and to have had the names of the nine Muses given to the nine books of his history, has been disproved. The story is founded upon a small piece by Lucian, entitled "Herodotus or Aëtion," which apparently was not intended by the writer himself as an historical truth; and, in addition to this, Herodotus was only about twenty-eight years old (Suid. s. v. Θουκυδίδης) when he is

Herodotus. (Visconti, *Iconog. Gr.* pl. 27, 2.)

said to have read to the assembled Greeks at Olympia a work which was the result of most extensive travelling and research, and which bears in every part of it evident marks of the hand of a man of mature age. The Olympic recitation is not even alluded to by Plutarch, in his treatise on the "malignity" of Herodotus. Furthermore, it is certain that the division of his work into books was not known to Herodotus himself, but was probably due to the Alexandrian grammarians. It is first mentioned by Diodorus Siculus. At a later period Herodotus read his history, as we are informed by Plutarch and Eusebius, at the Panathenaean festival at Athens, and the Athenians are said to have presented him with the sum of ten talents for the manner in which he had spoken of the deeds of their nation. The account of this second recitation may be true.

With a simplicity which characterizes his whole work, Herodotus makes no display of the great extent of his travels. He frequently avoids saying in express terms that he was at a place, but he uses words which are as conclusive as any positive statement. He describes a thing as standing behind the door (ii. 182), or on the right hand as you enter a temple (i. 51); or he was told something by a person in a particular place (ii. 28); or he uses other words equally significant. In Africa he visited Egypt (see Budinger, *Die ägyptische Forschung Herodot's* [Vienna, 1873]), from the coast of the Mediterranean to Elephantiné, the southern extremity of the country (ii. 29); and he travelled westward as far as Cyrené (ii. 32, 181), and probably farther. (See Neumann, *Nordafrika nach Herodot* [1893]). In Asia he visited Tyre, Babylon, Ecbatana (i. 98), Nineveh, and probably Susa (v. 52 foll., vi. 119). He also travelled to various parts of Asia Minor, and probably went as far as Colchis (ii. 104). In Europe he visited a large part of the country along the Black Sea, between the mouths of the Danube and the Crimea, and went some distance into the interior. He seems to have examined the line of the march of Xerxes from the Hellespont to Attica, and certainly had seen numerous places on this route. He was well acquainted with Athens (i. 98, v. 77), and also with Delphi, Dodona, Olympia, Delos, and many other places in Greece. That he had visited some parts of Southern Italy is clear from his work (iv. 99, v. 44). The mention of these places is sufficient to show that he must have seen many more. (See Hildebrandt, *De Itineribus Herodoti Europaeis et Africanis* [Leipzig, 1883].) So wide and varied a field of observation has rarely been presented to a traveller, and still more rarely to any historian of either ancient or modern times; and, if we cannot affirm that the author undertook his travels with a view to collecting materials for his great work, a supposition which is far from improbable, it is certain that, without such advantages, he could never have written it, and that his travels must have suggested much inquiry, and supplied many valuable facts, which afterwards found a place in his history.

The nine books of Herodotus contain a great variety of matter, the unity of which is not perceived till the whole work has been thoroughly examined; and for this reason, on a first perusal, the history is seldom well understood. But the subject of that history was conceived by the author both clearly and comprehensively. His aim was to combine a general history of the Greeks and the barbarians (i. e. those not Greeks) with the history of the wars between the Greeks and Persians. Accordingly, in the execution of his main task, he traces the course of events from the time when the Lydian kingdom of Croesus fell before the arms of Cyrus, the founder of the Persian monarchy (B.C. 546), to the capture of Sestus (B.C. 478), an event which completed the triumph of the Greeks over the Persians. The great subject of his work, which is comprised within the space of sixty-eight years, advances, with a regular progress and truly dramatic development, from the first weak and divided efforts of the Greeks to resist Asiatic numbers, to their union as a nation, and their final triumph in the memorable battles of Thermopylae, Salamis, Plataea, and Mycalé. But with this subject, which has a complete unity, well maintained from its commencement to its close, the author has interwoven, conformably to his general purpose, and by way of occasional digression, sketches of the various people and countries which he had visited in his wide-extended travels. The more one contemplates the difficulty of thus combining a kind of universal history with a substantial and distinct narrative, the more one must admire, not so much the art of the historian, as his happy power of bringing together and arranging his materials, which was the result of the fulness of his information, the distinctness of his knowledge, and his clear conception of the subject. These numerous digressions are among the most valuable parts of his work; and, if they had been omitted or lost, barren indeed would have been modern investigation in the field of ancient history, over which the labour of this one great writer now throws a clear and steady light. The anecdotes, also, that sparkle through his pages are fascinating in their variety and in the illustrations they afford of the life and manners of the age that he describes.

The style of Herodotus is simple, pleasing, and highly picturesque; often, indeed, poetical both in expression and sentiment, and bearing evident marks of belonging to a period when prose composition had not yet become a finished art. That he was a close student of Homer is evident in every page of the history, since his phrases and expressions are everywhere coloured by the Homeric influence. Hence, Dionysius of Halicarnassus calls him Ὁμήρου ζηλωτής, and Longinus μόνος Ὁμηρικώτατος. So graceful and winning was his style that Athenaeus describes him as ὁ μελίγηρυς. His information is apparently the result of his own experience. In physical knowledge he was somewhat behind the science of even his own day. He had, no doubt, reflected on political questions; but he seems to have formed his opinions mainly from what he himself had observed. To pure philosophical speculations he had no inclination, and there is not a trace of such in his writings. He had a strong religious feeling bordering on superstition, though even here he clearly distinguished the gross and absurd from that which was reasonable. He seems to have viewed the manners and customs of all nations in a more truly philosophical way than many so-called philosophers, considering them all as various forms of social existence under which happiness might be found. He treats with respect the religious observances of every nation; a decisive proof of his great good sense. Until lately there was a strong tendency to exaggerate the credulity of Herodotus; but a fuller knowledge of the countries described by him has justified many of the statements once regarded as absurd. Moreover, a distinction must be drawn between the things he tells of his own knowledge and those which he merely relates as having been told him by other persons. The exquisite lines quoted by Prof. Merriam in his introduction are wonderfully descriptive of the whole tone and spirit of Herodotus:

> "He was a mild old man and cherished much
> The weight dark Egypt on his spirit laid;
> And with a sinuous eloquence would touch
> Forever at that haven of the dead.
> Single romantic words by him were thrown
> As types on men and places, with a power
> Like that of shifting sunlight after shower
> Kindling the cones of hills and journeying on.
> He feared the gods and heroes and spake low
> That Echo might not hear in her light room."

Plutarch accused Herodotus of partiality, and composed a treatise on what he termed the "spitefulness" of this writer (Περὶ τῆς Ἡροδότου Κακοηθείας), taxing him with injustice towards the Thebans, Corinthians, and Greeks in general; but the whole monograph is weak and frivolous.

Herodotus had planned to write a work on Assyrian history (i. 106, 184), but whether or not he ever carried out his intention is not known. A life of Homer has been commonly ascribed to Herodotus, and appears in some editions of his history; but it is now deemed spurious. See Schmidt, *De Herodotea quae fertur Vita Homeri*, 2 pts. (1874–75).

MANUSCRIPTS.—Of forty-six MSS. containing a whole or a portion of Herodotus, five, which are of superior age and excellence, form the basis of the accepted text. These represent two "families," to one of which belong the Codex Florentinus or Mediceus of the Laurentian Library at Florence, dating from the tenth century, a Codex Romanus of the eleventh century, and a second Codex Florentinus, also of the eleventh century. To the other family belong a Codex Parisinus, beautifully written, of the thirteenth century, and a third Codex Romanus of the fourteenth century, lacking, however, the Fifth Book. Of this, also, the text of the First Book has been considerably altered, possibly in order to adapt the work to the use of schools. An account of the MSS. is given by Stein in his edition mentioned below.

BIBLIOGRAPHY.—The *editio princeps* of Herodotus is that of Aldus (1502). Standard critical editions are those of Schweighäuser, 5 vols. (Strassburg, 1816); Gaisford (Oxford, 1840); Stein (Berlin, 1869); and Dietsch (Leipzig, 1874). Good commentaries are those of Bähr in Latin (Leipzig, 1856); Blakesley (London, 1854); Stein in German (Berlin, 1877), and Rawlinson (London, 1858); also Abicht in German (1876). English translations have been made by Rawlinson, 4 vols. (2d ed. 1862), and G. C. Macaulay, 2 vols. (London, 1890). A valuable *Lexicon Herodoteum* is that of Schweighäuser (London, 2d ed. 1824). Very useful are the appendices to Prof. Sayce's edition of Bks. I.–III. (London, 1883). On the dialect, see Abicht, *Uebersicht über den herodoteischen Dialect* (3d ed. Leipzig, 1874); and Merzdorf, *Quaestiones Grammaticae de Dialecto Herodotea* (Leipzig, 1875). Stein's introduction on the dialect in his school edition is admirable; also Smyth in his *Sounds and Inflections of the Greek Dialects* (1894). On the sources of his history, see the monographs of Panofsky (1865) and K. W. Nitzsch (1871). On his travels, see the works already cited in the text.

(2) A physician of Tarsus, of the empiric school, and successor to Menodotus of Nicomedia. A work of his, entitled "The Physician," is mentioned by Galen.

Heron. See HERO.

Herondas (Ἡρώνδας) or **Herōdas** (Ἡρώδας). A Greek writer of iambics, who lived probably at Cos in the third century B.C., and of whose verses little was known before the recent discovery among the papyri in the British Museum of a MS. containing seven poems. Previous to this discovery there existed only ten quotations from him (one in iambic dimeter and nine in choliambics), five of which are found in the British Museum MS., and served to identify the author, as his name is not there given. These seven complete poems contain from 85 to 129 lines apiece, and are entitled (1) Προκυκλίς ἤ Μαστροπός, "The Matchmaker or the Go-between;" (2) Πορνοβοσκός, "The Pimp;" (3) Διδάσκαλος, "The Schoolmaster;" (4) Ἀσκληπιῷ ἀνατιθεῖσαι καὶ θυσιάζουσαι, "A Visit to Asclepius;" (5) Ζηλότυπος, "The Jealous Woman;" (6) Φιλιάζουσαι ἤ Ἰδιάζουσαι, "Affectionate Friends, or the Confidantes;" (7) Σκυτεύς (?), "The Cobbler." The titles of two more poems are found in the MS.—Ἐνύπνιον, "The Dream;" and Ἀπονηστιζόμεναι, "Ladies at Breakfast." The poems are difficult to read, abounding in words found hitherto only in Hesychius, and containing some that are entirely unknown. Many of these strange vocables are probably the result of copyists' errors, having been written in Egypt whence the MS. came, while others are doubtless colloquialisms.

The previously extant fragments of Herondas can be found in Meineke's *Ceterorum Poetarum Choliambi*, appended to Lachmann's *Babrius* (Berlin, 1845). The recently discovered poems have been published unamended with autotype facsimiles of the MS. by the Trustees of the British Museum, and collated by F. G. Kenyon (London, 1891). An edition with a translation into Latin and a most admirable index has been published by Prof. Bücheler of Bonn (1892). An improved text with short notes by Rutherford appeared simultaneously with Mr. Kenyon's text. The latest edition is that of Crusius (Leipzig, 1894). Valuable edition by Meister in *Ber. der sächs. Geschichte der Wiss.* (Leipzig, 1893).

Herōon (ἡρῷον). The shrine of a hero. See HEROS.

Heroöpŏlis (Ἡρώων πόλις) or **Hero** (Ἡρώ). A city in Lower Egypt, standing on the border of the desert east of the Delta, upon the canal connecting the Nile with the western head of the Red Sea, which was called from it Sinus Heroöpoliticus (Κόλπος Ἡρώων). The country about it is considered to be the Goshen of the Bible.

Herophĭlē (Ἡροφίλη). The Erythraean Sibyl. See SIBYLLA.

Herophĭlus (Ἡρόφιλος). A celebrated physician, a native of Chalcedon, of the family of the Asclepiades, and a disciple of Praxagoras. Herophilus lived under Ptolemy Soter, and was contemporary with the philosopher Diodorus, and the celebrated physician Erasistratus, with whose name his own is commonly associated in the history of anatomical science. As a physician, Herophilus is mentioned with praise by both the ancient and the early modern writers. Galen says that he carried anatomy to the highest degree of perfection. With such zeal, indeed, did Herophilus pursue this science, that he is said to have dissected 700 subjects, and it was against him and Erasistratus that the charge was first made of having frequently opened living criminals that they might discover the secret springs of life (Celsus, *Praef.*). From the peculiar advantages which the school of Alexandria presented by this authorized dissection of the human body, it gained, and for many centuries preserved, the first reputation for medical education, so that Ammianus Marcellinus, who lived about 650 years after its establishment, says that it was sufficient to secure credit to any physician if he could say that he had studied at Alexandria (Amm. Marc. xxii. 16). Herophilus made great discoveries in anatomy, and Fallopius calls him "the evangelist of anatomists." He is to be regarded as the inventor of pathological anatomy, having been the first that thought of opening the bodies of men after death in order to ascertain the nature of the malady which had caused their dissolution. His principal discoveries have reference to the nervous system, which he acknowledged as the seat of the sensations. The description which Herophilus gave of the brain itself was far superior to those of previous authors. He also noticed the lacteals, though he was not aware of their use. He pointed out that the first division of the intestinal canal is never more than the breadth of twelve fingers in length, and from this fact proposed for it a name (δωδεκαδακτύλη ἔκφυσις), the Latin form of which (*duodenum*) is still applied to it. He described with great exactness the organ of sight, and gave to its various membranes the names which have still, in a great measure, remained to them. He operated on the cataract by extracting the crystalline humour. Herophilus was the first, also, that had correct notions respecting the pulse, of which his master, Praxagoras, had taught him some of the value as a means of discriminating diseases (Galen, *De Diff. Puls.* ii. p. 24; Pliny, *H. N.* xi. 37, xxix. 1). It was he who first showed that paralysis is an affection of the nervous system. His commentary on Hippocrates still exists. All his other works are lost. See Marx, *De Herophili Vita* (Göttingen, 1840); Berdoe, *Origin and Growth of the Healing Art* (London, 1893); and the articles CHIRURGIA; MEDICINA.

Heros (ἥρως, "a hero"). In Homer, a descriptive title given to princes and nobles, but also applied to men of mark sprung from the people. Hesiod reserves the name for mortals of divine origin, who are therefore known as demigods. Many of these he places on the Islands of the Blessed, where, under the sovereignty of Cronus, they lead a life of happiness. Hesiod makes no allusion to the influence of heroes upon the life of man, or to the worship due to them in consequence. But in later times this belief spread throughout the whole of Greece. The heroes are in most respects like men and suffer death; but death puts them in a more exalted rank, and they then have power to do men good as well as harm. The most distinguished warriors of prehistoric times were accounted heroes, being generally regarded as the offspring of gods by mortal women; to their souls another destiny was accordingly assigned than that allotted to the souls of mortals. But even among the heroes of old time there were some who, without being children of the gods, nevertheless so distinguished themselves by their virtue that they appeared to participate in the divine nature, and therefore to deserve a higher distinction after death. Even in later times such men were not unknown, when personages recently deceased were actually exalted to the ranks of heroes, as in the case of Leonidas at Sparta, and Harmodius and Aristogiton at Athens. The founders of colonies and cities (ἀρχηγέται, κτίσται) were especially considered worthy of worship as heroes;

when the true founder was unknown, then some appropriate hero was selected instead. Formerly there were many such fictitious heroes; to this class properly belong all the titular ancestors of the noble and priestly families of Attica and the founders of particular arts and trades, as Daedalus, Triptolemus, etc. Many heroes of historical times were originally gods, who, in course of time, were divested of their primitive dignity. There was no town or district of Greece in which a host of heroes was not worshipped by the side of the higher divinities; many as special tutelary spirits of the country, others as the heroes of the country, as the Dioscuri at Sparta, the Aeacidae at Aegina, and Theseus in Attica. There were festivals in their honour everywhere, many of them small and unimportant, and only celebrated in a restricted circle, others observed by the State as festivals of the people in general, and not at all inferior in wealth of equipment to the most important festivals in honour of the gods. This was especially the case with the heroes of the country. Many heroes (e. g. Adrastus, Theseus) had shrines, known as Heroa, which were generally erected over their graves (Herod. v. 67). The altars of heroes were lower than those of gods, and were commonly designated sacrificial hearths; they were generally on a level with the ground, and on the west side—the region of the nether world—were provided with a hollow, into which the libations were poured. Like offerings to the dead, these consisted of honey, wine, water, milk, oil, and blood which had been shed by sacrificial victims; the flesh of the animals sacrificed was burned. In the period of decadence it became customary to treat the living with heroic honours. Such honours were paid to the Spartan Lysander by the towns in Asia Minor, and were afterwards accorded to kings—e. g. to Antigonus and his son Demetrius at Athens.

The Greek ἥρως is used as an equivalent of the Latin *divus*, as applied to those who once were mortal, and hence opposed to *deus*, one who was from the first a god. It is therefore used of the deified Roman emperors. See APOTHEOSIS.

Herostrătus (Ἡρόστρατος). An Ephesian who set fire to the Temple of Artemis at Ephesus on the same night that Alexander the Great was born, B.C. 356, in order to immortalize himself. The Ephesians passed a decree condemning his name to oblivion, but as might naturally be expected, this only increased his notoriety, and made him more absolutely certain of the attainment of his object (Plut. *Alex.* 3; Val. Max. viii. 14, 5; Gell. ii. 6).

Hersé (Ἕρση). See AGRAULUS; CECROPS; ERECHTHEUS.

Hersilia. One of the Sabine women carried away by the Romans at the celebration of the Consualia. She was given to Romulus as a wife, and, after his death, became herself a divinity, under the name of Hora (Youth) (Livy, i. 11; Gell. xiii. 22; Plut. *Romul.* 14). Others make her the wife of Hostus Hostilius, grandfather of king Tullus Hostilius of Rome (Macrob. *Sat.* i. 6).

Hertha. A goddess worshipped by the ancient Germans, and, according to Tacitus (*Germ.* 40), the same with the earth. She was supposed to take part in human affairs, and even sometimes to come among mortals. She had a sacred grove in an island of the ocean, and a chariot, covered with a veil, standing in the grove and consecrated to her service. Whenever it was known that the goddess had descended into this her sanctuary, her car was got ready, cows were yoked to it, and the deity was carried around in the covered vehicle. Festivity reigned in every place which the goddess honoured with her presence; wars ceased, arms were laid aside, and peace and harmony prevailed, until the priest declared that the goddess was sated with human society, and once more enclosed her within the temple. The island mentioned by Tacitus is supposed by many to have been that of Rügen, in the Baltic, while others have placed it in the Northern Ocean. See Rabus, *De Dea Hertha* (Augsburg, 1842).

Herŭli or **Erŭli**. A powerful German race, which was said to have come originally from Scandinavia. It attacked the Roman Empire on its decline. Under the command of Odoacer, who is said to have been an Herulian, the Heruli destroyed the Western Empire, A.D. 476.

Hesiŏdus (Ἡσίοδος). A celebrated Greek poet, supposed to have been born at Ascra in Boeotia (*Op. et D.* 633 foll.). His father, it seems, had migrated to Ascra in consequence of his poverty, and resided at the latter place for some time, though without obtaining the rights of a citizen. Still, however, he left at his death a considerable property to his two sons, Hesiod, and a younger one named Perses. The brothers divided the inheritance; but Perses, by means of bribes to the judges, contrived to defraud his elder brother. Hesiod thereupon migrated to Orchomenus, as Göttling supposes, and the harsh epithets which he applies to his native village were, in all probability, prompted by resentment at the wrong which he had suffered from the Ascraean judges. From a passage in the proëm to his *Theogony*, it has been inferred that Hesiod was literally a shepherd, and tended his flocks on the side of Helicon. He was evidently born in an humble station, and was himself engaged in rural pursuits; and this perfectly accords with the subject of the poem which was unanimously ascribed to him—namely, the *Works and Days* (Ἔργα καὶ Ἡμέραι), which is a collection of reflections and precepts relating to husbandry and the regulation of a rural household, interwoven with fables, allegories, etc., forming, as has been said, "a Boeotian shepherd's-calendar." The only additional fact that can be gathered from Hesiod's writings is that he went over to the island of Euboea, on occasion of a poetical contest at Chalcis, which formed part of the funeral games instituted in honour of Amphidamas; that he obtained a tripod as the prize, and consecrated it to the Muses of Helicon. This latter passage is suspected by Wolf; but it seems to have formed a part of the poem from time immemorial; and it may not be unreasonable to infer its authenticity from the tradition respecting an imaginary contest between Homer and Hesiod.

The following legendary account is given as to the manner of Hesiod's death. He is said to have consulted the oracle of Delphi as to his future destinies, and the Pythia directed him, in reply, to shun the grove of Nemean Zeus, since there death awaited him. There were at Argos a temple and a brazen statue of Zeus; and Hesiod, believing this to be the fatal spot, directed his course to Oenoë, a town of the Locri; but the ambiguity of the oracle had deceived him, for this place also, by obscure report, was sacred to the same god. He was here the guest of two brothers. It happened that their sister Clymené was violated in the night-time by the person who had accompanied Hesiod, and hanged herself in consequence of the outrage. This man they accordingly slew; and, suspecting the connivance of Hesiod, killed him also, and threw his body into the sea. The murder is said to have been detected by the sagacity of Hesiod's dog; though by some it is related that his corpse was brought to the shore by a company of dolphins, at the moment that the people were celebrating the festival of Poseidon. The body of Hesiod was recognized, the houses of the murderers were razed to the foundation, and the murderers themselves cast into the sea. Another account states them to have been consumed by lightning; a third, to have been overtaken by a tempest while escaping to Crete in a fishing-boat, and to have perished in the wreck.

The only works that remain under the name of Hesiod are: (i.) Ἔργα καὶ Ἡμέραι ("Works and Days"); (ii.) Θεογονία ("Theogony"); (iii.) Ἀσπὶς Ἡρακλέους ("The Shield of Heracles"). The *Works and Days* (which, according to Pausanias, the Boeotians regarded as the only genuine production of Hesiod) is entirely occupied with the events of common life. The poem consists of advice given by Hesiod to his brother Perses, on subjects relating for the most part to agriculture and the general conduct of life. The object of the first portion of the poem is to improve the character and habits of Perses, and to incite him to a life of labour, as the only source of permanent prosperity. Mythical narratives, fables, descriptions, and moral apophthegms, partly of a proverbial kind, are ingeniously chosen and combined, so as to illustrate and enforce the principal idea, and served as a model for Vergil in his *Georgics*. In the second part Hesiod shows Perses the succession in which his labours must follow, if he determines to lead a life of industry. The poet speaks of the time of life when a man should marry, and how he should look out for a wife. He recommends all to bear in mind that the immortal gods watch over the actions of men; in all intercourse with others to keep the tongue from idle and provoking words, and to preserve a certain purity and care in the commonest occurrences of every-day life. At the same time, he gives many curious precepts, which resemble sacerdotal rules, with respect to the decorum to be observed in acts of worship, and which, moreover, have much in common with the symbolic rules of the Pythagoreans, that ascribed a spiritual import to many acts of ordinary life. Of a very similar nature is the last part of the poem, which treats of the days on which it is expedient or inexpedient to do this or that business.

The *Theogony* (Θεογονία) consists of an account of the origin of the world, including the birth of the gods, and makes use of numerous personifications. Even as early as the time of Pausanias (viii. 18, ix. 31) it was doubted whether Hesiod was actually the author of this poem, though its genuineness is expressly asserted by Herodotus (ii. 53), and all the internal evidence is in favour of this view. According to Hermann, it is a species of *mélange*, formed by the union of several poems on the same subject, and which has been effected by the same copyists or grammarians. The *Theogony* is interesting as being the most ancient monument that we have of the Greek mythology. When we consider it as a poem, we find no composition of ancient times so stamped with a rude simplicity of character. It is without luminous order of arrangement, abounds with dry details, and only occasionally rises to any particular elevation of fancy. It exhibits that crude irregularity and that mixture of meanness and grandeur which characterize a strong but uncultivated genius. The censure of Quintilian that "Hesiod rarely soars, and a great part of him is occupied in mere names," is undoubtedly merited. The sentence just quoted, however, refers plainly to the *Theogony* alone, while the following seems exclusively applicable to the *Works and Days*: "Yet he is distinguished by useful sentences of morality, and an admirable sweetness of diction and expression, and he deserves the palm in the middle style of writing." The passage relating to the battle of the gods, however, can not surely be classed among the specimens of the middle style. This passage, together with the combat of Zeus and Typhoëus, astonishes the reader by sudden bursts of enthusiasm, for which the prolix and nerveless narrative of the general poem has little prepared him. Mahaffy speaks of it as having "a splendid crash and thunder about it," and even as "far superior in conception, though inferior in execution, to the battle of the gods in the *Iliad*." Milton has borrowed some suggestions from these descriptions; and the arming of the Messiah for battle in *Paradise Lost* is obviously imitated from the magnificent picture of Zeus summoning all the terrors of his omnipotence for the extirpation of the Titans.

We have also, under the name of Hesiod, a fragment of 480 lines from a poem entitled the Ἡρωογονία or the genealogy and history of the demigods. To this poem some unknown rhapsodist has attached a piece on the combat between Heracles and Cycnus, containing a description of the hero's shield. It is from this part that the fragment in question bears the title of the *Shield of Heracles* (Ἀσπὶς Ἡρακλέους). Modern critics think that to the *Heroögony* of Hesiod belonged two works which are cited by the ancients—the one under the title of *Catalogue of Women* (Κατάλογος Γυναικῶν), a sort of Greek Debrett, giving the history of those mortal women who had become the mothers of demigods, and the other under the title of the Μεγάλαι Ἠοῖαι, so named because the history of each woman or heroine mentioned therein commenced with the words ἢ οἵη ("or such as"). There are scholia on Hesiod by Proclus, John Tzetzes, Moschopulus, and John Protospatharius; but the commentary by Aristophanes of Byzantium is lost. Tzetzes has also left a life of the poet, which is printed in Flach's edition of Hesiod.

The *editio princeps* of Hesiod appeared at Milan in 1493. Other memorable editions are those of Gaisford (1814–20), Lehrs (1862), Schömann (1869), Koechly (1878), and Fick (1887); and with explanatory notes, those of Paley, in English (1861), and of Göttling (1843) and Flach, in Latin (1878). The fragments are collected by Markscheffel (Leipzig, 1840). There is an English prose translation of Hesiod with Callimachus and Theognis in the Bohn Library; and a spirited verse translation by Elton. See also Rzach's monograph on the language of Hesiod, *Der Dialect des Hesiodus* (1876);

and on the mythology, Gruppe, *Die griech. Kulte und Mythen*, i. 567–612.

Hesiŏnē (Ἡσιόνη). The daughter of Laomedon, king of Troy, and of Leucippé. By her death she was to appease the wrath of Poseidon, who, on account of her father's breaking his word, was devastating the land with a marine monster. Heracles destroyed the monster and set the maiden free; but Laomedon wished to break his promise to the hero, and to deprive him of his stipulated payment. Heracles took Troy, slew Laomedon and his sons, and gave Hesioné to his companion Telamon, to whom she bore a son, Teucer.

Hesperia (Ἑσπερία). The Western Land (from ἕσπερος, *vesper*), the name given by the Greek poets to Italy, because it lay west of Greece. In imitation of them, the Roman poets gave the name of Hesperia to Spain, which they sometimes called Ultima Hesperia (Hor. *Carm.* i. 36, 4) to distinguish it from Italy, which they occasionally called Hesperia Magna. See ITALIA.

Hesperĭdes (Ἑσπερίδες). "The Western Maidens," three celebrated nymphs, whose genealogy is differently given by various writers. According to Hesiod (*Theog.* 215), they were the daughters of Night, without a father. Diodorus, on the other hand, makes them to have had for their parents Atlas and Hesperis, daughter of Hesperus (Diod. Sic. iv. 27), an account which is followed by Milton in his *Comus* (981). Others, however, to assimilate them to their neighbours the Graiae and Gorgons, call the Hesperides the offspring of Phorcys and Ceto. Apollonius gives their names as Aeglé, Hespera, and Erytheïs (iv. 1427); while Apollodorus, who increases the number to four, calls them Aeglé, Erythea, Hestia, and Arethusa (ii. 5, 11). Hesiod makes them to have dwelt "beyond the bright ocean," opposite to where Atlas stood supporting the heavens (*Theog.* 518); and when Atlas had been fixed as a mountain in the extremity of Libya, the dwelling of the Hesperides was usually placed in his vicinity, though some set it in the country of the Hyperboreans (Apollod. l. c.).

According to the legend, when the bridal of Zeus and Heré took place, the different deities came with nuptial presents for the latter, and among them the goddess of Earth, with branches having golden apples growing on them (Hyg. *Poet. Astron.* ii. 3). Heré, greatly admiring these, begged of Earth to plant them in her gardens, which extended as far as Mount Atlas. The Hesperides, or daughters of Atlas, were directed to watch these trees; but, as they were somewhat remiss in discharging this duty, and frequently plucked off the apples themselves, Heré sent thither a large serpent to guard the precious fruit. This monster was the offspring of Typhon and Echidna, and had a hundred heads, so that it never slept. According to Pisander, the name of the reptile was Ladon. One of the tasks imposed upon Heracles by Eurystheus was to bring him some of this golden fruit. For the legend, see HERACLES, p. 791.

Hesperĭdum Insŭlae. See HESPERIUM; HESPERIDES.

Hespĕris. See BERENICÉ.

Hesperium (Ἑσπέριον, Ἑσπέρον κέρας). The modern Cape Verde or Cape Roxo, a headland on the west coast of Africa, was one of the farthest points along that coast to which the knowledge of the ancients extended. At a day's journey from it was a group of islands called Hesperidum Insulae, wrongly identified by some with the Fortunatae Insulae. They are either the Cape de Verde islands, or, more probably, the Bissagos, at the mouth of the Rio Grande.

Hesperius Sinus. A bay on the western coast of Africa.

Hespĕrus (Ἕσπερος). The evening star, son of Astraeus and Eos (Aurora), of Cephalus and Eos, or of Atlas. He was also regarded as the same as the morning star. See LUCIFER.

Hestia (ἑστία). See FOCUS.

Hestia (Ἑστία; Ionic, Ἱστίη). The goddess of the hearth, which is the emblem of the settled home. She was deemed the founder and maintainer of the family and the State, of civic concord and of public reverence for the gods. She was the daughter of Cronus and of Rhea; sister of Zeus, Poseidon, Hades, Heré, and Demeter; one of the twelve Olympian deities, from the rest of whom she was distinguished by the fact that, as the abiding goddess of the household, she never left Olympus. In Homer, although the sanctity of the hearth is indeed recognized, as yet we find no mention of the goddess. It is a matter of discussion whether this was by accident, or because in that period the personification of the worship of the hearth had not attained its full perfection. Having been wooed by Apollo and Poseidon, she took an oath of perpetual virginity; so Zeus granted her the honour of being worshipped, as a tutelary goddess, at every hearth, in human habitations as well as in the temples of the gods, and of being called to mind amid libations at the beginning and end of every sacrifice and every festal entertainment. Hence it was that every sacrifice began and ended with a libation to Hestia, so that she had a share in all festivities; and in every prayer, as well as in all the public forms of solemn oaths, her name was recited before the name of any other god. Just as in the home her consecrated hearth formed the central point of family life, at which family festivals were celebrated and where both strangers and fugitives found a hospitable asylum, so also in the prytaneum, or town hall, where the sacred fire was ever burning, her hearth was the centre of the life of the city, indeed of the whole State, and of the colonies which had gone forth from it. Here, as representative of the State, the highest officials sacrificed to her, just as in every private house the father or mother of the family provided for her worship. Here also were held the public deliberations, and the public banquet given to deserving citizens and to foreign ambassadors. Hither repaired all who besought the protection of the State. Hence also the colonists, bound for distant shores, took the fire for the public hearth of their new community. In some respects, the centre of the religious life of Greece was the fire on the hearth of Hestia in the Delphic temple, where was the sacred ὀμφαλός

Vesta Giustiniani.

(navel), which the Greeks considered to be the central point of the inhabited earth. Hestia stands in close connection with Zeus as the guardian of the law of hospitality and of the oath. She was also much associated with Hermes and often invoked in conjunction with him; Hestia, as the goddess of quiet domesticity, and Hermes, as the restless god of trade on the public streets and roads, representing between them the two principal varieties of human life. According to a view that afterwards became current, under the influence of philosophers and mystics, she was regarded as personifying the earth, as the fixed centre of the world, and was identified with Demeter and Cybelé. The corresponding deity among the Romans was Vesta (q. v.). The statues placed in the prytanea represented her, in accordance with her nature, as a being with grave and yet gentle expression, sitting or standing in an attitude of rest, with a sceptre as her attribute. She is never represented as nude, whence perhaps so few statues of her have been found. The most celebrated of her existing statues is known as the Vesta Giustiniani, in the Torlonia collection at Rome, and ascribed conjecturally to Calamis—a form robed in simple drapery, with hair unadorned and wearing a veil; her right hand rests on her hip, and her left hand, which is pointing upwards, once held a long staff as her sceptre. It represents the earlier Greek conception of divinity, austere and rigid, yet stately and imposing, blending simplicity and severity with grace and tenderness. See Preuner, *Hestia-Vesta* (Tübingen, 1864).

Hestiaeōtis (Ἑστιαιῶτις). (1) According to Strabo, that portion of Thessaly which lies near Pindus, and between that mountain and Upper Macedonia. This district was originally the country of the Dorians, who are stated by Herodotus (i. 56) and others to have once occupied the regions of Pindus. See THESSALIA. (2) Or HISTIAEA. A district of Euboea, whose inhabitants are said to have peopled the Thessalian Hestiaeotis.

Hestiāsis (ἑστίασις). A species of liturgy which consisted in giving a feast to one of the tribes at Athens by some person belonging to the tribe, who was known as ἑστιάτωρ. See Harpocration, s. v. ἑστιάτωρ.

Hesus. A deity among the Gauls, the same as Mars of the Romans (Lucan, i. 445). Lactantius (*Div. Inst* i. 21) writes the name *Heusus*.

Hesychius (Ἡσύχιος). (1) A Greek grammarian of Alexandria, who lived probably towards the end of the fourth century A.D. He composed, with the assistance of the works of earlier lexicographers (especially the Περιεργοπένητες of Diogenianus), a lexicon (Γλῶσσαι), which has come down to us in a very confused form, but is nevertheless among the most important sources of our knowledge of the Greek language, and throws much light on the interpretation and criticism of Greek poets, orators, historians, and physicians. Editions by Alberti and Ruhnken (Leyden, 1746–66), with additions by Schon (Leipzig, 1792); and by M. Schmidt (5 vols. 1858–61). The Christian glosses, which are interpolations, have been separately edited by Ernesti (Leipzig, 1785). See Ranke, *De Lex. Hesych. Vera Origine* (Quedlinburg, 1831). (2) A Milesian, called Illustris, who lived about A.D. 540, and wrote an *Onomasticon* or biography of illustrious men (ed. by Orelli, 1820), and a *Chronicon* or synopsis of universal history, in six parts, beginning with Belus, the alleged founder of the Assyrian State, and ending with the death of the Byzantine emperor, Anastasius I. (A.D. 518). The latter work is lost. See Krumbacher, *Grundriss der byzantinischen Literatur* (in I. Müller's *Handbuch*, vol. ix.), pp. 110 foll.

Hetaerae (ἑταῖραι). See MERETRIX.

Hetaeri (ἑταῖροι, "comrades"). The designation of all free Macedonians who were ready to join in the defence of their country; especially the noblemen who composed the heavy cavalry, as contrasted with the infantry (πεζεταῖροι) of the royal guard.

Hetaerīae (ἑταιρεῖαι). The common name in Greece for all associations having any particular object, but chiefly for political clubs, often of a secret character, for the advancement of certain interests in the State. In many cases their members only aimed at assisting one another as candidates for public office or in lawsuits; but occasionally they also worked for the victory of their party and for a change in the constitution. See ERANOS.

Hetricŭlum. A town of the Bruttii.

Hetruria. See ETRURIA.

Hexaēmĕron. See DRACONTIUS.

Hexaphŏrum. See LECTICA.

Hexapŏlis. See DORIS; LESBOS; LINDUS.

Hexastȳlos. A temple or like building having six columns in front. See TEMPLUM.

Heyne, CHRISTIAN GOTTLOB. A German classical scholar, born at Chemnitz in Saxony, September 25, 1729. His father was a poor weaver, and for a number of years the son struggled with poverty and disappointment, being sometimes reduced almost to actual starvation. In 1753, however, he secured the position of under-clerk in the Brühl Library at Dresden, and before long published an edition of Tibullus (1755), and one of the *Enchiridion* of Epictetus (1756), works which won for him the notice of the great Dutch scholar Ruhnken of Leyden. The Seven Years' War occurring at this time unfortunately threw Heyne out of employment, and reduced him to his former straits, his only source of income being the hack-work which he did for the booksellers. This period of want, however, was finally ended by his appointment, through the favour of Ruhnken, to the chair of Eloquence at the University of Göttingen, an office which he held until his death, and in which his profound scholarship and stimulating lectures raised the reputation of Göttingen to an unquestioned pre-eminence among the universities of Germany. It is said that he trained and sent forth more than 130 professors. He died on July 14, 1812. Heyne's principal works are his edition of Vergil (4 vols. 1767, new ed. 1830–44); of Pindar (1773), of Apollodorus (1782, 2d ed. 1802), and of the *Iliad* in eight vols. (1802). He also put forth a number of translations of the classics; six volumes of miscellanies in his *Opuscula Academica* (1785–1812); and between 7000 and 8000 book reviews in the *Göttinger Gelehrte Anzeiger*, of which he was the editor for more than thirty years. His life has been written by his son-in-law Heeren (Göttingen, 1813). See also Carlyle, *Miscellanies*, vol. ii. and Bursian, *Geschichte der class. Philologie*, pp. 476–500 (Munich, 1883).

Hibernia (also called **Iernê, Iverna,** and **Iuverna**; Ἰέρνη, Ἰερνὶς νῆσος, Ἰουερνία; Keltic, *Eri*). The ancient name of Ireland, which is said to have been derived from the name of the early inhabitants of its southern coast, the Iuverni (Ἰούερνοι). It is mentioned in the pseudo-Orphic poem on the Argonautic expedition (line 1164), and by Aristotle (*De Mundo*, 3), who describes it as lying in the ocean beyond the Pillars of Hercules. Strabo says that it is too cold to be more than barely habitable; whereas Mela speaks of its herbage as so rich as to cause the cattle to eat until they burst with it. Solinus mentions the fact that there are no snakes in the island, and pictures the inhabitants as so warlike that on the birth of a male child the mother places the first bit of food in its mouth on the point of a sword. Ptolemy gives the names of the rivers and promontories, and describes the outline of the coast with surprising accuracy. He also names the principal tribes of the island—the Vennicnii in Ulster, the Nagnatae in Connaught, the Uterni in Munster, and the Brigantes and others in Leinster. On the coast were two towns—Menapia and Eblana (Dublin). The Romans made no attempt to conquer the island, though they gained some knowledge of it from the British traders who visited its coast.

Hicesia (Ἱκεσία). One of the Aeoliae Insulae (q.v.).

Hicĕtas (Ἱκέτας or Ἱκέτης). (1) A Syracusan, contemporary with the younger Dionysius and Timoleon. He was at first a friend of Dion, after whose death (B.C. 353) his wife Aretê and his sister Aristomachê placed themselves under the care of Hicetas; but he was persuaded, notwithstanding, to consent to their destruction. A few years later he became tyrant of Leontini. He carried on war against the younger Dionysius, whom he defeated, and had made himself master of the whole city, except the island citadel, when Timoleon landed in Sicily, B.C. 344. Hicetas then opposed Timoleon and called in the aid of the Carthaginians, but he was defeated and put to death by Timoleon, B.C. 339 or 338. (2) Tyrant of Syracuse, during the interval between the reign of Agathocles and that of Pyrrhus. He defeated Phintias, tyrant of Agrigentum, and was himself defeated by the Carthaginians. After a reign of nine years (B.C. 288–279), he was expelled from Syracuse.

Hiempsal. (1) Son of Micipsa, king of Numidia, and grandson of Masinissa, murdered by Iugurtha, soon after the death of Micipsa, B.C. 118. (2) King of Numidia, grandson or great-grandson of Masinissa, and father of Iuba. He appears to have received the sovereignty of part of Numidia after the Jugurthine War. He was expelled from his kingdom by Cn. Domitius Ahenobarbus, the leader of the Marian party in Africa, but was restored by Pompey in 81. Hiempsal wrote some works in the Punic language, which are cited by Sallust (*Iugurtha*, 17).

View of the Phrygian Hierapolis from the City Gates.

Hiĕra. (1) See AEOLIAE INSULAE. (2) See AEGATES.

Hierapŏlis (Ἱεράπολις). (1) A city of Great Phrygia, near the Maeander, and an early seat of Christianity, mentioned in St. Paul's Epistle to the Colossians (iv. 13). Here Cybelê was worshipped. Epictetus was a native of Hierapolis. (2) Formerly BAMBYCÊ (Βαμβύκη), a city in the northeast of

Syria, one of the chief seats of the worship of Astarté.

Hieratic Writing. See HIEROGLYPHICS.

Hiero (Ἱέρων). (1) A Sicilian who succeeded his brother Gelon as tyrant of Syracuse, B.C. 478. He committed many acts of violence, encouraged spies, and kept a mercenary guard around his person. He was ambitious of extending his dominion, and his attempts proved successful. After the death of Theron of Agrigentum, Hiero defeated his son Thrasydaeus, who was soon afterwards expelled by his countrymen. He took Naxus and Catana, and, having driven away the inhabitants from both towns, replaced them by Syracusan and Peloponnesian colonists. He changed the name of Catana to Aetna, and he himself assumed the title of Aetnaeus (Αἰτναῖος). Having joined his fleet to that of the people of Cumae, he succeeded in clearing the Tyrrhenian Sea of the Etruscan and other pirates who infested it. His chariots repeatedly won the prize at the Olympic Games, and his success on those occasions formed the theme of several of the odes of Pindar, who was his guest and friend. Aeschylus, Simonides, Bacchylides, and Epicharmus were also well received at the court of Hiero, who was fond of the society of learned men. His intimacy with Simonides is the subject of Xenophon's dialogue entitled Ἱέρων. Hiero died at Catana, B.C. 467, and was succeeded by his brother Thrasybulus, who had all his faults without any of his good qualities, and was at last driven away by the Syracusans, who restored the government to the commonwealth (Diod. Sic. xi. 48 foll.). (2) The second of the name, son of Hierocles, a wealthy citizen of Syracuse, and a descendant of Gelon, distinguished himself in early life by his brilliant qualities, and served with distinction also under Pyrrhus in his Sicilian campaigns. After Pyrrhus had suddenly abandoned Sicily, the Syracusans found themselves threatened on one side by the Carthaginians and on the other by the Mamertines, a band of Campanian mercenaries, who had treacherously taken possession of Messana. The Syracusan troops, being in want of a trusty leader, chose Hiero by acclamation, and the Senate and citizens, after some demur, ratified the choice, B.C. 275. After various successful operations against the Mamertines, Hiero returned to Syracuse, where, through the influence of Leptines, his father-in-law, a leading man among the aristocratic party, he was proclaimed king, B.C. 270. Shortly afterwards the Mamertines at Messana quarrelled with the Carthaginians, who had managed to introduce a garrison into the citadel, and drove them out, upon which the Carthaginians invited Hiero to join his forces to theirs, in order to drive the Mamertines out of Sicily. Hiero having assented, encamped under the walls of Messana on one side, and the Carthaginians fixed their camp on the other, while their squadron guarded the strait. The Mamertines, meanwhile, had applied to the Romans for assistance, claiming a common origin with them, as being descended from Mars, called Mamers in the Oscan language; and Rome eagerly seized this opportunity of obtaining a footing in Sicily. The consul Appius Claudius marched to Rhegium, and, having contrived to pass the strait in the night unobserved by the Carthaginian cruisers, he surprised Hiero's camp, routed the soldiers, and obliged the monarch himself to seek safety in flight. The consul next attacked the Carthaginian camp with the same success, and this was the beginning of the First Punic War, B.C. 265. In the following year the Romans took Tauromenium and Catana and advanced to the walls of Syracuse, when Hiero sued for peace, which he obtained on condition of paying 100 talents of silver and supplying the Roman army with provisions. He punctually fulfilled his engagements, remaining faithful to Rome during the whole of the war, and by his supplies was of great service to the Roman armies, especially during the long sieges of Agrigentum and Lilybaeum. Hiero was included in the peace between Rome and Carthage, by which his territories were

Coin of Hiero II.

secured to him, and he remained in friendship with both States. He even assisted Carthage at a very critical moment by sending her supplies of provisions during the war which she had to sustain against her mercenaries. The period of peace which elapsed between the end of the First and the beginning of the Second Punic Wars, from B.C. 241 to 218, was most glorious for Hiero and most prosperous for Syracuse. Commerce and agriculture flourished, and wealth and population increased to an extraordinary degree. Hiero paid particular attention to the administration of the finances, and made wise regulations for the collection of the tithe or tax on land, which remained in force throughout Sicily long after his time, and are mentioned with praise by Cicero as the *lex Hieronica*. Hiero introduced the custom of farming out the tax every year by auction. He embellished and strengthened Syracuse, and built large ships. Archimedes lived under Hiero's reign. When the Second Punic War broke out, Hiero continued true to his Roman alliance, and, after the Trasimenian defeat, he sent a fleet to Ostia with provisions and other gifts, and a body of light troops to the assistance of Rome. He lived to see the battle of Cannae, after which his son Gelon embraced the part of the Carthaginians. Gelon, however, died, not without suspicion of violence, and Hiero himself, being past ninety years of age, ended his days soon afterwards (B.C. 216), leaving the crown to his grandson, Hieronymus.

Hiero (Ἱέρων ἢ Τυραννικός). A dialogue of Xenophon between King Hiero and the poet Simonides. Separate editions by Breitenbach (1847), and Holden (1888).

Hierŏcles (Ἱεροκλῆς). (1) A rhetorician of Alabanda, in Caria, who lived in the beginning of the first century before the Christian era. He excelled in what Cicero termed the Asiatic style of eloquence (Cic. *De Orat.* ii. 23.) (2) A lawyer, who wrote a work on veterinary medicine, addressed to Cassianus Bassus, of which three chapters are preserved in the sixteenth book of the "Geoponica." (See GEOPONICI.) (3) Styled "the grammarian," for distinction's sake from the philosopher of the same name, a Greek writer supposed to have been contemporary with Justinian, but of whom one thing at least is certain—that he was anterior to the tenth century. He composed, under the title of Συνέκδημος ("Travelling Companion"), a description of the sixty-four provinces that formed the Byzantine Empire and of the cities situated in them. Ed. by Parthey (Berlin, 1866). (4) A New Platonist, who flourished at Alexandria about the middle of the fifth century A.D. He has left a commentary on the Golden Verses of Pythagoras and a treatise on Providence, Destiny, and Free-will. The aim of Hierocles is to show the agreement which exists in respect of these doctrines between Plato and Aristotle and to refute the systems of Epicurus and the Stoics. We have only extracts from this latter work made by Photius and an abridgment by an unknown hand. Stobaeus has preserved for us fragments of a work of Hierocles on the worship of the gods and of several other productions of his. There exists also, under the name of Hierocles, a collection of amusing anecdotes (Ἀστεῖα, *Facetiae*), giving an account of the ridiculous actions and sayings of book-learned men and pedants (σχολαστικοί). Among them are to be found the originals of several professedly modern jokes, and they furnish a model for the innumerable German witticisms at the expense of the typical Herr Professor. The best edition of the commentary on the Golden Verses and of the fragments, etc., is that of Warren (London, 1742). (5) A prefect of Bithynia, and afterwards of Alexandria, who is said by Lactantius to have been the principal adviser of the persecution of the Christians in the reign of Diocletian (Lactant. *Inst. Div.* v. 2; *De Morte Persec.* 17). He also wrote two works against Christianity, entitled Λόγοι Φιλαλήθεις πρὸς τοὺς Χριστιανούς ("Truth-loving words to the Christians"), in which, according to Lactantius, he endeavoured to show that the Scriptures overthrow themselves by the contradictions with which they abound. He also reviled Paul, Peter, and the other disciples, as propagators of falsehood. He endeavoured to destroy the effect of the Saviour's miracles, though he did not deny the truth of them. He also aimed to show that like things, or even greater, had been done by Apollonius of Tyana. See the chapter on Apollonius of Tyana in Dyer's *Gods in Greece*, pp. 257–266 (London, 1891), and Professor Gildersleeve's essay.

Hierodūli (ἱερόδουλοι, "temple servants"). The name for all who were closely connected with the service of a sanctuary, and especially such as were bound to perform certain services, obligations, and duties to the same, and in part lived as a kind of bondmen upon its land. We find them forming a considerable population in Asia; e. g. at Comana in Cappadocia, there were more than 6000 of them, who with their descendants belonged as slaves to the goddess called Enyo by the Greeks. They served as labourers on the estates of the temple, and performed the humblest offices as hewers of wood and drawers of water. See AEDITUUS.

The Delphic sanctuary of Apollo had similar ministrants from a very early date, as had also the temple of Aphroditē on Mount Eryx in Sicily. In the same manner Aphroditē of Corinth, in the flourishing times of that city, had over 1000 girls dedicated to her service. They added brilliancy and lustre to her worship, and living as prostitutes paid a portion of their earnings to the goddess as tribute. See MERETRIX.

Hieroglyphics (ἱερογλυφικά, sc. γράμματα) or **Hieroglyphs** (in Egyptian, called *Neter kharu* or "divine words"). Pictures of objects used to express either sounds, words, or ideas. Hieroglyphs have been used by several nations, among them the Mexican Aztecs, but the word is oftenest employed of the system of the ancient Egyptians. Their invention in Egypt was ascribed to the god Thoth. Pliny the Elder speaks of Menon as their inventor. There is no evidence that any of the early Greeks acquired an understanding of them, but Philo in his *Vita Moysis* says that Moses could read them. In Egypt they were universally employed by the educated classes, but were practically a mystery to the people at large, whence a belief in their divine origin prevailed. Democritus of Abdera (B.C. 460), in a work now lost, described both the hieroglyphs of Egypt and the Assyrian cuneiform; and under the Greek rulers of Egypt (after B.C. 300) considerable attention was paid to the language and literature of the country. Under the Romans, Chaeremon, librarian in the Serapeum, compiled a dictionary of hieroglyphs, and they are spoken of by Diodorus, Strabo, Tacitus, Ammianus Marcellinus, Iulius Valerius, and the novelist Heliodorus (about A.D. 400), who in his romance *Aethiopica*, describes a letter written in hieroglyphs by Queen Candacē. Clemens Alexandrinus (A.D. 211) is the first writer to speak of the twofold nature of the hieroglyphs, which he divides into phonetic and symbolic characters.

After the sixth century A.D. all knowledge of them was lost until about the beginning of the seventeenth century when the learned Jesuit, Athanasius Kircher, endeavoured to interpret them, but had little success owing to his theory that the signs were purely ideographic. That they were at least partly phonetic was asserted by Zoega in 1787, and a certain clue to their decipherment was found in 1799 by the discovery of the celebrated Rosetta Stone during the Napoleonic occupation of Egypt. This is a slab of black basalt inscribed with (1) hieroglyphics; (2) demotic (enchorial, cursive), and (3) Greek. It gives a decree of the priests of Memphis in honour of Ptolemy V. The labour of many scholars was devoted to the study of these inscriptions. Dr. Young in 1818 partly proved that the characters were alphabetic, a fact surely established in 1822 by the French scholar Champollion, who used for comparison an inscription found on an obelisk at Philae. His methods were subsequently used and his discoveries largely extended by Rosellini, Salvolini (1832), Lepsius (1837), and more recently by Bunsen, De Rougé, Birch, Chabas, Brugsch, and others.

Hieroglyphs are either ideographic (representing ideas) or phonetic (representing sounds). Phonetic signs are found dating back at least as early as B.C. 3800, and are partly alphabetic and partly syllabic. There are found in the earliest hieroglyphic writing 24 alphabetic signs. In all, there are about 1700 different hieroglyphic characters. Many of them are used as determinatives, that is as signs which aid in determining the meaning of the phonetic symbols which have preceded them. Thus after the phonetic signs for "dog," is placed a picture of a dog; after those for "tree," the picture

The Rosetta Stone. (British Museum.)

granite, porphyry, basalt, and sandstone; and cut or carved on wood and plaster. They were also written upon papyrus and leather. (See PAPYRUS.) In writing upon papyrus, a reed pen (*qash*) was employed. The colours most used were black, red, and green, and the inks were held when in use in a sort of wooden or ivory palette, with holes hollowed out of it as receptacles. On the Ani papyrus in the British Museum, thirteen colours are employed. The characters are written either in horizontal lines or in perpendicular columns, and are read in the order in which the pictures face. See ALPHABET.

On the subject of the hieroglyphics, see Birch, *Introduction to the Study of the Hieroglyphics* (London, 1857); Brugsch, *Grammaire Démotique* (Berlin, 1855); Bunsen, *Egypt's Place* (vol. v. 1867). There are dictionaries of hieroglyphics by Birch and Pierret, and in German by Brugsch. See also Berger, *Histoire de l'Ecriture dans l'Antiquité* (Paris, 1891), and Taylor, *The Alphabet* (2 vols. London, 1883). A very full account of the Rosetta Stone is given in Budge's work *The Mummy* (London, 1893).

of a tree, etc. Abstract ideas are expressed by some figures which symbolize them or denote the objects which possess and illustrate them. Thus, "joy" is pictured in a man dancing; "craft" by a jackal, etc. Many of these determinatives get to be largely conventional, as where all actions of moving, standing, or stretching are signified by Λ, originally representing two legs. There are about 150 of these determinative signs in all, and they have their fellows in the cuneiform system of the Assyrians. In the cuneiform, however, the determinatives precede the word and in Egyptian follow it. The Egyptian determinatives are also more numerous and oftener used than the Assyrian.

There are two cursive or running forms of the hieroglyphs. The first, which is known as the *hieratic*, which was very extensively used, being found in legal and governmental documents, accounts, in nearly all books and rituals, and in private accounts and memoranda. Its characters were fewer in number than the hieroglyphs proper, and the vocalic complements of the consonants are regularly employed to prevent ambiguity. For a specimen of hieratic writing, see the article AEGYPTUS, p. 28.

The second cursive form is known as the *demotic*, used as early as the sixth century B.C., and continuing down to the third century A.D. It was the last native form of writing to survive in Egypt, and was gradually supplanted by the characters of the Greek alphabet introduced by the Christians. It appears on the Rosetta Stone side by side with the hieroglyphs. A specimen of it will be found on p. 494.

The language of the hieroglyphs is best represented by the Coptic, which ceased to be spoken about a century ago, but in which the services of the Egyptian Christians are still conducted. The Coptic forms are largely those of the ancient Egyptian, modified by phonetic decay.

Hieroglyphs have been found inscribed upon

Hieromantēa (*ἱερομαντεία*). See DIVINATIO.

Hieromenia (*ἱερομηνία*). The Greek term for the holy time of the month—i. e. that portion of each month which was kept as a festival. It differed in the several months according to the number and duration of the festivals. During this time there was a suspension of all business and even of lawsuits, and executions and warrants were in abeyance; in short, everything that was likely to interrupt the universal peace and the celebration of the festival was set aside. For the greater feasts a "truce of God" was proclaimed. See EKECHEIRIA.

Hieromnēmon (*ἱερομνήμων*). The recorder or officer in charge of sacred business at the meetings of the Amphictyonic Council. See AMPHICTYONES.

Hiĕron. See HIERO.

Hieronȳmus (*Ἱερώνυμος*). (1) Of Cardia, accompanied Alexander the Great to Asia, and after the death of that monarch (B.C. 323) served under his countryman Eumenes. He afterwards fought under Antigonus, his son Demetrius, and grandson Antigonus Gonatas. He survived Pyrrhus, and died at the advanced age of 104. Hieronymus wrote a history of the events from the death of Alexander to that of Pyrrhus, if not later. (2) King of Syracuse, succeeded his grandfather, Hieron II., B.C. 216, at fifteen years of age, and was assassinated after a short reign of only thirteen months. (3) Of Rhodes, a Peripatetic philosopher, and a disciple of Aristotle. (4) Saint Jerome, one of the best known of the Christian Fathers, born at Stridon on the borders of Dalmatia about A.D. 340. His full name was EUSEBIUS HIERONȲMUS SOPHRONIUS. As a boy he studied Greek and Latin rhetoric and philosophy under Aelius Donatus at Rome, where he was baptized. After residing in Gaul, he settled at Aquilea in A.D. 370, with his friend Rufinus. From 374 to 378 he lived in the desert of Chalcis undergoing penance and studying the Hebrew language. In 379 he was admitted to the priesthood at Antioch, where he was the friend of Gregory Nanzianzenus. In 382, in which year he visited Rome and became secretary to Pope Damasus, he began his great version of the Bible into Latin, known as the Vulgate, undertaken at the pope's request. From a linguistic point of view this version is of very great interest, as containing many lexical and grammatical forms not found in the classical language, but peculiar to the popular speech (*sermo plebeius*). In 386 he fixed his residence at Bethlehem, whither two noble Roman ladies, Paula and her daughter Eustochium, followed him and founded four convents, one of which Jerome himself governed. He died Sept. 30, 420. His writings comprise, besides the Vulgate, letters, treatises, and commentaries on the Scriptures. Important is his translation of the Chronicle of Eusebius (q. v.), which he revised and enlarged, bringing it down to the year A.D. 378. A complete edition of the works of St. Jerome is that of Vallarsi (Verona, 1734–42), reprinted by Migne in 8 vols. (Paris, 1845). See the special works by Zöckler (Gotha, 1865), Cutts (London, 1878), and Goelzer (Paris, 1886).

Hierophantes (ἱεροφάντης, "discloser of sacred things"). The chief priest in the Eleusinian Mysteries. See ELEUSINIA.

Hieropoei (ἱεροποιοί, "managers of the sacrifices"). The Greek term for certain officials, who, besides having the care of the sacrifices, had also the superintendence of the economic details of the sanctuary, and the charge of the money and treasures of the temple. In Athens, besides such officials attached to the several temples, there was a board of ten men, yearly appointed by lot, who had to attend to the celebration of the extraordinary and quinquennial sacrifices, the cost of which was defrayed by the public treasury. Another college of three or ten hieropoei, appointed by the Areopagus, superintended the sacrifices offered to the Eumenides by the State.

Hieroscopia (ἱεροσκοπία, "viewing the sacrifice"). A form of divination by means of the entrails of sacrificed beasts. See MANTIKÉ.

Hierosolȳma (τὰ Ἱεροσόλυμα). Jerusalem, a celebrated city of Palestine, the capital of Iudaea. The history of Abraham mentions that Melchizedek, king of Salem, came forth to meet him when he returned from the slaughter of the kings (Gen. xiv. 18), and it has been generally supposed that this Salem was the original of the city which we are now considering. It is more certain, however, that when the Israelites entered Canaan they found the place in the occupation of the Jebusites, a tribe descended from Jebus, a son of Canaan, and the city then bore the name of Jebus or Jebusi (Josh. xv. 63, xviii. 28). The lower city was taken and burned by the children of Judah (Jud. i. 8) after the death of Joshua; but the Jebusites had so strongly fortified themselves in the upper city, on Mount Zion, that they maintained themselves in possession of it till the time of David. That monarch, after his seven years' rule over Judah in Hebron, became king of all Israel, on which he expelled the Jebusites from Mount Zion, and established here the metropolis of his kingdom. The city now took the name of Jerusalem (Yerushalaïm), a term which denotes "the abode of peace," or (according to another derivation) "the people of peace" (Gesenius, *Hebr. Lex.* s. v.). Yakût, the Mohammedan geographer, gives other forms of the name (Urishallum, Urishalum, and Shallam). The Septuagint version gives Ἱερουσαλήμ as the form of the name, while by the Greek and Roman writers the place is called Hierosolyma. At present this city is known throughout Western Asia by the Arabic name of El-Kuds, which signifies "The Holy." See CADYTIS.

Jerusalem was built on several hills, the largest of which was Mount Sion, which formed the southern part of the city. A valley towards the north separated this from Acra, the second or lower city, on the east of which was Mount Moriah, the site of the Temple of Solomon. Northeast of Mount Moriah was the Mount of Olives, on the south was the valley of Hinnom, and at the north Mount Calvary, the scene of Christ's crucifixion.

Passing over the earlier history of this celebrated city, so fully detailed in the Scriptures, we come to the memorable period of its capture and destruction by Titus. The date of this event was the 8th of September, A.D. 70. During this siege and capture 1,100,000 persons are said to have perished, and 97,000 to have been made prisoners and afterwards either sold for slaves or exposed to the fury of wild beasts. In fact, the population, not only of Jerusalem, but that of the adjacent districts —many who had taken refuge in the city, more who had assembled for the feast of unleavened bread— had been shut up by the sudden formation of the siege. The ardent zeal of the Jewish nation for their holy city and temple soon caused both to be again rebuilt; but fresh commotions compelled the emperor Hadrian to interfere and ordain that no Jew should remain in, or even approach near Jerusalem, on pain of death. On the ruins of their temple the same emperor caused a temple in honour of Iupiter Capitolinus to be erected, and the image of a hog to be cut in stone over the gate leading to Bethlehem, as a standing insult to the religious feelings of this unfortunate people. The name of the city was also changed to Aelia Capitolina, the first part of the name alluding to the family of the Roman emperor. The more peaceful Christians were permitted, however, to establish themselves within the walls, and Aelia became the seat of a flourishing church and bishopric. This latter name became afterwards the ordinary name of the city, and Jerusalem became nearly obsolete. Upon the ascension to the throne, however, of the Christian emperors the earlier name revived. Jerusalem, thus restored, was much less in compass than the ancient city, Mount Sion and Bezetha being excluded.

The following description of Jerusalem, as it appeared just before the siege by Titus, is taken, with a few alterations, from Dean Milman (*History of the Jews*, vol. iii. pp. 17 foll.): "Jerusalem, at this period, was fortified by three walls, in all those parts where it was not surrounded by abrupt and impassable ravines; there it had but one. Not that these walls stood one within the other, each in a narrower circle running round the whole city; but each of the inner walls defended one of the several quarters into which the city was divided, or, it might be almost said, one of the separate cities. Since the days in which David had built his capital on the rugged heights of Sion, great alterations had taken place at Jerusalem. That eminence was still occupied by the upper city; but, in addition, first the hill of Moriah was taken in, on which the temple stood, then Acra, which was originally, although a part of the same ridge, separated by a deep chasm from Moriah. This chasm was almost entirely filled up, and the top of Acra levelled by the Asmonean princes, so that Acra and Moriah were united, though on the side of Acra the temple presented a formidable front, connected by several bridges or causeways with the lower city. To the south the height of Sion, the upper city, was separated from the lower by a ravine, which ran right through Jerusalem, called the Tyropoeon, or the valley of the cheesemongers; at the edge of this ravine, on both sides, the streets suddenly broke off, though the walls in some places must have crossed it, and it was bridged in more than one place. To the north extended a considerable suburb called Bezetha, or the new city. The first or outer wall encompassed Bezetha. Agrippa the First had intended to make this wall of extraordinary strength; but he had desisted from the work on the interference of the Romans, who seem to have foreseen that this refractory city would hereafter force them to take up arms against it. Had this wall been built according to the plan of Agrippa, the city, in the opinion of Iosephus, would have been impregnable. This wall began at the tower of Hippicus, which stood, it seems, on a point at the extreme corner of Mount Sion. It must have crossed the western mouth of the valley of Tyropoeon, and run directly north to the tower of Psephina. The wall then bore towards the monument of Helena, ran by the royal caverns of the Fuller's Monument, and was carried into the valley of Kedron or Jehoshaphat, where it joined the old or inner wall under the temple. The wall, however it fell short of Agrippa's design, was of considerable strength. The stones were 35 feet long, so solid as not easily to be shaken by battering engines, or undermined. The wall was 17½ feet broad. It had only been carried to the same height by Agrippa, but it had been hastily run up by the Jews to 35 feet; on its top stood battlements 3½ feet high, and pinnacles 5¾; so the whole was nearly 45 feet high. The second wall began at a gate in the old or inner one, called Gennath, the gate of the gardens; it intersected the lower city, and, having struck northward for some distance, turned to the east and joined the northwest corner of the tower of Antonia. The Antonia stood at the northwest corner of the temple, and was separated from Bezetha by a deep ditch, which probably protected the whole northern front of the temple as well as of the Antonia. The old or inner wall was that of Sion. Starting from the southwestern porticos of the temple to which it was united, it ran along the ridge of the Tyropoeon, passed first the Xystus, then the council-house, and abutted on the tower

View of Jerusalem.

Hippicus, whence the northern wall sprang. The old wall then ran southward through Bethso to the gate of the Essenes, all along the ridge of the valley of Hinnom, above the pool of Siloam, then eastward again to the pool of Solomon, so on through Opha, probably a deep glen. It then joined the eastern portico of the temple. Thus there were, it might seem, four distinct towns, each requiring a separate siege. The capture of the first wall only opened Bezetha; the fortifications of the northern part of the temple, the Antonia, and the second wall still defended the other quarters. The second wall forced, only a part of the lower city was won; the strong rock-built citadel of Antonia and the temple on one hand, and Sion on the other, were not the least weakened. The whole circuit of these walls was guarded with towers, built of the same solid masonry with the rest of the walls. They were 35 feet broad and 35 high; but above this height were lofty chambers, and above those again upper rooms and large tanks to receive the rain-water. Broad flights of steps led up to them. Ninety of these towers stood in the first wall, 14 in the second, and 60 in the third. The intervals between the towers were about 350 feet. The whole circuit of the city, according to Iosephus, was 33 stadia, rather more than 4 miles. The most magnificent of all these towers was that of Psephina, opposite to which Titus encamped. It was 122½ feet high, and commanded a noble view of the whole country of Iudea, to the border of Arabia, and to the sea. It was an octagon. Answering to this was the tower Hippicus, and following the old wall stood those of Phasaëlus and Mariamné, built by Herod, and named after his wife and his brother and friend. These were stupendous, even as works of Herod. Hippicus was square, 43¾ feet each way. The whole height of the tower was 140 feet; the tower itself 52½, a deep tank or reservoir 35, two stories of chambers 43¾, battlements and pinnacles 8¾. Phasaëlus was a solid square of 70 feet. It was surrounded by a portico 17½ feet high, defended by breastworks and bulwarks, and above the portico was another tower, divided into lofty chambers and baths. It was more richly ornamented than the rest with battlements and pinnacles, so that its whole height was above 167 feet. It looked from a distance like the tall pharos of Alexandria. Mariamné, though not equal in elevation, was more luxuriously fitted up; it was built of solid wall 35 feet high, and of the same width; on the whole, with the upper chambers, it was about 76¾ feet high. These lofty towers appeared still higher from their situation. They were built on the old wall, which ran along the steep brow of Sion. Their masonry was perfect. They were built of white marble, cut in blocks 35 feet long, 17½ wide, 8¾ high, so fitted that the towers seemed hewn out of the solid quarry. High above the whole city rose the temple, uniting the commanding strength of a citadel with the splendour of a sacred edifice. According to Iosephus, the esplanade on which it stood had been considerably enlarged by the accumulation of fresh soil since the days of Solomon, particularly on the north side. It now covered a square of a furlong on each side. Solomon had faced the precipitous sides of the rock on the east, and perhaps the south, with huge blocks of stone; the other sides likewise had been built up with perpendicular walls to an equal height. These walls in no part were lower than 300 cubits (525 feet), but their whole height was not seen excepting on the eastern and perhaps the southern sides, as the earth was heaped up to the level of the streets of the city. Some of the stones employed in this work were 70 feet square. On this gigantic foundation ran, on each front, a strong and lofty wall without, within a spacious double portico or cloister 52½ feet broad, supported by 162 columns, which upheld a ceiling of cedar, of the most exquisite workmanship. The pillars were entire blocks hewn out of solid marble, of dazzling

View of the Interior of Jerusalem.

Golden Gate of Jerusalem.

whiteness, 43¾ feet high. On the south side the portico or cloister was triple. This quadrangle had but one gate to the east, one to the north, two to the south, four to the west; one of these led to the palace, one to the city, one at the corner to the Antonia, one down towards the gardens. The open courts were paved with various inlaid marbles. Between this outer court of the Gentiles and the second court of the Israelites ran rails of stone, but of beautiful workmanship, rather more than 5 feet high. Along these, at regular intervals, stood pillars, with inscriptions in Hebrew, Greek, and Latin, warning all strangers, and Jews who were unclean, from entering into the Holy Court beyond. An ascent of fourteen steps led to a terrace 17½ feet wide, beyond which rose the wall of the inner court. This wall appeared on the outside 70 feet, on the inside 43¾; for, besides the ascent of 14 steps to the terrace, there were 5 more up to the gates. The inner court had no gate or opening to the west, but four on the north, and four on the south, two to the east, one of which was for the women, for whom a portion of the inner court was set apart, and beyond which they might not advance; to this they had access likewise by one of the northern and one of the southern gates, which were set apart for their use. Around this court ran another splendid range of porticos or cloisters; the columns were quite equal in beauty and workmanship, though not in size, to those of the outer portico. Nine of these gates, or, rather, gateway towers, were richly adorned with gold and silver, on the doors, the door-posts, and the lintels. The doors of each of the nine gates were 52½ feet high, and half that breadth. Within, the gateways were 52½ feet wide and deep, with rooms on each side, so that the whole looked like lofty towers; the height from the base to the summit was 70 feet. Each gateway had two lofty pillars 21 feet in circumference. But what excited the greatest admiration was the tenth, usually called 'the Beautiful,' gate of the temple. It was of Corinthian brass of the finest workmanship. The height of the Beautiful Gate was 87½, its doors 70 feet. Within this quadrangle there was a further separation, a low wall which divided the priests from the Israelites; near this stood the great brazen altar. Beyond, the temple itself reared its glittering front. The porch or propylon, according to the design of the last, or Herod's temple, extended to a much greater width than the temple itself. In addition to the former width of 105 feet, it had two wings of 35 feet each, making in the whole 175 feet. The great gate of this last quadrangle, to which there was an ascent of twelve steps, was called that of Nicanor. The gateway tower was 132½ feet high, 43¾ wide; it had no doors, but the front was covered with gold, and through its spacious arch was seen the Golden Gate of the temple, glittering with the same precious metal, with large plates of which it was sheeted all over. Above this gate hung the celebrated golden vine. This extraordinary piece of workmanship had bunches, according to Iosephus, as large as a man. The Rabbins add that, 'like a true natural vine, it grew greater and greater; men would be offering—some, gold to make a leaf; some, a grape; some, a bunch; and these were hung up upon it; and so it was increasing continually.' The temple itself, excepting in the extension of the wings of the propylon, was probably the same in its dimensions and distribution with that of Solomon. Its roof had been set all over, on the outside, with sharp golden spikes, to prevent the birds from settling on and defiling the roof, and the gates were still sheeted with plates of the same splendid metal. At a distance the whole temple looked literally like a mountain of snow, fretted with golden pinnacles."

See Besant and Palmer, *Jerusalem* (2d ed. London, 1888); and Warren and Conder's *Jerusalem*, with a fine collection of plates (1884). The work of Le Strange, *Palestine under the Moslems*, gives a valuable résumé of the Arabic authorities regarding the city. On the temple, see De Vogüé, *Le Temple de Jérusalem.*

Hierosolymitānum Itinerarium. See ITINERARIA.

Hierosylias Graphé (ἱεροσυλίας γραφή). An action in the Athenian courts directed against one who robbed a temple (Dem. *c. Eubul.* p. 1318, § 64).

Highwayman. See LATRO.

Hilaria (ἱλάρια). (1) In Greece, any day a season of rejoicing. (2) At Rome, one of the *feriae stativae* held March 25th, in honour of Cybelé (Macrob. *Sat.* i. 21, § 7). See RHEA.

Hilarius. (1) A Christian writer born at Poitiers of pagan parents. He was elected bishop of his native place in A.D. 350. In 356, his strong polemics against the Arians led to his banishment by Constantine, who allowed him, however, to return from Phrygia, the place of his exile, and resume his office. He died in 368. His works consist of polemics against the Arians and addresses to the emperor. The best edition of his works is that of Coutant (2d ed. 1844–45). For his life see Cazenove's *St. Hilary of Poitiers* (1883). (2) Bishop of Arelaté (Arles) from A.D. 429 to 449. He wrote the life of Honoratus and a few other works.

Hilarotragoedia (ἱλαροτραγῳδία, "comic tragedy"). A species of comedy invented by Rhinthon of Tarentum, and consisting of a travesty of tragic themes. See RHINTHON; TRAGOEDIA.

Hildesheim, TREASURE OF. A number of drinking-vessels, plates, and cooking-utensils of silver, most of them embossed in high relief, found at Hildesheim in 1868. These important products of Roman art of the time of Augustus, are now deposited in the Berlin Museum. They probably belonged to the table service of some wealthy Roman, and had been hidden in the ground by Germans who had taken them as the spoils of victory. Artistically the most important pieces are a bowl shaped like a bell, and gracefully decorated externally with arabesques and figures of children, and four magnificent saucers decorated with a gilt Minerva seated on a rock, and half-length figures of the young Hercules slaying the serpents, of Cybelé, and of Attis; also two cups adorned with masks and all kinds of emblems of the worship of Bacchus. See Wieseler, *Der hildesheimer Silberfund* (Bonn, 1888), and the article CAELATURA.

Hilleviōnes. According to Pliny (*H. N.* iv. 27), a general term for the inhabitants of Scandinavia.

Himation (ἱμάτιον). Part of the outdoor dress of Greeks of free birth, worn over the χιτών, and reaching at least as far as the knees. It was an oblong piece of drapery, one end of which was first thrown over the left shoulder, then brought forward and held fast by the left arm; the garment was then drawn over the shoulder to the right side in such a manner that the right side was completely covered up to the shoulder, according to the more elegant fashion. Otherwise it went on under the right arm, and left the right shoulder exposed. Women wore the himation in the same manner, but some drew it over the head, so as to leave only the face visible. See CHLAMYS; PALLIUM; TRIBON.

Himation. (Stackelberg, *Gräber d. Hellenen,* taf. lxvii.)

Himĕra (Ἱμέρα). (1) Now Fiume Salso; one of the principal rivers in the south of Sicily, at one time the boundary between the territories of the Carthaginians and Syracusans, receives near Enna the water of a salt spring, and hence has salt water as far as its mouth. (2) A smaller river in the north of Sicily, flowing into the sea between the towns of Himera and Thermae. (3) A celebrated Greek city on the north coast of Sicily, west of the mouth of the river Himera (2), was founded by the Chalcidians of Zanclé, B.C. 648, and afterwards received Dorian settlers, so that the inhabitants spoke a mixed dialect, partly Ionic (Chalcidian), and partly Doric. In B.C. 409 it was taken by the Carthaginians, and was levelled to the ground. It was never rebuilt; but on the opposite bank of the river Himera the Carthaginians founded a new town, which, from a warm medicinal spring in its neighbourhood, was called THERMAE (Termini). The poet Stesichorus was born at the ancient Himera, and the tyrant Agathocles at Thermae.

Himerius (Ἱμέριος). A Greek sophist, born at Prusa in Bithynia, about A.D. 315, and educated at Athens, where, after extending his knowledge by travelling, he became a teacher of rhetoric. As such, he was so successful that he received the rights of citizenship and became a member of the Areopagus. Among his pupils were Basil the Great and Gregory of Nazianzus; for, although himself a pagan, nevertheless, like Libanius, he exhibited no animosity against Christians. He was summoned to Antioch by Julian, and appointed his private secretary. On the emperor's death (363), he returned to his earlier occupation at Athens, and there died, after becoming blind in his old age, about 386. Of his speeches and declamations twenty-four exist in a complete form, ten in fragments, and thirty-six in the summaries and excerpts preserved by Photius. His style is ornate, turgid, and overladen with erudition. He owes his special importance solely to the fact that his speeches contain material for the history of the events and of the manners of his time. The complete works of Himerius have been edited by Wernsdorf (Göttingen, 1790) and Dübner (1849).

Himĕros (Ἵμερος). The personification of longing and desire, and companion of Eros (q. v.).

Himilco (equivalent in Punic to *gratia Milcaris*, "the favour of Milcar"). The Greek form is Ἱμίλκων. The name of several Carthaginians. (1) A Carthaginian commander, who is said by Pliny (ii.

67) to have been contemporary with Hanno the navigator. He was sent by his government to explore the northwestern coast of Europe. A few fragments of this voyage are preserved by Avienus (*Ora Marit.* i. 90), in which the Hiberni and Albioni are mentioned, and also a promontory, Oestrymnis, and islands called Oestrymnides, which are usually considered to be Cornwall and the Scilly Islands. (2) A Carthaginian, who took Agrigentum in 406, and commanded in the wars with Dionysius I., tyrant of Syracuse, B.C. 405–368. Himilco was an able and successful general. He took Gela, Messana, and many other cities in Sicily, and at length besieged Syracuse by sea and land, but was finally defeated by Dionysius, who burned most of the Carthaginian vessels (Diod. Sic. bks. xiii. and xiv.). Hamilco, in his despair, ended his life by voluntary starvation. (3) A supporter of the Barcine party at Carthage (Livy, xiii. 12). He was sent by the Carthaginian government to oppose Marcellus in Sicily (Livy, xxiv. 35 foll., xxv. 23 foll.).

Hindustan. See INDIA.

Hinges. See CARDO.

Hippagrĕtae (ἱππαγρέται). The three officers chosen at Lacedaemon by the ephors to command the horsemen who formed the body-guard of the kings.

Hippăna (τὰ Ἵππανα). A town in the north of Sicily near Panormus.

Hipparchus (ἵππαρχος). The Greek name for a commander of cavalry. (See HIPPEIS.) In the Aetolian and Achaean Leagues, this name was borne by an officer charged with other functions besides, who was in rank second only to the στρατηγός.

Hipparchus (Ἵππαρχος). (1) A son of Pisistratus. (See PISISTRATIDAE.) (2) A Greek mathematician, the founder of scientific astronomy. He was born at Nicaea in Bithynia about B.C. 160, lived chiefly at Rhodes and Alexandria, and died about B.C. 120. He discovered the precession of the equinoxes, settled more accurately the length of the solar year, as also of the revolution of the moon, and the magnitude and distances of the heavenly bodies. He placed mathematical geography on a firmer basis, by teaching the application of the latitude and longitude of the stars to marking the position of places on the surface of the earth. He is also regarded as having invented trigonometry. In plane trigonometry he constructed a table of chords of arcs, which is practically the same as one of natural sines; and in spherical trigonometry he had some methods of solving triangles. Of his numerous writings we possess only his commentary on the *Phaenomena* of Eudoxus and Aratus and a catalogue of 1026 fixed stars. The famous *Almagest* of Ptolemy (Μεγίστη Σύνταξις) is founded on the writings of Hipparchus. See Ball, *Short Hist. of Mathematics*, pp. 79–81, 90 (London, 1888).

Hippăris (Ἵππαρις). A river in the south of Sicily, now Camarina.

Hipparmostes (ἱππαρμοστής). A leader of the Spartan cavalry. See HIPPEIS.

Hippăsus (Ἵππασος). A native of Metapontum and follower of the Pythagorean doctrine. He is said to have excelled in the application of mathematical principles to music, statics, and mensuration. In common with others of the same school, he held that fire was the originating cause of all things. He taught also that the universe is finite, is always changing, and undergoes a periodical conflagration. In consequence of his having made known the sphere consisting of twelve pentagons, which was a secret of the Pythagoreans, he is said to have been drowned as an impious person (Diog. Laërt. viii.).

Hippeis (ἱππεῖς). The Greek term for horsemen and knights. (1) Among the Athenians, the citizens whose property qualified them for the second class. (2) Among the Spartans, the royal guard of honour, consisting of 300 picked young men under the age of thirty, who, although originally mounted, afterwards served as heavy-armed foot-soldiers.

The cavalry of Athens, which was first formed after the Persian War, and then consisted of 300 men, from the time of Pericles onwards consisted of 1200 men—viz. 200 mounted bowmen (ἱπποτόξοται), who were slaves belonging to the State, and the 1000 citizens of the two highest classes. They were kept together in time of peace, and carefully drilled; at the great public festivals they took part in the processions. They were commanded by two ἵππαρχοι, each of whom had five φυλαί under him and superintended the levy. Subordinate to these were the ten φύλαρχοι in command of the ten phylae. Both sets of officers were drawn from the two highest classes. It was the duty of the council to see that the cavalry was in good condition, and also to examine new members in respect of their equipment and their eligibility.

The number of horsemen to be despatched to the field was determined by the decree of the popular assembly. Every citizen-soldier received equipment-money on joining, and during his time of service a subsidy towards keeping a groom and two horses; this grew to be an annual grant from the State, amounting to forty talents ($10,400 in intrinsic value), but regular pay was only given in the field.

At Sparta it was not until B.C. 404 that a regular body of horse was formed, the cavalry being much neglected as compared with the infantry. The rich had only to provide horses, equipment, and armour; for the actual cavalry service in time of war, only those unfitted for the heavy-armed infantry were drafted off and sent to the field without any preliminary drill. In later times every μόρα of heavy-armed infantry seems to have had allotted to it a μόρα of cavalry, of uncertain number. By enlisting mercenaries and introducing allies into their forces, the Spartans at length obtained better cavalry.

The utility of the Greek citizen-cavalry was small on account of their heavy armour, their metal helmet, and their coat of mail, their kilt fringed with metal flaps, their cuisses reaching to the knee, and their leather leggings. They did not take shields into action. As weapons of offence they had the straight two-edged sword and a spear, used either as a lance or a javelin. Shoeing of horses was unknown to the Greeks, as was also the use of stirrups. If anything at all was used as a saddle, it was either a saddle-cloth or a piece of felt, which was firmly fastened with girths under the horse's belly.

The Thessalians were considered the best riders. Cavalry became really important for the first time in the Macedonian army under Philip and his son

Alexander the Great. Although in earlier times the number of horsemen in the Greek forces was only very small, in the army which Alexander marched into Asia they formed nearly a sixth part of the infantry. The Macedonian cavalry was divided into heavy and light, both consisting of squadrons (ἶλαι) of an average strength of 200 men. Of the heavy cavalry the choicest troops were the Macedonian and Thessalian horsemen, armed in the Greek fashion, who were as formidable in onslaught as in single combat; in order and discipline they far surpassed the dense squadrons of the Asiatic cavalry, and even in attacking the infantry of the enemy they had generally a decisive effect. The light cavalry, which was constituted under the name of πρόδρομοι (skirmishers), consisted of Macedonian σαρισσοφόροι, so called from the *sarissa*, a lance from fourteen to sixteen feet long (Polyb. xviii. 12), and of Thracian horsemen. The heavy cavalrymen had each a mounted servant and probably a led horse for the transport of baggage and forage. In the time after Alexander there came into existence what were called the *Tarentini equites*, or light-armed spearmen, with two horses each (B.C. 192, Livy, xxxv. 28, 29). See EXERCITUS.

Hippias (Ἱππίας). (1) A Greek sophist of Elis and a contemporary of Socrates. He taught in the towns of Greece, especially at Athens. He had the advantage of a prodigious memory, and was deeply versed in all the learning of his day. He attempted literature in every form which was then extant. He was among the first to undertake the composition of dialogues. In the two Platonic dialogues named after him (*Hippias Maior* and *Hippias Minor*), he is represented as excessively vain and arrogant. See the study by Osann in the *Rhein. Museum* for 1843, p. 495 foll., and P. Leja, *Der Sophist Hippias* (1893). (2) A son of Pisistratus. See PISISTRATIDAE.

Hippĭcon (ἱππικόν, sc. στάδιον). A Greek measure of distance, equal to four stadia, or about 2426 English feet. According to Plutarch, it was mentioned in the laws of Solon (Plut. *Sol.* 23). See HIPPODROMUS; STADIUM.

Hippo (Ἱππών). (1) HIPPO REGIUS, a city on the coast of Numidia, once a royal residence, and afterwards celebrated as the bishopric of St. Augustine. (2) HIPPO DIARRHYTUS or ZARITUS (now Biserta), a city on the north coast of the Carthaginian territory west of Utica. (3) A town of the Carpetani in Hispania Tarraconensis, south of Toletum (Toledo).

Hippobŏtae (ἱπποβόται). "The feeders of horses." The name of the nobility of Chalcis in Euboea, corresponding to the ἱππεῖς in other Greek States. On the conquest of the Chalcidians by the Athenians in B.C. 506, these Hippobotae were deprived of their lands, and 4000 Athenian cleruchi sent to take possession of them (Herod. v. 77, vi. 100; Plut. *Pericl.* 23; Aelian, *V. H.* vi. 1; Grote, ch. 31, iii. 145).

Hippocampus (ἱππόκαμπος). A fabulous animal, having the fore-quarters and body of a horse, but ending in the tail of a fish, like the following illustration, from a Pompeian painting, which the poets and artists of antiquity commonly attach to the marine car of Neptune and the Tritons. See Naev. and Lucil. *ap.* Non. s. v. p. 120.

Hippocampus. (Pompeian painting.)

Hippocentaurus (ἱπποκένταυρος). A horse-centaur, half-horse and half-man (Cic. *N. D.* ii. 2), as opposed to the fish-centaur, half-man and half-fish (ἰχθυοκένταυρος), under which form the giants who waged war against the gods, were represented (Apollod. i. 6, 1). See CENTAURUS.

Hippocoön (Ἱπποκόων). The son of Oebalus of Sparta and of the nymph Batea. He drove his brothers Tyndareus and Icarius from home. Afterwards, in consequence of his slaying the young Oeonus, a kinsman of Heracles, he himself, with his twenty sons, was slain by Heracles in alliance with King Cepheus of Tegea. Tyndareus was thereby restored to the inheritance of his father's kingdom.

Hippocrătes (Ἱπποκράτης). (1) The father of Pisistratus, the Athenian tyrant. (2) A famous Greek physician, was born in the island of Cos (an ancient seat of the worship of Asclepius), about B.C. 460. He was the son of Heraclides and of Phaenaretē, and sprang from the race of the Asclepiadae, a priestly family, who in the course of time had gathered and preserved medical traditions,

Hippocrates. (Louvre.)

which were secretly handed down from father to son. Like many of the Asclepiadae, he practised his art while travelling in different parts of Greece. He is said to have been at Athens at the time of the Peloponnesian War, and to have taken advantage of the instructions of the sophists Gorgias and Prodicus; Democritus of Abdera is also named as one of his teachers. The value he himself set upon philosophic education is proved by his remark that "a philosophic physician resembles a god." Towards the end of his life he lived chiefly in Thessaly and on the island of Thasos. He died about B.C. 377 (or later) in the Thessalian Larissa, where his tomb was to be seen as late as the second century A.D. All through his long life his activity was unceasing in its efforts to increase the amount of his knowledge on all subjects, by both practical and theoretical investigations, and his practical knowledge was as great as his theoretical. Some of his fragments and epigrammatic dicta have passed into the literature of all time, as, for instance, the famous saying, "Life is short, and Art is long." He was the founder of the school of a scientific art of healing, and, as in the case of Homer, numerous writings of unknown authorship, proceeding from the school which followed his system, were attributed to him. Seventy-two works, great and small, in the Ionic and old Attic dialects, bear his name, and, apparently, formed a single collection, even before they came under the consideration of the critics of Alexandria. But it is clear that, as the ancients themselves were aware, only a small portion, which can no longer be precisely defined, really belongs to him. It is highly probable that his nearest relations, who were also distinguished physicians, contributed their share to the collection, and that it contains works by his sons Thessalus and Dracon, his son-in-law Polybus, and his two grandsons, the sons of Thessalus and Dracon, who bore his own name. The best known of these works are the aphorisms (Ἀφορισμοί), which, in antiquity and in mediæval times, were held in high esteem, and have been freely commented on by Greeks, Romans, and Arabs; they consist of short sentences upon the nature of illnesses, their symptoms and crises, and their final issue. One of his treatises (Περὶ Ἀέρων, Ὑδάτων, Τόπων), which is of general interest, and is in all respects among the best, is that on the influence of the climate, the water, and the configuration of a country upon the physical and intellectual life of its inhabitants. In the second portion of this work are found the first beginnings of a comparative ethnography, which at once surprise us by the acuteness and intelligence of its observation, and attracts us by the simplicity and clearness of its style. Many ancient physicians wrote commentaries on the works of Hippocrates, the most celebrated being those of Galen.

The first edition of the Greek text of Hippocrates is the Aldine (Venice, 1526). The best modern editions are those of Littré, with a French translation, 10 vols. (Paris, 1839–61), and that of Ermerius, with a Latin version (Utrecht, 1859–65). A good English translation is that by Adams, 2 vols. (1849). See Berdoe, *Origin and Growth of the Healing Art* (London, 1893), and the article MEDICINA.

Hippocrēnē (Ἱπποκρήνη or Ἱππουκρήνη, "the fountain of the steed"). The fount of the Muses, which was struck out of Mount Helicon, in Boeotia, by the hoof of the winged steed Pegasus. See MUSAE; PEGASUS.

Hippodameia (ἱπποδάμεια, sc. ἔργα). An adjective derived from the name of the architect Hippodamus of Miletus, who is said to have been the first of the Greeks who built whole cities on a regular architectural plan; and hence the word is applied to such cities, and to the public places and buildings in them. The Piraeus, for example, was designed by Hippodamus, and its market-place was called Ἱπποδάμειος ἀγορά, Ἱπποδαμεία ἀγ., or simply ἡ Ἱπποδαμεία. Hippodamus flourished during the second half of the fifth century B.C.

Hippodamīa (Ἱπποδάμεια). (1) A daughter of Oenomaüs, king of Pisa, in Elis, who married Pelops, son of Tantalus. (See PELOPS, where the full legend is given.) (2) A daughter of Adrastus, king of Argos, who married Pirithoüs, king of the Lapithae. The festivity which prevailed on the day of her marriage was interrupted by the violent conduct of the Centaurs, which led to their conflict with the Lapithae. (See CENTAURI; LAPITHAE.) (3) See BRISEÏS.

Hippodămus (Ἱππόδαμος). A Greek architect, born at Miletus in the second half of the fifth century B.C. He was the first inventor of a system of laying out towns on geometrical principles, carried out, under his direction, in the laying out of the Piraeus (q. v.), the harbour-town of Athens, and also at the building of Thurii (B.C. 443) and of Rhodes (408); it was also used in subsequent times in the foundation of new towns.

Hippodrŏmus (ἱππόδρομος). The name by which the Greeks designated the place appropriated to the horse-races, both of chariots and of single horses, which formed a part of their games. The word was also applied to the races themselves.

The mode of fighting from chariots, as described by Homer, involves the necessity of much previous practice; and the funeral games in honour of Patroclus present us with an example of the chariot-race, occupying the first and most important place in those games (*Il.* xxiii. 262–650). In this vivid description the nature of the contest and the arrangements for it are very clearly indicated. There is no artificially constructed hippodrome; but an existing landmark or monument (σῆμα) is chosen as the goal (τέρμα), round which the chariots had to pass, leaving it on the left hand, and so returning to the Greek ships on the sea-shore, from which they had started. The course thus marked out was so long that the goal, which was the stump of a tree, could only be clearly seen by its having two white stones leaning against it, and that, as the chariots return, the spectators are uncertain which is first (450 foll.: the passage furnishes a precedent for betting at a horse-race, 485). The ground is a level plain, but with its natural inequalities, which are sufficient to make the light chariots leap from the ground, and to threaten an overthrow where the earth was broken by a winter torrent, or a collision in the narrow hollow way thus formed. The chariots were five in number, each with two horses and a single driver, who stood upright in his chariot. See CURRUS.

In a race of this nature, success would obviously depend quite as much on the courage and skill of the driver as on the speed of the horses. At starting, it was necessary so to direct the horses as, on the one hand, to avoid the loss of time by driving wide of the straightest course, and on the other not to incur the risk of a collision in the crowd of chariots, nor to make so straight for the goal as to leave insufficient room to turn it. Here was the critical point of the race, to turn the goal as sharply as possible, with the nave of the near wheel almost grazing it, and to do this safely;

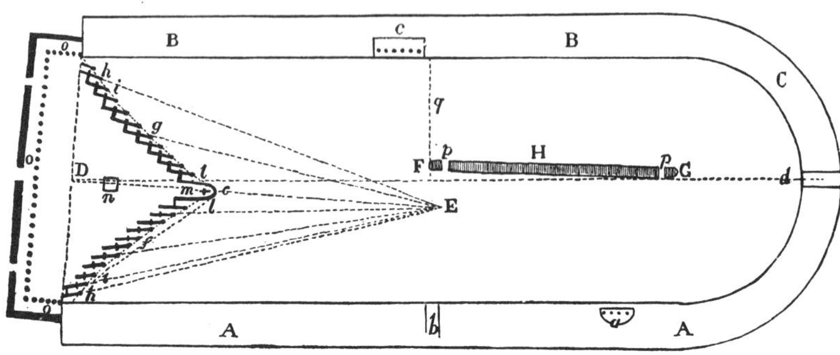

Ground-plan of Hippodrome at Olympia. (Hirt.)

very often the driver was here thrown out, and the chariot broken in pieces. There was another danger at this point, which deserves particular notice as connected with the arrangements of the hippodrome of later times. As the horse is easily scared, it can readily be understood that the noise and crush of many chariots turning the goal together, with the additional confusion created by the overthrow of some of them, would so frighten some of the horses as to make them unmanageable; and this is expressly referred to by Homer. Among the other disasters to which the competitors were liable were: the loss of the whip; the reins escaping from the hands; the breaking of the pole; the light chariot being overturned, or the driver thrown out of it, through the roughness of the ground, or by neglecting to balance the body properly in turning the goal, and the being compelled to give way to a bolder driver, for fear of a collision; but it was considered foul play to take such an advantage. The prizes, as in the other Homeric games, were of substantial value, and one for each competitor. The charioteer accused of foul play was required to lay his hand upon his horses, and to swear by Poseidon, the patron deity of the race, that he was guiltless. This description is shown by the following illustration from an antique Greek vase, in which is seen the goal as a mere stone post, with a fillet wound round it; the form of the chariots and the attitude of the drivers is well shown; each has four horses, as in the earliest Olympic chariot-race; and the vividness of the representation is increased by the introduction of the incident of a horse having got loose from the first chariot, the driver of which strives to retain his place with the others (Panofka, *Bilder antiken Lebens*, pl. iii. No. 10).

In no other writer is there a description, at once so vivid and so minute, of the Greek chariot-race as this of Homer's; and it may be safely assumed that, with a few points of difference, it will give an equally good idea of a chariot-race at Olympia or any other of the great games of later times. The chief points of difference were the greater compactness of the course, in order that a large body of spectators might view the race with convenience, and the greater number of chariots. The first of these conditions involved the necessity of making the race consist of several double lengths of the course, instead of only one; the second required some arrangement by which the chariots might start without confusion and on equal terms. It is now to be seen how these conditions were satisfied in the hippodrome at Olympia, of which the only description we possess is in two passages of Pausanias (v. 15, § 4; vi. 20, § 7 foll.).

The following is the ground-plan which Hirt (pl. xx. fig. 8) has drawn out from the description of Pausanias: A, B, the sides; C, the rounded end of the hippodrome, with raised seats for the spectators (the dotted line D *d* is the axis of the figure); *a*, place of honour for the magistrates and musicians; *b*, side door, perhaps for the exit of disabled chariots and horses; *c*, seats for the Hellanodicae, the judges of the games; *d*, principal entrance, corresponding to the *porta triumphalis* in a Roman circus; D, the starting-place; *e*, its apex; *f*, *g*, its curved sides; *h*, *i*, etc., up to *l*, stations of the chariots, their directions converging towards the point E; F, G, the goals, or turning-posts; H, the spina; *p*, *p*, small intervals between the spina and the goals; *q*, the winning line; *m*, dolphin used as a signal; *n*, altar, with eagle for signal; *o*, *o*, *o*, portico of Agnaptus.

The general form of the hippodrome was an oblong, with a semicircular end, C, and with the right side, A, somewhat longer than the left, B, for a reason to be stated presently. The right side, A, was formed by an artificial mound; the left, B, by the natural slope of a hill. The base of the fourth side, D, was formed by the portico of Agnaptus, so called from its builder. At this end of the hippodrome was the starting-place (*ἄφεσις*), in the form of the prow of a ship, with its apex, *e*, towards the area, and each of its sides more than 400 feet long. Along both of these sides were stalls (*οἰκήματα*) for the chariots about to start, like the *carceres* in the Roman circus; and it was in the arrangement of these stalls that the peculiarity of the Greek starting-place consisted. According to the view which we follow, the stalls were so arranged as that the pole of each chariot, while standing in its stall, was directed to a normal point E, at which, as nearly as possible, each chariot ought to fall into its proper course. As this point, E, was necessarily on the right side of

Chariot-race. (From a Vase-painting.)

the area (in order to turn the goal on the left hand), and as the corresponding stalls on each side were required to be equidistant from the apex, *e* (as will presently be seen), and of course also from the point E, it follows that the base of the *aphesis* must have been perpendicular to the line E *e*, and therefore oblique to the axis D *d;* and this is the reason why the side A was longer than the side B. The curvature of the sides of the aphesis, *f*, *g*, is a conjectural arrangement, assumed as that which was probably adopted to give more space to each chariot at starting. The front of each stall had a cord drawn across it, and the necessary arrangements were made for letting these cords fall at the right moments. On the signal being given for the race to begin, the cords in front of the two extreme stalls, *h*, *h*, were let fall simultaneously, and the two chariots started; then those of the next pair; and so on, each pair of chariots being liberated at the precise moment when those which had already started came abreast of their position; and when all the chariots formed an even line abreast of the apex of the *aphesis*, *e*, it was a fair start. This arrangement of the *aphesis* was the invention of the statuary Cleoetas, and was improved by Aristeides, perhaps the famous painter.

Precisely the same arrangements were made for the start in the race of single horses (κέλητες);

Race-horse. (Mosaic found near Constantine.) Inscription: *Vincas non vincas te amamus, Polidoxe.*

and in both cases, as in the race described by Homer, the stalls were assigned to the competitors by lot. How many chariots usually started cannot be determined, but that the number was large is proved by the well-known story that Alcibiades alone sent to one race seven chariots. Sophocles (*Elect.* 701–708) mentions ten chariots as running at once in the Pythian games; and the number at Olympia was no doubt greater than at any of the other games. This is probably the reason why the arrangements of a starting-place were so much more complicated in the Greek hippodrome than they were in the Roman circus. (See CIRCUS.) About the centre of the triangular area of the *aphesis* there was an altar, *n*, of rough brick, which was plastered afresh before each festival, surmounted by a bronze eagle with outstretched wings; and above the apex of the *aphesis* was a bronze dolphin, *m*. As the signal for the race to begin, the eagle was made to soar aloft, so as to be seen by all the spectators, and the dolphin sank to the ground.

Race of Single Horses. (Panofka.)

The chariots, thus started, had to pass several times round two goals (νύσσαι), the distinction between which is one of the difficult points in the description of Pausanias. On the whole, it seems most probable that the one which he describes as having a bronze statue of Hippodameia holding out the victor's fillet as if about to crown Pelops with it, was the one nearer to the *aphesis*, and abreast of the winning line, F; and that the other, G, round which the chariots made their first turn, was that which Pausanias calls "Taraxippus, the terror of the horses." This was a round altar, dedicated to Taraxippus, who was supposed to strike a supernatural terror into the horses as they passed the spot, and whom, therefore, the charioteers sought to propitiate, before the race began, by offering sacrifices and making vows at this altar. Pausanias gives various accounts as to who this Taraxippus was; some modern scholars take the word for an appellation of Poseidon Hippius. He was similarly honoured in the Isthmian hippodrome. At Nemea there was no such hero, but above the turning-point of the course there was a bright-red rock, which was supposed to frighten the horses. There are several vase-paintings on which chariots or single horses are exhibited turning the goal, which is represented as a Doric or Ionic column. (See Panofka, *Bilder antiken Lebens*, pl. iii.) One of these is shown in the following illustration, which exhibits a vivid picture of a race of single horses. The last rider has been unlucky in turning the goal.

There is no authority in the account of Pausanias for the connecting wall, H, between the goals, nor does he state that the winning line, *q*, was marked out as a white line; but these details are inserted from the analogy of the Roman circus. So also is the oblique position of the line of the goals, as compared with the axis of the figure: of course the greatest space was required at E, where the chariots were all nearly abreast of each other.

Respecting the dimensions of the Olympic Hippodrome there is no precise information; but from the length of the measure called ἵππικον and on other grounds, it seems probable that the distance from the starting-place to the goal, or perhaps, rather, from one goal to the other, was two stadia, so that one double course was four stadia. How many such double courses made up the whole race is not known. The width must have been at least as great as the length of each side of the *aphesis*—namely, more than 400 feet.

The chief points of difference between the Greek hippodrome and the Roman circus are the smaller width of the latter, as only four chariots ran at once, and the different arrangement of the *carceres*. The periods at which the Olympic horse-races were instituted are mentioned under OLYMPIA.

Among the Romans the term was also applied to an enclosed space for riding and driving in, attached to a garden or villa, and planted with trees (Pliny, *Epist.* v. 6, §§ 19, 32; Mart. xii. 50, 5, with Paley's note). See CIRCUS; CURRUS.

Hippolȳté (Ἱππολύτη). (1) Queen of the Amazons, daughter of Ares and of Otrera; slain in battle by Heracles, when he went at the bidding of Eurystheus to fetch the girdle given her by Ares. (See HERACLES.) In some accounts she is said to have been married to Theseus, and to have been the mother of Hippolytus (q. v.). (2) Or ASTYDAMIA, wife of Acastus, who fell in love with Peleus. He rejected her proposals, and was in consequence accused by her to Acastus. She was subsequently slain by Peleus. See ACASTUS: PELEUS.

Hippolȳtus (Ἱππόλυτος). The Joseph of classical literature, a son of Theseus and Hippolyté, or, according to others, of Theseus and Antiopé. Theseus, after the death of his first wife, married Phaedra, the daughter of Minos and sister of Ariadné. This princess was seized with a criminal affection for the son of the Amazon, an affection produced by the wrath of Aphrodité against Hippolytus for neglecting her divinity and for devoting himself solely to the service of Artemis; or else against Phaedra as the daughter of Pasiphaë (q. v.). During the absence of Theseus, the queen made advances to her step-son, which were indignantly rejected. Filled with fear and hate, on the return of her husband she accused Hippolytus of an attempt on her honour. Without giving the youth an opportunity of clearing himself, the monarch, calling to mind that Poseidon had promised him the accomplishment of any three wishes that he might form, cursed and implored destruction on his son from the god. As Hippolytus, leaving Troezen, was driving his chariot along the seashore, a monster, sent by Poseidon from the deep, terrified his horses; they burst away in fury, heedless of their driver, dashed the chariot to pieces, and dragged along Hippolytus, entangled in the reins, until he died. Phaedra ended her days by her own hand; and Theseus, when too late, learned the innocence of his son. Euripides has founded his tragedy, *Hippolytus*, on this subject, but the legend assumes a somewhat different shape with him. According to the plot of his play, Phaedra hangs herself in despair when she finds that she is slighted by her step-son, and Theseus, on his return from his travels, finds, when taking down her corpse, a writing attached to it, in which Phaedra accused Hippolytus of having attempted her honour. According to another legend, Aesculapius restored Hippolytus to life, and Artemis transported him, under the name of Virbius, to Italy, where he was worshipped in the grove of Aricia. (See VIRBIUS; Apollod. iii. 10, 3.) The story of Hippolytus forms the subject of a play by Euripides with that title, of a Latin tragedy by Seneca, and the *Phèdre* of Racine.

Hippomĕdon (Ἱππομέδων). A son of Aristomachus and Mythidicé, was one of the seven chiefs that went against Thebes. He was killed by Ismarus, son of Acastus, or by Ismaeus (Apollod. iii. 6; Aesch. *Sept.* 490; Pausan. ii. 36).

Hippomĕnes (Ἱππομένης). (1) Son of Megareus and great-grandson of Poseidon. He conquered Atalanta in a foot-race. (See ATALANTA.) (2) A descendant of Codrus, the fourth and last of the decennial archons. Incensed at the barbarous punishment which he inflicted on his daughter and her paramour, the Attic nobles deposed him.

Hippomolgi, or, more correctly, **Hippemolgi** (Ἱππημολγοί). A people of Scythia, who, as the name imports, lived on the milk of mares (Dionys. *Perieg.* 309).

Hippōna. A goddess who presided over horses. Her statues were placed in horses' stables (Juv. viii. 157).

Hippōnax (Ἱππῶναξ). A Greek iambic poet of Ephesus, who about B.C. 540 was banished to Clazomenae by Athenagoras and Comas, tyrants of his native city. At Clazomenae, two sculptors, Bupalus (Hor. *Epod.* vi. 14) and Athenis, made the little, thin, ugly poet ridiculous in caricature; but he avenged himself in such bitter iambic verses that, like Lycambes and his daughter, who were persecuted by Archilochus (q.v.), they hanged themselves.

The burlesque character of the poems which he composed in the Ionic dialect found an appropriate form in his favourite metre, which was probably invented by himself. This metre is known as the *choliambus* ("the halting iambus"), or the *scazon* ("limping"), from its having a spondee or trochee in the last place, instead of the usual iambic foot. He is also reckoned among the very first to produce parodies of epic poetry, and in his satire he spared neither his own parents nor the gods. Of his poems we have only a few fragments, which are collected by Bergk in his *Poetae Lyrici Graeci* (4th ed. 1878).

Hipponīcus. See CALLIAS.

Hipponium. See VIBO.

Hipponoüs. The original name of Bellerophon, who changed it on slaying the Corinthian Bellerus. See BELLEROPHON.

Hippopērae (ἱπποπῆραι). Saddle-bags. This appendage to the saddle (*ephippium*) was made of leather or untanned hide (Fest. s. v. *Bulgae*), and seems not to have changed its form and appearance in ancient or modern times. Its proper Latin name was *bisaccium* (Petron. *Sat.* 31, 9), which gave origin to *bisaccia* in Italian and *besace, bissac* in French. By the Gauls, saddle-bags were called *bulgae*. See BULGA.

Hippotădes (Ἱπποτάδης). A son of Hippotes, and hence = Aeolus. From him the Aeoliae Insulae are called Hippotadae Regnum (Ovid, *Met.* xiv. 86).

Hippŏtes (Ἱππότης). (1) The father of Aeolus (q. v.). (2) Son of Phylas by a daughter of Iolaüs, and hence a great-grandson of Heracles. He was banished for ten years because of his having killed the prophet Carnus during the invasion of the Peloponnesus by the Heraclidae. As an expiation for this murder, the Spartans are said to have established the festival of the Carnea (q. v.).

Hippothoön (Ἱπποθόων). An Attic hero, son of Poseidon and Alopé, daughter of Cercyon. After him one of the Attic tribes was called Hippothoöntis. He had a shrine at Athens.

Hippothoüs (Ἱππόθοος). Son of Cercyon, and father of Aepytus, king of Arcadia.

Hippotoxŏta (ἱπποτοξότης). A mounted archer (Hirt. *B. Afr.* 19); in most cases characteristic of foreign nations, as the Syrians (Caes. *B. C.* iii. 4),

Persians (Herod. ix. 49), etc.; but men thus equipped appear to have been used among the light horse of the Greeks (Aristoph. *Av.* 1179), and of the Romans; at least under the Empire.

Hippys (of Rhegium). One of the Greek Logographi (q. v.).

Hira or **Alexandrīa**. A town of Asia in Babylonia, situated on a lake, a short distance from the western bank of the Euphrates. It was the residence of a dynasty of rulers (the Alamundari), who aided the Persians and Parthians against the Romans.

Hirpīni. A Samnite people, dwelling in the south of Samnium, between Apulia, Lucania, and Campania. Their chief town was Aeculanum. The name, Hirpini, is said to have been derived from the Sabine *hirpus*, "a wolf."

Hirtius, AULUS. A friend of Caesar, and one of his companions in arms as in politics. In B.C. 58 he was Caesar's legate in Gaul, was praetor in 46, and consul in 43, when, acting for Octavian, he defeated Antony at Mutina. He completed Caesar's *Commentarii de Bello Gallico* by adding an eighth book (Suet. *Iul.* 56). According to the dedication to Cornelius Balbus prefixed to that book, he contemplated the continuation of Caesar's account of the Civil War to Caesar's death. This intention he never carried out, as he fell in battle at Mutina, April 27, B.C. 43, when he was consul. Of the three works, the *Bellum Alexandrinum*, *Bellum Africanum*, and *Bellum Hispaniense*, which have come down to us with Caesar's commentaries, the first may have been written by him. Of the other two, it has been conjectured that they were composed at his request, in preparation for his intended work on military commanders, and that having been found at his death among his papers, they were added, with his own writings, to the works of Caesar himself. A short letter of Hirtius to Cicero is found in Cic. *Ad Att.* xv. 6. He is known to have written, at Caesar's instigation, an answer to Cicero's panegyric on Cato (Cic. *Ad Att.* xii. 40. 1, 41. 4, 44. 1, 45. 3, 47. 3). See CAESAR.

Hirtulēius. An able general under Sertorius in Spain. He fell at Italica in Baetica (B.C. 78), routed by the troops of Metellus. See SERTORIUS.

Hispălis, more rarely **Hispal**. The modern Seville, a town of the Turdetani in Hispania Baetica, founded by the Phœnicians, and situated on the left bank of the Baetis, and in reality a seaport, for, although 500 stadia from the sea, the river is navigable for the largest vessels up to the town. Under the Romans it was an important place, with the name IULIA ROMŬLA or ROMULENSIS, and was surpassed in size by Corduba (Cordova) and Gades alone. Under the Goths and Vandals it was the chief town in the south of Spain; and under the Arabs the capital of a separate kingdom.

Hispania (Ἱσπανία). An extensive country, forming a kind of peninsula, in the southwest of Europe; the modern Spain and Portugal. It was bounded on the north by the Pyrenees and Sinus Cantabricus or Bay of Biscay, on the west by the Atlantic, on the south by the Atlantic, Fretum Herculeum or Strait of Gibraltar, and the Mediterranean, which last bounds it also on the east. By the Romans, Spain was represented by the figure of a woman with a rabbit at her side. The Romans borrowed the name Hispania, appending their own termination to it, from the Phœnicians, through whom they first became acquainted with the country. The Greeks called it Ἰβηρία (Lat. Iberia), but attached at different periods different ideas to the name. Up to the time of the Achaean League and their more intimate acquaintance with the Romans, they understood by this name all the sea-coast from the Pillars of Hercules to the mouth even of the Rhodanus (Rhone) in Gaul (Polyb. iii. 37). The coast of Spain on the Atlantic they called Tartessis (Herod. i. 163). The interior of the country they termed Celticé (Κελτική), a name which they applied, in fact, to the whole northwestern part of Europe. The Greeks in after-ages understood by Iberia the whole of Spain. The name Iberia is derived from the Iberi (Ἴβηρες) of whom the Greeks had heard as one of the most powerful nations of the country The Roman poets called the country Hesperia Ultima. For a map of Hispania, see the article PROVINCIA.

The origin of the ancient population of Spain is altogether uncertain. The Iberi, according to the ancient writers, were divided into six tribes; the Cynetes, Gletes, Tartessii, Elbysinii, Mastieni, and Calpiani. Diodorus Siculus (v. 31 foll.) mentions the invasion of Spain by the Kelts. The Iberi made war against them for a long time, but, after an obstinate resistance on the part of the natives, the two people entered into an agreement, according to which they were to possess the country in common, bear the same name, and remain forever united; such, says the same historian, was the origin of the Celtiberi in Spain. These warlike people, continues Diodorus, were equally formidable as cavalry and infantry; for, when the horse had broken the enemy's ranks, the men dismounted and fought on foot. Their dress consisted of a *sagum*, or coarse woollen mantle; they wore greaves made of hair, an iron helmet adorned with a red feather, a round buckler, and a broad two-edged sword, of so fine a temper as to pierce through the enemy's armour. Although they boasted of cleanliness in both their food and dress, it was not unusual for them to wash their teeth and bodies with urine, a custom which they considered favourable to health. Wine was brought into the country by foreign merchants. The land was equally distributed, and the harvests were divided among all the citizens; the law punished with death the person who appropriated more than his just share. They sacrificed human victims to their divinities, and the priests pretended to read future events by inspecting the entrails. At every full moon they celebrated the festival of a god without a name; from this circumstance, their religion has been considered a sort of deism.

The Phœnicians were the first people who established colonies on the coast of Spain. Tartessus was perhaps the most ancient; at a later period they founded Gades (Cadiz). They carried on there a very lucrative trade, inasmuch as the country was unknown to other nations; but, in time, the Rhodians, the Samians, the Phocaeans, and other Greeks established settlements on different parts of the coast. Carthage had been founded by the Phœnicians; but the inhabitants, regardless of their connection with that people, took possession of the Phœnician stations, and conquered the whole of maritime Spain. The government of these people was still less supportable. The Carthaginians were unable to form any friendly intercourse with the

Spaniards in the interior. The ruin of Carthage paved the way for new invaders, and Spain was considered a Roman province two centuries before the Christian era. Those who had been the allies became masters of the Spaniards, and the manners, customs, and even language of the conquerors were introduced into the peninsula. But Rome paid dearly for her conquest; the north—or the present Old Castile, Aragon, and Catalonia—was constantly in a state of revolt. The mountaineers shook off the yoke, and it was not before the reign of Augustus that the country was wholly subdued.

The peninsula was then divided into HISPANIA CITERIOR and HISPANIA ULTERIOR. Hispania Citerior was also called TARRACONENSIS, from Tarraco, its capital, and extended from the foot of the Pyrenees to the mouth of the Durius (Douro), on the Atlantic shore; comprehending all the north of Spain, together with the south as far as a line drawn below Carthago Nova (Carthagena), and continued in an oblique direction to Salamantica (Salamanca), on the Durius. Hispania Ulterior was divided into two provinces; Baetica, on the south of Spain, between the Anas (Guadiana) and Citerior, and above it Lusitania, corresponding in a great degree, though not entirely, to Portugal. In the age of Diocletian and Constantine, Tarraconensis was subdivided into a province towards the limits of Baetica, and adjacent to the Mediterranean, called Carthaginiensis, from its chief city Carthago Nova, and another, north of Lusitania, called Gallaecia from the Callaici. The province of Lusitania was partly peopled by the Cynetes or Cynesii. The Celtici possessed the land between the Anas and the Tagus. The Lusitani, a nation of freebooters, were settled in the middle of Estremadura. The part of Baetica near the Mediterranean was peopled by the Bastuli Poeni. The Turduli inhabited the shores of the ocean, near the mouth of the Baetis. The Baeturi dwelt on the Montes Mariani, and the Turdetani inhabited the southern slope of the Sierra de Aracena. The last people, more enlightened than any other in Baetica, were skilled in different kinds of industry long before their neighbours. When the Phœnicians arrived on their coasts, silver was so common among them that their ordinary utensils were made of it. The people in Gallaecia, a subdivision of Tarraconensis, were the Artabri, who derived their name from the promontory of Artabrum, now Cape Finisterre; the Bracari, whose chief town was Bracara, the present Braga; and lastly the Lucenses, the capital of whose country was Lucus Augusti, now Lugo. These tribes and some others formed the nation of the Callaici or Callaeci. The Astures, now the Asturians, inhabited the banks of the Asturis, or the country on the east of the Gallaecian mountains. Their capital was Asturica Augusta, now Astorga. The Vaccaei, the least barbarous of the Celtiberians, cultivated the country on the east of the Astures. The fierce Cantabri occupied Biscay and part of Asturias. The Vascones, the ancestors of the present Gascons, were settled on the north of the Iberus or Ebro. The Iacetani were scattered over the Pyrenaean declivities of Aragon. The Ilergetes resided in the country round Lerida. As to the country on the east of these tribes, the whole of Catalonia was peopled by the Ceretani, Indigetes, Ausetani, Cosetani, and others. The lands on the south of the Ebro were inhabited by the Arevaci and Pelendones; the former were so called from the river Areva; they were settled in the neighbourhood of Arevola, and in the province of Segovia: the latter possessed the high plains of Soria and Moncayo. The space between the mountains of Albaracino and the river was peopled by the Edetani, one of the most powerful tribes of Spain. The Ilercaones, who were not less formidable, inhabited an extensive district between the upper Jucar and the lower Ebro. The country of the Carpetani, or the space from the Guadiana to the Somo-Sierra, forms at present the archiepiscopal see of Toledo. The people on the south of the last were the Oretani, between the Guadiana and the Montes Mariani; and the Olcades, a small tribe near the confluence of the Gabriel and Jucar. Hispania Carthaginiensis, a subdivision of Tarraconensis, was inhabited by two tribes: the Bastitani, in the centre of Murcia, and the Contestani, who possessed the two banks of the Segura, near the shores of the Mediterranean.

Under the Romans all the arts of Latin civilization flourished. Latin was spoken by the educated, and many of the great writers of the Silver Age were Spaniards—Martial, Seneca, Quintilian, Lucan, Silius Italicus, Columella, Pomponius Mela, as also Prudentius and Isidorus in later times. The emperor Trajan was of Spanish birth.

The different tribes were confounded while the Romans governed the country; but, in the beginning of the fifth century, the Suevi, Vandals, and Visigoths invaded the Peninsula, and, mixing with the Kelts and Iberians, produced the different races which the ethnologist still observes in Spain. The first-mentioned people, or Suevi, descended the Durius under the leadership of Ermeric, and chose Braga for the capital of their kingdom. Genseric led his Vandals to the centre of the peninsula, and fixed his residence at Toletum (Toledo); but fifteen years had not elapsed after the settlement of the barbarous horde when Theodoric, conquered by Clovis, abandoned Tolosa (Toulouse), penetrated into Spain, and compelled the Vandals to fly into Africa. During the short period that the Vandals remained in the country, the ancient province of Baetica was called Vandalusia, and all the country, from the Ebro to the Strait of Gibraltar, submitted to them. The ancient Celtiberians, who had so long resisted the Romans, made then no struggle for liberty or independence; they yielded without resistance to their new masters. Powers and privileges were the portion of the Gothic race, and the title of *hijo del Goda*, or "son of the Goth," which the Spaniards changed into *hidalgo*, became the title of a noble or a free and powerful man among a people of slaves. A number of petty and almost independent States were formed by the chiefs of the conquering tribes; but the barons or freemen acknowledged a liege lord. Spain and Portugal were thus divided, and the feudal system established.

See Dunham, *History of Spain and Portugal*, 5 vols. (London, 1832); Mariana, *The General History of Spain from the Earliest Times* (Eng. trans. by Stephens, London, 1699), a very valuable work; Romey, *Histoire d'Espagne*, 9 vols. (Paris, 1839–50); and Hübner, *La Arqueologia de España* (Barcelona, 1888).

Hister. See ISTER.

Histion (ἱστίον). A sail. See NAVIS.

Historia (ἱστορία, "investigation"). I. GREEK.—The composition of history, and indeed of all forms of prose composition among the Greeks, originated with the Ionians of Asia Minor, who also created the epos, the elegy, and iambic poetry. It was among them, in the sixth century B.C., that the Logographi (q. v.) made their appearance. These writers treated the materials supplied by family traditions and local legends in a style which gradually approached more and more to prose, but without any attempt at critical investigation or scientific arrangement. The most important writers in this style and also its latest representatives were Hecataeus of Miletus and Hellanicus of Lesbos. The latter was a contemporary of Herodotus of Halicarnassus (about B.C. 485–424), called by Cicero the Father of History. His work, also written in the Ionic dialect, was founded upon a vast collection of historical and geographical material gathered in his extensive travels, and through the researches of many years. This mass of information he, with great art, moulded into a homogeneous work, the leading theme of which is the struggle of the Greeks against the barbarians. The narrative is simple, but always attractive. See HERODOTUS.

The line of historians who wrote in the Attic dialect is headed by the Athenian Thucydides, whose history of the Peloponnesian War is a masterpiece of the first order, noble alike in style and in matter. A continuation of Thucydides was written by his countryman Xenophon (about B.C. 431–355) in his *Hellenica*. In his *Anabasis*, Xenophon described the famous retreat of the Ten Thousand in a style which won for him the name of "the Attic Bee." In the *Cyropaedia* he gives a picture, much idealized, but not without a foundation of fact, of the history of the Persian Cyrus. His contemporary Ctesias of Cnidus, writing in Ionic Greek, introduced his countrymen to the formal history of the Persian Empire. At the same time Philistus of Syracuse, an imitator of Thucydides, compiled the history of Sicily from the earliest times down to his own. In the second half of the fourth century B.C. appeared two celebrated historians, Theopompus of Chios and Ephorus of Cymé, both disciples of the rhetorician Isocrates. The chief work of Theopompus was a history of Philip of Macedon, from his accession to his death. Ephorus, in a great work embracing the whole course of events from the invasion of the Peloponnesus by the Heraclidae, to B.C. 345, was the first writer who attempted a universal history. To this period belong the numerous chronicles of Attic history, called *Atthides*. (See ATTHIS.) In these, comparatively little regard was paid to style—less, certainly, than was paid by the historians just mentioned as succeeding Xenophon.

The period of Alexander the Great and his successors was very fertile in historical writing. One may mention Callisthenes, Aristobulus, Chares, Onesicritus, Clitarchus, and Hieronymus, who narrated contemporary events in a style sometimes plain and simple, and sometimes rhetorically exaggerated. This was the age of the Sicilian Timaeus, whose great work on the history of his native island, in some forty books, won him little recognition, but who simplified chronology by introducing the method of reckoning by Olympiads, and thus established a lasting claim on the gratitude of historians. Among the better histories should be named also the great work of Phylarchus (about B.C. 210), which began with the invasion of the Peloponnesus by Pyrrhus, and ended with the death of Cleomenes.

The Alexandrian scholar Eratosthenes conferred a great boon on scientific historical investigation by his attempt to place chronology on the firm foundation of mathematics and astronomy. His labours were continued by Apollodorus, whose *Chronica* was the most important work on chronology produced in antiquity. This was a brief enumeration of the most important events, from the taking of Troy (by him assigned to the year B.C. 1183) down to his own time (B.C. 144). Only isolated fragments of the histories written after Xenophon have, in the greater number of instances, come down to us; but we have a considerable part of the work of Polybius of Megalopolis, who died about 122. This was a general history of the known world from the beginning of the Second Punic War to the destruction of Carthage. Its style has no just claim to artistic merit, but its contents make it one of the most remarkable of ancient Greek histories. About the year B.C. 40, the Sicilian writer Diodorus compiled a valuable general history from the works of Greek and Roman writers now lost. Of this a considerable part still remains. Nicolaüs of Damascus, who lived a little later, was the author of a great general history, in 144 books, of which we have considerable fragments. Dionysius of Halicarnassus composed, a few years before Christ, his *Roman Archaeology* (Ῥωμαϊκὴ Ἀρχαιολογία), about half of which has survived. This was the history of Rome from the earliest period down to the First Punic War. It was written with taste and care. In the second half of the first century A.D. the Hebrew Iosephus wrote a work on Jewish archaeology and a history of the Jewish War. At the beginning of the second century, Plutarch of Chaeronea produced his fascinating biographies of famous Greeks and Romans. In the course of the same century appeared the *Anabasis* of Alexander the Great, written after the best authorities by Arrian of Nicomedia, the *Strategemata* of the Macedonian Polyaenus, a number of examples of military stratagems collected from older writers; and a part of the Roman history of the Alexandrian Appian, ethnographically arranged. At the beginning of the third century Dio Cassius of Nicaea conceived and executed his great work on Roman history, which has unfortunately come down to us in a very mutilated form. His younger contemporary, Herodianus, composed in eight books an interesting history of the Caesars, which still survives, from the death of Marcus Aurelius to Gordian (A.D. 180–238). Ancient chronology is much indebted to the *Chronicle* (Χρονικά) of Eusebius, bishop of Caesarea. This was written in the fourth century A.D., and only survives in quotations and an Armenian translation. Among later writers we may mention Zosimus (in the second half of the sixth century), the author of a history of the Roman emperors, from Augustus to A.D. 410. For a bibliography of the great writers, see the separate articles in this dictionary. The fragments of their lost works will be found in the *Historicorum Graec. Fragmenta*, ed. by C. and Th. Müller for the Didot series, 5 vols. (Paris, 1868–74). The text of the minor historians is edited by L. Dindorf, 2 vols. (Leipzig, 1870–71).

II. ROMAN.—The beginnings of Roman history date from about B.C. 200. The form of composition was, until the first half of the first century B.C., almost exclusively that of annals (*annales*), and the historians previous to that period are, in consequence, usually mentioned under the term "annalists." They confined themselves exclusively to the history of their country in its widest extent, from the earliest times to their own. In later times, but not till then, Roman historians undertook to write on the events of special periods, generally on those of their own time. At first they wrote in Greek only. Among the greatest of these annalists are Fabius Pictor, L. Cincius Alimentus, C. Acilius, and Postumius Albinus. The first annalist to write in Latin was Cato the Censor (B.C. 184) in his *Origines*, now unfortunately lost. His example was followed by Cassius Hemina, L. Calpurnius Piso, Sempronius Tuditanus, and many others. The early annalistic writers of Latin had no style. It is not until the knowledge of Greek literature and the development of style had reached a higher stage in the second half of the second century B.C. that one finds any attempt at good writing. In the age of Cicero, good prose was at last attained, and many men of distinction, such as Varro, Atticus, Hortensius, and Cicero himself, wrote historical works and memoirs. Some even sought to include foreign history, as was the case with C. Cornelius Nepos in his well-known collection of biographies entitled *De Viris Illustribus*. The biographies which remain are mostly those of non-Roman generals. Iulius Caesar and Sallust surpass all the other historical writers of this period both in form and matter. Sallust is an imitator of Thucydides, and the first Roman historian who can lay any claim to finished execution. The other historians of the time whose works have come down to us are Aulus Hirtius, who continued Caesar's commentaries, and the unknown authors of the Alexandrian, African, and Spanish Wars.

The Augustan Age produced the Roman history of Livy, a work as remarkable for its comprehensiveness as for its delightful literary finish. The greater part of it is unhappily lost. The first general history written in Latin, by Trogus Pompeius, belongs to the same period, but is preserved only in an epitome by Iustinus.

The first century A.D. was fruitful in historical literature, but only a certain number of works have survived, including a short sketch of Roman history by Velleius Paterculus, which is unduly animated by the adulating spirit of the courtier; a collection of historical anecdotes by Valerius Maximus; a very rhetorical history of Alexander the Great, by Q. Curtius Rufus; and a number of instances of military stratagems by Iulius Frontinus. The great history of the Empire comprised in the *Annales* and *Historiae* of Tacitus, one of the most important monuments of Roman literature, was written partly in the first and partly in the second century A.D. Dating from the beginning of the second century A.D. we have the lives of the twelve Caesars, by C. Suetonius Tranquillus, and the panegyrical account of Roman history by Florus.

After this period, Suetonius becomes the model of historians, and their favourite subject is the doings of the emperors and of the imperial court. These lost writings were the main sources of the *Historia Augusta*, a collection of biographies of the emperors from Hadrian to Numerian (A.D. 117–284), abounding in personal details often scandalous and disgusting. (See AUGUSTAE HISTORIAE.) For the history of the fourth century, the excellent work of Ammianus Marcellinus survives. At this time, writers began to content themselves with merely epitomizing and revising the books of their greater predecessors. Among the authors of historical summaries of this sort are Vopiscus, Eutropius, Orosius, St. Jerome, and Cassiodorus. There are valuable special histories by Iordanis (relating to the Goths), and by Gregory of Tours (relating to the Franks).

See Peter, *Zur Kritik der Quellen d. ält. röm. Geschichte* (Halle, 1879); Vossius, *De Historicis Latinis* (Leyden, 1627; 2d ed. 1651); Schäfer, *Quellenkunde d. griech. und röm. Geschichte*, ed. by Nissen (Leipzig, 1885); and the chapters on Roman literature in Mommsen's *History of Rome*. The fragments of lost historical works are collated by H. Peter in his *Historicorum Romanorum Reliquiae* (Leipzig, 1870), and *Historicorum Rom. Fragmenta* (Leipzig, 1883). For bibliographies of the great writers, see the special articles in this Dictionary.

Historia Augusta. See AUGUSTAE HISTORIAE SCRIPTORES.

Historia Miscella. See PAULUS.

Historia Naturālis. See PLINIUS.

Historiae. See TACITUS.

Histrio (ὑποκριτής). An actor. (1) GREEK. The steps by which ὑποκρίνομαι, ὑποκριτής acquired their dramatic meaning have been variously traced. The primitive sense of "answering" (i. e. of the quick repartee of dialogue between the actor and the chorus—ὑποκρίνεσθαι implying a more ready and instantaneous reply than ἀποκρίνεσθαι) seems quite sufficient for the purpose (Poll. iv. 123).

It is shown in the articles CHORUS and DIONYSIA that the Greek drama originated in the chorus which at the festivals of Dionysus danced around his altar, and that at first one person detached himself from the chorus and, with mimetic gestures, related his story either to the chorus or in conversation with it. If the story thus acted required more than one person, they were all represented in succession by the same choreutes. Thespis, who was regarded in antiquity as the inventor of tragedy, was the first to employ an actor distinct from the chorus; the latter still took the most important part in the performance, but lost something of its original character by becoming an interlocutor in the dialogue. Aeschylus therefore added a second actor, so that the action and the dialogue became independent of the chorus, and the dramatist at the same time had an opportunity of showing two persons in contrast with each other on the stage (Aristot. *Poet.* 4, § 16). Sophocles took the final step by adding a third actor (Aristot. l. c.); and towards the close of his career, Aeschylus found it necessary to follow the example of his younger rival, and to introduce a third actor, as is seen in the *Agamemnon*, *Choëphori*, and *Eumenides* (Poll. iv. 110). This number of three actors was also adopted by Euripides, and remained the limit scarcely ever exceeded in any Greek drama, at least in tragedy. In comedy a somewhat greater license was taken; and though Cratinus kept to the regular three performers, Aristophanes sometimes, and notably in the *Thesmophoriazusae*, employed a larger number.

Some real or apparent exceptions to this rule in tragedy have been keenly discussed, and demand a short notice. For instance, the *Prometheus* is a piece for two actors, yet in the opening scene there are four persons upon the stage—Prometheus, Hephaestus, and the allegorical Κράτος and Βία. But Βία does not speak, and mute actors were unquestionably not reckoned; while Prometheus himself, there can be no doubt, was represented by a gigantic lay figure, "so contrived that an actor standing behind the pictorial mountain could speak through the mask. No protagonist could have been expected to submit to the restraint of such an attitude throughout the whole of the play, to say nothing of the catastrophe at the end, when the rocks fall asunder, and Prometheus is dashed down into Tartarus" (Donaldson, *Theatre of the Greeks*, 7th ed. p. 286). In the *Choëphori* Aeschylus had three actors, but in 900 foll. a fourth seems required, where Pylades, who has been present most of the time as a mute actor, begins to speak. The notion of the Scholiast that the οἰκέτης, who has only just quitted the stage, reappears as Pylades, is rejected by A. Müller on the ground that the actor has not had time to change his dress. It may be remarked, however, that the Greek tragic actor, in order to assume another character, had only to change an upper garment, a mask, and perhaps a wig. There were none of the minute toilet accessories of the modern "make-up," and the operation may have been got through with much greater rapidity. Once more, in the *Oedipus at Colonus*, a fourth actor must be assumed unless the part of Theseus is divided among all three performers. The former alternative is supported by C. O. Müller (*Diss. on Eumen.* p. 127) and A. Müller (p. 175, n. 4); the latter by K. F. Hermann (*De Distributione Personarum inter Histriones in Tragoediis Graecis*, Marburg, 1840, p. 42) and Donaldson, who observes that "the mask and the uniformity of tragic declamation would make it as easy for two actors to represent one part as for one actor to sustain several characters" (p. 268 n.). The terms παρασκήνιον and παραχορήγημα here come in for explanation. The usual meaning of παραχορήγημα is of course a subordinate chorus or ἕτερος χορός; but the statement that the word was also applied to the part taken by a fourth actor rests only on the authority of Pollux (iv. 109, 110), where there is almost certainly some confusion in the text. It is more likely that a supernumerary who spoke a few words only, such as the children in the *Medea*, or the above cases of a fourth actor being required, was called παρασκήνιον.

The three regular actors were distinguished by the technical names of πρωταγωνιστής, δευτεραγωνιστής, and τριταγωνιστής, indicating the more or less prominent part each had to play in the drama. Certain conventional means were also devised, by which the spectators, as soon as an actor appeared on the stage, were enabled to judge which part he was going to perform; thus the protagonist regularly came from a door in the centre, the deuteragonist from one on the right, and the tritagonist from a door on the left-hand side (Poll. iv. 124). The protagonist naturally undertook the character in which the interest of the piece was intended to centre; not always the title-rôle, unless it were that of the real hero or heroine. It is true that, in six out of the seven extant plays of Sophocles, the title-rôle is also the leading part; but in the *Cresphontes* and *Oenomaüs* of Euripides the title-rôle was only a third-class part, and as such was taken by Aeschines (Dem. *De Cor.* p. 288, § 180). The conjecture is also unfounded that the protagonist was always the principal messenger (ἄγγελος), or again that the narrative of a death (e. g. of Hippolytus or Pentheus) was necessarily assigned to the actor of the dead man's part (K. F. Hermann, *op. cit.* p. 33). It is an ingenious but rather fanciful notion of K. O. Müller's (*Griech. Lit.* ii. 57) that the deuteragonist regularly took sympathetic parts as a friend of the hero or heroine, whereas the tritagonist was generally "an instigator who was the cause of the sufferings of the protagonist, while he himself was the least capable of depth of feeling or sympathy;" in popular language, that he was the "villain of the piece." This is supported by the recorded fact that Creon in the *Antigone* was a tritagonist's part, and by an arrangement of the characters in the Orestean trilogy of Aeschylus which gives the part of Clytaemnestra throughout to the tritagonist. It is a fact not without significance that the thirty-two extant tragedies contain no "hero" who is also a "villain," like *Macbeth* or *Richard the Third;* but the titles of lost plays show an *Ixion* of Aeschylus, an *Acrisius* and an *Atreus* of Sophocles; and it would seem that the villain-hero, though rare, was not altogether unknown. It is safer to say with Donaldson that the second and third performers "seem to have divided the other characters between them, less according to any fixed rule than in obedience to the directions of the poet, who was guided by the exigencies of his play." As on the modern stage, parts were written for particular actors; a proof that the author, notwithstanding the many conventional restrictions imposed by the sacred character of the Attic drama, had some influence over the choice of his actors.

The number of supernumeraries was unlimited. They were usually silent, but sometimes spoke a few words, especially when a fourth interlocutor was required as above; in which case the speaker was occasionally placed behind the scenes, or sheltered from view by the chorus, that the limit of three actors might not be obtrusively violated. Persons of rank and dignity always came upon the stage suitably attended, just as no Athenian lady or gentleman in real life went out without at least one slave: the body-guards of royal personages were a conspicuous feature, so that δορυφόρος or δορυφόρημα became an equivalent to κωφὸν πρόσωπον, and in one or two instances (the opening scene of the *Oedipus Tyrannus* and probably that of the *Acharnians*) we have a regular "stage-mob" of citizens like those in *Julius Caesar* and *Wilhelm Tell.*

The acting of female characters by men was greatly assisted by the use of masks; there was no need to assign such parts to beardless youths, as in England in the Shakespearian times. In early days the dramatic poets themselves acted in their own plays, and doubtless as protagonists. Of Aeschylus it is further recorded that he was his own ballet-master, and trained his choruses to dance without the aid of a professional ὀρχηστοδιδάσκαλος (Ath. i. 21 e). Sophocles appeared only twice on the stage; as Thamyris in the play of that name, accompanying a song on the *cithara*, and as Nausicaa playing at ball, in the Πλύντριαι: he then gave up acting on account of the weak-

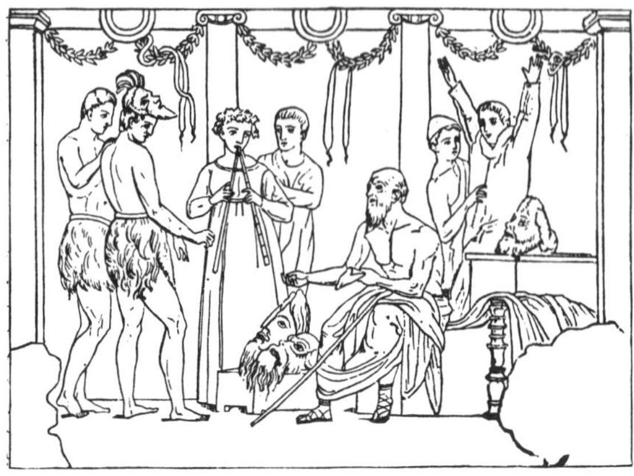

Green-room of an Ancient Theatre.

ness of his voice. After his time it became exceptional for the poet to be also an actor. Aeschylus, who seems to have been usually protagonist in his own plays, employed Cleander as his deuteragonist, and subsequently (after the introduction of a third actor) Mynniscus as tritagonist (*Vit. Aesch.* p. 3, l. 75 Dind.). Cleidemides and Tlepolemus were similarly associated with Sophocles, and Cephisophon with Euripides. Actors sometimes received enormous salaries, occasionally as much as a talent ($1180) for two or even one day's performance (Gell. xi. 9, § 2).

No social stigma attached to the actor's calling (Corn. Nep. *Praef.* 5). Distinguished Athenian citizens appeared on the stage as amateurs, and the rôle of a τριταγωνιστής, notwithstanding the scurrilous and exaggerated invectives of Demosthenes, did not detract from Aeschines' position as a soldier and orator. Bad actors, however, to whatever station in life they belonged, were not, on that account, spared; displeasure was shown by whistling or hissing (συρίττειν, Demosth. *De Cor.* p. 315, § 265); another word is θορυβεῖν, probably denoting uproar against the author rather than the actor. For the throwing of fruit or nuts in theatres, and sometimes even of stones, cf. [Andoc.] *c. Alcib.* § 20; Demosth. *De Cor.* p. 314, § 262. On the other hand, the practice of encoring (αὖθις) is inferred from Xen. *Symp.* 9, § 4.

At a later time, when Greece had lost her independence, we find regular troops of actors, who were either stationary in particular towns of Greece, or wandered from place to place, and engaged themselves wherever they found it most profitable. They formed regular companies or guilds (σύνοδοι) with their own internal organization, with their common officers, property, and sacra. There are a number of inscriptions belonging to such companies. They can be traced at Athens, Thebes, Argos, Teos, Cyprus, and Rhegium. But these actors are generally spoken of in very contemptuous terms; they were perhaps in some cases slaves or freedmen, and their pay was sometimes as low as seven drachmas ($1.25) for a performance (Lucian, *Icaromen.* 29). The language of Lucian must, however, be received with caution. He has evidently confused the old Greek estimate of the profession with the much lower Roman one of his own time; and in one passage (*Apol.* 5) writes as though Polus and Aristodemus, free Greeks of the highest consideration, had been liable to the *ius virgarum in histriones.*

On Greek actors in general, cf. Müller, *Gr. Lit.* chap. 22; Donaldson, *Theatre of the Greeks*, 7th ed., book iii. chaps. 1, 2; Becker-Göll, *Charikles*, iii. 195–200; and especially Alb. Müller, *Bühnenalterth.* in Hermann-Blümner, § 14, pp. 170–188: on the "guilds of the artists of Dionysus," § 26, pp. 392–414.

(2) ROMAN. The word *histriones*, by which the Roman actors were called, is said to have been formed from the Etruscan *hister*, which signified a *ludio* or dancer (Livy, vii. 2). The origin of scenic representations at Rome has been related under COMOEDIA. The name *histrio* thenceforward lost the signification of a dancer, and was now applied to the actors in the drama. Only the Atellanae (q. v.) and *exodia* were played by freeborn Romans, while the regular drama was left to the histriones, who formed a distinct class of persons.

In the times of Plautus and Terence we find the actors gathered into a company (*grex, caterva*), under the control of a manager (*dominus gregis*, also called *actor* in a technical sense, though *actor* is of course also a synonym of *histrio*). It was through the manager that a magistrate who was giving games, of which stage-plays formed a part, engaged the services of a company. Brutus, who was praetor in the year of Caesar's death, tried to regain the popularity he had lost through the murder by giving the Ludi Apollinares with unusual splendour; and he went all the way to Naples to negotiate with actors, who seem to have been Greeks, besides getting his friends to use their interest in his behalf (Plut. *Brut.* 21). So in imperial times a public singer is said *vocem vendere praetoribus* (Juv. vi. 379). The pay (*merces*) was on as varied a scale as in modern times. In the first century of the Empire an ordinary actor seems to have received five denarii and his food (Sen. *Ep.* 80, § 7); while at an earlier period "stars" like Roscius and Aesopus, the contemporaries and friends of Cicero, made ample fortunes. Cicero tells us that Roscius could have honourably made 6,000,000 sesterces ($240,000) in ten years had he chosen to do so (*Pro Rosc. Com.* 8, § 23); and Pliny gives half a million ($20,000) as his annual earnings. The tradition preserved by Macrobius (*Sat.* iii. 14, §§ 11–13) is that Roscius alone received 1000 denarii ($175) for every day's performance; while Aesopus left a fortune of 20,000,000 sesterces ($800,000), acquired solely by his profession. This was afterwards squandered by his son (Hor. *Sat.* ii. 3, 239).

It is clear from the words of Livy (vii. 2) that the histriones were not citizens; that they were not contained in the tribes, nor allowed to be enlisted as soldiers in the Roman legions; and that, if any citizen entered the profession of histrio, he, on this account, was excluded from his tribe. The histriones were therefore usually either freedmen, foreigners, or slaves; the latter specially educated for the stage to their master's profit. Even if *ingenui*, they were legally *infames* (Edict. Praet. *ap. Dig.* 3, 2, 1; cf. Cic. *De Rep.* iv. *fr.* 10 *ap.* Aug. *De Civ. Dei*, ii. 13), and socially in low estimation (Cic. *Pro Arch.* 5, § 10; Corn. Nep. *Praef.* 4; Suet. *Tib.* 35). Aesopus seems to have been a freedman of the Claudian gens; but Roscius, the *amor et deliciae* of Cicero, was certainly *ingenuus*, and probably of good birth. Sulla gave him the gold ring of equestrian rank. Towards the close of the Republican period, a few men of position and Greek culture raised themselves above the prejudices of their countrymen, and valued the person no less than the genius of great artists. When Caesar forced Laberius (q. v.), a knight advanced in years, to appear on the stage in his own mimes, he was thought to have exceeded the powers even of a dictator, and his victim took a dignified revenge (Macrob. *Sat.* ii. 7, § 3 foll.). Under the emperors men of equestrian rank often appeared, with or without compulsion (Suet. *Aug.* 43; Dio Cass. liii. 31; Suet. *Tib.* 35); and this circumstance, together with the increasing influence of Greek manners, tended to improve the social position of the actors. At the very beginning of the reign of Tiberius it had become necessary to check the extravagant compliments paid them (Tac. *Ann.* i. 77). Their legal status remained the same as regards *infamia* and exclusion from office; even provincial honours are denied them in the Lex Iulia Municipalis of B.C. 45, where they are coupled with gladiators (*C. I. L.* p. 123); though inscriptions show that the rule was not always enforced (Orelli, 2625). But the old law was now somewhat modified, by which the Roman magistrates were empowered to coerce the histriones at any time and in any place, and the praetor had the right to scourge them (*ius virgarum in histriones*). Augustus entirely did away with the *ius virgarum*, and limited the interference of the magistrates to the time when, and the place where (*ludi et scaena*), the actors performed (Suet. *Aug.* 45). But he nevertheless inflicted, of his own authority, very severe punishments upon those actors who, either in their private life or in their conduct on the stage, committed any impropriety. After these regulations the only legal punishments that could be inflicted upon actors for improper conduct seem to have been imprisonment and exile (Tac. *Ann.* iv. 14, xiii. 28).

Comic Actor. (From an Engraved Ring.)

The competition of the actors for public favour was carried to extraordinary lengths, and stirred up factions like those of the Circus. If not as early as the time of Plautus himself, yet at the time when the existing Plautine prologues were composed (probably about B.C. 150–100), we find partisanship (*ambitio*) in full operation (Plaut. *Poen.* prol. 37 foll.). At first palms and inexpensive crowns of gold or silver tinsel were the reward of popularity (Pliny, *H. N.* xxi. § 6); afterwards, under the Empire, presents of money and rich garments (Juv. vii. 243 with Schol.). There was a regularly organized and paid *claque* (the *theatrales operae* of Tac. *Ann.* i. 16; cf. Mart. iv. 5, 8); and over and above that the backers (*fautores*) resorted to actual violence and even bloodshed. Hence Tiberius on one occasion found himself obliged to expel all histriones from Italy (Tac. *Ann.* iv. 14); but they were recalled and patronized by his successor. The emperors as a rule tolerated, sometimes encouraged, and occasionally checked the excesses of the stage. We read of the emperor's private companies who performed during dinner-time (Suet. *Aug.* 74), and were sometimes allowed also to play in the theatres before the people. The practice of giving immoderate sums to actors was restricted by Tiberius (Tac. *Ann.* i. 77; Suet. *Tib.* 34); again by M. Aurelius, and by Alexander Severus. Aurelius ordained a maximum payment of five aurei ($25.50) to each actor, and that no *editor* should exceed the sum of ten aurei ($51); this must mean that there were to be *editores* in number equal to half the actors, for it cannot be thought that he reduced the actors to two for each performance. The restrictions of the Greek stage as to the number of actors never prevailed upon the Roman.

Hobgoblin. See LARVA.

Hodopoei (ὁδοποιοί). Public officials at Athens, charged with the care of the roads (Phot. *Lex.* s. h. v.).

Hoe. See LIGO; MARRA.

Hogshead. See DOLIUM.

Holosphyrāton. Made of beaten metal.

Homeric Question. See HOMERUS.

Homerĭdae. See HOMERUS.

Homērus (Ὅμηρος). The ancient Greeks never doubted the historical existence of Homer. He was to them "the poet" (ὁ ποιητής) in a special sense, but they knew nothing of him as a person. Eight Greek biographies of him are still extant—one under the name of Plutarch, another falsely ascribed to Herodotus—but none of them have any historic value; most of them belong to the Christian era. The early Greeks had no more interest in literary biography than the English contemporaries of Chaucer, and later generations supplied the lack of knowledge from vague tradition and from uncertain indications in the works attributed to the poet. They did not require scientific accuracy of statement, and enjoyed a good story too well to question its truth. A large variety of manifestly fictitious genealogical trees is presented for Homer, in many of which he is brought into some connection with Hesiod. Some made him a descendant of Orpheus. He was called by some Melesigenes, as the son of the river-god Meles, near Smyrna. Others called him Maeonides, either as the son of Maeon or the son of Maeonia (Lydia). A well-known epigram emphasizes the uncertainty with regard to his birthplace. More than seven cities claimed him as their own. Some thought he was born at Smyrna, and near that city a grotto was shown in which they said he composed his poems. Simonides (*Frag.* 85) called him a Chian, doubtless partly on the strength of the verse in the Hymn to Delian Apollo, 172, τυφλὸς ἀνήρ, οἰκεῖ δὲ Χίῳ ἔνι παιπαλοέσσῃ, which is quoted by Thucydides (iii. 104)—a verse which at least supported the popular belief in the poet's blindness. The great critic Aristarchus thought him an Athenian, basing his arguments upon characteristics of the Homeric dialect. Aristodemus of Nyssa believed him to be a Roman, because of the similarity of certain Roman customs with those described by the poet. Others would make an Ithacan of him. Others thought him an Aegyptian. Lucian called him a Babylonian, but doubtless in merry jest. It was reserved for an English scholar, however, to suggest that if Homer's name were read backwards, in Hebrew style, ΟΜΗΡΟΣ would become ΣΟΡΗΜΟ, which was only another form for Solomon; thus the Homeric poems were ascribed to the Hebrew king. He was generally assumed to have lived about a century or a century and a half after the Trojan War (B.C. 1183). Others made him flourish about B.C. 976. He was set by Herodotus (ii. 53) not more than four hundred years before his time, or B.C. 850. The church fathers, Clemens Alexandrinus and Tatian, inclined to set the date of his birth as late as possible, in order to sustain their claim that the wisdom of the Greeks was derived from the Hebrews.

Scholars no longer ask where Homer was born or when he lived, but in what regions and tribes of Greece epic poetry was perfected, and in what centuries the *Iliad* and *Odyssey* received their present form. Not that all would deny that any poet Homer ever lived to whom we owe the *Iliad* or *Odyssey*, or both, but all authentic information regarding him has perished beyond recovery. Even in his poems his personality is kept entirely in the background.

The meaning of the name Homer is uncertain. Many stories were invented to account for it as meaning "a hostage." Half a century ago it was explained as "the uniter" (ὁμοῦ ἀραρίσκω), and thus it was made to sustain the view that the poems are only a conglomeration of distinct and independent lays. Georg Curtius showed that, according to analogy, the name should mean "the united," not "the uniter." The plural Ὅμηροι would then be used of the members of a guild of poet-singers. The next generation would be Ὁμηρίδαι, and from this patronymic an assumption was made of an original Ὅμηρος. This pro-

Ideal Head of Homer. (Sans Souci Palace, Potsdam.)

cess has been playfully but fairly illustrated by the succession in English: "fellows" (ὅμηροι), "the fellows' guild" (ὁμηρίδαι), "the Fellows guild" (Ὁμηρίδαι), which last assumes a Mr. Fellows (Ὅμηρος) as its founder. But very possibly the name had nothing to do with the profession of song.

Homer was to the early Greeks the personification of epic poetry. All the old epic poems were attributed to him, as all great achievements were assigned to Heracles—not only what are extant, but also what are known as the cyclic poems: the *Cypria* (τὰ Κύπρια, in eleven books, of the judgment of Paris, the rape of Helen, and other events which immediately preceded the Trojan War—ascribed by others to Stasinus of Cyprus), the *Aethiopis* and *Iliupersis* (Αἰθιοπίς, in five books, of the arrival of the Amazons and the Aethiopian Memnon, the defence of Troy, and the death of Achilles; and Ἰλίου Πέρσις, in two books, of the device of the wooden horse and the capture of the city —generally ascribed to Arctinus of Miletus), the *Little Iliad* (Ἰλιὰς Μικρά, in four books, in which Philoctetes and Achilles' son Neoptolemus were brought to the help of the Greeks—by Lesches of Mitylené), the *Nosti* (Νόστοι, in five books, of the adventures of the Greeks on their return from Troy—by Agias of Troezen), and the *Telegonia* (Τηλεγονία, in two books, a sort of conclusion of the story of the *Odyssey*—by Eugammon of Cyrené).

When Aeschylus said that his tragedies were but crumbs from the rich feast of Homer (Athen. viii. 347 E, τὰς αὑτοῦ τραγῳδίας τεμάχη εἶναι ἔλεγε τῶν Ὁμήρου μεγάλων δείπνων), he probably had in mind not only the *Iliad* and *Odyssey*, but also the other poems of the Trojan cycle, from which he borrowed suggestions, as is seen from the titles of his plays. Herodotus was the first, so far as is known, to deny the Homeric authorship of the *Cypria*. This he did (ii. 117) on the ground of the inconsistency that the poet of the *Cypria* made Paris reach Troy on the third day from Sparta, while the poet of the *Iliad* represented him as driven on a devious course to Sidon; and the historian remarks that nowhere else does Homer contradict himself (οὐδαμῇ ἄλλῃ ἀνεπόδισε ἑωυτόν). Thucydides (iii. 104) seems to have acknowledged or assumed the Homeric authorship of the so-called Homeric Hymns. Plato and Xenophon mean our *Iliad* and *Odyssey* when they speak of Homer; but Aristotle (*Nicom. Eth.* 1141 a) quotes from the *Margites* (ὥσπερ Ὅμηρός φησιν ἐν τῷ Μαργίτῃ). The earliest Alexandrian editor of Homer, Zenodotus, seems to have assigned to him only the *Iliad* and *Odyssey*.

Among the minor poems of Homer are generally placed the *Hymns, Battle of the Frogs and Mice* (Βατραχομυομαχία), *Jests* (παίγνια), and *Margites*. The *Hymns* are not hymns in the modern sense of the term; they are rather epic than lyric. They number thirty-four in all, but ten are brief, having only three to six lines each. The first two, to Apollo, were counted as one until the critic Rhunken in 1749 convinced scholars that the first was in praise of Delian (178 verses) and the second of Pythian Apollo (368 verses). The latest editor endeavours again to show that the two are simply parts of one. The third Hymn (580 verses) tells of the birth of Hermes and the exploits and tricks of the new-born babe: how he found a tortoise and invented the seven-stringed lyre (φόρμιγξ), how he stole the cattle of Apollo and then returned to his cradle, finally appeasing Apollo's wrath by the gift of the lyre. This and the one immediately following are distinctly secular, not religious, in their character. The fourth Hymn (293 verses) tells of Aphrodité and her love for Anchises. The fifth Hymn (495 verses), to Demeter, has a more serious tone than the preceding. It seems to have been intended to state the mythical foundation for the Eleusinian Mysteries. It tells how Persephoné, Demeter's daughter, was carried off by

Hades as she was plucking flowers ("herself a fairer flower"), and of the disconsolate wanderings of the mother in search of her daughter until she found a temporary home at Eleusis; on her departure thence a temple was built in her honour, and at last the mother and daughter were united. No one of the other Hymns has more than sixty verses. They are "introductions," proems (*προοίμια*), intended to be sung before the rhapsodist's recital of some other lay (perhaps at some rhapsodic contest), as a sort of "grace before meat"—in the same spirit which made every Greek festivity sacred to some divinity. No external evidence exists for the date of these Hymns. They contain many Homeric formulas and tags of verses which give an antique flavour even to what is comparatively modern. Parts of the poems may go back to a remote antiquity; the Hymn to Demeter may have been composed about B.C. 650; more date from the fifth and sixth centuries. After the fifth century, the interest in epic recitations was so slight that these proems would not be composed.

The *Batrachomyomachia* is a comic epic poem of 303 verses, giving a burlesque account of the battle between the frogs and mice, when Puff-cheek (*Φυσίγναθος*), king of the frogs, caused the death of Crumb-snatcher (*Ψιχάρπαξ*), a promising young mouse, inviting him and bearing him on his back to visit his home, but deserting him in the midst of the waters on the approach of a water-snake. The story is composed with humour and some ingenuity, but is a light production. It was ascribed to Pigres, son of Lygdamis and nephew of the Artemisia who distinguished herself in the battle of Salamis; but if it were composed by him, it was interpolated and worked over later. Very possibly it was composed in the Alexandrian period, in mockery of the revival of epic poetry after the ancient spirit was lost. The epigrams and jests are entirely insignificant, both in quantity and quality. The only one of any note is the answer of Arcadian fishers to the question as to their luck: "All that they took, they left; what they did not take, they brought with them" (*ὅσσ' ἕλομεν, λιπόμεσθ'· ὅσα δ' οὐχ ἕλομεν φερόμεσθα*). The *Margites* was a comic poem of considerable fame in antiquity, part in dactylic hexameter and part in iambic trimeter verse, with the story of a stupid (*μάργος*), bashful fellow, who had all manner of ridiculous adventures and attempted many things which were beyond his powers. As long as critics are not agreed as to what works are rightly attributed to Chaucer, and even as to the authorship of some of the plays which have been ascribed to Shakespeare, no one can wonder that little is known of the history of the incunabula of Greek poetry, composed in the imaginative age, long before the classical period.

The *Iliad* and the *Odyssey* contain the story of parts of the Trojan cycle of myths.

The *Iliad* opens with a scene in the last of the ten years of the Siege of Troy, and the action of the poem continues for only seven weeks. With great ingenuity (as it would seem) just enough incidental indications are given of the early history of the war to supply the needed basis for an intelligent appreciation of the story. As Horace says, Homer *semper ad eventum festinat et in medias res, | non secus ac notas auditorem rapit.* The judgment of Paris and the assignment of the prize of beauty to the Goddess of Love are referred to in the Homeric poems but once, and that in a doubtful passage, xxiv. 29, 30. Paris (his Greek name Alexander is more frequent in the poems), the voluptuous son of Priam, king of Ilios (the later Ilium), in the Trojan land, on the southwestern shore of the Hellespont, had sailed to Lacedaemon and carried away Helen, the beautiful wife of Menelaüs, the king, and many of her possessions. In order to avenge this insult and to recover the woman and her treasures, Menelaüs and his brother Agamemnon, king of Mycenae, gathered an army at Aulis, and with 1186 ships (and perhaps 100,000 men) set sail for the plain of Troy. For ten years they besiege the city. They bring with them no supplies, and spend much of their time in making forays on the neighbouring districts and more formal expeditions against the adjoining towns. The captured men are slain or sold to distant islands; the women are kept as slaves. The Trojans are not closely barred within their walls, but they are unable to cultivate their fields and are obliged to send their treasures to their neighbours, in order to buy provisions and to hire mercenaries. The loss of men does not seem to have been very great on either side in the early years of the war. At the opening of the *Iliad*, an old priest of Apollo, Chryses, comes to the Greek camp to ransom his daughter, who had been captured by the Greeks and given as a prize of honour to Agamemnon. The king refuses the request, and Apollo avenges the slight to his priest by sending a pestilence upon the Greek camp. After nine days an assembly of the army is called, and the seer Calchas declares the cause of the god's anger. The rude language used by Achilles, the mightiest of the Greek warriors, arouses the wrath of Agamemnon, and a quarrel follows. Achilles "sulks in his tent," while his mother, the goddess Thetis, persuades Zeus to grant victory to the Trojan arms. The action of the *Iliad* includes only four days of battle. In the first, ii.–vii. 380, neither side gains any great advantage; in the second, viii., the tide of battle often turns and the gods interfere again and again, but at last the Trojans drive the foe to their camp, and bivouac on the plain, near the Greek watch-fires. In the third day of battle, xi.–xviii., the Trojans break into the Greek camp and begin to set fire to the fleet; but as soon as Achilles sees the flickering flame he sends his comrade Patroclus with his Myrmidons, enjoining upon him to drive the Trojans from the camp, but not to attempt to capture the city. Patroclus forgets the warning of his chief, and filled with the spirit of the combat presses on too far; Apollo strikes him (the only instance in the poems of such direct interference of a divinity), and Hector slays him. Achilles now becomes more angry at Hector than he had been at Agamemnon, and takes an active part in the fourth day of battle, xix.–xxii., in which he drives the Trojans in confusion into their city, and slays Hector. The twenty-third book is devoted to the funeral games in honour of Patroclus, in accordance with the curious ancient custom of honouring the dead with horse-races and foot-races and contests in wrestling, boxing, putting the shot, and shooting the bow. In the twenty-fourth book old Priam comes to the Greek camp and ransoms the body of Hector from Achilles, who here appears in a gentler mood. The poem closes very simply: "Thus these were busy with the burial of Hector."

After the action of the *Iliad*, the Aethiopian Memnon comes with his men to the help of Troy, while Philoctetes with the bow of Heracles and Neoptolemus, the son of Achilles, after his father's death, come to aid the Greeks. The alliance of the Amazons with the Trojans is not mentioned in the poems. Odysseus plans the Wooden Horse, by which the city is captured. Athené's wrath is kindled against the Greeks by their conduct after the capture of the city, and she sends upon them a storm, which scatters their fleets. Menelaüs is driven to Crete and Egypt, and with Helen reaches his home in Sparta only in the eighth year of their wandering. Odysseus is driven first to the land of the lotus-eaters, then to the island of the Cyclopes, where Polyphemus slays and devours six of his comrades (and is blinded by him), thence to the land of the Laestrygonians (where all but one of his ships are destroyed), and to Circe's island, where he passes a year. He then visits Hades, in order to consult the soul of the blind Theban seer, Teiresias. In Hades he sees the shade of his mother and those of many of the Greek heroes. On his return the dangers of Scylla and Charybdis are met. His comrades slay one of the cattle of the Sun, and their boat is wrecked. Odysseus himself is borne to the island of the sea-nymph Calypso, who cares for him tenderly, and would make him immortal and her husband. The scene of the *Odyssey* opens in the tenth year after the close of the Trojan War and the twentieth after the departure of Odysseus from his home on Ithaca. He has been absent so long that no expectation is entertained of his return. His home is filled by more than a hundred young princes, each eager to win the hand of the faithful and prudent wife, Penelopé; and thus to become the king of the realm. The goddess Athené pities Odysseus, who is weary of his sojourn in the grotto of Calypso and longing for his home, and secures the decree of Zeus for his return. Meanwhile she sends his son Telemachus to Nestor and Menelaüs, asking for tidings of his father. Odysseus sets out from Calypso's island, eighteen days' sail to the west, but as he approaches Greece he is wrecked by the sea-god Poseidon, whose son Polyphemus he had blinded, and is cast on the shore of the Phaeacians (identified by the ancients with Corcyra, the modern Corfu), who convey him to his home. Finding his palace in the possession of haughty suitors, he returns in the guise of a beggar, but with the help of his son and two faithful servants (and Athené) he slays the suitors and regains his kingdom and faithful wife.

The action of the *Odyssey* covers only six weeks —less even than that of the *Iliad*—yet the events of the ten years of wandering are comprised in the stories which are put into the mouth of Nestor, Menelaüs, and Odysseus himself. This device of introducing a full account of events which are not included in the time of the proper action of the poem was followed by Vergil in his account of the capture of Troy (as told by Aeneas), and by Milton in his account of the war in heaven (told by Raphael). Many matters which are merely touched upon in the poem were discussed more fully in the lesser epic poems, and the question has been raised whether these brief mentions in the *Iliad* and *Odyssey* were allusions to the fuller accounts, already familiar to the hearer, or rather were the fruitful germs which were later developed into the *Cypria*, the *Nosti*, etc. In some cases the latter alternative seems certain—e. g. on the death of Hector, his wife Andromaché despairs of safety for herself and her son Astyanax; "he will either accompany her into slavery, or some Greek will seize him by the arm and hurl him from the wall." This seems to have suggested to a later poet the detailed description of such a death for the boy.

The influence of the Homeric poems upon the Greeks was very great. Pindar says that Odysseus had more fame than he deserved because of the sweet-voiced Homer (*Nem.* vii. 20, *ἐγὼ δὲ πλέον' ἔλπομαι λόγον Ὀδυσσέος ἢ πάθαν διὰ τὸν ἁδυεπῆ γενέσθ' Ὅμηρον*). Herodotus (ii. 53) even asserts that Homer and Hesiod fixed the theogony of the Greeks, distributing to the gods their epithets, arts, and honours. Appeal was made to the Homeric poems to settle questions of precedence and of title to territory. These poems were in large measure the basis of the Greek youth's education. A fragment of a play of Aristophanes (*Frag.* 222) shows us a father examining his son, to prove his diligence in school, on the meaning of certain obsolete Homeric words: *τί καλοῦσι κόρυμβα; τί καλοῦσ' ἀμενηνὰ κάρηνα;* In the *Symposium* of Xenophon (iii. 5), Niceratus says that his father, the noted Athenian general Nicias, in his desire to make a good man of him, compelled him to learn all the poems of Homer, and that he could repeat the entire *Iliad* and *Odyssey* from memory. At the Panathenaic festival from the time of Solon early in the sixth century, for at least two hundred years the recitation of portions of the Homeric poems had a prominent place (Lycurg. *Leocrates*, 102). The Platonic dialogue *Ion* reports a conversation between Socrates and the Ephesian rhapsode Ion, who visits Athens after taking the prize in the Homeric recitation at Epidaurus, and expects the same honour from the Panathenaic festival. This Ion was a Homeric specialist; he claimed no unusual familiarity with Hesiod and Archilochus, but asserted that no one equalled him as an interpreter of Homer. Such men naturally magnified their office and represented the poet as the teacher of much occult wisdom—finding in his works the best maxims for war and for peace, for the statesman, the philosopher, and the general. Even Aristophanes represents Aeschylus as saying, "From what has divine Homer received his fame except from his most excellent instructions with regard to tactics, brave deeds, and the arming of men?" (*Frogs*, 1034, *ὁ δὲ θεῖος Ὅμηρος | ἀπὸ τοῦ τιμὴν καὶ κλέος ἔσχεν πλὴν τοῦδ' ὅτι χρήστ' ἐδίδαξεν | τάξεις ἀρετὰς ὁπλίσεις ἀνδρῶν*). The words of Horace are familiar: at Praeneste he read again Homer, who taught what was base and what was honourable more fully and better than the Stoic Chrysippus or the Academic philosopher Crantor (*Epist.* i. 2. 1, *Troiani belli scriptorem . . . relegi;* | *qui quid sit pulchrum, quid turpe, quid utile, quid non,* | *plenius ac melius Chrysippo et Crantore dicit*). Plato (*Rep.* x. 599 c) refutes the view that Homer had special wisdom in regard to "wars, generalships, administration of cities, and the education of men," thus showing the prevalence of that belief.

According to an uncertain story, Pythagoras was said to have seen Homer in Hades, suffering torments in return for his statements about the gods. But the first definite criticism of Homer, so far as is known, was that of Xenophanes (*Frag.* 7), at the close of the sixth century B.C., that Homer and Hesiod attributed to the gods all actions which are regarded as shameful by men. Heraclitus, Xenophanes' contemporary, would have Homer driven from the musical contests. Plato, in his *Republic* (ii. 377 d–iii. 391 c), enters into a detailed examination of the moral effect exerted by the Homeric poems, and declares that the youths who are in process of training to be the guardians of his ideal State must not be rendered impious by hearing what would degrade the gods in their eyes; lest they should fear death more than defeat and flight, they must not hear Zeus lamenting the death of Sarpedon (*Il.* xvi. 433 foll.), and Achilles declaring that he would rather serve a poor man on earth than rule over all the dead in the home of Hades (*Od.* xi. 488 foll.); they must not be taught insubordination and insolence to commanding officers by hearing Achilles call Agamemnon a coward (*Il.* i. 225); and they must not learn to give free rein to their passions from the wantonness of Zeus (*Il.* xiv. 314 foll.) and from Odysseus' enjoyment of food and drink (*Od.* ix. 5 foll.). Thus, although with much regret because of his old regard and affection for the poet, the works of Homer are not allowed in Plato's ideal State. The reader is at a loss to know how seriously he is to understand these words of the philosopher, who is fond of clinching an argument or giving a higher literary flavour to a sentence by a quotation from the "inspired poet." Allegory was already employed in the interpretation of the most offensive passages, but Plato says that the young person cannot distinguish between what is allegorical and what is not (*Rep.* ii. 378 d). In the *Phaedrus* (243 a) he playfully suggests that the poet may have lost his sight because of his false statements with regard to the gods. Plutarch, in his treatise on "How a young man should study poetry," makes a formal reply to Plato without naming him, urging that the young should be taught to discriminate between what is admirable in itself and what is an admirable imitation of the offensive or even base. The rhetorician Zoïlus received the nickname of Homer's Scourge (Ὁμηρομάστιξ) because of his severe criticisms on the poet; but these were meant very likely merely as a paradox, just as other rhetoricians showed their ingenuity in maintaining the guilt of Socrates, the innocence of Busiris, and the advantages of fever and vermin.

The old Greek commentaries (*scholia*, *σχόλια*) on Homer mention editions by Antimachus of Colophon (himself an epic poet, a contemporary of Plato), and by Aristotle, who was said to have prepared an edition expressly for the use of his distinguished pupil, Alexander the Great (Plut. *Alex.* 8). Athenian school-masters prepared also lists of obsolete Homeric words. The critical study of Homer, however, began at Alexandria, in connection with the great library and "Museum" which were established by the Ptolemies. These kings of Egypt had abundant means with which to encourage the arts and sciences, and desired by the help of Greek civilization to break down the barriers which existed between the different races of their subjects and to exalt their kingdom. They gathered men of literary talent from all lands and set apart a portion of the palace for a great library. Strenuous efforts were made to secure copies of all works of Greek literature, and, in fact, of all literature, including, according to the story, the Greek translation of the Hebrew Scriptures. In the time of Ptolemy Philadelphus (who reigned B.C. 285–247), the library was said to contain 400,000 volumes (rolls)—perhaps equal to about 40,000 modern octavo volumes—such a collection as had never existed before. It possessed copies of Homer from Marseilles, Chios (the seat of the Homeridae), Sinope on the Black Sea, Argos, Cyprus, Crete. The Homeric poems formed the centre of the literary studies of the Alexandrian scholars. The first careful editor and reviser of the Homeric text was Zenodotus, the earliest of the librarians. He had before him copies of the poems with variations which extended over whole verses and clauses, as well as to words and forms. A critical procedure was necessary. Even the same manuscript must have shown marked inconsistencies of grammatical forms. The first critical edition, in the nature of the case, must have been an experiment. The editor can have had no fixed principles with regard to the formation of words and the characteristics of the Homeric dialect. Zenodotus is thought to have been the first to divide the *Iliad* and the *Odyssey* each into twenty-four books. In earlier times this division was unknown. So, for example, Herodotus (ii. 116) speaks of *Iliad* vi. 289–292 as ἐν Διομήδεος ἀριστείῃ. Aelian (*Varia Hist.* xiii. 14) writes in detail of this ancient custom of reference by the subject of each particular portion of the poems. The ancient titles are preserved, though with some possible inaccuracies and no definite authority, as the headings of the books in ordinary editions of the poems. The division into books became necessary at this particular time, because then parchment was replaced by papyrus as the ordinary writing material. The comparatively frail papyrus was not suited for long rolls. Hence the works of Plato, Xenophon, Thucydides, and Herodotus were divided, also. Zenodotus seems to have composed no commentary to accompany his edition of the poems, but tradition preserved his views of certain passages. He was not led to reject or change for grammatical reasons, but seems to have been guided in many changes rather by a sense of propriety. Thus he rejected *Il.* iii. 424, where Aphroditê took a chair and set it for Helen, for the goddess to do menial service was ἀπρεπές in his eyes; verses *Il.* i. 28–30 were unworthy of a king; in *Il.* i. 260, where Nestor says, "I have been associated with better men than you" (ἀρείοσιν ἠέ περ ὑμῖν), Zenodotus read "than we" (ἡμῖν), in order to make the expression more courteous. But the work of this critic is coming to honour, and it is at present fashionable in some quarters to praise him at the expense of Aristarchus.

The edition of Zenodotus formed the basis of that of his successor, Aristophanes of Byzantium, a little after B.C. 200, who is noteworthy as the first to introduce to general use the marks of accentuation and the signs of quantity, which are still in use. His chief work was in lexicography.

Unquestionably the greatest of the literary critics of Alexandria was Aristarchus, who was born in the island of Samothrace, but came to Alexandria and studied under Aristophanes, whom he succeeded in the care of the library. He prepared two revised editions of the Homeric text, with critical marks in the margin, and wrote eight hundred tracts on many subjects, largely connected with our poet. He founded a school of critics which continued active until the time of the early

Roman emperors. Many of his notes have been preserved to us in the Greek scholia, and prove his learning and his caution. The watchword and battle-cry of his school was *analogy*, opposed to the rival school of the Stoic Crates at Pergamum, who was more free in the admission of *anomalies* in the construction of sentences and in the formation and meaning of words. Crates indulged in allegorical interpretation, paying little attention to grammatical studies, and making Homer a philosopher and an orator, while Aristarchus was more conservative and sober in his views.

The basis of our scholia to the *Iliad* is an epitome made about A.D. 200, of four works. Of these the most important was a work by Didymus (called Χαλκέντερος and Βιβλιολάθας from his unwearied industry and literary productivity), of the time of Augustus, in which Didymus aimed at giving a full report of the readings of the editions of Aristarchus, in so far as they varied from others. Next in importance was a work by an earlier contemporary, Aristonicus, who endeavoured to explain the use of the critical signs of Aristarchus, and the reasons for their employment in each case. Less full and important were the extracts from a treatise by Herodian on Accentuation (ἡ Ἰλιακὴ Προσῳδία) and one by Nicanor on Punctuation (Περὶ Στιγμῆς). The epitome of these four works has suffered serious losses in its transmission to the present time, and considerable additional matter of little value and authority has been added. The component parts of these scholia have been carefully analyzed and separated, and scholars no longer speak of the statement of the scholiast, but of that of Didymus, of Nicanor, etc. The extant scholia to the *Odyssey* are far less extensive and important than those to the *Iliad*.

The Homeric text of the MSS. does not seem to be so distinctly under the control of the text of Aristarchus as was to be expected. In many particulars it differs from his editions—so widely that it seems that the vulgate text was only indirectly and slightly influenced by his work. Many scholars now regard the restoration of the Aristarchean text as the ultimate, or at least the immediate, aim of Homeric text-criticism. But Bekker's edition of 1858 attempted to present the text as it was sung—not as it stood in the old MSS.—inserting the lost *vau* where the editor believed it had once been pronounced. Bekker had been preceded by a wholly unscientific attempt of the same kind in 1820, by R. Payne Knight, who inserted *vaus* with more zeal than discretion, printing as the title of the *Iliad* ϜΙΛϜΙΑΣ, and Tydeus as ΤΥϜΔΕϜΣ, but who with many absurdities had many ideas which have been confirmed by modern investigations. Bekker has been followed by others, notably Nauck, who has made a scientific edition of Homer such as he believes the poems to have been before the forms were subjected to later Attic influence.

That the Homeric text of Plato and Aristotle was not exactly like that of the present day is extremely probable, but these seem to have quoted so freely that exact inferences are difficult. The view that they quoted from memory is strengthened by the fact that each of the two makes a careless reference to the Homeric story: Plato (*Rep.* iii. 405 e) speaks of Eurypylus where he means Machaon, confusing two similar incidents in the same book of the *Iliad* (xi. 638–641, 822–848); and Aristotle (*Nicom. Eth.* ii. 1109, a 31) puts into the mouth of Calypso a command of Odysseus which was given in accordance with advice of Circé (*Od.* xii. 219). In the summer of 1891 the British Museum published a collation of several very ancient papyrus texts of the *Iliad*, containing fragments of several hundred lines. With the exception of two or three details, the most important teaching of these MSS., one of which is from the very beginning of our era, is that the ordinary texts of to-day are rather more accurate and intelligible than those of two thousand years ago, but certain verses may not have been recognized as Homeric then which are in modern texts.

For the last century the vexed and ever-burning Homeric Question has been with regard to the composition and original form of the Homeric poems—whether they were the creations of one poetic genius or the remnants of the songs of many bards; whether their composition was organic or atomic; whether they can be compared with Vergil's *Aeneid* and Milton's *Paradise Lost*, or whether they were at first only short, scattered songs, grouped around central personages and events, and gradually developed into longer poems with unity. The heat and length of the discussion have made clear the fact that the question is difficult, and no hypothesis has been presented free from grave objections. Scholars are more nearly agreed than half a century ago, however. Probably no one who has a right to an opinion on the subject now holds to the strict unity of the poems in the old sense—that all of the *Iliad* and *Odyssey* was composed by one man—yet comparatively few would deny a certain unity in the poems, however it was secured. The ancient Alexandrians had their Separatists (χωρίζοντες), Xeno and Hellanicus, who denied that the *Odyssey* was composed by the author of the *Iliad*, and Perizonius in 1684 called attention to the late use of writing for literary purposes. The great Bentley in 1713 said that "Homer wrote a sequel of songs and rhapsodies to be sung by himself for small earnings and good cheer, at festivals and other days of merriment; the *Iliad* he made for the men, and the *Odysseïs* for the other sex. These loose songs were not collected together in the form of an epic poem till about five hundred years after." Vico of Naples in 1725 expressed his view that Homer never existed—that he was the personification of the early songs of the Greeks. Robert Wood, in *An Essay on the Original Genius of Homer* (1769), declared his belief that the art of writing was not known to Homer. But the modern discussion of the Homeric Question dates from the *Prolegomena ad Homerum* of Friedrich August Wolf, published in 1795. The *Prolegomena* excited much attention, and probably has had greater influence than any other work on the methods of historical and philological study, although its ideas were not wholly novel. The poet Herder and the philologist Heyne each claimed that his thunder had been stolen. The book owed its great success largely to its clear and attractive presentation of the subject, and it is more valuable now for its method than for its particular arguments. Wolf planned to give a critical history of the Homeric poems through six periods, the first of which extended from the composition of the poems (about B.C. 950, according to him) to the age of Pisistratus, tyrant of Athens in the sixth century B.C., who, according to an uncertain tradition, first collected and arranged them in their present form; the second period extended from Pisistratus to Zenodotus, the earliest of the Alexandrian critics. Wolf never completed his work beyond these first two periods. He attempted to show (*a*) that the Homeric poems were not committed to writing by the poet, but were intrusted to the memory of the rhapsodes, who were gathered in schools, like the Hebrew prophets; thus before the poems were written they were exposed to many and unintentional changes—from lapse of memory, and from a singer's desire to improve a passage or suit it more perfectly to a special occasion. Writing was unknown in Greece in Homer's time, and no class of readers existed for whom a poem should be written. (*b*) After the poems had been committed to writing, many more additional changes were made in them, in order to remove inconsistencies and to give them the polish of an age advanced in culture and poetic art. (*c*) The *Iliad* and *Odyssey* in their present form are due not to the poetic genius of Homer, but to the intelligence of a later age—to the united efforts of Pisistratus and the poets of his court. (*d*) The songs themselves, of which the *Iliad* and *Odyssey* are composed, are not by the same poet. These last two theses were never publicly discussed by Wolf in detail. He only urged that if the poems were not to be committed to writing at the time when they were composed, the songs were not originally parts of one long work; no one would have thought of making a poem which could not be read and which was too long to be sung or recited at a single sitting. A bond of union would be valueless between lays which were to be sung in no regular order on different occasions. The Homeric poems unquestionably possess a certain unity beyond what is found in Hesiod or in the late poet Quintus Smyrnaeus, but this unity must be due to the editors of the Pisistratean age. Discrepancies are found which could not occur in a single poem, but might very well be overlooked in the combination of independent lays. Entire rhapsodies (e. g. *Iliad* x.) seem to be due to some other than the poet of the greater part of the *Iliad*.

The views of Wolf were received with intense interest, but with varied approval. The poet Schiller said that the man was a barbarian who would tear asunder the Homeric poems and believe that they were put together long after their composition. Goethe, while at first an enthusiastic admirer of the *Prolegomena*, soon declared that he believed in the unity of the *Iliad* more heartily than ever. On the whole, however, the work of Wolf was convincing, at least in large part, to most scholars of Germany. Theologians received it with special interest, on account of the applications of Wolf's principles to the study of the Old Testament. But a reaction took place. Opponents urged that the use of writing in Greece was much earlier than Wolf claimed; but they made the fatal concession that such long poems would be impossible without the aid of writing. Both sides claimed too much. Writing was certainly known in Greece earlier than Wolf allowed, but was not used for extensive literary purposes until long after the time alleged by his opponents. The power of the human memory to retain accurately long poems had been underrated. The external arguments against the original unity of the Homeric poems have yielded rather than advanced since Wolf's time. The evidence in support of the story of the work of Pisistratus in collecting and arranging the scattered Homeric poems is considered weak, as well as that for the existence of schools of rhapsodists corresponding to the schools of the prophets.

Only a beginning had been made of the attempt to disprove the unity of the Homeric poems from internal evidence when Lachmann, of Berlin, in 1837, applied to the *Iliad* the analysis which had been applied not much earlier to the *Nibelungenlied*. He set to work to discover contradictions and inconsistencies which would indicate the different authorship of different parts. The discussion of the unity of the poems was conducted mainly on his principles for half a century, and no one now lays stress on the external evidence, one way or the other. In the first book of the *Iliad* he determined an original lay (1–347), complete in itself, and two independent and inconsistent continuations (430–492; and 348–429, 493–611). The beginning of the second book (he says) cannot have been part of the same lay as the close of the first book; at the close of book i., Zeus sleeps, with Hera by his side, while at the beginning of book ii., Zeus cannot sleep and has an interview with the Dream God, in which he tells much that he would not have Hera know. In the third day of battle, which begins book xi. 1 and continues through book xviii. 240, the sun comes twice to the zenith (at xi. 86 and xvi. 777, nearly 4000 verses later). The twenty-third book of the *Iliad* cannot have been intended to follow immediately upon the twenty-second—the one ending, "Thus she spake weeping, and the women groaned in response," while the next begins, "Thus these were groaning throughout the city." Following such indications, Lachmann marked out the boundaries of eighteen distinct lays in the *Iliad*. Köchly, following in Lachmann's footsteps, published in 1851 an edition of the *Iliad*, in sixteen lays (omitting books x., xix.–xxiii., and parts of some others)—not agreeing with Lachmann in the divisions so well as in the number of the songs. The advocates of the theory that the Homeric poems are but a conglomeration of independent lays have not succeeded in coming to essential agreement with regard to the original songs. Their lines of cleavage do not agree. Contradictions certainly exist: Odysseus' hair is blonde (*Od.* xiii. 431), but black (*Od.* xvi. 176). Diomed and Odysseus are seriously wounded and retire from the conflict (*Il.* xi. 369 foll., 428 foll.), but two days later take part in the games in honour of Patroclus—Odysseus wrestling with Telamonian Ajax (*Il.* xxiii. 709), and winning the prize in the foot-race (*Il.* xxiii. 778). Most noted of all is the case of Pylaemenes; he is slain at *Il.* v. 576, but follows the corpse of his son from the battle (*Il.* xiii. 658). Some inconsistencies may be considered as trifles about which the poet did not concern himself; he was composing for hearers rather than for critical readers who can turn backward and forward, and compare statements. Other inconsistencies may have been caused by interpolations; the incident of Pylaemenes in *Il.* xiii. 658 may have been added by a later poet in order to give increased pathos to the scene. Possibly the Homeric Greeks were not so much disturbed as some moderns at such inconsistencies. Similar discrepancies are found in the works of Vergil and other poets.

In 1846, the historian Grote, declaring that "the

idea that a poem as we read it grew out of atoms not originally designed for the places which they now occupy, involves us in new and inextricable difficulties when we seek to elucidate either the mode of coalescence or the degree of existing unity," proposed the theory that the present *Iliad* was made up by the combination of an original *Iliad* (books ii.–vii., ix., x., xxiii.–xxiv.) with an *Achilleïd* (books i., viii., xi.–xxii.). This latter poem on the Wrath of Achilles gives all that is "really necessary to complete the programme in the opening proem of the poem."

In 1878, Professor Geddes of Aberdeen, following in Grote's footsteps, declared that "the Homeric corpus of *Iliad* and *Odyssey* falls asunder into two great sections, on the one hand the *Achilleïd*, and on the other the non-Achilleïd, *plus* the Odyssey." "A poet, who is also the author of the *Odyssey*, has engrafted on a more ancient poem, the *Achilleïd*, splendid and vigorous saplings of his own, transforming and enlarging it into an *Iliad*." This view was maintained by many indications: Achilles is more gentle in the Odyssean books; Helen is not mentioned in the *Achilleïd;* the dog is more honoured in the Odyssean books, the horse in the *Achilleïd*, etc.

Organic development from a brief epic poem was claimed for the *Odyssey* by Kirchhoff of Berlin, in 1859. He considers the original part to be the old *Return* (Νόστος) *of Odysseus*, of just 1200 verses; to this simple story was added a longer story of 3560 verses, narrating the adventures of Odysseus after his return to Ithaca; still later were added (7185 verses) the *Telemachia*, or account of the journey of Telemachus to Pylus and Sparta, the experiences of Odysseus in Phaeacia, and his adventures in the cave of Polyphemus, in the island of Circé, in the realm of Hades, etc.

Christ of Munich published in 1884 an edition of the *Iliad* in which he divided the poem into forty lays, and indicated by the use of four different styles of Greek type his view of the relative order of composition of the different parts of the poem. Immediately after the first book he places the eleventh, the Bravery of Agamemnon, believing that the intermediate books were composed after the poet saw what a rich vein he had struck, and to what a magnificent growth his germ might be developed. He holds that most of the poem proves a poet revolving a great plan in his mind, and arranging the parts to form a whole.

Von Wilamowitz-Moellendorff published in 1884 an important work on this subject, *Homerische Untersuchungen*, dedicated to the well-known Biblical scholar Wellhausen. Just as Wolf's *Prolegomena* stimulated the investigation of the historical sources and of the age of the Old Testament Scriptures, so the method of the recent analysis of the Pentateuch has been applied to the Homeric poems. Wilamowitz rejects Lachmann's lays as being fragments, unintelligible when separated. He bases his work upon that of Kirchhoff, yet rejects many of the latter's views. He follows him in putting the *Odyssey* in the front of the discussion. Until Kirchhoff, no scholar had seriously attempted the critical dissection of this poem, of which the artistic plan was not doubted. Two of Wilamowitz's conclusions are that the *Telemachia* (*Od.* ii. 1–iv. 619) was composed in Asia Minor, and that the *Odyssey* was brought into its present form in Greece proper —probably near Corinth or in Euboea.

The Homeric Question is clearly full of difficulties. No theory has been proposed which meets with general acceptance. The poems doubtless contain a great mass of very ancient material. Professor Percy Gardner writes, in his *New Chapters in Greek History* (1892), "There is a broad line dividing mythical from political Hellas, a line which seems to coincide with the great break made in the continuity of Hellas by the Dorian invasion. . . . The Homeric poetry may have been reduced to form after the splendour of the Ionian and Achaean chiefs had passed away. . . . In using the name of Homer, we do not, of course, assert that the Homeric poems had a single author. But we do assert the antiquity of those poems. Homer reflects the pre-historic age of Greece as truly as does Herodotus the Greece of the Persian Wars, or Pausanias the Greece of the age of the Antonines." The poet does not profess to have seen Priam's Troy; he is clearly conscious that he belongs to a degenerate age, and that he is dependent on the muse for his information. No one supposes that the poems are an accurate record of a particular war. The recent excavations, however, establish the fact that at Mycenae, the home of the Homeric Agamemnon, and on the shore of the Hellespont, the home of the Homeric Priam, stood at the same period, flourishing from about B.C. 1400 to about B.C. 1000, cities of wealth and power, of similar culture. A war between these cities, which may have suggested the Homeric story, is by no means an impossibility. The details, however, and perhaps every name of a person, are due to the poet's imagination. The view that the poems were essentially in their present condition before the historical period in Greece began, early in the eighth century B.C., is moderate.

The Homeric dialect is artificial—that is, such as was never spoken by any Greek tribe. It con-

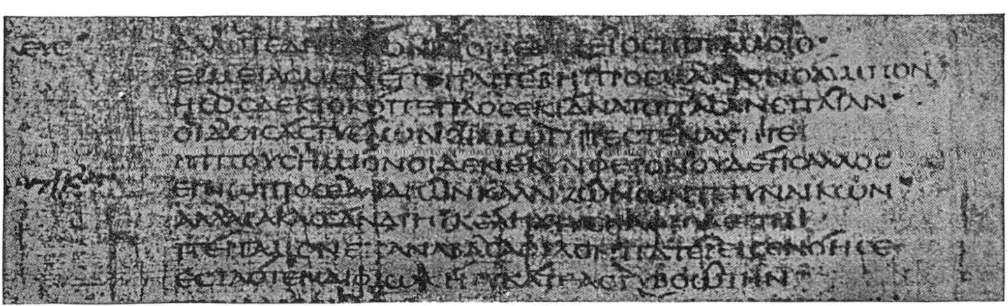

Bankes Papyrus of the Second Century B.C. (*Il.* xxiv. 692–700.)

tains many ancient elements, but is far from being the ancestor of all the later historical dialects. It is not even the source of the Attic or Ionic dialects. The Aeolic element in it is so strong as to suggest to Fick the view that the older parts of the poems were composed in the Aeolic dialect and were afterwards translated into that of the Ionic. The formulaic character of many of the Aeolic words and phrases, the large number of Homeric proper names found in historical times in Northern Greece, the traditions with regard to the seats of the Pierian Muses, and the prominence given to the Thessalian hero, Achilles, make probable the view that epic poetry was first cultivated by the Aeolians in Northern Greece, but was afterwards brought to perfection by the Ionians in Asia Minor. The dialect certainly indicates a long course of development. Obsolete words and forms were retained by the poets in certain connections after they had been dropped from the ordinary speech of the people. Certain late forms appear in the ordinary texts in sufficient number to suggest to Paley the theory that the poems were brought into their present form in the age of Pericles at Athens; but most of these forms can be explained easily as the work of a careless copyist, who substituted a form which he heard every day for one which was found only in old poems—just as a half-educated man would do to-day in copying the works of Chaucer, unless he were specially warned and trained to be accurate in this matter. If the Homeric poems were thoroughly worked over, revamped, in the time of Solon or of Pericles, some clear trace would have been left of the culture and political relations of that time. A strong indication of the falsity of the story that Pisistratus gathered the poems and caused interpolations to be made to the glory of Athens, is the simple fact that Athens is so insignificant in the *Iliad* and *Odyssey*. If the unity of the poems were really due to Pisistratus, and he ordered the poets of his court to insert passages which would honour Athens, we should find greater distinction given to Athenian heroes and more myths of the Attic cycle. The two or three verses assigned by the ancient critics to Athenian interpolators are absolutely trifling.

Fortunately the Homeric poems *exist*, even though scholars have not settled the question when and how they came into being. Destructive criticism has not been able to disturb the fact that they remain the greatest epic poems the world has seen—admired by many ages and peoples of different civilizations. They stand unrivalled. In comparison with them the vast epics of India are as shapeless as the Hindoo idols, and are in their luxuriance like to a tropical jungle; while the work of Vergil and of Milton, who take Homer as their master, is artificial and unnatural in comparison with his—the "clearest-souled of men."

BIBLIOGRAPHY.—The best MS. of the *Iliad* is Venetus A, now in the library of San Marco at Venice, written in the eleventh century on 327 large leaves of parchment. The best MS. of the *Odyssey* is Codex Harleianus, now in the British Museum, written in the thirteenth century on 150 folio leaves of parchment.

The best introduction to Homer, with a delightful literary flavour, is Professor Jebb's *Homer* (1887). This treats of the general literary characteristics of the poems, the Homeric world, Homer in antiquity, and the Homeric question.

For the Homeric question, see Wolf, *Prolegomena ad Homerum* (1795); Lachmann, *Betrachtungen über Homers Ilias* (1837, 1865); Kirchhoff, *Die homerische Odyssee und ihre Entstehung* (1859, 1879); Grote, *History of Greece*, vol. ii.; Geddes, *Problem of the Homeric Poems* (1878); Bonitz, *Origin of the Homeric Poems* (1880); Wilamowitz-Moellendorff, *Homerische Untersuchungen* (1884).

The best critical edition of the poems, with brief notes, is that of Nauck, 2 vols. (1874–79); the most complete critical apparatus for the *Iliad* is in the edition of La Roche (1873), and for the *Odyssey* in the edition of Ludwich (1889); the best exegetical commentary is that of Ameis-Hentze (with German notes, in twelve parts, of different dates — three parts as yet published with English notes); the best complete edition of the *Iliad* with English notes is that of Leaf, 2 vols. (1886–88); the best edition of the *Odyssey* with English notes is that of Hayman, 3 vols. (1866–82). Convenient text editions are those of Dindorf-Hentze and Cauer, both published at Leipzig. The most complete lexicon for Homer is the *Lexicon Homericum* of Ebeling, 1700 pages (1871–85); admirable is the *Index Homericus* of Gehring (1891); Keep's Autenrieth's *Homeric Dictionary* (1891) is capitally convenient; more elaborate than the last mentioned is Capelle's *Wörterbuch über die Gedichte des Homeros und die Homeriden* (1889). The best work in its department is Monro's *Homeric Grammar* (1882, 1891).

For Homeric antiquities, see Buchholz, *Homerische Realien*, 3 vols. (1871–85); Helbig, *Das homerische Epos aus den Denkmälern erklärt* (1884, 1887); Inghirami, *Galleria Omerica*, 3 vols. (1829); Anderson's Engelmann's *Pictorial Atlas to Homer* (1892). For Schliemann's work in connection with Homer, see Schuchhardt, *Schliemann's Excavations* (1891) and Gardner's *New Chapters in Greek History* (1892). The old Greek commentaries (Scholia) are published best by Dindorf and Maass, 8 vols. (1855–1887); for their illustration, see Lehrs' *De Aristarchi Studiis Homericis* (3d ed. 1882), and Ludwich's *Aristarchs Homerische Textkritik* (1884–85).

Very many translations have been made, and different tastes will like different translations. See Matthew Arnold's essay *On Translating Homer*. The translations of Chapman and Pope are classics in their way. Within the last few years two good prose translations of the *Odyssey* have appeared—one by Palmer, the other by Butcher and Lang. That of the *Iliad* by Lang, Leaf, and Myers, is not so good: Worsley's verse is enjoyed by some, and Bryant's by others. Leaf has published a *Companion to the Iliad* (1892), and Andrew Lang a work entitled *Homer and the Epic* (1892), in connection with their versions.

Homoioi (ὅμοιοι, "peers"). A name given to the Spartiatae (q. v.) in allusion to their having equal political rights with one another (Xen. *Hell.* iii. 3. 5) as opposed to the ὑπομείονες, whose position was in some respects subordinate. See SPARTA.

Homŏlé (Ὁμόλη). (1) A lofty mountain in Thessaly, near Tempé, with a sanctuary of Pan. (2) Or HOMOLIUM (Ὁμόλιον). A town in Magnesia in Thessaly, at the foot of Mount Ossa, near the Peneus.

Honor or **Honos**. The personification of honour at Rome, to whom temples were built both by Marcellus (B.C. 212) and by Marius (B.C. 101), close to the temples of Virtus. Marcellus also built one to Virtus; and the two deities are frequently mentioned together. Honor and Virtus are represented on coins as youthful figures—Honor wearing a bay-leaf chaplet, and Virtus a helmet. See VIRTUS.

Honorarii Ludi. See LUDI.

Honorarium Ius. See EDICTUM.

Honōres. (1) A term used of any compliment or honour conferred by the Roman Senate or any public body (Cic. *Pro Planc.* 26, 64; *Ad Fam.* i. 9, 14). (2) A commission or rank in the army (Caes. *B. C.* i. 77). (3) Technically the name denotes actual magistrates whether of the Populus Romanus, the Plebs, or of a municipality, excluding, however, the office of *iudex*, senator, and priest (Mommsen, *Staatsrecht*, i. p. 8), and possibly the *principatus* (q. v.). The *ius honorum* was a part of the rights of one who was a free citizen and might be withheld when all the other rights were granted (Tac. *Ann.* xi. 23). (See MUNUS.) (4) *Cursus honorum* is an expression of Roman official life which may be defined as the career of public service through which a citizen must pass before attaining to the position of the highest rank. In the early Roman Republic there existed in an informal way a principle of official promotion by which those who had held inferior magistracies were understood to be eligible for higher positions after the lapse of a certain interval of time (Callist. *Dig.* 50, 4, 14, 5). The order, *certus ordo magistratuum*, in which the various magistracies should be held, was, however, formally defined in B.C. 180 by the Lex Villia Annalis. The *cursus honorum* thus legally determined consisted of the quaestorship, curule aedileship, praetorship, consulship. A preliminary military service of ten years was required before the career of magistracies could be begun. Since enrollment by the censors took place at the census next following the attainment of the age of seventeen years, allowing for the ten years of military service, we may place the earliest age at which the quaestorship could be held as twenty-eight years. An interval of at least two years was required between the holding one office and the following, so that the aedileship could be held at thirty-one years, the praetorship at thirty-four, and the consulship at thirty-seven. Since the holding of the curule aedileship was optional, the praetorship might directly follow the quaestorship, and the consulship might thus be reached at thirty-four years.

The principle of an *ordo honorum* found, however, its most important application in the development of the imperial government under Augustus and his successors.

In the imperial period there were three careers of official service. The republican magistracies formed the *cursus honorum* for those of senatorial rank—i. e. senators, sons of senators, or those raised to senatorial rank by the emperor, all possessing the requisite property of one million sesterces.

To a select body of the knights invested by the emperor with membership in the equestrian troop through the conferring of the knight's horse, were assigned the offices of administration, the various procuratorships and *praefecturae* which formed the equestrian *cursus honorum*.

To the commonalty were assigned the subordinate offices, civil and military.

SENATORIAL CURSUS HONORUM.

I. Preliminary service.
   (*a*) Annual tenure of one of a group of minor offices, known as *vigintiviri*: *triumvir capitalis, triumvir monetalis, quattuorvir viarum curandarum, decemvir stlitibus iudicandis.*
   (*b*) A year's service as *tribunus militum laticlavius.*

II. Quaestorship—at twenty-five years.
   Interval of at least one year.

III. Aedileship or tribunate of the plebs.
   Interval of at least one year.

IV. Praetorship—at thirty years.
   Interval of at least two years.

V. Consulship.
   A patrician being ineligible for the tribunate of the plebs or the plebeian aedileship could pass directly from the quaestorship to the praetorship.

EQUESTRIAN CURSUS HONORUM.

I. Preliminary service.
   (*a*) Military service. No special military service appears to have been regularly required, although Claudius determined upon three positions—(1) *praefectura cohortis;* (2) *praefectura alae;* (3) *tribunatus legionis;* and these *tres militiae equestres* became the usual preliminary service in the second century. In the inscriptions the *tribunatus* regularly holds the second place.
   (*b*) Civil service. Through the reforms of Hadrian, training in state affairs was recognized as equivalent to service in the army—e. g. those who had served as *advocati fisci* or *ab commentariis praefecti praetorio* were eligible for the procuratorships and praefectures.

II. Procuratorships of various kinds and grades.

III. Praefecturae.
   The highest offices open to those of the equestrian order given in ascending order were: *praefectura classis, praefectura vigilum, praefectura annonae, praefectura Aegypti, praefectura praetorio.*

OFFICIALS OF THE THIRD CLASS.

These were of great number and variety, being made up mainly of subordinate officers of administration in Rome and the provinces, attendants of public officials, officers of the army and the fleets, magistrates of the coloniae and municipia, and the officers of the collegia. The inscriptions show that these subordinate offices were arranged in a *cursus honorum* on the same principle prevailing in the senatorial and equestrian *cursus.*

See T. Mommsen, *Römisches Staatsrecht*, vol. i. 523–577; and O. Hirschfeld, *Untersuchungen auf dem Gebiete der römischen Verwaltungsgeschichte*, vol. i. 240.

Honoria. See ATTILA.

Honorius Flavius. A Roman emperor of the West, A.D. 395–423, the second son of Theodosius the Great. During his minority the able Stilicho was regent, but in 408 was charged with treason and put to death. In the reign of Honorius, Alaric (q. v.) took and plundered Rome (410), while the emperor led a life of ease at Ravenna.

Coin of the Emperor Honorius.

Honos. See Honor.

Hood. See Cucullus; Mitra.

Hoop. See Trochus.

Hoplītae (ὁπλῖται). Heavy-armed soldiers. See Exercitus, p. 649.

Hoplomăchi (ὁπλομάχοι). See Gladiatores.

Hora. See Dies.

Horae (Ὧραι). The goddesses of order in nature, who cause the seasons to change in their regular course, and all things to come into being, blossom, and ripen at the appointed time. In Homer, who gives them neither genealogy nor names, they are mentioned as handmaidens of Zeus, intrusted with the guarding of the gates of heaven and Olympus — in other words, with watching the clouds. Hesiod calls them the daughters of Zeus and Themis, who watch over the field operations of mankind; their names are Eunomia (Good Order), Diké (Justice), and Irené (Peace), names which show that the divinities of the three ordinary seasons of the world of nature—Spring, Summer, and Winter—are also, as daughters of Themis, appointed to superintend the moral world of human life. This is especially the case with Diké, who is the goddess who presided over legal order, and, like Themis, was enthroned by the side of Zeus. According to Hesiod, she immediately acquaints him with all unjust judicial decisions, so that he may punish them. In the tragic poets she is mentioned with the Erinyes, and as a divinity who is relentless and stern in exacting punishment. (See Astraea.) At Athens, two Horae were honoured —Thallo, the goddess of the flowers of spring; and Carpo, the goddess of the fruits of summer. Nevertheless the Horae were also recognized as four in number, distinguished by the attributes of the seasons. They were represented as delicate, joyous, lightly moving creatures, adorned with flowers and fruits, and, like the Graces, often associated with other divinities, such as Aphrodité, Apollo, and Helios. As the Hora specially representing spring, we have Chloris, the wife of Zephyrus, and goddess of flowers, identified by the Romans with Flora (q. v.).

Horatia. The sister of the Horatii, killed by her surviving brother for deploring the death of her betrothed, one of the Curiatii, and for reproaching him with the deed by which she had lost her lover. See Horatius.

Horatia Gens. One of the most ancient of the patrician gentry at Rome. See Horatius.

Horatii. See Horatius.

Horatius. (1) The name of three brave Roman brothers, who fought, according to the old Roman legends, against the Curiatii, three Alban brothers, about 667 years before the commencement of our era. Mutual acts of violence committed by the citizens of Rome and Alba had given rise to a war. The armies were drawn up against each other at the Fossa Cluilia, where it was agreed to avert a battle by a combat of three brothers on either side —namely, the Horatii and Curiatii. It is evident that we have here types of the two nations regarded as sisters and of the three tribes in each. In the first onset, two of the Horatii were slain by their opponents; but the third brother, by joining address to valour, obtained a victory over all his antagonists. Pretending to fly from the field of battle, he separated the three Curiatii, and then, attacking them one by one, slew them successively. As he returned triumphant to the city, his sister Horatia, who had been betrothed to one of the Curiatii, met and reproached her brother bitterly for having slain her intended husband. Horatius, incensed at this, stabbed his sister to the heart, exclaiming, "So perish every Roman woman who bewails a foe." For this murder he was adjudged by the duumvirs to be scourged with covered head and hanged on the accursed tree. Horatius appealed to his peers, the burghers or *populus;* and his father pronounced him guiltless, or he would have punished him by the paternal power. The populus acquitted Horatius, but prescribed a symbolical punishment. With veiled head, led by his father, Horatius passed under a yoke or gibbet—*tigillum sororium,* "sisters' gibbet." (See Livy, i. 26.) (2) Cocles. See Cocles.

The Horae bringing Wedding Gifts to Peleus. (Relief in the Louvre.)

(3) Quintus Horatius Flaccus, a celebrated Roman poet, born at Venusia, December 8th, B.C. 65, during the consulship of L. Aurelius Cotta and L. Manlius Torquatus (*Carm.* iii. 21, 1; *Epod.* 13, 6). His father, who was a freedman of the Horatian family, had gained considerable property as a *coactor*, a name applied to the servant of the money-brokers, who attended at sales at auction, and collected the money from the purchasers (*Sat.* i. 6, 86). With these gains he purchased a farm in the neighbourhood of Venusia, on the banks of the Aufidus. In this place Horace appears to have lived until his eleventh or twelfth year, when his father, dissatisfied with the country school of Flavius, removed with his son to Rome, where he was placed under the care

Monument of the Horatii and Curiatii. (Von Falke.)

of a celebrated teacher, Orbilius Pupillus, of Beneventum, whose life has been written by Suetonius. After studying the ancient Latin poets, Horace acquired the Greek language. He also enjoyed, during the course of his education, the advice and assistance of his father, who appears to have been a sensible man, and who is mentioned by his son with the greatest esteem and respect. It is probable that, soon after he had assumed the *toga virilis* at the age of seventeen, he went to Athens to pursue his studies, where he appears to have remained till the breaking out of the Civil War during the second triumvirate. In this contest he joined the army of Brutus, was promoted to the rank of military tribune, and was present at the battle of Philippi, his flight from which he compares to a similar act on the part of the Greek poet Alcaeus.

Though the life of Horace was spared by the imperial party, his paternal property at Venusia was confiscated, and he repaired to Rome, with the hope of obtaining a living by his literary exertions. Some of his poems attracted the notice of Vergil and Varius, who introduced him to Maecenas, and the liberality of that statesman quickly relieved the poet from all pecuniary difficulties. From this eventful epoch the current of his life flowed on in a smooth and gentle course. Satisfied with the competency which his patron had bestowed, Horace declined the offers made him by Augustus, to take him into his service as private secretary, and steadily resisted the temptation thus held out of rising to wealth and political consideration; advantages which would have been dearly purchased by the sacrifice of his independence. That he was really independent in the noblest sense of the word, in freedom of thought and action, is evidenced by that beautiful epistle (i. 7) to Maecenas, in which he states that if the favour of his patron is to be secured by a slavish renunciation of his own habits and feelings, he will at once say farewell to fortune and welcome poverty.

Not long after his introduction to Maecenas the journey to Brundisium took place (*Sat.* i. 5), and the gift of his Sabine farm soon followed. Rendered independent by the bounty of Maecenas, high in the favour of Augustus, courted by the proudest patricians of Rome, and blessed in the friendship of his brother poets, Vergil, Tibullus, and Varius, it is difficult to conceive a state of more perfect temporal felicity than Horace must have enjoyed. This happiness was first seriously interrupted by the death of Vergil, which was shortly succeeded by that of Tibullus. These losses must have sunk deeply into his mind. The solemn thoughts and serious studies which, in the first epistle of his first book, he declares shall henceforward occupy his time, were, if we may judge from the second epistle of the second book, confirmed by those sad warnings of the frail tenure of existence. The severest blow, however, which Horace had to encounter, was inflicted by the death of his early friend and best patron Maecenas. He had declared that he could never survive the loss of one who was "part of his soul" (*Carm.* ii. 17, 5), and his prediction was verified. The death of the poet occurred only a few weeks after that of his friend, on the 27th of November, B.C. 8, when he had nearly completed his fifty-eighth year. His remains were deposited next to those of Maecenas, on the Esquiline Hill.

Horace. (From a Gem in the British Museum.)

When at Rome, Horace lived in a small and plainly-furnished mansion on the Esquiline. When he left the city, he either betook himself to his Sabine farm or his villa at Tibur, the modern Tivoli. When in the country, as the whim seized him, he would either study hard or be luxuriously idle. The country was his favourite abode, and here he displayed all the genial simplicity of his nature.

If we may believe Horace himself, his own preference was for a country life; and some of the truest poetry that he ever wrote deals with themes drawn from his love of rural scenes—the peaceful meadows of Apulia, the Bandusian fountain, the cattle resting in the flickering shade through the long summer afternoon, the siesta by the brook-side, the cool vistas of the forest glades with the young deer browsing among the trees. His own homely tastes are delightfully set forth in the passages where he tells of his sitting about the fire at evening with his rustic neighbours, exchanging stories and cracking jokes over the mellow wine.

Horace is described as short and stout, so that Augustus rallied him on his corpulency; of a rather quick temper, yet easily placated; and given to ease and the enjoyment of the good things of life. This disposition is perfectly reflected in his writings, which embody a genial, if not very deep, philosophy of life, and a good sense which robbed Epicureanism of its selfishness and Stoicism of its sourness and severity.

The productions of Horace are divided into Odes, Epodes, Satires, and Epistles. The Epodes (*Epodi*) are the earliest of his works, and are written in various forms of iambic and dactylic verse. They were not published as a collection until B.C. 29, after the publication of his first book of Satires (*Sermones*), which had appeared about the year B.C. 35, dedicated to Maecenas. At about the time of the publication of the Epodes appeared the second book of Satires. The Odes (*Carmina*) were written in part as early as B.C. 29, but their formal appearance in three books is to be assigned to the year B.C. 20 or thereabouts. These three books were also dedicated to Maecenas. Following them came a continuation of the Satires in a new form, that of letters addressed each to a single person, and called Epistles (*Epistulae*). These are in two books, the first having been published soon after the first publication of the Odes, and the second not long before the poet's death in B.C. 8. In B.C. 17, the *Carmen Saeculare* or Secular Hymn was composed at the request of Augustus for the celebration of the Ludi Saeculares (q. v.). Horace likewise, being in a way the Poet Laureate of Augustus, celebrated the victories of the emperor's stepsons, Tiberius and Drusus, in several new Odes, which he published with a number of others, as a fourth book of Odes in B.C. 13. The famous bit of literary criticism, the *Epistula ad Pisones*, usually known as the *Ars Poetica*, and perhaps unfinished, is of uncertain date, but is to be assigned with much probability to the year B.C. 20.

Horace, as a poet, does not show the inspiration and *Geist* that would rank him with the great masters of lyric verse—Pindar, Alcaeus, Sappho—whom he imitates; and he is himself thoroughly aware of his own poetic limitations. When he attempts the flight of the Theban eagle and when he writes in his *rôle* of Poet Laureate, he is never at his best; but, like Tennyson in his official verse, invariably suggests a person ill at ease

Augustus. Maecenas. Agrippa. Horace.

Augustus and his Friends. (From a wall-painting from the Palace of the Caesars, discovered in 1737.)

over a perfunctory task. His temperament and tastes marked out for him a far different sphere, in which he is inimitable. When he gets away from battles and triumphs, and gods and heroes, and the whole machinery of Olympus, and turns to the familiar world in which he lives, he plays with a master hand upon the chords that vibrate in the breast of all men. Tenderness, humour, a lively and picturesque fancy, a sympathetic love of external nature in her familiar aspects, a keen insight into human nature in its varying moods—all these are his in a high degree, and joined with them is an undercurrent of occasional melancholy that not infrequently touches the source of tears. In those Odes where he depicts the lighter side of love, the genial intercourse of friends, and natural scenery, or in which he sets forth his amiable philosophy of life, he is quite inimitable. Words cannot do justice to the exquisite polish of his verse, the crispness and terse vigour of his phrases, and the perfect choice of words, which Petronius, in the following century, characterized as *Horatii curiosa felicitas*. He has filled the pages of modern literature with a host of sparkling epigrams, phrases, and proverbial lines—"jewels five words long"—more numerous, in fact, than those that have been taken from all the rest of Latin literature put together. No other writer in any language so abounds in pregnant phrases. His *carpe diem* is an epitome in two words of the whole practical teaching of Epicureanism. His *nil desperandum*, twisted out of its context, has almost become an English phrase. So, too, the expressions *consule Planco—damnosa quid non—nunc vino pellite curas—post equitem sedet atra cura—non omnis moriar—semper avarus eget—sapere aude—nil admirari—sub iudice lis est—disiecti membra poetae*—and a hundred others.

It is in his Satires and Epistles that the true Horace is most clearly seen, freed from the uncomfortable trappings of the grand style, and, as it were, chatting at ease among his friends. Here he most winningly sets forth his shrewd and kindly views of men and things, laughing good-humouredly at the foibles of his friends and at his own as well, like Thackeray, except that in the laugh of Horace there is no subacid tone of even a pretended cynicism. The whole tenour of his teaching is moderation—the *mediocritas aurea,* the *modus in rebus*—which he preaches incessantly alike to the ambitious, the pleasure-loving, and the philosopher. Not even virtue itself is to be pursued beyond what is reasonable. This is essentially the philosophy of "good form," of the man of the world, enlivened by a sense of humour that is fatal alike to the fanaticism of the "crank" and the priggish solemnity of the Philistine. It is the philosophy of the average man, and it explains the constant popularity of Horace in all ages and all nations, and the fact that he is today, at the end of the nineteenth century, the most modern writer that literature can show us. He, more than any other, makes antiquity live for us again; and, stripping off the superficial differences of time and place and language, flashes upon the mind a conviction of the essential unity of the present and the past. He is thus the most human of all the classic writers, and the one whose wit and wisdom linger in the mind of the most idle student long after the lines of Aeschylus and Vergil and even Homer have been forgotten. Hence we find him admired, translated, and imitated by men of such different types as Pope, Byron, Gladstone, and Eugene Field. His nearest representative in English literature is Pope; but, as Mr. Mackail well says, to suggest a true parallel we must unite in thought the excellence of Pope and Gray with the easy wit and cultured grace of Addison.

From an early date Horace's poems were used in Roman schools as a text-book, and were expounded by Roman scholars, especially by Acron and Porphyrion. His use as a school-text has perpetuated the order in which his works are now always printed, that being the order in which the Roman school-boys read them. As Horace has been continuously popular, there exist a very large number of MSS. (about 250) of the text—none, however, older than the ninth century A.D. The oldest is the Codex Bernensis (denoted as B), written in Ireland. This is incomplete. A separate source of Horace is represented by the Codex Blandinius (*Vetustissimus* or V), in part collated by Cruquius (Jacques de Crusques) at Blankenberg, but destroyed about 1566. (See CRUQUIUS.) The best representative of this "family" is probably the Codex Gothanus (G), dating from the year 1456. The Horatian MSS. are enumerated in Keller and Holder's preface.

Q. Horatius Flaccus. (From a Gem.)

BIBLIOGRAPHY.—The *editio princeps* of Horace is said to have appeared at Milan in 1470. Great editions are those of Lambinus (Leyden, 1561, reprinted at Paris in 1567, 1579, 1587, and at Coblentz in 1829); Cruquius (first printed as a whole at Antwerp, 1578); Heinsius (Leyden, 1612); the great epoch-making work of Bentley (Cambridge, 1711, reprinted at Amsterdam, 1713, and lately at Berlin, 1869); Wakefield (London, 1794); Orelli and Baiter (1850–52; last ed. Berlin, 1885 foll.); Dillenburger (1881); Nauck and Krüger (Leipzig, 1885); Schütz (Berlin, 1880–83); Kiessling (Berlin, 1884–1888); the text alone by Meineke (Berlin, 1854); Keller and Holder (Leipzig, 1864–70); Haupt and Vahlen (4th ed. Leipzig, 1881); L. Müller (last ed. Chicago, 1882); with illustrations from gems, by King, text by H. A. J. Munro (London, 1869); French commentary by Waltz (Paris, 1887); English commentaries by Macleane (London, 1869); Wickham (vol. i. Odes and Epodes, 1874; vol. ii. Satires and Epistles, 1891). Separate editions are those of the Odes by Page, with an off-hand commentary of much literary merit (4th ed. London, 1890), and Wickham (2d ed. London, 1887); of the Satires by Palmer (London, 1883) and L. Müller (Vienna, 1891); of the Epistles by Wilkins (3d ed. London, 1889), Shuckburgh (Cambridge, 1888), L. Müller (Vienna, 1893); of the Satires and Epistles together by Kirkland, after Kiessling (Boston and N. Y. 1893). The *Ars Poetica* is edited separately by Hofmann-Peerlkamp (Leyden, 1845) and Albert (Paris, 1886), and discussed by Weissenfels (Görlitz, 1880), and Bonino (Turin, 1888).

No translation of Horace does any kind of justice to the original, though some of the imitations in English by Pope are very clever. There are translations by Sir Philip Francis, by Professor Conington (in verse), by Sir Theodore Martin (Odes and Satires), by Clark (Odes), by Sargent (Odes), and Sir Stephen De Vere (selected Odes and Epodes)—the last two in 1893. There is a fair prose translation by Lonsdale and Lee.

The life of Horace has been written in English by Milman (1853) and Hovenden (1877); in German by L. Müller (1880); in French by Walckenaer, 2 vols. (1858), and Des Vergers (1855); in Italian by Onesolto (Padua, 1888). A valuable life of the poet by Suetonius has come down to us with some discreditable interpolations, in the MSS. of the poet. Valuable criticism of Horace will be found in Teuffel's *Charakteristik des Horaz* (Leipzig, 1842); Gerlach, *Leben und Dichtung des Horaz* (Basle, 1867); Weissenfels, *Horaz* (Berlin, 1885); Vogel, *Die Lebensweisheit des Horaz* (Meissen, 1868); Beck, *Horaz als Kunstrichter und Philosoph* (Mainz, 1875); Weise, *De Horatio Philosopho* (Colberg, 1881); Maier, *D. philosoph. Standpunkt des Horaz* (Kremsier, 1888); and Sellar, *Roman Poets of the Augustan Age: Horace* (1892).

The scholia to Horace have been edited by Fabricius (Basle, 1555), with additions by Pauly (Prague, 1858 and 1877), and by Hauthal (Berlin, 1864–66). See the account of the scholia by Usener (Berne, 1863). There is a lexicon to Horace by Koch (2d ed. Hanover, 1879). On the language, etc., of Horace, see Ernesti's *Clavis Horatiana* (2d ed. Leipzig, 1823); Barta, *Sprachliche Studien*, etc. (Linz, 1879 and 1881); Habenicht, *Alliteration bei Horaz* (Eger, 1885); Waltz, *Des Variations de la Langue et de la Métrique d'Horace*, etc. (Paris, 1881); and the introduction to Kirkland's edition of the Satires and Epistles (1893). On Horace as a satirist, see R. Y. Tyrrell in *Hermathena*, iv. 355; id. *Latin Poetry* (1895); and the article SATIRA.

Hordicidia. See FORDICIDIA; TELLUS.

Horesti. A people of Scotland, mentioned by Tacitus. In Agricola's time they seem to have been the inhabitants of what is now Angus (Tac. *Agric.* 38).

Horistae (ὁρισταί). Officials at Athens and some other places, e. g. Chios, whose duty it was to settle boundaries, especially of sacred precincts.

Hormisdas. See SASSANIDAE.

Horn. See CORNU.

Horologium (ὡρολόγιον). A name given to various instruments by means of which the ancients measured the time of the day and night. The earliest and simplest horologia of which mention is made were called πόλος and γνώμων. Herodotus (ii. 109), who ascribes their invention to the Babylonians, mentions the πόλος and γνώμων as two distinct instruments. Both, however, divided the day into twelve parts, and were a kind of sun-c. 17; *Somn. s. Gall.* c. 9). In later times the name gnomon was applied to any kind of sundial, and especially to its finger, which threw the shadow, and thus pointed to the hour. Even the clepsydra is sometimes called gnomon (Athen. ii. p. 42).

The gnomon was evidently a very imperfect instrument, and it was impossible to divide the day into twelve equal spaces by it. The πόλος or ἡλιοτρόπιον, on the other hand, seems to have been a more perfect kind of sundial; but it appears, nevertheless, not to have been much used, as it is but seldom mentioned (Aristoph. *ap.* Poll. ix. 46). It consisted of a basin (λεκανίς), in the middle of which the perpendicular staff or finger (γνώμων) was erected, and in it the twelve parts of the day were marked by lines (Lucian, *Lexiph.* 4).

Another kind of horologium was the *clepsydra* (κλεψύδρα). It derived its name from κλέπτειν and ὕδωρ, as in its original and simple form it consisted of a vessel with several little openings (τρυπήματα) at the bottom, through which the water contained in it escaped, as it were, by stealth. This instrument seems at first to have been used only for the purpose of measuring the time during which persons were allowed to speak in the courts of justice at Athens. The time of its invention or introduction is not known; but in the age of Aristophanes (see *Acharn.* 692) it appears to have been in common use. Its form and construction may be seen very clearly from a passage of Aristotle (*Problem.* xvi. 8). The clepsydra was a hollow globe, probably somewhat flat at the top part,

Horologium. (Pompeii.)

dial. The γνώμων, which was also called στοιχεῖον, was the more simple of the two, and probably the more ancient. It consisted of a staff or pillar standing perpendicular, in a place exposed to the sun (σκιάθηρον), so that the length of its shadow might be easily ascertained. The shadow of the gnomon was measured by feet, which were probably marked on the place where the shadow fell (Poll. i. 72). The gnomon is almost without exception mentioned in connection with the δεῖπνον or the bath; and the time for the former was towards sunset, or at the time when the shadow of the gnomon measured ten or twelve feet (Aristoph. *Eccles.* 652, with the Schol.; Poll. l. c.). The longest shadow of the gnomon, at sunrise and sunset, was twelve feet. The time for bathing was when the gnomon threw a shadow of six feet (Lucian, *Cronos*, where it had a short neck (αὐλός), like that of a bottle, through which the water was poured into it. This opening might be closed by a lid or stopper (πῶμα), to prevent the water running out at the bottom. The clepsydra which Aristotle had in view was probably not of glass or of any transparent material, but of bronze or brass, so that it could not be seen in the clepsydra itself what quantity of water had escaped. As the time for speaking in the Athenian courts was thus measured by water, the orators frequently use the term ὕδωρ instead of the time allowed to them (ἐν τῷ ἐμῷ ὕδατι, Demosth. *De Coron.* p. 274, § 139). Aeschines (*c. Ctesiph.* § 197), when describing the order in which the several parties were allowed to speak, says that the first water was given to the accuser, the second to the accused, and the third to the judges. An especial officer (ὁ ἐφ' ὕδωρ) was appointed in the courts for the purpose of watching the clepsydra, and stopping it when any documents were read, whereby the speaker was interrupted. The time, and consequently the quantity of water allowed to a speaker depended upon the importance of the case; and we are informed that in a γραφὴ παραπρεσβείας the water allowed to each party amounted to eleven amphorae (Aeschin. *De Fals. Leg.* § 126), whereas in trials concerning the right of inheritance only one amphora was allowed (Demosth. c. *Macart.* p. 1052, § 8). Those actions in which the time was thus measured to the speakers are called by Pollux (viii. 113) δίκαι πρὸς ὕδωρ: others are termed δίκαι ἄνευ ὕδατος, and in these the speakers were not tied down to a certain space of time.

The clepsydra used in the courts of justice, however, was, properly speaking, not a horologium; but smaller ones, made of glass, and of the same simple structure, were undoubtedly used very early in families for the purposes of ordinary life, and for dividing the day into twelve equal parts. In these glass clepsydrae the division into twelve parts must have been visible, either on the glass globe itself, or in the basin into which the water flowed. These instruments, however, did not show the time quite correctly all the year round: first, because the water ran out of the clepsydra sometimes quicker and sometimes slower, according to the different temperature of the water (Plut. *Quaest. Nat.* 7); and secondly, because the length of the hours varied in the different seasons of the year. To remove the second of these defects the inside of the clepsydra was covered with a coat of wax during the shorter days, and when they became longer the wax was gradually taken away again (Aen. Tact. c. 22, § 10). Plato is said to have used a νυκτερινὸν ὡρολόγιον in the shape of a large clepsydra, which indicated the hours of the night, and seems to have been of a complicated structure. This instance shows that at an early period improvements were made on the old and simple clepsydra. But all these improvements were excelled by the ingenious invention of Ctesibius (q. v.), a celebrated mathematician of Alexandria (about B.C. 135). It is called ὡρολόγιον ὑδραυλικόν, and is described by Vitruvius (ix. 9). Water was made to drop upon wheels which were thereby turned. The regular movement of these wheels was communicated to a small statue, which, gradually rising, pointed with a little stick to the hours marked on a pillar which was attached to the mechanism. It indicated the hours regularly throughout the year, but still required to be often attended to and regulated. This complicated clepsydra seems never to have come into general use, and was probably found only in the houses of very wealthy persons. The sundial or gnomon, and a simpler kind of clepsydra, on the other hand, were much used down to a very late period. The twelve parts of the day were not designated by the name ὥρα until the time of the Alexandrian astronomers, and even then the old and vague divisions, described in the article DIES, were preferred in the affairs of common life. At the time of the geographer Hipparchus, however (about B.C. 150), it seems to have been very common to reckon by hours.

There is still existing, though in ruins, a horological building, which is one of the most interesting monuments at Athens. It is the structure formerly called the Tower of the Winds, but now known as the Horological Monument of Andronicus Cyrrhestes. It is expressly called *horologium* by Varro (*R. R.* iii. 5, § 17). This building is fully described by Vitruvius (i. 6, § 4), and the following illustration shows its ground-plan. For the elevation see the article ANDRONICUS.

Ground-plan of the Horological Monument of Andronicus Cyrrhestes at Athens.

The structure is octagonal, with its faces to the points of the compass. On the northeast and northwest sides are distyle Corinthian porticos, giving access to the interior; and to the south wall is affixed a sort of turret, forming three-quarters of a circle, to contain the cistern which supplied water to the clepsydra in the interior. On the summit of the building was a bronze figure of a Triton, holding a wand in his hand; and this figure turned on a pivot, so that the wand always pointed above that side of the building which faced the wind then blowing. The directions of the several faces were indicated by figures of the eight winds on the frieze of the entablature. On the plain wall below the entablature of each face, lines are still visible which, with the gnomons that stood out above them, formed a series of sundials. In the centre of the interior of the building was a clepsydra, the remains of which are still visible, and are shown on the plan, where the dark lines represent the channels for the water, which was supplied from the turret on the south, and escaped by the hole in the centre. Three other Athenian horologia are extant, one in the monument of Thrasyllus, another that of Phaedrus in the British Museum (*C. I. G.* 522), a third in the theatre of Dionysus, besides others from different parts of Greece.

The first horologium with which the Romans became acquainted was the sundial (*solarium*, or *horologium sciothericum*), and was, according to some writers, brought to Rome by Papirius Cursor twelve years before the war with Pyrrhus, and placed before the temple of Quirinus (Pliny, *H. N.* vii. § 213). Varro stated that it was brought to Rome from Catina in Sicily, at the time of the First Punic War, by the consul M. Valerius Messala, and erected on a column behind the Rostra. But this solarium, being made for a different latitude, did not show the time at Rome correctly. Ninety-nine years afterwards, the censor Q. Marcius Philippus erected by the side of the old solarium a new one, which was more carefully regulated according to the latitude of Rome. But as sundials, however perfect they might be, were useless when the sky was cloudy, P. Scipio Nasica, in his censorship, B.C. 159, established a public clepsydra, which indicated the hours both of day and night. This clepsydra was in after-times generally called *solarium* (Cic. *De N. D.* ii. 34, 87). The word *hora* for hour was introduced at Rome at the time when the Romans became acquainted with the Greek horologia, and was in this signification well known at the time of Plautus (*Pseud.* 1307). After the time of Scipio Nasica, several horologia, chiefly solaria, seem to have been erected in various public places at Rome. A magnificent horologium was erected by Augustus in the Campus Martius. It was a gnomon in the shape of an obelisk; but Pliny (*H. N.* xxxvi. § 73) complains that in the course of time it had become incorrect. Horologia of various descriptions seem also to have been commonly kept by private individuals (Cic. *Ad Fam.* xvi. 18, 3); and at the time of the emperors, the wealthy Romans used to keep slaves whose special duty it was to announce the hours of the day to their masters (Juv. x. 216, with Mayor's note; Mart. viii. 67; Petron. 26).

From the number of solaria which have been discovered in modern times in Italy (thirteen having been discovered in the neighbourhood of Rome alone), we must infer that they were very generally used among the ancients. The following illustrations represent one of the simplest horologia which have been discovered; it seems to bear great similarity to that the invention of which Vitruvius ascribes to Berosus. It was discovered in 1741, on the hill of Tusculum, and is described by Zuzzeri (Venice, 1746), and by G. H. Martini, in his *Abhandlung von den Sonnenuhren der Alten*, p. 49 (Leipzig, 1777).

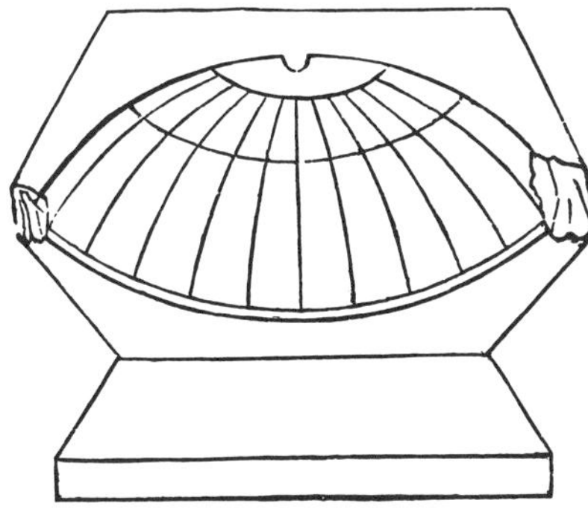

Horologium. (From Tusculum.)

The following illustration shows the same solarium as restored by Zuzzeri:

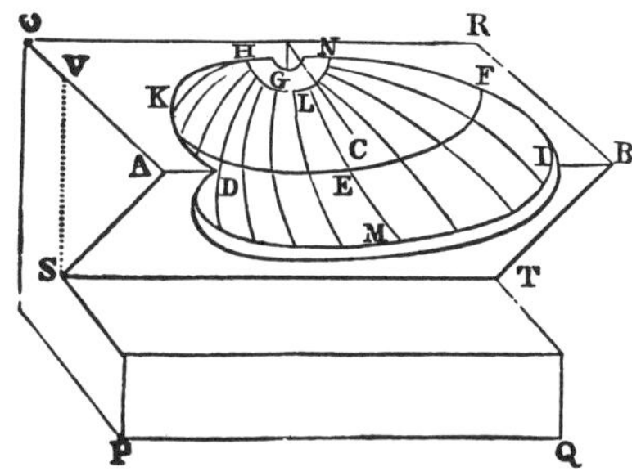

The same restored.

The breadth as well as the height (A O and P A) are somewhat more than eight inches, and the length (A B) a little more than sixteen inches. The surface (A O R B) is horizontal. S P Q T is the basis of the solarium, which, originally, was probably erected upon a pillar. Its side (A S T B) inclines somewhat towards the basis. This inclination was called ἔγκλιμα, or *inclinatio solarii* and *enclima succisum* (Vitruv. l. c.), and shows the latitude or polar altitude of the place for which the solarium was made. The angle of the enclima is about 40° 43′, which coincides with the latitude of Tusculum. In the body of the solarium is the almost spherical excavation (H K D M I F N), which forms a double hemicyclium. Within this excavation the eleven hour-lines are marked which pass through three semicircles (H L N, K E F, and D M I). The middle one (K E F) represents the equator, the two others the tropic lines of winter and summer. The curve representing the summer tropic is somewhat more than a semicircle, the other two curves somewhat smaller. The ten middle parts or hours in each of the three curves are all equal to one another; but the two extreme ones, though equal to each other, are by one-fourth smaller than the rest. In the middle (G) of the curve (D K H N I I), there is a little square hole, in which the gnomon or pointer must have been fixed, and a trace of it is still visible in the lead by means of which it was fixed. It must have stood in a perpendicular position upon the surface (A B R O), and at a certain distance from the surface it must have turned in a right angle above the spheric excavation, so that its end (C) extended as far as the middle of the equator, as it is restored in the last illustration.

Clepsydrae were used by the Romans in their camps, chiefly for the purpose of measuring accurately the four watches into which the night was divided (Caes. *B. G.* v. 13).

The custom of using clepsydrae as a check upon the speakers in the courts of justice at Rome is said to have been introduced by a law of Cn. Pompeius, in his third consulship (Tac. *De Clar. Orat.* 38), who adds, before that time the speakers had been under no restrictions, but spoke as long as they deemed proper. But there is some inaccuracy here, as Cicero in B.C. 70 (*In Verr.* i. 9, 25) speaks of his *legitimae horae;* in B.C. 63 (*Pro Rab. Perd.* 2, 6) his defence is limited to half an hour; and in B.C. 59 (*Pro Flacc.* 33, 82) six hours are allotted. At Rome, as at Athens, the time allowed to the speakers depended upon the importance of the case. Pliny (*Epist.* ii. 11) states that on one important occasion he spoke for nearly five hours, ten large clepsydrae having been granted to him by the judices, but the case was so important that four others were added. (Cf. Pliny, *Epist.* vi. 2.) The law of Pompeius only limited the time during which the accuser was allowed to speak to two hours, while the accused was allowed three hours in the case of prosecutions *de vi.* It is clear from the case of Pliny (*Epist.* iv. 9) and others that this restriction was not observed on all occasions. An especial officer was at Rome as well as at Athens appointed to stop the clepsydra during the time when documents were read (Apul. *Apolog.* i. and ii.). See Ernesti, *De Solariis*, in his *Opuscul. Philolog. et Crit.* pp. 21–31; Wöpcke, *Disquisitiones Arch. Math. Circa Solaria Veterum* (Berlin, 1842); Becker-Göll, *Gallus*, ii. pp. 407 foll.; and especially Marquardt, *Privatl.* pp. 370 foll.

Horoscŏpus. A horoscope. See ASTRONOMIA, p. 146.

Horreum (ὡρεῖον, σιτοφυλακεῖον, ἀποθήκη). (1) A granary, especially at Rome a public granary, in which grain was stored at the expense of the State for distribution to the people. (See FRUMENTARIAE LEGES.) (2) A warehouse or storehouse where anything might be deposited for safe-keeping. These were common at Rome under the Empire, and were used for the storage of securities, money, goods, etc. (*Cod.* iv. 24, 9; *Dig.* i. 15, 3). Keepers of *horrea* in either sense of the word were called *horrearii* or *vilici ex horreis*.

Horse-races. See CIRCUS; HIPPODROMUS.

Horta or **Hortānum.** Now Orte; a town in Etruria, at the junction of the Nar and the Tiber, so called from the Etruscan goddess Horta, whose temple at Rome always remained open. (Cf. Müller, *Die Etrusker*, ii. p. 62.)

Hortălus. See HORTENSIUS (2).

Hortātor (κελευστής). On board ship, the officer who gave out the chant (κέλευσμα), which was sung or played to make the rowers keep the stroke, and, as it were, encourage them at their work (Ovid, *Met.* iii. 619; cf. Verg. *Aen.* v. 177; Serv. *ad loc.*), whence the name (*solet hortator remiges hortarier*, Plaut. *Merc.* iv. 2, 5). He sat on the stern of the vessel, with a truncheon in his hand, which he used to beat the time, as represented in the above illustration.

Hortator. (From the Vatican Vergil.)

Hortensia. The daughter of the orator Hortensius (q. v.), who inherited her father's eloquence. When the members of the Second Triumvirate had imposed a heavy tax upon the Roman matrons and no one of the other sex dared to espouse their cause, Hortensia appeared as their advocate, and made so able a speech that a large portion of the burden was removed (Val. Max. viii. 3, 3). This harangue was extant in Quintilian's time, who speaks of it with praise (Quint. i. 1, 6).

Hortensius, QUINTUS. (1) A celebrated orator, who began to distinguish himself by his eloquence in the Roman Forum at the age of nineteen. He was born of a plebeian family, B.C. 114, eight years before Cicero. He served at first as a common soldier, and afterwards as military tribune, in the Social War. In the contest between Marius and Sulla he remained neutral, and was one of the twenty quaestors established by Sulla. He afterwards obtained in succession the offices of aedile, praetor, and consul. As an orator he for a long time shared the reputation of Cicero; but, as his orations are lost, we can only judge of him by the account which his rival gives of his abilities. "Nature had given him," says Cicero, in his *Brutus* (88), "so splendid a memory that he never had any need of committing to writing any discourse which he had thought over; while, after his opponent had finished speaking, he could recall, word by word, not only what the other had said, but also the authorities which had been cited against himself. His industry was indefatigable. He never let a day pass without speaking in the Forum, or preparing himself to appear on the morrow; oftentimes he did both. He excelled particularly in the art of dividing his subject, and in then reuniting it in a luminous manner, adapting, at the same time, even some of the arguments which had been urged against him. His diction was noble, elegant, and rich; his voice strong and pleasing; his gestures carefully studied." The eloquence of Hortensius would seem, in fact, to have been of the showy species called Asiatic, which flourished in the Greek colonies of Asia Minor, and was infinitely more florid and ornamental than the oratory of Athens, or even of Rhodes, being full of brilliant thoughts and sparkling expressions. This glowing style of rhetoric, though deficient in

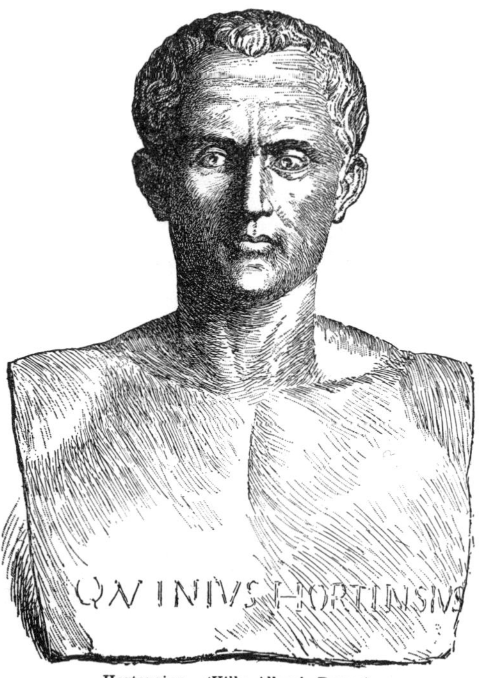

Hortensius. (Villa Albani, Rome.)

solidity and weight, was not unsuitable in a young man; and, being further recommended by a beautiful cadence of periods, met with great applause. But Hortensius, as he advanced in life, did not correct this exuberance; and his somewhat tawdry taste in phraseology, which, even in his earliest years, had occasionally excited ridicule among the senators, being now totally inconsistent with his advanced age and dignity, his reputation in consequence waned. Possibly, too, from his declining health and strength, which greatly failed in his latter years, he may not have been able to give its full effect to that showy rhetoric in which he had indulged. A constant toothache and swelling in the jaws greatly impaired his powers of elocution and utterance, and became at length so severe as to accelerate his end. A few months, however, before his death, which happened in B.C. 50, he pleaded for his nephew Messala, who was accused of illegal canvassing, and acquitted more in consequence of the exertions of his uncle than the justice of his cause. So discreditable, indeed, was the case esteemed that, though the speech of Hortensius had been much admired, he was received, on entering the theatre on the following day, with loud hisses (Cic. *Ad Fam.* viii. 2). The speech, however, revived all the admiration of the public for his oratorical talents, and convinced them that, had he possessed the same perseverance as Cicero, he would not have been inferior to that orator.

It appears from Macrobius that Hortensius was much ridiculed by his contemporaries on account of his affected gestures. In pleading, his hands were constantly in motion, whence he was often attacked by his adversaries in the Forum for resembling an actor; and on one occasion he received from his opponent the appellation of Dionysia, the name of a celebrated dancing-girl (Aul. Gell. i. 5). The actors Aesopus and Roscius frequently attended his pleadings to catch his gestures and imitate them on the stage (Val. Max. viii. 10). Such, indeed, was his exertion in action that it was commonly said that it could not be determined whether people went to hear or to see him. Like Demosthenes, he selected and put on his dress with the most studied care and neatness. He is said not only to have prearranged his gestures, but also to have adjusted the folds of his toga before a mirror when about to go to the Forum. He so arranged his gown that the folds did not fall by chance, but were formed with great care by help of a knot carefully tied and concealed by his robe, which apparently flowed carelessly around him (Macrob. *Sat.* iii. 13). Macrobius also records a story of his instituting an action of damages against a person who had jostled him while walking in this elaborate dress, and had ruffled his toga when he was about to appear in public with his drapery adjusted according to his favourite arrangement.

Hortensius stood, for thirteen years, at the head of the Roman bar; and being, in consequence, engaged during that long period on one side or other in every case of importance, he soon amassed an enormous fortune. He lived, too, with a magnificence corresponding to his wealth. His house at Rome formed the nucleus of the imperial palace, which was enlarged from the time of Augustus to that of Nero, till it nearly covered the whole Palatine Mount and branched over other hills. (See PALATIUM.) Besides his mansion in Rome, he possessed villas at Tusculum, Bauli, and Laurentum, where he was accustomed to give the most elegant and elaborate entertainments. His olive plantations he is said to have regularly moistened with wine; and, on one occasion, during the hearing of an important case in which he was engaged with Cicero, he begged the latter to change with him the previously arranged order of pleading, as he was obliged to go to the country to pour wine on a favourite plane-tree, which grew near his Tusculan villa (Macrob. *Sat.* iii. 13). Notwithstanding this profusion, his heir found no less than 10,000 casks of wine in his cellar after his death (Pliny, *H. N.* xiv. 14). Besides his taste for wine and fondness for plantations, he indulged in a passion for pictures and fish-ponds. At his Tusculan villa he built a hall for the reception of a painting of the expedition of the Argonauts, by the painter Cydias, which cost the sum of 144,000 sesterces. At his country-seat near Bauli, on the sea-shore, he vied with Lucullus and Philippus in the extent of his fish-ponds, which were constructed at an immense cost, and so formed that the tide flowed into them (Varr. *R. R.* iii. 3); yet such was his reluctance to diminish the supply that when he gave entertainments at Bauli he generally sent to the neighbouring town of Puteoli to buy the fish; and Varro declares that a friend could more easily get his chariot-mules out of his stable than a mullet from his ponds. He was more anxious about the welfare of his fish than the health of his slaves, and less solicitous that a sick servant might not take what was unfit for him than that his fish might not drink water which was unwholesome. It is even said (Pliny, *H. N.* ix. 55) that he was so passionately fond of a particular lamprey as to shed tears for its untimely death. At his Laurentan villa, Hortensius had a wooded park of fifty acres encompassed with a wall. This enclosure he called a nursery of wild beasts, all of which came for their food at a certain hour on the blowing of a horn. See Forsyth, *Hortensius* (London, 1879). (2) Son of the preceding, called also HORTĂLUS, a dissipated person who fought on Caesar's side in the Civil War. In B.C. 44, after Caesar's death, he joined Brutus and put to death C. Antonius, brother of the triumvir. After the battle of Philippi, Hortalus was himself taken and slain.

Hortus (κῆπος). A garden. Gardens among the ancients were usually of a strictly utilitarian character. Even the mythical garden of Alcinoüs, described in the *Odyssey* (vii. 112–130), is divided into a fruit-garden, a vineyard, and a kitchen-garden, with no mention of flowers; and when, in later times, flower-gardens are spoken of (e. g. κήπους εὐώδεις, Aristoph. *Aves*, 1066), they are probably gardens in which flowers were cultivated for profit. The ancients, in fact, had much less love of landscape beauties than the moderns, and some of their garden arrangements seem shocking to modern taste. Longus (*Pastoralia*, ii. 3) describes a garden in which flowers were mingled with fruits; and Plutarch says that the beauty of roses and violets is enhanced by planting them side by side with onions and leeks! The suburbs of Athens abounded in market-gardens, which supplied the city with both flowers and vegetables (Pliny, *H. N.* xxxvi. 18). Plato speaks of books on gardening (*Min.* p. 316 E).

Roman gardens are described in two letters of the Younger Pliny (ii. 17; v. 6), from which it appears that they were rather prim and formal in their plan, with regular walks (*ambulationes*) lined by closely-clipped hedges of box, yew, and cypress; and diversified with statues, pyramids, and summer-houses (*diaetae*). As in modern Italy and in France under Louis XV., so at Rome the trees and shrubs were often cut into figures of animals, ships, letters, and grotesque forms (*ars topiaria*), so that the regular name for an ornamental gardener is *topiarius*. (Cf. Pliny, *H. N.* xvi. 140; xxi. 68; xxii. 76.) The principal flowers known to the ancients were the rose, violet, crocus, narcissus, lily, iris, poppy, amaranth, and gladiolus.

Conservatories with windows closed by *specularia* (windows of talc) are mentioned by the writers of the first century A.D. (Mart. viii. 14 and 68; Sen. *Epist.* 90; Pliny, *Epist.* ii. 17). Columella speaks of forcing-houses for grapes and melons. For flowers in private houses see DOMUS.

Ornamental gardens were called *viridaria.* The regular name for a gardener is *cultor hortorum, vilicus, viridarius,* and *topiarius.*

HORTUS PENSĬLIS is a term meaning (1) a hanging (i. e. terraced) garden (see BABYLON); and (2) a frame like our frames for melons and cucumbers, and used for forcing vegetables and fruits. See Pliny, *H. N.* xix. 64.

Horus (Ὧρος, Egyptian *Har*). An Egyptian god, the son of Osiris and Isis. At the death of his father he was still a child, but when he had grown to be a stalwart youth (Harver—i. e. "stronger Horus"), he overcame and captured Typhon, the murderer of his father, after a combat lasting over many days, and handed him over to Isis, who, however, let him go free. By the Egyptians he was deemed the victorious god of light, who overcame darkness, winter, and drought, and was identified with Apollo by the Greeks. He is often represented with the head of a sparrow-hawk, which was sacred to him. He must be distinguished from a younger Horus, the Harpocrates of the Greeks (in Egyptian Harpechruti—i. e. "Har, the Child"), who was received by Isis from Osiris in the under-world, and is the representative of the winter-sun, and also the image of early vegetation, and therefore identified with Priapus (q. v.). Statues represent him as a naked boy with his finger on his mouth. Misunderstanding this symbol of childhood, the Greeks made him the god of Silence and Secrecy. Afterwards, in the time when mysteries were in vogue, his worship was widely extended among the Greeks, and also among the Romans. See Beauregard, *Les Divinités Égyptiennes* (Paris, 1866); and ISIS.

Hostia. A victim. See SACRIFICIUM.

Hostilia. Now Ostiglia; a small town in Gallia Cisalpina, on the Po, and on the road from Mutina Verona; the birthplace of Cornelius Nepos.

Hostilius, TULLUS. See TULLUS HOSTILIUS.

Hostis. See HOSPITIUM in Appendix.

Hostius. A Roman poet, perhaps a contemporary of Lucilius the satirist. He wrote a poem on the Istrian War, which took place in B.C. 178. Some fragments of this have reached our time. Hostius wrote also metrical annals, after the manner of Ennius. See Bergk, *Kl. Schr.* i. 252.

Hotels. See CAUPONA.

Hounds. See CANIS.

Hour-glass. See HOROLOGIUM.

House. See DOMUS.

House-breakers. See EFFRACTOR.

Household Gods. See LARES; PENATES.

House-rent. See DOMUS, p. 541.

Hunnĕric. King of the Vandals in Africa (A.D. 477–484), succeeding his father Genseric. His reign is memorable for his persecution of the Christians.

Hunni (Οὖννοι, Χοῦνοι). An Asiatic people who dwelt for some centuries in the plains of Tartary, and were formidable to the Chinese Empire long before they were known to the Romans. It was against them, in fact, that the famous Chinese wall was built. A portion of the nation crossed into Europe, and were allowed by Valens to settle in Thrace, A.D. 376. Under their king, Attila (A.D. 434–453), they devastated the fairest portions of the Empire; but a few years after Attila's death their power was completely destroyed by the Turks.

The Huns were probably remotely descended from the Hiung-nu, a race of Turkish ("Turanian") stock, though fable declared them to be the offspring of the Scythian witches and the unclean and infernal spirits with whom these witches consorted in the desert. They are described as being dark, stunted, and uncouth, with shrill voices. Like the Mongolians, they were a race of horseman, fighting with bone-tipped javelins and with slings and lassoes. They ate meat nearly raw, and herbs; and wore the hides of wild beasts. See De Guignes, *Histoire Générale des Huns* (1756); Neumann, *Die Völker des südlichen Russland* (2d ed. 1855); Thierry, *Histoire d'Attila* (4th ed. 1874); and Howorth, in the *Journal of the Anthropological Institute* (English) for 1872–74.

Hunting. See VENATIONES.

Hyacinthia (τὰ Ὑακίνθια). A festival, celebrated for three days in the summer of each year, at Amyclae, in honour of Apollo and his unhappy favourite Hyacynthus (q. v.). Müller gives strong reasons for supposing that the Hyacinthia was originally a festival of Demeter. Like other festivals in honour of nature, the festival of the Hyacinthia, celebrated by the Spartans at Amyclae for three days in July, down to the time of the Roman emperors, was connected with the expression of grief at the death of vegetation, of joy over the harvest, and of cheerful trust in the re-awakening of nature. On the first day, which was dedicated to silent mourning, sacrifice to the dead was offered at the grave of Hyacinthus, which was under the statue of Apollo in the temple at Amyclae. The following day was spent in public rejoicing in honour of Apollo, in which all the populace, including the slaves, took part. They went in festal procession with choruses of singing boys and girls, accompanied by harps and flutes, to the temple of Apollo, where games and competitions, sacrifices and entertainments to one another took place, and a robe, woven by the Spartan women, was offered to the god.

Hyacinthus (Ὑάκινθος). (1) Son of King Amyclas, of Amyclae in Laconia, and of Diomedes. He was beloved for his beauty by Apollo and Zephyrus. As Apollo was one day teaching the boy how to play at quoits, on the banks of the river Eurotas, the wind-god in his jealousy drove the quoit with such violence against the head of Hyacinthus that the blow killed him. From his blood Apollo caused a flower of the same name to spring up, with the exclamation of woe, AI, AI, marked upon its petals. (See AIAX.) Hyacinthus, like Adonis, is a personification of vegetation, which flourishes in the spring-time, but is scorched and killed by the glowing heat of the summer sun, which is symbolized by the quoit or discus. (2) The flower sprung from the blood of Hyacinthus, described in the older poets as dark but later as rather light; so that several flowers have been included under the name. (3) The jacinth, or perhaps the sapphire.

Hyădes (Ὑάδες). According to some, the daughters of Atlas and sisters of the Pleiades. The best accounts, however, make them to have been the nymphs of Dodona, to whom Zeus confided the nurture of Bacchus. Pherecydes gives their names as Ambrosia, Coronis, Eudora, Dioné, Aesula, and Polyxo. Hesiod, on the other hand, calls them Phaesula, Coronis, Cleea, Phaeo, and Eudora. The names generally given to the seven stars are Ambrosia, Eudora, Pedilé, Coronis, Polyxo, Phyto, and Dioné or Thyené. The Hyades went about with their divine charge, communicating his discovery to mankind, until, being chased with him into the sea by Lycurgus, Zeus, in compassion, raised them to the skies and transformed them into stars. According to the more common legend, however, the Hyades, having lost their brother Hyas, who was killed by a bear or lion, or, as Timaeus says, by an asp, were so disconsolate at his death that they pined away and died; and after death they were changed into stars (Hyg. *Fab.* 192). The stars called Hyades (Ὑάδες) derived their name from ὕειν, "to make wet," "to rain," because their setting, at both the evening and morning twilight, was for the Greeks and Romans a sure presage of wet and stormy weather, these two periods falling respectively in the latter half of April and November. Horace, with a double allusion to both fable and physical phenomena, calls the stars in question *tristes Hyadas* (*Carm.* i. 3, 14). The Roman writers sometimes call these stars by the name of Suculae, "little pigs," for which epithet Pliny assigns a singular derivation. According to this writer, the Roman farmers mistook the etymology of the Greek name Hyades, and deduced it, not from ὕειν, "to rain," but from ὗς, "a sow" (Pliny, *H. N.* xviii. 26). It is more probable, however, that Suculae was the oldest Roman name, given before the Greek appellation was known, and to be compared with our popular astronomical terms such as "the Dipper," "Charles's Wain," etc. Isidorus derives the term Suculae from *succus*, in the sense of "moisture" or "wet" (*a succo et pluviis*, Isidor. *Orig.* iii. 70), an etymology which has found its way into many later works. Some grammarians, again, sought to derive the name Hyades from the Greek Υ (upsilon), in consequence of the resemblance which the cluster of stars bears to that letter.

The Hyades, in the celestial sphere, are at the head of the Bull (ἐπὶ τοῦ βουκράνου).

Hyălos (ὕαλος). Glass. See VITRUM.

Hyampēa (Ὑάμπεια). One of the two lofty rocks which rose perpendicularly from behind Delphi, and obtained for Parnassus the epithet of δικόρυφος, or the two-headed (Eurip. *Phoen.* 234; Herod. viii. 39). The other was called Nauplea. It was from these elevated crags that culprits and sacrilegious criminals were hurled. See PARNASSUS.

Hyampŏlis (Ὑάμπολις). A town in Phocis, east of the Cephissus, near Cleonae, founded by the Hyantes. It was first destroyed by Xerxes, and afterwards rebuilt to be destroyed again in part by Philip and the Amphictyons.

Hyantes (Ὕαντες). The ancient inhabitants of Boeotia, from which country they were expelled by the Cadmeans. Part of the Hyantes emigrated to Phocis, where they founded Hyampolis and part to Aetolia. The poets use the adjective Hyantius as equivalent to Boeoticus.

Hyas (Ὕας). The son of Atlas, and father or brother of the Hyades (q. v.), and said to be the ancestor of the Hyantes (q. v.).

Hybla (Ὕβλη). Three towns in Sicily. (1) MAIOR (ἡ μεγάλη), on the southern slope of Mount Aetna and on the river Symaethus, was originally a town of the Siculi. (2) MINOR (ἡ μικρά), afterwards called Megara. (3) HERAEA, in the south of the island, on the road from Syracuse to Agrigentum. It is doubtful from which of these three places the Hyblaean honey came, so frequently mentioned by the poets.

Hybreas (Ὑβρέας). (1) A Carian, a native of Mylasa, who was well known as an orator in the time of M. Antonius, the triumvir. (2) A Cretan lyric poet, the author of a drinking-song preserved in Athenaeus and edited by Gräfenhan (Mulhausen, 1834).

Hybreōs Graphé (ὕβρεως γραφή). In Attic law, a criminal prosecution for assault or personal violence of any kind. In it any penalty might be demanded, and in extreme cases, death. The case was tried before a Heliastic court.

Hyccăra (τὰ Ὕκκαρα). A town of the Sicani on the north coast of Sicily, west of Panormus, taken by the Athenians, and its inhabitants sold as slaves, B.C. 415. Among the captives was the beautiful Timandra, the mistress of Alcibiades and the mother of Laïs. The place was said to get its name from the fish ὕκαι.

Hydarnes (Ὑδάρνης). One of the seven Persians who conspired against the Magi, B.C. 521. See PERSIA.

Hydaspes (Ὑδάσπης). The modern Jhelum; the northernmost of the five great tributaries of the Indus, which, with the Indus itself, water the great plain of northern India, which is bounded on the north by the Himalaya range, and which is now called the Punjab—i. e. five rivers. The Hydaspes falls into the Acesines (Chenâb), which itself falls into the Indus. The epithet *fabulosus*, which Horace applies to the Hydaspes, refers to the marvellous stories current among the Romans, who knew next to nothing about India. See INDIA.

Hydra. See HERACLES, p. 790.

Hydraōtes (Ὑδραώτης). A tributary to the Indus, now the Raví. Strabo and Quintus Curtius call it the Hyarotes or Hyarŏtis.

Hydraulus (ὕδραυλος). A water-organ. According to Athenaeus, it was the invention of Ctesibius of Alexandria (q. v.), who evidently took the idea of his organ from the syrinx or Pandean pipes, a musical instrument of the highest antiquity among the Greeks. His object being to employ a row of pipes of great size, and capable of emitting the most powerful as well as the softest sounds, he contrived the means of adapting keys with levers (ἀγκωνίσκοι), and with perforated sliders (πώματα) to open and shut the mouths of the pipes (γλωσσόκομα), a supply of wind being obtained, without intermission, by bellows, in which the pressure of water performed the same part which is fulfilled in the modern organ by a weight (Hero, *Spirit.* 228). On this account the instrument invented by Ctesibius was called the water-organ (ὕδραυλις, ὑδραυλικὸν ὄργανον, Heron, *Spirit.*; *hydraulica machina*, Vitruv. x. 13; *hydraulus*, Pliny, *H. N.* ix. § 24; Cic. *Tusc.* iii. 18, § 43). It is described in an epigram by the emperor Julian (Brunck, *Anal.* ii. 403 = *Anth. Pal.* ix. 365), who mentions the swift fingers of the performer, but not the water-bellows; and more clearly in the lines of Claudian (*De Manl. Theod. Cons.* 316–319). We have here the keys, the innumerable pipes of metal, the lever as large as a beam which sets the water in motion. Its pipes were partly of bronze (χαλκειὴ ἄρουρα, Julian; *seges aëna*, Claudian), and partly of reed (δόνακες, Julian). The number of its stops, and consequently of its rows of pipes, varied from one to eight, so that Tertullian (*De Anima*, 14) describes it with reason as an exceedingly complicated instrument. We are still in the dark as to the exact part played by the water, which, besides, must have rendered the instrument much less portable. As invented by Ctesibius, the organ was doubtless hydraulic: but the epigram of Julian omits all mention of the water, and probably, in later times, the mechanism was simplified and the bellows blown directly by the pedal, as in the modern harmonium.

The organ was well adapted to gratify the Roman people in the splendid entertainments provided for them by the emperors and other opulent persons. Nero was very curious about organs, both in regard to their musical effect and their mechanism (Suet. *Ner.* 41, 54). A contorniate coin of this emperor in the British Museum (see illustration) shows a small organ with a sprig of laurel on one side and a man standing on the other. The general form of the organ is also clearly exhibited in a poem by Publilius Porphyrius Optatianus, describing the instrument, and composed of verses so constructed as to show both the lower part which contained the bellows, the wind-chest which lay upon it, and over this the row of twenty-six pipes. These are represented by twenty-six lines, which increase in length each by one letter, until the last line is twice as long as the first (Wernsdorf, *Poetae Lat. Min.* vol. ii. pp. 394–413).

Organ, from a coin of Nero. (British Museum.)

There can be little doubt that ὑδραύλης, *hydraula* or *hydraules*, denotes the organist (Suet. *Ner.* 54; Petron. *Sat.* 36). See MUSICA.

Hydrĕa (Ὑδρέα). The modern Hydra; a small island in the Gulf of Hermionê, off Argolis (Herod. iii. 59; and E. Curtius, *Peloponnesos*, ii. p. 456).

Hydria (ὑδρία). (1) A vessel for holding water. (2) A balloting-urn in the Attic law-courts. (See SITELLA.) (3) A cinerary urn.

Hydriaphoria (ὑδριαφορία). "The carrying of a water-pot," a service performed by the wives of resident aliens at the Panathenaea (q. v.). See SCIADEPHORIA.

Hydromĕli (ὑδρόμελι). See VINUM.

Hydruntum or **Hydrus** (Ὑδροῦς). The modern Otranto. One of the most ancient towns of Calabria, situated on the southeast coast, near a mountain of the same name. It had a good harbour, from which persons frequently crossed over to Epirus.

Hygiēa (Ὑγίεια). In Greek mythology, the goddess of Health, daughter of Asclepius (Aesculapius), with whom she is often worshipped. In works of art she is represented by his side, as a maiden of kindly aspect, with a serpent to whom she is giving drink from a saucer. As the giver of mental health, she is sometimes confused with Athenê Hygiea (Aesch. *Eumen.* 522). By the Romans she was identified with Salus (q. v.).

Hygīnus. (1) GAIUS IULIUS. A celebrated grammarian. He is mentioned by Suetonius as a native of Spain, though some have supposed him an Alexandrian, and to have been brought to Rome after the capture of that city by Caesar. Hyginus was a freedman of Augustus Caesar, and was put by that emperor in charge of the library on the Palatine Hill. (See BIBLIOTHECA.) He also gave instruction to numerous pupils. Hyginus was intimately acquainted with Ovid and other writers of the day, and was said to be the imitator of Cornelius Alexander, a Greek grammarian. Some suppose him to have been the faithless friend of whom Ovid complains in his *Ibis*. His works, which were numerous, are frequently quoted by the ancients with great respect. The principal ones appear to have been: (*a*) *De Situ Urbium Italicarum;* (*b*) *De Troianis Familiis;* (*c*) *De Claris Viris;* (*d*) *De Proprietatibus Deorum;* (*e*) *De Diis Penatibus;* (*f*) A commentary on Vergil; (*g*) A treatise on Agriculture. These are all lost. Those which are extant, and are ascribed to Hyginus, were possibly written by another individual of the same name. These are: (*a*) *Fabularum Liber*, a collection of 277 fables, taken for the most part from Grecian sources, and embracing all the most important legends of antiquity. It is written in a very inferior style, but is still of great importance for the mythologist. Text by Schmidt (Jena, 1872), and see the paper by Wölfflin, *Zur Kritik von Hyg. Fabeln*, in the *Philologus*, x. 303. (*b*) *De Astrologia*, also called *Poetica Astronomia.* This, like the previous work, is in prose, and consists of four books, being partly astronomical and mathematical, partly mythological and philosophical in its character, since it gives the origin of the Catasterisms according to the legends of the poets. The proëm of the work is addressed to a certain Quintus Fabius. This work is written in a careless manner, but is very important for obtaining a knowledge of ancient astronomy, and for a correct understanding of the poets. Text by Bunte (Dresden, 1875), and see Robert's edition of the *Catasterismi* of Eratosthenes (Berlin, 1878). (2) A gromatic writer of whom nothing is known, but to whom are often ascribed two works—one on legal boundaries (*De Limitibus Constituendis*), and one on castrametation (*De Munitionibus Castrorum*), though they are really by two different writers, as the language shows. They are to be assigned to the third century A.D. The text is to be found in the Lachmann-Rudorff editions of the *Agrimensores* (Berlin, 1848).

Hyksos Kings. See AEGYPTUS, p. 28.

Hylaeus (Ὑλαῖος, i. e. "the Woodman"). The name of an Arcadian centaur who was slain by Atalanta when he pursued her. According to some legends, Hylaeus fell in the fight against the Lapithae, and according to others he was one of the centaurs slain by Heracles.

Hylas (Ὕλας). Son of Theodamas, king of the Dryopes, and the nymph Menodicê. He was a favourite of Heracles, whom he accompanied on the Argonautic expedition. When Heracles disembarked upon the coast of Mysia to cut himself a fresh oar, Hylas followed him to draw water from a fountain, whose nymphs drew the youth down into the water. The Argonauts having gone on their way, Heracles, with his sister's son Polyphemus, remained behind to search for him. On failing to find him, he did not leave until he had taken hostages from the Mysians, and made them promise that they would produce the boy either dead or alive. After that, the inhabitants of Cios (founded by Polyphemus and afterwards called Prusias) continually sought for Hylas, and sacrificed to him every year at the fountain, thrice calling him by name. The story of Hylas suggested a song of Thomas Moore's, and is the subject of a poem, *Hylas*, by Bayard Taylor. See Calverly's translation of the thirteenth idyl of Theocritus.

Hylé (Ὕλη) and **Hylae** (Ὗλαι). A small town in Boeotia, situated on Lake Hylicé, which was called after this town.

Hylias. A river in Bruttium, separating the territories of Sybaris and Croton.

Hylĭcé (ἡ Ὑλικὴ λίμνη). See HYLÉ.

Hylĭcus (Ὕλικος). A small river in Argolis near Troezen.

Hyllus (Ὕλλος). The son of Heracles and Deïanira, and husband of Iolé. When he and the rest of the children of Heracles, at their father's death, were pursued everywhere by the enmity of Eurystheus, they at last found succour from Theseus, or his son Demophon. When Eurystheus drew near with his army to compel the Athenians to give them up, Macaria, daughter of Heracles, freely offered herself up as a sacrifice for her brethren, who, aided by the Athenians, defeated the enemy, Eurystheus being slain as a fugitive by Hyllus himself. Having withdrawn from Attica to Thessaly, Hyllus was adopted by the Dorian prince Aegimius, whom Heracles had once assisted in the war between the Lapithae and the Dryopes, under promise of his abdication of the royal power, together with a third part of the kingdom. Thus the rule over the Dorians passed to him and his descendants. When commanded by the Delphic oracle to attempt to conquer the kingdom of Eurystheus immediately after "the third fruit," he endeavoured after the lapse of three years to invade the Peloponnesus by way of the Isthmus. He was, however, repulsed by Atreus, the successor of Eurystheus, and fell in single combat with Echemus, king of Tegea. It was in the "third generation" after him that the sons of his grandson Aristomachus — viz. Temenus, Cresphontes, and Aristodemus—at last conquered the Peloponnesus, which was then under the rule of Tisamenus, son of Orestes. See HERACLIDAE.

Hyllus (Ὕλλος). A river of Lydia, falling into the Hermus on its north side.

Hymenaeus (Ὑμέναιος) or **Hymen** (Ὑμήν). The Greek god of marriage and of the marriage-song named after him. He is sometimes described as the son of Apollo and a Muse (either Terpsichoré, Urania, or Calliopé), who had vanished on his own wedding-day, and was consequently always sought for at every wedding. He is also described as a son of the Thessalian Magnes and of the Muse Calliopé, and as beloved by Apollo and Thamyris; or as the son of Dionysus and Aphrodité, who lost his voice and life while singing the nuptial song at the marriage of Dionysus and Ariadné. According to Attic tradition, he was an Argive youth who, in the disguise of a girl, followed to the feast of Demeter at Eleusis a young Athenian maiden whom he loved without winning the consent of her parents. Hymenaeus and some of the maidens who were celebrating the festival, were carried off by pirates, whom he afterwards killed in their sleep, and henceforth became the champion of all women and damsels. In art he is represented like Eros, as a beautiful, winged youth, only with a more serious expression, and carrying in his hand the marriage torch and nuptial veil. The marriage-song called *Hymenaeus*, which is mentioned as early as Homer (*Il.* xviii. 493), was sung by young men and maidens, to the sound of flutes, during the festal procession of the bride from the house of her parents to that of the bridegroom. In character it was partly serious and partly humorous. The several parts always ended with an invocation of Hymenaeus. (See Catullus, 61 and 62, with the rendering by Sir Theodore Martin; and the article EPITHALAMIUM.) On the Roman god of weddings, see TALASSIO.

Hymettus (Ὑμηττός). A mountain in Attica, about three miles south of Athens, celebrated for its marble and its honey (Herod. vi. 137). See ATHENAE.

Hymnus (ὕμνος). In general, an invocation of the gods, especially in the form of an ode sung by a choir, to the accompaniment of the cithara, while they stood round the altar. For the so-called Homeric Hymns (to Aphrodité, Hermes, Demeter, etc.), see the article HOMERUS. For wedding hymns, see EPITHALAMIUM. For the Orphic Hymns, see ORPHEUS. Many of the Pindaric odes, written in lyric measures, are to be classed as ὕμνοι. (Cf. Aristoph. *Eq.* 530.) Famous among Greek hymns is the noble hymn to Zeus by the Stoic Cleanthes (q. v.). See MUSICA.

In Latin, examples of hymns in the older sense are the songs of the Salii (*carmina Saliaria*), sung by the priests of Mars (see SALII); the hymn of the Arval Brethren (see FRATRES ARVALES); the hymns composed by Horace (*carmen saeculare*) for the Ludi Saeculares in B.C. 17, and sung in honour of Diana and Apollo (see LUDI SAECULARES); and some of later date, like the poem called *Laus Herculis*, in 137 hexameters, by an anonymous author (see Bährens in the *Neue Jahrbücher für Philologie*, etc., 105, 52. 503); the *Hymnus Claudii ad Lunam* (*Poet. Lat. Min.*, ed. Bährens, iii. 163); and the parodic hymn to Pan (id. iii. 170).

The early Christian hymns in Greek and Latin are interesting. Of those in Greek, only a comparatively few are written in the classic metres—e. g. those by Clemens Alexandrinus (about A.D. 220), Englished by Dr. Dexter in his "Shepherd of Early Youth;" Gregory of Nanzianzus (A.D. 360), Synesius (A.D. 400), and Sophronius (A.D. 629). Others, and especially those used by the Eastern Church, are strongly Oriental in style, due to the constant study of the Jewish Psalter. No authors of Latin hymns are mentioned earlier than A.D. 325, the date of the Council of Nice. Soon after, however, two great hymnologists—St. Hilary and St. Ambrose—appear, both in the fourth century, followed by Prudentius (A.D. 350–410), whose poems in 1860 reached a sixty-third edition; Sedulius of the same period; Venantius Fortunatus (A.D. 530–609), and Gregory the Great (A.D. 540–604). Some of the most magnificent of the Latin hymns are of unknown authorship. Such are the famous *Veni, Creator Spiritus*, popularly ascribed to Charlemagne, but really of earlier date; the hymn beginning *Verbum Dei, Deo Natum;* and, above all, the sublime *Dies Irae*, the despair of translators, which is often attributed to Thomas of Celano, but on no sure authority (Mohnike, *Hymnologische Forschungen*, i. pp. 1–24).

The Latin hymns are interesting from a linguistic and metrical standpoint, as usually reverting to the older and more natural accentual system of prosody instead of preserving the artificial and unpopular distinctions of syllabic quantity. Among the common people, in their folk-songs (e. g. the songs of the soldiers in their barracks and during the triumphs, the chants, spells, and nursery songs), the accentual system still survived, and, as in the *Instructiones* of Commodianus, written in the third century A.D., the popular system sometimes made its way even into written literature. It was natural that the Christian hymns, being composed not for the learned and fastidious, but for the common people—for provincials and non-Romans—should avail themselves of the far freer range allowed by the loose laws of accent. Thus St. Augustine, even in the title of one of his psalms (*Psalmus contra Partem Donati*), shows his desire to escape from the rigid restrictions of the Augustan prosody—in other words, to write a *canticum* and not a *carmen*. In the later hymns, many metrical ingenuities are introduced, such as the so-called leonine and other rhymes (see LEONINI VERSUS), of which a good account will be found in the introduction and notes to Archbishop Trench's *Sacred Latin Poetry* (London, 1874).

For the Greek Christian hymns, see Christ and Paranika's *Anthologia Graeca Carminum Christianorum* (1871); Chatfield's *Hymns of the Eastern Greek Christian Poets* (1876)—the former giving the original text and the latter the English reading; and Petra, *Hymnographie de l'Église-Grecque* (1867); *Analecta Sacra Inedita* (Paris, 1876). On the Latin hymns, see the work of Trench already cited; Cardinal Newman's *Carmina Ecclesiae* (1876); Du Méril, *Poésies Populaires Latines* (1843); Mone, *Hymni Latini*, 3 vols. (1853–55); and Duffield (1888).

There is a dictionary of Hymnology by Julian (1888). On the versification of the Christian hymns (usually trochaic and iambic metres with a special preference for the iambic dimeter, with rhyme and frequent alliteration), see Schuch, *De Poësis Latinae Rhythmis et Rimis* (1851); Hümer, *Der iamb. Dimeter bei den christl.-lat. Hymnendichtern der vorkaroling. Zeit* (Vienna, 1876); id. *Die ältesten lat.-christl. Rhythmen* (Vienna, 1879); and the article RHYME.

Hypacȳris, Hypacăris, or **Pacăris.** A river in European Sarmatia, flowing through the country of the nomad Scythians and falling into the Sinus Carcinites in the Euxine Sea.

Hypaea. See STOECHADES INSULAE.

Hypaepa (Ὕπαιπα). A city of Lydia, on the southern slope of Mount Tmolus, near the north bank of the Caÿster.

Hypaethral Temple. A temple not covered by a roof, and in form usually decastyle. See Dörpfeld in the *Mittheilungen d. deutschen archäol. Inst. zu Athen* for 1891, pp. 334–344; and the article TEMPLUM.

Hypăna (τὰ Ὕπανα) and **Hypănê** (Ὑπάνη). A town in Elis belonging to the so-called Pentapolis.

Hypănis (Ὕπανις). The modern Bog; a river in European Sarmatia, falling into the Euxine Sea west of the Borysthenes (Herod. iv. 17, etc.).

Hypaspistae (ὑπασπισταί). The shield-bearers in the Greek army, who followed the heavy-armed warriors and carried a portion of their burdensome equipment, principally the shield, the necessary baggage, and the usual provision for three days. Among the Macedonians the light infantry were so called to distinguish them from the heavy φαλάγγιται (see HOPLITES) and the archers. They wore a round felt hat (see CAUSIA), a linen jerkin, and had a long dagger and a short hand-pike. They were a standing body of 6000 men, and in war formed the king's body-guard. See EXERCITUS.

Hypăta (τὰ Ὕπατα). A town of the Aenianes in Thessaly, south of the Spercheus, whose inhabitants were notorious for witchcraft. It is now Neopatra (Turk. Batrajik).

Hypatia (Ὑπατία). A mathematician of Alexandria, daughter of Theon, and still more celebrated than her father. She was born about the end of the fourth century. In her studies she applied herself in particular to the philosophy of Plato. Following the example of her master, she resolved to add to her information by travelling; and, having reached Athens, attended there the lectures of the ablest instructors. On her return to her native city, she was invited by the magistrates to give lectures in philosophy, and Alexandria beheld a woman succeed to that long line of illustrious teachers which had rendered its school one of the most celebrated in the world. She was an Eclectic; but the exact sciences formed the basis of all her instruction, and she applied their demonstrations to the principles of the speculative sciences. She numbered among her disciples many celebrated men, among others Synesius, afterwards bishop of Ptolemaïs, who preserved during his whole life the most friendly feelings towards her, although she constantly refused to become a convert to Christianity. Hypatia united to a masculine intellect many of the attractions and all the virtues of her sex. Her dress was remarkable for its simplicity; her conduct was always above suspicion; and she knew well how to compel the respect of those of her auditors who felt the influence of her charms. All idea of marriage was constantly rejected by her as threatening to interfere with her devotion to her favourite studies. Orestes, governor of Alexandria, admired the talents of Hypatia, and frequently had recourse to her for advice. He was desirous of repressing the too ardent zeal of St. Cyril, who saw in Hypatia one of the principal supports of paganism. The partisans of the bishop, on their side, beheld in the measures of the governor the result of the counsels of Hypatia; the most fanatical of their number, in March, A.D. 415, seized upon Hypatia as she was proceeding to her school, forced her to descend from her chariot, and dragged her into a neighbouring church, where, stripped of her vestments, she was put to death by her brutal foes. Her body was hacked to pieces with oyster-shells, and the bloody remains were dragged through the streets and finally burned.

The works of Hypatia were lost in the burning of the Alexandrian Library. In the number of these were a commentary on Diophantus, an Astronomical Canon, and a commentary on the Conics of Apollonius of Perga. The very names of her other productions are lost. The Greek Anthology contains an epigram in praise of Hypatia, attributed to Paulus Silentiarius. Canon Kingsley's historical romance (London, 1853) has done much to make her name familiar to English readers. See the exhaustive monograph on Hypatia by Hoche in the *Philologus*, xv. 435 foll. (1860).

Hypatodōrus (Ὑπατόδωρος). A Theban sculptor, who flourished about B.C. 372.

Hyperbŏlus (Ὑπέρβολος). An Athenian demagogue in the Peloponnesian War, of servile origin. In order to get rid of either Nicias or Alcibiades, Hyperbolus called for the exercise of the ostracism. But the parties endangered combined to defeat him, and the vote of exile fell on Hyperbolus himself—an application of that dignified punishment by which it was thought to have been so debased that the use of it was never recurred to. Some years afterwards he was murdered by the oligarchs at Samos, B.C. 411 (Thuc. viii. 74).

Hyperborei (Ὑπερβόρεοι, lit. "dwellers beyond the north wind"). A people of Greek legend, whose existence was denied by some of the ancients, while others endeavoured to define their position more precisely. They were said to dwell far in the North, where the sun rose and set only once a year—a fancy due, perhaps, to some dim report of the long arctic summer day. The fruits of the earth ripened quickly with them; they lived in unbroken happiness, knowing no violence or strife, and reached the age of a thousand years; any who were weary of life casting themselves from a sacred rock into the sea. The myth is connected with the worship of the god of light, Apollo, who during the dark winter was supposed to visit them, as his priestly people, in a chariot drawn by swans; returning to Delphi for the summer. There was a tradition in Delos that in earlier times they used to send to that island the first-fruits of their harvests by way of Dodona, Thessaly, and Euboea.

Hyperborei Montes. Originally the mythical name of an imaginary range of mountains in the north of the earth. It was afterwards applied by the geographers to various chains; as, for example, the Caucasus, the Rhipaei Montes, and others.

Hyperesia (Ὑπερεσίη). The more ancient name of Aegira in Achaia. Pausanias (vii. 26) relates the story which accounts for the subsequent change of name.

Hyperīa (Ὑπέρεια). A fountain of Thessaly, placed by some in the vicinity of Argos Pelasgicum, while others think that it was near Pherae.

Hyperīdes (Ὑπερείδης and Ὑπερίδης). One of the Ten Attic Orators, born about B.C. 390, son of the Athenian Glaucippus. He was a pupil of Plato and Isocrates, and won for himself an important position as a forensic and political orator, although his private life was not unblemished. As a statesman, he decidedly shared the views of Demosthenes, and was his steadfast ally in the struggle against the Macedonian party. It is true that he afterwards (B.C. 324) took part in the prosecution of Demosthenes, when accused of having taken bribes from Alexander's treasurer, Harpalus, and that he contributed to his condemnation on that charge. After the destruction of Thebes by Alexander (335) it was only with difficulty that he and Demosthenes escaped being given up to the Macedonians. After the death of Alexander (323) he was the chief instigator of the Lamian War, at the unfortunate conclusion of which he and Demosthenes (who had been reconciled to one another in the meantime) and other patriots were condemned to death by the Macedonian party. He fled for sanctuary to a temple in Aegina, but was dragged away from it by force, and by order of Antipater put to death at Corinth in 322.

Of the seventy-seven speeches which were known to antiquity as the work of Hyperides, only a few fragments were known until recent times; but in 1847, in a tomb at Thebes, in Egypt, extensive fragments were found of his speech against Demosthenes, together with a speech for Lycophron, and the whole of his oration for Euxenippus. In 1856 there was a further discovery in Egypt of an important part of the funeral oration delivered in 322 over those who had fallen in the siege of Lamia. In 1889 M. Eugène Revillout announced the purchase by the Louvre of a papyrus containing portions of the first oration of Hyperides against Athenogenes (*Revue des Études Grecques*, Jan.–March, 1889).

Though the speeches of Hyperides never attain to the force and depth of those of Demosthenes, nevertheless they were valued highly on account of the skill of their construction and the grace and charm of their expression. They are the productions of a practical pleader who is thoroughly in command of all his powers, and who is, above all, an accomplished man of the world—slightly indolent, witty, refined, with a delicious fund of irony, of perfect taste, entertaining and urbane. He is, oratorically speaking, to Demosthenes what Lord Salisbury is to Mr. Gladstone.

The text of Hyperides is edited by Blass in the Teubner series; and there is a good edition of the orations for Lycophron and Euxenippus by Babington, with fac-similes of the MSS. (Cambridge, 1853). The best account of his oratory is that of Blass in his *Attische Beredsamkeit*, iii. 2. 1–72 (1877). See, also, Hager's *Quaestiones Hyperideae* (Leipzig, 1870); Caffiaux, *Hypéride* (Valenciennes, 1860); Jebb, *The Attic Orators*, ii. pp. 381–92 (London, 1876); and Böhnecke, *Demosthenes, Lykurgos, Hyperides und ihr Zeitalter* (Berlin, 1874).

Hyperīon (Ὑπερίων). One of the Titans, father of the Sun-god Helios, who himself is also called Hyperion in Homer. See TITANES.

Hypermnestra (Ὑπερμνήστρα). (1) The only one of the daughters of Danaüs who spared her husband, Lynceus. (See DANAÜS.) (2) Daughter of Thestius and Eurythemis, wife of Oïcles, and mother of Amphiaraüs.

Hyperōōn (ὑπερῷον). The upper story of a Greek house. See DOMUS.

Hyphăsis (Ὕφασις), **Hypăsis** (Ὕπασις) or **Hypănis** (Ὕπανις). A river of India, now the Gharra, falling into the Acesines. See HYDASPES.

Hypius (Ὕπιος). A river and mountain in Bithynia.

Hypnos (Ὕπνος). The god of sleep.

Hypocaustum. See BALNEAE.

Hypocrĭtes (ὑποκριτής). An actor. See HISTRIO.

Hypodēma (ὑπόδημα). See CALCEUS.

Hypogaeum. A tomb or vault underground.

Hyponŏmus. See EMISSARIUM.

Hyporchēma (ὑπόρχημα). A species of lyric, choral song in lively rhythms; its subject was generally gay, and contained imitative dance movements. Like the paeans, these choral odes were mostly sung in honour of Apollo.

Hyposcenium. See THEATRUM.

Hypothēca. See PIGNUS.

Hypozōma (ὑπόζωμα). See NAVIS.

Hypsas (Ὕψας). A river of Sicily falling into the Crinisus.

Hypseus (Ὑψεύς). A son of Peneüs and Creüsa. He was king of the Lapithae (q. v.) and father of Cyrené.

Hypsĭcles (Ὑψικλῆς). An astronomer of Alexandria, who flourished under Ptolemy Physcon, about B.C. 146. He is considered by some to have been the author of the fourteenth book appended to Euclid's *Elements*, in which he discussed the regular solids. No one, however, disputes his claim to a small work entitled Περὶ τῆς τῶν Ζωδίων Ἀναφορᾶς, in which he gives a method, far from exact, of calculating the risings of each sign or portion of the ecliptic.

Hypsipȳlé (Ὑψιπύλη). Daughter of Thoas of Lemnos. The Lemnian women had, from jealousy of their Thracian maids, killed all the men of the island; Hypsipylé alone spared her father Thoas, having been the means of aiding his flight. When the Argonauts landed at Lemnos and united with the women, Hypsipylé bore twin sons to Iason—Euneus, who in Homer figures as king of Lemnos and carries on trade with the Greeks before Troy; and Thoas (also called Deïphilus and Nebrophonus), who is sometimes described as a son of Dionysus. When the news of her father's escape was rumoured among the Lemnian women, Hypsipylé was forced to flee for her life, and was captured by pirates, who sold her to Lycurgus of Nemea. There, as the nurse of Opheltes, the infant son of the king, she accidentally caused his death by a snake (see SEVEN AGAINST THEBES), and was exposed to the greatest danger, from which she was only rescued by the intervention of her sons, who were sent to her aid by Dionysus.

Hypsus (Ὑψοῦς). A town in Arcadia on a mountain of the same name.

Hyrcania (Ὑρκανία). A province of the ancient Persian Empire, on the south and southeast shores of the Caspian or Hyrcanian Sea, and separated by mountains on the west, south, and east from Media, Parthia, and Margiana. It flourished most under the Parthians, whose kings often resided in it during the summer.

Hyrcānum or **Hyrcanium Maré.** See CASPIUM MARÉ.

Hyrcānus (Ὑρκανός). (1) IOANNES, prince and high-priest of the Jews, was the son and successor of Simon Maccabaeus, the restorer of the independence of Iudaea. He succeeded to his father's power B.C. 135, and died in 106. Although he did not assume the title of king, he may be regarded as the founder of the monarchy of Iudaea, which continued in his family till the accession of Herod. (2) High-priest and king of the Jews, was the eldest son of Alexander Iannaeus and his wife Alexandra, and was frequently engaged in war with his brother Aristobulus, who was, however, taken to Rome as a prisoner by Pompey in B.C. 63. Hyrcanus was put to death by his successor, Herod, in B.C. 30.

Hyria (Ὑρία). (1) A town in Boeotia near Tanagra. (2) A town in Apulia. (3) A city in Calabria.

Hyrieus (Ὑριεύς). (1) An Arcadian monarch, for whom Agamedes and Trophonius constructed a treasury. The story about this treasury resembles the one told by Herodotus (ii. 121) of the treasury of the Egyptian king Rhampsinitus. In the construction of the treasury of Hyrieus, Agamedes and Trophonius contrived to place one stone in such a manner that it could be taken away outside, and thus formed an entrance to the treasury, without any one perceiving it. Agamedes and Trophonius now constantly robbed the treasury; and the king, seeing that locks and seals were uninjured while his treasures were constantly decreasing, set traps to catch the thief. Agamedes was thus ensnared, and Trophonius cut off his head to avert the discovery. After this Trophonius was immediately swallowed up by the earth. On this spot there was afterwards, in the grove of Lebadea, the cave of Agamedes with a column by the side of it. Here, also, was the oracle of Trophonius. A tradition mentioned by Cicero (*Tusc.* i. 47) states that Agamedes and Trophonius, after building the temple of Apollo at Delphi, prayed to the god to grant them in reward for their labour what was best for men. The god promised to do so on a certain day, and when the day came, the two brothers died. (2) A peasant of Hyria in Boeotia, whose name is connected with the legend of the birth of Orion. See ORION.

Hyrminé (Ὑρμίνη). The daughter of Neleus (or Nycteus), wife of Phorbas, and mother of Actor.

Hyrtăcus (Ὕρτακος). A Trojan, to whom Priam gave his own first wife Arisba on marrying Hecuba. Homer makes him the father of Asius, called Hyrtacides. In Vergil, Nisus and Hippocoön are also represented as sons of Hyrtacus.

Hysiae (Ὑσιαί). (1) A town in Argolis, south of Argos, destroyed by the Spartans in the Peloponnesian War. (2) A town in Boeotia, east of Plataeae, called by Herodotus (v. 74) a demus of Attica, but probably belonging to Plataeae.

Hystaspes (Ὑστάσπης). (1) Father of the Persian king, Darius I. He had been satrap of Persis under Cambyses. (2) The son of Darius I. and Atossa. He commanded a force of Bactrians and Sacae in the army of his brother Xerxes.

I

I, as a symbol.

In Greek.—Only as a numeral either = 9 (in the earlier system) or = 10, τὸ Ι = τὸ δέκατον (*C. I. G.* 2020); Ι = 10,000.

In Latin.—I = Ianuarius, itur, Iulius, iunior.

I·A = in agro.

I·D = invictus deus, iure dicundo.

I·E = index esto.

I·A·P = in agro pedes.

I·F·P = in fronte pedes.

I·L·H = ius liberorum habens.

I·O·C = Iupiter optimus Capitolinus.

I·Q·P = idemque probavit.

I·S·E = (h)ic situs est.

I·D·Q·C·P = iure dicundo quinquennalis censoriae potestatis.

I·E·V·Q·I·S·S = in ea verba quae infra scripta sunt.

I·O·M·C·O·D·I = Iupiter optimus maximus cetérique omnes dii immortales.

I·O·M·F·F = Iupiter optimus maximus fulminator fulgurator.

I·O·M·I·R·M·T·M = Iupiter optimus maximus Iuno regina Minerva Terra mater.

I·O·S·P·D = Iupiter optimus Sol praestantissimus dignus.

I·S·M·R = Iuno sospes magna regina.

I·T·M·F·C = idem testamento monumentum faciendum curavit.

I·V·E·E·R·P·F·S·V·E = ita utei eis e re publica fideve sua videbitur esse.

Iaccetāni. A people in Hispania Tarraconensis between the Pyrenees and the Iberus.

Iacchus (Ἴακχος). The solemn name of Bacchus in the Lesser Eleusinian Mysteries, whose name was derived from the boisterous song called Iacchus. In these mysteries Iacchus was regarded as the son of Zeus and Demeter, and was distinguished from the Theban Bacchus (Dionysus), the son of Zeus and Semelé. In some traditions Iacchus is even called a son of Bacchus, but in others the two are identified. See the chapter on "Dionysus at Athens" in Dyer's *Gods in Greece* (Lond. and N. Y. 1891); and the articles Dionysus; Eleusinia.

Iaculatōres. See Exercitus, p. 651.

Iacŭlum. A dart or javelin lighter than the *hasta* (q. v.).

Iadĕra (Ἰάδερα) or **Iader.** A town on the coast of Illyricum with a good harbour.

Ialĕmus (Ἰάλεμος). The personification of a sort of dirge, as was Linus (q. v.), and as Hymenaeus personified the marriage song. He is called a son of Apollo and Calliopé, and was the inventor of a melancholy song which bore the name of ἰάλεμος.

Ialmĕnus (Ἰάλμενος). The son of Ares and Astyoché and brother of Ascalaphus. He was one of the Argonauts and a suitor of Helen. After the destruction of Troy he wandered about with his followers, the Orchomenians, and founded colonies in Colchis.

Ialȳsus (Ἰάλυσος). One of the three ancient Dorian cities in the island of Rhodes, on the northwestern coast of the island, about sixty stadia southwest of Rhodes. It was one of the six members of the so-called Dorian Hexapolis, and was said to have derived its name from that of the hero Ialysus, grandson of Helios. See Doris.

Iambé (Ἰάμβη). A Thracian servant-maid of Metanira, wife of Celeus, king of Eleusis, who succeeded by her tricks and jests in making Demeter (q. v.) smile when the goddess was full of distress at the loss of her daughter (Apollod. i. 5, 1). She was the daughter of Pan and Echo. From Iambé, the metrical foot known as the *iambus* (⏑–) gets its name, as being light and adapted to playful themes. Such, at any rate, was the tradition, but the story of Iambé is of probably later date than the nomenclature of the verse.

Iamblĭchus (Ἰάμβλιχος). (1) A Syrian who lived in the time of the emperor Trajan. He wrote in Greek a romance called Βαβυλωνικά on the loves of Rhodané and Sinonis, which is now lost, though an epitome of it is given by Photius. (See Novels and Romances.) (2) A Neo-Platonic philosopher, a native of Chalcis in Coele-Syria. He died about A.D. 330. He was a pupil of Porphyry and a follower of Plotinus; but pushing their teachings to the point of absurdity, became a mere charlatan and impostor, seeking the reputation of a magician and wonder-worker. His writings include (i.) a life of Pythagoras (Περὶ τοῦ Πυθαγορικοῦ Βίου) in ten books, of which four parts are extant, edited by Nauck (1884); (ii.) a work on mathematics (Περὶ Κοινῆς Μαθηματικῆς Ἐπιστήμης), edited by Friès (1790); (iii.) two treatises on mystical arithmetic (Περὶ Νικομάχου Ἀριθμητικῆς Εἰσαγωγῆς and Τὰ Θεολογούμενα τῆς Ἀριθμητικῆς), the latter edited by Ast (1817); (iv.) a treatise on the Egyptian mysteries (Περὶ Μυστηρίων), and intending to prove their divine origin, edited by Parthey (1857); and (v.) a sort of introduction to the study of Plato (Προτρεπτικοὶ Λόγοι εἰς Φιλοσοφίαν), edited by Kiessling (1813). The treatise on the mysteries and those on arithmetic are possibly not the work of Iamblichus. On the *De Mysteriis*, see Harles, *Das Buch von d. ägypt. Myst.* (Munich, 1858). It has been rendered into English by Thomas Taylor with the life of Pythagoras (2d ed. Chiswick, 1821). The best account of Iamblichus will be found in Zeller, *Philosophie der Griechen*, iii. 2, pp. 613 foll. in the second edition; and in Vacherot, *Histoire Critique de l'École d'Alexandrie*, ii. pp. 57 foll. (Paris, 1851).

Iambus. See Iambé.

Iamĭdae. Certain prophets among the Greeks, descended from Iamus, a son of Apollo and Evadné, who received the gift of prophecy from his father (Pausan. vi. 2).

Iamnīa (Ἰάμνεια, Ιαμνία). In the Old Testament Jabneel, Jabneh; a considerable city of Palestine, between Diospolis and Azotus, near the coast, with a good harbour. After the destruction of Jerusalem it became the seat of the Sanhedrim and of a celebrated school of Jewish learning.

Iămus (Ἴαμος). The son of Apollo and Evadné. He received the art of prophecy from his father, and was regarded as the ancestor of the famous family of seers, the Iamidae at Olympia.

Iana. See IANUS.

Ianicŭlum. A hill of Rome, across the Tiber, and connected with the city by means of the Sublician bridge. From its sparkling sands it obtained the name of Mons Aureus, now by corruption Montorio. There was an ancient tradition that Ianus, king of the Aborigines, contemporary with Saturn, who then inhabited the Capitoline Hill, founded a city opposite to the residence of Saturn, and, dying, left his name to the hill on which he had built (Verg. *Aen.* viii. 355 foll.; Serv. *ad loc.*). Ancus Marcius joined it to the Aventine by a bridge and a wall, lest an enemy should make it a citadel for attack.

The summit of the Ianiculum was seen from the Comitia, and also from the place of popular assemblies in the Campus Martius. At the earliest period of the Republic, when the Romans were surrounded by foes, and feared lest, while they held these assemblies, the enemy might come upon them unawares, they placed some of their citizens upon the Ianiculum to guard the spot, and to watch for the safety of the state; a standard was erected upon the top of the hill, and the removal of it was a signal for the assembly immediately to dissolve, because the enemy was near (Dio Cassius, xxxvii. 28). This act afterwards became a mere formal ceremony; it was, however, made subservient to the designs of factions in later times; and the taking down of the standard on the Ianiculum more than once put a stop to public proceedings at the Comitia.

Ianthé (Ἰάνθη). (1) The daughter of Oceanus and Tethys, and one of the companions of Pemphoné. (2) See IPHIS.

Ianua (*θύρα*). A door; denoting more especially the first entrance to the house through which one entered from the street. This door was also called by the Romans *anticum*, and by the Greeks *θύρα αὔλεια*, *αὐλία*, etc. The back-door was termed *posticum*, *postica*, and *posticula;* in Greek, *παράθυρος*, dim. *παραθύριον*, and *κηπαία* (*θύρα*). The doors of the inner apartments were called *ostia*, and in Greek *μέσαυλοι* or *μέταυλοι*, etc. A secret door was styled *pseudothyrum* (*ψευδόθυρον*).

The complete doorway consisted of the four indispensable parts—threshold (*limen*, *βηλός*, *οὐδὸς ὀδός*), lintel (*iugumentum*, *limen superum*), and jambs (*postes*, *σταθμοί*). Vitruvius speaks of the jambs as *antepagmenta*. For the hinges, see CARDO. The door itself was called *foris*, *valva*, and in Greek *σανίς*, *κλισίας*, *θύρετρον*. It was regularly bivalve or double, and hence spoken of in the plural.

The threshold was an object of reverence, and it was thought unlucky to tread on it with the left foot. On this account the steps leading into a temple were of an uneven number, because the worshipper, after placing his right foot on the bottom step, would then place the same foot on the threshold also (Vitruv. iii. 4). The doors of Greek houses regularly opened inward, and of Roman houses always so, with the single exception of the house of M. Valerius Publicola (Pliny, *H. N.* xxxvi. § 112), who was exempted from the usual rule as a special honour.

As early as Homer we find mention of a contrivance for bolting or unbolting a door from the outside, which consisted in a leathern thong (*ἱμάς*) inserted through a hole in the door, and by means of a loop, ring, or hook (*κλείς*, *κληΐς*), which was the origin of keys, capable of laying hold of the bolt so as to move it in the manner required (*Odyss.* i. 442; iv. 802). The bolt by the progress of improvement was transformed into a lock, and the keys found at Herculaneum and Pompeii and those attached to rings prove that among the Greeks and Romans the art of the locksmith (*κλειδοποιός*) approached very nearly to its present state. See CLAVIS.

Temple Door. (Roman bas-relief.)

By night the front door of the house was further secured by means of a wooden and sometimes an iron bar (*sera*, *repagula*, *μοχλός*) placed across it, and inserted into sockets, on each side of the doorway. Hence it was necessary to remove the bar in order to open the door (*reserare*). Even chamber doors were secured in the same manner (Heliodor. vi. 9); and here also, in case of need, the bar was employed as a further security in addition to the two bolts (Eurip. *Orest.* 1551, 1571; *Iph. Aul.* 345; *Androm.* 951). Where, as in the case of tyrants, midnight assassination was especially dreaded, we read of a bedchamber secured with a portcullis (Plut. *Arat.* 26). To fasten the door with the bolt was *ianuae pessulum obdere*, with the bar, *ianuam obserare*. At Athens a jealous husband sometimes even sealed the door of the women's apartment (Aristoph. *Thesm.* 427; Menand. *Incert.* 1, 11). The door of a bedchamber was occasionally covered with a curtain (*velum*). See DOMUS.

Ianual. The sacrifice offered to Ianus (q. v.) and consisting of barley, incense, and wine (Paul. *ex* Fest. p. 104, Müller).

Ianus and **Iana.** Two ancient Latin divinities, who were worshipped as the sun and moon. The names Ianus and Iana were thought to be other forms of Dianus and Diana (Varro, *R. R.* i. 37, 3; Macrob. i. 9), which words contain the same root as *dies*, day. The ancients, however, also connected the words with *ianua*, a door, which itself contains the root of *ire*, "to go." Ianus occupied an important place in the Roman religion. He presided over the beginning of everything, and was therefore always invoked first in every undertaking, even before Iupiter. He opened the year and the seasons, and hence the first month of the year was called after him (*mensis Iani*, Ovid, *Fasti*, ii. 51). He was the porter of heaven, and therefore bore the surnames Patulcus or Patulcius (*pateo*), "the opener," and Clusius or Clusivius (*cludo*), "the shutter" (Ovid, *Fasti*, 130). On earth, also, he was the guardian deity of gates, and hence is commonly represented with two heads, because every door looks two ways (*Ianus bifrons*). He is sometimes represented with four heads (*Ianus quadrifrons*), because he presided over the four seasons. At Rome, Numa is said to have dedicated to Ianus the covered passage bearing his name, which is commonly, but erroneously, called a temple. It stood close by the Forum. A temple to Ianus was built by Duilius, to take the place of this passage; and was restored by Augustus. It appears to have been left open in war to indicate symbolically that the god had gone out to assist the Roman warriors, and to have been shut in time of peace that the god, the safeguard of the city, might not escape. The gates of Ianus were closed only three times from Numa to Augustus, and twice by Augustus. On New-year's day, which was the principal festival of the god, people gave presents to one another, consisting of sweetmeats and copper coins, showing on one side the double head of Ianus (see illustration under BIFRONS) and on the other a ship. The general name for these presents was *strenae*, the modern French *étrennes*.

Temple of Ianus. (Coin of Nero.)

The connection of Ianus with the year was indicated by representing him with three fingers of his right hand bent so as to suggest the numeral CCC (300), while the fingers of the left hand were spread for the numerals L+V (55), and in later times L+V+V+V (65), for the 355 days of the old Roman year and 365 of the Julian year (Pliny, *H. N.* xxxiv. 7).

Ianus. An arch, as distinct from *ianua*, a door or gate.

Iapetĭdae. See IAPETUS.

Iapĕtus (Ἰαπετός). A son of Uranus and Gaea, and one of the Titans. According to the *Theogony* (v. 507 foll.), he married Clymenē, a daughter of Oceanus, by whom he became the father of four sons, Atlas, Menoetius, Prometheus, and Epimetheus. Some authorities made him to have married Aethra, others Asia, others again Libya: the last two refer to the abodes of Prometheus and Atlas. He was thrown into Tartarus for rebelling against Zeus. (See Hom. *Il.* viii. 479, and the article TITANES.) The Greeks regarded him as the ancestor of the human race. (See PROMETHEUS.) His descendants are often designated as Iapetidae and Iapetionidae.

Iāpis. The son of Iasus. He was loved by Apollo, who taught him the healing art and prophecy. Iapis cured Aeneas of a wound received by him in his war with Latinus (Verg. *Aen.* xii. 391).

Iapȳdes (Ἰάπυδες and Ἰάποδες). A warlike and barbarous people in the north of Illyricum, between the rivers Arsia and Tedanius. They were a mixed race, partly Illyrian and partly Celtic, who tattooed their bodies. They were subdued by Augustus. Their country was called IAPYDIA.

Iapygia (Ἰαπυγία). A division of Italy, forming what is called the heel. It was called also Messapia, and contained two nations, the Calabri on the northeast, and the Salentini on the southwest side. The name of Iapygia was not known to the Romans, except as an appellation borrowed from the Greeks, to whom it was familiar. Among the many traditions current with the latter people may be reckoned their derivation of this name from Iapyx, the son of Daedalus (Pliny, *H. N.* iii. 11). This story, however, belongs rather to fable than to history. There is no positive evidence regarding the origin of the Iapyges, but their existence on these shores prior to the arrival of any Grecian colony is recognized by the earliest writers of that nation, such as Herodotus (vii. 170) and Hellanicus of Lesbos (*ap.* Dion. Hal. i. 22). Thucydides evidently considered them as barbarians (vii. 33), as did also Scylax, in his *Periplus*, and Pausanias (x. 1). It may be noticed that the name of the Iapyges appears on one of the Eugubine Tables under the form *Iapuscom*, which might lead one to suppose that some connection once existed between this people and the Umbri. See TABULAE IGUVINAE; and for further observations, the articles ITALIA; MESSAPIA.

Iapygium, or **Salentīnum, Promontorium.** A famous promontory of Italy, at the southern extremity of Iapygia, now Capo di Leuca. When the art of navigation was yet in its infancy, this great headland presented a conspicuous landmark to mariners bound from the ports of Greece to Sicily, of which they always availed themselves (Thuc. vi. 44). It formed, with the opposite Cape of Lacinium, the entrance to the Tarentine Gulf.

Iapȳgum Tria Promontoria. Three capes on the coast of Magna Graecia, to the south of the Lacinian promontory. They are now called Capo delle Castello, Capo Rizzuto, and Capo della Nave.

Iāpyx (Ἰάπυξ). (1) Son of Lycaon and brother of Daunius and Peucetius, who went as leaders of a colony to Italy. According to others, he was a Cretan and a son of Daedalus. (2) The west-northwest wind blowing off the coast of Iapygia (Apulia), in the south of Italy, and consequently favourable to persons crossing over to Greece. It was called by the Greeks ἀργέστης.

Iarbas, also **Hiarbas.** A son of Iupiter and the Libyan nymph Garamantis. He was king of Gaetulia, and a suitor of Dido, queen of Carthage. See DIDO.

Iardănes (Ἰαρδάνης). King of Lydia, and father of Omphalē, who is hence called Iardanis (Apollod. ii. 6, § 3).

Iardănes (Ἰαρδάνης) or **Iardănus** Ἰάρδανος). (1) A river in Elis. (2) A river in the north of Crete, which flowed near the town Cydonia.

Iasĭdes. A patronymic given to Palinurus, as descended from a person of the name of Iasius (Verg. *Aen.* v. 843).

Iasion or **Iasius** (Ἰασίων or Ἰάσιος). (1) Son of Zeus and Electra, beloved by Demeter, who, in a thrice-ploughed field (τρίπολος), became by him the mother of Pluto or Plutus in Crete. He was slain by Zeus with a thunderbolt. From Iasion came the patronymic Iasides, a name given to Palinurus, as a descendant of Atlas.

Ĭăsis. A name given to Atalanta (q. v.), daughter of Iasus.

Iāso (Ἰασώ, from ἰάομαι, "to heal"). A personification of recovery from illness, and called the daughter of Aesculapius and sister of Hygiea.

Iason (Ἰάσων). (1) Son of Aeson and Polymedé or Alcimedé. He was the celebrated leader of the Argonauts. His father, Aeson, who reigned at Iolcus in Thessaly, was deprived of the kingdom by his half-brother Pelias, who attempted to take the life of the infant Iason. He was saved by his friends, and intrusted to the care of the centaur Chiron. When he had grown up he came to Iolcus, and demanded the kingdom, which Pelias promised to surrender to him, provided he brought the golden fleece, which was in the possession of King Aeëtes in Colchis, and was guarded by an ever-watchful dragon. Iason willingly undertook the enterprise, and set sail in the ship Argo, accompanied by the chief heroes of Greece. He obtained the fleece with the assistance of Medea, whom he made his wife, and along with whom he returned to Iolcus. The history of his exploits on this enterprise is related elsewhere. (See ARGONAUTAE.) In order to avenge the death of his father, who had been slain by Pelias during his absence, Medea, at the instigation of Iason, persuaded the daughters of Pelias to cut their father to pieces and boil him, in order to restore him to youth and vigour, as she had before changed a ram into a lamb, by boiling the ram in a caldron. Pelias thus perished miserably; and his son Acastus expelled Iason and Medea from Iolcus. They then went to Corinth, where they lived happily for several years, until Iason deserted Medea, in order to marry Glaucé (or Creüsa), daughter of Creon, the king of the country. Medea fearfully revenged this insult. She sent Glaucé a poisoned garment, which burned her to death when she put it on. Creon likewise perished in the flames. Medea also killed her children by Iason, and then fled to Athens in a chariot drawn by winged dragons. (See MEDEA.) The death of Iason is related variously. According to some, he made away with himself from grief; according to others, he was crushed by the poop of the ship Argo, which fell upon him as he was lying under it. (2) Tyrant of Pherae, elected Tagus or military chief of Thessaly, B.C. 374. He possessed great power, and aspired to the sovereignty of Greece, but was assassinated in 370. He was a man of much ability and culture, and was the friend of Isocrates and admirer of Gorgias.

Iasonium Promontorium. A promontory of Pontus, northeast of Polemonium. It was so called from the ship Argo having anchored in its vicinity (Xen. *Anab.* vi. 2. 1).

Iassĭcus Sinus (Ἰασικὸς κόλπος). A gulf of Caria, deriving its name from the city of Iassus, situated at its head (Thuc. viii. 26).

Iassus (Ἴασσος and Ἴασος). A city of Asia Minor, situated on a small island near the coast of Caria, and giving to the adjacent bay the name of Sinus Iassicus. It was a rich and flourishing city, and the inhabitants were chiefly occupied with fisheries along the adjacent coasts (Livy, xxxii. 33; xxxvii. 17).

Ĭăsus (Ἴασος). The father of Atalanta (q. v.).

Iatralipta and **Iatraliptes** (ἰατραλείπτης). A physician who used a system which combined the use of unguents and friction (massage) with dieting and gymnastic exercise (Celsus, i. 1). See MEDICINA; MEDICUS.

Iatraliptĭcé (ἰατραλειπτική). Iatraliptic practice. See IATRALIPTA.

Iātros (ἰατρός). A physician. See MEDICUS.

Iatrosophista (ἰατροσοφιστής). A professor of medicine. See MEDICINA.

Iavolēnus Priscus. A Roman jurist born about A.D. 79. He was one of the council of Antoninus Pius and a man of much ability. As a jurist he belonged to the Sabinian school. His opinions are cited more than two hundred times in the *Digest.* The younger Pliny gives some personal anecdotes of him (*Epist.* vi. 15).

Iaxartes (Ἰαξάρτης). The modern Syr Daria, or Sihûn; a great river of Central Asia, flowing northwest into the Sea of Aral; the ancients supposed it to fall into the north side of the Caspian, not distinguishing between the two seas. It divided Sogdiana from Scythia. On its banks dwelt a Scythian tribe called Iaxartae.

Iazȳges (Ἰαζύγες). A powerful Sarmatian people, who originally dwelt on the coast of the Pontus Euxinus and the Palus Maeotis, but in the reign of Claudius settled near the Quadi in Dacia, in the country bounded by the Danube, the Theiss, and the Sarmatian mountains. In the fifth century A.D., they were conquered by the Goths.

Ibēri. A powerful nation of Spain, dwelling along the Iberus, and who, mingling with Keltic tribes, took the name of Celtiberi. See HISPANIA.

Iberia (Ἰβηρία). (1) A country of Asia, bounded on the west by Colchis, on the north by Mount Caucasus, on the east by Albania, and on the south by Armenia. It answers now to Georgia, the country of the Gurians, etc. The Cyrus (Kûr) flowed through Iberia. Ptolemy enumerates several towns of this country, such as Agiuna, Vasaeda, Varica, etc. The Iberians were allies of Mithridates, and were therefore attacked by Pompey, who defeated them in a great battle, and took many prisoners. Plutarch makes the number of slain to have been not less than 9000, and that of the prisoners 10,000. (2) One of the ancient names of Spain, derived from the river Iberus. See HISPANIA.

Ibērus (Ἴβηρος and Ἴβηρ). The modern Ebro; the principal river in the northeastern part of Spain, rising among the mountains of the Cantabri, and falling into the Mediterranean near Dertosa (Tortosa), after forming a delta. See HISPANIA.

Ibis. (1) A bird worshipped by the Egyptians, and called by them *Hab* or *Hib.* It was supposed from the colour of its feathers to symbolize the light and shade of the moon; and to be the avatar of the god Thoth (Hermes). It appeared at the time of the rise and departed at the inundation of the Nile, and was supposed to deliver Egypt from the serpents which came from Arabia. Its purity was celebrated, and its flesh was regarded as incorruptible. Ibises were kept in temples, and after death were mummied after the fashion of human mummies, wrapped in linen bandages. See

Herodotus, ii. 65, 67, 75, 76; Wilkinson, *Manners and Customs of the Ancient Egyptians* (1847); and Renouf, *Hibbert Lectures* (1880). (2) A poem by Ovid, written in exile, and denouncing some unnamed person at Rome who had sought to injure the poet's interests. It is in elegiac verse, and is an imitation of a similar poem of Callimachus. There is a separate edition by Robinson Ellis (Oxford, 1881). See OVIDIUS.

Ibȳcus (Ἴβυκος). A Greek lyric and erotic poet of Rhegium in Lower Italy, who flourished about B.C. 530. Like Anacreon, he led a roving life, and spent much of his time at the court of Polycrates of Samos. According to his epitaph, he died in his native town; but according to the legend made familiar by Schiller's poem, he was slain on a journey to Corinth, and his murderers were discovered by means of a flock of cranes, which, as he died, he had invoked as his avengers. The story goes that, after his murder, when the Corinthians were gathered in the theatre, the cranes appeared; whereupon one of the assassins who was present cried out, "See the avengers of Ibycus!" thus giving a clue to their detection. Hence arose the expression used of the cranes, Ἰβύκου γέρανοι. His poems, which were collected into seven books, survive in scanty fragments only. They dealt partly with mythological themes in the metres of Stesichorus and partly with love-songs in the spirit of Aeolic lyric poetry, full of glowing passion and sensibility. It was mainly to the latter that he owed his fame. The fragments are given in Schneidewin's *Delectus Poesis Graecorum Elegiacae* (1833), and Bergk's *Poetae Lyrici Graeci* (vol. ii.). See Holsten, *De Stesichori et Ibyci Dialecto et Copia Verborum* (1884).

Icaria (Ἰκαρία). (1) An island of the Aegean, near Samos, west from Ampelos, the western promontory of the latter. Mythology derived the name of this island from Icarus (q. v.), son of Daedalus, whose body was washed upon its shores after the unfortunate termination of his flight. The modern name is Nicaria. (2) Also ICARIUS (Ἰκάριος). A deme of Attica belonging to the tribe Aegeïs. Here Dionysus is said to have taught Icarius the cultivation of the vine.

Icăris and **Icariōtis**. Names given to Penelopé, as daughter of Icarius.

Icarium Maré. A part of the Aegean Sea, near the islands of Myconus and Gyarus. The ancient mythologists derive the name from Icarus (q. v.), who fell into it and was drowned. See, however, the article ICARIA.

Icarius (Ἰκάριος). (1) An Athenian, father of Erigoné. Having been taught by Dionysus the culture of the vine, he gave some of the juice of the grape to certain shepherds, who, thinking themselves poisoned, killed him. When they came to their senses they buried him; and his daughter Erigoné, being shown the spot by his faithful dog Maera, hanged herself through grief (Apollod. iii. 14, 7; Hyg. *Fab.* 130). Icarius was fabled to have been changed after death into the constellation Boötes, Erigoné into Virgo, while Maera became the star Procyon. (See AEORA; ERIGONÉ.) (2) A son of Oebalus of Lacedaemon. He gave his daughter Penelopé in marriage to Odysseus, king of Ithaca, but he was so tenderly attached to her that he wished her husband to settle at Lacedaemon. Odysseus refused; and when he saw the earnest petitions of Icarius, he told Penelopé, as they were going to embark, that she might choose freely either to follow him to Ithaca or to remain with her father. Penelopé blushed in silence, and covered her head with her veil. Icarius, upon this, permitted his daughter to go to Ithaca, and immediately erected a temple to the goddess of modesty, on the spot where Penelopé had covered her blushes with her veil.

Icărus (Ἴκαρος). (1) A son of Daedalus (q. v.). (2) See ICARIA.

Icĕlus. A dream-god (Ovid, *Met.* xi. 640).

Icēni. A powerful people in Britain, dwelling north of the Trinobantes, in the modern countries of Suffolk and Norfolk. Their revolt from the Romans, under their heroic queen, Boadicea, is celebrated in history. (See BOADICEA.) Their chief town was Venta Icenorum (Caister), about three miles from Norwich. Ptolemy calls them SIMĔNI (Σιμενοί).

Ichnae (Ἴχναι) and **Ischnae** (Ἴσχναι). A town of Macedonia, placed by Herodotus in Bottiaea, and situated probably at the mouth of the Ludias (Herod. vii. 123). From other authors, cited by Stephanus, it appears that the name was sometimes written Achne. (2) A city of Thessaly, near Phyllus, and in the district of Phthiotis. The goddess Themis was especially revered here.

Ichnographia (ἰχνογραφία). A ground-plan or map used by architects, surveyors, etc. (Vitruv. i. 2, 2). A good example of Roman chartography is the plan of Rome engraved on marble and originally part of the temple of Romulus and Remus. Fragments of it are still preserved in the Capitol.

Ichnūsa (Ἰχνοῦσα). An ancient name of Sardinia, which it is said to have received from its likeness to a human foot (*ἴχνος = vestigium*) (Pausan. x. 17). It was also called Sandaliotis, from its resemblance to a sandal (*σανδάλιον*). See SARDINIA.

Ichthyocentauri (ἰχθυοκένταυροι). See TRITON.

Ichthyophăgi (Ἰχθυοφάγοι, "fish-eaters"). A vaguely descriptive name given by the ancients to various peoples on the coasts of Asia and Africa, of whom they knew but little. Thus we find Ichthyophagi (1) in the extreme southeast of Asia, in the country of the Sinae; (2) on the coast of Gedrosia; (3) on the northeastern coast of Arabia Felix; (4) in Africa, on the coast of the Red Sea, above Egypt; (5) on the western coast of Africa.

Ichthyophagōrum Sinus. A bay on the northeastern coast of Arabia Felix.

Icilius. The name of a celebrated Roman family, the most distinguished members of which were (1) SPURIUS ICILIUS, one of the three plebeian envoys who treated with the Senate at the time of the secession to the Sacred Mount (B.C. 494); and (2) LUCIUS ICILIUS, tribune of the plebs, B.C. 456 and 455. He was one of the chief leaders in the revolt against the Decemviri, B.C. 449, Virginia having been betrothed to him. See VIRGINIA.

Iconium (Ἰκόνιον). The modern Koniyeh; the capital of Lycaonia, in Asia Minor, and when visited by St. Paul a flourishing city. During the Middle Ages it was of great importance in the history of the Crusades.

Ictīnus (Ἰκτῖνος). One of the most famous architects of Greece; he flourished in the second half of the fifth century B.C., and was a contemporary of Pericles and Phidias. His most famous works were the Parthenon on the Acropolis at Athens, and the temple of Apollo at Bassae, near Phigalia in Arcadia. Of both these edifices important remains are in existence. Most of the columns of the temple at Bassae are still standing. In the judgment of the ancients, it was the most beautiful temple in the Peloponnesus, after the temple of Athené at Tegea, which was the work of Scopas (Pausan. viii. 41, § 8). See PARTHENON.

Ida (Ἴδη, Dor. Ἴδα). (1) Now Ida or Kas-Dagh; a mountain range of Mysia, in Asia Minor, which formed the southern boundary of the Troad; extending from Lectum Promontorium in the south-western corner of the Troad, eastwards along the northern side of the Gulf of Adramyttium, and further east into the centre of Mysia. Its highest summits were Cotylus on the north and Gargara on the south; the latter is about 5700 feet high, and is often capped with snow. Lower down, the slopes of the mountain are well wooded; and lower still, they form fertile fields and valleys. The sources of the Scamander, the Simoïs, and the Granicus, besides other rivers and numerous brooks, are on Ida. The mountain is celebrated in mythology, as the scene of the rape of Ganymedes, whom Ovid (*Fasti*, ii. 145) calls *Idaeus puer*, and of the judgment of Paris, who is called *Idaeus iudex* by Ovid (*Fasti*, vi. 44), and *Idaeus pastor* by Cicero (*Ad Att.* i. 18). In Homer, too, its summit is the place from which the gods watch the battles in the plain of Troy. Ida was also an ancient seat of the worship of Cybelé, who obtained from it the name of *Idaea Mater.* (2) Now Psilorati; a mountain in the centre of Crete, belonging to the mountain range which runs through the whole length of the island. Mount Ida is 8055 feet above the level of the sea. It was closely connected with the worship of Zeus, who is fabled to have been reared in a cave in this mountain. See CURETES; ZEUS.

Idaea Mater. See IDA; RHEA.

Idaei Dactÿli (Ἰδαῖοι Δάκτυλοι). See DACTYLI.

Idalium (Ἰδάλιον). A town in Cyprus, sacred to Aphrodité, who hence bore the surname Idalia.

Idas (Ἴδας) and **Lynceus** (Λυγκεύς). The sons of Aphareus of Messenia and of Arené; two brothers as heroic and inseparable as their cousins Castor and Pollux (Polydeuces). The nymph Marpessa, daughter of the Acarnanian river-god Euenus, was wooed by Apollo, when Idas carried her off in a winged chariot given him by Poseidon. When Apollo overtook the fugitives in Messenia, Idas, who was then the strongest of living men (Hom. *Il.* ix. 556), stretched his bow against Apollo. Zeus interposed and gave the girl her choice of suitors; she decided in favour of the mortal, as she feared that Apollo would desert her. After that the god detested her; and both she and her beautiful daughter Cleopatra or Alcyoné, wife of Meléager, and also their daughter, all died young, and brought misfortune on those that loved them. Idas and Lynceus, who could see even into the heart of the earth, joined in the Calydonian hunt and the Argonautic expedition. They met their deaths fighting Castor and Pollux, with whom they had been brought up. As they were all returning from a raid into Arcadia, Idas was appointed to divide the cattle they had captured; he divided an ox into four portions and decided that whosoever devoured his portion first was to have the first half of the spoil, and he who finished his next, the second half. He finished his own and his brother's share first, and then drove the cattle away. The Dioscuri were enraged and hid themselves from the brothers in a hollow oak-tree; but the keen sight of Lynceus detected their lurking-place, and Idas stabbed Castor in the tree. Thereupon Pollux pierced Lynceus through, while Idas was slain by the lightning of Zeus. For another account of the origin of the quarrel, see DIOSCURI.

Idistavīsus Campus. A plain in Germany near the Weser, probably in the neighbourhood of the modern Minden, memorable for the victory of Germanicus over the Cherusci, A.D. 16.

Idmon (Ἴδμων). The son of Apollo and of Asterié, daughter of Coronus; a seer who took part in the Argonautic expedition, although he foresaw that it would lead to his own death. He was killed by a wild boar in the land of the Mariandyni, in Bithynia, and was worshipped as a hero by the inhabitants of the town of Heraclea in Pontus, which was built around his grave by command of Apollo (Apollon. Rhod. i. 139).

Idomĕneus (Ἰδομενεύς). (1) The son of Deucalion of Crete, and grandson of Minos. Being one of Helen's suitors, he and Meriones, the son of his half-brother, went with eighty ships to Troy, where he appears in Homer as among the bravest of heroes. He is described by Homer (*Od.* iii. 191) as one of those who safely returned to his native land. According to a later story, he was caught in a storm on his way home, and vowed to Poseidon that, if he returned in safety, he would sacrifice to the god whatever he should first meet on his landing. His son came out to meet him, and was accordingly sacrificed; a plague thereupon broke out, he was banished by the Cretans, and betook himself to Calabria. He afterwards withdrew to Colophon in Asia, where he is said to have been buried. His tomb, however, was shown by the Cretans at Cnosus, where he and Meriones were worshipped as heroes. (2) An Epicurean philosopher of Lampsacus, who flourished about B.C. 260. He wrote several historical and philosophical works that are now lost.

Idothea (Εἰδόθεα). A daughter of Proetus, king of Argos. She was cured of insanity, together with her sisters, by Melampus (q. v.).

Idrieus (Ἰδριεύς) and **Hidrieus** (Ἱδριεύς). A king of Caria, brother of Mausolus (q. v.), who ascended the throne on the death of his brother's widow Artemisia. His own widow, Ada, was allowed by Alexander the Great to retain the government of Caria.

Idubĕda. A range of mountains in Spain, commencing among the Cantabri, and extending nearly in a southeastern direction through Spain until it terminates on the Mediterranean coast, near Saguntum.

Idumaea (Ἰδουμαία). The Greek form of the Scriptural name EDOM. In the Old Testament, Edom is the district of Mount Seir, that is, the mountainous region extending from the Dead Sea to the eastern head of the Red Sea. The decline of the kingdom of Iudaea enabled the Edomites to extend their power over the southern part of Iudaea as far as Hebron, while their original territory was taken possession of by the Nabathaean Arabs. Thus the Idumaea of the later Jewish and of the Roman history is the southern part of Iudaea, and a small portion of the north of Arabia Petraea, extending from the Mediterranean to the west side of Mount Seir. Antipater, the father of Herod the Great, was an Idumaean. The Roman writers of the Augustan and of later ages use Idumaea and Iudaea as equivalent terms. Both the old Edomites and the later Idumaeans were a commercial people, and carried on a great part of the traffic between the East and the shores of the Mediterranean.

Idus. A word said to be derived from the Etruscan. The thirteenth (in March, May, July, and October the fifteenth) day of the Roman month. It was sacred to Iupiter. See CALENDARIUM.

Idȳia (Ἰδυῖα). Wife of the Colchian king Aeëtes, and mother of Medea (q. v.). See Hes. *Theog.* 352.

Idyllium (εἰδύλλιον, diminutive of εἶδος, "form," "a small picture"). A poetic sketch of character, especially, though not necessarily, in connection with pastoral life. For the chief ancient writers of idylls, see AUSONIUS; BION; CALPURNIUS; CLAUDIANUS; EPICHARMUS; MOSCHUS; THEOCRITUS; VERGILIUS; and the article BUCOLICA.

Ientacŭlum (ἀκράτισμα). Breakfast. See CENA.

Ierĭcho (Ἱεριχώ) or **Hierĭchus** (Ἱεριχοῦς). A city of the Canaanites, in a plain on the west side of the Jordan, near its mouth, destroyed by Joshua, but afterwards rebuilt.

Iernē (Ἰέρνη). See HIBERNIA.

Iĕtae (Ἰεταί). A town in the interior of Sicily, on a mountain of the same name, southwest of Macella.

Igilgĭlis (Ἰγιλγιλί). A town of Mauretania Caesariensis, west of the mouth of the river Ampsagas, and north of Cirta (Amm. Marcell. xxix. 5).

Igilium. The modern Giglio; a small island off the Etruscan coast, opposite Cosa.

Ignatius (Ἰγνάτιος). A martyr who suffered at Rome during the third persecution of the Christians. He was a Syrian by birth, and an immediate disciple of St. John the Evangelist, who, in A.D. 67, committed the church at Antioch to his pastoral superintendence, as successor to Euodius. Over this bishopric he presided for upwards of forty years, when the emperor Trajan, after his triumph over the Dacians, entering the city, exercised many severities towards those who professed the Christian faith, and summoned the prelate himself before him, on which occasion Ignatius conducted himself with such boldness in the imperial presence that he was sent to Rome, and ordered to be exposed in the amphitheatre to the fury of wild beasts. This dreadful death he underwent (October 17) with great fortitude, having availed himself of the interval between his sentence and its execution to strengthen, by his exhortations, the faith of the Roman converts. After his decease, which took place A.D. 107, or, according to some accounts, A.D. 116, his remains were carried to Antioch for interment.

It is reported that Ignatius was one of the little children whom Jesus took up in his arms and blessed, whence he was called Theophorus or "God-borne"; and it is certain that he conversed familiarly with the Apostles, and was perfectly acquainted with their doctrine. Of his works there remain seven genuine epistles, on the various forms of which see Zahn, *Ignatios von Antiochien* (1873), and Bishop Lightfoot, *The Apostolic Fathers*, pt. ii. 2d ed. (1889).

Igniaria (πυρεῖα). Fire-sticks. One of the earliest methods of producing fire was by the friction of two specially prepared sticks—a method which Lucretius (v. 199) supposes the primitive peoples to have learned from the ignition of forest trees by friction. (Cf. Thuc. ii. 77; Pliny, *H. N.* xvi. 208). It was the means prescribed by Roman usage for relighting the vestal fire when by any oversight it became extinguished. In Greece, the sacred flame was rekindled from the sun's rays by the use of burning-glasses (Plut. *Numa*, 9). Seneca (*Nat. Quaest.* ii. 22) speaks of producing fire from flints, and also from *igniaria*. These last were (1) a block of soft wood with a hollow in it, and called ἐσχάρα, and (2) a bit of hard wood (τρύπανον). The τρύπανον was whirled around in the hollow of the former. The sparks produced by this friction were caught in a sort of tinder made of dried grass and shavings. Instead of this primitive tinder the ancients also used bits of wood smeared with sulphur (*ramenta sulpurata*), such as were common in modern times until the invention of lucifer matches in the present century. With these, the sparks produced from the *igniaria* or from the flints were caught; and these more quickly and surely ignited than the ordinary tinder, saving both time and breath. See Seneca, *Nat. Quaest.* i. 1, 8; Mart. x. 3; Juv. xiii. 145; Stat. *Silv.* i. 6, 73; Pliny, *H. N.* xxxvi. 138; Blümner, *Technologie*, ii. 353, and iv. 407; Tylor, *Early Hist. of Mankind*, p. 237 (1865); and Dr. M. H. Morgan in the *Harvard Studies in Classical Philology*, vol. i. (1890).

Ignobĭles. See NOBILES.

Ignominia. See INFAMIA.

Iguvīnae Tabŭlae. See TABULAE IGUVINAE.

Iguvium. Now Gubbio or Eugubio, a town in Umbria on the southern slope of the Apennines. Here were found the famous Eugubine Tables (*Tabulae Iguvinae*), which form so important a factor in our knowledge of the Umbrian dialects, and of which an account is given in the article TABULAE IGUVINAE. See also UMBRIA.

Ilaïra (Ἰλάειρα). The daughter of Leucippus and Philodicé and sister of Phoebé. She and her sister, who are called by the poets Leucippidae, were carried off by the Dioscuri. Ilaïra became the wife of Castor.

Ilarches (ἰλάρχης). See ILÉ.

Ilba or **Ilva.** The modern Elba. An island of the Tyrrhenian Sea, off the coast of Etruria, and about ten miles from the promontory of Populonium. It was early celebrated for its rich iron mines; but by whom they were first discovered and worked is uncertain, as they are said to exhibit the marks of labour carried on for an incalculable time (Pliny, *H. N.* xxxiv. 14).

Ilé (ἴλη or εἴλη, "a troop"). (1) The Spartan term for a company of boys of the same age, who were brought up together. (See EDUCATION.) (2) In the organization of the Macedonian army, a squadron of cavalry, generally 200 strong, under the command of an *ilarches*. See HIPPEIS.

Ilerda. A town of the Ilergetes in Hispania

Tarraconensis, situated on a height above the river Sicoris (Segre), which was here crossed by a stone bridge. It was here that Afranius and Petreius, the legates of Pompey, were defeated by Caesar (B.C. 49). Its modern name is Lerida.

Ileracŏnes (Ἰλερκάονες). A people of Hispania Tarraconensis on the western coast. Their chief town was Dertosa.

Ilergētes (Ἰλέργητες). A people in Hispania Tarraconensis, between the Iberus and the Pyrenees.

Ilia. Daughter of Numitor. According to the legend, Romulus and Remus were her sons by Mars. See RHEA SILVIA; ROMULUS.

Iliad (Ἰλιάς). See HOMERUS; TROJAN WAR.

Iliad, THE LATIN. See SILIUS ITALICUS.

Ilienses. An ancient people of Sardinia.

Iliŏna (Ἰλιόνη). Daughter of Priam and Hecuba, wife of Polymnestor or Polymestor, king of the Thracian Chersonesus, to whom she bore a son, Deïpylus. As to her connection with Polydorus, see POLYDORUS.

Iliŏneus (Ἰλιονεύς). A son of Niobé, whom Apollo would have liked to save, because he was praying; but the arrow was no longer under the control of the god (Ovid, *Met.* vi. 261). See NIOBÉ.

Ilios (Ἴλιος). The scene of the *Iliad* is laid before the walls of Ilios or Troy, described by the poet as a populous and warlike city, mistress of the Troad, or northwest promontory of Asia Minor, and ruled by King Priam. In the Greek myths Ilios was founded by Ilus, son of Tros and great-grandson of Dardanus. In the reign of Laomedon, son of Ilus, the city was fortified with huge walls by Poseidon and Apollo; but as Laomedon refused to pay the price agreed upon for this service, he incurred the hostility of his mighty assistants. Laomedon was succeeded by his son Podarces, or Priam, who became a great monarch, with fifty sons, including Hector and Paris, and twelve daughters. Paris, by the help of Aphrodité, carried off Helen, wife of Menelaüs, king of Sparta; and to avenge this insult an army of Achaeans besieged the city for ten years, and finally captured and destroyed it. For a fuller account of the mythical history of Troy, see DARDANUS; ILUS; LAOMEDON; PARIS; TROJAN WAR.

It is impossible to determine how much, if any, of historical truth is contained in these legends, and particularly in the Homeric account of the Trojan War. But recent excavations have done much to show that the siege of Troy was not all a myth. Where the ancient city stood, or where the poet conceived that it stood, has been the subject of endless discussion. A brief history of this controversy will be the best introduction to an account of the present state of the question.

Long after the assumed date of the fall of Troy, but before the Persian wars, the Greek town of (Novum) Ilium was founded at the low mound of Hissarlik (pl. i.), nearly four miles from the Hellespont at Sigēum and about three miles from the nearest point on the coast. Its inhabitants asserted that the city of Priam had never been completely destroyed and that their own town was the immediate successor of Homeric Ilios. This claim seems to have been generally allowed. Hellanīcus expressly approved it, and Herodotus describes, without dissent, the visit of Xerxes to the spot, to which he was drawn by its legendary fame. The Spartan admiral Mindarus, during the Peloponnesian War, and Alexander the Great, almost a century later, each offered sacrifice to the Ilian Athené, in recognition of the ancient glory of the town. But in the second century B.C. Demetrius of Scepsis advanced the theory that Homeric Troy could not have stood on the site of (Novum) Ilium. His chief reasons were: (1) that the plain between Ilium and the sea was an alluvial deposit, and must have been far too small, in the days of Homer, for the mighty combats described in the *Iliad;* (2) the flight of Hector from Achilles three times around the walls of the city could not have taken place at the site of Ilium, for the mound on which the latter stands (the modern Hissarlik) was not an isolated hill, but a spur from Mount Ida, so that at one point the runners would have had to ascend a considerable incline. Demetrius would look for ancient Ilios apparently at a site now called Hanaï-tepeh, opposite Bunárbashi (pl. i.). In these opinions he was followed by Strabo, our chief authority for the geography of the Troad; and most modern scholars, until recent years, including such men as Welcker, Kiepert, Von Moltke, E. Curtius, and Jebb, have agreed with them. It has been the accepted belief that it was impossible to separate truth from fiction in the *Iliad*, and that we must not therefore hope to find anywhere a site exactly corresponding to the poet's description. According to this modern view, the ancient capital of the Troad was situated on a high hill called Bali Dagh, much farther inland than Hissarlik, and this mountain fortress was transformed, by the poet's imaginaton, into a great city—the capital of a mighty empire. George Grote almost alone, with his usual perspicacity, maintained that there was "every reason for presuming that the Ilium visited by Xerxes and Alexander was the holy Ilium present to the mind of Homer;" and the excavations of the last two decades have rendered it quite certain that he was right in his adherence to the general opinion of antiquity.

But before giving an account of these excavations, it may be well to glance at some of the circumstances which seem to favor the Hissarlik site. Its distance from the coast is such as to agree with the Homeric conception of the rapid ebb and flow of the tide of battle between the ships and the city walls, and the frequent and speedy journeys of messengers, and king Priam himself. The situation on the level plain, but with the low mound of from fifty to sixty-five feet in height for the citadel, is more favourable for a great and wealthy city than the almost inaccessible steep of Bali Dagh; while the latter is too far from the coast (over ten miles) to meet the conditions mentioned above. Professor Virchow has shown that the river Scamander (Menderé), which now discharges near Cape Sigēum, must formerly have followed the course of the present Kalifatli-Asmak, farther north, thus bringing it between the city and the ships, and providing for its union with the Simois (Dumbrek-su); and so removing all objection to the Hissarlik site on this score. The view of Demetrius, that the plain is an alluvial deposit (see above), is clearly founded on Herodotus ii. 11, where it is stated that the plain was originally a bay. But Herodotus manifestly did not think that the plain lay under water in the Trojan period, for he could not, in that case, have believed in the identity of Troy and Ilium, as his recital of the visit of Xerxes would seem to indicate that he did. The statement, if true, must refer to some remote period of antiquity, for Scylax (*Peripl.* 94) makes the distance of Ilium from the sea almost precisely the same as the distance from Hissarlik to-day, showing that the alluvial deposit has not materially extended the plain in the last 2000 years, at least. The objection to the Hissarlik site, based upon the flight of Hector around the walls, amounts to nothing, since this whole story is manifestly a poetic exaggeration, like the battle of Achilles with the Scamander; and we need not expect to find the exact spot where such fictitious and impossible occurrences took place. But if importance is attached to this point, it may be added that recent excavations prove that this ridge was originally about forty feet lower than at present, as it was gradually raised by the clearing away of debris from the citadel mound. At its former insignificant height it might easily have been surmounted by the two stout warriors. It may be added that the ruins on the Bali Dagh consist of nothing more than the remains of a small circuit wall, indicating that we have to do with an unimportant mountain fortress, which may have commanded the Scamander gorge—a fortress which could never have been described as a great and populous city "on the plain" (*Iliad*, xx. 217).

It would thus appear that on topographical grounds alone the question, though a difficult one, might fairly be decided in favour of the Hissarlik site. It remains to show how recent discoveries have converted this probability into a practical certainty. In 1870 Dr. Heinrich Schliemann (q. v.), a retired German merchant and enthusiastic archæologist, began his excavations at Hissarlik. These excavations were continued, with various interruptions, until his death in 1890. During their progress, the scholarly world, incredulous at first, gradually came more and more to the belief that the Homeric Ilios had actually been found. After 1882 Schliemann had the coöperation of Dr. W. Dörpfeld, afterwards secretary of the German Archæological Institute at Athens, whose adhesion added much to the weight of authority in favour of Schliemann's views. The remains which have been unearthed were found in no less than seven different layers, of which the uppermost contained what could be positively identified as ruins of the Hellenistic and Roman city of Ilium. The four layers below this contained nothing but traces of small and mean buildings of a village character. It was in the two lowest layers that the most interesting discoveries were made. The lowest settlement of all was built upon the solid rock, and the remains consisted of fortification walls eight feet thick, built of rough limestone (pl. ii. fa, fb, fc), with house walls (f f f), two to three feet in thickness, of small stones cemented with clay. Utensils were found, very rarely of metal, but usually of stone, with vases of black baked clay. The potter's wheel was apparently known to the inhabitants of this settlement, but was not so often employed as later. The debris of this first city, which Schliemann decided to be pre-Homeric, is about eight feet in depth. Above this was a layer of earth nearly two feet in thickness, showing a long period of desertion, and over this the great layer of debris, in which were found the remains of the second city, now generally believed to be Homeric Ilios.

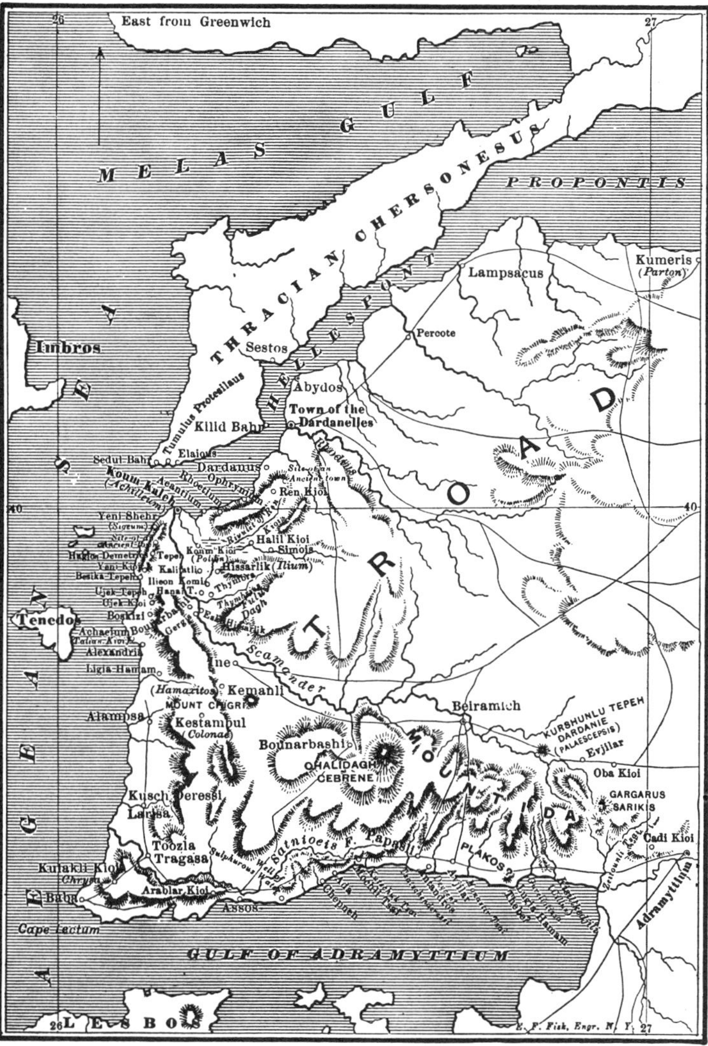

Map of the Troad.

Here the great citadel walls (c, b) were discovered. These consisted of a stone substructure 13 feet wide at the top, which is level, the depth varying according to the irregularities of the surface below. On this was built a wall of brick, from 11 to 13 feet in thickness, and rising originally, as well as can be estimated, to a height of 13 feet. These bricks are sun-dried, and measure 18×9×3½ inches. In the walls were found long, hollow channels, one foot square, which Dr. Dörpfeld first considered to have been made for the purpose of conducting heat to bake the bricks after the wall had been built. But this theory has now been abandoned, and it is generally believed that the marks of heat about these channels were caused, at the time of the destruction of the city, by the burning of beams which had been imbedded in the walls to give them stronger cohesion. These circuit walls seem to have formed an equilateral of about 165 feet on each side, with projecting bastions at the corners. The walls are pierced by several gates, of which the central one on the south side is the oldest (NF). This consists of a tower 130 feet long by 59 feet broad, and projecting 59 feet beyond the wall. Through this tower the road to the citadel passed, and by means of the projecting wing was protected all the way from the foot of the acropolis hill. The side walls of this passage were buttressed with thick wooden braces, which were probably connected at the top, thus forming a continuous flat roof over the whole gateway. Such a roofed gate we may suppose the poet to have had in mind in *Iliad*, iii. 145, when he describes the elders as sitting "on the Scaean gates." The other two gates (FM, OX) cannot be described for lack of space.

In the centre of the citadel lies the building, which is generally considered to be the palace. The ruins consist of a gateway (C), opening upon the courtyard, beyond which stand the chief apartments of the palace, the megaron or men's apartment on the left (A) and the women's apartments on the right (B). The megaron is 66 feet in depth, with an entrance hall 37 feet square in front of it, and in its centre are slight remains of a large round hearth, which thus occupied the central point of the whole palace, as described in the *Iliad* and *Odyssey* (*Od.* xiv. 158).

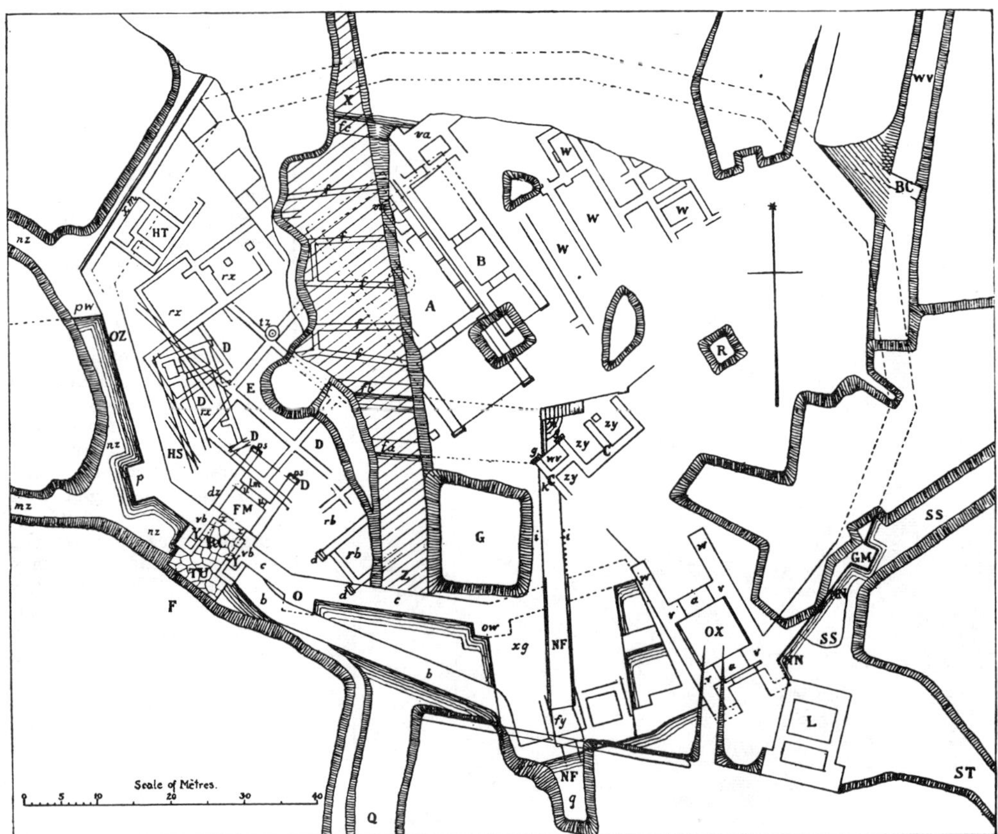

Plan of the Acropolis of the Second Ilios. (Schuchhardt.)

The women's apartment is considerably smaller, consisting of a series of three rooms 15 feet wide and 20, 24, and 29 feet long respectively.

But besides these remains of walls and buildings, numerous articles of gold and silver were found by Dr. Schliemann, showing conclusively that the ruins were those of a prosperous and wealthy city. In May, 1873, the so-called "great treasure" was found buried within the fortification wall, near the southwestern gate (F). This consisted of a great variety of articles, packed into one another in the form of a rectangular mass, apparently placed originally in a wooden chest, and stored for safe keeping in a hollow in the wall.

The most valuable were two large diadems of gold, formed of a number of small pendant chains of beautiful workmanship. Gold earrings were found in large numbers, as well as cups, vases, bracelets, and other ornaments of gold or silver, with spear-heads, battle-axes, and knife blades, and numerous other articles of various kinds.

Space will not allow a description of the remains found in the five upper layers, which are not materially different from those of the same period elsewhere. But in general it may be said that these excavations show that the hill of Hissarlik was inhabited, without serious interruption, from the late Graeco-Roman period back to a time before the dawn of history. At a date so early that we cannot estimate it even approximately the hill was covered with fortifications and palaces. Captain E. Bötticher, to be sure, has attempted to prove that the so-called citadel is nothing but a huge fire-necropolis, and even went so far as to accuse Schliemann of ill faith in describing what he found. But a conference of scholars, which met at Hissarlik in March, 1890, at Schliemann's invitation, decided: (1) that the site was well suited for a fortress; (2) that traces of fortifications of different epochs can be seen there; (3) that the "corridors" of Bötticher did not exist; (4) that the hill did not consist of a series of artificial terraces, each smaller than the one below. On the contrary each layer occupies more space than the one below it (showing the gradual extension by the accumulation of debris); (5) that the ruins in the second layer resemble those at Tiryns and Mycenae; (6) that the numerous upright jars which were found contained grain and not human bones; (7) that no traces were found of the burning of corpses. This decision overthrew the theory of Bötticher (who was indeed compelled to withdraw his accusation of bad faith), and went far to satisfy scholars that Schliemann's discoveries have actually revealed the site of Homeric Ilios.

BIBLIOGRAPHY.—Grote's *History of Greece*, pt. i. ch. xv.; Le Chevalier, *Voyage de la Troad* (Paris, 1802); Schliemann's *Troy* (1875), *Ilios* (1880), *Troja* (1884); Forchhammer, *Erklärung der Ilias auf Grund der Eigenthümlichkeiten der troischen Ebene* (Kiel, 1884); Bötticher, *La Troie de Schliemann une Nécropole à Incinération;* Le Museon (Louvain), viii. i. pp. 101–131; N. 2, pp. 226–246; Schuchhardt, *Schliemann's Investigations*, translated by Eugénie Sellers (London and New York, 1891); Georges Perrot, *Les Fouilles de Schliemann à Troie, Journal des Savants* (Paris, June, August, October, December, 1891).

Ilĭpa. A town in Hispania Baetica, on the right bank of the Baetis, which was navigable to this place with small vessels.

Ilissus (Ἰλισσός and Εἰλισσός). A small river in Attica, rising on the north slope of Mount Hymettus, flowing through the east side of Athens, and losing itself in the marshes, in the Athenian plain. See ATHENAE.

Ilithyia (Εἰλείθυια). The goddess of the Greeks who aided women in childbirth when she was propitious to them, but protracted the labour-pains if she was displeased. In the *Iliad* the Ilithyiae (in the plural) are called the daughters of Heré; but in the *Odyssey* and in later poets there is only one goddess of this name. In an ancient hymn she is called the mother of Eros. See IUNO.

Ilium. See ILIOS.

Illibĕris (Ἰλλιβερίς). (1) The modern Tech, called TICHIS or TECHUM by the Romans, a river in Gallia Narbonensis in the territory of the Sardones, rising in the Pyrenees and falling, after a short course, into the Mare Gallicum. (2) A town of the Santones, on the above-mentioned river, at the foot of the Pyrenees. Constantine changed its name into HELĒNA, whence the modern Elne.

Illĭcis. A city of the Contestani in Spain, northeast of Carthago Nova (Mela, ii. 6).

Illicitānus Sinus. A bay on the southeast coast of Spain, extending from Carthago Nova to the Dianium Promontorium. It is now the Bay of Alicante (Mela, ii. 6).

Illiturgis, Ilitŭrgis, or **Ilīturgi.** A city of Spain, not far from Castulo and Mentesa, and five days' march from Carthago Nova. It was situated near the Baetis, on a steep and rugged rock, and was called in Roman times Forum Iulium. The place was destroyed by Scipio B.C. 210 (Livy, xxviii. 19), but was soon afterwards repeopled. It is now Andujar.

Illustres. A name given by Diocletian and Constantine to magistrates and officials belonging to the first of the three classes into which they were divided, the other two being *Spectabiles* and *Clarissimi.* Among the Illustres were the consuls, *patricii*, *praefectus praetorio*, *praefectus urbi*, *praepositus sacri cubiculi*, the *magister officiorum*, and some of the *comites*. See Walter, *Geschichte des röm. Rechts*, § 380, 2d ed.

Illyrĭcum or **Illȳris,** more rarely **Illyria** (τὸ Ἰλλυρικόν, Ἰλλυρίς, Ἰλλυρία), included, in its widest signification, all the land west of Macedonia and east of Italy and Rhaetia, extending south as far as Epirus, and north as far as the valleys of the Savus and Dravus, and the junction of these rivers with the Danube. This wide extent of country was inhabited by numerous Illyrian tribes, all of whom were more or less barbarous. They were probably of the same origin as the Thracians. (See INDO-EUROPEAN LANGUAGES.) The country was divided into two parts. (1) ILLYRIS BARBĂRA or ROMĀNA, the Roman province of ILLYRĬCUM, extended along the Adriatic sea from Italy (Istria), from which it was separated by the Arsia, to the river Drilo, and was bounded on the east by Macedonia and Moesia Superior, from which it was separated by the Drinus, and on the north by Pannonia, from which it was separated by the Dravus. It thus comprehended a part of the modern Croatia, the whole of Dalmatia, almost the whole of Bosnia, and a part of Albania. It was divided in ancient times into three districts, according to the tribes by which it was inhabited—Iapydia, the interior of the country on the north, from the Arsia to the Tedanius; Liburnia, along the coast from the Arsia to the Titius; and Dalmatia, south of Liburnia, along the coast from the Titius to the Drilo. The Liburnians submitted at an early time to the Romans; but it was not till after the conquest of the Dalmatians, in the reign of Augustus, that the entire country was organized as a Roman province. From this time the Illyrians, and especially the Dalmatians, formed an important part of the Roman legion. (2) ILLȲRIS GRAECA, or ILLYRIA PROPRIA, also called EPĪRUS NOVA, extended from the Drilo, along the Adriatic, to the Ceraunian Mountains, which separated it from Epirus proper; it was bounded on the east by Macedonia. It thus embraced the greater part of the modern Albania.

It was a mountainous country, but possessed some fertile land on the coast. Its principal rivers were the Aoüs, Apsus, Genusus, and Panyasus. In the interior was an important lake, the Lychnitis. On the coast there were the Greek colonies of Epidamnus, afterwards Dyrrhachium, and Apollonia. It was at these places that the celebrated Via Egnatia commenced, which ran through Macedonia to Byzantium. The country was inhabited by various tribes—Atintanes, Taulantii, Parthini, Dassaretae, etc. In early times they were troublesome and dangerous neighbours to the Macedonian kings. They were subdued by Philip, the father of Alexander the Great, who defeated and slew in battle their king, Bardylis, in B.C. 359. After the death of Alexander the Great, most of the Illyrian tribes recovered their independence. At a later time the injury which the Roman trade suffered from their piracies brought against them the arms of the Republic. The forces of their queen, Teuta, were easily defeated by the Romans, and she was obliged to purchase peace by the surrender of part of her dominions and the payment of an annual tribute (B.C. 229). The second Illyrian war was finished by the Romans with the same ease. It was commenced by Demetrius of Pharos, who was guardian of Pineus, the son of Agron, but he was conquered by the consul Aemilius Paulus in 219. Pineus was succeeded by Pleuratus, who cultivated friendly relations with the Romans. His son Gentius formed an alliance with Perseus, king of Macedonia, against Rome; but he was conquered by the praetor L. Anicius, in the same year as Perseus (168); whereupon Illyria, as well as Macedonia, became subject to Rome. See Bahr, *Illyrien* (Leipzig, 1876).

In the new division of the Empire under Constantine, Illyricum formed one of the great provinces. It was divided into ILLYRICUM OCCIDENTALÉ, which included Illyricum Propria, Pannonia, and Noricum, and ILLYRICUM ORIENTALÉ, which comprehended Dacia, Moesia, Macedonia, and Thrace.

Ilus (Ἶλος). The son of Tros, and great-grandson of Dardanus, brother of Assaracus and Ganymede, and father of Laomedon. He once went from his native town of Dardania upon Mount Ida to Phrygia, where he was victorious in an athletic contest held by the king of the country. Besides fifty youths and fifty maidens, the prize of the contest, the king gave him, at the command of an oracle, a spotted cow, and directed him to found a city on the spot where she lay. He accordingly founded on the hill of the Phrygian Até, the town which after him was called Ilios, and also Troy (Troia) after his father. When he demanded a sign of Zeus, on the following morning he found the statue known as the Palladium (q. v.) before his tent.

Ilva. See ILBA.

Ilvātes. A people in Liguria, south of the Po, in the modern Montferrat.

Imachăra (Ἱμιχάρα). A town in Sicily, in the Heraean mountains.

Imagĭnes. The Roman portrait-masks of deceased members of a family; they were made of wax and painted, and probably fastened to the busts. They were kept in small wooden shrines let into the inner walls of the *atrium*. Inscriptions under the shrines recorded the names, merits, and exploits of the persons they referred to. The images were arranged and connected with one another by means of coloured lines, in such a way as to exhibit the pedigree (*stemma*) of the family. On festal days the shrines were opened, and the busts crowned with bay-leaves. These portrait-masks must have been originally used for covering the faces of the dead, like the light metal masks of Phœnicia, Carthage, and Mycenae. (See PERSONA.) At family funerals, there were persons specially appointed to walk in procession before the body, wearing the masks of the deceased members of the family, and clothed in the *insignia* of the rank which they had held when alive. The right (*ius imaginum*) of having these ancestral images carried in procession was one of the privileges of the nobility, and distinguished the *nobilis* from the *novus homo*. If a person died not being in the possession of full civic rights, his image could not be exhibited, as in the case of Brutus and Cassius (Polyb. vi. 53; Pliny, *H. N.* xxxv. 2, §§ 6, 7; Tac. *Ann.* iii. 76; Mommsen, *Hist. of Rome*, book iii. chap. xiii.).

Imagĭnes. See VARRO, M. TERENTIUS.

Imagĭnum Ius. See IMAGINES.

Imăus (τὸ Ἴμαον ὄρος). The name of a great mountain range of Asia; one of those terms which the ancient geographers appear to have used indefinitely for want of exact knowledge. In its most definite application, it appears to mean the western part of the Himalaya, between the Paropamisus and the Emodi Montes; but when it is applied to some great chain, extending much farther to the north and dividing Scythia into two parts—Scythia intra Imaum and Scythia extra Imaum—it must either be understood to mean the Altai Mountains, or else some imaginary range, which cannot be identified with any actually existing mountains.

Imbrăsus (Ἴμβρασος). A river in the island of Samos.

Imbrĭces. See TEGULA.

Imbros (Ἴμβρος). An island in the north of the Aegaean Sea, near the Thracian Chersonesus, about twenty-five miles in circumference. Like the neighbouring island of Samothrace, it was one of the chief seats of the worship of the Cabeiri. See CABEIRIA.

Immissarium. A basin, trough, or other contrivance built upon the ground, of stone or brick, and intended as a cistern to contain a body of wa-

Immissarium. (Pompeii.)

ter flowing from the reservoir (*castellum*) of an aqueduct, for the accommodation of the adjacent neighbourhood (Vitruv. viii. 6, 1). It differs from *cisterna*, which was underground, and is shown by the preceding illustration. The high vaulted building is the reservoir, from which the water flowed through the small dark aperture at its bottom into the square stone trough (*immissarium*) on the level of the pavement. See AQUAEDUCTUS.

"Immortals" (οἱ ἀθάνατοι). A body of 10,000 picked troops in the Persian army. They were equipped with great magnificence, and all vacancies in their ranks were filled by successors previously appointed (Herod. vii. 83).

Impeachment. See EISANGELIA.

Impedimenta (τὰ σκεύη). The baggage of an army (Caes. *B. G.* i. 26). The word often includes also the pack-animals and the wagons (Caes. *B. G.* vii. 45). See EXERCITUS.

Impedīti. Troops who marched with all their arms, provisions, and personal baggage (*sarcina*), as Roman soldiers usually did (Caes. *B. G.* i. 12). See EXERCITUS; EXPEDITI.

Imperatīvae Feriae. See FERIAE.

Imperātor. A Roman title, originally the designation of each separate possessor of an independent command (*imperium*). In the course of time

Augustus. (Glyptothek, Munich.)

it became customary to assume the title after a man had gained his first great victory, usually after having been greeted as imperator either by the soldiers on the battlefield, or by the decree of the Senate. Under the Empire the title, which was seldom conferred by Augustus, was granted for the last time by Tiberius, A.D. 22. It was usually followed by a triumph, and ceased when the triumph was over. As a permanent title, it was first assumed by Caesar, whose adopted son and heir, Octavian (Augustus), bore it as an inherited cognomen, and from the year B.C. 40 onwards, according to a custom that arose at that time, substituted it for his previous praenomen Gaius, instead of Caesar Imperator (Mommsen, *Staatsr.* ii.[3] pp. 767–770). His immediate successors, Tiberius, Caligula, and Claudius abstained from using this praenomen; Nero used it frequently, but it first became permanent with Vespasian. The emperors also took the title Imperator, in its earlier signification, after a victory won by themselves or on their behalf. See IMPERIUM.

Imperium. The full kingly power among the Romans, the royal authority over all members of the State. It was conferred on the newly-elected king by the Comitia Curiata, a formal assembly of the patricians comprising the *curiae*, and it consisted of the rights of levying the citizens for military service, of leading the army, of celebrating a triumph, of exercising civil and criminal jurisdiction, and of inflicting punishment on the citizens, whether corporal or capital, or such as affected either their property or their liberty. A symbol of this authority was the axe and the bundle of rods borne by the lictors. See FASCES.

At the establishment of the Republic the imperium was transferred to the two consuls, as the successors of the kings; but the full power of the imperium was then limited by the fact that both possessed the same power, and that, in the penalties they inflicted in times of peace, they were subject to the right of appeal (see PROVOCATIO), and to the intervention of the tribunes of the people, after the institution of that office. When the consulship was deprived of its civil jurisdiction and the praetorship instituted for this purpose, the praetors also received the imperium; nevertheless it was more limited (*minus*) than that of the consuls, who, in contrast with the praetors and all other magistrates except the tribunes, had the right of ordering and forbidding. The imperium in its undivided and unlimited form was conferred on those who in exceptional cases were appointed dictators. It was also possessed by the *interrex*, but for five days only. For consuls and praetors the imperium could be prorogued, i. e. prolonged beyond their time of office; but the imperium thus prolonged was *finitum*, i. e. bounded within the limits of their province. In the Republic it could also be conferred by means of the Comitia Curiata, but this act fell into a mere formality. Under the Empire the term imperium included the highest military authority, which resided in the emperor and was the foundation of all his power. It was taken up either at the instance of the Senate or the troops. Its full validity depended on its recognition by both. See PRINCEPS.

Impluvium. A depression in the floor of the Roman *atrium* made for the purpose of receiving the rain which came in through the open roof. See DOMUS, p. 544.

Imprisonment. See CARCER.

Impūbes. In Roman law, persons were classed as follows with reference to their age in its legal aspect: (1) *Infantes*, from birth to the end of the seventh year; (2) *Infantiā maiores*, from the end of seven years to the age of puberty, which was fixed at twelve for a girl and fourteen for a boy; (3) *Adulescentes, adulti, puberes*, or *minores* (sc. *xxv annis*); (4) *maiores*, above the age of twenty-five. The first two classes were generally styled *impuberes*.

An *infans* could not perform any legal act whatever, nor incur any liability; but one who was *infantiā maior* and not in the power of a father (see PATRIA POTESTAS) could do any legal act with the sanction (*auctoritas*) of his guardian (*tutor*). Without that assent he could do only such acts as were legally beneficial, and not those that were to his disadvantage—e. g. he could not release another from a debt due him, though he could enter into a contract looking to his own release from debt. He could enter into a betrothal (*sponsalia*) alone, because the *auctoritas* of the *tutor* had reference only to property; and *sponsalia* did not give rise to any liability to be sued. An impubes could not without the sanction of his *tutor* be plaintiff or defendant in a suit. He could acquire the ownership of property alone, but he could not alienate it or manumit a slave unless with the concurrence of his *tutor*. See CURATORES; TUTOR.

Inachĭdae. A name given to the first eight successors of Inachus (q. v.) on the throne of Argos.

Inachĭdes. A patronymic of Epaphus, as grandson of Inachus (Ovid, *Met.* i. 704).

Inăchis (Ἰναχίς). A patronymic of Io (q. v.) as daughter of Inachus (Ovid, *Fasti*, i. 454). The goddess Isis (q. v.) is also called Inachis, as being identified with Io.

Inăchus (Ἴναχος). A son of Oceanus and Tethys, and father of Io. He was said to have founded the kingdom of Argos, and was succeeded by his son Phoroneus, B.C. 1807. Inachus is said, in the old legend, to have given his name to the principal river of Argolis. Hence, probably, he was described as the son of Oceanus, the common parent of all rivers. They who make Inachus to have come into Greece from beyond the sea regard his name as a Greek form for the Oriental term *Enak*, denoting "great" or "powerful," and this last as the base of the Greek ἄναξ, "a king." The foreign origin of Inachus, however, or, rather, his actual existence, is very problematical. According to the mythological writers, Inachus became the father of Io by his sister, the ocean-nymph Melia (Apollod. ii. 1, 1), and he is also described as the father of Aegialeus, Argus, and Rhegeus.

Inăchus (Ἴναχος). (1) A river of Argolis, flowing at the foot of the Acropolis of Argos, and emptying into the Bay of Nauplia. Its real source was in Mount Lyrceus, on the confines of Arcadia; but the poets, who delighted in fiction, imagined it to be a branch of the Inachus of Amphilochia, which, after mingling with the Acheloüs, passed under ground, and reappeared in Argolis. (2) A river of the Amphilochian district in Acarnania.

Inarĭmē. See AENARIA.

Inăros (Ἰνάρως, Ἴναρος). Son of Psammetichus, a Libyan, and the leader of a revolt of the Egyptians against the Persians in B.C. 461. He was at first successful, and formed an alliance with the Athenians, but was eventually defeated by the Persians, taken prisoner, and crucified in 455. See AEGYPTUS.

Inauguratio. A Roman ceremony by which the augurs obtained, or endeavoured to obtain, the sanction of the gods to something which had been decreed by man—e. g. to the election of the magistrates, who continued to be inaugurated under the Republic (Dionys. ii. 6), and for this purpose were summoned by the augurs (*condictio, denuntiatio*) to appear on the Capitol on the third day after their election (Serv. *ad* Verg. *Aen.* iii. 117). The inauguratio conferred no priestly dignity upon the magistrates, but was merely a method of obtaining the sanction of the gods to their election, and gave them the right to take the *auspicia;* and in important emergencies it was their duty to make use of this privilege. At the time of Cicero, however, this duty was scarcely ever observed (Cic. *De Div.* ii. 36, 76).

A building was "inaugurated" only when it was to be used for meetings of the Senate, or when the rites to be performed there required it should be a *templum*. The *inauguratio* hallowed the site, and the *consecratio* the building. Thus the Aedes Vestae was consecrated, but not inaugurated, and meetings of the Senate were never held there. See AUGUR; TEMPLUM.

Inauris (ἐλλόβιον, ἐνώτιον, ἕρμα). An ear-ring fastened, as in modern times, to the ear through the hole (*fenestra*) bored in the lobe. They were worn in Greece and Italy by women, and among ultra-fashionable men it appears to have been the practice to wear a single ear-ring, much as the "smart" set in London at one time favoured the wearing of a single bracelet by men. Ear-rings were of every conceivable pattern and value, and were often set with precious stones, and sometimes with drops (*stalagmia*).

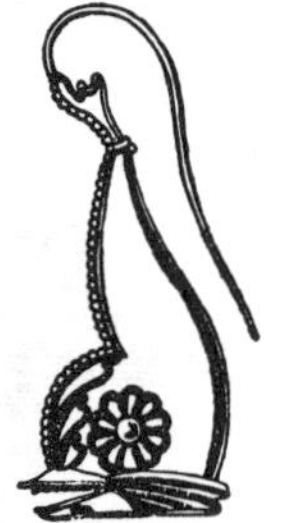

Ear-ring of B.C. 350, found at Tarentum. (Castellani Collection.)

Etruscan Ear-ring. (Blacas Collection.)

Incaustum. A name given to black ink. See PALAEOGRAPHY.

Incendium. The crime of causing a fire by which the property of another was endangered. It was thus more comprehensive than our "arson." As to the methods of extinguishing fires, and regulations relating to fires, see SIPHO; VIGILES.

Incense. See TUS.

Incensus. One who voluntarily absented himself from the census at Rome—an offence severely punished by law. See CENSUS.

Incestum. The crime of incest. See VESTALES.

Incitēga (ἐγγυθήκη, ἀγγοθήκη). A stand for holding bottles, cruets, decanters, and other like vessels

(Fest. s. h. v.). They were made of wood or earthenware.

Incitegae. (British Museum.)

Inclinatio. See CLIMA.

Incubāre (ἐγκοιμᾶσθαι). A verb especially used of sleeping in a sanctuary where oracular responses were sought through dreams or necromancy. (See ORACULUM.) It was with a view to obtaining in a dream a revelation either from the god of the sanctuary, or by conjuring up the spirit of some dead person. Certain preliminaries had generally to be performed, in particular the sacrifice of some animal, on whose skin it was often customary to sleep. These incubations, which were in vogue among the Greeks from the earliest times, but were not extensively practised among the Romans until under the Empire, generally took place in the temple of Aesculapius, the god of healing.

Child in Swaddling Clothes. (Roman bas-relief.)

Incunabŭla. (1) A cradle and layette. (2) A cradle alone (Livy, iv. 36). See CUNAE. (3) A name applied to all specimens of printed books issued prior to the year 1500. See EDITIO PRINCEPS.

Incus (ἄκμων). An anvil (Verg. *Aen.* vii. 629), exactly similar in appearance to those in use at the present day.

Anvil. (From a gem in the Louvre.)

Indāgo. A Roman sporting term, expressive of the surrounding of a wood or cover with nets to prevent the escape of the game at a *battue* (Verg. *Aen.* iv. 121).

Index (σίλλυβος). (1) The title of a book (Cic. *Ad Att.* iv. 4). See LIBER. (2) An inscription upon the base of a statue or slab, or upon any object indicative of the purpose for which the object was erected (Livy, xli. 28).

India (Ἰνδία). India is the middle one of the three great land-masses that jut southward from the mainland of Asia. In shape it is somewhat like a lozenge or diamond, with land-boundaries to the north and water-boundaries to the south. The northern half is wedged in between the Himalayan and the Sulaiman ranges, which thus form respectively its northeastern and northwestern frontiers; while the southern half, tapering to a point at Cape Comorin, projects into the Indian Ocean, and is washed by the Arabian Sea on the southwest and by the Bay of Bengal on the southeast. Its area is nigh 1,500,000 square miles—that is, nearly one-half (about $\frac{5}{12}$) that of the United States, or almost equal to that of all Europe less Russia.

In respect of physical configuration, India may be divided into three very distinct parts: the Himalayan region; the river plains of the Indus and Ganges, or the Indo-Gangetic plain; and Peninsular India. The last is a triangular plateau which forms the southern half of the "lozenge." The Himalaya shuts off India from Central Asia by an almost impassable barrier on the north. The Indus, flowing northwest, drains the back of the western half of the range; then, turning a right angle to the left, it breaks through the mountains, and receiving the affluents which with it drain the Punjab (Persian, *Panj-āb,* "Five-river" land) flows in a general southwesterly direction to the Arabian Sea. The Ganges, with its feeders, drains the southern slopes of the range and flows in a general southeasterly direction into the Bay of Bengal. The watershed between the drainage basins of the Indus and the Ganges is scarce a thousand feet above sea-level, and the slope on each side is imperceptible. The "basins," therefore, form one practically continuous "plain." This Indo-Gangetic plain is a vast alluvial formation, made by deposits of rich silt brought down by the rivers, and has accordingly been the principal scene of Indic civilization.

The home of the earliest and most primitive Indic civilization, as indicated by the geographical allusions of the Vedas, was the Punjab, the region of the middle Indus and its tributaries. Later, the scene shifts to the southeast, to the valley of the Ganges and its most important affluent, the Jumna. This is the "Middle Country" (Sanskrit, *Madhya-deça*), the fertile region in which occur the chief events of the great Epic period and of the rise and bloom of Buddhism.

For the country above defined as India, there is no comprehensive name in the oldest native literature. Later books call it *Jambu-dvīpa,* "Land of the Rose-apple;" and the great Gangetic region is named "The Bhāratan" (Sanskrit, *Bhārata*), or also *Ārya-āvarta,* "Home of the Aryans." The French take their name for Germany—Allemagne—from that of the region of the tribe—the Alemanni—nearest themselves, and then extend it to the whole country. Similarly the Greeks. Their names for India—ἡ Ἰνδία, ἡ Ἰνδική—apply properly only to the westernmost part of India, the region of the Indus. In Sanskrit, *Sindhu-s* (the *Hindu-sh* of the ancient Persians) means "stream," and then "*The* Stream," that is, "The Indus, ὁ Ἰνδός" (*incolis Sindus appellatus,* says Pliny), and finally also "The region on the Indus."

Subjoined are the names of the tributaries of the Indus in order from west to east—first the Sanskrit form, then the Greek, and then the modern name:

Vitastā	Ὑδάσπης	Jehlam
Asiknī ("Black")	Ἀκεσίνης	Chenāb
Irāvatī ("Refreshing")	Ὑδραώτης	Rāvi
Vipāç ("Unfettered")	Ὕφασις	Beas
Çatadru ("Hundred-runs")	Ζαδάδρης	Sutlej

The Asiknī was known later as the Chandrabhāgā, a name to the Macedonian ears so ominously like Σανδαρο-φάγος ("Xander-devourer"), that Alexander changed it to Ἀκεσίνης ("The Healing"), with a bright play on its older name Asiknī. *Σανδαροφάγος ὑπὸ Ἀλεξάνδρου ποταμὸς μετωνομάσθη καὶ ἐκλήθη Ἀκεσίνης*, says Hesychius.

The names of the Ganges and its greatest tributary, the Jumna, are easily recognized in their ancient forms—*Γάγγης* and *Διάμουνα*; Sanskrit, *Gangā* and *Yamunā*. The mountain names Ἡμωδό-ς (Strabo, 689) and *Haemodes* (Mela, i. 81) correspond closely to the vernacular form of the Sanskrit *Haimavata-s*, synonymous with *Hima-vant*, "The Snow-y" range, and with *Hima-ālaya*, "Abode of Snow." The Hindu, in telling the points of the compass, faces the east. The Sanskrit name for Peninsular India, south of the Vindhya Mountains (*τὸ Οὐίνδιον ὄρος*) is, accordingly, *Dakshinā-patha*, "Region to the right (*δεξιά*) or the south," *Δαχιναβάδης* of the Periplus (§ 50), our Dekkan.

The recent science of Comparative Grammar has proved that the ancestors of Hindus and Iranians and Greeks and of the Slavic, Germanic, Italic, and Keltic races are of one stock, called Aryan or Indo-European, which once had a common language and home. The Indic branch of this stock were not the aboriginal inhabitants of India; these were the dark-skinned tribes or *Dasyus*, whom the more gifted Aryan invaders, entering India from the extreme northwest, forced constantly to retire to the east and southeast. These non-Aryan tribes are now represented in part by the Dravidian races of the Dekkan. Of the Aryans, numerous tribes are mentioned in the Vedic literature, among them the *Pūrus*, the *Bharatas*, the *Kuru-Panchālas;* but the physical form of the Indo-Gangetic plain, free as it is from mountain barriers, is not favourable to the maintenance of tribal identity, and the floods of foreign invasion have had a similarly unfavourable tendency.

The language of the Indic Aryans shows three principal stages of development: (1) Old Indic or Sanskrit; (2) Middle Indic or Prākrit; and (3) New Indic or Bhāshā. The first is represented by the Vedic, the Epic, and the Classical Sanskrit; the second, chiefly by the Pāli and by the Prākrit proper, or languages respectively of the sacred books of the Southern Buddhists and of the Jains; the third, chiefly by the nine principal Aryan tongues of modern India, Mahratti, Bengali, etc.

Of all these, as indeed of all recorded Aryan tongues, the language of the Vedas is the most ancient; and it has, on the whole, conserved the greatest number of antique features. Note, for example, the retention in Sanskrit of the primitive sibilant in *sū-s* as compared with the cognate ὗ-ς and English *sow;* in *jánas-as* = γένε(σ)-ος, *gener-is;* in *ás-mi*, "I am" = Lesbian ἔμ-μι; in *á-srava-t*, "it flowed" = ἔρρεε, for *ἐ-σρεϝε-τ, root *sru* = ῥυ.

The structure of the Sanskrit forms of derivation and inflection is so transparent as to shed much light on the corresponding forms of the allied languages. Thus it has two equivalent endings for the passive participle, *-na-s* and *-ta-s;* and likewise a root *mah*, "Be great," with an older form, *magh*—facts which, considered together, furnish an easy bond of connection for *μέγ-α*, *măg-nu-s*, and *māc-tu-s*, "Magnified." In *ichāmi dā-tu-m*, "I wish to give," the infinitive is simply the accusative of a verbal noun-stem *dā-tu*, of which various other case-forms occur. Such facts make clear the nature of the Latin supines: *īre datum*, "Be going to give;" *lepida memorātuī*, "Nice for telling, nice to tell;" *redīre opsōnātu*, "Come back from marketing." Take *quo-d* and *πό-θεν* by themselves, and the stem is obscure; but in the light of the Sanskrit *ka-d*, Gothic *hva*, English *wha-t*, Ionic *κό-θεν*, it is plain that the pronominal stem began originally with the *k*-sound, not with the *p*.

An extensive Sanskrit literature has come down to us from the Hindus. Oldest and most important are the four Vedas, chiefly metrical. The Rigveda is a collection of over a thousand hymns, the most ancient of which may antedate our era by twenty centuries, and are therefore the oldest recorded documents of Aryan antiquity. Next come the Brahmanas, in prose, and containing, besides mystical discussions of the sacrifice and ritual, those theosophic speculations which culminated in the doctrines of the Upanishads, and thus became the basis of the later philosophical systems, notably of the pantheistic system of the Vedanta. In another stream from the Vedas flow the books of ceremonial, of custom, and of law. The legends of the Heroic Age are embodied in the vast epic called the Great Bharata Story (*Mahā-bhārata-ākhyāna*, or, more briefly, the Mahā-bhārata); and also in the lesser epic called Rāmāyana. Notable, besides, are especially the drama (Kālidāsa's Çakuntalā) and the beast-fable (Pancha-tantra).

The Pāli literature embraces the legends of the life and teachings of Buddha, the books of the doctrine and order which grew therefrom, and the great collection of charming folk-stories called the Jātaka, or tales of the anterior births of Gotama Buddha.

The early Indic Aryans of the Punjab were a sturdy, life-loving race. Their religion was a primitive polytheism, whose deities were personifications of the phenomena of nature, such as the wind and the sun. Thus *agnis* was the element (Latin *ignis*), while *Agnis* was the fire-god, who bore aloft the sacrifice to the other gods. To Hindu, as to Greek and Roman, the sky (*dyaus*, Ζεύς, *Diēs-piter*) was father and the earth was mother. As the Aryans advanced southeastward down the Ganges valley, the hot and humid climate wrought a profound change in their character. Their religion degenerated into a most elaborate and soul-deadening ritualism. The growth of individuality and so of great and public-spirited personalities was estopped by the rigid system of caste. The belief in the transmigration of souls became general. And the institutions of monkish life and asceticism developed to a degree which astonished the Greeks beyond measure, and is perhaps without a parallel elsewhere. Religious nostrums were doubtless many in the "Middle Country" in the sixth century B.C.; and so were the religious teachers or saviours, each with his following greater or less. Of all the latter, only two have left any great mark in the world's history—namely, Nātaputta the Nigantha and the great monk Gotama.

Nātaputta was contemporary with Gotama, but somewhat older; and he was the reformer of Jainism, or the religion of the "Conqueror" (*Jina*), which, since it still flourishes in India, may not unfairly be deemed the oldest Aryan sect in the world. Gotama, whose death at the age of eighty may be set at about B.C. 480, seems to be the greatest personality that India has ever produced. He taught not only a pure and gentle and noble morality, but also that all things are transitory, are misery, are unreal; and that the supreme goal is escape from the bonds of existence and rebirth. His religion, vastly modified by influences of time and locality, has spread to the Extreme Orient; and has meanwhile become displaced in India by Hinduism and the worship of the gods Vishnu and Çiva.

The customs of the ancient Hindus may be learned with much fulness from the treatises of household usages called *Grihya-sūtras*; and, when studied in the light of the corresponding classical or Germanic customs, will form a most important and interesting chapter of Aryan comparative philology. Since birth, reproduction, and death are the three great facts of human existence, the marriage and funeral customs naturally take a prominent place in these pictures of ancient life. The joining of right hands was the most significant feature of the nuptial ceremonies; and this was not lacking with the Romans (*dextrarum iunctio*). The walking about the altar with the right side towards it (ἐπιδέξια), or the sunwise circumambulation, finds its analogies among other Aryan races: compare the Roman *dextratio* and the Gaelic "walking the deasil." The *confarreatio* and the *pellis lanata* may be traced to India. At a funeral the circumambulation was reversed, in Italy (Statius, *Theb.* vi. 215) as well as on the Ganges. The above may serve as examples of coincidences of usage. It is likely that a considerable body of these customs go back to Aryan antiquity.

Ancient India has no history, in the ordinary acceptation of the word. If all things are transitory, are misery—why fix the thoughts on them? The events of its past do not show the working of noble and mighty personalities. Its loftiest souls are absorbed in religious and philosophical speculation. The history of India is a history of thought, of religion. The Vedas and the Epics yield us abundant and invaluable evidence concerning the life and civilization of the times to which they belong; but for any records of events in orderly sequence and with fixed chronology we look in vain.

Yet two great events — the appearance of Buddha and the invasion of Alexander — are exceptions. The one was of profoundest importance to India; the other, of great importance for our knowledge of India. Indeed, it is to foreign invaders and pilgrims that we owe some of our most valuable knowledge about India. Darius (521–485), on an inscription at Persepolis, mentions the Indus region among his conquered provinces. Nearly two centuries later, B.C. 326, Alexander the Great crossed the Indus (Arrian, *Anab.* v. 4) and the Hydaspes (v. 12); and, after defeating the Indian king Porus (v. 17), advanced to the Hyphasis. On the bank of this Indian stream the world-conqueror was forced to turn back; and, without even entering the Gangetic plain, he set out for Persis.

After his death (June, 323), one of his great generals, Seleucus Nicator, invaded India again (about 305), and made a treaty with the famous Sandrokottos (or Σανδρόκυπτος, Sanskrit *Chandra-gupta*), the founder of the Mauryan dynasty of Magadha. The Magadhan empire extended from Lower Bengal to the Indus, and its capital was Παλίβοθρα (Sanskrit *Pātaliputra*), on the Ganges at the old confluence of the Sone. The Pāli books call him Chandagutta the Moriya (Μωριεύς); and there is no other ancient Hindu about whom there is so much concurrent evidence from Indian and classical sources. (See Justin, xv. 4.) It was to his court that Seleucus sent his friend Megasthenes as ambassador. Megasthenes was a careful observer, and had a most unusual opportunity for observing; so that the book which he wrote was probably the most valuable work of antiquity on India. As if to show how deplorable is its loss, considerable excerpts from it have been preserved by Strabo, Arrian, and others.

Chandragupta's grandson Açoka (B.C. 259–222) was the greatest monarch of ancient India. Many rock-inscriptions containing his edicts are still extant, and are of priceless worth, as being the oldest of their kind. Some of them are especially interesting because they mention the Greeks, for example, "Antiyoka, king of the Yonas," and "Antikina." The former is Antiochus II., and the latter Antigonus Gonatas. The Yonas or Yavanas are of course the Ἴωνες or Ἰάονες, that is, the Greeks. The rock-cut edicts are found in Orissa, Gujarat, and the extreme north of the Punjab—places so wide apart as to show that Açoka's empire embraced the whole Indo-Gangetic region. Perhaps the most notable event of his reign was his conversion to Buddhism. He was mild and tolerant, but zealous withal for the promotion of the faith. See Senart's "Un roi de l'Inde," in the *Revue des Deux Mondes*, March 1, 1889.

The century from B.C. 326 to 222, accordingly—including, as it does, Alexander's invasion and death, the reigns of Chandragupta and Açoka, and the culmination of the Magadhan empire—is the most notable one of Indian antiquity. It includes also the rise of the Graeco-Bactrian kingdom, from which Hellenic kings made repeated conquests of parts of Western India. There followed the Graeco-Indian sovereigns, chief of whom was Menander (Pāli *Milinda*), about B.C. 100. Some fifteen years later the dynasty was overthrown by the Çakas or Scythians, and the power of the Greeks put to an end. The greatest of the Caka kings was Kanishka; and it is probably his consecration in A.D. 78 that forms the starting-point of the Caka era, which is still in use.

The Imperial Gupta dynasty, beginning A.D. 320 and lasting till about 480, deserves mention as bearing a national Indian character. It gave to India a respite from the inroads of the northern barbarians and an excellent administration of government. Among regents of the sixth century, Harsha of Ujjain, with the title Vikramāditya, is famous because of the traditional connection of his name with that of the greatest of all Hindu poets, Kālidāsa. In the seventh century, Çilāditya of Kanauj became very powerful; and it was during his long reign that the illustrious Chinese Buddhist pilgrim, Hiuen Tsiang, made his travels in India (A.D. 629–645). The history of modern India begins with the invasion made by Mahmud of

Ghazni, A.D. 1000, and embraces the period of the Mohammedan conquerors and that of British rule.

Bibliography. — Geography: H. F. Blanford, *Elementary Geography of India, Burma, and Ceylon* (New York, 1890). The best map of ancient India is Colonel Yule's, in William Smith's *Atlas of Ancient Geography*. See, also, in the *Journal of the Royal Asiatic Society* for 1889 the map facing p. 527. An admirable modern atlas is *Constable's Hand Atlas of India* (London, 1893). Language: W. D. Whitney, *Sanskrit Grammar* (2d ed. Boston, 1889); C. R. Lanman, *Sanskrit Reader, with Vocabulary and Notes* (Boston, 1888); Victor Henry, *Short Comparative Grammar of Greek and Latin* (Eng. trans. New York, 1890). Literature and Civilization: A. Kaegi, *The Rigveda* (Boston, 1886); L. von Schroeder, *Indiens Literatur und Cultur in historischer Entwickelung* (Leipzig, 1887). Religion: A. Barth, *The Religions of India* (2d ed. London, 1890); H. Oldenberg, *Buddha: his Life, his Doctrine, his Order*, trans. by W. Hoey (also 2d German ed., Berlin, 1893). Greek Knowledge of India: see, especially, J. W. M'Crindle's *Ancient India as described by the Classical Authors, being a series of copiously annotated translations of all the Greek and Roman texts which relate to India*. Five volumes have appeared. Vol. I. Megasthenes, and Arrian's *Indica*, i.–xvii. Vol. II. Commerce and navigation of the Erythraean Sea, being a translation of the *Periplus* and of Arrian's account of the voyage of Nearchus (*Indica*, xviii.–xliii.). Vol. III. The *Indica* of Ctesias, the Cnidian (the abridgment by Photius, and the fragments). Vol. IV. The *Geography* of Claudius Ptolemaeus (the chapters on India, etc.). Vol. V. The invasion of India by Alexander the Great, as described by Arrian, Q. Curtius, Diodorus, Plutarch, and Justin (London, 1893). Texts: Megasthenes's *Indica*, fragments ed. by E. A. Schwanbeck (Bonn, 1846). Also, in C. Müller's *Fragmenta Historicorum Graecorum*, ii. pp. 397–439 (Paris, 1848); Strabo's *Geography*, xv. pp. 685–720; Arrian's *Anabasis*, iv. 22 to vi. 28; and Porphyrius, *De Abstinentia*, iv. 17–18.

Indibĭlis. See Mandonius.

Indĭca. See Ctesias; Megasthenes.

Indicētae or **Indigētes.** A people in the northeast corner of Hispania Tarraconensis, close upon the Pyrenees. Their chief town was Emporium (q. v.).

Indicopleustes. See Cosmas.

Indĭcus Oceănus. See Erythraeum Maré.

Indigĕtes. The name of those indigenous gods and heroes at Rome who once lived on earth as mortals, and were worshipped after their death as gods. Thus Aeneas, after his disappearance on the banks of the Numicus, became a *deus indiges*, *pater indiges*, or Iupiter Indiges; and in like manner Romulus became Quirinus, and Latinus, Iupiter Latiaris.

Indigitamenta. The Latin term for an official collection of forms of prayer belonging to the *libri pontificii*. (See Pontifex). In them were set forth the various powers of each god who was to be summoned to aid in particular cases; and none of these divinities could be passed over, if the prayer was to receive a favourable answer. Only those portions of the collection were made public which bore direct reference to private life; prayers at marriages, at births, for a blessing on the children at different times of life, and for the beginning of all kinds of work, especially agriculture. The names of the gods of earliest childhood were as follows: Potina and Educa, who taught the child when weaned to eat and drink; Cuba, who protected the child when taken out of the cradle and put to bed; Ossipaga, who strengthened the bones; Carna, who strengthened the flesh; Levana, who helped it to rise from the ground; Statanus, Statilinus, or Dea Statina, who taught it to stand; Abeona and Adeona, who supported its first walking; Fabulinus, Farinus, who assisted it to talk. All collective occupations, all parts of the house, all different spots had their particular gods, who were invoked in these forms of prayer. Often the various names only indicate the different characteristics of a single divinity—e. g. Maia was invoked under the names of Bona, Fauna, Ops, and Fatua. In course of time the different attributes came to be regarded as separate divinities. The names of these divinities are quoted from Varro's *Antiquitates Rerum Divinarum* by Tertullian *Ad Nat.* ii. 11, 15; *De Anima*, 37, 39; and by Augustine, *De Civitate Dei*, iv. 11, 21; iv. 8, 10; vi. 9; vii. 23.

Indo-European Languages or **Aryan Languages.** Names used to designate those languages and dialects of Europe and Asia which can be grouped together as showing by their vocabularies and general grammatical structure a strong linguistic relationship to one another. The term Indo-Germanic is also frequently applied to the same family. The languages in question are conveniently arranged in eight groups.

I. The Indian and Iranian Group.—(1) *Indian.* Of these, Sanskrit, the ancient literary language of the priestly caste of the Brahmins, is the chief. In its oldest form it is found in the Vedas, or sacred hymns, from about B.C. 1500. Later it was modified by the native grammarians. (2) *Iranian* or *Persian.* This is found in the cuneiform inscriptions of Persia (Old Persian) and in the Avesta, or sacred books of Zoroaster (Avestan, Zend, Old Bactrian). See Cuneiform; Persia; Zoroaster.

II. Armenian Group.—This group includes the dialects of Armenia, and its main point of difference as compared with the Indian and Iranian tongues lies in its possession of the vowel *e*.

III. Hellenic Group.—This comprises the dialects of ancient Greece and the modern dialects descended from them. Roughly, the ancient Hellenic dialects are divided into Ionic and non-Ionic, but oftener into Doric, Aeolic, and Ionic. The dialects of modern Greece are known as Romaic. For a fuller account, see Dialects.

IV. Albanian or Skipetar.—A tongue of which little is definitely known, though it is classed as distinct from the Greek, and regarded as representative of the ancient Illyrian.

V. Italic Group.—These are the Indo-European dialects developed out of those spoken in Italy. They are to be roughly divided: (1) *Umbro-Oscan*, (2) *Latin*, and (3) the modern *Romance Languages* sprung from the vulgar Latin (Italian, French, Provençal, Spanish, Portuguese, Catalan [in North Spain], Rhaeto-Romanic [in the Tyrol, etc.], and Roumanian or Wallachian). See Italia; Osci; Umbria.

VI. Keltic Group.—The Keltic dialects are subdivided into two: (1) *Northern Keltic* (Irish, Gaelic [Scotland], Manx [in the Isle of Man]); and (2) *Southern Group* (Cymric [Wales], Cornish [Cornwall], and Armorican [Brittany]). See Celtae.

VII. Teutonic Group.—This is subdivided into (1) *Eastern Teutonic* (Ancient Gothic and Scandinavian), and (2) *Western Teutonic* (English, Frisian, Saxon, High German, Low German).

VIII. Baltic and Sclavonic Group.—(1) *Baltic* (Old Prussian, Lithuanian, and Lettish); (2) *Russian* (Bulgarian, Servian, Croatian, Czechish, and Polish).

Comparative philologists have long speculated over the probable separation and development of these different languages. Two main theories have been put forward. The older is that known as the Genealogical Theory, best stated by Schleicher, but now generally abandoned. According to this view there was a parent-language (*Ursprache*) spoken by a single people dwelling together in the original home of the race. From these "there hived off swarms which, on geographical disjunction, began to develop differences in language that separated them from the other members of their stock—swarms, however, which still comprised two or three more peoples that for a long period were linguistically one." Hence were assumed an Italo-Graeco-Keltic period, a Graeco-Latin period, and a Lithu-Slavo-Teutonic period, to account for special points of agreement observed between certain members of the family—e. g. Latin and Greek, Latin and Keltic, etc. The relation between the divisions of the Indo-European language according to the genealogical theory is shown in the following table based upon Schleicher.

At the present time, the Wave Theory or Transition Theory of Johannes Schmidt, which has the support of Brugmann, Paul, and Schrader, has supplanted the genealogical theory, as it presents fewer difficulties and contradictions when tested by known facts. According to Schmidt, the primitive Indo-European peoples were strictly homogeneous, not packed closely together into a limited territory, but settled at considerable distances though with facility of intercourse. Thus differences of dialect would be evolved and accentuated in many parts of the whole territory, and, having been so evolved, spread in waves or undulations over the immediate neighbourhood. Adjacent peoples partook of one another's linguistic peculiarities, and neighbouring dialects borrowed from one another, while those widely separated had no close mutual connection, but became more and more unlike. The relation of different languages is thus explained partly by geographical as well as by genealogical conditions. This can be illustrated in the special group of Greek dialects in later times. In Attic, Boeotian, and Euboean Greek alone an original $\tau\iota$ became $\tau\tau$, because Attica, Boeotia, and Euboea are geographically contiguous; and so, in later Laconian, σ is changed to ρ (Rhotacism) by the influence of the usage of Elis, the neighbour of Laconia. There are, in fact, three kinds of resemblances to be noted in the Indo-European tongues—resemblances inherited from the original tongue, resemblances due to long-continued geographical proximity, and resemblances that come from accidental contact with different neighbours at different points, perhaps during a gradual migration from place to place. This last is important, for it will account for the fact that languages which have no especial closeness of relation often exhibit curious special coincidences. Thus, as noted above, Armenian agrees with its European rather than with its Asiatic congeners in possessing *e*; Sanskrit and Letto-Slavonic assibilate the palatal guttural; Latin and Keltic alone have *r* as a passive sign.

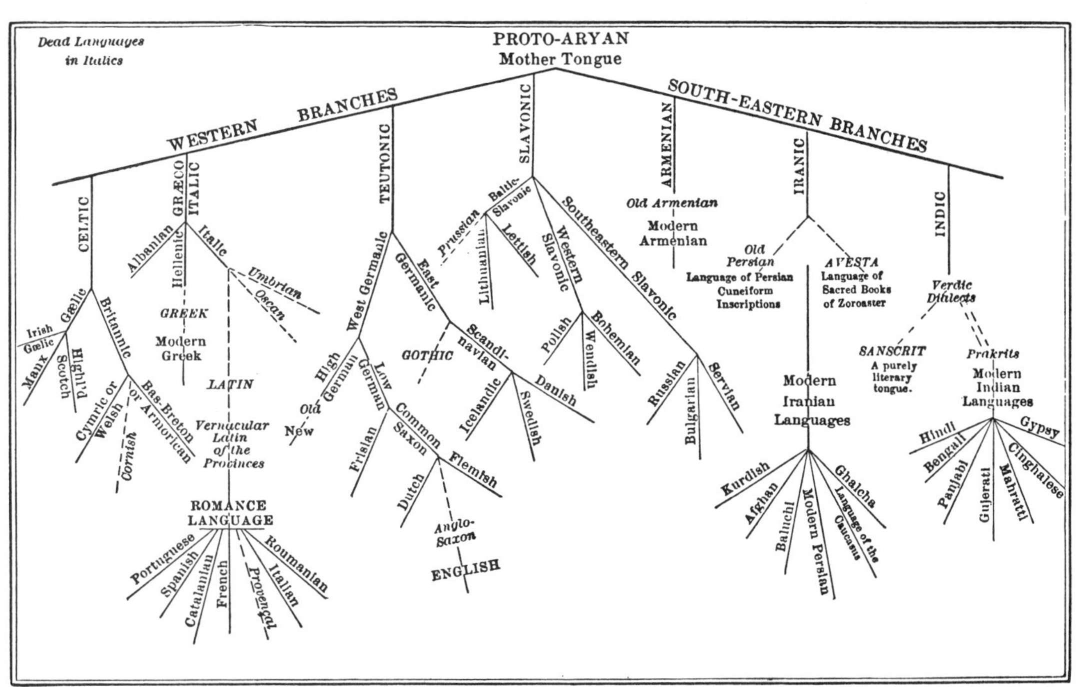

Plan illustrating Schleicher's Genealogical Theory.

It is not possible to say that any one of the existing Aryan languages has a predominance of archaic traits; and attempts to reconstruct the primitive tongue from comparative evidence are always unsatisfactory and frequently fanciful. As to the early home of the race before its separation and dispersion, several theories have been held. The old view placed it in Asia among the mountains of the Hindu-Kush (Max Müller). Other suppositions have been vigorously urged. Latham argues that the whole people must have dwelt where the majority of its parts are now found—i. e. in Europe. Benfey supported the same conclusion, arguing from the absence of common names for beasts of prey, and fixed upon the country north of the Black Sea. Geiger and Cuno urge the claims of Germany; Pösche holds to Western Russia; Penka, appealing to craniology, declares Scandinavia to have been the original home; Schrader defends a site partly European and partly Asiatic. The first is the territory bounded on the south by the Danube and the Black Sea, on the west by the Carpathian Mountains, on the east by the Dnieper, and on the north by the forests and swamps of Volhynia. This he regards as the seat of the common European culture, and for the common Indo-Iranian development he selects ancient Sogdiana and Bactriana.

See Brugmann, *Comparative Grammar of the Indo-Germanic Languages* (1888–95); Curti, *Die Sprachschöpfung* (1890); Schrader, *Prehistoric Antiquities of the Aryan Peoples* (Eng. trans. 1890); Taylor, *The Origin of the Aryans* (1889); Wilser, *Die Herkunft der Deutschen* (1886); an article by Hirt, "Die Urheimat der Indo-Germanen," the introduction to Clark's *Manual of Linguistics* (1893); various papers in Brugmann's *Indogermanische Forschungen;* and also the article PHILOLOGIA in this Dictionary.

Inducŭla. A woman's undergarment, probably the same as a chemise (Plaut. *Epid.* ii. 2, 41).

Indumentum. A word derived from *induo;* hence anything put on—e. g. a mask (Gell. v. 7); a garment (Gell. xvi. 19. 3; a tunic (Aurel. Vict. *Caes.* 12), etc.

Indus (Ἰνδός; Skt. *Sindhu*). (1) A river of India frequently mentioned in the classics. It rises in Thibet, and after taking a northwesterly course, turns to the south and finally empties into the Indian Ocean. Its total length is something more than 1800 miles, and the area of its drainage-basin 372,000 square miles. At a distance of 812 miles from its source it receives the waters of the five streams of the Punjab—Hydaspes, Acesines, Hydrastes, Hyphasis, and Xeradrus. These all unite and flow into the Indus through the single channel of the Panjnad, a fact maintained by Ptolemy but long disbelieved. The delta of the Indus covers an area of some 3000 square miles. (2) A river of Asia Minor rising in the southwestern part of Phrygia and emptying into the Mediterranean opposite Rhodes.

Indusium. A woman's frock worn over the chemise (*subucula*). It had short sleeves and a loose belt over it (Varro, *L. L.* v. 131).

Indutiomārus or **Induciomārus.** One of the leading chiefs of the Treviri in Gaul who opposed the Romans, but was defeated and slain by Labienus, B.C. 54. See CINGETORIX.

Indūtus (ἔνδυμα). Any kind of close-fitting garment as distinguished from *amictus* (q. v.), which is generally expressive of loose clothing. It is oftenest applied to the underclothing of both men and women (Alciphr. *Epist.* iii. 42; Tac. *Ann.* xvi. 4). See AMICTUS; TUNICA.

Inessa. See AETNA (2).

Infamia (ἀτιμία). The Latin term for the loss of certain political rights; resembling, but not identical with, *deminutio capitis* (q. v.). It was the direct consequence of dishonourable conduct, or of some shameless act (such as a widow not observing the usual year of mourning, bigamy, bankruptcy, going on the stage, or becoming a gladiator, pandering, or becoming a prostitute, etc.). It also resulted from a condemnation for felony, robbery, fraud, embezzlement of a deposit, whether belonging to a society or a ward, or, in fact, for any criminal offence. The *infamis* was expelled from his tribe, lost his vote and his capacity for filling public offices (*ius suffragii* and *ius honorum*), and could not appear in a court of law either on his own account or on behalf of another. See Mommsen, *Römisches Staatsrecht,* ii. 1, pp. 375 foll.; and cf. the article ATIMIA.

Infāmis. See INFAMIA.

Infans. See CURATORES; IMPUBES.

Infantry. See EXERCITUS.

Infĕri (οἱ κάτω, οἱ χθόνιοι, οἱ ὑπὸ γαῖαν, οἱ ἔνερθε). The gods of the nether world, in contradistinction from the Superi, or the gods of heaven. But the word Inferi is also frequently used to designate the dead, and therefore comprises all the inhabitants of the lower world, both the gods—viz., Hades or Pluto, his wife Persephoné (Proserpina), the Erinyes or Furies, and also the souls of departed men. See HADES.

Inferiae. See FUNUS.

Infĕrum Maré. See TYRRHENUM MARÉ.

Infŭla. A flock of wool dyed red and white and knotted at intervals with a ribbon (*vitta*). It was worn by Roman priestesses and vestals, and by the victim at a sacrifice (Lucret. i. 87). The plural INFŬLAE is sometimes used.

Infundibŭlum (χώνη). (1) A funnel for transferring liquids from one vessel to another (Cato, *R. R.* 13. 3). (2) A hopper through which the corn to be ground was poured into a mill (Vitruv. x. 5, 2).

Ingaevōnes. See GERMANIA.

Ingauni. A people in Liguria on the coast, whose chief town was Albium Ingaunum.

Ingenui, Ingenuĭtas. In Roman law, ingenui are those persons sprung from free parents. The word is therefore opposed in meaning to *libertini,* which denoted those who were only themselves free. At one time those only whose parents were freeborn were styled ingenui, but by the time of Justinian any child born of a free mother was ingenuus. See Mommsen, *Röm. Staatsr.* iii. pp. 72 foll., 518, 519; ii. 2, p. 518; and the article LIBERTINUS.

Ingenuus. One of the Thirty Tyrants, slain in Pannonia by Gallienus, A.D. 258. See THIRTY TYRANTS.

Ingrātus. See PATRONUS.

Inheritance. See HERES.

Iniuria. In general, iniuria is whatever is not *ius;* hence a violation of law. In a special sense, it denotes a wrong against one's person as distinguished from a wrong against one's property. It involves an insult (ὕβρις, *contumelia*) and must include an intent to act unlawfully (*dolus*). Instances of iniuria are assault, noisy abuse (*convicium*), libellous writings, insulting gestures, spitting at a man (Cic. *Ad Q. Fratr.* ii. 3, 2), dunning him for a debt in such a way as to injure his credit, etc. Iniuria to a wife was also iniuria to her husband. No iniuria could be done to a slave, though iniuria to his master might be done upon the person of a slave. See SERVUS.

The penalty of twenty-five *asses*, which was provided by the Twelve Tables for iniuria, was subsequently found insufficient in many cases, and so an action was established by the praetor (*actio iniuriarum aestimatoria*), in which the injured party was allowed to claim such damages as he thought he was entitled to, and the *iudex* might give the full amount or less. This became the ordinary remedy on account of iniuria, but a Lex Cornelia gave a special action in cases of *pulsatio, verberatio*, and forcible entry into a man's house. The person who committed the iniuria was styled *iniurius* and later *iniustus*.

Iniuriārum Actio. See INIURIA.

Ink. See ATRAMENTUM; WRITING AND WRITING-MATERIALS.

Inns. See CAUPONA.

Ino (Ἰνώ). The daughter of Cadmus, and wife of Athamas (q. v.). Being followed by the latter after he had been seized with madness, she fled to the cliff Moluris, between Megara and Corinth, and there threw herself into the sea with her infant son Melicertes. At the isthmus, however, mother and child were carried ashore by a dolphin, and, from that time forward, were honoured as marine divinities along the shores of the Mediterranean, especially on the coast of Megara and at the Isthmus of Corinth. Ino was worshipped at Leucothea, and Melicertes as Palaemon. They were regarded as divinities who aided men in peril on the sea. As early as Homer, we have Ino mentioned as rescuing Odysseus from danger by throwing him her veil (*Od.* v. 333–353). Among the Romans Ino was identified with Matuta (q. v.).

Inōa (Ἰνῶα). Festivals celebrated at Megara, at Epidaurus Limera (in Laconia), and on the Corinthian Isthmus in honour of Ino (q. v.) (Pausan. i. 42, § 8; iii. 23, § 5).

Inofficiōsum Testamentum. See TESTAMENTUM.

Inōpus (Ἰνωπός). A river of Delos, watering the plain in which the town of Delos stood. It was said to rise and fall at the same time as the Nile, and hence was supposed to be in some way connected with that river (Val. Fl. v. 105).

Inōus. A name of both Melicertes and of Palaemon, as being sons of Ino (q. v.) (Verg. *Aen.* v. 823).

Insania, Insānus. See CURATORES.

Inscriptions. See EPIGRAPHY.

Inscriptus, sc. *servus.* A branded slave. See SERVUS.

Insignĕ. (1) In general, any kind of badge or decoration—e. g. the crest of a helmet, the *bulla* of a child, the sceptre of a king, the device on a shield. (2) (παράσημον) The figure-head of a ship. See NAVIS.

Instĭta (περιπόδιον). (1) A flounce or hem attached to the *stola* (q. v.) of the Roman matron at the bottom of the skirt (Hor. *Sat.* i. 2, 29; Ovid, *A. A.* i. 32). (2) A train. (3) A fillet or ribbon tied to the Bacchic *thyrsus* (Stat. *Theb.* vii. 654). (4) (τόνοι, ἐπίτονοι). The bands of a bedstead used to support the mattress (Petron. 97). (5) Any band or bandage (Petron. 20).

Instĭtor (παλιγκάπηλος). One who sells for another on commission (Livy, xxii. 25; Ovid, *A. A.* i. 421).

Institoria Actio. An action brought against one for business debts contracted by whatever person (son, slave, or freeman) he had made his *institor* or business agent. See ACTIO; MANDATUM.

Institutio Oratoria. See QUINTILIANUS.

Institutiōnes. A student beginning the study of Roman law was instituted in the subject (*institui*); that is, he went through an elementary course of legal instruction under the direction of a competent lawyer. Such introductory study led to the publication of law books of an educational kind, which were called *Institutiones.* There were various institutional works written by the Roman jurists. Thus Callistratus, who lived under Septimius Severus and Antoninus Caracalla, wrote three books of *Institutiones;* Aelius Marcianus wrote sixteen books of *Institutiones,* under Caracalla, or shortly afterwards; Florentinus, who probably lived in the time of the Antonines, wrote twelve books of *Institutiones,* from which there are forty-two excerpts in the *Digest;* Paulus also wrote two books of *Institutiones.* There still remain fragments of the *Institutiones* of Ulpian. But the most important treatise of this kind that we know of was the *Institutiones* of Gaius, in four books or commentaries, of which the first relates to persons, the second and third to property, and the fourth to actions. (See GAIUS.) On the *Institutiones* of Justinian, see CORPUS IURIS CIVILIS; IUSTINIANUS.

Instragŭlum. See STRAGULUM.

Insŭbres. A Gallic people, who crossed the Alps and settled in Gallia Transpadana in the north of Italy. Their chief town was Mediolanum (Milan). They were conquered by the Romans, shortly before the commencement of the Second Punic War. See CELTAE.

Insubŭlum (ἀντίον). The cloth-beam of a weaver's loom, still called by the Italians *il subbio.*

Insŭla. See DOMUS, p. 541.

Insŭla. A part of Syracuse separated from the rest of the city by a narrow arm of the sea (Livy, xxiv. 21).

Insŭla Batavōrum. See BATAVI.

Insula Gallinaria. See GALLINARIA.

Insŭla Sacra. An island formed at the mouth of the Tiber, by the separation of the two branches of that river.

Insŭla Tiberīna. An island in the river Tiber within the city of Rome. It was united to the left bank of the river by the Pons Fabricius and to the right bank by the Pons Cestius. See PONS.

Insŭlae Fortunātae. See FORTUNATAE INSULAE.

Insularii. (1) Persons who lived in a hired lodging (*insula*). See DOMUS, p. 541. (2) Slaves who acted as house-agents or *concierges* for the owners of *insulae*. See DOMUS, p. 541.

Intabulamentum. Entablature (from *tabula*). In the Greek styles, the whole of the structure above the columns, with the exception of the gable. The entablature has three members—(1) the epistyle or architrave which joins the columns; (2) the frieze; and (3) the terminal cornice.

Entablature of the Parthenon at Athens.

Intemelii. A people in Liguria on the coast, whose chief town was Albium Intemelium (Ventimiglia).

Intemelium or **Albium Intemelium.** The capital of the Intemelii.

Intentio. See ACTIO in the Appendix.

Interamna. The name of several towns in Italy, so called from their lying between two streams. (1) (Terni), in Umbria, situated on the Nar, and surrounded by a canal flowing into this river, whence its inhabitants were called Interamnates Nartes. It was the birthplace of the historian Tacitus. (2) In Latium, at the junction of the Casinus with the Liris, whence its inhabitants were called Interamnates Lirinates.

Intercalation. See CALENDARIUM.

Intercatia. A town of the Vaccaei in Hispania Tarraconensis, on the road from Asturica to Caesaraugusta.

Intercessio. (1) The Latin term for the interference of a higher officer with some public act on the part of one lower in rank—e. g. calling a meeting of the commons. The tribune of the people could thus interfere with the praetor, quaestor, and aedile, so that it was even open to the tribunes of the people to refuse a triumph to a consul or a praetor. (2) The quashing of an official act. As in (1), this might be issued by a higher official against a lower one; and also by one colleague against another—e. g. by tribune against tribune. It was necessary that the intercessio should be made in person, and in general immediately after the act in question. It was employed against judicial decisions, administrative ordinances (solely on the appeal of the person concerned); also against decrees of the Senate and motions in the popular assembly. The later species of intercessio early became a special right of the *tribuni* (q. v.). (3) In general legal procedure, intercessio means the assumption by one person of another's debt. To become an *intercessor*, he must incur liability by entering into a contract or other similar transaction with the other person's creditors. See Gaius, iii. 110–127, ed. Poste.

Intercidōna. The name given by the Italian tribes to one of the three divinities who, during child-bed, protected mother and child from being tormented by the wood-god Silvanus (Varr. *ap.* Aug. *De Civ. Dei*, vi. 9). See PICUMNUS.

Intercīsa or **Petra Pertūsa.** A town in Umbria, named from its road cut through the rocks by order of Vespasian.

Intercīsi Dies. See DIES.

Intercolumnium (*μεσοστύλιον*). The space left between one column and another in a colonnade (Cic. *Verr.* ii. 1. 19). See PORTICUS.

Interdictio Aquae et Ignis. The Roman term for exclusion from the common use of fire and water, which were the symbols of the community. See EXSILIUM.

Interdictum. The intervention by the praetor or proconsul in certain legal controversies to command the abstention from some act—e. g. to forbid the disturbance of some possessions or the desecration of consecrated ground. An order requiring the performance of some act is called *decretum.* Orders of restitution are styled *restitutoria;* of production, *exhibitoria;* of abstention, *prohibitoria.* (Cf. Gaius, iv. 139, 140, with Poste's note.) The interdict probably arose in cases where there was no statutory action, but where the intervention of the supreme authority was necessary to maintain law and order. In later times, the praetor ceased to intervene absolutely, but made his action conditional, referring the case to a *iudex* and directing the interested parties to stake a wager (*sponsio*) on the question at issue. See Machelard, *Théorie des Interdits;* and Muirhead, *Historical Introduction to the Private Law of Rome,* § 73.

Interest of Money. See FENUS.

Intermetium. The barrier between the *metae* or goals of a race-course; the same as the *spina.* See CIRCUS, pp. 352, 353.

Intermontium. See article in the Appendix.

Internum Maré. The Mediterranean Sea, extending on the west from the Strait of Hercules, which separated it from the Atlantic, to the coasts of Syria and Asia Minor on the east. It was called by the Romans, Maré Internum or Intestinum; by the Greeks, *ἡ ἔσω θάλαττα*, or *ἡ ἐντὸς θάλαττα*, or, more fully, *ἡ ἐντὸς Ἡρακλείων στηλῶν θάλαττα*, and by Herodotus, *ἥδε ἡ θάλαττα;* and from its washing the coasts both of Greece and Italy, it was also called, by both Greeks and Romans, Our Sea (*ἡ ἡμετέρα θάλαττα, ἡ καθ' ἡμᾶς θάλαττα*, Maré Nostrum). The term Maré Mediterraneum is not used by the best classical writers, and occurs first in Solinus. The ebb and flow of the tide are perceptible in only a few parts of the Mediterranean, such as in the Syrtes on the coast of Africa, in the Adriatic, etc. The different parts of the Mediterranean are called by different names, which are spoken of in separate articles. See AEGEUM MARÉ; HADRIATICUM MARÉ; SICULUM MARÉ; TYRRHENUM MARÉ.

Internundĭnum. The Roman week. See CALENDARIUM; NUNDINAE.

Interpres. An interpreter; used by the foreign embassies at Rome; by Roman merchants in foreign cities; and by the Roman officials in the provinces. See Pliny, *H. N.* vi. 15; Val. Max. ii. 2, § 2.

Interrēges (μεσοβασιλεῖς). The name given by the Romans to the senators who, between the death of one king and the election of another, held regal authority, during the *interregnum*, for successive periods of five days each. One of these interreges had to conduct the election itself. Even under the Republic an interrex was nominated by the Senate to hold the Comitia for the election of consuls, whenever the consuls had died, or resigned, or if the election had not been completed by the end of the year. If five days did not suffice, the retiring interrex named another to succeed him. See Mommsen, *Röm. Staatsrecht*, vol. i. 647–660.

Interregnum. See INTERREGES.

Interrex. See INTERREGES.

Interscalmium. The space between thowl and thowl on the side of a vessel (Vitruv. i. 2, 4); consequently represented on the outside by the space between one oar, or oar-port, and another.

Interscalmia. (From Rich after a Roman fresco.)

Intertignium. The space between the ends of the tie beams (*tigna*, B B B in the illustration) which rest upon the architrave (*trabs*, A) in the timber work of a roof (Vitruv. iv. 2, 2, and 4). Six of these are here shown; and in the earliest buildings these intervals were left open; but, subsequently, they were covered over with slabs of marble, so as to form part of a continuous frieze (*zophorus*), or to form a metope (*metopa*) in the Doric order.

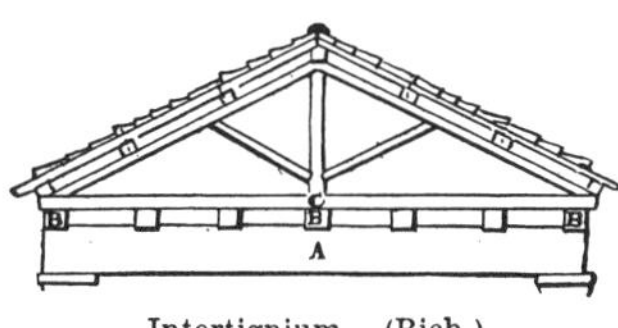

Intertignium. (Rich.)

Interŭla. See TUNICA.

Intestātus. One who has made no will. See HERES; TESTAMENTUM.

Intonsus. "The unshorn." An epithet applied to Apollo and Bacchus with reference to their eternal youth.

Inui Castrum. See CASTRUM (1).

Inuus. See FAUNUS.

Inventarium. A list or inventory.

Inventio Crucis. See HELENA.

Investis. A Roman who has not yet assumed the *toga virilis*. See IMPUBES.

Io (Ἰώ). The beautiful daughter of Inachus, and the first priestess of Heré at Argos. As Zeus loved her, she was changed by the jealousy of Heré into a white heifer, and Argus of the hundred eyes was appointed to watch her. When Hermes, at the command of Zeus, had killed Argus, Heré maddened the heifer by sending a gad-fly which perpetually pursued her. Io thus wandered through the continents of Europe and Asia, by land and by sea. Each of the different straits she swam across was named after her Bosporus, or Ox-ford. At last in Egypt she recovered her original shape, and bore Epaphus to Zeus. Libya, the daughter of Epaphus, became by Poseidon the mother of Belus, who in turn was father of Aegyptus, Danaus, Cepheus, and Phineus. The Greek legend of Io's going to Egypt is probably to be explained by her having been identified with the Egyptian goddess Isis, who is always represented with cow's horns. Io ("the wanderer") is generally explained as a moon-goddess wandering in the starry heavens, symbolized by Argus of the hundred eyes; her transformation into a horned heifer representing the crescent moon.

Ioannes. The name of several Byzantine emperors. See BYZANTINUM IMPERIUM.

Ioannes Chrysostŏmus. See CHRYSOSTOMUS.

Ioannes Chrysolōras. See CHRYSOLORAS.

Ioannes Laurentius. See LYDUS.

Ioannes Secundus (JAN EVERARD). A Dutch artist and scholar, justly celebrated for his Latin verse. He was born at the Hague, November 11, 1511, and died at Utrecht, September 24, 1536. He won some success for his painting and sculpture, and was one of the suite of Charles V. in his expedition to Tunis. His Latin verses are written with classical purity and show an exquisite felicity of expression, which has led to their translation and imitation in many languages. The finest is the *Basia* ("Kisses"), published at Utrecht in 1539. It consists of separate poems, each descriptive of a kiss. The grace and melody of the lines and their voluptuous warmth of feeling have led them to be compared with the love-lyrics of Catullus, and the comparison is fully justified. There is a translation in prose and verse, with notes, in the Bohn series (London, 1858). The collected works of Everard, comprising elegies, odes, and epigrams, were published under the title *Opera Poetica* by his brothers at Paris in 1541, and have since been reprinted (Göttingen, 1748; Leyden, 1821).

Iobātes (Ἰοβάτης). A king of Lycia, father of Anteia, and son-in-law of Proetus, king of Tiryns, by whom he was commissioned to kill Bellerophon (q. v.).

Iocasté or Iocasta (Ἰοκάστη, called Ἐπικάστη in Homer). The wife of Laïus, and mother of Oedipus. See OEDIPUS.

Iocus. A joke. See JESTS.

Iol. See CAESAREA (2).

Iolāus (Ἰόλαος). Son of Iphicles, the half-brother of Heracles, and the faithful companion and charioteer of that hero. For his help in destroying the Lernaean hydra and in the fight with Cycnus, Heracles transferred to him his first wife Megara. The friendship he had devoted to the father he continued to the children of Heracles in defending them against Eurystheus. As the comrade of Heracles he was worshipped beside him in Thebes, where the gymnasium was named after him, and where the inhabitants used to swear by his name.

Iolcus (Ἰωλκός). An ancient town in Magnesia in Thessaly, at the top of the Pagasean Gulf, about a mile from the sea. It was celebrated in mythology as the residence of Pelias and Iason, and as the place from which the Argonauts sailed in quest of the golden fleece.

Ion (Ἴων). (1) According to the Attic story, the son of Apollo and Creüsa, daughter of the Athenian king Erechtheus. He was exposed at his birth by his mother in a grotto on the cliff of the Acropolis, whence he was taken by Hermes to Delphi and brought up by the Pythian priestess to be an attendant in his father's temple. Creüsa afterwards married Xuthus, who had migrated from Thessaly, and was son of Hellen and brother of Aeolus and Dorus. As this marriage was childless, the pair went to Delphi to consult the god as to the cause. Xuthus received the command to consider as his son the first person he should meet in front of the temple. This happened to be Ion, who had meanwhile grown up, and was at once accepted by Xuthus as his son. But Creüsa, fancying he was her husband's son by a former union, resolved to poison him. Ion detected her design in time and would have killed Creüsa, who, however, took refuge at the altar of the god. Then the Pythian priestess produced the cradle in which he had been exposed as an infant, and thus brought about recognition and reconciliation between mother and son. Ion married Helicé, the daughter of Selinus, king of the Aegialeans on the north coast of the Peloponnesus. At the death of this king he became monarch of the land, and the inhabitants assumed the name of Ionians after him. Afterwards being called upon by the Athenians to help them against Eumolpus and the Eleusinians, he conquered the enemy and was made king of Athens. From the four sons who are attributed to him, Geleon, Aegicores, Argades, and Hoples, were descended the four Ionic tribes. (2) Of Chios. A Greek author of rare versatility for his time. He composed historical writings, among them a kind of memoirs of men of mark he had met, such as Sophocles; also lyric poems of the most varied types, and thirty or forty tragedies which were more remarkable for elegance and erudition than for elevation of style. When in B.C. 452 he won a dramatic victory at Athens, he is said to have presented every Athenian with a flask of Chian wine. He died at Athens in B.C. 422. There remain only scanty fragments of his works.

Iōnes (Ἴωνες). Ionians; one of the two great original divisions of the Hellenic race, the other being the Doric. Their ancestors at an early period spread over the coasts of Asia Minor, and there established a people of great commercial and intellectual activity, while the ancestors of the Dorians settled in the highlands of Northern Greece. In Asia the Ionians came into close contact with the Semitic peoples, especially at Miletus, and from them received an impulse towards civilization which they in turn imparted to their kinsmen on the other side of the Aegaean. Their name (under the form Ἰάονες) occurs only once in the *Iliad* (xiii. 685), but not long after this we find them in Attica and in a part of the Peloponnesus. Their name was by them derived from that of the mythical Ion, adopted son of Xuthus (cf. Herod. viii. 44). The Oriental peoples called the Greeks indiscriminately by the name "Ionians" (Schol. on Aristoph. *Acharn.* 104). See HELLAS; HERACLIDAE; IONIA; PELASGI.

Ionia (Ἰωνία) and **Iōnis** (in Latin poetry). A district on the west coast of Asia Minor, so called from the Ionian Greeks who colonized it earlier than any distinct historical records. The mythical account of "the great Ionic migration" relates that in consequence of the disputes between the sons of Codrus, king of Athens, about the succession to his government, his younger sons, Neleus and Androclus, resolved to seek a new home beyond the Aegean Sea. Attica was at the time over-peopled by numerous exiles, whom the great revolution, known as "the return of the Heraclidae," had driven out of their own States, and the chief of whom were the Ionians who had been expelled from Peloponnesus by the Dorian invaders. A large portion of this superfluous population went forth as Athenian colonists, under the leadership of Androclus and Neleus, and of other chieftains of other races, and settled on that part of the western shores of Asia Minor which formed the coast of Lydia and part of Caria, and also in the adjacent islands of Chios and Samos, and in the Cyclades. The mythical chronology places this great movement 140 years after the Trojan War, or 60 years after the return of the Heraclidae—that is, in B.C. 1060 or 1044, according to the two chief dates imagined for the Trojan War.

Passing from mythology to history, the earliest authentic records show us the existence of twelve great cities on the above-named coast, claiming to be (though some of them only partially) of Ionic origin, and all united into one confederacy, similar to that of the twelve ancient Ionian cities on the north coast of the Peloponnesus. The district they possessed formed a narrow strip of coast, extending between, and somewhat beyond, the mouths of the rivers Maeander on the south, and Hermus on the north. The names of the twelve cities, going from south to north, were Miletus, Myus, Prienē, Samos (city and island), Ephesus, Colophon, Lebedus, Teos, Erythrae, Chios (city and island), Clazomenae, and Phocaea; the first three on the coast of Caria, the rest on that of Lydia. The city of Smyrna, which lay within this district, but was of Aeolic origin, was afterwards (about B.C. 700) added to the Ionian confederacy. The common sanctuary of the league was the Panionium (πανιώνιον), a sanctuary of Poseidon Heliconius, on the north side of the promontory of Mycalé, opposite to Samos; and here was held the great national assembly (πανήγυρις) of the confederacy, called Panionia (πανιώνια). It is important to observe that the inhabitants of these cities were far from being exclusively and purely of Ionic descent. The traditions of the original colonization and the accounts of the historians agree in representing them as peopled by a mixture, not only of Hellenic races, but also of these with the earlier inhabitants, such as Carians, Leleges, Lydians, Cretans, and Pelasgians; their dialects, Herodotus expressly tells us, were very different, and nearly all the cities were founded on the sites of pre-existing native settlements. The religious rites, also, which the Greeks of Ionia observed, in addition to their national worship of Poseidon, were borrowed in part from the native peoples; such were the worship of Apollo Didymaeus at Branchidae near Miletus, of Artemis at Ephesus, and of Apollo Clarius at Colophon. All these facts point to the conclusion that the Greek colonization of this coast was effected, not by one, but by successive emigrations from different States, but chiefly of the Ionic race.

The central position of this district, its excellent harbours, and the fertility of its plains, watered by the Maeander, the Caÿster, and the Hermus, combined with the energetic character of the Ionian race to confer a high degree of prosperity upon these cities; and it was not long before they began to send forth colonies to many places on the shores of the Mediterranean and the Euxine, and even to Greece itself. During the rise of the Lydian Empire, the cities of Ionia preserved their independence until the reign of Croesus, who subdued those on the mainland, but relinquished his design of attacking the islands. When Cyrus had overthrown Croesus, he sent his general, Harpagus, to complete the conquest of the Ionian Greeks, B.C. 557. Under the Persian rule, they retained their political organization, subject to the government of the Persian satraps, and of tyrants who were set up in single cities, but they were required to render tribute and military service to the king. In B.C. 500 they revolted from Darius Hystaspis, under the leadership of Histiaeus, the former tyrant of Miletus, and his brother-in-law Aristagoras, and supported by aid from the Athenians. The Ionian army advanced as far as Sardis, which they took and burned; but they were driven back to the coast, and defeated near Ephesus, B.C. 499. The reconquest of Ionia by the Persians was completed by the taking of Miletus, in 496, and the Ionians were compelled to furnish ships and to serve as soldiers, in the two expeditions against Greece. After the defeat of Xerxes, the Greeks carried the war to the coasts of Asia, and effected the liberation of Ionia by the victories of Mycalé (479), and of the Eurymedon (469). In 387 the peace of Antalcidas restored Ionia to Persia; and after the Macedonian conquest, it formed part, successively, of the kingdom of Pergamus and of the Roman province of Asia. For the history of the several cities, see the respective articles.

In no country inhabited by the Hellenic race, except at Athens, were the refinements of civilization, the arts, and literature more highly cultivated than in Ionia. The restless energy and free spirit of the Ionians, the riches gained by commerce, and the neighbourhood of the great seats of Asiatic civilization, combined to advance with rapidity the intellectual progress and the social development of its people; but these same influences, unchecked by the rigid discipline of the Doric race, or the simple earnestness of the Aeolic, imbued their social life with luxury and license, and invested their works of genius with enchanting beauty at the expense of severe good taste and earnest purpose. Out of the long list of the authors and artists of Ionia, we may mention Mimnermus of Colophon, the first poet of the amatory elegy; Anacreon of Teos, who sang of love and wine to the music of the lyre; Thales of Miletus, Anaxagoras of Clazomenae, and several other early philosophers; the early annalists, Cadmus, Dionysius, and Hecataeus, all of Miletus. In the fine arts, besides being the home of that exquisitely beautiful order of architecture, the Ionic, and possessing many of the most magnificent temples in the world, Ionia was the native country of that refined school of painting, which boasted the names of Zeuxis, Apelles, and Parrhasius. The most flourishing period in the history of Ionia is that during which it was subject to Persia; but its prosperity lasted till the decline of the Roman Empire, under which its cities were among the chief resorts of the celebrated teachers of rhetoric and philosophy. The important place which some of the chief cities of Ionia occupy in the early history of Christianity is attested by the Acts of the Apostles, and the epistles of St. Paul to the Ephesians, and of St. John to the seven churches of Asia.

Ionian School of Philosophy. The earliest school of Greek philosophy, devoted to physical research, the problem before them being the discovery of the *ἀρχή* or first principle of all things. The great names of this school are those of Thales of Miletus (B.C. 640–550), Anaximander of Miletus (B.C. 611–547), Anaximenes of Miletus (about B.C. 520), and Heraclitus of Ephesus (about B.C. 510). To this list some add Pythagoras of Samos (about B.C. 500), though he properly belongs to another division. See PHILOSOPHIA.

Ionic Dialect. See DIALECTS.

Ionic Order of Architecture. See ARCHITECTURA; CAPITULUM; COLUMNA.

Ionic Tribes. The four original divisions (*φυλαί*) of the inhabitants of Attica, said by the ancients to have descended from the mythical Ion, adopted son of Xuthus, after whose four sons they were said to have got their names—*Γελέοντες*, *Αἰγικορεῖς*, *Ἀργαδεῖς*, and *Ὅπλητες*. It is fairly certain, however, that the names are in reality descriptive of the respective functions of those composing each: *γελέοντες*, "the shining"—i. e. the noble; *αἰγικορεῖς*, "the goat-herds;" *ἀργαδεῖς*, "the artisans;" and *ὅπλητες*, "the warriors." See PHRATRIA.

Ionium Maré (*Ἰόνιος πόντος*). The sea between Italy and Greece south of the Adriatic, beginning on the west at Hydruntum in Calabria, and on the east at Oricus in Epirus, or at the Ceraunian Mountains. In more ancient times the Adriatic was called the Ionian Gulf; while at a later time the Ionium Maré itself was included in the Adriatic. In its widest signification the Ionium Maré included the Maré Siculum, Creticum, and Icarium. Its name was usually derived by the ancients from the wanderings of Io, but it was more probably so called from the Ionian colonies which settled in Cephallenia and the other islands off the western coasts of Greece.

Iŏphon (*Ἰοφῶν*). Son of Sophocles by Nicostraté. He was a distinguished tragic poet. For the celebrated story of his undutiful charge against his father, see SOPHOCLES.

Ioppé, IOPPA; O. T. Japho; Japha. An ancient maritime city of Palestine, lying south of the boundary between Iudaea and Samaria.

Iordānes (*Ἰορδάνης*). The modern Jordan. A river of Palestine, rising at the southern foot of Mount Hermon (the southernmost part of Anti-Libanus), flowing south into the Sea of Galilee (Lake of Tiberias), and thence into Lake Asphaltites (Dead Sea), where it is finally lost.

Iordānis (less correctly JORNANDES). An Alanian by birth. He wrote about the year A.D. 551 two historical works: (1) a compendium of universal history (*De Summa Temporum Gentis Romanorum*) down to A.D. 551; and (2) an abstract of Cassiodorus' history of the Goths (*De Rebus Geticis* or *De Origine Actibusque Getarum*), which, though done in a cursory and unskilful manner, is nevertheless of great value, owing to the loss of the original work. The principal edition of both works is that of Mommsen (Berlin, 1882). There is a translation of the *Getica* and of part of the *De Summa Temporum,* into German, by Martens (Leipzig, 1884). See also Jordan, *Iordanes' Leben und Schriften* (Ansbach, 1843).

Ios (Ἴος). An island in the Aegean Sea, to the north of Thera. Here, according to some accounts, Homer was interred (Pliny *H. N.* iv. 12). It was also said that the poet's mother was a native of this island. The modern name is Nio.

Iosēphus, FLAVIUS (Φλάβιος Ἰώσηπος). A celebrated Jewish historian, born at Jerusalem in A.D. 37, inheriting on his father's side the priestly office and being descended through his mother from the Asmonaean princes. After receiving an excellent education, he was sent to Rome at the age of twenty-six to plead before Nero the cause of several Jewish priests whom the procurator Felix had sent there as prisoners. After securing their release, he returned to Jerusalem, which he found on the eve of a revolt against the Romans. He endeavoured to dissuade his countrymen from the attempt, but failing in this, he entered into their plans and took the field as one of their generals. On the approach of Vespasian with a Roman army, Iosephus retired with his forces into Iotapata, where, for forty-seven days, he sustained a siege, surrendering, however, in the end. His life was spared by Vespasian through the intercession of Titus. Iosephus thereupon assumed the character of a prophet, and predicted to Vespasian that the Empire should one day be his and his son's. Vespasian treated him with respect, but did not release him from captivity until he was proclaimed emperor nearly three years afterwards (A.D. 70). Iosephus was present with Titus at the siege of Jerusalem, and afterwards accompanied him to Rome. He received the freedom of the city from Vespasian, who assigned him, as a residence, a house formerly occupied by himself, and treated him with great regard to the end of his reign. The same favour was extended to him by Titus and Domitian as well. He assumed the name of Flavius, as a dependant of the Flavian family. His time at Rome appears to have been employed mainly in the composition of his works. He died about A.D. 100.

The works of Iosephus are written in Greek of such pleasing style as to win for him the title of "the Greek Livy." They are: (1) A History of the Jewish War (Περὶ τοῦ Ἰουδαϊκοῦ πολέμου ἢ Ἰουδαϊκῆς Ἱστορίας περὶ Ἁλώσεως), in seven books, published about A.D. 75. Iosephus first wrote it in Hebrew, and then translated it into Greek. It commences with the capture of Jerusalem by Antiochus Epiphanes in B.C. 170, runs rapidly over the events before Iosephus's own time, and gives a detailed account of the fatal war with Rome. (2) On Jewish Antiquities (Ἰουδαϊκὴ Ἀρχαιολογία), in twenty books, completed about A.D. 93, and addressed to Epaphroditus. The title as well as the number of books may have been suggested by the Ῥωμαϊκὴ Ἀρχαιολογία of Dionysius of Halicarnassus. It gives an account of Jewish History from the creation of the world to A.D. 66, in which the Jews were goaded to rebellion by Gessius Florus. In this work Iosephus seeks to reconcile the Jewish religion with heathen tastes and prejudices. Thus he speaks of Moses and his law in a tone which might be adopted by any disbeliever in his divine mission. He says that Abraham went into Egypt (Gen. xii.), intending to adopt the Egyptian views of religion, should he find them better than his own. He speaks doubtfully of the preservation of Jonah by the fish. He intimates a doubt of there having been any miracle in the passage of the Red Sea, and compares it with the passage of Alexander the Great along the shore of the sea of Pamphylia. He interprets Exod. xxii. 28 as if it conveyed a command to respect the idols of the heathen. Many similar instances might be quoted from his work. (3) His own life, in one book. This is a supplement to the *Archaeologia*, and is addressed to the same Epaphroditus. It was not written earlier than A.D. 97, since Agrippa II. is mentioned in it as no longer living. (4) A treatise on the Antiquity of the Jews, or against Apion, in two books, also addressed to Epaphroditus. It is in answer to such as impugned the antiquity of the Jewish nation, on the ground of the silence of Greek writers respecting it. (See APION.) The treatise exhibits extensive acquaintance with Greek literature and philosophy. (5) Εἰς Μακκαβαίους ἢ περὶ Αὐτοκράτορος Λογισμοῦ, in one book. Its genuineness is doubtful. It is a declamatory account of the martyrdom of Eleazar (an aged priest), and of seven youths and their mother, in the persecution under Antiochus Epiphanes. The best editions of Iosephus are by Hudson (Oxford, 1720), Havercamp (Amsterdam, 1726), Dindorf (Paris, 1845–47), Bekker, 6 vols. (Leipzig, 1855–1856), and Niese (Berlin, 1886 foll.). Excellent translations into English are those of Maynard (1800), Traill and Taylor (1851), and Shilleto's revision of Whiston, 5 vols. (1889–90).

Ioviānus, FLAVIUS CLAUDIUS. A Roman emperor, born A.D. 331, the son of Veronianus, of an illustrious family of Moesia, who had filled important offices under Constantine. Iovianus served in the army of Julian, in his unlucky expedition against the Persians; and when that emperor was killed, A.D. 363, the soldiers proclaimed him successor. His first task was to save the army, which was surrounded by the Persians, and in great distress for provisions. After repelling repeated attacks of the enemy, he willingly listened to proposals for peace, and accepted conditions offensive to Roman pride. Iovianus gave up the city of Nisibis to the Persians, the inhabitants withdrawing to Amida. On his arrival at Antioch, Iovianus, who was of the Christian faith, revoked the edicts of Julian against the Christians. He also supported the orthodox or Nicene creed against the Arians, and showed his favour to the bishops who had previously suffered from the Arians, and especially to Athanasius, who visited him at Antioch. Having been acknowledged over the whole Empire, Iovianus set off during the winter to Constantinople. At Ancyra he assumed the consular dignity; but, a few days after, being at a place called Dadastana, in Galatia, he was found dead in his bed, having been suffocated, as some say, by the vapour of charcoal burning in his room; according to others, by the steam of the plaster with which it had been newly laid; while others, again, suspected him of having been poisoned or killed by some of his guards. He died February 16, A.D. 364, after a reign of only seven months. The army proclaimed Valentinianus as his successor (Amm. Marcell. xxv. 5 foll.).

Iovīnus. A person born of a noble family of Gaul who assumed the imperial title under the weak reign of Honorius, and, placing himself at the head of a mixed army of Burgundians, Alemanni, Alani, etc., took possession of part of Gaul, A.D. 411. Ataulphus (Athawulf), king of the Visigoths, offered to join Iovinus, and share Gaul between them; but the latter having declined his alliance, Ataulphus made peace with Honorius, attacked and defeated Iovinus, and, having taken him prisoner, delivered him to Dardanus, prefect of Gaul, who had him put to death at Narbo (Narbonne), A.D. 412.

Iphianassa (Ἰφιάνασσα). See IPHIGENIA.

Iphias (Ἰφιάς). Evadnē, a daughter of Iphis, and wife of Capaneus.

Iphĭcles (Ἰφικλῆς) and **Iphĭclus** (Ἴφικλος). (1) A son of Amphitryon and Alcmenē, born at the same birth with Heracles. The children were but eight months old when Herē sent two huge serpents into the chamber to devour them. Iphicles alarmed the house by his cries, but Heracles raised himself up on his feet, caught the two monsters by the throat, and strangled them (Theocr. *Idyll.* 24; Apollod. ii. 4). Iphicles, on attaining to manhood, was slain in battle during the expedition against the sons of Hippocoön, who had beaten to death Oeonus, the son of Licymnius (Pausan. iii. 15. 4). (2) A king of Phylacē in Phthiotis, whose name is connected with one of the legends relative to Melampus (q. v.). (3) One of the Argonauts, distinguished for his speed in running.

Iphicrătes (Ἰφικράτης). A famous Athenian general, son of a shoemaker. He introduced into the Athenian army the peltastae or targeteers, a body of troops possessing, to a certain extent, the advantages of heavy and light armed forces. This he effected by substituting a small target for the heavy shield, adopting a longer sword and spear, and replacing the old coat of mail by a linen corselet. At the head of his targeteers he defeated and nearly destroyed a Spartan mora, in B.C. 392, an exploit which became very celebrated throughout Greece. He also defeated Anaxibius at the Hellespont (388), aided the Persians in subduing Egypt (377), reduced Cephallonia (373), and commanded in the Social War. He married the daughter of Cotys, king of Thrace, and died shortly before 348.

Iphigenīa (Ἰφιγένεια, in Homer Ἰφιάνασσα). Daughter of Agamemnon and of Clytaemnestra, or (according to another account) of Theseus and Helen (q. v.), and brought up by Clytaemnestra as her own child to hide her sister's shame. When the Greek ships were detained at Aulis by the calm caused by the wrath of Artemis against Agamemnon for killing a hind sacred to that goddess, and boasting that he was superior to her in the chase, the seer Calchas announced that the goddess could be appeased only by the sacrifice of Iphigenia. According to another story, Agamemnon had vowed, before the birth of Iphigenia, that he would sacrifice to the goddess whatever the year brought forth that was loveliest, but had neglected to keep his vow. After a long struggle Agamemnon finally gave way to the pressure put upon him by Menelaüs, and sent for his daughter to come to Aulis under the pretext of betrothing her to Achilles. During the sacrifice Artemis substituted a hind for her, and carried her off in a cloud to the land of the Tauri (the modern Crimea), where, as priestess of the goddess, it fell to her lot to offer up as victims all strangers who were shipwrecked on the coast. Orestes, who,

Sacrifice of Iphigenia. (Pompeian Painting.)

commanded by the oracle, had gone there to bring to Attica the image of the goddess, was on the point of being sacrificed by her, when she recognized him as her brother and allowed herself to be carried off by him together with the image. At Delphi her sister Electra wanted to put her eyes out, on hearing that the Tauric priestess had slain Orestes; but was prevented from doing so by her brother's arrival. She is said to have brought the image of the Tauric Artemis to the Attic deme of Brauron, and to have died and been buried there as its priestess. She was even introduced into Attic legend as daughter of Theseus and Helen. In other places also, such as Sparta, the image was shown, and she was regarded as a priestess who had brought it to Greece from among the Scythians. In all probability Iphigenia was originally a designation of Artemis herself, and out of this epithet of the goddess the personality of the priestess was in time evolved. Her grave was also shown at Megara. According to another legend, she is said to have been made immortal by Artemis, and to have lived on in the island of Leucē as the wife of Achilles under the name of Orsilochia. Two plays of Euripides (*Iphigenia at Aulis* and *Iphigenia among the Tauri*) deal with her story.

Iphimedīa (Ἰφιμέδεια) or **Iphimĕdē** (Ἰφιμέδη). The wife of Aloeus. She became by Poseidon the mother of the Aloadae, Otus and Ephialtes. See ALOADAE.

Iphis (Ἶφις). (1) A youth in love with Anaxaretê (q. v.). (2) A Cretan girl, brought up as a boy, and, on being betrothed to Ianthê, metamorphosed by Isis into a youth (Ovid, *Met.* ix. 665, etc.).

Iphĭtus (Ἴφιτος). (1) A son of Eurytus, king of Oechalia. (See HERACLES.) (2) A king of Elis, son of Praxonides, in the age of Lycurgus. He re-established the Olympic Games 470 years after their first institution, or B.C. 884. It was not, however, until 108 years after this (B.C. 776) that the custom was introduced of inscribing in the gymnasium at Olympia the names of those who had borne off the prize in the stadium. (Pausan. v. 4, 5).

Ipsus (Ἶψος). A small town in Great Phrygia, celebrated for the great battle in which Antigonus was defeated and slain by Seleucus and Lysimachus, B.C. 301. See ANTIGONUS.

Ira (Εἶρα, Ἰρά). A mountain stronghold in Messenia, in which Aristomenes defended himself for eleven years against the Spartans in the Second Messenian War. See ARISTOMENES; MESSENIA.

Iranian Languages. See INDO-EUROPEAN LANGUAGES.

Ireland. See HIBERNIA.

Iren (εἴρην and ἰρήν). See EDUCATION, p. 570.

Irenaeus (Εἰρηναῖος). A native of Greece, disciple of Polycarp, and bishop of Lyons, in France. The time of his birth and the precise place of his nativity cannot be satisfactorily ascertained. On the martyrdom of Photinus, his predecessor in the see of Lyons, Irenaeus, who had been a distinguished member of the church in that quarter, was appointed his successor in the diocese, A.D. 177, and presided in that capacity at two councils held at Lyons, in one of which the Gnostic heresy was condemned and in another the Quartodecimani. He also went to Rome, and disputed there publicly with Valentinus, Florinus, and Blastus, against whose opinions he afterwards wrote with much zeal and ability. He wrote on different subjects; but there remains only a barbarous Latin version of a work, *Adversus Haereses*, in five books, written to confute the Gnostics and Ebionites. Fragments of his works in Greek are, however, preserved, which prove that his style was simple, though clear and often animated. His opinions concerning the soul are curious. He is said to have suffered martyrdom about A.D. 202. His day is the 28th of June.

The *editio princeps* of the *Adversus Haereses* is that of Erasmus (Basle, 1526). The best editions are those of Stieren (Leipzig, 1851-53) and Harvey (Cambridge, 1857). There is an English translation in Clark's *Ante-Nicene Library*. On the views of Irenaeus, see Werner, *Der Paulinismus des Irenaeus* (1890).

Irēné (Εἰρήνη), called Pax by the Romans. The goddess of peace was, according to Hesiod, a daughter of Zeus and Themis and one of the Horae. (See HORAE.) She was worshipped at Athens and Rome; and in the latter city a magnificent temple was built to her by the emperor Vespasian. Pax is represented on coins as a youthful female, holding in her left arm a cornucopia and in her right hand an olive branch or the staff of Mercury. See HORAE.

Irēné (Εἰρήνη). See BYZANTINUM IMPERIUM.

Iris (Ἶρις). Daughter of Thaumas (whence she is called Thaumantias) and of Electra, and sister of the Harpies. In the *Iliad* she appears as the messenger of the gods; but in the *Odyssey*, Hermes (Mercury) is the messenger of the gods, and Iris is never mentioned. Iris was originally the personification of the rainbow, which was regarded

Iris. (Parthenon frieze.)

as the swift messenger of the gods. In the earlier poets Iris appears as a virgin goddess; but in the later she is the wife of Zephyrus and the mother of Eros (Amor). Iris is represented in works of art, dressed in a long and wide tunic, over which hangs a light upper garment, with wings attached to her shoulders, carrying the herald's staff in her left hand, and sometimes also holding a vase. See Bergstedt, *Studia Archaeologica* (Upsala, 1881).

Iris (Ἶρις). The modern Yeshil-Irmak; a considerable river of Asia Minor, rising on the north side of the Anti-Taurus and flowing through Pontus into the Sinus Amisenus in the Euxine.

Iron. See METALLUM.

Irpex. A heavy rake or harrow set with teeth and drawn over the ground by cattle to tear up the weeds (Varr. *L. L.* v. 136).

Irus (Ἶρος). (1) A beggar of Ithaca, remarkable for his large stature and unusual gluttony. His original name was Arnaeus, but he received that of Irus, as being the messenger of the suitors of Penelopé. Irus attempted to obstruct the entrance of Odysseus into the palace, under the mean disguise assumed by the latter on his return home, and in presence of the whole court challenged him to fight. Odysseus immediately brought him to the ground with a single blow (*Odyss.* xviii. 1 foll.). (2) The son of Actor and father of Eurydamus and Eurytion. He purified Peleus (q. v.) after the latter had killed Phocus. During the Calydonian boar-hunt, Peleus accidentally slew Eurytion.

Is (Ἴς). The modern Hit; a city in the south of Mesopotamia, eight days' journey from Babylon, on the west bank of the Euphrates, and upon a little river of the same name. In its neighbourhood were the springs of asphalt from which was obtained the bitumen that was used, instead of mortar, in the walls of Babylon. (Herod. i. 179).

Isădas (Ἴσαδας). A young Spartan, who, when Epaminondas and the Thebans had attacked Lacedaemon and the city was in danger of falling into their hands, rushed forth from his dwelling stark naked and newly anointed with oil, having nothing but a spear in one hand and a sword in the other, and in this condition contended valiantly against the foe. The Ephori honoured him with a chaplet for his gallant achievement, but at the same time fined him 1000 drachmas for having dared to appear without his armour (Plut. *Ages.*).

Isaeus (Ἰσαῖος). One of the ten Attic orators. He was born at Chalcis, and came to Athens at an early age. He wrote judicial orations for others and established a rhetorical school at Athens, in which Demosthenes is said to have been his pupil. He lived between B.C. 420 and 348. Eleven of his orations are extant, all relating to questions of inheritance. They afford considerable information respecting this branch of the Attic law, of which he was a master, and are marked by intellectual acumen, clearness of statement, and vigour of style. Edited with the other orations by Reiske (1773), Bekker (1823–28), Dobson (1828), Baiter and Sauppe (1839–43); and separately by Schömann (1831); with notes by Burmann (1883), and by Scheibe in the Teubner series. See Blass, *Attische Beredsamkeit*, vol. ii.; May, *Les Plaidoyers d' Isée* (Paris, 1876); and on the style, Lincke, *De Elocutione Isaei* (1884).

Isagŏras (Ἰσαγόρας). The leader of the oligarchical party at Athens, opposing Clisthenes, B.C. 510. He was finally expelled from Athens by the party of the people. See CLISTHENES.

Isăra. The modern Isère; a river in Gallia Narbonensis, descending from the Graian Alps, and flowing into the Rhone north of Valentia.

Isauria (Ἰσαυρία). A district of Asia Minor, on the northern side of the Taurus, between Pisidia and Cilicia, whose inhabitants, the Isauri, were daring robbers. They were defeated by the Roman consul, L. Servilius, in B.C. 75, who received in consequence the surname of Isauricus. Two Byzantine emperors (Zeno I. and Leo III.) were Isaurians. See BYZANTINUM IMPERIUM.

Isca. (1) A town of the Damnonii or Dumnonii in Britain, now Axminster or Exeter. (2) A town of the British Silures, now Caerleon.

Ischys. See AESCULAPIUS.

Iselastĭci Ludi. The four great games of Greece—i. e. the Olympian, Isthmian, Nemean, and Pythian. They were so called because the victors, after the contests were over, entered their native towns crowned and in a triumphal chariot (εἰσήλασαν) drawn by four horses (Pliny, *Epist.* x. 118; cf. Suet. *Nero*, 25). In later times the reward given by the Roman emperors to the victors at the Iselastic Games was called *iselasticum* (Trai. *ad* Pliny, *Epist.* x. 119).

Isidōrus (Ἰσίδωρος). A Spaniard who, from the beginning of the seventh century, was bishop of Seville (in Latin *Hispalis*, whence he is called Hispalensis). He died about A.D. 636. He possessed a width of reading which was remarkable for his time, and an extraordinary faculty for collecting information. Next to Boëtius and Cassiodorus, he exercised the most important influence upon the general culture and literature of the Middle Ages. Besides works on grammar, theology, and history (including a chronicle of the world to his own day, and histories of the Goths, Vandals, and Suevi), he composed in the last years of his life his greatest and most important work—an immense but imperfect encyclopaedic survey of all knowledge, in twenty books, entitled the *Etymologiae* or *Origines*, from its often very capricious and marvellous explanations of the various subjects of which it treats. Though it is only a vast congeries of collected excerpts, devoid of a single original idea, it is nevertheless important owing to the variety of its contents and its citations from writings now lost, such as those of Suetonius. Another work, which is similarly a compilation, but was greatly used in the Middle Ages, is his *De Natura Rerum*, a handbook of natural history.

The complete text of Isidorus is given in the Abbé Migne's *Patrologia Latina*, 4 vols., reprinted from Arevalo (1850). The *De Natura Rerum* is edited separately by G. Becker (Berlin, 1857), and the *Origines* in Lindemann's *Corpus Grammaticorum Veterum* (Leipzig, 1833), by Otto.

Isionda (Ἰσιόνδα). A city of Pisidia in Asia Minor, near Termessus.

Isis (Ἶσις). The divinity most extensively worshipped, with her brother and husband Osiris, by the Egyptians, among whom she represented the feminine, receptive, and producing principle in nature. As the goddess of procreation and birth her symbol was the cow. On monuments she is mostly represented as of youthful appearance with a cow's horns on her head, between the horns the orb of the moon, and with a sceptre of flowers and the emblem of life in her hands. Her greatest temple stood at Busiris (i. e. Pe-Osiri, or Abode of Osiris) in the midst of the Delta of the Nile, where, amidst the fruitful fields, the inhabitants worshipped the mightiest god and goddess with ceremonies which typified the search and discovery of Osiris by his mourning wife after his murder by Typhon. Like Osiris she was a divinity who ruled over the world below. In the course of the fusion of religions which took place under the Ptolemies, Isis and Osiris were confounded with all manner of Asiatic and Greek gods. In process of time she became in her power the most universal of all goddesses, ruling in heaven, on earth, and on the sea, and in the world below, decreeing life and death, deciding the fate of men, and dispensing rewards and punishments. Her worship spread over Greece, and after the Second Punic War obtained a firm footing in Rome in spite of repeated interference by the State. In the days of the Empire it obtained recognition by the State and established itself in all parts of the Roman dominions. The attractiveness of the service of Isis lay in the religious satisfaction which it was calculated to insure. Through

Egyptian Isis and Horus (Harpocrates). (Berlin Museum.)

abstinence from food and from sensual pleasures, and through expiations and purifications, it promised to lead its votaries to sanctification of life and to a true perception of the life divine. The ritual consisted in part of a morning and evening service to the god, partly in annual festivals celebrated in spring at the return of the season for navigation, and also in the late autumn before the advent of winter. At the former festival, held on the fifth of March, and called the ship of Isis (*Isidis navigium*), in recognition of her being the patroness of navigation, and inventress of the sail, the people in general, with the devotees and priests of Isis, went in solemn procession down to the seashore, where a sailing-vessel painted in the Egyptian manner and laden with spices, was committed to the sea (Apul. *Met.* xi. 8–17, esp. 11; Firm. Matern. *De Err. Prof. Relig.* 2).

Isis. (Cairo Museum.)

The other feast was emblematic of the grief of Isis at her loss and her joy at finding again her husband Osiris and her son Horus. Besides these popular feasts there were also certain special mysteries of Isis, which in all their essentials were borrowed from the Eleusinian mysteries of Demeter. (See MYSTERIA.) In these, all who were called thereto by the goddess in a dream were admitted to the select circle of the worshippers of Isis. These devotees, like the priests, were recognized by their linen robes and their shaven heads, and had to devote themselves to an ascetic life. Oracular responses received in dreams were as much associated with the temples of Isis as with those of Serapis (q. v.). In Greek art the goddess is represented as similar to Heré. Her attributes are a serpent, a cornucopia, ears of corn, lotus, moon and horns, as well as the *sistrum* (q. v.), a metal rattle, specially employed in her service.

See Chantepie de la Saussaye, *Lehrbuch der Religionsgeschichte*, vol. i. (1887); R. Lepsius, *Ueber den ersten ägyptischen Götterkreis* (1851); Brugsch Pasha, *Religion und Mythologie der alten Aegypter*, vol. i. (1884); Lefébure, *Étude de la Religion Égyptienne* (1886).

Ismărus (Ἴσμαρος) or **Ismăra**. A town in Thrace, near Maronea, situated on a mountain of the same name, which produced excellent wine. It is mentioned in the *Odyssey* as a town of the Cicones. The poets frequently use the adjective Ismarius as equivalent to Thracus. Near Ismarus was Lake Ismaris.

Ismēné (Ἰσμήνη). The daughter of Oedipus and Iocasta and sister of Antigoné (q. v.).

Ismenias (Ἰσμηνίας). (1) A celebrated musician of Thebes. When he was taken prisoner by the Scythians, Atheas, the king of the country, observed that he liked the neighing of his horse better than all the music of Ismenias. (2) A Theban general, sent to Persia on an embassy by his countrymen. As none were admitted into the king's presence without prostrating themselves at his feet, Ismenias, when he was introduced, dropped his ring, and the motion he made to recover it from the ground being mistaken for the required homage, Ismenias had a satisfactory audience with the monarch (Aelian, *V. H.* i. 21).

Ismēnus (Ἰσμηνός). A small river in Boeotia, rising in Mount Cithaeron, flowing through Thebes, and falling into the lake Hylica. The brook from the fountain Dircé, so celebrated in Theban story, flowed into the Ismenus. From this river Apollo was called Ismenius.

Ismēnus (Ἰσμηνός). The son of Amphion and Niobé. Being struck by one of Apollo's arrows, he fell into the Theban river Ladon, which after this was called from him Ismenus. See NIOBÉ.

Isocrătes (Ἰσοκράτης). The fourth among the ten Attic orators (q. v.). He was born at Athens in B.C. 436, the son of Theodorus, the wealthy proprietor of a flute manufactory, who provided for his son a thorough education. Accordingly, he had the advantage of being instructed by Prodicus, Protagoras, Theramenes, and above all by Gorgias; his character was also moulded by the influence of Socrates, although he never belonged to the more restricted circle of that philosopher's pupils.

Bashfulness and a weak voice prevented him from taking part in public life. After the fall of the Thirty, as his father had lost his means in the calamitous years that closed the Peloponnesian War, he turned his attention to composing forensic speeches for others. After having taught rhetoric at Chios (probably about B.C. 404), he returned to Athens in 403, and there opened a regular school of rhetoric about 392. It was largely attended by both Athenians and non-Athenians, and gained for him considerable wealth. The total number of his pupils has been given at one hundred, including Timotheus, son of Conon, the orators Isaeus, Hyperides, and Lycurgus, and the historians Ephorus and Theopompus. Each pupil paid him 1000 drachmae. Isocrates also had friendly relations with foreign princes, especially with Evagoras of Cyprus and his son Nicocles, who loaded him with

Isocrates (Villa Albani.)

favours. He kept himself completely aloof from any personal share in the public life of his day; yet attempted to influence the political world, not only within the narrow bounds of his native land, but also throughout the whole of Greece, by a series of rhetorical declamations, not intended to be delivered, but only to be read. This he did in the first place in his *Panegyricus* (Πανηγυρικός), which he published in B.C. 380, after spending ten or, according to another account, as many as fifteen years over its preparation. It is a kind of festal oration, eulogizing the services of Athens to Greece, exhorting the Spartans peacefully to share the supremacy with Athens, and calling on the Greeks to lay aside all internal dissensions and to attack the barbarians with their united strength. In the ninetieth year of his age, in a discourse addressed to Philip in B.C. 346, he endeavoured to induce that monarch to carry out his policy by reconciling all the Greeks to one another and leading their united forces against the Persians. Other discourses relate to the internal politics of Athens. Thus, in the *Areopagiticus* (B.C. 354), he recommends his fellow-citizens to get rid of the existing weaknesses in their political constitution by returning to the democracy as founded by Solon and reconstituted by Clisthenes, and by reinstating the Areopagus as the supreme tribunal of censorship over public decorum and morality. He retained his mental and bodily powers unimpaired to an advanced age, and in his ninety-eighth year completed the *Panathenaicus*, a discourse in praise of Athens. He lived to see the total wreck of all his hopes for a regeneration of Greece, and died B.C. 338, a few days after the battle of Chaeronea. He is said to have died of voluntary starvation, owing to his despair at the downfall of Greek liberty; but this account of his death, made familiar to the English world by Milton in his fifth English sonnet, must be considered as doubtful.

There were sixty compositions bearing his name known to antiquity, but less than half that number were considered genuine. Of the twenty-one which have come down to us, the first, the letter to Dominicus, is often regarded as spurious, but there is no reason to doubt the genuineness of nine of the ten other letters. It is only the letter prefixed to the nine in the older editions that is not genuine, having been really written by Theophylact Simocatta early in the seventh century A.D. Of the speeches, six are forensic orations, written to be delivered by others; the rest are declamations, chiefly on political subjects. By his mastery of style, Isocrates had a far-reaching influence on all subsequent Greek prose, which is not confined to oratorical composition alone. His chief strength lies in a careful choice of expression, not only in his vocabulary, but also in the rhythmical formation of his flowing periods, in a skilful use of the figures of speech, and in all that lends euphony to language. Even in Latin the oratorical prose of Cicero is, on its formal side, based chiefly on that of Isocrates; and as modern literary prose has, in its turn, been largely modelled on that of Cicero, the influence of Isocrates has endured to the present day.

The first separate edition of Isocrates is that of Demetrius Chalcocondylas (Milan, 1493). The best modern editions are those of Lange (Halle, 1803); G. S. Dobson, with a Latin rendering, notes, and scholia, 2 vols. (London, 1828); Baiter and Sauppe, 2 vols. (Zürich, 1850); and separately by Benseler-Blass (Leipzig, 1882). There are good editions, with English notes, of the *Demonicus* and *Panegyricus* by Sandys (London, 1872); of the *Areopagiticus*, with German notes by Rauchenstein (5th ed. Berlin, 1882); of the *Philippus* by Schneider (1875). There is an *Index Graecitatis* by Mitchell (Oxford, 1827). See Henn, *De Isocrate Rhetore* (1861); Gehlert, *De Elocutione Isocratea* (1874); Spengel, *Isokrates und Platon* (1855); Susemihl, *De Vita Isocratis* (1884); Blass, *Attische Beredsamkeit;* and Jebb, *Attic Orators*, vol. ii. pp. 1–34.

Isodŏmos (ἰσόδομος). A style of masonry adopted by Greek builders, in which every stone was cut and squared to the same height. Hence, when laid, the courses were all equal (Pliny, *H. N.* xxxvi. 51).

Isopoliteia. See POLITEIA.

Isoteleia (ἰσοτέλεια, "equality in tax and tribute"). At Athens, the position of partial equality with the citizens which was granted to the more deserving of the *metoeci* (q. v.).

Issa (Ἴσσα). The modern Lissa; a small island in the Adriatic Sea, with a town of the same name, off the coast of Dalmatia, said to have derived its name from Issa, daughter of Macareus of Lesbos, who was beloved by Apollo. (Ovid, *Met.* vi. 124). The island was inhabited by a hardy race of sailors, whose barks (*lembi Issaei*) were much prized.

Issedŏnes (Ἰσσηδόνες). A Scythian tribe in Great Tartary, near the Massagetae, whom they resembled in their manners. They are represented as extending to the borders of Serica. (Herod. iv. 26).

Issĭcus Sinus. See Issus.

Issoria (Ἰσσωρία). A name given to Artemis from her shrine at Mount Issorion in Laconia.

Issus (Ἰσσός). A city in the southeastern extremity of Cilicia, near the head of the Issicus Sinus (Gulf of Iskenderûn), and at the northern foot of the pass of Mount Amanus, called the Syrian Gates; memorable for the great battle in which Alexander defeated Darius Codomannus (B.C. 333), which was fought in a narrow valley near the town. See ALEXANDER; DARIUS.

Battle of Issus. (Pompeian Mosaic in the Naples Museum.)

Istaevŏnes. See GERMANIA.

Ister (Ἴστρος) and **Danubius** (Δανούβιος), also **Danuvius.** The greatest river in southeastern Europe; now the Danube, Germ. *Donau.* Its sources are at Donaueschingen near the Mons Abnoba, and after a long course through Vindelicia, Noricum, Pannonia, and Dacia, it separates into a delta of three branches and empties into the Pontus Euxinus (Black Sea). Among its 400 tributaries are the Dravus (Drave), Savus (Save), Pathiseus or Tibiseus (Theiss?), and Margus (Morava). The early writers, such as Pindar, had only the vaguest notions about the sources of this stream, and even in later times it was supposed to empty into the Adriatic. Ister was said to be its Keltic name and Danubis its Thracian. The syllable Dan is that found in Rho-dan-us, Tan-aïs, Eri-dan-us, etc., and is said to mean "river." The most ancient name of the stream was said to be Matoas. Some writers use Ister of the lower Danube, and Danubius of the upper from its source as far as Vindobona (Vienna). The total length of the river is 1740 miles.

Ister. A Greek historian, at one time the slave of Callimachus (q. v.). He wrote, in the third century B.C., a number of works, of which an *Atthis*, or history of Attica, was especially important. The fragments are given in Müller's *Frag. Hist. Graec.* i. pp. 418–427.

Isthmia (τὰ Ἴσθμια). One of the four great national festivals of the Greeks, held on the Isthmus of Corinth, in a grove of pine-trees sacred to Poseidon, near the shrines of the Isthmian Poseidon and of Melicertes. From B.C. 589, they were held in the first month of spring, in the second and fourth years of each Olympiad. According to legend, the Isthmian Games were originally funeral games in memory of Melicertes (q. v.); another tradition relates that they were established by Theseus either in honour of Poseidon, or in commemoration of his victory over Sciron and Sinis. In any case, the Athenians were specially interested in the festival from the earliest times. It was alleged that, from the days of Theseus downwards, they had what was called the προεδρία, the right of occupying the most prominent seats at the games, and, in accordance with a law attributed to Solon, they presented to those of their citizens who were victors in the contests a reward amounting to 100 drachmae. The only occasion when Socrates was absent from Athens, except with the army, was to attend this festival. The inhabitants of Elis were completely excluded from the games, being debarred from either sending competitors or festal envoys. The Corinthians had the presidency, which was transferred to the Sicyonians after the destruction of Corinth (B.C. 146), but at the rebuilding of Corinth (B.C. 46) it was restored to that city. The contests included gymnastic exercises, horse-races, and competitions in music. The former two differed in no essential way from the Olympian Games; in the third, besides musicians, poets of either sex contended for the prize. Besides the customary palm, the prize in Pindar's time consisted of a wreath of dry σέλινον (often translated "parsley," but more probably identical with the "wild celery," *apium graveolens*). The σέλινον was a symbol of funeral games. After the destruction of Corinth, a crown of pine needles was substituted for it. The games long continued to be held, even under the Roman Empire. (Cf. Plut. *Timoleon*, 26; *Sympos.* v. 3, 1–3).

Isthmus (ἰσθμός). A small neck of land which joins a country to another and prevents the sea from making them separate, such as that of Corinth joining the Peloponnesus to Greece prior to 1893, when it was cut by a canal. This is often called "the Isthmus" by way of eminence. See CORINTHIACUS ISTHMUS.

Istria or **Histria.** A peninsula at the northern extremity of the Adriatic, separated from Venetia by the river Timavus, and from Illyricum by the river Arsia. Its inhabitants, the Istri or Histri, were a warlike Illyrian race, who carried on several wars with the Romans, till their final subjugation by the consul C. Clodius Pulcher, B.C. 177. Their chief towns were Tergesté and Pola.

Istropŏlis (Ἰστρόπολις), **Istros** (Ἴστρος), or **Istria** (Ἰστρίη). A town in Lower Moesia, not far from the mouth of the Danube; a colony from Miletus. Its modern name is Istére.

Ităla. The name given to a Latin version of the Scriptures, used by Tertullian in his Biblical quotations. (Cf. St. August. *Doctr. Christ.* ii. 15.) It followed the Septuagint in the Old Testament, and mingled Graecisms, Hebraisms, and plebeian Latin. Its form largely influenced the existing Vulgate. See H. Rönsch, *Itala und Vulgata* (2d ed. Marburg, 1875); Linke, *Studien z. Itala* (Breslau, 1889); and the articles HIERONYMUS; SERMO PLEBEIUS.

Italia. See PROVINCIA.

Italia (Ἰταλία). A country of Europe, bounded on the north by the Alps, on the south by the Ionian Sea, on the northeast by the Adriatic or Maré Superum, and on the southwest by the Maré

Tyrrhenum or Inferum. It was called HESPERIA (Ἑσπερία, "Land of the West") by the Greeks, from its western situation in relation to Greece (Verg. *Aen.* i. 530), and received also from the Latin poets the appellation of AUSONIA (Verg. *Aen.* vii. 54), SATURNIA (Verg. *Georg.* ii. 173), and OENOTRIA (Οἰνωτρία, "Land of Wine"). The name ITALIA some writers derive from Italus, a chief of the Oenotri or Siculi (Thuc. vi. 2). Others find the origin of the term in the Greek word ἰταλός, or the Latin *vitulus* (Oscan *vitlu*), which corresponds to it (Varr. *R. R.* ii. 5; Dion. Hal. i. 35; and Mommsen, *Hist. of Rome*, i. p. 185). Some make the name to have belonged originally to a small section of Calabria, and to have been gradually applied to the whole country.

When the Greeks first became acquainted with this country, they observed it to be peopled with several distinct nations, as they thought; and hence we find it divided by them about the time of Aristotle into six regions—Ausonia or Opica, Tyrrhenia, Iapygia, Ombria, Liguria, and Henetia. Thucydides, in speaking of Cumae, says that it is situated in Opica; and Aristotle, cited by Diony-

sius of Halicarnassus, made Latium a part of this same Opica. As regards the original use of the name Italia, the truth appears to be that the appellation was first given by the early Greeks to Calabria Ulterior, or that southern extremity of the boot which is confined between the Sinus Terinaeus and the Sinus Scyllacius. Such, at least, is the account of Aristotle (*Polit.* vii. 10). This was not done because the name was in strictness confined to that section of the country, but because the Greeks knew at that early period very little, comparatively speaking, of the interior. The nations in the south of Italy, with whom the Greeks first became acquainted, were found by them to be descended from the Itali, or, rather, they found this name in general use among them: hence they called their section of the country by the name of Italia. As their knowledge of the interior became more enlarged, other branches of the same race were successively discovered, and the name Italia thus gradually progressed in its application until it reached the southern limits of Cisalpine Gaul. To this latter country the name of Gallia Cisalpina was originally given, because it was peopled principally by Gauls. (See GALLIA.) Towards the end of the third century B.C., Italia designated all the countries south of the Tiber and Aesis. At length, in Polybius, we find the name given to all Italy up to the foot of the Alps. The inclusion of Cisalpine Gaul under this appellation was an act of policy on the part of the Second Triumvirate, who were afraid lest, if it remained a province, some future proconsul might imitate Caesar, and overthrow with his legions the authority of the Republic. At a still later period, Augustus divided Italy into eleven regions (see below). It is somewhat remarkable that the name Italia, after having gradually extended to the Alps, should at a subsequent epoch be limited in its application to the northern parts alone. When the emperor Maximian, towards the close of the third century A.D., transferred his residence to Milan, the usage prevailed in the West of giving the name of Italy exclusively to the five provinces of Æmilia, Liguria, Flaminia, Venetia, and Istria. It was in this sense that the kings of the Lombards were styled kings of Italy.

Italy was never inhabited by a single race. It contained a number of different peoples, who had migrated into the country at a very early period. They may be classified under the following five divisions:

(1) THE ILLYRIANS.—These were the people usually spoken of as the Veneti, dwelling at the head of the Adriatic (cf. Herod. i. 196), and regarded by ethnologists as Indo-European and probably allied to the Albanians in their racial type as in their language. Of the speech of these people there exist, in addition to geographical and personal names, several hundred inscriptions, largely dedications on bronzes and pottery, and all of them very brief. Other offshoots of the same branch are probably to be found in the Iapygians of southeastern Italy, of whom the Messapii are the most noted group. Of the last there exist some 165 stone inscriptions. See Pauli, *Die Veneter* (Leipzig, 1891); and the article MESSAPIA.

(2) THE ETRUSCANS.—This curious people extended from the mouth of the Tiber between its right bank on the sea to the Alps in the north. For a full account of the theories regarding them, see the article ETRURIA.

(3) THE GREEKS.—Southern Italy was colonized by Greeks at an early period, and there existed in that part of the peninsula (called MAGNA GRAECIA or GRAECIA MAIOR) rich and flourishing cities long before Rome had risen to power. Among them were Tarentum, Sybaris, Croton, Siris (Heraclea), Metapontum, Locri, and Rhegium, and their inhabitants exerted considerable influence upon both the purely Italic peoples of Italy and upon the Latin language, contributing to it a number of non-Ionic word-forms. See Lenormant, *La Grande-Grèce*, 3 vols. (Paris, 1881).

(4) THE KELTS.—These first appeared in Italy only in historic times, in the early years of the fourth century B.C. Keltic inscriptions have been found in Italy as far south as Todi in Umbria. See CELTAE; GALLIA CISALPINA; INDO-EUROPEAN LANGUAGES.

(5) THE ITALIANS PROPER.—These are the branch of the Indo-European race that became specifically identified with Italy, and of which the Latin subdivision finally dominated the whole peninsula and in fact the known world. Grouped linguistically, there are two principal divisions: (*a*) *Latin-Faliscan* and (*b*) *Oscan-Umbrian* or *Umbro-Sabellian.* The Oscan-Umbrian is subdivided into many minor dialects, their general relations being sufficiently well indicated in the foregoing diagram; see, also, the separate articles OSCI; UMBRIA.

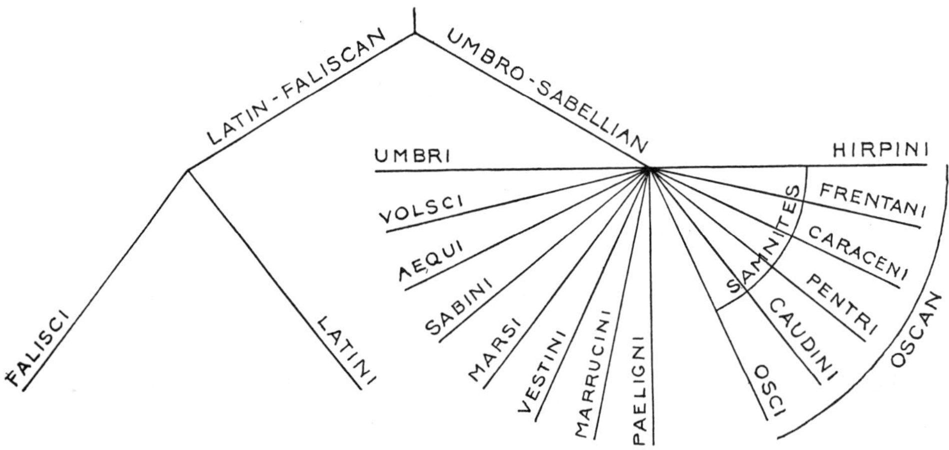

Diagram of the Italic Peoples.

At the time of Augustus the following were the chief divisions of Italy, an account of which is also given in separate articles: (1) UPPER ITALY, which extended from the Alps to the rivers Macra on the west and Rubico on the east. It comprehended (*a*) Liguria; (*b*) Gallia Cisalpina; (*c*) Venetia, including Carnia; (*d*) Istria. (2) CENTRAL ITALY, sometimes called ITALIA PROPRIA (a term not used by the ancients), to distinguish it from Gallia Cisalpina or Upper Italy, and Magna Graecia or Lower Italy, extended from the rivers Macra on the west and Rubico on the east, to the rivers Silarus on the west and Frento on the east. It comprehended (*a*) Etruria; (*b*) Umbria; (*c*) Picenum; (*d*) Samnium, including the country of the Sabini, Vestini, Marrucini, Marsi, Paeligni, etc.; (*e*) Latium; (*f*) Campania. (3) LOWER ITALY, or MAGNA GRAECIA, included the remaining part of the peninsula, south of the rivers Silarus and Frento. It comprehended, (*a*) Apulia, including Calabria; (*b*) Lucania; (*c*) Bruttium.

Augustus divided Italy into the following eleven Regiones: I. Latium and Campania. II. The land of the Hirpini, Apulia, and Calabria. III. Lucania and Bruttium. IV. The land of the Frentani, Marrucini, Paeligni, Marsi, Vestini, and Sabini, together with Samnium. V. Picenum. VI. Umbria and the district of Ariminum, in what was formerly called Gallia Cisalpina. VII. Etruria. VIII. Gallia Cispadana. IX. Liguria. X. The eastern part of Gallia Transpadana, Venetia, Carnia, and Istria. XI. The western part of Gallia Transpadana. See Desjardins, *Les Onze Régions d'Auguste* (1875).

See Curtius, *De Antiquis Italiae Incolis* (Greifswald, 1829); Diefenbach, *Origines Europaeae* (Frankfurt-on-the-Main, 1861); Bugge, *Altitalische Studien* (Christiania, 1878); Deecke, *Die Falisker* (Strassburg, 1885); Czörnig, *Die alten Völker Oberitaliens* (Vienna, 1885); Nissen, *Italische Landeskunde* (Berlin, 1883); Deecke, *Die italischen Sprachen* in Gröber's *Grundriss der romanischen Philologie;* Mommsen, *Die unteritalischen Dialekte* (Leipzig, 1850); Conway, *The Italic Dialects* (announced in 1895); and the articles CELTAE; DIALECTS; ETRURIA; GALLIA; INDO-EUROPEAN LANGUAGES; OSCI; ROMA; UMBRIA.

Italĭca. Now Sevilla la Vieja in Spain. A municipium in Hispania Baetica on the west bank of the Baetis, founded by Scipio Africanus in the Second Punic War. It was the birthplace of both Trajan and Hadrian.

Italĭcus, SILIUS. See SILIUS.

Ităłus (Ἰταλός). A fabled monarch of early Italy, said to have been the son of Telegonus by Penelopé. See Thuc. vi. 2, and ITALIA.

Itănus (Ἴτανος). A town on the eastern coast of Crete, of Phœnician origin.

Iter. See SERVITUTES; VIAE.

Iterdūca or **Interdūca.** An epithet of Iuno. See Mart. Capell. ii. § 149 (Grot.).

Ithăca (Ἰθάκη). Now Thiaki; an island in the Ionian Sea, off the coast of Epirus, celebrated as the birthplace of Odysseus. It is about twelve miles long, and four in its greatest breadth, and is divided into two parts, which are connected by a narrow isthmus not more than half a mile across. In each of these parts there is a mountain ridge of considerable height—the one in the north called Neritum, and the one in the south Neium. The city of Ithaca, the residence of Odysseus, was situated on a precipitous, conical hill, now called Aëto, or "eagle's cliff," occupying the whole breadth of the isthmus mentioned above. Its summit is still surrounded by Cyclopean walls and shows traces of fortifications. The chief town of the island is now called Vathý. See Warsberg, *Odysseische Landschaften* (Vienna, 1879); Partsch, *Kephallenia und Ithaka* (Gotha, 1890); and La Roche, *Ithaka* (1892).

Ithacesiae. (1) Three islands opposite Vibo, on the coast of Bruttium. They are thought to answer to the modern Braces, Praca, and Torricella. (2) Baiae is called by Silius Italicus *sedes Ithacesia Baii,* because founded by Baius, the pilot of Odysseus, according to the poetic legends of antiquity (Sil. Ital. viii. 539).

Ithăcus (Ἴθακος). The son of Pterolaüs. He was the hero after whom Ithaca was said to have been named (*Odyss.* xvii. 207).

Ithōmé (Ἰθώμη). (1) A town of Thessaly, in the vicinity of Metropolis. (2) A fortress of Messenia, on a mountain of the same name. It was celebrated for the long and obstinate defence (ten years) which the Messenians there made in their last revolt against the Spartans. The mountain was said to have derived its name from Ithomé, one of the nymphs that nourished Zeus. On the summit was the altar of Zeus Ithometes, to whom the mountain was especially dedicated. Strabo compares the Messenian Acropolis to the Acrocorinthus, being situated, like that citadel, on a lofty and steep mountain, enclosed by fortified lines which connected it with the town. Hence these were justly deemed the two strongest places in the Peloponnesus. When Philip, the son of Demetrius, was planning the conquest of the peninsula with Demetrius of Pharos, the latter advised him to seize first the horns of the heifer, which would secure to him possession of the animal. By these enigmatical expressions he designated the Peloponnesus and the two strongholds above mentioned (Polyb. vii. 11). Remains of the ancient fortress still exist, the towers being magnificent specimens of military architecture and engineering.

Itineraria. The Roman name for (1) compendious lists of the names and distances of the different stations on the public roads, after the manner of our road-books (*itineraria adnotata* or *scripta*); and (2) chartographic representations similar to our travelling maps (*itineraria picta,* Veget. iii. 6). Of the former kind we have: (i.) the two ANTONINE ITINERARIES, the basis of which belongs to the time of the emperor Antoninus Caracalla; but the edition which has come down to us dates from the beginning of the fourth century. They contain lists of routes by land and sea in the Roman Empire; (ii.) the ITINERARIUM BURDIGALENSÉ or HIEROSOLYMITĀNUM, A.D. 333, the route of a pilgrimage from Burdigala (Bordeaux) to Jerusalem; (iii.) the ITINERARIUM ALEXANDRI, an abstract of the Persian expedition of Alexander the Great, drawn up mainly from Arrian for the expedition of the emperor Constantius against the Persians (A.D. 340–345).

At Vicarello in Etruria have been found four silver travelling-cups shaped like mile-stones, and having marked upon them a list of stations and distances from Gades (Cadiz) to Rome.

Of the other kind of itineraries, in the form of maps, there exists a specimen in the Peutinger map (*tabula Peutingeriana*), now in Vienna. It received its name from a former possessor, Konrad Peutinger, a councillor of Augsburg. It was painted at Kolmar in 1265 on the model of an original map which dates back to the middle of the third century A.D., and consists of twelve broad strips of parchment, on which are delineated all those parts of the world which were known to the Romans; only the pieces which should contain Spain and Britain are lost, with the exception of part of Kent. It is probably derived from Agrippa's map. (See GEOGRAPHIA.) It is disproportionately elongated in the direction of east to west, the ratio of its height to its breadth being 1:21. The distances from town to town are marked on lines running from east to west, and the relative sizes of the towns are indicated by distinctive marks. An excellent fac-simile has been published by O. Maier of Ravensburg (1888), and the table is represented on a small scale in the very convenient little *Atlas Antiquus* of Justus Perthes (Gotha, 1893). See D'Urban, *Recueil des Itinéraires Anciens*, with ten maps (Paris, 1845); Renier, *Itin. Romains de la Gaule* (Paris, 1850); and NOTITIA REGIONUM.

Itius Portus. A harbour of the Morini, on the north coast of Gaul, from which Caesar set sail for Britain; probably Vissant, or Witsand, near Calais.

Iton. See ITONIA.

Itonia (Ἰτωνία), **Itonias** (Ἰτωνιάς), or **Itōnis** (Ἰτωνίς). A surname of Athenê, derived from the town of Iton, in the south of Phthiotis in Thessaly. Here the goddess had a celebrated sanctuary, and hence is called by the Roman poets *incola Itoni.*

Itūna, or **Itūnae**, AESTUARIUM. Now Solway Firth, in Scotland.

Ituraea (Ἰτουραία) or **Ityraea.** A country of Palestine, so called from Itur or Ietur, one of the sons of Ishmael, who settled in it; but whose posterity were either driven out or subdued by the Amorites, when it is supposed to have formed part of the kingdom of Bashan. It lay on the north-eastern side of the land of Israel, between it and the territory of Damascus or Syria. The Itureans being subdued by Aristobulus, the high-priest and governor of the Jews, B.C. 106, were forced by him to embrace the Jewish religion, and were at the same time incorporated into the State. They again became independent, but were again subdued by Pompey. Many of them entered the Roman armies and won renown by their skill in horsemanship and archery. Philip, one of the sons of Herod the Great, was tetrarch or governor of this country when John the Baptist commenced his ministry (Ioseph. *Ant. Jud.* xiii. 19; Epiphan. *Haeres.* 19; Luke, iii. 1). See PALAESTINA.

Itȳlus (Ἴτυλος). See AËDON.

Itys (Ἴτυς). (1) See TEREUS. (2) A companion of Aeneas, slain by Turnus in Italy (Verg. *Aen.* ix. 574).

Iuba (Ἰόβας). (1) King of Numidia and son of Hiempsal. He joined Pompey's party, and gained a victory over Curio, Caesar's legate, B.C. 49. He afterwards fought with Scipio against Caesar; and after the battle of Thapsus (B.C. 46) put an end to his own life. (2) Son of the preceding. He was a child at the time of his father's death, and was carried by Caesar to Rome, where he received an excellent education. He became one of the most learned men of his day, and wrote numerous works on historical and other subjects. In B.C. 30, Augustus reinstated him in his paternal kingdom of Numidia, and gave him in marriage Cleopatra, otherwise called Selenê, the daughter of Antony and Cleopatra. Five years afterwards (25) Augustus gave him Mauretania in exchange for Numidia, which was reduced to a Roman province. He died in Mauretania, about A.D. 19. Plutarch calls him ὁ πάντων ἱστορικώτατος βασιλέων (*Sert.* 9), and he appears to have attempted (in Greek) many kinds of literary and scientific work; but the titles alone have descended to us. Among these are an African history (Λιβυκά), a Roman history (Ῥωμαϊκὴ Ἱστορία), and a history of painting (Περὶ Γραφικῆς). There is an epigram by Iuba preserved in Athenaeus (viii. p. 343). See the account of Iuba by the Abbé Sevin in the *Mémoires de l'Académie des Inscriptions*, iv. p. 457 foll.; and for the fragments, Müller's *Frag. Hist. Graec.* iii. pp. 465–484.

Iudaea. See PALAESTINA.

Iudaei (Hebr. *Yehudim*). The Jews came into historical contact with the Greeks during the Asiatic campaigns of Alexander the Great, who in 332, on his march through Palestine, spared Jerusalem and its temple at the intercession of Jaddua the high-priest. During the following century, when Iudaea became subject to Alexander's successors, the Ptolemies and Seleucidae in Egypt and Syria, Greek philosophy and Greek culture were widely diffused among the Jews. The Sadducees appear to have been largely influenced by the Epicurean doctrines, and the stricter Pharisees by the Stoic. Even the worship of the Grecian gods made considerable progress in Iudaea, and the Greek language came into common use. Many Jews were drawn to Alexandria soon after the founding of that city, and enjoyed these unusual privileges under both Ptolemy I. and Ptolemy II. (B.C. 323–247). Under the latter the celebrated translation of the Old Testament, known as the Septuagint, was made by a body of Jewish scholars, seventy in number, and this Greek version was even used in the synagogues. In B.C. 198 the Jews aided Antiochus the Great in expelling the Egyptians from Palestine; but found to their sorrow that, under the new régime of the Seleucidae, their lot was much less favourable, for an attempt was soon made to Hellenize the Empire at the expense of some of the most cherished Jewish traditions. The treasury of the temple at Jerusalem was several times robbed of its treasures; and in 169, owing to a revolt against the king of Syria, a general massacre of the inhabitants of that city occurred. At the same time its walls were destroyed, the image of Antiochus was placed in the temple, swine were sacrificed on its altar, the Jewish Scriptures were publicly burned, shrines to Zeus were erected, and great cruelty was shown to the surviving inhabitants. This savage rule was checked by the great revolt headed by the Maccabees, the priest Mattathias and his five sons, under whom the Jews freed the land for a time (167–63) and defeated the Syrian armies, forming alliances with the Romans.

In B.C. 63 a civil war between the Jewish claimants for political power led to the intervention of Pompey, who had been invoked as arbiter. He laid siege to Jerusalem, violated the temple, even entering the Holy of Holies, and finally reduced

Iudaea to the form of a Roman province. In 39 Herod the Great, having won the favour of the Second Triumvirate, was installed as king of Iudaea, and kept himself in power by his servile flattery of M. Antonius. (See HERODES.) At the death of Herod, Augustus Caesar divided his territories among his sons—Archelaüs, Philip, and Herodes Antipas; but a state of anarchy ensued, and the country was re-annexed to the Roman dominions. Under the emperors, the Jews suffered greatly from the oppression of their governors. Their religion was insulted, and their property wrung from them by the exactions of the procurators. Under Nero, a great revolt took place, owing to the severities of the governor Gessius Florus; and Jerusalem fell into the hands of the insurgents. The Roman governor of Syria, Cestius Gallus, was routed by the Jewish army. The revolt, however, was crushed by Vespasian, who took Jerusalem after a memorable siege (A.D. 68), in which the sufferings of the besieged and the ferocity of their defence are immortalized in the narrative of Iosephus (q. v.). The city was razed to the ground; and a new city, reared under Hadrian, received the name Aelia Capitolina. Into this no Jew was allowed to enter.

The Romans seem to have felt considerable interest in the Jews, being attracted by their monotheistic religion, though failing to understand it rightly, and accepting many strange stories regarding it. Thus, it was asserted that the Jews worshipped clouds and thunder (Juv. xiv. 97, with Mayor's note); that they adored an ass's head (Apion in Ios. ii. 7); that they ate human flesh (Apion, *Fr.* 19, Didot); that they made it a practice annually to cook and eat a Greek, swearing hostility to the Greek race (Apion in Ios. ii. 7). Nevertheless, the spiritual beauty of the Jewish faith impressed many serious minds among both the Greeks and Romans. Tacitus, in his *Historiae*, pays a high tribute to the Jews; and there are many instances recorded of acts of reverence paid by the Romans to the Mosaic religion. Thus, Cumanus ordered the execution of a soldier who had torn and burned the book of the law; Agrippa, the son-in-law of Augustus, visited the temple daily during his stay in Jerusalem, and offered sacrifices there; Iulius Caesar, before this, had removed restrictions set upon the practice of the Jewish faith, so that at his funeral rites the Jews took a conspicuous part in the public mourning (Suet. *Iul.* 84, with Peck's note). They were regarded as especially given to making proselytes (cf. Hor. *Sat.* i. 4, 43; Ioseph. *Ant. Jud.* vii. 3, 3), and were successful in spreading their religion (Dio Cass. lxvii. 14, § 2), especially among women (Juv. vi. 542 foll.; Ovid, *A. A.* i. 76). When the Romans began to import Oriental rites, the Sabbath was superstitiously observed by many (Plut. *De Superst.* iii. p. 166 *a*; cf. Hor. *Sat.* i. 9, 69). From the similarity of many of their usages, the Jews and Christians were often regarded as identical.

The heathen accounts of the Jews are carefully collected by Meyer, *Judaica* (Jena, 1832); Gill, *Notices of the Jews*, etc. (2d ed. London, 1872); and reference may be made to the following works: Göser, in the *Tüb. Quartalschr.* (1868); Friedländer, *Sittengeschichte Roms*, vol. iii. (Leipzig, 1890); Langen, *Das Judenthum in Palästina zur Zeit Christi* (1866); Huidekoper, *Judaism at Rome* (New York, 1876); Derenbourg, *Essai sur l'Histoire, etc., de la Palestine*, ch. xiv. (Paris, 1867); Lecky, *Hist. of European Morals*, ch. iii.; Döllinger, *Heidenthum und Judenthum* (Regensburg, 1857); and Mayor's elaborate notes to Juvenal, xiv. 96–106. See PALAESTINA.

Iudex. In the Roman constitution a general designation of all judges, whether officials exercising judicial functions or individuals in a private position intrusted on oath with the duty of deciding in either civil or criminal trials. For standing and for extraordinary criminal courts (see QUAESTIO) the iudices were at first chosen from the number of the senators by agreement of the parties concerned. Gaius Gracchus first introduced a list of iudices (*album*) for the permanent tribunals (*quaestiones perpetuae*). At first this list was permanent, but afterwards it was published annually by the *praetor urbanus*, who had to swear that he would be impartial in his selection of names. Under the Empire, as long as the *quaestiones perpetuae* existed, it was published by the emperor, who nominated the iudices to hold office for life, and from time to time revised and completed the list. By the lex Sempronia of Gaius Gracchus (B.C. 123), the office of judge was taken away from the senators, who had held it previously, and transferred to the possessors of the knight's census (the *equites*). In B.C. 80 a lex Cornelia of L. Cornelius Sulla restored it to the Senate. In B.C. 70 the office was equally divided between the senators, the knights, and the *tribuni aerarii*. These last were once more excluded by Caesar. Augustus formed four *decuriae*, or divisions, of iudices. Of these the first three were obliged to possess the knight's census, and the last the half of it. Caligula added a fifth decuria.

Under the Empire the judicial functions, hitherto confined to certain definite classes, had become so general in their obligations that it was considered a privilege to be freed from them. This exemption was granted to a man with many children, and, afterwards, to those following the professions of grammarians and teachers. The requisite qualifications, apart from that of property, were that a person should be by birth a citizen, and not less than thirty years of age (after Augustus, not less than twenty-five). The other requirements were bodily and mental capacity, an unblemished reputation, and a long residence in Italy. Under the Republic the number of those who were sworn in varied at different times; under the Empire it was fixed at 4000, and later at 5000. For every court of justice the judges were taken from the general list by lot, and out of this special list the presiding magistrate appointed a definite number for each trial. Out of these a certain number might be challenged and rejected by either side; perhaps the president filled up the vacancies by again drawing lots. The swearing in took place before the trial. When the number of the praetors appointed for the *quaestiones* was not sufficiently large, a *iudex quaestionis* was appointed, generally one who had served as aedile.

In civil cases it was customary from early times for the judicial magistrates—i. e. the praetors—to depute the investigation and decision to a person instructed by them and appointed by consent of both sides, who was styled *iudex pedaneus* (χαμαι δικαστής), and corresponded with the referee of New York state law. The terms *arbiter*, *iudex delegatus*, and *iudex specialis* are also used of such a person. From the time of Augustus a single judge (*iudex unus*) was appointed in each case from the general *album* of sworn iudices, but for certain cases several judges were introduced. (See RECUPERATORES; JUDICIAL PROCEDURE, II.) The *iudices centumviri* formed the single great judicial body for trying civil cases. (See CENTUMVIRI.) Concerning the *iudices litibus iudicandis*, who were also appointed in civil cases, see VIGINTI-SEX VIRI.

Iudex Pedaneus. See IUDEX.

Iudex Quaestiōnis. See IUDEX.

Iudicāti Actio. A defendant who had been condemned in an action was under an obligation to satisfy the judgment—i. e. to pay to the plaintiff the sum of money which the iudex had awarded; and the actio iudicati was the mode which the successful party had to adopt in order to compel the defendant to fulfil his obligation. The ground of the actio iudicati being the judgment debt, the defendant was not allowed to go behind the judgment and dispute the original claim, but might set up the plea that the judgment was invalid. If defeated in the action he was mulcted in double the original amount.

Iudĭces. See IUDEX.

Iudicium. See IUDEX; JUDICIAL PROCEDURE.

Iudicium Publĭcum. In Roman law, a sort of application of civil procedure, in some of its points, to criminal cases. The presiding officers were usually a civil magistrate (the praetor), and the case was heard before a bench of *iudices*. It differed from ordinary civil process in that the magistrate sat with the *iudices*, directed their decision, and pronounced the verdict. The earliest notice of the iudicium publicum is found in the Lex Bantina of about B.C. 130. (See TABULA BANTINA.) Reference may be made to Mommsen, *Röm. Staatsrecht*, i. pp. 168 and 182 foll.; ii. pp. 223 and 569 foll.

Iugatio. A word which implies the training of vines to a rail or trellis, which was practised in two ways: either in single lines, like an espalier, then termed *iugatio directa*, or over a frame formed with uprights and tie-bars at the top (Varro, *R. R.* i. 8, 2).

Iugĕrum and **Iugus.** A Roman measure of surface = 240 × 120 feet, or 28,800 square feet, and hence = ⅝ of an English acre. It was the common measure of land, two iugera forming an *heredium*, one hundred *heredia* forming a *centuria*, and four *centuriae* a *saltus*.

Iugum (ζυγόν and ζυγός). (1) In architecture, a cross-beam (Vitruv. x. 8, 19). (2) The beam which united the upright posts of a loom. (3) The cross-rail of a trellis. (4) The cross-bar of a lyre. (5) A scale-beam, and hence, by metonymy, a pair of scales = *libra*. (6) The thwart or cross-bench of a boat. (7) A yoke, often fastened to the horns of a beast (Columell. *R. R.* ii. 2). The yoke was tied to the pole (ῥυμός, *temo*) by a rope or strap (ζυγόδεσμον). Cf. Hom. *Il.* xxiv. 268–274, with Leaf's discussion in the *Journal of the Hellen. Soc.* v. 185 foll. See CURRUS.

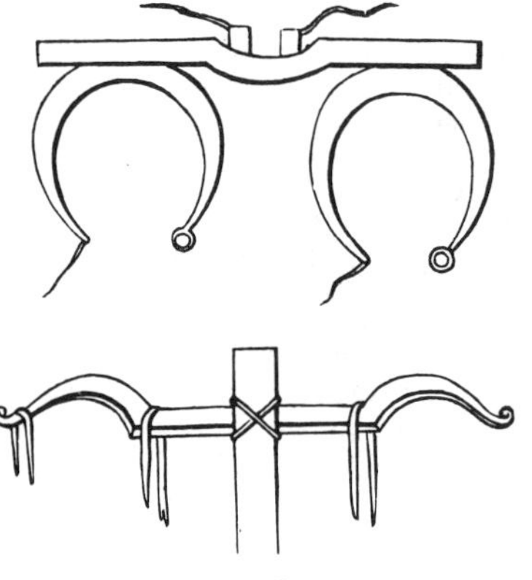

Ancient Yokes.

Iugumentum (ζύγωμα). The lintel of a doorway (Cato, *R. R.* xiv. 1, 4). See IANUA.

Iugurtha (Ἰουγούρθας). An illegitimate son of Mastanabal, and grandson of Masinissa. He lost his father at an early age, but was brought up by Micipsa with his own sons, Hiempsal and Adherbal. Iugurtha was a brave, able, and ambitious prince, and distinguished himself greatly while serving under Scipio against Numantia, in B.C. 134. Micipsa, on his death in 118, bequeathed his kingdom to Iugurtha and his two sons, Hiempsal and Adherbal, in common. Iugurtha aspired to the sole sovereignty. He assassinated Hiempsal soon after his father's death, and a division of the kingdom between Iugurtha and Adherbal was then made by the Roman Senate; but shortly afterwards Iugurtha attacked Adherbal, took him prisoner, and put him to death (112). The Romans had previously commanded Iugurtha to abstain from hostilities against Adherbal; and as he had paid no attention to their commands, they now declared war against him. The consul L. Calpurnius Bestia was sent into Africa (111); but by large sums of money Iugurtha purchased from him a favourable peace—a disgraceful proceeding which excited the greatest indignation at Rome. The peace was disowned, and the war renewed under the command of the consul Sp. Postumius Albinus; but during the absence of the consul, his brother Aulus was defeated by Iugurtha (110). Next year (109) the consul Q. Caecilius Metellus, an able general and incorruptible man, was sent into Africa at the head of a new army. In the course of two years Metellus frequently defeated Iugurtha, and at length drove him to take refuge among the Gaetulians. In 107 Metellus was succeeded in the command by Marius. The cause of Iugurtha was now supported by his father-in-law, Bocchus, king of Mauretania; but Marius defeated their united forces, and Bocchus purchased the forgiveness of the Romans by surrendering his son-in-law to Sulla, the quaestor of Marius (106). Iugurtha was carried a prisoner to Rome, and after adorning the triumph of Marius (January 1, 104), was thrown into a dungeon, and there starved to death. The history of the Jugurthine War was written by Sallust, and is a masterpiece of historical composition. See SALLUSTIUS.

Iulia. (1) A daughter of Iulius Caesar by Cornelia, celebrated for her beauty and excellent character. She had been affianced to Servilius Caepio, and was on the point of being given to him in marriage, when her father bestowed her upon Pompey (Plut. *Pomp.* 47; Appian. *B. C.* i. 14). Iulia possessed great influence over both her father and her husband, and as long as she lived prevented any outbreak between them. Her sudden death, however, in childbed, severed the tie that had in some degree bound Pompey to his father-in-law, and no private considerations any longer existed to allay the jealousies which political disputes might arouse between them. The amiable character of Iulia, and her constant affection for her husband, gained for her the general regard of the people; and this they showed by insisting on celebrating her funeral in the Campus Martius, a compliment scarcely ever paid to a woman before (Suet. *Iul.* 21, 26, 84). (2) The sister of Iulius Caesar. She married M. Atius Balbus, and became by him the mother of Octavia Minor and Augustus (Suet. *Iul.* 74; *Aug.* 4, 8). (3) The aunt of Iulius Caesar. At her decease, her nephew pronounced a eulogy from the Rostra over her remains (Suet. *Iul.* 6). (4) The daughter of Augustus by his first wife Scribonia. As he had no children by Livia, whom he had subsequently espoused, Iulia remained his sole heiress, and the choice of her husband became a matter of great importance. She was first married to her cousin M. Marcellus (B.C. 25), the nephew of Augustus by his sister Octavia, and the person celebrated by Vergil in the famous lines of the sixth *Aeneid*. But Marcellus dying young and without children, Augustus selected for the second husband of his daughter his oldest friend and most useful adherent, M. Vipsanius Agrippa. This marriage seemed to answer all the wishes of Augustus, for Iulia became the mother of five children—Gaius, Lucius, Iulia, Agrippina, and Agrippa Postumus. Agrippa died B.C. 12, and Iulia was married, for the third time, to Tiberius Claudius Nero, the son of Livia, and afterwards emperor. Tiberius subsequently thought proper to withdraw from Rome to the island of Rhodes, where he lived in the greatest retirement. During his absence, his wife Iulia was guilty of such gross infidelities towards him that Augustus himself divorced her in the name of his son-in-law, and banished her to the island of Pandataria, off the Campanian coast, where she was closely confined for some time, and treated with the greatest rigour; nor would Augustus ever forgive her, or receive her again into his presence, although he afterwards removed her from Pandataria to Rhegium, and somewhat softened the severity of her treatment. When her husband Tiberius ascended the throne (A.D. 14) she was again severely dealt with, and soon died of ill-treatment and starvation. (5) The granddaughter of Augustus, and daughter of Agrippa and Iulia (4). She was married to L. Paulus, but, imitating the licentious conduct of her mother, was banished by Augustus for her adulterous practices to the island of Tremerus, off the coast of Apulia, where she continued to live for the space of twenty years, and where at last she died (Tac. *Ann.* iv. 71). (6) A daughter of Germanicus and Agrippina, married in A.D. 33 to M. Vinicius. She was cut off by the intrigues of Messalina, who accused her of adultery with the philosopher Seneca (Dio Cass. lix. 3, 8). (7) Daughter of Caligula and Milonia Caesaria. Her father carried her to the temples of all the goddesses, and dedicated her to Minerva, as the patroness of her education. She showed in her infancy strong indications of the cruelty that branded both her parents. She suffered death with her mother after the assassination of Caligula (Suet. *Calig.* 25, 59). (8) See DOMNA. (9) Daughter of Titus the son of Vespasian, and married to Flavius Sabinus, Vespasian's nephew. She lived in criminal intercourse with the emperor Domitian, and died of an abortion caused by him. (10) See DRUSILLA. (11) See MAESA.

Iulia, daughter of Augustus.

Iulia, daughter of Titus. (Gem in the King Collection.)

Iulia Gens, one of the most ancient patrician houses at Rome. It was of Alban origin, and was removed to Rome by Tullus Hostilius upon the destruction of Alba Longa. It claimed descent from the mythical Iulus, the son of Venus and Anchises. The most distinguished family in the gens is that of Caesar.

Iuliae Leges. See LEX.

Iuliānus, DIDIUS. See DIDIUS.

Iuliānus, FLAVIUS CLAUDIUS. A Roman emperor, popularly known as "Julian the Apostate" (ὁ ἀποστάτης). He was born at Constantinople in A.D. 331, the youngest son of Iulius Constantius, half-brother to Constantine the Great. On the death of Constantine there was a general massacre of the male members of the younger line of the Flavian family, and among those so put to death was Julian's father, Julian being spared only on account of his extreme youth. He was reared under close and vexatious surveillance at Macellum in Cappadocia and at Nicomedia, and the treatment which he and his family had received from nominal Christians both embittered him and led him to reject Christianity, he being also won back to paganism by the teaching of his Neoplatonic master Maximus. In 355 he studied at Athens, among his fellow-students being the future bishops Basil and Gregory Nau-

Iulianus.

zianzenus. In November of the same year Julian was summoned to Milan to assume the rank of Caesar. He married the emperor's sister Helena.

During the next five years he joined the army in Germania and defeated the Alemanni near Argentoratum (Strassburg), and also subdued the Franks along the Rhine, winning at the same time the affections of the people by his courage, mildness, and simplicity. In April, 360, the emperor, becoming alarmed at Julian's popularity, ordered away some of his best troops, upon which his soldiers revolted, and proclaimed him as Augustus. Soon after, he sent forward the greater part of his army by way of Rhaetia and Noricum, and himself with a picked body of 3000 men plunged into the Black Forest, sailing down the Danube to Sirmium in Pannonia Inferior, which he had made the rendezvous of his forces. Here he heard of the death of the emperor (November 3, 361), and here he openly proclaimed himself a pagan, sacrificing to the old gods of Rome. Though he tolerated the Jewish and the Christian religions, he did all that lay in his power to cripple the spread of the latter. He confiscated the revenues of the churches, and ordered that those who had assisted in pulling down the heathen temples should rebuild them. This was the signal for a fearful reaction and persecution against the Christians in the provinces, where many were imprisoned, tormented, and even put to death. Julian restrained or punished some of these disorders, but with no very zealous hand. There was evidently a determined struggle throughout the Empire between the old and the new religion, and Julian wished for the triumph of the former. He forbade the Christians to read, or teach to others, the works of the ancient classic writers, saying that, as they rejected the gods, they ought not to avail themselves of the learning and genius of those who believed in them. He also forbade their filling any office, civil or military, and subjected them to other disabilities and humiliations.

In July, 362, he resolved upon war with the Persians, and spent some months at Antioch. Gibbon has given a powerful, though no doubt too highly coloured, picture of the emperor—awkward, shy, and unkempt, with ink-stained fingers, long nails, and vermin-infested beard—at whom the citizens of this luxurious capital sneered and aimed lampoons. Against them in reply he directed his satire *Misopogon* (Μισοπώγων, "beard-hater"), and gave them a rapacious governor.

It was during his residence at Antioch that Julian undertook to aim what he thought would prove a deadly blow to Christianity. An order was issued for rebuilding the great temple of Jerusalem. The Jews were invited from all the provinces of the Empire to assemble on the holy mountain of their fathers, and a bold attempt was thus made to falsify the language of prophecy and annul the decree which the Christians believed to have been pronounced by the Almighty against his once chosen, but now rejected, people. The accomplishment of this design was intrusted to Alypius, who had been governor of Britain, and every effort was made to insure its success as well on the part of the "imperial sophist" as on that of the Jews themselves. But the attempt was an unavailing one, and is said to have been signally and miraculously interrupted. Few historical facts, indeed, rest on more abundant testimony. The narratives of Gregory Nanzianzenus and of Rufinus are confirmed in the fullest manner by Ammianus Marcellinus, himself a heathen writer. "When Alypius," observes Ammianus, "was plying the work vigorously, and the governor of the province was lending his aid, fearful globes of fire, bursting forth repeatedly from the earth close to the foundations, scorched the workmen, and rendered the place, after frequent trials on their part, quite inaccessible." The Jewish rabbis, in their annals, attest the same fact; and even Gibbon, though in his solemnly sneering way he styles it a "splendid and specious miracle," is obliged to treat the evidence with respect. See Newman, *Essay on the Miracles in Early Ecclesiastical History* (1842).

In March, 363, Julian set out on his expedition against the Persian king Sapor, and advanced upon Ctesiphon. Proceeding still farther, with a treacherous guide and under a burning sun, he was continually assailed by the Persian cavalry; and in one of their onslaughts the emperor was wounded by a spear-thrust in the side and fell from his horse, the blood spurting from the wound. Theodoretus relates that as he saw the ghastly injury the dying man exclaimed, "Thou hast conquered, Galilaean; yet still do I renounce thee!" He passed away at midnight of June 26, 363.

Julian's life is one of much pathetic interest, and is a sad instance of noble views distorted and of powers misapplied, with failure as the inevitable result; for, as Beugnot says, it was an accident, after which events reverted to their natural channel. Christianity was scarcely checked for a single moment in its spread, and the ill-success of its imperial opponent only added to his prestige. Julian's extant writings are as follows: seventeen *Epistles;* nine *Orations;* a satirical sketch called *Caesares* (Καίσαρες ἢ Συμπόσιον), in which the deified Romulus gives a banquet to the gods and, at a separate table, to the Caesars, who are made to pass in review before Silenus, who comments upon them; and finally, the Μισοπώγων already mentioned. His work against the Christians is now lost. It was answered by Apollinarius of Laodicea and others. To the reply of Apollinarius, Julian put forth this *jeu de mots*, Ἀνέγνων, ἔγνων, κατέγνων ("I have read it, understood it, and condemned it"). On this, St. Basil remarked, Ἀνέγνως ἀλλ' οὐκ ἔγνως · εἰ γὰρ ἔγνως οὐκ ἂν κατέγνως ("Thou hast read it, but hast not understood it; for hadst thou done so, thou wouldst not have condemned it").

Of Julian's works, a good edition is that of Hertlein (Leipzig, 1875). See also Neander, *Kaiser Julian und sein Zeitalter* (1813; Eng. trans. 1850); De Broglie, *L'Église et l'Empire Romain*, vols. iii. and iv. (1856–69); Mücke, *Flavius Claudius Iulianus nach den Quellen* (1867–69); and Rendall, *The Emperor Julian*, with an excellent bibliography (1879).

Iuliānus, Salvius. A Roman jurist under Hadrian and the Antonines, who was *praefectus urbi* and twice consul. He drew up at Hadrian's request the *edictum perpetuum*, on which see the articles Edictum; Iurisprudentia.

Iulias (Ἰουλίας). The Bethsaida of the Bible; a city of Palestine on the eastern bank of the Jordan. It

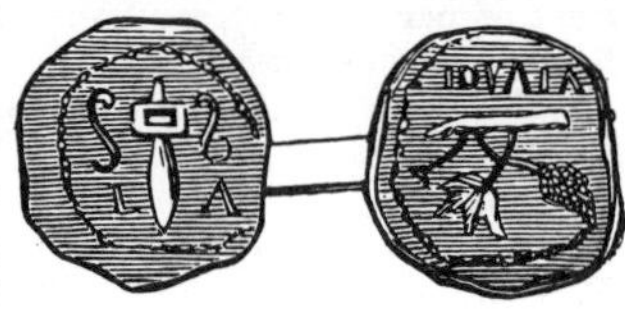

Coin of Iulias.

was named in honour of Iulia, the daughter of Augustus.

Iulii. See Iulia Gens.

Iuliomăgus. A city of Gaul, the capital of the Andecavi, situated on a tributary of the Liger (Loire), near its junction with that river, and to the northeast of Namnetes (Nantes). It was afterwards called Andecavi, from the name of the people, and is now Angers.

Iuliopŏlis (Ἰουλιόπολις). (1) A city of Galatia. See Gordium. (2) See Tarsus.

Iulis (Ἰουλίς). The chief town in Ceos; the birthplace of Simonides. See Ceos.

Iulius Caesar. See Caesar.

Iulus. (1) Son of Aeneas, usually called Ascanius. See Ascanius. (2) The eldest son of Ascanius, who claimed the government of Latium, but was obliged to give it up to his brother Silvius.

Iunia Gens. An ancient patrician house at Rome, to which belonged the celebrated M. Iunius Brutus, who took such an active part in expelling the Tarquins. But afterwards the gens appears as only a plebeian one. The chief families were those of Brutus, Bubulcus, Gracchanus, Norbanus, Pullus, and Silanus.

Iunia Lex. See Lex.

Iuno. A name which contains the same root div, "to shine," as the name Iupiter (q. v.). As Iupiter was the king of heaven and of the gods, so Iuno was, in the Roman mythology, the queen of heaven, or the female Iupiter. She was worshipped as the queen of heaven, from early times, with the surname of Regīna. At a later period her worship was solemnly transferred from Veii to Rome, where a sanctuary was dedicated to her on the Aventine. As Iupiter was the protector of the male sex, so Iuno watched over women, accompanying every woman through life, from the moment of birth to that of death. Hence she bore the special surnames of Virginālis and Matrōna, as well as the general ones of Opigĕna and Sospĭta, and under the last-mentioned name she was worshipped at Lanuvium. On their birthday women offered sacrifices to Iuno surnamed Natālis, just as men sacrificed to their *genius natalis*. The great festival, celebrated by all the women, in honour of Iuno, was called Matronalia, and took place on the 1st of March. Her protection of women, and especially her power of making them fruitful, is further alluded to in the festival Populifugia (q. v.), as well as in the surname of Febrŭlis, Februāta, Febrŭta, or Februālis. Iuno was further, like Saturn, the guardian of the finances, and under the name of Monēta she had a temple on the Capitoline Hill, which contained the mint. The most important period in a woman's life is that of her marriage, and Iuno was therefore believed especially to preside over marriage. Hence she was called Iuga or Iugālis, and had a variety of other names, such as Pronŭba, Cinxia, Lucīna, etc. The month of June, which is said to have been originally called Iunonius, was considered to be the most favourable period for marrying. Women in childbed invoked Iuno Lucina to help them, and newly-born children were likewise under her protection; hence she was sometimes confounded with the Greek Artemis or Ilithyia. In Etruria she was worshipped under the name of Cupra. She was also worshipped at Falerii, Lanuvium, Aricia, Tibur, Praenesté, and other places. In the representations of the Roman Iuno that have come down to us, the type of the Greek Heré is commonly adopted. See Heré.

Iunōnes. A sort of feminine equivalent to the *genius* (q. v.) of men. The Iunones were to the Romans guardian spirits who watched over women. They are represented in art as young girls, winged, and wholly draped (Pliny, *H. N.* ii. 5; Sen. *Epist.* 110).

Iunonia. One of the Canary Islands, or Insulae Fortunatae. It is now Palma (Pliny, *H. N.* vi. 32).

Iunōnis Promontorium. A promontory of Spain, on the Atlantic side of the Strait of Gibraltar. It is now Cape Trafalgar (Mela, ii. 6).

Iupĭter (Iuppĭter). The chief of the gods in the Roman mythology. He was originally an elemental divinity, and his name signifies the father or lord of heaven, being a contraction of *Diovis pater*, or *Diespiter* (Skt. *Dyāus pitar;* cf. the Teutonic *Tiu* or *Zio*). Being the lord of heaven, he was worshipped as the god of light, rain, storms, thunder, and lightning, whence he had the epithets of Lucetius, Imbricĭtor, Serenātor, Pluvius, Fulgurātor, Tonitruālis, Tonans, and Fulminātor. As the pebble or flint stone was regarded as the symbol of lightning, Iupiter was frequently represented with such a stone in his hand instead of a thunderbolt. In concluding a treaty, the Romans took the sacred symbols of Iupiter—i. e. the sceptre and flint stone—together with some grass from his temple, and the oath taken on such an occasion was expressed by *per Iovem Lapidem jurare.* In consequence of his possessing such powers over the elements, and especially of his always having the thunderbolt at his command, he was regarded as the highest and most powerful among the gods. Hence he is called the Best and Greatest (*Optimus Maximus*). His temple at Rome stood on the lofty hill of the Capitol, whence he derived the surnames Capitolīnus and Tarpēius. The Ides of each month were sacred to him. He was regarded as the special protector of Rome. As such he was worshipped by the consuls on entering upon their office; and the triumph of a victorious general was a solemn procession to his temple. He therefore bore the surnames of Imperātor, Victor, Invictus, Stator, Opitŭlus, Feretrius, Praedātor, Triumphātor, and the like. Under all these surnames he had temples or statues at Rome; and two temples, viz. those of Iupiter Stator and of Iupiter Feretrius, were believed to have been built in the time of Romulus. Under the name of Iupiter Capitolinus, he presided over the great Roman games; and under the name of Iupiter Latialis or Latiaris, over the Feriae Latinae.

Iupiter, according to the belief of the Romans, determined the course of all human affairs. He foresaw the future, and the events happening in it were the results of his will. He revealed the future to men through signs in the heavens and the flight of birds, which are hence called his messengers, while the god himself is designated as Prodigiālis—that is, "sender of prodigies." For the same reason the god was invoked at the beginning of every undertaking, whether sacred or profane, together with Ianus, who blessed the beginning itself. Iupiter was further regarded as the guardian of law and as the protector of justice and virtue. He maintained the sanctity of an oath, and presided over all transactions which were based upon faithfulness and justice. Hence Fides was his companion on the Capitol along with Victoria; and hence a traitor to his country; and persons guilty of perjury were thrown down from the Tarpeian Rock.

As Iupiter was the lord of heaven, and consequently the prince of light, the white colour was sacred to him, white animals were sacrificed to him, his chariot was believed to be drawn by four white horses, his priests wore white caps (*albogaleri*), and the consuls were attired in white when they offered sacrifices in the Capitol the day they entered on their office. The worship of Iupiter at Rome was under the special care of the Flamen Dialis, who was the highest in rank of all the flamens. (See FLAMEN.) The Romans, in their representations of the god, adopted the type of the Greek Zeus (see ZEUS); but the Roman conception of Iupiter differs from the Greek conception of Zeus in being more purely animistic as distinct from anthropomorphic. Hence we do not find Iupiter as the subject of plastic art until the later (Graeco-Roman) period. Cf. Mommsen, *Hist. of Rome*, i. pp. 41, 52, 53 (Amer. ed. 1888).

Iura or **Iurassus Mons.** Now Iura; a range of mountains running north of the Lake Lemanus as far as Augusta Rauracorum (August, near Bâle), on the Rhine, forming the boundary between the Sequani and Helvetii (Caes. *B. G.* i. 2).

Iure, CESSIO IN. A method used under the forms of Roman law, by which the transfer of rights was accomplished by means of a fictitious suit. See Gaius, ii. 24 foll.

Iuridĭci Conventus. See PROVINCIA.

Iuris Consulti and **Iure Consulti.** See IURISPRUDENTIA.

Iuris Perīti. See IURISPRUDENTIA.

Iurisdictio. The term used in Roman law of the power belonging to the king or magistrate of administering justice in suits between private persons (*inter privatos*), which was a part of the *imperium* or supreme executive power. The plebeian and inferior magistrates did not possess iurisdictio, except that the curule aediles exercised it in matters relating to the markets.

Very strictly used, the term iurisdictio means the same as *iudicis datio*, or the right of a magistrate to appoint a *iudex*. See ACTIO; IMPERIUM; IUDEX; JUDICIAL PROCEDURE; MAGISTRATUS.

Iurisprudentia. A post-classical term defined by the *Digest* (i. 1, 10) as the knowledge of what is legally right and wrong (*iusti atque iniusti scientia*). The science of law is the one branch of Roman literature which had a purely national development. From an early date there were definite legal ordinances in Rome, and shortly after the expulsion of the kings a collection of *leges regiae* was made by a certain Gaius Papirius. These consisted of archaic customary laws of a strongly sacerdotal character, and arbitrarily attributed to individual kings (known as the *Ius Papirianum*). However, the foundation of the collective legal life of the Romans was primarily the well-known law of the Twelve Tables, B.C. 451–450. (See TWELVE TABLES.) This put an end to the want of a generally known law; for the knowledge of previous legal decisions, like the whole of the judicial procedure, had been hitherto kept in the exclusive possession of the patricians. The administration of the law remained as formerly in the hands of the patricians alone, for they kept from the plebeians all knowledge of the *dies fasti* and *nefasti*—i. e. the days on which legal proceedings might or might not be taken, as also the forms of pleading which were regularly employed (*legis actiones*). The latter were so highly important that the least infraction of them would involve the loss of the cause. This condition of things existed for a long time, until Appius Claudius Caecus drew up a calendar of the days on which causes could be pleaded, and a list of the forms of pleading. These were made public about B.C. 304 by his secretary, Gnaeus Flavius, after whom they were then called *Ius Flavianum.* By these means a knowledge of the law became generally attainable. It soon had eminent representatives among the plebeians in the persons of Publius Sempronius Sophus and Tiberius Coruncanius. In ancient days, however, the work of the jurists was purely practical. It was considered an honourable thing for men learned in the law (*iuris periti*) to allow people to consult them (*consulere*, hence *iuris*, or *iure consulti*) either in the Forum or at appointed hours in their own houses, and to give them legal advice (*responsa*). It was mainly by a kind of oral tradition that the knowledge of law was handed down, as the most eminent jurists allowed younger men to be present at these consultations as listeners (*auditores* or *discipuli*).

The beginning of literary activity in this department, as in others, dates from the Second Punic War. It begins with the earliest exposition of existing law. Sextus Aelius Catus published in B.C. 204 a work named *Tripertita* (from its being divided into three parts) or *Ius Aelianum*, which consisted of the text of the laws of the Twelve Tables together with interpretations, and the legal *formulae* for carrying on suits. From the middle of the second century it became common to make collections of the *responsa* of eminent jurists, and to use them as a source of legal information. Among others, Marcus Porcius Cato, the son of Cato the Elder, made a collection of this kind. In some families knowledge of the law was in a measure hereditary, as in those of the Aelii, Porcii, Sulpicii, and Mucii. A member of the last family, the pontifex Quintus Mucius Scaevola (died B.C. 82), was the first who, with the aid of the formal precision of the Stoic philosophy, gave a scientific and systematic account of all existing law, in his work, *De Iure Civili.* Servius Sulpicius Rufus, the contemporary and friend of Cicero, further advanced this new and more methodical treatment of law by his numerous writings and by training up pupils, such as Aulus Ofilius and Publius Alfenus Varus. The former rendered great assistance to Caesar in his scheme for forming the whole of the *Ius Civile* into a single code. Besides these there were several eminent jurists at the close of the Republic: Gaius Trebatius Testa, Quintus Aelius Tubero, Gaius Aelius Gallus, and Aulus Cascellius.

While under the Republic the learned jurist had held an inferior position to the orator in influence and importance, there is no doubt that under the Empire public eloquence became subordinate, and the position of the jurists was the most coveted and influential in the State, especially when Augustus decreed that the opinions of jurists authorized by the head of the State were to have the validity of law. It was from the jurists as advisers of the emperor that all legislation now proceeded. They had access to all the highest offices of the court and of the State. Accordingly men of the highest gifts and character betook themselves naturally to this profession, and even introduced into the laws an increased unity, consistency, and systematic order. Under Augustus two jurists were pre-eminent, Quintus Antistius Labeo and Gaius Ateius Capito, the founders of the two later schools, named, after their pupils Sempronius Proculus and Masurius Sabinus, the "Proculiani" and "Sabini" respectively. Labeo sought to extend his professional knowledge, while Capito held fast to the traditions of former jurists. A third school was that of the Cassiani, who took their name from the jurist Cassius Longinus (Pliny, *Epist.* vii. 24, 8), and represented a mean between the conservatism of Capito and the innovating spirit of Labeo.

The first scientific collection of laws was made under Hadrian by the Sabinian lawyer Salvius Iulianus, with his *Edictum Perpetuum*, a classified collection of the praetorian edicts from the times of the Republic. (See EDICTUM.) Sextus Pomponius, his somewhat younger contemporary, composed among other things a history of the law till the time of Hadrian.

Under the Antonines jurisprudence was able to claim a remarkable representative in the Asiatic Gaius, but it received its completion and conclusion in the first half of the third century A.D. through Aemilius Papinianus, Domitius Ulpianus, and Iulius Paulus. After their time there were no jurists of great and original capacity. In the fourth century literary activity revived again, but confined itself to the collection of legal authorities, especially that of imperial ordinances. Thus the *Codex Theodosianus*, finished in A.D. 438, contains an official record of all the enactments decreed by the emperors from the time of Constantine. Under Justinian I. (A.D. 527–565) the last and most complete Roman collection of laws was made, under the name of the *Corpus Iuris Civilis* (q. v.).

See Bach, *Historia Iurisprudentiae Romanae* (rev. by Stockmann, Leipzig, 1796); Bremer, *Die Rechtslehrer und Rechtsschulen im röm. Kaiserreich* (Berlin, 1868); Krüger, *Quellen und Lit. des röm. Rechts;* and on the law language, Kalb, *Das Juristlatein* (Nürnberg, 1886).

Ius. (1) In the widest sense, right or justice (so *ius reddere*); and, derivatively, the place where justice is dispensed, the tribunal of the praetor (cf. ACTIO); but usually law, the system of social order enforced by the community. More strictly, human law as contrasted with *fas*, the divine law. (Nevertheless, the body of ancient rules which regulated the intercourse of the city-states of Italy, and which seems to have been a part of *fas*, was termed *ius fetiale.*) *Ius*, in the sense of human law, may be either customary in its origin (*ius moribus constitutum*) or statutory (cf. LEX). The two make up the *ius civile* or municipal law of each State. *Ius civile*, unqualified, usually means the civil law of Rome, more precisely designated as the law of the Quirites (*ius Quiritium*). Such principles of law as were common to all the Mediterranean States, and were applied by the Romans in cases where others than Roman citizens were concerned, were termed *ius gentium*. This *ius gentium* was often identified with natural law, but in the early Imperial period *ius naturale* commonly designated the postulates of natural reason and the sense of right. Closely analogous, therefore, is the conception of *ius aequum* as opposed to *ius strictum.* It was the acceptance and development of *ius gentium* and *ius naturale* that gave to the Roman law of the Imperial period its character of universality. The chief agencies in this development were (*a*) the edicts of the praetors (cf. EDICTUM) during the last two centuries of the Republic, and (*b*) the writings of the great jurists (*iurisperiti, iurisprudentes*), especially of those to whose opinions the emperors gave legal authority by granting them the *ius respondendi.* The edict law was sometimes distinguished from the *ius* (sc. *civile*), as English lawyers contrast "equity" and "law"; but the distinction, as in English law, was essentially historical. The real authority of the edict and the source of its authority—viz. the *imperium* of the praetor — were well expressed in terming it *ius honorarium* (Dig. i. 1, 7, § 1, *honor* = office). The juristic literature of the second and third centuries was cited in the later Empire as the sole authority for all the older law (*ius vetus*), and was commonly described as the *ius*, in antithesis to the *leges* promulgated by the emperors.

Ius publicum embraces all those rules of law which primarily subserve public interests; *ius privatum* those which primarily subserve individual interests (Dig. i. 1, 1, § 2). *Ius privatum* covers the law of the family and of property. *Ius singulare*, as opposed to *ius commune*, denotes a special rule contrary to the general spirit and tenor of the law (Dig. i. 3, 16).

(2) A right, in the sense of a privilege granted to a special community or class. So the *ius Latii*, by which allies (*socii*) of Rome gained *commercium* and, in some cases, full Roman citizenship (cf. LATINITAS); the *ius Italicum*, by which, in the Imperial period, provincial cities obtained the same rights as those commonly possessed by Italian cities—viz. municipal self-government and exemption from poll and land taxes; the *ius liberorum*, by which the mother of at least three children was emancipated from guardianship and obtained a special capacity of inheritance.

(3) A right in the ordinary legal sense, which may be political, like the *ius suffragii* or *ius honorum*, or private, like family and property rights. In the family relations, *ius* is frequently equivalent to *potestas;* wife and children are *alieno iuri subjecti*, an independent person is *sui iuris.* Property rights the Roman jurists divided into real and personal according as they were enforcible by *actio in rem* or only by *actio in personam* (cf. ACTIO). *Ius nudum* was a right without a remedy. The praetor could not make any person *heres* or *dominus* who was not *heres* or *dominus* by the old civil law; but he could give such a person *bonorum possessio* and the actions necessary to protect his possession; and by refusing to give actions to the civil-law owner, he made the latter's right *ius nudum.*

Ius Aeliānum. See ACTIO.

Ius Anulōrum or **Ius Anŭli Aurei.** See EQUITES.

Ius Civilĕ. See IUS; CORPUS IURIS.

Ius Edicendi. See EDICTUM.

Ius Flaviānum. See IURISPRUDENTIA.

Ius Gentium. See IUS.

Ius Gladii. See GLADIUS.

Ius Italĭcum. See IUS.

Ius Latii. See LATINI.

Ius Liberōrum. See LEX IULIA.

Ius Naturālĕ. See IUS.

Ius Oscŭli. See COGNATIO.

Ius Papiriānum. See IURISPRUDENTIA.

Ius Pontificium. See IUS; PONTIFEX.

Ius Privātum. See IUS.

Ius Publĭcum. See IUS.

Ius Quiritium. See CIVITAS; IUS.

Ius Respondendi. See IURISPRUDENTIA.

Ius Scriptum. See IUS.

Ius Suffragii. See CIVITAS; SUFFRAGIUM.

Ius, Vocatio in. See ACTIO.

Iusiurandum (ὅρκος). An oath, either formally and solemnly pronounced as a part of a religious or legal act, or loosely used in common life. Among the GREEKS oaths were taken on important occasions, such as treaties, alliances, and other compacts, in making vows, in ratifying promises; and on many other occasions, such as the registry of a youth as an Athenian citizen (see EPHEBI), the assumption of public office by kings and ephors in Sparta, and by archons, generals, judges, and other officials at Athens, by judges of the games, by both accuser and defendant in the ἀνάκρισις (see ANACRISIS), and by witnesses (see MARTYRIA).

Oaths were sworn in the name of all the gods together, or by the special deity appropriate to the special occasion, as when virgins swore by Artemis, married women by Herê, etc. Women had also their own peculiar oaths, μὰ τὼ θεώ ("by the two goddesses," i. e. Demeter and Persephonê), νὴ τὴν Ἀφροδίτην, etc. The Spartans swore by Castor and Pollux as their national demigods, and the Athenians by their deities (Zeus, Poseidon, and Athenê), much as in the age of chivalry the nations of Europe swore by their national saints. The Greeks also swore by whatever was especially dear to them—e. g. Achilles by his sceptre, warriors by their weapons, friends by their friendship. The most solemn oaths, however, were those that were sworn by Zeus (hence styled ὅρκιος), who punished perjury both in this life and after death (*Il.* xix. 260; Pind. *Ol.* ii. 71). The gods themselves swore by the Styx as the most terrible of oaths (*Il.* xv. 36 foll.). In taking an oath men usually stood, lifting up the hands and eyes to heaven, the oath being a sort of prayer; and sacrifices and libations were the accompaniments of the most solemn adjurations. To give them especial sanctity, oaths were often taken in temples, shrines, or sacred groves.

Among the ROMANS, oaths were taken by the magistrates and other persons who entered the service of the State, by soldiers, by the *fetiales* in ratifying treaties with foreign powers, by the parties to a legal action before the praetor, by witnesses, and loosely by persons in the ordinary speech of common life. Under the Empire, oaths of allegiance were commonly taken by all subjects of the emperor, and on the recurrence of the day on which such an oath had been taken, it was customary to renew it, and also on the first day of each year. The form of this oath of allegiance was probably the same as that of the *sacramentum* (see below). Vestal virgins and the Flamen Dialis were not allowed to swear on any occasion. Men swore by the gods, much as did the Greeks, by their genii, or by the genius of the emperor, and also by individuals or objects most dear to them. Favorite oaths were *Hercle* or *Mehercle* (i. e. *ita me Hercules iuvet*); *Pol, Perpol, Aedepol* (i. e. *per Pollucem, ah di Pollux*); *per Iovem* and *per Iovem Lapidem; per superos; per deos immortales; medius fidius* (i. e. *ita me deus Fidius iuvet*); *ita me dii ament.* Women never swore by Hercules nor men by Castor (Gell. xi. 6). The form called *exsecratio* was common. Thus, *di me perdant ni . . .; dispeream; di me interficiant; ne vivam; ne salvus sim,* etc.

The oath taken in legal actions was called *iusiurandum in iure* and also *iusiurandum necessarium* as being required, and hence opposed to the *iusiurandum voluntarium* out of court. The oath taken by the Roman soldier was called *sacramentum.* It was taken on enlisting for a campaign, and first gave the soldier the right of using arms against the enemy. It thus distinguished legitimate warfare (*militia*) from mere rapine (*latrocinium*). It contained an *exsecratio,* and he who broke it was accursed (*sacer*). The formula of a *sacramentum* is given by Gellius (xvi. 4).

The ancients, especially the Greeks, tried to check the indiscriminate use of oaths in daily life. To allow men to relieve their feelings without profanity, Rhadamanthus is said to have ordained swearing by the names of animals, much as in modern times resort is had to such expressions as "By Jingo!" "Thunder!" "Great Scott!" etc. Thus Socrates swore by the dog, Lampon by the goose, and such elliptical expressions as μὰ τὸν (with the name of the deity suppressed) were common, just as in English men say "I swear!" (Aristoph. *Ran.* 1374). See Lasaulx, *Ueber den Eid bei den Griechen;* Brissonius, *De Formulis,* etc.; and the article SPONSIO.

Iusta Funĕra. See FUNUS.

Iustinianēus Codex. See CODEX IUSTINIANEUS.

Iustiniāna. (1) PRIMA, a town in Illyria, near Tauresium, was the birthplace of Justinian, and was built by that emperor. It became the residence of the archbishop of Illyria, and, in the Middle Ages, of the Servian kings. (2) SECUNDA, also a town in Illyria, previously called Ulpiana, was enlarged and embellished by Justinian.

Iustiniānus. (1) FLAVIUS ANICIUS. A Roman emperor of the East, born in Illyria A.D. 482 or 483, of servile parentage. He was nephew on his mother's side to Iustinus, afterwards emperor. His original name was Uprauda. The elevation of his uncle to the throne, A.D. 518, decided the fortune of Justinian, who, having been educated at Constantinople, had given proofs of considerable capacity and application. Iustinus was ignorant and old, and the advice and exertions of his nephew were of great service to him during the nine years of his reign. He adopted Justinian as his colleague, and at length a few months before his death, feeling that his end was approaching, crowned him in presence of the patriarch and senators, and made over the imperial authority to him, in April, 527. Justinian was then in his forty-fifth year, and he ruled more than thirty-eight years, till November, 565, when he died. His long reign forms a remarkable epoch in the history of the world. Although himself unwarlike, by means of his able generals, Belisarius and the eunuch Narses, he completely defeated the Vandals and the Goths, and restored Italy and Africa to the Empire. Justinian was the last emperor of Constantinople who, by his dominion over the whole of Italy, reunited in some measure the two principal portions of the ancient Empire of the Caesars. In the East, his arms repelled the inroads of Chosroës and conquered Colchis; and the Negus, or king of Abyssinia, entered into an alliance with him. On the Danubian frontier, the Gepidae, Langobardi, Bulgarians, and other hordes were either kept in check or wholly routed. The wars of his reign are related by Procopius and Agathias.

Iustinianus. (From a medal.)

Justinian must be viewed also as the administrator and legislator of a vast empire. In the first capacity he did much good and considerable harm. He was both profuse and penurious. Personally inclined to justice, he often overlooked, through weakness, the injustice of subordinates. He established monopolies of certain branches of industry and commerce, and increased the taxes; but he introduced the culture of silkworms into Europe, and the numerous edifices which he raised, and the towns which he repaired or fortified, attest his love for the arts, and his anxiety for the security and welfare of his dominions. Procopius gives a notice of the towns, churches (St. Sophia among the rest), convents, bridges, roads, walls, and fortifications constructed or repaired during his reign. The same Procopius, however, wrote a secret history (Ἀνέκδοτα) of the court and reign of Justinian and his wife Theodora, both of whom he paints in the darkest colours. Theodora, previous to her marriage, indeed, had been a dissolute woman, but one of some ability, and she exercised till her death in 548, a great influence over the mind of Justinian. Many acts of oppression and cruelty were committed by her orders. At the same time the *Anecdota* of Procopius cannot be implicitly trusted, as many of his charges are evidently misrepresentations or malignant exaggerations.

Justinian was easy of access, patient of bearing, courteous and affable in discourse, and perfect master of his temper. In the conspiracies against his authority and person he often showed both justice and clemency. He was chaste and temperate, frequently fasting, and allowing himself little time for sleep. His restless application to business and to study, as well as the extent of his learning, have been attested even by his enemies (Procop. viii. 13). He adorned Constantinople with many magnificent structures, among them the great church (now mosque) of St. Sophia. He was, or professed to be, a poet and philosopher, a lawyer and theologian, a musician and architect; but the greatest act of his reign is the codification of the Roman law, which has immortalized his name, and an account of which will be found under the articles CORPUS IURIS and TRIBONIANUS. He was, however, much more than a codifier, for the following fundamental changes were introduced by him: (*a*) a great amelioration of the condition of slaves (see SERVUS); (*b*) a change in the law of intestate succession by which *cognati* or relations on the mother's side inherited equally with *agnati* or relations on the father's side; (*c*) the introduction of a system of small-debt courts. Unfortunately, his love of theological controversy led him to interfere with the consciences of his subjects; and his penal enactments against Jews and heretics displayed a spirit of intolerance. He was succeeded by his nephew, Iustinus IV. See the biographies by Isambert (1856) and Body (6th ed. 1889); also Roby's *Introduction to the Digest* (1884).

(2) The second of the name, the son of Constantine III., and lineal descendant of the emperor Heraclius. He succeeded his father on the throne of Constantinople, A.D. 685, but his reign, which lasted ten years, was marked chiefly by wars with the Saracens, and by the exactions and oppressions of his ministers. At last, his general Leontius drove him from the throne, and, having caused his nose to be cut off, banished him to the Crimea, A.D. 695. Leontius, however, was soon after himself deposed and banished by Tiberius Apsimerus, who reigned for seven years. Meantime Justinian had escaped from the Crimea and married the daughter of chief of the Gazari, a tribe of Turks; and he afterwards, with the assistance of the Bulgarians, entered Constantinople, and put to death both Leontius and Tiberius, along with many others. He ordered also many of the principal people of Ravenna to be killed. Justinian was finally dethroned and slain by Philippus Bardanes, A.D. 711.

Iustīnus, M. IUNIĀNUS. A Latin historian, generally supposed to have flourished in the age of the Antonines. Nothing is known of the particulars of Justin's life. He made an epitome or selection of extracts from the *Historiae Philippicae* of Trogus Pompeius, written under Augustus. This epitome is entitled, *Historiarum Philippicarum et Totius Mundi Originum, et Terrae Situs ex Trogo Pompeio Excerptarum Libri XLIV. a Nino ad Caesarem Augustum*, and it is best described as a history of the world down to the Roman conquest of the East. In making his extracts, Justin gave the preference to those facts and those passages which he considered peculiarly interesting. Other events are only mentioned briefly, and by way of transition. Chronology is entirely neglected in the work of Justin, as in the greater part of the ancient writers. His style is correct, simple, and elegant, but unequal; though preferable to that of Florus.

The value of Justin's history chiefly depends on the circumstance of Trogus's work having been compiled from some of the best of the ancient historical writers, such as Theopompus, Herodotus, Ctesias, Hieronymus of Cardia, Timaeus, Phylarchus, Polybius, Posidonius, etc.

In the Middle Ages the work of Justin was much read and copied, though not used in schools. The *editio princeps* appeared at Venice and Rome in 1470. Good editions are those of Fittbogen, with notes (Halle, 1835), Johanneau and Dübner, revised by Jeep (Leipzig, 1860), with critical commentary, and Rühl (Leipzig, 1886). There is an index in the Delphin edition (by Cantel) and in the Lemaire edition, from Wetzel.

Iustitium. The term by which the Romans designated a legal vacation, or cessation from business in the courts of justice, in the sittings of the Senate, and even in private life, when all the shops were closed. This took place on extraordinary occasions, such as famine, or during the perils of war, and, under the Empire, on the death of a member of the imperial family. It was decreed by the highest magistrate present in Rome, subject to the approval of the Senate. When the occasion had passed by, it was removed by a special edict on the part of the magistrate (Mommsen, *Römisches Staatsrecht*, i. pp. 263–266).

Iustus (Ἰοῦστος). A Jewish historian of Tiberius in Galilee. He was a contemporary of Iosephus, who was unfriendly towards him. Iustus wrote a history of the Jewish kings from Moses down to the death of Herod in the third year of the reign of Trajan, but it has not survived.

Iuthungi. A German tribe dwelling north of the Danube between Vindobona (Vienna) and the site of the modern Pesth (Ammian. Marc. xvii. 6).

Iuturna. The nymph of a fountain in Latium, famous for its healing qualities, whose water was used in many of the sacrifices. A pond in the Forum, between the temples of Castor and Vesta, was called Lacus Iuturnae. The nymph is said to have been beloved by Iupiter, who rewarded her with immortality and dominion over the waters. Vergil calls her the sister of Turnus. See Serv. *ad Aen.* xii. 139; Varr. *L. L.* v. 71; Ovid, *Fast.* i. 463; Arnob. iii. 29.

Iuvāvum or **Iuvavia.** Now Salzburg; a town in Noricum, on the river Iuvavus (Isonta, Salzach). It was founded by Hadrian, and made the residence of the Roman provincial governor. It was destroyed by the Heruli in the fifth century, but afterwards rebuilt.

Iuvenalia and **Iuvenāles Ludi.** Scenic games instituted by Nero in A.D. 59 in honour of the first shaving of his beard. They were celebrated in a private theatre, and consisted of a great variety of plays acted by distinguished amateurs (Pliny, *H. N.* xxxvii. 19; Dio Cass. lxvii. 14).

Iuvenālis, Decĭmus Iunius. The fourth in order of time and of literary development of the great writers of Roman satire, his predecessors being Lucilius, Horace, and Persius. Of his life there are known but few particulars. His ancient biographers relate that he was either the son or foster-son of a rich freedman, and was born at Aquinum (cf. Juv. iii. 319) at a date that can not be determined, but which may be approximately given as between A.D. 57 and 67. He is said to have studied rhetoric, and began writing satire not earlier than A.D. 100, for in his first satire (i. 49) he mentions the exile of Marius Priscus, which took place in that year. He lived a simple life at his country estate near Tibur (xi. 65). He tells us himself that he visited Egypt at some period of his life; and according to an inscription dedicated by him to Ceres Helvina, found at Aquinum, he held at various times the offices of tribune of a cohort, duumvir of Aquinum, and *flamen.* (*C. I. L.* x. 5382). Tradition explains his military office and his visit to Egypt as having been in reality a form of exile for having attacked the imperial favourite, Paris, in his satires (cf. Sidon. Apoll. viii. 270). Another tradition makes Britain to have been his place of exile. Of the date and place of his death, nothing is known; but he must have died later than A.D. 127, as he mentions Aemilius Iunius (xv. 27). He was a friend of Martial, who speaks of him in friendly terms (vii. 24 and 91; xii. 18).

There remain to us sixteen satires of Juvenal, the last of which is probably a fragment, and is by some regarded as spurious. All are written in dactylic hexameters. They represent the final development of satire among the Romans, and answer the modern definition of satiric composition, being passionate, scornful, and filled with the language of indignant denunciation and bitter invective. His subject is not, as with Horace, the foibles and venial follies of the age, but those darker vices whose prevalence taints the history of the times in which he wrote. His tone is, therefore, not that of the indulgent man of the world, but of the stern censor who hates the hideous sins that he looks upon, and scourges them with a whip of scorpions. Yet there is much of the rhetorician's exaggeration in his invective, and it may be questioned whether the passion is not partly simulated. Moreover, the painful minuteness with which he draws the details of abnormal vice, and the excessive crudity of his language in at least two of the satires (the Second and Sixth) seem inconsistent with the professed morality of the writer, and excite a strong suspicion of pruriency. He is at his best in the Third and Tenth, in which he touches the less loathsome faults of contemporary Rome, and where one finds here and there a noble bit of poetry. It is these two satires that Dr. Samuel Johnson paraphrased in English in his two poems, *London* and *The Vanity of Human Riches*, with a fire and force and epigrammatic terseness of language that are in no respect inferior to the original. Juvenal is very modern in his mental attitude as well as in his phrasing. An English scholar has recently declared that we are to see in him the first instances in literature of American humour—the humour that derives its effect from bringing together unexpectedly two ludicrously inappropriate ideas, or in applying to the most solemn subjects the familiar language of every-day life. In this, Juvenal has been hailed as the prototype of Hosea Biglow and Mark Twain; and his "waxing over the knees of the gods" and his offering "the sacred sausages of a little white pig" have perhaps to many obscured the other passages of great nobility and beauty that are not far to seek. Of pregnant phrases and epigrammatic sentences, he has made some striking contributions to literature. *Probitas laudatur et alget—facit indignatio versum—res angusta domi —scribendi cacoëthes — stemmata quid faciunt?— Cantabit vacuus coram latrone viator—Orandum est ut sit mens sana in corpore sano—Maxima debetur puero reverentia*—are perhaps the most famous of his many famous epigrams.

The best MS. of Juvenal is the Codex Pithoeanus of the ninth century, preserved at Montpellier in France. The other MSS. are enumerated by Jahn in his edition. The *editio princeps* of Juvenal appeared at Rome in 1470, but undated. Standard editions with notes are those of Ruperti (2d ed. Leipzig, 1819); Lemaire (Paris, 1823); Weber (Weimar, 1825); Heinrich, with scholia (Bonn, 1839); Jahn (Berlin, 1851) revised by Bücheler (Berlin, 1886); Friedländer, 2 vols. (1895); of thirteen satires with English notes, Macleane and Long (2d ed. London, 1867); Simcox (2d ed. London, 1873); Hardy (London, 1883); Pearson and Strong, with good introduction (Oxford, 1887); but especially by J. E. B. Mayor (4th ed. of vol. i. London, 1886; 3d ed. of vol. ii. 1881); of satires i. and ii. by Nash (Boston, 1893). There is a spirited verse translation by Gifford (London, 1817; reprinted in the Bohn Library); and a prose by J. D. Lewis, with text and notes (2d ed. London, 1882); by Strong and Lesper (London, 1882). On Juvenal, see Widal, *Juvénal et ses Satires* (Paris, 1869); and an article by Boissier in the *Revue des Deux Mondes* for June, 1870. On the coincidences between Juvenal and Martial, see a monograph in the introduction to Pearson and Strong's edition. See also the article SATIRA.

Iuvencus, GAIUS VETTIUS AQUILĪNUS. A Spanish presbyter, who, under Constantine, composed a version of New Testament history in heroic metre, modelling his diction on the Roman epic poets, especially Vergil. He shows considerable taste and technical skill. In the best MSS. the work is styled *Evangeliorum*, Liber i.–iv. In the story, Iuvencus follows chiefly St. Matthew. Edition by Reusch (Frankfort, 1710). On the language, etc., see the monograph by Hatfield (Bonn, 1890).

Iuventas. The Roman goddess of youth. See HEBÉ.

Iuvernia (Ἰουερνία). A name for Ireland, found among the Greek writers (Agathem. ii. 4; Ptol. ii. 2). See HIBERNIA; IERNÉ.

Ivory. See ELEPHAS.

Ixīon (Ἰξίων). The son of Antion or Peision, or, according to some, of Phlegyas. Others, again, gave him the god Ares for a father. He obtained the hand of Dia, the daughter of Deïoneus, having promised his father-in-law large gifts; but he did not keep his agreement and Deïoneus seizing his horses detained them as a pledge. Ixion then sent messengers to say that the gifts were ready if he would come to bring them. Deïoneus accordingly came, but his treacherous son-in-law had prepared in his house a pit filled with fire and carefully covered over, into which the unsuspecting man fell and perished. After this deed Ixion was stricken with madness, and the atrocity of his crime was such that neither gods nor men would absolve him, till at length Zeus took pity on him and purified him, and admitted him to Olympus. Here again, incapable of good, Ixion cast a lustful eye on Heré, the wife of his divine benefactor. She, however, in concert with Zeus, formed a cloud in the likeness of herself, which Ixion embraced. Having boasted of his good-fortune, Zeus precipitated him into Erebus, where Hermes fastened him with brazen bands to an ever-revolving fiery wheel, lying upon which he is forever scourged and forced to cry out "Benefactors should be honoured!" The offspring of Ixion and the cloud was a son, Centaurus, who afterwards, having intercourse with the mares of Magnesia, begot the race of centaurs. See CENTAURI.

The myth of Ixion is probably of great antiquity, as the customs on which it is founded only prevailed in the Heroic Age. Its chief object seems to have been to inspire a horror of the violation of hospitality on the part of those who, having committed homicide, were admitted to the house and table of the one who had consented to perform the rites by which the guilt of the offender was supposed to be removed. On Ixion, see the poem by Robert Browning in his *Jocoseria*.

Ixionĭdes. A patronymic applied to Pirithoüs, the son of Ixion (q. v.). The Centaurs are also called Ixionidae (Lucan, vi. 386).

Ixios (Ἴξιος). A name applied to Apollo, and derived from a district in Rhodes called Ixiae or Ixia.

Iynx (Ἴυγξ). Daughter of Peitho and Pan (or Echo). She was changed into a bird by Heré, as a punishment for endeavoring to fascinate Zeus. She is the symbol of restless, passionate love.

J

J. For Latin words beginning with J (consonantal I), see under I. For the character, see ALPHABET, p. 62.

Jacobs, CHRISTIAN FRIEDRICH WILHELM, a distinguished classicist, was born at Gotha, October 6, 1764. He studied philology, theology, and philosophy at the universities of Jena and Göttingen, and in 1785 became an instructor in the Gymnasium at Gotha, with a position after 1802 in the Public Library of that city. In 1807 he accepted the office of classical teacher in the Munich Lyceum, returning, however, to Gotha in 1810 to assume full charge of the Library and of the collection of numismatics and antiques. From 1831 to 1842 he was director of the art collections of Gotha. He died March 30, 1847. Besides many special editions of the classics, including the *Carmina Iliaca* of Tzetzes, Aelian, Achilles Tatius, and the *Imagines* of the Philostrati, Jacobs was a prolific contributor to general literature and a frequent translator. His essays on topics relating to classical philology were published at various times with the title *Vermischte Schriften*, and make eight volumes in all (1823–44). His most important classical work is an edition of the *Anthologia Graeca*, 13 vols. (1794–1814). He also made numerous translations from the Anthology, which he published under the title of *Tempe*, in 2 vols. (1803). His elementary book on Greek (*Elementarbuch der griechischen Sprache*), published in 1805, was long popular. Of his other writings may be mentioned the *Geschichte des weiblichen*

Geschlechts. See Bursian, *Geschichte der class. Philol. in Deutschland*, pp. 635–640.

Jahn, Otto, distinguished as an archaeologist and classical scholar, was born at Kiel, June 16, 1813. He pursued his university studies at Kiel, Leipzig, and Berlin, and after travelling extensively in Italy, took up his residence for a time at Rome, whence he was called to lecture at Kiel and later at Greifswald. In 1847 he became Professor of Archaeology at the University of Leipzig, where he founded the Archaeological Society and acted himself as Director of the Archaeological Museum. Having taken part with Mommsen and other distinguished men in the political agitation of 1848–1849, he was deprived of his university offices in 1851. Four years later he received a call to Bonn as Professor of "Alterthumswissenschaft" and Director of the Art Museum, resigning in 1867 to succeed Gerhard at Berlin, but died before actually commencing to lecture there, September 9, 1869.

Jahn was a most prolific writer, and possessed a versatile mind coupled with acuteness and power. His contributions to literature comprise many works that are of the first importance. Such are his editions of Persius (1843), Censorinus (1845), Florus (1852), *Pausaniae Descriptio Arcis Atheniensis* (1860), the *Brutus* of Cicero (1849), Juvenal (1851), the *Periochae* of Livy (1853), the *Psyche et Cupido* of Apuleius (1856), the *Electra* of Sophocles (1861), the *Symposium* of Plato (1864), and Longinus (1867). Purely archaeological are the following works: *Die hellenische Kunst* (1846); *Peitho* (1846); a description of the antique vases in the Royal Bavarian Collection (1854); *Die Wandgemälde des Columbariums in der Villa Pamfili* (1859); a work on the evil eye (1855); and *Darstellungen griechischer Dichter auf Vasenbildern* (1861). Other works are the elaborate and able biography of Mozart (1856–60); the *Gesammelte Aufsätze über Musik* (1866); his *Biographische Aufsätze* (1866); and *Ludwig Uhland* (1853). See the sketch of Jahn by Vahlen (Vienna, 1870).

Jail. See Carcer.

Jamb. See Ianua; Postis.

Janitor. See Domus.

January. See Calendarium.

Jar. See Amphora; Cadus; Dolium; Olla; Seria; Urceus; Vitrum.

Javelin. See Iaculum; Pilum.

Jerome. See Hieronymus.

Jerusalem. See Hierosolyma.

Jesters. See Balatro; Scurra.

Jests (*ἀστεῖα, σκώμματα, ioci, iocularia, facete dicta*). In their fun-making, the Greeks and Romans seem to have differed somewhat as do the French and the English of to-day—the Greeks inclining more to wit and the Romans to humour. The Greeks admired what was neat in form, terse, pointed, sparkling; the Romans what was provocative of laughter. This is, in fact, the essential difference between the *sal Atticum* and the *acetum Italicum*. (See Epigramma.) The witty sayings of the most famous Greeks, preserved for us in the pages of Diogenes Laërtius and Plutarch, have a higher quality about them than mere fun. Such is that of Diogenes the Cynic, who, when journeying from Sparta to Athens, was asked where he was going, and replied, "From the men's apartments to the women's." The same person, observing the son of a courtesan throwing stones among a crowd, said to him, "Take care lest you hit your father!" A stock joke of modern times is told of him, for seeing an unskilful archer practising, he went and sat by the target, saying, "Now I shall be out of harm's way." Clever, also, is the saying of Aristotle on being told that a person had been abusing him in his absence: "He may even beat me, if he likes, in my absence." Two of his sayings anticipate two famous passages of the New Testament. Being asked how we should treat our friends, he replied, "As we should wish our friends to treat us." And to one who inquired how students should get on, he said, "Pressing on upon those who are before and not waiting for those who are behind."

Parody and burlesque flourished among the Greeks from very early times, witness the mock-heroics of the *Batrachomyomachia* (q. v.) and the other ludicrous imitations of the Homeric poems, and so in Latin in the pseudo-Vergilian comic epic *Culex*. As early as Epicharmus (in the fifth century B.C.) tragic themes were burlesqued, as in later times by Rhinthon (q. v.), who gave his name to this species of composition (*fabula Rhinthonica*); while Aristophanes (q. v.) has filled his comedies with the richest kind of drollery based upon the presentation of serious subjects in a comic light. Lucian's dialogues are remarkable examples of clever burlesque and keen irony, which spares neither men nor gods. See Lucianus; Parodia.

In later times special collections of *facetiae* were made, one of the best known being the Ἀστεῖα ascribed to Hierocles. This is the source of many jokes that are professedly modern, and deals principally with the absurd doings of pedants (*σχολαστικοί*), which bear a strong family likeness to many of the jokes that appear in the *Fliegende Blätter*. The following will serve as specimens of these ancient jests:

"A bookworm, wishing to teach his horse to be a small eater, gave him no food at all. Finally the horse starved to death, whereupon the bookworm exclaimed, 'What a loss I have suffered! Just as he had learned to live without eating, he has gone and died!'"—a story which reappears in modern fiction in Sir Walter Scott's *Waverley*, where it is put into the mouth of Evan Dhu Maccombich.

"A bookworm, meeting another of his own kind, said, 'Why, I heard you were dead!' 'And yet,' replied the other, 'you see that I am alive.' 'Well,' said the first, with a puzzled air, 'I really don't know what to believe, for the party who told me is a much more reliable person than you are.'"

Quintilian devotes a part of his treatise (vi. 3) to the discussion of humour, giving copious examples from Roman sources. In it he deprecates the use of puns as being only a cheap form of wit; yet punning was much practised by the Romans. Cicero was an inveterate punster, much to the disgust of Pompey when they were associated together in the Civil War. Many of these cheap jokes of his are preserved by Macrobius (ii. 2), by Plutarch in his life of the orator, and Quintilian mentions a collection of them as having been made and published (vi. 3, 5) by Cicero's freedman Tiro. Another collection of them was made by C. Trebonius (Cic. *Ad Fam.* xv. 21, 1–3). Like books were made of Caesar's *ἀποφθέγματα*. (Cf. C. F. W. Müller's ed. of Cicero, iv. 3, 341; and for examples, the article describing Puns in this Dictionary.) Cato the Censor is said to have published a joke-book, but not, however, of his own sayings (Plut. *Cat. Mai.* 2). For satirical wit, see SATIRA.

Jet. See GAGATES.

Jewellery. See ANULUS; ARGENTUM; ARMILLA; AURUM; CAELATURA; GEMMA; INAURIS; MONILÉ.

Jews. See IUDAEI; PALAESTINA.

Jockeys. See CIRCUS; HIPPODROMUS.

Jokes. See JESTS.

Journal. See ACTA; CODEX ACCEPTI ET EXPENSI; COMMENTARII; EPHEMERIS.

Jove. See IUPITER.

Judge. See DICASTES; IUDEX.

Judicial Procedure. I. AT ATHENS.—A clear distinction was drawn at Athens between public (γραφαί) and private actions (δίκαι). But it must be remarked that the public actions included more offences than those which directly affected the State. Injuries to individuals might form matter for a public prosecution, if (as, e. g., in a case of theft or damage to property) the wrong to a citizen in his honour or property admitted of being viewed as an attack upon the honour of the citizens or the security of property in general. The difference, both in public and private actions, was essential, whether we consider (*a*) the right of prosecution, or (*b*) the consequences of condemnation.

(*a*) Any one might institute a public prosecution, even if he had himself suffered no wrong. The only condition was that he must be of full age and in possession of all civic rights. It was only in cases of murder that the right of prosecution was limited to the relations of the murdered person. Private prosecutions, on the other hand, could only be undertaken by the injured person or his legal representative, in the case of a ward by his guardian, in that of a married woman by her husband, in that of strangers by their πρόξενος, in that of resident aliens by their patrons.

(*b*) In the case of public prosecutions, if a fine was inflicted the amount went into the public treasury; in the case of a private prosecution, to the prosecutor. At public trials other penalties than fines could be inflicted: death, imprisonment, deprivation of civic rights, banishment with confiscation of property. This was not the case in private causes, though in them the State had the right of increasing the penalty. For instance, a prosecution for false witness was not public, but private; yet if a person was convicted three times, the State could inflict deprivation of civil rights. In public causes the prosecutor ran the risk of being himself fined 1000 *drachmae* ($166) if he failed to carry at least one third of the votes of the jurymen, besides which he lost his right of instituting a similar action again. In private causes the prosecutor, if he failed to establish his case, was fined in an amount generally equal to one sixth of the sum in dispute. A distinction was drawn between assessed and non-assessed causes. The non-assessed were those in which the amount of the fine was already fixed by law, and any further estimate was therefore unnecessary; the assessed causes were all those in which the amount of fine had to be settled according to the character of the offence, or the magnitude of the damage; in other words, those which required that the punishment should be fixed for the occasion. Besides those prosecutions, the object of which was to get a person punished for an actual breach of law, there were others which merely aimed at settling a disputed right. These were naturally, for the most part, private causes; but there were public prosecutions of this kind as well. For instance, any one who proposed and carried a new law was liable for a whole year after it had passed to prosecution and punishment for making an illegal proposal. But after the year had elapsed, his personal responsibility came to an end, and only the new law could be attacked. Private causes could be settled by arrangement, but the law forbade the accuser in a public cause to drop the case. If he did, he was liable to the same punishment as if he had failed to carry one third of the votes. This was the principle, but it was not always carried out in practice. In certain public causes in which a reward was offered by the State, the prosecutor, if successful, received a share of the fine. The costs of private causes (πρυτανεῖα) were paid by both parties in advance, and returned to the successful suitor by his adversary. These fees amounted, if the sum in dispute were less than 1000 drachmae, to three drachmae (about $0.50); if greater, to thirty drachmae (about $5.00). The costs of public prosecutions were not paid by the accused. They were paid by the accuser in one case only—namely, if, in the event of the accused being condemned, the accuser received part of the fine imposed. In testamentary suits, supposing a person to claim an inheritance already assigned to another, or to lay exclusive claim to one which was claimed by several others, the tenth part of the amount was deposited before the trial. If the suit was instituted against the State, supposing the question affected confiscated property, a fifth part of the amount was deposited. The successful litigant in either case received the amount deposited.

As above mentioned, the Athenian law allowed the prosecutor, in many cases, to institute the same suit in various forms. A case of personal injury might be treated either as a private action for assault or as a public action for outrage. In the latter case the prosecutor could make no claim for personal compensation. If the injury was accompanied by aggravating circumstances, supposing, for instance, that the person injured were performing a public function, either form of action was open.

Private actions were often decided by Diaetetae, or arbitrators (see DIAETETAE)—an important body. For the convenience of persons living outside Athens, thirty (in later times forty) local magistrates were appointed by lot, whose business it was to go from place to place and decide petty cases of debt, or damage, or assault. In cases of murder the jurisdiction belonged to the Ephetae, in certain other cases to the Senate, the Ecclesia, the Strategi, the Archons, and the Eleven. (See HENDEKA.) The greater number of cases came before the court of the Heliaea. See DICASTES; DIKÉ.

The most general name for a public charge was γραφή, or a statement in writing. The γραφή was resorted to only in cases of offences already recognized by law, and was always brought before a court of law, never before a political body, such as the Senate or Public Assembly. On the special forms of public prosecution, see APAGOGÉ; EISANGELIA; ENDEIXIS; PHASIS; PROBOLÉ. Δίκη (suit) was the term for a civil process. Under both forms of action the proceedings were very much the same. Except in certain cases affecting the religious mysteries, they were public, and involved a great many formalities. By way of introducing his case, the prosecutor applied to the president of the court, who fixed the date for the preliminary investigation. The summons was made by the prosecutor in a public place and in the presence of witnesses. Aliens were obliged to give security for their appearance; citizens were not, except in case of ἀπαγωγή, ἔνδειξις, or εἰσαγγελία; and in these cases a special summons was sometimes dispensed with, and the accused might be immediately arrested. The charge having been handed in, the presiding judge decided, when the day mentioned in the summons came round, whether he should admit it or not. Various reasons might lead him to dismiss it: the non-appearance of the accused, there being no sufficient evidence to show that he had been summoned; or if the accuser appeared, on the whole, not justified in bringing the charge; or if the forms were not duly observed. If the charge were admitted, it was publicly posted up on a tablet in the neighbourhood of the court, with a notification of the day when the trial would come on. If the accuser failed to appear on the appointed day, the charge fell through *ipso facto;* if the accused failed without putting in a valid plea for postponement, he was proceeded against *in contumaciam.* If the parties came into court, they were both put on their oath, the accuser with respect to his charge, the accused with regard to his answer. They then paid the court fees.

The accused generally tried, if possible, to prevent the trial coming on. There were many ways of doing this. He might, or another might for him, dispute the admissibility of the charge on various grounds—e. g. the legal inability of the prosecutor to prosecute, limitation, want of jurisdiction on the part of the authorities, absence of any law to serve as a basis for the charge, and so on. A witness was usually put forward in cases of disputed inheritance to prove that the prosecutor had no claim. In either case the trial was postponed until a decision had been come to upon the objection raised by the accused or upon the charge of false testimony brought by him against the witness. If the decision went against the accuser he was obliged to retire from the case. After a decision was given on the objection raised by the accused, the party to whom it was unfavourable had to pay his adversary a fine amounting to a sixth part of the value of the object in dispute.

All the material necessary for the trial, the passages to be quoted from laws, documents, and testimony, had to be prepared by the parties. The evidence consisted of written statements which were given in among the records. The witnesses who were responsible for these might either have made them in person before the magistrates, or in their absence before other witnesses. The witnesses were either willing or unwilling. If a person had at first offered to give evidence and afterwards refused to do so, he might be prosecuted by the person affected by his conduct. If any person, even without having bound himself to appear, refused to give evidence after being formally summoned by the herald, he had to pay into the public treasury a fine of 1000 drachmae.

The statements of slaves were only accepted as evidence when given under torture in the presence of witnesses, who had to take them down. The owners of slaves offered to submit them to the torture, either of their own will or on the demand of the opposite party, with which, however, they were not bound to comply. The oath was regarded as the ultimate test of truth. (See IUSIURANDUM.) It might either be taken by both parties on their own proposal, or be exacted by one party from the other. The taking of the oath or the refusal to take it was put into writing as evidence and enrolled among the archives. These documents were kept by the magistrate in a sealed box, and brought by him into court on the day of trial. In certain cases, such as those relating to commerce, mining, and dowries, the duration of the proceedings was legally limited to thirty days; but in other causes trials would sometimes drag themselves out through a whole year. If one of the parties failed to appear in court on the day appointed, his reason had to be stated on oath by a representative. The other party was free to declare on oath that the reasons alleged were insufficient: if the judge took this view, the proceedings went on *in contumaciam,* and the absent party lost in the suit. In the opposite case the accuser had to propose another date for the trial. In private cases an arrangement might be made, even in court. The charge and the answer having been read by the clerk, both parties delivered their speeches. These had often been composed for them, for, according to strict law, the parties could not be represented by advocates. In practice, however, they often contented themselves with a short introductory address of their own, and then asked for permission to employ an advocate.

The first speech and reply were often followed by a second, but the whole number of speeches on each side was not allowed to exceed a certain time measured by the water-clock. The pieces of written evidence were read out by the clerk, during the speaking, in their proper places, but the time which they took was not counted against the speaker. The judge alone had the right of interrupting the speaker. It was usual to introduce the evidence of parents, wives, children, and influential persons. The voting was secret. Every judge received a black and a white pebble (the black for condemnation and the white for acquittal), and put the pebble (ψῆφος) which indicated his vote into a metal urn (ὑδρία), the other into a wooden one. Stones bored through or left entire, mussel shells, beans, or metal balls were also used for voting.

The verdict was decided by the majority of votes: if they were equal, the accused was acquitted. If the cause was assessed (ἀγὼν τιμητός), a second voting followed, to decide between the punishment proposed by the accuser and the counter-proposal of the accused. There was no appeal, at least against the decision of the public court of the Heliastae. The utmost that was possible was to get the verdict set aside by proving that the proceedings *in contumaciam* had been illegal, or that the winner had gained the case by suborning false witnesses. The magistrates were, in the case of public actions, responsible for carrying out the punishment. Capital sentences were usually carried out (by poison or strangulation) in prison by the executioner commissioned by the Eleven. (See HENDEKA.) The corpses of great criminals were thrown down a precipice or removed over the border. If the sentence were banishment, the condemned person had to leave the country within a certain time at the peril of his life; his property was confiscated. If ἀτιμία were inflicted, and the condemned person attempted to usurp the rights of which he had been deprived, he was liable to severe, even to capital, punishment. In case of a fine being inflicted, a man was ἄτιμος till it was paid: if he failed to pay by the time appointed, he was liable to a double punishment, and ultimately to the confiscation of his property. If the amount of his property exceeded the fine, the surplus was returned to him; if it fell short of it, he and his descendants were debtors to the State and ἄτιμοι. Imprisonment seems to have served only as an increase of sentence or as a means of enforcing sentence. Loss of freedom and sale were only inflicted on non-citizens for usurping civic rights. In private actions the ultimate means of compelling the condemned person to the fulfilment of his obligation was an executory mandate, by which he was declared a debtor to the State in the same sum that he owed the prosecutor, and made ἄτιμος till it was paid.

II. At Rome. Criminal jurisdiction, until the establishment of the Republic, belonged to the kings, and on their commission to the *quaestores parricidii* and the *duo viri perduellionis*. (See Parricidium; Perduellio.) After the expulsion of the kings it passed over immediately to the consuls, until the public courts (*iudicia populi*) were gradually developed. In capital cases, even in the time of the kings, an appeal was allowed, as an act of grace, from their verdict to the representative assembly, at first to the Comitia Curiata, and after Servius Tullius to the Comitia Centuriata. (See Provocatio.) After the establishment of the Republic, it was, in B.C. 509, legally provided that an appeal might be made, in capital cases, from the sentence of the magistrate to the decision of the Comitia Centuriata as a court of appeal. Condemned persons, as a rule, naturally made use of this right, and the magistrates consequently brought their verdict before the Comitia Centuriata, in the form of a charge with reasons to support it. Thus these comitia acquired a jurisdiction, dependent, it is true, on a previous judgment of the magistrates, and limited to capital cases which admitted of appeal. The jurisdiction of the Comitia Tributa was developed in the same way. At first these comitia had merely served as a court of appeal against the fines imposed by the tribunes for violation of their authority. (See Multa.) But they soon acquired jurisdiction in all cases involving fines, and quite overshadowed the Comitia Centuriata in importance. The judicial power of the latter was gradually more and more restricted by the increasing habit of referring cases of common offences to the exceptional commissions. At last actions brought under the name of *perduellio* were the only ones in which they retained their judicial competence. But the greatest possible number of cases were brought before the Comitia Tributa, notably those of a political character in which illegal or mischievous administration was in question. Only the name of *perduellio* was avoided. The distinction between the judicial competence of the two assemblies was founded, not so much on differences in the offences, as in those of the penalties. Whether the Comitia Centuriata or Comitia Tributa were to take cognizance of an offence depended on the light in which the magistrates regarded it. If they thought less seriously of it, it would go before the Comitia Tributa, which had only the power of inflicting fines to the amount of half the property; if more seriously, before the Comitia Centuriata, which could only pass capital sentences; in early times death, in later times the *interdictio aquae et ignis*, and the confiscation of property which accompanied them. See Exsilium.

The proceedings in the assembly were opened by the accusing magistrate. In the Comitia Centuriata this would be a consul or praetor, in the Comitia Tributa a tribune, aedile, or quaestor. The trial began with the *diei dictio*, or fixing of a day for the proceedings. The accused was then either put into prison, or left free on giving bail for his appearance. To give the people some means of arriving at a conclusion on the guilt or innocence of the accused, a preliminary investigation was held in three *contiones* at intervals of some days. Before these the accused was allowed to defend himself against the charge of the magistrate. At the last *contio* the magistrate pronounced a provisional verdict, which, if adverse, was taken as a definite charge. At the same time he fixed the day for the meeting of the Comitia, always allowing an interval of thirty days. At the meeting of the Comitia, supposing nothing had occurred to stop the proceedings—i. e. supposing the accused had gone into voluntary exile, or a tribune had interposed his veto, or the accuser had withdrawn the charge—the accuser made his proposal (*rogatio*) to punish the accused. Thereupon the accused (or his advocate) spoke in his defence, the evidence of the witnesses who had been previously called was shortly gone through, and the proofs laid before the assembly. Finally the votes were taken in the usual manner, and the result at once made known. An action which remained unfinished at the expiration of the appointed time was not continued, but the accused was regarded as acquitted. The condemnation of the accused was followed by the immediate infliction of the penalty. The sentence could only be reversed by a subsequent resolution of the people. (See Restitutio.) The popular tribunals fell gradually into disuse; the standing judicial courts or *quaestiones* arose, the first of which was instituted in B.C. 149. In Cicero's time there were eight of those commissions, each presided over by a praetor or his representative. These courts were respectively appointed to try the following offences: (1) *Repetundae*, or official extortion; (2) *Maiestas*, or offences against the majesty of the State; (3) *Peculatus*, or embezzlement; (4) *Ambitus*, or attempt to gain office by unlawful means; (5) *Vis*, or violence; (6) *De Sicariis*, or murder; (7) *Adulterium*, or adultery; (8) *Falsum*, or forgery. (See Ambitus; Maiestas; Peculatus; Repetundae; Vis.) Any citizen, not an official, might bring the charge. On the proceedings, see Quaestio.

The Comitia Tributa were, after this, only set in motion in cases for which there was no *quaestio perpetua*, or for which it was thought improper to institute a *quaestio extraordinaria*. The popular tribunals of the Comitia came to an end with the Republic, but the *quaestiones* continued until the second century A.D. to act as the regular criminal courts. Under the Empire the Senate and the emperor had an extraordinary jurisdiction in criminal cases. The senatorial court, which met under the presidency of the consuls, followed the procedure of the *quaestiones*, but its proceedings were not public. The cases which it tried were usually those which affected persons of high standing charged with political or official offences. The decision of the court took the form of a *senatus consultum*, but had all the force of a legal sentence. The emperor, in virtue of his tribunician authority, had the power of neutralizing it by his veto. An interval of ten days occurred between sentence and execution, in pursuance of an order of Tiberius made in A.D. 22. But up to that time the sentence was carried out immediately after being passed, even in capital cases. Capital punishment had in the republican times been practically abolished, but was at once reinstated under the imperial régime. The emperor himself usually exercised his jurisdiction only over his own procurators and the higher officers of the army, notably in the case of strictly military offences. He acted as sole judge even when he invited the assistance of a jury (*consilium*). No formal act of accusation was required. Actions which he was unwilling to settle himself he would generally hand over to the *quaestiones* or the senatorial tribunals. The power of inflicting sentence of death on Roman citizens was confined originally to the emperor and Senate; but in later times the emperor, by a special mandate, transferred it for purposes of provincial administration to the governors of the provinces, whose jurisdiction extended to all citizens, with the exception of the high military officers, senators, and the *decuriones* of a *municipium*. (See DECURIO.) The criminal jurisdiction in Rome and its neighbourhood for a radius of 100 miles was given to the *praefectus urbi*, whose court ended by becoming the chief criminal court in the capital. The rest of Italy was placed under the jurisdiction of the praefect of the Praetorian Guard. From the decision of these representatives of the imperial authority an appeal was allowed to the emperor. But, after the third century A.D., the appeal mostly came before the praefect of the body-guard, whose judgment was generally final. The senatorial court came finally to acting only on the motion of the emperor.

The Roman civil jurisdiction, like the criminal, belonged originally to the king, from whom it passed to the consuls. With them it remained until a special magistracy, the praetorship, was instituted for it. (See PRAETOR.) According to ancient usage, the highest judicial authorities did not superintend the case from beginning to end. Their action was usually confined to the preparation of the case and such measures as its course made absolutely necessary, as (supposing their interference was required) in ordering execution of sentence. The investigation proper, and the passing of judgment, they as a rule handed over (with the consent of the parties) either to a single judge (see IUDEX) or *recuperatores* (see RECUPERATORES) appointed for the occasion, or to the judicial *collegia* of the *iudices decemviri* and *centumviri*, appointed, independently of special cases, for the whole year. As an introduction of the case, the suitor (*petitor*) was required to bring the defendant (*reus*) before the tribunal of the magistrate (*in ius*). In the case of the praetor, this would be his tribunal in the Forum. If the accused failed either to obey the personal summons of the prosecutor (*in ius vocatio*) or to appear by his representative (*vindex*), the prosecutor could, after calling a witness to attest that his summons was in order, take him before the praetor by force. In later time, to meet the cases in which the accused was unable to answer the summons immediately, the *vadimonium* was introduced. This was a promise, given by the accused on the security of sureties, that he would appear in court on a certain day, or if he failed would pay a sum of money, the amount of which depended on the nature of the question in dispute. The proceedings *in iure*, or before the magistrate, took place according to certain definite formal rules, the so-called *legis actiones*, the commonest of which was the *actio sacramenti*. This was accompanied by the utterance of a solemn formula partly by the magistrate, partly by the parties, and by certain symbolical acts. The smallest departure from the traditional formula involved the loss of the suit. The trial thus commenced, the next step was the *iudicis datio*, or appointment of a judge to try it. The case came on before the appointed *iudex* (*in iudicio*) on a day appointed. It was first shortly stated; the parties or their advocates made their speeches, the evidence was tested and judgment pronounced. See ACTIO; IUDEX.

The cumbrous machinery of the *legis actiones* gave way afterwards, in all cases but a few, to the procedure of *formula*. The *formula* was a document written out by the praetor, in which he, after hearing the parties, summed up the points of the accusation and the replies of the accused, appointed the judge, and gave him the materials for investigation and judgment. The proceedings *in iudicio* were then opened with the production of the formula. The question of the debt being settled, the judge proceeded to make a valuation of the object in dispute, in case a definite amount had not been mentioned in the formula. On the procedure in case of default, see CONTUMACIA. The judgment was irreversible. It was only in certain exceptional cases, notably if it appeared that any deception or force had been employed, that the magistrate who had appointed the judge, or his successor in office, could set it aside by *restitutio in integrum*. If the condemned party refused to make the payment, the magistrate who had prepared the case could order personal arrest or seizure of goods. See MANUS INIECTIO and BONORUM EMPTIO.

The only weapon against abuse of judicial authority in the republican age was the right of appeal to a magistrate with the power of veto. See APPELLATIO; PROVOCATIO.

The system of civil jurisdiction continued to exist in the imperial period, though with many modifications in detail, until the third century A.D. After that, the exceptional procedure (*extra ordinem*), in which the magistrate superintended the case till its conclusion and pronounced judgment at the end of it, became the usual one. The emperor, as supreme judge, had the power of deciding every case, criminal or otherwise, if his decision was appealed to. Further, he could interfere by his decree during the course of the trial, and either quash the verdict himself, or lay the appeal for decision before an authority constituted by himself for the purpose. In later times this authority was the *praefectus urbi*. A further appeal from this authority back to the emperor was allowed.

Jug. See URCEUS.

Juggler. See CIRCULATOR.

Julian Calendar. See CALENDARIUM.

July. See CALENDARIUM.

June. See CALENDARIUM.

Jurisprudence. See IURISPRUDENTIA.

Jury. See IUDICES.

K

For Greek and Latin words commencing with K, and for K as a symbol, see under C.

Kammermeister, JOACHIM. See CAMERARIUS.

Keel. See NAVIS.

Keg. See DOLIUM.

Kettle. See AENUM; CACCABUS; CORTINA.

Key. See CLAVIS.

Kiln. See FICTILÉ; FORNAX.

King. See REX.

Kissing, RIGHT OF. See COGNATI.

Kitchen. See CULINA.

Kitchen-gardens. See HORTUS.

Knapsack. See PERA; SARCINA.

Knights. See EQUITES; HIPPEIS.

Knives. See CULTER.

Knob. See BULLA.

Koppa. See C at the beginning.

L

L (Λ), as a symbol.

IN GREEK.—Λ=Λούκιος or Λεύκιος. The Lacedaemonians bore Λ upon their shields, as the Sicyonians Σ and the Messenians M. (See CLIPEUS, and cf. Eupolis, *Frag. Incert.* 37; Theopomp. [com.] *Frag. Incert.* 16.) As a numeral it stands for 11 (old system), or 30. ͵λ=30,000.

IN LATIN.—L=latum, legio, lex, libertus, librarius, locus, Lucius.

L·A·D·D=libens animo donum dat.

L·B=libertus bonus.

L·C=laticlavius, locus concessus.

L·D=libens dat, libero damno, locum dedit (loco dato, locus datus)—very frequent.

L·F=Latinae fuerunt, laudabilis femina, liberti fecerunt.

L·L=legatus legionis, libens laetus, liberto libertae, librarius legati (legionis), Lucii (duo).

L·M=libens merito, libertus meus, ludus magnus.

L·P=Liber pater, libertus patrono, libens posuit.

L·R·P=legas rogo praeteriens.

L·V=luna quinta.

L·V·S=libens votum solvit.

L·D·D·C·F·C=locus datus decreto collegii fabrum centurionum.

L·D·D·D·D·D=loco dato decreto decurionum dono dederunt.

L·F·D·D=ludos fecerunt decurionum decreto.

L·L·P·E=libertis libertabus posterisque eorum.

L·P·P·P=loco publico pecunia publica.

Labărum (λάβαρον and λάβουρον). The sacred banner or standard borne before the Roman emperors in war from the time of Constantine. It is described as a long pike intersected by a transverse beam. A silken veil, of a purple colour, hung down from the beam, and was adorned with precious stones, and curiously inwrought with the images of the reigning monarch and his children. The summit of the pike supported a crown of gold, which enclosed the monogram at once expressive of the figure of the cross, and the two initial letters (X and P) of the name of Christ. The safety of the Labarum was intrusted to fifty guards of approved valour and fidelity. In the Second Civil War, Licinius felt the power of this consecrated banner, the sight of which, in the stress of battle, animated the soldiers of Constantine with an invincible enthusiasm, and scattered terror and dismay through the adverse legions. Eusebius (*Vit. Const.* i. 2, 7 foll.) introduces the Labarum before the Italian expedition of Constantine; but his narrative seems to indicate that it was never shown at the head of an army till Constantine, about ten years afterwards, declared himself the enemy of Licinius and the deliverer of the Church. The Christian emperors, who respected the example of Constantine, displayed in all their military expeditions the standard of the cross; but when the successors of Theodosius had ceased to appear in person at the head of their armies, the Labarum was deposited as a venerable but useless relic in the palace of Constantinople. Its form is still preserved on the medals of the Flavian family; and there is extant a medal of the emperor Constantius, where the standard of the Labarum is accompanied with these memorable words: "By this sign thou shalt conquer."

Labarum.

The history of this standard is a curious one. A contemporary writer (Caecilius) affirms that in the night which preceded the last battle against Maxentius (A.D. 312), Constantine was admonished in a dream to inscribe the shields of his soldiers with the "celestial sign of God," the sacred monogram of the name of Christ; that he executed the command, and that his obedience was rewarded by a decisive victory at the Milvian bridge. The dream of Constantine may be naturally explained either by the enthusiasm or the policy of the emperor. While his anxiety for the approaching day, which must decide the fate of the Empire, was suspended by a short and interrupted slumber, the revered form of the Saviour and the well-known symbol of his religion might forcibly offer themselves to the active fancy of a prince who reverenced the name, and had, perhaps, secretly implored the power of the God of the Christians. As readily, on the other hand, might a consummate statesman indulge himself in the use of one of those military stratagems, one of those pious frauds, which Philip and Sertorius had employed with such art and effect.

The account given by Eusebius, however, is different from this. According to his statement, Constantine is reported to have seen with his own eyes the luminous trophy of the cross placed above the meridian sun, and inscribed with the following words in Greek: Ἐν τούτῳ νίκα. This appearance in the sky astonished the whole army, as well as the emperor himself, who was yet undetermined in the choice of a religion; but his astonishment was converted into faith by the vision of the ensuing night. The Saviour appeared before his eyes, and displayed the same celestial sign of the cross, directing Constantine to frame a similar standard, and to march, with an assurance of victory, against Maxentius and all his enemies.

The form of the Labarum and monogram may be seen, as we have already said, on the medals of the Flavian family. The etymology of the term itself has given rise to many conflicting opinions. Some derive the name from *labor;* others from εὐλάβεια, "reverence"; others from λαμβάνειν, "to take"; and others, again, from λάφυρα, "spoils." One writer makes Labarum to be like S.P.Q.R., only a *notatio*, or combination of initials to represent an equal number of terms; and thus, L.A.B.A.R.V.M. will stand for *Legionum aquila Byzantium antiqua Roma urbe mutavit.*

Labdacĭdae (Λαβδακίδαι). See LABDACUS.

Labdacĭdes (Λαβδακίδης). A name given to Oedipus as descended from Labdacus. See OEDIPUS.

Labdăcus (Λάβδακος). A son of Polydorus by Nycteïs, the daughter of Nycteus, king of Thebes. His father and mother died during his childhood, and he was left to the care of Nycteus, who, at his death, left his kingdom in the hands of Lycus, with orders to restore it to Labdacus as soon as of age. On succeeding to the throne, Labdacus, like Pentheus (q. v.), opposed the cult of Bacchus, and underwent a similar fate. He was father to Laïus, and his descendants were called Labdacidae. See LAÏUS.

Labdălum (Λάβδαλον). See SYRACUSAE.

Labeātes. A warlike people in Dalmatia, whose chief town was Scodra, and in whose territory was the Labeatis Palus (Lake of Scutari), through which the river Barbana (Bogana) runs.

Label. See SCHEDA; TITULUS.

Labeo, ANTISTIUS. (1) A Roman jurist, one of the murderers of Iulius Caesar. He put an end to his life after the battle of Philippi, B.C. 42. (2) A son of the preceding, and a still more eminent jurist. He adopted the republican opinions of his father, and was in consequence disliked by Augustus. It is probable that the *Labeone insanior* of Horace was a stroke levelled against the jurist in order to please the emperor. Labeo wrote a large number of works, which are cited in the *Digest.* He was the founder of one of the two great legal schools spoken of under IURISPRUDENTIA. He died A.D. 17.

Laberius, DECĬMUS. A Roman knight of good family, born about B.C. 107. He was famed for his talent in writing mimes, in the composition of which productions he occasionally amused himself. He was at length requested by Iulius Caesar, in B.C. 45, to appear on the stage and act the mimes which he had written (Macrob. *Sat.* ii. 7). Laberius was sixty years of age when this occurrence took place. Aware that the entreaties of a dictator were equivalent to commands, he complied; but, in the prologue to the first piece which he acted, he complained bitterly to the audience of the degradation to which he had been subjected. The whole prologue, consisting of twenty-nine lines, which have been preserved by Macrobius, is written in a lofty vein and with all the high spirit of a Roman citizen. He is said to have represented the feigned character with inimitable grace and spirit; yet in the course of the performance he could not refrain from expressing strong sentiments of freedom and detestation of tyranny. In one of the scenes he personated a Syrian slave; and, while escaping from the lash of his master, he exclaimed,

"Porro, Quirites, libertatem perdidimus;"

and shortly after he added,

"Necesse est multos timeat quem multi timent,"

on which the whole audience turned their eyes towards Caesar, who was present in the theatre (Macrob. l. c.). It was not merely to entertain the people, who would have been as well amused with the representation of any other actor; nor to wound the private feeling of Laberius that Caesar forced him on the stage. His sole object was to degrade the Roman knighthood, to subdue their spirit of independence, and to strike the people with a sense of his unlimited sway. This policy formed part of the same system which afterwards led him to persuade a senator to fight in the ranks of the gladiators. Though Laberius complied with the wishes of Caesar in exhibiting himself on the stage, and acquitted himself with ability as a mimetic actor, it would appear that the dictator had been hurt and offended by the freedoms which he used in the course of the representation, and, either on this or some subsequent occasion, bestowed the dramatic crown on Publilius Syrus in preference to the Roman knight. Laberius submitted with good grace to this fresh humiliation; he pretended to regard it merely as the ordinary chance of theatric competition. He did not long survive, however, this double mortification, but retired from Rome, and died at Puteoli about ten months after the assassination of Caesar. The titles and fragments of forty-three of the mimes of Laberius are still extant; but, excepting the prologue already cited, none is important. They will be found collected in Ribbeck's *Comicorum Romanorum Fragmenta*, pp. 279–302 (Leipzig, 1873).

Labials. See GRIMM'S LAW.

Labīci, Lavīci, or **Labīcum.** The modern Colonna; an ancient town in Latium, on a hill of the Alban mountain, fifteen miles southeast of Rome, west of Praenestĕ, and northeast of Tusculum. It was taken by the Romans B.C. 418, and by them colonized (Livy, iii. 25; iv. 45).

Labiēnus. (1) TITUS, one of Caesar's lieutenants in the Gallic war. In the beginning of the civil war he left Caesar for Pompey (*B. C.* iii. 13), escaped from the battle of Pharsalia, and was killed in that at Munda (*B. H.* 31). Labienus appears to have parted with almost all his former success on abandoning the side of his old commander. (2) QUINTUS, a son of the preceding, who inherited all his father's hatred of the party of Caesar. After the defeat of Brutus and Cassius, he refused to submit to the triumvirs, and retired to Parthia, where he was invested with a military command, and proved very serviceable to his new allies in their contests with the Romans. He was made prisoner in Cilicia, and probably put to death. Labienus caused medals to be struck, having on the obverse his head, with this legend, Q. LABIENUS PARTHICUS IMPER., and on the reverse a horse caparisoned after the Parthian manner. (3) TITUS, an orator and author of the time of Augustus, who distinguished himself by his bitter opposition to the imperial régime. The Senate decreed that his writings should be publicly burned; whereupon he shut himself up in his ancestral tomb and died there, about A.D. 12 (Suet. *Cal.* 16).

Laborīnus Campus. See PHLEGRAEI CAMPI.

Labours of Heracles. See HERACLES.

Labrădeus (Λαβραδεύς). A surname of Zeus at Labranda near Mylassa in Caria. The name was derived, according to Plutarch, from λάβρυς, the Lydian term for a hatchet, which the statue of Zeus held in its hand, and which had been offered up by Arselis of Mylassa from the spoils of Candaules, king of Lydia (Plat. *Quaest. Gr.*).

Labranda (τὰ Λάβρανδα). A town in Caria to the north of Mylae, celebrated for its temple of Zeus Stratios or Labrandenus.

Labrōnis Portus or **Portus Hercŭlis Liburni.** A harbour of Etruria, below the mouth of the Arnus. It is now Livorno (Leghorn). Cicero calls it Portus Labronis (*Ad Q. frat.* ii. 6).

Labrum. See BALNEAE, p. 191.

Labynētus (Λαβύνητος). A name common to several of the Babylonian monarchs, seems to have been a title rather than a proper name. The Labynetus mentioned by Herodotus (i. 74) as arranging a peace between Cyaxares and Alyattes is the same with Nebuchadnezzar. The Labynetus mentioned by Herodotus (i. 77) as a contemporary of Cyrus and Croesus is the same with the Belshazzar of the prophet Daniel. By other writers he is called Nabonadius or Nabonidus. He was the last king of Babylon.

Labyrinthus (Λαβύρινθος). A name given to a species of structure full of intricate passages and windings, so that when once entered, it is next to impossible for an individual to extricate himself without the assistance of a guide. The origin of the term will be considered at the close of the article. There were four very famous labyrinths among the ancients—one in Egypt near the Lake Moeris, another in Crete, a third at Lemnos, and a fourth near Clusium in Italy. (1) THE EGYPTIAN. This was situated in Lower Egypt, near Lake Moeris, and in the vicinity of Arsinoë or Crocodilopolis. The accounts which the ancient writers give of it are very different from each other. Herodotus, who saw the structure itself, assigns to it twelve courts (Herod. ii. 148). Pliny, whose description is much more highly coloured and marvellous than the former's, makes the number sixteen (*H. N.* xxxvi. 19); while Strabo, who, like Herodotus, beheld the very structure, gives the number of courts as twenty-seven. The following imperfect sketch, drawn from these different sources, may give some idea of the magnitude and nature of this singular structure: A large edifice, divided, most probably, into twelve separate palaces, stretched along with a succession of splendid apartments, spacious halls, etc., the whole adorned with columns, gigantic statues, richly carved hieroglyphics, and every other appendage of Egyptian art. With the northern side of the structure were connected six courts, and the same number with the southern. These were open places surrounded by lofty walls, and paved with large slabs of stone. Around these courts ran a vast number of the most intricate passages, lower than the corresponding parts of the main building; and around all these again was thrown a large wall, affording only one entrance into the Labyrinth; while at the other end, where the Labyrinth terminated, was a pyramid forty fathoms high, with large figures carved on it, and a subterraneous way leading within. According to Herodotus, the whole structure contained 3000 chambers, 1500 above ground, and as many below. The historian informs us that he went through all the rooms above the surface of the earth, but that he was not allowed by the Egyptians who kept the place to examine the subterraneous apartments, because in these were the bodies of the sacred crocodiles and of the kings who had built the Labyrinth. "The upper part, however," remarks the historian, "which I carefully viewed, seems to surpass the art of men; for the passages through the buildings and the variety of windings afforded me a thousand occasions of wonder, as I passed from a hall to a chamber, and from the chamber to other buildings, and from chambers into halls. All the roofs and walls within are of stone, but the walls are further adorned with figures of sculpture. The halls are surrounded with pillars of white stone, very closely fitted."

According to Herodotus, the Labyrinth was built by twelve kings, who at one time reigned over Egypt, and it was intended as a public monument of their common reign (Herod. ii. 148). Others make it to have been constructed by Psammetichus alone, who was one of the twelve; others again, by Ismandes or Petosuchis. Mannert assigns it to Memnon. Opinions are also divided as to the object of this singular structure. Some regard it as a burial-place for the kings and sacred crocodiles, an opinion very prevalent among the ancients. Others view it as a kind of Egyptian Pantheon. Others, again, make it to have been a place of assembly for the deputies sent by each of the twelve nomes of Egypt; while another class think that the Egyptian Mysteries were celebrated here. According to Galterer, however, the Labyrinth was an architectural symbolical representation of the zodiac and the course of the sun through the same. The twelve palaces are the twelve zodiacal signs; the one half of the building above ground and the other below is a symbol of the course of the sun above and below the horizon.

As regards the name Labyrinth itself, much diversity of opinion exists. By a sort of antiphrasis it was formerly derived ἀπὸ τοῦ μὴ λαβεῖν θύραν, from its difficulty of egress; but very probably from λαύρα (λάϝρα), "a passage-way;" the termination being found in such words as μήρινθος, ὑάκινθος. Others, finding in Manetho that an Egyptian king, named Lachares or Labaris, had erected the structure in question, make the term equivalent to "the abode of Labaris." Brugsch regards it as the corruption of an Egyptian word meaning "the building at the entrance to a reservoir" (*Egypt under the Pharaohs*).

The position of the Egyptian Labyrinth is clearly indicated by the words of Herodotus, "a little above the Lake Moeris." It is now certain that the remains of the Labyrinth must be sought for near Sakkara in the district called Fayûm. Vast piles of rubbish are here to be seen, and the destruction is supposed to be owing to the Arabs, who may have thought that treasures were concealed under ground here. The ruins were first carefully explored, and an imperfect idea of their original plan made out by the Prussian expedition of 1843, of which Prof. Lepsius was the head. More recent expeditions are those of Mr. Petrie, to whose work the reader is referred (*Hawâra, Biahma, and Arsinoë* [1889]).

(2) For an account of the CRETAN and ETRURIAN labyrinths, consult the articles PORSENA and THESEUS respectively.

Lacedaemon (Λακεδαίμων). (1) A son of Zeus and Taÿgetê, the daughter of Atlas, who married Sparta, the daughter of Eurotas, by whom he had Amyclas, Asinê, and Eurydicê, the wife of Acrisius. He was the first who introduced the worship of the Charites into Laconia, and who built them a temple. From Lacedaemon and his wife the capital of Laconia was called Lacedaemon and Sparta (Apollod. iii. 10; Hyg. *Fab.* 155). (2) A city of the Peloponnesus, the capital of Laconia, called also Sparta. See SPARTA.

Lacedaemonii (Λακεδαιμόνιοι) and **Lacedaemŏnes** (Λακεδαίμονες). The inhabitants of Lacedaemon. See SPARTA.

Lacēdas (Λακήδας) or **Leocēdes**. A king of Argos, father of Melas (Herod. vi. 127).

Lacerna (practically identical with the Greek χλαμύς). The Latin term for a coarse, dark-coloured cloak, fastened on the shoulder by a brooch, which was in use as a protection against rain. It was provided with a hood. In later times the name was given to a light and elegant mantle, either white or dyed in Tyrian purple, which was worn over the toga to complete the costume at games or other outdoor occasions. In the time of Augustus, who forbade its use in the Forum or Circus, it formed part of the military uniform. It was afterwards commonly worn even in Rome itself.

Lacerna. (From the Column of Trajan.)

Lacetāni. A people in Hispania Tarraconensis, at the foot of the Pyrenees.

Lachăres (Λαχάρης). An Athenian popular leader who in B.C. 296 made himself supreme in Athens at the time when that city was besieged by Demetrius. When the city was about to capitulate, Lachares escaped to Thebes with a great treasure, and was there murdered for his wealth (Pausan. i. 25, 7).

Laches (Λάχης). An Athenian general who fell at the battle of Mantinea, B.C. 418. A dialogue of Plato bears his name. See PLATO.

Lachĕsis (Λάχεσις). One of the Fates. See MOERAE.

Lachmann, KARL KONRAD FRIEDRICH WILHELM. One of the greatest of modern philologists and text-critics, born at Brunswick, March 4, 1793. He began his studies at the Katharineum in Brunswick, and at once showed an extraordinary aptitude for classical literature and linguistics. In 1809 he entered the University of Leipzig, where he studied philology and theology, soon, however, transferring himself to the University of Göttingen, where the stimulating influence of Heyne and Dissen powerfully affected his intellectual development. Besides working hard at classical philology, he pursued with much ardour the scientific study of Italian, English, and Old German. In 1815, carried away by the patriotic enthusiasm which swept over Germany, he enlisted as a volunteer in the army which in that year marched upon Paris; but he had no part in active fighting.

In 1816 he took the position of assistant master in the Friedrich Werder Gymnasium at Berlin, and, soon after, habilitated at the University of that place, publishing a dissertation on the *Nibelungennoth*, and almost simultaneously an edition of Propertius. Receiving an appointment as master in the Fridericianum of Königsberg, he assisted his colleague Köpke in editing Rudolf von Monfort's text of *Barlaam and Josaphat* (1818), and also in preparing notes for an edition of Walther von der Vogelweide. In January, 1818, he was appointed Professor Extraordinarius of Classical Philology in the University of Königsberg, where he had Lobeck for a colleague, and where he also lectured on Middle High German literature and Old German grammar. In 1824, having received leave of absence for this purpose, he devoted some time to a thorough search through the libraries of Germany, especially of Southern Germany, for unpublished material relating to these subjects. In February, 1825, he was called to the University of Berlin as Professor Extraordinarius of Classical and German Philology, and in 1827 was promoted to Professor Ordinarius. He died March 13, 1851.

Lachmann was one of the most truly scientific scholars that Germany has ever produced, and possessed a mind of singular originality, sagacity, and subtle power. In both classical and Germanic philology, and in New Testament criticism as well, his independent work has justly been styled "epoch-making." "His influence," says Nettleship, "on the general course of philological study has probably been greater than that of any single man during the present century. Many scholars who never saw him, and to whom he is only known by his books, have been inspired by the extraordinary impulse which he gave to critical methods. Greek, Latin, and German philology have alike felt the touch of the magician."

His chief classical works are the following: Editions of Propertius (1816), Catullus (1829), Tibullus (1829), Genesis (1834), Terentianus Maurus (1836), Babrius (1845), Avianus (1845), Gaius (1841–1842), the *Agrimensores Romani* (1848–52), Lucilius, and, above all, Lucretius (1850). Of this last great work, Professor Munro has justly said that it is "a work which will be a landmark for scholars as long as the Latin language continues to be studied." In his *Betrachtungen über die Ilias* (1837, 1841), he attempted to show that the *Iliad* consists of sixteen independent "lays" that were subsequently enlarged and altered. (See HOMERUS.) In New Testament criticism he first carried out the plan first put forth by Richard Bentley (q. v.) of restoring the ancient readings current in the Eastern MSS., using the Latin authorities (and West Greek) as evidence in case of a divergence of readings in the oldest Eastern MSS. His smaller edition of the New Testament appeared in 1831 (3d ed. 1846); the larger one, in two volumes (*Novum Testamentum Graece et Latine*), in the preparation of which he was aided by Philip Buttmann, in 1842–50. Of his work in Germanic philology and literature it is not necessary to speak here. Lachmann's life has been written by M. Hertz, *Karl Lachmann, eine Biographie* (Berlin, 1851); and see Bursian, *Geschichte der class. Philol.*, etc., pp. 789–800 (Munich, 1883).

Lacia (Λακία) or **Laciădae** (Λακιάδαι). A deme of Attica belonging to the tribe Oeneïs.

Lacinia. A surname of Iuno, from her temple at Lacinium in Italy.

Lacinia. The angular extremity of the toga, one end of which was thrown over the left shoulder. See TOGA.

Lacinium (Λακίνιον ἄκρον). A promontory on the eastern coast of Bruttium, a few miles south of Croton, and forming the western boundary of the Tarentine Gulf. It possessed a celebrated temple of Iuno, who was worshipped here under the surname of Lacinia. The ruins of this temple have given the modern name to the promontory, Capo delle Colonne.

Lacmon (Λάκμων) or **Lacmus** (Λάκμος). The northern part of Mount Pindus, in which the river Aoüs takes its origin (Herod. ix. 92).

Lacobrĭga. (1) A town of Spain, near the Sacrum Promontorium, now Lagoa (Mela, iii. 1). (2) A town of Spain, among the Vaccaei, now Lobera (Pliny, *H. N.* iii. § 4).

Laconĭca (Λακωνική, sc. γῆ), called by the Roman writers **Laconia.** A country of the Peloponnesus, situated at its southern extremity, having Messenia on the west, and Arcadia and Argolis on the north. The extent of Laconia from east to west, where it reached farthest, was 1° 45′, but it became narrower towards the north, and its extent from north to south was about fifty miles. As the southern parts were encompassed by the sea, and the east and northeast parts by the Sinus Argolicus, it had a great number of promontories, the chief of which were those of Malea and Taenarum, now Capes Malio and Matapan. The sea-coast of Laconia was furnished with a considerable number of seaports, towns, and commodious harbours, the chief of which were Trinnassus, Acria, Gytheum, and Epidaurus. The Laconian coasts were famous for yielding a shellfish (*murex*) whence was obtained a beautiful purple dye, inferior only to that which was brought from the Red Sea and Phœnicia. The mountains of Laconia were numerous, the most famous being Taÿgetus. The principal river was the Eurotas, on which stood the capital, Sparta or Lacedaemon. The soil was very rich, especially in the low grounds, and, being well watered, was excellent for pasture; but the number of its mountains and hills prevented its being tilled so well as it might otherwise have been. See SPARTA.

Laconĭcum (λακωνικόν). A species of dry sweating-bath, introduced from Greece by the Romans towards the end of the Republic. See BALNEAE, p. 191.

Laconĭcus Sinus (Κόλπος Λακωνικός). A gulf in the south of the Peloponnesus, into which the Eurotas falls.

Lactantius. (1) FIRMIĀNUS (in some MSS. called LUCIUS CAECILIUS or CAELIUS). An eminent Christian writer of the early part of the fourth century, whose birthplace is uncertain. He taught rhetoric at Nicomedia in Bithynia, and it was probably there that he became converted to Christianity. About the year 313 he was invited by Constantine the Great to act as tutor to his son Crispus. He died about 325. His chief work is a defence of Christianity, in seven books, entitled *Institutiones Divinae*, written in reply to an attack upon the faith made by two pagan writers. He also wrote treatises *De Ira Dei* and *De Opificio Dei*, the latter being an account of anthropology from the Christian standpoint. A fourth book, by some not credited to him, is entitled *De Mortibus Persecutorum*, in which he tries to show that all the persecutors of the Christians have met with violent deaths. There exists, also, an epitome of the *Institutiones Divinae*, made by Lactantius. His Latinity is so pure that he is styled "the Christian Cicero." During the Middle Ages his writings were extremely popular, and the MSS. of them are very numerous. The first book ever printed in Italy (1465) was a Lactantius. The earlier texts are enumerated by Dufresnoy in his edition (2 vols. 1748). Lactantius has also been edited by Gersdorf, in the *Bibl. Pat. Eccles. Lat.* (Leipzig, 1842–1844); by Migne in vols. vi. and vii. of his *Patrologia* (Paris, 1844); and by Laubmann and S. Brandt (Vienna, 1891). On his life, see P. Brandt, *Das Leben des Lactantius* (Vienna, 1890). (2) PLACĬDUS. The author of a collection of scholia on the *Thebaïs* of Statius, probably the same as the glossator Luctatius (?) Placidus, who has left a book of glosses with Latin commentaries. They are chiefly on Plautus and Lucilius. See Goetz, *De Placidi Glossis* (Jena, 1886), Onions in the (Eng.) *Journal of Philology*, xi. 75, xii. 77, and xv. 167; and the article GLOSSA.

Lactarius. See PISTOR.

Lactarius Mons or **Lactis Mons.** A mountain in Campania near which the eunuch Narses defeated the Goths in A.D. 553.

Lacūna. The name given to a gap found in classical MSS., and due to erasures, accidental obliterations, the tearing of the pages, loss of pages, etc. On the importance of the lacunae as a means of determining the "family" to which a MS. belongs, see TEXTUAL CRITICISM.

Lacunaria, Lacuaria, or **Laquearia.** The Latin

name for the panelled ceilings of rooms which were formed by placing planks across the beams of the roof, whereby hollow spaces were produced. These spaces were covered with wood or ivory, or ornamented with sculptured reliefs or pictures; occasionally they were even gilded or inlaid with plates of gold (Hor. *Carm.* ii. 18, 1). In banqueting-rooms they were sometimes so formed that the panels could be slipped aside to let flowers, wreaths, and other complimentary presents fall in showers on the guests below. See Suet. *Nero*, 31; and the article PALATIUM.

Lacus. (1) See FONS. (2) A bath (βαφή) into which the armourer plunged the hot iron to give it a greater hardness (Verg. *Georg.* iv. 172). See Blümner, *Technologie*, iv. 342–350.

Lacȳdes (Λακύδης). A philosopher of Cyrené, who filled the chair of the Platonic School at Athens after the death of Arcesilaüs. He assumed this office about the year B.C. 245. He is said to have been the founder of a new school, not because he introduced any new doctrines, but because he changed the place of instruction, and held his school in the garden of Attalus, still, however, within the limits of the Academic grove. He died of a palsy occasioned by excessive drinking about B.C. 215 (Diog. Laërt. iv. 59 foll.; Aelian, *V. H.* ii. 41).

Ladas (Λάδας). A swift runner of Laconia, whose speed became proverbial. There were statues to him in Argos and Arcadia (Pausan. ii. 19, 7; Catull. lv. 25; Juv. xiii. 97).

Ladders. See SCALAE.

Ladé (Λάδη). An island off the west coast of Caria, opposite to Miletus and to the bay into which the Maeander falls (Herod. vi. 8).

Ladle. See COCLEAR; CYATHUS; TRULLA.

Ladon (Λάδων). (1) A dragon sprung from Typhon and Echidna (or from Phorcys and Ceto). He guarded the golden apples of the Hesperides, but was slain by Heracles. See HERACLES; HESPERIDES. (2) The husband of Stymphalis and father of Daphné and Metopé.

Ladon (Λάδων). (1) A river in Arcadia, rising near Clitor, and falling into the Alpheus, between Heraea and Phrixa. (2) A small river in Elis, rising on the frontiers of Achaia, and falling into the Peneus.

Laeëtani. A people on the eastern coast of Hispania Tarraconensis, near the mouth of the river Rubricatus, the same as the Laletani, whose country, Laletania, produced good wine, and whose chief town was Barcino.

Laelaps (Λαῖλαψ). The storm-wind, personified as the swift dog, which Procris had received from Artemis and gave to her husband, Cephalus. When the Teumessian fox was sent to punish the Thebans, Cephalus sent the dog Laelaps against the fox. The dog overtook the fox, but Zeus changed both animals into a stone, which was shown in the neighbourhood of Thebes. See Hyg. *Fab.* 28; Ovid, *Met.* vii. 771; and TEUMESSUS.

Laeliānus. One of the Thirty Tyrants, who was proclaimed emperor in Gaul (A.D. 267), but was slain in the course of a few months by his own soldiers, who then set up Victorinus in his stead (Eutrop. ix. 7).

Laelius, GAIUS. (1) The friend of Scipio Africanus the elder. He fought under the latter in almost all his campaigns. He was consul B.C. 190. (2) Surnamed SAPIENS, son of the preceding. His intimacy with Scipio Africanus the younger was as remarkable as his father's friendship with the elder, and it obtained an imperishable monument in Cicero's treatise, *Laelius sive de Amicitia.* He was born about 186; was tribune of the plebs in 151, praetor in 145, and consul in 140. He was celebrated for his love of literature and philosophy, and cultivated the society and friendship of the philosopher Panaetius, of the historian Polybius, and of the poets Terence and Lucilius. Laelius is the principal interlocutor in Cicero's dialogue *De Amicitia*, and is one of the speakers in the *De Senectute* and in the *De Republica.* His two daughters were married—the one to Q. Mucius Scaevola, the augur, the other to C. Fannius Strabo.

Laena (χλαῖνα). An ancient Roman garment worn by the Flamines, fastened with a bronze clasp (Cic. *Brut.* 14, 56). It was a woollen mantle, of a coarse, shaggy material, twice as thick as an ordinary toga. Under the Empire it was very generally worn as an outer cloak by all classes of society, especially on going out to supper. It was sometimes scarlet, and sometimes violet, but in these colours it appears to have been used only by the rich. (Cf. Juv. iii. 283 with Mayor's note; and Pers. i. 32.)

Laenas. The name of a family of the gens Popilia, its members being distinguished for their sternness and haughty pride. The most famous of them was GAIUS POPILIUS LAENAS, consul in B.C. 172. He was afterwards sent as ambassador to Antiochus, king of Syria, whom the Senate wished to abstain from hostilities against Egypt. Antiochus was just marching upon Alexandria, when Popilius gave him the letter of the Senate, which the king read and promised to take into consideration with his friends. Popilius straightway described with his cane a circle in the sand around the king, and ordered him not to stir out of it before he had given a decisive answer. This boldness so impressed Antiochus that he at once yielded to the demand of Rome. (Livy, xlv. 12.)

Laërtes (Λαέρτης). King of Ithaca, son of Acrisius, husband of Anticlea, and father of Odysseus, who is hence called Laërtiades. Some writers call Odysseus the son of Sisyphus. (See ANTICLEA.) Laërtes took part in the Calydonian hunt, and in the expedition of the Argonauts. He was still alive when Odysseus returned to Ithaca, after the fall of Troy. See ODYSSEUS.

Laërtius, DIOGENES. See DIOGENES.

Laestrygŏnes (Λαιστρυγόνες). A savage race of cannibals, whom Odysseus encountered in his wanderings. (See Hom. *Od.* x. 119.) They were governed by Antiphates and Lamus. They belong to mythology rather than to history. The Greeks placed them on the east coast of Sicily, in the plains of Leontini, which are therefore called Laestrygonii Campi. The Roman poets, who regarded the promontory Circeium as the Homeric island of Circé, transplanted the Laestrygones to the southern coast of Latium, in the neighbourhood of Formiae, which they supposed to have been built by Lamus, the king of this people. Hence Horace speaks of *Laestrygonia Bacchus in amphora*—that is, Formian wine; and Ovid calls Formiae *Laestrygonis Lami urbs.* See FORMIAE.

Laetoria Lex. See LEX.

Laevi or **Levi.** A Ligurian people in Gallia Transpadana, on the river Ticinus, who, in conjunction with the Marici, built the town of Ticinum (Pavia).

Laevīnus, VALERIUS. (1) PUBLIUS, consul B.C. 280, defeated by Pyrrhus on the banks of the Siris. (See PYRRHUS.) (2) MARCUS, praetor in B.C. 215, when he carried on war against Philip in Greece; and consul in B.C. 210, when he carried on the war in Sicily, and took Agrigentum.

Lagōna, Lagūna, Lagoena, or **Lagēna** (λάγυνος). An earthenware jar having a long, narrow neck, a rather wide mouth and a swelling body, with one handle. It was used for wine and was set on the table like a modern decanter (Juv. v. 29), and in Gaul for beer.

Lagos. A town in Great Phrygia (Livy, xxxviii. 15).

Lagus (Λάγος). A Macedonian who married Arsinoë, a concubine of Philip of Macedon. She was said to be pregnant at the time of the marriage, so that their son Ptolemy, who afterwards founded the Egyptian monarchy, was by many regarded as the son of Philip (Pausan. i. 6, § 2). See PTOLEMAEUS.

Lagūsa. (1) An island in the Sinus Glaucus, near the northern coast of Lycia. (2) Or LAGUSSAE, an island, or, more properly, a cluster of islands off the coast of Troas, to the north of Tenedos (Pliny, v. 31).

Laïădes. A patronymic of Oedipus, son of Laïus (Ovid, *Met.* vi. 18).

Laïs (Λαΐς). The name of two celebrated Grecian hetaerae, or courtesans. (1) The elder, a native probably of Corinth, lived in the time of the Peloponnesian War, and was celebrated as the most beautiful woman of that age. She was notorious also for her avarice and caprice. One of her lovers was the Cyrenaic philosopher Aristippus, two of whose works were inscribed with her name. In her old age she took to drink. At her death she was buried in Corinth, and over her was placed a monument representing a lioness tearing a ram. So much was her reputation a part of that of her city that there arose the proverb οὐ Κόρινθος οὔτε Λαΐς. A number of anecdotes regarding her are preserved in Athenaeus. (2) The younger daughter of Timandra, probably born at Hyccara in Sicily. According to some accounts she was brought to Corinth when seven years old, having been taken prisoner in the Athenian expedition to Sicily, and bought by a Corinthian. This story, however, involves numerous difficulties, and seems to have arisen from a confusion between this Laïs and the other woman of the same name. She was a contemporary and rival of Phrynē (q. v.). She became enamoured of a Thessalian named Hippolochus, or Hippostratus, and accompanied him to Thessaly, where, it is said, some Thessalian women, jealous of her beauty, enticed her into a temple of Aphroditē, and there stoned her to death (Pausan. ii. 2, 5).

Laïus (Λάϊος). King of Thebes, son of Labdacus, husband of Iocasta, and father of Oedipus, by whom he was slain. See OEDIPUS.

Lalăgē. A common name of courtesans, from the Greek λαλαγή, "prattling," used as a term of endearment—"little prattler." See Hor. *Carm.* i. 22, 23.

Laletāni. A people in the eastern part of Hispania Tarraconensis, whose country, Laletania, produced good wine. Their chief town was Barcino (Barcelona). The correct form of the name is probably LAEĔTANI.

Lamăchus (Λάμαχος). An Athenian, the colleague of Alcibiades and Nicias in the great Sicilian Expedition, B.C. 415. He fell under the walls of Syracuse, in a sally of the besieged. In Aristophanes he is represented as a brave but blustering soldier (*Acharn.* 565, etc.).

Lambīnus, DIONYSIUS. The pseudo-classical form of DENYS LAMBIN, one of the greatest of French scholars in the sixteenth century. He was born at Montreuil-sur-Mer in 1516, and after lecturing and teaching for many years in the provinces with much success, was called to Paris to take the chair of Greek Literature in the Collège Royal. In this office he achieved a great reputation for the soundness and accuracy of his scholarship, being, in fact, so noted for attention to minute details that his opponents coined from his name the verb *lambiner*, which is still retained in French to denote the work of a pedant. His chief published works are the *Oratio de Recta Pronunciatione Linguae Graecae* (1568); emendations on Cicero (1577); a life of Cicero (1578); and editions with notes of Horace (1561); Lucretius, his *magnum opus* (1564); Cicero, 4 vols. (1566); Nepos (1569); Demosthenes (1570); and Plautus (1577). Lambinus died in 1572, it is said of grief at the loss of his friend Ramus, who was killed in the affair of St. Bartholomew's Day.

Lambrus or **Lamber.** A river of Cisalpine Gaul, issuing from the Eupilis Lacus, and falling into the Olona, one of the tributaries of the Po. It is now the Lambro or Lambrone (Pliny, iii. 19).

Lamia. A town in Phthiotis, in Thessaly, situated on the small river Acheloüs, fifty stadia inland from the Maliac Gulf. It has given its name to the war which was carried on by the confederate Greeks against Antipater after the death of Alexander, B.C. 323. When Antipater was defeated by the confederates under the command of Leosthenes, the Athenian, he took refuge in Lamia, where he was besieged for some months. During the siege Leosthenes was killed, and soon after Antipater, being joined by Craterus, defeated the confederates at Cranon, ending the war (Polyb. ix. 29).

Lamia, AELIUS. A Roman family, which claimed descent from the mythical hero Lamus. L. AELIUS LAMIA, the friend of Horace (see *Carm.* i. 26, 8), was consul in A.D. 3, and the son of the Lamia who supported Cicero in the suppression of the Catilinarian conspiracy.

Lamiae (Λαμίαι). Fabulous monsters, the vampires of ancient legend, commonly represented with the head and breast of a woman and the body of a serpent. According to some, they changed their forms at pleasure, and, when about to ensnare their prey, assumed such appearances as were most seductive and calculated to please. The blood of young persons was believed to possess peculiar attractions for them, and for the purpose of quaffing this they were wont to take the forms of beautiful women, the better to allure young men. The Lamiae possessed also another means of accomplishing their object. This was a species of hissing sound emitted by them, so soothing and attractive in its nature that persons found themselves irresistibly allured by it. When not in disguise and when they had sated their horrid appetites, their form was hideous, their visages glowed like fire, their bodies were besmeared with blood, and their feet appeared of iron or of lead. Sometimes they showed themselves completely blind; at other times they had a single eye, either in the forehead or on one side of the visage. The popular belief made them frequent Africa and Thessaly, in both of which countries they watched along the main roads and seized upon unwary travellers.

The fable of Queen Lamia has some analogy to this fiction, and both, in all probability, owe their origin to one and the same source. Lamia, according to Diodorus Siculus and other ancient authorities, was a queen of Africa, remarkable for beauty, who, on account of her cruel disposition, was eventually transformed into a wild beast. Having lost, it seems, her own children by the act of Heré, who was jealous of Lamia's intercourse with Zeus, she sought to console her sorrow by seizing the children of her subjects from their mothers' arms, and putting them to death. Hence the transformation inflicted upon her by the gods (Diod. Sic. xx. 41; Wesseling, *ad* Diod. l. c.). The Lamiae figured extensively in the nursery-legends of antiquity, and their names and attributes were standing objects of terror to the young (Diod. l. c.; cf. Hor. *A. P.* 340; Aristoph. *Vesp.* 1177). See also EMPUSA; LEMURES; MORMOLYCÉ.

Lampadedromia (*λαμπαδηδρομία*, also *λαμπαδηφορία*). A torch-race, such as were celebrated at Athens, Corinth, Ceos, Syros, Amphipolis, Byzantium, and other places, in honour of different deities, and probably at any great funeral games. At Athens it took place on five special occasions: at the Promethea, in honour of Prometheus; at the Panathenaea, in honour of Athené; after the Apaturia, in honour of Hephaestus; and in honour of Bendis.

Torch used in the race. (Coin in Mionnet, pl. 49, fig. 6.)

The race was run usually on foot, but sometimes on horses by *ephebi*. The torches were of two kinds—one a sort of candlestick, shown in the above illustration, and the other one of a more conventional kind, like that shown in the article FAX. There were two different methods of conducting the race. The first or earlier system required lines of runners (*λαμπαδισταί* or *λαμποδηφόροι*), posted at intervals, the first in each line who receives the torch, or takes it from the altar, running at his best speed and handing it to the second in his own line, and the second to the third, until the last in the line is reached, who runs with it up to the appointed spot. Of course, if any torch went out, the line to which it belonged was out of the race. The victory (*νικᾶν λαμπάδι*) fell to that line of runners whose torch first reached the goal alight. Assuming that all the gymnasiarchs contended on each occasion, there would be ten such lines (or, after B.C. 307, twelve), one for each tribe; but it is possible that each gymnasiarch performed his service only once a year, and that only a certain number were told off for each festival. All the runners in the winning line or chain contributed to the victory, and this may possibly be the explanation of the well-known line of Aeschylus (*Ag.* 314), "the last and the first (i. e. all alike in the chain) are successful." The beacons are all victorious, because all belong to the successful chain of light, as in the torch-race each person in the line shares the victory.

A different kind of torch-race is described by Pausanias (i. 30, § 2), in which there was no handing of the torch from one to another, but several torch-bearers started, possibly one for each tribe; the first who reached the goal with his torch alight won; the competition was individual, not one chain of runners against another; and it is no doubt to such a race that inscriptions, which speak of a single victor with a single prize, refer. The race in honour of Bendis was run on horseback.

The starting-point of the race at Athens was the altar of Prometheus in the Academy, and the course was through the Ceramicus to the city, a little more than a mile. The archon basileus presided and awarded the prize.

The origin of the custom is probably to be found in the honour paid to the giver of fire, Prometheus, and after him to the deities associated with the arts in which fire is used—Athené, Hephaestus, etc. See Preller, *Griech. Mythol.* p. 80 (1872).

Lampas (*λαμπάς*). A general term for any thing which shines or gives light, as a torch (see FAX), a lamp (see LUCERNA); but especially a light which was carried by the youth of Athens in the Lampadedromia (q. v.).

Lampĕdo. (1) A Lacedaemonian woman, wife of Archidamus II., king of Sparta, and mother of Agis. She was celebrated as being the daughter, wife, sister, and mother of a king. (2) A queen of the Amazons (Justin, ii. 4).

Lampetia (*Λαμπετίη*). Daughter of Helios (the sun) and sister of Phaëthon (*Odyss.* xii. 132).

Lampon (*Λάμπων*). An Athenian soothsayer and interpreter of dreams and oracles. With Xenocritus, he founded Thurii in Italy B.C. 443 (Diod. xii. 10).

Lamponīa (*τὰ Λαμπώνεια*). A city of Mysia, in the interior of the Troad, near the borders of Aeolia.

Lampra (*Λάμπρα*). An Attic deme belonging to the tribe Erechtheïs.

Lampridius, AELIUS. A Latin historian, who flourished in the early part of the fourth century, under Diocletian and Constantine the Great. Of his works there are extant the lives of the emperors Antoninus, Marcus Aurelius, Lucius Verus, Pertinax, Albinus, Macrinus, etc. The life of Alexander Severus, which, according to the Palatine manuscript, is the work of Spartianus, has been by some authorities ascribed to him. The lives are to be found in the collection of the *Historiae Augustae Scriptores*. See AUGUSTAE HISTORIAE SCRIPTORES.

Lampsăcus (*Λάμψακος*). An important city of Mysia in Asia Minor, on the coast of the Hellespont; a colony of the Phocaeans; celebrated for its wine, and the chief seat of the worship of Priapus. Here were born Anaximenes, Charon, the historian, and the philosophers Adimantus and Metrodorus.

Lamus. Son of Poseidon and king of the Laestrygones, said to have founded Formiae in Italy. See FORMIAE; LAESTRYGONES.

Lamus (Λάμος). A river and town of Cilicia.

Lancea (λόγχη). A lance. See ARMA; HASTA.

Lancia. The name of two towns in Lusitania, distinguished by the appellations of Oppidana and Transcudana. The first was on the frontiers of the Lusitani, near the sources of the river Munda (Mondego). It is now La Guarda. The latter lay to the east of the former, and is now Ciudad Rodrigo. It was called Transcudana, because it lay beyond the Cuda.

Lancŭla. Diminutive of *lanx* (q. v.); and especially the scale, which was appended when necessary to one end of a Roman steelyard (*statera*) (Vitruv. x. 3, 4).

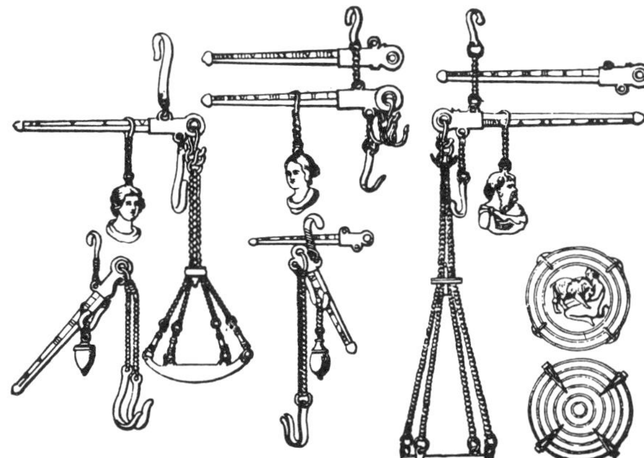

Lances and Lanculae. (Pompeii.)

Langobardi or **Longobardi**, "those dwelling along the river-plains (Börde)," corrupted into Lombards, a German tribe of the Suevic race, dwelt originally on the banks of the Elbe, and after many migrations eventually crossed the Alps (A.D. 568), and settled in the north of Italy, which has ever since received the name of Lombardy. The kingdom of the Lombards existed for upwards of two centuries, till its overthrow by Charlemagne. In A.D. 643, the Lombard king, Rothari, and his successors, embodied the legal customs of the Lombards in a code written in Latin and called *Leges Lombardorum*. The earliest historian of the Lombards is Paulus Diaconus, whose works in Latin still survive. See PAULUS.

Lanīcé (Λανίκη). The nurse of Alexander the Great (Arrian, iv. 9).

Lanista. The Roman name for a fencing-master or trainer of gladiators. See GLADIATORES.

Lantern of Demosthenes. A mediæval name for the Monument of Lysicrates (q.v.).

Lanterna, and in late Latin, **Laterna** (ἰπνός, λυχνοῦχος; in late Greek, φανός). A lantern. Two bronze lanterns have been found in the ruins of Herculaneum and Pompeii. One of them is represented in the foregoing illustration. Its form is cylindrical. At the bottom is a circular plate of metal, resting on three balls. Within is a bronze lamp attached to the centre of the base, and provided with an extinguisher, shown on the right hand of the lantern. The plates of translucent horn, forming the sides, probably had no aperture; but the hemispherical cover may be raised so as to admit the hand and to serve instead of a door, and it is also perforated with holes through which the smoke might escape. To the two upright pillars supporting the frame-work, a front view of one of which is shown on the left hand of the lantern, chains are attached for carrying the lantern by means of the handle at the top.

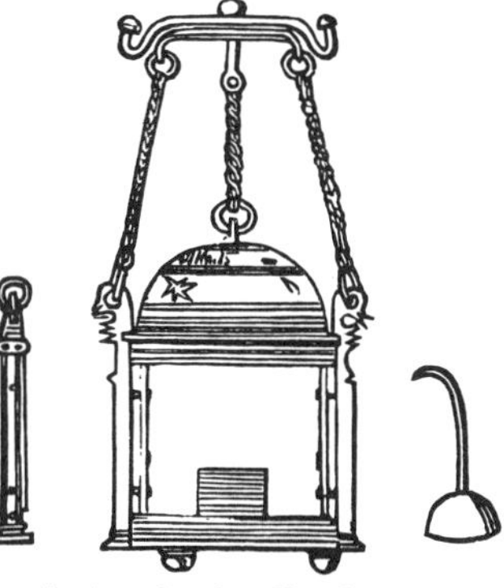

Lantern found at Herculaneum.

We learn from Martial (xiv. 61, 62) that bladder was used for lanterns as well as horn. Some centuries later glass was also substituted. The most transparent horn lanterns were brought from Carthage (*lanternae Punicae*). When the lantern was required for use the lamp was lighted and placed within it. It was carried by a slave, who was called the *lanternarius* or *servus praelucens*. When a lantern was not at hand, a basket (σπυρίδιον), as a cheaper and commoner utensil, was taken to hold the lamp.

Lanuvium. The modern Lavigna; an ancient city in Latium, situated on a hill of the Alban Mount, not far from the Appia Via; possessed an ancient and celebrated temple of Iuno Sospita; and was the birthplace of the emperor Antoninus Pius.

Lanx. (1) Originally a large dish, probably flat. The name is thus generally applied to all sorts of plates and platters, of various forms and sizes. It was probably always of metal, often silver (Marquardt, *Privatleben*, 654). (2) The metal dishes of the Roman balance (*libra*) also received the name *lances;* and the balance itself is sometimes called *libra bilanx*. See LANCULA.

Laocoön (Λαοκόων). A son of Priam and Hecuba, or, according to others, of Antenor, and a priest of Apollo during the Trojan War. While offering, in the exercise of his sacerdotal office, a bullock to render Poseidon propitious to the Trojans, two enormous serpents issued from the sea, and, having first destroyed his two sons, whom he vainly endeavoured to save, attacked Laocoön himself, and, winding themselves round his body, crushed him to death in their folds. This dreadful punishment was inflicted by the goddess Athené for the part Laocoön had taken in endeavouring to dissuade the Trojans from admitting into Troy the famous wooden horse, which the Greeks had consecrated to Athené (Verg. *Aen.* ii. 40 foll.).

An enduring fame has been gained for the story of Laocoön, from its forming the subject of one of the most remarkable groups in sculpture which time has spared to us. It represents the agonized father and his youthful sons, one on each side of him, writhing and expiring in the folds of the serpents. The figures are naked, the drapery that is introduced being used only to support and fill up the composition. This superb work of art, which Pliny describes inaccurately as consisting of only

Laocoön. (Group in the Vatican.)

picted there, but it is rather the exhibition of mental anguish than of the repulsive and undignified contortions of mere physical pain. The whole of this figure displays the most intimate knowledge of anatomy and of outward form; the latter selected with care, and freed from any vulgarity of common individual nature. Indeed, the single figure of Laocoön may be fairly referred to as one of the finest specimens existing of that combination of truth and beauty which is so essential to the production of perfect sculpture, and which can alone insure for it lasting admiration. The sons are of a smaller standard than the proportion of the father—a liberty hardly justifiable, but taken, probably, with the view of heightening the effect of the principal figure by the so-called "pyramidal" arrangement. The right arm of Laocoön is a restoration; but so ably done,

a single block of marble, originally ornamented the baths of Titus, among the ruins of which it was found in the year 1506. The names of the sculptors who executed it are also recorded. They are Agesander, Polydorus, and Athenodorus, natives of Rhodes. Pliny (*H. N.* xxxvi. 5) says: "The Laocoön, which is in the palace of the emperor Titus, is a work to be preferred to all others, either in painting or sculpture. Those great artists, Agesander, Polydorus, and Athenodorus, Rhodians, executed the principal figure and the sons and the wonderful folds of the serpents out of one block of marble."

This group is justly considered, by all competent judges, to be a masterpiece of art. It combines, in its class, all that sculpture requires, and both admits of, and may truly be studied as, a canon. The subject is of the most affecting and interesting kind; and the expression in every part of the figures reaches, but does not exceed, the limits of propriety. Intense mental suffering is portrayed in the countenances, while the physical strength of all the three figures is evidently sinking under the irresistible power of the huge reptiles wreathed around their exhausted limbs. One son, in whose side a serpent has fixed his deadly fangs, seems to be fainting; the other, not yet bitten, tries to disengage one foot from the serpent's embrace. The father, Laocoön, himself, is mighty in his sufferings: every muscle is in extreme action, and his hands and feet are convulsed with painful energy. Yet there is nothing frightful, disgusting, or contrary to beauty in the countenance. Suffering is faithfully and strongly de-

though only in plaster, that the deficiency is said to be scarcely a blemish. Some antiquarians have thought that the original action of the arm was not extended, but that this limb was bent back towards the head; and they have supported their hypothesis by the fact of there being a rough and broken surface where they think the hand, or perhaps a fold of the serpent, may have come in contact with the hair. This view is rendered still more probable by a smaller figure of Laocoön, now in the Museum at Naples. Though much mutilated, it is evidently copied from the famous group, and is sufficiently preserved to show that the arms were drawn back, as described above.

For a criticism of the work, see Lessing's *Laocoön* (1766, new ed. by Blümner, 1880); the monograph by Kekulé (1883); and Perry's *Greek and Roman Sculpture*, pp. 520–527 (1882).

Laodămas (Λαοδάμας). (1) The son of Alcinoüs, king of the Phaeacians, and Areté. (2) The son of Eteocles, and king of Thebes, in whose reign the Epigoni marched against Thebes. In the battle against the Epigoni he slew their leader Aegialeus, but was himself slain by Alcmaeon. Others related that after the battle was lost Laodamas fled to the Encheleans in Illyricum (Herod. v. 61).

Laodamīa (Λαοδάμεια). (1) A daughter of Acastus and Astydamia, and wife of Protesilaüs. (See PROTESILAÜS.) When she received intelligence of the death of her husband in the Trojan War, she caused an image of him to be formed, which she would never allow to be out of her sight. Her father ordered the image to be burned, that her thoughts might be diverted from her loss; but Laodamia threw herself into the flames, and perished along with it. Thence probably the tradition adopted by some poets that the gods restored life to Protesilaüs for three hours, and that this hero, finding the decree irreversible, by which he was to return to the shades below, prevailed on Laodamia to accompany him thither. She was also called Phylacea (Verg. *Aen.* vi. 447; Ovid, *Her.* 13; Hyg. *Fab.* 104). (2) A daughter of Bellerophon by Achemoné, the daughter of king Iobates. She had a son by Zeus called Sarpedon. See SARPEDON.

Laodĭcé (Λαοδίκη). (1) Daughter of Priam and Hecuba, and wife of Helicaon (Pausan. x. 26). (2) The name given by Homer to the daughter of Agamemnon and Clytaemnestra, who is called Electra by the tragic poets (*Il.* ix. 146). (3) The name of several Greek princesses of the family of the Seleucidae, one of whom was the mother of Seleucus Nicator, the founder of the Syrian monarchy.

Laodicēa (Λαοδίκεια). The name of several Greek cities in Asia, called after the mother of Seleucus I., Nicator, and other Syrian princesses of this name. (1) LAODICĒA AD LYCUM, a city of Phrygia, near the river Lycus, a tributary of the Maeander, founded by Antiochus II. Theos. It became one of the most prosperous cities in Asia Minor, and was the seat of a flourishing Christian church as early as the apostolic age. (2) LAODICĒA CATACECAUMĒNÉ or COMBUSTA—i. e. the burned; the reason of which epithet is doubtful. A city of Lycaonia, north of Iconium. (3) LAODICĒA AD MARÉ, a city on the coast of Syria, about fifty miles south of Antioch, built by Seleucus I., and had the best harbour in Syria. (4) LAODICĒA AD LIBĂNUM, a city of Coelé-Syria, at the north entrance to the narrow valley, between Libanus and Anti-Libanus.

Copper Coin (medallion) of Laodicea, with Head of Commodus.

Laodŏcus (Λαοδόκος). The son of Bias and Pero. He took part in the Argonautic expedition and in that of the Seven against Thebes.

Laomĕdon (Λαομέδων). (1) King of Troy, son of Ilus, and father of Priam, Hesioné, and other children. Poseidon and Apollo, who had displeased Zeus, were doomed to serve Laomedon for wages. Accordingly, Poseidon built the walls of Troy, while Apollo tended the king's flocks on Mount Ida. When the two gods had done their work, Laomedon refused them the reward he had promised them, and expelled them from his dominions. Thereupon Poseidon sent a marine monster to ravage the country, to which the Trojans were obliged, from time to time, to sacrifice a maiden. On one occasion it was decided by lot that Hesioné, the daughter of Laomedon, should be the victim; but she was saved by Heracles, who slew the monster, upon Laomedon promising to give him the horses which Tros had once received from Zeus as a compensation for Ganymedes. But when the monster was slain, Laomedon again broke his word. Thereupon Heracles sailed with a squadron of six ships against Troy, killed Laomedon, with all his sons except Priam, and gave Hesioné to Telamon. Priam, as the son of Laomedon, is called Laomedontiades; and the Trojans, as the subjects of Laomedon, are called Laomedontiadae. (2) A general of Alexander the Great who after the king's death received the government of Syria, of which he was subsequently deprived by Nicanor, Ptolemy's general (Diod. xviii. 39).

Laomedontēus. An epithet applied to the Trojans from their king Laomedon (Verg. *Aen.* iv. 542, vii. 105, viii. 18).

Laomedontiădae. A patronymic given to the Trojans from Laomedon (q. v.) their king (Verg. *Aen.* iii. 248).

Lapēthus (Λάπηθος). A town on the northern coast of Cyprus on a river of the same name.

Laphria. A name given to Artemis as worshipped at a festival called Λάφρια, celebrated at Patrae in Achaia (Pausan. iv. 31, § 6).

Laphystium (Λαφύστιον). A mountain in Boeotia, about twenty stadia to the north of Coronea, on which Zeus had a temple, whence he was called Laphystius. It was here that Athamas prepared to immolate Phrixus and Hellé, whom Zeus saved by sending them a golden ram (Pausan. ix. 34, § 5).

Lapicidīnae. See LAUTUMIAE.

Lapidei Campi and **Lapidōsus Campus**. See HERACLES, p. 791.

Lapĭthae (Λαπίθαι). A mythical people inhabiting the mountains of Thessaly. They were governed by Pirithoüs, who, being a son of Ixion (q. v.), was a half-brother of the Centaurs. The latter, therefore, demanded their share in their father's kingdom; and, as their claims were not satisfied, a war arose between the Lapithae and Centaurs, which, however, was terminated by a peace. But when Pirithoüs married Hippodamia, and invited the Centaurs to the marriage feast, the latter, fired by wine, and urged on by Ares, attempted to carry off the bride and the other women. Thereupon a bloody conflict ensued, in which the Centaurs were defeated by the Lapithae. The Lapithae are said to have been the inventors of bits and bridles for horses.

Laquearia. See LACUNARIA.

Laquearius. See GLADIATORES.

Lar or **Lars**. An Etruscan praenomen, borne, for instance, by Porsena and Tolumnius. From the Etruscans it passed over to the Romans, whence we read of Lar Herminius, who was consul B.C. 448. This word signified "lord," "king," or "hero" in the Etruscan. See LARES.

Lara. (1) See MANIA. (2) See LARES.

Laranda (*τὰ Λάρανδα*). A considerable town in the south of Lycaonia, at the northern foot of Mount Taurus, used by the Isaurian robbers as one of their strongholds.

Lararia. See LARES.

Lararium. A part of the Roman house set apart for the worship of the Lares (q. v.). Originally it was in the *atrium* (see DOMUS), but, in later times, in the kitchen, dining-room, or peristyle.

Larentalia. See ROMULUS.

Larentia. See ACCA LARENTIA; FRATRES ARVALES; ROMULUS.

Lares. Gods of inferior power worshipped at Rome, of human origin and presiding over houses and families. There were various classes of them, such as URBĀNI, to preside over the cities; FAMILIĀRES, over houses; RUSTĬCI, over the country; COMPITĀLES, over crossways; MARĪNI, over the sea; VIĀLES, over roads, etc. The Lares were originally human beings themselves, who lived upon the earth, and, becoming pure spirits after death, loved still to hover round the dwelling which they once inhabited, to watch over its safety, and to guard it with as much care as the faithful dog does the possessions of its master. They keep off, therefore, danger from without, while the Penates (q. v.), residing in the interior of the dwelling, pour forth benefits upon its inmates. The fundamental idea, on which rests the doctrine of the Lares, is intimately connected with all the psychology and pneumatology of the ancient Italians. According to Apuleius the *daemones* which once had inhabited, as souls, human bodies, were called Lemures: this name therefore designated, in general, the spirit separated from the body. Such a spirit, if it adopted its posterity—if it took possession, with favourable power, of the abode of its children—was called LAR FAMILIARIS. If on the contrary, by reason of the faults committed in life, it found in the grave no resting place, it appeared to men as a phantom; inoffensive to the good, but terrible to the wicked. Its name was in that case LARVA. As, however, there was no way of precisely ascertaining what had been the lot of a deceased person, whether he had become, for example, a Lar or a Larva, it was customary to give to the dead the general appellation of MANES. The mother of the Lares was called Lara or Larunda (Arnob. *Adv. Gent.* iii. 41; Macrob. i. 7). This conception of the Lares, as the souls of fathers and of forefathers, protectors of their children, and watching over the safety of their descendants, necessarily gave rise to the custom of burying the dead within the dwelling (Serv. *ad* Verg. *Aen.* v. 64; vi. 152; Isid. *Orig.* xv. 11). Men wished to have near them these tutelary genii, in order to be certain of their assistance and support. In process of time, however, this custom was prohibited at Rome by the laws of the Twelve Tables.

The Etrurians, and the Romans after them, had their LARES PUBLĬCI and LARES PRIVĀTI. The Lares were supposed to assist at all gatherings of men, at all public assemblies or reunions, in all transactions of men, and in all the most important affairs of State as well as of individuals. As each individual had his Lar, his genius, his guardian spirit, even the infant at the breast, so entire families, and whole races and nations, were equally under the protection of one of these tutelar deities. Here the Lares became in some degree confounded with the Heroes, that is, with the spirits of those who, having deserved well of their country while on earth, continued to watch over and protect it. It would seem, too, that at times the worship of these public Lares, like that of the public Penates, was not without some striking resemblance to that rendered to the great national divinities.

All that the house contained was confided to the superintending care of these vigilant genii: they were set as a watch over all things large and small, and hence the name of PRAESTĬTES, which is sometimes given them (Ovid, *Fast.* v. 128, 132). Hence the dog was the natural symbol of the Lares; an image of this animal was placed by the side of their statues, or else these were covered with the skin of a dog. The ordinary altar on which sacrifices were offered to the Lares was the domestic hearth. The victims consisted of a hog (Hor. *Carm.* iii. 23, 4) or a fowl; sometimes, with the rich, of a young steer; to them were also presented the first fruits of the season, and libations of wine were poured out. In all the family repasts, the first thing done was to cast a portion of all the viands into the fire that burned on the hearth, in honour of the Lares. In the form of marriage, called *coëmptio*, the bride always threw a piece of money on the hearth to the Lares of her family, and deposited another in the neighbouring cross-road, in order to obtain admission, as it were, into the dwelling of her husband. Young persons, after their fifteenth year, consecrated to the Lares the bulla which they had worn from infancy (Pers. v. 31). Soldiers, when their time of service was once ended, dedicated to them the arms with which they had fought (Ovid, *Trist.* iv. 8, 21). Captives and slaves restored to freedom consecrated to the Lares the fetters from which they had just been freed (Hor. *Sat.* i. 5). Before undertaking a journey, or after a successful return, homage was paid to these deities, their protection was implored, or thanks were rendered for their guardian care (Ovid, *Trist.* i. 3, 33). The new master of a house crowned the Lares, in order to render them propitious; a custom which was of the most universal nature, and which was perpetuated to the latest times (Plaut. *Trinum.* i. 2, 1). The proper place for worshipping the Lares, and where their images stood, was called Lararium, a sort of domestic chapel in the atrium, where were also to be seen the images and busts of the family ancestors. The rich had often two Lararia, one large and the other small; they had also "Masters of the Lares," and "Decuries of the Lares"—namely, slaves specially charged with the care of these domestic chapels and the images of their divinities. As to the poor, their Lares had to be content with the simple hearth, where honours not less simple were paid to them. Certain public festivals were also celebrated in honour of the Lares, called LARARIA and COMPITALIA. The period for their celebration fell in the month of December, a little after that of the Saturnalia. The Compitalia, dedicated to the Lares Compitales, were celebrated in the open air, in the cross-roads. The day of their celebration was not fixed. They were introduced at Rome by Servius Tullius, who left to the Senate the care of determining the period when they should be held. In early times, children were immolated to the goddess Mania, the mother, according to some, of the Lares, to propitiate her favour for the protection of the family. This barbarous rite was subsequently abolished, and little balls of wool were hung up in the stead of human offerings at the gates of dwellings. Macrobius (*Sat.* i. 7, 34) informs us that it was Junius Brutus who, after the expulsion of the Tarquins, introduced a new form of sacrifice, by virtue of which heads of garlic and poppies were offered up in place of human heads, *ut pro capitibus capitibus supplicaretur*, in accordance with the oracle of Apollo.

As regards the forms under which the Lares were represented, it may be observed that it dif-

Lares. (Duruy.)

fered often but little from that of the Penates. Thus, on the coins of the Caesian family, they are represented as two young men, seated, their heads covered with helmets, and holding spears in their hands, while a dog watches at their feet. Sometimes, as has already been remarked, the heads of the Lares are represented as covered with, or their mantle as formed of, the skin of a dog. At other times we find the Lares resembling naked children, with the bulla hanging from the neck.

Largitio. See AMBITUS; FRUMENTARIAE LEGES.

Largus, SCRIBONIUS. See SCRIBONIUS.

Larīnum. A town of the Frentani (whence the inhabitants are sometimes called Frentani Larinates, on the river Tifernus, and near the borders of Apulia.

Larissa (Λάρισσα). The name of several Pelasgian places, whence Larissa is called in mythology the daughter of Pelasgus. (1) An important town of Thessaly in Pelasgiotis, situated on the Peneus, in an extensive plain, and once the capital of the Pelasgi. (2) Surnamed CREMASTÉ, another important town of Thessaly in Phthiotia, distant twenty stadia from the Maliac Gulf. (3) An ancient city on the coast of the Troad. (4) L. PHRICŌNIS, a city on the coast of Mysia, near Cymé, of Pelasgian origin, but colonized by the Aeolians. It was also called the Egyptian Larissa, because Cyrus the Great settled in it a body of his Egyptian mercenary soldiers. (5) LARISSA EPHESIA, a city of Lydia, in the plain of the Caÿster. (6) In Assyria, an ancient city on the eastern bank of the Tigris, some distance north of the mouth of the river Zabatus or Lycus. It was deserted when Xenophon saw it. The name Larissa is in this case no doubt a corruption of some Assyrian name (perhaps Al-Assur), which Xenophon naturally confounded with Larissa, through his familiarity with the word as the name of cities in Greece.

Larissaeus. An epithet applied by Vergil (*Aen.* ii. 197, xi. 404) to Achilles, either with reference to the town of Larissa Cremasté, which lay within his dominions (see LARISSA), or as equivalent generally to Thessalicus.

Larissus (Λάρισσος). A small river, forming the boundary between Achaia and Elis, and flowing into the Ionian Sea (Xen. *Hell.* iii. 21, 23).

Larius Lacus. The modern Lake Como; a beautiful lake in Gallia Transpadana (Northern Italy), running from north to south, through which the river Adda flows. Pliny had several villas on the banks of the lake (Pliny, *Epist.* ix. 7).

Lars or **Lartes Tolumnius**. See TOLUMNIUS.

Lartia Gens. A patrician gens, distinguished at the beginning of the Republic through two of its members, T. Lartius, the first dictator, and Sp. Lartius, the companion of Horatius Cocles (q. v.) on the wooden bridge.

Lartius Florus. (1) TITUS, a consul, who appeased a sedition raised by the poorer citizens, and was the first dictator ever chosen at Rome, B.C. 498 (Livy, ii. 18). (2) SPURIUS, one of the three Romans who withstood the fury of Porsenna's army at the head of a bridge while the communication was being cut down behind them. His companions were Cocles and Herminius (see COCLES; Livy, ii. 10, 18; Val. Max. iii. 2).

Larunda or **Lara**. Daughter of Almon, the nymph who informed Iuno of the connection between Iupiter and Iuturna: hence her name was connected with λαλεῖν. Iupiter deprived her of her tongue, and ordered Mercury to conduct her into the lower world. On the way thither Mercury fell in love with her, and she afterwards gave birth to two Lares (Ovid, *Fasti*, ii. 599 foll.; Macrob. i. 7, 34). See LARES.

Larvae. In Roman belief the Larvae, in contrast to the Lares (the good spirits of the departed), were the souls of dead persons who could find no rest, either owing to their own guilt, or from having met with some indignity, such as a violent death. They were supposed to wander abroad in the form of dreadful spectres, skeletons, etc., and especially to strike the living with madness. Similar spectres of the night are the LEMURES. To expel them from the house, peculiar expiatory rites were held on three days of the year, the 9th, 11th, and 13th of May, the Lemuria, when all the temples were closed, and marriages avoided.

Las (Λᾶς). An ancient town of Laconia, on the east side of the Laconian Gulf, ten stadia from the sea, and south of Gytheum (Thuc. viii. 91).

Lasaea (Λασαία). A town in the south of Crete,

not far from the Promontorium Samonium mentioned in the Acts of the Apostles (xxviii. 8).

Lasthĕnes (Λασθένης). An Olynthian who, with Euthycrates, betrayed his country to Philip of Macedon for a bribe in B.C. 347 (Demos. *Philip.* iii. p. 126; Diod. xvi. 53). See OLYNTHUS.

Lasus (Λᾶσος). A native of Hermioné in Argolis, a lyric poet and the teacher of Pindar. He lived at Athens under the patronage of Hipparchus. His works have perished See Herod. vii. 6.

Later (πλίνθος). A brick. For brickmaking, see FICTILÉ. The term *later crudus* signifies a brick dried in the sun; and *later coctus* a brick baked by fire.

Lateraria. A brick-field (Pliny, *H. N.* vii. 57). A painting at Thebes in Egypt represents an Egyptian brick-field, and shows exactly the same process as still pursued; the men at the bottom are digging up the brick earth, and loading it in baskets, while the one at the top lays the bricks already made in wooden moulds. See FICTILÉ.

Laterculus. See POLEMIUS SILVIUS.

Latiālis or **Latiāris.** A surname of Iupiter as the protecting divinity of Latium. The Latin towns and Rome celebrated to him every year the Feriae Latinae on the Alban Mount, which were conducted by one of the Roman consuls

Latifundium. The Latin term for an extensive landed estate which was worked by means of slaves. Lands of the State (see AGER PUBLICUS) taken into permanent use by *occupatio* formed the foundation of these properties, and their possessor enlarged them by obtaining contiguous property either by purchase or by forcible appropriation. This system of *latifundia* gradually caused the utter ruin of the Italian peasantry, and involved in it the general destruction of the community (*latifundia perdidere Italiam*, Pliny, *H. N.* xviii. 35).

Latin Language. See ITALIA.

Latin League. See LATIUM.

Latin, PRONUNCIATION OF Three methods of pronouncing Latin are in use in this country at the present time, described respectively as the English method, the Continental method, and the Roman or Phonetic method.

I. THE ENGLISH METHOD, in general, pronounces Latin words as though they were English. The tendency of this system is frequently to obscure the vowel sounds. Thus, before *r* final, or followed by another consonant, *e*, *i*, and *u* are scarcely distinguishable from one another. Between *qu* and *rt*, *a* receives a sound like *o*—e. g. in *quartus.* The quantities of unaccented syllables are not carefully rendered. The diphthongs *æ* and *œ* are sounded like *ē* in *be; au,* as in *author; eu,* as in *neuter; ui,* like *ī* in *like*—e. g. *cui, huic,* etc. *C* and *g* are pronounced soft (like English *s* and *j*) before *e, i, y, ae,* or *oe.* *Ch* is hard, like *k; c, s,* and *t,* in such words as *socius, militia, Alsium, anxius,* receive the sound of *sh.* *G* and *m* are silent before *n* (e. g. *Gnaeus, Mnemon*); *ch* and *ph* before a mute (e. g. *Chthonia, Phthia*); *p* before *s* or *t* (e. g. *Psyche, Ptolemaeus*); and *t* before *m* (e. g. *Tmolus*).

The English method is falling into desuetude in this country, and will probably soon be wholly obsolete. In England, the leading Latinists have long since repudiated it in theory, but the conservatism of the schools clings to it as being the old historic usage of English scholarship; whereas it is nothing of the kind, but a comparatively modern innovation, as shown below.

II. THE CONTINENTAL METHOD gives to the consonants in general the same sounds as in the English method, and to the vowels the following sounds: *a,* as in *father; e,* like *a* in *make; i,* as in *machine; o,* as in *go; u,* like *oo* in *moo; y,* like *e* in *me; ae* and *oe,* like *a* in *make; au,* like *ou* in *out.* The tendency of this method also is to neglect difference of quantity in unaccented syllables.

The name "Continental Method" is rather a misnomer, as there is on the continent of Europe no uniform system, the scholars of each nation pronouncing the consonants as in their own language. Thus, a German pronouncing *Cicero,* says *Tsitsĕro;* an Italian, *Chichĕro;* a Frenchman, *Sisĕro;* a Spaniard, *Thithĕro,* and so on. Yet the practical identity of the vowel-sounds in all the chief continental languages and the fact that only a few of the consonants vary in pronunciation, make the so-called Continental System, as used in this country, one that is easily intelligible to any Continental Latinist. It is used by the Catholic clergy and in a number of colleges, and is substantially the system that has always prevailed at the Scotch universities.

III. THE ROMAN or PHONETIC METHOD aims to reproduce, so far as our present knowledge makes such a thing possible, the pronunciation used by the Romans themselves in the classical period. It distinguishes very carefully between long and short vowels, even in syllables where the natural vocalic quantities are obscured by their position before two consonants.

ā, as in *father; ă,* as in *Cuba.*
ē, as in *they; ĕ,* like *a* in *Senate.*
ī, as in *machine; ĭ,* as in *pin.*
ō, as in *note; ŏ,* as in *obey.*
ū, like *oo* in *moo; ŭ,* like *oo* in *hood.*
ae=*ah-ee* quickly spoken.
au, like *ou* in *out.*
ei, as in *eight.*
oe=*oh-ee* quickly spoken.
ui, like *wee* in *sweet* (nearly).
eu, as in *feud* (nearly).
ȳ, like German *ü; y̆,* the same sound short.

The pronunciation of the consonants is as follows:

b=*b* in English; before *s* or *t*=*p.*
c=*k* (always).
ch, as in German.
d=*d* in English; at the end of words nearly=*t.*
f=*f* in English.
g=*g* in *get* (always hard).
h=*h* in English.
j (*i*-consonant)=*y* in English.
l=*l* in English.
m=*m* in English.
n=*n* in English; but before *c, q, g,* or *x*=*ng* in *linger.*
p=*p* in English.
q=*q* in English. (It is always, in Latin, followed by *u.*)
r=*r* in English with a slight trill.
s=*s* in *sit.*
t=*t* in English, and never assibilated.
v (*u*-consonant)=*w* in English.
x=*x* in English.
z=*z* in English.

Our knowledge of how the Romans pronounced

their own language is derived from several sources: (*a*) from the statements of the Roman writers themselves, especially of the grammarians; (*b*) from the orthography of the language, which was, in the main, phonetic (Quint. i. 7, 11); (*c*) from the way in which the Greeks represented Roman sounds in Greek characters—spelling by ear; (*d*) from a comparison of all the modern languages derived from the Latin with reference to the points which they possess in common; (*e*) from the spelling of the Latin words taken into German, Gothic, and Anglo-Saxon at an early period; (*f*) from the traditions of scholars as set forth in the treatises of Erasmus, Lipsius, and others, as cited below; (*g*) from the traditions of the Roman Catholic Church, which has employed Latin in its rites from the first century to the present time; (*h*) from the general principles of the science of phonology. These sources were very carefully investigated, and the results they yield were correlated by Dr. Wilhelm Corssen (q. v.) in his great work, *Ueber Aussprache, Vokalismus, und Betonung der lateinischen Sprache*, 2 vols. (Leipzig, 1858–59; 2d ed. 1868–70), since the appearance of which the ancient system of pronunciation has made steady progress in gaining the acceptance of scholars all over the world. In 1859, Professor J. F. Richardson, of the University of Rochester, put forth an excellent little volume advocating the true method; and in 1872, Professors Munro and Palmer in England, at the request of the head-masters of the public schools, prepared and published a condensed statement of the Roman system, entitled *A Syllabus of Latin Pronunciation* (Oxford and Cambridge, 1872), which received the approval of the two great universities and of all the leading Latinists of England. The Roman system has now practically supplanted the other two in the leading schools, colleges, and universities of the United States. This is not due to the greater willingness of Americans to accept what is new, but to practical considerations that will readily occur to any one. In the United States, the inconveniences of having no standard system have been very great. New England, being wholly settled from Old England, long continued the English system of pronouncing Latin. In the Middle States, the Germans and Dutch introduced their own methods; in the South and West, the French pronunciation came in quite frequently; and all over the Union, the Catholic clergy in their schools and colleges have propagated the traditional usage of their Church. Hence, a Babel of pronunciations and systems existing and practised side by side in a picturesque confusion such as no European country ever knew; and hence the general willingness to accept a single method, especially one that is based upon historic truth.

The advantages of the Roman system, briefly stated, are these: (*a*) It is approximately the system used by the Romans themselves. (*b*) It is more musical and harmonious in sound, and makes the structure of Latin verse clear even to the beginner. (*c*) It is simpler than the English system, giving as it does but one sound to each alphabetical character, and thus always distinguishing words of different orthography and meaning by their sounds, while the English system often confuses them—e. g. *census* and *sensus*; *caedo*, *cedo*, and *sedo*; *circulus* and *surculus*; *cervus* and *servus*; *amici* and *amisi*. (*d*) It makes the connection of Latin words with their Greek cognates plain at once, and renders easier the study of Greek, of the modern Romance languages, and of the science of Comparative Philology.

Advocates of other systems have made their chief assault upon the Roman method because of its dictum regarding the pronunciation of *c* and *v*. They say that Latin *c* must have had a modified sound before *e* and *i*, because every modern language derived from the Latin has so modified it.

But it must be remembered that the modern Romance languages are the children, not of the classical Latin spoken in the days of Cicero, but of the provincial Latin spoken five or six centuries later. There is no doubt that at this late period Latin *c* had become modified before *e* or *i* so as to be equivalent to *s* or *z*. Latin words received into German at this time represent *c* before *e* or *i* by *z*. But had this modification been a part of the usage of the classical language, it would have been noticed by the grammarians, who discuss each letter with great minuteness. Now, no grammarian ever mentions more than one sound for Latin *c*. Again, if Latin *c* had ever had the sound of *s*, surely some of the Greeks, ignorant of Latin and spelling by ear, would at least occasionally have represented Latin *c* by σ—a thing which none of them has ever done, always using κ. It is probable that the modification of *c* which is noticed in the modern languages was a characteristic of the Umbrian and Oscan dialects (the Umbrian had a special character to denote the modified sound), and so prevailed to some extent in the provinces; but there is absolutely not the slightest evidence to show that it formed a part of the pronunciation of cultivated men at Rome. On the other hand, words taken into Gothic and Old High German from the Latin at an early period invariably represent Latin *c* by *k*: thus, Latin *carcer* gives the Gothic *karkara* and the German *Kerker*; Latin *Caesar* gives the German *Kaiser*; Latin *lucerna* gives the Gothic *lukarn*; the Latin *cellarium* gives the German *Keller*; the Latin *cerasus* gives the German *Kirsche*. Also in late Hebrew, Latin *c* is regularly represented in transliteration by the hard consonant *kôph*. In Latin inscriptions, also, *c* alternates with *k*, showing it to have had the same sound. Thus we find *Caelius* and *Kaelius*, *Cerus* and *Kerus*, *decembres* and *dekembres*. (See, also, Quint. i. 7, 10).

As to *v*, the Greeks transliterated it by ου, writing Οὐαλήριος for *Valerius*, Οὐόλσκοι for *Volsci*, etc., while it passes easily into *u* in such forms as *cautum* for *cavitum*, *fautor* for *favitor*, etc.

"It is not always remembered that only very gradually was the true pronunciation of Latin lost in Europe. Scholars long retained the essential features of it, and by the fact of their constant intercourse long prevented the growth of local and national variations from the established method. Great teachers like Erasmus passed from country to country, lecturing in Latin at the universities of Italy, Germany, Holland, France, and England; teaching pupils of all nationalities, and being everywhere understood without any difficulty, for Latin was the *lingua franca* of the educated, and one general pronunciation of it prevailed. Even in England, it was only after that country's isolation, political and religious, in the sixteenth century, that an 'English pronunciation' arose, and this was long protested against—e. g. by Cardinal

Wolsey, by Milton, and as late as the last century by Ainsworth (1746) and Philipps (1750). For the Continental traditions, see Justus Lipsius in his *Dialogus de Recta Pronunciatione Linguae Latinae;* and Erasmus, *De Recta Latini Graecique Sermonis Pronunciatione* (Basle, 1528). In Scotland, the Continental sound of the vowels was long retained, on which see the incident imagined by Sir Walter Scott in his novel *The Fortunes of Nigel*, ch. ix." (Peck).

BIBLIOGRAPHY.—Besides the works already cited, reference may be made to the following: Haldeman, *Elements of Latin Pronunciation* (Philadelphia, 1851); Tafel, *Latin Pronunciation* (N. Y. 1860); Blair, *Latin Pronunciation* (N.Y. 1874); Ellis, *The Quantitative Pronunciation of Latin* (London, 1874); King, *Latin Pronunciation* (N.Y. and Boston, 1880); Edon, *Écriture et Prononciation du Latin* (Paris, 1882); Seelmann, *Die Aussprache des Latein* (Heilbronn, 1885); and H. T. Peck, *Latin Pronunciation: a Short Exposition of the Roman Method* (2d ed. N. Y. 1894). See, also, articles by Prof. Max Müller and Mr. Munro in the *Academy* for Feb. 15, 1871; Dec. 15, 1871; Jan. 11, 1872; and by Prof. J. C. Jones in *Classical Review* for February, 1893; and Lindsay, *The Latin Language* (Oxford, 1894).

Latin War. See LATIUM.

Latīnae Feriae. See FERIAE

Latīni. See LATINITAS.

Latinĭtas or **Ius Latii** designated, in the later republican and early imperial period, a special legal status conferred upon the inhabitants of many provincial municipalities — a status midway between that of Roman citizens (*cives*) and that of aliens (*peregrini*). Historically, the Latin allies of Rome had always enjoyed special treaty rights; and when the people of Latium received full citizenship, similar rights were bestowed upon certain colonies in other parts of Italy. After the Social War and the extension of Roman citizenship on the entire peninsula, *Latini colonarii* were found only in the provinces. Where *minus ius Latii* was conferred upon a municipality, all its citizens who were chosen as municipal magistrates became *ipso facto* Roman citizens; where *maius ius Latii* was given, the *decuriones* or municipal senators also became Roman citizens. In both cases all free inhabitants of the municipality enjoyed *commercium* with Rome, but not *conubium* —i. e. the Roman law of property could be invoked by them, but they had no part in Roman family law. With the edict of Caracalla, conferring citizenship upon all the free inhabitants of the Roman Empire, the *Latini colonarii* disappeared.

A second and distinct class of Latins was established in the early imperial period by a *lex Iunia* or *Iunia Norbana* (A.D. 19?). This law enacted that freedmen (*liberti*) who had been informally manumitted from slavery, and who were free only by virtue of praetorian protection (*tuitione praetoris*) should have, with some exceptions, the status of *Latini colonarii*. These *Latini Iuniani* were not citizens, and had no political rights; they had no *conubium*, and their marriages, like those of slaves, were purely *de facto* matters, creating neither *manus* over the wife nor *patria potestas* over the children; and they had only a restricted *commercium—inter vivos*, but not *mortis causa*. Their contracts were perfectly valid, but they could neither take inheritances or legacies nor dispose of their property by testament. Their estates, in fact, were treated as *peculia* or slave-estates, and went at death to the former master or his heirs. There were, however, several methods in which this *Latina libertas* might be converted into full citizenship (cf. Ulpian, *Fragmenta*, iii. 1–6). The *Latini Iuniani* were unaffected by the edict of Caracalla, but disappeared under the legislation of Justinian (Gaius, *Inst.* i. §§ 23 foll., iii. §§ 85 foll.; Codex, 7, 6, 1, § 1).

Latīnus. (1) Son of Faunus and of the nymph Marica (or, according to another story, of Heracles and Fauna, or of Odysseus and Circé). He was king of Latium and father of Lavinia, the wife of Aëneas (q. v.). (2) A mime-player, a favourite of the emperor Domitian, mentioned by Juvenal and Martial (Juv. i. 35; Mart. ii. 72, etc.).

Latium (from *latus*, "the level land"). A country of Italy, lying south of Etruria, from which it was separated by the Tiber. The earliest records of Italian history, as we are assured by Dionysius of Halicarnassus (i. 9), represented the plains of Latium as first inhabited by the Siculi, a people of obscure origin, but who would be entitled to our notice from the circumstance above mentioned, even had they not acquired additional historical importance from their subsequent migration to the celebrated island from them named Sicily. (See SICULI.) Ancient writers do not seem agreed as to the name of the people who compelled the Siculi to abandon Latium. Dionysius informs us that Philistus ascribed their expulsion to the Umbri and Pelasgi. Thucydides refers the same event to the Opici; while Antiochus of Syracuse, a still more ancient writer, represents the Siculi as flying from the Oenotri. Notwithstanding this apparent discrepance, it is pretty evident that under these different names of Umbri, Opici, and Oenotri, the same people are designated whom Dionysius and the Roman historians usually term Aborigines (*Ant. Rom.* i. 10). The Aborigines, intermixing with several Pelasgic colonies, occupied Latium, and soon formed themselves into the several communities of Latini, Rutuli, Hernici, and Volsci, even prior to date of the supposed arrival of Aeneas.

The name Prisci Latini was first given to certain cities of Latium (see PAGUS), supposed to have been colonized by Latinus Silvius, one of the kings of Alba, but most of which were afterwards conquered and destroyed by Ancus Marcius and Tarquinius Priscus (Livy, i. 3). In the reign of Tarquinius Superbus the Latin nation was united under the form of a confederate Republic, and acknowledged that ambitious king as the protector of their league (Livy, i. 50). After the expulsion of the tyrant from Rome, we are told that the Latins, who favoured his cause, experienced a total defeat near the Lake Regillus, and were obliged to sue for peace (Dion. Hal. vi. 18). According to this historian, the Latins received the thanks of the Roman Senate, some years afterwards, for having taken no advantage of the disturbances at Rome, which finally led to the secession of the people to Mons Sacer, and for having, on the contrary, offered every assistance in their power on that occasion; he adds, also, that a perpetual league, known as the Latin League, was formed at that time between the Romans and the Latins. However, about 143 years afterwards, we find the latter openly rebelling, and refusing to supply the usual quota of troops which they had agreed to furnish as allies of Rome. Their bold demand, which was urged through L. Annius Setinus, in the Roman Senate, that one of the consuls at least should be chosen out of their nation, led to an open rupture. A war followed (B.C. 340–338), known as the Latin War, which was rendered remarkable from the circumstances of the execution of the young Manlius by order of his father, and the devotion of Decius. (See DECIUS.) After having been defeated in several encounters, the Latins were reduced to subjection, with the exception of a few towns, which experienced greater lenity, and Latium thenceforth ceased to be an independent State (Livy, viii. 14; Pliny, xxxiv. 5). At that time the rights of Roman citizens had been granted to a few only of the Latin cities; but at a later period the Gracchi sought to level all such distinctions between the Latins and the Romans. This measure, however, was not carried. The Social War followed; and though the confederates were finally conquered, after a long and desperate contest, the Senate thought it advisable to decree that all the Latin cities which had not taken part with the allies should enjoy the rights of Roman citizens. Many of these towns were, however, deprived of their privileges by Sulla; and it was not till the close of the Republic that the Latins were admitted generally to participate in all the rights and immunities enjoyed by the Quirites. See FOEDERATAE CIVITATES.

The name of Latium was at first given to that portion of Italy only which extends from the mouth of the Tiber to the Circeian promontory, a distance of about fifty miles along the coast; but subsequently this latter boundary was removed to the river Liris, whence arose the distinction of *Latium Antiquum* or *Vetus* and *Novum* or *Adiectum* (Pliny, *H. N.* iii. 59). At a still later period, the southern boundary of Latium was extended from the Liris to the mouth of the river Vulturnus and the Massic Hills. See ITALIA.

Latmĭcus Sinus (Λατμικὸς κόλπος). A gulf on the coast of Ionia in Asia Minor, into which the river Maeander fell, named from Mount Latmus, which overhangs it.

Latmus (Λάτμος). A mountain in Caria, extending in a southeast direction from the Sinus Latmicus. It was the mythological scene of the story of Selenê (Luna) and Endymion, who is hence called by the Roman poets *Latmius heros* and *Latmius venator.*

Latobrĭgi. A people in Gallia Belgica, neighbours of the Helvetii, probably dwelling near the sources of the Rhine in Switzerland (Caes. *B. G.* i. 5, 29).

Latomiae. See LAUTUMIAE.

Latōna. See LETO.

Latopŏlis (Λατόπολις). A city of Egypt in the Thebaïd, between Thebes and Apollinopolis Magna. It derived its Greek name from the fish *latos* worshipped there, which was regarded as the largest of all the fishes of the Nile. The later writers drop the term πόλις, and call the place merely Laton (Λάτων, Hierocles); and therefore, in the *Itin. Anton.* and *Notitia Imperii,* the ablative form *Lato* occurs.

Latrīna. In early language the name for a bath or washing-place, corrupted from *lavatrina* (Varr. *L. L.* ix. 68; Lucil. *ap.* Non. s. v. p. 212); but subsequently also used to designate a water-closet in a private house (Columell. x. 85; Suet. *Tib.* 58; Apul. *Met.* i. p. 13), several of which are still to be seen at Pompeii; and all, like that shown in the article DOMUS, p. 546, contiguous to the kitchens. The two small arches on the right are the kitchen stove; four steps lead down to the room, and had a hand-rail by their side to assist the ascent or descent, the mark of which remains against the wall. The recess on the left is the *latrina,* originally closed by a wooden door, which has left the marks of its hinges and bolt on the edge of the door frame; and the mouth of the pipe through which the place was supplied with water is observable in the right-hand corner. See FORICAE.

Latro (cognate with λάτρις). An armed highwayman. The term for highway robbery was *latrocinium,* and was punishable with death. Unarmed robbers were called *grassatores,* but the distinction is not always observed (Juv. iii. 305).

Latruncŭli (πεσσοί, ψῆφοι, *calces, calculi*). A game of skill not unlike our game of checkers or draughts. It was played in a variety of ways by both the Greeks and the Romans; and in Egypt there have been found paintings representing the game, while checkers of metal, glass, etc., have been taken from the tombs. Homer represents the suitors of Penelopê as playing the game (*Odyss.*

Egyptian Checker-player. (Papyrus at Leyden of B.C. 1700.)

i. 107), which was traditionally said to have been invented by Palamedes, to whom dice are also ascribed (Soph. *Frag.* 380, 381 Dind.). The older form of the Greek game was the game of five lines (πέντε γραμμαί, Poll. ix. 97). It is probable that in this the object of the player was to hem in the enemy's men or place one of them between two of his, in which case it could be removed from the board; and thus the game was won when all the enemy's pieces had been taken or else so hemmed in as to be unable to move. The men were perhaps moved along lines rather than squares; but Liddell and Scott suggests that the five lines marked off thirty-six squares (i. e. divided by five lines each way).

The other kind of Greek πεττεία was called πόλεις, this name indicating the χῶραι or squares, which in this form of the game are distinctly mentioned (Poll. ix. 98). Here, too, the pieces are of different colours and are called κύνες ("dogs"). The object in this form of the game was the same as in the other—to bring the opponent to a standstill or to capture all his men.

In the Roman forms of the game we find mention of some pieces more powerful than the others, like the "kings" of modern checkers. The latrunculi are sometimes called *latrones* and sometimes *milites*, and the game was regarded as representing a combat between two armies. The pieces stood on squares and not on lines (Varro, *L. L.* x. 22). The phrase for blocking an opponent's moves is *ad incitas* (*calces*) *redigere;* to attack his *ligare*, *obligare* or (more usually) *adligare*.

See Salmasius *ad* Vopisc. *Proc.* 13 (1671), where there is a copious citation of authorities; Becq de Fouquières, *Les Jeux des Anciens* (2d ed. 1873); and especially Falkener, *Games Ancient and Oriental* (1892).

Laughing Philosopher. See DEMOCRITUS.

Laureăcum. A fortified town of Noricum Ripensê, the station of a Roman fleet on the Danube, and the headquarters of the second legion. It lay to the east of the junction of the Oenus and Danube.

Laurentes Agri. The country in the neighbourhood of Laurentum (Tibull. ii. 5, 41).

Laurentia. See ACCA; FRATRES ARVALES; ROMULUS.

Laurentius Lydus. See LYDUS.

Laurentum. An ancient town of Latium, the residence of the mythical Latinus, situated on a height between Ostia and Ardea, not far from the sea, and surrounded by a grove of laurels, whence it was supposed to have derived its name. The younger Pliny and the emperor Commodus had villas at Laurentum. Later it was united with Lavinium, six miles distant, under the name LAUROLAVINIUM, a compound suggesting the American Texarkana.

Lauretānus Portus. A harbor of Etruria (Livy, xxx. 39).

Laurĭum (Λαύριον and Λαύρειον). A mountain in the south of Attica, a little north of the promontory Sunium, celebrated for its silver mines, which in early times were very productive, so that each Athenian citizen received ten drachmae ($1.60) annually; but in the time of Augustus they yielded nothing. See METALLUM.

Lauron. A town in the east of Hispania Tarraconensis, near the sea and the river Sucro. Here the younger Cn. Pompeius was put to death after the battle of Munda (Plut. *Pomp.* 18).

Lāus (Λᾶος). A Greek city in Lucania, near the mouth of the river Laüs, which formed the boundary between Lucania and Bruttium.

Laus Pompēia. A town of Cisalpine Gaul, next in importance to Mediolanum (Milan), and situated to the southeast of that place, near the river Lambrus. It was founded, as Pliny reports, by the Boii (iii. 17), and afterwards probably colonized by Pompeius Strabo, father of the great Pompey. In a letter of Cicero to his brother, it is simply called Laus (ii. 15).

Lausus. (1) Son of Mezentius (q. v.), king of the Etruscans, slain by Aeneas. (2) Son of Numitor and brother of Ilia, killed by Amulius.

Lautŭlae. A village of the Volsci in Latium, in a narrow pass between Tarracina and Fundi.

Lautumiae or **Latomiae.** A name properly denoting a quarry, and derived from the Greek λᾶας, "a stone," and τέμνω, "to cut" or "quarry." This appellation was particularly applied to certain quarries near Syracuse, one of which still bears the name of "The Ear of Dionysius," because it is said to have been used by that tyrant for a prison, and to have been so constructed that all the sounds uttered in it converged to and united in one particular point, termed, in consequence, the tympanum. This point communicated with an apartment (the famous "Ear of Dionysius"), where Dionysius placed himself, and thus overheard all that was said by his unsuspecting captives. There is no doubt that these quarries actually served as places of imprisonment, and Cicero reproaches Verres with having employed them for this purpose in the case of Roman citizens (Cic. *Verr.* v. 27). Aelian informs us that some of the workmen in the quarries near Syracuse remained so long there as to marry and rear families in them, and that some of their children, having never before seen a city, were terrified on their coming to Syracuse, and beholding for the first time horses and oxen (Aelian, *V. H.* xii. 44). See CARCER, p. 278.

Laverna. The Roman goddess of thieves and impostors (Hor. *Epist.* i. 16, 60), from whom the Porta Lavernalis derived its name. A grove on the Via Salaria was consecrated to her. See Petron. 140.

Lavernium. A temple of Laverna, near Formiae (Cic. *Ad Att.* vii. 8).

Lavīcum. See LABICUM.

Lavinia. The daughter of Latinus and Amata, betrothed to Turnus, but married to Aeneas (Livy, i. 1). See TURNUS.

Lavinium. An ancient town of Latium, three miles from the sea, and six miles east of Laurentum, on the Via Appia, founded by Aeneas, and called Lavinium in honour of his wife Lavinia (Livy, i. 1). It was the sanctuary of the Latin Penates. See LAURENTUM.

Leaena (Λέαινα). The mistress of Aristogiton or of Harmodius (q. v.). On the murder of Hipparchus she was tortured, but refused to betray her friends, and, according to one account, bit off her own tongue to make any revelation impossible. She died of her sufferings, and in her memory the Athenians erected on the Acropolis a bronze lioness (λέαινα) without a tongue (Pausan. i. 23, 2).

Leander (Λέανδρος or Λείανδρος). A youth of Abydos, who was in love with Hero, the priestess of Aphroditê in Sestus, and swam every night across the Hellespont to visit her, and returned before daybreak. Once during a stormy night he perished in the waves. Next morning his corpse was washed on the coast of Sestus, whereupon Hero threw herself into the sea. This story was the subject of the poem of Musaeus (q. v.), entitled *De Amore Heroïs et Leandri*, and is also mentioned by Ovid (*Her.* xviii. 19) and Vergil (*Georg.* iii. 258). In modern times the story has been used by Marlowe, Schiller, Leigh Hunt, and Grillparzer.

Learchus. See ATHAMAS.

Lebadēa (Λεβάδεια). A town in Boeotia, between Chaeronea and Mount Helicon, at the foot of a rock, in a cave of which was the celebrated oracle of Trophonius (Herod. viii. 34).

Lebĕdus (Λέβεδος). One of the twelve Ionic

cities, situated on the coast of Lydia, between Colophon and Teos (Herod. i. 142). It was nearly deserted in the time of Horace.

Lebes (λέβης). (1) A kettle of iron or copper of any size, put over the fire to cook (Hom. *Il.* xxi. 362; Thuc. iv. 100). (2) A basin, usually of silver, used by guests at dinner for washing their hands, which were held over it while water was poured over them from above. (3) Any vessel, as an urn for ashes (Aesch. *Agam.* 444), a bath-tub, etc.

Lebinthus (Λέβινθος). An island in the Aegean Sea, one of the Sporades (q. v.).

Lechaeum. See CORINTHUS, p. 413.

Lectīca (φορεῖον, σκιμπόδιον). A sort of litter, or palanquin, introduced into Greece and Italy from the East; at first, as an article of luxury for women, but afterwards very generally used for men as well. The body consisted of a wooden case with low sides to it, like the bier (*capulus, ferentum*), upon which a corpse was carried out (Aul. Gell. x. 3, 2); with uprights which supported a wooden tester, like the *pluteus*. This roof was covered with leather (Mart. xi. 98), and curtains (*vela, plagae, plagulae*) were suspended from it, which might be closed all round (Suet. *Tit.* 10), or drawn back, as in the illustration, when it was said to be open (*aperta*, Cic. *Phil.* ii. 24);

Supposed form of Lectica. (Ginzrot.)

but in some cases it was a close conveyance (*clausa*), having the sides fitted with panels and windows, which could be opened or shut at pleasure (Juv. iii. 242). The inmate reclined upon a soft mattress or feather-bed (Juv. l. 159), with a bolster to support the back (*cervical*), so that he could read, write, or sleep within it. According to the wealth of the owner and the size of the *letica*, it was borne by two, four, six, or eight tall slaves (*lecticarii*). Fragments of a lectica were found at Rome on the Esquiline in 1874.

Lecticarii (φορειαφόροι). See LECTICA.

Lections. See TEXTUAL CRITICISM.

Lectisternium. A festival of Greek origin, first ordered at Rome by the Sibylline Books in B.C. 399. It was held on exceptional occasions, particularly in times of great distress. Images of the gods (probably portable figures of wood draped with robes, and with their heads made of marble, clay, or wax) were laid on a couch (called the *lectus* or *pulvinar*). A table was placed before them, on which was laid out a meal, always a free-will offering. At the first Lectisternia, there were three *lecti* arranged for three pairs of non-Roman divinities—Apollo and Latona, Heracles and Artemis (Diana), Hermes (Mercury), and Poseidon (Neptune). Afterwards, this sacrifice was offered to the six pairs of Roman gods, who corresponded to the twelve great gods of the Greeks: Iupiter, Iuno, Neptune, Minerva, Mars, Venus, Apollo, Diana, Vulcan, Vesta, Mercury, and Ceres. These banquets to the gods generally took place at festivals of prayer and thanksgiving, which were called Sup-

Pulvinar (Munich).

plicationes (q. v.), and were performed in the market-places or at appointed temples, in which the arrangements for the purpose were on a permanent footing. It was customary to have connected with this a domestic feast, to which both strangers and friends were invited, and in which even those imprisoned for debt were allowed to participate. From the commencement of the third century B.C. a banquet was regularly given to the three Capitoline divinities, Iupiter, Iuno, and Minerva, on every 13th of November, in conjunction with the Plebeian Games. Under the Empire, the celebration was on the 13th of September, and was associated with the Roman games. From B.C. 196 it was provided by the college of Epulones (q. v.). The images of the three gods were decked with curls, and tricked out with colours. Iupiter was placed reclining on a cushion, with a goddess on each side of him seated on a chair; and the divinities were invited to a banquet, in which the whole Senate participated.

Lectisternium. (From a terracotta lamp.)

Lectonia. A land thought by some to have existed in the Mediterranean, and to have connected Greece with Asia. According to the Pseudo-Orphic account, Poseidon being angry with Zeus, struck Lectonia with his trident and buried it in the sea, leaving only scattered islands to recall its past. This tradition has been received with credence by some geographers and scholars, who regard the numerous small islands between Greece and Asia Minor as making probable a former land-connection which facilitated the early immigration from Asia into Europe. See Pliny, *H. N.* ii. 90; Diod. Sic. v. 47.

Lectum (τὸ Λέκτον). The southwestern promontory of the Troad, formed by Mount Ida jutting out into the sea (Herod. ix. 114).

Lectus (λέκτρον). (1) A bed to sleep upon was called LECTUS CUBICULĀRIS (Cic. *Div.* ii. 65). The ancient bedsteads were of considerable height, requiring a footstool (*scamnum*), or a set of steps (*gradus*) to get into them; and were made like our largest-sized sofas, with a head-board (*anaclinterium*), sometimes a corresponding one against the feet, and a high back (*pluteus*) on the farther side, but entirely open on the one at which the occupants entered (*sponda*). The frame was strung with girths (*fasciae, restes, institae*), which supported a thick mattress (*torus, culcita*), on which were placed a bolster and pillow (*cubital, cervical*).

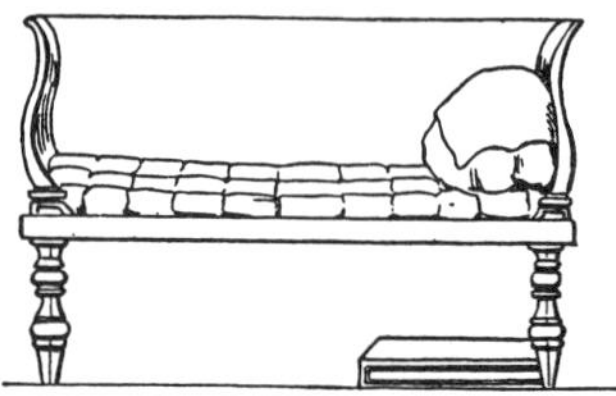

Lectus. (British Museum.)

A bed inferior in size and in materials was called by the diminutive name LECTŬLUS or LECTICŬLA, which also denoted a sofa, forming part of the usual furniture in a study (Pliny, *Ep.* v. 5, 5; Ovid, *Trist.* i. 11, 39), and on which it was a common practice to recline at length while reading, and even writing, the tablet being placed against one knee, which was raised up as a support for the purpose.

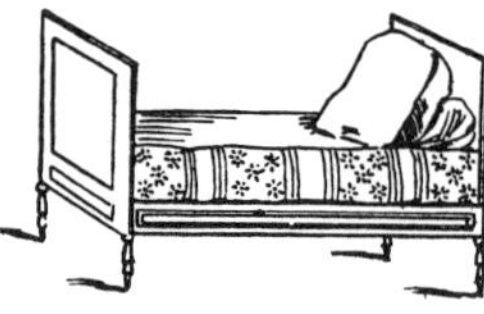

Lectulus. (Pompeii.)

The lectus was also used instead of seats in dining-rooms, the guests reclining at table. The usual number of couches at a table was three—*summus, medius,* and *imus.* For a full treatment of the table-arrangements, see TRICLINIUM.

(2) LECTUS GENIĀLIS or IUGĀLIS, denotes the marriage-bed (εὐνή), to which the wife was conducted on the eve of her marriage by the *pronuba*, after she had retired from the bridal feast. (See MATRIMONIUM.) It was a large bed, handsomely decorated, and raised to a very great height from the ground, as is indicated by the flight of steps at the foot in the illustration given in the article GRADUS, p. 744, which represents the *lectus genialis* of Dido, in the Vatican Vergil.

Lectus Funebris. (Rich.)

(3) LECTUS FUNĒBRIS is the name of the bier upon which dead bodies were carried out to the funeral pile, or to their place of sepulture, as shown by the annexed illustration from an ancient tombstone.

Lecȳthus (λήκυθος). See AMPULLA.

Lecȳthus (Λήκυθος). A town in the peninsula of Sithonia taken by Brasidas (Thuc. iv. 115).

Leda (Λήδα). A daughter of King Thestius and Eurythemis, who married Tyndareos, king of Sparta. According to the common account, she became, by Zeus (who assumed for that purpose the form of a swan), the mother of Pollux and Helen, and on the same night by her own husband, the parent of Castor and Clytaemnestra. Two eggs, it seems, were brought forth by her, from which respectively came the children just named, Pollux and Helen being in one, and Castor and Clytaemnestra in the other. Other versions, however, are given of the legend, for which consult Homer (*Od.* xi. 298) and the articles DIOSCURI and HELENA. See also Calverley's *Sons of Leda*, from Theocritus. The story of Leda and the swan has formed the subject of many beautiful works of art in both ancient and modern times.

Ledaea. An epithet given to Hermioné, and sometimes to Helen, and others, as related to Leda (Verg. *Aen.* iii. 328).

Ledaei Dii. Castor and Pollux, the sons of Leda.

Ledon (Λέδων). A town in Phocis, the birthplace of Philomelus, who led the Phocians in the Sacred War, at which time it was destroyed.

Ledus and **Ledum.** Now Lez or Les, a river of Gaul, near the modern Montpellier (Mela, ii. 5).

Legacies. See HERES; LEGATUM.

Legae (Λῆγαι) and **Leges** (Λῆγες). A people on the southern shore of the Caspian Sea.

Legātum. A legacy; a term of Roman law defined in the *Digest* (31, 1, 36), as *donatio testamento relicta*—i. e. a legatum implies a formal testament and universal succession. A legacy could only be given in the Latin language. If given unconditionally, it was said to be given *pure;* if otherwise, *sub condicione.*

There were four forms in which a legacy could be left: *per vindicationem, per damnationem, sinendi modo, per praeceptionem.*

A legatum *per vindicationem* was given in these words: *Hominem Stichum do, lego,* or the words might be with reference to the legatee, *Capito, sumito, sibi habeto.* A legatum *per vindicationem* was so called with reference to the legal means by which the legatee asserted his right to the legacy against the heir or any possessor, which was by a *vindicatio* (q. v.) or an *actio in rem* (see ACTIO); for as soon as the *hereditatis aditio* had taken place, the legatee had the quiritary (*ex iure Quiritium*) ownership of the legacy. If the same thing was given to more than one person, either jointly (*coniunctim*), so as to make them *collegetarii*, or severally (*disiunctim*), each took an equal share. A legatum was given *coniunctim,* thus: *Titio et Seio hominem Stichum do, lego; disiunctim,* thus: *Titio hominem Stichum do, lego; Seio eundem hominem do, lego.* If one *collegatarius* failed to take, his portion went to the others.

The formula *per damnationem* was this: *Heres meus Stichum servum meum dare damnas esto;* but the word dato was equally effective. A thing which belonged to another (*aliena res*) could be thus left, and the heres was bound to procure the thing for the legatee, or to pay him the value of it. A thing not in existence at the date of the will might be left by this form—i. e. the future produce of a female slave (*ancilla*). The legatee did not acquire the quiritary ownership of the legacy by virtue of the *hereditatis aditio;* the thing still remained the property of the heir, and the legatee could only sue for it by an *actio in personam.* If it was a thing *mancipi*, the legatee could only acquire the quiritary ownership of it by *mancipatio* or in *iure cessio* from the heir; if it was merely delivered, the *legatarius* only acquired the complete ownership (*plenum ius*) by *usucapion* (q. v.).

The form of legacy *sinendi modo* was *Haeres*

meus damnas esto sinere L. Titium hominem Stichum sumen sibique habere, by which formula the testator could bequeath anything that belonged to himself or to his heir, at the time of his decease; and as in the previous case, the legatee had merely an *actio in personam* against the heir, though it was doubted whether the form of bequest imposed any active duty on the latter, it being argued that his only obligation was to allow the legatee to "take" the object bequeathed to him.

The *legatum per praeceptionem* was in this form: *Lucius Titius hominem Stichum praecipito*—i. e. "take first." The Sabiniani were of opinion that a legacy could only thus be left to one who was also made an heir; but a *senatus consultum* of Nero made the legacy good, even if it was thus left to another than the heir, provided the legatee was a person to whom a legacy could be left in any of the three other modes.

By the Twelve Tables, a man could dispose of his property as he pleased, and he might exhaust (*erogare*) the whole *hereditas* by legacies and bequests of freedom to slaves, so as to leave the heir nothing. The consequence was that in such cases the heirs refused to take the *hereditas*, and there was, of course, an intestacy. The first legislative measure on this subject was the Lex Furia Testamentaria (B.C. 183), which did not allow a testator to give as a *donatio mortis causa* or as a legacy more than a thousand asses to one person, certain relatives excepted. But this measure did not prevent a man from giving as many several thousands to as many persons as he pleased, and so exhausting his estate. The Lex Voconia (B.C. 169) afterwards enacted that no person should take, by way of legacy or *donatio mortis causa*, more than the heirs (severally, as it seems); but this was also ineffectual; for, by distributing the *hereditas* among numerous legatees, the heir might have so small a portion as not to make it worth his while to assume the burdens attached to the inheritance. The Lex Falcidia (B.C. 40) at last took away all means of evasion by declaring that a testator should not give more than three fourths in legacies, and thus a fourth was secured to the heir. The Lex Falcidia applied to the wills of persons who died in captivity (*apud hostes*), for a previous Lex Cornelia had given to the wills of such persons the same force as if they had died *cives*.

Legata were *inutilia* or void if they were given before an heir was instituted by the will, for the will derived all its legal efficacy from such institution; there was the same rule as to a gift of freedom. It was void if in form the gift was given after the death of the heir, but it might be given on the event of his death; it was also void if given in form on the day before the death of the testator. A legatum could not be left in the way of a penalty (*poenae nomine*)—that is, for the purpose of compelling the heir to do, or restraining him from doing, any particular act. A legacy could not be left to an uncertain person (*incerta persona*). The notion of an uncertain person was not of a person who could never be ascertained, but the notion of the uncertainty was referred to the mind of the testator at the time of making his testament. Accordingly, the person was not considered uncertain where he was one of a certain class, such as *cognati*, though the individual of the class might be uncertain till the event happened which was to determine who out of the class was intended by the testator. Such a form of bequest was called a *certa demonstratio incertae personae*. A legacy could not be left to a *postumus alienus*, nor could such a person be a *heres institutus*, for he was an *incerta persona*. It has been explained elsewhere who is a *postumus* (see TESTAMENTUM); a *postumus alienus* is one who, when born, cannot be among the *sui heredes* of the testator.

Legātus. An envoy from one State to another; an ambassador. (1) Envoys were sent from Rome, in the regal period, by the king; in the republican period by the consuls, with the advice and authority of the Senate. In the later Republic the sending and receiving of *legati* was practically an exclusive function of the Senate. In the Empire these rights passed to the emperor. In the royal and early Republican periods envoys were always taken from the college of fetial priests. (See FETIALES; IUS FETIALE.) When the Senate gained substantial control of foreign affairs, *legati* were always chosen from the senatorial order. Like the fetials, the secular *legati* were neutral and inviolable persons (*iure gentium*). In the last century of the Republic, senators travelling on private business or for pleasure were frequently invested with the character of *legati* without the least pretence of an actual mission, the appointment assuring them not merely special consideration and protection, but also free transportation at the cost of the State.

(2) Envoys were also sent by the Senate to convey tidings or counsel to magistrates in the field. When an important treaty was to be concluded by such a magistrate, a board of senatorial legati was frequently sent, nominally to advise the general, actually to settle the terms of the treaty. When conquered territory began to be organized into provinces (see PROVINCIA), it became customary to send out one or more senatorial legati with the magistrate to whom the government of a province was intrusted. These legati were legally under the command of the governor, and served as his assistants in military, administrative, and judicial matters; but they also represented the authority of the Senate, and the necessity of hearing their advice operated as a check upon the governor's arbitrary powers. In the last two centuries of the Republic, legati were regularly appointed to accompany consuls or praetors charged with important military operations; and these legates, often nominated by the general in command, served as corps commanders. As the military power began to overshadow that of the Senate, the generals obtained free hand in selecting their legati (cf. the Lex Gabinia, B.C. 66, which gave Pompey the selection of his own legati for the conduct of the war against the pirates), and the way was prepared for the development of the imperial office of *legatus*. This whole evolution from envoy to officer is indicated, according to Mommsen, in the successive forms of expression: *legatus ad aliquem, legatus alicui, legatus alicuius*.

The Republican legatus had no *imperium* and bore no *fasces*. The symbol and credential of his office was a ring. Here again the Gabinian law marked an innovation: the legati of Pompey had propraetorian powers. The same was true of the legates of Iulius Caesar in Gaul (*B. G.* i. 21).

(3) In the Early Empire certain provinces were

assigned to the *princeps*, and these provinces he governed through legati of his own selection. These legates had propraetorian powers and bore *fasces* (not of twelve or six rods, like the consuls and praetors, but of five—*legati quinquefascales*). Similar powers and insignia were accorded to the legates in the senatorial provinces, who were now selected by the governor with the approval of the emperor. In the imperial system, accordingly, the *legati pro praetore* are vice-governors, subordinated in the provinces of Augustus to the emperor and in the other provinces to the senatorial governor. Besides these, the emperors appointed other *legati pro praetore* without fixed provinces and with purely military duties.

Still other legates were appointed for the provinces with special military or judicial duties, the *legati legionis* and the *legati iuridici*. These had no *imperium*, and were subordinated to the provincial governors and vice-governors. Cf. Mommsen's *Römisches Staatsrecht*, esp. ii. 675–701.

Leges. See LEX.

Legio. In the time of Romulus, the united armed forces of Rome went by the name of *legio*. The legion then consisted of 300 knights (*celeres*), under the command of a *tribunus celerum*, appointed by the king, and 3000 foot soldiers, under the command of three *tribuni militum*. Each of the three ancient tribes provided a third of this force and one tribune. With the increase of the military forces of Rome the name of *legio* was given to each of the subdivisions equivalent in numbers to the original army.

The military system of King Servius Tullius made the infantry the most important part of the military forces, instead of the cavalry as heretofore. The five classes included in the *census* (q. v.) were obliged to serve in the army at their own expense; those who were not comprised in these classes—viz. the *proletarii*—were freed from service, and, when they were enlisted, received their equipment from the State. The *iuniores*, those who were from 17 to 46 years old, were appointed for field service, and the *seniores*, those from 47 to 60, for the defence of the city.

The first and second lines of the legion, drawn up in unbroken order like the Greek phalanx, consisted of citizens of the first class, equipped with helmet, cuirass, round shield (*clipeus*), and greaves, all of bronze. The third and fourth lines were from the second class, and had no cuirass, but had the helmet and greaves and large oblong shields (*scutum*). The fifth and sixth were armed similarly, but without greaves, and were drawn from the third class. The fourth class was armed with the *scutum* as its only weapon of defence, but, like the others, provided with spear (*hasta*) and sword. It either filled the seventh and eighth lines, or, with the fifth class, formed the *rorarii*, who opened the battle with slings and other light missiles.

An important alteration, ascribed to Camillus (about B.C. 390), was the abolition of the phalanx and introduction of the manipular formation, which prevailed till the time of Marius (end of the second century B.C.). In the flourishing days of the Republic, the normal strength of a legion, which could be increased in time of need, consisted of 300 knights (*equites*) and 4200 foot soldiers (*pedites*). In respect to the weapons used, the latter were divided into four kinds, according to their length of service and familiarity with warfare: (1) 1200 *hastati*, all in early manhood; (2) 1200 *principes*, in the full vigour of life; (3) 600 *triarii*, who were proved veterans; and (4) 1200 *velites*, who were lightly armed, and were drawn from the lowest classes of the census. The first three classes had a bronze helmet (*cassis*) with a lofty plume of feathers, a *scutum*, a leathern cuirass (*lorica*, q. v.), greaves, and a sword (*gladius*), which, after the Second Punic War, was of the Spanish kind, being short, strong, and two-edged, fitted for thrusting rather than cutting, and worn on the right side. There was also a spear, which in the first two divisions was a *pilum* (q. v.), and among the *triarii* a lance (Polyb. vi. 23). The *velites* were armed with a leather helmet (*galea*), a light shield (*parma*), and a sword and several light javelins. The 3000 heavily armed men were divided into 30 *manipuli*, numbering 120 men each among the *hastati* and *principes*, and 60 each among the *triarii*, and were again subdivided into two bodies called *centuriae*, and led by centurions (q. v.). Of the 1200 *velites*, 20 were allotted to each century, and they formed the final complement of each maniple. On the field of battle the maniples were drawn up in open order, separated laterally from one another by intervals corresponding to the breadth of each maniple in front. The arrangement of the maniples would thus resemble that of the black squares on a chess-board. They fell into three divisions—the *hastati* in the front rank, with the *principes* behind them, and the *triarii* in the rear. If the first division, the *hastati*, were compelled to give way, then the second division, the *principes*, advanced through the intervals left by the maniples of the first division; if the *principes*, in their turn, had to retreat, then the third division, the *triarii*, who had been previously kneeling, protected by their shields, allowed the *hastati* and *principes* to fall back into the intervals separating the maniples of the *triarii*, and themselves, closing their ranks, pressed forward to meet the enemy. The 300 knights of the legion were divided into 10 *turmae* of 30 men each, and were equipped with a bronze cuirass, leathern greaves, helmet, shield, a long sword for attacking, and a long lance provided at both ends with an iron point. Each *turma* was under three decurions and three under-officers (*optiones*). The legion, as a whole, was under the command of six *tribuni militum* (q. v.).

The consular army consisted of two legions. Four legions were regularly levied in each year; in other words, 16,800 foot soldiers and 1200 cavalry. This levy of citizens was further swelled by the Italian allies (*socii*), a body of 20,000 foot soldiers and 3600 cavalry, thus adding to each of the two consular armies 10,000 foot soldiers and 1800 cavalry. The former were in twenty cohorts (see COHORS), each consisting of 420 men. Ten of these cohorts fought on the right wing and ten on the left wing of the legions. Besides these, four cohorts of 400 men each were formed into a picked body. The cavalry were in six squadrons (*alae*) of 300 men each. Four of these belonged to the main army, and two to the picked body. In wars beyond the limits of Italy there were also auxiliary forces (*auxilia*), consisting either of soldiers raised in the country where the war was being carried on, or of light-armed troops furnished by allied kings and nations. Besides the ordinary component parts of the legion there was also the bodyguard of the commander-in-chief, the *cohors praetoria*. See COHORS.

In the course of the first century B.C. the organization of the legion was essentially altered. In the first place, in the time of Marius, the census ceased to be the basis of the levy, and all the citizens collectively were placed on the same footing in respect to their military service and the uniform which they wore. All the soldiers of the legion alike received the heavy equipment and the *pilum*, while the light-armed *velites* were done away with. After the right of citizenship had been conferred on the Italian allies, these no longer formed a separate part of the legions, but were incorporated with them. Thus the Roman army now consisted only of heavy-armed legions and of light-armed auxiliary troops. The latter were partly raised in the provinces and divided into cohorts, and partly enlisted as slingers and archers. The cavalry of the legions ceased to exist. Like the light-armed soldiers, the whole of the cavalry consisted of auxiliary troops, who were partly enlisted and partly levied from the provinces, while some were supplied according to agreement by allied nations and princes. A further important novelty introduced by Marius was the use of the cohort-formation, instead of the maniple-formation, which broke up the front too much. The legion was now divided into ten cohorts, in each of which there were three maniples of *hastati*, *principes*, and *triarii*, designations which now only concerned the relative rank of the six centurions of the cohort. The customary battle array was in three divisions, the first being formed of four cohorts, and the second and third of three each. Again, while in earlier times the obligation of service extended at the most in the infantry to twenty campaigns and in the cavalry to ten, from the days of Marius the soldier remained uninterruptedly for twenty years with the army, an earlier dismissal being only exceptional. For this reason the well-to-do classes sought to withdraw themselves from the general military service, and it thus came to pass that the legions were for the greater part manned by means of conscriptions from the lowest ranks of the burgher population of Italy, in which the service was regarded simply as a means of livelihood. Thus from the original army of citizens there was gradually developed a standing army of mercenaries.

Under the Empire we find what is really a standing army, bound to the emperor by oath. (See SACRAMENTUM.) Apart from the legions this army consisted of the *auxilia* (q. v.), the guards stationed in Rome and the neighbourhood (see PRAETORIANI), and the city-cohorts (see COHORS), the artillery and the corps of workmen (see FABRI), the marines (see CLASSIARII), and the municipal and provincial militia. The legions are now once more provided with a corps of cavalry 120 strong, and are designated not only by numbers, but also by distinctive names. Together with the auxiliary troops they form the garrison of the imperial provinces under the command of the imperial *legati legionum* (see LEGATI), whose place was taken in the middle of the third century A.D. by the *praefecti legionum*. (See PRAEFECTI.) The strength of the legion now amounted to 5000–6000 men, raised partly by a regular levy, partly by drawing recruits from the Roman citizens of all the provinces beyond the bounds of Italy. As under the Republic, it was divided into 10 cohorts of 6 centuries each; the first cohort was, however, twice the strength of the remainder. It was not until the second half of the third century A.D. that a new division of the 10 cohorts into 55 centuries came into use, with 10 centuries in the first cohort, and 5 in each of the rest. At the death of Augustus, the number of the legions was 25; it was then increased to 30, and this number was maintained until the end of the second century, when three new legions were added by Septimius Severus. From the beginning of the fourth century it gradually rose to about 175, each of them, however, mustering a considerably smaller contingent. In course of time, and especially after the second century, owing to the conflicts with the barbarians, the legion was drawn up more and more after the manner of the Greek phalanx, without intervals in its line and with a division of troops in its rear. In its equipment there was an important alteration beginning with the second half of the third century, when all the soldiers of the legion carried long swords (*spathae*), and the first five cohorts two *pila*, one larger and another smaller, while the last five had *lanceae*, or javelins serving as missiles, and fitted with a leather loop to help in hurling them with precision. See Pfitzner, *Geschichte der röm. Kaiserlegionen* (Leipzig, 1881).

The military music of the Romans was provided by *tubicines* (see TUBA), *cornicines* (see CORNICEN), *bucinatores* (see BUCINA), and *liticines* (see LITUUS). The accompanying illustration from the Column of Trajan represents the soldiers of a legion on the

Roman Legionaries on the March. (Relief from the Column of Trajan, Rome.)

march, carrying their helmets close to the right shoulder, and their "kit" at the top of a pole resting on the left. On standards or ensigns, see SIGNUM; VEXILLUM. On levy, oath of allegiance, pay, and discharge from service, see DELECTUS; MISSIO; SACRAMENTUM; STIPENDIUM. For the army as a whole, see Brissaud, *De l'Organization Militaire chez les Romains* (Paris, 1891); and EXERCITUS.

Legio Septĭma Gemĭna. A Roman military colony in Spain among the Astures, northeast of

Asturica. It is now Leon. Ptolemy calls it Legio Septima Germanorum (ii. 6).

Legis Actio. See ACTIO.

Legislation. See COMITIA; LEX; SENATUS.

Lehrs, KARL. A German classical scholar, born at Königsberg in 1802. He studied at the university of his native place, in which he himself became, after teaching for some time in various gymnasia, Privat-Docent (1831), Extraordinary Professor (1835), and Ordinary Professor (1845). He died in 1878.

His most valuable work is the treatise on early Homeric criticism, *De Aristarchi Studiis Homericis* (Königsberg, 1833; 3d ed. 1882). Of his other writings it is most necessary to mention *Quaestiones Epicae* (1837); *Herodiani Tria Scripta Minora* (1848); *Die Pindarscholien* (1873); besides an edition of the Odes of Horace this is remarkable for the extreme length to which Lehrs carried his subjective criticism of the text. See Kammer, *Karl Lehrs* (Berlin, 1879); and TEXTUAL CRITICISM.

Leiturgia. See LITURGIA.

Lelantine War. A war waged between Eretria and Chalcis, probably for the possession of the plain of Lelantus (q. v.). E. Curtius has assumed as the date of this contest B.C. 704, which Professor Mahaffy thinks too early. Some of the most powerful States of Greece joined in the struggle, especially Samos and Miletus. See Strabo, pp. 58, 447; Herod. v. 99; Thuc. i. 15; Hermann in the *Rheinisches Museum*, i. p. 85; and especially Mahaffy in *Hermathena*, iv. p. 325.

Lelantus Campus (τὸ Λήλαντον πεδίον). A plain lying between the two cities of Eretria and Chalcis in Euboea and an object of contention to them. It was noted for its copper and iron mines and warm springs.

Lelegēïs. A name applied to Miletus, because once possessed by the Leleges (Pliny, *H. N.* v. 29).

Lelĕges (Λέλεγες). An ancient race, frequently mentioned with the Pelasgians as the prehistoric inhabitants of Greece. The Leleges were described as a warlike and migratory race, who first took possession of the coasts and the islands of Greece, and afterwards penetrated into the interior. Piracy was probably their chief occupation; and they are represented as the ancestors of the Teleboans and the Taphians, who were notorious for their piracies. The name of the Leleges was derived by the Greeks from an ancestor, Lelex, who is called king of either Megaris or Lacedaemon (Pausan. iii. 1, 1). They must be regarded as a branch of the great Indo-Germanic race, who became gradually incorporated with the Hellenes, and thus ceased to exist as an independent people. They are spoken of as inhabiting Acarnania and Aetolia, and afterwards Phocis, Locris, Boeotia, Megaris, Elis, and Laconia, which last was originally called Lelegia; also (in Asia Minor) Ionia, the southern part of the Troad, and Caria (Herod. i. 171). See Deimling, *Die Leleger* (Leipzig, 1862).

Lelex (Λέλεξ). See LELEGES.

Lemannus or **Lemānus Lacus.** The modern Lake of Geneva; a large lake formed by the river Rhodanus (Rhône), and constituting the boundary between the old Roman province in Gaul and the land of the Helvetii. It is fifty-five miles long, and its maximum width is six miles.

Lembus (λέμβος). A swift light vessel, also called *dromo*. The *lembus* varied in size from a mere cat-boat to a fast-sailing transport (Plaut. *Merc.* i. 2, 81; Polyb. li. 3).

Lemnia Terra, also called **Sigillāta.** A species of reddish earth found in Lemnos, and highly esteemed down to modern times for its supposed virtues as an antidote against snake-bites and as a remedy for dysentery. It was gathered on only one day of the year (Aug. 6) with religious ceremonies.

Lemniscus. See CORONA, p. 415.

Lemnos or **Lemnus** (Λῆμνος). One of the largest islands in the Aegaean Sea, situated nearly midway between Mount Athos and the Hellespont. Its area is about 180 square miles. It was sacred to Hephaestus, who is said to have fallen here when he was hurled down from Olympus. Hence the workshop of the god is sometimes placed in this island. The legend appears to have arisen from the volcanic nature of Lemnos. Its earliest inhabitants, according to Homer, were the Thracian Sinties, a name which probably signifies "robbers," from σίνομαι. When the Argonauts landed at Lemnos, they found it inhabited only by women who had murdered all their husbands, and had selected Hypsipylé as their queen. (See HYPSIPYLÉ.) By the Lemnian women some of the Argonauts became the fathers of the Minyae, who inhabited the island till they were expelled by the Pelasgians. Lemnos was conquered by one of the generals of Darius; but Miltiades delivered it from the Persians, and made it subject to Athens. Pliny (*H. N.* xxxvi. 13) speaks of a remarkable labyrinth in Lemnos, of which, however, no remains are to be found at the present day. See Tozer, *Islands of the Aegean* (1890).

Lemonia. One of the country tribes at Rome, named after a village Lemonium, situated on the Via Latina beyond the Porta Capena.

Lemonium. See LEMONIA.

Lemovīces. A people in Gallia Aquitanica, between the Bituriges and Arverni, whose chief town was Augustoritum, subsequently called Lemovices, the modern Limoges (Caes. *B. G.* vii. 4).

Lemovii. A people of Germany, mentioned together with the Rugii as inhabiting the shores of the Baltic in the modern Pomerania (Tac. *Germ.* 43).

Lemuralia. See LEMURES.

Lemŭres. The spectres or spirits of the dead. Some writers describe Lemures as the common name for all the spirits of the dead, and divide them into two classes: the Lares, or the souls of good men, and the Larvae, or the souls of wicked men. But the common idea was that the Lemures and Larvae were the same. They were said to wander about at night as spectres, and to torment and frighten the living. In order to propitiate them, the Romans celebrated the festival of the Lemuralia or Lemuria in the month of May (the 9th, 11th, and 13th). It was said to have been originally instituted by Romulus to appease the spirit of Remus (Ovid, *Fast.* v. 473, etc.). At this festival it was the custom to appease or expel the evil spirits by walking barefoot and throwing black beans over the shoulder at night (Ovid, *Fasti*, v. 473 foll.). Because of this festival to the dead, the whole month of May was supposed to be unlucky for marriages, whence the proverb *Mense Maio malae nubent.* See Preller, *Röm. Myth.* 499.

Lemuria. See LARES; LEMURES.

Lenaea. See DIONYSIA.

Lenaeon (Ληναιών). The Ionic name of the Attic month Gamelion (q. v.), in which the Lenaea were held. (See DIONYSIA.) It was the fifth month of the Asiatic Greeks and the seventh of the Attic Greeks. See CALENDARIUM.

Lenaeus (Ληναῖος). A surname of Dionysus, derived from ληνός, the wine-press or the vintage.

Leno. A pimp. See MERETRIX.

Lenocinium. The trade of a procurer. See MERETRIX.

Lentia. The modern Linz; a town of Noricum on the Danube.

Lenticular Gems. See GEMMA.

Lentienses. A tribe of the Alemanni dwelling along the northern shore of the Lacus Brigantinus (Constance), in the modern Linzgau.

Lentŭlus. A haughty patrician family of the Cornelia gens (Cic. *Ad Fam.* iii. 7), of which the most important persons were: (1) P. CORNELIUS LENTULUS SURA, the person of chief note among Catiline's conspirators. He was quaestor to Sulla B.C. 81; praetor in 75; consul in 71. In the next year he was ejected from the Senate, with sixty-three others, for infamous life and manners. It was this, probably, that led him to join Catiline and his band. From his distinguished birth and high rank, he calculated on becoming chief of the conspiracy; and a prophecy of the Sibylline Books was applied by flattering haruspices to him. Three Cornelii were to rule Rome, and he was the third after Sulla and Cinna; the twentieth year after the burning of the Capitol, etc., was to be fatal to the city. To gain power and recover his place in the Senate, he became praetor again in 63. When Catiline quitted the city for Etruria, Lentulus was left as chief of the home conspirators, and his irresolution probably saved the city from being fired; for it was by his over-caution that the negotiation with the ambassadors of the Allobroges was entered into, and these unstable allies revealed the secret to the consul Cicero. The sequel will be found in the article CATILINA. Lentulus was deposed from the praetorship, and was strangled in the Capitoline prison on the 5th of December. (2) P. CORNELIUS LENTULUS SPINTHER, curule aedile in B.C. 63, praetor in 60, and consul in 57. In his consulship he moved for the immediate recall of Cicero, and afterwards received Cilicia as his province. On the breaking out of the Civil War in 49 he joined the Pompeian party. (3) L. CORNELIUS LENTULUS CRUS, praetor in 58, and consul in 49, when he took a very active part against Caesar. After the battle of Pharsalia, he fled to Egypt, and was put to death by the young Ptolemy's ministers. (4) GNAEUS, called GAETULĬCUS, consul in A.D. 26, commanded the imperial legions in Upper Germany. His great popularity with the soldiers excited the jealousy of the emperor Caligula, who had him put to death in A.D. 39. He was a writer of both verse and prose, and to him have been ascribed nine epigrams in the Greek anthology, inscribed with the name Gaetulicus.

Leo or **Leon** (Λέων). (1) Also called LEONĪDES (Λεωνίδης), of Heraclea on the Pontus, a disciple of Plato. He was one of the conspirators who, with their leader, Chion, assassinated Clearchus, tyrant of Heraclea, B.C. 353. (2) DIACŎNUS, or the Deacon, a Byzantine historian of the tenth century. His history, in ten books, includes the period from the Cretan expedition of Nicephorus Phocas, in the reign of the emperor Romanus II. (A.D. 959), to the death of Ioannes I. Zimisces (975). The style of Leo is corrupt; he employs unusual and inappropriate words, many of them borrowed from Homer, Agiathias the historian, and the Septuagint, in the place of common ones; and he abounds in tautological phrases. His history, however, is a valuable contemporary record of a stirring time, honestly and fearlessly written. It is edited by Migne (Paris, 1863). (3) GRAMMATĬCUS, one of the continuators of Byzantine history from the period when Theophanes leaves off. His work, entitled *Chronographia*, extends from the accession of Leo V. the Armenian (813) to the death of Romanus Lecapenus (944). (4) Archbishop of Thessalonica, an eminent Byzantine philosopher and ecclesiastic of the ninth century. His works are lost, but he is frequently mentioned in terms of the highest praise by the Byzantine writers, especially for his knowledge of geometry and astronomy. (5) MAGENTĒNUS, a commentator on Aristotle, flourished during the first half of the fourteenth century. He was a monk, and afterwards archbishop of Mitylené. Several of his commentaries on Aristotle are extant, and have been published (6) Leo was also the name of six Byzantine emperors. Of these, Leo VI., "the philosopher," who reigned 886–911, is celebrated in the history of the later Greek literature. He wrote a treatise on Greek tactics, and several other works, which are still extant. He is also celebrated in the history of legislation. As the Latin language had long ceased to be the official language of the Eastern Empire, Basil, the father of Leo, had formed and partly executed the plan of issuing an authorized Greek version of Iustinian's legislation. This plan was carried out by Leo. The Greek version is known under the title of Βασιλικαὶ Διατάξεις, or shortly, Βασιλικαί; in Latin, *Basilica*, which means "Imperial Constitutions," or "Laws." See BASILICA.

Leochăres (Λεωχάρης). A Greek sculptor, of Athens, who (about B.C. 350) was engaged with Scopas in the adornment of the Mausoleum (q. v.) of Halicarnassus. One of his most famous works was the bronze group of Ganymede and the Eagle, a work remarkable for its ingenious composition, which boldly ventures to the verge of what is allowed by the laws of sculpture, and also for its charming treatment of the youthful form as it soars into the air. It is apparently imitated in a well-known marble group in the Vatican, half life-size. See Perry, *Greek and Roman Sculpture*, ch. xxxix. (London, 1882).

Leonĭdas (Λεωνίδας). (1) A celebrated king of Lacedaemon, of the family of the Eurysthenidae, sent by his countrymen to maintain the pass of Thermopylae against the invading army of Xerxes (B.C. 480). A narrative of the affair will be found in the article THERMOPYLAE. (2) Son of Cleonymus, of the line of the Agidae, succeeded Areus II. on the throne of Sparta, B.C. 257. Agis, his colleague in the sovereignty, having resolved to restore the institutions of Lycurgus to their former vigour, Leonidas opposed his views, and became the main support of those who were inclined to a relaxation of ancient strictness. He was convicted, however, of having transgressed the laws, and was obliged to yield the supreme power to Cleombrotus, his son-in-law. Not long after he was reestablished on the Spartan throne, and avenged the affront which he had received at the hands of Agis, by impeaching him and effecting his condemnation (Pausan. ii. 9; iii. 6). He died about B.C. 236. (3) A relative of Olympias, the mother of Alexander the Great. He had charge of Alexander's education before he became the pupil of Aristotle. Afterwards when king, Alexander said that Leonidas had furnished him with two excellent cooks — a night's march to give zest to his breakfast, and a scanty breakfast to give zest to his dinner. (4) A native of Alexandria, who flourished at Rome as a grammarian towards the close of the first century of the Christian era. He wrote, among other things, epigrams denominated *ἰσόψηφα*, arranged in such a manner that the numerical value of all the letters composing any one distich is equal to that of the letters of any other. He was very probably the inventor of this learned species of trifling. (5) A native of Tarentum, who flourished about B.C. 275. He left behind a hundred epigrams in the Doric dialect, and which belong to the best of those that have been preserved to modern times.

Leonidēa (Λεωνιδεῖα). A solemn feast annually celebrated in Sparta in honour of Leonidas and the three hundred Spartans who fell at Thermopylae. See THERMOPYLAE.

Leonīni Versus. A name given especially to a form of the Latin hexameter and pentameter rhymed in the middle and at the end. They are ascribed to Leoninus, Canon of the Church of St. Victor in Paris about the middle of the twelfth century, and by some to Pope Leo II.; but they occur in the classical Latin writers of the Augustan Age. Such is the line of Vergil:

> "Limus ut hic durescit et haec ut cera liquescit;"

and this from Ovid:

> "Quot caelum stellas, tot habet tua Roma puellas."

In the Middle Ages, however, they were systematically written and chiefly by poets who let their rhyme take the place of syllabic quantity. Many famous old couplets are leonine. Such is the original of "When the devil was ill," etc.—

> "Daemon languebat, monachus tunc esse volebat:
> Ast ubi convaluit, mansit ut ante fuit."

And the famous epitaph of Bede in Durham Cathedral:

> "Hac sunt in fossa, Bedae venerabilis ossa."

And this skit on the legal profession:

> "Dirue iuristas, Deus, ut Satanae citharistas;
> O Deus extingues hos pingues atque bilingues!"

And the punning line on the Fair Rosamond:

> "Hic iacet in hac tumba rosa mundi non rosa munda."

For a full account of the leonine verse, with abundant specimens, see J. Grimm, *Lat. Gedichte;* Trench's introduction to his *Sacred Latin Poetry;* Leyser, *Historia Poetarum Medii Aevi*, pp. 832–837; and, especially, Eberhard's *Labyrinthus*, a sort of mediæval *Ars Poetica*. Cf. also the article RHYME in this Dictionary.

Leonnātus (Λεοννάτος). A Macedonian of Pella, one of Alexander's generals. At the assault on the city of the Malli in India he saved Alexander's life. He crossed over into Europe in B.C. 322, to assist Antipater against the Greeks; but was defeated by the Athenians and their allies, and fell in battle (Diod. xviii. 12–15).

Leontiădes (Λεοντιάδης). (1) A Theban who commanded the forces sent by Thebes to the Greek army at Thermopylae, B.C. 480. (See THERMOPYLAE.) (2) A Theban who, in B.C. 382, aided the Spartans in seizing the citadel of Thebes, the Cadmea. He was slain by Pelopidas in 379 (Diod. xv. 25).

Leontīni (Λεοντῖνοι). The modern Lentini, a town in the east of Sicily, about five miles from the sea, northwest of Syracuse, founded by Chalcidians from Naxos, B.C. 730, but never attained much political importance in consequence of its proximity to Syracuse. The rich plains north of the city, called Leontini Campi, were some of the most fertile in Sicily, and produced abundant crops of most excellent wheat. It was the birthplace of Gorgias, "the Nihilist."

Leontium (Λεόντιον). An Athenian woman, originally a courtesan, although afterwards the wife of Metrodorus, the most eminent friend and disciple of Epicurus. Many slanders were circulated respecting her intercourse with the philosopher and his followers. She herself composed works on philosophy (Diog. Laert. x. 7; Cic. *N. D.* i. 33). Her daughter Danaë was a prostitute of some celebrity.

Leontium (Λεόντιον). A town in Achaia, between Pharae and Aegium.

Leontopŏlis (Λεοντόπολις, Λεόντων πόλις). (1) A city in the Delta of Egypt, the capital of the Nomos Leontopolites. (2) See NICEPHORIUM.

Leoprepĭdes. The poet Simonides, as son of Leoprepes (Herod. vii. 228).

Leos (Λεώς). An eponymous hero of Athens, who is described as son of Orpheus. Once, when Athens was suffering from famine or plague, the Delphic oracle demanded that the daughters of Leos should be sacrificed, and the father complied with the command of the oracle. The maidens were afterwards honoured by the Athenians, who erected the Leocorium (from Λεώς and κόραι) to them. Their names were Praxithea, Theopé, and Eubulé (Pausan. i. 5, 2; x. 10, 1). From Leos the tribe Leontis got its name.

Leosthĕnes (Λεωσθένης). An Athenian commander of the combined Greek army in the Lamian War, slain by a stone while besieging Antipater in the town of Lamia, B.C. 322. His funeral discourse was pronounced by Hyperides.

Leotychĭdes (Λεωτυχίδης). (1) King of Sparta, B.C. 491–469. He commanded the Greek fleet in 479, and defeated the Persians at the battle of Mycalé. (2) The reputed son of Agis II., excluded from the throne in consequence of his being suspected to be the son of Alcibiades by Timaea, the queen of Agis. His uncle, Agesilaüs II., was therefore substituted in his stead (Xen. *Hellen.* iii. 3).

Lepĭda. (1) AEMILIA, daughter of Manius Lepidus and wife of Drusus Caesar. She was engaged in an adulterous intercourse with Seianus, and was suborned by that ambitious and profligate minister to become the accuser of her own husband to Tiberius. Notwithstanding her crimes, she was protected during her father's life; but, being afterwards made a subject of attack by the informers of the day, she put an end to her own existence (Tac. *Ann.* iv. 20; vi. 40). (2) DOMITIA, daughter of Drusus and Antonia. She was grandniece of Augustus and aunt of Nero, who destroyed her by poison (Tac. *Ann.* xiii. 19). (3) DOMITIA, daughter of Antonia the younger, by Lucius Domitius Ahenobarbus. She was the wife of Valerius Messala and mother of Messalina, and is described as having been a woman of debauched character and of a violent temper. In point of beauty and vice, she was the rival of Agrippina, Nero's mother. She was condemned to death through the influence of the same Agrippina (Tac. *Ann.* xi. 37, xii. 64; Suet. *Claud.* 26; *Ner.* 7).

Lepĭdus. (1) LUCIUS AEMILIUS PAULUS, brother of M. Lepidus, the triumvir. His surname of Paulus was probably given him by his father, in honour of the celebrated Aemilius Paulus, the conqueror of Macedonia; but since he belonged to the family of the Lepidi, and not to that of the Pauli, he is mentioned in this place and not under the title PAULUS. Aemilius Paulus commenced his public career by supporting the aristocratic party. His first public act was the accusation of Catiline in B.C. 63. He was quaestor in Macedonia in 59; aedile, 55; praetor, 53; and consul, 50, with M. Claudius Marcellus. Paulus was raised to the consulship, on account of his being one of the most determined enemies of Caesar, but Caesar gained him over to his side by a bribe of 1500 talents, which he is said to have expended on the completion of a magnificent basilica commenced by him in his aedileship. After the murder of Caesar (B.C. 44), Paulus joined the senatorial party. He was one of the senators who declared M. Lepidus a public enemy, on account of his having joined Antony; and, accordingly, when the Second Triumvirate was formed, his name was set down first in the proscription list by his own brother. The soldiers, however, who had been ordered to kill him, allowed him to escape. He passed over to Brutus in Asia, and after the death of the latter repaired to Miletus, where he remained, and refused to go to Rome, although he was pardoned by the triumvirs. (2) M. AEMILIUS, the triumvir, son of the M. Lepidus, consul B.C. 78, who took up arms to rescind the laws of Sulla, but was defeated by Pompey and Catulus. The son was praetor in 49, and supported Caesar in the Civil War. In 46 he was consul with Caesar, and in 44 he received from the latter the government of Narbonese Gaul and Nearer Spain. He was in the neighbourhood of Rome at the time of the dictator's death; and having the command of an army, he was able to render M. Antony efficient assistance. Lepidus was now chosen pontifex maximus, which dignity had become vacant by Caesar's death, and then repaired to his provinces of Gaul and Spain. Antony, after his defeat at Mutina (43), fled to Lepidus, who espoused his cause against the Senate. They crossed the Alps at the head of a powerful army, and were joined in the north of Italy by Octavian (afterwards Augustus). In the month of October the celebrated Second Triumvirate was formed, by which the Roman world was divided between Augustus, Antony, and Lepidus. In the fresh division of the provinces after the battle of Philippi (42), Lepidus received Africa, where he remained till 36. In this year Augustus summoned him to Sicily to assist him in the war against Sex. Pompey. Lepidus obeyed; but, tired of being treated as a subordinate, he resolved to make an effort to acquire Sicily for himself. He was easily subdued by Augustus, who spared his life, but deprived him of his triumvirate, his army, and his provinces; and commanded that he should live at

Lepidus, the Triumvir. (Duruy.)

Circeii, under strict surveillance. He allowed him, however, to retain the office of pontifex maximus. He was not privy to the conspiracy which his son formed to assassinate Augustus in 30. He died in 13. Augustus succeeded him as pontifex maximus.

Lepontii. An Alpine people, dwelling near the sources of the Rhine, on the southern slope of the St. Gothard and the Simplon. Their name is still retained in the Val Loventina. Their chief town was Oscela (Domo d'Ossola).

Lepreum (Λέπρεον). A town of Elis in Triphylia, situated forty stadia from the sea (Herod. iv. 148). Its name was derived from Leprea, daughter of Pyrgeus, or from Lepreus, son of Poseidon, and rival of Heracles, by whom he was slain (Pausan. v. 5, 4).

Leptĭnes (Λεπτίνης). An Athenian, known only as the proposer of a law taking away all special exemptions from the burden of public charges (ἀτέλειαι τῶν λειτουργιῶν), against which the oration of Demosthenes is directed, usually known as the Oration against Leptines, B.C. 355. The argument of Demosthenes is directed to the repeal of the law, and was successful in its object. See DEMOSTHENES.

Leptis (Λεπτίς). (1) LEPTIS MAGNA or NEAPŎLIS, a city on the coast of North Africa, between the Syrtes, east of Abrotonum, was a Phœnician colony, with a flourishing commerce, though it possessed no harbour. With Abrotonum and Oea it formed the African Tripolis. It was the birthplace of the emperor Septimius Severus. (2) LEPTIS MINOR or PARVA, usually called simply LEPTIS, a Phœnician colony on the coast of Byzacium in North Africa.

Lepton. See OBOLUS.

Leria. A variety of *limbus* (q. v.).

Lerīna or **Planasia**. A small island in the Mediterranean, on the coast of Gallia Narbonensis, south of Nicaea (Nice) (Tac. *Ann.* i. 3).

Lerna (Λέρνα) or **Lerné** (Λέρνη). A district in Argolis, not far from Argos, in which was a marsh and a small river of the same name. It was celebrated as the place where Heracles (q. v.) killed the Lernaean Hydra.

Lernaea (τὰ Λερναῖα). Mysteries in honour of Dionysus and Demeter, celebrated at Lerna in Argolis (Pausan. ii. 36, 37; viii. 15).

Lernaean Hydra. See HERACLES.

Leros (Λέρος). A small island, one of the Sporades, opposite to the mouth of the Sinus Iassius, on the coast of Caria (Herod. v. 125). Here the sisters of Meleager were said to have been transformed into guinea-pigs (μελεαγρίδες). See MELEAGER.

Lesbia. See CATULLUS; CLODIA.

Lesbōnax (Λεσβῶναξ). (1) A Greek rhetorician who lived early in the first century of our era. He composed political declamations on imaginary topics. Two of these have come down to us, exhorting the Athenians in the Peloponnesian War to be bold in battle against the Thebans and the Spartans. They have been separately edited by Orelli (Leipzig, 1820). (2) A Greek grammarian of uncertain date, though later than the preceding. There exists a work of his on figures of grammar (Περὶ Σχημάτων). See R. Müller, *De Lesbonacte Grammatico* (1890).

Lesbos (Λέσβος). A large island in the Aegaean, off the coast of Mysia in Asia Minor. It was colonized by Aeolians, who founded in it an Hexapolis, consisting of the six cities Mitylené, Methymna, Eresus, Pyrrha, Antissa, and Arisbé, afterwards reduced to five through the destruction of Arisbé by the Methymnaeans. The chief facts in the history of Lesbos are connected with its principal city, Mitylené. (See MITYLENÉ.) The island is most important in the early history of Greece as the native region of the early school of lyric poetry. It was the birthplace of the poets Terpander, Alcaeus, Sappho, and Arion, of the sage Pittacus, of the historian Hellanicus, and of the philosophers Theophrastus and Phanias. See Newton, *Travels and Discoveries in the Levant*, 2 vols. (1865); Koldewey, *Die Antiken Baureste der Insel Lesbos;* and Tozer, *Islands of the Aegean* (1890).

Lesbus (Λέσβος). A son of Lapithus, grandson of Aeolus, who married Methymna, daughter of Macareus. He succeeded his father-in-law, and gave his name to the island over which he reigned.

Lesché (λέσχη). A word of uncertain etymology, perhaps connected with λέγω (Curt. *Gk. Etym.* 366), and denoting a lounging-place, a resort for idlers, such as the porticoes at Rome, the bakeshops, and the bath-houses. In the Dorian countries it was the name of a sort of club-room (Plut. *Lyc.* 25). See Curtius, *Hist. of Greece*, Engl. trans., i. p. 205.

Lesches (Λέσχης) or **Lescheus** (Λέσχευς). A Cyclic poet, a native of Mitylené or Pyrrha, in the island of Lesbos, and considerably later than Arctinus. The best authorities concur in placing him in the time of Archilochus, or about B.C. 708–676. Hence the account which we find in ancient authors, of a contest between Arctinus and Lesches, can only mean that the latter competed with the earlier poet in treating the same subjects. His poem, in four books, which was attributed by many to Homer, and, besides, to very different authors, was called the "Little Iliad" (Ἰλιὰς Μικρά), and was clearly intended as a supplement to the great *Iliad*. It is learned from Aristotle (*Poët.* 23) that it comprised the events before the fall of Troy, the fate of Aiax, the exploits of Philoctetes, Neoptolemus, and Odysseus, which led to the taking of the city, as well as the account of the destruction of Troy itself; which statement is confirmed by numerous fragments. The last part of this (like the first part of the poem of Arctinus) was called the "Destruction of Troy" (Ἰλίου Πέρσις), from which Pausanias makes several quotations with reference to the sacking of Troy and the partition and carrying away of the prisoners. See CYCLICI POETAE; HOMERUS.

Lethaeus (Ληθαῖος). (1) A river of Ionia emptying into the Meander. (2) A river of Crete.

Lethé (Λήθη, "the river of oblivion"). A river of Hades (q. v.), out of which the souls of the departed drink oblivion of all their early existence. Oblivion was also personified in a goddess called by Hesiod the daughter of Eris (*Theog.* 227).

Leto (Λητώ), called by the Romans **Latōna**. According to Hesiod, a daughter of the Titan Coeus and Phoebé, a sister of Asteria. She was the mother of Apollo and Artemis by Zeus, to whom she was married before Heré. Homer likewise calls her the mother of Apollo and Artemis by Zeus; he mentions her in the story of Niobé, who paid so dearly for her conduct towards Leto, and he also describes her as the friend of the Trojans in the war with the Greeks. In later writers these elements of her story are variously embellished, for they do not describe her as the lawful wife of Zeus, but merely as his mistress, who was persecuted by Heré during her pregnancy. All the world being afraid of receiving Leto on account of their dread of Heré, she wandered about till she came to Delos, which was then a floating island, and bore the name of Asteria or Ortygia. When Leto arrived there, Zeus fastened it by adamantine chains to the bottom of the sea, that it might be a secure resting-place for his beloved, and here she gave birth to Apollo and Artemis. The tradition is also related with various other modifications. Some said that Zeus changed Leto into a quail (ὄρτυξ), and that in this state she arrived in the floating island, which was hence called Ortygia. Others related that Zeus was enamoured of Asteria, but that she, being metamorphosed into a bird, flew across the sea; that she was then changed into a rock, which, for a long time, lay under the surface of the sea; and that this rock arose from the waters and received Leto when she was pursued by Python. Leto was generally worshipped only in conjunction with her children. Delos was the chief seat of her worship, and in the sanctuary devoted to her honour she was represented by a shapeless wooden image. See APOLLO; DAEDALA.

It is probable that the name of Leto belongs to the same class of words as the Greek λήθη and the *lateo*, as typifying night. Leto would therefore signify "the obscure" or "concealed," not as a physical power, but as a divinity yet quiescent and invisible, from whom issued the visible divinity with all his splendour and brilliancy. This view is supported by the account of her genealogy given by Hesiod. (See Preller, *Röm. Myth.* i. 190; Lang, *Myth, Ritual*, etc., ii. 199.) From their mother Apollo is frequently *Letoïus* or *Latoïus*, and Artemis (Diana), *Letoïa*, *Letoïs*, *Latoïs*, or *Latoë*.

Letter-carriers. See TABELLARIUS.

Letters. (1) See ALPHABET. (2) See EPISTOLA.

Leuca (τὰ Λευκά). A town at the extremity of the Iapygian Promontory in Calabria with a foul-smelling spring, under which tradition made the giants slain by Heracles to have been buried (Strabo, p. 281).

Leucae (Λεῦκαι) and **Leuca** (Λεύκη). A small town on the coast of Ionia in Asia Minor, near Phocaea, built by the Persian general Tachos in B.C. 352. Here was fought a battle between the Roman consul Licinius Crassus and Aristonicus in B.C. 131.

Leucas (Λευκάς sc. πέτρα) or **Leucadia** (Λευκαδία). The modern Santa Maura. An island in the Ionian Sea, off the western coast of Acarnania, about twenty miles in length and from five to eight miles in breadth. It derived its name from the numerous calcareous hills which cover its surface. It was originally united to the mainland at its northeastern extremity by a narrow isthmus. Homer speaks of it as a peninsula, and mentions its well-fortified town Nericus. It was at that time inhabited by the Teleboans and Leleges. Subsequently the Corinthians under Cypselus, between B.C. 665 and 625, founded a new town called Leucas. They also cut a canal through the isthmus, and thus converted the peninsula into an island. This canal was afterwards filled up by deposits of sand, but was opened again by the Romans. At present the channel is dry in some parts, and has from three to four feet of water in others. During the war between Philip and the Romans, Leucas was the place where the meetings of the Acarnanian League were held. The other towns of the island were Hellomenum and Phara.

At the southern extremity of the island, opposite Cephallenia, was the celebrated promontory, variously called LEUCAS, LEUCĀTAS, LEUCĀTES, or LEUCĀTĒ, on which was a temple of Apollo Leucadius. At the annual festival of the god it was the custom to cast down a criminal from this promontory into the sea; birds were attached to him in order to break his fall; and if he reached the sea uninjured, boats were ready to pick him up. This appears to have been an expiatory rite; and it gave rise to the well-known story that lovers leaped from this rock in order to seek relief from the pangs of love. Thus Sappho is said to have leaped down from this rock when in love with Phaon. See SAPPHO.

Leucātē (Λευκάτας). See LEUCAS.

Leucé (Λευκή). An island in the Euxine Sea, near the mouth of the Borysthenes. It derived its name from its white, sandy shores. According to the poets, the souls of the ancient heroes were placed here as in the Elysian fields, and enjoyed perpetual felicity. Here, too, the shade of Achilles is fabled to have been united to that of Helen.

Leuci. A people in the southeastern part of Gallia Belgica, south of the Mediomatrici, between the Matrona and Mosella. Their chief town was Tullum (Toul).

Leuci (Albi) Montes. A range of snow-covered mountains in the western part of Crete.

Leucippé. The sister of Alcithoë, and with her changed into a bat. See ALCITHOË.

Leucippĭdes (Λευκιππίδες). See LEUCIPPUS (2).

Leucippus (Λεύκιππος). (1) Son of Oenomaüs, the lover of Daphné. (2) Son of Perieres, prince of the Messenians, and father of Phoebé and Hilaïra, usually called Leucippides, who were betrothed to Idas and Lynceus, the sons of Aphareus, but were carried off by Castor and Pollux, who married them. (3) A Grecian philosopher, the founder of the atomic theory of philosophy, which was more fully developed by Democritus (Diog. Laërt. ix. 30, 34). His date is uncertain. See DEMOCRITUS; EPICURUS.

Leucon (Λεύκων). (1) The son of Poseidon or Athamas and Themisto, and father of Erythrus and Evippé. (2) A powerful king of Bosporus, who reigned B.C. 393–353. He was in close alliance with the Athenians, whom he supplied with corn in great abundance, and who, in return for his services, admitted him and his sons to the citizenship of Athens (Diod. xiv. 93). (3) An Athenian poet of the old comedy, a contemporary and rival of Aristophanes (Suidas, s. v.).

Leuconoë (Λευκονόη). The same as Leucippé (q. v.).

Leucopĕtra (Λευκοπέτρα). The modern Capo dell' Armi; a promontory in the southwest of Bruttium, on the Sicilian Strait, and a few miles south of Rhegium. It derived its name from the white colour of its rocks.

Leucŏphrys (Λευκόφρυς). (1) A city of Caria, close to a curious lake of warm water, and having a renowned temple of Artemis Leucophryné (Xen. *Hell.* iii. 2, 19). (2) Another name for the island of Tenedos (q. v.).

Leucosia (Λευκωσία) or **Leucasia.** The modern Piana; a small island in the south of the Gulf of Paestum, off the coast of Lucania, said to have been called after one of the Sirens.

Leucosȳri (Λευκόσυροι—i. e. White Syrians). A name given by the Greeks to the inhabitants of Cappadocia, who were of the Syrian race, in contradistinction to the Syrian tribes of a darker colour beyond the Taurus. Later, the name was applied to the people in the north of the country between the rivers Halys and Iris (Xen. *Anab.* v. 6).

Leucothĕa (Λευκοθέα). The name of the deified Ino. See INO.

Leuctra (τὰ Λεῦκτρα). A small town in Boeotia, on the road from Plataeae to Thespiae, memorable for the victory of Epaminondas and the Thebans over the Spartans in B.C. 371. See EPAMINONDAS.

Leuctrum (Λεῦκτρον). (1) A town of Messenia, on the coast, sixty stadia from Cardamyle (Pausan. iv. 26). In consequence of its frontier situation, it became a source of dispute between the Messenians and Laconians. Philip, the son of Amyntas, who acted as umpire, awarded the place to the Messenians. It is called Leuctra by Thucydides (v. 54) and Xenophon. The latter informs us it was situated above the promontory of Malea. It was said to have been founded by Pelops. (2) A small town of Achaia, on the Sinus Corinthiacus, above Aegium, and in the vicinity of Rhypae, on which latter place it was dependent (Pausan. vii. 24). (3) A town of Arcadia, below Megalopolis (Pausan. viii. 27).

Levee. See SALUTATIO.

Levy. See DILECTUS; EXERCITUS.

Lex. (1) A statute; a rule of law (*ius*) laid down by some authorized organ of the State. In the royal period the kings are said to have exercised legislative power (whether the assent of the Comitia Curiata was required, is disputed; cf. Dionysius, 4, 13; *Dig.* 1, 2, 2, §§ 1, 2); but the so-called *leges regiae* seems to be mainly rules of the old religious law formulated by the priests. A collection of the *leges regiae*, made towards the end of the Republic by Sextus Papirius, was called, from its editor, the *ius Papirianum* (*Dig.* 1, 2, 2, § 2; 50, 16, 144). With the establishment of the Republic the initiative in legislation passed to the magistrates, but their proposals (*rogationes*) required the assent of the Comitia Centuriata (*uti rogas* = yes; *antiquo* = no). All the earlier leges of the Republic, including the Twelve Tables, were thus enacted. The tribunes might similarly propose bills to the assembly of the *plebs;* but these, if ratified (*plebiscita*), originally bound the plebeians only. By a *lex Hortensia* (B.C. 286) *plebiscita* became binding on the whole people, and the Comitia Tributa thus obtained concurrent legislative power. In the last centuries of the Republic the *plebiscita* were more numerous and more important than the leges voted by the Comitia Centuriata. Within the limits of their respective powers, resolves of the Senate and edicts of the magistrates had also the force of laws. In the Empire all legislative power was practically vested from the outset (by the *lex de imperio*, also called *lex regia*) in the emperor. Bills were still submitted by Augustus to the popular assembly and by his successors to the Senate; but the imperial measures were invariably approved, and the jurists often cited laws voted by the Senate not as *senatus consulta*, but as *orationes principis*. The emperors had also the full *ius edicendi*, or right of issuing edicts, which had been exercised by the republican magistrates. As late as the third century, however, the jurists confined the term *leges*, in the stricter sense, to the enactments of the Comitia Centuriata, distinguishing between these and all other forms of law (cf. Gaius Iust. i. 5; *Dig.* 1, 1, 7, pr.; 1, 4, 1, pr.). In a wider sense *plebiscita, Senatus consulta, edicta praetorum*, and *constitutiones principum* were all termed *leges* (cf. *Dig.* 9, 2, 1, § 1; 14, 6, 9, § 4; 38, 8, 1, § 2; 1, 4, 1, § 1). In the later Empire *leges* designated primarily the imperial constitutions, all the earlier statutes having become a part of the *ius* (cf. IUS [1]). A complete collection of all the older leges and fragments of leges that have come down to us in texts or inscriptions (including reconstructions of the *leges regiae* and the Twelve Tables) is to be found in Bruns and Mommsen, *Fontes Iuris Romani Antiqui* (5th ed. 1887).

(2) In a looser sense any rule of law, even of customary origin, is occasionally termed *lex* (cf. *Dig.* 1, 5, 24; 1, 3, 32, § 1); and in the later imperial constitutions *leges* is occasionally used in a collective sense, as equivalent to *ius* or the whole body of the law (so *legum scientia, legum prudentes*). (3) *Lex* was also used, from the earliest period, to denote the rule which private persons impose upon themselves and their successors by contracts or other legal acts. So *lex contractus* (*Dig.* 16, 3, 24), *lex donationis* (*ib.* 1, 5, 22), for the provisions or conditions of a contract, gift, etc., and *legum testamento dicere* (*ib.* 28, 1, 14). *Lex commissoria* was a clause in a contract by which one of the parties reserved the right of annulling the contract. So in sales it was frequently agreed that if the price were not paid at a certain time *res inempta fuerit.* In mortgages *lex commissoria* was an agreement that if the debtor failed to pay at a stipulated time the mortgagee need not sell the property and account for any surplus, but might simply appropriate it. Such an agreement Constantine declared null.

The following list of the principal laws is given for the convenience of the student:

ACILIA. See REPETUNDAE.

ACILIA CALPURNIA or CALPURNIA. See AMBITUS.

AEBUTIA, of about B.C. 170, which, with two *Iuliae leges*, put an end to the *legis actiones*, except in certain cases. See IUDEX; ACTIO.

This, or another law of the same name, prohibited the proposer of a law which created any office or power (*curatio ac potestas*) from having such office or power, and even excluded his colleague, *cognati* and *affines* (Cic. *De Domo*, 20, 51).

AELIA. This law, and a *Fufia lex*, passed about the end of the first century B.C., gave to all the magistrates the *obnuntiatio*, or power of preventing or dissolving the Comitia, by observing the omens and declaring them to be unfavourable.

AELIA SENTIA. This law (of A.D. 4) contained various provisions as to the manumission of slaves. See MANUMISSIO.

AEMILIA. A law passed in the dictatorship of Mamercus Aemilius (B.C. 433), by which the censors were elected for a year and a half instead of a whole *lustrum*. After this law they had accordingly only a year and a half allowed them for holding the census and farming out the public works.

AEMILIA BAEBIA. See CORNELIA BAEBIA.

AEMILIA LEPĬDI, AEMILIA SCAURI. See SUMTUARIAE LEGES.

AGRARIAE. See AGRARIAE LEGES.

AMBĬTUS. See AMBITUS.

ANNĀLES. Statutes prescribing the age at which a man might be a candidate for the various offices. The first law of this kind was a *lex Villia* (B.C. 80).

ANTIA. See SUMTUARIAE LEGES.

ANTONIAE, the name of various enactments proposed or passed by the influence of M. Antonius, after the death of the dictator I. Caesar. Another law that was promulgated allowed an appeal to the people after conviction for *vis* or *maiestas.* Various other measures proposed by M. Antonius are mentioned by Cicero, Dio Cassius, and Appian.

APULĒIA (of B.C. 102), gave a surety an action against his cosureties for whatever he had paid above his share.

APULĒIA AGRARIA, proposed by the tribune L. Apuleius Saturninus, B.C. 101 (Livy, *Epit.* 69).

APULĒIA FRUMENTARIA, proposed about the same time by the same tribune.

APULĒIA MAIESTĀTIS. See MAIESTAS.

AQUILIA. A law relating to *damnum* (q. v.).

ATERNIA TARPĒIA (B.C. 454). This law empowered all magistrates to fine persons who resisted their authority; but it fixed the highest fine at two sheep and thirty oxen. See MULTA.

ATIA DE SACERDOTIIS (B.C. 63), proposed by the tribune T. Atius Labienus, repealed the *lex Cornelia de sacerdotiis.*

ATILIA. See IULIA LEX ET TITIA; TUTOR.

ATINIA (of perhaps B.C. 198), allowed no usucapion in a stolen thing. See USUCAPIO.

ATINIA, of uncertain date, was a *plebiscitum* which gave the rank of senator to a tribune. The measure perhaps originated with C. Atinius, who was tribune B.C. 130 (Gell. xiv. 8).

AURELIA. See TRIBUNUS.

AURELIA IUDICIARIA. See IUDEX.

BAEBIA (B.C. 192), enacted that four praetors and six praetors should be chosen alternately; but the law was not observed (Livy, xl. 44).

CAECILIA DE CENSŌRIBUS or CENSORIA (B.C. 52), proposed by Metellus Scipio, repealed a *Clodia lex* (B.C. 58) which had prescribed certain regular forms of proceeding for the censors in exercising their functions as inspectors of morals, and had required the concurrence of both censors to inflict the *nota censoria*. When a senator had been already convicted before an ordinary court, the law permitted the censors to remove him from the Senate in a summary way.

CAECILIA DE VECTIGALĬBUS (B.C. 62), released lands and harbours in Italy from the payment of taxes and dues (*portoria*). The only vectigal remaining after the passing of this law was the *vicesima*. See PORTORIUM.

CAECILIA DIDIA (B.C. 88) forbade the proposing of a *lex Satura*, on the ground that the people might be compelled either to vote for something which they did not approve, or to reject something which they did approve, if it was proposed to them in this manner. This law was not always operative.

CAELIA TABELLARIA. See TABELLARIAE LEGES.

CALPURNIA DE AMBĬTU. See AMBITUS.

CALPURNIA DE CONDICTIŌNE. See ACTIO.

CALPURNIA DE REPETUNDIS. See REPETUNDAE.

CANULĒIA (B.C. 445) established *conubium* between the patres and plebs, which had been refused by the law of the Twelve Tables (Livy, iv. 1, 6).

CASSIA (B.C. 104), proposed by the tribune L. Cassius Longinus, did not allow a person to remain a senator who had been convicted in a *iudicium populi*, or whose *imperium* had been abrogated by the people.

CASSIA, empowered the dictator Caesar to add to the number of the patricians, to prevent their extinction (Tac. *Ann.* xi. 25).

CASSIA AGRARIA, proposed by the consul Sp. Cassius, B.C. 486.

CASSIA TABELLARIA. See TABELLARIAE LEGES.

CASSIA TERENTIA FRUMENTARIA (B.C. 73), for the distribution of corn among the poor citizens and the purchasing of it.

CINCIA or MUNERĀLIS, a plebiscitum carried by the tribune M. Cincius Alimentus in B.C. 204. It provided (1) that gifts beyond a maximum amount should not be made; but imposed no penalty for the violation of this provision, and was therefore a *lex imperfecta;* (2) it prescribed a set form of gift.

CLAUDIA, a law passed in the time of the emperor Claudius, taking away the *agnatorum tutela* in the case of women, not *in potestate* or *in manu* (Gaius, i. 57, 171–72).

CLODIAE, the name of various *plebiscita*, proposed by Clodius when tribune, B.C. 58.

CLODIA DE AUSPICIIS prevented the magistratus from dissolving the Comitia Tributa by declaring that the auspices were unfavourable. This law, therefore, repealed the Aelia and Fufia. It also enacted that a law might be passed on the *dies fasti*. See AELIA LEX.

CLODIA DE CENSORĬBUS. See CAECILIA.

CLODIA DE CIVĬBUS ROMĀNIS INTEREMPTIS, to the effect that *qui civem Romanum indemnatum interemisset ei aqua et igni interdiceretur.* It was in consequence of this law that the interdict was pronounced against Cicero, who considers the whole proceeding as a *privilegium* (q. v.).

CLODIA FRUMENTARIA, by which the corn, which had formerly been sold to the poor citizens at a low rate, was given. See FRUMENTARIAE LEGES.

CLODIA DE SODALITATĬBUS or DE COLLEGIIS, restored the *sodalicia*, which had been abolished by a *senatus consultum* of the year B.C. 64, and permitted the formation of new *sodalicia*.

There were other so-called *leges Clodiae*, which were, however, *privilegia*.

COELIA. See TABELLARIAE LEGES.

CORNELIAE. Various leges passed in the dictatorship of Sulla, and by his influence, are so called.

AGRARIA, by which many of the inhabitants of Etruria and Latium were deprived of the complete *civitas* and retained only the *commercium*, and a large part of their lands were made *publicum* and given to military colonists.

DE FALSIS. See FALSUM.

DE INIURIIS. See INIURIA.

IUDICIARIA. See IUDEX.

MAIESTATIS. See MAIESTAS.

NUMMARIA. See FALSUM.

DE PROSCRIPTIŌNE. See PROSCRIPTIO.

DE PARRICIDIO. See CORNELIA LEX DE SICARIIS.

DE SACERDOTIIS. See SACERDOTIUM.

DE SICARIIS ET DE VENEFĬCIS. A law passed about B.C. 81 inflicting penalties not only for actual killing, but for carrying weapons with a murderous purpose, for arson, for selling poisons for the destruction of human life, for perjury in a capital case, etc. Under Antoninus Pius this law was further extended to cover the killing of slaves without just cause (see SERVUS), and the castration of men.

SUMTUARIAE. See SUMPTUARIAE LEGES.

TESTAMENTARIA. See FALSUM.

UNCIARIA appears to have been a law which lowered the rate of interest, and to have been passed about the same time with the *leges sumtuariae* of Sulla.

DE VADIMONIO. See VADIMONIUM.

There are other *leges Corneliae*, such as that *de sponsoribus* (see INTERCESSIO), which may be laws of L. C. Cinna.

There were also *leges Corneliae* which were proposed by the tribune C. Cornelius about B.C. 67, and limited the edictal power by compelling the praetors *ius dicere ex edictis suis perpetuis*. See EDICTUM.

Another law of the same tribune enacted that no one *legibus solveretur*, unless such a measure was agreed on in a meeting of the Senate at which two hundred members were present, and afterwards approved by the people; and it enacted that no tribune should put his veto on such a *senatus consultum*.

There was also a *lex Cornelia* concerning the wills of those Roman citizens who died in captivity (*apud hostes*). See LEGATUM.

DE VI PUBLĬCA. See VIS PUBLICA.

CORNELIA BAEBIA DE AMBĬTU, proposed by the consuls P. Cornelius Cethegus and M. Baebius Tamphilus, B.C. 181. This law is sometimes, but erroneously, attributed to the consuls of the preceding year, L. Aemilius and Cn. Baebius. See AMBITUS.

CORNELIA CAECILIA DE CN. POMPĒIO. A law of B.C. 57 giving Pompey extraordinary powers for five years for the management of the corn supply of Rome (Cic. *Ad Att.* iv. 1, 7).

DECEMVIRĀLIS. See TWELVE TABLES.

DIDIA. See SUMPTUARIAE LEGES.

DOMITIA DE SACERDOTIIS. See SACERDOTIUM.

DUILIA (B.C. 449), a *plebiscitum* proposed by the tribune Duilius, which enacted *qui plebem sine tribunis reliquisset, quique magistratum sine provocatione creasset, tergo ac capite puniretur* (Livy, iii. 55).

DUILIA MAENIA *de unciario fenore*, B.C. 357. The same tribunes, Duilius and Maenius, carried a measure which was intended in future to prevent such unconstitutional proceedings as the enactment of a law by the soldiers out of Rome, on the proposal of the consul.

DUODĔCIM TABULĀRUM. See TWELVE TABLES.

FABIA DE PLAGIO. See PLAGIUM.

FALCIDIA. See LEGATUM.

FANNIA. See SUMPTUARIAE LEGES.

FLAMINIA was an agrarian law for the distribution of lands in Picenum, proposed by the tribune C. Flaminius in B.C. 228 according to Cicero, or in B.C. 232 according to Polybius.

FLAVIA AGRARIA (B.C. 60), for the distribution of lands among Pompey's soldiers, proposed by the tribune L. Flavius, who committed the consul Caecilius Metellus to prison for opposing it.

FRUMENTARIAE. Various leges were so called which had for their object the distribution of grain among the people at a low price or gratuitously. See FRUMENTARIAE LEGES.

FUFIA DE RELIGIŌNE (B.C. 61) was a *privilegium* which related to the trial of Clodius.

FUFIA CANINIA (about A.D. 4) limited the number of slaves to be manumitted by testament. See MANUMISSIO.

FURIA TESTAMENTARIA. See LEGATUM.

GABINIA TABELLARIA. See TABELLARIAE LEGES.

There were various Gabinian laws, some of which were *privilegia*, as that for conferring extraordinary power on Cn. Pompeius for conducting the war against the pirates.

A Gabinian law (B.C. 58) forbade all loans of money at Rome to *legationes* from foreign parts (*Salaminii cum Romae versuram facere vellent, non poterant, quod lex Gabinia vetabat*). The object of the law was to prevent money being borrowed for the purpose of bribing the senators at Rome.

GELLIA CORNELIA (B.C. 72), which gave to Cn. Pompeius the extraordinary power of conferring Roman citizenship on Spaniards in Spain, with the advice of his council (*de consilii sententia*).

GENUCIA (B.C. 343) forbade altogether the taking of interest for the use of money. See FENUS.

HIERONĬCA was not a law properly so called. Before the Roman conquest of Sicily, the payment of the tenths of wine, oil, and other produce had been fixed by Hiero, and the Roman quaestors, in letting these tenths to farm, followed the practice which they found established. See DECUMA.

HORATIA, proposed by M. Horatius (B.C. 449), made the persons of the tribunes, the aediles, and others *sacrosancti*. Another *lex Horatia* mentioned by Gellius (vi. 7, 2–4) was a *privilegium*.

HORTENSIA DE PLEBISCĪTIS. See PLEBISCITUM.

Another *lex Hortensia* enacted that the *nundinae*, which had hitherto been *feriae*, should be *dies fasti*. This was done for the purpose of accommodating the inhabitants of the country.

ICILIA (B.C. 456), by which the Aventine Hill was assigned to the plebs as a dwelling-place. This was the first instance of the public land being assigned to the plebs.

Another *lex Icilia*, proposed by the tribune Sp. Icilius, B.C. 469, had for its object to prevent all interruption to the tribunes while acting in the discharge of their duties. In some cases the penalty was death.

IULIAE. Most of these were passed in the time of Iulius Caesar and Augustus. The following are the most important:

AGRARIA (B.C. 59), providing for the assignment of lands in Campania to the veterans of Pompey and to poor citizens, especially to those who had three children.

DE ADULTERIIS. See ADULTERIUM.

DE ANNŌNA, against those who tried to raise the price of grain—to "corner the market."

DE BONIS CEDENDIS. See BONORUM CESSIO.

DE FENŌRE (B.C. 49), compromising the claims of creditors and debtors (Caes. *B. C.* iii. 1).

DE MARITANDIS ORDINĬBUS. See IULIA ET PAPIA POPPAEA.

DE PROVINCIIS, limiting the praetorian governor of a province to one year and the consular to two.

IULIAE IUDICIARIAE, one depriving the *tribuni aerarii* of their share in the *iudicia publica* (Suet. *Iul.* 41) and the other instituting a select list of *iudices* for trying civil cases (Suet. *Aug.* 32).

IULIA MAIESTĀTIS. See MAIESTAS.

IULIA MUNICIPĀLIS, also called the TABŬLA HERACLEENSIS, found on a bronze in the fragments at Tarentum (Heraclea) in 1732 and 1735, and now in the Naples Museum. On one side is a Greek ψήφισμα of the town of Heraclea; on the other is a part of a Roman law containing various police regulations of the city of Rome, and rules for the constitution of colonies, muncipalities, etc. A lithographed copy of the table is given by Ritschl, tab. xxxiii., xxxiv. For the text, see Spangenberg's *Monumenta Legalia* (1830).

IULIA ET PAPIA POPPAEA. Augustus appears in his sixth consulate (B.C. 28) to have issued an edict (Tac. *Ann.* iii. 28) on the subject of marriage, which he followed up (B.C. 18) by proposing a law to the Senate regulating certain marriages, imposing disabilities on unmarried persons (*caelibes*), and establishing rewards for those who had married and reared children (Dio Cass. liv. 16). This he carried, with difficulty, through the Senate; but, apparently owing to the organized resistance of the *equites*, it was rejected at the Comitia (Suet. *Aug.* 34). Towards the end of his reign, however (A.D.

3), he succeeded in passing it, with its rewards increased and its penalties mitigated; it is referred to in the *Carmen Saeculare* of Horace, which was written B.C. 17, and is mentioned under the name *lex Iulia de maritandis ordinibus* in *Dig.* 38, 11; 23, 2. The opposition of the knights was overcome by a provision that it should not come into force for three, a period subsequently extended to six, years; and taking advantage of this, Augustus passed, in A.D. 9, another statute (called Papia Poppaea from the *consules suffecti* for the year, M. Papius Mutilus and Q. Poppaeus Secundus: Dio Cass. lvi. 1–10), containing further enactments on the same subject. Sometimes they are cited by reference to their various chapters—e. g. *lex Caducaria*, *lex Decimaria*, *lex Miscella*, etc.

Many commentaries were written on these laws by the Roman jurists, of which considerable fragments are preserved in the Digest. Gaius wrote fifteen books, Ulpian twenty, and Paulus at least ten. The joint statute contained at least thirty-five chapters (*Dig.* 22, 2, 19); but, as a rule, it is impossible to say to which of the two laws, included under the general title of *lex Iulia et Papia Poppaea*, the several provisions, as now known to us, belong.

Among the enactments of these statutes are the following:

(*a*) Prohibition of certain marriages under penalties: viz. of *ingenui* and *infames* (e. g. actresses and prostitutes); and of senators or their children with freedwomen, freedmen, and actors' daughters. Marriages between a senator or his issue and *libertini* were declared void by a *senatus consult* passed under M. Aurelius, and the rule was subsequently extended to actors and actresses (*Dig.* 42, 1).

(*b*) Avoidance of conditions against marriage annexed to legacies and inheritances.

(*c*) Provisions to encourage marriage. *Caelibes* were disabled by the *lex Iulia* from taking either as heirs or as legatees under a will, unless the testator was related to them within the sixth degree, or unless they married within 100 days. *Spadones* and Vestal Virgins were exempted from the operation of the statute, as were widows for twelve months, and divorced women for six. Again, the penalty of the statute could be evaded by an engagement to marry, if carried out within two years (Suet. *Oct.* 34). Finally, males were released from its provisions in this respect on attaining sixty, women on attaining fifty years of age; but a *senatus consultum Persicianum*, passed under Tiberius, enacted that they should be regarded as *caelibes* in perpetuity if they postponed marrying till so late in life. A *senatus consultum Claudianum* so far modified the strictness of the new rule as to give a man who married after sixty the same advantage that he would have had if he had married under sixty, provided he married a woman who was under fifty; but it was enacted by a *senatus consultum Calvisianum* under Nero, that if a woman over fifty married a husband under sixty, even the latter should not escape the disabilities imposed by the statute. Similarly, by the *lex Papia*, *orbi* (persons who had married, but had no children living) were disqualified from taking more than half of what was left them by way of either inheritance or legacy, unless related to the testator within the sixth degree. Males escaped the penalties of *orbitas* by having a single (even adoptive) child (Iuv. xix. 83, 86–89), but by a *senatus consultum Memmianum* adoption was deprived of this effect when resorted to merely in order to evade the statute; but women were not so well off, *ingenuae* being released only by three, *libertinae* only by four children. There were exceptions to these rules if the wife was under twenty or over fifty, or the husband under twenty-five or over sixty, and also if the husband was residing away from the wife *reipublicae causa*. Legacies and inheritances which could not be taken either in whole or part, owing to these provisions of the *lex Iulia* or *lex Papia Poppaea*, became *caduca* (see BONA CADUCA), the law upon which subject was considerably modified by these statutes.

(*d*) Among other provisions may be noticed the rule giving a preference to candidates for office according to the number of their children; the release of *ingenuae* with three and *libertinae* with four children from tutela; and of *libertini* with a certain number of children from *operarum obligationes* (*Dig.* 38, 1). The exemption of persons from discharging the office of tutor or curator *iure liberorum* was based on these statutes.

After the enactment of the *lex Papia Poppaea*, it became not unusual to obtain a grant of a fictitious *ius liberorum* by special favour from the Senate, and later from the emperor, whereby those who had no children, or not enough, were enabled to escape its disabilities and even enjoy most of its benefits. This privilege is mentioned in some inscriptions, on which the abbreviation I. L. H. (*ius liberorum habens*) sometimes occurs. The emperor Marcus Aurelius enacted that children should be registered by name within thirty days of their birth with the Praefectus Aerarii Saturni.

The penalties of *caelibatus* and *orbitas* were abolished by Constantine and his sons, and little is left of these statutes in the law of Justinian.

IULIA ET TITIA (about B.C. 31), assigning to the *praesides* of provinces the duty of appointing guardians for women and *impuberes* who were not in *patria potestate*, or already provided with one.

PAPIRIA. See PAPIRIA.

SUMPTUARIA. See SUMPTUARIAE LEGES.

THEATRĀLIS, allowing Roman knights, in case either they or their parents had ever had a knight's fortune, to sit in the fourteen rows of seats at the theatre set apart for *equites* by the *lex Roscia theatralis* (Suet. *Aug.* 40).

VICESIMARIA. See VICESIMA.

IUNIA DE PEREGRĪNIS, proposed B.C. 126 by M. Iunius Pennus, a tribune, banished *peregrini* from the city.

A law of C. Fannius, consul, B.C. 122, contained the same provisions respecting the Latini and Italici; and a law of C. Papius, perhaps B.C. 65, contained the same respecting all persons who were not domiciled in Italy.

IUNIA LICINIA. See LICINIA IUNIA.

IUNIA NORBĀNA, of uncertain date, but probably about A.D. 19, enacted that when a Roman citizen had manumitted a slave without the requisite formalities, the manumission should not in all cases be ineffectual, but the manumitted person should have the status of a Latinus. See LATINITAS; LIBERTUS.

IUNIA REPETUNDĀRUM. See REPETUNDAE.

IUNIA VELLĒIA (A.D. 10) allowed a *posthumus* to be instituted *heres*, if he should be born in the life-time of the testator. It also so far modified the old law that a person who, by the death of a *heres institutus*, after the testator had made his will, became a *heres quasi agnascendo*, did not break the will if he was instituted *heres*.

LAETORIA. See CURATOR.

Sometimes the law proposed by Volero for electing plebeian magistrates at the Comitia Tributa is cited as a lex Laetoria (Livy, ii. 56, 57).

LICINIA DE SODALICIIS. See AMBITUS.

LICINIA IUNIA or, as it is sometimes called, IUNIA ET LICINIA, passed in the consulship of L. Licinius Murena and Iunius Silanus, B.C. 62, enforced the Caecilia Didia, in connection with which it is sometimes mentioned.

LICINIA MUCIA DE CIVĬBUS REGUNDIS, passed in the consulship of L. Licinius Crassus and Q. Mucius Scaevola, B.C. 95, which enacted a strict examination as to the title to citizenship, and deprived of the exercise of civic rights all those who could not make out a good title to them. This measure partly led to the Marsic War.

LICINIA SUMTUARIA. See SUMPTUARIAE LEGES.

LICINIAE ROGATIŌNES. See ROGATIONES LICINIAE.

LIVIAE were various enactments proposed by the tribune M. Livius Drusus, B.C. 91, for establishing colonies in Italy and Sicily, distributing corn among the poor citizens at a low rate, and admitting the *foederatae civitates* to Roman citizenship. He is also said to have been the mover of a law for adulterating silver by mixing with it an eighth part of brass. Drusus was assassinated, and the Senate declared that all his laws were passed contrary to the auspices, and were therefore not at all.

MAENIA LEX is only mentioned by Cicero, who says that M. Curius compelled the patres *ante auctores fieri*, in the case of the election of a plebeian consul, "which," adds Cicero, "was a great thing to accomplish, as the *lex Maenia* was not yet passed." The law, therefore, required the *patres* to give their consent, at least to the election of a magistrate; or, in other words, to confer, or agree to confer, the *imperium* on the person whom the Comitia should elect. It was probably proposed by the tribune Maenius, B.C. 287.

MAIESTĀTIS. See MAIESTAS.

MANILIA, proposed by the tribune C. Manilius, B.C. 66, was a *privilegium*, by which was conferred on Pompey the command in the war against Mithridates. The law was supported by Cicero when praetor. See POMPEIUS.

The LEGES MANILIĀNAE, mentioned by Cicero, were evidently not leges proper, but probably forms which it was prudent for parties to observe in buying and selling.

MANLIA, also called LICINIA (B.C. 196), created the *triumviri epulones*.

MANLIA DE VICESĬMA. See VICESIMA.

MARCIA, probably about the year B.C. 352, against usury (Gaius, iv. 23).

MARIA, proposed by Marius when tribune, B.C. 119, for narrowing the *pontes* at elections. See PONS.

MENSIA. This law enacted that if a woman who was a Roman citizen (*civis Romana*) married a *peregrinus*, the offspring was a *peregrinus*. If there was *conubium* between the *peregrinus* and the woman, the children, according to the principle of *conubium*, were *peregrini*, as the legal effect of *conubium* was that children followed the condition of their father (*liberi semper patrem sequuntur*). If there were no *conubium*, the children, according to another rule of law, by which they followed the condition of the mother, would have been Roman citizens; and it was the object of the law to prevent this.

MINUCIA (B.C. 46) created the *triumviri mensarii*.

MUNERĀLIS. See CINCIA; IULIAE.

OGULNIA, proposed by the tribunes B.C. 300, increased the number of pontifices to eight and that of the augurs to nine; it also enacted that four of the pontifices and five of the augurs should be taken from the plebeians.

OPPIA (B.C. 215). See SUMPTUARIAE LEGES.

ORCHIA (B.C. 171). See SUMPTUARIAE LEGES.

OVINIA, of uncertain date, was a *plebiscitum*, which gave the censors certain powers in regulating the lists of the senators (*ordo senatorius*); the main object seems to have been to exclude all improper persons from the Senate, and to prevent their admission, if in other respects qualified.

PAPIA DE PEREGRĪNIS. See IUNIA DE PEREGRINIS.

PAPIA POPPAEA. See IULIAE LEGES.

A *lex Papia* on the manner of choosing the Vestal Virgins is mentioned by Gellius; but the reading appears to be doubtful, and perhaps it ought to be called *lex Popilia* (Gell. i. 12).

PAPIRIA or IULIA PAPIRIA DE MULTĀRUM AESTIMATIŌNE (B.C. 430) fixed a money value, as an equivalent for fines, which formerly were paid in sheep and cattle. Gellius and Festus make this valuation part of the Athenian law.

PAPIRIA (B.C. 89), by which the *as* was made *semuncialis*, one of the various enactments which tampered with the coinage.

PAPIRIA (B.C. 332), proposed by the praetor Papirius, gave the Acerrani the *civitas* without the *suffragium*. It was properly a *privilegium*, but is useful as illustrating the history of the extension of the *civitas Romana*.

PAPIRIA (B.C. 303) enacted that no *aedes* should be consecrated without a *plebiscitum* (*iniussu Plebis*).

PAPIRIA PLAUTIA, a *plebiscitum* of the year B.C. 89, enacted that all citizens and inhabitants of *foederatae civitalis* (q. v.) who at the date of the statute were domiciled in Italy should be qualified to obtain Roman citizenship on giving in their names to the *praetor urbanus* within sixty days (Cic. *Pro Archia*, 4, 7).

PAPIRIA POETELIA. See POETELIA.

PAPIRIA TABELLARIA. See TABELLARIAE LEGES.

PEDUCAEA (B.C. 114), a *plebiscitum*, seems to have been merely a *privilegium* relating to Vestal Virgins, and not a general law against incest.

PESULANIA provided that if an animal did any damage, the owner should make it good or give up the animal. There was a general provision to this effect in the Twelve Tables, and it might be inferred from Paulus that this law extended the provisions of the old law to dogs.

PETRĒIA, a law under this title, DE DECIMATIŌNE MILĬTUM, in case of mutiny, is mentioned by Appian. See DECIMATIO.

PETRONIA, probably passed in the reign of Augustus, and subsequently amended by various *senatus consulta*, forbade a master to deliver up his slave to fight with wild beasts. If, however, the master thought that his slave deserved such a punishment, he might take him before the authorities (*iudex*), who might condemn him to fight if he appeared to deserve it.

PINARIA related to the giving of a *iudex* within a limited time (Gaius, iv. 15).

PLAETORIA. See CURATOR.

PLAUTIA or PLOTIA DE VI. See VIS.

PLAUTIA or PLOTIA IUDICIARIA (B.C. 89) is mentioned by Asconius as having enacted that fifteen persons should be annually taken from each tribe to be placed in the list of *iudices*.

POETELIA (B.C. 358), a *plebiscitum*, and noted as the first law against *ambitus*. See AMBITUS.

POETELIA PAPIRIA (B.C. 326) made an important change in the liabilities of the *nexi*. See NEXUM.

POMPĒIAE. There were various leges so called:

POMPĒIA, proposed by Cn. Pompeius Strabo, the father of Cn. Pompeius Magnus, probably in his consulship (B.C. 89), gave the *ius Latii* or *Latinitas* to all the towns of the Transpadani, and probably the *civitas* to the Cispadani.

POMPĒIA DE AMBĬTU. See AMBITUS.

POMPĒIA DE IURE MAGISTRATUUM forbade a person to be a candidate for public offices (*petitio honorum*) who was not at Rome; but Iulius Caesar was excepted. This was, doubtless, the old law, but it had apparently become obsolete (Suet. *Iul.* 28).

POMPĒIA IUDICIARIA. See IUDEX.

POMPĒIA DE PARRICIDIIS. See CORNELIA DE SICARIIS; PARRICIDIUM.

POMPĒIA TRIBUNICIA (B.C. 70) restored the old *tribunicia potestas*, which Sulla had nearly destroyed. See TRIBUNUS.

POMPĒIA DE VI was a *privilegium*, and only referred to the case of Milo (q. v.).

POPILIA. See PAPIA.

PORCIA DE CAPĬTE CIVIUM or DE PROVOCATIŌNE (B.C. 197) enacted that a Roman citizen should not be scourged or put to death.

PORCIA DE PROVINCIIS (about B.C. 198). The passage in Livy (*Sumptus quos in cultum praetorum*, etc.) is supposed to refer to a Porcian law, to which the *plebiscitum de thermensibus* refers; and the words quoted by Cicero (*Ne quis emat mancipium*) are taken, as it is conjectured, from this Porcian law.

PUBLICIA permitted betting at certain games which required strength, as running and leaping.

PUBLILIA DE SPONSŌRIBUS. See INTERCESSIO.

PUBLILIAE of the dictator Q. Publilius Philo, B.C. 339. See PUBLILIAE LEGES.

PUBLILIAE LEGES of the tribune Q. Volero Publilius, B.C. 472. See PUBLILIAE LEGES.

PUPIA (B.C. 224), mentioned by Cicero, seems to have enacted that the Senate could not meet on days when the Comitia were held.

QUINTIA was a law proposed by T. Quintius Crispinus, consul B.C. 9, and enacted by the *populus* for the preservation of the aqueducts.

REGIA. See REGIA LEX.

REGIAE. See LEX.

REPETUNDĀRUM. See REPETUNDAE.

RHODIA. The Rhodians had a maritime code which was highly esteemed. Some of its provisions were adopted by the Romans, and have thus been incorporated into the maritime law of European states. Strabo speaks of the wise laws of Rhodes and their admirable policy, especially in naval matters; and Cicero to the same effect. The *Digest* contains so much of the *lex Rhodiorum* as relates to *iactus*, or the throwing overboard of goods in order to save the vessel or remainder of the cargo. This *lex Rhodiorum de Iactu* is not a law in the proper sense of the term. See Schryver, *Sur la Loi Rhodia de Iactu* (Brussels, 1884).

ROSCIA THEATRĀLIS, proposed by the tribune L. Roscius Otho (B.C. 67), which gave the *equites* a special place at the public spectacles in fourteen rows or seats (*in quattuordecim gradibus sive ordinibus*) next to the place of the senators, which was in the orchestra. This law also assigned a certain place to spendthrifts (*decoctores*). The phrase, *sedere in quattuordecim ordinibus*, is equivalent to having the proper *census equestris* which was required by the law. There are numerous allusions to this law, which is sometimes simply called the law of Otho, or referred to by his name.

RUBRIA. The province of Gallia Cisalpina ceased to be a province, and became a part of Italia about the year B.C. 49 or 42. When this change took place, it was necessary to provide for the administration of justice, as the usual modes of provincial administration would cease with the determination of the provincial form of government. This was effected by a law, the name of which is unknown, but a large part of it, on a bronze tablet, is preserved in the Museum at Parma. This law arranged the judiciary establishment of the former province, and appointed *duo viri* and *quattuor viri iure dicundo; a praefectus Mutinensis* is also mentioned in the law. In two passages of this law a *lex Rubria* is mentioned, which, according to some, is an earlier law, by which Mutina was made a *praefectura;* and, according to others, the *lex Rubria* is this very *lex de Cisalpina.* This subject is discussed by Savigny and by Puchta.

This law has been published several times; the text is lithographed in Ritschl's volume of inscriptions, i. taf. 32.

RUPILIAE LEGES (B.C. 131) were the regulations established by P. Rupilius and ten *legati* for the administration of the province of Sicily after the close of the first Servile War. They were made in pursuance of a *consultum* of the Senate. Cicero speaks of these regulations as a *decretum* of Rupilius, which, he says, they call *lex Rupilia;* but it was not a law proper. The powers given to the commissioners by the *lex Iulia municipalis* were of a similar kind.

SACRĀTAE, mentioned by Livy (ii. 33) and by Cicero (*De Leg.* ii. 7, 18). Leges were properly so called which had for their object to make a thing or person *sacer*. The *consecratio* was, in fact, the sanction by which a law was to be enforced. In the latter case, it was the opinion of the *jurisconsults* that the law did not make *sacrosancti* the persons for whose protection it was designed, but that it made *sacer* (*sacrum sanxit*) any one who injured them; and this interpretation is consistent with the terms of the law. An example of a *lex sacrata* is that making the tribunes of the people sacred (Livy, ii. 8).

A *lex sacrata militaria* is also mentioned by Livy.

SATŬRA. See LEX.

SCANTINIA, proposed by a tribune. The date and contents are not known, but its object was to suppress unnatural crimes. It existed in the time of Cicero. The *lex Iulia de adulteriis* considered this offence as included in *stuprum*, and it was punishable with a fine; but by the later imperial constitution the punishment was death (Suet. *Domit.* 8).

SCRIBONIA. The date and whole import of this law are not known; but it enacted that a right to *servitutes* should not be acquired by usucapion, from which it appears that the law was once different. See SERVITUS.

SEMPRONIA DE FENŎRE (B.C. 193) was a *plebiscitum* proposed by the tribune M. Sempronius, which enacted that the law (*ius*) about money lent (*pecunia credita*) should be the same for the Socii and Latini (*Socii ac nomen Latinum*) as for Roman citizens. The object of the law was to prevent Romans from lending money in the name of the *Socii*, who were not bound by the *fenebres leges*. The law could obviously only apply within the jurisdiction of Rome.

SEMPRONIAE. Various *leges* proposed by the Gracchi were so named. See AGRARIAE LEGES.

SEMPRONIA DE CAPĬTE CIVIUM, carried by C. Gracchus (B.C. 123), reaffirming the old principle that no judgment involving the life or freedom of a citizen should be valid without the assent of the Roman people (Gell. x. 3).

SERVILIA AGRARIA, proposed by the tribune P. Servilius Rullus in the consulship of Cicero (B.C. 63), was a very extensive agrarian law. It was successfully opposed by Cicero; but it was in substance carried by Caesar (B.C. 59), and is the law called by Cicero *lex Campana*, from the public land called Ager Campanus being assigned under this law.

SERVILIA GLAUCIA DE REPETUNDIS. See REPETUNDAE.

SILIA. The *legis actio* called *condictio* was established by this law in the case when the demand was a determinate sum of money (*certa pecunia*). See ACTIO.

SULPICIAE, proposed by the tribune P. Sulpicius Galba, a supporter of Marius (B.C. 88), enacted the recall of the exiles, the distribution of the new citizens and the *libertini* among the thirty-five tribes, that the command in the Mithridatic War should be taken from Sulla and given to Marius, and that a senator should not contract debt to the amount of more than 2000 *denarii* ($100). The last enactment may have been intended to expel persons from the Senate who should get into debt. All these laws were repealed by Sulla.

SULPICIA SEMPRONIA (B.C. 304). No name is given to this law by Livy, but it was probably proposed by the consuls. It prevented the dedication of a temple or altar without the consent of the Senate or a majority of the tribunes.

SUMTUARIAE. See SUMPTUARIAE LEGES.

TABELLARIAE. See TABELLARIAE LEGES.

TARPEIA ATERNIA. See ATERNIA TARPEIA.

TERENTILIA, proposed by the tribune C. Terentilius (B.C. 462) but not carried, was a *rogatio* which had for its object an amendment of the constitution, though in form it only attempted a limitation of the consular imperium. This rogatio probably led to the subsequent legislation of the Decemviri. See TWELVE TABLES.

TESTAMENTARIAE. Various laws, such as the Cornelia, Falcidia, Furia, and Voconia, regulated testamentary dispositions. See LEGATUM; TESTAMENTUM.

THORIA. The importance of this law requires that it should have a separate notice. See THORIA LEX.

TITIA. Similar in its provisions to the *lex Publicia.*

TITIA DE TUTŌRIBUS. See IULIA ET TITIA; and cf. Gaius, i. 195.

TREBONIA, a *plebiscitum* proposed by L. Trebonius (B.C. 448), which enacted that if the ten tribunes were not chosen before the Comitia were dissolved, those who were elected should not fill up the number (*coöptare*), but that the Comitia should be continued till the ten were elected.

TRIBUNICIA. See TRIBUNUS.

TULLIA DE LEĠATIŌNE LIBĔRA. See LEGATUS.

VALERIA HORATIA. See PLEBISCITUM.

VARIA. See MAIESTAS.

VATINIA DE PROVINCIIS (B.C. 59) was the enactment by which Caesar obtained the province of Gallia Cisalpina with Illyricum for five years, to which the Senate added Gallia Transalpina. This *plebiscitum* was proposed by the tribune Vatinius. A *Trebonia lex* subsequently prolonged Caesar's *imperium* for five years.

VATINIA. See REPETUNDAE.

VATINIA DE COLŌNIS, under which the Latina Colonia (cf. LATINITAS) of Novum-Comum in Gallia Cisalpina was planted, B.C. 59.

LEGES DE VI. See VIS.

VICESIMARIA. See VICESIMA.

VILLIA ANNĀLIS. See ANNALES LEGES.

VISELLIA (A.D. 23) made a man liable to a criminal prosecution who, being a Latinus, assumed to exercise the rights of an *ingenuus*.

VOCONIA. See VOCONIA LEX.

Lexiarchi (ληξίαρχοι). At Athens a board of six members, who, with thirty assistants, saw that only properly qualified persons attended meetings of the ἐκκλησία, and also compelled their attendance by the aid of the police (τοξόται). They also entered young citizens on the list of their deme when they came of age. See ECCLESIA.

Lexicography. See LEXICON.

Lexĭcon (λεξικόν, sc. βιβλίον). A Greek name for a word-book, probably first used in the ninth century A.D. The Latin equivalent *dictionarium* appears about three centuries later. Chinese writers pretend that lexicons have been known in their language for 3000 years. But the conception of a condensed digest of a branch of knowledge, classified and ordered for convenient reference, is traced by authentic records to that source of all ideas which have been fruitful of intellectual growth, the great age of Greece. In Plato's time, the Homeric poems were a text-book for the study of the youth of Athens, and collections of peculiar words and phrases, with explanations, were made for the use of teachers. At first the notes were written in the order of the text, but convenience soon dictated other arrangements, by subjects or by alphabetical sequence. Before B.C. 400 Democritus of Abdera discussed the vocabulary of Homer, and is even said to have compiled an Homeric dictionary. Clearchus of Soli, a pupil of Aristotle, prepared a treatise on the mathematical terms in Plato's *Republic*. Near the end of the fourth century B.C., Philetas of Cos, celebrated as a poet by Theocritus and Propertius, wrote a famous book, ἄτακτα or γλῶσσαι, on the meanings of words, especially of poetical and dialectic forms. His successors of the Alexandrian school of grammarians industriously compiled special dictionaries or glossaries, now to particular authors, as Homer, Plato, and the dramatists, now of the language of tragedy or comedy, again of dialectic conceptions, which encroached on the province of good Attic words, and even of the technical terms of particular arts. Thus Zenodotus of Ephesus, about B.C. 280, prepared an elaborate glossary (γλῶσσαι) to Homer; Artemidorus of Byzantium soon after made a dictionary of cookery (γλῶσσαι ὀψαρτυτικαί); and scores of others collected extensive word-lists of Plato's writings, of tragedy, of comedy, of history, of medicine. Didymus of Alexandria, an indefatigable compiler of the first century B.C., published at least twenty-eight "books" (rolls?) on tragic diction (περὶ τραγῳδουμένης λέξεως), a work of similar extent on the language of comedy, seven "books" on words of ambiguous or doubtful meaning, and a treatise on corrupt expressions. Pollux and Athenaeus name twenty-one writers on terms peculiar to cookery. In short, through the many generations of grammatical activity which succeeded the creative period of Greek literature, the interpretation of words assumed ever greater prominence, until Zopyrion and Pamphilus, near the end of the reign of Augustus, attempted to bring together the rich materials thus furnished, in a comprehensive lexicon of the language (95 books, περὶ γλωσσῶν). An abridgment of this great work by Diogenianus of Heraclea (A.D. 130?) is said, on doubtful authority, to have been the basis of the dictionary ascribed to Hesychius of Alexandria (A.D. 380?), which is a principal source of information upon the Greek language and literature (best ed. by Moritz Schmidt, 4 vols. 4to, Jena, 1858–64). The important lexicon called that of Suidas, and ascribed to the eleventh century, is a miscellany of lexicographical and literary excerpts and comments made by many hands in successive ages (best editions by Gaisford, 3 vols. fol., Oxford, 1834; by Bernhardy, 4to, Halle, 1834). The first attempt systematically to explain Greek words in Latin was perhaps the glossary of Philoxenus, A.D. 550 (first printed, fol., Paris, 1573, included in Valpy's ed. of Stephens' *Thesaurus*, London, 1816), but for 800 years afterwards the Greek language was almost forgotten in Catholic Europe.

Upon the revival of learning an earnest demand for such helps was felt, and old vocabularies and glossaries were eagerly copied and enlarged. In 1483 the first Greek-Latin vocabulary was printed, that of John Crastenus. It passed through several editions, growing in size. In 1497 appeared a much more important work from the press of Aldus, Venice (*Dictionarium Graecum Copiosissimum cum Interp. Lat.*), and was rapidly followed by similar lexicons in the names of Julius Pollux, Budaeus, Münster, Gillius, Gessner, Grynaeus, Dasypodius, Constantine, and others. Each of these copied most of his work from his latest predecessor, but often with important, though irregular additions. Thus the dictionary of Budaeus (first published at Paris, 1529; reprinted at Basle, 1530; reëdited and much enlarged by Robert Stephens, Paris, 1548) was copious and exact in explaining legal and forensic terms. Montanus, in 1539, gave to scholars the first Latin-Greek vocabulary, for use in writing Greek. Robert Constantine's lexicon (Geneva, 1562: a marked improvement on earlier ones in accuracy) was especially valuable in illustrations of Thucydides. But in 1572 Henry Stephens published his *Thesaurus Linguae Graecae* (5 vols. fol., Paris), containing more than 100,000 Greek words, with references to authorities; a work of surpassing industry and scholarship, which remained unrivalled for nearly 250 years. It was reproduced in magnificent form, and with additions, by Valpy (London, 1816 foll.), and again by Hase and Dindorf (Paris, 1836 foll.). The Greek manuals of Scapula (Paris, 1579), Hederich (2 vols. 8vo, Leipzig, 1766), and others, in common use until the early years of this century, were hardly more than extracts of the great *Thesaurus*. Several special lexicons, however, such as those of Portus to Herodotus (Frankfort, 1603; reprinted London, 1825) and to Pindar (1606), of Seber to Homer (1604), of Damm to Homer and Pindar (1765–1774), of Ernesti for the technical terms of rhetoric (1795), of Reiske to Theocritus (1765), of Sturz to Xenophon (1801–4), of Schweighäuser to Herodotus (1824), and of Wyttenbach to Plutarch (Oxford, 1843), collected the results of more accurate criticism in parts of the field. The first general lexicon which exhibited a marked improvement upon Stephens in method, and the first which defined Greek words in a modern language, was the critical Greek-German lexicon of Schneider (2 vols. 8vo, 1797–98). It passed through three editions, besides abridgments, and was then reconstructed with admirable skill by Passow (1819–23). The latest revision of Passow's *Handwörterbuch*, by Rost and five well-equipped associates (3 vols. 4to, 1841–1857), is still the standard of Greek exegesis in Germany, though the rival works of Pape (1842–1845; 3d ed. by Sengebusch, 1880), of Jacobitz and Seiler (1839–46), and of Suhle and Schneidewin (Leipzig, 1875), have peculiar merits and strong eulogists. Students whose mother-tongue was English had no trustworthy general dictionary of Greek until 1848, when Liddell and Scott published at Oxford their Greek-English lexicon, drawn mainly from Passow; which was improved and enlarged, first by Drisler (N. Y. 1850), and later by the original editors, aided by several American scholars, so that it now renders the student for most purposes independent of the *Thesaurus* and of special lexicons to the Greek classics (7th ed. London and New York, 1883). Of such special lexicons, the most complete and accurate are Ast's dictionary to Plato (3 vols. Leipzig, 1835–38), Bétant's to Thucydides (2 vols. 1843–49), the index of Bonitz to Aristotle (Berlin, 1870), the Lexicon Sophocleum of Ellendt (best ed. Berlin, 1872), Bindseil's Concordantia to Pindar (1875), the Lexicon Aeschyleum of Dindorf (1876), the Lexicon Theocriteum (1879), the Lexicon Pindaricum (1883) of Rumpel, and, above all, the Lexicon Homericum of Capelle and several associates (1874–83).

The lexicography of the Greek Testament and of ecclesiastical writers has long formed a distinct and very extensive branch of the science, important epochs in which have been marked by Pasor's *Lexicon Graec.-Lat.* in *Novum Testamentum* (1636; best ed. by Fischer, Leipzig, 1767); Suicer's *Thesaurus Ecclesiasticus* (Amsterdam, 1682; often reprinted and abridged); Wahl's *Clavis Novi Testamenti* (1819; translated by Robinson, New York, 1825; best ed. Leipzig, 1853); Schirlitz, *Griech.-deutsches Wörter-*

buch zum N. T. (1851–58); Robinson's *Lexicon of the New Testament* (New York, 1836; rewritten, New York, 1850); Cremer's *Biblisches-theologisches Wörterb.* (3d and best ed. Gotha, 1881–82); Grimm's *Lexicon zum Neuen Testament* (Leipzig, 1862–68; best ed. 1879); translated and much improved by Thayer (New York, 1887). The Glossary of later and Byzantine Greek, by Sophocles (Cambridge, 1860), enlarged into a Greek lexicon of the Roman and Byzantine periods (Boston, 1870), is the standard in its department. By far the most complete and useful English-Greek lexicon is that by Yonge (London, 1849; best ed. New York, 1870).

The beginnings of Latin lexicography are ascribed to Verrius Flaccus, whom Augustus made the tutor of his grandsons. His great work, *De Significatu Verborum*, is supposed to have been abridged, some generations later, by Pompeius Festus, under the same title; and extensive fragments of the abridgment, besides unintelligent excerpts from it by Paulus Diaconus of the eighth century, are still preserved (best ed. by C. O. Müller, Leipzig, 1839; reprinted 1880). There are also curious remnants of verbal exegesis in the fragments of Nonius Marcellus (about A.D. 300; best eds. by Mercier, Leipzig, 1825; by Quicherat, Paris, 1871) and of Isidore (A.D. 600; best ed. by Arevalo, 7 vols. Rome, 1797–1803). Glossaries and vocabularies were common in the ages before printing; but were compiled as needed, copied, abridged, corrected, and enlarged, according to the knowledge or ignorance of each new compiler, or the special need to be met. None of them were regarded as literary works, to be studied and preserved, in deference to the author's authority, or in respect to his fame. Many of these remain in old libraries. One of the best, a glossary of the ninth century, in the national library at Paris, has been admirably edited, with a commentary containing the substance of twelve others, by Professor G. F. Hildebrand (Göttingen, 1854). A learned description of the works of this class, which were still unedited, was given by G. Löwe, in his *Prodromus Glossariorum Latinorum* (Leipzig, 1876), and much light was thrown by him upon their origin and value. His project for a collection of the extant glossaries has been carried on with energy since his death, under the auspices of the Royal Literary Society of Saxony, by George Goetz, who has published four volumes (*Corpus Glossariorum Latinorum*, II., III., IV., V., 1886–94) of the nine which are necessary to complete it. These vocabularies explained rare and obscure words, ambiguous terms, forms of doubtful authority, or of dialectic or foreign origin; and it was but slowly that the conception was formed of a complete vocabulary of the language. About A.D. 1063, Papias, the Lombard, finished his *Elementarium Doctrinae Erudimentum* (printed, Venice, 1491), intended for an encyclopaedia of instruction, a large part of which was devoted to defining words. A century later the monk Osborn of Gloucester followed with the *Panorama*, an attempt at an etymological dictionary (published in Mai's *Classicorum Auctorum*, tom. viii. Rome, 1836). About A.D. 1200, Hugutio, Bishop of Ferrara, wrote a *Liber Derivationum*. On the works of Papias and Hugutio was founded the famous *Catholicon*, by Balbi of Genoa (Joannes Januensis), finished A.D. 1286, and published at Mayence in 1460, containing, besides a manual of grammar, rhetoric, and criticism, a copious lexicon, especially of ecclesiastical Latin. Johann Reuchlin enlarged this in his *Vocabularius Breviloquus* (Basle, 1475), which passed through twenty-three editions, the last in 1504. The *Cornucopiae* of Nicholas Perotti, though in form a commentary on Martial, is lexicographical in substance, and has an alphabetic index (1482 and often). In 1502 appeared at Reggio, in Italy, the *Dictionarium* of Ambrosius Calepinus, the first attempt to represent the classical language as a whole, with illustrative citations from the literature. Its fame grew rapidly. For many years labourers in this department of learning accepted it as a standard, and sought only to supply its omissions. Twenty editions were published within a generation, and "Calepinus" became the common name for a lexicon. In 1539 Jacobus Montanus added to the definitions the Greek equivalents. In 1546 a Calepinus Pentaglottus was issued at Venice; in 1581 a Calepinus Septem Linguarum at Leyden; and successive editors added new languages, until the Calepinus of 1603 was a parallel lexicon of eleven. Meanwhile, in 1531, Robert Stephens, *princeps lexicographorum*, gave to the world his *Thesaurus Linguae Latinae;* but used it as the basis of a far more comprehensive and accurate work under the same title, which he completed in 1548. This long remained the unrivalled storehouse of the language, and every important dictionary of classical Latin was substantially a reprint (3 vols. Venice, 1551; 4 vols. Leyden, 1573), or an abridgment of it. From the first edition was compiled the *Promptuarium* of Trebellius (Basle, 1545); from the second, the extensive *Thesaurus Linguae Latinae* of Caelius Secundus (Basle, 1561), the useful *Thesaurus* of Faber Soranus (Leipzig, 1571; 2d ed. 1587; abridged, Leipzig, 1594, and Heidelberg, 1608), the *Lexicon Criticum* of Pareus (Nuremberg, 1645), and many more. The most important original work of this period in lexicography was the *Glossarium ad Scriptores Mediae et Infimae Latinitatis* of DuCange (Paris, 1678), which has been several times reprinted (ed. by Hendschel, 7 vols. Paris, 1840–1850; ed. by Favre, 10 vols. Niort, 1883–88; a good abridgment by Migne, Paris, 1866; and very important supplements by Diefenbach, Frankfurt, 1857 and 1867). (See DuCange.) An association of Cambridge scholars reëdited the great *Thesaurus*, at the end of its second century of preëminence, with large additions (4 vols. London, 1734–35). Antony Birrius recovered the collections Henry Stephens had made for a new edition of his father's work, and surpassed the English reprint in the accuracy of his reproduction (4 vols. Basle, 1740–43). Finally, J. M. Gessner, after preparing an enlarged edition of Faber (Leipzig, 1726), spent twelve years in revising the *Thesaurus* of Stephens, correcting and completing its classical citations, while excluding much ecclesiastical and semi-barbarous material (4 vols. Leipzig, 1749). But in Italy, Calepinus retained the primacy, undergoing many revisions and enlargements before that of Sartori (Padua, 1708), which brought its imperfections to the notice of two of the most eminent Latinists of the day, then at the University of Padua. With the supervision and aid of Facciolati, his pupil Forcellini devoted three years to its correction and extension (*Septem linguarum Calepinus, hoc est Lexicon Latinum, variarum linguarum interpretatione adiecta*, Pavia, 1718), and his important edition was eleven times reprinted. The last appearances of this lexicon, which held its place in the schools for nine generations, were at Venice, 1778, and at Pavia, 1779. But Forcellini's labours on Calepinus taught him the need of a more perfect dictionary, and he undertook to construct it mainly from the original texts. For forty years, with some interruptions from church-work, he toiled, with rare intelligence and persistence; and at his death, in 1768, left complete in manuscript the greatest contribution to this department of science ever achieved by a single hand (*Totius Latinitatis Lexicon*, 2 vols. fol. Padua, 1771). It has been several times reprinted (4 vols. Padua, 1805, etc.), sometimes with uncritical additions (ed. Bailey, London, 1827; ed. Schumann, Schneeberg, 1835), sometimes with diligence and literary skill (ed. Furnaletti, 4 vols. 4to, Padua, 1827–33; ed. De Vit, 5 vols. fol. Prato, 1858–75); but none of these editions has conformed the citations to the improved critical texts of the classical authors. The latest (ed. Corradini, Padua, 1864, completed to the word STELLIO, 1894) is by far the best in this respect, though still defective in etymology and arrangement. Scheller's Latin-German Lexicon (Leipzig, 1783) was at first an abridgment of Forcellini's, but was rapidly improved by the compiler in successive editions (3d ed. 5 vols. Leipzig, 1804). His condensed hand-lexicon (Leipzig, 1792) was reëdited many times by Lünemann, aided in the seventh edition (Leipzig, 1831) by Georges, who issued the eighth edition (Leipzig, 1837) alone, and then reconstructed the work, under his own name, in the *Ausführliches Handwörterbuch der lateinischen Sprache*, whose seventh edition (Leipzig, 1879–80) is the reliance and the delight of all who study Latin through German, though it omits, in most cases, specific local references to texts. Klotz's *Handwörterbuch der lateinischen Sprache* (2 vols. Brunswick, 1853–57) is distinguished for fulness of illustration in many articles, especially under the earliest letters of the alphabet; but it was hastily finished, and is defective in uniformity and in typographical accuracy. Freund's *Handwörterbuch* (4 vols. Leipzig, 1834), also founded on Forcellini, introduced a principle, the historical arrangement of meanings in each article, which has since been fruitful in all departments of lexicography. A revised translation by Andrews (New York, 1850), substantially reprinted as Dr. Smith's Latin Dictionary (London, 1853), was for many years the standard in the United States and Great Britain. An enlarged translation into French by Theil (2 vols. Paris, 1866) is valuable for its full notices of terms of natural history. The same work was revised and enlarged by Riddle and White (London, 1870), and entirely reconstructed by Lewis and Short (Harper's Latin Dictionary, New York, 1879). The best English-Latin dictionary is that of Smith and Hall (London, 1870; New York, 1871); the most complete and critical work in which a modern language is explained in Latin is the *Deutsches-latein. Wörterbuch* of Georges (6th ed. 2 vols. Leipzig, 1870). In recent years German scholars have shown new zeal in constructing complete word-books (concordances) to Latin classics. Merguet's *Lexicon zu den Reden des Cicero* (4 vols. 4to, Jena, 1877–84) has been followed by the full dictionaries to Caesar of Merguet (Jena, 1884–1886), Menge and Preuss (Leipzig, 1884–90), and Meusel (Berlin, 1884–93); by that of Preuss to the pseudo-Caesarian books of Hirtius and others (Erlangen, 1884); while complete verbal indexes to the fragments of Plautus, the works of Sallust, and those of several minor poets have been added to recent editions of the texts. A complete lexicon to the philosophical writings of Cicero by Merguet (Jena, vols. i. ii. 1887–93, vol. iii. in the press), one by Gerber and Greef to Tacitus (fasciculi i. to xi. Leipzig, 1887–93), and one on an enormous scale to Livy by Fügner (fasciculi i. to vi. Leipzig, 1889–94) are slowly appearing. The principles and methods of constructing a complete thesaurus of the language have been actively discussed in Germany for two generations. In 1857 the king of Bavaria offered to contribute 10,000 gulden if the completion of such a work could be insured; Carl Halm of Munich, with Ritschl and Fleckeisen, undertook to organize an association of scholars, and Bücheler was selected as editor-in-chief; but political and military troubles smothered the scheme. The critical restoration of many texts, the reform of orthography, the multiplication of special lexicons, and the great advances made in philology and in the study of inscriptions have since vastly increased and improved the materials available for a *Thesaurus*. In 1884 E. Wölfflin announced his *Archiv für lateinische Lexicographie und Grammatik . . . als Vorarbeit zu einem Thesaurus Linguae Latinae*, and under the patronage of the Bavarian Academy of Sciences began its publication in quarterly numbers, containing collections, notices, reviews, and model articles, as contributions to the most complete digest of a great language ever planned. With the aid of many competent scholars, this periodical has been continued through eight years, and has done much to awaken interest in the subject. The last number for 1893 contained a plan, *zur Begründung eines Thesaurus Linguae Latinae*, in twelve volumes of 1000 large quarto pages each, under the auspices of the five great academies of science in Berlin, Göttingen, Leipzig, Munich, and Vienna, to be finished in twenty years, at an estimated cost of 605,000 marks (about $150,000). The five academies have sanctioned the plan, with Messrs. Bücheler, Wölfflin, and Leo as editorial directors, and there is reasonable hope of its success.

See also Gräfenhan, *Gesch. d. klassischen Philologie im Alterthum*, 3 vols. (1843 foll.); Mahn, *Darstellung der Lexicographie nach allen ihren Seiten* (Rudolstadt, 1817); Hübner, *Grundriss zu Vorlesungen über die latein. Grammatik* (2d ed. Berlin, 1880), and *Grundriss zu Vorlesungen über Gr. Syntax* (Berlin, 1883); *Lexicographie der griechischen und lateinischen Sprache*, by Drs. G. Autenrieth and F. Heerdegen (in Iwan Müller's *Handbuch*, Nördlingen, 1885); Pökel, *Philolog. Schriftsteller-lexicon* (1882); Ebert, *Allgemeine Gesch. der Literatur des Mittelalters im Abendlande*, 2 vols. (Leipzig, 1884, 1880); De Vit, *Preface to the Lexicon of Forcellini* (Prato, 1879); Wölfflin, *Archiv für latein. Lexicographie* (Leipzig, 1884–93); "Greek Lexicography," by J. E. B. Mayor, in the *Journal of Philology*, vols. vi., vii. (Cambridge, 1876–77); "Notes on Latin Lexicography," by H. Nettleship, *Journal of Philology*, vol. xii. (Cambridge, 1883).

Lex Metalli Vipascensis. A summary of rules for the management of a mine, of which a fragment was found in 1876, at Aljustrel in the south of Portugal. It is engraved on bronze, and has been published by Hübner in the *Ephem. Epigraph.* iii. 165. See Soromenho, *La Table de Bronze d'Aljustrel* (Lisbon, 1877); Flack, *La Table d'Aljus-*

trel (Paris, 1880); and Wilmanns in the *Zeitschrift für Bergrecht* (1877).

Lexis (λῆξις). See DIKÉ.

Lexovii or **Lexobii.** A people in Gallia Lugdunensis, on the ocean, west of the mouth of the Sequana. Their capital was Noviomagus (Lisieux).

Lex Tappŭla. See VALENTINUS; VALERIUS.

Libanius (Λιβάνιος). A Greek rhetorician of Antioch in Syria, born A.D. 314. His education was begun in his native city and completed at Athens, where he became a public teacher at the early age of twenty-five. Called from Athens to Constantinople in 340, he met with extraordinary success; at the same time he excited the envy of his rivals, whose slanders led to his expulsion in 345. After being actively engaged for five years as a public teacher in Nicomedia in Bithynia, he was recalled to Constantinople, where he was again remarkably popular, but found himself compelled by the continued persecutions of his detractors to leave the capital once more in 353. He withdrew to his native city of Antioch, where he was for many years actively employed in the exercise of his profession and in promoting the interests of his fellow-citizens; but even here he was much persecuted by his opponents. Apart from bodily sufferings caused by his being struck by a flash of lightning, his old age was saddened by the decline of learning and the fall of paganism, which he had foreseen would follow the lamented death of his admirer and patron, Julian. He died about A.D. 393, honoured and admired by his pupils, among whom were included Christians such as Basil the Great and Iohannes Chrysostomus.

Libanius gives us information about his own life and work in a series of letters and in a speech "on his own fortune," written in his sixtieth year, but completed at a later date. There remains sixty-seven of his speeches, the majority of which refer to the events of his time; also fifty declamations; a considerable series of rhetorical exercises of various kinds, among them narratives, sketches of character and descriptions of works of art (some of them important in connection with the history of ancient art), and also arguments to the speeches of Demosthenes. There are, further, about 2000 letters addressed to friends, pupils, rhetoricians, scholars, statesmen, etc., which give us a vivid picture of his times. A fourth part of them, however, only exist in a Latin translation, and some of them are of doubtful genuineness. His style, which is formed on the best Attic models, is pure and has a certain elegance, although it is not always free from the affected and unnatural mannerism of his age.

The most complete edition of the orations and declamations is that of Reiske, 4 vols. (1791–97); of the letters, that of Wolf (1738). The life of Libanius has been written by Petri (Paris, 1866), and in German by Sievers (Berlin, 1868).

Libănus (Λίβανος). A range of mountains on the confines of Syria and Palestine, dividing Phoenicé from Coelé-Syria. Its highest summits are covered with perpetual snow, and its sides were in ancient times clothed with forests of cedars. It is considerably lower than the opposite range of Anti-Libanus. In the Scriptures the word Lebanon is used for both ranges and for either of them; but in classical authors the names Libanus and Anti-Libanus are distinctive terms, being applied to the west and east ranges respectively (Ptol. v. 15).

Libatio. See SACRIFICIUM.

Libella. (1) The diminutive of *libra*, the Roman pound, and used of the sum in silver, which expresses the value of the pound of copper. (See As.) It was, as a monetary term, originally equal to one-tenth of a denarius and later one-tenth of a sestertius. It was never coined, however, but was a mere "money of account," like the guinea in England to-day. The half of a libella was called *sembella* (Varr. v. 174). (2) (διαβήτης, σταφυλή). A carpenter's level (*libella fabrilis*). It is represented in the illustration under the article CIRCINUS (p. 350), in the left-hand lower corner, where it is partly inverted.

Libellus (in form the dim. of *liber*). (1) A small book, i. e. roll, usually a book of verse (cf. Birt, *Das antike Buchwesen*, p. 22 [Berlin, 1882]). (2) A memorial of any kind, whether an accusation or petition. (3) A pasquinade, lampoon, or satirical skit (whence our word "libel"), intended to ridicule or defame (*libellus famosus*). Such were severely punished by the Twelve Tables, and later they were often publicly burned (Dio Cass. lvi. 27); but they were always numerous at Rome, especially in times of political excitement. (See Rein, *Das Criminalrecht der Römer*, pp. 378 foll., 531.) (4) See ORATIONES PRINCIPUM. (5) A notice of appeal (*libellus appellatorius*; cf. *Dig.* 40, 1). (6) A hand-bill or programme of the gladiatorial games (*libellus gladiatorius* or *munerarius*). (7) A hand-bill or public notice of any sort posted up in the most frequented parts of the city (Cic. *Pro Quint.* 6, 15, 9; Sen. *De Benef.* iv. 12; Plaut. *Rud.* v. 2, 7).

Liber. The Italian god of wine, afterwards identified with the Greek Dionysus (q. v.). A feminine deity, Libera, was worshipped with him. See DIONYSIA; LIBERALIA.

Liber. A free man. See CIVIS; DIMINUTIO CAPITIS; LIBERTUS; SERVUS.

Liber (βίβλος, βιβλίον). A book; but among the Greeks and Romans, until a very late period, to be understood as referring to a roll. The modern book shape was used for the *codex* (τεῦχος) only, as explained in the article CODEX. The Latin name *liber* meant originally the bark, rind, or bust of a tree, which was early used for writing material, as afterwards for the manufacture of paper (*charta*). (For an account of the writing materials used in ancient times, see PALAEOGRAPHY.) The same meaning is found in the Greek term βίβλος, properly "rind" or "bark" (βύβλος). For the preparation of papyrus of which the pages of books were made, see PAPYRUS. The pages (σελίδες, *paginae*) having been prepared, they were pasted together (*conglutinatae*) to form a long roll; but sometimes the pages were written first and pasted into a roll afterwards, for which purpose some people kept *glutinatores* (Cic. *Ad Att.* iv. 4). The writing was in columns, so that the lines of writing were parallel to the sides of the roll: on each page there was a column, and there was a blank space between each column. Down to the time of Caesar, however, it was the custom to write official documents *transversa charta*; that is to say, across the whole breadth of the roll, so that the lines of writing were at right angles to the sides of the roll. This explains the passage in Suet.

Jul. 56. The shape and appearance of Greek and Roman books will be understood from the following illustration.

Liber.

The roll was sometimes of considerable length. The Scholiasts, indeed, speak of Thucydides and Homer as being written each in one long roll. The roll of Thucydides is estimated at about 578 pages, nearly 100 yards—surely an incredible length; and a Homer roll, 120 yards in length, is said to have been in existence at Constantinople. But this was not the usual system, and the roll rarely exceeded 100 pages (cf. Mart. viii. 44), and was usually much smaller. It was customary to divide a long work (*opus* or *corpus*) into several books (*libri*), each *liber* being in one roll (*volumen;* in Greek, *τομός* or *κύλινδρος*). Greek writers sometimes called these *libri* or divisions of a work *βίβλια*, sometimes *λόγοι*, and in the later Empire *συγγράμματα*. Thus, in contrast to the huge roll of Homer, said to have been at Constantinople, we have the papyrus of the twenty-fourth book of the *Iliad* from Elephantiné, so that the complete *Iliad* would have been in twenty-four rolls or volumes. The pages were numbered, or at any rate the total number was usually put on the *titulus:* even the total number of verses, or of lines in a prose work, were sometimes written on it. The price of the book was in part estimated by this number (*C. I. L.* iii. p. 831).

The writing was usually only on one side of the paper. The other side in old books was utilized for school-boys' exercises (Mart. iv. 86); or as scribbling paper (Mart. viii. 62). Both sides were, however, sometimes used for the original work, and the books were then called *opisthographi* (Pliny, *Epist.* iii. 5). Sometimes the writing was sponged out (as in a parchment palimpsest) and the paper used over again.

The roll was protected against worms by being smeared with cedar oil, which gave the paper a yellow tinge (Ovid, *Trist.* iii. 1, 13; Mart. iii. 2; Hor. *A. P.* 331); then the last leaf was pasted on to a thin piece of wood called the *umbilicus* or *ὄμφαλος* (the *umbilicus* is found also made of tightly-folded paper). Hence the last page is called *eschatocollion* (Mart. ii. 6); and the expression *ad umbilicum adducere* means to finish (*ad cornua*, Mart. xx. 107). The edges (*frons*) of the roll were carefully cut, and also smoothed with pumice-stone (Ovid, *Trist.* iii. 1, 13; Mart. i. 67; viii. 72). As a further decoration, the ends (*cornua*) of the *umbilicus* were sometimes gilded as far as they projected (Mart. viii. 61). The edges themselves (*frons*) were also coloured. A strip of parchment on which the title or subject of the book, and sometimes its number of pages or even lines, was written, was pasted on to the roll. This strip was called *titulus* or *index* (*σίττυβοι* or *σίττυβαι*). This *titulus* or index was often painted a bright colour. Finally, a cover for the roll (*membrana, διφθέρα*) was made of parchment coloured red or yellow. If one work was in several *libri*, they were tied in a bundle (*fasces, fasciculus*, Gell. ix. 4, or *δέσμη*). The only other addition to be noticed is that occasionally the portrait of the author was placed on the first page of the book (Sen. *De Tranq. An.* 9; Mart. xiv. 186).

In reading, the roll (*liber* or *volumen*) was held in both hands and unrolled with one, while the other rolled it up. The unrolling was called *evolvere, revolvere*, or *volvere;* going right through was called *explicare;* rolling up again, *convolvere, replicare*, or *complicare.* In rolling it up tightly, it was convenient to do so by holding the *umbilicus* with both hands while the first page was pressed under the chin. This is the meaning of *quae trita duro non inhorruit mento* (Mart. i. 66; cf. x. 93). The apparatus of a book is given completely by Martial (iii. 2):

> "Cedro nunc licet ambules perunctus
> Et frontis gemino decens honore
> Pictis luxurieris umbilicis;
> Et te purpura delicata velet
> Et cocco rubeat superbus index."

The multiplication of books at Rome began after the conquest and pacification of Italy; but booksellers' shops were not known until the end of the Republic. The earliest mention of such shops is in Cicero (*Ad Q. Fr.* iii. 4) and Philo (ii. 9, 21); but they were then still uncommon, and we find Atticus selling books, for the copying of which he had a large number of slaves (Cic. *Ad Att.* ii. 4). Booksellers were called *librarii* and also *bibliopolae*, and in Greek *βιβλιοκάπηλοι*. Horace gives us the name of the Sosii Brothers (*Epist.* i. 20, 2). Martial names several, and specifies Argiletum as the booksellers' quarter (i. 3, 117); there were also the Vicus Sandaliarius and the Sigillaria. There were booksellers, too, in the provincial towns—e. g. at Lugdunum (Pliny, *Epist.* ix. 11) and at Brundisium (Gell. ix. 4). As to the price, we have no very clear information; but it would seem that a book was not necessarily, as regards the cost of production, very expensive, though it might, from special circumstances, command a large price. Gellius (ii. 3) speaks of the second book of the *Aeneid* being bought for *viginti aurei* = nearly $90; but it was an antiquarian curiosity, as being reputed Vergil's own copy; and as a literary tradition, possibly untrue, it was said that Aristotle gave three talents for an autograph MS. of Speusippus, and Plato nearly two for three books of Philolaüs (Gell. iii. 17). Such instances merely show that bibliophiles lived

Libri. (From paintings at Pompeii.)

then as now, and price was regulated by fashion and rarity. Trustworthy copies of Ennius, for instance, were so rare in the time of Gellius that one of undoubted authority was hired for a large sum to decide a dispute as to a reading (Gell. xvii. 5). That, on the other hand, the real cost of production was not great, may be seen from the fact that Statius (*Silv.* iv. 9, 9) speaks of a book in a neat purple cover costing about ten cents. The first book of Martial, in the shop of Atrectus, cost five *denarii* (Mart. i. 117); but even that was dear, for the bookseller Tryphon could sell it at a profit for two (Mart. xiii. 3). The author's profit could be made (1) by selling his original copy to a bookseller (Sen. *De Ben.* vii. 6; Suet. *Gram.* 8), (2) by selling copies made by his own slaves; but in the absence of all legal protection, the gains so to be made were very small, and the author who sought profit from his writing depended mainly on the liberality of rich patrons.

How early or to what extent booksellers existed at Athens is a matter of dispute. It is not unreasonable to deduce, from the mention of βιβλιογράφοι in Cratinus (Poll. vii. 211), that they existed as early as B.C. 430. This name, for which βιβλιοπώλης was afterwards used, would imply that the first booksellers were copyists who both copied and sold books. We have a book-market (τὰ βιβλία) at Athens in the time of Eupolis (Poll. ix. 47); and the same may be inferred from the mention of the book-collector Eudemus in Xenophon (*Mem.* iv. 2).

BIBLIOGRAPHY.—The standard work on ancient books is Birt's *Das antike Buchwesen* (Berlin, 1882); and the following are also valuable: Buchsenschutz, *Besitz und Erwerb im griechischen Alterthum* (Leipzig, 1879); Géraud, *Les Livres dans l'Antiquité* (Paris, 1840); Louisy, *Le Livre* (Paris, 1886); Wehle, *Das Buch* (Leipzig, 1879); Blümner, *Technologie*, 4 vols. (Leipzig, 1875–87); and Thompson, *Hand-book of Greek and Latin Palaeography* (London, 1893). For an account of the book-trade and literary property in antiquity, see the introduction to Clement's *Étude sur le Droit des Auteurs* (Grenoble, 1867); Haenny, *Schriftsteller und Buchhändler im alten Rom* (Leipzig, 1885); Romberg, *Études sur la Propriété Artistique et Littéraire* (Brussels, 1892); Schmitz, *Schriftsteller und Buchhändler in Athen* (Heidelberg, 1876); and the interesting but inaccurate work by Putnam, *Authors and their Public in Ancient Times* (New York, 1894).

Līber. The Italian Bacchus. See DIONYSUS.

Libĕra. The wife of the Italian wine-god Liber, identified with the Greek Persephoné.

Liberāles Artes. The origin of the liberal arts is to be sought in the school education of the Greeks. As early as the time of Solon, the distinction between γυμναστική, the training of the body, and μουσική, the training of the soul, is to be met with. Out of μουσική was gradually developed the body of studies which embraced as its chief content the so-called liberal arts. By the time of Aristotle (B.C. 384–322) the educational doctrine of the Greeks reached its highest development, and his references to the liberal arts may be taken as exhibiting this doctrine in a representative and authoritative manner. He defines the liberal arts (*Politics*, viii. 1) as the proper studies for freemen who seek intellectual and moral excellence in general rather than what is immediately practical as the end of their education, thus drawing a distinction between liberal and technical education, and perhaps foreshadowing in his identification of liberal with general culture the contrast between a general and a specialized training.

No exclusive list of seven or any other definite number of arts is to be found in any Greek writer, nor any reference to seven as the proper number of the liberal arts. However, it is plain that grammar was the inevitable first study in the list, and that it was followed by instruction in rhetoric and dialectics (logic). After these came the study of one or more of the following subjects: Arithmetic, geometry, music, astronomy. Yet besides these seven, which long afterwards came to be known as the seven liberal arts, we find mention of medicine as a liberal art and of architecture as a liberal art, while philosophy, which was the goal and completion of all the arts, is sometimes styled the liberal art *par excellence* (Aristot. *Met.* i. 2).

By the time of Varro (B.C. 116–27) and Cicero (B.C. 106–43), the liberal arts of the Greeks had become the recognized ground-work for the education of the Roman *liber homo*, or gentleman, and were commonly known as *artes liberales*, *studia liberalia*, *liberales disciplinae*, or *liberales scientiae*—terms which are not always identical in meaning, but which were used loosely to indicate the school studies of the Greeks. Of these expressions, *artes liberales* is the chief. The repository of information for the Romans regarding the Greek studies was Varro's monumental work, now lost, entitled *Libri Novem Disciplinarum.* According to Ritschl (*Opusc.* iii. 371), Varro's nine "disciplines" were grammar, dialectics, rhetoric, geometry, arithmetic, astrology, music, medicine, and architecture. Astrology, of course, answers to astronomy, and Varro's list accordingly embraces medicine and architecture in addition to the seven arts previously enumerated.

Passing on to the time of the early Empire, the course of the liberal arts may be traced with considerable clearness in the writings of the younger Seneca (B.C. 4–A.D. 65) and Quintilian (A.D. 35–95), and in Philo Iudaeus. By this time the liberal arts had become closely coördinated as a body of school instruction known as ἐγκύκλιος παιδεία, or "encyclical education;" and although we have no evidence that their number was then consciously limited to seven, it is quite possible that Alexandrian influences were beginning to operate towards such a limitation.

With the promulgation of Christianity the history of the liberal arts entered on a new phase. In the Western Church particularly there was a strong spirit of antagonism at the first, which gradually passed into qualified tolerance, and finally changed to active encouragement of the liberal arts on the ground that they ministered to higher spiritual truth. This transition is to be clearly seen in the writings of Augustine (A.D. 354–430), and it is also interesting to notice that although Varro is Augustine's great authority in all matters pertaining to the history of the liberal arts, he does not adhere to Varro's number of "disciplines." Instead of Varro's nine, we find that Augustine's enumeration embraces only seven and yet without expressly limiting the arts to that number. In the famous treatise of Martianus Capella of Carthage, written before A.D. 439 and entitled *De Nuptiis Philologiae et Mercurii*, we find for the first time an express limitation of the arts to seven, though without attaching any significance to that number. The book of Martianus was a popularized account of Varro's nine disciplines, and from this list of nine Martianus explicitly excludes medicine and architecture on the ground that they were not liberal but utilitarian studies (Eyssenhardt's edition, pp. 332, 336). No mention of the number of the arts is to be found in Boethius (A.D. 480–525), although the name *quadrivium* for the four later studies of arithmetic, geometry, music, and astronomy appears in his writings, and it is possible that the word *trivium* as the name for the three earlier studies—grammar, rhetoric, and dialectics—dates back to his time. Cassiodor(i)us (A.D. 480–575), in his work *De Artibus ac Disciplinis Liberalium Litterarum*, not only follows Martianus in limiting the arts to seven, but finds a mystical hint of their excellence in the text, "Wisdom hath builded her house; she hath hewn out her seven pillars" (Prov. ix. 1). The liberal arts thus became the seven supports of *Sapientia*, the higher spiritual philosophy. Isidore of Seville (died A.D. 636) copies after Cassiodor(i)us and expressly recognizes the arts as seven. Alcuin (A.D. 735–804), in the preface to his *Grammatica*, presses the interpretation of the text suggested by Cassiodor(i)us and finds the liberal arts in the Scriptures as a matter of direct interpretation. Alcuin's pupil, Rabanus Maurus, in his book *De Clericorum Institutione* (iii. 27), written in the year 819, after a full description of each of the seven arts, calls them *septem artes liberales*, apparently the first instance in history of the use of this term. The *septem artes liberales* are thus the ancient *artes liberales* Christianized, and to the end of the Middle Ages they remained the substance of school instruction, not being disturbed until the Renaissance.

Grammar, rhetoric, and dialectics, which composed the *trivium*, were also named "arts" as distinguished from the four "disciplines" which made up the *quadrivium*. The term *artes sermocinales*, or the arts pertaining to expression, is another name for the *trivium*, and *artes reales*, or the substantial sciences, another name for the *quadrivium*. Still another name for the *quadrivium* is "mathematics." Moreover, inasmuch as the seven arts culminated in the higher study of philosophy, it is clear that the ancient and mediæval world not only entertained the distinction between literary studies, on the one side, and sciences, on the other, as well as the notion that both find their goal and completion in philosophical studies, but that in so doing they likewise laid down the lines upon which European university education was to be subsequently modelled.

Liberalia. A festival celebrated annually in honour of Liber, the Italian Bacchus, and not to be confounded with the Greek Dionysia. It took place on the 17th of March. It was on this day that boys who assumed the *toga virilis* (see TOGA) marched in procession to the Capitol, where they made an offering of cakes (*liba*). See Varr. *L. L.* vi. 4; Marquardt, *Staatsverwaltung*, iii. 363; and the article DIONYSUS.

Liberālĭtas. See AMBITUS.

Liberōrum Ius. See LEX IULIA ET PAPIA POPPAEA, p. 943.

Libertas. Among the Romans the personification of Liberty; she had a temple on the Aventine. Her name was also given to the Atrium Libertatis, a place of public business which served, among other purposes, as an office of the censors. After it had been burned down under Augustus, it was rebuilt by Asinius Pollio, and the first public library in Rome was established within its walls. On coins Libertas is represented as a beautiful and richly adorned matron. At the end of the Republic, after the assassination of Caesar, she appears with a dagger and a cap of Liberty, or laurel wreath.

Libertīnus. See LIBERTUS.

Libertus (ἀπελεύθερος). A freedman. I. GREEK. The Greeks had no special legal form for the process of emancipating slaves, and consequently no legal differences in the status of freedmen. At Athens they took the position of resident aliens (μέτοικοι), and lay under certain obligations to their liberators as patrons. They could be called to legal account for any injury done to their patrons, and if condemned could be given back to them as slaves, or sold by the State. In the latter case the price was paid to their liberators. Occasionally the State set free a slave or a body of slaves who had rendered an important public service, as in the case of those who fought in the battle of Arginusae and at Chaeronea (Aristoph. *Ran.* 33, 192, 693; Dio Chrys. xv. 21). In such cases the owners of the slaves received compensation. The Greek inscriptions record the emancipation of more female than male slaves.

II. ROMAN. As a class, freedmen were called by the Romans *libertini*, but in relation to their former masters *liberti* (i. e. *liberati*). Slaves were emancipated either formally or informally. There were four kinds of formal emancipation: (1) By the *manumissio vindicta*, according to which the owner brought the slave before the praetor or some other competent official. In his presence a free citizen (usually an officer of the court) laid a staff (*vindicta*) on the slave's head and declared him free. The master, who was holding the slave by the hand, thereupon released him as symbolizing his assent (*manu misit*). (2) The *manumissio censu*, when the master formally caused the slave's name to be enrolled in the official list of citizens. (3) The *manumissio testamento*, where the master either bequeathed his freedom to the slave by will, or stipulated that the heir to the estate should free him. (4) In later times, a form called *manumissio in ecclesia* was introduced by the emperor Constantine. Here the owner emancipated the slave in the presence of the congregation.

Informal mancipation was emancipation brought about by a verbal statement of the master in the presence of friends (*manumissio inter amicos*), or by letter (*per epistulam*), or by an invitation to the slave to dinner (*in convivio*).

After formal emancipation freedmen at once became Roman citizens and members of the city tribes and of the lowest classes in the *centuriae*, with full right of voting; but, not being free born, they were not eligible to office, and were excluded from military service. The latter was, however, the case only till the first century B.C. They obtained the right to be enrolled in the country tribes several times in the republican period, but not permanently till the imperial age. Their descendants, however, were, as being free-born (*ingenui*), admitted into all the tribes, and in the second, or at least in the third generation, eligible to office. Informal emancipation conferred only practical freedom without civic rights. It was not until A.D. 17, under Tiberius, that freedmen of this kind won the *commercium*, or the right of acquiring and transferring property. Even then they had no power of testamentary bequest, and their property, at their death, went to their liberators. It was permissible, however, to pronounce a formal emancipation after their death.

To obviate abuses, and to check the excessive increase in the number of freedmen, the right of manumission was limited in several directions under Augustus. Among other things, if a slave under thirty years of age was to be manumitted *vin dicta*, a proof of sufficient reason was required; and, in case of testamentary manumission, the number was limited to a certain proportion of the whole number of slaves, and never allowed to exceed one hundred.

A mutual obligation continued to exist between the freedman and his liberator, based on the fact that the freedman belonged to the family of his patron. This is seen in the circumstance that the freedman assumed the *nomen* and the *praenomen* of his patron. In and after the first century B.C. we generally find a Greek *cognomen* added. A well-known freedman of Lucius Cornelius Sulla, for instance, was called Lucius Cornelius Epicadus. The *patronus* was bound on his side to care for his *libertus*, and in consequence either retained him altogether in his home and service, or supplied him with a farm and capital to start it; buried him in the family tomb after his death, and took charge of his children if not grown up. On the other side the freedman was bound to support his *patronus*, in case of need, out of his own resources, and if he was reduced to poverty to maintain him. If the freedman died childless, the patron inherited his property; but the rights of the patron in respect to his freedman did not pass to his patron's heirs. If a freedman neglected his duty towards his patron, he was liable to severe punishment, and in some cases might be sold for his patron's benefit, or re-enslaved to him.

The manumission of slaves was a source of much profit to the State, as a tax of five per cent. on the value of the slave was paid into the treasury after his liberation.

On the status of freedmen who were not full Roman citizens, see DEDITICII and LATINITAS. See also the articles MANUMISSIO; SERVUS.

Liberty Cap. See PILLEUS.

Libēthra (τὰ Λείβηθρα or Λίβηθρα). (1) A city of Macedonia, situated, according to Pausanias (ix. 30), on the declivity of Olympus, and not far from the tomb of Orpheus. An oracle declared that when the sun beheld the bones of the poet the city should be destroyed by a boar (ὑπὸ συός). The inhabitants of Libethra ridiculed the prophecy as a thing impossible; but the column of Orpheus's monument having been accidentally broken, a gap was made by which light broke in upon the tomb, when the same night the torrent named Sus, being prodigiously swollen, rushed down with violence from Mount Olympus upon Libethra, overthrowing the walls and all the public and private edifices, and every living creature in its furious course. Whether Libethra recovered from the devastation occasioned by this inundation is not stated in any writer, but its name occurs in Livy as a town in the vicinity of Dium before the battle of Pydna (xliv. 5). It would seem that the name of Libethrius was given to the summit of Olympus, which stood above the town, and probably transferred thence to the Boeotian Mountains, afterwards styled Libethrius Mons (Pausan. ix. 34). Hence the muses were surnamed Libethrides as well as Pierides (Verg. *Ecl.* vii. 21). (2) A fountain of Thessaly on Mount Homolé, in the district of Magnesia, at the northern extremity (Mela, ii. 3).

Libethrĭdes (Λειβηθρίδες). See LIBETHRA.

Libethrius Mons. See LIBETHRA.

Libēthrum. The same as LIBETHRA (q. v.).

Libitīna. An ancient Italian goddess of voluptuous delight and of gardens, vineyards, and vintages, originally connected with Venus, and therefore often called Venus Libitina. She was also regarded as the goddess of death and of the departed, and was therefore afterwards identified with Proserpina. By an ancient ordinance, ascribed originally to Servius Tullius, for every person who died in Rome a piece of money was deposited in her temple. Everything requisite for burials was kept there, and had to be bought or borrowed from it. Hence a person undertaking the burial of a person (an undertaker) was called *libitinarius*, and his business *libitina;* whence the expression *libitina funeribus non sufficiebat*—i. e. they could not all be buried. Owing to the connection of Libitina with the dead, the Roman poets frequently employ her name in the sense of death itself.

Libitinarii. See FUNUS, p. 698; LIBITINA.

Libo, SCRIBONIUS, a plebeian family. (1) LUCIUS, tribune of the plebs, B.C. 149, accused Ser. Sulpicius Galba on account of the outrages which he had committed against the Lusitanians. (See GALBA [1]). It was perhaps this Libo who consecrated the *Puteal Scribonianum* or *Puteal Libonis*, of which we so frequently read in ancient writers (Hor. *Sat.* ii. 6, 35). (See PUTEAL.) (2) LUCIUS, the father-in-law of Sex. Pompey, the son of Pompey the Great. On the breaking out of the Civil War in B.C. 49, he naturally sided with Pompey, and was intrusted with the command of Etruria. Shortly afterwards he accompanied Pompey to Greece, and was actively engaged in the war that ensued. On the death of Bibulus (B.C. 48) he had the chief command of the Pompeian fleet. In the Civil Wars which followed Caesar's death, he followed the fortunes of his son-in-law Sex. Pompey. In B.C. 40 Octavianus married his sister Scribonia, and this marriage was followed by a peace between the triumvirs and Pompey (39). When the war was renewed in 36, Libo for a time continued with Pompey, but, seeing his cause hopeless, he deserted him in the following year. In 34 he was consul with M. Antonius.

Libon (Λίβων). An architect of Elis, who built the temple of Olympian Zeus, in the sacred grove Altis, out of the proceeds of the spoil taken from the Pisaeans and some other people (Pausan. v. 10, 3). This temple was built in the Doric style, and it must have been erected about B.C. 444-440. See OLYMPIA.

Libra. The Roman unit of weight, nearly equal to twelve ounces avoirdupois. The libra of copper was also the unit of value, and was called *as*. See AS; PONDERA.

Libra (σταθμός). (1) A balance or pair of scales, whose principal parts were (*a*) the beam, *iugum*, ζυγόν; (*b*) the scales, *lances*, τάλαντα. When the beam had a tongue working in an "eye" (*agina*), the tongue was called *examen* and *ligula*. This sort of balance was called TRUTĬNA (τρυτάνη). A steelyard was called STATĒRA. (2) A constellation (Ζυγός) placed in the Zodiac at the equinox when days and nights are equally balanced. (3) An instrument for ascertaining the level of the water in an aqueduct (Vitruv. viii. 5, 1).

Libra. (Millin, *Peint. de Vases Ant.*)

Libraries. (1) For ancient libraries see BIBLIOTHECA. (2) For the benefit of the student is given the following list of the great libraries that contain important collections of Greek and Latin MSS. or of early editions of the classic authors: (*a*)

Vatican Library.

ITALY. The *Vatican Library* at Rome, founded by Pope Nicholas V. (1447–1455), the most magnificent collection in the world, though not the largest. Here are the majority of the MSS. from the convent at Bobbio, in the Middle Ages one of the richest collections in Europe. Here are also 3000 MSS. brought to the Vatican from Heidelberg in 1623. In 1655 the greater part of the library of Duke Federigo of Urbino was purchased by Pope Alexander VII. The collection of Queen Christina of Sweden added 1900 MSS. The last great addition was in 1856, when Pope Pius IX. added 40,000 volumes that had belonged to Cardinal Mai. In 1894, the whole number of MSS. of all kinds in the Vatican Library was more than 26,000, of which some 19,000 are Latin, 4000 Greek, and 2000 Oriental. The printed books number about 220,000. No complete catalogue has yet been made.—The *Laurentian Library* at Florence, founded in 1444 by Cosimo de Medici, contains some 10,000 Greek and Latin MSS., among them early codices of Vergil (fourth or fifth century), Tacitus, Cicero's letters *ad familiares*, the Pandects, and Aeschylus. It has however, only 4000 printed volumes.—The *Ambrosian Library* at Milan, founded in 1609 by the Cardinal Archbishop Federigo Borromeo, has 8000 MSS., among them some valuable palimpsests, and 170,000 printed books.—The *Marcian Library* or *Library of St. Mark* in Venice was founded in 1362, and established as a library by Cardinal Bessarion in the following century. Its Greek MSS. are very valuable, especially those of Aristophanes, Sophocles, Euripides, and Homer. (See HOMERUS.)—The *Biblioteca Nazionale* at Naples, opened as late as 1804 in conjunction with the remarkable *Museo*

Nazionale, has over 4000 MSS. and 200,000 printed volumes, all catalogued. Among the former are codices of Lycophron, Quintus Smyrnaeus, the half-burned MS. of Festus, a Charisius, etc.—The *Biblioteca Casanatense* at Rome has lately been united with the *Biblioteca Vittorio Emanuelo*, which contains the great collections made by the Jesuits of the old Collegio Romano. The united library contains upwards of 6000 MSS. and 500,000 printed volumes.

(*b*) FRANCE. France possesses the largest library in the world in the great *Bibliothèque Nationale* at Paris, founded by Charles V. (d. 1380). It contains nearly 100,000 MSS. and over 3,000,000 printed volumes, not systematically catalogued. The library is arranged in four departments—(1) Books and Maps; (2) Manuscripts; (3) Engravings; (4) Medals and Antiques. The collection illustrative of Latin Palaeography is wonderfully complete; and among the MSS. are famous ones of Sophocles, Euripides, Theocritus, Herodotus, Xenophon (the best), Plato, Demosthenes, Lucian, Catullus, Cicero, Ovid, Caesar, Sallust (the best), Livy, etc.—Many of the provincial libraries in France have valuable MSS., which have been catalogued at the expense of the French government (1849 foll.).

(*c*) GERMANY AND AUSTRIA. The *Royal Library* at Berlin, founded by the Elector Frederick William in 1661, has over 15,000 MSS. and nearly 1,000,000 volumes.—The largest library in Germany is the *Royal Library* at Munich, founded by Duke Albrecht V. of Bavaria (1550–1579). It is particularly rich in first editions of the classics derived from the monasteries, and has 30,000 MSS. and over 1,000,000 printed volumes. Among the MSS. are important ones of Demosthenes (A), Ovid, and Sallust. The *University Library* at Munich has some 1800 MSS. and 250,000 volumes.—The *Royal Library* at Dresden, founded by the Elector Augustus (d. 1586), has 4000 MSS. and 475,000 printed volumes, besides a very remarkable collection of dissertations, numbering fully 400,000. It has also a set of incunabula, 2000 in number.—The *Royal Public Library* at Stuttgart, founded in 1765, has 3800 MSS. and nearly 500,000 volumes.—The *Ducal Library* of Gotha, dating from the seventeenth century, has more than 6000 MSS., many of which are of great value (see CODEX), and 250,000 volumes.—Most of the German universities have admirable collections of classical material, especially *Heidelberg* (400,000 volumes and many famous MSS.) and *Strassburg*, which, though founded as late as 1871, has over 500,000 volumes and some good codices.—The *Imperial Library* at Vienna, founded by the emperor Frederick III. (or by his son Maximilian) about 1440, has 20,000 MSS., among them the only codex containing the Fifth Decade of Livy's history. There are also 6800 incunabula, and 400,000 other volumes.—There are many monastic libraries in Austria with MSS. of importance, besides large collections of incunabula. Those at Salzburg, Kremsmünster, and Lembach are the best.

(*d*) BELGIUM AND HOLLAND. Brussels has in the *Bibliothèque Royale* one of the finest libraries of Europe, with 30,000 MSS. and 400,000 volumes. There are several famous *codices Bruxellenses*. The *University Library* at Ghent (1600 MSS., 275,000 volumes) and that at Liège (1550 MSS., 160,000 volumes) are also important.—In Holland the *Royal Library* at the Hague (4000 MSS., 250,000 volumes), the *University Library* at Leyden (founded by William I. of Orange, 1575; 5600 MSS., 350,000 volumes), and the *University Library* at Amsterdam have codices of great importance to classical scholars.

(*e*) DENMARK. The *Royal Library* at Copenhagen, founded in the sixteenth century by Christian III., has many important classical MSS. (*codices Haunienses*) and 500,000 volumes.

(*f*) ENGLAND. The library of the *British Museum* in London, founded by Sir Hans Sloane in 1753, is one of the largest in the world, and in point of system and accessibility the most admirable. It contains more than 1,500,000 printed volumes, and upwards of 50,000 MSS. of all kinds—Greek, Latin, Oriental, and Mediaeval. Most important among the classical MSS. are two codices of Homer, one containing the *Iliad* and one the *Odyssey* (*codices Townleiani*), both among the earliest in existence.—At Oxford is the *Bodleian Library*, founded by Sir Thomas Bodley in 1602. It contains nearly 500,000 printed volumes and 30,000 MSS., many of them Oriental. Its collection of *editiones principes* of Greek and Latin authors is one of the finest in Europe.—The *University Library* at Cambridge was established in the early part of the fifteenth century. It has nearly 6000 MSS. and a number of printed books with MS. notes, among them being some by Bentley (q. v.). Its printed volumes number about 250,000.—The library of Trinity College at the same university is also unusually rich in Greek and Latin MSS. and early editions.

(*g*) UNITED STATES. The American libraries that are richest in classical works are those of *Harvard University* (400,000 volumes) and *Yale University* (more than 200,000 volumes). In the library of *Columbia College* (200,000 volumes) the early and rare printed editions of Greek and Latin authors are well represented.

See Petzholdt, *Bibliotheca Bibliographica* (Leipzig, 1866); Madan, *Books in Manuscript* (London, 1893); Montfaucon, *Bibliothèque des Bibliothèques des Manuscrits* (Paris, 1739); and Reinach, *Manuel de Philologie Classique*, i. pp. 23, 24 (Paris, 1883).

Librarius. The Latin name for (1) a copyist of books (Hor. *A. P.* 354); and (2) for a bookseller. See LIBER.

Librātor. (1) An expert in the construction of sewers, aqueducts, etc., called so from the hydrostatic balance (*libra aquaria*) used by him (Pliny, *Epist.* x. 70; Frontin. *De Aquaed.* 105). (2) A soldier who worked the *tormentum* (q. v.).

Libri Lintei. See article in the Appendix.

Librĭpens. See COEMPTIO.

Libui. A Gallic tribe in Gallia Cispadana, to whom the towns of Brixia and Verona formerly belonged, from which they were expelled by the Cenomani (Livy, xxi. 38).

Libum. A sort of cake made of flour, milk, eggs, oil, and sometimes honey, used as an offering to the gods, or as a birthday present (Cato, *R. R.* 75; Mart. x. 24).

Liburna and **Liburnĭca** (λιβυρνίς). A kind of light war-vessel, with two banks of oars and of little draught, carrying a mast amidships. Its shape was long and narrow, pointed at both ends, with a heavy ram. The pattern was taken by the Romans from the Liburnians, a piratical tribe on the Dalmatic coast. They are described in Aul. Gell. xvii. 3. See LIBURNIA; NAVIS.

Liburnia (Λιβουρνία). A district of Illyricum, along the coast of the Adriatic Sea, separated from Istria by the river Arsia, and from Dalmatia by the river Titius. Its inhabitants, the Liburni, supported themselves chiefly by commerce and navigation. They were celebrated at a very early period as bold and skilful sailors. Their ships were remarkable for their swift sailing; and hence vessels built after the same model were called *Liburnicae* or *Liburnae naves*. It was to light vessels of this description that Augustus was mainly indebted for his victory over Antony's fleet at the battle of Actium. (See ACTIUM.) The Liburnians were the first Illyrian people who submitted to the Romans. See ILLYRICUM.

Liburnĭdes. Islands off the coast of Liburnia, said to amount to the number of forty.

Liburnus. A chain of mountains near Apulia, crossed by Hannibal in his march from Samnium and the Peligni into Apulia. It is stated that, before he arrived in the latter province, he crossed this chain; which probably answers to the branch of the Apennines bordering on the valley of the Tifernus to the north, and known by the name of Monte della Serra (Polyb. iii. 101).

Libya (Λιβύη). The Greek name for (1) the continent of Africa in general (see AFRICA); and (2) for a district of Northern Africa (Λιβύης νομός), between Egypt and Marmarica, once an Egyptian nomos. It also bore the Roman name of Libya Exterior. See D'Avezac, *Afrique* (Paris, 1883).

Libўcum Marĕ. That part of the Mediterranean which lies along the coast of Libya, extending eastward as far as the island of Crete (Mela, i. 4).

Libyphoenīces (Λιβυφοίνικες). The inhabitants of the cities founded by the Phœnicians on the coast of the Carthaginian territory, and so called from their being a mixed race of the Libyan natives with the Phœnician settlers. See CARTHAGO.

Libyssa (Λίβυσσα). A small village of Bithynia, west of Nicomedia, and near the shores of the Sinus Astacenus. It is rendered memorable for containing the tomb of Hannibal, whence, no doubt, its name (Pliny, *H. N.* v. 148).

Licātes. A people of Vindelicia, on the eastern bank of the Licus, in the modern Oberdonaukreis, to the northeast of Füssen (Pliny, iii. 20).

Lichădes. See LICHAS.

Līchas (Λίχας or Λείχας). An attendant of Heracles, who brought his master the poisoned garment of Nessus, and was hurled by him into the sea. The Lichades (Λιχάδες)—three small islands between Euboea and Locris—were believed to have derived their name from him. See HERACLES, p. 792.

Licinia Gens. A Roman house to which belonged the distinguished families of Crassus, Lucullus, and Murena.

Licinia Lex. See LEX.

Licinian Rogations. See ROGATIONES LICINIAE; LICINIUS (1).

Licinius. (1) C. LICINIUS CALVUS, surnamed STOLO, a name said to be derived from the care with which he dug up the shoots (*stolones*) from the roots of his vines. He brought the contest between the patricians and plebeians to a happy termination, and thus became the founder of Rome's greatness. He was tribune of the people from B.C. 376 to 367, and was faithfully supported in his exertions by his colleague, L. Sextius. The laws which he proposed were: (*a*) That in future no more consular tribunes should be appointed, but that consuls should be elected, one of whom should always be a plebeian. (*b*) That no one should possess more than 500 *iugera* of the public land, or keep upon it more than 100 head of large, and 500 of small cattle. (*c*) A law regulating the affairs between debtor and creditor. (*d*) That the Sibylline Books should be intrusted to a college of ten men (*decemviri*), half of whom should be plebeians. These rogations were passed after a vehement opposition on the part of the patricians, and L. Sextius was the first plebeian who obtained the consulship, 366. Licinius himself was elected twice to the consulship, 364 and 361. Some years later he was accused by M. Popilius Laenas of having transgressed his own law respecting the amount of public land which a person might possess. He was condemned and sentenced to pay a heavy fine (Livy, vi. 35; vii. 1, 9, 16; Val. Max. viii. 6, 3). (2) C. LICINIUS MACER, an annalist and orator, who was impeached of extortion by Cicero, and, finding that the verdict was against him, committed suicide, B.C. 66. (3) C. LICINIUS MACER CALVUS, son of the last, a distinguished orator and poet, was born B.C. 82, and died about 47 or 46, in his thirty-fifth or thirty-sixth year. His most celebrated oration was delivered against Vatinius, who was defended by Cicero, when he was only twenty-seven years of age. His elegies were very warmly extolled by Catullus, Propertius, and Ovid. All his works are lost. He was very short of stature, so that Catullus calls him (53) *Salaputium disertum*, "the eloquent Tom Thumb." (Cf. Quint. x. 1, 115.) (4) A Roman emperor, ruling A.D. 307–324. He was a Dacian peasant by birth, and was raised to the rank of Augustus by the emperor Galerius. He afterwards had the dominion of the East. He carried on war first with Maximinus II., whom he defeated A.D. 314, and subsequently with Constantine, by whom he was in his turn defeated, 315. A second war broke out between Licinius and Constantine in 323, in which Licinius was not only defeated, but deprived of his throne. In the following year he was put to death by Constantine, 324. See CONSTANTINUS.

Licĭnus. (1) A Gaul by birth, who was taken prisoner in war, and became a slave of Iulius Caesar, whose confidence he gained so much as to be made his *dispensator* or steward. Caesar gave him his freedom. He also won the favour of Augustus, who appointed him, in B.C. 15, governor of his native country, Gaul. By the plunder of Gaul and by other means, he acquired enormous wealth, and hence his name is frequently coupled with that of Crassus. He lived to see the reign of Tiberius. (2) CLODIUS, a Roman annalist, who lived about the beginning of the first century B.C., wrote the history of Rome from its capture by the Gauls to his own time. This Clodius is frequently confounded with Q. Claudius Quadrigarius (q. v.).

Lictor (ῥαβδοῦχος, ῥαβδοφόρος). An attendant who bore the *fasces* (q. v.) before such Roman magistrates as had a right to these insignia. The king had twelve; the officiating consul, twelve (see CONSUL); the dictator, twenty-four (Polyb. iii. 87). The *magister equitum* had six; the praetor at Rome, two; the provincial praetor, six; proconsuls outside of Rome, twelve; the quaestor, five. They were generally freedmen, and formed in Rome a corps consisting of three *decuriae* under ten presidents. From these *decuriae*, the first of which was exclusively reserved for the consuls, the magistrates in office drew their lictors, while the provincial office-bearers nominated their own for their term of power. There was besides another decuria of thirty *lictores curiati* to attend on the public sacrifices, to summon the Comitia Curiata, and, when these meetings became little more than formal, to represent in them the thirty *curiae;* from this *decuria* probably were also chosen the lictors of the *flamen dialis* and of the Vestals. It was the duty of the lictors to accompany the magistrate continually, whenever he appeared in public. On these occasions they marched before him in single file, last in order and immediately preceding him being the *lictor proximus*, also called *lictor primus*, who was superior in rank. All passers-by, with the exception of matrons and Vestals, were warned by the lictors to stand aside and make due obeisance. The space required for official purposes was kept clear by them. Sentences of punishment were also executed by them. Their dress corresponded to that of the magistrate; inside the city the toga; outside, and in a triumph, the red military cloak (*sagulum*). See Mommsen, *Staatsrecht*, i. 374 foll.; and the articles ACCENSUS; VIATOR.

Lictors.

Licymnĭus (Λικύμνιος). (1) A son of Electryon and the Phrygian slave Midea, and consequently half-brother of Alcmenê. He was married to Perimedê, by whom he became the father of Oeonus, Argeus, and Melas. He was a friend of Heracles, whose son Tlepolemus slew him, according to some unintentionally, and according to others in a fit of anger. (2) Of Chios, a distinguished dithyrambic poet, of uncertain date. Some writers place him before Simonides; but it is perhaps more likely that he belonged to the later Athenian dithyrambic school about the end of the fourth century B.C. (3) Of Sicily, a rhetorician, the pupil of Gorgias, and the teacher of Polus.

Lidê (Λίδη). A mountain of Caria, above Pedasus.

Ligarius, QUINTUS. A Roman who fought on the side of the Pompeian party in Africa, and was defended by Cicero before Caesar in a speech still extant, and which secured a pardon from the dictator. Ligarius joined the conspirators who assassinated Caesar in B.C. 44, and perished in the proscription by the triumvirs in 43.

Liger or **Ligĕris**. The modern Loire; a large river in Gaul, rising in Mount Cevenna, flowing through the territories of the Arverni, Aedui, and Carnutes, and falling into the ocean between the territories of the Namnetes and Pictones (Caes. *B. G.* vii. 5).

Light-armed Troops. See EXERCITUS; LEGIO.

Light-houses. See PHAROS.

Lighting. See CANDELABRUM; DOMUS; FAX; LAMPAS; LANTERNA; LUCERNA.

Ligo (δίκελλα, μάκελλα). A hoe made with either one or two prongs, and with a long handle, used in weeding, etc. (Colum. x. 89).

Ligŭla. (1) A Roman liquid measure containing one fourth of the *cyathus* (q. v.). The word is also used generically, like our "spoonful," of a small quantity. (2) A spoon larger than the *cochlear* (q. v.), and like our dessert-spoon. (3) The leather tongue of a shoe, also written LINGŬLA (Poll. ii. 109).

Ligŭres. The inhabitants of Liguria. See LIGURIA.

Liguria (ἡ Λιγυστική and Λιγυστίνη). A district of Italy, bounded on the west by the river Varus and the Maritime Alps, which separated it from Transalpine Gaul; on the southeast by the river Macra, which separated it from Etruria; on the north by the river Po, and on the south by the Marê Ligusticum. The Maritime Alps and the Apennines run through the greater part of the country. The inhabitants were called by the Greeks Ligyes (Λίγυες) and Ligystini (Λιγυστῖνοι), and by the Romans LIGŬRES (sing. *Ligus*, more rarely *Ligur*). They were in early times widely spread, and inhabited the coasts of Gaul and Italy from the mouth of the Rhone to Pisae in Etruria. They were divided by the Romans into Ligures Transalpini and Cisalpini. The names of the principal tribes were: On the west side of the Alps, the Salyes or Salluvii, Oxybii, and Deciates; on the east side of the Alps, the Intemelii, Ingauni, and Apuani near the coast, the Vagienni, Salassi, and Taurini on the upper course of the Po, and the Laevi and Marisci north of the Po. The Ligurians were small of stature, but strong, active, and brave. In early times they served as mercenaries in the armies of the Carthaginians, and they were not subdued by the Romans till after a long and fierce struggle. Their chief city was Genua. The ethnic affinities of the Ligurians are uncertain; but they are regarded as having been a non-Aryan people, like the Iberians. See Bormann, *Ligustica* (3 pts. 1864–68).

Ligustĭcum Marê. See LIGUSTICUS SINUS.

Ligustĭcus Sinus. A gulf forming the upper part of the Marê Tyrrhenum. It is now the Gulf of Genoa (Flor. iii. 6). It was also called Ligusticum Marê (Colum. viii. 2).

Ligўes (Λίγυες). (1) A people of Asia, mentioned by Herodotus (vii. 72). The historian informs us that the Ligyes, Mariandyni, and Cappadocians, forming part of the army of Xerxes, were under the same commander. (2) See LIGURIA.

Lilaea (Λίλαια). An ancient town in Phocis, near the sources of the river Cephissus.

Lilybaeum (Λιλύβαιον). The modern Marsala; a town in the west of Sicily, with an excellent harbour, situated on a promontory of the same name, opposite to the Promontorium Hermaeum or Mercurii (Cape Bon) in Africa, the space between the two being the shortest distance between Sicily and Africa. The town was founded by the Car thaginians about B.C. 397, and was the strongest fortress possessed by them in Sicily, having massive walls surrounded by a huge moat forty feet in depth and some sixty feet wide. It was besieged by the Romans in the First Punic War, but they failed to take it, and it was only given up to them later as a part of the concessions made in the final treaty of peace.

Lima (ῥίνη). A file, practically identical with our own (Pliny, *H. N.* ix. 109).

Limaea, Limia, or **Limius.** Now the Lima; a river in Spain between the Durius (Douro) and the Minius (Minho), flowing into the Atlantic Ocean. It was also called Flumen Oblivionis or "River of Forgetfulness," from the legend that the Turduli and Kelts once lost their leader at this river and forgot the object of their expedition (Pliny, *H. N.* iv. 115; Sil. Ital. i. 235, xvi. 476; Plut. *Quaest. Rom.* 34).

Limbus (παρυφή). The border of a tunic or a scarf, chiefly in a woman's dress. Various patterns were used in weaving of the limbus, which was usually of a piece with the garment itself. See Serv. *ad* Verg. *Aen.* ii. 676.

Limen. See IANUA.

Limes Germanĭcus. A part of the gigantic scheme of defence established by the Romans, and extending from the mouth of the Rhine to the mouth of the Danube. The *limes Germanicus* was the part which especially protected the Agri Decumates (q. v.). See Bury's *Student's Roman Empire*, pp. 403–405 (1893); and the article LIMITES ROMANI; RHAETIA.

Limes Rhaetĭcus. See RHAETIA.

Limĭtes Romāni. The name of a continuous series of fortifications, consisting of castles, walls, earthen ramparts, and the like, which the Romans erected to protect their possessions along the Rhine and the Danube from the attacks of the Germans. Its whole length was 350 miles, between Cologne and Ratisbon. Part of it was a huge stone wall, of which extensive portions still remain. See RHAETIA.

Limnae (Λίμναι). (1) A town in Messenia, on the frontiers of Laconia, with a temple of Artemis Limnatis. (2) See SPARTA.

Limnaea (Λιμναία). A town in the north of Acarnania, near the Ambracian Gulf, on which it had a harbour.

Limonum. See PICTONES.

Limus. The apron worn by the *popa*, or person who did the killing at sacrifices, and by other *servi publici*, who were in consequence spoken of as *limo cincti*. See Serv. *ad* Verg. *Aen.* xii. 120; *C. I. L.* v. 3401; Isid. *Orig.* xix. 33.

Limȳra (τὰ Λίμυρα). A city in the southeast of Lycia, on the river Limyrus.

Lindum or **Lindum Colonia.** The modern Lincoln; a town of the Coritani in Britain, on the road from Londinium (London) to Eboracum (York), and a Roman colony. Among the Roman remains still to be seen at Lincoln are an altar (in St. Swithin's Church), part of a basilica, and part of a city gate, now known as "Newport Arch," etc. The modern name Lincoln has been formed out of Lindum Colonia (Ptol. ii. 3, 30).

Remains of a Roman Arch at Lincoln.

Lindus (Λίνδος). One of the three Dorian cities in the island of Rhodes, situated on the eastern coast. Its modern name is Lindo. It is mentioned by Homer (*Il.* ii. 656), with its kindred cities, Ialysus and Camirus. These three cities, with Cos, Cnidus, and Halicarnassus, formed the original Hexapolis, in the southwest corner of Asia Minor. Lindus stood upon a mountain in a district abounding in vines and figs, and had two celebrated temples, one of Athenê surnamed Λινδία and one of Heracles. It was the birthplace of Cleobulus, one of the seven wise men. It retained much of its consequence even after the foundation of Rhodes. Inscriptions of some importance have been found in its Acropolis.

Linea. A thread. (1) (ὁρμιά). A fish-line made of strong hair (*seta*) or flax (Mart. iii. 58, 28; Ovid, *Met.* xiii. 923). (2) (στάθμη). A carpenter's chalked line (Vitruv. 3, 5).

Lingŏnes. (1) A powerful people in Transalpine Gaul, bounded by the Treviri on the north and the Sequani on the south. Their chief town was Andematurinum, afterwards Lingones (Langres). (2) A branch of the above-mentioned people, who migrated into Cisalpine Gaul along with the Boii, and dwelt in the neighbourhood of Ravenna.

Linguistics. See GRAMMATICA; PHILOLOGY.

Lingŭla. See LIGULA.

Linter. (1) Originally a sort of "dug-out," a small flat-bottomed boat used in shallow water. It was rowed by oars and was chiefly used in ferrying people over small rivers, etc. (Livy, xxi. 27; Caes. *B. G.* vii. 60).

Linternum. See LITERNUM.

Linus (Λίνος). The personification of a dirge or lamentation, and therefore described as a son of Apollo by a Muse (Calliopê, or by Psamathê or Chalciopê) or of Amphimarus by Urania. Both Argos and Thebes claimed the honour of his birth. An Argive tradition related that Linus was exposed by his mother after his birth, and was brought up by shepherds, but was afterwards torn to pieces by dogs. Psamathé's grief at the occurrence betrayed her misfortune to her father, who condemned her to death. Apollo, indignant at the father's cruelty, visited Argos with a plague; and, in obedience to an oracle, the Argives endeavoured to propitiate Psamathé and Linus by means of sacrifices and dirges, which were called *lini*. According to a Boeotian tradition, Linus was killed by Apollo because he had ventured upon a musical contest with the god. The Thebans distinguished between an earlier and later Linus; the latter is said to have instructed Heracles in music, but to have been killed by the hero.

Lions, GATE OF. See MYCENAE.

Lipăra and **Liparenses Insŭlae.** See AEOLIAE.

Lipŏgram (from λιπογράμματος, "wanting a letter"). A name given to any literary work which is characterized by the exclusion of some particular letters of the alphabet. The first known writer of lipograms was the Greek poet Lasus (about B.C. 500). Tryphiodorus of Egypt, a writer of the same period, is said to have written an *Odyssey* in twenty-four books, from each of which in succession one of the letters of the Greek alphabet was excluded. A curious instance in Latin is found in the prose history (*De Aetatibus Mundi*) of the Christian writer Fulgentius (q. v.). In modern times this sort of fooling is found principally in Spanish literature—an inheritance, perhaps, from Rome. Lope de Vega wrote five novels from each of which one of the vowels is carefully excluded. See Wheatley, *Anagrams* (1862).

Lipography. See HAPLOGRAPHY.

Liponautiou Graphé (λιποναυτίου γραφή). See ASTRATEIAS GRAPHÉ.

Lipostratiou Graphé (λιποστρατίου γραφή). See ASTRATEIAS GRAPHÉ.

Lipotaxiou Graphé (λιποταξίου γραφή). See ASTRATEIAS GRAPHÉ.

Lips (λίψ). The southwest wind (Herod. ii. 25), corresponding to the Latin Africus.

Lips. (Tower of the Winds, Athens.)

Lipsius, JUSTUS, the Latinized form of JOEST LIPS. A great humanist, born at Overyssche in Brabant, October 18, 1547. Educated at the Jesuit College of Cologne and the University of Louvain, he obtained, at the age of twenty, the office of Latin Secretary to Cardinal Granvella, to whom he had dedicated his first work, *Variarum Lectionum Libri III.* (1567). With the cardinal he visited Rome, and for two years studied the Latin classics and collected inscriptions in that city. He also familiarized himself with the great collection of MSS. in the Vatican, and his book, published in 1575, *Antiquarum Lectionum Libri V.*, showed his familiarity with some of the greater principles and methods of text criticism—the collation, emendation, and classification of codices.

After making the acquaintance in Rome of such scholars as Muretus, Paulus Manutius, and Fulvio Orsini, he travelled in 1570 over Burgundy, Germany, Austria, and Bohemia, for the sake of meeting the great classicists of those countries. A little later he taught at the University of Jena for a year, and in 1579 received a call to the University of Leyden as Professor of History. This chair he held for eleven years, during which period his literary productiveness was very great, his numerous works being issued from the celebrated press of Plantin of Antwerp. In 1591 he left Leyden because of his failing health, and after travelling about from place to place, and refusing many calls from the courts and universities of Italy, Austria, and Spain, accepted the Latin chair at the Collegium Buslidianum at Louvain, with the understanding that he was not to be required to teach. With this appointment he coupled that of Privy-Councillor and Historiographer to the king of Spain. He died at Louvain, March 23, 1606.

Lipsius was the master of an epigrammatic and fascinating Latin style, and his writings were always readable. His great favourite of the classical authors was Tacitus, the whole of whose writings he could repeat from memory, and used to offer to do so with a dagger at his breast to stab him if he made a single error. His range as a scholar, however, was limited. He knew little Greek, though ostentatiously parading Greek quotations in his Latin letters, and he was wholly un-Ciceronian in his Latinity. He had no ear for metre and cared little for the poets. His general knowledge of classical antiquity was also comparatively slight. Nevertheless, he was ranked among the most noted scholars of his age, and with Scaliger and Casaubon formed the so-called "Triumvirate." His chief strength lay in his knowledge of the Roman histories and of Roman antiquities in the narrow sense of the word. His two most elaborate works are his edition of Tacitus (1574), which was five times revised by him, the last edition appearing in 1606; and of Seneca (Antwerp, 1605). The former work is almost epoch-making in the completeness and elaboration of its exhaustive commentary. He also edited Valerius Maximus (Antwerp, 1585) and Velleius Paterculus (Leyden, 1591, and 1607). His complete works appeared in 4 vols. at Antwerp in 1637, reprinted at Wesel in 1675 with his life by Le Mire. A bibliographical list of forty-eight separate publications is given by Nicéron in his *Mémoires*, xxiv. p. 118. See De Reiffenberg, *De Justi Lipsi Vita et Scriptis* (Brussels, 1823); and L. Müller, *Geschichte d. class. Phil. in den Niederlanden*, pp. 249 foll. (Leipzig, 1869).

Liquentia. The modern Livenza, a river in Venetia, in the north of Italy, flowing into the Sinus Tergestinus.

Liris. The modern Garigliano, more anciently called CLANIS or GLANIS; one of the principal rivers in Central Italy, rising in the Apennines west of Lake Fucinus, flowing into the Sinus Caietanus near Minturnae, and forming the boundary between Latium and Campania. Its stream was sluggish, whence the *Liris quieta aqua* of Horace (*Carm.* i. 31).

Lissus (Λισσός). A town in the south of Dalmatia, at the mouth of the river Drilon, founded by

Dionysius of Syracuse, B.C. 385, and possessing a strongly fortified acropolis called Acrolissus, which was considered impregnable.

Lista. The old capital of the Aborigines, in the country afterwards settled by the Sabines. The town was surprised by the Sabines in an expedition by night, and the inhabitants were driven out (Dion. Hal. i. 14).

Lita. Now Litani; a river of Syria rising near Heliopolis (Baalbek) and emptying into the Mediterranean a little north of Tyre.

Litai. See ATÉ.

Litāna Silva. A large forest on the Apennines in Cisalpine Gaul, southeast of Mutina. Here the Romans were defeated by the Gauls in B.C. 216. The modern name is Silva di Luge.

Liternum or **Linternum.** The modern Patria; a town on the coast of Campania, at the mouth of the river Clanis or Glanis, which in the lower part of its course takes the name of LITERNUS, and which flows through a marsh to the north of the town, called LITERNA PALUS. It was to this place that the elder Scipio Africanus retired when the tribunes attempted to bring him to trial, and here he is said to have died.

Litterārum Obligatio. See OBLIGATIO.

Little Iliad. See LESCHES.

Liturgia (λειτουργία—i. e. "service performed for the public"). A term applied at Athens to either an ordinary or extraordinary service, which the State imposed on its wealthier citizens in accordance with a regular rotation. The ordinary services, which citizens whose property amounted to more than three talents ($3500) were required to perform, are: (1) The CHOREGIA (χορηγία), the most expensive service of this kind, involving the equipment of a chorus (q. v.) for its musical competitions at public festivals, which were accompanied by theatrical and musical performances. (2) The GYMNASIARCHIA (γυμνασιαρχία), which imposed the obligation of training in the Gymnasia the competitors for the gymnastic contests, supplying them with proper diet while they were in training, and providing at the games themselves for the requisite arrangement and decoration of the scene of the contest. The most expensive type of this form of service was the lampadarchy (λαμπαδαρχία), the equipment of the torch race (q. v.), which in one instance (recorded in Lysias, *Or.* 21, § 3) cost twelve *minae* ($200). (3) The ARCHITHEORIA (ἀρχιθεωρία), or superintendence of the sacred embassies (θεωρίαι), sent to the four great national festivals, or to Delos and other holy places. In this case the State contributed part of the expense. There were other liturgies confined to the separate tribes and demes, such as the entertainment of members of the clan on festal occasions.

The most expensive of all was the extraordinary liturgy called the TRIERARCHIA (τριηραρχία), which was necessary mainly in times of war. This involved the equipment of a ship of war, and was required of the wealthiest citizen only. Before the Persian Wars the equipment of the forty-eight to fifty ships of the Athenian navy of that time devolved on the *naucrariae* (q. v.). When the number of the fleet was increased, the necessary number of trierarchs was nominated in each year by the strategi. The State provided the vessel—i. e. the hull and mast; and every trierarch had to fit out this vessel with the necessary equipment, to keep it in readiness for the year, and to man it with a complete crew of oarsmen and others. The State supplied pay and provision for the crew, though the sum paid did not always suffice for the purpose; it afterwards supplied the furniture of the vessel also. To lighten the expense, which amounted to between forty minae and a talent ($665–$1180), it became allowable, about B.C. 411, for two persons to share it. Afterwards, in 358, twenty *symmoriae* (q. v.) were instituted—i. e. companies consisting of sixty citizens each, with a committee of the 300 wealthiest citizens at their head; the 300 distributed the expense over the individual *symmoriae* in such sort that the cost of a single trireme was shared by a greater or less number of citizens. Lastly, about B.C. 340, the incidence of the burden was regulated by a law introduced by Demosthenes, whereby all citizens, with the exception of the poorer classes, bore the expense in proportion to their property. Thus property (or rather taxable capital) amounting to ten talents imposed the obligation of equipping one vessel, twenty talents two vessels, and so on. Those who had less than ten talents were to club together and to make up that amount among them.

The time of service lasted, as has been already stated, for one year. On its expiration, the trierarch, who had looked after the vessel, was responsible to the Logistae (q. v.) for the condition of the vessel, and had to hand in his account of the expenditure of the sums paid by the State. Another board, the *epimeletae* of the *neoria* (the inspectors of the dock-yards), superintended the regular fulfilment of the duties of the trierarchs, and were armed for this purpose with compulsory powers.

No one was compelled to undertake more than one liturgy at the same time, or two in two immediately successive years. The only persons exempt from the trierarchy were the archons, unmarried heiresses, and orphans up to the end of the first year after they had come of age. The obligation to see that the liturgy was discharged in each particular case fell on the tribe concerned. If any one considered that he had been unfairly chosen for this duty, and a wealthier person passed over, he could resort to the form of challenge to exchange properties known as the *antidosis* (q. v.). See the introduction to the oration of Demosthenes, *Adv. Leptinem*, in the edition of Sandys, pp. ii.–xviii.; and Wolf's *Prolegomena* to the same oration.

Augur with Lituus. (Inghirami, *Mon. Etrusc.*)

Lituus. A word probably containing the root of *clino*, κλίνω, and hence = (*c*)*lituus*, "the bent instrument." (1) The crooked staff used by the Roman augurs. With it they divided the expanse of heaven for purposes of divination, as explained in the articles AUGUR; DIVINATIO; TEMPLUM. It is probably the original of the archiepiscopal crosier of the Roman Church. On the derivation, see Müller, *Die Etrusker*, iv. 1, 5. An alternative etymology makes it from *litare*, "to get good omens."

(2) A trumpet slightly curved at the end (Gell. v. 8). It differs from both the *tuba*, which was straight, and the *cornu*, which was spiral. The *lituus* was chiefly used for cavalry-signals.

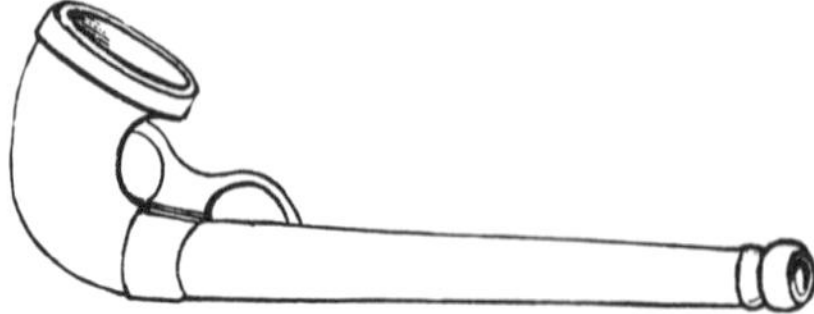

Lituus or Trumpet. (Fabretti.)

Lityerses (Λιτυέρσης). A son of Midas, said to have lived at Celaenae in Phrygia and to have forced all strangers who passed his fields to work at his harvest. If they failed to surpass him, he cut off their heads and hid their bodies in the sheaves, over which a reaping-song was sung. Heracles overcame him and killed him. His memory was preserved in a harvest-song called Lityerses (Suidas, s. v.; Schol. *ad* Theocr. x. 41).

Livia. (1) A sister of M. Livius Drusus, the celebrated tribune, B.C. 91. She was married first to M. Porcius Cato, by whom she had Cato Uticensis, and subsequently to Q. Servilius Caepio, by whom she had a daughter, Servilia, the mother of M. Brutus, who killed Caesar. (2) LIVIA DRUSILLA, the daughter of Livius Drusus Claudianus. She was married first to Tib. Claudius Nero, and afterwards to Augustus, who compelled her husband to divorce her in B.C. 38. She had already borne her husband one son, the future emperor Tiberius, and at the time of her marriage with Augustus was six months pregnant with another, who subsequently received the name of Drusus. She never had any children by Augustus, but she retained his affection till his death. On the accession of her son

Livia, wife of Augustus. (Naples Museum.)

Tiberius to the throne, she at first attempted to obtain an equal share in the government; but this the jealous temper of Tiberius would not brook, and he commanded her to cease meddling in public affairs. From that time he showed towards her only hatred, refusing even to visit her when she was dying. She died in A.D. 29, at the age of 82 or 86. (3) LIVILLA, the wife of the younger Drusus, son of the emperor Tiberius. She was seduced by Seianus, who persuaded her to poison her husband, A.D. 23. (4) IULIA LIVILLA, daughter of Germanicus and Agrippina. See IULIA.

Livia Gens. An important plebeian gens at Rome, whose most distinguished names are those of Drusus (q. v.) and Salinator (q. v.).

Liviae Leges. Laws proposed by M. Livius Drusus, a tribune, B.C. 92, about transplanting colonies to different parts of Italy and Sicily, and granting corn to poor citizens at a low price; also, that the *iudices* should be chosen indiscriminately from the senators and equites, and that the allied States of Italy should be admitted to the freedom of the city. Drusus was a man of great eloquence and of the most upright intentions; but, endeavouring to reconcile those whose interests were diametrically opposite, he was crushed in the attempt, being murdered by an unknown assassin in his own house, upon his return from the Forum, amid a number of clients and friends. No inquiry was made about his death. The States of Italy considered this event the signal for a revolt, and endeavoured to extort by force the privileges which they could not obtain voluntarily. Above 300,000 men fell in the contest in the space of two years. At last the Romans, although upon the whole they had the advantage, were obliged to grant the freedom of the city, first to the allies, and afterwards to all the States of Italy (Vell. Paterc. ii. 13 foll.; Flor. iii. 18).

Livius. (1) ANDRONĪCUS. An early writer who is regarded as the founder of Roman epic and dramatic poetry. He was by birth a Greek of Southern Italy, and was brought as a slave to Rome, after the conquest of Tarentum in B.C. 272, while still a young man. His master, a Livius (perhaps Livius Salinator), whose name he bears, gave him his liberty, and he became an instructor in the Greek and Latin languages. This employment probably gave occasion for his translation of the *Odyssey* into Saturnian verse, which, in spite of its imperfections, remained a school-book in Rome for centuries. The first verse runs as follows:

"Virum mihi, Camena, insece versutum."

In B.C. 240 he brought upon the Roman stage the first drama composed after a Greek model, and with such success that thenceforward dramatic poetry was well established in Rome. According to ancient custom he appeared as an actor in his own pieces. His dramatic compositions, tragedies, and comedies were faithful but undoubtedly imperfect translations of Greek originals. He attempted lyric poetry also, for he was commissioned by the State to write a march in honour of Iuno Regina. Scanty remains of his works are all that have come down to us; and these are collected by Ribbeck in his *Scaenicae Romanorum Poesis Fragmenta* (Leipzig, 1873), and Bährens, *Frag. Poetarum Romanorum*, pp. 37–43 (Leipzig, 1886). See, also, Wordsworth's *Fragments and Specimens of Early Latin* (Oxford, 1874). (2) TITUS. One of the greatest and certainly the most popular of the Roman writers of history. He was born at Patavium (B.C. 59), of good family, and, after being carefully educated, betook himself early (before B.C. 31) to Rome, where he soon became acquainted with the most distinguished men of the day. Even Augustus entertained friendly relations towards him in spite of his openly expressed republican convictions, for which he called him a partisan of Pompey. He does not seem to have taken public office, but to have lived exclusively for literature. He was esteemed by his contemporaries so highly that a Spaniard is said to have travelled from Gades (Cadiz) to Rome merely to see him (Pliny, *Epist.* ii. 3). He died in his native town in A.D. 17. He must have begun his great historical work between B.C. 27 and 25; it can only have been completed shortly before his death, as he did not publish the first twenty-one books until after the death of Augustus (A.D. 14). It recounts the history of Rome in 142 books, extending from the foundation of the city (whence the title *Ab Urbe Condita Libri*) to the death of Drusus (A.D. 9). His own death must have prevented its continuation to the death of Augustus, as he doubtless had proposed. He published the work, called by himself *Annales* (xliii. 13), from time to time, in separate parts, arranging his material—at least for the first ninety books—as far as possible in decades (portions consisting of ten books), and half-decades; the division into decades was, however, first carried through in the fifth century, probably for convenience of handling so vast a series of books. There still remain only the first decade (to B.C. 293), the third, fourth, and half of the fifth decade (218–167); and of the remainder, with the exception of a fairly large portion of the ninety-first book, only inconsiderable fragments. We also possess from an unknown pen, epitomes (*periochae*) of all the books except 136 and 137, and a scanty extract from the account of the portents (*prodigia*), which appeared in B.C. 249 and following year. This is by a certain Iulius Obsequens, and perhaps dates from the fourth century.

Livy's importance rests more on the magnitude of his patriotic undertaking and the charm of his style than on his acquisitions as a scientific historian. He is, in fact, best regarded as a remarkable story-teller, who possessed a diction almost perfect in its way, and an unusual power of graphic narrative. For writing history, however, he had no special training, and his knowledge of Roman law and of the Roman military system was but slight. In selecting his authorities, also, he showed little discrimination, basing his judgment of them on *a priori* assumptions. Thus he follows Valerius Antias in the first decade with no mistrust (cf. vii. 36; ix. 27, 37, 43), but later denounces him as a falsifier (xxvi. 49; xxx. 19; xxxiii. 10, etc.). He does, however, use Polybius, besides Licinius Macer, Quadrigarius, and Caelius Antipater, but often draws different portions of his narrative from conflicting accounts, so that there are frequent inconsistencies to be noticed. It is evident that he had never read the *Leges Regiae* or even many important laws of later times. His purpose, however, was not at all to write a critical history, but rather, by a lively and brilliant narrative, to rekindle the patriotic spirit among his countrymen and to inspire them with a desire to emulate the deeds of their heroic ancestors. From this standpoint, his history deserves the highest praise, and justly won for him the name of "the Roman Herodotus." The only criticism of any account that has come down to us is that of Asinius Pollio recorded by Quintilian (i. 5, 56 and viii. 1, 3), which charges the historian with displaying in his writings a certain Patavinity (*Patavinitas*, from Patavium, Padua, Livy's birthplace). Just what this criticism was meant to imply is not clearly known. It may have been intended to characterize the style as being more florid than was consistent with the reserve of a Roman gentleman, or it may refer to the presence of provincialisms, which we are not now able to detect as such. It may, as some think, have marked the enthusiasm of the writer as opposed to the polished and self-contained *urbanitas* of the metropolis. On this point, see Wiedemann, *De Patavinitate Livii* (Görlitz, 1848–54); and Moritz Haupt, *Opuscula*, ii. 69.

Of Livy's history, the first decade (books one to ten) is entire. It embraces the period from the foundation of the city to the year B.C. 294, when the subjugation of the Samnites may be said to have been completed. The second decade (books eleven to twenty) is altogether lost. It embraced the period from 294 to 219, comprising an account, among other matters, of the invasion of Pyrrhus and of the First Punic War. The third decade (books twenty-one to thirty) is entire. It embraces the period from 219 to 201, comprehending the whole of the Second Punic War The fourth decade (books thirty-one to forty) is entire, and also one half of the fifth (books forty-one to forty-five). These fifteen books embrace the period from 201 to 167, and develop the progress of the Roman arms in Cisalpine Gaul, in Macedonia, Greece, and Asia, ending with the triumph of Aemilius Paulus. Of the other books nothing remains except inconsiderable fragments, the most notable being a few chapters of the ninety-first book, concerning the fortunes of Sertorius. The composition of so vast a work necessarily occupied many years; and we find indications which throw some light upon the epochs when different sections were composed. Thus, in the first book (ch. 19), it is stated that the temple of Ianus had been closed twice only since the reign of Numa—for the first time in the consulship of T. Manlius (B.C. 235), a few years after the termination of the First Punic War; for the second time by Augustus Caesar, after the battle of Actium, in 29. But we know that it was shut again by Augustus, after the conquest of the Cantabrians, in 25; and hence it is evident that the first book must have been written between the years 29 and 25. Moreover, since the last book contained an account of the death of Drusus, it is evident that the task must have been spread over seventeen years, and probably occupied a much longer time.

The discovery of the lost books of Livy has been a dream of scholars for many centuries, and may yet be realized. In the sixteenth century a complete Livy was reported to be in existence in a monastery in Denmark, where two travellers independently professed to have seen it; but inquiry failed to verify the claim.

Among the most famous MANUSCRIPTS of Livy now in existence are a Codex Mediceus and a Codex Parisinus, each of the eleventh century. Portions of bks. iii.–vi. are preserved in a very old palimpsest at Verona. The third decade is preserved in a MS. now in Paris (the Codex Puteaneus) of the eighth century, and in a Mediceus of the eleventh century. The fourth decade is known from a Codex Moguntinus (Mayence), now lost, and from a MS. at Bamberg. What is preserved of the fifth decade is in a sixth-century MS. at Vienna.

The *editio princeps* of Livy appeared at Rome about 1469 (bks. xxxiii. and xli.–xlv. omitted). The first critical edition was that of J. F. Gronovius (Leyden, 1645). Great editions are those of Drakenborch with variorum notes and supplements (7 vols. Amsterdam, 1738–46; reprinted at Stuttgart, 1820–28, and edited by Bekker and Raschig, Berlin, 1829 foll.); Madvig, Ussing, and Luchs, not yet finished (Berlin, 1888 foll.); and Weissenborn and Müller, with German notes (Berlin, 1867–1888). Good editions of separate portions are the following: Bk. i., by Seeley (Oxford, 1876), Purser (Dublin, 1881), Stephenson (London, 1886); bk. iv., Stephenson (London, 1890); bk. v., Whibley (London, 1890), Prendeville, 13th ed. (London, 1890); bks. v.–vii., Cluer and Matheson (London, 1881); bks. vii.–viii., Luterbacher (Leipzig, 1890); bks. xxi.–xxii., Lord (Boston, 1891); bks. i., xxi.–xxii., Westcott (Boston, 1891); bks. xxi.–xxv., Harant (Paris, 1886); bks. xxvi.–xxx., Riemann (Paris, 1889).

On Livy's language, see Riemann, *Études sur la Langue et la Grammaire de Tite Live* (Paris, 1884). There is a vast lexicon to Livy, preparing by Fügner, of which in 1894 six parts had appeared. On the sources of Livy's history, see Lachmann, *De Fontibus Historiarum T. Livii* (Göttingen, 1821); H. Peter, *Hist. Reliquiae*, i. 89, 198, 225; and Kieserling, *De Rerum Romanarum Scriptoribus Quibus T. Livius Usus Est* (Berlin, 1858).

There is a translation of the whole of Livy into Elizabethan English by Philemon Holland (London, 1600); of bks. xxi.–xxv., by Church and Brodribb (2d ed. London, 1890); and of the whole into German by Klaiber and Teuffel, in 6 vols. (2d ed. Stuttgart, 1854–56). See HISTORIA.

Lixae. Sutlers or traders who followed the Roman army (Livy, v. 8; Hirt. *Bell. Afr.* 75). They bought up the plunder taken by the soldiers, and sold their own wares to the troops at bazaars or booths (*canabae*) outside the camp.

Lixus (Λίξος). A city on the west coast of Mauretania Tingitana in Africa, at the mouth of a river of the same name. It was a place of some commercial importance.

Lobeck, CHRISTIAN AUGUST. A distinguished Greek scholar, born at Naumburg, June 5, 1781. He was Corrector at Wittenberg, 1802; Professor Extraordinarius, 1810–14; and Professor Ordinarius and Librarian at Königsberg, 1814–60. His principal writings consist of contributions to the study of Greek grammar and mythology, including *Paralipomena Grammaticae* (2 vols. 1837); *Aglaophamus* (2 vols. 1829); and *Pathologiae Sermonis Graeci Prolegomena* (1843). The *Aglaophamus* treats especially of the Orphic sect and literature, and is a monument of accurate and exhaustive scholarship. He also edited some Greek texts, among them the *Ajax* of Sophocles, with a good commentary. See Bursian, *Geschichte der class. Philologie in Deutschland*, pp. 572–575, 711–713 (Berlin, 1883).

Locatio Conductio. Letting and hiring; one of the four forms of Roman contract. (1) *Locatio conductio rerum*, the letting or hiring of anything that can be bought or sold. (2) *Locatio conductio operarum*, the letting or hiring of a free man for his services. See Gaius, iii. 142–147.

Lochāgus (λοχαγός). The commander of a λόχος. See LOCHUS.

Lochus (λόχος). The Greek designation of a body of foot soldiers. Among the Spartans it denoted in early times the largest divisions into which the whole population capable of bearing arms was grouped. Each of these (according to Thuc. v. 66 and 68) comprised four πεντηκοστύες of four ἐνωμοτίαι each, an ἐνωμοτία containing on an average thirty-two men. The name also denoted the individuals comprised therein. Later (Xen. *Rep. Lac.* ii. 4) it was the name of the four subdivisions of a mora (q. v.). In Greek mercenary troops a lochus was a company of one hundred men under a separate commander. Several of these companies were united under the superior command of a στρατηγός (q. v.).

Locks. See CLAVIS.

Locri (Λοκροί), sometimes called LOCRENSES by the Romans. The inhabitants of two districts in Greece called LOCRIS (Λοκρίς). (1) EASTERN LOCRIS, extending from Thessaly and the pass of Thermopylae along the coast to the frontiers of Boeotia, and bounded by Doris and Phocis on the west. It was a fertile and well-cultivated country The northern part was inhabited by the LOCRI EPICNEMIDII, who derived their name from Mount Cnemis. The southern part was inhabited by the LOCRI OPUNTII, who derived their name from their principal town, Opus. The two tribes were separated by Daphnus, a small slip of land, which at one time belonged to Phocis The Epicnemidii were for a long time subject to the Phocians, and were included under the name of the latter people; whence the name of the Opuntii occurs more frequently in Greek history. (2) WESTERN LOCRIS, or the country of the LOCRI OZŎLAE, was bounded on the north by Doris, on the west by Aetolia, on the east by Phocis, and on the south by the Corinthian Gulf. The country is mountainous, and for the most part unproductive. Mount Corax from Aetolia and Mount Parnassus from Phocis occupy the greater part of it. The Locri Ozolae were a colony of the Western Locrians, and were more uncivilized than the latter. They resembled their neighbours, the Aetolians, both in their predatory habits and in their mode of warfare. Their chief town was Amphissa.

Locri Epizephyrii (Λοκροὶ Ἐπιζεφύριοι). An ancient Greek city in Lower Italy, situated in the southeast of Bruttium, north of the promontory of Zephyrium, from which it was said to have derived its surname Epizephyrii, though others suppose this name was given to the place simply because it lay to the west of Greece. It was founded by the Locrians from Greece, B.C. 683. The inhabitants regarded themselves as descendants of Aiax Oïleus; and as he resided at the town of Naryx among the Opuntii, the poets gave the name of Narycia Locri. For the same reason the pitch of Bruttium is frequently called Narycia. Locri was celebrated for the excellence of its laws, which were drawn up by Zaleucus soon after the foundation of the city. (See ZALEUCUS.) Near the town was an ancient and wealthy Temple of Persephonē.

Locris. See LOCRI.

Locŭli (dim. of *locus*). A small box, coffer, or casket with compartments, whence the word is used only in the plural. In Hor. *Sat.* i. 6, 74 the word is used of a schoolboy's satchel and = *capsa* (q. v.) or *theca*.

Locŭlus. See COLUMBARIUM.

Locuplētes, also called ADSIDUI. Roman freeholders of land who were included in the five classes of Servius as liable for summons to service or *tributum* (Cic. *De Rep.* ii. 22, 40).

Locusta, or more correctly, **Lucusta**. A famous female poisoner, employed by Agrippina in poisoning the emperor Claudius, and by Nero for dispatching Britannicus. She was put to death in the reign of Galba (Tac. *Ann.* xii. 66; xiii. 15).

Lodgings. See INSULA.

Lodix and **Lodicŭla** (σάγιον). A small, shaggy blanket used as a bed-covering (Suet. *Aug.* 83), or as a floor-covering (Petron. 20).

Logeion (λογεῖον, "speaking-place"). In the ancient theatre, the front of the stage occupied by the actors. In Latin it was called *pulpitum*. See THEATRUM.

Logistae (λογισταί, "auditors of accounts"). The name given at Athens to a board consisting originally of thirty, subsequently of ten members, who, in conjunction with another board, the ten εὔθυνοι, and their twenty assessors, received from magistrates, at the expiration of their term of office, the accounts of their administration. (See EUTHYNÉ.) This was especially important with those magistrates through whose hands public money passed. Both boards were originally chosen by show of hands; later by lot. One member was elected from each φυλή; the assessors of the εὔθυνοι were appointed by free choice. The logistae were the supreme authority to whom outgoing magistrates submitted their accounts The εὔθυνοι examined the several details, notified, when necessary, those who were liable, and returned the accounts to the logistae, with a report on their merits. Magistrates who had nothing to do with public money only gave an assurance to the logistae that they had received and paid nothing. If the accounts were approved, and no charge was brought after the public proclamation by the logistae, they gave the magistrate his discharge. In the other alternative they referred the case to a court of justice in which they were themselves presidents. The prosecution was intrusted to ten συνήγοροι, or counsel for the State, who were chosen by lot and sat with the logistae. The final decision rested with the Heliastic court. See HELIAEA.

Logistĭca (λογιστική, sc. τέχνη). The art of reckoning. See NUMERI.

Logogrăphi (λογογράφοι, i. e. writers in prose). The name given to the oldest Greek historians, who by their first attempts at disquisitions in prose marked the transition from narrative poetry to prose history (Thuc. i. 21). As in the case of epic poetry, so these earliest historical writings emanated from Ionia, where the first attempts at an exposition of philosophic reflections in prose were made at about the same time by Pherecydes, Anaximander, and Anaximenes; and, in both cases alike, it was the Ionic dialect that was used. This class of writing long preserved in its language the poetic character which it inherited from its origin in the epic narrative. It was only by degrees that it approached the tone of true prose. It confined itself absolutely to the simple telling of its story, which was largely made up of family and local traditions. It never classified its materials from a more elevated point of view, or scrutinized them with critical acumen. The logographers flourished from about B.C. 550 down to the Persian Wars. Their latest representatives extend, however, down to the time of the Peloponnesian War. When true history arose with Herodotus, they soon lapsed into oblivion, whence they were rescued in Alexandrian days. Many of the works ascribed to them were, however, believed to be spurious, or at least interpolated. There remain fragments only of a few. The larger number of the historic writers who are described as logographers were Asiatic Greeks, e. g. Cadmus of Miletus, author of a history of the founding of Miletus and the colonization of Ionia (he lived about B.C. 540, and was considered the first writer of historic prose); further, Dionysus of Miletus, a writer of Persian history; Hecataeus (q. v.) of Miletus (550–476); Xanthus of Sardis (about 496), a writer of Lydian history; Hellanicus (q. v.) of Lesbos (about 480–400); Charon of Lampsacus (about 456), a compiler of Persian history and annals of his native town; Pherecydes of the Carian island Leros (died about B.C. 400), who lived at Athens, and in his great collection of myths in ten books treated chiefly of the early days of Attica. Some belonged to the colonies in the West—e. g. Hippys of Rhegium, at the time of the Persian War the oldest writer on Sicily and Italy. The only representative from Greece itself is Acusilaüs of Argos in Boeotia, the author of a genealogical work. The scanty remains of the logographers are collected by Müller in his *Fragmenta Historicorum Graecorum* (Paris, 1856). See HISTORIA.

Loidorias Diké (λοιδορίας δίκη). See KAKEGORIAS DIKÉ.

Lollia Paulīna. A granddaughter of M. Lollius, mentioned below, and heiress to his immense wealth. She was married to C. Memmius Regulus; but the emperor Caligula sent for her, divorced her from her husband, and married her, and soon divorced her again. After Claudius had put to death his wife Messalina, Lollia was one of the candidates for the vacancy, but she was put to death by means of Agrippina. Pliny the Elder speaks of her magnificent jewels (*H. N.* ix. 58).

Lollius, MARCUS. A Roman who was consul, B.C. 21, governor of Gaul, B.C. 16, and appointed by Augustus as tutor to his grandson, C. Caesar, whom he accompanied to the East, B.C. 2. Horace addressed an Ode (iv. 9) to Lollius, and two Epistles (i. 2 and 18) to the eldest son of Lollius.

Lonché (λόγχη). A lance. See HASTA.

Londinium or **Londīnum**. The modern London, the capital of the Cantii in Britain, originally situated on the southern bank of the Thames in the modern Southwark. It afterwards spread over the north side of the river, and was hence called a town of the Trinobantes. It is first mentioned in the reign of Nero as a flourishing and populous town, much frequented by Roman merchants. It was taken and its inhabitants massacred by the Britons when they revolted under Boadicea, A.D. 62. The quarter on the north side of the river was surrounded with a wall and ditch by Constantine the Great or Theodosius, the Roman governor of Britain. This wall probably commenced at a fort near the present site of the Tower, and continued along the Minories to Cripplegate, Newgate, and Ludgate. London was the

Remains of a Roman Wall, London.

central point from which all the Roman roads in Britain diverged. It possessed a *Milliarium Aureum*, from which the miles on the roads were numbered; and a fragment of this Milliarium, the celebrated London Stone, may be seen affixed to the wall of St. Swithin's Church in Cannon Street. This is almost the only monument of the Roman Londinium still extant, with the exception of coins, tesselated pavements, and the like, which have been found buried under the ground.

Roman Tesselated Pavement, London.

The Roman name Londinium represents the early Keltic *Llyn din*, "fort on the pool," the pool being a widening of the Thames at this point. The British London was probably a collection of huts on a dry spot surrounded by a marsh, and defended by an earthwork and a ditch. London is mentioned by Ptolemy (Λονδίνιον, ii. 3, 27), Tacitus (*Ann.* xiv. 33), Eumenius (*Paneg. Const.* 17), and Ammion. Marc. (xx. 1; xxviii. 3). See Besant, *London* (1892).

Longimănus (the Roman rendering of Μακρόχειρ). A surname of Artaxerxes I. Plutarch states that this appellation was given him because his right hand was longer than his left; but Strabo says that he was so called from the extraordinary length of his arms, which, on his standing upright, could reach his knees. See ARTAXERXES.

Longīnus. (1) DIONYSIUS CASSIUS (Λογγῖνος). A Greek rhetorician, born at Athens about A.D. 213, who studied Neoplatonism at Alexandria, and practised as teacher of philosophy, grammar (i. e. literary criticism), and rhetoric, in his native city, from about 260, until the accomplished queen Zenobia of Palmyra summoned him as minister to her court. As he persuaded her to resist the Roman yoke, the emperor Aurelian caused him to be executed after Zenobia's overthrow in 273. He possessed such an extent of learning that Eunapius called him a living library and a walking museum. His versatility is proved by compositions on philosophy, grammar, rhetoric, chronology, and literature. Of these, only fragments are extant, for example, the introduction to a commentary on Hephaestion's handbook of metres, and a short Rhetoric incomplete at the beginning. A brief treatise *On the Sublime* (Περὶ Ὕψους), commonly ascribed to him, is more probably to be assigned to an unknown writer about the Christian era. It treats and illustrates by classic examples the characteristics of the lofty style from a philosophical and aesthetic point of view. It is written in a vigorous manner. Good editions are those of Weiske (1820), Egger (1837), both with excellent notes; and Jahn (1867; revised by Vahlen, 1887). On the question of authorship, see Buchenau, *De Scriptore Libri Περὶ ὕψους* (Marburg, 1849); Martens, *De Libello Περὶ ὕψους* (Bonn, 1877); and Egger, *Essai sur l'Histoire de la Critique chez les Grecs* (Paris, 1886). (2) See CASSIUS.

Longobardi. See LANGOBARDI.

Longŭla. A town of the Volsci in Latium, not far from Corioli

Longus (Λόγγος). A writer who probably lived in the third century A.D. He was the author of a Greek pastoral romance, *Daphnis and Chloë*, in four books. It is considered the best of all ancient romances which have come down to us, on account of its deep and natural feeling, its grace of narrative, and the comparative purity and ease of its language. It has suggested many imitations by Italian, French, German, and English writers, the more famous being Bernardin de St. Pierre's *Paul et Virginie.* The rare translation by John Day of the French version of Amyot was reprinted in 1890. The Greek text is edited by Hirschig with a Latin version in the *Erotici Scriptores* of the Didot collection (Paris, 1856). Translation by Smith (London, 1855). See NOVELS AND ROMANCES.

Longus, P. CONSIDIUS. A propraetor in Africa, who left his province shortly before the breaking out of the Civil War, B.C. 49, intrusting the government to Q. Ligarius. He returned to Africa soon afterwards, and held Adrumetum for the Pompeian party. After the defeat of the Pompeians at Thapsus, he attempted to fly into Mauretania, but was murdered by the Gaetulians (Pseud. Caes. *Bell. Afr* 93).

Lophos (λόφος). A helmet-crest See GALEA.

Lorarii Persons who wielded the thong (*lorum*) in the punishment of slaves. See SERVUS.

Lorīca. (1) The leathern corselet of the Roman legionary. It consisted of thongs (*lora*) of shoe-leather faced with metal. These were fastened one upon another in such a way that they formed a covering for the body with two shoulder-pieces. Below the latter a plate of iron 9⅓ inches square was placed over the region of the heart. Of the early citizen-soldiers, the more wealthy wore also coats of chain-armour (*lorica hamata*) and corselets of mail (*lorica squamata*), in which the joints were further covered with metal plates; the latter were also worn by the praetorians in imperial times. (2) The breastworks on walls and on redoubts.

Legionary with Lorica. (Arch of Severus.)

Lorium or **Lorii.** A small place in Etruria on the Via Aurelia, where Antoninus Pius was brought up and where he died.

Lorўma (τὰ Λώρυμα). A city on the southern coast of Caria, opposite Ialysus in Rhodes.

Lotis. A nymph, who, to escape the embraces of Priapus, was metamorphosed into a tree, called after her *lotus* (Ovid, *Met.* ix. 347).

Lotophăgi (Λωτοφάγοι—i. e. lotus-eaters). Homer, in the *Odyssey*, represents Odysseus as coming in his wanderings to a coast inhabited by a people who fed upon a fruit called *lotus*, the taste of which was so delicious that every one who ate it lost all wish to return to his native country. Afterwards, in historical times, the Greeks found that the people on the north coast of Africa, between the Syrtes, used to a great extent, as an article of food, the fruit of a plant which they identified with the lotus of Homer, and they called these people Lotophagi (Herod. iv. 177). They carried on a commercial intercourse with Egypt and with the interior of Africa by the very same caravan routes which are used to the present day. The legend in the *Odyssey* suggested Tennyson's exquisite poem, *The Lotus Eaters*.

Lotus (λωτός). The lotus. (1) A plant known to botanists as the *Zizyphus lotus*, or jujube. See LOTOPHAGI. (2) A species of water-lily (*Nymphaea lotus*) found on the Nile and regarded by the ancient Egyptians as sacred. It appears as a symbol of the Egyptian deities and is very prominent in works of art, especially in the capitals of columns, the prows of vessels, etc. See Goodyear, *A Grammar of the Lotus* (N. Y. 1892).

Lotus Capital. (Goodyear.)

Loutron (λουτρόν). See BALNEAE.

Loxias (Λοξίας). A title given to Apollo as the god of oracles, from the base of λέγειν or perhaps from λόξα.

Lua, also called **Lua Mater** or **Lua Saturni.** One of the early Italian divinities, to whom were dedicated the arms taken in battle (Gell. xiii. 23, 1).

Luca. The modern Lucca; a Ligurian city in Upper Italy, at the foot of the Apennines and on the river Ausus, northeast of Pisae.

Lucāni. The inhabitants of Lucania. See LUCANIA.

Lucania. A district in Lower Italy, bounded on the north by Campania and Samnium, on the east by Apulia and the Gulf of Tarentum, on the south by Bruttium, and on the west by the Tyrrhene Sea. It was separated from Campania by the river Silarus, and from Bruttium by the river Laus. Lucania was celebrated for its excellent pastures; and its oxen were the finest and largest in Italy. Hence the elephant was at first called by the Romans a Lucanian ox (*Lucas bos*). The coast of Lucania was inhabited chiefly by Greeks, whose cities were numerous and flourishing. The interior of the country was originally inhabited by the Chones and Oenotrians. The Lucanians proper were Samnites, a brave and warlike race, who left their mother country and settled both in Lucania and Bruttium. They not only expelled or subdued the Oenotrians, but they gradually acquired possession of most of the Greek cities on the coast. They were subdued by the Romans after Pyrrhus had left Italy. The chief cities of Lucania were Heraclea, Metapontum, Thurii, Elea or Velia, Paestum (Posidonia), and Buxentum.

Lucanĭca. A sort of sausage, a favourite article of food among the Lucani. Its composition is given by Apicius (ii. 4).

Lucānus, OCELLUS. See OCELLUS.

Lucānus, M. ANNAEUS, usually called LUCAN, a Roman poet, was born at Corduba in Spain, A.D. 39. His father was L. Annaeus Mella, a brother of M. Seneca, the philosopher. Lucan was carried to Rome at an early age, where his education was superintended by the most eminent preceptors of the day. His talents developed themselves at a very early age, and excited such general admiration as to awaken the jealousy of Nero, who, unable to brook competition, forbade him to recite in public. Stung to the quick by this prohibition, Lucan embarked in the famous conspiracy of Piso, was betrayed, and, by a promise of pardon, was induced to turn informer. He began by denouncing his own mother, Acilia or Atilia, and then revealed the rest of his accomplices without reserve. He received, however, a traitor's reward. After the more important victims had been despatched, the emperor issued a mandate for the death of Lucan, who, finding escape hopeless, caused his veins to be opened. When, from the rapid effusion of blood, he felt his extremities becoming cold, he began to repeat aloud some verses which he had once composed, descriptive of a wounded soldier perishing by a like death; and, with these lines upon his lips, expired A.D. 65, in the twenty-sixth year of his age.

Lucan wrote various poems, the titles of which

are preserved, and also prose works; but the only extant production is an epic poem, in ten books, entitled *Pharsalia,* in which the progress of the struggle between Caesar and Pompey is fully detailed, the events, commencing with the passage of the Rubicon, being arranged in regular chronological order. The tenth book is imperfect, and the narrative breaks off abruptly in the middle of the Alexandrian War; but it is not known whether the conclusion has been lost, or whether the author ever completed his task. The whole of what now remains was certainly not composed at the same time, for the different parts do not by any means breathe the same spirit. In the earlier portions we find liberal sentiments expressed in very moderate terms, accompanied by open and almost fulsome flattery of Nero; but as we proceed, the blessings of freedom are loudly proclaimed, and the invectives against tyranny are couched in language the most offensive, evidently aimed directly at the emperor. The work contains great beauties and great defects. It is characterized by copious diction, lively imagination, and a bold and masculine tone of thought; but it is at the same time disfigured by extravagance, far-fetched conceits, and forced similes. The hero of the poem is Cato, of whom the following very famous line of Lucan is written:

Victrix causa diis placuit sed victa Catoni.

The oldest MS. of Lucan is a palimpsest, perhaps as early as the fourth century, the leaves of which are distributed between Vienna, Naples, and Rome. There are editions of the *Pharsalia* with notes by Grotius (Antwerp, 1614); Oudendorp (Leyden, 1728); Burmann (Leyden, 1740); Weber (3 vols. Leipzig, 1821–31); Lemaire (2 vols. Paris, 1830); and Haskins (London, 1889). It was translated into English verse by N. Rowe (London, 1719); and there are German versions by Bothe (Stuttgart, 1855) and Krais (Stuttgart, 1863). On the style, etc., see Körber, *De Lucani Usu Syntactico* (St. Petersburg, 1874); Berthold, *De Elocutione Poetica* (Grimma, 1879); and Obermeier, *Sprachgebrauch des Lucanus* (Munich, 1886). See also the introduction by Heitland to the edition of Haskins cited above.

Lucar. Money paid from the Roman treasury to the persons who presided over the *ludi scaenici,* as a contribution towards the expense. It was originally the money derived from the sacred groves (*luci*); but, because it was used for the expenses of the *ludi,* the word *lucar* usually bears the secondary meaning of money devoted to the payment of actors, etc. (Tac. *Ann.* i. 77). By a regulation of Servius Tullius, on each death a piece of money had to be presented to the goddess Libitinae (*lucar Libitinae,* cf. Dionys. iv. 15).

Lucceius. (1) Lucius. An old friend and neighbour of Cicero, was an unsuccessful candidate for the consulship with Iulius Caesar, in B.C. 60. He wrote a contemporaneous history of Rome, commencing with the Social or Marsic War. (2) Hirrus. A tribune who in B.C. 53 proposed that Pompey be made dictator. He afterwards fought in the Civil War on the side of Pompey (Caes. *B. C.* i. 15; iii. 82).

Lucenses. See Hispania, p. 828.

Lucĕres. One of the three old patrician tribes in Rome. See Patricii.

Luceria. A city of Apulia, about twelve miles to the west of Arpi. It was a place of great antiquity, and was said to have been founded by Diomedes.

Lūcerna (λύχνος). An oil-lamp. The Greeks and Romans originally used candles, but in later times candles were chiefly confined to the houses of the lower classes. A large number of ancient lamps have come down to us, the greater part of which are made of terra-cotta (τροχήλατοι), but also a considerable number of bronze. Most of the lamps are of an oval form and flat upon the top, on which there are frequently figures in relief. In the lamps there are one or more round holes, according to the number of wicks (*ellychnia*)

Dimyxos Lucerna. (*Museo Borbonico,* iv. 14.)

burned in it; and as these holes were called, from an obvious analogy, μυκτῆρες or μύξαι, literally, nostrils or nozzles, the lamp was also called *monomyxos, dimyxos, trimyxos,* or *polymyxos,* according as it contained one, two, three, or a greater number of nozzles or holes for the wicks.

The next illustration of a lamp, with a figure of Silenus, represents one of the most beautiful bronze lamps that have yet been found.

Lucerna. (*Museo Borbonico,* i. 10.)

The lamps sometimes hung in chains from the ceiling of the room (Verg. *Aen.* i. 726), but generally stood upon a stand. (See Candelabrum.) Sometimes a figure holds the lamp, which also exhibits the needle or instrument which served to trim the wick, and is attached to the figure by means of a chain.

We read of *lucernae cubiculares, balneares, tricliniares, sepulcrales,* etc., which were named from the places where they were used, but were not distinguished in their shapes.

Having no contrivance like ours for consuming the smoke of their lamps, the ancients were much troubled by the resulting soot and smell. To obviate this they often used perfumed oils (Petron. 70). See Becker-Göll, *Charicles,* iii. 86; id. *Gallus,* ii. 390.

Luciānus (Λουκιανός), usually called LUCIAN. A Greek writer, born at Samosata, the capital of Commagené, in Syria. The dates of his birth and death are uncertain; but it has been conjectured, with much probability, that he was born about A.D. 120, and that he lived till towards the end of that century. We know that some of his more celebrated works were written in the reign of M. Aurelius. Lucian's parents were poor, and he was at first apprenticed to his maternal uncle, who was a statuary. He afterwards became an advocate, and practised at Antioch. Being unsuccessful in this calling, he employed himself in writing speeches for others, instead of delivering them himself. But he did not remain long at Antioch; and at an early period of his life he set out upon his travels, and visited the greater part of Greece, Italy, and Gaul. At that period it was customary for professors of the rhetorical art to proceed to different cities, where they attracted audiences by their displays, much in the same manner as musicians or itinerant lecturers in modern times. He appears to have acquired a good deal of money as well as fame. On his return to his native country, probably about his fortieth year, he abandoned the rhetorical profession, the artifices of which, he tells us, were foreign to his temper. He now devoted most of his time to the composition of his works. He still, however, occasionally travelled; for it appears that he was in Achaia and Ionia about the close of the Parthian War, 160–165, on which occasion, too, he seems to have visited Olympia, and beheld the self-immolation of Peregrinus. About the year 170, or a little previously, he visited the false oracle of the impostor Alexander, in Paphlagonia. Late in life he obtained the office of procurator of part of Egypt, which office was probably bestowed upon him by the emperor Commodus.

The nature of Lucian's writings inevitably made for him many enemies, by whom he has been painted in the darkest colours. According to Suidas, he was surnamed "the Blasphemer," and was torn to pieces by dogs, as a punishment for his impiety; but to this account no credence can be given. Other writers state that Lucian apostatized from Christianity; but there is no proof in support of this charge; and the dialogue entitled *Philopatris*, which would appear to prove that the author had once been a Christian, was certainly not written by Lucian, and was probably composed in the reign of Julian the Apostate.

As many as eighty-two works have come down to us under the name of Lucian; but some of these are spurious. The most important of them are his *Dialogues*. They are of very various degrees of merit, and are treated in the greatest possible variety of style, from seriousness down to the broadest humour and buffoonery. Their subjects and tendency, too, vary considerably; for while some are employed in attacking the heathen philosophy and religion, others are mere pictures of manners without any polemic drift. Our limits only allow us to mention a few of the more important of these dialogues: The *Dialogues of the Gods* (Θεῶν Διάλογοι), twenty-six in number, consist of short dramatic narratives of some of the most popular incidents in the heathen mythology. The reader, however, is generally left to draw his own conclusions from the story, the author only taking care to put it in the most absurd point of view.—In the *Zeus Convicted* (Ζεὺς Ἐλεγχόμενος) a bolder style of attack is adopted; and the cynic proves to Zeus's face that everything being under the dominion of fate, he has no power whatever. As this dialogue shows Zeus's want of power, so the *Zeus the Tragedian* (Ζεὺς Τραγῳδός) strikes at his very existence, and that of the other deities.—The Βίων Πρᾶσις, or *Sale of the Philosophers*, is an attack upon the ancient philosophers. In this humorous piece the heads of the different sects are put up for sale, Hermes being the auctioneer.—*The Fisherman* (Ἁλιεύς) is a sort of apology for the preceding piece, and may be reckoned among Lucian's best dialogues. The philosophers are represented as having obtained a day's life for the purpose of taking vengeance upon Lucian, who confesses that he has borrowed the chief beauties of his writings from them.—*The Banquet* (Συμπόσιον) is one of Lucian's most humorous attacks on the philosophers. The scene is a wedding feast, at which a representative of each of the principal philosophic sects is present. A discussion ensues, which sets all the philosophers by the ears, and ends in a pitched battle.—The *Nigrinus* is also an attack on philosophic pride; but its main purpose is to satirize the Romans, whose pomp, vainglory, and luxury are unfavourably contrasted with the simple habits of the Athenians.

The more miscellaneous class of Lucian's dialogues, in which the attacks upon mythology and philosophy are not direct but incidental, or which are mere pictures of manners, contains some of his best. At the head must be placed *Timon*, which may perhaps be regarded as Lucian's masterpiece.—The *Dialogues of the Dead* (Νεκρικοὶ Διάλογοι) are perhaps the best known of all Lucian's works. The subject affords great scope for moral reflection and for satire on the vanity of human pursuits. Wealth, power, beauty, strength, not forgetting the vain disputations of philosophy, afford the materials. Among the moderns these dialogues have been imitated by Fontenelle, Lord Lyttelton, and Walter Savage Landor.—The *Icaro-Menippus* is in Lucian's best vein and a masterpiece of Aristophanic humour. Menippus, disgusted with the disputes and pretensions of the philosophers, resolves on a visit to the stars for the purpose of seeing how far their theories are correct. By the mechanical aid of a pair of wings he reaches the moon, and thence surveys the miserable passions and quarrels of men. Thence he proceeds to Olympus, and is introduced to the Thunderer himself. Here he is witness of the manner in which human prayers are received in heaven. They ascend by enormous vent-holes, and become audible when Zeus removes the covers. Zeus himself is represented as a partial judge, and as influenced by the largeness of the rewards promised to him. At the end he pronounces judgment against the philosophers, and threatens in four days to destroy them all.—*Charon* is a much admired dialogue, but of a graver turn than the preceding. Charon visits the earth to see the course of life there, and what it is that always makes men weep when they enter his boat. Hermes acts as his cicerone. For his *True History* (Ἀληθὴς Ἱστορία) and *Asinus* (Λούκιος ἢ Ὄνος), see NOVELS AND ROMANCES.

Lucian's merits as a writer consist in his knowledge of human nature, his strong common-sense, the fertility of his invention, the raciness of his humour, and the simplicity and Attic grace of his diction. There was very much to justify his attacks in the systems against which they were directed. Yet he establishes nothing in their stead. His aim is only to pull down; to spread a universal scepticism. Nor were his assaults confined to religion and philosophy, but extended to everything old and venerated, the poems of Homer and Hesiod, and the history of Herodotus.

The best editions of Lucian are by Hemsterhuis and Reitz, 4 vols. (Amsterdam, 1743); by Lehmann, 9 vols. (Leipzig, 1822–29); by Dindorf, with a Latin version, but without notes (Paris, 1840); critical text by Jacobitz (1874); Fritzsche (incomplete, 1882–85); Sommerbrodt (in progress, 1892 foll.); select dialogues edited by Abbott (1877); Heitland (1878); and Jerram (1879).

Lucĭfer or **Phosphŏrus** (Φωσφόρος, "the bringer of light"). The name of the planet Venus, when seen in the morning before sunrise. The same planet was called Hesperus, Vesperugo, Vesper, Noctifer, or Nocturnus, when it appeared in the heavens after sunset. Lucifer as a personification is called a son of Astraeus and Aurora or Eos, of Cephalus and Eos, or of Atlas By Philonis he is said to have been the father of Ceÿx. He is also called the father of Daedalion and of the Hesperides. Lucifer is also a surname of several goddesses of light, as Artemis, Aurora, and Hecaté.

Lucilius, Gaius. (1) The creator of the Roman satire. He was born at Suessa Auruncorum, B.C. 180, of good family; served in the Numantine War in Spain, under Scipio; and, returning to Rome, lived on familiar terms with that general and with his friend Laelius (Hor. *Sat.* ii. 1). He was the maternal uncle or (less probably) the maternal grandfather of Pompey the Great. He died at Naples, B.C. 103.

It was Lucilius that first developed the *satira*, which had before his time been a name applied to miscellaneous verse (see Satira) into the form in which it is afterwards found in Horace, Persius, and Juvenal. He boldly and even fiercely assailed the faults of living contemporaries (Hor. *Sat.* i. 4, 6; i. 10, 1; Pers. i. 114; Juv. i. 165). Horace criticises him for the carelessness and haste with which he wrote, and which always left something to be desired.

"Cum flueret lutulentus, erat quod tollere velles."

Of his thirty books of satires, some 300 lines are preserved in a fragmentary state, giving us but a slight clue to his style and method; yet it is evident that he was a boldly original, almost eccentric, genius. He affected a cosmopolitanism unusual in a Roman of his time. "I write for the people of Cosentia and Tarentum and Sicily," he says; and his Latin is liberally interlarded with Greek in a macaronic fashion. His vocabulary, in fact, is a very unusual one, abounding in strange words, disgusting expressions, and plebeian forms.

The fragments are collected by L. Müller (Leipzig, 1872); Lachmann and Vahlen (Berlin, 1876); and Bährens (Leipzig, 1886). See also L. Müller's *Leben und Werke des Gaius Lucilius* (Leipzig, 1876); and for the language, Fischer, *De Vocibus Lucilianis* (Halle, 1881).

(2) Lucilius Iunior. Probably the author of a poem entitled *Aetna* (q. v.). He was procurator of Sicily and a friend of Seneca the philosopher, who addresses to him his *Epistolae*, *Quaestiones Naturales*, and his *De Providentia*.

Lucilla. A daughter of the emperor Marcus Aurelius and of Faustina, born A.D. 146. At the age of seventeen she was given in marriage to Lucius Verus, at that time commanding the Roman armies in Syria. Verus came as far as Ephesus to meet her, and the union was celebrated in that city, but, habituated to debauchery, Verus soon relapsed into his former mode of life; and Lucilla, finding herself neglected, took a woman's revenge, and entered on a career of similar licentiousness. Returning subsequently with her husband to Rome, she caused him to be poisoned there; and afterwards, in accordance with her father's directions, contracted a second marriage with Claudius Pompeianus, an aged senator, of great merit and probity. Her licentious conduct, however, underwent no change, and she was banished to the island of Capreae by her brother Commodus, against whom she had formed a conspiracy Not long after, Commodus sent a centurion to her place of exile, who put her to death, in the thirty-eighth year of her age, A.D. 184 (Dio Cass. lxxi. 1; lxxii. 4; Iul. Cap. *Aurel.* 7).

Lucīna. The goddess of light (*lux*), or rather the goddess that brings to light, and hence the goddess that presides over the birth of children. It was therefore used as a surname of both Iuno and Diana. Lucina corresponded to the Greek goddess Ilithyia (q. v.). See Hor. *Carm. Saec.* 15.

Lucretia. See Tarquinius.

Lucretīlis. A mountain range in the country of the Sabines. It is now Monte Corrignaleto.

Lucretius Carus, Titus. A Roman poet and philosopher who was born probably in B.C. 98 or 96; the year is uncertain. Of his birthplace and parentage nothing is known. St. Jerome is authority for the statement that he was made insane by a love-philter, and finally committed suicide, having composed some books in the intervals of his madness. According to Donatus, he died on the same day that Vergil assumed the *toga virilis*—October 15, B.C. 55.

Lucretius left but one work, the *De Rerum Natura*, a didactic poem in six books containing in all nearly 7500 hexameter lines. The purpose of the poem is to set forth the Epicurean system of philosophy, particularly those portions dealing with the origin of the world and the operations of natural forces. The poet's aim in writing was, as he tells us, to free men's minds from the baneful influence of superstition and of the belief in the hereafter, to which he attributed the greater portion of the fears and troubles of life. He endeavoured to explain how, without the direction or intervention of supernatural agencies in any degree, all natural phenomena may be accounted for. In Book I he lays down as fundamental truths the propositions that nothing can come from nothing, and that to nothing nought returns. The universe is made up of matter and void, or space. It has no centre; for matter exists in infinite quantity, and space is without limit. Matter is composed of atoms, which are inconceivably minute, perfectly solid, and indestructible. Book II. is devoted to an elaborate discussion of the atoms, treating of their movements, shapes, and combinations. Sensation and feeling are declared to be an accident of atomic combination, a result of the coming together of atoms of certain shapes in certain ways. The subject of the third book is the mind and soul, which, according to the poet, are inseparably united and of material nature, being composed of the finest and roundest atoms. Many reasons are brought forward to prove that the soul perishes at the same time with the body. Book IV. deals with the phenomena of sense-perception. From the surface of all objects thin films of matter are continually flying off, preserving the general outline of that from which they come. These impinge upon our senses, and perception is an immediate result. Yet in the adaptation of the senses to their functions there is no evidence of design, no sign of creative intelligence. The fifth book sets forth the perishable nature of the world, its formation from a fortuitous concourse of atoms, the origin of life by spontaneous generation, the preservation of animal life in accordance with the law of the survival of the fittest, and the development of man in civilization out of a condition of brutish savagery. In Book VI. the poet attempts to explain the natural phenomena which seem most terrible and inexplicable, particularly thunder and lightning, earthquakes, volcanic eruptions, the changes of the Nile, and the power of the magnet. The poem ends abruptly with a description of the plague at Athens, and was evidently given to the world before it had received the final revision of the author.

In the matter of the poem Lucretius followed closely the teachings of Epicurus, whom he revered as guide and master. With a truly Roman spirit he laid more emphasis upon the reign of law in the universe than his teacher; but he made no contribution in the way of doctrine to the Epicurean system. Whether he intended to bring his work to a close with a presentation of the ethical views of Epicurus it is impossible to determine; but numerous references show that in these, also, the poet was fully in sympathy with his master. The form of the *De Rerum Natura* was perhaps suggested by that of the poem of Empedocles, *On Nature.* The thought and manner of expression reveal the influence of several Greek poets besides Empedocles (notably Homer and Euripides), and of the early Roman poets (particularly Ennius), as well as of Cicero's *Aratea.* Yet the poem throughout bears the stamp of a marked individuality. Believing deeply himself in the mission of Epicureanism as a cure-all for human ills, Lucretius proclaimed its teachings with an almost religious fervor. Previous to his time this system of philosophy had received only scanty treatment in Latin, that, too, in barbarous prose. From the multitude of its technical details and the absence of a supernatural element, it seemed incapable of poetic handling. Nevertheless, Lucretius succeeded not only in presenting the main features of Epicurean physics and psychology with admirable clearness, but even in clothing them with a highly poetic form. There are, indeed, passages of unequal merit, and now and then the lack of the poet's finishing touches becomes unpleasantly apparent; yet from beginning to end the poem carries the reader along with a kind of epic movement and interest. It possesses a unity and continuity inconsistent with the tradition that it was composed "in lucid intervals;" still it is not impossible that the story of the poet's insanity and self-destruction may reflect some tragic event of his life. The legend of the madness of Lucretius was elaborated by Tennyson in a well-known poem.

The *De Rerum Natura* ranks not only as one of the finest poems in the Latin language, but also as undoubtedly the greatest didactic poem of all literature. It is masterly in its grasp and handling of the subject-matter, elevated in tone, and finely poetic in expression and suggestion. As an earnest attempt to adapt Epicureanism to the needs of the Roman life, the *De Rerum Natura*—apart from its value and inspiration as literature—is of especial interest at the present time, when atomic materialism under a new form is again challenging the attention of the philosophic world. Its doctrines form a curious and instructive parallel to those of the advocates of materialistic evolution, and sometimes foreshadow in a striking manner the conclusions of modern science.

The existing manuscripts of Lucretius are all derived from a single archetype, which has long since disappeared. From this at least three copies were made. One of these, a beautiful folio of the ninth century, is now at Leyden (called A by Munro). Another was the parent of a quarto MS. of the tenth century (B), also at Leyden, and of two others of which there are considerable fragments at Copenhagen and Vienna. The third copy was taken by Poggio to Italy in the fifteenth century, and became the ancestor of the numerous Italian MSS. of the *De Rerum Natura.* The *editio princeps* of the poem was published about 1473 by Ferandus of Brescia. The most important of the early editions are the first Aldus (1500), edited by Avancius, the Jiunta (1512) by Candidus, and those by Lambinus (Paris, 1563; 2d ed. 1565; 3d ed. 1570, often reprinted). Recent editions are those by Lachmann (Berlin, 1850; 4th ed. of the text, 1871; of the commentary, 1882), Bernays (text, Leipzig, 1852), Bockemüller (text with commentary, 2 vols., Stade, 1873–74), Kelsey (text of Munro, with notes to Books I., III., and V., Boston, 1884), but especially by H. A. J. Munro (text, commentary, translation; 4th ed. 3 vols., London, 1886). For the poet's philosophy, see Masson, *The Atomic Theory of Lucretius contrasted with Modern Doctrines of Atoms and Evolution* (London, 1884); Woltjer, *Lucretii Philosophia cum Fontibus Comparata* (Groningen, 1877); Bruns, *Lucrez-Studien* (Freiburg, 1884); Royer, *Les Arguments du Matérialisme dans Lucrèce* (Paris, 1883); Lange, *History of Materialism*, vol. i. For his language, see Holtze, *Syntaxis Lucretianae Lineamenta* (Leipzig, 1868); Städler, *De Sermone Lucretiano* (Jena, 1869); Kühn, *Quaestiones Lucr. Grammaticae et Metricae* (Breslau, 1869); Kraetsch, *De Abundanti Dicendi Genere Lucretiano* (Berlin, 1881). For his rank as a poet, see Sellar's *Roman Poets of the Republic* (3d ed. 1889); Martha, *Le Poème de Lucrèce—Morale, Religion, Science* (Paris, 4th ed. 1885).

Lucrīnus Lacus. Properly the inner part of the Sinus Cumanus or Puteolanus, a bay on the coast of Campania, between the promontory Misenum and Puteoli, running a considerable way inland. But at a very early period the Lucrine Lake was separated from the remainder of the bay by a dike eight stadia in length, and thus assumed the character of an inland lake. Its waters still remained salt, and were celebrated for their oyster beds. Behind the Lucrine Lake was another lake called LACUS AVERNUS. In the time of Augustus,

Agrippa made a communication between Lake Avernus and the Lucrine Lake, and also between the Lucrine Lake and the Sinus Cumanus, thus forming out of the three the celebrated Julian Harbour. The Lucrine Lake was filled up by a volcanic eruption in 1538, when a conical mountain rose in its place, called Monte Nuovo.

Lucullus, L. LICINIUS. A Roman celebrated as the conqueror of Mithridates. He fought on the side of Sulla in the Civil Wars with the Marian party, was praetor B.C. 77, and consul in 74. In the latter year he received the conduct of the war against Mithridates, which he carried on for eight years with great success (see MITHRIDATES), but being unable to bring the war to a conclusion in consequence of the mutinous disposition of his troops, he was superseded in the command by Acilius Glabrio, B.C. 67. Glabrio, however, never took the command; but in the following year (66) Lucullus had to resign the command to Pompey, who had been appointed by the Manilian law to supersede both him and Glabrio. On his return to Rome, Lucullus devoted himself to a life of indolence and luxury, and lived in a style of extraordinary magnificence. He died in B.C. 57 or 56. He was the first to introduce cherries into Italy, which he had brought with him from Cerasus in Pontus.

Lucullus. (Duruy.)

The name of Lucullus became and has continued proverbial for extravagant and studied luxury. His gardens in the suburbs of the city were extraordinary for their splendour; his villas at Tusculum and Naples were laid out with such lavish disregard of expense in constructing fishponds (*piscinae*), cutting through hills and rocks, and throwing out moles into the sea, that Pompey called him, in derision, "the Roman Xerxes." His domestic service was on a scale of equal magnificence. A single dinner cost him $10,000.

Lucullus was not, however, a mere sensualist. He collected a fine library, which was open to the public; he enjoyed the conversation of philosophers and scholars, and himself wrote a work on the history of the Marsic War, composed in Greek. He was also the patron of the poet Archias, the friend of Cicero. His life was written by Plutarch, and in it may be found many curious anecdotes of this very remarkable and interesting man.

Lucŭmo. The title applied to the hereditary chiefs who ruled over each of the twelve independent tribes of the Etrurian nation. It would seem, also, to have been given to the eldest sons of noble families, who, by their right of primogeniture, would have a fairer claim to public offices and the honours of the State. The original Etruscan term was *Lauchme*, and hence among the Latin writers we sometimes meet with the form *Lucmo*, as in Propertius (iv. 1, 29). See ETRURIA; TARQUINIUS.

Ludi. A term applied to the various contests and spectacles held in the Roman Circus and amphitheatre (*ludi circenses*) and those of the theatre (*ludi scaenici*) and stadium.

Games were either public (*publici*) or private (*privati*). PUBLIC GAMES were originally ceremonials connected with religion, the oldest being the Equirria, in honour of Mars, and the Consualia, in honour of Consus. (See EQUIRRIA; CONSUALIA.) Games were frequently exhibited in fulfilment of a vow (*ludi votivi*). Such were the seven great celebrations of the republican period—the Ludi Magni (or Maximi), the Ludi Plebeii, the Ludi Cereales, the Ludi Apollinares, the Ludi Megalenses, the Ludi Florales, and the Ludi Victoriae Sullanae. (See below.) Under the Empire many new games were introduced—in honour of the emperor's birthday (*ludi natalicii*) and games instituted at the conclusion of a great war (e. g. *ludi Parthici*, *ludi Alemannici*, *ludi Sarmatici*, etc.).

PRIVATE GAMES were those given by private individuals, and not by the emperor or by the State. The most usual private games were the *ludi funebres*, celebrated on the ninth day after death, and hence called *ludi novendiales*. Private games were also given by persons of high rank on any occasion of public thanksgiving (*ludi honorarii*.) Games given by the emperor for the benefit of invited guests alone were also classed as *ludi privati*.

Games were given in the Circus and amphitheatre, or in the theatre. Those in the Circus were races (see CIRCUS); those in the amphitheatre were gladiatorial contests (see GLADIATORES), or beast-baiting (see VENATIONES). (For the theatrical games and contests, see COMOEDIA; HISTRIO; MIMUS; PANTOMIMUS; THEATRUM; TRAGOEDIA.) There were also contests imported from Greece and called *agones*, either musical or athletic in their nature, for which, see ATHLETAE; CURSUS; HIPPODROMUS; PALAESTRA; PUGIL; STADIUM.

The games originally lasted for one day only; but in the later days of the Republic the duration of them was greatly extended — e. g. the Ludi Magni, or Romani, to sixteen days, the Ludi Plebeii to fourteen, the Ludi Cereales to eight, etc. Under the Empire the games were often continued through the night—a custom which probably began with the Floralia (Ovid, *Fasti*, v. 361 foll.).

The observance opened with a regular ritual, which was carefully carried out; and if it appeared that the *instauratio* had been in any way defective in form, the games were repeated (see Weissenborn on Livy, xxiii. 30, 16). The great games were administered by the consuls until B.C. 366, the date of the first creation of curule aediles. Down to the Empire, the praetors had charge of the Ludi Apollinares. The gladiatorial contests were frequently given under the direction of the quaestors.

The cost of the games was partly defrayed by the State from a special fund (*lucar*) originally formed from the income received from the sacred groves. The rest of the expense was borne by the giver of the games—i. e. the officials whose duty it was to administer them. The outlay was often so great as to deter many persons from aspiring to the curule offices (Dio Cass. liii. 2). Martial tells us that the chariot-races sometimes cost 400,000 sesterces ($16,000). Symmachus spent nearly $400,000 in this way; and Justinian's games cost $1,000,000. For an account of the magnificence of these exhibitions, see Calpurnius, *Ecl.* vii.; Dio Cass. lxviii. 15; Gibbon, ii. 58–60; and Friedländer, *Sittengeschichte*, ii. 319 foll. (2d ed.).

At the games, the emperor occupied a private box (*cubiculum*), and it is probable that seats were reserved by law for magistrates (consuls, praetors, tribunes, etc.) and priests and Vestals. Free seats were sometimes given in perpetuity to a distinguished man and his descendants (Cic. *Philipp.* ix. 7, 16). At ordinary games seats were (1) sold by the exhibitor to those who wished to avoid the crush; (2) given by him to his friends and to those who had by law a right to reserved places; or (3) opened free to the general public. Tickets for the first class of seats were often secured by speculators (*locarii*) and sold at a considerable advance. In early times, slaves were not allowed to attend the games; but this prohibition was afterwards either withdrawn or ignored. Roman citizens were obliged to wear the toga at the games; magistrates appeared in official costume. The exhibitor often gave presents to the spectators in the shape of things to be scrambled for (*missilia*). Cloaks could be worn over the toga in bad weather, and hats (*causiae*) as a protection from the sun. When the weather was bad and the wind so high that the awning (*velarium*) could not be used, the spectators were allowed to hold up their umbrellas (*umbracula*).

The following are the principal games mentioned by the ancient writers:

(1) Ludi Actiăci (Ἄκτια). Games in honour of the Actian Apollo, decreed by Augustus in B.C. 31 after his victory over Antony at Actium. They consisted at Rome of horse-races, gymnastic contests, and occasionally of gladiatorial contests. They were held every fourth year (Dio Cass. li. 19). See Actia.

(2) Ludi Apollinăres. Games established in B.C. 212, in accordance with a prophecy of the seer Marcius, in honour of Apollo, the averter of evil. They were originally *ludi votivi*, and were given by the *praetor urbanus* (Livy, xxv. 12, 2). They were, to a large degree, a Greek festival. The *decemviri sacris faciundis* sacrificed with victims after the Greek fashion; the State supplied the victims, and also gave 12,000 *asses* to defray the expenses of the games, and the people aided with a small subscription (Livy, xxv. 12, 12–14). The next year the praetor L. Calpurnius Piso proposed that the games should be vowed each year, and hence the Calpurnii have the head of Apollo on their denarii (Mommsen, *Röm. Münzwesen*, pp. 580, 626). After this they were celebrated every year, but till B.C. 208 on no definite day. In consequence of a pestilence in that year, the praetor P. Licinius Varus voted that they should be held every year on a fixed day. That day was July 13, which always continued to be the last day on which these games were held. The number of days gradually increased from one till it finally reached eight, or perhaps nine. They were, for the most part, theatrical exhibitions from the very beginning (see the interesting story in Festus, s. v. *Thymelici*, p. 326 Müller); but sometimes there was a *venatio*, and Dio Cassius (xlviii. 33) speaks of a horse-race. In the Apollinarian games, held by Agrippa in B.C. 40, two days were given to the games of the Circus, during one of which the *ludus Troiae* was exhibited (Dio Cass. xlviii. 20).

(3) Ludi Augustăles. See Augustales.

(4) Ludi Capitolīni. Livy states (v. 50, 4) that in the year B.C. 390 (better 388), after the defeat of the Gauls, on the motion of Camillus, a decree of the Senate was passed that Ludi Capitolini should be instituted, inasmuch as Iupiter, the best and greatest, had preserved his settlement and citadel in a serious crisis, and that the dictator M. Furius should appoint for that purpose a *collegium*, consisting of those who dwelt in the Capitol and citadel (cf. Livy, v. 52, 11). As being administered by a *collegium*, the Capitoline games were like the Circensian games of the Fratres Arvales. After B.C. 384, when Marius Capitolinus was condemned, a motion was brought before the people that no patrician should dwell in the citadel or the Capitol (Livy, vi. 20, 3), so that from this time only plebeians could be members of this *collegium*.

For the guild of the Capitolini, see Cic. *Q. Fr.* ii. 5, 2. They had *magistri* of their own. Preller (*Röm. Myth.* 202) thinks this is a very old festival in honour of Iupiter Capitolinus, so old that it was attributed to Romulus (cf. Tert. *Spect.* 5). A curious ceremony was performed at these Capitoline games, from their supposed connection with a triumph of Romulus over Veii; or, as Mommsen holds, with the capture of Veii by Camillus in B.C. 396. An old man, who was considered to represent the king of Veii, was led through the Forum to the Capitol, dressed in regal attire and wearing a *bulla* suspended from his neck; and a herald accompanying him proclaimed the "sale of the Sardians," because the Veientines, being Etruscans, were supposed to have come from Sardis, in Lydia (Plut. *Quaest. Rom.* 53, p. 227).

(5) Ludi Cereăles or Ceriăles. See Ceres.

(6) Ludi Compitalicii. See Compitalia.

(7) Ludi Florăles. See Floralia.

(8) Ludi Funĕbres. See above, p. 972.

(9) Ludi Honorarii. See above, p. 972.

(10) See Iuvenalia.

(11) Ludi Liberăles. See Dionysia, p. 521.

(12) Ludi Magni. See above, p. 972.

(13) Ludi Martiăles or Martis Ultōris. Games celebrated annually by the consuls (Dio Cass. lx. 5; lvi. 46), in honour of Mons Ultor. They included sometimes a mock sea-fight, *venationes*, etc.

(14) Ludi Megalenses. See Megalesia.

(15) Ludi Natalicii. See above, p. 972.

(16) Ludi Novendiāles. See above, p. 972.

(17) Ludi Palatīni. Theatrical exhibitions held on the 21st, 22d, and 23d of each January in a private theatre and before a specially invited audience, in honour of the divinity of Augustus (Dio Cass. lvi. 46; lix. 16; Tac. *Ann.* i. 73).

(18) Ludi Plebeii. Games held in the Circus Flaminius, and mentioned as early as B.C. 216 (Livy, xxiii. 30, 17). Now, as the Circus Flaminius was built in B.C. 220 (Livy, *Epit.* xx.), we may assign the establishment of the Ludi Plebeii to the same date, and also the *Iovis epulum* on the Ides (for all Ides were sacred to Iupiter) which is connected with these games (Livy, xxv. 2, 10; xxvii. 3, 9). We find from the Calendar of Philocalus (A.D. 354) that the Ludi Plebeii lasted till the fourth century. The date of them was originally Nov. 15, just as that of the Ludi Romani was Sept. 15 (*C. I. L.* i. 401). They were celebrated by the plebeian aediles; and already in B.C. 207 they lasted for more than one day (Livy, xxviii. 10, 7). In some early calendars—e. g. the Fasti Maffeiani—they are put down as lasting from Nov. 4 to Nov. 17. Dramatic performances formed a part of these games, as is seen from the didascalia to the *Stichus* of Plautus.

(19) Ludi Pontificāles. The same as the Ludi Actiaci. See above, p. 973.

(20) Ludi Romāni. Games held in honour of Iupiter, and said to have been established by Tarquinius Priscus on the occasion of his conquest of the Latin Apiolae (Livy, i. 35, 9); though Dionysius and Cicero refer their establishment to the victory over the Latins at Lake Regillus. At first they lasted for one day only; a second day was added on the expulsion of the kings in B.C. 509; a third after the first secession, B.C. 494. From the year 191 to 171 they lasted ten days (Livy, xxxvi. 2; xxxix. 22, 1), and shortly before Caesar's death they appear to have been a fifteen-day festival—from Sept. 5 to 19. After Caesar's death a day was added: this day must have been Sept. 4; and so it appears in the calendars of the Augustan period, the days of the games being Sept. 4 to 19. There was the *epulum Iovis* on the 13th, and the *equorum probatio* on the 14th. The games in the Circus lasted from the 15th to the 19th. In the Calendar of Philocalus (A.D. 354) they run from Sept. 12 to 15. The celebration was in the hands, at first, of the consuls; afterwards of the curule aediles.

We must not suppose that these games were regularly established as annual from the beginning. Games, as already stated, in many cases began from a vow made by the commander, and were celebrated as a special festival after his triumphal procession. As the army, however, used to go forth, as a general rule, each summer, it became customary, when it returned in autumn, to celebrate such games, though connected with no triumph, and though no signal victory had been gained. But still, in all cases, they were celebrated as extraordinary games, and not as games regularly established by law. They were *sollemnes*, "customary," but had not yet become *annui*. *Ludi magni* is the term applied to extraordinary games originating in a vow (*ludi votivi*), while *ludi Romani* is that applied to the games when they were regularly established as annual (*ludi stati*). The latter term—i. e. *ludi Romani*—is first used by Livy in viii. 40, 2 (see Weissenborn *ad loc.*); and after that the terms varied according as the games are *stati* (e. g. x. 47, 7; xxv. 2, 8) or *votivi* (xxii. 9, 10; 10, 7; xxvii. 33, 8; xxxvi. 2, 2; xxxix. 22, 2, etc.; Suet. *Aug.* 23). The final establishment of these games must lie between B.C. 367 and B.C. 322; and the year B.C. 367, when so many changes were effected, and when we are told a day was added to these games and curule aediles appointed to superintend them, seems most reasonable to assume.

The actual Ludi Romani consisted of, first a solemn procession (*pompa*); then a chariot-race, in which each chariot, in Homeric fashion, carried a driver and a warrior, the latter, at the end of the race, leaping out and running on foot (Dionys. vii. 72). This was a practice confined to the Ludi Romani. In the exhibitions of riding, each rider had a second horse led by the hand, as it appears the Roman horsemen, in early times, were in the habit of using two horses in battle (cf. Gran. Licinian. bk. xxvi.), like the Tarentini in Greek warfare (Livy, xxxv. 28, 8). Such riders were called *desultores* (Livy, xxiii. 29, 5). Originally, in all probability, there was only one contest of each kind, and only two competitors in each contest, as "may be inferred from the circumstance that, at all periods in the Roman chariot-race, only as many chariots competed as there were so-called factions; and of these there were originally only two—the white and the red" (Mommsen, *R. H.* i. 301, note). These few events allowed further minor exhibitions, such as boxers, dancers, competition in youthful horsemanship (*ludus Troiae*), etc. It was allowed that the wreath the victor won should be put on his bier when dead (Twelve Tables, 10, 7). During the festival, too, the successful warrior in real warfare wore the spoils he had won from the enemy, and was crowned with a chaplet. After the introduction of the drama in B.C. 364, plays were acted at the Ludi Romani. In B.C. 161 the *Phormio* of Terence was given at these games. See Mommsen, *Römische Forschungen*, ii. 42–57.

(21) Ludi Saeculāres. Games originally known as Ludi Terentīni. *Terentum* (from *terere*) was a volcanic cleft in the Campus Martius, at which even under the monarchy the Valerian gens sacrificed dark victims to Dis and Proserpina. Valerius Maximus (ii. 5, 2) tells a story of a certain Valesius who got his sons cured of a serious illness by giving them water from the Tiber boiled over this cleft; and these sons saw in the sleep that restored them to health a vision which ordered the sacrifice of dark-coloured victims to Dis and Proserpina on an altar to be found in the Terentum, and the celebration of *lectisternia* and nocturnal games for three nights in their honour. The altar was found deep buried, the sacrifice was offered, and from this sacrifice date the Ludi Terentini. We are told that P. Valerius Poplicola, first consul, in a case of pestilence offered the same sacrifice and held the same games, and thereby saved the State (Val. Max. l. c.). But this latter is a very old mistake, due to the confusion of the first consul with the L. Valerius Poplicola, consul in B.C. 449; for though we cannot be certain of any celebration of these games in B.C. 349, we have the most distinct evidence for their being held in B.C. 249 (cf. Varro *ap.* Censor. *De Die Natali*, 17, 18). The next celebration was not in B.C. 149, but in 146 (Censor. *op. cit.* 17, 11, who quotes contemporary authorities, Piso, Gellius, and Hemina). In the year

B.C. 49 religion was silent amid the turmoil of the Civil War, and the games were not solemnized till the well-known celebration of Augustus in B.C. 17. But why in that year?

There were many Greek myths (Lobeck, *Aglaoph.* 791 foll.) of certain ages of the world—the Golden Age, the Silver Age, etc.—mixed up with astronomical theories of the whole order of the universe beginning anew when the planets returned to their original positions after what was called the *magnus annus*. The same series of people would reappear on earth and repeat again the various exploits of their lives (cf. Verg. *Ecl.* iv. 34 foll.). Among these myths was one that the cycle began anew after four periods of 110 years each (cf. Probus *ad* Verg. l. c.; and Varro *ap.* St. August., *De Civ. Dei*, xxii. 28). Again, there was an influence from Etruria. Just as at Rome at the end of every five years there was a propitiatory offering made to the gods for the people, so in Etruria a similar sacrifice was made at the beginning of what they considered a *saeculum*—i. e. that space of time which embraced even the longest life. The propitiatory offering was made for all alive at the time: when that whole race had passed away, the gods signified that the cycle was over by sending prodigies, and a new sacrifice had to be offered (Censor. *op. cit.* 17, 5). The first four *saecula* of the Etruscans lasted 100 years each, the fifth 123, the sixth and seventh 119 (Varro *ap.* Censor. l. c.): so that something over 100 years was the average *saeculum*. The definite Greek theory that the *saeculum* lasted 110 years was taken up by the Quindecimviri (Hor. *Carm. Saec.* 21), and in the interest of Augustus they proceeded to invent celebrations for B.C. 456, 346, 236, 126, Augustus's games being celebrated in the last year of the *saeculum*, B.C. 17.

The successors of Augustus celebrated the secular games according to different kinds of computation. Claudius, says Gibbon, did not treat the oracle with implicit respect. He celebrated the games, "which none had ever seen before," in the eight hundredth year of the city (A.D. 47), with an actor who had taken part in the secular games of Augustus (Pliny, *H. N.* vii. § 159). Domitian celebrated them in A.D. 87, six years too early if they were to be 110 years after those of Augustus. (See Suet. *Domit.* 4; Tac. *Ann.* xi. 11.) Antoninus Pius in the year 900 of the city (A.D. 147) celebrated them (Aurel. Vict. *Caes.* 15, 4), while Sept. Severus held them 220 years after Augustus, in A.D. 204. The last celebration was in the thousandth year of the city (A.D. 247) by the emperor Philip (Eutrop. 9, 3; Eckhel, vii. 323, 324). It may be that Gallienus in A.D. 257 (Eckhel, vii. 409; viii. 22) held them as an extraordinary solemnity in a period of great trouble (Trebell. Pollio, *Gall.* 5), and Maximian, in A.D. 304, certainly intended to hold them, but does not appear to have carried out his intention: so from Philip's time we may say that the secular games disappear till they were revived in the Middle Ages as the Papal Jubilees instituted by Pope Boniface VIII. in the year 1300 (Gibbon, i. 327, 328; viii. 217, ed. Smith).

The Ludi Terentini, then, and their continuation, the Ludi Saeculares, are not a really genuine Roman ceremony. They rest on reference to the Sibylline Books (Hor. *Carm. Saec.* 5), are celebrated by the Quindecimviri outside the Pomoerium (that the gods of the lower world might not be brought inside the city), the gods honoured are not Roman, and the Roman antiquarians considered the solemnities to be derived from Etruria (Censor. *l. c.*).

The rites of the celebration are given by Zosimus (ii. 5), who also quotes *verbatim* the Sibylline oracle ordering the celebration. His account is as follows: Heralds summoned the people to the spectacle they had never seen before and never would see again. Then in the Capitoline temple of Iupiter and the Palatine temple of Apollo, the Quindecimviri gave to all present (slaves excluded) purificatories (καθάρσια, *suffimenta*), consisting of torches, sulphur, and bitumen; and in the same temples, and that of Diana on the Aventine, wheat, barley, and beans were given to the people to make an offering with, though Zosimus says these were to be given to the actors in the games. Then began the feast, which lasted three nights and three days. Offerings were made to Iupiter, Iuno Lucina, Apollo, Latona and Diana, the Fates, Demeter (*Tellus*, Hor. *Carm. Saec.* 29), Pluto, and Proserpina. On the first night, at the second hour, the emperor, with the assistance of the Quindecimviri, sacrificed to the Fates, at the Terentum, on the border of the Tiber, three rams on three altars, letting the blood flow all over the altars, and then thoroughly burned the victims. A stage was then erected, the people lighted torches, a newly-composed hymn was sung, and splendid shows exhibited: for the oracle had said that the grave was to be mingled with the gay. On the next day a sacrifice was made on the Capitol of white bulls to Iupiter and a white cow to Iuno, in accordance with the oracle, and then in the theatre there were dramatic representations in honour of Apollo. On the second night a white pig and a white sow were sacrificed to Tellus, in accordance with the oracle, and dark victims offered to Dis and Proserpina, at an altar of which some remains were discovered in the winter of 1886–87. On the second day the matrons offered supplications and sang hymns to Iuno on the Capitol; and on the third day in the Palatine temple of Apollo there was a sacrifice of white oxen, and thrice nine noble boys and maidens whose parents were still alive (ἀμφιθαλεῖς, *patrimi ac matrimi*) sang hymns in Greek and Latin for the preservation and prosperity of the Roman Empire. Such a hymn was called *Carmen Saeculare*, and we still possess the one which Horace wrote for the celebration of the games by Augustus.

A most interesting inscription containing an official report of the Augustan pageant was discovered September 20, 1890. It was cut upon a block of marble and contained 168 lines of minute writing. The inscription has been edited by Prof. Mommsen (Rome, 1891), and is the subject of an excellent popular article by Prof. Lanciani in the *Atlantic Monthly* for February, 1892.

(22) LUDI SEVIRĀLES. The same as the Ludi Martiales.

(23) LUDI TAURII. Games in honour of the infernal gods (*Fest.* p. 350, Müller). They included a chariot-race in the Circus. The name is possibly derived from *taura* or *taurea*, a barren cow sacrificed to Proserpina. For an absurd etymology, see Varro, p. 351.

(24) LUDI TERENTĪNI. See LUDI SAECULĀRES above.

(25) LUDI VICTORIAE CAESĂRIS or LUDI VENĔRIS GENETRĪCIS. Games first celebrated by Iulius Caesar in B.C. 46, on the dedication of the temple of Venus Genetrix, which had been vowed at the

battle of Pharsalia. (See Suet. *Aug.* 10; Dio Cass. xlix. 42.) They were held in July, from the 20th to the 30th. Venus Genetrix was in these identified with Victoria, on which see Gellius, x. 1, 7, and Mommsen in the *C. I. L.* i. 397.

(26) LUDI VICTORIAE SULLĀNAE. Games established by Sulla in B.C. 82 (Vell. Paterc. ii. 27).

(27) LUDI VOLCANALĬCI. Games established probably after the recovery of the standards of Crassus from the Parthians by Augustus. They were celebrated in the temple of Vulcan outside the city, on the 23d of August (Plut. *Quaest. Rom.* 47; Mommsen, *C. I. L.* i. 400).

(28) LUDI VOTĪVI. See above, p. 972.

On the games in general, see Friedländer's *Sittengeschichte*, ii. 263–289, 3d ed.; id. in Marquardt, *Röm. Staatsverwaltung*, iii. 462–475; and Mommsen in the *C. I. L.* i. pp. 293–412.

Ludi Actiăci. See ACTIA.

Ludias. See LYDIAS.

Ludus Litterarius (διδασκαλεῖον). A school.

I. GREEK. Of education in the Homeric Age one cannot affirm anything with certainty. Achilles is represented as having a sort of rhetorical training under Phoenix (*Il.* ix. 414), and in music and the healing art under the Centaur, Chiron; and noble youths are spoken of as undergoing a course of instruction in arms and martial exercises. Cf. Plut. *De Educ. Liberis*, 12.

In later times, the Ionic States of Greece paid great attention to literary as well as to physical culture. Herodotus (vi. 27) speaks of a boys' school at Chios as early as B.C. 500 with 120 pupils. A decree of the Mitylenaeans is given by Aelian (vii. 15) in which the prohibition of schools is made a punishment for disloyal allies. Diodorus (xii. 12) states that Charondas (*circa* B.C. 550) passed a law for Thurii giving to all boys a literary training at the public cost. (See Polyb. xxxi. 17; Hirschfeld in *Hermes*, ix. 501; and Plato, *Crit.* 50 D.) The Spartans, on the other hand, and in fact the Dorians in general, paid much more attention to physical than to mental training, and any literary education was given to a boy at the expense of his parents and not by the State. Cf. Plato, *Hipp. Maior*, p. 285 C; and the articles BIDIAEI; EDUCATION; PAEDONOMI.

For the purposes of the present article we may take the schools of Athens as representing the higher development of secondary education in ancient Greece. There is no positive evidence that at Athens the State exercised any direct control over the schools, though a law of Solon required parents and guardians to provide boys with a suitable education (Plato, *Crit.* 50 D). There were no girls' schools at Athens, but such training as the daughters of a family received was from their mothers, and consisted chiefly of the domestic arts of sewing, spinning, etc.

School Period.—From the age of six, a boy was intrusted to a *paedagogus* (q. v.), who conducted him everywhere—to school, to the palaestra, etc.—carrying his books, tablets, and other school requisites. This is explained by Plato, who says that, if animals have care-takers, of course the boy must, "being the most unmanageable of all animals" (*De Leg.* vii. 808 D). The school began early in the morning, and ended at sunset, according to Solon's law, but there was an interval for luncheon at mid-day. In grammar-schools the Musea was a school festival, and there were holidays at great festivals, so much so that in the month Anthesterion there was comparatively little time for school (Theophr. 22).

Subjects of Study.—The regular school course (ἐγκύκλιος παιδεία) was intended to convey, besides mere reading and writing, a knowledge of the poets, and proficiency in music and gymnastics. In the time of Socrates some mathematical training was added, and at least a knowledge of simple arithmetic was universally imparted. This mere reckoning, however, was taught mainly at home by means of a calculating-table (see ABACUS; MATHEMATICA); and accordingly Aristotle (*Pol.* v. or viii. 1) speaks of three usual subjects, γράμματα, γυμναστική, and μουσική, the last including γράμματα. The elementary reading-lesson was sometimes made easy and attractive by methods like those of the modern kindergarten, the use of ivory letters, etc. (Cf. Plato, *De Leg.* vii. 819 D.) Grasberger cites from Philostratus (*Vit. Soph.* ii. p. 240) a device of Herodes, who gives to a dull pupil twenty-four companions named from the letters of the alphabet to aid his memory.

For the method of teaching writing, see Plato, *Protag.* 326 D. The literary course consisted of reading and explaining the best poets, such as Homer, Hesiod, Theognis, Phocyllides; but more especially Homer. In Xen. *Symp.* iii. 5, Niceratus says, "My father, to make me a good man, compelled me to learn all the poems of Homer, and now I could say by heart the whole *Iliad* and *Odyssey*." This poetical training was intended to impart a knowledge of mythology and philosophy (especially through the maxims), as well as taste and power of expression. Of course time was less occupied than now, since there was no language, natural science, or history to be learned.

To this literary course was sometimes added special teaching in tactics and strategy for those who looked to a military career; and drawing was taught before the time of Aristotle, having been, according to Pliny, introduced by Pamphilus (the teacher of Apelles), first at Sicyon, whence it spread over Greece, and was regarded for all sons of citizens a most important branch of education—slaves might not learn it (Pliny, *H. N.* xxxv. § 77). It was chiefly correct outline drawing without colour, on boxwood tablets. The musical teaching began at twelve or thirteen, and was so managed that the pupils might appreciate and accompany lyric poetry. It should be observed that the instrument taught was the lyre: the flute, a favourite instrument at Thebes, and once commonly learned at Athens, was tabooed, except for professionals, about the time of the Peloponnesian War. The διδασκαλεῖα lasted till ἥβη—i. e. till sixteen; and afterwards for those of the richer classes, who wished for advanced learning, came the schools of the rhetoricians and sophists, who taught various departments of knowledge.

Place of Education.—The school-room itself was called διδασκαλεῖον or παιδαγωγεῖον; also φωλεόν, or φωλεός. Some, indeed, maintain that the παιδαγωγεῖον was only an ante-room, where the paedagogi sat and waited; but Grasberger (vol. ii. 207) remarks that it was unlikely that so poor a school as that of Elpias would have an ante-room, and cites Philostratus (*Vit. Soph.* ii. 263) to show that the paedagogi sat with their charges. In Roman times certainly we have Remmius Palae-

Athenian School. (From the Duris Vase.)

mon, as paedagogus, learning more than the schoolboys from the lesson (Suet. *Gr.* 23). Some schools had not even one room, but were held in the open air, as by Dionysius the Younger (Gell. xxi. 5). This, however, is only in the case of the very poor; even the father of Aeschines is described by Demosthenes as in a school-room, and Demosthenes contrasts that establishment with the respectable (*προσήκοντα*) schools to which he went himself. The boys sat on benches (*βάθρα*), the master on a chair (*θρόνος*). See the rather unattractive picture in Libanius (iv. p. 868), where we are told that the master "sits aloft, like a dicast, with an awful frown and an expression of implacable wrath, before which the pupil must tremble and cringe." In the vase-picture given above we see the various departments, each group representing a class: (1) repetition of poetry; (2) music lesson on the lyre (where both teacher and pupil sit, and both have laid aside the *himation* to give free play to the arms); (3) the writing-master with a tablet (or possibly a master correcting an exercise); (4) a singing-lesson, where the master is not teaching the forbidden flute (see above), but giving a note from it. On the walls are articles of the school apparatus—book-roll, tablets, lyre, geométrical instrument (?), drinking-vessel, basket for books. It is a disputed question whether the seated spectators are government inspectors, paedagogi, or parents, and the question is so impossible to decide that the picture unfortunately cannot be made an argument for the presence of any one of the three at the lesson.

School-fees.—The poor status of the Athenian school-master (*γραμματιστής*) is sufficiently established. He was ill-paid, and often did not receive his payment at all. This does not apply to the sophists in the more advanced schools, who were able to charge as much as 100 minae ($1800) for their complete course to each pupil; and the chairs founded in later times by Hadrian had a stipend of 100 minae a year attached to them. See EDUCATION, p. 572.

II. ROMAN. At Rome, education, though not made obligatory by any law, was always considered important. In early days, however, the father himself generally taught his son (Pliny, *Ep.* viii. 14; cf. Plaut. *Most.* i. 2, 42). So Servius Tullius is said to have been taught by King Tarquin; and of Cato the Elder it is said, as part of his conservatism, that he taught and trained his own son (Plut. *Cat. Mai.* 20). This old training no doubt consisted much in living with the father and learning his business of public life; but there was also direct instruction in reading, writing, and arithmetic (i. e. reckoning), and in saying by heart the Twelve Tables (q. v.), which formed a sort of catechism to the Roman of the old school. But it of course often happened that the father lacked either the ability or the inclination to teach his son, and so arose the custom of wealthy parents employing educated slaves or freedmen as private tutors at home. Livius Andronicus, late in the third century B.C., was so employed by Livius Salinator; Augustus so employed the freedman Verrius Flaccus to teach his grandsons; and in some cases, when the teacher was a slave, his master let him teach a class of outsiders and so made a profit (Plut. *Cat. Mai.* 20). It is probable, however, that even in the earliest times there were schools to which those who could neither teach themselves, nor provide competent slaves as teachers, sent their children, boys and girls alike. Plutarch (*Rom.* 6) represents Romulus and Remus as learning at a school at Gabii; and, in less purely legendary times, there is no reason to discredit the account of Virginia going to school (Livy, iii. 44), or of the schools at Falerii (Livy, v. 44) and Tusculum (Livy, vi. 25) early in the fourth century B.C.

Against this has been adduced by some the passage of Plutarch (*Quaest. Rom.* 59), which states that Spurius Carvilius was the first person who opened a school (*γραμματοδιδασκαλεῖον*) at Rome, B.C. 231; but Plutarch probably only means that Carvilius was the first *grammaticus* or teacher of the more advanced literary schools, which came in along with the influence of Greek literature, and he does not thereby negative the elementary schools mentioned by Livy (and indeed by himself elsewhere) as existing much earlier. It is necessary, therefore, to distinguish (1) *litterator*, or *magister litterarius* (= *γραμματιστής*), the elementary school-master; (2) *grammaticus* (also *litteratus*), a more advanced teacher; (3) *rhetor* (Apul. *Flor.* 20). Private teachers were employed in later as in older times by many men of high station; but still, except the imperial family, it was common for those of the highest rank to send their sons to schools. Thus we find Sulla sending his son Faustus to the school in which Cassius also was being educated; and Ausonius, a man of the highest rank in the State, recommends school education in a passage cited below. The question whether home or school education is to be preferred is discussed by Quintilian (*Inst. Or.* i. 2), with a result in favour of the latter, and the arguments on either side have a striking resemblance to those which are used at the present day.

Place.—The elementary schools and those of the *grammatici* were usually in a veranda partly open to the street, and the school-room is accordingly called *pergula*, *taberna*, or *porticus* (Suet. *Gr.* 18; Juv. xi. 137; Livy, iii. 44, vi. 25; Eumen. *Pro Inst. Schol.* 20). Hence the noise of teaching and of punishing was audible through the street and annoying to the neighbours (Mart. xii. 57). Boys and girls were taught in the same school, as is shown alike by passages such as Mart. viii. 3, ix.

68; Ovid, *Trist.* ii. 369; and by old paintings which have been discovered.

School-hours.—The school began early, even before dawn (Mart. ix. 68); so that the boys brought lamps with them (Juv. vii. 226). There was a break for the prandium, after which the school was continued. Each boy was accompanied from his home by his paedagogus, or slave, who acted as a sort of private tutor both in regard to control and not unfrequently in teaching, also called *custos*, and by an inferior slave called *capsarius*, carrying the books and tablets. Juvenal (vii. 222 foll.) describes for us the school-room; the busts of the poets blackened by smoke from the scholars' lamps, the master seated on his chair (*cathedra*), while his class stood before him or sat on benches (*subsellia*). We hear also of wall-maps in a remarkable passage of Eumenius, a teacher at Autun at the end of the third century: "The boys should have daily before their eyes on the walls all lands and seas, all cities and peoples, comprehended under our Empire; for the name and position of places, the distances between them, the source and outflow of rivers, the coast-line with all its sea-board, its gulfs and its straits, are better taken in by the eye than by the ear" (*Pro Inst. Schol.* 20; cf. Propert. v. 3, 37). There were also tables of authors and of dates hung up (see Marquardt, *Privatleben*, 109).

Discipline.—That this was generally severe may be seen from the line of Juvenal (i. 15), *et nos ergo manum ferulae subduximus*, and from the abundant illustrations given by Professor Mayor on that passage. Zonaras mentions that the prince Arcadius was flogged by Arsenius without apparently any objection from the emperor Theodosius. Arsenius, however, seems to have been a private tutor, teaching only the emperor's children. Quintilian (i. 3, 14) argues against corporal punishment altogether. On the other hand, prizes were given to encourage the industrious—some valuable or prettily got-up book (Suet. *Gr.* 17). Prizes are mentioned also at Athens in the Roman period for the best ἐγκώμιον or essay. Few passages will better give an idea of a Roman school than the idyl (iv.) which Ausonius (once tutor to Valentinian's sons, but afterwards a count of the Empire and consul) addresses to his grandson, just going to school.

School Flogging.

School-time and Holidays.—The Roman school year began on March 24, after the Quinquatria, when the new boy brought his entrance-fee (*Minerval*). Sometimes the money for the whole previous year was brought then (Juv. vii. 242), but (as appears from Hor. *Sat.* i. 6, 72) it was usually paid each month; and this is prescribed by an edict of Diocletian (*C. I. L.* iii. 831). The regular holidays or vacation were the week at the Saturnalia in December and the five days at the Quinquatria in March, but there was also a holiday on each of the *nundinae* (Suet. *Gr.* 7), and at the time of the important games.

Subjects of Study.—The school life began usually at seven years of age (Quint. i. 1, 15); but no doubt in most cases there was some earlier home instruction. Tacitus (*Dial.* 29) mentions, with no approval, the custom of having a Greek maid, like a *bonne*, for children to give them an early familiarity with the Greek language. In the elementary schools the course consisted of reading, writing, and simple arithmetic. Quintilian mentions the system of making the reading-lesson attractive by using ivory letters, as mentioned above in Greek schools. The writing-lesson was on a wax tablet, with lines or furrows (*sulci*) to guide the hand (Quint. i. 1, 27). Arithmetic was of great importance in the Roman judgment, and we find from an edict of Diocletian that the arithmetic master (*calculator*) was paid more highly than the teacher of reading and writing. In the schools of the grammarians came the study of poets. This school differed from the elementary school, because that was training merely for the bare necessities of practical life, while the grammar school (if we may so term it) was nearer the ideal Greek training, an *eruditio liberalis* or "liberal education" (Cic. *Tusc.* ii. 11, 27). The central point was to read with full explanation Greek and Latin poets; the boy must first learn to read the poet with understanding and with correct emphasis. It is clear that the Romans, like the Greeks, laid the greatest stress on elocution, for eloquence under the Republic was the only avenue to power (Tac. *Dial.* 37), and the school was intended to train the utterance as well as to supply a flow of words.

With this object the master read over the passage and made the class repeat it (*reddere dictata*); expressed also by the word *praelegere* (Mart. i. 36; Quint. i. 8, 8). Besides this, however, the passage was thoroughly threshed out as to its meaning, its metre, and the questions of geography, history, mythology, and ethics connected with it (Quint. i. 4, 4; Cic. *Verr.* i. 18, 47; Tac. *Dial.* 30). The questions raised were, however, often extremely trivial, "the name of Anchises' nurse," etc. (Juv. vii. 235, with Mayor's note). There were also learning by heart and practice in verse composition: prose belonged to the rhetorical school, when that was established as separate from the grammatical. As regards the authors read, Homer universally held the first place (Hor. *Epist.* ii. 2, 42; Quint. i. 5, 8; Pliny, *Epist.* ii. 14), and next, perhaps, the favourite was Menander (Ovid, *Trist.* ii. 23), and then the great tragedians. We have an account of the books read in the school kept by the father of Statius at Naples, and the list comprises Homer, Hesiod, Theocritus, Pindar, Ibycus, Stesichorus, Sappho, Corinna, Callimachus. It is possible, as Friedländer remarks, that at Naples, as a town preserving Greek life and habits, Greek literature might be more deeply studied than elsewhere. The Latin authors most read in the first century were Vergil, Horace, and Lucan. A reaction took place as to the literature in vogue about A.D. 100, and, in place of the authors of the Augustan Age, the older prose writers and the poets of the third century B.C. —Gracchus, Naevius, Ennius, Plautus, Attius, and Lucilius—were adopted as school-books. This was at the time when Hadrian preferred Cato to Cicero, Ennius to Vergil. Fronto, the teacher of Marcus Aurelius, was a leader in the depreciation of the Augustan writers. Music began to be studied towards the end of the first century—a mark of Greek influence (Sen. *Epist.* 88, 9; Suet. *Tit.* 3); and the above course, with the addition of geometry, formed what Quintilian calls the *ἐγκύκλιος παιδεία*, with which the majority were content. Many, however, proceeded to the school of the *rhetor*. Like the school of the *grammaticus*, this was originally formed after the Greek pattern. The early Latin rhetors, Plotius, etc., were not approved, and the censors in B.C. 92 closed the Latin schools of rhetoric, because, as they alleged, they were a pretence for idleness (Suet. *Rhet.* 1). In these schools prose authors took the place of poets; but the principal part was the prose exercise, which, for the beginner a mere prose narrative, passed on to the *declamatio*. The easier kind of *declamatio* was *suasoria*, on some historical and mythological subject, adopting some view on this or that story or point of history and arguing it. They advanced to *controversiae* or declamations on some legal point.

The status and emoluments of the school-masters, *grammatistae* and *grammatici* alike, were low. What their ordinary fee was, cannot, however, be determined. In Diocletian's time (when their position was probably better than when Juvenal wrote), the maximum fee for the *grammatistes* from each pupil was 50 denarii a month, and for the *grammaticus* 200 (*C. I. L.* iii. 831). The *rhetor* seems to have received twice as much as the *grammaticus*, and his emoluments were increased by the State endowments begun by Vespasian (Suet. *Vesp.* 18). Remmius Palaemon is cited as an instance of a wealthy *grammaticus*, and by a *rhetor* wealth was more often acquired. There were, besides, the turns of fortune, of which Juvenal speaks (vii. 197, with Mayor's note), and of which the emperor Pertinax (once a *grammaticus*) and Ausonius afford instances.

See Grasberger, *Erziehung und Unterricht im classischen Alterthum* (Würzburg, 1864–80), which is the most complete modern authority; with the works cited at the end of the article EDUCATION in this Dictionary.

Ludus Troiae. See TROIAE LUDUS.

Lugdunensis Gallia. A part of Gaul, which received its name from Lugdunum (Lyons), the capital city of the province. See GALLIA.

Lugdūnum. (1) A city of Gaul, situated near the confluence of the Rhodanus (Rhône) and the Arar (Saône) (Pliny, *H. N.* iv. 18). It was one of the places conquered by Caesar, and, a short time after his death, Munatius Plancus received orders from the Roman Senate to re-assemble at Lugdunum the inhabitants of Vienna (Vienne), who had been driven out of their city by the Allobroges (Dio Cass. xlvi. 50). In a little while it became very powerful, so that Strabo says it was not inferior to Narbo (Narbonne) in the number of its inhabitants. The ancient city did not occupy exactly the same spot as the modern one, but lay on the west side of the Rhône and Saône, while the chief part of Lyons is on the east side, at the very confluence of the two streams. At the extremity of the point of land formed by the two streams, and, of course, precisely corresponding with the southern extremity of the modern city, stood the famous altar erected by sixty Gallic nations in honour of Augustus (Livy, *Epit.* 137). At Lugdunum was established the gold and silver coinage of the province, and from this city, as a centre, the main roads diverged to all parts of Gaul. Here, too, was an immense aqueduct, remains of which still exist. The Palais des Arts of the modern city contains many specimens of Roman bronzes and other antiques found in the vicinity. The city was the seat of Irenaeus when bishop, and had witnessed severe persecutions of the Christians. In the third century it declined in importance, on account of the vicinity and rapid growth of Arelaté and Narbo. Lugdunum is said by Strabo to have been situate at the foot of a hill. In Keltic, *dun* signifies "a hill," and from this comes the Latin termination *dunum*. The earlier name is said by Dio Cassius (*l. c.*) to have been Lugudunum (Λουγούδουνον). (2) A city of the Batavi, in Germania Inferior, now Leyden. The modern name is said to be derived from that of Leithis, which it took in the Middle Ages. (See BATAVA.) (3) CONVENĀRUM. The chief town of the Convenae in Aquitania, now St. Bertrand de Comminges. See CONVENAE.

Luggage. See IMPEDIMENTA.

Lumĭna. See SERVITUTES.

Luna. The goddess of the Moon. See SELENÉ.

Luna. Now Luni; an Etruscan town, situated on the left bank of the Macra, about four miles from the coast, that once formed part of Liguria, but became the most northeasterly city of Etruria when Augustus extended the boundaries of the latter country as far as the Macra. It possessed a large and commodious harbour at the mouth of the river called LUNAE PORTUS (Gulf of Spezzia). In B.C. 177 Luna was made a Roman colony. It was celebrated for its white marble, from the time of Iulius Caesar. The quarries now take their name from the neighbouring town of Carrara.

Lunae Montes. Mountains believed by ancient geographers to extent through the interior of Africa, covered with snow, and containing the sources of the Nile (Ptol. iv. 8, 3, 6).

Lunch. See CENA; PRANDIUM.

Lupa. A she-wolf; an animal held in great veneration at Rome, because Romulus and Remus were fabled to have been suckled by one. See ROMULUS.

Lupa. A prostitute. See MERETRIX.

Lupānar. A brothel. See MERETRIX.

Lupātum. A curb-bit with sharp prickers resembling the teeth of a wolf (*lupus*); hence the name. See FRENUM.

Luperca. See LUPERCALIA.

Lupercal. A cave at the foot of the Palatine Hill, consecrated by Evander to the god Pan, who was identified with Lupercus by the Latins, as protecting the flocks from wolves (*lupos arcens*) (Serv. *ad Aen.* viii. 343). See LUPERCALIA.

Lupercalia. A festival held in Rome from time immemorial on February 15. It was in honour of Faunus, who was worshipped under the name Lupercus in the Lupercal, a grotto in the Palatine Mount. His wife LUPERCA or LUPA was sometimes identified with Acca Larentia. (See ACCA LARENTIA; FRATRES ARVALES.) The object of the festival was, by expiation and purification, to give new life and fruitfulness to fields, flocks, and people. The cult was originally administered by two confraternities, which were chosen from the members of the Fabian and Quintilian families, and were named in consequence Luperci Fabiani and Luperci Quintiliani. To these was added in B.C. 44 that of the Luperci Iulii in honour of Caesar. In consequence of the Civil Wars the cult fell into desuetude, but was renewed by Augustus. In imperial times the members of these *collegia* were commonly of equestrian standing, and retained the name of Luperci even after leaving the body. The festival was observed until A.D. 494, in which year Bishop Gelasius I. changed it into the Feast of the Purification. See Fleury, *Hist. Ecclés.* xxx. 41.

The procedure at the Lupercalia was as follows: After the Flamen Dialis had sacrificed some he-goats and a dog, two youths were touched on the forehead with a knife, smeared with the blood of the goats. It was then immediately wiped off with wool dipped in milk, whereupon they were bound to laugh. After the sacrificial feast the Luperci, crowned and anointed, and naked, except for an apron of goat-skin, ran round the ancient city on the Palatine with thongs cut from the skin of the sacrificed goats in their hands. On their course, women used to place themselves in their way to receive blows from the thongs, which was believed to be a charm against barrenness. (See Mannhardt, *Mythologische Forschungen*, pp. 113 foll.) The thongs were called *februa*, from the old word *februare*, "to purify"; the day, *dies februatus*, "the day of purification"; and the whole month, *Februarius*, "the month of purification." For the possible connection with totem-worship, see A. Lang, *Myth, Ritual, and Religion*, ii. 177 and 213.

Luperci. See LUPERCALIA.

Lupercus or **Sulpicius Lupercus Servastus Iunior.** A poet, who appears to have lived during the latter period of the Western Empire. He has left an elegy on cupidity and a sapphic ode on old age, printed in the *Poetae Latini Minores* of Bährens, iv. 107.

Lupiae or **Luppiae.** A town in Calabria between Brundisium and Hydruntum.

Luppia or **Lupia.** The modern Lippe; a river in the northwest of Germany, falling into the Rhine at Wesel in Westphalia, and on which the Romans built a fortress of the same name.

Lupus Ferreus. A grappling-iron used in repelling the attacks of a ram. See Livy, xxxiii. 3.

Lupus, RUTILIUS. The author of an extant rhetorical treatise in two books, entitled *De Figuris Sententiarum et Elocutionis.* He appears to have lived in the time of Nero. His work is chiefly valuable for well-translated extracts from Greek orations now lost. It is probably an abridged translation of one of the rhetorical works of Gorgias, but in its present shape is incomplete. It is printed in the *Rhetores Latini Minores* of C. Halm, pp. 3–21 (Leipzig, 1863), and has been edited with explanatory notes by Jacob (Lübeck, 1837) and Draheim (Berlin, 1874). See C Schmidt, *De Rutilio Lupo* (Breslau, 1865).

Lurco, M. AUFIDIUS. The maternal grandfather of Livia, wife of Augustus Caesar. He was tribune of the plebs in B.C. 61, and is also remembered for having been the first person at Rome who dealt in peacocks on a large scale, fattening them for food.

Luscīnus. See FABRICIUS.

Luscius Lavinius or **Lanuvīnus.** A Roman playwright only known to us as the bitter critic of Terence, who calls him *malevolus vetus poeta.* See Ter. *Andr.* prol. 15; *Heaut.* 16; *Phorm.* prol. 1; *Eun.* prol. 9; *Adelph.* 1.

Lusitania, Lusitāni. See HISPANIA.

Lusōnes. A tribe of the Celtiberi in Hispania Tarraconensis.

Lustratio (κάθαρσις). A purification (1) as preliminary to entering holy places; (2) to remove the taint of blood-guiltiness; (3) at birth, marriage, and death; (4) a purification of houses, temples, cities, or people on special occasions—e. g. in Greece at each meeting of the Ecclesia (q. v.), at the Mysteries (see ELEUSINIA), and at Rome at the Lupercalia (q. v.) or the formal *lustrum* (q. v.). See Tylor, *Primitive Culture*, ii. 388, and LUSTRUM.

Lustrum, among the Romans, was the purification, or absolution from sin, of the entire people. It took place at the close of each census (q. v.), commonly in May of the year following the censors' accession to office. The host of the people, horse and foot, in their newly constituted classes, was drawn up in full armour on the Campus Martius under the leadership of the censor to whom this duty fell by lot. The *Suovetaurilia*—a pig, ram, and bull—were carried three times round the whole army, and thereupon sacrificed to Mars, accompanied by a prayer of the censor in which he besought that the power of the Roman people might be increased and magnified, or, as it ran later, might be maintained entirely undiminished. The censor then led the army under his banner to the city gate, where he dismissed them, while he himself, as a token of the completed *lustrum,* drove a nail into the wall of a temple and deposited the new roll of citizens in the Aerarium. The last *lustrum* took place in A.D. 74, under Vespasian.

Lutatius Catŭlus. See CATULUS.

Lutatius Cerco, QUINTUS. A Roman consul who in B.C. 241 subdued a revolt of the Falisci.

Lute. See TIBIA.

Lutetia, or, more commonly, **Lutetia Parisiōrum** (Paris). The capital of the Parisii in Gallia Lugdunensis, was situated on an island (now La Cité) in the Sequana (Seine), and was connected with the banks of the river by two wooden bridges. Under the emperors it became a place of importance, and the chief naval station on the Sequana. Here Julian was proclaimed emperor, A.D. 360, at which time the name of the place was changed to Parisii. Remains of a great Roman bath belonging to a palace still exist near the Boulevard St. Michel. See Caes. *B. G.* vi. 3; vii. 58; Ammian. Marcel. xvii. 2, 8; xx. 4; and Hoffbauer, *Paris à travers les Ages* (1891 foll.).

Luxorius (also written **Luxurius,** and **Lusorius**). A Roman epigrammatic poet, who lived in Africa about the beginning of the sixth century A.D., during the Vandal domination. He sought to imitate Martial. We still possess eighty-eight of his epigrams, mostly in elegiac metre, which are often coarse and always dull. He also wrote a Vergilian cento, and *versus serpentini*. See the *Poetae Latini Minores* of Bährens, iv. 267, 331, and 386 foll.; and the monograph by Klapp, *De Anthologiae Lat. Carminibus Nonnullis* (Wandsbeck, 1874).

Lyaeus (Λυαῖος, "care-dispeller"). A name of Dionysus (q. v.).

Lycabettus (Λυκαβηττός). The modern Mount St. George, a mountain in Attica, belonging to the range of Pentelicus, close to the walls of Athens on the northeast of the city. See ATHENAE.

Lycaea (τὰ Λύκαια). A festival celebrated in honour of Zeus on the Lycaean Mount in Arcadia. In the sacred enclosure on its highest peak, where, according to popular belief, no object cast a shadow, there was an altar of heaped-up earth, and before it two columns with gilt eagles on top of them, looking to the east. At the festivals, probably celebrated every ninth year, the priests, who alone were allowed to enter the precincts, offered mysterious sacrifices to the god, including a human sacrifice. These were said to have been instituted by Lycaon (q. v.), and were kept up till the second century A.D. The man who had been chosen by lot to perform the sacrifice was afterwards compelled to flee, and wandered about for nine years; like Lycaon, in the shape of a wolf, so the people believed. In the tenth he was allowed to return and regained his human form—i. e. the taint was removed. Besides the festival there were also athletic contests. See Pausan. viii. 38.

Lycaeus (Λυκαῖος) or **Lycēus**. A lofty mountain in Arcadia, northwest of Megalopolis, one of the chief seats of the worship of Zeus and of Pan, each of whom was therefore called Lycaeus. See LYCAEA.

Lycambes (Λυκάμβης). See ARCHILOCHUS.

Lycaon (Λυκάων). A mythical king of Arcadia, son of Pelasgus and Meliboea (daughter of Oceanus) or Cyllenė, and father of Callisto. He is said to have founded on Mount Lycaeum the town Lycosura, the oldest that the sun looked upon, and to have sacrificed a child to Zeus on the altar he had raised on the highest peak of the mountain, on account of which he was changed into a wolf. (See LYCAEA.) Another legend relates that he had fifty impious sons. When Zeus came to them in the guise of a beggar, in order to put their contempt of the gods to the test, they followed the advice of Maenalus, the eldest, and set before him the entrails of a boy which had been mixed with the sacrifice. The god, however, threw the table over and killed Lycaon and his sons with lightning, with the exception of Nyctimus, the youngest, whom Gaea saved by firmly holding the right hand of Zeus. During the reign of Nyctimus the deluge connected with the name of Deucalion covered the land as a punishment for the impiety of Lycaon and his sons. See Pausan. viii. 2.

Lycaonia (Λυκαονία). A district of Asia Minor, forming the southeastern part of Phrygia. The people were, so far as can be traced, an aboriginal race, speaking a language which is mentioned in the Acts of the Apostles (xiv. 4) as a distinct dialect; they were warlike, and especially skilled in archery. Lycaonia belonged successively to the Persians, Syrians, Greeks, and Romans. Under Trajan it was united with the province of Cappadocia, but in the fourth century was made a separate province. Its chief town was Iconium.

Lycēum (Λύκειον). A sacred enclosure at Athens, dedicated to Apollo, where the polemarch originally held his court. It was decorated with fountains, plantations, and buildings, by Pisistratus, Pericles, and Lycurgus, and became the usual place of exercise for the Athenian youths who devoted themselves to military pursuits (Pausan. i. 19). Nor was it less frequented by philosophers, and those addicted to retirement and study. We know that it was more especially the favourite walk of Aristotle and his followers, who thence obtained the name of Peripatetics (Cic. *Acad.* i. 4). Here was the fountain of the hero Panops, and a plane-tree of great size and beauty, mentioned by Theophrastus (*Hist. Pl.* i. 11). The position commonly assigned to the Lyceum is on the right bank of the Ilissus. See GYMNASIUM.

Lycēus (Λύκειος). A surname of Apollo, the meaning of which is not quite certain. Some derive it from λύκος, a wolf, so that it would mean "the wolf-slayer;" others from λύκη, light, according to which it would mean "the giver of light;" and others again from the country of Lycia. See APOLLO.

Lychnĭdus (Λύχνιδος), more rarely **Lychnidium** (Λυχνίδιον) or **Lychnis** (Λυχνίς). The ancient capital of the Dessaretii in the interior of Illyricum, situated on a height on the northern bank of Lake Lychnitis. In the Middle Ages it was the residence of the Bulgarian kings. The modern name is Achrita.

Lychnītis (Λυχνῖτις). See LYCHNIDUS.

Lycia (Λυκία). A small district on the south side of Asia Minor, between Caria and Pamphylia. According to tradition, the most ancient name of the country was Milyas, and the earliest inhabitants were called Milyae, and afterwards Solymi; subsequently the Termilae, from Crete, settled in the country; and lastly, the Athenian Lycus, the son of Pandion, fled from his brother Aegeus to Lycia, and gave his name to the country. Homer, who gives Lycia a prominent place in the *Iliad*, represents its chieftains, Glaucus and Sarpedon, as descended from the royal family of Argos (Aeolids). He speaks of the Solymi as a warlike race, inhabiting the mountains, against whom the Greek hero Bellerophontes is sent to fight by his relative the king of Lycia. Besides the legend of Bellerophon and the Chimaera, Lycia is the scene of another popular Greek story, that of the Harpies and the daughters of Pandareos; and memorials of both are preserved on the Lycian monuments now in the British Museum. On the whole, it is clear that Lycia was colonized by the Greeks at a very early period, and that its historical inhabitants were Greeks, though with a mixture of native blood. The earlier names were preserved in the district in the north of the country called Milyas, and in the mountains called Solyma. The Lycians always kept the reputation they have in Homer as brave warriors. They and the Cilicians were the only people west of the Halys whom Croesus did not conquer, and they were the last who resisted the Persians. The principal rivers are the Xanthus (Echen-Chai) and the Limyrus. The principal cities were Xanthus, Patara, Pinara, Olympus, Mira, and Tlos. Since 1840 much has been done in the way of exploration and excavation among the ruined cities of Lycia, especially by Sir Charles Fellows, who in 1846 brought back the remarkable sculptures now in the Lycian Room at the British Museum. The linguistic affinities of the Lycian language are as yet not certainly determined. See Savelsberg, *Beiträge zur Erklärung der lykischen Sprache* (1875–78). The few Lycian inscriptions are collected in the *Corpus Inscript. Lyc.* of Schmidt (1868). See Treuber, *Geschichte der Lykier* (1887).

Lycius. See APOLLO.

Lycomēdes (Λυκομήδης). A king of Scyros, an island in the Aegean Sea, son of Apollo and Parthenopé. He was secretly intrusted with the care of young Achilles, whom his mother Thetis had disguised in feminine attire to prevent his going to the Trojan War, where she knew he must perish. (See ACHILLES.) Lycomedes rendered himself infamous for his treachery to Theseus, who had implored his protection when driven from the throne of Athens by the usurper Mnestheus. Lycomedes, as it is reported, either envious of the fame of his illustrious guest, or bribed by the emissaries of Mnestheus, led Theseus to an elevated place on pretence of showing him the extent of his dominions, and perfidiously threw him down a precipice, where he was killed. According to another account, however, his fall was accidental (Plut. *Thes.;* Pausan. i. 17; vii. 4; Apollod. iii. 13). See THESEUS.

Lycon (Λύκων) (1) OF TROAS. A distinguished Peripatetic philosopher and the disciple of Straton, whom he succeeded as the head of the Peripatetic school, B.C. 272. (2) An orator and demagogue who, with Anytus and Meletus, accused Socrates. He was afterwards banished for his share in the prosecution. See SOCRATES.

Lycŏphron (Λυκόφρων). A grammarian and poet who was a native of Chalcis in Euboea, and lived at Alexandria under Ptolemy Philadelphus (B.C. 285–247). He was the author of an extant poem in 1474 iambic lines, entitled *Cassandra* or *Alexandra*, in which Cassandra is made to prophesy the fall of Troy, with numerous other events. The obscurity of this work is proverbial, and it is filled with obsolete words and long compounds. Among the numerous ancient commentaries on the poem, the most important are the scholia of Isaac and John Tzetzes, which are far more valuable than the poem itself. The earliest edition is that which appeared at Venice in 1513. It has since been edited by Bachmann (Leipzig, 1828), Kinkel (1880), and Scheer (1881). There is an English version by Lord Royston.

Lycophron also wrote a work on the history of Greek comedy and the comic poets, and composed tragedies now lost.

Lycopŏlis (ἡ Λύκων πόλις). A city of Upper Egypt, on the west bank of the Nile, between Hermopolis and Ptolemaïs. Its name was said to be derived from the fact that in its vicinity an Aethiopian army was once routed by wolves (Diod. ii. 88; Ael. *H. A.* x. 28), but more probably from its worship of the jackal (wolf) god Anubis.

Lycorēa (Λυκώρεια). An ancient town at the foot of Mount Lycorea, which was the southern of the two peaks of Mount Parnassus. (See PARNASSUS.) Hence Apollo derived the name of Lycoreus.

Lycōris. See CYTHERIS.

Lycosūra (Λυκόσουρα). A town of Arcadia, on the slope of Mount Lycaeus, regarded by Pausanias (viii. 2, 4, 38) as the most ancient city in the world. It still contained some few inhabitants when he made the tour of Arcadia.

Lyctus (Λύκτος) or **Lyttus** (Λύττος). An important town in the east of Crete, situated on a height, eighty stadia from the coast. It is said to have been a Spartan colony.

Lycurgus (Λυκοῦργος). (1) A king of Thrace, who, when Bacchus was passing through his country, assailed him so furiously that the god was obliged to take refuge with Thetis. Bacchus avenged himself by driving Lycurgus mad, and the latter thereupon killed his own son Dryas with a blow of an axe, taking him for a vine-branch. The land became, in consequence, sterile; and his subjects, having been informed by an oracle that it would not regain its fertility until the monarch was put to death, bound Lycurgus, and left him on Mount Pangaeus, where he was destroyed by wild horses (Apollod. iii. 5, 1). (2) King in Arcadia, son of Aleus and Neaera, brother of Cepheus and Augé, husband of Cleophilé, Eurynomé, or Antinoë, and father of Ancaeus, Epochus, Amphidamas, and Iasus. Lycurgus killed Areïthoüs, who used to fight with a club. Lycurgus bequeathed this club to his slave Ereuthalion, his sons having died before him. (3) Son of Pronax and brother of Amphithea, the wife of Adrastus. He took part in the war of the Seven against Thebes, and fought with Amphiaraüs. He is mentioned among those whom Aesculapius called to life again after their death. (4) King of Nemea, son of Pheres and Periclymene, brother of Admetus, husband of Eurydicé or Amphithea, and father of Opheltes.

(5) A Spartan legislator of whose personal history we have no certain information; and there are such discrepancies respecting him in the ancient writers that many modern critics have denied his real existence altogether. The more generally received account about him was as follows: Lycurgus was the son of Eunomus, king of Sparta, and brother of Polydectes. The latter succeeded his father as king of Sparta, and afterwards died, leaving his queen with child. The ambitious woman proposed to Lycurgus to destroy her offspring if he would share the throne with her. He seemingly consented; but when she had given birth to a son (Charilaüs), he openly proclaimed him king, and as next of kin acted as his guardian. But to avoid all suspicion of ambitious designs, with which the opposite party charged him, Lycurgus left Sparta, and set out on his celebrated travels, which had been magnified to a fabulous extent. He is said to have visited Crete, and there to have studied the wise laws of Minos. Next he went to Ionia and Egypt, and is reported to have penetrated into Libya, Iberia, and even India. In Ionia he is said to have met either with Homer himself, or at least with the Homeric poems, which he introduced into the mother-country. The return of Lycurgus to Sparta was hailed by all parties. Sparta was in a state of anarchy and turbulence, and he was considered as the man who alone could cure the growing diseases of the State. He undertook the task; yet before he set to work he strengthened himself with the authority of the Delphic oracle and with a strong party of influen-

tial men at Sparta. The reform seems not to have been carried altogether peaceably. The new division of the land among the citizens must have violated many existing interests. But all opposition was overborne, and the whole constitution, military and civil, was remodelled. After Lycurgus had obtained for his institutions an approving oracle of the national god of Delphi, he exacted a promise from the people not to make any alterations in his laws before his return, and then he left Sparta to finish his life in voluntary exile, in order that his countrymen might be bound by their oath to preserve his constitution inviolate forever. Where and how he died nobody could tell. He vanished from the earth like a god, leaving no traces behind him but his spirit; and he was honoured as a god at Sparta with a temple and yearly sacrifices down to the latest times. The date of Lycurgus is variously given, but it is impossible to place it later than B.C. 825. Lycurgus was regarded through all subsequent ages as the legislator of Sparta, and therefore almost all the Spartan institutions were ascribed to him as their author. See SPARTA.

(6) An Athenian orator, and one of the warmest supporters of the democratic faction in the contest with Philip of Macedon. The time of his birth is uncertain, but he was older than Demosthenes; and if his father was put to death by order of the Thirty Tyrants, he must have been born previous to B.C. 404. But the words of the biographer are, as Clinton has justly remarked, ambiguous (*Fast. Hell.* ii. p. 151), and may imply that it was his grandfather who was put to death by the Thirty. Lycurgus is said to have derived instruction from Plato and Isocrates. He took an active part in the management of public affairs, and was one of the Athenian ambassadors who succeeded (B.C. 343) in counteracting the designs of Philip against Ambracia and the Peloponnesus. He filled the office of treasurer of the public revenue for three periods of five years (Diod. Sic. xvi. 88); and was noted for the integrity and ability with which he discharged the duties of his office. Böckh considers that Lycurgus was the only statesman of antiquity who had a real knowledge of the management of finance. He raised the revenue to twelve hundred talents, and also erected, during his administration, many public buildings, and completed the docks, the armory, the theatre of Bacchus, and the Panathenaic course. So great confidence was placed in the honesty of Lycurgus that many citizens confided to his custody large sums; and, shortly before his death, he had the accounts of his public administration engraved on stone, and set up in a part of the wrestling-school. An inscription, preserved to the present day, containing some accounts of a manager of the public revenue, is supposed by Böckh to be a part of the accounts of Lycurgus. After the battle of Chaeronea (B.C. 388), Lycurgus conducted the accusation against the Athenian general Lysicles. He was one of the orators demanded by Alexander after the destruction of Thebes (B.C. 335). He died about B.C. 323, and was buried in the Academia (Pausan. i. 29, 15). Fifteen years after his death, upon the ascendency of the democratic faction, a decree was passed by the Athenian people that public honours should be paid to Lycurgus. A brazen statue of him was erected in the Ceramicus, which was seen by Pausanias (i. 8, 3), and the representative of his family was allowed the privilege of dining in the Prytaneum. This decree, which was proposed by Stratocles, has come down to us at the end of the lives of the Ten Orators. Lycurgus is said to have published fifteen orations, of which only one has been preserved. This oration, which was delivered B.C. 331, is an accusation of Leocrates (Κατὰ Λεωκράτους), as Athenian citizen, for abandoning Athens after the battle of Chaeronea, and settling in another Grecian State. The best editions of Lycurgus are those of Osann (Jena, 1821), Mätzner (1836), Kiessling and Meier (1847), Rehdantz (1876), and Thalheim (1880). See also Dürrbach, *L'Orateur Lycurgue* (1890). Another excellent text is that of Bekker, in his *Oratores Attici*. The oration of Lycurgus is also found in the collections of Reiske and Dobson.

Lycus (Λύκος). (1) Son of Poseidon and the Pleiad Celaeno, married to Dircé. He assumed the government of Thebes after his brother Nycteus, for Labdacus, who was a minor; and, after the death of Labdacus, for his son Laïus. He was either killed by Amphion (q. v.) and Zethus, or (according to another account) handed the government of Thebes over to them at the behest of Hermes. (2) Son of Poseidon, tyrant of Thebes, killed by Heracles for murdering his father-in-law Creon during his absence and for plotting against his wife Megara and his children.

Lydda (τὰ Λύδδα). A town of Palestine, southeast of Joppa and northwest of Jerusalem, subsequently called Diospolis. Here St. George was said to have been born.

Lydia (Λυδία). A district of Asia Minor, in the middle of the western side of the peninsula, between Mysia on the north and Caria on the south, and between Phrygia on the east and the Aegean Sea on the west. Its boundaries varied so much at different times that they cannot be described with any approach to exactness till we come to the time of the Roman rule over western Asia. At that time the northern boundary, towards Mysia, was the range of mountains which form the northern margin of the valley of the Hermus, called Sardené, a southwestern branch of the Phrygian Olympus; the eastern boundary, towards Phrygia, was an imaginary line; and the southern boundary, towards Caria, was the river Maeander, or, according to some authorities, the range of mountains which, under the name of Messogis (Kastane Dagh), forms the northern margin of the valley of the Maeander, and is a northwestern prolongation of the Taurus. From the eastern part of this range, in the southeast corner of Lydia, another branches off to the northwest, and runs to the west far out into the Aegean Sea, where it forms the peninsula opposite to the island of Chios. This chain, which is called Tmolus (Kisilja Musa Dagh), divides Lydia into two unequal valleys, of which the southern and smaller is watered by the river Caÿster, and the northern forms the great plain of the Hermus; these valleys are very beautiful and fertile, and that of the Hermus especially is one of the most delicious regions of the earth. The eastern part of Lydia and the adjacent portion of Phrygia, about the upper course of the Hermus and its tributaries, is an elevated plain, showing traces of volcanic action, and hence called Catacecaumené (κατακεκαυμένη). In early times the country had another name, MAEONIA (Μῃονίη, Μαιονία), by which alone it is known to Homer, who is himself sometimes spoken of as Maeonides; and this name was afterwards applied specifically to the eastern and southern part of Lydia; and then, in contradistinction to it, the name Lydia was used for the northwestern part.

In the mythical legends the common name of the people and country, Lydi and Lydia, is derived from Lydus, the son of Atys, the first king. The Lydians appear to have been a race closely connected with the Carians and the Mysians, with whom they observed a common worship in the temple of Zeus Carius at Mylasa; they also practised the worship of Cybelé, and other Phrygian customs. Amid the uncertainties of the early legends, it is clear that Lydia was a very early seat of Asiatic civilization, and that it exerted a very important influence on the Greeks. The Lydian monarchy, which was founded at Sardis before the time of authentic history, grew up into an Empire, under which the many different tribes of Asia Minor west of the river Halys were for the first time united. Tradition mentioned three dynasties of kings: the Atyadae, which ended (according to the backward computations of chronologers) about B.C. 1221; the Heraclidae, which reigned 505 years, down to 716; and the Mermnadae, 160 years, down to 556. Only the last dynasty can be safely regarded as historical, and the fabulous element has a large place in the details of their history; their names and computed dates were: (1) Gyges, B.C. 716–678; (2) Ardys, 678–629; (3) Sadyattes, 629–617; (4) Alyattes, 617–560; (5) Croesus, 560 (or earlier) – 546, under whose names an account is given of the rise of the Lydian Empire in Asia Minor and of its overthrow by the Persians under Cyrus. Under these kings the Lydians appear to have been a highly civilized, industrious, and wealthy people, practising agriculture, commerce, and manufactures, and acquainted with various arts; and exercising, through their intercourse with the Greeks of Ionia, an important influence on the progress of Greek civilization. Among the inventions or improvements which the Greeks are said to have derived from them were the weaving and dyeing of fine fabrics; various processes of metallurgy; the use of gold and silver money, which the Lydians are said first to have coined, the former from the gold found on Tmolus and from the golden sands of the Pactolus (now Sarabat); and various metrical and musical improvements, especially the scale or mode of music called the Lydian, and the form of the lyre called the *magadis*. (See LYRA; MUSICA.) The Lydians had, also, public games similar to those of the Greeks. Their high civilization, however, was combined with a lax morality; and after the Persian conquest, when they were forbidden by Cyrus to carry arms, they sank gradually into a by-word for effeminate luxuriousness, and their very name and language had almost entirely disappeared by the commencement of our era. Under the Persians, Lydia and Mysia formed the second satrapy. After the Macedonian conquest Lydia belonged first to the kings of Syria, and next (after the defeat of Antiochus the Great by the Romans) to those of Pergamus, and so passed, by the bequest of Attalus III., to the Romans, under whom it formed part of the province of Asia.

The chief cities of Lydia were Sardes (Sart), Magnesia (Manissa), Thyatira (Ak Hissar), Philadelphia (Ala Shehir), and Hypaipa (Birghé). See Stark, *Nach dem griechischen Orient* (1874); Prof. Sayce, in the *Journal for Hellenic Studies* (1880); and Gregorovius, *Kleine Schriften zur Geschichte und Cultur*, vol. i. (1887). For the art of Lydia, see Perrot and Chipiez, *Hist. of Art in Phrygia, Lydia*, etc., pp. 232–301 (Lond. and N. Y. 1892). For Lydian numismatics, see Head, *The Coinage of Lydia and Persia* (London, 1874–77). For the supposed connection of the Lydians with the Etruscans, who were sometimes called Lydi (e. g. Verg. *Aen.* ii. 781), see the article ETRURIA, p. 625.

Lydiădes (Λυδιάδης). A citizen of Megalopolis, who, though of an obscure family, raised himself to the sovereignty of his native city about B.C. 244. In 234 he voluntarily abdicated the sovereignty, and permitted Megalopolis to join the Achaean League as a free State. He was elected several times general of the Achaean League, and became a formidable rival to Aratus. He fell in battle against Cleomenes in B.C. 226.

Lydias or Ludias (Λυδίας; Ion. Λυδίης, Λουδίας). Now Mavronero; a river in Macedonia which rises in Eordaea, passes Edessa, and, after flowing through the lake on which Pella is situated, falls into the Axius a short distance from the Thermaic Gulf. In the upper part of its course it is called the Eordaean River (Ἐορδαϊκὸς ποταμός) by Arrian.

Lydus (Λυδός). A son of Atys and Callithea, and brother of Tyrrhenus. He is said to have been the mythical ancestor of the Lydians.

Lydus, IOANNES LAURENTIUS. A Greek writer, born at Philadelphia in Lydia, A.D. 490. At the age of twenty-one he went to Constantinople in order to study philosophy, entered the service of the State, and rose to high office. About 552 he was dismissed by Justinian, and took a post as teacher in the imperial school. Here he devoted himself to literature, and died in 565. We still possess some of his writings, which are derived from ancient sources now lost: (1) on the State offices of Rome (Περὶ Ἀρχῶν, *De Magistratibus*); (2) on portents in the sky, etc., and the doctrine of auguries (Περὶ Διοσημειῶν, *De Ostentis*); (3) extracts from a work on the Roman months and the festivals held in them (Περὶ Μηνῶν, *De Mensibus*). Edition by Becker (Bonn, 1837).

Lygdămis (Λύγδαμις). (1) A Naxian, who aided Pisistratus in recovering his authority at Athens, and received as a recompense the government of his native island (Herod. i. 61, 64). (2) The father of Artemisia, the celebrated queen of Halicarnassus (Herod. vii. 99). (3) A tyrant of Caria, son of Pisindelis, who reigned in the time of Herodotus at Halicarnassus. He put to death the poet Panyasis. Herodotus fled from his native city in order to avoid his tyranny, and afterwards aided in deposing him. See HERODOTUS.

Lygii or Ligii. An important people in Germany, between the Viadus (Oder) and the Vistula (Tac. *Germ.* 43).

Lygȳes. See LIGURIA.

Lyncestis (Λυγκηστίς). A district in the southwest of Macedonia, upon the frontiers of Illyria, inhabited by the Lyncestae, an Illyrian people. The ancient capital of the country was Lyncus, though Heraclea at a later time became the chief town in the district. Near Lyncus was a river, whose waters are said to have been as intoxicating as wine (Ovid, *Met.* xv. 329).

Lynceus (Λυγκεύς). (1) The son of Aphareus, was among the hunters of the Caledonian boar, and was also one of the Argonauts. According to the old legend, he was so sharp-sighted as to have been able to see through the earth, and also to distinguish objects at the distance of many miles. He was slain by Pollux. (See DIOSCURI.) (2) One of the fifty sons of Aegyptus. He obtained Hypermnestra for his bride, and was the only one of the fifty whose life was spared by his spouse. (See DANAÜS; HYPERMNESTRA.) (3) A Samian pupil of Theophrastus who was a rival of Menander as a writer of comedy (Suid. s. v.).

Lyncus. A king of Scythia, who endeavored to murder Triptolemus, who came to him with the gifts of Demeter. He was metamorphosed by the goddess into a lynx (Ovid, *Met.* v. 650).

Lyra (λύρα, pure Latin, *fides*). A stringed musical instrument, said to have been invented by Hermes, who stretched four strings across the shell of a tortoise. In historical times a whole tortoise-shell was used for the sounding-bottom, the curved horns of a goat or pieces of wood of a similar shape were inserted in the openings for the front legs, and joined near the upper ends by a transverse piece of wood called the yoke. On the breast-plate of the shell was a low bridge, across which the strings (usually seven) ran all at the same height to the yoke, and were either simply wound round it or fastened to pegs; at the other end they were tied in knots and fastened to the sounding-board. It was ordinarily played with the left hand, while to produce louder and longer notes the strings were struck by the right hand with the *plectrum*, the point of which was usually like the leaf of a tree, and sometimes in the shape of a heart or like a little hammer.

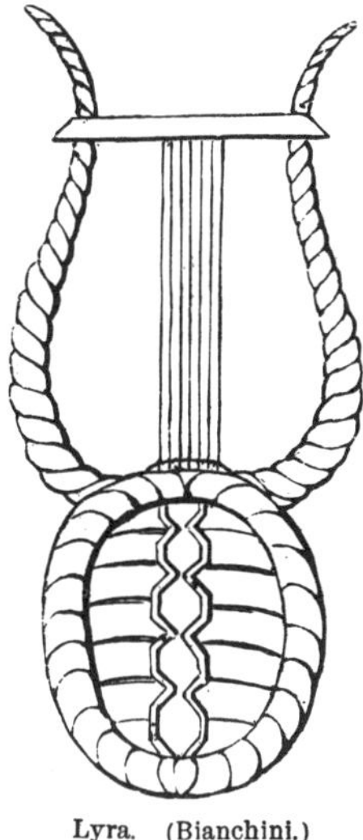

Lyra. (Bianchini.)

The cithara differed from the lyra in replacing the shell by a wooden case either square or angular, and instead of the so-called horns (*cornua*) the sides of the case were prolonged upwards, as shown in the accompanying illustration. The cithara, therefore, represents an advance in point of construction over the lyre. The φόρμιγξ of Homer is probably the lyre rather than the cithara, though the word λύρα is post-Homeric; and the κίθαρις does not appear to have been different (Ammon. *De Diff. Voc.* p. 82). In later times, the cithara took on a form not unlike the modern guitar, the word guitar, in fact, being a derivation of *cithara* through the Italian *chitarra*. See Von Jan, *De Fidibus Graecorum* (Berlin, 1859), and the works mentioned in the article MUSICA.

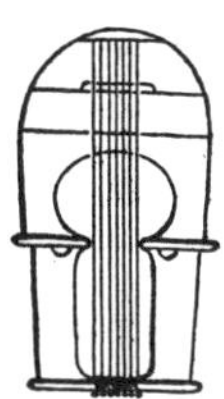

Cithara. (Guhl and Koner.)

Lyrcēa (Λυρκεία) or **Lyrcēum** (Λύρκειον). A small town in Argolis, situated on a mountain of the same name.

Lyre. See LYRA.

Lyric Poetry. While among the GREEKS the elegiac and iambic poetry, which forms the transition from epic to lyric composition, was practised by the Ionians, lyric poetry proper, or, as it was more commonly called, melic poetry (μέλος, "a song")—viz., the song accompanied by music, was cultivated by the Aeolians and Dorians. This is due to the talent for music peculiar to these races. That playing on stringed instruments and singing were cultivated even in mythical times in Aeolia, in the island of Lesbos, is shown by the legend that the head and lyre of Orpheus, who had been torn to pieces by Thracian women, were washed ashore on that island, and that the head was buried in the Lesbian town of Antissa. Antissa was the native place of Terpander (q. v.), who gave artistic form to the νόμος, or hymn to Apollo, by elaborating the laws of its composition. Settling at Sparta in B.C. 676, he laid the foundation of the Dorian music. While he had closely followed Homeric poetry in the texts which he wrote for his musical compositions, there afterwards arose a greater variety in the kinds of songs, corresponding to the greater variety of musical forms, springing from the foundation laid by him. In the AEOLIAN lyric the pathetic prevails, as might be expected from the passionate nature of the people; the feelings of love and hatred, joy and sorrow are their principal themes. As to the metrical form we find short lines with a soft, melodious rhythm, which make up a small number of short strophes. They are written in the Aeolic dialect; we may suppose that they were solos sung to the accompaniment of stringed instruments. In Lesbos the Aeolian lyric was brought to its highest perfection by Alcaeus of Mitylené (about 600), and by his contemporary Sappho, also a Lesbian, and teacher of the poetess Erinna. The joyous poems of Anacreon of Teos (born about 550), whose subjects are love and wine, were also in the Aeolian style, but in the Ionic dialect. An echo of the Aeolian lyric are the *scolia*. See SCOLIUM.

It was among the DORIANS, however, that the lyric poetry of the Greeks reached the highest degree of its development. It is also called choral lyric, because the Dorian songs were intended to be sung at the public festivals, especially those of the gods, by a dancing choir to the accompaniment of stringed instruments and flutes. Intended, therefore, to be public, it naturally had on the whole an earnest, objective character, and is thus distinguished from the Aeolian lyrics that expressed the personal feelings of the poet. Their form shows further points of difference. Instead of the diminutive Aeolian strophes of short lines, unsuitable for dancing, the Dorian lyrics have ampler strophes, usually with longer lines, and the combination of strophes is again subdivided into strophe, antistrophe, and epode, of which the first two are exactly parallel, while the last differs from both in its structure. While the number of the Aeolian metres is fixed, every Dorian song has its own metre, the rhythm of which depends on the tune suitable to the subject. As to the kinds of songs, there is also a great variety in the Dorian lyric: there are paeans, *hyporchemata*, hymns, *prosodia*, *parthenia*, dithyrambs, *encomia*, *epinicia*, *hymenaea*, *epithalamia*, *threnoi*; drinking-songs and love songs are also not wanting. They are written in the old epic dialect, influenced by Doric.

With regard to their historical development, Alcman (about 660), a Lydian who had become a citizen of Sparta, was the first to compose longer and more varied poems on the lines laid down by Terpander and his school. The Dorian lyric received its later artistic form from the Sicilian Stesichorus of Himera (about 600), whose contemporary Arion first gave a place in literature to the dithyramb. (See DITHYRAMBUS.) In the sixth century choral poetry became the common property of all Greeks, and so flourished more and more. Of its older representatives we have still to mention Ibycus of Rhegium (about 540), in whose choral songs the erotic element prevails. This class of poetry was brought to its greatest perfection at the time of the Persian Wars by Simonides of Ceos, by his nephew, Bacchylides, and above all by Pindar of Thebes. Besides these, Timocreon of Ialysus, and the poetesses Myrtis, Corinna, Praxilla, and Telesilla deserve mention. Of the productions of Aeolian and Dorian lyric poetry, only fragments have been preserved, except the epinician odes of Pindar. (See PINDARUS.) These fragments are edited by Bergk, *Poetae Graeci Lyrici* (1878).

With the ROMANS, the first attempts to imitate the forms of the Greek "melic" date from the last years of the Republic. Laevius wrote mythological poems in a great variety of metres, the *Erotopaegnia* ("Diversions of Love"), which, however, seem to have attracted little attention. Catullus also wrote some poems in melic measures. This kind of poetry was perfected in the age of Augustus by Horace, who introduced the forms of Aeolian lyric. None of the succeeding poets were of even secondary importance, in spite of the great skill with which they handled the various melic metres; one of them, the Christian poet Prudentius, wrote as late as the fourth century. The Dorian lyric never obtained a footing among the Romans.

See Deventer, *Zu den griechischen Lyrikern* (1887); Führer, *Sprache u. Entwicklung d. griech. Lyrik* (1885); Mattel, *Die griechischen Lyriker* (1892); and for the Christian lyrics, the article HYMNUS.

Lyrnessus (Λυρνησσός). A town in the Troad, the birthplace of Briseïs, and often mentioned by Homer (*Il.* ii. 690).

Lysander (Λύσανδρος). (1) A Spartan, who rose to eminence towards the end of the Peloponnesian War, and was placed in command of the Lacedaemonian troops, on the coast of Asia Minor, B.C. 407. Having about him little of the old Spartan severity, and being ready to sacrifice that personal and national pride and inflexibility, which were the peculiar characteristics of the Spartan institutions, to personal or national interests, he gained in an unusual degree the regard and confidence of his Persian allies. This he used to the best advantage, by seizing a favourable moment to obtain from the younger Cyrus, the Persian viceroy in Asia Minor, in place of any personal advantage, the addition of an obolus daily (somewhat more than two cents of our money) to every seaman in the Peloponnesian fleet. During his year's command he defeated the Athenian fleet commanded by Antiochus, as lieutenant of Alcibiades, at Notium. In September, B.C. 406, he was superseded by Callicratidas, who was defeated and slain in the memorable battle of Arginusae. The allies then petitioned that Lysander might be reappointed. It was contrary to Spartan law to intrust a fleet twice to the same person; but this difficulty was evaded by nominating another individual as commander-in-chief and sending Lysander as lieutenant with the command in Asia. He soon justified the preference by gaining the decisive victory of Aegospotami, in the Hellespont, where 170 Athenian ships were taken. This, in effect, finished the war. Receiving, as he went, the submission of her allies, Lysander proceeded leisurely to Athens, and blockaded her ports, while the Spartan kings marched into Attica and invested the city, which, unassaulted, was reduced by the sure process of famine. The capitulation being settled, B.C. 404, Lysander had the proud satisfaction of entering as victor the Piraeus or harbour of Athens, which had been unviolated by the presence of an enemy since the Persian invasion. His services and reputation gained for him corresponding weight at Sparta; and, on occasion of the contested succession, his influence was powerful in raising Agesilaüs to the throne. He accompanied that eminent statesman and soldier during his first campaign in Asia, where his popularity and renown threw his superior into the shade and an estrangement resulted, in which Lysander conducted himself with temper and wisdom. About B.C. 396 he returned to Sparta. In the following year, on occasion of a quarrel with Thebes, he was sent into Phocis to collect contingents from the northern allies, a task for which his name and popularity rendered him peculiarly fit. Having done this, and being on his way to join the Lacedaemonian army, he was surprised and slain by the Thebans at Haliartus in Boeotia. The force which he had collected was dispersed, and the war at once came to an end, with no credit to the Lacedaemonians, B.C. 395.

It is said that, urged by ambitious hopes, he meditated a scheme for abolishing the hereditary right of the descendants of Heracles, and rendering the Spartan throne elective, and that he had tampered largely with different oracles to promote his scheme. Xenophon, however, a contemporary historian, makes no mention of this rumour. The subject has been discussed by Thirlwall, in an appendix to the fourth volume of his *History of Greece*. This writer thinks that Lysander actually formed such a project; and that the same motive which induced the Spartan government to hush up the affair would certainly have led Xenophon carefully to avoid all allusion to it. There is a life of Lysander by Plutarch, and another by Nepos. (2) One of the ephori in the reign of Agis. (3) A grandson of Lysander (Pausan. iii. 6).

Lysĭas (Λυσίας). One of the ten Athenian orators. He was born at Athens, B.C. 458 or 459. His father, Cephalus, was a native of Syracuse, who settled at Athens during the time of Pericles. Cephalus was a person of considerable wealth, and lived on intimate terms with Pericles and Socrates; and his house is the supposed scene of the celebrated dialogues related in Plato's *Republic*. Lysias, at the age of fifteen, went to Thurii in Italy, with his brother Polemarchus, at the first foundation of the colony. Here he remained for thirty-two years; but, in consequence of his supporting the Athenian interests, he was obliged to leave Italy after the failure of the Athenian expedition to Sicily. He returned to Athens, B.C. 411, and carried on, in partnership with his brother Polemarchus, an extensive manufactory of shields, in which they employed as many as 120 slaves. Their wealth excited the cupidity of the Thirty Tyrants; their house was attacked one evening by an armed force while Lysias was entertaining a few friends at supper; their property was seized, and Polemarchus was taken to prison, where he was shortly after executed (B.C. 404). Lysias, by bribing some of the soldiers, escaped to the Piraeus, and sailed thence to Megara. He has given us a graphic account of his escape in his oration against Eratosthenes, who had been one of the Thirty Tyrants. Lysias actively assisted Thrasybulus in his enterprise against the Thirty; he supplied him with a large sum of money from his own resources and those of his friends, and hired a considerable body of soldiers at his own expense. In return for these services Thrasybulus proposed a decree by which the rights of citizenship should be conferred upon Lysias; but, in consequence of some informality, this decree was never carried into effect. He was, however, allowed the peculiar privileges which were sometimes granted to resident aliens (namely, ἰσοτέλεια). Lysias appears to have died about B.C. 378.

The author of the *Life of Lysias*, attributed to Plutarch, mentions 425 orations of his, 230 of which were considered to be genuine. There remain only 34, which are all forensic, and remarkable for the method which reigns in them. The purity, the perspicuity, the grace and simplicity which characterize the orations of Lysias, would have raised him to the highest rank in the art had they been coupled with the force and energy of Demosthenes. His style is elegant without being overornate, and is regarded as a model of the "plain" style. In the art of narration, Dionysius of Halicarnassus considers him superior to all orators in being distinct, probable, and persuasive; but, at the same time, admits that his composition is better adapted to private litigation than to important causes. The text of his harangues, as we now have it, is extremely corrupt. His masterpiece is the funeral oration in honour of those Athenians who, having been sent to the aid of the Corinthians under the command of Iphicrates, perished in battle. Lysias is said to have delivered only one of the orations which he wrote—that against Eratosthenes.

Lysias has been edited by Reiske (1772), Bekker (1828), Baiter and Sauppe (1850), Cobet (1863), and Scheibe (1886); and there are selections edited by Rauchenstein-Fuhr (with German notes), Frohberger, and (with English notes) by Shuckburgh, Stevens, and Bristol. There is an English translation by Gillies. See Jebb's *Attic Orators*, i. pp. 142–312.

Lysicrătes, Monument of. One of the most graceful relics of Greek antiquity, raised in memory of a victory in the dramatic contests won by Lysicrates when he was *choregus* (see Chorus) in B.C. 334. From a slender square basement, 12 feet high by 9 feet wide, rises a small but elegant round temple. Six engaged Corinthian columns surround its circular wall and support the entablature, on the frieze of which there is a delicate and life-like representation of a scene in the legend of Dionysus—the changing of the Tyrrhenian pirates into dolphins, for having by mistake laid hands on the god. Over the entablature is a flat dome made of a single block of marble, and from the centre of the roof rises a finial of acanthus leaves, formerly crowned by the tripod which was the prize of victory. The monument is 35 feet high, and the diameter of the inside is about 6 feet. The reliefs of the frieze are of great value, as they belong to the new Attic school of Scopas and Praxiteles. According to a tradition (which is without foundation) that Demosthenes used to study here, the monument used to be called the Lantern of Demosthenes—a name familiar to Michael Acominatos, in the second half of the twelfth century (Gregorovius, *Mirabilien der Stadt Athen*, p. 357). The true name was first restored by Transfeldt about 1674 (id. *Athen im Mittelalter*, ii. 357). See Perry's *Greek and Roman Sculpture*, pp. 473–475.

Lysimachĭa (Λυσιμαχία or Λυσιμάχεια). An important town of Thrace, on the Gulf of Melas, and on the isthmus connecting the Thracian Chersonesus with the mainland, founded B.C. 309 by Lysimachus, who removed to his new city the inhabitants of the neighbouring town of Cardia.

Lysimăchus (Λυσίμαχος). One of Alexander's generals, who obtained Thrace in the division of the provinces after Alexander's death (B.C. 323), and assumed the title of king in B.C. 306. He joined the other generals of Alexander in opposing Antigonus, and it was he and Seleucus who gained the decisive victory at Ipsus over Antigonus, in which the latter fell (B.C. 301). In B.C. 291 Lysimachus was taken prisoner by Dromichaetes, king of the Getae, whose country he had invaded, but he was restored to liberty by the latter. In B.C. 287 Lysimachus and Pyrrhus expelled Demetrius from Macedonia. Pyrrhus, for a time, obtained possession of the Macedonian throne; but in the following year he was driven out of the country by Lysimachus, who now became king of Macedonia. Towards the end of his reign the aged Lysimachus put to death his son Agathocles, at the instigation of his wife, Arsinoë, daughter of Ptolemy Soter. This bloody deed alienated the minds of his subjects, and Seleucus invaded the dominions of Lysimachus. The two monarchs met in the plain of Corus (Corupedion), and Lysimachus fell in the battle that ensued, B.C. 281, in his eightieth year.

Lysippus (Λύσιππος). A native of Sicyon, and one of the most famous Greek artists, a contemporary of Alexander the Great. He was originally a worker in metal, and taught himself the art of the sculptor by studying nature and the *canon* of Polyclitus (q. v.). His works, which were said to amount to 1500, were all statues in bronze, and were remarkable for their lifelike characterization and their careful and accurate execution, shown particularly in the treatment of the hair. He aimed at representing the beauty and harmony more especially of the male human body; and substituted for the proportions of Polyclitus a new ideal, which kept in view the effect produced, by giving the body a more slender and elegant shape, and by making the head smaller in comparison with the trunk, than is the case with the actual average man. The most famous among his stat-

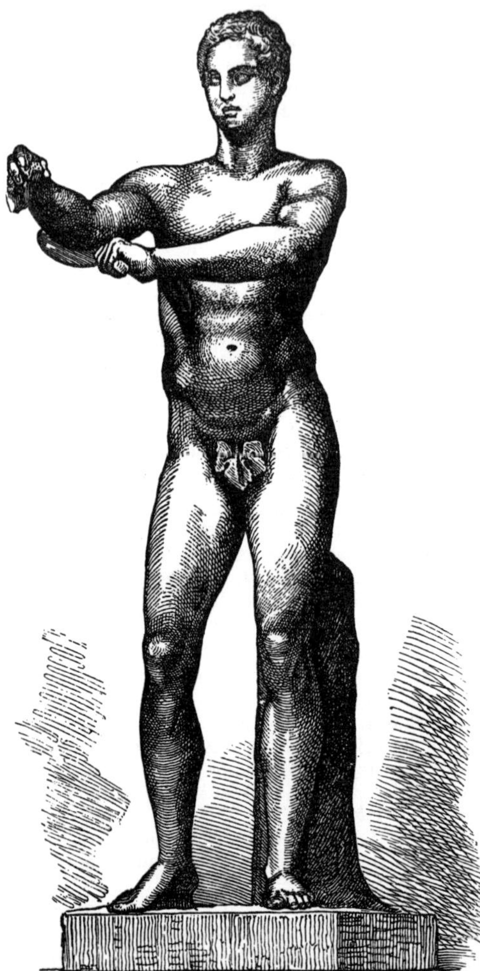

Marble Copy of the Apoxyomenos of Lysippus. (Vatican Museum, Rome.)

ues of gods were the colossal forms of Zeus and Heracles, at Tarentum of which the former was second in size only to that at Rhodes, while the latter was afterwards brought to the Capitol at Rome, and then to the Hippodrome at Constantinople, where it was melted down in A.D. 1022; and, lastly, the sun-god on the four-horse chariot at Rhodes (Pliny, *H. N.* xxxiv. §§ 40, 63).

The first example of pure allegory in Greek art was his Καιρός, the "Favourable Moment"—a delicate youth with modest look standing on a ball, with his foot winged, and holding shears and a balance in his hands. The hair hung down in front, while it was so short behind that it could not be grasped (*Anthol. Gr.* ii. 49, 13; Callist. *Statuae*, 6).

By far the greater number of his statues were portraits. Of these the various representations of Alexander the Great from boyhood onwards were of marked excellence (Pliny, *H. N.* xxxiv. 64). Indeed, the king would have no sculptor but Lysippus to represent him, even as he would have no other painter than Apelles (Pliny, *H. N.* vii. 125; Hor. *Epist.* ii. 1, 240; Cic. *Ad Fam.* v. 12, 13).

Among his large groups were Craterus saving the life of Alexander chasing the lion (Pliny, *H. N.* xxxiv. 64), and the portraits of twenty-five horsemen and nine foot soldiers who fell at the first assault in the battle of the Granicus (Arrian, *Anab.* i. 16, § 7; Plut. *Alex.* 16). The excellent copy in marble, at the Vatican, of the *Apoxyomenos*, a youth removing the dust of the palaestra with a strigil, affords an idea of his skill in representing beautiful and perfectly developed bodies of delicate elasticity and graceful suppleness (Pliny, *H. N.* xxxiv. 62). See Perry's *Greek and Roman Sculpture*, pp. 478–488.

Lysis (Λῦσις). An eminent Pythagorean philosopher, the teacher of Epaminondas (Pausan. ix. 13).

Lysistrătus (Λυσίστρατος). A statuary of Sicyon, who flourished in the 114th Olympiad. He was the brother of the celebrated Lysippus (Pliny, *H. N.* xxxv. 12, 44). He is said to have been the first artist who made use of gypsum moulds for casts of the human face.

Lystra (ἡ Λύστρα). A city of Lycaonia, on the confines of Isauria, celebrated as one chief scene of the preaching of Paul and Barnabas (Acts, xiv. 8). See Sterrett, *The Wolfe Expedition to Asia Minor* (Boston, 1888).

M

M, as a symbol.

IN GREEK.—

M = μιλλιάριον (*Bull. de Corr. Hell.* ii. 597), μηνός (*Mittheil d. ath. Inst.* iii. 57), μέσος (*Arch. Zeit.* 1876, p. 57), μνημεῖον (*C. I. G.* 5628), μονάρψου (*Bull. de Corr. Hell.* viii. 43), Μάρκος. As a numeral = 12 (old system), or 40 (M̄). Also = μυριάς or μυριάς μία (M). ,μ = 40,000.

MNΔ = μέγας νέος Διόνυσος (*C. I. G.* 2278).

IN LATIN.—

M = Macedonica, magister, maiestas, maiora, Manes, manu, Marcus, marmora, Martia (legio), mas, maritus, Mars, mater, Mercurius, metalla, miles, Minerva, minus, missus, modius, muliebris, municipium.

MM = Marci (duo), memoriae.

M·A = Mercurius Augustus, militavit annos.

M·C = mater castrorum, memoriae causa.

M·D = Manibus diis, Mater deum, mater dulcissima.

M·E = merita eius.

M·F = magister fani, mater (monumentum, memoriam) fecit, miles factus, munere functus.

M·L = miles legionis.

Ꟶ·L = mulieris libertus.

M·M = magister Mercurialis, malis male, Mater magna, municipes municipii.

M·N = metalla nova, milia nummum.

M·O = matri optimae.

M·P = magister pagi, maior pars, mater (memoriam) posuit, mille passus (milia passuum).

M·A·G·S = memor animo grato solvit.

M·B·M·F = maritus bene merenti fecit.

M·D·A·N = metalla domini Augusti nostri.

M·D·M·A = monumento dolus malus abesto.

M·D·M·I = mater deum magna Idaea.

M·H·F·C = memoriam (monumentum) heres faciundum curavit.

M·H·N·S = monumentum heredem non sequetur.

M·P·D·M = monumentum positum dis Manibus.

As a numeral, M = 1000. See NUMERI.

Macae (Μάκαι). (1) A people on the eastern coast of Arabia Felix, probably near Muscat. (2) An inland people of Libya, in the part of northern Africa between the Syrtes.

Macalla (Μάκαλλα). A town on the eastern coast of Bruttium. Here Philoctetes was said to have been buried (Lycophron, *Alex.* 927).

Macăreus (Μακαρεύς). A son of Aeolus, who committed incest with his sister Canacé. (See CANACÉ). Hence Issé, the daughter of Macareus, is called Macareïs. After the suicide of Canacé, Macareus fled to Delphi, where he became the priest of Apollo. His story is told by Ovid in the *Heroides*, xi.

Macaria (Μακαρία). The daughter of Heracles and Deïanira. When Eurystheus, after the death of Heracles, made war upon the Heraclidae and their allies, the Athenians, an oracle declared that the descendants of Heracles would be victorious if one of them should devote himself to death. This lot Macaria voluntarily accepted, and the oracle was fulfilled in the success of the Athenians by whom Macaria was therefore held in great honour. A fountain at Marathon was called by her name (Pausan. i. 32).

Macaria (Μακαρία). (1) A name used by the poets for several of the Grecian islands—e. g. Cyprus, Rhodes, and Lesbos. (2) An island in the southern part of the Red Sea.

Maccabaei. See IUDAEI, p. 894.

Macĕdo (Μακεδών). A son of Osiris (q. v.), and worshipped by the Egyptians, who represented him as clothed in a wolf's skin. The hero who gave his name to Macedonia (q. v.) was by some regarded as identical with this Egyptian, but by some was held to be the grandson of Deucalion (q. v.). His name is also given as Macednus. See Apollod. iii. 8, 1.

Macedonia (Μακεδονία). A country in Europe, north of Greece, said to have been originally named EMATHIA. Its boundaries before the time of Philip, the father of Alexander, were, on the south, Olympus and the Cambunian Mountains, which separated it from Thessaly and Epirus; on the east, the river Strymon, which separated it from Thrace; and on the north and west, Illyria and Paeonia. Macedonia was greatly enlarged by the conquests of Philip. He added to his kingdom Paeonia on the north; a part of Thrace on the east as far as the river Nestus, which Thracian district was usually called Macedonia Adiecta; the peninsula Chalcidicé on the south; and on the west a part of Illyria as far as Lake Lychnitis. On the conquest of the country by the Romans, B.C. 168, Macedonia was divided into four districts, independent of one another; but the whole country was formed into a Roman province after the conquest of the Achaeans in 146.

Macedonia may be described as a large plain, surrounded on three sides by lofty mountains. Through this plain, however, run many smaller ranges of mountains, between which are wide and fertile valleys, extending from the coast far into the interior. The chief mountains were Scordus, or Scardus, on the northwest frontier, towards Illyria and Dardania; further east Orbelus and Scomius, which separated it from Moesia; and Rhodopé, which extended from Scomius in a southeasterly direction, forming the boundary between Macedonia and Thrace. On the southern frontier were the Cambunii Montes and Olympus. The chief rivers were in the direction of east to west—the Nestus, the Strymon, the Axius, the largest of all, the Ludias or Lydias, and the Haliacmon. The chief cities were Aegae and Pella, the capitals, and Pydna, Potidaea, Olynthus, Amphipolis, and Philippi. The great bulk of the inhabitants of Macedonia consisted of Thracian and Illyrian tribes. At an early period some Greek tribes settled in the southern part of the country. They are said to have come from Argos, and to have been led by the three sons of Temenus, the Heraclid. Perdiccas, the youngest of the three, was looked upon as the founder of the Macedonian monarchy. A later tradition, however, regarded Caranus, who was also a Heraclid from Argos, as the founder of the monarchy. These Greek settlers intermarried with the original inhabitants of the country. The dialect which they spoke was akin to the Doric, but it contained many barbarous words and forms; and the Macedonians accordingly were never regarded by the other

Silver Coin of Macedonia after the Roman Conquest.

Greeks as genuine Hellenes. Moreover, it was only in the south of Macedonia that the Greek language was spoken. See Brugmann, *Comp. Gram.* vol. i. p. 7.

Very little is known of the history of Macedonia till the reign of Amyntas I., who was a contemporary of Darius Hystaspis; but from that time their history is more or less intimately connected with that of Greece, till at length Philip, the father of Alexander the Great, became the virtual master of the whole of Greece. The conquests of Alexander extended the Macedonian supremacy over a great part of Asia; and the Macedonian kings continued to exercise their sovereignty over Greece till the conquest of Perseus by the Romans, in B.C. 168, brought the Macedonian monarchy to a close. See Abel, *Makedonien vor König Phillipp* (Leipzig, 1847); Döll, *Geographie der alt. Makedoniens* (1891); Heuzey and Daumet, *Mission Archéologique de Macédonie*, 2 vols. (Paris, 1876); Curteis, *Rise of the Macedonian Empire* (N. Y. 1878); and the articles ALEXANDER; PERDICCAS; PHILIPPUS.

Macedonĭcus. A name given to Q. Caecilius Metellus, who made Macedonia a Roman province. See Vell. Peterc. i. 11, and the article METELLUS.

Macella (Μάκελλα). A small fortified town in the west of Sicily, southeast of Segesta.

Macellarii. See MACELLUM.

Macellum (ὀψοπωλία, ὀψοπωλεῖον, and κρεοπωλεῖον). A market for provisions of all kinds—

meat, fish, poultry, fruit, etc. At Athens, the separate kinds of wares were sold in the divisions of the market-place, called κύκλοι. The opening of a sale was announced by the ringing of a bell. See Mahaffy, *Social Life in Greece*, ch. x., and the article AGORA.

At Rome, there were originally separate markets for the sale of each kind of food, thus the Forum Boarium for meat, Olitorium for vegetables, Piscatorium for fish, etc., but in B.C. 179 a great Macellum, or general market, was built north of the Forum Romanum (Fest. s. v. *macellum*), and afterwards, a number of other macella arose, such as the Macellum Augusti mentioned on a coin of Nero (Eckhel, vi. 273), and the Macellum Livianum near the Porta Esquilina. The market-men were called *macellarii* (Suet. *Iul.* 26).

Macer, AEMILIUS. (1) A Roman poet, a native of Verona, who died in Asia, B.C. 16. He wrote a poem upon birds, snakes, and medicinal plants, the fragments of which are given in Bährens, *Frag. Poet. Rom.* 345. (2) We must distinguish from Aemilius Macer of Verona, a poet Macer who wrote on the Trojan War, and who must have been alive in A.D. 12, since he is addressed by Ovid in that year (*Epist. ex Pont.* ii. 10, 2). (3) A Roman jurist of the time of Alexander Severus.

Macer, LICINIUS. See LICINIUS.

Macestus (Μάκηστος). A river of Mysia, rising in Phrygia and flowing north through Mysia into the Rhyndacus.

Macĕtae (Μακέται). Another name of the Macedonians (Μακεδόνες). See MACEDONIA.

Machaera (μάχαιρα). See CULTER; PUGIO.

Machaerus (Μαχαιροῦς). A fortified place in the southern part of Peraea in Palestine. Tradition makes John the Baptist to have been beheaded here.

Machanĭdas (Μαχανίδας). A tyrant of Lacedaemon, who succeeded Lycurgus about B.C. 210. He was defeated and slain by Philopoemen, acting for the Achaean League, in 207.

Machāon (Μαχάων). A son of Aesculapius, and surgeon of the Greeks in the Trojan War. He led, with his brother Podalirus, troops from Trica, Ithomé, and Oechalia. He was killed by Eurypylus, the son of Telephus, and received divine honours after his death in Messenia, of which he was by some called the king. See Verg. *Aen.* ii. 263, 426.

Machon (Μάχων). A comic poet, who flourished at Alexandria about B.C. 175. He was a native of Corinth (or Sicyon), and is said to have taught the grammarian Aristophanes of Byzantium.

Macistus (Μάκιστος). A town of Elis, originally called PLATANISTUS.

Macorāba (Μακοράβα). Now Mecca; a city in the western part of Arabia Felix. Even before the time of Mohammed it appears to have been regarded with veneration by the Arabs, who worshipped the Deity there in the shape of a meteoric stone. The town before the time of Mohammed was held by the Kosuites and then by the Koreish, from whom the Prophet took it in A.D. 627. See the article by Prof. Robertson Smith in the *Encyclopaedia Britannica* (1883).

Macra. The modern Magra; a small river rising in the Apennines and flowing into the Ligurian Sea near Luna, which, from the time of Augustus, formed the boundary between Liguria and Etruria.

Macrae Petrae (Μακραὶ Πέτραι). "The Long Rocks;" on the northwestern side of the Athenian Acropolis at its foot, with a grotto sacred to Apollo and Pan (Eurip. *Ion*, 13).

Macri Campi (Μακροὶ Κάμποι). "The Long Plains." A strip of country between Parma and Modena in Italy, famous for the fine wool of its sheep.

Macriānus. One of the (Roman) Thirty Tyrants (q. v.); slain by Aureolus, A.D. 262.

Macrīnus, MARCUS OPILIUS SEVĒRUS. A Roman emperor from April, A.D. 217, to June 218. Born of humble parentage at the Mauretanian Caesarea, he became praetorian praefect under Caracalla, whom he accompanied against the Parthians, and whose death he procured, in order that he might become his successor. As emperor he won considerable popularity by the remission of certain oppressive taxes, but suffering at Nisibis a defeat at the hands of the Parthians, and losing the love of his soldiers by his severe discipline, he was attacked by the forces who had proclaimed Elagabalus as emperor and defeated by them. Escaping in disguise, he was taken prisoner in Chalcedon and put to death. His life has come down to us written by Capitolinus.

Macro, NAEVIUS SERTORIUS. A favourite of the emperor Tiberius, whose minister Seianus (q. v.) he undermined and finally destroyed. By prostituting his wife Ennia to Caligula he won, for a time, the tolerance of that emperor; but, becoming disliked, he was finally forced to take his own life in the year A.D. 38 (Suet. *Tib.* 73).

Macrobii (Μακρόβιοι, "long-lived"). An Aethiopian people in Africa, placed by Herodotus (iii. 17) on the shores of the Southern Ocean, and said to live to the age of 120 years (Herod. iii. 23).

Macrobius, AMBROSIUS THEODOSIUS. A grammarian probably of Greek extraction, since he says in the preface to his *Saturnalia* that Latin was to him a foreign tongue. He lived in the fourth century A.D., and was probably a pagan. His extant works are: (1) *Saturnaliorum Conviviorum Libri VII.*, consisting of a series of discussions on history, mythology, criticism, and various points of antiquarian research, supposed to have been delivered during the holidays of the Saturnalia at the house of Vettius Praetextatus, who was invested with the highest offices of State under Valentinian and Valens. The form of the work is avowedly copied from the dialogues of Plato, especially the *Banquet:* in substance it bears a strong resemblance to the *Noctes Atticae* of Gellius; and the material of it is drawn from a great variety of sources, such as Suetonius, Seneca, Plutarch, and Athenaeus. The first book treats of the festivals of Saturnus and Ianus, of the Roman calendar, etc. The second book commences with a collection of bon mots, ascribed to the most celebrated wits of antiquity; to these are appended a series of essays on matters connected with the pleasures of the table. The following four books are devoted to criticisms on Vergil. (See VERGILIUS.) The seventh book is of a more miscellaneous character than the preceding. The *Saturnalia* contains the first pagan mention of the Slaughter of the Innocents at Bethlehem (ii. 4). (2) *Commenta-*

rius ex Cicerone in Somnium Scipionis, a work in his book much studied during the Middle Ages. The Dream of Scipio, contained in the sixth book of Cicero's *De Republica*, is taken as a text, which suggests a succession of discourses on the physical constitution of the universe, according to the views of the New Platonists, together with notices of some of their peculiar tenets on mind as well as matter. (3) *De Differentiis et Societatibus Graeci Latinique Verbi*, a treatise purely grammatical, of which only an abridgment is extant, compiled by a certain Ioannes.

The best editions of the works of Macrobius are by Gronovius (Leyden, 1670); Jan (Quedlinburg, 1848–52); Eyssenhardt (Leipzig, 1868; rev. 1893). There is no English version of Macrobius, but a French translation by De Rosoy appeared at Paris in 1826.

Macrocōlum. Paper of a large size. See PAPYRUS.

Macrōnes (Μάκρωνες). A powerful and warlike Caucasian people on the northeastern shore of the Pontus Euxinus.

Madaura, also MEDAURA, AD MEDĒRA. A town on the confines of Numidia and Gaetulia, the birthplace of Apuleius (q. v.).

Madyes (Μαδύης). A Scythian chief who conquered Cyaxares in the year B.C. 623, and for a long time held sway over portions of Asia Minor (Herod. i. 103).

Madȳtus (Μάδυτος). A sea-port town on the Thracian Chersonesus.

Maeander (Μαίανδρος). A river in Asia Minor, proverbial for its wanderings, rising in the south of Phrygia, close to the source of the Marsyas, flowing between Lydia and Caria, of which it forms the boundary, and at last falling into the Icarian Sea between Myus and Prienê. Its chief tributaries are the Marsyas, Cludrus, Lethaeus, and Gaeson on the right (northern) side; and the Obrimas, Lycus, Harpasus, and a second Marsyas on the left (southern) side. In its course it was said to describe the Greek letters ϵ, ζ, ξ, σ, and ω; and from it Daedalus was imagined to have received the idea of his famous Labyrinth. (See Herod. ii. 29; Verg. *Aen.* v. 254; Lucan, v. 208; vi. 471; Ovid, *Met.* viii. 105; Mela, i. 17.) As a god, Maeander is described as the father of the nymph Cyanê, who was the mother of Caunus. Hence the latter is called by Ovid, *Maeandrius iuvenis.*

Maecēnas, GAIUS CILNIUS. A famous statesman, courtier, and patron of literature of the Augustan Age at Rome. The date of his birth is uncertain, but is to be placed between the years B.C. 73 and 63, on the 13th of April (Hor. *Carm.* iv. 11). His family was of Etruscan origin—a great subject of boasting in a society where Etruscomania was as great a fad as is Anglomania in certain American communities to-day—and was even traced to Porsena, so that we find Augustus addressing him in his somewhat ironical style as *berylle Porsenae* (Macrob. *Sat.* ii. 4).

He received a careful education, and was well versed in both Greek and Roman literature, to which he himself contributed in verse as well as prose. He is thought to have been with Octavius in Apollonia at the time of the assassination of Iulius Caesar, perhaps as the director of his studies; and from this time his name appears continually in conjunction with that of the future emperor. He assisted in arranging a marriage between Augustus and Scribonia, the daughter of Libo, and negotiated the peace of Brundisium by which Antony and Augustus were temporarily reconciled, and which led to the marriage of Antony with Octavia, the sister of Augustus (Dio Cass. xlviii. 16; App. *B. C.* v. 64). In B.C. 36 he accompanied Augustus to Sicily in the campaign against Sextus Pompeius, from which he was twice sent back to Rome to suppress revolts that had there broken out. So well did he discharge the task that he was soon after placed in charge first of Rome and then of the administration of all Italy. In this capacity he crushed out the dangerous conspiracy of the younger Lepidus, which contained the germs of a disastrous civil war; and in every way he so justified the confidence reposed in him as to have received from Augustus his seal and a commission to act with Agrippa as the personal representative of the young Caesar in all negotiations with the Senate.

After the establishment of the Empire he continued for a long time to exercise a supreme influence in the counsels of Augustus. By his advice, against that of Agrippa, Augustus decided not to restore the Republic (Dio Cass. lii. 14); and it was Maecenas who brought about the marriage of Iulia, the daughter of Augustus, with Agrippa. The influence of Maecenas over his master continued undiminished until about the year B.C. 18, when by his own choice the former withdrew from any active participation in matters of State. This withdrawal was coincident with a coolness that arose between the two men, which rendered their personal intercourse one of much restraint, and which, though it has been often explained as due to the predominance of Agrippa in the favour of the emperor, is much more certainly to be ascribed to the seduction by Augustus of Terentia, the wife of Maecenas. This woman, beautiful and accomplished, was the object of her husband's passionate love, and to a nature such as his—sensitive, ardent, and honourable—the thought of her continued infidelity was not to be endured with the complaisant toleration that so many Roman husbands appear to have exhibited. The city was filled with the pasquinades in which the wits of the day jeered at the progress of this amour. Even Augustus, who was remarkably thick-skinned, is said by Tacitus to have made a journey to Gaul on one occasion (B.C. 16) to escape the shower of epigrams, jests, and lampoons, and it is easy to surmise what torture they must have inflicted upon the statesman who felt himself to be at once injured and made a public laughing-stock. (See Dio Cass. liv. 19; lv. 7; Suet. *Aug.* 68, in which last passage the Terentilla alluded to in Antony's indecent letter is undoubtedly Terentia.) Maecenas died in B.C. 8, leaving no children.

Maecenas is best known as the fosterer of literature and literary men, so much so that his very name has passed into all languages as a generic term for a munificent patron of letters. His enormous fortune (Tac. *Ann.* xiv. 53, 55) made it possible for him to give a princely protection and support to poets, wits, and, in fact, to all the virtuosi of distinction, who were received with magnificent hospitality at his mansion on the Esquiline, with its beautiful gardens, in which he spent nearly all the year, visiting the country but seldom

(Tac. *Ann.* xiv. 53). So lavish was his entertainment that it became open to the charge of being too indiscriminate, so that Augustus called his table *mensa parasitica* (Suet. *Vit. Horat.*). It must be recollected, however, that he drew the line very sharply between his general hospitality and his private friendship, which last was reserved for the select few, such as Vergil and Horace, who were possessed of the fine culture and delicate feeling so essential to familiar intercourse among gentlemen.

Much of the personal eccentricity which Maecenas exhibited must be ascribed to the condition of his health. He suffered for many years from insomnia and nervous prostration, and resorted to many devices to secure sleep, listening to soft music and to the plash in his house of artificial waterfalls; and his luxurious indolence was perhaps only the self-indulgence of an invalid, seeking distraction from the thought of his own condition. His passionate clinging to life is best expressed in a short verse of his that has come down to us in the pages of Seneca, and whose frantic eagerness is at once pathetic and repulsive:

"Debilem facito manu
Debilem pede, coxa;
Tuber adstrue gibberum
Lubricos quate dentes:
Vita dum superest, bene est.
Hanc mihi vel acuta
Si sedeam cruce sustine."

The life of Maecenas has been many times written: in Latin by Meibom (Leyden, 1653), Lion (Göttingen, 1846); in Italian by Cenni (Rome, 1684), Dini (Venice, 1704), Santa Viola (Rome, 1816); in German by Bennemann (Leipzig, 1744), Frandsen (Altona, 1843); in French by Richer (Paris, 1746); and in English by Schomberg (London, 1766). See, also, Weber's *Horaz* (Jena, 1844); Friedländer, *Sittengeschichte Roms* (iii. 389). His poetical fragments are collected in the *Fragmenta Poetarum Romanorum* by Bährens (Leipzig, 1886). See also Harder, *Fragmente des Mäcenas* (Berlin, 1889); and the article HORATIUS.

Maecius Tarpa. See TARPA.

Maedi (Μαῖδοι). See MAEDICA.

Maedĭca (Μαιδική). The country of the Maedi, a powerful people in the west of Thrace, on the western bank of the Strymon (Livy, xxvi. 25).

Maelius, SPURIUS. The richest of the plebeian knights, who employed his fortune in buying up corn in Etruria in the great famine at Rome in B.C. 439. This corn he sold to the poor at a small price, or distributed it gratuitously. The patricians accused him of aiming at the kingly power, and appointed L. Quinctius Cincinnatus, then eighty years of age, as dictator. C. Servilius Ahala, the master of the horse, summoned Maelius to appear before the tribunal of the dictator; but as he refused to go, Ahala rushed into the crowd and slew him. His property was confiscated and his house pulled down; its vacant site, which was called the Aequimaelium, continued to subsequent ages a memorial of his fate. See Mommsen, *Hist. of Rome*, i. p. 378.

Maenădes (Μαινάδες). A name of the Bacchantes, from μαίνομαι, "to rave," because they were frenzied in the worship of Dionysus. See BACCHANTES.

Maenălus (τὸ Μαίναλον). A mountain in Arcadia, extending from Megalopolis to Tegea, celebrated as the favourite haunt of the god Pan. The Roman poets frequently use the adjectives Maenalius and Maenalis as equivalent to Arcadius.

Maeniānum. See MAENIUS; DOMUS, p. 542.

Maenius. (1) GAIUS. Consul B.C. 338, with L. Furius Camillus. The two consuls completed the subjugation of Latium; they were both rewarded with a triumph, and equestrian statues were erected to their honour in the Forum. The statue of Maenius was placed upon a column, called Columna Maenia, which appears to have stood near the end of the Forum, on the Capitoline. Maenius, in his censorship (B.C. 318), allowed balconies to be added to the various buildings surrounding the Forum, in order that the spectators might obtain more room for beholding the games which were exhibited there: these balconies were called after him MAENIĀNA (sc. *aedificia*). (2) The proposer of a law, about B.C. 286, which required the *patres* to give their sanction to the election of the magistrates before they had been elected, or, in other words, to confer, or agree to confer, the imperium on the person whom the comitia should elect. (3) A contemporary of Lucilius. He was a great spendthrift, who squandered all his property, and afterwards supported himself by playing the buffoon. He possessed a house in the Forum, which Cato in his censorship (184) purchased of him for the purpose of building the Basilica Porcia. Some of the scholiasts on Horace relate that when Maenius sold his house, he reserved for himself one column, the Columna Maenia, from which he built a balcony that he might thence witness the games. The true origin of the Columna Maenia and of the balconies called Maeniana has been explained above.

Maenŏba. A town in the southeastern part of Hispania Baetica, near the coast.

Maenus. A river in Germany, now the Main, emptying into the Rhine at Mainz (Mogontiacum).

Maeon (Μαίων). The son of Haemon of Thebes. With Lycophontes he led a band which lay in ambush for Tydeus in the war of the Seven against Thebes. Tydeus spared his life, and was in return buried by Maeon after Tydeus had been slain (*Il.* iv. 394).

Maeonia (Μαιονία). The ancient name of Lydia. Hence Vergil gives the name of Maeonia to Etruria, because the Etruscans were said to be descended from Lydians. Hence also Homer, as a native of Maeonia, is called *Maeonides* and *Maeonius senex*, and his poems the *Maeoniae chartae*, or *Maeonium carmen*. (See LYDIA.) *Maeonis* likewise occurs as a surname of Omphalé and of Arachné, because both were Lydians.

Maeonĭdes. See MAEONIA.

Maeŏnis. An epithet applied to Omphalé (q. v.) as queen of Lydia or Maeonia.

Maeōtae (Μαιῶται). See MAEOTIS PALUS.

Maeōtis Palus (Μαιῶτις Λίμνη). The modern Sea of Azov; an inland sea on the borders of Europe and Asia, north of the Pontus Euxinus (Black Sea), with which it communicates by the Bosporus Cimmerius. The Scythian tribes on its banks were called by the collective name of Maeotae or Maeotici. The sea had also the names of Cimmerium or Bosporicum Maré. The Amazons are called Maeotides, as living near by.

Maera (Μαῖρα). (1) The dog of Icarius, the father

of Erigonė. See ICARIUS. (2) The daughter of Proetus and Antea and companion of Artemis, by whom she was killed after becoming the mother of Locrus by Zeus (*Odyss.* xi. 325).

Maesa, IULIA. The sister-in-law of Septimius Severus, aunt of Caracalla, and grandmother of Elagabalus and Alexander Severus. She was a native of Syria, born at Emesa, and after her sister Iulia Domna had married Septimius Severus, lived at the Roman court until the death of Caracalla. Being a woman of remarkable force and ability, and possessed of great wealth, she conceived and carried out a plot for the overthrow of Macrinus (q. v.), and the enthroning of her grandson Elagabalus. Her courage and pertinácity did much to bring her plan to its successful issue. When the downfall of Elagabalus became certain, she persuaded him to adopt her other grandson, his cousin, Alexander Severus. By the latter, after his accession to the throne, she was treated with great respect and received the title Augusta.

Maevius or **Mevius**. See BAVIUS; VERGILIUS.

Magăba. A mountain in Galatia, east of Ancyra.

Magădis (μάγαδις). A lyre with frets so that the player could divide the notes. It had twenty strings. See LYRA.

Magalia and **Mapalia**. Words said to be borrowed from the Punic language, in which they denoted the cottages, huts, and hovels of the peasants, made of reeds or canes (Serv. *ad* Verg. *Aen.* i. 420; iv. 259; Sil. Ital. xvii. 88–89). They are described as being sometimes conical or circular

Magalia. (Column of Antoninus.)

in shape, and sometimes oblong with bulging sides. Both these forms are common in the primitive structures of other peoples, and the circular variety is represented in the accompanying illustration, reproduced from the Column of Antoninus. See Sall. *Iug.* 211.

Magas (Μάγας). A king of Cyrenė. He was the stepson of Ptolemy Soter, being the son of Berenicė by a former husband. In B.C. 308 he received the command of an expedition to recover Cyrenė after the death of Ophellas (q. v.), and, being successful, was made by Ptolemy governor of the country. He ruled it at first as a dependency of Egypt, but after the death of Ptolemy Soter he not only assumed the character of an independent monarch, but even made war on the king of Egypt. He married Apama, daughter of Antiochus Soter, by whom he had a daughter, Berenicė, afterwards the wife of Ptolemy Euergetes. He died B.C. 258 (Pausan. i. 7; Just. xxvi. 3).

Magazine. See HORREUM.

Magdăla (Μάγδαλα). A village of Palestine on the Sea of Galilee.

Magdŏlum (Μάγδολος, Old Test. MIGDOL). A city of Lower Egypt, near the northeastern frontier, where Pharaoh Necho defeated the Syrians (Herod. ii. 159).

Magella. A town in the central part of the island of Sicily.

Magetobria. The modern Moigte de Broie, on the Saône. A town on the western frontiers of the Sequani, near which the Gauls were defeated by the Germans shortly before Caesar's arrival in Gaul (Caes. *B.G.* i. 31).

Magi (Μάγοι). A religious sect or class among the Persians, devoted to the worship of fire. See PERSIA; ZOROASTER; and for their share in the politics of Persia, SMERDIS.

Magister. A Latin word very generally applied to any person who has command or authority as the chief over a number of others. The following are the principal officials and others who were styled *magistri:*

(1) MAGISTER ADMISSIŌNUM. See ADMISSIO.

(2) MAGISTER BIBENDI. See SYMPOSIUM.

(3) MAGISTER A CENSĪBUS. An official who examined the qualifications of candidates for enrolment among the *equites*.

(4) MAGISTER COLLEGII. The presiding officer of a *collegium* (q. v.).

(5) MAGISTER EPISTOLĀRUM or AB EPISTŎLIS. The emperor's private secretary (Orelli, *Inscr.* 2352).

(6) MAGISTER EQUĬTUM. The assistant to the Roman dictator appointed by him immediately on taking office and bound to obey him in everything implicitly. In the absence of the dictator he acted as his representative. In battle he commanded the cavalry, as the dictator did the infantry, whence his peculiar title. He was attended by six lictors, and had the *sella curulis* and the *praetexta*. See DICTATOR.

(7) MAGISTER LIBELLŌRUM or A LIBELLIS. A clerk or secretary who read and replied to petitions (*libelli*) addressed to the emperor.

(8) MAGISTER MEMORIAE. An official who made known the emperor's pleasure on any subject (Ammian. Marc. xv. 5).

(9) MAGISTER MILĬTUM. The title of two officers under Constantine. They had command of all the imperial forces, one taking charge of the infantry and one of the cavalry. Later, their number was increased and their functions modified (Zosim. ii. 33; iv. 27).

(10) MAGISTER OFFICIŌRUM. See ADMISSIO.

(11) MAGISTER PAGI. See PAGUS.

(12) MAGISTER POPŬLI. See DICTATOR.

(13) MAGISTER A RATIONĬBUS, also called *procurator*. One who had charge of the emperor's private expenses. See FISCUS.

(14) MAGISTER SOCIETĀTIS. See SOCIETAS.

(15) MAGISTER VICŌRUM. See VICUS.

Magistrātus, at Rome, designated alike the office and the office-holder, the magistracy and the magistrate.

I. THE REPUBLICAN MAGISTRATES. In the widest sense the term *magistratus* included all the governmental officers of the State, elected and appointed, civil and military. In a narrower sense it was restricted to the officials elected by the Roman people, excluding the promagistrates (proconsuls, propraetors, etc.), whose authority rested on decrees of the Senate, and the subordinate officers with delegated powers who were appointed by the magistrates. In the narrowest and most usual sense the term was not extended to include the subordinate military officers (*tribuni militum*) or the city officials below the rank of quaestor (*vigintisexviri, curatores*, etc.), in spite of the fact that these were elected by the people. On the other hand the dictator or *magister populi* and his lieutenant, the *magister equitum*, although not elected, were always regarded and described as magistrates.

1. *Historical Development.* In the early Republic the only regular or ordinary magistrates were the consuls and the quaestors; the only extraordinary magistrates the dictator and his lieutenant. The tribunes and aediles of the plebs, officials whose right and duty it was to protect their order against the regular magistrates, were not regarded as magistrates until the struggle between the orders had come to an end. The *decemviri legibus scribendis* (B.C. 451–449) and the military tribunes (B.C. 444–367), who for a time replaced the consuls and exercised consular powers, were regarded as magistrates; and so also were the censors, praetors, and curule aediles, officials who were first elected during or at the close of the conflict between the orders. With the termination of this conflict and the recognition of the plebeian tribunes and aediles as representatives of the whole people, the list of magistrates, as the term was commonly employed, was closed. For fuller description, see the special article upon each magistracy. For the promagistracy, fully developed only towards the end of the Republic, see PROVINCIA.

From the period of the conflict between the orders dates the division of magistracies into "patrician" and "plebeian." In the later Republic the term patrician magistracy was merely an historical reminiscence: it designated the offices from which the plebeians had formerly been excluded. The term plebeian magistracy, on the other hand, continued to express a fact; the offices of tribune and of plebeian aedile were never thrown open to the patricians.

2. *The Relation of the different Magistrates to each other* was not determined, at Rome, by assigning to each office special and distinct powers and duties; nor were the different magistrates protected against each other's interference. The earliest magistrates, the consuls, held an undifferentiated complex of military, judicial, and administrative powers; and the creation of new magistracies was not at first accompanied (except in the case of the censors) by any logical separation of these powers. The trend of development, especially in the later Republic, was towards a division of *provinciae* or spheres of power; but the separation never became complete. Powers of interference were so general as to amount to a fundamental principle of the constitution—a principle which found its extreme expression in the tribunate.

The Romans themselves classed their magistrates not according to the kind of power, but according to the degree of power, which each exercised. Their term for general power was *imperium.* The dictator and his lieutenant, the consuls and the praetors, all had imperium. The consular imperium was *minus* as regarded the dictator and his lieutenant, *maius* as compared with that of the praetors. The other magistrates (censors, tribunes, aediles, quaestors, etc.) had not imperium—i. e. their powers were not general, but special. These, therefore, strictly speaking, were all lower or lesser magistrates (*magistratus minores*). The censors, however, by reason of the importance of their duties, were regularly classed among the *magistratus maiores;* and so also, on more technical grounds, were the curule aediles.

Maior potestas. In principle, any magistrate with imperium might issue commands and prohibitions to any magistrate without imperium. The exceptions to this rule were as follows: neither the tribunes nor the censors were subject to the commands or prohibitions of the magistrates with imperium; and the tribunes might intervene negatively, by prohibitions, against the acts of all magistrates except the dictator, his lieutenant, and the censors. The exceptional position of the censors was due to their possession of a distinct field of duties. They had no occasion to interfere with other magistrates, and no other magistrates were permitted to interfere with them. The peculiar position of the tribunes was a survival from the period of the conflict between the orders. Negatively the tribunes had *maior potestas* as against the consuls; but no Roman would have so expressed it, for the Romans meant by *potestas* power to act rather than power to prevent.

In principle, again, a magistrate with *maius imperium* might issue commands to a magistrate with *minus imperium;* so that a dictator might command and restrain a consul, and a consul might similarly direct or check a praetor.

Par potestas. Further possibilities of interference resulted from the fact that every magistracy except the dictatorship was held by two or more persons. Between such colleagues there was, in principle, no division of power; each possessed all the powers of the office. Each, therefore, might act alone, and without regard to the views or wishes of his colleague or colleagues; and if they remained passive, his act was valid and effective. But if a colleague stepped in (*intercessit*) and forbade the act, then equal power stood opposed to equal power and the result was a deadlock. This was true not merely as between two colleagues, but also when a larger number held the same magistracy; majority rule was not recognized; the negative will of one was as powerful as the positive will of any larger number. A veto, therefore, could not be vetoed—a rule which was of peculiar importance in the tribunate. In that body one tribune could prevent the other nine from doing any positive act—e. g. from presenting a bill to the people; but nine tribunes could not prevent one from vetoing the act of a consul or other magistrate.

Provinciae. In principle, therefore, the positive powers of each magistracy could be exercised only when the colleagues were of one mind; and this unanimity was necessary for each single act. In fact, however, some division of power, by agreement or by lot, was customary from the earliest period of the Republic (e. g. one consul sometimes took the field with an army while the other governed the city); but it does not appear that in the early Republic any such division of the field of consular duties was made for the year. The assignment to a single magistrate of a distinct field of power for his full annual term apparently dates from the establishment of the praetorship. The praetor was not simply a judicial officer, nor was his authority limited to the city; but by force of constant custom civil jurisdiction within the city became his peculiar "province." When a second praetorship was instituted, B.C. 242, a division of the judicial field became usual; but the assignment to each praetor of his special competence was made after election and by lot. The same system prevailed when the number of praetors was successively increased to four, six, and eight, and when such distinct functions as the government of subject provinces and the presidency of special criminal courts (*quaestiones*) were attached to the office. No Roman was ever elected to a special praetorship; he was simply elected praetor, and his special duties were determined by lot. The same system was extended to the quaestors, and gradually, in the later Republic, to the consuls. For some time after the establishment of the city praetorship the consuls acted jointly. They even took the field together, the supreme command alternating day by day. But as foreign wars became more numerous they began, often by the advice of the Senate, but technically, in every case, by agreement, to divide the legions and the field of military operations, and to draw lots for their respective armies and "provinces." The Senate indeed might recommend or the people decree the assignment of a particular campaign or territory to a particular magistrate *extra sortem;* but this was unusual.

From the fact that all magistrates of equal rank were colleagues with equal powers and that the division of functions here described was primarily a *de facto* rather than a legal division, it followed, in principle, that either consul could interfere with the other in the field of military operations, and that any praetor could intercede against the act of any other praetor in the city. Such interference was practically impossible outside of the city, if different fields of activity had been assigned to the consuls, because of the rule that intercession must be made in person; and within the city it was regularly excluded by custom (but see Cicero, *Verr.* i. 46, 119).

3. *Powers of the Magistrates.* The imperium conferred upon the higher magistrates was, in principle, the same sort of power that had been exercised by the kings (*imperium regium*). It was primarily military power (*imperium militiae*), and was understood to include all governmental power not distinctly withheld by custom or law. Special limitations were first imposed in the field of justice, criminal and civil. The royal power of capital punishment has been practically annulled, according to Roman tradition, by the recognition of a right to appeal to the assembly (*provocatio*); and in the early Republican period this power passed wholly to the people, the magistrate retaining only the power to investigate and accuse. The power of the magistrates to fine was also limited by law. Civil cases were regularly referred, for decision, to a private *iudex* or *arbiter*, or a board of elected *iudices*. All these limitations, however, were confined to the city; and the restrictions afterwards imposed upon imperium out of the city (e. g. right of appeal in capital cases) were less extensive. Outside of the city, moreover, the magistrates with imperium were freed from the interference of the tribunes. The Romans accordingly came to distinguish *imperium militiae* from *imperium domi*, the complete power exercised beyond the city limits from the restricted power exercised within the city. The dictator alone had *imperium militiae* within the city—i. e. by the appointment of a dictator the city was placed under martial law.

Practically, of course, the governmental power of the higher magistracy was lessened by the multiplication of magistrates, by their short terms of office, and by their accountability to the people after the expiration of their terms. The power of the single magistrates was also practically diminished, in the later Republic, by the assignment of special fields of action to special magistrates; but in spite of all these facts, no magistrate clothed with imperium was ever regarded as an officer of special, designated powers. Imperium was always, in theory, general power; and every magistrate with imperium had, as against the people, all powers not legally denied him. The consuls, by virtue of their higher imperium, had residuary governmental power, not only as against the people, but also as against the magistrates with lower imperium and those without imperium—i. e. a consul could do whatever law and custom had neither forbidden to him nor assigned to the exclusive competence of another magistrate.

Special powers included in imperium, many of which were exercised also by magistrates without imperium, were as follows: (1) *Ius agendi cum populo*—i. e. the right of summoning and presiding over the meetings of the people (*comitia centuriata*), submitting proposals to them, causing a vote to be taken and announcing the result. Whether the business of the meeting was legislation, criminal justice, or the election of magistrates for the ensuing year, the initiative was wholly in the magistracy. The magistrates determined the form of a bill and accepted or rejected proposed amendments. They decided whether accusation should be brought against a person suspected of crime, and what penalty the people should be asked to impose. They submitted the list of candidates to be voted for, and no names could be brought before the people without their assent. This *ius agendi cum populo* belonged exclusively to the magistrates with imperium. The tribunes, however, had similar control over the meetings of the plebeians; and when the *concilia plebis* had developed into the *comitia tributa* and had obtained concurrent powers of legislation, a limited criminal jurisdiction and the right of electing the lower magistrates, the *ius agendi cum plebe* gave the tribunes an initiative similar to that of the consuls and praetors. The analogous right of summoning the Senate and obtaining an expression of its opinion, originally an exclusive right of the magistrates with imperium, was also extended to the tribunes. In the field of legislation the power of the tribunate thus became legally equivalent to that of the magistrates with imperium. Practically it was greater; for if a consul or a praetor proposed a bill to the popular assembly or a resolution to the Senate, the tribunes could veto the proposal and thus arrest legislative action, while they themselves were not subject to such interference from the other magistrates. It is therefore not surprising that the most important laws of the later Republic were *plebiscita* proposed by the tribunes.

(2) *Ius edicendi.* The people alone could establish a law (*lex*); but all magistrates had power to issue commands and prohibitions (*edicta, interdicta*) and means of punishing disobedience. Their ordinances, therefore, had the force of law (*legis vicem*), at least during the terms of the magistrates who

issued them. In principle there was nothing to prevent a magistrate from invading by his edicts the field of general legislation. In the later Republic the development and the reform of the private law were chiefly accomplished by the edicts of the praetors, and important contributions to the law of sale were made by the aediles. As a rule, however, the ordinances of the magistrates were not intended to override the general law, but to secure its observance; and the edicts and interdicts of each set of magistrates were commonly confined to that sphere of administration which law and custom allotted them.

(3) *Ius coercendi.* The means by which the magistrates enforced obedience to their commands were as follows: (*a*) *prensio*, arrest; (*b*) *in vincula ductio*, imprisonment; (*c*) *verberatio*, scourging; (*d*) *multae dictio*, imposition of a fine; (*e*) *pignoris captio*, seizure of movable property. All of these powers were included in imperium; the second and third were accorded only to magistrates with imperium. Imprisonment ordered by a magistrate was probably limited to his term of office; from a sentence of scourging *in urbe* a *lex Valeria* authorized an appeal to the people. The power to arrest was held by the tribunes and by the censors. The powers of fining and of seizing property were apparently exercised by all the magistrates,* and constituted the ordinary and normal method of coercion. That it was a very ancient method is shown by numerous Aryan analogies, and by the fact that among the Romans fines were originally levied in sheep and oxen. The power to fine was first limited by the rule that the fine must not exceed the half of the estate of the delinquent; later laws (*Aeternia Tarpeia, Menenia Sestia* [?]) confined *multae dictio* to a definite maximum (two sheep and thirty oxen; two sheep and five oxen. For an ingenious explanation of these numbers, see Karlowa, pp. 167–169). The magistrate who wished to fine beyond the legal maximum had to obtain the consent of the assembly (*multae irrogatio*). By the *lex Iulia Papiria* money fines were introduced and a pecuniary maximum substituted, the sheep being reckoned at ten as, the ox at one hundred. *Pignoris captio*, like imprisonment, might be employed to secure the payment of a fine; but it was often (and perhaps originally) used as a milder means of constraint, the property being restored to the owner if he promptly purged himself of contempt and subjected himself to the commands of the magistrate.

The fact that the tribunes could arrest (*prendere*) other magistrates, while the *leges sacratae* protected them against all coercion, was the key to their peculiar position in the Roman State.

(4) *Auspicia.* Before taking any important step, it was the right and the duty of the magistrates to ascertain whether the act in contemplation was favoured by the gods. (See AUGUR.) The magistrate who acted without proper auspices, or in defiance of unfavourable auspices, took the risk of punishment at the end of his term; and if his act was of a legal nature (e. g. the calling of *comitia*), it was the right and duty of the Senate, after obtaining the expert opinion of the augurs, to rescind the act and annul its results (e. g. the passage of a *lex* or the choice of magistrates). Auspices were regularly taken, at least in the earlier Republic, by the augurs; but the answer of the gods, as interpreted by these priests, referred to the inquiry of the magistrate at whose instance the auspices were taken. It was, of course, possible that the gods should be consulted on the same matter by different magistrates, and that different answers should be obtained. The result was then determined by the relative authority of the magistrates: *maiora auspicia* (i. e. auspices taken at the instance of a magistrate with *maior potestas*) overrode *minora*. As between colleagues with *par potestas*, unfavourable auspices prevailed over those of a favourable character.

It is a plausible hypothesis that in the early Republic, when the entire constitution had a sacral colour, the doctrine of *maior* and *par potestas* was worked out by the priests in the form of a doctrine of auspices. It accords with this theory that the lower patrician magistrates were under the auspices of the higher, and that the non-magistrate, who exercised delegated powers, was said to act under the auspices of the magistrate who appointed him.

4. *Responsibility.* The lower magistrates, as we have seen, were generally subject to the control of the higher, and the higher magistrates to the negative control of the tribunate; but the magistracy, as a whole, was not subject to the direct control of the people, or even to the control of the law. It enjoyed regal irresponsibility. During their terms of office the higher magistrates could not be made defendants in civil actions (*in ius vocari*), nor could criminal proceedings be instituted against them. In the later Republic magistrates were occasionally deposed by a vote of the assembly which had created them, but such action was contrary to the spirit of the constitution.

An indirect control of a moral character was exercised by the *consilia* of the magistrates (see below) and by the Senate (q. v.); and a very strong indirect control lay in the unlimited responsibility of the magistrates after their terms of office had expired. Not only did they then become liable to ordinary civil and criminal proceedings, but they might be punished by the people on purely political grounds.

5. *Expenses.* The republican magistrates received no pay; the technical term for office was *honour;* but they were not expected to waste their substance in the service of the State. They were provided with an ample force of paid assistants and attendants. (See APPARITORES; SCRIBAE.) If their duties called them out of the city, they received a liberal outfit from the treasury, and were entitled to transportation and sustenance *sumptu publico.* What they could not obtain by requisition from the subjects of Rome, they paid for; and for such outlays they were reimbursed from the treasury. In the later Republic it was not unusual to grant round sums by way of allowance for expenses, without requiring any account to be rendered.

6. *Insignia, attendants,* etc. The quasi-royal position held by the magistrates was strikingly expressed in the ceremonial and formal distinctions accorded them. The years were designated by the names of the consuls. The higher magistrates were accompanied, within and without the city, by numerous public attendants. Before the

* The power of the quaestors to fine is disputed by Mommsen. But even *curatores* could fine. (See Karlowa, *Rechtsgeschichte*, p. 171.)

highest magistrates, those clothed with imperium, marched lictors, bearing the symbols of punitive power. When a magistrate approached, the citizens rose from their seats, dismounted from their horses, descended from their carriages. The lower magistrates observed the same respect towards those of higher authority. Public business was transacted by a seated magistracy in the presence of a standing people. Magistrates who acted singly had chairs or stools (*sellae*); those who, like the tribunes, acted collectively, as a board, sat on benches (*subsellia*). The higher magistrates had stools of a special pattern (the *sella curulis*), and their garments were distinguished from those of the ordinary citizens. On ceremonial occasions ex-magistrates were permitted to resume the distinctive apparel of their office, and it was ostentatiously associated with their memory by their descendants (*ius imaginum*). For details, see APPARITORES; INSIGNIA.

7. *Consilia.* It was a principle of Roman law, private and public, that he who exercised power over others should not act unadvised. It was equally a principle of the law that advice was not binding. The power to act was not impaired by the dissent of advisers, nor did their assent diminish or divide responsibility.

The Senate, which had been the council of the kings, was also, in a broad sense, the council of the whole higher magistracy; but each magistrate had a special *consilium.* This always included any lower magistrates who were assigned to the same "province," or field of administration, and the principal assistants or deputies selected by the magistrate himself; but it also included persons chosen by him as advisers simply. The choice was limited, by custom, to the senatorial and equestrian orders. It was often based on personal friendship, but chiefly on the reputation of the persons chosen for knowledge and experience of affairs. In the administration of justice the urban and peregrine praetors and the provincial governors were regularly assisted by the counsel of the most eminent Roman jurists.

8. *Election, terms,* etc. All the magistrates, except the dictator, were elected (*creati*) by the people; the higher magistrates, including the censors and curule aediles, by the *comitia centuriata;* the tribunes, plebeian aediles, quaestors, vigintisexviri, curatores, and military tribunes, by the *comitia tributa.* All except the censors were elected annually; the censors every fifth year. All were elected during the year preceding their assumption of office, the magistrates in office (consuls, praetors, or tribunes) summoning and directing the *comitia* in which their successors were chosen. The election of tribunes took place in July; that of the other magistrates later in the year. See COMITIA.

The term of office, except in the case of the dictator and in that of the censors, was one year. The dictatorship was limited to six months. The censors originally held office until their work was done; later, the rule was established that their work must be done in eighteen months. The annual terms, in the early Republic, did not begin at any fixed date; in case of abdication or death of both consuls, their successors were chosen, not for the residue of the term, but for a full year. In the later Republic the practice was changed; at the close of the third century B.C. the official year began on the 15th of March; in the second century it began on the 1st of January. The quaestors, however, took office December 5th, and the tribunes December 10th.

Lex curiata de imperio. According to Roman tradition, the king-elect had no imperium until it was granted him by a special law. Under the Republic the consuls and praetors, at the beginning of their terms of office, were obliged to summon the old patrician assembly (*comitia curiata*) and obtain from it a similar grant. The necessary law seems always to have been voted as a matter of course; and in the late Republic its adoption was a singularly empty form, the *curiae* being represented by lictors. At some intermediate period the theory that a formal grant of power should follow election and accompany the assumption of office was extended to some of the officials without imperium—e. g. a *lex curiata* was regularly passed for the benefit of the quaestors. In the case of the censors, a law authorizing them to enter upon the discharge of their duties was voted by the centuriate assembly. No *lex curiata* or other confirmatory law was ever passed in the case of the plebeian magistrates.

9. *Eligibility* (*ius honorum*). The power of the magistrates to strike unfit persons from the list of candidates could never have been exercised on purely political grounds without serious risk of subsequent punishment; and in the course of the republican period the grounds of exclusion were defined, by custom or statute, with considerable exactness. Non-citizens, lunatics, and persons afflicted with serious bodily infirmities were, of course, excluded; so also were women. Condemnation for political offences (and for ordinary crimes and torts when the condemnation carried with it *infamia*) operated as a bar to office; and it lay in the power of the magistrate to exclude those whose occupations made them infamous. Freedmen and their sons were ineligible, and originally their grandsons also; but in the later Republic the grandsons were eligible. Tradesmen were regularly excluded, trade on a small scale being regarded as an illiberal occupation.

At different periods in the history of the Republic candidacy for office was made conditional on the previous performance of military duty, upon the observance of a definite order of advancement with intervals between the different offices, and upon the attainment of certain age limits. For details, see HONORES.

Re-election. As early as B.C. 342 a plebiscite forbade re-election to the same office until ten years had elapsed; but from this rule frequent dispensations seem to have been granted. Re-election to the censorship was absolutely forbidden. In the year B.C. 151 the same rule was established for the consulate, but it was abrogated seventy years later.

10. *Vacancies and Representatives.* The fact that every magistracy was held by a number of persons, each of whom possessed all the powers of the office, and the further fact that the consuls possessed residuary governmental power, excluded the assumption that a vacancy was created by the death or resignation of any single magistrate. Even when a distinct field of administration had been allotted to such a magistrate, his duties could be assigned to a colleague or assumed by one of the consuls. Cases even occurred where

the duties associated with one magistracy were temporarily assigned by the Senate to another (e. g. duties of an aedile to a praetor).

The death or abdication of both consuls (if at the time there was no dictator) meant more than a mere vacancy in the consular office: it meant the temporary disappearance of the ordinary government. By the sacral tradition praetors, curule aediles, and even quaestors were bound to resign their offices; the auspices under which they held their respective positions were extinguished, and it was necessary to institute a new administration with new auspices. The situation was the same as that produced in the royal period by the death of the king: there was an *interregnum*. As in the royal period, the auspices were with the Senate, and the Senate designated the temporary holders of supreme power—one *interrex* after another, each holding for five days—until the centuries could be assembled and new magistrates elected. As soon as a single consul was chosen, the *interregnum* was at an end. The *interregnum* exercised no influence upon the plebeian magistrates, for they were not under the same auspices.

In case of the simultaneous absence from the city of both consuls, it was customary, in the early Republic, for them to appoint a temporary governor. See PRAEFECTUS URBI.

II. THE REPUBLICAN MAGISTRATES UNDER THE EMPIRE. According to the official theory, promulgated by Augustus and accepted by his successors, the establishment of the *principatus* left the republican constitution intact, and in the early Empire republican forms were scrupulously observed. The magistrates were elected, during the reign of Augustus, by the people; under Tiberius and his successors they were "created" by the Senate and "announced" in the popular assembly. Under both systems they were selected by the *princeps*, and however independent they might be in theory, in fact they were unable to cross the imperial purposes. They were not, however, the real agents of the imperial government. The emperors preferred to exercise the more important powers of sovereignty through officers whom they appointed openly and directly, and whose authority was theoretically as well as actually a delegated authority. The real officials of the Empire were the prefects and legates of Augustus. The republican magistrates were loaded with honours, but they were quietly deprived, from the start, of all their political powers and confined to the exercise of judicial and administrative functions; and, later on, these functions also were gradually absorbed by the imperial officials—police powers and criminal justice first, minor administrative duties and civil jurisdiction last. The development of the new official hierarchy was practically completed in the second century. The republican magistracies became mere titles, earned by heavy outlays for the amusement of the people. In this form they continued to exist throughout the principate, and were even transferred to the Eastern Empire. Allusions to the tribunate occur in the fifth century; and as late as 541 an "Oriental consul" was elected at Constantinople, and for a quarter of a century the years were officially dated from his consulate.

III. MUNICIPAL MAGISTRATES. With the development of self-governing colonies and the extension to allied and subject cities of Roman citizenship and municipal autonomy, there appeared, at the close of the republican period, a municipal magistracy closely modelled on that of Rome. (See MUNICIPIUM.) Under the principate, this system, first worked out for Italy, was gradually extended throughout the Empire, until the municipal magistrates became everywhere the regular organs of local government. In the legal literature of the Empire, therefore, *magistratus* regularly refers to the municipal magistracy, the titular dignitaries of Rome being distinguished as *magistratus populi Romani*.

BIBLIOGRAPHY. See Madvig, *Verfassung und Verwaltung des römischen Staates* (1881–82); Herzog, *Geschichte und System der römischen Staatsverfassung* (1884–87); Mommsen, *Römisches Staatsrecht* (3d ed. 1887–88); Karlowa, *Römische Rechtsgeschichte*, Bd. I. (1885); Willems, *Droit Public Romain* (6th ed. 1889).

Magna Graecia. See GRAECIA MAGNA.

Magna Mater. A Roman name of the goddess Cybelé or Rhea (q. v.).

Magnentius. A German by birth who conspired against the life of the emperor Constans, whom he caused to be murdered in his bed. Subsequently, being pursued by the vengeance of Constantius, and defeated by him at the battle of Mursa (A. D. 351), he took his own life by falling on his sword. His reign lasted from A.D. 350 to 353. His full name was Flavius Popilius Magnentius. See Victor, *Caes.* 41 and 42.

Magnes (Μάγνης). (1) One of the first founders of Attic comedy, B.C. 460. See COMOEDIA. (2) A youth said by some to have been the slave of Medea and to have been changed by her into a magnet. The more generally accepted story states that once, while walking over a mine, he found himself detained by the iron nails in his shoes which became attached to the lodestones over which he was attempting to pass. From him, as the first discoverer, the magnet received its name (Orph. *De Lapid.* x. 7).

Magnesia (Μαγνησία). (1) A narrow strip of country along the eastern coast of Thessaly, extending from the Peneus on the north to the Pagasaean Gulf on the south. Its inhabitants, the Magnetes, are said to have founded the two cities in Asia mentioned below. (2) MAGNESIA AD SIPY̆LUM, a city in the northwest of Lydia, at the foot of Mount Sipylus, and on the south bank of the Hermus, famous as the scene of the victory gained by Scipio Asiaticus over Antiochus the Great, B.C. 190. (3) MAGNESIA AD MAEANDRUM, a city in the southwest of Lydia, situated on the river Lethaeus, a tributary of the Maeander. It was destroyed by the Cimmerians (probably about B.C. 700), and rebuilt by colonists from Miletus. It was celebrated for its beautiful temple of Artemis, ruins of which still exist.

Magnopŏlis (Μαγνόπολις) or **Eupatoria Magnopŏlis**. A city of Pontus in Asia Minor near the union of the rivers Lycus and Iris. It was begun by Mithridates Eupator and finished by Pompey the Great (Appian, *Mithr.* 78, 115).

Mago (Μάγων). (1) A Carthaginian general sent against Dionysius, the Sicilian tyrant, over whom he obtained a victory, but was subsequently slain in battle. (2) A son of the preceding, who succeeded his father in command of the Carthaginian army. He laid siege to Syracuse, but fled on the approach of Timoleon. Being impeached for cowardice by the Senate of Carthage, he escaped execution by committing suicide. After his death, his body was gibbeted and exposed in public. (3) See PUNIC WARS.

Magontiăcum. See MOGONTIACUM.

Maharbal (Μαάρβας). A son of Himilco, and one of the most distinguished officers of Hannibal in the Second Punic War. He is first mentioned at the siege of Saguntum. After the battle of Cannae he urged Hannibal to push on at once with his cavalry upon Rome itself; and on the refusal of his commander, he is said to have observed that Hannibal knew how to gain victories, but not how to use them (Livy, xxi., xxii.; Florus, ii. 6).

Maia (Μαῖα). The daughter of Atlas and Pleioné, one of the Pleiades (q. v.), and mother of Hermes by Zeus. The Romans identified her with an old Italian goddess of spring, Maia Maiestas (also called Fauna, Bona Dea, Ops), who was held to be the wife of Vulcan, and to whom the flamen of that god sacrificed a pregnant sow on the first of May.

Maiestas, in Roman criminal law, meant the inviolable dignity or sovereignty of the State; and all conduct derogatory to the dignity or power of the people, or of those to whom the people had intrusted power, was *crimen imminutae maiestatis* (Cic. *De Invent.* ii. 17, 53). This particular conception of treason appeared late in the history of the Republic, and was at first supplementary to the older conception of *perduellio*. An attack upon the existence of the State was *perduellio*; anything less than this was the crime of impaired majesty. The Republican laws *de maiestate* were all passed in a period of bitter, and often bloody, political strife, and all the prosecutions under these laws were essentially partisan. The expression *imminuta maiestas* seems first to have been used in the *lex Apuleia* (B.C. 103?); and the principal object of this law, apparently, was to protect the sovereignty of the people as incorporated in the tribunate. The conception was further developed by a *lex Varia* (B.C. 90?) and (in the conservative interest) by a *lex Cornelia* of Sulla (B.C. 80), until the crime against majesty practically covered and included *perduellio*. In a *lex Iulia* (ascribed by some authorities to Julius Caesar, by others to Augustus, while others again hold that there were two *leges Iuliae de maiestate*), the two crimes were fused, and *perduellio* thenceforward meant simply a grave case of lese-majesty (cf. *Inst.* 3, 1, 5; *Dig.* 48, 4, 11; Codex, 9, 50, 2). This *lex Iulia* remained the basis of the law of treason through the Imperial period, but the number of possible offences against majesty was greatly increased by succeeding statutes. The *maiestas publica* was primarily and chiefly embodied in the person of the emperor (*maiestas principatus, augusta*); and the *crimen laesae maiestatis* included not only acts injurious to the State, but all plots against the emperor and his family, and all acts derogatory to his dignity and honour. Thus libels upon the emperor, destruction of his statues, false or violated oaths *per genium principis*, and, under some of the more tyrannic rulers, hostile and even disrespectful speech were punished as lese-majesty. Arcadius, who repealed all laws of the last-mentioned character, extended the law of treason to include plots against the higher officials of the Empire (A.D. 397).

Trials for *perduellio*, under the Republic, were always *in comitiis*—i. e. prosecution took the form of a bill, and the decision lay with the popular assembly. Prosecutions *de maiestate*, on the other hand, were conducted before special courts (*quaestiones*). In the early Imperial period cases of treason were tried by the Senate; later by the emperor himself or his praefects. Accusation could be brought, even under the Republic, by slaves, infamous persons, and others who were debarred in ordinary criminal cases; and under the emperors torture was applied to freemen and even to persons of rank (*honorati*) for the purpose of obtaining evidence.

The penalty in the Republican period was exile, or rather outlawry (*aquae et ignis interdictio*). In the Empire it varied, according to the gravity of the offence, the social position of the offender, and the temper of the reigning emperor, from death in various forms (*humiliores vestiis obiiciuntur vel vivi exuruntur, honestiores capite puniuntur*, Paul, v. 29, 1) to scourging or simple *relegatio*. In both periods the extreme penalty carried with it the escheat or confiscation of the criminal's property, and, under the Empire, attainder of the blood, so that the sons of the criminal could neither hold office nor take inheritances or legacies (Codex, 9, 8, 5). The same results attached to condemnation when prosecution was instituted after the death of the criminal (*damnatio memoriae*). See Zumpt, *Das Criminalrecht der röm. Republik* (1868), ii. 1, 226–237, 249–258, 376–392; and Rein, *Das Criminalrecht der Römer* (1844), 506–597.

Maiūma. A May-day festival celebrated at Rome by the inhabitants, who on this occasion made up excursion parties to visit the sea-shore at Ostia and bathe in the salt-water. The name is not found in the early Latin writers, but the *Cod. Theod.* (xv. 6, 1 and 2) speaks of it as an old custom revived in later times.

Malăca. The modern Malaga; an important town on the coast of Hispania Baetica and on a river of the same name, founded by the Phœnicians. Near Malaca was found in 1851 a bronze tablet containing the LEX MALACENSIS, a statute regulating the city's municipal constitution. It was granted by Domitian (A.D. 81–84). It is given in the *C. I. L.* ii. 1964, and in Bruns. See SALPENSA.

Malchus (Μάλχος). A Byzantine historical writer and rhetorician of Philadelphia in Syria. He wrote a history of the Eastern Empire covering a short period in the fifth century. The remains are edited by Bekker and Niebuhr (Bonn, 1829).

Malĕa (Μαλέα). (1) A promontory on the southeast of Laconia, separating the Argolic and Laconic gulfs. At this point the sea is so rough as to give rise to the proverb, *Cum ad Maleam deflexeris, obliviscere quae sunt domi* (Mela, ii. 3). (2) A promontory on the coast of Lesbos.

Malĕlas or **Malălas**, IOANNES (Ἰωάννης ὁ Μαλέλα or Μαλάλα). A Byzantine historian born at Antioch who flourished in the sixth century A.D. He was the author of a universal history from the creation of the world through the reign of Justinian. It has been edited by Dindorf (Bonn, 1831).

Malia. A city of Phthiotis, near Thermopylae. In its vicinity were hot mineral springs, and from it the neighbouring gulf was called Maliacus Sinus.

Maliăcus Sinus. See Malis.

Malis (Μαλίς, Μηλίς). A district in the south of Thessaly, on the shores of the Maliacus Sinus, and opposite the northwestern point of the island of Euboea. It extended as far as the pass of Thermopylae. Its inhabitants, the Malienses, were Dorians, and belonged to the Amphictyonic League.

Malleŏlus. A sort of rocket or torch, used in naval warfare, having a mass of lighted pitch or tar at one end. It was employed to set fire to the enemy's rigging; or in sieges, like the more modern fire-ball. See Cic. *Cat.* i. 13, 32; Livy, xlii. 64.

Malleus, dimin. **Malleŏlus** (σφῦρα). A hammer or mallet. In Greek, σφῦρα is the generic term, and ῥαιστήρ and κέστρα denote the heavy hammer used by smiths, while κροταφίς is a hammer with one end sharpened like a pick. In Latin, the heavy hammer is called *marcus*, and the

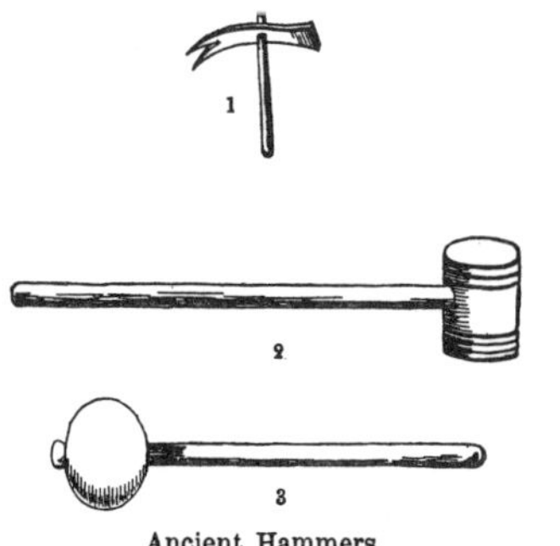

Ancient Hammers.

(1) Carpenter's Hammer. (2) Smith's Hammer. (3) Butcher's Hammer.

smaller varieties *marculus* and *marcellus*. The smith's hammer, shown in no. 2, is of wood, bound with iron. The butcher's hammer or mallet in no. 3 was used in slaughtering oxen, and also by the *popa* (q. v.) at sacrifices.

Malli (Μαλλοί). An Indian people on both sides of the Hydraotes. Their capital is supposed to have been on the site of the celebrated fortress of Mooltan (Arrian, *Anab.* vi. 7–14).

Mallophŏra (Μαλλοφόρα). "Wool-bearing." An epithet of Demeter, as worshipped at Megara, whose inhabitants she was fabled to have taught the use of wool (Pausan. i. 44).

Mallus (Μαλλός). A very ancient city of Cilicia, on a hill east of the mouth of the river Pyramus, said to have been founded at the time of the Trojan War by Mopsus and Amphilochus.

Malluvia (from *manus* + *luo*). A basin used for washing the hands, and called by the Greeks χειρόνιπτρον and χέρνιβον (*Il.* xxiv. 304). The accompanying illustration shows the basin upon its stand, with a towel beside it.

Malluvia. (Aldobrandini fresco, Vatican.)

Mālus. The mast of a ship. See Navis.

Malus Ocŭlus. See Fascinum.

Mamaea, Iulia. A Syrian, a native of Emesa, the daughter of Iulia Maesa and mother of the emperor Alexander Severus, whom he reared with much care. When her son was put to death by the soldiers in A.D. 235, she shared his fate. See Elagabalus; Maesa; Severus.

Mamercus. The name of a distinguished family of the Aemilia gens in the early times of the Roman Republic (Livy, iv. 17–34).

Mamers. The Oscan name of the god Mars (q. v.).

Mamertine Prison. See Carcer, p. 278.

Mamertīni. See Messana; Punic Wars.

Mamertīnus, Claudius. A Latin panegyrist, the author of a speech addressed to the emperor Iulian on January 1, A.D. 362, at Constantinople, thanking him for conferring the consulate on him. It gives a pretty accurate picture of the personality of the emperor and of his administration. An older Mamertinus is assumed to be the author of two panegyrics in praise of Maximianus, co-regent with Diocletian, which were delivered in A.D. 289 and 291 at Trèves. See Panegyricus.

Mamilius. The name of a distinguished family in Tusculum. It was to a member of this family, Octavius Mamilius, that Tarquinius betrothed his daughter; and on his expulsion from Rome his son-in-law roused the Latin people against the infant Republic, and perished in the great battle at Lake Regillus. The Mamilii afterwards removed to Rome.

Mamurius. The mythical maker of the *ancilia*. See Ancilé; Salii.

Mamurra. A Roman knight, born at Formiae. He was the commander of the engineers (*praefectus fabrum*) in Iulius Caesar's army in Gaul, and amassed great riches. Horace calls Formiae, in ridicule, *Mamurrarum urbs*, from which we may infer that the name of Mamurra had become a by-word of contempt (*Sat.* i. 5, 37).

Manceps. One who acquired possession of a thing by the form of conveyance known as *mancipatio* (q. v.).

Mancīnus, C. Hostilius. A Roman who was consul in B.C. 137. He was defeated by the Numantines, and purchased his safety by making a peace with them. The Senate refused to recognize it, and went through the hypocritical ceremony of delivering him over to the enemy, who refused to accept him. On his return to Rome he was expelled from the Senate by the tribune P. Rutilius on the ground that he had lost his citizenship, as being still technically a prisoner (see Postliminium); but his rights were restored by a special law (Vell. Pat. ii. 1).

Mancipatio (from *manus* + *capio*, "a taking with the hand"). A formal mode of purchase among the Romans, which seems to go back to a time when the price of purchase was weighed out in bars of copper. In the presence of six Roman citizens of the age of puberty, one of whom, called the *libripens* (weigher), held a copper balance, the purchaser took hold of the thing and uttered certain prescribed words. He then struck the balance (*libra*) with a small piece of copper (*aes* or *raudusculum*), which he gave to the seller as symbol of the price. This mode of purchase *per aes et libram* was employed in the case of *res mancipi*—i. e. estates in Italy or provinces with Italian law, in the country or in towns, slaves, and domestic animals and beasts of burden needed for agricultural purposes; also in a certain kind of testaments, in the form of marriage called *coëmptio*, and in transferring one's power over a person (*manus*) to another. See Adoptio; Emancipatio; Mancipium; Manus.

Mancipium. The right of possession obtained through *mancipatio* (q. v.), and the possession itself, which none but the head of the family has a right to dispose of. *Homines liberi in mancipio* are free men, whom their father has given into the power of another man by *mancipatio*—e. g. in compensation for some damage they have done to the latter. Their position differed from that of slaves in this, that they retained the right of personality, could complain if their masters treated them badly, and regained all the rights of a free-born man on leaving their position of dependence. This was effected in the same way as the liberation of slaves *vindicta*, *censu*, and *testamento*. (See LIBERTUS.) After the repeal of the severe laws making imprisonment the penalty of convicted debtors, the same relation as that mentioned above existed between debtor and creditor until the money was paid. See NEXUM.

Mandānē. The mother of Cyrus the Great of Persia. See CYRUS.

Mandonius and **Indibĭlis.** Two brothers, and chiefs of the Spanish tribe of the Ilergetes, who played an important part in the war between the Romans and Carthaginians in Spain during the Second Punic War. For some years they were faithful allies of the Carthaginians; but in consequence of the generous treatment which the wife of Mandonius and the daughters of Indibilis received from P. Scipio, when they fell into his hands, the two brothers deserted the Carthaginian cause, and joined Scipio in B.C. 209 with all the forces of their nation. But in B.C. 206 the illness and reported death of Scipio gave them hopes of shaking off the yoke of Rome, and they excited a general revolt not only among their own subjects, but the neighbouring Celtiberian tribes also. They were defeated by Scipio, and upon suing for forgiveness were pardoned. But when Scipio left Spain in the next year (B.C. 205) they again revolted. The Romans attacked them; Indibilis was slain in battle, and Mandonius was soon after captured and put to death (Livy, xxix. 1; Appian, *Hisp.* 38).

Mandra. A checker-board. See LATRUNCULI.

Mandubii. A people in Gallia Lugdunensis, in the modern Burgundy, whose chief town was Alesia.

Manduria. A town in Calabria, on the road from Tarentum to Hydruntum (Livy, xxvi. 15).

Mānes (from *mānus*, "good"). A name euphemistically given by the Romans to the spirits of the dead, which were held to be immortal like the gods, and hence designated as such (*dii manes*). They dwelt below the earth, and only came forth at certain seasons of the year. On the Mons Palatinus at Rome, there was, as in other Italian towns, a deep pit with the shape of an inverted sky, known as *mundus*, the lowest part of which was consecrated to the infernal gods and also to the Manes, and was closed with a stone, *lapis manalis*, thought to be the gate of the nether world. This stone was lifted up three times a year (August 24, October 5, November 8), and the Manes were then believed to rise to the upper world; on this account those days were *religiosi*—i. e. no serious matter might be undertaken on them. Sacrifices were made to the Manes as to the dead; water, wine, warm milk, honey, oil, and the blood of black sheep, pigs, and oxen were poured on the grave; ointments and incense were offered; and the grave was decked with flowers, roses and violets by preference. Oblations, which chiefly consisted of beans, eggs, lentils, bread and wine, were placed on the grave, and the mourners partook of a meal in its neighbourhood. Besides the private celebrations there was also a public and universal festival, the Parentalia, which lasted from the 13th to the 21st of February, the last month of the older Roman year; the last day had the special name Feralia. During these days all the temples were closed, marriages were prohibited, and the magistrates had to appear in public without the tokens of their office. The festival of the dead was followed by that of the relations on February 22, called Caristia (q. v.). This was celebrated throughout the town by each individual family, the members of which exchanged presents and met at festal banquets. See Ovid, *Fasti*, ii. 617; LARES; and PARENTALIA.

Manĕtho (Μανεθώς or Μανεθών). An Egyptian, a priest at Heliopolis in the reign of the first Ptolemy (B.C. 283–246), and who was the first Egyptian to give in Greek an account of the history and religion of his native country. One work was entitled Τῶν Φυσικῶν Ἐπιτομή, dealing with the theology of the Egyptians and with the origin of the world; the second was styled Αἰγυπτιακὴ Ἱστορία, and in three books treated of Aegyptian chronology and history. The first book covers the mythical period prior to the eleventh dynasty; the second, from the eleventh to the twentieth; the third, from the twentieth dynasty to the reign of Nectanebus, the last native Egyptian king. The original works of Manetho are lost, but copious extracts remain preserved by the ecclesiastical writers, especially Iulius Africanus, Eusebius, and Georgius Syncellus. The sources of Manetho's history were the early archives and sacred books of Egypt, and in recent years much corroborative evidence of the truth of what he wrote has been derived by Egyptologists from the hieroglyphics and other sources. The fragments of Manetho are collected and edited by C. Müller in his *Frag. Hist. Graec.* (Paris, 1856). A long astrological poem in six books and entitled Ἀποτελεσματικά, once ascribed to Manetho, is now regarded as written several centuries later than his time. It is edited by Axt and Rigler (Cologne, 1832), and Köchly (1858).

Mango. A slave-dealer. See SERVUS.

Mania. See LARES.

Manĭca (χειρίς). (1) A sleeve worn either separately (Pallad. *R. R.* i. 43) or sewn to the tunic (Curt. iii. 7). The latter was long regarded as effeminate (Verg. *Aen.* ix. 616; Gell. vi. 12), but in the later Empire was regularly worn. It appears to have been developed from a species of

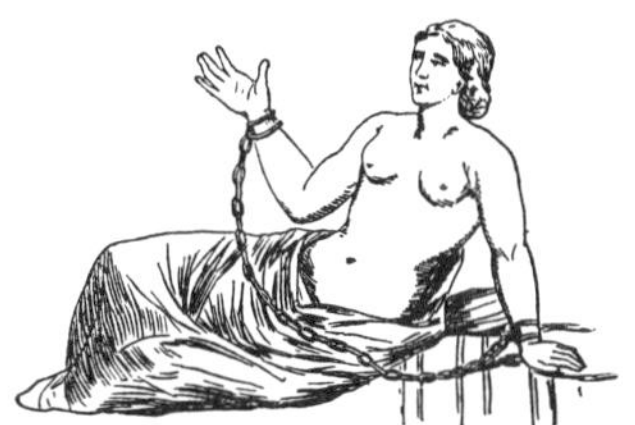

Manicae. (Rich.)

glove with gauntlets, originally used by hedgers and huntsmen to protect the hands and arms from briars and thistles. Such were probably the χειρίδες of Homer (*Od.* xxiv. 228, 229), differing only from gloves in not having fingers. (See DIGITALIA.) (2) A handcuff, generally spoken of in the plural (*manicae*), of which the preceding illustration gives an example (Plaut. *Most.* v. 1, 17). (3) A grappling-iron used in naval battles (Lucan. iii. 565). See HARPAGO.

Manilius. (1) GAIUS, a tribune of the plebs (B.C. 66), who proposed the law (Manilia Lex) granting to Pompey the command of the war against Mithridates, and which Cicero supported in an extant oration. (2) The reputed author of a Latin didactic poem upon astronomy and astrology (*Astronomica*), in five books, the first of which was written under Augustus, after the battle in the Saltus Teutoburgiensis (A.D. 9), and the fifth under Tiberius. The first two books treat of astronomy as the foundation of astrology; the rest of the influence of constellations on human destiny. The author certainly intended to write a sixth book, but it has either been lost or was never written. The poet, who shows extensive knowledge, frequently boasts of having been the first among Roman poets to treat the subject, and handles his difficult theme with a dexterity and a moral earnestness that recall Lucretius, whose language he has frequently imitated. In metrical skill he is on a par with the best poets of the Augustan Age. The *editio princeps* of Manilius appeared at Nüremberg about 1472; the best texts are those of Bentley (London, 1739), and Jacob (Berlin, 1846). See Woltjer, *De Manilio Poeta* (Groningen, 1881); Lanson, *De Manilio Poeta eiusque Ingenio* (Paris, 1887); and Kraemer, *De Manilii Astronomicis* (Marburg, 1890).

Manipŭlus (literally, "a handful"). A subdivision of the Roman legion (q. v.), which had thirty of them (three in each of the ten cohorts). The manipulus consisted of two centuries. The name is derived from *manus* + *plenus*, and originally signified those who rallied around the handful of hay or grain carried at the end of a pole, which formed the primitive standard. See SIGNUM.

Manipulus. (From a terra-cotta lamp.)

Manlia Gens. A Roman patrician family, of which the chief branches were those of Acidinus, Torquatus, and Vulso.

Manlius, MARCUS. A Roman who was consul in B.C. 392, took refuge in the Capitol when Rome was taken by the Gauls in 388 (Mommsen). One night, when the Gauls endeavored to ascend the Capitol, Manlius was roused from his sleep by the cackling of the geese; collecting hastily a body of men, he succeeded in driving back the enemy, who had just reached the summit of the hill. From this heroic deed he is said to have received the surname of Capitolinus. In 385 he defended the cause of the plebeians, who were suffering severely from the harsh and cruel treatment of their patrician creditors. In the following year he was charged with high treason by the patricians; and being condemned to death by the people, he was hurled down the Tarpeian Rock by the tribunes. The members of the Manlia gens accordingly resolved that none of them should ever bear in future the praenomen of Marcus. See Mommsen, *Hist. of Rome*, i. pp. 380, 381, 429 (Amer. ed. 1888).

Manlius Torquātus. See TORQUATUS.

Mannus. A god of the ancient Germans, and by them regarded as one of the founders of the race. See GERMANIA, p. 726.

Mannus. A familiar Latin word for a horse, derived from the Keltic, and used like our "nag" or perhaps even more slangily like "plug."

Mansio (σταθμός). A posting-station. See CURSUS PUBLICUS.

Mansions. See DOMUS.

Mantēlé. (1) A towel or napkin used by the Roman priests in their sacrificial rites (Ovid, *Fast.* iv. 933). (2) In imperial times a table-cloth (Mart. xii. 29. 12). In this sense it is not employed earlier than the time of Martial, and in an earlier age the table was not covered, the grain of the wood being an object of admiration. See MAPPA.

Mantiāna Palus. A great lake in the southern part of Armenia Maior. It was also called Arsissa.

Mantĭca (πήρα, θύλακος). A wallet, satchel, or travelling-bag carried by hand, or slung over the shoulder, or strapped on behind the saddle of a horse (Hor. *Sat.* i. 6, 106). A larger kind of bag was called *averta* (*Cod. Theod.* viii. 5, 47).

Mantĭké (μαντική, sc. τέχνη). The name given by the Greeks to the gift or art of divination. The belief of the ancients that it was possible to find out what was hidden or what was going to happen sprang from the idea that the gods, when implored by prayer, or even when unimplored, graciously communicated revelations to men by means of direct inspiration or through signs requiring interpretation. Hence the ancients distinguished between natural and artificial divination.

Divination is natural when a man receives the supposed inspiration in a dream or in an ecstatic state. The belief in divine inspiration in dreams is of the greatest antiquity, and continued to be held when the natural causes of dreams had been ascertained. The meaning of prophetic dreams cannot, however, always be immediately comprehended; they are mostly symbolical, and therefore require an interpretation. As a guide to this, there arose in the course of time certain rules resulting from experience, which produced a special art—that of interpreting dreams—of which some idea is given by the Ὀνειροκριτικά, on the interpretation of dreams, by Artemidorus (q. v.). Similarly, the dreams obtained by sleeping at holy places (*incubatio*), which were always considered prophetic, usually needed a priest to interpret them.

The power of more or less clearly seeing in waking hours things concealed from ordinary vision was believed by the Greeks to be a special gift of Apollo. It is from him that Homer makes Calchas receive his revelations, although no mention is made of his being in the ecstatic state usually connected with this kind of soothsaying. At the oracles this state was usually produced by external influences (see ORACULUM); women were held to be particularly susceptible to them. Besides oracles and persons reputed to be inspired, use was made of various collections of older oracular sayings and pretended predictions of prophets and prophetesses of former times, such as the Branchidae of Miletus, the Iamidae of Olympia, the Eumolpidae of Athens, and the Sibyls. Such collections were not only in the possession of States and priesthoods, but also in that of private individuals, called *χρησμολόγοι*, who drew on their store when paid to do so by those who believed in them, and often also explained the dark sayings. Like the prophets by immediate inspiration, those also were called seers who interpreted according to certain rules the divine signs which formed the subject of the artificial variety of the art of divination.

From the very oldest times special importance was attached to omens of birds (whether in answer to prayer or not), which were discriminated from one another by various rules, with regard partly to the kind of birds, partly to the manner of their appearing — e. g. direction (favourable from the right, unfavourable from the left), flight, alighting, singing, and anything else they did. The principal birds consulted were the birds of prey that fly highest and alone—the eagle (the messenger of Zeus), the heron, the hawk, the falcon, and the vulture; in the case of ravens and crows, the cawing was an omen.

Second in importance were the various phenomena of the sky considered as divine signs. Whether thunder and lightning were favourable or not was also decided by the direction, right or left, from which they came. At Sparta, shooting stars were thought to show that the gods were displeased with the kings. Eclipses of the sun and moon, comets, and meteors were signs that inspired terror. Prophesying from the stars, however, did not become known in Greece till the time of Alexander the Great.

In important enterprises, especially in war, recourse was had to an examination of the condition of sacrificed animals or *ἱεροσκοπία*—oxen, sheep, and also pigs being most frequently the victims. The points observed were: normal or abnormal nature of the entrails, especially the liver, with the gall-bladder, and also the heart, spleen, and lungs. The various kinds of entrails and their abnormal conditions were made the subject of a highly elaborate system, so that no Greek army could dispense with a skilled interpreter of signs. When the omens were unfavourable, the sacrifice was repeated till they were favourable, or the enterprise was postponed. The manner, too, in which animals went to be sacrificed, whether willingly or with reluctance (Juv. xii. 5, with Mayor's note), was looked upon as an omen, as also the way in which the sacrifice burned on the altar, the burning of the flame itself, the rising or sinking of the smoke, etc. These signs drawn from fire were the subject of *πυρομαντεία*.

There was, indeed, a general inclination to regard all striking and unusual events as hints from the gods, and to interpret them one's self, or to have them interpreted by skilled seers. From ancient times the chance utterances of others were thought to be prophetic in so far as they applied to the circumstances of the moment. For such omens also the gods were asked. Besides these, lots and dice were used for predictions. There were many other artificial varieties of the art of divination, some of them very strange, which were in special favour in the lower classes of the people and in later times; as, for instance, soothsaying with a sieve suspended by threads, for the purpose of finding out thieves, or remedies for illness, etc., that name being thought the one required, at mention of which the sieve ceased to turn round. As early as Aristotle allusion is made to chiromancy, or palmistry. See Bouché-Leclercq, *Histoire de la Divination dans l'Antiquité*, 4 vols. (Paris, 1879–82); and the articles AUGUR; DIVINATIO; ORACULUM; SIBYLLA; SORTES VERGILIANAE.

Mantinēa (Μαντίνεια). One of the most ancient and important towns in Arcadia, situated on the small river Ophis, near the centre of the eastern frontier of the country. It is celebrated for the great battle fought under its walls between the Spartans and Thebans, in which Epaminondas fell, B.C. 362. In consequence of its treachery to the Achaeans, Aratus put to death its leading citizens, sold the rest of its inhabitants as slaves, and changed its name into ANTIGONIA, in honour of Antigonus Doson. The emperor Hadrian restored to the place its ancient name.

Mantius (Μαντίος). A son of Melampus (q. v.).

Manto (Μαντώ). (1) The daughter of the seer Tiresias, and herself a prophetess, at first of the Ismenian Apollo at Thebes. After the capture of the town by the Epigoni she was presented to the oracle at Delphi as part of the booty, and sent by the god to Asia, in order to found the oracle of the Clarian Apollo in the neighbourhood of what was afterwards Colophon. Here she bore Mopsus (q. v.) to the Cretan seer Rhacius. (2) The daughter of Heracles and also a prophetess. From her the town of Mantua received its name (Verg. *Aen.* x. 199).

Mantua. A town in Gallia Transpadana, on an island in the river Mincius. It was not a place of importance; but is celebrated because Vergil, who was born at the neighbouring village of Andes, regarded Mantua as his birthplace. See VERGILIUS.

Mantuan Vase. See GEMMA.

Manubiae. See SPOLIA.

Manum, CONVENTIO IN. See MANUS; MATRIMONIUM.

Manumissio. The legal act by which slaves and persons *in mancipii causa* were released from the *manus* of their masters and presented with freedom. There were three kinds of manumission: (*a*) *vindictā*, (*b*) *censu*, (*c*) *testamento*, on which classification see Gaius, i. 17.

(*a*) Manumissio by *vindicta* was probably the earliest form (Livy, ii. 5), and was the assertion before a magistrate of the slave's freedom to which the owner made no defence, whereupon the magistrate declared the slave a freeman. The ceremony was as follows: The master brought his slave before the praetor, since it was his province to exercise jurisdiction in civil causes. The praetor's lictor, who came to be used as *adsertor libertatis*, in order to save the trouble of bringing a person to take this part, holding a rod (*vindicta* or *festuca*) with one hand, and with the other laying hold of the slave, said, *Hunc ego hominem ex iure Quiritium liberum esse aio*, at the same time touching him with the rod; the master then using the same formalities, and turning the slave round and releasing his hold of him, as seems to have been the custom (Pers. *Sat.* v. 78), admitted his freedom, either expressly or by his silence, which was followed by the *pronuntiatio* of the magistratus, *Quandoque Numerius Nigidius non contra vindicat, hunc ego hominem ex iure Quiritium liberum esse dico.*

Addicere is the technical term to express this act of a magistrate by which he pronounced in favour of a right, in this case a right to freedom (Cic. *Ad Att.* vii. 2). This form of manumission derived its name from the *vindicta* or rod, otherwise called *festuca*, which was used in the proceeding (Plaut. *Mil.* iv. 1, 15).

(*b*) Ulpian (1, 8) thus describes manumissio by the *census:* "Slaves were formerly manumitted by census, when at the lustral census (*lustrali censu*) at Rome they gave in their census at the bidding of their masters." The slave must of course have had a sufficient *peculium*, or the master must have given him property, so that he might become a taxpayer.

(*c*) The Twelve Tables confirmed freedom that was granted by will (*testamento*). There were three kinds of testamentary manumission—when the master freed the slave by will and made him a *heres;* when the master gave his slave his freedom as a direct legacy; and when a person requested his heir or legatee to manumit the slave.

Manumission according to legal form not only freed a slave, but made him a citizen. There were other informal ways of manumitting—e. g. *inter amicos*, which was a declaration by the master in the presence of witnesses that the slave was free. An invitation to dinner sent to a slave was regarded as such a declaration. For restrictions on manumission, see SERVUS.

The legal act of manumission was often followed by a religious ceremony in the temple of Feronia, where the freedman appeared clad in the toga or dress of a Roman citizen, and with a *pileus*, or particular kind of cap, on his shaven head. This last circumstance explains the expression *servos ad pileum vocare* (Liv. xxiv. 32), which means to promise slaves their liberty in order to induce them to join in some civil disturbance (cf. Plaut. *Amph.* iii. 4, 16; *Poen.* v. 2, 2; Serv. *Ad Aen.* viii. 564). The *pileus* was still worn in the time of Justinian, since he declares that slaves who attend the funeral of their master with the cap of freedom on their heads (*pileati*) become Roman citizens.

Manus. In its wider sense, the name given by the Romans to the power of the chief of a family over the whole of that family, especially the power of the husband over his wife, whose person and property were so completely his own that he was legally responsible for her actions, but at the same time had the right to kill, punish, or sell her. As in this respect, so also with respect to the right of inheritance, the wife was placed on a level with the children, as she obtained the same share as they. For marriages without manus, see MATRIMONIUM.

Manus Ferrea. See HARPAGO.

Manūs Iniectio (laying on of the hand). In the oldest Roman legal procedure a kind of execution levied on the person of one who had been condemned to pay a certain sum. If this was not done within thirty days of the condemnation, the plaintiff could seize the debtor and bring him before the praetor, who handed him over to the creditor with the word *addico* (I hand over), unless he paid there and then, or a *vindex* came forward to pay for him or to show there was no ground for complaint. The creditor kept the debtor in chains at his house for sixty days; if his claims had not been satisfied during this period, he might kill him or sell him as a slave in foreign parts. From the fourth century onwards a less severe arrangement was usual; the relation of the *addictus* to his creditor was that of a *homo liber in mancipio.* See Bekker, *Die Actionen des röm. Privatrechts*, vol. i.; Karlowa, *Der röm. Civilprocess*, i. § 45; and MANCIPIUM.

Manuscripts. See CODEX; PALAEOGRAPHY; TEXTUAL CRITICISM.

Mapalia. See MAGALIA.

Mappa (χειρόμακτρον). (1) A table-napkin used by the Romans, as in modern times. It was considered vulgar to fasten it under the chin to protect the clothes from stains (Petron. 32). As a rule, the guests brought their own *mappae* to an entertainment (Mart. xii. 29, 11), and occasionally carried away from the table such dainties as they did not consume at the time (id. vii. 20). (2) A cloth which the magistrate presiding over the Circensian races threw down as a signal for the start (Juv. xi. 191; Suet. *Nero*, 22). The custom is said by Cassiodorus (Varro, *Ep.* iii. 51) to have originated with the emperor Nero; but Quintilian (i. 5, 57) ascribes it to the Phœnicians, and it is doubtless of great antiquity.

Mappa. (From a Pompeian Painting.)

Maps. See GEOGRAPHIA; ICHNOGRAPHIA; ITINERARIA.

Maracanda (τὰ Μαράκανδα). The modern Samarcand; the capital of Sogdiana, where Alexander the Great killed his friend Clitus.

Maraphii (Μαράφιοι). One of the noble tribes of the ancient Persians, the other two being the Maspii and Pàsargadae.

Marătha (Μάραθα). A town of Arcadia at the source of the Buphagus.

Marathesium (Μαραθήσιον). A town of Ionia, between Ephesus and Neapolis. It originally belonged to the people of Samos, but they gave it to the Ephesians in exchange for Neapolis, which was nearer to Samos.

Marăthon (Μαραθών). A deme of Attica, belonging to the tribe Leontis, was situated near a bay on the east coast of Attica, twenty-two miles from Athens by one road, and twenty-six miles by another. It originally belonged to the Attic tetrapolis, and is said to have derived its name from the hero Marathon. This hero, according to one account, was the son of Epopeus, king of Sicyon, who having been expelled from Peloponnesus by the violence of his father, settled in Attica; while, according to another account, he was an Arcadian who took part in the expedition of the Tyndaridae against Attica, and devoted himself to death before the battle.

The site of the ancient town of Marathon was probably not at the modern village of Marathon, but at a place called Vraná, a little to the south of Marathon. Marathon was situated in a plain, which extends along the sea-shore, about six miles in length, and from three miles to one mile and a half in breadth. It is surrounded on the other three sides by rocky hills and rugged mountains. Two marshes bound the extremity of the plain; the northern is more than a square mile in extent, but the southern is much smaller, and is almost dry at the conclusion of the great heats. Through the centre of the plain runs a small brook. In this plain was fought the celebrated battle between the Persians and Athenians, August 12th, B.C. 490. The Persians, numbering some 100,000 men, were drawn up on the plain, and the Athenians, 10,000 strong, under Miltiades, on some portion of the high ground above the plain; but the exact ground occupied by the two armies cannot be identified, notwithstanding the investigations of modern travellers. The Athenians lost 192 men, the Persians 6400. The tumulus or mound, raised over the Athenians who fell in the battle, is still to be seen. It is an isolated knoll in the plain, about 40 feet in height and 600 feet in circumference. Excavations made by Schliemann and others yielded nothing until 1890, when, under the direction of the Greek Archaeological Society, a number of vases of the fifth century B.C. and burned bones were found, undoubtedly those of the Athenians slain in the battle. The mound is now called the Sorós. On the battle, see Herod. vi. 106, 107; and Schauer, *Die Schlacht bei Marathon* (1893).

Marăthus (Μάραθος). An important city on the coast of Phœnicia, opposite to Aradus and near Antaradus.

Marble. See STATUARIA ARS.

Marcella. (1) The sister of Augustus Caesar, and married first to M. Vipsanius Agrippa; next to Iulius Antonius, son of the triumvir; at last to Sextus Apuleius, consul A.D. 14. (2) The second wife of the poet Martial.

Marcellīnus. See AMMIANUS MARCELLINUS.

Marcellus. The name of an illustrious plebeian family of the Claudia gens. (1) M. CLAUDIUS MARCELLUS, celebrated as having been five times consul and commander of Syracuse. In his first consulship, B.C. 222, Marcellus distinguished himself by slaying in battle with his own hand Britomartius or Virdomarus, the king of the Insubrian Gauls, whose spoils he afterwards dedicated as *spolia opima* in the temple of Iupiter Feretrius. This was the third and last instance in Roman history in which such an offering was made. Marcellus was one of the chief Roman generals in the Second Punic War. He took Syracuse in B.C. 212, after a siege of more than two years, in which all his powerful military engines were rendered wholly unavailing by the superior skill and science of Archimedes, who directed those of the besieged. On the capture of the city Archimedes was one of the inhabitants slain by the Roman soldiers. Marcellus fell in battle against Hannibal in 208, and was buried by the enemy with military honours. (2) M. CLAUDIUS MARCELLUS, consul B.C. 51 and a bitter enemy of Caesar. In B.C. 46 he was pardoned by Caesar on the intercession of the Senate; whereupon Cicero returned thanks to Caesar in the oration *Pro Marcello*, which has come down to us. Marcellus, who was then living at Mitylené, set out on his return; but he was murdered at the Piraeus by one of his own attendants, P. Magius Chilo. (3) C. CLAUDIUS MARCELLUS, brother of the preceding and also an enemy of Caesar. He was consul in 49, when the Civil War broke out. (4) C. CLAUDIUS MARCELLUS, first cousin of the two preceding and, like them, an enemy of Caesar. He was consul in 50, but he did not join Pompey in Greece, and was therefore readily pardoned by Caesar. (5) M. CLAUDIUS MARCELLUS, son of the preceding and of Octavia, the daughter of C. Octavius and sister of Augustus. He was born B.C. 43. Augustus, who had probably destined him for his successor, adopted him as his son, and gave him his daughter Iulia in marriage (B.C. 25). In 23 he was curule ædile, but died in the same year, to the great grief of Augustus as well as of his mother Octavia. The memory of Marcellus is immortalized by the well-known passage of Vergil (*Aen.* vi. 860–886), which was recited by the poet to Augustus and Octavia. In his honour, Augustus built the great theatre near the Forum Olitorium, remains of which still exist. See VERGILIUS.

Marcellus Empirĭcus (so called from his empirical work on medical remedies), of Burdigala (Bordeaux). Marshal of the household (*magister officiorum*) to Theodosius I., he compiled about A.D. 410 a dispensatory for the poor (*De Medicamentis*), which is chiefly founded on Scribonius Largus (q. v.), with many superstitious additions. It has a poetical epilogue of seventy-eight hexameters. The text is given in Ackermann's *Parabilium Medicamentorum Script. Antiq.* (Nürnberg, 1788), and lately edited by Helmreich (Leipzig, 1889). On Marcellus Empiricus, see Helmreich in the *Blätter für das bayerische Gymnasialschulwesen*, xviii. 392, 460.

Marcellus, NONIUS. See NONIUS.

March. See CALENDARIUM.

Marcia. (1) The wife of M. Regulus (q. v.). (2) The wife of Cato Uticensis. (3) The daughter of Cremutius Cordus (q. v.). (4) The favourite mistress of Commodus (q. v.).

Marcia Aqua. See AQUAEDUCTUS.

Marcia Gens. A Roman gens which claimed descent from Ancus Marcius, fourth king of Rome, so that one of its branches afterwards took the name of Rex. The name of its most distinguished families are Censorinus, Philippus, Rex, and Rutilus.

Marciāna Carmĭna. See MARCIUS.

Marcianopŏlis (Μαρκιανούπολις). A city in the interior of Moesia Inferior, west of Odessus (Varna). It was founded by Trajan, and named in honour of his sister Marciana.

Marciānus (Μαρκιανός). (1) A Greek geographer, who lived at Heraclea in Bithynia. With the aid of the best sources of information from Hanno and Scylax down to Ptolemaeus he compiled, about A.D. 400, a description of the Western and Eastern Ocean in two books, not completely preserved. Edition by Hoffmann (Leipzig, 1841). It is of particular importance for ancient geography, as the distances in stadia are given. (2) AELIUS. A Roman jurist, who lived under Caracalla and Alexander Severus, and who is frequently cited in the *Digest*. (3) Emperor of the East, A.D. 450–457. He was a native of Thrace or Illyricum, and served for many years as a common soldier in the imperial army. Of his early history we have only a few particulars; but he had attained such distinction at the death of Theodosius II. in 450 that the widow of the latter, the celebrated Pulcheria, offered her hand and the imperial title to Marcian, who thus became emperor of the East. Marcian was a man of resolution and bravery; and when Attila sent to demand the tribute which the younger Theodosius had engaged to pay annually, the emperor sternly replied, "I have iron for Attila, but no gold." Attila swore vengeance; but he first invaded the Western Empire, and his death, two years afterwards, saved the East. In 451 Marcian assembled the Council of Chalcedon, in which the doctrines of the Eutychians were condemned. He died in 457, and was succeeded by Leo. (4) MARCIĀNUS CAPELLA. See CAPELLA.

Marcius. (1) See MARCIA GENS. (2) An Italian seer, whose prophetic verses (*Carmina Marciana*) were discovered in B.C. 213, and were preserved in the Capitol with the Sibylline Books. Some writers mention only one person of this name, but others speak of two brothers—the Marcii. See Livy, xxv. 12; Symmach. *Epist.* 4, 34.

Marcomanni. "Men of the marches (borders)." One of the divisions of the Suevi (q. v.).

Marcus. See MALLEUS.

Marcus Aurelius. See ANTONINUS.

Mardēné (Μαρδηνή) or **Mardyēné** (Μαρδυηνή). A district of Persis extending from Taocené to the sea-coast.

Mardi (Μάρδοι). A warlike tribe dwelling on the southern shore of the Caspian Sea.

Mardonius (Μαρδόνιος). A distinguished Persian, son of Gobryas and son-in-law of Darius Hystaspis. In B.C. 492 he was sent by Darius to punish Eretria and Athens for the aid they had given to the Ionians; but his fleet was destroyed by a storm off Mount Athos, and the greater part of his land forces was destroyed on his passage through Macedonia by the Brygians, a Thracian tribe. On the accession of Xerxes he was one of the chief instigators of the expedition against Greece. After the defeat of the Persians at Salamis (480) he was left by Xerxes with a large army to conquer Greece; but he was defeated in the following year (479), near Plataeae, by the combined Greek forces under the command of Pausanias, and was slain in the battle (Herod. vi. 43, 94; vii. 5, 9, 82; viii. 100–144; ix. 165).

Mardyēné. See MARDENÉ.

Marēa (Μάρεια, Μαρία, Μαρέη). A town of Lower Egypt, which gave its name to the district and lake of Mareotis. The lake was separated from the Mediterranean by the neck of land on which Alexandria stood, and supplied with water by the Canopic branch of the Nile and by canals. It served as the port of Alexandria for vessels navigating the Nile.

Mareōtis (Μαρεῶτις). See MAREA.

Mares (Μᾶρες). An Asiatic people dwelling on the southern coast of the Euxine, mentioned by Herodotus as serving in the army of Xerxes.

Marēsa (Μαρησά) or **Marescha** (Μαρεσχά). An ancient fortress of Palestine, in the south of Iudaea, of some importance in the history of the early kings of Judah and of the Maccabees.

Margiāna (Μαργιανή). A province of the ancient Persian Empire, bounded on the east by Bactriana, on the northeast and north by the river Oxus, and on the west by Hyrcania. It received its name from the river Margus, which flows through it. On this river stood the capital of the district, Antiochia Margiana, which was founded by Alexander the Great and rebuilt by Antiochus I. Margiana corresponds to the southern part of Khiva and Bokhara and the northeastern part of Khorassan. Its chief inhabitants were the Derbices, Dahae, and Mardi.

Margītes. See HOMERUS, p. 835.

Margum or **Margus.** A fortified place in Moesia Superior on the river Margus where it joins the Danube.

Margus (Μάργος). See MARGIANA.

Maria. See MAREA.

Mariaba (Μαρίαβα). A town of the Sabaei in the southwestern part of Arabia.

Mariamma (Μαριάμμη). A city of Coele-Syria, west of Emesa.

Mariamné. See HERODES.

Mariamné Turris. See HIEROSOLYMA.

Mariānae Fossae. See FOSSA.

Mariandȳni (Μαριανδυνοί). An ancient people living in the northeast of Bithynia in Asia Minor.

Mariānus Mons. Now the Sierra Morena; a range in Hispania Baetica, the eastern part of which was called the Saltus Castulonensis from the town Castulo.

Marīca. A nymph, the mother of Latinus by Faunus, according to the Roman legend. She was worshipped by the people of Minturnae on the river Liris (Hor. *Carm.* iii. 17, 7).

Marīnus (Μαρῖνος). (1) A Tyrian geographer, who lived about the middle of the second century A.D. He was the first mathematical geographer, and was largely followed by Ptolemy. (See PTOLEMAEUS.) (2) A philosopher and rhetorician of Flavia Neapolis in Palestine. He succeeded Proclus (q. v.), and wrote his life, which is still extant. Edited by Boissonade (Leipzig, 1814).

Marius. (1) GAIUS, a distinguished Roman general and statesman, who was born near Arpinum in B.C. 157 of an obscure family in humble circumstances. His father's name was C. Marius, and his mother's Fulcinia; and his parents, as well as Marius himself, were clients of the noble plebeian house of the Herennii. So indigent, indeed, is the family represented to have been, that young Marius is said to have worked as a common peasant for wages, before he entered the ranks of the Roman army. (Cf. Juv. viii. 246.) The meanness of his origin has probably been somewhat exaggerated; but, at all events, he distinguished himself so much by his valour at the siege of Numantia in Spain (134) as to attract the notice of Scipio Africanus, who is said to have foretold his future greatness. His name does not occur again for fifteen years; but in 119 he was elected tribune of the plebs, when he was thirty-eight years of age. In this office he came forward as a popular leader, and proposed a law to give greater freedom to the people at the elections; and when the Senate attempted to overawe him, he commanded one of his officers to carry the consul Metellus to prison.

Marius now became a marked man, and the aristocracy opposed him with all their might. He lost his election to the aedileship, and with difficulty obtained the praetorship; but he acquired influence and importance by his marriage with Iulia, the sister of C. Iulius Caesar, who was the father of the future ruler of Rome. In 109 Marius crossed over into Africa as lieutenant of the consul Q. Metellus. Here, in the war against Iugurtha, the military genius of Marius had ample opportunity of displaying itself, and he was soon regarded as the most distinguished officer in the army. He also ingratiated himself with the soldiers, who praised him in the highest terms in their letters to their friends at Rome. His popularity became so great that he resolved to return to Rome, and become at once a candidate for the consulship; but it was with great difficulty that he obtained from Metellus permission to leave Africa. On his arrival at Rome he was elected consul with an enthusiasm which bore down all opposition before it; and he received from the people the province of Numidia and the conduct of the war against Iugurtha (107). On his return to Numidia he carried on the war with great vigour; and in the following year (106) Iugurtha was surrendered to him by the treachery of Bocchus, king of Mauretania. (See IUGURTHA.) Marius sent his quaestor Sulla to receive the Numidian king from Bocchus. This circumstance sowed the seeds of the personal hatred which afterwards existed between Marius and Sulla, since the enemies of Marius claimed for Sulla the merit of bringing the war to a close by obtaining possession of the person of Iugurtha.

Meantime Italy was threatened by a vast horde of barbarians, who had migrated from the north of Germany. The two leading nations of which they consisted were called Cimbri and Teutoni, the former of whom are supposed to have been Celts, and the latter Gauls. To these two great races were added the Ambrones, and some of the Swiss tribes, such as the Tigurini. The whole host is said to have contained three hundred thousand fighting men, besides a much larger number of women and children. They had defeated one Roman army after another, and it appeared that nothing could check their progress. The utmost alarm prevailed throughout Italy; all party quarrels were hushed. Every one felt that Marius was the only man capable of saving the State, and he was accordingly elected consul a second time during his absence in Africa. Marius entered Rome in triumph on the first of January, 104, the first day of his second consulship. Meanwhile, the threatened danger was for a while averted. Instead of crossing the Alps, the Cimbri marched into Spain, which they ravaged for the next two or three years. But as the return of the barbarians was constantly expected, Marius was elected consul a third time in 103, and a fourth time in 102. In the latter of these years the Cimbri returned into Gaul. The barbarians now divided their forces. The Cimbri marched round the northern foot of the Alps, in order to enter Italy by the northeast, crossing the Tyrolese Alps by the defiles of Tridentum (Trent). The Teutoni and Ambrones, on the other hand, marched against Marius, who had taken up a position in a fortified camp on the Rhône. The decisive battle was fought near Aquae Sextiae (Aix). The carnage was dreadful. The whole nation was annihilated, for those who did not fall in the battle put an end to their own lives. The Cimbri, meantime, had forced their way into Italy. Marius was elected consul a fifth time (101), and joined the proconsul Catulus in the north of Italy. The two generals gained a great victory over the enemy on a plain called the Campi Raudii, near Vercellae (Vercelli). The Cimbri met with the same fate as the Teutoni; the whole nation was destroyed. Marius was received at Rome with unprecedented honours. He was hailed as the saviour of the State; his name was coupled with the gods in the libations and at banquets, and he received the title of third founder of Rome.

Hitherto the career of Marius had been a glorious one; but the remainder of his life is full of

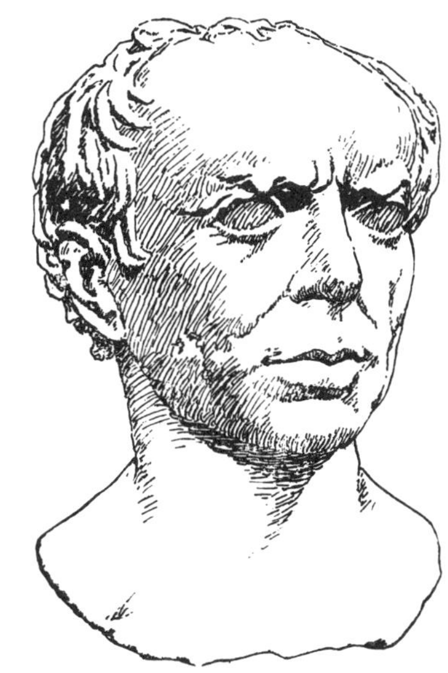

Gaius Marius. (Duruy.)

horrors, and brings out the worst features of his character. In order to secure the consulship the sixth time, he entered into close connection with two of the worst demagogues that ever appeared at Rome, Saturninus and Glaucia. He gained his object, and was consul a sixth time in 100. In this year he drove into exile his old enemy Metellus; and shortly afterwards, when Saturninus and Glaucia took up arms against the State, Marius crushed the insurrection by command of the Senate. (See SATURNINUS.) His conduct in this affair was greatly blamed by the people, who looked upon him as a traitor to his former friends. For the next few years Marius took little part in public affairs. He possessed none of the qualifications which were necessary to maintain influence in the State during a time of peace, being an unlettered soldier, rude in manners, and arrogant in conduct. The Social War again called him into active service (90). He served as legate of the consul P. Rutilius Lupus; and after the latter had fallen in battle, he defeated the Marsi in two successive engagements. Marius was now sixty-seven, and his body had grown stout and unwieldy; but he was still as greedy of honour and distinction as he had ever been. He had set his heart upon obtaining the command of the war against Mithridates, which the Senate bestowed upon the consul Sulla at the end of the Social War (88). In order to gain his object, Marius allied himself to the tribune, P. Sulpicius Rufus, who brought forward a law for distributing the Italian allies, who had just obtained the Roman franchise, among all the Roman tribes. As those new citizens greatly exceeded the old citizens in number, they would of course be able to carry whatever they pleased in the Comitia. The law was carried, notwithstanding the violent opposition of the consuls; and the tribes, in which the new citizens now had the majority, appointed Marius to the command of the war against Mithridates. Sulla fled to his army, which was stationed at Nola; and when Marius sent thither two military tribunes, to take the command of the troops, Sulla not only refused to surrender the command, but marched upon Rome at the head of his army. Marius was now obliged to take to flight. After wandering along the coast of Latium, and encountering terrible sufferings and privations, which he bore with unflinching fortitude, he was at length taken prisoner in the marshes formed by the river Liris, near Minturnae. The magistrates of this place resolved to put him to death, in accordance with a command which Sulla had sent to all the towns in Italy. A Gallic or Cimbrian soldier undertook to carry their sentence into effect, and with a drawn sword entered the apartment where Marius was confined. The part of the room in which Marius lay was in the shade; and to the frightened barbarian the eyes of Marius seemed to dart out fire, and from the darkness a terrible voice exclaimed, "Man, durst thou murder C. Marius?" The barbarian immediately threw down his sword, and rushed out of the house. Straightway there was a revulsion of feeling among the inhabitants of Minturnae. They got ready a ship, and placed Marius on board. He reached Africa in safety, and landed at Carthage; but he had scarcely put his foot on shore before the Roman governor sent an officer to bid him leave the country. This last blow almost unmanned Marius; his only reply was, "Tell the praetor that you have seen C. Marius a fugitive sitting on the ruins of Carthage." Soon afterwards Marius was joined by his son, and they took refuge in the island of Cercina.

During this time a revolution had taken place at Rome, in consequence of which Marius was enabled to return to Italy. The consul Cinna (87), who belonged to the Marian party, had been driven out of Rome by his colleague Octavius, and had subsequently been deprived by the Senate of the consulate. Cinna collected an army, and resolved to recover his honours by force of arms. As soon as Marius heard of these changes he left Africa, and joined Cinna in Italy. Marius and Cinna now laid siege to Rome. The failure of provisions compelled the Senate to yield, and Marius and Cinna entered Rome as conquerors. The most frightful scenes followed. The guards of Marius stabbed every one whom he did not salute, and the streets ran with the blood of the noblest of the Roman aristocracy. Among the victims of his vengeance were the great orator M. Antonius and his former colleague Q. Catulus. Without going through the form of an election, Marius and Cinna named themselves consuls for the following year (86). But he did not long enjoy the honour: he was now in his seventy-first year; his body was worn out by the fatigues and sufferings he had recently undergone; and eighteen days after his assumption of the consulate he died of an attack of pleurisy. See Plutarch's life of Marius; Beesly, *The Gracchi, Marius, and Sulla* (N. Y. 1878); and Mommsen, *Hist. of Rome*, vol. iii.

(2) GAIUS, son of the preceding by adoption. He was consul in B.C. 82, when only twenty-seven years of age. He resisted Sulla for some time, but at last, being defeated, took his own life (Vell. Pat. ii. 26, 27).

(3) M. AURELIUS MARIUS, one of the Thirty Tyrants (q. v.).

(4) MARIUS MAXĬMUS, a Roman historian, who is repeatedly cited by the Augustan historians. He probably flourished under Alexander Severus, and appears to have written the biographies of the Roman emperors, beginning with Trajan and ending with Elagabalus.

(5) MARIUS MERCĀTOR, an ecclesiastical writer, distinguished as a zealous antagonist of the Pelagians and the Nestorians. He appears to have commenced his literary career during the pontificate of Zosimus, A.D. 418, at Rome, and he afterwards repaired to Constantinople. The works of Mercator refer exclusively to the Pelagian and Nestorian heresies.

(6) MARIUS VICTORĪNUS. See VICTORINUS.

Marius Maxĭmus. A Latin historian. See SUETONIUS.

Market. See AGORA; MACELLUM.

Market, CLERKS OF THE. See AGORANOMUS.

Markland, JEREMIAH. An English classicist and text-critic, born October 29, 1693, and educated at London and Cambridge. He died July 7, 1776. His work included a number of emendations of the text of Lysias and of Euripides, and a great edition of the very difficult *Silvae* of Statius (London, 1728; last ed. Dresden, 1824). He attacked the authenticity of Cicero's letters to Brutus, and of the Ciceronian orations *Pro Domo Sua, Post Reditum in Senatu, Ad Quirites,* and the *De Haruspicum Responsis*, in which he was afterwards followed by F. A. Wolf. See Wolf, *Analecten*, ii. 370–391.

Marmarĭca (Μαρμαρική). A district of Northern Africa, between Cyrenaïca and Egypt, extending inland as far as the Oasis of Ammon. Its inhabitants were called Marmaridae.

Marmarium (Μαρμάριον). A place in the south-western part of Euboea with celebrated quarries of marble and a temple of Apollo Marmarius.

Maro, VERGILIUS. See VERGILIUS.

Maroboduus (Marbod). King of the Marcomanni, a Suevian by birth, and brought up at the court of Augustus. After his return to his native country he succeeded in establishing a powerful kingdom in Central Germany along the northern bank of the Danube. (See SUEVI.) Having become an object of suspicion to the other German tribes, he was expelled from his dominions by the Goth Catualda about A.D. 19, and took refuge in Italy, where Tiberius allowed him to remain until his death, which took place at Ravenna in A.D. 35 (Tac. *Ann.* ii. 44–46; Vell. Pat. ii. 108).

Maron. In Homer, the hero of sweet wine, son of Evanthes and priest of Apollo in Maronea in Thrace. He gave Odysseus the cask which the hero carried with him to the Cyclops (*Odyss.* ix. 197).

Maronēa (Μαρώνεια). A town on the southern coast of Thrace, on the lake Ismaris, belonged originally to the Cicones, but afterwards colonized from Chios. It was celebrated for its excellent wine, and is mentioned by Homer as the residence of Maron, son of Evanthes, grandson of Dionysus and Ariadné, and priest of Apollo.

Marpessa (Μάρπησσα). Daughter of Evenus and Alcippé. See IDAS.

Marpessa (Μάρπησσα). A mountain in Paros, from which the celebrated Parian marble was obtained. Hence Vergil speaks of *Marpesia cautes* (i. e. Parian).

Marra. A hoe or rake with a broad head and teeth, used in Roman husbandry for clearing the ground of weeds and other encumbrances (Columella, x. 70, 88; Juv. xv. 166.)

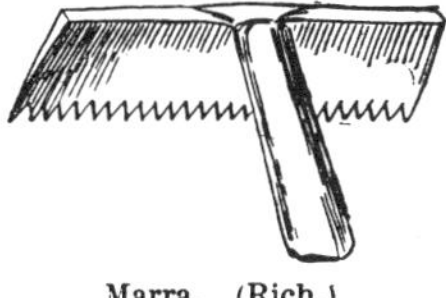
Marra. (Rich.)

Marriage. See CONUBIUM; MATRIMONIUM.

Marrucīni or **Marucīni.** A brave and warlike people in Italy, of the Sabellian race, occupying a narrow slip of country along the right bank of the river Aternus, and bounded on the north by the Vestini, on the west by the Peligni and Marsi, on the south by the Frentani, and on the east by the Adriatic Sea. Their chief town was Teaté. With their neighbours the Marsi, Peligni, etc., they submitted to the Romans in B.C. 304 (Livy, ix. 41).

Marruvium or **Maruvium.** The chief town of the Marsi (who are therefore called *gens Maruvia* by Vergil), situated on the east bank of the lake Fucinus.

Mars (also MAVORS, MAMERS). After Iupiter the principal deity of the inhabitants of Italy, and therefore honoured with particular reverence by the Latins and Romans from the very earliest times, especially as the latter regarded him as the father of Romulus, the founder of Rome. He was held to be the son of Iuno, who bore him in consequence of touching a wonderful spring-flower, and the husband of Nerio or Nerienė, a goddess of strength. Through the emphasizing of one of his attributes he gradually came to be considered as, above all, the god of war; for originally he was at the same time one of the mightiest gods of nature, the Vedic Marut, who accords fertility and protection to fields and herds.

The first month of the old Roman year was dedicated to him as the fertilizing god of spring; in the very ancient chant of the Arval Brothers (see FRATRES ARVALES), at the May-day festival of the Dea Dia, the help and protection of Mars were demanded. In earlier times he was also invoked at the hallowing of the fields (see AMBARVALIA), that he might bless the family, the field, and the cattle, and keep off sickness, bad weather, and all else that did harm. (Cf. ROBIGUS.) In later times the names of Ceres and Bacchus were substituted for his on this particular occasion. At the festival on 15th October a horse was sacrificed to him to insure the fair growth of the seed that had been sown. As god of war (cf. QUIRINUS), his symbols were the ravenous wolf, the prophetic and warlike woodpecker, and the lance. When war broke out, the general solemnly invoked his aid, by smiting his holy lance and the holy shields (*ancilia;* see SALII) with the cry, "Mars, awake!" (*Mars vigila!*) Many sacrifices were also offered to him during the campaign and before battle; and in his name military honours were conferred. The Field of Mars (Campus Martius) was dedicated to him as the patron god of warlike exercises; contests with battle-steeds, called Equirria, were there held in his honour on the 27th February, 14th March, and 15th October. On the last-mentioned day the horse on the right of the victorious team was sacrificed on his altar in the Field of Mars; it was known as the horse of October (*October equus*), and its blood was collected and preserved in the temple of Vesta, and used at the Palilia for purposes of purification. The cult of Mars was entrusted to a special priest, the flamen Martialis (see FLAMEN), and the college of the Salii (q. v.), which worshipped him more particularly as god of war. His principal festival was in March, the month sacred to him. As early as the time of King Tullus Hostilius, Pavor and Pallor (Fear and Pallor) are said to have been worshipped as his companions in the fight, in sanctuaries of their own. Augustus caused him to be honoured in a new form, as Mars Ultor (the avenger of Caesar), in the magnificent temple in the Forum Augusti, consecrated B.C. 2, where statues of him and of Venus, as the two divine ancestors of the Julian family, were set up. In later times he was identified completely with the Greek Ares. See ARES.

Mars, FIELD OF. See CAMPUS MARTIUS.

Mars' Hill. See AREOPAGUS.

Marsacii. A people in Gallia Belgica, on one of the islands formed by the Rhine.

Marsi. (1) An Italian people of Sabellian race, living on the high land in which Lake Fucinus is situated, and surrounded by the Apennines. Their chief town was Marruvium. Owing to their knowledge of herbs, which they used medicinally, they got a reputation for a skill in magic (Verg. *Aen.* vii. 750–758; Gell. xvi. 11), and were said to be descended from the enchantress Circé. In B.C. 304, the Marsi, Peligni, and others concluded a peace with Rome, but later took a prominent part in the Social War for the Roman franchise, which from their bravery is often called the Marsic War. In imperial times they furnished a valuable contingent to the Roman army (Hor. *Carm.* ii. 20, 18; iii. 5, 9). (2) A German people, dwelling by the Amisia (Ems). They were allied with the Cherusci.

Marsigni. A people in the southeast of Germany, of Suevic extraction (Tac. *Germ.* 43).

Marsupium.

Marsupium (μαρσύπιον). A money-bag or purse, often represented in ancient works of art in the hands of Mercury, the god of gain (cf. Plaut. *Rud.* v. 2, 26).

Marsus, DOMITIUS. A Roman poet of the Augustan Age, who wrote a collection of epigrams (*Cicuta*), a treatise on the use of wit in oratory (*De Urbanitate*), and in epic (*Amazonis*). He died about B.C. 4. He is mentioned several times by Martial (e. g. iv. 29, 7; and vii. 29, 7). The few fragments of his works that remain will be found in the *Fragmenta Pöet. Lat.* of Bährens, 346 (Leipzig, 1886).

Marsȳas (Μαρσύας). A Silenus of Phrygian legend (really god of the river of the same name near the old Phrygian town Celaenae), son of Hyagnis or of Olympus. He was the typical player on the flute. Among the Phrygians the flute entered into the worship of Cybelé and Dionysus, and Marsyas is said to have instructed Olympus in playing upon that instrument. According to a Greek legend, Athené had invented the flute, and then cast it aside because it distorted the features of the player. Marsyas took it up, and became so skilful as to challenge Apollo, the patron god of the lyre. The Muses having declared him vanquished, the god flayed him; his skin was hung up in the cave from which the river Marsyas issued, and was said to move about joyfully when a flute was played. King Midas, who had decided in his favour, received as punishment from Apollo a pair of ass's ears. The contest was a favourite subject in art. See MIDAS.

Marsўas (Μαρσύας). (1) A small but rapid river of Phrygia, emptying into the Maeander at Celaenae. (2) A river of Caria, falling into the Maeander nearly opposite Tralles. (3) A tributary of the Orontes in Syria. (4) The plain of Syria, through which the upper Orontes flows.

Martiālis. (1) M. VALERIUS, a writer of Latin epigrams, was born at Bilbilis in Spain, in the third year of Claudius, A.D. 43. He came to Rome in the thirteenth year of Nero, 66; and after residing in the metropolis thirty-five years, he returned to the place of his birth, in the third year of Trajan, 100. He lived there for upwards of three years at least, on the property of his wife, a lady named Marcella, whom he seems to have married after his return to Bilbilis. His death cannot have taken place before 104. His fame was extended, and his books were eagerly sought for not only in the city, but also in Gaul, Germany, and Britain; he secured the patronage of the emperors Titus and Domitian, obtained by his influence the freedom of the State for several of his friends, and received for himself, although apparently without family, the privileges accorded to those who were the fathers of three children (*ius trium liberorum*), together with the rank of tribune and the rights of the equestrian order. His circumstances appear to have been easy during his residence at Rome, for he had a mansion in the city, whose situation he describes, and a suburban villa near Nomentum, to which he frequently alludes with pride.

The extant works of Martial consist of a collection of short poems, all included under the general appellation *Epigrammata*, upwards of 1500 in number, divided into fourteen books. Those which form the last two books, usually distinguished respectively as *Xenia* and *Apophoreta*, amounting to 350, consist of couplets, descriptive of a vast variety of small objects, chiefly articles of food or clothing, such as were usually sent as presents among friends during the Saturnalia and on other festive occasions. In addition to the above, nearly all the printed copies include thirty-three epigrams, forming a book apart from the rest, which has been commonly known as *Liber de Spectaculis*, because the contents relate to the shows exhibited by Titus and Domitian; but there is no ancient authority for the title. The different books were collected and published by the author, sometimes singly and sometimes several at one time. The *Liber de Spectaculis* and the first nine books of the regular series involve a great number of historical allusions, extending from the games of Titus (80) down to the return of Domitian from the Sarmatian expedition, in January, 94. All these books were composed at Rome, except the Third, which was written during a tour in Gallia Togata. The Tenth Book was published twice: the first edition was given hastily to the world; the second, that which we now read (x. 2), celebrates the arrival of Trajan at Rome, after his accession to the throne (99). The Eleventh Book seems to have been published at Rome, early in 100, and at the close of the year he returned to Bilbilis. After keeping silence for three years (xii. prooem.), the Twelfth Book was despatched from Bilbilis to Rome (xii. 3, 18), and must therefore be assigned to 104. Books xiii. and xiv., *Xenia* and *Apophoreta*, were written chiefly under Domitian, although the composition may have been spread over the holidays of many years. It is well known that the word epigram (ἐπίγραμμα), which originally denoted simply "an inscription," was, in process of time, applied to any brief metrical effusion, whatever the subject might be, or whatever the form under which it was presented. Martial, however, first placed the epigram upon the narrow basis which it now occupies, and from his time the term has been in a great measure restricted to denote a short poem, in which all the thoughts and expressions converge to one sharp point, which forms the termination of the piece. See EPIGRAMMA.

Martial's epigrams are distinguished by singular fertility of imagination, prodigious flow of wit, and delicate felicity of language; and from no source do we derive more copious information on the national customs and social habits of the Romans during the first century of the Empire. But, however much we may admire the genius of the author, we can feel no respect for one whose fulsome servility towards the great is equalled only by the frightful obscenity of much that he has written—an obscenity scarcely conceivable in modern times. He himself seems to feel a certain shame for so pandering to the corrupt tastes of his rich and dissolute patrons, and in one epigram he tries to draw the line between his life and his writings. "My Muse is wanton, but my life is pure" (i. 4, 8); and in the prose dedication to the First Book he explains that he is only following out the traditions of this form of literature; but these are excuses which, to many minds, only heighten the enormity of his offence.

The principal value of Martial's epigrams is in the insight they give us into the daily life of the times, since they abound in personal details, and are an indispensable contribution towards the *Culturgeschichte* of Ancient Rome. In modern literature they have been continually imitated and translated, but rarely equalled except now and then by the French.

The MSS. fall into three "families," of which the typical representatives are a Paris Codex (T) of the ninth century, a Codex Palatinus (P) of the fifteenth century, and an Edinburgh Codex (E) of the tenth century. See the critical account in the editions of Schneidewin and Friedländer. The best texts are those of Schneidewin (Grimma, 1842), Friedländer, 2 vols. (Leipzig, 1886), with a list of words; Gilbert (Leipzig, 1886). Friedländer's edition contains explanatory notes, but the best commentary on the subject-matter is his *Sittengeschichte Roms*, 3 vols (6th ed. Leipzig, 1888–1890). Editions of selected epigrams with English notes are those of Paley and Stone (London, 1881); Sellar and Ramsay (Edinburgh, 1884); Stephenson (2d ed. London, 1888); and one (announced) by C. Knapp (N. Y. 1895). See Brandt, *De Martialis Poetae Vita* (Berlin, 1853); Van Stockum, *De Martialis Vita et Scriptis* (The Hague, 1884); and on his language, etc., Paukstadt, *De Martiale Catulli Imitatore* (Halle, 1876); Zingerle, *Martials Ovidstudien* (Innsbruck, 1877); and Stephani, *De Martiale Verborum Novatore* (Breslau, 1889).

(2) Q. Gargilius Martiālis, a Roman writer and a contemporary of Alexander Severus, who is cited by Vopiscus (*Prob.* ii. 7). There are extant some fragments on veterinary surgery and husbandry, bearing the name of Gargilius Martialis; and Angelo Mai discovered on a Neapolitan palimpsest a part of a work on gardens. The fourth book of the *Medicina Plinii*, or extracts on medicine from Pliny, was made up of citations from Gargilius Martialis. The same person also wrote a sketch of Alexander Severus. The greater part of the botanical fragments was printed in Lüneburg in 1832; and the veterinary fragments by Schuch (Donaueschingen, 1857).

Martiālis Flamen. See Flamen.

Martiānus Capella. See Capella.

Martiniānus. A Roman allied with Licinius during the last struggle of the latter with Constantine. Constantine put him to death in A.D. 323. See Constantinus.

Martius Campus. See Campus Martius.

Martyria (*μαρτυρία*). Testimony given by witnesses; a deposition. The following legal terms are those most used with reference to the act of giving testimony: *μαρτυρεῖν τινι*, to testify in one's favour; *κατὰ μαρτυρεῖν τινος*, to testify against one; *μαρτύρεσθαι*, to call a witness; *διαμαρτύρεσθαι*, to call upon those present to notice what is transpiring, so as to swear to it afterwards; *κλητεύειν*, to subpœna a witness; *ἐξόμνυσθαι*, to swear that one knows nothing of the facts in question; *ἐπιορκεῖν*, to perjure one's self; *ψευδομαρτυρεῖν*, to testify falsely (not on oath); *μάρτυς*, a witness; *νόμιμος ὅρκος*, a legal oath. See Anacrisis; Diké; Iusiurandum; Judicial Procedure.

At Athens only freemen, males, and adults were legally entitled to bear witness in court; except that a slave could testify in a case of murder, and their evidence could also be accepted after torture. A woman could take an oath if offered her as a challenge (*πρόκλησις*). Disfranchised citizens (*ἠτιμωμένοι*) could not appear as witnesses; and neither party to a suit could testify on his own behalf, but must answer such questions as were asked him by the other side. No other persons could refuse to testify, as this duty was regarded as one claimed by the State. As to depositions made by those unable to attend in court, see Ecmartyria. A person thrice convicted of giving false witness was *ipso facto* disfranchised. For examination after torture (*βάσανος*), see Tormentum.

Martyropŏlis (Μαρτυρόπολις). A city of Sophenē in Armenia Maior, strongly fortified under Justinian.

Marullus, Gaius Epidius. A tribune of the people who, with his colleague L. Caesetius Flavus, removed the diadem that had been placed upon the statue of Iulius Caesar. He also tried to bring to trial the persons who had saluted Caesar as king, but the dictator deprived him of the tribunician power and expelled him from the Senate (Suet. *Iul.* 79).

Maruvium. See Marruvium.

Masăda (Μάσαδα). A fortress on the Dead Sea built by Jonathan Maccabaeus and strengthened by Herod. After the capture of Jerusalem it fell into the hands of the Romans after the garrison had all committed suicide.

Mascas (Μασκᾶς). An eastern tributary of the Euphrates in Mesopotamia.

Masinissa (Μασσανάσσης). A king of the Numidians, son of Gala, king of the Massylians, the easternmost of the two great tribes into which the Numidians were at that time divided. In the Second Punic War he at first fought on the side of the Carthaginians in Spain (B.C. 212), but afterwards deserted their cause and joined the Romans. On his return to Africa he was attacked by the Carthaginians and his neighbour Syphax, and with difficulty maintained his ground till the arrival of Scipio in Africa (B.C. 204). He rendered important service to Scipio, and reduced Cirta, the capital of Syphax. Among the captives that fell into his hands on this occasion was Sophonisba, the wife of Syphax, who had been formerly promised in marriage to Masinissa himself. The story of his hasty marriage with her, and its tragical termination, is related elsewhere. (See Sophonisba). In the decisive battle of Zama (B.C. 202) Masinissa commanded the cavalry of the right wing. On the conclusion of the peace between Rome and Carthage he was rewarded with the greater part of the territories which had belonged to Syphax, in addition to his hereditary dominions. For the next fifty years Masinissa reigned in peace. He died in the second year of the Third Punic War, B.C. 148, at the advanced age of 90, having retained in an extraordinary degree his bodily strength and activity to the last. He left three sons—Micipsa, Mastanabal, and Gulussa—among whom Scipio Africanus the Younger divided the kingdom.

Masks. See Persona.

Massa, Baebius or Bebius. A Roman accused by Pliny the Younger and Herennius Senecio of plundering the province of Baetica, of which he had been governor, A.D. 93. He was condemned, but escaped punishment by the favour of Domitian; and from this time became one of the informers and favourites of the tyrant.

Massa (Μάσσα). (1) A river on the western coast of Libya Interior. (2) Massa Veternensis. A city of Etruria northeast of Populonium.

Massaesȳli. See Mauretania; Numidia.

Massăga (τὰ Μάσσαγα). The capital of the Indian people called the Assaceni.

Massagĕtae (Μασσαγέται). A wild and warlike people of Central Asia, north of the Iaxartes (the Araxes of Herodotus) and the Sea of Aral, and on the peninsula between this lake and the Caspian. Herodotus appears to include under the name all the nomad tribes of Asia east of the Caspian. It was in an expedition against them that Cyrus the Great was defeated and slain. See Cyrus.

Massĭcus Mons. A mountain in the northwest of Campania, near the frontiers of Latium, celebrated for its excellent wine, the produce of the vineyards on the southern slope of the mountain. The famous Falernian wine came from the eastern side of this mountain. See VINUM.

Massicўtus and **Massicўtes** (Μασσικύτης). An extensive mountain chain of Lycia.

Massilia, called by the Greeks Μασσαλία (Marseilles). A Greek city in Gallia Narbonensis, on the coast of the Mediterranean, in the country of the Salyes, founded by the Phocaeans of Asia Minor about B.C. 600. It was situated on a promontory, connected with the mainland by a narrow isthmus, and washed on three sides by the sea. Its excellent harbour (Lacydon) was formed by a small inlet of the sea, about half a mile long and a quarter of a mile broad. This harbour had only a narrow opening, and before it lay an island, where ships had good anchorage. At an early period the Massilienses cultivated the friendship of the Romans, to whom they always continued faithful allies. Massilia was for many centuries one of the most important commercial cities in the ancient world, and founded a number of other towns, such as Antipolis (Antibes) and Nicaea (Nice). In wealth and power it even excited the jealousy of Carthage, which led to a war between the two cities, in which the Massilienses won a naval victory (Thuc. i. 13). Because of its friendship for Rome, the Romans left it independent with its own constitution and government, which was aristocratic or oligarchic, the city being ruled by a Senate of 600 called Timuchi, who acted through smaller councillors (Cic. *De Rep.* i. 27, 43). In the civil war between Caesar and Pompey (B.C. 49) it espoused the cause of the latter, but after a protracted siege, in which it lost its fleet, it was obliged to submit to Caesar. Its inhabitants had long paid attention to literature and philosophy; and under the early emperors it became one of the chief seats of learning, to which the sons of many Romans resorted in order to complete their studies.

Massīva. (1) A Numidian, grandson of Gala, king of the Massylians, and nephew of Masinissa, whom he accompanied into Spain. (2) Son of Gulussa, and grandson of Masinissa. He was assassinated at Rome by order of Iugurtha, because he had put in a claim to the kingdom of Numidia.

Massurius Sabīnus. See SABINUS.

Massўli (Μασσυλεῖς). See MAURETANIA; NUMIDIA.

Mastanăbal or **Manastăbal.** The youngest of the three legitimate sons of Masinissa (q. v.). He was the father of Iugurtha (q. v.).

Master. See DOMINUS; SERVUS.

Mastiffs. See CANIS.

Masts. See NAVIS.

Masurius Sabīnus. See SABINUS.

Matches. See IGNIARIA.

Materialists. See EPICURUS; PHILOSOPHIA.

Mater Matūta. See MATUTA.

Maternus Firmĭcus. See FIRMICUS.

Matho. A leader of the Carthaginian mercenaries in their revolt after the First Punic War, B.C. 241. He was at last made prisoner and put to death. See CARTHAGO; HAMILCAR.

Matiāna (Ματιανή). The southwesternmost district of Media Atropatenē, along the mountains separating Media from Assyria, inhabited by the Matiani.

Matīnus. A mountain in Apulia, running out into the sea, one of the offshoots of Mount Garganus, and frequently mentioned by Horace, in consequence of his being a native of Apulia.

Matisco. The modern Mâcon; a town of the Aedui in Gallia Lugdunensis, on the Arar.

Matius Calvēna, GAIUS. A Roman knight, the friend of Caesar and Cicero, and after Caesar's death, an adherent of Augustus. It is possibly this person who translated the *Iliad* of Homer into Latin verse; and he certainly wrote a gastronomic work in three books, entitled respectively *Cocus*, *Cetarius*, and *Salmagarius*, the fragments of which were edited by Zell (Stuttgart, 1829). A letter of his to Cicero will be found in the collection *Ad Familiares* (xi. 28). A hash was named after him (*minutal Matianum*). Cf. Apic. iv. 174; Pliny, *H. N.* xv. 49.

Matrālia. The festival of mothers at Rome. See MATUTA.

Matrimonium, also **Nuptiae** (γάμος). Marriage.

I. GREEK.—Athenian tradition ascribed the introduction of the marriage relation to Cecrops (Athen. xiii. 2), before whose time men were said to have had wives in common, as was the case in historic times among the non-Hellenic tribes on the borders of the Greek world—e. g. the Massagetae, Nasamones, and Ausenses (Herod. i. 126; iv. 172, 180). In the rest of Greece monogamy was of slow growth as against promiscuity of sexual relation; yet in the *Iliad* and *Odyssey* the households described are monogamistic, even though concubines are mentioned. (See CONCUBINA.) Throughout the greater part of Greece the position of the married women was a very subordinate one, the chief exception being found in the usage of Sparta, and to a less degree of Crete and Cyrenē and, in general, the Doric States. (See Aristot. *Polit.* ii. 9; Plut. *Lac. Apophtheg.*) As to illicit relations between the sexes, see MERETRIX.

We may now consider the subject of Athenian marriage. Marriage at Athens was made compulsory by Solon (Plut. *De Amore Prol.* 2); but the law fell into disuse. A youthful citizen was not allowed to marry until his name was entered in the tribal register (ληξιαρχικὸν γραμματεῖον). The restrictions as to whom he might marry differed from those imposed in modern times, being in part looser, in part more severe. Prohibitions on the ground of consanguinity were less numerous than with us. A man might not marry a direct ancestor or descendant; nor might he marry step-mother or step-daughter, mother-in-law or daughter-in-law; nor, with an exception to be noticed, his sister. The marriage of Oedipus was looked on with horror, and the fact that it was accidental was not regarded as an alleviation. On the other hand, the marriage of a brother with a half-sister on the father's side did sometimes occur (Demosth. *c. Eubul.* p. 1304, § 20; Plut. *Themist.* 32). Marriage with a niece was common; with an aunt naturally less so, but there was nothing to forbid it.

The prohibition of marriage between a citizen and an alien belongs to a different class from the prohibition by reason of relationship. It would hardly seem to have existed in the early period of Athenian history (Herod. vi. 130). The influx of foreigners into Athens in the time of Pericles was doubtless the cause that necessitated a more stringent law—namely, that both the parents of a citizen must be citizens; whence it resulted that marriage with an alien was forbidden (Plut. *Pericl.* 37).

Marriage at Athens took place in two ways: either by *ἐγγύησις* or by *ἐπιδικασία*. Ἐγγύησις was the ordinary method, and meant the act of the father or guardian (*κύριος*) of a maiden in giving her in betrothal to her future husband. The act was a solemn one, the relatives of either side being witnesses. Whenever any woman had a *κύριος*, marriage could take place by no other method than this. If, however, a woman were left an heiress (*ἐπίκληρος*) without having a *κύριος*, then the next of kin might claim her in marriage, preference being given to kindred on the father's side; such a claim was called *ἐπιδικασία*, and was brought in the first instance before the archon. (See EPICLERUS.) The public interest in such a claim being allowed lay in the danger of dissensions being caused by rival suitors, of which Aristotle (*Polit.* v. 4) gives instances. If the heiress were poor (*θῆσσα*), it was likely that no claimant would come forward; in this case the archon was bound to compel the next of kin either himself to marry the heiress or to portion her and give her in marriage (Demosth. *c. Macart.* p. 1067, § 51). It is to be inferred that the next of kin was regarded as *κύριος* of the heiress in such a case as this. Legitimate children at Athens were invariably the offspring of a marriage ratified according to one of these forms.

At the time of the betrothal the dowry of the bride was settled, and this was a most important point for her future welfare. For the wife was reckoned to have no claim at all on her husband's property. Supposing her husband died, even the most distant cousin might inherit from him; but the wife, never. Nay, she might not even continue to reside in his house after his death, unless she pleaded pregnancy; in that case she would come under the protection of the archon, and would remain undisturbed until the child was born (Demosth. *c. Macart.* p. 1076, § 75). Hence the dowry was the only security to the wife against extreme poverty in the event of her husband's death, or if she were divorced; the husband, therefore, had to give a guarantee for its return in the shape of some piece of landed property. It would, however, be incorrect to suppose that the dowry would ever become the wife's absolute property; it would in the case supposed revert to her *κύριος*, who would either support her from it or give her in marriage again. But as against her husband or his creditors, it was absolutely hers. The dowry, as has been said, did not exist in Homer's time, and was a gradual growth; Plato disapproved of it (*De Leg.* vi. 777 A) as tending to produce avarice; in early times it was small.

The marriage ceremonial at Athens, among the higher classes, was more elaborate than with us. The consecration of all girls to Artemis, when they were ten years old, at the festival Brauronia, stood in intimate relation with it. When the marriage itself drew near, the sacrifice to the tutelar gods of marriage (*θεοὶ γαμήλιοι*) took place. This was performed by the father, and might take place some days before the marriage, or on the day itself. As to who the tutelary deities were, custom appears to have varied. Diodorus Siculus (v. 73) names Zeus and Heré; but Pollux names Heré, Artemis, and the Fates (iii. 38): Artemis is also mentioned in relation to Boeotia and Locris in Plutarch (*Aristid.* 20); and the Nymphs are mentioned in Plutarch (*Amat. Narr.* 1). The sacrifice itself was called *προτέλεια γάμων*, or *προγάμεια*, and it was regarded as a dedication of the bride to the deities named, some locks of the bride's hair (*ἀπαρχαί*) being offered as a symbol of the dedication. On the wedding day itself bride and bridegroom bathed in water drawn from a particular fountain of running water: at Athens this was the fountain Callirrhoë, also called *ἐννεάκρουνος* (Thuc. ii. 15). The water from this fountain was carried either by a boy or a girl, from which custom was probably derived that other custom of placing over the tombs of those who died unmarried the image of a girl carrying water. Late in the evening of the wedding day the bridegroom brought his bride from her parents' house on a car (*ἅμαξα*) drawn by horses, mules, or oxen; on either side of her sat the bridegroom and his "best man" (*παράνυμφος* or *πάροχος*, Arist. *Av.* 1735). In front of the car went the torch-bearing procession (*δᾷδες νυμφικαί*), the nuptial torch having been lit by the mother of the bride or of the bridegroom; bride and bridegroom were crowned with chaplets, and clothed in festal attire, as also were the attendants, the bride being covered with a long veil; congratulations were poured out by relations, friends, and well-wishers, and the cry Ὑμὴν Ὑμέναι' ὦ resounded to the sweet melody of flutes (Aristoph. *Pax*, 1316–1356). On their reaching the bridegroom's house, a peculiar custom prevailed in Boeotia: the axle of the car was burned, to symbolize the irreversible step taken. The bridegroom who had been married before could not bring his bride home in this exultant way; a friend (*νυμφαγωγός*) in that case brought the bride to him from her house. At the entrance to the bridegroom's house sweetmeats (*καταχύσματα*) were thrown upon the wedded pair; the doors of the house were covered with garlands, as were those of the bride's house.

Then followed the wedding-feast (*θοίνη γαμική*), usually in the house of the bridegroom—one of the most important parts of the entire ceremonial; for the guests were in fact witnesses to the marriage, and their testimony was the final and single proof that it had taken place, since documentary evidence was not looked for or provided (Demosth. *c. Onet.* p. 869, § 20; Athen. v. p. 185 a). At the wedding-feast women were allowed to be present, though at different tables from the men (Lucian, *Conviv.* 8). Sesame-cakes, symbolical of a fertile marriage, formed a part of the feast. At the conclusion of the feast the bride was conducted, veiled, into the bridal-chamber; the bridegroom closed the door; and a law of Solon enjoined that the bride and bridegroom should eat a quince together, to symbolize the sweetness of their conversation (Plut. *Sol.* 20). The epithalamium (q. v.) was then sung before the door of the bridal-chamber by a chorus of maidens, and the song was accompanied with dancing. But the Scholiast on this passage tells us that some epithalamia were sung in the early morning to wake the wedded pair, the two kinds being called *κατακοιμητικά* and *διηγερτικά* respectively.

On the second or third day after the marriage the bride for the first time showed herself without a veil, and the gifts which she on that day received from her relatives were thence called *ἀνα-*

καλυπτήρια or ὀπτήρια. Among them was a garment (ἀπαυλιστηρία) presented by the bride to the bridegroom, who, on the succeeding night, did not sleep with his bride, but in his father-in-law's house, the bride being unveiled, and the ἀνακαλυπτήρια presented the day after.

An offering to Aphrodité was made by the wedded pair, either on the wedding-day or on the day after. Another ceremony observed after marriage was the sacrifice which the husband offered up on the occasion of his bride being registered among his own phrateres.

Marriages generally took place in the winter (Aristot. *Polit.* vii. 16); and the month Gamelion (our January) derived its name from the favour in which it was held for this purpose. The fourth day of the month, according to Hesiod (*Op.* 800), was the most favourable day; and as in a lunar month this would be the day on which the first crescent of the new moon appeared, the interpretation of Proclus seems correct: that the day when sun and moon met in the same quarter of the heavens was the day when man and woman might best meet in wedlock. Pindar, however (*Isthm.* vii. 44), and Euripides (*Iph. in Aul.* 717) prefer the full moon.

After marriage the wife lived with the other female inmates of the house in the γυναικωνῖτις, or women's apartments: in a large house these would be a separate building, connected by a passage with the men's rooms. The wife then had the superintendence of the entire household: she had charge of the education of the boys till they were put under a master, of the girls till they were married; she tended the sick, whether free or slave; the kitchen, the furniture, the stores came under her; and last, not least, the ταλάσια ἔργα (Xen. *Oecon.* vii. 6), all that related to the spinning and weaving of wool and the making of clothes, for it must be remembered that the clothes of an ancient household were mostly made within the house itself. If the establishment were a large one, the wife would have a house-keeper (ταμία) to assist her. If the husband were alone, the wife would dine with him, and familiar jesting would pass between them (Lysias, l. c.), or perhaps even serious conversation on politics (Demosth. *c. Neaera*, p. 1382, § 142); but if the husband had other male friends with him, it was thought indecorous for the wife to appear.

It will be seen that the wife had no lack of duties, but they were duties that would naturally be felt to be monotonous; and it is interesting to find that religious exercises were then, as in later times, one of the chief resources of the married woman.

II. Roman.—Marriage was among the Romans a complete union for life between a man and one woman, which had for its main object the procreation of children (*liberûm quaesundûm gratia*). To marry and beget children, who could keep up the *sacra familiaria*, was the religious duty of a Roman, and also a duty to the State.

The only marriage recognized in early Roman law was that which was conformable to the Ius Civile, and which was called *iustae nuptiae*, in later times also *iustum matrimonium* (Ulpian, v. 1, 2). To this marriage of *ius civile* the *matrimonium iuris gentium*, or marriage according to gentile law, came to be opposed (Gaius, i. 87). The word *matrimonium* seems to have been used originally to signify a marriage which was not a civil marriage, the child of such marriage following the condition of his mother instead of that of his father, as would have been the case if he had been born from *iustae nuptiae*.

A Roman civil marriage was either *cum conventione uxoris in manum viri*, or it was *sine in manum conventione* (Ulpian, xxvi. 7). The marriage *cum conventione in manum* differed from that *sine conventione*, in the effect which it had on the condition of the wife.

By the marriage *cum conventione*, the wife came into the power (*manus*) of her husband, or, if he were a *filiusfamilias*, of his *paterfamilias;* leaving her own *familia*, she passed into the *familia* of her husband, and was to him in the relation of a *filiafamilias* (Cic. *Top.* 3, 14; Gaius, ii. 159). In marriage *sine conventione* the wife did not pass into the power of her husband; she was, as it were, a stranger (*extranea*) in his household, her relation to her own family remaining as before the marriage; she did not share in the *familiaria sacra* of her husband, and bore no civil relation to her own children. See Manus.

A marriage *cum conventione* was a necessary condition to make a woman a materfamilias in the strict sense of the word. In the marriage *sine conventione* the wife was merely *uxor;* that is, a wife and nothing more (Cic. l. c.).

The right of entering into a valid civil marriage is called the *ius conubii*. The *ius conubii* belonged only to Roman citizens; the cases in which it at any time existed between parties not both Roman citizens, were exceptions to the general rule. "Roman men citizens," says Ulpian (*Fragm.* 5, 4, 11), "have *conubium* with Roman women citizens (*Romanae cives*), but with Latinae and Peregrinae only in those cases where it has been permitted. With slaves there is no *conubium*."

Originally there was no *conubium* between the patricians and plebeians, but this was granted by the Lex Canuleia. See Lex, p. 941.

The Lex Iulia et Papia Poppaea placed certain restrictions on marriage as to the parties between whom it could take place. (See Lex, p. 942.) Thus certain marriages were prohibited on account of disparagement, as marriages between senators and freedwomen. The law allowed free-born persons (*ingenui*) to marry freedwomen (*libertinae*). Persons within certain prohibited degrees of relationship could not intermarry. A union of persons within the prohibited degrees was an incestuous one. Relations who had the *ius osculi*, or right to kiss one another, could not marry one another. See Klenze, *Das Familienrecht der Cognaten und Affinen nach röm. und verwandten Rechten*, p. 16; and Muirhead, *Roman Law*, iii. p. 26.

In early times there could be no marriage between cognates within the seventh degree, but subsequently the prohibited circle was made less wide. There could be no marriage between ascendants and descendants, whether the relation was natural or by adoption; and a man could not marry an adopted daughter or granddaughter, even after he had emancipated her. Brothers and sisters, whether of the whole or half blood, could not marry, but a man might marry a sister by adoption after her emancipation, or after his own emancipation. It became legal to marry a brother's daughter after Claudius had set the example by marrying Agrippina; but the rule was not carried further than the example, and in the time of Gaius it remained unlawful for a man to marry his sister's daughter (Gaius, i. 62; Tac. *Ann.* xii. 5; Sueton. *Claud.* 26). Constantine prohibited a marriage between a man and his brother's daughter. Marriages between first cousins were in later times recognized.

Betrothal was a necessary preliminary to marriage, on which see SPONSALIA.

A marriage *cum conventione* might be effected by *confarreatio, coemptio*, or *usus*. *Confarreatio* was a form of marriage peculiar to the patricians, while *coemptio* seems to have been originally confined to the plebeians; but when *conubium* was extended to the plebeians, *coemptio* became a common form of intermarriage between the two orders. *Confarreatio* or *farreum* was a religious form of marriage, which principally consisted in an offering, with solemn words, of spelt bread (*panis farreus*) to Iupiter Farreus, in the presence of ten witnesses, the Pontifex Maximus and Flamen Dialis taking part in the ceremony. See COEMPTIO; USUS.

It remains to describe the actual ceremonies of Roman marriage: and it must be premised (1) that there was some difference according to the precise form of marriage adopted, though this distinction gradually disappeared and (2) that, as was said above, the greater part of marriage formality was voluntary, and that then, as in our own day, there might be weddings of a far simpler character. When therefore the complete ceremony of the most elaborate kind is described, it must be understood that a great deal of it was often omitted, and the marriage rites narrowed to little beyond the procession. In the choice of the wedding-day, superstition played a large part. May (as by many even now) and the first half of June were unlucky for marriages (Ovid, *Fasti*, v. 487; vi. 225). The reason was that the month of May took its general character from the festivals of the Lemuria (q. v.). In the first part of June came *dies religiosi* connected with the worship of Vesta. Besides these periods, it was necessary to avoid the *dies parentales*, Feb. 13–21; the first half of March; the three days of the opening of the lower world (*mundus patet*), viz.: Aug. 24, Oct. 5, Nov. 8; and also the days of Kalends, Ides, and Nones.

At the *sponsalia*, besides the formal words of the parent or guardian, *Spondesne? Spondeo* (Plaut. *Aul.* ii. 2, 78), the bridegroom gave the bride a present, as an earnest or pledge (*arra, pignus*), which was often a ring placed on the fourth finger of the left hand (our "ring finger"), which Gellius (x. 10) says is connected by a nerve with the heart.

On the day before the marriage the bride put aside her *toga praetexta*, which, with other belongings of childhood, was laid before the Lares, and put on the *tunica recta*, or *regilla*, which was woven in one piece in the old-fashioned way at the upright loom. The bride wore this dress also at the marriage, and a flame-coloured veil (*flammeum*), with which she was said *nubere caput*. The dress was fastened by a woollen girdle (*cingulum*) in the *nodus Herculeus*, as to the significance of which there is some difference of opinion. It has been explained by some as intended to secure a fruitful marriage, because Hercules had many children: Göll takes it to be an amulet against the evil eye (*fascinum*). But it is perhaps nearer the truth to take it to be the symbol of a stable marriage, and perhaps the original of the "true lovers' knot." The hair was arranged in six locks (*sex crines*) parted by the point of a spear (*hasta caelibaris*), and held in place by *vittae* or bands. Hence the words *crines* and *vitta* are used by poets as a synonym for marriage. The custom of parting it with a spear is perhaps a relic of the old marriage by capture, and may convey the idea of the word δορίληπτος. The bride had also a wreath of flowers and sacred herbs (*verbenae*) gathered by herself, and the bridegroom wore a similar wreath (Plut. *Pomp.* 55). As an account of the dressing of the bride, the passage in Claudian, *VI. Cons. Hon.* 523–528, is well worth reading.

In the house of the bride, which was decked with garlands (Juv. vi. 227; Stat. *Silv.* i. 2, 230), were assembled the relations, friends, and clients, as an *officium* (Juv. ii. 132). Then the omens were taken and announced by the *auspices* (Cic. *Pro Cluent.* 4, 14; Juv. x. 336), with the sacrifice of a sheep (cf. Verg. *Aen.* iv. 56). It had always been the custom to begin the sacred ceremony of *confarreatio* by consulting the omens, and the practice probably was as a rule extended to all marriages (Cic. *De Div.* i. 16, 28; Plaut. *Cas. Prol.* 85; Plin. *H. N.* x. § 21). Valerius Maximus (ii. 1, 1) says that in his time the *auspices* formed in name part of the attendance, though no *auspicia* for marriage were any longer taken. After these preliminaries, the omens being favourable, the marriage ceremonies began. They were in four main parts: (1) the contract; (2) the giving away of the bride, with whatever sacred rites were used; (3) the conducting (*deductio*) to her husband's house (the only *invariable* part); (4) her reception there. First the marriage tablets (*tabulae nuptiales* or *dotales*) were signed before witnesses (*signatores*), though the marriage was valid without this formality. When the form of marriage called *coemptio* was adopted (when either or both were plebeians), the formalities of an imaginary sale were gone through before not less than five witnesses, and a *libripens* (who held the scales at a sale): questions and answers as to the willingness on both sides followed, and with that ended this distinctive part of the marriage *per coemptionem;* the other ceremonies followed which were usual in all marriages. After the *coemptio*, or, where that was not used, after the signing of the *tabulae nuptiales*, a married woman, who must have been married only once, acting as *pronuba*, led the bride up to the bridegroom and joined their right hands. It seems probable that there was always some formal expression of willingness to marry, in the old patrician rite of *confarreatio* the set form of response from the bride was *Quando tu Gaius, ego Gaia*, which form of words was used also in the *coemptio* (Cic. *Pro Muren.* 12, 27). When the rite of *confarreatio* was followed the bloodless offering was made: a cake of spelt (*farreum libum*) was offered by the Pontifex Maximus and the Flamen Dialis to Iupiter: ten witnesses were present. With the offering to Iupiter a prayer was recited by the Flamen to Iuno as the goddess of marriage, and the deities of the country and its fruits — Tellus, Picumnus, and Pilumnus. During this ceremony the bride and bridegroom sat together upon two seats, which were placed side by side and covered with the skin of the sheep sacrificed before for the auspices: they sat to the left of the altar in the atrium and looked towards it: meanwhile a *camillus*, i. e. an attendant boy who was *patrimus et matrimus*, held (perhaps) all that was required by the priest for the offering in a covered basket called *cumerus*. Sir John Lubbock suggests that the wedding-cake cut by the bride is a survival of the *farreum* in this rite; but the original for that will be found, if anywhere in the Roman marriage, in the *mustaceum*. The rite of *confarreatio* suggests rather the sacramental view of marriage.

In what follows, marriages in general of all forms are described. The prayer where there was no *confarreatio* (and therefore no Flamen Dialis) was pronounced by the *auspex*, and was addressed to five deities—Iupiter, Iuno, Venus, Suadela, and Diana. It would seem that sometimes, at least, a victim was here offered. There was next a formal congratulation from the wedding guests in the word *feliciter* (which, if there was no sacred rite, came directly after the contract). Then came the *cena nuptialis*, which was certainly, as a rule, given by the bride's father, and therefore before the procession (Catull. 62, 3; Dio Cass. xlviii. 44; Capitol. *Ant. Pius*, 10). But, as in modern weddings, the place of the wedding-feast might be altered from considerations of space or economy, and it seems sometimes to have been in the bridegroom's house. The wedding-cake (*mustaceum*), which was made of meal steeped in *must* and placed on bay-leaves (Pliny, xv. § 127), was cut up and distributed to the guests. Afterwards came the procession (*deductio*), the invariable part of the marriage. This took place usually at dusk, whence arose the custom of having torches (Catull. 62, 1). The bride was taken with simulated force from her mother's arms—clearly a survival of the marriage by capture, or, as the Romans themselves put it, a reminiscence of the Sabine marriage. Flute-players and torch-bearers went in front. The bride was conducted by three boys, *patrimi et matrimi*, two leading her by the hand, the third carrying a torch of whitethorn for luck. In the procession, besides the general crowd, there came also the *camillus* with his *cumerus*, and the bride's spindle and distaff were carried after her. Fescennine songs were sung during the procession (Catull. 61, 126), with interjections of *Talasse*. As to this deity of the wedding-day, reference may be made to Marquardt, *Privatl.* p. 54; Preller, *Röm. Myth.* p. 584 foll. He appears as Talasius, Talasio, Talassus, Thalassius, Thalassio. Livy (i. 9) gives us as bearing that name a companion of Romulus prominent in the rape of the Sabines, and derives the cry *Talasse* from him: but Talus (Fest. p. 359) is an old Sabine name, and Talassius may have been a Sabine deity of marriage: Varro connects him with τάλαρος, a work-basket. On the whole a Sabine origin is most probable. The part of the bridegroom in the procession was to scatter nuts for the boys in the crowd (Verg. *Ecl.* viii. 30; Catull. 61, 131). Though Catullus says that it shows the putting away of childhood, it is much more likely that the nuts symbolized fruitfulness of marriage and plenty. The custom, which may be compared with the Greek καταχύσματα, has its representative in the throwing of rice at the present day. When the bridal train reached the bridegroom's house, the bride bound the door-posts with wool, probably as dedicating her work to it, and anointed them with oil or fat to signify health and plenty. All these actions were, so to speak, personified in a Dea Iterduca, Domiduca, and Unxia. The bride was lifted over the threshold (Plaut. *Cas.* iv. 4, 1; Catull. 61, 166), which, according to some, symbolizes the marriage by capture: others suppose the object to be the prevention of the bad omen, which would be caused by her stumbling on it. Sir John Lubbock (*op. cit.* p. 97) adopts the former view, and finds a similar custom among such widely divided races as the American Indians, the Chinese, and the Abyssinians. At the entrance the wife repeated the formula *ubi tu Gaius, ego Gaia;* and the husband met her bearing fire and water, to signify that he admitted her to a share in the family hearth and the family lustral rites: the bride, on her part, brought three coins; one she gave as symbol of the dowry to her husband, another to the Lares of the house, a third was dropped in the neighbouring street as an offering for the Lares Compitales. The torch of whitethorn seems to have been scrambled for by the guests as a lucky possession, and the ceremonies were over. The *lectus genialis* had been prepared by the *pronuba* in the atrium. On the following day the second wedding-feast, called *repotia*, was given to the friends and relations in the new home (Hor. *Sat.* ii. 2, 60; Gell. ii. 24, 14), and the bride as a *matrona* offered at the family shrine.

BIBLIOGRAPHY.—See Newman's *Aristotle*, vol. i. pp. 168–198 (Oxford, 1887); Lenz, *Geschichte der Weiber im heroischen Zeitalter;* Mahaffy, *Social Life in Greece*, pp. 170–194; Van den Es, *De Iure Familiarum apud Athenienses* (1864); Westermarck, *History of Human Marriage*, Eng. trans. (London, 1891); Tylor, *Primitive Culture*, 3d ed. (London, 1891); Hearn, *The Aryan Household* (London, 1879); Baecker, *Le Droit de la Femme dans l'Antiquité* (Paris, 1880); Bader, *La Femme Grecque* (Paris, 1873); id. *La Femme Romaine* (Paris, 1877); Karlowa, *Die Formen der röm. Ehe und Manus;* E. Holder, *Die röm Ehe;* and the articles DONATIO; HERES; MANUS; USUS.

Matron (Μάτρων). A celebrated writer of parodies on Homer. He lived about the year 380 B.C. at Pitana in Mysia. He is frequently quoted by Eustathius and Athenaeus, and the latter writer has preserved a line relating to a dinner which parodies the opening verse of the *Odyssey:*

Δεῖπνα μοι ἔννεπε, Μοῦσα, πολύτροφα καὶ μάλα πολλά.

The fragments of his parodies are printed in Brunck's *Analecta*, ii. p. 245 foll. See the dissertation by Moser, *Ueber Matron den Parodiker*.

Matrōna. A name applied by the Romans to every honourable married woman. She enjoyed the highest esteem; the way was cleared for her in the street, in which she could not appear unaccompanied, and she was not allowed to be touched even when cited before a law court. She was distinguished by the long white *stola*, the cloak called *palla*, and her hair divided into six plaits, with woollen ribbons (*vittae*) wound round it.

Matrŏna. The modern Marne, a river in Gaul, falling into the Sequana, a little south of Lutetia (Paris).

Matronalia. The chief festival of Iuno (q. v.), celebrated on the first day of March, when all the matrons of Rome marched in procession to the temple of the goddess on the Esquiline to offer flowers and libations.

Mattiăci. A people in Germany, dwelling on the east bank of the Rhine, between the Main and the Lahn. They were a branch of the Chatti. Their chief towns were Aquae Mattiacae (Wiesbaden) and Mattiacum (Marburg).

Mattium. The modern Maden, the chief town of the Chatti, situated on the Adrana (Eder).

Mattrass. See LECTUS; STRAGULUM.

Mattya (ματτύη). Dainties of any kind.

Matŭla and **Matella** (ἀμίς). A chamber utensil (Plaut. *Most.* ii. 1, 39).

Matūta (usually MATER MATUTA). An old Italian goddess of dawn and of birth, also goddess of harbours and of the sea, and hence identified with the Greek Leucothea (q. v.). In her temple at Rome in the Forum Boarium, on the 11th of June, the Matralia, or festival of mothers, was celebrated in her honour by the women of Rome; no slaves were admitted to it, and only a matron who had not been married before was allowed to place a wreath on the statue of the goddess. The women first prayed for the well-being of their nephews and nieces, and then for that of their own children. This custom was referred to the myth of Ino-Leucothea, who tended Dionysus, the son of her sister Semelé.

Mauretania and **Mauritania** (Μαυρουσία, from μαῦρος, "black") (Pausan. i. 33, § 5; viii. 43, § 3). The most westerly of the principal divisions of northern Africa, lying between the Atlantic on the west, the Mediterranean on the north, Numidia on the east, and Gaetulia on the south; but the districts embraced under the names of Mauretania and Numidia respectively were of very different extent at different periods. The earliest known inhabitants of all northern Africa west of the Syrtes were the Gaetulians, who were displaced and driven inland by peoples of Asiatic origin, who are found, in the earliest historical accounts, settled along the northern coast under various names; their chief tribes being the Mauri or Maurusii, west of the river Malva or Malucha (Muluia); thence the Massaesylii to (or nearly to) the river Ampsaga (Wady-el-Kebir), and the Massylii between the Ampsaga and the Tusca (Wady-Zain), the western boundary of the Carthaginian territory. Of these people, the Mauri, who possessed a greater breadth of fertile country between the Atlas and the coasts, seem to have applied themselves more to the settled pursuits of agriculture than their kindred neighbours on the east, whose unsettled warlike habits were moreover confirmed by their greater exposure to the intrusions of the Phœnician settlers. Hence arose a difference, which the Greeks marked by applying the general name of Νομάδες to the tribes between the Malva and the Tusca; whence came the Roman names of Numidia for the district, and Numidae for its people. (See NUMIDIA.) Thus Mauretania was at first only the country west of the Malva, and corresponded to the later district of Mauretania Tingitana, and to the modern empire of Morocco, except that the latter extends further south; the ancient boundary on the south was the Atlas.

The Romans first became acquainted with the country during the war with Iugurtha in B.C. 106. From 106 to 33 the kingdom of Mauretania was increased by the addition of the western part of Numidia, as far as Saldae, which Iulius Caesar bestowed on Bogud, as a reward for his services in the African war. A new arrangement was made about 25, when Augustus gave Mauretania to Iuba II., in exchange for his paternal kingdom of Numidia. Upon the murder of Iuba's son, Ptolemaeus, by Caligula (A.D. 40), Mauretania became finally a Roman province, and was formally constituted as such by Claudius, who added to it nearly half of what was still left of Numidia—namely, as far as the Ampsaga, and divided it into two parts, of which the western was called Tingitana, from its capital Tingis (Tangier), and the eastern Caesariensis, from its capital Iulia Caesarea (Zershell), the boundary between them being the river Malva, the old limit of the kingdom of Bocchus I. The latter corresponded to the western and central part of the modern French department of Algiers. These "Mauretaniae duae" were governed by an equestrian procurator. In the later division of the Empire under Diocletian and Constantine, the eastern part of Mauretania Caesariensis, from Saldae to the Ampsaga, was erected into a new province, and called Mauretania Sitifensis from the inland town of Sitifi (Setif); at the same time the western province, Mauretania Tingitana, seems to have been placed under the same government as Spain, so that we still find mention of the two Mauretanias, meaning now, however, Caesariensis and Sitifensis. From A.D. 429 to 534 Mauretania was in the hands of the Vandals, and in 650 and the following years it was conquered by the Arabs. Its ancient inhabitants still exist as powerful tribes in Morocco and Algeria, under the names of Berbers, Kabyles, and Tuariks. Under the later Roman emperors Mauretania was remarkable for the great number of its episcopal sees. See Chénier, *Recherches Historiques sur les Maures* (1787); Gibbon, *Decline and Fall*, chapters 41 and 43.

Mauri (Μαυρούσιοι, Μαῦροι). See MAURETANIA.

Mauriciānus, IUNIUS. A Roman jurist under Antoninus Pius (A.D. 138–161).

Maurĭcus, IUNIUS. A friend of the younger Pliny, banished by Domitian, but restored by Nerva.

Mauritania. See MAURETANIA.

Maurus, TERENTIĀNUS. See TERENTIANUS.

Mausolēum (Μαυσωλεῖον). A splendid sepulchre at Halicarnassus, built in honour of King Mausolus of Caria, who died B.C. 353, by his wife Artemisia, and reckoned by the ancients one of the seven wonders of the world (Pliny, *H. N.* xxxvi. §§ 30, 31). It consisted of an oblong substructure surrounded by thirty-six columns, with a circuit of 440 feet, crowned by a pyramid diminishing by twenty-four steps to its summit, on which stood a marble *quadriga*, the work of Pythis (or Pythius, Brunn, *Gr. Künstler*, ii. 377, first ed.). The height of the whole building, gorgeous with the most varied colours, was 140 feet. Satyrus and Pythius were the architects, and the sculptures on the four sides were executed by Scopas, Bryaxis, Timotheus, and Leochares. In the twelfth century after Christ the work was still in a good state of preservation; in succeeding centuries it fell to pieces more and more, until the Knights of St. John used it as a quarry from the time when they built their castle on the site of the old Greek acropolis in 1402, down to the repair of their fortifications in 1522, when they made lime of its marble sculptures. In 1845, a number of reliefs were extracted from the walls

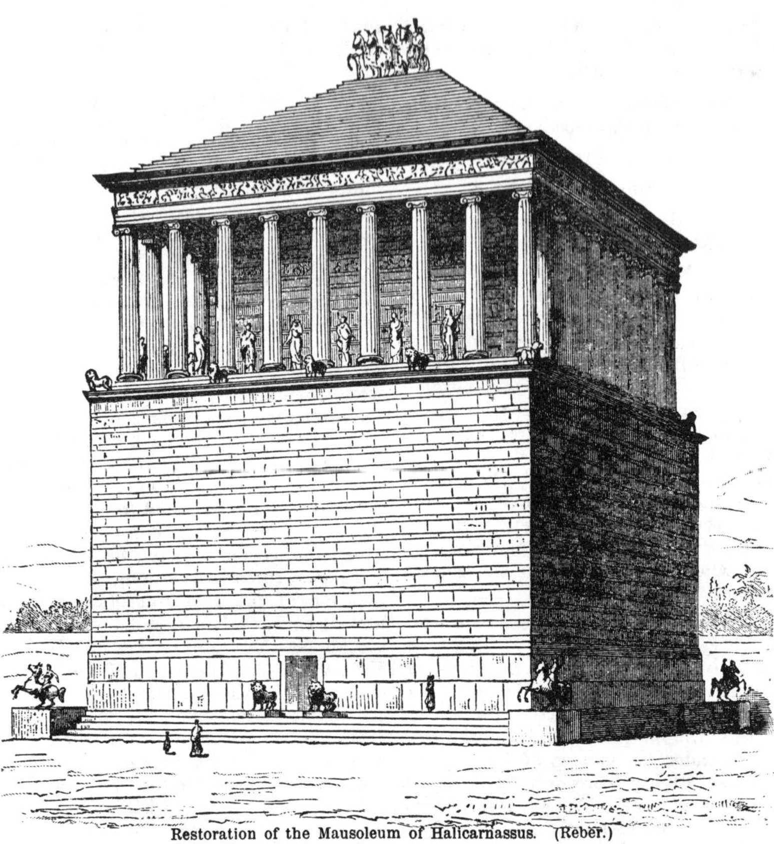

Restoration of the Mausoleum of Halicarnassus. (Reber.)

of the castle and placed in the British Museum. In 1857 the site was discovered by Newton, acting under a commission from the English government, and the sculptures thus unearthed, including the statue of Mausolus and important fragments of the marble *quadriga*, were removed to the British Museum. See Newton's *History of Discoveries at Halicarnassus*, etc., 1862; *Travels and Discoveries*, ii. 84–137; and for a restoration, the article ARCHITECTURA in this Dictionary, p. 113.

The Romans gave the name of Mausoleum to all sepulchres which approached that of Mausolus in size and grandeur of execution, as, for instance, (1) that erected by Augustus for himself and his family, the magnificence of which is attested by the still extant walls inclosing it, on the Via de' Pontefici in Rome (see AUGUSTUS, p. 170); and (2) the sepulchre of Hadrian, which is in part preserved in the Castle of S. Angelo, a circular building of 220 feet in diameter and 72 feet high, resting on a square base, the sides of which are almost 100 yards long. It was originally covered with Parian marble, and profusely ornamented with colonnades and statues, and probably had a pyramid on the top.

Present Appearance of the Mausoleum of Hadrian at Rome.

Mausōlus (Μαύσωλος). A king of Caria and eldest son of Hecatomnus. He reigned B.C. 377–353. In 362 he joined in a revolt against Artaxerxes Mnemon, and thereby added to his dominions. In 358 he aided the Rhodians and their allies against Athens, and died in the year 353, leaving no children. He was succeeded by his wife and sister Artemisia, who erected to his memory the costly monument called from him the Mausoleum. See ARTEMISIA; MAUSOLEUM.

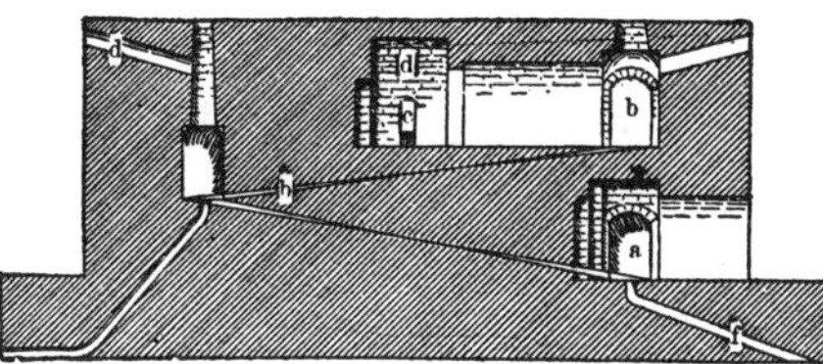

Section of Hadrian's Mausoleum.

a. Entrance, with Statue of Hadrian. b. Ventilating Passage. c. Central Tomb-chamber. d. Ventilating Channel. f. Drainage Outlet.

Mavors. See MARS.

Maxentius, M. AURELIUS VALERIUS. A Roman emperor, who ruled A.D. 306–312. He was passed over in the division of the Empire which followed the abdication of his father Maximianus and Diocletian in A.D. 305; but he seized Rome, where he was proclaimed emperor in 306. He reigned till 312, when he was defeated by Constantine at Saxa Rubra, near Rome. He tried to escape over the Milvian Bridge into Rome, but perished in the river. Maxentius is represented by all historians as a monster of rapacity, cruelty, and lust. See CONSTANTINUS.

Maxilūa. A town of Hispania Baetica, where bricks were said to be made of such lightness as to swim in water (Pliny, *H. N.* xxxv. 14).

Maxĭma Caesariensis. See BRITANNIA.

Maximianopŏlis. (1) The later name of PORSŬLAE in Thrace, east of Abdera. (2) The Hadad Rimmon of the Old Testament; a town in Palestine in the valley of Megiddo.

Maximiānus, M. AURELIUS VALERIUS. (1) A Roman emperor, who ruled A.D. 286–305, originally a Pannonian soldier. He was made by Diocletian his colleague in the Empire, but was compelled to abdicate along with the latter. (See DIOCLETIANUS.) When his son Maxentius assumed the imperial title in the following year (306), he resided some time at Rome; but being expelled from the city by Maxentius, he took refuge in Gaul with Constantine, who had married his daughter Fausta. Here he was compelled by Constantine, against whom he is said to have conspired, to put an end to his own life in 310. (2) GALERIUS MAXIMIĀNUS, usually called GALERIUS, Roman emperor, A.D. 305–311. He was first made Caesar by Diocletian, whose daughter he had married; and upon the abdication of Diocletian and Maximianus (305), he became Augustus or emperor. He died in 311, of the disgusting disease known in modern times by the name of *morbus pediculosus*. He was a cruel persecutor of the Christians. (3) MAXIMIĀNUS of Etruria. A Latin poet in the beginning of the sixth century after Christ. He is the author of six amatory elegies, modelled on classical poets, from whom he borrowed largely. His chief theme is a lament for the prospective loss of his youth. Edited first by Gauricus (Venice, 1501), who ascribed the elegies to Cornelius Gallus; and lately by Bährens in his *Poetae Latini Minores*, v. 316; and Petschenig (Berlin, 1890). See Professor Robinson Ellis in the *American Journal of Philology* (1884).

Maximīnus. (1) GAIUS IULIUS VERUS. A Roman emperor who reigned from A.D. 235 to 238. He was born in a village on the confines of Thrace, of barbarian parentage, his father being a Goth, and his mother a German from the tribe of the Alani. Brought up as a shepherd, he attracted the attention of Septimius Severus by his gigantic stature and marvellous feats of strength, and was permitted to enter the army. He eventually rose to the highest rank in the service; and on the murder of Alexander Severus by the mutinous troops in Gaul (235) he was proclaimed emperor. He immediately bestowed the title of Caesar on his son Maximus. During the three years of his reign he carried on war against the Germans with success, but his government was characterized by a degree of oppression and sanguinary excess hitherto unexampled. The Roman world became at length tired of this monster. The Senate and the provinces gladly acknowledged the two Gordiani, who had been proclaimed emperors in Africa, and after their death the Senate itself proclaimed Maximus and Balbinus emperors (238). As soon as Maximinus heard of the elevation of the Gordians, he hastened from his winter-quarters at Sirmium. Having crossed the Alps he laid siege to Aquileia, and was there slain by his own soldiers along with his son Maximus in April. The most extraordinary tales are related of the physical powers of Maximinus, which seem to have been almost incredible. His height exceeded eight feet. The circumference of his thumb was equal to that of a woman's wrist, so that the bracelet of his wife served him for a ring. It is said that he was able single-handed to drag a loaded wagon, could with his fist knock out the teeth, and with a kick break the leg of a horse; while his appetite was such that in one day he could eat forty pounds of meat and drink an amphora of wine. (2) A Roman emperor (305–314), originally called DAZA, and subsequently GALERIUS VALERIUS MAXIMĪNUS. He was the nephew of Galerius by a sister, and in early life followed the occupation of a shepherd in his native Illyria. Having entered the army, he rose to the highest rank in the service; and upon the abdication of Diocletian in 305, he was adopted by Galerius and received the title of Caesar. In 308 Galerius gave him the title of Augustus, and on the death of the latter, in 311, Maximinus and Licinius divided the East between them. In 313 Maximinus attacked the dominions of Licinius, who had gone to Milan for the purpose of receiving in marriage the sister of Constantine. He was, however, defeated by Licinius near Heraclea, and fled to Tarsus, where he soon after died. Maximinus possessed no military talents. He owed his elevation to his family connection. He surpassed all his contemporaries in the profligacy of his private life, in the general cruelty of his administration, and in the furious hatred with which he persecuted the Christians. An account of the two Maximini is given by Iulius Capitolinus in the *Augusta Historia.*

Maxims. See PROVERBIUM.

Maxĭmus, FABIUS. See FABIUS.

Maxĭmus, MAGNUS CLEMENS. A Roman emperor, A.D. 383–388, in Gaul, Britain, and Spain, was a native of Spain. He was proclaimed emperor by the legions in Britain in 383, and forthwith crossed over to Gaul to oppose Gratian, who was defeated by Maximus, and was shortly afterwards put to death. Theodosius found it expedient to recognize Maximus as emperor of Gaul, Britain, and Spain, in order to secure Valentinian in the possession of Italy. Maximus, however, aspired to the undivided empire of the West, and accordingly, in 387, he invaded Italy at the head of a formidable army. Valentinian was unable to resist him, and fled to Theodosius in the East. Theodosius forthwith prepared to avenge his colleague. In 388 he forced his way through the Noric Alps, which had been guarded by the troops of Maximus, and shortly afterwards took the city of Aquileia by storm and there put Maximus to death. Victor, the son of Maximus, was defeated and slain in Gaul by Arbogastes, the general of Theodosius.

Maxĭmus, PETRONIUS. A Roman emperor, A.D. 455, belonged to a noble Roman family, and enjoyed some of the highest offices of State under Honorius and Valentinian III. In consequence of the violence offered to his wife by Valentinian, Maximus formed a conspiracy against this emperor, who was assassinated, and Maximus proclaimed emperor in his stead. His reign, however, lasted only two or three months. Having forced Eudoxia, the widow of Valentinian, to marry him, she resolved to avenge the death of her former husband, and accordingly Genseric was invited to invade Italy. When Genseric landed at the mouth of the Tiber, Maximus prepared to fly from Rome, but was slain by a band of Burgundian mercenaries, commanded by some old officers of Valentinian.

Maxĭmus, PLANŪDES. A learned Greek monk of the Byzantine period, and distinguished as a theologian and philologist. He lived from A.D. 1260 to 1330, and took some part in public life, being sent by Andronicus II. in 1327 as ambassador to Venice. His writings comprise treatises on grammar and syntax, scholia to Theocritus and Hermogenes, a collection of excerpts from Plato, Aristotle, Strabo, Dio Cassius, etc., and translations from Latin into Greek (e. g. Caesar's *De Bello Gallico*, Cicero's *Somnium Scipionis*, the *Metamorphoses* and *Heroides* of Ovid, and Boethius, *De Consolatione*); but, above all, he is remembered for his famous collection known as the *Anthologia Planudea*, which was the only Greek anthology known to Western Europe until 1606, when Salmasius discovered the older and richer collection of Cephalas at Heidelberg. See Professor Alfred Gudeman in Calvary's *Berl. Stud.* viii. 3 (1888), and in the *Proc. of the American Philological Assoc.* xx. pp. 6 foll.; also M. Treu's commentary on the *Epistulae* of Planudes (Breslau, 1890); A. Palmer, *Ovid's Heroides* (Oxford, 1894); and the article ANTHOLOGY.

Maxĭmus Tyrius. A native of Tyre, a Greek rhetorician and Platonic philosopher, who lived during the reigns of the Antonines and of Commodus, and was the author of forty-one extant dissertations (Διαλέξεις or Λόγοι) on philosophical subjects, written in an easy and pleasing style. There is an edition by Reiske (Leipzig, 1774–75), in two volumes.

Maxĭmus, VALERIUS. See VALERIUS MAXIMUS.

Maxŭla. The name of the Roman city built upon the site of the older Carthaginian Adis, on the modern Bay of Tunis.

Mazăca. See CAESAREA (3).

Mazăra (Μαζάρα). Now Mazzara; a town on the western coast of Sicily.

Mazĭces (Μάζικες). A people of Northern Africa, in Mauretania Caesariensis.

Mazonŏmum (μαζονομεῖον). (1) A round wooden trencher on which barley-cakes were served (Hesych.). (2) A bronze or golden salver for incense (Athen. v. 27). (3) A large dish for game-pies (Hor. *Sat.* ii. 8, 86).

Meals. See CENA.

Mecyberna (Μηκύβερνα). A town of Macedonia in Chalcidicé, at the head of the Toronaic Gulf, east of Olynthus, of which it was the sea-port.

Medaura, Madaura, Ad Medĕra, or **Amedĕra**. A city of Northern Africa, on the borders of Numidia and Byzacena. It was the birthplace of Apuleius. It is probably to be identified with the MADAURA, to which St. Augustine was sent to be educated (*Confess.* ii. 3).

Meddix Tutĭcus (also MEDIX, MAEDIX). "Community-manager." The title of the chief magistrate in the Oscan and Sabellian towns in Italy. So we find the name used at Pompeii, Herculaneum, and Bovianum, and at Capua after the Samnites got possession of the city. The word *meddix* is probably cognate with μέδω, and *tuticus* with the Oscan *tauta, tuta*, "a town." See Mommsen, *Unterital. Dialekte*, p. 278; Curtius, *Gk. Etym.* p. 225; and Mommsen, *Hist. of Rome*, i. p. 321 (Amer. ed.).

Medēa (Μήδεια). The daughter of Aeëtes, king of Colchis, by the Oceanid Idyia, or, according to others, by Hecaté, the daughter of Perses. She was celebrated for her skill in magic. The principal parts of her story are given under ABSYRTUS, ARGONAUTAE, and IASON. It is sufficient to state here that, when Iason came to Colchis to seek the Golden Fleece, she fell in love with the hero, assisted him in accomplishing the object for which he had visited Colchis, and afterwards fled with him as his wife to Greece; that, having been deserted by Iason for the youthful daughter of Creon, king of Corinth, she took fearful vengeance upon her faithless husband by murdering the two children whom she had borne to him and by destroying his young wife by a poisoned garment; and that she then fled to Athens in a chariot drawn by winged dragons. So far her story has been related elsewhere. (See IASON.) At Athens she is said to have married King Aegeus, or to have been beloved by Sisyphus. Zeus himself is said to have sued for her, but in vain, because Medea dreaded the anger of Heré; and the latter rewarded her by promising immortality to her children. Her children are, according to some accounts, Mermerus, Pheres, or Thessalus, Alcimenes, and Tisander; according to others, she had seven sons and seven daughters, while others mention only two children, Medus (some call him Polyxenus) and Eriopis, or one son Argus. Respecting her flight from Corinth, there are different traditions. Some say, as stated above, that she fled to Athens and married Aegeus; but

Medea. Pompeian Painting. (Overbeck.)

when it was discovered that she had laid snares for Theseus, she escaped and went to Asia, the inhabitants of which were called after her Medes (Μῆδοι). Others relate that she first fled from Corinth to Heracles at Thebes, who had promised her his assistance while yet in Colchis, in case of Iason being unfaithful to her. She cured Heracles, who was seized with madness; and as he could not afford her the assistance he had promised, she went to Athens. She is said to have given birth to her son Medus after her arrival in Asia, where she had married a king; whereas others state that her son Medus accompanied her from Athens to Colchis, where her son slew Perses, and restored her father Aeëtes to his kingdom. The restoration of Aeëtes, however, is attributed by some to Iason, who accompanied Medea to Colchis. At length Medea is said to have become immortal, to have been honoured with divine worship, and to have married Achilles in Elysium. The story of Medea is the subject of plays by Euripides (q. v.) and Seneca (q. v.).

Medeon (Μεδεών). (1) A town in the interior of Acarnania, near the road which led from Limnaea to Stratos. (2) A town on the coast of Phocis, near Anticyra. (3) A town in Boeotia, near Onchestus and Lake Copaïs. (4) A town of the Labeates in Dalmatia, near Scodra.

Media (Μηδία). An important country of Asia above Persia, and bounded on the north by the Araxes, on the west and southwest by the range of mountains called Zagros and Parachoatras (Mountains of Kurdistan and Louristan), which divided it from the Tigris and Euphrates valley; on the east by the Desert; and on the northeast by the Caspii Montes (Elburz Mountains). It was a fertile country, well peopled, and one of the most important provinces of the ancient Persian Empire. After the Macedonian conquest it was divided into two parts—Great Media and Atropatené. See ATROPATENÉ.

The earliest history of Media is involved in much obscurity. Herodotus reckons only four kings of Media, namely: (1) Deioces, B.C. 710–657; (2) Phraortes, 657–635; (3) Cyaxares, 635–595; (4) Astyages, 595–560. The last king was dethroned by a revolution, which transferred the supremacy to the Persians, who had formerly been the subordinate people in the united Medo-Persian Empire. (See CYRUS.) The Medes made more than one attempt to regain their supremacy; the usurpation of the Magian pseudo-Smerdis was no doubt such an attempt (see SMERDIS); and another occurred in the reign of Darius II., when the Medes revolted, but were soon subdued (B.C. 408). With the rest of the Persian Empire, Media fell under the power of Alexander; it next formed a part of the kingdom of the Seleucidae, from whom it was conquered by the Parthians in the second century B.C., from which time it belonged to the Parthian, and then to the later Persian Empire. See PERSIA, with bibliography there given.

It is important to notice the use of the names Medus and Medi by the Roman poets for the nations of Asia east of the Tigris in general and for the Parthians in particular.

Mediae Murus (τὸ Μηδίας τεῖχος). An artificial wall which ran from the Euphrates to the Tigris, at the point where they approach nearest, and divided Mesopotamia from Babylonia. It is described by Xenophon (*Anab.* ii. 4) as being 20 parasangs long, 100 feet high, and 20 thick, and as built of baked bricks, cemented with asphalt. Its erection was ascribed to Semiramis.

Medials (μέσα). In phonetics, the voiced non-aspirate explosives—*g*, *d*, *b*.

Mediastīni. Slaves of all work (Schol. *ad* Hor. *Epist.* i. 14, 14) in either city or country. See SERVUS.

Medicamĭna Faciēi. See OVIDIUS.

Medicīna (ἰατρική). The ancients ascribed the origin of the medical art to the gods (Pliny, *H. N.* xxix. 2), and Prometheus, Chiron, and Asclepius were among those who made it known to men. It was also believed to have been improved by the observation of the remedies instinctively sought out by animals when suffering from injuries or disease (Pliny, *H. N.* viii. 97). Thus, dogs taught the Egyptians the use of purgatives, bleeding was learned from the hippopotamus, and enemata from the ibis. Sheep and cattle led men to the use of the natural saline and chalybeate waters. The results of these and various other observations of cures were recorded on tablets, and suspended by the priests in the temples of the gods both in Egypt and in Greece. These tablets were the beginnings of medical literature.

The Asclepiadae, to which family Hippocrates belonged, were, in a way, hereditary physicians (see AESCULAPIUS), and founded a number of medical schools, of which the most famous in early times were those of Rhodes, Cnidos, and Cos (Galen, *De Meth. Med.* i. 1). From the second came the collection of medical observations called Κνίδιαι Γνῶμαι, "Cnidian Maxims," which long enjoyed a considerable repute. The school of Cos was, however, the best known of the three, and one of its representatives was Hippocrates himself. Herodotus mentions other schools at Crotona in Italy and Cyrené in Africa (iii. 131). Of the different medical sects that sprang up at different times, the following deserve especial mention: (1) The DOGMATĬCI or HIPPOCRATĬCI, founded about B.C. 400 by Thessalus, the son, and Polybus, the son-in-law of Hippocrates; (2) the EMPIRĬCI, founded in the third century B.C., and so called because they professed to base their knowledge and practice on experience alone; (3) the METHODĬCI, founded in the first century B.C. by Themison, who taught doctrines partly theoretical and partly empirical; (4) the PNEUMATĬCI, founded by Athenaeus in the first century A.D.; and (5) the ECLECTĬCI, founded at about the same time by Agathinus of Sparta, or perhaps his pupil Archigenes.

For further details regarding ancient medicine, see the articles CELSUS; CHIRURGIA; DIOSCORIDES; GALENUS; HIPPOCRATES; and MEDICUS.

Medicīna Pliniāna. The title of an anonymous compilation on medical topics drawn chiefly from bks. xx.–xxxii. of the *Historia Naturalis* of Pliny the Elder. (See PLINIUS.) It was made in the fourth century A.D., and was much used in succeeding centuries as a book of reference. It is edited by Rose (Leipzig, 1875).

Medĭcus (ἰατρός). A physician or surgeon, the name being indiscriminately used of either. In Greece and Asia Minor, physicians were held in higher repute than at Rome, probably because of the traditional association of medicine with religion. A law of the Locrians quoted by Aelian (*Var. Hist.* ii. 37), punished with death the patient who disobeyed the orders of his physician. Hippocrates was treated as a demigod by the Athenians, if the account of Soranus be true.

The Greek physician compounded his own medicines, and either sat in his consulting-room (ἰατρεῖον) or visited his patients, in the latter duty being often accompanied by his pupils or assistants. There is only one mention of a Greek hospital prior to the Roman period. (See VALETUDINARIA.) State physicians were employed in Greece, receiving a salary and their expenses, but no fees (Aristoph. *Aves*, 587; *Acharn.* 994). Thus Democedes received from the public treasury of Aegina about $1400 per annum, and from Athens afterwards a salary of some $2000 (Herod. iii. 131). A physician who cured King Antiochus received from him a fee of over $100,000 (Pliny, *H. N.* vii. 123; xxix. 5). State physicians attended gratis any one who called for them.

In the early days of the Republic, Rome had no regular physicians. The haruspices and augurs pretended to some knowledge of medicine; but when a man fell ill, he was usually treated by the

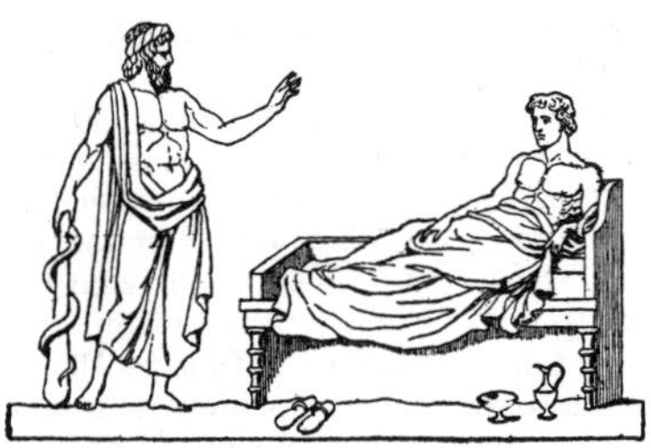

Aesculapius and a Sick Man. (Millin.)

old women with their simples; or if the disease was a very serious one, he trusted to religious rites, vows, and sacrifices for his recovery. The various deities of disease were propitiated by temples and altars. In Varro's time there were in Rome three temples to the goddess of Fever; in the Esquiline quarter, an altar to Mefitis, the goddess Malaria; in the centre of the Forum Romanum, an altar to Cloacina, "the goddess of typhoid" (so Lanciani), and near the Praetorian Camp, an altar to Verminus, the god of disease-germs. Cf. Lanciani, *Ancient Rome*, pp. 49–73.

At a later period, among the Greeks who first came in numbers to Rome in the second century B.C., were many professed physicians; and from that time the practice of medicine became a lucrative profession among the Romans, though the chief practitioners remained Greeks, a fact to which the Latin vocabulary bears witness in that its medical terms are nearly all of Greek origin. The elder Pliny gives some interesting details regarding the fees received by the leading doctors. The native physicians of celebrity, Cassius, Calpetanus, and Arruntius, received, he estimates, an income of not less than 250,000 sesterces ($10,000) a year. Quintus Stertinius, a fashionable physician, was asked by the emperor to give up his private practice and devote himself to the imperial family alone. Stertinius said that, as an especial favour, he would do it if he could receive a salary of 500,000 sesterces ($20,000). This struck the emperor as an exorbitant demand, but Stertinius showed from his books that his private practice was worth to him at least 600,000 sesterces per annum. The brother of this Stertinius had a sort of partnership with him, and when they died, which they did at about the same time, they left a property of 30,000,000 sesterces ($1,200,000), though they had lived very expensively, and given large sums to public objects. The Greek physicians at Rome probably earned still larger sums. An ex-praetor paid 200,000 sesterces ($8000) as a single fee to the practitioner who treated him for leprosy. Pliny mentions one Thessalus, of whom he says: "No popular actor, no famous jockey, had a greater throng attending him when he appeared in public."

Nothing is known of the course of study necessary to qualify a man for medical practice. That there were medical students and clinical lectures is seen from Martial (v. 9). It is probable that the profession was open to all kinds of quacks and impostors, for we read of men taking up medicine as they would any form of trade, with no mention of any special qualification. It is, in fact, likely that, in the main, ancient medicine was little better than quackery, and that the best physicians were men like Crinas who made a careful study of dietetics, and like Asclepiades, who said "Nature is the true physician." How absurd much of the treatment must have been is shown in the list of remedies given by Pliny in his *Historia Naturalis* (bk. xxix.). The patent medicines of to-day sink into insignificance beside them. Thus, we read of a mysterious preparation called *Theriaca* with 600 ingredients, and of another known as "the Mithridatic antidote" with 450. Pliny mentions 35 nostrums prepared from wool, 22 from eggs, and also several pastes of which the principal constituent was pounded bugs. The notion, which is still largely prevalent among the laity, that the efficacy of a drug is in direct proportion to its nastiness seems to have had a strong hold on the minds of the ancients. Dog's blood was given for narcotic poisons; urine for gout; goat's gall for ophthalmia; bull's gall and garlic for ear-ache. Superstition entered largely into the treatment. A person afflicted with hiccoughing was gravely advised to touch his lips to a mule's nostrils and be cured. Hydrophobia was treated by applying to the bite the ashes of the dead dog's hair. A still more effectual remedy for the same disease was to cut out the liver of the dog and to eat it raw, applying at the same time to the wound, horse-dung sprinkled with vinegar.

All these prescriptions are the serious advice of men of reputation. It is not surprising if, on the whole, the profession was less esteemed than others. Pliny the Elder sums up the matter in the following sentences:

"There is no doubt that physicians in pursuit of celebrity, by the introduction of some novelty or other, purchase it at the cost of human life. Hence these woful discussions, these consultations at the bedside of the patient; hence, too, the ominous inscription to be read upon a tomb—'I perished by the multitude of physicians' . . . And there is, moreover, no law to punish the mistakes of a physician, and no instance before us of any punishment so inflicted. They acquire skill at our risk, and put us to death for the sake of making an experiment; for a physician is the only person who is licensed to kill."

Other scandals besides those due to ignorance

were not unknown. So many unprincipled persons entered the profession that it is not surprising to find complaints made of their conduct. Even the palace of the Caesars was the scene of strange occurrences, for it is recorded that both Livia, the wife of Drusus, and the empress Messalina were criminally intimate with their medical attendants. It is not remarkable, therefore, to find a Roman writer concluding a discussion of the subject with the words: "Medicine is the only one of the arts of Greece that, lucrative though it be, Roman dignity still refuses to cultivate."

Nevertheless, medicine flourished, and its followers kept increasing in number. We hear of the practice of specialties. General practitioners were known as *medici;* surgeons as *chirurgi* and *vulnerarii*. There were also oculists (*ocularii*) and dentists (*medici a dentibus*). We even read of female physicians (Orell. *Inscript.* 4320–31), and, of course, of numerous midwives (*obstetrices*). Pharmacies existed, their sign being the Aesculapian snake; and though physicians usually furnished their own drugs, they also gave signed prescriptions (Duruy). The physicians attached to the imperial household were under the direction of a chief styled *archiater* (ἀρχίατρος), or in pure Latin *dominus medicorum*. The name *archiater* was also applied to the dispensary-physicians who gave their services to the people (*archiatri populares*). See Goldhorn, *De Archiatris Romanis* (Leipzig, 1841).

Surgery was the branch of medicine most scientifically pursued, and successful operations were performed by the ancient surgeons for stone and cataract, while trephining was not unknown. See CHIRURGIA.

For a full discussion of the subject of ancient medicine, see Daremberg, *Histoire des Sciences Médicales* (Paris, 1870–73); Watson, *The Medical Profession in Ancient Times* (N. Y. 1856); Dunglison, *History of Medicine* (Philadelphia, 1872); and Berdoe, *Origin and Growth of the Healing Art* (London, 1894).

Medimnus (*μέδιμνος* or *μέδιμνος σιτηρός*). The principal dry measure of the Greeks. It contained 6 *hectes*, 12 *hemiecta*, 48 *choenices*, 96 *xestae* (= *sextarii*), 192 *cotylae*, and 1152 *cyathi*. The Attic medimnus = 2 Rom. *amphorae* = 52.53 litres = 12 gallons (nearly) or 1½ bushel. The Sicilian medimnus was the same as the Attic, but the Aeginetan was about half as much again. See Hultsch, *Metrologie*, pp. 104, 503.

Mediolānum (Μεδιολάνιον). (1) The modern Milan; the capital of the Insubres in Gallia Transpadana. It was taken by the Romans B.C. 222, and afterwards became both a municipium and a colony. From the time of Diocletian till its capture by Attila it was the usual residence of the emperors of the West. It is celebrated in ecclesiastical history as the see of St. Ambrose. When the Western Empire fell it became the residence of Theodoric the Great and the capital of the Ostrogothic kingdom. At one time it surpassed Rome in population. It was taken and partly destroyed by the Goth Vitiges in A.D. 539. (2) The modern Saintes; a town of the Santones in Aquitania, northeast of the mouth of the Garumna; subsequently called Santones after the people, whence its modern name. (3) The modern Evreux, a town of the Aulerci Eburovices in the northern part of Gallia Lugdunensis. It was subsequently called Civitas Ebroicorum, whence came its present name.

Mediomatrĭci. A people in the southeast of Gallia Belgica, on the Moselle, south of the Treviri. Their chief town was Divodurum (Metz).

Mediterraneum Maré. See INTERNUM MARÉ.

Meditrīna. A Roman goddess of the healing art, whose festival, the MEDITRINALIA, was observed annually on October 11. See Varro, *L. L.* vi. 21.

Medoăcus or **Meduăcus**. A river in Venetia, in the north of Italy, falling into the Adriatic Sea near Edron, the harbour of Patavium.

Medobrēga. A town in Lusitania, on the road from Emerita to Scalabis. It is now Marvao.

Medon (Μέδων). (1) Son of Codrus, the first archon. (See CODRUS.) (2) A Lacedaemonian statuary, who made the chryselephantine statue of Athené for the Heraeum at Olympia.

Medŭli. A people in Aquitania, on the coast of the ocean, south of the mouth of the Garumna, in the modern Médoc. There were excellent oysters found on their shores.

Medulli. A people on the eastern frontier of Gallia Narbonensis and in the Maritime Alps, in whose country the Druentia (Durance) and Duria (Doria Minor) took their rise.

Medullia. A colony of Alba, in the land of the Sabines, situated between the Tiber and the Anio.

Medullus. A mountain in Hispania Tarraconensis near the Minius (Minho).

Medus (Μῆδος). Son of Aegeus and Medea (q. v.).

Medūsa (Μέδουσα). See GORGO.

Megabazus (Μεγάβαζος) or **Megabyzus** (Μεγάβυζος). One of the seven Persian nobles who conspired against the magian Smerdis (q. v.), B.C. 521. He afterwards subdued Perinthus and other cities on the Hellespont and the coast of Thrace (Herod. iii. 70; iv. 143; v. 1–16).

Megăcles (Μεγακλῆς). (1) A name borne by several of the Athenian family of the Alcmaeonidae. The most important of these was the Megacles who put to death Cylon and his adherents after they had taken refuge at the altar of Athené, B.C. 612. (See CYLON.) (2) Son of Alcmaeon, son-in-law of Clisthenes, leader of the Alcmaeonidae in the time of Solon. At first he was opposed to Pisistratus, and expelled him from Athens; but afterwards he became reconciled to him, gave him his daughter Coesyra in marriage, and assisted in his restoration to Athens. Pisistratus not having treated his wife in a proper manner, Megacles resented the affront, and again drove the former out of Athens; with the aid of large sums from the Thebans and other States, Pisistratus again raised an army, defeated his opponents, and drove Megacles and the partisans of the Alcmaeonidae into exile. (3) A Syracusan, brother of Dion, and brother-in-law of the elder Dionysius. He accompanied Dion in his flight from Syracuse, B.C. 358, and afterwards returned with him to Sicily.

Megaera (Μέγαιρα). See EUMENIDES.

Megalesia. A Roman festival in honour of Rhea (q. v.). These games are also styled MEGALENSIA and MEGALENSES LUDI. The name is derived from the title of Cybelé, ἡ μεγάλη θεός (Cic. *De Harusp. Resp.* 12, 24), whose image, a black stone, was brought to Rome in the year B.C. 204 at the time of the Second Punic War, and placed in the temple of Victory on the Palatine.

The games were scenic and probably *circenses* (Mommsen, *C. I. L.* i. 391), and were held on the Palatine and later in the theatres. They were directed by the curule aediles till B.C. 22, when Augustus placed them in charge of the praetor. At the celebration, the *galli* or eunuch priests of Cybelé carried the sacred ensign in procession through the city, singing Greek hymns and collecting coins from the people in the streets. This procession is described by Lucretius (ii. 618 foll.). The ceremony lasted seven days, on the third of which the scenic exhibitions especially took place, and the whole celebration ended with a grand carnival. The date of the Megalesia was April 4th to April 10th. Four of the existing plays of Terence were first performed at the Megalesia. See Marquardt, *Staatverwaltung*, pp. 367–374.

Megalia or **Megăris.** A small island in the Tyrrhenian Sea, opposite Neapolis.

Megalopŏlis (Μεγαλόπολις). (1) The most recent but the most important of the cities of Arcadia, was founded on the advice of Epaminondas after the battle of Leuctra, B.C. 371, and was formed out of the inhabitants of thirty-eight villages. It was situated in the district Maenalia, near the frontiers of Messenia, on the river Helisson, which flowed through the city. It became afterwards one of the chief cities of the Achaean League. Philopoemen and the historian Polybius were natives of Megalopolis. (2) A town in Caria. (See APHRODISIAS.) (3) A town in Pontus. (See SEBASTIA.) (4) A town in the north of Africa.

Megăra (τὰ Μέγαρα). (1) The town of Megara, the capital of Megaris, a small district in Greece between the Corinthian and Saronic Gulfs, bounded on the north by Boeotia, on the east and northeast by Attica, on the south by the territory of Corinth, and situated a mile from the sea, opposite the island of Salamis. Its citadel was called Alcathoë, from its reputed founder, Alcathoüs, son of Pelops. Its seaport was Nisaea, which was connected with Megara by two walls, built by the Athenians when they had possession of Megara, B.C. 461–445. In front of Nisaea lay the small island Minoa, which added greatly to the security of the harbour. In ancient times Megara formed one of the four divisions of Attica. It was next conquered by the Dorians, and was for a time subject to Corinth; but it finally asserted its independence, and rapidly became a wealthy and powerful city. Its power at an early period is attested by the flourishing colonies which it founded, of which Selymbria, Chalcedon, and Byzantium, and the Hyblaean Megara in Sicily, were the most important. After the Persian wars, Megara was for some time at war with Corinth, and was thus led to form an alliance with Athens, and to receive an Athenian garrison into the city, B.C. 461; but the oligarchical party having got the upper hand, the Athenians were expelled, B.C. 441. Megara is celebrated in the history of philosophy as the seat of a philosophical school, usually called the Megarian, which was founded by Euclid, a native of the city. See EUCLIDES (2). (2) A town in Sicily on the east coast north of Syracuse, founded by Dorians from Megara in Greece, B.C. 728, on the site of a small town, Hybla, and hence called MEGARA HYBLAEA, and its inhabitants Megarenses Hyblaei. From the time of Gelon it belonged to Syracuse.

Megăreus (Μεγαρεύς). The son either of Onchestus or of Poseidon, and father of Hippomenes and Evaechmé.

Megăris (Μεγαρίς). See MEGARA.

Megăron (μέγαρον). In many Greek temples a space divided off and sometimes subterranean, which only the priest was allowed to enter. (See TEMPLUM.) The word originally denoted the large hall or chief room in the early (Homeric) Greek house, with the roof supported by columns, the light entering through the doors, the smoke-hole, and the apertures (ὀπαῖα) just under the roof. See DOMUS, p. 537.

Megaron of Early Greek House. (Autenrieth.)

Megasthĕnes (Μεγασθένης). A Greek historian, who stayed for a considerable time, as ambassador of King Seleucus Nicator, at the court of the Indian king Sandracus or Sandracottus (B.C. 315–291), at Palibothra on the Ganges. From information about the country and the people, obtained while he occupied that position, he compiled a historical and geographical work about India (τὰ Ἰνδικά), the chief treatise on that country left us by the ancients. On it are founded the accounts of Diodorus and Arrian; beyond this only fragments are preserved. His record of the state of India at the time has been discredited; but recent investigations have, to a great extent, shown its trustworthiness. The remains of Megasthenes have been edited by Schnaubeck (Bonn, 1846), and cf. Müller's *Frag. Hist. Graec.* (Paris, 1868–74).

Megiddo (Μαγεδδώ). A considerable city of Palestine, on the river Kishon, in a valley of the same name, on the confines of Galilee and Samaria.

Megistāni. An Armenian people dwelling near the Euphrates.

Mela. See MELLA.

Mela. (1) M. ANNAEUS. Youngest son of M. Annaeus Seneca, the rhetorician, brother of L. Seneca, the philosopher, and father of the poet Lucan. (2) POMPONIUS. A native of Tingentera in Spain, under Claudius or Caligula, and author of an excellent Latin work on geography, entitled *De Situ Orbis Libri III.*, containing a description of the world as known to the Romans of his time. It is written in a clear and simple style; and, though very concise, is enlivened by bits of interesting description of manners and customs. The number of geographical names mentioned by Mela amounts to more than 1500. The principal MS. of the work is in the Vatican, and dates from the tenth century. Editions are those of Voss (last ed. Franeker, 1700); A. Gronovius (Leyden, 1696); Tzschucke (Leipzig, 1807), revised by Parthey (Berlin, 1867); and Frick (Leipzig, 1880). See Fink, *Pomponius Mela und seine Chorographie* (1881); and the article GEOGRAPHIA.

Melaena Acra (ἡ Μέλαινα Ἄκρα). "Black Cape." (1) The northwestern promontory of the peninsula of Ionia, formed by Mount Mimas. (2) The northwestern promontory of the island of Chios. (3) A promontory of Bithynia, east of the Bosporus.

Melampus (Μελάμπους). (1) The son of Amythaon (see AEOLUS) and of Idomené; brother of Bias, the oldest Greek seer, and ancester of the family of seers called Melampodidae. The brothers went with their uncle Neleus from Thessaly to Pylus in Messenia, where they dwelt in the country. Melampus owed his gift of soothsaying to some serpents, which he had saved from death and reared, and who in return cleansed his ears with their tongues when he slept; on awaking he understood the voices of birds, and thus learned what was secret. When Neleus would only give Bias his beautiful daughter Pero on condition that he first brought him the oxen of Iphiclus of Phylacé in Thessaly, which were guarded by a watchful dog, Melampus offered to bring the oxen for his brother, though he knew beforehand that he would be imprisoned for a year. He was caught in the act of stealing them, and kept in strict confinement. From the talk of the worms in the woodwork of the roof he gathered that the house would soon fall to pieces. He thereupon demanded to be taken to another prison; and this was scarcely done when the house broke down. When, on account of this, Phylacus, father of Iphiclus, perceived his prophetic gifts, he promised him the oxen, if, by his art, he would find out some way of curing his son's childlessness. Melampus offered a bull to Zeus, cut it in pieces, and invited the birds to the meal. From these he heard that a certain vulture, that had not come, knew how it could be effected. This vulture was made to appear, and related that the defect in Iphiclus was the result of a sudden fright at seeing a bloody knife, with which his father had been castrating some goats; he had dug the knife into a tree, which had grown round about it; if he took some of the rust scraped off it, for ten days, he would be cured. Melampus found the knife, cured Iphiclus, obtained the oxen, and Bias received Pero for his wife.

Afterwards he went to Argos, because, according to Homer (*Od.* xv. 225–240), Neleus had committed a serious offence against him in his absence, for which he had taken revenge; while, according to the usual account, he had been asked by king Proetus to heal his daughter, stricken with madness for acting impiously towards Dionysus or Heré. He had stipulated that his reward should be a third of the kingdom for himself, another for Bias; besides which Iphianassa became his wife, and Lysippé that of Bias, both being daughters of Proetus. A descendant of his son Antiphates was Oïcles, who was a companion of Heracles in the expedition against Troy, and was slain in battle by Laomedon; he again was ancestor of the seer and hero Amphiaraüs. Descendants of his other son Mantius were Cleitus, whom Eos, the goddess of dawn, carried off on account of his beauty, and Polypheides, whom, after the death of Amphiaraüs, Apollo made the best of seers. The son of Polypheides was the seer Theoclymenus, who, flying from Argos on account of committing a murder, met Telemachus at Pylus, was led by him to Ithaca, and announced to Penelopé the presence in Ithaca of Odysseus and to the suitors their approaching death. The seer Polyidus (q. v.) was also said to be a great-grandson of Melampus. At Argos Melampus was held to be the first priest of Dionysus, and originator of mysterious customs at festivals and at ceremonies of expiation.

(2) The author of two short works in Greek on divination, who lived in the third century B.C. at Alexandria. Edition by Franz (Altenburg, 1780).

Melan (μέλαν). Ink. It was made of the liquid of the cuttle-fish, or of soot and gum, or gall-apples. (See ATRAMENTUM.) An inkstand was called μελανδόχον (*atramentarium*).

Melanchlaeni (Μελάγχλαινοι). A people in the north of Asia, about the upper course of the river Tanaïs (Don), resembling the Scythians in manners, though of a different race. Their Greek name was derived from their dark clothing.

Melăneus (Μελανεύς). A son of Apollo. He was king of the Dryopes, and was a famous archer. He founded the town of Oechalia, which he named after his wife.

Melanippé (Μελανίππη). Daughter of Chiron, also called Evippé. Being with child by Aeolus, she fled to Mount Pelion, and was there metamorphosed by Artemis into a mare, and placed among the stars as a constellation (Hyg. *Fab.* 86).

Melanippĭdes (Μελανιππίδης). A celebrated Greek lyric poet in the department of the dithyramb, who flourished about B.C. 440 at Melos. His fragments will be found in Bergk, *Poet. Lyric. Graec.* See DITHYRAMBUS.

Melanippus (Μελάνιππος). A Theban, who mortally wounded Tydeus in the fight of the Seven against Thebes, and was himself slain by Amphiaraüs. See TYDEUS.

Melanogaetūli. A black race of mixed blood dwelling in Gaetulia.

Melanthius (Μελάνθιος). (1) A goat-herd of Odysseus. (2) An Athenian tragic poet attacked by Aristophanes (*Pax*, 796, and elsewhere). (3) A Greek painter of the Sicyonian School, contemporary with Apelles (B.C. 332), with whom he studied under Pamphilus (Pliny, *H. N.* xxxv. 50).

Melanthus (Μέλανθος). A king of Messenia driven out by the Heraclidae (Herod. i. 147).

Melas (Μέλας). The name of several rivers, whose waters were a dark colour. (1) A small river in Boeotia, flowing between Orchomenus and Aspledon. (2) A river of Thessaly, in the district Malis, falling into the Malic Gulf. (3) A river of Thessaly in Phthiotis, falling into the Apidanus. (4) A river of Thrace, falling into the Melas Sinus. (5) A river in the northeast of Sicily, flowing into the sea between Mylae and Naulochus, through excellent meadows, in which the oxen of the Sun are said to have fed. (6) A river in Asia Minor, the boundary between Pamphylia and Cilicia.

Melas Sinus (Μέλας Κόλπος). A gulf between the coast of Thrace and the Thracian Chersonesus. See MELAS.

Meldi or **Meldae**. A people in Gallia Lugdunensis, upon the river Sequana (Seine).

Meleāger (Μελέαγρος). (1) The son of Oeneus of Calydon and Althaea, husband of Cleopatra (see IDAS), one of the most celebrated heroes of Greek legend. He took part in the expedition of the Argonauts, and brought about the celebrated chase of the Calydonian boar (see OENEUS), to which he invited the most renowned heroes of the time, Admetus, Amphiaraüs, Iason, Idas, Lynceus, Castor and Pollux, Nestor, Theseus, and Pirithous, Peleus, Telamon, and others. Many lost their lives, till at last Meleager slew the monster. However, Artemis thereupon stirred up a furious strife between the Calydonians and the Curetes who dwelt at Pleuron, about the head and skin of the

Meleager. (From a Painting at Pompeii.)

boar, the prize of victory. The Calydonians were victorious as long as Meleager fought at their head; but when he slew the brother of his mother, she invoked a terrible curse on him, and he retired sullenly from the fray. The Curetes immediately forced the Calydonians to retreat, and were already beginning to climb the walls of Calydon, when, at the height of their distress, he yielded to the prayers of his wife, and again joined in the fight to ward off destruction from the city; but he did not return alive, for the Erinys had accomplished the curse of his mother. According to a later legend, the Moerae appeared to his mother on the seventh day after his birth, and announced to her that her son would have to die when a log of wood on the hearth was consumed by the flame; whereupon Althaea immediately snatched the log from the fire and concealed it in a chest. At the Calydonian Hunt, Meleager fell in love with Atalanté (q. v.), and gave her (who had inflicted the first wound) the prize, the skin of the animal which he had killed. He slew the brothers of his mother, the sons of Thestius, when they were lying in wait for the virgin to rob her of the boar's hide. Overcome by pain at the death of her brothers, Althaea set fire to the log, and Meleager died a sudden death. His mother and wife hanged themselves; his sisters wept so bitterly for Meleager, that Artemis for pity changed them into guinea-hens (μελεαγρίδες). Legends relate that even in the nether world Meleager retained his dauntless courage; for when Heracles descended to Hades, all the shades fled before him except Meleager and Medusa. (2) A Greek epigrammatist of Gadara in Palestine, who flourished about B.C. 60. His collection of epigrams, by himself and others, entitled *Stephanos* (wreath), formed the nucleus of the Greek anthology. Of his own poems there remain 131, in which amatory themes are cleverly and wittily treated. See ANTHOLOGY.

Meles (Μέλης). A small stream in Ionia, on whose banks near Smyrna Homer was said to have been born. Hence he is styled Μελησιγένης. One legend makes Meles, the river-god, to have been the poet's father. See HOMERUS.

Melĕtē. See MUSAE.

Melētus (Μέλητος) or **Melītus** (Μέλιτος). An obscure tragic poet, but notorious as one of the accusers of Socrates (q. v.). It was he who made the formal accusation before the archon; but he was really the least important of the three accusers, and is said to have been bribed to take part in the proceedings. After the death of Socrates, Meletus was stoned to death by the people, in the revulsion of feeling which they experienced (Plat. *Apol.*; Diod. xiv. 37; Diog. Laërt. ii. 43).

Melia (Μελία). A nymph, daughter of Oceanus, who became by Inachus the mother of Phoroneus and Aegialeus; by Silenus, the mother of the centaur Pholus (q. v.); by Poseidon, the mother of Amycus; and by Apollo, the mother of Ismenus and of the prophet Tenerus. She was worshipped at Thebes in the Ismenium.

Meliae (Μελίαι) and **Meliădes** (Μελιάδες). (1) The nymphs who, with the Gigantes and Erinnyes, sprang from the drops of blood that fell from Uranus and were received by Gaea. (2) The nymphs who nursed the infant Zeus (q. v.).

Meliboea (Μελίβοια). (1) A town on the coast of Thessaly in Magnesia, between Mount Ossa and Mount Pelion, where Philoctetes reigned, who is hence called by Vergil, *dux Meliboeus.* It was noted for its purple dye (Lucret. ii. 499). (2) An island at the mouth of the river Orontes in Syria.

Melicertes (Μελικέρτης). In Greek mythology the son of Athamas and Ino, and changed after his death by drowning into the marine deity Palaemon, while his mother became Leucothea. (See INO.) His name (=*Melkart*), however, shows him to have been originally a Phœnician god. Like Ino-Leucothea, he was worshipped on all the coast of the Mediterranean, especially on that of Megara and at the Isthmus of Corinth, where he was so closely connected with the cult of Poseidon that the Isthmian Games, originally instituted in honour of this god, came to be looked upon as the funeral games of Melicertes. The Romans regarded him as a beneficent god of the sea, and identified him with Portunus, the god of harbours.

Melĭna. A bag or pouch made of the skin of the badger (*meles*) (Plaut. *Epid.* i. 21).

Mĕlinno (Μελιννώ). A Greek poetess, the author of an ode to Rome consisting of five Sapphics usually ascribed to Erinna. See Welcker's *Kleine Schriften*, ii. p. 160.

Melissa (Μέλισσα). (1) A nymph who was said to have discovered the use of honey, and from whom bees were believed to have received their name (μέλισσαι). There can be no doubt, however, that her name really came from μέλι, "honey," and was hence given to nymphs. The name was commonly given to priestesses of Demeter, Persephoné, Apollo, and Artemis. (2) The wife of Periander and daughter of Procles. She was slain by her husband.

Melissa (Μέλισσα). A village of Phrygia Magna containing the tomb of Alcibiades, of whom the emperor Hadrian caused a marble statue to be erected there.

Melissus (Μέλισσος). (1) A Samian philosopher of Eleatic tendencies. He is probably not the person who commanded the fleet opposed to Pericles in B.C. 440, but of earlier date. Only fragments of his work remain. (2) A Latin grammarian and comic poet, the freedman of Maecenas. Augustus intrusted him with the arrangement of a library in the portico of Octavia (Suet. *Gramm.* 21).

Melĭta or **Melĭté** (Μελίτη). (1) The modern Malta, an island in the Mediterranean Sea, about seventeen miles long and nine in breadth. It was colonized by the Phœnicians, and afterwards belonged to the Carthaginians, from whom it was taken by the Romans in the Second Punic War (B.C. 216). It is celebrated as the island on which the Apostle Paul was shipwrecked; though some writers erroneously suppose that the Apostle was shipwrecked on the island of the same name off the Illyrican coast. The inhabitants manufactured fine cloth (*Melitensia*, sc. *vestimenta*); and the lapdogs (*catuli Melitaei*) were much petted by Roman ladies. Cicero speaks of it as the home of pirates (*Verr.* iv. 46, 47), but himself often thought of making it a place of exile. The Ogygia of Homer is sometimes identified with Malta. In the fifth century A.D. it was taken by the Vandals, then by the Goths, and in 870 by the Arabs. See Caruana, *Reports on Phœnician and Roman Antiquities in Malta* (1881–1882); and James Smith, *Voyage and Shipwreck of St. Paul* (1866). (2) Now Meleda, a small island in the Adriatic Sea, off the coast of Illyria (Dalmatia), northwest of Epidaurus. (3) A deme of Attica which gave its name to one of the city gates. (4) A lake in Aetolia.

Melitaea (Μελιταία), **Melitēa** (Μελίτεια), or **Melitia** (Μελιτία). A town in Thessaly in Phthiotis, on the northern slope of Mount Othrys, and near the river Enipeus (Thuc. iv. 78).

Melĭté (Μελίτη). A nymph, one of the Nereïdes, a daughter of Nereus and Doris.

Melitēné (Μελιτηνή). A city and district of Armenia Minor, between the Anti-Taurus and the Euphrates. It was known for its fruit, oil, and wine, and under the Roman Empire was the station of a legion and the capital of the province. Here the Romans defeated the Persians in A.D. 577.

Melitensia Vestimenta. See MELITA.

Melĭto (Μελίτων). A bishop of Sardes under Marcus Aurelius, to whom he inscribed a defence of the Christians, fragments of which are extant.

Melium. A leather dog-collar studded with nails (Varr. *R. R.* ii. 9. 15). See MILLUS.

Mella or **Mela.** The modern Mella, a river in Gallia Transpadana, flowing by Brixia (Brescia), and falling into the Ollius (Oglio).

Mellaria. (1) A town of the Bastuli in Hispania Baetica, between Belon and Calpé. (2) A town in the same province, considerably north of the former.

Melodūnum. The modern Melun; a town of the Senones in Gallia Lugdunensis, on an island of the Sequana (Seine) (Caes. *B. G.* vii. 58).

Melos (Μῆλος). An island in the Aegaean Sea, the most westerly of the Cyclades. It was first colonized by the Phœnicians, who called it Byblos or Byblis, and afterwards by the Lacedaemonians, or at least by Dorians. Hence, in the Peloponnesian War, it embraced the side of Sparta. In B.C. 416 it was taken by the Athenians, who killed all the adult males, sold the women and children as slaves, and peopled the island with an Athenian colony. The length of the island is about fourteen miles from east to west, and its breadth from north to south eight miles. In 1820, among the ruins of the ancient city of Melos near the theatre was found the exquisite statue usually called the Venus of Milo (Venere di Milo), now in the Louvre at Paris, having been purchased by the Marquis de Rivière, and by him presented to Louis XVIII. It is composed of two blocks of marble, which unite just above the garment which covers the legs. See illustration on p. 96; and Perry, *Greek and Roman Sculpture*, pp. 600–605 (London, 1882). Melos was the birthplace of Diagoras the Atheist, whence Aristophanes calls Socrates also "the Melian" (*Nub.* 830).

Melpomĕné (Μελπομένη, from μέλπομαι). "The singing goddess." One of the nine Muses, and presiding over Tragedy. (See illustration on next page.) See MUSAE.

Membrāna (διφθέρα). Parchment. See LIBER; PALEOGRAPHY; WRITING AND WRITING MATERIALS.

Memmia Gens. A Roman family (plebeian), whose members pretended to be descended from the Trojan Mnestheus (cf. Verg. *Aen.* v. 117).

Memmius. The name of a Roman gens, which claimed descent from the Trojan Mnestheus. (1) C. MEMMIUS, tribune of the plebs B.C. 111, an ardent opponent of the oligarchical party at Rome during the Jugurthine War. He was slain by the mob of Saturninus and Glaucia while a candidate for the consulship in 100. (2) C. MEMMIUS GEMELLUS, tribune of the plebs in B.C. 66, curule aedile in 60, and praetor in 58, was impeached for bribery, and withdrew from Rome to Mitylené. Memmius married Fausta, a daughter of the dictator Sulla, by whom he had a son. He was eminent both in literature and in eloquence, though profligate in his private character. Lucretius dedicated to him his poem *De Rerum Natura*.

Memnon (Μέμνων). (1) The beautiful son of Tithonus and Eos (Aurora), was king of the Ethiopians, and came to the assistance of Priam towards the end of the Trojan War. He wore armour

Melpomenê. (Vatican.)

made for him by Hephaestus at the request of his mother. He slew Antilochus, the son of Nestor, but was himself slain by Achilles after a long and fierce combat. While the two heroes were fighting, Zeus weighed their fates, and the scale containing Memnon's sank. To soothe the grief of his mother, Zeus conferred immortality upon Memnon, and caused a number of birds to issue out of the funeral pile, which fought over the ashes of the hero. These birds were called Memnonides, and were said to have visited every year the tomb of the hero on the Hellespont. The Greeks gave the name of Memnonium and Memnonia to certain very ancient buildings and monuments in Europe and Asia, which they supposed to have been erected by or in honour of Memnon. Of these the most celebrated was a great temple of Thebes, behind which was a colossal statue (called the statue of Memnon, τὸ Μεμνόνιον), which, when struck by the first rays of the rising sun, was said to give forth a sound like the snapping asunder of a chord. It appears, however, that the statue represented in reality the Egyptian king Amenophis. The citadel of Susa was also called Memnonion by the Greeks. On the musical statue, cf. Pliny, *H. N.* xxxvi. 58; Pausan. i. 42; and a paper in the *Edinburgh Review* for July, 1886. (2) A native of Rhodes, who had the command of the western coast of Asia Minor when Alexander invaded Asia. He was an able officer, and his death, in B.C. 333, was an irreparable loss to the Persian cause. (3) A native of Heraclea Pontica who wrote an elaborate history of that city, extracts from which have been preserved by Photius and are separately edited by Orelli (Leipzig, 1816).

Weighing the Fates of Achilles and Memnon.

Memnonium (Μεμνόνιον). See MEMNON.

Memorabilia. See XENOPHON.

Memphis (Μέμφις; in the Old Testament, *Moph*). A great city of Egypt, second in importance only to Thebes, after the fall of which it became the capital of the whole country, a position which it had previously shared with Thebes. It is said to have been founded by Menes. It stood on the left bank of the Nile, about ten miles above the Pyramids. See AEGYPTUS.

Menaechmi. A play of Plautus's (q. v.), from which Shakespeare derived the plot of his *Comedy of Errors*. Recent edition, with English notes, by Fowler (Boston, 1889).

Menaenum or **Menae.** A town on the eastern coast of Sicily, south of Hybla, the birthplace and residence of the Sicel chief Ducetius (q. v.), who long made himself a terror to the Greek cities of Sicily.

Menageries. See VIVARIUM.

Menalippus. See MELANIPPUS.

Menander (Μένανδρος). (1) The chief representative of the New Comedy. He was born in B.C. 342, at Athens, of a distinguished and wealthy family, received a careful education, and led a comfortable and luxurious life, partly at Athens, and partly at his estate in the Piraeus, the harbour of Athens, enjoying the intimate friendship of his contemporary and the friend of his youth, Epicurus, of Theophrastus, and of Demetrius Phalereus. He declined an invitation from King Ptolemy I. of Egypt, so as not to have his comfort disturbed. At the height of his poetic productiveness he was drowned while bathing in the Piraeus, at the age of fifty-two. His uncle Alexis had given him some preparatory training in dramatic composition. As early as 322 he made his first appearance as an author. He wrote above a hundred pieces, and worked with the greatest facility; but he only obtained the first prize for eight comedies, in the competition with his popular rival Philemon. The admiration accorded him by posterity was all the greater: there was only one opinion about the excellence of his work. His principal merits were remarkable inventiveness, skilful arrangement of plots, life-like painting of character, a clever and refined wit, elegant and graceful language, and a copious supply of maxims based on a profound knowledge of the world. These last were collected in regular anthologies, and form the bulk of the extant fragments. Unfortunately not one of his plays has survived, although they were much read down to a late date. However, apart from about seventy-three titles, and numerous fragments (some of considerable length), we have transcripts of his comedies (in which, of course, the delicate beauties of the original are lost), in a number of Latin plays by Plautus (*Bacchides, Stichus, Poenulus*) and Terence (*Andria, Eunuchus, Heauton Timorumenos, Adelphi*). Lucian also, in his Conversations of Hetaerae, and Alciphron in his epistles, have made frequent use of Menander. Menander's most popular play seems to have been the *Thais*, a line of which is quoted by St. Paul (1 Cor. xv. 33). The fragments of Menander were printed in the collections of Meineke (1841) and Kock (1880). See the monographs by Guizot (1855), Horkel (1857), and Lübke (1892). (2) A Greek rhetorician of Laodicea, who probably lived at the end of the third century after Christ. He is the author of two treatises about speeches for display, which add to our knowledge of the theory of the sophistic type of oratory. They can be found in Spengel's *Rhetores Graeci*, iii. 331–446. (3) A Byzantine historian of the sixth century A.D., who wrote a history of the Empire from 559–582, in eight books, of which some portions are preserved, edited by Bekker and Niebuhr (Bonn, 1830).

Menander. (Vatican.)

Menapii. A powerful people in the north of Gallia Belgica. They originally dwelt on both banks of the Rhine, but were afterwards driven out of their possessions on the right bank by the Usipetes and Tenchteri, and inhabited only the left bank near its mouth, and west of the Mosa. Their country is described as heavily wooded, and with great swamps and marshes. They had a fortified place on the Mosa (Meuse) called Castellum Menapiorum, the modern Cassel.

Menas (Μηνᾶς). A familiar form of Menodōrus (Μηνόδωρος). A freedman of Pompey the Great and one of the principal commanders of the fleet of Sextus Pompey against Antony and Octavianus (B.C. 40). In B.C. 39 he tried in vain to dissuade his master from concluding a peace with Octavianus and Antony; and, at an entertainment given to them by Sextus on board his ship at Misenum, Menas suggested to him to cut the cables of the vessel, and, running it out to sea, despatch both his rivals. The treacherous proposal, however, was rejected by Pompey. On the breaking out of the war again in B.C. 38, Menas deserted Pompey and went over to Octavianus. In B.C. 36 he returned to his old master's service; but in the course of the same year he again played the deserter, and joined Octavianus. In B.C. 35 he accompanied Octavianus in the Pannonian campaign, and was slain at the siege of Siscia. According to the old scholiasts, this Menas is the person so vehemently attacked by Horace in the Fourth Epode.

Mendé (Μένδη) or **Mendae.** A town on the west coast of the Macedonian peninsula Pallené and on the Thermaic Gulf, a colony of the Eretrians, and celebrated for its wine (Pausan. x. 5, 27).

Mendes (Μένδης). A city of the Delta of Egypt, on the bank of one of the lesser arms of the Nile, named after it the Mendesian mouth (Μενδήσιον στόμα). Here was worshipped a deity of the Egyptians, called Mendes, and identified by Herodotus (ii. 42, 46) with the Arcadian Pan.

Mendīcus (πτωχός). A beggar. Beggars abounded in ancient times, but were less numerous, apparently, in Greece than in Italy, where the beggar's trade was, in ancient as in modern times, a recognized profession. The bridges over the Tiber were favourite resorts for mendicants (Juv. iv. 116; xiv. 134), as also the vicinity of the theatres and the temples (Orelli, *Inscr.* 4097), and the great *viae* in the neighbourhood of Rome. Children were trained up as beggars, and were often mutilated to excite compassion, after the manner of the *comprachicos* of later days (Sen. *Controv.* 33). Blind beggars were led by a dog (Mart. xiv. 81), as shown in the accompanying illustration from a painting found at Herculaneum and given by Rich. The

Roman Beggar. (Herculaneum.)

priests of Cybelé were a sort of mendicant order, and lived on the alms of the charitable (Hor. *Sat.* i. 2, 2).

Menĕcles (Μενεκλῆς). (1) Of Barcé in Cyrené, an historian of uncertain date. (2) Of Alabanda, a celebrated rhetorician. He and his brother Hierocles taught rhetoric at Rhodes, where the orator M. Antonius heard them, about B.C. 94.

Menecrātes (Μενεκράτης). (1) A Syracusan physician at the court of Philip, king of Macedon, B.C. 359–336. He made himself ridiculous by calling himself "Zeus," and assuming divine honours. There is a tale that he was invited one day by Philip to a magnificent entertainment, where the other guests were sumptuously fed, while he himself had nothing but incense and libations, as not being subject to the human infirmity of hunger. He was at first pleased with his reception; but afterwards, perceiving the joke and finding that no more substantial food was offered him, he left the party in disgust (Athen. p. 289). (2) TIBERIUS

CLAUDIUS MENECRĂTES, a physician mentioned by Galen, composed more than 150 medical works, of which only a few fragments remain.

Menedēmus (Μενέδημος). A Greek philosopher, a native of Eretria. Though of noble birth, he was poor, and worked for a livelihood either as a builder or as a tent-maker. According to one story, he seized the opportunity afforded by his being sent on some military service to Megara to hear Plato, and abandoned the army to addict himself to philosophy; but it may be questioned whether he was old enough to have heard Plato before the death of the latter. According to another story, he and his friend Asclepiades got their livelihood as millers, working during the night that they might have leisure for philosophy in the day (Athen. p. 168). The two friends afterwards became disciples of Stilpo at Megara. From Megara they went to Elis, and placed themselves under the instruction of some disciples of Phaedo. On his return to Eretria Menedemus established a school of philosophy, which was called the Eretrian. He did not, however, confine himself to philosophical pursuits, but took an active part in the political affairs of his native city, and came to be the leading man in the State. He went on various embassies to Lysimachus, Demetrius, and others; but being suspected of the treacherous intention of betraying Eretria into the power of Antigonus, he quitted his native city secretly, and took refuge with Antigonus in Asia. Here he starved himself to death in the seventy-fourth year of his age, probably about B.C. 277. Of the philosophy of Menedemus little is known, except that it closely resembled that of the Megarian School, on which see EUCLIDES, p. 630.

Menelāï Portus (Μενελάïος λίμην). An ancient city on the coast of Marmarica in Northern Africa, founded, according to tradition, by Menelaüs, and where Agesilaüs died.

Menelaïum (Μενελάïον). A mountain in Laconia near Therapné, where the *heroum* of Menelaüs was situated.

Menelāüs (Μενέλαος and Μενέλεως). A son of Atreus, and younger brother of Agamemnon, with whom he was exiled by Thyestes, the murderer of Atreus, and fled to King Tyndareos, at Sparta, whose daughter Helen he married, and whose throne he inherited after the death of Helen's brothers, Castor and Polydeuces (Pollux). When Paris had robbed him of his wife and of great treasures, he went with Odysseus to Troy to demand restitution, and they were hospitably received there by Antenor. His just claims were refused, and his life was even put in danger. He and Agamemnon accordingly called on the Greek chieftains to join in an expedition against Troy, and himself furnished sixty ships. At Troy he distinguished himself in counsel and in action, and was specially protected by Athené and Heré. In the single combat with Paris he was victorious, but his opponent was rescued and carried off by Aphrodité. On demanding that Helen and the treasures should be restored, he was wounded by an arrow shot by the Trojan Pandarus. He was also ready to fight Hector, and was only prevented by the entreaties of his friends. When Patroclus had fallen, he shielded the dead body, at first alone, and then with the aid of Aiax, and bore it from the field of battle with Meriones. He was also one of the heroes of the wooden horse. Having recovered Helen he hastened home, but on rounding the promontory of Malea was driven to Egypt with five ships, and wandered about for eight years among the peoples of the East, where he was kindly received everywhere, and received rich presents. He was finally detained at the isle of Pharos by contrary winds, and with the help of the marine goddess Eidothea artfully compelled her father Proteus to prophesy to him. He thus learned the reason for his being detained at the island, and was also told that, as husband of the daughter of Zeus, he would not die, but enter the Elysian plains alive. After appeasing the gods in Egypt with hecatombs, he returned prosperously to his home, where he arrived on the very day on which Orestes was burying Aegisthus and Clytaemnestra. He spent the rest of his life quietly with Helen, in Lacedaemon. Their only daughter Hermioné was married to Neoptolemus, son of Achilles. See HELENA; TROJAN WAR.

Menenius Lanātus. (1) AGRIPPA. Roman consul in B.C. 503. It was owing to his mediation that the first great rupture between the patricians and plebeians, when the latter seceded to the Sacred Mount, was brought to a happy and peaceful termination in B.C. 493; and it was upon this occasion he is said to have related to the plebeians the well-known fable of the belly and the members. (2) TITUS. A Roman who as consul in B.C. 477 was defeated by the Etruscans. He had previously, by his treacherous neglect, allowed the Fabii to be destroyed by the enemy. Being tried by the tribunes, he was fined, and, by constant brooding over his disgrace, pined away and died (Livy, ii. 51).

Menes (Μήν and Μήνης). The first king of Egypt, according to the Egyptian traditions, and the one who introduced into Egypt the worship of the gods, sacrifices, and many of the usages of advanced civilization (Herod. ii. 4, 99). His date is given as between B.C. 4500 and 4000. See AEGYPTUS, p. 28.

Menestheus (Μενεσθεύς). (1) The son of Peteos, who seized the government of Attica, while Theseus pined away in the nether world, and commanded the Athenians before Troy, where he fell. (See DEMOPHOÖN; THESEUS.) (2) The charioteer of Diomedes. (3) The son of the Athenian general Iphicrates. With his father and his father-in-law he was impeached by their colleague Chares for misconduct in their command during the Social War (B.C. 356); but Iphicrates and Menestheus were acquitted (Diod. xvi. 21).

Menexĕnus (Μενέξενος). An Athenian, the son of Demophoön, introduced by Plato as one of the interlocutors in his dialogues *Lysis* and *Menexenus*.

Meninx (Μῆνιγξ) or **Lotophagītis** (Λωτοφαγῖτις). An island close to the coast of Africa Propria, at the southeastern extremity of the Lesser Syrtis. It was the birthplace of the Roman emperors Vibius Gallus and Volusianus.

Menippé (Μενίππη). A daughter of Orion, who offered to die with her sister Metioché, when a pestilence was raging in Boeotia, and the oracle demanded the sacrifice of two virgins. (See ORION.) They were changed into comets by Pluto and Persephoné, and had a sanctuary near Orchomenus (Ovid, *Met.* xiii. 685).

Menippus (Μένιππος). (1) A Greek philosopher of Gadara in Syria, who flourished about B.C. 250. He was originally a slave, and afterwards an adherent of the Cynic School of philosophy. His writings (now completely lost) treated of the follies of mankind, especially of philosophers, in a sarcastic tone. They were a medley of prose and verse, and became models for the satirical works of Varro (hence called *Saturae Menippeae*), and afterwards for those of Lucian. (See SATIRA.) (2) A Carian orator of Cicero's time, and regarded by many as almost equal to the great Attic orators. (3) A geographer of Pergamus, who, in the Augustan Age, wrote a *Periplus*, of which an abridgment was made by Marcianus (q. v.).

Menodōrus. See MENAS.

Menoeceus (Μενοικεύς). (1) Grandson of Pentheus of Thebes, father of Hipponomé, Creon, and Iocasta. (2) The grandson of the above, son of Creon. At the siege of Thebes by the Seven, Tiresias prophesied that the Thebans would conquer if the wrath of Ares at the slaying of the dragon by Cadmus were appeased by the voluntary death of a descendant of the warriors that had sprung from the dragon's teeth. Menoeceus, one of the last of this race, slew himself, in spite of his father's prohibition, on the castle wall, and fell into the chasm which had once been the haunt of the dragon that guarded the spring Dircé.

Menoetius (Μενοίτιος). Son of Actor and Aegina and father of Patroclus, who is hence called Menoetiades.

Menon (Μένων). A Thessalian adventurer, one of the generals of the Greek mercenaries in the army of Cyrus the Younger, when the latter marched into Upper Asia against his brother Artaxerxes, B.C. 401. After the death of Cyrus he was apprehended along with the other Greek generals by Tissaphernes, and was put to death by lingering tortures, which lasted for a whole year. His character is drawn in the blackest colours by Xenophon. He is the same as the Menon introduced in the dialogue of Plato which bears his name.

Mens. Under this name the Romans personified intelligence and prudence. After the battle at Lake Trasimenus, which was lost through the carelessness of the Romans, a temple was erected to her on the Capitol. The anniversary of its foundation was celebrated on the eighth of June.

Mensa (τράπεζα). (1) Originally a board or plank, and then a table, which the ancients had in all varieties and shapes. The simplest table was one with three legs and a round top (*cilliba*), used in wine-shops. The Greek table was originally four-legged, as the name τράπεζα implies. Tables were made of white marble (Hor. *Sat.* i. 6, 16) and of wood, and in the houses of the rich at Rome were very costly, being regarded as heirlooms. The most valued woods were the maple (*acerna*) and the *citrus*, whose roots and tubers were used, displaying when cut a great variety of markings and curling veins. These were called *tigrinae* or *pantherinae* from their spots, and also *pavoninae* (Mart. xiv. 85) as suggesting the "eyes" in a peacock's tail. Enormous sums were paid for fine tables. Pliny (*H. N.* xiii. 91–99) speaks of Cicero as paying 500,000 sesterces ($20,000) for one, and Pollio as giving 1,000,000 sesterces ($40,000). A table with a single leg was called *monopodium; orbis* denotes any round table. The feet were often of ivory, beautifully carved; and the tables themselves were often overlaid with plates of gold, silver, or bronze (Petron. 73; Mart. iii. 31), and were inlaid with jewels.

Three-legged Table. (Pompeii.)

The table was a little lower than the couches surrounding it. Among the Greeks and later Romans it was covered by a cloth (*mantele*), and was cleaned by sponges or woollen cloths.

(2) MENSA PRIMA (πρώτη τράπεζα), the first course at dinner. In early times, the whole table was carried away at the end of each course, whence the expressions *mensam ponere, auferre, tollere, removere.*

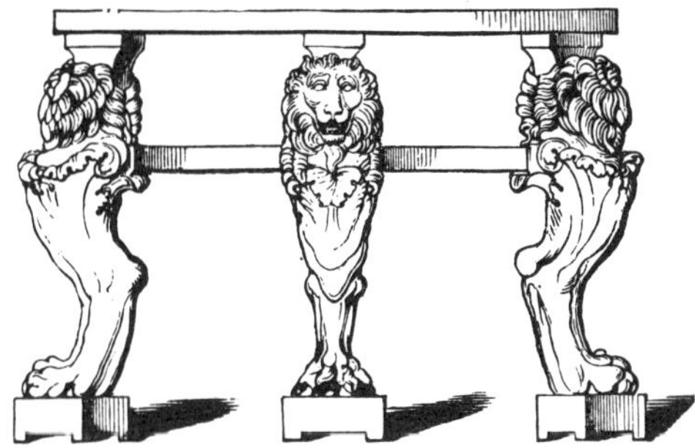
Marble Table. (Overbeck.)

(3) MENSA SECUNDA (δεύτερα τράπεζα), the last course of a meal, i. e. the dessert. See CENA.

(4) MENSA DELPHĬCA, an ornamental table as a part of the furniture of a house. See ABACUS.

(5) MENSA SACRA, a table used as an altar (Verg. *Aen.* ii. 764).

(6) MENSA ARGENTARIA, a broker's counter.

(7) MENSA PUBLĬCA, a bank (Cic. *In Pison.* 36).

(8) See CATASTA.

(9) A square flat gravestone laid over a grave and with a hole in the centre for sacrificial oils, etc. (Cic. *De Leg.* ii. 26).

Mensarii. See TRAPEZITAE.

Mensis. A month. See CALENDARIUM.

Mensōres. Persons employed in taking any kind of measurements, such as (1) land-surveyors (see GROMATICI); (2) the persons who marked out the various divisions of the camp (see CASTRA); (3) house-builders (Pliny, *Epist.* x. 19, 5); and (4) *mensores frumentarii*, officials who measured out the corn brought to the public granaries. See FRUMENTARII LEGES; HORREA.

Menstruum. See SERVUS.

Mensularii. See TRAPEZITAE.

Mensūra (μέτρον). Measure. The earliest measures known are probably those derived from parts of the human body (Vitruv. iii. 1, 5), and were at first, naturally, less definite and exact than those employed in later times. Thus, the foot, the finger, the palm of the hand, the forearm were all employed as primitive units of length and breadth. Units of capacity were generally based upon such natural objects or measures as were approximately uniform. The Jews and some of the Kelts employed the hen's egg as a unit; the natives of Zanzibar the gourd; the Romans a mussel-shell (*cochlear*). Possibly the Greek κύαθος was originally a pod or gourd of some kind. The filled hand also is mentioned as serving as a measure of capacity. Afterwards a more precise system was adopted and ratified by law. Thus Phidon of Argos fixed the standard measure for the people of the Peloponnesus (Herod. vi. 127), Solon for the Athenians (Andoc. 11, 25), and Augustus for the later Romans.

The principal measure of length among the Greeks was the foot (πούς), there being three different standards, the Attic, the Olympic, and the Aeginetan. The first was 295.7 millimetres; the second, 320.5 mill.; the third, 330 mill. In Western Europe there were three kinds of foot (*pes*), the Italian (275 mill.), the Roman (296 mill.), and the *pes Drusianus* (333 mill.). In both the Greek and the Roman systems the unit (μονάς) was the finger-breadth (δάκτυλος, *digitus*). The *palmus* (δοχμή) was four *digiti*. The foot was regarded as equal to 16 *digiti*. The cubit (πῆχυς, *cubitus*) was the distance from the point of the elbow to the point of the middle finger, and = 24 *digiti*.

The fathom (ὀργυιά, *ulna* or *tensum* in Low Lat.) was the length of the extended arms = six feet. The πλέθρον (Oscan and Umbr. *vorsus*) was about 100 feet. The Roman *actus* was 120 feet. Among the itinerary measures the *stadium* (στάδιον) was 600 feet; the ἱππικόν, or race-course, was four *stadia;* the parasang (παρασάγγης), a Persian measure, was 30 *stadia* or four Roman miles; the *millarum* (μίλιον) was 1000 feet (*milia passuum*).

Of land measures were the Homeric unit γύης (γύη), about 60 feet; the square plethrum = 10,000 sq. ft.; the *scripulum* = 100 sq. ft.; the *iugerum* = 288 sq. rods; the *heredium* = 2 *iugera;* the *centuria* = 200 *iugera* (perhaps originally 100); the *saltus* = 800 *iugera*.

Of liquid and dry measures, the chief are the κύαθος = .08 of an Eng. pint; the κοτύλη = 6 *cyathi;* the Roman *sextarius* (ξέστης) = 12 *cyathi*, nearly an Eng. pint; the χοῦς, *congius* = 12 *cyathi*, or about six pints; the ἀμφορεύς, *amphora* = 8 *congii* or 48 *sextarii*, about 22 quarts; and the *culleus* = 20 *amphorae*. Distinctly for dry measure were the χοῖνιξ = four κοτύλαι, or about one quart; the μόδιος, *modius* = about a peck; the μέδιμνος = 6 *modii*.

See the standard work by Hultsch, *Griechische und römische Metrologie* (Berlin, 1882); R. Lepsius, *Längenmasse der Alten* (Berlin, 1884); Queipo, *Essai sur les Systèmes Métriques Monétaires des Anciens Peuples* (Paris, 1859); and for a full list of equivalents, the tables given in the Appendix to this Dictionary.

Mentĕsa. (1) Called Bastia, a town of the Oretani in Hispania Tarraconensis. (2) A small town of the Bastuli in the south of Hispania Baetica.

Mentor (Μέντωρ). (1) Son of Alcimus of Ithaca, friend of Odysseus, who, on departing for Troy, confided to him the care of his house and the education of Telemachus (*Odyss.* ii. 225). His name has hence become a proverbial one for a wise and faithful adviser or monitor. Athené assumed his shape when she brought Telemachus to Pylus, and when she aided Odysseus in fighting the suitors and made peace between him and their relatives. (2) The most celebrated master of the toreutic art among the ancients (Pliny, *H. N.* xxxiii. § 154). As some of his works were destroyed at the burning of the temple of Artemis at Ephesus, in B.C. 356, obviously he lived before that event, and probably flourished in the best period of Greek art, though he is never mentioned by any earlier Greek writer than Lucian (*Lexiphanes*, 7). He worked mainly in silver. The orator Crassus paid 100,000 sesterces ($4000) for two cups chased by his hand, but, from regard to their value, refrained from using them. Varro possessed a statue wrought by him in bronze; and one Diodorus at Lilybaeum, two fine cups in the style of those adorned with figures of animals by Thericles, the Corinthian potter. Martial (iii. 41) mentions a cup with a lifelike representation of a lizard, and often refers to him (cf. Juv. viii. 104). (3) A Rhodian Greek who with his brother Memnon served the Persian Artabazus and later King Nectanabis of Egypt. He aided Tennes, king of Sidon, against Darius Ochus, and, when Tennes went over to the Persians, entered the service of Darius, who made him satrap of the western part of Asia Minor (Arrian, *Anab.* vii. 419).

Menŭsis (μήνυσις). An accusation made by a disqualified person or by an unwilling witness. See ECCLESIA; EISANGELIA.

Mercenarii (μισθωτοί, μισθοφόροι, ξένοι, and collectively τὸ ξενικόν). Mercenary troops. Apart from a few earlier examples of the employment of mercenaries, a regular organization of such troops was formed among the Greeks in the course of the Peloponnesian War, especially by the Arcadians, who were compelled by the poverty of their own country to utilize their strength and courage by seeking employment outside it. It was most easily found by serving as soldiers in the continual wars between the Grecian States. When the mercenary system was at its height, Arcadians formed by far the larger portion of the mercenary forces, even as early as in the first great army of mercenaries of 13,000 men, which the younger Cyrus led against his brother Artaxerxes, king of Persia, in B.C. 401. In Greece in the fourth century the ground became more and more favourable to the growth of the mercenary body, and the citizens of the Greek States, instead of bearing arms themselves, became more and more inclined to leave their wars to be fought out by mercenaries, especially since it had become a trade to form troops of mercenaries, and to let them out wholesale for service, no matter whether to Greeks or barbarians. Even prominent men, such as Agesilaüs and Philopoemen, did not consider it beneath their dignity to fight for strangers at the head of mercenaries. One of the chief recruiting places in the fourth century was Corinth, and afterwards for a time the district near the promontory of Taenarum in Lacedaemon. The generals of mercenaries were called στρατηγοί; their captains, through whom they raised companies of different kinds of troops, known as λόχοι, one hundred men in number, λοχαγοί. The usual monthly pay of a common soldier was on the average a gold daric (= 20 silver drachmae or $3 in intrinsic value of silver, but in intrinsic value of the gold contained in it a little more than $5). Out of this he had to maintain himself entirely, to buy his armour, and keep it in good condition. The pay of the λοχαγοί was double and of the στρατηγοί four times that amount. In later times the στρατηγοί, when they entered with complete armies into the service of some power at war, seem to have generally received considerable sums at the conclusion of the contract. The Romans also employed foreign mercenaries after the Second Punic War, especially as archers and slingers, and after the time of Marius a recruited army of mercenaries (see LEGIO) had sprung out of the earlier levied army of citizens; but the mercenary organization never took among the Romans a form similar to that among the Greeks.

Mercurii Promontorium. See HERMAEUM.

Mercurius. See HERMES.

Mercurius Trismegistus. See HERMES TRISMEGISTUS.

Merenda. Breakfast or luncheon. See CENA.

Merĕtrix (πόρνη). A woman of loose character. There are a number of words in Greek and Latin to designate the harlot; ἑταίρα and *concubina* usually implying one who has a quasi-recognized connection with a single man, while πόρνη, *meretrix*, *scortum*, etc., designate the common prostitute: παλλακή, παλλακίς, and *pellex* usually imply the kept mistress of a married man. See CONCUBINA.

I. GREEK.—In Greece the State not only tolerated but protected the public courtesans. Solon is said to have established a brothel (πορνεῖον) from whose profits he built a temple to Aphroditê Pandemos. In later times the number of such places increased and were licensed (πορνικὸν τέλος), as in Paris and other Continental cities to-day. Women living by themselves also paid a regular tax like the *filles inscrites*. The keepers of houses of ill-fame were known as πορνοβοσκοί. Private courtesans were very numerous at Athens and especially at Corinth, which last city was proverbial for its loose morals and the beauty of its *hetaerae*. Some of these persons were famous throughout Greece for their wit and accomplishments, and seem to have prided themselves on their mental gifts. Thus the Arcadian Lasthenea was a pupil of Plato, Leontion of Epicurus, and Aspasia (q. v.) is said to have instructed Sophocles and Pericles. For other famous courtesans, see the articles HARMODIUS; LAÏS; PHRYNÊ.

As virtuous women in Greece (outside of Sparta and a few Dorian communities) were kept strictly at home and possessed few accomplishments, we find the *hetaera* occupying often the influential position which in modern times belongs to the lawful wife; and so long as the husband did not altogether neglect his wife, any associations that he might have outside his own home with *hetaerae* were not regarded with severity. It is probable that the indulgence with which women of this class were looked upon sprang in part from the semi-religious character of the prostitute as being associated with the worship of Aphroditê. At Corinth, for instance, a large number of these women were formally dedicated to the service of that goddess and were styled ἱερόδουλοι. Few citizens ever entered the ranks of the πορναί, and whenever such a case happened loss of citizenship was the penalty, as also for a person who kept a πορνεῖον.

II. ROMAN.—In the early days of the Roman Republic prostitution was little known, and when recognized was branded with infamy. It seems to have been first introduced as a regular profession from Etruria, and at last assumed frightful proportions and had little or no legal restriction. Its growth was fostered by the spread of slavery among the Romans, since from the slave-markets both men and women, bred in the midst of Oriental corruption, came from Asia and Africa to taint the old-time purity of Rome by their influence. The pages of Ovid, Petronius, Juvenal, and Martial supply a mass of information regarding the frightful prevalence of the social evil. Under the Empire, so lightly was public debauchery regarded that ladies of noble birth voluntarily abandoned their rank in order to enroll themselves in the police-registers as courtesans; while Juvenal states that the empress Messalina, the wife of Claudius, used to steal away from the imperial palace at night and under the assumed name of Lycisca occupy a harlot's cell (Juv. vi. 638). Dancing-girls, actresses, musicians, and professional women in general were regularly classed as *meretrices;* and there were both those who occupied public houses (*lupanaria*) and those who lived in private lodgings. The parts of the city that were most frequented by them were the Suburra (q. v.), the Vicus Tuscus, the Vicus Patricius, the baths, the Summoenium (near the walls), and the arcades of the Circus Maximus, where remains of their low-vaulted cells (*cellae*) still exist. These places were small and a little lower than the sidewalk, and were also known as *fornices* from the arch (*fornix*) that formed their roof. At the entrance to each was usually a sign (*titulus*) bearing the name of the *meretrix* and her price. The wording of one of them has been preserved for us in the *Apollonius Tyrius* (ch. xxx.). Besides the names given above, these women were called *lupae*, "wolves," *prostibulae* (*pro* + *stabulum*), *prosedae* (*pro* + *sedeo*), *bustuariae* (as plying their trade near the *bustae* or cemeteries), *diobolariae*, *alicariae* (from the bakeries), and *nonariae* (as forbidden to appear on the streets before the *hora nona*, 3 p. m.).

Some few attempts were made to control and regulate this evil. *Meretrices* were forbidden to wear the *stola* of the matron, but dressed in a dark toga; and the city praetor had power to imprison, scourge, or banish them without a trial. Yet the restraint put upon them was only nominal, and as they were publicly recognized in some of the great festivals, such as the Floralia (q. v.), they may be said to have had a sort of official standing.

BIBLIOGRAPHY.—See Dufour, *Histoire de la Prostitution*, 6 vols. (Paris, 1853); Lecky, *Hist. of European Morals*, vol. i. (N. Y. 1884); Becker-Göll, *Charikles*, vol. ii. pp. 85–104; vol. iii. pp. 306–398; Fr. Jacobs, *Vermischte Schriften*, vol. iv. (1844). The ancient authorities for Roman prostitution are carefully collected by Jeannel, *La Prostitution* (Paris, 1874). A Roman *lupanar* is among the houses excavated at Pompeii, where it is now shown to visitors. The paintings on the walls are still too plainly preserved. The other objects found in this house are now kept in the Raccolta Pornografica of the Museo Nazionale at Naples.

Merga. An agricultural implement used in the harvest, but of uncertain form. Plautus (*Poen.* v.

2, 58) speaks of it as used for reaping, but Festus as a sort of fork (*furca*).

Merges. A bundle or sheaf of grain. The quantity taken up or cut by a *merga* (Verg. *Georg.* ii. 517).

Meridiāni. See GLADIATORES.

Meriŏnes (Μηριόνης). Son of Molus, a half-brother of Idomeneus of Crete, whom he accompanied to Troy with eighty ships. In Homer we read that he was there one of the bravest in the fight, and with Teucer specially distinguished in archery, an art in which the Cretans had always excelled. According to a later legend, on his return from Troy his vessel was driven to Engyion in the north of Sicily, which was supposed to be a Cretan settlement. At Gnossus in Crete his grave was shown, and both he and Idomeneus, his friend and companion in battle, were honoured as heroes (Diod. iv. 79).

Merměrus (Μέρμερος). (1) One of the Centaurs present at the wedding of Pirithoüs. (2) Son of Iason and Medea. He, with his brother Pheres, was murdered by his mother at Corinth. He is also called MACĂREUS and MORMŎRUS.

Mermessus (Μερμησσός) and **Myrmessus** (Μυρμησσός); also **Marmessus** and **Marpessus.** A town of Mysia near Polichus; famous as the home of a sibyl (Pausan. x. 12, 2).

Merobaudes, FLAVIUS. A rhetorician born in Spain and distinguished as a general, and also as a Latin poet, in the first half of the fifth century after Christ. Besides a short hymn, *De Christo* (or *Laus Christi*), there are preserved fragments of five secular poems, the longest being part of a panegyric on the third consulate of Aëtius (A.D. 446), with a preface in prose, discovered by Niebuhr on a palimpsest at St. Gallen and published by him at Bonn in 1824. They prove him to be no unskilful imitator of Claudian; in language and metre he possesses an elegance rare in his time. The bust of a statue exhumed in the Forum of Ulpian in 1813 contained an inscription eulogizing Merobaudes. See Winnefeld, *Sortes Sangallenses Ineditae* (Bonn, 1887).

Meroë (Μερόη). The island formed by the rivers Astapus (Blue Nile) and Astaboras (Atbarah), and the portion of the Nile between their mouths, was a district of Ethiopia. Its chief city, also called Meroë, became at a very early period the capital of a powerful State. The priests of Meroë were closely connected in origin and customs with those of Egypt; and, according to some traditions, the latter sprang from the former, and they from India. From Meroë in the eighth century B.C. sprang the Ethiopian dynasty of Egypt (the twenty-fifth), reigning at Thebes. See AECYPTUS; AETHIOPIA; THEBAE.

Merom Lacus. See SEMECHONITIS.

Merŏpé (Μερόπη). (1) One of the Heliades or sisters of Phaëthon. (2) Daughter of Atlas, one of the Pleiades, wife of Sisyphus of Corinth and mother of Glaucus. In the constellation of the Pleiades she is the seventh and the least visible star, because she is ashamed of having had intercourse with a mortal man (Apollod. i. 9, 3; iii. 10, 1). (3) Daughter of Cypselus, wife of Cresphontes, and mother of Aepytus. See AEPYTUS.

Merops (Μέροψ). (1) A king of the Ethiopians, by whose wife, Clymené, Helios (Sol) became the father of Phaëthon. (2) A king of Cos, husband of the nymph Ethemea, and father of Eumelus. His wife was slain by Artemis for neglect of her worship; whereupon Merops wished to take his own life, but was changed by Heré into an eagle and placed among the stars (Hyg. *Astr.* ii. 16). (3) King of Rhyndacus on the Hellespont. He is also called MACAR or MACAREUS, and was a famous seer. His children were Clité, Arisbé, Amphius, and Adrastus.

Merŭla, L. CORNELIUS. A flamen Dialis who, on the deposition of Cinna in B.C. 87, was elected consul, but committed suicide on the capture of Rome by Marius and Cinna (Plut. *Mar.* 41, 45).

Merŭla, PAULUS (PAUL VAN MERLE). A Dutch classical scholar, born at Dordrecht in 1558, and Professor of History from 1592. Because of ill-health he went to Rostock, where he died in 1607. He edited Eutropius, and, for the first time, the fragments of Ennius, besides writing other works of less importance. See ENNIUS.

Merum (ἄκρατον). Unmixed wine. See VINUM.

Mesambria (Μεσαμβρίη). A peninsula on the coast of Persis.

Meschěla (Μεσχέλα). A large city on the northern coast of Africa, and said to have been founded by the Greeks while returning from the Trojan War.

Mesembria (Μεσημβρία). (1) A celebrated town of Thrace on the Pontus Euxinus, and at the foot of Mount Haemus, founded by the inhabitants of Chalcedon and Byzantium in the time of Darius Hystaspis, and hence called a colony of Megara, since those two towns were founded by the Megarians. (2) A town in Thrace, but of less importance, on the coast of the Aegaean Sea, and in the territory of the Cicones, near the mouth of the Lissus.

Mesēné (Μεσηνή). "Midland." The part of Babylonia which consisted of the great island formed by the Euphrates, the Royal Canal, and the Tigris.

Mesoa or **Messoa.** See SPARTA.

Mesōgis. See LYDIA.

Mesomēdes (Μεσομήδης). A Greek lyric poet of Crete, who lived about A.D. 130, and was a freedman of Hadrian. Three small poems of his have come down to us (*Anthologia Graeca*, xiv. 63; xvi. 323). They are not unattractive, and the one on Nemesis is of peculiar interest, as its musical composition is indicated according to the ancient notation. See Brunck's *Analecta*, iii. 292; Bellermann, *Hymnen des Dionysius und Mesomedes*, pp. 13, 26.

Mesopotamia (Μεσοποταμία). A district of Asia, named from its position between the Euphrates and the Tigris, divided by the Euphrates from Syria and Arabia, and by the Tigris from Assyria. On the north it was separated from Armenia by a branch of the Taurus, called Masius, and on the south from Babylonia by the Median Wall. The name was first used by the Greeks in the time of the Seleucidae. In earlier times the country was reckoned a part, sometimes of Syria, and sometimes of Assyria. In the division of the Persian empire it belonged to the satrapy of Babylonia. The northern part of Mesopotamia was divided into the districts of Mygdonia and Osroëné. In a wider sense, the name is sometimes applied to the whole country between the Euphrates and the Tigris.

Mesostic Verse. See ACROSTICHA.

Mespila (Μέσπιλα). A city of Assyria, on the eastern side of the Tigris, which, in the time of Xenophon, had fallen into decay (*Anab.* iii. 4).

Messa (Μέσσα). A town and harbour in Laconia, near Cape Taenarum.

Messabatēnē (Μεσσαβατηνή) and **Messabatĭcē** (Μεσσαβατική). A district on the southeastern margin of the Tigris and Euphrates Valley.

Messāla or **Messalla.** The name of a distinguished family of the Valeria gens at Rome. The first who bore the name of Messala was M'. VALERIUS MAXĬMUS CORVĪNUS MESSALA, consul B.C. 263, who carried on the war against the Carthaginians in Sicily, and received this cognomen in consequence of his relieving Messina. The most celebrated member of the family was M. VALERIUS MESSĀLA CORVĪNUS. He fought on the republican side at the battle of Philippi (B.C. 42), but was afterwards pardoned by the triumvirs, and became one of the chief generals and friends of Augustus. He was consul B.C. 31, and proconsul of Aquitania in 28, 27. He died about B.C. 3–A.D. 8. Messala was a patron of learning, and was himself an historian, a poet, a grammarian (Quint. i. 7, 37), and an orator; but none of his works are extant. His friendship for Horace and his intimacy with Tibullus are well known. In the elegies of the latter poet the name of Messala is continually introduced.

Messalīna and **Messallīna.** (1) STATILIA, granddaughter of T. Statilius Taurus, consul in A.D. 11. She was the third wife of the emperor Nero, who married her in A.D. 66. She had previously espoused Atticus Vestinus, whom Nero put to death without accusation or trial merely that he might marry Messalina. (2) VALERIA, daughter of M. Valerius Messala Barbatus and of Domitia Lepida. She

Supposed Bust of Messalina. (Capitoline Museum, Rome.)

was the third wife of the emperor Claudius. She married Claudius, to whom she was previously related, before his accession to the Empire. Her profligacy and licentiousness were notorious; and the absence of virtue was not concealed by a lingering sense of shame or even by a specious veil of decorum, inasmuch as she often visited the public brothels (Juv. vi. 115). She was as cruel as she was profligate, and many members of the most illustrious families of Rome were sacrificed to her fears or her hatred. She long exercised an unbounded empire over her weak husband, who alone was ignorant of her infidelities. For some time she was supported in her career of crime by the freedmen of Claudius; but when Narcissus, the most powerful of the emperor's freedmen, perceived that he should probably fall a victim to Messalina's intrigues, he determined to get rid of her. The insane folly of Messalina furnished the means of her own destruction. Having conceived a violent passion for a handsome Roman youth, C. Silius, she publicly married him with all the rites of a legal connubium during the absence of Claudius at Ostia, A.D. 48. Narcissus persuaded the emperor that Silius and Messalina would not have dared such an outrage had they not determined also to deprive him of empire and life. Claudius wavered long, and at length Narcissus himself issued Messalina's death-warrant. She was put to death by a tribune of the guards in the gardens of Lucullus (Tac. *Ann.* xi. 26–38; Suet. *Claud.* 17–39; Juv. x. 333).

Messāna (Μεσσήνη). The modern Messina; a celebrated town of Sicily, on the strait separating Italy from this island, which is here about four miles broad. The Romans called the town Messana, according to its Doric pronunciation, but Messenē was its more usual name among the Greeks. It was originally a town of the Siceli, and was called Zanclē, or a sickle, on account of the shape of its harbour, which is formed by a singular curve of sand and shells. It was first colonized by Chalcidians, and was afterwards seized by Samians, who had come to Sicily after the capture of Miletus by the Persians (B.C. 494). The Samians were shortly afterwards driven out of Zanclē by Anaxilas, who changed the name of the town into Messana or Messenē, both because he was himself a Messenian and because he transferred to the place a body of Messenians from Rhegium. In B.C. 396 it was taken and destroyed by the Carthaginians, but was rebuilt by Dionysius. It afterwards fell into the hands of Agathocles. Among the mercenaries of this tyrant were a number of Mamertini, an Oscan people from Campania, who had been sent from home, under the protection of the god Mamers, or Mars, to seek their fortune in other lands. These Mamertini were quartered in Messana; and after the death of Agathocles (B.C. 282) they made themselves masters of the town, killed the male inhabitants, and took possession of their wives, their children, and their property. The town was now called MAMERTĪNA, and the inhabitants Mamertini; but its ancient name of Messana continued to be in more general use. The new inhabitants could not lay aside their old predatory habits, and in consequence became involved in a war with Hieron of Syracuse, who would probably have conquered the town had not the Carthaginians come in to the aid of the Mamertini, and, under the pretext of assisting them, taken possession of their citadel. The Mamertini had at the same time applied to the Romans for help, who gladly availed themselves of the opportunity to obtain a footing in Sicily. Thus Messana was the immediate cause of the First Punic War, 264. The

Mamertini expelled the Carthaginian garrison, and received the Romans, in whose power Messana remained till the latest times. See Siefert, *Zankle-Messana* (1854); and Axt, *Topographie v. Messana* (1887).

Messapia (Μεσσαπία). The Greek name of Calabria (q. v.).

Messapii (Μεσσαπιοί). A name given to the early inhabitants of southeastern Italy, often regarded as the earliest historical inhabitants of the peninsula. They are the same as the Iapyges or Iapygii, and are also loosely described as Peucetii, Dauni, Bruttii, Sallentini, Paediculi, etc. They perhaps represent an early migration from Hellas into Italy, though the remains of their language contained in a comparatively few inscriptions show that they were not Greeks proper. Scholars generally hold them to have been of the same stock as the Illyrians (Albanians). Their inscriptions have not been deciphered. The most noticeable features of their language appear to have been the genitive endings *-aihi* and *-ihi* (Skt. *-asya*, Gk. *-οιο*), the use of the aspirated consonants, and the avoidance of final *m* and *t*. See Mommsen, *Hist. of Rome*, i. pp. 31–33 (Amer. ed.); id. *Unteritalische Dialekte* (1850); Nissen, *Italische Landeskunde*, vol. i. (1883); Deecke in the *Rheinisches Museum*, vols. xxxvi., xxxviii., and xl.; and the articles INDO-EUROPEAN LANGUAGES; ITALIA.

Messenia (Μεσσηνία). A country in Peloponnesus, bounded on the east by Laconia, from which it was separated by Mount Taygetus, on the north by Elis and Arcadia, and on the south and west by the sea. In the Homeric times the western part of the country belonged to the Neleid princes of Pylos, of whom Nestor was the most celebrated; and the eastern to the Lacedaemonian monarchy. On the conquest of Peloponnesus by the Dorians, Messenia fell to the share of Cresphontes, who became king of the whole country. Messenia was more fertile than Laconia; and the Spartans soon coveted the territory of their brother-Dorians; and thus war broke out between the two people. The First Messenian War lasted twenty years, B.C. 743–723; and notwithstanding the gallant resistance of the Messenian king, Aristodemus, the Messenians were obliged to submit to the Spartans after the capture of their fortress Ithomé. (See ARISTODEMUS.) After bearing the yoke thirty-eight years, the Messenians again took up arms under their heroic leader, Aristomenes (q. v.). The Second Messenian War lasted seventeen years, B.C. 685–668, and terminated with the conquest of Ira and the complete subjugation of the country. Most of the Messenians emigrated to foreign countries, and those who remained behind were reduced to the condition of Helots or serfs. In this state they remained till 464, when the Messenians and other Helots took advantage of the devastation occasioned by the great earthquake at Sparta to rise against their oppressors. This Third Messenian War lasted ten years (464–455), and ended by the Messenians surrendering Ithome to the Spartans on condition of being allowed a free departure from Peloponnesus. When the supremacy of Sparta was overthrown by the battle of Leuctra, Epaminondas collected the Messenian exiles, and founded the town of Messené (B.C. 369), at the foot of Mount Ithomé, which formed the acropolis of the city. Messené was made the capital of the country. Messenia was never again subdued by the Spartans, and it maintained its independence till the conquest of the Achaeans and the rest of Greece by the Romans (B.C. 146). See Niese, *Die älteste Geschichte Messeniens* (1891).

Mēstra (Μήστρα). Daughter of Erysichthon (q. v.). She supported her famished father by employing the power to change herself into any form she pleased, the gift of her lover Poseidon. She let herself be sold in various forms, and then always returned to her father (Ovid, *Met.* viii. 738–878).

Meta. The columns at the upper and lower end of the Roman Circus, round which the competitors usually had to drive seven times. See CIRCUS.

Meta Sudans. The name given to the partly restored brick interior of a beautiful fountain erected by the emperor Domitian near the Colosseum at Rome. It is shown in the illustration on p. 73. It was originally a tall marble cone spouting water from the top and from several jets below (Sext. Ruf. *De Reg. Urb.* 4).

Metăbus. A chief of the Volsci, father of Camilla (q. v.).

Metageitnia (μεταγείτνια). An Athenian festival in honour of Apollo (q. v.).

Metageitnion (Μεταγειτνιών). The second Attic month, nearly equivalent to our August. See CALENDARIUM.

Metal, Artistic Work in. See CAELATURA; TOREUTICA.

Metallum (μέταλλον). In Greek, a mine; in Latin, either a mine or a metal.

It is the purpose of this article to give a brief list of the metals known and used in antiquity, and of the working of mines.

I. METALS.

(*a*) Gold. See AURUM.

(*b*) Silver. See ARGENTUM.

(*c*) Copper. See AES.

(*d*) Brass. See ORICHALCUM.

(*e*) Electrum or gold alloyed with silver; "white gold." See ELECTRUM.

(*f*) Iron (σίδηρος, *ferrum*). Iron is one of the latest metals to come into use owing to the difficulty of working it (Hesiod, 150); but it had begun to be employed in the Homeric Age (*Il.* xviii. 34) for swords and also for ploughshares, though bronze was much commoner. In Hesiod's *Shield of Heracles* hot iron is plunged into water to harden it. By the time of Croesus (i. e. the sixth century B.C.) iron had supplanted bronze for weapons (Herod. i. 67; Pausan. iii. 3, 6). Pliny (*H. N.* xiv. 139) implies that the Romans used iron in the time of Porsena; and in the early Gallic invasions the Roman weapons of iron were a source of superiority over the Gauls, whose weapons were easily bent. Later, in the first century B.C., the Cimbri who invaded Italy had swords, javelins, and even corselets of iron, according to Plutarch. In Greece, Cyprus and the cities of Chalcis and Lacedæmon were celebrated for their iron ware; but external nations like the Chalybes of Pontus surpassed the best work of the Hellenic smiths (Xen. *Anab.* v. 5, 1). Iron was sometimes used in art, as we learn that Aecon made an iron statue of Heracles. The people of Sparta (q. v.) and of Byzantium used iron in their coinage (Pollux, ix. 78).

(*g*) Lead (*μόλυβδος, plumbum nigrum*). Being easy to work, lead was much employed in ancient times, especially for coffins, water-pipes, etc. It was recognized also in ancient medicine. See Pliny, *H. N.* xxxiv. 156 foll., for a full account.

(*h*) Tin (*κασσίτερος, plumbum album*). Tin was very widely used and is found employed in the Homeric Age in the adornment of arms. Herodotus (iii. 115) speaks of it as produced in the islands of the Western Sea, the Cassiterides, perhaps the Scilly Isles (see CASSITERIDES); Diodorus mentions the coast of Britain as its source; while Pliny (*H. N.* xxxiv. 156) says that it came from Spain. It is probable that the Phœnicians were the principal purveyors and importers of it. The name *κασσίτερος* suggests the Sanskrit *kastîra*, so that it may first of all have been brought from India.

(*i*) *Stannum*, an alloy of silver with lead, used for plating bronze (Pliny, *H. N.* xxxiv. 159).

(*j*) Mercury or quicksilver (*ὑδράργυρος, argentum vivum*) was produced by the ancients from cinnabar and used in gold-mining (Pliny, *H. N.* xxxiii. 97).

(*k*) Zinc. Zinc is not specifically mentioned in the ancient writings, but was known to the Romans at any rate, for an analysis of Roman coins shows its presence to a considerable extent (Mommsen, *Römisches Münzwesen*, p. 763).

(*l*) Nickel, a metal also not named, but found in the coins of some of the Greek kings of India in the third century B.C. (*Numismatic Chronicle* for 1868, p. 305).

II. MINING. Information regarding the ancient mines is scanty, the chief authorities dealing only with the lead and silver mines of Attica and the gold and silver mines of Spain. The most satisfactory source is Xenophon's treatise *De Vectigalibus* (iv. 2), which deals with the Attic mines. The mines had shafts and adits. The ores were smelted with charcoal (*ἄνθρακες*). Fuller explanations regarding the Roman mines are given by Pliny (*H. N.* xxxiii.), Diodorus Siculus (v. 36), and Strabo (iii. pp. 146 foll.). Shafts, galleries, pumps, cross-drains, etc., were elaborate and scientific. In Spain gold was obtained in large quantities by washing, as in modern placer mining; while gold found in nuggets was refined by being first treated with an astringent and afterwards by heat.

In Greece the mines were the property of the State, which leased them for various terms, but only to citizens and *ἰσοτελεῖς*. The labour was performed by slaves. Under the Roman Republic mines were private property, but under the Empire were worked for the emperor and yielded a considerable revenue to the *fiscus*. (See FISCUS.). The workmen were usually slaves, criminals, or soldiers.

See the essay by Boeckh given as an appendix to his *Public Economy of Athens*; Lenz, *Mineralogie der alten Griechen und Römer* (1861); Marquardt, *Staatsverwaltung*, ii. 252 foll.; and the article VECTIGALIA.

Metanīra (*Μετάνειρα*). The wife of Celeus, and mother of Triptolemus. See CELEUS.

Metapontium (*Μεταπόντιον*) and **Metapontum**. A celebrated Greek city in Lucania, and on the Tarentine gulf, originally called Metabum (*Μέταβον*). It was founded by the Greeks at an early period, was afterwards destroyed by the Samnites, and was repeopled by a colony of Achaeans. It fell into the hands of the Romans with the other Greek cities in the south of Italy in the war against Pyrrhus; but it revolted to Hannibal after the battle of Cannae (Livy, xxii. 61), and soon after disappears from history. Pythagoras died at Metapontium, whither he had transferred his school.

Metatōres. See CASTRA.

Metaulos (*μέσαυλος*). The inner door of a house. See DOMUS.

Metaurum. See METAURUS (2).

Metaurus. (1) Now Metaro; a small river in Umbria, flowing into the Adriatic Sea, memorable by the defeat and death of Hasdrubal, the brother of Hannibal, on its banks, B.C. 207. (2) Now Marro; a river on the eastern coast of Bruttium, at whose mouth was the town of Metaurum.

Metella, CAECILIA. (1) The daughter of L. Metellus Dalmaticus, consul B.C. 119. She was first married to M. Aemilius Scaurus, consul in 115, and afterwards to the dictator Sulla, who avenged upon Athens an affront put upon her by the Athenians (Plut. *Sulla*, 6, 13, 22, 35). She fell ill in 81, during the celebration of Sulla's triumphal feast; and as her recovery was hopeless, Sulla for religious reasons sent her a bill of divorce, and had her removed from his house, but honoured her memory with a splendid funeral. (2) The daughter of Metellus Creticus, and daughter-in-law of Crassus, the triumvir. In her memory, the magnificent tomb on the Appian Way was erected.

Tomb of Caecilia Metella, on the Appian Way.

Metellus. A distinguished plebeian family of the Caecilia gens at Rome. (1) L. CAECILIUS METELLUS, consul B.C. 251, carried on the war in Sicily against the Carthaginians. In the following year he gained a great victory at Panormus over Hasdrubal, the Carthaginian general. The elephants which he took in this battle were exhibited in his triumph at Rome. Metellus was consul a second time in 249, and was elected pontifex maximus in 243, and held this dignity for twenty-two years. He must, therefore, have died shortly before the

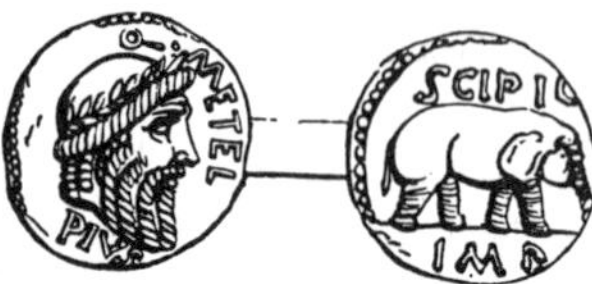

Coin of Caecilius Metellus, referring to the Battle of Panormus.

commencement of the Second Punic War. In 241 he rescued the Palladium when the Temple of Vesta was on fire, but lost his sight in consequence. He was dictator in 224 for the purpose of holding the comitia. (2) Q. Caecilius Metellus, son of the preceding, was plebeian aedile B.C. 209; curule aedile 208; served in the army of the consul Claudius Nero 207, and was one of the legates sent to Rome to convey the joyful news of the defeat and death of Hasdrubal; and was consul with L. Veturius Philo, 206. In his consulship he and his colleague carried on the war against Hannibal in Bruttium, where he remained as proconsul during the following year. In 205 he was dictator for the purpose of holding the comitia. Metellus survived the Second Punic War many years, and was employed in several public commissions. (3) Q. Caecilius Metellus Macedonĭcus, son of the last, was praetor in B.C. 148, and carried on war in Macedonia against the usurper Andriscus, whom he defeated and took prisoner. He next turned his arms against the Achaeans, whom he defeated at the beginning of 146. On his return to Rome in 146, he triumphed, and received the surname of Macedonicus. Metellus was consul in 143, and received the province of Nearer Spain, where he carried on the war with success for two years against the Celtiberi. He was succeeded by Q. Pompeius in 141. Metellus was censor 131. He died 115, full of years and honours. He is frequently quoted by the ancient writers as an extraordinary instance of human felicity. He had filled all the highest offices of the State with reputation and glory, and was carried to the funeral pile by four sons, three of whom had obtained the consulship in his lifetime, while the fourth was a candidate for the office at the time of his death. (4) L. Caecilius Metellus Calvus, brother of the last, consul B.C. 142. (5) Q. Caecilius Metellus Balearĭcus, eldest son of No. 3 was consul B.C. 123, when he subdued the inhabitants of the Balearic Islands, and received in consequence the surname of Balearicus. He was censor B.C. 120. (6) L. Caecilius Metellus Diademātus, second son of No. 3, has been frequently confounded with Metellus Dalmaticus, consul B.C. 119. Metellus Diadematus received the latter name from his wearing for a long time a bandage round his forehead, in consequence of an ulcer. He was consul B.C. 117. (7) M. Caecilius Metellus, third son of No. 3, was consul B.C. 115, the year in which his father died. In 114 he was sent into Sardinia as proconsul, and suppressed an insurrection in the island, in consequence of which he obtained a triumph in B.C. 113 on the same day as his brother Caprarius. (8) C. Caecilius Metellus Caprarius, fourth son of No. 3. The origin of his surname is quite uncertain. He was consul B.C. 113, and carried on war in Macedonia against the Thracians, whom he subdued. He obtained a triumph in consequence in the same year and on the same day with his brother Marcus. He was censor B.C. 102 with his cousin Metellus Numidicus. (9) L. Caecilius Metellus Dalmatĭcus, elder son of No. 4, and frequently confounded, as has been already remarked, with Diadematus, was consul B.C. 119, when he subdued the Dalmatians, and obtained in consequence the surname Dalmaticus. He was censor with Cn. Domitius Ahenobarbus in 115; and he was also pontifex maximus. He was alive in 100, when he is mentioned as one of the senators of high rank who took up arms against Saturninus. (10) Q. Caecilius Metellus Numidĭcus, younger son of No. 4, was one of the most distinguished members of his family. The character of Metellus stood very high among his contemporaries; in an age of growing corruption, his personal integrity remained unsullied; and he was distinguished for his abilities in war and peace. He was one of the chief leaders of the aristocratic party at Rome. He was consul B.C. 109, and carried on the war against Iugurtha in Numidia with great success. (See Iugurtha.) He remained in Numidia during the following year as proconsul; but as he was unable to bring the war to a conclusion, his legate C. Marius industriously circulated reports in the camp and the city that Metellus designedly protracted the war for the purpose of continuing in the command. These rumours had the desired effect. Marius was raised to the consulship, Numidia was assigned to him as his province, and Metellus saw the credit of finishing the war snatched from his grasp. (See Marius.) On his return to Rome in 107 he was received with the greatest honour. He celebrated a splendid triumph, and received the surname of Numidicus. In 102 he was censor with his cousin Metellus Caprarius. In 100 the tribune Saturninus and Marius resolved to ruin Metellus. Saturninus proposed an agrarian law, to which he added the clause that the Senate should swear obedience to it within five days after its enactment, and that whosoever should refuse to do so should be expelled from the Senate and pay a heavy fine. Metellus refused to take the oath, and was therefore expelled from the Senate; but Saturninus, not content with this, brought forward a bill to punish him with exile. The friends of Metellus were ready to take up arms in his defence; but Metellus quitted the city and retired to Rhodes, where he bore his misfortune with great calmness. He was, however, recalled to Rome in the following year (99) on the proposition of the tribune Q. Calidius. The orations of Metellus are spoken of with praise by Cicero, and they continued to be read with admiration in the time of Fronto. (11) Q. Caecilius Metellus Nepos, son of Balearicus and grandson of Macedonicus, appears to have received the surname of Nepos because he was the eldest grandson of the latter. Metellus Nepos exerted himself in obtaining the recall of his kinsman Metellus Numidicus from banishment in B.C. 99, and was consul in 98 with T. Didius. In this year the two consuls carried the lex Caecilia Didia. (12) Q. Caecilius Metellus Pius, son of Numidicus, received the surname of Pius on account of the love which he displayed for his father when he besought the people to recall him from banishment in B.C. 99. He was praetor B.C. 89, and was one of the commanders in the Marsic or Social War. He was still in arms in 87, prosecuting the war against the Samnites, when Marius landed in Italy and joined the consul Cinna. The Senate, in alarm, summoned Metellus to Rome; but as he was unable to defend the city against Marius and Cinna, he crossed over to Africa. After remaining in Africa three years, he returned to Italy and joined Sulla, who also returned to Italy in 83. In the war which followed against the Marian party, Metellus was one of the most successful of Sulla's generals, and gained several important victories both in Umbria and in Cisalpine Gaul. In 80 Metellus was consul with Sulla himself; and in the following year (79) he went as proconsul into Spain, in order to prosecute the war against Sertorius, who adhered to the Marian party. Here he remained for the next eight years, and found it so difficult to obtain any advantages over Sertorius that the Senate sent Pompey to his assistance with proconsular power and another army. Sertorius, however, was a match for them both, and would probably have continued to defy all the efforts of Metellus and Pompey if he had not been murdered by Perperna and his friends in 72. (See SERTORIUS.) Metellus was pontifex maximus, and, as he was succeeded in this dignity by Iulius Caesar in 63, he must have died either in this year or at the end of the preceding. (13) Q CAECILIUS METELLUS CELER, elder son of Nepos. In B.C. 66 he served as legate in the army of Pompey in Asia; and was praetor in 63, the year in which Cicero was consul. During his year of office he afforded warm and efficient support to the aristocratic party. He prevented the condemnation of C. Rabirius by removing the military flag from the Ianiculum. He coöperated with Cicero in opposing the schemes of Catiline; and, when the latter left the city to make war upon the Republic, Metellus had the charge of the Picentine and Senonian districts. By blocking up the passes he prevented Catiline from crossing the Apennines and penetrating into Gaul, and thus compelled him to turn round and face Antoninus, who was marching against him from Etruria. In the following year, 62, Metellus went with the title of proconsul into the province of Cisalpine Gaul, which Cicero had relinquished because he was unwilling to leave the city. In 60 Metellus was consul with L. Afranius, and opposed all the efforts of his colleague to obtain the ratification of Pompey's acts in Asia and an assignment of lands for his soldiers. He died in 59, and it was suspected that he had been poisoned by his wife Clodia, with whom he lived on the most unhappy terms, and who was a woman of the utmost profligacy. (14) Q. CAECILIUS METELLUS NEPOS, younger son of the elder Nepos (No. 11). He served as legate of Pompey in the war against the pirates and in Asia from B.C. 67 to 64. He returned to Rome in 63 in order to become a candidate for the tribunate, that he might thereby favour the views of Pompey. His election was opposed by the aristocracy, but without success. His year of office was a stormy one. One of his first acts in entering upon his office on the 10th of December, 63, was a violent attack upon Cicero. He maintained that the man who had condemned Roman citizens without a hearing ought not to be heard himself, and accordingly prevented Cicero from addressing the people on the last day of his consulship, and only allowed him to take the usual oath, whereupon Cicero swore that he had saved the State. In the following year (62) Metellus brought forward a bill to summon Pompey, with his army, to Rome, in order to restore peace; but on the day on which the bill was to be read, the two parties came to open blows; and Metellus was obliged to take to flight. He repaired to Pompey, with whom he returned to Rome in 61. He was praetor in 60, and consul in 57 with P. Lentulus Spinther. Notwithstanding his previous enmity with Cicero, he did not oppose his recall from exile. In 56 Metellus administered the province of Nearer Spain, where he carried on war against the Vaccaei. He died in 55. Metellus did not adhere strictly to the political principles of his family. He did not support the aristocracy, like his brother; nor, on the other hand, can he be said to have been the leader of the democracy. He was rather the faithful henchman of Pompey, opposing or supporting Cicero as his master required. (15) L. CAECILIUS METELLUS CRETĬCUS, tribune of the people in B.C. 49 and a supporter of the aristocracy. At the outbreak of the Civil War he did not leave the city when Pompey fled, but remained and opposed Caesar, who demanded possession of the sacred treasury. Metellus yielded only on compulsion (Plut. *Caes.*, *Pomp.;* Caes. *B. C.* i. 33).

Methāna. See METHONÉ (3).

Metharmé (Μεθάρμη). A daughter of King Pygmalion and wife of Cinyras (q. v.).

Methōné (Μεθώνη). (1) A town at the southwest corner of Messenia, with an excellent harbour, protected from the sea by a reef of rocks, of which the largest was called Mothon. (2) A town in Macedonia on the Thermaic Gulf, founded by the Eretrians, and celebrated from Philip having lost an eye at the siege of the place. (3) Or METHĀNA, an ancient town in Argolis, situated on a peninsula of the same name, opposite the island of Aegina.

Methŏra (Μέθορα). Matra, the sacred city of Krishna; a city of India on the river Iomanes (Jumna). It was the seat of the Indian god whom the Greeks identified with Heracles (Arrian, *Ind.* 8).

Methydrium (Μεθύδριον). A town of central Arcadia (Thuc. v. 58).

Methymna (Μήθυμνα and Μέθυμνα, the first form being the better). The second city of Lesbos, standing at the northern extremity of the island. It was the birthplace of the poet Arion and of the historian Hellanicus. The celebrated Lesbian wine grew in its neighbourhood. In the Peloponnesian war it remained faithful to Athens, even during the great Lesbian revolt (see MITYLENÉ); afterwards it was sacked by the Spartans (B.C. 406), and never recovered its former prosperity.

Metiŏché (Μητιόχη). See MENIPPÉ; ORION.

Metion (Μητίων). The son of Erechtheus and Praxithea and husband of Alcippé. His sons, the Metionidae, expelled their cousin Pandion (q. v.) from Athens, of which he was king, but were themselves afterwards expelled by his sons (Apollod. iii. 15; Pausan. i. 5, 3).

Metis (Μῆτις, "counsel"). A daughter of Oceanus, first wife of Zeus, by whom she was devoured, as he feared she would bear a son mightier than himself; whereupon Athené (q. v.) sprang from the head of the god. See ATHENÉ.

Metius. See METTIUS.

Mĕtoeci (*μέτοικοι*). The name given at Athens to aliens (other than slaves) resident in Attica. When the State was most flourishing, they numbered 10,000 adult men (B.C. 309). The favourable position of Athens for commerce and the rich opportunities for carrying on trade and for selling merchandise induced both Greeks and barbarians to settle there. The Athenians besides had the reputation among the Greeks of being friendly towards foreigners. For the legal protection granted them by the State, they paid a sum of twelve drachmae ($2) annually for each man, and half as much for each independent woman; and they had to choose a patron (*προστάτης*) to conduct their dealings with the State in all public and private affairs — e. g. the bringing of an action. Whoever failed to do the one or the other was summoned before a law court, and, if guilty, sold as a slave. They were prohibited from marrying citizens and from obtaining landed property; but they could follow any trade they pleased, on payment of a tax (*μετοίκιον*). They also had to pay the extraordinary taxes for war (*εἰσφοραί* and *λειτουργίαι*), and were obliged to serve either in the fleet or in the army; they might be hoplites, but not knights. At festivals (e. g. the Panathenaea) it was their duty to follow the processions, carrying sunshades, pitchers, and bowls or trays filled with honey or cakes. A decree of the people could, in return for special services, confer on them the *ἰσοτέλεια*, which placed them on a level with the citizens with regard to liturgies, or public burdens, freed them from the necessity of having a patron or paying a tax for protection, and gave them the right of holding property in land and of transacting business with the people or the authorities without an intermediary; but even this privileged class did not possess the active rights of a citizen.

Resident aliens were found in most other cities and States besides Athens. (See the list given by Schenkl in the *Wiener Studien* for 1880, ii. pp. 163 foll.) At Sparta, however, they were not allowed to settle (Xen. *Resp. Lac.* xiv. 4), and so, possibly, Apollonia (Ael. *V. H.* xiii. 16).

Meton (Μέτων). A Greek astronomer of Athens, who instituted in B.C. 432 the cycle of nineteen years called after him; it was intended to reconcile the lunar and the solar year: 235 lunar months of 29 or 30 days (on an average $29\frac{25}{47}$) = 19 solar years of $365\frac{5}{19}$ days. This cycle was not adopted at Athens till much later, probably in B.C. 330. (See CALENDARIUM.) He is said to have feigned insanity in order to avoid going on the ill-fated Sicilian expedition in the Peloponnesian War (Diod. xii. 36).

Metŏpae (*μετόπαι*, Vitruv. iv. 2, § 4; literally, "interstices between two beam-ends"). A name given in Doric architecture to the spaces between the triglyphs (q. v.) in the frieze. They were originally left open. Thus, Orestes manages to make his way into the Tauric temple of Artemis through one of these openings (Eurip. *Iph. T.* 113). They were afterwards filled with panels of wood, which were in course of time superseded by plain slabs of marble, as in the temples at Paestum, etc. These slabs were sometimes slightly ornamented with a round shield in low relief, as in the frieze of the temple of Zeus at Olympia. More frequently they were filled with figures in relief, as in those of Selinus (see SCULPTURE), and of the Theseum and the Parthenon (q. v.). The term is also applied to similarly sculptured slabs not placed between the triglyphs, but on the wall of the *cella*, as in the temple of Zeus at Olympia. See OLYMPIA.

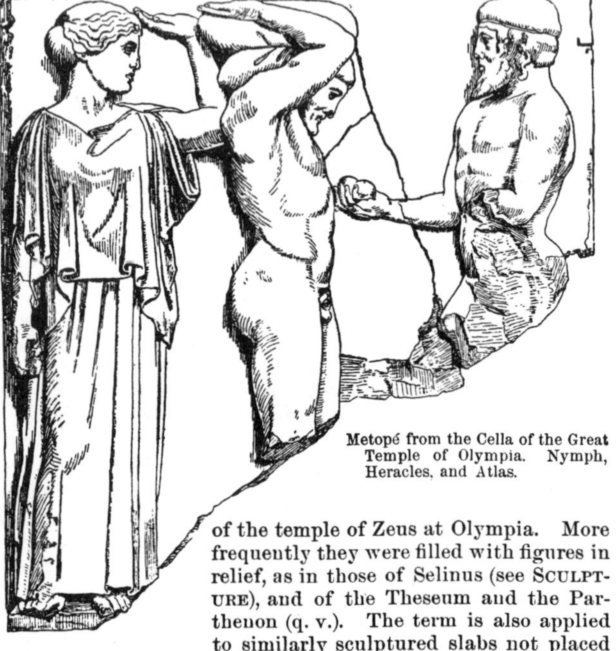

Metopé from the Cella of the Great Temple of Olympia. Nymph, Heracles, and Atlas.

Metoposcŏpus (*μετωποσκόπος*). A physiognomist; one who told fortunes by studying the face (Suet. *Tit.* 2).

Metragyrti. The vagrant begging priests of Rhea (q. v.). See AGYRTI.

Metrētes (*μετρητής*), or **amphŏra metrētes.** The largest liquid measure of the Greeks, a little less than nine gallons. Its chief subdivisions were the Greek *χοῦς* ($\frac{1}{12}$), *ξέστης* ($\frac{1}{72}$), *κοτύλη* ($\frac{1}{144}$), *κύαθος* ($\frac{1}{864}$). The name is also given to a large earthenware vessel for oil (Cato, *R. R.* 100).

Metrodōrus (Μητρόδωρος). A name of several Greek philosophers, the most important of whom was a native of Lampsacus or Athens, an Epicurean philosopher, and the most distinguished of the disciples of Epicurus, with whom he lived on terms of the closest friendship. He died 277, in the fifty-third year of his age, seven years before Epicurus, who would have appointed him his successor had he survived him. The philosophy of Metrodorus appears to have been of a more grossly sensual kind than that of Epicurus. Perfect happiness he made to consist in having a well-constituted body. He found fault with his brother Timocrates for not admitting that the stomach was the test and measure of every thing that pertained to a happy life. He was the author of several works, quoted by the ancient writers.

Another Metrodorus, of Scepsis, was raised to a

Metrodorus, the Epicurean.

position of great influence and trust by Mithridates Eupator, being appointed supreme judge without appeal even to the king. Subsequently he was led to abandon his allegiance, when sent by Mithridates on an embassy to Tigranes, king of Armenia. Tigranes sent him back to Mithridates, but he died on the road. According to some accounts he was despatched by order of the king; according to others he died of disease. In consequence of his hostility to the Romans he was surnamed "the Roman-hater" (Cic. *De Orat.* ii. 88, 360; Strabo, p. 609).

Metronŏmi (*μετρονόμοι*). Officers chosen by lot from among the Athenian police and assigned to the duty of seeing that proper weights and measures were used in the market. They also prosecuted those whom they found using false measures. They were probably ten in number, one from each tribe. Their subordinates were called *prometretae*. See Schömann, *Antiquities of Greece*, pp. 416, 420.

Metrōon (*μητρῷον*). The temple of the Mother of the Gods in Athens, in which the public archives were kept in charge of the president of the Boulé. See Curtius, *Das Metroön in Athen* (1868).

Metropŏlis (*μητρόπολις*). The mother State. A name given to a city or State in relation to its colonies. Thus, Athens was the metropolis of the Ionians, Meropé of the Aethiopians, Corinth of the Corcyraeans, etc. See Colonia.

Metropŏlis (Μητρόπολις). A town of Thessaly in Histiaeotis, near the Peneus, and between Gomphi and Pharsalus. There were several other cities of this name, one in Phrygia, one in Lydia, and one in Acarnania.

Mettius or **Metius**. (1) Curtius. See Curtius. (2) Fuffetius, dictator of Alba, and torn asunder by chariots driven in opposite directions by order of Tullus Hostilius, third king of Rome, on account of his treachery towards the Romans (Livy, i. 23–28).

Metŭlum. The chief town of the Iapydes in Illyricum, situated on the twin peaks of a high mountain. Here the emperor Augustus nearly lost his life in reducing the place (Dio Cass. xlix. 35).

Mevania. The modern Beragna; an ancient city in the interior of Umbria on the river Tinea, situated in a fertile country, and celebrated for its breed of beautiful white oxen. According to some accounts, Propertius was a native of this place (Pliny, *H. N.* xxxv. 173).

Mezentius (Μεσέντιος) or **Medientius**. A king of Caeré in Etruria. He aided Turnus of Ardea against Aeneas, but was killed in battle by the latter or by his son Ascanius (Verg. *Aen.* viii. 480; x. 689, 785, 800). Dionysius, however, relates that Mezentius finally concluded a peace with Ascanius and became his ally (Dionys. i. 64). Still another tradition states that Mezentius demanded of the Latini the produce of their vineyards, but that they vowed the firstfruits to Iupiter and thereby won the victory (Plut. *Quaest. Rom.* 45). See Mommsen, *Hist. of Rome*, i. 173 (Amer. ed.).

Micāre Digĭtis. To play a game that was popular among the Romans, and still survives in modern Italy under the name *morra* (in French, *la mourre*). It is also mentioned by Aristotle (*De Insomn.* 2), but seems not to have been very common in Greece. It was played by two persons, who simultaneously held up their right hands with one, more than one, or none of the fingers extended. At the same time each called out a number which represented his guess at the sum of all the fingers extended by both players. The correct guesser, of course, won; or, as sometimes played, the one whose successful guesses first amounted to five in number was the winner (Nonius, xxxiii. 77). A proverbial expression for a thoroughly honest man describes him as one with whom you would be willing to play *morra* in the dark (*quicum in tenebris mices*, Cic. *De Off.* iii. 19; Petron. 44). The game was the modern equivalent of throwing dice or matching coins. See Marquardt, *Privatleben*, 836.

Game of Morra. (Baumeister.)

Micipsa (Μικίψας). A king of Numidia, the eldest of the sons of Masinissa (q. v.), on whose death (B.C. 148) Scipio divided the supreme power between Micipsa and his two brothers, Gulussa and Mastanabal. The death of his brothers soon made him sole monarch of Numidia, which he ruled mildly and with wisdom until his death (Sall. *Iug.* 5–11; Florus, iii. 2). He died B.C. 118, leaving two sons, Adherbal and Hiempsal. See IUGURTHA.

Micon (Μίκων). An Athenian painter, who flourished about B.C. 460. He was also known as a sculptor (Pausan. vi. 6, 1).

Midaēum (Μιδάειον). A city of Phrygia Epictetus where Sex. Pompeius was captured by the troops of Antony, B.C. 35 (Dio Cass. xlix. 18).

Midas (Μίδας). The son of Gordius and Cybelé. He was the wealthy but effeminate king of Phrygia, a pupil of Orpheus, and a great patron of the worship of Dionysus. His wealth is alluded to in a story connected with his childhood, for it is said that while a child, ants carried grains of wheat into his mouth to indicate that one day he should be the richest of all mortals. Midas was introduced into the satyric drama of the Greeks, and was represented with the ears of a Satyr, which were afterwards lengthened into the ears of an ass. He is said to have built the town of Ancyra, and as king of Phrygia he is called *Berecynthius heros* (Ovid, *Met.* xi. 106).

There are several stories connected with Midas, of which the following are the most celebrated: Silenus, the companion and teacher of Dionysus, had gone astray in a state of intoxication, and was caught by country people in the rose-gardens of Midas. He was bound with wreaths of flowers and led before the king. These gardens were in Macedonia, near Mount Bermion or Bromion, where Midas was king of the Bruges, with whom he afterwards emigrated to Asia, where their name was changed into Phryges. Midas received Silenus kindly; and, after treating him with hospitality, he led him back to Dionysus, who allowed Midas to ask a favour of him. Midas in his folly desired that all things which he touched should be changed into gold. The request was granted; but as even the food which he touched became gold, he implored the god to take his favour back. Dionysus accordingly ordered him to bathe in the source of Pactolus near Mount Tmolus. This bath saved Midas, but the river from that time had an abundance of gold in its sand.

Midas, who was himself related to the race of Satyrs, once had a visit from a Satyr, who indulged in all kinds of jokes at the king's expense. Thereupon Midas mixed wine in a well; and when the Satyr had drunk of it, he fell asleep and was caught. This well of Midas was at different times assigned to different localities. Xenophon (*Anab.* i. 2, § 13) places it in the neighbourhood of Thymbrium and Tyraeum, and Pausanias at Ancyra. Once when Pan and Apollo were engaged in a musical contest on the flute and lyre, Midas was chosen to decide between them. The king decided in favour of Pan, whereupon Apollo changed his ears into those of an ass. Midas contrived to conceal them under his Phrygian cap, but the servant who used to cut his hair discovered them. The secret so much harassed this man that, as he dared not betray it to a human being, he dug a hole in the earth, and whispered into it, "King Midas has ass's ears." He then filled the hole up again, and his mind was relieved. But on the same spot a reed grew up, which in its whispers betrayed the secret. Midas is said to have killed himself by drinking the blood of an ox. (Strabo, p. 61.)

So-called Tomb of Midas.

A tomb found at Dogan-lu, in Phrygia, is called "the tomb of Midas" from the one legible word, MIDAI, upon it.

Milanion (Μειλανίων). The faithful lover of Atalanta (q. v.).

Miles Gloriōsus. "The Braggart Soldier." An amusing play of Plautus. See PLAUTUS.

Milesian Tales. See NOVELS AND ROMANCES.

Miletopŏlis (Μιλητόπολις). (1) A city of Mysia. (2) See BORYSTHENES.

Milētus (Μίλητος). The son of Apollo and Aria of Crete, who fled from Minos to Asia, where he built the city of Miletus. Ovid (*Met.* ix. 442) calls him a son of Apollo and Deïoné, and hence Deïonides.

Milētus (Μίλητος). (1) One of the greatest cities of Asia Minor. It belonged territorially to Caria and politically to Ionia, being the southernmost of the twelve cities of the Ionian confederacy. The city stood upon the southern headland of the Sinus Latmicus, opposite to the mouth of the Maeander, and possessed four distinct harbours, protected by a group of little islands; its territory was rich in flocks, and the city was celebrated for its woollen fabrics, the *Milesia vellera*. At a very early period it became a great maritime State, and founded numerous colonies, especially on the shores of the Euxine. Among these were Abydos, Tomi, Olbia, Cyzicus, and Odessus; and in Egypt, Naucratis. It was the birthplace of the philosophers Thales, Anaximander, and Anaximenes, and of the historians Cadmus and Hecataeus. It was the centre of the great Ionian revolt against the Persians, after the suppression of which it was destroyed (B.C. 494). (See ARISTAGORAS; HISTIAEUS.) It recovered sufficient importance to oppose a vain resistance to Alexander the Great, which brought upon it a second ruin. Under the Roman Empire it still appears as a place of some consequence. The earlier name of Miletus is said to have been PITYŪSA (Πιτυοῦσα) or ANACTORIA (Ἀνακτορία). See Herod. i. 17–20, 141; vi. 6; Arrian, *Anab.* i. 18; and Rayet and Thomas, *Milet et le Golfe Latmique* (Paris, 1877). (2) A town in Crete on the northeastern coast.

Milĭchus (Μείλιχος). A river in Achaia flowing by the town of Patrae, on whose banks victims were in early times sacrificed to Artemis (Pausan. vii. 19, 9).

Milĭtes. See EXERCITUS.

Milliarium. The Roman milestone, a stone column, such as were set up at intervals of a thousand (*mille*) *passus* = 5000 Roman feet, on the military roads, partly during the last years of the Republic, and regularly since Augustus. They gave in numbers, usually preceded by M.P. (*milia passuum*), the distance from the place from which the measurement was made, besides its name and those of the persons who had constructed the road or erected the milestone, and of the emperor in whose reign the road had been made. A great number of these milestones in every part of the Roman Empire has been preserved, and also the base of the central column of the gilded one (*milliarium aureum*) erected by Augustus in the Forum near the temple of Saturn, and said to have been regarded as the centre of the Empire; but this cannot be taken literally, as the distances were really measured from the city gates (Macer, *Dig.* l. 16, 154). It is probable that each of the chief cities of the Empire had its own milliarium.

Milliarium. (Capitol at Rome; originally a stone marking the first mile out of Rome.)

Millus. A dog-collar fitted with spikes (Fest. s. h. v.).

Milo or **Milon** (Μίλων). (1) Of Crotona, a celebrated athlete, six times victor in wrestling at the Olympic Games, and as often at the Pythian. He was one of the followers of Pythagoras, and also commanded the army which defeated the Sybarites, B.C. 511. Many stories are related of his extraordinary feats of strength: such as his carrying a heifer four years old on his shoulders through the stadium at Olympia, and afterwards eating the whole of it in a single day. Passing through a forest in his old age, he saw the trunk of a tree which had been partially split open by wood-cutters, and attempted to rend it further, but the wood closed upon his hands, and thus held him fast, in which state he was attacked and devoured by wolves (Gell. xv. 16). (2) TITUS ANNIUS MILO PAPINIĀNUS, was born at Lanuvium, of which place he was in B.C. 53 dictator or chief magistrate. As tribune of the plebs, B.C. 57, Milo took an active part in obtaining Cicero's recall from exile; and from this time he carried on a fierce and memorable contest with P. Clodius. In 53 Milo was candidate for the consulship, and Clodius for the praetorship of the ensuing year. Each of the candidates kept a gang of gladiators, and there were frequent combats between the rival ruffians in the streets of Rome. At length, on the 20th of January, 52, Milo and Clodius met apparently by accident at Bovillae, on the Appian Way. An affray ensued between their followers, in which Clodius was slain. At Rome such tumults followed upon the burial of Clodius that Pompey was appointed sole consul in order to restore order to the State. Milo was brought to trial. He was defended by Cicero; but was condemned, and went into exile at Massilia (Marseilles). The soldiers who lined the Forum intimidated Cicero, and he could not deliver the oration which he had prepared. Milo returned to Italy in 48, in order to support the revolutionary schemes of the praetor, M. Caelius; but he was slain under the walls of an obscure fortress in Thurii. Milo, in 57, married Fausta, a daughter of the dictator Sulla, a worthless woman with whom the historian Sallust carried on an intrigue, for which he was soundly beaten by Milo. See the articles CICERO; CLODIUS; POMPEIUS.

Milo, VENUS OF. See APHRODITÉ.

Miltiădes (Μιλτιάδης). (1) The son of Cypselus. He was a man of considerable distinction in Athens in the time of Pisistratus. The Doloncians, a Thracian tribe dwelling in the Chersonesus, being hard pressed in war by the Absinthians, applied to the Delphic oracle for advice, and were directed to admit a colony led by the man who should be the first to entertain them after they left the temple. This was Miltiades, who, eager to escape from the rule of Pisistratus, gladly took the lead of a colony under the sanction of the oracle, and became tyrant of the Chersonesus, which he fortified by a wall built across its isthmus. In a war with the people of Lampsacus he was taken prisoner, but was set at liberty on the demand of Croesus. He died without leaving any children, and his sovereignty passed into the hands of Stesagoras, the son of his half-brother Cimon. Sacrifices and games were instituted in his honour, in which no Lampsacene was suffered to take part (Herod. vi. 34, 38, 103).

(2) The son of Cimon and brother of Stesagoras. He became tyrant of the Chersonesus on the death of the latter, being sent out by Pisistratus from Athens to take possession of the vacant inheritance. By a stratagem he got the chief men of the Chersonesus into his power and threw them into prison, and took a force of mercenaries into his pay. In order to strengthen his position still more, he married Hegesipylé, the daughter of a Thracian prince named Olorus. He joined Darius Hystaspis on his expedition against the Scythians, and was left with the other Greeks in charge of the bridge over the Danube. When the appointed time had expired, and Darius had not returned, Miltiades recommended the Greeks to destroy the bridge and leave Darius to his fate. Some time after the expedition of Darius, an inroad of the Scythians drove Miltiades from his possessions; but after the enemy had retired the Doloncians brought him back. It appears to have been between this period and his withdrawal to Athens, that Miltiades conquered and expelled the Pelasgian inhabitants of Lemnos and Imbros and subjected the islands to the dominion of Attica. Lemnos and Imbros belonged to the Persian dominions; and it is probable that this encroachment on the Persian possessions was the cause which drew upon Miltiades

the hostility of Darius, and led him to fly from the Chersonesus, when the Phœnician fleet approached, after the subjugation of Ionia. Miltiades reached Athens in safety, but his eldest son Metiochus fell into the hands of the Persians. At Athens Miltiades was arraigned, as being amenable to the penalties enacted against tyranny, but was acquitted. When Attica was threatened with invasion by the Persians under Datis and Artaphernes, Miltiades was chosen one of the ten generals. Miltiades by his arguments induced the polemarch Callimachus to give the casting vote in favour of risking a battle with the enemy, the opinions of the ten generals being equally divided. Miltiades waited till his turn came, and then drew his army up in battle array on the ever-memorable field of Marathon. (See MARATHON.) After the defeat of the Persians, Miltiades endeavoured to urge the Athenians to measures of retaliation, and induced them to intrust to him an armament of seventy ships, without knowing the purpose for which they were designed. He proceeded to attack the island of Paros, for the purpose of gratifying a private enmity. His attacks, however, were unsuccessful; and after receiving a dangerous hurt in the leg, while penetrating into a sacred enclosure on some superstitious errand, he was compelled to raise the siege and return to Athens, where he was impeached by Xanthippus for having deceived the people. His wound had turned into a gangrene, and, being unable to plead his cause in person, he was brought into court on a couch, his brother Tisagoras conducting his defence for him. He was condemned; but on the ground of his services to the State the penalty was commuted to a fine of fifty talents, the cost of the equipment of the armament. Being unable to pay this, he was thrown into prison, where he not long after died of his wound. The fine was subsequently paid by his son Cimon. See Herod. iv. 137; vi. 41, 132–136; Pausan. i. 15, 3; Nepos, *Miltiades*.

Miltiades.

Milvius Pons. See PONS; ROMA.

Milyas (Μιλυάς). A name originally given to all Lycia (Herod. i. 173), but afterward restricted to the table-land in the north of that country. It became a part of the dominions of Eumenes, king of Pergamus (Livy, xxxviii. 39), and finally a part of the Roman province of Pamphylia. See LYCIA.

Mimallŏnes (Μιμάλλονες) or **Mimallonĭdes.** The Macedonian name of the Bacchantes, formed from the name of Mt. Mimas.

Mimas (Μίμας). One of the giants who warred against the gods and was slain by a flash of lightning. See GIGANTES; PROCHYTÉ.

Mimas (Μίμας). A promontory and mountain in Ionia, opposite the island of Chios.

Mimetic Words. See ONOMATOPOEIA.

Mimnermus (Μίμνερμος). A native of Colophon or Smyrna; and creator of the erotic type of Greek elegy, an older contemporary of Solon. He flourished about B.C. 630–600. He gave his collection of love elegies the name of the beautiful flute-player Nanno, who on account of his advanced age would not return his love. There are only a few fragments of his poems left; their chief themes are the melancholy complaint of old age abandoned by love, the transitoriness of the life of man, and the exhortation to enjoy youth, the age of love. His language is simple and tender, and the ancients therefore called him "the sweet singer" (Λιγυαστάδης, in Solon's lines to Mimnermus; Bergk's *Poëtae Lyrici*, Solon, *fragm.* 20). The remains of Mimnermus have been separately edited by Bach (Leipzig, 1826).

Mimus (μῖμος). Literally "imitation" or "imitator"; hence applied both to the play and the actor.

I. GREEK.—A sort of popular composition full of slang, dialect, and aphorism, and written in a sort of rhythmic prose (Mahaffy, *Greek Lit.* § 240), performed as a private comedy. This sort of literature in Greece apparently originated with Sophron of Syracuse in the fifth century B.C., and was written also by his son Xenarchus. Plato the comedian was fond of the mime, and is said to have kept a copy of Sophron under his pillow. He also imitated him. The fragments of Sophron were collected by Botzon (1867). See Fuhr, *De Mimis Graecorum* (1860).

II. ROMAN.—The Roman mimus was a more or less unconventional character-play of every-day life acted without masks or buskins. It deals more with town life than the Atellanae, which it somewhat resembles, and was developed among the Latins out of the character-dances that were originally performed between the acts at the theatres or in private houses (Mommsen, *Hist. of Rome*, iv. 689). The mimus became very popular at Rome, and was finally made a sort of afterpiece (*exodium*). It was acted in front of the curtain (*siparium*) by an actor (also called *mimus*) who wore no buskins, and was hence styled *planipes*. He also had no mask, but wore a sort of harlequin coat of many colours (*centunculus*) and a *phallus*. The chief characters were the *archimimus*, or hero, and the *stupidus* or *parasitus*, the butt of the hero. The female parts were played by women (*mimae*). Dancing, largely of an indecent and suggestive character, formed a feature of the mime, and horse-play was the rule. (See Mayor on Juv. v. 171.) Contrary to the usual rule of the Roman stage, political criticism was allowed in the dialogue of the mimes. The subjects were very miscellaneous, ranging from seduction to ghost-stories. The greatest writer of mimes was Publilius Syrus (q. v.), who was famous for the maxims (*sententiae*) with which he furnished his text. Some 500 lines ascribed to him are collected by Ribbeck in his *Com. Lat. Reliquiae.* See Patin, *Études sur la Poésie Latine*, ii. 346–365 (Paris, 1875); Grysar, *Der röm. Mimus* (1854); and Friedländer, *Sittengeschichte Roms*, vol. ii.

Mina (μνᾶ; Lat. *mina*). An old Greek weight, and a sum of coined money equal to it, the sixtieth part of a talent, like which it varied in value. The weight of the *mina* (=100 *drachmae*) was 1¼ lb., and the intrinsic value of the Attic mina of silver was about $16.

Minaei (Μιναῖοι). A people dwelling on the western coast of Arabia Felix (Pliny, *H. N.* xii. 54).

Minas Sabbătha (Μείνας Σαβαθά). A late Roman fortress in Babylonia, built on the site of Seleucia.

Mincius. Now the Mincio; a river in Gallia Transpadana, flowing through Lake Benacus (Lago di Garda), and falling into the Po a little below Mantua.

Mindărus (Μίνδαρος). A Lacedaemonian who succeeded Astyochus in command of the Spartan fleet, B.C. 411; and who was defeated and slain by the Athenians near Cyzicus the next year (Thuc. viii. 85, 104).

Minerva, originally **Menerva** (Etruscan, Menfra). One of the great Roman divinities, the goddess of wisdom; identified with the Greek Athené (q. v.). Her name contains the same root as *mens*, *me-min-i*, *mentio*, etc., and she is accordingly the thinking, calculating, and inventive power personified. Iupiter was the first, Iuno the second, and Minerva the third in the number of the Capitoline divinities. Tarquin, the son of Demaratus, was believed to have united the three divinities in one common temple, and hence, when repasts were prepared for the gods, these three always went together. She was the daughter of Iupiter, and is said to have sometimes wielded the thunderbolts of her father. As Minerva was a virgin divinity, and her father the supreme god, the Romans easily identified her with the Greek Athené, and accordingly all the attributes of Athené were gradually transferred to the Roman Minerva; but we confine ourselves at present to those which were peculiar to the Roman goddess. Being a maiden goddess, her sacrifices consisted of calves which had not borne the yoke. She is said to have invented numbers; and it is added that the law respecting the driving in of the annual nail was for this reason attached to her temple. (See CLAVUS.) She was worshipped as the patroness of all the arts and trades, and at her festival she was particularly invoked by all who desired to distinguish themselves in any art or craft, such as painting, poetry, the art of teaching, medicine, dyeing, spinning, weaving, and the like. This character of the goddess may be perceived also from the proverbs "to do a thing *pingui Minerva*," i. e. to do a thing in an awkward or clumsy manner; and *sus Minervam* (*docet*) of a stupid person who presumed to set right an intelligent one. Minerva, however, was the patroness, not only of women, on whom she conferred skill in sewing, spinning, weaving, etc., but she also guided men in the dangers of war, where victory is gained by cunning, prudence, courage, and perseverance. Hence she was represented with a helmet, shield, and a coat of mail; and the booty made in war was frequently dedicated to her. Minerva was further believed to be the inventor of musical instruments, especially wind instruments, the use of which was very important in religious worship, and which were accordingly subjected to a sort of purification every year on the last day of the festival of Minerva. This festival lasted five days, from the 19th to the 23d of March, and was called *Quinquatrus*, because it began on the fifth day after the Ides of the month. On this date the Roman boys brought to their teachers the school fee (*Minerval*). This number of days was not accidental, for we are told that the number five was sacred to Minerva. The most ancient temple of Minerva at Rome was probably that on the Capitol; another existed on the Aventine; and she had a chapel at the foot of the Caelian Hill, where she bore the surname of CAPTA—a title borrowed from the Faliscans, but of doubtful import (Ovid, *Fasti*, iii. 843).

Minerva. (Gem in the King Collection.)

Minervae Castrum or **Minervium.** Now Castro; a hill on the coast of Calabria, the traditional landing-place of Aeneas in Italy.

Minervae Promontorium. A rocky promontory in Campania, running out a long way into the sea, six miles southeast of Surrentum, on whose summit was a temple of Minerva, said to have been built by Odysseus. Here the Sirens are reported to have dwelt.

Minerval. The school fee among the Romans. See EDUCATION; LUDUS LITTERARIUS; QUINQUATRUS.

Mines and **Mining.** See METALLUM.

Minio. Now Mignone; a small river in Etruria, falling into the Tuscan Sea, between Graviscae and Centum Cellae.

Minius. Now the Minho; a river in the northwestern part of Hispania, deriving its name from the *minium* (vermilion) carried down by its stream. It was also called BAENIS.

Minōa (Μινώα). (1) See MEGARA. (2) A town on the eastern coast of Laconia. (3) A town on the northern coast of Crete. (4) A town on the northeastern coast of Crete. (5) See HERACLEA.

Minor. See CURATOR; INFANS.

Minos (Μίνως). The son of Zeus and Europa, brother of Rhadamanthus, was the king and legislator of Crete. After his death he became one of the judges of the shades in Hades. He was the father of Deucalion and Ariadné; and, according to Apollodorus, the brother of Sarpedon. Some traditions relate that Minos married Itoné, daughter of Lyctius, by whom he had a son, Lycastus, and that the latter became, by Ida, the father of another Minos. But it should be observed that Homer and Hesiod know of only one Minos, the ruler of Cnossus, and the son and friend of Zeus; and that they relate nearly the same things about him which later traditions assign to a second Minos, the grandson of the former. In this case, as in many other mythical traditions, a rationalistic criticism attempted to solve contradictions and difficulties in the stories about a person, by assuming that the contradictory accounts must refer to two different personages.

Assuming, however, the fact of a second Minos, he was also a king and lawgiver of Crete. He is described as the husband of Pasiphaë, a daughter of Helios; and as the father of Catreus, Deucalion, Glaucus, Androgeos, Acallé, Xenodicé, Ariadné, and Phaedra. After the death of Asterius, Minos aimed at the supremacy of Crete, and declared that it was destined to him by the gods; in proof of which, he asserted that the gods always answered his prayers. Accordingly, as he was offering up a sacrifice to Poseidon, he prayed that a bull might come forth from the sea, and promised to sacrifice the beast. The bull appeared and Minos became king of Crete. Minos, however, admiring the beauty of the bull, did not sacrifice him, but substituted another in his place, whereupon Poseidon rendered the bull furious, and made Pasiphaë conceive a passion for the animal. Daedalus enabled Pasiphaë to gratify her passion, and she became by the bull the mother of the Minotaurus, a monster with a human body and a bull's head, or, according to others, with a bull's body and a human head. The monster was kept in the labyrinth at Cnossus, constructed by Daedalus. Daedalus fled from Crete to escape the wrath of Minos and took refuge in Sicily. Minos followed him to Sicily, and was there slain by Cocalus and his daughters.

Minos is further said to have divided Crete into three parts, and to have ruled nine years. The Cretans traced their legal and political institutions to Minos. He is said to have been instructed in the art of legislation by Zeus himself; and the Spartan Lycurgus was believed to have taken the legislation of Minos as his model. In his time Crete was a powerful maritime State; and Minos not only checked the piratical pursuits of his contemporaries, but made himself master of the Greek islands of the Aegean. The most ancient legends describe Minos as a just and wise lawgiver, whereas the later accounts represent him as an unjust and cruel tyrant. In order to avenge the wrong done to his son Androgeos (q. v.) at Athens, he made war against the Athenians and Megarians. He subdued Megara, and compelled the Athenians either every year or every nine years to send him as a tribute seven youths and seven maidens, who were devoured in the labyrinth by the Minotaurus. The monster was slain by Theseus. See ARIADNÉ; THESEUS.

It is generally held that the tradition of Minos embodies a certain amount of historical truth, and that there really was a king of that name who ruled Crete before the Dorian migration, and developed a formidable sea-power, which he used in putting down piracy. Cf. Thuc. i. 4, 8; Aristotle, *Polit.* ii. 10; iv. 10; and see the article NISUS.

Minotaurus. See MINOS; THESEUS.

Mintha or **Minthé** (Μίνθη). A daughter of Cocytus, beloved by Hades, and metamorphosed by Demeter, or Persephoné (Proserpina), into a plant called after her *mintha*, or mint. A hill near Pylos bore this name, and at its foot was a temple of Pluto and grove of Demeter.

Minturnae. An important town in Latium, on the frontiers of Campania, situated on the Via Appia, and on both banks of the Liris, and near the mouth of this river. It was an ancient town of the Ausones or Aurunci, but surrendered to the Romans of its own accord, and received a Roman colony B.C. 296. In its neighbourhood was a grove sacred to the nymph Marica, and also extensive marshes (*Paludes Minturnenses*), formed by the overflowing of the river Liris, in which Marius (q. v.) was taken prisoner. Here are now the remains of an aqueduct and the ruins of an amphitheatre, at the modern Trajetta.

Minuciānus (Μινουκιανός). An Athenian, son of Nicagoras, and known as a rhetorician. He flourished under the Roman emperor Gullienus (A.D. 260–263), and wrote several works in Greek. A portion of his Τέχνη Ῥητορική still exists and is included in Walz's *Rhetores Graeci* (Stuttgart, 1832–36).

Minucius. The name of a Roman gens, of whom the most celebrated was M. Minucius Rufus, *magister equitum* to the dictator Q. Fabius Maximus (B.C. 217), in the war against Hannibal. He fell at the battle of Cannae. Others of the gens are MARCUS MINUCIUS, who, in B.C. 121, when serving as tribune of the plebs, brought forward a bill to repeal the laws of C. Gracchus (Florus, iii. 15); and who with his brother Quintus is mentioned in an interesting inscription (*C. I. L.* i. 199); and QUINTUS MINUCIUS, who built the Porticus Minucia near the Circus Flaminius at Rome in memory of his triumph over the barbarians in Thrace, B.C. 110. MINUCIUS ANGURĪNUS, who was consul in B.C. 305, constructed the Via Minucia from Rome to Brundisium (Cic. *Ad Att.* ix. 6). MINUCIUS BASĬLUS was one of Caesar's assassins (Appian, *B. C.* iii. 96).

Minucius Felix, MARCUS. The first Latin Christian author, a man of excellent education, and a distinguished lawyer at Rome. After becoming a Christian at an advanced age, he wrote in the second half of the second century a dialogue entitled *Octavius*, and carried on by one Caecilius, a heathen, and Octavius, a Christian, in which the aim is to refute the objections raised against Christianity. The work is marked by purity of diction and by acuteness and precision of argument. The oldest MS. is one at Paris, of the ninth century. The text is printed in Migne's *Patrologia* (Paris, 1844), and is edited by Bährens (Leipzig, 1886). A version in German is given by Dombart (2d ed. Erlangen, 1882), accompanied by the Latin text.

Minucius Thermus. See THERMUS.

Minutio Capĭtis. See DEMINUTIO CAPITIS.

Minyădes (Μινυάδες). The daughters of Minyas, the rich king of Orchomenus and mythical ancestral hero of the race of the Minyae; their names were Alcathoë (Alcithoë), Leucippé, and Arsippé. When the worship of Dionysus was introduced into Boeotia, and all the other women wandered in frenzy over the mountains in honour of the god, they alone remained at home, and profaned the festival by working at their looms, in spite of the warning of the god, who had appeared to them in the shape of a maiden. It was not till he had assumed the shapes of a bull, a lion, and a panther, had made milk and wine flow from the yarnbeams, and had changed their weft into grapes and vine-leaves, that they were terrified and drew lots who should offer a sacrifice to the god; and Leucippé, on whom the lot fell, tore her own son Hippasus to pieces in her Bacchic fury. They then raged about on the mountains till they were transformed into bats. With this legend was connected the custom, that at the annual festival of Dionysus the priest of the god was allowed to pursue the women of the Minyan race with a drawn sword and kill them (Aelian, *V. H.* iii. 42; Plutarch, *Quaest. Gr.* 38; Ovid, *Met.* iv. 1–40, 390–415).

Minўae (Μινύαι). An ancient Greek race, originally dwelling in Thessaly. Their ancient hero, Minyas, is said to have migrated from Thessaly into the north of Boeotia, and there to have established the empire of the Minyae, with the capital of Orchomenus. (See ORCHOMENUS.) As the greater part of the Argonauts were descended from the Minyae, they are themselves called Minyae. The Minyae founded a colony in Lemnos, called Minyae, whence they proceeded to Elis Triphylia, and to the island of Thera.

Minўas (Μινύας). The son of Chryses. He was the ancestral hero of the Minyae (q. v.). There are many and conflicting accounts of his genealogy. (See the schol. *ad* Pind. *Ol.* xiv. 4; *Pyth.* iv. 69.) His tomb was shown at Orchomenus.

Mirrors. See SPECULUM.

Misēnum. Now Punta di Miseno. A promontory in Campania, south of Cumae, said to have derived its name from Misenus, the companion and trumpeter of Aeneas, who was drowned and buried here. The bay formed by this promontory was converted by Augustus into an excellent harbour, and was made the principal station of the Roman fleet on the Tyrrhenian Sea. A town sprang up around the harbour. Here was the villa of C. Marius, which afterwards passed into the hands of the emperor Tiberius, who died at this place (Suet. *Tib.* 72).

Missio. The Roman term for the dismissal of soldiers from service, whether on account of illness (*missio causaria*) or of some dishonourable offence (*missio ignominiosa*), or at the expiration of their period of service. The last-mentioned, *missio honesta* or honourable dismissal, carried with it, under the Empire, the maintenance of the dismissed soldier. At first a fixed sum of money was given him; afterwards a parcel of land in Italy or the provinces was assigned. He also received the rights of citizenship, if he did not already possess them, and the privilege of contracting a legal marriage. The imperial decree which contained a list of those dismissed, arranged according to the subdivisions of the army and with the privileges granted, was posted on a public building on the Capitol or in the Forum, and each one of those specified received an extract from this document, made out in the presence of seven witnesses and inscribed on a bronze *diptychon* (q. v.). Sixty-two such military diplomas have been preserved completely or in part. (See EXERCITUS.) The same term was used of the release of gladiators from the gladiatorial school. See GLADIATORES, p. 733.

Misthophŏri (μισθοφόροι). See MERCENARII.

Misthoseos Phasis (μισθώσεως φάσις). An action in Attic law brought against a guardian for having neglected to make a profitable use of the property of his ward, or for having made no use of it at all. Complaints of this sort were made before the first archon. See EPITROPUS.

Mithras (Μίθρας). The Persian god of created light and of all earthly wisdom. In the course of time he became identified with the sun-god, who conquers all demons of darkness. In the time after Alexander the Great, his worship, mixed with various customs peculiar to Western Asia, was extended over all the Oriental kingdoms. In the first half of the first century B.C. it is said to have been introduced into the Roman provinces in the West by the Cilician pirates who were at that time masters of the Mediterranean (Plut. *Pomp.* 24). There are traces of his worship at Rome under Tiberius; and in the beginning of the second century after Christ, under the Antonines, it became common throughout the whole Roman Empire, and was kept up till the end of the fourth century. Mithras was a special favourite of the Roman armies. Being born from the rocks, he was worshipped in natural or artificial caves, such as have been found in every part of the Roman Empire. He is represented as a young man in Oriental dress and as an invincible hero, stabbing a bull with his dagger, or standing upon a bull that he has thrown down. The sacrifice of a bull and the purification of his worshippers with bull's blood formed a part of the rites of Mithras. See TAUROBOLIUM.

Specimens of a Mithras group may be seen in the Louvre, in the British Museum, and elsewhere. The cave itself was explained by the ancients to signify the world, into which the human soul must descend, that it may be purified by many trials before leaving it. Before any one was initiated into the mysteries of Mithras, it was necessary for the person to undergo a series of (it is said eighty) trials of increasing difficulty; and an undaunted,

Mithras. (Louvre.)

unsubdued spirit had to be maintained in fire and water, hunger and thirst, scourging, and solitude, and the aspirant was thus prepared for the initiation. It consisted of seven degrees, that of the ravens, the secret, the fighters, the lions or she-lions (for women were also received), the Persians, the sun-runners, and the fathers (κόρακες, κρύφιαι, λέοντες or λέαιναι, Ἡλιόδρομοι, *patres* or ἀετοί). Various Christian rites seem also to have been introduced into the mysteries of Mithras. Epithets like "Lord and Creator of all things," "Father and source of all life," enable us to recognize Mithras as one of the pantheistic divinities of declining heathendom.

See Hammer-Purgstall, *Mithriaca* (1833); Windischmann, *Mithra* (1857); Lajard, *Recherches sur le Culte Publique et les Mystères de Mithra* (Paris, 1847–1867).

Mithridātes (Μιθριδάτης) and **Mithradātes** (Μιθραδάτης). A name given to certain kings of Parthia and Persia. The name is derived from the Persian *Mithra*, "the sun," and probably means "sun-given."

(1) MITHRIDĀTES I., king or, more properly, satrap of Pontus, was son of Ariobarzanes I., and was succeeded by Ariobarzanes II., about B.C. 363. The kings of Pontus claimed to be lineally descended from one of the seven Persians who had conspired against the Magi, and who was subsequently established by Darius Hystaspis in the government of the countries bordering on the

Euxine Sea. Very little is known of their history until after the fall of the Persian Empire. (2) MITHRIDATES II., king of Pontus (337–302), succeeded his father Ariobarzanes II., and was the founder of the independent kingdom of Pontus. After the death of Alexander the Great, he was for a time subject to Antigonus; but during the war between the successors of Alexander he succeeded in establishing his independence. He died at the age of eighty-four. (3) MITHRIDATES III., king of Pontus (302–266), son and successor of the preceding. He enlarged his paternal dominions by the acquisition of great part of Cappadocia and Paphlagonia. He was succeeded by his son Ariobarzanes III. (4) MITHRIDATES IV., king of Pontus (about 240–190), son and successor of Ariobarzanes III. He gave his daughter Laodicé in marriage to Antiochus III. He was succeeded by his son Pharnaces I. (5) MITHRIDATES V., king of Pontus (about 156–120), surnamed EUERGĔTES, son and successor of Pharnaces I. He was the first of the kings of Pontus who made an alliance with the Romans, whom he assisted in the Third Punic War and in the war against Aristonicus (131–129). He was assassinated at Sinopé by a conspiracy among his own immediate attendants. (6) MITHRIDATES VI., king of Pontus (120–63), surnamed EUPĂTOR, also DIONȲSUS, but more commonly "the Great," was the son and successor of the preceding, and was only eleven years old at the period of his accession. We have very imperfect information concerning the earlier years of his reign, and much of what has been transmitted wears a suspicious aspect. It is said that immediately on ascending the throne he found himself assailed by the designs of his guardians, but that he succeeded in eluding all their machinations, partly by displaying a courage and address in warlike exercises beyond his years, partly by the use of antidotes against poison, to which he began thus early to accustom himself. In order to evade the designs formed against his life, he also devoted much of his time to hunting, and took refuge in the remotest and most unfrequented regions, under pretence of pursuing the pleasures of the chase. Whatever truth there may be in these accounts, it is certain that when he attained to manhood he was not only endowed with consummate skill in all martial exercises, and possessed of a bodily frame inured to all hardships as well as a spirit to brave every danger, but his naturally vigorous intellect had been improved by careful culture. As a boy, he had been brought up at Sinopé, where he had probably received the elements of a Greek education; and so powerful was his memory that he is said to have learned not less than twenty-two languages, and to have been able in the days of his greatest power to transact business with the deputies of every tribe subject to his rule in their own peculiar dialect.

The first steps of his career were marked by blood. He is said to have murdered his mother, to whom a share in the royal authority had been left by Mithridates Euergetes; and this was followed by the assassination of his brother. In the early part of his reign he subdued the barbarian tribes between the Euxine and the confines of Armenia, including the whole of Colchis and the province called Lesser Armenia, and even extended his conquests beyond the Caucasus. He assisted Parisades, king of the Bosporus, against the Sarmatians and Roxolani, and rendered the whole of the Tauric Chersonesus tributary to his kingdom. After the death of Parisades the kingdom of Bosporus itself was incorporated with his dominions. He was now in possession of such great power that he began to deem himself equal to a contest with Rome itself. Many causes of dissension had already arisen between them, but Mithridates had hitherto submitted to the mandates of Rome. Even after expelling Ariobarzanes from Cappadocia and Nicomedes from Bithynia in 90, he offered no resistance to the Romans when they restored these monarchs to their kingdom. But when Nicomedes, urged by the Roman legates, invaded the territories of Mithridates, the latter made preparations for immediate hostilities. His success was rapid and striking. In 88 he drove Ariobarzanes out of Cappadocia and Nicomedes out of Bithynia, defeated the Roman generals who had supported the latter, made himself master of Phrygia and Galatia, and at last of the Roman province of Asia. During the winter he issued the sanguinary order to all the cities of Asia to put to death, on the same day, all the Roman and Italian citizens who were to be found within their walls. So hateful had the Romans rendered themselves, that these commands were obeyed with alacrity by almost all the cities of Asia, and eighty thousand Romans and Italians are said to have perished in this fearful massacre. Meantime Sulla had received the command of the war against Mithridates, and crossed over into Greece in 87. Mithridates, however, had resolved not to await the Romans in Asia, but had already sent his general Archelaüs into Greece at the head of a powerful army. The war proved unfavourable to the king. Archelaüs was twice defeated by Sulla with immense loss near Chaeronea, and Orchomenus in Boeotia (86). About the same time Mithridates was himself defeated in Asia by Fimbria. (See FIMBRIA.) These disasters led him to sue for peace, which Sulla was willing to grant, because he was anxious to return to Italy, which was entirely in the hands of his enemies. Mithridates consented to abandon all his conquests in Asia, to pay a sum of two thousand talents, and to surrender to the Romans a fleet of seventy ships. Thus terminated the First Mithridatic War (84). Shortly afterwards Murena, who had been left in command of Asia by Sulla, invaded the dominions of Mithridates (83) under the pretext that the king had not yet evacuated the whole of Cappadocia. In the following year (82) Murena renewed his hostile incursions, but was defeated by Mithridates on the banks of the river Halys. But shortly afterwards Murena received peremptory orders from Sulla to desist from hostilities, in consequence of which peace was again restored. This is usually called the Second Mithridatic War. Mithridates, however, was well aware that the peace between him and Rome was in fact a mere suspension of hostilities, and that the Republic would never suffer the massacre of her citizens in Asia to remain ultimately unpunished. No formal treaty was ever concluded between Mithridates and the Roman Senate; and the king had in vain endeavoured to obtain the ratification of the terms agreed on between him and Sulla.

The death of Nicomedes III., king of Bithynia, at the beginning of 74, brought matters to a crisis.

That monarch left his dominions by will to the Roman people; and Bithynia was accordingly declared a Roman province; but Mithridates asserted that the late king had left a legitimate son by his wife Nysa, whose pretensions he immediately prepared to support by his arms. He had employed the last few years in forming a powerful army, armed and disciplined in the Roman manner; and he now took the field with one hundred and twenty thousand foot soldiers, sixteen thousand horse, and a vast number of barbarian auxiliaries. This was the commencement of the Third Mithridatic War. The two Roman consuls, Lucullus and Cotta, were unable to oppose his first irruption. He traversed Bithynia without encountering any resistance, and when at length Cotta ventured to give him battle under the walls of Chalcedon, the consul was totally defeated both by sea and land. Mithridates then proceeded to lay siege to Cyzicus both by sea

Coin of Mithridates the Great.

and land. Lucullus marched to the relief of the city, cut off the king's supplies, and eventually compelled him to raise the siege early in 73. On his retreat Mithridates suffered great loss, and eventually took refuge in Pontus. Hither Lucullus followed him in the next year. The new army which the king had collected was entirely defeated by the Roman general; and Mithridates, despairing of opposing the further progress of Lucullus, took refuge in the dominions of his son-in-law Tigranes, the king of Armenia. Tigranes at first showed no disposition to attempt the restoration of his father-in-law; but being offended at the haughty conduct of Appius Claudius, whom Lucullus had sent to demand the surrender of Mithridates, the Armenian king not only refused this request, but determined to prepare for war with the Romans. Accordingly, in 69, Lucullus marched into Armenia, defeated Tigranes and Mithridates near Tigranocerta, and in the next year (68) again defeated the allied monarchs near Artaxata. The Roman general then turned aside into Mesopotamia, and laid siege to Nisibis. Here the Roman soldiers broke out into open mutiny, and demanded to be led home; and Lucullus was obliged to raise the siege, and return to Asia Minor. Meanwhile Mithridates had taken advantage of the absence of Lucullus to invade Pontus at the head of a large army. He defeated Fabius and Triarius, to whom the defence of Pontus had been committed; and when Lucullus returned to Pontus, he was unable to resume the offensive in consequence of the mutinous spirit of his own soldiers. Mithridates was thus able, before the close of 67, to regain possession of the greater part of his hereditary dominions. In the following year (66) the conduct of the war was intrusted to Pompey. Hostilities were resumed with greater vigour than ever. Mithridates was obliged to retire before the Romans; he was surprised and defeated by Pompey; and as Tigranes now refused to admit him into his own dominions, he resolved to plunge with his small army into the heart of Colchis, and thence make his way to the Palus Maeotis and the Cimmerian Bosporus. Arduous as this enterprise appeared, it was successfully accomplished; and he at length established himself without opposition at Panticapaeum, the capital of Bosporus. He had now nothing to fear from the pursuit of Pompey, who turned his arms first against Tigranes, and afterwards against Syria. Unable to obtain peace from Pompey, unless he would come in person to make his submission, Mithridates conceived the daring project of marching round the northern and western coasts of the Euxine, through the wild tribes of the Sarmatians and Getae, and, having gathered round his standard all these barbarous nations, to penetrate into Italy itself. But meanwhile disaffection had made rapid progress among his followers. His son Pharnaces at length openly rebelled against him. He was joined both by the whole army and the citizens of Panticapaeum, who unanimously proclaimed him king; and Mithridates, who had taken refuge in a strong tower, saw that no choice remained to him but death or captivity. Hereupon he took poison, which he constantly carried with him; but his constitution had been so long inured to antidotes that it did not produce the desired effect, and he was compelled to call in the assistance of one of his Gaulish mercenaries to dispatch him with his sword. He died in 63. His body was sent by Pharnaces to Pompey at Amisus, as a token of his submission; but the conqueror caused it to be interred with regal honours in the sepulchre of his forefathers at Sinopé. He was sixty-eight or sixty-nine years old at the time of his death, and had reigned fifty-seven years, of which twenty-five had been occupied, with only a few brief intervals, in one continued struggle against the Roman power. The estimation in which he was held by his adversaries is the strongest testimony to his great abilities: Cicero calls him the greatest of all kings after Alexander, and in another passage says that he was a more formidable opponent than any other monarch whom the Roman arms had yet encountered. See Reinach, *Mithridate Eupator* (Paris, 1890).

(7) Kings of Parthia. (See Arsaces.) (8) Of Pergamus, son of Menodotus; but his mother having had an amour with Mithridates the Great, he was generally looked upon as, in reality, the son of that monarch. The king himself bestowed great care on his education; and he appears as early as 64 to have exercised the chief control over the affairs of his native city. At a subsequent period he served under Iulius Caesar in the Alexandrian War (48); and after the defeat of Pharnaces in the following year (47) Caesar bestowed upon Mithridates the kingdom of the Bosporus, and also the tetrarchy of the Galatians. But the kingdom of the Bosporus still remained to be won; for Asander, who had revolted against Pharnaces, was, in fact, master of the whole country, and Mithridates, having attempted to expel him, was defeated and slain.

Mithridātis Regio (Μιθριδάτου χώρα). A district of Sarmatia Asiatica, on the western side of the river Rha (now Volga), so called because it was the place of refuge of the last Mithridates in the reign of Claudius.

Greek Mitra. (Rich.)

Mitra (μίτρα). (1) A band of of any kind. (2) A head-dress, something like a turban. (3) A kerchief which women wore round the head. See CALANTICA; COMA.

Mitra (Μίτρα). The Persian Aphroditê (Herod. i. 131).

Mitylēnê (Μιτυλήνη) or **Mytilēnê** (Μυτιλήνη), the latter being the earlier form. The chief city of Lesbos, stood on the east side of the island opposite the coast of Lesbos, upon a promontory which was once an island, and both sides of which formed excellent harbours. Its first foundation is ascribed to Carians and Pelasgians. It was early colonized by the Aeolians. Important hints respecting its political history are furnished by the fragments of the poetry of Alcaeus, whence (and from other sources) it seems that, after the rule and overthrow of a series of tyrants, the city was nearly ruined by the bitter hatred and conflicts of the factions of the nobles and the people, till Pittacus was appointed to a sort of dictatorship, and the nobles were expelled. (See ALCAEUS; PITTACUS.) Meanwhile, the city had grown to great importance as a naval power, and had founded colonies on the coasts of Mysia and Thrace. At the beginning of the seventh century B.C. the possession of one of these colonies, Sigeum, at the mouth of the Hellespont, was disputed in war between the Mitylenaeans and Athenians, and assigned to the latter by the award of Periander, tyrant of Corinth. Among the other colonies of Mitylenê were Achilleum, Assos, and Antandrus. Mitylenê submitted to the Persians after the conquest of Ionia and Aeolis, and furnished contingents to the expeditions of Cambyses against Egypt and of Darius against Scythia. It was active in the Ionian revolt, after the failure of which it again became subject to Persia, and took part in the expedition of Xerxes against Greece. After the Persian War it formed an alliance with Athens, and remained one of the most important members of the Athenian confederacy, retaining its independence till the fourth year of the Peloponnesian War (B.C. 428), when it headed a revolt of the greater part of Lesbos, the progress and suppression of which forms one of the most interesting episodes in the history of the Peloponnesian War. This event destroyed the power of Mitylenê. Its subsequent fortunes cannot be related in detail here. It fell under the power of the Romans after the Mithridatic War. See Leithäuser, *Der Abfall Mytilenes von Athen* (1874); Cichorius, *Rom und Mytilene* (Leipzig, 1888); Conze, *Reise auf der Insel Lesbos*, and LESBOS.

Mixta Actio. See ACTIO, in the Appendix.

Mna (μνᾶ). See MINA; TALENTUM.

Mnaseas (Μνασέας). A native of Patara in Lycia, who studied under Eratosthenes of Alexandria, and became noted as a grammarian. He wrote two works—one a *Periplus* and one on the oracles given at Delphi (Athen. pp. 158, 296, 530).

Mnemăta (μνήματα), **Mnemeia** (μνημεῖα). See SEPULCRUM.

Mnemé (Μνήμη). See MUSAE.

Mnemosȳné (Μνημοσύνη). Daughter of Uranus and Gaea (Heaven and Earth) and one of the Titanides, the goddess of memory, by Zeus, mother of the Muses, in company with whom she was usually worshipped. See MUSAE.

Mnesarchus (Μνήσαρχος). (1) See PYTHAGORAS. (2) A Stoic philosopher, a pupil of Panaetius, who taught at Athens about B.C. 110 (Cic. *De Fin.* i. 2, 6).

Mnesĭcles (Μνησικλῆς). A Greek architect, the builder of the Propylaea (q. v.) of the Athenian Acropolis.

Mnesitheüs (Μνησίθεος). An Athenian physician of the fourth century B.C., who is frequently mentioned by Galen and others.

Mnester (Μνήστηρ). A pantomimic actor, who was one of the lovers of Messalina, wife of the emperor Claudius, and who was put to death on her downfall (Tac. *Ann.* ix. 4, 36).

Mnestheüs (Μνησθεός). A Trojan, who accompanied Aeneas to Italy, and is said to have been the ancestral hero of the Memmii (Verg. *Aen.* v. 117).

Moabite Stone. A stone discovered by Klein in 1868 at Dhibân, the ancient Dibon. It was of

Moabite Stone. (Ginsburg.)

black basalt of the shape shown in the illustration, of a height of 3 feet 10 inches, a thickness of 14½ inches, and a breadth of 2 feet. It was covered by an inscription in Hebrew Phœnician characters, extending to thirty-four lines. After its discovery it was broken up by the Arabs, but has been pieced together again, and the whole is now in the Louvre at Paris. The inscription is a record relating to Mesha, king of Moab, and relates to his successful revolt against the Jewish king (cf. 2 Kings, ch. iii.). See Ginsburg, *The Moabite Stone* (2d ed. 1871); Smend and Socin, *Die Inschrift des Königs Mesa* (Freiburg, 1886).

Moabītis (Μωαβῖτις, Μόβα), called Moab in the Old Testament. A district of Arabia Petraea, east of the Dead Sea. The Moabites were frequently at war with the Israelites. They were conquered by David, but afterwards recovered their independence.

Mochlus (μοχλός). See Ianua.

Modestīnus, Herennius. A late Roman jurist and pupil of the great lawyer Ulpian, who flourished A.D. 222–244. There are 345 extracts from his writings given in the *Digest.*

Modestus. (1) Iulius. A Roman grammarian of the first century A.D. (Gell. iii. 9, 1). (2) A Roman military writer, whose treatise on military terms (*De Vocabulis Rei Militaris*) is still extant. It is dedicated to the emperor Tacitus (A.D. 275).

Modicia. A town of Gallia Transpadana, north of Mediolanum (Milan), where Theodoric built a palace and the Lombard queen Theodolinda a church, the latter still remaining.

Modin (Μοδεΐν). A mountain village in the northwestern part of Iudaea, famous as being the birthplace of the Maccabaei (Ios. *Ant. Iud.* xii. 8, 1).

Modius and **Modium.** The principal dry measure of the Romans, equal to nearly two gallons, a sixth part of the Greek medimnus. It was divided into 16 *sextarii*, 32 *heminae*, 64 *quartarii*, 128 *acetabula*, 192 *cyathi.*

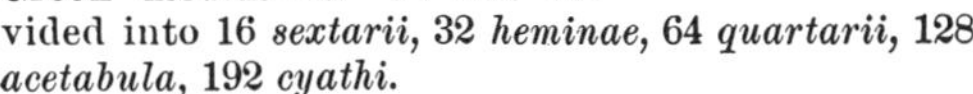

Modius. (From a terra-cotta lamp.)

Moenia. See Murus.

Moenus, Moenis, Maenus, Menus. Now the Main; a river of Germany. It flowed through the territory of the Hermunduri and the Agri Decumates, emptying into the Rhine opposite Moguntiacum (Mainz). See Tac. *Germ.* 28.

Moerae (Μοῖραι). The Greek goddesses of fate. Homer, in one passage (*Il.* xxiv. 209), speaks generally of the Moera, that spins the thread of life for men at their birth; in another (ib. 49), of several Moerae; and elsewhere (*Od.* vii. 197), of the Κλῶθες, or Spinners. Their relation to Zeus and other gods is no more clearly defined by Homer than by the other Greeks. At one time fate is a power with unlimited sway over men and gods, and the will of fate is searched out and executed by Zeus with the other gods (*Il.* xix. 87; *Od.* xxii. 413); at another, Zeus is called the highest ruler of destinies; or again, he and the other gods can change the course of fate (*Il.* xvi. 434), and even men can exceed the limits it imposes (*Il.* xx. 336). In Hesiod, they are called in one passage (*Theog.* 211–17) daughters of night and sisters of the goddesses of death (Κῆρες), while in another (*Theog.* 904) they are the daughters of Zeus and Themis and sisters of the Horae, who give good and bad fortunes to mortals at their birth; their names are Clotho (the Spinner), who spins the thread of life; Lachĕsis (Disposer of Lots), who determines its length, and Atrŏpos (Inevitable), who cuts it off. As exerting power at the time of birth, they are connected with Ilithyia, the goddess of birth, who was supposed to stand beside them, and was invoked together with them, these and the Keres being the powers that decided when life should end. As at birth, they determine men's destinies in life; they are also able to predict them. While, on the one hand, they are regarded as the impartial representatives of the government of the world, they are, on the other hand, sometimes conceived as cruel and jealous, because they remorselessly thwart the plans and desires of men.

Clotho, Atropos, and Lachesis. (Roman relief, in Schloss Tegel, near Berlin.)

In art, they appear as maidens of grave aspect. Clotho is usually represented with a spindle; Lachesis with a scroll, or a globe; and Atropos with a pair of scales, or shears, or else drawing a lot (as in the illustration). The Romans identified the Moerae with their native goddesses of fate—the Parcae. These were also called Fata, and were invoked, at the end of the first week of an infant's life, as Fata Scribunda, the goddesses that wrote down men's destiny in life.

Moeris (Μοῖρις) or **Myris** (Μύρις). A supposed king of Egypt, who is said to have dug, about B.C. 1350, the great lake known by his name. It covered over sixty square miles at the entrance to the Fayûm; and was really constructed by Amenemhat III. of the Twelfth Dynasty about B.C. 2300. It was employed for storing the water of the Nile for irrigation, and is now properly to be identified with the natural lake Borket-el-Kurûn. Herodotus says that the king erected two pyramids in the lake, one supporting a statue of himself and the other a statue of his wife. Remains of these pyramids have been discovered in modern times. The name *Moeris* is the Egyptian *meri,* "a lake," and no such king as Moeris ever lived. See Herod. ii. 13, 101, 149; Diod. i. 52; Pliny, *H. N.* v. 9, 50; xxxvii. 12, 76; and Linant Bey, *Mémoire sur le Lac Moeris* (1843).

Moeris, AELIUS. Known as "the Atticist" (MOERIS ATTICISTA). A Greek grammarian of the second century A.D. He was the author of an Attic lexicon (Λέξεις 'Αττικαί), a list, in alphabetical order, of a number of expressions and forms used by Attic writers, with the parallel expressions used in his own time, and in other dialects. It is edited by Pierson (1759) and Bekker (1833).

Moeris Lacus. See MOERIS.

Moero (Μοιρώ) or **Myro** (Μυρώ). A Byzantine poetess, mother of the grammarian and tragic poet Homerus. She lived about B.C. 300, and wrote epic, elegiac, and lyric verse (Athen. p. 490).

Moesia (Μοισία). A country of Europe, called by the Greeks MYSIA (Μυσία ἡ ἐν Εὐρώπῃ). It was bounded on the south by Thrace and Macedonia, on the west by Illyricum and Pannonia, on the north by the Danube, and on the east by the Pontus Euxinus, thus corresponding roughly to the present Servia and Bulgaria. This country was subdued in the reign of Augustus (B.C. 29), and was made a Roman province at the commencement of the reign of Tiberius. It was afterwards formed into two provinces, called Moesia Superior and Moesia Inferior, the former being the western and the latter the eastern half of the country. When Aurelian surrendered Dacia to the barbarians and removed the inhabitants of that province to the south of the Danube, the middle part of Moesia was called Dacia Aureliani.

Moeso-Goths. See GOTHI.

Mogontiăcum, Moguntiăcum, or **Magontiăcum.** The modern Mainz or Mayence; a town on the left bank of the Rhine, opposite the mouth of the river Moenus (Main). It lay within the territories of the Vangiones, and finally became the capital of Germania Prima. (See GERMANIA.) It was strongly fortified by Drusus, and until the downfall of the Roman Empire remained one of the chief of the Rhenish fortresses (Tac. *Hist.* iv. 15, 24; Amm. Marc. xv. 11).

Moicheias Graphé (μοιχείας γραφή). A suit brought to punish adultery. See ADULTERIUM.

Moirae. See MOERAE.

Mola (μύλη). The generic term for a mill. The following varieties may be specified: (1) MOLA MANUARIA or TRUSATĬLIS (χειρομύλη), a hand-mill, used for grinding wheat, beans, and other farinaceous products. Several of these have been found in the bakers' shops at Pompeii (see PISTOR), and all of them show the same general construction.

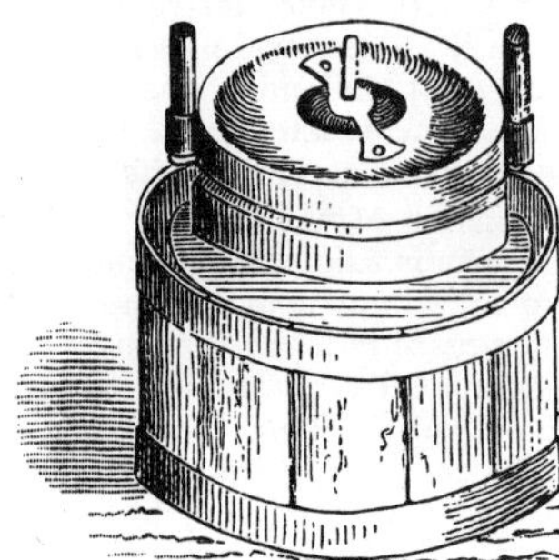

Hand-mill.

Pompeian Hand-mills.

The base is a cylindrical stone of some five feet in diameter and one in height, out of which rises a conical projection two feet high, forming the lower millstone (*meta*). This has an iron pivot fastened at its top. The outer stone (*catillus*) is formed in the shape of an hour-glass, so that one half fits like a cap upon the conical surface of the lower stone, receiving the iron pivot mentioned above in a socket made in the centre of the narrowest part between the two hollow cones. The grain was poured into the hollow cup at the top, which served as a hopper, and ran gradually down through from holes pierced in it to the solid cone beneath, where it was ground to flour between the outer surface of the cone and the inner surface of its cap as the latter was turned round and round (*lapis lapidem terit,* Plaut. *Asin.* i. 1, 16). The turning was done by slaves, with the aid of a wooden bar inserted in each of its sides, for which a socket was provided. The flour, when ground, fell from the bottom into a receptacle cut round the base. (2) MOLA BUXEA. A smaller hand-mill, used

Mola Machinaria. (From a marble in the Vatican.)

Mola Versatilis. (From a Gem.)

for grinding pepper (Petron. 74). (3) MOLA MACHINARIA or ASINARIA. A mill constructed like a hand-mill, but so large as to require an ass, ox, or horse to work it, as shown in the illustration (Cat. *R. R.* 11, 4). (4) MOLA VERSATĬLIS. A species of grindstone worked by the foot, as at the present time. The use of it is attested by the engraved gem, from which the illustration is taken; but there is no certain reference to it in the classical writers.

Moliŏné (Μολιόνη). See MOLIONIDAE.

Moliŏnes. See MOLIONIDAE.

Molionĭdae (Μολιονίδαι) and **Moliŏnes** (Μολίονες). Eurytus and Cteatus, the sons of Actor (whence they were also called ACTORĬDAE), or else of Poseidon and Molioné. (Homer [*Il.* xi. 750] calls them by the dual and double name Actorione Molione.) As boys they fought against Nestor and the men of Pylos. When they had grown up, they defeated the army of Heracles that threatened their uncle Augeas, but were killed by the former near Cleonae in Argolis. In Homer their sons Thalpius and Antimachus are the chieftains of the Epeians before Troy. A later legend describes them as having only one body but two heads (Athen. ii. 58).

Molo. A very celebrated Greek rhetorician of Rhodes, under whom both Caesar and Cicero studied oratory.

Molochath. See MULUCHA.

Molon (Μόλων). A satrap of Media under Antiochus the Great, against whom he revolted, and by whom he was defeated near Babylon (B.C. 220), upon which he put an end to his own life (Polyb. v. 40–54).

Molossi (Μολοσσοί). A people of Epirus, inhabiting a narrow strip of country, called after them MOLOSSIA or MOLOSSIS, which extended along the western bank of the Arachthus as far as the Ambracian Gulf. They were the most powerful people in Epirus, and their kings gradually extended their dominion over the whole of the country. The first of their kings, who took the title of King of Epirus, was the Alexander who perished in Italy B.C. 326. (See EPIRUS.) Their capital was Ambracia. The Molossian hounds were celebrated in antiquity (Verg. *Georg.* iii. 405).

Molus (Μόλος). The son of Deucalion and father of Meriones (q. v.).

Molycrīum (Μολύκρειον). A town in the south of Aetolia, at the entrance of the Corinthian Gulf.

Momus (Μῶμος). In Greek mythology the evil spirit of blame and mockery, according to Hesiod (*Theog.* 214) the son of Night. According to Lucian (*Hermotimus*, 20), he found fault with the man formed by Hephaestus for not having little doors in his breast, so as to allow of his secret thoughts being seen. In Philostratus (*Ep.* 21=37) the only faults he finds in Aphrodité are that she is too talkative and that her sandals make too much noise.

Mona (Μόνα). The modern Anglesey (Angles Ey, "Englishman's island"); an island off the coast of the Ordovices in Britain, one of the chief seats of the Druids. Caesar erroneously describes this island as half way between Britannia and Hibernia (*B. G.* v. 13). Hence it has been supposed by some critics that the Mona of Caesar is the Isle of Man; but it is more probable, on account of the celebrity of Mona in connection with the Druids, that he had heard of Anglesey, and that he received a false report respecting its real position. The island was taken in A.D. 61 by Suetonius Paulinus, who broke the power of the Druids; and was again subdued by Agricola in A.D. 78 (Tac. *Agric.* 18; *Ann.* xiv. 29). See MONAPIA.

Monaeses. A Parthian general mentioned by Horace, probably the same as Surenas, the general of Orodes, who defeated Crassus (*Carm.* iii. 6, 9).

Monapia or **Monarīna**. The Isle of Man; an island lying between Britannia and Hibernia (Pliny, *H. N.* iv. 103). It is probably this island that Caesar intends in speaking of Mona. See MONA.

Monarchia (μοναρχία). A form of government in which the supreme functions of political administration are vested in a single person, no matter whether this person is an hereditary or an elective ruler, or one who has usurped power. When he appoints all the other officials, Aristotle speaks of the form of government as παμβασιλεία. Plutarch describes the Roman dictatorship as μοναρχία. See Aristot. *Polit.* iii. 14.

Monda or **Munda**. Now the Mondego; a river in Spain between the Tagus and Durius. It empties into the ocean (Mela, iii. 1, 7).

Monēta (ἀργυροκοπεῖον). A mint. In Persia the king enjoyed the sole right of issuing gold money (see DARICUS); but the cities on the coast of Asia Minor coined copper, silver, and even electrum coins at pleasure; and the different satraps struck silver money bearing their own names. In Greece proper and the Greek colonies each State or πόλις issued such money as it chose, so that a great variety of Greek coins have come down to us. Fully 2000 mints are known to have existed prior to the fall of the Roman Empire (A.D. 410). Sicily had more than fifty different mints, and even the little island of Ceos had three. The cities of Magna Graecia in Italy issued coins of a general uniformity, as did the Aetolian and Achaean Leagues. Under the Romans the Greek cities ceased to coin silver money, except a few favoured ones like Antioch, the Cappadocian Caesarea, and Tarsus, though copper coins were still struck in many towns of Greece and Asia.

As the Roman dominion extended over Italy, the State gradually put down the rival issues of Oscan, Etruscan, and other non-Latin coinages, and introduced a uniform system. At Rome, however, various personages at different times controlled the mintage. In the city, money was usually struck under the direction of three officials, the *triumviri monetales*; but generals in the field and abroad issued money as they found it necessary, placing upon it not only their names but their effigies. When Augustus assumed the supreme power he took to himself the sole right to issue gold and silver coins, leaving to the Senate the mintage of copper. Hence copper coins of the Empire bore the letters S. C., indicating that they were issued by authority of the Senate.

The ancient processes of minting were very simple. One engraved die was let into an anvil, another into the end of a metal bar. Between the two was placed the blank, roughly cast into the required shape and size and heated red hot. A single blow of a heavy hammer on the upper end of the bar usually finished the coin, which was then removed by a pair of tongs. Collars and milling were unknown. See NUMISMATICS.

Monēta. A name given to Iuno (q. v.) as the goddess of good counsel (from *moneo*), under which title a temple was built to her on the Capitol. Attached to it was the mint (Livy, vii. 28), which on this account received the name of *moneta.*

Iuno Moneta.

Money. See MONETA; NUMISMATICS.

Money-changers. See TRAPEZITAE.

Monīlé (ὅρμος, μάννος). A necklace. In Homer, necklaces of gold and amber are mentioned (*Odyss.* xv. 460; xviii. 295), and in later times necklaces were in common use among both the Greeks and Romans, being worn by men as well as by women, though for men to wear them was regarded as effeminate. They were especially in vogue as bridal ornaments (Lucan, ii. 361). The simplest form was that of the bead necklace (*monile bacatum*), in which small globes of gold, silver, amber, crystal, and glass were strung together, often in rows. Very costly necklaces of exquisite workmanship were also made for the wealthy, with pendants and clasps, often adorned with pearls, rubies, and other precious stones. The ornamentation also included disks, rosettes, lozenges, lotus-buds, heads of animals, ivy-leaves, etc. The hooks or fastenings at the back of the neck were called

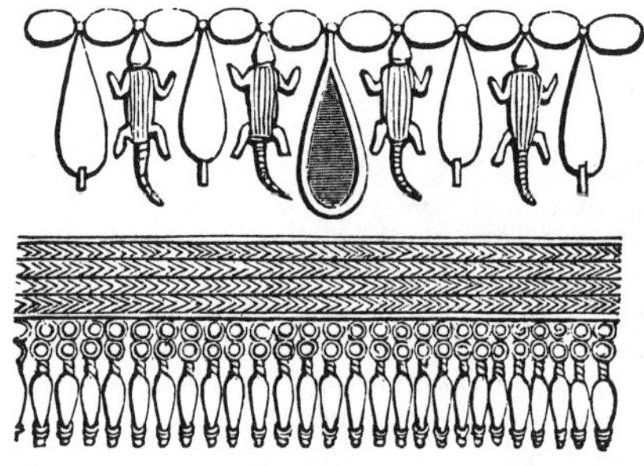
Necklaces. (Naples.)

clusurae. See the articles ARMILLA; CAELATURA (with illustration, p. 243); CATENA; GEMMA; TORQUES. The name *monile* is also applied to a collar or necklace placed about the neck of a horse or other favourite animal (Verg. *Aen.* vii. 278).

Monochromăta (μονοχρώματα). Paintings tinged with a single colour upon a dark ground, as frequently upon vases (Pliny, *H. N.* xxxiii. 39; xxxv. 36).

Monoeci Portus, also **Herculis Monoeci Portus.** The modern Monaco; a port-town on the coast of Liguria, founded by the Massilians, was situated on a promontory (hence the *arx Monoeci* of Vergil), and possessed a temple of Hercules Monoecus, from whom the place derived its name (Verg. *Aen.* vi. 801).

Monogrammăta. Paintings drawn in outline (Pliny, *H. N.* xxxv. 5).

Monopodium. A one-legged table. See MENSA.

Monoptĕros (μονόπτερος). An epithet descriptive of a round temple with its columns arranged in a circle and supporting a cupola. See TEMPLUM.

Montānus. (1) CURTIUS. A Roman exiled by Nero, A.D. 67; but soon afterwards recalled at his father's petition. On the accession of Vespasian he vehemently attacked in the Senate the notorious informer, Aquilius Regulus. (2) VOLTIĒNUS, an orator and declaimer in the reign of Tiberius. From his propensity to refine upon thought and diction, he was named "the Ovid of the rhetorical schools." He was convicted on a charge of treason, and died an exile in the Balearic Islands, A.D. 25. (3) A noted heresiarch, who appeared in A.D. 156 at Ardaban in Phrygia, professing to have a mission to reform the Church. See TERTULLIANUS.

Montfaucon, BERNARD DE. A French classical scholar, born in 1655. After serving in the army he entered the Benedictine Order and gave his time to the study of classical antiquity. He died at Paris in 1741. He was the author of critical editions of several of the Greek Fathers and of the following great works: *Palaeographia Graeca* (1708); *L'Antiquité Expliquée et Representée en Figures* (15 vols. 1719–1724); and *Bibliotheca Bibliothecarum MSS. Nova* (2 vols. 1739). The first establishes palaeography as a science, and is based upon a careful examination of nearly 12,000 manuscripts. The second is still consulted by all archaeologists; and the third is a list of the manuscripts examined by him in the course of forty years of study. See De Broglie, *La Société de l'Abbaye de St. Germain* (2 vols. 1891).

Months. See CALENDARIUM.

Monumentum. See SEPULCRUM.

Monumentum Adulitānum. A monument at Adulé in Aethiopia on a bay of the Red Sea, bearing inscriptions in Greek letters, commemorating the tribute received from the Arabs and Aethiopians by Ptolemy Euergetes (B.C. 247–222), and also the conquests of a certain Aethiopian king whose name is not given. The monument is of white marble in the shape of a throne. The inscriptions were copied in the sixth century A.D. by Cosmas Indicopleustes, and have been edited by Buttmann in the *Museum der Alterthumswissenschaft.* ii. 1, p. 105.

Monumentum Ancyrānum. See ANCYRANUM MONUMENTUM; AUGUSTUS CAESAR, p. 171.

Moon, GODDESS OF THE. See LUNA; SELENÉ.

Mopsia or **Mopsopia** (Μοψοπία). An ancient name of Attica, whence Mopsopius is frequently used by the poets as equivalent to Athenian.

Mopsia or **Mopsopia.** A name of Pamphylia derived from that of Mopsus, a mythical leader of a band of Greeks who were reputed to have settled in that country after the Trojan War.

Mopsium (Μόψιον). A town of Thessaly in Pelasgiotis, on a hill of the same name.

Mopsucrēné (Μόψου κρήνη). A city of Cilicia, on the southern slope of the Taurus. Here the emperor Constantine died, A.D. 364.

Mopsuestia (Μόψου ἑστία, also Μόψου πόλις and Μόψος). Now Messis; an important city of Cilicia Campestris, on both banks of the river Pyramus, twelve Roman miles from its mouth, on the road from Tarsus to Issus, in the beautiful plain called τὸ Ἀλήϊον πεδίον, was a *civitas libera* under the Romans. The two parts of the city were connected by a handsome bridge built by Constantius over the Pyramus. In ecclesiastical history, it is notable as the birthplace of Theodore of Mopsuestia. In the Middle Ages it was called Mampsista.

Mopsus (Μόψος). (1) The son of Ampyx or Ampycus by the nymph Chloris. Being a seer, he was also called a son of Apollo by Himantis. He was one of the Lapithae of Oechalia or Titaeron in Thessaly, and took part in the combat at the wedding of Pirithoüs. He was one of the Calydonian hunters, and also one of the Argonauts. He died in Libya of the bite of a snake, and was buried there by the Argonauts. He was afterwards worshipped as an oracular hero. (2) The son of Apollo and Manto, the daughter of Tiresias, and also a celebrated seer. He contended in prophecy with Calchas at Colophon, and showed himself superior to the latter in prophetic power. He was believed to have founded Mallos in Cilicia in conjunction with the seer Amphilochus. A dispute arose between the two seers respecting the possession of the town, and both fell in combat by each other's hands. Mopsus had an oracle at Mallos, which existed as late as the time of Strabo. See CALCHAS.

Mora (μόρα). One of the six principal divisions of the army at Sparta, which included all Spartans and Perioeci that were obliged to serve. It was under the command of a polemarch, and consisted of four *lochi*, eight *pentecostyes*, and sixteen *enomotiae*, which were under as many *lochagi*, *pentecosteres*, and *enomotarchi*. These divisions were never sent on a campaign in their full strength, but only the men of particular years, specified in each case. The polemarch always took the command of the first levy. See EXERCITUS.

Mora. In Roman law, a term used of a delay in the discharge of a legal duty. A debtor was not *in mora* if he had a good excuse for the nonperformance of his obligation; but when mora could be legally imputed to a man, he was bound to make good to his creditor whatever loss had been sustained in consequence of the delay. Delay on the part of the creditor is called *mora accipiendi;* on the part of the debtor, *mora solvendi.* See Madai, *Die Lehre von der Mora;* and Wolff, *Zur Lehre von der Mora.*

Morētum. "The Country Breakfast." A poem in 124 hexameters, usually ascribed to Vergil and perhaps translated by him from a Greek original. It describes a peasant, Simylus, rising in the morning, baking bread, and preparing a mess of herbs in a mortar before going to work. See Barth, *Sprache und Versbau des Moretum* (Horn, 1879); Egli, *Pseudo-Verg. Gedichte* (Leipzig, 1886); and the article VERGILIUS.

Morgantium (Μοργάντιον), **Morgantīna** (Μοργαντίνη), **Murgantia, Morgentia.** A town in Sicily, southeast of Agyrium, and near the Symaethus, founded by the Morgetes, after they had been driven out of Italy by the Oenotrians.

Morgētes (Μόργητες). An ancient people in the south of Italy. According to Strabo, they dwelt in the neighbourhood of Rhegium, but being driven out of Italy by the Oenotrians crossed over to Sicily and there founded the town of Morgantium. According to Dionysius of Halicarnassus, Morges was the successor of the Oenotrian king Italus, and hospitably received Siculus, who had been driven out of Latium by the Aborigines, in consequence of which the earlier Oenotrians were called Italietes, Morgetes, and Siculi; according to this account, the Morgetes ought to be regarded as a branch of the Oenotrians.

Moria or **Morĭia** (Μώριον ὄρος). A mountain of Iudaea, within the city of Jerusalem, on the summit of which the Temple was built. See HIEROSOLYMA.

Moriměné (Μοριμενή). The northwestern district of Cappadocia, on the banks of the Halys, assigned under the Romans to Galatia.

Morĭni. The most northerly people in all Gaul, whence Vergil calls them *extremi hominum* (*Aen.* viii. 727). They dwelt on the coast, at the narrowest part of the channel between Gaul and Britain (*fretum Morinorum*). Their chief town was Gesoriacum (q. v.), now Boulogne.

Morio. A buffoon. See NANI.

Mormo (Μορμώ) and **Mormolȳcé** (Μορμολύκη). A female spectre, whose name was used by the Greeks to frighten children (Aristoph. *Ach.* 582; *Pax*, 474; Theoc. xv. 40). cf. LAMIAE.

Morpheus (Μορφεύς, "the moulder" or "fashioner"). The Greek god of dreams (Ovid, *Met.* xi. 635).

Mors. See THANATOS.

Morsĭmus (Μόρσιμος). A tragic poet, ridiculed by Aristophanes (*Ran.* 181).

Mortarium (ὅλμος, θύεια), in Latin also **Pila.** A mortar, used in early times for pounding grain, over which act the domestic deity Pilumnus (q. v.) presided. They were made of either wood or stone, and occasionally of baked white clay. Besides its primitive use, the mortar was also employed in pounding drugs, making perfumes, paint, plaster, and drugs, and in some of the processes of ancient metallurgy. The philosopher Anaxarchus was pounded to death in a mortar with iron pestles. See MOLA; PILA.

Mortgage. See PIGNUS.

Morȳchus (Μόρυχος). A tragic poet, ridiculed by Aristophanes for his gluttony (*Vesp.* 504).

Mos. See IUS.

Mosa. Now the Maas or Meuse; a river in Gallia Belgica, rising in Mount Vogesus and falling into the Vahalis, or west branch of the Rhine.

Mosaic. See MUSIVUM OPUS.

Moscha (Μόσχα). Now Muscat; a seaport on the northwestern coast of Arabia Felix. It was an important seat of the trade between Arabia and India (Ptol. vi. 7).

Moschi (Μόσχοι). A people of Asia, dwelling in the southern part of Colchis.

Moschĭci Montes (τὰ Μοσχικὰ ὄρη). A range of mountains forming the boundary between Colchis and Iberia. They were named from the Moschi who dwelt among them.

Moschion (Μοσχίων). A Greek gynaecologist, who lived about the second century A.D. A short treatise of his remains is edited by Dewez (Vienna, 1793).

Moschus (Μόσχος). A Greek bucolic poet, who lived in Syracuse about B.C. 150. Four longer and four shorter poems have been handed down as his; they show the greatest elegance of expression without the truth to nature and the dramatic power of his model, Theocritus. His lament for Bion is marked by melody and genuine pathos. Edited with Bion (q. v.) by Jacobs (1795); Wakefield (1795); Hartung (1858); and Ahrens (1875).

Mosella. The Moselle, a river in Gallia Belgica, rising in Mount Vogesus, and falling into the Rhine at Confluentes (Coblenz). The name gives its title to a graceful poem by Ausonius in 483 hexameters, a translation of which into English has been made by C. T. Brooks in Waring's *Bride of the Rhine* (Boston, 1878).

Mosquito-netting. See CONOPEUM.

Mostellaria. "The Ghost Story." A play of Plautus. Edited with English notes by Ramsay (1880) and Morris (1881). See PLAUTUS.

Mostēni (Μοστηνοί). A city of Lydia, southeast of Thyatira.

Mosy̆chlus (Μόσυχλος). A mountain in Lemnos regarded by the ancients as a volcano.

Mosynoeci (Μοσύνοιχοι). A barbarous people on the northern coast of Asia Minor, in Pontus, so called from the conical wooden houses in which they dwelt (Xen. *Anab.* iv. 4; v. 4).

Mothăces. See HELOTAE.

Mothōnē. See METHONĒ.

Motoria (sc. *fabula*). A comedy of a lively character as opposed to a *fabula statoria*, which has little or no action. The *Phormio* of Terence is a good specimen of a *fabula motoria;* the *Andria* of the other kind.

Motūca (Μότουκα). A town in the south of Sicily, west of the promontory Pachynus. The inhabitants were called Motycenses.

Moty̆a (Μοτύη). An ancient town in the northwest of Sicily, situated on a small island (now S. Pantaleo) near the coast, with which it was connected by a mole. It was founded by the Phœnicians, and next belonged to the Carthaginians, who transferred its inhabitants to the town of Lilybaeum, B.C. 397 (Thuc. vi. 2).

Mound. See AGGER; TUMULUS.

Mountebank. See CIRCULATOR.

Moustache. See BARBA; MUSTAX.

Mucia. The daughter of Q. Mucius Scaevola, the augur, consul B.C. 95, married Cn. Pompey, by whom she had two sons, Gneius and Sextus, and a daughter, Pompeia. She was divorced by Pompey in 62. She next married M. Aemilius Scaurus, a stepson of the dictator Sulla. In 39, Mucia went to Sicily to mediate between her son Sex. Pompey and Augustus. She was living at the time of the battle of Actium, 31. Augustus treated her with great respect (Dio Cass. xxxvii. 49; lvi. 38).

Muciānus. (1) P. LICINIUS CRASSUS DIVES MUCIĀNUS, the son of P. Mucius Scaevola, and adopted by P. Licinius Crassus Dives. He was consul B.C. 131, and carried on the war against Aristonicus in Asia, but was defeated by the latter. He succeeded Scipio Nasica as pontifex maximus. He was distinguished both as an orator and a lawyer. (2) C. LICINIUS MUCIĀNUS, three times consul in A.D. 52, 70, and 75. On Nero's death, in 68, Mucianus had the command of the province of Syria; and he rendered efficient aid to Vespasian, when the latter resolved to seize the imperial throne. As soon as Vespasian was proclaimed emperor, Mucianus set out for Europe to oppose Vitellius; but the Vitellians were entirely defeated by Antonius Primus before Mucianus entered Italy. Antonius, however, had to surrender all power into the hands of Mucianus upon the arrival of the latter at Rome. Mucianus was an orator and an historian. His powers of oratory are greatly praised by Tacitus. He made a collection of the speeches of the republican period, which he published in eleven books of *Acta* and three of *Epistolae.* The subject of his history is not mentioned; but it appears to have treated chiefly of the East. He is frequently quoted by Pliny the Elder. See Peter, *Hist. Reliq.* p. cccli.; and Brunn, *De Gaio Licinio Muciano* (Leipzig, 1870).

Mucinum or **Mucinium.** A handkerchief for wiping the nose (Arnob. ii. 5). See SUDARIUM.

Mucius Scaevŏla. See SCAEVOLA.

Mucro. The point of any weapon, especially of the sword, though a spear-point is *cuspis.*

Mulcĭber. An epithet of Vulcanus (q. v.).

Mulcta. See MULTA.

Mulctra, Mulctrālē, and **Mulctrum** (ἀμολγεύς). A milk-pail (Verg. *Ecl.* iii. 30).

Muli Mariāni. A nickname given to soldiers who carried a heavy kit (Festus, s. h. v.).

Mulio. (1) A muleteer (Suet. *Nero,* 30). (2) A person who keeps mules to hire (Suet. *Vesp.* 4).

Müller, KARL OTFRIED. A remarkable archæologist and classical scholar, born at Brieg, in Silesia, August 28, 1797. He was educated at Breslau and at Berlin under Boeckh, and when only twenty-two years of age was made Professor Extraordinarius of Archæology and Director of the Philological Seminary at the University of Göttingen (1819), and Professor Ordinarius in 1823. In 1840, while in Greece, he died from the effects of a fever contracted at Delphi, where he had been copying inscriptions. Müller was the author of a number of works that were really epoch-making, in that they opened up questions upon which several generations of scholars have since been continuously at work, and he may be said to have permanently established archæology upon a scientific basis. His chief works in this field are *Orchomenos und die Minyer* (1820); *Die Dorier* (2 vols. 1824; Eng. tr. 1829); *Die Etrusker,* which received a prize from the Berlin Academy (2 vols. 1828; 2d ed. revised by Deecke, 1877), on which see the article ETRURIA; a treatise on the Macedonians (1825); *Prolegomena zu einer wissenschaftlichen Mythologie* (1825); *Handbuch der Archäologie der Kunst* (1830, last ed. 1878; Eng. tr. 1847); and a *History of the Literature of Ancient Greece,* undertaken at the request of the British Society for the Diffusion of Useful Knowledge (1841, published by Dr. Müller's brother), of which the English version is by Sir George Cornewall Lewis and Dr. Donaldson, the latter continuing it through the Byzantine Period (last ed. 1882–84). He also edited the *Eumenides* of Aeschylus (1833–35), with valuable excursus on questions of scenic antiquities—a work that involved him in a bitter polemic with Gottfried Hermann, "the despot of Leipzig"; Varro, *De Lingua Latina* (1833); and Festus (1839), until lately the standard edition. See the memoirs by Lücke (1841) and F. Ranke (1870); and Bursian, *Geschichte* *der classischen Philologie in Deutschland*, pp. 1007–1028 (Munich, 1883).

Mulleus. See CALCEUS.

Mulsum. See VINUM.

Multa (also spelled *mulcta*, and possibly from *mulgeo*, "a milking"). The Roman term for a fine, inflicted either by a magistrate for disobedience or insubordination, or at the motion of an official by the decision of the people at the Comitia Tributa, or prescribed in laws, wills, etc., in case any one contravened them. It originally consisted in cattle, sheep, or oxen; then, after B.C. 430, the Lex Iulia Papiria permitted the payment in money according to a fixed scale (a sheep = 10 *asses*, an ox = 100 *asses*). The lowest amount of the *multa* inflicted by a magistrate in virtue of his office was a sheep; when acts of disobedience were repeated, the fine could be raised to 30 oxen (*suprema multa*). Against heavier penalties, such, in particular, as were imposed by the tribunes of the people on account of political crimes—e. g., when a general had waged war unskilfully or had exceeded the limits of his power—an appeal to the Comitia Tributa was granted, and they were decided by that body in the regular legal manner. The fines imposed by the people were always, and those imposed by the magistrates usually, set apart for sacred purposes; otherwise they fell to the Treasury, as was the rule under the Empire. This also received a part of the penalties fixed by laws; the other was given to the plaintiff. Fines for contravention of the clauses of a will were either paid to the funds of a temple or to the community to which the testator belonged, and at Rome to the Treasury. See Huschke, *Die Multa* (Leipzig, 1882); and the article POENA.

Mulŭcha and **Molŏchath** (Μολοχάθ). A river in the north of Africa, rising in the Atlas Mountains and forming the boundary between Mauretania and Numidia.

Mummius. (1) LUCIUS. A tribune of the plebs B.C. 187, and praetor 177. (2) LUCIUS, surnamed ACHAĬCUS, son of the last, was praetor 154, when he carried on the war successfully in further Spain against the Lusitanians. He was consul in 146, when he won for himself the surname of Achaicus by the conquest of Greece and the establishment of the Roman province of Achaia. After defeating the army of the Achaean League at the isthmus of Corinth, he entered Corinth without opposition. The city was burned, razed, and abandoned to pillage; the native Corinthians were sold for slaves, and the rarest specimens of Grecian art were given up to the rapacity of an ignorant conqueror. Polybius, the historian, saw Roman soldiers playing at draughts upon the far-famed picture of Dionysus by Aristides; and Mummius himself was so unconscious of the real value of his prize that he sold the rarer works of painting, sculpture, and carving to the king of Pergamus, and took bonds from the masters of vessels who conveyed the remainder to Italy to replace by equivalents any picture or statue lost or injured in the passage (Polyb. iii. 32; xl. 7–11; Vell. Paterc. i. 13). He remained in Greece during the greater part of 145 with the title of proconsul. He arranged the fiscal and municipal constitution of the newly-acquired province, and won the confidence and esteem of the provincials by his integrity, justice, and equanimity. He triumphed in 145. He was censor in 142 with Scipio Africanus the younger. The political opinions of Mummius inclined to the popular side. (3) SPURIUS, brother of the preceding, and his legate at Corinth in 146–145, was an intimate friend of the younger Scipio Africanus. In political opinions Spurius was opposed to his brother Lucius, and was a noted aristocrat. He composed ethical and satirical epistles, which were extant in Cicero's day, and were probably in the style which Horace afterwards cultivated so successfully. (4) A writer of Atellanae, who flourished later than B.C. 90 (Macrob. *Sat.* i. 10, 3).

Munatius Plancus. See PLANCUS.

Munda. (1) A Roman colony and an important town in Hispania Beatica, situated on a small river, and celebrated on account of two battles fought in its neighbourhood, the victory of Cn. Scipio over the Carthaginians in B.C. 216, and the important victory of Iulius Caesar over the sons of Pompey in 45. The town had fallen into decay as early as the time of Pliny. The site of the ancient town is usually supposed to be the modern village of Monda, southwest of Malaga; but Munda was more probably in the neighbourhood of Cordova, and there are ruins of ancient walls and towers between Martos, Alcandete, Espejo and Baena, which are conjectured to be the remains of Munda (Livy, xxiv. 42). (2) See MONDA.

Munerātor. See GLADIATORES, p. 732.

Munĭceps. The Latin term for an inhabitant of a free town; a burgher. See FOEDERATAE CIVITATES; MUNICIPIUM.

Municipium. Originally the Roman term for a town the inhabitants of which, called *municipes*, possessed only part of the rights of Roman citizenship—viz., the private rights of *commercium* and *conubium*, while they were excluded from the political rights, the *ius suffragii* and the *ius honorum*, the right to elect and to be elected to office. As Roman citizens, they did not serve (like the allies) in cohorts under a prefect, but in the legions under tribunes; they were, however, assigned to legions distinct from the others, since they were not inscribed on the lists of the Roman tribes, and therefore could not be levied in accordance with those lists. After the dissolution of the Latin League in B.C. 338, the allied towns were put into the position of municipia.

At first there were two classes of municipia, according as they retained an independent communal constitution or not. The second class, which had no senate, magistrates, or popular assembly of its own, and was governed directly by Rome, consisted of the *praefecturae* (q. v.). As the municipia gradually obtained the full rights of citizenship, their nature changed; all persons were now called *municipes*, who did not belong to the town of Rome by birth, but were full Roman citizens; and hence belonged to a Roman tribe, were registered at Rome, could elect and be elected to office, and served in the Roman legions.

The Lex Iulia of B.C. 90 made all the towns of Italy municipia with full civic rights, and every Italian country town was now called a Roman municipium. Gradually the towns in the provinces received municipal rights, till finally Caracalla made all towns of the Empire municipia. Originally one class of municipia had retained their own laws and their own constitution; this arrangement underwent a change when they were received into the Roman citizenship, inasmuch as the Roman law then became binding upon them, and a regularly organized administration on the Roman model was introduced. The citizens were divided into *curiae*, and at their Comitia Curiata passed all kinds of decrees, and chose officers; most of these rights, however, passed into the hands of the local senate towards the end of the first century. This senate usually consisted of 100 life-members, called *decuriones*, and in every fifth year the vacancies were filled up from those who had held office or were qualified by their property. The highest officials were the *duo viri*, who were judges and presided at the assemblies of the people, especially at elections, and in the senate; the two *quinquennales*, chosen for a year, once in five years, and corresponding to the Roman censors; and *quaestores* and *aediles*, officials with similar duties to the Roman officials of the same name. (See MAGISTRATUS.) Besides the decuriones, whose position became hereditary at the end of the Empire, there were, under the heathen emperors, a second privileged class, known as Augustales, chosen by decree of the local senate and next to that body in rank. They made up a collegium, which was originally dedicated to the worship of the Julian family, and in later times seems to have extended its functions to the worship of the other emperors. The decline of the municipal system, the prosperity of which had depended on the liberty and independence of the administration, set in at the end of the second century after Christ, when the emperors began to transfer to the municipia the burdens of the State, and the decuriones gradually became mere imperial officials, who were more especially responsible for the collection of the tribute imposed.

Munro, HUGH ANDREW JOHNSTONE. A brilliant classical scholar, born at Elgin, in Scotland, in 1819. He was educated at Shrewsbury and the University of Cambridge, and was elected to a fellowship in 1843. From 1869 to 1872 he filled the Latin chair at Cambridge. He died at Rome, March 30, 1885. Professor Munro's greatest work is his edition of Lucretius (2 vols. 1864; 4th ed. 1885), a remarkable monument of learning, taste, and critical skill, and accompanied by a prose translation that is itself a classic. He also edited Horace (1869), and wrote *Criticisms and Elucidations of Catullus* (1878), besides publishing many minor papers and a good deal of excellent Greek and Latin verse. See a memoir in the (English) *Journal of Philology* for 1885.

Munus. See HONORES; GLADIATORES, p. 732.

Munychia (Μουνυχία). A hill in the peninsula of Piraeus, which formed the citadel of the ports of Athens. It was strongly fortified, and is frequently mentioned in Athenian history. At its foot lay the harbour of Munychia, one of the three harbours in the peninsula of Piraeus, fortified by Themistocles. The names of these three harbours were Piraeus, Zea, and Munychia. The entrance to the harbour of Munychia was very narrow, and could be closed by a chain. The hill of Munychia contained several public buildings. Of these the most important were: (1) a temple of Artemis Munychia, in which persons accused of crimes against the State took refuge; (2) the Bendideum, the sanctuary of the Thracian Artemis Bendis, in whose honour the festival of the Bendidea was celebrated; (3) the theatre on the northwestern slope of the hill, in which the assemblies of the people were sometimes held (Pausan. i. 1, 4).

Munychia (τὰ μουνύχια). A festival celebrated in April, in honour of Artemis Munychia, as goddess of the full moon shining alone by night, and instituted to commemorate the defeat of the Persians at Salamis (Plut. *De Gloria Ath.* p. 349 F).

Munychion (Μουνυχιών). The tenth month of the Attic year, corresponding to our April. It had twenty-nine days. See CALENDARIUM.

Mural Crown. See CORONA.

Muratori, LODOVICO ANTONIO. A distinguished archaeologist, born at Vignola, October 21, 1672. Though he took orders at an early age, his time was principally given to historical and antiquarian research, being appointed, when twenty-three years of age, director of the Ambrosian Library at Milan. Here he published a collection of hitherto unedited Greek and Latin fragments, *Anecdota Graeca* and *Anecdota Latina*. In 1700 he was placed in charge of the great D'Este Library and of the ducal archives at Modena. In 1723 he began to publish his first collection, entitled *Rerum Italicarum Scriptores*, the twenty-eighth and last volume of which appeared in 1723. Most important to classical scholars is his collection of inscriptions, in six volumes, which appeared between 1739 and 1743, supplanting the collections of Gruter and earlier epigraphists. He died at Modena, January 28, 1750. See his life by G. F. Muratori (Omer, 1758).

Muratorian Fragment. A fragment of 85 lines first published by Muratori from a MS. of the eighth century, in Milan. It is a list of the writings in the New Testament, and is interesting from the evidence it gives of the corrupt condition of the Latin language at the time when it was written, such forms as *Spaniam* (*Hispaniam*), *desceplina* (*disciplina*), *seconda* (*secunda*) occurring in it. A fac-simile is printed by Tregelles (Oxford, 1867).

Murcia, Murtea, or **Murtia.** A surname of Venus at Rome, where she had a chapel in the circus, with a statue. This surname, which is said to be the same as Myrtea (from *myrtus*, a myrtle), was believed to indicate the fondness of the goddess for the myrtle-tree. See VENUS.

Murcus. A nickname given by the Roman soldiers to a malingerer, one who maimed himself by cutting off his thumbs, in order to be excused from military service (Amm. Marcel. xv. 12, 5; Suet. *Aug.* 24). Compare the English word "poltroon"; Ital. *poltrone* (*pollice trunco*).

Murcus, L. STATIUS. A legate of Iulius Caesar, B.C. 48, and praetor 45. He went to Syria after his year of office expired, and after Caesar's death became an active supporter of the Republican party. Cassius appointed him praefect of the fleet. After the ruin of the Republican party at Philippi, in 42, Murcus went over to Sex. Pompey in Sicily. Here he was assassinated by Pompey's order at the instigation of his freedman Menas, whom Murcus had treated scornfully (Caes. *B. C.* iii. 15; Dio Cass. xlviii. 19; Vell. Paterc. ii. 77).

Murēna, LICINIUS. The name Murena (not Muræna) is said to have been given in consequence of one of the family having a great liking for the lamprey (*murena*), and building tanks (*vivaria*) for them. (1) PUBLIUS, a man of some literary knowledge, lost his life in the wars of Marius and Sulla, B.C. 82, and (2) LUCIUS, brother of the preceding, served under Sulla in Greece in the Mithridatic War. After Sulla had made peace with Mithridates (84), Murena was left as propraetor in Asia. Anxious for distinction, Murena sought a quarrel with Mithridates; and after carrying on the war for two years, was at length compelled, by the strict orders of Sulla, to stop hostilities. Murena returned to Rome, and had a triumph in 81. He probably died soon after. (3) LUCIUS, son of the last, served under his father in the Second Mithridatic War and also under Lucullus in the Third Mithridatic War. In 65 he was praetor, in 64 propraetor of Gallia Cisalpina, and in 63 was elected consul with D. Iunius Silanus. Serv. Sulpicius, an unsuccessful candidate, instituted a prosecution against Murena for bribery (*ambitus*), and he was supported in the matter by M. Porcius Cato, Cn. Postumius, and Serv. Sulpicius the Younger. Murena was defended by Q. Hortensius, M. Tullius Cicero, who was then consul, and M. Licinius Crassus. The speech of Cicero, which is extant, was delivered in the latter part of November. The orator handled his subject skilfully by joking about the formulae and the practice of the lawyers, to which class Sulpicius belonged, and with the paradoxes of the Stoics, to which sect Cato had attached himself. Murena was acquitted, and was consul in the following year, 62. (4) A. TERENTIUS VARRO MURĒNA, probably the son of the preceding, was adopted by A. Terentius Varro, whose name he took, according to the custom in such cases. In the Civil Wars, he is said to have lost his property, and C. Proculeius, a Roman knight, is said to have given him a share of his own property. This Proculeius is called the brother of Varro; but, if we take the words of Horace literally (*Carm.* ii. 2), Proculeius had more than one brother. It is conjectured that this Proculeius was a son of the brother of No. 3, who had been adopted by one Proculeius. This would make Proculeius the cousin of Varro. It was common enough among the Romans to call cousins by the name of brothers (*frater patruelis* and *frater*). In 25 Murena subdued the Salassi in the Alps, and founded the town of Augusta (*Aosta*) in their territory. He was consul suffectus in 23. In 22 he was involved in the conspiracy of Fannius Caepio, and was condemned to death and executed, notwithstanding the intercession of Proculeius and Terentia, the sister of Murena and wife of Maecenas.

Murētus, MARCUS ANTONIUS (MARC ANTOINE MURET). A celebrated French classical scholar, born at Muret, April 12, 1526. In early life he studied jurisprudence and lectured on the civil law, but later took up literature. In 1576 he entered the priesthood, and then resided in Rome until his death, which occurred June 4, 1585. Muretus was a brilliant stylist of the Italian or "Ciceronian" school of modern Latinity, and wrote Latin with the ease and purity of an ancient Roman. Many of his orations are absolutely faultless, so that for many generations they were read in the schools of Europe side by side with Cicero and Livy. His Latin verse was also very graceful and fluent, though now little read. He published five volumes of *Variae Lectiones*, full of much acute criticism and still often referred to. His works have been edited by Ruhnken (1789), Frotscher (1834–41), and two volumes of selected writings by Frey (1871–73). See the life in French by Dejob (Paris, 1881); and the paper by Pattison in his *Essays* (Oxford, 1889).

Murex. A shell-fish with a sharp-pointed shell, used to ornament grottos (Ovid, *Met.* viii. 563), some of which have been found at Pompeii. A species of murex (*murex trunculus* or *murex brandaris*) was crushed to produce the famous Tyrian purple, so called (Pliny, *H. N.* ix. 36, 60). The name is also used of any sharp substance, as a stone (Verg. *Aen.* v. 205), a bridle-bit (Stat. *Achill.* i. 221), and especially of a "caltrop," called also *tribulus* (τρίβολος), a ball furnished with spikes, used to impede the advance of cavalry (Val. Max. iii. 7, 2).

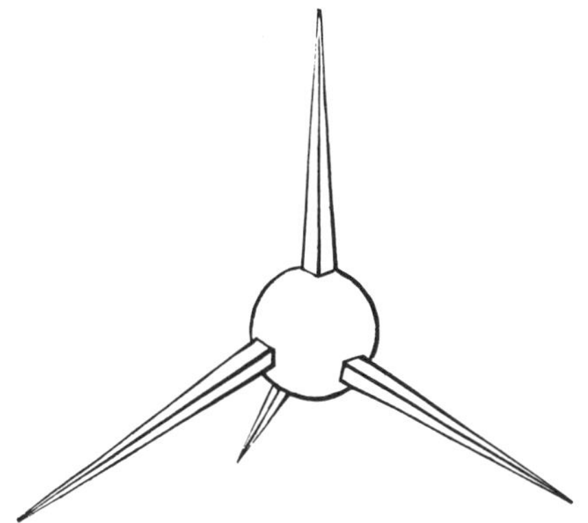

Murex or Tribulus. (Caylus, *Recueil*, iv. pl. 98.)

Murgantia. (1) See MORGANTIUM. (2) A town in Samnium.

Muropolium (μυροπώλιον). A perfumer's shop (Plaut. *Epist.* ii. 2, 17).

Murrhīna or **Murrea** (VASA). A name given by the Romans to vessels made of an oriental mineral called *murra*, which only occurred in small plates, opaque, of dull lustre and changing colours, and very brittle. The first vessels of this kind were brought to Rome by Pompey in B.C. 61 among the spoils of King Mithridates (Pliny, *H. N.* xxxvii. 18). In Rome, enormous prices were paid for them on account of their material, which is unknown to us, but is held by many to have been a rare kind of fluor spar, while others identify it with porcelain (Propert. iv. 5, 26) or agate. Nero paid for his cup with a handle, made of murra, the sum of a million sesterces, about $50,000 (Pliny, *H. N.* xxxvii. § 20). Murra, as well as every variety of precious stone, was imitated in glass. See Mayor's notes on Juvenal (vii. 133), and King, *Nat. Hist. of Precious Stones and Gems*, pp. 237–245 (London, 1864).

Mursa or **Mursia**. A town in Pannonia Inferior, on the Dravus. Here Magnentius was defeated by Constantius II., A.D. 351.

Murus or **Moenia** (τεῖχος). A wall surrounding an unroofed enclosure, as opposed to *paries* (τοῖχος), the wall of a building. The word *maceria* denotes a boundary wall, fence-wall. Cities were enclosed by walls at a very early period of Greek history, as is shown by the epithet used by Homer —"well-walled"—of Tiryns, Mycenae, etc., and the massive remains of those cities have also demonstrated the fact So vast, in truth, are some of these structures as to have induced a belief among the ancients that they were the work of Cyclopes.

Part of the Wall at Pompeii. (Overbeck.)

(See CYCLOPES.) The following principal species of city walls are to be distinguished: (*a*) those in which the masses of stone are of irregular shape and put together loosely, the interstices being filled by smaller stones, as in the wall at Tiryns (see TIRYNS); (*b*) those in which polygonal stones are carefully fitted together, and their faces cut so as to give the whole a comparatively smooth surface, as in the walls at Larissa and at Cenchreae (see the second illustration on page 452); and (*c*) those in which the blocks are laid in horizontal courses more or less regular with the vertical joints either perpendicular or oblique, and are more or less accurately fitted together, as in the walls beside the "Lion Gate" at Mycenae. See MYCENAE.

Brick was largely used in Egypt, Assyria, and Chaldaea, and also in Greece and Italy; but was often defended against the weather by an outer casing of stone, when the bricks were sun-dried instead of burned. (See FICTILÉ.) After the first Persian War the Athenians began to use marble for their finest buildings, as in the Propylaea (q. v.) and the Parthenon. A century later marble was also used for facing walls of brick. Less important structures were made of smaller stones, rough or square, flints, or bricks.

At Rome there were several kinds of masonry. (See CAEMENTUM.) (*a*) Blocks of stone were laid in alternate courses, lengthwise in one course and crosswise in the next. (*b*) The stones in each course were laid alternately along and across. (*c*) The stones were laid all lengthwise. (*d*) The stones entirely crosswise. (*e*) The courses were alternately higher and lower than each other. The earliest walls at Rome, largely of Etruscan origin, were built of huge quadrangular stones, hewn, and placed together without cement. Such were the Carcer Mamertinus (see CARCER), the Cloaca Maxima (see CLOACA), and the Servian Walls (see ETRURIA, p. 628). The Romans also used small rough stones, not laid in courses, but held together by mortar (*opus incertum*) and courses of flat tiles. Tiles were also introduced in the stone and brick walls. Brick covered with painted stucco was a very common material at Rome, and even columns were so constructed.

See Blümner, *Technologie und Terminologie* (Leipzig, 1875–87); Schliemann's works on Tiryns, Troy, and Mycenae; and Middleton, *Remains of Ancient Rome*, vol. i. (London, 1892).

Mus, DECIUS. See DECIUS.

Musa, ANTONIUS. A celebrated physician at Rome just before the beginning of the Christian era. He was brother to Euphorbus, the physician to King Iuba, and was himself the physician to the emperor Augustus. He had been originally a slave. When the emperor was seriously ill, and had been made worse by a hot regimen and treatment, B.C. 23, Antonius Musa succeeded in restoring him to health by means of cold bathing and cooling drinks, for which service he received from Augustus and the Senate a large sum of money and permission to wear a gold ring; and also had a statue erected in his honour by public subscription near that of Aesculapius. He seems to have been attached to this mode of treatment, to which Horace alludes (*Epist.* i. 15, 3), but failed when he applied it to the case of M. Marcellus, who died under his care a few months after the recovery of Augustus, B.C. 23. He wrote several pharmaceutical works, which are frequently quoted by Galen, but of which nothing except a few fragments remains, edited by Caldani (Bassano, 1800). There are, however, two short Latin medical works ascribed to Antonius Musa, but they are universally considered to be spurious. See Pliny, *H. N.* xxx. 117.

Musa or **Muza** (Μοῦσα, Μοῦζα, probably Moushid, north of Mokha). A celebrated port of Arabia Felix, on the western coast, near its southern extremity, or, in other words, on the eastern shore of the Red Sea, near the Strait of Bab-el-Mandeb.

Musae (Μοῦσαι). In Greek mythology the Muses were originally the nymphs of springs, whose waters gave inspiration, such as Hippocrené, Castalia, etc.; then goddesses of song in general; and afterwards the representatives of the various kinds of poetry, arts, and sciences. In Homer, who now speaks of one, and now of many Muses, but without specifying their number or their names, they are considered goddesses dwelling in Olympus, who at the meals of the gods sing sweetly to the lyre of Apollo, inspire the poet and prompt his song. Hesiod (*Theog.* 52–76) calls them the nine daughters of Zeus and Mnemosyné, born in Pieria, and mentions their names, to which we shall at the same time add the province and the attributes afterwards assigned to each. (1) CALLIŎPÉ (she of the fair voice), in Hesiod the noblest of all, the Muse of epic song; among her attributes are a wax tablet and a pencil. (2) CLIO (she that extols), the Muse of history; with a scroll. (3) EUTERPÉ (she that gladdens), the Muse of lyric song; with the double flute. (4) THALĪA (she that flourishes), the Muse of comedy and bucolic poetry; with the comic mask, the ivy wreath, and the shepherd's staff. (5) MELPOMĔNÉ (she that sings), the Muse of tragedy; with tragic mask, ivy wreath, and occasionally with attributes of individual heroes—e. g. the club, the sword. (6) TERPSICHŎRÉ (she that rejoices in the dance), the Muse of dancing; with the lyre. (7) ERĂTO (the lovely one), the Muse of erotic poetry; with a smaller lyre. (8) POLYMNIA or POLYHYMNIA (she that is rich in hymns), the Muse of serious sacred songs; usually represented as veiled and pensive. (9) URANIA (the heavenly), the Muse of astronomy; with the celestial globe. See the separate articles on the Muses.

Three older Muses were sometimes distinguished from these. Meleté (Meditation), Mnemé (Remembrance), Aoidé (Song), whose worship was said to have been introduced by the Aloadae, Otus and Ephialtes, near Mount Helicon. Thracian settlers in the Pierian district at the foot of Olympus and of Helicon in Boeotia are usually mentioned as the original founders of this worship. At both these places were their oldest sanctuaries. According to the general belief, the favourite haunts of the Muses were certain springs, near which temples and statues had been erected in their honour: Castalia, at the foot of Mount Parnassus, and Aganippé and Hippocrené, on Helicon, near the towns of Ascra and Thespiae. After the decline of Ascra, the inhabitants of Thespiae attended to the worship of the Muses and to the arrangements for the musical contests in their honour that took place once in five years. They were also adored in many other places in Greece. Thus the Athenians offered them sacrifices in the schools, while the Spartans did so before battle. As the inspiring nymphs of springs they were early connected with Dionysus; the god of poets, Apollo, is looked on as their leader (Μουσαγέτης), with whom they share the knowledge of past, present, and future. As beings that gladden men and gods with their song, Hesiod describes them as dwelling on Olympus along with the Charites and Himeros. They were represented in art as virgin goddesses with long garments of many folds, and frequently with a cloak besides; they were not distinguished by special attributes till comparatively later times. See *Die Musen in der antiken Kunst* (Berlin, 1887).

The Roman poets identified them with the Italian CAMĒNAE, prophetic nymphs of springs and goddesses of birth, who had a grove at Rome outside the Porta Capena. (See EGERIA.) The Greeks gave the title of Muses to their nine most distinguished poetesses: Praxilla, Moero, Anyté, Erinna, Telesilla, Corinna, Nossis, Myrtis, and Sappho.

Musaeus (Μουσαῖος). (1) A mythical singer, seer, and priest, who appears especially in Attic legends. He is said to have lived in pre-Homeric times, and to have been the son of Selené and Orpheus or Linus or Eumolpus. Numerous oracular sayings, hymns, and chants of dedication and purification were ascribed to him which had been collected, and also interpolated, by Onomacritus, in the time of the Pisistratidae. His tomb was shown at Athens on the Museum Hill, southwest of the Acropolis (Pausan. i. 22, x. 9). See Eberhard, *De Pampho et Musaeo* (1864). (2) A grammarian and Greek poet, who, in the beginning of the sixth century after Christ, wrote, in imitation of Nonnus (q. v.), a short epic of love, on the subject of Hero and Leander, which shows intense warmth of feeling, and has touches that are almost modern. It is edited by Passow (Leipzig, 1810), Schaefer (Leipzig, 1825), and Dilthey (Bonn, 1874). See Schwabe, *De Musaeo Nonni Imitatore* (Tübingen, 1876).

Musagĕtes (Μουσαγέτης, leader of the Muses). A title of Apollo, the god of poets, but sometimes given to Heracles. See HERACLES, p. 793.

Muscŭlus. The Latin name of a shelter used by soldiers while engaged in undermining the walls of a hostile fortification. It was made of wood with a sloping roof, and is fully described by Caesar, *B. C.* ii. 10. See TESTUDO; VINEA.

Musēa (Μούσεια). (1) A festival in honour of the Muses celebrated with contests on the slopes of Mount Helicon, near Aganippé, every fifth year (Pausan. ix. 29, 1, etc.). (2) A festival celebrated in schools (Theophrast. 25, 11). It appears to have been a sort of school-exhibition.

Museion (Μουσεῖον). See MUSEUM.

Musēum (Μουσεῖον). Originally a temple of the Muses, then a place dedicated to the works of the Muses. In this sense the most remarkable and most important museum of antiquity was that established at Alexandria by Ptolemy Philadelphus in the first half of the third century B.C., or perhaps by his father, Ptolemy Soter. This institution contributed very largely towards the preservation and extension of Greek literature and learning. It was a spacious and magnificent edifice, supplied with everything requisite for its purpose, such as an observatory, a library, a portico (περίπατος), a public lecture-room (ἐξέδρα), and a large hall or common-room where the professors dined together. There were also botanical and zoölogical gardens. It lay near the royal palace and communicated immediately with the temple of the Muses. Noted men of erudition were there supported at the cost of the State, to enable them to devote themselves to their learned studies without interruption. They were under the supervision of principals chosen from their own body, while the priest of the Muses was at their head. The Museum was practically, therefore, a great university. Its scholars formed four faculties—letters, mathematics, astronomy, and medicine; and there are said to have been at one time as many as 14,000 students in attendance. Under the Roman emperors, when Egypt had become a province of the Empire, it was still continued as an imperial institute and the centre of all learning, especially in mathematics and astronomy (Strabo, p. 794). Caracalla confiscated the pensions of the learned men attached to it, and the institution itself was completely destroyed during the Civil Wars under Aurelian in the third century.

The Alexandrian Museum was probably suggested by the Museum at Athens founded in accordance with the will of Theophrastus, the pupil of Aristotle (Diog. Laërt. v. 5). This may have taken its name from the earlier Μουσεῖον at Stagira, Aristotle's birthplace. The Athenian Museum was like that of Alexandria in its general purpose, though on a much smaller scale. See EDUCATION, p. 572; and for the Alexandrian Library attached to the Museum, the article BIBLIOTHECA. On the influence of the two, see ALEXANDRIAN SCHOOL; CANON ALEXANDRINUS. The following works may also be consulted: Parthey, *Das alexandrinische Museum* (Berlin, 1838); Ritschl, *Opuscula*, i. pp. 1–70, 123–172, 197–237; Susemihl, *Gesch. der alexandrin. Literatur*, i. pp. 327 foll.

MODERN MUSEUMS.—The modern museums that

are of the greatest interest to the classical student because of the value of their archaeological collections, are the following: (1) the various collections of the *Vatican* at Rome, comprising the Museo Chiaramonte, the Museo Pio-Clementino (in which are the Apollo Belvidere, the Laocoön group, the so-called statue of Antinoüs, the most beautiful statue in the world, and the tomb of Scipio Barbatus), the Braccio Nuovo, opened in 1820; the Museo Gregoriano, with a superb collection of Etruscan antiquities, and the Egyptian Museum; (2) the *Palazzo dei Conservatori* on the Capitol, containing the famous Capitoline Wolf, with Romulus and Remus, and many Etruscan terra-cottas; (3) the *Capitoline Museum*, founded by Innocent X., and containing the so-called Dying Gladiator, the Satyr of Praxiteles (a copy), a fine collection of busts of celebrated characters of antiquity, a collection of the busts of the Roman emperors, the mosaic called the Capitoline Doves, and the Capitoline Venus; (4) the *Kircherian Museum*, founded by the Jesuit, Kircher, about 1680, containing the Cista Ficoroniana (q. v.) and the famous caricature of the crucifixion (see GRAFFITI); (5) the *Museum of the Lateran* (Museum Gregorianum Lateranense), established in 1843 by Pope Gregory XVI., and containing a famous statue of Sophocles; (6) the *Museo Nazionale* at Naples, formerly the *Museo Reale Borbonico*, famous for its immense collection of objects found at Herculaneum and Pompeii, for its collection of inscriptions, and for the statues of the Farnese Hercules, the Farnese Bull, Venus Callipygé, etc.; (7) the collections of the *Galleria degli Uffizi* at Florence, containing the Venus de' Medici, the Wrestlers (see p. 758), and numerous inscriptions, bronzes, and gems; (8) the *Louvre* in Paris, with a splendid collection of inscriptions, the Venus de Milo, the Borghese Athlete, the Victory of Samothrace, the Melpomené, the Polymnia, and remarkable terra-cottas, fragments of sculptures from the Parthenon, Olympia, and Assos, with many painted vases; (9) the *British Museum* in London, opened in 1759, and containing the Elgin Marbles, the Phigalion Marbles, the Xanthian (Lycian) Marbles, the Halicarnassian Marbles, besides immense treasures of art in the shape of statuary, with inscriptions, etc., making it perhaps the finest collection in the world; (10) the *Glyptothek* at Munich, with a remarkable collection of some 1300 ancient vases; (11) the *Royal Museum* at Berlin, with objects found at Troy and Pergamus; (12) the *Imperial Museum* at Vienna, with an especially fine collection of bronzes; (13) the *Museum of the Hermitage* at St. Petersburg, rich in vases and jewels; (14) the *Museum at Athens*, with marbles from the Theseum, objects from Mycenae, and funerary remains. The most noted museum in America is the *Metropolitan Museum* in New York, containing a fine collection of objects from Cyprus, collected by Gen. di Cesnola. See CYPRUS.

Musĭca (μουσική, sc. τέχνη, "art of the Muses"). A term which included among the Greeks everything that belonged to a higher intellectual and artistic education. Plato (*Rep*. p. 136), while discussing education, speaks of "gymnastic for the body and music for the soul," and ranks literature under the head of music. Music in the narrower sense was regarded by the Greeks both as an agreeable amusement and as one of the most effective means of cultivating the feelings and the character. The great importance they attached to music is also shown by their idea that it was of divine origin; Hermes or Apollo is said to have invented the lyre, Athené the simple flute, Pan the shepherd's pipe. Besides these gods and the Muses, Dionysus also was connected with music. Numerous myths, as, for instance, those concerning Amphion and Orpheus, tell of its mighty power, and testify to the Greeks having cultivated music at a very early epoch. It was always intimately allied to poetry. Originally epic poems were also sung to the accompaniment of the cithara, and the old masters of poetry, such as Orpheus and Musaeus, are at the same time masters of music, just as in historical times the lyric and dramatic poets were at the same time the composers of their works. It was not until the Alexandrian Age that the poet ceased to be also a musician. Owing to its connection with poetry, music developed in the same proportion and flourished at the same period as lyric and dramatic poetry. Of the Greek races, the Dorians and Aeolians had a special genius and capacity for music, and among both are found the first traces of its development as an art.

The actual foundation of the classical music of the Greeks is ascribed to Terpander (q. v.), of the Aeolian island of Lesbos, who, in Dorian Sparta (about B.C. 675), first gave a truly artistic form to song accompanied by the cithara, and especially to the citharodic νόμος. In the Peloponnesian school of the Terpandridae, who followed his teaching and formed a closely united guild, κιθαρῳδική received its further artistic development. What Terpander had done for κιθαρῳδική was done not long afterwards by Clonas of Thebes or Tegea for αὐλῳδική, or song accompanied by the flute. The artistic flute-playing which had been elaborated by the Phrygian Olympus in Asia, was introduced by Clonas into the Peloponnesus, which long remained the principal seat of all musical art. Of the two kinds of independent instrumental music, which throughout presupposes the development of vocal music and always adapts itself to this as its model, the earlier is the music on the flute (αὐλητική), which was especially brought into favourable notice by Sacadas of Argos (about B.C. 580), while the music on stringed instruments (κιθαριστική) is later. Music was much promoted by the contests at the public festivals, above all by those at the Pythian Games. Its highest point of development was attained in the time of the Persian Wars, which seems to have seen the completion of the ancient system as it had been elaborated by the tradition of the schools. The lyric poets of this time, as Pindar and Simonides, the dramatists, as Phrynichus and Aeschylus, were held by the critics to be unsurpassable models. What was added in subsequent times can hardly be called a new development of the art. Athens in her golden age was the central city where professional musicians met one another—Athens the home of Greek dramatic poetry. At this time vocal combined with instrumental music largely prevailed over instrumental music alone. The latter was chiefly limited to solo performances.

Ancient vocal music is distinguished in one important point from ours: throughout classical times part-singing was unknown. There was at most a difference of octaves, and that only when men and boys sang in the same choir. Theoretically, however, the Greeks were acquainted with some of the effects upon which harmonic systems are based, though in practice the nature of their harmonics was extremely simple, with no sure trace of chords or groups of more than two notes. Again, in classical times, the music was subordinate to the words, and was therefore necessarily much simpler than it is now. It is only in this way that we can explain the fact that an ancient audience could follow the musical representation of the often intricate language of the odes, even when the odes were sung by the whole choir. Critics regarded it as a decline of art when, at the end of the Peloponnesian War, the music began to be the important element instead of the poetry. This change took place at first in single branches of the art, as in the solos (μονῳδίαι) in tragedy and in the dithyrambic choruses. Thenceforward ancient music, like modern music, raised itself more and more to a free and independent position beside that of poetry.

The first place among the various kinds of music was assigned to the indigenous citharodic art, which was connected with the first development of the musical art; and, indeed, stringed instruments were always more esteemed than wind instruments, in part on account of the greater technical difficulties which had to be overcome, and which led to musicians giving particular attention to them. Moreover, playing on the flute

was limited to certain occasions, as its sound seemed to the ancients to arouse enthusiasm and passion (Arist. *Polit.* viii. 3). There is evidence that, on the one hand, the ancient theory of singing and of instrumentation, in spite of the primitive nature of the instruments, was brought to a high degree of perfection; and that, on the other hand, the public must have possessed a severely critical judgment in matters of music. The characteristic feature of ancient music is the great clearness of its form, resulting, above all, from the extreme precision of the rhythmic treatment.

This was not the only point in which ancient music differed from modern music; it also differed from it in the number of its modes. The modes were distinguished from one another by the place of the semitones in the octave. While modern music has only two modes, the major and the minor, the Greek had seven. These seven modes, the names of which are taken from the three great Greek races and the neighbouring Asiatic nations (Dorian, Aeolian or Hypodorian, Ionian or Hypophrygian, Phrygian, Lydian, Mixolydian, and Hypolydian), were all employed at some time in the classical period, though they did not all of them come into use at the same date. It is significant of the distinction between ancient and modern music that of these modes the Dorian, which was the oldest and the lowest in pitch, and is described as dignified, severe, and grave, was most extensively used in all kinds of music.

As the basis of every melodic series of sounds the ancients had the *tetrachord*, a scale of four notes, to which, according to tradition, the earliest music was limited. The *heptachord* was certainly in use before Terpander, who is said to have given the lyre seven strings instead of four (Strabo, p. 618); but Pausanias (iii. 12, § 10) states with greater accuracy that he added four strings to the previously existing seven. The heptachord consisted of two tetrachords, as the central note was at once the highest of the first and the lowest of the second tetrachord.

Next came the *octachord* or octave, and at last, after various additions, the following scale of notes was formed:

From the lowest *b* onward, this scale was divided into tetrachords in such a way that the fourth note was always also regarded as the first of the following tetrachord; the intervals between the sounds of the tetrachord were, in ascending order, semitone, tone, tone. This sequence was called the "diatonic genus." Besides this there was also the "chromatic," the tetrachords of which were as follows: *b c ♭d e f ♭g a* (the intervals in this case were semitone, semitone, tone and a half). Thirdly, there was the "enharmonic," the tetrachord of which had for its intervals ¼ tone, ¼ tone, 2 tones, and accordingly cannot be expressed in modern notation.

The musical notation (σημασία) of the Greeks consisted of two distinct systems of signs—one for the voice, the other for the instrument. The vocal signs are taken from the common or Ionic alphabet. The notes of the middle part of the scale are denoted by the letters in their usual order; those of the lower part by an alphabet of inverted or otherwise altered letters; the upper notes are distinguished by accents—an accent signifying that the note is an octave higher than that of the unaccented letter. The following is a brief summary of Westphal's discoveries:

(1) The instrumental notation was derived from the first fourteen letters of a Peloponnesian alphabet, possessing *digamma*, Ϝ, the old form of *iota*, ϟ, and two forms of *lambda*, < and ⊢. In a few cases the forms of the letters have been modified: thus *alpha* (originally ⋈) appears as ɥ, *beta* as ⊏, *delta* as ᒣ, *theta* as C, *my* (originally M) as P, *iota* as Һ. By treating the two forms of *lambda* as distinct characters the number is raised to fifteen.

(2) These characters are applied to denote a scale of two octaves, as follows:

H Һ E ⊢ Γ P F C K ᒣ < ⊏ N Z ɥ

The arrangement of the letters is worth notice. The inventor began by taking *alpha* for the highest note of his scale. Then he took the other characters in pairs, ⊏ Γ, ᒣ E, F Z, H C, Һ K, < ⊢, P N, and made each pair stand for the extreme notes of an octave. This scale may be regarded as the framework of the system of notation.

(3) A character may be varied by being reversed—i. e. written from right to left (ἀπεστραμμένον), or by being turned half round backward (ἀνεστραμμένον, ὕπτιον). When reversed, it denotes a note half a tone higher; when half reversed, it denotes a note a quarter of a tone higher. The

combination of the two varieties evidently gives an Enharmonic πυκνόν, or group obtained by dividing a semitone—e. g. if we take the four "stable" notes of the central octave, Γ C K ⊏, we complete the scale in the Enharmonic genus by inserting the varieties of Γ and K, thus obtaining Γ L ⅂ C K ⋎ ꓘ ⊏.

In some cases this method of varying the letters is impracticable—e. g. H reversed does not change; N half-reversed becomes Z, and vice versa. Other modifications are accordingly employed, and we have the groups M ⲩ ⋎, Z ⋋ ⋌, N / \, ⅂ ⊲ Δ, and H Ħ Ħ.

(4) In the Diatonic genus the second lowest note of a tetrachord is not represented, as we should expect, by the reversed letter, but by the half-reversed one, the same character as the second lowest Enharmonic note.

(5) In the Chromatic genus the characters used are the same as in the Enharmonic, but the reversed letter is distinguished by an accent. Thus the Chromatic tetrachord *e f f ♯a* is written Γ L ⅂ ′C or (in the upper octave) ⊏ ⊔ ⊐ ′M.

(6) The system was enlarged by the addition of two tones, each with the corresponding πυκνόν, at the lower end of the scale, and an octave, except the highest note, at the upper end. The two groups were denoted by the characters ⊾ ⊱ T and Є ω Э, which are evidently invented on the analogy of the letters already in use. The new upper notes were denoted by accented letters, K′ to Z′, repeating the scale from K to Z an octave higher.

Fragment found at Delphi in 1893 with part of a Hymn to Apollo in musical notation.

We now have only seven pieces of ancient music whose authenticity is practically undisputed—the beginning of the First Pythian Ode of Pindar (see Boeckh's Pindar, *De Metris Pindari*, iii. 12); two hymns to Calliopé and Apollo, ascribed to one Dionysius (q. v. 4); a papyrus fragment of the music of a chorus of Euripides (*Orestes*, 338–344); an inscription found at Tralles in 1883, giving a musical setting to four short gnomes; a hymn of Mesomedes (q. v.) of the second century after Christ, published, with fac-similes, in Bellermann's *Hymnen des Dionysius und Mesomedes* (Berlin, 1840); and the fragments of a hymn found inscribed at Delphi in 1893. This last appears to be composed in a mood identical with the modern minor. It was composed after the repulse of the Gauls from Delphi in B.C. 279 and was first published in the *Bulletin de Correspondance Hellénique*, xvii. 569–610. The fragments of this hymn are fourteen in number; and from them various reconstructions of the piece reduced to the modern system of notation have been published, one of which was performed before the king of Greece at Athens not long after the discovery of the inscription. See the work by Monro cited at the end of the article.

Besides the pieces cited above there are also a few passages in the nature of short instrumental exercises; and a hymn to Demeter, first published by the Venetian composer Marcello, but regarded by Gevaert and other scholars as of very doubtful authenticity.

With regard to the musical instruments it may be mentioned that only stringed instruments (see especially CITHARA and LYRA) and the flute, which closely resembled our clarionet, were employed in music proper (see TIBIA); and that the other instruments, such as trumpets (see SALPINX), Pan's pipes (see SYRINX), cymbals (*cymbala*), and kettle-drums (see TYMPANUM), were not included within its province.

In proportion to the amount of attention paid to music by the Greeks, it early became the subject of learned research and literary treatment. The philosopher Pythagoras occupied himself with musical acoustics; he succeeded in representing numerically the relations of the octave, the fifth, and the fourth. For representing the symphonic relations the Pythagorean School invented the monochord or canon, a string stretched over a sounding-board and with a movable bridge, by means of which the string could be divided into different lengths; it was on this account known as the school of the Canonici as opposed to the Harmonici, who opposed this innovation and continued to be satisfied with a system of scales ("harmonics") sung by the sole guidance of the ear. Among the Canonici were philosophers such as Philolaüs, Archytas, Democritus, Plato, and Aristotle. Lasus of Hermioné, the master of Pindar, is mentioned as the first author of a theoretical work on music. The "harmonic" Aristoxenus (q. v.) Tarentum, a pupil of Aristotle, was held by the ancients to be the greatest authority on music; from his numerous works was drawn the greatest part of subsequent musical literature. Of other writers on music we may mention the well-known mathematician Euclid, and the great astronomer Claudius Ptolemaeus, who perfected musical acoustics.

Among the Romans a native development of music was completely wanting. They had, indeed, an ancient indigenous musical instrument, the short and slender Latin flute with four holes; but their national art of flute-playing was, at an early period, thrown into the background by the Etruscan, which was practised as a profession by foreigners, freedmen, and people of the lowest classes of the Roman population. Among the nine old guilds, said to have been instituted by King Numa, there was one of flute-players (*tibicines*), who assisted at public sacrifices. With the Greek drama, Greek dramatic music was also introduced; it was, however, limited to flute-playing. Stringed instruments were not originally known at Rome, and were not frequently employed till after the Second Punic War. Indeed, as Greek usages and manners in general gained ground with the beginning of the second century, so also did Greek music. Greek dances and musical entertainments became common at the meals of aristocratic families, and the younger members of respectable households received instruction in music as in dancing. Though it was afterwards one of the subjects of higher education, it was never considered a real and effective means of training. Entertainments like our concerts became frequent towards the end of the Republic, and formed part of the musical contests instituted by Nero, a great lover of music, in A.D. 60, on the model of the Greek contests. Domitian had an "Odeum" built on the Campus Martius for the musical entertainments of the Agon Capitolinus, instituted by him in A.D. 86, and celebrated at intervals of four years to the end of the classical period. Passages bearing on music in Roman literature have no independent value, as they are entirely drawn from Greek sources, as in the writings of Martianus Capella and Boetius. See the general histories of music by Naumann, 2 vols. (London, 1882–86); Ambros (2d ed. Leipzig, 1880–81); and Fétis (5 vols. unfinished, Paris, 1868–76). Also Westphal, *Die Musik des griechischen Alterthums* (Leipzig, 1883); Fortlage, *Das musikalische System der Griechen* (Leipzig, 1847); Chappell, *History of Music* (1874); Paul, *Boetius und die griechische Harmonik* (Leipzig, 1872); Engel, *The Music of the Most Ancient Nations* (London, 1864); Gevaert, *Histoire et Théorie de la Musique dans l'Antiquité* (Ghent, 1881); and Monro, *Modes of Ancient Greek Music* (Oxford, 1894).

Musīvum Opus. Mosaic. The term mosaic is usually derived from a post-classical word *musivum* (*μουσεῖον*), occurring in Spartianus (*Vit. Pescenn.* 6, *pictum de musivo*), and St. Augustine (*De Civ. Dei*, xvi. 8, *hominum genera musivo picta*). It is the art of arranging small cubes or *tesserae* of marble, coloured stone, terra-cotta, glass, or some other artificial substance, so as to produce an ornamental pattern or picture, and to provide a durable form of decoration for walls and pavements. The only mosaic hitherto found in Greece Proper is that discovered in 1829, in the floor of the east portico of the temple of Zeus, at Olympia, possibly little later than the first half of the fourth century B.C. It is formed of rough round pebbles of various colours from the bed of the Alpheus, and it represents Tritons of graceful design surrounded by a tasteful border of palmettes and meandering lines.

The earliest mosaics mentioned in literature are those made for the ship of Hiero II., about the middle of the third century, with scenes from the *Iliad*, which took 300 skilled workmen a whole year to execute (Athenaeus, 206 D). To the same age belongs the only artist in mosaic whose name is recorded in literature, Sosus of Pergamun, famous as the inventor of a kind of mosaic called the *ἀσάρωτον* (the "unswept" floor), in which the floor of a room is inlaid with representations of fruits, fishes, and fragments of food that have fallen from the table (Pliny, *H. N.* xxxvi. § 184; cf. Statius, *Silvae* i. 3, 36). Mosaics of this type have been found not only at Pompeii, but also at Aquileia and in Algiers (see p. 825). According to Pliny, the original design by Sosus included a remarkable representation of a dove drinking and casting the shadow of its head on the water beneath, while several other doves were to be seen sunning themselves on the rim of the bowl. The best-known copy of this is that called "The Capitoline Doves," found at Hadrian's Villa near Tivoli. It is entirely composed of cubes of marble, without any admixture of coloured glass.

The art of reproducing paintings in mosaic probably originated in Egypt, and thence found its way to Greece and Italy. It is doubtless connected in its origin with the brick-work and tiling of Egypt and Mesopotamia. In fact, just as wall-paintings were first suggested by tapestries, so mosaic work is a natural development from carpets. All these arts, indeed, were closely related, and the subjects of paintings are also used by the makers of mosaic. One of the finest pieces of mosaic at Pompeii, signed by Dioscorides of Samos, reproduces a wall-painting found in the same city. The largest mosaic picture of Roman workmanship is that executed for the temple

The Capitoline Doves. (Rome, Capitoline Museum.)

of Fortune at Praenestê, restored by Sulla (Pliny, *H. N.* xxxvi. 189). This was discovered in 1640, and is generally supposed to represent a popular *fête* on the occasion of an inundation of the Nile. It probably belongs to the time of Hadrian.

Among the mosaics of Pompeii the most famous is that identified as the "Battle of Issus," possibly a copy of the painting of the same subject by a female artist, Helena, "daughter of Timon the Egyptian," which was placed in the Temple of Peace in the time of Vespasian (Photius, *Bibl.* p. 482). It represents the critical moment when Alexander is charging, bare-headed, in the thick of the fray, and has just transfixed with his lance one of the leaders of the Persians; while Darius, with his lofty tiara and red chlamys, is extending his right hand in an attitude of alarm and despair. In the mosaic itself the lower border represents a river, apparently the Nile, with a crocodile, hippopotamus, ichneumon, ibis, etc., thus confirming the conjecture as to the Egyptian origin of the design. See illustrations, pp. 296 and 890.

Mosaics bearing the artist's name are seldom found. The two finest of this class are those from Pompeii inscribed with the name of Dioscorides of Samos. One of these represents four masked figures playing on various instruments. The work is composed of very small pieces of glass, of the most beautiful colours and in various shades. (See Dyer's *Pompeii*, p. 276). Another of similar construction portrays a rehearsal for a satyric drama. The ground is black, the drapery mainly white, but the robe of the flute-player is bordered with purple, the lips are a bright red, and the flutes and ornaments coloured like gold. The finest mosaic of the early part of the second century A.D. is the highly pictorial centaur-mosaic now at Berlin, found at the Villa of Hadrian (Baumeister's *Denkmäler*, fig. 941). The most celebrated works of a later date include that in the Thermae of Caracalla, with numerous gladiatorial figures of colossal size and ungraceful drawing (ib. fig. 174); and that of the Roman villa at Nennig, near Trèves. The dimensions of the latter are fifty feet by thirty-three, and the design includes several groups of figures enclosed in a square or hexagonal framework of tessellated marble (ib. figs. 1001–2343). Among the mosaics in the British Museum are an Amphitritê and Tritons, with Dionysus, Meleager, and Atalanta, all from Halicarnassus, and of Roman times, since figures of Dido and Aeneas were found in the same villa (Newton's *Travels and Discoveries*, ii. 76). Among mosaics still preserved in England may be mentioned those at Woodchester, Bignor, and Brading.

Mosaic pavements are known by different names descriptive of certain varieties of structure. (1) A *pavimentum sectile* is composed of thin plates of coloured marble of various sizes, cut (*secta*) into slices of regular form and arranged in an ornamental geometrical pattern including triangles, hexagons, etc. (Vit. vii. 1, 3, 4; Suet. *Caes.* 46 fin.). (2) The epithet *tessellatum* describes a pavement of the same general kind, but made up of regular square dies (*tesserae, tessellae, tesserulae*), forming rectangular designs. (3) *Vermiculatum* is applied to a design formed of small pieces of marble in various colours, arranged so as to imitate the object represented with a high degree of pictorial effect. The dies are of different shapes, so as to allow of their following the wavy contours of the outline of the object. The name owes its origin to the fact that the general effect of such an arrangement resembles the contortions of a cluster of worms (*vermes*). (Cf. Pliny, *H. N.* xxxv. 2; and Lucilius, quoted in Cicero's *Orator*, 149.) (4) The term *lithostrotum* (Varro, *R. R.* iii. 2, § 4; 1, § 10; Pliny, *H. N.* xxxvi. 189) was probably applied to a pavement made of small pieces of stone or marble of natural colours, and distinguished from those of coloured glass or some other artificial composition. Mosaics of glass were used to decorate ceilings.

Threshold in Mosaic. (Pompeii.)

The gilt *tesserae* used in Christian mosaics for the background of the pictures were formed by applying to a cube of earthenware two thin plates of glass with a film of gold-leaf between them, and vitrifying the whole in a furnace. It was this discovery that led to the extensive application of mosaic for the decoration of the walls, and more particularly the apses, of Christian churches. After the ninth century the art of working in mosaic ceased for a while in Rome and in Italy in general, to be revived at a later date in the church of S. Cyprian at Murano (1109) and the basilica of St. Mark's at Venice (in and after the eleventh century), and afterwards at Rome itself. In Sicily, the mosaics of the Cappella Palatina in the Royal Palace at Palermo were finished in 1143, while those of the cathedral at Monreale were begun in 1172.

The reader is referred to Marquardt, *Das Privatleben der Römer*, 625–632; Blümner's *Technologie*, iii. 323–343; Von Rohden on *Mosaik* in Baumeister's *Denkmäler;* Gerspach, *La Mosaïque* (1883); and Morgan, *Romano-British Mosaic Pavements* (1886).

Musonius Rufus, Gaius. A Stoic philosopher, son of a Roman knight. He was banished by Nero in A.D. 66 to the island of Gyaros for his alleged share in the conspiracy of Piso. When Galba became emperor, the philosopher returned to Rome, and continued there under Vespasian, whose favour he had secured (Tac. *Ann.* xv. 71; Dio Cass. lxvi. 13).

Mustaceum. A wedding-cake which was cut up and divided among the guests as the bride and groom left the feast. It was made of flour mixed with new wine (*mustum*), cheese, and anise-seed, and was laid upon bay-leaves while baking (Juv. vi. 202; Cato, *R. R.* 121).

Mustax (μύσταξ). A moustache; also called ὑπήνη. The Greeks took pride in well-developed moustaches, as indicative of manly vigour (Theocr. xiv. 4; Pollux, ii. 80, x. 120). At Sparta, however, the people were required by the ephors to shave their moustaches (Plut. *Cleom.* 9). See BARBA.

Muster. See DELECTUS.

Mustum. New wine. See VINUM.

Muta. The same as Mania. See LARES.

Mutatiōnes. Posting-stations at which relays of horses were kept for the public service (see CURSUS PUBLICUS) and for the use of travellers. From twenty to forty horses were usually in readiness at these stations. See MANSIO.

Mutātor. The same as *desultor* (q. v.).

Muthul. Now Melleg; a river of Numidia which formed the boundary between the kingdoms of Iugurtha and Adherbae (Sall. *Iug.* 48).

Mutĭlus, C. PAPIUS. A Samnite general in thé Marsic War (B.C. 90–89).

Mutĭna. Now Modena; an important town in Gallia Cispadana, originally a town of the Boii, and afterwards a Roman colony. It is celebrated in the history of the Civil War after Caesar's death. Decimus Brutus was besieged here by M. Antonius from December, B.C. 44 to April, 43; and under its walls the battles were fought in which the consuls Hirtius and Pansa perished. Hence this war is called the BELLUM MUTINENSÉ.

Mutŭlus. See COLUMNA.

Mutunus Tutunus. A deity of the primitive Italians presiding over fruitful marriage, and resembling the later Priapus (q. v.) (Arnob. iv. 7). See PHALLUS.

Mutuum. The Latin word for a loan.

Mycălé (Μυκάλη). A mountain in the south of Ionia in Asia Minor, north of the mouth of the Maeander, and opposite the island of Samos. On the north side of the promontory near Priené was a great temple of Poseidon, where the Pan-Ionic festival was held (Pausan. v. 7, 3). Here a great victory was gained by the Greeks over the Persian fleet on the same day as the battle of Plataea, B.C. 479.

Mycalessus (Μυκαλησσός). An ancient city in Boeotia, on the road from Aulis to Thebes. In B.C. 413 it was sacked by some Thracian mercenaries in the pay of Athens. Here was a famous temple of Demeter, who was in consequence called Mycalessia (*Il.* ii. 498; Pausan. ix. 19).

Mycēnae and **Mycēné** (Μυκῆναι, Μυκήνη). A city at the head of the plain of Argolis, reputed in Greek tradition to have been the residence of Agamemnon. Its most flourishing period probably fell within the latter half of the second thousand years before Christ. At that time the seat of wealthy and powerful chieftains, it subsequently fell under the power of Argos, and was during the historical period a place of no importance. The wall of the citadel and several "bee-hive" tombs have always been visible. Excavations, carried on by Schliemann in 1876, and later by the Greek Archæological Society, have enormously increased our knowledge of Mycenae and of the early civilization which it represents.

The first illustration shows in the middle distance the acropolis of Mycenae, with a portion of its encompassing wall. This wall, for the most part, resembles in its construction that of Tiryns (q. v.), though the blocks are not so gigantic. In places, however, we find an outer facing of approximately regular ashlar masonry (so, e. g., at the Lion Gate); in other places, of carefully jointed polygonal work. The principal entrance, the so-called Lion Gate, is shown in the third illustration. It consists of two upright posts surmounted by an enormous flat lintel. The relieving triangle above the lintel is filled by a relief representing

Acropolis at Mycenae and Mount St. Elias. (From a photograph.)

two lions (or lionesses) facing one another, and having between them an object of doubtful interpretation. There is, in addition, a smaller gate on the north side of the citadel.

Within the Lion Gate is a circular enclosure, nearly ninety feet in diameter. This was formed by two concentric rows of upright slabs, the space between the two rows being covered by horizontal slabs. Within the enclosure are six rectangular graves of various sizes, sunk in the rock at various depths below the double ring of slabs. The graves when opened contained the remains of from one to five corpses each (buried unburned), or nineteen in all, together with gold masks and ornaments, vessels of gold and of bronze, bronze weapons, pottery of the so-called Mycenae type, etc. Above the graves (in precisely what positions it is now difficult to make out) stood a number of grave-stones, partly unsculptured, partly sculptured with rude reliefs.

At the summit of the acropolis remains of a palace, similar in plan to that of Tiryns, but less well preserved, were discovered in 1886 by the Greek Archæological Society. The great *μέγαρον* or hall, with its circular hearth surrounded by four pillars and its double vestibule, is easily recognizable. Above the palace, and partly upon its ruins, are remains of what is thought to have been an early Doric temple.

Outside the acropolis was the city, consisting apparently of several detached settlements. In this region eight large subterranean buildings, doubtless tombs, of bee-hive form, are known to exist. The most imposing of these is the so-called "Treasury of Atreus" or "Tomb of Agamemnon," of which a vertical section is shown on p. 452. It is approached by a passage-way or *δρόμος*, walled at the sides, but open above. Then comes the doorway, once closed by heavy doors. The principal inner chamber is about fifty feet in diameter at the bottom and the same in height. It is built of great stones, laid in horizontal courses, each course pushed a little farther inward than the one below; compare the construction of the relieving triangle over the Lion Gate. There is, besides, a smaller side-chamber, cut in the rock. The other seven bee-hive tombs are built in a similar fashion, but with smaller stones. In addition to these, upwards of sixty smaller tomb-chambers, excavated in the solid rock and approached likewise by *δρόμοι*, have been discovered and opened.

Principal Approach to Citadel of Tiryns.

The prehistoric civilization to which the Mycenaean remains bear witness must have been, in comparison with what meets us at the dawn of the historical period in Greece, a brilliant one. That it was powerfully influenced by the earlier civilizations of the East, and especially by that of Egypt, there is abundant evidence to show. But the whole subject of its relations to what went before and what came after is in too uncertain a state to be treated in a sketch like the present.

Lion Gate, Mycenae. (From a photograph.)

See Steffen, *Karten von Mykenai* (Berlin, 1884); Schliemann, *Mycenae* (London, 1878); Πρακτικὰ τῆς Ἀρχαιολογικῆς Ἑταιρίας (1886); Ἐφημερὶς Ἀρχαιολογική (1887, 1888, 1891); Furtwängler und Loeschke, *Mykenische Thongefässe* (Berlin, 1879), and *Mykenische Vasen* (Berlin, 1886); Schuchhardt, *Schliemann's Ausgrabungen* (2d ed. Leipzig, 1891; Engl. trans. *Schliemann's Excavations*, London, 1891); Gardner, *New Chapters in Greek History* (London, 1892); Tsountas, Μυκῆναι (Athens, 1893).

Mycēnē (Μυκήνη). A daughter of Inachus and wife of Arestor. From her the city of Mycenae was said to have derived its name (Pausan. ii. 16, 3).

Mycerīnus (Μυκερῖνος). A son of Cheops, king of Egypt, succeeded his uncle Chephren on the throne, and reigned with justice. He began to build a pyramid, but died before it was finished. The Egyptian form of the name is Men-Kau-Ra. A pyramid erected by him is in the plain of Gizeh; and the coffin containing the body of the king is in the British Museum. See Herod. ii. 129–34; Diod. i. 64.

Mycŏnus (Μύκονος). A small island in the Aegaean Sea, one of the Cyclades, east of Delos, is celebrated in mythology as one of the places where the giants were defeated by Heracles. The island was popularly supposed to contain an unusual number of bald persons (Pliny, *H. N.* xi. 130).

Mygdon (Μύγδων). The son of Acmon, who fought against the Amazons, and from whom some of the Phrygians are said to have been called Mygdonides (Pausan. x. 27).

Mygdonia (Μυγδονία). (1) A district in the east of Macedonia, bordering on the Thermaic Gulf and the Chalcidic peninsula. (2) A district in the east of Mysia and the west of Bithynia, named after the Thracian people, Mygdones, who formed a settlement here, but were afterwards subdued by the Bithyni. (3) The northeast district of Mesopotamia, between Mount Masius and the Chaboras, which divided it from Osroënê.

Myia (Μυῖα). (1) A daughter of Pythagoras and Theano, and wife of the great athlete Milo of Crotona. (2) See CORINNA.

Myinda (μυῖνδα). The game of blindman's-buff, in which one person was blindfolded and was obliged to keep his eyes shut (μύειν). It was played in two ways: the blindfolded person (καταμύων), after crying φυλάττου ("look out"), tries to catch one of the players, who must then be blindfolded in his place; or else the καταμύων stands still and tries to guess the identity of those who touch him. In still another form of the game the players struck the blindfolded person with whips of papyrus. See Pollux, ix. 113; and Becq de Fouquières, *Les Jeux des Anciens*, p. 84.

Mylae (Μυλαί). A town on the eastern part of the north coast of Sicily, founded by Zanclê (Messana), and situated on a promontory running out into the sea. It was off Mylae that C. Duilius won his victory over the Carthaginians in B.C. 260, and that Agrippa defeated the fleet of Sex. Pompeius (B.C. 36).

Mylāsa (τὰ Μύλασα) or **Mylassa**. A flourishing inland city of Caria, in a fertile plain.

Myndus (Μύνδος). A Dorian colony on the coast of Caria, situated at the western extremity of the same peninsula on which Halicarnassus stood.

Myonnēsus (Μυόννησος). A promontory of Ionia, with a town and a little island of the same name, forming the northern headland of the Gulf of Ephesus. Here the Romans defeated Antiochus the Great in B.C. 190 (Livy, xxxviii. 27).

Myos Hormos (ὁ Μυὸς ὅρμος, i. e. "Musselport"), an important port-town of Upper Egypt, built by Ptolemy II. Philadelphus, on the Red Sea, six or seven days' journey from Coptos. It was afterwards called VENĔRIS PORTUS (Ἀφροδίτης ὅρμος).

Myra (τὰ Μύρα) and **Myron** (Μύρων). One of the chief cities of Lycia, built on a rock two miles from the sea. Remarkable ruins still exist here.

Rock-cut Tombs at Myra.

Myriandrus (Μυρίανδρος). A Phœnician colony in Syria, on the east side of the Gulf of Issus, a little south of Alexandria.

Myrii (μυρίοι). The name of the popular assembly of the Arcadians, established after the battle of Leuctra. See Grote, *Hist. of Greece*, x. p. 318.

Myrīna (Μυρίνα). (1) An ancient and important city of the Aeolians on the western coast of Mysia. At Gryneum, which belonged to it, was a famous oracle of Apollo The city was also called SMYRNA, and in Roman times SEBASTOPŎLIS. (2) A town in Lemnos.

Myrlēa (Μύρλεια). A city of Bithynia, not far from Prusa, founded by the Colophonians, and almost rebuilt by Prusias I., who called it APAMEA, after his wife.

Myrmĭdon (Μυρμιδών). A son of Zeus and Eurymedusa, daughter of Clitos, to whom Zeus managed to obtain access in the form of an ant (μύρμηξ). He was the legendary ancestor of the Thessalian Myrmidones; and was by Pisidicé the father of Antiphus and Actor (Apollod. i. 7, 3; Apoll. Rhod. i. 56).

Myrmidŏnes (Μυρμιδόνες). A race in Southern Thessaly, said to have originally dwelt in the island of Aegina and to have emigrated from it with Peleus. They fought before Troy under their chieftain Achilles. For a legend about their origin, see AEACUS.

Myrmillo. See GLADIATORES.

Myron (Μύρων). One of the most celebrated Greek artists of Eleutherae, in Attica, an older contemporary of Phidias and Polyclitus, and, like them, a pupil of Ageladas. His works, chiefly in bronze, were numerous and very varied in subject — gods, heroes, and especially athletes and representations of animals, which were admired by the ancients for their life-like truth to nature. Most famous among these were his statue of the Argive runner Ladas; of Marsyas, of which a marble copy is now in the Lateran at Rome; his "Discobolus," or quoit-thrower (see DISCUS), which we are enabled to appreciate in several copies in marble, the best being that in the Palazzo Massimi and one in bronze in the Palazzo Lancelotti in Rome; and his "Cow on the Market-place at Athens," which received the very highest praise among the ancients, was celebrated in thirty-six extant epigrams in the Greek anthology, all quoted in Overbeck's *Schriftquellen*, §§ 550–588, and may be regarded as his masterpiece. He was also the first to represent what is really a genre portrait in his "Drunken Old Woman" (Pliny, *N. H.* xxxvi. 32); but this is now attributed to another artist, one Socrates (Overbeck, § 2092). See Collignon, *Histoire de la Sculpture Grecque* (Paris, 1892).

Myrrha (Μύρρα), also called **Smyrna** (Σμύρνα). Mother of Adonis by her own father Cinyras, for whom she entertained an unnatural passion, in consequence of which she was changed into a myrtle-tree. See ADONIS; CINYRAS.

Myrrhĭnūs (Μυρρινοῦς). A deme on the eastern coast of Attica, belonging to the tribe Pandionis (Pausan. i. 31, 4).

Myrsĭlus (Μύρσιλος). (1) See CANDAULES. (2) A Lesbian historical writer of uncertain date; one of the sources used by Dionysius of Halicarnassus in his account of the Pelasgians (i. 23).

Myrsĭnus. See MYRTUNTIUM.

Myrtĕa. See MURCIA.

Myrtĭlus (Μυρτίλος). Son of Hermes, by Cleobulé or Myrto. He was the charioteer of Oenomaüs, whose defeat by Pelops in the race was due to his treachery. When he demanded the reward that had been settled, the half of the realm of Oenomaüs, Pelops threw him into the sea near Geraestus, in Euboea, and that part of the Aegean was thence called the Myrtoan Sea. He was placed among the stars as the constellation Auriga. See OENOMAÜS; PELOPS.

Myrtis (Μύρτις). A lyric poetess of Anthedon, in Boeotia, who is said to have been the teacher of Pindar, to which there is an allusion in an extant fragment of Corinna (*Anthol. Pal.* ix. 26). See PINDARUS.

Myrtōum Maré (τὸ Μυρτῷον πέλαγος). The part of the Aegaean Sea south of Euboea, Attica, and Argolis, which derived its name from the small island Myrtus, though others suppose it to come from Myrtilus, whom Pelops threw into the sea. (See PELOPS.) The name of Mygdonia was first introduced after the Macedonian conquest.

Myrtuntium (Μυρτούντιον), called **Myrsĭnus** in Homer. A town of the Epeans in Elis, on the road from Elis to Dymé.

Myrtus. See MYRTOUM MARÉ.

Mys (Μῦς). A famous toreutic artist who engraved the "Battle of the Centaurs" on the inside of the shield of the Athené Promachos of Phidias. The work was executed after a design by Parrhasius (Pausan. i. 28, 2), a generation after Phidias. It was Parrhasius also who designed the "Capture of Troy" for a cup embossed by Mys (Athen. p. 782 b; see also Pliny, *H. N.* xxxiii. 154).

Myscĕlus (Μύσκελος). A native of Achaia, who founded Croton in Italy, B.C. 710, by order of the Delphic oracle, which had commanded him to build a city, where he should find rain with fine weather. For a long time he thought it impossible to fulfil the command of the oracle, till at length he found in Italy a beautiful woman in tears; whereupon he perceived that the oracle was accomplished, and straightway founded Croton on the spot (Dionys. ii. 59).

Mysia (τὰ Μύσια). A festival held in honour of Demeter Mysia at Pellené in Arcadia (Pausan. vii. 27, 9). It lasted for seven days.

Mysia (Μυσία). A district of Asia Minor, called also the Asiatic Mysia (Μυσία ἡ Ἀσιανή), in contradistinction to Moesia on the banks of the Danube. Originally, it meant the territory of the Mysi; but in the usual division of Asia Minor, as settled under Augustus, it occupied the whole of the northwestern corner of the peninsula between the Hellespont on the northwest, the Propontis on the north, the river Rhyndacus and Mount Olympus on the east, which divided it from Bithynia and Phrygia, Mount Temnus and an imaginary line drawn from Temnus to the southern side of the Elaïtic Gulf on the south, where it bordered upon Lydia, and the Aegean Sea on the west. It was subdivided into five parts: (1) MYSIA MINOR (ἡ μικρά), along the northern coast; (2) MYSIA MAIOR (ἡ μεγάλη), the southeastern inland region, with a small portion of the coast between the Troad and the Aeolic settlements about the Elaïtic Gulf; (3) TROAS (ἡ Τρωάς), the northwestern angle, between the Aegean and Hellespont and the southern coast along the foot of Ida; (4) AEŎLIS or AEOLIA (ἡ Αἰολίς or Αἰολία), the southern part of the western coast around the Elaïtic Gulf, where the chief cities of the Aeolian confederacy were planted; but applied in a wider sense to the western coast in general; and (5) TEUTHRANIA (ἡ Τευθρανία), the southwestern angle, between Temnus and the borders of Lydia, where, in very early times, Teuthras was said to have established a Mysian kingdom, which was early subdued by the kings of Lydia; this part was also called Pergamené, from the celebrated city of Pergamus, which stood in it. This account applies to the time of the early Roman Empire; the extent of Mysia and its subdivisions varied greatly at other times.

In the Heroic Age we find the great Teucrian monarchy of Troy in the northwest of the country and the Phrygians along the Hellespont; as to the Mysians, who appear as allies of the Trojans, it is not clear whether they were Europeans or Asiatics. The Mysia of the legends respecting Telephus is the Teuthranian kingdom in the south, only with a wider extent than the later Teuthrania. Under the Persian Empire, the northwestern portion, which was still occupied in part by Phrygians, but chiefly by Aeolian settlements, was called Phrygia Minor, and by the Greeks Hellespontus. Mysia was the region south of the chain of Ida; and both formed, with Lydia, the second satrapy. In the division of the Empire of Alexander the Great, Mysia fell, with Thrace, to the share of Lysimachus, B.C. 311, after whose defeat and death, in 281, it became a part of the Graeco-Syrian kingdom, with the exception of the southwestern portion, where Philetaerus founded the kingdom of Pergamus (280), to which kingdom the whole of Mysia was assigned, together with Lydia, Phrygia, Caria, Lycia, Pisidia, and Pamphylia, after the defeat of Antiochus the Great by the Romans in 190. With the rest of the kingdom of Pergamus, Mysia fell to the Romans in 133 by the bequest of Attalus III., and formed part of the province of Asia. Under the later Empire, Mysia formed a separate proconsular province under the name of Hellespontus.

The country was, for the most part, mountainous, its chief chains being those of Ida, Olympus, and Temnus, which are terminal branches of the northwestern part of the Taurus chain, and the union of which forms the elevated land of southeastern Mysia. Their prolongations into the sea form several important bays and capes—namely, among the former, the great Gulf of Adramyttium (Adramytti), which cuts off Lesbos from the continent, and the Sinus Elaïticus (Gulf of Chandeli); and, among the latter, Sigeum (Cape Yenicheri) and Lectum (Gulf of Baba), at the northwestern and southwestern extremities of the Troad, and Cane (Cape Coloni) and Hydria (Fokia), the northern and southern headlands of the Elaïtic Gulf. Its rivers are numerous; some of them considerable, in proportion to the size of the country; and some of first-rate importance in history and poetry; the chief of them, beginning on the east, were Rhyndacus and Macestus, Tarsius, Aesepus, Granicus, Rhodius, Simoïs and Scamander, Satnoïs, Evenus, and Caïcus. The peoples of the country, besides the general appellations mentioned above, were known by the following distinctive names: the Olympieni or Olympeni (Ὀλυμπιηνοί, Ὀλυμπηνοί), in the district of Olympené at the foot of Mount Olympus; next to them, on the south and west, and occupying the greater part of Mysia proper, the Abretteni, who had a native divinity called by the Greeks Ζεὺς Ἀβρεττηνός; the Trimenthuritae, the Pentademitae, and the Mysomacedones, all in the region of Mount Temnus.

Mystae (μύσται). The Greek term for those who had been initiated into the mysteries of the Lesser Eleusinia. Opposed to ἐπόπται, who were those admitted to the third or higher grade. See ELEUSINIA.

Mystagōgus (μυσταγωγός). One who performs the initiation into the Mysteries. See ELEUSINIA.

Mysteria (τὰ μυστήρια). The Mysteries, also called ὄργια. The term τελεταί is likewise employed, and the Latin equivalent is INITIA (Cic. *De Leg.* ii. 14, 36). The Mysteries were ceremonies in the ancient religions practised in seclusion and known only to bodies of initiates. They were held at certain fixed seasons and were largely symbolical in their character, though their origin is not very satisfactorily understood. It is held by many that they were intended to strengthen men's hopes in a future life in which the good who fail of a reward here should there receive it, while punishment should be visited upon the wicked. Hence a part of the ceremonial had to do with the resurrection of the gods and heroes; and we find some remarkable passages in the Greek poets that support this view. Thus Pindar (*Frag.* 137): "Blessed is he who has seen them before he goes below the earth;" and the inscription (*Ephem. Arch.* 1883): "To the initiated, death is not an evil; it is a gain." Cf. also Soph. *Frag.* 719; and Aristoph. *Ran.* 455.

The Mysteries consisted of purifications, sacrifices, processions, songs, dances, dramatic spectacles, and similar ceremonies. The formulae or liturgies (δεικνύμενα, λεγόμενα, δρώμενα) were kept profoundly secret, to be revealed only to those who had been fully initiated. The *mystagogi*, or priests of the Mysteries, had undoubtedly at their command an abundance of mechanical devices to produce effects most startling and convincing to the credulous worshippers. All the arts, in fact, were taxed to the utmost to astonish, dazzle, and appal. Marvels of light, sound, and colour were displayed. Mysterious harmonies stole upon the ears of the attendant throngs; sighs and whispers were audible amid the intervals of awful silence; lights gleamed in strangely beautiful colours; and dazzling figures appeared and disappeared. In the earlier times the fame of the Mysteries was very great. Herodotus speaks of some 30,000 persons attending them (viii. 65); but in later times they degenerated, the secrecy was removed, and they became orgies in the modern sense of the word, at which the most shameless indecencies were practised, until under the Romans they had to be suppressed as public nuisances.

The most important Mysteries were those of Eleusis and the Thesmophoria, both symbolizing the rape of Persephoné and the search for her by her mother Demeter (see ELEUSINIA; THESMOPHORIA); those of Cybelé and Aphrodité, referring to the mystery of procreation (see APHRODISIA; RHEA); those of Orpheus, who was regarded as the founder of all Mysteries (see ORPHICA); of Bacchus (see DIONYSIA); of Zeus in Crete; of the foreign gods Mithras (see MITHRAS), Sabazius (see SABAZIUS), the Cabeiri (see CABEIRIA), and Isis (see ISIS). The most famous Mysteries of Roman origin were those of the Bona Dea (see BONA DEA) and of the Arval Brethren (see FRATRES ARVALES).

The principal works in modern times relating to the Mysteries are those of Creuzer, *Symbolik und Mythologie der alten Völker* (1810–12), which regards their nature as wholly symbolical; the profoundly learned treatise of Lobeck, *Aglaophamus* (1829), anti-symbolistic and lacking in the religious sense; Preller, *Demeter und Persephoné* (1837); Lenormant, *Voie Sacrée Eleusinienne* (1864); Strabo,

Studien über den Bilderkreis von Eleusis (1872); Förster, *Der Raub und die Rückkehr der Persephone* (1874); Haggenmacher, *Die eleusinischen Mysterien* (1880); Stengel, *Griechische Kultusalterthümer* (1890), Rubensohn, *Die Mysterienheiligthümer in Eleusis und Samothrake* (1892); and Gardner, *New Chapters in Greek History*, pp. 381–402 (1892).

Mystīlé (*μυστίλη*). A sort of spoon used by the Greeks. See CENA, p. 311.

Mytilēné. See MITYLENÉ.

Mystrum (*μύστρον*, "a spoonful"). A Greek liquid measure of two sizes—the small = $\frac{1}{50}$ of an English pint, the large being variable, but usually about $\frac{1}{4}$ more than the small one.

Mythologia (*μυθολογία*, Plato, *De Rep.* 394 B). Mythology; a term sometimes used of the collected myths of a race or nation, and sometimes of the scientific study of such myths. A myth (*μῦθος*) is a story, more or less poetic, related of gods or heroes. It is not a pure product of the imagination, but is best regarded as in a way related to fact, whether the fact be a preceding reality or some often-recurring phase of nature. The Greeks, a people most prolific in the development and elaboration of myths, themselves took the view that there is necessarily some meaning in a myth, either an historical occurrence disguised and exaggerated or an operation of nature veiled in an allegory. Thus Anaxagoras regarded the true meaning of most of the myths to be psychological; Empedocles, philosophical. Euhemerus (q. v.) gave a rationalistic turn to mythology, stripping away the element of the supernatural altogether; though Gruppe takes the ground that the work of Euhemerus is best regarded as a work of pure fiction, with no ulterior motive behind it. The Stoics at Rome tried to explain all myths as allegorical descriptions of physical facts, but this failed to account for just those myths which most required explanation—the hideously immoral and bestial myths that troubled the minds of men like Plato.

It is safe to say that most myths are the result of man's observations of nature, whose various forms are personified as powerful beings by the imaginations of primitive men. These forms were regarded as in part hostile and in part friendly to man. A more advanced stage of mental development elaborated these crude conceptions, and began to regard these beings as acting in accordance with fixed moral laws and endowed with human forms. Thus we have Anthropomorphism. Poets and story-tellers brought the gods into connection with one another by inventing genealogies for them and building up a whole political system, presided over by Zeus, the father alike of gods and men. Around the earlier and ruder fancies a wonderful maze was now woven, adorned by all the arts of poetry and prose and embedded in the nation's literature. Among the Romans the cruder and simpler notion prevailed much longer—in fact, throughout the whole period of purely national development. To them the gods were still only the natural forces—beings strangely impersonal and making little demand upon the imagination or the affection. They were to be propitiated, but not loved. Their worship was a State affair, and the early Roman performed his religious duties in much the same spirit as he paid his taxes. This is shown in the very nature of the deities at Rome—gods not only of the sky and the earth, the sea and the world below, but gods of thievery and lust, of typhoid fever and sewers. Later, when the Romans came into contact with the Greeks and began the systematic study of their literature, they adopted the Greek conception of the gods and the genealogies worked out by Hesiod and others. They transplanted the Greek myths and told them of such of their own gods and goddesses as bore the closest likeness to those of the Greeks, identifying Zeus with Iupiter, Heré with Iuno, Ares with Mars, Athené with Minerva, and so on. For some of their deities, as, for instance, Ianus, they could find no Hellenic prototype.

In modern times the Graeco-Roman mythology has been differently viewed. Creuzer made it wholly symbolical and allegorical; Lobeck overthrew this doctrine in its extreme form and paved the way for a thoroughly scientific study of the subject. The brothers Grimm taught that mythology was not, as Creuzer implied, the work of the superior few, of a learned caste, but was the way in which the multitude expressed their religious feeling. This view is supported by the fact that in peoples widely apart the same myth is found, varying in its form, but identical in its main outlines. Hence arose the study of Comparative Mythology, the creation of two scholars—Adalbert Kuhn (1812–81) in Germany, and Max Müller in England. The object of this study is to trace all myths back to the pre-historic period when the Indo-European peoples were united; and, having done so, to determine the original forms and the original meanings. More recent mythologists, such as Mannhardt (1831–89), view the folk-tales as the earliest stratum accessible to the comparative mythologist, rejecting the Sanskrit Vedas as a later and literary compilation. Gruppe, one of the very latest investigators, rejects the comparative method altogether, and thinks that myths have been simply borrowed by one nation from another, and not handed down from a common ancestry at all.

For a discussion of the theory of myths, the standard works are: Creuzer, *Symbolik und Mythologie* (1810–12); Lobeck, *Aglaophamus* (1829); Max Müller, *Comparative Mythology* (1856); Schrader, *Prehistoric Antiquities of the Aryan Peoples* (Engl. trans. 1890); Gruppe, *Die griechischen Culte und Mythen* (1887); Mannhardt, *Wald- und Feldkulte* (1876); Tylor, *Primitive Culture* (3d Amer. ed. 1888); A. Lang, *Custom and Myth* (1884); id. *Myth, Ritual, and Religion* (1887).

Good descriptive works of the Greek and Roman systems of mythology are: Preller, *Griechische Mythologie* (4th ed. 1887); id. *Römische Mythologie* (3d ed. 1883); Gayley, *Classic Myths* (popular, 1893); Guerber, *Myths of Greece and Rome* (popular, 1893); Seelmann, *The Mythology of Greece and Rome* (elementary; Engl. trans. 1892). There is a dictionary of mythology giving the latest views, in German, by Roscher, *Ausführliches Lexicon der griechischen und römischen Mythologie* (Leipzig, still in course of publication). See also RELIGIO.

Myus (Μυοῦς). The least city of the Ionian confederacy. It stood in Caria, on the bank of the Maeander.

N

N, as a symbol.

In Greek.—

N = νεώτερος.

NX = νομίσματος χαλκοῦ.

N̊ = Νουμήνιος or Νουμήριος.

NΦ = νομοφύλαξ.

As a numeral = 13 (old system) or 50. ͵ν = 50,000.

In Latin.—

N = natalis, natus, nauta, nefastus, nepos, niger, nonae, noster, novus.

N·A·S = numini Augusti sacrum.

N·D = numen deorum.

N·D·A·N·M = nullum dolorem accepit nisi morte.

N·I = natione Itala.

N·M = numerus militum, Noricum mediterraneum.

N·M·Q·E·D = numini maiestatique eius dicatissimus.

N·M·V = nobilis memòriae vir.

N·P(V) = Neptunus, nobilissimus puer (vir).

N·S·S·I·M = numen sanctum Solis invicti Mithrae.

Naarmalcha (Νααρμάλχας). "The King's Canal"; a great canal connecting the Euphrates and the Tigris, near the northern boundary of Babylonia (Herod. i. 193; Pliny, *H. N.* vi. 120).

Nabalia or **Navalia**. Now the Yssel; a river flowing into the Flevum (Zuyder Zee). See Tac. *Hist.* v. 26.

Nabarzānes (Ναβαρζάνης). A Persian who conspired with Bessus (q. v.) against Darius, the last king of Persia.

Nabataei, Nabăthae (Ναβαταῖοι, Ναβάται). An Arabian race said to have descended from Ishmael. They originally dwelt in the northwestern part of Arabia, east of the Moabites; but later occupied the Sinaitic peninsula. Their capital in Roman times was Petra (q. v.). At first they were a roving pastoral people; but, as their position gave them the command of the trade between Arabia and the west, they prosecuted that trade with great energy, establishing regular caravans between Leucé Comé, a port of the Red Sea, and the port of Rhinocolura (El-Arish) on the Mediterranean, upon the frontiers of Palestine and Egypt. Sustained by this traffic, a powerful monarchy grew up, which resisted all the attacks of the Greek kings of Syria, and which, sometimes at least, extended its power as far north as Syria. Thus, in the reign of Caligula, even after the Nabathaeans had nominally submitted to Rome, we find even Damascus in possession of an ethnarch of "Aretas the king," i. e. of the Nabathaean Arabs: the usual names of these kings were Aretas and Obodas. Under Augustus the Nabathaeans are found, as nominal subjects of the Roman Empire, assisting Aelius Gallus in his expedition into Arabia Felix, through which, and through the journey of Athenodorus to Petra, Strabo derived important information. Under Trajan the Nabathaeans were conquered by A. Cornelius Palma, and Arabia Petraea became a Roman province, A.D. 105–107. In the fourth century it was considered a part of Palestine, and formed the diocese of a metropolitan, whose see was at Petra. The Mohammedan conquest finally overthrew the power of the Nabathaeans. See C. Doughty, *Documents Épigraphiques Recueillis dans le Nord de l'Arabie* (1884).

Nabis (Νάβις). A person who succeeded in making himself tyrant of Lacedaemon on the death of Machanidas, B.C. 207. He carried his tyranny to the furthest possible extent. All persons possessed of property were subjected to incessant exactions, and the most cruel tortures if they did not succeed in satisfying his rapacity. One of his engines of torture resembled "the Maiden" of more recent times. It was a figure resembling his wife Apega, so constructed as to clasp the victim and pierce him to death with the nails with which the arms and bosom of the figure were studded (Polyb. xiii. 7). The money which he got by these means and by the plunder of the temples enabled him to raise a large body of mercenaries, whom he selected from among the most abandoned and reckless villains. With these forces he was able to extend his sway over a considerable part of Peloponnesus; but his further progress was checked by Flamininus, who after a short campaign compelled him to sue for peace (B.C. 195). The tyrant, however, was allowed to retain the sovereignty of Sparta, and soon after the departure of Flamininus from Greece he resumed hostilities. He was opposed by Philopoemen, the general of the Achaean league; and though Nabis met at first with some success, he was eventually defeated by Philopoemen, and was soon afterwards assassinated by some Aetolians who had been sent to his assistance, B.C. 192 (Livy, xxxv. 12–35; Pausan. viii. 50).

Nabla (νάβλα). A kind of lyre. See Lyra.

Nabonassar (Ναβονάσαρος). A king of Babylon, who lived about the middle of the eighth century before the Christian era, and who gave name to what is called the Nabonassarian Era. The origin of this era is thus represented by Syncellus from the accounts of Polyhistor and Berosus, the earliest writers extant in Chaldaean history and antiquities: "Nabonassar, having collected the acts of his predecessors, destroyed them, in order that the computation of the reigns of the Chaldaean kings might be made from himself." It began, therefore, with the reign of Nabonassar (February 26, B.C. 747). The form of year employed in it is the movable year of 365 days, consisting of twelve equal months of thirty days, and five supernumerary days, which was the year in common use among the Chaldaeans, Egyptians, Armenians, Persians, and the principal Oriental nations from the earliest times. This year ran through all the seasons in the course of 1461 years. The freedom of the Nabonassarean Year from intercalation rendered it peculiarly convenient for astronomical calculation. Hence it was adopted by the early Greek astronomers Timochares and Hipparchus, and by those of the Alexandrian school, Ptolemy, etc. In consequence of this, the whole historical catalogue of reigns has been commonly, though improperly, called Ptolemy's Canon, because he probably continued the original table of Chaldaean and Persian kings, and added thereto the Egyptian and Roman down to his own time.

Nabopolassar (Ναβοπωλάσαρος). A king of Babylon, who united with Astyages against Assyria, which country they conquered, and, having divided it between them, founded two kingdoms, that of the Medes under Astyages, and that of the Chaldaeans under Nabopolassar, B.C. 626. Necho, king of Egypt, jealous of the power of the latter, declared war against and defeated him. Nabopolassar died after a reign of twenty-one years.

Nacolīa (Νακόλεια, Νακώλεια, and Νακολία). A town of Phrygia Epictetus on the river Thymbrius, where the Roman emperor Valens defeated his rival Procopius in A.D. 366 (Ammian. Marc. xxvi. 6).

Naenia. See NENIA.

Naevius, GNAEUS. A Roman epic and dramatic poet. He was probably born in Campania, about B.C. 270; served in the Roman army during the First Punic War; and, settling after this at Rome, brought out his first play in 235, soon after the first appearance of Livius Andronicus. Owing to the recklessness with which he attacked the Roman nobles, especially the Metelli, he was thrown into prison, and though liberated by the tribunes of the people (Gell. iii. 3), was afterwards banished from Rome. He died in exile at Utica about the year 199. See the epitaph in Gellius (i. 24).

His poetical account of the First Punic War (*Bellum Punicum*), written when an old man in the Saturnian verse, made him the creator of the Roman national epic. (See EPOS.) This work originally formed one continuous whole, but in a later age was divided into seven books by the scholar Octavius Lampadio (Suet. *Gram.* 2). The fragments preserved give the impression of its having been little more than a chronicle in verse. Even in its plan, it bears a close resemblance to the prose chronicles of the Roman annalists; for here, as there, the real subject of the poem was preceded by an account of the early history of Rome, dating from the flight of Aeneas from Troy. Naevius also made an important departure in the province of dramatic poetry by creating a national drama. Besides imitations of Greek tragedies, of which seven alone are known by name and by extant fragments, it was he who first attempted to adapt the materials of Roman history to the dramatic form handed down by the Greeks. Thus, in the *Romulus* or *Lupus*, he treated of the youth of Romulus and Remus; and, in the play *Clastidium*, of a contemporary historical event. From the number of titles of his comedies still preserved (thirty-three), and from the verdict of antiquity, we may infer that his forte lay in that species of composition; and he appears to have been no mere translator of his Greek originals, but to have handled them with considerable freedom. It was in his comedies especially that he introduced his attacks on men and events of the day. The fragments of Naevius will be found in Ribbeck's *Poeseos Scenicae Fragmenta.* See De Moor, *Cn. Névius* (Tournai, 1877); and Mommsen's *Hist. of Rome*, ii. pp. 519, 538, 540 (American ed.).

Naevius Macro. See MACRO.

Nägelsbach, KARL FRIEDRICH. A German classical scholar, born near Nuremberg in 1806. He became Professor in the University of Erlangen in 1842; and died in 1859. He wrote *Die homerische Theologie* (1861); *Die nachhomerische Theologie* (1857); and edited the *Agamemnon* of Aeschylus (ed. by List, 1863); but is best known by his elaborate treatise, *Lateinische Stilistik* (1846; last ed. by I. Müller, 1890).

Naharvăli. A tribe of the Lygii in Germany, probably dwelling on the banks of the Vistula (Tac. *Germ.* 43).

Nahrmalcha. See NAARMALCHA.

Naïădes (Νηΐδες). Inferior deities who presided over rivers, brooks, springs, and fountains. Their name is derived from ναίω, "to flow," as indicative of the gentle motion of water. The Naiades are generally represented as young and beautiful virgins, leaning upon an urn, from which flows a stream of water. They were held in great veneration among the ancients, and sacrifices of goats and lambs were offered them, with libations of wine, honey, and oil. Sometimes they received only offerings of milk, fruit, and flowers. See NYMPHAE.

Nails. See CLAVUS.

Naïsus, Naïssus, or **Naesus** (Ναΐσος, Ναϊσσός, Ναΐσσος). The modern Nisch; a town of Upper Moesia, situated on an eastern tributary of the Margus, and celebrated as the birthplace of Constantine the Great, who enlarged and beautified it.

Namatiānus, RUTILIUS CLAUDIUS. A Roman poet, by birth a Gaul and a pagan, who was *praefectus urbi* under the emperor Honorius. After the sack of Rome by Alaric, he returned to his native country, then overrun by the Visigoths, and described his journey home in a poem in two books, *De Reditu Suo*, of which a portion of the first and the end of the second have perished. The poem is pure and correct in language and metrical form, and is interesting on account of its pathetic description of the misfortunes of the time. He detests the Jews (i. 383), and speaks of Christianity as *deterior Circaeis secta venenis* (i. 525). His philosophy is Stoic. See F. Müller, *De Namatiano Stoico* (1882). There is an edition by L. Müller with an introduction (Leipzig, 1870); and a (German) translation with notes by Reumont (Berlin, 1872).

Names. See NOMEN.

Namnētae (Ναμνηταί) or **Namnētes.** A people on the west coast of Gallia Lugdunensis, on the north bank of the Liger. Their chief town was Condivincum, afterwards Namnetes (Nantes) (Caes. *B. G.* iii. 9).

Nana. The mother of Attis. See ATTIS; RHEA.

Nani (νάννοι, νᾶνοι, σκωπαῖοι, στίλπωνες). Pygmies or dwarfs, beings of diminutive stature, kept for amusement and as rarities among the number of State slaves (Suet. *Tib.* 61), both males and females (*nanae*) (Lamprid. *Alex. Sev.* 34). They were neither always distorted in figure, nor always of mental imbecility, like the *moriones*, for they were taught music and other accomplishments (Propert. iv. 8, 41). Deformity, however, added to their value; and this was often caused by artificial means, children being kept in a casting or frame to stunt their growth (Longin. *De Sublim.* 44, 5). See Mayor on Juv. viii. 32; Marquardt, *Privatleben*, 152; and PUMILIO.

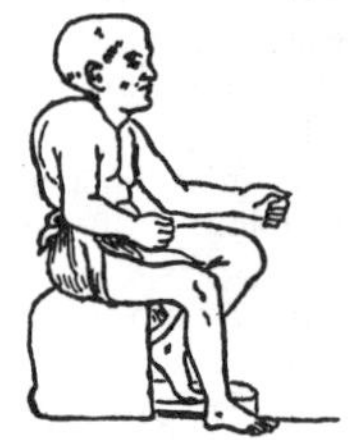

Nanus. (Rich.)

Nantuātae or **Nantuātes.** A people in the southeast of Gallia Belgica, at the eastern extremity of the Lacus Lemannus (Lake of Geneva). See Caes. *B. G.* iv. 10.

Naos (*νάος*). The Greek term for the inner portion of a temple. See TEMPLUM.

Napaeae (*Ναπαῖαι*). Nymphs haunting forests, groves, and glens. See NYMPHAE.

Napăta (*τὰ Νάπατα*). The capitol of an Aethiopian kingdom, at the great bend of the Nile between the fourth and fifth cataracts (Strabo, p. 820).

Napkins. See MAPPA.

Napōca or **Napūca.** Now Clausenberg; a Roman colony in Dacia (*C. I. L.* iii. 860, 865).

Nar. The modern Nera; a river in Central Italy, rising in Mount Fiscellus, forming the boundary between Umbria and the land of the Sabini, and falling into the Tiber, not far from Ocriculum. It was celebrated for its sulphureous waters and white colour (Verg. *Aen.* vii. 517).

Naragăra (*Ναράγαρα*). An important inland city of Numidia, where Scipio had an interview with Hannibal before the battle of Zama (Livy, xxx. 29).

Narbo Martius, afterwards **Narbōna.** The modern Narbonne; a town in the south of Gaul and the capital of the Roman province of Gallia Narbonensis, situated on the river Atax (Aude). It was made a Roman colony by the consul Q. Marcius or Martius B.C. 118, and hence received the surname Martius. It was the first colony founded by the Romans in Gaul, and gave the name Narbonensis to a part of that country. See Vell. Paterc. i. 15; Eutrop. iv. 3.

Narbonensis Gallia. See GALLIA.

Narcissus (*Νάρκισσος*). (1) The beautiful son of the river-god Cephissus. He rejected the love of the nymph Echo (q. v.), and Nemesis punished him for this by inspiring him with a passion for the reflection of himself which he saw in the water of a fountain (Ovid, *Met.* iii. 341–510; Pausan. ix. 10). He pined away in the desire for it; and to see one's reflection in the water was hence considered as a presage of death. The flower of the same name, into which he was changed, was held to be a symbol of fragility and death, and was sacred to Hades, the divinity of the world below. Persephonē had just gathered a narcissus, when she was carried off by Hades (Hom. *Hymn. Ad Cer.* 15; see PERSEPHONĒ). (2) A freedman of the emperor Claudius. He afterwards became his private secretary, and in the exercise of this office acquired immense riches by the most odious means. Messalina, jealous of his power, endeavoured to remove him, but her own vices made her fall an easy victim to this unprincipled man, who betrayed to Claudius her intrigue with C. Silius. (See MESSALINA.) Agrippina, however, was more successful. She was irritated at his having endeavoured to prevent her ascending the imperial throne; while Narcissus, on his side, espoused the interests of the young Britannicus, and urged Claudius to name him as his successor. Apprised of these plans, Agrippina drove Narcissus into a kind of temporary exile by compelling him to go to the baths of Campania for his health; and, having taken advantage of his absence from Rome to poison the emperor, she next compelled Narcissus to put himself to death. He is said to have amassed a fortune of 400,000,000 sesterces or $16,000,000 (Tac. *Ann.* xi. 30–35, xii. 57, xiii. 1; Suet. *Claud.*). (3) An athlete who strangled the emperor Commodus (A.D. 192), and was exposed to the lions by Severus (Dio Cass. lxxii. 22; lxxiii. 16).

Narcissus. (Naples Museum.)

Narisci or **Varisci.** A Suevic people in the south of Germany, in the Upper Palatinate and the country of the Fichtelgebirge (Tac. *Germ.* 42).

Narmalcha. See NAARMALCHA.

Narnia. The modern Narni; a town in Umbria, situated on a lofty hill, on the southern bank of the river Nar, originally called NEQUĪNUM, and made a Roman colony B.C. 299, when its name was changed into Narnia, after the river (Livy, x. 9).

Naro or **Nar.** The Narenta; a river in Dalmatia emptying into the Adriatic Sea (Ptol. ii. 16, 5).

Narōna. A Roman colony in Dalmatia, situated on the river Naro (Ptol. ii. 16, 5).

Narses (*Ναρσῆς*). A eunuch of the emperor Justinian I. at Constantinople. The place of his birth is unknown. He so ingratiated himself with the emperor, that he appointed him his chamberlain and private treasurer. In A.D. 538 he was placed at the head of an army destined to support Belisarius in the expulsion of the Ostrogoths from Italy; but the dissensions which soon arose between them occasioned his recall. In 552 he was again sent to Italy, to check the progress of Totila the Goth, and, after vanquishing Totila, he captured Rome. He also conquered Teias, whom the Goths had chosen king in the place of Totila, and, in the spring of 554, Bucellinus, the leader of the Alemanni. After Narses had cleared nearly all Italy of the Ostrogoths and other barbarians, he was appointed governor of the country, and ruled it fifteen years. During this time he endeavoured to enrich the treasury by all the means in his power, and excited the discontent of the provinces subject to him, who laid their complaints before the emperor Justin. Narses was deposed in disgrace, and sought revenge by inviting the Lombards to invade Italy, which they did in 568, under their king Alboin. After his deposition he lived at Naples, and died at an advanced age at Rome, in 568 (Procop. *B. G.* ii. 13; iii. and iv.).

Naryx (Νάρυξ), **Narȳcus** (Νάρυκος), or **Narycium** (Ναρύκιον). A town of the Locri Opuntii, on the Euboean Sea, described as the birthplace of Aias, son of Oïleus, who is hence called *Narycius heros.* Since Locri Epizephyrii, in the south of Italy, claimed to be a colony from Naryx, in Greece, we find the town of Locri called Narycia by the poets, and the pitch of Bruttium was also named Narycia (Verg. *Aen.* iii. 399).

Nasamōnes (Νασαμῶνες). A powerful, but savage, Libyan people, originally inhabiting the shores of the Great Syrtis, but driven inland by the Greek settlers of Cyrenaïca, and afterwards by the Romans (Herod. iv. 172; cf. ii. 32). Like the Chinese, they worshipped their ancestors. See NIGEIR.

Nasīca, SCIPIO. See SCIPIO.

Nasidiēnus. A wealthy Roman, who gave a supper to Maecenas, which Horace ridicules in one of his satires (*Sat.* ii. 8).

Nasidius, QUINTUS (LUCIUS?). A Roman sent by Pompey in B.C. 49 with a squadron to relieve Massilia (Marseilles) when besieged by Decimus Brutus. Brutus routed him, and he fled to Africa, where he continued to serve Pompey as a naval commander, and afterwards Sex. Pompey in Sicily. In the contest of Antony with Octavianus, he sided with the former (Caes. *B. C.* ii. 3–7; App. *B. C.* v. 139).

Naso, P. OVIDIUS. See OVIDIUS.

Nassa (κημός, κύρτη). A weel, or basket for snaring fish, made of wicker work with a wide funnel-shaped mouth, long body, and narrow throat, constructed as our own are, in such a manner that the fish could enter it, but not get out again. See Festus, s. v. and Sil. Ital. v. 48, where the form and manner of making it are described at length.

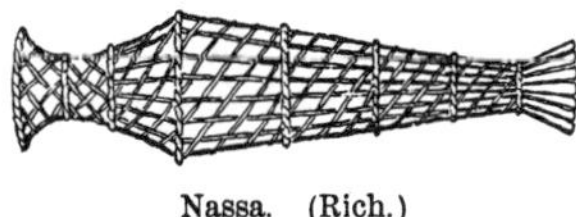
Nassa. (Rich.)

Nassiterna. A vessel for carrying water (Plaut. *Stich.* ii. 2, 28), described by Festus, s. h. v., as wide, and having handles.

Nasus or **Nesus.** See OENIADAE.

Natalicii Ludi. See LUDI.

Natatio or **Natatorium.** See BALNEAE, p. 191.

Natĭso. A river of Venetia, in Cisalpine Gaul, rising in the Alps and falling into the Adriatic near Aquileia. It is now the Natisone (Pliny, *H. N.* iii. 126).

Natta or **Nacca.** "A fuller;" the name of an ancient family of the gens Pinaria. The Natta satirized by Horace for his dirty habits was perhaps a member of the Pinarian family, and therefore attacked by the poet for such conduct; but more likely the name was given to heighten a contrast between the appellation and the manners of the man (Hor. *Sat.* i. 6, 124).

Nauarchus (ναύαρχος, "commander of a ship"). The Spartan term for the commander of the fleet, chosen for one year; also a general term for the captain of a ship, and regularly so used in the fleets of the Roman Empire (Veget. iv. 32, 43). At Athens the name was used only of the commander of the sacred triremes. See THEORIS.

Nauck, AUGUST. A classical scholar born at Auerstadt, in Germany, in 1822. He was educated at the University of Halle, and taught for some years at several gymnasia in Berlin. In 1856 he received a position as Member Extraordinary of the Imperial Academy of Sciences in St. Petersburg, and made that city his home until his death, which occurred in 1892. As a text-critic and editor, Nauck must be ranked among the greatest of the century, and his writings in this field are very numerous. As a controversialist he was often too harsh in his language. The following are his best-known works: An edition of the fragments of Aristophanes of Byzantium (1848); the complete works of Euripides, with the fragments (1854; last ed. 1877); an annotated edition of Sophocles based upon Schneidewin (1867); the *Odyssey* and *Iliad* of Homer (1874–77); Iamblichus on Pythagoras (1884); select works of Porphyrius (1886); and greatest of all his *Tragicorum Graecorum Fragmenta* (1856), with a lexicon or rather index (1892). This is now the standard edition. Nauck's writings are enumerated and his life told by Zielinski in his monograph, *August Nauck* (Berlin, 1894).

Naucraria (ναυκραρία). An early administrative division at Athens, dating from prehistoric times, for taxation for military purposes. They were forty-eight in number, twelve from each of the old phylae. Each of them was obliged to furnish two horsemen and a ship towards the army and navy. The naucrari, who were at their head, seem to have formed a college or corporate body, who occupied themselves especially with all military and financial affairs, while current business was managed by the πρυτανεῖς, whose office was the Prytaneum. Clisthenes raised their number to fifty, five from each of the ten new phylae, and probably restricted in functions to the services of the State, and especially the fleet. It is likely that they were given up after the fleet had been increased by Themistocles, and that their place was probably taken by the trierarchies. See LITURGIA.

Naucrătes (Ναυκράτης). A Greek rhetorician of Erythrae, a pupil of Isocrates. With others he competed for a prize offered by Artemisia (q. v.) to the orator who should deliver the best funeral discourse in honour of her husband Mausolus, and which was won by Theopompus (Gell. x. 18).

Naucrătis (Ναύκρατις). A city in the Delta of Egypt, on the eastern bank of the Canopic branch of the Nile. It was a colony of the Milesians, flourishing in the reign of Amasis, about B.C. 550, and remained a purely Greek city. It was the only place in Egypt where Greeks were permitted to settle and trade. Its importance was lessened after Alexandria was founded. It was the birthplace of Athenaeus and Iulius Pollux. Important excavations were made here by Mr. Flinders Petrie in 1885 and 1886, with the result of adding greatly to our knowledge of the Graeco-Egyptian period. Naucratis possessed a temple to Aphroditê, one to Herê, and a smaller one to Castor and Pollux, besides a very great one, the Panhellenion, the central religious meeting-place of all the Greeks in Egypt. In the heart of the city stood the oldest temple of all, dedicated to the Milesian Apollo.

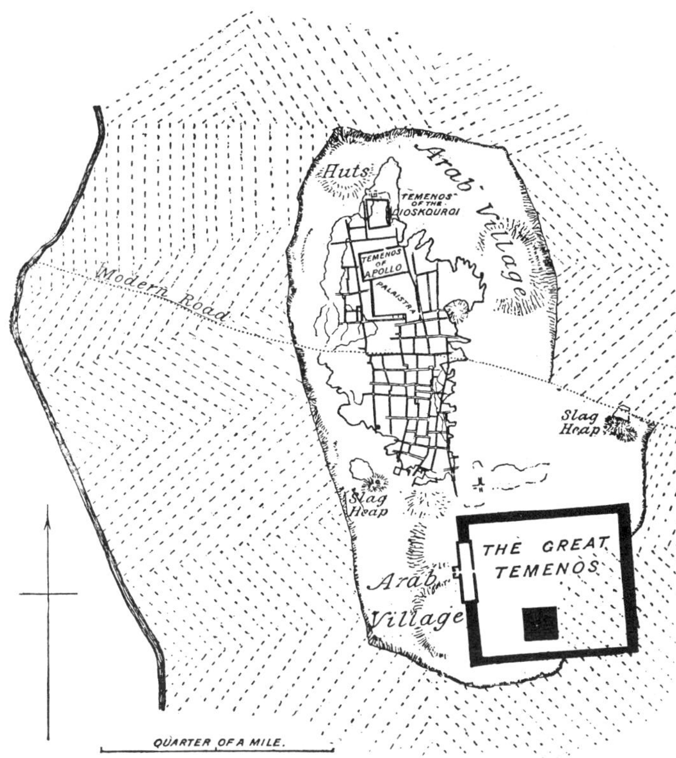

Plan of Naucratis.

The recent discoveries have added to our knowledge of the relations of Greece with earlier Egypt, and the writing found here is of great value in the study of the Greek alphabet. An ancient factory for making Greek imitations of the Egyptian scarabs is one of the curious things revealed by Mr. Petrie's researches. For an account of Petrie's archaeological discussions and of the temple-ruins, see his monograph *Naukratis* (1886); and his *Ten Years' Digging in Egypt* (1895).

Naulŏchus (Ναύλοχος). (1) A naval station on the eastern part of the northern coast of Sicily, between Mylae and the promontory Pelorus. (2) An island off the coast of Crete (Pliny, *H. N.* iv. § 12). (3) The port of the town of Bulis in Phocis (Pliny, *H. N.* iv. 3).

Naumachia (*ναυμαχία*). A name given by the Romans to a contest between ships, represented for the amusement of the people, and commemorating naval engagements famous in history. The first representation of this kind was given by Caesar in B.C. 46 in a basin dug out for this purpose on the Campus Martius, on which occasion a Tyrian and an Egyptian fleet fought against each other, each with 2000 oarsmen and 1000 marines on board. In B.C. 2 Augustus, at the dedication of the Temple of Mars Ultor, had a sea-fight between Athenians and Persians, represented with thirty ships. The greatest of all naumachiae was that of Claudius in A.D. 52; it took place on the Lacus Fucinus, and 19,000 men in the dress of Rhodians and Sicilians fought in 100 fully armed men-of-war. For similar contests the arena of the amphitheatre was sometimes filled with water. The crews of the ships consisted of gladiators, prisoners, and criminals who had been condemned to death. See Friedländer, *Sittengeschichte*, ii. 367 foll.; Marquardt, *Privatleben*, iii. 558 foll.; and the article AMPHITHEATRUM, p. 73.

Naumachia. (From a Medal of Domitian.)

Naupactus (Ναύπακτος). The modern Lepanto; an ancient town of the Locri Ozolae, near the promontory Antirrhium, possessing the best harbor on the northern coast of the Corinthian Gulf. It is said to have derived its name from the Heraclidae having here built the fleet with which they crossed over to the Peloponnesus (from *ναῦς* + *πήγνυμι*) (Apollod. ii. 7, 2). After the Persian Wars it fell into the power of the Athenians, who settled here the Messenians who had been compelled to leave their country at the end of the Third Messenian War, B.C. 455. During the Peloponnesian War it was the military base of the Athenians in their operations against Western Greece (Thuc. i. 103; ii. 83). In later times, Philip of Macedon assigned it to Aetolia, and the Romans to Locris (Livy, xxxvi. 30).

Nauplia (Ναυπλία). The port of Argos, situated on the Saronic Gulf. It was never a place of importance in antiquity, but is at the present day one of the chief commercial centres of Greece, with handsome buildings, and still retaining its ancient name. The name of Nauplius, its alleged founder, and his sons Oeax (steersman) and Nausimedon (shipmaster), prove its early maritime importance. See NAUPLIUS.

Nauplius. (1) Son of Poseidon and Amymoné (see DANAÜS; Pausan. ii. 38), founder of Nauplia (q. v.), and a famous navigator. (2) A king of Euboea, husband of Clymené. (See CATREUS.) After the unjust execution of his son Palamedes (q. v.) at the siege of Troy, the Greeks refused to give him the satisfaction he demanded. Thereupon he avenged his son's death by raising deceptive fire-signals, and stranding the returning Greeks among the breakers near the cliffs of Caphareus in Euboea. He thus caused the shipwreck and destruction of a large number, while he also put many others to the sword (Apollod. ii. 1, 4; iii. 2, 2; Hyg. *Fab.* 116). He is said to have finally thrown himself into the sea.

Nauportus. Now Ober or Upper Laibach; an important town of the Taurisci, situated on the river Nauportus (Laibach), a tributary of the Savus, in Pannonia Superior (Vell. Paterc. ii. 110). The name was traditionally derived from the legendary landing of the Argonauts at this place, where they are said to have founded the town, afterwards carrying their vessel across the Alps to the Adriatic. See ARGONAUTAE.

Nausicăa (Ναυσικάα). A daughter of Alcinoüs, king of the Phaeacians, and Areté, who conducted Odysseus to the court of her father when he was shipwrecked on the coast of Scheria. The passages in which Nausicaa is introduced are among the most pleasing and graceful of any in Homer. See *Od.* bks. vi., vii., viii.

Nausithoüs (Ναυσίθοος). The son of Poseidon and Periboea, and father of Alcinoüs, king of the Phaeacians. See CORCYRA; PHAEACES; SCHERIA.

Naustathmus (Ναύσταθμος). (1) A port and harbour in Sicily, at the mouth of the river Cacyparis, below Syracuse; now Asparanetto. (2) A village and anchoring-place of Cyrenaïca, between Erythron and Apollonia (Mela, i. 8). (3) An anchoring-place on the coast of the Euxine, in Asia Minor, about ninety stadia from the mouth of the Halys.

Nauta. See NAVIS.

Nautes. See NAUTIA GENS.

Nautia Gens. A patrician gens at Rome, claiming descent from Nautes, one of the companions of Aeneas, who was said to have brought with him the Palladium from Troy, which was placed under the care of the Nautii at Rome. All the Nautii had the surname Rutilus (Verg. *Aen.* v. 704; Dionys. vi. 4).

Nautĭcon (ναυτικόν). See FENUS.

Nautodĭcae (ναυτοδίκαι). Commercial judges. At Athens a judicial board, having cognizance in disputes between traders and suits against foreigners who pretended to be citizens. The former class of cases they settled themselves; the latter they prepared and brought before the Heliastic court. In Demosthenes' time they had ceased to exist, and both kinds of suits came under the jurisdiction of the Thesmothetae.

Nava. The modern Nahe; a tributary of the Rhine, falling into it at Bingen.

Navalia. See NABALIA.

Navalia (νεώρια). Dry-docks in which vessels were drawn up for repairs or when out of commission. Those at the Piraeus (Athens) were built by Pericles. At Rome the chief docks were in the upper bend of the Tiber, above the Aventine (Livy, iii. 26; viii. 15).

Navālis Corōna. See CORONA.

Navarchus. See NAUARCHUS.

Navia. See CAPITA AUT NAVIA.

Navigium (πλοῖον). Any kind of a craft, whether used for sailing or rowing. See NAVIS.

Navis (ναῦς). A ship. It is doubtless owing to the fact that the Mediterranean suffers from frequent calms lasting for days at a time, that the characteristic implements of navigation in that sea were oars, and that the chief problems of ancient shipbuilding were problems relating to the use of oars. The art of rowing is historically first discernible upon the river Nile. The earliest representation of rowing found on the Egyptian monuments dates from at least B.C. 2500, and there is evidence that paddling was the older practice. Among the Greeks, the generic term for the oars of a ship was τάρσος, a word applicable to the wing of a bird; so that the name sufficiently indicates the earliest "wings" of a ship to have been its oars. In the *Iliad*, ships of twenty rowers and fifty rowers are often mentioned, and in the *Odyssey* as well. In the so-called Homeric "Catalogue of Ships" there is mention of vessels with as many as 118 oarsmen. In the course of time, since the ships could not be indefinitely lengthened as the number of oarsmen increased, the oars began to be arranged in two and then in three banks, one above the other. Two-banked ships-of-war were used by the Phœnicians as early as B.C. 700, for they are represented in the Assyrian sculptures of that date, and Herodotus states that three-banked war-ships were built in Egypt about B.C. 600. Among the Greeks the first vessels of this type were not generally employed until about B.C. 500, chiefly in Sicily and Corfu. Ships with four banks of oars were built by the Athenians a little earlier than B.C. 330, and ships of five banks in B.C. 325.

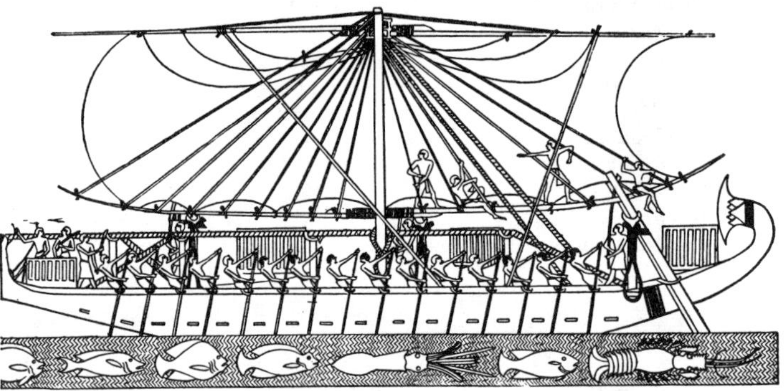

Egyptian Ship (Mariette).

Pliny the Elder speaks of ships having six banks as built at Syracuse; Quintus Curtius says that seven-banked ships were built by Alexander, and Pliny also speaks of ships having ten banks of oars. Plutarch tells of a thirteen-banked ship built by Demetrius in B.C. 301, and of fifteen, and sixteen-banked ships in B.C. 288. Polybius and Plutarch mention a sixteen-banked ship belonging to the Macedonians as arriving in the Tiber in B.C.

167, and as giving a name to one of the docks at Rome. Under the Ptolemies in Egypt, ships of twenty, thirty, and forty banks of oars are spoken of by Pliny and Plutarch, and these statements are apparently confirmed by an inscription discovered in Cyprus some years ago.

While, however, the art of rowing was developed before the art of sailing, in later times the use of oars was in general restricted to ships-of-war, which were thus made independent of the wind. In merchant vessels, on the other hand, sails were generally used, thus requiring a much smaller crew and thereby securing an economy of men. Ships-of-war, however, were also rigged with sails, though in a somewhat peculiar manner. The mast was low and carried a square sail attached to a yard. This mast was unshipped during a battle and in its stead a small foremast with a similar sail was used in place of it. Only merchant vessels appear to have carried three sails, and were very much more seaworthy than ships-of-war, being built heavier and of greater depth. The helm was usually strengthened by a stay made of two strong beams stretched between the two ends of the vessel; the bow and stern were built after the same form, and were usually the only parts of the ship to be covered with half-decks, the middle of the vessel being left open except in later times, though merchant vessels occasionally had the regular full deck.

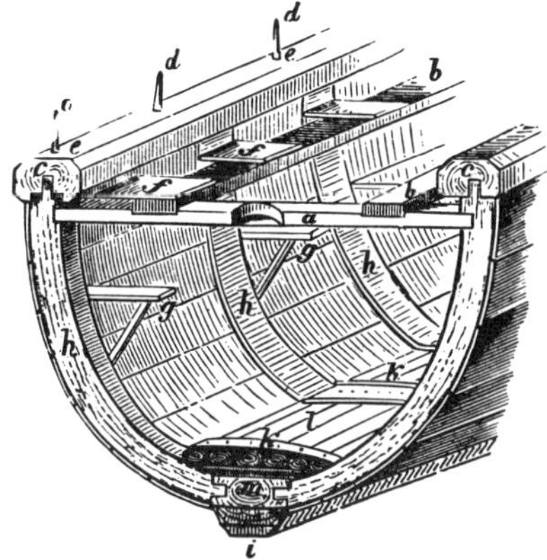

Part of the Hull of an Homeric Ship.

[*a*, μεσόδμη, mast-box; *b*, beams parallel to *c*, the gunwale; *d*, κληῖδες, row-locks; *e*, bed of the oar; *f*, ζύγα, thwarts (should cross the hold); *g*, θρῆνυς, braces for the feet; *h*, ἴκρια, ribs; *i*, τρόπις, keel; *k*, ἁρμονιαί, slabs sustaining the floor; *l*, ἔδαφος, floor; *m*, keelson.]

Homeric Ship.—The Homeric ship or galley had a sharp black hull, but was not as yet provided with a ram. The keel (τρόπις) was probably first laid upon short upright banks (δρύοχοι) of timber, laid level at suitable intervals. From the keel sprang the stem-post (στεῖρα), carried upward to a good height, as was also the stern-post. The sides (τοῖχοι) were held together by the thwarts (ζύγα), which formed the seats for the oarsmen. At the bow was a raised platform or deck (ἴκρια πρώρης), on which stood the fighting men of the ship; and there was a similar deck at the stern, on which the arms were kept, and under which there was room for stowage. The length of the fifty-oared galley is calculated to have been about 90 to 100 feet from stem to stern, with a breadth amidships of 10 to 12 feet. The galley was propelled by oars and sails together, the mast (ἱστός) being raised or lowered as stated above. When raised it was held in a sort of box (μεσόδμη), and kept in its place by forestays (πρότονοι). When lowered it rested on a sort of crutch (ἱστοδόκη). There was also a backstay (ἐπίτονος). The sail was hoisted on a yard (ἐπίκριον) having braces (ὑπέραι) and halyards (κάλοι). The sails were square in shape and white in colour. The ropes were of thong; but larger cables (ὅπλα) were made of byblus (*Odyss.* xxii. 391), occasionally of hemp or rushes (σπάρτα). The ship was steered by paddles (πηδάλια). The oars (ἐρετμά) were of fir-wood, the parts being the handle (κώπη) and blade (πηδόν). The oars were fastened to thowls (σκαλμοί) by thongs, and when not in use were drawn in, leaving the blade projecting. The master of the ship (κυβερνήτης) had his place on the forward deck. At times a long pole for pushing (κοντός) was used as an instrument of propulsion.

The Post-Homeric Ship.—As civilization and commerce grew and extended, various types of vessel were evolved. The two-banked ship (διήρης, *biremis*) and the three-banked ship (τριήρης, *triremis*) now appear to replace the earlier μονήρης, and are soon developed into the ship of many banks (πολυήρεις) mentioned above. In the bireme the second row of oarsmen sat a little lower than the first row, nearer the water-line, and with shorter oars. (From their being more in the hold (θάλαμος) of the vessel, they get the name of θαλαμῖται.) This was a great step in advance, as it doubled the motive power without adding appreciably to the length or bulk of the vessel. In the trireme we have merely an extension of the principle. The arrangement of the oarsmen in this type of ship and in those in which the number of banks of oars was still larger is not definitely known, and the question involves great difficulties. It is really impossible to conceive how the thirty or forty banked ships could have been worked, since the longest oars would have had a length of 38 cubits, or say 57 English feet. Mr. Ridgeway ingeniously suggests (*Class. Review*, June, 1895) that the word στοῖχος, rendered "bank" or "tier," really refers to the *rows* of men viewed from stem to stern, five or six oarsmen pulling each oar, and not to banks of oars at all. He calls attention to the significant fact that no representation of a many-banked ship has come down to us on coins, medals, etc. All that we do know is that the rowers in the three-banks were not separated by decks; that the whole rowing strength of the trireme was 170 men; and that the crew was densely packed, so that Cicero says that not a single additional person could enter. Each man had a cushion (ὑπηρέσιον), and the rowing port-holes were protected by leather bags (ἀσκώματα), intended to prevent the wash in a rough sea from entering the hold.

The oarsmen having the longest oars were called θρανῖται, and were 62 in number; those with the next longest were called ζύγιοι or ζυγῖται, 54 in number; and those with the shortest oars, θαλαμῖται, 54 in number. They all entered in regular order, and took their places with the strictest regard to discipline, and thus also they disembarked. The whole complement of an Athenian trireme was about 210 persons—170 oarsmen, 15 to 20 sailors, and 10 to 12 marines (ἐπιβάται), besides the officers.

The normal dimensions of the Attic trireme are differently estimated by different archaeologists. Cartault regards the length over all as 113 feet,

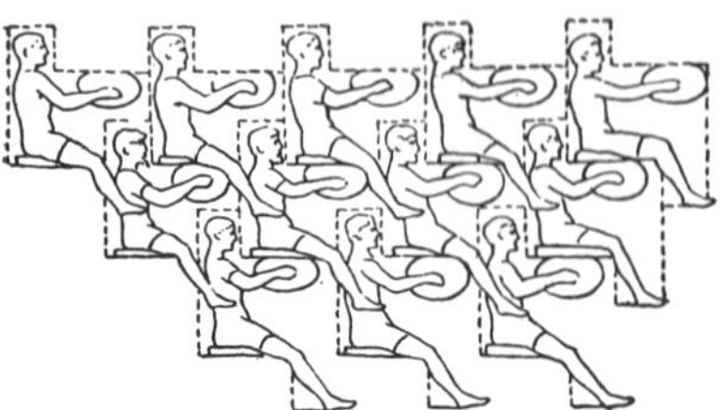

Supposed Arrangement of Oarsmen in a Trireme. (Cartault.)

with a maximum breadth of about 15½ feet, height of deck above water 10 feet, and draught 6 feet. Graser puts the length at 149 feet, the maximum breadth at 18 feet, a deck height of 11 feet, a draught of 8½ feet, and a capacity of 232½ tons.

constructed of wicker-work, and sometimes merely of canvas. Later ships have deck-houses all along the upper deck, and these were sometimes fitted up very luxuriously, like the *cabines de luxe* on a modern transatlantic liner, having paintings, statuary, marble-baths, and even libraries in the saloons. Alongside ran covered promenades, lined with rows of vines, and even trees planted in tubs (Athen. v. 41; Suet. *Calig.* 37). But these vessels partook probably more of the nature of barges than of actual ships. A decked ship was called *κατάφρακτος*; an open ship, *ἄφρακτος*.

War-vessels carried turrets on their upper decks, whence missiles might be showered upon an enemy; and these are also found on merchant-vessels that traversed waters infested by pirates. These turrets were movable. Some ships carried as many as eight; and they were often of several stories. The colours in which they were painted

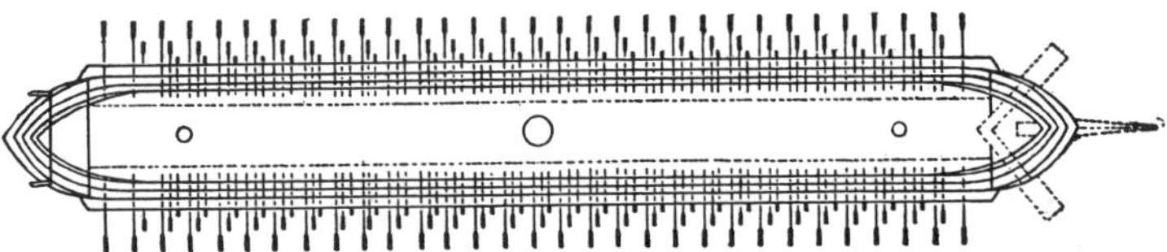

Supposed Plan of a Trireme. (Graser.)

There were developed, roughly speaking, in the post-Homeric times, three types of ship: (1) the trading-vessel, propelled principally by sail-power, roomy, wide, and safe; (2) the pirate-vessel, using both sails and oars, swift, sharp, yet with sufficient room for storing the plunder; and (3) the man-of-war (*ναῦς μακρά, navis longa*), intended first of all for fighting. This last was high out of water, less steady than the trader, having bulwarks of great strength running the whole length of the ship, propelled principally by oars. This type finds its highest expression in the Athenian trireme.

A ship with a single bank of oars (*μονήρης*) was also named according to the number of oarsmen employed—thus, *πεντηκόντορος*, with fifty rowers; *ἑξηκόντορος*, with sixty rowers, etc.

Trading-ship. (From a Vase in the British Museum.)

Decks.—The earliest Greek ships were decked over at the stem and at the stern, as described above; but towards B.C. 500 the ships appear without poop. Occasionally about this time the forecastle is represented as supporting the forepart of a hurricane-deck and enclosing a cabin below. The stern now held a tier of seats for the steerer and for officers. There was also usually a deck-house at the stern for the commander, oftenest lightly

identified the squadron to which they belonged. Lest the ships should be made top-heavy by these turrets, large quantities of ballast were carried at the bottom of the hold, usually gravel or sand or

Pirate-ship. (From a Vase in the British Museum.)

stone. Vessels were baled by a machine worked by a sort of tread-mill (Athen. v. 43), but in early times by buckets (*ἀντλητήρια, sentinacula*). Drinking-water was carried in cisterns.

Rams.—The forepart of war-ships was constructed largely with regard to the use of the ram (*ἔμβολος, rostrum*), being built very strongly, with massive cat-heads projecting far enough to tear away the upper works of a hostile ship. There were auxiliary rams besides the principal one. Rams were

Ram. (Montfaucon.)

usually of bronze, but sometimes of iron. The principal ram of a trireme weighed some 170 pounds. It usually had three prongs, and often sloped downward, as the one shown above. Before the use of rams, heads of animals had usually been carved upon the prows as figure-heads, the subject corresponding to the name of the ship. Thus, a crocodile would go with a ship named *Nilus;* a mountain with one named *Ida,* etc. There were regular national emblems so used, as the statue of Pallas Athené by Athenian ships and a head of Ammon by the Carthaginians. In Roman ships of about A.D. 50 a gilded swan or goose was common. The stern was often ornamented by a painting or relief, and by a carving resembling originally the Egyptian lotus, but developed, in time, into a sort of plume or fan. On the bow of the ship there was also generally a huge eye, or sometimes a pair of eyes.

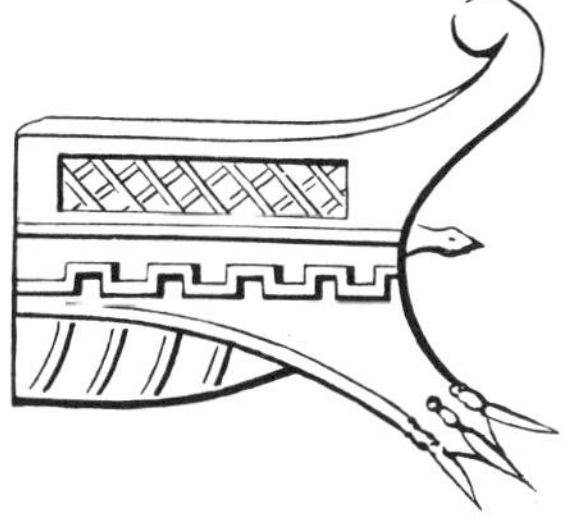
Ram. (From a medal.)

Rudders.—See GUBERNACULUM.

Anchors.—In early times the anchors (ἀγκύρα, *ancora*) were stones (εὐναί). The metal anchor with arms was said to be the invention of Anacharsis (B.C. 600). They were first of iron and later of lead with a wooden shank. The remains of one lately found near Cyrené afford evidence that for a ship of some 200 tons the anchor weighed some 1400 pounds. The anchor was often slung over the stern, and when in use had its position marked by cork buoys (σημεῖα ἀγκύρας). The cables (τὰ σχοῖνα, *ancoralia*) were sometimes of chain, but usually of rope.

Anchor. (Column of Trajan.)

Sails.—The sail (ἱστίον) was often made of pieces of canvas stitched together, whence the plural ἱστία often means only a single sail. They were sometimes strengthened by strips of leather sewn over the stitching. At the lower extremities of the sail were the sheets (πόδες) and tacks (πρόποδες). Instead of reefing the sails the ancients appear rather to have brailed them up (στέλλειν, παραιρεῖν) to reduce the area exposed to the wind. In battle the war-ships depended wholly upon their oars.

Brailing the Sails of a Ship. (Mazois, *Pomp.* i. 22.)

Material for Ships.—The hull was usually of pine or fir; cedar and cypress are also mentioned. The keels were of pine and the false keels of oak or beech. Barbarian ships of leather (Caes. *B. C.* i. 54) are mentioned. The masts and yards were made of fir or pine, and so also the oars. The seams of the ship were calked by packing them with tow fastened by wax or tar; and the whole outer planking was protected by a coating of similar materials, coloured. Pliny (*H. N.* xxxv. 31 and 41) mentions seven colours as used; but in later times a colour resembling that of the sea-water was employed, probably to enable the vessel to escape observation from enemies, a device employed in modern navies. The timbers were held together by wooden pegs and metal nails.

THE ROMAN SHIP.—The Romans, though not a seafaring people, appear from the treaty with Carthage to have been familiar with the sea, and to have had maritime interests as early as the time of the kings. The existence of *duumviri navales,* officers charged with repairing the fleet, the right of electing whom was transferred to the people in B.C. 311, proves that the State had, at that time and previously, some naval force; and coins of a date as early as B.C. 350 bear the representation of the bows of a ship of a type more rude than the Greek, but still very possibly borrowed from the Greek cities in Magna Graecia. In the instances exhibited by the coins, which belong to the half-century preceding the First Punic War, there are apparently two varieties of construction. In one the depression of the beak is remarkable, and the timbers which support it appear to be compacted with cross-pieces. These vessels were probably triremes. In the year B.C. 303 a treaty was made with the Tarentines, by which the Lacinian Promontory was made the boundary beyond which the Roman war-ships were not to pass. L. Cornelius in B.C. 282 violated that treaty, and was defeated by the Tarentines with the loss of half his fleet. The Samnite Wars seem to have diverted the attention of the Romans entirely from maritime affairs, and at the beginning of the Punic Wars they were practically without a fleet. They then first seem to have realized the fact that in the conflict which was before them the mastery of the Mediterranean was an absolute necessity, not only for the protection of their own coasts, which already had suffered from the descents of the Carthaginian fleets, but also as the first step towards empire (Polyb. i. 20, 21). Hence, in the year B.C. 260, when a Carthaginian quinquereme which had been driven on shore fell into their hands, they determined to construct a fleet of similar vessels. No less than 100 were built in six weeks, while their future crews were practised rowing in frame-work set up on land. Cn. Cornelius with seventeen of these vessels sailed in advance to attack the Carthaginians, but was himself attacked and taken with all his vessels. Duilius, who then took the command of the fleet, by the invention of the *corvus* (Polyb. i. 22, 23)—a swinging bridge with a heavy iron spike, which, when let fall on the enemy's deck, not only grappled his vessel, but gave the boarders access to it—was enabled to neutralize the ramming tactics of the Carthaginians and their superior naval skill. The battles of Mylae and of Ecnomus, in which the Carthaginians were defeated with great loss, were the prelude of maritime dominion to Rome. The importance of the ram was thus much diminished, and in the coins of the century following we see the ram much less projecting and apparently less strongly supported. On the other hand, the δελφίς, great beams and great grappling hooks, iron hands, and *falces* with curved steel heads, such as those with which the sailing vessels of the Veneti were crippled by Caesar off the coast of Gaul (Caes. *B. G.* iii. 14), came into favour. Huge towers (*turres*) were placed in the bows—whence our term "forecastle"—from which missiles could be showered on the enemy's deck. The main object of Roman tactics seemed to be to leave as little as possible to seamanship and skill, and to come to close quarters and a hand-to-hand fight as soon as possible. In a word, boarding tactics superseded ramming tactics. See Polyb. i. 61; Livy, xxxvi. 44, 45; xxxvii. 24, 30.

As early as B.C. 413 the use of fire (Thuc. vii. 53) in a naval action is mentioned. Later, catapults, the precursors of artillery, launched Greek fire rocket-fashion against the enemy.

The Liburnian galleys were biremes (Lucan, iii. 534). The name seems to have been taken from the vessels of the Liburnians, an Illyrian race, inhabiting the islands of that coast and much given to piracy. The name Liburnian, in the same way as the name trireme, came afterwards to be used for any ship of war.

In the time of Trajan some attempt was made to build larger rates than biremes, and Valentinian had quinqueremes constructed. But in the Byzantine period no vessels with more banks than two appear; and the tendency is to return to single banks, which, according to the emperor Leo (*Tactica*), are called γαλαῖαι, "galleys."

Under the emperors two great naval stations were established for the fleets that were intended to keep the peace of the Mediterranean—(1) at Ravenna, for the east; and (2) at Misenum, on the Campanian coast, for the west. There were also guard-ships regularly stationed on the coast of Gaul at Forum Iulii (Fréjus) and Portus Herculis Monoeci (Monaco). But after Actium there is little to interest us in naval affairs, with the exception perhaps of Germanicus's operations in the North Sea, and at a later date the war with the Vandals, for which Procopius is our authority, until the time of the Byzantine emperor Leo (A.D. 960). In the following centuries came the invention of the *apostis* (a projecting framework, upon the edge of which were set the thowlpins, thus enabling oars of greater length to be used) and the birth of the mediæval galley, which, with its long sweeps worked by several men, was a vessel distinct from the ancient men-of-war.

Sailors and Marines.—The Athenian fleet was manned in its best days by freemen. Xenophon tells us that the seafaring habits of the Athenians were such that every one knew how to handle an oar, and that the crew of a trireme could be got together at once. At the time of the Peloponnesian War the pay of an ordinary oarsman was three obols a day, increased towards the end of the war to four obols. The pay of the *thranitae* was higher, their services being valued at a drachma. Raising the pay of seamen during hostilities was a favourite expedient with a view to induce the enemy's crews to desert. There were, however, many causes that led to the employment of forced labour, and with it to the deterioration and unpopularity of sea-service. The unavoidable discomfort in a decked ship must have been extreme. In a hot climate, with little ventilation, the participation with 200 or 300 human beings, all stark naked and packed closely in a laborious mechanical toil, could only have been voluntarily endured under the pressure of some great necessity or sense of duty. The heat, the smell, the drudgery, must have been terrible. Besides the discomfort, the actual danger was very great. The crews might at any time be drowned or burned, or, as at Sybota (Thuc. i. 50), butchered perhaps in cold blood. We have only to think of the moment of conflict—the crash of the beak through the timbers, and the mangled mass of humanity hurled into the bilge, while the water swiftly followed the blow, the *thranitae*, perhaps, escaping, but the lower ranks almost certainly drowned — and it is easy to understand how the service was avoided by the free and left to slaves. The marines (ἐπιβάται) varied in number, the Athenian ship carrying few, and the Chians, at the battle of Ladé, for instance, as many as forty to each vessel.

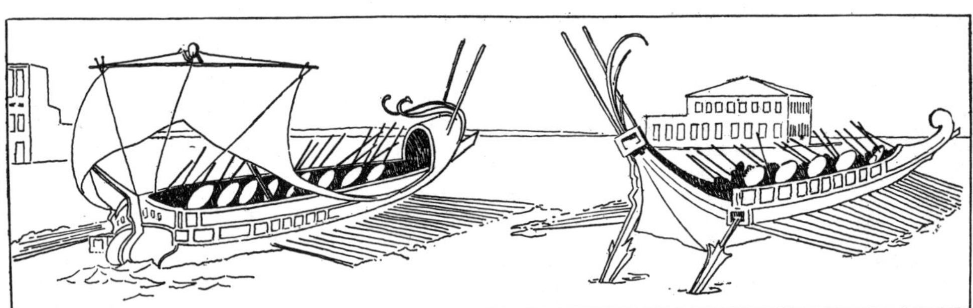

Naval Battle. (Pompeian Painting.)

The Romans manned their fleet by levies from the lowest orders and forced service of the allies. The greater proportion of the crews were slaves contributed as substitutes, and it is this fact, perhaps, which explains the equanimity with which such wholesale loss of life at sea as is recorded by Polybius was endured. Among the Romans themselves service on board ship was most unpopular;

and it is not surprising to find discontented *classiarii* wishing to be transferred to the legions. The Roman term for marines is *classiarii milites*. They were held in less esteem than regular soldiers.

Roman Marines. (Scheffer.)

BIBLIOGRAPHY.—See Scheffer, *De Militia Navali Veterum* (Upsala, 1654); Graser, *De Re Navali Veterum* (Berlin, 1864); id. *Die Gemmen des königlichen Museums zu Berlin* (1867); id. *Die ältesten Schiffsdarstellungen auf antiken Münzen* (Berlin, 1870); id. *Das Modell eines alt-griechischen Kriegsschiffes* (Berlin, 1873); De la Gravière, *La Marine des Anciens*, 2d ed. (Paris, 1887); Sestier, *De la Piraterie de l'Antiquité* (Paris, 1880); Cartault, *La Trière Athénienne* (Paris, 1882); Breusing, *Die Nautik der Alten* (Bremen, 1886); Vars, *L'Art Nautique dans l'Antiquité* (Paris, 1887); Serre, *Études sur l'Histoire Militaire et Maritime* (Paris, 1888); and Torr, *Ancient Ships* (Cambridge, 1894). For special types of ships and boats, see the following articles: ACATUS; APHRACTUS; BARIS; CATAPHRACTI; CATASCOPIUM; CELOX; CYMBA; HEMIOLIA; LEMBUS; LINTER; RATIS; SCAPHA; THALAMEGUS.

Navius, ATTUS or ATTIUS. A renowned augur in the reign of Tarquinius Priscus, who opposed the project of the king to double the number of the equestrian centuries. Tarquin then commanded him to divine whether what he was thinking of at the time could be done; and when Navius declared that it could, the king held out a whetstone and a razor to cut it with. Navius immediately bade him apply the razor to the stone, which he did; and the blade passed through the flint with so much force as to cut the king's hand. The statue of Navius was placed in the Comitium, and beside it was preserved the whetstone (Livy, i. 36; Dionys. iii. 70; Cic. *Nat. Deor.* ii. 3; *De Div.* i. 17).

Naxos (Νάξος). (1) Now Naxia; an island in the Aegaean Sea, the largest of the Cyclades, especially celebrated for its wine. It is about eighteen miles in length and twelve in breadth. It was also called DIA, STRONGY̆LE, and DIONYSIAS. Here Dionysus is said to have come to Ariadné after she had been deserted by Theseus. (See ARIADNÉ.) It was colonized by Ionians, who had emigrated from Athens. After the Persian Wars, the Naxians were the first of the allied States whom the Athenians reduced to subjection (B.C. 471). The chief town of the island was also called Naxos. See Dugit, *De Insula Naxo* (Paris, 1867); and Tozer, *Islands of the Aegean* (Oxford, 1890). (2) A Greek city on the eastern coast of Sicily, founded B.C. 735 by the Chalcidians of Euboea, and the first Greek colony established in the island. In B.C. 403 the town was destroyed by Dionysius of Syracuse; but nearly fifty years afterwards (358) the remaining Naxians scattered over Sicily, were collected by Andromachus, and a new city was founded on Mount Taurus, to which the name of Tauromenium was given. See TAUROMENIUM.

Nazareth (Ναζαρέθ) or **Nazăra** (Ναζαρά). A city of Galilee in Palestine, south of Cana.

Nazarius. A Latin panegyric writer; the author of a eulogy on the emperor Constantine, delivered A.D. 321. Text in Bährens' edition of the Panegyrici (Leipzig, 1874). His daughter Eunomia is also said to have won fame by her eloquence. See PANEGYRICUS.

Nazianzus (Ναζιανζός). A city of Cappadocia, celebrated as the diocese of a distinguished Father of the Church—Gregory Nazianzenus.

Neaera (Νέαιρα). The name of several nymphs and maidens mentioned by the poets.

Neaethus (Νέαιθος). Now Nieto; a river in Bruttium, falling into the Tarentine Gulf a little north of Croton. Here the captive Trojan women are said to have burned the ships of the Greeks, from which circumstance some of the ancients fancifully derived the name of the place (qs. ναῦς + αἴθω). See Strabo, p. 262.

Neanthes (Νεάνθης). A Greek of Cyzicum, who flourished in the third century B.C. He was a voluminous writer on historical topics, and some of his fragments have come down to us, for which see Müller's *Fragment. Hist. Graecorum.*

Neapŏlis (Νεάπολις). The name of a number of ancient cities.

I. EUROPEAN.—(1) Now Napoli (Naples); a city of Campania in Italy on the western slope of Mount Vesuvius and the river Sebethus (Maddalena). It was founded about B.C. 1056 by Aeolian Chalcidians of Cumae, on the site of an ancient place called PARTHENŎPÉ (Παρθενόπη), after the Siren of that name. Hence we find the town called Parthenopé by Vergil and Ovid. The year of the foundation of Neapolis is not recorded. It was perhaps called the "New City," because regarded simply as a new quarter of the neighbouring city of Cumae. When the town is first mentioned in Roman history it consisted of two parts, divided from each other by a wall, and called respectively Palaeopolis and Neapolis. This division probably arose after the capture of Cumae by the Samnites,

Coin of the Campanian Neapolis (about B.C. 300.)

when a large number of the Cumaeans took refuge in the city they had founded; whereupon the old quarter was called Palaeopolis, and the new quarter, built to accommodate the new inhabitants, was named Neapolis. There has been a dispute respecting the site of these two quarters; but it is probable that Palaeopolis was situated on the west side near the harbour, and Neapolis on the east side near the river Sebethus. In B.C. 327 the town was taken by the Samnites, and in 290 it passed into the hands of the Romans, who allowed it, however, to retain its Greek constitution. At a later period it became a municipium, and finally a Roman colony. Under the Romans the two quarters of the city were united, and the name of Palaeopolis disappeared. It continued to be a prosperous and flourishing place till the time of the Empire; and its beautiful scenery and the luxurious life of its Greek population made it a favourite residence with many of the Romans. In the reign of Titus the city was destroyed by an earthquake, but was rebuilt by this emperor in the Roman style. The modern city of Naples does not stand on exactly the same site as Neapolis. The ancient city extended farther east than the modern city, since the former was situated on the Sebethus, whereas the latter does not reach so far as the Fiume della Maddalena; but the modern city, on the other hand, extends farther north and west than the ancient one, since the island of Megaris, on which the Castel del Ovo now stands, was situated in ancient times between Pausilypum and Neapolis. In the neighbourhood of Neapolis there were warm baths, the celebrated villa of Lucullus, and the Villa Pausilypi or Pausilypum, bequeathed by Vedius Pollio to Augustus, and which has given its name to the celebrated grotto of Posilippo between Naples and Pozzuoli, at the entrance of which what is called the tomb of Vergil is still shown. Augustus frequently visited the city, and Tiberius, Claudius, Nero, Titus, and Hadrian favoured it in many ways. In 536 it was taken by Belisarius, and in 543 by the Goths under Totila. Naples is a city of much interest to archaeologists, both because of its proximity to Pompeii and Herculaneum, and because of its remarkable collection of ancient works of art and industry preserved in the Museo Nazionale. (See MUSEUM.) (2) A part of Syracuse. (See SYRACUSAE.) (3) Napoli, a town on the west coast of the island of Sardinia, celebrated for its warm baths. (4) Kavallo, a sea-port town in Thrace, subsequently Macedonia adjecta, on the Strymonic Gulf, between the Strymon and Nessus.

II. ASIATIC.—(1) A small Ionian city, on the coast of Lydia, north of Mycalé and southwest of Ephesus. The Ephesians, to whom it at first belonged, exchanged it with the Samians for Marathesium. (2, 3) Two towns of Caria, the one near Harpasa, the other on the coast, perhaps the new town of Myndus. (4) In Pisidia, south of Antioch; afterwards reckoned to Galatia. (5) In Palestine, the SYCHEM or SYCHAR of Scripture (Συχέμ, Συχάρ, Σικίμα, Nablous), one of the most ancient cities of Samaria, stood in the narrow valley between Mounts Ebal and Gerizim, and was the religious capital of the Samaritans, whose temple stood on Mount Gerizim before its destruction by Hyrcanus, B.C. 129. Its full Roman name was FLAVIA NEAPŎLIS. Here was born Justin Martyr.

III. AFRICAN.—(1) A town in North Africa on the coast west of the Great Syrtis, and by some identified with the modern Tripoli. (2) A Phœnician colony, now Nabal, on the eastern coast of Zeugitana near the northern end of the gulf called from it Sinus Neapolitanus.

Nearchus (Νέαρχος). A Greek writer of Crete, resident afterwards at Amphipolis. He was a friend of Alexander the Great in his youth, and, participating in his youthful intrigues, was banished by Philip. Later he administered the satrapy of Lycia for five years after the battle of the Granicus (B.C. 334). He then took part in the Indian expedition (B.C. 327), and returned, as commander of the fleet, down the Indus and along the coast of Asia to the mouth of the Tigris. After Alexander's death he attached himself to Antigonus, and under him governed the provinces of Lycia and Pamphylia. He wrote an account (Παράπλους) of his voyage, which was rich in geographical discoveries. Of this we possess, besides fragments, an abstract in Arrian's *Indica*. The investigations of later times have in many respects confirmed the trustworthiness of his statements concerning ancient India. See INDIA.

Nebo. The name of an Assyrian deity who presided over learning and had many of the attributes of the Greek Hermes. See p. 143.

Nebo. A mountain in Palestine opposite Jericho, on the eastern side of the Jordan.

Nebris (from νεβρός). A faun-skin; worn originally by hunters, but assumed by Bacchanals:

Priestess of Bacchus with a Nebris. (Hamilton's vases, i. 37.)

and in works of art forming a part of the attire of Pan and of the satyrs.

Nebrissa, or **Colonia Venerea Nebrissa.** A town of the Turdetani, in Hispania Baetica, northeast of Gades and southwest of Hispalis. It is now Lebrija.

Nebrŏdes. The principal chain of mountains in Sicily, running through the whole of the island, and forming a continuation of the Apennines.

Necessĭtas (Ἀνάγκη). A goddess regarded as superior even to the gods themselves, since she represented the Inevitable. At Corinth there was a

Necessitas. (Causei, *Museum Romanum.*)

temple dedicated to Ἀνάγκη and Βία (Force), which no one was permitted to enter (Pausan. ii. 4, 6). Among the Romans her symbol is the nail, as fixing fast the decrees of Fate. See Hor. *Carm.* i. 35, 17.

Necklace. See MONILÉ.

Neco or **Necho** (Νεκώς, Νεχώς, Νεκαῦς, Νεχαώς: in Egyptian, *Neku*). (1) An Egyptian, the grandfather (or father) of Psammetichus. He was defeated and imprisoned by Sardanapalus; but being at length released, became king of Saïs and Memphis (Herod. ii. 152). (2) The son of Psammetichus, succeeding his father on the throne of Egypt in B.C. 612. He attempted to cut a canal to connect the Nile with the Arabian Gulf—a project that had interested his predecessors, Seti I. and Rameses II. The attempt was abandoned after he had lost 120,000 men and had received a warning from an oracle to the effect that he was only labouring for the barbarians (Herod. ii. 158). In his reign it is reported that Phœnicians in his service circumnavigated the continent of Africa, setting sail from the Arabian Gulf, and, at the end of two years, entering the Mediterranean through the Strait of Gibraltar (Herod. iv. 42). See AFRICA.

Necrodeipnon (νεκρόδειπνον). See FUNUS, p. 697.

Necropŏlis (from νεκρός, "dead," and πόλις, "city"). The city of the dead; a name applied to the cemeteries in the neighbourhood of many of the ancient cities, such as Thebes in Egypt, Cyrené, Alexandria, etc.

Nectanăbis (Νεκτάναβις: Egyptian, *Nekt-Hor-Heb*). (1) A king of Egypt (B.C. 378–364), who successfully resisted the invasion of the Persian force under Pharnabazus and Iphicrates. He was succeeded by Tachos. (2) The nephew of Tachos, deprived the latter of the sovereignty in B.C. 361, with the assistance of Agesilaüs. He was defeated by the Persians in 350, and fled into Aethiopia. He was the last king of Egypt of the Egyptian race. See Diod. Sic. xv. 92; xvi. 48 foll.; Pausan. iii. 10.

Nectar. The drink of the Greek gods (see AMBROSIA), which Homer describes as a red beverage (*Il.* xix. 38) poured out by Hebé for the immortals (*Il.* iv. 3).

Neda (Νέδα). A river in the Peloponnesus, rising in Arcadia and emptying into the Ionian Sea (Pausan. iv. 20, 1).

Needles. See ACUS.

Nefasti Dies. See DIES.

Negligentia. A term in Roman law to denote carelessness in performing any obligation; a breach of duty; the opposite of *diligentia*. See CULPA.

Negotiatōres (πραγματευόμενοι). Provincial citizens who lent money on interest and bought grain on speculation (Caes. *B. G.* vii. 3). Transactions of the former sort were, however, their principal occupation, so that *negotiator* meant, as a rule, the same thing in the provinces as *argentarius* or *fenerator* at Rome. Senators were not allowed to be negotiatores, so that, like the *publicani*, these were of the equestrian order. See the monograph by Ernesti, *De Negotiatoribus* in his *Opuscula Philologica*; Marquardt, *Staatsverwaltung*, vol. i. p. 542 (2d ed.); and the articles FENUS; PUBLICANI; TRAPEZITAE.

Roman Aqueduct at Nemausus.

Nekysia (τὰ νεκύσια). A feast in honour of the dead. See FUNUS.

Neleus (Νηλεύς). (1) The son of Poseidon and Tyro, daughter of Salmoneus, and brother of Pelias. The brothers were exposed after birth by their mother, who afterwards married Cretheus of Iolcus; they were found by a herdsman and brought up by him until they grew up and were acknowledged by their mother. After Cretheus's death they quarrelled about the possession of Iolcus; and Neleus, together with Melampus and Bias, the sons of his half-brother Amythaon, retired into exile in Messenia, where Aphareus, Tyro's cousin, allowed them to occupy Pylus. By Chloris, daughter of Amphion, the king of the Minyan Orchomenus (it is only a later myth that identifies him with Amphion of Thebes), he became father of twelve sons, of whom Periclymenus and Nestor (q. v.) were the most celebrated, and one daughter, the beautiful Pero, bride of Bias. (See MELAMPUS.) On his refusing to purify Heracles from the murder of Iphitus, Heracles invaded his country and slew all his sons, except Nestor, who chanced to be absent from home at the time. Nestor became the champion and avenger of the aged Neleus when the Epeans and their king Augeas, emboldened by his misfortune, ventured on acts of injustice towards him. According to one account, it was Neleus who renewed the Olympian Games, and died at Corinth, where, it was said, he was buried at the isthmus; according to others, he was slain along with his sons by Heracles. (2) The younger son of Codrus, who disputed the right of his elder brother Medon to the throne. The Delphic oracle declared against him, and he migrated to Ionia, where he founded the city of Miletus (Herod. ix. 97). (3) A disciple of Aristotle and Theophrastus. See ARISTOTELES, p. 129.

Nelīdes (Νηλείδης) or **Neleïădes** (Νηληιάδης). Patronymics of Neleus, by which both Nestor, the son of Neleus, and Antilochus, his grandson, are designated.

Nemausus. The modern Nîmes; an important town of Gallia Narbonensis, the capital of the Arecomici and a Roman colony. It was situated west of the Rhone on the high-road from Italy to Spain.

The Roman remains at Nîmes are among the most perfect found north of the Alps, and include the so-called Maison Carrée, which is a Corinthian temple admirably preserved, and the splendid Roman aqueduct, the Pont du Gard, some fourteen miles from the town. It consists of three rows of arches, 180 feet in height, and spans the little river Gard. Its construction is traditionally ascribed to Agrippa, the general of Augustus. There are also an amphitheatre, built to seat 20,000 people, a Nymphaeum, baths, a mausoleum, and two ancient gates.

Neméa (Νεμέα) or **Nemeë** (Νεμέη). A valley in Argolis between Cleonae and Phlius, celebrated in mythical story as the place where Heracles slew the Nemean lion. (See HERACLES.) In this valley there was a splendid temple of Zeus Nemeus surrounded by a sacred grove, in which the Nemean Games were celebrated every other year. See NEMEA.

Neměa (τὰ Νέμεα or Νέμεια). The Nemean Games; one of the four Greek national festivals, which was celebrated in the valley of Nemea in the territory of the Argive town Cleonae. In historic times the festival was held in honour of Zeus, who had here a temple with a sacred grove. Originally it is said to have consisted of funeral games, instituted by the Seven during their expedition against Thebes (Apollod. iii. 6, 4), in memory of the boy Archemorus as an ἀγὼν ἐπιτάφιος. (See SEVEN AGAINST THEBES.) Heracles afterwards changed it into a festival in honour of Zeus. From about B.C. 575 onwards, athletic competitions were added to the festival, after the model of those at Olympia; and, like the latter, it was only gradually that it developed into a general Hellenic celebration. It was held twice in a period of four years—once in August, every fourth year; once in winter, every second or first Olympic year. It is more probable, however, that the so-called "Winter Nemea" were only local games held in Argos, and that the Panhellenic Nemea were celebrated in alternate years at the end of every first and third Olympic year, at a time corresponding to our July. The question is discussed by Unger in the *Philologus* (xxxiv. 50), but Droysen, in *Hermes* (xiv. 1), considers it still unsettled. The management of the festival was originally possessed by the Cleonaeans, but soon passed, together with the possession of the sanctuary, into the hands of the Argives. The games, which lasted more than one day (Livy, xxvii. 31), consisted of gymnastic, equestrian, and musical contests (for the two former, see OLYMPIA); the prize was a palm-branch and a garland of fresh σέλινον, often rendered "parsley," but more probably identical with the "wild celery." See Krause, *Pythien, Nemeen, und Isthmien*, and the scholiasts on Pindar.

Nemean Lion. See HERACLES.

Nemesīa (τὰ Νεμέσεια). The same as the Genesia (τὰ γενέσια). A festival celebrated at Athens on the fifth of Boedromion, of which no particulars are known. See A. Mommsen, *Heortologie*, p. 209; and the article FUNUS.

Nemesiānus, MARCUS AURELIUS OLYMPIUS, of Carthage. A Roman poet famous in his own times, belonging to the end of the third century A.D. He flourished under the emperor Carus and his sons (212–284). We possess by him the first 325 hexameter lines of a well-written poem on the chase (*Cynegetica*), and four eclogues, in which he has closely followed Calpurnius (q. v.). Editions by Stein (Leipzig, 1832), and by Bährens in his *Poetae Latini Minores* (Leipzig, 1879).

Neměsis (Νέμεσις). A post-Homeric personification of the moral indignation felt at all derangements of the natural equilibrium of things, whether by extraordinarily good fortune or by the arrogance usually attendant thereon. According to Hesiod (*Theog.* 223) she is the daughter of Night (Nyx), and with Aidos, the goddess of Modesty, left the earth on the advent of the Iron Age. A legend makes her to have been by Zeus the mother of Helen and the Dioscuri (Athen. p. 334). As goddess of due proportion she hates every transgression of the bounds of moderation, and restores the proper and normal order of things. As, in doing this, she punishes wanton boastfulness, she is a divinity of chastisement and vengeance. She enjoyed special honour in the Attic district of Rhamnus (where she was believed to be the daughter of Oceanus), and is often called the Rhamnusian goddess. Her statue there (of which fragments were found in 1890) was said to have been executed by Phidias out of a block of Parian marble which the Persians had brought with them in presumptuous confidence to Marathon, to erect a trophy of victory there. She was also called Adrastia, that name appropriate only to the Phrygian Rhea-Cybelé, being interpreted as a Greek word with the meaning, "She whom none can escape." She was also worshipped at Rome, especially by victorious generals, and was represented as a meditative, thoughtful maiden with the attributes of proportion and control (a measuring-rod, a bridle, and a yoke), of punishment (a sword and scourge), and of swiftness (wings, a wheel, and a chariot drawn by griffins).

Neměsis. A lady loved by Tibullus and celebrated by him in his verse. See Doncieux, *De Tibulli Amoribus* (Paris, 1887), and the article TIBULLUS.

Nemesius (Νεμέσιος). The author of a treatise in Greek on the nature of man (Περὶ Φύσεως Ἀνθρώπου). He was bishop of Emesa in Syria, and lived in the fourth or early in the fifth century A.D. Edition by Matthaei (Halle, 1802).

Nemetăcum or **Nemetocenna.** See ATREBATES.

Nemētes or **Nemētae.** A people in Gallia Belgica on the Rhine, whose chief town was Noviomagus, subsequently Nemetae (Speyer or Spires). Cf. Caes. *B. G.* i. 51; Tac. *Germ.* 28.

Nemorensis. An epithet of Diana (q. v.).

Nemorensis Lacus. See ARICIA.

Nemossus. The chief town of the Arverni, a Gallic people in the modern Auvergne. It was situated on the Elaver (Allier), with a citadel known in the early Middle Ages as Clarus Mons, whence the modern name of the town—Clermont. As the capital of the Arverni it replaced the earlier capital Gergovia (Caes. *B. G.* i. 45; vi. 7 foll.).

Nenia (better than NAENIA). A name given by the Romans to the funeral dirge in honour of the dead, sung to the accompaniment of flutes, at first by the relatives, in later times by hired mourners (*praeficae*). There was also a goddess so called, the dirge personified, who had a chapel outside the Porta Viminalis. See FUNUS, p. 699.

Neobūlé. See ARCHILOCHUS.

Neocaesarēa (Νεοκαισαρεία). A city of Pontus in Asia Minor, standing on the river Lycus. It was the native place of Gregory Thaumaturgus. The modern name is Niksar.

Neocŏrus (νεωκόρος). A Greek term, corresponding to the Latin *aedituus* (q. v.); a verger who has the charge of a temple, and the objects contained in it; and whose duty it was to attend to the sweeping and cleaning of the same. Hence the inhabitants of the Greek towns often styled themselves the νεωκόροι of their patron divinity; and in later times, as a piece of refined flattery, of the Roman emperor; thereby intending to express devotion and piety towards the sovereign, and at the same time insinuate his divinity (Firm. Math. 3, 7, n. 9).

Neodamōdeis (νεοδαμώδεις). See HELOTAE.

Neon (Νέων). An ancient town in Phocis, at the eastern side of Mount Tithorea, a branch of Mount Parnassus, destroyed by the Persians under Xerxes, but rebuilt and named Tithorea (Τιθορέα), after the mountain on which it was situated (Herod. viii. 33).

Neontīchos (Νέον Τεῖχος, "New Wall"). (1) One of the twelve cities of Aeolis, on the coast of Mysia. (2) A fort on the coast of Thrace, near the Chersonesus (Xen. *Anab.* vii. 5, 8).

Neoplatonism. A form of later Greek philosophy, founded upon Plato. See PHILOSOPHIA.

Neoptolĕmus (Νεοπτόλεμος, also called PYRRHUS; i. e. the ruddy). (1) The son of Achilles and Deïdamia. He was brought up by his grandfather Lycomedes in Scyros. After Achilles' death, however, he was led by Odysseus to Troy, since, according to the prophecy of Helenus, that town could be taken only by a descendant of Aeacus. Here, like his father, he distinguished himself above all by a courage which none could withstand. He slew Eurypylus, son of Telephus, and was one of the heroes in the wooden horse, where he alone remained undaunted. Later legend depicts him as fierce and cruel: at the taking of Troy he killed the aged Priam at the altar of Zeus, hurled Hector's son, Astyanax, down from the walls, and offered up Polyxena upon his father's tomb. In Homer he arrives safely with much booty at Phthia, his father's home, and weds Menelaüs's daughter Hermioné, who was promised him during the siege of Troy (*Od.* iv. 5). Later legend represents him as accompanied by Andromaché, Hector's wife, who is allotted him as a part of his booty, and Helenus, and then, on the strength of a prophecy of Helenus, as going to Epirus and settling there. It was to a son of his by Lanassa, granddaughter of Heracles, that the later kings of Epirus traced back their descent, and accordingly styled themselves Aeacidae; while from his son by Andromaché, Molossus, the district of Molossia was said to derive its name (Pausan. i. 11). He afterwards went to Phthia, to reinstate his grandfather Peleus in his kingdom whence he had been expelled by Acastus and wedded Hermioné. He soon, however, met his death at Delphi, whither, according to one story, he had gone with dedicatory offerings, or, according to another, to plunder the temple of Apollo in revenge for his father's death. The accounts of his death vary, some attributing it to Orestes, the earlier lover of Hermioné; others to the Delphians, at the instance of the Pythian priestess; others again to a quarrel about the meat-offerings. The scene of his death was the altar, a coincidence which was regarded as a judgment for his murder of Priam. His tomb was within the precincts of the Delphic temple, and in later times he was worshipped as a hero with annual sacrifices by the Delphians, as he was said to have vouchsafed valuable assistance against the Gauls when they threatened the sacred spot (B.C. 279) (Pausan. x. 23). (2) A king of Epirus, father of Alexander I. and of Olympias, the mother of Alexander the Great. He died about B.C. 360. (3) A king of Epirus, the son of Alexander I. and grandson of the preceding (Plut. *Pyrr.*). (4) A general of Alexander the Great. He obtained the government of Armenia after Alexander's death. He was slain in battle by Eumenes (q. v.) (Plut. *Eum.* 4, 7). (5) A general of Mithridates (App. *Mith.* 17).

Neoterĭci and **Novelli.** A name applied to the minor poets who sprang up in great numbers during and after the reign of Hadrian and who wrote pretty little poems on trifling themes of no great merit. See Diomedes in the *Grammatici Latini* (Keil), i. 514 foll.; and Schultz in *Hermes*, xxii. 274; and Leo, ib. xxiv. 294.

Nepa. According to Festus, an African word, and equivalent to the Latin *sidus.* Cicero often employs it in his translation of Aratus, and it occurs in Manilius (ii. 32) and elsewhere. Plautus uses it (*Casin.* ii. 8, 7) for Cancer, and Cicero (*De Fin.* v. 15) for Scorpio. This latter writer, moreover, who, in his translation of Aratus, commonly employs *Nepa* in the sense of *Scorpio*, in one passage (v. 460) uses it in the sense of *Cancer.* In Columella, also (xi. 2, 30), *Nepa* occurs for *Cancer,* according to some, but perhaps with more correctness for *Scorpio.*

Nepĕté or **Nepé.** The modern Nepi. An ancient town of Etruria, situated near the Saltus Ciminius. It was an important strategic point (Livy, vi. 9).

Nephĕlé (Νεφάλη). Wife of Athamas and mother of Phrixus and Hellé. Hence Hellé is called by Ovid, Nepheleïs. See ATHAMAS.

Nepos. (1) CORNELIUS. A Roman historical writer, born in Northern Italy about B.C. 100. He was the friend of Cicero, Atticus, and of the poet Catullus, who dedicated to him a volume of poems. He died about B.C. 24. Besides erotic poems, three books of *Chronica*, five books of *Exempla* (probably an account of the men who were typical of the early Roman virtues), biographies of Cato and Cicero, and a geographical treatise, all of which, except a few fragments, are lost, he wrote a series of biographies in at least sixteen books (*De Viris Illustribus*), in which the lives of famous Greeks and Romans were narrated in parallel arrangement. Of this work there remain the part treating of foreign generals and the biographies of Cato and Atticus. The style of Nepos is not good, as it borders on the colloquial; but the biographies are of considerable historical value, as being fair, sympathetic, and well arranged. The best MS. of Nepos is the Codex Parcensis at Louvain, dating from the fifteenth century. Others of a greater age exist, but are of an inferior "family," and very corrupt. Principal editions are those of Lambinus (Paris, 1569); Bremi (4th ed. Zürich, 1827); Roth (Basel, 1841); with commentary by Nipperdey (Leipzig, 1849; rev. ed.

by Lupus, Berlin, 1879); Siebelis (11th ed. 1885); with index by Gitlbauer (Freiburg, 1883); Weidner (2d ed. Prague, 1888); with English notes by O. Browning (Oxford, 1868); and by Lindsay (last ed. New York, 1895). There is a lexicon in Halm's ed. by Haacke (9th ed. Leipzig, 1887), by Jahr in Andresen's ed. (Prague, 1884); and by Koch and Georges (5th ed. Hanover, 1885).

(2) IULIUS. A Roman emperor of the West, the last but one, reigning A.D. 474–475. He was placed on the throne by the Byzantine emperor Leo, the usurper Glycerius being deposed. Nepos, however, was, in his turn, soon deposed by his general Orestes, who soon crowned his own son Romulus Augustulus. Nepos went into exile in Dalmatia, where he was killed in A.D. 480.

Nepotiānus, FLAVIUS POPILIUS. A son of Eutropia, the half-sister of the emperor Constantine. He proclaimed himself emperor (A.D. 350) after the death of his cousin Constans, marched to Rome with a body of gladiators and other disreputable followers, defeated Anicetus, the praetorian prefect, and pillaged the city. He enjoyed his usurped power only twenty-eight days, at the end of which period he was defeated and slain by Marcellinus, one of the lieutenants of Magnentius.

Neptūnus. The Italian god of the sea, husband of Salacia, the goddess of salt water (Varro, *L. L.* v. 72), and identified by the Romans with the Greek Poseidon. This identification dated from B.C. 399, when a *lectisternium* (q. v.) was ordained in his honour by the Sibylline Books (Livy, v. 13). Like Poseidon, he was worshipped as god of the sea and of equestrian accomplishments. As such he had a temple in the Circus Flaminius, while in the Circus Maximus the old Italian god Consus had an altar in a similar capacity. In after-times Agrippa built a temple and portico to Neptune on the Field of Mars, in honour of his naval victory over Sextus Pompeius and Antonius. A festival of Neptune (Neptunalia), accompanied by games, was celebrated on July 23. The old harbour-god of the Romans was Portunus (q. v.). The original conception of Neptunus was of a god presiding over rivers and springs, as the early Romans had little to do with the sea. The wider view which made him primarily a sea-god is possibly due to the influence of the Etruscan religion in which Neptune (Nethuns) was so regarded. See POSEIDON.

Nereïd Monument. A sculptured temple at Xanthus in Lycia, discovered in 1838 by Sir Charles Fellows. The sculptures with which it was adorned are now in the British Museum. The name was given from ten draped female figures, whose moist, clinging garments and the accompanying sea-weed and shells led many archæologists to regard them as Nereïds. See Perry's *Greek and Roman Sculpture*, pp. 501 foll., where illustrations are given.

Nereïdes (Νηρηΐδες). The nymphs of the sea, daughters of Nereus (q. v.) and Doris. They were said to be fifty in number, though Propertius (iii. 5, 33) makes them a hundred. The best known were Amphitrîtê, wife of Poseidon, Thetis, Galatea, Doto, etc. They were originally represented as having sea-grown hair and descending into a fish-like form, like the mermaids of later times. See Pliny, *H. N.* ix. 4; and the articles NAIADES; NYMPHAE; OCEANIDES.

Nereïd. (Pompeii.)

Nerēïus. A name given by the poets to any descendant of Nereus, such as Phocus and Achilles.

Nerētum. Now Narbo; a town of the Salentini in Calabria.

Nereus (Νηρεύς). The eldest son of Pontus and Gaea, husband of Doris, daughter of Oceanus, father of fifty (according to a later account, a hundred) beautiful sea-nymphs, the Nereids. He is described as a venerable old man, of a kindly disposition towards mortals, and as dwelling in a resplendent cave in the depths of the Aegean. Like all gods of water, he had the gift of prophecy and of transforming himself into any shape he chose to assume. He was represented as an old man with the leaves of sea-weed for hair and a sceptre or trident. His daughters were likewise benevolent beings, well disposed to mortals (*Il.* xviii. 141; *Odyss.* xxiv. 58). The myths related of Nereus strongly suggest those told of Glaucus (q. v.) and Proteus (q. v.).

Nerĭcus. See LEUCAS.

Nerīnê. Equivalent to Nereïs, a daughter of Nereus. See NEREÏDES.

Nerio, Neriēnê or **Neriēnis.** See MARS.

Nerĭtos. A mountain in Ithaca, and also a small rocky island near Ithaca (Hom. *Odyss.* i. 21). The adjective Neritius is often used by the poets as equivalent to Ithacan or Odyssean.

Nerium Celtĭcum. A promontory of Spain, the same as Artabrum; now Cape Finisterre.

Nerius, GNAEUS. A Roman who accused P. Sestius of *vis* in the case defended by Cicero in his oration *Pro Sestio* (Cic. *Q. Fratr.* ii. 3, 5).

Nero. A Sabine word meaning "brave," cognate with ἀνήρ. (1) TIBERIUS, a son of Appius Claudius, from whom all the Claudii Nerones were descended. (2) A general in the Second Punic War, who defeated and slew the Carthaginian Hasdrubal at the battle of the Metaurus, thus probably saving Rome from capture (B.C. 207). (3) TIBERIUS, father of the emperor and a partisan of Iulius Caesar and afterwards of Antony. He surrendered his beautiful wife Livia (q. v.) to Octavianus (Augustus), who married her. Nero died soon after (Tac. *Ann.* i. 10; v. 1; Dio Cass. xlviii. 44). (4) CLAUDIUS CAESAR. The sixth of the Roman emperors, born at Antium, in Latium, A.D. 37, nine months after the death of Tiberius. He was the son of Domitius Ahenobarbus and Agrippina, the daughter of Germanicus, and was originally named Lucius Domitius. After the death of Ahenobarbus, and a second husband, Crispus Passienus, Agrippina married her uncle, the emperor Claudius, who gave his daughter Octavia in marriage to her son Lucius, and subsequently adopted him with the formal sanction of a *lex Curiata*.

The education of Nero was carefully attended to in his youth. He was placed under the care of the philosopher Seneca, and appears to have applied himself with considerable perseverance to study. He is said to have made great progress in Greek, of which he gave a specimen in his sixteenth year, by pleading in that tongue the rights of the Rhodians, and of the inhabitants of Ilium (Suet. *Nero*, 7; Tac. *Ann.* xii. 58). At the death of Claudius (A.D. 54), while Agrippina, by flatteries and lamentations, detained Britannicus, the son of Claudius and Messalina, within the palace, Nero, presenting himself before the gates, was lifted by the guard-in-waiting into the covered chariot used for the purpose of carrying in procession an elected emperor, and was followed by a multitude of the people, under the illusion that it was Britannicus. He entered the camp, promised a donative to the cohorts, was saluted emperor, and pronounced before the Senate, in honour of Claudius, a panegyric composed by his preceptor Seneca.

Coin of Nero.

Agrippina soon endeavoured to obtain the chief management of public affairs; and her vindictive and cruel temper would have hurried Nero, at the commencement of his reign, into acts of violence and bloodshed, if her influence had not been counteracted by Seneca and Burrus, to whom Nero had intrusted the government of the State. Through their counsels the first five years of Nero's reign were distinguished by justice and clemency; and an anecdote is related of him, that, having on one occasion to sign an order for the execution of a malefactor, he exclaimed, "Would that I could not write!" (Suet. *Nero*, 10). He discouraged public informers, refused the statues of gold and silver which were offered him by the Senate and people, and used every art to ingratiate himself with the latter. But his mother was enraged to find that her power over him became weaker every day, and that he constantly disregarded her advice and refused her requests. His neglect of his wife Octavia, and his criminal love of Acté, a woman of low birth, still farther widened the breach between him and his mother. She frequently addressed him in the most contemptuous language; reminded him that he owed his elevation solely to her, and threatened that she would inform the soldiers of the manner in which Claudius had met his end, and would call upon them to support the claims of Britannicus, the son of the late emperor. The threats of his mother only served to hasten the death of Britannicus, whose murder forms the commencement of that long catalogue of crimes which afterwards disgraced the reign of Nero. But while the management of public affairs appears, from the testimony of most historians, to have been wisely conducted by Burrus and Seneca, Nero indulged in private in dissipation and profligacy. He was accustomed, in company with other young men of his own age, to sally into the streets of Rome at night, in order to rob and maltreat passengers, and even to break into private houses and carry off the property of their owners. But these extravagances were comparatively harmless; his love for Poppaea, whom he had seduced from Otho, led him into more serious crimes. Poppaea, who was ambitious of sharing the imperial throne, perceived that she could not hope to attain her object while Agrippina was alive, and, accordingly, induced Nero to consent to the murder of his mother. The entreaties of Poppaea appear to have been supported by the advice of Burrus and Seneca; and the philosopher did not hesitate to justify the murder of a mother by her son (Tac. *Ann.* xiv. 11; Quint. viii. 5).

In the eighth year of his reign, Nero lost his best counsellor, Burrus; and Seneca had the wisdom to withdraw from the court, where his presence had become disliked, and where his enormous wealth was calculated to excite the envy even of the emperor. About the same time Nero divorced Octavia and married Poppaea, and soon after put to death the former on a false accusation of adultery and treason. In the tenth year of his reign (A.D. 64) Rome was almost destroyed by fire. Of the fourteen districts into which the city was divided, four only remained entire. The fire originated at that part of the Circus which was contiguous to the Palatine and Coelian Hills, and raged with the greatest fury for six days and seven nights; and, after it was thought to have been extinguished, it burst forth again, and continued for two days longer. Nero appears to have acted on this occasion with the greatest liberality and kindness; the city was supplied with provisions at a very moderate price; and the imperial gardens were thrown open to the sufferers, and buildings erected for their accommodation. But these acts of humanity and benevolence were insufficient to screen him from the popular suspicion. It was generally believed that he had set fire to the city himself, and some even reported that he had ascended the top of a high tower in order to witness the conflagration, where he amused himself with singing the "Destruction of Troy." From many circumstances, however, it appears improbable that Nero was guilty of this crime. His guilt, indeed, is asserted by Suetonius (*Nero*, 38) and Dio Cassius (lxii. 17), but Tacitus admits that he was not able to prove the truth of the accusation (*Ann.* xv. 38). In order, however, to remove the suspicions of the people, Nero spread a report that the Christians were the authors of the fire, and numbers of them, accordingly, were seized and put to death. Their execution served as an amusement to the people. Some were covered with skins of wild beasts, and were torn to pieces by dogs; others were crucified; and several were smeared with pitch and other combustible materials, and burned in the imperial gardens in the night: "Whence," says the historian, "pity arose

Nero. (Bust in the Louvre.)

and the Senate pronounced sentence of death against Nero, who had fled from Rome as soon as he heard of the revolt of the Praetorian Guards. Nero, however, anticipated the execution of the sentence which had been passed against him, by requesting one of his attendants to put him to death, after making an ineffectual attempt to do so with his own hands. He died A.D. 68, in the thirty-second year of his age, and the fourteenth of his reign. See the chapter in Baring-Gould's *Tragedy of the Caesars*, vol. ii. (1892).

Neronēa. A name given to Artaxata by Tiridates, who had been restored to his kingdom by Nero. See ARTAXATA.

Neronia. See QUINQUENNALIA.

Nertobrīga. (1) A city of Hispania Baetica, some distance to the west of Corduba. It was also called Concordia Iulia, and is now Valera la Vieja (Pliny, *H. N.* iii. 14). (2) A city of Hispania Tarraconensis, in the territory of the Celtiberi, between Bilbilis and Caesaraugusta. It is now Almuña.

for the guilty (though they deserved the severest punishments), since they were put to death, not for the public good, but to gratify the cruelty of a single man" (Tac. *Ann.* xv. 44).

In the following year (A.D. 65) a powerful conspiracy was formed for the purpose of placing Piso upon the throne, but it was discovered by Nero, and the principal conspirators were put to death. Among others who suffered on this occasion were Lucan and Seneca; but the guilt of the latter is doubtful. (See SENECA.) In the same year Poppaea died, in consequence of a kick which she received from her husband while she was in an advanced state of pregnancy. A long list of victims is to be found in the pages of the annalists. The distinguished general Domitius Corbulo, Thrasea Paetus, and Barea Soranus are among these.

During the latter part of his reign, Nero was principally engaged in amateur theatricals, and in contending for the prizes at the public games. He had previously appeared as an actor on the Roman stage; and he now visited in succession the chief cities of Greece, and received no less than 1800 crowns for his victories in the public Grecian games. He also began the canal across the Isthmus of Corinth, but ordered the work to be stopped (Dio Cass. lxiii. 6 foll.), leaving its completion to our own times (1893). On his return to Italy he entered Naples and Rome as a conqueror, and was received with triumphal honours. But while he was engaged in these extravagances, Vindex, who commanded the legions in Gaul, declared against his authority; and his example was speedily followed by Galba, who commanded in Spain. The praetorian cohorts espoused the cause of Galba,

Nerva. (1) MARCUS, the grandfather of the emperor Nerva. He was consul in A.D. 22, and starved himself to death in the year 33. He was a famous lawyer, and is often cited in the *Digest.* He also had charge of the public works under Tiberius, and originated the tunnel (Grotta di Posilipo) near Naples. (2) MARCUS, the son of the preceding and father of the emperor. He won distinction as a jurist, and is quoted in Gaius and the Digest under the name of Nerva Filius. (3) MARCUS COCCĒIUS. The thirteenth Roman emperor, was born at Narnia, in Umbria, A.D. 27 according to Eutropius (viii. 1), or A.D. 32 according to Dio Cassius (lxviii. 4). His family originally came from Crete; but several of his ancestors rose to the highest honours of the Roman State. His grandfather, Cocceius Nerva, who was consul A.D. 22, and a great favourite of the emperor Tiberius, was one of the most celebrated jurists of his age. Nerva is first mentioned in history as a favourite of Nero, who bestowed upon him triumphal honours, A.D. 66, when he was praetor elect. The poetry of Nerva, which is mentioned with praise by Pliny and Martial, appears to have recommended him to Nero; and he was employed in offices of trust and honour during the reigns of Vespasian and Titus, though he incurred the suspicion of Domitian, who banished him to Tarentum. On the assassination of Domitian, A.D. 96, Nerva succeeded to the sovereign power, through the influence of Petronius Secundus, commander of the praetorian cohorts, and of Parthenius, the chamberlain of the palace.

The mild and equitable administration of Nerva is acknowledged and praised by all ancient writers, and forms a striking contrast to the bloody reign of his predecessor. He discouraged informers, recalled the exiles from banishment, relieved the people from some oppressive taxes, and tolerated the Christians. Many instances of his liberality and clemency are recorded by the younger Pliny; he allowed no senator to be put to death during his reign; and he practised the greatest economy, in order to relieve the wants of the poorer citizens. But his impartial administration of justice met with little favour from the Praetorian Guard,

Nerva. (Bust in the Vatican.)

which had been allowed by Domitian to indulge in excesses of every kind. Enraged at the loss of their benefactor and favourite, they compelled Nerva to deliver into their hands Parthenius and their own commander Petronius, both of whom they put to death. The excesses of his guards convinced Nerva that the government of the Roman Empire required greater energy both of body and mind than he possessed, and he accordingly adopted Trajan as his successor, and associated him with himself in the sovereignty. Nerva died A.D. 98, after a reign of sixteen months and nine days. His life is sketched by Suetonius.

Nervii. A powerful and warlike people in Gallia Belgica, whose territory extended from the river Sabis (Sambre) to the ocean. Their chief towns were Bagacum (Bavia), Camaracum (Cambray), and Turnacum (Tournay) (Caes. *B. G.* v. 39). In B.C. 58 they were defeated by Iulius Caesar with terrible slaughter (Caes. *B. G.* ii. 15; v. 38; vi. 2).

Nervus. (1) (*ξύλον, ποδοκάκκη, χοῖνιξ*). A sort of stocks or pillory for the confinement of criminals and the punishment of refractory slaves. Festus speaks of it as confining both the neck and the feet; but its form is uncertain. All that is known is that it had a framework of wood, with holes for hands, neck, and feet. See Plaut. *Poen.* v. 4, 99; Gell. xx. 1; and Aristoph. *Eq.* 1047. (2) (*νεῦρον*). The string of a musical instrument. (3) A bowstring.

Nesis. The modern Nisita; a small island off the coast of Campania, between Puteoli and Neapolis. It was a favourite residence of the Roman nobles (Stat. *Silv.* iii. 1, 148).

Nessōnis (*Νεσσωνίς*). A lake in Thessaly, a little south of the river Peneus, usually reduced in summer to a mere marsh. The ancients regarded it as the remains of a vast body of water which they supposed to have at one time covered the whole of Thessaly and finally to have been drawn off through the vale of Tempê (Strabo, p. 430).

Nessotrophīum (*νησσοτροφεῖον*). A duck-yard with a pond (Varro, *R. R.* iii. 10).

Nessus (*Νέσσος*). A Centaur, who used to ferry travellers over the river Evenus. On attempting to outrage Deïanira, the wife of Heracles, he was shot by the latter with one of his poisoned arrows. Upon this he presented Deïanira with a portion of his poisoned blood, professedly to enable her to regain her husband's affections, should he prove false to her. A robe smeared with this blood proved fatal to Heracles, as related in the article HERACLES, p. 792. See Sophocles, *Trachiniae*, 558, 1141.

Nestor (*Νέστωρ*). Son of Neleus and Chloris, ruler of the Messenian and Triphylian Pylus, and later also, after the extinction of the royal family there, of Messenia. He was married to Eurydicé, by whom he had seven sons and two daughters. He was the only one of twelve sons of Neleus who escaped being slain by Heracles, since he was, it is said, living at the time among the Gerenians in Messenia, from whom he derives the name *Γερήνιος*, given him in Homer. After this disaster, the king of the Epeans, Augeas, illegally kept back a four-horse chariot which Neleus had sent to Elis to compete in a contest. Nestor, as yet hardly a youth, retaliated by driving off the herds of the Epeans; upon which the latter with a large army besieged the Pylian fortress of Thyroessa on the Eurotas. Nestor formed one of the relieving army, serving as a foot-soldier, owing to his father's having, from regard to his youth, had the war-horses concealed from him. He slew in battle Augeas's son-in-law, and, fighting from the dead man's chariot, won a most brilliant victory, so that the Pylians offered thanks to him among men just as they offered them to Zeus among the gods. In like manner in the war against the Arcadians, when he was the youngest of all the combatants, he killed the gigantic and much-dreaded hero Ereuthalion. He also took an important part in the battle between the Centaurs and the Lapithae, and is mentioned as among the Argonauts (Val. Flac. i. 380). In old age, when he was ruling over the third generation of his people, he was involved in the expedition against Troy, owing, as the story went, to the obligation incurred by his son Antilochus as a suitor of Helen; with Odysseus he gained the help of Achilles and Patroclus for the undertaking, and himself sailed, in the company of his sons Antilochus and Thrasymedes, with ninety ships to the seat of war at Ilium. Here, according to Homer, "Nestor the horseman," in spite of his great age, took a prominent part among the heroes in council and battle alike: the qualities which adorned him were wisdom, justice, eloquence, "from his lips flows language sweeter than honey" (*Il.* i. 248), experience in war, unwearied activity, and courage. All valued and loved him, and none more than Agamemnon, who wished that he had ten such counsellors: in which case, he said, Troy would soon fall (*Il.* ii. 372). He is so great a favourite with Homer that in ancient times it was conjectured that the poet was himself a native of Pylos. After the destruction of Troy he returned in safety with his son Thrasymedes to Pylos, Antilochus (q. v.) having for the sake of his father, who was in sore peril, sacrificed his own life in battle against Memnon. Ten years afterwards, Telemachus found him still at Pylos, amidst his children, in the enjoyment of a cheerful and prosperous old age. On the "cup of Nestor," see TOREUTICÉ.

Nestorĭdes (Νεστορίδης). A patronymic applied to a son of Nestor—e. g. Antilochus or Pisistratus.

Nestorius (Νεστόριος). A native of Germanicia in Northern Syria, who from his eminence as a zealous and eloquent priest was made Patriarch of Constantinople (A.D. 428). He is famous for his views on the divine and human natures of Christ, and by his connection with the sect that took his name. He held that the Virgin was the mother of Christ (Χριστοτόκος), and that while the divinity of the Word (λόγ s) is to be distinguished from the temple of his flesh enshrining it, yet there still remained but one true Person. His opponents charged him, however, with teaching the doctrine of a duality of Persons—the human person of Christ and the divine person of the Logos. He was denounced by Cyril of Alexandria in twelve anathemas, and at a grand council held at Ephesus in A.D. 431, Nestorius was condemned and deposed. He died in exile somewhere in Egypt, the date and place of his death being alike unknown. See Anderson's *Oriental Churches* (1872).

Nestus (Νέστος), sometimes **Nessus**. A river in Thrace, rising in Mount Rhodopé, and falling into the Aegean Sea opposite the island of Thasos. The Nestus formed the eastern boundary of Macedonia from the time of Philip and Alexander the Great.

Nesus. The fortress of Oeniadae. See OENIADAE.

Net. See RETÉ.

Netum (Νέητον). A town in Sicily, southwest of Syracuse.

Neuri (Νεῦροι, Νευροί). A people of Sarmatia Europaea, to the northwest of the sources of the Tyras (Dniester). See Herod. iv. 17, 51, 100, 125.

Neuron. See NERVUS.

Neurospasta. A doll worked by wires. See PUPA.

Nevirnum. See NOVIODUNUM.

New Academy, also called the THIRD ACADEMY. The form which the Academic philosophy of Plato received at the hands of Carneades. (See CARNEADES.) It was largely skeptical in its teaching, denying the possibility of aiming at absolute truth or at any certain criterion of truth. Carneades argued that if there were any such criterion it must exist in reason (λόγος) or sensation (*αἴσθησις*) or conception (*φαντασία*); but as reason depends on conception and this in turn on sensation, and as we have no means of deciding whether our sensations really correspond to the objects that produce them, the basis of all knowledge is always uncertain. Hence, all that we can attain to is a high degree of probability, which we must accept as the nearest possible approximation to the truth. The New Academy teaching is in the nature of modern agnosticism, and represents the spirit of an age when religion was decaying, and philosophy itself, losing its earnest and serious spirit, was becoming merely a vehicle for rhetoric and dialectical ingenuity. Cicero's speculative philosophy was in the main in accord with the teachings of Carneades, looking rather to the probable (*illud probabile*) than to certain truth. See his *Academica*.

Newspapers. See ACTA.

Nexum. In the old Roman legal system *nexum* was the solemn process of entering upon a relationship of debtor and creditor under the form of *mancipatio* (q. v.). In the formula used therein the borrower gave the lender, in case of non-fulfilment of the obligation incurred, the right to seize him (cf. MANUS INIECTIO) without more ado as his bondsman, since he stood in the position of a defendant against whom judgment had already been given (*iudicatus*), or who had admitted his liability in open court (*in iure confessus*). There was no limit in respect of time to the right of the creditor over a debtor whose person thus became forfeit to him: it consisted in the fact that the creditor could keep the *nexus* in his private dungeon and make him work as a slave for him. The latter, however, continued to be a citizen; but, as long as the debt existed, was considered dishonoured, and was accordingly excluded from service in the legion and voting in the assemblies of the people. After the Lex Poetilia Papiria of B.C. 326 had, in the interest of the plebeians, for the most part abolished personal security, the *nexum* gradually passed into a mere contract of loan. Varro defines it as *quodcumque per aes et libram geritur* (*L. L.* vii. 105).

In Nettleship's *Lectures and Essays*, pp. 363–66 (Oxford, 1885), there is a note which attempts to show that the proper meaning of *nexum* is "a thing pledged (bound)," and of *nexus* (second declension), "a prisoner"; that the evidence for making *nexum* mean "a solemn process" is weak; and that *nexus -ūs* is the proper word for the contract or bond between debtor and creditor. In almost all the passages where *nexum -i* is supposed to mean "a process," it might as well come from *nexus* (fourth declension). Cicero, however, in the oration *Pro Caecina* 102, has *nexa atque hereditates;* and in *De Rep.* ii. 59, *propter unius libidinem omnia nexa civium liberata nectierque postea desitum.* See Bachofen, *Das Nexum* (1843); Huschke, *Ueber das Recht des Nexum* (1846); and Giraud, *Des "Nexi,"* etc. (1847).

Nicaea (Νικαία). (1) A celebrated city of Asia, situated on the eastern side of Lake Ascania (Isnik) in Bithynia, built (about B.C. 300) by Antigonus, king of Asia, and originally called Antigonea; but Lysimachus soon after changed the name into Nicaea, in honour of his wife. Under the kings of Bithynia it was often the royal residence; and under the Romans it continued to be one of the chief cities of Asia; and at the time of the Byzantine emperors it was a great military outpost of Constantinople against the Turks. It fell in A.D.

1330, being taken by the Turk Orchan, the son of Ottoman. The great double walls of the ancient city still exist, and there are ruins of an aqueduct, a theatre, a gymnasium, and the two moles of the ancient harbour. It is famous in ecclesiastical history as the seat of the great Oecumenical Council which Constantine convoked in A.D. 325, chiefly for the decision of the Arian controversy, and which drew up the Nicene Creed. See Stanley's *History of the Eastern Church* (1861). The modern name is Isnik (εἰς Νίκαιαν). (2) A fortress of the Epicnemidian Locrians on the sea, near the pass of Thermopylae, which it commanded. (3) The modern Nizza or Nice; a city on the coast of Liguria, to the east of the river Var; a colony of Massilia, and subject to that city.

Nicander (Νίκανδρος). (1) A king of Sparta, father of Theopompus. He reigned about B.C. 809–770. (2) A Greek poet, born at Colophon, in Asia, about B.C. 150. He was an hereditary priest of Apollo, as well as a physician, and lived a great deal in Aetolia as well as later in Pergamum. He wrote numerous works, such as those on agriculture, of which considerable fragments are still preserved, and on mythological metamorphoses (used by the Roman poet Ovid). Two of his poems, written in a dull and bombastic manner, are still extant: the Θηριακά, on remedies against the wounds inflicted by venomous animals; and the Ἀλεξιφάρμακα, on poisons taken in food and drink, with their antidotes. These poems are edited by Schneider, and revised by Keil (1856).

Nicānor (Νικάνωρ). (1) A Macedonian officer of Alexander the Great, who, on the death of Perdiccas, received the government of Cappadocia. Antigonus made him governor of Media and its adjacent provinces, but in 312 he was deposed by Seleucus. (2) A Macedonian officer under Cassander, by whom he was secretly despatched, immediately on the death of Antipater in B.C. 319, to take the command of the Macedonian garrison at Munychia. Nicanor arrived at Athens before the news of Antipater's death, and thus readily obtained possession of the fortress. Soon afterwards he surprised the Piraeus also, and placed both fortresses in the hands of Cassander on the arrival of the latter in Attica in 318. Nicanor was afterwards despatched by Cassander with a fleet to the Hellespont, where he gained a victory over the admiral of Polysperchon. On his return to Athens he incurred the suspicion of Cassander, and was put to death (Diod. xviii. 64 foll.; Plut. *Phoc.* 33).

Nicarchus (Νίκαρχος). A writer to whom are ascribed thirty-eight epigrams in the Greek Anthology. Of his personality nothing is known.

Nicātor (Νικάτωρ—i. e. "Victor"). A surname assumed by Seleucus I., the founder of the Syrian monarchy. See SELEUCUS.

Nicephorium (Νικηφόριον). (1) A fortified town of Mesopotamia, on the Euphrates, and due south of Edessa, built by order of Alexander the Great, and probably completed under Seleucus. It is identical with CALLINĪCUS. Still later it was called LEONTOPŎLIS. (2) A fortress on the Propontis.

Nicephorius (Νικηφόριος). A river of Armenia Maior, on which Tigranes built his residence Tigranocerta. It was a tributary of the Upper Tigris, probably identical with the CENTRĪTES, or a small tributary of it.

Nicephŏrus (Νικηφόρος). (1) CALLISTUS XANTHOPŪLUS, the author of an ecclesiastical history, was born in the latter part of the thirteenth century, and died about 1450. His ecclesiastical history was originally in twenty-three books, of which there are eighteen extant, extending from the birth of Christ down to the death of the tyrant Phocas, in 610. Although Nicephorus compiled from the works of his predecessors, he entirely remodelled his materials, and his style is vastly superior to that of his contemporaries. (2) GREGŎRAS. (See GREGORAS.) (3) PATRIARCHA, originally the notary or chief secretary of state to the emperor Constantine V. Copronymus, subsequently retired into a convent, and was raised to the patriarchate of Constantinople in 806. He was deposed in 815, and died in 828. Several of his works have come down to us, of which the most important is entitled *Breviarium Historicum*, a Byzantine history, extending from 602 to 770, and one of the best works of the Byzantine period. It is edited by Gedner (1832).

Nicer. Now the Neckar, a river in Germany falling into the Rhine at Mannheim (Auson. *Mosell.* 423).

Nicētas (Νικήτας). (1) EUGENIĀNUS, author of one of the poorest of the Greek romances that have come down to us. He appears to have lived not long after Theodore Prodromus, whom, according to the title of his work as given in a Paris manuscript, he selected for his model. He wrote of the loves of Drosilla and Chariclea. Boissonade gave to the world an edition of this romance, published in 1819 at Paris (2 vols.). (2) ACOMINĀTUS, surnamed CHONIĀTES, from his having been born at Chonae, or Colossae, in Phrygia. He filled many posts of distinction at Constantinople, under the emperor Isaac II. (Angelus). About A.D. 1189 he was appointed by the same monarch governor of Philippopolis, an office of which Alexius V. deprived him. He died A.D. 1216 at Nicaea, in Bithynia, to which city he had fled after the taking of Constantinople by the Latins. He wrote a history of the Byzantine emperors, in twenty-one books, commencing A.D. 1118 and ending A.D. 1206. It is edited by Bekker (1835) and Migne (1865). (3) An ecclesiastical writer, who flourished during the latter half of the eleventh century. He was at first bishop of Serrae in Macedonia (whence he is sometimes surnamed Serrariensis), and afterwards metropolitan of Heraclea, in Thrace. He is known by his commentary on sixteen discourses of St. Gregory Nazianzen and by other works connected with theology and sacred criticism. He was the author, likewise, of some grammatical productions, of which, however, only a small remnant has come down to us, in the shape of a treatise, "On the Names of the Gods" (Εἰς τὰ Ὀνόματα τῶν Θεῶν), edited by Creuzer (Leipzig, 1817).

Niceterium (νικητήριον). A badge or reward of victory, worn on the breast or neck (Juv. iii. 68). It was not, as Rich appears to think, of a military character, but denoted athletic prowess, like the modern medals given in amateur contests.

Nicia. A small river of Cisalpine Gaul, rising in the territory of the Ligures Apuani and falling into the Po at Brixellum. The Aemilian Way crossed it a little before Tanetum.

Nicias (Νικίας) (1) An Athenian general who was a man of birth and fortune; but one in whom a generous temper, popular manners, and considerable political and military talent were marred by unreasonable diffidence and an excessive dread of responsibility. Nicias, however, signalized himself on several occasions He took the island of Cythera from the Lacedaemonians, subjugated many cities of Thrace which had revolted from the Athenian sway, shut up the Megarians within their city-walls, cutting off all communications from without, and taking their harbour Nisaea. When the unfortunate expedition against Syracuse was undertaken by Athens, Nicias was one of the three commanders who were sent at its head, the other two being Alcibiades and Lamachus. He had previously, however, used every effort to prevent his countrymen from engaging in this affair, on the ground that they were only wasting their resources in distant warfare and multiplying their enemies. After the recall of Alcibiades, the natural indecision of Nicias, increased by ill-health and dislike of his command, proved a principal cause of the failure of the enterprise. In endeavouring to retreat by land from before Syracuse, the Athenian commanders, Nicias and Demosthenes (the latter had come with re-enforcements), were pursued, defeated, and compelled to surrender. The generals were put to death (B.C. 414); their soldiers were confined at first in the quarry of Epipolae, and afterwards sold as slaves. There is a life of Nicias by Plutarch. (2) An Athenian painter, a son of Nicomedes, and a pupil of Euphranor's pupil Antidotus. He lived during the latter half of the fourth century B.C., and was a younger contemporary of Praxiteles. The latter, when asked which of his works in marble he specially approved, was in the habit of answering, "Those that have been touched by the hand of Nicias"—such importance did he attribute to that artist's method of tinting, or "touching up with colour," *circumlitio* (Pliny, *H. N.* xxxv. 133). He painted mainly in encaustic, and was especially distinguished by his skill in making the figures on his pictures appear to stand out of the work by means of a proper treatment of light and shade. He was celebrated for his painting of female figures and other subjects which were favourable to the full expression of dramatic emotions, such as the rescue of Andromeda and the questioning of the dead by Odysseus in the lower world. This latter picture he presented to the city of his birth, after Ptolemy I. had offered sixty talents (about $60,000) for it (Pliny, *H. N.* xxxv. §§ 130–133). He insisted on the importance of an artist's choosing noble themes, such as cavalry engagements and battles at sea, instead of frittering away his skill on birds and flowers (Demet. *De Elocutione*, 76). (3) The younger, an Athenian painter, son of Nicomedes, and pupil of Euphranor. He began to practise his art about B.C. 320. Nicias is said to have been the first artist who used burnt ochre in his paintings (Pliny, *H. N.* xxxv. 6, 20). (4) The physician of Pyrrhus, king of Epirus, who offered to poison that monarch for a sum of money to be paid by the Romans. The Roman general, Fabricius, rejected this offer with scorn, and delivered Nicias over to Pyrrhus (Gell. iii. 8).

Niche. See AEDICULA.

Nicknames. See NOMEN.

Nico. An architect and geometrician, father of Galen, who lived in the beginning of the second century of the Christian era (Suid. s. v. Γαληνός).

Nicochăres (Νικοχάρης). An Athenian poet of the Old Comedy, and contemporary with Aristophanes.

Nicŏcles (Νικοκλῆς). (1) A king of Paphos, in the island of Cyprus. He owed his throne to the kindness of Ptolemy I., king of Egypt, who continued thereafter to bestow upon him many marks of favour. Having learned, however, at last, that Nicocles had formed an alliance with Antigonus, Ptolemy sent two emissaries to Cyprus, with orders to despatch Nicocles in case his treachery should be clearly proved. These persons, having taken with them a party of soldiers, surrounded the palace of the king of Paphos, and compelled him to destroy himself, although he protested his innocence (B.C. 310). His wife Axiothea, when she heard of her husband's death, killed her daughters with her own hand, and then slew herself. The other female relatives followed her example. The brothers of Nicocles also, having shut themselves up in the palace, set fire to it, and then fell by their own hands (Diod. Sic. xx. 21). (2) King of Salamis, in Cyprus, succeeding his father Evagoras B.C. 374. He celebrated the funeral obsequies of his parent with great splendour, and engaged Isocrates to write his eulogy. (See ISOCRATES.) (3) A tyrant of Sicyon, deposed by Aratus in B.C. 251.

Nicocreon (Νικοκρέων). A tyrant of Cyprus in the age of Alexander the Great. A fabulous story is related of his having caused the philosopher Anaxarchus to be pounded alive in a mortar (Diod. xix. 59–79; Cic. Tusc. ii. 22, 52; Diog. Laërt. ix. 59).

Nicolāus (Νικόλαος). (1) Called DAMASCĒNUS. A Greek historian of Damascus. At the suggestion of the Jewish king, Herod the Great, whose intimate friend he was, and who had recommended him to Augustus (B.C. 6), he wrote an autobiography, of which fragments remain; a comprehensive history of the world down to his own times in 144 books, which is partly preserved in fragments exhibiting an agreeable style. A portion of his panegyrical biography of Augustus has come down to us. The remains of Nicolaüs are edited by Dindorf in the *Hist. Graeci* (1870). See Steinmetz, *Herod und Nicolaus* (1861). (2) Called CHALCOCONDȲLES, a Byzantine historian of the fifteenth century A.D., who wrote a history of the Empire from 1298 to 1463, including the capture of Constantinople (1453). It is in ten books.

Nicomăchus (Νικόμαχος). (1) A scribe at Athens, who, in transcribing the laws of Solon, altered them for a bribe (Xen. *Hellen.* i. 7, 35). (2) A Greek painter, probably of Thebes, about B.C. 360. He was celebrated as an artist who could paint with equal rapidity and excellence, and was regarded as rivalling the best painters of his day. A famous painting of his was "The Rape of Persephoné" (Pliny, *H. N.* xxxv. 108). (3) The father of Aristotle (q. v.). (4) The son of Aristotle, by a slave-girl, Herpyllis. He wrote some philosophical works; and some of Aristotle's writings are called the *Nicomachean Ethics* (Ἠθικὰ Νικομάχεια). (See ARISTOTELES.) (5) Of Gerasa, in Arabia, a follower of the Pythagorean philosophy, about A.D. 150. He composed an introduction to mathematics in two books and a hand-book on harmony, of which only the first book is preserved entire, the second consisting of two fragments, which cannot be said, with certainty, to come from Nicomachus. The first-mentioned work gives valuable information as regards the arithmetic of the Greeks in earlier times. It was translated into Latin by Boëtius, and has been edited by Hoche (1863). The musical work was edited by Meibomius (Amst. 1652).

Nicomēdes (Νικομήδης). (1) NICOMĒDES I., king of Bithynia, was the eldest son of Zipoetes, whom he succeeded, B.C. 278. With the aid of the Gauls, whom he invited into Asia, he defeated and put to death his brother Zipoetes, who had for some time held the independent sovereignty of a considerable part of Bithynia. The rest of his reign appears to have been undisturbed, and under his sway Bithynia rose to a high degree of power and prosperity. He founded the city of Nicomedia, which he made the capital of his kingdom. The length of his reign is uncertain, but he probably died about 250. He was succeeded by his son Zielas. (2) NICOMĒDES II., surnamed EPIPHĂNES, king of Bithynia, reigned B.C. 149–91. He was the son and successor of Prusias II., and fourth in descent from the preceding. He was brought up at Rome, where he succeeded in gaining the favour of the Senate. Prusias, in consequence, became jealous of his son, and sent secret instructions for his assassination. The plot was revealed to Nicomedes, who thereupon returned to Asia, and declared open war against his father. Prusias was deserted by his subjects, and was put to death by order of his son, B.C. 149. Of the long and tranquil reign of Nicomedes, few events have been transmitted to us. He courted the friendship of the Romans, whom he assisted in the war against Aristonicus, 131. He subsequently obtained possession of Paphlagonia, and attempted to gain Cappadocia by marrying Laodicé, the widow of Ariarathes VI. He was, however, expelled from Cappadocia by Mithridates; and he was also compelled by the Romans to abandon Paphlagonia, when they deprived Mithridates of Cappadocia. (3) NICOMĒDES III., surnamed PHILOPATOR, king of Bithynia (B.C. 91–74), son and successor of Nicomedes II. Immediately after his accession, he was expelled by Mithridates, who set up against him his brother Socrates; but he was restored by the Romans in the following year (90). At the instigation of the Romans, Nicomedes now proceeded to attack the dominions of Mithridates, who expelled him a second time from his kingdom (88). This was the immediate occasion of the First Mithridatic War, at the conclusion of which (84) Nicomedes wăs again reinstated in his kingdom. He reigned nearly ten years after this second restoration. He died at the beginning of B.C. 74, and, having no children, by his will bequeathed his kingdom to the Roman people. (4) A geometrician famous for the invention of the "conchoid curve," much used by the ancients in solid geometry. See Ball's *Short History of Mathematics*, p. 78 (London, 1888).

Nicomedīa (Νικομήδεια). A celebrated city of Bithynia, built by King Nicomedes I. (B.C. 264), at the northeastern corner of the Sinus Astacenus. Under the Romans it was a colony, and a favourite residence of several of the later emperors, especially of Diocletian and Constantine the Great. It is memorable in history as the scene of Hannibal's death, and was the birthplace of the historian Arrian.

Nicon (Νίκων). A citizen of Tarentum, who betrayed his native city to Hannibal (B.C. 212). When the Romans retook the place, he was put to death (B.C. 209). See Livy, xxv. 8; Polyb. viii. 26.

Niconia or **Niconium**. A town in Scythia on the right bank of the Tyras (Dniester).

Nicopŏlis (Νικόπολις). A city at the southwestern extremity of Epirus, on the point of land which forms the north entrance to the Gulf of Ambracia, opposite to Actium. It was built by Augustus in memory of the victory (νίκη) of Actium, and was peopled from Ambracia, Anactorium, and other neighbouring cities, and also with settlers from Aetolia. (See ACTIUM.) There were cities of the same name in Moesia Inferior, Armenia Minor, Cilicia, Lower Egypt (now Kars), and Thrace.

Nicostrătus (Νικόστρατος). One of the sons of Aristophanes, and ranked among the poets of the Middle Comedy. The titles of some of his own and his brothers' comedies are preserved in Athenaeus (pp. 108, 118, 230, 597). The names of his brothers were Araros and Philippus.

Niebuhr, BARTHOLD GEORG. A great historian and critic, born at Copenhagen, August 27, 1776. He studied at the Universities of Kiel and Göttingen, and entered the Danish public service in 1796, holding various offices. In 1806 he removed to Berlin, where he served the Prussian governor in the bureau of finance; but owing to various personal disputes resigned, and in 1810 was made Historiographer to the King of Prussia, delivering in the same year the first of a course of lectures in the newly founded University of Berlin. The subject of this course was the early history of Rome, and his treatment of the subject was so new, so brilliant, and so profoundly learned as to excite widespread notice. He applied to the hitherto accepted narrative the laws of evidence and the searching methods of historical research, demonstrating that the whole account of the founding and the early regal period is purely mythical and legendary. This demonstration he elaborated more fully in his *Römische Geschichte*, 3 vols. (1811–32), which carries the story of Rome down to the First Punic War. The negative and destructive part of his work has completely revolutionized the views of Rome's historians, so that all writers now accept the view of Niebuhr in the main as sound; his constructive work, however, has been generally rejected, especially his "epic hypothesis," which traces the source of the Roman legends to ballads and sagas which he assumes to have existed. Niebuhr inaugurated a new epoch in the study of history by establishing and demonstrating a fundamental difference between legend and history, and his critical methods have been universally adopted as sound.

Barthold Georg Niebuhr.

Niebuhr's later life was one of great activity. From 1816–22 he served as Prussian ambassador to the papal court at Rome; and in the latter year accepted a call to the chair of History in the University of Bonn. Here he founded the *Rheinisches Museum* (1827), and took part with Bekker in the publication of the *Corpus Scriptorum Historiae Byzantinae*, besides issuing *Kleine historische und philologische Schriften*, 2 vols. (1828), an edition of Fronto (1816), and *Griechische Heroengeschichte* (1842). His Roman history has been translated into English by Hare, Thirlwall, and Smith, and a volume of lectures on Roman history appeared in 1850, edited by Leonhard Schmitz. Dr. Schmitz also published English editions of Niebuhr's lectures on ancient history (1852), and on ancient ethnography and geography (1853). See Winkworth, *Life and Letters of Niebuhr*, 3 vols. (London, 1852); Eyssenhardt, *Barthold Georg Niebuhr* (Gotha, 1886); and Bursian, *Geschichte der class. Philologie in Deutschland*, pp. 647–663 (Munich, 1883).

Niger, Nigir, Nigris (Νίγειρ, Νίγιρ). A great river of Aethiopia Interior, which modern usage has identified with the river called Joli-ba (i. e. Great River) and Niger in West Africa. Many of the ancients imagined the Niger to be a branch of the Nile (Pliny, *H. N.* v. 30; viii. 77). Ptolemy states that a branch of the Niger communicated with Lake Libya (probably Lake Tchad), and mentions a city Thamondocana (Timbuctoo?) as situated on the river itself (Ptol. iv. 6, 14). The name seems to be based upon an African word *geir*, *gar*, or *jir*, "river." See AFRICA.

Niger, GAIUS PESCENNIUS. A Roman of humble origin, but one whose great military talents recommended him successively to the notice of Marcus Aurelius, Commodus, and Pertinax, by whom he was employed in offices of trust and honour. He was consul together with Septimius Severus, and obtained the government of Syria. On the murder of Pertinax, A.D. 193, the Empire was exposed for sale by the Praetorian Guards, and was purchased by Didius Iulianus, whom the Senate was compelled to acknowledge as emperor. The people, however, did not tamely submit to this indignity, and three generals, at the head of their respective legions—Septimius Severus, who commanded in Pannonia; Clodius Albinus in Britain, and Pescennius Niger in Syria—refused to acknowledge the nomination of the Praetorians, and each claimed the Empire. Of these Niger was the most popular, and his cause was warmly espoused by all the provinces of the East. But instead of hastening to Italy, he quietly remained at Antioch, while Severus marched to Rome, dethroned Didius, and made active preparations for prosecuting the war against Niger in Asia. Roused at length from his inactivity, Niger crossed over to Europe, and established his headquarters at Byzantium; but he had scarcely arrived at this place, before his troops in Asia were defeated near Cyzicus by the generals of Severus. He was soon, however, able to collect another army, which he commanded in person; but, being defeated successively near Nicaea and at Issus, he abandoned his troops and fled towards the Euphrates, with the intention of seeking refuge among the Parthians. Before he could reach the Euphrates, he was overtaken by a detachment of the enemy, and put to death on the spot (Spartian. *Vit. Nig.*; Eutrop. viii. 10).

Night, GODDESS OF. See NYX.

Nigidius Figŭlus, PUBLIUS. See FIGULUS.

Nigir. See NIGER.

Nigrītae (Νιγρῖται). An African people dwelling on the banks of the Niger (Ptol. iv. 6, 16).

Nigrītis Lacus (Νιγρῖτις λίμνη). An African lake probably the same as Lake Debu, south of Timbuctoo. Ptolemy incorrectly regards it as the source of the Niger (iv. 6, 27).

Niké (Νίκη). The Greek goddess of victory, according to Hesiod, daughter of Pallas and Styx, by whom she was brought to Zeus to assist him in his struggle with the Titans; thenceforward she remained always with Zeus on Olympus. She is the sister of Zelos (zeal), Cratos (power), and Bia (force). Sculptors often represent her in connection with divinities who grant victory: thus the Olympian Zeus and the Athené on the Acropolis at Athens held in one hand a statue of Niké. She was generally represented as winged and with a wreath and a palm-branch. As herald of victory she also bore the wand of Hermes. This mode of representing her was adopted for the statues of the goddess specially revered by the Romans under the name Victoria. Vica Pota ("Victorious Issue") was an earlier designation of the same goddess. Such statues were erected chiefly on the Capitol by triumphant generals. The most famous was the statue, brought from Tarentum and therefore probably the work of a Greek artist, which Augustus dedicated to her in the Curia Iulia, in memory of his victory at Actium. When the Curia Iulia had been destroyed by fire in the reign of Titus and rebuilt by Domitian, the statue was placed in the new building, and was adored as the guardian goddess of the Senate until Christianity became the religion of the Empire. Athené was also styled Niké as giving victory, and the Niké Apteros or Wingless Victory, to whom the famous temple at Athens was built (see illustration on p. 1097), was Athené, she being thus distinguished from Niké proper, who was conventionally represented with wings. See Baudrillart, *Les Divinités de la Victoire en Grèce et en Italie* (Paris, 1894).

Nilupŏlis (Νείλου πόλις) or **Nilus** (Νεῖλος). A city of Middle Egypt in the Nomos Heracleopolites, built on an island of the Nile. There was a temple here in which the Nile was worshipped.

Nilus (Νεῖλος). The Nile, a great river of Egypt. The name is probably cognate with the Semitic *Nahar* or *Nahal*, "river." Homer calls it Αἴγυπτος (*Od.* iv. 477); and the name Νεῖλος occurs first in Hesiod (*Theog.* 338) and Hecataeus (*Frag.* 279). The Jews called it Nahal-Misraim, "River of Egypt." The Nile takes its rise in the two lakes Victoria Nyanza and Albert Nyanza, which are themselves fed by various streams. For three hundred miles after leaving the former, it flows with a swift current in rapids and cataracts and between high walls of rock. It leaves the northern end of Lake Albert Nyanza, where it is known as the Bahr-el-Jebel, and flows in a northerly course towards the Mediterranean Sea. The first six score miles are through a level country, then for another equal distance is contracted into a narrow stream (in places not more than a quarter of a mile in width), and then, being forced over the Yarbovah Rapids, it enters the plains and flows in a sluggish stream to Khartoum, distant some 800 miles. In

Temple of Niké Apteros. (Acropolis at Athens.)

7° 30′ north latitude it divides into two streams, the so-called White Nile (Bahr-el-Abiad) and the Bahr-el-Jebel. In 9° 30′ north latitude the latter receives the Bahr-el-Ghazal from the west. At Khartoum (15° 37′ north latitude) the White Nile and the Blue Nile (Bahr-el-Azrak) unite, and the great stream then flows on, taking up the Black Nile (Bahr-el-Aswad), whose black sediment makes the Delta so remarkable for its fertility. The point of junction is the apex of the island Meroë, where the river has a breadth of two miles. Thence it flows through Nubia in a rocky valley, falling over six cataracts, the northernmost being known as the First Cataract, and marking now, as in antiquity, the southern boundary of Egypt. See AEGYPTUS.

The Nile emptied into the Mediterranean by three channels, parted into seven, of which, according to Herodotus, two were artificial and five natural. From these seven channels come the names applied to it by Moschus (ἑπτάπορος), Catullus (*septemgeminus*), and Ovid (*septemplex*). Most of the seven mouths had names derived from their cities (i. e.

View on the Nile. (From a photograph.)

the Canopic, Bolbitic, Sebennytic, Pathmetic or Bucolic, Mendesian, Tanitic or Saïtic, and Pelusiac). At the present time there are only two principal mouths, known as the Rosetta on the west and the Damiat on the east. From the dark sediment deposited by the river came the native name of Egypt—Chemi or Kemi, "the black land." A great artificial canal (Bahr-Yussouf, i.e. "Joseph's Canal") runs parallel to the river, at the distance of about six miles, from Diospolis Parva in the Thebais to a point on the west mouth of the river about half-way between Memphis and the sea. Many smaller canals were cut to regulate the irrigation of the country. A canal from the east mouth of the Nile to the head of the Red Sea was commenced under the native kings, and finished by Darius, son of Hystaspes. There were several lakes in the country, respecting which see BUTO, MAREOTIS, MOERIS, SIRBONIS, and TANIS. For the use of the Nile in irrigation, see AEGYPTUS, p. 24.

The ancients knew little of the Nile beyond the First Cataract at Meroë. It was generally believed that the great river originated in Mauretania and flowed for a long distance underground until it came to the southern part of Aethiopia, whence it flowed northward as the Astapas. The emperor Nero undertook to discover its sources, and sent out two expeditions for that purpose, which succeeded only in reaching the confluence of the Sobat and the White Nile, some thirty miles beyond the junction of the White Nile with the Bahr-el-Zereb. Ptolemy, however, speaks of the river as issuing from two great lakes six and seven degrees respectively south of the equator, and fed by the melting snows of the Mountains of the Moon, lately identified by Stanley with Gordon Bennett, Ruwenzovi, and adjacent peaks. This is about as much as any one had learned until the present century, when the discoveries of Speke (1858 and 1862), Baker (1864), Schweinfurth (1868–71), and Stanley (1875 and 1889) solved bit by bit the mystery of the ages.

The Nile was deified by the Egyptians and worshipped as a god. A famous statue in the Vatican at Rome represents the river deity as a reclining figure pillowed on a sphinx and holding a cornucopia (typical of the fertility caused by the river's overflow), while sixteen children, representing the affluents of the Nile, play about. The work belongs to the Graeco-Egyptian period.

See Herod. ii. 19–26; Pliny, *H. N.* v. 51, 58; viii. 77; Dio Cass. lxxv. 13; Solin. 35; and on the deification of the river by the Egyptians, Herod. ii. 101; Diod. i. 6–26. See also Budge, *The Nile* (1890).

The God of the Nile. (Vatican.)

Nimrod or **Nimroud.** See BABYLONIA.

Nineveh. See NINUS.

Nīnus (Νῖνος) or **Nĭnus** (Νίνος). The reputed founder of the city of Ninus, or Nineveh, and the husband of Semiramis (q. v.). Ninus is doubtless a mystical personage, but Semiramis is probably to be identified with Sammuramat, wife of Ramman-Nirari III. (B.C. 811–782).

Ninus (Νῖνος), **Ninĭvé** (Νινεύη, Νινευί), in Assyrian NINUA (cf. Herod. i. 193; ii. 150). The name is perhaps derived from the Assyrian *nûnu*, "fish." Nineveh, the capital of the great Assyrian monarchy, standing on the eastern side of the Tigris, at the upper part of its course, in the district of Aturia. The prophet Jonah (B.C. 825) describes it as "an exceeding great city, of three days' journey," and as containing "more than 120,000 persons that cannot discern between their right and their left hand," which, if this phrase refer to children, would represent a population of 600,000 souls. Diodorus also describes it as an oblong quadrangle of 150 stadia by 90, making the circuit of the walls 480 stadia (more than fifty-five miles); if so, the city was nearly twice as large as London, with its suburbs. In judging of these statements, not only must allowance be made for the immense space occupied by palaces and temples, but also for the Oriental mode of building a city, so as to include large gardens and other open spaces within the walls. The walls of Nineveh are described as 100 feet high, and thick enough to allow three chariots to pass each other on them; with 1500 towers, 200 feet in height. The city is said to have been entirely destroyed by fire when it was taken by the Medes and Babylonians, about B.C. 606; and frequent allusions occur to its desolate state. Under the Roman Empire, however, we again meet with a city Nineva, in the district of Adiabené; but this must have been some later place built among or near the ruins of the ancient Nineveh.

Of all the great cities of the world, none was long thought to have been more utterly lost than the capital of the most ancient of the great monarchies. Tradition pointed out a few shapeless mounds opposite Mosul on the Upper Tigris as all that remained of Nineveh; but within the last fifty years, especially since 1870, those shapeless mounds have been shown to contain the remains of great palaces. The excavations conducted by Layard, Botta, and Smith have brought to light the sculptured remains of immense palaces, not only at the traditional site of Nineveh, namely, Kouyunjik and Nebbi-Younus, opposite to Mosul, and at Khorsabad, about ten miles to the northeast, but also in a mound, eighteen miles lower down the river, in the tongue of land between the Tigris and the Great Zab, which still bears the name of Nimroud. Which of these ruins corresponds to the true site of Nineveh, or whether that vast city may have extended all the way along the Tigris from Kouyunjik to Nimroud and to a corresponding breadth northeast of the river as far as Khorsabad, are questions still under discussion. Some splendid fragments of sculpture, obtained by Layard from Nimroud, are now to be seen in the British Museum. The moat and wall of the city are still discernible, and their ruined temples, a palace built by Shalmaneser I. and destroyed by Sennacherib, a palace of Tiglath-Pileser III. (B.C. 745–727), a palace built by Shalmaneser I. (B.C. 1320), a temple of Nebo, and palaces of Ramman-Nirari and Sennacherib, are among the buildings buried in the vast mound. These palaces were of great magnificence and were adorned with the finest products of Oriental art. See ASSYRIA; BABYLONIA; CUNEIFORM INSCRIPTIONS.

Ninyas (Νινύας). See SEMIRAMIS.

Niŏbé (Νιόβη). The daughter of Tantalus and Dioné. She was the sister of Pelops and wife of Amphion of Thebes. Like her father, she stood in close connection with the gods, especially with Leto, the wife of Zeus, and fell into misfortune by her own arrogance. In her maternal pride for her numerous progeny of six sons and six daughters, the ill-fated woman ventured to compare herself to Leto, who had only two children. To punish this presumption Apollo and Artemis slew with their arrows all Niobé's children in their parents' palace. For nine days they lay in their blood without any one to bury them, for Zeus had changed all people into stone. On the tenth day the gods buried them. Niobé, who was changed to stone on the lonely hills of Sipylus, could not, even in this form, forget her sorrow. So runs Homer's account (*Il.* xxiv. 612), in which we have the earliest reference to "a colossal relief roughly carved on the rocks" of Mount Sipylus, in Lydia, the face of which is washed by a stream in such a manner that it appears to be weeping (cf. Jebb on Soph. *Antig.* 831). Pausanias (i. 21, 5) declares that he saw this relief which modern archaeologists now regard as referable to the art of the Hittites.

The accounts of later writers vary greatly in respect of the number of the daughters of Niobé and of the scene of her death. Sometimes the spot where the disaster occurs is Lydia, sometimes Thebes, where, moreover, the grave of Niobé's children was pointed out; the sons perish in the chase, or on the race-course, while the daughters die in the royal palace at Thebes, or at the

Niobé. (Uffizi Gallery, Florence.)

burial of their brethren. This story describes Niobé as returning from Thebes to her home on Sipylus, and as there changed into a stone by Zeus, at her own entreaty. The fate of Niobé was often, in ancient times, the theme both of poetry and of art. The group of the children of Niobé, discovered at Rome, near the Lateran Church, in 1583, and now (since 1775) at Florence, is well known; it is probably the Roman copy of a Greek work which stood in Pliny's time in a temple of Apollo at Rome, and with regard to which it was a mooted point with the ancients whether it was from the hand of Scopas or of Praxiteles (Pliny, *H. N.* xxxvi. 28). See Stark, *Niobe und die Niobiden* (1863).

Niphātes (Νιφάτης—i. e. "Snow Mountain"). A mountain chain of Armenia, forming an eastern prolongation of the Taurus.

Nireus (Νιρεύς). Son of Charopus and Aglaïa, a native of the island of Symé, near Rhodes, and the handsomest among the Greeks at Troy. He was slain by Aeneas or Eurypylus (Hom. *Il.* ii. 671; Diod. v. 53).

Nisaea (Νίσαια). See MARGIANA; MEGARA.

Nisaeus Campus (τὸ Νίσαιον πεδίον). A plain in the north of Great Media, near Rhagae, celebrated for its breed of horses (Strabo, pp. 529, 536).

Nisĭbis (Νίσιβις), also called ANTIOCHIA MYGDONIAE. A celebrated city of Mesopotamia, and the capital of the district of Mygdonia, stood on the river Mygdonius in a very fertile district. It was of great importance as a military post. Its name was changed into Antiochia, but it soon resumed its original name. In the successive wars between the Romans and the Parthians and Persians, it was several times taken and retaken, until at last it fell into the hands of the Persians in the reign of Jovian (Strabo, pp. 522, 747; Ammian. Marcell. xxv. 9).

Nisus (Νῖσος). (1) A son of Hyrtacus, born on Mount Ida, near Troy. He came to Italy with Aeneas, and was attached to Euryalus, son of Opheltes. During the war with Turnus, Nisus, to whom the defence of one of the entrances of the camp was intrusted, sallied forth in search of Aeneas, and Euryalus accompanied him. Fortune at first aided their efforts, but they were at length surprised by a Latin detachment. Euryalus was cut down by Volscens; the latter was as immediately despatched by Nisus, who, however, overpowered by numbers, soon shared the fate of his friend (Verg. *Aen.* ix. 176 foll.; cf. v. 334 foll.). (2) A king of Megara. In the war waged by Minos, king of Crete, against the Athenians, on account of the death of Androgeus (see ANDROGEUS), Megara was besieged, and it was taken through the treachery of Scylla, the daughter of Nisus. This prince had a golden or purple lock of hair growing on his head, and as long as it remained uncut, so long was his life to last. Scylla, having seen Minos, fell in love with him, and resolved to give him the victory. She cut off her father's precious lock as he slept, and he immediately died; the town was then taken by the Cretans. But Minos, instead of rewarding the maiden, disgusted with her unnatural treachery, tied her by the feet to the stern of his vessel, and thus dragged her along until she was drowned (Apollod. iii. 15, 1). Another legend adds that Nisus was changed into the bird called the Sea-eagle (ἁλιάετος) and Scylla into that named Ciris (κεῖρις), and that the father continually pursues the daughter to punish her for her crime (Ovid, *Met.* viii. 145; Verg. *Cir.*). According to Aeschylus (*Choëph.* 609 foll.), Minos bribed Scylla with a golden collar.

Nisȳrus (Νίσυρος). A small island in the Carpathian Sea, off Caria. Its volcanic nature gave rise to the fable respecting its origin that Poseidon tore it off the neighbouring island of Cos to hurl it upon the giant Polybotes. (See POLYBOTES.) It is now Nikero.

Nitaquest. See NITOCRIS (2).

Nitiobrīges. A Keltic people in Gallia Aquitanica, between the Garumna (Garonne) and the Liger (Loire). Their chief town was Aginnum (Agen).

Nitōcris (Νίτωκρις). (1) A queen of Babylon, generally supposed to have been the wife of Nebuchodonosor or Nebuchadnezzar (B.C. 604–562), and grandmother, consequently, to Labynetus or Nabonedus, who is called in Daniel Belshatzar or Beltzasar. Wesseling, however, and others make her the queen of Evilmerodach, son of Nebuchadnezzar. Herodotus informs us that Nitocris, in order to render her territories more secure from the Medes, altered the course of the Euphrates, and made it so very winding that it came, in its course, three times to Ardericca. She also faced the banks of the Euphrates, where it passed through Babylon, with burned bricks, and connected the two divisions of the city by a bridge of stone (Herod. i. 186). The historian likewise informs us that she prepared a sepulchre for herself over the most frequented gate of the city, with an inscription to this effect: that if any of her successors should find himself in want of money, he should open this sepulchre and take as much as he might think fit; but that, if he were not reduced to real want, he ought to forbear; otherwise he would have cause to repent. This monument remained untouched till the reign of Darius, who, judging it unreasonable that the gate should remain useless to the inhabitants (for no man would pass under a dead body), and that an inviting treasure, moreover, should be rendered unserviceable, broke open the sepulchre; but, instead of money, he found only the remains of Nitocris, and the following inscription: "Hadst thou not been insatiably covetous, and greedy after the most sordid gain, thou wouldst not have violated the sepulchres of the dead" (Herod. i. 187). Plutarch tells the same story of Semiramis. (2) Also called NITAQUEST, a queen of Egypt, who succeeded her brother. The Egyptians, having dethroned and put to death the latter, set her over them. She took a singular revenge, however, for the death of her brother; for, having constructed a large subterranean apartment, and having invited to an entertainment in it those individuals who had been most concerned in her brother's murder, she let in the river by a secret passage and drowned them all. She then destroyed herself (Herod. ii. 100).

Nitriae (Νιτρίαι) or **Nitrariae** (Νίτραιαι). The celebrated natron lakes ("nitre-producing") in Lower Egypt, which lay in a valley on the southwestern margin of the Delta (Pliny, *H. N.* xxxi. 111).

Nitzsch, GREGOR WILHELM. A distinguished Homeric scholar, born at Wittenberg, November 22, 1790. He was Professor of Ancient Literature in the University at Kiel from 1827 to 1852, and later Professor of Classical Philology at Leipzig. He died, July 22, 1861. His principal works are: *Erklärende Anmerkungen zu Homers Odyssee*, 3 vols. (1826–40); *Meletemata de Historia Homeri*, 2 vols. (1837); *Die Sagenpoesie der Griechen* (1852); and *Geschichte der epischen Poesie der Griechen* (1862). Nitzsch was perhaps the most eminent of those who argue for the essential unity of authorship of the two great Homeric poems. See the critical estimate of his work by Lübker, *G. W. Nitzsch in seinem Leben und Wirken* (Jena, 1864), and the article HOMERUS, pp. 838 foll.

Nivaria. (1) One of the Fortunatae Insulae, off the western coast of Mauritania Tingitana. It is now the island of Teneriffe. The name Nivaria has reference to the snows which cover the summits of the island for a great part of the year. It was also called CONVALLIS (Pliny, *H. N.* iv. 32). (2) A city of Hispania Tarraconensis, in the territory of the Vaccaei, and to the north of Cauca.

Nixi Dii. Male deities, by some supposed to aid Iuno Lucina in her task of presiding over childbirth (Ovid, *Met.* ix. 294), but this view is regarded as erroneous.

Nobĭles, Nobilĭtas. The aristocracy of office, which, at Rome, took the place of the patrician aristocracy of birth, after the admission of the plebeians to all the offices of State and the levelling of the distinction between patricians and plebeians consequent thereon. It comprised those patrician and plebeian families whose members had held one of the curule magistracies. These families, for the most part the most illustrious and wealthy, had the influence and money, which afforded them the necessary means to canvass for and hold an office. Thus, in spite of the theoretical equality of rights now existing, they almost completely excluded from the higher magistracies all citizens who had neither wealth nor noble relatives to support them. It was quite exceptional for a man who did not belong to the nobility to be fortunate enough to attain to them. If he did so, he was styled a *novus homo* ("new man," "parvenu"), and his condition *novitas*. It was one of the privileges of the nobility that they enjoyed the right (*ius imaginum*) to possess images of their ancestors, and this was the chief external distinction between the *nobiles* and the *ignobiles*. See IMAGINES.

Nobilior. The name of a distinguished family of the Fulvia gens. The most distinguished member of the family was M. Fulvius Nobilior, consul B.C. 189, when he conquered the Aetolians, and took the town of Ambracia. He had a taste for literature and art, and was a patron of the poet Ennius, who accompanied him in his Aetolian campaign (Cic. *Tusc.* i. 2).

Noctilūca. A Roman surname of Diana, as indicating the goddess that shines during the night season. The epithet would also appear to have reference to her temple's being adorned with lights during the same period. This temple was on the Palatine Hill. Cf. Varro, *L. L.* iv. 10.

Nola (in Oscan, *Nuvia*). The modern Nola; one of the most ancient towns in Campania, twenty-one Roman miles southeast of Capua, celebrated as the place where the emperor Augustus died. In the neigbourhood of the town some of the most beautiful Campanian vases have been found in modern times. The town was destroyed by Genseric in A.D. 455.

Nomădes (Νομάδες). A name given by the Greeks to the pastoral nations of antiquity, who lived in wandering tribes, as the Scythians, Arabs, etc. Sallust makes the Numidians to have obtained their name in this way (*Iug.* 18), but without the least propriety. The term Numidae is evidently of Phœnician origin.

Nomen (ὄνομα). I. GREEK. The Greeks had no names denoting family, and so corresponding to modern surnames (Pausan. vii. 7, 4). Hence the name of the new-born child was left to the free choice of the parents, like the Christian name with us. The child usually received it on the tenth day (δεκάτη) after birth, the occasion being a family festival. (See AMPHIDROMIA.) According to the most ancient custom, the son, especially the first-born, received the name of his grandfather, sometimes that of his father, or a name derived from it (Phocus=Phocion) or similarly compounded (Theophrastus=Theodorus). Girls, in like manner, received the name of the grandmother (Isae. *De Pyrrh. Herod.* 30). As a rule, a Greek had only one name, to which was added that of his father, to prevent confusion—e. g. Ἀλκιβιάδης ὁ (sc. the son) Κλεινίου. Sometimes, also, the name of the country was added in the form of an adjective—e. g. Θουκυδίδης ὁ Ἀθηναῖος. A great many names were compounded with the names of gods (Heracleitus, Herodotus, Artemidorus, Diogenes), or derived from them (Demetrius, Apollonius). Frequently names of good omen for the future of the child were chosen. Sometimes a new name was afterwards substituted for the original one; so Plato was originally called Aristocles, and Theophrastus, Tyrtamus. Slaves were usually called after their native country, or their physical or moral peculiarities. See Becker-Göll, *Charikles*, ii. p. 26.

II. ROMAN. The development of the Roman name was co-ordinate with the growth and development of the Roman State. In the early period, when, in the small community, the individual was all-important, the strictly personal name was prominent; but as the community increased in size and consequence, added importance was given to certain determinatives, which marked the individual as a member of society and distinguished him from his fellows. These determinatives probably belonged to the name in its early history, notwithstanding the statement, *Varro simplicia in Italia nomina fuisse ait*, found in the fragment *De Praenominibus*, assigned to Valerius Maximus by Julius Paris of the fourth century. This statement is there supported by reference to Romulus and Remus, names belonging to a mythology of late origin, but is controverted by reference to Rhea Silvia and Silvius Numitor. The first of these early determinatives was the word, indicating *potestas, manus, mancipium*, in the genitive case—e. g. Marcus Marci, Caecilia Crassi—followed later, as shown in the inscriptions, by *f(ilius)* or *f(ilia)*, *uxor*, or *s(ervus)*. The second early determinative was the word indicating the family (*gens*) distinguished from the other elements by the suffix *-ius*. Thus the three elements of the early name were the individual name, the name of the one in authority, and the name of the family. Among the Romans the order of the last two was reversed, while among the Greeks, Umbrians, and Volscians the original order was maintained.

In the course of time the necessity of still further identifying the individual led to the use of other elements, the name of the tribe and the *cognomen*, an additional personal name. The latter afterwards came to indicate the branch or family, *stirps*, of the *gens*. The name of a free-born citizen then consisted of a *praenomen, nomen, cognomen*, with the insertion in formal usage, before the *cognomen*, of the words denoting filiation and descent, followed by *filius, nepos, pronepos, abnepos, adnepos*, and of the name of the tribe. The order indicated—*praenomen, nomen, cognomen*—is violated in the inscriptions only for metrical reasons, or because of Greek influence or rustic usage. In literature the same order is observed in prose of the good period, even in Livy, when the *praenomen* is given; but if the *praenomen* is omitted the older order, that followed by Cicero, is *cognomen, nomen;* while the later order, that followed by Caesar, is *nomen, cognomen.* In social intercourse children, clients, slaves, addressed the master of the house by his *praenomen*, while strangers used his *cognomen.* In more formal address both *nomen* and *cognomen* were employed.

Praenomen.—The strictly personal name was conferred by parents upon their children on the *dies lustricus*, the ninth day after birth in case of boys and the eighth in case of girls. The assertion of Q. Scaevola, as given in *De Praenominibus*, to the effect that boys did not receive the *praenomen* until they assumed the *toga virilis*, or girls before their marriage, must refer to the formal conferring of the name, for the inscriptions of persons dying in childhood often contain the *praenomina.*

Eighteen *praenomina* were employed by the patrician families: A., Aulus; D., Decimus; C., Gaius; CN., Gnaeus; K., Kaeso; L., Lucius; M'., Manius; M., Marcus; P., Publius; Q., Quintus; SER., Servius; SEX., Sextus; S., Spurius; TI., Tiberius; T., Titus; AP., Appius; MAM., Mamercus; N., Numerius. Certain of these were selected by the individual patrician families; thus, the Cornelii used A., CN., L., M., P., SER., TI.; but the Cornelii Scipiones, CN., L., P. (see table given by Momm. *Röm. Forschungen*, p. 15). Other *praenomina* were employed, some of which fell into disuse at an early period, and are known from the *fasti* or from statements of authors, while others were of foreign origin and rare occurrence. Varro, in *De Praenom.* § 3, names fourteen ancient *praenomina* not used at his time: Agrippa, Ancus, Caesar, Faustus, Hostus, Lar, Opiter, Postumus, Proculus, Sertor, Statius, Tullus, Volero, Vopiscus.

Cognomina were used at times as *praenomina*, particularly in Gallia Cisalpina — e. g. Maximus, Rufus; also in the imperial family in the employment of such names as Cossus, Drusus, and Germanicus. The word *imperator* in the time of Augustus became a *praenomen* in the imperial name. *Nomina* also served as *praenomina*—e. g. Aelius, Aurelius—after the middle of the second century, and even suffered abbreviation.

Nomen.—The second determinative in the early Roman name belonged to all members of the same family, and was at first identified with a certain locality. The *nomina* of the old Roman families ended in *-ius* and the closely related terminations *-aius*, *-eius*, *-eus*, *-aeus*. *Nomina* with other terminations may be assigned to the localities to which they originally belonged—e. g. *-arna*, *-erna*, *-enna*, *-ina*, *-inna* show Etruscan origin, while *-as*, *-anas*, *-enas*, *-inas* testify to Umbrian derivation. Other *nomina* are directly derived from names of places —e. g. Acerranus (*Acerrae*); Verres, of Roman origin, stands by itself, and may have been originally a *cognomen*.

Cognomen.—This last addition to the Roman name was first used as a strictly personal name employed as appropriate to the individual—e. g. Albus, Barbatus, Severus, Siculus. The position of the *cognomen* after the name of the tribe indicates a time of introduction subsequent to the Servian Constitution; and judging from its use in inscriptions the custom of writing *cognomina* dates back to the fifth century of the city, while its regular use may be assigned to the latter part of the seventh century. The *cognomen* afterwards served as an indication of the family of the *gens*, so of the *gens Cornelii* there were the Cethegi, Lentuli, Scipiones, while of the Scipiones there were the Nasicae; also as an indication of nobility, being employed by patrician families and certain of the plebeian. In the late republican period the *cognomen* was given to all free-born citizens and frequently to freedmen, and at this time served as an indication of freedom. The custom of using more than one *cognomen* became very common in the early days of the Empire, and prevailed generally in the second and third centuries. These additional *cognomina* were regarded by the grammarians after the fourth century as new elements, and were termed by them *agnomina*. Of this class were the *cognomina ex virtute*—e. g. Caudinus, Hispanus—and names, indicating the parentage of those adopted, made with the termination *-anus*—e. g. Aemilianus.

Names of Women.—The names of women in the early period consisted of an individual name, *praenomen*, followed by the *nomen* of the father and the genitive case of his *praenomen*, or by the *nomen* of the husband and the genitive case of his *praenomen*—e. g. Maior Anicia C. f(ilia). Subsequently the *praenomen* disappeared, and the female name consisted of merely the *nomen gentile* of the father or husband alone—e. g. Aemilia, or accompanied, when more formal, by the genitive of the *praenomen* of the father or husband—e. g. Acilia C. f(ilia); cf. also Curtia Rosci (uxor). At the close of the Republic *cognomina* were used with names of women —e. g. Caecilia Metella; and from the middle of the first century the custom prevailed generally —e. g. Furia Sabinia Tranquillina.

Names of Slaves.—The name of the slave originally consisted simply of the name of his master in combination with the word *puer;* as, Marcipor= *Marci puer.* In the republican period the slave was known by an individual name, often of foreign origin, followed by the *nomen* and afterwards the *praenomen* of his master, both in the genitive case. His servile condition was indicated by the word *servus*, abbreviated in the inscriptions S. or SER. Thus, Helenus Hosti Q. s. = Helenus, slave of Quintus Hostius. In the imperial period the name of the owner is given in full—as, Martialis C. Oli(i) Primi s(ervus). The transfer of a slave to a new master was indicated by the use of an additional name, made from the *cognomen* of his former master, with termination *-anus* — e. g. Epitynchanus Caes(aris) n(ostri) ser(vus) Candidian(us).

Names of Freedmen.—Originally the freedman received the *nomen* of his *patron*, and selected his *praenomen*, which might be his early servile name. His former state was indicated, as shown in the inscriptions, by the word *servus*, following the genitive case of his patron's *praenomen*—e. g. C. Sextius V(ibi) s(ervus). In the seventh century of the city a freedman received his patron's *nomen*, a Roman *praenomen* (regularly that of his master), and used his former slave name as a *cognomen*. His former state was indicated, as shown in the inscriptions, by the word *libertus*, abbreviated L. or LIB.—e. g. P. Helvidius P. l. Hermes. When freedmen were liberated by the emperor, the expression Aug(usti) l(ibertus) or Caes(aris) n(ostri) l(ibertus) took the place of the *praenomen* of the patron. Freedmen of women took the *nomen* of their patroness and the *praenomen* of her father—e. g. M. Livius Aug(ustae) l(ibertus) Menophilus. Freedmen of a *colonia* or *municipium* formed *nomina* out of the word *publicus*, since they had been *servi publici*, or from the name of the *colonia* or *municipium*.

Bibliography.—Ellendt, *De Cognomine et Agnomine Romano* (Königsberg, 1853); Th. Mommsen, *Römische Forschungen*, art. *Die römischen Eigennamen* (Berlin, 1864); J. Marquardt, *Das Privatleben der Römer*, 2d ed. (Leipzig, 1886); Cagnat, *Cours d'Épigraphie Latine*, 2d ed. (Paris, 1890); E. Hübner, *Handbuch der klassischen Altertumswissenschaft*, vol. i. 2d ed. art. *Römische Epigraphik* (Munich, 1892).

NICKNAMES.—Nicknames were freely given by both the Greeks and Romans, based upon any bodily or mental defect or peculiarity, or upon some well-known circumstance of the individual's career. Thus Demosthenes, from his childhood, was called Βάτταλος, because of his stuttering (Aesch. *C. Timarch.* 126, 141); and Aristophanes gives several names of birds that were used as nicknames (*Av.* 1291). Dionysius of Heraclea was popularly styled Μεταθέμενος, or "turn-coat," from his abandonment of the Stoic philosophy; and Hegesias of Cyrené got the name of Πεισιθάνατος, or "Death's Advocate," from his gloomy view of life. Epicrates was styled Σακεσφορός, from his large beard; and one of the Ptolemies Φύσκων, from his paunch. Collections of Greek nicknames are given by Athenaeus (vi. p. 242); and cf. Xen. *Hellen.* ii. 2, 31; Lucian, *Symp.* 6; and Athen. x. p. 436).

As already shown, many of the Roman family names were originally nicknames; as, Naso, "big-nose"; Flaccus, "flop-ear"; Varus, "bandy-legs"; and Scaurus, "knock-kneed." The Rufi were named from a red-headed ancestor; and the name Cicero is said to have been due to a wart like a pea (*cicer*) on the face. Some of the nicknames were accepted by their subjects as formal names, and hence passed into history, as Cunctator ("slow-coach") and Caligula. The last emperor of the West, Romulus Augustus, was, because of his insignificance, styled Augustulus, just as Victor Hugo dubbed the Third Napoleon, *Napoléon le Petit.* Pompey was nicknamed "Sampsiceramus" by Cicero, after a petty prince of Emesa (Cic. *Ad Att.* ii. 14, 16). The bibulous tastes of Tiberius led the people to change his name from Tiberius Claudius Nero to Biberius Caldius Mero (from *bibo*, *calda*, and *merum*). Sometimes a whole phrase was applied as a nickname, as *Cedo alteram* (Tac. *Ann.* i. 23, 41) and *Manus ad ferrum* (Lamprid. *Aurel.* 6), much as in modern times "Cœur de Lion," "Rough and Ready," and "Me Too" have been so applied. The Latin term for a nickname is *signum* or *vocabulum* (Capitol. *Gord.* iv. 8; Tac. *Ann.* i. 41).

Nomenclātor (*nomenculator*). A sort of usher; a slave kept by great personages, whose business it was to make himself acquainted with the names and persons of every one who was in the habit of attending his master's levees, so that when the great man met any of them out of doors, the nomenclator, who accompanied him, announced their names, and enabled him to address them personally, or pay them some little appropriate compliment; for to pass a client without notice, even inadvertently, might be regarded as an affront, and possibly be resented at the next elections (Cic. *Ad Att.* iv. 1; Hor. *Epist.* i. 6, 50–52). In great houses, where the acquaintances and hangers-on were very numerous, the nomenclator arranged the order of precedence among the guests, announced the name of each dish as it was served up, and enumerated its peculiar excellences (Pet. *Sat.* 47, 8; Sen. *Ep.* 19; Pliny, *H. N.* xxxii. 21). The name is properly written *nomenculator*, as is shown on the evidence of glosses and MSS. See Mart. x. 30, 30; Suet. *Aug.* 19; *Calig.* 41; *Claud.* 34.

Nomentum. Now Mentana; a Latin town founded by Alba, but subsequently a Sabine town, fourteen (Roman) miles from Rome. Its neighbourhood was celebrated for its wine (Mart. x. 48).

Nomia (τὰ Νόμια). A mountain in Arcadia on the frontiers of Laconia.

Nominatio. The first stage of the appointment of a person to the office of augur. Under the law of Labienus (B.C. 63), when a vacancy occurred in the augural college, each of the augurs nominated a candidate for the post, and the choice between these was made by seventeen tribes chosen by lot. The word is also used of the approval by the emperor of any candidate for office.

Nomius (Νόμιος). "The Pasturer;" a name given to divinities protecting the pastures and shepherds, such as Apollo, Pan, Hermes, and Aristaeus.

Nomophylăces (νομοφύλακες, "Guardians of the Laws"). A board found in different States of Greece, which had to see to the observance of the requirements of the law, especially in the deliberative assemblies. At Athens, after the abolition of the Areopagus as a board of supervision (about B.C. 461), a body of seven nomophylaces was introduced as a check upon the Senate, the public assembly, and the magistrates. They also provide for the safe custody of the laws and public archives (*C. I. G.* 3794). At Sparta the number of monophylaces was five. See Gilbert, *Greek Constitutional Antiquities*, pp. 155, 160 (Eng. trans. London, 1895); and PARANOMON GRAPHÉ.

Nomos (νόμος). (1) Originally an ancient kind of solo in epic form in praise of some divinity. It was either "aulodic" or "citharodic"—that is, it was sung to the accompaniment of the flute or the cithara. The citharodic nomos was from ancient times used at the festivals of Apollo, whom the Dorians especially worshipped. It received its artistic form from Terpander (about B.C. 675) principally by a systematic distribution into five or seven parts, of which three were the essential portions, the middle one forming the cardinal point of the whole. It formed an important element in the Delphian festival of the Pythian Apollo. On the other hand, the aulodic nomos, which Clonas of Tegea had introduced in imitation of the nomos of Terpander, was early excluded from this festival. By the side of the ancient nomoi, in which the words were sung to an instrumental accompaniment, there arose another variety formed on the same model. In this the song was dramatically recited to the tune of the flute or cithara, according as the nomos was "aulodic" or "citharodic." Of the former kind was the nomos introduced by the flute-player Sacadas of Argos (about B.C. 580) at the Pythian Games, and hence called the *Pythian nomos*, a musical representation of the destruction of the dragon Pytho by Apollo. At a later period the province of the nomos was more and more extended and secularized, until it became the most important part of the musician's profession. See Plut. *De Mus.* cap. iii.–x.; and the article MUSICA. (2) A general term for a law. See ECCLESIA.

Nomothĕtae (νομοθέται). At Athens a commission for the examination of proposed laws. Their number was fixed by the popular assembly and they were chosen by lot from among the Heliasts. (See HELIAEA.) This number was often a very large one (e. g. a thousand, Poll. viii. 101), but varied according to the importance of the laws under consideration. See Schöll, *Ueber attische Gesetzebung* (Munich, 1886); and Gilbert, *Greek Constitutional Antiquities*, p. 255. See ECCLESIA.

Nonăcris (Νώνακρις). A town in the north of Arcadia, surrounded by lofty mountains, in which the river Styx took its origin. From this town Evander is called *Nonacrius*, Atalanta *Nonacria*, Callisto *Nonacrina virgo*, and Hermes *Nonacriates*, in the general sense of Arcadian (Pausan. viii. 18; Pliny, ii. § 104; Ovid, *Fasti*, v. 97).

Nonae. The Roman name for the fifth day of the month, or in the months of March, May, July, and October the seventh day. See CALENDARIUM.

Nonius Marcellus. A Latin grammarian, born at Thubursicum Numidarum in Africa (*C. I. L.* viii. 4878), who composed, in the beginning of the fourth century A.D., a manual of miscellaneous information on points of lexicography, grammar, and antiquities, bearing the title of *De Compendiosa Doctrina*. It consisted originally of twenty books, of which the sixteenth is lost. It is evidently founded on the works of earlier scholars, and in some parts exhibits verbal coincidences with Aulus Gellius. Though not showing the least genius or critical acumen, the work is of considerable importance, owing to its numerous quotations from lost authors, especially of the archaic period. The chief editions are those of Mercier (Paris, 1583; reprinted, Leipzig, 1825); Quicherat (Paris, 1871); and L. Müller (Leipzig, 1888). See Nettleship's *Lectures and Essays*, pp. 277–331 (London, 1885).

Nonius Sufēnas. See SUFENAS.

Nonnus (Νόννος). A Greek poet of Panopolis, in Egypt, belonging to the fifth century A.D. As a pagan, he wrote, with poetic talent and in a spirited though highly rhetorical style, a vast epic, called the *Dionysiaca* (Διονυσιακά) or *Bassarica* (Βασσαρικά), in forty-eight books, one of the chief sources of our knowledge of the Dionysiac cycle of legends. After becoming a Christian, he composed a paraphrase of the gospel of St. John in Greek hexameters. A good edition of the *Dionysiaca* is that of Graefe (Leipzig, 1819–26), in 2 vols., and Köchly (Leipzig, 1858). The paraphrase has been edited by Passow (Leipzig, 1834).

Nora (τὰ Νῶρα). (1) A city of Sardinia, on the coast of the Sinus Caralitanus. (2) A mountain fortress of Cappadocia, on the borders of Lycaonia, noted for the siege sustained in it by Eumenes against Antigonus (Plut. *Eum.* 10).

Norba. (1) A town in Latium, now Norma, on the slope of the Volscian Mountains and near the sources of the Nymphaeus, originally belonging to the Latin, and subsequently to the Volscian, League. As early as B.C. 492 the Romans founded a colony at Norba. (2) Named CAESARĒA (Cacere), a Roman colony in Lusitania, on the left bank of the Tagus. The bridge, 600 feet in length, built by order of Trajan over the Tagus at this place is still extant.

Norbānus, GAIUS. One of the leaders of the Marian party in the war with Sulla, and consul B.C. 83, in which year he was defeated by Sulla at Capua. In the following year he joined forces with the consul Carbo in Cisalpine Gaul, but was again routed by Metellus Pius. He then escaped from Italy, and fled to Rhodes, where he committed suicide (Appian, *B. C.* i. 82–91; Plut. *Sulla*, 27).

Norēia. Now Neumarkt, in Styria; the ancient capital of the Taurisci or Norici, in Noricum, from which the whole country derived its name. It is celebrated as the place where Carbo was defeated by the Cimbri, B.C. 113.

Norĭcum. A Roman province south of the Danube, bounded on the north by the Danube, on the west by Rhaetia and Vindelicia, on the east by Pannonia, and on the south by Pannonia and Italy. It thus corresponds to the greater part of Styria and Carinthia, and to a part of Austria, Bavaria, and Salzburg. One of the main branches of the Alps, the Alpes Noricae (in the neighbourhood of Salzburg), extended through the province. In those mountains a large quantity of excellent iron was found; and the Noric swords were celebrated in antiquity. The inhabitants of the country were Kelts, divided into several tribes, of which the Taurisci, also called Norici, after their capital Noreia, were the most important. They were conquered by the Romans in the reign of Augustus, after the subjugation of Rhaetia by Tiberius and Drusus, and their country was formed into a Roman province. The chief towns were Virunum (Mariasaal), Ovilava, and Iuvavum (Salzburg).

Norma (κανών, γωνία). A square for measuring right angles; employed by carpenters, masons, builders, etc., to prove that the angles are true (Vitruv. vii. 3; Pliny, xxxvi. 51). It was formed in two ways, either by two rules (*regulae*) joined together at right angles, or by a flat piece of board with a right angle cut out of it; both of which are exhibited in the illustration, from sepulchral marbles. See AMUSSIS; RUBRICA.

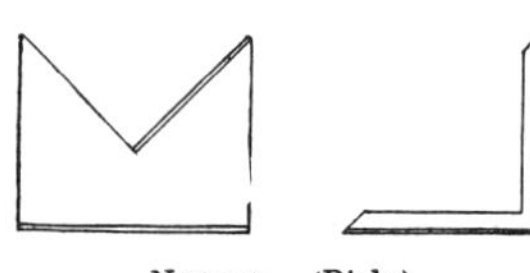

Normae. (Rich.)

North Wind. See BOREAS.

Nortia or **Nurtia.** An Etruscan goddess of Fortune worshipped at Volsinii (Livy, vii. 3). See CLAVUS ANNALIS.

Nossis (Νοσσίς). A Greek poetess of Locri in Italy who lived in the fourth century B.C., and wrote twelve epigrams preserved in the Greek Anthology.

Nota Censoria. The punishment inflicted by the Roman censors who by a mark of disapproval branded dishonourable or discreditable acts, such as unjustifiable divorce, ill treatment of one's family, excessive luxury and extravagance of life, the pursuit of disgraceful gain, legacy hunting, etc. The terms NOTATIO and ANIMADVERSIO CENSORIA are also used. See CENSOR; CENSUS.

Notae (σημεῖα). A word used technically of signs and abbreviations, as (1) for secret writing, cipher; (2) for rapid writing, short-hand, stenography; and (3) for critical purposes in texts (σημεῖα κριτικά).

I. There is no mention of cryptography, properly so called, among the Greeks of the classical period, though they had various devices for concealing a written message and making it unintelligible except to the person for whose eyes it was intended. Among such devices was the σκυτάλη, mentioned by Plutarch as in use among the Spartans, and of which an account is given in the article SCYTALĒ. At Rome towards the end of the Republican period we find mention of cipher writing, though it was of a simple sort and one that would not long baffle the scrutiny of an ingenious investigator. Thus, we are told of Caesar's private correspondence, that he had an agreement with the persons to whom he was writing by which the letters of the words were to be interchanged. Suetonius says that this system consisted in making D stand for A, E for B, and so on through the alphabet, and that Augustus used a similar system (Suet. *Iul.* 56; *Aug.* 88; Becker-Göll, *Gallus*, i. 62).

II. Whether the use of short-hand arose first

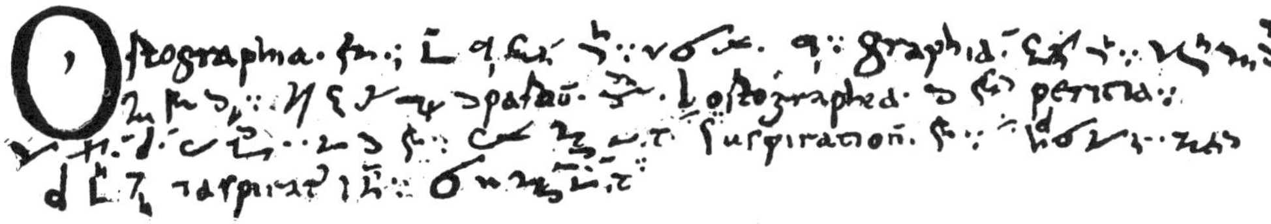

Specimen of Roman Notae. (From MS. in the Vatican Library.)

among the Greeks or among the Romans there is no definite information. A passage in Diogenes Laertius (ii. 48) seems to imply that Xenophon took down lectures by some stenographic process, but there is no direct mention of it earlier than the time of Cicero, who employed it frequently, as we learn from Plutarch (*Cat. Min.* 23) and others. Thus, at the trial of the Catilinarian conspirators, Cato's speech was taken down by writers whom Cicero had instructed "to use certain signs which in small and brief characters comprehended the force of many letters. . . . For the Romans at that time were not accustomed to employ and did not possess what are known as short-hand writers, but it is said that it was on this occasion that they first conceived the idea." Dio Cassius (lv. 7) ascribes the invention of the art to Maecenas, but this probably means that Maecenas made some improvements in the existing system. An explanation is given by Isidorus, who ascribes the invention of short-hand to one Ennius (not the poet), who is said to have used 1100 signs. He also says that Tiro, the confidential freedman and secretary of Cicero, was the first person to use these signs at Rome, but implies that this short-hand consisted of abbreviations or arbitrary signs only for particles of frequent occurrence, and that additional signs were added successively by Vipsanius, Philargyrus, and Aquila, the freedmen of Maecenas, until finally Seneca reduced the whole to a regular system and increased the number of signs to about 5000. It is probable, however, from what Cicero says (*Ad Fam.* xvi. 4), that the main structure of the system is due to Tiro, and in fact the traditional name for short-hand signs (*notae Tironianae*) seems to justify this belief (cf. Gell. vi. 3, 8). However this may be, from the time of Cicero and his immediate successors the use of stenography spread among the Romans. It was used both for taking down public speeches and for the use of students in the lecture-room, and many Romans kept slaves who were trained as short-hand writers (*notarii*). The emperor Titus was a skilful stenographer, and often instituted contests in rapid writing with his secretaries (Suet. *Tit.* 3). After the Christian era began, short-hand was much used among the Christians for taking down sermons and ecclesiastical speeches, and St. Augustine (*Epist.* 141) speaks of an episcopal assemblage held at Carthage at which eight stenographers were employed in relays of two. Such ancient manuscripts as are written in the Tironian short-hand remained undecipherable until 1747, when the French scholar Charpentier succeeded in reading them and published an account of them.

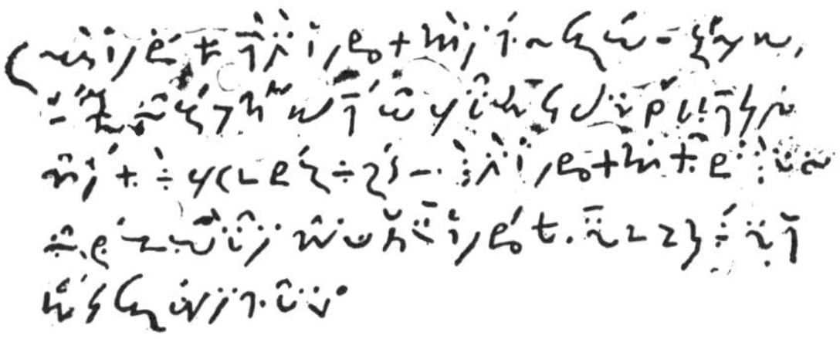

Greek Notae.

The ancient system consisted first of an alphabet more cursive than the ordinary Roman alphabet and especially modified so as to facilitate the juncture of letters. In the second place, it represented terminations by arbitrary characters used in conjunction with a point—thus, B. stood for *bam* and .B for *bant*. In the third place, all sorts of abbreviations (*sigla*) independently of the character used were employed. Finally, as in modern stenography, a number of arbitrary signs were employed for words in common use.

III. The Alexandrian grammarians appear to have originated the use of critical signs by which to indicate certain judgments in their recension and study of texts. Aristophanes of Byzantium (B.C. 257–180) published an edition of Homer with such signs, and these were developed by his successors, especially Aristarchus. The most important of these were the *obelus*, —, used to denote a spurious passage; the *diplé* (διπλῆ), ⊱, used to call attention to something special; the *dotted diplé* (διπλῆ περιεστιγμένη), ⊱̈, to denote variant readings; the *asterisk*, ✱, to mark genuine verses if repeated; the *antisigma*, Ↄ, and the *stigmé*, ■, both used to denote repetitions of the same idea; the *ceraunion* (κεραύνιον), used when a large number of lines were to be rejected. Other signs and symbols of a different character, such as marks of punctuation, accents, breathings, etc., will be found treated under PALAEOGRAPHY; and TEXTUAL CRITICISM.

For ancient short-hand, see Kopp, *Palaeographia Critica*, vol. i. (Mannheim, 1817); and Anderson, *History of Short-hand* (London, 1882). On the *notae criticae*, see Reifferscheid's *Suetonii Reliquiae*, pp. 137–144 (Leipzig, 1890); Schrader, *De Notatione Critica*, etc. (Bonn, 1863); and Römer, *Die Notation der alexandr. Philol.* etc. in the *Bayr. Acad. Cl. I.*, vol. xix. (1892).

Notarii. Short-hand writers. See NOTAE.

Notation. See NUMERI.

Notitia Dignitātum. A Byzantine official hand-book, containing a list of court appointments, civil and military, with statistics, etc.—a sort of statesman's year-book—compiled about A.D. 410. It is edited by Seeck (Berlin, 1876). See Jullian in the *Mélanges d'Archéologie*, i. 284; iii. 80.

Notitia Regiōnum. A survey of the fourteen *regiones* into which Augustus divided Rome. It was made in the time of Constantine (A.D. 315?), and specifies the principal buildings in the quarters. It is contained in two lists, the first being called *Notitia* and the second *Curiosum Urbis Romae Regionum XIV*. See Jordan, *Topographie der Stadt Rom*, vol. ii. (Berlin, 1871), and id., *Forma Urbis Romae Regionum XIIII.* (Berlin, 1874).

Notus (Νότος), called AUSTER by the Romans, the south wind, or strictly the southwest wind, bringing with it fogs and rain.

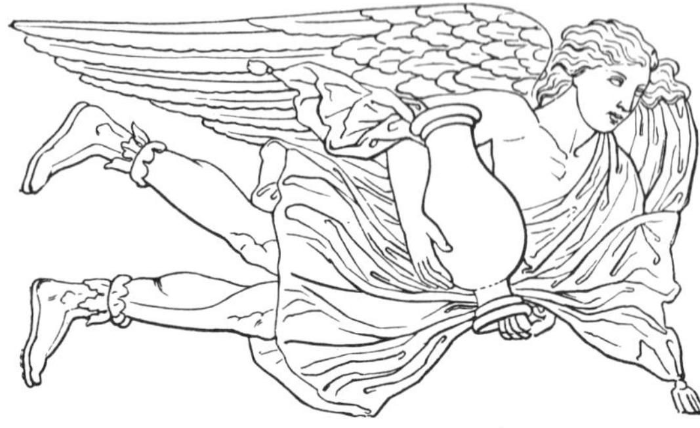

Notus. (Temple of the Winds, Athens.)

Nouns. See GRAMMATICA.

Novacŭla (ξυρόν). A knife with a very sharp edge, employed for shaving the hair of the head or beard, like our razor (Petron. 103, 1; Mart. ii. 66; Suet. *Cal.* 23; Alciph. *Ep.* iii. 66, 9; cf. CULTELLUS; CULTER; and especially TONSOR). Martial (vii. 61) applies the same name to the assassin's knife (*sica*).

Novaria. Now Novara; a town in Gallia Transpadana, situated on a river of the same name (Gogna), and on the road from Mediolanum (Milan) to Vercellae.

Novatio. A renewed bond. See OBLIGATIONES.

Novellae. See CORPUS IURIS CIVILIS.

Novelli Poetae. See POETAE NOVELLI.

Novels and Romances. Fiction in its origin is with difficulty separated from myth — myth, however, being unconscious and due to a desire to give concrete form to various beliefs that spring up in the primitive mind; while fiction, as a literary motive, originates in a desire to amuse and occasionally to instruct. Hence, the earliest form of fiction is the Beast Fable, which is found in every quarter of the earth and at every period of history. A papyrus dating from B.C. 1200 gives an Egyptian version of the Aesopic fable of the Lion and Mouse; the inscribed Babylonian bricks afford examples of the same thing, and the Hindus probably originated most of the fables which Aesop, Babrius, and Phaedrus made popular in Europe. Akin to conscious fiction and at the same time allied to myth are the folk-tales of nymphs, satyrs, ghosts, fairies, demons, and vampires which Greeks and Romans alike propagated, but which have nearly all been lost to us because they seemed to the ancients unworthy of preservation in formal literature; so that we have now only here and there tantalizing half-glimpses and vanishing suggestions of the curious and fascinating legends told by the common people. Such bits as remain, however, are quite sufficient to prove the existence of a great unwritten literature, and examples of these may still be found, though no longer preserved in their original simplicity, in the stories of the love of Echo for Narcissus, the legend of Hylas and the Naiads, of Cupid and Psyché, and in the various allusions to the monsters known as the Lamiae, Mormolycé, Incubus, and Empusa, the spectre with the brazen leg and the ass's hoof. Ghosts figure in Greek literature as early as Homer, and are introduced with striking effect in the *Odyssey*, as also by the Romans Attius and Vergil, and in the famous story preserved by Pliny the Younger. To this informal fiction belong also the tales of the Lares and the Larvae.

The earliest form of literary prose fiction, however, is to be found in the short stories collected by Herodotus, most of which have their origin in the East, the home of story-telling. Such are the famous anecdotes of Candaules (i. 8–12), of Arion and the Dolphin (i. 24), of Rhampsinitus and the Robber (ii. 121), and of Polycrates and the Ring (iii. 39), all being admirable instances of the short story in its earliest form—brief, simple, and embodying a single incident.

Of a more formal type are the so-called Milesian Tales (Μιλησιακά), a generic term for the short anecdotes which were produced in great numbers in the luxurious cities of Asia Minor prior to the second century B.C., and first ascribed to one Aristides, who is said to have written six books of them. No actual examples are known to exist, though their nature may be judged of by the short stories found in later writers, especially Petronius, from which it would appear that they were very much like the stories told in the *Decameron* of Boccaccio and the *Cent Nouvelles Nouvelles* of Louis XI. of France—brief, witty, and indecent. The choice of subjects in these early novelettes is seen in the existing collection of Parthenius of Nicaea, who taught Vergil Greek. From him have come down thirty-six skeleton stories, or rather hints for stories gathered by Parthenius for the use of Cornelius Gallus, and intended to be treated by him poetically. They can be found in both Greek and Latin versions in the Didot Collection (Paris, 1856). Other stories of this sort, written in other cities than Miletus, were produced by a host of story-writers who gave to their collections the titles Ephesian, Babylonian, Cyprian, Egyptian, Sybaritic, Naxian, Lydian, Trojan, and Bithynian Tales, though these do not seem to have differed, except in name, from those of Miletus. Some of them are preserved in epitome by Photius (q. v.). One of the most important writers of them after Aristides was Conon, from whom Cervantes borrowed an episode in his *Don Quixote*. While the short story was reaching its full development, it was used philosophically by Plato in the story of Er, and by Prodicus in his epilogue on the Choice of Heracles.

At about this time fiction underwent a further development as a result of the contact of the Greeks with the East at the time of the Persian Wars and of the spirit of adventure resulting from the conquests of Alexander. We now have instances of the historical romance in the *Atlantis* of Plato and the *Cyropaedia* of Xenophon, which find their echo in modern times in the Utopia of Sir Thomas More and the *New Atlantis* of Francis Bacon. The *Cyropaedia* contains the first romantic love-story in Greek fiction. These works, however, are partly political, and are of less literary consequence than the romance of adventure which was afterwards introduced, and which finds an illustration in the novel entitled Τὰ Ὑπὲρ Θούλην Ἄπιστα (Marvels Beyond Thulé), by one Antonius Diogenes, the Munchausen of antiquity. It relates to the love-adventures of an Arcadian youth, Dinias, with a Tyrian girl, Dercyllis, and abounds with most extraordinary incidents. It is, in reality, nothing more than a collection of short stories or episodes strung together by a very slender plot. More homogeneous and artistic are the later romances of Lucius of Patrae of uncertain date called *Metamorphoses*, drawn upon by Lucian and Apuleius; of Iamblichus of Syria, who wrote Βαβυλωνικά, the adventures of a married pair, Sinonis and Rhodanes, with a double plot; of Xenophon of Ephesus, author of Ἐφησιακά, the loves of Abrocomas and Anthia, the ultimate source of *Romeo and Juliet;* and especially of Heliodorus of Emesa, in the fourth century A.D., whose Αἰθιοπικά is still in existence, and is regarded as the best of the novels of adventure produced by the Greeks. It is in ten books, and relates the adventures of two lovers, Theagenes and Chariclea. It has some quite interesting episodes, is regularly developed, and contains one curious passage on the influence of pre-natal conditions upon the unborn child. It was much read in its day, and again in the seventeenth century, when it was the favourite novel of the French poet, Racine. See HELIODORUS.

Other instances of the romantic novel are those of Achilles Tatius of Alexandria, entitled Τὰ κατὰ Λευκίππην καὶ Κλειτοφῶντα (The Loves of Leucippé and Clitophon) in eight books; the *Chaereas and Callirrhoë* of Chariton of Aphrodisias; and the novelette called *Apollonius Tyrius*, of unknown authorship, preserved only in a Latin version, in which it was much read in the Middle Ages, and suggested a part of Gower's *Confessio Amantis* (iii. 284 foll.), and probably Shakespeare's *Pericles, Prince of Tyre.* Of very late origin are the trashy Greek novels by Theodorus Prodromus of Constantinople, and the imitation of this by Nicetas Eugenianus (both in doggerel verse), and last of all the eleven books on the adventures of Hysminé and Hysminias, perhaps the original source of the story of Don Juan.

Early in the Christian era, fiction was written in the form of letters by Alciphron, a Greek sophist, of whose imaginary epistles 118 are still preserved and give valuable pictures of low life in Athens during the second century A.D. They are very lively and entertaining, and are the best character sketches that Greek fiction can show us. Other writers of the same class are Aristaenetus of Nicaea (?), the author of two books of erotic letters written in a cynical spirit; and Theophilus of Simocatta (A.D. 610), from whom we have 85 letters, rhetorical and epigrammatic, but of no literary merit.

The prose pastoral was created by Longus (perhaps not the author's name), whose romance Ποιμενικὰ τὰ κατὰ Δάφνιν καὶ Χλόην, usually called *Daphnis and Chloë*, is one of the most original and pleasing things in ancient literature. Its theme is the growth of the sexual instinct in two children, a boy and a girl, who have been brought up together in a state of perfect innocence. Its physico-psychological motive makes it unique in the history of early fiction, and the warmth and beauty of its descriptions of nature are also very striking. It has been many times translated into all the modern languages, and is the original of Bernardin de St. Pierre's *Paul et Virginie*, of Allan Ramsay's *Gentle Shepherd*, and of many other less important works.

The Romans have left us only two specimens of true prose fiction—the *Satiricon* of Petronius Arbiter and the *Metamorphoses* of Apuleius; but these are in many ways superior to anything of their kind in Greek. The *Satiricon*, in fact, though incomplete, is one of the first great novels of our time, and is remarkable for its modern tone, its subtle touches of character, its wit, its vivid pictures of life in the Roman provincial towns, and for the grace and elegance of its style. It also gives us some of the best existing specimens of the *sermo plebeius*, the colloquial Latinity of uneducated men. (See PETRONIUS; SERMO PLEBEIUS.) The *Metamorphoses* of Apuleius is based upon the *Metamorphoses* of Lucius of Patrae, and possibly upon the Λούκιος ἢ Ὄνος of Lucian, the contemporary of Apuleius; but it is more likely that both Apuleius and Lucian drew independently from the earlier writer. The novel of Apuleius, which is in eleven books, tells the story of one Lucius, who, by a mistake, swallowed a magic potion which turned him into an ass, in which form he passed through a maze of curious and amusing adventures, until at last he regained his natural shape. The novel is highly diverting and is told with much cleverness, though often with a disregard for even an elemental sense of propriety. Among its episodes is the very famous one giving the story of Cupid and Psyché, one of the most exquisite things in literature and one that has inspired innumerable works of art. See APULEIUS; PSYCHÉ.

In the Middle Ages, when the knowledge of ancient literature and history became lost to Western Europe, confused recollections of them still existed in the minds of men, and, together with many Teutonic folk-tales, became blended into a curious collection of stories known as the *Gesta Romanorum*, which were told and retold in many forms by the mediævals. They mingle together the characters of antiquity in a most remarkable way, having no chronological or historical accuracy, but reproducing the legends of the past in a sort of literary mirage. Vergil, Homer, Alexander the Great, the Roman emperors, and Hercules, Romulus, and Remus, appear and reappear side by side with knights and wizards and dragons; but the tales have a certain value in literary history as forming the connecting link between the fiction of Greece and Rome and the fiction of modern times, which took its early themes largely from those monkish legends.

The ancient novel is far inferior to the modern, because (1) it was developed only after literature had entered upon its decline; (2) because of the difference in the social spirit of antiquity which made impossible the modern romantic treatment of the relations of men and women; and (3) because the true fiction of the Greeks was to be found, not in prose, but in the great epics which more perfectly represented the highest manifestation of the Hellenic imagination.

BIBLIOGRAPHY.—For the general subject of the origin of pure fiction, see Clauston's *Popular Tales and Fictions* (London, 1887); Rutherford's introduction to his edition of Babrius (1883); Rhys-Davids, *Buddhist Birth-Stories* (1880); Benfey's introduction to the *Panchatantra* (1859); Bedier, *Les Fabliaux* (1893); and Lang, *Custom and Myth* (1885). On the Greek and Roman novels, see Dunlop, *History of the Novel* (last ed. London, 1887); Salverte, *Le Roman dans la Grèce Ancienne* (Paris, 1893); Chauvin, *Les*

Romanciers Grecs et Latins (Paris, 1862); Chassang, *Histoire du Roman dans l'Antiquité Grecque et Latine* (Paris, 1862); Rohde, *Der Griechische Roman* (Leipzig, 1876); Warren, *History of the Novel* (N. Y. 1895). The principal Greek romances are printed in the *Erotici Graeci* of the Didot Collection (Paris, 1856); and the epistolographers in the *Epistolographi Graeci* of the same collection. For special texts, translations, etc., see the separate articles in this Dictionary on the writers named above. The *Gesta Romanorum* will be found edited by Oesterley (Berlin, 1872); and translated into English by Swan, revised by Hooper (London, 1877).

November. See CALENDARIUM.

Novensīles or **Novensīdes Dii** (from *novus* + *insideo*, "the newly-settled gods"). A name used by the Romans in contrast to *dii indigetes* or native gods, to denote those deities introduced from non-Roman sources and of late introduction (Livy, viii. 9). Such were, for example, Apollo, Mercury, and in later times Cybelé; while the *dii patrii* or *indigetes* were of a less poetic and magnificent character, and are in general the deities presiding over special functions—e. g. Parca, presiding at birth; Rumina, who watched the suckling of the child; Levana, who saw it adopted by the father; Cuba and Cunina, who protected it in the cradle, etc. In solemn formulae, the *dii indigetes* and the *dii novensiles* are invoked together (Livy, *l. c.*).

Novesium. The modern Neuss; a fortified town of the Ubii on the Rhine, and on the road leading from Colonia Agrippina (Cologne) to Castra Vetera (Xanten) (Ammian. Marcell. xxvii.).

Novi Homĭnes. See NOBILES.

Noviodūnum. A name given to many Celtic places from their being situated on a hill (*dun*). (1) Nouan; a town of the Bituriges Cubi in Gallia Aquitanica. (2) Nevers; a town of the Aedui in Gallia Lugdunensis, at the confluence of the Niveris and the Liger, afterwards called Nevirnum. (3) A town of the Suessones in Gallia Belgica, probably the same as Augusta Suessonum (Soissons). (4) Nion; a town of the Helvetii in Gallia Belgica, on the north bank of the Lacus Lemanus (Lake of Geneva).

Noviomāgus or **Neomāgus** or **Noviomāgum.** (1) A city of the Batavi, now Nymegen. In the Peutinger Table it is called Niumaga. (2) The capital of the Lexubii or Lixovii, in Gallia Lugdunensis. According to Mannert, it corresponds to the modern Caen; others, however, are in favour of the modern Lisieux. (3) Or Augusta Nemetum, the capital of the Nemetes, now Spires. (4) A city of the Bituriges Vivisci, in Gallia Aquitanica. According to Mannert, it is now Castillon, not far from the mouth of the Gironde. Reichard, however, decides in favour of Castelnau de Médoc. (5) A city of Britain, the capital of Regni, the remains of which may be traced at Woodcote, near Croydon. (6) A city of the Treveri, on the Mosella, now Numagen or Neumagen. (7) A city of the Veromandui, in Belgica Secunda, now Noyon. It is also called Novionum or Noviomum.

Novĭtas. See NOBILES.

Novius, QUINTUS (?). A celebrated writer of Atellan plays, a contemporary of the dictator Sulla (Macrob. i. 10, 3).

Novum Comum. A name at one time given to Comum, when Iulius Caesar settled there 6000 colonists. See COMUM.

Novus Homo. See NOBILES.

Nox. See NYX.

Noxa. See NOXALIS ACTIO.

Noxālis Actio. A "noxal action" was a suit brought by one who had been injured by a son or slave of another citizen. He could bring no action directly against the person who had been guilty of the *noxa*, as he was not *sui iuris* (see IUS), but, instead, sued the father of the youth or the owner of the slave. The father or the owner, as the case might be, could either pay damages to the plaintiff or could give up the offender (*noxae dare*) to him. If the father or owner made no defence to the suit, the offender was given up to the injured person by decree of the praetor. Justinian abolished the *noxae datio* in the case of children. See Gaius, iv. 74–79; and cf. Ihering, *Geist des römischen Rechts*, i. p. 131.

Nubae (Νοῦβαι) or **Nubaei** (Νουβαῖοι). An African people, south of Egypt, in modern Nubia, south of Meroë (Ptol. iv. 7, 30).

Nubilarium. A large shed or barn, open on one side, and situated close to the threshing-floor (*area*), which was in the open air, in order to house grain until it was threshed out, and shelter it from sudden or partial showers (Varro, *R. R.* i. 13, 5; Columell. ii. 21, 3).

Nuceria. (1) Styled ALFATERNA (Nocera), a town in Campania on the Sarnus (Sarno), and nine Roman miles from the coast. (2) Styled CAMELLARIA (Nocera), a town in the interior of Umbria on the Via Flaminia. (3) The modern Luzzara, a small town in Gallia Cispadana on the Po, northeast of Brixellum. (4) A town in Apulia, more correctly called Luceria.

Nuces. Nuts. Several games of skill were played by the Greeks and Romans with nuts. So identified with childhood and its sports were nuts that *nuces relinquere* was the conventional phrase used for "putting away childish things." The games in question were as follows:

(1) Pitching nuts into a hole, from a given distance—a game possibly called in Latin *orca*, from the jar which was often used as the receptacle of the nuts thrown (Pers. iii. 50). The Greeks also pitched the nuts into a circle drawn on the ground (ὦμιλλα), or into a hole (βόθρος) dug in the ground (Poll. ix. 102 and 103). The nuts that fell outside the jar, circle, or hole were forfeited.

(2) A second game was called *castellum*, which was somewhat as follows: three nuts were placed on the ground, with a fourth resting on them, making a sort of pyramid. Then the player aimed his nut so as to scatter the pyramid (*dilaminare*), and, having done this, he had one or two

Roman Boys playing Castellum. (Relief in the Blundell Collection.)

more shots, the object of which was to cannon on the nuts, as boys do in playing marbles. The first shot was taken standing (*rectus*), the next kneeling (*pronus*), the next being flipped, as in the "knuckle-down tight" of modern boys. Sometimes, however, the nuts were rolled down a board (*tabula*), as in the accompanying illustration, where the kneeling boy is probably arranging the *castellum*, or pyramid.

(3) A third game with nuts was called *delta*. In this a triangle (*delta*) was chalked on the ground, and marked across with lines and bars (*virgae*) drawn parallel to the base. The player then flipped nuts into the triangle, and won as many nuts as he crossed bars, provided that he did not roll them out of the triangle, in which case they were forfeited. The best play was, therefore, that which drove the nut exactly to the apex of the delta.

(4) For various games of chance, odd or even, played with nuts, see PAR IMPAR and on the general subject of the games briefly described above, see Becq de Fouquières, *Les Jeux des Anciens*.

Nudipedalia. A name given to a procession of barefooted matrons, as an *obsecratio*, in time of great drought (Tertull. *De Ieiun.* 16; *Apol.* 40; Petron. *Sat.* 44). The magistrates laid aside their insignia, the fasces were reversed, and a sacrifice was offered at the Temple of Iupiter, the pontifices bearing at the head of the procession a sacred stone called the *lapis manalis*, from the Temple of Mars outside the Porta Capena (Non. p. 547; Fest. pp. 2. 128; Marquardt, *Staatsverw.* iii. 261).

Nudus (γυμνός). Unclad; in the ordinary sense, denoting absolute nakedness; thence, in common language, scantily or imperfectly clad, denoting a person of either sex who is divested of

Nudi. (Rich.)

all clothing except that which is worn next the skin—the Roman of his *toga*, the Greek of his *pallium*—as we say "in undress," "negligé," of a man without his coat, or of a woman without her gown. But the Latin *nudus*, as well as the Greek γυμνός, appear to have indicated something more precise than the mere absence of an outer garment (*amictus*) over the tunic; for both words are particularly used in describing the hard-working population, agricultural labourers, ploughmen, etc. (Hesiod, *Op.* 391; Verg. *Georg.* ii. 299). See EXOMIS.

Nuithōnes. A people of Germany dwelling on the right bank of the Albis (Elbe), in the modern Mecklenburg-Schwerin (Tac. *Germ.* 40).

Numa, MARCIUS. (1) An intimate friend of Numa Pompilius, whom he is said to have accompanied to Rome, where Numa made him the first Pontifex Maximus. Marcius aspired to the kingly dignity on the death of Pompilius, and starved himself to death on the election of Tullus Hostilius. (2) Son of the preceding. He is said to have married Pompilia, the daughter of Numa Pompilius, and to have become by her the father of Ancus Marcius. Numa Marcius was appointed by Tullus Hostilius *praefectus urbi*.

Numa Pompilius. The second king of Rome whose name belongs to legend rather than to history. He was a native of Cures, in the Sabine country, and was elected king one year after the death of Romulus, when the people became tired of the interregnum of the Senate. He was renowned for his wisdom and his piety; and it was generally believed that he had derived his knowledge from Pythagoras. His reign was long and peaceful, and he devoted his chief care to the establishment of religion among his rude subjects. He was instructed by the Camena Egeria, who visited him in a grove near Rome, and who honoured him with her love. He was revered by the Romans as the author of their whole religious worship. It was he who first appointed the pontiffs, the augurs, the flamens, the virgins of Vesta, and the Salii. He founded the Temple of Ianus, which remained always shut during his reign. The length of his reign is stated differently. Livy makes it forty-three years; Polybius and Cicero, thirty-nine years. The sacred books of Numa, in which he prescribed all the religious rites and ceremonies, were said to have been buried near him in a separate tomb, and to have been discovered by accident, 500 years afterwards, in B.C. 181. They were carried to the city-praetor Petilius, and were found to consist of twelve or seven books in Latin on ecclesiastical law and the same number of books in Greek on philosophy; the latter were burned by the command of the Senate, but the former were carefully preserved. The story of the discovery of these books is evidently a forgery; and the books, which were ascribed to Numa, and which were extant at a later time, were evidently nothing more than works containing an account of the ceremonial of the Roman religion. See Plutarch, *Numa*; Dionys. ii. 58.

Numantia. The capital of the Arevacae or Arevaci, in Hispania Tarraconensis, and the most important town in all Celtiberia. It was situated near the sources of the Durius (Douro), on a precipitous hill. It was taken by Scipio Africanus the Younger after a long siege (B.C. 133) (Flor. ii. 18).

Numasios Inscription. See PRAENESTINE BROOCH.

Numbers. See NUMERI.

Numenius (Νουμήνιος). (1) A Greek philosopher of the Platonic School, who is supposed to have flourished about the end of the second century of our era. He was born at Apamea, in Syria, and was regarded as an oracle of wisdom. He was the author of a treatise, entitled Περὶ τῆς τῶν Ἀκαδημαϊκῶν περὶ Πλάτωνα διαστάσεως ("Of the Disagreement among the Academic Philosophers respecting Plato"). Eusebius has preserved some fragments of this work. (2) A Greek rhetorician, who flourished in the time of the Antonines. He wrote two works, which have been printed in the Aldine Rhetorical Collection. (3) An epigrammatic poet; a native of Tarsus.

Numĕri (ἀριθμοί). Numbers; numerals. The use of signs to denote numbers is older than writing; yet most of the existing numerical signs in Greek and Latin are alphabetic modifications; because very primitive peoples, being able to count no higher than ten or so, need few symbols of number, so that the characters for large numbers are of late origin. The earliest visible signs were probably the extended fingers. The early system was in fact one based upon five, the number of fingers on one hand, traces of which survive in the Greek words πεμπάζειν, πεμπαστής from πέντε, "five" (cf. Hom. *Odyss.* iv. 412–415); and our denary system is due to the fact that the total number of our fingers is ten (cf. our English "-teen" as a termination). Finger-counting was very highly developed by the ancients, and many fairly complicated arithmetical operations could be denoted by finger-signs, as is still done in the Oriental bazaars, where the venders can reckon on their ten digits sums involving five places of figures. This system is fully described by Nicolaüs Smyrnaeus, a Greek of the thirteenth century A.D., in a treatise entitled Ἔκφασις τοῦ Δακτυλικοῦ Μέτρου, which was printed at Paris in 1636. Units and tens were represented by the fingers of the left hand, and hundreds or thousands by the fingers of the right. The thumb and forefinger of the left hand were devoted to tens, those of the right to hundreds; the remaining fingers of the left hand belonged to the units, those of the right to thousands. The fingers might be straight (ἐκτεινόμενοι), bent (συστελλόμενοι), or closed (κλινόμενοι). In the left hand, bending the fourth finger marked 1; bending the third and fourth, 2; the middle, third, and fourth, 3; the middle and third only, 4; the middle only, 5; the third only, 6. Closing the fourth finger gave 7; the fourth and third fingers, 8; the middle, third, and fourth, 9. The same motions on the right hand indicated thousands, from 1000 to 9000. The motions of the forefinger and thumb, in representing tens and hundreds, on the left and right hands respectively, are more difficult to describe. Various combinations were also indicated by placing the hands upon the breast, the hips, etc. This system was taught in the Greek and Roman schools. (See Plut. *Apophth.* 1746; Dio Cass. lxxi. 32; *Anth. Pal.* xi. 72; and the works cited below.) Reckoning was also performed by pebbles or counters arranged in sets of ten—a system which was developed into the calculating-instrument known as the *abacus*, and still used by the Chinese, who call it *swan-pan*. See ABACUS.

For recording numbers, a system of single strokes was first used as the most obvious; but this, of course, would be too cumbrous when applied to large numbers. Hence, additional symbols came into use for 5, 10, 100, and 1000; and after alphabetical writing was invented these signs were employed as numerals, either following the order of the letters, or taking the initial letter of the word for its symbol. Thus, in Greek, the inscriptions give I for "one," Π (πέντε) for "five," Δ (δέκα) for "ten," H (old sign for rough breathing, ἕκατον) for "one hundred," X (χίλιοι) for "one thousand," and M (μύριοι) for "ten thousand." (See the articles on each letter of the alphabet in this Dictionary.) Then, a Π with a Δ inscribed in it stood for $5 \times 10 = 50$, or with H inscribed in it for 500, etc. The twenty-five letters of the Ionic alphabet were used also for the simple numbers, 1 to 24. In the third century B.C. a new system called the Herodian or Alexandrian was introduced, by which the cursive alphabet was divided into three groups, of which the first did duty for the units, the second for the tens, and the third for the hundreds. This required 27 instead of 24 letters; so the old characters *digamma* (q. v.), *koppa* (q. v.), and the old sibilant *sampi* (ϡ) were revived, the first representing 6, the second 90, and the third 900. Intermediate numbers like 11 were represented by the sum of 10 and 1, etc., as ιά. This gave a notation for all numbers up to 999, and by a system of suffixes and indices the system was extended to represent numbers as high as 100,000,000. Until a comparatively late period these signs were used only to record results got by the use of the abacus; but at last they were employed in actual operations like our own. Long lists of multiples were learned by heart, and various operations of multiplication and division were obtained by repeated addition (σύνθεσις) and subtraction (ἀφαίρεσις). As late as the year 944 we find a scholar multiplying 400 by 5 by means of addition. A few skilled mathematicians like Hero of Alexandria and Theon multiplied as we do. Thus, to multiply 18 by 13 the operation was as follows:

$$\begin{aligned}\iota\gamma \times \iota\eta &= (\iota + \gamma)\,(\iota + \eta) \\ &= \iota(\iota + \eta) + \gamma(\iota + \eta) \\ &= \rho + \pi + \lambda + \kappa\delta \\ &= \sigma\lambda\delta\end{aligned} \qquad \begin{aligned}13 \times 18 &= (10 + 3)\,(10 + 8) \\ &= 10\,(10 + 8) + 3\,(10 + 8) \\ &= 100 + 80 + 30 + 24 \\ &= 234\end{aligned}$$

In the Alexandrian system thousands could be made by subscribing an ι beneath the units; thus, ͵α = 1000; ͵αωθα = 1891. A sort of algebraic method was also used for very large numbers—e. g. βM = $(2 \times 10{,}000) = 20{,}000$.

The Roman system is, in its ordinary use, familiar to all readers. It is thought that **V** denotes the opening between the thumb and the forefinger; **X** is two **V**'s with the angles together; **C** is possibly for *centum*, but probably an original ⊖ assimilated to **C**; **M** (ↀ) may be for *mille*, but probably for ⦶ modified; **L** is from an old Chalcidian form of **X**, inscribed for lapidary purposes as ⊥, and then simplified. Others believe **M** to be from a circle with a vertical stroke, and the **C** from a circle with a cross ⊕, from which last **V**, **X**, and **L** would also be derived. The Romans, like the Greeks, used the system of finger-signs, and did arithmetical operations by aid of the *abacus*. (See ABACUS.) Their arrangement of the latter was more complete than the Greek, and allowed very elaborate calculations; and, in fact, the Romans were, in general, better arithmeticians than the Greeks. There is a book by one Victorius of the fifth century B.C. entitled *Calculus*, which is a sort of "ready-reckoner" of sums, differences, products, quotients, reductions, etc.

Fractions (λεπτά) are variously represented in MS., but the most common way is to write the denominator over the numerator (the reverse of our method), or to write the numerator once with one accent and the denominator twice with two accents. Thus, $\overset{\kappa\alpha}{\iota\zeta}$, or ιζ′ κα″ κα″. The Romans treated fractions as did the Greeks, and attempted quite difficult operations, which were often very inexactly performed (Pliny, *H. N.* vi. 38).

On ancient numerals and arithmetic, see Delambre, *Die Arithmetik der Griechen*, rev. by Hoffmann (Mainz, 1817); Benloew, *Sur l'Origine des Noms de Nombre* (Giessen, 1861); Hoefer, *Histoire des Mathématiques*, 3d ed. (Paris, 1886); Martin, *Les Signes*

Numéraux, etc. (Rome, 1864); Friedlein, *Die Zahlzeichen*, etc. (Erlangen, 1869); Taylor, *The Alphabet*, ii. pp. 263–268 (London, 1883); and Treutlein, *Geschichte unserer Zahlzeichen* (1875).

As to the history of mathematics among the Greeks and Romans, it may be said that the earliest Greek school of mathematics was that founded by Thales of Miletus (B.C. 640–550), who studied astronomy and geometry in Egypt, and, after returning to Miletus, taught them to his disciples. (See THALES.) His geometrical teaching was largely deductive, and the following theorems of Euclid are ascribed to him: i. 5; i. 15; i. 26; vi. 4 (vi. 2?); iii. 31. He also wrote a treatise on astronomy. His philosophical follower, Anaximander, wrote a treatise on spherical geometry and constructional globes. This school, known as the Ionian School, flourished till about B.C. 400. It really gave more attention to astronomy than to geometry, which as an actual part of a liberal education, dates from Pythagoras (B.C. 569–500), whose philosophy and even whose ethics rested on a mathematical basis. He first arranged the leading problems of geometry in logical order, and carried arithmetic beyond the mere needs of the trader. (See Hoffmann, *Der pythagorische Lehrsatz* [Mainz, 1821].) Archytas, a follower of Pythagoras (about B.C. 400) and head of the school, applied mathematics to mechanics, and also worked in astronomy, teaching that the earth is a sphere revolving on its axis once in twenty-four hours. He attacked one of the most famous problems in antiquity—to find the side of a cube whose volume should be double that of a given cube. Two other well-known mathematical schools were the Eleatic, whose great name was Zeno's (B.C. 495–435), and the Atomistic School of Democritus of Abdera (B.C. 460–370). In the fourth century Athens became a great centre for mathematical study, and the scholars Anaxagoras (B.C. 500–428), Hippocrates of Chios, Eudoxus, Plato, and Theaetetus are among its greatest names. Hippocrates wrote the first text-book on geometry, and attempted the quadrature of the circle. Eudoxus founded the School of Cyzicus, to which Menaechmus and Aristaeus also gave distinction. Aristotle (B.C. 384–322) did much to stimulate the study of mathematics, and especially of mechanics. The establishment of a great university in Alexandria (see ALEXANDRIAN SCHOOL) made that city an intellectual centre; and there three of the greatest mathematicians of antiquity flourished—Euclid (B.C. 330?–275), Archimedes (B.C. 287–212), and Apollonius (B.C. 260–200). (See APOLLONIUS; ARCHIMEDES; EUCLIDES.) After these came Hipparchus, the most eminent of Greek astronomers (B.C. 160), whose work is preserved in Ptolemy's great treatise known as the *Almagest*. He determined the true length of the year, and placed the study of astronomy on a truly scientific basis. Hero of Alexandria (about B.C. 125) did the same for land-surveying and engineering. The Roman occupation of Egypt seriously interrupted the studies of the Alexandrian School; and no mathematicians of equal eminence with those already mentioned are afterwards found. The most original works subsequently published are the treatise by Serenus (A.D. 70) on the plane sections of the cone and cylinder, and that by Menelaüs on spherical trigonometry. About A.D. 100 the Jewish scholar Nicomachus wrote an arithmetic which, in a Latin version, remained the standard treatise on the subject for a thousand years. Ptolemy of Alexandria, who died in the year A.D. 168, was the author of a great work on astronomy; Pappus, in the third century, published a useful synopsis of Greek mathematics. In the fourth century geometrical studies decline, and algebra begins to be pursued, though possibly not unknown. It was probably at first what is called "rhetorical algebra"—i. e. the problems were solved by a process of reasoning expressed in words rather than in symbols. Diophantus of Alexandria (probably a non-Greek) introduced a system of signs and abbreviations. He lived in the fourth century A D. (See Heath, *Diophantos of Alexandria* [Cambridge, 1885].) His work is called *Arithmetica*, but is really an algebra. The last of the Alexandrian mathematicians are the famous Hypatia (q.v.) and Theon, her father. In the fifth century there were some Athenian geometricians of repute, such as Proclus, Damascius, and Eutocius; and in the sixth century the Roman Boëtius forms the link between the mathematical studies of antiquity and those of the Middle Ages. He wrote a geometry which contained the problems of the first book of Euclid and a few other selected propositions, and an arithmetic founded on that of Nicomachus. Cassiodorus (A.D. 470–566), and Isidorus of Seville (A.D. 570–636), also wrote in an elementary way of the various mathematical sciences.

See Hankel, *Zur Geschichte der Mathematik* (Leipzig, 1874); Hoefer, *Histoire des Mathématiques*, 3d ed. (Paris, 1886); Gow, *A Short History of Greek Mathematics* (Cambridge, 1884); and Ball, *A Short History of Mathematics* (London and New York, 1888).

Numeriānus, MARCUS AURELIUS. A Roman who succeeded to the imperial throne conjointly with his elder brother Carinus, after the death of their father Carus, at the beginning of A.D. 284. Numerianus was with the army in Mesopotamia at the death of Probus; but, instead of following up the advantage which his father had gained over the Persians, he was compelled by the army to abandon the conquests which had been already made, and to retreat to Syria. During the retreat, a weakness of the eyes obliged him to confine himself to a litter, which was guarded by the praetorians. The administration of all affairs, civil as well as military, devolved on Arrius Aper, the praetorian prefect, his father-in-law. The army was eight months on its march from the banks of the Tigris to the Thracian Bosporus, and during all that time the imperial authority was exercised in the name of the emperor, who never appeared to his soldiers. Reports at length spread among them that their emperor was no longer living; and when they had reached the city of Chalcedon they could not be prevented from breaking into the imperial tent, where they found only his corpse. Suspicion naturally fell upon Arrius; and an assembly of the army was accordingly held, for the purpose of avenging the death of Numerianus and electing a new emperor. Their choice fell upon Diocletian, who, immediately after his election, put Arrius to death with his own hands, without giving him an opportunity of justifying himself, which might, perhaps, have proved dangerous to the new emperor. The virtues of Numerianus are mentioned by most of his biographers. His manners were mild and affable; and he was celebrated among his contemporaries for eloquence and poetic talent. The Senate voted him a statue, with the inscription, "To Numerianus Caesar, the most powerful orator of his times" (Vopisc. *Numerian.*; Aurel. Vict. *De Caes.* 38; Eutrop. ix. 12).

Numĕrus. (1) See NUMERI. (2) The name of a body-guard of the later Roman emperors.

Numĕrus Italĭcus. See SATURNIUS VERSUS.

Numicia Via. See VIAE.

Numicius or **Numīcus.** Now Numico or Rio Torto; a small river in Latium flowing into the Tyrrhenian Sea near Ardea, on the banks of which was the tomb of Aeneas.

Numidia (Νουμιδία, Νομαδία, and Νομαδική). A country of Africa, bounded on the east by Africa Propria, on the north by the Mediterranean, on the south by Gaetulia, and on the west by Mauretania. The Roman province of Numidia was, however, of somewhat smaller extent. Intersected by a chain of the Lesser Atlas, and watered by the streams running down from it, it abounded in fine pastures, which were early taken possession of by wandering tribes of Asiatic origin, who from their occupation as herdsmen were called by the Greeks, here as elsewhere, Νομάδες, and this name was perpetuated in that of the country. A sufficient account of these tribes, and of their connection with their neighbours in the west, is given under MAURETANIA. The fertility of the country, inviting to agriculture, gradually gave a somewhat more settled character to the people; and, at their first appearance in Roman history, we find their two great tribes, the Massylians and the Massaesylians, forming two monarchies, which were united into one under Masinissa, B.C. 201. (See MASINISSA.) On Masinissa's death in 148, his kingdom was divided, by his dying directions, between his three sons, Micipsa, Mastanabal, and Gulussa; but it was soon reunited under Micipsa, in consequence of the death of both his brothers. His death, in 118, was speedily followed by the usurpation of Iugurtha, an account of which and of the ensuing war with the Romans is given under IUGURTHA. On the defeat of Iugurtha in 106, the country became virtually subject to the Romans, but they permitted the family of Masinissa to govern it, with the royal title (see HIEMPSAL; IUBA), until B.C. 46, when Iuba, who had espoused the cause of Pompey in the Civil Wars, was defeated and dethroned by Iulius Caesar, and Numidia was made a Roman province. It seems to have been about the same time or a little later, under Augustus, that the western part of the country was taken from Numidia, and added to Mauretania, as far east as Saldae. In B.C. 30 Augustus restored Iuba II. to his father's kingdom of Numidia; but in B.C. 25 he exchanged it for Mauretania, and Numidia—that is, the country between Saldae on the west and the Tusca on the east—became a Roman province. It was again diminished by near a half under Claudius; and henceforth, until the Arab conquest, the senatorial province of Numidia denoted the district between the river Ampsaga on the west and the Tusca on the east; its capital was Cirta (Constantin). The country, in its later restricted limits, is often distinguished by the name of New Numidia or Numidia Proper. The Numidians are known to military history as furnishing the best light cavalry in the Carthaginian and Roman armies.

Numidĭcus Sinus (Νουμιδικὸς κόλπος). A great gulf on the north of Numidia.

Numismatics (from νόμισμα, *numus* or *nummus*, "a coin"). The science which has to do with the study of coins and, in its widest acceptance, of medals also. The value of the science is not only historical and chronological, but artistic and archaeological in the broadest sense of the word. Coins furnish very valuable clues to the names, governments, etc., of many obscure cities and peoples of whom other remains are often unknown. They also give information concerning the development of the alphabet and writing; and they record the progress of art through all its stages of development and decline.

The ancient names for money are various. The Greeks use χρήματα of wealth in general, not merely coined money; ἀργύριον denotes money of any kind (originally silver money only); νομίσματα (from νόμος, "law"), legal-tender money (Herod. i. 94). The Romans employ *nummus* in various ways, but when not qualified it usually refers to the *sestertius*, which was the standard coin. In Late Latin *moneta* is the generic term for money, whence the modern word; but in the earlier usage *pecunia* is the word employed.

The principal materials for money were gold, silver, bronze; sometimes *electrum* (gold alloyed with silver), iron (at Sparta and some of the other Peloponnesian cities), nickel (used by the Greek kings in India), and rarely pure copper. We also read that Polycrates made coins of lead (Herod. iii. 56), Dionysius of tin (Pollux, ix. 79), and the Laconians of leather (Sen. *De Benef.* v. 14). See AES; ARGENTUM; AURUM; ELECTRUM; METALLUM; MONETA.

Greek coins are variously inscribed, having the name of the city or ruler issuing them; that of the monetary official or officials, and sometimes that of the artist who cut the die. The earliest of all bear no legend. Later, the names of cities appear, or of the people of the city in the genitive case—e. g. Συρακοσίων; or else the genitive adjective is used—e. g. Ἀρκαδικόν (sc. νόμισμα.) Names of kings are usually in the genitive. When magistrates' names are given they are sometimes in the nominative case and sometimes in the genitive preceded by ἐπί. At Athens, during the later days of her independence, every coin bears the names of three distinct magistrates. Other Greek coins (e. g. the later coins of Rhodes and Ephesus, and the copper money of the Achaean League) exhibit the name of only one magistrate. Artists' signatures occasionally occur, oftenest upon Sicilian coins. See Von Sallet, *Künstlerinschriften auf griech. Münzen* (1871); and Lenormant, *La Monnaie dans l'Antiquité*, iii. p. 255.

The earliest gold and silver money of the Romans bears only the word ROMA or ROMANO, with the mark of value; and by the time of Sulla the name of the city and the indication of value both disappear as unnecessary. There are used the names of the *triumvir monetalis* (this as early as B.C. 190), and from B.C. 100 legends explanatory of the "types" of the coins—e. g. P. P. (*Penates Publici*); or, fully written, SALVS beside the head of their deity. Under the Empire, coins regularly show the effigy of the emperor with his name and title, and the other side a date or an inscription referring to some historical event, or to a "type" with a like allusion

—e. g. FECVNDITATI AVGVSTAE, when the empress had just borne a child; FIDES MILITVM, when the soldiers had just presented a loyal address, etc. A word of explanation as to the terms "type" and "symbol" in their technical sense is necessary. "Type" is used of the principal device or subject on either obverse or reverse; "symbol" is applied to a minor figure. Thus the "type" belongs to the city or State; the "symbol" to the monetary magistrate.

GREEK COINS.—In Homer's time, cattle served as a medium of exchange and a standard of value (*Il.* xi. 211; xxi. 385); but metals were also used in the same way, and their value was decided by weight. The balance in which they were weighed was called τάλαντον, and the same name was given to the weight. The gold τάλαντον or talent of Homer was probably equivalent to the value of an ox, and in weight=2 drachmae. At an early date the idea arose of giving the metal so used a special form, but just when money was first coined with an official stamp is not known. As early as the fifth century B.C. a highly elaborated and artistic system of coinage was in existence. Various Greek standards of value were developed —in several gradations, it is true—from the gold and silver standard of Asia Minor. It was not until a later time that the standard of the Persian gold money was in some cities transferred to the silver coinage. The proportion of gold to silver was commonly reckoned among the Greeks as 10:1, so that a gold piece weighing 2 drachmae

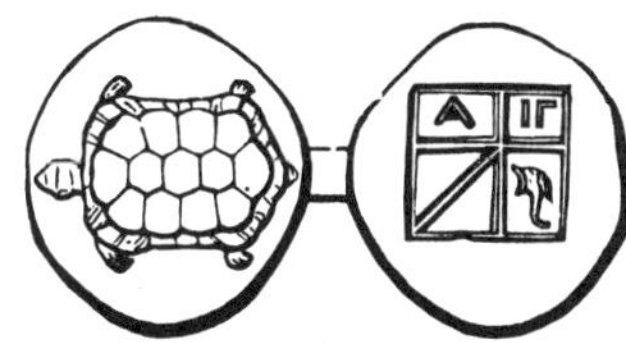

Aeginetan Drachma, actual size. (British Museum.)

was = 20 silver drachmae. But in commerce the proportion assumed was 12:1, and this was the average generally observed in the Roman Empire. The measure of weight most commonly current was the talent, which contained 60 minae. Like the talent, the mina was not a real coin, but a standard of measurement. The unit of coinage

Attic Drachma, actual size. (British Museum.)

was the drachma, 100 drachmae being reckoned to the mina. The drachma, again, contained 6 obols. In ancient times the commonly accepted standard was that of Aegina. The coins of the island of Aegina were stamped on one side with the figure of a tortoise, on the other side with a roughly executed incuse square. The largest silver coin was the στατήρ or *didrachmon* (=about $0.52, the Aeginetan drachma being=$0.26). Solon abolished this standard in Attica, and introduced a lighter drachma equal to about $0.16. The Attic talent (=6000 drachmae) was thus worth about $1000, the mina about $16. The silver coins of Attica bore on the front the head of Pallas, and on the reverse the figure of an owl. The principal coin was the τετράδραχμον or 4 drachmae, the largest (which was

Tetradrachmon of Athens. (Time of the Persian Wars.)

only issued occasionally) the δεκάδραχμον or 10 drachmae. The δίδραχμον (2 drachmae) was in like manner issued rarely. The τριώβολον (3 obols), the ὀβολός, and the ἡμιωβόλον (½ obol) were small silver coins; the τεταρτημόριον (¼ obol) the smallest of all.

The Greek States always adopted a silver currency, gold being rarely issued. The largest gold piece was the *didrachmon* or golden στατήρ (=20 silver drachmae). Besides this we find drachmas, triobols, obols, half-obols, quarter-obols, and even eighth-obols in gold. The gold money most com-

Gold Daric, actual size. (British Museum.)

monly current in Greece was, down to the Macedonian age, the royal Persian coin called δαρεικός, or daric. It was stamped on one side with a crowned archer, on the other with an oblong incuse. This corresponded with the gold stater of Attica and of the cities of Asia Minor. Among these should be especially mentioned the stater of Cyzicus or the *Cyzicenus*=28 silver drachmae. The earliest copper coin issued at Athens was the χαλκοῦς = ⅛ of a silver obol (B.C. 440). In the time of Alexander the Great the silver coinage stopped at the triobolus, and it therefore became necessary to represent the smaller fractions in copper. The silver money of Attica was in very general use, but the Attic standard was not adopted in Greece Proper. It spread westward, however, in quite early times. In the greater part of Sicily, and in Tarentum and Etruria, the coinage was from the

Silver Daric, actual size. (British Museum.)

first regulated in accordance with the Attic standard. But the wide diffusion of this standard was mainly due to the action of Philip II. of Macedon and Alexander the Great. The former adopted it when introducing his gold coinage (Φίλιππος), the latter for his silver money (see illustration); and even after Alexander's death this standard held its ground in the kingdoms of the Macedonian Empire, except in Egypt, where the Ptolemies maintained the old coinage of the country. Macedonian influence extended the Attic currency into many other States—e. g. Epirus, the coasts of the

Head of Apollo.

Victorious *biga*.

Gold Stater of Philip II. of Macedon.

Black Sea, and even Parthia. The largest Greek gold coin is the twenty-stater piece of the Graeco-Bactrian king Eucratides, now preserved in Paris;

Head of Heracles.

Zeus.

Tetradrachmon of Alexander the Great.

the largest silver coins are the ten-drachma pieces of Athens, Syracuse, and Alexander the Great.

Hellenic coins are important as giving an admirable idea of the development of the plastic art among the Greeks. In the Greek cities of Italy and Sicily, in particular, the art of stamping coins had attained considerable importance as early as

Coin of Chios.

the fifth century B.C., and in the fourth century, with its lifelike characterizations, and with the rich variety and noble perfection of its forms, it reached the highest degree of finish.

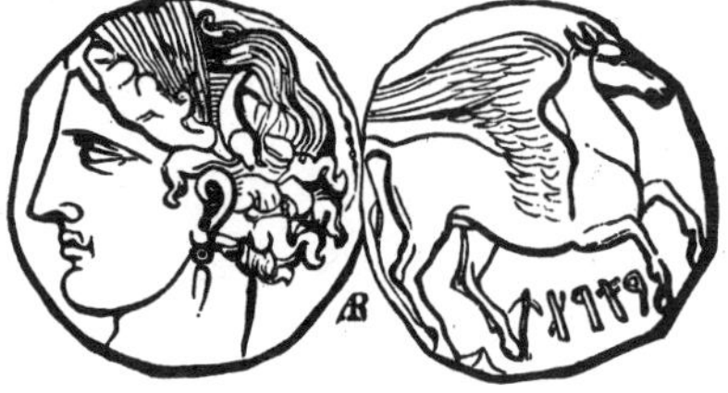

Coin of Carthage.

ROMAN COINS.—As in Greece, so at Rome, oxen and sheep were originally the medium of exchange. The oldest pecuniary fines were exacted in cattle, and the Latin word for money (*pecunia*), is derived from *pecus*. In later times unwrought copper (*aes rude*), given in pieces according to weight, took the place of oxen. Bars of cast copper marked on both sides with some figure (as of an ox, pig, or fowl) are said to have been introduced by King Servius Tullius when he took in hand the regulation of weights and measures. The first demonstrable example of a coin is from the age of the decemvirs (about B.C. 450). The unit of coinage was the *as* of cast copper, carrying the nominal weight of the Roman pound (*libra* = 12 *unciae*).

Roman *As* of Cast Copper.

The *as* (*aes grave*) bore the image of Ianus; the coins representing its fractions were all stamped on the reverse side with the figure of a ship's prow. These were *semis*, with the head of Iupiter = $\frac{1}{2}$ *as* or 6 *unciae; triens*, with the head of Minerva, $\frac{1}{3}$ of an *as* = 4 *unciae; quadrans*, with the head of Heracles, $\frac{1}{4}$ *as* = 3 *unciae; sextans*, with the head of Mercury, $\frac{1}{6}$ *as* = 2 *unciae; uncia*, with the head of Roma, $\frac{1}{12}$ *as*. As in the course of time the copper money became lighter, the smaller fractional coins were first struck, and afterwards all the fractions. This copper currency was intended exclusively for the home trade, so that it was easily allowed to suffer a continuous depreciation, at first to 4, then to 2, after B.C. 217 to 1 ounce, after B.C. 89 to $\frac{1}{2}$ an ounce, and under the Empire even to $\frac{1}{4}$ an ounce. In B.C. 269 a silver currency was intro-

Denarii, actual size. (British Museum.)

duced, and a mint for it set up on the Capitoline Hill in the temple of Iuno Moneta. The silver fractional coins struck according to the Athenian and Sicilian standard were the *denarius* (about $0.19) = 10 *asses* of 4 ounces; the *quinarius* = 5 *asses;* and the *sestertius* = $2\frac{1}{2}$ *asses*. These coins were denoted by the characters X, V, and HS (II.S [*semis*] respectively. There is displayed on the obverse the head of Roma personified, wearing a winged helmet, and on the reverse the Dioscuri on horseback. Later we find Diana Victoria in a *biga* or two-horse chariot, or Iupiter in a quadriga, but from the middle of the first century there is no fixed device for the reverse. The *sestertius* was the equivalent of the old *as*. Payments were made in *denarii*, but calculated in *sestertii*, whence, as stated above, the word *nummus* (coin) is generally synonymous with *sestertius*.

Sestertius.

The reduction of the copper *as* to 1 *uncia* in B.C. 217 degraded the copper money to the position of small coin, and silver currency drove out the copper. The *denarius* sank at the same time to the value of about $0.15, which it maintained till the time of Nero. The *denarius* was reckoned as = 16 *asses*, the *quinarius* as 8, and the *sestertius* (nearly $0.03) = 4. At about the same period a temporary effort was made to introduce gold coinage. This movement was not taken up again till towards the end of the Republic, when Caesar struck a large number of gold coins (*aurei*) equal in weight to $\frac{1}{40}$ of the Roman pound, and in value 25 *denarii* or 100 *sestertii* (a little over $5). No regular coinage was carried on in the time of the Republic, but the necessary money was minted as occasion required. This was done in Rome at the commission of the Senate under the superintendence of certain officials intrusted with the duty. A permanent board of three persons (*tres viri monetales*) was at last appointed for the purpose. In the provinces money was coined by the Roman generals and governors. From the time of Augustus the emperor retained the exclusive privilege of coining gold and silver money, the copper coinage being left to the Senate. The standard of the imperial coinage was the *aureus* of Caesar, the weight of which sank with many variations lower and lower, until Constantine (A.D. 312) fixed it at $\frac{1}{72}$ of a pound (about $3). The *aureus* now got the name of *solidus*, and was stamped, first with the Roman numeral LXXII, and later with the Greek numeral OB = 72. It remained in use down to the fall of the Eastern Empire, the name surviving in modern times in the Italian *soldo*. Of the silver pieces of the Republic, the *denarius* and the *quinarius* alone remained in use under the Empire, all the rest being stamped in copper. The *denarius* remained of the value of $0.17, as fixed in B.C. 217, until Nero's time, when it was reduced in weight and fineness until it was worth only about $0.12. During the second century it fell to $0.06, and the silver coinage in consequence was changed to small money. Diocletian, about A.D. 292, reformed the currency, issuing a new silver coin, the *argenteus*, equal in weight to Nero's *denarius*. This was in use until A.D. 360, when a new system of silver coinage on the basis of the gold *solidus* was instituted.

Aureus of Marcus Aurelius.

The copper coins, as issued by the authority of the Senate, bore the letters S. C. (*senatus consulto*). The following small coins were issued under the Empire: *sestertius* = 4 *asses*; *dupondius* = 2 *asses*; *semis* = ½ *as*; and the *quadrans* = ¼ *as*. The *sestertius* and the *dupondius* were of brass; the *semis* and *quadrans* of copper. The *quadrans* was disused under Trajan; the *dupondius*, *as*, *semis*, and *sestertius* under Diocletian.

Gold Solidus.

BIBLIOGRAPHY.—See Eckhel, *Doctrina Numorum* (1792–98); Head, *Historia Numorum* (Oxford, 1887); id., *A Guide to the Principal Gold and Silver Coins of the Ancients* (3d ed. London, 1889); Mionnet, *Description des Médailles Grecques* (Paris, 1807–37); Mommsen, *Geschichte des röm. Münzwesens* (Berlin, 1860); Babelon, *Monnaies de la République Romaine* (Paris, 1885); Cohen, *Description Historique des Monnaies Frappées sous l'Empire Romain*, 7 vols. (2d ed. Paris, 1880–88); and Stephenson, *Dictionary of Roman Coins* (London, 1889). For Byzantine and mediæval coins, see Sabatier, *Monnaies Byzantines* (Paris, 1862); and Serrure, *Traité de Numismatique du Moyen Âge* (Paris, 1891). On the mintage, see MONETA.

Numĭtor. See ROMULUS.

Nummularii. See TRAPEZITAE.

Nummus or **Numus**. A special name for the commonest coin at Rome, which generally served as the unit of reckoning—the *sestertius*. See NUMISMATICS (Roman); SESTERTIUS.

Nuncupatio. See TESTAMENTUM.

Nundĭnae (Old Lat. *noundinae*). The Roman term for the market day held on the last day of the week of eight days, on which countrymen rested from labour and came to Rome to buy and sell, as well as to do other business. Accordingly the Nundinae were used for public announcements especially concerning public assemblies and the business to be conducted in them. The actual holding of the assemblies on these days was avoided, so as not to prevent the people from attending to the business of the market. Originally, too, no legal business was conducted on them, and it was not till the beginning of the third century B.C. that it was introduced. The Nundinae, though not a regular feast-day, were nevertheless celebrated in private life by inviting strangers to one's table and exempting children from going to school. The form *nundinum* (sc. *tempus*) or *inter nundinum* means the whole period of eight days. In late Latin, *nundinium* means the period of the consulship (Mommsen, *Staatsrecht*, ii. 84; iii. 375). See DIES.

Nupta (νύμφη). A bride. See MATRIMONIUM.

Nuptiae. See MATRIMONIUM.

Nursia. A town of the Sabines, situated near the sources of the Nar and amid the Apennines, whence it is called by Vergil *frigida Nursia* (*Aen.* vii. 716). It was the birthplace of Sertorius and of the mother of Vespasian.

Nuts, GAMES PLAYED WITH. See NUCES.

Nux. The title of an elegiac poem in 182 lines often ascribed to Ovid, and probably of a date not much later than that poet. It voices the complaint of a nut-tree concerning ill-treatment and the degeneracy of the times. It is based upon a poem in the Greek anthology (*Anthol. Palat.* ix. 3), and is written in an ornate but graceful style. It is edited with a commentary by Lindemann (Zittau, 1844); critical text in Bährens, *Poetae Lat. Minores*, i. 90 (Leipzig, 1886).

Nyctēis (Νυκτηΐς). See NYCTEUS.

Nycteus (Νυκτεύς). Son of Hyrieus and Clonia and father of Antiopé, who is hence called Nycteïs. Antiopé was carried off by Epopeus, king of Sicyon; whereupon Nycteus, who governed Thebes, as the guardian of Labdacus, invaded Sicyon with a Theban army. Nycteus was defeated, and died of his wounds, leaving his brother Lycus guardian of Labdacus. See Hyg. *Fab.* 7, and LYCUS.

Nyctimĕné. Daughter of Epopeus, king of Lesbos. Having been dishonoured by her father, she concealed herself in the shade of forests, where she was metamorphosed by Athené into an owl (Ovid, *Met.* ii. 590; Hyg. *Fab.* 204).

Nymphae (Νύμφαι, properly "the young maidens"). Inferior divinities of nature dwelling in groves, forests, and caves, beside springs, streams, and rivers; in some cases, too, on lonely islands, like Calypso and Circé. The nymphs of the hills, the forests, the meadows, and the springs (called in Homer daughters of Zeus, while Hesiod makes the nymphs of the hills and the forests, together with the hills and the forests, children of earth) appear as the benevolent spirits of these spots, and lead a life of liberty, sometimes weaving in grottoes, sometimes dancing and singing, sometimes hunting with Artemis, or revelling with Dionysus. Besides these divinities it is especially Apollo, Hermes, and Pan who are devoted to them and seek after their love; while the wanton satyrs are also continually lying in wait for them. They are well disposed towards mortals, and ready to help them; they even wed with them. According to the various provinces of nature were distinguished various kinds of nymphs: nymphs of rivers (Ποταμηΐδες) and springs, the Naiads (Νηΐδες), to whom the Oceanids (Ὠκεανίδες) and Nereïds (Νηρηΐδες) are closely related; nymphs of the hills, Oreads (Ὀρειάδες); nymphs of the forests and trees, Dryads (Δρυάδες) or Hamadryads (Ἁμαδρυάδες); besides this they often received special names after certain places, hills, springs, and grottoes. The Naiads, as the goddesses of the nourishing and fructifying water, were especially rich in favours, giving increase and fruitfulness to plants, herds, and mortals. Hence, they were also considered as the guardian goddesses of marriage, and the besprinkling of the bride with spring-water was one of the indispensable rites of the marriage ceremony. On the same principle, legendary lore represents them as nursing and bringing up the children of the gods, as, for instance, Zeus and Dionysus. Further, owing to the healing and inspiring power of many springs, they belong to the divinities of healing and prophesying, and can even drive men into a transport of prophetic and poetic inspiration. The Muses themselves are, in their origin, fountain-nymphs. Popular belief assigned to the nymphs in general an exceedingly long life, without actual immortality. The existence of Dryads, it was supposed, was closely bound up with the origin and decay of the tree in which they dwelt. They enjoyed divine honours from the earliest times, originally in the spots where they had power, at fountains, and in groves and grottoes. In later times shrines of their own, hence called Nymphaea, were built to them, even in cities. These eventually became very magnificent buildings, in which it was customary to celebrate marriages. Goats, lambs, milk, and oil were offered to them. Works of art represented them in the form of charming maidens, lightly clothed or naked, with flowers and garlands; the Naiads drawing water, or carrying it in an urn. They appear as the attendants of Hermes, the deity of herdsmen; of Pan, of Artemis, and of Apollo—this last in the prophetic character.

Nymphaeum (Νυμφαῖον). (1) A mountain, with perhaps a village, by the river Aoüs, near Apollonia, in Illyricum. (2) A port and promontory on the coast of Illyricum. (3) The southwestern promontory of Acté or Athos, in Chalcidicé. (4) A seaport town of the Tauric Chersonese (Crimea), on the Bosporus. (5) A place on the coast of Bithynia. (6) A place in Cilicia.

Nymphaeum (νυμφαῖον). A room forming a part of the Flavian Palace at Rome. (See PALATIUM, p. 1159.) The name in general designates a grand and lofty chamber, decorated with columns, statues, and pictures, and having a stream of spring-water, gushing from a fountain, in its centre, so as to form a cool and agreeable retreat for the resort of a luxurious population (Philostr. iv. 8). Many edifices of this description are enumerated by P. Victor (*Urb. Rom.*) in the city of Rome; and other writers generally speak of them in connection with the public baths (Ammian. xv. 7, 3; Capitol. *Gord.* 32).

Nymphaeus (Νύμφαιος). (1) A small river of Latium (now the Ninfa) falling into the sea above Astura, and contributing to the formation of the Pomtine marshes. (2) A small river of Armenia, a tributary of the Upper Tigris.

Nymphis (Νύμφις). The son of Xenagoras of Heraclea, who flourished about B.C. 250. He wrote a work on Alexander the Great and his successors in twenty-four books (Suid. s. v.).

Nymphodōrus (Νυμφόδωρος). A Syracusan of the time of Alexander the Great. He wrote a *Periplus* of Asia and a work on Sicily.

Nysa (Νύσα). The legendary scene of the nurture of Dionysus (Bacchus), who was therefore called Nysaeus, Nysius, Nyseïus, Nyseus, Nysigena, etc. Hence the name was applied to several places sacred to that god: as (1) in India, at the northwest corner of the Punjab, near the confluence of the rivers Cophen and Choaspes. (2) NYSSA, a city of Caria, on the southern slope of Mount Messogis, famous for its wine. (3) A city of Cappadocia, near the Halys, the bishopric of St. Gregory of Nyssa. (4) A town in Aethiopia near Meroë (Herod. iii. 97, 111). (5) A village on the slopes of Helicon, in Boeotia.

Nysaeus. See NYSA.

Nyseïdes or **Nysiădes.** The Nymphs of Nysa, who are said to have reared Dionysus, and whose names are Cisseïs, Nysa, Erato, Eriphia, Bromia, and Polyhymno (Apollod. iii. 4, 3).

Nyx (Νύξ), by the Romans called **Nox**. One of the most ancient deities, daughter of Chaos. From her union with her brother Erebus, she gave birth to the Day and the Light. She was also the mother of the Moerae, Hesperides, Hypnos, Nemesis, Discord, Thanatos, Momus, Fraus, etc. She is called by some of the poets the mother of all things, of gods as well as of men, and was worshipped with great solemnity. A black sheep and a cock, the latter as announcing the approach of day, were sacrificed to her.

Night was represented under various forms: as riding in a chariot preceded by the constellations, with wings, to denote the rapidity of her course; as traversing the firmament seated in her car, and covered with a black veil studded with stars. Sometimes her veil seems to be floating on the wind, while she approaches the earth to extinguish a flaming torch which she carries in her hand. She has often been confounded with Artemis, or the moon; and her statue was placed in the temple of that goddess at Ephesus (Hyg. *Praef.*; Serv. *ad* Verg. *Aen.* vi. 250; Tibull. iii. 4, 17; Verg. *Aen.* v. 721, etc.).

O

O, as a symbol.

IN GREEK.—

O = ὀβολός. OO = 2 ὀβολοί, etc.

As a numeral, o = 15 (old system) or 70 (ō), ͵o = 70,000.

IN LATIN.—

O = optio, horae, ovum, obiit.

O·B·Q·T = ossa bene quiescant tibi.

O·C = opus constat.

O·C·S = ob cives servatos.

O·H·F = omnibus honoribus functus.

O·M = ob memoriam.

O·M·C·P·F·V·C·C·T = oppidum municipium colonia praefectura forum vicus conciliabulum castellum territorium.

O·N·F = omnium nomine faciundum.

O·O·D = ornatus ornamentis decurionalibus.

O·S = ossa sita.

O·S·T·T·L = opto sit tibi terra levis.

O·T(V)·B·C(Q) = ossa tibi (volo), bene cubent (quiescant).

O·V = oro vos, ornatus vir.

O·V·F·D·R·P·O·V·F = oro vos faciatis, dignum re publica, oro vos faciatis.

Oănus (Ὤανος). The modern Frascolari; a river in Sicily near Camarina.

Oars. See NAVIS; REMUS.

Oărus (Ὄαρος). A river of Sarmatia, rising in the country of the Thyssagetae, and falling into the Palus Maeotis (Herod. iv. 123). This river has not yet been satisfactorily identified.

Oăsis (Ὄασις and Αὔασις). The Greek form of the Egyptian word *Uah*, which was used to denote an island in the sea of sand of the great Libyan Desert. These oases are preserved from the shifting sands by steep hills of limestone round them, and watered by springs, which make them fertile and habitable. The name is applied especially to two of these oases on the west of Egypt, which were taken possession of by the Egyptians at an early period. (1) OĂSIS MAIOR (Ὄασις μεγάλη), the Greater Oasis, was situated seven days' journey west of Abydos, and belonged to Upper Egypt. This oasis contains numerous ruins of the ancient Egyptian and Roman periods. (2) OASIS MINOR (Ὄασις μικρά), the Lesser or Second Oasis, was a good day's journey from the southwestern end of Lake Moeris, and belonged to the Heptanomis, or Middle Egypt. (3) A still more celebrated oasis than either of these was that called AMMON, HAMMON, AMMONIUM, HAMMŌNIS ORACŬLUM, from its being a chief seat of the worship and oracle of the god Ammon. It is now called Siwah. Its distance from Cairo is twelve days, and from the northern coast about 160 English miles. The Ammonians do not appear to have been subject to the old Egyptian monarchy. Cambyses, after conquering Egypt in B.C. 525, sent an army against them, which was overwhelmed by the sands of the desert. In B.C. 331, Alexander the Great visited the oracle, which hailed him as the son of Zeus Ammon (Q. Curt. iv. 33). Cato the Younger also made a journey to the place. Ruins of the temple of Ammon still exist.

Oath. See IUSIURANDUM; SACRAMENTUM.

Oaxes. See OAXUS.

Oaxus (Ὄαξος), called **Axus** (Ἄξος) by Herodotus. A town in the interior of Crete on the river Oaxes (Herod. iv. 154).

Obae. See TRIBUS.

Obba (ἄμβιξ). A drinking-cup made of earthenware or wood (Pers. v. 148; Varro *ap.* Non. p. 545 Müll.), and of uncertain shape. The epithet *sessilis* applied to it by Persius (Conington's "squab noggin") suggests a vessel with a broad bottom.

Obeliscus (ὀβελίσκος). Literally, a small spit, diminutive of ὀβελός; whence applied to other things which possess a sharp or pointed extremity, like a spit; and especially to the tall, slender, rectangular columns, upon a narrow base, and terminating in a point at the top, which were originally invented by the Egyptians, and retain their ancient name with us (Pliny, *H. N.* xxxvi. 13; Ammian. xvii. 4, 6). The obelisk served in Egyptian art the same purpose as the στήλη of the Greeks and the *columna* of the Romans, marking the triumphs or the honours of some prince. They are monoliths, cut in four faces, and are broader at the base than at the top, near which the sides form the base of a pyramid in which the obelisk terminates. The sides are very slightly concave, in order to increase the impression of height, which varies from 25½ inches to a hundred feet. Upon them are usually cut inscriptions in hieroglyphics and pictures recording the names and titles of kings. They were transported in rafts from their quarries at the time of the inundation of the Nile, and raised by means of inclined planes aided by machinery. Some of the obelisks give evidences of having originally had their tips covered with gilded bronze or gold. The use of obelisks antedates history, and has continued to modern times. Most of the Egyptian obelisks date from the eighteenth and nineteenth dynasties (B.C. 1800–1300). The most famous two once stood at Heliopolis, whence they were brought by Rameses II. to Alexandria. These are the ones

Ancient Obelisk.

popularly known as "Cleopatra's Needles," of which one was taken to London in 1878 and set up on the Thames Embankment, and the other to New York in 1881, where it is now one of the ornaments of Central Park. There are several at Rome—in the Piazza della Trinità, the Piazza di Monte Citorio, the Piazza del Quirinale, the Piazza dell' Esquilino, the Piazza della Minerva, the Circo Agonale (Piazza Navona), the Piazza di San Giovanni in Laterano, the Piazza del Popolo, and the Piazza di San Pietro, and others of no historical importance. The last named was brought from Heliopolis by Caligula, and is the only one at Rome that has never been broken. Its height is 132 feet. There are also ancient obelisks at Florence, Constantinople, Arles, Catana, and Paris, and one (Lepsius's) at Berlin, this being at once the oldest and the smallest of all, having a height of only 2 feet 1½ inches. Of these small obelisks other specimens are to be seen in various European museums. No ancient obelisk ever attained the height of the modern American obelisk at Washington, though this, of course, is not a monolith. See Birch, *Notes upon Obelisks* (London, 1853); and Gorringe, *Egyptian Obelisks* (New York, 1885).

Obĕlus. See NOTAE.

Obex. A generic Latin term for a door-fastening, applicable alike to bolt, bar, lock, and latch (Ovid, *Met.* xiv. 780; Tac. *Hist.* iii. 30). See IANUA.

Obligatio. A legal bond by which one is bound to the performance of some act at the behest and for the benefit of another person (*Inst.* iii. 13). It may, however, be of a negative character, in which case the persons bound must abstain from some specified act. Obligationes to be binding must satisfy their creditors: (1) they must be lawful in nature and form; (2) they must have a money value to the person in whose favour they are assumed; and (3) they must be definite and specific. See Savigny's *Obligationenrecht* (2 vols. 1851–53).

Obligatio Litterārum. One of the four modes of incurring contractive obligations was "by letters" (*litteris*, Gaius, iii. 137). The contract was made by the creditor's entry in his account-book (*codex accepti et expensi*) under the head of *expensum* to the debtor. To this entry the debtor's assent was necessary (Val. Max. viii. 2, 2), but he need not actually have received the money. The items of receipt and expenditure appear to have been entered without distinction, in the order of their occurrence, in a day-book (*adversaria*), and transcribed at the end of each month into a ledger (*tabulae, codex accepti et expensi*), the precise form and character of which is much disputed, though most probably it was arranged in two sides or columns after the fashion of an ordinary banker's pass-book. The entry in this ledger (*nomen facere*) made the contract, and bound the debtor to repay the specified sum: it was not merely evidence, admitting of the possibility of rebuttal. We are told by Gaius (iii. 131) that if an entry were made in the codex of an actual money loan, the obligation to repay it arose *re*, not *litteris*, and the debt was called specifically *nomen arcarium*, the written record serving merely as evidence. It follows that wherever a genuine money debt was created *litteris* it must have been under the fiction of a loan, as appears to have been the case in two instances of debts originally incurred in this manner of which we have a record (Cic. *Ad Att.* iv. 18; Val. Max. viii. 2, 2).

Obliviōnis Flumen. See LIMAEA.

Obŏlus (ὀβολός). A piece of money (Greek) originally of silver, but in later times (after B.C. 400) of bronze. The Attic obolus was worth about three cents American; and the Aeginetan obolus, about five cents. There were also *tetroboli, trioboli,* and *dioboli;* and fractional denominations, such as the *hemiobolus, tetartimorion,* etc. The Attic obolus = 8 *chalci*. See CHALCUS; NUMISMATICS (Greek).

Obrĭmas. An eastern tributary of the Maeander in Phrygia (Livy, xxxviii. 15).

Obringa (Ὀβρίγκας). A western tributary of the Rhine, identified by modern geographers with the Ahr, which joins the Rhine between Bonn and Andernach (Ptol. ii. 10, 17).

Obsĕquens, IULIUS. The author of a work entitled *De Prodigiis* or *Prodigiorum Libellus*, of which a portion is extant. Of the writer nothing is known save that he flourished about the year A.D. 369. He gives us a record of the prodigies and portents in Roman history, arranged in chronological order from B.C. 190 to B.C. 11. The writer borrows largely from Livy. It is edited by O. Jahn (Leipzig, 1863); and in Weissenborn-Müller's Livy, vol. x. (2d ed. Berlin, 1881).

Crepida with Obstragulum.

Obsidionālis Corōna. See CORONA.

Obsonium. See VICTUS.

Obstragŭlum. The flat leather strap used in fastening on the shoe known as the *crepida* (q. v.).

Obturacŭlum and **Obturamentum.** A stopper for closing the mouth of a jar or bottle. It was sometimes of cork and sometimes of glass (Marcell. Empir. 35; Pliny, *H. N.* xvi. § 13).

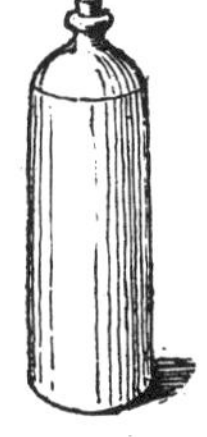
Glass Bottle with Obturaculum. (Found at Pompeii.)

Ocalea (Ὠκαλέα). An ancient town in Boeotia, situated on a river of the same name falling into Lake Copaïs (Strabo, p. 410).

Occatio (βωλοκοπία). Harrowing. It was effected by drawing a hurdle (*crates*) over the land, or a wooden frame set with teeth (*dentata*), similar to our harrow, often weighted by the driver standing upon it; and in very stiff soils the clods were broken and levelled by hand, with a heavy pronged instrument (*rastrum*), possessing the properties of a rake and hoe (Verg. *Georg.* i. 94, 95).

Occult Sciences. See ASTROLOGIA; MAGUS.

Occupatio. The taking possession of a thing which belongs to no one (*res nullius*), with the intention of appropriating it: the property in it is thereby *ipso facto* vested in him who takes possession (Cic. *De Off.* i. 7, 21). Among the things of which one can become owner in this fashion are wild animals, birds, bees, and fishes (Just. *Inst.* ii. 1, 12-16), enemies' property on Roman soil (*ib.* 17), stones and pebbles found on the sea-shore (*ib.* 18), islands which rise in the sea (*ib.* 22), treasure-trove (*ib.* 39), and *res derelictae*, property abandoned by its former owner (*ib.* 47).

Oceanĭdes. See NYMPHAE.

Oceănus (Ὠκεανός). (1) The god of the stream Oceanus, earlier than Poseidon. He was the first-born of the Titans, the offspring of Uranus and Gaea, or Heaven and Earth. Oceanus espoused his sister Tethys, and their children were the rivers of the earth and the three thousand Oceanides or Nymphs of Ocean (Hesiod, *Theog.* 337 foll.). This is all the account of Oceanus that is given in the *Theogony*. Homer speaks of him and Tethys as the father even of the gods (*Il.* xiv. 201, 246, 302). When Zeus placed his sire in Tartarus, Rhea committed her daughter Heré to the charge of Oceanus and Tethys, by whom she was carefully nurtured. The abode of Oceanus was in the West (*Il.* xiv. 200, 301). He dwelt, according to Aeschylus, in a grotto palace, beneath his stream, as it would appear (*Prom. Vinct.* 300). In the *Prometheus Vinctus* of this poet, Oceanus comes borne through the air on a hippogriff, to console and advise the heroic sufferer; and from the account given of his journey, it is manifest that he came from the West. When Heracles was crossing his stream in the cup of the Sun-god to procure the oxen of Geryon, Oceanus rose, and, by agitating his waters, tried to terrify him; but, on the hero's bending a bow at him, he retired.

(2) Besides being the name of a deity, the term Oceanus (Ὠκεανός) occurs in Homer in another sense also. It is made to signify an immense stream, which, according to the rude ideas of that early age, circulated around the terraqueous plain, and from which the different seas ran out in the manner of bays. This opinion, which is also that of Eratosthenes, was prevalent even in the time of Herodotus (iv. 36). Homer terms the ocean ἀψόρροος, because it thus flowed back into itself. This same river Oceanus was supposed to ebb and flow thrice in the course of a single day, and the heavenly bodies were believed to descend into it at their setting and emerge from it at their rising. Hence the term ὠκεανός is sometimes put for the horizon. In Homer, therefore, ὠκεανός and θάλασσα always mean different things, the latter merely denoting the sea in the more modern acceptation of the term. On the shield of Achilles the poet represents Oceanus as encircling the rim or extreme border of the shield, in full accordance with the popular belief of the day, whereas in Vergil's time, when this primitive meaning of the term was obsolete, and more correct geographical views had come in, we find the sea (the idea being borrowed, probably, from the position of the Mediterranean) occupying in the poet's description the *centre* of the shield of Aeneas. Herodotus (ii. 23; iv. 8) rejects the notion that Oceanus is a stream. See GEOGRAPHIA.

It is remarkable that one of the oldest names of the Nile among the Greeks was ὠκεανός.

Ocēlis (Ὄκηλις). Now Ghela; a harbour and mart in Arabia Felix, at the entrance of the Red Sea (Ptol. i. 7, 4).

Ocellāta. A sort of marble used in play by the Roman children (Suet. *Aug.* 83), and probably so called from *oculus*, either because of their shape or colour, or both—the "allies" of our school-boys. See NUCES.

Ocellus (Ὄκελλος). An Italian Greek of Lucania, who wrote a work on the nature of the Whole (Περὶ τῆς τοῦ Παντὸς Φύσεως). His date is uncertain. There is an edition of the work by Mullach (1846).

Ocĕlum. (1) A town in the Cottian Alps, now Oulx. It was the last place in Cisalpine Gaul before entering the territories of King Cottius. (2) A town in the northeastern part of Lusitania. (3) A promontory of Britain, perhaps Spurn Head (Ptol. ii. 3, 6).

Ocha (Ὄχη). The highest mountain in Euboea in the south of the island near Carystus. The name Ocha was once applied to the whole island (Strabo, pp. 445, 446).

Ochlocratia (ὀχλοκρατία). The dominion of the rabble, or "mobocracy." It is a name of later origin than the time of Aristotle, and applied to that perversion of a democracy which extends the idea far beyond that of a State where all have equal legal rights and equal franchise, so that the natural and wholesome inequalities of society were removed or counteracted by the introduction of devices, such as paying citizens for attendance in the popular assembly, or increasing the number and restricting the duration and authority of public offices. Hence the exercise of all the highest functions of government came to be practically in the hands of a mere faction, consisting of the lowest and poorest, though most numerous, class of citizens, who were thus tempted to adopt as their vocation that which they would formerly have delegated to others; and the State came to be regarded as a *property* of which each citizen was entitled to an equal share. In some respects, therefore, it most nearly represents the modern idea of a socialistic State (Aristot. *Pol.* iv. 5).

Ochus. A surname of Artaxerxes III., king of Persia, who reigned B.C. 359–338. In order to secure his throne, he began his reign with a merciless extirpation of the members of his family. He himself was a cowardly and reckless despot; and the great advantages which the Persian arms gained during his reign were owing only to his Greek generals and mercenaries. These advantages consisted in the conquest of the revolted satrap Artabazus and in the reduction of Phœnicia, of several revolted towns in Cyprus, and of Egypt, B.C. 350. The reins of government were entirely in the hands of the eunuch Bagoas and of Mentor the Rhodian. At last he was poisoned by Bagoas, and was succeeded by his youngest son, Arses. See PERSIA.

Ochus (Ὄχος). A great river of Central Asia, supposed by some to be the same as the Oxus (Pliny, *H. N.* vi. 48).

Ocrea (κνημίς). A greave; a piece of defensive armour covering the shin from the ankle to a little above the knee, and fastened by buckles or straps at the back of the leg which was left uncovered (Varro, *L. L.* v. 116). It was made of metal (tin or bronze), and often ornamented, embossed, or chased with various designs. That the greaves were an important feature of the warrior's equipment is

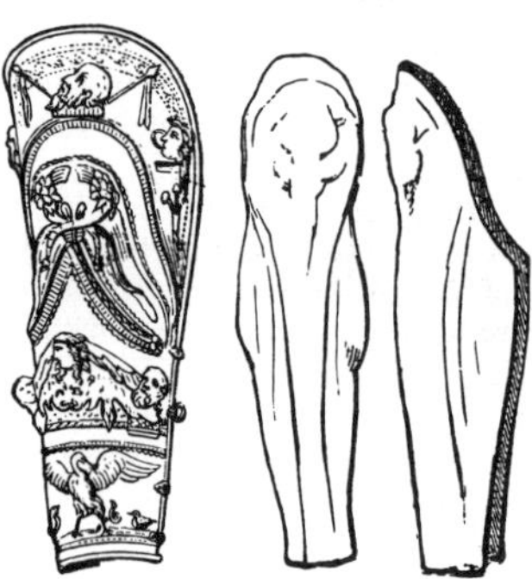

Bronze Greaves found at Pompeii.

seen by the epithet εὐκνημῖδες continually applied by Homer to the Greeks, and from the minuteness with which he describes their various parts, especially the ankle-rings (ἐπισφύρια), which were often of silver (*Il.* iii. 331). Several species of bronze greaves have been found at Pompeii, probably belonging to the gladiators.

Greek Warrior wearing Greaves. (Hope.)

Ocricŭlum. See OTRICULUM.

Ocrisia. The mother of Servius Tullius (q. v.).

Octastȳlus (ὀκτάστυλος). A term applied to a temple having a row of eight columns in front of the *pronaos* (Vitruv. iii. 3, 7).

Octāvae. See VECTIGALIA.

Octavia. (1) A daughter of Gaius Octavius and Accia, and sister to the emperor Augustus. All the historians praise the beauty and virtues of this celebrated woman. She was first married to Marcus Marcellus, a man of consular rank, and every way worthy of her; and after his death she became the wife of M. Antonius, this latter union being deemed essential to the public welfare, as a means of healing existing differences between Antonius and Octavianus. It was with this view that the Senate abridged the period of her widowhood and of her mourning for her first husband, who had been dead little more than five months. Antonius, however, was incapable of appreciating the excellence of her character. After her marriage she followed him to Athens, where she passed the winter with him (B.C. 39), though keeping far aloof from the dissolute pleasures to which he abandoned himself. Without her interposition, civil war would even then have broken out between Octavianus and Antonius. By urgent prayers she appeased her husband, who was incensed against her brother for his suspicions, and then, disregarding the difficulties of the journey and her own pregnancy, she went with his consent from Greece to Rome, and induced her brother to consent to an interview with Antonius, and to come to a reconciliation with him. When Antonius went to make war against the Parthians, she accompanied him to Corcyra, and at his order returned thence to remain with her brother. New quarrels arose between Octavianus and Antonius. To have a pretext for a rupture, the former ordered his sister to go to her husband, in the expectation that he would send her back. This actually happened. Antonius was leading a life of pleasure with Cleopatra at Leucopolis, when letters from Octavia at Athens informed him that she would soon join him with money and troops. The prospect of this visit was so unwelcome to Cleopatra that she persisted in her entreaties until Antonius sent his wife an order to return. Even now, however, she endeavoured to pacify the rivals. Octavianus commanded her to leave the house of a husband who had treated her so insultingly; but, feeling her duties as a wife and a Roman, she begged him not, for the sake of a single woman, to destroy the peace of the world, and of two persons so dear to her, by the horrors of war. Octavianus granted her wish; she remained in the house of Antonius, and occupied herself with educating, with equal care and tenderness, the children she had borne him and those of his first wife Fulvia. This noble behaviour of hers increased the indignation of the Romans against Antonius. At last, when war broke out between Antonius and Octavianus, he divorced her, and ordered her to leave his mansion at Rome. She obeyed without complaint, and after his death reared the children he had had by Fulvia and Cleopatra. She died in B.C. 11. Her children numbered five—three by Marcellus and two by Antonius, the last being daughters. Her son, M. Marcellus, was adopted by Augustus, and was intended by him for his successor; but he died in B.C. 23. (See MARCELLUS.) Her elder daughter by Antonius was the grandmother of the emperor Nero, and the younger was the mother of the emperor Claudius and grandmothor of Caligula.

Octavia. (Porphyry Bust in the Louvre.)

(2) The daughter of the emperor Claudius, born A.D. 42. She was first betrothed by Claudius to L. Silanus, who put an end to his life, as Agrippina had destined Octavia to be the wife of her son, afterwards the emperor Nero. She was married to Nero in A.D. 53, but was soon deserted by her young and profligate husband for Poppaea Sabina. After living with the latter as his mistress for some time, he resolved to recognize her as his legal wife; and accordingly he divorced Octavia on the alleged ground of sterility, and then married Poppaea, A.D. 62. Shortly afterwards Octavia was falsely accused of adultery, and was banished to the little island of Pandataria, where she was put to death. Her untimely end excited general commiseration. Octavia is the heroine of a tragedy, found among the works of Seneca, but the author of which was more probably Curiatius Maternus.

Octaviānus. See AUGUSTUS.

Octavius. (1) NEPOS, CN., Roman praetor B.C. 168, and appointed to the command of the fleet against Perseus. He pursued this monarch, after his defeat by Aemilius Paulus, to the island of Samothrace, and there obtained his surrender. For this he was rewarded with a naval triumph. In B.C. 165 he was consul with M. Torquatus. Having been sent, three years after this, into Syria, at the head of a deputation to act as guardians to the young king, Antiochus Eupator, he was assassinated by order, as was supposed, of Lysias, a relative of the previous monarch, who claimed the regency during the minority of Antiochus. The arrogant and haughty conduct of Octavius appears to have hastened his fate. The Senate, however, erected a statue to his memory. (2) CN., was consul B.C. 87, along with Cinna. Being himself attached to the party of Sulla, and having the support of the Senate, he drove his colleague out of the city. Marius, however, having returned this same year and re-entered Rome with Cinna, Octavius was put to death. (3) GAIUS, the father of Augustus, was praetor B.C. 61, and distinguished himself by the correctness and justice of his decisions. After his praetorship he was appointed governor of Macedonia, and defeated the Ressi and other Thracian tribes, for which he received from his soldiers the title of Imperator. He died at Nola, on his return from his province. Octavius married Atia, the sister of Iulius Caesar, and had by this union Octavius (afterwards Augustus) and Octavia, the wife of Antonius. (4) The name of the emperor AUGUSTUS before his adoption by Iulius Caesar. See AUGUSTUS.

Octōber. See CALENDARIUM.

Octōber Equus. A Roman rite originally held in honour of Mars. On the Ides of October in each year there was held a race of two-horse chariots (*bigae*) in the Campus Martius, after which the off-horse of the winning chariot was sacrificed by the Flamen Martialis. The tail was cut off (Arnob. vii. 24), and taken to the Regia, while the blood from it was sprinkled on the hearth of Vesta. The inhabitants of the Via Sacra and the Subura had a rough-and-tumble fight for the possession of the head. This contest was symbolical of the rivalry between the two halves of the older city. See Mommsen, *Hist. of Rome*, i. 53; Burn, *Rome and the Campagna*, p. 38; and Marquardt, *Staatsverwaltung*, iii. 334 foll.

Octodūrus. Now Martigny; a town of the Veragri in the country of the Helvetii. Here Galba, Caesar's officer, was attacked by the Gauls and forced to retreat (Caes. *B. G.* iii. 1).

Octogēsa. A town of the Ilergetes in Hispania Tarraconensis, near the Iberus, probably south of the Sicoris (Caes. *B. C.* i. 61).

Octolŏphus. A town of Macedonia.

Octophŏron. A litter (*lectica*) carried by eight slaves. See LECTICA.

Oculariarius. A dealer in artificial eyes. These were made of glass, silver, and even of precious stones; but were inserted not in human heads, but in the heads of statues (*Inscr. Grut.* 645, 1; Fabretti, *Inscr.* p. 641, no. 357).

Ocularius. An oculist; a medical specialist who devoted himself to the treatment of the eyes (Scrib. *Comp.* 37; Cels. vi. 6, 8). At Rome these practitioners were generally Greek, and appear not to have been numerous before the first century A.D. A number of seals belonging to these physicians have been found, and are described by Villefosse Thédenat, *Les Cachets d'Oculistes Romains* (Paris, 1882). See also Grotefend, *Die Stempel der Augenärzte* (Hanover, 1867); and Fröhner in the *Phil. Suppl.* v. 87.

Ocypĕté (Ὠκυπέτη). "The swift-footed." One of the Harpies. See HARPYIAE.

Ocyrhoë (Ὠκυρόη). (1) A daughter of the Centaur Chiron, who possessed the gift of prophecy. She is said to have been changed into a mare. (2) A daughter of Oceanus and Tethys.

Ode. See CARMEN.

Odenăthus. The ruler of Palmyra who checked the victorious career of the Persians after the defeat and capture of Valerian, A.D. 260 (Procop. *Pers.* ii. 5). In return for these services, Gallienus bestowed upon Odenathus the title of Augustus. He was soon afterwards murdered, and was succeeded by his wife Zenobia, A.D. 266. See PALMYRA; ZENOBIA.

Odessus (Ὀδησσός). (1) Now Varna; a Greek town in Thracia (in the later Moesia Inferior), on the Pontus Euxinus. It was founded by the Milesians, and carried on an extensive commerce. (2) A seaport in European Sarmatia, northeast of the modern Russian city of Odessa.

Odēum. See THEATRUM.

Odoăcer, usually styled king of the Heruli, was the leader of the barbarians, who overthrew the Western Empire, A.D. 476. He took the title of King of Italy, and reigned till his power was overthrown by Theodoric, king of the Goths. Odoacer was defeated in three decisive battles by Theodoric (489–490), and then took refuge in Ravenna, where he was besieged for three years. He at last capitulated on condition that he and Theodoric should be joint kings of Italy; but Odoacer was soon afterwards murdered by his rival. See Procop. *B. G.* i. 1; Iornand. *De Reb. Goth.* pp. 128–141; and Hodgkin, *Italy and her Invaders* (1880–95).

Odrȳsae (Ὀδρύσαι). The most powerful people in Thrace, dwelling in the plain of the Hebrus, whose king, Sitalces, in the time of the Peloponnesian War, exercised dominion over almost the whole of Thrace. (See THRACIA.) The poets often use the adjective *Odrysius* in the general sense of *Thracicus*.

Odyssēa (Ὀδύσσεια). A town of Hispania Baetica, north of Abdera, and reported to have been founded by Odysseus (Strabo, pp. 149, 157).

Odysseia (Ὀδύσσεια). The *Odyssey*. See ODYSSEUS; HOMERUS.

Odysseus (Ὀδυσσεύς; the Latin equivalent being ULIXES; erroneously written ULYSSES). King of Ithaca, son of Laërtes and Anticlea, the daughter of Autolycus. In post-Homeric legends he is called a son of Sisyphus, conceived by Anticlea before her marriage with Laërtes. According to Homer, his name ("the hater," from ὀδύσσομαι) was given him by his grandfather Autolycus, because he himself had so often cherished feelings of hatred during his life (*Od.* xix. 402). His wife Penelopé (or Penelopea), daughter of Icarius (see PENELOPÉ), is said by later legends to have been obtained for him by her uncle Tyndareos in gratitude for counsel given by him. (See TYNDAREOS.) When his son Telemachus was still an infant, Agamemnon and Menelaüs, as Homer tells us, prevailed on him to take part in the expedition against Troy. Their task was hard, as it had been predicted to him that it would be twenty years before he saw his wife and child again. Later writers relate that he was bound, as one of Helen's suitors, to take part in the scheme, but tried to escape his obligation by feigning madness, and among other acts yoked a horse and an ox to his plough and so ploughed a field. When, however, Palamedes, who, with Nestor and Menelaüs, was desirous of taking him to Troy, proceeded to place Telemachus in the furrow, he betrayed himself, and had to accompany them to the war. Odysseus led the troops of Ithaca and the surrounding islands to Troy in twelve vessels. In contrast to the later legend, which represents him as a cowardly, deceitful, and intriguing personage, he always appears in Homer among the noblest and most respected of the heroes, and, on account of his good qualities, he is the declared favourite of Athené. He combines in his person courage and determined perseverance with prudence, ingenuity, cunning, and eloquence. Accordingly, he is employed by preference as a negotiator and a spy. Thus, after the disembarkation, he goes with Menelaüs into the enemy's city to demand the surrender of Helen. Again, he is among those who are despatched by the Greeks to reconcile with Agamemnon the enraged Achilles. With Diomedes, who delights in his company, he captures the spy Dolon and surprises Rhesus; with the same hero he is said by later legend to have stolen the Palladium from Troy. When Agamemnon faint-heartedly thinks of flight, he opposes this idea with the utmost decision. Everywhere he avails himself of the right time and the right place, and, where courage and cunning are needed, is ever the foremost. After Achilles' death, in the contest with Aiax, the son of Telamon, he received the hero's arms as a recognition of his services, and by his ingenuity brought about the fall of Troy. Shortly before it, he stole into the city in the garb of a beggar, in order to reconnoitre everything there; he then climbed with the others into the wooden horse, and contrived to control the impatient and the timid alike until the decisive moment. See TROJAN WAR.

His adventures during the return from Troy and on his arrival in his native country form the contents of the *Odyssey* of Homer. Immediately after the departure Odysseus was driven to the Thracian Ismarus, the city of the Cicones, and, though he plundered it, he lost in a surprise seventy-two of his companions. When he was desirous of rounding the promontory of Malea, the southeast point of the Peloponnesus, he was caught by the storm and carried in nine days to the coast of North Africa, on to the land of the Lotophagi (lotus-eaters), whence he had to drag his companions by force to prevent their forgetting their homes for love of the lotus-food. Thence the voyage passed into the legendary world of the Western Sea, then little known to the Greeks. Odysseus came first to the country of the Cyclopes (q. v.), where, with twelve of his comrades, he was

Odysseus offering wine to the Cyclops. (Vatican Museum, Rome.)

shut up in a cavern by Polyphemus. The monster had already devoured half of Odysseus's companions before the latter intoxicated him, deprived him of his one eye, and by his cunning escaped with his comrades. From this time the anger of Poseidon, on whom Polyphemus called for revenge, pursued him and kept him far from his country. On the island of Aeolus, the Keeper of the Winds (q. v.), he found hospitable entertainment, and received on his departure a leathern bag, in which were enclosed all the winds except the western. The latter would have carried him in nine days to the coast of Ithaca; but, while Odysseus was resting, his comrades opened the bag, which they imagined to contain treasure, and the winds thus released carried them back to Aeolus. He ordered them off from his island, regarding them as enemies of the gods. On coming to Telepylus, the city of Lamus, King Antiphates and his Laestrygones, cannibals of immense stature, shattered eleven of their vessels, and the twelfth was saved only by Odysseus's wariness. On the island of Aeaea the sorceress Circé turned part of his crew into swine, but with the help of Hermes, who gave him an antidote against her charms, he compelled her to restore them to their human shape, and spent a whole year with her in pleasure and enjoyment. When his companions urged him to return home, Circé bade him first sail towards the farthest west, to the entrance into the lower world on the farther bank of Oceanus, and there question the shade of the seer Tiresias concerning his return. (See HADES.) From the latter he learned that it was the malice of Poseidon that prevented his return, but that nevertheless he would attain his object if his comrades spared the cattle of Helios on the island of Thrinacia; otherwise, it would be only after a long time, deprived of all his comrades and on a foreign ship, that he would reach his home. Odysseus next returned to the isle of Circé and set out on his homeward voyage, supplied by her with valuable directions and a favouring wind. Passing the isles of the Sirens, who tried to lure his vessel upon the rocks by their sweet songs, but whom Odysseus resisted by filling his sailors' ears with wax and lashing himself to the mast, and sailing through Scylla and Charybdis (q. v.), he reached the island of Thrinacia, where he was compelled to land by his comrades. They were there detained for a month by contrary winds; at length his comrades, overcome by hunger, in spite of the oath they had sworn to him, slaughtered, during his absence, the finest of the cattle of Helios. Scarcely were they once more at sea, when a terrible storm broke forth, and Zeus split the ship in twain with a flash of lightning, as a penalty for the offence. All perished except Odysseus, who clung to the mast and keel, and was carried back by the waves to Scylla and Charybdis, and after nine days reached the island of Ogygia, the abode of the nymph Calypso, daughter of Atlas. For seven years he dwelt here with the nymph, who promised him immortality and eternal youth, if he would consent to remain with her and be her husband. But the yearning for his wife and home made him proof against her snares. All the day long he sat on the shore gazing through his tears across the broad sea; anxious to catch a glimpse, were it only of the rising smoke of his home, and thereafter die. So his protectress, Athené, during Poseidon's absence, prevailed on Zeus, in an assembly of the gods, to decree his return, and to send Hermes to order Calypso to release him. Borne on a raft of his own building, he came in eighteen days near to Scheria, the island of the Phaeacians, when Poseidon caught sight of him and shattered his raft in pieces. However, with the aid of the veil of Ino Leucothea (q. v.), he reached land in safety, and met with Nausicaa, the king's daughter, who conducted him into the Phaeacian city before her parents Alcinoüs (q. v.) and Areté. He received the most hospitable treatment, and was then brought by the Phaeacians loaded with presents on board one of their marvellous vessels to his own country, which he reached after twenty years' absence, while asleep. He arrived just in time to ward off

Odysseus and the Sirens. (Vase in British Museum.)

the disaster that was threatening his house. After his mother Anticlea had died of grief for her son, and old Laërtes had retired to his country estate in mourning, more than a hundred noble youths of Ithaca and the surrounding isles had appeared as suitors for the hand of the fair and chaste Penelopé, had persecuted Telemachus, who was now growing up to manhood, and were wasting the substance of the absent Odysseus. Penelopé had demanded a respite from making her decision until she had finished weaving a shroud intended for her father-in-law, and every night unravelled the work of the day. In the fourth year one of her attendants betrayed the secret; she had to complete the garment, and when urged to make her decision promised to choose the man who should win in a shooting-match with Odysseus's bow, hoping that none of the wooers would be able even so much as to bend it. Just before the day of trial, Odysseus landed on the island disguised by Athené as a beggar. He betook him-

Odysseus and Penelopé. (Pompeian Painting.)

self to the honest swineherd Eumaeus, one of the few retainers who had remained true to him, who received his master, whom he failed to recognize, in an hospitable manner. To the same spot Athené brought Telemachus, who had returned in safety, in spite of the plots of the suitors, from a journey to Nestor at Pylus, and to Menelaüs and Helen in Sparta. Hereupon Odysseus made himself known, and, together with his son and retainer, concerted his plan of revenge. In the shape of a beggar he betook himself to the house, where he manfully controlled his anger at the arrogance of the suitors which was displayed towards himself, and his emotion on meeting Penelopé. Next day the shooting-match took place. This involved shooting through the handles of twelve axes with the bow of Eurytus (q. v.), which the latter's son Iphitus had once presented to the young Odysseus. None of the suitors could bend the bow, and so Odysseus took hold of it, and bent it in an instant, thus achieving the master-shot. Supported by Telemachus, Eumaeus, and the herdsman Philoetius, and with the aiding presence of Athené, he shot first the insolent Antinoüs, and then the other suitors. He next made himself known to Penelopé, who had meanwhile fallen into a deep sleep, and visited his aged father. In the meantime the relatives of the murdered suitors had taken up arms, but Athené, in the form of Mentor (q. v.), brought about a reconciliation. The only hint of Odysseus's end in Homer is in the prophecy of Tiresias—that in a calm old age a peaceful death will come upon him from the sea.

In later poetry Telegonus, the son of Odysseus by Circé, is sent forth by his mother to seek out his father. He lands at Ithaca, and plunders the island. Odysseus proceeds to meet him, is wounded by him with a poisonous sting-ray, given by Circé to her son as a spear-point, and dies a painful death, which thus comes "from the sea." On Telegonus discovering that he had killed his father, he carried the dead body home with him, together with Penelopé and Telemachus, and there the latter lived a life of immortality, Telemachus becoming husband of Circé, and Telegonus of Penelopé. Besides Telegonus, the legend told of two sons of Odysseus by Circé, named Agrius and Latinus, who were said to have reigned over the Etruscans. Telegonus, in particular, was regarded by the Romans as the founder of Tusculum (Ovid, *Fasti*, iii. 92) and Praenesté (Hor. *Od.* iii. 29, 8). In later times the adventures of Odysseus were transferred, as a whole, to the coast of Italy: the promontory of Circeii was regarded as the abode of Circé, and Formiae as the city of the Laestrygones. Near Surrentum was found the island of the Sirens; near Cape Lacinium that of Calypso, while near to Sicily were the isle of Aeolus, Scylla, and Charybdis, and, on the Sicilian shore, the Cyclopes. Odysseus is generally represented as a bearded man, wearing a semi-oval cap like that of a Greek sailor, as in the first illustration. See HOMERUS.

Oea. (1) (Ἑώα). A city on the northern coast of Africa with a mixed population of Libyans and Sicilians. Under the Romans it was a colony with the name Aelia Augusta Felix (Tac. *Hist.* iv. 50). It is perhaps the same as the modern Tripoli. (2) (Οἴα). A town in the island of Aegina.

Oeăgrus or **Oeăger** (Οἴαγρος). King of Thrace and father of Orpheus and Linus. Hence *Oeagrius* is used by the poets as equivalent to *Thracicus*.

Oeanthé (Οἰάνθη) or **Oeanthīa** (Οἰανθεία). A town of the Locri Ozolae, near the entrance of the Crissaean Gulf.

Oeax (Οἴαξ). A son of Nauplius and Clymené, and brother of Palamedes and Nausimedon (Apollod. ii. 1). See PALAMEDES.

Oebălus (Οἴβαλος). (1) King of Sparta and father of Tyndareos. The patronymics Oebalides, Oebalis, and the adjective Oebalius are not only applied to his descendants, but to the Spartans generally. Hence Tarentum is termed *Oebalia arx*, because it was founded by the Lacedaemonians; and since the Sabines were, according to one tradition, a Lacedaemonian colony, we find the Sabine king Titus Tatius called Oebalius Titus, and the Sabine women, *Oebalides matres*. (2) Son of Telon by a nymph of the stream Sebethus, near Naples. He ruled in Campania.

Oechalia (Οἰχαλία). (1) A town in Thessaly, on the Peneus, near Tricca. (2) A town in Messenia, on the frontier of Arcadia. (3) A town of Euboea, in the district Eretria. The ancients were divided in opinion as to which of these places was the residence of Eurytus, whom Heracles defeated and slew. The original legend probably belonged to the Thessalian Oechalia, and was thence transferred to the other towns.

Oecus (οἶκος). (1) A house. (See DOMUS.) (2) A special apartment in a house resembling the *atrium*, but having no *compluvium*, being wholly roofed over. It was frequently used as a dining-hall, and was of four kinds: (*a*) the *oecus tetrastylus* with four columns; (*b*) *oecus Corinthius* with a vaulted roof, supported upon columns at a certain distance from the side-walls; (*c*) *oecus Aegyptius*, a more magnificent apartment than the last, having its roof supported by a double row of columns like a *basilica* (q. v.); (*d*) *oecus Cyzicenus*, on which see DOMUS, p. 546.

Oedĭpus (Οἰδίπους). The son of Laïus, king of Thebes, and of Iocasta (called in the *Odyssey* Epicasté), the daughter of Menoeceus. An oracle had warned Laïus against having children, declaring that he would meet his death by means of his offspring; and the monarch accordingly practised continence until, after some lapse of time, having indulged in festivity, he forgot the injunction of the god, and Iocasta gave birth to a son. The father immediately delivered the child to his herdsman to expose on Mount Cithaeron. The herdsman, moved to compassion, according to one account (Soph. *Oed. Tyr.* 1038), gave the babe to a neat-herd belonging to Polybus, king of Corinth; or, as others say (Eurip. *Phoeniss.* 28), the neat-herds of Polybus found the infant after it had been exposed, and brought it to Periboea, the wife of Polybus, who, being childless, reared it as her own, and named it Oedipus, on account of its swollen feet (from οἰδέω, "to swell," and πούς, "a foot"); for Laïus, previous to its exposure, had pierced its ankles, and had inserted through the wound a leathern thong. The foundling Oedipus was brought up by Polybus as his heir. Happening to be reproached by some one at a banquet with being a supposititious child, he besought Periboea to inform him of the truth; but, unable to get any satisfaction from her, he went to Delphi and consulted the oracle. The god directed him to shun his native country, or else he would be the slayer of his father and the sharer of his mother's bed. He therefore resolved never to return to Corinth, where so much crime, as he thought, awaited him, and he took his road through Phocis. Now it happened that Laïus, at this same time, was on his way to Delphi, for the purpose of ascertaining whether the child which had been exposed had perished or not. He was in a chariot, accompanied by his herald Polyphontes; a few attendants came after. The father and son, total strangers to each other, met in a narrow road in Phocis. Oedipus was ordered to make way, and, on his disregarding the command, the charioteer endeavoured to crowd him out of the path. A contest thereupon ensued, and both Laïus and the charioteer, together with all the attendants except one, who fled, were slain by the hand of Oedipus.

Immediately after the death of Laïus, Heré, always hostile to the city of Bacchus, sent a monster named the Sphinx to ravage the territory of Thebes. It had the face of a woman, the breast, feet, and tail of a lion, and the wings of a bird. This monster had been taught riddles by the Muses, and she sat on the Phicean Hill, and propounded one to the Thebans. It was this: "What is that which has one voice, is four-footed, two-footed, and at last three-footed?" or, as others give it, "What animal is that which goes on four feet in the morning, on two at noon, and on three at evening?" The oracle told the Thebans that they would not be delivered from her until they had solved her riddle. They often met to try their skill; and when they had failed, the Sphinx always carried off and devoured one of their number. At length Haemon, son of Creon, having become her victim, the father offered by public proclamation the throne, to which he had succeeded on the death of Laïus, and the hand of his sister Iocasta, to whoever should solve the riddle of the Sphinx. Oedipus, who was then at Thebes, hearing this, came forward and answered the Sphinx that it was Man, who, when an infant, creeps on all fours; when he has attained to manhood, goes on two feet; and when old, uses a staff, a third foot. The Sphinx thereupon flung herself down to the earth and perished; and Oedipus now unknowingly accomplished the remainder of the oracle. He had by his mother two sons, Eteocles and Polynices, and two daughters, Antigoné and Ismené.

After some years Thebes was afflicted with famine and pestilence; and the oracle being consulted, ordered the land to be purified of the blood which defiled it. Inquiry was set on foot after the murder of Laïus, and a variety of concurring circumstances brought the guilt home to Oedipus. Iocasta, on the discovery being made, hung herself, and her unhappy son and husband, in his grief and despair, put out his eyes. He was banished from Thebes; and, accompanied by his

Oedipus and the Sphinx. (Fragment of an archaic Greek Vase found at Daphnae.)

daughters, who faithfully adhered to him, he came, after a tedious period of miserable wandering, to the grove of the Eumenides at Colonus, a village not far from Athens, and there found the termination of his wretched life, having mysteriously disappeared from mortal view, and been received into the bosom of the earth, the secret of his death and burial being known to Theseus only. The history of his sons will be found under the articles ETEOCLES; POLYNICES.

Such is the form in which the history of Oedipus has been transmitted to us by the Attic dramatists. We will now consider its most ancient shape. The hero of the *Odyssey* says: "I saw (in Erebus) the mother of Oedipodes, the fair Epicasta, who, in her ignorance, did an awful deed, marrying her own son; and he married, having slain his own father, and immediately the gods made this known unto men. Now he ruled over the Cadmaeans in desirable Thebes, suffering woes through the pernicious councils of the gods; but she, oppressed with grief, went to the abode of Aïdes, the strong gate-keeper, having fastened a long halter to the lofty roof, and left to him many woes, such as the avenging furies of a mother produce" (*Od.* xi. 271 foll.). In the *Iliad* (xxiii. 679) the funeral games are mentioned which were celebrated at Thebes in honour of the "fallen Oedipodes." Hesiod (*Op. et D.* 162) speaks of the heroes who fell fighting at the seven-gated Thebes, on account of the sheep of Oedipodes. It would also seem that, according to the above passage of the *Odyssey* and to the epic poem, the *Oedipodea* (Pausan. ix. 5, 11), Epicasta had not any children by her son; Eurygenia, the daughter of Hyperphas, being the mother of his well-known offspring. According to the cyclic *Thebaïs*, the fatal curse of Oedipus on his sons had the following origin: Polynices placed before his father a silver table which had belonged to Cadmus, and filled a golden cup with wine for him; but when Oedipus perceived the heir-looms of his family thus set before him, he raised his hands and prayed that his sons might never divide their inheritance peaceably, but ever be at strife. Elsewhere (*ap.* Schol. *ad* Soph. *Oed. Col.* 1440) the *Thebaïs* said that his sons, having sent him the loin, instead of the shoulder, of the victim, he flung it to the ground, and prayed that they might fall by each other's hands.

The story of Oedipus forms the subject of two plays of Sophocles, the *Oedipus Tyrannus* and the *Oedipus Coleneus;* and was also taken by Aeschylus as the subject of a trilogy, of which only the third play, the *Seven against Thebes*, remains. Seneca also wrote a Latin tragedy, the *Oedipus*, following the first play of Sophocles with considerable fidelity. In French, Corneille and Voltaire, and in English, Dryden, have also treated the same theme dramatically. See ANTIGONÉ; CREON; SEVEN AGAINST THEBES; and also AESCHYLUS; SOPHOCLES.

Oeneus (Οἰνεύς). A king of Calydon in Aetolia, son of Portheus or of Porthaon. He married Althaea, the daughter of Thestius, by whom he had, among other children, Meleager and Deïanira. After Althaea's death, he married Periboea or Melanippé, the daughter of Hipponoüs, by whom he became the father of Tydeus, though others made Tydeus his son by his own daughter Gorgé. In a sacrifice which Oeneus made to all the gods, upon reaping the rich produce of his fields, he forgot Artemis, and the goddess, to revenge this neglect, sent a wild boar to lay waste the territory of Calydon. The animal was at last killed, by Meleager and the neighbouring princes of Greece, in a celebrated chase known by the name of the chase of the Calydonian boar. (See MELEAGER.) After the death of Meleager, Oeneus was dethroned and imprisoned by the sons of his brother Agrius. Diomedes, having come secretly from the city of Argos, slew all the sons of Agrius but two, who escaped to the Peloponnesus; and then, giving the throne of Calydon to Andraemon, son-in-law of Oeneus, who was himself now too old to reign, led the latter with him to Argolis. Oeneus was afterwards slain by the two sons of Agrius, who had fled into the Peloponnesus. Diomedes buried him in Argolis, on the spot where the city of Oenoë, called after Oeneus, was subsequently erected. Oeneus is said to have been the first that received the vine from Bacchus. The god taught him how to cultivate it, and the juice of the grape was called after his name (οἶνος, "wine") (Apollod. i. 8; Hyg. *Fab.* 129).

Oeniădae (Οἰνιάδαι). A town of Acarnania, near the mouth of the Acheloüs, and surrounded by marshes. The fortress Nesus or Nasus, belonging to the territory of Oeniadae, was situated in a small lake near Oeniadae. (Diod. xviii. 8).

Oenīdes. A patronymic from Oeneus, and hence given to Meleager, son of Oeneus, and Diomedes, grandson of Oeneus.

Oenochoë (οἰνοχόη). (1) A vessel or ladle for distributing wine from the bowl to the cups (Eurip. *Tro.* 820). (2) A wine-jug. See VAS.

Oenochoë. (Schliemann.)

Oenochoë (οἰνοχόη). A female cup-bearer.

Oenoë (Οἰνόη). (1) A deme of Attica belonging to the tribe Hippothoöntis, near the frontier of Boeotia (Herod. v. 74). (2) A deme of Attica, near Marathon, belonging to the tribe Aeantis. (3) A town of Argolis, west of Argos. Here the Argives and Athenians defeated the Lacedaemonians, B.C. 388. (4) A town of Elis. (5) A town in the island of Icaria. (6) A fortress of the Corinthians on the Gulf of Corinth.

Oenomaüs (Οἰνόμαος). (1) King of Pisa in Elis, son of Ares and father of Hippodamia. An oracle had warned him that he should perish by the hands of his son-in-law; and as his horses were swifter than those of any other mortal, he declared that all who came forward as suitors for Hippodamia's hand should contend with him in a chariot-race, that whoever conquered should receive her, and that whoever was conquered should suffer death. The race-course extended from Pisa to the altar of Poseidon, on the Corinthian Isthmus. The suitor started with Hippodamia in a chariot, and Oenomaüs then hastened with his swift horses after the lovers. He had overtaken and slain many a suitor, when Pelops, the son of Tantalus, came to Pisa. Pelops bribed Myrtilus, the charioteer of Oenomaüs, to take out the linch-pins from the wheels of his master's chariot, and Pelops received from Poseidon a golden chariot and horses of great swiftness. In the race which followed, the chariot of Oenomaüs broke down, and he fell out and was killed. Thus Pelops obtained Hippodamia and the kingdom of Pisa.

There are some variations in this story, such as that Oenomaüs was himself in love with his own daughter, and for this reason slew her lovers. Myrtilus also is said to have loved Hippodamia, and as she favoured the suit of Pelops, she persuaded Myrtilus to take the linch-pins out of the wheels of her father's chariot. As Oenomaüs was breathing his last, he pronounced a curse upon Myrtilus. This curse had its desired effect, for as Pelops refused to give to Myrtilus the reward he had promised, or else because Myrtilus had attempted to dishonour Hippodamia, Pelops thrust him down from Cape Geraestus. Myrtilus, while dying, likewise pronounced a curse upon Pelops, which was the cause of all the calamities that afterwards befell his house. (See PELOPS.) The tomb of Oenomaüs was shown on the river Cladeus, in Elis. His house was destroyed by lightning, and only one pillar of it remained standing. (2) Of Gadara, a Cynic philosopher, who flourished in the reign of Hadrian, or somewhat later. He wrote a work to expose the oracles, of which considerable fragments are preserved by Eusebius (*Praep. Ev.* v. 18; vi. 7).

Oenōné (Οἰνώνη). A nymph of Mount Ida, daughter of the river Cebrenus in Phrygia. Paris, when a shepherd on Mount Ida, and before he was discovered to be a son of Priam, had united himself in marriage with Oenoné; and as she had received from Apollo the gift of prophecy, she warned her husband against the consequences of his voyage to Greece. She at the same time told him to come to her if ever he was wounded, as she alone could cure him. Paris came to her, accordingly, when he had been wounded by one of the arrows of Philoctetes, but Oenoné, offended at his desertion of her, refused to aid him, and he died on his return to Ilium. Repenting of her cruelty, Oenoné hastened to his relief; but, coming too late, she threw herself on his funeral pile and perished (Apollod. iii. 12, 6). The story of Oenoné is the subject of an exquisite poem by Lord Tennyson. See PARIS.

Oenōné or **Oenopia**. The early name of the island of Aegina (q. v.).

Oenophŏrum (οἰνόφορον). A vessel for holding wine. It had two handles, and was larger than a mere drinking-cup (Juv. vi. 425).

Oenophȳta (τὰ Οἰνόφυτα). A town in Boeotia, on the left bank of the Asopus, memorable for the victory gained here by the Athenians over the Boeotians, B.C. 456 (Thuc. i. 108; iv. 95).

Oenopia. The ancient name of Aegina (q. v.).

Oenopĭdes (Οἰνοπίδης). An astronomer and mathematician of Chios, who obtained from the Egyptian priests a knowledge of the obliquity of the ecliptic, of which he subsequently claimed to be the discoverer. He fixed the length of the solar year at 365 days, less nine hours. To him are ascribed the demonstrations of the twelfth and twenty-third propositions in Euclid, and the quadrature of the meniscus. He flourished in the fifth century B.C. (Diod. i. 98; Ael. *V. H.* x. 7).

Oenopion (Οἰνοπίων). Son of Dionysus and husband of the nymph Helicé, and father of Meropé, with whom the giant Orion fell in love. See ORION.

Oenopolium (οἰνοπώλιον). A wine-shop. See CAUPONA; POPINA.

Oenōtri (Οἰνωτροί). See OENOTRIA.

Oenotria (Οἰνωτρία). A name derived from the ancient race of the Oenotri, and in early use among the Greeks, to designate a portion of the south-eastern coast of Italy. The name is derived by some from οἶνος, "wine," and they maintain that the early Greeks called the country Oenotria, or "the wine-land," from the number of vines they found growing there when they first became acquainted with the region. With the poets of a later age it is a general appellation for all Italy. The Oenotri, as they were called, appear to have been spread over a large portion of Southern Italy. See ITALIA.

Oenotrĭdes (Οἰνωτρίδες νῆσοι). Two small islands in the Tyrrhenian Sea, off the coast of Lucania, and opposite the town of Elea or Velia and the mouth of the Helos (Pliny, *H. N.* iii. 85).

Oenōtrus (Οἴνωτρος). A son of Lycaon. He was fabled to have passed with a body of followers from Arcadia into Southern Italy, and to have given the name of Oenotria to that part of the country where he settled (Verg. *Aen.* i. 532). But see OENOTRIA.

Oenus (Οἰνοῦς). (1) A town of Laconia, supposed to have been situated on the river of the same name flowing near Sellasia (Livy, xxxiv. 28). (2) Or AENUS, a river of Germany, separating Noricum from Vindelicia, and falling into the Danube at Boiodurum (Passau). It is now the Inn.

Oenūsae (Οἰνοῦσαι) or **Oenussae** (Οἰνοῦσσαι). (1) Small islands in the Aegean Sea, between Chios and the mainland, now Egonuses (Herod. i. 165). (2) Small islands off the coast of Messenia, and nearly facing the city of Methoné. They are two in number, and are now called Sapienza and Cabrera.

Oeōnus (Οἰωνός). The son of Licymnius of Midea in Argolis, the first victor at Olympia in the foot-race. He was killed at Sparta by Hippocoön, and avenged by his kinsman Heracles (Pausan. iii. 15).

Oestrus. (οἶστρος). A gad-fly; especially the one that tormented Io. See IO.

Oeta or **Oeté** (Οἴτη). Now Katavothra; a rugged pile of mountains in the south of Thessaly, an eastern branch of Mount Pindus, extending along the southern bank of the Sperchius to the Maliac Gulf at Thermopylae, thus forming the northern barrier of Greece proper. Respecting the pass of Mount Oeta, see THERMOPYLAE. Oeta was celebrated in mythology as the mountain on which Heracles burned himself to death. From this range, the southern part of Thessaly was called OETAEA (Οἰταία).

Oetȳlus (Οἴτυλος), also **Tylus** (Τύλος). An ancient town in Laconia on the Messenian Gulf.

Ofella, Q. LUCRETIUS. A Roman who originally belonged to the Marian party, but deserted to Sulla, who appointed him to the command of the army employed in the blockade of Praenesté, B.C. 82. Ofella became a candidate for the consulship in the following year, although he had not yet been either quaestor or praetor, thus acting in defiance of one of Sulla's laws. He was in consequence put to death by Sulla's orders (Plut. *Sulla*, 29, 33; Vell. Pat. ii. 27).

Offendix. The string used in fastening the *apex*, or priestly cap. See APEX.

Officīna (ἐργαστήριον). A manufactory or workshop where things were made, as contrasted with *taberna*, the place where they were sold; and with *apotheca*, where they were stored.

Ofilius. A Roman jurist and friend of Caesar and Cicero. His works are often cited in the *Digest*.

Oglasa. Now Monte Cristo; a small island off the coast of Etruria (Pliny, *H. N.* iii. 80).

Ogy̆ges (Ὠγύγης) or **Ogy̆gus**. Son of Boeotus, and the first ruler of Thebes, which was called after him OGYGIA. In his reign a great deluge is said to have occurred. The name of Ogyges is also connected with Attic story, for in Attica an Ogygian flood is likewise mentioned. He was said to be the father of the Athenian hero Eleusis. From Ogyges the Thebans are called by the poets *Ogygidae*, and *Ogygius* is used in the sense of Theban.

Ogygia (Ὠγυγία). The mythical island inhabited by the enchantress Calypso (q. v.), placed by Homer as lying in the very centre of the sea, away from all lands (*Od.* i. 50; v. 55, etc.).

Ogy̆gus. See OGYGES.

Oïcles (Ὀϊκλης) or **Oïcleus** (Ὀϊκλεύς). The son of Antiphates, grandson of Melampus and father of Amphiaraüs, of Argos. He is also called a son of Amphiaraüs, or a son of Mantius, the brother of Antiphates. Oïcles accompanied Heracles on his expedition against Laomedon of Troy, and was there slain in battle. According to other traditions, he returned home from the expedition, and dwelt in Arcadia, where he was visited by his grandson Alcmaeon, and where his tomb was shown.

Oikias Diké (οἰκίας δίκη). An action to recover a house (Att. *Proc.* ed. Lips. p. 674).

Oil. See OLEUM.

Oïleus (Ὀϊλεύς). The son of Hodoedocus and Laonomé, grandson of Cynus, and great-grandson of Opus, was a king of the Locrians, and married to Eriopis, by whom he became the father of Aiax, who is hence called Oïlides, Oïliades, and Aiax Oïlei. Oïleus was also the father of Medon by Rhené. He is mentioned among the Argonauts.

Oinos (οἶνος). See VINUM.

Ointment. See UNGUENTUM.

Olba or **Olbé** (Ὄλβη). A city of Cilicia said to be founded by Aiax, son of Teucer. In later times it was called ORŎPI.

Olbia (Ὀλβία). (1) Now Eoubes near Hyères; a colony of Massilia (Marseilles), on a hill called Olbianus, east of Telo Martius (Toulon). (2) A city near the northern end of the eastern side of the island of Sardinia, with the only good harbour on this coast; and therefore the usual landing-place for persons coming from Rome. It is now Terra Nuova. (3) See BORYSTHENES.

Olcădes. A people in Hispania Tarraconensis, near the sources of the Anas, in a part of the country afterwards inhabited by the Oretani. Their chief town was Althaea (Livy, xxi. 5).

Olcinium. Now Dulcigno; a town on the coast of Illyria.

Olea. See OLEUM.

Oleărus. See OLIARUS.

Olen (Ὠλήν). A mythical poet of Lycia belonging to early Greek times, standing in connection with the worship of Apollo in Delos and represented as having composed the first hymns for the Delians. The legend which was especially attributed to him was that of Apollo's sojourn among the Hyperboreans (Herod. iv. 35; Pausan. i. 18, 5; ii. 13, 3).

Olĕnus (Ὤλενος). The husband of Lethaea, and changed with her into a stone. He was the father of the nymphs Aegé and Helicé, who reared the youthful Zeus.

Olĕnus (Ὤλενος). (1) A town in Aetolia, near New Pleuron, destroyed by the Aetolians at an early period. (2) A town in Achaia, between Patrae and Dyme. The goat Amalthaea, which suckled the infant Zeus, is called *Olenia capella* by the poets, either because the goat was supposed to have been born near the town of Olenus, and to have been subsequently transferred to Crete, or because the nymph Amalthaea, to whom the goat belonged, was the daughter of Olenus.

Oleum (ἔλαιον). Oil; a substance very extensively used in ancient times. Apart from its employment as an article of food and for burning in lamps, it served to anoint the body after the bath and in the *palaestra*. The oil most used was that obtained by means of olive-presses from the olive-tree (ἐλάα, ἐλαία), which seems to have been transplanted from Syria to Greece and thence to Italy. The best olive-oil produced among the Greek States was that of Attica; here the olive-tree was considered a gift of the national goddess Athené, who, by means of it, had obtained the victory in her contest with Poseidon for the possession of the country. Here, also, the olive-tree was under the special protection of the State; no one was allowed to cut down olive-trees on his own plot of land, except for specified purposes, and then only a specified number. Moreover, many olive-trees standing on private ground were regarded as the property of the goddess of the State, and it was therefore forbidden, on pain of death, to cut them down. They were under the special control of the Areopagus, which had them inspected from time to time by certain officials, and they were farmed out by the State (Lysias, *Or.* ix.). Part of the oil thus obtained had to be sold by the farmer to the State at a fixed price; this was only used for festive purposes, especially to be distributed in prizes to the victors in the Panathenaic contests (Pindar, *Nem.* x. 35).

In Italy the olive-tree, which spread thence to France and Spain, grew so well that the Italian oil, especially from the neighbourhood of the South Italian cities Venafrum and Tarentum, and that from the Sabine country (hence *baca Sabella*), was considered the finest in the world, and so met with a ready sale abroad. The best kind was considered to be oil from unripe olives, especially the first from the press (Pliny, *H. N.* xv. 1–34). See Blümner, *Technologie*, i. 348 foll.

For the preparation and use of fragrant oils and perfumes, see UNGUENTUM.

Oliărus (Ὠλίαρος) or **Oleărus** (Ὠλέαρος). A small island in the Aegaean Sea; one of the Cyclades west of Paros.

Oligarchia (ὀλιγαρχία, "the rule of the few"). A name given in Greek writers to that form of constitution where a portion of the community, privileged either by reason of nobility of birth or by wealth, are exclusively, or at least in preference to others, in possession of power. The former case is an example of an absolute despotism; the latter resulted where the magistracies, though filled exclusively from the privileged classes, nevertheless depended on popular election; or where the mass of the people possessed a share in deliberation or in the drawing up of decrees, while to the privileged body was reserved the right of making proposals, convoking and presiding over the assemblies, and ratifying the decrees. See Polyb. vi. 4; Aristot. *Pol.* iv. 4; Wachsmuth, *Hellenische Alterthumskunde;* and Whibley, *Greek Oligarchies* (N. Y. 1896).

Olisĭpo. Now Lisbon. A town in Lusitania, near the mouth of the Tagus. It was famous in antiquity for its fine horses. The name is sometimes written ULYSSĬPO (Mela, iii. 1, 6), from a belief that it was founded by Ulysses.

Olīva (ἐλαία). The olive. See OLEUM.

Olla, and (anciently) **Aula** (χύτρα). A jar or pot of earthenware (rarely of metal) with a flat bottom, a wide mouth, with a lid, used by the ancients for a variety of purposes: (1) for cooking and preserving fruits; and (2) for preserving the bones (*olla ossuaria*) and ashes (*olla cineraria*) of the dead (see CINERARIA; COLUMBARIUM; FUNUS; OLLARIUM); and (3) for exposing infants—this last in Greece (Aristoph. *Ran.* 1188, with scholia).

Olla. (British Museum.)

Ollarium. A niche in a burial-vault, in which the cinerary urns (*ollae*) were deposited. See COLUMBARIUM.

Olŏrus (Ὄλορος). A king of Thrace whose daughter married Miltiades (q. v.).

Olpae (Ὄλπαι) or **Olpé** (Ὀλπή). (1) A town of the Amphilochae in Acarnania on the Ambracian Gulf. (2) A town of the Locri Ozolae.

Olybrius, ANICIUS. A Roman emperor placed on the imperial throne by Ricimer, the Suebian, in succession to Anthemius (A.D. 472). He reigned only three months and thirteen days, when he died, and was succeeded by Glycerius.

Olympia (τὰ Ὀλύμπια). The Olympian Games; the chief national festival of the Greeks, celebrated in honour of Zeus at Olympia, in the Peloponnesian district Pisatis, belonging to the Eleans, at the point where the Cladeus runs into the Alpheus. The institution of this ancient festival is sometimes referred to Pisus, the mythical founder of the city Pisa, which was afterwards destroyed by the Eleans, and before whose gates lay the sanctuary of Zeus; sometimes to Pelops, in whose honour funeral games were held at this point on the banks of the Alpheus.

These were restored, it is said, by Heracles, who instituted the regular order of the festival. This opinion did not become current until the Dorian States, established after the immigration of the Heraclidae into the Peloponnesus, had been admitted to a share in the festival, which was originally frequented only by the Pisitans and their immediate neighbours. This admission dates from Lycurgus of Sparta and Iphitus of Elis, who, at the direction of the Delphic oracle, restored the festival of Zeus, now fallen into oblivion, and established the sacred Truce of God (see EKECHEIRIA), which insured a safe conduct at the time of the festival for all strangers resorting thither, even through hostile territory. In course of time the membership extended itself further, over all the Hellenic States in and out of Greece; and the festival was not only visited by private individuals, but also received sacred envoys from the several states. Through all the assaults of time it lasted on, even during the Roman rule, and was not abolished until A.D. 394, under the reign of Theodosius.

From the time of the above-mentioned restoration by Iphitus and Lycurgus it was a quinquennial celebration—that is, it was held once in every four years, in midsummer (July to August), about the beginning or end of the Greek year. A regular and continuous list of the victors was kept from B.C. 776, when Coroebus won the race in the Stadium, and with this year begins the Olympiad reckoning prevalent among the historians from the time of Timaeus (q. v.). The duration of the festival was in course of time extended to at least five days.

The place where the festival was celebrated was the Altis (see plan), a sacred precinct at the foot of the hill of Cronus (Κρόνος), 403 feet high. The precinct, which was about 750 feet long by 570 feet broad, was surrounded by a wall ascribed to Heracles, having entrances at the northwest and southwest. The centre, both by position and by religious association, was formed by the great sacrificial altar of Zeus, which rose on an elliptical base 128 feet in circumference to a height of 32 feet, and was composed of the ashes of the victims mingled with the water of the Alpheus. Round it were grouped the four most important sanctuaries—the temples of Zeus, Hera (Ἡραῖον), the Mother of the Gods (Μητρῷον), and the holy enclosure of Pelops (Πελόπιον)—besides a multitude of altars consecrated some to gods and some to heroes, and a countless host of dedicatory offerings and statues of every kind, among them, southeast of the temple of Zeus, the Niké of Paeonius (q. v.).

The temple of Zeus, which was begun about B.C. 572 by the Elean Libo, was not completed in its main outline until about 450. It was a Doric hypaethral building, having no roof over the *cella* or temple proper; and it was also peripteral—that is, it was surrounded by a single row of columns. It was built of the local conchyliferous limestone (called πῶρος by Pausanias, v. 10, § 2). In its more finished parts it was overlaid with fine stucco, giving the appearance of marble, and was also richly decorated with colour. It was 210 feet in

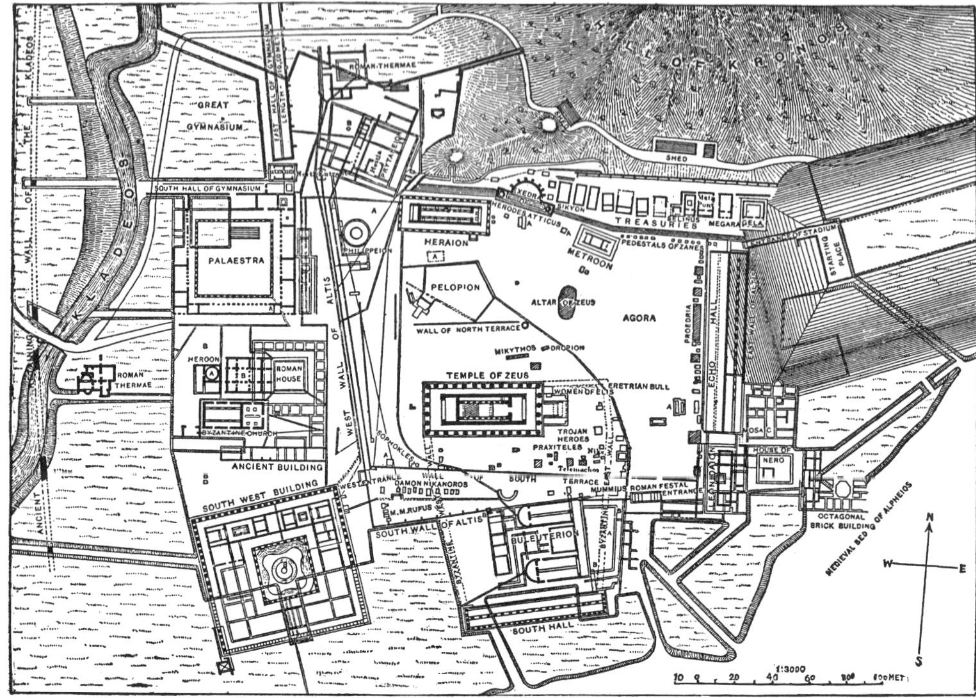

Plan of Olympia (after Dörpfeld).

length, 91 in breadth, and 65 in height. The outer hall had 6 columns along its breadth and 13 along its length (each 34 feet high), while the inner hall had a double row of nine columns. The eastern pediment was occupied by a representation of the contest between Pelops and Oenomaüs, with Zeus as the centre (fig. 1); the western, by one of the battle between the Centaurs and Lapithae, with Apollo as centre (fig. 2). The former was designed by the already-mentioned Paeonius; the latter, by Alcamenes of Athens.

The accompanying illustrations indicate the figures belonging to the two pediments, so far as their fragmentary portions were recovered in the excavations begun by the German archaeologists in 1875. While the outer metopes beneath these pediments had no ornament except a large plain boss on each, twelve other metopes sculptured with reliefs adorned the outer walls at each end of the *cella* or temple proper, six over the door of the πρόναος, and six over that of the ὀπισθόδομος. All these have been discovered—four by the French in 1829, and eight by the Germans in 1875–79. Their subjects are the labours of Heracles. The best preserved of the series, and one of them which, as compared with the rest, is apparently the work of a mature and well-trained school of sculpture, is that representing Heracles bearing the heavens. Atlas stands by, offering to Heracles the apples of the Hesperides, and on the other side one of the daughters of Atlas is touching the hero's burden with her arm, as though endeavouring to aid him in sustaining it. In the chamber at the western end of the *cella* stood the greatest work of Greek art, the statue of Zeus, wrought in gold and ivory by Phidias (q. v.). Outside the sacred enclosure, though still in direct connection with it, were, to the west, the Gymnasium, and to the east the Hippodrome and the Stadium. The Hippodrome has been washed away by the encroachments of the Alpheus. The Stadium, which was 600 Olympic feet in length, has been excavated to an extent sufficient to determine the length of the single course, between the starting-place and the goal,

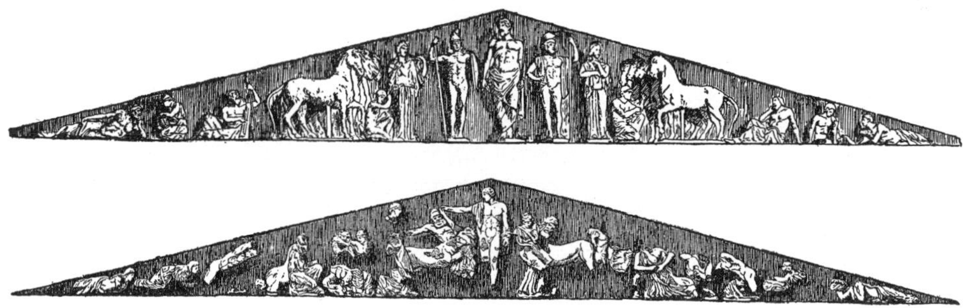

Pediments of the Temple of Zeus at Olympia.

to be 192.27 metres = 630.81845073 English feet. The Olympic foot therefore measured .3204 of a metre = 1.05120036 feet. The parallel grooves in the slabs of stone at each end of the Stadium still show the spot where the feet of the competitors in the foot-race were planted at the moment immediately preceding the start. There is room for twenty at either end, separated from one another by posts at intervals of four Olympic feet from one another.

The festival consisted of two parts—(1) the presentation of offerings, chiefly, of course, to Zeus, but also to the other gods and heroes, on the part of the Eleans, the sacred embassies, and other visitors to the feast; and (2) the contests. In the first Olympiad the contest consisted of a simple match in the Stadium (race-course), which had a length of a trifle more than 210 yards. The runners ran in heats of four, and then the winners in each heat competed together, the first in the final heat being proclaimed victor. About B.C. 724 the double course (δίαυλος) was introduced, in which the runners had to make a circuit of the goal and return to the starting-point; about 720 came the δόλιχος or long race, where the distance of the Stadium had to be covered either 6, 7, 8, 12, 20, or 29 times (Schol. on Soph. *Electra*, 691); in 708, the πένταθλον, or fivefold contest, consisting of leaping, running, quoit (δίσκος) and spear throwing, and wrestling (the last being also practised by itself); in 688, boxing. In 680 chariot-racing on the Hippodrome was introduced, and, though this was twice as long as the Stadium, it had to be traversed from eight to twelve times in both directions (at first with four horses, after 500 with mules, and after 408 with two horses). From 648 there were races in which the horsemen, towards the end of the race, had to leap from their horses and run beside them with the bridle in their hands. With the same year began the practice of the παγκράτιον (a combination of wrestling and boxing); with 520, the race in armour, with helmet, greaves, and shield, though afterwards the shield alone was carried. Competitions between heralds and trumpeters also found a place here. Originally it was only men who took part in the contests; but after 632, boys also shared in them.

Metopé from the Cella of the Great Temple at Olympia. (Reber)

The contests were open only to freemen of pure Hellenic descent, provided that no personal disgrace had in any way attached to them; but after the Romans came into closer relationship with Greece they were opened to them also, and indeed (as is well known) the Romans were not officially considered barbarians. Even to barbarians, however, and to slaves, permission was given to view them, while it was refused to all married women (Pausan. vi. 20, § 9), or more probably all women whatsoever, except the priestess of Demeter, who even received a place of honour among the spectators. Those who took part in the competitions had to take a solemn oath at the altar of Zeus to the effect that they had spent at least ten months in preparation for the games, and that they would not resort to any unfair trick in the course of their contest: this oath was taken for boy competitors by an older relative. Special practice for thirty days at Elis was also usual, but probably only for those who were coming forward for the first time. The duties of heralds and judges were discharged by the Hellanodicae (Ἑλλανοδίκαι), appointed by popular election from among the Eleans themselves. Their number rose in course of time from 1 to 2, 9, 10, and 12, but after 348 it was always 10. Distinguished by purple robes, wreaths of bay-leaves, and a seat of honour opposite the Stadium, they kept guard over the strict observance of all the minute regulations for the contests, and in general maintained order. In these duties they were supported by a number of attendants provided with staves. Transgressions of the laws of the games, and unfairness on the part of competitors, were punished by forfeiture of the prize or by fines of money, which went to the revenue of the temple. Out of the money from penalties of this kind, a whole row of bronze images of Zeus (called Ζανές) was erected in front of the eleven treasure-houses along the eastern end of the northern wall of the Altis.

The games were opened with the sound of trumpets and the proclamation of heralds, the marshalling of the various competitors in the Stadium, accompanied by the announcement of their name and country by the herald, and the appointment by lot of the pairs of combatants. The victors in the several pairs of competitors had then apparently to contend in couples with each other until one couple alone remained, and the winner in this was declared victor. If the number of combatants had been uneven, so that one of them

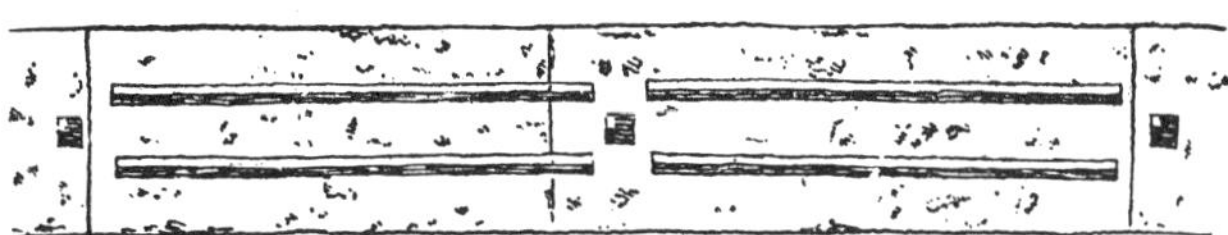

Starting-place in the Stadium. (Seyffert.)

had remained without an opponent, he had finally to meet this rival. The contests were accompanied by the music of flutes. The name of the victor (and one whom no adversary had come forward to meet counted for victor) as well as his home were proclaimed aloud by the herald, and a palm-branch presented to him by the Hellanodicae. The actual prize he only received at the general and solemn distribution on the last day of the festival. This was originally some article of value; but at the command of the Delphic Oracle this custom was dropped, and the victors were graced by a wreath of the leaves of the sacred wild-olive, said to have been originally planted by Heracles, which had been cut with a golden knife by a boy of noble family with both parents living. After about 540 the victors also possessed the right to put up statues of themselves in the Altis.

The festival ended with a sacrifice made by the victors wearing their crowns at the six double altars of the hill of Cronus, and with a banquet in the Prytaneum of the Altis. Brilliant distinctions awaited the victor on his return home, for his victory was deemed to have reflected honour on his native land at large. He made his entry, clad in purple, upon a chariot drawn by four white horses, amid the joyous shouts of all the people, and then rode amid an exultant escort to the temple of the highest god, and there deposited his wreath as a votive offering. During the ride, as also at the banquet which followed thereupon, the song of victory, often composed by the most celebrated poets, was chanted by choral bands. There was no lack of other rewards: at Athens the Olympian victor received 500 drachmae, the right to a place of honour at all public games, and board in the Prytaneum for the rest of his life. The opportunity afforded by the assembling of so vast a crowd from all parts of Greece at Olympia was utilized, from about the middle of the fifth century before Christ, by authors, orators, poets, and artists to make themselves known in the widest circles by the recital or exhibition of their works. When the compliment of a crown was offered by one State to another, the distinction was made generally known by being proclaimed by the heralds at the Olympian Games.

The buildings that formerly stood upon the Olympian plain are described by Pausanias in the sixth book of his work; and since the German archaeologists began in 1875 their explorations and excavations on its site, the ground-plans of nearly all these structures have been traced from existing remains. A good account of these excavations and of their discoveries will be found in the article by Flasch in Baumeister's *Denkmäler*, cited below. In 1895 preparations were begun in Athens under the patronage of the king of Greece for a celebration of the ancient games to be held in 1896.

For more elaborate details regarding the Games, see Krause, *Olympia* (1836); Bötticher, *Olympia* (1883); Baumeister, *Denkmäler des klassischen Alterthums* (1888); Laloux and Monceaux, *Restauration de l'Olympie* (1889); and Curtius and Adler, *Olympia, die Ergebnisse der Ausgrabungen* (1891).

Olympia (Ὀλυμπία). A small plain in Elis where the Olympian Games were held. It was surrounded on the north by the hill Cronus or Cronius, on the south by the river Alpheus, and on the west by the river Cladeus. Within its limits was the sacred precinct of Zeus called Ἄλτις (a dialectic form of ἄλσος, "grove"). For particulars regarding the Games, see the preceding article.

Olympias (Ὀλυμπιάς). A period of four years from one celebration of the Olympian Games (see OLYMPIA) to another. The Olympiads were counted from the victory of Coroebus (B.C. 776); the last, the 283d, ended A.D. 394, with the abolition of the Olympian Games. This method of reckoning never passed into everyday life, but is of importance, inasmuch as, through the historian Timaeus, about B.C. 240, it became the one generally used by the Greek historians.

Subjoined for the use of the student is a list of the Olympiads with the years of the Christian era corresponding to them from the beginning of the Olympiads to A.D. 301. To save space the separate years of each Olympiad, with the corresponding years B.C., are only given from the 47th to the 126th Olympiad, as this is the most important period of Grecian history; in the other Olympiads the first year only is given. In consulting the following table it must be borne in mind that the Olympic Games were celebrated about midsummer, and that the Attic year commenced at about the same time. If, therefore, an event happened in the second half of the Attic year, the year B.C. must be reduced by 1. Thus Socrates was put to death in the first year of the 95th Olympiad, which corresponds in the following table to B.C. 400; but as his death happened in Thargelion, the 11th month of the Attic year, the year B.C. must be reduced by 1, which gives us B.C. 399, the true date of his death.

B.C.	Ol.		B.C.	Ol.		B.C.	Ol.		B.C.	Ol.	
776.	1.	1.	589.		4.	540.	60.	1.	491.		2.
772.	2.	1.	588.	48.	1.	539.		2.	490.		3.
768.	3.	1.	587.		2.	538.		3.	489.		4.
764.	4.	1.	586.		3.	537.		4.	488.	73.	1.
760.	5.	1.	585.		4.	536.	61.	1.	487.		2.
756.	6.	1.	584.	49.	1.	535.		2.	486.		3.
752.	7.	1.	583.		2.	534.		3.	485.		4.
748.	8.	1.	582.		3.	533.		4.	484.	74.	1.
744.	9.	1.	581.		4.	532.	62.	1.	483.		2.
740.	10.	1.	580.	50.	1.	531.		2.	482.		3.
736.	11.	1.	579.		2.	530.		3.	481.		4.
732.	12.	1.	578.		3.	529.		4.	480.	75.	1.
728.	13.	1.	577.		4.	528.	63.	1.	479.		2.
724.	14.	1.	576.	51.	1.	527.		2.	478.		3.
720.	15.	1	575.		2.	526.		3.	477.		4.
716.	16.	1.	574.		3.	525.		4.	476.	76.	1.
712.	17.	1.	573.		4.	524.	64.	1.	475.		2.
708.	18.	1.	572.	52.	1.	523.		2.	474.		3.
704.	19.	1.	571.		2.	522.		3.	473.		4.
700.	20.	1.	570.		3.	521.		4.	472.	77.	1.
696.	21.	1.	569.		4.	520.	65.	1.	471.		2.
692.	22.	1.	568.	53.	1.	519.		2.	470.		3.
688.	23.	1.	567.		2.	518.		3.	469.		4.
684.	24.	1.	566.		3.	517.		4.	468.	78.	1.
680.	25.	1.	565.		4.	516.	66.	1.	467.		2.
676.	26.	1.	564.	54.	1.	515.		2.	466.		3.
672.	27.	1.	563.		2.	514.		3.	465.		4.
668.	28.	1.	562.		3.	513.		4.	464.	79.	1.
664.	29.	1.	561.		4.	512.	67.	1.	463.		2.
660.	30.	1.	560.	55.	1.	511.		2.	462.		3.
656.	31.	1.	559.		2.	510.		3.	461.		4.
652.	32.	1.	558.		3.	509.		4.	460.	80.	1.
648.	33.	1.	557.		4.	508.	68.	1.	459.		2.
644.	34.	1.	556.	56.	1.	507.		2.	458.		3.
640.	35.	1.	555.		2.	506.		3.	457.		4.
636.	36.	1	554.		3.	505.		4.	456.	81.	1.
632.	37.	1.	553.		4.	504.	69.	1.	455.		2.
628.	38.	1.	552.	57.	1.	503.		2.	454.		3.
624.	39.	1.	551.		2.	502.		3.	453.		4.
620.	40.	1.	550.		3.	501.		4.	452.	82.	1.
616.	41.	1.	549.		4.	500.	70.	1.	451.		2.
612.	42.	1.	548.	58.	1.	499.		2.	450.		3.
608.	43.	1.	547.		2.	498.		3.	449.		4.
604.	44.	1.	546.		3.	497.		4	448.	83.	1.
600.	45.	1.	545.		4.	496.	71.	1.	447.		2.
596.	46.	1.	544.	59.	1.	495.		2.	446.		3.
592.	47.	1.	543.		2.	494.		3.	445.		4.
591.		2.	542.		3	493.		4.	444.	84.	1.
590.		3.	541.		4.	492.	72.	1.	443.		2.

B.C.	Ol.		B.C.	Ol.		B.C.	Ol.		B.C.	Ol.	
442.		3.	363.		2.	284.	124.	1.	4.	194.	1.
441.		4.	362.		3.	283.		2.			
440.	85.	1.	361.		4.	282.		3.	A.D.	Ol.	
439.		2.	360.	105.	1.	281.		4.	1.	195.	1.
438.		3.	359.		2.	280.	125.	1.	5.	196.	1.
437.		4.	358.		3.	279.		2.	9.	197.	1.
436.	86.	1.	357.		4.	278.		3.	13.	198.	1.
435.		2.	356.	106.	1.	277.		4.	17.	199.	1.
434.		3.	355.		2.	276.	126.	1.	21.	200.	1.
433.		4.	354.		3.	275.		2.	25.	201.	1.
432.	87.	1.	353.		4.	274.		3.	29.	202.	1.
431.		2.	352.	107.	1.	273.		4.	33.	203.	1.
430.		3.	351.		2.	272.	127.	1.	37.	204.	1.
429.		4.	350.		3.	268.	128.	1.	41.	205.	1.
428.	88.	1.	349.		4.	264.	129.	1.	45.	206.	1.
427.		2.	348.	108.	1.	260.	130.	1.	49.	207.	1.
426.		3.	347.		2.	256.	131.	1.	53.	208.	1.
425.		4.	346.		3.	252.	132.	1.	57.	209.	1.
424.	89.	1.	345.		4.	248.	133.	1.	61.	210.	1.
423.		2.	344.	109.	1.	244.	134.	1.	65.	211.	1.
422.		3.	343.		2.	240.	135.	1.	69.	212.	1.
421.		4.	342.		3.	236.	136.	1.	73.	213.	1.
420.	90.	1.	341.		4.	232.	137.	1.	77.	214.	1.
419.		2.	340.	110.	1.	228.	138.	1.	81.	215.	1.
418.		3.	339.		2.	224.	139.	1.	85.	216.	1.
417.		4.	338.		3.	220.	140.	1.	89.	217.	1.
416.	91.	1.	337.		4.	216.	141.	1.	93.	218.	1.
415.		2.	336.	111.	1.	212.	142.	1.	97.	219.	1.
414.		3.	335.		2.	208.	143.	1.	101.	220.	1.
413.		4.	334.		3.	204.	144.	1.	105.	221.	1.
412.	92.	1.	333.		4.	200.	145.	1.	109.	222.	1.
411.		2.	332.	112.	1.	196.	146.	1.	113.	223.	1.
410.		3.	331.		2.	192.	147.	1.	117.	224.	1.
409.		4.	330.		3.	188.	148.	1.	121.	225.	1.
408.	93.	1.	329.		4.	184.	149.	1.	125.	226.	1.
407.		2.	328.	113.	1.	180.	150.	1.	129.	227.	1.
406.		3.	327.		2.	176.	151.	1.	133.	228.	1.
405.		4.	326.		3.	172.	152.	1.	137.	229.	1.
404.	94.	1.	325.		4.	168.	153.	1.	141.	230.	1.
403.		2.	324.	114.	1.	164.	154.	1.	145.	231.	1.
402.		3.	323.		2.	160.	155.	1.	149.	232.	1.
401.		4.	322.		3.	156.	156.	1.	153.	233.	1.
400.	95.	1.	321.		4.	152.	157.	1.	157.	234.	1.
399.		2.	320.	115.	1.	148.	158.	1.	161.	235.	1.
398.		3.	319.		2.	144.	159.	1.	165.	236.	1.
397.		4.	318.		3.	140.	160.	1.	169.	237.	1.
396.	96.	1.	317.		4.	136.	161.	1.	173.	238.	1.
395.		2.	316.	116.	1.	132.	162.	1.	177.	239.	1.
394.		3.	315.		2.	128.	163.	1.	181.	240.	1.
393.		4.	314.		3.	124.	164.	1.	185.	241.	1.
392.	97.	1.	313.		4.	120.	165.	1.	189.	242.	1.
391.		2.	312.	117.	1.	116.	166.	1.	193.	243.	1.
390.		3.	311.		2.	112.	167.	1.	197.	244.	1.
389.		4.	310.		3.	108.	168.	1.	201.	245.	1.
388.	98.	1.	309.		4.	104.	169.	1.	205	246.	1.
387.		2.	308.	118.	1.	100.	170.	1.	209.	247.	1.
386.		3.	307.		2.	96.	171.	1.	213.	248.	1.
385.		4.	306.		3.	92.	172.	1.	217.	249.	1.
384.	99.	1.	305.		4.	88.	173.	1.	221.	250.	1.
383.		2.	304.	119.	1.	84.	174.	1.	225.	251.	1.
382.		3.	303.		2.	80.	175.	1.	229.	252.	1.
381.		4.	302.		3.	76.	176.	1.	233.	253.	1.
380.	100.	1.	301.		4.	72.	177.	1.	237.	254.	1.
379.		2.	300.	120.	1.	68.	178.	1.	241.	255.	1.
378.		3.	299.		2.	64.	179.	1.	245.	256.	1.
377.		4.	298.		3.	60.	180.	1.	249.	257.	1.
376.	101.	1.	297.		4.	56.	181.	1.	253.	258.	1.
375.		2.	296.	121.	1.	52.	182.	1.	257.	259.	1.
374.		3.	295.		2.	48.	183.	1.	261.	260.	1.
373.		4.	294.		3.	44.	184.	1.	265.	261.	1.
372.	102.	1.	293.		4.	40.	185.	1.	269.	262.	1.
371.		2.	292.	122.	1.	36.	186.	1.	273.	263.	1.
370.		3.	291.		2.	32.	187.	1.	277.	264.	1.
369.		4.	290.		3.	28.	188.	1.	281.	265.	1.
368.	103.	1.	289.		4.	24.	189.	1.	285.	266.	1.
367.		2.	288.	123.	1.	20.	190.	1.	289.	267.	1.
366.		3.	287.		2.	16.	191.	1.	293.	268.	1.
365.		4.	286.		3.	12.	192.	1.	297.	269.	1.
364.	104.	1.	285.		4.	8.	193.	1.	301.	270.	1.

See CALENDARIUM.

Olympias (Ὀλυμπιάς). Daughter of Neoptolemus, king of Epirus, and wife of Philip, king of Macedon, by whom she had Alexander the Great. The conduct of Olympias had given rise to the suspicion that Alexander was not the son of Philip; and the brilliant career of the Macedonian conqueror made his flatterers assign to him for a parent the Father of the Gods. Olympias herself, in the intoxication of female vanity, sanctioned the story, and Zeus was said to have approached her under the form of a serpent. The haughtiness of Olympias, or, more probably, her infidelity, led Philip to repudiate her, and contract a second marriage with Cleopatra, the niece of King Attalus. The murder of Philip, which happened not long after, has been attributed by some to her intrigues, though with no great degree of probability. Alexander, after his accession to the throne, treated her with great respect, but did not allow her to take part in the government. At a subsequent period, after the death of Antipater (B.C. 319), Polysperchon, in order to confirm his power, recalled Olympias from Epirus, whither she had fled, and confided to her the guardianship of the young son of Alexander. She now cruelly put to death Arridaeus, son of Philip, with his wife Eurydicé, as also Nicanor, the brother of Cassander, together with many leading men of Macedonia who were inimical to her interests. Her cruelties, however, did not remain long unpunished. Cassander besieged her in Pydna, and she was obliged to surrender after an obstinate siege, and was put to death (B.C. 316). See Diod. xix. 11–51; Just. xiv. 5, 6; Pausan. ix. 7, 2; and the article CASSANDER.

Olympiēum (Ὀλυμπιεῖον). The temple of Olympian Zeus at Athens, in the southern part of the city, between the Acropolis and the Ilissus. It was built on the site of an ancient temple of Zeus, said to have been erected by Deucalion. The architects were Antistates, Callaeschrus, Antimachides, and Porinus. It was begun by Pisistratus about B.C. 535, continued by the Syrian king Antiochus Epiphanes (B.C. 175–164), and completed by the Roman emperor Hadrian (A.D. 125–130). See Pausan. i. 18, 6–8, and the monograph by Bevier in the *Papers of the American Classical School at Athens*, i. 183–222 (1885). Illustrations of its ruins are given on pp. 152 and 155 of this Dictionary.

Olympiodōrus (Ὀλυμπιόδωρος). A name common to many individuals. The most deserving of notice are the following: (1) A native of Thebes, in Egypt, who flourished in the beginning of the fifth century of our era. He continued the history of Eunapius from A.D. 407 to 425. His work, entitled Ὕλη Ἱστορίας ("Materials for History"), or Ἱστορικοὶ Λόγοι ("Historical Narratives"), consisted of twenty-two books. Only a fragment of it has been preserved by Photius. The work began with the seventh consulship of the emperor Honorius, and was brought down to the accession of Valentinian. It was dedicated to the younger Theodosius. (2) An Alexandrian philosopher, who flourished about the year B.C. 430. He is celebrated for his knowledge of the Aristotelian doctrines, and was the master of Proclus, who attended upon his school before he was twenty years of age. (3) A Platonic philosopher, who flourished towards the close of the sixth century. He was the author of commentaries on four of Plato's dialogues—the *First Alcibiades*, the *Phaedon*, *Gorgias*, and *Philebus*. The first of these contains a life of Plato, in which we meet with certain particulars relative to the philosopher not to be found elsewhere. This Olympiodorus was a native of Alexandria. The title which his commentaries bear appears to indicate by the words ἀπὸ φωνῆς ("from the mouth" of Olympiodorus) that they were copied down by the hearers of the philosopher. (4) A native of Alexandria, a Peripatetic, who flourished during the latter half of the sixth century A.D. He was the author of a commentary on the meteorology of Aristotle, still extant.

Olympius (Ὀλύμπιος). A name applied especially to Zeus as the chief of the gods who lived upon Olympus. See OLYMPUS; ZEUS.

Olympius Nemesiānus. See NEMESIANUS.

Olympus (Ὄλυμπος). (1) A mountain situated in Thessaly, the summit of which (nearly 10,000 feet above the sea) rises from the region of the earth's atmosphere into the sky, and was, according to the earliest popular belief of the Greeks, the abode of the higher (hence named Olympian) gods. Below the summit, which, according to Homer's description, is never ruffled by winds or drenched with rain, but is always radiant in cloudless splendour (*Od.* vi. 42–45), comes the region of clouds, which Zeus at one time gathers together and at another dispels; it forms the boundary between the celestial region and that of the earth, and, accordingly, Homer elsewhere implies that the clouds are the gates of heaven, which are guarded by the Horae (*Il.* v. 749). On the highest peak Zeus has his throne, and it is there that he summons the assemblies of the gods. The abodes of the other gods were imagined to be placed on the precipices and in the ravines of the mountain. When the height of the vault of heaven came to be regarded as the abode of the gods, the name Olympus was transferred to the sky. See Henzey, *Le Mont Olympe* (Paris, 1860); and Tozer, *The Highlands of Turkey*, vol. ii. (London, 1869). (2) A chain of mountains in Mysia, Bithynia, Galatia, Paphlagonia, and Pontus. (3) A volcano on the eastern coast of Lycia. (4) A mountain in Cyprus. (5) A mountain in Lesbos.

Olympus (Ὄλυμπος). One of the mythic poets and musicians belonging to Phrygian mythology, pupil of Marsyas. The art of flute-playing, invented by Marsyas, was supposed to have been perfected by Olympus. A Phrygian family, in which the art of flute-playing was hereditary, traced their descent from him. The Phrygian Olympus, who lived about the seventh century before Christ, invented the auletic νόμος, and brought it into esteem among the Asiatic Greeks, was said to be descended from the mythical Olympus (Plut. *De Mus.* p. 1133).

Olynthiacs. See DEMOSTHENES; OLYNTHUS.

Olynthus (Ὄλυνθος). A town of Chalcidicé, at the head of the Toronaic Gulf, and the most important of the Greek cities on the coast of Macedonia. It was at the head of a confederacy of all the Greek towns in its neighbourhood, and maintained its independence, except for a short interval, when it was subject to Sparta (379–375), till it was taken and destroyed by Philip, B.C. 347. The Olynthiac orations of Demosthenes were delivered by the orator to urge the Athenians to send assistance to the city when it was attacked by Philip. When the supremacy of Sparta was destroyed by the Thebans, Olynthus recovered its independence, and even received an accession of power from Philip, who was anxious to make Olynthus a counterpoise to the influence of Athens in the north of the Aegean. With this view Philip gave Olynthus the territory of Potidaea, after he had wrested this town from the Athenians in 356. But when he had sufficiently consolidated his power to be able to set at defiance both Olynthus and Athens, he threw off the mask, and laid siege to the former city. The Olynthians earnestly besought Athens for assistance, and were warmly supported by Demosthenes in his Olynthiac orations; but as the Athenians did not render the city any effectual assistance, it was taken and destroyed by Philip, and all its inhabitants sold as slaves (347). Olynthus was never restored. Olynthus used the town of Mecyberna as its port. See DEMOSTHENES; PHILIPPUS.

Omăna (Ὄμανα) and **Omănum** (Ὄμανον). (1) A seaport of Arabia Felix, on a gulf of the same name. (2) A seaport in the eastern part of the Persian province of Carmania. It was a great mart for the Indian, Persian, and Arabian trade (Pliny, *H. N.* vi. 149).

Ombi (Ὄμβοι). The last great city of Upper Egypt, except Syené. It stood on the eastern bank of the Nile, in the Ombites Nomos, and was celebrated as one of the chief seats of the worship of the crocodile. Juvenal's Fifteenth Satire is founded on a religious war between the people of Ombi and those of Tentyra, who hated the crocodile (Ptol. iv. 5, 73; Aelian, *H. A.* x. 21).

Omen (for *osmen*, *ausmen*, from the root of *audio*, "something heard"). The Roman term for a favourable or unfavourable sign, especially a word spoken by chance, so far as it drew the attention of the hearers to itself and appeared to be a prognostic. An omen could be accepted or repudiated, and even taken in an arbitrary sense, except in the case of words which already had in themselves a favourable or unfavourable signification. For example, when Crassus was embarking on his unfortunate expedition against the Parthians, and a man in the harbour was selling dry figs from Caunus with the cry *Cauneas*, which sounded like *cave ne eas*, "beware of going," this was an evil omen (Cic. *De Div.* ii. 84). Men often changed an apparently evil omen into one more favourable. Thus when Caesar landed in Africa, he stumbled and fell, whereupon he embraced the earth, exclaiming, "Thus do I take possession of thee, Africa." On festal occasions care was taken to protect oneself from evil omens; for example, when sacrifice was being made, by veiling the head, by commanding silence, and by music that drowned any word spoken. People were particularly careful at solemn addresses, Near Year greetings, and the like. On the other hand, for the sake of the good omen, it was usual to open levies and censuses by calling out those names that were of good import, such as Valerius (from *valere*), Salvius, from *salvere*, etc. (Cic. *Pro Scauro*, 30). On one occasion the Roman soldiers refused to be led by an officer named Atrius Umber, whose name De Quincey well styles "a pleonasm of darkness." People also made New Year's presents (*strenae*) to one another, so that the year might begin with a good omen. The Greeks also paid a good deal of attention to omens; and Socrates criticises this superstition (Xen. *Mem.* i.).

Omphălé (Ὀμφάλη). The daughter of the Lydian king Iardanus, and wife of Tmolus, on whose death she governed the kingdom herself. When Heracles was cursed with a dangerous disease as a punishment for the slaying of Iphitus, the oracle informed him that he could only be cured by serving for hire for a period of three years. To effect the cure, Hermes sold him to Omphalé, with whom he fell in love, and to please her put on her garments and spun wool, while she wore his lion skin. By him she had several children (Diod. iv. 31; Apollod. ii. 6, 3; Ovid, *Fasti*, ii. 305; *Her.* ix. 53).

Heracles and Omphalé. (Naples Museum.)

Omphălus (ὀμφαλός). Literally "the navel" (*umbilicus*), and applied to anything like the navel, round—e. g the knobs or bosses on a shield (see CLIPEUS), a knob on the yoke of a horse for fastening the reins, and, figuratively, the centre of anything. Thus Ogygia, the island of Calypso, is called ὀμφαλὸς θαλάσσης, and Delphi (q. v.) was also called ὀμφαλός, as being the supposed centre of the earth, from which, according to the myth, Zeus once despatched two eagles, one flying eastward and the other westward, with the result that they met again at Delphi. A marble boss marked the exact spot where they met.

On. The Hebrew name of the Egyptian Heliopolis (q v.).

Onăger A catapult for hurling stones. See TORMENTUM.

Onātas (Ὀνάτας). A Greek artist, the chief representative of the Aeginetan school of sculpture in bronze, about B.C. 460. Besides statues of the gods, such as an Apollo at Pergamon, admired for its size and execution (Pausan. viii. 42, § 7), we hear of groups of his, rich in figures, drawn either from the heroic epoch—as, for example, the ten Greek heroes casting lots as to who should undertake the battle with Hector—or from contemporary history, such as the votive offering of the Tarentines, containing equestrian and pedestrian combatants, and consecrated at Delphi for their victory over the barbarian Peucetians. He also executed a group representing Hiero of Syracuse with the chariot in which he had been victorious at Olympia. His most remarkable work was the bronze figure of the black Demeter, in a cavern thirty stadia from Phigalea, in the southeast corner of Elis (Pausan. viii. 42, 1).

Oncae (Ὄγκαι). A Boeotian village near Thebes. One of the city gates of Thebes was named from it (Ὀγκαῖαι).

Oncēum (Ὄγκειον). A town in Arcadia on the river Ludon (Pausan. viii. 25, 4).

Onchesmus (Ὄγχησμος) or **Onchismus** (Ὄγχισμος). A seaport town of Epirus, opposite Corcyra.

Onchestus (Ὄγχηστος). (1) An ancient town of Boeotia, situated a little south of Lake Copaïs, near Haliartus, said to have been founded by Onchestus, son of Poseidon. (2) A river in Thessaly, flowing by Cynoscephalae, and falling into Lake Boebeïs.

Oneraria Navis. See NAVIS.

Onesander (Ὀνήσανδρος, wrongly ONOSANDER). A Greek philosopher, the author of a work dedicated to Q. Veranius, consul in A.D. 49, and dealing with the duty of a general (Στρατηγικὸς Λόγος), in which he treats the subject in philosophical commonplaces, without any practical acquaintance with it, and simply from an ethical point of view. The work is edited by Köchly (Leipzig, 1860).

Onesicrĭtus (Ὀνησίκριτος). A Greek historian, of the island of Astypalaea or of Aegina. In mature years he was a pupil of the Cynic Diogenes, and then accompanied Alexander the Great upon his expedition. By order of Alexander he investigated, with Nearchus, the route by sea from India to the mouths of the Euphrates and Tigris. He afterwards lived at the court of Lysimachus, king of Thrace. During Alexander's life he began a comprehensive history of that personage, which fell into disrepute, owing to its exaggerations and its false accounts of distant lands (Strabo, p. 628). Only scanty fragments of it are preserved.

Oningis. See ORINGIS.

Onirocritĭcé (Ὀνειροκριτική, sc. τέχνη). The art of interpreting dreams. See MANTIKÉ.

Onīros (Ὄνειρος). The god of dreams. Dreams dwelt on the shores of the Western Ocean, false dreams coming out of an ivory gate and true dreams from a gate of horn (*Odyss.* xix. 562; xxiv. 12). Dreams were controlled by Hermes, the god of messages. Ovid calls them the children of Sleep, and names three of them—Morpheus, Icelus (or Phobetor), and Phantasus (Met. xi. 633). For dream-oracles, see ORACULA.

Onomacrĭtus (Ὀνομάκριτος). An Athenian, who lived at the court of Pisistratus and his sons (about B.C. 520–485). At the request of Pisistratus, he is said to have prepared an edition of the Homeric poems. He was an industrious collector, and also a forger of old oracles and poems. Those which go under the name of Orpheus are regarded as, for the most part, concocted by Onomacritus. He was detected in forging an oracle of Musaeus, and banished from Athens by the Pisistratidae; but he was afterwards reconciled to them, and in their interest induced Xerxes, by alleged oracular responses, to decide upon his war with Greece (Herod. vii. 6).

Onomarchus (Ὀνόμαρχος). A general of the Phocians in the Sacred War, succeeded his brother Philomelus in this command, B.C. 353. In the following year he was defeated in Thessaly by Philip, and perished in attempting to reach by swimming the Athenian ships, which were lying off the shore. His body fell into the hands of Philip, who caused it to be crucified, as a punishment for his sacrilege (Diod. xvi. 41–61).

Onomatopoeia (ὀνοματοποιΐα) and **Onomatopoeēsis** (ὀνοματοποίησις), called by the Roman linguists FICTIO NOMĬNIS (Quint. viii. 6, 31). Literally, "word-making"; (1) the coining of a word to imitate some natural sound; and (2) a word so made. Both Greek and Latin possess many imitative words, the greater part of which mimic the sounds made by animals, birds, and insects. Such are the Greek βῆ βῆ (the English "baa"), κρώζω ("to croak"), γρῦ ("a grunt"), πιπίζω ("to peep," of birds), κοάξ (the sound made by frogs), κοΐ, κοΐζω (of swine, "queek"), ὠρύω ("to roar"), τιτίζω ("to twitter"), ὑλάω ("to howl"). Other excellent imitative words are βαβάζω ("to babble"), βόμβος ("a booming"), κρόταλον ("a rattle"), χάω ("to yawn"), πτύω ("to spit"), χρέμπτομαι ("to hawk"), πτάρνυμαι ("to sneeze"), ῥοφέω ("to suck"). In Latin, though Quintilian (l. c.) regards the language as poor in onomatopoeias, the number is really very large. Good examples are *baubor* ("bow-wow"), *bee* ("baa"), *bubo* ("owl"), *cachinno* ("to cackle"), *cocococo* ("cluck"), *crocio* ("croak"), *flo* ("to blow"), *glut-glut* ("gurgle"), *hinnio* ("whinny"), *minurrio* ("to coo"), *raucus* ("hoarse"), *stloppus* ("a slap"), *susurrus* ("a whisper"), *zinzala* ("a mosquito").

Onomatopoeia of a higher type than mere word-making is found in literature, where the poets, especially, often make the sound of their lines harmonize with the sense most effectively. Homer is rich in such verses. Thus, the falling of the sea has been much admired (*Il.* i. 34):

βῆ δ' ἀκέων παρὰ θῖνα πολυφλοισβοῖο θαλάσσης

and this of the galloping of horses (*Il.* x. 535):

ἵππων μ' ὠκυπόδων ἀμφὶ κτύπος οὔατα βάλλει.

The latter is imitated and surpassed by Vergil (*Aen.* viii. 596):

Quadrupedante putrem sonitu quatit ungula campum.

The following (*Georg.* iv. 174) is written of the Cyclopes at the forge, and is the Anvil Chorus of antiquity:

Illi inter sese magna vi bracchia tollunt.

Again, Vergil writes of the flight of a dove (*Aen.* v. 217):

Radit iter liquidum celeres neque commovet alas;

where the dactylic movement and the recurrent liquids give the exact effect desired.

A late Latin poem, called *De Philomela*, collects all the words used in imitation of the sounds made by animals; and Suetonius, in his *Pratum*, made an even longer list, which is preserved in a fragment edited by Reifferscheid (Leipzig, 1890).

On the mimetic vocabulary of the Greeks and Romans, see Lenormant, *Comment. sur le Cratyle de Platon* (Athens, 1861); Nodier, *Dictionnaire des Onomatopées* (Paris, 1828); Wackernagel, *Voces Variae Animantium* (Basel, 1869); and H. T. Peck, *Onomatopoetic Words in Latin* (in *Classical Studies in Honour of Henry Drisler*) (N. Y. 1894). On the theory which makes onomatopoeia the original principle of language-making (the so-called "bow-wow theory"), see Voigtman, *Die Bau-wau Theorie* (Leipzig, 1865); Steinthal, *Der Ursprung der Sprache* (Berlin, 1858); id. *Philologie, Geschichte und Psychologie* (Berlin, 1864); and Strong, Logeman, and Wheeler, *Principles of Language* (New York, 1893).

Onosander. See ONESANDER.

Onyx. See GEMMA.

Opa (ὀπή). The Greek equivalent of *columbarium* (q. v.).

Opalia and **Opeconsīva**. Feasts of the Roman goddess Ops (q. v.).

Opals. See GEMMA.

Operculum (πῶμα). A lid or cover of a jar (Cato, *R. R.* 104).

Ophelion (Ὠφελίων). An Athenian comic poet, probably of the Middle Comedy, B.C. 380.

Ophellas (Ὀφέλλας). A native of Pella, in Macedonia. He was one of the generals of Alexander the Great, after whose death he followed the fortunes of Ptolemy. In B.C. 322 he conquered Cyrené for Ptolemy, of which city he held the government on behalf of the Egyptian king for some years. But soon after 313 he threw off his allegiance to Ptolemy, and continued to govern Cyrené as an independent state for nearly five years. In 308 he formed an alliance with Agathocles, and marched against Carthage; but he was treacherously attacked by Agathocles near this city, and was slain (Diod. xx. 40–42).

Opheltes (Ὀφέλτης). The son of Lycurgus, king of Nemea. Hypsipylé, the Lemnian princess, whom her countrywomen had sold into slavery, was nurse to the infant Opheltes, when the army of Adrastus marched to Nemea, on its way to Thebes. She undertook to guide the new-comers to a spring; and, for that purpose, left the child lying on the grass, where a serpent found and killed it. The Argive leaders slew the serpent and buried the child. Amphiaraüs, the famous soothsayer and warrior, augured ill-luck from this event, and called the child ARCHEMŎRUS ("Fate-beginner"), as indicative of the evils that were to befall the chieftains. His other name, Opheltes, was derived, according to the mythologists, from ὄφις, as he died by the bite of a serpent.

Ophīon (Ὀφίων). (1) One of the Titans. (2) One of the companions of Cadmus. (3) Father of the centaur Amycus, who is hence called Ophionides.

Ophiūsa (Ὀφιόεσσα) or **Ophiussa** (Ὀφιοῦσσα). A name given to many ancient places from their abounding in snakes. It was an ancient name of both Rhodes and Cyprus, whence Ovid speaks of *Ophiusia arva*.

Opĭci. See OSCI.

Opilio (οἰοπόλος). A shepherd.

Opilius, AURELIUS. The freedman of an Epicurean, taught at Rome, first philosophy, then rhetoric, and, finally, grammar. He gave up his school upon the condemnation of Rutilius Rufus (B.C. 92), whom he accompanied to Smyrna, and there the two friends grew old together in the enjoyment of each other's society. He composed several learned works, one of which, named *Musae*, is referred to by A. Gellius (i. 25).

Opilius Macrīnus. See MACRINUS.

Opīma Spolia. Spoils taken by a Roman general from a general of the enemy whom he had slain in battle. They were dedicated to Iupiter Feretrius and suspended in his temple. These spoils were obtained only thrice before the fall of the Republic. The first by Romulus, who slew Acron, king of the Caeninenses; the next by A. Cornelius Cossus, who slew Lars Tolumnius, king of the Veientes, B.C. 436; and the third by M. Claudius Marcellus, who slew Viridomarus, a king of the Gauls, B.C. 224.

Opimius. (1) QUINTUS, consul B.C. 154, when he subdued some of the Ligurian tribes north of the

Alps, who had attacked Massilia. He was notorious in his youth for his riotous living. (2) LUCIUS, son of the preceding, was praetor in B.C. 125, in which year he took Fregellae, which had revolted against the Romans. He belonged to the high aristocratic party, and was a violent opponent of C. Gracchus. He was consul in 121, and took the leading part in the proceedings which ended in the murder of Gracchus. Opimius and his party abused their victory most savagely, and are said to have killed more than 300 persons. (For details, see GRACCHUS.) In the following year (120) he was accused of having put Roman citizens to death without trial; but he was defended by the consul C. Papirius Carbo, and was acquitted. In 112 he was at the head of the commission which was sent into Africa in order to divide the dominions of Micipsa between Iugurtha and Adherbal, and was bribed by Iugurtha, to assign to him the better part of the country (Sall. *Iug.* 16, 40). Three years after he was condemned under the law of the tribune C. Mamilius Limetanus, by which an inquiry was made into the conduct of all those who had received bribes from Iugurtha. Opimius went into exile to Dyrrhachium in Epirus, where he lived for some years, hated and insulted by the people, and where he eventually died in great poverty. He richly deserved his punishment, and met with a due recompense for his cruel and ferocious conduct towards C. Gracchus and his party. Cicero, on the contrary, who, after his consulship, had identified himself with the aristocratic party, frequently laments the fate of Opimius. The year in which Opimius was consul (121) was remarkable for the extraordinary heat of the autumn, and thus the vintage of this year was of an unprecedented quality. This wine long remained celebrated as the *vinum Opimianum* (Cic. Brut. 83, 287).

Opinatōres. Officers under the Roman emperors who were sent to demand arrears of the *annona militaris*. The regular collector was termed *exactor;* the opinator was an extraordinary official sent to coerce overdue supplies, and was for the army what the *compulsor* was for other tribute. The name is probably derived from *opinari*, in the sense of *aestimare*, because they assessed what the due amounted to (Cod. 12, tit. 38, s. 11).

Opis (Ὦπις). A city of Assyria, in the district Apolloniatis, where the Physcus River joined the Tigris (Herod. i. 189).

Opisthodŏmus (ὀπισθόδομος). A chamber built at the back of a temple, like a modern sacristy (Fronto, *ad* M. Caes. i. 8, Mai's ed.). See TEMPLUM.

Opisthogrăphus (ὀπισθόγραφος). Written on both sides of the paper, a practice not usual with the ancients, but sometimes practised for motives of economy. See Pliny, *Epist.* iii. 5, 17; and the article LIBER.

Opitergium. Now Oderzo; a Roman colony in Venetia, in the north of Italy, on the river Liquentia.

Oppiānus (Ὀππιανός). (1) A Greek didactic poet of Anazarbus, in Cilicia. In the second half of the second century A.D., under the emperor Marcus Aurelius, he composed a didactic poem *Halieutica* (Ἁλιευτικά), in five books, on the habits of fishes and the method of capturing them. It is written in an ornate, though often bombastic, style. He was formerly confounded with (2) Oppianus, the author of a didactic poem on the chase, consisting of four books, and entitled *Cynegetica* (Κυνηγετικά), written in a harsh, dry style and in halting verse. The author of the *Cynegetica* lived under Caracalla about the end of the second century, and came from Apamea, in Syria. A poem on bird-catching, *Ixeutica* (Ἰξευτικά), preserved to us only in a paraphrase by Eutechnius, was also wrongly ascribed to the author of the *Halieutica*. Both the *Halieutica* and *Cynegetica* are edited together by Lehrs (1846).

Oppĭdum. (1) Originally, the stronghold, commonly overlooking the plain (*ob pedum*), which served as a refuge in times of danger for the inhabitants of the surrounding district; and later, the town which grew up about the stronghold. (2) In a special sense the mass of buildings occupying the straight end of a Circus, which included the stalls for the horses and chariots (*carceres*), the row of seats above, where the musicians and spectators sat, the gate between them, through which the Circensian procession entered the course (*porta pompae*), and the towers which flanked the whole on either side, all which together presented the appearance of a town.

Restoration of the Oppidum in the Circus of Maxentius. (Rich.)

Oppius. (1) C. OPPIUS, a tribune of the plebs B.C. 213, who carried a law to curtail the expenses and luxuries of Roman women. (See SUMPTUARIAE LEGES.) (2) C. OPPIUS, an intimate friend of C. Iulius Caesar, whose private affairs he managed in conjunction with Cornelius Balbus, and whose biography he wrote. He has by some been regarded as the author of the pseudo-Caesarian treatises *De Bello Alexandrino*, *De Bello Africano*, and *De Bello Hispaniensi*. As to the first of these, his authorship is possible but not probable; as to the other two it is impossible. See Nipperdey, *De Supplementis Commentariorum Caesaris* (Berlin, 1846); and Teuffel, *Rom. Lit.* i. pp. 338–341 (Eng. trans. 1891).

Ops. The wife of Saturnus. She was the Roman goddess of plenty and fertility, as is indicated by her name, which is connected with *opimus*, *opulentus*, *inops*, and *copia*. She was especially the protectress of agriculture; and was also the goddess of the world below, so that in worshipping her, persons stooped and touched the ground (Macrob. *Sat.* i. 10, 12; iii. 9, 12). She was honoured by the Fratres Arvales (q. v.) in the three days' festival held by them in summer, and in the Opalia, December 17, at the time of the Saturnalia. She was regarded as the wife of Saturnus, and her worship was closely connected with his and also with that of Ceres. As the goddess of seedtime, she was styled OPS CONSĪVA, and was also called by the name DEA DIA.

Optatiānus. See PORPHYRIUS.

Optimātes ("those belonging to the best or noblest"). At Rome, in the last century of the Republic, a title borne by the adherents of the "best" men, in a political sense (i. e. the conservatives), working in the interests of the Senate and the aristocracy of office (*nobiles*) and in opposition to the democrats (*populares*). See NOBILES.

Optostrōtum. A flooring of bricks (*Not. Tires.* p. 164).

Opūs (Ὀποῦς). A town of Locris, from which the Opuntian Locrians derived their name. It was the birthplace of Patroclus. The bay of the Euboean Sea, near Opus, was called OPUNTIUS SINUS.

Ora. A hawser or cable (Livy, xxii. 19).

Oracŭla (μαντεῖα, "oracular responses," or the "seats of oracles"; χρηστήρια is used in the same senses, and also of victims offered by persons consulting an oracle). The seats of the worship of some special divinity, where prophecies were imparted with the sanction of the divinity, either by the priests themselves or with their co-operation. There were many such places in all Greek countries, and these may be divided, according to the method in which the prophecy was made known, into four main divisions: (1) oral oracles, (2) oracles by signs, (3) oracles by dreams, and (4) oracles of the dead.

(1) The most revered oracles were those of the first class, where the divinity, almost invariably the god Apollo, orally revealed his will through the lips of inspired prophets or prophetesses. The condition of frenzy was produced, for the most part, by physical influences: the breathing of earthy vapours or drinking of the water of oracular fountains. The words spoken while in this state were generally fashioned by the priests into a reply to the questions proposed to them. The most famous oracle of this kind was that of Delphi (see further below). Besides this there existed in Greece Proper a large number of oracles of Apollo, as at Abae in Phocis, in different places of Boeotia, in Euboea, and at Argos, where the priestess derived her inspiration from drinking the blood of a lamb, one being killed every month. Not less numerous were the oracles of Apollo in Asia Minor. Among these that of the Didymaean Apollo at Miletus traced its origin to the old family of the Branchidae, the descendants of Apollo's son Branchus. Before its destruction by Xerxes, it came nearest to the reputation of the Delphian. Here it was a priestess who prophesied, seated on a wheel-shaped disc, after she had bathed the hem of her robe and her feet in a spring, and had breathed the steam arising from it. The oracle at Clarus, near Colophon (see MANTO), was also very ancient. Here a priest, after simply hearing the names and the number of those consulting the oracle, drank of the water of a spring, and then gave answer in verse.

(2) The most venerated among the oracles where prophecy was given by signs was that of Zeus of Dodona (q. v.), mentioned as early as Homer (*Od.* xiv. 327–xix. 296), where predictions were made from the rustling of the sacred oak, and at a later time from the sound of a brazen cymbal. Another mode of interpreting by signs, as practised especially at the temple of Zeus at Olympia by the Iamidae, or descendants of Iamus, a son of Apollo, was that derived from the entrails of victims and the burning of the sacrifices on the altar. There were also oracles connected with the lot or dice, one especially at the temple of Heracles at Bura, in Achaia; and prophecies were also delivered at Delphi by means of lots, probably only at times when the Pythia was not giving responses. The temple of the Egyptian Ammon, who was identified with Zeus, also gave oracles by means of signs.

(3) Oracles given in dreams were generally connected with the temples of Asclepius. After certain preliminary rites, sick persons had to sleep in these temples; the priests interpreted their dreams, and dictated, accordingly, the means to be taken to insure recovery. The most famous of these oracular shrines of the healing god was the temple at Epidaurus, and next to this the temple founded thence at Pergamum, in Asia Minor. Equally famous were the similar oracles of the seer Amphiaraüs at Oropus, of Trophonius at Lebadea, in Boeotia, and of the seers Mopsus and Amphilochus at Mallus, in Cilicia (q. v.). In later times such oracles were connected with all sanctuaries of Isis and Serapis.

(4) At oracles of the dead (ψυχομαντεῖα) the souls of deceased persons were evoked in order to give the information desired. Thus, in Homer (*Od.* xi), Odysseus betakes himself to the entrance of the lower world to question the spirit of the seer Tiresias. Oracles of this kind were especially common in places where it was supposed there was an entrance to the lower world; as at the city of Cichyrus in Epirus (where there was an Acherusian lake as well as the rivers of Acheron and Cocytus, bearing the same names as those of the world below), at the promontory of Taenarum in Laconia, at Heraclea in Pontus, and at Lake Avernus, near Cumae, in Italy. At most of them oracles were also given in dreams; but there were some in which the inquirer was in a waking condition when he conjured up the spirits whom he wished to question.

While oracles derived either from dreams or from the dead were chosen in preference by superstitious people, the most important among oral oracles and those given by means of signs had a political significance. On all serious occasions they were questioned on behalf of the State in order to ascertain the divine will: this was especially the case with the oracle of Delphi. In consequence of the avarice and partisanship of the priests, as well as the increasing decline of belief in the gods, the oracles gradually fell into abeyance, to revive again everywhere under the Roman emperors, though they never regained the political importance they had once had in ancient Greece.

Such investigation of the divine will was originally quite foreign to the Romans. Even the mode of prophesying by means of lots (see SORTES), practised in isolated regions of Italy, and even in the immediate neighbourhood of Rome, as at Caeré, and especially at Praenesté, did not come into use, at all events for State purposes, and was generally regarded with contempt. The Romans did not consult even the Sibylline verses in order to forecast the future. On the other hand, the growth of superstition in the imperial period not only brought the native oracles into repute, but caused a general resort to foreign oracles besides. The inclination to this kind of prophecy seems never to have been more generally spread among the masses of the people than at this time. Apart from the Greek oracular deities, there were the oriental deities, whose worship was nearly everywhere combined with predictions. In most of the famous sanctuaries the most various forms of prophecy were represented, and the stranger they were the better they were liked. In the case of the oral oracles, the responses in earlier times were, for the most part, composed in verse; on the decay of poetic productiveness, they began to take the form of prose, or of passages from the poets, the Greeks generally adopting lines of Homer or Euripides; the Italians, lines of Vergil. The public declaration of oracles ended with the official extermination of paganism under Theodosius at the end of the fourth century.

The following is a list of the most celebrated oracles:

(1) Of Zeus: at Dodona, in Epirus, the most ancient of all; at Olympia, with the Iamidae and Clytiades as its priests; and of Zeus Ammon in a Libyan oasis in the northwest of Egypt.

(2) Of Apollo: at Delphi (see below); at Abae, in Phocis; at Tegyraia, in Boeotia; at Mount Ptoön, near Acraephia; of Apollo Ismenius, near Thebes, the national oracle of the Thebans; of Hysiae, at the base of Mount Cithaeron; at Eutresis, near Leuctra; of Apollo Didymaeus, in the territory of Miletus, with the Branchidae as its ministers; at Claros, north of Miletus; at Patara, in Lycia; at Cyaneae, in Lycia; of Apollo Sarpedonius at Seleucia, in Cilicia; at Hybla, in Magnesia; at Grynea or Grynium, in Asia Minor; at Methymna, in Lesbos; at Chalcedon; at Delos; at Argos; at Daphne, in Syria (in later times).

(3) Of Gaea (the Earth): at Aegira, in Achaia, and at Patrae; of Pluto and Persephoné at Acharaca, in Asia Minor, near Tralles; of Bacchus, at Amphiclea, in Phocis, and at Satrae, in Thrace; of Hermes, at Pharae, in Achaia; and of the Nymphs on Mount Cithaeron.

(4) There were also oracles of heroes—e. g. of Asclepius, at Epidaurus and Pergamus; of Trophonius, at Lebadea; of Tiresias, at Orchomenus; of Amphiaraüs, near Thebes and near Oropus; of Mopsus, at Mallos, in Cilicia; of Calchas and Podalirius, on Mount Dion, in Southern Italy; of Protesilaüs, at Elaeus, in the Thracian Chersonesus; of Autolycus, the Argonaut, at Sinopé; and of Odysseus, in Aetolia.

(5) There were Italian oracles of Faunus at Albunea and of Fortuna at Praenesté and Antium (Cic. *De Div.* ii. 41, 85). At Caeré and at Falerii there were "lots" (*sortes*), from which oracles or perhaps omens were inferred (Livy, xxii. 1).

As the Delphic oracle is by far the most famous and the one to which allusion is oftenest made in literature, a somewhat more detailed account of it may be of interest. Its seat was on the southwestern spur of Parnassus in a valley of Phocis. In historical times the oracle appears in possession of Apollo; but the original possessor, according to the story, was Gaea (Aesch. *Eumen.* 1, 2). Then it was shared by her with Poseidon (Eurip. *Ion*, 446), who gave up his part in it to Apollo in exchange for the island of Calauria, Themis, the daughter and successor of Gaea, having already given Apollo her share. According to the Homeric hymn to the Pythian Apollo, the god took forcible possession of the oracle soon after his birth, slaying with his earliest bow-shot the serpent Pytho, the son of Gaea, who guarded the spot. To atone for his murder, Apollo was forced to fly and spend eight years in menial service before he could return forgiven. A festival, the Septeria, was held every year, at which the whole story was represented: the slaying of the serpent, and the flight, atonement, and return of the god. Apollo was represented by a boy, both of whose parents were living. The dragon was symbolically slain, and his house, decked out in costly fashion, was burned. Then the boy's followers hastily dispersed, and the boy was taken in procession to Tempé, along the road formerly followed by the god. Here he was purified and brought back by the same road, accompanied by a chorus of maidens singing songs of joy. The oracle proper was a cleft in the ground in the innermost sanctuary, from which arose cold vapours, which had the power of inducing ecstasy. Over the cleft stood a lofty gilded tripod of wood. On this was a circular slab, upon which the seat of the prophetess was placed. The prophetess, called Pythia, was a maiden of honourable birth; in earlier times a young girl, but in a later age a woman of over fifty, still wearing a girl's dress, in memory of the earlier custom. In the prosperous times of the oracle two Pythias acted alternately, with a third to assist them. In the earliest times the Pythia ascended the tripod only once a year, on the birthday of Apollo, the seventh of the Delphian spring month Bysius. But in later years she prophesied every day, if the day itself and the sacrifices were not unfavourable. These sacrifices were offered by the supplicants, adorned with laurel crowns and fillets of wool. Having prepared herself by washing and purification, the Pythia entered the sanctuary, with gold ornaments in her hair and flowing robes upon her; she drank of the water of the fountain Cassotis, which flowed into the shrine, tasted the fruit of the old bay-tree standing in the chamber, and took her seat. No one was present but a priest, called the προφήτης (and προφῆτις), who explained the words she uttered in her ecstasy, and put them into metrical form, generally hexameters. In later times the votaries were contented with answers in prose. The responses were often obscure and enigmatical, and couched in ambiguous and metaphorical expressions, which themselves needed explanation. The order in which the applicants approached the oracle was determined by lot, but certain cities, as Sparta, had the right of priority.

The reputation of the oracle stood very high throughout Greece until the time of the Persian Wars, especially among the Dorian tribes, and among them pre-eminently the Spartans, who had stood from of old in intimate relation with it. On all important occasions, as the sending out of colonies, the framing of internal legislation or religious ordinances, the god of Delphi was consulted, and that not only by Greeks, but by foreigners, especially the people of Asia and Italy. After the Persian Wars the influence of the oracle declined, partly in consequence of the growth of unbelief, partly from the mistrust excited by the partiality and venality of the priesthood, who sometimes were bribed into giving oracles favourable to the inquirer, and in the case of Philip of Macedon, when Demosthenes said, ἡ πυθία φιλιππίζει. But it never fell completely into discredit, and from time to time its position rose again. In the first half of the second century A.D. it had a revival, the result of the newly awakened interest in the old region. It was abolished at the end of the fourth century A.D. by Theodosius the Great.

The oldest stone temple of Apollo was attributed to the mythical architects, Trophonius and Agamedes. It was burned down in B.C. 548, when the Alcmaeonidae, at that time in exile from Athens, undertook to rebuild it for the sum of 300 talents, partly taken from the treasure of the temple, and partly contributed by all countries inhabited by Greeks and standing in connection with the oracle. They put the restoration into the hands of the Corinthian architect Spintharus, who carried it out in a more splendid style than was originally agreed upon, building the front of Parian marble instead of limestone. The groups of sculpture in the pediments represented, on the eastern side, Apollo with Artemis, Leto, and the Muses; on the western side, Dionysus with the Thyiades and the setting sun; for Dionysus was worshipped here in winter during the imagined absence of Apollo. These were all the work of Praxias and Androsthenes, and were finished about B.C. 430. The temple was, on account of its vast extent, a hypaethral building—that is, there was no roof over the space occupied by the temple proper. The architecture of the exterior was Doric, of the interior Ionic, as may still be observed in the surviving ruins. On the walls of the entrance-hall were short texts written in gold, attributed to the Seven Sages. One of these was the celebrated "Know Thyself" (*γνῶθι σεαυτόν*, Pausan. x. 24, 1). In the temple proper stood the golden statue of Apollo, and in front of it the sacrificial hearth with the eternal fire. Near this was a globe of marble covered with fillets, the Ὀμφαλός, or centre of the earth. In earlier times two eagles stood at its side, representing the two eagles which fable said had been sent out by Zeus at the same moment from the eastern and western ends of the world. These eagles were carried off in the Phocian War, and their place filled by two eagles in mosaic on the floor. Behind this space was the inner shrine, lying lower, in the form of a cavern over the cleft in the earth. Within the spacious precincts (*περίβολος*) stood a great number of chapels, statues, votive offerings, and treasure-houses of the various Greek states, in which they deposited their gifts to the sanctuary, especially the tithes of the booty taken in war. Here, too, was the council-chamber of the Delphians. Before the entrance to the temple was the great altar for burnt-offerings, and the golden tripod, dedicated by the Greeks after the battle of Plataea, on a pedestal of brass, representing a snake in three coils, and of which the greater part now stands in the Hippodrome at Constantinople. Besides the treasures accumulated in the course of time, the temple had considerable property in land, with a population consisting mainly of slaves (*ἱερόδουλοι*), bound to pay contributions and to render service to the sanctuary. The management of the property was in the hands of priests chosen from the noble Delphian families, at their head the five *ὅσιοι* or consecrated ones. Since the first spoliation of the temple by the Phocians in B.C. 355, it was several times plundered on a grand scale. Nero, for instance, is said to have carried off 500 bronze statues. Yet some 3000 statues were to be seen there in the time of the elder Pliny.

On the oracles in general, see Bouché-Leclercq, *Hist. de la Divination dans l'Antiquité* (Paris, 1879–1882); Maury, *Histoire des Religions de la Grèce Antique* (Paris, 1857); E. Curtius, *Die hellenische Mantik* (Göttingen, 1864); Fontaine, *De Divinitatis Origine et Progressu* (Rostock, 1867); Stengel, *Griechische Sacralalterthümer*, §§ 44–50 (1890); Hartung, *Die Religion der Römer*, vol. i. pp. 96 foll. (1836); and Hoffmann, *Das Orakelwesen im Alterthume* (1877). The oracles that have descended to us are collected by Henders, *Oracula Graeca Quae Exstant* (1877).

On particular oracles, see A. Mommsen, *Delphika* (Leipzig, 1878); Hüllmann, *Würdigung des delphischen Orakels* (Bonn, 1837); Kayser, *Delphi* (Darmstadt, 1855); Götte, *Das delphische Orakel* (Leipzig, 1839); Carapanos, *Dodone et des Ruines* (Paris, 1878); id. *Mémoire sur Dodone* (1877); Von Lassaulx, *Das pelasgische Orakel des Zeus zu Dodona* (Würzburg, 1840); Arneth, *Ueber das Taubenorakel von Dodona* (Vienna, 1840); Von Gerlach, *Dodona* (Basel, 1859); and Perthes, *Die Peleiaden zu Dodona* (Merseburg 1869). On the temple at Delphi, see a paper by Prof. Middleton in the *Journal of Hellenic Studies*, vol. ix. pp. 282 foll.

Orae. See ORITAE.

Orarium. See SUDARIUM.

Orātiōnes Princĭpum. (1) Messages to the Senate sent to announce any important event—e.g. a victory. (2) Memoranda sent by the emperor suggesting the adoption of laws (Gaius, ii. 285). (3) Such a suggestion, embodied in a letter (*epistola*) or book (*libellus*), and having the form of law. This was the final development of the *oratio principis*, and was due to the unwillingness of the obsequious Senate even to discuss a measure proposed by the emperor. See Dirksen in the *Rhein. Museum für Jurisprudenz*, vol. ii.

Orātor. The word *orator* (also *patronus*), of one who pleads the case of a client (*cliens*), is not at all identical in meaning with *iuris consultus* (q. v.), or even *advocatus* (q. v.). He need not be skilled in legal lore, which the jurisconsults possessed, but depended largely for his success upon voice, gesture, and the eloquence of his language. The earliest orators at Rome got their knowledge practically by observing the pleadings of the older men and by advice, experience, and trial of themselves. Under the Empire the principal speakers were trained in the schools of the rhetoricians (see RHETORICA), and thus gradually lost the power and form of the earlier style of speaking (Petron. i). In the republican period oratory was the noblest of the professions, awarding the key to political power and influence; but when freedom was lost, the art declined, and became a mere plaything for the young. See Cicero, *Brut.* 91 foll.; the *Dialogus* of Tacitus; and Westermann, *Geschichte d. röm. Beredsamkeit* (Leipzig, 1835); also Berger and Cucheval, *Histoire de l'Eloquence Latine jusqu' à Cicéron*, 2 vols. (Paris, 1872).

Orātor. A treatise of Cicero's fully styled *Orator ad M. Brutum*, giving his ideal of a perfect orator. Edited by Sandys (London, 1885).

Orbicŭlus. A roller or pulley worked by a rope (Vitruv. x. 2).

Orbilius Pupillus. A Roman grammarian and schoolmaster, best known to us from his having been the teacher of Horace, who gives him the epithet of *plagosus*, from the severe floggings which his pupils received from him (Hor. *Epist.* ii. 1, 71). He was a native of Beneventum, and after serving as an *apparitor* of the magistrates, and also as a soldier in the army, he settled at Rome in the fiftieth year of his age, in the consulship of Cicero, B.C. 63. He lived to be nearly 100 years of age (Suet. *Gram.* 9).

Orbis. A circular table. See MENSA.

Orbōna. An ancient goddess of the Italians who slew children and thus made parents childless (*orbi*). She was invoked and propitiated in the Indigitamenta (q. v.). See Cic. *N. D.* iii. 25, 63.

Orca (ὄρχη and ὕρχα). A vessel of earthenware shaped like an *amphora* (q. v.), but somewhat smaller, used for holding pickles, oil, wine, or figs. It was also employed by children in playing a game of skill (τρόπα; Anglicé, "cherry-pit," "pitch-in-the-hole"), in which the player tried to pitch nuts or cherry-pits into the narrow opening from a distance. See Persius, iii. 50, with Gildersleeve's note, and Shakspeare, *Twelfth Night*, iii. 4.

Orca. (Rich.)

Orcădes Insŭlae. Now the Orkney and Shetland Isles. A group of several small islands off the north coast of Britain, with which the Romans first became acquainted when Agricola sailed round the northern extremity of Britain (Tac. *Agric.* 10).

Orchēsis (ὄρχησις). See SALTATIO.

Orchestic. See SALTATIO.

Orchestra (ὀρχήστρα). Literally "the dancing place," from ὀρχέομαι. The space of the Greek theatre situated in front of the stage, in which the chorus went through its evolutions. In the Roman theatre it was absorbed in the area occupied by the audience. See CHORUS; THEATRUM.

Orchomĕnus (Ὀρχόμενος). (1) An ancient, wealthy, and powerful city of Boeotia, the capital of the Minyans in the ante-historical ages of Greece, and hence called by Homer the Minyan Orchomenos. It was situated northwest of the lake Copaïs, on the river Cephissus. Sixty years after the Trojan War it was taken by the Boeotians, and became a member of the Boeotian League. It continued to exist as an independent town till B.C. 367, when it was taken and destroyed by the Thebans; and though subsequently rebuilt by the Phocians, the Thebans again demolished it. Philip of Macedon once more restored it (B.C. 338), but it never recovered its former prosperity. It was famous for its musical festival in honour of the Charites, who were worshipped here (Theoc. xvi. 104). In the vicinity of Orchomenos Sulla defeated Archelaüs, the general of Mithridates, in B.C. 85. In 1880, 1881, and 1886 extensive excavations were made here by Dr. Schliemann, who exhumed an ancient "treasury" or mausoleum larger even than the famous one discovered by him at Mycenae (q. v.). See K. O. Müller, *Orchomenos und die Minyer* (1844); Schliemann, *Orchomenos* (1881); and Schuchhardt, *Schliemann's Excavations* (Eng. tr. London, 1891). (2) An ancient town of Arcadia, situated northwest of Mantinea.

Orcīnus Libertus. A slave set free by the death of his owner. See MANUMISSIO.

Orcīnus Senātor. See SENATUS.

Orcus. See HADES.

Ordessus (Ὀρδησσός). A tributary of the Danube of uncertain identity (Herod. iv. 48).

Ordinarius Iudex. See IUDEX.

Ordo. In a general sense, a row or series of objects. Hence (1), in naval language, a row or tier of oars in a ship, as to which, see NAVIS. (2) In Roman political language, the word is applied to any body of men forming a distinct and separate class in the community, either as possessing special privileges, or as pursuing some special occupation. Thus, the senators are spoken of collectively as the *ordo senatorius*, the knights as the *ordo equester;* the priests (*sacerdotes*) as *ordo sacerdotalis.* The plebeians, however, are now spoken of as an ordo. The Senate, being the august body, is sometimes called *amplissimus ordo* at Rome, and in colonies and *municipia* the local Senate is *ordo decurionum.* (See DECURIONES.) The *libertini* formed a separate ordo, and so did the *scribae*, the *tribuni aerarii*, and the *publicani.* At Rome the Senate and equestrians are often styled *uterque ordo*, as being *the* orders *par excellence.* (3) In military language, the word is applied to a company or troop of soldiers, and is used as equivalent to *centuria*, as the first centuries in a legion are sometimes called *primi ordines.* See LEGIO.

Ordovīces. A people of Britain, occupying what would correspond at the present day to the northern portion of Wales, together with the island of Anglesey (Tac. *Hist.* xii. 33). It was probably owing to the nature of their country and to the vicinity of Deva, now Chester, where a whole Roman legion was quartered, that the Romans had so few towns and stations among the Ordovices. Mediomanium was their capital, and was probably situated at Maywood or Meifad, in Montgomeryshire.

Ore. See AES; AURUM; METALLUM.

Oreădes (Ὀρειάδες). See NYMPHAE.

Oreae (χαλινός). A snaffle-bit (Fest. s. h. v.). Its nature is seen in the following example from a bronze original, which is jointed:

Oreae. (Rich.)

Orelli, JOHANN KASPAR. A classical scholar born at Zürich, Switzerland, February 13, 1787. After entering the Church and preaching for some time at Bergamo, he became a teacher in a school at Coire, and in 1819 at Zürich. When the university in his native city was founded, Orelli was called to the chair of classical philology (1833). He died at Zürich January 6, 1849. Orelli is best known as an editor of classical texts, especially of Cicero in 8 vols. (1826–31), Horace (1837–38, 4th ed. 1892, with a lexicon), and Tacitus (1746–47, last ed. completed in 1894). He also compiled an *Onomasticon Tullianum* to Cicero (ed. by Halm and Baiter, 1851), and a collection of Latin inscriptions, entitled *Inscriptionum Latinarum Selectarum Collectio* (3 vols. 1856; revised by Henzen, with indexes).

See Adert, *Essai sur la Vie et les Travaux de J. G. Orelli* (Geneva, 1849).

Orestae (Ὀρέσται). A people of northern Epirus, originally independent of the Macedonian kings, though afterwards subjected to their dominion. At a later period, having revolted under the protection of a Roman force, they were declared free on the conclusion of peace between Philip and the Romans (Livy, xxxiii. 34). Their country apparently contained but few towns. Among these Orestia is named by Stephanus Byzantinus, who declares it to have been the birthplace of Ptolemy, the son of Lagus. Its foundation was ascribed by tradition to Orestes.

Orestēa (Ὀρεστεία). A collective name given to the Orestean trilogy by Aeschylus. See AESCHYLUS; ORESTES.

Orestes (Ὀρέστης). (1) The son of Agamemnon and Clytaemnestra. On the assassination of Agamemnon, Orestes, then quite young, was saved from his father's fate by his sister Electra, who had him removed to the court of their uncle Strophius, king of Phocis. There he formed an intimate friendship with Pylades, the son of Strophius, and with him concerted the means, which he successfully adopted, of avenging his father's death by slaying his mother and Aegisthus. (See AEGISTHUS; CLYTAEMNESTRA.) After the murder of Clytaemnestra, the Furies drove Orestes into insanity; and when the oracle at Delphi was consulted respecting the duration of his malady, an answer was given that Orestes would not be restored to a sane mind until he went to the Tauric Chersonesus, and brought away

Orestes and Aegisthus. (From a vase.)

from that quarter the statue of Artemis to Argos. It was the custom in Taurica to sacrifice all strangers to this goddess, and Orestes and Pylades, having made the journey together, and having both been taken captive, were brought as victims to the altar of Artemis. Iphigenia, the sister of Orestes, who had been carried off by Artemis from Aulis when on the point of being immolated (see AULIS; IPHIGENIA), was the priestess of the goddess among the Tauri. Perceiving the strangers to be Greeks, she offered to spare the life of one of them, provided he would carry a letter from her to Greece. This occasioned a memorable contest of friendship between them, which should sacrifice himself for the other, and it ended in Pylades' yielding to Orestes and agreeing to be the bearer of the letter. The letter was for Orestes, and a discovery was the consequence. Iphigenia, thereupon, on learning the object of their visit, contrived to aid them in carrying off the statue of Artemis, and all three arrived safe in Greece with the statue. After his return to the Peloponnesus, Orestes took possession of his father's kingdom at Mycenae, which had been usurped by Aletes or Menelaüs. When Cylarabes of Argos died without leaving any heir, Orestes also became king of Argos. The Lacedaemonians likewise made him their king of their own accord, because they preferred him, the grandson of Tyndareus, to Nicostratus and Megapenthes, the sons of Menelaüs by a slave. The Arcadians and Phocians increased his power by allying themselves with him. He married Hermioné, the daughter of Menelaüs, and became by her the father of Tisamenus. The story of his marriage with Hermioné, who had previously been married to Neoptolemus, is related elsewhere. (See HERMIONÉ; NEOPTOLEMUS.) He died of the bite of a snake in Arcadia, and his body, in accordance with an oracle, was afterwards carried from Tega to Sparta, and there buried. His bones are said to have been found at a later time in a war between the Lacedaemonians and Tegaetans, and to have been conveyed to Sparta (Herod. i. 67). According to one story, Orestes spent the time of his madness in Arcadia, where, in his frenzy, he gnawed off one of his fingers (Pausan. viii. 34, 2). The story of Orestes is the subject of an existing trilogy by Aeschylus (the *Agamemnon*, *Choephoroe*, and *Eumenides*), and is treated by Sophocles in his *Electra* and by Euripides in the remaining plays *Electra*, *Orestes*, and *Iphigenia in Tauris*. See Becker, *Die Orestessage der Griechen* (Wittenberg, 1858). See PYRRHUS.

Such is the ordinary form of the legend of Orestes. The tragic writers, of course, introduced many variations. Thus it is said that when the Furies of his mother persecuted him, he fled to Delphi, whose god had urged him to commit the deed, and thence went to Athens, where he was acquitted by the court of Areopagus. Orestes had by Hermioné two sons, Tisamenus and Penthilus, who were driven from their country by the Heraclidae. (2) A Pannonian who acted as regent of Italy during the short reign of his infant son Romulus Augustulus, in favour of whom he had deposed the emperor Iulius Nepos (A.D. 475). In the following year he was defeated and put to death by Odoacer, king of the Heruli. See AUGUSTULUS; ODOACER.

Oresteum (Ὀρέστειον) or **Orestheum** (Ὀρέσθειον), also called ORESTHASIUM (Ὀρεσθάσιον) by Pausanias (viii. 3). A town of Arcadia, southeast of Megalopolis, in the district of Oresthis. Its ruins, according to Pausanias, were to be seen to the right of the road leading from Megalopolis to Tegaea (viii. 44). Orestes died here.

Orestheus (Ὀρεσθεύς). A legendary king of the Locri, whose dog brought forth a log of wood. This he buried, but from it came forth shoots (ὄζοι) of vine, whence the people got the name of Ozolae (Pausan. x. 31, 1).

Orestia. The country of the Orestae (q. v.) and also one of their towns.

Orestias. The primitive name of Adrianopolis (q. v.) in Thrace, and which the Byzantine authors frequently employ in speaking of that city. The name is derived from the circumstance of Orestes having purified himself on this spot after the murder of his mother.

Orestilla, Aurelia. The wife of Catiline. As she objected to marrying him because he had a grown son, he is said to have killed the young man in order to secure her favour.

Oretāni. A powerful people in the southwestern part of Hispania Tarraconensis. Their chief town was Castulo. See Pliny, *H. N.* iii. 25.

Oreus (Ὠρεός). A town in the north of Euboea, originally called Hestiaea or Histiaea. After the Persian Wars it became subject to Athens, but having revolted from the Athenians in B.C. 445, it was taken by Pericles, its inhabitants expelled, and their place supplied by 2000 Athenians (Thuc. i. 114). It was an important place down to the dissolution of the Achaean League.

Orgănum (ὄργανον). A generic term for any machine or implement for saving labour, but differing from *machina* in that it always implies skill as well as strength in its use. It frequently denotes a musical instrument (Quint. ix. 4, 10), on which see the article Hydraulus.

Orgeōnes (ὀργέωνες). The Athenian term for the members of a society for the observance of a cult not belonging to the State religion, especially those who, without belonging to the old families (see Gennetae), nevertheless like them formed a family union originating in descent from the same ancestors, and possessing a special family worship. The adoption of the children of families belonging to such a religious society occurred, as with the Gennetae, at the same time as their enrolment into the phratries at the feast of the Apaturia (q. v.).

Orgetŏrix. A noble Helvetian, the most conspicuous for rank and riches of any of his countrymen. He attempted to possess himself of the chief power in his native State (B.C. 61), and was, in consequence, summoned to trial. His retainers, however, assembled in great numbers, and prevented the case from being heard. He died not long after, having fallen, as was supposed, by his own hands (Caes. *B. G.* i. 2, 26; Dio Cass. xxxviii. 31).

Orgia (τὰ ὄργια). The ordinary Greek term for ceremonies, generally connected with the worship of a divinity, but especially secret religious customs to which only the initiated were admitted, and equivalent in meaning to "mysteries." It was customary to designate as orgies the mysteries of the worship of Dionysus in particular. These were sometimes celebrated with wild and extravagant rites. See Dionysia; Mysteria.

Oribasius (Ὀρειβάσιος and Ὀριβάσιος). A native of Pergamus, born about A.D. 325, the physician and adviser of the emperor Julian the Apostate, after whose death (A.D. 363) he was banished by the emperors Valens and Valentinianus, and lived among the barbarians. He was afterwards recalled. He seems not to have died before the beginning of the fifth century. At the suggestion of Julian he composed, on the plan of abstracts from earlier works, a medical treatise (Συναγωγαὶ Ἰατρικαί) in seventy-two books, of which some twenty-two are preserved, partly in the Greek original and partly in a Latin rendering. He himself prepared for his son Eustathius a conspectus (Σύνοψις) of the larger work in nine books, only part of which has been published. Another manual of Oribasius is the Εὐπόριστα, also a medical treatise, in four books. The best edition of Oribasius is that by Daremberg, in 6 vols. (Paris, 1851–76).

Orichalcum (ὀρείχαλκος). Brass (i. e. an alloy of copper and zinc). Existing specimens of brass are chiefly coins (*sestertii* and *dupondii*) of Augustus and his successors, though the alloy was probably made as early as the second century B.C. (Pliny, *H. N.* xxxiv. 2, 4; and cf. Cic. *De Off.* iii. 23, 92). The word ὀρείχαλκος ("mountain copper") occurs first in the Homeric Hymns (*In Ven.* 9), and in the early writers it probably designated any bright metal that had the appearance of gold. See Rossignol, *Les Métaux dans l'Antiquité* (Paris, 1863); and Blümner, *Technologie*, iv. pp. 91, 192 (note), and 193 foll.

Orĭcum (Ὤρικον) or **Orĭcus** (Ὤρικος). An important Greek town on the coast of Illyria, near the Ceraunian Mountains and the frontiers of Epirus. It was said to have been founded by the Euboeans who were here cast ashore on their return from the Trojan War.

Origĕnes, usually called Orĭgen. A learned Christian Father, born at Alexandria in A.D. 185. He was converted to Christianity by Clement of Alexandria, and after the martyrdom of his father, Leonides, Origen opened a school in which at first he taught Greek literature only, but soon after Christian doctrine also. Being made head of the catechetical school of Alexandria, he became distinguished for his severe asceticism as for his profound learning, not only in theology, but also in Greek philosophy and Hebrew, which he learned at Rome. In A.D. 228, during a visit to Palestine, he was ordained presbyter, but Bishop Demetrius of Alexandria refused his assent to this both as not being given by himself as diocesan bishop and because Origen, through a fanatical interpretation of Matt. xix. 12, had castrated himself. Later, the controversy which began over this decision led to a close investigation of Origen's theological views, and these were condemned by a synod in A.D. 231. Many Eastern bishops, however, supported him, and he reopened his school at Caesarea. During the later persecutions of the Christians by Maximinus and Decius he suffered greatly, so that, his health breaking down, he died at Tyre in A.D. 254. His most controverted teachings were those on the subject of the ultimate salvation of all, as he taught that even the devils would finally be redeemed—a doctrine known as Restorationism. His writings in all numbered some 6000, of which comparatively few have been preserved. An important one (the *De Principiis*) survives only in a Latin version by Rufinus. There are also a treatise on martyrdom and a defence of Christianity against Celsus; and of his *Hexapla*—an edition of the Old Testament in six parallel columns in Hebrew, Hebrew transliterated in Greek letters, and the four versions by Aquila, Symmachus, the Septuagint, and Theodotion—a number of fragments remain. Editions of Origen by Migne (vols. xi.–xvii.), and Lommatzsch in 25 vols. (Berlin, 1831–48). Separate editions of the *De Principiis* by Redepenning (Leipzig, 1836); of the *Hexapla* by Field (Oxford, 1875). Translations of some of the works in Clark's Ante-Nicene Library. See Freppel, *Origène* (Paris, 1868); and Farrar's *Lives of the Fathers* (1889).

Originarii. A name given to children in a colony whose parents were both *coloni* (*Cod. Th.* 10, 38).

Origĭnes. See Cato, p. 300; and Isidorus.

Oringis or **Oningis** or **Aurinx**. A town of Hispania Baetica with silver-mines (Pliny, *H. N.* iii. 3).

Orīon (Ὠρίων). A celebrated giant, said by one legend to have been the son of Poseidon and Euryalé. His father, according to this same account, gave him the power of wading through the depths of the sea, or, as others say, of walking on its surface. He married Sidé, whom Heré cast into Erebus for contending with her in beauty (Apollod. i. 4, 3). Another and more common account makes Hyria, a town of Boeotia, to have been the birthplace of Orion, and the story of his origin is told as follows: As Zeus, Poseidon, and Hermes were taking a ramble upon earth, they came, late in the evening, to the house of a farmer named Hyrieus. Seeing the wayfarers, Hyrieus, who was standing at his door, invited them to enter, and pass the night in his humble abode. The gods accepted the kind invitation, and were hospitably entertained. Pleased with their host, they inquired if he had any wish which he desired to have gratified. Hyrieus replied that he once had a wife whom he tenderly loved, and that he had sworn never to marry another. She was dead; he was childless; his vow was binding; and yet he was desirous of being a father. The gods took the hide of his only ox, which he, on discovering their true nature, had sacrificed in their honour: they buried it in the earth; and ten months afterwards a boy came to light, whom Hyrieus named Urion or Orion (ἀπὸ τοῦ οὐρεῖν, Ovid, *Fasti*, v. 495 foll.; Hyg. *Fab.* 195). This legend owes its origin to the name Orion, and was the invention of the Athenians (Müller, *Orchom.* p. 99). In Hyginus, Hyrieus is Byrseus, from the hide (βύρσα).

When Orion grew up, he went, according to this same account, to the island of Chios, where he became enamoured of Aero or Meropé, the daughter of Oenopion, son of Dionysus and Ariadné. He sought her in marriage; but, while wooing, seized a favourable opportunity and offered her violence. Her father, incensed at this conduct, and having made Orion drunk, blinded him, and cast him on the seashore. The blinded hero contrived to reach Lemnos, and came to the forge of Hephaestus, who, taking pity on him, gave him Cedalion (Guardian), one of his men, to be his guide to the abode of the Sun. Placing Cedalion on his shoulder, Orion proceeded to the East; and there, meeting the sun-god, was restored to vision by his beams. Anxious for revenge on Oenopion, he returned to Chios; but the Chians, aware of his intention, concealed the object of his search under the ground, and Orion, unable to find him, returned to Crete. The death of Orion is variously related. As all the legends relating to him are evidently later than the time of Homer, none ventures to assign any other cause to it than the goddess Artemis, whose wrath (though Homer rather says the contrary) he drew on himself. Some said that he attempted to offer violence to the goddess herself; others to Opis, one of her Hyperborean maidens, and that Artemis slew him with her arrows; others, again, that it was for presuming to challenge the goddess at the discus. It was also said that, when he came to Crete, he boasted to Leto and Artemis that he was able to kill anything that would come from the earth. Indignant at his boast, they sent a scorpion, which stung him, and he died. It was said, finally, that Artemis loved Orion, and was even about to marry him. Her brother was highly displeased, and often reproached her, but to no purpose. At length, observing one day Orion wading through the sea with his head just above the waters, he pointed it out to his sister, and maintained that she could not hit that black thing on the water. To show her skill she took aim and hit it, thus slaying Orion (Hyg. *Astr.* ii. 34). Asclepius attempted to restore him to life, but was slain by Zeus with a thunderbolt.

Orīon (Ὠρίων). A Greek scholar, a native of the Egyptian Thebes, who flourished in the fifth century A.D., and wrote at Alexandria or Constantinople an etymological lexicon and an anthology of gnomes or maxims from the Greek poets. The lexicon is edited by Sturz (Leipzig, 1820).

Orītae (Ὠρεῖται) or **Orae** (Ὦραι). A people of Gedrosia, in what is now Beluchistan (Q. Curt. ix. 10, 6).

Orithyia (Ὠρείθυια). Daughter of Erechtheus, king of Athens, and of Praxithea, who was seized by Boreas, and carried off to Thrace, where she became the mother of Cleopatra, Chioné, Zetes, and Calaïs. See BOREAS.

Ormĕnus (Ὄρμενος). Son of Cercaphus and father of Amyntor. Hence Amyntor is called Ormenides, and Astydamia, his granddaughter, Ormenis. He was said to have founded the town of Ormenium in Thessaly.

Ornamenta Triumphalia. See TRIUMPHUS.

Ornātrix. A hair-dresser. See COMA.

Orneae (Ὀρνεαί). An ancient town of Argolis, near the frontier of the territory of Phlius, subdued by the Argives in the Peloponnesian War, B.C. 418 (Thuc. vi. 7).

Ornīthon (ὀρνιθών). A chicken-house (Columel. viii. 3). See GALLINA.

Oroanda (Ὀρόανδα). A city of Pisidia, from which the tract of country known as OROANDĬCUS TRACTUS derived its name (Livy, xxxviii. 18).

Orobiae (Ὀροβίαι). A town on the coast of Euboea near Aegae. It had an oracle of Apollo.

Orōdes (Ὀρώδης). The names of two kings of Parthia. See ARSACES.

Oroetes (Ὀροίτης). A Persian who, under Cyrus and Cambyses, was satrap of Sardis. In B.C. 522 he decoyed Polycrates (q. v.) into his power, and put him to death (Herod. i. 69, iii. 39; Thuc. i. 18). He was himself executed by order of Darius, who suspected his loyalty (Herod. iii. 120).

Orontes (Ὀρόντης). The largest river of Syria, rising in the Anti-Libanus, flowing past Antioch, and falling into the sea at the foot of Mount Pieria. Its earlier name was TYPHON (Strabo, p. 750).

Orōpi. See OLBA.

Orōpus (Ὠρωπός). A town on the eastern frontiers of Boeotia and Attica; was long an object of contention between the Boeotians and Athenians. It finally remained permanently in the hands of the Athenians. Its seaport was Delphinium.

Orosius, PAULUS. A Spanish presbyter in Lusitania who, about A.D. 417, and at the wish of St. Augustine, whom he had sought out in Africa, composed a history against the heathen (*Historiae contra Paganos*) in seven books, the first attempt at a Christian universal history, from Adam to the year A.D. 417. The theory of his work is that the whole history of mankind is directed by the one God who created them, and it aims at refuting the charges brought against Christianity by showing that it was not to Christianity and the abolition of the heathen religion that the calamities of the time were due, but that such calamities had always existed, and to a still greater degree before Christian times. His chief authority is Justin, besides whom he mainly used Livy, Tacitus, Suetonius, and Eutropius. His view of the four kingdoms of the world—Babylon, Macedon, Carthage, and Rome—prevailed throughout the whole of the Middle Ages; and Alfred the Great caused it to be translated into Anglo-Saxon. The history is edited by Zangemeister (Vienna, 1882), with a commentary; and translated into English by Sweet (1883). See Méjean, *Orose et son Apologétique* (Strassburg, 1862). Besides the *Historiae*, Orosius also wrote two polemical treatises against the theology of the Pelagians and Priscillianists.

Orpheus (Ὀρφεύς). A mythical personage, regarded by the Greeks as the most celebrated of the early poets, who lived before the time of Homer. His name does not occur in the Homeric or Hesiodic poems; but it had already attained to great celebrity in the lyric period. There were numerous legends about Orpheus, but the common story ran as follows: Orpheus, the son of Oeagrus and Calliopé, lived in Thrace at the period of the Argonauts, whom he accompanied in their expedition. Presented with the lyre by Apollo and instructed by the Muses in its use, he enchanted with its music not only the wild beasts, but the trees and rocks upon Olympus, so that they moved from their places to follow the sound of his golden harp. The power of his music caused the Argonauts to seek his aid, which contributed materially to the success of their expedition; at the sound of his lyre the Argo glided down into the sea; the Argonauts tore themselves away from the pleasures of Lemnos; the Symplegades, or moving rocks, which threatened to crush the ship between them, were fixed in their places; and the Colchian dragon, which guarded the Golden Fleece, was lulled to sleep; other legends of the same kind may be read in the *Argonautica*, which bears the name of Orpheus. After his return from the Argonautic expedition he took up his abode in a cave in Thrace, and employed himself in the civilization of its wild inhabitants. There is also a legend of his having visited Egypt. The legends respecting the loss and recovery of his wife, and his own death, are very various. His wife was a nymph named Agriopé or Eurydicé. In the older accounts the cause of her death is not referred to. The legend followed in the well-known passages of Vergil and Ovid, which ascribes the death of Eurydicé to the bite of a serpent, is no doubt of high antiquity; but the introduction of Aristaeus into the legend cannot be traced to any writer older than Vergil himself. He followed his lost wife into the abodes of Hades, where the charms of his lyre suspended the torments of the damned, and won back his wife from the most inexorable of all deities; but his prayer was only granted upon this condition: that he should not look back upon his restored wife till they arrived in the upper world; at the very moment when they were about to pass the fatal bounds, the anxiety of love overcame the poet; he looked round to see that Eurydicé was following him; and he beheld her caught back into the infernal regions. (See illustration, p. 643.) His grief for the loss of Eurydicé led him to treat with contempt the Thracian women, who, in revenge, tore him to pieces under the excitement of their Bacchanalian orgies. After his death the Muses collected the fragments of his body, and buried them at Libethra at the foot of Olympus, where the nightingale sang sweetly over his grave. His head was thrown into the Hebrus, down which it rolled to the sea, and was borne across to Lesbos, where the grave in which it was interred was shown at Antissa. His lyre was also said to have been carried to Lesbos; and both traditions are simply poetical expressions of the historical fact that Lesbos was the first great seat of the music of the lyre; indeed, Antissa itself was the birthplace of Terpander, the earliest historical musician. The astronomers taught that the lyre of Orpheus was placed by Zeus among the stars at the intercession of Apollo and the Muses. Orpheus is spoken of as the first diviner, the first to employ the rites of expiation, the inventor of letters and of the heroic metre—in fact, as the first civilizer of early Thracia and Greece. In these legends there are some points which are sufficiently clear. The invention of music, in connection with the services of Apollo and the Muses, its first great application to the worship of the gods, which Orpheus is therefore said to have introduced, its power over the passions, and the importance which the Greeks attached to the knowledge of it, as intimately allied with the very existence of all social order, are probably the chief elementary ideas of the whole legend. But here comes in one of the dark features of the Greek religion, in which the gods envy the advancement of man in knowledge and civilization, and severely punish any one who transgresses the bounds assigned to humanity. In a later age the conflict was no longer viewed as between the gods and man, but between the worshippers of different divinities; and especially between Apollo, the symbol of pure intellect, and Dionysus, the deity of the senses; hence Orpheus, the servant of Apollo, falls a victim to the jealousy of Dionysus and the fury of his worshippers. The story of Orpheus and Eurydicé is found in a reversed form in the ancient Keltic tale of the three daughters of King O'Hara. (See Curtin, *Myths and Folk-lore of Ireland* [Boston, 1890].) It has been the theme of many works of modern literature, of which (in English) may be mentioned the following poems: Wordsworth, *The Power of Music;* Browning, *Orpheus and Eurydicé;* W. Morris, *Orpheus and the Sirens;* J. R. Lowell, *Eurydicé;* Dowden, *Eurydicé;* Gosse, *The Waking of Eurydicé;* and R. Buchanan, *Orpheus the Musician*. The story of Orpheus is the subject of a series of ten fine paintings by Burne-Jones. For the so-called Orphic sect, see ORPHICA.

Orphĭca (τὰ Ὀρφικά). Orpheus (q. v.) gave his name to a kind of monastic order which sprang up in later times in Greece calling themselves *οἱ Ὀρφικοί*, who, under the pretended guidance of Orpheus, dedicated themselves to the worship of Dionysus. They performed the rites of a mystical worship; but instead of confining their notions to the initiated, they published them to others, and committed them to literary works. The Dionysus with whose worship the Orphic rites were connected was Dionysus Zagreus, closely connected with Demeter and Cora (Persephoné). The Orphic legends and poems related in great part to this

Dionysus, who was combined, as an infernal deity, with Hades; and upon whom the Orphic theologians founded their hopes of the purification and ultimate immortality of the soul. But their mode of celebrating this worship was very different from the popular rites of Bacchus. The Orphic worshippers of Bacchus did not indulge in unrestrained pleasures and frantic enthusiasm, but rather aimed at an ascetic purity of life and manners, abstaining from meat, though not from wine, dressing in white, practising frequent purifications, expiations, and incantations, and professing a creed, in which the doctrine of the transmigration of souls (metempsychosis) held an important place. This sect degenerated by the time of the early Roman Empire into a mere fraternity of jugglers, and died out finally amid general contempt.

All the part of the mythology of Orpheus which connects him with Dionysus must be considered as a later invention, quite irreconcilable with the original legend, in which he is the servant of Apollo and the Muses; but it is almost hopeless to explain the transition.

Connected with the Orphic cult is the so-called Orphic literature. Many poems ascribed to Orpheus were current as early as the time of the Pisistratidae. (See ONOMACRITUS.) They are often quoted by Plato, and the allusions to them in later writers are very frequent. The extant poems, which bear the name of Orpheus, are the forgeries of grammarians and philosophers of the Alexandrian School; but among the fragments, which form a part of the collection, are some genuine remains of that Orphic poetry which was known to Plato, and which must be assigned to the period of Onomacritus, or perhaps a little earlier. To the original portions, which grew under the hands of the Orphici into a vast literature, were added also interpretations and liturgies by the Pythagoreans, some of whose doctrines were akin to those of the Orphic brotherhood. Aristotle and even Herodotus attacked the pretended antiquity of the Orphic works, yet the myths and songs retained their acceptance as antiques down to the third and fourth centuries A.D., when we find them quoted by the Fathers. The Orphic literature, which, in this sense, may be called genuine, seems to have included hymns, a theogony, oracles, etc. The principal productions which have come down to us are: (1) *Argonautica*, an epic poem in 1394 hexameters, giving an account of the expedition of the Argonauts; (2) *Hymns*, eighty-seven or eighty-eight in number, in hexameters, evidently the productions of the Neo-Platonic School; (3) *Lithica* (Λιθικά) treating of properties of stones, both precious and common, and their uses in divination; (4) fragments, chiefly of the *Theogony* (Θεογονία), which show the influence of Hesiod. It is in this class that we find the genuine remains of the literature of the early Orphic theology, but intermingled with others of a much later date. There are also a number of other poems, of which a list is given in Christ's *Griechische Litteraturgeschichte* (pp. 658, 659).

On the Orphic brotherhood, see especially Lobeck's *Aglaophamus* (1829); Gruppe, *Die Griechischen Kulte und Mythen*, i. 612–674 (1887); Maury, *Les Religions de la Grèce Antique*, iii. 300–337 (1859); Lenormant in the *Gazette Archéologique* for 1879, pp. 18–37; and Gerhard, *Orpheus und die Orphiker* (1861). On the Orphic literature, see Hermann's *Orphica* (1805); Tyrwhitt's *Lithica* (1781); Abel's *Orphei Lithica* (1881); id. *Orphica* (1886); Kern, *De Orphei, Epimenidis, Pherecydis, Theogoniis* (1888); Buresch, *Klaros* (1890); and Rohde in *Psyche*, ii. 395 foll. See also the article MYSTERIA.

Orphĭci (Ὀρφικοί). See ORPHICA.

Orsilochia. See IPHIGENIA.

Orthia (Ὀρθία). A name given to Artemis, as worshipped at Limnaeum, in Laconia, where boys were severely scourged at her altar (Pausan. iii. 16, 7). See DIAMASTIGOSIS.

Orthosia (Ὀρθωσία). A city of Caria, on the Maeander, where the Rhodians defeated the Carians, B.C. 167 (Livy, xlv. 25).

Orthrus (Ὄρθρος). The two-headed dog of Geryones (q. v.), begotten by Typhon and Echidna, and slain by Heracles.

Ortygia (Ὀρτυγία). (1) The ancient name of Delos. Since Artemis and Apollo were born at Delos, the poets sometimes call the goddess Ortygia, and give the name of *Ortygiae boves* to the oxen of Apollo. The ancients connected the name with ὄρτυξ, a quail. (2) An island near Syracuse. (See SYRACUSAE.) (3) A grove near Ephesus, in which the Ephesians pretended that Apollo and Artemis were born. Hence the Caÿster, which flowed near Ephesus, is called Ortygius Caÿster. See EPHESUS.

Orus. See HORUS; ORION.

Osca. Now Huesca, in Arragonia. An important town of the Ilergetes, and a Roman colony in Hispania Tarraconensis, on the road from Tarraco to Ilerda, with silver mines.

Oscan Plays. See ATELLANAE; COMOEDIA; DRAMA.

Oschophoria (τὰ ὀσχοφόρια). At Athens a festival in honour of Dionysus. See, further, DIONYSIA.

Osci or **Opĭci.** The name Opiscan or Oscan, properly Opscian language (φωνὴ Ὀπικῶν; τῶν Ὄσκων ἡ διάλεκτος), was first applied by the Greek colonists of the coast of Campania to the dialect of the Italic race of Ὀπικοί (*Opici*) or Ὄσκοι (*Opsci*, prop. *Opisci*) whom they found to be the chief inhabitants of that region. The Opici have been occasionally identified with the Ausones, also inhabiting Campania, and certainly closely related to them, and to the Aurunci, living on the neighbouring coast of Latium, and probably also to the Sidicini, who settled the middle valley of the Volturnus. The association of the Aurunci, on the other hand, with the aborigines, once living farther north in Southern Sabini, about Reaté, appears to be more than doubtful. The Oscans were not unsusceptible to Greek civilization; they constructed an excellent alphabet of twenty-one characters from the Greek: *a, b, g, d, e, v, z, h, i, k, l, m, n, p, r, s, t, w, f, í* (sound between *i* and *e*), and *ú* (sound between *w* and *o*). The signs for *d* and *r* are interchangeable, according to pronunciation indicating either letter; the peculiar Italic spirant *f* takes the place of the aspirates; the *z* is vocal *s* as well as sibilant-dental (=*ts, ds*); rewritten in Greek and Latin, *ú* is regularly represented by *o* (ω), *í* occasionally by ε (ει), *e*.

The Etruscan supremacy in Campania from about B.C. 800 to 400 appears, as in Rome, to have been exercised by a small military aristocracy, and therefore very superficial. We have no written traces of them other than a number of inscriptions on vases, partly in a mixed language mainly Oscan, so that it may be inferred that the Etruscan supremacy, even if it broke the national power of the Oscans, yet rather advanced than suppressed their language and culture.

But when the Romans reached the region, about B.C. 380, the Oscan race, as well as the Ausones, had disappeared, absorbed by the Campanians, closely related to the Samnites, who had rushed down from the mountains, and made a sudden end of the Etruscan rule. From that time the Romans designated by the name *lingua Opsca* or *Osca* (also *Obsca*, by a leaning to *obscaenus*) not only the language of these Campanians, but that of the whole Samnite race, which then spread extensively over Southern Italy. And, in fact, the monuments of the language that have come down to us, and which are recognizable as Oscan, are found in an area of about 1000 square miles, almost as extensive as the Samnite territory—i. e. in Samnium proper (the land of the Caraceni, the Pentri, and Caudini), in the provinces of their descendants the Frent(r)ani in the east, the Hirpini in the south, as well as the adjacent parts of Apulia and Lucania, which they subdued, and above all, most numerously in Campania, whence the Mamertini carried the language to Bruttium (Vibo) and Sicily (Messana). The Oscan inscription of Nesce (Nersae) farther north, in the territory of the Aequicoli, is iso-

Oscan Inscription from Pompeii.

votive inscription (more properly an "inventory of temenos") of Agnoné; and the lead plate of Capua with the Curse of Vibia.

Chronologically these remains extend from about B.C. 400 to the early Empire. Only the inscriptions found north of the Aufidus and Silarus show the Oscan alphabet; the southern have Greek or, as in the case of the Tabula Bantina, Latin characters. However, as their name shows and tradition confirms, the Samnite tribes were derived from the Sabines: *Samnium=Sab(i)nium, Saf(i)nium;* on the coins of the Social War, *Safinum* (not gen. pl.); cf. the softening in Greek Σαυνῖται, Σαυνῖτις χώρα. According to an old tradition, the Sabines in a war with the Umbrians sent out their finest young soldiers as *ver sacrum* (q. v.), who formed the stock of the Samnite race, and who again continued its extension in Southern Italy by like means. This Samnite people must therefore have originally used a Sabellian dialect; but the language of none of the Oscan remains can pass as such. If this difficulty be solved, nothing remains but to assume that after the Campanians the other Samnites appropriated the language of the more civilized Oscans and kindred tribes whom they had conquered, so that they both used and propagated it.

The Oscan language, with a well-developed phonetic system and series of forms, held its own uncorrupted till its latest days. In Campania, where Capua once dared to dispute with Rome the sovereignty of Italy, arose an extensive and diversified literature, as shown by the example of the *ludi Atellani*, a kind of popular farce, which the Romans eagerly adopted, and to which they gave a peculiar form of their own.

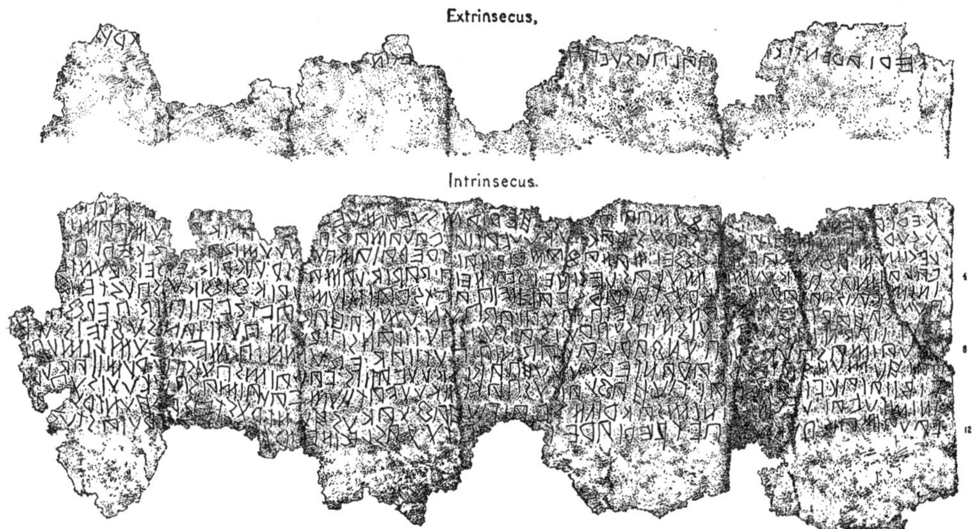

Oscan Inscription known as "The Curse of Vibia." (Leaden plate found at Capua in 1876.)

lated. Finally, the coins of the Aurunci, who were perhaps conquered long before, have Oscan words and characters. The entire number of Oscan remains is about 200, and of these only four are important—the so-called municipal laws of Bantia (*tabula Bantina*); the treaty of temple-boundary between Nola and Abella (*cippus Abellanus*); the

As an example of the Oscan dialect the following from the Tabula Bantina may be cited:

PON CENSTVR BANSAE TOVTAM CENSAZET, PIS CEVS BANTINS FVST, CENSAMVR ESVF IN EITVAM, POIZAD LIGVD IOSC CENSTVR CENSAVM ANGETVZET.

In Latin:

Cum censores Bantiae populum censebunt quis civis Bantinus erit censetor ipse et pecuniam quoia lege ii censores censere proposuerint (?)

These few lines afford instances of the principal peculiarities of Oscan, some of which are found also in the Old Latin. Such are the *p* for *c* (*q*), the use of *s* for the future sign, the ending *-d* in the ablative, the ending *-s* in the nominative plural of the second declension, the infinitive in *-m*, etc. Other characteristic features of the language are the retention of the diphthongs in all positions (whereas the Umbrian regularly loses them), the dative and ablative plural in *-ais* (Gk. *-αις*) and *-ois* (Gk. *-οις*), the locative singular in *ei* (Gk. *-ει*, as in *οἴκει*), and the genitive singular of *u*-stems in *-ous* (*us*). The vowel-system of the Oscan is the most elaborate of any of the European languages except the Greek, and the weakening of the vowels in unaccented syllables (so characteristic of the Latin) is almost unknown to it.

On the Oscan language see the chapter in Gröber's *Grundriss der romanischen Philologie*, vol. i. (Strassburg, 1893); Mommsen, *Die unteritalischen Dialekte* (Leipzig, 1850); Buck, *Vocalismus der oskischen Sprache* (Leipzig, 1892); Bronisch, *Die oskischen I und E Vocale* (Leipzig, 1892); Von Planta, *Grammatik der oskisch-umbrischen Dialekte* (Strassburg, 1892); and Conway, *The Italic Dialects* (announced in 1895). The Oscan inscriptions are edited by Zvetaieff in his *Sylloge Inscriptionum Oscarum*, with plates and a vocabulary (St. Petersburg, 1878), and cf. his *Inscriptiones Italiae Mediae Dialecticae* (Leipzig, 1884); and *Inscriptiones Italiae Inferioris Dialecticae* (Moscow, 1886). See also the articles ITALIA; TABULA BANTINA.

Oscillātio. A swing. See AEORA.

Oscillum. A diminutive of *os*, and applied to the small mask or image (usually of Bacchus) suspended by the country people in their vineyards, so that the wind might turn it around in different

Oscilla. (Left-hand figure from marble in British Museum; right-hand figure from Maffei, *Gemmae Ant.* iii. 64.)

directions. The belief which led to this practice was that the spot upon which the god looked would become fruitful (Macrob. *Sat.* i. 7).

Oscĭnes. See AUGUR.

Osīris (Ὄσιρις). An Egyptian god, who, with his sister and wife Isis (q. v.), enjoyed in Egypt the most general worship of all the gods (Herod. ii. 42). He is the male god of the fructification of the land. From him comes every blessing and all life; he gives light and health; he causes the Nile to overflow with its fertilizing waters, and all things to continue in their established order. He is always represented in human shape and with a human head, as in the annexed illustration. His hue, as that of a god who bestows life, is green; his sacred tree is the ever-green tamarisk. The Greeks identified him with Dionysus. Originally he ruled as king over Egypt, where he introduced agriculture, morality, and the worship of the gods, until his brother Typhon (Set) contrived by deceit to shut him up in a chest and put him to death by pouring in molten lead. The murderer cast the chest into the Nile, which carried it into the sea. After long search the mourning Isis found the chest on the coast of Phœnicia at Byblus, and carefully concealed it. Nevertheless Typhon discovered it in the night, and cut the corpse into fourteen pieces, which he scattered in all directions. Isis, however, collected them again, and buried them in Philae or Abydus, in Upper Egypt. When Horus, the son of Osiris and Isis, grew up, he took vengeance upon Typhon when, after a most obstinate struggle, he had defeated him in battle. Although Osiris lived no longer upon the earth, he was ever regarded as the source of life. In the upper world he continues to live and work by the fresh power of his youthful son Horus, and in the lower world, of which he is king, the spirits of those who are found to be just are awakened by him to new life. His hue as ruler of the lower world is black, his robes white, and his symbol an eye opened wide as a sign of his restoration to the light of day.

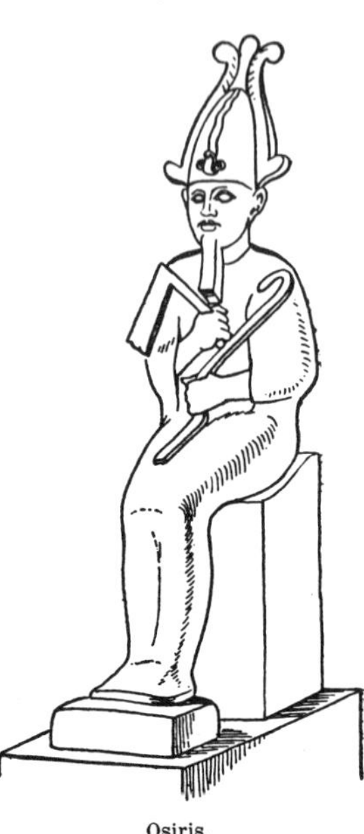

Osiris.

Osiris, by his ever-renewed incarnation in the form of the black bull Apis, the symbol of generative power, assured for the Egyptians the endurance of his favour, and the consequent continuance of their life in this world and the next. In this incarnation he was called *Osarhapi* (Osiris-Apis), the origin of the Greek Serapis (q. v.) or Sarapis. The fortunes of Osiris were celebrated in magnificent annual festivals connected with mourning ceremonies, in which the Egyptians, as is observed by the ancients (e. g. Plutarch, *De Iside et Osiride*, 32, and Aelian, *De Nat. Animalium*, 10, 46), lamented in Osiris the subsidence of the Nile, the cessation of the cool north wind (whose place was taken for a time by the hot wind Typhon), the decay of vegetation, and the shortening of the length of the day. The rites of Osiris find their counterpart in those of Dionysus-Zagreus held in Crete. See Wiedemann, *Die Religion der alten Aegypter* (1890); AEGYPTUS; HORUS; ISIS; TYPHON; ZAGREUS.

Osroēnē (Ὀσροηνή). A district in the north of Mesopotamia, separated by the Chaboras from Mygdonia on the east, and from the rest of Mesopotamia on the south. Its capital was Edessa.

Ossa (Ὄσσα). A celebrated mountain in the north of Thessaly, connected with Pelion on the southeast, and divided from Olympus on the northwest by the vale of Tempê. It is mentioned in the legend of the war of the Giants, respecting which see GIGANTES; TITANES.

Ossarium and **Ossuarium.** A receptacle of stone or other material which held the vase containing the bones and ashes of the dead, when deposited in sepulchral chambers. See COLUMBARIUM.

Ossarium of Agrippina. (Capitoline Museum.)

Ostia. A town at the mouth of the river Tiber, and the harbour of Rome, from which it was distant sixteen miles by land, situated on the left bank of the left arm of the river. It was founded by Ancus Martius, the fourth king of Rome, who is said to have established salt-works there, was a Roman colony, and became an important and flourishing town. The emperor Claudius constructed a new and better harbour on the right arm of the Tiber, which was enlarged and improved by Trajan. This new harbour was called simply Portus Romanus or Portus Augusti, and around it there sprang up a flourishing town, also called Portus. The old town of Ostia, whose harbour had been already partly filled up by sand, now sank into insignificance, and only continued to exist through its salt-works (*salinae*), which had been established by Ancus Martius. The modern town bears the same name as the old.

Ostia Nili. See NILUS.

Ostiarium. A tax called by Cicero (*Ad Fam.* iii. 8, 5) *exactio ostiorum*, and imposed in Cilicia, Syria, and probably other provinces. It was laid upon the doors of a house as indicating by their number the value of the property. The window-tax in England and France is a like impost in modern times.

Ostiarius. A janitor. See DOMUS.

Ostium. (1) The entrance-hall in the Roman dwelling-house. (See DOMUS.) (2) (θύρα). The inner door as opposed to the street door (*ianua*) on which cf. Vitruv. vi. 3; and Plaut. *Pers.* v. 1, 6. (See IANUA.) (3) The door which closed the front of the stalls in which the horses and chariots were stationed in the Circus. See illustration in article CIRCUS, pp. 352, 353.

Restoration of Entrance to Pompeian House, showing outer and inner Doors. (Rich.)

Ostorius Scapŭla. See SCAPULA.

Ostra. A town of Umbria (Ptol. iii. 1, 51).

Ostracismus (ὀστρακισμός, i. e. vote by potsherd, ὄστρακον). A mode of judgment by the people practised in various Greek States (Argos, Megara, Miletus), and especially at Athens, by which persons whose presence appeared dangerous to liberty were banished for a certain period, without, however, thereby suffering any loss in reputation or property. Ostracism was introduced at Athens in B.C. 509. It was applied (among others) to Themistocles, Aristides, Cimon, and Alcibiades, and was last exercised in 417 against a demagogue, one Hyberbolus, whose insignificance made the measure ridiculous, and so brought about its abolition (Thuc. viii. 73; Plut. *Nicias*, 11, *Alcibiades*, 13). Every year the question was put to the people, whether the measure appeared necessary: if they so decided (and it was only exceptionally that there was occasion for it), the citizens who possessed the franchise assembled in the market-place, and each wrote upon a sherd (ὄστρακον) the name of the person whose banishment he deemed desirable. The man whose name was found upon not less than 6000 sherds had to leave the country in ten days at latest, for ten or (later) five years. He could, however, at any time be recalled by a decree of the people; and the question, as before, was decided by not less than 6000 votes. (See Arist. *Pol.* iii. 13 § 15, 17 § 7, v. 3 § 3; Plut. *Arist.* 7; cf. Grote's *History of Greece*, chap. xxxi.).

Ostrakinda (ὀστρακίνδα) A game played by children in Greece, as follows: Two sets of boys stand facing one another, divided by a line drawn on the ground; a boy throws up a shell or a dish, white on one side and coloured black on the other, and each set of boys has one or other of these colours allotted to it. As he throws the shell, he calls νὺξ ἡμέρα: and if the white (i. e. day) side falls uppermost, the set which represents the day pursues, and the other set runs away; if the "night" side falls uppermost, the fugitives and pursuers are reversed. As soon as any boy is caught he is called ὄνος, and is out of the game (Plato, *Theaet.* p. 146 A). It is not precisely stated whether the game went on until all the fugitives were caught, nor whether there was a point of safety to be reckoned, but it is very likely that the game was played with varying rules at different times and places. The expression ὀστράκου περιστροφή seems to have become proverbial for a turn of fortune (Plato, *Rep.* vii. p. 521 C). See Pollux, ix. 111; Eustath. *ad Il.* xviii. 543; Plato, Com. in Meineke, *Fr. Com.* ii. 2, 664; see also Becq de Fouquières, *Les Jeux des Anciens*, p. 79; Grasberger, *Erziehung*, p. 57; and Becker-Göll, *Charikles*, ii. 37.

Otacilius. See VOLTACILIUS.

Otacilius Crassus. (1) A Roman who as consul in B.C. 263 besieged Syracuse and forced Hiero into a treaty with Rome. He was again consul in B.C. 246 (Ptol. i. 16). (2) A Roman general who in B.C. 215, at the time of the Second Punic War, ravaged the Carthaginian coast. He died in B.C. 211. (3) OTACILIUS PILŬTUS. See VOLTACILIUS.

Otānes (Ὀτάνης). (1) A Persian who was the

first to suspect the imposture of Smerdis (q. v.), the Magian, and organized a conspiracy against him in B.C. 521. Later he invaded Samos for the purpose of placing Syloson, brother of Polycrates, at the head of the Samian government (Herod. iii. 68 and 141). (2) A Persian, the son of Sisamnes, who in B.C. 506 took command of the forces on the coast in place of Megabyzus. He captured Byzantium, Chalcedon, Lamponium, Antandros, and the islands of Lemnos and Imbros (Herod. v. 102; vi. 6).

Otho, L. Roscius. A tribune of the plebs in B.C. 67, when he carried the law (*lex Roscia*) which gave to the *equites* a special place at the public spectacles, in fourteen rows or seats (*in quattuordecim gradibus sive ordinibus*), next to the place of the senators, which was in the orchestra. This law was very unpopular; and in Cicero's consulship (B.C. 63) there was such a riot occasioned by the obnoxious measure that it required all his eloquence to allay the agitation (Vell. Paterc. ii. 32; Cic. *Ad Att.* ii. 1).

Otho, M. Salvius. A Roman emperor from Jan. 15 to April 16, A.D. 69, who was born in 32. He was one of the companions of Nero in his debaucheries; but when the emperor took possession of his wife, the beautiful but profligate Poppaea Sabina, Otho was sent as governor to Lusitania, which he administered with credit during the last ten years of Nero's life. Otho attached himself to Galba, when he revolted against Nero, in the hope of being adopted by him, and succeeding to the Empire. But when Galba adopted L.

Otho. (Bust in British Museum.)

Piso, on the tenth of January, 69, Otho formed a conspiracy against Galba, and was proclaimed emperor by the soldiers at Rome, who put Galba to death. Meantime, Vitellius had been proclaimed emperor at Cologne by the German troops on the third of January. When this news reached Otho, he marched into the north of Italy to oppose the generals of Vitellius. He at first won several victories over Caecina, the general of Vitellius, but his army was defeated by Caecina and Valens in a decisive battle near Bedriacum, whereupon he put an end to his own life at Brixellum, in the thirty-seventh year of his age. His life is given by Suetonius and Plutarch.

Othryădes (Ὀθρυάδης). (1) A patronymic given to Panthoüs or Panthus, the Trojan priest of Apollo, as the son of Othrys. (2) The survivor of the 300 Spartan champions who fought with the 300 Argives for the possession of Thyrea. Being left on the field as dead, he was afterwards ashamed to return to Sparta as the only survivor, and slew himself on the spot (Herod. i. 82).

Othrys (Ὄθρυς). A lofty range of mountains in the south of Thessaly, extending from Mount Tymphrestus, or the most southerly part of Pindus, to the eastern coast. It shut in the great Thessalian plain on the south.

Otricoli, Zeus of. See Otriculum.

Otricŭlum. Now Otricoli; a town in Umbria, situated on the Tiber, near its confluence with the Nar, and six miles from Horta (Orte). Many interesting remains of antiquity have been excavated here, the most famous being the bust of Zeus, known as the Zeus of Otricoli, now in the Vatican Museum at Rome, and of which a representation will be found in the article Zeus.

Otus (Ὦτος). One of the two Aloadae. See Aloadae.

Oudendorp, Franz von, a famous Dutch classical scholar, was born July 31, 1696, at Leyden, in the University of which place he received his training. In 1724 he was made Rector of the school at Nymegen, and in 1726 of the more important school at Haarlem, leaving the latter to accept a chair at Leyden as Professor of Eloquence and History (1740). He died Feb. 14, 1761.

Oudendorp was the last of the old school of Latinists which had flourished at Leyden from the time of Gronovius (q. v.), and his commentaries follow the stereotyped methods of his predecessors. He published an *Oratio de Litterariis C. Iulii Caesaris Studiis* (inaugural address, Leyden, 1740), and editions of the following classics: Iulius Obsequens (Leyden, 1720); Lucan (Leyden, 1728); Frontinus (Leyden, 1731; 2d ed. 1779); Caesar (Leyden, 1737); and Suetonius (2 vols. Leyden, 1751). After his death appeared his edition of Apuleius in 3 vols. (1785–1823).

Ounce. See Uncia.

Ousias Diké (οὐσίας δίκη). The same as Enoikiou Diké (q. v.).

Ovatio. See Triumphus.

Oven. See Furnus.

Overcoat. See Amictus; Paenula.

Ovidius Iuventīnus, Albius. See Philomela.

Ovidius Naso, Publius. A very popular Roman poet, born March 21, B.C. 43, at Sulmo (now Solmona), in the country of the Paeligni, son of a wealthy Roman of an old equestrian family. He came at an early age to Rome, to be educated as a pleader, and enjoyed the tuition of the most famous rhetoricians of the time—Porcius Latro and Arellius Fuscus. It was not long before the instinct for poetry awoke in him with such power that it needed all his father's resolution to keep him to his legal studies; his oratorical exercises were simply poems in prose, as is testified by one of his fellow-students—the elder Seneca (*Controv.* ii. 10, 8). After he had visited Greece and Asia to complete his education, he entered into political life at his father's desire, and filled several subordinate offices. But he soon withdrew again from public business, partly from an inclination to idleness, and lived only for poetry, in the society of the poets of his day, among whom he was especially intimate with Propertius. He came into note as a poet by a tragedy called the *Medea*, which is now lost, but is much praised by ancient literary critics; and about the same time he produced a series of amatory, and in some parts extremely licentious, poems.

When little more than a mere boy, as he says himself (*Tristia*, iv. 10, 69), he had a wife given him by his father; but this marriage, like a second one, ended in a divorce. He derived more satisfaction, as well as the advantage of contact with the court and with men of the highest distinction, from a third marriage, with a widow of noble family and high connections. To her influence, perhaps, should be referred the fact that he turned his attention to more important and more serious works. He had almost completed his best known work, the *Metamorphoses*, when suddenly, in A.D. 8, he was banished for life by Augustus to Tomi (Kustindje), on the Black Sea, near the mouths of the Danube. The cause for this severity on the part of the emperor is unknown; Ovid himself admits that there was a fault on his side, but only an error, not a crime (*Tristia*, i. 3, 37). At all events, the matter directly affected Augustus; and as Ovid describes his eyes as the cause of his misfortune, it is conjectured that he had been an unintentional eye-witness of some offence on the part of the frivolous granddaughter of the prince, the younger Iulia, and had neglected to inform the emperor of the matter. His indecent amatory poems, to which he also points as the source of the emperor's displeasure, can at most only have been used as a plausible excuse in the eyes of the public, as they had been published more than ten years before. See Deville, *Sur l'Exil d'Ovide* (Paris, 1859); Appal, *Quibus de Causis Ovidius Relegatus Sit* (Leipzig, 1872); Körber, *De Ovidii Relegationis Causis* (St. Petersburg, 1883); and Thomas in the *Revue de Philologie*, xiii. 47.

After a perilous voyage Ovid reached the place of his exile in the winter of A.D. 10–11; and there, far from his beloved wife and his daughter Perilla, who had inherited the poetic talent of her father, far from his friends and all intercourse with men of genius, he had to pass the last years of his life in desolation among the barbarous Getae. Even in his exile his poetic talent did not fail him. It was then that he composed his poems of lamentation, entitled the *Tristia*, and his letters from Pontus, which afford touching proofs of his grief, though also of his failing powers. His ceaseless prayers and complaints had succeeded in softening Augustus, when the latter died. All his efforts to gain forgiveness or some alleviation of his condition met with no response from Tiberius, and he was compelled to close his life, broken-hearted and in exile, A.D. 17 or 18.

His extant works are: (1) Erotic poems (*Amores*), published about B.C. 14, in five books, and again about B.C. 2, in three books. The latter edition is the one we possess; some of its forty-nine elegies depict, in a very sensual way, the poet's life, the centre of which is the unknown Corinna, who by later writers was identified with Iulia, the daughter of Augustus (Sid. Apoll. xxiii. 159), but with no probability. (2) Letters (*Epistulae*), also called *Heroïdes*, rhetorical declamations in the form of love-letters sent by heroines to their husbands or lovers, twenty-one in number; the last six of these, however, and the fourteenth, are considered spurious. (3) Methods for beautifying the face (*Medicamina Faciei*), advice to women respecting the art of the toilette; this poem has come down to us in an incomplete form. (4) The Art of Love (*Ars Amandi* or *Amatoria*), in three books, published about B.C. 2, advice to men (books i. and ii.) and women (book iii.) as to the methods of contracting a love-affair and insuring its continuance—a work as licentious as it is original and elaborate. (5) Cures for Love (*Remedia Amoris*), the pendant to the previous work, and no less offensive in substance and tone. (6) The fifteen books of the Transformations (*Metamorphoses*), his most important work. It is composed in hexameter verse; the material is borrowed from Greek and (to a less extent) from Roman sources, being a collection of legends of transformations, very skilfully combining jest and earnest in rapid alternations, and extending from chaos to the apotheosis of Caesar. When it was completed and had received the last touches, the work was cast into the flames by Ovid in his first despair at banishment, but was afterwards rewritten from other copies. (7) A Calendar of Roman Festivals (*Fasti*), begun in the last years before his banishment, and originally in twelve books, corresponding to the number of the months. Of these only six are preserved, probably because Ovid had not quite completed them at Rome, and had not the means to do so at Tomi. It was originally intended for dedication to Augustus. After Augustus's death the poet began to revise it, with a view to its dedication to Germanicus; he did not, however, proceed with his revision beyond the first book. It contains, in elegiac metre, the most important celestial phenomena and the festivals of each month, with a description of their celebration and an account of their origin according to the Italian legends. (8) Poems of Lament (*Tristia*), to his family, to his friends, and to Augustus, belonging to the years A.D. 9–13, in five books; the first of these was written while he was still on his journey to Tomi. (9) Letters from Pontus (*Epistulae ex Ponto*), in four books, only distinguished from the previous poems by their epistolary form. (10) *Ibis*, an imitation of the poem of the same name by Callimachus, who had attacked, under this name, Apollonius of Rhodes, consisting of imprecations on a faithless friend at Rome, written in the learned and obscure style of the Alexandrian poets. (11) A short fragment of a didactic poem on the fish in the Black Sea (*Halieutica*), written in hexameters. Besides these Ovid wrote, during his exile, numerous poems which have been lost, among them a eulogy of the deceased Augustus in the Getic tongue—a sufficient proof of the strength of his irrepressible love for poetry. In fact, in this respect he is distinguished above all other Roman poets. Perhaps no one ever composed with less exertion; yet at the same time no one ever used so important a faculty for so trivial a purpose. His poetry is for the most part simply entertaining; in this kind of writing he proves his mastery by his readiness in language and metre, by his unwearied powers of invention, by his ever-ready wit, elegance, and charm, though, on the other hand, he is completely wanting in deep feeling and moral earnestness. By his talent, Ovid as well as Vergil has had great influence on the further development of Roman poetry, especially with regard to metre. Many imitated his style so closely that their poems were actually attributed to himself. Among these, besides a number of *Heroïdes* (see above), we have the *Nux*, the nut-tree's complaint of the ill-treatment it met with, a poem in elegiac verse, which was at all events written about the time of Ovid; a poem on cosmetics, *De Medicamine Faciei*, the *Consolatio ad Liviam* on the death of Drusus; and a number of jointed skits such as the *De Pulice, De Vetula*, various Priapeia, etc.

BIBLIOGRAPHY.—Of the MSS. of Ovid the best are the Codex Petavianus of the eighth century (Vatican); the Codex B (Arundelianus) of the ninth century (British Museum); two at Munich (D and E) and one (G) at Göttingen of the twelfth century; the Codex Puteaneus of the tenth century (Paris), which is said to be one of the best classical MSS. in existence; the Codex Marcianus of the eleventh century (Florence). For an elaborate account of the MSS. and a vast collection of variant readings, see the edition of N. Heinsius cited below.

Editions of the whole of Ovid are those by D. Heinsius, 3 vols. (Leipzig, Leyden, 1629); N. Heinsius, 3 vols. (Amsterdam, 1652; revised 1661); Burmann, 4 vols. (Amsterdam, 1727); Merkel and Ehwald (Leipzig, 1888 foll.); Reise, last ed. 3 vols. (Leipzig, 1889 foll.); and by Zingerle and others (Prague, 1883 foll.). Separate editions of the different works, with notes, are as follows: of the *Amores* by L. Müller (Leipzig, 1867); of the *Heroïdes* by Palmer (London, 1874) and Shuckburgh (London, 1879); of the *Ars Amatoria* by Herzberg (with translation, Stuttgart, 1854) and Williams (London, 1884); of the *Metamorphoses* by Zingerle (Prague, 1885); of the *Fasti* by Merkel (Berlin, 1841), Peter (Leipzig, 1879), Keightley (London, 1848), and Paley, 3d ed. (London, 1888); of the *Tristia* by Owen (London, 1889); of the *Epistolae ex Ponto* by Korn, critical notes (Leipzig, 1868), and bk. i. by Keene (London, 1887); of the *Halieutica* by Haupt (Leipzig, 1838); of the *Ibis* by R. Ellis (Oxford, 1881); of the *Nux* by Lindemann (Zittau, 1844). The spurious Ovidiana were collected and printed in Goldast's *Catalecta Ovidii* (Frankfort, 1610), some of them being of mediæval origin. On Ovid's life see Nageotte, *Ovide* (Dijon, 1872), and especially Leutsch in Ersch and Gruber's *Encyclopädie* (1836). No authentic portraits of the poet are known to exist. On Ovid's verse see L. Müller, *De Re Metrica*, xci. 408; and Schmidt, *De Ovidii Hexametris* (Cleves, 1856).

Ovīlé. Literally "sheep-fold." An enclosure in the Campus Martius at Rome in which the tribes and centuries were separately assembled before giving their votes at the Comitia (Livy, xxvi. 22). It was partitioned off with a railing, and from it the voters passed out over a bridge or gangway (*pons suffragiorum*) to throw their ballots (*tabellae*) into the voting basket (*cista*). See COMITIA.

Voters passing out from the *Ovilé*. (Coin of Nerva.)

Ovum. An egg. See CIRCUS, p. 353. For eggs as an article of diet, see VICTUS. They formed the first course at a dinner; hence the phrase *ab ovo usque ad mala*, "from beginning to end" (Hor. *Sat.* i. 3).

Oxia Palus or **Oxiānus Lacus.** Now the Sea of Aral; a lake or sea formed by the rivers Iaxartes and Oxus (Ammian. Marc. xxiii. 6, 59).

Oxus (Ὦξος). The Jihoun or Amou. A great river of Central Asia, forming the boundary between Sogdiana on the north and Bactria and Margiana on the south, and falling into the Caspian. The Jihoun now flows into the southwestern corner of the Sea of Aral; but there are still distinct traces of a channel in a southwesterly direction from the Sea of Aral to the Caspian, by which at least a portion, and probably the whole, of the waters of the Oxus found their way into the Caspian. The Oxus occupies an important place in history, having been in nearly all ages the extreme boundary between the great monarchies of southwestern Asia and the hordes which wander over the central steppes. Herodotus does not mention the Oxus by name, but it is supposed to be the river which he calls Araxes.

Oxybăphum (ὀξυβάφον). A liquid measure of the Greeks containing about fifteen drams. It was the same as the Roman *acetabulum* (q. v.).

Oysters. See VICTUS.

Ozŏlae (Ὀζόλαι). See LOCRI.

P

P, as a symbol.

IN GREEK.—Π = Πούβλιος, πρεσβύτερος (*Arch. Zeit.* 1876, p. 57).

ΠΟ = ποδῶν.

ΠΑ = Πάναμος. ΠΒ = Πάναμος δεύτερος.

ΠΟ Π = Ποπιλίου.

ΠΠ = Πριμιπιλάριος (Waddington, *Le Bas*, 1963), πραιπώσιτος (*Rev. Arch.* ii. 263, 1884).

ΠΠ = πατρὶ πατρίδος.

As a numeral = 16 (old system), π′ = 80, ͵π = 80,000, but in inscriptions frequently Π = 5—e. g. ΠΔ, ΠΗ, ΠΧ, ΠΜ = πεντάκις δέκα, π. ἕκατον, π. χίλιοι, π. μύριοι.

IN LATIN.—P = pagina, pagus, pars, patria, Parthica, per, periit, posteri, praefectus, praetor, prima, princeps, pro, probum, proconsul, procurator, provincia, Publius, pagani, pater, patronus.

Ꟊ = puella, Publia.

P·A = pondo argenti, provincia Africa.

P·B·M = parentes (patrono) bene merenti.

P·C = patres conscripti, patronus civitatis (coloniae, collegii, corporis), pia constans (legio), pietatis causa, post consulatum, potestate censoria.

P·D·D = posuit dedicavitque, publice decreto decurionum.

P·D·D·E = populo dare damnas esto.

P·D·D·P·P = posuerunt decreto decurionum pecunia publica.

P·F = pater filio, pia fidelis, pius felix.

P·F·K·F = pater filio carissimo fecit.

P·G·S = provincia Germania superior.

P·H·O·ADQ·E·R·P·V = placere huic ordini atque e re publica videri.

P·I = pons iussit.

P·K = praetor candidatus.

P·L·L = posuit laetus libens, pro ludis luminibus.

P·M = patronus municipii, plus minus, pontifex maximus, (et) post mortem (nihil), pro meritis.

P·N = patrimonii nostri, praeses noster, provincia Numidia.

P·O = post obitum, praetorio, princeps optimus.

P·P = pater patriae, pater posuit, parentes prissimae, patronus perpetuus, pecunia publica, populo postulante, portorium publicum.

P·P·C = prentissimo ponendum curavit.

P·P·K = praepositus castris.

P·P·L = Publiorum duorum liberti.

P·P·P = pater pius posuit, proconsul pater patriae, pro pretate posuit, propria pecunia posuerunt, praepositus praeses provinciae, primipilaris pro parte, proprio publice positus.

P·P·P·C = primipilaris patronus coloniae.

P·P·P·F = patri pro pietate fuerunt.

P·Q = pedes quadrati, populusque.

P·Q·Q·V = pedes quoquoversus.

P·Q·S = posterisque suis.

P·R = populus Romanus, post reditum, provincia Raetia, publice restituit.

P·S = pater sacrorum, proprio sumptu, proxumis suis.

P·S·P·D = pecunia sua posuit dedicavit.

P·S·R = pecunia sua restituit, procurator summarum rationum.

P·T·M = posuit titulum memoriae.

P·V = praefectissimus vir, pia vindex (legio), portus uterque, praefectus urbi.

P·V·A = pius vixit annos.

Pacăris. See HYPACYRIS.

Pacatiāna. See PHRYGIA.

Pacātus, LATĪNUS DREPANIUS. A Roman rhetorician of Burdigala (Bordeaux), a younger contemporary and friend of the poet Ausonius. We possess from his pen a panegyric on the emperor Theodosius the Great, delivered before the Senate at Rome in B.C. 389. It is distinguished beyond the other speeches of this class by a certain vigour of thought resembling Tacitus, and is also of value as an historical authority. It is edited, with notes, by Arntzen (Amsterdam, 1753), and by Bährens (Leipzig, 1874).

Paccius Antiŏchus. A physician of the first century A.D., who made a fortune from a prescription which he used very successfully and the secret of which he bequeathed to the emperor Tiberius, who ordered it to be placed in all the public libraries (Scribon. Larg. *De Compos. Medicam.* ch. xxiii. p. 97).

Paches (Πάχης). An Athenian commander who, in the Peloponnesian War, took Mitylené and Lesbos (B.C. 427). On his return home an accusation was brought against him, the purport of which is not now known. Perceiving his condemnation to be certain, he stabbed himself in the presence of his judges (Thuc. iii. 18–49; Plut. *Nic.* 6).

Pachymĕres, GEORGIUS. A Byzantine historian, born about A.D. 1242 at Nicaea. He wrote an account of the emperors Michael Palaeologus and Andronicus Palaeologus the Elder, in thirteen books, which have been edited by Bekker (Bonn, 1835).

Pachȳnus (Πάχυνος) or **Pachȳnum** (Πάχυνον). A promontory at the southeastern extremity of Sicily. Its modern name is Capo Passaro. See SICILIA.

Pacŏrus. (1) A son of Orodes I.; king of Parthia. His history is given under ARSACES XIV. (2) A king of Parthia. See ARSACES XXIV.

Pactōlus (Πακτωλός). A small but celebrated river of Lydia, rising on Mount Tmolus, and flowing past Sardis into the Hermus. The golden sands of Pactolus have passed into a proverb, and were one of the sources of the wealth of ancient Lydia (Herod. v. 101; Verg. *Aen.* x. 142). For the fabulous origin of the gold, see MIDAS.

Pactyé (Πακτύη). A town in the Thracian Chersonesus, on the Propontis, to which Alcibiades retired when he was banished by the Athenians, B.C. 407 (Herod. vi. 36).

Pacuvius, MARCUS. A Roman tragedian, born about B.C. 220 at Brundisium. He is described as being the son of Ennius's sister, and pupil of the poet (Euseb. *Chron.* 156, 3; Cic. *Brut.* 64). He spent most of his life at Rome, where he gained his livelihood as a dramatic poet and as a painter. In his old age he returned to Lower Italy, and died there, at the age of ninety, about B.C. 130 (Gell. i. 24). He is the first Roman dramatist who confined himself to the composition of tragedies. Titles and fragments of some thirteen of his imitations of Greek plays are preserved, as well as fragments of a *fabula praetexta* entitled *Paulus,* whose hero was probably the victor of Pydna, Aemilius Paulus. If this small number justifies any opinion on his poetical activity, he was far less productive than his predecessor Ennius and his successor Attius. Nevertheless, he and Attius were considered the most important tragedians of Rome. In the judgment of literary critics, who followed the traditions of the Ciceronian Age, he was preferred to Attius for finish and learning, but Attius excelled him in fire and natural power (Hor. *Epist.* ii. 1, 55, 56; Quint. x. 1, 97). His style was praised for its copiousness, dignity, and stateliness, though Cicero (*Brutus,* 258) declines to give him credit for pure and genuine Latinity. Even in Cicero's time, however, the revival of his plays was often welcomed by Roman audiences, and for his dignity and command of language he was often styled *doctus.* Pacuvius was also successful in his painting, and one of his works in the temple of Hercules in the Forum Boarium was greatly admired (Gell. xiii. 2, 2).

The dramatic fragments of Pacuvius are edited by Ribbeck (Leipzig, 1871). See a paper by Prof. Nettleship in the (English) *Journal of Philology,* xviii. 263 foll.; and Mommsen, *Hist. of Rome,* iii. p. 536 (American ed.).

Padus. Now the Po; the chief river of Italy, identified by the Roman poets with the fabulous ERIDĂNUS, from which amber was obtained. This notion appears to have arisen from the Phœnician vessels receiving at the mouths of the Padus the amber which had been transported by land from the coasts of the Baltic to those of the Adriatic.

The name is said to be derived from the Keltic *padi*, "pine-tree" (Pliny, *H. N.* iii. 122). By the Ligurians it was called BODENCUS. The Padus rises on Mount Vesula (Monte Viso), in the Alps, and flows in an easterly direction through the great plain of Cisalpine Gaul, which it divides into two parts, Gallia Cispadana and Gallia Transpadana. It receives numerous affluents, which drain the whole of this vast plain, descending from the Alps on the north and the Apennines on the south. These affluents, increased in the summer by the melting of the snow on the mountains, frequently bring down such a large body of water as to cause the Padus to overflow its banks. The whole course of the river, including its windings, is about 450 miles. About twenty miles from the sea the river divides itself into two main branches, and falls into the Adriatic Sea by several mouths (the ancients enumerated seven), between Ravenna and Altinum. Strabo believed the Padus to be the largest river in Europe after the Danube, and Vergil calls it *fluviorum rex* (*Georg.* i. 482).

Padūsa. A canal running from the Padus to Ravenna, and now called the Canal of St. Alberti (Verg. *Aen.* xi. 457).

Paean (Παιάν, Παιήων, Παιών, "the healer," "helper"). In Homer (*Il.* v. 401, 899) the physician of the Olympian gods; then an epithet of gods who grant recovery and deliverance, especially of Apollo. The paean, which appears in Homer (*Il.* i. 473; xxii. 391), was connected originally with Apollo and his sister Artemis. It was a solemn song for several voices, either praying for the averting of evil and for rescue, or giving thanks for help vouchsafed. The name was, however, also used in an extended sense for invocations to other gods. The paean was struck up by the generals before the battle and by armies on the march against the enemy as well as after the victory. Similarly it was sounded when the fleet sailed out of a harbour. Paeans were sung at entertainments between the meal and the carousal, and eventually also at public funerals.

Paeania (Παιανία). A deme of Attica belonging to the tribe Pandionis. It was the deme of Demosthenes, the orator.

Paedagōgus (παιδαγωγός, "boy-leader"). The name among the Greeks for the slave who had the duty of looking after the son of his master while in boyhood, instructing him in certain rules of good manners, and attending him whenever he went out, especially to school and to the palaestra and gymnasium. With the Romans in earlier times it was an old slave or freedman who had a similar duty as *custos*; but after it became the custom to have even children taught to speak Greek, his place was filled by a Greek slave, who bore the Greek name and had the special duty of instructing his pupils in Greek. See EDUCATION; LUDUS LITTERARIUS.

Paedonŏmus (παιδονόμος). At Sparta, the overseer of the education of the young. See EDUCATION.

Paedotrībes (παιδοτρίβης). In Greece, the master who imparted gymnastic instruction in the palaestra. See ATHLETAE; EDUCATION; GYMNASIUM; PALAESTRA.

Paemāni. A Germanic people in Gallia Belgica (Caes. *B. G.* ii. 4).

Paenŭla (φαινόλης). The Roman name for a mantle of shaggy frieze or leather, thick and dark-coloured, without sleeves, buttoned or stitched up in front, in the direction of its length. A hood (*cucullus*) was generally fastened on to it, and drawn over the head (Pliny, *H. N.* xxiv. 88). It was chiefly worn by people of low rank and slaves, but also by the higher classes, and even by ladies, in bad weather, on a journey, and in the country.

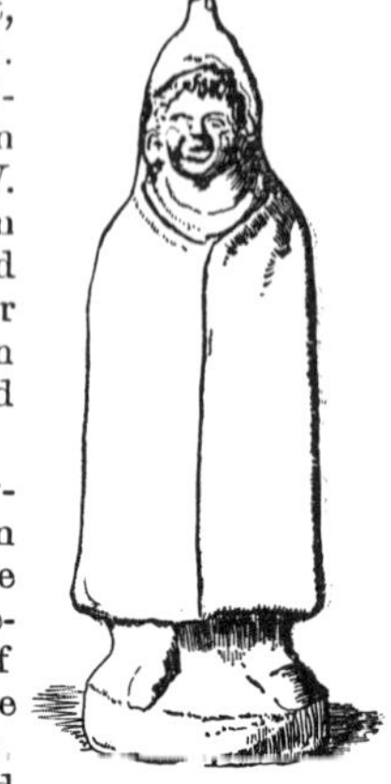
Paenula. (Statuette in the British Museum.)

Paeŏnes (Παίονες). A powerful Thracian people who, in historical times, inhabited the whole of the north of Macedonia from the frontiers of Illyria to some little distance east of the river Strymon. Their country was called PAEONIA (Παιονία). They were troublesome neighbours to the Macedonians, whose territories they frequently raided; but Philip, the father of Alexander the Great, at last subdued them (Diod. xix. 2, etc.).

Paeonius (Παιώνιος). (1) A Greek sculptor of Mendé in Thrace. About B.C. 436 he was employed in the decoration of the temple of Zeus in Olympia. According to Pausanias (v. 10 § 6), he was the sculptor of the marble groups in the front, or eastern, pediment of the temple, representing the preparations for the chariot-race between Pelops and Oenomaüs. (See OLYMPIA.) Important portions of these have been brought to light by German excavators. He was also the sculptor of the figure of Niké, more than life-size, dedicated by the Messenians (Pausan. v. 26 § 1), which has been restored to us by the same means. With the exception of the head, it is in fairly good preservation. (2) See EUTROPIUS. (3) An architect of Ephesus who, with Demetrius, completed the great temple of Artemis in that city. With Daphnis, a Milesian, he began the so-called Didymaeum or temple of Apollo Didymus at Miletus—a structure, however, which was never finished (Herod. vi. 19; Pausan. vii. 5, 4). See EPHESUS.

Paeŏplae (Παιόπλαι). A people of Paeonia on the Strymon (Herod. v. 15; vii. 113).

Paerisădes (Παιρισάδης) or **Parisădes** (Παρισάδης). The name of two kings of Bosporus, the first of whom ruled in the fourth century B.C. and the second in the first century B.C. The latter ceded his kingdom to Mithridates the Great (Strabo, p. 310).

Paestānus Sinus. See PAESTUM.

Paestum, called **Posidonia** (Ποσειδωνία) by the Greeks. A city in Lucania, situated four or five miles south of the Silarus, and near the bay, which derived its name from the town (Paestanus Sinus: Gulf of Salerno). It was colonized by the Sybarites about B.C. 524, and soon became a powerful and flourishing city. It was captured by the Lucanians about B.C. 430 and gradually lost its Greek characteristics. Under the Romans it gradually sank in importance, and in the time of Augustus it is mentioned only on account of the beautiful roses grown in its neighbourhood. The ruins of

Ruined Temple at Paestum.

two Doric temples at Paestum are among the most remarkable remains of antiquity. See Labrouste, *Les Temples de Paestum* (1877), and TEMPLUM.

Paetus. A cognomen in many Roman gentes; it signified a person who had a slight cast in the eye. This was regarded by the Romans as giving piquancy to beauty, and was ascribed by them to Venus, as in the line from the *Priapea:*

"Minerva flavo lumine est, Venus paeto"

which explains the passage in Horace (*Sat.* i. 3, 45), where the fond father calls his squinting son *paetus*, i. e. "Venus-eyed."

Paetus Thrasea. See THRASEA.

Paganalia. In Italy, a movable festival of the old village communities (see PAGUS), celebrated after the winter-sowing in January, on two days separated by an interval of a week. On this occasion a pregnant sow was sacrificed to Tellus or to Ceres, who, at a later period, was worshipped together with Tellus.

Paganĭca, sc. PILA. A ball stuffed with down and covered with leather. See PILA.

Pagānus. See PAGUS.

Pagăsae (Παγασαί) or **Pagăsa.** A town of Thessaly, on the coast of Magnesia, and on the bay called after it SINUS PAGASAEUS or PAGASĬCUS. It was the port of Iolcos, and afterwards of Pherae, and is celebrated in mythology as the place where Iason built the ship Argo. Hence the adjective *Pagasaeus* is applied to Iason, and is also used in the general sense of Thessalian. Apollo is called Pagasaeus from having a temple at the place.

Pagĭna. See PAPYRUS.

Pagus (πάγος). In Italy, in ancient times, the pagus was a country district with scattered hamlets (*vici*). The same name was given to its fortified centre, which protected the sanctuaries of the district and served as a refuge in time of war. The separate districts were members of a larger community. After cities had developed out of the places where the people of these districts assembled, the pagi were either completely merged in their territorium or continued to exist merely as geographical districts, without importance for administration, or as subordinate village communities. In Rome the earliest population consisted of the *montani*, the inhabitants of the seven hills of the city, and the *pagani*, the inhabitants of the level ground of the city. Out of the two Servius Tullius made the four city tribes. The country tribes doubtless arose similarly out of pagi, the names of which were in some cases transferred to them. Like the old division into *pagani* and *montani*, the old districts under the authority of *magistri* long continued to exist for sacred purposes. They had their special guardian deities, temples, and rites, which survived even the introduction of Christianity. To the district festivals belonged especially the Paganalia (q. v.), the Ambarvalia (q. v.), at which the festal procession carefully traversed the old boundaries of the district; and, lastly, the Terminalia (see TERMINUS). The word *paganus* is sometimes used as equivalent to *armatus* or *sagatus* = *miles*, and hence opposed to *togatus*. Cf. Pliny, *Epist.* x. 86, 2; *Hist.* iii. 24; and see further Peck's note on Suet. *Aug.* xxvii. On the pagus in general, see Mommsen, *Hist. of Rome*, i. pp. 63 foll. (Amer. ed.).

Pagus (Πάγος). A conical hill some 500 to 600 feet high, a little to the north of Smyrna. Here was a shrine of Nemesis and a celebrated spring.

Pail. See SITULA.

Painting. See PICTURA.

Pala. (1) A spade with an iron blade used for gardening and digging in the earth (Colum. x. 45). (2) A modern shovel of the same form, used for winnowing grain (Cato, *R. R.* 11). The shape of the pala is shown in the accompanying illustration. (3) The bezel of a ring (Cic. *De Off.* iii. 9).

Pala. (Fabretti, *Inscr. Ant.* p. 574.)

Palace of the Caesars. See PALATIUM.

Palaemon (Παλαίμων). A Greek sea-god. See MELICERTES.

Palaemon (Παλαίμων), QUINTUS REMMIUS. A Latin grammarian of Vicetia (Vicenza), the son of a female slave. He acquired a learned education while accompanying his master's son to school, and, after he had been set free, taught at Rome in the first half of the first century after Christ, under Tiberius and Claudius, with extraordinary success in spite of his thoroughly disreputable character. The earlier scholars, and especially Varro, had made the older literature the centre of their linguistic studies. Palaemon, as head of a new school, devoted himself especially to Vergil, just as Greek literary criticism had concentrated itself on Homer. He seems to have treated grammar in the practical spirit of a clever schoolmaster, and to have done his best to deride the scientific labours of Varro. His grammar (*ars*, Juv. vii. 251) was doubtless much consulted by later grammarians. It is now lost. The grammar that bears his name is wrongly attributed to him. (See Prof. Nettleship in the [English] *Journal of Philology*, xv. 192). Palaemon is to be remembered for having first introduced Vergil as a text-book into the Roman schools.

Palaeography (from παλαιός + γράφειν). The science which has to do with the study of ancient manuscripts, comprising their decipherment, and the determination of their date, genuineness, and origin. Strictly speaking, palaeography deals only with the external characteristics of a codex, while the study and criticism of its internal characteristics fall under the general department of Textual Criticism. (See TEXTUAL CRITICISM.) Palaeography also differs from epigraphy in being concerned with writings upon leather, papyrus, vellum, and other soft substances, while epigraphy treats of writing engraved upon stone, metal, etc. See EPIGRAPHY.

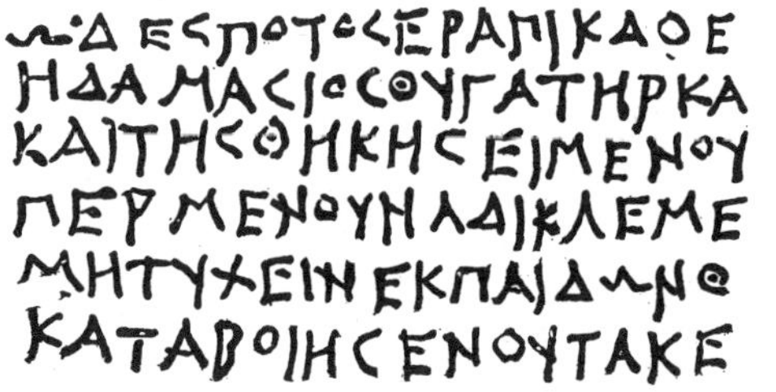

Papyrus of Artemisia. (Third Century, B.C.)

The oldest existing manuscripts are the papyri found in the Egyptian tombs, the most ancient of all being the so-called Papyrus Prisse, which is the oldest book in the world, dating from the eleventh dynasty, and therefore earlier than the date at which the Book of Exodus was composed. The oldest classical manuscript is the papyrus containing the Greek text of the *Antiope* of Euripides, which dates from about the second century B.C. See PAPYRUS, p. 1173.

The subject matter of palaeography is the

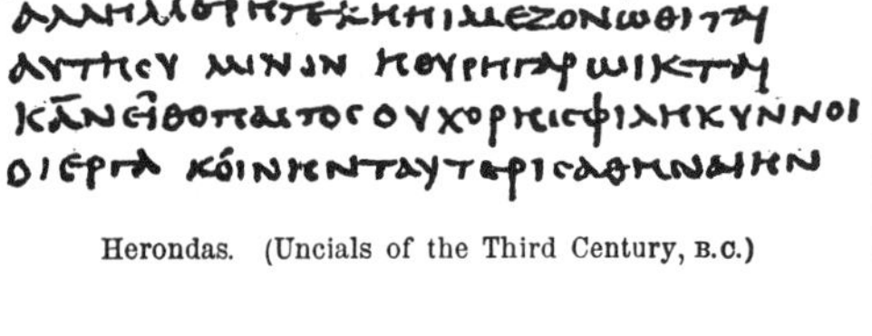

Herondas. (Uncials of the Third Century, B.C.)

substance on which the writing was done and the instruments which the writers used. The writing materials were papyrus (πάπυρος), early used in Egypt; skins of animals, used by the Egyptians as early as the fourth dynasty and by the Greeks (Herod. v. 58); parchment and vellum (διφθέραι, *membrana Pergamena*), used by both Greeks and Romans (Boissonade, *Anecd.* i. 420; Cic. *Ad Att.* xiii. 24; Martial, xiv. 184 and 186); and paper made of the cotton-plant (ξυλοχάρτιον,

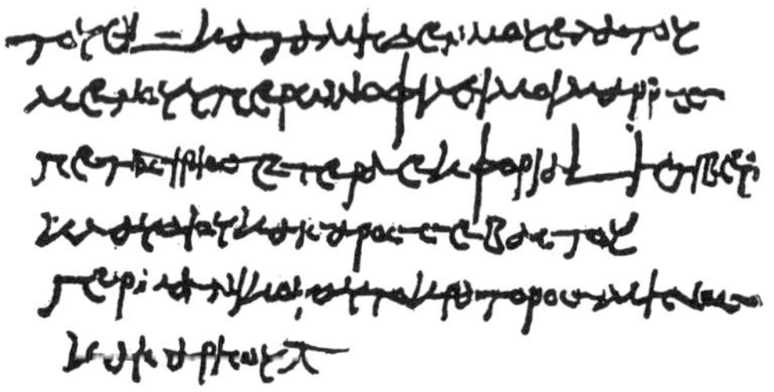

Receipt in Greek Cursive. (A.D. 20.)

ξυλότευκτον, *charta bombycina, gossypina, Damascena*), first imported from the East by the Greeks, but hardly used before the twelfth century A.D. (Theoph. *Sched. Divers. Artium*, i. 24, ed. Hendrie). The implements used for writing on these substances were the reed-pen (κάλαμος, δόναξ γραφεύς, σχοῖνος, *calamus, canna*), the use of which survived in Italy to the thirteenth century; the brush (κονδίλιον, *peniculus, penicillus*), used for writing in gold; and the quill-pen (*penna*), not mentioned before the fourth century (Ammian. Marcell. *Excerp.* ed. Gronovius, p. 512, 1693; Isid. *Orig.* vi. 13).

Ink, usually black, but sometimes brown, red, and purple, and in the Middle Ages green, yellow, etc., was called μέλαν or γραφικὸν μέλαν, μελάνιον, *atramentum* (*librarium*), and *incaustum*. Red ink was μελάνιον κόκκινον, *minium, rubrica*. Gold writing-fluid and (rarely) silver ink were used in ornamentation. Other collateral implements were the ruler (κυκλοτερὴς μόλιβδος, *regula*), the knife-eraser (*rasorium, novacula*), the pen-knife (σμίλη, *scalprum librarium*), and pricker or compass (διαβάτης, *circinus*). For the removal of recent writing, a sponge was used (Martial, iv. 10). A pointed piece of lead (μόλυβδος, *plumbum*) performed the office of the modern *lead*-pencil. See CIRCINUS; CODEX; PAPYRUS; WRITING AND WRITING MATERIALS.

The earliest form of manuscript was the roll. For full details, see LIBER. From the manuscript, the writing was often erased to make room for new matter. In this case it was called a palimpsest (παλιμψηστος). See PALIMPSESTUS.

The copyists of the manuscripts (γραμματεῖς, *scribae*) were in classical times usually slaves especially trained; in the Middle Ages, monks. For short-hand writers (*notarii*), see NOTAE.

There are four sorts of Greek writing: capitals, uncials, cursives, and minuscules. The capitals are found chiefly in manuscripts, in letters and initial letters. The uncials are the most common form of letters in ancient books, and resemble the modern capital. The breathings and accents are generally omitted, and the iota subscript is written by the side of its vowel—at the right. The cursive was gradually developed out of the uncial, from which it differed more and more. It is found in manuscripts of the second century B.C. and as late as the seventh century A.D. Minuscules prevail after the ninth century A.D.

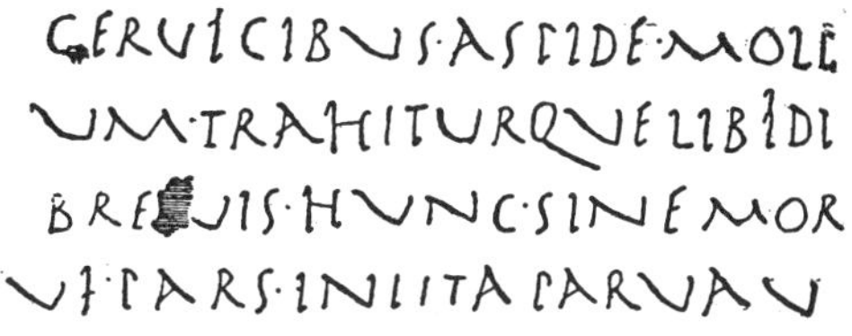

Latin Poem on the Battle of Actium. (Before A.D. 79.)

There are also the same four varieties of writing in Latin manuscripts. The capitals appear in a poem by Rabirius (?) on the battle of Actium found at Herculaneum, in the Vatican and Florence Vergils, and in the Paris Prudentius. The uncials, which are distinguished by the rounded forms of the letters (especially U), were perfected in the fourth century A.D. and lasted till the ninth. The Veronese palimpsest of Livy is in uncials. There are many specimens of the Roman cursive in the *graffiti* of Pompeii (see vol. iv. of the *Corp. Inscrip. Lat.*) and elsewhere. It varied at different periods, and gave rise to different mediæval forms of writing — e. g. the Lombardic, Visigothic, etc. The Roman minuscules were not developed until the end of the eighth century A.D.

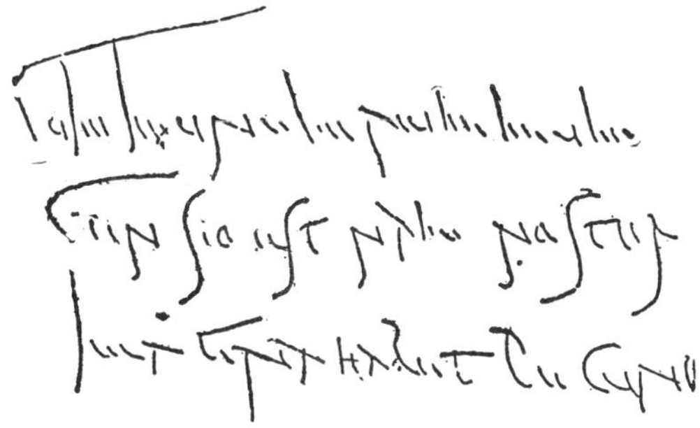

Pompeian Wall Inscription. (First Century, A.D.)

in the school of Alcuin, and reached their perfection in the twelfth century. They are the source of the earliest Italic characters. If a Latin manuscript is wholly in capitals, it is earlier than the eighth century; and when the words are not spaced it is earlier than the seventh. Stiff, upright characters denote a late date. The uncial writings are usually earlier than the eighth century; the minuscule prevails after the ninth; a great number of abbreviations indicates the eleventh century. If a text is written in cursive that has great facility in its ligatures, it is presumably antique. See ALPHABET.

The greatest difficulty in deciphering manuscripts comes from the contractions, abbreviations, and ligatures which they contain. Thus, the copyists in mediæval France used more than 5000 forms of contraction. The following are a few that are common, and hence may serve as illustrations: *qm̄* = *quum* or *quoniam; qūō* = *quomodo;* ·*n*· = *enim;* ÷ = *est; om̄s* = *omnes; hōīn̄* = *hominum; āūt* = *autem; ā* = *annos;* p = *prae;* pp. =

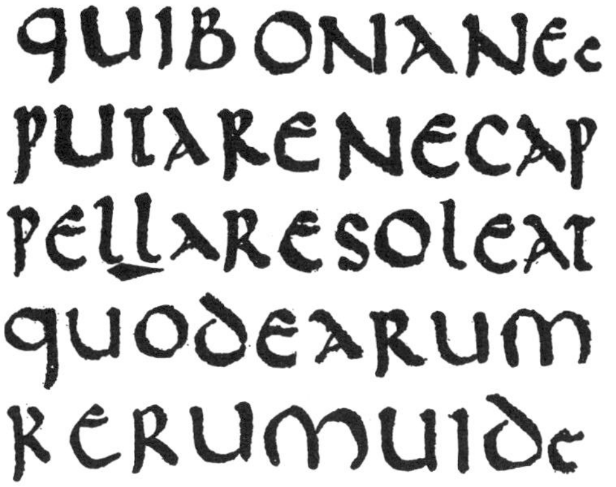

Cicero, De Republica. (Roman Uncials of the Fourth Century, A.D.)

prope. Some of the mediæval abbreviations we still find in common use, as *e. g.* for *exempli gratia; i. e.* for *id est; viz.* for *videlicet.*

BIBLIOGRAPHY. — See Gardthausen, *Griechische Paläographie* (Leipzig, 1879); Wattenbach, *Anleitung zur griechischen Paläographie* (Leipzig, 1877); id. *Anleitung zur lateinischen Paläographie* (4th ed. Leipzig, 1886); Chatelain, *Paléographie des Classiques Latins* (Paris, 1884, still appearing); the monograph "Paläographie," by Blass, in Iwan Müller's *Handbuch* (2d ed. Munich, 1892); Wailly, *Éléments de Paléographie,* 2 vols. (Paris, 1838); and for the student especially Maunde Thompson's *Handbook of Greek and Latin Palaeography* (London and New York, 1893). See also Chassang, *Paléographie des Chartes et des Manuscrits* (8th ed. Paris, 1885). For abbreviations, consult Allen, *Notes on Abbreviations in Greek MSS.* (Oxford, 1889) and Chassang, *Dictionnaire des Abréviations du Moyen Âge* (Paris, 1884), with Wattenbach's *Schriftwesen im Mittelalter* (2d ed. Leipzig, 1875). For fac-similes of ancient texts, see Silvestre, *Paléographie Universelle* (London, 1850); the collec-

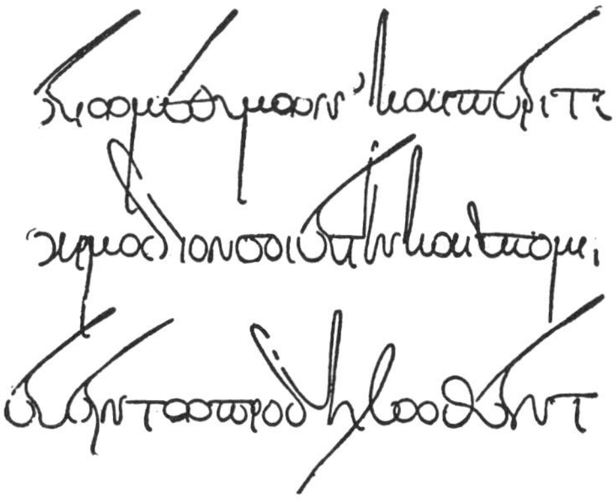

Imperial Letter in Greek Cursive. (A.D. 756.)

tions by Omont (Paris, 1890 and 1892); Wattenbach, *Scripturae Graecae Specimina* (Berlin, 1883); and Zangemeister, *Exempla Codicum Latinorum* (Heidelberg, 1876, 1879).

Palaeopŏlis (Παλαιόπολις). See NEAPOLIS.

Palaephătus (Παλαίφατος). (1) A Greek author who followed the Peripatetic philosophy. He composed in the fourth century B.C. an historical and allegorical explanation of Greek myths in several books. Of this work we possess only a short abstract, probably composed in the Byzantine Age, under the title *On Incredible Tales* (Περὶ Ἀπίστων). In former times it was a favourite school-book. It has been edited by Westermann in his *Mythographi* (Brunswick, 1843). (2) An Egyptian or Athenian Greek, a rhetorician, whose best-known work called *Troica* (Τρωϊκά) is frequently mentioned by the ancient grammarians.

Palaerus (Παλαιρός). A town on the coast of Acarnania near Leucas (Thuc. ii. 30).

Palaesté (Παλαίστη). A town on the coast of Epirus, and a little south of the Acroceraunian Mountains, where Caesar landed when he crossed over to Greece to carry on the war against Pompey (Lucan, v. 460).

Palaestīna (Παλαιστίνη, ἡ Παλαιστίνη Συρία). The Greek and Roman form of the Hebrew word which was used to denote the country of the Philistines, and which was extended to the whole country. The Romans called it IUDAEA, extending to the whole country the name of its southern part. It was regarded by the Greeks and Romans as a part of Syria. It was bounded by the Mediterranean on the west, by the mountains of Lebanon on the north, by the Jordan and its lakes on the east, and by the deserts which separated it from Egypt on the south. The Romans did not come into contact with the country till B.C. 63, when Pompey took Jerusalem. From this time the country was really subject to the Romans. At the death of Herod his kingdom was divided between his sons as tetrarchs; but the different parts of Palestine were eventually annexed to the Roman province of Syria, and were governed by a procurator. The Jews were by no means well disposed, however, to the rule of the Romans, and in the first century A.D. broke out with a general rebellion which was crushed out by Vespasian and Titus with merciless severity. The latter general took Jerusalem and destroyed it in A.D. 70. Under Constantine, Palestine was divided into three provinces—Palaestina Prima in the centre, Palaestina Secunda in the north, and Palaestina Tertia in the south. See Tristram, *Land of Israel* (3d ed. 1876); Thomson, *The Land and the Book* (2d ed. 1880–85); Merrill, *Galilee in the Time of Christ* (1881); Derenbourg, *Essai sur l'Histoire, etc., de la Palestine* (Paris, 1867); and the articles HERODES; HIEROSOLYMA; IUDAEI.

Palaestra (παλαίστρα). A private training-school where boys received regular instruction in gymnastics and physical culture, and thus differing from gymnasia, which were public establishments for the training of men (Becker-Göll, *Charikles*, ii. 239; Grasberger, *Erziehung und Unterricht*, i. 252; and Iwan Müller, *Handbuch*, iv. 451 c). The training-master (παιδοτρίβης) was paid by the parents of the boys whom he taught, and he trained all who did not intend either to enter the games in competition or to become professional athletes. The latter were trained by the γυμναστής, whose work was of a more special and scientific character. The exercises practised in the palaestra were running, jumping, wrestling, throwing the discus, and spear-throwing (i. e. the *pentathlon*), and in a mild way boxing and the *pancration*. Boys were also taught to walk properly and to have a graceful carriage. The Romans did not support the institution of the palaestra to any great extent (Plut. *Quaest. Rom.* 40; Sen. *Epist.* 88, 18; Pliny, *Epist.* x. 40, 2). Among them, as among the later Greeks, the word is often used of the part of a gymnasium especially devoted to wrestling and often as a synonym for gymnasium (Vitruv. v. 11). The details of the institution are not known with certainty, but it may be assumed that they differed from those of the gymnasium only in being milder and less exacting. See ATHLETAE; GYMNASIUM.

Palamēdes (Παλαμήδης). (1) The son of Nauplius and brother of Oeax, a hero of the post-Homeric cycle of Trojan legend. Odysseus envied his wisdom and ingenuity, and was bent on avenging himself on Palamedes for detecting his feigned madness. Accordingly he is said to have conspired with Diomedes and drowned him while engaged in fishing; or (according to another account) they persuaded him to enter a well, in which treasure was said to be concealed, and then overwhelmed him with stones. According to others, Agamemnon also hated him as head of the peace party among the Greeks. He accordingly got Odysseus and Diomedes to conceal in his tent a letter purporting to be written by Priam, as well as some money, and then accuse him as a traitor; whereupon he was stoned to death by the people. His brother Oeax informed his father of the sad event by writing the news on an oar and throwing it into the sea, upon which he took a terrible vengeance on the returning Greeks. (See NAUPLIUS.) Palamedes was considered by the Greeks as the inventor of the alphabet and of lighthouses; also of measures and weights, and of dice and draughts and the discus. (2) A Greek grammarian mentioned by Athenaeus, who makes him one of the speakers in his book.

Palatīnus Mons. See ROMA.

Palatium. A name originally applied to one of the seven hills of Rome, the Mons Palatinus, upon which the earliest city was built (see ROMA); but from the time when Augustus made his permanent residence there the word came to mean "a palace," and *par excellence* the imperial palace of the Caesars.

The house of Augustus (*domus Augustana*) was built upon the southwestern edge of the Palatine Hill and overlooked the Circus Maximus. He had at first purchased the house of the orator Hortensius, also on the Palatine, and when it was struck by lightning he consecrated the spot to a temple of Apollo, and bought some neighbouring buildings, where he built a house for himself (Vell. Pat. ii. 81; Dio Cass. xlix. 15; Suet. *Aug.* 29, 72).

The house of Tiberius (*domus Tiberiana*) on the Palatine is mentioned as distinct from that of Augustus, though it adjoined it, the palace of Augustus being more conspicuous towards the Forum, while that of Tiberius formed the back front. Its situation is indicated by the statements of the ancient writers that Otho descended through the back of the palace of Tiberius into the Velabrum (Tac. *Hist.* i. 27; Suet. *Otho*, 6), and that Vitellius surveyed from it the conflagration of the Capitol (Suet. *Vitell.* 6). During the reign of Augustus, Tiberius lived first in the house of Pompey in the Carinae, and afterwards in that of Maecenas on the Esquiline, but when he became emperor he probably resided in this house on the Palatine till he withdrew to Capreae. In later times this palace was the residence of Antoninus Pius and Marcus Aurelius, and a library was established there (Gell. xiii. 19). The palaces of Augustus and Tiberius were destroyed in the fire of Nero; but they were rebuilt, as they are mentioned as separate buildings in the *Notitia;* and Josephus tells us that the different parts of the complex of buildings forming the imperial palace were named after their respective founders (*Ant.* xix. 1, § 15).

The palace of Augustus was excavated in 1775, and drawings made of it by Guattani (*Monumenti Antichi di Roma*, 1785); the whole was soon covered in again, and no part is now visible. That part of the plan shown here, which represents the palace of Augustus, is taken from Guattani's plan.

This palace, which was of very modest size, had a number of small rooms in two stories grouped round one peristyle: its comparative simplicity must have formed a striking contrast to the stately splendour of the public halls, libraries, and temples in the adjoining Area Apollinis, all built by Augustus, and adorned by him with countless works of art of every kind. Nevertheless, though the palace

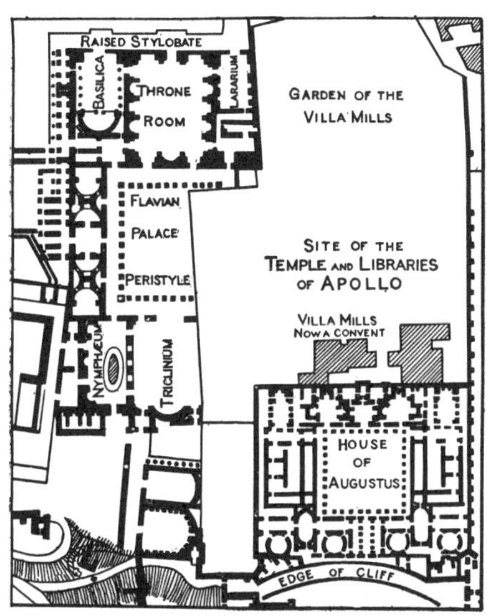

Plan of the Palace of Augustus and the Flavian Emperors.

of Augustus was small, yet it appears to have been designed with great taste, and decorated with considerable richness in its mixture of white and coloured marbles. That it was a very carefully designed architectural affair is shown by the base plan with its domed and vaulted halls and small apse-like recesses arranged with some complications and much ingenuity.

The Flavian Palace, which is shown on the same plan, was built by Domitian, adjoining the Area of Apollo and the Palace of Augustus on the northwest side (Plut. *Popl.* 15; Mart. viii. 36; Stat. *Silv.* iii. 4, 47; iv. 2). Extensive remains of this building still exist, and are among the most conspicuous of the imperial palaces on the Palatine. It was a very different building from that of Augustus, being not so much a place of residence as a magnificent series of State apartments intended for public use. Hence Nerva had the words *aedes publicae* inscribed on it (Pliny, *Panegyr.* 47). At one end is a very splendid throne-room, with a *lararium* or imperial chapel on one side and a *basilica* for judicial business on the other. At the other end of the peristyle is the *triclinium* for State banquets, and beyond it a series of stately halls, which may possibly be libraries (*bibliothecae*), and an *Academia* for recitations and other literary purposes. A sort of *Nymphaeum*, or room containing a fountain, with flowers, plants, and statues of nymphs and river-gods, was placed at one side of the *triclinium*, if not on both, so that the murmur and coolness of the water and the scent of the flowers might refresh the wine-heated guests. The whole of this magnificent palace was adorned with the greatest richness, both of design and materials, with floors, wall-linings, and columns of Oriental marbles, alabaster, and red and green porphyry. Even the rows of colossal statues which decorated the throne-room were made of the very refractory basalts and porphyry from the quarries of Egypt, at a cost of an almost incredible amount of labour: remains of these were found early in the last century. The position of the Flavian palace is remarkable; it is built on an immense artificial platform which bridges over a deep valley or depression in the summit of the Palatine.

Remains of a lofty building of Republican date still exist deep below the floor-level of the so-called libraries; and a small house of early imperial date, richly decorated with marbles and paintings, can still be seen buried under the great peristyle. In many parts of the palace traces are distinctly visible of restorations made by Severus after the great fire in the reign of Commodus (A.D. 191), which devastated a large portion of the imperial palaces. The cracked and partly calcined marbles which suffered in the fire were broken up, and used to make concrete for the new walls of Severus; and thus, in many places, the somewhat curious sight is to be seen of concrete made of the most costly Oriental marbles and porphyries.

The enormous palace of Caligula occupied the northern corner of the Palatine Hill and the adjoining slopes as far as the Forum, covering the ground once occupied by the houses of Clodius, Cicero, and other wealthy Romans (Dio Cass. lix. 28; Suet. *Cal.* 22; Pliny, *H. N.* xxxvi. § 111). The equally large palace of Severus occupied the opposite end of the Palatine. They are both remarkable for the gigantic substructures on which they stand, constructed so as to form at the foot of the hill a basement for State rooms on a level with the highest part of the ground, or, in other words, at both places the Palatine itself was enlarged by the construction of an artificial hill of massive concrete walls and vaults. On one side Severus used the stately palace of Hadrian as a sort of platform on which to extend his new palace at the higher level; and so we see the rough concrete walls of Severus's substructure cutting through and rendering useless the richly ornamented halls of Hadrian. The enormous height of the palace of Severus must have made it one of the most imposing of all the buildings of Rome: its southern part, which stood at the foot of the Palatine Hill, not only equalled the hill in height, but towered high above its summit. In costliness of material, though not in delicacy of design, this palace more than equalled the buildings of the earlier emperors, with the exception of that which Nero built. Some additions and improvements were made to the palace of Sep-

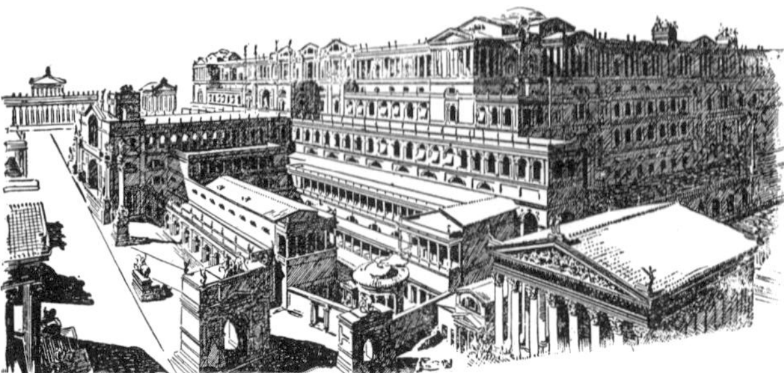
Palace of the Caesars. (Restoration by Benvenuti.)

timius Severus by Elagabalus and Alexander Severus (Lamprid. *El.* iii. 3, 8, 24; *Alex. Sev.* 24, 25).

The Golden House (*domus aurea*) of Nero, which covered part of the Palatine and Esquiline hills and the great valley between them, must have been a building of the most marvellous splendour and extent. It was nearly a mile in length, and included large gardens and parks for wild animals, all surrounded by a triple *porticus* or colonnade of marble. The interior was decorated in the most lavish way with gold, ivory, and jewels (Tac. *Ann.* xv. 42; Suet. *Nero*, 31; Mart. *Spect.* 2). Some rooms, according to Suetonius, were entirely plated with gold and studded with precious stones and pearls. The supper-rooms were vaulted with ivory panels (*lacunaria*), from openings in which flowers and perfumes were scattered on the guests. An enormous number of works of art of every class collected from Greek cities were brought to adorn the palace, and others were made by Nero's orders, such as the bronze colossal statue of himself, 120 feet high, the work of the Greek sculptor Zenodorus, and a painted portrait on canvas of the same ridiculous size. See COLOSSUS.

The destruction of the Golden House and the restoration of most of its site to public uses were among the most popular acts of the Flavian emperors. Both the Colosseum and the great Thermae of Titus stand on part of the site of Nero's palace, of which a small portion was used, after being stripped of its rich marble linings, to form the substructures of part of the Thermae of Titus. This is almost the only part which now exists: remains of a large peristyle and the lofty rooms round it are still fairly well preserved; the vaults are richly decorated with stucco reliefs and paintings, which are rapidly perishing. It was the discovery of these elaborate ornaments early in the sixteenth century which gave so great an impulse to the growing love for classical methods of decoration. Raphael and his pupils with great skill copied the stucco-work, and painted arabesques in the Vatican palace, in the Villa Madama, and in a large number of other buildings. Owing to these magnificent rooms having been used as the substructures of the baths of Titus, most writers on the subject have described the paintings as being part of the work of Titus. But, though the walls of these two structures are mixed in a somewhat complicated way, it is very easy to distinguish one from the other. Titus's walls are of plain brick-faced concrete, without any stucco covering, while Nero's are in all cases either coated with painted stucco or with the cement backing of the missing marble lining. Even where the stucco has in some places fallen off Nero's walls, clear evidence as to its former existence is given by the marble plugs with which the wall-surface was studded to form a key for the plastering.

See Lanciani, *Ancient Rome*, pp. 106–133 (Boston, 1888); and Middleton, *Remains of Ancient Rome*, vol. i. pp. 158–219 (London and Edinburgh, 1892).

Palé (Πάλη). A city of Cephallenia opposite Zacynthus (Polyb. v. 3).

Pales. The Italian goddess of shepherds and pastoral life. Her festival, the Palilia or Parilia, held on April 21st, was properly a herdsmen's festival to promote the fruitfulness of the flocks and to purify the sacred groves and fountains from all unintentional injury or pollution caused by the herds. It was deemed the anniversary of the founding of Rome, the former abode of shepherds. Accordingly, it was celebrated at Rome, as in the villages, by the whole of the inhabitants, with the ancient rites of a shepherds' festival. It was customary to purify house, steading, and sheep with sulphur, and, as a special means of expiation, to offer incense, together with a mixture of the blood of the *October equus* (q. v.), the ashes of the unborn calf which was burned at the feast of Tellus, and bean-straw which was obtained from the Vestals. When these solemn purifications were over, the cheerful part of the festival began. Bonfires were made of straw and hay; the shepherds leaped across them thrice; cakes of millet were also offered to the goddess; and the festival was concluded by a feast in the open air. After the second century of our era the festival was combined with that of Dea Roma, and was celebrated as her birthday with festal processions and Circensian games, which continued till the fifth century A.D.

There seems to have been at one time a male deity of the name Pales (Arnob. iii. 40), but the masculine form had fallen into disuse in classical times. The word contains the root of the verb *pasco*, and hence means "the Feeder" or "Pasturer."

Palīcé (Παλική). A town in Sicily founded by Ducetius (q. v.) near the sulphurous lake of the Palici, west of Leontini. It was destroyed soon after the death of the founder (Diod. xi. 88, 90).

Palīci (Παλικοί). Two spirits worshipped in the neighbourhood of Mount Aetna in Sicily, as benevolent deities and protectors of agriculture. They are sometimes described as sons of Adranus, a native hero honoured through the whole of Sicily; sometimes, of Hephaestus and the nymph Aetna; sometimes, of Zeus and Thalia, a daughter of Hephaestus, who concealed herself in the earth from fear of Heré's jealousy, whereupon two hot sulphur springs burst out of the ground (Aesch. *ap.* Macrob. v. 19). Beside these springs solemn oaths were taken, especially in legal proceedings, the swearer, who must have previously kept himself from all defilement, touching the brink; if the oath were false, blinding or instantaneous death followed. According to another account, a tablet inscribed with the oath was thrown into the water, and swam on the surface if the oath were true, but sank in the contrary case, while flames devoured the perjurer. The neighbouring sanctuary of the

Palici served as an oracle and also as a shelter for fugitive slaves. See Diod. xi. 79; Cic. *N. D.* iii. 22; Verg. *Aen.* ix. 585.

Palilia. A feast among the Romans, held in honour of the goddess Pales on the 21st of April. See PALES.

Palimpsest (from πάλιν + ψέω). The name given to a manuscript from which the original writing has been rubbed off, in order that the leaves may be used again for fresh writing. This process is occasionally repeated, so that the leaves receive a third text. The MS. is then called a double palimpsest. The word *palimpsestus* is found in Catullus (22. 5) and Cicero (*Ad Fam.* vii. 18, 2), and the Greek form παλίμψηστος in Plutarch (*Cum Princip. Philosoph.* ad fin.). From vellum and strong substances the writing was removed by scraping or rubbing, but from the delicate papyrus leaves by washing, usually with a sponge (Mart. iv. 10; Suet. *Aug.* 85). These erasures were often so carelessly done that the original text can usually be restored and read, at least in part, especially when chemicals are used to intensify the traces that remain. Of these chemicals, the one oftenest employed is the hydrosulphuret of ammonia. Many important texts, both classical and biblical, have been recovered from palimpsests when they have been erased for the purpose of writing less valuable matter. Among these are portions of the *De Republica* of Cicero of the fourth century, hidden under a work of St. Augustine on the Psalms (Vatican); the *Commentarii* of the jurist Gaius under St. Jerome (Verona); fragments of Plautus, written in rustic capitals in the fourth (?) century (Milan); and part of the first decade of Livy (from bks. iii.–vi.), under the *Moralia* of Gregory the Great (Verona). No work as a whole, however, has ever been recovered from a palimpsest. Many fac-similes of these palimpsest MSS. are given by Zangemeister in his *Exempla Codicum Latinorum* (Heidelberg, 1876, 1879 foll.) and by Wattenbach. See also Thompson, *Handbook of Greek and Latin Palaeography*, pp. 75–77 (1893); and the article PALAEOGRAPHY.

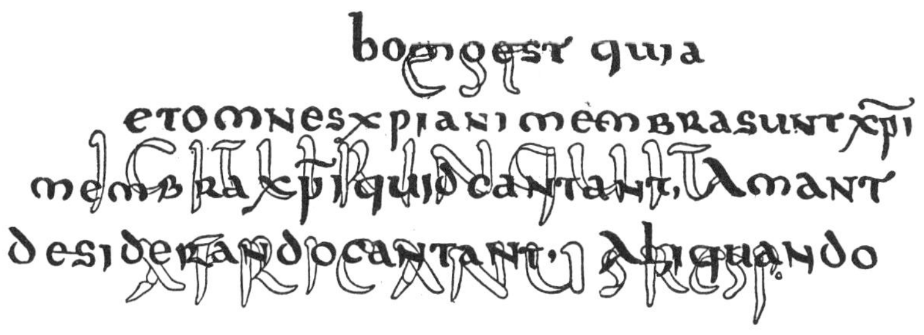

Palimpsest with St. Augustine's Commentary on the Psalms, written over Cicero's Treatise *De Republica*. (Codex in the Vatican.)

Palindrome. The name given to a verse which is the same when read either backwards or forwards. Such verses were written in the decadence of Greek and Latin literature, and similar compositions amused the readers of the Middle Ages. The following is an elaborate example:

Si bene te tua laus taxat sua laute tenebis
Et necat eger (i. e. *aeger*) amor non Roma rege tacente
Roma reges una non anus eger amor.

A Roman lawyer is said to have produced the following:

Si nummi immunis.
"Give me your fee, and go scot-free."

For further examples, see ECHOÏCI VERSUS; and the work by Clark entitled *Palindromes* (Glasgow, 1887).

Palinūrus. Now Cape Palinuro; a promontory on the west coast of Lucania, said to have derived its name from Palinurus, pilot of the ship of Aeneas, who fell into the sea, and was murdered on the coast by the natives (*Aen.* v. 833, vi. 337).

Palla (ξυστίς, πέπλος). A Roman mantle worn by women, consisting of a square piece of cloth, which matrons wore over the *stola*, in the same way as the men wore the toga. They let one third fall down in front over the left shoulder, but drew the rest away over the back, and then either brought it forward over the right shoulder, or drew it under the right arm, but in either case threw the end back over the left arm or shoulder. The palla could also be drawn over the head, just like the toga. Other women, who were not privileged to wear the stola, wore the palla over the tunic, folded together about the body, fastened together on the shoulders with buckles, and open on the right side, or held together in the same way with buckles. It then lay double over the breast and back, but fell down in one thickness to the feet.

Livia, wearing the Palla.

Pallacŏpas (Παλλακόπας). A canal running through Babylonia from the Euphrates to a point some eighty miles distant, on the edge of the Arabian desert, where it lost itself amid marshland (Arrian, vii. 21, 1).

Pallădas (Παλλάδας). A writer of epigrams in the fifth century A.D.

Palladium (Παλλάδιον). A name generally applied to any image of Pallas Athenê, but specifically to the one which was kept secretly hidden as insuring the safety of the town possessing it. The most famous effigy of this sort was the carved image preserved jealously in the citadel of Troy. It is described as of three cubits in height, the feet placed close together, holding a spear in its right hand, and either a distaff or a shield in its left. It was traditionally said to have been given by the goddess herself to Chrysé, the bride of Dardanus, who brought it to Dardania, whence Ilus carried it to Troy. Another legend makes Zeus to have sent it to Ilus from heaven. It was believed that Troy could not be taken so long as the image remained in the city; whereupon Odysseus and Diomedes stole it away and carried it to Argos (Conon, *Narrat.* 34; Verg. *Aen.* ii. 164). Later tradition makes Troy to have had two Palladia, one being stolen by Diomedes and one to have been carried by Aeneas into Italy; so that a number of cities in Italy afterwards claimed to possess it. These were Rome, Lavinium, Siris, and Luceria. (See Plut. *Camill.* 120; Tac. *Ann.* xv. 41; Serv. *ad Aen.* ii. 166; Strabo, p. 264.) The Roman Palladium was preserved in the temple of Vesta. See VESTA.

Palladius, RUTILIUS TAURUS AEMILIĀNUS. A Latin author of the fourth century A.D., who, by borrowing from the writings of his predecessors and from his own experience, composed a work upon husbandry in fourteen books. Of these the first contains general precepts; books ii.–xiii. give the operations of agriculture in each of the successive months, while the fourteenth treats of the grafting of trees, in eighty-five elegiac couplets. His book, though written in dry and feeble language, was much used in the Middle Ages on account of its practical arrangement. There is a modern edition of bk. i. by Schmitt (Würzburg, 1876), and of bk. xiv. also by Schmitt (Münnerstadt, 1877). Text of the whole in Schneider's *Script. Rei Rusticae* (Leipzig, 1794–97).

Palla Gallĭca is the name given to a short, close-fitting jerkin slit up before and behind (Mart. i. 93). It was also called *caracalla* (q. v.).

Pallantia. Now Palencia. The chief town of the Vaccaei, in the north of Hispania Tarraconensis, and on a tributary of the Durius (Douro).

Pallantias and **Pallantis**. Patronymics given to Aurora, the daughter of the giant Pallas. See Eos.

Pallantium (Παλλάντιον). An ancient town of Arcadia, near Tegea, said to have been founded by Pallas, son of Lycaon. Evander is said to have come from this place, and to have called the town which he founded on the banks of the Tiber Pallantēum (afterwards Palantium and Palatium), after the Arcadian town (Pausan. viii. 43, 44). Hence Evander is called *Pallantius heros*.

Pallas (Παλλάς). (1) Pallas Athenê. (See ATHENÉ.) (2) Son of the Titan Crius, husband of Styx, father of Niké. (3) Son of Pandion, who robbed his brother of the dominion of Athens, but was, together with his fifty gigantic sons, slain by the youthful Theseus. (4) A giant who, according to some traditions, was the father of the goddess Athené, who is said to have slain him when he attempted to violate her (Cic. *N. D.* iii. 23, 59).

Pallas. A favourite freedman of the emperor Claudius, under whom, in conjunction with Narcissus, he administered the affairs of the Empire. It was Pallas who persuaded Claudius to marry Agrippina, and to adopt Domitius, afterwards the emperor Nero. By Nero he was deprived of his offices in A.D. 56, and owing to his immense wealth, which excited the jealousy of the emperor, he was destroyed by poison in the year 63 (Tac. *Ann.* xi. 29; xii. 2, 25, 65; xiii. 23). His riches were so great as to become proverbial, as can be seen by the line in Juvenal (i. 107).

Pallas Lacus. See TRITON.

Pallēnē (Παλλήνη). (1) The most westerly of the three peninsulas running out from Chalcidicé in Macedonia. (2) A deme of Attica belonging to the tribe Antiochis.

Palliastrum. A by-form of *pallium*, denoting a *pallium* of coarse material worn by the poorer classes and by such philosophers as affected simplicity of dress (Apul. *Flor.* ii. 14).

Palliāta (sc. *fabula*). A branch of Roman comedy. See COMOEDIA.

Palliŏlum. The diminutive of *pallium* (q v.).

Pallium (ἱμάτιον, φᾶρος). The Roman name for a large Grecian cloak or blanket of wool, which was also worn by Romans among the Greeks. It was especially the garb of the philosophers. In Rome it was also worn by courtesans. In a general sense the word also denotes any large rectangular cloth used for a covering as a pall (Apul. *Flor.* i. 4); a counterpane for a bed (Juv. vi. 236); a curtain (Prudent. *ad Symm.* ii. 726), etc. See Studniczka, *Beiträge zur Geschichte der altgriechischen Tracht* (Vienna, 1886); Baumeister, *Denkmäler*, s. v. "Himation."

Lady in Out-door Dress. (From a terra-cotta in the British Museum.)

Pallor and **Pavor** ("Paleness" and "Fright"). The Roman personifications of terror, and companions of the war-god Mars. As early as the time of King Tullus Hostilius sanctuaries are said to have been erected in their honour. On coins Pallor was represented as a boy with dishevelled hair and perturbed bearing, and Pavor as a man with an expression of horror and with bristling hair.

Palma. The palm branch bestowed by both Greeks and Romans upon victorious athletes and drivers in the race-course (Livy, x. 49; Cic. *Brut.* 47). In works of art, therefore, it symbolizes victory.

Palmăta Tunĭca. See TUNICA.

Palmŭla (ταρσός). The blade of a small oar (Catull. 4. 4).

Palmus and **Palma**. A Roman measure properly the breadth of the four fingers, reckoned in classical times as three inches. See MENSURA.

Palmȳra (Πάλμυρα; the O. T. Tadmor). A celebrated city of Syria, standing in an oasis of the great Syrian Desert, which from its position was a halting-place for the caravans between Syria and Mesopotamia. Here Solomon built a city, which was called in Hebrew Tadmor—that is, "a city of palm-trees." Of this name the Greek Palmyra is a translation. Under Hadrian and the Antonines it was highly favoured, and reached its greatest splendour. The history of its temporary elevation to the rank of a capital, in the third century of the Christian era, is related under ODENATHUS and ZENOBIA. After its capture by Aurelian in A.D. 270 it was partly destroyed, but was made a frontier fortress, and under Justinian was strongly fortified. When the Arabs overran the country it was taken by them, and in the year 1400 was plundered by the Tartars under Tamerlane. Its splendid ruins, which form a most striking object in the midst of the desert, are of the Roman period. They resemble those of Heliopolis (q. v.), though less fine. Among them are the remains of a temple of the Sun (or Baal), a great colonnade which originally consisted of some 1500 columns of the Corinthian order, and was nearly a mile in length. There are also a number of square sepulchral towers of much interest; and the streets can still be traced. Several inscriptions in Greek, Latin, Hebrew, and the Palmyrean dialect are still extant. See Wood, Bouverie, and Dawkins, *The Ruins of Palmyra* (1753); Seiff, *Reisen in der asiatischen Türkei* (1875); and Wright, *An Account of Palmyra and Zenobia* (London, 1895).

Palmyrēnē (Παλμυρήνη). The district of Syria comprising the Syrian Desert from the eastern border of Coele-syria to the Euphrates.

Palton (παλτόν). The lance of the Greek cavalry. (See ARMA.) Also a light spear used by the Persian cavalry (Xen. *Cyrop.* iv. 3, 9; vi. 2, 16).

Paludamentum. The short, red mantle of Roman generals, fastened on the left shoulder and worn over the armour. They assumed it on the Capitol on their departure to the war, but on their return exchanged it for the toga, the garb of peace, before entering into the city (Pliny, *Paneg.* 56, 4). Under the Empire, when the emperor was the commander-in-chief, the purple paludamentum became exclusively a token of imperial power. It became the usual attire of the emperors in the first century after Christ (Suet. *Claud.* 31). Accordingly after that time entrance on imperial power was termed "assuming the purple" (Eutrop. ix. 8).

Roman Emperor in Paludamentum. (Maffei.)

Palus (πάσσαλος). A pole or stake used by the Romans in their military exercises. It was thrust into the ground and then attacked by the raw recruit (*tiro*), who was equipped with a heavy wicker shield and wooden sword (Vegetius, *Mil.* i. 11).

Pamboeotia (Παμβοιώτια). A festival of all the Boeotians, as the Panathenaea was a festival of all the Attic Greeks and the Panionia of all the Ionians. It was held near Coronea and had for its object the worship of Athenē Itonia (Pausan. ix. 34, 1; Gilbert, *Staatsalterthümer*, ii. 53).

Pambōtis Lacus (Παμβῶτις λίμνη). A lake in Epirus not far from Dodona.

Pamīsus (Πάμισος). (1) A river flowing into the Peneus in Thessaly. (2) The chief river of Messenia emptying into the Messenian Gulf. (3) A river of Laconia also emptying into the Messenian Gulf near Leuctra.

Pammachium (παμμάχιον). The same as *pancratium* (q. v.).

Pammĕnes (Παμμένης). A Theban, the lieutenant of Epaminondas, who intrusted him with the defence of Megalopolis (B.C. 371), and again in B.C. 352 (Pausan. viii. 27; Diod. xv. 14; Plut. *Pelop.* 26).

Pamphĭla (Παμφίλη). A woman writer of history. She lived in the time of Nero and wrote an historical miscellany (Συμμίκτων Ἱστορικῶν Ὑπομνημάτων λόγοι). She is variously described as a Greek and as an Egyptian. See Aulus Gellius, xv. 23, where he cites her eleventh book.

Pamphĭlus (Πάμφιλος). (1) A Greek painter of Amphipolis in Macedonia, who lived in the first half of the fourth century B.C., chiefly at Sicyon, as head of the school there founded by his master Eupompus. He is the originator of the scientific teaching of art: he traced back all practice of art to scientific principles. He maintained that painting could not be brought to perfection without arithmetic and geometry. In spite of the fact that his fee for instruction was one talent ($1180), the number of his pupils was considerable, the greatest among them being Apelles. Through his influence instruction in drawing was introduced among the subjects of Greek education (Pliny, *H. N.* xxxv. 74, 76). The only work of this artist now known to us by name is his picture of the "Suppliant Heraclidae," to which Aristophanes alludes in the *Plutus*, 385. (2) A disciple of Plato whose lectures Epicurus attended as a young man (Cic. *N. D.* i. 26, 70). (3) An Alexandrian grammarian who wrote a lexical treatise in ninety-five books, epitomized by Vestinus and Diogenianus in five books, and supposed to have been the basis of the lexicon of Hesychius (q. v.) See Weber, *Philol. Suppl.* iii. 467 foll.

Pamphlets. See LIBELLUS.

Pamphȳli. (1) See DORIS. (2) See PAMPHYLIA.

Pamphylia (Παμφυλία). A narrow strip of the southern coast of Asia Minor, extending in a sort of arch along the Sinus Pamphylius (Gulf of Adalia), between Lycia on the west and Cilicia on the east, and on the north bordering on Pisidia. The inhabitants were a mixture of races, whence their name Pamphyli (Πάμφυλοι), "of all races." There were Greek settlements in the land, the foundation of which was ascribed to Mopsus. It was successively a part of the Persian, Macedonian, Greco-Syrian, and Pergamene kingdoms, and passed by the will of Attalus III. to the Romans (B.C. 130), under whom it was made a province; but this province of Pamphylia included also Pisidia and Isauria, and afterwards a part of Lycia. Under Constantine Pisidia was again separated from Pamphylia.

Pamphylia was in early times called MOPSOPIA, as its early settlements were ascribed to Mopsus (q. v.), the famous seer (Pliny, *H. N.* v. 96), as stated above.

Pamphylium Maré or **Pamphylius Sinus** (τὸ Παμφύλιον πέλαγος). See PAMPHYLIA.

Pan. See PATINA; SARTAGO.

Pan (Πάν). The Greek god of flocks and shepherds, described as the son of the Arcadian shepherd deity Hermes and Dryops, by others as the son of Hermes and Penelopé (Herod. ii. 145), and by still others as the offspring of Penelopé by all the suitors. (See PENELOPÉ.) The Homeric hymn describes him as delighting *all* the gods, and thus getting his name. He was perfectly developed from his birth; and when his mother saw him she ran away through fear; but Hermes carried him to Olympus, where all the gods were delighted with him, especially Dionysus. He was originally only an Arcadian god; and Arcadia was always the principal seat of his worship. From this country his name and worship afterwards spread over other parts of Greece; but at Athens his worship was not introduced until the time of the battle of Marathon. In Arcadia he was the god of forests, pastures, flocks, and shepherds, and dwelt in grottoes, wandered on the summits of mountains and rocks, and in valleys, either amusing himself with the chase, or leading the dances of the nymphs. As the god of flocks, both of wild and tame animals, it was his province to increase and guard them; but he was also a hunter, and hunters owed their success or failure to him. The Arcadian hunters used to scourge the statue of the god if they had been disappointed in the chase (Theocr. vii. 107). During the heat of midday he used to slumber, and was very indignant when any one disturbed him. As the god of flocks, bees also were under his protection, as well as the coast where fishermen carried on their pursuit. As the god of everything connected with pastoral life, he was fond of music, and the inventor of the syrinx or shepherd's flute, which he himself played in a masterly manner, and in which he instructed others also, such as Daphnis. He is thus said to have loved the poet Pindar, and to have sung and danced his lyric songs, in return for which Pindar erected a sanctuary to him in front of his house.

Pan, like other gods who dwelt in forests, was dreaded by travellers, to whom he sometimes appeared, and whom he startled with sudden awe or terror. Thus, when Phidippides, the Athenian, was sent to Sparta to solicit its aid against the Persians, Pan accosted him, and promised to terrify the barbarians if the Athenians would worship him. Hence, sudden fright without any visible cause was ascribed to Pan, and was called a Panic fear (πανικὸν δεῖμα). He is further said to have had a terrible voice, and by it to have frightened the Titans in their fight with the gods. It seems that this feature—namely, his fondness of noise and riot—was the cause of his being considered the minister and companion of Cybelé and Dionysus. He was at the same time believed to be possessed of prophetic powers, and to have even instructed Apollo in this art. While roaming in the forests, he fell in love with the nymph Echo, by whom, or by Pitho, he became the father of Iynx. His love of Syrinx, after whom he named his flute, is well known from Ovid (*Met.* i. 691 foll.). Fir-trees (πίτυες) were sacred to him, since the nymph Pitys, whom

Pan and the Nymph Echo. (Baumeister.)

he loved, had been metamorphosed into that tree; and the sacrifices offered to him consisted of cows, rams, lambs, milk, and honey. Sacrifices were also offered to him in common with Dionysus and the nymphs. The various epithets which are given him by the poets refer either to his singular appearance, or are derived from the names of the places in which he was worshipped. The Romans identified with Pan their own god Inuus, and also Faunus, which name is merely another form of Pan. In works of art Pan is represented as a voluptuous and sensual being, with horns, snub-nose, and goat's feet, sometimes in the act of dancing, and sometimes playing on the syrinx. His attendant deities or demons were known as PANES or PANISCI (Πανίσκοι). Famous representations of Pan in sculpture are the so-called Barberini Faun at Munich, the Dancing Pan at Naples, and the Pan (or Faun) of Praxiteles at Rome, which suggested to Hawthorne his famous romance, *The Marble Faun.* In English literature, besides this romance, Pan is the subject of Landor's *Pan and Pitys* (see above), *Cupid and Pan*, Buchanan's *Pan*, Browning's *Pan and Luna*, and Swinburne's *Pan and Thalassius.* See SATYRI.

Panăca. A drinking-cup. The name is only given as a title of one of Martial's epigrams (xiv. 100).

Panacēa (Πανάκεια, "the all-healing"). A daughter of Asclepius, who had a temple at Oropus (Pausan. i. 34, 2).

Panachaïcus Mons (τὸ Παναχαϊκὸν ὄρος). A mountain in Achaia, 6300 feet high, immediately behind Patrae.

Panacra (Πάνακρα). A mountain in Crete; a branch of Mount Ida.

Panactum (Πάνακτον). A town on the frontiers of Attica and Boeotia, originally belonged to Boeotia, and after being a frequent object of contention between the Athenians and Boeotians, at length became permanently annexed to Attica (Pausan. i. 25, 6).

Panaenus (Πάναινος). A distinguished Athenian painter, who flourished B.C. 448. He was the nephew of Phidias, whom he assisted in decorating the Temple of Zeus at Olympia. He was also the author of a series of paintings, of the battle of Marathon, in the Stoa Poecilé at Athens (Pausan. v. 11, 5).

Panaetius (Παναίτιος). A Greek philosopher of Rhodes, born about B.C. 180; the most important representative of Stoicism in his time. From Athens, where he had received his education, he went to Rome, about B.C. 156. Being there received into the circle of the younger Scipio and of Laelius, he was able to gain numerous adherents among the Roman nobles by his skill in softening the harshness and subtlety of the Stoic teaching, and in representing it in a refined and polished form. After Scipio's death (129) he returned to Athens, where he died, as the head of the Stoic school, about 111. Only unimportant fragments of his writings remain. The most important of them, the *Treatise on Duty* (Περὶ τοῦ Καθήκοντος), in three books, supplied the groundwork of the *De Officiis* of Cicero. See Thiancourt, *Essai sur les Traités Philosophiques de Cicéron et leurs Sources Grecques* (Paris, 1885).

Panaetolium (Παναιτώλιον). A mountain in Aetolia, near Thermon, in which town the panegyric festival of the Aetolians was held. See AETOLIA; PANEGYRIS.

Panariŏlum. A basket for bread (Mart. v. 105).

Panarium (ἀρτοθήκη). A closet for storing bread. A pantry (Varro, *L. L.* v. 105).

Panathenaea (τὰ Παναθήναια). The most ancient and most important of Athenian festivals. It was celebrated in honour of Athené, the patron deity of Athens. Related to have been founded in early times by Erichthonius, it is said to have been originally named only Athenaea, and to have first received the name of Panathenaea at the time when Theseus united all the inhabitants of Attica into one body. In memory of the union itself was kept the festival of the συνοικία, or συνοίκησις, on the 16th of Hecatombaeon (July–August), which may be regarded as a kind of preparatory solemnity to the Panathenaea. There was a festival of the ordinary or lesser Panathenaea celebrated every year, and from the time of Pisistratus, the great Panathenaea held every fifth year, and in the third year of every Olympiad, from the 24th to the 29th of Hecatombaeon. Pisistratus, in the year B.C. 566, added to the original chariot and horse-races athletic contests in each of the traditional forms of competition. He, or his son Hipparchus, instituted the regulation that the collected Homeric poems should be recited at the Feast of Rhapsodes. In 446 Pericles introduced musical contests, which took place on the first day of the festival, in the Odeum, which he had built. Competitions of cyclic choruses and other kinds of dances, torch-races and trireme-races added to the splendour of the festival. The care and direction of all these contests were committed to ten stewards (ἀθλοθέται), who were elected by the people for four years, from one great Panathenaic festival to the next (Pollux, viii. 93). In the musical contests the first prize was a golden crown; in the athletic, the prize was a garland of leaves from the sacred olive-trees of Athené, together with large and beautiful vases filled with oil from the same trees. Many specimens of these Panathenaic vases have been found in Italy, Sicily, Greece, and at Cyrené. They have the figure of Athené on one side and a design indicating the contest for which they are awarded on the other. Most of them belong to the fourth century B.C., 367–318; the so-called "Burgon Vase," in the British Museum, to the sixth century. The tribe whose ships had been victorious received a sum of money, part of which was expended upon a sacrifice to Poseidon.

The culminating-point of the festival was the 28th day of the month, the birthday of the goddess, when the grand procession carried through the city the costly, embroidered, saffron-coloured garment, the *peplus* (πέπλος). This had been woven in the preceding nine months by Attic maidens and matrons, and was embroidered with representations from the battle of the gods and giants. It was carried through the city, first of all, as a sail for a ship moving on wheels, and was then taken to the Acropolis, where it adorned one of the statues of Athené Polias. The procession is represented in a vivid manner in the well-known frieze of the Parthenon. It included the priests and their attendants, leading a long train of animals festally adorned for sacrifice; matrons and maidens bearing in baskets the various sacrificial implements (see CANEPHORI); old men in festal attire, with olive-branches in their hands, whence came their name, θαλλοφόροι; warriors, with spear and shield, in splendid array; young men in armour; the cavalry under the command of both the ἵππαρχοι; the victors in the immediately preceding contests; the festal embassies of other States, especially of the colonies; and, lastly, the aliens resident in Athens. Of these last the men bore behind the citizens trays with sacrificial cakes, the women water-pots, and the maidens sunshades and stools for the citizens' wives; while on the freedmen was laid the duty of adorning with oak-leaves the market-places and streets through which the procession moved. The feast ended with the great festal sacrifice of a hecatomb of oxen, and with the general banqueting which accompanied it. At the yearly minor Panathenaea, on the 28th and 29th of Hecatombaeon, contests, sacrifices, and a procession took place, but all in a more simple style, under the direction of the ἱεροποιοί. (See HIEROPOEI.) In later times the festival was removed to the spring, perhaps in consequence of Roman influence, in order to make it correspond to the Quinquatrus (q. v.) of Minerva. All the ancient authorities are collected by Michaelis in his work, *Der Parthenon*, pp. 318–333 (1875); see also Mommsen, *Heortologie der Athener*, pp. 116–205 (1875); and H. A. Müller, *Panathenaica* (1837); with the articles LAMPADEDROMIA; PYRRHICA; SKIADAPHORIA.

Pancratiastae. See PANCRATIUM.

Pancratium (παγκράτιον). The combination of boxing and wrestling in Greek gymnastics, getting its name from the fact that it called into play all the powers (πᾶν + κράτος) of the fighter. At Sparta the name was applied to any rough, irregular fighting that was not conducted according to any

Wrestlers in the Pancratium. (Krause, *Gymnastik.*)

rules, but in which even biting and scratching were not uncommon. The Greeks ascribed the invention of the pancratium to Theseus, who thus fought against the Minotaur. (See the Schol. on Pind. *Nem.* v. 49; and THESEUS.) It made its way into the four great games of Greece, and there was a pancratium for boys as well as for men (Pausan. v. 8 *fin.*). It was fought partly standing and partly on the ground, and the boxing was the chief feature of it (Pind. *Nem.* iii. 17; Lucian, *Anach.* 8, 24). The *caestus* (q. v.) was not used, however, and the blows were given, not with the closed fist, but with the hands curved, as in the second illustration. When two παγκρατιασταί began to fight, they stood with outstretched arms, feeling for an opening, and each tried to get the other into such a position as to have the sun shine in his eyes. With the clinch the real fight began. Biting and butting were against the rules (Lucian, *Demon.* 47). The victory was not decided until one of the combatants was killed, or held up a finger in token of defeat (Philostr. *Imag.* ii. 6).

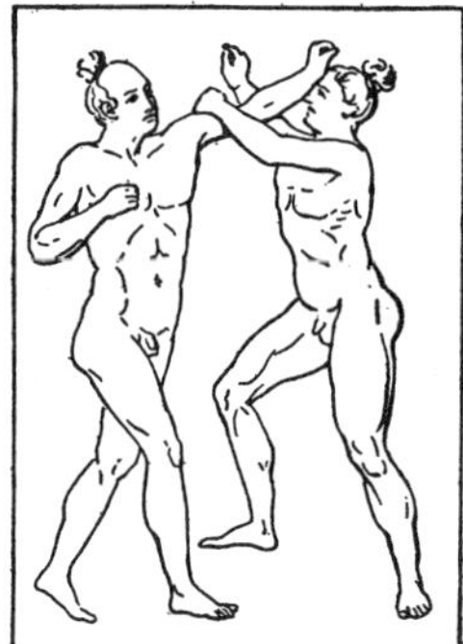

Pancratium. (Krause, *Gymnastik.*)

At Rome the pancratium is first mentioned in the time of Caligula (Dio Cass. lix. 13), and it soon became very popular.

For the training of the fighters, see ATHLETAE. The chief works are those of H. Mercurialis, *De Arte Gymnastica*, and Krause, *Die Gymnastik und Agonistik der Hellenen*, i. pp. 534–556.

Panda. A river of Sarmatica Asiatica (Tac. *Ann.* xii. 16).

Pandareōs (Πανδάρεως). A native of Miletus, the son of Merops, who stole from Minos of Crete a living dog made of gold, the work of Hephaestus, which was the guardian of the temple of Zeus, and gave it to Tantalus to keep it safely. When Zeus demanded the dog back, Pandareos fled with his wife Harmothoë to Sicily, where both were turned into stones. (For his daughter Aëdon, see AËDON.) Of his two other daughters (Meropé and Cleodora, or Camira and Clytea), Homer (*Od.* xx. 66–78) relates that they were brought up by Aphrodité after their early bereavement, and were endowed by Heré with beauty and wisdom, by Artemis with lofty stature, and by Athené with skill in handiwork; but while their foster-mother went to Olympus to implore Zeus to grant the maidens happy marriages, they were carried off by the Harpies, and delivered to the Erinyes as servants, and thus expiated their father's guilt (*Odyss.* xx. 65–78; Pausan. x. 30, 1).

Pandărus (Πάνδαρος). (1) A Lycian hero, son of Lycaon. He led the troops of Zelea (on Mount Ida) in the Trojan War, and was distinguished as an archer, having received his bow from Apollo. He was slain by Diomedes (*Il.* ii. 824, v. 290). (2) A companion of Aeneas slain by Turnus (Verg. *Aen.* ix. 672, 758).

Pandataria. Now Vendutené; a small island off the coast of Campania, to which Iulia (q. v.), the daughter of Augustus, was banished.

Pandectae. See CORPUS IURIS CIVILIS.

Pandēmos. See APHRODITÉ, p. 96.

Pandīa (τὰ Πανδῖα). A festival held at Athens in the middle of the month Elaphebolion. It is doubtful whom it originally commemorated, and the ancients themselves disputed this question—whether it was in honour of Pandion (q. v.), Pandia, the moon-goddess, or Zeus, the all-divine. Hermann regards it as the feast of the old tribe Dias; Welcker inclines to the Zeus hypothesis; and Mommsen and Preller think it originated in the worship of Pandia = Selené. (See SELENÉ.) Cf. Mommsen, *Heort.* pp. 61, 389, 396; and Preller, *Griech. Mythologie*, i. 347.

Pandīon (Πανδίων). (1) The son of Erichthonius, father of Procné, Philomela, Butes, and Erechtheus (q. v.). (2) Son of Cecrops and Metiadusa, grandson of Erechtheus, king of Athens. Driven into exile by the sons of his brother Metion, he went to Megara, where he married Pylia, the daughter of King Pylas, and inherited the kingdom. His sons, Aegeus, Lycus, Pallas, and Nisus (known as the PANDIONĬDAE), regained Attica from the Metionidae, and the first three shared it among themselves, while Nisus (q. v.) received Megara.

Pandokeion (πανδοκεῖον). See CAUPONA, p. 304.

Pandōra (Πανδώρα). The Greek Eve; the first woman on earth. After Prometheus (q. v.) had stolen the heavenly fire, Zeus in revenge caused Hephaestus to make a woman of exquisite beauty who should bring sorrow upon the human race. From her perfection of loveliness and intellect she was called Pandora, "the All-gifted." She became the wife of Epimetheus, brother of Prometheus, though Epimetheus had been advised to accept nothing that came from Zeus. In the house of Epimetheus stood a closed box or jar containing all the evils possible for man; and this box Pandora out of curiosity opened. The evils poured out when the lid was raised, and though she closed it hastily, she only succeeded in preventing the escape of Hope, which was also in the box (Hesiod. *Theog.* 571; *Op.* 50). In later times the story was differently told. The box was then said to contain blessings which were thus secured to the human race; but by opening it, Pandora lost them all except Hope (Hyg. *Fab.* 142).

Pandosia (Πανδοσία). (1) A town of Epirus, in the district Thesprotia, on the river Acheron. (2) A town in Bruttium, near the frontiers of Lucania, situated on the river Acheron. It was here that Alexander of Epirus fell, B.C. 326, in accordance with an oracle (Livy, viii. 25; Iustin. xii. 2). (3) A town of Lucania near Heraclea.

Pandrŏsos (Πάνδροσος). "All bedewing." A daughter of Cecrops of Athens, first priestess of Athené, honoured together with her in a sanctuary of her own, the Pandroseion, on the Acropolis of Athens. See CECROPS.

Pandūra (πανδοῦρα). A stringed instrument with three chords (Pollux, iv. 60).

Panēas. See CAESAREA (4).

Panegyrĭcus (πανηγυρικός). The name given among the Greeks to a speech delivered before a πανήγυρις—that is, an assembly of the whole nation on the occasion of the celebration of a festival, such as the Panathenaea and the four great national games. This oration had reference to the feast itself, or was intended to inspire the assembled multitude with emulation by praising the great deeds of their ancestors, and also to urge them to unanimous co-operation against their common foes. The most famous compositions of this kind which have been preserved are the *Panegyricus* and *Panathenaïcus* of Isocrates, neither of which, however, was actually delivered in public. In later times eulogies upon individuals were so named. This kind of composition was especially cultivated under the Roman Empire by Greeks and Romans. In Roman literature the most ancient example of this kind which remains is the eulogy of the emperor Trajan, delivered by the younger Pliny in the Senate, A.D. 100, thanking the emperor for conferring on him the consulate—a model which subsequent ages vainly endeavoured to imitate. It forms, together with eleven orations of Mamertinus, Eumenius, Nazarius, Pacatus Drepanius, and other unknown representatives of the Gallic school of rhetoric from the end of the third and the whole of the fourth centuries A.D., the extant collection of the *Panegyrici Latini.* Besides these we possess similar orations by Symmachus, Ausonius, and Ennodius. There are also a considerable number of poetical panegyrics—e. g. one upon Messala, composed in the year B.C. 31, and wrongly attributed to Tibullus; one by an unknown author of the Neronian time upon Calpurnius Piso; and others by Claudian, Sidonius Apollinaris, Merobaudes, Corippus, Priscian, and Venantius Fortunatus (q. v.).

There are editions of the panegyrici by Beatus Rhenanus (Basle, 1520), Livineius (Antwerp, 1599), Rittershusius, with notes (Frankfort, 1607), Schwarz (Altdorf, 1739–48), Arntzen (Utrecht, 1790–95), and Bährens (Leipzig, 1874). See Rühl, *De Panegyricis Duodecim Latinis* (Greifswald, 1868).

Panegȳris (Πανήγυρις). A name applied by the Greeks to any gathering of the whole people at a fixed period. Examples are the Panionia (q. v.), the great national meetings on the occasion of the Olympian, Pythian, Nemean, and Isthmian Games; and in later times, the popular fairs, etc. On these occasions, besides other features, formal orations (λόγοι πανηγυρικοί) were delivered. See PANEGYRICUS.

Panēum or **Panium** (Πάνειον, Πάνιον). "Pan's home"; a cave in the southern extremity of the range of Antilibanus, out of which the river Jordan flows (Ioseph. *Ant. Iud.* xv. 10).

Pangaeum (Παγγαῖον) or **Pangaeus** (Πάγγαιος). A mountain range in Macedonia between the Strymon and the Nestus. It was famous for its mines of gold and silver, and for its roses (Herod. v. 16; Pliny, *H. N.* iv. 42).

Panhellenia (Πανελλήνια). A gathering (πανήγυρις) of all the Hellenes instituted by the Roman emperor Hadrian (Philostr. *Vit. Soph.* ii. 1, 5).

Panhellenius. See ZEUS.

Panionia (Πανιώνια). A great gathering (πανήγυρις) of the Ionian peoples, held on Mount Mycalé near Priené, and between Ephesus and Miletus. At this feast the national god Poseidon Heliconius, whose sanctuary at this place was called Panionium, was worshipped with magnificent sacrifices (Herod. i. 148; Pausan. vii. 24; Diod. xv. 49). The meetings had also a political colour, as when the assembled Ionians discussed dangers threatening their country and passed resolutions of general political importance (Herod. i. 141, 170). See Grote, *Hist. of Greece,* iii. pp. 229 foll.

Panionium. A spot on the north of the promontory of Mycalé, with a temple to Poseidon, which was the place of meeting for the cities of Ionia. See MYCALÉ.

Panis. (1) Bread. See PISTOR. (2) PANIS GRADĬLIS. Bread distributed gratuitously to the populace at Rome from the top of a flight of steps (*gradus*), near the bakers' shops (Prudent. *In Symm.* i. 584; ii. 984).

Panisci. See PAN.

Panium (Πάνιον). A town on the coast of Thrace.

Pannonia. A Roman province between the Danube and the Alps, separated on the west from Noricum by the Mons Cetius, and from Upper Italy by the Alpes Iuliae, on the south from Illyria by the Savus, on the east from Dacia by the Danube, and on the north from Germany by the same river. It corresponded, therefore, to the eastern part of Austria, Carinthia, Styria, Carniola, and Hungary with Slavonia and part of Croatia and Bosnia.

The Pannonians (Pannonii) were probably of Illyrian origin. They were a brave and warlike people, and were conquered by the Romans in the time of Augustus (about B.C. 33). In A.D. 7 the Pannonians joined the Dalmatians and the other Illyrian tribes in their revolt from Rome, but were conquered by Tiberius after a struggle which lasted three years (A.D. 7–9). Pannonia was originally only one province, but was afterwards divided into two provinces, called Pannonia Superior and Pannonia Inferior. The principal towns were Carnuntum, Siscia (Sissek), Poetovio (Pettau), Sopianae (Fünfkirchen), and Aquincum (Altofen).

Panomphaeus (Πανομφαῖος). The author of all signs and omens; a surname of Zeus (*Il.* viii. 250).

Panŏpé (Πανόπη). A sea-nymph, daughter of Nereus and Doris.

Panŏpeus (Πανοπεύς). The son of Phocus and Asteropaea, who accompanied Amphitryon on his expedition against the Taphians or Teleboans, and took an oath not to embezzle any part of the booty; but having broken his oath, he was punished by his son Epeus becoming unwarlike. He is also mentioned among the Calydonian hunters (*Il.* xxiii. 665). Cf. Pausan. ii. 29, 4; Ovid, *Met.* viii. 312.

Panŏpeus (Πανοπεύς), **Panopeae** (Πανοπέαι), or **Panŏpé** (Πανόπη). An ancient town in Phocis on the Cephissus and near the frontiers of Boeotia, twenty stadia west of Chaeronea, said to have been founded by Panopeus, son of Phocus (Herod. viii. 34).

Panoplia (πανοπλία). The full armour of a hoplite. See ARMA.

Panopŏlis. See CHEMMIS.

Panoptes. See ARGUS.

Panormus (Πάνορμος). (1) Now Palermo; an important town on the north coast of Sicily, founded by the Phœnicians, and which at a later time

Coin of Panormus in Sicily.

received its Greek name from its excellent harbour. From the Phœnicians it passed into the hands of the Carthaginians, and was taken by the Romans in the First Punic War, B.C. 254. Cicero speaks of it as a place of considerable commercial importance (*Verr.* ii. 26). See Schubring, *Historische Topographie von Panormos* (1870). (2) A harbour on the east coast of Attica. (3) A harbour in Achaia. (4) A harbour on the northern coast of Crete. (5) A harbour in Epirus. (6) The outer harbour of Ephesus.

Pansa, GAIUS VIBIUS. A friend of Caesar's, tribune of the plebs in B.C. 51 and governor of Gaul in 46, in which office he was the successor of Marcus Brutus. He was consul with Hirtius in 43, and fell before Mutina in that year. See HIRTIUS.

Pansa, HOUSE OF. See DOMUS, p. 549; POMPEII.

Pan's Pipe. See PAN; SYRINX.

Pantagias, Pantacÿas (Παντακύας), or **Pantagies.** A small river on the eastern coast of Sicily, flowing into the sea between Megara and Syracuse.

Pantaleon (Πανταλέων). (1) A king of Pisa in Elis, son of Omphalion. In B.C. 644 he seized upon Olympia by force, and being supported by his troops declared himself sole umpire of the Olympian Games. Hence, the Eleans afterwards refused to reckon this Olympiad (the thirty-fourth) in the regular calendar. Pantaleon also aided the Messenians in the Second Messenian War (Pausan. vi. 21, 22; Strabo, p. 362). (2) A Bactrian king who ruled in the second century B.C.

Panthēa. The heroine of the first Greek love-story in prose, embodied in Xenophon's historical romance, the *Cyropaedia.* See ABRADATAS; NOVELS AND ROMANCES.

Panthēon (Πάνθειον, "all divine") or **Panthēum.** The Pantheon, the only ancient edifice at Rome whose walls and vaulting have been perfectly preserved. The original statues that adorned it have long ago been removed, but the mighty dome-like building with its vast colonnade attests better than any existing work the massive strength and splendour of the architecture of imperial Rome. The purpose for which the temple was first built is not known, but we learn from an inscription on the porch that it was erected by M. Vipsanius Agrippa in B.C. 27. (M. AGRIPPA L. F. COS. TERTIVM FECIT.) At a later time the name Pantheon was thought to mean "the temple of all the gods," a notion which led Pope Boniface IV. to dedicate the building, in A.D. 609, as a Christian church to the memory of all the martyrs, under the name of *S. Maria ad Martyres* (now S. Maria Rotonda, or simply La Rotonda). The building had been already repeatedly enlarged in ancient times by Domitian, Hadrian, and last of all, in A.D. 202, by Septimius Severus and Caracalla. It consists of a circular structure, 140 feet 6 inches in height and inner diameter, with

The Pantheon. (From a photograph.)

a portico 103 feet long formed by sixteen Corinthian columns 39 feet high. Eight of these in front supported a massive pediment, behind which rose another pediment of still higher elevation, resting against the square projection which connects the portico with the dome. The other columns divide the portico into three parallel portions, originally vaulted over. In the interior of the portico on each side of the entrance are two niches, which formerly contained colossal statues of Augustus and Agrippa. The massive walls of the great rotunda, which is completely circular in form, are divided by ring-cornices into two stories, an upper and a lower. Above these springs a cupola of concrete, of vaster dimensions than any that had been attempted in previous times. The diameter of this lofty cupola corresponds to that of the vast cylindrical building on which it rests. The walls of the latter are 19 feet thick. The interior of the cupola is divided into five rows of deeply sunk panels (*lacunaria*), 28 in each row. At its vertex an opening about 30 feet in diameter lights the whole of the interior. The gilt-bronze tiles of the roof were taken by the emperor Constans II. to Constantinople in A.D. 655. The remains of the costly marble wall-linings of the interior, which dated from the last restoration, and consisted of 56 compartments, divided by 112 Corinthian columns, and covered with white marble, porphyry, serpentine, and pavonazetto, were not carried off until 1747. In 1632 the great bronze tubes which supported the roof of the portico were melted down by Pope Urban VIII. (Barberini) to be cast into pillars for the *baldacchino* in St. Peter's and into cannon for the castle of S. Angelo—which led to Pasquin's famous epigram, *Quod non fecerunt barbari fecerunt Barberini*. The Pantheon now contains the tomb of King Victor Emmanuel. See an article by Lanciani in the *Atlantic Monthly* for June, 1893.

Panthoüs (Πάνθοος) and **Panthūs** (Πάνθους). One of the Trojan elders. By his wife, Phrontis, he was the father of Euphorbus, Polydamas, and Hyperenor, who are therefore called Panthoides. Panthoüs was originally a priest of Apollo at Delphi, and was brought to Troy by Antenor, who was captivated by his beauty (*Iliad*, iii. 146; xiv. 450; xvii. 24, 40, 81; Verg. *Aen*. ii. 319).

Panticapaeum (Παντικάπαιον). A town in the Tauric Chersonesus, situated on a hill on the Cimmerian Bosporus, was founded by the Milesians about B.C. 541, and became the residence of the Greek kings of the Bosporus, and was hence itself sometimes called Bospŏrus (Procop. *Aed*. iii. 7). A number of interesting remains of Greek art are found here, and preserved in the museum at St. Petersburg. See the *Comtes Rendus de la Commission Archéologique de St. Pétersbourg*.

Panticăpes (Παντικάπης). A river of European Sarmatia, perhaps the same as the Samara. Cf. Herod. iv. 18, 47, 54.

Pantomīmus (παντόμιμος). The representation of a dramatic subject by dancing and rhythmic gesticulation alone, as practised by the Romans. It originated in the custom of the ancient Roman drama, of allowing one actor on the stage to make only the necessary movements of dancing and gesticulation, while another actor sang the recitative to the accompaniment of the flute. This recitative was called *canticum*, and was a monologue composed in rhythmical form. The illustrative dance was raised to a separate, independent branch of art by Pylades and Bathyllus under Augustus, B.C. 22. There were comic and tragic pantomimes, but the latter variety prevailed on the stage of the Empire. The subjects were chiefly taken from tragedies founded on mythological love stories (e. g. those of Iupiter and Leda, of Mars and Venus, of Cinyras and Myrrha, etc.), and treated so that the chief situations were included in a series of *cantica*. All of these were represented by a single pantomimus, the dancer as well as the performer being designated by that name. He thus had to represent several characters, male and female, in succession, while a chorus, accompanied by flutes and other instruments, sang the corresponding song. The pauses necessary for the change of mask and costume for each successive part were apparently filled up with the recital of music by the chorus, which served to connect the chief scenes with each other. Because of the prominence given to dancing in them the pantomimes were known as *fabulae salticae*. In imperial times the best poets wrote them—e. g., Lucan and Statius (Juv. vii. 92).

It was only in the latest times of the Empire that women were employed in pantomime. Pantomime, aiming at sensual charm alone, went beyond all bounds of decorum in the representation of delicate subjects. As an understanding of the subtleties of the art required a cultivated taste, pantomime was specially favoured by the higher classes, while the *mimus*, with his buffoonery, was more pleasing to the multitude. On the true dramatic ballet of imperial times, see Pyrrhica; and on the whole subject, Friedländer, *Sittengeschichte*, ii. 427–442.

Panyasis (Πανύασις, the quantity of the penult is doubtful) and **Panyassis**. A Greek poet of Halicarnassus, uncle of Herodotus, the historian. He was put to death by the tyrant Lygdamis about B.C. 454 for being the leader of the aristocratic party. He composed a poem in fourteen books and 9000 verses, entitled *Heraclea* (exploits of Heracles), which was reckoned by later writers among the best epics. The few fragments preserved are in an elegant and graceful style. Another poem of his, the *Ionica* (Ἰωνικά), contained 7000 lines, and relates the history of Neleus, Codrus, and the Ionian colonies. Panyasis was ranked by the Alexandrian School (q. v.) with the great epic poets. The fragments of Panyasis are edited by Gaisford (1823) and Dübner (1840). There was another person of the same name, possibly the grandson of the poet, who wrote a work in two books on dreams (Suid. s. v.).

Paper. See Papyrus; Pergamentum; Writing and Writing Materials.

Paphlagonia (Παφλαγονία). A country of Asia Minor, bounded by Bithynia on the west, by Pontus on the east, by Phrygia and afterwards by Galatia on the south, and by the Euxine on the north. In the Trojan War the Paphlagonians are said to have come to the assistance of the Trojans, from the land of the Heneti, under the command of Pylaemenes. The Paphlagonians were subdued by Croesus, and afterwards formed part of the Persian Empire. Under the Romans, Paphlagonia formed part of the province of Galatia, but it was made a separate province by Constantine. The principal rivers were the Halys, the Sesamus, the

Ochosbanes, the Evarchus, the Zalecus, and the Amnius. The principal cities (mostly on the coast) were Amastris, Cromna, Aegealius, Abonitichos, Cimolis, Stephané, Potami, Sinopé, Pompeiopolis, and Gangra.

Paphus (Πάφος). Son of Pygmalion, and founder of the city of the same name.

Paphus (Πάφος). The name of two towns on the west coast of Cyprus, called "Old Paphos" (Παλαίπαφος) and "New Paphos" (Πάφος Νέα), the former near the promontory of Zephyrium, ten stadia from the coast; the latter more inland, sixty stadia from the former. Old Paphos was the chief seat of the worship of Aphrodité, who is said to have landed at this place after her birth among the waves, and who is hence frequently called the Paphian goddess (Paphia). Here she had a celebrated temple, the high-priest of which exercised a kind of religious superintendence over the whole island. The priests were supposed to be descendants of Cinyras (q. v.). The image of the goddess was a conical stone (Serv. *ad Aen.* i. 724), which was anointed with oil at the time of worship, and this, with other testimony derived from excavations made since 1887 by English explorers, makes it evident that the cult of the Paphian Aphrodité was Semitic rather than Hellenic. The very temple, with its large open courts and small chambers, had the characteristics of a Phœnician structure. New Paphos, on the other hand, was of Greek foundation, and the traditions ascribed it to Agapenor (Pausan. viii. 5, 2).

In the reign of Augustus Old Paphos was destroyed by an earthquake, and when rebuilt by order of the emperor received the name of Augusta (Dio Cass. lxiv. 23).

Papias (Παπίας). A bishop of Hierapolis in Phrygia, who flourished in the first half of the second century A.D., and suffered martyrdom at Pergamus in the year 163 (or 156). He wrote a work entitled Λογίων Κυριακῶν Ἐξήγησις, of which only fragments remain, preserved in the writings of Irenaeus, Eusebius, and others who quote them. They are collected and edited by Routh in vol. i. of his *Reliq. Sacr.* (1846).

Papilio. Literally, "a butterfly;" a name applied by the Romans to a tent whose curtains, when opened and fastened in front, resembled a butterfly's wings (Veget. *Mil.* i. 3).

Papiniānus, Aemilius. The most important among the Roman jurists; born about A.D. 140, a contemporary and friend of the emperor Septimius Severus, whom he accompanied on his expedition to Britain in the capacity of *praefectus praetorio.* Severus, on his death-bed at York, left to him the guardianship of his sons Geta and Caracalla; yet the latter caused Papinianus to be put to death in the next year, 212, on the day after the murder of his brother Geta (Spart. *Sev.* 21, 8). Of all his works, the thirty-seven books of *Quaestiones* (legal questions) and the nineteen books of *Responsa* (legal decisions) were considered the most important. Till the time of Justinian these formed the nucleus of that part of jurisprudence which was connected with the explanation of the original authorities on Roman law. We possess only fragments of them, in the form of numerous excerpts in the *Digest;* and lately a few have been discovered belonging to the fifth and ninth books of the *Responsa,* on a few leaves of a MS. written in uncials in the fifth (?) century. See Brinz, *Die Berlin. Frag. vorjustinianischer Rechtsquellen* (Munich, 1884), and the article Corpus Iuris Civilis.

Papinius Statius. See Statius.

Papiria Gens. A gens divided between patricians and plebeians. The families of Crassus, Cursor, Maso, and Mugillanus were patrician; those of Carbo, Paetus, and Turdus were plebeian.

Papirius. See Iurisprudentia.

Papirius Carbo. See Carbo.

Papirius Cursor, Lucius. (1) A Roman general who in the Second Samnite War frequently defeated the enemy. He was five times consul (B.C. 333, 320, 319, 315, 313), and twice dictator (B.C. 325, 309). He was a very severe disciplinarian, so that in spite of his victories he was not liked by his troops (Livy, viii. and ix.). (2) The son of the preceding, who was twice consul, and in his second consulate (B.C. 272) brought the Third Samnite War to a successful end (Livy, x. 31–47).

Papius Mutĭlus, Gaius. A Samnite general in the Marsic War (B.C. 90–89).

Papposilēnus. See Silenus.

Pappūa (Παππούα). A high mountain in Numidia near the city of Melitené.

Pappus (Πάππος). A geometrician of Alexandria who flourished in the fourth century A.D. A treatise of his on mathematical collections (Μαθηματικῶν Συναγωγῶν βιβλία) is still in existence, and has been edited by Hultsch (Berlin, 1875–78). It was originally in eight books, but the first and part of the second are lost. The work was intended to be a synopsis of Greek mathematics. See Ball's *Short History of Mathematics,* pp. 92–93 (London, 1888).

Pappus (πάππος). A name given to a stock character of the Atellan plays (*Atellanae fabulae*). Pappus is the prototype of the Pantaloon of modern pantomime—a foolish, credulous old man, who is always gulled and tricked by Dossennus, the sharper. See Munk, *De Fabulis Atellanis* (Breslau, 1840); and Friedländer, *Sittengeschichte,* ii. 435 (6th ed. Leipzig, 1889).

Paprēmis (Πάπρημις). A city of Lower Egypt in the Nomos Papremites. It was sacred to a god whom the Greeks identified with Ares (Herod. ii. 71).

Papȳrus (πάπυρος). Information as to the papyrus reed, celebrated in antiquity as providing material for writing, is obtained from the study of existing plants believed to belong to the same genus, and also from the statements of ancient writers.

There are two species of the papyrus plant (*Cyperus Papyrus,* cf. κύπειρος, "a reed") recognized to-day. One, the *Cyperus Syriacus,* mentioned by Theophrastus as growing with the sweet-scented calamus on the borders of a Syrian lake, was transplanted to Sicily by the Arabs in the tenth century, and is found at the present time in various parts of that island. The other species is found in Nubia and Abyssinia. This is the descendant of the old Egyptian papyrus which was cultivated in antiquity in the delta of the Nile. Herodotus (ii. 92, 96) and Strabo (799 foll.) speak of papyrus as belonging to lower Egypt. Since, however, it has disappeared from what was anciently believed to be its home, it is probable that its presence there was originally due to transplanting and assiduous cultivation. These two species differ from each other mainly in the length of the stalk—that of the former growing much higher than that of the latter. Other minor differences are also noticeable.

The most valuable description given by ancient writers is that of Theophrastus, the successor of Aristotle in charge of the Lyceum, in his *Historia Plantarum* (Περὶ Φυτῶν Ἱστορία, iv. 8, 3). He describes the papyrus as growing along the Nile in water of about two cubits (three feet) in depth, with a root as thick as a man's arm and of ten cubits (fifteen feet) or more in length. This root, rising somewhat above the soil, sends forth slender shoots into the mud. The stalks (*πάπυροι*) are about four cubits (six feet) in height, and are of triangular shape. These bear no fruit, but produce a soft, hair-like tuft as a head. The roots are used for firewood and for making various articles of furniture. The papyrus itself (Theophrastus refers to the stalk) is put to many uses. Boats are made from it, and from the *βίβλος* (the substance within the stalk) sails, mats, clothing, coverings, and ropes. The *βιβλία* (*chartae*, or sheets made of *βίβλος*) are most familiar to people of other lands. Above all, this plant is useful as a means of subsistence, since the inhabitants chew it either raw, boiled, or roasted, drawing the juice and rejecting the fibre.

Papyrus Plant.

Pliny (*H. N.* xiii. 12, 77 foll.) repeats the statements of Theophrastus, but enlarges his mere reference to *βιβλία* into an extended account of the manufacture of paper from the papyrus plant. The following description is based upon the statements of Pliny; but that author's general and unscientific treatment of his subject and the inaccuracies in the text have caused much uncertainty concerning various points.

Paper was made from the pith or cellular tissue within the stalk. It was once believed that the material was the outer rind of the plant. The word *liber*, which refers to bark (once used for writing material), and Pliny's use of *philyrae*, in his description of the thin strips of web-like material, are misleading. Pliny elsewhere describes *philyra* as the inner bark of the lime-tree. Ulpian, of the third century A.D. (*Dig.* 32, 52), sets apart *philyrae* as of different material from *chartae*. Cassiodorus (sixth century), in his *Variae*, uses the following expressions, which show that the pith or inner tissue is designated: *viscera nivea viventium herbarum mollities in medullis; bibula teneritudine spongeum lignum.* This tissue was cut into strips (*schidae*, *σχίζειν*) or *inae* (Fest. p. 104: *ina quae pars chartae est tenuissima;* p. 81, 4: *a tenuitate inarum quas Graeci in chartis ita appellant*), which were made as broad and thin as possible. Those taken from the centre of the stalk were the best, while the quality became poorer the nearer the rind was approached. The strips (*schidae*) were arranged in parallel lines upon a board (*tabula*) wet with Nile water. They were then moistened with paste and overlaid with strips placed at right angles. Thus *texitur* is used of the process and *plagula* first of the unfinished page opposed to *pagina* the completed page, although both words afterwards were used for the page (*σελίς*) of the roll. These two layers of strips were pressed closely together until they formed one sheet. The remainder of the process consisted in drying in the sunlight and polishing with a shell (Mart. xiv. 209) or some instrument of ivory. While the *paginae* (*σελίδες*) might be used separately, they were regularly joined with others to form a roll (*volumen*, *τόμος*). The chief defects which were to be avoided were roughness (*scabritia*), dampness (*humor*), spots (*lentigines*), and streaks (*taeniae*), running down the middle of the *pagina* and rendering the paper spongy. The paste used was made of flour and boiling water, with the addition of a little vinegar. Ordinary glue, or workman's paste (*glutinum fabrile*), was not useful for this purpose, as it made the paper brittle. Pliny states that the separation of the pith into strips was accomplished by the use of the needle (*acu*). It is a question whether broad and thin strips could be obtained by the use of a needle. Birt (*Antike Buchwesen*, p. 231) suggests that *acu* may be a translation of some Greek expression, as, perhaps, *ὀξεῖ τινι ὀργάνῳ*. The language of Pliny, as commonly interpreted, indicates that the water of the Nile, when muddy, served as glue (*turbidus liquor vim glutinis praebet*). This is correct if *glutinis* is a genitive, but Birt shows that Pliny knew only *glutinum-i*, and *glutinis* is then a dative; and the inference is that paste was used, and water served to make it effective in uniting the strips. Pliny also states that in making the roll the best sheets were placed first, while those of poorer quality were at the end of the roll. Such an arrangement was most natural, as the most durable sheets would be on the outside; and if a portion of the roll alone was used the best would come first.

The manufacture of paper from papyrus belonged almost exclusively to Egypt and in particular to the city of Alexandria. One kind of paper, the Fanniana, was made in Rome, but the process was merely additional treatment of a paper manufactured in Egypt. Papyrus *chartae* differed in form, quality, and the care bestowed in preparation. The essential difference was that of form, as it will be seen that difference in form implied a difference in quality and care in manufacture. This form was determined by the breadth of the single sheet before it became part of a roll, and not by the height of the page, as was once believed. The height varied from eight to thirteen inches (Birt, *Antike Buchwesen*, pp. 252–253). The breadth depended upon the number of *schidae* which were placed side by side to form the lower layer of the *plagula*. The broader the page the greater the advantage both to writer and reader, as there was less interruption to the continuity of the writing. In bound books the strain comes upon the binding; in the rolls, however, the individual page must stand the strain. Hence, the poorer the quality the narrower the page, as the liability to tear was greater in the large sheets than in the small. The great object in manufacturing paper was the attainment of the greatest breadth (*latitudo*) and thinness (*tenuitas*) consistent with toughness (*densitas*) and strength. Whiteness (*candor*) and smoothness of surface (*levitas*) were also desirable in papyrus paper. Pliny mentions nine varieties of paper. (*a*) The Augusta. This was the best quality known in Pliny's days, though previously the best quality had been called Hieratica. It was thirteen *digiti* (nine and one-half inches) wide. (*b*) The Livia. This was of the same breadth as the former, though the quality was somewhat inferior to it. (*c*) The Hieratica. This name was given to the third quality in the time of the Empire, probably after the death of Augustus. It was eleven *digiti* (eight inches) broad. (*d*) The Amphitheatrica. This was so called because of its being manufactured near the Amphitheatre of Alexandria. It was nine *digiti* (six and one-half inches) broad. (*e*) The Fanniana. This was the Amphitheatrica remade in Rome into a finer and broader paper. It was ten *digiti* (seven inches) broad. (*f*) The Saïtica, from Saïs, in Egypt, was eight *digiti* (five to six inches) broad. (*g*) The Taeniotica, named from a tongue (ταινία) of land near Alexandria. It was sold by weight and not by quality. (*h*) The Emporetica, which had a rough surface, and was used as wrapping-paper. It was six *digiti* (four and three-eighths inches) wide. (*i*) The Claudia. The emperor Claudius made a combination of the first two qualities by placing strips (*schidae*) of the first over those of the second, producing, thus, a new paper—better, in certain respects, than the Augusta. Claudius also increased the width until it reached a full Roman foot (eleven and one-half inches). The Claudia was preferred to all others, though the Augusta was still used for correspondence. The Claudia was of such a quality that both sides of the paper could be used (*opisthographa*). The usual custom was to write only on one side of the page (cf. Juv. i. 5; Mart. viii. 62; Pliny, *Epist.* iii. 5, 17).

For letters and documents single pages (*paginae*), termed *schidae* or *schidulae* (Mart. iv. 89), were used. However, even for these purposes, but particularly for books, a number of sheets were joined to form a roll (*volumen*). The length of these rolls varied from a few pages to a large number. The reading *vicenae* in Pliny (*H. N.* xiii. 77: *numquam plures scapo quam vicenae*) is corrupt. Birt suggests *ducenae*. Egyptian papyri have been found to vary in length from 70 to 140 feet. Birt considers 39 feet the average length of a classical book-roll. A roll containing the entire history of Thucydides, which required 578 pages, or a length of 265 feet, has been mentioned by the scholiast. In like manner a roll containing the *Iliad* and *Odyssey* of Homer, and another, the *Odyssey* of Livius Andronicus, are said to have existed. On the other hand, one literary work might be separated into smaller rolls. The fourth book of the *Rhetoric* of Philodemus was arranged in two rolls, and the Homeric papyrus of Elephantiné contained only the twenty-fourth book of the *Iliad*. The size of the volume corresponded to the character of the contents. Letters and poetry were written on small rolls; history, on rolls of larger size (Isidor. *Orig.* vi. 12, 1).

The first page of the roll was termed πρωτόκολλον (*protocollum*); the last, ἐσχατόκολλιον (Mart. 2, 6, 3). The term *macrocollum*, employed by Cicero in designating the paper used by himself (Cic. *Ad Att.* xiii. 25, xvi. 3), was applied in his time to the Hieratica and the finer grades of papyrus. Pliny's statement (*H. N.* xiii. 80, *Erat et cubitalis macrocollis*) means that the *macrocolla* might reach the breadth of a cubit (eighteen inches). To Pliny all kinds of paper superior in quality to the Saïtica were *macrocolla*. The writing was as a rule in columns, so that each page represented a column. The term σελίδες, originally of the rowing-benches of a galley, then of the columns of writing, finally was used as equivalent to *paginae*. The portion of the roll which marked the joining of the sheets was not used. However, in public documents before Caesar, the writing ran across the combined sheets, not in *paginis*, but *transversa charta* (cf. Suet. Caes. 56). Among the Ravenna diplomata of the fifth to the tenth centuries there are papyri written *transversa charta* (Marini, *Pap. Dipl.*).

The standard of measurement in a roll was the page (σελίς, *pagina*), as this was closely related to the size of the roll. The number of pages was regularly marked at the end of the book, but in some cases each page was numbered. In other rolls the number of pages is found on the *titulus*. In estimating the contents of a roll, it was customary to use lines as a standard of reckoning, not chapters or pages. This method of reckoning is the so-called stichometry. The number of lines (στίχοι and ἔπη, *versus*) in prose-writing and of verses in poetry was given at the close of the writing. This στίχος was the normal hexameter line of thirty-five letters on the average (Birt, p. 197), or sixteen syllables (Diels, *Herm.* xvii. p. 377 foll.). The normal hexameter verse required the broad papyrus, so that the lines of narrow pages were estimated only as parts of the normal line. Theopompus states the length of his orations as 20,000 ἔπη, and of his historical works as of 150,000 ἔπη; so the emperor Iustinian calculates 150,000 *versus* in his *De Confirmatione Digestorum*.

In making the rolls the last sheet was folded upon a strip of wood termed *umbilicus*, ὀμφαλός (cf. *ad umbilicum adducere*, "to finish a work," Hor. *Epod.* 14, 8; Mart. iv. 89). The ends of the *umbilicus* were gilded (Mart. iii. 2, 9), and the edges (*frons*) of the cylinder were polished (Ovid, *Trist.* iii. 1, 13; Mart. i. 67, 10; Catull. 22, 8) and coloured (*nigra frons*) (Ovid, *Trist.* i. 1, 8). The roll was stained with cedar-oil, as a protection against moths (Vitruv. ii. 9, 13; Mart. iii. 2); in consequence, the roll had a yellow colour (Ovid, *Trist.* iii. 1, 13). There was fastened to the roll a strip of parchment, which contained the title of the book. This was termed *titulus* or *index* (σίττυβος = a strip of leather, or σίλλυβος = an index). The roll was usually enveloped in a parchment cover (*membrana*, διφθέρα), outside of which the *titulus* hung. In the case of the papyri of Herculaneum the envelope itself was of papyrus. If several rolls belonged to the same work, it was customary to bind these in a bundle (*fasces*). In reading, the roll was held with both hands.

There are in existence to-day Egyptian papyri of great age. (See illustration, p. 28.) The oldest, the Prisse papyrus, which is kept in Paris, is estimated as dating from 1800 to 2000 years B.C. The earliest Greek papyri in existence, containing the fragments of the *Antiope* of Euripides, date about the second century B.C. Others dating from the last century B.C. contain orations of Lycophron and Euxenippus.

The earliest Latin papyri are those of Herculaneum, which certainly date from the early part of the first century A.D. After these come the deeds of Ravenna dating fifth–tenth century and papal documents of the eighth–tenth century. In 1752 there were discovered in the Villa Suburbana at Herculaneum a large number of blackened rolls which, though at first disregarded, were finally recognized as literary works. It was not until 1754 that any success was attained in opening the rolls. In that year a monk, Piaggio, unrolled what proved to be a portion of a work of Philodemus. (See De Jorio, *Officina de' Papiri, Real Museo Borbonico*, Naples, 1825.)

In the forty-eight years following only seventeen rolls were opened. The authorities of Naples took little interest in the matter, and the first publication did not appear until 1793. In 1800, George IV., then Prince of Wales, sent Bishop Hayter to Italy to copy the papyri. Bishop Hayter was driven from Italy in the French war of 1806, but managed to save one hundred lead-pencil fac-similes and an engraving of the *Carmen Latinum*. These are preserved in the Bodleian Library at Oxford. The British Museum possesses several opened and unopened rolls. This library on papyrus was found to contain the works of Epicurean philosophers — Epicurus, Demetrius, Polystratus, Colotes, and particularly of Philodemus; also notes on Chrysippus, the Stoic. There were found twenty-four Latin rolls all in one *capsa* (book-box). Of these Latin rolls only one, No. 817 (*Carmen Latinum de Bello Actiaco*), has been opened. (See page 1157.) As the larger number of the rolls appear to have been written by Philodemus, and as no rolls save the Latin are of later date than Philodemus, it is possible that the library originally belonged to him. The Latin rolls were probably a chance addition in the time of the early Empire to a library of an earlier date. Various opinions have been expressed as to the authorship of the *Carmen Latinum*. Varius or Rabirius, or a little-known Albinius, has at different times been mentioned as the author. It was, at any rate, the work of some insignificant poet of the early Empire. The following works contain the poem: Kreyssig, *Commentatio de Sallustii Historiae Fragmentis*, vol. iii. (1835); Riese, *Anthol. Lat.* vol. i. (1870); Baehrens, *Poetae Latini Minores*, vol. i. pp. 212 foll. (Leipzig, 1819): Baehrens used the Oxford plates loaned him by the Bodleian librarian; Comparetti, *Relazione sui Papiri Ercolanesi*: *Reale Acad. dei Lincei*, 1879; Spengel, *Die Hercul. Rollen* (*Philologus*, 1863, sup. vol.); Gompertz, *Hercul. Studien* (Leipzig, 1865–66); *Herculanensium Voluminum quae Supersunt* (Naples, 1793–1809, 2 vols. *Collectio altera*, 1862–76); Scott, *Fragmenta Herculanensia* (Oxford, 1885).

BIBLIOGRAPHY.—Guilandini, *Comment. in Plin. de Papyro Capita* (Venice, 1572); Montfaucon, *Diss. sur la Plante Appelée Papyrus* in *Mém. de l'Acad. d. Inscr.* vi. p. 592 foll.; Baumstark, *Pauly's Real-encycl.* v. p. 1154 foll.; Sprengel and Krause in Ersch and Gruber's *Encyclop.*; Parlatore, *Mém. de l'Acad. des Sciences*, xii. p. 469 foll. (Paris, 1854); Dureau de la Malle, "Mémoire sur le Papyrus et la Fabrication du Papier chez les Anciens," in *Mém. de l'Institut*, vol. xix. i. p. 140; Wilkinson, *Manners and Customs of the Ancient Egyptians*, vol. iii. pp. 146–151 (1837); Blümner, *Technologie und Terminologie der Gewerbe und Künste der Griechen und Römern*, vol. i. p. 308 foll.; Wattenbach, *Das Schriftwesen im Mittelalter*, p. 80 (1875); Marquardt, *Das Privatleben der Römern*, p. 784 foll. (1879); Birt, *Das antike Buchwesen* (1882); and the article "Papyrus" in the *Encyclopaedia Britannica*.

Parabăsis (παράβασις). A characteristic, though not indispensable, part of the chorus in the Old Attic comedy. About the middle of the piece, when the action of the play had been developed up to a certain point, the chorus, which had up to this time turned towards the actors on the stage, now turned to the audience. This stepping forward towards the audience is itself also termed *parabasis*. In this position they made an appeal to the public on behalf of the poet, who could thus give expression to his personal views and wishes, and offer advice, as well as explain the purport of his play, etc. This address stood wholly outside the action of the play. When the *parabasis* was complete, which was seldom the case, it consisted of seven parts, partly spoken by the leader of the chorus, partly sung by the chorus. One of these parts was called the *parabasis* in a narrower sense, and consisted chiefly of anapaestic tetrameters. One feature of the parabasis was the introduction of lines relating to topics of the day, which Professor Mahaffy has compared with the "topical songs" of the modern burlesque. See Müller, *Hist. of the Lit. of Ancient Greece*, Eng. trans. i. p. 401, and Professor Brander Matthews in *Classical Studies in Honour of Henry Drisler*, pp. 177–178 (N. Y. 1894).

Parabŏlon (παράβολον). A fee paid by the appellant on an appeal (ἔφεσις) from an arbitrator or magistrate to the dicasts, or from the Senate to the Assembly, or from the Assembly to the Heliasts (Pollux, viii. 62 foll.).

Paracatabŏlé (παρακαταβολή). A deposit required from a plaintiff or petitioner in certain cases as security that the complaint or demand was not a frivolous one. See *Att. Process*, ed. Lipsius, pp. 800, 814–822.

Paracatathēké (παρακαταθήκη) and **Parathēké** (παραθήκη). A deposit made with a friend or other person for the benefit of the owner of the deposit; as when money is deposited at the banker's on interest. An action brought to recover such property from the person holding it was called παρακαταθήκης δίκη. See *Att. Process*, ed. Lipsius, pp. 700 foll.

Paracheloītis (Παραχελωῖτις). The plain in Acarnania and Aetolia traversed by the river Achelоüs. See ACHELOÜS.

Parachoāthras (Παραχωάθρας). (1) A part of the mountain chain forming the boundary between

Susiana and Media. (2) Another part of the same range, forming the boundary between Parthia and the Desert of Carmania (Ptol. vi. 2, 3).

Paradīsus (*παράδεισος*). A word obtained by the Greeks from the Persians (Pollux, ix. 13), and applied by them to any park or plaisance which surrounded the country-houses of the Persian nobles. They were often of very great extent, and were usually stocked with wild animals for the chase, beautified by trees and streams, and enclosed by a wall. (Cf. Xen. *Anab.* i. 4, § 10; ii. 4, § 16; Gell. ii. 10). They were introduced into Greece at the time of the successes of Alexander. (See I. Müller's *Handbuch*, iv. p. 468.) For similar enclosures among the Romans, see VIVARIUM.

Paradoxa. A philosophical treatise of Cicero setting forth six striking theorems of the Stoic system. It was composed in B.C. 46. Edited by Orelli (with the Tusculans) (Zürich, 1829); and by Möser (Göttingen, 1846).

Paraetacēnē (Παραιτακηνή). (1) A mountainous region on the borders of Media and Persis (Arrian, iii. 19). (2) A district on the borders of Bactria and Sogdiana (Q. Curt. viii. 14)

Paraetonium (Παραιτόνιον) or **Ammonia** (Ἀμμωνία). An important city on the northern coast of Africa, belonging politically to Egypt: hence this city on the west and Pelusium on the east are called *cornua Aegypti*. The adjective *Paraetonius* is used by the poets in the general sense of Egyptian.

Paragrăphé (*παραγραφή*). An Attic law-term that may be approximately rendered "a plea"; an objection raised by the defendant to the admissibility of the plaintiff's action—not quite a "demurrer," which is an objection arising from the plaintiff's own statement of his case, but rather a "special plea" depending on facts set forth by the defendant himself. It was given in writing; and if it went further than a mere denial of the plaintiff's allegations, the issue raised by it was tried as a proceeding preliminary to the principal cause. It was, therefore, a means of delaying the case. See *Attische Process*, ed. Lipsius, pp. 849–854, 948.

Parăli (*πάραλοι*). "The people of the coastland." See ATTICA; SOLON.

Paralia. See ATTICA.

Parălus. See THEORIS.

Parălus (Πάραλος). The younger of the two legitimate sons of Pericles. He and his brother Xanthippus died in the great plague which afflicted Athens B.C. 429. The Athenians gave each brother the name of *βλιττομάμμας* or "booby." See Plutarch, *Pericles*, 24, 36.

Paranoias Diké (*παρανοίας δίκη*). A suit brought at Athens by a son or relation acting for a son against a person who had become mentally incapable of managing his own affairs. It therefore resembled our writ *de lunatico inquirendo*. If the suit was successful, the person against whom it was brought was inhibited from the further care of his property. Such a suit is said to have been instituted against the dramatic poet Sophocles; but see SOPHOCLES.

Paranŏmon Graphé (*παρανόμων γραφή*). An indictment brought against any person who proposed or carried an unconstitutional *ψήφισμα*, or law, whether its unconstitutionality consisted in form, contents, or both together. Such was the proposal of Androtion to award a crown to the outgoing senators, though they had failed to build the required number of triremes. This was improper as not having first been submitted to the Senate (Demosth. *C. Androt.* p. 594, § 5). A law was also unconstitutional if it contravened an existing law (Andoc. *De Myst.* § 87). The indictment could also be brought against one who proposed laws that were generally inexpedient or contrary to public policy (Poll. viii. 87). Any citizen might prefer the indictment, and if he declared on oath his intention of doing so this acted as a means of suspending the vote upon a proposed law; or if it had already been adopted, as a temporary suspension of its operation. If the indictment was sustained, the person proceeded against might suffer death or a fine, and his law was repealed; but if the person bringing the indictment failed to secure a fifth of the votes at the trial (as Aeschines did in his famous prosecution of Ctesiphon), he incurred a fine of 1000 drachmae and lost the right of instituting a similar prosecution in the future.

Paranymphus. The "best man" at a wedding. See MATRIMONIUM, p. 1013.

Parapetasma (*παραπέτασμα*). See VELUM.

Parapherna (*τὰ παράφερνα*). A term applied to whatever property a bride brought with her over and above her dower. See PHERNÉ; PROÏX

Parapotamii (Παραποτάμιοι). A town of Phocis, on the left bank of the river Cephissus. It was destroyed by Xerxes in the Persian War, but later rebuilt, only to be again destroyed in the Sacred War (Herod. viii. 33; Pausan. x. 3, 1).

Parapresbeia (*παραπρεσβεία*). A Greek term used of any corrupt conduct or neglect of duty on the part of an ambassador (*πρέσβυς, πρεσβυτής*). For such misfeasance he was liable to be recalled and prosecuted (Demosth. *De Falsa Leg.* p. 430, § 278 foll.). Ambassadors who acted contrary to their instructions were liable to such a charge, but on their recall first made a report to the Senate and then to the Assembly, where, if their defence seemed satisfactory, they received a vote of thanks and an invitation to dinner in the Prytaneum. See Aeschin. *De Falsa Leg.* §§ 45, 53.

Parasanga (*παρασάγγης*). A parasang; a Persian measure of distance equal to thirty stadia (Herod. vi. 42) or some 3½ or 4 English miles. The length of the parasang varied in later times (Pliny, *H. N.* vi. 30), but the name survives in the modern Persian *farsang*, in which distances are still reckoned in Asia, and which is approximately the same as that of the time of Herodotus.

Parascenium (*παρασκήνιον*) and **Parascenia** (*παρασκήνια*). The space at the sides of the stage. See THEATRUM.

Parasēmon (*παράσημον*). See INSIGNÉ.

Parasītus (*παράσιτος*, "table companion"). A word which among the Greeks denoted originally the priest's assistant, who, like the priest, received his support from the offerings made to the temple, in return for certain services. These services included the collection and care of supplies of corn due to the temple, assistance at certain sacrifices, and the preparation of the banquets connected with certain festivals. The assistants of civil officials, who were maintained at the expense of the State, were also called parasites in many places. The word received another meaning in the Middle and New Greek comedy, where it means the hanger on, who plays the flatterer and buffoon, with a view to getting invited to dinner. The parasite was transferred as a standing character to the Roman imitations of Greek comedy, and figures largely in the plays of Plautus. Good examples of the stage parasite will be found in his *Captivi* and *Menaechmi* and in the *Phormio* of Terence. See Know, *Die Parasiten bei den Griechen* (1876).

Parăstas (*παραστάς*). See ANTAE.

Parastătae (*παραστάται*). Officials who served under the Eleven at Athens, as jailers, executioners, or torturers. See HENDEKA.

Paravaei (Παραύαιοι). A tribe of Epirus on the Aoüs (Thuc. ii. 80).

Parazonium. See ZONA.

Parcae. See MOERAE.

Parechēsis. See RHYME.

Parĕdri (*πάρεδροι*). "Assessors"; officers at Athens attached to the three chief archons, the euthyni and the Hellenotamiae. Each of the three archons had the right to two assessors, whom he chose himself as advisers and general assistants; and they were usually his personal friends. Before entering upon their duties, the paredri had to pass an examination (*δοκιμασία*) in the Senate and also before a commission of judges. Besides acting as advisers of the archons, etc., the paredri had authority to keep order in the theatres and at the public festivals, and could punish the disorderly with fines (Demosth. *C. Mid.* p. 572, § 179). Paredri might be dismissed by their principals for cause. See Gilbert, *Greek Constit. Antiq.*, Eng. trans. pp. 225, 228, 252, 254, 255; and EUTHYNA; HELLENOTAMIAE.

Parengrapti (*παρέγγραπτοι*) and **Parengrăphi** (*παρέγγραφοι*). A term given at Athens to those whose names were enrolled among the citizens without their being such by birth (*φύσει*) or special grant (*δωρεᾷ*). Such a person might be prosecuted by any Athenian citizen, the prosecution being called *ξενίας γραφή*, and if condemned his person and property were forfeited to the State, and he was sold as a slave (Demosth. *Epist.* iii. p. 1481, § 28). The *δημόται* had authority to strike from the rolls any such person who, if he acquiesced in their action, was merely relegated to the position of an alien; but if he appealed to the dicasts, and they refused to sustain his appeal, the heavier penalty was enforced.

Parentalia. The general festival in honour of deceased relatives, celebrated by the Romans from February 13th to 21st. See FUNUS; MANES; SEPULCRUM.

Parian Chronicle (Χρονικὸν Παριανόν, or MARMOR PARIUM). A marble tablet found at Paros in 1627, now placed among the Arundel Marbles in the University Galleries at Oxford. It is written chiefly in the Attic, but partly in the Ionian dialect, and consists of ninety-three lines, some of which are no longer complete. It originally contained a number of dates of the political, but chiefly of the religious and literary, history of the Greeks, from the Athenian king Cecrops to the Athenian archon Diognetus, B.C. 264; in its present condition, however, it only goes down to B.C. 354. All the dates are given according to Attic kings and archons, and the historical authorities on which it depends must have been Attic authors. The origin and aim of the tablet are unknown. It was first published by Selden in 1628; it has since been printed by Boeckh (*C. I. G.* ii. 2374), who considers the leading authority followed to be Phanias of Eresus.

Paries (*τοῖχος*). A wall belonging to a roofed building and thus distinguished from *murus* (q. v.). PARIES SOLĬDUS is a wall unpierced by doors or windows. PARIES COMMŪNIS is a party-wall common to two houses. PARIES DIRECTUS is a cross-wall between rooms. PARIES FORNICĀTUS is a wall pierced by arches.

Parietarian Inscriptions. See GRAFFITI.

Parilia. See PALILIA.

Par Impar Ludĕre (*ἀρτιασμός, ἄρτια ἢ περιττὰ παίζειν, ζυγὰ ἢ ἀζυγὰ παίζειν, ζυγὰ μόνα παίζειν*, or *ποσίνδα*). The game of "odd or even," much played by both Greeks and Romans. A person held in his hand a number of dice, nuts, coins, or other objects, and his opponent guessed whether the number of them was odd or even. The amount won or lost was either the objects themselves or a sum of money staked upon the guess (Pollux, ix. 101; Apollon. iii. 115; Aristoph. *Plut.* 816; Becker-Göll, *Gallus*, iii. 477).

Paris (Πάρις), also called **Alexander** (Ἀλέξανδρος). The second son of Priam, king of Troy, by his wife Hecuba. When his mother, being about to give birth to a son, had dreamed that she brought forth a torch which set all Ilium in flames, the soothsayer Aesacus declared that the child would prove the ruin of his country, and recommended its exposure (Eurip. *Andr.* 298; Cic. *Div.* i. 21). As soon as born, the child was given to a servant to be left on Ida to perish. He obeyed, but, on returning at the end of five days, he found that a bear had been nursing the infant. Struck with this strange event, he took home the infant, reared him as his own son, and named him Paris. When Paris grew up he distinguished himself by his strength and courage in repelling robbers from the flocks, and the shepherds, in consequence, named him Alexander ("Man-protector"), or, according to the Greek form, Ἀλέξανδρος (*ἀπὸ τοῦ ἀλέξειν τοὺς ἄνδρας*). In this state of seclusion, too, he united himself to the nymph Oenoné, whose fate is elsewhere related. (See OENONÉ.) Their happiness was soon disturbed. At the marriage of Peleus and Thetis, the goddess of Discord, who had not been invited to partake of the entertainment, showed her displeasure by throwing into the assembly of the gods who were at the wedding celebration a golden apple, on which were written the words Ἡ *καλὴ λαβέτω*, "Let the beauty (among you) take me." Heré, Athené, and Aphrodité laying claim to it, and Zeus being unwilling to decide, the god commanded Hermes to lead the three deities to Mount Ida, and to intrust the decision of the affair to the shepherd Alexander, whose judgment was to be final. The goddesses appeared before him, and each, to influence his decision, made him an alluring offer of future advantage, Heré by the promise of a kingdom, Athené by the gift of intellectual superiority and martial renown, and Aphrodité by offering him the fairest woman in the world for his wife. To Aphrodité he assigned the prize, and brought upon

Paris. (Aeginetan Marbles.)

himself, in consequence, the unrelenting enmity of her two disappointed rivals, which was extended also to his whole family and the entire Trojan race.

Soon after this event, Priam proposed a contest among his sons and other princes, and promised to reward the conqueror with one of the finest bulls on Mount Ida. Persons were sent to procure the animal, and it was found in the possession of Paris, who reluctantly yielded it up. The shepherd, desirous of obtaining again this favourite animal, went to Troy, and entered the lists of the combatants. Having proved successful against every competitor, and having gained an advantage over Hector himself, that prince, irritated at seeing himself conquered by an unknown stranger, pursued him closely, and Paris must have fallen a victim to his brother's resentment had he not fled to the altar of Zeus. This place of refuge preserved his life; and Cassandra, the daughter of Priam, struck with the similarity of the features of Paris to those of her brothers, inquired his birth and his age. From these circumstances she soon discovered that he was her brother, and as such she introduced him to her father and to his children. Priam, thereupon, forgetful of the alarming predictions of Aesacus, acknowledged Paris as his son, and all enmity instantly ceased between the newcomer and Hector. Not long after this, at the instigation of Aphroditē, who had not forgotten her promise to him, Paris proceeded on a voyage to Greece, from which the soothsaying Helenus and Cassandra had in vain endeavoured to deter him. The ostensible object of the voyage was to procure information respecting his father's sister Hesionē, who had been given in marriage by Hercules to his follower Telamon, the monarch of Salamis. The real motive, however, which prompted the enterprise, was a wish to obtain, in the person of Helen, then the fairest woman of her time, a fulfilment of what Aphroditē had offered him when he was deciding the contest of beauty. Arriving at Sparta, where Menelaüs, the husband of Helen, was reigning, he met with a hospitable reception; but, Menelaüs soon after having sailed away to Crete, the Trojan prince availed himself of his absence, seduced Helen, and bore her away to his native city, together with a large portion of the wealth of her husband. Hence ensued the war of Troy, which ended in the total destruction of that ill-fated city. See TROJAN WAR.

Paris, though represented in general as effeminate and vain of his personal appearance, yet distinguished himself during the siege of Troy by wounding Diomedes, Machaon, Antilochus, and Palamedes, and subsequently by discharging the dart which proved fatal to Achilles. Aphroditē took him under her special protection, and, in the single combat with Menelaüs, rescued him from the vengeance of the latter. On the capture of Troy, Paris was wounded by Philoctetes with one of the arrows of Heracles, and, falling ill, returned to Oenonē, whom he had so long before abandoned. Resenting her wrongs she refused to heal him, and he returned to Troy, where he died.

Paris. (1) A pantomimic actor in the reign of Nero, who greatly liked him and issued a special edict declaring him free-born (*ingenuus*), though in reality he had been the slave of the emperor's aunt, Domitia, and had purchased his freedom with a large sum of money. Later, when Nero himself began acting in pantomimes, he became jealous of the superior art of Paris and put him to death (Tac. *Ann.* xiii. 19–27; Suet. *Nero*, 54). (2) An actor at Rome in the reign of Domitian, whose favourite he was until detected in an intrigue with the empress Domitia, when he was put to death (Dio Cass. lxvii. 3; Suet. *Domit.* 3, 10).

Parisii. Paris. See LUTETIA PARISIORUM.

Parium (Πάριον). A city of Mysia, on the Propontis, founded by a colony from Miletus, Paros, and Erythrae. It was known for its local worship of Apollo, Dionysus, and Eros. Under Augustus it was made a Roman colony.

Parma. Now Parma. A town in Gallia Cispadana, situated on a river of the same name, between Placentia and Mutina, on the Via Aemilia; originally a town of the Boii, but made a Roman colony B.C. 183. It was celebrated for its wool (Mart. xiv. 155).

Parma. The circular leathern shield of the Roman light infantry. See CLIPEUS.

Parmenīdes (Παρμενίδης). A Greek philosopher and poet, born of an illustrious family about B.C. 510, at Elea in Lower Italy. He was held in high esteem by his fellow-citizens on account of his excellent legislation, to which they ascribed the prosperity and wealth of the town; and also on account of his exemplary life. A "Parmenidean life" was proverbial among the Greeks (Cebes, *Tabula*, 2). Little more is known of his biography than that he stopped at Athens on a journey in his sixty-fifth year, and there became acquainted with the youthful Socrates. He is the chief representative of the Eleatic philosophy. Like his great teacher, Xenophanes, he also formulated his philosophical views in a didactic poem, *On Nature* (Περὶ Φύσεως), the form of which was considered inartistic (Cic. *Acad.* ii. 74). According to the proëm, which has been preserved (while we only possess fragments of the rest), the work consisted of two divisions. The first treated of the truth, the second of the world of illusion; that is, the world of the senses and the erroneous opinions of mankind founded upon them. In his opinion truth lies in the perception that existence is, and error in the idea that non-existence also can be. Nothing can have real existence but what is conceivable; therefore to be imagined and to be able to exist are the same thing, and there is no development; the essence of what is conceivable is incapable of development, imperishable, immutable, unbounded, and indivisible; what is various and mutable, all development, is a delusive phantom; perception is thought directed to the pure essence of being; the phenomenal world is a delusion, and the opinions formed concerning it can only be improbable. The best edition of the fragments is that in Karsten's *Philosophorum Graecorum Reliquiae* (Amsterdam, 1835). They have been rendered into English hexameter by T. Davidson (*Journal of Speculative Philosophy*, St. Louis, 1870), and paraphrased in prose by Courtney in his *Studies in Philosophy* (1882). See PHILOSOPHIA.

Parmenion (Παρμενίων). (1) The son of Philotas, a distinguished Macedonian general in the service of Philip of Macedon and Alexander the Great. Philip held him in high esteem, and used to say of him that he had never been able to find more than one general, and that was Parmenion. In Alexander's invasion of Asia, Parmenion was regarded as second in command. At the three great battles of the Granicus, Issus, and Arbela, while the king commanded the right wing of the army, Parmenion was placed at the head of the left, and contributed essentially to the victory on all those memorable occasions. The confidence reposed in him by Alexander appears to have been unbounded, and he is continually spoken of as the most attached of the king's friends, and as holding, beyond all question, the second place in the State. But when Philotas, the only surviving son of Parmenion, was accused in Drangiana (B.C. 330) of being privy to the plot against the king's life, he not only confessed his own guilt, when put to the torture, but involved his father also in the plot. Whether the king really believed in the guilt of Parmenion, or deemed his life a necessary sacrifice to policy after the execution of his son, he caused his aged friend to be assassinated in Media before the latter could receive the tidings of his son's death. The death of Parmenion, at the age of seventy years, will ever remain one of the darkest stains upon the character of Alexander. It is questionable whether even Philotas was really concerned in the conspiracy, and we may safely pronounce that Parmenion had no connection with it. (2) Of Macedonia, an epigrammatic poet, whose verses were included in the collection of Philip of Thessalonica; whence it is probable that he flourished in, or shortly before, the time of Augustus.

Parmularius. A gladiator who carried the small shield known as the *parma* (Suet. *Domit.* 10).

Parnassus (Παρνασσός). A name applied (1) to a range of mountains extending from Oeta and Corax southeast through Doris and Phocis, and terminating at the Corinthian Gulf between Cirrha and Anticyra where it was called Cirphis (Κίρφις); and (2) to the highest part of the range a little north of Delphi (q. v.), where it attains an elevation of some 8000 English feet. Its twin peaks are called Tithorea (Τιθορέα) and Lycorea (Λυκώρεια). Here the mountain forms a crescent-shaped curve of cliffs, known as Φαιδριάδες or "the resplendent," since they face south and receive the full rays of the sun during the heat of the day. On the southern slope of Parnassus lay Delphi. The modern name is Liákoura.

On the sides of Parnassus were many caves, romantic grottoes, and ravines, and it was regarded as a principal abode of Apollo and the Muses. On Mount Lycorea was the Corycian cave of the latter, and just above Delphi lay the famous Castalian spring flowing from between the two cliffs known as Nauplia and Hyamplia. Between Parnassus proper and Mount Cirphis was the valley of the Plistus, with the sacred road which ran from Delphi to Daulis and Stiris. At the branch of this road where the two ways parted, Oedipus slew his father Laïus. See OEDIPUS.

(3) A town in northwestern Cappadocia, between Ancyra and Archelaïs.

Parnes (Πάρνης). A mountain in the northeastern part of Attica, was a continuation of Mount Cithaeron, and formed part of the boundary between Boeotia and Attica. It was well wooded, abounded in game, and on its lower slopes produced excellent wine. On the summit were altars and a statue of Zeus (Pausan. i. 32, 1).

Parnon (Πάρνων). A mountain which separated Laconia from the Arcadian district Tegeatis. Its height is about 6500 feet.

Parŏchi. Commissaries employed by the Roman State to furnish all necessary supplies to officials who were travelling on public business. They were distributed among the chief posting-stations throughout Italy and the provinces. (See CURSUS PUBLICUS; MANSIO.) A law passed in B.C. 59 by Iulius Caesar defined the supplies which these persons were compelled to furnish, and limited them to the barest necessaries, such as firewood, shelter, beds, etc. See Hor. *Sat.* i. 5, 46; Cic. *Ad Att.* v. 16; xiii. 2; Marquardt, *Privatleben der Römer*, 199.

Parodia (παρῳδία). Parody, burlesque. Parody among the Greeks is ascribed by Aristotle to Hegemon of Thasos (*Poët.* ii. 5; Athen. 698 B), who flourished at the time of the Peloponnesian War, and is frequently cited by Athenaeus, who mentions his nickname of Φακῆ or "Lentil." His parodies are based upon the Greek epics which he burlesqued. Mention is especially made of his parody of the *Gigantomachia.* (See Athen. i. p. 5; iii. p. 108; ix. pp. 406–407; and Meineke, *Hist. Crit. Com. Graec.* pp. 214–215.) Another Greek, Matron of Pitana, wrote burlesques of Homer, from one of which Athenaeus has preserved a long fragment which parodies the beginning of the *Odyssey.* He flourished in the fourth century B.C. (See Athen. iv. pp. 134–137; Eustath. *ad* Hom. pp. 1067, 1571, etc., and the monograph by Moser, *Ueber Matron den Parodiker* in Daub and Kreuzer's *Studien*, vi. pp. 293 foll.). Matron gave a gastronomical turn to his fun, as the first line of the passage mentioned above plainly shows:

Δεῖπνα μοι ἔννεπε, Μοῦσα, πολύτροφα καὶ μάλα πολλά.

In this he was followed by Archestratus of Gela, whose Ἡδυπάθεια was afterwards translated into Latin by Ennius. Another famous Homeric parody is the *Batrachomyomachia* or "Battle of the Frogs and Mice," commonly ascribed to Pigres. See BATRACHOMYOMACHIA; HOMERUS.

The philosophical writers were parodied first by Timon of Phlius, a skeptic of the school of Pyrrho (about B.C. 280), who was a writer of very great ability. His parodies were known as *Silli* (Σίλλοι), a word of uncertain derivation, and were in three books, partly in dialogue, and written in hexameters in the epic style. They ridiculed the dogmatic philosophers, but also parodied the Homeric language, as in the following line in imitation of *Iliad*, ii. 484:

Ἔσπετε νῦν μοι ὅσοι πολυπράγμονές ἐστε σοφισταί.

Some have ascribed the *Silli* to Xenophanes of Colophon as the originator whom Timon introduces in his dialogue, but of this there is no definite proof. These compositions by Timon were regarded by the Greeks as so important that commentaries were afterwards written on him, notably by Apollonides of Nicaea; and were imitated by various writers, such as Sotades, Blaesus, Salerias, and Sopater of Paphos. See Diog. Laërt. ix. ch. 12; Brunck, *Analecta*, ii. pp. 67 foll.; Langenreich, *Dissertationes Tres de Timone Sillographo* (Leipzig, 1720–21); Wölcke, *De Graecorum Sillis* (Berlin, 1820); and F. Paul, *De Sillis* (Berlin, 1821).

Burlesques of the dramatic writers were apparently first written by Rhinthon (q. v.) of Tarentum (or Syracuse), whose thirty-eight dramas parodied the classic tragedy and gave rise to the so-called ἱλαροτραγῳδία, which became very popular among the Greeks of Southern Italy. Rhinthon belongs to the Ptolemaic period, and therefore lies beyond the domain of classic Greek literature; but the comedies of Aristophanes contain many scenes that are evidently written in mockery of the tragedians and that contain many touches of subtle banter.

Among the Romans parody was early written, the most complete specimen that we have being the *Amphitruo* of Plautus, which is the only remaining model that we have of the Rhinthonic play. The burlesque epic is well represented in the pseudo-Vergilian *Culex* (q. v.). Bucolic poetry was ridiculed in the *Antibucolica* of one Numitorius, who in them poked fun at Vergil's *Eclogues* (Serv. *ad Ecl.* vi. 43). A line or two of these have been preserved—e. g. the following in ridicule of *Ecl.* i. 1:

Tityre si toga calda tibi, quo tegmine fagi?

Parody flourished most, however, in the period of the decline. The first satire of Persius parodies a number of lines from the popular poetry of the day; and Juvenal occasionally amuses himself by burlesquing a Vergilian line, as in i. 25, which recalls Verg. *Ecl.* i. 28; and he often falls into the mock-heroic vein, as did Horace at times. (Cf. Hor. *Sat.* i. 5, 9–10; 53; Juv. iv. 58.) Petronius burlesqued the *improvvisatori*. Legal forms are ridiculed in the *Testamentum Porcelli* ("Last Will and Testament of a Little Pig"); and in the *Lex Tappula* of the strange humorist Valerius Valentinus. See Fest. 363; Bücheler, *Bonner Ind. Lect.* (1877); Ribbeck, *Römische Dichter*, i. 232.

In modern times burlesques of classical subjects were made popular by Scarron in his *Virgile Travestié*, which was the first of a number of such works, most of them, however, being very dreary.

See Moser in *Heidelb. Studien*, vi. 2, pp. 267 foll., and Delapierre, *La Parodie chez les Grecs, les Romains, et les Modernes* (London, 1871).

Parodos (πάροδος). A technical term of the Greek drama, used to denote (1) the entrance of the chorus upon the orchestra; (2) the song which they sang while entering; (3) the passage by which they entered. See CHORUS; THEATRUM.

Paronomasia. See PUNS.

Paropamīsus (Παροπάμισος). The part of the great chain of mountains in Central Asia lying between the Sariphi Mountains (Mountains of Kohistan) on the west and Mount Imaus (Himalaya) on the east, or from about the sources of the river Margus on the west to the point where the Indus breaks through the chain on the east. The Greeks sometimes called them the Indian Caucasus (*Caucasus Indicus*), a name which has come down to our times in the native form of Hindu Kush. Its inhabitants were called Paromisadae or Paropanisii, the former name being also given to their territory, which was approximately the eastern part of Afghanistan and part of the Punjab west of the Indus.

Paropsis. See CATINUS.

Parorēa (Παρώρεια). (1) A town in Thrace on the frontiers of Macedonia. (2) A town in Southern Arcadia, founded by Paroreus, the grandson of Lycaon (Pausan. viii. 27, 3; 35, 6).

Parorios. See PHRYGIA.

Paros (Πάρος). An island in the Aegaean Sea, one of the larger of the Cyclades, was situated south of Delos and west of Naxos, being separated from the latter by a channel five or six miles wide. It is about thirty-six miles in circumference. It was inhabited by Ionians, and became so prosperous, even at an early period, as to send out colonies to Thasos and to Parium on the Propontis. In the first invasion of Greece by the generals of Darius, Paros submitted to the Persians; and after the battle of Marathon Miltiades attempted to reduce the island, but failed in his attempt, and received a wound of which he died. (See MILTIADES.)

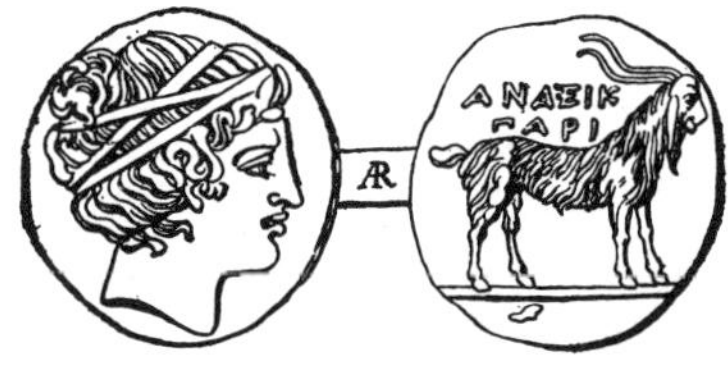

Coin of Paros.

After the defeat of Xerxes, Paros came under the supremacy of Athens, and shared the fate of the other Cyclades. The most celebrated production of Paros was its marble, which was extensively used by the ancient sculptors. It was chiefly obtained from a mountain called Marpessa. Paros was the birthplace of the poet Archilochus.

In Paros was discovered the celebrated inscription called the Parian Chronicle (q. v.). The modern name of the island is Paro. See Becker, *De Paro Insula* (1868).

Parrhasia (Παρρασία). A district in the south of Arcadia. The adjective *Parrhasius* is frequently used by the poets as equivalent to Arcadian.

Parrhasius (Παρράσιος). A famous Greek painter of Ephesus, who with Zeuxis was the chief representative of the Ionic school. He lived about B.C. 400 at Athens, where he seems to have received the citizenship. According to the accounts of ancient writers, he first introduced into painting the theory of human proportions, gave to the face delicate shades of expression, and was a master in the careful drawing of contours (Pliny, *H. N.* xxxv. 67, 68). His skill in indicating varieties of psychological expression could be appreciated in the picture representing the Athenian State or Δῆμος, in which, according to ancient authors, he distinctly portrayed all the conflicting qualities of the Athenian national character. Another of his pictures represented two boys, one of whom seemed to personify the pertness, and the other the simplicity, of boyhood. His inclination to represent excited states of mind is attested by the choice of subjects like the feigned madness of Odysseus, and the anguish of Philoctetes in Lemnos. His supposed contest with Zeuxis is well known. The grapes painted by Zeuxis deceived the birds, which flew to peck at them; while the curtain painted by Parrhasius deceived Zeuxis himself (Pliny, ib. 65). See PICTURA; ZEUXIS.

Parricidium. (According to the usual, but very doubtful explanation derived from *patricidium*, "murder of a father," but better from *par+caedo*, the murder of a peer, i. e. a citizen). A term used among the Romans for the murder of any relative with whom one is united by bonds of blood or duty, but sometimes also for treason and rebellion against one's country. In earlier times the examination in trials for homicide was conducted by two *quaestores parricidii*, on whom it was also incumbent to bring the accusation before the comitia for trial. Sulla transferred the decision in all cases of parricide to a standing tribunal (see QUAESTIO PERPETUA), which had also to try cases of assassination and poisoning. The punishment for parricide was drowning in a leathern sack (*culleus*), into which were sewn, besides the criminal, a dog, a cock, a viper, and an ape (Cic. *Rosc. Am.* 70; Juv. viii. 214). The murder of relations in other degrees of relationship was punished by exile (*interdictio aquae et ignis*). See EXSILIUM; INTERDICTIO.

Parsii. One of the tribes comprising the Pampamisadae. See PARAPAMISUS.

Parthēni. See PATHINI.

Partheniae (παρθενίαι). A word meaning literally "children of unmarried women," but usually applied to a distinct class of citizens at Sparta after the First Messenian War. The tradition goes that after the Messenian War had lasted a number of years, the Spartan women sent an embassy to the camp to the effect that they were weary of so long an abstention from the pleasures of married life, and representing also that the State would suffer if the increase of population should cease. Their husbands, who had taken an oath not to return home until the Messenians were conquered, sent back all the young men who were in camp with permission to cohabit with the maidens at Sparta. The children thus begotten were called παρθενίαι; and after the return of the army from the war, these were not treated as citizens, and therefore joined the Helots for a war against the ruling class. This, however, appearing impracticable, they migrated to Italy, where they founded the colony of Tarentum. (See Ephorus *ap.* Strabo, vi. p. 279, and cf. the article EPEUNACTI.) Hesychius, on the other hand, says that the Partheniae were the children of Spartan citizens and female slaves; and Antiochus that they were the sons of those Spartans who took no part in the Messenian War, and who were in consequence degraded to the position of Helots. See Grote, *Hist. of Greece*, i. p. 332; iii. p. 519.

Parthenium (Παρθένιον). (1) A town in Mysia, south of Pergamum. (2) A promontory in the Chersonesus Taurica, on which stood a temple of the Tauric Artemis, from whom it derived its name. It was in this temple that human sacrifices were offered to the goddess. See TAURI.

Parthenium Maré (τὸ Παρθενικὸν πέλαγος). The southeastern part of the Mediterranean Sea between Egypt and Cyprus (Ammian. Marc. xiv. 8, 10).

Parthenius (Παρθένιος). A Greek grammarian and poet, of Nicaea in Bithynia, who was brought captive to Rome during the war with Mithridates. After his release, he lived there till the time of Tiberius, esteemed as a scholar and poet, especially as a writer of elegiac verse. He was acquainted with Vergil, whom he taught Greek, and one of his poems is said to have been the model for the *Moretum* (q. v.); but he was more closely connected with the elegiac poet, Cornelius Gallus. For Gallus he composed the only work of his which has survived, under the title, *Erotic Experiences* (Περὶ Ἐρωτικῶν Παθημάτων). This is a collection of thirty-six prose stories of unhappy lovers, compiled from ancient poets, especially from those of the Alexandrian school. They are in reality only sketches and were intended to be developed by Gallus into poems of passion. Apart from the light which the work throws on the Alexandrine poets, of whose productions it contains fragments, it has a special interest as a precursor of the Greek novel. Edited by Hirschig in the Didot collection (Paris, 1856). See NOVELS AND ROMANCES.

Parthĕnon (Παρθενών, "the maiden's chamber"), particularly a temple of Athené Parthenos (the virgin goddess), especially that on the Acropolis of Athens, distinguished by the grandeur of its dimensions, the beauty of its execution, and the splendour of its artistic adornment; so that it is usually regarded as the most perfect specimen of Grecian architecture. There was an earlier temple of Athené immediately to the south of the Erechtheum (see plan under ACROPOLIS), and the foundations of a new temple were laid after the Persian War, probably in the time of Cimon. This temple was never completed; on the same site there was built a temple of less length, but greater breadth, which is usually called the Parthenon. It was built at the command of Pericles by the architects Ictinus and Callicrates. It took about five years in building, and was finished in B.C. 438. Its further adornment with sculptures in the pediments, and with metopes and frieze was completed under the direction of Phidias, who himself took part in the work. The temple, built wholly of Pentelic marble, is 65 feet high. The στυλοβάτης, or platform, on which the columns stand, is 228 feet in length, and 101 feet in breadth ($=225 \times 100$ in Attic feet, giving 9 : 4 as the ratio of length to breadth). Under the stylobate is the κρηπίδωμα, or basis proper, formed of three steps resting on a massive substructure, 250 feet long and 105 feet broad, and founded on the rock at the highest part of the plateau of the Acropolis. The temple is peripteral, its walls being entirely surrounded by a colonnade of forty-six Doric columns, about 35 feet high, eight at each end, and fifteen on each side. The architrave from the first was adorned with ninety-two metopes sculptured in high relief. Shields and votive inscriptions were subsequently placed there by Alexander the Great, in B.C. 338 (Plut. *Alex.* 16). The subjects were: on the east,

The Parthenon in 1892. (From a Photograph.)

the battle of the gods and giants; on the south, that of the Centaurs and Lapithae; on the west, the victory of the Athenians over the Amazons; and on the north, the destruction of Troy. The sculptures of the eastern pediment represented the birth of the goddess, those of the western the strife of Athené with Poseidon for the possession of Attica. These pediments are 93 feet long, and 11 feet 4 inches high. The *cella*, or temple proper, is 194 feet long, and 69½ feet wide, with six columns at each end, 33 feet in height. Opposite the outermost columns at each end are *antae*, formed by the prolongation of the side walls of the *cella* (see plan under ACROPOLIS). Along the top of the outer wall of the *cella* ran a continuous frieze, 524 feet in length, with representations of the Panathenaic procession carved in very low relief. At the east end of the *cella*, the *pronaos*, or portico, led into the eastern chamber, which was 100 Greek feet in length, and was therefore called the ἑκατόμπεδος. It was divided longitudinally into three parts by two rows of nine columns each, and above these was a second row of columns forming an upper story. The central space was open to the sky (hypaethral). At its western end, under a protecting canopy, stood the statue of the goddess, wrought in gold and ivory, the masterpiece of Phidias (see ATHENÉ, near the end). The western chamber of the *cella* was fronted by a portico, and was called by the special name of the Parthenon. Within this smaller chamber were kept vessels for use in the sacred processions, with various small articles of gold or silver. Modern writers have hitherto generally identified this small chamber with the ὀπισθόδομος (lit. back-chamber), which was used as the treasury, or State bank, of Athens; but it is held by Dörpfeld that this term should be confined to the corresponding chamber of the early temple south of the Erechtheum.

In the Middle Ages the temple was converted into a church, dedicated to the Virgin Mary, and then into a mosque, and remained in good preser-

From the Frieze of the Parthenon.

vation till 1687. In that year, during the siege of Athens by the Venetians, the building was blown up by a bomb which fell into a powder magazine that the Turks had stored there, and, with the exception of the two pediments, it was almost completely destroyed. Most of the sculptures preserved from the pediments and metopes, and from the frieze of the temple chamber, are now among the Elgin Marbles (q. v.) in the British Museum. See Michaelis, *Der Parthenon*, with plates (1875); and the Dilettanti Society's *Athenian Architecture* (2d ed. 1889). See ATHENAE.

Parthenopaeus (Παρθενοπαῖος). One of the Seven against Thebes (q. v.). He was the son of Ares (or Milanion) and Atalanta, or of Talaüs and Lysimaché. His son, variously styled Promachus, Stratolaüs, Thesimenes, or Tlesimenes, was one of the Epigoni (q. v.).

Parthenŏpé (Παρθενόπη). See NEAPOLIS.

Parthia (Παρθία), **Parthyaea** (Παρθυαία), and **Parthyēné** (Παρθυηνή). A country, southeast of the Caspian Sea, in Asia. Its extent varied greatly at different times, and the name is often used indefinitely by the ancient writers; but it may be regarded as bordering upon Hyrcania, Asia, Carmania, Persis, Susiana, and Media. It was largely a mountainous and semi-desert country, whose people were noted warriors, celebrated especially for their skill in archery and horsemanship. Their tactics, of which the Romans had fatal experience in their first wars with them, became so celebrated as to pass into a proverb. Their mail-clad horsemen spread like a cloud around the hostile army, and poured in a shower of darts; and then evaded any closer conflict by a rapid flight, during which they still shot their arrows backward upon the enemy.

Under the Persian Empire, the Parthians, with the Chorasmii, Sogdii, and Arii, formed the sixteenth satrapy: under Alexander and the Greek kings of Syria, Parthia and Hyrcania together formed a satrapy. About B.C. 250 they revolted from the Seleucidae, under a chieftain named Arsaces, who founded an independent monarchy, the history of which is given under ARSACES. During the period of the downfall of the Syrian kingdom, the Parthians overran the provinces east of the Euphrates, and about B.C. 130 they overthrew the kingdom of Bactria, so that their empire extended over Asia from the Euphrates to the Indus, and from the Indian Ocean to the Paropamisus, or even to the Oxus; but on this northern frontier they had to maintain a continual conflict with the nomad tribes of Central Asia. On the west their progress was checked by Mithridates and Tigranes, till those kings fell successively before the Romans, who were thus brought into collision with the Parthians. After the memorable destruction of Crassus and his army, B.C. 53 (see CRASSUS, p. 424), the Parthians threatened Syria and Asia Minor; but their progress was stopped by two signal defeats, which they suffered from Antony's legate Ventidius, in 39 and 38. The preparations for renewing the war with Rome were rendered fruitless by the contest for the Parthian throne between Phraates IV. and Tiridates, which led to an appeal to Augustus, and to the restoration of the standards of Crassus, B.C. 20; an event to which the Roman poets often allude in terms of flattery to Augustus, almost as if he had conquered the Parthian Empire. It is to be observed that the poets of the Augustan Age use the names Parthi, Persae, and Medi indifferently.

Parthians. (From a Roman Coin.)

Coin of Arsaces.

The Parthian Empire had now begun to decline, owing to civil contests and the defection of the governors of provinces, and had ceased to be formidable to the Romans. There were, however, continual disputes between the two empires for the protectorate of the kingdom of Armenia. In consequence of one of these disputes Trajan invaded the Parthian Empire (A.D. 115–117), and obtained possession for a short time of Mesopotamia; but his conquests were surrendered under Hadrian, and the Euphrates again became the boundary of the two empires. There were other wars at later periods, which resulted in favour of the Romans, who took Seleucia and Ctesiphon, and made the district of Osroëné a Roman province. The exhaustion which was the effect of these wars at length gave the Persians the opportunity of throwing off the Parthian yoke. Led by Artaxerxes (Ardshir), they put an end to the Parthian kingdom of the Arsacidae, after it had lasted 476 years, and established the Persian dynasty of the Sassanidae, A.D. 226. See ARSACES; SASSANIDAE.

The Parthians were of Scythic origin, but during the more flourishing period of the Empire adopted many of the usages of Greek civilization, including the Greek language (as the official form of speech) and to some extent the Greek religion. As the Empire declined, however, this superficial cultivation wore off, and by the second century A.D. even the Greek language fell into total disuse.

See the histories of Parthia by Schneiderwirth (1874), Spiegel (1887), and G. Rawlinson (1893).

Parthīni. See PATHINI.

Paryadres (Παρυάδρης). A mountain chain of Asia, connecting the Taurus and the mountains of Armenia, and considered as the boundary between Cappadocia and Armenia.

Paryēti Montes (τὰ Παρυητῶν ὄρη). From the Indian *paruta*, "mountain." A great mountain-chain running north and south on the western side of the valley of the Indus. It now divides

Beluchistan and Afghanistan from Scinde and the Punjab.

Parysătis (Παρύσατις or Πιρυσάτις). The daughter of Artaxerxes I. Longimanus, king of Persia. She was given by her father in marriage to her own brother Darius, surnamed Ochus, who, in B.C. 424, succeeded Xerxes II. on the throne of Persia. The feeble character of Darius threw the chief power into the hands of Parysatis, whose administration was little else than a series of murders. Four of the sons grew up to manhood. The eldest of these, Artaxerxes Mnemon, was born before Darius had obtained the sovereign power, and on this pretext Parysatis sought to set aside his claims to the throne in favour of her second son Cyrus. Failing in this attempt, she nevertheless interfered after the death of Darius, in B.C. 405, to prevent Artaxerxes from putting Cyrus to death, and prevailed upon the king to allow him to return to his satrapy in Asia Minor. After the death of Cyrus at the battle of Cunaxa (B.C. 401), she did not hesitate to display her grief for the death of her favourite son by bestowing funeral honours on his mutilated remains; and she subsequently succeeded in getting into her power all the authors of the death of Cyrus, whom she put to death by the most cruel tortures. She afterwards poisoned Statira, the wife of Artaxerxes. The feeble and indolent king was content to banish her to Babylon; and it was not long before he recalled her to his court, where she soon recovered all her former influence. Of this she availed herself to turn his suspicions against Tissaphernes, whom she had long hated as having been the first to discover the designs of Cyrus to his brother, and who was now put to death by Artaxerxes at her instigation (B.C. 396). She appears to have died soon afterwards. See Xen. *Anab.* i. 1; Ctes. *Pers.* 57; Plut. *Artax.*, and Diod. xiv. 80.

Pasargăda (Πασαργάδα). The older of the two capitals of Persis (the other and later being Persepolis), is said to have been founded by Cyrus the Great on the spot where he gained his great victory over Astyages. The tomb of Cyrus stood here in the midst of a beautiful park. The exact site is doubtful. Most modern geographers identify it with Murghab, northeast of Persepolis, where there are the remains of a great sepulchral monument of the ancient Persians. See PERSIA, p. 1212.

Pasargădae (Πασαργάδαι). The noblest of the three chief tribes of ancient Persia, the other two being the Maraphii and the Maspii (Herod. i. 125).

Pasceŏlus (φάσκωλος). A leathern bag for carrying money, clothes, etc. (Plaut. *Rud.* v. 2, 27).

Pasion (Πασίων). A rich Athenian banker, originally a slave, but manumitted as a reward for his fidelity. He also manufactured shields. Being accused of fraudulently withholding a sum of money intrusted to him by a foreigner from the Euxine, he was prosecuted, and accused in an oration by Isocrates, which is still extant. Pasion showed much public spirit in the use of his money, and was, in consequence, rewarded with the freedom of the city, and was enrolled in the deme of Acharnae. He died in B.C. 370, when his elder son Apollodorus squandered a large part of his fortune. See the oration of Demosthenes for Phormion.

Pasiphaë (Πασιφάη). A daughter of Helios (the Sun) and Perseïs, and a sister of Circé and Aeëtes. She was the wife of Minos, by whom she became the mother of Androgeos, Catreus, Deucalion, Glaucus, Acallé, Xenodicé, Ariadné, and Phaedra. Hence Phaedra is called *Pasipheïa* (Ovid, *Met.* xv. 500). As a punishment for Minos who had failed to carry out a vow that he had made, Pasiphaë was inspired by Poseidon with a violent passion for a bull. By a device of the artisan Daedalus, who enclosed her in a wooden cow, Pasiphaë was enabled to gratify her desires, and became by the bull the mother of the monster Minotaurus, a creature half man and half bull. (See MINOS; THESEUS.) There is a poem *De Pasiphaë* of twenty-two lines in the Latin Anthology, ascribed to Rufinus Antiochensis (Bährens, *Poet. Lat. Min.* v. 108).

Pasitĕles (Πασιτέλης). A Greek artist of the first century B.C., a native of southern Italy. He was actively engaged at Rome on important works in marble, ivory, silver, and bronze, and was also an author. He originated a new school, which was not immediately connected with any of the existing tendencies of art, but was founded on a careful study of nature and the masterpieces of earlier sculptors. It aimed above all things at correctness of form, combined with elegance of representation and a mastery of technique. Pasiteles chased in silver a representation of the infant Roscius (Cic. *De Div.* i. 79), and executed an ivory statue of Iupiter for the temple dedicated by Metellus (Pliny, *H. N.* xxxvi. 40). According to his contemporary Varro, he never executed any work without modelling it first (ib. xxxv. 156). Among his pupils was Stephanus, who in his turn was the master of Menelaüs.

Pasithea (Πασιθέα). One of the Charites, or Graces, also called AGLAIA. See GRATIAE.

Pasitigris (Πασίτιγρις). A river rising on the confines of Media and Persis, and flowing through Susiana into the head of the Persian Gulf, after receiving the Eulaeus on its western side. Some geographers make the Pasitigris a tributary of the Tigris.

Passăron (Πασσάρων). A town of Epirus in Molossia, and the ancient capital of the Molossian kings.

Passiēnus. (1) CRISPUS, the husband of Agrippina and step-father of the emperor Nero (Quint. x. i, 24). (2) See PAULUS.

Passus. The pace, or double step, a Roman measure of length = 5 Roman feet (*pes*) or 1.479 metres (= 4 English feet 10¼ inches). 1000 *passus* formed a Roman mile, 1478.70 metres (or 1616 yards, 2 feet, 2 inches, or about 143 yards less than an English mile. The *passus* is sometimes estimated as 1.48 metre; 1000 *passus* being then 1480 metres or 1618 yards—i. e. 142 yards less than an English mile).

Pastillus (τροχίσκος). A small round ball of flour or paste, or of perfumed and aromatic ingredients used to impart an agreeable odour to the breath, like our "cachous" and similar preparations (Pliny, *H. N.* xiii. 43).

Pastinatio. The preparation of the soil of vineyards by digging and ditching for the purpose of planting young vines (Columel. iii. 13, 12).

Pastīnum. A species of dibble or instrument for planting young vines. It was a stick with two prongs at the end between which the plum was held and pressed into the ground (Columel. iii. 18, 1).

Pastophŏri (παστοφόροι). Egyptian priests who carried in processions small shrines (παστοί) of their god (Apul. *Met.* xi. 17).

Pataeci (Πάταικοι). Phœnician deities whose figures were attached to the Phœnician ships either in the prows or stems (Herod. iii. 37).

Patagium (παταγεῖον). A broad stripe of purple or gold on the front of a woman's tunic, like the *clavus* (q. v.) worn by men (Fest. s. v.).

Patăla, Patalēné. See PATTALA, PATTALENÉ.

Patăra (τὰ Πάταρα). One of the chief cities of Lycia, situated on the coast a few miles east of the mouth of the Xanthus. It was early colonized by Dorians from Crete, and became a chief seat of the worship of Apollo, who had here a very celebrated oracle, which uttered responses in the winter only. Hence Apollo is called by Horace *Delius et Patareus Apollo* (*Carm.* iii. 4, 64).

Patavinĭtas. See LIVIUS, p. 963.

Patavium. Now Padova or Padua. An ancient town of the Veneti in the north of Italy, on the Medŏacus Minor, and on the road from Mutina to Altinum, said to have been founded by the Trojan Antenor. Under the Romans it was the most important city in the north of Italy, and by its commerce and manufactures (of which its woollen stuffs were the most celebrated) it attained great opulence. It is celebrated as the birthplace of the historian Livy. Near Patavium were the Aquae Patavinae, on which see APONI FONS.

Patchwork. See CENTO.

Patella. See PATINA.

Patēna. A manger for horses (Veget. *Vet.* ii. 28, 3).

Patĕra (φιάλη.) The broad, flat dish or saucer used by the ancients for drinking and for offering

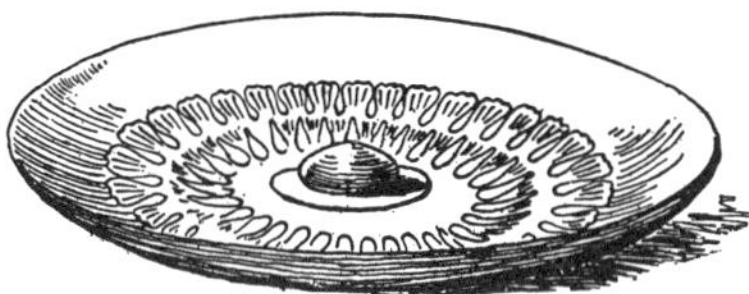

Greek Φιάλη. (British Museum.)

libations. It had no foot or stem, and thus resembled a large saucer. Among the Romans, one form of patera had a handle, as shown in the second

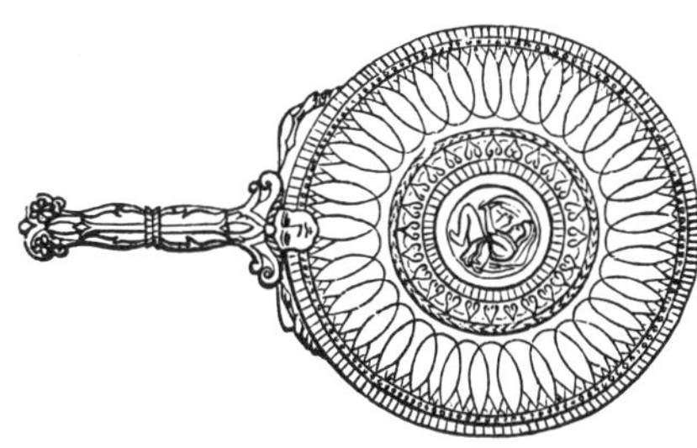

Roman Patera. (Pompeii.)

illustration. The post-Homeric φιάλη seems to have had a small knob in the centre like an acorn, and was hence called βαλανωτή and καρυωτή (Athen. xi. 502 b). The patera was made of earthenware or metal (gold, silver, bronze). See CALIX; SACRIFICIUM; VAS.

Paterculus, GAIUS VELLÉIUS. A Roman historian born about B.C. 19 of a distinguished Campanian family. Entering the army, he accompanied Gaius Caesar, the grandson of Augustus, on an expedition to the East (A.D. 2). Two years later he served with Tiberius in Germany, attaining the rank of military tribune and *praefectus equitum.* With Tiberius he remained for some eight years and became *legatus* (*C. I. L.* viii. 10311) and quaestor (A.D. 7). In A.D. 12 he returned to Rome and took part in the triumph of Tiberius. In A.D. 15 he and his brother, Magius Celer, were praetors.

In the year 30, he wrote his history at the request of the consul M. Vinicius, and probably died in the following year. It is believed that he was executed because of his connection with Seianus (q. v.). The history is in two books, of which a portion is lost after the eighth section of the first book, and also the opening. The title of the work is *Historiae Romanae ad M. Vinicium Consulem Libri Duo.* It is a succinct compendium of universal history (with especial reference to the history of Rome), beginning with the settlement of Magna Graecia and extending to his own times. The latter portion of the narrative is more diffuse than the first part. His method is to seize upon the striking points of his subject and to dwell upon them, leaving less important events in abeyance. His treatment is therefore rather that of an annalist than an historian, and his style is unfinished. His facts are in the main trustworthy, but his fulsome praise of Tiberius detracts from the value of the narrative of his own times. The text is in a very unsatisfactory condition. Only one MS. survived to modern times, and was lost in the seventeenth century, after being copied by Beatus Rhenanus at Amerbach. There are editions of the text by Orelli (Leipzig, 1835); Kritz (annotated) (Leipzig, 1840); Haase (2d ed. Leipzig, 1858); Halm (Leip. 1876); Rockwood (Eng. notes) (Boston, 1893).

Pater Familias. The master of a house among the Romans. (See FAMILIA.) PATER PATRĀTUS, the spokesman of the *fetiales* (q. v.). PATER MATUTĬNUS, a special name of Ianus (q. v.).

Paternus, TARRUTĒNIUS. A Roman jurist, probably the person who as praetorian praefector was put to death by Commodus for alleged treason (Lamprid. *Comm.* 4). He wrote a treatise in four books called *Militarium,* or *De Re Militari,* quoted in the Digest. See Dirksen in his *Hinterlassen Schriften,* ii. 412.

Pathīni (Παθινοί) or **Parthēni** (Παρθηνοί). An Illyrian people in the neighbourhood of Dyrrhachium.

Patibŭlum. A sort of wooden fork used for the punishment of criminals. It was placed upon the neck so that the prongs should project in front, and to these the hands of the culprit were tied fast. In that condition he was beaten through the city (Plaut. *Mil.* ii. 4, 7). It was probably often a straight piece of wood, the arms then being stretched over from the sides. The word is often roughly used as equivalent to *crux.* See CRUX; FURCA.

Patĭna (λεκάνη, τρύβλιον, λοπάς), dimin. **Patella.** A deep dish used both for cooking and for serving food at table; sometimes covered. When used for cooking it was generally of earthenware, but for table-service it was often of silver, sometimes with delicate chasing, so that the actor Aesopus had one valued at 100,000 sesterces, or $4000 (Pliny, *H. N.* xxxv. 163). Vitellius had one of earthenware so large that the special oven built to contain it cost 1,000,000 sesterces, or $40,000 (Pliny, l. c.; Suet. *Vitell.* 13).

Patmos (Πάτμος). One of the islands called Sporades, in the Icarian Sea, celebrated as the place to which the Apostle John was banished, and in which he wrote the Apocalypse (Pliny, *H. N.* iv. 69). See Tozer, *Islands of the Aegean* (1890).

Patrae (Πάτραι). Now Patras. One of the twelve cities of Achaea, and situated west of Rhium, near the opening of the Corinthian Gulf. It was the only Achaean city that sided with Athens in the Peloponnesian War (Thuc. v. 52). Augustus made it the chief city of Achaia.

Patres. See PATRICII; SENATUS.

Patria Potestas. See FAMILIA; MANCIPIUM; MANUS.

Patricii (literally the relatives of the *patres*, or heads of families of the old tribes. [See GENS.]). In the oldest times of Rome the actual citizens who constituted the *populus Romanus*. They were divided into three tribes—*Ramnes*, *Tities*, and *Luceres*, each consisting of ten *curiae*. (See CURIA.) The union of these latter formed the national assembly, the Comitia Curiata. (See COMITIA.) Besides these there were originally only *clientes*, settlers enjoying no legal rights, with the citizens for their protectors (or *patroni*). Afterwards, when a new element of the population, endowed with partial citizenship, called the plebs (q. v.), sprang up from the settlement of subjugated Latin tribes, the *patricii* stood in contrast to them as old citizens possessing full rights. Later, the plebeians received a fuller citizenship through the centurial constitution framed by Servius Tullius (see CENTURIA), while they gained at the same time the right of voting in the Comitia Centuriata, composed of patricians and plebeians, together with the obligation of serving in the field and paying taxes, hitherto obligatory on the patricians alone. In contrast to the plebeians, the patricians thus formed a hereditary aristocracy, with the exclusive right to hold public offices, whether civil or religious. Nothing short of a decision by the Comitia Curiata could either remove any one from the patrician body or (on rare occasions) enrol a plebeian among the patricians. The contraction of marriages between patricians and plebeians was not allowed till B.C. 445. A violent struggle arose between the two parties, after the establishment of the Republic in B.C. 510, on the subject of the admission of the plebeians to State offices. This struggle lasted till B.C. 300, and the patricians were, step by step, forced to give up their exclusive right to one office after another. First of all, they had to give up the quaestorship (B.C. 409), then the consulate (367), the dictatorship (356), the censorship (351), the praetorship (338), and finally the most important priestly offices, the pontificate and the augurship (300). Only politically unimportant offices were left reserved for them, the temporal office of *interrex*, and the priestly offices of *rex sacrorum* and the three *flamines maiores*. The political importance which the patrician Comitia Curiata possessed, through its right to confirm the decisions of the Comitia Centuriata, was lost in B.C. 286. The Comitia Tributi, in which the *plebs* had the preponderance, thus became the most important organ of the democracy.

An aristocracy of holders of public offices was thus formed, consisting of the patricians together with the more important plebeian families. The members of such families, whether patrician or plebeian, were called *nobiles*. The number of patrician families dwindled greatly owing to the Civil Wars (on their number towards the end of the Republic, see GENS). Caesar and Augustus increased them by introducing plebeian families, and subsequent emperors gave the patriciate as a distinction. Under Constantine the Great *patricius* became a personal title, which conferred a rank immediately below the consuls. The external distinctive marks of a patrician were the *tunica laticlavia* (see TUNICA) and a peculiar sort of shoe (see CALCEUS) adorned with an ivory crescent (*lunula*).

Patrīmi et Matrīmi (ἀμφιθαλεῖς). Children whose parents were both alive (Festus, s. h. v.); though the name is also applied to children whose parents had been married by the ceremony called *confarreatio*, and were still alive (Serv. *ad Verg. Georg.* i. 32). For the religious functions, at which the services of *patrimi et matrimi* were required, see ARVALES; CAMILLUS; MATRIMONIUM.

Patrŏcles (Πατροκλῆς). A Macedonian general in the service of Seleucus I. and Antiochus I., kings of Syria. Patrocles held, both under Seleucus and Antiochus, an important government over some of the eastern provinces of the Syrian Empire. During the period of his holding this position, he collected accurate geographical information, which he afterwards published to the world; but though he is frequently cited by Strabo, who placed the utmost reliance on his accuracy, neither the title nor exact subject of his work is mentioned. It seems clear, however, that it included a general account of India as well as of the countries on the banks of the Oxus and the Caspian Sea. Patrocles regarded the Caspian Sea as a gulf or inlet of the ocean, and maintained the possibility of sailing thither by sea from the Indian Ocean (Strabo, ii. p. 69).

Patrŏcli Insŭla (Πατρόκλου νῆσος). A small island off the southwestern coast of Attica, near Sunium.

Patroclus (Πάτροκλος) and **Patrocles** (Πατροκλῆς). The penult is almost always long in the *Iliad*, PATRŎCLUS once only in vocative (*Il.* xix. 287). Son of Menoetius and Sthenelé, the bosom friend of Achilles. While still a boy Patroclus involuntarily slew Clysonymus, son of Amphidamas. In consequence of this accident he was taken by his father to Peleus at Phthia, where he was educated together with Achilles. He is said to have taken part in the expedition against Troy on account of his attachment to Achilles. He fought bravely against the Trojans until his friend withdrew from the scene of action, when Patroclus followed his example. But when the Greeks were hard pressed, he begged Achilles to allow him to put on his armour, and with his men to hasten to the assistance of the Greeks. Achilles granted the request, and Patroclus succeeded in driving back the Trojans and extinguishing the fire which was raging among the ships. He slew many enemies, and thrice made an assault upon the walls of Troy; but he was suddenly struck by Apollo, and became senseless. In this state Euphorbus ran him through with his lance from behind, and Hector gave him the last and fatal blow. Hector also took possession of his armour. A long struggle now ensued between the Greeks and Trojans for the body of Patroclus; but the former obtained possession of it, and brought it to Achilles, who was deeply grieved, and vowed to avenge the death of his friend. Thetis protected the body with ambrosia against decomposition until Achilles had leisure solemnly to burn it with funeral sacrifices. His ashes were collected in a golden urn which Dionysus had once given to Thetis, and were deposited under a mound, where the remains of Achilles were subsequently buried. Funeral games were celebrated in his honour. Achilles and Patroclus met again in the lower world; or, according to others, they continued after their death to live together in the island of Leucé. See ACHILLES; HECTOR; TROJAN WAR.

Patrol. See VIGILES.

Patron. An Epicurean philosopher, who lived for some time in Rome, where he became acquainted with Cicero and others. From Rome he removed to Athens, and there succeeded Phaedrus as head of the Epicurean school, B.C. 52.

Patrōnus. The Roman term for the protector of a single client, or of a whole community (see CLIENTES); the emancipator in relation to his freedman (see LIBERTUS); and the judicial representative of accuser or accused. (See ORATOR.) For the distinction between *patronus* and *advocatus*, see the articles ADVOCATUS; JUDICIAL PROCEDURE.

Pattăla. See PATTALENÉ.

Pattalēné (Παττaληνή) or **Patalēnē** (Παταληνή). The name of the great delta formed by the two principal arms by which the Indus falls into the sea. At the apex of the delta stood the city Pattala or Patala, the Sanskrit *patâla*, which means "the western country," and is applied to the western part of northern India about the Indus, in contradistinction to the eastern part about the Ganges.

Patulcius. A name applied to Ianus (q. v.).

Patūmus (Πάτουμος). The Egyptian Pa-Thmu; O. T. Pithom. A town in the Egyptian Delta between Bubastis and Succoth, built by the Jews in their captivity (Exod. i. 11; cf. Herod. ii. 158).

Paulīna or **Paullīna.** (1) See LOLLIA. (2) POMPĒIA, the wife of the philosopher Seneca. When her husband was condemned to death by Nero, she severed her veins, but Nero ordered them to be bound up, so that she lived for several years longer. See Tac. *Ann.* xv. 63, 64; and the article SENECA.

Paulīnus or **Paullīnus.** (1) POMPĒIUS, commanded in Germany with L. Antistius Vetus in A.D. 58, and completed the dam to restrain the inundations of the Rhine, which Drusus had commenced sixty-three years before. Seneca dedicated to him his treatise *De Brevitate Vitae;* and the Pompeia Paullina, whom the philosopher married, was probably the daughter of this Paullinus. (2) C. SUETONIUS, propraetor in Mauretania, in the reign of the emperor Claudius, A.D. 42, when he conquered the Moors who had revolted, and advanced as far as Mount Atlas. He had the command of Britain in the reign of Nero from A.D. 59 to 62. For the first two years all his undertakings were successful; but during his absence on an expedition against the island of Mona (Anglesey), the Britons rose in rebellion under Boadicea (A.D. 61). They at first met with great success, but were conquered by Suetonius on his return from Mona. (See BOADICEA.) In A.D. 66 he was consul; and after the death of Nero in 68 he was one of Otho's generals in the war against Vitellius. It was against his advice that Otho fought the battle of Bedriacum. He was pardoned by Vitellius after Nero's death. (3) Of MILAN (*Mediolanensis*), the secretary of St. Ambrose, after whose death he became a deacon, and repaired to Africa, where, at the request of St. Augustine, he composed a biography of his former patron. This biography, and two other small works by Paullinus, are still extant. (4) MEROPIUS PONTIUS ANICIUS PAULLĪNUS, bishop of Nola, and hence generally designated Paullinus Nolanus, was born at Bordeaux, or at a neighbouring town, which he calls Embromagum, about A.D. 353. His parents were wealthy and illustrious, and he received a careful education, enjoying in particular the instruction of the poet Ausonius. After many years spent in worldly honours he withdrew from the world, and was eventually chosen Bishop of Nola in A.D. 409. He died in 431. The works of Paullinus are still extant, and consist of prose *Epistolae* (51 in number), *Carmina* (36 in number, composed in a great variety of metres), and a short tract entitled *Passio S. Genesii Arelatensis.* The works of Paullinus are edited by Migne (Paris, 1847.)

Paulus (Παῦλος). The name of several Greek writers. (1) AEGINĒTA, a celebrated medical writer, of whose personal history nothing is known except that he was born in Aegina, and that he travelled a good deal, visiting, among other places, Alexandria. He probably lived in the latter half of the seventh century after Christ. He wrote several medical works in Greek, of which the principal one is still extant, with no exact title, but commonly called *De Re Medica Libri Septem.* This work is chiefly a compilation from former writers. The Greek text has been edited by Brian (Paris, 1855). There is an English translation by Adams (London, 1834 foll.). (2) Of ALEXANDRIA, wrote, in A.D. 278, an introduction to Astrology (Εἰσαγωγὴ εἰς τὴν ἀποτελεσματικήν), which has come down to us, edited by Schatus or Schato (Wittenberg, 1586). (3) Of SAMOSATA, a celebrated heresiarch of the third century, was made bishop of Antioch, about A.D. 260. He was condemned and deposed by a council held in 269. Paulus denied the distinct personality of the Son of God, and maintained that the Word came and dwelt in the man Jesus. (4) SILENTIARIUS, so called, because he was chief of the *silentiarii*, or secretaries of the emperor Justinian. He wrote various poems, of which the following are extant: (*a*) A Description of the Church of St. Sophia (Ἔκφρασις τοῦ ναοῦ τῆς ἁγίας Σοφίας), consisting of 1029 verses, of which the first 134 are iambic, the rest hexameter. This poem gives a clear and graphic description of the superb structure which forms its subject, and was recited by its author at the second dedication of the church (A.D. 562), after the restoration of the dome, which had fallen in. Edited by Graefe (Leipzig, 1822) and by Bekker (Bonn, 1837), in the Bonn edition of the Byzantine historians. (*b*) A Description of the Pulpit (Ἔκφρασις τοῦ ἄμβωνος), consisting of 304 verses, a supplement to the former poem. It is printed in the editions mentioned above. (*c*) Epigrams, 83 in all, given in the *Anthologia*. Among these is a poem on the Pythian Baths (Εἰς τὰ ἐν Πυθίοις θέρμα).

Paulus or **Paullus**, AEMILIUS. (1) MARCUS, consul B.C. 302, and *magister equitum* to the dictator Q. Fabius Maximus Rullianus in 301. (2) MARCUS, consul 255 with Ser. Fulvius Paetinus Nobilior, about the middle of the First Punic War. (3) LUCIUS, son of No. 2, consul B.C. 219, when he conquered Demetrius off the island of Pharos in the Adriatic, and compelled him to fly for refuge to Philip, king of Macedonia. He was consul a second time in 216 with C. Terentius Varro. This was the year of the memorable defeat at Cannae. (See HANNIBAL.) The battle was fought against the advice of Paulus; and he was one of the many distinguished Romans who perished in the engagement, refusing to fly from the field when a tribune of the soldiers offered him his horse. Hence we find in Horace (*Carm.* i. 12) *animaeque magnae prodigum Paulum, superante Poeno.* Paulus was a stanch adherent of the aristocracy, and was raised to the consulship by the latter party to counterbalance the influence of the plebeian Terentius Varro. (4) LUCIUS, afterwards surnamed MACEDONĬCUS, son of the last, was born about 230 or 229, since at the time of his second consulship (168) he was upwards of sixty years of age. He was one of the best specimens of the high Roman nobles. He would not condescend to flatter the people for the offices of the State, maintained with strictness severe discipline in the army, was deeply skilled in the law of the augurs, to whose college he belonged, and maintained throughout life a pure and unspotted character. He was elected curule aedile in B.C. 192; was praetor in 191, and obtained Further Spain as his province, where he carried on war with the Lusitani; and was consul in 181, when he conquered the Ingauni, a Ligurian people. For the next thirteen years he lived quietly at Rome, devoting most of his time to the education of his children. He was consul a second time in 168, and brought the war against Perseus to a conclusion by the defeat of the Macedonian monarch, near Pydna, on the 22d of June. Perseus shortly afterwards surrendered himself to Paulus. (See PERSEUS.) Paulus remained in Macedonia during the greater part of the following year as proconsul, and arranged the affairs of Macedonia in conjunction with ten Roman commissioners, whom the Senate had despatched for the purpose. Before leaving Greece he marched into Epirus, where, in accordance with a cruel command of the Senate, he gave to his soldiers seventy towns to be pillaged because they had been in alliance with Perseus. The triumph of Paulus, which was celebrated at the end of November, 167, was the most splendid that Rome had yet seen. It lasted three days. Before the triumphal car of Aemilius walked the captive monarch of Macedonia and his children, and behind it were his two illustrious sons, Q. Fabius Maximus and P. Scipio Africanus the younger, both of whom had been adopted into other families. But the glory of the conqueror was clouded by family misfortune. At this very time he lost his two younger sons; one, twelve years of age, died only five days before his triumph, and the other, fourteen years of age, only three days after his triumph. The loss was all the severer, since he had no son left to carry his name down to posterity. In 164 Paulus was censor with Q. Marcius Philippus, and died in 160, after a long and tedious illness. The fortune he left behind him was so small as scarcely to be sufficient to pay his wife's dowry. The *Adelphi* of Terence was brought out at the funeral games exhibited in his honour. Aemilius Paulus was married twice. By his first wife, Papiria, the daughter of C. Papirius Maso, consul 231, he had four children—two sons, one of whom was adopted by Fabius Maximus and the other by P. Scipio, and two daughters, one of whom was married to Q. Aelius Tubero, and the other to M. Cato, son of Cato the censor. He afterwards divorced Papiria; and by his second wife, whose name is not mentioned, he had two sons, whose death has been recorded above, and a daughter, who was a child at the time that her father was elected to his second consulship. (5) IULIUS. A Roman jurist of high repute in the beginning of the third century A.D., contemporary with Papinianus and Ulpian. With the former he was legal assessor to the emperor Septimius Severus. With the latter he was *praefectus praetorio* under Alexander Severus, after he had been sent into exile by Elagabalus. He was most productive as a legal author, but in literary skill and finish stood far below his two contemporaries. The extracts from his numerous monographs or more comprehensive works form a sixth part of the *Digest*. Besides these extracts, his *Sententiae*, a very popular compendium of undisputed principles on the most frequent points of law, has been preserved in a shortened form. (6) PAULUS DIACŎNUS. The Latin name of Paul Warnifrid, a Lombard who became a monk at Monte Casino about A.D. 775. He wrote a history of the Lombards; compiled a Roman history largely from Eutropius; and abridged the glossary of Festus which was itself epitomized from the lexicon of Verrius Flaccus. He also wrote ecclesiastical works. His Roman history was in sixteen books, but was subsequently (about A.D. 1000) enlarged by Landolfus Sagax, who drew upon various sources for his additions, especially upon Orosius and St. Jerome. This enlarged work got the name *Historia Miscella*, by which it is now known. On the abridgment of Festus, see FESTUS; VERRIUS FLACCUS.

Pausanias (Παυσανίας). (1) A Spartan of the Agid branch of the royal family, the son of Cleombrotus and nephew of Leonidas. Several writers incorrectly call him king; but he only succeeded his father Cleombrotus in the guardianship of his cousin Plistarchus, the son of Leonidas, for whom he exercised the functions of royalty from B.C. 479 to the period of his death. In 479, when the Athenians called upon the Lacedaemonians for aid against the Persians, the Spartans sent a body of 5000 Spartans, each attended by seven Helots, under the command of Pausanias. At the Isthmus, Pausanias was joined by the other Peloponnesian allies, and at Eleusis by the Athenians when he took command of the united armies, the other Greek generals forming his council. The allied forces numbered 110,000 men. Near Plataeae in Boeotia Pausanias defeated the Persians under Mardonius, and thus assured the independence of Greece. For his own reward, Pausanias received one tenth of the spoils (Herod. ix. 10–85; Diod. xi. 29–33).

In the year 477 the Greeks sent out a fleet under Pausanias to drive the Persians from the islands. He attacked Cyprus and subdued the greater part, and then sailed to Byzantium, which he succeeded in taking. After this victory Pausanias began to aim at personal dominion for himself rather than success for his country, being evidently dazzled by his unbroken and brilliant successes. His ambition seems to have looked for a tyranny over the whole of Greece, and to have conceived the plan of securing the aid of the Persian king in the accomplishment of this design. Among the prisoners taken at Byzantium were some Persians connected with the royal family. These he sent to the king, with a letter, in which he offered to bring Sparta and the rest of Greece under his power, and proposed to marry his daughter. His offers were gladly accepted, and whatever amount of troops and money he required for accomplishing his designs. Pausanias now set no bounds to his arrogant and domineering temper. The allies were so disgusted by his conduct that they all, except the Peloponnesians and Aeginetans, voluntarily offered to transfer to the Athenians that pre-eminence of rank which Sparta had hitherto enjoyed. In this way the Athenian confederacy first took its rise. Reports of the conduct and designs of Pausanias reached Sparta, and he was recalled and put upon his trial; but the evidence respecting his meditated treachery was not yet thought sufficiently strong. Shortly afterwards he returned to Byzantium, without the orders of the ephors, and renewed his treasonable intrigues. He was again recalled to Sparta, was again put on his trial, and again acquitted. But even after this second escape he still continued to carry on his intrigues with Persia. At length a man, who was charged with a letter to Persia, having his suspicions awakened by noticing that none of those sent previously on similar errands had returned, counterfeited the seal of Pausanias and opened the letter, in which he found directions for his own death. He carried the letter to the ephors, who prepared to arrest Pausanias; but he took refuge in the temple of Athenē Chalcioecus. The ephors stripped off the roof of the temple and built up the door; the aged mother of Pausanias is said to have been among the first who laid a stone for this purpose. When he was on the point of expiring, the ephors took him out lest his death should pollute the sanctuary. He died as soon as he got outside, B.C. 470. He left three sons behind him, Plistoanax, afterwards king, Cleomenes, and Aristocles. See Bulwer's unfinished novel, *Pausanias the Spartan.* (2) Son of Plistoanax, and grandson of the preceding, was king of Sparta from B.C. 408 to 394. In 403 he was sent with an army into Attica, and secretly favoured the cause of Thrasybulus and the Athenian exiles, in order to counteract the plans of Lysander. In 395 Pausanias was sent with an army against the Thebans; but in consequence of the death of Lysander, who was slain under the walls of Haliartus, on the day before Pausanias reached the spot, the king agreed to withdraw his forces from Boeotia. On his return to Sparta he was impeached, and seeing that a fair trial was not to be hoped for, went into voluntary exile, and was condemned to death. He was living at Tegea in 385, when Mantinea was besieged by his son Agesipolis, who succeeded him on the throne. (3) King of Macedonia, the son and successor of Aeropus. He was assassinated in the year of his accession by Amyntas II., 394. (4) A pretender to the throne of Macedonia, made his appearance in 367, after Alexander II. had been assassinated by Ptolemaeus. Eurydicē, the mother of Alexander, sent to request the aid of the Athenian general, Iphicrates, who expelled Pausanias from the kingdom. (5) A Macedonian youth of distinguished family, from the province of Orestis. Having been shamefully treated by Attalus, he complained of the outrage to Philip; but as Philip took no notice of his complaints, he directed his vengeance against the king himself. He shortly afterwards murdered Philip at the festival held at Aegae, 336, but was slain on the spot by some officers of the king's guard. Suspicion rested on Olympias and Alexander of having been privy to the deed; but with regard to Alexander, at any rate, the suspicion is probably totally unfounded. There is a story that Pausanias, while meditating revenge, having asked the sophist Hermocrates which was the shortest way to fame, the latter replied, that it was by killing the man who had performed the greatest achievements. (6) A celebrated Greek traveller and geographer, a native of Lydia. He explored Greece, Macedonia, Asia, and Africa; and then, in the second half of the second century A.D., settled in Rome, where he composed a *Periegesis* (Περιήγησις) or Itinerary of Greece in ten books. Book I. includes Attica and Megaris; II., Corinth with Sicyon, Phlius, Argolis, Aegina, and the other neighbouring islands; III., Laconia; IV., Messenia; V., VI., Elis and Olympia; VII., Achaea; VIII., Arcadia; IX., Boeotia; X., Phocis and Locris. The work is founded on notes, taken on the spot, from his own observation and inquiry from the natives of the country, on the subject of the religious cults and the monuments of art and architecture. Together with these there are topographical and historical notices, in working up which Pausanias took into consideration the accounts of other authors, especially of Polemon (A.D. 150), poets as well as prose writers. Although his account is not without numerous inaccuracies, omissions, and mistakes, it is yet of inestimable value for our knowledge of ancient Greece, especially with regard to its mythology, folk-lore, and religious cults, but above all for the history of Greek art. The composition of his work, especially in the earlier books, shows little skill in plan, execution, or style, and, while accurate, shows that he did not grasp the distinction between legend and history.

The best editions of Pausanias are those of Siebelis, 5 vols. (Leipzig, 1822–28); and Schubart and Walz, 3 vols. (1838–40; reprint by Teubner, Leipzig, 1862 and 1881). English translations by Taylor (1793–94); Shilleto (2 vols. 1886). See Kalkmann, *Pausanias der Perieget* (Berlin, 1886); Gurlitt, *Pausanias* (Gratz, 1890); and Miss Verrall's *Mythology and Monuments of Ancient Athens* (1890).

Pausarius. The officer in a ship who led at the song and beat the time for the rowers (Sen. *Epist.* 56). He was also styled *hortator.*

Pausias (Παυσίας). A Greek painter, a pupil of Pamphilus and a follower of the Sicyonian school. He lived about 360–330 B.C. at Sicyon, and invented the art of painting vaulted ceilings, and also of foreshortening; he brought encaustic painting with the *cestrum* to perfection. He painted chiefly children and flowers. One of his most famous pictures was the Flower Girl (Στεφανοπλόκος), representing the flower girl Glycera, of whom he was enamoured in his youth (Pliny, *H. N.* xxxv. 123–127). See PICTURA.

Pausilȳpum (Παυσίλυπον, "grief-assuaging"). The name of a villa near Neapolis (Naples) which Vedius Pollio left by will to Augustus (Dio Cass. liv. 23; Pliny, *H. N.* ix. 167). The name has been given in modern times under the corrupted form Posilipo to the grotto between Naples and Pozzuoli, cut through the rock by the engineer Cocceius at the desire of Agrippa. See NEAPOLIS.

Pausilȳpus Mons. Now Posilipo; a ridge in the rear of Naples, forming a barrier between Neapolis and Puteoli. It was pierced by a tunnel called the Crypta Neapolitana, now the Grotta di Posilipo, 2244 feet in length, 21 feet broad, and with a maximum height of 70 feet.

Pauson (Παύσων). A Greek painter whom Aristotle contrasts with Polygnotus in terms implying that the former was a caricaturist (*Poët.* 2, § 2). Elsewhere Aristotle says that young people should not look at the pictures of Pauson, but rather at those of Polygnotus or of any other "ethical" artist (*Polit.* viii. 5, § 7). He is improbably identified with the Pauson who is mentioned with contempt by Aristophanes (*Ach.* 854, *Thesm.* 948, and *Plutus*, 602). See PICTURA.

Pavicŭla. A rammer for beating down the earthen flooring of a room or other place (Cato, *R. R.* 91).

Pavimentum (ἔδαφος, δάπεδον). A flooring composed of small pieces of brick, tiling, stone, and shells, placed in a bed of cement and beaten down solid by a rammer (*pavicula*). The name is also applied to artificial flooring composed of coloured marbles, often of elaborate workmanship and design. Such were (1) the *pavimentum sectile* of marbles cut (*secta*) into sets of regular form and size, such as squares, hexagons, etc.; (2) *pavimentum tessellatum* of marbles cut in regular dies without the admixture of other forms; (3) *pavimentum vermiculatum*, a mosaic flooring representing natural objects, animate or inanimate; and (4) *pavimentum scalpturatum*, on which designs were produced by engraving or inlaying. Another kind of flooring (*pavimentum testaceum*) was made of broken pieces of pottery (*testae*).

Pavimentum Sectile. (Ancient Floor in the Church of S. Croce, Rome.)

Pavimentum Tessellatum. (Baths of Caracalla, Rome.)

Pavimentum Vermiculatum. (Rich.)

Pavor. See PALLOR.

Pax. See IRENÉ.

Pax Iulia or **Pax Augusta.** Now Beja; a Roman colony in Lusitania (Pliny, *H. N.* iv. 117).

Paxi. The name of two small islands, now Paxo and Antipaxo, between Corcyra and Leucas, on the western coast of Greece.

Pearls. See GEMMA.

Peck. See MODIUS.

Pecten (κτείς). A comb for the hair made of boxwood (Mart. xiv. 25) or ivory. A comb with large teeth was called *rarus pecten*. For an illustration of an ancient comb, see the article DENS.

Pectorālé. The front plate of a cuirass. See LORICA.

Peculātus. The Roman term for misappropriation of public property, whether by officials (e. g. in the delivery of booty) or by private persons. Such offences, which seldom occurred in the more ancient times of the Republic, were then judged by the national tribunal. In later times they must have become more frequent, since various laws were issued against them, and a special court of justice (see QUAESTIO) was appointed to try them. Besides the payment of compensation, the condemned person suffered disgrace and banishment (*interdictio aquae et ignis*, see EXSILIUM), and, in the time of the Empire, transportation. See DEPORTATIO.

Peculium. The Romans considered the master of the house (*pater familias*) the lawful owner of all the earnings of the members of the family under his control, whether bond or free. (See FAMILIA; SERVUS.) Whatever sum of money he gave to a grown-up son or to a slave for his own use was called the *peculium* of the latter. This gift could be revoked at pleasure, and could not be disposed of by will. Augustus first granted this right to soldiers, in the case of property won in war (*peculium castrense*, cf. Juv. xvi. *fin.*), and Constantine extended it to that gained in a civil office (*peculium quasi castrense*). See SERVUS.

Pecunia. See AS; NUMISMATICS; PONDERA.

Pecuniae Repetundae. See REPETUNDAE.

Pedalium (Πηδάλιον). (1) A promontory of Caria, called also ARTEMISIUM. (2) A promontory on the eastern coast of Cyprus.

Pedaneus Iudex. See IUDEX.

Pedarii. Those members of the Roman Senate who had occupied no office of State, and hence took a lower rank. They might share in the voting, but did not enjoy the right of expressing individual opinions. See SENATUS.

Pedăsa (τὰ Πήδασα). A very ancient city of Caria, originally a chief abode of the Leleges. The district about it was called PEDĂSIS.

Pedăsus (Πήδασος). A town of Mysia, on the Satnioïs, mentioned several times by Homer.

Pediaeus (Πεδιαῖος). A river of Cyprus, near Salamis.

Pediānus, ASCONIUS. See ASCONIUS.

Pedĭca (πέδη). (1) A trap or snare for animals (Verg. *Georg.* i. 307). (2) A fetter for men (Plaut. *Poen.* iii. 1, 11).

Pedieis. See SOLON.

Pedigree. See IMAGINES; STEMMA.

Pedisĕqui. Slaves whose duty it was to follow their master on foot. The slave who preceded him was called *anteambulo.* A similar class of female slaves had the name *pedisequae* (Cic. *Ad Att.* ii. 16; Plaut. *Asin.* i. 3, 31).

Pedius. (1) QUINTUS, the great-nephew of the dictator C. Iulius Caesar, being the grandson of Iulia, Caesar's eldest sister. He served under Caesar in Gaul as his legatus, B.C. 57. In 55 he was a candidate for the curule aedileship with Cn. Plancius and others, but he lost his election. In the Civil War he fought on Caesar's side. He was praetor in 48, and in that year he defeated and slew Milo in the neighbourhood of Thurii. In 45 he served against the Pompeian party in Spain. In Caesar's will Pedius was named as one of his heirs along with his two other great-nephews, C. Octavius and L. Pinarius, Octavius obtaining three fourths of the property, and the remaining one fourth being divided between Pinarius and Pedius: the latter resigned his share of the inheritance to Octavius. After the fall of the consuls, Hirtius and Pansa, at the battle of Mutina in April, 43, Octavius marched upon Rome at the head of an army, and in the month of August he was elected consul along with Pedius. The latter forthwith proposed a law, known by the name of the *Lex Pedia,* by which all the murderers of Iulius Caesar were punished with *aquae et ignis interdictio.* Pedius was left in charge of the city while Octavius marched into the north of Italy. He died towards the end of the year shortly after the news of the proscription had reached Rome. (2) SEXTUS, a Roman jurist, living just before the reign of Hadrian in the second century A.D. His works and opinions are frequently cited by the later writers, such as Paulus and Ulpian.

Pednelissus (Πεδνηλισσός). A city in the interior of Pisidia.

Pedo, ALBINOVĀNUS. See ALBINOVANUS.

Pedum. An ancient town of Latium, on the Via Labicana, which fell into decay at an early period.

Pedum (κορύνη). A shepherd's crook. It is the usual attribute of Thalia as the Muse of Pastoral Poetry, and is sometimes ascribed to Pan (Verg. *Ecl.* v. 88).

Roman Shepherdess with Pedum. (*Antich. d'Ercolano,* iii. tav. 53.)

Pegae. See PAGAE.

Pegasĭdes (Πηγασίδες). The Muses. See PEGASIS.

Pegăsis (Πηγασίς). A name applied to the fountain Hippocrenê (the *fons caballinus* of Persius), as having been made by the hoof of Pegasus. From this fountain the Muses got their name Pegasides. See HIPPOCRENÊ; PEGASUS.

Pegăsus (Πήγασος). The celebrated winged horse, whose origin is thus related: When Perseus struck off the head of Medusa, with whom Poseidon had had intercourse in the form of a horse or a bird, there sprang from her Chrysaor and the horse Pegasus. The latter received this name because he was believed to have made his appearance near the sources (πηγαί) of Oceanus. He ascended to the seats of the immortals, and afterwards lived in the palace of Zeus, for whom he carried thunder and lightning. According to this view, which is apparently the most ancient, Pegasus was the thundering horse of Zeus; but later writers describe him as the horse of Eos, and place him among the stars. Pegasus also acts a prominent part in the combat of Bellerophon against the Chimaera. In order to kill the Chimaera, it was necessary for Bellerophon to obtain possession of Pegasus. For this purpose the soothsayer Polyidus at Corinth advised him to spend a night in the temple of Athenê. As Bellerophon was asleep in the temple, the goddess appeared to him in a dream commanding him to sacrifice to Poseidon, and gave him a golden bridle. When he awoke he found the bridle, offered the sacrifice, and caught Pegasus while he was drinking at the well Pirenê. According to some, Athenê herself tamed and bridled Pegasus, and surrendered him to Bellerophon. After he had conquered the Chimaera he endeavoured to rise up to heaven upon his winged horse, but fell down upon the earth. (See BELLEROPHON.) Pegasus was also regarded as the horse of the Muses, and in this connection is more celebrated in modern times than in antiquity; for with the ancients he had no connection with the Muses, except producing with his hoof the inspiring fountain Hippocrenê.

The story about this fountain runs as follows: When the nine Muses engaged in a contest with the nine daughters of Pierus on Mount Helicon, all became darkness when the daughters of Pierus began to sing; whereas, during the song of the

Muses, heaven, the sea, and all the rivers stood still to listen, and Helicon rose heavenward with delight, until Pegasus, on the advice of Poseidon, stopped its ascent by kicking it with his hoof. From this kick there arose Hippocrené, the inspiring well of the Muses, on Mount Helicon, which, for this reason, Persius calls *fons caballinus*. Others, again, relate that Pegasus caused the well to gush forth because he was thirsty. Pegasus is often seen represented in ancient works of art with Athené and Bellerophon.

Pegăsus. A Roman jurist, one of the followers or pupils of Proculus, and *praefectus urbi* under Domitian (Juv. iv. 76).

Pegma (πῆγμα). (1) Planks joined to make shelves—e. g. in the atrium of a house for the *imagines* or for book-shelves (Auson. *Epigr.* 26, 10; Cic. *Ad. Att.* iv. 8). (2) A wooden structure of several stages (four are sometimes mentioned) which could be raised or lowered by weights and pulleys (Sen. *Epist.* 89). The pegmata were used in the Roman amphitheatres and spectaculas in various ways; for effecting sudden transformation, like the double stage of the old Madison Square Theatre in New York City; and sometimes for letting off fireworks (Vopisc. *Carin.* 15).

Pegmāres. Gladiators introduced by means of a *pegma* (Suet. *Calig.* 26).

Peiraeĭcus. See PIRAEICUS.

Peiso Lacus. See PELSO LACUS.

Peitho (Πειθώ). See PITHO.

Pelagius. Probably a native of Britain, who was celebrated as the propagator of those heretical opinions which have derived their name from him, and which were opposed with great energy by his contemporaries Augustine and Jerome. He first appears in history about the beginning of the fifth century A.D., when we find him residing at Rome. In the year 409 or 410, when Alaric was threatening Rome, Pelagius, accompanied by his disciple and ardent admirer Caelestius, passed over to Sicily, from thence proceeded to Africa, and leaving Caelestius at Carthage, sailed for Palestine. The fame of his sanctity had preceded him, for upon his arrival he was received with great warmth by St. Jerome and many other distinguished fathers of the Church. Soon afterwards the opinions of Pelagius were denounced as heretical; and in A.D. 417 Pelagius and Caelestus were anathematized by Pope Innocentius. Their doctrines included a denial of the tenet of original sin; a belief in the possibility of a sinless life on earth; and a rejection of the teaching of the Church with regard to grace. Pelagius also believed in the freedom of the human will. The date and circumstances of his death are not known. A very few only of the numerous treatises of Pelagius have descended to us. They are printed with the works of St. Jerome. There are special monographs on Pelagius by Wiggers (Eng. tr. Andover, 1840); Jacobi (1842); Wörter (1866); and Klasen (1882).

Pelagonia (Πελαγονία). (1) A district and city in Macedonia, inhabited by the Pelagones, and situated south of Paeonia, upon the Erigon. (2) A district in Thessaly, situated west of Olympus, and belonging to Perrhaebia.

Pelănor (πέλανορ). A Spartan coin of iron of about twenty Troy ounces in weight (Plut. *Apophtheg. Lacon.* p. 903); and worth four *chalci* or half an Attic obol (i. e. from two to four cents).

Pelasgi (Πελασγοί). A name given to the earliest (prehistoric) inhabitants of Greece. In Homer the name applied now to a people in Asia Minor dwelling near Ilium (*Il.* ii. 840), and now to people inhabiting various parts of Greece. Thus, Argos is called Pelasgian (id. ii. 681), and the god worshipped at Dodona is the "Pelasgian" Zeus (id. xvi. 233). Pelasgians are also spoken of as dwelling in Crete (*Odyss.* xix. 177). Herodotus tells us that the earliest name that Greece bore was Πελασγία, and ascribes a Pelasgic origin to some of the Greek peoples, as the Arcadians, Athenians, Aeolians, etc. (cf. Herod. i. 146; vii. 94, 95; viii. 44). He draws a definite distinction between the Pelasgi and the Hellenes proper, as being different in both race and language (i. 56, 58). Thucydides agrees with Herodotus, and goes a step further in identifying them with the Tyrrheni. He also mentions them as found in the island of Lemnos, on which see the article ETRURIA, p. 625.

Modern scholars, in general, regard the Pelasgi as a prehistoric people, probably non-Aryan in their racial affinities, and possibly to be identified with the same branch as the Etruscans, who came to Greece from Asia at a period earlier than that of the Indo-European migration. Still others use the name as designating the Indo-Europeans before the time of their separation into Greeks and Italians. To them are usually ascribed certain religious cults, which are in their origin non-Hellenic, such as that of the Cabeiri (q. v.) and of Zeus at Dodona; and also the architectural remains popularly called Cyclopean. The ancient authorities on the subject of the Pelasgi are collected by Bruck in his monograph *Quae Veteres de Pelasgis Tradiderunt* (1884). See also Eissner, *Die Alten Pelasger* (Leipzig, 1825); Hesselmeyer, *Die Pelasgerfrage;* Flor, *Zur Geschichte der Pelasger* (1859); and the articles CYCLOPES; HELLAS; INDO-EUROPEAN LANGUAGES; MYCENAE.

Pelasgia (Πελασγία). See PELASGI.

Pelasgiōtis (Πελασγιῶτις). A district in Thessaly, between Hestiaeotis and Magnesia. See THESSALIA.

Pelasgus (Πέλασγος). The mythical ancestor of the Pelasgi, by some regarded as sprung from the earth, but by others described as the son of Zeus (Pausan. ii. 14, 3; Apollod. ii. 1, 1); or of Phoroneus (Pausan. i. 14, 2), or of Poseidon and Larissa (Dionys. i. 17). See PELASGI.

Pelătae (πελάται). Free labourers working for hire like the θῆτες. The word is used by some of the later Greek writers to describe the Roman *clientes*, who had, however, a very different position. See CLIENTES.

Peleiădes. Priestesses at Dodona (q. v.).

Pelendŏnes. A people in Hispania Tarraconensis between the sources of the Durius and the Iberus (Ptol. ii. 6, 54).

Pelethronium (Πελεθρόνιον). A mountainous district in Thessaly, part of Mount Pelion, where the Lapithae dwelt (Verg. *Georg.* iii. 115).

Peleus (Πηλεύς). A king of Thessaly, son of Aeacus, monarch of Aegina, and the nymph Endeïs, the daughter of Chiron. Having been accessory, along with Telamon, to the death of their brother Phocus, he was banished from his native island, but found an asylum at the court of Eurytus, son of Actor, king of Phthia in Thessaly. He married Antigoné, the daughter of Eurytus, and received with her, as a marriage portion, the third part of the kingdom. Peleus was present with Eurytus at the chase of the Calydonian boar; but having unfortunately killed his father-in-law with the javelin which he had hurled against the animal, he was again doomed to be a wanderer. His second benefactor was Acastus, king of Iolcos; but here again he was involved in trouble through a false charge brought against him by Astydamia, or, as Horace calls her, Hippolyte, the queen of Acastus. (See ACASTUS.) To reward the virtue of Peleus, as fully shown by his resisting the blandishments of Astydamia, the gods resolved to give him a goddess in marriage. The spouse selected for him was the sea-nymph Thetis, who had been wooed by Zeus himself and his brother Poseidon; but Themis having declared that her child would be greater than his sire, the gods withdrew (Pind. *Isth.* viii. 58 foll.). Others say that she was courted by Zeus alone till he was informed by Prometheus that, if he had a son by her, that son would dethrone him. Others, again, maintain that Thetis, who was reared by Heré, would not assent to the wishes of Zeus, and that the god, in his anger, condemned her to espouse a mortal; or that Heré herself selected Peleus for her spouse (*Il.* xxiv. 59). Chiron, being made aware of the will of the gods, advised Peleus to aspire to the favour of the nymph of the sea, and instructed him how to win her. He therefore lay in wait, and seized and held her fast, though she changed herself into every variety of form, becoming fire, water, a serpent, and a lioness. The wedding was solemnized on Mount Pelion; the gods all honoured it with their presence, and bestowed armour on the bridegroom. Chiron gave him the famous ashen spear afterwards wielded by his son; and Poseidon bestowed on him the immortal Harpy-born steeds Balius and Xanthus. The offspring of this union was the celebrated Achilles. According to one account, Peleus was deserted by his goddess-wife for not allowing her to cast the infant Achilles into a caldron of boiling water, to try if he were mortal. (See ACHILLES.) This, however, is a post-Homeric fiction, since Homer represents Peleus and Thetis as dwelling together all the lifetime of their son. Of Peleus it is farther related that he survived his son and even grandson (*Od.* xi. 493), and died in misery in the island of Cos. It was at the wedding of Peleus and Thetis that the goddess of Discord threw the apple of gold into the middle of the assembled deities, with which was connected so much misfortune for both the Trojans and the Greeks. See HELENÉ; PARIS.

Peliădes (Πελιάδες). The daughters of Pelias (q. v.).

Pelias (Πελίας). A son of Poseidon and Tyro, a daughter of Salmoneus. Poseidon once visited Tyro in the form of the river-god Enipeus, with whom she was in love, and she became by him the mother of Pelias and Neleus. To conceal her shame, their mother exposed the two boys, but they were found and reared by some countrymen. They subsequently learned their parentage; and after the death of Cretheus, king of Iolcus, who had married their mother, they seized the throne of Iolcus, to the exclusion of Aeson, the son of Cretheus and Tyro. Pelias soon afterwards expelled his own brother Neleus, and thus became sole ruler of Iolcus. After Pelias had long reigned over Iolcus, Iason, the son of Aeson, came to Iolcus and claimed the kingdom as his right. In order to get rid of him, Pelias sent him to Colchis to fetch the golden fleece. Hence arose the celebrated expedition of the Argonauts. After the return of Iason, Pelias was cut to pieces and boiled by his own daughters (the Peliades), who had been told by Medea that in this manner they might restore their father to vigour and youth. His son Acastus held funeral games in his honour at Iolcus, and expelled Iason and Medea from the country. (See ARGONAUTAE; IASON; MEDEA.) The names of several of the daughters of Pelias are four, the best known of which is that of Alcestis (q. v.).

Pelīdes (Πηλείδης). "Son of Peleus," a patronymic which usually designates Achilles, but sometimes the son of Achilles, Neoptolemus.

Peligni or **Paeligni**. A brave and warlike people, of Sabine origin, in Central Italy, bounded by the Marsi, the Marrucini, the Samnites, and the Frentani. They took an active part in the Social War (B.C. 90–89), and their chief town, Corfinium, was destined by the allies to be the new capital of Italy in place of Rome. See ITALIA.

Pelinaeus Mons (τὸ Πελιναῖον ὄρος). The highest mountain in Chios, near the city of Chios. It had a celebrated temple of Zeus.

Pelinna (Πελίννα) and **Pelinnaeum** (Πελινναῖον). A town of Hestiaeotis in Thessaly (Livy, xxxvi. 10, 14).

Pelion (τὸ Πήλιον ὄρος), more rarely **Pelios** (Πήλιος). A lofty range of mountains in Thessaly, in the district of Magnesia, situated between the lake Boebeïs and the Pagasaean Gulf. Its sides were covered with wood, and on its summit was a temple of Zeus Actaeus. Mount Pelion was celebrated in mythology. Near its summit was the cave of the Centaur Chiron. The Giants, in their war with the gods, are said to have attempted to heap Ossa and Olympus on Pelion, or Pelion and Ossa on Olympus, in order to scale heaven. (See GIGANTES.) On Pelion the timber was felled with which the ship Argo was built. See ARGONAUTAE.

Pella (Πέλλα). (1) An ancient town in Macedonia, in the district Bottiaea, situated upon a lake formed by the river Lydias. Philip the Great made it his residence and the capital of the Macedonian monarchy. It was the birthplace of Alexander the Great. Hence the poets give the surname of Pellaea to Alexandria in Egypt, because it was founded by Alexander the Great, and also use the adjective in a general sense as equivalent to Egyptian. See MACEDONIA. (2) A city of Palestine, east of the Jordan, in Peraea. It was the place of refuge of the Christians who fled from Jerusalem before its capture by the Romans. (3) A city of Syria on the Orontes, afterwards called Apamea (q. v.). (4) A city of Phrygia. See PELTAE.

Pellāna. See PELLENÉ (2).

Pellēné (Πελλήνη). (1) The most easterly of the twelve cities of Achaia, near the frontiers of Sicyonia, and situated on a hill sixty stadia from the city. The inhabitants of the peninsula of Pallené, in Macedonia, professed to be descended from the Pellenaeans in Achaia, who were shipwrecked on the Macedonian coast on their return from Troy. (2) Often called PELLĀNA, a town in Lucania on the Eurotas, northwest of Sparta.

Pellex or **Paelex** (παλλακή). A mistress kept by a married man. See CONCUBINA, p. 399.

Pellis. A skin. For skins as clothing, see VESTIS.

Pelluvia (ποδανιπτήρ). A basin for washing the feet, and hence opposed in meaning to *malluvia* (q. v.).

Pelopia. See AEGISTHUS; THYESTES.

Pelopĭdae. See PELOPS.

Pelopĭdas (Πελοπίδας). A Theban general and statesman, son of Hippoclus. He was descended from a noble family, and inherited a large estate, of which he made a liberal use. He lived always in the closest friendship with Epaminondas, to whose simple frugality, as he could not persuade him to share his riches, he is said to have conformed his own mode of life. He took a leading part in expelling the Spartans from Thebes, B.C. 379; and from this time until his death there was not a year in which he was not intrusted with some important command. In 371 he was one of the Theban commanders at the battle of Leuctra, so fatal to the Lacedaemonians, and joined Epaminondas in urging the expediency of immediate action. In 369 he was also one of the generals in the first invasion of the Peloponnesus by the Thebans. (See EPAMINONDAS.) In 368 Pelopidas was sent again into Thessaly, on two separate occasions, in consequence of complaints against Alexander of Pherae. On his first expedition Alexander of Pherae sought safety in flight, and Pelopidas advanced into Macedonia to arbitrate between Alexander II. and Ptolemy of Alorus. Among the hostages whom he took with him from Macedonia was the famous Philip, the father of Alexander the Great. On his second visit to Thessaly, Pelopidas went simply as an ambassador, not expecting any opposition, and unprovided with a military force. He was seized by Alexander of Pherae, and was kept in confinement at Pherae till his liberation in 367 by a Theban force under Epaminondas. In the same year in which he was released he was sent as ambassador to Susa to counteract the Lacedaemonian and Athenian negotiations at the Persian court. In 364 the Thessalian towns again applied to Thebes for protection against Alexander, and Pelopidas was appointed to aid them. His forces, however, were dismayed by an eclipse of the sun (June 13), and, therefore, leaving them behind, he took with him into Thessaly only three hundred horse. On his arrival at Pharsalus he collected a force which he deemed sufficient, and marched against Alexander, treating lightly the great disparity of numbers, and remarking that it was better as it was, since there would be more for him to conquer. At Cynoscephalae a battle ensued, in which Pelopidas drove the enemy from their ground, but he himself was slain as, burning with resentment, he pressed rashly forward to attack Alexander in person. The Thebans and Thessalians made great lamentations for his death, and the latter, having earnestly requested leave to bury him, celebrated his funeral with extraordinary splendour.

Peloponnesian War. A name given to the great contest between Athens and her allies on the one side, and the Peloponnesian confederacy, headed by Sparta, on the other, which lasted from B.C. 431 to 404. The war, which is one of the most memorable and epoch-making in the history of Europe, was a consequence of the jealousy with which Sparta and Athens regarded each other, as States each of which was aiming at supremacy in Greece, as the heads respectively of the Dorian and Ionian races, and as patrons of the two opposite forms of civil government, oligarchy and democracy. The war was eagerly desired by a strong party in each of those States, but it was necessary to find an occasion for commencing hostilities, especially as a truce for thirty years had been concluded between Athens and Sparta in the year B.C. 445. Such an occasion was presented by the affairs of Corcyra and Potidaea. In a quarrel, which soon became a war, between Corinth and Corcyra, respecting Epidamnus, a colony of the latter State (B.C. 436), the Corcyreans applied to Athens for assistance. Their request was granted, as far as the conclusion of a defensive alliance between Athens and Corcyra, and an Athenian fleet was sent to their aid, which, however, soon engaged in active hostilities against the Corinthians. Potidaea, on the isthmus of Pallené, was a Corinthian colony, and, even after its subjection to Athens, continued to receive every year from Corinth certain functionaries or officers (ἐπιδημιουργοί). The Athenians, suspecting that the Potidaeans were inclined to join in a revolt, to which Perdiccas, king of Macedon, was instigating the towns of Chalcidicé, required them to dismiss the Corinthian functionaries, and to give other pledges of their fidelity. The Potidaeans refused, and, with most of the other Chalcidian towns, revolted from Athens and received aid from Corinth. The Athenians sent an expedition against them, and, after defeating them in battle, laid siege to Potidaea (B.C. 432). The Corinthians now obtained a meeting of the Peloponnesian confederacy at Sparta, in which they complained of the conduct of Athens with regard to Corcyra and Potidaea. After others of the allies had brought their charges against Athens, and after some of the Athenian envoys, who happened to be in the city, had defended the conduct of their State, the Spartans first, and afterwards all the allies, decided that Athens had broken the truce, and they resolved upon immediate war; King Archidamus alone recommended some delay.

In the interval necessary for preparation, an attempt was made to throw the blame of commencing hostilities upon the Athenians by sending three several embassies to Athens with demands of such a nature as could not be accepted. In the assembly which was held at Athens to give a final answer to these demands, Pericles, who was now at the height of his power, urged the people to engage in the war, and laid down a plan for the conduct of it. He advised the people to bring all their movable property from the country into the city, to abandon Attica to the ravages of the enemy, and not to suffer themselves to be provoked to give them battle with inferior numbers, but to expend all their strength upon their navy, which might be employed in carrying the war into the enemy's territory, and in collecting supplies from subject States; and further, not to attempt any new conquest while the war lasted. His advice was adopted, and the Spartan envoys were sent home with a refusal of their demands, but with an offer to refer the matters in difference to an impartial tribunal, an offer which the Lacedaemonians had no intention of accepting. After this the usual peaceful intercourse between the rival States was discontinued. Thucydides (ii. 1) dates the beginning of the war from the early spring of the year B.C. 431, the fifteenth of the thirty years' truce, when a party of Thebans made an attempt, which at first succeeded, but was ultimately defeated, to surprise Plataea.

The truce being thus openly broken, both parties addressed themselves to the war. The Peloponnesian confederacy included all the States of Peloponnesus except Achaia (which joined them afterwards) and Argos, and without the Peloponnesus, Megaris, Phocis, Locris, Boeotia, the island of Leucas, and the cities of Ambracia and Anactorium. The allies of the Athenians were Chios and Lesbos, besides Samos and the other islands of the Aegaean which had been reduced to subjection (Thera and Melos, which were still independent, remained neutral), Plataea, the Messenian colony in Naupactus, the majority of the Acarnanians, Corcyra, Zacynthus, and the Greek colonies in Asia Minor, in Thrace and Macedonia, and on the Hellespont. The resources of Sparta lay chiefly in her land forces, which, however, consisted of contingents from the allies, whose period of service was limited; the Spartans were also deficient in money. The Athenian strength lay in the fleet, which was manned chiefly by foreign sailors, whom the wealth collected from the allies enabled them to pay. Thucydides informs us that the cause of the Lacedaemonians was the more popular, as they professed to be deliverers of Greece, while the Athenians were fighting in defence of a dominion which had become odious through their tyranny, and to which the States which yet retained their independence feared to be brought into subjection.

In the summer of the year B.C. 431 the Peloponnesians invaded Attica under the command of Archidamus, king of Sparta. Their progress was slow, as Archidamus appears to have been still anxious to try what could be done by intimidating the Athenians before proceeding to extremities. Yet their presence was found to be a greater calamity than the people had anticipated; and when Archidamus made his appearance at Acharnae, they began loudly to demand to be led out to battle. Pericles firmly adhered to his plan of defence, and the Peloponnesians returned home. Before their departure the Athenians had sent out a fleet of a hundred sail, which was joined by fifty Corcyrean ships, to waste the coasts of Peloponnesus; and towards the autumn Pericles led the whole disposable force of the city into Megaris, which he laid waste. In the same summer the Athenians expelled the inhabitants of Aegina from their island, which they colonized with Athenian settlers. In the winter there was a public funeral at Athens for those who had fallen in the war, and Pericles pronounced over them an oration, the substance of which is preserved by Thucydides (ii. 35–46). In the following summer (B.C. 430) the Peloponnesians again invaded Attica under Archidamus, who now entirely laid aside the forbearance which he had shown the year before, and left scarcely a corner of the land unravaged. This invasion lasted forty days. In the meantime, a grievous pestilence broke out in Athens, and raged with the more virulence on account of the crowded state of the city. Of this terrible visitation Thucydides, who was himself a sufferer, has left a minute and apparently faithful description (ii. 46 foll.). The murmurs of the people against Pericles were renewed, and he was compelled to call an assembly to defend his policy. He succeeded so far as to prevent any overtures for peace being made to the Lacedaemonians, but he himself was fined, though immediately afterwards he was reëlected general. While the Peloponnesians were in Attica, Pericles led a fleet to ravage the coasts of Peloponnesus. In the winter of this year Potidaea surrendered to the Athenians on favourable terms (Thuc. ii. 70). The next year (B.C. 429), instead of invading Attica, the Peloponnesians laid siege to Plataea. The brave resistance of the inhabitants forced their enemies to convert the siege into a blockade. In the same summer, an invasion of Acarnania by the Ambracians and a body of Peloponnesian troops was repulsed; and a large Peloponnesian fleet, which was to have joined in the attack on Acarnania, was twice defeated by Phormion in the mouth of the Corinthian Gulf. An expedition sent by the Athenians against the revolted Chalcidian towns was defeated with great loss.

In the preceding year (B.C. 430) the Athenians had concluded an alliance with Sitalces, king of the Odrysae in Thrace, and Perdiccas, king of Macedon, on which occasion Sitalces had promised to aid the Athenians to subdue their revolted subjects in Chalcidicé. He now collected an army of 150,000 men, with which he first invaded Macedonia, to revenge the breach of certain promises which Perdiccas had made to him the year before, and afterwards laid waste the territory of the Chalcidians and Bottiaeans, but he did not attempt to reduce any of the Greek cities. About the middle of this year Pericles died. The invasion of Attica was repeated in the next summer (B.C. 428), and immediately afterwards all Lesbos except Methymné revolted from the Athenians, who laid siege to Mitylené. The Mitylenaeans begged aid from Sparta, which was promised, and they were admitted into the Spartan alliance. In the same winter a body of Plataeans, amounting to 220, made their escape from the besieged city in the night, and took refuge in Athens. In the summer of B.C. 427 the Peloponnesians again invaded Attica, while they sent a fleet of forty-two galleys, under Alcidas, to the relief of Mitylené. Before the fleet arrived Mitylené had surrendered, and Alcidas, after a little delay, sailed home. In an assembly which was held at Athens to decide on the fate of the Mitylenaeans, it was resolved, at the instigation of Cleon, that all the adult citizens should be put to death, and the women and children made slaves; but this barbarous decree was repealed the next day. The land of the Lesbians (except Methymné) was seized and divided among Athenian citizens, to whom the inhabitants paid a rent for the occupation of their former property. In the same summer the Plataeans surrendered; they were massacred, and their city was given up to the Thebans, who razed it to the ground. In the year B.C. 426 the Lacedaemonians were deterred from invading Attica by earthquakes. An expedition against Aetolia, under the

Athenian general Demosthenes, completely failed; but afterwards Demosthenes and the Acarnanians routed the Ambracians, who nearly all perished. In the winter (B.C. 426–425) the Athenians purified the island of Delos, as an acknowledgment to Apollo for the cessation of the plague.

At the beginning of the summer of B.C. 425 the Peloponnesians invaded Attica for the fifth time. At the same time the Athenians, who had long directed their thoughts towards Sicily, sent a fleet to aid the Leontini in a war with Syracuse. Demosthenes accompanied this fleet, in order to act, as occasion might offer, on the coast of Peloponnesus. He fortified Pylus on the coast of Messenia, the northern headland of the modern Bay of Navarino. In the course of the operations which were undertaken to dislodge him, a body of Lacedaemonians, including several noble Spartans, got blockaded in the island of Sphacteria, at the mouth of the bay, and were ultimately taken prisoners by Cleon and Demosthenes. Pylus was garrisoned by a colony of Messenians, in order to annoy the Spartans. After this event the Athenians engaged in vigorous offensive operations, of which the most important was the capture of the island of Cythera by Nicias early in B.C. 424. This summer, however, the Athenians suffered some reverses in Boeotia, where they lost the battle of Delium, and on the coasts of Macedonia and Thrace, where Brasidas, among other exploits, took Amphipolis. The Athenian expedition to Sicily was abandoned, after some operations of no great importance, in consequence of a general pacification of the island, which was effected through the influence of Hermocrates, a citizen of Syracuse. In the year B.C. 423 a year's truce was concluded between Sparta and Athens, with a view to a lasting peace. Hostilities were renewed in B.C. 422, and Cleon was sent to cope with Brasidas, who had continued his operations even during the truce. A battle was fought between these generals at Amphipolis, in which the defeat of the Athenians was amply compensated by the double deliverance which they experienced in the death both of Cleon and Brasidas. In the following year (B.C. 421) Nicias succeeded in negotiating a peace with Sparta for fifty years, the terms of which were a mutual restitution of conquests made during the war and the release of the prisoners taken at Sphacteria. This treaty was ratified by all the allies of Sparta except the Boeotians, Corinthians, Eleans, and Megarians. This peace never rested on any firm basis. It was no sooner concluded than it was discovered that Sparta had not the power to fulfil her promises, and Athens insisted on their performance. The jealousy of the other States was excited by a treaty of alliance which was concluded between Sparta and Athens immediately after the peace, and intrigues were commenced for the formation of a new confederacy, with Argos at the head. An attempt was made to draw Sparta into alliance with Argos, but it failed. A similar overture subsequently made to Athens met with better success, chiefly through an artifice of Alcibiades, who was at the head of a large party hostile to the peace, and the Athenians concluded a treaty offensive and defensive with Argos, Elis, and Mantinea for one hundred years (B.C. 420). In the year B.C. 418 the Argive confederacy was broken up by their defeat at the battle of Mantinea, and a peace, and soon after an alliance, was made between Sparta and Argos. In the year B.C. 416 an expedition was undertaken by the Athenians against Melos, which had hitherto remained neutral. The Melians surrendered at discretion; all the males who had attained manhood were put to death; the women and children were made slaves; and subsequently five hundred Athenian colonists were sent to occupy the island (Thuc. v. 116).

The fifty years' peace was not considered at an end, though its terms had been broken on both sides, till the year B.C. 415, when the Athenians undertook their daring and tragic expedition to Sicily. (See SYRACUSAE.) Sicily proved a rock against which their resources and efforts were fruitlessly expended. And Sparta, which furnished but a commander and a handful of men for the defence of Syracuse, soon beheld her antagonist reduced, by a series of unparalleled misfortunes, to a state of the utmost distress and weakness. The accustomed procrastination of the Spartans, and the timid policy to which they ever adhered, alone preserved Athens in this critical moment, or at least retarded her downfall. Time was allowed for her citizens to recover from the panic and consternation occasioned by the news of the Sicilian disaster; and instead of viewing hostile fleets, as they had anticipated, ravaging their coasts and blockading the Piraeus, they were enabled still to dispute the empire of the sea and to preserve the most valuable of their dependencies. Alcibiades, whose exile had proved so injurious to his country, since it was to his counsels alone that the successes of her enemies are to be attributed, now interposed in her behalf, and by his intrigues prevented the Persian satrap, Tissaphernes, from placing at the disposal of the Spartan admiral that superiority of force which must at once have terminated the war by the complete overthrow of the Athenian Republic (Thuc. viii.). The temporary revolution which was effected at Athens by his contrivance also, and which placed the State at variance with the fleet and army stationed at Samos, afforded him another opportunity of rendering a real service to his country by moderating the violence and animosity of the latter. The victory of Cynossema and the subsequent successes of Alcibiades, now elected to the chief command of the forces of his country, once more restored Athens to the command of the sea, and, had she reposed that confidence in the talents of her generals which they deserved and her necessities required, the efforts of Sparta and the gold of Persia might have proved unavailing. But the second exile of Alcibiades, and, still more, the iniquitous sentence which condemned to death the generals who fought and conquered at Arginusae, sealed the fate of Athens; and the battle of Aegos Potamos at length terminated a contest which had been carried on, with scarcely any intermission, during a period of twenty-seven years, with a spirit and animosity unparalleled in the annals of warfare. Lysander now sailed to Athens, receiving as he went the submission of the allies, and blockaded the city, which surrendered after a few months (B.C. 404) on terms dictated by Sparta, with a view of making Athens a useful ally by giving the ascendency in the State to the oligarchical party.

The history of the Peloponnesian War was written by Thucydides, upon whose accuracy and impartiality, as far as his narrative goes, we may place the fullest dependence. His history ends abruptly in the year B.C. 411. For the rest of the war we have to follow Xenophon and Diodorus. The value of Xenophon's history is impaired by his prejudice, and that of Diodorus by his carelessness.

Peloponnēsus (Πελοπόννησος). Now the Morea; the southern part of Greece, or the peninsula, which was connected with Hellas proper by the isthmus of Corinth. It is said to have derived its name—Peloponnesus, or the "island of Pelops"—from the mythical Pelops. (See PELOPS.) This name does not occur in Homer. In his time the peninsula was sometimes called Apia, from Apis, son of Phoroneus, king of Argos, and sometimes Argos, which names were given to it on account of Argos being the chief power in Peloponnesus at that period. On the east and south there are three great gulfs—the Argolic, Laconian, and Messenian. The ancients compared the shape of the country to the leaf of a plane-tree; and its modern name, the Morea, which first occurs in the twelfth century of the Christian era, was given to it on account of its resemblance to a mulberry-leaf. Peloponnesus was divided into various provinces, all of which were bounded on one side by the sea, with the exception of Arcadia, which was in the centre of the country. These provinces were Achaia in the north, Elis in the west, Messenia in the west and south, Laconia in the south and east, and Corinthia in the east and north. An account of the geography of the peninsula is given under these names. The area of Peloponnesus is computed to be 7779 English square miles, and it probably contained a population of upwards of a million in the flourishing period of Greek history.

The Peloponnesus was originally inhabited by Pelasgians. Subsequently the Achaeans, who belonged to the Aeolic race, settled in the eastern and southern parts of the peninsula, in Argolis, Laconia, and Messenia; and the Ionians in the northern part, in Achaia; while the remains of the original inhabitants of the country, the Pelasgians, collected chiefly in the central part, in Arcadia. Eighty years after the Trojan War, according to mythical chronology, the Dorians, under the conduct of the Heraclidae, invaded and conquered Peloponnesus, and established Doric States in Argolis, Laconia, and Messenia, whence they extended their power over Corinth, Sicyon, and Megara. Part of the Achaean population remained in these provinces as tributary subjects to the Dorians, under the name of Perioeci; while others of the Achaeans passed over to the north of the Peloponnesus, expelled the Ionians, and settled in this part of the country, which was called after them Achaia. The Aetolians, who had invaded the Peloponnesus along with the Dorians, settled in Elis, and became intermingled with the original inhabitants. The peninsula remained under Doric influence during the most important period of Greek history, and opposed to the great Ionic city of Athens. After the conquest of Messenia by the Spartans it was under the supremacy of Sparta till the overthrow of the power of the latter by the Thebans at the battle of Leuctra, B.C. 371. See Curtius, *Peloponnesos* (Gotha, 1851–52); Clark, *Peloponnesus* (London, 1858); Gell, *Itinerary of the Morea* (London, 1827); Beulé, *Études sur le Péloponèse* (Paris, 1875); Leake, *Peloponnesiaca* (London, 1846); Wyse, *Excursion in the Peloponnesus* (London, 1865); Bursian, *Geographie von Griechenland*, ii. pp. 1–343 (Leipzig, 1872); and the articles DORIS; HERACLIDAE; and HELLAS.

Pelops (Πέλοψ, "Black-face"). A grandson of Zeus and son of Tantalus and Dioné, the daughter of Atlas. Some writers call his mother Euryanassa or Clytia. He was married to Hippodamia, by whom he became the father of Atreus, Thyestes, Dias, Cynosurus, Corinthius, Hippalmus (Hippalcmus or Hippalcimus), Hippasus, Cleon, Argius, Alcathoüs, Aelius, Pittheus, Troezen, Nicippé, and Lysidicé, known collectively as the Pelopidae. By Axioché or the nymph Danaïs he is said to have been the father of Chrysippus. Pelops was king of Pisa in Elis, and from him the great southern peninsula of Greece was believed to have derived its name Peloponnesus. According to a tradition which became very general in later times, Pelops was a Phrygian, who was expelled by Ilus from Phrygia (Ovid, *Met.* viii. 622), and thereupon migrated with his great wealth to Pisa. Others describe him as a Paphlagonian, and call the Paphlagonians themselves Πελοπήϊοι. Others again represent him as a native of Greece; and there can be little doubt that in the earliest traditions Pelops was described as a native of Greece and not as a foreign immigrant; in them, also, he is called the tamer of horses and the favourite of Poseidon. The legends about Pelops consist mainly of (*a*) the story of his being cut to pieces and boiled; (*b*) of his contest with Oenomaüs and Hippodamia; and (*c*) of his relation to his sons, to which may be added the honours paid to his remains.

(*a*) The first tells how Tantalus, the favourite of the gods, once invited them to a repast, and on that occasion killed his own son, and having boiled him set the flesh before them that they might eat it. But the immortal gods, knowing what it was, did not touch it; Demeter alone, being absorbed by grief for her lost daughter, consumed the shoulder of Pelops. Hereupon the gods ordered Hermes to put the limbs of Pelops into a caldron, and thereby restore him to life. When the process was over, Clotho took him out of the caldron, and as the shoulder consumed by Demeter was wanting, the goddess supplied its place by one made of ivory; his descendants (the Pelopidae), as a mark of their origin, were believed to have one shoulder as white as ivory.

(*b*) As an oracle had declared to Oenomaüs that he should be killed by his son-in-law, he refused giving his daughter Hippodamia in marriage to any one. But since many suitors appeared, Oenomaüs declared that he would bestow her hand upon the man who should conquer him in the chariot-race, but that he should kill all who were defeated by him. Among other suitors Pelops also presented himself; but when he saw the heads of his conquered predecessors stuck up above the door of Oenomaüs he was seized with fear, and endeavoured to gain the favour of Myrtilus, the charioteer of Oenomaüs, promising him half the kingdom if he would assist him in conquering his master. Myrtilus agreed, and drew out the linchpins of the chariot of Oenomaüs. In the race the chariot of Oenomaüs broke down, and he was thrown out and killed. Thus Hippodamia became the wife of Pelops. But as Pelops had now gained his object, he was unwilling to keep faith with Myrtilus; and accordingly, as they were driving along a cliff, he threw Myrtilus into the sea. As Myrtilus sank he cursed Pelops and his whole race. Pelops returned with Hippodamia to Pisa in Elis, and soon also made himself master of Olympia, where he restored the Olympian Games with greater splendour than they had ever been celebrated before.

(*c*) Chrysippus was the favourite of his father, and was, in consequence, envied by his brothers. The eldest two among them, Atreus and Thyestes, with the connivance of Hippodamia, accordingly murdered Chrysippus, and threw his body into a well. Pelops, who suspected his sons of the murder, expelled them from the country. Hippodamia, dreading the anger of her husband, fled to Midea in Argolis, whence her remains were afterwards conveyed by Pelops to Olympia.

Pelops, after his death, was honoured at Olympia above all other heroes. His tomb, with an iron sarcophagus, existed on the banks of the Alpheus, not far from the temple of Artemis, near Pisa. The spot on which his sanctuary (Πελόπιον) stood in the Altis was said to have been dedicated by Heracles, who also offered to him the first sacrifices. The magistrates of the Eleans likewise offered to him there an annual sacrifice, consisting of a black ram, with special ceremonies. The name of Pelops was so celebrated that it was constantly used by the poets in connection with his descendants and the cities they inhabited. Hence we find Atreus, the son of Pelops, called *Pelopeïus Atreus*, and Agamemnon, the grandson or great-grandson of Atreus, called *Pelopeïus Agamemnon*. In the same way Iphigenia, the daughter of Agamemnon, and Hermioné, the wife of Menelaüs, are each called by Ovid *Pelopeïa virgo*. Vergil (*Aen*. ii. 193) uses the phrase *Pelopea moenia* to signify the cities in Peloponnesus which Pelops and his descendants ruled over; and in like manner Mycenae is called by Ovid *Pelopeïades Mycenae*.

Peloria (Πελώρια). A Thessalian festival resembling the Roman Saturnalia (q. v.). In it sacrifices were offered to Zeus Pelorius; banquets open even to strangers were given; and slaves enjoyed the utmost freedom, being waited upon by their masters. See Athen. xiv. p. 639.

Pelōris (Πελωρίς), **Pelorias** (Πελωριάς), or **Pelorus** (Πελωρός). Now Cape Faro. The northeast point of Sicily and one of the three promontories which formed the triangular figure of the island. According to the usual story, it derived its name from Pelorus, the pilot of Hannibal's ship (Val. Max. ix. 8, 1); but the name was more ancient than Hannibal's time, being mentioned by Thucydides (iv. 25).

Pelso or **Peiso**. Now the Plattensee; a great lake in Pannonia which the emperor Galerius connected with the Danube (Aurel. Vict. *Caes*. 40).

Pelta (πέλτη). A small, round shield made of wicker-work or wood, covered with hide or leather (Xen. *Anab*. ii. 1, 6). The name is also given to the Thracian shield, which was rectangular in shape (Schol. *in* Thuc. ii. 29). See CETRA; CLIPEUS.

Amazons with Peltae. (Rich.)

Peltae (Πέλται). An ancient and flourishing city in the north of Phrygia (Xen. *Anab*. i. 2, 10).

Peltastae (πελτασταί). The Greek light-armed foot-soldiers, forming an arm intermediate between the heavily equipped hoplites and the sharp-shooters (γυμνῆτες). The name is taken from the πέλτη, a light shield of Thracian origin. (See CLIPEUS.) For attack they had a javelin, or ἀκόντιον, and a long sword. These troops originated in Thrace and North Greece, and the peltastae serving in the Peloponnesian War and in the armies of the younger Cyrus and Agesilaüs belonged to those countries. Iphicrates equipped his mercenaries with this kind of armament, introducing at the same time linen doublets and, instead of greaves, what were called after him ἰφικρατίδες, something between boots and leggings (Diod. xv. 44). In the Macedonian army their place was taken by the ὑπασπισταί. See EXERCITUS.

Pelusium (Πηλούσιον, Old Test. Sin; both names are derived from nouns meaning "mud"). A celebrated city of Lower Egypt, standing on the east side of the easternmost mouth of the Nile, which was called after it the Pelusiac mouth, twenty stadia (about two miles) from the sea, in the midst of morasses, from which it obtained its name. As the key to Egypt on the northeast, and the frontier city towards Syria and Arabia, it was strongly fortified, and was the scene of many battles and sieges. It was the birthplace of the geographer Ptolemaeus.

Pelvis (ποδανιπτήρ). A vessel for washing the feet (Varro, *L. L.* v. 19). It was of pottery, bronze, or even silver. Other names applied to it are PELLUVIA and PELLUVIUM. The POLLUBRUM was used for either hands or feet. See MALLUVIUM.

Pelvis. (Pompeian painting.)

Pen. See PALAEOGRAPHY; STILUS.

Penātes. With VESTA and LAR, the household gods of the Romans; strictly the guardians of the store-room (*penus*), which in old Roman houses stood next the atrium; in later times, near the back of the building (*penetralia*). They were two in number, and presided over the well-being of the house, their blessing being shown in the fulness of the store-room. This chamber, therefore, as being sacred to them, was holy, and not to be entered except by chaste and undefiled persons. The hearth of the house was their altar, and on it were sculptured the figures of the two Penates beside that of the Lar. Often they were represented dancing and raising a drinking-horn to symbolize a joyful and prosperous life. The offerings to them were made jointly with those to the Lar. (See LARES.) There were also Penates belonging to the State. These at first had their temple in the Velian Quarter, where their statues stood below those of the Dioscuri. Afterwards it was supposed that the original Penates, brought from Samothrace to Troy, and thence conveyed by Aeneas to Lavinium, were identical with certain symbols kept with the Palladium in a secret part of the temple of Vesta. The Penates of the Latin League, which were at first regarded as the Trojan Penates, were enshrined in the sanctuary at Lavinium. Annual offerings were brought to them by the Roman priests, and also by consuls, praetors, and dictators on assuming or laying down office, and by generals on their departure for their provinces.

Peneleōs (Πηνέλεως). One of the Argonauts, son of Hippalcmus and Asteropé. He was numbered among the suitors of Helen and was the father of Opheltes. He led the Boeotians in the Trojan War, slaying Ilioneus and Lycon; and was himself wounded by Polydamus and killed by Eurypylus, son of Telephus. See Pausan. ix. 5, 8; Apollod. i. 9, 16; *Il.* ii. 494; xix. 487.

Penelŏpé (Πηνελόπη and Πενελόπη). A princess of Greece, daughter of Icarius, brother of Tyndarus, king of Sparta, and of Polycasté or Periboea. She became the wife of Odysseus (q. v.), monarch of Ithaca, and her marriage was celebrated about the same time with that of Menelaüs and Helen. Penelopé became by Odysseus the mother of Telemachus, and was obliged soon after to part with her husband, whom the Greeks compelled to go to the Trojan War. Twenty years passed away, and Odysseus did not return to his home. Meanwhile his palace at Ithaca was crowded with numerous and importunate suitors, aspiring to the hand of the queen. Her relatives also urged her to abandon all thoughts of the probability of her husband's return, and not to disregard, as she had, the solicitations of the rival aspirants to her favour. Penelopé, however, exerted every resource which her ingenuity could suggest to protract the period of her decision: among others she declared that she would make choice of one of them as soon as she should have completed a web that she was weaving (intended as a funeral ornament for the aged Laërtes); but she baffled their expectations by undoing at night what she had accomplished during the day. This artifice has given rise to the proverb of "Penelopé's web," or "to unweave the web of Penelopé" (*Penelopes telam retexere*), applied to whatever labour appears to be endless. For three years this artifice succeeded, but on the beginning of a fourth a disclosure was made by one of her female attendants; and the faithful and unhappy Penelopé, constrained at length by the renewed importunities of her persecutors, agreed, at their instigation, to bestow her hand on him who should shoot an arrow from the bow of Odysseus through a given number of axe-eyes placed in succession. An individual disguised as a beggar was the successful archer. This was no other than Odysseus, who had just returned to Ithaca. The hero then directed his shafts at the suitors, and slew them all. The character of Penelopé has been variously represented, some writers saying that she was unfaithful to Odysseus with all the suitors, and that from this intercourse was born Pan; but it is the more general version that she is to be considered as a model of conjugal and domestic virtue.

Penelopé. (*Ant. Denkm.* i. 3, p. 17.)

Penestae (Πενέσται). In Thessaly the descendants of the older population subdued by the Thessalians and occupying a position analogous to that of the Helots of Laconia. They managed the property of the owners as serfs bound to the soil, paying a moderate tax, and being also liable to be called out for military service; but their lords could not remove them from the land nor put them to death. See Grote, *Hist. of Greece*, ii. pp. 373–376.

Penēus (Πηνειός). (1) Now the Salambria; the principal river in Thessaly, rising in Mount Lacmon; after receiving the waters of the Enipeus, Lethaeus, and Titaresius rivers, it passes through the Vale of Tempé between Mounts Ossa and Olympus, and empties into the sea. (See TEMPÉ.) The river-god Peneus was the son of Oceanus and Tethys (Hes. *Theog.* 343). By the Naiad Creüsa he became the father of Hypseus, Stilbé, and Daphné. He was also the father (by some called the husband) of Cyrené. (2) Now the Gastuni, a river of Elis.

Penicillus (ῥαβδίον). A painter's brush, some being made with hair (Pliny, *H. N.* xxviii. 71) and some with sponge (id. ix. 69). See PICTURA.

Penicŭlus. (1) The same as *penicillus* (q. v.). (2) A brush for dusting (Plaut. *Men.* i. 1, 1).

Penius. A little river of Pontus, falling into the Euxine (Ovid, *Epist. ex Ponto*, iv. 10).

Penna. (1) A quill; used for various purposes, as for toothpicks (Mart. xiv. 22). (2) A pen; so only after the fourth century A.D. See Isidor. *Orig.* xiv. 3; Beckmann, *Hist. of Inventions*, i. p. 408 (London, 1846); and WRITING AND WRITING MATERIALS.

Pennīnae Alpes. See ALPES.

Pensum (from *pendo*) That which is weighed out as a task, especially of a portion of wool given to female slaves to spin (Iustin. i. 3).

Pentacosiomedimni (πεντακοσιομέδιμνοι). The first of the four classes of citizens instituted at Athens by Solon. See EISPHORA; SOLON.

Pentapŏlis (Πεντάπολις). The name for any association of five cities, but applied specifically to the five chief cities of Cyrenaïca in North Africa —Cyrené, Berenicé, Arsinoë, Ptolemaïs, and Apollonia.

Pentathlon (πένταθλον). In Greek gymnastics a contest compounded of the five events (running, jumping, wrestling, throwing the discus, and the javelin). After each separate event the defeated stood out, till finally two contested the victory in the wrestling. See ATHLETAE; DISCUS; GYMNASIUM; QUINQUERTIUM.

Pentecontŏrus (πεντηκόντορος). A kind of Greek ship in which there were fifty oarsmen arranged in a single row. See NAVIS.

Pentecosté (πεντηκοστή). A custom duty of one fiftieth (two per cent.) levied on imports and exports at Athens (Harpocr. s. h. v.) On imports the duty was paid upon unloading (Demosth. *Lacrit.* p. 932, § 29), and on exports probably at the time when the goods were shipped. The collection of the customs was farmed out, probably from year to year, by the πωληταί to the highest bidder. The persons so receiving the right to receive them were called τελῶναι (see TELONAE), whose chief officer was called ἀρχώνης (Andoc. 17). The collectors of the duty were called πεντηκοστολόγοι. Two other taxes of a like nature were paid by merchants—the ἐλλιμένιον, probably a harbour-due, and the ἑκατοστή, a tax of one per cent., as to which no details are known. Smuggling was practised to some extent (Demosth. l. c. § 28). Nothing is said by the ancient writers of customs duties imposed on articles brought by land. See Boeckh, *Staatshaushaltung*, i. pp. 384–387, 390; ii. p. 77 (3d edition).

Pentecostys (πεντηκοστύς). In the Spartan army a division of the λόχος. See LOCHUS.

Pentelĭcus (τὸ Πεντελικὸν ὄρος). A mountain in Attica, celebrated for its marble; a branch of Mount Parnes, from which it runs in a southeasterly direction between Athens and Marathon to the coast. It was also called BRILESSUS (Βριλησσός, Thuc. ii. 23). See ATHENAE.

Pentēres (πεντήρης). A quinquereme, i. e. the form of Greek ship in which there were five rows of oarsmen one above the other. See NAVIS.

Penthesilēa (Πενθεσίλεια). A celebrated queen of the Amazons, daughter of Ares, who came to the aid of Priam in the last year of the Trojan War, and was slain by Achilles after having displayed great acts of valour. Achilles, after he had slain Penthesilea, admiring the prowess which she had exhibited, and struck by the beauty of the corpse, wished the Greeks to erect a tomb to her. Thersites (q. v.) thereupon both ridiculed the grief which the hero testified at her fall and indulged in other remarks so grossly offensive that Achilles slew him on the spot. Diomedes, the relative of Thersites, in revenge for his death, dragged the dead body of the Amazon out of the camp, and threw it into the Scamander. Other accounts say that Achilles buried it on the banks of the Xanthus (Tzetz. *ad* Lyc. 997).

Pentheus (Πενθεύς). The son of Echion by Agavé, daughter of Cadmus. He was the successor of Cadmus as king of Thebes, and on the introduction of the Bacchic worship resisted it. It is said that Pentheus concealed himself in a tree in order to witness secretly the orgies of the Bacchanals, and on being discovered by them was taken for a wild beast, and torn in pieces by his own mother and his two sisters, Ino and Autonoë, in their Bacchic frenzy. The scene of this occurrence was said to be Mount Cithaeron or Mount Parnassus. The story forms the subject of the *Bacchae* of Euripides. (See EURIPIDES.) The Corinthians had a tradition that the tree in which Pentheus hid was afterwards carved into images of the god Dionysus and worshipped (Pausan. ii. 6, 6). Hence some have tried to connect the story of Pentheus with the primitive tree-worship.

Pentri. One of the most important of the tribes in Samnium. Their chief town was Bovianum. They were the only Samnites who remained loyal to the Romans in the Second Punic War (Livy, ix. 31; xxii. 61).

Peos Artemĭdos (Πέος Αρτεμίδος). Now Beni Hassan. A city of Middle Egypt on the east bank of the Nile, nearly opposite Hermopolis. It is the site of some remarkable catacombs, hewn out of the solid rock, and having walls covered with paintings and sculptures.

Peparēthus (Πεπάρηθος). A small island in the Aegaean Sea, off the coast of Thessaly, and east of Halonesus. It produced a considerable quantity of wine.

Pephrēdo (Πεφρηδώ). One of the Graiae (q. v.).

Peplus (πέπλος). (1) A Greek woman's garment, large, broad, hanging in folds, and usually richly embroidered. It was thrown over the rest of the clothing, and wrapped round the whole of the body. (2) In particular, the State robe of Athené, which was a work of art, embroidered with groups from the battle of the Giants, representations of the exploits of heroes under Athené's guidance, scenes of Attic history, and portraits of celebrated men. It was woven by the wives and maidens of Attica for the statue of Athené as goddess of the State, and presented at the Panathenaic festival. See PANATHENAEA.

Pera (πήρα). A wallet or bag slung over the shoulder and hanging under the arm at the side. It was carried by beggars and peasants. See BULGA.

Peraea (Περαία, i. e. "the country on the opposite side"). A general name for any district belonging to or closely connected with a country, from the main part of which it was separated by a sea or river. (1) The part of Palestine east of the Jordan. (2) PERAEA RHODIŌRUM, a district in the south of Caria, opposite to the island of Rhodes, and subject to the Rhodians, extending from Mount Phoenix on the west to the frontier of Lycia on the east. (3) PERAEA TENEDIŌRUM, a strip of the western coast of Mysia, near Adramyttium, one of the colonies of the Mitylenaeans.

Percentage. See FENUS.

Percōté (Περκώτη). A very ancient city of Mysia, between Abydos and Lampsacus, near the Hellespont.

Perdiccas (Περδίκκας). (1) The founder of the Macedonian monarchy according to Herodotus (viii. 137). He and his two brothers Gauanes and Aëropus were Argives who settled near Mount Bermius, whence they gradually conquered a part of the territory that was later known as Macedonia. Other writers, however, make Caranus the founder of the kingdom and Perdiccas only the fourth among the early kings. (See CARANUS.) Perdiccas was succeeded by his son Argaeus. See MACEDONIA. (2) The son and successor of Alexander I. of Macedonia, reigning from B.C. 454 to 413. Shortly before the Peloponnesian War, Perdiccas was at war with the Athenians, who sent a force to support his brother Philip, and Derdas, a Macedonian chieftain, against the king, while the latter espoused the cause of Potidaea, which had shaken off the Athenian yoke, B.C. 432 (Diod. Sic. xii. 34). In the following year peace was concluded between Perdiccas and the Athenians, but it did not last long, and he was during the greater part of his reign on hostile terms with the Athenians. In B.C. 429 his dominions were invaded by Sitalces, king of the powerful Thracian tribe of the Odrysians, but the enemy was compelled, by want of provisions, to return home (Diod. Sic. xii. 50). It was in great part at his instigation that Brasidas in B.C. 424 set out on his celebrated expedition to Macedonia and Thrace. In the following year (B.C. 423), however, a misunderstanding arose between him and Brasidas; in consequence of which he abandoned the Spartan alliance, and concluded peace with Athens (Thuc. iv. 82). Subsequently we find him at one time in alliance with the Spartans and at another time with the Athenians; and it is evident that he joined one or other of the belligerent parties according to the dictates of his own interest at the moment. (3) PERDICCAS III., king of Macedonia, B.C. 364–359, was the second son of Amyntas II., by his wife Eurydicé. On the assassination of his brother Alexander II., by Ptolemy of Alorus, B.C. 367, the crown of Macedonia devolved upon him by hereditary right, but Ptolemy virtually enjoyed the sovereign power as guardian of Perdiccas till B.C. 364, when the latter caused Ptolemy to be put to death, and took the government into his own hands (Just. vii. 4). Of the reign of Perdiccas we have very little information. We learn only that he was at one time engaged in hostilities with Athens on account of Amphipolis, and that he was distinguished for his patronage of men of letters. He fell in battle against the Illyrians in B.C. 359. (4) Son of Orontes, a Macedonian of the province of Orestis, was one of the most distinguished of the generals of Alexander the Great. He accompanied Alexander throughout his campaign in Asia; and the king, on his death-bed, is said to have taken the royal signet ring from his finger and given it to Perdiccas (Q. Curt. x. 5, 4). After the death of the king (B.C. 323), Perdiccas had the chief authority intrusted to him under the command of the new king Arrhidaeus, who was a mere puppet in his hands, and he still further strengthened his power by the assassination of his rival Meleager. (See MELEAGER.) The other generals of Alexander regarded him with fear and suspicion; and at length his ambitious schemes induced Antipater, Craterus, and Ptolemy to unite in a league and declare open war against Perdiccas. Thus assailed on all sides, Perdiccas determined to leave Eumenes in Asia Minor, to make head against their common enemies in that quarter, while he himself marched into Egypt against Ptolemy. He advanced without opposition as far as Pelusium, but found the banks of the Nile strongly fortified and guarded by Ptolemy, and was repulsed in repeated attempts to force the passage of the river; in the last of which, near Memphis, he lost great numbers of men. Thereupon his troops, who had long been discontented with Perdiccas, rose in mutiny and put him to death in his own tent (Diod. xviii. 14–36).

Perdix (Πέρδιξ). The sister of Daedalus, and mother of Talos, or, according to others, the sister's son of Daedalus, figures in the mythological period of Greek art as the inventor of various implements, chiefly for working in wood. Perdix is sometimes confounded with Talos or Calos, and it is best to regard the various legends respecting Perdix, Talos, and Calos as referring to one and the same person—namely, according to the mythographers, a nephew of Daedalus. The inventions ascribed to him are the saw, the idea of which is said to have been suggested to him by the back-bone of a fish, or the teeth of a serpent; the chisel; the compasses; the potter's wheel. His skill excited the jealousy of Daedalus, who threw him headlong from the temple of Athené on the Acropolis, but the goddess caught him in his fall, and changed him into the bird which was named after him, πέρδιξ, the partridge. See TALOS.

Perduellio. The Roman term for all acts whereby an individual within the State showed himself an enemy (*perduellis*) of the established constitution. It included attempts at despotic power, usurpation or abuse of magisterial powers (*e. g.* the execution of a citizen), violation of the sanctity of the *tribuni plebis*, etc. In the time of the kings, the king himself tried crimes of the kind, or handed over the decision to two deputies appointed in each instance by himself, *duoviri capitales* or *perduellionis*, from whom an appeal lay to the people; after Servius Tullius, to the Comitia Centuriata. Under the Republic, duoviri were still appointed as presiding judges, till this gradually fell into disuse, and trials of the kind came in general to be dealt with by the popular court. In earlier times the penalty was death by hanging on a tree, by throwing from the Tarpeian Rock, or by beheading; later, banishment, and after the tribunes brought cases of perduellio before the Comitia Tributa, fines as well. From the latter half of the second century B.C. the less important cases began to be treated as offences of *maiestas;* and by Caesar's Julian law, B.C. 46, all cases of *perduellio* were included under this name. See MAIESTAS, p. 999.

Peregrīnus. The description in Roman law of any foreigner or person other than a citizen sojourning or domiciled within Roman territory. Originally peregrini were entirely without rights, unless they obtained a *patronus*, except in cases where there was a treaty (*foedus*) with the State to which they belonged, regulating the legal position of the subjects of the two States respectively. But the increasing intercourse between Rome and other States, and the consequent growth in the number of peregrini in Rome, made it necessary to grant to all foreigners a definite competency to acquire property, enter into obligations, and the like; and for the decision of civil suits between foreigners and citizens, or of foreigners among themselves, a special praetor (q. v.) was appointed. From the public, private, and sacrificial law of Rome they were always excluded. See Morey, *Outlines of Roman Law* (N. Y. 1891), and the article CIVITAS.

Peregrīnus Proteus. A Cynic philosopher of Parium who flourished during the reign of the Antonines in the second century A.D. As a young man he was a notorious profligate, but afterwards turned Christian during a visit to Palestine. Later he became a Cynic and travelled about from place to place seeking notoriety. He finally decided to burn himself to death in public at the Olympic Games, and executed this purpose in A.D. 165. An account of his life was written by Lucian, who was present at his death-scene. See Gell. xi. 13.

Perenna, Anna. See Anna Perenna.

Perennis. A praefect of the Praetorian Guard at Rome who succeeded Paternus as sole commander in A.D. 183. As the emperor Commodus was wholly given up to debauchery, Perennis was practically supreme in the State; but having incurred the hatred of his troops, he was massacred by them in A.D. 186 or 187. Opinions differ as to the character of Perennis—Dio Cassius eulogizing him and other historians accusing him of complicity in the evil actions of the emperor (Dio Cass. lxxii. 9; *Vit. Commod.* 5, 6).

Perfumes. See Unguentum.

Perga (Πέργη). An ancient and important city of Pamphylia, a little inland, northeast of Attalia, between the rivers Catarrhactes and Cestrus, sixty stadia (six geographical miles) from the mouth of the former. It was a celebrated seat of the worship of Artemis. It was the first place in Asia Minor visited by the Apostle Paul on his first missionary journey (Acts, xiii. 13).

Pergăma and **Pergamia**. See Pergamum.

Pergamēna. Parchment. See Palaeography; Writing and Writing Materials.

Pergamene Sculptures. A group of sculptures discovered by the architect Humann in 1871, and excavated by Conze, R. Bohn, and others in 1878 and the following years, with the aid of the German government. They belonged to the acropolis at Pergamum (q. v.). They comprise a piece representing a battle of the Giants, mentioned in Ampelius (*Liber Memorialis*). The piece is colossal, occupying the upper part of a marble altar which is nearly forty feet in height. The sculptures are now in the Museum at Berlin. See Ars; Statuaria.

Pergamēnum. See Writing and Writing Materials.

Pergămum (Πέργαμον) or **Pergămus** (Πέργαμος). The former by far the most usual form in the classical writers, though the latter is more common in English, probably because of its use in our version of the Bible (Rev. ii. 12). The word is significant, connected with πύργος, "a tower." (1) The citadel of Troy, and used poetically for Troy itself; the poets also use the forms Pergăma (τὰ Πέργαμα) and Pergamia (ἡ Περγαμία, sc. πόλις). (2) A celebrated city of Asia Minor, the capital of the kingdom of Pergamum, and afterwards of the Roman province of Asia, was situated in the district of South Mysia called Teuthrania, on the north bank of the river Caïcus, about twenty miles from the sea. The kingdom of Pergamum was founded about B.C. 280 by Philetaerus, who had been intrusted by Lysimachus with the command of the city. The successive kings of Pergamus were: Philetaerus, B.C. 280–263; Eumĕnes I., 263–241; Attălus I., 241–197; Eumĕnes II., 197–159; Attălus II. Philadelphus, 159–138; Attălus III. Philomētor, 138–133. The kingdom reached its greatest extent after the defeat of Antiochus the Great by the Romans, in B.C. 190, when the Romans bestowed upon Eumenes II. the whole of Mysia, Lydia, both Phrygias, Lycaonia, Pisidia, and Pamphylia. It was under the same king that the celebrated library was founded at Pergamus, which for a long time rivalled that of Alexandria, and the formation of which occasioned the invention of parchment, *charta Pergamena*. This library became the centre of a school of great importance in the history of ancient learning; among its leaders were such distinguished men as Crates of Mallos, who introduced philological studies into Rome. (See Philologia.) The Pergamene Library was afterwards presented by Antony to Cleopatra and united with the Alexandrian. On the death of Attalus III., in B.C. 133, the kingdom, by a bequest in his will, passed to the Romans. The city was an early seat of Christianity, and is one of the Seven Churches of Asia to which the Apocalyptic epistles are addressed. Among the celebrated natives of the city were the rhetorician Apollodorus and the physician Galen. The place is now called Bergama; and here were excavated in 1875–86, by Humann, Bohn, Conze, and others for the German government, many remains of magnificent buildings, such as temples, porticoes, theatres, baths, etc.

Pergé (Πέργη). See Perga.

Pergŭla (from *pergo*, hence something projecting). A name given to (1) a veranda, roofed over, but open at the sides, used for a teacher's lecture-room, a painter's studio, or a shop (Juv. xi. 137; Pliny, *H. N.* xxxv. 84; Auson. *Epist.* iv. 6); (2) a covered balcony projecting from the upper part of a house (Suet. *Aug.* 94); and (3) the *cella* of a prostitute (Plaut. *Pseud.* i. 2, 78).

Periactos. See Theatrum.

Periander (Περίανδρος). (1) Son of Cypselus, whom he succeeded as tyrant of Corinth in B.C. 625, and reigned forty years, to B.C. 585. His rule was mild and beneficent at first, but afterwards became oppressive. According to the common story, this change was owing to the advice of Thrasybulus, tyrant of Miletus, whom Periander had consulted on the best mode of maintaining his power, and who is said to have taken the messenger through a cornfield, cutting off as he went the tallest ears, and then to have dismissed him without committing himself to a verbal answer. The action, however, was rightly interpreted by Periander, who proceeded to rid himself of the most powerful nobles in the State. He made his power respected abroad as well as at home; and besides his conquest of Epidaurus, mentioned below, he kept Corcyra in subjection. He was, like many of the other Greek tyrants, a patron of literature and philosophy, and Arion and Anacharsis were in favor at his court. He was very commonly reckoned among the Seven Sages, though by some he was excluded from their number, and Myson of Chenae in Laconia was substituted in his place.

The private life of Periander was marked by misfortune and cruelty. He married Melissa, daughter of Procles, tyrant of Epidaurus. She bore him two sons, Cypselus and Lycophron, and was passionately beloved by him; but he is said to have killed her by a blow during her pregnancy, having been roused to a fit of anger by a false accusation brought against her. His wife's death embittered the remainder of his days, partly through the remorse which he felt for the deed, partly through the alienation of his younger son Lycophron, inexorably exasperated by his mother's fate. The young man's anger had been chiefly excited by Procles, and Periander, in revenge, attacked Epidaurus, and, having reduced it, took his father-in-law prisoner. Periander sent Lycophron to Corcyra; but when he was himself advanced in years, he summoned Lycophron back to Corinth to succeed to the tyranny, seeing that Cypselus, his elder son, was unfit to hold it, from deficiency of understanding. Lycophron refused to return to Corinth as long as his father was there; thereupon Periander offered to withdraw to Corcyra if Lycophron would come home and take the government. To this he assented; but the Corcyraeans, not wishing to have Periander among them, put Lycophron to death. Periander shortly afterwards died of despondency, at the age of eighty, and after a reign of forty years, according to Diogenes Laërtius. He was succeeded by a relative, Psammetichus, son of Gordias. See Herod. iii. 48–53; v. 92; Aristot. *Pol.* v. 12. (2) Tyrant of Ambracia, and contemporary with his more famous namesake of Corinth, to whom he was also related, being the son of Gorgus, who was son or brother to Cypselus. Periander was deposed by the people about B.C. 585 (Ael. *V. H.* xii. 35).

Periboea (Περίβοια). (1) The wife of Icarius and mother of Penelopé. (2) The wife of Telamon and mother of Teucer and Aiax. She is also called ERIBOEA. (3) The daughter of Hipponoüs and wife of Oeneus, by whom she became the mother of Tydeus.

Peribŏlus (περίβολος). The court of a Greek temple. See TEMPLUM.

Peribolus in the Temple of Apollo at Pompeii. (Overbeck.)

Perĭcles (Περικλῆς). (1) The greatest of Athenian statesmen. He was the son of Xanthippus and Agaristé, both of whom belonged to the noblest families of Athens. The fortune of his parents procured for him a careful education, which his extraordinary abilities and diligence turned to the best account. He received instruction from Damon, Zeno of Elea, and Anaxagoras. With Anaxagoras he lived on terms of the most intimate friendship till the philosopher was compelled to retire from Athens. From this great and original thinker Pericles was believed to have derived not only the cast of his mind, but the character of his eloquence, which, in the elevation of its sentiments and the purity and loftiness of its style, was the fitting expression of the force and dignity of his character and the grandeur of his conceptions. Of the oratory of Pericles no specimens remain to us, but it is described by ancient writers as characterized by singular force and energy. He was described as thundering and lightening when he spoke, and as carrying the weapons of Zeus upon his tongue (Quint. x. 1, 82).

In B.C. 469 Pericles began to take part in public affairs, forty years before his death, and was soon regarded as the head of the more democratic part in the State in opposition to Cimon. He gained the favour of the people by the laws which he succeeded in passing for their benefit. Thus it was enacted through his means that the citizens should receive from the public treasury the price of their admittance to the theatre, amounting to two oboli apiece; that those who served in the courts of the Heliaea should be paid for their attendance; and that those citizens who served as soldiers should likewise be paid. It was at his instigation that his friend Ephialtes proposed, in 461, the measure by which the Areopagus was deprived of those functions which rendered it formidable as an antagonist to the popular party. This success was followed by the ostracism of Cimon, who was charged with Laconism, and Pericles was thus placed at the head of public affairs at Athens. Pericles was distinguished as a general as well as a statesman, and frequently commanded the Athenian armies in their wars with the neighbouring States. In 454 he commanded the Athenians in their campaigns against the Sicyonians and Acarnanians; in 448 he led the army which assisted the Phocians in the Sacred War; and in 445 he rendered the most signal service to the State by recovering the island of Euboea, which had revolted from Athens. Cimon had been previously recalled from exile without any opposition from Pericles, but had died in 449. On his death the aristocratic party was headed by Thucydides, the son of Melesias; but on the ostracism of the latter in 444 the organized opposition of the aristocratic party was broken up, and Pericles was left without a rival. Throughout the remainder of his political course no one appeared to contest his supremacy; but the boundless influence which he possessed was never perverted by him to sinister or unworthy purposes. So far from being a mere selfish demagogue, he neither indulged nor courted the multitude. The next important event in which Pericles was engaged was the war against Samos, which had revolted from Athens, and which he subdued after an arduous campaign, 440. The poet Sophocles was one of the generals who fought with Pericles against Samos (Thuc. i. 115–117).

Pericles. (Vatican.)

For the next ten years, till the outbreak of the Peloponnesian War, the Athenians were not engaged in any considerable military operations. During this period Pericles devoted especial attention to the Athenian navy, as her supremacy rested on her maritime superiority, and he adopted various judicious means for consolidating and strengthening her empire over the islands of the Aegaean. The funds derived from the tribute of the allies and from other sources were, to a large extent, devoted by him to the erection of those magnificent temples and public buildings which rendered Athens the wonder and admiration of Greece. Under his administration the Propylaea and the Parthenon and the Odeum were erected as well as numerous other temples and public buildings. With the stimulus afforded by these works architecture and sculpture reached their highest perfection, and some of the greatest artists of antiquity were employed in erecting or adorning the buildings. The chief direction and oversight of the public edifices was intrusted to Phidias. (See PHIDIAS.) These works, calling into activity almost every branch of industry and commerce at Athens, diffused universal prosperity while they proceeded, and thus contributed in this, as well as in other ways, to maintain the popularity and influence of Pericles. But he still had many enemies, who were not slow to impute to him base and unworthy motives. From the comic poets Pericles had to sustain numerous attacks. They exaggerated his power, spoke of his party as Pisistratids, and called upon him to swear that he was not about to assume the tyranny. His high character and strict probity, however, rendered all these attacks harmless. But as his enemies were unable to ruin his reputation by these means, they attacked him through his friends. His friends Phidias and Anaxagoras, and his mistress Aspasia (q. v.), were all accused before the people. Phidias was condemned and cast into prison; Anaxagoras was also sentenced to pay a fine and leave Athens (see ANAXAGORAS); and Aspasia was only acquitted through the entreaties and tears of Pericles (Plut. *Per.* 24).

The Peloponnesian War has been falsely ascribed to the ambitious schemes of Pericles. It is true that he counselled the Athenians not to yield to the demands of the Lacedaemonians, and he pointed out the immense advantages which the Athenians possessed in carrying on the war; but he did this because he saw that war was inevitable; and that as long as Athens retained the great power which she then possessed, Sparta would never rest contented. On the outbreak of the war in 431 a Peloponnesian army under Archidamus invaded Attica; and upon his advice the Athenians conveyed their movable property into the city and their cattle and beasts of burden to Euboea, and allowed the Peloponnesians to desolate Attica without opposition. Next year (430), when the Peloponnesians again invaded Attica, Pericles pursued the same policy as before. In this summer a plague made its appearance in Athens. The Athenians, being exposed to the devastation of the war and the plague at the same time, began to turn their thoughts to peace, and looked upon Pericles as the author of all their distresses, inasmuch as he had persuaded them to go to war. Pericles attempted to calm the public ferment; but such was the irritation against him that he was sentenced to pay a fine (Thuc. ii. 64). The ill-feeling of the people having found this vent, Pericles soon resumed his accustomed sway, and was again elected one of the generals for the ensuing year (429). Meantime Pericles had suffered in common with his fellow-citizens. The plague carried off most of his near connections. His son Xanthippus, a profligate and undutiful youth, his sister, and most of his intimate friends died of it. Still he maintained unmoved his calm bearing and philosophic composure. At last his only surviving legitimate son, Paralus, a youth of greater promise than his brother, fell a victim. The firmness of Pericles then at last gave way; as he placed the funeral garland on the head of the lifeless youth, he burst into tears and sobbed aloud. He had one son remaining, his child by Aspasia; and he was allowed to enroll this son in his own tribe and give him his own name. In the autumn of 429 Pericles himself died of a lingering sickness. He survived the commencement of the war two years and six months. The name of the wife of Pericles is not mentioned. She had been the wife of Hipponicus, by whom she was the mother of Callias. She bore two sons to Pericles, Xanthippus and Paralus. She lived unhappily with Pericles, and a divorce took place by mutual consent, when Pericles connected himself with Aspasia. Of his strict probity he left the decisive proof in the fact that at his death he was found not to have added a single drachma to his hereditary property. His greatest fault as a statesman was his inability to see that personal government in the long run is injurious to a nation; for it impairs the capacity of the people for self-government, and on the death of the chief leaves them helpless and inexperienced. On his death-bed his friends were commenting on his victories and triumphs, when he interrupted them with the remark, "That which you have left unnoticed is that of which I am the proudest; no Athenian ever wore mourning through any act of mine." His life is sketched for us by Thucydides and Plutarch. See also the sketch by E. Abbott (London, 1891); and for a comprehensive account of his times, Lloyd, *The Age of Perikles* (London, 1875); Filleul, *Histoire du Siècle de Periclès* (Paris, 1873); also Frey, *Leben des Perikles* (Bern, 1889). (2) Son of the preceding, by Aspasia, was one of the generals at the battle of Arginusae, and was put to death by the Athenians with the other generals, B.C. 406.

Periclymĕnus (Περικλύμενος). (1) Son of Neleus and Chloris, brother of Nestor. He is the chief hero of the defence of Pylos against Heracles, to whom he gave much trouble by his prowess as well as by his power of transforming himself, like the sea-gods, into every possible shape. This power had been given him by Poseidon, who was reputed to be his father. Finally he succumbed to the arrows of Heracles, and by his death sealed the doom of Pylos. (2) A Theban, son of Poseidon and Chloris, daughter of the seer Tiresias. In the war of the Seven against Thebes he slew Parthenopaeus, and was in pursuit of Amphiaraüs at the moment when the latter sank into the earth. See SEVEN AGAINST THEBES.

Periegētae (περιηγηταί, "those who guide strangers about," and show them what is worth notice). A term applied by the Greeks to the authors of travellers' guide-books enumerating and describing what was worthy of note, especially buildings or monuments, in the several cities or countries. This kind of literature was especially in vogue from the third century B.C. onwards. Its chief representatives are Polemon of Troas (about 200), whose numerous works are now unfortunately preserved in fragments only; and after him the Athenian Heliodorus, author of a great work on the Acropolis, likewise lost. Larger fragments survive of a hand-book to Greece by a certain Heraclides, and of the interesting work on Alexandria by Callixenus of Rhodes. The only complete work of this kind remaining is the valuable description of Greece by Pausanias (q. v.) in the second century A.D.

Periēres (Περιήρης). A king of Messenê, son of Aeolus and Enaretê, and father of Aphareus and Leucoppus by Gorgophonê. Some accounts make him also the father of Tyndareos and Icarius (Pausan. iv. 2, 2).

Perilāus (Περίλαος). The son of Icarius and brother of Penelopê (Pausan. viii. 34, 2).

Perillus (Πέριλλος). An artist who is said to have made the great bronze bull for the tyrant Phalaris (see PHALARIS), and to have been himself the victim of his own invention (Ovid, *A. A.* i. 653).

Perimeridia (περιμηρίδια) and **Parameridia** (παραμηρίδια). Armour for covering the thighs. They were made of metal and resembled the *ocreae* or greaves. See OCREAE.

Perinthus (Πέρινθος). An important town of Thrace on the Propontis, founded by the Samians about B.C. 559, and situated twenty-two miles west of Selymbria on a small peninsula. At a later time it was called Heraclea, and sometimes Heraclea Thraciae or Heraclea Perinthus.

Periŏcha (περίοχη). Literally, "the contents," from περιέχω. A name given to any short summary or digest of the contents of a book, or of the plot of a play. An example of the first is found in the *Periochae T. Livii Omnium Librorum*, which is a short summary of Livy's history, including the books now lost, in their original form (except bks. cxxxvi. and cxxxvii., which have been accidentally lost). This was made in the fourth century A.D. from an earlier and fuller digest now lost. Of these there is an edition by Jahn (Leipzig, 1853). See also Wöfflin's paper in the *Commentationes in Honorem Th. Mommsenii* (Berlin, 1886). Of the dramatic periochae, a familiar example is the short metrical summary of the plot prefixed to the several plays of Terence, and written by Sidonius Apollinaris in the fifth century A.D.

Perioeci (περίοικοι, "those dwelling about," from περιοικέω). A name used by Greek writers of a subject population dwelling in the vicinity of some particular dominant city, or in the rural provinces under its control, personally free but devoid of political rights. The name is more properly applied to a class found in Laconia who were probably in their origin partly representatives of the original Achaian stock conquered by the Dorian invaders and partly a mixed race resulting from the marriage of the Dorians with the Achaians. (See E. Curtius, *History of Greece*, Eng. trans. ii. ch. i.) They possessed lands, and are stated to have been settled in a hundred towns (Strabo, viii. p. 557), among which were Gythium on the coast, Thyrca, and Amyelae. Clinton (*Fasti Hellenici*, App. ch. xxii.) estimates roughly their number at the time of the Persian Wars as between 60,000 and 70,000 souls.

The perioeci were engaged partly in farming, partly in manufacturing and in trade. They paid taxes to the State, and were bound to perform military service either as hoplites or as light-armed troops. The perioecic inhabitants of Sciritis formed a special body of light infantry. After the Peloponnesian War the perioeci constituted the bulk of the Spartan army, and they were eligible to the inferior commands. Having no civil rights, they were completely subject to the Spartans proper, and in case of insubordination they could be put to death by the ephors without trial. On rare occasions a perioecus is found in a high office, as in the case mentioned by Thucydides (viii. 22), where one of them was admiral of an allied Chian fleet; but they seem never to have been put over Spartans. The name περίοικοι is also used of other subject populations as a convenient term (cf. Herod. iv. 159), but these were not perioeci in the Laconian sense of the word.

See Arnold's *Thucydides*, i. App. ii.; Müller, *Dorier*, bk. iii.; Grote, *History of Greece*, pt. ii. ch. vi.; and Gilbert, *Constitutional Antiquities of Greece*, Eng. trans. (1895).

Peripatetĭci (περιπατητικοί, literally, "persons given to walking about"). The followers of Aristotle's philosophy. They derived their name from Aristotle's habit of walking with his disciples in the shady avenues of the Athenian Gymnasium, called the Lyceum, while he discussed the problems of philosophy. See also ARISTOTELES; PHILOSOPHIA.

Perĭphas (Περίφας). One of the autochthones of Attica, who was a priest of Apollo and also king of the country before the time of Cecrops. Zeus is said to have wished to destroy him, being jealous of his eminence; but at Apollo's request changed him into an eagle (Ovid, *Met.* vii. 400)

Periphētes (Περιφήτης). A son of Hephaestus; a monster at Epidaurus, who slew the passers-by with an iron club (whence he was called κορυνήτης, or "club-bearer") till he was himself slain by the young Theseus (q. v.).

Peripŏli (περίπολοι). Troops on patrol duty; a name given to the Athenian ἔφηβοι during two years of their ἐφηβεία (Plato, *De Leg.* vi. 760 C), so that this part of their service is called περιπολία.

See Philippi in the *Rheinisches Museum* (new series), xxxiv. 613; and the article EPHEBI.

Periptĕros (περίπτερος). An epithet describing a temple completely surrounded by a colonnade supporting the entablature. See TEMPLUM.

Periscĕlis (περισκελίς). An anklet worn by women among the Greeks and Romans. The plebeian women at Rome wore anklets of silver and the patricians anklets of gold (Pliny, *H. N.* xxxiii. 39). The purely Latin word is *compes* (Pliny, l. c.), and Tertullian uses the form *periscelium* (*De Cult. Fem.* ii. 13). See ARMILLA.

Peristȳlum (περίστυλος). A court surrounded by columns. See DOMUS; TEMPLUM.

Permessus (Περμησσός). A river in Boeotia, descending from Mount Helicon, and falling into Lake Copaïs near Haliartus.

Pero (Πηρώ). The daughter of Neleus and Chloris, famous for her beauty. She was married to Bias (Pausan. x. 31, 9).

Pero (ἀρβύλη). The shoe of the ordinary Roman citizen. See CALCEUS.

Perpendicŭlum (κάθετος, μολυβδίς, στάθμη). A plumb-line, or string with a piece of lead attached, used by carpenters, masons, and other artisans to test the correctness of their perpendicular lines (Vitruv. vii. 3, 5). The line used in measuring horizontally was called *linea* (κανών).

Perperēna (Περπερήνα). A small town of Mysia, south of Adramyttium.

Perperna or **Perpenna**. (1) MARCUS, a Roman consul in B.C. 130, who defeated Aristonicus in Asia, and took him prisoner. He died at Pergamum in the following year (Livy, *Epist.* 59; Vell. Paterc. ii. 4). (2) MARCUS, son of the preceding, consul in B.C. 92 and censor in 86. He lived to the age of ninety-eight years (Pliny, *H. N.* vii. 156). (3) M. PERPERNA VENTO, son of the preceding. He was a follower of Marius in the Civil War, and fled to Sicily when Sulla conquered Italy in B.C. 82. On the death of Sulla, in 78, Perperna joined the consul M. Lepidus in his attempt to overthrow the new aristocratical constitution, and retired with him to Sardinia on the failure of this attempt. Lepidus died in Sardinia in the following year (77), and Perperna with the remains of his army crossed over to Spain and joined Sertorius (q. v.). Perperna was jealous of the ascendency of Sertorius, and after serving under him some years he and his friends assassinated Sertorius at a banquet in B.C. 72. His death soon brought the war to a close. Perperna was defeated by Pompey, was taken prisoner, and was put to death (App. *B. C.* i. 107–115; Plut. *Pomp.* 10, 20).

Perpetua Actio. See ACTIO in the Appendix.

Perrhaebi (Περραιβοί) and **Peraebi** (Περαιβοί). A powerful and warlike Pelasgic people in the north of Thessaly. Homer places the Perrhaebi in the neighbourhood of the Thessalian Dodona and the river Titarosius; and at a later time the name of Perrheabia was applied to the district bounded by Macedonia and the Cambunian Mountains on the north, by Pindus on the west, by the Peneus on the south and southeast, and by the Peneus and Ossa on the east. The Perrhaebi were members of the Amphictyonic League.

Perrhĭdae (Περρίδαι). A deme of Attica belonging to the tribe Antiochis.

Persae (Πέρσαι). A play of Aeschylus first produced in B.C. 472, in a tetralogy of which the other three plays were the *Phineus*, *Glaucus Pontius*, and Prometheus Πυρκαεύς. The plot deals with the time of the Second Persian War, and the scene is laid at Susa. Separate edition by Prickard (1885).

Persé (Πέρση). The daughter of Oceanus and wife of Helios, by whom she became the mother of Aeëtes and Circé (*Odyss.* ix. 139; Hes. *Theog.* 356, 956). Others speak of her as also the mother of Perses and Pasiphaë.

Persēïs. See HECATÉ.

Persephŏné (Περσεφόνη), called **Proserpĭna** by the Romans; the daughter of Zeus and Demeter. In Homer she is called PERSEPHONĪA (Περσεφόνεια); the form Persephoné first occurs in Hesiod. But besides these forms of the name, we also find PERSEPHASSA, PHERSEPHASSA, PERSEPHATTA, PHERSEPHATTA, PHERREPHASSA, PHEREPHATTA, and PHERSEPHONĪA, for which various etymologies have been proposed. The Latin Proserpina is only a corruption of the Greek, though the Romans derive it from *proserpo*. In Attica she was worshipped under the name of CORA (Κόρη, Ion. Κούρη) —that is, "the Daughter," namely, of Demeter; and the two were frequently called "the Mother

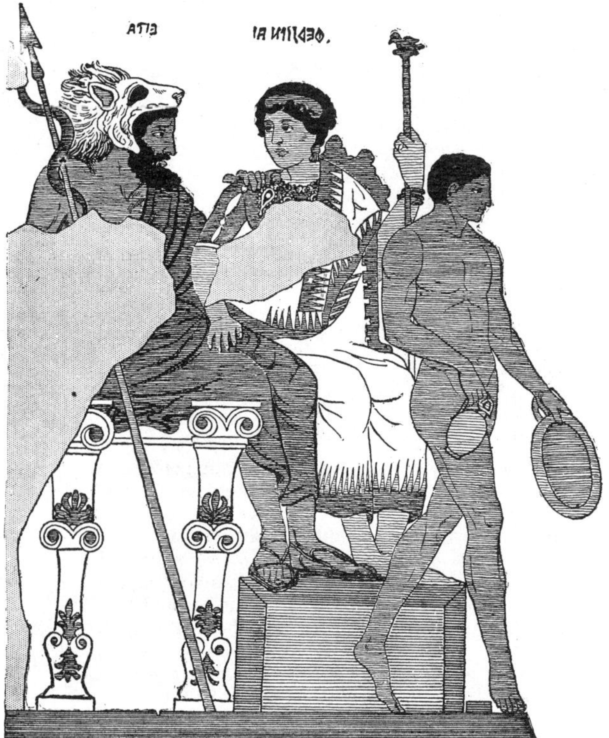

Hades and Persephoné. (Etruscan painting, Dennis.)

and the Daughter" (ἡ Μητὴρ καὶ ἡ Κόρη). Being the infernal goddess of death, she is also called a daughter of Zeus and Styx. In Arcadia she was worshipped under the name of Despoena, and was called a daughter of Poseidon Hippius and Demeter, said to have been brought up by the Titan Anytus. Homer describes her as the wife of Hades, and the formidable, venerable, and majestic queen of the Shades, who rules over the souls of the dead, along with her husband. Hence she is called by later Roman writers Iuno Inferna, Averna, and Stygia; and the Erinyes are said to have been her daughters by Pluto. Groves sacred to her are placed by Homer in the western extremity of the earth, on the borders of the lower world, which is itself called the house of Persephoné. The story of her being carried off by Hades or Pluto against her will is not mentioned by Homer, who simply describes her as the wife and queen of Hades. Her abduction is first mentioned by Hesiod. The account of it, which is the most celebrated part of her story, and the wanderings of her mother in search of her, and the worship of the two goddesses in Attica at the festival of the Eleusinia, are related under DEMETER and ELEUSINIA. In the mystical theories of the Orphics, Persephoné is described as the all-pervading goddess of nature, who both produces and destroys everything; and she is therefore mentioned along, or identified with, other mystic divinities, such as Isis, Rhea, Gê, Hestia, Pandora, Artemis, and Hecaté. This mystic Persephoné is further said to have become by Zeus the mother of Dionysus, Iacchus, Zagreus, or Sabazius.

Persephoné frequently appears in works of art. She is represented either with the grave and severe character of an infernal Heré or as a mystical divinity with a sceptre and a little box, in the act of being carried off by Pluto. Her symbols are a torch or torches, a cornucopia, ears of corn, pomegranates, or a cock as heralding the dawn (i. e. a new life).

Persepŏlis (Περσέπολις, Περσαίπολις; in the Middle Ages, Istakhar; now Takhti-Jemshid, i. e. "Throne of Jemshid," or Chil-Minar, i. e. "Forty Pillars"). The Greek name, probably translated from the Persian name which is not recorded, of the great city which succeeded Pasargada as the capital of Persis and of the Persian Empire. From the circumstance, however, of the conquest of the Babylonian Empire taking place about the time when Persepolis attained this dignity, it appears to have been seldom used as the royal residence. Neither Herodotus, Xenophon, Ctesias, nor the sacred writers during the Persian period, mention it at all; though they often speak of Babylon, Susa, and Ecbatana as the capitals of the Empire. It is only from the Greek writers after the Macedonian conquest that we learn its rank in the Empire, which appears to have consisted chiefly in its being one of the two burial places of the Persian kings (the other being Pasargada), and also a royal treasury; for Alexander found in the palace immense riches, which were said to have accumulated from the time of Cyrus. Its foundation is sometimes ascribed to Cyrus the Great, but more generally to his son Cambyses. It was greatly enlarged and adorned by Darius I. and Xerxes, and preserved its splendour till after the Macedonian conquest, when it was burned; Alexander, as the story goes, setting fire to the palace with his own hand at the end of a revel by the instigation of the courtesan Thaïs in B.C. 331. It was not, however, so entirely destroyed as some historians represent. It appears frequently in subsequent history, both ancient and mediæval. It is now deserted, but its ruins are considerable, though too dilapidated to give any good notion of Persian architecture, and they are rich in cuneiform inscriptions. In the days of its splendour a great plaza or species of platform was crowned with palaces, halls, and altars. Here were stored the treasures which Alexander rifled; and here was kept the copy of the Avesta (see ZOROASTER), written on 12,000 oxhides in letters of gold.

Ruins of Persepolis.

Among the ruins still existing three groups are distinguished by archaeologists: first, the Forty Pillars proper, with the so-called "Mountain of Tombs" or "Throne of Jamshid," after a fabulous king who is said to have founded the city; second, the Naksh-in-Rustam, a collection of tombs; and third, a building now called "the Haram of Jamshid." The first group is the most important, being the terrace already mentioned, built of cyclopean masonry, and extending 1500 feet in one direction and 800 in another. It was once surrounded by triple walls of a height varying from about 48 to 100 feet. There are still to be distinguished on the central platform the so-called "Great Hall of Xerxes," the Palace of Xerxes, and the Palace of Darius. The stone used for these structures is dark grayish marble cut into enormous square blocks, and highly polished. The ascent to this platform is by two double flights of steps nearly 22 feet in width and only 3½ inches high, so that they have been ascended in modern times on horseback. The portals still exhibit huge figures of animals, 15 feet high, and not unlike the Assyrian bulls of Nineveh. The cuneiform inscriptions are ascribed to Xerxes.

Perseus and Andromeda. (Marble relief in the Naples Museum.)

Persepolis was situated in the heart of Persis, in the part called Hollow Persis (κοίλη Περσίς), not far from the border of the Carmanian Desert, in a beautiful and healthy valley, through which runs the river Araxes. After Alexander's time the place was of secondary importance. It was plundered by Antiochus in B.C. 164, and later was the residence of a Persian viceroy. See Fergusson, *The Palaces of Nineveh and Persepolis Restored;* Vaux, *Nineveh and Persepolis;* Mme. Dieulafoy, *La Perse et la Susiane;* and especially Stölze and Noldeke, *Persepolis*, with fine photographic views (Berlin, 1882).

Perses (Πέρσης). (1) The son of the Titan Crius. He became by Asteria the father of Hecaté (Hes. *Th.* 409). (2) The son of Perseus and Andromeda, and regarded by the Greeks as the founder of the Persian people (Herod. vii. 61). (3) The son of Helios and Persé, and brother of Aeëtes and Circé (Apollod. ii. 4, 5).

Perseus (Περσεύς). Son of Zeus and Danaë, the daughter of Acrisius. A sketch of his fabulous history has already been given under a previous article (see DANAË); and it remains here but to relate the particulars of his enterprise against the Gorgons. When Perseus had made his rash promise to Polydectes, by which he bound himself to bring the latter the Gorgon's head, he retired full of grief to the extremity of the island of Scyros, where Hermes came to him, promising that he and Athené would be his guides. Hermes brought him first to the Graiae (see PHORCYDES), whose eye and tooth he stole and would not restore until they had furnished him with directions to the abode of the nymphs who were possessed of the winged shoes, the magic wallet, and the helmet of Pluto which made the wearer invisible. Having obtained from the Graiae the requisite information, he came to the nymphs, who gave him their precious possessions: he then flung the wallet over his shoulder, placed the helmet on his head, and fitted the shoes to his feet. Thus equipped, and grasping the short curved sword (ἅρπη) which Hermes gave him, he mounted into the air, accompanied by the gods, and flew to the ocean, where he found the three Gorgons asleep. (See GORGONES.) Fearing to gaze on their faces, which changed the beholder to stone, he looked on the head of Medusa as it was reflected on his shield, and, Athené guiding his hand, he severed it from her body. The blood gushed forth, and with it the winged steed Pegasus and Chrysaor, the father of Geryon, for Medusa was at that time pregnant by Poseidon. Perseus took up the head, put it into his wallet, and set out on his return. The two sisters awoke, and pursued the fugitive; but, protected by the helmet of Pluto, he eluded their vision, and they were obliged to give over the bootless chase (Hes. *Scut.* 220–230; Pausan. v. 18, 1). Perseus pursued his aërial route, and after having, in the course of his journey, punished the inhospitality of Atlas (q. v.) by changing him into a rocky mountain (Ovid, *Met.* iv. 626 foll.), he came to the country of the Ethiopians. Here he liberated Andromeda (see ANDROMEDA), whom he married. He is also said to have come to the Hyperboreans, by whom he was hospitably received. On his return to Seriphos, he found his mother with Dictys in a temple, whither they had fled from the violence of Polydectes. Perseus then went to the palace of Polydectes, and metamorphosed him and all his guests, and, some say, the whole island, into stone (Pind. *Pyth.* xii. 10). He then presented the kingdom to Dictys. He gave the winged sandals and the helmet to Hermes, who restored them to the nymphs and to Pluto, and the head of Gorgon to Athené, who placed it in the middle of her shield or breast-plate. Perseus then went to Argos, accompanied by

Danaë and Andromeda. Acrisius, remembering the oracle, escaped to Larissa, in the country of the Pelasgians; but Perseus followed him, in order to persuade him to return. Some writers state that Perseus, on his return to Argos, found Proetus, who had expelled his brother Acrisius, in possession of the kingdom; and that Perseus slew Proetus, and was afterwards killed by Megapenthes, the son of Proetus. The more common tradition, however, relates that when Teutamidas, king of Larissa, celebrated games in honour of his guest Acrisius, Perseus, who took part in them, accidentally hit the foot of Acrisius with the discus, and thus killed him. Acrisius was buried outside the city of Larissa, and Perseus, leaving the kingdom of Argos to Megapenthes, the son of Proetus, received from him in exchange the government of Tiryns. According to others, Perseus remained in Argos, and successfully opposed the introduction of the Bacchic orgies. Perseus is said to have founded the towns of Midea and Mycenae. By Andromeda he became the father of Perses, Aïcaeus, Sthenelus, Heleus, Mestor, Electryon, Gorgophoné, and Autochthé. Perseus was worshipped as a hero in several places in Greece and even in Egypt (Herod. ii. 91).

Perseus or **Perses** (Περσεύς). The last king of Macedonia, the eldest son of Philip V. He reigned eleven years, from B.C. 178 to 168. Before his accession he persuaded his father to put to death his younger brother Demetrius, whom he suspected that the Roman Senate intended to set up as a competitor for the throne on the death of Philip. Immediately after his accession he began to make preparations for war with the Romans, which he knew to be inevitable, though seven years elapsed before actual hostilities commenced. The war broke out in B.C. 171. The first year of the war was marked by no striking action. The consul P. Licinius Crassus first suffered a defeat in Thessaly in an engagement between the cavalry of the two armies, but subsequently gained a slight advantage over the king's troops. The second year of the war (B.C. 170), in which the consul A. Hostilius Mancinus commanded, also passed over without any important battle, but was, on the whole, favourable to Perseus. The third year (B.C. 169), in which the consul Q. Marcius Philippus commanded, again produced no important results. The length to which the war had been unexpectedly protracted, and the ill success of the Roman arms, had by this time excited a general feeling in favour of the Macedonian monarch; but the ill-timed avarice of Perseus, who refused to advance the sum of money which Eumenes, king of Pergamus, demanded, deprived him of this valuable ally; and the same unseasonable niggardliness likewise deprived him of the services of twenty thousand Gallic mercenaries, who had actually advanced into Macedonia to his support, but retired on failing to obtain their stipulated pay. He was left to carry on the contest against Rome single-handed.

The fourth year of the war (B.C. 168) was also the last. The new consul, L. Aemilius Paulus, defeated Perseus with great loss in a decisive battle fought near Pydna, on June 22, B.C. 168. Perseus took refuge in the island of Samothrace, where he shortly afterwards surrendered with his children to the praetor Cn. Octavius. When brought before Aemilius he is said to have degraded himself by the most abject supplications; but he was treated with kindness by the Roman general. The following year he was carried to Italy, where he was compelled to adorn the splendid triumph of his conqueror (November 30, B.C. 167), and afterwards cast into a dungeon, from whence, however, the intercession of Aemilius procured his release, and he was permitted to end his days in an honourable captivity at Alba. He survived his removal thither a few years, and died, according to some accounts, by voluntary starvation, while others, fortunately with less probability, represent him as falling a victim to the cruelty of his guards, who deprived him of sleep. Perseus had been twice married; the name of his first wife, whom he is said to have killed with his own hand in a fit of passion, is not recorded; his second, Laodicé, was the daughter of Seleucus IV. Philopator. He left two children —a son, Alexander, and a daughter, both apparently by his second marriage, as they were mere children when carried to Rome. Besides these, he had adopted his younger brother Philip, who appears to have been regarded by him as the heir to his throne, and who became the partner of his captivity. See Livy, bks. xl.–xliv.; and Polyb. bks. xxiv., xxvi., xxvii., xxix.

Coin of Perseus, King of Macedonia.

Persia (Περσική, sc. γῆ, Περσίς; Lat. PERSIS, more rarely PERSIA; old Pers. *Pārsa*). The original home of the ancient Persians, and later the chief province of the great Persian Empire, is the small territory in the southwestern corner of the Iranian tableland. In this limited and original sense, Persia corresponds exactly to the present Province of Fārs or Fārsistān with the capital Shīrāz. On the north it was bounded by Media, on the east by Karmania, on the southwest by the Persian Gulf, and on the northwest by the province of Susiana. The latter had from the time of Cyrus been closely united with Persia (Strabo, p. 727). Persis was separated from Media by the Parachoathras Mountains, the most southerly spur of the Taurus. Persia is a highland rising in terraces to a height of 5000 metres, intersected by many clefts, with approaches on most sides only by difficult rocky passes. In consequence of its isolated position, the oriental peoples, before the time of Alexander, had only a scanty knowledge of the land. The flat coast line was intolerably hot, sandy, and unfruitful; but in the interior the climate was everywhere favorable, temperate, and for the latitude almost raw, on account of the elevated position; the valleys and plains productive and well watered, with many clear rivers and lakes, where all kinds of waterfowl made their homes, covered with fertile meadows and gardens, and pasturage for horses and cattle, and, in parts, with forests and game. Wine and all fruits except olive oil were produced. The northern portion of Persia, on the other hand, is cold and snow is frequent. As a whole, Persia was intended by nature more for a grazing than for an agricultural country. The largest inland river is the Araxes (now Bundemir), which empties into a salt lake, with its tributary the Medos (now Pulvar). In the fruitful plain of the Medos in the centre of the country, sixty kilometres northeast of the present Shīrāz, over 1000 metres high, in a mild and healthful climate, lay the capital Persepolis (later Istakhr). Next to Susa, Persepolis was the largest and most beautiful city in the land. Here stood the costly and strong royal citadel (τὰ βασίλεια), the extensive ruins of whose walls, terraces, halls, and state apartments are still extant. Twelve kilometres down the river was the rock-hewn grave city of the Achaemenids (now Naksh-i-Rustem). Persepolis remained the nominal capital of the kingdom even after the kings had moved their residence to Susa and in mid-summer to Ecbatana. The original seat of the dynasty lay two days' journey northeast of Persepolis, in the so-called lower Persis, on the little river Cyrus, the present Murghāb. There stood the ancient royal city of Pasargadae with the palace and the still preserved tomb of Cyrus (Strabo, p. 727 ff.; Arrian, *Indica*, 40; Ptol. vi. 7, 8). In a wider sense the name Persia embraces the whole Persian nation of Iranian race, which should rather be called Irān. The broad highland of Irān, from the Tigris to the Indus, from the Indian Ocean to the Oxus and the Caspian Sea, is divided into halves by the great salt desert in its midst —western Irān with the States of Media and Persia, and northeastern Irān with Sogdiana, Chorasmia, Bactria, Areia, and Arachosia. These divisions are united only in the north by a narrow inhabitated strip, Hyrcania. The old geographers confined the term Ἀριανή to Eastern Irān. The feeling of national unity existed in all the tribes; their common name was once that of Aryan. Darius emphasizes first of all the fact that he is a Persian, the son of a Persian, and secondarily that he is an Aryan, of Aryan race. The Medes, too, according to Herodotus (vii. 62), anciently called themselves Aryans. The national unity of all Irān, a national dream even in the old heroic legends, was fully realized only once, under the Achaemenids. The empire of the Sassanids did not succeed in recovering the whole east of Irān. The present Persia fully includes only western Irān, and extends eastward not far beyond the eastern edge of the salt desert. The greater part of the ancient eastern Irān is occupied by Afghans and Turcomans.

ETHNOLOGY.—The inhabitants of Persis were originally a genuine mountain race of shepherds. Herodotus, Xenophon, and others describe the ancient Persians (old Pers. Pārsa, formerly, according to Herod. vii, 61, called Atrei) as an energetic, brave, contented race, of inordinate self-esteem, accustomed to hardships but not lacking in finer traits, fond of rude pleasures, of strict discipline, with a certain sense of justice, and of sound morals. The Persian sculptures show a noble profile, with long, straight nose, and carefully arranged beard. They ate only once a day, but then heartily, and drank wine freely. The life of men of station was consumed in hunting, travelling, archery, and war. The Persians served in the army from the twentieth to the fiftieth year. The soldiers wore the characteristic pointed felt hat (τιάρα), a coloured coat and breeches, and carried a light shield, a short spear, a long bow with thirty arrows, and the short dagger-sword (ἀκινάκης). Commerce was unknown among them, as were also rapine and thieving; lying, developed in the East to a virtue, they abhorred, at least in theory. Next to lying, incurring debt was considered the greatest disgrace. Polygamy and pæderasty were customary. Large families of children were esteemed honourable and the king offered yearly prizes for them. Education was undertaken by the State; the sons of nobles were brought up as pages at the court, where they were prepared for the high State offices. All kinds of bodily exercise and truthfulness were required of the youth, and they were early accustomed to hardship and watchfulness. They studied the sciences, traditions, natural history, and arboriculture (Herod. i. 133 ff.; Xen. *Anab.* i. 9; *Cyrop.* i. 2; viii. 8). Even Herodotus blames their fatal eagerness to imitate foreign customs. Thus in place of their ancient simple leather garments, they took from the more civilized Medes a more highly adorned dress (purple caftan, necklaces, and bracelets, *Cyrop.* i. 3, 2), false hair, and a blasé air of fashion, and wherever they heard of a new form of amusement they introduced it. With their growing dominion and under the influence of foreign customs the Persians rapidly deteriorated. Luxury, debauchery, and effeminacy destroyed their former discipline and bodily excellence. Cruelty and barbarity on the part of those in authority, extortion, crime, and injustice became the order of the day (Agathias, ii. 30; Xen. *Cyrop.* viii. 8, 6). The traditional origin of the Persian satraps is quite incredible.

The Persian nation was divided into various tribes, each possessing its own special portion of farming and pasture land. Of the ruling nobility, to which all other classes were subject, there were according to Herodotus three orders: the Pasargadae, Maraphii, and Maspii. Of these the Pasargadae were the highest; from them sprang the dynasty of the Achaemenids, who raised themselves from petty tribal chiefs and princes to national sovereigns. The king was permitted to select his wives only from the six highest families of the land, and the six "First of the Persians" had free access to the king.

The Iranian languages belong to the Indogermanic stock. In spite of strong dialectic differences, a specific Iranian type is unmistakably noticeable in all. Their common characteristic marks are the change of s to h, the preference for fricatives, and the great development of sibilants. Old-Pers. hanti ("they are")=Skt. santi, Lat. sunt; hindu (Indus)=Skt. Sindhu; fra=Skt. pra, πρό; thri (three)=mod. Pers. si=Skt. tri.

Old Persian stands on a very primitive stage, still very close to Sanskrit. The sentence from an inscription "Aüramazdā hya imām bumim adā hya avam asmānam adā hya martīyam adā" ("Ormuzd, who created this earth, who created that heaven, who created man"), would read in Sanskrit "Asuro medhasvi ya imām bhūmim adhād yo 'mum açmānam adhād yo martyam adhāt." Characteristic is the change of the Iranian z to d; adam (I)=Avestan azem; and f for Eastern Iranian hv: Vindafarnā (Ἰνταφέρνης) = Avestan Vindaṭ-hvarenāo. The final syllable is greatly maimed: abara = Skt. abharat ("he bore").

The ancient Persians left no real literature. Remains of a lost heroic epic of Eastern Irān are to be found in the Avestā. But we have a fairly accurate knowledge of the language of the old Persians from the rock-inscriptions in which Darius I. and his successors perpetuated their deeds in plain, almost clumsy style. The most extensive of these inscriptions are those of Darius on the smoothed rock-face of Mount Behistān in Media, 426 lines, with a twofold translation. These Persian inscriptions are written in the simplest form of cuneiform, and, so far as they are not destroyed by the action of the weather or wantonly, they have been almost completely deciphered. (See CUNEIFORM.) Of the language of the Medes we know only a few words through the Greeks; it probably resembled Old Persian. The dog was called by the Medes spakō (Herod. i. 110), in the Avestā spā. The home of the very primitive language of the Avestā cannot be determined.

From the Old Persian was developed the Middle Persian or Pahlavī, the literary and official language under the Sassanids. A peculiar cryptographic system (with Semitic ideograms), and a very defective and ambiguous alphabet, make this language unnecessarily difficult. While the Old Persian is still rich in grammatical forms, the Pahlavī shows great poverty. Still further poverty is shown in the Modern Persian (from the tenth century A.D. the national language of modern Persia), the last stage of development in the local speech of the Persians. The purest Modern Persian is still spoken around Shīrāz.

Among the arts architecture and sculpture hold the first place. Monumental structures are confined exclusively to the numerous royal palaces, and of their former magnitude the ruins of Susa and the far more imposing remains of Persepolis are silent witnesses. Their luxury and extravagance were a source of amazement to the Greeks. Founded by Darius, most of them were enlarged and finished by his successors. According to the detailed description of Polybius (x. 27), the palace in Ecbatana at the time of the Achaemenids (whether during the period of the Medes is questionable) was covered with silver tiles, and a great part of the interior was coated with gold and silver plates. And so it may have been in Persepolis. But while the Median palace was a wooden structure, the material in Persepolis is a durable stone. The treatment of the stone shows a high degree of workmanship; walls and columns are ornamented with reliefs and inscriptions. The architectural style was drawn from the Babylonian and Assyrian, but was not a slavish imitation. The palace of Persepolis lay on a terrace of ten metres in height, with the rear towards a mountain. It was protected by an ingenious threefold wall and brazen doors. The interior contained the dwelling and reception rooms of the king and his highest officials, as well as the treasure-chambers. (Cf. the description of Diod. xvii. 71.) The slender columns are twenty metres high and end in lofty, delicate capitals. The whole produced an effect of towering and imposing elegance and gigantic dimensions.

The numerous sculptures excavated do not depict single episodes in the life of the king, but form a common symbolic picture-language, glorifying the splendour of the kingdom and its far-reaching might. The composition is in general stiff and monotonous, but is carefully elaborated in details; the faces expressionless, but the forms lifelike and natural, the dress, weapons, etc., reproduced with great fidelity.

Specimen of Persian Sculpture from Persepolis.

RELIGION.—The Perso-Iranian national religion has from the oldest times been the Zoroastrian, with its belief in a good and an evil spirit (Ormuzd, ahurō mazdāo; Ahriman, aṅro mainyush), worship of moral and natural powers (Asha, "law"; Rashnu, "justice"; Mithra, "sun"), purity of body and soul, after death a strict balancing of good and evil deeds, with the rewards of paradise or the punishments of hell, a last judgment, resurrection of the dead, marriage of relatives, etc. In all probability the teachings of Zoroaster (q. v.) originated in the East and spread westward into Media. The external and internal history of the Zoroastrian doctrine until it became a fully developed national church is still dark. In Media the Magi, one of the Median orders, became the privileged priestly class. The Magi, doubtless under the Median supremacy, carried the religious movement to Persis, and there also remained in exclusive and lasting possession of the priestly dignity. Without Magi no one could make a sacrifice (Herod. i. 132), for they alone possessed the priestly mysteries; they also were soothsayers and interpreters of dreams. They had great respect and influence in public and private affairs; they conducted the education of the princes from the seventh year and constantly surrounded the king's person. They dressed in white and wore a felt turban, the cheek-pieces of which concealed the mouth (Avesta, paitidāna).

Cyrus was undoubtedly an orthodox Zoroastrian; the belief in the resurrection arose under

Cambyses (Herod. iii. 62). Darius in his inscriptions constantly emphasizes the fact that he is ruler through the grace of Aüramazda; Ahriman is naturally not mentioned by name. The cult of the goddess Anaitis (Anāhita) and that of Mithra, which afterwards became almost international, was not officially introduced into Persia until the time of Artaxerxes II.

In their descriptions of Persian sacrificial rites, the details given by Western writers agree in all essentials with the ordinances of the Avesta (Herod. i. 131; Strabo, p. 732; Plut. *De Is.* 46). The Persians had neither images of the gods nor real temples. They offered a garlanded sacrificial animal under the open heavens, while the Magi, holding in their hands a bundle of tamarisk twigs (the barsom), chanted the sacred passages. They sacrificed to the highest god, Ormuzd; to the sun and moon, but especially to fire and water—to fire, by burning dry wood and dropping fat on it; they offered worship to water, by some lake, river, or spring. The dog and the birds were sacred creatures; the dog they held as inviolable as men. On the other hand, it was considered a righteous deed to kill as many harmful animals as possible.

The Perso-Iranian funeral rites are the strict consequence of the belief that all dead things were unclean and forfeited to the evil spirit. It was a mortal sin to defile the pure elements, fire and water. (Fire could not even be blown upon, under penalty of death.) The ecclesiastical prescriptions concerning burial, as later set down in the Avesta, seem for a long time to have been repugnant to the Persians, and only gradually to have supplanted the old customs. According to Xenophon (*Cyrop.* viii. 7, 25), Cyrus, when dying, ordered his body to be buried. Herodotus (i. 140) tells of the Magi that they do not bury their dead until dogs and birds have torn them. Whether the Persians did the same is not certain; at any rate they buried the corpse only after having covered it with wax. But the prescription of the Avesta indicates that the naked corpse was exposed to the vultures on an elevation (dakhma) outside the city, and that only subsequently the bones were buried in the open field. Not until the Sassanid period did this become the usual practice, as the description in Agathias, ii. 21, 22 proves. Procopius relates that a Persian who had buried his wife was sentenced to death (*Bell. Pers.* i. 7). When Damassius and his companions covered a body lying on the ground with earth, the latter had disappeared in the morning, and during the night a spirit appeared to them in a dream, warning them to bury the dead, because the earth, the mother of all, received no tribute (Agathias, ii. 31). Evidence is not wanting that the custom existed as early as the time of Alexander, at least in Bactria. Alexander's Grecian governor in Bactria was almost driven out because he wished to forbid the exposure of the dead (Porphyr. *De Abst.* iv. 21).

The Zoroastrian priesthood and sect fell into decay with the fall of the Achaemenid dynasty. Under the Sassanids it was restored, and under the royal protection reached a position of power as the organized State religion which it had never possessed before. It gradually succumbed to the advance of Islam, and in the Persia of to-day there are very few Zoroastrians. More numerous are the adherents of the old national religion, who have found refuge in and about Bombay—the Parsees.

Persian Soldiers. (Relief from the Palace of Darius at Persepolis.)

HISTORY.—The history of Persia is lost in the little-known period of Median supremacy. The Persian kings are vassals of the Median kings, who, on their side, freed themselves from Assyrian dominion after long struggles. The founder of the Median dynasty is Deioces, who, in the first half of the seventh century B.C., raised the Median tribes from confusion and anarchy to an organized state under a central royal power (Herod. i. 96 foll.), for a time probably still a tributary vassal of the Assyrian king, but paving the way for the Median war of independence from the Assyrian yoke. He built the royal capital Ecbatana (old Pers. Hagmatāna, later Hamadān). His son Phraortes (646–625) was the real founder of the Median supremacy. He subdued Persis and portions of the rest of Irān ("all Asia, one tribe after the other," Herod. i. 102), and finally entered into an attack on Assyria, for which, however, he paid with his life. His successor Cyaxares (624-585) was the most important king of Media, and raised the young nation to the highest power. He gave the country a firm organized military system. His expedition against Assyria, which brought him victorious before Nineveh, had to be broken off, as the Scythians were meantime invading and devastating all Irān. Cyaxares freed his land from this plague by stratagem (Herod. i. 106). Even then he made Armenia and Cappadocia as far as the Halys subject to himself, and is said to have pushed his dominion eastward over Hyrcania, Parthia, and Bactria. In alliance with Nabopolassar of Babylon, he destroyed Nineveh, and divided the Assyrian Empire among his allies. His son Astyages (584–550) was the last king of his race. Herodotus tells only of his fall, which was brought about by the son of his vassal in the small but energetic district of Persis.

Cyrus (Kūrush), 559–530, belonged to the highest order of Persian nobility — the Pasargadae. His family, which already occupied a leading position in Persis, traced its origin to Achaemenes (Hakhāmani). Xenophon (*Cyrop.* i. 2, 1), in opposition to Herodotus (i. 91–107), makes the father of Cyrus king of Persia. Babylonian inscriptions call his great-grandfather Teispes "king of the city of Anshan." According to this, the Achaemenids had long ruled as kings in Persis under the suzerainty of the great kings of Media.

Myths early gathered about the youth of Cyrus and his ascension to the throne. The romantic story in Herodotus (i. 107–130) is familiar. The Persians under Cyrus revolt against Astyages; he sends against them Harpagus, who, however, from private enmity, is favourable to Cyrus. A large part of the Median army goes over to Cyrus, and Astyages is conquered and taken alive. The *coup d'état* is told differently in Nicol. Damascenus, *Fragm.* 66 (after Ctesias). But Xenophon's account makes Cyrus gain the power most easily of all by marrying the daughter and heiress of the last Median king Cyaxares, a son of Astyages, receiving Media as a dowry (*Cyrop.* viii. 5, 19). But Herodotus and Xenophon agree that Cyrus, on his mother's side, was a grandson of Astyages. The account of Herodotus is corrected and in part confirmed by the Babylonian inscriptions (cf. Rawlinson in the *Journal of the Royal Asiatic Soc. XII.*, new series, p. 70; Th. Pinches, *Transactions of the Soc. of Bibl. Arch. VII.*, Ad. Bauer, *Sitzungsberichte der Wiener Akademie*, 1882, p. 497).

In these inscriptions it is related that Astyages took the field against Cyrus, but his soldiers revolted and surrendered him to Cyrus. Briefly, therefore, the circumstances were probably the following: In the year 559 Cyrus succeeds his father Cambyses as viceroy in Persis. He frees Persis and Susia, which was connected with it, from the Median suzerainty, and so becomes the first sovereign king of Persis and Susia. Astyages makes war upon him, and in the decisive battle at Pasargadae (Strabo, p. 730) loses his liberty and his Empire (550). After a short existence and rapid growth the Median sovereignty had given place to the Persian. In Media itself the acquirement of Ecbatana, which was shortly afterwards accomplished, seems to have completed the transfer of the powers without any long resistance; the Medes soon became reconciled to the new order. For them the change meant not a foreign domination, but only a change of dynasty; the political aim of the Median Empire—the conquest of Asia—remained undisturbed. Since all accounts agree that Astyages had no son, Cyrus was the natural pretender for the throne, and only anticipated his time somewhat. And with the new Persian sovereign the place of the unloved Astyages (cf. Herod. i. 123; Aristot. *Polit.* v 8, 15) was occupied by a man who combined daring energy with paternal kindness. The Persian nobles, indeed, played the first parts, and Persian soldiers formed the military nucleus of the Empire. On the other hand, the less civilized victors willingly submitted themselves to the higher culture of the conquered. The Persians adopted their dress, customs, and vices from the Medes, together with the whole system of court and State, as they had already adopted their religion. Although to foreign eyes the Median name long retained its lustre, the national wall of division between Persians and Medes seems gradually to have fallen away and both races to have been mingled in a national unity. The court resided for a portion of the year in Media. Medes occupied high State positions and commands. From this time Persia, Susia, and Media formed the powerful kernel of the nation.

Not so willingly did the other vassal States of the Median kingdom give their adherence to their new lords; their revolts caused Cyrus many wars (Herod. i. 177; Just. i. 7). Even before Cyrus was involved in the second great war, the former vassal countries westward to the Halys were subject to him. Here followed at once the collision with his powerful neighbour Lydia. Once already, under Cyaxares, a bloody war had broken out between the two rival Empires, which continued with varying results for five years, and was finally calmed through the diplomatic intervention of the kings of Babylon and Cilicia (Herod. i. 74). The fall of his brother-in-law and the rapid rise of the insatiable Cyrus forced the ruler of Sardis, Croesus, into war. After assuring himself of the alliance of Babylon, Egypt, and Sparta (Herod. i. 77 foll.), he crossed the Halys in the year 547, anticipating an attack of Cyrus, and carried devastation into Cappadocia, a Persian protectorate (Herod. i. 76). The first battle occurred at Pteria, but was not decisive (Herod. i. 76). There Croesus began the return march, to occupy winter-quarters in Lydia. Cyrus pursued with forced marches, gained a decisive victory over the Lydians at Sardis before the auxiliaries which had been requested arrived, and shut the king up in the capital, which, after a siege of two weeks, was stormed and plundered. Cyrus eventually showed mercy to the captured Croesus, and took him with him to court in Persia, leaving the complete subjection of Lydia to his Median governors Mazares and Harpagus (Herod. i. 162). Not alone all the Greek towns on the west coast of Asia Minor, which were tributary to Lydia, but also Miletus, Lycia, Caria, and Cilicia recognized the Persian authority either willingly or by force. Cyrus himself, immediately after the capture of Sardis, was summoned to the eastern part of the monarchy, to Bactria, by new

Tomb of Cyrus near Pasargadae.

revolts. All of Upper Asia to the eastern border of Irān is from this time on under his sway. Sardis became the firm centre of the western half of the Empire. Lydia was divided into two provinces, the governors of which resided at Sardis and Dascyleion (Herod. iii. 120).

Now, when his Empire reached from the Iaxartes to the west coast of Asia Minor, only Babylon stood between him and the supreme power in Asia. In the year 539 Cyrus made an incursion into Babylonian territory (Herod. i. 190 foll.; Berosus, *Fragm.* 14). In the very first battle the troops of the enemy mutinied. King Nabonidus of Babylon fled. The strong capital surrendered without resistance, and the whole Babylonian territory, together with the vassal States, of which Syria was the most important, yielded willingly to Cyrus (Herod. iii. 19), who, in this case also, showed himself not as a barbarous, oppressive conqueror, but as the new father of the country. He allowed the sanctuaries and palaces of Babylon to remain unharmed. It was quite in the character of the ancient Persians, who were not in the least religious fanatics, that he should tolerate and protect the old Babylonian religion. Cyrus was accustomed to treat the dispossessed princes with consideration, and to retain them in his service as governors. Through his wise policy, he was able to make moral conquests, and became the least sanguinary of the great conquerors of the Orient. His followers also, notably Darius, pursued this moderate policy in cases of conquest, not of rebellion.

The crown treasures of the conquered lands Cyrus took as spoils of war and stored up in his palaces, thus laying the foundation of the inexhaustible reserves of money of the later Persian Empire. These supplies indirectly benefited the Persians, for it is said that as often as Cyrus entered the territory of Persia he gave a piece of gold to every Persian man and woman (Xen. *Cyrop.* viii. 5, 19; Nicod. Damas. *Fragm.* 66). To his Persians he was always the national king; the heads of the nobility of Persis were nearest to the throne, and their counsel was of weight in important decisions.

Cyrus is said to have met his death in an expedition against a nomad race beyond the Iaxartes—the Massagetae, according to Herodotus, the Derbiccae, according to Ctesias. At all events, it was one of the wild Turanian tribes which, with their plundering inroads, had long been the scourge of Northern Irān. But the reports are conflicting. His military science probably failed in the inhospitable steppes of Central Asia before the crafty tactics of these rider hordes. His army was cut to pieces; Herodotus says that he himself fell in the battle, Ctesias that he died from the wounds received there. His body was entombed at Pasargadae, in the shade of the park, in a chamber upon a small stone pyramid. There Alexander saw his golden coffin (Strabo, p. 730). Cyrus had two sons, Cambyses and Smerdis, by his wife Cassandané, who died before him. Of his daughters, Atossa is best known.

He was succeeded by his eldest son, Cambyses (Kabujiya), B.C. 529–522, an imperious, passionate man, whose notorious intemperance (Herod. iii. 34) at times developed into delirium. While the Persians considered Cyrus as their father, they looked on the new sovereign as their master (Herod. iii. 89). Cambyses inherited the active disposition of his father. His first expedition against Egypt involved immense armies. The Phœnician ports, as well as Cyprus, which had recently revolted from Egypt and voluntarily submitted to Persia (Herod. iii. 19), were obliged to mobilize their fleets to afford naval support to the land attack. Samos also at the time entered into voluntary alliance with Persia (Herod. iii. 44). Cambyses first caused his younger brother Smerdis (Bardiya), whose loyalty he distrusted, to be murdered secretly by Prexaspes. A Greek fugitive, Thanes, led the army through the Arabian Desert (Herod. iii. 4). At Pelusium Cambyses met the army of Psammetichus III., who had shortly before succeeded King Amasis. The Egyptian army was completely vanquished, Memphis was taken after a short siege, and Psammetichus made prisoner. In the year 525 the old kingdom of the Pharaohs was made a province of the Persian Empire. In general, Cambyses held to the policy of recognizing and respecting foreign nationality; no change was made in religion or government except that a satrap took the place of the Pharaohs. But the unbridled king personally outraged the people by brutal excesses, such as the desecration of the corpse of Amasis (Herod. iii. 16) and his private mockery of their sacred things.

From Egypt Cambyses planned great expeditions to the west and south. The naval expedition against Carthage was abandoned, because the Phœnicians refused to move against their own colony. A land force perished utterly in the sands of the Libyan Desert (Herod. iii. 26). The expedition under his own command against Aethiopia was not entirely fruitless, but entailed heavy losses (Herod. iii. 25). These failures increased his madness to a still higher point; he killed the bull Apis in rage (Herod. iii. 27), and by ill-treatment caused the death of his own sister, whom he had married according to Persian custom.

Cambyses remained in Egypt until the year 522, when suddenly disquieting reports came from Persia, which, in consequence of his long absence, seems for a long time to have been in a state of fermentation. A Magian, Gaumāta, whose brother was the steward of Cambyses, took advantage of the universal dissatisfaction, and, favoured by a certain resemblance to the murdered Smerdis (Herod. iii. 61 even gives him the same name), proclaimed himself to be the latter, and inflamed the land against the rightful king. Only a few initiated persons knew of the murder of Smerdis. Through great mildness and still greater promises the usurper quickly succeeded. Persia, Media, and the provinces gave him their allegiance, and Cambyses was practically a dethroned prince. From this point we can test the statements of Herodotus by the inscriptions of Darius. While on his homeward journey to punish the usurper, he met his death in Syria by his own hand, or through carelessness, as Herodotus (iii. 64) thinks. The position of the Achaemenid dynasty was precarious. The people considered the pretender the real Bardiya, who would now have been the legitimate successor to the throne, as Cambyses died childless. Certain expressions of doubt seem to have been checked by the new tyrant with great cruelty. He must have feared most of all being unmasked by the Persian grandees, and therefore he never received them, nor allowed himself to be seen publicly, which was quite contrary to etiquette. Herodotus makes him reside in Susa, but according to the inscriptions his fate overtook him in a Median fortress. Seven Persian nobles, with Darius at their head, who had secretly discovered the truth, formed a conspiracy, surprised the castle, and struck Gaumāta down.

Persian Intaglio Cylinder. (Dieulafoy.)

It had been neither a Median revolt against Persian sovereignty (Herod. i. 130) nor a religious uprising of the Magi, but the game of chance of a political adventurer, whom fortune favoured for a short time through a rare combination of circumstances. But for the moment the whole wrath of the insulted Persian nobility was turned against the Magi, and it would have needed little to end the day with a night of St. Bartholomew for all the Magi (Herod. iii. 79). Darius, the head of the conspiracy, was proclaimed king. The story of Herodotus that the choice was to be made among the seven by lot or chance is a later addition. In fact Darius was the only rightful heir to the throne. He was descended from a collateral branch of the Achaemenids, which from the time of Teïspes had separated from the now extinct chief line. The genealogy of the family, according to Herodotus and the inscriptions, is the following:

When he ascended the throne as governor of Persis his father was still alive (Herod. iii. 70), but appears to have resigned all claim to the succession to the avenger of his order. The other conspirators were rewarded with hereditary privileges.

The new king, Darius I. (Dārayavaüsh), (521–485), was in his thirtieth year. He entered into the inheritance of the Achaemenids at a critical period. The short interregnum had relaxed the empire of Cyrus in all its points. The provinces were everywhere uneasy—rebels and pretenders sprang up in every direction. The revolt first broke out in Susiana, but was quickly repressed. The uprising in Babylon was more serious, where a pretended son of Nabonidus placed himself at the head of the rebels; the fortress was taken only after a hard siege—according to Herodotus, through the craft of Zopyrus. While Darius was still fighting in Babylonia, Persia and Media revolted at the same time. The rebellion spread eastward to Margiana, westward over Armenia and Assyria, only the outer provinces remaining quiet. It seemed that the end of the empire had come, but the young king remained unshaken through all the storms, and the Persian and Median armies stood faithful. Only a great man could meet this gigantic task. Through years of sharp fighting he forced the seceding countries to return, one after the other, and disarmed the rebels. Later on he set up a proud memorial of these deeds in the great rock-inscriptions of Behistan.

By the end of the year 519 the great rebellion had been crushed forever; the Empire, twenty-three countries from the Nile to the Iaxartes, was again under his undisputed sway. He proceeded at once to unite the Empire more closely by reorganizing the government, and in accordance with the traditions of his house to extend his boundaries. To the east the Empire was extended to the Indus after he had carefully explored the lands of the Indus by ship (Herod. iv. 44), and the same were annexed (Herod. iii. 139).

The great expedition to the Danube against the Scythians, on the other hand, was only partially successful. There were probably various reasons for this expedition. Perhaps those mysterious, restless savages, who, from the time of Cyaxares, had been held in hostile memory, again attracted attention; perhaps this far-seeing man intended to surround Greece from the north, and so wished to secure first the right flank. Darius is said to have placed 700,000 men in the field, while his Ionian subjects supplied 600 ships (Herod. iv. 87). From the latter the Samian engineer Mandrocles constructed the famous bridge of ships over the Bosporus, on which in 515 Darius crossed to Europe. While the land force travelled north over the Balkan, the Ionians received command to break up the bridge, to put into the Danube, and to construct another bridge there. On the Danube the Getae alone offered an obstinate resistance, and he proceeded across the river into a wholly unknown region, while the Ionians were to wait sixty days for his return, and hold the bridge during that period. Most of the operations in the present Bessarabia were brought to nothing by the skilful equestrian tactics of the enemy, who came and disappeared with the speed of lightning, and never allowed themselves to be grasped. The Persian army was thus led deeper and deeper into the inhospitable steppes, and at last forced by lack of supplies and exhaustion to return. After heavy losses Darius succeeded in getting back to the bridge over the Danube, which fortunately, thanks to the faithfulness of Histiaeus of Miletus, had not yet been broken up. The sole result was the subjugation of the Thracian cities by Megabazus (Herod. v. 10), followed by that of the Grecian ports Paeonia and Macedonica (Herod. v. 15, xxvi. 18).

Persia and Greece had thus come into dangerous proximity, and the inevitable collision from the Persian side must have been long foreseen. A slight cause set the stone rolling. Exiled Greeks from Naxos applied to Aristagoras, governor of Miletus, for Persian aid against their city, whose freedom they were willing to sacrifice to their private revenge. The Persian king gave them assistance through the satrap of Sardis. The command was, however, divided between Aristagoras and Megabates, and the rivalry of the two generals caused the failure of the undertaking. The offended Aristagoras revenged himself: in the year 500 he gave the signal for a general uprising of the Ionian cities, which he had for some time been planning with Histiaeus. In the freedom-loving Greek cities the tyrants introduced by Persia (cf. Herod. iv. 98) had long been found a burden, and the spirit of revolt found in them ample nourishment. First a republic was proclaimed in Miletus, and the fleet returning from Naxos was seized. At the same time aid was asked from the mother-country, but only Athens and Eretria responded with twenty-five ships, which were the beginning of all misfortune for Greeks and barbarians (Herod. v. 97). The forces of Aristagoras moved upon Sardis and burned the city. Next the Greek cities on the Hellespont and almost the whole of Cyprus and Caria joined the revolt. But soon the Persian army was in the field, operating in conjunction with the fleet provided by Phœnicia. Cyprus was first reconquered, and the revolt suppressed in Asia Minor by three Persian armies after battles of varying results. The decisive naval battle occurred at Ladé, where the Ionian fleet was completely overcome by the combined Phœnician, Cyprian, and Egyptian fleets. Miletus, the home of the revolt, was taken and destroyed, after holding out for six years, 500–494 (Herod. vi. 20). The vengeance of the victors was terrible; Milesian maidens were carried off to the Persian harems, the men banished, and the flourishing country of the Ionians devastated and depopulated. For the Athenians and Eretrians also the Persian monarch had planned a similar chastisement. In the spring of 492 the land forces under Mardonius set out, supported by an enormous fleet. But the army had little success in Thrace, and the fleet was shipwrecked at Athos. A second and larger expedition started in 490 under Datis and Artaphernes, this time by sea only. The course was laid past Naxos, which was conquered. Then Eretria was burned, and its inhabitants carried off to the interior of Asia. This expedition came to its end on the memorable Plain of Marathon (490). The Greek victory has evidently been greatly exaggerated. Probably the Greeks, after having avoided battle for a long time, fell upon the Persians as they were departing, when the greater part of the army, especially the powerful cavalry, had already embarked. The Persian generals contented themselves with the results in Naxos and Euboea and abandoned the campaign. If Darius had commanded in person, the result would probably have been a different one.

Another piece of bad news troubled the closing days of the king's life. Egypt, which up to this time had borne the easy yoke, now rose against Persia. Thus the unyielding monarch saw himself confronted with a twofold war, but in the midst of extensive preparations he was overtaken by death after a reign of thirty-six years (485). With him died the greatest ruler that Irān ever produced, the ideal of an enlightened despot, trained in a hard school, filled with his high calling, wise in his choice of means and persons, fitted by his energy and wariness for the greatest achievements.

Darius was not alone a conqueror like Cyrus, an augmenter of his Empire, which he raised from twenty-three to thirty lands, but also a wise and practical organizer. His predecessors had appointed governors (satraps) as need arose; Darius divided the kingdom into fixed governmental districts (satrapies), and regulated the powers of the satraps (*khshathrapāvan*). They held a prince's court in the provincial capitals, and were the chief heads of the government, the law, and the military in their provinces. They were responsible immediately to the sovereign. In order to prevent any possible schemes of independence, Darius caused them to be watched by persons in whom he reposed special confidence. He himself made annual tours of inspection. The commanders of fortresses in the provinces were appointed directly by the king. Besides, he fixed definitely the tax to be imposed on each province, and so assured the Empire as well as the crown a definite revenue, whereas formerly the taxes had consisted in so-called presents (Herod. iii. 89)—i. e. voluntary tribute. Only the original Persia was untaxed. The rest of the provinces paid a land tax in proportion to the yield of the soil, Babylonia being taxed most heavily. There were, besides, indirect taxes, duties, taxes on products, etc. The direct taxes alone amounted annually to about twelve million dollars.

Intercourse and trade were fostered by Darius by means of military roads and canals. His courier post was renowned, by means of which he sent his commands through the whole Empire in the shortest possible time (Herod. viii. 98).

His descendants were quite numerous. Some of his sons were born when he was still a private citizen. The succession descended according to Persian custom to Xerxes, the first son born after his accession to the throne.

Xerxes (Khshayārsha) (485–465) was the eldest son of the imperious Atossa, the daughter of Cyrus, who had been successively the wife of Cambyses, Pseudo-Smerdis, and Darius. Soon after his accession Egypt was subdued (484). He was at first little disposed to continue the war against Greece, but finally followed the promptings of the war-party under the ambitious Mardonius, and for fully four years was actively employed in making preparations. The army was concentrated at Sardis. In the spring of 480 Xerxes marched with the land forces through Thrace and Macedonia, while the fleet sailed to Therma. The defeat of the Spartans at Thermopylae, where the Persians avenged Marathon, and the doubtful result of the sea-fight at Artemisium, were compensated by the brilliant victories of Salamis, Plataeae, and Mycalé. The chances of war were by no means so unfavourable to Greece as they had appeared in the momentary discouragement at first. The numerical advantage of the Persians was very great; but the patriotic legend has enormously exaggerated the number of actual combatants in making it reach the total of two and a half millions (Herod. vii. 185). It was, moreover, a contest between a people fighting for their country and a soldiery brought together from all quarters, partly by force, who had little to lose by defeat. The boastful Persian generals committed a mistake in wholly undervaluing their antagonists. In organization, tactics, and generalship the Greeks were far superior to the Asiatics, and the great masses of the Persian army could not be used to the best advantage in the Grecian territory. Even before Plataeae Xerxes had lost all courage and quickly removed his Persians to a place of safety, leaving Mardonius with the choicest Persian troops. He retired at once to his luxurious capitals in the interior, sinking into the inactive life of the harem, while the Greeks, especially under the leadership of Timon, made greater and greater progress in the liberation of their countrymen on the islands and the Asiatic coast. The European possessions of the Persians were lost forever.

In the year 465 Xerxes and his eldest son Darius were murdered in a revolt in the palace. Under Xerxes began the chain of misrule, seldom interrupted, which slowly undermined the existence of the nation. The fate of the dynasty was determined almost alone by palace revolts, court intrigues, and the rule of women and favourites. The inner history of the Empire, its growing decay, is hidden from our knowledge, as Herodotus, the fullest source of information, breaks off with the battle of Mycalé, and the Persian inscriptions after Xerxes become more and more scanty. In its external history the Greeks remain the chief factor; Persian money and intrigues play an important part in Greece.

Xerxes was succeeded by his youngest son Artaxerxes I. Longimanus (Artakhshathra) (464–425). In his long reign only two events are important—a revolt in Egypt, supported by Athens, but repressed by the battle of Memphis, and the conclusion of peace with Athens (449), through which the Aegean and the Greek colonies in Asia were taken from the Persian dominion.

Seal of Artaxerxes I. (Dieulafoy.)

His only legitimate son, Xerxes II., was murdered after a very short reign by his half-brother, Secydianus; but the murderer was himself put to death by another illegitimate son of Artaxerxes, Orthus, previously satrap of Hyrcania. Orthus himself ascended the throne as Darius II. (Nothus), (423–405). In his reign an opportunity was offered to Persia of regaining its lost power in the Aegean and the whole west coast. When in the Peloponnesian War the hegemony of Persia's hereditary enemy, Athens, was broken, the Persian court entered into relations with Sparta through the satraps Tissaphernes of Lydia and Pharnabazus of Phrygia. In return for subsidies Sparta was to give over to Persia all the coast region lost by the peace of 449. For a long time the alliance accepted by Sparta could not be put into effect, owing to the rivalry of the two satraps and the perfidy of Tissaphernes, and the Athenians for a time had a decided advantage. A change came only when the Persian prince, Cyrus, an energetic and ambitious young man, received the chief command of the troops of Asia Minor. He sought a close alliance with Sparta; subsidies were freely given, and with this assistance Sparta was enabled to force Athens to a peace.

About this time Darius II. died, and his death occasioned the well-known contest for the throne. His wife Parysatis, an imperious, intriguing woman, had borne him two sons, the elder, Arsicas, before his accession, and younger, Cyrus, when queen. Her efforts to gain the succession for her younger and far more gifted favourite son Cyrus, as being the real king's son, had no result. Arsicas ascended the throne as Artaxerxes II. (Mnemon) in 405. He placed his younger brother as satrap over Asia Minor. But Tissaphernes, the professed friend of Cyrus, defamed him to his brother, and it was only through the protection of his mother that he escaped imprisonment. Returning to his satrapy, he assured himself of troops from every side in Greece, in order to gain forcible possession of the throne. In the spring of 401 he began an expedition with 13,000 Greek auxiliaries and his own army of Asiatics, ostensibly against rebels in his own satrapy. Again he was betrayed by Tissaphernes. At Cunaxa Cyrus met an enormous royal army. The mere appearance of the Greek soldiers put the Asiatics to terror and flight; but Cyrus ventured too far into the conflict, and fell. The sudden end of this knightly youth, who was entitled to great hopes, is tragic. The adventurous return of 10,000 Greeks is familiar from Xenophon's *Anabasis*.

Sparta had openly sided with Cyrus against the great king, and the relations between the two States were therefore strained. Tissaphernes, returned to his post of satrap in Asia Minor, demanded submission from all the Ionian cities which had gone over to Cyrus. They refused, and asked help of Sparta, which, in spite of the still existing alliance, forbade Tissaphernes to attack the cities; and, as Tissaphernes paid no attention to this prohibition, war broke out in 401 between Sparta and Persia. The war dragged along, and the Spartans gained no important results until Agesilaus received the chief command, when they invested the provinces of Asia Minor. In its difficulties the Persian court now made use of Athenian aid. The Athenian admiral Conon commanded the newly equipped Persian fleet, and conquered the Spartans at Cnidos (397). Mutual exhaustion ended the war with the peace of Antalcidas (387), which the Persian king practically dictated. In it Persia claimed the whole Asiatic sea-coast and some islands, such as Cyprus, as its property.

The last years of Artaxerxes were occupied with numerous revolts among the satraps. Personally he is said to have been mild and peace-loving (Thuc. *Artax.* 30). He showed fatal weakness towards the women of the court, and his life was a series of intrigues and quarrels. In his last days he named his oldest son Darius as his successor, but the latter became involved in a conspiracy against his father, and was beheaded. His ambitious son Ochus caused the murder of two older brothers who stood in his way, and after his father's death in 358 ascended the throne as Artaxerxes III. He was a thorough despot, pursuing his ends without scruple, shrinking at no cruelty. By his severity and by his wise policy he lifted the decaying kingdom once more to its former power. At his accession all the western part of the Empire was in turmoil. Hardly was the rebellious satrap of Phrygia conquered when Phœnicia and Cyprus revolted. His generals were unsuccessful in their operations against the rebelling king Tennes of Sidon and Mentor of Rhodes. The monarch placed himself at the head of a large army, which was strengthened by Greek soldiers supplied in accordance with the terms of the alliance. Sidon fell through the treachery of Tennes, and was fearfully punished. The fall of the capital soon reduced the rest of Phœnicia, and Cyprus was reconquered.

The most important task before Artaxerxes was to reconquer Egypt, which, for more than sixty years, had remained independent. His two generals Bagoas and Mentor, who had come over to his side, operated so skilfully under his command on the field, and not less with threats, that king Nectanebus of Egypt soon abandoned his cause as lost and fled to Aethiopia. The defenceless land, after a severe punishment, was again made part of the Persian Empire. Mentor became satrap of the sea-coast of Asia Minor; Bagoas remained near the king as minister, and appears to have been the originator of the plot to kill the king by poison, which was carried out in 338; Bagoas, who remained master of the situation, placed Arses, the youngest son of Artaxerxes, on the throne (338–336). But as the latter did not show himself pliant, he was removed in the third year of his reign.

Bagoas now placed on the throne a distant relative of the murdered king, Darius III. (Codomannus), a great-grandson of Darius II. (336–320). When Bagoas once more attempted his old manoeuvre, he was himself forced to drink the poison. Darius was perhaps the most worthy of the Achaemenids at the time to fill the high station, but he was not man enough to ward off the threatening evils. Even at the time of his accession there was imminent danger of war from the uprisings in Macedonia. The *casus belli*, if, indeed, any was needed, dated from the time of Artaxerxes III. When, in the year 340, Philip was besieging the town of Perinthus, opposite the Persian territory, Persian auxiliaries, in union with Athens, had relieved the town. Philip himself had planned an expedition against the Persian king, ostensibly as the avenger of Greece. On the threshold of his undertaking Philip was assassinated, apparently not without instigation on the part of Persia (Arrian, *Anab.* ii. 14). The young Alexander, whom Darius at first wholly undervalued, at once took up the great plans of his father as soon as Greece was completely pacified. Darius in vain sought to counteract his extensive preparations. Darius's right-hand and first general was the Rhodian Memnon, a brother of Mentor, a man as skilful and energetic as his renowned brother. He alone planned earnestly for the safety of the Empire, when indecision, suspicion, and great egoism controlled the other Persian commanders.

In the spring of 334 Alexander crossed the Hellespont with not more than 30,000 infantry, 4500 horsemen, and 182 ships. At the Granicus, where, against the advice of Memnon and with no plan of action, the Persian army offered battle, Alexander gained his first brilliant victory. Sardis capitulated without a blow. In Ephesus he was greeted as a liberator; Miletus and Halicarnassus alone defended themselves bravely. At the end of the year Alexander was in possession of Asia Minor as far as the Taurus. Only Memnon threatened him with danger. Memnon crossed to the sea unhindered, and was on the point of carrying the war into Europe behind Alexander's back when death overtook him. His death was the most severe blow to the Persian cause. Nothing now obstructed Alexander's victorious course. In an unfavourable position at Issus, Darius himself opposed him with an immense army, and was completely routed with great losses (333). The Persian army was scattered, and Darius fled across the Euphrates. In order to protect the rear, Alexander occupied Phœnicia and Egypt (332). In the spring of 331 he marched towards the heart of the Persian monarchy, after having rejected various overtures of peace from the Persian king. Darius had concentrated in Assyria another immense army from the inexhaustible resources of the Persian Empire. The decisive battle of Arbela and Gaugamela completely shattered the Persian colossus. Darius did not even await the issue of the day, but was among the first to flee to Media. Without a blow, Babylon and Susa opened their gates. In the middle of the winter Alexander stood before the passes of Persis, in which the satrap Ariobarzanes, with a small army, successfully opposed him. Alexander imitated the Persian manoeuvre of Thermopylae. Persepolis capitulated, and immense treasures fell into Alexander's hands. At his command the royal citadel was burned, and the town was given over to plunder. Persis was completely reduced to subjection. In the spring of 330 Alexander went to Ecbatana, and pressed hard in pursuit of the fleeing Darius. Meantime Bessus, satrap of Bactria, had gained possession of the government of all Ariana, and had been taken prisoner by Darius in his retreat. When Alexander was close at his heels Bessus struck Darius down. Alexander found only the corpse of the last of the Achaemenids. Bessus for a time maintained himself as King Artaxerxes IV. in the far east of Irān, and organized the defence of Bactria and Sogdiana with much skill. But beyond the Oxus he was surrendered by his own people, and later on was crucified in Ecbatana. Bactria quickly yielded, but Sogdiana for a long time offered stout resistance, and not until 327 did it, the last bulwark of Iranian independence, fall completely into the hands of the great Macedonian.

Persian history from this time is absorbed in the history of Alexander, the Diadochi, and the Parthian kingdom under the Arsacids. Not until the year A.D. 224 was a new Persian nation born, under the dynasty of the Sasanids.

BIBLIOGRAPHY.—Rawlinson, *The Five Great Monarchies*, vols. ii., iii. (London, 1871); Spiegel, *Iranische Alterthumskunde* (Leipzig, 1871); Duncker, *Geschichte des Alterthums*, vol. iv.; Eduard Meyer, *Geschichte des Alterthums*, vol. i. (Stuttgart, 1884); Nöldeke, *Aufsätze zur Persischen Geschichte* (Leipzig, 1887); Spiegel, *Die Altpersischen Keilinschriften* (Leipzig, 1862; 2d ed. 1881); Darmesteter, *Études Iraniennes* (Paris, 1883); Flandin and Coste, *Voyage en Perse* (Paris, 1843–54); Stolze, *Persepolis*, 2 vols. (Berlin, 1882).

Persĭca Māla. "Persian apples"; a name given by the Romans to peaches. The peach-tree was called *Persicus arbor*.

Persĭci Montes. See PARSICI MONTES.

Persĭcus Sinus (Περσικὸς κόλπος) or **Persĭcum Maré** (Περσικὴ θάλασσα). The name given by the later geographers to the great gulf of the Maré Erythraeum (Indian Ocean), extending between the coast of Arabia and the opposite coast of Susiana, Persis, and Carmania, now called the Persian Gulf.

Persīdes (Περσείδης). A patronymic given to the descendants of Perses (q. v.).

Persis. See PERSIA.

Persius Flaccus, AULUS. A well-known Roman satirist, the third in order among the writers of that form of literature. He was born A.D. 34 at Volaterrae, in Etruria, of a good equestrian family. Losing his father when six years old, at the age of twelve he went to Rome, and enjoyed the instruction of the most eminent teachers, more especially of one for whom he had the greatest reverence, Annaeus Cornutus (q. v.), who initiated him in the Stoic philosophy and introduced him to the acquaintance of Lucan. After the first poetic attempts of his youth, which he himself burned, his energies were directed to satiric verse, under the influence of Lucilius and Horace. On his early death, in the year 62, the six satires which he left, after some slight revision by Cornutus, were published by his friend, the poet Caesius Bassus. A short introduction in fourteen scazonic trimeters is possibly spurious. In these Persius deals with the moral corruption of his age, from the standpoint of a Stoic preacher of ethics. Both in thought and expression a tendency to echo Horace is constantly apparent. (See Werther, *De Persio Horatii Imitatore* [Halle, 1883].) He composed slowly, and appears to be himself conscious that he has no true poetic faculty. His mode of expression is frequently difficult and involved to the verge of obscurity. The need of explanations was accordingly felt in comparatively early times; but the collection of scholia bearing the name of Cornutus shows hardly any traces of ancient learning. Many of the terse phrases and lines of Persius have passed into literature, the most famous being the *O quantum est in rebus inane* (i. 1); *pulchrum est digito monstrari* (i. 28); *rara avis* (i. 46); *tecum habita; noris quam sit tibi curta supellex* (iv. 52); and the striking lines in the Third Satire (35–38). In fact, many of the epigrammatic lines of Juvenal seem to have been suggested by the earlier satirist. (See Wilcke's monograph [Stendal, 1869].) The language of Persius is often tinged with the vocabulary and usage of the plebeian Latin, as he writes in the character of a plain, blunt man—the very opposite of his real self. See SERMO PLEBEIUS.

The best MSS. of Persius are the Codex Montepessulanus (of Montpellier) and a Codex Vaticanus, of the ninth or tenth centuries. Few classic authors are represented by so many codices, as the moral tone of Persius made him a favourite throughout the Middle Ages. Famous editions are those of Pithœus (Paris, 1585); Casaubon (Paris, 1605; ed. by Dübner with many additions, Leipzig, 1833); Orelli (Zürich, 1833); Hauthal (Leipzig, 1837); and especially Jahn (Leipzig, 1843, and Berlin, 1886), the last ed. by Bücheler; Hermann (Leipzig, 1854); and Gildersleeve (New York, 1875). An excellent idiomatic (prose) translation is that of Conington, with commentary (London, 1874), ed. by Nettleship. On Persius as a philosopher, see Knickenberg, *De Ratione Stoica in Persio* (Münster, 1869), and Schlüter, *De Sat. Pers. Natura et Indole* (Andernach, 1886).

Persōna (πρόσωπον and προσωπεῖον). A mask; an artificial covering for the face worn among many peoples in all ages of history and for different purposes, but more frequently in Greece and Italy (1) for covering the faces of the dead and (2) by actors in theatrical performances.

Death-masks of gold have been found in tombs at Mycēnae and elsewhere; at Carthage masks of clay were also similarly used. In Egypt they were placed upon the case containing the mummy. See also IMAGINES.

Mask from Mummy-case of Rameses II.

For theatrical purposes, masks were made of linen, of bark, of leather, and sometimes of wood. Their introduction in dramatic performances is ascribed to Choerilus (q. v.) of Samos about B.C. 500, and to Aeschylus (q. v.); but their use really goes back to the mummery in honour of Dionysus, at whose festivals in early Greece the face was painted with the lees of wine or covered with leaves. The opening for the eyes was not larger than the pupil of the actor's eyes behind the mask. The masks themselves sometimes merely covered the face, like masks in modern times; but sometimes, also, they covered the whole head down to the shoulders. The wig worn by the tragic actors was usually if not always a part of the mask. Phrynichus is said by Suidas (s. v.) to have first made comic masks. The varieties of masks were very numerous, representing every possible sort of character, age, sex, and condition. Pollux (iv. 133, etc.) enumerates twenty-eight typical kinds of mask, six for old men, eight for young men, eleven for women, and three for slaves. Gellius thinks that the mouth of the mask was arranged so as to intensify the sound of the actor's voice (v. 7); but this is doubtful.

Masks in British Museum.

At Rome masks were not used in early times, but only wigs. They were probably first introduced in B.C. 110 by Roscius, who was homely and had a squint. When the audiences hissed an actor he was obliged to remove his mask, except when acting in the *Atellanae fabulae* (Macrob. *Sat.* ii. 7).

See the articles DRAMA and SATYRICA FABULA.

Pertĭnax, HELVIUS. A Roman emperor who ruled from January 1 to March 28, A.D. 193, having been reluctantly persuaded to accept the Empire on the death of Commodus. But having attempted to check the license of the Praetorian Guards, he was slain by the latter, who then put up the Empire for sale. See Capitolin. *Pertinax;* and Krakauer, *Commodus und Pertinax* (Breslau, 1883).

Pertinax.

Perusia. Now Perugia; an ancient city in the eastern part of Etruria between the lake Trasimenus and the Tiber, and one of the twelve cities of the Etruscan confederacy. (See ETRURIA.) It was situated on a hill, and was strongly fortified by nature and by art. It is memorable in the Civil Wars as the place in which L. Antonius, the brother of the triumvir, took refuge when he was

Masks. (Pompeii.)

no longer able to oppose Octavianus (Augustus) in the field, and where he was kept closely blockaded by Octavianus from the end of B.C. 41 to the spring of 40. Famine compelled it to surrender; but one of its citizens having set fire to his own house, the flames spread, and the whole city was burned to the ground. It was rebuilt by Augustus. Portions of the ancient walls and several of the gates of Perusia still remain, the best preserved of the latter being the so-called Arco d'Augusta, which bears the inscription AUGUSTA PERUSINA over the arch. A number of tombs with Etruscan relics have been found near the city.

Pervigilium (lit. "a night-watch"). A nocturnal festival in honour of a divinity, especially that of the Bona Dea, at which originally only married women were allowed to be present. In imperial times, when the presence of men was permitted, a nocturnal festival to Venus was also instituted. Such a festival, extending over three nights in the spring, is referred to in an anonymous poem called the PERVIGILIUM VENĔRIS, of the second or third century A.D. It consists of ninety-three trochaic septenarii, separated into unequal strophae by the recurring refrain, *Cras amet qui nunquam amavit, quique amavit cras amet.* It celebrates in a lively strain the power of Venus, particularly as displayed in springtime, lauding her as the giver of life to all, and as the ancestress and patroness of Rome. The *editio princeps* is that of Pithoeus (Paris, 1577). An edition with notes and emendations is that of Bücheler (Leipzig, 1859); it is also given in Bährens's *Unedierte lat. Gedichte* (Leipzig, 1877); and there is an *édition de luxe* by Owen (1893).

Pes. See MENSURA.

Pescennius Niger. See NIGER.

Pessi (πεσσοί). See LATRUNCULI.

Pessīnus (Πεσσινοῦς) or **Pesīnus** (Πεσινοῦς). A city in the southwest corner of Galatia, on the southern slope of Mount Dindymus or Agdistis, was celebrated as a chief seat of the worship of Cybelé, under the surname of Agdistis, whose temple, crowded with riches, stood on a hill outside the city. In this temple was an image of the goddess, which was removed to Rome to satisfy an oracle in the Sibylline Books. See RHEA.

Pessŭlus. See IANUA.

Petăsus (πέτασος). A flat felt hat, with a broad and round brim, usually worn among the Thessalians. The brim is often parted into four bow-shaped indentations. It is said to have been introduced into Greece along with the chlamys as a distinguishing mark of the *ephebi*. Hermes is usually represented with the winged petasus. The Romans wore a similar hat in the country, and when travelling; in the city it was generally used only in the theatre, as a protection from the sun (Suet. *Aug.* 82). See PILLEUS.

Petasi. (Pompeian Painting.)

Petauristae. See PETAURUM.

Petaurum (πέταυρον). (1) A perch or roost for fowls (Pollux, x. 156). (2) A spring-board for acrobats (Juv. xiv. 265), who were called *petauristae*. From the petaurum the acrobats sometimes leaped through blazing hoops (Petron. 53, with Friedländer's note).

Petelia (Πετηλία) or **Petilia.** Now Strongoli; an ancient Greek town on the eastern coast of Bruttium, founded, according to tradition, by Philoctetes (Verg. *Aen.* iii. 402). It was taken by Hannibal after a desperate resistance, and by him colonized with Bruttians; but the Romans restored it to its own people (App. *Ann.* 29, 57).

Petilius Capitolīnus. See CAPITOLINUS.

Petitio Consulātus. See CICERO (3).

Petītor. See ACTOR.

Petorrĭtum or **Petorĭtum.** A four-wheeled carriage which, like the later form of the *essedum* (q. v.) and some other vehicles, the Romans adopted from the Gauls. The name itself is Keltic (*petvar*= *quattuor*, and *rit*=*rota*). It was strongly built and better adapted for rough roads than the *reda* (q. v.). On journeys the family usually rode in a *reda* and the servants in a petorritum. See the Schol. Cruq. *ad* Hor. *Epist.* ii. 1, 192; Ginzrot, *Die Wagen der alten Völker*, i. 224; and Marquardt, *Privatleben*, 734.

Petosīris (Πετόσιρις). An Egyptian priest said to be the founder of astrology. His name was often used as a generic term for an astrologist (Juv. vi. 580).

Petovio. See POETOVIO.

Petra (ἡ Πέτρα). The name of several cities built on rocks, or in rocky places, of which the most celebrated was in Arabia Petraea, the capital, first of the Idumaeans, and afterwards of the Nabathaeans. It lies in the midst of the mountains of Seir, just half way between the Dead Sea and the head of the Aelanitic Gulf of the Red Sea, in a valley or, rather, ravine, surrounded by almost inaccessible precipices, which is entered by a narrow gorge on the east, the rocky walls of which approach so closely as in some places hardly to permit two horsemen to ride abreast. On the banks of the river which runs through this ravine stood the city itself, and some fine ruins of its public buildings still remain. These ruins are chiefly of the Roman period, when Petra had become an important city as a centre of the caravan traffic of the Nabathaeans. It maintained its independence under the Romans till the time of Trajan, by whom it was taken. It was the chief city of Arabia Petraea; and under the later Empire the capital of Palaestina Tertia. The rocks about it were honeycombed with tombs.

Other cities of the name were situated in Sicily (Cic. *Verr.* iii. 39), Elis (Pausan. vi. 24, 5), Macedonia (Livy, xlv. 41), and Illyricum (Caes. *B. C.* iii. 42).

Petrēius, MARCUS. A person of great military experience, first mentioned in B.C. 62, when he served as legatus to the proconsul C. Antonius, and commanded the army in the battle in which Catiline perished. He belonged to the aristocratic party; and in 55 he was sent into Spain along with L. Afranius as legatus of Pompey, to whom the provinces of the two Spains had been granted. Soon after the commencement of the Civil War in 49, Caesar defeated Afranius and Petreius in Spain, whereupon the latter joined Pompey in Greece. After the loss of the battle of Pharsalia (48), Petreius crossed over to Africa, and took an active part in the campaign in 46, which was brought to an end by the decisive defeat of the Pompeian army at the battle of Thapsus. Petreius then fled with Iuba, and, despairing of safety, they fell by each other's hands (Caes. *B. C.* i. 38, 63).

Petrīnus and **Petrīnum**. A mountain near Sinuessa, on the confines of Latium and Campania, on which good wine was grown (Hor. *Epist.* i. 5, 5).

Petrocorii. A people in Gallia Aquitanica, in the modern Perigord. Their chief town was Vesunna (Périgueux) (Caes. *B. G.* vii. 75).

Petronius, GAIUS, or (possibly) TITUS. A Roman novelist probably to be identified with an accomplished voluptuary at the court of Nero. He was one of the chosen companions of Nero, and was regarded as director-in-chief of the imperial pleasures, the judge whose decision upon the merits of any proposed scheme of enjoyment was held as final (*elegantiae arbiter*). The influence thus acquired excited the jealous suspicions of Tigellinus. Petronius was accused of treason; and believing that destruction was inevitable, he resolved to die as he had lived, and to excite admiration by the frivolous eccentricity of his end. Having caused his veins to be opened, he from time to time checked the flow of blood by the application of bandages. During the intervals he conversed with his friends, and even showed himself in the public streets of Cumae, where these events took place; so that at last, when he collapsed from exhaustion, his death (A.D. 66), although compulsory, appeared to be the result of natural and gradual decay. He is said to have despatched in his last moments a sealed document to the emperor, taunting him with his brutal excesses (Tac. *Ann.* xvi. 18, 19; Pliny, *H. N.* xxxvii. 20).

The remarkable work which is traditionally ascribed to this person and which has come down to modern times in an incomplete form, was originally written in at least 16 books, with the title *Satira* or *Satiricon*. It is in prose, with many passages in verse scattered through it as quotations, or as compositions of characters introduced in the novel. The book is a sort of comic romance, in which the adventures of a certain Encolpius and his companions in the south of Italy, chiefly in Puteoli or its environs (on the place see H. W. Hayley in *Harvard Studies in Class. Philology* for 1892), are made a vehicle for exposing the false taste and vices of the age. Unfortunately the vices of the personages introduced are depicted with such fidelity that we are perpetually disgusted by the obscenity of the descriptions. The longest section is generally known as the Dinner of Trimalchio (*Cena Trimalchionis*), presenting us with a caricatured account of a fantastic banquet, such as the gourmands of the Empire were wont to exhibit on their tables. Next in interest is the well-known tale of the Ephesian Matron, which is really older than the time of Petronius, and is found in various forms in the literature of many peoples, even in the Chinese; and which in English is introduced into one of the sermons of Jeremy Taylor. It is probably the best if not the only remaining specimen of a Milesian Tale. (See NOVELS AND ROMANCES.) The novel is also remarkable for its pictures of low life, and for the specimens which it gives of the Latin of the uneducated classes (*sermo plebeius*), of which it is the most important literary example. The dialogue is amusing, abounding in idiomatic expressions, popular maxims, ungrammatical language, and slang. See SERMO PLEBEIUS.

A remarkable attempt at fraud by one François Nodot in the seventeenth century is associated with the history of the text of Petronius. Nodot professed to have got possession of a complete copy of Petronius with no *lacunae*, found, he said, at the sack of Belgrade. His text was printed at Rotterdam in 1693, but was at once seen to be a forgery; yet as it gives a continuous narrative instead of the fragmentary one of the genuine text its additions are sometimes printed (in different type) in editions of Petronius.

There are twenty-one existing manuscripts of Petronius, the most important being the Codex Traguriensis in the Bibliothèque Nationale at Paris. It was found at Trau in Dalmatia in 1663, and contains the *Cena Trimalchionis*. See Beck, *The Age of Petronius* (Cambridge, Mass., 1856), and the account of the MSS. in Bücheler's large edition.

The best editions are those of Burmann (2d ed. Amsterdam, 1743); Reiske (Leipzig, 1748); Bücheler, ed. maior (Berlin, 1862); and Bücheler, ed. minor, text only (Berlin, 1886; last ed. 1895); De Guerle, with translation into French (Paris, 1862); of the *Cena*, with German translation and notes (Leipzig, 1892); and Waters, with English notes (announced, 1895). On the language, see Ludwig, *De Petronii Sermone Plebeio* (Leipzig, 1870); von Guericke, *De Lingua Vulgari apud Petronium* (Königsberg, 1875); Cesareo, *De Petronii Sermone* (Rome, 1887); Schuchardt, *Der Vokalismus des Vulgärlateins* (Leipzig, 1866–68); and Cooper, *Word Formation in the Roman Sermo Plebeius* (N. Y. and Boston, 1895). For criticism, etc., see Pétrequin, *Récherches sur Pétrone* (Paris, 1869); Gaston Boissier in the *Revue des Deux Mondes* for November, 1874; Thomas, *La Société Romaine d'après Pétrone* (Paris, 1892); and H. W. Hayley, *Harvard Studies in Classical Philology*, iii. pp. 1–40 (1892).

Peucé (Πεύκη). An island in Moesia Inferior, formed by the two southern mouths of the Danube, inhabited by the Peucini, who were a tribe of the Bastarnae, and took their name from the island (Ptol. iii. 10, 2).

Peucestas (Πευκέστας). A Macedonian, who was a distinguished officer of Alexander the Great. He had the chief share in saving the life of Alexander in the assault on the city of the Malli in India, and was afterwards appointed by the king to the satrapy of Persia. In the division of the provinces after the death of Alexander (B.C. 323), he obtained the renewal of his government of Persia. He fought on the side of Eumenes against Antigonus (317–316), but displayed both arrogance and insubordination in these campaigns. Upon the surrender of Eumenes by the Argyraspids, Peucestas fell into the hands of Antigonus, who deprived him of his satrapy (Arrian, *Anab.* vi. 9–30; vii. 23).

Peucetia. See APULIA.

Peucīni. See PEUCÉ.

Peutinger Tablet (*Tabŭla Peutingeriāna*). A chartographic representation of the Roman world now preserved at Vienna. See ITINERARIA.

Pezetaeri (πεζέταιροι). In the Macedonian army, the free but not noble class of the population, who formed the heavy infantry (ὁπλῖται). See EXERCITUS.

Phacium (Φάκιον). Now Alifaka; a mountain fortress of Thessaly on the right bank of the Peneus (Thuc. iv. 78; Livy, xxxii. 13).

Phacūsa. A town called Goshen in the Old Testament. It was sacred to the god Supt or Horus, and was hence called Pe-Supt.

Phacussa (Φακοῦσσα). Now Fecussa; an island in the Aegaean Sea, one of the Sporades.

Phaea (Φαιά). The sow of Crommyon, in Megaris, which ravaged the country till slain by Theseus. See Plut. *Thes.* 9; and THESEUS.

Phaeăces (Φαίακες, Φαίηκες). A fabulous people in Homer, to whom Odysseus came in his wanderings (*Od.* vi.–viii.). They were as like to the gods as the Giants and Cyclopes, seeing them face to face. Originally settled in Hyperia, they were compelled, by the violence of their neighbours, the Cyclopes, to migrate, under their king Nausithoüs, son of Poseidon and Periboea, daughter of Eurymedon, the last king of the Giants, to the happy island of Scheria, where they built a city. On the arrival of Odysseus, their ruler was Alcinoüs, the son of Nausithoüs; his wife was Areté, his brother's daughter, and besides many sons he was the father of the fair Nausicaa, Odysseus's preserver. Far from the turmoil of the world, the Phaeaces are described as leading a life of undisturbed happiness, in the enjoyment of the goods wherewith they are richly blessed; above all, Alcinoüs, who had the fairest of orchards and a most beautiful palace. Their business was solely with the sea, with shipping, and the provision of all that belongs to it. Their ships were of wondrous sort. Without steersman or rudder, divining of themselves the wishes and thoughts of all men, and knowing all lands, they traversed the sea swift as a bird or a thought, wrapped in mist and darkness, yet never suffered wreck or loss. When the ship, that brought the sleeping Odysseus in one night to Thrace, returned, Poseidon, of whose envious malice a prophecy had long ago bidden them beware, changed it to a rock in sight of harbour, and the Phaeaces were in fear that the rest of the saying would come true, and mountains rise up all round their city. Though it is obvious that the Phaeaces and their abodes, Hypĕria and Scheria, are purely mythical, the kingdom of Alcinoüs was early identified as Corcyra (Corfu). He had a shrine there, and the harbour was named after him. Near the island was also shown the petrified ship. Hence the later Argonautic legends made even Iason and Medea touch at Corcyra on their flight from Aeëtes, and, like Odysseus, find protection and help from Alcinoüs. (See ARGONAUTAE.) The Phaeacian episode of the *Odyssey* has been edited separately by Prof. A. C. Merriam in his *Phaeacians of Homer* (New York, 1880).

Phaeax (Φαίαξ). An Athenian orator and statesman and a contemporary of Nicias and Alcibiades (Plut. *Alcib.* 13). Some critics maintain that the extant speech against Alcibiades, once commonly attributed to Andocides, was written by Phaeax; but it is now generally held to be the work of a later sophist.

Phaecasium (φαικάσιον). A white shoe worn by the Athenian gymnasiarchs, and also by the priests of Greece and Alexandria, which finally came to be used by other persons of both sexes (Petron. 67; Sen. *Epist.* 113).

Phaedon (Φαίδων). A Greek philosopher, was a native of Elis, and of high birth, but was taken prisoner, probably about B.C. 400, and was brought to Athens. It is said that he ran away from his master to Socrates, and was ransomed by one of the friends of the latter. Phaedon was present at the death of Socrates, while he was still quite a youth. He appears to have lived in Athens some time after the death of Socrates, and then returned to Elis, where he became the founder of a school of philosophy. He was succeeded by Plistanus, after whom the Elean School was merged in the Eretrian (Gell. ii. 18). The dialogue of Plato, which contains an account of the death of Socrates, bears the name of Phaedon. See SOCRATES.

Phaedra (Φαίδρα). The daughter of Minos by Pasiphaë or Crete, and the wife of Theseus. She was the step-mother of Hippolytus, the son of Theseus, with whom she fell in love; but having been repulsed by Hippolytus, she accused him to Theseus of having attempted her dishonour. After the death of Hippolytus his innocence became known to his father, and Phaedra made away with herself. The story forms the subject of plays by Euripides (the *Hippolytus*), Seneca (the *Phaedra*), and in French by Racine (the *Phèdre*). For details, see HIPPOLYTUS.

Phaedriădes. See PARNASSUS.

Phaedrus (Φαῖδρος). (1) An Epicurean philosopher, who was head of the Epicurean School at Athens while Cicero was a student there (B.C. 80). He died in the year 70, and was succeeded by Patron. He wrote a treatise on the gods (Περὶ Θεῶν), a fragment of which was found at Herculaneum in 1806. (Edition by Petersen [Hamburg, 1883].) From it Cicero largely drew his materials for the first book of the *De Natura Deorum.* See Schwenke in Jahn's *Neue Jahrbücher*, 119, 49; 129. (2) A Roman writer of poetical fables. By birth a Macedonian of the district of Pieria, he came early to Rome as a slave, and acquired a knowledge of Roman literature while still a boy. If the traditional title of his five books of fables after Aesop is to be trusted (*Phaedri, Augusti liberti, fabulae Aesopiae*), he was set free by Augustus. To Phaedrus belongs the credit of introducing fable-writing into Latin poetical literature—a fact of which he was fully conscious, but which secured him neither relief from his miserable position, nor recognition on the part of the educated public; his patrons seem to have been only freedmen like himself. In fact, he even drew upon himself, by his two first published books, the ill-will and persecution of the all-powerful favourite of Tiberius, Seianus, who suspected in them malicious reference to contemporary events. In consequence, he did not publish the remaining books till after the fall of Seianus in A.D. 31 and the death of Tiberius in 37.

The five books are preserved, though not in a complete form. Whether the further collection of thirty-two fables, transcribed from a MS. in the fifteenth century by Archbishop Nicolo Perotti (*Fabulae Perottianae*)—and published at Naples in 1809—are a genuine work of Phaedrus, is doubtful. The matter of the fables is only to a small extent borrowed from Aesop. Some include stories from history, partly referring to the present or immediate past. In relation to the Greek originals, the material is not always skilfully used, especially in the "morals." The drawing of the characters is at first very cramped, but is afterwards more broadly treated; the language fluent and, in general, correct; the metre, too (iambic senarius), used with strictness, though wanting the purity which, in this kind of verse, became general from the time of Catullus. About the tenth century an author, calling himself Romulus, drew up a prose version of Phaedrus, which served as a model for the mediæval collections of fables.

The *editio princeps* of Phaedrus is that by Pithoeus (Autun, 1596). Other editions are those of Burmann (Amsterdam, 1698; re-edited with a commentary, Leyden, 1727); Bentley, with Terence (London, 1726); Schwabe, with commentary, 2 vols. (last ed. Brunswick, 1806); Orelli (Zürich, 1831); Dressler (Leipzig, 1850); Eyssenhardt (Berlin, 1867); Ramorius (Turin, 1884); L. Müller, with lexicon by Schaubach (Leipzig, 1888); Riese (Leipzig, 1885). Larger critical ed. by L. Müller (Leipzig, 1877). School edition, with English notes and vocabulary, by Schmitz; selections by Walford (London, 1873). See Hervieux, *Les Fabulistes Latins*, 2 vols. (Paris, 1884).

Phaenarētē. See SOCRATES.

Phaenias. See PHANIAS.

Phaestus (Φαιστός). (1) A town in the southern part of Crete, near Gortyna, twenty stadia from the sea, with a port-town Matala, said to have been built by Phaestus, son of Heracles (Pausan. ii. 6, 7). It was the birthplace of Epimenides. (2) A town of Thessaly.

Phaëthon (Φαέθων, "the shining"). A name that occurs in Homer as an epithet or surname of Helios (the Sun), and is used by later writers as a proper name for Helios; but it is more commonly known as the name of a son of Helios by the Oceanid Clymené, the wife of Merops. The genealogy of Phaëthon, however, is not the same in all writers, for some call him a son of Clymenus, the son of Helios by Meropé, or a son of Helios by Proté, or, lastly, a son of Helios by the nymph Rhodé or Rhodos. He received the significant name of Phaëthon from his father, and was afterwards presumptuous and ambitious enough to request his father to allow him, for one day, to drive the chariot of the sun across the heavens. Helios was induced, by the entreaties of his son and of Clymené, to yield; but the youth being too weak to check the horses, they rushed out of their usual track, and came so near the earth as almost to set it on fire. Thereupon Zeus killed him with a flash of lightning, and hurled him down into the river Eridanus. His sisters, the Heliades or Phaëthontiades, who had yoked the horses to the chariot, were metamorphosed into poplars, and their tears into amber. See Baugert, *De Fabula Phaëthontea* (Halle, 1885); and HELIADAE.

Phaëthon. (Zannoni, *Gal. di Firenzi*, ser. 4. vol. ii.).

Phagres (Φάγρης). A town of the Pierians in Macedonia (Herod. vii. 112).

Phaininda (φαινίνδα). A Greek game of ball in which the players tried always to throw it to one who was not expecting it. It is described in Antiphon, *Incant.* 8.

Phalaecus (Φάλαικος). (1) A son of Onomarchus, succeeding his uncle Phaÿllus as leader of the Phocians in the Sacred War (B.C. 351). In order to secure his own safety, he concluded a treaty with Philip, by which he was allowed to withdraw into the Peloponnesus with a body of eight thousand mercenaries, leaving the unhappy Phocians to their fate, B.C. 346. Phalaecus now assumed the part of a mere leader of mercenary troops, in which character we find him engaging in various enterprises. He was slain at the siege of Cydonia in Crete. (2) A lyric and epigrammatic poet, from whom the hendecasyllabic metre, called *Phalaecian*, took its name. Five of his epigrams are preserved in the Greek Anthology. His date is uncertain, but he was probably one of the principal Alexandrian poets (Athen. p. 440).

Phalaesiae (Φαλαισίαι). A town in Arcadia, south of Megalopolis, on the road to Sparta, twenty stadia from the Laconian frontier.

Phalanga (φάλαγξ). See PHALANGARII.

Phalangarii or **Palangarii.** Porters who carried burdens by means of a pole (*phalanga*) resting on their shoulders and supporting the load which was hung from it. Four, six, or eight phalangarii were often so employed for a single burden (Vitruv. x. 3, 7).

Phalangītes (φαλαγγίτης). A soldier of the Macedonian phalanx. See PHALANX.

Phalanna (Φάλαννα). A town of the Perrhaebi, in the Thessalian district of Hestiaeotis (Livy, xlii. 54).

Phalanthus (Φάλανθος). See TARENTUM.

Phalanx (φάλαγξ). The Greek term for the order of battle in which heavy infantry were drawn up, in an unbroken line, several ranks deep. (See EXERCITUS.) The most famous phalanx was that formed by King Philip, constituting the chief strength of the Macedonian army. It was first eight, afterwards twelve to sixteen deep. In the eight-rank formation, the lances (σάρισσαι) being eighteen feet long, those of all ranks could be presented to the enemy. They were grasped with the right hand at the butt, and, with the left, four feet from the butt end; hence, the lances of the first rank projected fourteen feet, while the spear-heads of the last rank were level with, or just in front of, the men in the front rank. In the deeper formation, and after the reduction of the length of the sarissa to fourteen feet, only the first five ranks presented their weapons to the front; the rest held them slanting over the shoulders of their comrades in front. The name phalanx, or τάξις, was also applied to the separate regiments of the φαλαγγῖται. The line of each such phalanx was divided, from front to rear, into four chiliarchies (χιλιαρχίαι), each chiliarchy into four syntagmata (συντάγματα), each syntagma into four tetrarchies (τετραρχίαι). The importance of this formation lay in its power of resistance to hostile onset, and in the weight with which it fell, when impelled against the enemy's lines. Its weaknesses were want of mobility, the impossibility of changing front in face of the enemy, and unsuitability for close, hand-to-hand engagement. The Roman legions also fought in phalanx in the older times before Camillus. Under the emperors the phalanx was used, after about the second century A.D., in fighting against barbaric nations.

Phalăra (τὰ Φάλαρα). A town of Phthiotis in Thessaly; the harbour of Lamia.

Phalăris (Φάλαρις). The infamous tyrant of Agrigentum, notorious for his cruelty; he was killed in a popular revolt in B.C. 549. His reign probably commenced about B.C. 570, and is said to have lasted sixteen years. He was a native of Agrigentum, and appears to have been raised by his fellow-citizens to some high office in the State, of which he afterwards availed himself to assume a despotic authority. He was engaged in frequent wars with his neighbours, and extended his power and dominion on all sides, though more frequently by stratagem than open force. He perished by a sudden outbreak of the popular fury, in which it appears that Telemachus, the ancestor of Theron, must have borne a conspicuous part. No circumstance connected with Phalaris is more celebrated than the brazen bull in which he is said to have burned alive the victims of his cruelty, and of which we are told that he made the first experiment upon its inventor, Perillus. This latter story has much the air of an invention of later times, but it is mentioned as early as Pindar (*Pyth.* i. 185). His name is affixed to 148 Greek letters, in which he appears as a gentle ruler, and a patron of art and poetry; but, as proved in Bentley's *Dissertation* in 1699 (ed. Wagner, 1883), they are really a worthless forgery, probably by a sophist of the second century A.D. See BENTLEY, RICHARD.

Phalĕrae (τὰ φάλαρα). The terms for bosses of thin bronze or silver, or of gold-leaf impressed in relief. They were loaded at the back with pitch, and fitted to a plate of copper, being fastened to it with leather straps. They served sometimes as

Collar formed of Phalerae. (Vienna.)

decorations for the harness on the head or breast of horses (Livy, ix. 46), sometimes as signs of military rank, worn across the whole coat-of-mail (Juv. xvi. 60).

Phalērum (Φάληρον). The most easterly of the harbours of Athens, and the one chiefly used by the Athenians before the time of the Persian Wars. After the establishment by Themistocles of the harbours in the peninsula of Piraeus, Phalerum was not much used.

Phallus (φαλλός). The male organ of generation; but most often the figure of that organ used by both Greeks and Romans as symbolizing the generative and creative force of nature, and therefore displayed as a sort of charm to promote manly vigour, to prevent decay, and to avert the displeasure of those spirits on whom the fertility of men, animals, and plants was supposed to depend. It was especially the symbol of Priapus (q. v.), whose image was provided with an enormous phallus, and was set up in gardens both to drive away birds, like the modern scarecrow (Hor. *Sat.* i. 8), and to secure productiveness. The most primitive use of the phallus was devoid of any indecent suggestion, but was regarded as harmless and natural; yet this was not true in later times, when it was worshipped as a part of the obscene cults that sprang up, and was depicted with pornographic intention. Thus it was used as a sign for houses of prostitution (see MERETRIX), and decorated the walls of drinking-shops. By the lower classes, small images of the same kind were worn about the neck as amulets (see AMULETUM), to avert the evil eye, as is the case in Italy to-day, where the peasants carry them made of coral. Pastry was made in the same form, and also lamps. A similar superstitious custom obtains in some parts of India, and the ancient Egyptians associated the phallus with the worship of Osiris. Many specimens of the phallus of various materials are preserved in the National Museum at Naples. See Plut. *De Is. et Osir.*; Augustin. *De Civ. Dei*, vi. 7, 9; vii. 21, 24; and Dulaure, *Des Divinités Génératrices; ou du Culte du Phallus* (Paris, 1805).

Stone cut in Phallic Form. (Schliemann.)

Phaloria (Φαλώρεια). A town of Histiaeotis in Thessaly (Livy, xxxii. 15).

Phanae (Φάναι). The southern point of the island of Chios, celebrated for its temple of Apollo and for its excellent wine (Strabo, p. 645).

Phanagoria (Φαναγόρεια). A Greek city on the Asiatic coast of the Cimmerian Bosporus, was chosen by the kings of Bosporus as their capital in Asia.

Phanaroea (Φανάροια). A very fertile plain in Pontus in Asia Minor, shut in by mountains (Strabo, p. 73).

Phanias (Φανίας) or **Phaenias** (Φαινίας). A native of Eresus in Lesbos, a pupil of Aristotle, and a countryman and friend of Theophrastus. He flourished about B.C. 336. He was a very prolific writer on philosophy, physics, and history. Only fragments of these works remain. He was also the author of a chronicle of his native city, entitled Πρυτάνεις Ἐρέσιοι. This is supposed to have been one of the principal authorities followed in the so-called Parian Chronicle (q. v.).

Phanŏcles (Φανοκλῆς). A Greek elegiac poet of the Alexandrine Period. He celebrated in erotic elegies (Ἔρωτες ἢ Καλοί) the loves of beautiful boys. A considerable fragment remaining describes the love of Orpheus for Calaïs, the beautiful son of Boreas, and his death ensuing therefrom at the hands of the Thracian women. The language is simple and spirited, and the versification melodious. The fragments have been edited by Bach (Halle, 1829), and also by Schneidewin in his *Delectus Poesis Graecae*, p. 158 foll.

Phanodēmus (Φανόδημος). The author of a work on the early legends of Attica (Dionys. i. 61). See ATTHIS.

Phantăsus. See SOMNIUM.

Phaon (Φάων). A boatman at Mitylené who is said to have been originally an ugly old man; but in consequence of his carrying Aphrodité across the sea without accepting payment, the goddess gave him youth and beauty. After this Sappho is said to have fallen in love with him, and to have leaped from the Leucadian rock, when he slighted her. See SAPPHO.

Pharae (Φαραί or Φῆραι). (1) One of the twelve Achaean cities in the western part of Achaea. See ACHAEAN LEAGUE. (2) A town of Messenia mentioned as early as Homer (*Il.* v. 543). (3) A town of Laconia in the valley of the Eurotas.

Pharĕtra (φαρέτρα). The quiver. See ARCUS.

Pharis (Φᾶρις). The same as PHARAE (3).

Pharmacōn Graphé (φαρμάκων γραφή). An indictment in Attic law for poisoning with criminal intent (πρόνοια), whether the poison was given to cause death or to aid in some felonious purpose. The punishment was death (Aelian, *V. H.* v. 18).

Pharmacopōla (φαρμακοπώλης). A vender of medicines (φάρμακα), described by Cato and Cicero as frequenting the market-places and haranguing the people on the merits of their nostrums like our modern travelling quacks. See Cato *ap.* Gell. i. 5, 3, and Cic. *Pro Cluent.* 14, with Hor. *Sat.* i. 2, 1.

Pharmacūsa (Φαρμακοῦσα). An island off the coast of Miletus, where Iulius Caesar was taken prisoner by pirates. (See Plutarch, *Caes.* 1 and 2.) Here, too, King Attalus died.

Pharmacussae (Φαρμακοῦσσαι). Two small islands off the coast of Attica near Salamis. On one of them was shown the tomb of Circé.

Pharnabāzus (Φαρνάβαζος). The son of Pharnaces, succeeding his father as satrap of the Persian provinces near the Hellespont. In B.C. 411 and the following years he rendered active assistance to the Lacedaemonians in their war against the Athenians. When Dercyllidas and, subsequently, Agesilaüs passed over into Asia to protect Asiatic Greeks against the Persian power, we find Pharnabazus connecting himself with Conon to resist the Lacedaemonians. In 374 Pharnabazus invaded Egypt in conjunction with Iphicrates; but the expedition failed, chiefly through the dilatory proceedings and the excessive caution of Pharnabazus. The character of Pharnabazus is eminently distinguished by generosity and openness. He has been charged, it is true, with the murder of Alcibiades; but the latter probably fell by the hands of others. See ALCIBIADES.

Pharnăces (Φαρνάκης). (1) A king of Pontus, the son of Mithridates IV., whom he succeeded on the throne, about B.C. 190. He carried on war for some years with Eumenes, king of Pergamum, and Ariarathes, king of Cappadocia, but was obliged to conclude with them a disadvantageous peace in 179. The year of his death is uncertain; it is placed by conjecture in 156. (2) King of Pontus, or, more properly, of the Bosporus, was the son of Mithridates the Great, whom he compelled to put an end to his life in 63. (See MITHRIDATES VI.) After the death of his father Pharnaces hastened to make his submission to Pompey, who granted him the kingdom of the Bosporus with the titles of friend and ally of the Roman people. In the Civil War between Caesar and Pompey, Pharnaces seized the opportunity to reinstate himself in his father's dominions, and made himself master of the whole of Colchis and the lesser Armenia. He defeated Domitius Calvinus, the lieutenant of Caesar in Asia, but was shortly afterwards defeated by Caesar himself in a decisive action near Zela (B.C. 47). The battle was gained with such ease by Caesar that he informed the Senate of his victory by the words, *Veni, vedi, veci.* In the course of the same year Pharnaces was again defeated, and was slain by Asander, one of his generals, who hoped to obtain his master's kingdom. See ASANDER.

Pharnacia (Φαρνακία). A flourishing city of Asia Minor, on the coast of Pontus, built near or actually on the site of Cerasus, probably by Pharnaces, the grandfather of Mithridates the Great.

Pharsalia (Φαρσαλία). (1) See PHARSALUS. (2) The title of an epic poem by the Roman writer Lucan. See LUCANUS.

Pharsālus (Φάρσαλος). A town in Thessaly, in the district Thessaliotis, west of the river Enipeus. Near Pharsalus was fought the decisive battle between Caesar and Pompey, B.C. 48, which made Caesar master of the Roman world. It is frequently called the battle of Pharsalia, which was the name of the territory of the town.

Pharus (Φάρος). (1) A small island off the coast of Egypt. When Alexander the Great planned the city of Alexandria, on the coast opposite to Pharus, he caused the island to be united to the coast by a mole seven stadia in length, thus forming the two harbours of the city. (See ALEXANDRIA.) The island was chiefly famous for the lofty tower built upon it by Ptolemy II. for a light-house, whence the name of *pharus* was applied to all similar structures. (2) An island of the Adriatic, off the coast of Dalmatia, east of Issa.

Pharus (φάρος). The light-house on the eastern summit of the small island of the same name in front of the harbour of Alexandria. It was a tower of white marble, built for Ptolemy Philadelphus by Sostratus of Cnidus, in B.C. 270, at a cost of 800 silver talents ($940,000), and accounted by the ancients one of the wonders of the world. It rose pyramidally in a number of decreasing stories of different forms (the lowest square, the next octagonal, the third circular). It was adorned with galleries and pillars to a considerable height. It was still standing, in great part, about A.D. 1300 (Caes. *B. C.* iii. 112; Pliny, *H. N.* xxxvi. 83). In later times all the light-houses were called after it, and large numbers of these were built by the Romans round Italy, and on all the coasts of the Empire, the best known being those at Brundisium, Capreae, Centum Cellae (Cività Vecchia), Ostia, and Ravenna. A Roman light-house still remains in England, and is now within the limits of Dover Castle. It is represented in the first figure given below. The tower at Ravenna approached the

Roman Light-houses in Great Britain.

Alexandrian in magnificence. Light-ships were also used by the ancients.

Phasēlis (Φασηλίς). A town on the coast of Lycia, near the borders of Pamphylia, founded by Dorian-colonists. It became afterwards the head-quarters of the pirates who infested the southern coasts of Asia Minor, and was therefore destroyed by P. Servilius Isauricus (Eutrop. vi. 3). Phaselis is said to have been the place at which light, quick vessels called *phaseli* were first built (Juv. xv. 127).

Phasis (Φᾶσις). (1) A celebrated river of Colchis, flowing into the eastern end of the Pontus Euxinus (Black Sea). It was famous in connection with the story of the Argonautic expedition. Hence Medea is called *Phasias*, and the adjective *Phasiacus* is used in the sense of *Colchicus*. (See ARGONAUTAE.) It has given name to the pheasant (*phasianus*), which is said to have been first brought to Greece from its banks. (2) Near the mouth of the river, on its southern side, was a town of the same name, founded by the Milesians.

Phasis (φάσις). A Greek legal term used to denote any kind of information, or, more strictly, one of the various methods by which public offenders at Athens might be prosecuted. Its peculiarity was its purely public nature, this offence being regarded as wholly affecting the State. The prosecutor received half the penalty (τίμημα). The offences subject to phasis are enumerated by Pollux (viii. 47), and refer to the infraction of mining laws, customs regulations, etc.

Phavorīnus. See FAVORINUS.

Phaÿllus (Φάϋλλος). (1) A celebrated athlete of Crotona, who had thrice gained the victory at the Pythian Games. He fought at the battle of Salamis, B.C. 480, in a ship fitted out at his own expense (Herod. viii. 47). (2) A Phocian, brother of Onomarchus, whom he succeeded as general of the Phocians in the Sacred War, B.C. 352. He died in the following year, after a long and painful illness. Phaÿllus made use of the sacred treasures of Delphi with a far more lavish hand than either of his brothers, and he is accused of bestowing the consecrated ornaments upon his wife and mistresses (Diod. Sic. xvi. 35–38, 61).

Phazania. Now Fezzan. A district of Libya Interior. See GARAMANTES.

Phegeus (Φηγεύς). A king of Psophis in Arcadia. He was the father of Arsinoë, Pronoüs, Agenor, Temenus, and Axion. He purified Alcmaeon (q. v.) after he had slain his mother, and gave him Arsinoë (or Alphesiboea) in marriage. Alcmaeon presented her with the necklace and peplus of Harmonia; but wishing to get them back for his new wife, Callirrhoë, he was slain by the sons of Phegeus at their father's bidding. The sons of Alcmaeon then put Phegeus to death (Pausan. vi. 17, 4; viii. 24, 4; ix. 41, 2; Apollod. iii. 7, 6).

Phellus (Φελλός). A city of Lycia (Strabo, p. 666).

Phemius (Φήμιος). A celebrated minstrel of Ithaca (*Odyss.* i. 54).

Phemonoë (Φημονόη). A mythical Greek poet, said to antedate Homer (Pausan. x. 5, 7; Strabo, p. 419).

Phenăcé (φενάκη). See COMA.

Pheneus (Φένεος). An ancient town in the northeast of Arcadia, at the foot of Mount Cyllené.

Pherae (Φεραί). An ancient town of Thessaly in the Pelasgian plain, ninety stadia from its port-town Pagasae, on the Pagasaean Gulf. It is celebrated in mythology as the residence of Admetus, and in history on account of its tyrants, who extended their power over nearly the whole of Thessaly. Of these the most powerful was Iason, who was made Tagus, or military chief, of Thessaly about B.C. 374.

Pherecrătes (Φερεκράτης). A native of Athens. He was one of the best poets of the Old Comedy, contemporary with the comic poets Cratinus, Crates, Eupolis, Plato, and Aristophanes, being somewhat younger than the first two, and somewhat older than the others. He gained his first victory B.C. 438, and imitated the style of Crates, whose actor he had been. Crates and Pherecrates very much modified the coarse satire and vituperation of which this sort of poetry had previously been the vehicle, and constructed their comedies on the basis of a regular plot and with more dramatic action. Pherecrates did not, however, abstain altogether from personal satire, for we see by the fragments of his plays that he attacked Alcibiades, the tragic poet Melanthius, and others. He invented a new metre, which was named, after him, the *Pherecratean*. The system of the verse is ⁄– – ⁄– ⏑ ⏑ ⁄– –, which may be best explained as a choriambus, with a spondee for its base and a long syllable for its termination. The metre is very frequent in the choruses of the Greek tragedies and in Horace. The extant titles of the plays of Pherecrates are eighteen, and the fragments are preserved by Meineke, *Frag. Com. Graec.*

Pherecȳdes (Φερεκύδης). (1) A Greek philosopher, of the isle of Syros, about B.C. 600–550; said to have been the first writer of prose. He wrote in the Ionic dialect of the origin of the world and the gods (*Cosmogonia* and *Theogonia*). The poetic element seems to have held a predominant place in his prose. He is also said to have been the first to maintain the doctrine of the transmigration of souls, which his pupil Pythagoras borrowed from him. (2) One of the best known of the Greek logographi (q. v.), and a contemporary of Hellanicus and Herodotus. His chief work was a mythological history in ten books, beginning with the genealogy of the gods, and passing on to an account of the Heroic Age and of the origins of the great families of his own time. Fragments edited by Sturz (Leipzig, 1824), and Müller (Paris, 1850).

Pheres (Φέρης). (1) The son of Cretheus and Tyro and brother of Aeson and Amythaon; he was married to Periclymené, by whom he became the father of Admetus, Lycurgus, Idomené, and Periapis. He was believed to have founded the town of Pherae in Thessaly. (2) Son of Iason and Medea. (3) A follower of Pallas, who fought on the side of Aeneas against Turnus, and was slain by Halesus.

Pheretiădes (Φερητιάδης). A son of Pheres; especially used as the name of Admetus (*Il.* ii. 763).

Pheretīma (Φερετίμα). The wife of Battus III. and mother of Arcesilaüs III., successive kings of Cyrené. After the murder of her son by the Barcaeans, Pheretima fled into Egypt to Aryandes, the viceroy of Darius Hystaspis; and representing that the death of Arcesilaüs had been the consequence of his submission to the Persians, she induced him to avenge it. On the capture of Barca by the Persian army, she caused those who had the principal share in her son's murder to be impaled, and ordered the breasts of their wives to be cut off. Pheretima then returned to Egypt, where she soon after died of a painful and loathsome disease (Herod. iv. 162, 200–205).

Pherné (φερνή). See MATRIMONIUM.

Pheron or **Pheros** (Φέρων, Φερῶς). A king of Egypt and son of Sesostris, Ramses II. He was visited with blindness, an hereditary complaint, though, according to the legend preserved in Herodotus, it was a punishment for his presumptuous impiety in throwing a spear into the waters of the Nile when it had overflowed the fields. By attending to the directions of an oracle he was cured; and he dedicated an obelisk at Heliopolis in gratitude for his recovery (Herod. ii. 111). Pliny tells us that this obelisk, together with another also made by him but broken in its removal, was to be seen at Rome in the Circus of Caligula and Nero at the foot of the Vatican Hill. Pliny (*H. N.* xxxvi. 74) calls the Pheron of Herodotus Nuncoreus or Nencoreus, a name corrupted, perhaps, from Menophtheus (Egyptian, Meneptah). Diodorus gives him his father's name, Sesoosis. Pheron is by some identified with the Pharaoh of the Book of Exodus.

Phiălé (φιάλη). The flat drinking-cup of the Greeks. See PATERA; VAS.

Phidias (Φειδίας). The greatest sculptor and statuary of Greece. Of his personal history we possess but few details. He was a native of Athens, was the son of Charmides, and was born about the time of the battle of Marathon, B.C. 490. He began to work as a statuary about 464, and one of his first great works was the statue of Athené Promachos, which may be assigned to about 460. This work must have established his reputation; but it was surpassed by the splendid productions of his own hand, and of others working under his direction, during the administration of Pericles. That statesman not only chose Phidias to execute the principal statues which were to be set up, but gave him the oversight of all the works of art which were to be erected.

Of these works the chief were the Propylaea (q. v.) of the Acropolis, and, above all, the temple of Athené on the Acropolis, called the Parthenon, on which, as the central point of the Athenian polity and religion, the highest efforts of the best of artists were employed. There can be no doubt that the sculptured ornaments of this temple, the remains of which form one of the glories of the British Museum (see ELGIN MARBLES), were executed under the immediate superintendence of Phidias; but the colossal statue of the divinity made of ivory and gold, which was enclosed within that magnificent shrine, was the work of the artist's own hand. The statue was dedicated in 438. Having finished his great work at Athens, he went to Elis and Olympia, which he was now invited to adorn. He was there engaged for about four or five years from 437 to 434 or 433, during which time he finished his statue of the Olympian Zeus, the greatest of all his works.

On his return to Athens he fell a victim to the jealousy against his great patron, Pericles, which was then at its height. The party opposed to Pericles, thinking him too powerful to be overthrown by a direct attack, aimed at him in the persons of his most cherished friends—Phidias, Anaxagoras, and Aspasia. (See PERICLES.) Phidias was first accused of peculation; but this charge was at once refuted, as, by the advice of Pericles, the gold had been affixed to the statue of Athené in such a manner that it could be removed and the weight of it examined. The accusers then charged Phidias with impiety, in having introduced into the battle of the Amazons, on the shield of the goddess, his own likeness and that of Pericles. On this latter charge Phidias was thrown into prison, where he died from disease, in 432.

Of the numerous works executed by Phidias for the Athenians the most celebrated was the statue of Athené in the Parthenon, to which reference has already been made. This statue was of that kind of work which the Greeks called "chryselephantine"—that is, the statue was formed of plates of ivory laid upon a core of wood or stone for the flesh parts, while the drapery and other ornaments were of solid gold. The statue stood in the foremost and larger chamber of the temple (πρόδρομος). It represented the goddess standing, clothed with a tunic reaching to the ankles, with her spear in her left hand and an image of Victory four cubits high in her right: she was girded with the aegis, and had a helmet on her head, and her shield rested on the ground by her side. The height of the statue was twenty-six cubits, or nearly forty feet, including the base. The eyes were of a kind of marble, nearly resembling ivory, perhaps painted to imitate the iris and pupil; there is no sufficient authority for the statement, which is frequently made, that they were of precious stones. The weight of the gold upon the

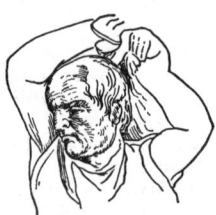

Head supposed to be that of Phidias. (From the Strangford Shield, British Museum.)

statue, which, as above stated, was removable at pleasure, is said by Thucydides to have been forty talents, or about $470,000 (ii. 13).

Still more celebrated than his statue of Athené was the colossal ivory and gold statue of Zeus, which Phidias made for the great temple of this god, in the Altis or sacred grove at Olympia. (See OLYMPIA.) This statue was regarded as the masterpiece not only of Phidias, but of the whole range of Grecian art, and was looked upon not so much as a statue, but rather as if it were the actual manifestation of the present deity. It was placed in the πρόδρομος, or front chamber, of the temple directly facing the entrance. It was only visible, however, on great festivals; at other times it was concealed by a magnificent curtain. The god was represented as seated on a throne of cedarwood, adorned with gold, ivory, ebony, stones, and colours, crowned with a wreath of olive, holding in his right hand an ivory and gold statue of Victory, and in his left hand supporting a sceptre, which was ornamented with all sorts of metals, and surmounted by an eagle. The throne was brilliant both with gold and stones and with ebony and ivory, and was ornamented with figures both painted and sculptured. The statue almost reached to the roof, which was about sixty feet in height. The idea which Phidias essayed to embody in this, his greatest work, was that of the supreme deity of the Hellenic nation no longer engaged in conflicts with the Titans and the Giants, but having laid aside his thunderbolt, and enthroned as a conqueror, in perfect majesty and repose, ruling with a nod the subject world. It is related that when Phidias was asked what model he meant to follow in making his statue, he replied that of Homer (*Il.* i. 528–530). This passage has been imitated by Milton, whose paraphrase gives no small aid to the comprehension of the idea (*Paradise Lost*, iii. 135–137):

> "Thus while God spake, ambrosial fragrance fill'd
> All heaven, and in the blessed spirits elect
> Sense of new joy ineffable diffused."

The statue was removed by the emperor Theodosius I. to Constantinople, where it was destroyed by a fire in A.D. 475. In 1888 a red vase was exhumed at Tanagra, bearing a signature which archæologists believe to be that of Phidias.

The distinguishing character of the art of Phidias was ideal sublimity, especially in the representation of divinities and of subjects connected with their worship. While on the one hand he freed himself from the stiff and unnatural forms which, by a sort of religious precedent, had fettered his predecessors of the archaic or hieratic school, he never, on the other hand, descended to the exact imitation of any human model, however beautiful; he never represented that distorted action, or expressed that vehement passion, which lie beyond the limits of repose; nor did he ever approach to that almost meretricious grace, by which some of his greatest followers, if they did not corrupt the art themselves, gave the occasion for its corruption in the hands of their less gifted and spiritual imitators. See Murray, *Greek Sculpture* (London, 1880); Waldstein, *The Art of Pheidias* (Cambridge, 1885); Collignon, *Phidias* (Paris, 1886); and the article STATUARIA ARS.

Phidippĭdes or **Philippĭdes** (Φειδιππίδης, Φιλιππίδης). A courier was sent by the Athenians to Sparta in B.C. 490 to ask for aid against the Persians, and arrived there on the second day from his leaving Athens. On his return to Athens he related that on his way to Sparta he had fallen in with Pan on Mount Parthenium, near Tegea, and that the god had bid him ask the Athenians why they paid him no worship, though he had been hitherto their friend, and ever would be so. In consequence of this revelation they dedicated a temple to Pan after the battle of Marathon, and honoured him thenceforth with annual sacrifices and a torch-race (Herod. vi. 105; Pausan. i. 28, 4).

Phiditia (τὰ φειδίτια). The Spartan name for the public meals. See SYSSITIA.

Phīdon (Φείδων). (1) The son of Aristodamidas, and king of Argos. He restored the supremacy of Argos over Cleonae, Phlius, Sicyon, Epidaurus, Troezen, and Aegina, and aimed at extending his dominions over the greater part of the Peloponnesus. The Pisans invited him (B.C. 748) to aid them in excluding the Eleans from their usurped presidency at the Olympic Games, and to celebrate them jointly with themselves. The invitation quite fell in with the ambitious pretensions of Phidon, who succeeded in dispossessing the Eleans and celebrating the games along with the Pisans; but the Eleans not long after defeated him, with the aid of Sparta, and recovered their privilege. Thus apparently fell the power of Phidon; but as to the details of the struggle we have no information. The most memorable act of Phidon was his introduction of copper and silver coinage, and a new scale of weights and measures, which, through his influence, became prevalent in the Peloponnesus, and ultimately throughout the greater portion of Greece. The scale in question was known by the name of the Aeginetan, and it is usually supposed that the coinage of Phidon was struck in Aegina; but there seems good reason for believing that what Phidon did was done in Argos, and nowhere else—that "Phidonian measures" probably did not come to bear the specific name of Aeginetan until there was another scale in vogue, the Euboic, from which to distinguish them—and that both the epithets were derived, not from the place where the scale first originated, but from the people whose commercial activity tended to make them most generally known—in the one case the Aeginetans, in the other case the inhabitants of Chalcis and Eretria. (2) An ancient Corinthian legislator of uncertain date.

Phigalia (Φιγαλία). A town in the southwest corner of Arcadia, on the frontiers of Messenia and Elis, which owes its celebrity in modern times to the remains of a splendid temple in its territory (i. e. at Bassae, some four miles distant), built in the time of Pericles. The sculptures, in alto-relievo, which ornamented the frieze in the interior, are now preserved in the British Museum. They represent the combat of the Centaurs and the Lapithae, and of the Greeks and the Amazons. The temple is, next to the Theseum at Athens, the most completely preserved architectural specimen of classic Greek art. It was built by Ictinus, one of the architects of the Parthenon, of gray stone and white marble. It was originally 125½ feet long and 48 feet wide. See Cockerell, *Temples of Aegina and Bassae* (1860).

Phila (Φίλα). The daughter of Antipater, regent of Macedonia, and celebrated as one of the noblest and most virtuous women of the age in which she lived. She was married to Craterus in B.C. 322, and after the death of Craterus, who survived his marriage with her scarcely a year, she was again married to the young Demetrius, the son of Antigonus. She shared with her husband his various vicissitudes of fortune; but when he was expelled from Macedonia in B.C. 287, she put an end to her own life at Cassandrea, unable to bear this unexpected reverse. She left two children by Demetrius—Antigonus, surnamed Gonatas, who became king of Macedonia; and a daughter, Stratonicé, married first to Seleucus, and afterwards to his son Antiochus (Plut. *Demetr.* 14–45; Diod. xx. 93).

Philadelphia (*Φιλαδελφία*). (1) A city of Lydia, at the foot of Mount Tmolus, built by Attalus Philadelphus, king of Pergamum. It was an early seat of Christianity, and its Church is one of the seven to which the Apocalypse of St. John is addressed. (2) A city of Cilicia Aspera, on the Calycadnus, above Aphrodisias.

Philadelphus. See PTOLEMAEUS II.

Philae (*Φιλαί*; Egypt. *Pālek*). An island in the Nile, near Assouan, just below the first cataract, on the southern boundary of the country towards Aethiopia. It was inhabited by Egyptians and Ethiopians jointly, and was covered with magnificent temples, whose splendid ruins still remain, so that the natives style it Jesiret-el-Birbeh, or "Temple Island." The ancient Egyptians regarded it as the birthplace of Isis and Osiris.

Philae is a granite rock about 1200 feet in length and 460 feet in breadth, fringed with rich verdure. The temples mentioned above are in the main of the Graeco-Roman period. The great temple of Isis was built by Ptolemy Epiphanes and his successors, though the oldest part (the great propylaeum or gateway) bears the name of Nectanebes II. (about B.C. 360). To the east of the island is a roofless house, popularly called Pharaoh's Bed, 63 feet in length and 48 in breadth. It has fourteen columns with diversified capitals. See Bénédicte, *Descr. et Hist. de Philae* (Paris, 1893).

View of Philae.

Philaeni (*Φίλαινοι*). Two Carthaginian brothers, of whom the following story is told: A contest had arisen between the Carthaginians and Cyreneans respecting the point where their respective territories met, and this was the more difficult to be determined, since the country on the borders of the two States was a sandy desert, and without anything that might serve as a common landmark. It was agreed at last that two individuals should set out at the same time from Carthage and Cyrené respectively, and that the spot where they might meet should be regarded as the common boundary of the two communities. The parties accordingly set out, the two Philaeni having been selected by the Carthaginians for this purpose; but the two Cyreneans travelled more slowly than their Carthaginian antagonists, and only met the Philaeni after the latter had advanced a considerable distance into the disputed territory. The Cyreneans thereupon accused the Philaeni of unfairness, and of having started before the appointed time. The Philaeni, on their part, offered to do anything to show that they had acted fairly, and the two Cyreneans then gave them their choice, either to be buried alive on the spot where they were standing, or else to allow them (the Cyreneans) to advance as far as they pleased into the disputed territory, and there be buried alive on their part. The Philaeni accepted the former part of the offer, and were accordingly entombed. The Carthaginians erected two altars on the spot, which were thenceforth regarded as the limits of their territory in this direction (Sall. *Iug.* 19, 79; cf. Strabo, pp. 171, 836). These altars stood in the innermost bend of the Syrtis Maior, and not, as Sallust erroneously states, to the west of both the Syrtes. The story of the Philaeni, moreover, as given by the Roman historian, seems to wear a doubtful appearance, from the circumstance of Cyrené's being so much nearer the point in question than Carthage.

Philammon (Φιλάμμων). A mythical poet and musician of the ante-Homeric period, was said to have been the son of Apollo and the nymph Chioné, or Philonis, or Leuconoë. By the nymph Agriopé, who dwelt on Parnassus, he became the father of Thamyris and Eumolpus. He is closely associated with the worship of Apollo at Delphi and with the music of the cithara. He is said to have established the choruses of girls, who, in the Delphian worship of Apollo, sang hymns in which they celebrated the births of Latona, Artemis, and Apollo. Pausanias relates that, in the most ancient musical contests at Delphi, the first who conquered was Chrysothemis of Crete, the second was Philammon, and the next after him his son Thamyris.

Philargyrius Iunius, or **Philargy̆rus**, or **Iunilius Flagrius**. An early commentator upon Vergil, who wrote upon the *Bucolics* and *Georgics*. His observations are less elaborate than those of Servius, and have descended to us in a mutilated condition. The period when he flourished is altogether uncertain. They are printed in the edition of Vergil by Burmann and in the edition of the commentaries of Servius by Lion (Göttingen, 1825–26).

Phileas (Φιλέας). (1) A Greek geographer of Athens, whose time cannot be determined with certainty, but who probably belonged to the older period of Athenian literature. He was the author of a *Periplus*, which was divided into two parts—one on Asia and the other on Europe. (2) Of Tarentum, having been sent as ambassador to Rome, he persuaded his countrymen, who were there detained as hostages, to make their escape, which they effected by his aid; but, having been overtaken at Terracina, they were brought back to Rome, scourged, and thrown from the Tarpeian Rock.

Philelphus. The Latinized name of Francesco Filelfo (1398–1481), an Italian scholar of the time of the Renaissance, known as an itinerant teacher and collector of manuscripts. See Symonds, *The Renaissance in Italy*, ii. pp. 267–289; and the article RENAISSANCE.

Philēmon (Φιλήμων) and **Baucis** (Βαυκίς). An old married couple in Phrygia, the Darby and Joan of classical antiquity. When Zeus and Hermes were wandering through the country in human form, and found no shelter with the richer inhabitants, the aged pair received them hospitably. The gods therefore, while destroying all the rest of the neighbourhood by floods in punishment for the inhospitable treatment they had met with, changed their miserable cottage into a magnificent temple. Here the two held the priestly office for the rest of their life, and finally, on their prayer that they might not be separated by death, were both at the same moment changed into trees (Ovid, *Met.* viii. 611–724).

Philēmon (Φιλήμων). A Greek poet of the New Attic Comedy, of Soli in Cilicia, or of Syracuse, born about B.C. 362. He came early to Athens, and first appeared as an author in the year 330. He must have enjoyed remarkable popularity, for he repeatedly won victories over his younger contemporary and rival Menander, whose delicate wit was apparently less to the taste of the Athenians of the time than Philemon's more showy comedy. To later times his successes over Menander were so unintelligible as to be ascribed to the influence of malice and intrigue. Except a short sojourn in Egypt with King Ptolemy Philadelphus, he passed his life at Athens. He there died, nearly a hundred years old, but with mental vigour unimpaired, in the year 262, according to the story, at the moment of his being crowned on the stage. Of his ninety-seven works, fifty-seven are known to us by titles and fragments, and two are preserved in the Latin version of Plautus (*Mercator* and *Trinummus*). The remains of Philemon are published in Meineke's collection, and by Bach (Halle, 1829).

Philes, MANUEL (Μανουὴλ ὁ Φιλῆς). A Byzantine poet, and a native of Ephesus, was born about A.D. 1275, and died about 1340. His poem, *De Animalium Proprietate*, chiefly derived from Aelian, is edited with a revised text by Lehrs and Dübner in the *Bucolici Graeci*, forming part of Didot's *Bibliotheca Graeca* (Paris, 1846), and his other poems on various subjects by Wernsdorf (Leip. 1768).

Philetaerus (Φιλέταιρος). The founder of the kingdom of Pergamum, a native of Paphlagonia (Strabo, pp. 543, 623). He had served in the army of Antigonus and later in that of Lysimachus, who put him in charge of the treasure stored at Pergamum. Philetaerus, shifting for himself, declared in favour of Seleucus (q. v.), but after the death of the latter (B.C. 280) practically established his own independence, and on his death (B.C. 263) left the government to his nephew Eumenes (Lucian, *Macrob.* 12).

Philētas (Φιλητᾶς). A Greek grammarian and poet, son of Telephus, of the island of Cos. He lived in the second half of the fourth century, latterly as tutor to Ptolemy II. (Philadelphus) in Alexandria. Besides epics he composed elegies on his favourite Battis, which were highly prized at Alexandria and Rome, and were imitated by Propertius (iv. 1, 1). We possess only scanty fragments of these elegies, published by Bach, with those of Hermesianax and Phanocles (Halle, 1829). See Couat, *La Poésie Alexandrine* (Paris, 1882).

Phileus. See PYTHIUS.

Philīnus (Φιλῖνος). (1) An Attic orator, the contemporary of Demosthenes and Lycurgus. (2) A Greek physician, the reputed founder of the Empirical School of medicine, in the third century B.C. See MEDICINA.

Philippēus (Φιλίππειος) and **Philippēum**. A gold stater struck by Philip II. of Macedonia between B.C. 359 and 336. Its value was 20 drachmae or about $4. It is represented on p. 1230.

Philippi (Φίλιπποι). A city of Macedonia, now Filibah. It was situated on the river Gangas or Gangites, and was founded by Philip on the site of an older town, Crenides (Κρηνίδες). In the vicinity were productive gold mines. Here Octavianus and Antony won a decisive victory over Brutus and Cassius in B.C. 42, and here the Apostle Paul first preached in Europe, in A.D. 53. The seaport of Philippi was Datus or Datum on the Strymonic Gulf.

Philippĭdes (Φιλιππίδης). (1) See PHIDIPPIDES. (2) An Athenian, one of the six great poets of the New Comedy, though his personal satire recalled the freedom of the Old Comedy (Plut. *Demetr.* 12, 36). He wrote about B.C. 323. The number of his plays is said to have been forty-five (Suidas, s. h. v.). Gellius (iii. 15) says that he died of joy over the unexpected success of one of his comedies.

Philippopŏlis (Φιλιππόπολις). Now Philippopoli; an important town in Thrace, founded by Philip of Macedon, was situated in a large plain, southeast of the Hebrus, on a hill with three summits, whence it was sometimes called Trimontium. Under the Roman Empire it was the capital of the province of Thracia.

Philippus (Φίλιππος). I. MINOR HISTORICAL PERSONS. (1) The son of Alexander I. of Macedonia, and brother of Perdiccas II., against whom he rebelled in conjunction with Derdas. The rebels were aided by the Athenians, B.C. 432. (2) The son of Herod the Great, king of Iudea, by his wife Cleopatra, was appointed by his father's will tetrarch of Ituraea and Trachonitis, the sovereignty of which was confirmed to him by the decision of Augustus. He continued to reign over the dominions thus intrusted to his charge for thirty-seven years (B.C. 4–A.D. 34). He founded the city of Caesarea, surnamed Paneas, but more commonly known as Caesarea Philippi, near the sources of the Jordan, which he named in honour of Augustus. (3) A son of Herod the Great, by Mariamné, whose proper name was Herodes Philippus. He must not be confounded with the preceding Philip. He was the first husband of Herodias, who afterwards divorced him, contrary to the Jewish law, and married his half-brother, Herod Antipas. It is Herod Philip, and not the preceding, who is meant by the Evangelists (Matt. xiv. 3; Mark, vi. 17; Luke, iii. 19), when they speak of Philip, the brother of Herod.

II. KINGS OF MACEDONIA. (1) PHILIPPUS I., son of Argaeus, was the third king, according to Herodotus and Thucydides, who, not reckoning Caranus and his two immediate successors (Cœnus and Thurimas or Turimmas), look upon Perdiccas I. as the founder of the monarchy. Philip left a son, named Aëropus, who succeeded him. (2) PHILIPPUS II., the youngest son of Amyntas II. and Eurydicé, reigned B.C. 359–336. He was born in 382, and was brought up at Thebes, whither he had been carried as a hostage by Pelopidas, and where he received a most careful education. Upon the death of his brother Perdiccas III., who was slain in battle against the Illyrians, Philip obtained the government of Macedonia, at first merely as regent and guardian to his infant nephew Amyntas; but at the end of a few months he was enabled to set aside the claims of the young prince, and to assume for himself the title of king. Macedonia was beset by dangers on every side. Its territory was ravaged by the Illyrians on the west, and the Paeonians on the north, while Pausanias and Argaeus took advantage of the crisis to put forward their pretensions to the throne. Philip was fully equal to the emergency. By his tact and eloquence he sustained the failing spirits of the Macedonians, while at the same time he introduced among them a stricter military discipline, and organized their army on the plan of the phalanx. He first turned his army against Argaeus, the most formidable of the pretenders, since he was supported by the Athenians. He defeated Argaeus in battle, and then concluded a peace with the Athenians. He next attacked the Paeonians, whom he reduced to subjection, and immediately afterwards defeated the Illyrians in a decisive battle, and compelled them to accept a peace, by which they lost a portion of their territory. Thus in the short period of one year, and at the age of twenty-four, had Philip delivered himself from his dangerous position, and provided for the security of his kingdom. But energy and talents such as his were not satisfied with mere security, and henceforth his views were directed not to defence, but to aggrandizement. His first efforts were directed to obtain possession of the various Greek cities upon the Macedonian coast. Soon after his accession he had withdrawn his garrison from Amphipolis, and had declared it a free city, because the Athenians had supported Argaeus with the hope of recovering Amphipolis, and his continuing to hold the place would have interposed difficulties in the way of a peace with Athens, which was at that time an object of great importance to him. But he had never meant seriously to abandon this important town; and accordingly, having obtained pretexts for war with the Amphipolitans, he laid siege to the town and gained possession of it in 358. The Athenians had sent no assistance to Amphipolis, because Philip, in a secret negotiation with the Athenians, led them to believe that he was willing to restore the city to them when he had taken it, and would do so on condition of their making him master of Pydna. After the capture of Amphipolis, he proceeded at once to Pydna, which seems to have yielded to him without a struggle, and the acquisition of which, by his own arms, and not through the Athenians, gave him a pretext for declining to stand by his secret engagement with them. The hostile feeling which such conduct necessarily excited against him at Athens made it most important for him to secure the good will of the powerful town of Olynthus, and to detach the Olynthians from the Athenians. Accordingly, he gave to the Olynthians the town of Potidaea, which he took from the Athenians in 356. Soon after this he attacked and took a settlement of the Thracians, called Crenides, and, having introduced into the place a number of new colonists, he named it Philippi after himself. One great advantage of this acquisition was, that it put him in possession of the gold mines of the district. From this point there is for some time a pause in the active operations of Philip. In 352 he took Methoné after a lengthened siege, in the course of which he himself

Gold Coin of Philip the Great.

lost an eye. The capture of this place was a necessary preliminary in any movement toward the south, lying as it did between him and the Thessalian border. He now marched into Thessaly to aid the Aleuadae against Lycophron, the tyrant of Pherae. The Phocians sent a force to support Lycophron, but they were defeated by Philip, and their general Onomarchus slain. This victory gave Philip the ascendency in Thessaly. He established at Pherae what he wished the Greeks to consider a free government, and then advanced southward to Thermopylae. The pass, however, he found guarded by a strong Athenian force, and he was compelled, or at least thought it expedient, to retire. He now turned his arms against Thrace, and succeeded in establishing his ascendency in that country also. Meanwhile Philip's movements in Thessaly had opened the eyes of Demosthenes to the real danger of Athens and Greece, and his first Philippic (delivered in 352) was his earliest attempt to rouse his countrymen to energetic efforts against their enemy; but he did not produce much effect upon the Athenians. In 349 Philip commenced his attacks on the Chalcidian cities. Olynthus, in alarm, applied to Athens for aid, and Demosthenes, in his three Olynthiac orations, roused the people to efforts against the common enemy, not very vigorous at first, and fruitless in the end. In the course of three years Philip gained possession of all the Chalcidian cities, and the war was brought to a conclusion by the capture of Olynthus itself in 347. In the following year (346) he concluded peace with the Athenians, and straightway marched into Phocis, and brought the Phocian War to an end. The Phocian cities were destroyed, and their place in the Amphictyonic council was made over to the king of Macedonia, who was appointed also, jointly with the Thebans and Thessalians, to the presidency of the Pythian Games. Ruling as he did over a barbaric nation, such a recognition of his Hellenic character was of the greatest value to him, especially as he looked forward to an invasion of the Persian empire in the name of Greece, united under him in a great national confederacy. During the next few years Philip steadily pursued his ambitious projects. From 342 to 340 he was engaged in an expedition in Thrace, and attempted to bring under his power all the Greek cities in that country. In the last of these years he laid siege to Perinthus and Byzantium; but the Athenians, who had long viewed Philip's aggrandizement with fear and alarm, now resolved to send assistance to these cities. Phocion was appointed to the command of the armament destined for this service, and succeeded in compelling Philip to raise the siege of both the cities (339). Philip now proceeded to carry on war against his northern neighbours, and seemed to give himself no further concern about the affairs of Greece. But meanwhile his hirelings were treacherously promoting his designs against the liberties of Greece. In 339 the Amphictyons declared war against the Locrians of Amphissa for having taken possession of a district of the sacred land; but as the general they had appointed to the command of the Amphictyonic army was unable to effect any thing against the enemy, the Amphictyons, at their next meeting in 337, conferred upon Philip the command of their army. Philip straightway marched through Thermopylae and seized Elatea. The Athenians heard of his approach with alarm; they succeeded, mainly through the influence of Demosthenes, in forming an alliance with the Thebans; but their united army was defeated by Philip in the month of August, 338, in the decisive battle of Chaeronea, which put an end to the independence of Greece. Thebes paid dear for her resistance, but Athens was treated with more favor than she could have expected. Philip now seemed to have within his reach the accomplishment of the great object of his ambition, the invasion and conquest of the Persian Empire. In a congress held at Corinth, which was attended by deputies from every Grecian State with the exception of Sparta, war with Persia was determined on, and the king of Macedonia was appointed to command the forces of the national confederacy. In 337, Philip's marriage with Cleopatra, the daughter of Attalus, one of his generals, led to the most serious disturbances in his family. Olympias and Alexander withdrew in great indignation from Macedonia; and though they returned home soon afterwards, they continued to be on hostile terms with Philip. Meanwhile, his preparations for his Asiatic expedition were not neglected, and early in 336 he sent forces into Asia, under Parmenion, to draw over the Greek cities to his cause. But in the summer of this year he was murdered at a grand festival which he held at Aegae, to solemnize the nuptials of his daughter with Alexander of Epirus. His murderer was a youth of noble blood, named Pausanias, who stabbed him as he was walking in the procession. The assassin was immediately pursued and slain by some of the royal guards. His motive for the deed is stated by Aristotle to have been private resentment against Philip, to whom he had complained in vain of a gross outrage offered to him by Attalus. Olympias and Alexander, however, were suspected of being implicated in the plot. (See OLYMPIAS.) Philip died in the forty-seventh year of his age and the twenty-fourth of his reign, and was succeeded by Alexander the Great. Philip had a great number of wives and concubines. Besides Olympias and Cleopatra, we may mention—(*a*) His first wife Audata, an Illyrian princess, and the mother of Cynané; (*b*) Phila, sister of Derdas and Machatas, a princess of Elymiotis; (*c*) Nicesipolis of Pherae, the mother of Thessalonica; (*d*) Philinna of Larissa, the mother of Arrhidaeus; (*e*) Meda, daughter of Cithelas, king of Thrace; (*f*) Arsinoë, the mother of Ptolemy I., king of Egypt, with whom she was pregnant when she married Lagus. To these numerous connections temperament as well as policy seems to have inclined him. He was strongly addicted, indeed, to sensual enjoyment of every kind; but his passions, however strong, were always kept in subjection to his interests and ambitious views. He was fond of science and literature, in the patronage of which he appears to have been liberal; and his appreciation of great minds is shown by his connection with Aristotle. In the pursuit of his political objects he was, as we have seen, unscrupulous, and ever ready to resort to duplicity and corruption; but when we consider his humanity and generous clemency, we may admit that he does not appear to disadvantage, even morally speaking, by the side of his fellow conquerors of mankind. See Curteis, *Rise of the Macedonian Empire* (New York, 1878). (3) The name of Philip was bestowed by the Macedonian army upon Arrhidaeus, the bastard son of Philip II., when he was raised to the throne after the death of Alexander the Great. He accordingly appears in the list of Macedonian kings as Philip III. For his life and reign see ARRHIDAEUS. (4) Eldest son of Cassander, whom he succeeded on the throne, B.C. 296. He reigned only a few months, and was carried off by a consumptive disorder. (5) Son of Demetrius II., reigned B.C. 220–178. He was only eight years old at the death of his father Demetrius (229); and the sovereign power was consequently assumed by his uncle Antigonus Doson, who, though he certainly ruled as king rather than merely as guardian of his nephew, was faithful to the interests of Philip, to whom he transferred the sovereignty at his death in 220, to the exclusion of his own children. Philip was only seventeen years old at the time of his accession, but he soon showed that he possessed ability and wisdom superior to his years. In consequence of the defeat of the Achaeans and Aratus by the Aetolians, the former applied for aid to Philip. This was granted; and for the next three years Philip conducted with distinguished success the war against the Aetolians. This war, usually called the Social War, was brought to a conclusion in 217, and at once gained for Philip a distinguished reputation throughout Greece, while his clemency and moderation secured him an equal measure of popularity. But a change came over his character soon after the close of the Social War. He became suspicious and cruel; and having become jealous

Coin of Philip V.

of his former friend and counsellor Aratus, he caused him to be removed by a slow and secret poison in 213. Meantime he had become engaged in war with the Romans. In 215 he concluded an alliance with Hannibal; but he did not prosecute the war with any activity against the Romans, who on their part were too much engaged with their formidable adversary in Italy to send any powerful armament against the Macedonian king. In 211 the war assumed a new character in consequence of the alliance entered into by the Romans with the Aetolians. It was now carried on with greater vigour and alternate success; but as Philip gained several advantages over the Aetolians, the latter people made peace with Philip in 205. In the course of the same year the Romans likewise concluded a peace with Philip, as they were desirous to give their undivided attention to the war in Africa. It is probable that both parties looked upon this peace as little more than a suspension of hostilities. Such was clearly the view with which the Romans had accepted it; and Philip not only proceeded to carry out his views for his own aggrandizement in Greece, without any regard to the Roman alliances in that country, but he even sent a body of auxiliaries to the Carthaginians in Africa, who fought at Zama under Hannibal. As soon as the Romans had brought the Second Punic War to an end, they again declared war against Philip, in 200. This war lasted between three and four years, and was brought to an end by the defeat of Philip by the consul Flamininus at the battle of Cynoscephalae in the autumn of 197. (See FLAMININUS.) By the peace finally granted to Philip (196), the king was compelled to abandon all his conquests, both in Europe and Asia, surrender his whole fleet to the Romans, and limit his standing army to 5000 men, besides paying a sum of 1000 talents. Philip was now effectually humbled, and endeavoured to cultivate the friendship of the all-powerful Republic. But towards the end of his reign he determined to try once more the fortune of war, and began to make active preparations for this purpose. His declining years were embittered by disputes between his sons Perseus and Demetrius; and the former, by forged letters, persuaded the king that Demetrius was plotting against his life, and induced him to order his execution. Philip afterwards learned of the trick that had been played upon him and was struck with such remorse as probably led to his death, which took place in B.C. 179 (Livy, xl. 6, 21, 54; Polyb. xxiv. 7, 8).

III. ROMAN CITIZENS. (1) Q. MARCIUS PHILIPPUS, praetor B.C. 188, with Sicily as his province and consul 186, when he carried on war in Liguria with his colleague Sp. Postumius Albinus. He was defeated by the enemy in the country of the Apuani, and the recollection of his defeat was preserved by the name of the Saltus Marcius. In 169 Philippus was consul a second time, and carried on the war in Macedonia against Perseus, but accomplished nothing of importance. (See PERSEUS.) In 164 Philippus was censor with L. Aemilius Paulus, and in his censorship he set up in the city a new sun-dial. (See HOROLOGIUM.) (2) L. MARCIUS PHILIPPUS was a tribune of the plebs 104, when he brought forward an agrarian law, and was consul in 91 with Sex. Iulius Caesar. In this year Philippus, who belonged to the popular party, opposed with the greatest vigour the measures of the tribune Drusus, who at first enjoyed the full confidence of the Senate. But his opposition was all in vain; the laws of the tribune were carried. Soon afterwards Drusus began to be regarded with mistrust and suspicion; Philippus became reconciled to the Senate, and on his proposition a senatus consultum was passed, declaring all the laws of Drusus to be null and void, as having been carried against the auspices. (See DRUSUS.) In the Civil Wars between Marius and Sulla, Philippus took no part. He survived the death of Sulla; and he is mentioned afterwards as one of those who advocated sending Pompey to conduct the war in Spain against Sertorius. Philippus was one of the most distinguished orators of his time (Hor. *Epist.* i. 7, 46). As an orator he was reckoned inferior only to Crassus and Antonius. He was a man of luxurious habits, which his wealth enabled him to gratify: his fish-ponds were particularly celebrated for their magnificence and extent, and are mentioned by the ancients along with those of Lucullus and Hortensius. Besides his son, L. Philippus, who is spoken of below, he had a step-son, Gellius Publicola. (See PUBLICOLA.) (3) L. MARCIUS PHILIPPUS, son of the preceding, was consul in 56. Upon the death of C. Octavius, the father of Augustus, Philippus married his widow Atia, and thus became the step-father of Augustus. Philippus was a timid man. Notwithstanding his close connection with Caesar's family, he remained neutral in the Civil Wars; and after the assassination of Caesar, he endeavoured to dissuade his step-son, the young Octavianus, from accepting the inheritance which the dictator had left him. He lived till his step-son had acquired the supremacy of the Roman world. He restored the temple of Hercules and the Muses, and surrounded it with a colonnade, which is frequently mentioned under the name of Porticus Philippi (Ovid, *Fasti*, vi. 801).

IV. ROMAN EMPERORS. (1) M. IULIUS PHILIPPUS I., Roman emperor A.D. 244–249, was an Arabian by birth, and entered the Roman army, in which he rose to high rank. He accompanied Gordianus III. in his expedition against the Persians; and upon the death of the excellent Misitheus (see MISITHEUS), he was promoted to the vacant office of praetorian praefect. He availed himself of the influence of his high office to excite discontent among the soldiers, who at length assassinated Gordian, and proclaimed Philippus emperor, 244. Philippus proclaimed his son Caesar, concluded a disgraceful peace with Sapor, founded the city of Philippopolis, and then returned to Rome. In 245 he was engaged in prosecuting a successful war against the Carpi on the Danube. In 248, rebellions, headed by Iotapinus and Marinus, broke out simultaneously in the East and in Moesia. Both pretenders speedily perished, but Decius, having been dispatched to recall the legions on the Danube to their duty, was himself forcibly invested with the purple by the troops, and compelled by them to march upon Italy. Philippus, having gone forth to encounter his rival, was slain near Verona either in battle or by his own soldiers. The great domestic event of the reign of Philippus was the exhibition of the Secular Games, which were celebrated with even more than the ordinary degree of splendour, since Rome had now, according to the received tradition, attained the thousandth year of her existence (A.D. 248). (2) M. IULIUS PHILIPPUS II., son of the foregoing, was a boy of seven at the accession (244) of his father, by whom he was proclaimed Caesar, and three years afterwards (247) received the title of Augustus. In 249 he was slain, according to Zosimus, at the battle of Verona, or murdered, according to Victor, at Rome by the Praetorians, when intelligence arrived of the defeat and death of the emperor.

V. WRITERS. (1) Of Medma, in the south of Italy, a Greek astronomer, and a disciple of Plato. His observations, which were made in the Peloponnesus and in Locris, were used by the astronomers Hipparchus, Geminus the Rhodian, and Ptolemy. (2) Of Thessalonica, an epigrammatic poet, who, besides composing a large number of epigrams himself, compiled one of the ancient Greek Anthologies. The whole number of epigrams ascribed to him in the Greek Anthology is nearly ninety; but of these, six (xxxvi.–xli.) ought to be ascribed to Lucillius, and a few others are manifestly borrowed from earlier poets, while others are mere imitations. He probably wrote in the reign of Trajan.

Philiscus (Φιλίσκος). (1) A Greek tragedian of Corcyra, in the first half of the third century B.C.; he was priest of Dionysus in Alexandria, and, as such, stood at the head of the Dionysiac guild of actors in that city. He was one of the "Pleiad" of Alexandrian tragic poets. His portrait is preserved in a relief in the Lateran Museum. He wrote forty-two dramas. (2) A Rhodian sculptor of about B.C. 146 (Pliny, *H. N.* xxxvi. 34).

Philistīnae Fossae. A canal connecting the Padus with the Athesis (Pliny, *H. N.* iii. 120).

Philistion (Φιλιστίων). A physician of the fourth century B.C., who was tutor to the astronomer and physician Eudoxus (Gell. xvii. 11).

Philistus (Φίλιστος). A Greek historian of Syracuse, born about B.C. 435. He encouraged the elder Dionysius, by advice and assistance, in securing and maintaining the position of despot in his native State; but was himself banished by Dionysius in 386, and lived a long while at Adria in Epirus, busied with historical studies. Recalled by Dionysius the younger, he counteracted the salutary influence of Dion and Plato at that tyrant's court, and brought about the banishment of both. As commander of the fleet against Dion and the revolted Syracusans, he lost a naval battle, and in consequence either committed suicide or was cruelly murdered by the angry populace (356). He left an historical work, begun in his exile, called *Sicelica* (Σικελικά), a history of Sicily in thirteen books. Books i.–vii. dealt with the events of the earliest times to the capture of Agrigentum by the Carthaginians in 406; viii.–xi., with the rule of the elder Dionysius; xii. and xiii., with that of the younger. The last portion, which remained incomplete owing to his death, was finished by his countryman Athanas. Only unimportant fragments of this have survived. According to the judgment of the ancients, he imitated Thucydides somewhat unsuccessfully, and betrayed in his work the one-sided attitude natural to his political views (Plut. *Dion*, 36; Dionys. *Ad Cn. Pompeium*, 5). The fragments of Philistus are edited by C. Müller in his *Frag. Hist. Graec.* (Paris, 1841).

Philo (Φίλων). (1) A sculptor; the son of Antipater. He flourished in the time of Alexander the Great. Among his works was the statue of Hephaestion, and that of Zeus Ourios, at the entrance of the Bosporus (Cic. *Verr.* iv. 58, 129). The dedicatory verses inscribed on the pedestal of the latter are now in the British Museum (quoted on p. 40 of Demosth. *Adv. Leptinem*, ed. Sandys). Pliny (xxxiv. 91) mentions him as one of the sculptors who made *athletas et armatos et venatores sacrificantesque*.

(2) An Athenian architect who built for Demetrius Phalereus, about B.C. 318, the portico to the great temple at Eleusis. It had twelve Doric columns in front, and its dimensions were 183 feet by 37½ feet. Under the administration of Lycurgus, he constructed an *armamentarium* or arsenal at Zea in the Piraeus, containing tackle, etc., for 1000 ships (Pliny, *H. N.* vii. 125). It was destroyed by Sulla, but apparently rebuilt, since it is described by Valerius Maximus (viii. 12, 2) as still existing. An inscription in the *Corpus Inscriptionum Atticarum* (ii. 1054) contains the contract for the work, with full details of its structure and fittings.

(3) Of Byzantium; a celebrated mechanician. He wrote, in the second century B.C., a work on mechanics, of which only one book, on the construction of engines of war, and portions of two others, on siege-warfare, are extant. Edited by Köchly and Rüstow (1853). See SEVEN WONDERS.

(4) Of Larissa; an Academic philosopher, a pupil of Clitomachus. He came to Rome in B.C. 88, being one of a number of eminent Greeks who fled

from Athens on the approach of its siege during the Mithridatic War. He was a man of versatile genius, and a perfect master of the theory and practice of oratory. Cicero had scarcely heard him before all inclination for Epicureanism was swept from his mind, and he surrendered himself wholly to the brilliant Academic (*Brutus*, § 306). One of his works, twice mentioned, though not by any definite title (*Acad.* i. 13, ii. 11), supplied Cicero with his historic account of the New Academy (*Academica*, ed. Reid, pp. 2, 52).

(5) Called IUDAEUS, "the Jew." Born of a priestly family at Alexandria, about B.C. 25, he carefully studied the different branches of Greek culture, and, in particular, acquired a knowledge of the Platonic philosophy, while in no way abandoning the study of the Scriptures or the creed of his nation. In A.D. 39 he went to Rome as an emissary to the emperor Caligula in the interest of his fellow-countrymen, whose religious feelings were offended by a decree ordering them to place the statue of the deified emperor in their synagogues. This embassy, which led to no result, is described by him in a work which is still extant, though in an incomplete form. Philo is the chief representative of the Graeco-Judaic philosophy. He wrote numerous Greek works in a style modelled on that of Plato. These are remarkable for moral earnestness, passionate enthusiasm, and vigour of thought. They include allegorical expositions of portions of the Scriptures, as well as works of ethical, historical, or political purport. Several of his works only survive in Armenian versions. His philosophy, especially his theology, is an endeavour to reconcile Platonism with Judaism. Eng. trans. by Yonge, 4 vols. (1854–55).

(6) PHILO BYBLIUS or HERENNIUS BYBLIUS. A Roman grammarian, born at Byblus in Phœnicia. His life extended from about the time of Nero to that of Hadrian (A.D. 61–141). A considerable fragment of his translation of the alleged Phœnician writer Sanchuniathon (q. v.) is preserved in the first book of the *Praeparatio Evangelica* of Eusebius; and he also wrote a work **Περὶ Πόλεων**, much used by the later grammarians, especially Hesychius and Stephanus of Byzantium.

(7) Q. PUBLILIUS. A distinguished Roman general in the Samnite Wars, and the author of one of the great reforms in the Roman constitution. He was consul in B.C. 339, with Ti. Aemilius Mamercinus, and defeated the Latins, over whom he triumphed. In the same year he was appointed dictator by his colleague Aemilius Mamercinus, and, as such, proposed the celebrated *Publiliae Leges*, which abolished the power of the patrician assembly of the curiae, and elevated the plebeians to an equality with the patricians for all practical purposes. (See PUBLILIAE LEGES.) In 337 Philo was the first plebeian praetor, and in 332 he was censor with Sp. Postumius Albinus. In 327 he was consul a second time, and carried on war in the south of Italy. He was continued in the command for the following year with the title of proconsul, the first instance in Roman history in which a person was invested with proconsular power. He took Palaepolis in 326. In 320 he was consul a third time, with L. Papirius Cursor, and carried on the war with success against the Samnites (Livy, viii. 15–26; ix. 7–15).

(8) L. VETURIUS. (1) L., consul B.C. 220, with C. Lutatius Catulus; dictator 217 for the purpose of holding the Comitia; and censor 210 with P. Licinius Crassus Dives, and died while holding this office. (2) L., praetor B.C. 209, with Cisalpine Gaul as his province. In 207 he served under Claudius Nero and Livius Salinator in the campaign against Hasdrubal. In 206 he was consul with Q. Caecilius Metellus, and in conjunction with his colleague carried on the war against Hannibal in Bruttium. He accompanied Scipio to Africa, and after the battle of Zama (B.C. 202) was sent to Rome to announce the news of Hannibal's defeat (Livy, xxviii. 9–11; xxx. 38–40).

Philochăres (Φιλοχάρης). A painter, possibly the brother of Aeschines, of whom Demosthenes spoke so scornfully (*Fals. Leg.* p. 329).

Philochŏrus (Φιλόχορος). A Greek historian, living at Athens between 306 and 260. As an upholder of national liberty he was among the bitterest opponents of Demetrius Poliorcetes and of his son Antigonus Gonatas, who put him to death after the conquest of Athens. Of his works, the *Atthis* was a history of Athens from the earliest times to B.C. 262, in seventeen books. It was highly esteemed and often quoted for its wealth of facts and thoroughness of investigation, especially as regards chronology. We still possess a considerable number of fragments. Edited separately by Siebelis (Leipzig, 1811).

Philŏcles (Φιλοκλῆς). (1) A Greek tragedian, son of Aeschylus's sister. He wrote a hundred plays in the manner of Aeschylus, and won the prize against Sophocles' *Oedipus Tyrannus*. Only scanty fragments of his plays remain. The drama was also cultivated by his sons Morsimus and Melanthius, by Morsimus's son Astydamas (about B.C. 399), and again by the sons of the latter, Astydamas and Philocles. (2) The joint commander with Conon of the Athenian fleet at the battle of Arginusae, and put to death by Lysander for having treated his prisoners with cruelty (Plut. *Lys.* 13).

Philocrătes (Φιλοκράτης). An Athenian orator, a paid partisan of the Macedonians against the patriotic party of Demosthenes (Demosth. *De Corona*, p. 230.

Philoctētes (Φιλοκτήτης). The son of Poeas, king of the Malians in Oeta, by Demonassa. He inherited the bow and arrows of Heracles (q. v.). He was leader of seven ships in the expedition against Troy; but, on the way out, was bitten by a snake at Lemnos, or the small island of Chrysé near Lemnos, and, on account of the intolerable stench caused by the wound, was abandoned at Lemnos on the advice of Odysseus. Here in his sickness he dragged out a miserable life till the tenth year of the war. Then, however, on account of Helenus's prophecy that Troy could only be conquered by the arrows of Heracles, Odysseus and Diomedes went to fetch him, and he was healed by Machaon. After he had slain Paris, Troy was conquered. He was one of the heroes who came safe home again. The story of Philoctetes was dramatized by Aeschylus and Euripides (B.C. 431), as well as by Sophocles (409), the last being still extant (ed. by Graves [Boston and N. Y. 1894]). It is also the theme of numerous monuments of ancient art. See Prof. Jebb's introduction to Soph. *Phil.*, p. xxxvii.

Philodēmus (Φιλόδημος). A native of Gadara, in Palestine, an Epicurean philosopher and epigrammatic poet, contemporary with Cicero. The Greek Anthology contains thirty-four of his Epigrams, which are chiefly of a light and amatory character, and which quite bear out Cicero's statements concerning the licentiousness of his matter and the elegance of his manner (Cic. *In Pis.* 28, 29). Considerable remains of Philodemus have come to light at Herculaneum, and are edited by Sudhaus.

Philolāus (Φιλόλαος). A distinguished Pythagorean philosopher. He was a native of Croton or Tarentum, a contemporary of Socrates, and the instructor of Simmias and Cebes at Thebes, where he appears to have lived many years. Pythagoras and his earliest successors did not commit any of their doctrines to writing, and the first publication of the Pythagorean doctrines is pretty uniformly attributed to Philolaüs. He composed a work on the Pythagorean philosophy in three books, which Plato is said to have procured at the cost of 100 minae through Dion of Syracuse, who purchased it from Philolaüs, who was at the time in deep poverty (Gell. iii. 17). Other versions of the story represent Plato as purchasing it himself from Philolaüs or his relatives when in Sicily. Plato is said to have derived from this work the greater part of his *Timaeus*.

Philologia (φιλολογία). The terms "philology" and "philological" are so convenient as frequently to be used in various senses in modern times; and this diversity of application is found also in the corresponding words among the ancients. Plato is the first Greek writer to employ the terms φιλολογία and φιλόλογος. In the *Theaetetus* (146 A) φιλολογία denotes a fondness for argument; in the *Laws* (641 E) φιλόλογος means one who is given to talking as opposed to the βραχύλογος Spartan. He develops the meaning a little further in the *Laches* (188 C), where it is applied to a person fond of philosophical discussion as opposed to μισόλογος. In Aristotle φιλολογία means a love of learning, and Cicero quotes the word in the same sense in a letter to Atticus (ii. 17). In a passage of Pericles, cited by Stobaeus (428, 53), it is opposed to ἀπαίδευτος, and in Plutarch (*Lucull.* 42) it is contrasted with πολιτικός. In the Alexandrian period (280 + B.C.) it is often restricted to the sense of a "scholar" and "a learned man," and was so applied to Eratosthenes, who was not, first of all, a student of language or literature, but a mathematician and astronomer. In Plutarch it is oftenest, however, used of a linguist (Plut. ii. 645 C). See Gudeman, *Outlines of the Hist. of Class. Philology*, pp. 1–5 (2d ed. Boston, 1894).

At Rome the prevailing sense was that of "a scholar," and it was so applied to Aelius Stilo, the teacher of Varro (Suet. *De Grammat.* p. 108 Reiff.). This comprehensive sense is also seen in a remarkable passage of Seneca (*Epist.* 108, 29), in which he distinguishes the respective standpoints of the philologist, the grammarian, and the philosopher. Hence we find that the word philology has, at different times, been understood to mean "a love of speaking," "the study of language," and finally "learning" in a wider sense of the word.

Language-study among the Greeks originated as an adjunct to psychological research. In an attempt to answer the question as to the nature of thought and the expression of thought, an endeavour was made to discover just what the nature of language is in its relation to the thought which it expresses; and this led to an investigation of the original meaning of words. Language-study, therefore, did not begin as a distinct science, but only as an adjunct to another branch of learning, and therefore it took the form of etymology. The Greeks never thought of connecting their own language with that of any other people, though Plato once came near to such an idea in a passage of his *Cratylus* (410), where he notes the similarity between the Greek and Phrygian names for certain common objects.

Such etymologizing as was done by the Greeks and Romans was largely in the nature of guess-work; but in the dialogue of Plato just mentioned some suggestions of considerable acuteness are put forth. In fact, this treatise embodies all that was best and truest in ancient linguistic speculation, and to it not much was added by writers on language down to the beginning of the present century. Plato is the first to draw attention to the distinction between simple and compound words; and his classification of the letters of the alphabet is the first that we find in any of the ancient writings. He separates them into "voiced" letters (φωνήεντα) or vowels and "voiceless" letters or consonants (ἄφωνα); the latter he subdivides into semi-vowels (ἡμίφωνα—i. e. λ, μ, ν, ρ, σ) and true mutes (ἄφθογγα).

The discussion as to the original meaning of words in course of time led to a consideration of the origin of human speech, as to which two schools arose. One set of scholars (the Anomalists) held that language arose by mere convention (θέσει), that words were arbitrarily assigned to objects, and that there was no inherent appropriateness in giving any particular object its name. The other set of thinkers (the Analogists), who were of the Eleatic School of philosophers, held that words are essentially and necessarily expressive of the objects which they describe, that they are made by nature (φύσει), that thought was stamped on words in their genesis, and that words have the same relation to things as exists between sensation and that which causes the sensation. Heraclitus illustrated his meaning by saying that the names of objects are, as it were, their shadows, representing them just as images in water represent the objects which they reflect. The theory of language which was put forth to explain this inherent appropriateness was the so-called mimetic or onomatopoetic theory (see ONOMATOPOEIA), which is found expressed in a passage of Epicurus, cited by Diogenes Laërtius (ix. 75) and by Lucretius (v. 1028). The mimetic theory they did not push very far, but merely asserted that there is something in the sound of primitive words appropriate to the sense. This Plato illustrates in his *Cratylus* by saying that, in order to arrive at the earliest meaning of a word, the word must be resolved not merely into its simplest form, but into the very letters which compose it; for these, or rather the sounds which they denote, possess a meaning. This fact, he says, was well known to the first makers of language, who observed that the sound of *a* denotes vastness and the sound of η denotes length; that ρ expresses motion, as in ῥέω, τρόμος, ῥυμβέω, because, in uttering this letter, the tongue is most agitated and least at rest; that φ, ψ, σ, and ζ require a great expenditure of breath, and are therefore used in the expression of such notions as are contained in ζέω, σεισμός, etc., and, in general, wherever the thought of air is involved; that the limpid movement of λ, in whose pronunciation the tongue slips easily along, enables that letter to express smoothness, as in λεῖος, λίπαρον: that the sound of γ detains the slipping tongue, so that when it is prefixed to λ there is given an impression of what is glutinous and clammy, as in γλισχρός, γλυκύς, γλοιώδης: that ν, being sounded within, gives the notion of inwardness, while ο suggests roundness. Thus, Plato says, the first language-makers impressed thought on names by giving them an imitative quality. Gesture is the method which a deaf-and-dumb person would use to make his meaning plain; and language is only vocal gesture—the gesture of the tongue. Yet, he adds, though thought was stamped on words in their genesis, the original meaning has in most cases been lost; so that the use of a word may now be metaphorical, accidental, or conventional, and thus may have no real relation to the thought or feeling of the speaker who uses it. Language has, therefore, both a natural element and a conventional element. In another portion of the *Cratylus* Plato ridicules many of the popular etymologies, such as *αἰθήρ* as a contraction of ἀειθεήρ (ἀεί + θέειν), "always running"; τέχνη from ἐχονόη, "possession of mind," on which Socrates says ironically that "you have only to take away the τ, insert ο between the χ and the ν, and another ο between the ν and the π," and thus you have ἐχονόη! (See Jowett's introduction to his translation of the *Cratylus*.)

The Sophists were much given to etymologizing, and made a great use of the so-called principle of Antiphrasis, which in later times was taken up by the Romans, and prevailed also to some extent in the Middle Ages. Antiphrasis explains names as being suggested by what is opposed to them in meaning, as when *aridus* ("dry") is derived from ἀρδεύειν: *bellum* from *bellus* ("fine"), because it is not a fine thing; *caelum* from *celare* ("to conceal"), because it conceals nothing; and the very famous etymology, which has in modern times become proverbial, *lucus a non lucendo*. The philosophical principle on which this notion was based is of course a sound one—i. e. that of two antithetical ideas one is apt to suggest the other, as light suggests darkness, as truth suggests falsehood, etc.; but the application of it to etymology was absurd. It appears to have been suggested to the ancients by the existence of certain well-known euphemisms, such as that which calls the Furies *Eumenides* or "the well-wishers," the left hand "the well-named," and so forth. They also observed in irony a similar principle; and, therefore, putting the two together, inferred that there is something in the human mind that instinctively describes objects by recalling their opposites. Among the writers who treated of etymological subjects at this period were Gorgias (Περὶ Ὀνομάτων), Protagoras (Περὶ Ὀρθοεπείας), Prodicus (Περὶ Ὀνομάτων), and Licymnius (Περὶ Λέξεων), the last of whom, in the course of his teaching, noted and partly classified synonyms, root-words, compounds, and cognates.

In the Alexandrian Period language was studied on its strictly grammatical side, and formal grammar arose at Alexandria in the writings of men like Zenodotus, Aristophanes, Aristarchus, and Tryphon, and at Pergamum with Crates of Mallos, who introduced philological study to the Romans, though formal grammar was first carefully studied at Rome after the time of Dionysius Thrax. (See GRAMMATICA.) At the same time lexicography was developed in the form of special glossaries, on which see LEXICON.

During the later Middle Ages speculation as to the origin and nature of language was a favourite amusement of scholars; but no advance was made by them in linguistics, owing to the fact that Greek and Latin were both supposed to be derived from the Hebrew. Upon the proof of this thesis an enormous amount of labour was wasted by generations of scholars, of whom Guichard and Gebelin may be taken as types. It was not until 1786, when Sir William Jones initiated the study of Sanskrit, that philology began to be set upon a scientific basis by a recognition of the fact that Sanskrit, Avestan, Greek, Latin, Gothic, and Keltic belong to the same family of languages; and soon after Franz Bopp (q. v.) became the founder of the special science of COMPARATIVE PHILOLOGY, which deals with the study of each language in its relation to the other members of the same family. His monumental treatise on Comparative Grammar dealt with the phonetic laws of the several languages, and traced their general forms back to a common origin in an Indo-European or "Aryan" speech now lost. Bopp's work was carried on and developed by such men as Jakob Grimm, who first scientifically studied the Teutonic languages; by Pott and by Benfey, the accomplished Sanskritist. The new science was applied to Greek by Georg Curtius, and to Latin by the German, Wilhelm Corssen (q. v.), and the Frenchman, Michel Bréal.

It now began to be accepted as a truth that the change which is always going on in languages is regulated by law; that in each form of speech there is a regular sequence of sound, which is not due to chance or to the conscious desire of those who speak it, but which has a definite, ascertainable course; and that the science of language is a science because the knowledge of these sequences can be acquired and understood. The most famous laws of sound-change are those known as Grimm's Law and Verner's Law. See GRIMM'S LAW; VERNER'S LAW.

Until comparatively recent years students of language held that the operation of phonetic law did not always exclude the possibility of what they called "sporadic change"—that is to say, changes that are found in some words, though not in every word in which the sound so affected occurs. To this notion of sporadic change the so-called New School of philologists vigorously objects. Brugmann, Paul, Osthoff, Ascoli, Leskien, and Verner (to mention only a few distinguished names) hold that phonetic change, so far as it is due to physical causes, is absolutely uniform in any one language at the same time; that the new form, when produced by such a change, invariably drives out the old one; and that in consequence there is no such thing as "sporadic change"; for phonetic law is as exact and definite as the law of any physical science. The "New School" of philologists has devoted itself very largely to an investigation of language on its inner or psychical side, and has therefore brought psychology into a close relation with the study of language. In so doing they have recognized the immense importance of the principle of analogy, which tends to reduce words of like function to a certain likeness of form, and thus conditions every new word that is made by the forms of like words that already exist. According to the New School, therefore, the two chief factors in word-formation are Phonetic Change due to the desire for euphony, and which is largely destructive, doing away with sounds or combinations which are inconvenient to pronounce; the other principle is Analogy, which comes from the imitative habit of the mind, and is rather restorative than destructive, constantly producing new forms on the analogy of old ones to supply each want that arises in the course of man's intellectual development.

At the present time the term "Linguistics" (Ger. *Linguistik*) is supplanting the word Philology in the sense of language-study pure and simple; while Philology, or rather CLASSICAL PHILOLOGY, is coming to be used as a comprehensive name for the general study of ancient life in all its various political, social, and intellectual phases, as handed down in the literary, epigraphic, and monumental remains of Greece and Rome. It embraces, then, not only Grammar, Lexicography, Text Criticism, and Hermeneutics, but Epigraphy, Numismatics, and Art; or as Karl Otfried Müller said: "Philology does not strive to establish isolated facts or to get an acquaintance with abstract forms, but to grasp the ancient spirit in its broadest meaning, in its works of reason, of feeling, and of imagination."

BIBLIOGRAPHY.—On the philological studies of the ancients, see Lersch, *Sprachphilosophie der Alten*, 3 vols. (Bonn, 1841); Gräfenhan, *Geschichte der classischen Philologie*, vol. i. (Bonn, 1843–50); Steinthal, *Geschichte der Sprachwissenschaft bei den Griechen und Römern*, 2 vols. (2d ed. Berlin, 1892); Urlichs in I. Müller's *Handbuch*, I. i. pp. 126 foll.; Sayce, *Introduction to the Science of Language*, vol. i. pp. 1–25; and Max Müller's *Science of Language*, vol. i. —On modern linguistics, see F. Müller's introduction to his *Grundriss der Sprachwissenschaft* (Vienna, 1876–1887); Delbrück, *Introduction to the Study of Language* (Eng. trans., London, 1882); Brugmann, *Zum heutigen Stand der Sprachwissenschaft* (Strassburg, 1885); La Grasserie, *Les Divisions de la Linguistique* (Paris, 1888); Strong, Logeman, and Wheeler, *Introduction to the Study of the History of Language*, based on Paul (New York and London, 1891); Collitz, *Die neueste Sprachforschung* (1886); Wheeler, *Analogy and the Scope of its Application in Language* (Ithaca, 1887); and Clark, *Manual of Linguistics* (New York and Edinburgh, 1893). See also BOPP; CORSSEN; CURTIUS; INDO-EUROPEAN LANGUAGES; POTT.

Philology. See PHILOLOGIA.

Philomēla (Φιλομήλα). The daughter of King Pandion in Attica, who, being dishonoured by her brother-in-law Tereus, was metamorphosed into a nightingale. The story is given under TEREUS.

Philomēla. The title of a Latin poem composed in the early Middle Ages, probably by a German monk, and giving in 66 elegiac lines the mimetic words used to imitate the sounds made by the different birds and beasts. The oldest MS. containing it dates from the eleventh century. It was ascribed by Goldast to a certain Albius Ovidius Iuventinus, who is probably an imaginary individual. The poem is printed with English notes in Peck and Arrowsmith's *Roman Life in Latin Prose and Verse* (New York, 1895). See an article by H. T. Peck on "Onomatopoetic Words in Latin" in *Classical Studies in Honour of Henry Drisler* (New York, 1894).

Philomelium or **Philomēlum** (Φιλομήλιον, or in the Pisidian dialect Φιλομηδή. A city of Phrygia Parorios, on the borders of Lycaonia and Pisidia, said to have been named from the numbers of nightingales in its neighbourhood. It is mentioned several times by Cicero. According to the division of the provinces under Constantine, it belonged to Pisidia. It is still found mentioned at the time of the Crusades by the name of Philomené (Strabo, p. 663).

Philomēlus (Φιλόμηλος). A general of the Phocians in the Phocian or Sacred War. He was the person who persuaded his countrymen to seize the temple of Delphi, and to apply the riches of the temple to the purpose of defending themselves against the Amphictyonic forces, B.C. 357. He commanded the Phocians during the early years of the war, but was slain in battle in 353. He was succeeded in the command by his brother Onomarchus (Diod. xvi. 22).

Philonīdes (Φιλωνίδης). An Athenian poet of the Old Comedy, who is, however, best known on account of his connection with the literary history of Aristophanes. It is generally stated that Philonides was an actor of Aristophanes, who is said to have committed to him and to Callistratus his chief characters; but the best modern critics have shown that this is an erroneous statement, and that the true state of the case is that several of the plays of Aristophanes were brought out in the names of Callistratus and Philonides. We learn from Aristophanes himself not only the fact that he brought out his early plays in the names of other poets, but also his reasons for so doing. In the parabasis of the *Knights* (v. 514), he states that he had pursued this course not from want of thought, but from a sense of the difficulty of his profession, and from a fear that he might suffer from that fickleness of taste which the Athenians had shown towards other poets, as Magnes, Crates, and Cratinus. It appears that Aristophanes used the name of Philonides probably for the *Clouds*, and certainly for the *Wasps*, the *Proagon*, the *Amphiaraüs*, and the *Frogs*. The *Daetaleis*, the *Babylonians*, the *Acharnians*, the *Birds*, and the *Lysistrata* were brought out in the name of Callistratus. Of the extant plays of Aristophanes, the only ones which he is known to have brought out in his own name are the *Knights*, the *Peace*, and the *Plutus*.

Philonŏmé. See TENES.

Philopoemen (Φιλοποίμην). A native of Megalopolis in Arcadia, one of the few great men that Greece produced in the decline of her political independence. The great object of his life was to infuse among the Achaeans a military spirit, and thereby to establish their independence on a firm and lasting basis. He was the son of Craugis, a distinguished man at Megalopolis, and was born about B.C. 252. He lost his father at an early age, and was brought up by Cleander, an illustrious citizen of Mantinea, who had been obliged to leave his native city, and had taken refuge at Megalopolis. He received instruction from Ecdemus and Demophanes, both of whom had studied the Academic philosophy under Arcesilaüs. At an early age he became distinguished by his love of arms and his bravery in war. His name, however, first occurs in history in B.C. 222, when Megalopolis was taken by Cleomenes, and in the following year (221) he fought with conspicuous valour at the battle of Sellasia, in which Cleomenes was completely defeated. In order to gain additional military experience, he soon afterwards sailed to Crete, and served for some years in the wars between the cities of that island. On his return to his native country, in 210, he was appointed commander of the Achaean cavalry; and in 208 he was elected *strategus*, or general of the Achaean League. In this year he defeated Machanidas, tyrant of Lacedaemon, and slew him in battle with his own hand. In 201 he was again elected general of the league, when he defeated Nabis, who had succeeded Machanidas as tyrant of Lacedaemon. Soon afterwards Philopoemen took another voyage to Crete, and assumed the command of the forces of Gortyna. He did not return to Peloponnesus till 194. He was made general of the League in 192, when he again defeated Nabis, who was slain in the course of the year by some Aetolian mercenaries. Philopoemen was reëlected general of the League several times afterwards; but the state of Greece did not afford him much further opportunity for the display of his military abilities. The Romans were now in fact the masters of Greece, and Philopoemen clearly saw that it would be an act of madness to offer open resistance to their authority. At the same time as the Romans still recognized in words the independence of the League, Philopoemen offered a resolute resistance to all their encroachments upon the liberties of his country, whenever he could do so without affording them any pretext for war. In 188, when he was general of the League, he took Sparta, and treated it with the greatest severity. He razed the walls and fortifications of the city, abolished the institutions of Lycurgus, and compelled the citizens to adopt the Achaean laws in their stead. In 183 the Messenians revolted from the Achaean League. Philopoemen, who was general of the League for the eighth time, hastily collected a body of cavalry, and pressed forward to Messenē. He fell in with a large body of Messenian troops, by whom he was taken prisoner and carried to Messenē. Here he was thrown into a dungeon, and was compelled by Dinocrates to drink poison. The news of his death filled the whole of Peloponnesus with grief and rage. An assembly was immediately held at Megalopolis; Lycortas was chosen general; and in the following year he invaded Messenia, which was laid waste far and wide; Dinocrates and the chiefs of his party were obliged to put an end to their lives. The remains of Philopoemen were conveyed to Megalopolis in solemn procession; and the urn which contained the ashes was carried by the historian Polybius. His remains were then interred at Megalopolis with heroic honours, and soon afterwards statues of him were erected in most of the towns belonging to the Achaean League. The life of Philopoemen is narrated by Plutarch. See also Pausan. viii. 49–52.

Philosophia (φιλοσοφία). I. GREEK PHILOSOPHY.—The beginnings of philosophy in Greece came from the Ionians of Asia; and it is in agreement with the character of that people, naturally inclined to the physical or sensualist view, that what the Ionian philosophers sought was the material principle (ἀρχή) of things, and the mode of their origin and disappearance. Thales of Miletus (about B.C. 640) is reputed the father of Greek philosophy. He declared water to be the basis of all things. Next came Anaximander of Miletus (about B.C. 611–547), the first writer on philosophy. He assumed as the first principle an undefined substance (τὸ ἄπειρον) without qualities, out of which the primary antitheses, hot and cold, moist and dry, became differentiated. His countryman and younger contemporary, Anaximenes, took for his principle air, conceiving it as modified, by thickening and thinning, into fire, wind, clouds, water, and earth. Heraclitus of Ephesus (about B.C. 535–475) assumed as the principle of substance aetherial fire. From fire all things originate, and return to it again by a never-resting process of development. All things, therefore, are in a perpetual flux (πάντα ῥεῖ).

Philosophy was first brought into connection with practical life by Pythagoras of Samos (about 582–504), from whom it received its name ("the love of wisdom"). Regarding the world as a perfect harmony, dependent on number, he aimed at inducing mankind likewise to lead a harmonious life. His doctrine was adopted and extended by a large following, especially in Lower Italy.

That country was also the home of the Eleatic doctrine of the One, called after the town of Elea, the headquarters of the school. It was founded by Xenophanes of Colophon (born about 570), the father of pantheism, who declared God to be the eternal unity, permeating the universe, and governing it by his thought. His great disciple, Parmenides of Elea (born about 511), affirmed the one unchanging existence to be alone true and capable of being conceived, and multitude and change to be an appearance without reality. This doctrine was maintained dialectically by his younger countryman Zeno in a polemic against the vulgar opinion, which sees in things multitude, becoming, and change. Empedocles of Agrigentum (born 492) appears to have been partly in agreement with the Eleatic School, partly in opposition to it: on the one hand, maintaining the unchangeable nature of substance; while, on the other, he supposes a plurality of such substances—i. e. the four elements, earth, water, air, and fire. Of these the world is built up, by the agency of two ideal principles as motive forces—viz., love as the cause of union, hate as the cause of separation.

Anaxagoras of Clazomenae (born about B.C. 500) also maintained the existence of an ordering principle as well as a material substance, and while regarding the latter as an infinite multitude of imperishable primary elements, qualitatively distinguished, conceived divine reason as ordering them. He referred all generation and disappearance to mixture and resolution respectively. To him belongs the credit of first establishing philosophy at Athens, in which city it reached its highest development, and continued to have its home for one thousand years without intermission. The first explicitly materialistic system was formed by Democritus of Abdera (born about B.C. 460). This was the doctrine of atoms—small primary bodies infinite in number, indivisible and imperishable, qualitatively similar, but distinguished by their shapes. Falling eternally through the infinite void, they collide and unite, thus generating existence, and forming objects which differ in accordance with the varieties, in number, size, shape, and arrangement, of the atoms which compose them.

The efforts of all these earlier philosophers had been directed somewhat exclusively to the investigation of the ultimate basis and essential nature of the external world. Hence their conceptions of human knowledge, arising out of their theories as to the constitution of things, had been no less various. The Eleatics, for example, had been compelled to deny the existence of any objective truth, since to the world of sense, with its multitude and change, they allowed only a phenomenal existence. This inconsistency led to the position taken up by the class of persons known as Sophists (see SOPHISTAE), that all thought rests solely on the apprehensions of the senses and on subjective impression, and that therefore we have no other standard of action than utility for the individual.

A new period of philosophy opens with the Athenian Socrates (469–399). Like the Sophists, he rejected entirely the physical speculations in which his predecessors had indulged, and made the subjective thoughts and opinions of men his starting-point; but whereas it was the thoughts and opinions of the individual that the Sophists took for the standard, Socrates endeavoured to extract from the common intelligence of mankind an objective rule of practical life. For this purpose he employed the two forms of philosophical inquiry of which he is the inventor, induction and definition. Such a standard he saw in knowledge, by which term he understood the cognition in thought of the true concept of an object, and identified it with virtue; that is to say, such action as proceeds from clear cognition of the concept appropriate to the circumstances. Thus, although Socrates did not himself succeed in establishing a genuine ethical principle, he is nevertheless the founder of ethics, as he is also of dialectic, the method of the highest speculative thought. Of Socrates' numerous disciples many either added nothing to his doctrine, or developed it in a one-sided manner, by confining themselves exclusively either to dialectic or to ethics. Thus while the Athenian Xenophon contented himself, in a series of writings, with exhibiting the portrait of his master to the best of his comprehension, and added nothing original, the Megarian School, founded by Euclides of Megara, devoted themselves almost entirely to dialectic investigation; whereas ethics preponderated both with the Cynics and Cyrenaics, although the position taken up by these two schools was in direct antithesis. For Antisthenes of Athens, the founder of the Cynics, conceived the highest good to be the virtue which spurns every enjoyment; while Aristippus of Cyrené, the founder of the Cyrenaics, considered pleasure to be the sole end in life, and regarded virtue as a good only in so far as it contributed to pleasure. See CYRENAÏCI.

Both aspects of the genius of Socrates were first united in Plato of Athens (428–348), who also combined with them all the principles established by earlier philosophers, in so far as they had been legitimate, and developed the whole of this material into the unity of a comprehensive system. The groundwork of Plato's scheme, though nowhere expressly stated by him, is the threefold division of philosophy into dialectic, ethics, and physics; its central point is the theory of ideas. This theory is a combination of the Eleatic doctrine of the One with Heraclitus's theory of a perpetual flux and with the Socratic method of concepts. The multitude of objects of sense, being involved in perpetual change, are thereby deprived of all genuine existence. The only true being in them is founded upon the ideas, the eternal, unchangeable (independent of all that is accidental, and therefore perfect) types, of which the particular objects of sense are imperfect copies. The number of the ideas is defined by the number of universal concepts which can be derived from the particular objects of sense. The highest idea is that of the Good, which is the ultimate basis of the rest, and the first cause of being and knowledge. Apprehensions derived from the impressions of sense can never give us the knowledge of true being—i. e. of the ideas. It can only be obtained by the soul's activity within itself, apart from the troubles and disturbances of sense; that is to say, by the exercise of reason. Dialectic, as the instrument in this process, leading us to knowledge of the ideas, and finally of the highest idea of the Good, is the first of sciences (*scientia scientiarum*). In physics, Plato adhered (though not without original modifications) to the views of the Pythagoreans, making Nature a harmonic unity in multiplicity. His ethics are founded throughout on the Socratic; with him, too, virtue is knowledge, the cognition of the supreme idea of the Good. And since in this cognition the three parts of the soul, cognitive, spirited, and appetitive, all have their share, we get the three virtues, Wisdom, Courage, and Temperance or Continence. The bond which unites the other virtues is the virtue of Justice, by which each several part of the soul is confined to the performance of its proper function. The school founded by Plato, called "the Academy," from the name of the grove of the Attic hero Academus, where he used to deliver his lectures, continued for long after. (See ACADEMIA.) In regard to the main tendencies of its members, it was divided into the three periods of the Old, Middle, and New Academy. The chief personages in the first of these were Speusippus (son of Plato's sister), who succeeded him as the head of the school (till 339), and Xenocrates of Chalcedon (till 314). Both of them sought to fuse Pythagorean speculations on number with Plato's theory of ideas. The two other Academies were still further removed from the specific doctrines of Plato. See PLATO.

The most important among Plato's disciples is Aristotle of Stagira (384–322), who shares with his master the title of the greatest philosopher of antiquity. But whereas Plato had sought to elucidate and explain things from the suprasensual standpoint of the ideas. his pupil preferred to start from the facts given us by experience. Philosophy to him meant science, and its aim was the recognition of the "wherefore" in all things. Hence he endeavours to attain to the ultimate grounds of things by induction—that is to say, by *a posteriori* conclusions from a number of facts to a universal. In the series of works collected under the name of *Organon*, Aristotle sets forth, almost in a final form, the laws by which the human understanding effects conclusions from the particular to the knowledge of the universal. Like Plato, he recognizes the true being of things in their concepts, but denies any separate existence of the concept apart from the particular objects of sense. They are inseparable as matter and form. In this antithesis, matter and form, Aristotle sees the fundamental principles of being. Matter is the basis of all that exists; it comprises the potentiality of everything, but of itself is not actually anything. A determinate thing only comes into being when the potentiality in matter is converted into actuality. This is effected by form, the idea existent not as one outside the many, but as one in the many, the completion of the potentiality latent in the matter. Although it has no existence apart from the particulars, yet, in rank and estimation, form stands first; it is of its own nature the most knowable, the only true object of knowledge. For matter without any form cannot exist, but the essential definitions of a common form, in which are included the particular objects, may be separated from matter. Form and matter are relative terms, and the lower form constitutes the matter of a higher (e. g. body, soul, reason). This series culminates in pure, immaterial form, the Deity, the origin of all motion, and therefore of the generation of actual form out of potential matter. All motion takes place in space and time; for space is the potentiality, time the measure of the motion. Living beings are those which have in them a moving principle, or soul. In plants the function of soul is nutrition (including reproduction); in animals, nutrition and sensation; in men, nutrition, sensation, and intellectual activity. The perfect form of the human soul is reason separated from all connection with the body, hence fulfilling its activity without the help of any corporeal organ, and so imperishable. By reason the apprehensions, which are formed in the soul by external sense-impressions, and may be true or false, are converted into knowledge. For reason alone can attain to truth either in cognition or action. Impulse towards the good is a part of human nature, and on this is founded virtue; for Aristotle does not, with Plato, regard virtue as knowledge pure and simple, but as founded on nature, habit, and reason. Of the particular virtues (of which there are as many as there are contingencies in life), each is the apprehension, by means of reason, of the proper mean between two extremes which are not virtues—e. g. courage is the mean between cowardice and foolhardiness. The end of human activity, or the highest good, is happiness, or perfect and reasonable activity in a perfect life. To this, however, external goods are more or less necessary conditions. See ARISTOTELES.

The followers of Aristotle, known as Peripatetics (Theophrastus of Lesbos, Eudemus of Rhodes, Strato of Lampsacus, etc.), to a great extent abandoned metaphysical speculation, some in favour of natural science, others of a more popular treatment of ethics, introducing many changes into the Aristotelian doctrine in a naturalistic direction. A return to the views of the founder first appears among the later Peripatetics, who did good service as expositors of Aristotle's works. The tendency of the Peripatetic School, to make philosophy the exclusive property of the learned class, thereby depriving it of its power to benefit a wider circle, soon produced a reaction; and philosophers returned to the practical standpoint of Socratic ethics. The speculations of the learned were only admitted in philosophy where immediately serviceable for ethics. The chief consideration was how to popularize doctrines, and to provide the individual, in a time of general confusion and dissolution, with a fixed moral basis for practical life.

Such were the aims of Stoicism, founded at Athens about 310 by Zeno of Cittium, and brought to fuller systematic form by his successors as heads of the school, Cleanthes of Assos, and especially Chrysippus of Soli, who died about 206. Their doctrines contained little that was new, seeking rather to give a practical application to the dogmas which they took ready-made from previous systems. With them philosophy is the science of the principles on which the moral life ought to be founded. The only allowable endeavour is towards the attainment of knowledge of things human and divine, in order to regulate life thereby. The method to lead men to true knowledge is provided by logic; physics embraces the doctrines as to the nature and organization of the universe; while ethics draws from them its conclusions for practical life. All knowledge originates in the real impressions of things on the senses, which the soul, being at birth a *tabula rasa,* receives in the form of presentations. These presentations, when confirmed by repeated experience, are syllogistically developed by the understanding into concepts. The test of their truth is the convincing or persuasive force with which they impress themselves upon the soul. In physics the foundation of the Stoic doctrine was the dogma that all true being is corporeal. Within the corporeal they recognized two principles, matter and force—i. e. the material, and the Deity permeating and informing it. Ultimately, however, the two are identical. There is nothing in the world with any independent existence: all is bound together by an unalterable chain of causation. The concord of human action with the law of nature, of the human will with the divine will, or life according to nature, is Virtue, the chief good and highest end in life. It is essentially one, the particular or cardinal virtues of Plato being only different aspects of it; it is completely sufficient for happiness, and incapable of any differences of degree. All good actions are absolutely equal in merit, and so are all bad actions. All that lies between virtue and vice is neither good nor bad; at most, it is distinguished as preferable, undesirable, or absolutely indifferent. Virtue is fully possessed only by the wise man, who is no way inferior in worth to Zeus; he is lord over his own life, and may end it by his own free choice. In general, the prominent characteristic of Stoic philosophy is moral heroism, often verging on asceticism. See ZENO.

The same goal which was aimed at in Stoicism was also approached, from a diametrically opposite position, in the system founded about the same time by Epicurus, of the deme Gargettus in Attica (342–268), who brought it to completion himself. Epicureanism, like Stoicism, is connected with previous systems. Like Stoicism, it is also practical in its ends, proposing to find in reason and knowledge the secret of a happy life, and admitting abstruse learning only where it serves the ends of practical wisdom. Hence, logic (called by Epicurus κανονικόν, or the doctrine of canons of truth) is made entirely subservient to physics, physics to ethics. The standards of knowledge and canons of truth in theoretical matters are the impressions of the senses, which are true and indisputable, together with the presentations formed from such impressions, and opinions extending beyond those impressions, in so far as they are supported or not contradicted by the evidence of the senses. In practical questions the feelings of pleasure and pain are the tests. Epicurus's physics, in which he follows in essentials the materialistic system of Democritus, are intended to refer all phenomena to a natural cause, in order that a knowledge of nature may set men free from the bondage of disquieting superstitions. In ethics he followed within certain limits the Cyrenaic doctrine, conceiving the highest good to be happiness, and happiness to be found in pleasure, to which the natural impulses of every being are directed. But the aim is not with him, as it is with the Cyrenaics, the pleasure of the moment, but the enduring condition of pleasure, which, in its essence, is freedom from the greatest of evils, pain. Pleasures and pains are, however, distinguished not merely in degree, but in kind. The renunciation of a pleasure or endurance of a pain is often a means to a greater pleasure; and since pleasures of sense are subordinate to the pleasures of the soul, the undisturbed peace of the soul is a higher good than the freedom of the body from pain. Virtue is desirable not for itself, but for the sake of pleasure of soul, which it secures by freeing men from trouble and fear and moderating their passions and appetites. The cardinal virtue is wisdom, which is shown by true insight in calculating the consequences of our actions as regards pleasure or pain. See EPICURUS.

The practical tendency of Stoicism and Epicureanism, seen in the search for happiness, is also apparent in the Sceptical School founded by Pyrrho of Elis (about 365–275). Pyrrho disputes the possibility of attaining truth by sensuous apprehension, reason, or the two combined, and thence infers the necessity of total suspension of judgment on things. Thus can we attain release from all bondage to theories, a condition which is followed, like a shadow, by that imperturbable state of mind which is the foundation of true happiness. Pyrrho's doctrine was followed by the Middle and New Academies (see above), represented by Arcesilaüs of Pitanè (316–241) and Carneades of Cyrene (214–129) respectively, in their attacks on the Stoics, for asserting a criterion of truth in our knowledge, although they considered that what they were maintaining was a genuine tenet of Socrates and Plato. The latest Academics, such as Antiochus of Ascalon (about B.C. 80), fused with Platonism certain Peripatetic and many Stoic dogmas, thus making way for Eclecticism, to which all later antiquity tended after Greek philosophy had spread itself over the Roman world. After the Christian era Pythagoreanism, in a resuscitated form, again takes its place among the more important systems; but the preëminence belongs to Platonism, which is notably represented in the works of Plutarch of Chaeronea and the physician Galen, while Scepticism is maintained by another physician, Sextus Empiricus.

The closing period of Greek philosophy is marked in the third century A.D. by the establishment in Rome, under Plotinus of Lycopolis in Egypt (205–270), of Neoplatonism, a scientific philosophy of religion, in which the doctrine of Plato is fused with the most important elements in the Aristotelian and Stoic systems and with Oriental speculations. At the summit of existences stands the One or the Good, as the source of all things. It generates from itself, as if from the reflection of its own being, reason, wherein is contained the infinite store of ideas. Soul, the copy of the reason, is generated by and contained in it, as reason is in the One, and, by informing matter in itself non-existent, constitutes bodies whose existence is contained in soul. Nature, therefore, is a whole, endowed with life and soul. Soul, being chained to matter, longs to escape from the bondage of the body and return to its original source. In virtue and philosophic thought it has the power to elevate itself above the reason into a state of ecstasy, where it can behold, or ascend up to, that one good primary Being whom reason cannot know. To attain this union with the Good, or God, is the true function of man, to whom the external world should be absolutely indifferent. Plotinus's most important disciple, the Syrian Porphyrius, contented himself with popularizing his master's doctrine. But the school of Iamblichus, a disciple of Porphyrius, effected a change in the position of Neoplatonism, which now took up the cause of polytheism against Christianity, and adopted for this purpose every conceivable form of superstition, especially those of the East. Foiled in the attempt to resuscitate the old beliefs, its supporters then turned with fresh ardour to scientific work, and especially to the study of Plato and Aristotle, in the interpretation of whose works they rendered great services. The last home of philosophy was at Athens, where Proclus (411–485) sought to reduce to a kind of system the whole mass of philosophic tradition, till in A.D. 529 the teaching of philosophy at Athens was forbidden by Justinian.

II. ROMAN PHILOSOPHY is throughout founded on the Greek. Interest in the subject was first excited at Rome in B.C. 155 by an Athenian embassy, consisting of the Academic Carneades, the Stoic Diogenes, and the Peripatetic Critolaüs. Of more permanent influence was the work of the Stoic Panaetius, the friend of the younger Scipio and of Laelius; but a thorough study of Greek philosophy was first introduced in the time of Cicero and Varro. In a number of works they endeavoured to make it accessible even to those of their countrymen who were outside the learned circles. Cicero chiefly took it up in a spirit of Eclecticism; but among his contemporaries Epicureanism is represented in the poetical treatise of Lucretius (q. v.) on the nature of things, and Pythagoreanism by Nigidius Figulus. In imperial times Epicureanism and Stoicism were most popular, especially the latter, as represented by the writings of Seneca, Cornutus, and the emperor Marcus Aurelius; while Eclectic Platonism was taken up by Apuleius of Madaura. One of the latest philosophical writers of antiquity is Boëthius, whose writings were the chief source of information as to Greek philosophy during the first centuries of the Middle Ages. See BOËTHIUS.

Useful works on the general history of the philosophy of Greece and Rome are the following: Ueberweg, *A History of Philosophy*, vol. i. (Eng. trans., N. Y. 1875), valuable for its bibliography; Ritter and Preller, *Historia Philosophiae*

Graecae et Romanae ex Fontium Locis Contexta (Berlin, 1878; ed. Schultess, Gotha, 1887); Schwegler, *History of Philosophy* (Eng. trans., N. Y. 1882); J. B. Mayor, *A Sketch of Ancient Philosophy from Thales to Cicero* (Cambridge, 1881); Burner, *Early Greek Philosophy* (London, 1892). Zeller's *Die Philosophie der Griechen in ihrer geschichtlichen Entwicklung dargestellt* is the fullest of all works yet published, 5 vols. with index (Berlin, 1874–79). A short syllabus is Scott's *Simple History of Greek Philosophy*, in 91 pp. (London, 1894).

For special periods, the following portions of Zeller's great work, in English translation, may be recommended: *Pre-Socratic Schools* (London, 1880); *Socrates and the Socratic Schools* (2d ed., London, 1877); *Stoics, Epicureans, and Skeptics* (London, 1870); *Plato and the Older Academy* (London, 1877); *Aristotle and the Elder Peripatetics* (London, 1882); *History of Eclecticism in Greek Philosophy* (London, 1883); also Teichmüller, *Xenophon und Platon* (1884); Lange, *History of Materialism*, 2 vols. (Eng. trans., London, 1878–81); Denis, *Histoire des Idées Morales dans l'Antiquité* (2d ed., Paris, 1879); Martha, *Les Moralistes sous l'Empire Romain* (Paris, 1872); Herbart, *Die Philosophie des Cicero* (Leipzig, 1842); Burmeister, *Cicero als Neuakademiker* (Oldenburg, 1860); Levin, *Lectures on the Philosophy of Cicero* (London, 1871); Holzherr, *De Philosophia Senecae* (Rastatt, 1858); Binde, *Seneca de Rerum Natura et Vita Humana* (Glogau, 1883); and Havet, *Le Christianisme et ses Origines* (Paris, 1873).

Philosophy. See PHILOSOPHIA.

Philostrătus (*Φιλόστρατος*). (1) FLAVIUS PHILOSTRĂTUS the elder, a Greek Sophist of Lemnos, son of a celebrated Sophist of the same name. He taught first in Athens, then at Rome till the middle of the third century A.D. By order of his great patroness Iulia Domna, the learned wife of the emperor Septimius Severus, he wrote (*a*) the romantic *Life of Apollonius of Tyana*. Besides this we have by him (*b*) a work entitled *Heroicus* (*Ἡρωικός*), consisting of mythical histories of the heroes of the Trojan War in the form of a dialogue, designed to call back to life the expiring popular religion; (*c*) lives of the Sophists (*Bίοι Σοφιστῶν*), in two books, the first dealing with twenty-six philosophers, the second with thirty-three rhetoricians of earlier as well as later times, a work important for the history of Greek culture, especially during the imperial age; (*d*) seventy-three letters, partly amatory in subject; (*e*) a fragment of a work intended to revive interest in the old *Gymnastic*; lastly (*f*), the *Imagines* (*Εἰκόνες*), in two books, being descriptions of sixty-six paintings on all possible subjects. Of these it is doubtful whether, as he pretends, they really belonged to a gallery at Naples, a statement accepted by Brunn, or whether their subjects were invented by himself, as maintained by Friederichs and Matz. Like all his writings, this work is skilful and pleasing in its manner, and the interest of its topic makes it particularly attractive. It is not so much designed to incite to the study of works of art as to exhibit the art of painting in a totally new field; and herein he is followed both by his grandson and namesake and by Callistratus (q. v.). The works of Philostratus are collected and edited by Kayser (Leipzig, 1870–71), and translated into English by Berwick (London, 1809). See Brunn, *Die Philostratischen Gemälde* (1861); and Bertrand, *Philostrate et son École* (1882). A new edition of the *Imagines* was published by the members of the Vienna Classical Seminary in 1893.

(2) PHILOSTRĂTUS THE YOUNGER, grandson of the preceding, of Lemnos. He lived chiefly at Athens, and died at Lemnos, A.D. 264. Following his grandfather's lead, he devoted himself to the rhetorical description of paintings; but fell considerably behind his model both in invention and descriptive power, as is proved by the sixteen extant *Imagines*, the first book of a larger collection. Printed in Kayser's edition of the preceding.

Philōtas (*Φιλώτας*). A son of Parmenio. He distinguished himself on many occasions as a commander of cavalry under Alexander the Great, but was at last accused of conspiring against the king's life. An informer said that he had at first told his secret to Philotas, who had daily access to Alexander, but who had taken no notice of it for two days, at the end of which time, through the means of another officer near Alexander's person, the information was conveyed to the king. This threw strong suspicion on Philotas, who, however, was not implicated by either the informer or any of the accused in their confessions. But Craterus, who was jealous of Philotas, on account of the favour which the latter enjoyed with the king, encouraged the suspicions of Alexander, who recollected what Philotas had said at the time when the former claimed Zeus Ammon for his father, that he pitied those who were doomed to serve a man that fancied himself to be a god. Craterus had also, for some time previous, bribed a courtesan intimate with Philotas, who reported to him, and, through him, to the king, all the expressions of discontent uttered by Philotas in his unguarded moments. In short, Alexander was induced to order Philotas to be tortured in consequence of the suggestions of Craterus, Hephaestion, and others of the king's companions. The torture was administered by Craterus himself, and Philotas, after enduring dreadful agonies, confessed, though in vague terms, that he had conspired against the life of Alexander, and that his father Parmenio was cognizant of it. This being considered sufficient evidence, Philotas was stoned to death; and Parmenio suffered not long after him. See PARMENIO.

Philoxĕnus (*Φιλόξενος*). (1) A famous Greek dithyrambic poet, of Cythera, born in B.C. 435. He came as a prisoner of war into the possession of the Athenian musician Melanippides, by whom he was educated and set free. He lived long at Syracuse, at the court of the tyrant Dionysius I., who threw him into the stone-quarries for outspoken criticism on his bad poems. On his escape from Sicily he revenged himself on the tyrant, who was short-sighted or perhaps blind of one eye, by witty raillery in the most famous of his twenty-four dithyrambs, the *Cyclops*, which describes the love of the one-eyed Polyphemus for the beautiful nymph Galatea. He died B.C. 380, at Ephesus, after visiting various places in Greece, Italy, and Asia Minor for the public performance of his compositions. These were celebrated among the ancients for originality of expression and rich variety of melody. We have only some considerable fragments of a lyric poem entitled *The Banquet* (*Δεῖπνον*), in which the burlesque subject affords a comic contrast to the dignified Doric rhythm. Edition by Bippart (Leipzig, 1843), and in Bergk, *Poet. Lyrici Graeci.* (2) A Macedonian officer of Alexander the Great who received from Perdiccas the government of Cilicia in B.C. 321. (3) An Alexandrian grammarian who taught in Rome and wrote on Homer and the Greek dialects, besides compiling a glossary which has been preserved and edited by H. Stephanus (Paris, 1573). See LEXICON.

Philus, FURĬUS. (1) PUBLIUS, was consul B.C. 223 with C. Flaminius, and accompanied his colleague in his campaign against the Gauls in the north of Italy. He was praetor in 216, when he commanded the fleet with which he proceeded to Africa. In 214 he was censor with M. Atilius Regulus, but died at the beginning of the following year. (2) LUCIUS, consul B.C. 136, received Spain as his province, and was commissioned by the Senate to deliver up to the Numantines C. Hostilius Mancinus, the consul of the preceding year. Philus, like his contemporaries Scipio Africanus the younger and Laelius, was fond of Greek literature and refinement. He is introduced by Cicero as one of the speakers in his dialogue *De Republica.*

Phily̆ra (Φιλύρα). One of the Oceanides, and the mother of Chiron by Cronos. The god, dreading the jealousy of his wife Rhea, changed Philyra into a mare and himself into a horse. The offspring of their love was the Centaur Chiron, half man, half horse. Philyra was so ashamed of the monstrous shape of the child that she prayed the gods to change her form and nature. She was accordingly metamorphosed into the linden-tree, called by her name among the Greeks (φιλύρα). (Hyg. *Fab.* 138.) See ACHERON; STYX.

Phily̆ra (φιλύρα). A thin strip cut from the inner coat of the papyrus and glued with others to form a page for writing. (See PAPYRUS.) The name is often given to a strip of linden bark used in making garlands of flowers *(coronae sutiles)*. See Hor. *Carm.* i. 38, 2; and CORONA.

Phimus (φιμός). A dice-box for which the Latin name is *fritillus*. See TESSERA.

Phineus (Φινεύς). (1) Son of Belus and Anchinoë, and brother of Cepheus. He was slain by Perseus. For details see ANDROMEDA and PERSEUS. (2) Son of Agenor, and king of Salmydessus in Thrace. He was first married to Cleopatra, the daughter of Boreas and Orithyia, by whom he had two children, Oryithus (Oarthus) and Crambis; but their names are different in the different legends: Ovid calls them Polydectus and Polydorus. Afterwards he was married to Idaea (some call her Dia, Eurytia, or Idothea), by whom he again had two sons, Thynus and Mariandynus.

Phineus was a blind soothsayer, who had received his prophetic powers from Apollo; but the cause of his blindness is not the same in all accounts. He is most celebrated on account of his being tormented by the Harpies, who were sent by the gods to punish him on account of his cruelty towards his sons by the first marriage. His second wife falsely accused them of having made an attempt upon her virtue, whereupon Phineus put out their eyes, or, according to others, exposed them to be devoured by wild beasts, or ordered them to be half buried in the earth, and then to be scourged. Therefore the gods struck him with blindness and sent the Harpies to torment him. Whenever a meal was placed before Phineus, the Harpies darted down from the air and carried it off; later writers add that they either devoured the food themselves or rendered it unfit to be eaten. When the Argonauts visited Thrace, Phineus promised to instruct them respecting their voyage, if they would deliver him from the monsters. This was done by Zetes and Calaïs, the sons of Boreas, and brothers of Cleopatra (Apollon. ii. 284). Phineus now explained to the Argonauts the further course they had to take, and especially cautioned them against the Symplegades. According to another story the Argonauts, on their arrival at Thrace, found the sons of Phineus half buried, and demanded their liberation, which Phineus refused. A battle thereupon ensued, in which Phineus was slain by Heracles. The latter also delivered Cleopatra from her confinement, and restored the kingdom to the sons of Phineus; and on their advice he also sent the second wife of Phineus back to her father, who ordered her to be put to death. Some traditions, lastly, state that Phineus was killed by Boreas, or that he was carried off by the Harpies into the country of the Bistones or Milchessians. Those accounts in which Phineus is stated to have put out the eyes of his sons add that they had their sight restored to them by the sons of Boreas, or by Asclepius.

Phintias (Φιντίας). (1) A Pythagorean, the friend of Damon, who was condemned to die by Dionysius the elder. For details, see DAMON. (2) A tyrant of Agrigentum, who established his power over that city during the period of confusion which followed the death of Agathocles (B.C. 289). He founded a new city on the southern coast of Sicily, to which he gave his own name, and whither he removed all the inhabitants from Gela, which he razed to the ground.

Phlebotŏmus (φλεβοτόμος). A lancet for opening a vein (Veget. *Vet.* i. 19).

Phlegĕthon (Φλεγέθων), "the flaming," and **Pyriphlĕgthon** (Πυριφλεγέθων), "flaming with fire." A river in the lower world, in whose channel flowed flames instead of water. See HADES.

Phlegon (Φλέγων). A Greek writer, of Tralles in Caria, freedman of the emperor Hadrian. He wrote in the first half of the second century A.D. a work entitled Περὶ Θαυμασίων ("On Wonderful Events"). It is a tasteless composition, but instructive as to the superstitions of antiquity. Also a dry catalogue of persons who attained a great age (Περὶ Μακροβίων). Of his great chronological work, a catalogue of victors at the Olympian games in 229 Olympiads (B.C. 776 to A.D. 137) in 17 books, only fragments remain. There is an edition of Phlegon by Westermann in his *Paradoxographi* (Brunswick, 1839), and Keller (1877).

Phlegra (τὰ Φλεγραῖα πεδία, PHLEGRAEI CAMPI, Phlegraean fields). The scene of the fight between the gods and the Giants. (See GIGANTES.) It was identified with the volcanic plain which extends along the coast of Campania from Cumae to Capua; and, because of its great productiveness, was called by the Romans Campus Laborinus and Laboriae (Pliny, *H. N.* xviii. 111).

Phlegra. See PALLENÉ.

Phliasia. See PHLIUS.

Phlius (Φλιοῦς). The chief town of a small province in the northeast of Peloponnesus, whose territory, PHLIASIA, was bounded by Sicyonia, Arcadia, and Argos. It was usually allied with Sparta, and under Cleonymus joined the Achaean League (Polyb. ii. 44).

Phobētor (Φοβήτωρ). A dream-god, son of Morpheus. See SOMNUS.

Phocaea (Φώκαια). The northernmost of the Ionian cities on the west coast of Asia Minor, celebrated as a great maritime State, and especially as the founder of the Greek colony of Massilia (q. v.) in Gaul. The name Phocaean is often used with reference to Massilia. It was said to have been founded by Phocian colonists under Philogenes and Damon. It was originally within the limits of Aeolis, in the territory of Cyme; but the Cymaeans voluntarily gave up the site for the new city, which was soon admitted into the Ionian Confederacy on the condition of adopting oecists of the race of Codrus. It was admirably situated, and possessed two excellent harbours, Naustathmus and Lampter. After the Persian conquest of Ionia, Phocaea had so declined that she could only furnish three ships to support the great Ionian revolt; but the spirit of her people had not been extinguished; when the common cause was hopeless, and their city was besieged by Harpalus, they embarked, to seek new abodes in the distant West, and bent their course to their colony of Aetalia in Corsica. During the voyage, however, a portion of the emigrants resolved to return to their native city, which they restored, and which recovered much of its prosperity, as is proved by the rich booty gained by the Romans, when they plundered it under the praetor Aemilius, after which it does not appear as a place of any consequence in history.

Care must be taken not to confound Phocaea with Phocis, or the ethnic adjectives of the former, **Φωκαεύς** and *Phocaeënsis*, with those of the latter, **Φωκεύς** and *Phocensis;* some of the ancient writers themselves have fallen into these mistakes.

Phocas (Φωκᾶς). Emperor of the East from A.D. 602 to 610. He was a Cappadocian of low origin, and began his career as a groom for the general Priscus (q. v.). He won his imperial rank by his reputation for brutal courage and his popularity with the soldiers. He was crowned in succession to Mauricius, against whose authority he had revolted, and whom he caused to be put to death. His short reign was distinguished by a bloody war with the Persians under their king Chosroïs, a war marked by many reverses for the Roman arms. Phocas, instead of taking the field in person, remained at Constantinople, giving himself up to sensual pleasures. A number of insurrections against him followed, and were put down with great severity by Phocas, until Heraclius, son of the exarch of Africa, led a force against Constantinople, which he took by storm, and caused Phocas to be beheaded.

Phocas, COLUMN OF. A pillar fifty-four feet in height, still standing in the Roman Forum, where it was disinterred from the rubbish that covered it, in 1813, at the expense of the Duchess of Devonshire. It was erected by the exarch Smaragdus in A.D. 608 in honour of the emperor Phocas (q. v.), whose gilded statue originally crowned it.

Phocion (Φωκίων). An Athenian general and statesman, son of Phocus. He was a man of humble origin, and appears to have been born in B.C. 402. He studied under Plato and Xenocrates. He distinguished himself for the first time under his friend Chabrias, in 376, at the battle of Naxos; but he was not employed prominently in any capacity for many years afterward. In 354 (according to others in 350) he was sent into Euboea in the command of a small force in consequence of an application from Plutarchus, tyrant of Eretria; and he was subsequently employed on several occasions in the war between the Athenians and Philip of Macedon. He frequently opposed the measures of Demosthenes, and recommended peace with Philip; but he must not be regarded as one of the mercenary supporters of the Macedonian monarch. His virtue is above suspicion, and his public conduct was always influenced by upright motives. When Alexander was marching upon Thebes in 335, Phocion rebuked Demosthenes for his invectives against the king; and after the destruction of Thebes he advised the Athenians to comply with Alexander's demand for the surrender of Demosthenes and other chief orators of the anti-Macedonian party. This proposal was indignantly rejected by the people, and an embassy was sent to Alexander, which succeeded in deprecating his resentment. According to Plutarch, there were two embassies, the first of which Alexander refused to receive, but to the second he gave a gracious audience and granted its prayer, chiefly from regard to Phocion, who was at the head of it. Alexander ever continued to treat Phocion with the utmost consideration, and to cultivate his friendship. He also pressed upon him valuable presents; but Phocion persisted in refusing his presents, begging the king to leave him no less honest than he found him, and only so far availed himself of the royal favour as to request the liberty of certain prisoners at Sardis, which was immediately granted to him. After Alexander's death Phocion opposed vehemently, and with all the caustic bitterness which characterized him, the proposal for war with Antipater. Thus, to Hyperides, who asked him tauntingly when he would advise the Athenians to go to war, he answered, "When I see the young willing to keep their ranks, the rich to contribute of their wealth, and the orators to abstain from pilfering the public money." When the Piraeus was seized by Alexander, the son of Polysperchon, in 318, Phocion was suspected of having advised Alexander to take this step; whereupon, being accused of treason by Agnonides, he fled, with several of his friends, to Alexander, who sent them with letters of recommendation to his father Polysperchon. The latter, willing to sacrifice them as a peace-offering to the Athenians, sent them back to Athens for the people to deal with them as they would. Here Phocion was sentenced to death. To the last he maintained his calm and dignified and somewhat contemptuous bearing. When some wretched man spat upon him as he passed to the prison, "Will no one," said he, "check this fellow's indecency?" To one who asked him whether he had any message to leave for his son Phocus, he answered, "Only that he bear no grudge against the Athenians." And when the hemlock which had been prepared was found insufficient for all the condemned, and the jailer would not furnish more until he was paid for it, "Give the man his money," said Phocion to one of his friends, "since at Athens one cannot even die for nothing." He perished in the year 317, at the age of eighty-five.

The Athenians are said to have repented of their conduct. A brazen statue was raised to the memory of Phocion, and Agnonides was condemned to death. Phocion was twice married, and his second wife appears to have been as simple and frugal in her habits as himself; but he was less fortunate in his son Phocus, who, in spite of his father's lessons and example, was a thorough profligate. As for Phocion himself, commendation of him must be almost wholly confined to his private qualities. His fellow-citizens may have been degenerate, but he made no effort to elevate them. His life is written by Plutarch. See also Morell, *Vita Phocionis* (Leyden, 1869); and Thirlwall, vii. pp. 256 foll.

Phocis (Φωκίς). A country in northern Greece, bounded on the north by the Locri Epicnemidii and Opuntii, on the east by Boeotia, on the west by the Locri Ozolae and Doris, and on the south by the Corinthian Gulf. At one time it possessed a narrow strip of country on the Euboean Sea, with the seaport Daphnus, between the territory of the Locri Epicnemidii and Locri Opuntii. It was a mountainous and unproductive country, and owes its chief importance in history to the fact of its possessing the Delphic oracle. Its chief mountain was Parnassus, situated in the interior of the country, to which, however, Cnemis, on its northern frontier, Cirphis, south of Delphi, and Helicon, on the southeastern frontier, all belonged. The principal river in Phocis was the Cephisus, the valley of which contained almost the only fertile land in the country, with the exception of the celebrated Crissaean Plain in the southwest, on the borders of the Locri Ozolae. Among the earliest inhabitants of Phocis we find mentioned Leleges, Thracians, Abantes, and Hyantes. Subsequently, but still in the ante-historical period, the Phlegyae, an Achaean race, a branch of the Minyae at Orchomenos, took possession of the country; and from this time the main bulk of the population continued to be Achaean, although there were Dorian settlements at Delphi and Bulis. The Phocians are said to have derived their name from an eponymous ancestor Phocus (q. v.), and they are mentioned under this name in the *Iliad*.

The Phocians played no conspicuous part in Greek history till the time of Philip of Macedon; but at this period they became involved in a war, called the Phocian or Sacred War, in which the principal states of Greece took part. The Thebans had long been inveterate enemies of the Phocians; and as the latter people had cultivated a portion of the Crissaean Plain, which the Amphictyons had declared in B.C. 585 should lie waste forever, the Thebans availed themselves of this pretext to persuade the Amphictyons to impose a fine upon the Phocians, and upon their refusal to pay it, the Thebans further induced the council to declare the Phocian land forfeited to the god of Delphi. Thus threatened by the Amphictyonic Council, backed by the whole power of Thebes, the Phocians were persuaded by Philomelus, one of their citizens, to seize Delphi, and to make use of the treasures of the temple for the purpose of carrying on the war. They obtained possession of the temple in B.C. 357. The war which ensued lasted ten years, and was carried on with various success on each side. The Phocians were commanded first by Philomelus, B.C. 357–353, afterward by his brother Onomarchus, 353–352, then by Phaÿllus, the brother of the two preceding, 352–351, and finally by Phalaecus, the son of Onomarchus, 351–346. The Phocians received some support from Athens, but their chief dependence was upon their mercenary troops, which the treasures of the Delphic temple enabled them to hire. The Amphictyons and the Thebans, finding at length that they were unable with their own resources to subdue the Phocians, called in the assistance of Philip of Macedon, who brought the war to a close in 346. The conquerors inflicted the most signal punishment upon the Phocians, who were regarded as guilty of sacrilege. All their towns were razed to the ground with the exception of Abae, and the inhabitants distributed in villages containing no more than fifty inhabitants. The two votes which they had in the Amphictyonic Council were taken away and given to Philip. See PHILIPPUS.

Phocus (Φῶκος). (1) The son of Aeacus and the nymph Psamathé, slain by his half-brothers Telamon and Peleus, who were therefore sent into banishment by Aeacus. From him the country Phocis derived its name (Pausan. ii. 29, 2). (2) The son of Ornytion of Corinth or of Poseidon. He colonized the territory about Mount Parnassus (Pausan. ii. 4, 3).

Phocylĭdes (Φωκυλίδης). An Ionian poet of Miletus, born B.C. 560. His poetry was chiefly gnomic (see EPOS), and only a few fragments of it survive, 18 in number. A poem in 217 hexameters, entitled Ποίημα Νουθετικόν, which has come down under his name, is a later forgery.

Phoebé (Φοίβη). (1) A special name of Artemis as moon-goddess. See ARTEMIS; SELENÉ. (2) The daughter of Uranus and Gaea, and mother by Coeus of Asteria and Leto (Hes. *Theog.* 136, 404). (3) A sister of Clytaemnestra (Ovid, *Heroid.* viii. 77).

Phoebus (Φοῖβος). A special name for Apolol (q. v.).

Phoenīcé (Φοινίκη); PHŒNICIA is found in only one passage (Cic. *De Fin.* iv. 20). Phœnicia; an Asiatic country on the Syrian coast. It was bounded on the north by the river Eleutherus, on the south by Mount Carmel, and on the east by Palestine and Coelesyria. It largely consisted of fertile, well-watered valleys, its chief rivers being the Eleutherus, the Sabbaticus, the Tripolis, the Adonis, the Lycus, the Magoras, the Tamyras, the Leo, the Lita, the Belus, and the Kishon. Its principal cities were Sidon, Tripolis, Byblus, Tyrus, Berytus, and Ptolemaïs. Phœnicia being little more than a narrow strip of coast, was almost necessarily a maritime country, and its cities for many centuries were at the head of naval power in ancient times. See SIDON; TYRUS.

Their commerce extended over the known world, and they became everywhere known for their traffic and dyestuffs, especially the Tyrian purple, glass, tin, and amber. They also, in connection with their commerce, established many colonies within the Mediterranean on various islands (see CYPRUS), on the north coast of Africa (see CARTHAGO), and even on the western coasts of Spain and Africa. They also had settlements on the Euxine Sea. In Gaul the city of Massilia was founded by the Phœnicians.

In race the Phœnicians must be classed as Semitic, as is evident from the language which they spoke and of which our knowledge is derived from a large number of inscriptions, mostly mortuary and votive, found in Phœnicia itself and more numerously on the site of Carthage and Citium. A number of Phœnician phrases are found transliterated in the comedy of Plautus mentioned below. The native Phœnician literature seems not to have been extensive, and of it nothing has been preserved except some fragments such as the Greek translation of Sanchuniathon and Hanno. The inscriptions, such as they are, cover, roughly speaking, a period extending from B.C. 600 to A.D. 250. Like the other Semitic languages the Phœnician is written without the vowel points. Some scholars have regarded the language as being so closely allied to Hebrew as to be almost capable of classification as a Hebrew dialect. Phœnician is more archaic in its structure, simpler in its syntax, and with an apparently limited vocabulary, but this last is perhaps an unsafe generalization owing to the fact that so little material has survived from which to judge of it. The Phœnician script is the prototype of the Greek and Roman alphabets as well as of the principal Semitic scripts. The oldest specimen of it is the Moabite Stone (q v.). The origin of the Phœnician itself is doubtful. Some scholars, like De Rouge, consider it a derivative from the Egyptian hieroglyphics. The language spoken in Carthage was practically the same as the original Phœnician, with differences in the pronunciation and orthography, and to some extent in the script. A curious bit of Phœnician exists in the *Poenulus* of Plautus, where one of the speakers utters some sentences in Carthaginian. The interpretation of the passage has puzzled scholars for generations. See POENULUS.

The influence of the Phœnicians upon Greek art has some importance, as from them the Greeks borrowed the types for all their early gold and silver work and for their vase patterns. The Greek religion was also influenced by them, on which see the article APHRODITÉ.

The internal history of Phœnicia is not very well known, nor is its form of government thoroughly understood. Particularism seems to have been its character, and the different cities of Phœnicia were practically independent of one another. Hence, at different periods, they fell an easy prey to invaders from Egypt, Assyria, Macedon, and Rome. At the earliest period of which we have any knowledge Phœnicia is found a dependency of Egypt, ruled by Egyptian governors and paying an annual tribute. About B.C. 1300 Egypt lost this hold owing to internal disturbances, which compelled her to give up her foreign possessions, and for several centuries after this the importance of the Phœnicians attains its height. About B.C. 800 the Assyrians obtained at least a nominal control and exacted tribute from the Phœnician cities, though without interfering with their commercial importance. Subsequently they were subdued by the Babylonians, the Persians, and the Macedonians, and under the Romans Phœnicia was incorporated into the province of Syria, while under the Empire it became the province of Phœnicé Libanensis.

For the history, see Rawlinson's *History of Phœnicia* (London, 1889); Mover, *Die Phönizier* (3 vols. Bonn, 1841–50); Prutz, *Aus Phönizien* (Leipzig, 1876); Duncker, *History of Antiquity*, Eng. trans. book iii. (London, 1877); Sayce, *Ancient Empires of the East* (London, 1884); Pietschmann, *Geschichte der Phönizier* (Berlin, 1889). On the language, see Levy, *Phönizische Studien* (Breslau, 1864); Schroeder, *Die phönizische Sprache* (Halle, 1869); and Bloch, *Phönizisches Glossar* (Berlin, 1891). The most complete collection of Phœnician inscriptions is that in vol. i. of the *Corpus Inscriptionum Semiticarum* (Paris, 1881–90).

Phoenīcé (Φοινίκη). Now Finiki; a city of Epirus on the coast, in the district Chaonia (Livy, xxix. 12).

Phoenicia. See PHOENICÉ.

Phœnicium Maré (τὸ Φοινίκιον πέλαγος). A name given to that part of the Mediterranean adjoining the coast of Phœnicia.

Phoenīcus (Φοινικοῦς). (1) Also called PHOENIX; a harbour on the southern shore of Crete (Acts, xxvii. 12). (2) A harbour in Messenia. (3) A harbour of Ionia. (4) A city of some size in the southern part of Lycia; on Mount Olympus, whence the city itself is also sometimes called OLYMPUS (Strabo, p. 666). Under the Romans it was a rendezvous for pirates and was destroyed by Servilius Isauricus. See VATIA.

Phoenicūsa. One of the Aeoliae Insulae (q. v.).

Phoenix (Φοίνιξ). A fabulous bird, of which Herodotus gives the following account in that part of his work which treats of Egypt (ii. 73): "The phœnix is another sacred bird, which I have never seen except in effigy. He rarely appears in Egypt; once only in five hundred years, immediately after the death of his father, as the Heliopolitans affirm. If the painters describe him truly, his feathers represent a mixture of crimson and gold, and he resembles the eagle in outline and size. They affirm that he does the following thing, which to me is not credible. They say that he comes from Arabia, and, bringing the body of his father inclosed in myrrh, buries him in the temple of the Sun; and that he brings him in the following manner: First, he moulds as great a quantity of myrrh into the shape of an egg as he is well able to carry; and, after having tried the weight, he hollows out the egg, and puts his parent into it, and stops up with some more myrrh the hole through which he had introduced the body, so that the weight is the same as before: he then carries the whole mass to the temple of the Sun in Egypt. Such is the account they give of the phœnix." Similar stories of marvellous birds are found in Persian literature (of the bird Simorg) and in Sanskrit literature (of the bird Semendar).

Phoenix (Φοίνιξ). Son of Amyntor, king of Argos, and the preceptor of Achilles, to whom he was so attached that he accompanied him to the Trojan War. According to the Homeric account (*Il.* ix. 447 foll.), Amyntor, having transferred his affections from his lawful wife, Hippodamia, to a concubine, the former besought her son Phœnix to gain the affections of his father's mistress, and alienate her from Amyntor. Phœnix succeeded in his suit, and his enraged father imprecated upon him the bitterest curses. The son, therefore, notwithstanding the entreaties and efforts of his relations to detain him at his parent's court, fled to Phthia, in Thessaly, where he was kindly received by Peleus, monarch of the country, who assigned him a territory on the confines of Phthia and the sway over the Dolopians. He intrusted him also with the education of his son Achilles.

Later writers, however, make Amyntor to have put out his son's eyes, and the latter to have fled in this condition to Peleus, who led him to Chiron, and persuaded the Centaur to restore him to sight. There was a play entitled *Phoenix* by Sophocles, another by Euripides, and a third by Ion.

After the death of Achilles, Phoenix, who had gone with him to the Trojan War, was one of those commissioned to return to Greece and bring young Pyrrhus to the war. On the fall of Troy he returned with that prince to Thessaly, in which country he continued to reside until his death.

Phoenix (Φοίνιξ). (1) A harbour in Crete. See PHOENICUS. (2) A river in Malis. (3) A river in the north of Thessaly.

Pholoë (Φολόη). A mountain forming the boundary between Arcadia and Elis; mentioned as one of the abodes of the Centaurs. See PHOLUS.

Pholus (Φόλος). A Centaur, son of Silenus and the nymph Melia. In the performance of his fourth task, which was to bring the Erymanthian boar alive to Eurystheus, Heracles (q. v.) took his road through Pholoë, where he was hospitably entertained by Pholus. The Centaur set before his guest roast meat, though he himself fared on raw. Heracles asking for wine, his host said he feared to open the jar, which was the common property of the Centaurs; but, when pressed by the hero, he consented to unclose it for him. The fragrance of the wine spread over the mountain, and soon brought all the Centaurs, armed with stones and pine sticks, to the cave of Pholus. The first who ventured to enter were driven back by Heracles with burning brands: he hunted the remainder with his arrows to Malea. When Heracles returned to Pholoë from this pursuit, he found Pholus lying dead along with several others; for, having drawn the arrow out of the body of one of them, while he was wondering how so small a thing could destroy such large beings, it dropped out of his hand and stuck in his foot, and he died immediately (Apollod. ii. 5, 4 foll.).

Phonetics. See PHILOLOGIA; GREEK, PRONUNCIATION OF; LATIN, PRONUNCIATION OF.

Phonos (φόνος). The Greek term for manslaughter, homicide. Originally in Greek the right of private vengeance was recognized, and only a ceremonious purification was required of those who thus took life (Antiph. *De Caede Herod.* 11). This primitive custom was disused at Athens as early as the time of the Draconian legislature, and survived in only a few special instances, as where the husband might kill the adulterer whom he caught in the act (see ADULTERIUM); personal chastity might also be defended by bloodshed. From this time, kinsmen of a deceased person, instead of becoming the lawful slayers of his murderer, were rather the legitimate prosecutors before the courts. In Attic law *φόνος ἑκούσιος* is the term for murder, and *φόνος ἀκούσιος* for manslaughter. All suits involving questions of homicide (*φονικαὶ δίκαι*) were under the jurisdiction of the Archon Basileus, assisted by the Ephetae. They were tried in the Court of the Areopagus, or in any of the four courts over which the Ephetae presided. The proceedings took place in the open air, lest the judges should be under the same roof with one accused of impiety. The Archon Basileus presided, and the trial occupied two days. On the third day the judges voted on the question of the acquittal of the accused. Wilful murder was punished with death (Antiph. l. c. 10); less serious cases by fine or exile. For details, see EPHETAE.

Phorbantia. See AEGATES.

Phorbas (Φόρβας). (1) The son of Lapithes and Orsinomé, and brother of Periphas. The Rhodians, in pursuance of an oracle, are said to have invited him into their island to deliver it from snakes, and afterwards to have honoured him with heroic worship. From this circumstance he was called Ophiuchus, and is said by some to have been placed among the stars (Diod. v. 54). According to another tradition, Phorbas went from Thessaly to Olenos, where Alector, king of Elis, made use of his assistance against Pelops, and shared his kingdom with him. Phorbas then gave his daughter Diogenia in marriage to Alector, and he himself married Hyrminé, a sister of Alector, by whom he became the father of Augeas and Actor. He is also described as a bold boxer, and is said to have plundered the temple of Delphi along with the Phlegyae, but to have been defeated by Apollo. (2) One of the followers of Aeneas, whose form was assumed by the god of Sleep to deceive Palinurus. (Verg. *Aen.* v. 842.)

Phorcus, Phorcys, or **Phorcyn** (Φόρκος, Φόρκυς, Φόρκυν). (1) A sea-deity, described by Homer as "the old man of the sea," to whom a harbour in Ithaca was dedicated, and is called the father of the nymph Thoosa. Later writers call him a son of Pontus and Gaea, and a brother of Thaumas, Nereus, Eurybia, and Ceto. By his sister Ceto he became the father of the Graeae and Gorgones, the Hesperian dragon, and the Hesperides; and by Hecaté or Crataïs, he was the father of Scylla. (2) The son of Phaenops, commander of the Phrygians of Ascania, assisted Priam in the Trojan War, but was slain by Aiax.

Phorcy̆des, Phorcĭdes, or **Phorcynĭdes**. See GORGONES; GRAEAE.

Phorminx (φόρμιγξ). A Greek stringed instrument. See LYRA.

Phormio. A comedy of Terence. See TERENTIUS.

Phormion (Φορμίων). (1) A celebrated Athenian general, the son of Asopius. He distinguished himself particularly in the command of an Athenian fleet in the Corinthian Gulf, where with far inferior forces he gained some brilliant victories over the Peloponnesian fleet in B.C. 429. In the ensuing winter he landed on the coast of Acarnania, and advanced into the interior, where he also gained some successes (Thucyd. ii. 80–92, 102; Diod. xii. 37–47). He was a man of remarkably temperate habits and a strict disciplinarian. (2) A Peripatetic philosopher of Ephesus, of whom is told the story that he discoursed for several hours before Hannibal on the military art and the duties of a general. When his admiring listeners asked Hannibal what he thought of him, the latter replied that of all the old fools whom he had ever seen, none could match Phormion (Cic. *De Orat.* ii. 18, 75).

Phormis (Φόρμις) or **Phormos** (Φόρμος). A Greek poet, writer of Dorian comedy. He was born in Arcadia, but removed to Sicily, where he became instructor to the children of the tyrant Gelon. After serving with success in the army under both Gelon and Hiero, he dedicated gifts to

Zeus at Olympia and to Apollo at Delphi as thank-offerings. Aristotle (*Poët.* 5) couples his name with that of Epicharmus (q. v.) as a founder of comedy. See COMOEDIA.

Phorōneus (Φορωνεύς). A son of Inachus and the Oceanid Melia or Archia, was a brother of Aegialeüs and the ruler of Argos. He was married to the nymph Laodicé, by whom he became the father of Niobé, Apis, and Car. According to other writers, his sons were Pelasgus, Iasus, and Agenor, who, after their father's death, divided the kingdom of Argos among themselves. Phoroneus is said to have been the first who offered sacrifices to Heré at Argos, and to have united the people, who, until then, had lived in scattered habitations, into a city which was called after him *ἄστυ Φορωνικόν* (Pausan. ii. 15, 5). The patronymic PHORONĬDES is sometimes used of the Argives in general, and especially to designate Amphiaraüs and Adrastus. Ovid (*Met.* i. 668) calls Io, who was a descendant of Phoroneus, *Phoronis*.

Phoros (φορος). The tribute paid by her allies to Athens. See DELOS, CONFEDERACY OF; HELLENOTAMIAE.

Photius (Φώτιος). A Greek scholar of the Byzantine Period, Patriarch of Constantinople A.D. 857–867 and 871–886. He died 891. Besides playing a prominent part in the ecclesiastical controversies of his time, he was conspicuous for his wide reading of ancient literature. Apart from theological writings, he left two works which are of great service to the student of antiquity. The one, the *Bibliotheca* (Μυροβίβλιον or Βιβλιοθήκη), is an account of 280 works, some of which are now lost, some only imperfectly preserved, which he read on his embassy to Assyria, with short notices and criticisms of matter and style, and in some cases more or less complete abstracts; the other, a *Lexicon* (Λέξεων Συναγωγή), or alphabetical glossary, of special value in connection with the Greek orators and historians. The *Bibliotheca* is edited by Bekker (Berlin, 1824–25); and the *Lexicon* by Hermann (Leipzig, 1808); from the papers of Porson (London, 1822); and by Naber, 2 vols. (1866). See also Hergenröther, *Photios* (1869); and the article LEXICON.

Phraāta or **Phraäspa** (τὰ Φράατα). A city of Media Atropatené, the winter residence of the Parthian kings (Dio Cass. xlix. 25).

Phraātes. The name of several Parthian kings. See ARSACES.

Phranza or **Phranzes** (Φραντζῆ or Φραντζῆς). The last and one of the most important of the Byzantine historians. He was frequently employed on important public business by Constantine XIII., the last emperor of Constantinople. On the capture of Constantinople by the Turks in 1453, Phranza was reduced to slavery, but succeeded in making his escape. He subsequently retired to a monastery, where he wrote his *Chronicon.* This work extends from 1259 to 1477, and is the most valuable authority for the history of the author's time, especially for the capture of Constantinople. It is edited by Alter (Vienna, 1796), and by Bekker, with a Latin translation (Bonn, 1838).

Phraortes (Φραόρτης). The second king of Media, and son of Deioces, whom he succeeded. He reigned from B.C. 656 to 634. He first conquered the Persians, and then subdued the greater part of Asia, but was at length defeated and killed while laying siege to Ninus (Nineveh), the capital of the Assyrian Empire. He was succeeded by his son Cyaxares (Herod. i. 73, 102).

Phratria (φρατρία, "brotherhood"). A word which denoted among the Greeks the subdivision of a φυλή (q. v.) embracing a number of families. In Attica the four old Ionic *phylae* contained three phratriae in each, twelve in all; and each phratria comprehended thirty families. (See GENNETAE.) When the old *phylae* were suppressed by Clisthenes, the phratriae remained in existence as religious associations for the observance of the ancient forms of worship, which did not admit of being suppressed. They had, however, no political importance, except that the sons (by birth or adoption) of a citizen had to be enrolled in the register of φράτορες, or members of the phratria of their natural or adoptive father. This was done by the φρατρίαρχοι (presidents) at the chief festival of the phratriae, the Apaturia (q. v.). Newly married husbands also introduced their wives into the phratria. Each phratria had a separate place of worship (φράτριον), with the altars of its deities (Pollux, iii. 52). Zeus and Athené were common to all, but each phratria worshipped other special deities of its own.

Phricōnis. A name given to Cymé in Aeolis. See also LARISSA.

Phrixa (Φρίξα). A town of Elis, on the borders of Pisatis, founded by the Minyae, and traditionally deriving its name from Phrixus (q. v.). See ARGONAUTAE.

Phrixus (Φρίξος). A son of Athamas and Nephelé and brother of Hellé. In consequence of the intrigues of his stepmother, Ino, he was to be sacrificed to Zeus; but Nephelé rescued her two children, who rode away through the air upon the ram with the golden fleece, the gift of Hermes. Between Sigeum and the Chersonesus, Hellé fell into the sea which was called after her the Hellespont; but Phrixus arrived in safety in Colchis, the kingdom of Aeëtes, who gave him his daughter Chalciopé in marriage. Phrixus sacrificed the ram, which had carried him, to Zeus Phyxius or Laphystius, and gave its fleece to Aeëtes, who fastened it to an oak-tree in the grove of Ares. This fleece was afterwards carried away by Iason and the Argonauts. (See ARGONAUTAE; IASON.) By Chalciopé Phrixus became the father of Argus, Melas, Phrontis, Cytisorus, and Presbon. Phrixus either died of old age in the kingdom of Aeëtes, or was killed by Aeëtes in consequence of an oracle, or returned to Orchomenus, in the country of the Minyans.

Phrixus (Φρίξος). A river in Argolis, which flows into the Argolic Gulf between Temenium and Lerna (Pausan. iii. 36, 6).

Phrygia (Φρυγία). A country of Asia Minor, which was of different extent at different periods. Under the Roman Empire Phrygia was bounded on the west by Mysia, Lydia, and Caria; on the south by Lycia and Pisidia; on the east by Lycaonia (which is often reckoned as a part of Phrygia) and Galatia (which formerly belonged to Phrygia), and on the north by Bithynia. The Phrygians are mentioned by Homer as settled on the banks of the Sangarius, where later writers tell us of the powerful Phrygian kingdom of Gordius and Midas. It would seem that they were a branch of the great Thracian family, originally settled in the northwest of Asia Minor as far as the shores of the Hellespont and Propontis, and that the successive migrations of other Thracian peoples, as the Thyni, Bithyni, Mysians, and Teucrians, drove them farther inland. They were not, however, entirely displaced by the Mysians and Teucrians from the country between the shores of the Hellespont and Propontis and Mounts Ida and Olympus, where they continued side by side with the Greek colonies, and where their name was preserved in that of the district under all subsequent changes—namely, Phrygia Minor or Phrygia Hellespontus. The kingdom of Phrygia was conquered by Croesus, and formed part of the Persian, Macedonian, and Syro-Grecian Empires; but, under the last, the northeastern part, adjacent to Paphlagonia and the Halys, was conquered by the Gauls, and formed the western part of Galatia; and under the Romans was included in the province of Asia. In connection with the early intellectual culture of Greece, Phrygia is highly important. The earliest Greek music, especially that of the flute, was borrowed in part, through the Asiatic colonies, from Phrygia. With this country also were closely associated the orgies of Dionysus and of Cybelé, the Mother of the Gods, the *Phrygia Mater* of the Roman poets. After the Persian conquest, however, the Phrygians seem to have lost all intellectual activity, and they became proverbial among the Greeks and Romans for submissiveness and stupidity. The Roman poets constantly use the epithet Phrygian as equivalent to Trojan.

But scanty remains of the Phrygian language survive, chiefly in the shape of brief inscriptions. It was probably an Indo-European dialect closely related to the Armenian, and some such relation is implied in the notices of Herodotus (vii. 73) and Strabo (p. 295).

On Phrygia, see Perrot and Chipiez, *Hist. of Art in Phrygia*, etc. (Eng. trans., London, 1892). On the language, see Fick, *Spracheinheit der indogermanischen Europas*, pp. 408 foll., and a paper in *Bezzenberger's Beiträge*, xiv. 50 foll.

Phrygia Mater. See PHRYGIA; RHEA.

Phrygio. An embroiderer, the Phrygians being famous for their skill in this art (Plaut. *Aul.* iii. 5, 34).

Phrȳné (Φρύνη). A celebrated Athenian courtesan, born at Thespis in Boeotia. She flourished in the times of Philip and Alexander the Great, and was the mistress of some of the most distinguished men of the day. She became so wealthy that she is said to have offered to rebuild the walls of Thebes, when destroyed by Alexander, if only she might inscribe upon the walls, "Alexander destroyed these; but Phryné, the *hetaera*, rebuilt them"—an offer which was rejected. The famous painting of Apelles, entitled "Aphrodité Anadyomené," or Aphrodité rising from the sea, is said to have had Phryné for its model. (See APELLES.) Praxiteles, the sculptor, who was another of her lovers, used her as a model for his "Cnidian Aphrodité." At one time she was accused of profaning the Eleusinian Mysteries, and was brought before the court of the Heliasts; but her advocate, Hyperides, threw off her veil, and exposed her breasts to the judges, who at once acquitted her amid the applause of the people, by whom she was carried in triumph to the temple of Aphrodité. See MERETRIX.

Phrynĭchus (Φρύνιχος). (1) A Greek tragic poet of Athens, an older contemporary of Aeschylus. He won his first victory as early as B.C. 511. He rendered a great service to the development of the drama by introducing an actor distinct from the leader of the chorus, and so laying the foundation for the dialogue. But the dialogue was still quite subordinate to the lyrics of the chorus. In this department he won extraordinary celebrity by the grace and melody of his verses, which continued to be sung at Athens long after. Besides mythical subjects, he dealt with events of contemporary history, as the conquest of Miletus (Μίλητου Ἅλωσις) by the Persians. At the representation of that event the audience burst into tears, and the poet was fined 1000 drachmae for recalling the disasters of his country, all further performance of the piece being prohibited (Herod. vi. 21). Again, in his *Phoenissae* (so named after the chorus of Sidonian women) he dealt with the battle of Salamis. This play, which was put on the stage by Themistocles in 478, was the model of Aeschylus's *Persae*. Phrynichus, like Aeschylus, is said to have died in Sicily. We possess only the titles of nine of his plays and a few fragments.

(2) A Greek poet of Athens; one of the less important writers of the Old Attic Comedy, and a frequent butt of the other comic poets. In B.C. 405, however, his *Musae* took the second prize after Aristophanes' *Frogs*. We have only fragments of about ten plays, ed. by Koch (1880 foll.).

(3) A Greek Sophist, who lived in the second half of the third century A.D. in Bithynia; author of a selection of Attic verbs and nouns (Ἐκλογὴ Ῥημάτων καὶ Ὀνομάτων Ἀττικῶν), compiled with great strictness in the exclusion of all but the best Attic forms. We have also notable excerpts from a work of his in thirty-seven books, dedicated to the emperor Commodus, and entitled *The Sophistic Armoury* (Παρασκευή). It was founded on the most comprehensive learning, and designed to supply the orator with everything necessary for good and pure expression. The arrangement is alphabetical, and it includes examples from the best authors, the different styles being carefully distinguished. The first work is edited by Lobeck (Leipzig, 1820); the second by Bekker (Berlin, 1814). See Rutherford's *New Phrynichus* (1881).

Phrynnis (Φρύννις) or **Phrynis** (Φρῦνις). A writer of dithyrambic verse, born at Mitylené, but a resident of Athens about the time of the Peloponnesian War. He is said to have added two strings to the heptachord, and to have been the first to conquer at the musical contests introduced into the Panathenaea by Pericles (cf. Aristoph. *Nub.* 971; Plut. *Mus.* p. 1146).

Phthia (Φθίη). See PHTHIOTIS.

Phthiōtis (Φθιῶτις). A district in the southeast of Thessaly, bounded on the south by the Maliac Gulf, and on the east by the Pagasaean Gulf, and inhabited by Achaeans. (See THESSALIA.) Homer calls it Phthia, and mentions a city of the same name, which was celebrated as the residence of Achilles. Hence, the poets call Achilles *Phthius heros*, and his father Peleus *Phthius rex*.

Phthira (τὰ Φθίρα). A mountain in Caria.

Phya. See PISISTRATUS.

Phycūs (Φυκοῦς). A promontory on the coast of Cyrenaïca, a little west of Apollonia.

Phylăcé (Φυλάκη). A small town of Thessaly in Phthiotis, the birthplace of Protesilaüs, hence called *Phylacides;* his wife Laodamia is also called *Phylaceïs.*

Phylarchus (Φύλαρχος). (1) A Greek historian, born probably at Naucratis, in Egypt, about B.C. 210, lived long at Sicyon, afterwards in Athens; author of a great historical work in twenty-eight books, dealing with the fifty years from the invasion of the Peloponnesus by Pyrrhus to the death of Cleomenes, king of Sparta (272–221). His enthusiastic admiration of that monarch appears to be the cause of the severe judgment passed on Phylarchus by Polybius (ii. 56), who represents the Achaean view. His style was lively and attractive, but sensational. His work was much used by Trogus Pompeius and by Plutarch in his lives of Cleomenes and Aratus. Only a few fragments remain, and have been edited by Müller in his *Fragmenta Hist. Graec.* (Paris, 1868).

Phylarchus (φύλαρχος). The Athenian term for (*a*) the president of a φυλή (see PHYLÉ); (*b*) one of the ten subordinate officers commanding the citizen cavalry. See HIPPEIS.

Phylas (Φύλας). (1) A king of the Dryopes, who was attacked and slain by Heracles, because he had violated the sanctuary of Delphi. By his daughter Midea, Heracles became the father of Antiochus. (2) Son of Antiochus and grandson of Heracles and Midea, was married to Deïphilé, by whom he had two sons, Hippotas and Thero. (3) King of Ephyra, in Thesprotia, and father of Polymelé and Astyoché, by the latter of whom Heracles was the father of Tlepolemus.

Phylé (Φυλή). Now Fili; a strongly fortified place in Attica, on the confines of Boeotia, and memorable as the place which Thrasybulus and the Athenian patriots seized soon after the end of the Peloponnesian War, B.C. 404, and from which they directed their operations against the Thirty Tyrants (q. v.) at Athens. It was an Attic deme. See THRASYBULUS.

Phylé (φυλή). The Greek term for a division of a nation, connected by (supposed) descent from a common ancestor of the stock. Thus the population of Attica, even before Solon, was divided into four phylae, tracing their origin from four legendary sons of Ion, and called Geleontes, Hopletes, Aegicores, and Argades. Probably the division was local, the names referring to the peculiarity or main occupation of the members of each division; for Hopletes appears to mean warriors, Aegicores, goat-herds, and Argades, agriculturalists. The meaning of Geleontes (or Teleontes) is perhaps "the shining." (See IONIC TRIBES.) Each phylé was presided over by a φυλοβασιλεύς (king of the phylé) and divided into three *phratriae* (brotherhoods, see PHRATRIA), each *phratria* being subdivided into thirty families. Each family contained about thirty households, and was named after a supposed common progenitor, in whose honour the households celebrated a common cult. Similarly the *phratriae* and phylae were united by the worship of special protecting deities. These old Ionic phylae were suppressed by Clisthenes, who divided the people into ten entirely different phylae, named after ancient heroes (Erechtheïs, Aegeïs, Pandionis, Leontis, Acamantis, Oeneïs, Cecropis, Hippothontis, Aiantis, Antiochis). They were subdivided into fifty *naucrariae* and one hundred *demi.* See DEMUS.

In B.C. 307, in honour of Demetrius Poliorcetes and his father Antigonis, the phylae were increased by two, called Demetrias and Antigonis, which names were afterwards changed, in honour of Ptolemy Philadelphus of Egypt and Attalus I. of Pergamon, into Ptolemais and Attalis. In later times, another, Adrianis, was added in honour of the emperor Hadrian. Besides priests for the cult of their eponymous hero, the phylae had presidents, called φύλαρχοι, and treasurers (ταμίαι). The assemblies were always held in Athens, and were concerned, not only with the special affairs of the phylé, but also with State business, especially the notification of the persons liable to State burdens. (See LITURGIA.) The ten phylae of Clisthenes served also as a foundation for the organization of the army. The forces were raised when required from the muster-roll of the phylae, and divided accordingly into ten battalions, which were themselves also called phylae.

The Dorian stock was generally divided into three phylae: Hylleis, Dymanes, and Pamphyli, purporting to be named after Hyllus, son of Heracles, and Dymas and Pamphylus, sons of king Aegimius. When families not of Dorian origin formed part of the forces of the State, they constituted an additional phylé. In the purely Dorian state of Sparta the three phylae were divided into thirty *obae,* answering to the families at Athens. See DORIS.

Phyllis (Φύλλις). (1) The daughter of Sithon, king of Thrace, and betrothed to Demophoön, son of Theseus, who, on his return from Troy, had stopped on the Thracian coast, and there became enamoured of the princess. A day having been fixed for their union, Demophoön set sail for Athens, in order to arrange affairs at home, promising to return at an appointed time. He did not come, however, at the end of the period which he had fixed, and Phyllis, fancying herself deserted, put an end to her existence. The trees that sprang up around her tomb were said at a certain season to mourn her untimely fate by their leaves withering and falling to the ground. (Hyg. *Fab.* 59.) According to another account, Phyllis was changed after death into an almond-tree, destitute of leaves; and Demophoön having returned a few days subsequently, and having clasped the tree in his embrace, it put forth leaves (φύλλα) as if conscious of the presence of a once-beloved object. Ovid has made the absence of Demophoön from Thrace the subject of one of his *Heroides.* It is said that Phyllis, when watching for the return of Demophoön, made nine journeys to the Thracian coast, whence the spot was called Ennea-Hodoi (Ἐννέα Ὁδοί) or "the Nine Ways." The true reason of the name, however, was the meeting here of as many roads from different parts of Thrace and Macedon. (2) A region of Thrace, forming part of Edonis, and situate to the north of Mount Pangaeus.

Phyllus (Φύλλος). A town of Thessaly in the district Thessaliotis. The poets use *Phylleïs* and *Phylleïus* in the sense of Thessalian.

Phylobasĭleis (φυλοβασιλεῖς), "Tribe-kings." Officers of the Athenian tribes (see PHYLÉ), of whose origin and functions little is known. They existed earlier than the time of Clisthenes, and were probably four in number, or one for each tribe. They presided in certain courts (e. g. the Prytaneum), and sat with the Archon Basileus in the Basileum. They were probably charged with religious rather than legal functions.

Phylon (φῦλον). See TRIBUS.

Physcon (Φύσκων). A surname of one of the Ptolemies, king of Egypt, from his great abdominal rotundity (φύσκων, "the paunch"; from φύσκη, "the lower belly"). See PTOLEMAEUS.

Physcus (Φύσκος). (1) A town of Caria, opposite Rhodes, and subject to that island. (2) A river of Lower Assyria flowing into the Tigris.

Physicians. See CHIRURGIA; MEDICINA; MEDICUS.

Picēni. See PICENUM.

Picentes. See PICENUM.

Picentia. Now Vicenza; a town in the south of Campania at the head of the Sinus Paestanus. The name of Picentini was not confined to the inhabitants of Picentia, but was given to the inhabitants of the whole coast of the Sinus Paestanus, from the promontory of Minerva to the river Silarus. They were a portion of the Sabine Picentes, who were transplanted by the Romans to this part of Campania after the conquest of Picenum, B.C. 268, at which time they founded the town of Picentia.

Picentīni. See PICENTIA.

Picēnum. A country in central Italy, was a narrow strip of land along the coast of the Adriatic, and was bounded on the north by Umbria, on the west by Umbria and the territory of the Sabines, and on the south by the territory of the Marsi and Vestini. It is said to have derived its name from the bird *picus*, which directed the Sabine immigrants into the land (Pliny, *H. N.* iii. 110). They were conquered by the Romans in B.C. 268, when a portion of them was transplanted to the coast of the Sinus Paestanus, where they founded the town of Picentia (Flor. i. 19; Eutrop. ii. 16). (See PICENTIA.) Picenum formed the fifth region in the division of Italy by Augustus. See ITALIA.

Picti. The Picts; a people inhabiting the northern part of Britain, who appear to have been either a tribe of the Caledonians, or the same people as the Caledonians, though under another name. They are said to have been called Picti ("painted men") by the Romans, from their practice of painting their bodies; but scholars now regard the word as the same with the other native terms Pictones, Pictavi, found in Gaul (cf. the French Poitou, Poictiers), and as therefore Keltic. The name, however, though not Latin, apparently coincides with the Latin in meaning, being cognate with *cicht*, "an engraver." Picts are first mentioned in A.D. 296 by Eumenius; and after this time their name frequently occurs in the Roman writers, and often in connection with that of the Scoti. See Skene, *Celtic Scotland*, vol. i. (Edinburgh, 1886); Rhys, *Celtic Britain* (London, 1884); and the article CALEDONIA.

Pictŏnes. A people of Aquitanic Gaul, a short distance below the Ligeris (Loire). Their territory corresponds to the modern Poitou. Ptolemy assigns them two capitals, Augustoritum and Limonum, but the former in strictness belonged to the Lemovices. The city of Limonum, the true capital, answers to the modern Poitiers. Strabo gives the name of this people with the short penult, Ptolemy with the long one. The short quantity is followed by Lucan (i. 436). Ammianus Marcellinus uses the form PICTĀVI (xv. 11). See PICTI.

Pictor. See FABIUS, p. 656.

Pictor. A painter. See PICTURA.

Pictūra (γραφή, ζωγραφία). Painting. Among the Greeks painting developed into an independent art much later than sculpture, though it was used very early for decorative purposes. This is proved by the evidence of painted vases belonging to the ages of the most primitive civilization, and by the mural paintings discovered by Schliemann at Tiryns. Many students of the subject regard it as suggested and developed by polychrome embroidery or textile work. Homer makes no mention of painting, but speaks of pictures woven on garments, as on the robe of Helen and the veil of Heré; while two of the earliest known artists of Greece (Acesas and Helicon) were weavers by trade. It is certain that the influence of Oriental tapestries is largely felt in Greek painting. Klein and Milchhöfer think that both painting and sculpture were preceded by coloured relief.

The scanty notices in ancient authors respecting the first discoveries in this art connect it with historical persons, and not with mythical names, as in the case of sculpture. Thus it is said (Pliny, *H. N.* xxxv. 16) that either Philocles, the Egyptian, or Cleanthes of Corinth was the first to draw outline sketches; that Telephanes of Sicyon developed them further; that Ecphantus of Corinth introduced painting in single tints (monochrome); and that Eumarus of Athens (in the second half of the sixth century) distinguished man and woman by giving the one a darker, the other a lighter colour. Cimon of Cleonae is mentioned as the originator of artistic drawing in profile (Pliny, *H. N.* xxxv. 56, cf. 90). It is further said of him that he gave variety to the face by making it look backwards or upwards or downwards, and freedom to the limbs by duly rendering the joints; also that he was the first to represent the veins of the human body, and to make the folds of the drapery fall more naturally (ib. 56).

Painting did not, however, make any decided advance until the middle of the fifth century B.C., though Pausanias states that in the sixth century, the Samiote Calliphon painted the Homeric battle of the ships. This advance was chiefly due to Polygnotus of Thasos, who painted at Athens, and with whom as a real art painting may be said to begin. Among other claims to distinction it is attributed to him that he gave greater variety of expression to the face, which hitherto had been rigidly severe. His works, most of them large compositions rich in figures, give evidence of a lofty and poetic conception; they appear to have been, in great part, mural paintings for decorating the interior of public buildings (Pausan. x. 25–31; i. 15, 22, § 6). The colours were first applied in uniform tints, so as to fill in the outlines, and fresh lines and touches were then added to indicate where the limbs and muscles began, and the folds of the garments. The drawing and the combination of colours were the chief considerations; light and shade were wanting, and no attention was paid to perspective. It is doubtful whether at this early time, besides mural paintings executed *al fresco* on carefully smoothed stucco-priming with plain water-colours, there were any pictures on panels, such as afterwards became common; but we may fairly assume it. These were painted on wooden panels *in tempera*—i. e. with colours mixed with various kinds of distemper, such as gum or size, to make them more adhesive. The art was still limited by its traditions, and each figure had its name carefully painted over it. A good deal of symbolism was tolerated—i. e. a single tree or a house or a piece of water was introduced to suggest a whole scene, which the spectator's imagination was supposed to supply. The range of colours was also still scanty, for Cicero tells us that Polygnotus used only four tints.

In the same century the encaustic method of painting was discovered, though not elaborated till the following century. The process, as described in Roman times by Vitruvius (vii. 9), was as follows: "The medium used was melted white wax (*cera punica*), mixed with oil to make it more fluid. The pot containing the wax was kept over a brazier while the painter was at work, in order to keep the melted wax from solidifying. The stucco itself was prepared by a coating of hot wax applied with a brush or *cestrum*, and it was polished by being rubbed with a wax candle, and finally with a clean linen cloth. After the picture was painted the wax colours were fixed, partly melted into the stucco, and blended with the wax of the ground by the help of a charcoal brazier, which was held close to the surface of the painting, and gradually moved over its whole extent." The encaustic method had several advantages over painting *in tempera*: it lasted longer and was more proof against damp, while the colouring was much brighter; on the other hand, it was much more laborious and slow, which explains the fact that the majority of encaustic paintings were of small size.

While the pictures of Polygnotus certainly did not deceive by too much truth to nature, it was his younger contemporary, the Samian Agatharchus, who practised scene-painting (σκηνογραφία) at Athens, and thus gave an impulse to the attempt at illusory effect and the use of perspective. He painted the scenery for a play of Aeschylus (Vitruv. vii. *praef.* 10), and decorated the interior of the house of Alcibiades (Andoc. *Alcib.* 17). The Athenian Apollodorus (about B.C. 420) was the actual founder of an entirely new artistic style, which strove to effect illusion by means of the resources of painting. He was the first to give his pictures the appearance of reality, the first to bring painting into just repute (Pliny, *H. N.* xxxv. 60). He also led the way in the proper management of the fusion of colours and their due gradation in different degrees of light and shade. It was to this that he owed his title of "shadow-painter" (σκιαγράφος).

The ATTIC SCHOOL flourished till about the end of the fifth century, when this art was for some time neglected at Athens, but made another important advance in the towns of Asia Minor, especially at Ephesus. The principal merits of this, the Ionic School, consist in richer and more delicate colouring, a more perfect system of pictorial representation, rendering on a flat surface the relief and variety of nature, and the consequent attainment of the greatest possible illusion. Its principal representatives were Zeuxis of Heraclea and Parrhasius of Ephesus; Timanthes also produced remarkable works, though not an adherent of the same school. It was opposed by the SICYONIAN SCHOOL, founded by Eupompus of Sicyon, and developed by Pamphilus of Amphipolis, which aimed at greater precision of technical training, very careful and characteristic drawing, and a sober and effective colouring (Pliny, l. c. 75, 76). Pausias, a member of this school, invented the art of foreshortening and of painting on vaulted ceilings, besides perfecting the encaustic art, which was much more favourable for purposes of illusion and picturesque effectiveness than painting *in tempera* (ib. 123–127). Greek painting reached its summit in the works of Apelles (q. v.) of Cos, in the second half of the fourth century; he knew how to combine the merits of the Ionian and the Sicyonian Schools, the perfect grace of the former with the severe accuracy of the latter.

After him the most famous artist was Protogenes of Caunus. The following contemporaries, some older and some younger than himself, deserve also to be mentioned: Nicomachus and Aristides of Thebes, Euphranor of Corinth, Nicias of Athens, the Egyptian Antiphilus, Theon of Samos, and Aëtion. After the age of Alexander the art of painting was characterized by a striving after naturalism, combined with a predilection for the representation of common, every-day scenes, and of still-life. Pictures of a small size came into favour, their models being objects taken from common life, such as barber-shops, cobblers' stalls, eatables, etc., such as one finds in the genre pictures and still-life paintings of the Netherlands. Lewd paintings also became popular, this branch of art being known as Pornographia, or Rhyparographia. At last, as art degenerated, even the floors were adorned with painting, and objects, such as melon-rinds, bits of food, etc., were delineated so as to produce the effect of a room in disorder. Such a curious bit of realism was the "Unswept Floor" (ἀσάρωτος οἶκος) at Pergamum, by Sosus. Callicles and Calates were famous painters of ob-

Still-life. (Pompeian Painting.)

scene pictures, while Piraeicus was noted for his scenes from still-life. Among painters of the loftier style the last noteworthy artist was Timomachus of Byzantium.

Among the Romans a few solitary names of early painters are mentioned—for instance, Fabius Pictor and the poet Pacuvius (Pliny, *H. N.* xxxv. 19); but nothing is known as to the value of their paintings, which served to decorate buildings. The way in which landscapes were represented by a certain S. Tadius (or Ludius (?), ib. 116; the best MS. has *studio*) in the reign of Augustus is mentioned as a novelty. These landscapes were mainly for purposes of decoration (Vitruv. vii. 5). Indeed, the love of display peculiar to the Romans, which had led them gradually to accumulate the principal works of the old Greek masters at Rome as ornaments for their public and private edifices, brought about an extraordinary development of decorative art, attested by the numerous mural paintings that have been found in Italy, chiefly at Pompeii and Herculaneum.

Landscape Painting from Pompeii. (Reber.)

These paintings were mostly executed *al fresco* on damp stucco, seldom with colours *in tempera* on the dry surface. The principal subjects represented are figures from the world of myth, such as Maenads, Centaurs male and female, Satyrs, etc.; scenes from mythology and heroic legends, frequently copies of famous Greek originals, one of the best examples of which is Achilles delivering Briseïs to the heralds (see p. 222); landscapes; still-life; animals, and also scenes from real life. From a technical point of view these works do not go beyond the limits of light decorative painting, and are especially wanting in correct perspective; but they show fine harmony, varied gradation, and delicate blending of colour, and frequently a surprising depth and sincerity of expression, qualities which must have characterized the lost masterpieces of the ancient artists to a much more remarkable degree, and cannot but give us a very high idea of them. One of the finest mural paintings is that known as the "Aldobrandini Marriage," discovered in 1606 near the Arch of Gallienus, now in the Library of the Vatican at Rome, and named after its first owner, Cardinal Aldobrandini. It is copied from an excellent Greek original, and represents, in the style of a relief, the preparations

The Aldobrandini Marriage. (Vatican.)

for a marriage. "It is composed," says Woermann (*History of Painting*, i. 115), "not pictorially, but yet with taste. It exhibits several individual motives of much beauty; its colouring is soft and harmonious; and it is instinct with that placid and serious charm which belongs only to the antique. In technical execution, however, the work is insignificant, and in no way rises above the ordinary handling of the Roman house-decorator in similar subjects." The Vatican Library also possesses an important series of landscapes from the *Odyssey*, found during the excavations on the Esquiline in 1848–1850. Landscapes of this kind are mentioned by Vitruvius (vii. 5), among the subjects with which corridors used to be decorated in the early times. They represent the adventure with the Laestrygones, the story of Circé, and the visit of Odysseus to the realm of Hades, thus illustrating a continuous portion of the poem (*Od.* x. 80, xi. 600). The predominant colours are a yellowish brown and a greenish blue, and the pictures are divided from one another by pilasters of a brilliant red. They furnish interesting examples of the landscape-painting of the last days of the Republic or the first of the Empire, and, in point of importance, stand alone among all the remains of ancient painting. On mosaic-painting and vase-painting, see MUSIVUM OPUS; VAS.

The ancients painted on stucco, wood (a thin slab called πίναξ, and in Latin *tabula*) which was primed with whitening (λελευκωμένος), stone, and marble. Canvas (*linteum*) was used but rarely (Pliny, *H. N.* xxxv. 51). When used it was stretched on wood or pasted in several layers.

The processes of painting are represented in several works of ancient art—e. g. in three mural paintings from Pompeii. Even some of the implements and materials used by artists have been discovered. Thus, in 1849, at St. Médard-des-Prés in La Vendée, a grave was opened containing a female skeleton surrounded by eighty small vessels of glass, in most of which remains of ancient pigments were still preserved. Besides these there was a small cup of brown glass (a); a knife of cedar-wood with its blade reduced to rust (b); a small bronze box (c) with a movable lid and four partitions, holding materials for pigments; a mortar of alabaster, and a smaller one of bronze (d); one or two elegant bronze spoons (e), either for removing colours from the palette or for adding some liquid to mix them; a small shovel, made of rock crystal, containing gold embedded in gum (f); and an oblong palette of basalt (g). There were also two small cylinders of amber and two brush-handles of bone. One of the glass vessels contained bits of resin; another, wax; a third, a mixture of both; a fourth, a mixture of lamp-black and wax, with traces of sebacic acid, possibly due to the presence of oil.

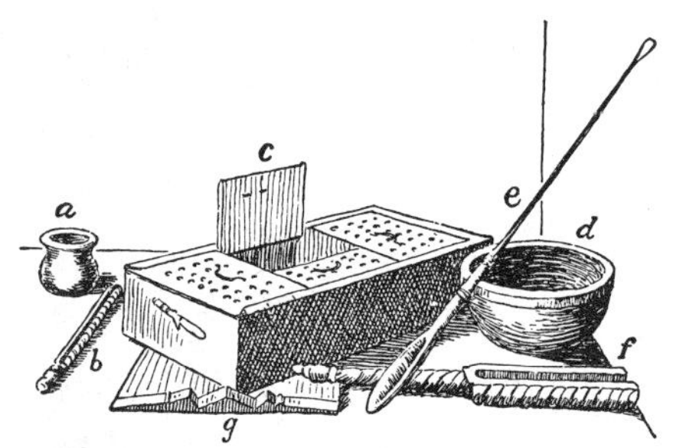

Paint-box and Implements for Painting. (First published by B. Fillon, *Description de la Villa et du Tombeau d'une Femme Artiste Gallo-romaine*, Fontenay, 1849.)

Our principal information about ancient pigments (φάρμακα, *medicamenta, pigmenta*) comes from Theophrastus (*De Lapidibus*), Dioscorides (bk. v.), Vitruvius (vii.), and the elder Pliny (*H. N.* xxxiii. and xxxv.). It is observed by Cicero in the *Brutus*, 70, that only four colours were used by Polygnotus, Zeuxis, Timanthes, and their contemporaries, as contrasted with their successors, Aëtion, Nicomachus, Protogenes, and Apelles. Pliny (*H. N.* xxxv. 50), who identified the colours as white (*melinum*), yellow (*sil Atticum*), red (*Sinopis Pontica*), and black (*atramentum*), even places Aëtion, Nicomachus, Apelles, and Melanthius under the same limitation. But it is hardly probable that such important colours as blue and green were dispensed with, even in the primitive art of Polygnotus, much less in the more advanced art of Zeuxis and his contemporaries, and least of all in that of Apelles and Protogenes. The earliest artists, however, may well have used comparatively few colours, and those of the simplest kind, the *colores austeri* of Pliny (*H. N.* xxxv. 30), as contrasted with the *colores floridi*, such as vermilion, "Armenian blue," "dragon's blood," malachite green, indigo, and purple. These were characteristic of later developments of art, and were so costly that they were not paid for by the artists, but by those who gave them their commissions (ib. 44; Vitruv. vii. 5, 8).

The pigments known to the ancients were as follows:

White.—The pigment used in Greece was a "pipe-clay" called *melinum*, found in veins in the island of Melos. It was not available for fresco-painting (Pliny, *H. N.* xxxv. 49). A white earth of Eretria was employed by Nicomachus and Parrhasius (ib. 38). A commoner pigment was the *creta Selinusia* of Selinus in Sicily, used for mural paintings (ib. 49, 194), and the *creta anularia*, made by mixing chalk with the glass composition worn in the rings of the poor (ib. 48). For fresco-painting they used *parætonium*, a hydrated silicate of magnesia, so called from a cliff on the African coast near Egypt (ib. 30), which in Rome was adulterated with *creta Cimolia* (ib. 36). For other purposes they employed white-lead (*ψιμύθιον, cerussa*), an artificial product, the finest sorts of which came from Rhodes, Corinth, and Sparta. It is carbonate of lead, and is still used under various names (e. g. ceruse). It is sold in its crude form as "Chemnitz or Vienna white," and mixed with sulphate of barium in "Dutch, Hamburg, and Venetian white." See CERUSSA.

Yellow.—The pigments in use were yellow ochre and orpiment. The best kind of yellow ochre (*ὤχρα*; Lat. *sil*) was found in the mines of Laurium. It was also found in Scyros, Achaia, Gaul, Cappadocia, Cyprus, and Lydia. The Attic variety was first used by Polygnotus and Micon; it was afterwards preferred for the high lights, while the kinds from Scyros and Lydia were reserved for the shadows (id. xxxiii. 158–160, xxxvii. 179). It is a diluted brown ochre or hydrated peroxide of iron, being composed of oxygen, water, and iron, mixed with more or less clay. Orpiment, or trisulphide of arsenic (*ἀρσενικόν*: *auripigmentum*), was of two kinds: (1) of a golden yellow, from Mysia on the coast of the Hellespont; and (2) a duller kind, from Pontus and Cappadocia (Dioscórides, v. 120). It could not be used for frescoes (Pliny, *H. N.* xxxv. 49). Yellow ochre and orpiment (under the name of "king's or Chinese yellow") are still in use.

Red.—One of the oldest pigments was ruddle (*μίλτος*; *rubrica*). This is a red earth coloured by sesquioxide of iron. In the Homeric age it was used to ornament the bows of ships. In later times the clay from which Greek vases were made owed its brilliant hue to the ruddle of Cape Colias on the Attic coast (Suid. s. v. Κωλιάδος κέραμος, and Pliny, *H. N.* xxxv. 152). The best kind came from Cappadocia, by way of Sinopé (hence called *Sinopis Pontica*, ib. 31, 36, xxxiii. 117), or through Ephesus (Strabo, p. 540). It was also found in North Africa (*cicerculum*, Pliny, *H.N.* xxxv. 32), especially in Egypt and at Carthage; also in Spain and the Balearic Islands, and Lemnos and Ceos. There was a treaty forbidding the export of ruddle from Ceos except only to Athens (Hicks, *Gr. Historical Inscriptions*, p. 186). It could be artificially produced by calcining yellow ochre, a discovery due to Cydias, a contemporary of Euphranor (Theophr. l. c. 53). Another mineral supplying a red, sometimes a yellow, pigment, was sandarach (*σανδαράχη*, *sandaraca*), found in Paphlagonia, probably disulphide of arsenic. As this mineral is poisonous, the mortality in the mines was very high. An artificial substitute, called *cerussa usta*, or *usta* alone, was therefore generally preferred. This was obtained by burning white lead, a discovery attributed to the painter Nicias (Pliny, *H. N.* xxxv. 38). The result is "red lead"—i. e. red oxide of lead. There was besides a colour compounded of equal parts of ruddle and sandarach, called *sandyx* (ib. 40), which is also the designation of a natural pigment of which little is known (Verg. *Ecl.* iv. 45). Of greater importance than these is cinnabar (Gr. originally *κιννάβαρι*, afterwards *ἄμμιον*: *minium*), found in Spain, especially at Sisapo (Pliny, *H. N.* xxxiii. 121). An artificial kind was made at Ephesus from the red sand of the *agri Cilbiani.* This discovery is assigned to Callias (ib. 113). The name *cinnabari* was often erroneously given to a red resin, now called dragon's-blood, and produced from the *calamus draco*, a kind of palm growing in the Sunda Islands and elsewhere. The ancients probably imported it from the island of Socotra, as it is a product of the Somali coast on the adjacent mainland of Africa.—A *purple* pigment (*ὄστρειον*; *ostrum*, *purpurissum*) was prepared by mixing *creta argentaria* with the purple secretion of the *murex* (see PURPURA); the best kind was made at Puteoli (Pliny, *H. N.* xxxv. 45).

Painter at Work. (Pompeian Caricature.)

Blue.—The pigment used from the earliest times was called in Greek *κύανος*, in Latin *caeruleum*, a blue silicate of copper, generally mixed with carbonate of lime (chalk). It is not to be confounded with the modern *caeruleum*, which is stannate of cobalt. *Κύανος* was found in small quantities in copper mines, and artificial kinds were made in Scythia, Cyprus, and Egypt (Theophr. l. c. 51, 55). Vitruvius mentions only the artificial *caeruleum* of Alexandria and Puteoli. The method of manufacturing it was brought from Egypt by Vestorius. It was prepared by heating strongly together sand, *flos nitri* (carbonate of soda), and filings of copper. This "Egyptian azure" was reproduced by Sir Humphry Davy, by taking fifteen parts by weight of carbonate of soda, twenty of powdered opaque flints, and three of copper filings, and heating them strongly for two hours. The product, when pulverized, supplied a fine deep sky blue. The "Alexandrian frit" is in part a species of artificial *lapis lazuli*, the colouring matter of which is naturally inherent in a hard siliceous stone. It was not available for fresco-painting, but could be used for painting *in tempera* (Pliny, *H. N.* xxxiii. 162). The name *κύανος* was given to a blue mineral, which is to be identified as *lapis lazuli*, a silicate of sodium, calcium, and aluminium, with a sulphur compound of sodium. This was pounded into a pigment, now known as ultramarine. *Κύανος* was also the name of the blue carbonate of copper from the copper mines of Cyprus, where *lapis lazuli* is not to be found. Artificial blue pigments were produced by colouring pulverized glass with carbonate of copper. "Armenian blue" (*Ἀρμένιον*) is described by Pliny (*H. N.* xxxv. 47) as made from a mineral like *chrysocolla* (malachite?) in colour, the best kinds being almost as good as *caeruleum.* It is probably a kind of ultramarine.—Indigo (*indicum*) was also used. The way in which it is men-

Specimen of Pompeian Mural-painting. (Reber.)

tioned in Vitruvius (vii. 9, 6, and 10, 4) implies that it had been recently introduced. It could not be used for frescoes. Modern experiment has proved that the colouring basis of the blue found in ancient mural paintings is oxide of copper. Cobalt has also been discovered in ancient specimens of transparent blue glass.

Green.—Several pigments were in use: (1) *chrysocolla* (or malachite (?), hydrated dicarbonate of copper), pounded and sifted, and mixed with alum and woad (*lutum*, Pliny, *H. N.* xxxiii. 87). Malachite green, sometimes called mountain, or Hungary, green, is also a modern pigment. (2) *Creta viridis*, the best kind of which came from Smyrna (Vitruv. vii. 7, 4). It is a species of ochre containing silica, oxide of iron, magnesia, potash, and water; and is still used under the names of terra verte, verdetta, green earth, Verona green, green bice, or holly green. (3) Verdigris (*ἰός*; *aerugo, aeruca*, Vitruv. vii. 12, 1). This is an acetate of copper (sometimes crystallized), i. e. a compound of acetic acid and oxide of copper. Malachite green and Verona green have both been traced in ancient paintings. Verdigris has not been found; hence it has been conjectured that what was originally a diacetate of copper has in the course of centuries changed into carbonate of copper (l. c. p. 112). It is described as "the least durable of copper greens; light fades it in water; damp and foul air first bleach it, and then turn it black."

Black.—The pigment (*μέλαν*: *atramentum*) was almost always produced by combustion. Polygnotus and Micon produced it by drying and burning the lees of wine (*τρύγινον*). Apelles was the discoverer of "ivory black" (*elephantinum*, Pliny, *H. N.* xxxv. 42). A common material was the smoke of burned resin (our lamp-black), or burned pine-twigs (Vitruv. vii. 10, 1). Pliny (*H. N.* xxxv. 41) also mentions a natural black pigment which is difficult to identify; it may be peat, or else oxide of iron, or oxide of manganese. The best black pigment was called *atramentum Indicum* (*μέλαν Ἰνδικόν*), doubtless the same as "Chinese black," which originally found its way to the West through India, and thus obtained its alternative name of "Indian ink." But it cannot be used for frescoes, and no traces of it have been found in the mural paintings of antiquity. The black in these paintings is always carbonaceous.

Some of the remains of ancient colours and paintings at Pompeii, and in the Baths of Titus and of Livia, and elsewhere, were analyzed by Sir Humphry Davy (*Phil. Trans. Royal Society*, 1815, pp. 97–124: *Some Experiments and Observations on the Colours used in Painting by the Ancients*). In an earthen vase from the Baths of Titus containing a variety of colours, the reds proved to be red oxide of lead, with two iron ochres of different tints, a dull red and a purplish red "nearly of the same tint as prussiate of copper;" all three were mixed with chalk or carbonate of lime (p. 101). The yellows were pure ochres mixed with carbonate of lime, and ochre mixed with red oxide of lead and carbonate of lime (p. 104). The blues were a kind of smalt, with carbonate of lime (p. 106). Of greens there were three varieties; "one, which approached to olive, was the common green earth of Verona; another, which was pale grass-green, had the character of carbonate of copper mixed with chalk; and a third, which was sea-green, was a green combination of copper mixed with blue copper frit" (p. 110). A pale, rose-coloured substance, found in the Baths of Titus, which in its interior "had a lustre approaching to that of carmine," was found to be either of vegetable or animal origin; if the latter, it was most probably a specimen of Tyrian purple (pp. 113–115). In the "Aldobrandini Marriage" the reds and yellows were all ochres; the greens, preparations of copper; the blues, "Alexandrian frit;" the purple, a mixture of red ochre and carbonate of copper; the browns, mixtures of ochres and black; the whites were all carbonates of lime.

Bibliography.—For further details regarding the history of painting, see Reber, *Hist. of Ancient Art*, Eng. trans. (N. Y. 1883); Lübke, *Hist. of Art*, vol. i. Eng. trans. (N. Y. 1877); C. O. Müller, *Ancient Art and its Remains*, Eng. trans. (London, 1852); Frank, *Geschichte der Kunst* (Leipzig, 1863);

Lübke and Lützow, *Denkmäler der Kunst* (5th ed. Stuttgart, 1884); Woltmann and Woermann, *Hist. of Painting*, Eng. trans. ed. by S. Colvin (New York, 1880); Overbeck, *Pompeii* (4th ed. 1884); Dyer, *Pompeii* (2d ed. 1875); Jones, *A Grammar of Ornament* (London, 1856); Parton, *Caricature and Other Comic Art* (N. Y. 1877); Wright, *A History of Caricature* (London, 1875); Woermann, *Die Landschaft in der Kunst der antiken Völker* (Leipzig, 1876); Helbig and Donner, *Wandgemälde der vom Vesuv verschütteten Städte* (1868); Urlichs, *Die Malerei in Rom vor Cäsars Dictatur* (Würzburg, 1876); Mau, *Geschichte der decorativen Wandmalerei in Pompeii* (1882); and the full list of works cited in Prof. E. Hübner's *Bibliographie der klassischen Alterthumswissenschaft* (Berlin, 1889); Bertrand, *Etude sur la Peinture et la Critique d'Art dans l'Antiquité* (Paris, 1893).—On the technique, etc., see Blümner, *Technologie und Terminologie der Gewerbe und Künste bei Griechen und Römern* (1874–1887); Baumeister, *Denkmäler des klassischen Alterthums*, s. v. "Malerei," "Polychromie;" Richter, *Ueber Technisches in d. Malerei der Alten* (Munich, 1885); Petrie, *Hawara, Biahmu, and Arsinoë* (1889); Cros and Henry, *L'Encaustique* (1884); Linton, *Ancient and Modern Colours* (London, 1852); and Church, *The Chemistry of Paints and Painting* (1890). See also POMPEII.

Picumnus. An old Italian god of agriculture, credited with the invention of the use of manure. He was said to be the husband of Pomona. His brother Pilumnus was honoured by bakers as the inventor of the pestle (*pilum*) for crushing corn; and the two together were protecting deities to women in child-bed and to new-born infants. Hence, in the country, festal couches were set for them in the *atrium* when children were safely brought to birth. According to another ancient view, there were three divinities protecting mother and child, who prevented the mischievous intrusion of Silvanus into the house. These powers (representing the triumph of civilization over the wild forest life) were impersonated by three men, who went round the house in the night, and knocked on the threshold of the front and back doors, first with a hatchet and then with a pestle, and lastly swept them with a broom (Serv. *ad* Verg. *Aen.* ix. 9; Isid. *Orig.* iv. 11).

The names of these deities were Intercidona, god of the hewing of timbers, Pilumnus, of the crushing of corn into meal by the pestle, and Deverra, of the sweeping together of grain (Varro, quoted by St. Augustine, *De Civitate Dei*, vi. 9). Picumnus, as appears in the name, is identical with Picus (q. v.).

Picus. An Italian god of agriculture, and especially of manure, hence called son of Stercutus ("the dunger"—i. e. Saturn). He also appears as a forest-god with prophetic powers, and as father of Faunus (Verg. *Aen.* viii. 48). In Latin legend he plays a prominent part as a warlike hero, the earliest king of Latium, of great wealth, who was finally changed into a woodpecker (*picus*) (ib. 187–190). According to Ovid (*Met.* xiv. 320–396), this was because he spurned the love of Circé and was faithful to the beautiful nymph Canens. Probably Picus was originally the woodpecker, the symbol of Mars as giver of fertility and warlike prowess, and from this symbol there was developed a separate deity.

Pieria (Πιερία). (1) A narrow strip of country on the southeastern coast of Macedonia, extending from the mouth of the Peneus in Thessaly to the Haliacmon, and bounded on the west by Mount Olympus and its offshoots. A portion of these mountains was called by the ancient writers PIĔRUS, or the Pierian Mountain. The inhabitants of this country, the Pieres, were a Thracian people, and are celebrated in the early history of Greek poetry and music, since their country was one of the earliest seats of the worship of the Muses, hence called PIERĬDES, and Orpheus is said to have been buried there. After the establishment of the Macedonian kingdom in Emathia in the seventh century B.C. Pieria was conquered by the Macedonians, and the inhabitants were driven out of the country. (2) A district in Macedonia east of the Strymon near Mount Pangaeum, where the Pierians settled, who had been driven out of their original abodes by the Macedonians, as already related. They possessed in this district the fortified towns of Phagres and Pergamus. (3) A district on the northern coast of Syria, so called from the mountain Pieria, a branch of the Amanus, a name given it by the Macedonians.

Pierĭdes (Πιερίδες). (1) See MUSAE; PIERIA. (2) The nine daughters of Pierus, king of Emathia, to whom he gave the name of the nine Muses. They entered into a contest with the Muses, and, being defeated, were changed into birds (Ovid, *Met.* v. 300–678; Pausan. ix. 29, 2).

Piĕrus (Πίερος). (1) See PIERIA. (2) See PIERIDES.

Piĕtas. The Roman goddess typifying loyalty and devotion, especially to parents. She is depicted on coins as a matron offering incense; and her symbol is the stork (Pliny, *H. N.* vii. 121).

Piĕtas Iulia. See POLA.

Pignus. In Roman law, a pledge seized by a creditor, or given to him, to secure the performance of an obligation.

I. If given, a contractual relation exists between the pledgor and pledgee (*pignori dans, accipiens*). The pledgee is bound to restore the pledge when the debt is paid; the pledgor is bound to reimburse the pledgee for necessary outlays. The pledgee had originally no right except to hold the pledge until the debt was paid. Even when the debtor was in default, the creditor could not sell the pledge (*pignus distrahere*) unless this had been specially agreed. At a later period such an agreement was presumed, and in the final development of the Roman law an agreement that the pledge should not be sold had no effect except that the creditor, before selling, was obliged to give the debtor three warnings (*denuntiationes*) instead of one. In case the sum realized by the creditor exceeded the amount due him, he was bound to restore the surplus (*superfluum, hyperocha*) to the pledgor. The pledgee had no right to use the property pledged unless this was specially agreed. If the property yielded *fructus* (as was the case, for example, with land), and if, as was not uncommon, it was agreed that the creditor should appropriate the yield in lieu of interest on the debt, the contract was termed *antichresis*.

Originally, the pledgee had no right against third persons. His possession was indeed protected: but if he lost possession, he could not recover as against an honest conveyee or pledgee in possession. The only method of giving him such a right of recovery was to break loose from the conception of pignus and make him owner, with an understanding that when the debt was paid he should reconvey the property to the debtor. This form of pledge (which did not require delivery of possession) was termed *fiducia* (q. v.). Towards the close of the republican period, however, the law of pignus was so developed as to admit lien without conveyance of ownership or delivery of possession, and to give the pledgee a right of recovery as against third persons. The first step was to recognize that a landlord (*locator fundi*) might obtain, by contract, a lien (*pignus*) on all the chattels which his tenant (*colonus*) brought upon the farm (*invecta et illata*). When the tenant was in arrears with his rent, summary proceedings were devised to put the landlord in possession (*interdictum Salvianum*). The next step was to enable the landlord to follow up any such chattels as were removed from the farm. This was done by the *actio Serviana.* A form of *pignus* was thus developed which operated *in rem*, and therefore created a *ius in re.* The third and last step was to extend the new principle to all contractual pledges, with or without possession. This was done by the *actio quasi Serviana.* A similar form of lien had been developed in Greece; and at the time of Cicero the term *hypotheca* was being naturalized among the Romans, and in the early Empire the jurists spoke of the *actio quasi Serviana seu hypothecaria.* The terms *pignus* and *hypotheca* were thenceforth used interchangeably, although the more careful writers restricted *pignus* to the pledge in possession (which was most frequent in the case of movables) and *hypotheca* to the pledge without possession.

In the earlier civil law it is probable that only corporeal things could be given *pignori.* In the later development of the law it was possible to create a lien on almost any property right, even on a right of action or debt (*pignus nominis*). The right of the pledgee might itself be pledged (*pignus pignoris*). It was finally recognized that all the assets of an estate might be hypothecated.

Successive hypothecations of the same property were possible. As between the different pledgees, the general rule was *prior potior.*

II. Pledges might be seized without the consent of the owners. For the *pignoris capio* of certain favoured creditors in early Roman law, see ACTIO in the Appendix. For the power of the magistrates to enforce obedience to their commands by *pignoris capio*, see MAGISTRATUS. Out of the latter power was gradually developed the seizure of property to satisfy judgment (*pignus in causa iudicati captum*).

Pigres (Πίγρης). A Greek poet of Halicarnassus, regarded by Baumeister and others as author of the *Batrachomyomachia* (q. v.). He is said to have been either the brother or son of Queen Artemisia (q. v.) of Caria. Besides the work mentioned, a poem called *Margites* is ascribed to him by Suidas (s. v.) and by Plutarch. He also inserted a pentameter line after each hexameter in the *Iliad*—a very curious literary freak. The following will serve as an illustration (*Il.* i. 1):

Μῆνιν ἄειδε θεὰ Πηληιάδεω Ἀχιλλῆος,
Μοῦσα γὰρ σὺ πάσης πείρατ᾽ ἔχεις σοφίης·

He is also said to have been the first poet to introduce the iambic trimeter. See HOMERUS.

Pigrum Maré. A name given by the Romans to the furthermost part of the North Sea, because its waters were supposed to be sluggish, or even half congealed (Tac. *Germ.* 45; Pliny, *H. N.* iv. 13).

Pīla. (1) (ἴγδη). A deep mortar in which substances of any kind, as drugs, were brayed and pounded with a pestle (*pilum*). It is chiefly distinguished from a *mortuarium* (q. v.) in being larger. (2) (πεσσός). A pillar used for architectural or other purposes, as the support of a bridge (Livy, xl. 51), a monument (Nepos, *Alcib.* 4), or the post in front of a book-shop, on which the publisher's announcements were hung (Hor. *Sat.* i. 4, 71). (3) (ἐνδόμησις). A pier or breakwater (Verg. *Aen.* ix. 711).

Pila or Mortar. (Pompeii.)

Pĭla. Pĭla Lusoria (σφαῖρα). (1) A ball. Ball-playing was a very favourite occupation among both Greeks and Romans, though regarded less as a game than as an exercise for strengthening the muscles and cultivating suppleness of limb. The earliest mention of such an exercise is found in two passages of the *Odyssey* (vi. 100; viii. 370). In the second passage, ball-tossing is an adjunct of the dance, and this choric ball-play was very popular at Sparta (Athen. i. 24 b), and long survived. In the Athenian gymnasia a special room (σφαιριστήριον) was devoted to this and similar exercises with balls. The practice was introduced at Rome only in the later days of the Republic (Hor. *Sat.* ii. 2, 10), but when once established it took a strong hold on persons of all classes and of all ages—old men as well as boys adopting it (Seneca, *De Brev. Vit.* 13; Sueton. *Aug.* 83; Pliny, *Epist.* iii. 1, 8).

The different kinds of balls in use were as follows: (*a*) the *harpastum* (μικρὰ σφαῖρα), a small hand-ball stuffed with hair; (*b*) the *pila trigonalis* (μέση σφαῖρα), the one most used, also a hand-ball stuffed with hair, but larger than the *harpastum;* (*c*) the *arenaria*, of doubtful nature; (*d*) the *paganica* (μεγάλη σφαῖρα), a large ball stuffed with feathers (Mart. xiv. 45); and (*e*) the *follis* (κενὴ σφαῖρα), a ball filled with air, like the modern football. There is nothing to show that in classical times the Greeks and Romans had any games of ball involving the use of a bat or racquet, though in one form of game the ball was struck with the palm of the hand (*lusus pilae cum palma,* Med. Lat.).

The following are the principal technical terms used in playing ball: διδόναι, βάλλειν, ἀφιέναι, *dare, mittere, iactare,* "to throw a ball;" λαμβάνειν, δέχεσθαι, *accipere, excipere, captare,* "to catch;" ἀντιπέμπειν, ἀνταφιέναι, *remittere, reddere,* "to throw *back* a ball to the sender;" οὐρανία, *datatim ludere,* "to play at catch;" ἀπόρραξις, "bounce-ball;" φενίνδα, *fallere,* "pretending to throw to one player when really throwing to another."

GAMES AT BALL (σφαιρομαχίαι). (*a*) The game called ἐπίσκυρος (also ἐφηβικὴ and ἐπίκοινος: Poll. ix. 104, Eustath. l. c.). In this game the ground was marked by two base lines (γραμμαὶ κατόπιν), and another line drawn parallel to them through the middle of the ground, presumably more than a stone's-throw from them, which was called σκῦρος or λατύπη, because it was marked with finely broken stones. The ball was placed upon this line (whence the name ἐπίσκυρος), and the players started at the same moment from their respective base-lines. The player who could first seize the ball threw it as far as he could towards the enemy's base-line: the object was to force the line of enemies back by constantly returning the ball farther and farther over their heads until they were driven over their own base-line. Clearly, getting the first throw by fast running at the start must have been an enormous advantage (cf. Schol. *ad* Plat. *Leg.* i. p. 633 C). It is not improbable, though there is no proof of it, that the contest of the *pagani* (whence the name *paganica* for the third-sized Roman ball) was a game of this kind. It seems to have been regarded as a game for the young (ἐφηβική), and for large numbers (ἐπίκοινος).

(*b*) *Harpastum* (or, by the older name, *Pheninda;* in Athen. and Eustath. φαινίνδα: in Clem. Alex. φενίνδα: in *Etym. Mag.* φεννίς, φενίνδα, φενακίνδα). This game cannot with certainty be reconstructed, but the following seems to us an outline most consistent with our authorities. (Galen, περὶ τῆς σμικρᾶς σφαίρας: Sidon. Apoll. v. 17; Mart. iv. 19; vii. 32; xiv. 48; Athen. i. p. 25; Eustath. l. c.; Poll. ix. 105). There were clearly two sides, for Galen lays stress on the fact that there is emulation (φιλοτιμία), which exercises the ψυχή, as well as movements which exercise the limbs and the eye: there are presumably base-lines as goals, without which it is hard to understand what he says about generalship (στρατηγία), and positions won and lost. The ground was then probably rectangular, the two ends being base-lines, and it was divided by a line in the centre (*trames*) into two equal camps. There was always one "middle player," a special feature of the game, called *medicurrens* (Sidon.), or ὁ μεταξύ (Galen: cf. *vagus*, Mart. vii. 32), each side being probably so represented in turn: how the "innings" of the *medicurrens* ended we do not know, but perhaps he gave up his place to one of the other side whenever a point was scored against his side. As to the identity of *pheninda* with *harpastum* we have the positive statement of Athenaeus that it was the old name of *harpastum*, the belief of Pollux that it was, and the fact that in some places it still went by that name; and, moreover, no writer mentions both games as distinct.

(*c*) *Trigon.* In this favourite game of the Romans there were no "sides," but each played for himself; still it was a legitimate game, played for winning and losing. The following description may, as it seems to us, best meet the accounts which we have: There were three players standing in the form of an equilateral triangle. Each player had one ball to start with, and played for his own score. He would wish both his fellow-players to miss their strokes, and drop the ball as often as possible. He might send his ball to either player (presumably there was some rule about sending it fairly within their reach), and he might do so either by catching the ball which came to him and throwing it, or by "fiving" it, so as either to strike it back to the sender (*repercutere*) or sideways to the third player (*expulsare*). Obviously the most disastrous position would be receiving three balls nearly at the same time — if, for instance, his own ball is smartly struck back to him, and almost simultaneously the two others have been sent to him; obviously, also, his easiest position was to receive only one ball at a time with a fair interval before the next. The winner was probably the player who allowed his ball to drop the fewest times. A fourth person stood by to count the misses (*numerare*). The ball used was a hard one, covered with leather and stuffed with hair, as stated above. See Becq de Fouquières, *Les Jeux des Anciens*, pp. 176–211.

(*d*) In very late times (i. e. in the Byzantine Period) a game of ball was played on horseback bearing a strong resemblance to our modern "polo" (Cinnamus, *Hist.* vi. 4). It was confined chiefly to princes and the higher nobles, who took sides and struck at a leather ball with a sort of curved stick provided with a catgut network, the object being for each party to drive the ball over the opponents' base-line (πέρας).

The word *pilicrepus*, so often found in Latin, means in general a professional ball-player as distinguished from an amateur, and is applied to teachers of scientific ball-playing and to those who juggled with balls. These last were also called *pilarii.* The following illustration, from the Baths of Titus at Rome, shows a *pilicrepus* (the person with a beard) giving a lesson in *trigon* to three young men:

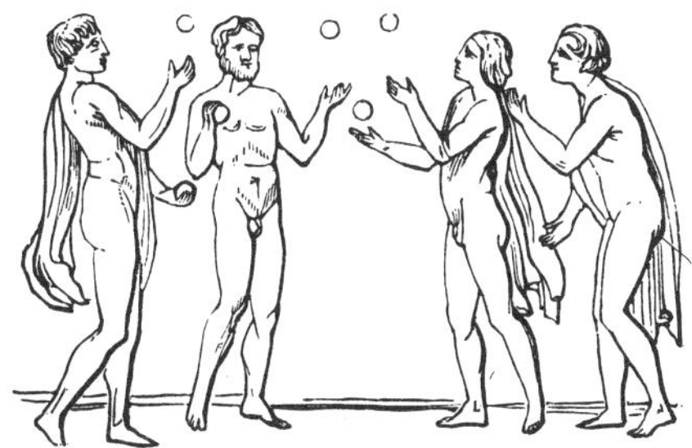

Lesson in Trigon. (From the Baths of Titus.)

There is an interesting wall-inscription from Pompeii which has been variously interpreted. It is an announcement of a ball-game, and reads as follows, the punctuation being that preferred by the present writer:

Amianthus, Epaphra, Tertius ludant cum Hedysio. Iucandus Nolanus petat. Numerent Citus et Iacus. Amianthus.

In this game, Hedysius is the *pilicrepus* who plays against any two of the three challengers first named. Iucandus of Nola picks up the dropped balls and pitches them back to the players. Citus and Iacus (the latter when not playing himself) keep the score—i. e. note the dropped balls. Amianthus signs the notice.

See Becq de Fouquières, *Les Jeux des Anciens* (1873); Marquardt, *De Sphaeromachiis Veterum* (1876); and Grasberger, *Erziehung und Unterricht*, pp. 88 foll. (1880).

(2) A balloting-ball; employed as a means for selecting what judge should try a cause, and prevent the packing of the bench against the interest of either party. For this purpose a certain number of balls, with the names of different judges inscribed on them, were put into a box, and thence drawn out by lot (Prop. iv. 11, 20; Ascon. *Argument. Milon.*).

(3) An effigy made out of old pieces of cloth stuffed with hay and employed to try the temper of some animals, bulls and buffaloes, when baited; or to infuriate them if they appeared tame and

impassive (Mart. *De Spect.* 19; Ascon. *ad* Cic. *Fragm. pro C. Cornel.*).

Pĭla Mattiăca. A ball of German pomade, employed by the ladies of Rome and young men of fashion to tinge the hair a light or fair colour. It was composed of goats' tallow and beechwood ashes made up into a ball, which received its distinguishing epithet from the town of Mattium (Wiesbaden) from whence it was imported (Mart. xiv. 27). See SAPO; SPUMA.

Pĭla Vitrea. A glass globe filled with water for the purpose of being placed between a person and the object he is contemplating, in order to magnify the object and render it clearer to the view—a custom still adopted in wood-engraving. It would also appear from a passage of Seneca (*Q. N.* i. 6) that this contrivance was sometimes employed by the ancients to assist an imperfect or failing sight, in the place of our spectacles. It must, however, be remembered that the ancients, who employed a numerous class of well-educated slaves in the character of readers, secretaries, and amanuenses, did not stand so much in need of an artificial aid to the eyesight as we moderns do.

Pīlāni. The original name by which the soldiers composing the third line or division of the old Roman legion were distinguished, because they alone at that time were armed with the heavy javelin or *pilum*, the other two using the spear or *hasta*. But when the *pilum* was adopted for all the three divisions, the title of *triarii* was substituted for that of *pilani*, with which it becomes thenceforth synonymous (Varro, *L. L.* v. 89; Paulus *ex* Fest. s. v.; Ovid, *Fast.* iii. 129). Subsequently, however, to this period, and towards the close of the Republic, when the custom obtained of drawing up an army by lines in cohorts, the distinctive character, as well as the name of *pilani* or *triarii* was abandoned, because it no longer represented any real distinction. See TRIARII.

Pilarius. One who exhibits feats of dexterity with a number of balls, similar to the Indian juggler (Quint. x. 7, 11; Inscript. *ap.* Fabrett. p. 250, n. 2), by throwing them up with both hands, catching them on, and making them rebound from, the palm. See PĬLA (1).

Pilarius. (From a Diptych at Verona.)

Pilentum. A sort of spring-cart, used chiefly at Rome by women of the upper classes. No representation of the Roman *pilentum* is known to exist, and hence its form is a matter of conjecture. It had, however, four wheels, was fitted with cushions, and was used on occasions of state for conveying the Roman matrons, *flamines*, and Vestals in processions and to the public games (Verg. *Aen.* viii. 666; Hor. *Epist.* ii. 1, 192; Livy, i. 21; Claud. *De Nupr. Honor.* 285; Isidor. *Orig.* xx. 12). It was covered at the top, but open at the sides. See Ginzrot, *Die Wagen der Alten*, ch. liv.

Pilia. The wife of T. Pomponius Atticus (q. v.), the friend of Cicero (Cic. *Ad Att.* iv. 16).

Pilicrĕpus. A word used to designate an expert ball-player (Seneca, *Epist.* 56). See PĬLA.

Pilleus, Pileus, or **Pilleum** (πῖλος, πῖλιον). A round felt cap with little or no brim, lying close to the temples. It was the mark of fishermen, sailors, and artisans; hence Castor and Pollux, Odysseus, Charon, Hephaestus, and Daedalus are represented with it. The upper classes wore it only in the country or when travelling; but it was worn in Rome by the whole people at the Saturnalia, and by freedmen as a sign of their new position. Hence the phrase *ad pilleos vocare* means "to set free." (Cf. Pers. iii. 106.) The first form of pilleus represented in the illustration is that which has become in modern times the "liberty cap." It was Phrygian in its origin. It was placed on the head of slaves when sold, as a sign that the vender undertook no responsibility. See SERVI.

Forms of the Pilleus.

The diminutive forms PILLEŎLUS and PILLEŎLUM are also used.

Pillow. See LECTUS.

Pilum. (1) (ὑσσός). The javelin of the Roman legionaries (about six feet long), which was hurled at the enemy's ranks at the beginning of the engagement, before proceeding to the use of the sword. It consisted of a wooden shaft three feet long, easily grasped in the hand, and an iron head of the same length, culminating in a barbed point, and provided with a socket to which the shaft was attached by iron rivets. Marius had the heads constructed of soft, weak iron, the point only being steeled. In this way, if the point stuck in the shield of an enemy, the iron was bent by the weight of the shaft, rendering the weapon useless and difficult to draw out, while it made the shield unmanageable so long as it remained in it (Plut. *Mar.* 25). When well thrown, the pilum would penetrate both shield and armour. (2) (κόπανον). A large instrument for braying substances in a mortar (*pila*). It was held in both hands, and was much heavier as well as longer than the *pistillum*. See PĬLA.

Pilum. (Mainz Museum.)

Pilumnus. One of the three deities conceived by the Italian tribes to protect women in childbed, and their offspring, from the mischief of the forest god Silvanus. See PICUMNUS; SILVANUS.

Pimplēa (Πίμπλεια). A town in the Macedonian province of Pieria, sacred to the Muses, who were hence called *Pimpleïdes*. Horace (*Carm.* i. 26, 9) uses the form *Pimplea* in the singular, and not *Pimpleïs*.

Pin. See ACUS; FIBULA.

Pinacothēca (πινακοθήκη). A picture gallery. At Rome pictures were first publicly exhibited by Marcellus after the capture of Syracuse (B.C. 212), from which he brought away many works of art.

Such objects were at first shown in the public buildings which they were used in decorating; but in the later years of the Republic private collections grew to considerable importance, and were kept in special galleries in the mansions of the rich (Cic. *Tusc.* v. 35, 102). See also Vitruv. i. 2, vi. 5, 7; Pliny, *H. N.* xxxv. 4; and Marquardt, *Privatleben,* 611; Becker-Göll, *Gallus,* ii. 275.

Pinăra (τὰ Πίναρα). An inland city of Lycia, where Pandarus (q. v.) was worshipped as a hero (Pliny, *H. N.* v. 101).

Pinaria Gens. One of the most ancient patrician gentes at Rome, tracing its origin to a time long previous to the foundation of the city. The legend related that when Hercules came into Italy he was hospitably received, on the spot where Rome was afterwards built, by the Potitii and the Pinarii, two of the most distinguished families in the country. The hero, in return, taught them the way in which he was to be worshipped; but as the Pinarii were not at hand when the sacrificial banquet was ready, and did not come till the entrails of the victim were eaten, Hercules, in anger, determined that the Pinarii should, in all future time, be excluded from partaking of the entrails of the victims, and that in all matters relating to his worship should be inferior to the Potitii (Livy, i. 7; Dionys. i. 40; Macrob. iii. 6, 12). These two families continued to be the hereditary priests of Hercules till the censorship of Appius Claudius (B.C. 312), who purchased from the Potitii the knowledge of the sacred rites, and intrusted them to public slaves; whereat the god was so angry that the whole Potitia gens, containing twelve families and thirty grown-up men, perished within a year, or, according to other accounts, within thirty days, and Appius himself became blind (Livy, ix. 29). The Pinarii did not share in the guilt of communicating the sacred knowledge, and therefore did not receive the same punishment as the Potitii, but continued in existence to the latest times. It appears that the worship of Hercules by the Potitii and Pinarii was a *sacrum gentilicium* belonging to these gentes, and that in the time of Appius Claudius these *sacra privata* were made *sacra publica.* The Pinarii were divided into the families of Mamercinus, Natta, Posca, Rusca, and Scarpus, but none of them obtained sufficient importance to require a separate notice.

Pinarius, Lucius. The great-nephew of Iulius Caesar, being the grandson of his sister Iulia. He was named as one of the heirs in Caesar's will (Suet. *Iul.* 83).

Pinărus (Πίναρος). A river of Cilicia, rising in Mount Amanus, and falling into the Gulf of Issus (Strabo, p. 676).

Pinax (πίναξ). (1) A tablet. See Tabula. (2) See Cebes.

Pincerna (οἰνοχόος). A cup-bearer (Inscr. Orell. 2881).

Pincers. See Forpex.

Pindărus (Πίνδαρος). The greatest of the Greek lyric poets, son of Daïphantos, was born at or near Thebes, B.C. 522. He belonged to a noble and priestly family and was carefully educated. His musical training was received from the best masters of the time, among whom is mentioned, perhaps without sufficient warrant, Lasos of Hermioné, the regenerator of the dithyramb. Familiar is the story of his unsuccessful contest with Corinna, and of the advice which she gave the youthful poet when he crowded the opening of one of his hymns with mythological figures: "Sow with the hand and not with the whole sack." Pindar began his career as a local poet early in life, and the Tenth Pythian, which is said to have been composed when he was only twenty years old, shows all the elements of his future greatness. By the time of the Persian War Pindar had risen to the position of a national poet, and though he was a good Theban and a stanch aristocrat, though he was bound by the ties of his family, which belonged to the old nobility, and by the ties of his people, who sided with the Persians, he was too true a Greek, too thoroughly Pan-Hellenic not to be proud of the victory of the Greeks of Attica over the Persians, and the victory of the Greeks of Sicily over the Carthaginians. According to the well-known story the high praise which he bestowed on Athens as the 'Stay of Greece' roused the indignation of the Thebans, who imposed on him a heavy fine, which the Athenians reimbursed twofold, adding, as is further reported, a statue and other honours. Like the other lyric poets of his time, Pindar travelled far and wide in fulfilment of his calling, though, doubtless, he often sent his song instead of going himself. A long sojourn in Sicily is beyond a doubt, and Aegina, which he loved only next to Thebes, must have been to him a second home; nor is it unlikely that he knew Macedon in the North and Cyrené in the South. He was received everywhere with veneration and bore himself as a peer of princes. And not only was he honoured by the highest on earth, but the gods themselves are said to have shown him special favour and to have sent him at last the boon of a swift and easy death as he rested his head on the lap of his favourite in the theatre or in the gymnasium of Argos. The date of that death we do not know with certainty, but his life can hardly have been prolonged much beyond the middle of the fifth century. The reverence felt for the poet in his lifetime was paid to his genius after his death, and when Thebes was pillaged and destroyed by the Macedonian soldiery in the next century, the house of Pindar was spared by the express order of Alexander the Great, whose ancestor he had celebrated in song.

Pindar was a consummate master of the whole domain of lyric poetry, as is shown by the fragments of his hymns (ὕμνοι), his paeans (παιᾶνες), his dancing-songs (ὑπορχήματα), his processional songs (προσόδια), his songs for choruses of virgins (παρθένια), his songs of praise (ἐγκώμια), his drinking-songs (παροίνια) and catches (σκολιά), his dithyrambs (διθύραμβοι) and dirges (θρῆνοι). These show the breadth of his genius; the height of it we must estimate by the one group of his poems which we have entire, the Songs of Victory (ἐπινίκια or ἐπίνικοι), composed to celebrate the successful contestants in the great national games of Greece, Olympian (Ὀλυμπιονῖκαι, sc. ὕμνοι), Pythian (Πυθιονῖκαι), Nemean (Νεμεονῖκαι), Isthmian (Ἰσθμιονῖκαι). In these poems, which were delivered by trained choruses, the poet is the spokesman, and this is an important point for the appreciation of the often intensely personal tone of the lyric chorus as compared with the chorus of the drama. A victory at one of the great games was a matter of joy and pride not only to the victor himself and to his kindred, but also to the community, so that there is a peculiar blending of the private with the public, of intimate allusion with wide scope. The elements are many: festal joy, wise and thoughtful counsel, the uplifting of the heart in prayer for prince and for people, the inspiration of a fervent patriotism; but the victory is the dominant theme, and that victory is raised to the high level of the eternal prevalence of the beautiful and the good over the foul and the base; the victor is transfigured into a glorious personification of his race, and the present is reflected, magnified, illuminated in the mirror of the mythic past. The epinician becomes the triumphal song of Hellenism and the triumphal song of idealized humanity. To understand this it is necessary to understand also the deep religious and ethical and artistic meaning of the great games of Greece, of which the Olympian Games were the crown; so that whatever else a man might achieve or suffer, an Olympian victory was sunshine for life. 'To spend and to toil'—this is the motto of him who would attain; a motto that means self-sacrifice, submission to authority, devotion to the public weal; and this motto is incarnate in the Pindaric Heracles, who is held up as the type of achievement and endurance in obedience to the divine will. Heracles is the Doric ideal, and Pindar his last prophet. Pindar still lives in the world of the old gods, still believes in the array of their shining forms, and if he rejects a myth that dishonours god, his faith is intact, the priestly temper conquers. Life was a serious thing to him. The melancholy strain that is not absent from Homer, that dominates Hesiod, makes itself heard in Pindar. We hear over and over again of the shortness and the sorrowfulness of human life, the transitoriness of its pleasures, our utter dependence upon the will of an envious god. And yet it is not a melancholy that degenerates into doleful brooding. It is 'a spur that the clear spirit doth raise' to noble action. But for noble action noble blood is necessary. Pindar is an aristocrat, and to him the blood of the gods is the true channel of the grace of the gods. Government fitly reposes only in the hands of those who are endowed by nature for the work of the ruler, and what is true of government is true also of art. Art is divine, and the eagle, the bird of Zeus, is its chosen symbol. Ineffectual chatter is all that can be expected of crows and daws. But the divine right of government, the divine right of genius, is not absolute, and is to be exercised only in obedience to divine law. Native endowment being god-given involves the duty of self-restraint, which is imposed by the giver. And this "measure," which is the summary of Pindaric ethics, brings with it the recompense of reward in that other world which Pindar sees and makes us see with a startling sense of reality.

Pindar was claimed by the ancient rhetoricians as an exemplar of the "austere" style, as belonging to the same order as Aeschylus in tragedy, as Thucydides in history. His style is the grand style, but grand after the antique pattern of grandeur, which combines weight and fulness of meaning with artistic exactness in every detail. The copiousness of Pindar is a commonplace, but the subtle art of Pindar is often overlooked in the earlier characterizations of his poetry, and it is safe to follow the poet himself, who bears ample witness to his own excellences. Opulence, elevation, force, cunning workmanship, vigorous execution—these are all claimed by the poet for himself; and his splendour, his loftiness, his wealth of imagery, his forceful concentration, his varied metaphor, his vivid narrative, his superb diction must be recognized at once, though the admiration of these characteristics is indefinitely enhanced by closer study. But what withdraws itself from the reader is the sequence of thought, the planfulness of the epinician, and yet this is a point which Pindar also insists on. This planfulness, though disregarded or denied by literary people ancient and modern, has been diligently sought after by the best commentators and by the most thoughtful students of Pindar, and while no consensus has been reached, much has been done to show sequence and balance, to reproduce the architectonic principle, to bring out the relations of the myth which forms the heart of every ode to the rest of the organism, to trace the thread of the thought and to make audible the burden of the song as revealed by the recurrence of significant words and significant sentiments. Despite much straining and much over-interpretation, Pindar is much nearer to us than he was ever before. The music and the dance are lost without which the full significance of a Pindaric ode cannot be appreciated, but the rhythm remains, and under the guidance of the rhythm we can penetrate into many of the recesses of Pindaric songs.

The great Pindaric MSS. are, according to Mommsen's notation, **A** (Ambrosianus A), twelfth century; **B** (Vaticanus B), also of the twelfth century; **C** (Parisinus G), belongs to the close of the twelfth century); **D** (Mediceus B) in the Laurentian Library at Florence, thirteenth or fourteenth century. The inferior MSS. are called Thomani, Moschopulei, Tricliniani, as they represent the editions of Thomas Magister, Moschopulos, and Triclinius. A good reading in them is a lucky accident.

The older scholia to Pindar go back to Didymus as Didymus goes back to an earlier time, and they have a certain value for the constitution of the text; the later scholia have very little value of any kind. A critical edition was begun by E. Abel with Nemeans and Isthmians in 1884.

Bibliography.—The *editio princeps* is an Aldine, 8vo (1513), followed by the *editio Romana* (1515). Then the ed. of H. Stephanus, 16mo (Paris, 1560), followed by five other Stephanus editions. Erasmus Schmidt (Wittenberg, 1616), elaborate, learned, with a fair proportion of successful emendations; Heyne (Göttingen, 1773; 2d ed. 1797), who revived the study of Pindar, enriched by the contributions of Gottfried Hermann; (3d ed. 1817) after the death of Heyne (1812). Hermann did much for Pindar, and Pindar was the favourite battle-ground of Hermann and his rival Boeckh, whose monumental edition of Pindar, two volumes in three parts (Leipzig, 1811–22), is still unexcelled for sagacious criticism, wide historical vision, reconstructive power. Metrical science dates from the *Metra Pindari* contained in this edition. Dissen, who prepared the commentary on the Nemeans and Isthmians for Boeckh, put forth a Pindar of his own (Gotha, 1830). Dissen is over-acute, sees too much, explains too much, analyzes too much. Schneidewin's edition of Dissen's Olympians and Pythians (1847) is a good advance. Bergk in the first volume of his *Poetae Lyrici Graeci* (4th ed.

1874) gives too much play to his rare acumen and brilliant conjectural talent. Tycho Mommsen (Berlin, 1864), also a small text edition (1866), is a model of completeness and system in the presentation of the critical apparatus. Donaldson's Pindar (new ed. 1868), based on Dissen, has been displaced by the excellent edition of C. A. M. Fennell (Olympians and Pythians, 2d ed. 1893; Nemeans and Isthmians, 1883). Fennell exhibits praiseworthy independence and nice scholarship. Christ's text ed. (Teubner, 1869) shows good judgment; the Latin commentary to his large ed. (1896) is hardly adequate. Mezger's commentary, without text (1880), is useful and suggestive but faddish. An elaborate edition by J. B. Bury is in progress (Nemeans, 1890; Isthmians, 1892). The editor lays too much stress on Mezger's "recurrent word," and is often the dupe of his own cleverness. To these editions may be added De Jongh's *Olympians* (Utrecht, 1855); Cookesley's *Olympians and Pythians*, 2 vols. (1850); Seymour's *Select Odes of Pindar* (1882); and Gildersleeve's *Olympians and Pythians* (1885).

TRANSLATIONS.—The best translation into English is the prose rendering of Ernest Myers (2d ed. 1884). The introductions and notes of Friedr. Thiersch's German translation (Leipzig, 1820) are still worth reading. Hartung's Pindar translation and text (Leipzig, 1855–56), contains interesting guesses. Fraccaroli's *Odi di Pindaro dichiarate e tradotte* (1894) is an important contribution to Pindaric studies.

AIDS.—Tafel, *Dilucidationes Pindaricae* (Berlin, 1824) has a great wealth of matter, relevant and irrelevant; Rauchenstein, *Zur Einleitung in Pindars Siegeslieder* (Aarau, 1843), excellent; Leopold Schmidt, *Pindars Leben und Dichtung* (Bonn, 1862), an attempt to reproduce the development of the poet; Alfred Croiset, *La Poésie de Pindare* (2d ed. Paris, 1886), a work of exceptional merit; Bindseil's concordance (Berlin, 1875); Rumpel, *Lexicon Pindaricum* (Leipzig, 1883). For the metres, besides Boeckh, see J. H. H. Schmidt in his *Eurythmie* (vol. i. of the *Kunstformen*, Leipz. 1868), and Moritz Schmidt, *Ueber den Bau der Pindarischen Strophen* (Leipzig, 1882).

Pindenissus (Πινδένισσος). A fortified town of Cilicia, which was taken by Cicero when he was proconsul of Cilicia (Cic. *Ad Att.* v.20).

Pindus (Πίνδος). (1) A lofty range of mountains in Northern Greece, a portion of the great backbone which runs through the centre of Greece from north to south. The name of Pindus was confined to that part of the chain which separates Thessaly and Epirus; and its most northerly and also highest part was called Lacmon. (2) One of the four towns in Doris, near the sources of a river of the same name.

Pinna (πτερόν). The blade of an oar. See GUBERNACULUM.

Pinna. The chief town of the Vestini, at the foot of the Apennines (Pliny, *H. N.* iii. 107).

Pinnes, Pinneus, or **Pineus.** The son of Agron, king of Illyria, by his first wife, Triteuta. At the death of Agron (B.C. 231) Pinnes, who was then a child, was left in the guardianship of his stepmother Teuta, whom Agron had married after divorcing Triteuta. When Teuta was defeated by the Romans, the care of Pinnes devolved upon Demetrius of Pharos; but when Demetrius in his turn made war against the Romans and was defeated, Pinnes was placed upon the throne by the Romans, but was compelled to pay tribute (Livy, xxii. 33).

Pinnirăpus. "Feather-snatcher," apparently a sort of slang Latin name for a gladiator who tries to pull the plume off his opponent's cap, as a trophy. The word is found only in Juv. iii. 158, on which see the scholia and Mayor's note.

Pintuaria (Πιντουαρία). Now Teneriffe; one of the Fortunatae Insulae (Canary Islands), also called CONVALLIS. From the perpetual snow on its peak, the name NIVARIA is also given to it.

Piper (πέπερι). Pepper; brought from India, and used by both Greeks and Romans as a seasoning (Pliny, *H. N.* xii. 26–29; Pers. v. 136). The word *piperatorium* is used of a pepper-box (Paul. *Sent.* iii. 6, 86). See the *Gazette Archéologique* for 1885, p. 335.

Piraeeus (Πειραιεύς) or **Piraeus.** Now Porto Leone or Porto Dracone. The most important of the harbours of Athens, was situated in the pen-

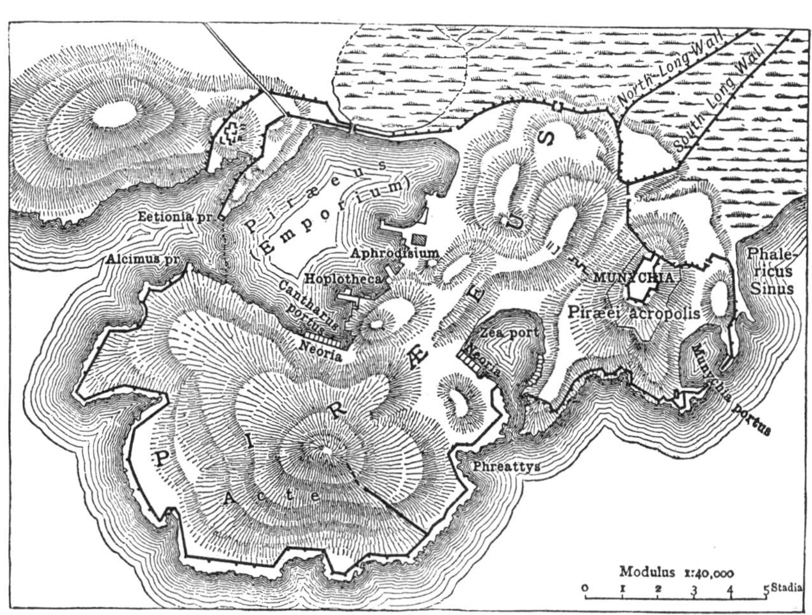

Plan of the Harbour of Athens.

insula about five miles southwest of Athens. This peninsula, which is sometimes called by the general name of Piraeeus, contained three harbours: PIRAEEUS proper on the western side, by far the largest of the three; ZEA on the eastern side, separated from the Piraeus by a narrow isthmus; and MUNYCHIA (Pharnari), still farther to the east. The northern part of the great harbour of the Piraeus was divided into three smaller harbours: Zea for corn-vessels, Aphrodisium for merchant-ships in general, and Cantharus for ships of war. It was through the suggestion of Themistocles that the Athenians were induced to make use of the harbour of Piraeeus. Before the Persian Wars their principal harbour was Phalerum, which was not situated in the Piraean peninsula at all, but lay to the east of Munychia. At the entrance of the harbour of the Piraeus there were two promontories—the one on the right-hand, called Alcimus (Ἄλκιμος), on which was the tomb of Themistocles (Pausan. i. 1, 2), and Eëtionea (Ἠετιώνεια), where the Four Hundred built a fortress (Thuc. viii. 90). The Piraeus had a good-sized population, especially of resident aliens, who were attracted by its facility for trade. The town was strongly fortified by Themistocles, and was connected with Athens by the Long Walls, due to Pericles. The narrow entrance to its harbour was protected by two great mole-heads, across which a huge chain could be drawn to keep out hostile ships.

The town had a fine agora, which stood in the centre of the place, and temples to Zeus Soter, Athené Soteira, and Aphrodité; and fine halls or *στοαί*.

Piraeïcus (Πειραϊκός). A Greek painter, probably of the time after Alexander the Great. He was the chief representative of what is called *ῥοπογραφία*, or the painting of petty subjects, such as still-life. He painted genre pictures in the Dutch style (barbers' and cobblers' shops), and subjects in still-life, of small size, but of proportionately careful execution (Propert. iii. 9, 12). In Pliny (*H. N.* xxxv. 112) the manuscript reading is *rhyparographos* ("rag-and-tatter-painter"). The word *rhopographia* is actually found in Cicero (*Ad Att.* xv. 16 *b*), and its opposite, *μεγαλογραφία*, in Vitruvius (vii. 4, § 4). See PICTURA.

Pirēné (Πειρήνη). The spring struck out by the winged steed Pegasus on the citadel of Corinth. (See PEGASUS.) It is also said to have sprung from Pirené, daughter of Oebalus, who melted into tears in sorrow for the loss of her son Cenchrias, accidentally slain by Artemis (Pausan. ii. 2, 3). It flowed from a rock in the Acrocorinthus (see CORINTHUS), and was conveyed by subterranean conduits down the hill to a marble reservoir, from which the city received a great part of its water-supply.

Pirithoüs (Πειρίθοος). The son of Ixion (or Zeus), and Dia, and king of the Lapithae in Thessaly. Pirithoüs once invaded Attica; but when Theseus came forth to oppose him, he conceived a warm admiration for the Athenian king; and from this time a most intimate friendship sprang up between the two heroes. When Pirithoüs was celebrating his marriage with Hippodamia, the intoxicated Centaur Eurytion or Eurytus carried her off, and this act occasioned the celebrated fight

Head of Pirithoüs. (West Pediment of the Temple of Zeus at Olympia.)

between the Centaurs and Lapithae, in which the Centaurs were defeated. Theseus, who was present at the wedding of Pirithoüs, assisted him in his battle against the Centaurs. Hippodamia afterwards died, and each of the two friends resolved to wed a daughter of Zeus. With the assistance of Pirithoüs, Theseus carried off Helen from Sparta. Pirithoüs was still more ambitious, and resolved to carry off Persephoné (Proserpina), the wife of the king of the lower world. Theseus would not desert his friend in the enterprise, though he knew the risk which they ran. The two friends accordingly descended to the lower world; but they were seized by Pluto and fastened to a rock, where they both remained till Heracles visited Hades. Heracles delivered Theseus, who had made the daring attempt only to please his friend; but Pirithoüs remained forever in torment (*Il.* i. 263; *Odyss.* xi. 630, xxi. 295; Hor. *Carm.* iii. 4, 80).

Pirus (Πεῖρος) or **Piĕrus** (Πίερος). The chief river of Achaia, falling into the Gulf of Patras.

Pisa (Πῖσα). The capital of PISĀTIS (Πισᾶτις), the middle portion of the province of Elis, in the Peloponnesus. (See ELIS.) Pisa itself was situated north of the Alphaeus, at a very short distance east of Olympia, and, in consequence of its proximity to the latter place, was frequently identified by the poets with it. The history of the Pisatae consists of their struggle with the Eleans, with whom they contended for the presidency of the Olympic Games. The Pisatae obtained this honour in the eighth Olympiad (B.C. 748), with the assistance of Phidon, tyrant of Argos, and also a second time in the thirty-fourth Olympiad (B.C. 644), by means of their own king Pantaleon. In the fifty-second Olympiad (B.C. 572) the struggle between the two peoples was brought to a close by the conquest and destruction of Pisa by the Eleans.

Pisae. Now Pisa. An ancient city of Etruria, and one of the twelve cities of the confederation. It was situated at the confluence of the Arnus and Ausar (Serchio), about six miles from the sea. According to some traditions, Pisae was founded by the companions of Nestor, the inhabitants of Pisa, in Elis, who were driven upon the coast of Italy on their return from Troy; whence the Roman poets give the Etruscan town the surname of Alphea. In B.C. 180 it was made a Latin colony. Its harbour, called Portus Pisanus, at the mouth of the Arnus (Arno), was much used by the Romans.

Pisander (Πείσανδρος). (1) An early Greek poet, born at Camirus, in the island of Rhodes, and supposed to have flourished about B.C. 650, although some made him earlier than Hesiod, and contemporary with Eumolpus. He wrote a poem, entitled *Heraclea* (Ἡράκλεια), on the exploits of Heracles, of which frequent mention is made by the grammarians. The Alexandrian critics assigned him a rank among epic poets after Homer, Hesiod, Panyasis, and Antimachus. (2) A Greek poet, born at Laranda, a city of Lycaonia, in Asia Minor, and who lived during the reign of Alexander Severus. He composed a long poem, entitled Ἡρωϊκαὶ Θεογαμίαι, in which he sang of the nuptials of gods and heroes. The sixteenth book of this poem is cited, and Suidas calls the whole production a history varied after the epic manner. One of the interlocutors in the *Saturnalia* of Macrobius (v. 2) accuses Vergil of having translated from Pisander almost all the second book of the *Aeneid*, and particularly the story of the wooden horse. (3) An epigrammatic poet, supposed by Jacobs to be the same with the native of Camirus above mentioned. Heyne, however, thinks that he was identical with the younger Pisander. (4) An Athenian, one of the leaders of the oligarchical party, and instrumental in bringing about the establishment of the Council of Four Hundred (Thuc. vi. 27, 60; viii. 49, 63, 89; Plut. *Alcib.*). (5) A Spartan admiral, in the time of Agesilaüs, slain in a naval battle with Conon near Cnidus, B.C. 394. (Xen. *Hellen.* iv. 3, 10).

Pisātis (Πισᾶτις). See PISA.

Pisaurum. Now Pesaro; an ancient town of Umbria, near the mouth of the river Pisaurus (Foglia), on the road to Ariminum. It was colonized by the Romans in B.C. 186.

Pisaurus. See PISAURUM.

Piscīna (literally, "fish-pond"). (1) (κολυμβήθρα). An artificial pond of either salt or fresh water for keeping fish. (See VIVARIUM.) (2) (λουτρόν). A pool or basin of water in Roman bath-rooms. See BALNEAE, p. 191.

Pisidia (ἡ Πισιδική). An inland district of Asia Minor, lying north of Lycia and Pamphylia. It was a mountainous region, inhabited by a warlike people, who maintained their independence against all the successive rulers of Asia Minor. The Romans never subdued the Pisidians in their mountain fortresses, though they took some of the towns on the outskirts of their country—for example, Antiochia, which was made a colony with the *ius Italicum.* In fact, the northern part, in which Antiochia stood, had originally belonged to Phrygia, and was more accessible and more civilized than the mountains which formed the proper country of the Pisidians. Nominally, the country was considered a part of Pamphylia, till the new subdivision of the Empire under Constantine, when Pisidia was made a separate province. The country is still inhabited by wild tribes, among whom travelling is dangerous; and it is therefore little known. Ancient writers say that it contained, amidst its rugged mountains, some fertile valleys, where the olive flourished; and it also produced the gum storax, some medicinal plants, and salt. On the southern slope of the Taurus several rivers flowed through Pisidia and Pamphylia into the Pamphylian Gulf, the chief of which were the Cestrus and the Catarrhactes; and on the northern the mountain streams form some large salt lakes—namely, Ascania (Hoiran and Egerdir), south of Antiochia, Caralius, or Pusgusa (Bei Shehr or Kereli), southeast of the former, and Trogitis (Soghla) further to the southeast, in Isauria. Special names were given to certain districts, which are sometimes spoken of as parts of Pisidia, sometimes as distinct countries—namely, CIBYRĀTIS, in the southwest, along the north of Lycia, and CABALIA, the southwest corner of Cibyratis itself; MILYAS, the district east of Cibyratis, northeast of Lycia and northwest of Pamphylia; and ISAURIA, in the east of Pisidia, on the borders of Lycaonia.

Pisistratĭdae (Πεισιστρατίδαι). The legitimate sons of Pisistratus. The name is used sometimes to indicate only Hippias and Hipparchus, and sometimes in a wider application, embracing the grandchildren and near connections of Pisistratus (as by Herod. viii. 52, referring to a time when both Hippias and Hipparchus were dead).

Pisistrătus (Πεισίστρατος). The youngest son of Nestor and Anaxibia. He was a friend of Telemachus, and accompanied him on his journey from Pylos to Menelaüs at Sparta.

Pisistrătus (Πεισίστρατος). An Athenian, son of Hippocrates, named after Pisistratus, the youngest son of Nestor, since the family of Hippocrates was of Pylian origin, and traced their descent to Neleus, the father of Nestor. The mother of Pisistratus (whose name we do not know) was first cousin to the mother of Solon. Pisistratus grew up equally distinguished for personal beauty and for mental endowments. The relationship between him and Solon naturally drew them together, and a close friendship sprang up between them. He assisted Solon (q. v.) by his eloquence in persuading the Athenians to renew their struggle with the Megarians for the possession of Salamis, and he afterwards fought with bravery in the expedition which Solon led against the island. When Solon, after the establishment of his constitution, retired for a time from Athens, the old rivalry between the parties of the Plain, the Highlands, and the Coast broke out into open feud. The party of the Plain, comprising chiefly the landed proprietors, was headed by Lycurgus; that of the Coast, consisting of the wealthier classes not belonging to the nobles, by Megacles, the son of Alcmaeon; the party of the Highlands, which aimed at more of political freedom and equality than either of the two others, was the one at the head of which Pisistratus placed himself, because they seemed the most likely to be useful in the furtherance of his ambitious designs. His liberality, as well as his military and oratorical abilities, gained him the support of a large body of citizens. Solon, on his return, quickly saw through the designs of Pisistratus, who listened with respect to his advice, though he prosecuted his schemes none the less diligently. When Pisistratus found his plans sufficiently ripe for execution, he one day made his appearance in the agora with his mules and his own person exhibiting recent wounds, pretending that he had been nearly assassinated by his enemies as he was riding into the country. An assembly of the people was forthwith called, in which one of his partisans proposed that a body-guard of fifty citizens, armed with clubs, should be granted to him. It was in vain that Solon opposed this; the guard was given him. Through the neglect or connivance of the people, Pisistratus took this opportunity of raising a much larger force, with which he seized the citadel, B.C. 560, thus becoming what the Greeks called τύραννος of Athens. See the account in Aristotle, *Ath. Pol.*

Having secured to himself the substance of power, he made no further change in the constitution or in the laws, which he administered ably and well. His first usurpation lasted but a short time. Before his power was firmly rooted, the factions headed by Megacles and Lycurgus combined, and Pisistratus was compelled to evacuate Athens. He remained in banishment six years. Meantime the factions of Megacles and Lycurgus revived their old feuds, and Megacles made overtures to Pisistratus, offering to reinstate him in the tyranny if he would connect himself with him by receiving his daughter in marriage. The proposal was accepted by Pisistratus, and the following stratagem was devised for accomplishing his restoration, according to the account of Herodotus: A maiden named Phya, of remarkable stature and beauty, was dressed as Athené in a full suit of armour, and placed in a chariot, with Pisistratus by her side. The chariot was then driven towards the city, heralds being sent on before to announce that Athené in person was bringing back Pisistratus to her Acropolis. The report spread rapidly, and those in the city believing that the woman was really their tutelary goddess, worshipped her, and admitted Pisistratus. Pisistratus nominally performed his part of the contract with Megacles; but, in consequence of the insulting manner in which he treated his wife, Megacles again made common cause with Lycurgus, and Pisistratus was a second time compelled to evacuate Athens. He retired to Eretria in Euboea, and employed the next ten years in making preparations to regain his power. At the end of that time he invaded Attica with the forces he had raised, and also supported by Lygdamis of Naxos with a considerable body of troops. He defeated his opponents near the temple of Athené at Pallené, and then entered Athens without opposition. Lygdamis was rewarded by being established as tyrant of Naxos, which island Pisistratus conquered (see LYGDAMIS).

Having now become tyrant of Athens for the third time, Pisistratus adopted measures to secure the undisturbed possession of his supremacy. He took a body of foreign mercenaries into his pay, and seized as hostages the children of several of the principal citizens, placing them in the custody of Lygdamis in Naxos. He maintained at the same time the form of Solon's institutions, only taking care, as his sons did after him, that the highest offices should always be held by some member of the family. He not only exacted obedience to the laws from his subjects and friends, but himself set the example of submitting to them. On one occasion he even appeared before the Areopagus to answer a charge of murder, which, however, was not prosecuted. Athens was indebted to him for many stately and useful buildings. Among these may be mentioned a temple to the Pythian Apollo, and a magnificent temple to the Olympian Zeus, which remained unfinished for several centuries, and was at length completed by the emperor Hadrian. Besides these, the Lyceum, a garden with stately buildings a short distance from the city, was the work of Pisistratus, as also the Fountain of the Nine Springs. Pisistratus also encouraged literature in various ways. It was apparently under his auspices that Thespis introduced at Athens his rude form of tragedy (B.C. 535), and that dramatic contests were made a regular part of the Attic Dionysia. It is to Pisistratus that tradition ascribes the first written text of the whole of the poems of Homer, as to which see Flach, *Peisistratos und seine literarische Thätigkeit* (Tübingen, 1885); and the article HOMERUS, pp. 838–39. Pisistratus is also said to have been the first person in Greece who collected a library, to which he generously allowed the public access.

By his first wife Pisistratus had two sons, Hippias and Hipparchus. By his second wife, Timonassa, he had also two sons, Iophon and Thessalus, who are rarely mentioned. He had also a bastard son, Hegesistratus, whom he made tyrant of Sigeum after taking that town from the Mitylenaeans. Pisistratus died at an advanced age in 527, and was succeeded in the tyranny by his eldest son Hippias; but Hippias and his brother Hipparchus appear to have administered the affairs of the State with so little outward distinction that they are frequently spoken of as though they had been joint tyrants. They continued the government on the same principles as their father. Thucydides (vi. 54) speaks in terms of high commendation of the virtue and intelligence with which their rule was exercised till the death of Hipparchus. Hipparchus inherited his father's literary tastes. Several distinguished poets lived at Athens under the patronage of Hipparchus, as, for example, Simonides of Ceos, Anacreon of Teos, Lasus of Hermioné, and Onomacritus.

After the murder of Hipparchus in 514, an account of which is given under HARMODIUS, a great change ensued in the character of the government. Under the influence of revengeful feelings and fears for his own safety, Hippias now became a morose and suspicious tyrant. He put to death great numbers of the citizens, and raised money by extraordinary imposts. His old enemies the Alcmaeonidae, to whom Megacles belonged, availed themselves of the growing discontent of the citizens; and after one or two unsuccessful attempts they at length succeeded, supported by a large force under Cleomenes, in expelling the Pisistratidae from Attica. Hippias and his connections retired to Sigeum in 510. The family of the tyrants was condemned to perpetual banishment, a sentence which was maintained even in after times, when decrees of amnesty were passed. Hippias afterward repaired to the court of Darius, and looked forward to a restoration to his country by the aid of the Persians. He accompanied the expedition sent under Datis and Artaphernes, and pointed out to the Persians the plain of Marathon as the most suitable place for their landing. He was now (490) of great age. According to some accounts, he fell in the battle of Marathon; according to others, he died at Lemnos on his return. Hippias was the only one of the legitimate sons of Pisistratus who had children; but none of them attained distinction. On Pisistratus, see the monographs by Flach (1885) and Töpffer (1886).

Piso, CALPURNIUS. The name of a distinguished plebeian family at Rome. The name of Piso, like many other Roman cognomens, is connected with agriculture, the noblest and most honourable pursuit of the ancient Romans: it comes from the verb *pisere* or *pinsere*, and refers to the pounding or grinding of corn. (1) A Roman who was taken prisoner at the battle of Cannae, B.C. 216; was praetor urbanus 211, and afterward commanded as propraetor in Etruria 210. Piso, in his praetorship, proposed to the Senate that the Ludi Apollinares, which had been exhibited for the first time in the preceding year (212), should be repeated, and should be celebrated in future annually. The Senate passed a decree to this effect. The establishment of these games by their ancestor was commemorated on coins by the Pisones in later times. (2) C., son of No. 1, was praetor 186, and received Further Spain as his province. He returned to Rome in 184, and obtained a triumph for a victory he had gained over the Lusitani and Celtiberi. He was consul in 180, and died during his consulship.

PISONES WITH THE AGNOMEN CAESONĪNUS. (3) L., received the agnomen Caesoninus because he originally belonged to the Caesonia gens. He was praetor in 154, and obtained the province of Further Spain, but was defeated by the Lusitani. He was consul in 148, and was sent to conduct the war against Carthage; he was succeeded in the command in the following year by Scipio. (4) L., son of No. 3, was consul 112 with M. Livius Drusus. In 107 he served as legatus to the consul, L. Cassius Longinus, who was sent into Gaul to oppose the Cimbri and their allies, and he fell together with the consul in the battle, in which the Roman army was utterly defeated by the Tigurini in the territory of the Allobroges. This Piso was the grandfather of Caesar's father-in-law, a circumstance to which Caesar himself alludes in recording his own victory over the Tigurini at a later time (Caes. *B. G.* i. 7, 12). (5) L., son of No. 4, never rose to any of the offices of State, and is only known from the account given of him by Cicero in his violent invective against his son. He married the daughter of Calventius, a native of Cisalpine Gaul, who came from Placentia and settled at Rome; and hence Cicero calls his son, in contempt, a semi-Placentian. (6) LUCIUS, son of No. 5, was an unprincipled debauchee, and a cruel and corrupt magistrate. He is first mentioned in 59, when he was brought to trial by P. Clodius for plundering a province, of which he had the administration after his praetorship, and he was only acquitted by throwing himself at the feet of the judges. In the same year Caesar married his daughter Calpurnia; and through his influence Piso obtained the consulship for 58, having for his colleague A. Gabinius, who was indebted for the honour to Pompey. Both consuls supported Clodius in his measures against Cicero, which resulted in the banishment of the orator. The conduct of Piso in support of Clodius produced that extreme resentment in the mind of Cicero which he displayed against Piso on many subsequent occasions. At the expiration of his consulship Piso went to his province of Macedonia, where he remained during two years (57 and 56), plundering the province in the most shameless manner. In the latter of these years the Senate resolved that a successor should be appointed, and in the debate in the Senate which led to his recall Cicero attacked him in the most unmeasured terms in an oration which has come down to us (*De Provinciis Consularibus*). Piso, on his return (55), complained in the Senate of the attack of Cicero, and justified the administration of his province, whereupon Cicero reiterated his charges in a speech which is likewise extant (*In Pisonem*). Cicero, however, did not venture to bring to trial the father-in-law of Caesar. In 50 Piso was censor with Appius Claudius Pulcher. On the breaking out of the Civil War (49) Piso accompanied Pompey in his flight from the city; and although he did not go with him across the sea, he still kept aloof from Caesar. He subsequently returned to Rome, and remained neutral during the remainder of the Civil War. After Caesar's death (44) Piso at first opposed Antony, but is afterwards mentioned as one of his partisans. (7) LUCIUS, son of No. 6, was consul B.C. 15, and afterwards obtained the province of Pamphylia; from thence he was recalled by Augustus in 11, in order to make war upon the Thracians, who had attacked the province of Macedonia. He was appointed by Tiberius *praefectus urbi*. While retaining the favour of the emperor, without condescending to servility, he at the same time earned the good-will of his fellow-citizens by the integrity and justice with which he governed the city. He died in A.D. 32, at the age of eighty, and was honoured by a decree of the Senate with a public funeral. It was to this Piso and his two sons that Horace addressed his epistle on the art of poetry (*Ars Poetica*).

PISONES WITH THE AGNOMEN FRUGI. (8) LUCIUS, received from his integrity and conscientiousness the surname of Frugi, which is perhaps nearly equivalent to our "man of honour." He was tribune of the plebs B.C. 149, in which year he proposed the first law for the punishment of extortion in the provinces. He was consul in 133, and carried on war against the slaves in Sicily. He was a staunch supporter of the aristocratic party, and offered a strong opposition to the measures of C. Gracchus. Piso was censor, but it is uncertain in what year. He wrote annals, which contained the history of Rome from the earliest period to the age in which Piso himself lived. (9) LUCIUS, son of No. 8, served with distinction under his father in Sicily in 133, and died in Spain about 111, whither he had gone as propraetor. (10) C., married Tullia, the daughter of Cicero, in 63, but was betrothed to her as early as 67. He was quaestor in 58, when he used every exertion to obtain the recall of his father-in-law from banishment; but he died in 57 before Cicero's return to Rome. He is frequently mentioned by Cicero in terms of gratitude on account of the zeal which he had manifested in his behalf during his banishment.

PISONES WITHOUT AN AGNOMEN. (11) C., consul B.C. 67, belonged to the high aristocratic party; and in his consulship opposed with the utmost vehemence the law of the tribune Gabinius, for giving Pompey the command of the war against the pirates. In 66 and 65, Piso administered the province of Narbonese Gaul as proconsul, and while there suppressed an insurrection of the Allobroges. In 63 he was accused of plundering the province, and was defended by Cicero. The latter charge was brought against Piso at the instigation of Caesar; and Piso, in revenge, implored Cicero, but without success, to accuse Caesar as one of the conspirators of Catiline. (12) M., usually called M. PUPIUS PISO, because he was adopted by M. Pupius, when the latter was an old man. He retained, however, his family-name Piso, just as Scipio, after his adoption by Metellus, was called

Metellus Scipio. On the death of L. Cinna, in 84, Piso married his wife Annia. In 83 he was appointed quaestor to the consul L. Scipio; but he quickly deserted this party, and went over to Sulla, who compelled him to divorce his wife on account of her previous connection with Cinna. After his praetorship, the year of which is uncertain, he received the province of Spain with the title of proconsul, and on his return to Rome in 69, enjoyed the honour of a triumph. He served in the Mithridatic War as a legatus of Pompey. He was elected consul for 61 through the influence of Pompey. In his consulship Piso gave great offence to Cicero, by not asking the orator first in the Senate for his opinion, and by taking P. Clodius under his protection after his violation of the mysteries of the Bona Dea. Cicero revenged himself on Piso, by preventing him from obtaining the province of Syria, which had been promised him. Piso, in his younger days, had so high a reputation as an orator, that Cicero was taken to him by his father, in order to receive instruction from him. He belonged to the Peripatetic School in philosophy, in which he received instruction from Staseas. (13) CN., a young noble who had dissipated his fortune by his extravagance and profligacy, and therefore joined Catiline in what is usually called his first conspiracy (66). (See CATILINA.) The Senate, anxious to get rid of Piso, sent him into Nearer Spain as quaestor, but with the rank and title of propraetor. His exactions in the province soon made him so hateful to the inhabitants that he was murdered by them. It was, however, supposed by some that he was murdered at the instigation of Pompey or of Crassus. (14) CN., fought against Caesar in Africa (B.C. 46), and after the death of the dictator, joined Brutus and Cassius. He was subsequently pardoned, and returned to Rome; but he disdained to ask Augustus for any of the honours of the State, and was, without solicitation, raised to the consulship in 23. (15) CN., son of No. 14, inherited all the pride and haughtiness of his father. He was consul B.C. 7, and was sent by Augustus as legate into Spain, where he made himself hated by his cruelty and avarice. Tiberius after his accession was chiefly jealous of Germanicus, his brother's son; and accordingly, when the eastern provinces were assigned to Germanicus in A.D. 18, Tiberius conferred upon Piso the command of Syria, in order that the latter might do everything in his power to thwart and oppose Germanicus. Plancina, the wife of Piso, was also urged on by Livia, the mother of the emperor, to vie with and annoy Agrippina. Germanicus and Agrippina were thus exposed to every species of insult and opposition from Piso and Plancina; and when Germanicus fell ill in the autumn of 19, he believed that he had been poisoned by them. Piso on his return to Rome (20) was accused of murdering Germanicus; the matter was investigated by the Senate; but before the investigation came to an end, Piso was found one morning in his room with his throat cut, and his sword lying by his side. It was generally supposed that, despairing of the emperor's protection, he had put an end to his own life, but others believed that Tiberius dreaded his revealing his secrets, and accordingly caused him to be put to death. The powerful influence of Livia secured the acquittal of Plancina. (See GERMANICUS.) (16) C., the leader of the well-known conspiracy against Nero in A.D. 65. Piso himself did not form the plot; but as soon as he had joined it, his great popularity gained him many partisans. He possessed most of the qualities which the Romans prized—high birth, an eloquent address, liberality, and affability; and he also displayed a sufficient love of magnificence and luxury to suit the taste of the day, which would not have tolerated austerity of manner or character. The conspiracy was discovered by Milichus, a freedman of Flavius Scevinus, one of the conspirators. Piso thereupon opened his veins, and thus died. There is extant a poem in 261 lines, containing a panegyric on a certain Calpurnius Piso, who is probably the same person as the leader of the conspiracy against Nero. (17) L., surnamed LICINIĀNUS, was the son of M. Licinius Crassus Frugi, and was adopted by one of the Pisones. On the accession of Galba to the throne, he adopted as his son and successor Piso Licinianus; but the latter only enjoyed the distinction four days, for Otho, who had hoped to receive this honour, induced the Praetorians to rise against the emperor. Piso fled for refuge into the Temple of Vesta, but was dragged out by soldiers, and despatched at the threshold of the temple, A.D. 69.

Pistor. The Roman word for a baker, the Greek terms being ἀρτοποιός, "bread-maker," and ἀρτοπώλης, "bread-seller." The Latin term is from *pinso*, and means literally "pounder." Bakers are first mentioned in Greece in the fifth century B.C., but do not appear in Rome before the early part of the second century. They were usually freedmen or citizens of the lower class; but, owing to the importance attached by the State to the trade, it became one of some standing. There was a *collegium* or guild of bakers under Augustus, which served the State, and under Trajan it was formally organized with 100 members and special privileges. It was under the supervision of the *praefectus annonae.* (See ANNONA.) Bread was distributed at Rome at the public expense, at first monthly, but in the third century daily; and at the beginning of the fourth century there were 254 public bakeries in the city. These made only the coarser kinds of bread, the finer sorts being produced at the private establishments.

Baker's Sign found at Pompeii. (Overbeck.)

Baking was sometimes done in furnaces, as in the bake-shop (*pistrina*) excavated at Pompeii; or in the *clibanus*, a clay vessel, in which the dough was placed and then buried in hot ashes (Petr[illegible]n. 35; see CLIBANUS). Wheat-bread (*panis sili[illegible]eus*) was the most common variety, as the ancients thought rye (*secale*) unfit to eat; and the quality of the flour determined the quality of the bread. Barley-bread (*panis hordeaceus*) was regarded as fit only for soldiers and slaves (Pliny, *H. N.* xviii. 74). Spelt (ζειά, *far*) was sometimes used for making a coarse bread.

The dough for bread was prepared by moistening the flour with water, by adding salt, and then by kneading (μάττειν, *subigere, depsere*) in a trough of wood or pottery. In large bakeries it appears to have been done by a sort of machine, the motive-power of which was supplied by an animal.

Baker selling Bread. (Pompeian Painting.)

The leaven (ζύμη, *fermentum*) was prepared from cakes of barley and water, or from the surplus dough of the preceding day's batch, which was kneaded with salt, put into water, and kept till it fermented. The dough was shaped either by hand or in moulds (*artoptae*), and then placed in the oven (ἰπνός, *furnus*) on a shovel (*pala*); but was sometimes baked on the hearth in the embers.

Cake and fancy-bread were made in various forms by special confectioners (πλακουντοποιοί, πεμματουργοί, *clibanarii*, *dulciarii*, *crustularii*, etc.), and were much used for sacrificial purposes. On these sweet preparations, see Athen. xiv. 643 e and f, and Pollux, vi. 75 foll. The sweetening was done with honey. See Blümner, *Technologie*, i. 1 foll.; and id. s. v. "Bäckerei" in Baumeister's *Denkmäler*.

Pistor. "Baker," a surname given to Iupiter by the Romans, because, when their city was taken by the Gauls, the god was believed to have inspired them with the idea of throwing down loaves from the Tarpeian Hill, where they were besieged, that the enemy might suppose that they were not in want of provisions, though, in reality, they were near surrendering through famine. This deceived the Gauls, and they soon withdrew (Ovid, *Fasti*, vi. 343; Lactant. i. 20, 33). This story is probably not the origin of the name *Pistor* as applied to Iupiter; but the name is best explained as "the Pounder" (*pinso*), referring to his smiting with thunderbolts.

Pistoria or **Pistorium.** Now Pistoia; a small place in Etruria, on the road from Luca to Florentia, rendered memorable by the defeat of Catiline in its neighbourhood. See CATILINA.

Pistrīnum and **Pistrīna** (μυλών). A place where grain was pounded (*pinso*) in a mortar; hence, a mill. See MOLA.

Pitănē (Πιτάνη). A seaport town of Mysia, on the coast of the Elaitic Gulf; the birthplace of the academic philosopher Arcesilaüs.

Pitcher. See URCEUS.

Pitchfork. See FURCA.

Pithecūsa. See AENARIA.

Pitho (Πειθώ). In Greek mythology the personification of persuasion. Like Eros and the Graces, with whom Hesiod mentions her (*Works and Days*, 73), she usually appears in the train of Aphroditê. She was, indeed, considered the daughter of the goddess, and was honoured together with her, as in Athens. She was also connected with Hermes as the god of eloquence. (See Herod. viii. 111; Pausan. ii. 7, 7.) The Romans called her **Suada** or **Suadēla** (Hor. *Epist.* i. 6, 38; Enn. *ap.* Cic. *Brut.* 15, 59).

Pithoegia (Πιθοίγια). The first day of the festival of the Anthesteria. See DIONYSIA.

Pithos (πίθος). A Greek wine-jar of earthenware, with a wide mouth and a close-fitting lid. See DOLIUM.

Pitĭnum. An Umbrian town on the river Pisaurus.

Pittacium (πιττάκιον). (1) A slip of parchment or leather used as a label, especially for a wine-jar, to give the date of the vintage, the quality of the wine, etc. (Petron. 34; id. 56). (2) A piece of linen spread with ointment for a plaster (Celsus, iii. 10).

Pittăcus (Πιττακός). A native of Mitylenê in Lesbos, and one of the so-called Seven Sages of Greece, was born about B.C. 650. Having obtained popularity among his countrymen by successfully opposing the tyrant Melanchrus, he was intrusted with the command of a fleet in a war with the Athenians concerning some territory which they had seized in the island. In the course of this war the Athenian commander Phryno, a man of uncommon size and strength, challenged him to single combat. Providing himself with a net, which he concealed under his buckler, he took the first opportunity to throw it over the head of his antagonist, and by this means gained an easy victory. According to Strabo's account, Pittacus came into the field armed with a casting-net, a trident, and a dagger; and it is said that from this stratagem of the Mitylenean was borrowed the mode of fighting practised by the Roman gladiators called *retiarii*. From this time Pittacus was held in high esteem among the Mityleneans, and was intrusted with the supreme power in the State (Aristot. *Polit.* iii. 15). Among other valuable presents, his countrymen offered him as much of the lands which had been recovered from the Athenians as he chose; but he only accepted of so much as he could measure by a single cast of a javelin; and one half of this small portion he afterward dedicated to Apollo, saying, concerning the remainder, that "the half is better than the whole." Cornelius Nepos says that the Mityleneans offered him many thousand acres, but that he took only a hundred. Pittacus displayed great moderation in his treatment of his enemies, among whom one of the most violent was the poet Alcaeus, who frequently made him the object of his satire. Finding it necessary to lay severe restrictions upon drunkenness, to which the Lesbians were particularly addicted, Pittacus passed a law which subjected offenders of this class to double punishment for any crime committed in a state of intoxication. When he had established such regulations as seemed to him satisfactory, he resigned his power, which he had held for ten years, and retired to private life.

Some of his famous sayings are as follows: "Power reveals the man;" "Whatever you do, do well;" "Watch for opportunities;" "Never talk of your plans before they are carried out." The life of Pittacus is given by Diogenes Laërtius. See SEVEN SAGES.

Pittheus (Πιτθεύς). A king of Troezen, and father of Aethra (hence called *Pittheïs*), the mother of Theseus (q. v.). He is said to have taught oratory, and even to have written a book on the subject (Pausan. ii. 30, 8).

Pityocamptes (πιτυοκάμπτης, "pine-bender"). A name applied to the robber Sinis (q. v.), who killed travellers by tying them between two pine-trees bent down so as nearly to meet, and then allowed to spring apart (Pausan. ii. 1, 3).

Pityūsae. A group of small islands in the Mediterranean, off the coast of Spain, and lying to the southwest of the Baleares. They derived their name from the number of pine-trees (πίτυς, "a pine") which grew in them. The largest is Ebusus (Ivica), and next to it is Ophiusa (Ias Columbretes). See Mela, ii. 7.

Placard. See LIBELLUS.

Placenta (πλακοῦς). A thin, flat cake of flour, mixed with cheese and honey. It was usually a large cake, so as to be cut up for a number of persons (Cato, *R. R.* 76; Hor. *Epist.* i. 10, 11). See PISTOR; SCRIBLITA.

Placentia. Now Piacenza; a Roman colony in Cisalpine Gaul, founded at the same time as Cremona, B.C. 219, and situated on the right bank of the Po, not far from the mouth of the Trebia. It was taken and destroyed by the Gauls in B.C. 200, but was soon rebuilt by the Romans, and became an important place.

Placidia, GALLA. See GALLA.

Placĭtus, SEXTIUS. The author of a short Latin treatise, in thirty-four chapters, treating of the medical properties supposed to reside in the bodies of certain animals. Its title is *De Medicina* (or *Medicamentis*) *ex Animalibus*. It is thought to have been written in the fourth century A.D. It is edited by Ackermann (Nürnberg, 1788).

Plaga (ἐνάδιον). A hunting-net. See RETÉ.

Plagium. Kidnapping; slave-stealing. A crime punishable by Roman law with a fine and *infamia*. The offence was a common one, but was severely dealt with by Augustus (Suet. *Aug.* 32). See Rein, *Das Criminalrecht der Römer*, p. 386, and the article SERVUS.

Plagunc̆ula (πλαγγών). A wax doll (Callim. *Dem.* 32). See PUPA.

Plaits. See COMA; SINUS.

Planaria (prob. also CANARIA). One of the Fortunatae Insulae (q. v.) or Canary Islands.

Planasia. Now Pianosa; an island between Corsica and the coast of Etruria, to which Augustus banished his grandson Agrippa Postumus.

Planciădes Fulgentius. See FULGENTIUS.

Plancīna, MUNATIA. See GERMANICUS; PISO.

Plancius, CN. A Roman who, as quaestor in Macedonia in B.C. 58, showed great kindness to Cicero when the orator came to Macedonia during his exile. (See CICERO.) Plancius was elected curale aedile in 54, but before taking office was accused of *sodalicium* or bribery of the tribes through illegal agencies. (See SODALICIUM.) Cicero defended him in orations still extant, and secured his acquittal. Plancius took the side of Pompey in the Civil War, and on Caesar's triumph went into exile in Corcyra (Corfu). See Cic. *Ad Fam.* iv. 14; xiv. 1, 3.

Plancus. (1) T. BURSA, tribune of the commons in B.C. 52. He took part in the troubles excited by the death of Clodius, and, on the expiration of his office, was accused and condemned, notwithstanding the interest made by Pompey in his behalf. (2) L. MUNATIUS, a native of Tibur, was in early life a pupil of Cicero's, and obtained considerable eminence in the oratorical art. He afterward commanded a legion under Caesar in Gaul. On the assassination of that individual Plancus acted at first a very equivocal part, and frequently changed sides, attaching himself successively to each party according as it became powerful. Thus we find him, after the victory at Mutina, affecting the utmost zeal for the cause of Brutus and freedom; and subsequently, when he saw Antony reestablished in power, he went over to him with four legions which he had at the time under his command. He obtained upon this the consulship along with Lepidus, B.C. 42. Tired at last of Antony, he sided with Octavius, who received him with the utmost cordiality. It was Plancus who proposed in the Senate that the title of Augustus should be bestowed on Octavianus. The ancient writers reproach him with an absurd performance at the court of Cleopatra, in Alexandria, when he appeared on the public stage in the character of a sea-god, having his person painted green, and in a state of almost complete nudity, wearing a crown of reeds on his head, and with the tail of a fish attached to his body behind. Plancus, however, appears to have been a man of literary tastes, and we have an ode addressed to him by Horace on one occasion, when he had become suspected of disaffection by Augustus, and was meditating his departure from Italy (Plut. *Ant.*; Vell. Paterc. ii. 63; Horat. *Carm.* i. vii). (3) LUCIUS, a friend of Iulius Caesar, under whom he served both in the Gallic and the Civil Wars. Caesar, shortly before his death, nominated him to the government of Transalpine Gaul for B.C. 44, with the exception of the Narbonese and Belgic portions of the province, and also to the consulship for 42, with D. Brutus as his colleague. After Caesar's death Plancus hastened into Gaul, and took possession of his province. Here he prepared at first to support the Senate against Antony; but when Lepidus joined Antony, and their united forces threatened to overwhelm Plancus, the latter was persuaded by Asinius Pollio to follow his example, and to unite with Antony and Lepidus. Plancus, during his government of Gaul, founded the colonies of Lugdunum and Raurica. He was consul in 42, according to the arrangement made by Caesar, and he subsequently followed Antony to Asia, where he remained for some years, and governed in succession the provinces of Asia and Syria. He deserted Antony in 32, shortly before the breaking out of the Civil War between the latter and Octavianus. He was favourably received by Octavianus, and continued to reside at Rome during the remainder of his life. It was on his proposal that Octavianus received the title of Augustus in 27; and the emperor conferred upon him the censorship in 22, with Paulus Aemilius Lepidus. Both the public and private life of Plancus were stained by numerous vices. One of Horace's odes (*Carm.* i. 7) is addressed to him.

Planĭpes. See MIMUS.

Planūdes Maxĭmus. See MAXIMUS.

Plastes (πλάστης). A modeller in clay or wax. See STATUARIA ARS.

Plastĭca. See STATUARIA ARS.

Plataea (Πλάταια), more commonly **Plataeae** (Πλαταιαί). An ancient city of Boeotia, on the northern slope of Mount Cithaeron, not far from the sources of the Asopus, and on the frontiers of Attica. It was said to have derived its name from Plataea, a daughter of Asopus. At an early period the Plataeans deserted the Boeotian Confederacy and placed themselves under the protection of Athens; and when the Persians invaded Attica, B.C. 490, they sent 1000 men to the assistance of the Athenians, and fought on their side at the battle of Marathon. Ten years afterward (480) their city was destroyed by the Persian army under Xerxes at the instigation of the Thebans; and the place was still in ruins in the following year (479), when the memorable battle was fought in their territory in which Mardonius was defeated, and the independence of Greece secured. In consequence of this victory, the territory of Plataea was declared inviolable. It now enjoyed a prosperity of fifty years; but in the third year of the Peloponnesian War (429) the Thebans persuaded the Spartans to attack the town, and after a siege of two years at length succeeded in obtaining possession of the place (427). Plataea was now razed to the ground, but was again rebuilt after the peace of Antalcidas (387). It was destroyed the third time by its inveterate enemies the Thebans in 374. It was once more restored under the Macedonian supremacy, and continued in existence till a very late period. See Wiegand, *Platää* (1886).

Plate. SEE CATINUS; LANX; PATINA.

Platēa (πλατεῖα, sc. ὁδός). The principal street in a town, suggesting the Broad Street and Broadway of modern cities (Ter. *Andr.* iv. 5, 1).

Platform. See CATASTA; ROSTRA; SUGGESTUS.

Plato (Πλάτων). The greatest of the Athenian philosophers. He was born May 26 (the seventh of Thargelion), B.C. 428, probably at Athens, though some say at Aegina (Diog. Laërt. iii. 2, 6). He was of an aristocratic family, his father Aristo claiming descent from Codrus, the last of the Athenian kings, and his mother Perictionê being of the family of Solon. His name was originally Aristocles, after his grandfather, but he was subsequently called Πλάτων, in consequence of his fluency of speech, or, as others say, because of his broad (πλατύς) forehead or his broad shoulders (Diog. Laërt. iii. 4). The traditions that have come down regarding his birth and career are largely mythical, and are given by Diogenes Laërtius. One story makes him the son of Apollo, and another tells how bees settled on his lips when a child, thus foreshadowing his honeyed eloquence (Cic. *Div.* i. 46, 78). Plutarch relates that he was humpbacked, but this, perhaps, was not a natural defect; it may have first appeared late in life as a result of his severe studies (Plut. *De Audiend. Poët.* 26, 53). Other ancient writers, on the contrary, speak in high terms of his manly and noble mien. The only authentic bust that we have of him is at present in the gallery at Florence. It was discovered near Athens in the fifteenth century, and purchased by Lorenzo de' Medici. In this bust the forehead of the philosopher is remarkably large. Plato first learned grammar, that is, reading and writing, from Dionysius. In gymnastics, Ariston was his teacher; and he excelled so much in these physical exercises that he entered, as is said, a public contest at the Isthmian and Pythian Games (Diog. Laërt. iii. 4). He studied painting and music under the tuition of Draco, a scholar of Damon, and Metellus of Agrigentum; but his favourite employment in his youthful years was poetry. The lively fancy and powerful style which his philosophical writings so amply display must naturally have impelled him, at an early period of life, to make some attempts at versification, which were assuredly not without influence on the beautiful form of his later works. After he had enjoyed the instruction of the most eminent teachers of poetry in all its forms, he proceeded himself to make an attempt in heroic verse; but when he compared his production with the masterpieces of Homer, he consigned it to the flames. He next tried lyric poetry, but with no better success; and finally turned his attention to dramatic composition. He elaborated four pieces, or a tetralogy, consisting of three separate tragedies and one satyric drama; but an accident induced him to quit this career, for which he was not probably fitted. A short time before the festival of Dionysus, when his pieces were to be brought upon the stage, he happened to hear Socrates conversing, and was so captivated by the charms of his manners as from that moment to abandon poetry, and apply himself earnestly to the study of philosophy. But, though Plato abandoned his poetic attempts, he still attended to the reading of the poets, particularly Homer, Aristophanes, and Sophron, as his favourite occupation; and he appears to have derived from them, in part, the dramatic arrangement of his dialogues. He had already heard the instructions of Cratylus, a disciple of the school of Heraclitus (Aristot. *Metaphys.* i. 6), and was now twenty years of age when he became acquainted with Socrates. He continued a professed disciple of that philosopher for the space of eight years, until the death of the latter. During all this period Socrates regarded him as one of his most faithful pupils, and Plato always cherished a deep affection and esteem for his master, so that when the latter was brought to trial he undertook to plead his cause; but the partiality and violence of the judges would not permit him to proceed. After the condemnation he presented his master with money sufficient to redeem his life, which, however, Socrates refused to accept. During his imprisonment Plato attended him, and was present at a conversation which he held with his friends concerning the immortality of the soul, the substance of which he afterwards committed to writing in the dialogue entitled *Phaedo*, not, however, without interweaving his own opinions and language. Upon the death of his master he withdrew, with several other friends of Socrates, to Megara, where they were hospitably entertained by Euclid, and remained till the *émeute* at Athens subsided. Brücker thinks that Plato received instruction in dialectics from Euclid. Cicero relates that the Megarean philosopher drew many of his opinions from Plato (Academ. Quaest. 4, 42).

Desirous of making himself master of all the wisdom and learning which the age could furnish, Plato, after this, travelled into every country which was so far enlightened as to promise him any recompense for his labour. He first visited that part of Magna Graecia where a celebrated school of philosophy had been established by Pythagoras. It is commonly believed that Plato formally became a scholar of the Pythagoreans, and many persons are expressly named as his teachers in the doctrines of that sect of philosophy. But this multitude of teachers is of itself sufficient to excite suspicion; and, besides, Plato must then have been at least thirty years old, and was undoubtedly acquainted with the Pythagorean system long before his Italian voyage. How long Plato remained in Italy cannot be determined, since all the accounts relative to this point are deficient. But so much is certain, that he did not leave this country before he had gained the entire friendship of the principal Pythagoreans, of which they subsequently gave most unequivocal proofs. From Italy Plato went to Cyrené, the celebrated Greek colony in Africa. It is not certain whether he visited Sicily in passing. According to Apuleius, the object of his journey was to learn mathematics of Theodorus. This mathematician, whose fame perhaps surpassed his knowledge, had given instruction to the youth of Athens in this branch of science; and Plato, in all probability, merely wished now to complete his knowledge on this subject. From Cyrené he proceeded to Egypt, and, in order to travel with more safety upon his journey to the last-named country, he assumed the character of a merchant, and, as a seller of oil, passed through the kingdom of Artaxerxes Mnemon. Wherever he came, he obtained information from the Egyptian priests concerning their astronomical observations and calculations. It has been asserted that it was in Egypt that Plato acquired his opinions concerning the origin of the world, and learned the doctrines of transmigration and the immortality of the soul; but it is more than probable that he learned the latter doctrine from Socrates, and the former from the school of Pythagoras. It is not likely that Plato, in the habit of a merchant, could have obtained access to the sacred mysteries of Egypt; for, in the case of Pythagoras, the Egyptian priests were so unwilling to communicate their secrets to strangers that even a royal mandate was scarcely sufficient in a single instance to gain this permission. Little regard is therefore due to the opinions of those who assert that Plato derived his system of philosophy from the Egyptians (Iamblich. *Myst. Aeg.* i. 2, p. 3). That Plato's stay in Egypt extended to a period of thirteen years, as some maintain, or even three years, as others state, is highly incredible; especially as there is no trace in his works of Egyptian research, and all that he tells us of Egypt indicates at most a very scanty acquaintance with the subject.

After leaving Egypt, he went to Sicily in order to see the volcano of Aetna, and visited Syracuse at the time when Dionysius the Elder was reigning. At the court of Dionysius Plato became acquainted with Dio, the brother-in-law of the tyrant, and Dio endeavoured to produce an influence upon the mind of Dionysius by the conversation of Plato. But the attempt failed, and had nearly cost the philosopher his life. Dionysius was highly incensed at the result of an argument in which he was worsted by Plato, who took occasion also to advance in the course of it some unpalatable truths; and in the first heat of his passion he would have punished the hardihood of the philosopher with death, had not Dio and Aristomenes together restrained him from it. They conceived, therefore, that Plato could no longer stay at Syracuse without hazard, and accordingly secured passage for him in a ship which was about to carry home Polis, a Lacedaemonian ambassador, or, according to Olympiodorus, a merchant of Aegina. Dionysius heard of it, and bribed Polis to sell him as a slave. He was accordingly sold by the treacherous Polis on the island of Aegina, which was then involved in war with Athens. According to some writers he was sold by the Aeginetans. A certain Anniceris, from Cyrené, ransomed him for twenty or thirty minae. Plato's friends and scholars (according to some, Dio alone) collected this sum in order to indemnify Anniceris, who, however, was so noble-minded that with the money he purchased a garden in the Academé, and presented it to the philosopher. When Plato had completed his travels, and had reached the end of his various dangers and calamities, he returned to Athens, and began publicly to teach philosophy in the Academy. He had inherited here a garden, which was purchased for five hundred drachmae. This garden remained the property of the philosophic school that he had founded. His memory was honoured by the Athenians and by foreigners with monuments and statues. Diogenes states that Plato taught philosophy first in the Academy, and also in a garden at Colonus. His Academy soon became celebrated, and was numerously attended by high-born and noble young men; for he had already, by means of his travels, and probably by some publications, acquired a distinguished name. Among these disciples, from whom he exacted no fee, were his nephew Speusippus, Xenocrates of Chalcedon, Aristotle, Heraclides of Pontus, Hestiaeus of Perinthus, and Philippus the Opuntian, while others, who were not regularly enrolled among his immediate followers, numbered such men as Iphicrates, Timotheus, Phocion, Lycurgus, Hyperides, Isocrates, and possibly Demosthenes (Cic. *De Orat.* i. 20, 89).

Plato. (Bust at Florence.)

Plato taught in the Academy for twenty-two years prior to his second journey to Syracuse, which he undertook at the instigation of Dio, who hoped, by the lessons of the philosopher, to influence the character of the new ruler of Syracuse. This prince, it is said, had been brought up by his father wholly destitute of an enlightened education, and it was now the task of Plato to form his mind by philosophy. It seems, at the same time, to have been the plan of Dio and Plato to bring about, by philosophical instruction, a wholesome reform of the Sicilian constitution, by giving it a more aristocratic character. But, whatever may have been their intentions, they were all frustrated by the weak and voluptuous character of Dionysius. Dio became the object of the tyrant's suspicion, and was conveyed away to the coast of Italy, without, however, forfeiting his possessions. In this condition of affairs, Plato did not long remain in Syracuse, where his position would at best have been ambiguous. He returned to Athens, but, in consequence of some fresh disagreement between Dionysius and Dio, with respect to the property of the latter, he was induced to take a third journey to Syracuse. The reconciliation, which it was his object to effect, completely miscarried; he himself came to an open rupture with Dionysius, and only obtained a free departure from Sicily through the active interposition of his Pythagorean friends at Tarentum. It does not appear that he took any part in the later conduct of Sicilian affairs, though his nephew and disciple Speusippus and others of the Academy, rendered personal assistance to Dio, in a warlike expedition against Dionysius. From this time Plato seems to have passed his old age in tranquillity in his garden, near the Academy, engaged with the instruction of numerous disciples, and the prosecution of his literary labours. He died while yet actively employed about his philosophical studies, in B.C. 347.

The philosophical writings of Plato have come down to us complete, and have always been admired as a model of the union of artistic perfection with philosophical acuteness and depth. They are in the form of dialogue; but Plato was not the first writer who employed this style of composition for philosophical instruction. (See DIALOGUS.) Zeno the Eleatic had already written in the form of question and answer. Alexamenus the Teian and Sophron in the mimes had treated ethical subjects in the same form. Xenophon, Aeschines, Antisthenes, Euclides, and other Socratics had also made use of the dialogical form; but Plato has handled this form not only with greater mastery than any one who preceded him, but, in all probability, with the distinct intention of keeping by this very means true to the admonition of Socrates, not to communicate instruction, but to lead to the spontaneous discovery of it. Moreover, the dramatic form gives great force and liveliness to the teaching, and was used by Plato with so much ability as to lead to the grouping of the dialogues into trilogies and tetralogies as though they had been actual dramas. The dialogues of Plato are closely connected with one another, and various arrangements of them have been proposed. Schleiermacher divides them into three series or classes. In the first he considers that the germs of dialectic and of the doctrine of ideas begin to unfold themselves in all the freshness of youthful inspiration; in the second those germs develop themselves further by means of dialectic investigations respecting the difference between common and philosophical acquaintance with things, respecting notion and knowledge (δόξα and ἐπιστήμη); in the third they receive their completion by means of an objectively scientific working out, with the separation of ethics and physics. The first series embraces, according to Schleiermacher, the *Phaedrus, Lysis, Protagoras, Laches, Charmides, Euthyphron,* and *Parmenides;* to which may be added as an appendix the *Apologia, Crito, Ion, Hippias Minor, Hipparchus, Minos,* and *Alcibiades II.* The second series contains the *Gorgias, Theaetetus, Meno, Euthydemus, Cratylus, Sophistes, Politicus, Symposium, Phaedo,* and *Philebus;* to which may be added as an appendix the *Theages, Erastae, Alcibiades I., Menexenus, Hippias Major,* and *Clitophon.* The third series comprises the *Republic, Timaeus, Critias,* and the *Laws.* This arrangement may be accepted as a matter of convenience, but scholars long ago ceased to think it possible to discover in the dialogues any satisfactory evidence of the order of their composition. The genuineness of many of the dialogues has been questioned, and the following are undoubtedly spurious: *Alcibiades II., Axiochus, Clitophon, Demadocus, Epinomis, Erastae, Eryxias, Hipparchus, De Iust., Minos, Sisyphus, Theages, De Virtute.* The following are probably spurious: *Hippias Minor, Alcibiades I., Menexenus.* The *Letters* are perhaps forgeries. (See Gudeman in *Classical Studies in Honour of Henry Drisler,* pp. 61–66 [New York, 1894].) The following are cited by Aristotle as having been written by Plato: *Republic, Timaeus, Laws, Phaedrus, Symposium, Gorgias, Meno, Hippias I.;* but obviously his silence as to the rest proves nothing.

It is impossible within any reasonable limits to give a satisfactory account of the Platonic philosophy. His attempt to combine poetry and philosophy (the two fundamental tendencies of the Greek mind) gives to the Platonic dialogues a charm which irresistibly attracts us, though we may have but a deficient comprehension of their subject matter. Plato, like Socrates, was penetrated with the idea that wisdom is the attribute of the Godhead; that philosophy, springing from the impulse *to know,* is the necessity of the intellectual man, and the greatest of the blessings which he possesses. When once we strive after Wisdom with the intensity of a lover, she becomes the true consecration and purification of the soul, adapted to lead us from the night-like to the true day. An approach to wisdom, however, presupposes an original communion with Being, truly so called; and this communion again presupposes the divine nature or immortality of the soul, and the impulse to become like the Eternal. This impulse is the love which generates in Truth, and the development of it is termed Dialectics. Out of the philosophical impulse which is developed by Dialectics, not only correct knowledge, but also correct action, springs forth. Socrates's doctrine respecting the unity of virtue, and that it consists in true, vigorous, and practical knowledge, is intended to be set forth in a preliminary manner in the *Protagoras* and the smaller dialogues attached to it. They are designed, therefore, to introduce a foundation for ethics by the refutation of the common views that were entertained of morals and of virtue; for although not even the words "ethics" and "physics" occur in Plato, and even dialectics are not treated of as a distinct and separate province, yet he must rightly be regarded as the originator of the threefold division of philosophy, inasmuch as he had before him the decided object to develop the Socratic method into a scientific system of dialectics, that should supply the grounds of our knowledge as well as of our moral action (physics and ethics), and therefore he separates the general investigations on knowledge and understanding, at least relatively, from those which refer to physics and ethics. Accordingly, the *Theaetetus*, *Sophistes*, *Parmenides*, and *Cratylus* are principally dialectical; the *Protagoras*, *Gorgias*, *Politicus*, *Philebus*, and the *Politics* principally ethical; while the *Timaeus* is exclusively physical. Plato's dialectics and ethics, however, have been more successful than his physics. Plato's doctrine of *ideas* (ἰδέαι) was one of the most prominent parts of his system. He maintained that the existence of things, cognizable only by means of conception, is their true essence, their *idea*. Hence he asserts that to deny the reality of ideas is to destroy all scientific research. He departed from the original meaning of the word idea (namely, that of form or figure), inasmuch as he understood by it the unities (ἑνάδες, μονάδες)which lie at the basis of the visible, the changeable, and which can only be reached by pure thinking. He included under the expression "idea" every thing stable amid the changes of mere phenomena, all really existing and unchangeable definitudes, by which the changes of things and our knowledge of them are conditioned, such as the ideas of genus and species, the laws and ends of nature, as also the principles of cognition and of moral action, and the essences of individual, concrete, thinking souls. His system of ethics was founded upon his dialectics, as is remarked above. Hence he asserted that, not being in a condition to grasp the idea of the good with full distinctness, we are able to approximate to it only so far as we elevate the power of thinking to its original purity.

The best MS. of the greater part of Plato is the Codex Clarkianus, secured in Patmos by Daniel Clarke, an Englishman, and now in the Bodleian Library (Oxford). It dates from A.D. 896, and does not include the *Republic*, of which the best copy is a Paris codex (Codex Parisinus A) of the eleventh century.

BIBLIOGRAPHY.—The principal editions of Plato are those of Aldus (Venice, 1513); H. Stephanus (Lausanne, 1587), from which the citations of Plato by page and letter are usually made; convenient texts by Stallbaum (1881 foll.), Orelli (1839), Hirschig (1873), K. F. Hermann (last ed. 1885 foll.); and a critical one is that of Schanz, not yet (1895) completed. Good editions of the separate dialogues with English notes are those of the *Protagoras* by Sihler (1881), the *Philebus* by Badham (1878), the *Theaetetus* by Campbell (1882), the *Phaedo* by Geddes (1885) and Andrew Hind (1883), the *Euthydemus* and *Symposium* by Badham (1866), the *Sophistes* and *Politicus* by Campbell (1867), the *Phaedrus* by Thompson (1868), the *Apology* by Wagner (1869) and by Riddell (1877), the *Gorgias* by Thompson (1871), the *Parmenides* by Maguire (1882) and by Waddell (1894), the *Republic* (bks. i.–v.) by Warren (1888), and complete by Jowett and Campbell (1894). There are notes on the *Cratylus* in French by Lenormant (1861), and on the *Republic* by Charpentier (1877).

The great translation of all of Plato's works into English, by Prof. Jowett (2d ed. Oxford, 1890), is itself a classic. There is a *Lexicon Platonicum* by Ast (1838) and a *Wörterbuch der Platonischen Philosophie* by Wagner (Göttingen, 1799). There is an immense mass of literature dealing with the Platonic philosophy, of which it is possible here to mention only the following for the general student: the introduction to the several dialogues in Jowett's translation; Grote's *Plato* (giving analyses of all the dialogues); Zeller, *Plato and the Old Academy* (Engl. trans. 1876); Stein, *Zur Geschichte des Platonismus* (1862–75); Auffarth, *Die Platonische Ideenlehre* (Berlin, 1883); Fouillée, *La Philosophie de Platon*, 4 vols. (Paris, 1888–89); Pater, *Plato and Platonism* (1895); and the chapters on Plato in the histories of philosophy by Ueberweg and Schwegler. See PHILOSOPHIA.

Platter. See PLATE.

Plaustrum (ἅμαξα). A wagon or two-wheeled cart. If it had four wheels, it was styled *plaustrum maius* (Cato, *R. R.* x. 2). It was used for

Plaustrum. (Ginzrot.)

heavy burdens, and was generally drawn by oxen, but sometimes by mules. The wheels of the plaustrum had no spokes.

Plausus. Applause which at Rome was reduced to a system, there being a trained *claque*. The different kinds of applause were *bombi*, "booming;" *imbrices*, clapping with hollowed hands; and *testae*, clapping with the palms of the hands, etc. (Suet. *Nero*, 20).

Plautia Gens, a plebeian gens at Rome. The name is also written PLOTIUS, the latter being the plebeian form. The gens was divided into the families of Hypsaeus, Proculus, Silvanus, Venno, Venox; and although several members of these families obtained the consulship, none of them is of sufficient importance to require a separate notice.

Plautiānus, FULVIUS, an African by birth, the fellow-townsman of Septimius Severus. He served as praefect of the praetorium under this emperor, who loaded him with honours and wealth, and virtually made over much of the imperial authority into his hands. Intoxicated by these distinctions, Plautianus indulged in the most despotic tyranny, and perpetrated acts of cruelty almost beyond belief. In A.D. 202 his daughter Plautilla was married to Caracalla; but having discovered the dislike cherished by Caracalla towards both his daughter and himself, and looking forward with apprehension to the downfall which awaited him upon the death of the sovereign, he formed a plot against the life both of Septimius and Caracalla. His treachery was discovered, and he was immediately put to death, 203. His daughter Plautilla was banished first to Sicily, and subsequently to Lipara, where she was treated with the greatest harshness. After the murder of Geta, in 212, Plautilla was put to death by order of her husband.

Plautilla. See PLAUTIANUS.

Plautius. (1) AULUS, a Roman of consular rank, who was sent by the emperor Claudius in A.D. 43 to subdue Britain. He remained in Britain four years, and subdued the southern part of the island. He obtained an ovation on his return to Rome in 47. (2) A Roman jurist, who lived about the time of Vespasian, and is cited by subsequent jurists.

Plautus, T. Maccius. The most celebrated comic poet of Rome. He was a native of Sarsina, a small village in Umbria. He used to be called M. Accius Plautus, but his real name, as Ritschl has shown, was T. Maccius Plautus. The date of his birth is uncertain, but it may be placed about B.C. 254. He probably came to Rome at an early age, since he displays so perfect a mastery of the Latin language, and an acquaintance with Greek literature which he could hardly have acquired in a provincial town. Whether he ever obtained the Roman franchise is doubtful. When he arrived at Rome he was in needy circumstances, and was first employed in the service of the actors. With the money he had saved in this inferior station he set himself up in business, but failed; he then returned to Rome, and his necessities obliged him to enter the service of a baker, who employed him in turning a hand-mill. While in this degrading occupation he wrote three plays, the sale of which to the managers of the public games enabled him to quit his drudgery and begin his literary career. He was then probably about thirty years of age (224), and therefore commenced writing comedies a few years before the breaking out of the Second Punic War. He continued his literary occupation for about forty years, and died in 184, when he was seventy years of age. His contemporaries at first were Livius Andronicus and Naevius, afterward Ennius and Caecilius: Terence did not rise into notice till almost twenty years after his death. During the long time that he held possession of the stage, he was always a great favourite of the people; and he expressed a bold consciousness of his own powers in the epitaph which he wrote for his tomb, and which has come down to us:

> "Postquam est mortem aptus Plautus, comoedia luget
> Scena deserta, dein risus, ludus iocusque
> Et numeri innumeri simul omnes collacrumarunt."

Plautus wrote a great number of comedies, and in the last century of the Republic there were 130 plays which bore his name. Most of these, however, were not considered genuine by the best Roman critics. There were several works written upon the subject; and of these the most celebrated was the treatise of Varro, entitled *Quaestiones Plautinae.* Varro limited the undoubted comedies of the poet to twenty-one, which were hence called the *Fabulae Varronianae.* These Varronian comedies are the same as those which have come down to our own time, with the loss of one. At present we possess only twenty comedies of Plautus; but there were originally twenty-one in the manuscripts, and the *Vidularia*, which was the twenty-first, and which came last in the collection, was torn off from the manuscript in the Middle Ages. The titles of the twenty-one Varronian plays are: (1) *Amphitruo*, (2) *Asinaria*, (3) *Aulularia*, (4) *Captivi*, (5) *Curculio*, (6) *Casina*, (7) *Cistellaria*, (8) *Epidicus*, (9) *Bacchides*, (10) *Mostellaria*, (11) *Menaechmi*, (12) *Miles*, (13) *Mercator*, (14) *Pseudolus*, (15) *Poenulus*, (16) *Persa*, (17) *Rudens*, (18) *Stichus*, (19) *Trinummus*, (20) *Truculentus*, (21) *Vidularia*. This is the order in which they occur in the manuscripts, though probably not the one in which they were originally arranged by Varro. The present order is evidently alphabetical; the initial letter of the title of each play is alone regarded, and no attention is paid to those which follow: hence we find *Captivi, Curculio, Casina, Cistellaria: Mostellaria, Menaechmi, Miles, Mercator: Pseudolus, Poenulus, Persa.* The play of the *Bacchides* forms the only exception to the alphabetical order. It was probably placed after the *Epidicus* by some copyist, because he had observed that Plautus, in the *Bacchides* (ii. 2, 36), referred to the *Epidicus* as an earlier work. The names of the comedies are either taken from some leading character in the play, or from some circumstance which occurs in it: those titles ending in *-aria* are adjectives, giving a general description of the play: thus *Asinaria* is the "Ass-Comedy."

The comedies of Plautus enjoyed unrivalled popularity among the Romans, and continued to be represented down to the time of Diocletian. The continued popularity of Plautus through so many centuries was owing, in a great measure, to his being a national poet. Though he founds his plays upon Greek models, the characters in them act, speak, and joke like genuine Romans, and he thereby secured the sympathy of his audience more completely than Terence could ever have done. Whether Plautus borrowed the plan of all his plays from Greek models, it is impossible to say. The *Cistellaria, Bacchides, Poenulus,* and *Stichus* were taken from Menander, the *Casina* and *Rudens* from Diphilus, and the *Mercator* and the *Trinummus* from Philemon, and many others were undoubtedly founded upon Greek originals. But in all cases Plautus allowed himself much greater liberty than Terence; and in some instances he appears to have simply taken the leading idea of the play from the Greek, and to have filled it up in his own fashion. It has been inferred from a well-known line of Horace (*Epist.* ii. 1. 58), *Plautus ad exemplar Siculi properare Epicharmi*, that Plautus took great pains to imitate Epicharmus. But there is no correspondence between any of the existing plays of Plautus and the known titles of the comedies of Epicharmus; and the verb *properare* probably has reference only to the liveliness and energy of Plautus's style, in which he bore a resemblance to the Sicilian poet. It was, however, not only with the common people that Plautus was a favourite; educated Romans read and admired his works down to the latest times. Cicero (*De Off.* i. 29) places his wit on a par with that of the old Attic comedy, and St. Jerome used to console himself with the perusal of the poet after spending many nights in tears on account of his past sins. The favourable opinion which the ancients entertained of the merits of Plautus has been confirmed by the judgment of the best modern critics, and by the fact that several of his plays have been imitated by many of the best modern poets. Thus the *Amphitruo* has been imitated by Molière and Dryden, the *Aulularia* by Molière in his *Avare*, the *Mostellaria* by Regnard, Addison, and others, the *Menaechmi* by Shakespeare in his *Comedy of Errors*, the *Trinummus* by Lessing in his *Schatz*, and so with others. Horace (*A. P.* 270), indeed, expresses a less favourable opinion of Plautus; but it must be recollected that the taste of Horace had been formed by a different school of literature, and that he undervalued the ancient poets of his country. Moreover, it is probable that the censure of Horace does not refer to the general character of Plautus's poetry, but merely to his inharmonious verses and to some of his jests. Plautus performed an important work in the enrichment of the Latin language. His genius for coining words was very remarkable, and in after-years the majority of his new terms were taken into the literary language by Cicero, who gave them the stamp of his authority. In this respect he stands out as a unique and important figure, and one whose influence has been too little recognized. See Peck's *History of the Latin Language*, pt. iii.; Besta, *De Verborum Compositione Plaut.* (Breslau, 1876); Ulrich, *Die Composita bei Plautus* (Halle, 1884); Georke, *Vocabula Graeca in Linguam Lat. Recepta* (Königsberg, 1868); and Rassow in *Jahn's Jahrbücher*, Suppl. xv. 589.

The MSS. of Plautus that are of especial importance are the Codex Ambrosianus (A) at Milan (a palimpsest) of the fourth or fifth century; the Codex Palatinus (B), now at Rome; the Codex Decurtatus (C) at Heidelberg; the Codex Vaticanus or Vetus (D); and the Codex Britannicus (J) in the British Museum. The last four are of about the eleventh or twelfth century, and represent a single archetype. No MS. contains all the plays.

The text of Plautus has come down to us in a very corrupt state. It contains many lacunae and interpolations. Thus the *Aulularia* has lost its conclusion, the *Bacchides* its commencement, etc. Of the present complete editions the best are by Lambinus (Paris, 1576); Pareus (Frankfort, 1610); Bothe, 2 vols. (Leipzig, 1834); Weise, 2 vols. (Quedlinburg, 1837–38; last ed. 1886); Ussing (Copenhagen, 1886); Leo (2 vols. Berlin, 1885–1896); Ritschl (Bonn, 1848–54; revised by Loewe, Goetz, and Schoell, 1894). There is no complete edition with English notes, but the following of separate plays are good: Wagner's *Aulularia* (1866); Hallidie's *Captivi* (1890); Ramsay's *Mostellaria*, incomplete (1869); Morris's *Mostellaria* (1880); Tyrrell's *Miles Gloriosus* (1885); Gray's *Epidicus* (1893); Sloman's *Trinummus* (1883); Fowler's *Menaechmi* (1889); Palmer's *Amphitruo* (1890); Morris's *Pseudolus* (1894); and Fennell's *Stichus* (1893). Foreign editions are those of the *Asinaria* by Richter (Nuremberg, 1833); of the *Captivi*, with critical apparatus, by Brix (4th ed. Leipzig, 1884); of the *Curculio* by Geppert (Berlin, 1845); of the *Casina* by Geppert (Berlin, 1866); of the *Cistellaria* by Benoist (Lyons, 1863); of the *Epidicus* by Geppert (Berlin, 1865); of the *Bacchides* by Ritschl (Halle, 1835); of the *Menaechmi* by Brix (3d ed. Leipzig, 1880) and Vahlen (Berlin, 1882); of the *Poenulus* by Geppert (Berlin, 1864); of the *Rudens* by Benoist (Paris, 1864); of the *Trinummus* by Brix (3d ed. Leipzig, 1879); and of the *Truculentus* by Spengel and Studemund (Göttingen, 1868). On the *Vidularia*, which was lost during the Middle Ages, see Studemund, *De Vidularia Plautina* (Greifswald, 1870); and Leo, *De Vidularia* (Berlin, 1892).

Playthings. See CREPUNDIA; NUCES; PUPA.

Plea. See ACTIO in the APPENDIX; DIKÉ; JUDICIAL PROCEDURE.

Plebeian Latin. See SERMO PLEBEIUS.

Plebeii Ludi. See LUDI PLEBEII, p. 974.

Plebiscītum. The Roman name for a decree of the Comitia Tributa on the rogation of a tribune. (See COMITIA.) Originally the plebiscitum required confirmation by the Senate, but by a *Lex Hortensia* (B.C. 286) the whole people (*universus populus*) were declared bound by the plebiscita. See LEX.

Plebs, Plebes. A part of the population of Rome, which derived its origin mainly from the conquered Latins settled on Roman territory by the kings Tullus Hostilius and Ancus Martius. At first these possessed only the passive rights of citizenship, being excluded from all its privileges as well as from service in war, and forming a community sharply separated from the old citizens, the patricians. In particular, they did not possess the right of concluding valid marriages with patricians, although they were otherwise equal in matters of private law. When, by the constitution of Servius Tullius, they were compelled to serve in war and to pay war-taxes, they obtained the right of voting with the patricians in the Comitia Centuriata. After the establishment of the Republic in B.C. 510, the plebeians began the struggle with the patricians, who were then in sole possession of the secular and priestly offices. The aim of the plebeians was to secure complete equality of rights, answering to their equality of duties. An important engine in this struggle was the tribunate of the people (see TRIBUNI PLEBIS) established in 491, as well as the Comitia Tributa. (See COMITIA.) The plebeians had the chief weight in that assembly, and after B.C. 448 it was invested with the right of passing decrees binding on the whole people. Among their first acquisitions was the right of entering into valid marriages with the patricians (B.C. 445). One after another, the plebeians gained admittance to the most important offices of State and the priesthoods, down to the year 300, so that only insignificant offices remained reserved for the patricians. (See PATRICII.) When the struggle of the orders was thus settled, the opposition between patricians and plebeians lost its practical importance. The two orders were completely blended together, and the place of the aristocracy of birth was taken by the aristocracy of office, the members of which were called *nobiles* (q. v.). From this time the name *plebs* passed to the lower ranks of the people, as contrasted with this nobler class. See Mommsen, *Römische Forschungen*, vol. i., and id. *Röm. Staatsrecht*, vol. iii.

Plectrum (πλῆκτρον). The instrument with which the lyre was struck. It was made of gold or ivory. See LYRA.

Pledge. See PIGNUS.

Pleiad, THE TRAGIC. See CANON ALEXANDRINUS; PLEIAS.

Pleiădes (Πλειάδες). The seven daughters of Atlas and the Ocean-nymph Pleionē, born on the Arcadian mountain Cyllenē, sisters of the Hyades. The eldest and most beautiful, Maia, became the mother of Hermes by Zeus; Electra and Taÿgetē, of Dardanus and Lacedaemon by the same; Alcyonē, of Hyrieus by Poseidon; Celaeno, of Lycus and Nycteus by the same; Steropē or Asteropē, of Oenomaüs by Ares; Meropē (i. e. "the mortal"), of Glaucus by Sisyphus. Out of grief, either for the fate of Atlas or for the death of their sisters, they killed themselves and were placed among the constellations. According to another legend, they were pursued for five years by the giant hunter Orion (q. v.), until Zeus turned the distressed nymphs and their pursuer into neighbouring stars. As the constellation of the seven stars, they made known by their rising (in the middle of May) the approach of harvest, and by their setting (at the end of October) the time for the new sowing.

Their rising and setting were also looked upon as the sign of the opening and closing of the sailing season. One of the seven stars is invisible; this was explained to be Meropé, who hid herself out of shame at her marriage with a mortal. The constellation of the Pleiades seems also to have been compared to a flight of doves (πελειάδες). Hence the Pleiades were supposed to be meant in the story told by Homer of the ambrosia brought to Zeus by the doves, one of which is always lost at the Planctae Rocks, but is regularly replaced by a new one (*Od.* xii. 62). Among the Romans, the constellation was called Vergiliae, the stars of spring. As being the daughters of Atlas, the name Atlantides is often used of them. See also HYADES.

Pleias (πλειάς, "a group of seven stars"). The name given by the Alexandrian critics to a group of seven tragic poets, who wrote at Alexandria under Ptolemy Philadelphus in the first half of the third century B.C. Their names were: Alexander Aetolus, Philiscus, Sositheus, Homerus, Aeantides, Sosiphanes, and Lycophron. See CANON ALEXANDRINUS.

Pleïŏnê (Πληιόνη). A daughter of Oceanus, and mother of the Pleiades by Atlas. See ATLAS; PLEIADES.

Plemmyrium (Πλημμύριον). A promontory on the southern coast of Sicily, immediately south of Syracuse.

Plemochoë (πλημοχόη). Literally, "an earthen vessel for water"; hence the name πλημοχόαι given to the last day of the Eleusinian festival, when this kind of vessel was used for pouring out water. See ELEUSINIA.

Plethrum (πλέθρον). (1) A measure of length among the Greeks = $\frac{1}{6}$ of a stadium = 100 Greek feet = little more than 101 English feet, or 33 yards 2 feet. (2) A unit of square measure, the square of 100 Greek feet, or 10,000 Greek square feet—i. e. an area of the extent of 10,226.2656 square feet, or about 1136.24 square yards—i. e. about two perches less than a rood, or quarter of an acre. See MENSURA.

Pleumoxii. A small tribe in Gallia Belgica, subject to the Nervii.

Pleurōn (Πλευρών). An ancient city in Aetolia, situated at a little distance from the coast. It was abandoned by its inhabitants when Demetrius II., king of Macedonia, laid waste the surrounding country, and a new city was built under the same name near the ancient one. The two cities are distinguished by geographers under the names of Old Pleuron and New Pleuron respectively.

Plinius. (1) GAIUS PLINIUS SECUNDUS, called the Elder. A Roman representative of encyclopaedic learning, born A.D. 23, at Novum Comum (Como), in Upper Italy. Although throughout his life he was almost uninterruptedly occupied in the service of the State, yet at the same time he carried on the most widely extended scientific studies to which he laboriously devoted all his leisure hours, and thus gained for himself the reputation of the most learned man of his age. Under Claudius he served as commander of a troop of cavalry (*praefectus alae*) in Germany; under Vespasian, with whom he was in the highest favour, he held several times the office of imperial governor in the provinces, and superintended the imperial finances in Italy. Finally, under Titus, he was in command of the fleet stationed at Misenum, when in A.D. 79, at the celebrated eruption of Vesuvius, his zeal for research led him to his death. For a detailed account of this event, as well as of his literary labours, we have to thank his nephew, the Younger Pliny (*Epist.* iii. 5; vi. 16).

Besides writings upon military, grammatical, rhetorical, and biographical subjects, he composed two greater historical works—a history of the Germanic wars in twenty books, and a history of his own time in thirty-one books. His last work was the Natural History (*Historia Naturalis*), in thirty-seven books, which has been preserved to us. This was dedicated to Titus, and was published in A.D. 77; but he was indefatigably engaged in amplifying it up to the time of his death. This encyclopaedia is compiled from 20,000 notices, which he had extracted from about 2000 writings by 474 authors. Book i. gives a list of contents and the names of the authors used; ii. is on astronomy and physics; iii.–vi., a general sketch of geography and ethnography, mainly a list of names; vii.–xix., natural history proper (vii., anthropology; viii.–xi., zoölogy of land and water animals, birds, and insects; xii.–xix., botany); xx.–xxxii., the pharmacology of the vegetable kingdom (xx.–xxvii.) and of the animal kingdom (xxviii.–xxxii.); xxxiii.–xxxvii., mineralogy and the use of minerals in medicine and in painting, sculpture, and the engraving of gems, besides valuable notices upon the history of art. A kind of comparative geography forms the conclusion.

Considering the extent and varied character of the undertaking, the haste with which the work was done, the defective technical knowledge and small critical ability of the author, it cannot be surprising that it includes a large number of mistakes and misunderstandings, and that its contents are of very unequal value, details that are strange and wonderful, rather than really important, having often unduly attracted the writer's attention. Nevertheless, the work is a mine of inestimable value in the information it gives us respecting the science and art of the ancient world; and it is also a splendid monument of human industry. Even the unevenness of the style is explained by the mosaic-like character of the work. At one time it is dry and bald in expression; at another, rhetorically coloured and impassioned, especially in the carefully elaborated introductions to the several books. On account of its bulk, the work was in early times epitomized for more convenient use. An epitome of the geographical part of Pliny's encyclopaedia, belonging to the time of Hadrian, and enlarged by additions from Pomponius Mela and other authors, forms the foundation of the works of Solinus and Martianus Capella. Similarly the *Medicina Plinii* is an epitome prepared in the fourth century for the use of travellers.

About two hundred manuscripts of Pliny are in existence, divided into two general classes—the *vetustiores*, all more or less incomplete, but truer to the original, and the *recentiores*, which are less fragmentary, but also less accurate. Of the former the best is the Codex Bambergensis of the tenth century, containing only bks. xxxii.–xxxvii. The *recentiores* are all of the same "family," going back to a single archetype now lost. See Fels, *De Codicibus Plinianis* (Göttingen, 1861).

Editions are those with notes by Barbari (Rome, 1492); by J. F. Gronovius, 3 vols. (Leyden, 1669);

by Hardouin (Paris, 1685); by Franz, 10 vols. (Leipzig, 1778–91); by Sillig, with critical notes and indices, 8 vols. (Gotha, 1853–55); by Jan, 6 vols. (Leipzig, 1854–65); 2d ed. by Mayhoff (1870 foll.); and by Detlefsen, 6 vols. (Berlin, 1866–73). There is a *Chrestomathia Pliniana* by Urlichs (Berlin, 1857); a good French translation by Grandsagne with notes by various scholars, 20 vols. (Paris, 1829–33); and a fair English one with good index in the Bohn Library (London, 1856). On the language and style of Pliny, see Wannowski, *Pliniana* (Posen, 1847); Grasberger, *De Usu Pliniano* (Würzburg, 1860); J. Müller, *Der Stil des älten Plinius* (Innsbruck, 1883); and Thüssing (Prague, 1890).

(2) Called the Younger, GAIUS PLINIUS CAECILIUS SECUNDUS, nephew and adopted son of the elder Pliny, born A.D. 62, at Novum Comum. After the early death of his father Caecilius, he was carefully brought up by his mother Plinia and by his adoptive father. He was trained in rhetoric under Quintilian, and began his public career as an advocate in the nineteenth year of his age. After serving in Syria as military tribune, he devoted himself under Domitian to the service of the State, and became the emperor's quaestor, and also a tribune of the people and praetor (A.D. 93). Under Trajan, he held the consulship in 100, and about 112 governed the province of Bithynia as imperial legate. He died about 114, very widely respected on account of his mild and benevolent character, his exemplary private life, his ability as an orator, his refined taste, and his services to letters. He was distinguished by the favour of the emperor, and was in friendly intercourse with the most celebrated men of his time and the representatives of literature. Among his friends appear Quintilian (*Epist.* ii. 14, § 9), Silius Italicus (iii. 7), Martial (iii. 21), Suetonius (i. 8; iii. 8; v. 10; ix. 34), and, above all, Tacitus (i. 6, 20; iv. 13; vi. 6, 16, 20; vii. 20, 33; viii. 7; ix. 10, 14), to whom he was bound by the most genuine mutual attraction.

Of his poems and forensic speeches, which he published himself, nothing has been preserved, with the exception of a panegyric addressed to Trajan, which he pronounced in the Senate in A.D. 100 in order to thank the emperor for the consulship conferred upon him. This he afterwards published in a revised form. It is composed in an affected and artificial style, and is full of the most exaggerated pieces of flattery addressed to the emperor; it served as a pattern for the later panegyrists. Besides this, we possess a collection of letters in nine books, dating from the year 97–108, edited by himself. To this collection there is added a tenth book, consisting of the official correspondence between him and Trajan, belonging chiefly to the time of his Bithynian governorship, published, we may presume, after his death. (The best-known letters in this book are that on the punishment of the Christians, No. 97, and the emperor's reply, No. 98.) His letters, in which he happily imitates Cicero, give a clear picture of his own personality, his studies, and his intercourse with his friends, as well as of the public, social, and literary life of his time, and are therefore valuable as authorities for the history of the same.

The only existing manuscript which contains all the nine books of Pliny is the Codex Laurentinus (Mediceus) of the ninth or tenth century, from which several others are derived. A very old manuscript, now lost, gave its readings to the editio Aldina of 1508.

The *editio princeps* (eight books only) appeared at Venice in 1471. The first complete edition is that of Aldus (Venice, 1508). Other editions are those of Gruter (1611); Veenhusen, with notes (Leyden, 1669); Döring (Freiburg, 1843); Waltz (Paris, 1833); of bk. iii. with English notes by Mayor (London, 1880); of bks. i. and ii. by Cowan (London, 1889). The best critical text is that of Keil, with indices, etc. by Mommsen (Leipzig, 1853). The Panegyric is edited by Dübner (Paris, 1843). There is a good English version of the Letters by Lewis (London, 1880). See Cauvet, *Étude sur Pline le Jeune* (Toulouse, 1857); Lagergren, *De Vita et Elocutione C. Plinii Secundi* (Upsala, 1872); Schöntag, *Plinius der Junger* (Hof, 1876); Kraut, *Syntax und Stil des jung. Plinius* (Schönthal, 1872); Morillot, *De Plinii Minoris Eloquentia* (Grenoble, 1888); and Platner in the *American Journal of Philology*, iv. pp. 214–218.

Plistus (Πλειστός). A small river in Phocis, rising in Mount Parnassus, and falling into the Crissaean Gulf.

Plostellum Poenĭcum or **Punĭcum.** A threshing-machine used by the Romans, consisting of several rollers fitted with iron spikes, which as they turned around threshed out the grain (Varro, *R. R.* i. 51). The same sort of contrivance is used by the modern Egyptians.

Plotīna. The wife of the emperor Trajan. See TRAIANUS.

Plotīnus (Πλωτῖνος). A Greek philosopher, born A.D. 205 at Lycopolis, in Egypt. In the twenty-eighth year of his life he applied himself to philosophy, and attended the lectures of the most celebrated men of that time in Alexandria. But none of these was able to satisfy him, until in Ammonius Saccas, the founder of Neo-Platonism, he discovered the teacher whom he had sought. With him he stayed for eleven years; then, in 243, he joined the expedition of the emperor Gordian against the Persians, in order to learn the Persian philosophy. In this object he failed, owing to the unsuccessful issue of the undertaking; he was even obliged to flee for his life to Antioch. In 244 he went to Rome, where he worked till 269 with great success, and gained the emperor Gallienus himself and his wife Salonina as converts to his teaching, so that he even dared to conceive the idea of founding an ideal city in Campania, with the approval and support of the emperor: this city was to be called Platonopolis, and its inhabitants were to live according to the laws of Plato. Gallienus was not disinclined to enter into the plan; but it was thwarted by the opposition of the imperial counsellors.

Plotinus died in 270, on the estate of a friend in Campania. With the fiftieth year of his age he had begun to reduce his teaching to a written form; the fifty-four treatises, which have been preserved to us, were published after his death by his pupil and biographer Porphyry, who revised their style and arranged them in order. They were published in six *Enneads*, or sets of nine books. Plotinus was the first to give a systematic development to the Neo-Platonic doctrine, or, at least, the first to put it forth in writing, not indeed with the charm of the Platonic dialogues, still less with their dialectic force, but nevertheless with depth of thought and in pithy, though at times careless and incorrect, language. It is true that there appears even in him a mystical tendency, especially in his doctrine of the ecstatic elevation of the soul to the divine being, to which he himself (according to the testimony of Porphyry) attained on four occasions; but he is still completely free from the fantastic and superstitious character of the later Neo-Platonism. See the works by Kirchner (1854); Brenning (1864); and Kleist (1884). The *Enneads* of Plotinus are edited by Kreuzer (1835); Kirchhoff (1856); and Müller (1878).

Plotius, MARIUS, called SACERDOS. A Latin grammarian, who wrote a work on grammar (*Ars Grammatica*) in the third century A.D. It was in three books, of which the third, *De Metris*, is preserved entire and the other two in part. It is given in Gaisford's collection of metrical writers (Oxford, 1837); the whole work in Keil's *Grammatici Latini*, vi. 427.

Plotius Tucca. See TUCCA.

Plough. See ARATRUM.

Ploxĕmum and **Ploxĕmus.** The body of a *cisium* or gig, made of leather or covered with this material. Quintilian speaks of the word as a provincial one (i. 5, 8). See CISIUM.

Plumae. The scales in a corselet or cuirass (Verg. *Aen.* xi. 771). See LORICA.

Plumbum (μόλυβδος). Lead. (See METALLUM.) The name is applied to (*a*) a water-pipe (see FISTULA); (*b*) a bullet (see GLANS); (*c*) the lumps on the lash of a whip (see FLAGRUM); (*d*) a plummet of lead for drawing lines; a *lead* pencil (Catull. 22, 8). See Beckmann, *Hist. of Inventions*, ii. p. 389 (London, 1846); and Thompson, *Greek and Latin Palaeography*, p. 53 (London, 1893).

Plutarchus (Πλούταρχος). A Greek writer of biographies and miscellaneous works, who was born at Chaeronea, in Boeotia, about A.D. 50. He came of a distinguished and wealthy family, and enjoyed a careful education. His philosophical training he received at Athens, especially in the school of the Peripatetic Ammonius (of Lamptrae in Attica), who is identified with Ammonius the Egyptian. After this he made several journeys, and stayed a considerable time in Rome, where he gave public lectures on philosophy, was in friendly intercourse with persons of distinction, and conducted the education of the future emperor Hadrian. From Trajan he received consular rank, and by Hadrian he was in his old age named procurator of Greece. He died about 120 in his native town, in which he held the office of archon and of priest of the Pythian Apollo.

His fame as an author is founded principally upon his *Parallel Lives* (Βίοι Παράλληλοι). These he probably prepared in Rome under the reign of Trajan, but completed and published late in life at Chaeronea. The biographies are divided into connected pairs, each pair (which makes a βιβλίον) placing a Greek and a Roman in juxtaposition, and generally ending with a comparative view of the two; of these we still possess forty-six: Theseus and Romulus; Lycurgus and Numa; Solon and Valerius Publicola; Themistocles and Camillus; Pericles and Fabius Maximus; Alcibiades and Coriolanus; Timoleon and Aemilius Paulus; Pelopidas and Marcellus; Aristides and the elder Cato; Philopoemen and Flamininus; Pyrrhus and Marius; Lysander and Sulla; Cimon and Lucullus; Nicias and Crassus; Eumenes and Sertorius; Agesilaus and Pompeius; Alexander and Caesar; Phocion and the younger Cato; Agis and Cleomenes and the two Gracchi; Demosthenes and Cicero; Demetrius Poliorcetes and Antonius; Dion and Brutus. To these are added the four specially elaborated lives of Artaxerxes Mnemon, Aratus, Galba, and Otho; a number of other biographies are lost. The sequels which follow most of the lives give a sort of balanced judgment (σύγκρισις) of the two men compared.

Plutarch's object was not to write history, but out of more or less important single traits to form distinct sketches of character. The sketches show, indeed, a certain uniformity, inasmuch as Plutarch has a propensity to portray the persons represented either as models of virtue in general, or as slaves of some passion in particular; but the lives are throughout attractive, owing to the liveliness and warmth of the portraiture, the moral earnestness with which they are penetrated, and the enthusiasm which they display for everything noble and great. For these reasons they have always had a wide circle of readers. More than this, their historical value is not to be meanly estimated, in spite of the lack of criticism in the use of the authorities and the manifold inaccuracies and mistakes, which, in the Roman lives, were in part the result of a defective knowledge of the Latin language. There are a large number of valuable pieces of information in which they fill up numerous gaps in the historical narratives that have been handed down to us. Besides this work eighty-three writings of various kinds (some of them only fragments and epitomes of larger treatises) are preserved under the name of Plutarch. These are improperly classed together under the title *Moralia* (ethical writings); for this designation is only applicable to a part of them. The form of these works is as diverse as their tenor and scope: some are treatises and reports of discourses; a large number is composed in the form of Platonic or Aristotelian dialogues; others again are learned collections and notices put together without any special plan of arrangement. A considerable portion of them are of disputable authenticity or have been proved to be spurious. About half are of philosophical and ethical tenor, and have for the most part a popular and practical tendency, some of them being of great value for the history of philosophy, such as the work on the opinions of the philosophers (*De Placitis Philosophorum*) in five books. Others belong to the domain of religion and worship, such as the works *On Isis and Osiris*, *On the Oracles of the Pythian Priestess*, and *On the Decay of the Oracles;* others to that of the natural sciences, while others again are treatises on history and antiquities, or on the history of literature, such as the *Greek and Roman Questions* and the *Lives of the Ten Orators*. This last is undoubtedly spurious. One of the most instructive and entertaining of all his works is the *Table-talk* (*Quaestiones Conviviales*) in nine books, which deal *inter alia* with a series of questions of history, archaeology, mythology, and physics. But even with these works his literary productiveness was not exhausted; for, besides these, twenty-four lost writings are known to us by their titles and by fragments. In his language he aims at attaining the pure Attic style, without, however, being able altogether to avoid the deviations from that standard which were generally prevalent in his time.

The entire works of Plutarch are edited by Reiske (12 vols. 1774–79); and in the Didot Collection, by Dübner-Döhner (5 vols. 1846–55). The best text of the *Lives* is that of Sintenis in the Teubner series (5 vols. Leipzig, 1874–81); of the *Moralia*, by Bernardakis, still in course of publication. The *Lives* are annotated by Held, Leopold, Siefert-Blass, and Sintenis-Fuhr, all in German; and by Holden in English. Translations in English are those of Langhorne, Dryden, and others (re-edited by A. H. Clough in 5 vols., 1874); and of the Roman lives by George Long. The *Moralia* are translated in a revision by Goodwin (Boston, 1874–78). See Trench, *A Popular Introduction to Plutarch* (London, 1873).

Pluteus and **Pluteum**. (1) A pent-house or mantlet used by the Romans in sieges. (2) The backboard of a bed, or the raised end of a couch. (3) A dwarf wall or parapet. (4) A bookshelf, bookcase, or desk.

Pluto (Πλοῦτων). In Greek mythology, the king of the underworld, identical with Hades. See HADES.

Plutus (Πλοῦτος). The Greek personification of riches; born in Crete as the son of Demeter and her beloved Iasion or Iasius, whom Zeus, out of jealousy, killed with lightning. He was supposed to have been blinded by Zeus, so that he might distribute his gifts without choice (Aristoph. *Plut.* 90). In Thebes and Athens he was represented as a child on the arm of Tyché and of Irené (q. v.) (Pausan. i. 8, 2; ix. 16, 2; ix. 26, 8).

Pluvius. A name given to Iupiter as the sender of rain (Tibull. i. 7, 26). Other like epithets are PLUVIĀLIS and IMBRICĬTOR. See IUPITER.

Plynteria (πλυντήρια). A festival at Athens in honour of Athené, goddess of the city, held in the month Thargelion. It lasted several days, probably from the 21st to the 25th (A. Mommsen, *Heort.* 436 foll.). See CALLYNTERIA.

Pnyx (Πνύξ). A place at Athens, no longer to be identified with certainty, in which the assemblies of the people were held. See ATHENAE; ECCLESIA.

Pocket. See SINUS.

Pocket-handkerchief. See MUCINUM; SUDARIUM.

Pocŭlum (ποτήρ). A cup. See CALIX.

Podalirius (Ποδαλείριος). The son of Asclepius and Epioné. Like his brother Machaon (q. v.), physician to the Greeks before Troy, and a brave warrior besides. He was honoured as a hero at Mount Dria.

Podarces (Ποδάρκης). (1) The original name of Priam. (2) The leader of the Thessalians of Phylacé against Troy (*Il.* ii. 695).

Podargé (Ποδάργη, "the swift-footed"). One of the Harpies. See HARPYIAE.

Podium. (1) A base projecting like a step from the wall of a room or building, and serving as a sort of low shelf for depositing any objects, as beehives, wine-jars, etc. (2) In the amphitheatre and circus it was a stage raised some eighteen feet from the arena, which it surrounded, and was reserved for the emperor, the Vestal Virgins, and the curule magistrates (Suet. *Nero*, 12; Juv. ii. 147). See AMPHITHEATRUM.

Poeas (Ποίας). King of the Malians at the foot of Mount Oeta. He set fire to the pyre of Heracles, in return for which the hero gave him his bow and his poisoned arrows. His son was Philoctetes (q. v.), who is hence called *Poeantius heros*.

Poecĭlé. A celebrated portico at Athens, which received its name from the paintings with which it was adorned (ποικίλη στοά, from ποικίλος, "diversified"). Its more ancient name is said to have been Peisianactius (Diog. Laërt. *Zen.*). The pictures were by Polygnotus, Micon, and Pamphilus, and represented the battle between Theseus and the Amazons, the contest at Marathon, and other achievements of the Athenians (Pausan. i. 15). Here were suspended also the shields of the Scioneans of Thrace, and those of the Lacedaemonians taken in the island of Sphacteria. It was in this portico that Zeno first opened his school, which was hence denominated the "Stoic," or "School of the Porch," from στοά. See STOICI.

Poemander (Ποίμανδρος). The father by Tanagra, daughter of Aeolus, of Ephippus and Leucippus. He was the reputed founder of the town of Tanagra, in Boeotia. See TANAGRA.

Poena (ποινή). A general name for punishment, while *multa* is a definite pecuniary punishment assigned to a particular offence. A poena was inflicted only by law, while the *multa* was imposed by the magistrate. See MULTA.

Poeni. A common name of the Carthaginians, cognate with PHOENIX, because they were a colony of Phœnicians. See CARTHAGO; PHOENICÉ.

Poenŭlus. A play of Plautus based upon a Greek play called Καρχηδόνιος, probably by Menander. The last scene exists in two separate texts which do not agree. The play is famous for a passage in it which gives in Latin characters a passage in the Phœnician language whose interpretation has exercised the ingenuity of many scholars. (See the programmes by Bellermann [Berlin, 1806–8], Wex [Schwerin, 1838], and Movers [Berlin, 1845].) The play is edited by Geppert (Berlin, 1864).

Poetovio or **Petovio**. Now Pettau; a town in Pannonia Superior on the river Dravus (Drave). It was made a Roman colony by Trajan, and was the station of the Twelfth Legion (*C. I. L.* iii. p. 439; Tac. *Hist.* iii. 1).

Poggio Bracciolini. See BRACCIOLINI.

Pogon (Πώγων). A name given to the harbour of Troezen from its shape, being formed by a curved strip of land which resembled a beard (πώγων): hence arose the proverbial joke, πλεύσειας εἰς Τροιζῆνα, which was addressed to those whose chins were but scantily provided. Herodotus says that the Greek ships were ordered to assemble there prior to the battle of Salamis. See TROEZEN.

Pola. A town in Istria, traditionally founded by the Colchians sent in pursuit of Medea. The modern place of the same name contains magnificent ruins (amphitheatre, triumphal arch, etc.), which attest its past prosperity.

Pole. See CONTUS.

Polemarchus (πολέμαρχος). (1) The third among the Athenian archons. (See ARCHON.) (2) Among the Spartans this was originally the designation of a high officer, who, without any specific command, was employed by the king for special duties. In later times it denoted the commander of a *mora* (q. v.).

Polemius Silvius. A Christian Latin writer of the fifth century A.D., who revised the official calendar, omitting everything that seemed to savour of paganism, and adding historical data and remarks on both grammar and meteorology (ed. by Mommsen, *C. I. L.* i. p. 335). He also wrote a work entitled *Laterculus*, given in the *Abhandl. der Sächs. Gesellsch d. Wissensch.* (1853).

Polĕmon (Πολέμον). (1) I. A king of Pontus and the Bosporus. He was the son of Zenon, the orator of Laodicea. As a reward for the services rendered by his father as well as himself, he was appointed by Antony in B.C. 39 to the government of a part of China; and he subsequently obtained in exchange the kingdom of Pontus. He accompanied Antony in his expedition against the Parthians in 36. After the battle of Actium he was able to make his peace with Octavian, who confirmed him in his kingdom. About the year 16 he was intrusted by Agrippa with the charge of reducing the kingdom of Bosporus, of which he was made king after conquering the country. His reign after this was long and prosperous; he extended his dominions as far as the river Tanaïs; but having engaged in an expedition against the barbarian tribe of the Aspurgians, he was not only defeated by them, but taken prisoner, and put to death. By his second wife Pythodoris, who succeeded him on the throne, he left two sons, Polemon II., and Zenon, king of Armenia, and one daughter, who was married to Cotys, king of Thrace. (2) II. Son of the preceding and of Pythodoris. He was raised to the sovereignty of Pontus and Bosporus by Caligula in A.D. 39. Bosporus was afterwards taken from him by Claudius, who assigned it to Mithridates, while he gave Polemon a portion of Cilicia in its stead, 41. In 62 Polemon was induced by Nero to abdicate the throne, and Pontus was reduced to the condition of a Roman province. (3) Of Athens, an eminent Platonic philosopher. He was the son of Philostratus, a man of wealth and political distinction. In his youth, Polemon was extremely profligate; but one day, when he was about thirty, on his bursting into the school of Xenocrates at the head of a band of revellers, his attention was so arrested by the discourse, which chanced to be upon temperance, that he tore off his garland and remained an attentive listener, and from that day he adopted an abstemious course of life, and continued to frequent the school, of which, on the death of Xenocrates, he became the head, B.C. 315. He died in 273 at a great age. He esteemed the object of philosophy to be, to exercise men in things and deeds, not in dialectic speculation. He placed the *summum bonum* in living according to the laws of nature.

Polĕmon (Πολέμων). The name of several Greek authors. (1) Called PERIEGĒTES, the most celebrated of that class of writers. (See PERIEGETAE.) Born in the district of Troas, he afterwards settled at Athens, where he was presented with the citizenship about B.C. 200. He there worked up the material which he had collected from inscriptions, dedications, and public monuments of all kinds into a number of works (*inter alia*, on Athens, and on the holy road from Athens to Eleusis), which, in succeeding times, were much quoted and highly valued as a mine of archaeological facts, and of important points connected with the history of art. The fragments which are preserved enable us to recognize him as a well-read author. (2) ANTONIUS POLĔMON, the Sophist or rhetorician; a native of Laodicea, who lived in the first half of the second century A.D., and presided over a flourishing school of rhetoric in Smyrna. He was much esteemed by his contemporaries and in high favour with the emperors Trajan, Hadrian, and Antoninus Pius. Towards the end of his life he was a martyr to the gout, and accordingly put an end to his life in his fifty-sixth year by causing himself to be buried alive in the tomb of his ancestors at Laodicea. His fame was founded principally on the pithiness and adroitness of his improvisations. There are preserved two declamations by him, artificial variations upon the same theme—funeral orations in honour of Cynaegirus and Callimachus, the generals who fell at Marathon. They have been edited by Orelli (Leipzig, 1819).

Polemonium (Πολεμώνιον). A city on the coast of Pontus, in Asia Minor, built by King Polemon (probably the second of the name), on the site of the older city of Sidé, and at the end of a deep gulf (Pliny, *H. N.* vi. 11).

Polenta. See PULS.

Polētae (πωληταί). A financial board at Athens, composed of ten members chosen yearly from the tribes by lot. Their chief duties were the leasing of the public taxes and the selling of confiscated goods (Aristot. *Polit. Ath.* § 47). See Gilbert, *Greek Const. Antiq.* pp. 131, 136 (Eng. trans. 1895).

Polias (Πολιάς) or **Poliūchus** (Πολιοῦχος, "Protectress of the city"). A special name of Athené (q. v.) in many Greek cities, but particularly at Athens.

Police. See VIGILES.

Polieus (Πολιεύς). "Protector of the city." A title given to Zeus at Athens, where he was worshipped on the Acropolis.

Polis (πόλις). See POLITEIA.

Politeia (πολιτεία). Citizenship, a citizen (πολίτης) being defined by Aristotle as one who is a sharer in the legislative and judicial power (μέτοχος κρίσεως καὶ ἀρχῆς). The character and meaning of citizenship differed in the various States of Greece, and in each State was not always the same. In the Homeric Age the notion of citizenship existed only so far as the condition of slaves and aliens was its negative. In the historical period there was a grand levelling up of the lower ranks, owing to (1) the overthrow of the monarchy, (2) the quarrels of the nobles who succeeded to the power of the kings, and (3) the growth of commerce and of wealth. Among the chief rights of a Greek πολίτης, and which were sometimes granted to πρόξενοι or closely allied aliens, were the right of intermarriage (ἐπιγαμία), the right of acquiring landed property (ἔκτησις), immunity from taxation (ἀτέλεια). These privileges were included under the general name of ἰσοτέλεια or ἰσοπολιτεία, and the non-citizens who obtained them were called ἰσοτελεῖς. The Greeks regarded the State (πόλις) as a definite entity intended to effect some one great end, as liberty (under a democracy), wealth (under an oligarchy), and education and training (under an aristocracy). This unity of purpose was most fully carried out in Sparta, where the one great aim of all the political institutions was to unite and solidify the governing body against the superior numbers of a subject population. (See HELOTES; SPARTA.) But in all the Greek governments the object was to draw the social bond as close as possible. See Gilbert, *Greek Constitutional Antiquities*, Eng. trans. (1895); METOECI; PERIOECI; PROXENUS.

Politiānus, ANGĔLUS, the Latinized name of ANGELO DE' AMBROGINI, of Monte Puliciano, usually known in English as POLITIAN, a distinguished Italian humanist of the fifteenth century. He was born at Monte Puliciano, in Tuscany, July 14, 1454, the son of a well-known jurist. At the age of ten he was sent to Florence, at that time the centre of the Renaissance movement, and pursued his studies under some of the most famous scholars of the day, among them the Greeks Argyropoulos and Callistus and the two great Italian teachers Landino and Ficino. As a student, Politianus evinced powers of an uncommon nature, especially in the classic languages. His brilliant epigrams in Greek and Latin, written in his sixteenth year, were universally admired and wondered at. When seventeen, he began the translation into Latin hexameters of the *Iliad*, carrying it as far as the fifth book, the first book having been already translated by another scholar. So great was his success in this rather audacious attempt that he won the notice and the favour of Lorenzo de' Medici, then supreme at Florence, who became the patron of the precocious boy then popularly known as "the Homeric youth." Aided alike by the patronage of Lorenzo and his own genius, he soon attained to the first place among the scholars of Italy. In 1484 he was made Professor of Greek and Latin in the University of Florence, whither his increasing fame drew students from all parts of Europe, among them Grocyn, Reuchlin, and Linacre, to whom England and Germany are so greatly indebted. Politian died in 1494, two years after the death of his patron, and during the temporary supremacy of Savonarola. He is buried in the Church of San Marco, Florence, and an inscription on his tomb styles him "an angel with one head and three tongues."

The original works of Politian in Latin fill a closely printed quarto, and consist of letters and miscellaneous papers in both prose and verse. His Latin style, while not of classical purity, is intensely individual, and shows that he used the language not as an imitator, but as a master. He likewise deserves an honourable distinction for the service rendered to his mother tongue, in which he wrote the first secular drama (*Orfeo*) that Italian literature has to show. Besides his translations of Homer mentioned above, he also made versions of Epictetus, Galen, Hippocrates, Herodian, of Plato's *Charmides*, and especially of Callimachus, besides editing the *Pandecta* of Justinian with such acuteness as to impress even modern students of the Roman law. His *praefationes* to Homer, Quintilian, Suetonius, and to the *Silvae* of Statius, as well as his *Praelectio in Persium*, also deserve mention.

The complete works of Politian were published at Florence in 1499, and at Lyons, 3 vols. (1536–46). On his personality, see Roscoe, *Life of Lorenzo de' Medici* (1796); Symonds, *The Renaissance in Italy*, vol. ii. pp. 345–355 (1877); Von Reumont, *Lorenzo de' Medici*, vol. ii. (Eng. trans. 1876); and Voigt, *Die Wiederbelebung des klass. Alterthums*, vol. i. p. 371, vol. ii. p. 199 (Berlin, 1881).

Polĭtĭci Versus (πολιτικοὶ στίχοι). A name given to verses written in popular metres and involving principles peculiar to the popular prosody, as rhyme, accentual quantity, etc. In this sense πολιτικός is used in reference to the general body of the citizens, the πολλοί or plebeians. See RHYME.

Politorium. A town in the interior of Latium, destroyed by Ancus Martius.

Polla, ARGENTARIA. The wife of the poet Lucan. See LUCANUS.

Pollentia. (1) Now Polenza; a town of the Statielli in Liguria, at the confluence of the Sturia and the Tanarus. It was celebrated for its wool. In its neighbourhood Stilicho gained a victory over the Goths under Alaric. (2) A town in Picenum.

Pollentia. An old Roman deity supposed to give strength to growing children (Livy, xxxix. 7).

Pollĭce Verso. See GLADIATORES, p. 733.

Pollinctor. An undertaker's assistant who washed and anointed the corpse, and prepared it either for burial or for the funeral pile (Mart. x. 97).

Pollio, GAIUS ASINIUS. A celebrated Roman poet, orator, and historian. He was born B.C. 75, and made his first public appearance by bringing an impeachment in B.C. 54. In the Civil Wars he fought on Caesar's side at Pharsalus and in Africa and Spain. After the murder of Caesar he at first inclined to the republicans, but in B.C. 43 joined Antony, and on the breaking up of the Triumvirate obtained Gallia Transpadana for his province. In the redistribution of lands there he saved the poet Vergil's paternal estate for him. After negotiating the Peace of Brundisium between Antony and Octavianus, B.C. 41, he became consul in 40, conquered the Parthini in Dalmatia in 39, and celebrated a triumph. He then retired from political life, and devoted himself to the advancement of learning. He served the cause of literature not only by his own writings, but by setting up the first public library at Rome, and by introducing the custom of reading new works aloud to a circle of experts before publication. (See RECITATIO.) He was himself a stern critic of others, as we see by his strictures on Cicero, Sallust, and Livy, though it was remarked that he was not always so severe upon himself. He was especially celebrated as an orator; yet his speeches, in spite of careful preparation, were devoid of elegance, and, as Quintilian remarks, might be supposed to have been written a century earlier than Cicero's. He wrote tragedies also, in which the same stiffness and dryness are complained of. He likewise composed a history of the Civil Wars in seventeen books, from the First Triumvirate to the battle of Philippi, which seems not to have been published in a complete form till after his death. Not one of his works has survived. The history of Caesar's African campaign, *Bellum Africanum*, has sometimes been attributed to him, but on insufficient grounds. He died in his eightieth year (A.D. 4). Three letters of his to Cicero are found among the Ciceronian collection, *Ad Familiares* (x. 31–33). Fragments of his history of the Civil Wars can be seen in St. Peter's *Historicorum Fragmenta*, 262. See Aulard, *De Asini Pollionis Vita et Scriptis* (Paris, 1877); and Schmalz, *Sprachgebr. des Asinius Pollio* (Munich, 1890).

Pollio, VEDIUS. A Roman knight and a friend of Augustus. He was by birth a freedman, and has obtained a place in history on account of his riches and his cruelty. He was accustomed to feed his lampreys with human flesh, and whenever a slave displeased him, the unfortunate wretch was forthwith thrown into the pond as food for the fish. On one occasion Augustus was supping with him, when a slave had the misfortune to break a crystal goblet, and his master immediately ordered him to be thrown to the fishes. The slave fell at the feet of Augustus, praying for mercy; and when the emperor could not prevail upon Pollio to pardon him, he dismissed the slave as an act of imperial power, and commanded all Pollio's crystal goblets to be broken and the fish-pond to be filled up. Pollio died B.C. 15, leaving a large part of his property to Augustus. It was this Pollio, who built the celebrated villa of Pausilypum (q. v.) near Naples.

Pollux (Πολυδεύκης). (1) See DIOSCURI. (2) IULIUS (Ἰούλιος Πολυδεύκης). A Greek rhetorician, a native of Naucratis in Egypt, in the latter half of the second century A.D., tutor of the emperor Commodus, from whom he received an appointment as a public teacher in Athens. His contemporaries, such as Lucian, ridiculed him for his small capacity. Lucian is supposed to have attacked him in his *Rhetorum Praeceptor* (Ῥητόρων Διδάσκαλος), his *Lexiphanes*, and his *De Saltatione*, chap. xxxiii. We possess from his hand a dictionary (Ὀνομαστικόν) in ten books, dedicated to his pupil. This is arranged, not in the order of the alphabet, but according to subjects. It spite of all its confusion and its want of critical acumen, it throws much light on the language, literature, and antiquities of Greece. It has been edited by I. Bekker (Berlin, 1846). See LEXICON.

Polo, THE GAME OF. See PILA, p. 1258.

Polus (Πῶλος). (1) A rhetorician of Agrigentum, introduced by Plato as a speaker in the *Gorgias*. (2) A Greek tragic actor of much repute. He is said to have acted in eight tragedies on four successive days when seventy years of age (Plut. *Dem.* 28).

Polyaenus (Πολύαινος). A Greek writer, who was born in Macedonia and lived about the middle of the second century A.D., as a rhetorician and advocate at Rome, under Marcus Aurelius and Lucius Verus. When the latter was setting out for the war against the Parthians in 162, Polyaenus, being prevented by his age from taking part in the campaign, addressed to him a collection of military stratagems compiled from old writers, under the title *Strategica*, or *Strategemata* (Στρατηγήματα), in eight books. In spite of many serious errors, this laborious and copious collection is not without value for purposes of historical research. It is edited by Casaubon (1589); Wölfflin (1860); and Wescher (1867).

Polybius (Πολύβιος). (1) One of the most important Greek historians, born about B.C. 204 at Megalopolis; the son of Lycortas, general of the Achaean League in 185–184 and after 183. Through his father, and his father's friend Philopoemen, he early acquired a deep insight into military and political affairs, and was afterwards intrusted with high federal offices, such as the commandership of the cavalry, the highest position next to the federal generalship. In this capacity he directed his efforts towards maintaining the independence of the Achaean League. As the chief representative of the policy of neutrality during the war of the Romans against Perseus of Macedonia, he attracted the suspicion of the Romans, and was one of the 1000 noble Achaeans who in 166 were transported to Rome as hostages, and detained there for seventeen years. In Rome, by virtue of his high culture, he was admitted to the most distinguished houses, in particular to that of Aemilius Paulus, the conqueror in the Macedonian War, who intrusted him with the education of his sons, Fabius and the younger Scipio. He was on terms of the most cordial friendship with the latter, whose counsellor he became. Through Scipio's intercession in 150, Polybius obtained leave to return to his home with those of the Achaeans who still survived; but in the very next year he went with his friend to Africa, and was present at the capture of Carthage, B.C. 146. After the destruction of Corinth in the same year, he returned to his native land, and made use of his credit with the Romans to lighten, as far as he could, the lot of his unfortunate countrymen. When Greece was converted into a Roman province, he was intrusted with the difficult task of organizing the new form of government in the Greek towns, and in this office gained for himself the highest recognition both from the conquerors and from the conquered, the latter rewarding his services by setting up statues to him and by other marks of honour (Polyb. *Epitome*, xl. 10; Pausan. viii. 9, 30, 37, 44, 48). The pedestal of such a statue has been discovered at Olympia. The succeeding years he seems to have spent in Rome, engaged on the completion of his historical work, and occasionally undertaking long journeys through the Mediterranean countries in the interest of his history, more particularly with a view to obtaining actual ocular knowledge of historical sites. After the death of his patron he returned to Greece, and died in 122, at the age of eighty-two, in consequence of a fall from his horse.

During his long sojourn in Rome, his study of the history and constitution of Rome, as well as his personal experiences, inspired him with the conviction that the Roman people owed the magnificent development of their power, not to fortune, but to their own fitness, and to the excellence of their political and military institutions, as compared with those of other States, and that therefore their rapid rise to world-wide dominion had been in some measure an historical necessity. In order to enlighten his countrymen on this point, and thereby to supply them with a certain consolation for their fate, he composed his history (Πραγματειά) of the period between B.C. 220 and 146, in forty books. Of these the first two are in the form of an Introduction, and give a compendium of events in Italy, Africa, and Greece, from the destruction of Rome by the Gauls to the First Punic War, thus recording the rise of the Roman supremacy. The first main division (books iii.–xxx.) contained in synchronistic arrangement the occurrences from 220 to 168—that is, of the time in which Rome was founding its world-wide dominion through the Hannibalian, Macedonian, Syrian, and Spanish Wars. The second (books xxxi.–xl.) described the maintenance and consolidation of this dominion against the attempts to overthrow it in the years 168–146. Of this work only books i.–v. have been preserved in a complete form; of the rest we possess merely fragments and epitomes. This is especially to be regretted in those parts in which Polybius narrates events which came within his own experience. He is the first representative of that particular type of historical composition, which does not merely recount the several facts and phenomena in chronological order, but goes back to the causes of events, and sets forth their results. His work rests upon a knowledge of the art of war and of politics, such as few ancient historians possessed; upon a careful examination of tradition, conducted with keen criticism; partly also upon what he had himself seen, and upon the communications of eye-witnesses and actors in the events. It sets forth the course of occurrences with clearness, penetration, sound judgment, and love of truth, and, among the circumstances affecting the result, lays especial stress on the geographical conditions. It belongs, therefore, to the greatest productions of ancient historical writing, though, in respect to language and style, it does not attain the standard of Attic prose. The language is often wanting in purity, and the style is stiff and inharmonious.

There are editions of Polybius by Schweighäuser, in 8 vols. (Leipzig, 1789–95); Bekker (Berlin, 1844); Dindorf (last ed. 1882); and Hultsch (2d ed. 1888); and of a part of the history, with good English notes, by Davidson (1890). There is a translation into English by Shuckburgh, 2 vols. (London, 1889). See Von Scala, *Die Studien des Polybius* (1891 foll.). (2) A favourite freedman of the emperor Claudius. He was the companion of the studies of Claudius; and on the death of his brother, Seneca addressed to him a *Consolatio*, in which he bestows the highest praises upon his literary attainments. Polybius was put to death through the intrigues of Messalina, although he had been one of her paramours.

Polybōtes (Πολυβώτης), one of the giants who fought against the gods. He was pursued by Poseidon across the sea as far as the island of Cos. There Poseidon tore away a part of the island, which was afterwards called Nisyrion, and throwing it upon the giant buried him under it.

Polybus (Πόλυβος). (1) A king of Corinth, foster-father of Oedipus (q. v.). (2) A physician, one of the pupils of Hippocrates. He founded the sect of the Dogmatici. See MEDICINA.

Polycarpus (Πολύκαρπος). One of the Apostolic Fathers, was a native of Smyrna. The date of his birth and of his martyrdom are uncertain. He is said to have been a disciple of the Apostle John, and to have been consecrated by this apostle bishop of the church at Smyrna. It has been conjectured that he was the angel of the church of Smyrna to whom Jesus Christ directed the letter in the Apocalypse (ii. 8–11); and it is certain that he was Bishop of Smyrna at the time when Ignatius of Antioch passed through that city on his way to suffer death at Rome, some time between 107 and 116. Ignatius seems to have enjoyed much this intercourse with Polycarp, whom he had known in former days, when they were both hearers of the Apostle John. The martyrdom of Polycarp occurred in the persecution under the emperors Marcus Aurelius and Lucius Verus. As he was led to death the proconsul offered him his life, if he would revile Christ. "Eighty and six years have I served him," was the reply, "and he never did me wrong: how then can I revile my King and my Saviour?" We have remaining only one short piece of Polycarp, his *Letter to the Philippians*, which is published along with Ignatius and the other apostolical writers. It is edited in Gebhard's *Patrum Apostolica Opera*, vol. ii. (1876). See Lightfoot's *Apostolic Fathers*, pt. ii. (2d ed. 1889); and IGNATIUS.

Polychromy. The ancient practice of colouring pieces of sculpture, as well as certain portions of the exterior and interior of buildings. See STATUARIA ARS.

Polўcles (Πολυκλῆς). The name of two artists. The elder Polycles was probably an Athenian, and flourished about B.C. 370. He appears to have been one of the artists of the later Athenian school, who obtained great celebrity by the sensual charms exhibited in their works. One of his chief works was a celebrated statue of an Hermaphrodite. The younger Polycles is placed by Pliny in B.C. 155, and is said to have made a statue of Juno, which was placed in the portico of Octavia at Rome, when that portico was erected by Metellus Macedonicus. But since most of the works of art with which Metellus decorated his portico were not the original productions of living artists, but the works of former masters, it has been conjectured that this Polycles may be no other than the Athenian artist already mentioned.

Polyclētus. See POLYCLITUS.

Polyclītus (Πολύκλειτος). (1) Next to his somewhat older contemporary Phidias, the most admired sculptor of antiquity. He was a native of Argos, and, like Phidias, a pupil of Ageladas. His name marks an epoch in the development of Greek art, owing to his having laid down rules of universal application with regard to the proportions of the human body in its mean standard of height, age, etc. In close accordance with these rules he fashioned a typical figure, the "Doryphorus," a powerful youth with a spear in his hand: this figure was called the κανών, and for a long time served as a standard for succeeding artists (Pliny, *H. N.* xxxiv. 55). The rules which he practically applied in the canon he also set forth theoretically in a written work (Galen, in Overbeck's *Schriftquellen*, §§ 958, 959). It is also said of him that when he made statues in an attitude of rest, instead of dividing the weight of the body equally between the two feet, according to the custom which had hitherto prevailed, he introduced the practice of causing them to rest upon one foot, with the other foot slightly raised, whereby the impression of graceful ease and calm repose was for the first time fully produced (Pliny, l. c. 56). Except the celebrated chryselephantine colossal statue of Heré (q. v.), which he made for the temple of the goddess at Argos (Pausan. ii. 17, § 4), when it was rebuilt after a fire in B.C. 423, he produced statues in bronze alone, and almost exclusively of men in the prime of youth, such as the "Doryphorus" already mentioned; the "Diadumenus," a

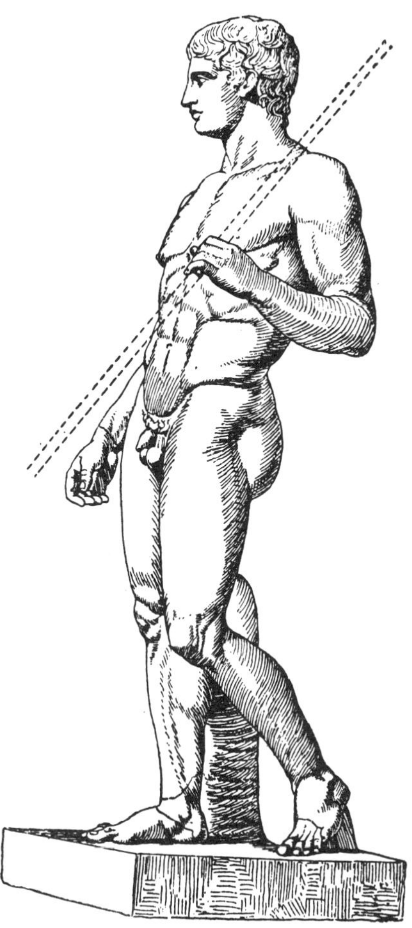

Copy of the Doryphorus of Polyclitus. (Naples.)

youth of softer lineaments, who is tying a band round his head (Pliny, l. c. 55; Lucian, *Philopseudes*, 18); and an "Amazon," which was preferred even to that of Phidias (Pliny, l. c. 53). These statues may still be identified in copies of a later time. He also worked as an architect. The theatre at Epidaurus (of which considerable remains still exist), the circular structure called the Tholos, and the temple of Asclepius (Pausan. ii. 27), are now generally assigned to the younger Polyclitus. (2) POLYCLĪTUS THE YOUNGER, a pupil of the Argive sculptor Naucydes. Among his works was a statue of the athlete Agenor (Pausan. vi. 6, § 2), and of Zeus Philios at Megalopolis, in which the god was represented with some of the attributes of Dionysus (id. viii. 31, § 4). The statues of Zeus Meilichios at Argos (id. ii. 20, § 1), and those of Apollo, Leto, and Artemis on Mount Lyconé near Argos (ib. 24, § 5), may possibly be assigned to the elder Polyclitus (Overbeck, *Schriftquellen*, §§ 941–943).

Polydămas (Πολυδάμας). (1) Son of Panthoüs and Phrontis. He was a Trojan hero, a friend of Hector, and brother of Euphorbus (*Il.* xvi. 534). (2) Of Scotussa in Thessaly, son of Nicias, conquered in the Pancratium at the Olympic Games in Ol. 93, B.C. 408. His size was immense, and the most marvellous stories are related of his strength, how he killed without arms a huge and fierce lion on Mount Olympus, and how he stopped a chariot at full gallop. His reputation led the Persian king, Darius Ochus, to invite him to his court, where he performed similar feats (Pausan. vi. 5, 4; vii. 27, 6). (3) Of Pharsalus in Thessaly. He was intrusted by his fellow-citizens, about B.C. 375, with the supreme government of their native town. He afterward entered into a treaty with Iason of Pherae. On the murder of Iason in 370, his brother Polyphron put to death Polydamas (Xen. *Hellen.* vi. 1, 2).

Polydectes (Πολυδέκτης). The son of Magnes, king of the island of Seriphus. He attempted to compel Danaë to marry him, but was turned into a stone by her son Perseus by the sight of the head of Medusa. See PERSEUS.

Polydeuces (Πολυδεύκης). See DIOSCURI.

Polydōrus (Πολύδωρος). (1) Son of Cadmus and Harmonia, father of Labdacus, and great-grandfather of Oedipus. (2) Youngest son of Priam and of Laothoë; his father's favourite son. He was killed while yet a boy by Achilles. The tragedians make him the son of Priam and Hecuba, who, before the fall of Troy, committed him with many treasures to the care of their guest-friend, the Thracian king Polymestor (or Polymnestor). After the capture of Troy, Polymestor put the boy to death, in order to get possession of the gold, and threw the body into the sea. The waves cast it up on the Trojan shore, and here Hecuba found it, just as Polyxena was on the point of being sacrificed. Out of revenge she, with the help of the captive Trojan woman, killed the two children of the murderer and blinded Polymestor himself. According to another version, Ilioné, Priam's daughter and Polymestor's wife, brought up the brother, who had been committed to her charge, as her own son, while she gave up her child Deïphilus (or Deïpilus) instead of Polydorus. The Greeks, who wished to exterminate the race of Priam, won over Polymestor by promising him the hand of Electra and a large present of money in return for the murder of Polydorus. Polymestor then murdered his own son, and was blinded and killed by Ilioné. (3) A Greek sculptor of the school of Rhodes, author (in conjunction with Agesander and Athenodorus) of the celebrated group of Laocoön (q. v.).

Polyeuctus (Πολύευκτος). An Athenian orator of the deme Sphettus. He was a political friend of Demosthenes, with whom he worked in resisting the Macedonian party (Plut. *Dem.* 10).

Polygnōtus (Πολύγνωτος). A celebrated Greek painter of the island of Thasos. He worked chiefly in Athens, whither he had been invited by Cimon about B.C. 460, and where he received the citizenship. His most celebrated paintings were the "Capture of Troy" and the "Descent of Odysseus into Hades," in the hall erected by the Cnidians at Delphi. We possess a description of them in considerable detail by Pausanias (x. 25–31). Other celebrated paintings by him (though several of his contemporaries were associated with him in their execution) were to be seen in the Stoa Poecilé, the "Capture of Troy" and the "Battle of Marathon" (ib. 15), and in the temples of the Dioscuri (ib. 18, § 1), and of Theseus at Athens. Though his works were only tinted outlines traced upon a coloured background, without shading and without any perspective, and sketched, as it were, in simple relief, all on the same plane, still his clear, rhythmical composition, the delicacy of his drawing, the impressiveness of his contours, and the nobility of his figures were highly celebrated. See Overbeck, *Schriftquellen*, 1067–1079.

Polyhymnia (Πολύμνια). The Muse of serious songs of adoration. See MUSÆ.

Polyhymnia. (Statue in the Louvre.)

Polyīdus (Πολύϊδος). The son of Coeranus, grandson of Abas, great-grandson of Melampus, father of Euchenor, Astycratia, and Manto; like his ancestor, a celebrated seer, who flourished, according to different accounts, either at Corinth or Argos or Megara. To his son he prophesied his death before Troy; and the son of Minos, Glaucus (q. v.), he raised from the dead. At Megara he cleansed Alcathoüs from the murder of his son Callipolis, and erected a temple of Dionysus.

Polymestor (Πολυμήστωρ). A Thracian king. He murdered Polydorus, the son of Priam, who had been intrusted to his protection, and was blinded by Hecuba and the captive Trojan women. See POLYDORUS.

Polymĭta. See TELA.

Polymnestus or **Polymnastus** (Πολύμνηστος). The son of Melos of Colophon. He was an epic, elegiac, and lyric poet, and a musician. He flourished B.C. 675–644. He belongs to the school of Dorian music, which obtained at this time at Sparta, where he carried on the improvements of Thaletas. The Attic comedians attacked his poems for their erotic character (Aristoph. *Eq.* 1287). As an elegiac poet, he may be regarded as the predecessor of his fellow-countryman, Mimnermus.

Polymnia. See POLYHYMNIA.

Polymyxus (πολύμυξος). See LUCERNA.

Polynīces (Πολυνείκης). Son of Oedipus and Iocasté, was driven out of Thebes by his brother Eteocles (see OEDIPUS), and fled to Adrastus (q. v.) of Argos, who gave him his daughter Argia in marriage, and brought about the expedition of the Seven against Thebes in order to restore him. He fell in single combat with Eteocles. His body, which had been thrown to the birds, was buried by his sister Antigoné (q. v.). His son was Thersander (q. v.). See SEVEN AGAINST THEBES.

Polyphēmus (Πολύφημος). The son of Poseidon and the nymph Thoösa; the one-eyed Cyclops, who held Odysseus prisoner in his cave and ate several of the companions, until the hero made him drunk and blinded him. Later legends made him the lover of the beautiful nymph Galatea. See ACIS; CYCLOPES; GALATEA; ODYSSEUS.

The Blinding of Polyphemus. (Etruscan Painting.)

Polyphontes (Πολυφόντης). A descendant of Heracles, who slew Cresphontes, king of Messené, and married his wife Meropé, taking also possession of the kingdom. He was slain by Aepytus, son of Cresphontes (Apollod. ii. 8, 4).

Polyptȳchon. See DIPTYCHA.

Polysperchon (Πολυσπέρχων). A Macedonian, and a distinguished officer of Alexander the Great (Arrian, *Anab.* iii. 11). In B.C. 323 he was appointed by Alexander II. in command of the army of invalids and veterans, which Craterus had to conduct home to Macedonia. He afterwards served under Antipater in Europe, and so great was the confidence which the latter reposed in him, that Antipater on his death-bed (319) appointed Polysperchon to succeed him as regent and guardian of the king, while he assigned to his own son Cassander the subordinate station of Chiliarch. Polysperchon soon became involved in war with Cassander, who was dissatisfied with this arrangement. It was in the course of this war that Polysperchon basely surrendered Phocion to the Athenians, in the hope of securing the adherence of Athens. (See PHOCION.) Although Polysperchon was supported by Olympias, and possessed great influence with the Macedonian soldiers, he proved no match for Cassander, and was obliged to yield to him the possession of Macedonia about 316. For the next few years Polysperchon is rarely mentioned, but in 310, he again assumed an important part by reviving the long-forgotten pretensions of Heracles, the son of Alexander and Barsiné, to the throne of Macedonia. Cassander marched against him, but distrusting the fidelity of his own troops, he entered into secret negotiations with Polysperchon, and persuaded the latter, by promises and flatteries, to murder Heracles (Diod. xx. 28). From this time he appears to have served under Cassander; but the period of his death is not mentioned.

Polytechnus. An artist of Colophon, who, according to one story, was the husband of Aëdon. See AËDON.

Polyxĕna (Πολυξένη). A daughter of Priam and Hecuba, the betrothed of Achilles, who, at his wedding with her in the temple of the Thymbraean Apollo, was treacherously killed by Paris (Eurip. *Hec.* 40; Hyg. *Fab.* 110). After the fall of Troy the shade of Achilles demanded the expiation of his death with her blood, and she was sacrificed on his funeral pyre. Another tradition makes Achilles and Polyxena to have fallen in love with one another when Hector's body was given up to Priam; that Polyxena fled from Troy and joined the Greeks; and that after the death of Achilles she slew herself upon his tomb (Philostr. *Her.* 19, 11).

Polyxo (Πολυξώ). (1) The nurse of queen Hypsipylé in Lemnos, and celebrated as a prophetess. (2) An Argive woman, married to Tlepolemus, son of Heracles, followed her husband to Rhodes, where, according to some traditions, she is said to have put to death the celebrated Helen. See HELENA.

Pomade. See PILA MATTIACA; SAPO; SPUMA; UNGUENTUM.

Pomerium and **Pomoerium**. A name given by the Romans to the space, originally along the city wall within and without, which was left vacant and reckoned holy. This space was marked off by stones, and in respect to the auspices formed the limit between city and country. (See Livy, i. 44, and Cicero, *Nat. D.* ii. 11, with the note of J. B. Mayor.) The form *Pomerium* is now generally approved (Mommsen in *Hermes*, x. 40), though the other spelling is more harmonious with the etymology of the word (*post-moerium*).

The old Pomerium remained unchanged until the time of Sulla; after him it was again extended by Claudius, Nero, Vespasian, and Titus, and probably also by Augustus, Trajan, and Aurelian. An extension of the Pomerium was only admissible on the ground of an extension of the legal boundaries of the Empire (Tac. *Ann.* xii. 23). See TEMPLUM.

Pomōna. An old Italian divinity presiding over the fruit of trees (*poma*). Her service was performed by a special priest (*flamen Pomonalis*), and she had a special sanctuary (*Pomonal*) between Ardea and Ostia. See Varro, *L. L.* vii. 45, and VERTUMNUS.

The Doric Peristyle of the Atrium of a House (reg. vi. ins. ix. n. 2), known as the *Casa del Meleagro*, from the subject of one of its finest paintings.

Pompēia. (1) The daughter of Q. Pompeius Rufus, son of the consul of B.C. 88, and of Cornelia, the daughter of the dictator Sulla. She married C. Caesar, subsequently the dictator, in 67, but was divorced by him in 61, because she was suspected of intriguing with Clodius (q. v.), who stealthily introduced himself into her husband's house while she was celebrating the mysteries of the Bona Dea. (2) The sister of Cn. Pompey, the triumvir. She married C. Memmius, who was killed in the war against Sertorius, in 75. (3) Daughter of the triumvir by his third wife Mucia. She married Faustus Sulla, the son of the dictator, who perished in the African War, B.C. 46. She afterwards married L. Cornelius Cinna, and her son by this marriage, Cn. Cinna Magnus, entered into a conspiracy against Augustus. As her brother Sextus survived her, she must have died before 35. (4) Daughter of Sex. Pompey, the son of the triumvir and of Scribonia. At the peace of Misenum in 39 she was betrothed to M. Marcellus, the son of Octavia, the sister of Octavian, but was never married to him. She accompanied her father in his flight to Asia, 36. (5) Paulina. See PAULINA.

Pompeii (Πομπήϊοι). A city in Campania, founded towards the sixth century B.C. by an Italic tribe, which left its native haunts in the Apennines to seek a happier home on the shores of Campania. They settled on a hill of volcanic origin between the river Sarno and the sea, and divided the land so that each *paterfamilias* should have a share of two *iugera* (57,600 square feet). The number of settlers is estimated by Fiorelli at 150 families. The city was inaugurated with the same political and religious rites which had been observed in the foundation of Rome; it was crossed by two main streets, the *cardo* running from south to north, the *decumanus* running from east to west. Two lanes parallel, one with the *cardo*, one with the *decumanus*, were added in course of time, by means of which the city was finally divided into nine quarters or wards (*regiones*), and each ward subdivided into blocks (*insulae*). The same division is maintained to-day. Thus the house of Lucius Popidius Secundus is marked house n. v., fourth insula, first region; that of Marius Epidius Rufus is n. xx., first insula, ninth region, and so on.

Towards B.C. 424 the city fell a prey to the Samnites. The new-comers, under the influence of Hellenic art and civilization, transformed the smoky huts of the conquered tribesmen into gay and commodious dwellings, levelled and paved the streets, and raised public and sacred edifices in the choicest forms of Doric architecture.

Towards the end of the Marsic War the Pompeians were defeated in the plains of Nola; their city and their territory were given up to a colony of veterans; the name was changed into that of Colonia Veneria Cornelia Pompeii. Under the benevolent rule of Augustus, Pompeii became the Newport of ancient Rome, and continued to enjoy the favour of the rich and pleasure-seeking patricians for more than a century. In A.D. 63, on February 5th, the *felix* Campania was shaken by an earthquake. Pompeii, Nuceria, Herculaneum, and Naples were seriously damaged; a flock of six hundred sheep disappeared in a fissure of the earth; statues fell from their pedestals; public edifices collapsed, and when the work of repairing the damages was nearly completed, and the recollections of the earthquake had almost died away, another by far more horrible catastrophe took place by which Pompeii, Herculaneum, and Stabia, as living cities, were wiped forever from the face of the earth.

Specimen of House Decorations of the Time of Augustus. The Mosaic-work is lined with Cornices of Shells, Pumice-stones, and Enamels. (From house, reg. vii. ins. ii. n. 38.)

The account of the eruption of Mount Vesuvius in A.D. 79 is given by Pliny the Younger in two well-known letters (vi. 16 and 20) to Tacitus. Other particulars are supplied by Dio Cassius, lxvi. 21; Suetonius, *Titus*, viii; Marcus Aurelius, iv. 48; and Tertullian, *Apol.* 40. The history of those eventful days has therefore been reconstructed in all the leading details. (See Dyer's chapter "History of Vesuvius," pp. 10–29.) Still there are a great many others, revealed by late excavations, which are less known to the general public. Thus, for instance, the year in which the eruption took place is well known (A.D. 79); not so the month and the day, as the text of Pliny which mentions them is undoubtedly corrupt. The Neapolitan scholars have favoured autumn (November) rather than summer (August), alleging the discoveries of carpets drawn over the mosaic and marble floors, of braziers placed in exposed corners, of dried figs and grapes, of chestnuts, pine-nuts, and other fruit belonging to the late autumn. On the other hand, it was alleged that in the hundred and fifty houses excavated since 1870, no carpet has been found, only a piece of matting which, however, seems to have been rolled, and not extended on the floor; that the braziers collected both from Pompeii and Herculaneum number scarcely fifty, and that they were used not for warming but for cooking purposes; and lastly that in Southern climates the fruit mentioned above ripens in August.

The controversy about the precise date of the destruction of Pompeii was settled on October 11th, 1889. While excavating a bed of volcanic ashes, a few steps outside the Porta Stabiana, Signor Ruggero discovered and moulded in plaster two human forms, and that of a trunk of a tree, 3.40 metres long, 0.40 m. in diameter. One of the human casts belonged to a middle-aged man clothed in an overcoat, and lying on his back with drawn-up legs, and arms outstretched, as if trying to protect his chest from the shower of burning ashes by which he was suffocated. The other belongs to an old woman suffocated and buried while attempting to raise herself from the ground by the joint action of hands and knees. By far more important is the cast of the trunk of the tree. The tree was still in its upright position, and must have been twenty-five or thirty feet high. The lower portion, embedded in pumice-stone, does not appear in the mould; the top also has disappeared, because, projecting above the bed of ashes, it must have been burned or cut away. The middle section of the trunk is wonderfully well preserved, together with many leaves and berries. Trunk, leaves, and berries belong undoubtedly to a species of *Laurus Nobilis*, the fruit of which comes to maturity towards the end of autumn. Prof. Pasquale, in a paper published in the *Notizie degli Scavi* for 1889, p. 408, proves that the berries discovered on October 11th were perfectly ripe. This Laurus Nobilis, therefore, so ingeniously brought back to life after a lapse of one thousand eight hundred and ten years, settles the controversy concerning the date of the eruption: it took place in the month of November, on November 23, A.D. 79. The catastrophe took the gay and thoughtless people by surprise. All over the town we find evidence of a sudden panic—of a wild rush for life. The writer has often noticed one of these striking examples in a corner of the Forum opposite to the temple of Iupiter. Some masons were engaged in raising an enclosure round a new altar of white marble; the mortar just dashed against the side of the wall was but half spread out; one can see the long sliding stroke of the trowel about to return and obliterate its own track; but it never did return: the hand of the workman was suddenly arrested. The city was not buried entirely, and concealed from the eyes of survivors. The top of the walls of private buildings, the colonnades of public edifices emerged from the words *Dumnos Pertusa* scratched above a hole cut through one of its walls to obtain a passage from room to room. The house of L. Caecilius Iucundus was found ransacked; its searching-party had left in one of the holes a lantern of the shape still in use among the Neapolitan peasantry. Yet there are a great many exceptions to the rule. Many wealthy houses have never been explored, and their valuable contents fall occasionally our prey, under the form of a treasure-trove. The writer remembers one which took place in 1881. While Michele Ruggero was excavating half-way between the Porta Stabiana and the coast, a building was found—perhaps a bathing establishment—comprising some twenty rooms gayly decorated with frescoes. Here a band of thirty-six Pompeians took refuge from the fury of the eruption, hoping to take to the boats; the fury of the sea, however,

Showing the thickness of the bed of pumice-stones and ashes under which Pompeii was buried, in comparison with the height of buildings. The view is taken from near the Gate to Herculaneum. In the almost perpendicular cutting of volcanic strata back of Hexedra on the left, the various layers of *lapilli* and *ceneri* are distinctly visible.

dreary waste, so that it was easy for the survivors to dig out the valuables left behind, and even the statues, marbles, fountains, and bronzes. Later eruptions and the work of nature and man obliterated the last traces of the city; a vague recollection of its site survived in the name of *Cività*, given to the hill in which it lay buried. The peasants of the Cività have searched for hidden treasure since time immemorial; to save the trouble and expense of an open excavation they tunnelled the bed of lapilli and scoriae, sometimes paying for their imprudence with their life. The skeletons of four men buried alive by the collapse of the *cuniculus* they were actually digging have been found in a house near the Via dell' Abbondanza. That of Papidius Priscus was searched likewise in the Byzantine period, as proved by the deprived the fugitives of their last chance of salvation. They were all buried alive; their skeletons were found mingled together, as they fell in their last struggle for a breath of air. They were wealthy people. Together with their bones the following objects lay scattered on the floor: five bracelets, six pairs of earrings, two necklaces, one chain, one brooch, seventeen finger-rings, fourteen pieces of gold, two hundred and eight of silver, besides engraved stones, pearls, mirrors, cameos, and copper coins.

In the following year (1882, October) a Lararium, or domestic chapel, was found in a house of the Via dell' Abbondanza in a wonderful state of preservation. On the steps of the altar there were seven statuettes of delicate workmanship. One had been taken away at the moment of the catastrophe by the fugitives, perhaps because it was the best or the most venerated of the group. The six others were found in their proper places. One represents Apollo Citharoedus, the figure being of bronze, the accessories of silver. The second, made of bronze, silver, and ivory, has undergone a curious transformation. At first it was made to represent Mercury, then, with the addition of proper clothing and attributes, it was turned into an Aesculapius. The others represent Mercury, Hercules, and two Lares.

On September 20, 1888, another remarkable discovery of silver-plate and other valuables took place in regio viii. insula ii. house xxiii. It seems that the owners of the house, having made a bundle of their plate, had put it on a stool, waiting, perhaps, for a lull in the shower of burning ashes in order to remove it to a safer place. However, in the hurry of flight, the bundle was left behind. Besides pieces of the stool on which it was laid, and of the coarse cloth in which it was enveloped, an exquisite silver set for four was found—viz., four large and four small cups and saucers, four egg-cups, one filter, and one jug, weighing nine pounds in all. There was also broken silverware and table-utensils, such as spoons, salt-cellars, etc. More important still was the discovery of three *libelli* (of wood coated with wax) containing family documents. The deeds, drawn up in A.D. 61, eighteen years before the eruption, belonged to two women—a Decidia Margaris and a Poppaea Noté. In the first deed Poppaea sells to Margaris two young slaves named Simplex and Petrinus. In the second she declares herself a debtor to Margaris for the sum of 1450 sestertii. The third document cannot be interpreted with certainty.

View of Pompeii.

Island of Reviglia no (Petra Herculis). Present line of coast. Ancient line of shore.

The question whether Pompeii was a sea-port town in the strict sense of the word, or whether it was separated from the sea by a strip of land more or less broad, has been fully discussed by Michele Ruggero in the volume published on the eighteenth centenary of the destruction of the ill-fated town. He declares the story of the discovery of a large three-masted ship (believed to be the flag-ship of Pliny) near the farm of Messigna, in 1833, to be devoid of foundation, because the would-be masts, seen by the naval engineer Giuseppe Negri, were but trunks of cypresses. Many such trees have been found since 1833: they are planted in quincunx, with the roots in the ancient vegetable soil, and the trunks buried in pumice-stone of the fatal eruption of 79. The average size of one hundred trees, measured by Palmieri and Scacchi, was 1.42 m. in circumference, 0.47 m. in diameter, which is the average size of cypresses thirty-six years old. Following the line of trees and of antique farm-houses, Ruggero was able to trace the line of the sea-coast before the eruption. It starts from Torre Annunziata, bends inland between the Salerno railway and the high-road to Castellamare, and crosses the river Sarno near the "molino di Rosa." The island of Revigliano, the *petra Herculis* of the Pompeians, which, before the eruption, was separated from the mainland by a channel 1.550 metres wide, comes now within 420 m. of the shore.

The foregoing view, taken from the north end of the excavations, shows the belt of land created by the shower of ashes and lapilli between the walls of the city and the Petra Herculis.

Of the inhabitants of Pompeii, whom Fiorelli puts down as about 12,000, the greater part fled on foot, on horseback, or in chariots. This is proved by the fact that, although the city contained many stables, two coaches only have been found—one in the court-yard of the house of Papidius Priscus and the other in the stables regio i. insula iv. n. 28. Eight skeletons of horses have been found in the space of eighteen years. In the same period of time 150 human bodies were discovered within the walls, the total number of victims being about 550, less than one in twelve. Many died in their own houses while waiting for the cessation of the shower of ashes; some were crushed by the fall of the roofs; some asphyxiated by the sulphuric vapours or by the fine dust; some starved to death or were buried alive in places from which there was no escape. The skeletons are generally found with a lamp close by, darkness, even in the day-time, having been dense; and they are seldom alone. The Pompeians died in family groups, as shown by the eighteen bodies discovered in the cellar of Diomede's villa; by the twelve in the atrium of house reg. i. ins. ii. n. 28. The fate of these last could not be explained at first, because it seemed so easy for them to have made an escape through the opening of the *impluvium*. On closer examination it was ascertained that a heavy iron grating had been laid across the *impluvium*, and that the unfortunate crowd had tried to force it without success.

Bodies crushed by falling ruins or buried in lapilli cannot be cast in plaster, being reduced to a shapeless heap of bones. Those buried in fine dust (hardened by water) are marvellously well preserved, and can be reproduced in plaster to perfection. Nothing is more impressive than the study of the various kinds of agonies suffered by these poor victims at the last moment of the struggle.

The first cast belongs to a man dashed against the pavement by the fall of the wooden ceiling of his shop-room. His fingers are clenched and his elbows drawn, as if trying to lift the weight under which he had fallen.

The following cast belongs to a workman of the Tanneries (Concia), who was left-behind or forgotten by his comrades, as he was lying ill in bed.

The poor wretch, whose legs and body appear emaciated, dragged himself as far as the court-yard of the establishment, and, perceiving no chance of deliverance or help, laid himself down to die quietly on the bare floor.

Women also seem to have died with resignation; they are generally found lying on the left side, with the *tunica* drawn over the face, as a

shelter from the ashes. The attitude of most of the men conveys the idea of energetic despair. Far from showing the abandonment of death, they fight to the last against their fate, raising hands and knees in a supreme effort, as shown by the following casts.

We must not forget the sad fate of a watch-dog, the casting of whose form is the most difficult and delicate yet accomplished in Pompeii, owing to the thinness of the legs and the extraordinary contortion of the body. The faithful animal was forgotten by his ungrateful master, L. Vesonius Prinius. He was left tied to a chain behind the street-door of the house, reg. vi. ins. xiv. n. 20. As the lapilli, pouring in from the door, began to fill the vestibule, the dog tried his best to break the ties. He was overtaken by death while lying on his back with outstretched legs.

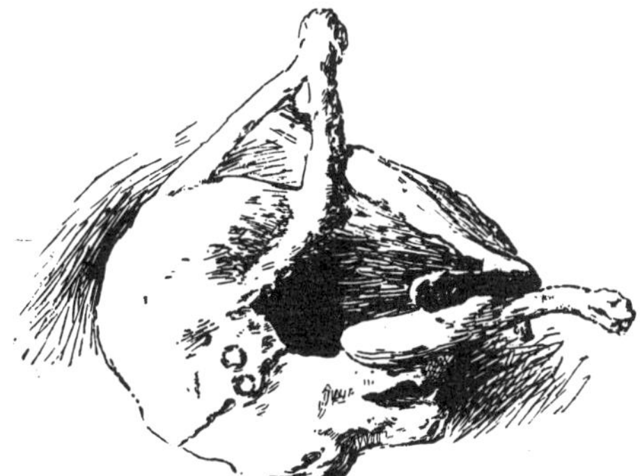

Watch-dog. Cast from nature. Discovered at the entrance of the prothyrum of the house of L. Vesonius Prinius.

Among the manifestations of Pompeian art which strike the visitor most forcibly, the wall-decorations in fresco or encaustic painting come first. There are many publications on this subject, one of the earliest being *Le Antichità di Ercolano e Pompei*, 9 fol. vols. (Napoli, 1755–1792). See also *Herculaneum et Pompei: Recueil général de peintures, bronzes, mosaïques, etc., découverts jusqu'à ce jour . . .*

gravé du trait sur cuivre par M. Roux aîné, et accompagné d'un texte explicatif par M. L. Barre, 8 large 8vo vols. (Paris, Didot); Raoul Rochette, *Choix de peintures de Pompéi, la plupart du sujet historique*, etc., with coloured plates, large fol. (Paris, 1844); E. O. Müller, *Wandgemälde aus Pompei und Herculanum, mit einem erlaüternden Texte* (Berlin, 1844); Wolfgang Helbig, *Wandgemälde der vom Vesuv verschütteten Städte Campaniens* (Leipzig, 1868). See Dilthey's criticism in the *Bullettino dell' Istituto* (1869), pp. 147–160. Professor Mau, of the German Institute, has been illustrating year by year the latest finds in this department, both in the *Bullettino* and the *Mittheilungen* of the German Institute.

The frescoes of Pompeian houses afford the best illustration that could be desired of ancient mythology, but they offer little of historical interest. Their value, as works of art, has been slightly exaggerated; at all events, they cannot bear comparison with the frescoes discovered in Rome, in Livia's Palatine house, in Livia's villa *ad Gallinas albas* (Prima Porta), in the Roman palace by la Farnesina, in Lamia's gardens (the Nozze Aldobrandine), in Nero's Golden House, etc. Among the few Pompeian frescoes connected with history the one discovered in the autumn of 1882 between the Via dell' Abbondanza, dei Teatri, e de xii. Dei, representing the Judgment of Solomon, took everybody by surprise. Who would ever have conceived that a scene inspired by the Bible should have been discovered on the walls of this purely pagan, dissolute, materialistic town? The picture belongs to the burlesque genre; and although the caricaturist has somewhat exaggerated the conventional deformity of his personages, still every particular of the Biblical account can be recognized. King Solomon, with the sceptre in his hand, sits on a platform between two assessors. He has already told the officer to make two portions of the infant; and while the pretended mother is waiting to receive her half in perfect indifference, the real one falls in a fit of despair.

Many conjectures have been proposed to explain the appearance of such a picture at Pompeii; the most satisfactory seems to be this: The Alexandrian School — after the translation of the Bible by the LXX.—was well acquainted with Hebrew archaeology, history, and tradition. The episode of Solomon's judgment may have become popular in Alexandrian circles. At Pompeii a large contingent of Alexandrians met every summer. No wonder if one of them chose to decorate his house with frescoes derived from legends so popular in his mother country. What renders the conjecture all the more probable is that, in the same apartment, there are other frescoes representing Egyptian scenes, such as crocodile-hunting, the land of the pygmies, etc.

Specimen of Pompeian fresco-paintings (The Wounded Adonis), showing the way they are cared for after their discovery. The cracks of the plaster are first filled with gluten, and then fastened with brass clasps shaped like a T. Sometimes the whole surface of the fresco is washed with a solution of wax.

A wine-shop was discovered in 1877, in regio vi. ins. xiv. n. 36, with several *tableaux de genre* painted on the white plastering of its walls. The first scene on the left represents a young man kissing a woman, who appears dressed in yellow garments with black shoes. She says, NOLO! CVM MVRTAL—"I don't want to be kissed; go to your Myrtalis." The second scene represents the same woman talking to Myrtalis. They both point their fingers at a third female, who brings in a great wine-jar and a cup, and says, QVI VOLT SVMAT OCEANE VENI BIBE—an invitation to partake of the drink. The third scene represents two gamblers seated, with the chessboard on their knees, on which several *latrunculi* are disposed in lines of different colours—yellow, white, and black. The one on the left throws the dice, and says, EXSI—"I am out." His partner, pointing to the dice, answers, NON TRIA · DVAS EST—"You only made two points, not three!" Both fight in the fourth scene. One says, NON ITA · ME TRIA · EGO FVI—"You lie; I made three points; I am out." The other retorts, ORTE FELLATOR · EGO FVI—"You . . . ! I have the game." At this moment the shop-keeper interferes, and, pushing the rioters outside, says, ITE FORAS RIXSATIS—"Go out in the street if you want to fight."

Landscapes are an utter failure; there is no colouring, no perspective, no appreciation of nature, no value of tones. Still, the study of the works of Pompeian landscape-painters is not without interest. Prof. O. Comes has compiled from them a catalogue of flowers, shrubs, ornamental and fruit-trees known to the Pompeians. It comprises seventy varieties. See Ruggero's *Pompei*, pp. 177–250.

The name of Pompeii was never forgotten in the Middle Ages. A chronicler of the ninth century, named Martinus Monachus, speaks of Sikkartol, prince of Benevento, having pitched his tents in a spot *qui a Pompeia urbe Campaniae, nunc deserta, nomen accepit* (named from Pompeii, a city of Campania, now deserted). Martinus refers not to Pompeii destroyed in A.D. 79, but to a village of the same name mentioned by the Tabula Pentingeriana at the time of Theodosius, which had in its turn been destroyed by later eruptions.

In 1594 Muzio Tuttavilla, Count of Sarno, while boring an underground channel to convey the waters of the Sarno itself to Torre dell' Annunziata, discovered remains of the amphitheatre, of the temple of Isis, of the Forum, of the *strada delle*

Tombe, to which, however, no attention was paid. Two inscriptions, dug up in the heart of the city, contained the name of Pompeii, of one of its prominent citizens (M. Popidius), of one of its prominent goddesses (Venus Physica Pompeiana); they were thrown aside and probably made use of as building materials. Regular investigation began a century and a half later, on April 1, 1748. I say regular, because the search was undertaken by the State; but there was no order, no regularity, no system. Holes were dug at random, more for the sake of official plunder in favour of the Naples museums than for topographical discovery. The merit of having brought Pompeian excavations to their actual efficiency belongs to Giuseppe Fiorelli, who was named superintendent in 1860. To him we are indebted for a thoroughly scientific organization of the work; since to his ingenuity we owe the invention of the casting in plaster the corpses of the Pompeians who lost their lives in that appalling catastrophe. (See Dyer's *Pompeii*, p. 475; *The Quarterly Review*, No. 230, p. 382.)

BIBLIOGRAPHY.—Works of general interest: Mazois (François), *Les Ruines de Pompéi dessinées et mesurées pendant les années 1809–1811*, 4 vols. (Paris, 1812–38), containing nearly 200 plates, and embracing the results of excavations from 1757 to 1821; Sir William Gell, *Pompeiana*, two series, each of two 8vo vols. (London, 1824–30), giving an account of excavations down to the year 1819; T. L. Donaldson, *Pompeii*, illustrated with picturesque views, engraved by W. B. Cooke, 2 fol. vols. (London, 1827); Breton, *Pompeia Décrite et Dessinée*, 2d ed. (Paris, 1855); Overbeck, *Pompeij in seinen Gebaüden, Alterthümern, und Kunstwerken* (Leipzig, 1856; 2d ed. in 2 vols. 1871); Fausto e Felice Niccolini, *Le Case ed i Monumenti di Pompei Disegnati e Descritti* (Naples, 1864–92); Giuseppe Fiorelli, *Pompeianarum Antiquitatum Historia* (Naples, 1860), in two 8vo vols., containing the diaries of excavations from their commencement in 1748 to 1860, with the reports printed verbatim in Spanish down to July, 1764, after that date in Italian; id. *Giornale degli Scavi di Pompei*, begun in 1861; id. *Descrizione di Pompei*, 4to (Naples, 1875), with a good map; Dyer, *Pompeii: its History, Buildings, and Antiquities*, 3d ed. (London, 1871), with nearly 300 engravings, maps, and plans; Michele Ruggero, *Pompei e la Regione Sotterrata dal Vesuvio nell' Anno LXXIX.*, a joint work of the directors of the Pompeian excavations, most excellent, and copiously illustrated (Naples, 1879); id. *Degli Scavi di Stabia dal MDCCXLIX. al MDCCLXXXII.* (Naples, 1881).

Besides these standard works many important accounts have appeared in archaeological journals, signed by Guaranta, Niccolini, Avellino, Minervini, Monnier, Helbig, Mau, Fiorelli, de Petra Sogliano. These contributions cannot be ignored by students wishing to obtain full knowledge of the subject. See *Il Real Museo Borbonico*, an illustrated serial of Neapolitan antiquities, begun in 1824; the Italian edition numbers fourteen 4to vols.; *Memorie della Reale Accademia di Archeologia di Napoli; Annali e Bullettino dell' Istituto di Corrispondenza Archeologica* (Rome and Paris, 1829–1885); *Jahrbuch und Mittheilungen des k. deutschen archäologischen Instituts* (Römische Abtheilung, 1886–92); Avellino and Minervini, *Bullettino Archeologico Napoletano; Giuseppe Fiorelli, Notizie degli Scavi di Antichità* (Rome, 1876–92). The first archaeological map of Pompeii was measured and designed by Antonio Bibent in 1827; the best is that of G. Fiorelli, entitled *Tabula Coloniae Veneriae Corneliae Pompei.* It is divided into 42 sheets, which, put together, form a superficies of 140 square palms, being the 333.3 part of the true area.

Pompeian epigraphy has been admirably illustrated by Mommsen, Zangemeister, Fiorelli, and others. See Theodor Mommsen, *Inscriptiones Regni Neapolitani*, p. 112 foll.; Raffaele Garrucci, *Graffiti di Pompei* (Paris, 1856); Giuseppe Fiorelli, *Monumenta Epigraphica Pompeiana, ad Fidem Archetyporum Expressa*, part first (Oscan inscriptions); Carl Zangemeister, *Corpus Inscriptionum Latinarum*, vol. iv. Inscriptiones Parietariae (Berlin, 1871); Theodor Mommsen, *Corpus Inscriptionum Latinarum*, vol. x. pars prior (Berlin, 1883); and the article GRAFFITI.

Pompeiopŏlis (Πομπηϊούπολις). See POMPELON; SOLOË.

Pompēius. (1) Q. POMPĒIUS, said to have been the son of a flute-player, was the first of the family who rose to dignity in the State. He was consul in B.C. 141, when he carried on war against the Numantines in Spain. Having been defeated by the enemy in several engagements, he concluded a peace with them; but on the arrival of his successor in the command, he disowned the treaty, which was declared invalid by the Senate. He was censor in 131 with Q. Metellus Macedonicus (App. *B.C.* vi. 76; Cic. *De Fin.* ii. 17, *Off.* iii. 30). (2) Q. POMPĒIUS RUFUS, either son or grandson of the preceding, was a zealous supporter of the aristocratic party. He was tribune of the plebs B.C. 100, praetor 91, and consul 88, with L. Sulla. When Sulla set out for the East, to conduct the war against Mithridates, he left Italy in charge of Pompeius Rufus, and assigned to him the army of Cn. Pompeius Strabo, who was still engaged in carrying on war against the Marsi. Strabo, however, who was unwilling to be deprived of the command, caused Pompeius Rufus to be murdered by the soldiers (Cic. *Pro Dom.* 31, *Brut.* 89; App. *B. C.* i. 57). (3) Q. POMPĒIUS RUFUS, son of No. 2, married Sulla's daughter, and was murdered by the party of Sulpicius and Marius in the Forum during the consulship of his father, B.C. 88 (Plut. *Sull.* 8). (4) Q. POMPĒIUS RUFUS, son of No. 3 and grandson of the dictator Sulla, was tribune of the plebs in B.C. 52, when he distinguished himself as the great partisan of the triumvir Pompey, whom he assisted to obtain the sole consulship. Rufus, however, on the expiration of his office, was accused of *vis*, was condemned, and went into exile at Bauli in Campania (Cic. *Ad Fam.* viii. 1, 4; Dio Cass. xi. 45). (5) Q. POMPĒIUS RUFUS, praetor B.C. 63, was sent to Capua and Apulia during Catiline's conspiracy. In 61 he obtained the province of Africa, with the title of proconsul. (6) SEX. POMPĒIUS, married Lucilia, a sister of the poet C. Lucilius. (7) SEX. POMPĒIUS, elder son of No. 6, never obtained any of the higher offices of the State, but acquired great reputation as a man of learning, and is praised by Cicero for his accurate knowledge of jurisprudence, geometry, and the Stoic philosophy (Cic. *Brut.* 47, 175). (8) SEX. POMPĒIUS, a descendant of No. 7, consul with Sex. Apuleius A.D. 14, in which year the emperor Augustus died. He seems to have been a patron of literature. Ovid addressed him several letters during his exile

(Ovid, *Pont.* iv. 1, 5). (9) Cn. POMPĒIUS STRABO, younger son of No. 6, and father of the triumvir. He was quaestor in Sardinia, B.C. 103, praetor 94, and propraetor in Sicily in the following year. He was consul in 89, when he carried on war with success against the allies, subduing the greater number of the Italian people who were still in arms. Towards the end of the year he brought forward the law (*Lex Pompeia*) which gave to all the towns of the Transpadani the *ius Latii* or *Latinitas*. He continued in the south of Italy as proconsul in the following year (B.C. 88), and when Pompeius Rufus was appointed to succeed him in the command of the army Strabo caused him to be assassinated by the troops. Next year (87) the Marian party obtained the upper hand. Strabo was summoned by the aristocratic party to their assistance; and, though not active in their cause, he marched to the relief of the city, and fought a battle near the Colline Gate with Cinna and Sertorius (Vell. Pat. ii. 21). Shortly afterwards he was killed by lightning. His avarice and cruelty had made him hated by the soldiers to such a degree that they tore his corpse from the bier and dragged it through the streets. Cicero describes him (*Brut.* 47) "as worthy of hatred on account of his cruelty, avarice, and perfidy" (cf. Flor. iii. 18); but he possessed some reputation as an orator, and still more as a general.

(10) Cn. POMPĒIUS MAGNUS, the TRIUMVIR, son of No. 9, was born on the 30th of September, B.C. 106, in the consulship of Atilius Serranus and Servilius Caepio, and was consequently a few months younger than Cicero (who was born on the 3d of January in the same year) and six years older than Caesar. He fought under his father in 89 against the Italians, when he was only seventeen years of age, and continued with him till his death two years afterwards. For the next few years the Marian party had possession of Italy; and accordingly Pompey, who adhered to the aristocratic party, was obliged to keep in the background, and was only saved from an indictment by the intervention of Carbo. But when it became known, in 84, that Sulla was on the point of returning from Greece to Italy, Pompey hastened into Picenum, where he raised an army of three legions. Although only twenty-three years of age, Pompey displayed great military abilities in opposing the Marian generals by whom he was surrounded; and when he succeeded in joining Sulla in the course of the year (83) he was saluted by the latter with the title of Imperator.

During the remainder of the war in Italy Pompey distinguished himself as one of the most successful of Sulla's generals; and when the war in Italy was brought to a close, Sulla sent Pompey against the Marian party in Sicily and Africa. Pompey first proceeded to Sicily, of which he easily made himself master (82): here he put Carbo to death. In 81, Pompey crossed over to Africa, where he defeated Cn. Domitius Ahenorbarbus and the Numidian king Hiarbas, after a hard-fought battle. On his return to Rome in the same year, he was received with enthusiasm by the people, and was greeted by Sulla with the surname of MAGNUS, a name which he bore ever afterwards, and handed down to his children. Pompey, however, not satisfied with this distinction, sued for a triumph, which Sulla at first refused, but at length, overcome by Pompey's importunity, he allowed him to have his own way. Accordingly, Pompey, who had not yet held any public office, and was still a simple *eques*, entered Rome in triumph in September, 81, and before he had completed his twenty-fifth year.

Pompey continued faithful to the aristocracy after Sulla's death (78), and supported the consul Catulus in resisting the attempts of his colleague Lepidus to repeal the laws of Sulla; and when Lepidus had recourse to arms in the following year (77), Pompey took an active part in the war against him, and succeeded in driving him out of Italy. The aristocracy, however, now began to fear the young and successful general; but since Sertorius in Spain had for the last three years successfully opposed Metellus Pius, one of the ablest of Sulla's generals, and it had become necessary to send the latter some effectual assistance, the Senate, with considerable reluctance, determined to send Pompey to Spain, with the title of proconsul, and with equal powers to Metellus. Pompey remained in Spain between five and six years (76–71); but neither he nor Metellus was able to gain any decisive advantage over Sertorius. But when Sertorius was treacherously murdered by his own officer Perperna in 82, the war was speedily brought to a close. Perperna was easily defeated by Pompey in the first battle, and the whole of Spain was subdued by the early part of the following year (71). Pompey then returned to Italy at the head of his army. In his march towards Rome he fell in with the remains of the army of Spartacus, which M. Crassus had previously defeated. Pompey cut to pieces these fugitives, and therefore claimed for himself, in addition to all his other exploits, the glory of finishing the Servile War.

Coin of Pompey.

Pompey was now a candidate for the consulship; and although he was ineligible by law, inasmuch as he was absent from Rome, had not yet reached the legal age, and had not held any of the lower offices of the State, still his election was certain. His military glory had charmed the people; and as it was known that the aristocracy looked upon Pompey with jealousy, they ceased to regard him as belonging to this party, and hoped to obtain, through him, a restoration of the rights and privileges of which they had been deprived by Sulla. Pompey was accordingly elected consul, along with M. Crassus; and on the 31st of December, B.C. 71, he entered the city a second time in his triumphal car a simple knight.

In his consulship (70), Pompey openly broke with the aristocracy, and became the great popular hero. He proposed and carried a law, restoring to the tribunes the power of which they had been deprived by Sulla. He also afforded his all-powerful aid to the Lex Aurelia, proposed by the praetor L. Aurelius Cotta, by which the *iudices* were to be taken in future from the Senate, knights, and tribunes of the treasury, instead of from the senators exclusively, as Sulla had ordained. In carrying both these measures Pompey was strongly supported by Caesar, with whom he was thus brought into close connection.

For the next two years (69 and 68) Pompey remained in Rome. In 67, the tribune A. Gabinius brought forward a bill, proposing to confer upon Pompey the command of the war against the pirates with extraordinary powers. This bill was opposed by the aristocracy with the utmost vehemence, but was notwithstanding carried. The pirates were at this time masters of the Mediterranean, and had not only plundered many cities on the coasts of Greece and Asia, but had even made descents upon Italy itself. As soon as Pompey received the command, he began to make his preparations for the war, and completed them by the end of the winter. His plans were formed with great skill and judgment, and were crowned with complete success. In forty days he cleared the western sea of pirates, and restored communication between Spain, Africa, and Italy. He then followed the main body of the pirates to their strongholds on the coast of Cilicia; and after defeating their fleet, he induced a great part of them, by promises of pardon, to surrender to him. Many of these he settled at Soli, which was henceforward called Pompeiopolis. The second part of the campaign occupied only forty-nine days, and the whole war was brought to a conclusion in the course of three months; so that, to adopt the panegyric of Cicero (*Pro Leg. Man.* 12), "Pompey made his preparations for the war at the end of the winter, entered upon it at the commencement of spring, and finished it in the middle of the summer." Pompey was employed during the remainder of this year and the beginning of the following in visiting the cities of Cilicia and Pamphylia, and providing for the government of the newly-conquered districts.

During his absence from Rome, Pompey had been appointed to succeed Lucullus in the command of the war against Mithridates (66). The bill, conferring upon him this command, was proposed by the tribune C. Manilius, and was supported by Cicero, in an oration which has come down to us (*Pro Lege Manilia*). Like the Gabinian law, it was opposed by the whole body of the aristocracy, but was carried triumphantly. The power of Mithridates had been broken by the previous victories of Lucullus, and it was only left to Pompey to bring the war to a conclusion. On the approach of Pompey, Mithridates retreated towards Armenia, but he was defeated by the Roman general; and as Tigranes now refused to receive him into his dominions, Mithridates resolved to plunge into the heart of Colchis, and from thence make his way to his own dominions in the Cimmerian Bosporus. Pompey now turned his arms against Tigranes; but the Armenian king submitted to him without a contest, and was allowed to conclude a peace with the Republic. In 65 Pompey set out in pursuit of Mithridates, but he met with much opposition from the Iberians and Albanians; and after advancing as far as the river Phasis (Faz), he resolved to leave these savage districts. He accordingly retraced his steps, and spent the winter at Pontus, which he reduced to the form of a Roman province. In 64 he marched into Syria, deposed the king Antiochus Asiaticus, and made that country also a Roman province. In 63 he advanced farther south, in order to establish the Roman supremacy in Phœnicia, Coele-Syria, and Palestine. The Jews refused to submit to him, and shut the gates of Jerusalem against him, and it was not till after a siege of three months that the city was taken. Pompey entered the Holy of Holies, the first time that any human being, except the high priest, had dared to penetrate into this sacred spot. It was during the war in Palestine that Pompey received intelligence of the death of Mithridates. (See MITHRIDATES [6].) Pompey spent the next winter in Pontus; and after settling the affairs of Asia, he returned to Italy in 62. He disbanded his army almost immediately after landing at Brundisium, and thus calmed the apprehensions of many, who feared that, at the head of his victorious troops, he would seize upon the supreme power. He did not, however, return to Rome till the following year (51), and he entered the city in triumph on the 30th of September. He had just completed his forty-fifth year, and this was the third time that he had enjoyed the honour of a triumph.

With this triumph the first and most glorious part of Pompey's life may be said to have ended. Hitherto his life had been an almost uninterrupted succession of military glory. But now he was called upon to play a prominent part in the civil commotions of the commonwealth, a part for which neither his natural talents nor his previous habits had in the least fitted him. It would seem that, on his return to Rome, Pompey hardly knew what part to take in the politics of the city. He had been appointed to the command against the pirates and Mithridates in opposition to the aristocracy, and they still regarded him with jealousy and distrust. At the same time, he was not disposed to unite himself to the popular party, which had risen into importance during his absence in the East, and over which Caesar possessed unbounded influence. The object, however, which engaged the immediate attention of Pompey was to obtain from the Senate a ratification for all his acts in Asia, and an assignment of lands which he had promised to his veterans. The Senate, however, glad of an opportunity to put an affront upon a man whom they both feared and hated, resolutely refused to sanction his measures in Asia. This was the unwisest thing the Senate could have done. If they had known their real interests, they would have sought to win Pompey over to their side, as a counterpoise to the growing and more dangerous influence of Caesar. But their short-sighted policy threw Pompey into Caesar's arms, and thus sealed the downfall of their party. Caesar promised to obtain for Pompey the ratification of his acts, and Pompey, on his part, agreed to support Caesar in all his measures. That they might be more sure of carrying their plans into execution, Caesar prevailed upon Pompey to become reconciled to Crassus, with whom he was at variance, but who, by his immense wealth, had great influence at Rome. The three agreed to assist one another against their mutual enemies, and thus was formed the so-called First Triumvirate. This union of the three most powerful men at Rome crushed the aristocracy for the time. Supported by Pompey and Crassus, Caesar was able in his consulship (59) to carry all his measures. Pompey's acts in Asia were ratified, and Caesar's agrarian law, which divided the rich Campanian land among the poorer citizens, enabled Pompey to fulfil the promises he had made to his veterans. In order to cement their union more closely, Caesar gave to Pompey his daughter Iulia in marriage.

Next year (58) Caesar went to his province in Gaul, but Pompey remained in Rome.

While Caesar was gaining glory and influence in Gaul, Pompey was gradually losing the confidence of all parties at Rome. The Senate hated and feared him; the people had deserted him for their favourite Clodius, and he had no other resource left but to strengthen his connection with Caesar. Thus he came to be regarded as the second man in the State, and was obliged to abandon the proud position which he had occupied for so many years. According to an arrangement made with Caesar, Pompey and Crassus were consuls for a second time in 55. Pompey received as his provinces the two Spains, Crassus obtained Syria, while Caesar's government was prolonged for five years more—namely, from the 1st of January, 53, to the end of the year 49. At the end of his consulship Pompey did not go in person to his provinces, but sent his legates, L. Afranius and M. Petreius, to govern the Spains, while he himself remained in the neighbourhood of the city. His object now was to obtain the dictatorship, and to make himself the undisputed master of the Roman world. Caesar's increasing power and influence had at length made it clear to Pompey that a struggle must take place between them, sooner or later. The death of his wife Iulia in 54, to whom he was tenderly attached, broke the link which still connected him with Caesar, and the fall of Crassus in the following year (53), in the Parthian expedition, removed the only person who had the least chance of contesting the supremacy with them. In order to obtain the dictatorship, Pompey secretly encouraged the civil discord with which the State was torn asunder; and such frightful scenes of anarchy followed the death of Clodius at the beginning of 52 that the Senate had now no alternative but calling in the assistance of Pompey, who was accordingly made sole consul in 52, and succeeded in restoring order to the State. Soon afterwards Pompey became reconciled to the aristocracy, and was now regarded as their acknowledged head.

The history of the Civil War which followed is related in the article CAESAR. It is only necessary to mention here that after the battle of Pharsalia (48) Pompey sailed to Egypt, where he hoped to meet with a favourable reception, since he had been the means of restoring to his kingdom the father of the young Egyptian monarch. The ministers of the latter, however, dreading Caesar's anger if they received Pompey, and likewise Pompey's resentment if they forbade him to land, resolved to release themselves from their difficulties by putting him to death. They accordingly sent out a small boat, took Pompey on board, and rowed for the shore. His wife and friends watched him from the ship, anxious to see in what manner he would be received by the king, who was standing on the edge of the sea with his troops; but just as the boat reached the shore, and Pompey was in the act of rising from his seat in order to step on land, he was stabbed in the back by Septimius, who had formerly been one of his centurions, and was now in the service of the Egyptian monarch. Pompey was killed on the 29th of September, B.C. 48, and had just completed his fifty-eighth year. His head was cut off, and his body, which was thrown out naked on the shore, was buried by his freedman Philippus, who had accompanied him from the ship. The head was brought to Caesar when he arrived in Egypt soon afterwards, but he turned away from the sight, shed tears at the melancholy death of his rival, and put his murderers to death. Pompey's untimely death excites pity; but no one who has well studied the state of parties at the close of the Roman commonwealth can regret his fall. There is abundant evidence to prove that, had Pompey's party gained the mastery, a proscription far more terrible than Sulla's would have taken place, and Italy and the provinces have been divided as booty among a few profligate and unprincipled nobles. From such horrors the victory of Caesar saved the Roman world. See Merivale, *The Roman Triumvirates* (London, 1887); Froude, *Caesar* (London, 1879); Mommsen, *Hist. of Rome*, vol. iv. (New York, 1877); and Baring Gould, *The Tragedy of the Caesars*, vol. i. (London, 1892).

(11) CN. POMPĒIUS MAGNUS, elder son of the triumvir by his third wife, Mucia. In the Civil War in 48 he commanded a squadron of the fleet in the Adriatic Sea. After his father's defeat at Pharsalia, he crossed over to Africa, and, after remaining there a short time, sailed to Spain in 47. In Spain he was joined by his brother Sextus and others of his party, who had fled from Africa after their defeat at Thapsus. Here the two brothers collected a powerful army, but were defeated by Caesar himself at the battle of Munda, fought on the 17th of March, 45. Cneius escaped from the field of battle, but was shortly afterwards taken prisoner and put to death. (12) SEXTUS POMPĒIUS MAGNUS, younger son of the triumvir by his third wife, Mucia, was born B.C. 75. After the battle of Pharsalia he accompanied his father to Egypt, and witnessed his murder. On the defeat at Munda and the death of his brother, Sextus lived for a time in concealment in the country of the Lacetani, between the Iberus and the Pyrenees; but when Caesar quitted Spain he collected a body of troops and emerged from his lurking-place. In the civil wars which followed Caesar's death the power of Sextus increased. He obtained a large fleet, became master of the sea, and eventually took possession of Sicily. His fleet enabled him to stop all supplies of corn which were brought to Rome from Egypt and the eastern provinces, and such scarcity began to prevail in the city that the triumvirs were compelled by the popular discontent to make peace with Pompey. This peace was concluded at Misenum in 39, but the war was renewed in the following year. Octavian made great efforts to collect a large and powerful fleet, which he placed under the command of Agrippa. In 36 Pompey's fleet was defeated off Naulochus, with great loss. Pompey himself fled from Sicily to Lesbos and from Lesbos to Asia. Here he was taken prisoner by a body of Antony's troops, and carried to Miletus, where he was put to death (35) probably by command of Antony, though the latter sought to throw the responsibility of the deed upon his officers (Dio Cass. xiv. 9; xlviii. 17; xlix. 11).

Pompēius Festus. See FESTUS.

Pompēius Trogus. A contemporary of Livy, author of the first Roman general history. He was of Gallic origin; his grandfather received the Roman citizenship from Pompeius in the Sertorian War, and his father served under Caesar, and discharged at the same time the offices of a secretary, an ambassador, and a keeper of the seals. His extensive work in forty-four books was drawn from Greek sources, and was a universal history entitled *Historiae Philippicae*, because the history of the various peoples was grouped round the Macedonian Empire founded by Philip; it began with Ninus, and reached down to his own time. With the historical narrative there were interwoven interesting descriptions relating to geography, ethnography, and natural science; and he is said to have also composed zoölogical and botanical works, derived largely from Aristotle and Theophrastus. Of the histories we now possess only lists of the contents of the several books (called the *prologi*) and the epitome of Iustinus. See Crohn, *De Trogi apud Antiquos Auctoritate* (Strassburg, 1882); and the article IUSTINUS.

Pompĕlōn. Now Pamplona; equivalent to POMPEIOPŎLIS, so called by the sons of Pompey. The chief town of the Vascones in Hispania Tarraconensis (Pliny, *H. N.* iii. 25).

Pompilius. See NUMA.

Pomponia. (1) The sister of T. Pomponius Atticus, and wife of Quintus Cicero, the brother of the orator. He divorced her in B.C. 45. (2) The daughter of T. Pomponius Atticus, also called Caecilia and Attica. She was married to M. Vipsanius Agrippa, and her daughter, Vipsania Agrippina, married Tiberius, the successor of Augustus.

Pomponiāna. See STOECHADES.

Pomponius. (1) LUCIUS POMPONIUS BONONIENSIS, i. e. of Bononia (Bologna), a Latin writer who flourished about B.C. 90. He was the first to raise the hitherto improvised popular plays called *Atellanae* (q. v.) to a higher plane by the introduction of written composition in the metrical forms of the Greeks. He is particularly praised for richness of fancy, liveliness in plays upon words, and readiness in the use of rustic and farcical language (Vel. Pat. ii. 9, § 6; Macrob. *Sat.* vi. 9, § 4; Sen. *Controv.* vii. 18, § 9). About seventy titles of plays by him are mentioned, a productiveness explained by the small compass of the Atellanae as being after-pieces. Some titles point to travesties of mythological subjects, such as the *Agamemnon Suppositus* and the *Armorum Iudicium.* The fragments are edited by Ribbeck in his *Comicorum Romanorum Fragmenta* (Leipzig, 1873). See Ribbeck, *Röm. Dichter.* i. 210.

(2) TITUS POMPONIUS ATTĬCUS. See ATTICUS.

(3) LUCIUS POMPONIUS SECUNDUS. The most important tragedian of the time of the Empire, probably the last who wrote for the stage. He lived under Tiberius and was a partisan of Seianus, after whose fall (A.D. 31) he had to submit to be kept in custody by his brother for six years, until Caligula gave him his freedom. In 44 he was consul; in 50 he fought with success against the Chatti, and received triumphal honours from Claudius. His poetical productions are highly spoken of by Tacitus (*Ann.* xii. 28) and Quintilian (x. 1, § 98). We possess only very scanty remains of his tragedies.

(4) POMPONIUS MELA. See MELA.

(5) SEXTUS POMPONIUS. A distinguished jurist of the first half of the second century A.D. He composed, among other works, a history of law and jurisprudence down to the time of Hadrian, which is frequently quoted in the *Digest.*

(6) POMPONIUS PORPHYRIO. A Roman grammarian, who lived in the first half of the second century A.D., and composed a commentary on Horace, a fragmentary abridgment of which is still preserved, and is edited by Meyer (Leipzig, 1874).

Pomptīnae (or **Pontīnae**) **Palūdes** (Ποντῖναι λίμναι). The Pontine Marshes. The name of a low, marshy plain on the coast of Latium, between Circeii and Terracina, said to have been so called after an ancient town Pontia, which disappeared at an early period. The marshes are formed chiefly by a number of small streams, which, instead of finding their way into the sea, spread over this plain. The miasmas arising from these marshes are exceedingly unhealthful in the summer. At an early period they either did not exist at all or were confined to a narrow district. We are told that originally there were twenty-three towns in this plain; and in B.C. 312 the greater part of it must have been free from the marshes, since the censor Appius Claudius constructed the celebrated Via Appia in that year through the plain, which must then have been sufficiently strong to bear the weight of this road. In the time of Augustus there was a navigable canal running alongside of the Via Appia from Forum Appii to the grove of Feronia, which was intended to carry off a portion of the waters of the marshes. Horace embarked upon this canal on his celebrated journey from Rome to Brundisium in B.C. 37. Juvenal (iii. 307) speaks of the marshes as the haunt of highway robbers. See ROMA.

Pomptorius, GAIUS. A Roman who was praetor in B.C. 63 when he aided Cicero in arresting the Allobrogian ambassadors who had been negotiating with the Catilinarian conspirators. In the year 61 he defeated the Allobroges, and in 54 triumphed (Sall. *Cat.* 45).

Pondĕra. See the tables of weights given in the Appendix.

Pondus (σταθμός). A weight used in weighing objects. The form of the weight was very similar to that employed in grocers' shops to-day, as is seen by the accompanying representation of one found at Herculaneum.

Roman Weight. (Herculaneum.)

Poniard. See SICA.

Pons (γέφυρα). A bridge. The earliest bridge mentioned in history is one built at Babylon across the Euphrates. It was of wood, and was constructed in the reign of Queen Nitocris, about B.C. 606 (Herod. i. 178–186). In GREECE the earliest bridges were temporary ones resting on floats like a pontoon, with cables of flax and papyrus tightly strained by windlasses to support the planking. These bridges were called σχεδίαι, and were for military purposes only. Such was the high bridge thrown across the Thracian Bosporus by a Samian Greek named Mandrocles at the order of the Persian king Darius (Herod. iv. 83, 85, 87, 88), and such also, though more carefully built, was that over the Hellespont connecting Sestos and Abydos, built for Xerxes when he invaded Greece in B.C. 480 (Herod. vii. 36). It was not, in fact, until Greece had fallen under Roman influence that permanent bridges were built over its streams, partly because these were so very narrow, and partly perhaps because of the feeling that to span a river with a bridge was an insult to the river-god. Later, however, the Roman engineers erected massive structures of stone of remarkable size, as that over the Acheron which was a thousand feet in length (Pliny, *H. N.* iv. 1), and that which united the island of Euboea to the mainland.

The ROMANS, in fact, were great bridge-builders, employing brick and concrete, or solid stone masonry fastened by iron clamps and lead. Roman bridges were usually quite narrow in proportion to their length. The central roadway for horses and vehicles was called *iter*. By the side of it ran footpaths, slightly raised and protected on the outside by a low wall. In the most elaborate bridges, such as the Pons Aelius at Rome, statues and columns were set at regular intervals along the parapet, while the main arches were decorated with mouldings. In some cases a tower was built as a defence at each end of the bridge.

Roman Bridge at Rimini.

Under the later Roman Empire the following bridges existed in the city of Rome:

(1) The PONS SUBLICIUS, which got its name from the wooden beams (*sublicae*) of which it was built. Until the second century B.C. this was the only bridge in Rome. It was said to have been built by Ancus Martius, and it connected the main city with the long walls leading from the right bank of the Tiber to the fortress on the Ianiculum. No traces of it now exist.

(2) The PONS AEMILIUS, also called the Pons Lapideus, which was the first stone bridge built in Rome. It was begun in B.C. 179 and completed about 146. It spanned the river near the theatre of Marcellus on the site now occupied by the Ponte Rotto.

(3) The PONS FABRICIUS, built in B.C. 62 by L. Fabricius, as is recorded in inscriptions cut across the face of its arches. It unites the Insula Tiberina with the left bank of the river. During the Middle Ages this bridge was called Pons Iudaeus, from its proximity to the Jewish quarter (Ghetto).

(4) The PONS CESTIUS, which unites the Insula Tiberina to the right side of the river. It was probably built in B.C. 46, and an inscription upon it records its restoration in A.D. 370.

(5) The PONS AELIUS, built in A.D. 135 by the emperor Hadrian to connect his Mausoleum with the Campus Martius. (See illustration, p. 1018.)

(6) The PONS AURELIUS, of uncertain date and probably on the site of the modern Ponte Sisto.

(7) The PONS NERONIĀNUS or VATICĀNUS, begun by Caligula and completed by Nero. The foundations of its piers are still visible in summertime a little below the Pons Aelius.

(8) The PONS MULVIUS, now called Ponte Molle, continues the Via Flaminia across the Tiber. It was built in B.C. 109 by the censor, M. Aemilius Scaurus. On this bridge Cicero caused the arrest of the ambassadors of the Allobroges at the time of Catiline's conspiracy, and in A.D. 312 it was the scene of the rout of Maxentius by Constantine. Under the Empire the Pons Mulvius was a favourite pleasure-resort for the lower classes of Rome (Tac. *Ann.* xiii. 47). Bridges in general were thronged by beggars who importuned the passers-by. See MENDICUS.

Among the best-preserved stone bridges built by the Romans and still preserved are the bridge at Rimini (Ariminum), shown in the accompanying illustration; the combined aqueduct and bridge near Nîmes, in France (see illustration under NEMAUSUS); the single-arched bridge near Brioude over the Allier; and (in a less complete condition) the bridges at Narni near Rome and at Alcantara across the river Tagus in Spain, this last being 670 feet in length.

The Romans showed great skill in constructing temporary bridges. The most famous of these was the bridge built by Caesar over the Rhine and described by him in a passage (*B. G.* iv. 17) whose translation and explanation are the terror of school-boys, and of some schoolmasters as well. This bridge was finished within ten days, and may be described as follows:

It was supported on a series of double piles, formed of two baulks of timber, each eighteen inches square (in section), pointed at one end, and driven into the bed of the river by machines called *fistucae;* they were set in a sloping direction, so as to resist the force of the current. A corresponding parallel row of piles was driven in at a distance of forty feet, thus forming a very wide roadway for the Roman army. The cross-pieces were two feet thick, and were supported by cross struts so as to diminish the bearing. A little higher up the stream a third row of piles was fixed to support "fenders," to secure the main structure from injury in case the enemy set heavy trees to float down the river and strike against the supports of the bridge.

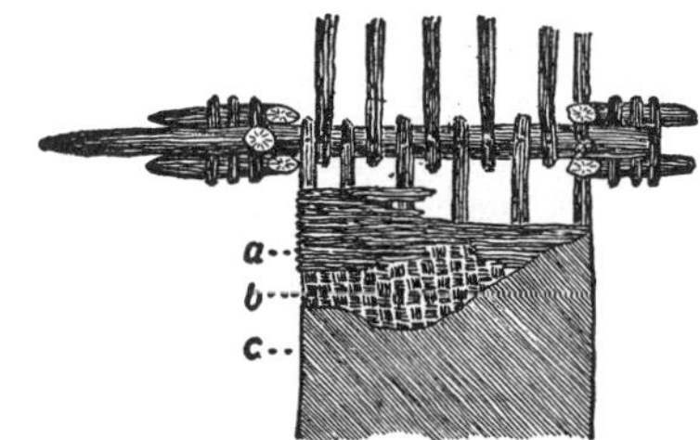

Plan of Caesar's Bridge over the Rhine.

(*a*) Rough joists. (*b*) Wattle-work. (*c*) Roadway of earth.

Transverse Section of Caesar's Bridge.

Longitudinal Section of Caesar's Bridge.

Other temporary bridges were supported by floating casks (*dolia, cupae*) or on boats (Veget. iii. 7; Florus, iii. 5). The accompanying illustration shows one of the latter bridges.

Bridge Supported on Boats. (Column of Trajan.)

See Mayerhöfer, *Die Brücken im alten Rom* (1884); Zippel in the *Jahrbücher für klass. Philologie*, pp. 481 foll. (1886); and Middleton, *Remains of Ancient Rome*, ii. 362–371 (1892).

The word *pons* also denotes any sort of wooden gangway, such as the *pons suffragiorum* through which the voters passed at the Comitia (see illustration under OVILE); and was applied to the gangplank (ἀποβάθρα) of a ship whence, by a species of metonymy, the deck itself is called *ponte* in modern Italian and *pont* in French.

Pons. A common name for towns or stations at important fords or places where rivers were crossed. Of these the best known were: (1) PONS AELIUS, now Newcastle-on-Tyne in England; (2) PONS AENI, now Pfünzen in Vindelicia on the river Inn; (3) PONS AUREŎLI, now Pontirolo, in Gallia Transpadana, named from Aureolus, one of the Thirty Tyrants, slain here (Aurel. Vict. *Caes.* 33); (4) PONS MOSAE, perhaps Maastricht, in the north of Gaul; (5) PONS SARĀVI, now Saarbrück, between the modern Metz and Strassburg.

Pontia. Now Ponza; a rocky island off the coast of Latium, opposite Formiae, taken by the Romans from the Volscians, and colonized B.C. 313. Under the Empire it was used as a place of banishment for State criminals (Suet. *Tib.* 54).

Pontĭcus. A Roman epic poet, the author of a poem on the legends of Thebes. He is best remembered as the friend of Ovid and Propertius (Ovid, *Trist.* iv. 10, 47).

Pontĭfex (γεφυροποιός). A member of the highest priestly *collegium* in Rome, to which belonged the superintendence over all sacred observances, whether performed by the State or by private persons. The meaning of the name is uncertain; for the interpretation which follows most obviously from the form of the word, that of "bridge-builder," referring in particular to the sacred bridge on piles (*pons sublicius*) over the Tiber (Varro, *L. L.* v. 83), is open to objection. (See Nettleship, *Lectures and Essays*, p. 27.) It is probable, however, that the pontifex got his name from the duty assigned him of performing rites for the propitiation of river deities on the building of bridges; for a widespread superstition regarded the spanning of a river by a bridge as in itself insulting to the divinity of the stream. See PONS.

The foundation of the college is ascribed to Numa. At first it probably consisted of six patrician members, with the addition of the king, whose place, after the abolition of the monarchy, was transferred to the Pontifex Maximus; from B.C. 300 it was composed of nine members (four patrician and five plebeian), from the time of Sulla of fifteen (seven patrician and eight plebeian); Caesar added another member; and the emperors also raised the number at their pleasure. The office was for life, as was also that of the president. While, in the time of the monarchy, the pontiffs were probably named by the king, under the Republic the college for a long time filled up its own numbers by coöptation, and also appointed the high-pontiff from among its members. From somewhere about B.C. 250 the election of the latter took place in the Comitia Tributa under the presidency of a pontiff, and, from B.C. 103, the other members were also elected in the Comitia out of a fixed number of candidates presented by the college. Under the Empire a preliminary election was held by the Senate, and merely confirmed by the Comitia.

Besides the pontiffs proper, there were also included in the college the *rex sacrorum*, the three higher *flamines* and the three *pontifices minores*, who assisted the pontiffs in transactions relating to sacrifices and in their official business, besides sharing in the deliberations and the banquets of the whole college: these ranked according to length of service. In earlier times an advanced age with freedom from secular offices was necessary for eligibility to the pontificate; the high-pontiff, among other restrictions, was not allowed to leave Italy, was obliged to have a wife without reproach, and might not enter upon a second marriage or see a dead body, much less touch one. As regards his position, he was, as spiritual successor of the king, the sole holder and exerciser of the pontifical power; and his official dwelling was in the king's house, the *regia* of Numa adjoining the Forum, the seat of the oldest State worship. The college existed by his side only as a deliberative and executive body of personal assistants. He appointed to the most important priestly offices of the State—those of *flamen*, of Vestal Virgin, and of *rex sacrorum;* he made public the authoritative decisions of the college. In matters which came within the limits of his official action, he had the right of taking auspices, of holding assemblies of the people, and of publishing edicts. He also exercised a certain jurisdiction over the persons subject to his high-priestly power, especially the flamens and Vestals, over whom his authority was that of an actual father. Owing to the great importance of the office, the emperors from the time of Augustus undertook it themselves until the year 382. As regards the functions of the college, besides performing a number of special sacrifices in the service of the household gods, they exercised (as already mentioned) a superintendence over the whole domain of the religious services recognized by the State, public and private. In all doubts which arose concerning the religious obligations of the State towards the gods, or concerning the form of any religious offices which were to be undertaken, their opinion was asked by the Senate and by the other secular bodies, which were obliged unhesitatingly to follow it. In the various religious transactions, expiatory offerings, vows, dedications, consecrations, solemn appropriations, undertaken on behalf of the State, their assistance was invited by the official bodies, in order that they might provide for the correct performance, especially by dictating the prayers. The knowledge of the various rites was handed down by the *libri pontificii*, which were preserved in the official dwelling of the high-pontiff and kept secret. These included the forms of prayer, the rules of ritual for the performance of ceremonial observances, the *acta pontificum*—i. e. the records relating to the official actions of the college—and the *commentarii pontificum*—i. e. the collection of opinions delivered, to which they were as a rule obliged to have recourse when giving new ones.

An important and, indeed, universal influence was exercised by the pontiffs, not only on religious, but also on civic life, by means of the regulation of the calendar, which was assigned to them as possessing technical knowledge of the subject, and by means of their superintendence over the observance of the holidays. Owing to the character of the Roman reckoning of the year, it was necessary from time to time to intercalate certain days, with a view to bringing the calendar into agreement with the actual seasons to which the festivals were originally attached; and special technical knowledge was needed, in order to be sure on what day the festivals fell. This technical knowledge was kept secret by the pontiffs as being a means of power. It was for the month actually current that they gave information to the people as to the distribution of the days, the festivals falling within the month, and the lawful and unlawful days (*fasti* and *nefasti;* see DIES) for civil and legal transactions. In B.C. 304 the calendar of the months was made public by Gnaeus Flavius; but the pontiffs still retained the right of regulating the year by intercalations, and thereby the power of furthering or hindering the aims of parties and individuals by arbitrary insertion of intercalary months. This they kept until the final regulation of the year introduced by Caesar as high-pontiff in B.C. 46. Closely connected with the superintendence of the calendar was the keeping of the lists of the yearly magistrates, especially of the consuls, since it was by their names that the years were dated, as well as the keeping of the yearly chronicle.

As experts in the law of ritual, the pontiffs had the superintendence over many transactions of private life, so far as ceremonial questions were connected with them, such as the conclusion of marriages, adoption by means of arrogation, and burial. Even upon the civil law they had originally great influence, inasmuch as they alone were in traditional possession of the solemn legal formulae, known as the *legis actiones,* which were necessary for every legal transaction, including the settlement of legal business and the forms for bringing lawsuits. They even gave legal opinions, which obtained recognition in the courts as customary law by the side of the written law, and grew into a second authoritative source of Roman law. Until the establishment of the praetorship (B.C. 366), a member of the college was appointed every year to impart information to private persons concerning the legal forms connected with the formulating of plaints and other legal business. The *legis actiones* were made public for the first time by the above-mentioned Flavius at the same time as the calendar. See Bouché-Leclercq, *Les Pontifes de l'Ancienne Rome* (Paris, 1871); Mommsen, *Röm. Staatsrecht,* ii. 18–70; and the article IURISPRUDENTIA.

Pontificium Ius. See IUS.

Pontius. (1) A special name of the sea-god Glaucus (q. v.). (2) GAIUS, a Samnite general who defeated the Romans in B.C. 321. (3) AQUĬLA, a friend of Cicero. He was one of the assassins of Iulius Caesar. He fell at the battle of Mutina, B.C. 43. (4) PILĀTUS. The sixth procurator of Iudaea (Tac. *Ann.* xv. 44). He held office for ten years under Tiberius, from A.D. 26 to 36, and during this period Christ was put to death. His tyrannical conduct in office and the consequent complaints made by the Samaritans led Vitellius, the governor of Syria, to depose him and send him to Rome for trial. He committed suicide in the reign of Caligula (Euseb. *H. E.* ii. 7). (5) TELESĪNUS. A Samnite, and commander of a Samnite army, with which he fought against Sulla. He was defeated by Sulla in a hard-fought battle near the Colline Gate, B.C. 82. He fell in the fight; his head was cut off, and carried under the walls of Praenesté, to let the younger Marius know that his last hope of succour was gone (Vell. Pat. ii. 27). (6) Brother of the preceding, was shut up in Praenesté with the younger Marius, when his brother was defeated by Sulla. After the death of the elder Pontius, Marius and Telesinus, finding it impossible to escape from Praenesté, resolved to die by one another's hands. Telesinus fell first, and Marius put an end to his own life or was slain by his slave. See MARIUS.

Ponto. (1) A large flat-bottomed boat used in ferrying cattle, soldiers, or passengers over a river (Caes. *B. C.* iii. 29). (2) A floating bridge or pontoon (Gell. x. 25). For illustrations, see PONS, pp. 1298, 1299.

Ponto. (Roman Painting.)

Pontus (Πόντος). The most northeasterly district of Asia Minor, along the coast of the Euxine, east of the river Halys, having originally no specific name, was spoken of as the country ἐν Πόντῳ, "on the Pontus" (Euxinus), and hence acquired the name of Pontus, which is first found in Xenophon's *Anabasis.* The name first acquired a political importance through the foundation of a new kingdom in it, about the beginning of the fourth century B.C., by Ariobarzanes I. This kingdom reached its greatest height under Mithridates VI., who for many years carried on war with the Romans. (See MITHRIDATES VI.) In A.D. 62 the country was constituted by Nero a Roman province. It was divided into the three districts of PONTUS GALATĬCUS in the west, bordering on Galatia; P. POLEMONIĂCUS in the centre, so called from its capital POLEMONIUM; and P. CAPPADOCIUS in the east, bordering on Cappadocia (Armenia Minor). Pontus was a mountainous country —wild and barren in the east, where the great chains approach the Euxine; but in the west watered by the great rivers Halys and Iris, and their tributaries, the valleys of which, as well as the land along the coast, are extremely fertile. The eastern part was rich in minerals, and contained the celebrated iron mines of the Chalybes. The inhabitants of Pontus were called generically Leucosyri (q. v.). See Meyer, *Geschichte d. Königr. Pontos* (Leipzig, 1879).

Pontus Euxīnus (Πόντος Εὔξεινος), or simply **Pontus** (Πόντος). Now the Black Sea. The great inland sea enclosed by Asia Minor on the south, Colchis on the east, Sarmatia on the north, and Dacia and Thracia on the west, and having no other outlet than the narrow BOSPŎRUS THRACIUS in its southwestern corner. Its length is about 700 miles, and its breadth varies from 400 to 160. The Argonautic legends show that the Greeks had some acquaintance with this sea at a very early period. It is said that they at first called it Ἄξενος ("inhospitable"), from the savage character of the peoples on its coast and from the supposed terrors of its navigation, and that afterwards, on their favourite principle of euphemism (i. e. abstaining from words of evil omen), they changed its name to Εὔξενος (Ion. Εὔξεινος), "hospitable." The Greeks of Asia Minor, especially the people of Miletus, founded many colonies and commercial emporiums on its shores.

Poop. See NAVIS; PUPPIS.

Popa (θύτης). The priest or attendant who at a sacrifice led the victim to the altar and there struck it a blow with a hammer or the back of an axe; whereas the person who slew it with a knife was called *cultrarius* (q. v.). The popa wore a short kilt, being otherwise unclothed (Suet. *Calig.* 32). See SACRIFICIUM.

Popănum (πόπανον). A flat, round cake used in the sacrifices (Juv. vi. 541).

Popillius Laenas. See LAENAS.

Popīna (=*coquina*, showing the Umbro-Oscan substitution of *p* for *q* and *c*). A Roman cookshop. See CAUPONA.

Poplicŏla. See PUBLICOLA.

Poplifugia. The festival of the flight of the people when the troops of Fidenae, Ficuleae, and other neighbouring communities appeared in arms against Rome. As this attack followed closely after the departure of the Gauls, the Romans were panic-stricken and fled (Varro, *L. L.* vi. 18). It was celebrated on the fifth of July. Macrobius (*Sat.* iii. 2) supposes the festival to refer to the flight of the Romans before the Etruscans, and Dionysius (ii. 76) thinks it commemorated the panic that prevailed when Romulus was translated to heaven. See Marquardt, *Staatsverwaltung*, iii. 325.

Poppaea Sabīna. See SABINA.

Poppaeus Sabīnus. See SABINUS.

Populāres. See NOBILES.

Populonia or **Populonium.** An ancient town of Etruria, situated on a lofty hill, sinking abruptly to the sea, and forming a peninsula. It was destroyed by Sulla in the Civil Wars, but parts of its walls still exist.

Popŭlus. A collective name for the whole body of Roman citizens of whatever rank or class. Originally it is likely that only the patrician Romans were regarded as fully possessed of citizenship; but from the time of the establishment of the Republic (B.C. 507) the plebeians were also restored as a part of the *populus Romanus.* See CIVITAS; COMITIA; PATRICII; PLEBS; QUIRITES; SUFFRAGIUM.

Porca. A ridge between the furrows of ploughed land (Varro, *R. R.* i. 29).

Porcelain. See MURRHA.

Porch. See PORTICUS; PRONAOS.

Porcia. (1) The sister of Cato Uticensis, married L. Domitius Ahenobarbus, consul B.C. 54, who was slain in the battle of Pharsalia. She died in 46. (2) The daughter of Cato Uticensis by his first wife Atilia. She was married first to M. Bibulus, consul B.C. 59, to whom she bore three children. Bibulus died in 48; and in 45 she married M. Brutus, the assassin of Iulius Caesar. She inherited all her father's republican principles, and likewise his courage and firmness of will. She induced her husband, on the night before the fifteenth of March, to disclose to her the conspiracy against Caesar's life, and she is reported to have wounded herself in the thigh in order to show that she had a courageous soul, and could be trusted with the secret. She put an end to her own life after the death of Brutus in 42. The common tale was, that her friends, suspecting her design, had taken all weapons out of her way, and that she therefore destroyed herself by swallowing live coals (Plut. *Brut.* 53). The real fact may have been that she suffocated herself by the vapour of a charcoal fire, which, as we know, was a frequent means of self-destruction among the Romans.

Porcius Cato. See CATO.

Porcius Festus. See FESTUS.

Porcius Latro. See LATRO.

Porcius Licĭnus. See LICINUS.

Pordoselēné (Πορδοσελήνη). The largest of the islands called Hecatonnesi near Lesbos (Pliny, *H. N.* v. 37).

Porfirius (Porphyrius) Optatiānus, PUBLILIUS. A Latin poet, who composed, about A.D. 330, a series of short poems in praise of Constantine, constructed in a highly artificial manner, in that the lines in each poem contain exactly the same number of letters. By this composition he obtained his recall from banishment, and won the favour of the emperor. The commendatory letter of Constantine as well as the thanks of the poet have come down to us with the poem. Edited by L. Müller (Leipzig, 1877).

Poristae (πορισταί). A financial board at Athens regarding whose functions little is known; but they probably had to do with raising extraordinary supplies (πόρους πορίζειν), i. e. a committee of ways and means. They are classed by Antiphon (*De Chor.* 14) with the *poletae* (q. v.).

Pork. See DIAETETA; VICTUS.

Pornae. See MERETRIX.

Porpé (πόρπη). The pin of a buckle or clasp; also the clasp itself. See FIBULA.

Porphyrion (Πορφυρίων). (1) One of the Giants. He tried to throw the island of Delos upon the gods, and was destroyed by Zeus at Heracles. See GIGANTES. (2) See POMPONIUS.

Porphyrius (Πορφύριος). (1) A Greek scholar and philosopher; in the latter capacity a votary of Neoplatonism. He was born A.D. 233 at Batanaea, in Syria, received his education at Tyre, and afterwards studied grammar, rhetoric, and philosophy at Athens with Longinus, who, instead of his Syrian name *Malchus* ("king"), gave him the Greek name Porphyrios ("clad in royal purple"). The fame of the Neoplatonist Plotinus (q. v.) drew him in 263 to Rome, where, after some initial opposition, he for six years enthusiastically devoted himself to the study of the Neoplatonic philosophy. Being attacked by a dangerous melancholy, the result of overwork, he went, on the advice of Plotinus, to Sicily, whence after five years he returned to Rome, strengthened in mind and body. Here, until his death (304), he taught philosophy in the spirit of Plotinus, especially by bringing the teaching of his master within the reach of general knowledge by his clear and attractive exposition. His most important scholar was Iamblichus. A man of varied culture, Porphyrius was particularly prolific as an author in the domain of philosophy, grammar, rhetoric, arithmetic, geometry, and music; however, most of his works, including the most important, are lost, among them a treatise against the Christians, in fifteen books, which was publicly burned under Theodosius II. (435). We have to lament the loss of his history of Greek philosophy before Plato, in four books, of which we now possess only the (certainly uncritical) life of Pythagoras, and that not complete. Besides this there are preserved a life of Plotinus; a compendium of the system of Plotinus, in the form of aphorisms; a work on abstaining from animal food (*De Abstinentia*), in four books, from the Pythagorean point of view, valuable for its fulness of information on philosophy, and on the religions, forms of ritual, and customs of various peoples; an introduction to the *Categories* of Aristotle, and a commentary on the same, in the form of questions and answers; a compendium of his own practical philosophy in the form of a letter to Marcella, a widow without property, and with seven children, whom Plotinus married in his old age on account of her enthusiasm for philosophy; scholia on Homer, discussions on a number of Homeric questions, an allegorical interpretation of the Homeric story of the grotto of the nymphs in the *Odyssey*, and a commentary on the *Harmonics* of Ptolemy. See the monograph by Bouillet (Paris, 1864). (2) See PORFIRIUS.

Porridge. See PULS.

Porrĭma. See CARMENTA.

Porsēna or **Porsenna,** LARS. A king of the Etruscan town of Clusium, who marched against Rome at the head of a vast army, in order to restore Tarquinius Superbus to the throne. He took possession of the hill Ianiculum, and would have entered the city by the bridge which connected Rome with the Ianiculum, had it not been for the superhuman prowess of Horatius Cocles, who kept the whole Etruscan army at bay while his comrades broke down the bridge behind him. (See COCLES.) The Etruscans proceeded to lay siege to the city, which soon began to suffer from famine. Thereupon a young Roman, named C. Mucius, resolved to deliver his country by murdering the invading king. He accordingly went over to the Etruscan camp, but, ignorant of the person of Porsena, killed the royal secretary instead. Seized, and threatened with torture, he thrust his right hand into the fire on the altar, and there let it burn, to show how little he heeded pain. Astonished at his courage, the king bade him depart in peace; and Scaevola, as he was henceforward called, told him, out of gratitude, to make peace with Rome, since three hundred noble youths had sworn to take the life of the king, and he was the first upon whom the lot had fallen. Porsena thereupon made peace with the Romans and withdrew his troops from the Ianiculum after receiving twenty hostages from the Romans. Such was the tale by which Roman vanity concealed one of the earliest and greatest disasters of the city (Livy, ii. 9–15). The real fact is, that Rome was completely conquered by Porsena. This is expressly stated by Tacitus (*Hist.* iii. 72), and is confirmed by other writers (Dionys. v. 34). Pliny tells us that so thorough was the subjection of the Romans that they were expressly prohibited from using iron for any other purpose but agriculture (*H. N.* xxxiv. 139). The Romans, however, did not long remain subject to the Etruscans. After the conquest of Rome, Aruns, the son of Porsena, proceeded to attack Aricia, but was defeated before the city by the united forces of the Latin cities, assisted by the Greeks of Cumae. The Etruscans appear, in consequence, to have been confined to their own territory on the right bank of the Tiber, and the Romans to have availed themselves of the opportunity to recover their independence. Remains of the magnificent tomb of Porsena still exist at Chiusi, the ancient Clusium. See TARQUINIUS.

Porson, RICHARD. The greatest of England's Greek scholars, born on Christmas Day, 1759. He was educated at Eton and at Trinity College, Cambridge, of which college he was elected a Fellow in 1782. He wrote several remarkable criticisms for *Maty's Review*, and in 1790 published *Notae Breviores ad Toupii Emendationes in Suidam*, which made his name known upon the Continent. In 1792 he became Regius Professor of Greek in the University of Cambridge. He published editions of Aeschylus (1795), of the *Hecuba, Orestes, Phoenissae*, and *Medea* of Euripides (1797–1801), and collated the Harleian MS. of the *Odyssey* for the Grenville Homer. In 1806 he added to his duties the care of the library of the London Institution, and two years later (September 25, 1808) died of apoplexy, and was buried in the chapel of Trinity College. After his death were published his *Adversaria* (1812), his notes on Aristophanes (1820), Pausanias (1820), Photius (1822), and Suidas (1834), besides *Tracts and Criticisms* (1815).

Porson was a man of astonishing erudition, a marvellous memory, great critical acuteness, and good sense, but all these qualities were marred by ill-health, indolence, and an incurable passion for strong drink amounting almost to insanity. His life is written by Watson (1861), and his correspondence has been edited by Luard (Cambridge, 1867).

Porta (πύλη). The gate of a city as opposed to *ianua* or *ostium*, the door of a house. City gates from very early times were flanked by bastions, which ultimately gave way to flanking towers. Additional security was given by double gates, an outer and an inner, with a space between. In some cities the gates had two passages close together, one for carriages entering and one for those leaving the place. There were also, as at Pompeii, small side-passages for persons on foot. Gateways usually had a small chamber on one side or both, for the use of the guard or porter, and resembling the *cella ostiaria* in a private house (Polyb. viii. 20, 23, 24). It was called πυλών. The contrivances for fastening a gate were about the same as those used for doors, only larger in proportion. See IANUA; and for illustrations of ancient gates the articles FALERII; MYCENAE; THORICUS; TREVIRI.

Porta Nigra. See TREVIRI.

Portentum. See PRODIGIUM.

Porthāon (Πορθάων). The son of Agenor and Epicasté. He was king of Pleuron and Calydon, in Aetolia, and married Euryté, by whom he had Agrius, Alcathoüs, Leucopeus, Melas, Oeneus, and Steropé. See OENEUS.

Porthmus (Πόρθμος). Now Porto Bufalo; a harbour in Euboea, opposite to Oropus (Pliny, *H. N.* iv. 64).

Portĭcus. The Roman name for a colonnade. The porticoes of ancient Rome must not be regarded as isolated structures, but as really forming a great connected maze of sheltered walks, in which one could cross, for instance, the whole Campus Martius, or go in a direct line from the Forum Boarium to the Mausoleum of Hadrian, a distance of more than two miles. Professor Lanciani estimates the space covered by the twelve larger porticoes of the Campus Martius as 4600 square yards, the surface protected from sun and rain as 28,000 square yards, and the total area of the porticoes, including the central gardens, as 100,000 square yards. These porticoes were decorated with columns of marble adorned with gilded bronze, and their pavements were inlaid with jasper and porphyry. Each one contained a gallery of sculpture and a collection of paintings, while the space which they enclosed was beautified by gardens, lakes, groves, fountains, and water-falls. There were also museums within their walls, such as one of natural history (in the Portico of the Septa), of Oriental curiosities (in the same), and of wigs and specimens of hair-dressing (in the Portico of Marcius Philippus). See Lanciani, *Ancient Rome*, ch. iv. (Boston, 1888); and STOA.

Portiscŭlus. A staff or truncheon used by the officer in charge of a ship's crew, to beat time to the song (*celeusma*) sung by them as they rowed (Plaut. *Asin.* iii. 1, 14).

Portĭtor (ἐλλιςμενιστής). A custom-house officer. See PORTORIUM; PUBLICANI.

Portland Vase. See GEMMA.

Portorium. The customs-duty levied by the Romans upon imports and exports; it was introduced as early as the time of the kings, and was generally leased to *publicani* (q. v.). In B.C. 60 it was abolished for Italy, but was re-introduced by Caesar for foreign goods, and after that time always continued to exist. Free and allied cities were, in earlier times, allowed to levy the customs for their own territory, but from these Romans were to be exempt. Under the emperors customs were levied not only at the frontier of the Empire, but also at the frontiers of the several provinces or of combinations of provinces united in one excise-district. The percentage on the purchasing price of articles was different in different districts. Besides this, export duties were levied on corn, oil, wine, salt, iron, and gold. See VECTIGALIA.

Portŭla (πυλίς, ῥινοπύλη). A wicket-gate, which opened in a valve of a larger one, to admit persons after the gates had been regularly closed (Livy, xxv. 9).

Portūnus or **Portumnus.** The Roman god of harbours, though originally of doors and gates (*portae*). Like Ianus (q. v.), the god of coming in and going out, he was represented with a key, and was perhaps only a personification of one attribute of Ianus. He had a special *flamen* in Rome (*Portunalis*), and at the harbour on the Tiber he had a temple, where a festival, the PORTUNALIA, was held in his honour every year on August 17th. In later times he was identified with the Greek Palaemon (q. v.).

Porus (Πῶρος). A king of the part of India lying east of the Hydaspes River. He was conquered by Alexander the Great in B.C. 327 in a very fiercely waged battle. Porus displayed great courage in the contest, and his reply to Alexander is justly celebrated. When Alexander asked him how, as a prisoner, he desired to be treated, he answered proudly, "Like a king." On this, his conqueror restored his dominions and gave him additional territory. In 321 he was put to death by the Greek general Eudemus (Curt. viii. 14; Arrian, *Anab.* v. 18; Plut. *Alex.* 60).

Posca (ὀξύκρατον). A drink of vinegar, water, and egg beaten together, much drunk by the lower classes at Rome and by the soldiers, and suggesting the New England "switchel" (Suet. *Vitell.* 12). It was this drink that was given to the Saviour on a sponge, as he hung upon the cross.

Poseidon (Ποσειδῶν). The god of the sea and the flowing waters—a name connected with the root of πότος, πόντος, and πόταμος. He was the son of Cronos and Rhea and dwelt in the sea, over which he ruled. With his brazen-hoofed horses he was said to ride over the waves, which became smooth as he approached, and the monsters of the deep recognized him and played around his chariot. Generally he yoked his horses to his chariot himself, but sometimes he was assisted by Amphitrité. Although he generally dwelt in the sea, still he also appears at Olympus in the assembly of the gods. Poseidon, in conjunction with Apollo, is said to have built the walls of Troy for Laomedon. (See ILIUM; TROIA.) Laomedon refused to give these gods the reward which had been stipulated, and even dismissed them with threats. Poseidon, in consequence, sent a marine monster, which was on the point of devouring Laomedon's daughter, when it was killed by Heracles; and he continued to bear an implacable hatred against the Trojans. He sided with the Greeks in the war against Troy, sometimes witnessing the contest as a spectator from the heights of Thrace, and sometimes interfering in person, assuming the appearance of a mortal hero and encouraging the Greeks, while Zeus favoured the Trojans. In the *Odyssey*, Poseidon appears hostile to Odysseus, whom he prevents from returning home in consequence of his having blinded Polyphemus, a son of Poseidon by the nymph Thoösa.

Being the ruler of the sea (the Mediterranean), he is described as gathering clouds and calling forth storms, but at the same time he has it in his power to grant a successful voyage and save those who are in danger; and all other marine divinities are subject to him. As the sea surrounds and holds the earth, he himself is described as the god

Poseidon. (Dolce Gem.)

who holds the earth (γαιήοχος), and who has it in his power to shake the earth (ἐνοσίχθων, κινητὴρ γᾶς). He was further regarded as the creator of the horse. It is said that when Poseidon and Athené disputed as to which of them should give the name to the capital of Attica, the gods decided that it should receive its name from the deity who should bestow upon man the most useful gift. Poseidon then created the horse, and Athené called forth the olive-tree, in consequence of which the honour was conferred upon the goddess. According to others, however, Poseidon did not create the horse in Attica, but in Thessaly, where he also gave the famous horses to Peleus. Poseidon was accordingly believed to have taught men the art of managing horses by the bridle, and to have been the originator and protector of horse-races. Hence he was also represented on horseback, or riding in a chariot drawn by two or four horses, and is designated by the epithets ἵππιος, ἵππειος, or ἵππιος ἄναξ. He even metamorphosed himself into a horse for the purpose of deceiving Demeter. The symbol of Poseidon's power was the trident, or a spear with three points, with which he used to shatter rocks, to call forth or subdue storms, to shake the earth, and the like. Herodotus states that the name and worship of Poseidon were brought into Greece from Libya; but he was probably a divinity of Pelasgian origin, and originally a personification of the fertilizing power of water, from which the transition to regarding him as the god of the sea was not difficult. The following legends respecting Poseidon deserve to be mentioned. In conjunction with Zeus he fought against Cronos and the Titans; and in the contest with the giants he pursued Polybotes across the sea as far as Cos, and there killed him by throwing the island upon him. He further crushed the Centaurs when they were pursued by Heracles, under a mountain in Leucosia, the island of the Sirens. He sued, together with Zeus, for the hand of Thetis; but he withdrew when Themis prophesied that the son of Thetis would be greater than his father. When Ares had been caught in the wonderful net by Hephaestus, the latter set him free at the request of Poseidon; but the latter god afterwards brought a charge against Ares before the Areopagus for having killed his son Halirrhothius. At the request of Minos, king of Crete, Poseidon caused a bull to rise from the sea, which the king promised to sacrifice; but when Minos treacherously concealed the animal among a herd of oxen, the god punished Minos by causing his wife Pasiphaë (q. v.) to fall in love with the bull.

Poseidon was married to Amphitrité, by whom he had three children, Triton, Rhodé, and Benthesicymé; but he had also a vast number of children by other divinities and mortal women. His worship extended over all Greece and Southern Italy, but he was more especially revered in Peloponnesus and in the Ionic towns on the coast. The sacrifices offered to him generally consisted of black and white bulls; but wild boars and rams were also sacrificed to him. Horse and chariot races were held in his honour on the Corinthian Isthmus. The Panionia, or the festival of all the Ionians near Mycalé, was celebrated in honour of Poseidon. In works of art, Poseidon may be easily recognized by his attributes, the dolphin, the horse, or the trident, and he was frequently represented in groups along with Amphitrité, Tritons, Nereïds, dolphins, the Dioscuri, Palaemon, Pegasus, Bellerophontes, Thalassa, Ino, and Galené. His figure does not present the majestic calm which characterizes his brother Zeus; but as the state of the sea is varying, so also is the god represented sometimes in violent agitation and sometimes in a state of repose. For the Roman god corresponding to Poseidon, see NEPTUNUS.

Posidippus (Ποσείδιππος). (1) One of the most eminent poets of the New Comedy at Athens, a native of Cassandrea, in Macedonia. He began to exhibit for the first time in the third year after the death of Menander, or in B.C. 289. Of his pieces, as many as forty are mentioned by name, but only fragments of them are preserved. It was probably in imitation of one of these that the *Menaechmi* of Plautus was written. (2) An Alexandrian writer of epigrams. Twenty-two of his poems are preserved in the Greek Anthology.

Posidium (Ποσείδιον). (1) A promontory on the coast of Lucania. (2) A promontory of Chios. (3) A promontory of Caria between Miletus and the Iassian Gulf. (4) A promontory of Bithynia.

Posidonia. See PAESTUM.

Posidonium (Ποσειδώνιον) or **Posidium.** A promontory on the southwestern coast of Pellené, in Macedonia.

Posidonius (Ποσειδώνιος). (1) A Stoic philosopher, a native of Apamea in Syria, and the last of the Stoics who belongs to the history of the Greek philosophy. He taught at Rhodes with such great success that Pompey came there, on his return from Syria, after the close of the Mithridatic War, for the purpose of attending his lectures. When the Roman commander arrived at his house, he forbade his lictor to knock, as was usual, at the door; the hero, who had subdued the Eastern and Western world, paid homage to philosophy by lowering the fasces at the gate of Posidonius (Cic. *Tusc.* ii. 25; Pliny, *Epist.* vi. 30). Posidonius studied natural as well as moral science; and, in order to represent the celestial phenomena, he constructed a kind of *planetarium*, by means of which he exhibited the apparent motions of the sun, moon, and planets round the earth (Cic. *N. D.* ii. 34). Cicero says that he himself attended upon this philosopher (*N. D.* i. 3). Posidonius was also known as an historical writer, having composed a supplement to the history of Polybius (Ἱστορία τῶν μετὰ Πολύβιον). It appears to have extended to B.C. 63, or the close of the Mithridatic War. This work is lost, but was one of Plutarch's sources. The fragments are edited by Bake (Leyden, 1810). (2) An astronomer and mathematician of Alexandria. He was the disciple of Zeno, and contemporary with, or else a short time posterior to, Eratosthenes. He probably flourished about B.C. 260. He is particularly celebrated on account of his having employed himself in endeavouring to ascertain the measure of the circumference of the earth by means of the altitude of a fixed star.

Postal Service. See CURSUS PUBLICUS.

Postĭcum. A back-door (Hor. *Epist.* v. 31).

Postilēna (ὑπουρίς). A crupper of wood or leather, encircling the hindquarters of a horse or pack-animal. The breast-strap was called *antilena* (Plaut. *Cas.* i. 1, 36).

Postis. See IANUA.

Postliminium, Postliminii Ius. When a Roman citizen during war came into the possession of an enemy, he sustained a *diminutio capitis maxima* (see CAPUT), and all his civil rights were in abeyance. Being captured by the enemy, he became a slave; but his rights over his children, if he had any, were not destroyed, but were said to be in abeyance (*pendere*) by virtue of the *ius postliminii:* when he returned, his children were again in his power; and if he died in captivity, they became *sui iuris.* Sometimes by an act of the State a man was given up bound to an enemy, and if the enemy would not receive him, it was a question whether he had the *ius postliminii.* This was the case with Sp. Postumius, who was given up to the Samnites, and with C. Hostilius Mancinus, who was given up to the Numantines, but the better opinion was that they had no *ius postliminii*, and Mancinus was restored to his civil rights by a special law (Cic. *De Orat.* i. 40, 141; *Off.* iii. 30, 109; *Top.* 8, 36; *Pro Caec.* 34, 98). It appears that the *ius postliminii* was founded on the fiction of the captive having never been absent from home—a fiction which was of easy application, for, as the captive during his absence could not perform any legal act, the interval of captivity was a period of legal non-activity, which was terminated on his reappearance. See Bechmann, *Das Ius Postliminii und die Fictio Legis Corneliae* (Erlangen, 1872).

Postsignāni. Soldiers stationed immediately behind the standard (*signum*) (Front. *Strat.* ii. 3, 17).

Postumia Gens. One of the oldest patrician gens at Rome, whose most distinguished family was that of Albus or Albinus.

Postŭmus, M. CASSIĀNUS LATINIUS, the second of the so-called Thirty Tyrants. While acting as governor of Gaul under Valerian in A.D. 258, he caused himself to be proclaimed emperor, and, being a very able ruler, maintained himself in power in Gaul for nearly ten years; but was slain by his own soldiers in A.D. 267, Labienus being proclaimed in his place (Trebell. Poll. *Trig. Tyr.* ii.).

Postverta or **Postvorta.** A goddess presiding over childbirth who was invoked when the infant was born feet first (Varro, *ap.* Gell. xvi. 16, 4). See ANTEVORTA; CARMENTA.

Potămi (Ποταμοί) or **Potămus** (Ποταμός). An Attic deme belonging to the tribe Leontis. Here the tomb of Ion was shown (Pausan. i. 31, 3).

Potentia. (1) A town of Picenum, on the river Flosis. (2) A town of Lucania.

Potestas. See PATRIA POTESTAS.

Potidaea (Ποτίδαια). A town in Macedonia, on the narrow isthmus of the peninsula Pallenē, was a colony of the Corinthians. It afterwards became tributary to Athens, and its revolt from the latter city, in B.C. 432, was one of the immediate causes of the Peloponnesian War (q. v.). It was taken by the Athenians in 429, after a siege of more than two years, its inhabitants expelled, and their place supplied by Athenian colonists. In 356 it was taken by Philip, who destroyed the city and gave its territory to the Olynthians. Cassander built a new city on the same site, to which he gave the name of CASSANDRĒA, and which soon became the most flourishing city in all Macedonia.

Potitii. See PINARIA GENS.

Potniae (Ποτνιαί). A small town in Boeotia, on the Asopus. The adjective *Potniades* is an epithet frequently given to the mares which tore to death Glaucus of Potniae. See GLAUCUS.

Pott, AUGUST FRIEDRICH. A great philologist, born at Nettelrede in Hanover, November 14, 1802. He received his philological training at Göttingen and Berlin, and in 1833 became Professor Extraordinarius of Linguistic in the University of Halle, and in 1839 Professor Ordinarius. He died at Halle, July 5, 1887. His principal works are the following: *Etymologische Forschungen auf dem Gebiet der indogermanischen Sprachen*, in 2 vols. (1833–36; 2d ed. in 6 vols. 1859–76); *Die Ziegeuner in Europa und Asien*, 2 vols. (1844–45); *Die Personennamen* (1853); *Die Ungleichheit der menschlichen Rassen vom Sprachwissenschaftlichen Standpunkt* (1856); *Doppelung als eins der wichstigsten Bildungsmittel der Sprache* (1862); *Anti-Kaulen oder mythische Vorstellungen*, etc. (1863); and *Die Sprachverschiedenheit in Europa* (1868).

In the development of language-study on a scientific basis, Pott stands next to Franz Bopp (q. v.), and in the vastness of his erudition and sympathetic insight was even his superior. His knowledge of anthropology was very effective in checking rash generalizations and hasty conclusions on the part of enthusiastic followers of the new science of comparative philology; and his *Etymologische Forschungen* was long a treasury of suggestive thought to students, though marred by lack of order and systematic presentation. See PHILOLOGIA.

Pottery. See FICTILÉ; VAS.

Pouch. See BULGA.

Poultry. See GALLINA.

Praaspa. See PHRAATA

Practŏres (πράκτορες). Subordinate officers at Athens, probably ten in number, who collected the fines and penalties (ἐπιβολαί, τιμήματα) imposed by magistrates and courts of justice, and payable to the State. See TIMEMA.

Praecia. A crier who went before the Flamens on holy days, ordering the people to cease from work while a procession was passing, lest the priests should see them, and thus the rites be profaned (Fest. s. h. v.).

Praecinctiōnes. See AMPHITHEATRUM; THEATRUM.

Praeco. The Latin term for a public crier, such as those who were employed in private life, especially at auctions. Their profession was eminently lucrative, but was not considered at all respectable. Similarly those employed by the State ranked as the most insignificant of its paid servants. (See APPARITOR.) Their duties were to summon the meetings of the people and the Senate, to command silence, to proclaim aloud the proposals under consideration, to announce the result of the individual votes, and also the final result; in legal proceedings, to cite the parties to the case, their counsel, and witnesses, to announce the close of the proceedings, and the jury's dismissal; to invite the people to funeral feasts and to games, and to assist at public auctions and other sales, etc. Consuls, praetors, and censors had three decuries of such attendants; quaestors, and probably also tribunes and aediles, one. They also attended on extraordinary magistrates and on governors of provinces. The term praeco was also applied to an auctioneer (Hor. *A. P.* 419; Cic. *Ad Att.* xii. 40). The office of praeco was called *praeconium*, and was regarded with contempt (Mart. v. 56, 10; Juv. iii. 33; vii. 6).

Praeco.

Praeconium. See PRAECO.

Praeda. A Latin word signifying movable things taken by an enemy in war. Such things were either distributed by the *imperator* among the soldiers or sold by the quaestors, and the produce was paid into the Aerarium or State treasury. The difference between praeda and *manubiae* lies in the fact that praeda means the things themselves that are taken in war, while *manubiae* is the money realized from their sale (Gell. xiii. 24). It was the practice to set up a spear at such sales, which was afterwards used at all sales of things by a magistratus in the name of the people. See SECTIO; SPOLIA.

Praedium. Originally any property which was made security to the State by a *praes* (q. v.) (Varro, *L. L.* v. 40). Later it means land or an estate in general.

Praefecti. Twelve officers appointed by the consuls to take command of the troops furnished by the allies. They ranked with the *tribuni* of the Roman legions (Caes. *B. G.* i. 39; iii. 7).

Praefectūra. An Italian township possessing no jurisdiction of its own, but having a prefect to administer justice (*praefectus iure dicundo*) sent to it every year, generally on the nomination of the *praetor urbanus*. When all Italian towns received full citizen rights, B.C. 90, these towns among the rest became *municipia* (see MUNICIPIUM), and retained the old name merely as a tradition.

Praefectus Aerarii. See AERARIUM.

Praefectus Annōnae. The praefect of the provisions at Rome, especially of the corn-market. He was not a regular magistrate under the Republic, but was appointed only in cases of extraordinary scarcity, when he seems to have regulated the prices at which corn was to be sold. Augustus created an officer under the title of *praefectus annonae*, who had jurisdiction over all matters appertaining to the corn-market, and, like the *praefectus vigilum*, was chosen from the knights, and was not reckoned among the ordinary magistrates. See FRUMENTARIAE LEGES.

Praefectus Aquārum. See AQUAE DUCTUS.

Praefectus Castrōrum. The praefect of the Roman camp. He is first mentioned in the reign of Augustus (Vell. Pat. ii. 112). There was one to each legion. See CASTRA; LEGIO.

Praefectus Classis. The commander of a Roman fleet. This title was frequently given under the Republic to the commander of a fleet; but Augustus appointed two permanent officers with this title, one of whom was stationed at Ravenna on the Adriatic, and the other at Misenum on the Tuscan Sea, each having the command of a fleet (Suet. *Aug.* 49).

Praefectus Fabrum. See FABRI.

Praefectus Legiōnis. See EXERCITUS; LEGIO.

Praefectus Praetorio. The commander of the troops who guarded the person of the Roman emperor. (See PRAETORIANI.) This office was instituted by Augustus, and was at first only military. It then had comparatively small power attached to it; but under Tiberius, who made Seianus commander of the Praetorian Guard, it became of much greater importance, till at length the power of these praefects became only second to that of the emperors. From the reign of Severus to that of Diocletian, the praefects, like the Oriental viziers, had the superintendence of all departments of the State, the palace, the army, the finances, and the law; and also had a court in which they decided cases. The office of Praefect of the Praetorium was not confined to military officers: it was filled by Ulpian and Papinian, and by other distinguished jurists. Originally there were two praefects; afterwards sometimes one and sometimes two; from the time of Commodus often three, and even four. They were, as a regular rule, chosen only from the knights; but from the time of Alexander Severus the rank of senator was always joined with their office.

Praefectus Urbi. The praefect or warden of the city of Rome. He was originally called CUSTOS URBIS (Lydus, *De Magistr.* i. 34, 38). The name *praefectus urbi* does not seem to have been used till after the time of the decemvirs. The dignity of *custos urbis*, being combined with that of *princeps senatus*, was conferred in early times by the king, as he had to appoint one of the *decem primi* as *princeps senatus*. The functions of the *custos urbis*, however, were not exercised except in the absence of the king from Rome; and then he acted as the representative of the king. He convoked the Senate, held the Comitia, if necessary, and on any emergency might take such measures as he thought proper; in short, he had the *imperium* in the city (Tac. *Ann.* vi. 11). During the kingly period, the office of *custos urbis* was probably for life. Under the Republic, the office and the title *custos urbis* remained unaltered; but in B.C. 487 it was elevated into a magistracy, to be bestowed by election. The *custos urbis* was, in all probability, elected by the *curiae*. Persons of consular rank alone were eligible. In the early years of the Republic the *custos urbis* exercised within the city all the powers of the consuls if they were absent; he convoked the Senate, held the Comitia, and, in times of war, even levied civic legions, which were commanded by him. When the office of *praetor urbanus* was instituted, the wardenship of the city was merged in it (Lydus, *De Mens.* 19); but as the Romans, by reason of their extreme conservatism, were at all times averse to dropping altogether any of their old institutions, a *praefectus urbi*, though a mere shadow of the former office, was henceforth appointed every year, only for the time that the consuls were absent from Rome for the purpose of celebrating the Feriae Latinae. This praefectus had neither the power of convoking the Senate nor the right of speaking in it; in most cases he was a person below the senatorial age, and was not appointed by the people, but by the consuls.

An office very different from this, though bearing the same name, was instituted by Augustus on the suggestion of Maecenas. This new Praefectus Urbi was a regular and permanent magistrate, whom Augustus invested with all the powers necessary to maintain peace and order in the city. He had the superintendence of butchers, bankers, guardians, theatres, etc.; and to enable him to exercise his power he had distributed throughout the city a number of *milites stationarii*, whom we may compare to modern police. (See VIGILES.) His jurisdiction, however, became gradually extended; and as the powers of the ancient republican Praefectus Urbi had been swallowed up by the office of the Praetor Urbanus, so now the power of the Praetor Urbanus was gradually absorbed by that of the Praefectus Urbi; and at last there was no appeal from his sentence, except to the person of the *princeps* himself, while any one might appeal from the sentence of any other city magistrate, and, at a later period, even from that of a governor of a province, to the tribunal of the Praefectus Urbi. Under the Eastern Empire, there was a Praefectus Urbi for the city of Constantinople as well as for Rome (Symmach. *Epist.* x. 37).

Praefectus Vigĭlum. See EXERCITUS; VIGILES.

Praefĭcae. Women who were hired to act as mourners at Roman funerals (Plaut. *Truc.* ii. 6, 14). They went before the corpse, with their heads bared, their locks dishevelled, uttering cries of lamentation and chanting dirges (*neniae*). See FUNUS.

Praefurnium. The mouth of a furnace, through which the fuel was introduced (Cato, *R. R.* 38, 1).

Praegustātor (προγευστής). A slave who tasted the dishes at table before offering them to his master, either to see whether they were properly seasoned, or as a precaution against poison (Xen. *Cyrop.* i. 3; Suet. *Claud.* 44).

Praeiudicium. A term used both in the sense of a precedent, in which case it is rather *exemplum* than *praeiudicium*, and also in the sense of a preliminary inquiry and determination about something which belongs to the matter in dispute (*iudiciis ad ipsam causam pertinentibus*), from whence also comes the name praeiudicium.

Praelusio. See GLADIATORES, p. 733.

Praenesté. Now Palestrina; one of the most ancient towns of Latium, situated on a steep and lofty hill about twenty miles southeast of Rome. It was said to have been founded by Telegonus, the son of Odysseus. It was strongly fortified by nature and by art, and frequently resisted the attacks of the Romans. Together with the other Latin towns, it became subject to Rome, and was at a later period made a Roman colony. It was here that the younger Marius took refuge, and was besieged by Sulla's troops. Praenesté possessed a celebrated temple of Fortuna, with an oracle, which is often mentioned under the name of *Praenestinae sortes*. (See ORACULUM.) In consequence of its lofty situation, Praenesté was a cool and healthy residence in the great heats of summer (hence *frigidum Praeneste*, in Horace).

Praenestīna Fibŭla. See next article.

Praenestine Brooch (FIBŬLA PRAENESTĪNA). The name given to a brooch (*fibula*) found at Praenesté in 1886, and believed by Bücheler to be as old as the sixth century B.C. A short inscription on it is the oldest specimen of Latin known to be in existence. It runs as follows:

MANIOS MED VHE VHAKED NVMASIOI
Manius me fe- facid (fecit) Numasio

The writing is retrograde (i. e. from right to left), and the characters are Greek. It is interesting in several ways: (1) as showing *-d* as an accusative

Fibula Praenestina with Numasios Inscription. (From a photograph.)

ending in use at so early a period of the language; (2) as exhibiting the attempt to represent the sound of Latin *f* in non-Latin characters; (3) as giving the reduplicated perfect in *fefacid*; (4) as separating the reduplicated syllable from the body of the verb (cf. *C. I. A.* 321); (5) as affording an example of the actual use of the dative in *-oi*, which had been postulated on the authority of Marius Victorinus (17, 20) and the analogy of the Greek dative, but had been questioned by Jordan (*Kritische Beiträge*, p. 241); and (6) as exploding a general belief that the retrograde writing in Latin had been used only in *devotiones* or sacred formulas where an element of secrecy was involved. See the *Wochenschrift für klass. Philologie* (Jan. 26, 1887); Wölfflin, *Archiv für lat. Lexicographie und Grammatik* (1887 pt. i. p. 143); the *Rheinisches Museum*, vol. xlii. p. 317; Darbishire in the (English) *Journal of Philology* (1886–87, pp. 196 foll.); the *Transactions of the Oxford Philological Society* (1887–89); Cortese, *Latini Sermonis Vetustioris Exempla* (Turin, 1892); Lindsay, *The Latin Language*, pp. 305, 504 (Oxford, 1894); and Egbert, *Latin Inscriptions*, p. 65 (New York, 1896).

Praenōmen. See NOMEN.

Praepĕtes. Birds of good omen. See AUGUR.

Praeposĭtus. A title given under the later Roman Empire to various officials, especially to the freedman who acted as chamberlain of the imperial palace (Cod. Theod. vi. tit. 8).

Praerogatīva. See COMITIA, p. 391.

Praes. In Roman law is a surety for one who buys of the State. The goods of a praes were called *praedia*. The *praediator* was a person who bought a *praedium*—that is, a thing given to the State as a security by a praes. See Walter, *Geschichte des röm. Rechts*, § 340.

Praescriptio or **Tempŏris Praescriptio.** A Latin term which signifies the *exceptio* or answer which a defendant has to the demand of a plaintiff, founded on the circumstance of the lapse of time. The word has properly no reference to the plaintiff's loss of right, but to the defendant's acquisition of a right by which he excludes the plaintiff from prosecuting his suit. This right of a defendant did not exist in the old Roman law.

Praeses. See PROVINCIA.

Praesul (*prae*+*salio*). The chief of the Salii or priests of Mars. See SALII.

Praetexta. See TOGA.

Praetexta or **Praetextāta** (sc. *fabula*). A class of Roman tragedies, which found its materials not in the Greek myths, but, in the absence of native legendary heroes, in ancient and contemporary Roman history. The name was derived from the fact that the heroes wore the national dress, the *toga praetexta*, the official garb, edged with purple, of the Roman magistrates. Naevius introduced them, and, following his example, the chief representatives of tragic art under the Republic, Ennius, Pacuvius, and Attius, composed, in addition to tragedies imitated from Greek originals, independent plays of this kind, which were, however, cast in the form they had borrowed from the Greeks. We also hear of some plays of this class written by poets of imperial times. The solitary example preserved to us is the tragedy of *Octavia*, wrongly ascribed to Seneca (q. v.), which, perhaps, may date from A.D. 1. See TOGATA.

Praetor (=στρατηγός, and derived by Cicero from *praeire*). Originally a title of the Roman consuls, but afterwards used to denote that magistrate to whom the administration of justice in Rome was transferred, when the consulship, to which this power had hitherto been attached, was thrown open to the commons in B.C. 366. At first reserved for the patricians, it became a plebeian office as early as 337. The praetor was elected in the Comitia Centuriata, with one of the consuls presiding, on the same day and with the same auspices as the consuls, who entered on their office simultaneously with him. On account of the increase in legal business, a second praetor was appointed in 242, to whom was transferred the hearing of the cases between citizens and foreigners (*inter cives et peregrinos*) and between foreigners (*inter peregrinos*), while the other decided between citizens. The latter, who ranked first, was called *praetor urbanus* (city praetor); the former, *praetor inter peregrinos* and (after the time of Vespasian) *praetor peregrinus*.

The praetors had their respective departments determined by lot after their election. While the *praetor peregrinus* might have a military command also intrusted to him, the city praetor, on account of the importance of his office, might not be absent from Rome, strictly speaking, for longer than ten days. He represented his absent colleague and also the consuls in their absence, presiding, as the highest magistrate present, at the public games, watching over the safety of Rome, summoning the Comitia Centuriata, holding the military levies, and the like. As early as 227 the number was further increased by two. To these was intrusted the administration of Sicily and Sardinia. Two others were added in 197 to administer the two provinces of Spain. In 149, on the establishment of the *quaestiones perpetuae*, a standing criminal court for certain stated offenders, the rule was introduced that the entire body of praetors should stay in Rome during their year of office; the praetors *urbanus* and *inter peregrinos* having jurisdiction in civil cases, as hitherto, while the others presided in the *quaestiones*, and had to instruct the jurors as to the case before the court, and to carry out the sentence passed. After the completion of their year of office, they all proceeded as propraetors or proconsuls to the praetorian provinces assigned them by lot. In consequence of the multiplication of the *quaestiones* and of the provinces, the number of praetors was raised by Sulla to eight, by Caesar to ten, fourteen, and sixteen. Under the Empire the praetorship lost its former importance, the civil jurisdiction of the *praetor urbanus* and *peregrinus* being in part transferred to the *praefectus urbi* and *praefectus praetorio*, while the criminal jurisdiction of the others ceased with the gradual decay of the *quaestiones*, and the praetors retained only particular departments of their judicial power and general administration. Their most important function was the management of the games, some of which had already, in republican times, been assigned to the *praetor urbanus*. When their year's office had expired, they went as proconsuls to the senatorial provinces. Their election was transferred to the Senate by Tiberius. Under the Republic the statutory age for the office was forty; under the Empire, thirty. The praetor's *insignia* were the *toga praetexta*, the *sella curulis*, and, in the provinces, six lictors; in Rome, probably two. Like the consul, he had the honour of a triumph open to him. See MAGISTRATUS.

Praetoriāni. The body-guard of the Roman emperor. Even in the armies of the Republic there had been a separate corps, the *cohors praetoria*, to guard the general, and protect the headquarters. The organization of a body-guard for the emperor, one of whose permanent powers was the

Praetoriani. (Relief in the Louvre.)

chief military command, was among the first administrative measures of Augustus. The supreme command was generally held by two *praefecti praetorio* in the emperor's name. The guard consisted of nine, and at a later time, of ten *cohortes praetoriae*, each composed of ten centuries of infantry and ten squadrons of cavalry (*turmae*), and commanded by a *tribunus* (see TRIBUNI MILITUM). They had higher rank and pay than the legions, and a shorter time of service (sixteen years instead of twenty). While the other cohorts were stationed at various places in Italy, where the emperors were in the habit of staying, there were quartered in Rome, to keep watch in the emperor's palace, three cohorts, which at first were billeted on separate parts of the city, until under Tiberius they were placed in a fortified camp (*castra praetoria*) to the northeast of the city, outside the walls. By being thus united, they gained such importance that they were often able to raise an emperor to the throne, and to overthrow him. To break down their influence and to make them simply a picked corps, Septimius Severus, towards the end of the second century, brought legions to Italy, and made a regulation that the Guard, which had hitherto been recruited exclusively from Italy and a few Romanized provinces, should have its ranks filled up from deserving legionary soldiers, and should serve for a longer time. To be thus transferred to the Guard was considered a promotion. The Guard was disbanded by Constantine the Great.

Praetorium. The headquarters in the Roman camp; a wide space, on which stood the general's tent, the altar of the camp, the *augurale*, and the *tribunal*. (See CASTRA.) In the provinces this name was given to the official residence of the governor (Cic. *Verr.* iv. 28, 65) and to any large country-house (Suet. *Calig.* 37).

Praevaricatio (literally, "deviation from the straight path"). The Latin term for the improper conduct of a case on the part of a prosecutor in favour of the defendant, or on the part of a *patronus* to the detriment of his client. The penalty was forfeiture of the right to prosecute and to act as an advocate. If the acquittal of the defendant was demonstrably due to *praevaricatio*, the case might be undertaken anew by a second prosecutor.

Prandium (ἄριστον). The second morning meal of the Romans. See CENA.

Prasiae (Πρασιαί). (1) Or PRASIA, a town on the eastern coast of Laconia (Thuc. ii. 56). (2) A deme of Attica belonging to the tribe Pandionis (Thuc. viii. 95).

Prasii (Πράσιοι), **Praesii**, or **Parrhasii** (Skt. Prachinas). A great people of India on the Ganges, whose capital was Palibothra (Patna) (Curt. ix. 2; Plut. *Alex.* 62). See SANDROCOTTUS.

Prasiniāni. See CIRCUS, p. 356.

Prasĭnus. A charioteer wearing the green colours in the Circus races. See CIRCUS, p. 356.

Prasum (Πράσον Ἀκρωτήριον, "Green Headland"). A promontory on the eastern coast of Africa. It appears to have marked the farthest limit of that country to the ancients. The neighbouring part of the Indian Ocean was called PROSŌDIS MARÉ (Προσώδης Κόλπος).

Pratinas. (Πρατίνας. The quantity of the penult is uncertain, probably long. See Fick, *Gr. Personen-Namen*, p. xxxv.) A Greek dramatist, of Phlius, who lived about B.C. 496 at Athens. He was a contemporary and rival of Aeschylus, and is believed to have invented the satyric drama. At any rate, he was a very prolific writer in this department of literature. He also wrote tragedies, dithyrambs, and *hyporchemata*, of which we possess a fairly long and highly original fragment, preserved by Athenaeus (xiv. 617). His son Aristias was also a dramatic poet.

Praxagŏras (Πραξαγόρας). A physician born in the island of Cos in the fourth century B.C. He was one of the school known as the Dogmatici (Pliny, *H. N.* xxvi. 10). See MEDICINA.

Praxias (Πραξίας). An Athenian sculptor of the age of Phidias, but more archaic than that great artist. He began the statues in the pediments of the great temple of Apollo at Delphi (Artemis, Lèto, and Apollo with the Muses, Dionysus, and the Thyades and Helios), but died leaving them unfinished (Pausan. x. 19, 3).

Praxidĭcé (Πραξιδίκη). The goddess who carried out the ends of justice. She is sometimes regarded as identical with Diké. In some traditions there appear to be three goddesses of the name forming a triad (Suidas, s. h. v.; Pausan. iii. 13, 3).

Praxilla (Πράξιλλα). A Greek poetess of Sicyon, about B.C. 450, who composed hymns and dithyrambs, but was especially famous for her *scolia*, or drinking-songs. We possess only insignificant fragments of her poems (Suidas, s. h. v.).

Praxiphănes (Πραξιφάνης). A Peripatetic philosopher, born either at Mitylené or Rhodes. He flourished about B.C. 322, and is said to have taught Epicurus. He paid much attention to grammatical study, and is hence classed with Aristotle as one of the founders of scientific grammar (Clem. Alex. i. p. 365). He wrote treatises on the poets, on history, and on poetry, and was the teacher of Aratus and Callimachus. See Preller, *De Praxiphane* (Berlin, 1864); Wilamowitz in *Hermes*, xii. 316 foll., and Hirzel in *Hermes*, xiii. 46 foll.

Praxitĕles (Πραξιτέλης). One of the most famous Greek sculptors, born at Athens about B.C. 390. He and his somewhat older contemporary, Scopas, were at the head of the later Attic school. He chiefly worked in marble, but at the same time occasionally used bronze. His recorded works exhibit every age and sex in the greatest variety of the divine and human form. Still, he paid most attention to youthful figures, which gave him the opportunity of displaying all the charm of sensuous grace in soft and delicate contours.

Hermes of Praxiteles. (From the Heraeum at Olympia.)

Among his most celebrated works the naked Aphrodité, of Cnidus, stands first—according to the enthusiastic descriptions of the ancients a masterpiece of the most entrancing beauty (e. g. Pliny, *H. N.* xxxvii. §§ 20, 21; cf. APHRODITÉ). Not less famous were his representations of Eros, among which the marble statue at Thespiae was esteemed most highly (ib. § 22; cf. EROS); his Apollo Sauroctonos (lizard-slayer) in bronze (ib. xxxiv. § 70); and a youthful Satyr in Athens (Pausan. i. 20, § 1). As to the group of Niobé's children, preserved at Rome in Pliny's time, it was disputed even among the ancients whether it was the work of Praxiteles or, as is more probable, of Scopas (*H. N.* xxxvi. § 28). Of all these only later copies have been preserved. An important original work by him (mentioned by Pausan. v. 17, § 3) was unearthed in 1877 by the German excavators at Olympia. It represents Hermes with the child Dionysus in his arms, and was set up in the *cella* of the temple of Heré. The arms and legs are partially mutilated, but otherwise it is in an excellent state of preservation. His sons, Cephisodotus the younger and Timarchides, were masters of some importance. See STATUARIA ARS.

Prayer. See PRECATIO.

Precatio. The act of praying. The Greeks and early Romans stood upright in prayer, extending both the arms, and bringing the hands together with the palms wide open (Verg. *Aen.* iii. 176; Lucret. v. 1199). In the imperial period the arms were thrown wide apart, though the suppliant still stood erect, as is seen from the figures on medals.

Precatio. (Vatican Vergil.)

Precatio. (Museo Pio-Clem. ii. 47.)

Prelum. (1) The beam of the press used for squeezing grapes or olives. (2) The press itself. (See VINUM.) (3) A clothes-press (Sen. *Q. N.* i. 3, 2). In modern Latin the word is also applied to the printing-press.

Prensatio. See AMBITUS.

Press. See PRELUM.

Pressorium. A clothes-press. (Plin. Vet. ii. 17.)

Priamĭdes. A patronymic applied to Paris, as being a son of Priam. It is also given to Hector, Deïphobus, and all the other children of the Trojan king (Verg. *Aen.* iii. 295 foll.).

Priămus (Πρίαμος). The last king of Troy. He was the son of Laomedon. When Heracles took the city of Troy Priam was in the number of his prisoners; but his sister, Hesioné, redeemed him from captivity, and he exchanged his original name of Podarces for that of Priamus, which signifies "bought" or "ransomed." (See HESIONÉ.) He was placed on his father's throne by Heracles, and employed himself in repairing, fortifying, and embellishing the city of Troy. He had married, by his father's orders, Arisba, whom now he divorced for Hecuba, the daughter of Dymas the Phrygian (Hom. *Il.* xvi. 718), or, according to others, of Cisseus (Eurip. *Hec.* 3). Hecuba bore him nineteen children (Hom. *Il.* xxiv. 496), of whom the chief were Hector, Paris or Alexander, Deïphobus, Helenus, Troïlus, Polites, Polydorus, Cassandra, Creüsa, and Polyxena. After he had reigned for some time in the greatest prosperity, Priam expressed a desire to recover his sister Hesioné, whom Heracles had carried into Greece, and married to Telamon, his friend. To carry this plan into execution, Priam manned a fleet, of which he gave the command to his son Paris, with orders to bring back Hesioné. Paris, to whom Aphrodité had promised the fairest woman in the world (see PARIS), neglected, in some measure, his father's injunctions, and, as if to make reprisals upon the Greeks, carried away Helen, the wife of Menelaüs, king of Sparta, during the absence of her husband. This violation of hospitality caused a general war. All the suitors of Helen, at the request of Menelaüs (q. v.), assembled to avenge the abduction of his wife, and the combined armament set sail for Troy. Priam might have averted the impending blow by the restoration of Helen; but this he refused to do when the ambassadors of the Greeks came to him for that purpose. Troy was accordingly beleaguered, and frequent skirmishes took place, in which the success was various. The siege was continued for ten successive years, and Priam had the misfortune to see the greater part of his sons fall in defence of their native city. Hector, the eldest of these, was the only one upon whom now the Trojans looked for protection and support; but he, too, fell a victim to his own courage, and was slain by Achilles. The father thereupon resolved to go in person to the Grecian camp, and ransom the body of the bravest of his children. The gods interested themselves in his behalf, and Hermes was directed to guide the aged monarch in safety amid the dangers of the way, and conduct him to the tent of Achilles. The meeting of Priam and Achilles was solemn and affecting. The conqueror paid to the Trojan monarch the reverence due to his dignity, his years, and his misfortunes; and Priam, as a suppliant, addressed the prince who had robbed him of the greatest and best of his sons. Achilles was moved by his tears and entreaties. He restored Hector, and permitted Priam a truce of twelve days for the funeral of his son. Some time after Troy was betrayed into the hands of the Greeks by Antenor and Aeneas, and Priam was slain by Neoptolemus, the son of Achilles, at the foot of the altar of Zeus Herceus; the wounded Polites, one of the sons of Priam, also fell, who, after the example of his father and mother, had fled thither for protection during the burning of the city (Hom. *Il.* xxiv. 139 foll.; Verg. *Aen.* ii. 507 foll.; Horace, *Carm.* x. 14; Hygin. *Fab.* 110). See HELENA; TROJAN WAR.

Priapeia. A collection of some eighty-six elegant but indecent Latin poems in various metres on the subject of Priapus. Judging from their execution, they may be referred to the time of Augustus, and may probably be traced to the circle of Messala, who, like other distinguished men of that age, occupied himself with amusements of this kind. Printed in Bücheler's Petronius (Berlin, 1886).

Priāpus (Πρίαπος). According to the usual account, son of Dionysus and Aphrodité, a god of the fruitfulness of the field and of the herds. Horticulture, vine-growing, goat and sheep-breeding, bee-keeping, and even fishing were supposed to be under his protection. The original seat of his worship lay in the towns of Asia Minor, situated on the Hellespont, especially Lampsacus, where it was said he was born. From here it afterwards spread over Greece and Italy. His statues were usually placed in gardens, generally in the form of rude *hermae* cut out of wood, stained with vermilion, with a club and sickle and a phallic symbol of the creative and fructifying powers of nature. The sacrifices offered to him included asses, as well as the first-fruits of the garden and the field. In the mystical interpretation of the myths, he was regarded as symbolizing the future life, and hence his image was placed upon tombs (*C. I. L.* v. 3634). Besides Lampsacus, he had as especial seats of his worship, Cyzicus, on the Hellespont, at Panium, (Catull. 18; Verg. *Georg.* iv. 110), and at Priapus in Mysia. See PHALLUS.

Priāpus (Πρίαπος). A Mysian city on the Propontis, a chief seat of the worship of the god Priapus. The surrounding district was called PRIĀPIS or PRIAPĒNÉ (Thuc. viii. 107).

Priēné. One of the twelve Ionian cities on the coast of Asia Minor, stood in the northwest corner of Caria, at the foot of Mount Mycalé. It was the birthplace of Bias, one of the Seven Sages of Greece. It was important from a religious point of view in connection with the Pan-Ionian festival on Mount Mycalé, where the people of Priené took precedence as being the supposed descendants of the inhabitants of Helicé in Hellas Proper (Strabo, p. 639).

Priest. See SACERDOS.

Primipīlus. The first centurion of the first maniple of the *triarii.* He had charge of the eagle, had the right of attending the general council of officers, and, in the absence of the tribune, took command of the men. See EXERCITUS; LEGIO.

Primus, M. ANTONIUS. A native of Tolosa in Gaul, who was condemned of forgery (*falsum*) in the reign of Nero, was expelled from the Senate, of which he was a member, and was banished from the city. After the death of Nero (68), he was restored to his former rank by Galba, and appointed to the command of the seventh legion, which was stationed in Pannonia. He was one of the first generals in Europe who declared in favor of Vespasian, and rendered him the most important services. In conjunction with the governors of Moesia and Pannonia, he invaded Italy, gained a decisive victory over the Vitellian army at Bedriacum, and took Cremona, which he allowed his soldiers to pillage and destroy. He afterwards forced his way into Rome, notwithstanding the obstinate resistance of the Vitellian troops, and had the government of the city till the arrival of Mucianus from Syria. (See MUCIANUS.) We learn from Martial, who was a friend of Antonius Primus, that he was alive at the accession of Trajan.

Princeps (ἡγεμών). The use of the word *princeps* as a title originated according to Tacitus (*Ann.* iii. 56) in the desire of Augustus to secure a term which should express the preëminence of the first citizen of the Republic (*princeps civitatis*), and imply the possession of all the functions belonging to him, and yet not suggest the idea of despotic rule (Tac. *Ann.* i. 1; ii. 53; *Hist.* iv. 3; Dio Cassius, lvii. 8). The word *princeps*, as thus used, was merely a title of courtesy; it does not appear in the titular list in the inscriptions, it was not official and did not refer to any definite function.

The origin of the title has been variously assigned to the phrases *princeps senatus* and *princeps civitatis*. The former was an honorary title indicating that the holder was first on the list of senators and was the first to be asked his opinion. We know from Monumentum Ancyranum (Gr. iv. 2) that Caesar was *princeps senatus* in B.C. 28. Nevertheless he is always termed simply *princeps* (Hor. *Car.* i. 2, 50) and thus speaks of himself (*me principe, Mon. Anc.* ii. 45; vi. 9). In the same inscription the Greek translation of the word is ἡγεμών. The title *princeps senatus* would certainly be too restricted in its application, indicating the relation to the Senate and not to the State.

The view that the word *princeps* as used of the emperor was an abridgment of the phrase *princeps senatus* which came to have a wider signification is best stated by Herzog in his *Geschichte und Syst. der röm. Staatsv.* ii. 134. The other view which is more generally accepted is held by Mommsen (*Staatsrecht*, ii. 733), and is clearly set forth by H. F. Pelham in *Jour. of Philol.* viii. p. 322. The expression *princeps civitatis* is found in classical writers and is applied by Cicero to Pompey, while *princeps*, evidently standing for the complete phrase, is used by Cicero of both Pompey and Caesar (*Ad Att.* viii. 9; *Ad Fam.* vi. 6), and by Sallust of Pompey (Hist. iii. 61 D or 81 K). Cf. also Suet. *Iul.* 26. See PRINCIPATUS.

Princeps Iuventūtis. See EQUITES.

Princeps Senātus. See SENATUS.

Principālis Porta. See CASTRA.

Principātus. In January of the year B.C. 27 (A.U.C. 727) Gaius Caesar Octavianus established the Roman Empire, or, as the new form of government at this stage of its existence may be more correctly termed, the principate. On the thirteenth day of that month he voluntarily laid aside the extra-constitutional powers granted him under the stress of civil disorder and on the sixteenth initiated a new system whose constitutional theory and plan were based upon the old republican form of government.

According to Augustus's own words, as given in *Mon. Anc.* vi. 83, *consulatu sexto* (B.C. 28) *et septimo* (B.C. 27) *rem publicam ex mea potestate in senatus populique Romani arbitrium transtuli*, in his sixth consulship he performed the initial act in the abolition of the provisional government by surrendering powers which he had received as triumvir, and which he had held alone after the deposing of Lentulus and after the hostility of Antonius. In January of the following year he completed the restoration of authority to the Senate and people, by what final act it is impossible to say, although at that time he may have surrendered the *proconsulare imperium* which was involved in the triumviral powers granted by the plebescite of P. Titius (*Mon. Anc. Lat.* vi. 13; Tac. *Ann.* iii. 28; Dio Cass. liii. 2). This voluntary return of intrusted powers was immediately followed by the renewal of the *proconsulare imperium* for a period of ten years and by the conferring, by the Senate and people, of the *cognomen Augustus*, which thus dignified and consecrated the new position assumed by Caesar in his relation to the State, and which became the distinctive title of the principate (*Mon. Anc. Lat.* vi. 16). The constitution of the principate thus dates from the renunciatory and reëstablishing enactments of January, B.C. 27.

Augustus still held, however, some form of the *tribunicia potestas* which had been given to him for life in B.C. 36 (A.U.C. 718) (Dio Cass. xlix. 15). He was also consul, for he succeeded himself each year from B.C. 31–23 (A.U.C. 723–731) in a series of nine consulships (Tac. *Ann.* i. 2). The *proconsulare imperium*, which was similar in character to that given to Pompey by the Gabinian and Manilian laws, implied the exclusive command of the armies and fleet, as well as the control of the most important border provinces. Inasmuch as Rome and Italy were not included under this *imperium*, Augustus relied upon the consulship which not only brought the city and Italy under his control, but rendered his *imperium* superior to that of other proconsuls. This is substantially the view of Mommsen as given in his *Staatsrecht*, vol. ii. Another theory stated by H. F. Pelham, *Jour. of Philol.* xvii., bases the new principate entirely on the consulship on the ground that in January, B.C. 27, Augustus, while consul, received from the people the *consulare imperium* involved in the conferring of the usual "province," which was in this case of very broad area, carrying with it control of armies, the direction of foreign relations, as well as the government of important provinces.

On the 27th of June, B.C. 23, Augustus, finding the consulship unsuited to his purpose, laid it aside (Dio Cass. liii. 32) and brought into prominence the *tribunicia potestas*, which, being perpetual, he made nominally annual by renewal from year to year. Thenceforward the title TR(*ibunicia*) POT(*estate*) appears in the inscriptions in the titular list followed by a numeral indicating the number of renewals (*Corpus Inscr. Latin.* indices, particularly vol. iii.). This tribunician power was the civil magistracy supplementing the authority given by the imperium, ranking higher moreover than the latter prerogative (Dio Cass. liii. 32; Momm. *Staatsr.* ii. 1050). Through its privileges the *princeps* had the right of *intercessio* or veto, also that of *coercitio* or power of compelling obedience, also *sacrosancta potestas*, so that his person was inviolable. This substitution of *tribunicia potestas* for the consulship involved the loss of *consulare imperium*, which gave authority in Rome and Italy although naturally it did not interfere with the *proconsulare imperium*. (According to Mr. Pelham's view stated above, the *consulare imperium* given Augustus in B.C. 27, which conferred such extensive powers, he now no longer holds as consul, but as proconsul, so that it really becomes *proconsulare imperium*.)

The renunciation of the consulship meant, however, the loss of an *imperium*, superior to that of other proconsuls, as well as most important prerogatives possessed by the consuls alone. This difficulty was met by special legislative action, whereby Augustus received from the Senate and people rights which belonged originally and legitimately to the consulship. These were, the enlargement of his *imperium* as *proconsul*, so that it became *maius* as compared with that of other proconsuls (B.C. 23), the privilege of introducing the first motion in the Senate (*ius primae relationis*) (B.C. 23), the right of convening the Senate (B.C. 22), the insignia of consular dignity—the twelve fasces and the curule chair between those of the consuls (B.C. 19). An inscription, *Lex de Imperio Vespasiani* (*Corp. Inscr. Lat.* vi. 930), engraved on a bronze tablet, which is extant in fragmentary form, confers upon Vespasian certain rights which were not included in the scope of his *imperium* or of his *tribunicia potestas*. In this *lex* we probably possess in documentary form the special legislative measures which were passed in favour of Augustus. For opposing views on this subject, see Mommsen (*Staatsr*. vol. ii.), who believes that the *lex de imperio* conferred the *tribunicia potestas* extended in its scope, and Herzog (*op. cit.* ii. 617–619), who holds the view expressed above.

The constitutional theory of the principate that the *princeps* was a citizen provided with exceptional powers by the Senate and people did not look to the transmission of this delegated power, but left the matter in the hands of the Senate and people in so far as the conferring of these remarkable powers was concerned. Thus at the death of the *princeps* the principate ended and was not renewed until similar powers had been delegated to his successor, the government being carried on by the consuls during the interregnum. Although there seems to have been no constitutional provision for the selection of a *princeps*, yet, theoretically at least, he was the creature of the people, and his appointment consisted in the conferring of the *imperium* and subsequently of the *tribunicia potestas* by the Senate and the people, the latter ratifying the action of the Senate in their Comitia. The final act was the bestowal of special privileges by the *lex de imperio*. In these acts the choice of the one thus honoured is implied and involved. Although the *princeps* was in theory elected, the choice, however, virtually depended upon certain influences which indicated and determined the selection, as, for example, in times of peace the designating of a son or near relative on the part of the reigning *princeps* and the investing such a one with powers of an imperial nature so as to confirm the choice. In time of civil strife other influences naturally prevailed, such as popularity with the Senate or army, or marked military ability. For opposing theories as to the election of the *princeps*, see Herzog, *Geschichte und Syst. der röm. Staatsv.* ii. 610 foll.; Momm. *Staatsr*. ii. 1038, and Pelham in the *Jour. of Philol.* xvii. 47.

This in outline is the constitution of the principate which recognized the existence of a republican form of government, and also the establishment of a new authority which, standing alongside of the consuls, theoretically the chief magistrates (Tac. *Ann.* iv. 19), held under the designation of *tribunicia potestate* powers equal to those of the consul at home and superior to them abroad. The government is practically in the hands of the *princeps* and the Senate, so that it has been aptly termed a dyarchy. The history of the first three centuries of the Christian era records the dissolution of this dyarchy by the absorption of all power by the *princeps*, and the disclosure of the imperial government in its true character as an absolute monarchy. The fictitious nature of the principate and the inevitable tendency under such a system to the centralization of power in the hands of Caesar may be more readily appreciated by considering the *princeps*, first in his relation to this second governing power, the Senate, and their mutual partition of governmental functions, and again in his personal position as ostensible magistrate but actual monarch, with all the attributes of kingly station.

The constitution of the Senate was controlled in various ways by the *princeps*. He was able to influence the election of magistrates in the assembly by certain privileges known as *nominatio* and *commendatio*. The former arose from the right, belonging to the magistrates (regularly the consuls) presiding at the elections, to canvass the names of the candidates and publish a list of those qualified to stand (Tac. *Ann.* i. 81). By accepting only a sufficient number to fill vacancies the *princeps* could easily control the election. Through the right of *commendatio* the princeps recommended his own candidates, *candidati Caesaris*, and naturally these persons were sure of election (Vell. ii., 124, 4; Tac. *Ann.* i. 15). See also the *Lex de Imperio*, 4, 12; Mommsen, *Staatsr*. ii. 865.

Again, while only those of senatorial rank could hold the office of *quaestor*, the initial office of the senatorial career, yet the emperor would admit to the preliminary service, the vigintivirate and the tribunate of the soldiers, those outside of the senatorial order who were thus placed in the line of promotion as prospective senators (Marquardt, *Staatsv.* ii. 354). By a process known as *adlectio* the *princeps* could place a non-senator in the senatorial order, assigning him to the performance of certain functions as those of quaestor or praetor. Hence we find in inscriptions *adlecti inter praetorios, inter tribunicios*, and rarely *inter quaestorios*, but after the third century *inter consulares*. In the meetings of the Senate the *princeps* had the privilege of voting first, also the right of introducing bills (*relatio*), and of receiving information as to the transactions.

The Senate under the principate discharged administrative functions in regard to religion, the affairs of Italy, and at first of the city itself; but its important control was over the senatorial provinces. In these provinces, however, the *princeps* had certain powers which resulted from his control of the troops, and again, because of the collection by imperial officers of the revenues which came to the *fiscus* of the emperor. Since his *imperium* was *maius*, all proconsuls were his subordinates and under his direction (Momm. *Staatsr.* ii. 227). The final result was the entire subordination of authority in the senatorial provinces to that of Caesar. This change is seen in the gradual modification in the relations existing between the *princeps* and the proconsuls of senatorial provinces. The former at first refused to control such officials of the Senate and people (Tac. *Ann.* ii. 47; iii. 60; Momm. *Staatsr.* iii. 1211), but in the latter part of the second century, Caesar, by virtue of his *maius imperium*, controlled proconsuls, and looked to them to follow his edicts as carefully as any of his own *legati* (*Lex de Imperio*, 6; Momm. *Staatsr.* ii. 843). What was true of the provinces was true of the general departments of administration in Italy and in Rome. They were gradually brought under the control of the *princeps*, so that officers of his own appointment, *praefecti* and *procuratores*, were in charge of public works, of the corn supply, and of the *viae*.

As regards judicial functions, Augustus made the Senate a high court of justice, in which he himself sat, and thus could influence decisions by his vote and by his right of *intercessio* (Tac. *Ann.* iii. 12; iv. 34; iii. 70). Although all criminal cases could be brought before this court, only those of the highest importance really fell to its jurisdiction. The emperor also had a private court of his own, before which only cases of political importance seem to have been brought (Suet. *Aug.* 32). The court of the praetors still existed in Rome and Italy, but the *princeps* often appointed the praetor and frequently sat at his side as *assessor* (Dio Cass. liii. 2, 3; Tac. *Ann.* i. 75). Appeals from senatorial provinces against the judicial decisions of governors were often heard by the *princeps* on the authority of his *maius imperium* (Mommsen, *Staatsr.* ii. 110).

The Senate, by the republican theory, had no direct legislative power, save through the acceptance of *senatus consulta* by the assembly of the people. Under the principate, however, the *senatus consulta*, enacted according to the wish of the emperor, became laws. The emperor, however, became the real source of law, for by special acts of the Senate (Cic. *Verr.* ii. 2, 49, 121) he was empowered to found colonies, grant charters, confer the Roman franchise (*leges datae*) (e. g. the Lex Malacitana, Bruns, *Fontes Iuris Romani*, vi. 147; *C. I. L.* ii. 876, 1964); and on his own authority he issued legislative documents (*constitutiones*), which were entirely of imperial origin. These were either *edicta, decreta, rescripta*, or *epistulae*. See Bruns, *op. cit.* 237 foll.

The financial affairs of the Empire were divided between the Senate and the *princeps*. There was a Senate treasury, known as the *aerarium*, and also the privy purse of the emperor, the *fiscus*. The latter was drawn upon not merely for the direct expenses of the emperor, but for provincial administration, the support of the army and fleet, and many public expenditures. The collection of taxes in all the provinces was at first farmed out on the old republican principle, but was ultimately conducted by the imperial officials. The coinage of gold and silver belonged at first to the Senate and emperor, but it was finally given exclusively to the emperor, and the coinage of copper was assigned to the Senate.

The falseness of the pretensions as to the magisterial character of the principate in the matter of limited tenure was disclosed at an early period in the acceptance by Tiberius and his successors of a life imperium, although the festival known as *decennalia* still recalled the periodical renewal. According to Dio Cassius (lix. 3, 2), Gaius received the powers of the principate by one grant, an act which showed still further the tendency to individualize the *princeps* in the possession of sole and permanent authority (Momm. *Staatsr.* ii. 744). Augustus refused the censorship consistently with his evident purpose; for a *princeps* possessed of the censor's power would be a monarch, inasmuch as he would absolutely control the constitution of the Senate. He indeed acted at times as censor, but only by virtue of his consular power. Domitian and his successors, however, performed the censorial functions simply by reason of their authority as *principes* (Mommsen, *Staatsr.* ii. 1018).

The name of the *princeps* was similar to that of an ordinary citizen, but differed in certain special features. The title *imperator* was substituted by Augustus for his *praenomen*, Gaius; and although the custom was disregarded by Tiberius, Gaius, and Claudius, it was resumed by Nero and regularly followed by his successors. The inscriptions show that it regularly took the position of a *praenomen*. A distinction must be made between this use of the word and the *acclamatio imperatoria* followed by the numeral of iteration, which appears among the titles. From the names of the early emperors, with the exception of the Claudii and Vitellius, the *nomen* was omitted, but its use was resumed by Hadrian. Caesar, the inherited *cognomen* of the Julian family, became a distinguishing mark of the reigning house, but from the time of Hadrian it was restricted to the emperor and his successor.

Augustus, the last word, strictly speaking, in the name of the *princeps*, was associated with the principate, and was conferred with the official granting of power by the Senate and people. From the latter part of the second century the word *Augustus* was preceded by additional surnames—e. g. *Pius, Pius Felix Invictus*—and from the beginning of the fourth century it was strengthened by *perpetuus* and *semper*. Special *cognomina ex virtute*—e. g. *Germanicus, Dacicus, Armeniacus*—were assumed by Vitellius and Nerva and regularly by Trajan and his successors. The following titles indicating *honores* also belonged to the imperial name: *Pontifex Maximus, Tribunicia Potestate, Imperator, Consul, Censor* (held only by Claudius, Vespasian, Titus, and Domitian), *Pater Patriae* (declined by Tiberius, Nero, Vespasian, Hadrian), *Proconsul* (in the names of Trajan, Hadrian, M. Aurelius, L. Verus, Septimius Severus, and his successors).

The emperors, because of the founding of the principate upon republican principles and precedents, had the right to use republican insignia, the curule chair, the laurel wreath and gold-embroidered toga of the *triumphator*, which were henceforth restricted to their use (Dio Cass. liii. 26), and the purple-bound toga of the magistrate (*Vita Hadriani*, 22). The right to wear the purple *paludamentum* was granted to Caesar as an indication of the supreme nature of his *imperium*, but it was rarely used in the first century, although it subsequently became the symbol of assumed authority (Momm. *Staatsr.* i. 349). As *imperator* the *princeps* had the privilege of carrying the sword of military power. For the personal safety of the *princeps* the *cohors praetoria* kept guard at the palace.

Consecration and deification of emperors testify to the unrepublican position they occupied. Iulius Caesar had permitted himself to be regarded as a god, but Augustus refused to allow worship of himself, at least in Rome and Italy. Like Iulius Caesar, however, he was placed among the gods of Rome after death, and with his deified successors received the title *divus*. Temples were built in Asia to Augustus and Tiberius during their lives, and the tendency to deify living emperors prevailed generally during the latter half of the second century.

Augustus and the early emperors endeavoured to follow republican principles in the natural dignifying and honouring of members of their families. Livia was an exception in the privileges she obtained (Dio Cass. xlix. 38), but at her death honours were restricted and deification was at first denied (Tac. *Ann.* v. 2). The title Augusta was conferred upon Livia by the will of Augustus, perhaps with some political significance; but though from the time of Domitian it was regularly given to the wife of the reigning prince, it became a general title of honour, being granted also to other relatives of the *princeps*. Later the wife of the reigning emperor was still more highly honoured by the granting of the appellation *mater castrorum*, e. g., to Faustina, wife of Marcus Aurelius, and *mater castrorum et senatus et patriae* to Iulia Domna, wife of Severus. The young men were made *principes iuventutis*, a title merely signifying entrance into the equestrian order, and whatever rank they obtained came through the holding of magistracies perhaps at an unusually early age, a favour granted, however, by a special decree alone. Notwithstanding this moderation on the part of the early emperors, there is a persistent endeavour to glorify the imperial family. In the *votorum nuncupatio* (Wilmanns, 2876) we find the *tota domus* associated with the names of the emperor Domitian, of Domitia and Iulia (Momm. *Staatsr.* ii. 776), and the phrase *tota domus Augusta* occurs in an inscription of the time of Hadrian (Wilm. 319), while *numina Augusti totiusque domus divinae* is seen in an inscription of the time of Commodus (Wilm. 120), and mention of the *domus divina* is very common thereafter (Momm. *Staatsr.* ii. 780–81).

As with his family, so with his associates and friends, Augustus endeavoured to prevent intimate relations with the *princeps* from implying undue influence and power (Suet. *Aug.* 56; Tac. *Ann.* ii. 34). It was inevitable, however, that the preëminence of the *princeps* should result in an exaggeration of the standing of those who had the honour of his friendship. The morning receptions, similar to those of other prominent citizens, became with the *princeps* the gatherings of magistrates and senators (Friedländer, *Sittengeschichte* I. ch. ii.). The *amici Caesaris* developed under Tiberius into a distinct and semi-official body (*cohors*) (Tac. *Ann.* vi. 9), arranged in classes with rank determined by degree of intimacy. The *renuntiatio amicitiae* on the part of the *princeps* was equivalent to sentence of banishment (Suet. *Tib.* 56; Tac. *Ann.* ii. 70; iii. 12, 24). The travelling companions (*comites*) of the *princeps* were chosen from this circle of *amici* (Suet. *Tib.* 46). After the first century *amici* became a general term, and included the regular attendants upon the emperor as well as any of high rank who were especially favoured. The term *comes* becomes more definite in its application, referring to those assigned to expeditions. These were supplied with special camp-quarters, and had precedence over provincial governors. A proof of the value assigned to appointment as *comes* is found in the appearance of the title in the inscriptions among the *honores*· (Friedländer, *Sittengeschichte*, i. 118 foll.). At first the agents of the *princeps* belonged strictly to his own household, and were either slaves or freedmen. The necessity of having a body of imperial representatives led to the formation of the equestrian *cursus honorum*. From a select class of the *equites* the *princeps* selected administrative officers, who were his agents, while the magistrates of the senatorial order were the officers of the State. The equestrian *cursus honorum* was introduced by a military service, which led to procuratorships of various grades and finally to the important praefectures. These imperial officers formed an organized service, which, spreading throughout the Empire, supplanted in many instances the representatives of the State, and brought the control of the provinces directly into the hands of the *princeps*, centralizing the governmental control in Caesar, and making him in this respect also a monarch. See Hirschfeld, *Verwaltungsgeschichte;* and the article HONORES.

BIBLIOGRAPHY.—J. B. Mispoulet, *Les Institutions Politiques des Romains*, 2 vols. (Paris, 1883); Th. Mommsen, *Res Gestae Divi Augusti* (Berlin, 1883); Ernst Herzog, *Geschichte und System der Römischen Staatsverfassung*, 2 vols. (Leipzig, 1884–87); A. Bouché-Leclercq, *Manuel des Institutions Romaines* (Paris, 1886); P. Willems, *Le Droit Public Romain* (Paris, 1888); Theodor Mommsen, *Römisches Staatsrecht*, 3 vols. (Leipzig, 1887–88).

Principia. The term for the headquarters of the Roman camp. Here the officers' tents were pitched, the standards reared, and the harangues (*contiones*) made to the troops (Livy, vii. 12; xxviii. 24). See CASTRA.

Prisciānus. (1) A Latin grammarian of Caesarea, in Mauritania, who lived, at the beginning of the sixth century A.D., as a teacher of the Latin language in Constantinople. He there compiled, in addition to a number of smaller grammatical works, his *Institutiones Grammaticae* in eighteen books, the fullest and completest systematic Latin grammar which has come down to us. This work, which is of great importance owing to its ample quotations from ancient literature, was for a long time, in the Middle Ages, the school-book in ordinary use in the shape of an epitome by Rabanus Maurus, and formed the foundation for the earlier treatises on Latin grammar in modern times. We also possess an insipid panegyrical poem written by Priscian on the emperor Anastasius, a translation of the Cosmography of the geographer Dionysius, in hexameter verse, besides a grammatical catechism on twelve lines of the *Aeneid* for school use, a treatise on accent, a treatise on declension, a treatise on symbols for coins and weights, a treatise on the metres of Terence, a translation of the Προγυμνάσματα (*Praeexercitamenta*) of Hermogenes, a poem *De Sideribus*, and two epigrams. The best editions of Priscianus are those of Krehl (Leipzig, 1819–20) in 2 vols. and Keil in his *Grammatici Latini* (1855). (See GRAMMATICA.) (2) A physician, who lived in the fifth century, named THEODŌRUS PRISCIĀNUS, has left us a *Medicina Praesentanea* (a book of rapid curatives) in five books. (3) LYDUS, a Neo-Platonic philosopher in the reign of Justinian. He wrote a paraphrase and commentary on the physics of Theophrastus (*Metaphrasis in Theophrastum*), and *Solutiones* to certain philosophic questions. His remains are edited by Bywater (1886).

Priscus (Πρίσκος). A Byzantine historian who was a native of Panium in Thrace, and was one of the ambassadors sent by Theodosius the Younger to Attila, A.D. 445. He died about 471. Priscus wrote an account of his embassy to Attila, enriched by digressions on the life and reign of that chief. The work was in eight books, but only fragments of it have come down to us. Priscus was an excellent and trustworthy historian, and his style was remarkably elegant and pure. The fragments are published with those of Dexippus and others, by Bekker and Niebuhr (Bonn, 1829), and by Müller in his *Frag. Hist. Graec.*

Priscus, HELVIDIUS. The son-in-law of Thrasea Paetus, and, like him, distinguished by his love of virtue, philosophy, and liberty. He was quaestor in Achaia during the reign of Nero, and tribune of the plebs A.D. 56. When Thrasea was put to death by Nero (66), Priscus was banished from Italy. He was recalled to Rome by Galba (68); but in consequence of his freedom of speech and love of independence, he was again banished by Vespasian, and was shortly afterwards put to death by order of this emperor. His life was written by Herennius Senecio at the request of his widow Fannia; and the emperor Domitian, in consequence of this work, subsequently put Senecio to death, and sent Fannia into exile (Pliny, *Epist.* vii. 19, 5; Dio Cass. lxvii. 13). Priscus left a son, Helvidius, who was put to death by Domitian.

Priscus, Servilius. The Prisci were an ancient family of the Servilia gens, and filled the highest offices of the state during the early years of the republic. They also bore the agnomen of Structus, which is always appended to their name in the Fasti, till it was supplanted by that of Fidenas, which was first obtained by Q. Servilius Priscus Structus, who took Fidenae in his dictatorship, B.C. 435, and which was also borne by his descendants.

Priscus, Tarquinius. See Tarquinius.

Prison. See Carcer.

Prista (πριστήρ). A sawyer. See Serra.

Privernum. An ancient town of Latium, on the river Amasenus.

Privilegium. See Lex.

Prize-fighters. See Pugilatus.

Proaeresius (Προαιρέσιος). A teacher of rhetoric, born in Armenia about A.D. 276. He studied at Athens and Antioch, and was afterwards the principal professor of rhetoric at Athens. He died in A.D. 368 (Suidas, s. h. v.).

Proba Faltonia or **Falconia.** A Roman lady who, in the fourth century A.D., put together a cento on the creation of the world, composed of verses gathered from Vergil. The poem, which is still extant, is printed in Migne's *Patrologia*, xix. pp. 803–817. (See Cento.) She also wrote an account of the war of Constantine against Magnentius, as is stated in the *subscriptio* to a MS. of the tenth century.

Probalinthus (Προβάλινθος). A deme of Attica, south of Marathon, and belonging to the tribe Pandionis (Strabo, p. 383).

Probŏlé (προβολή). A motion for a judicial prosecution. In Attic legal procedure it was a particular kind of public indictment. In the first assembly of every prytany, on the archon's inquiring whether the people were satisfied with the conduct of the magistrates, any citizen might accuse a magistrate of official misconduct. If the assembly considered there was foundation for the charge, the magistrate was temporarily suspended or even absolutely deposed from his office, and a judicial prosecution was instituted. Even against a private citizen, especially for doing an injury to magistrates, or to sacred persons or things, for interrupting a festival, embezzling public money, or instituting a vexatious prosecution, a complaint could be brought before the people in order to see whether they considered the case suitable for a judicial trial. The most celebrated example of this procedure is the case of Demosthenes against Midias for assaulting him in the discharge of public functions at the Dionysia. However, this neither bound the man who laid the complaint to bring forward an actual indictment nor the jury to follow in the formal trial the preliminary verdict of the people, although it would always influence them.

Probouli (πρόβουλοι). A name applied in Greece to any persons appointed to consult or take measures for the benefit of the people—e. g. delegates sent by the twelve Ionic cities to the Panionian Council (Herod. vi. 7) at the time of the Persian Wars. The word also denotes an oligarchical body which exercises the functions performed in a democracy by the βουλή, or is co-ordinate with the βουλή and a check upon it (Arist. *Pol.* vi. 15, 11).

Probus, M. Aurelius. A Roman emperor (A.D. 276–282). He was a native of Sirmium in Pannonia, and rose to distinction by his military abilities. He was appointed, by the emperor Tacitus, governor of the whole East, and, upon the death of that sovereign, the purple was forced upon his acceptance by the armies of Syria. The downfall of Florianus (q. v.) speedily removed his only rival, and he was enthusiastically hailed by the united voice of the Senate, the people, and the legions. The reign of Probus presents a series of the most brilliant achievements. He defeated the barbarians on the frontiers of Gaul and Illyricum and in other parts of the Roman Empire, and put down the rebellions of Saturninus at Alexandria, and of Proculus and Bonosus in Gaul. But, after crushing all external and internal foes, he was killed at Sirmium by his own soldiers, who had risen in mutiny against him, because he had employed them in laborious public works. Probus was as just and virtuous as he was warlike, and is deservedly regarded as one of the greatest and best of the Roman emperors. His life is given in the Historia Augusta; see also Zosim. i. 64.

Probus, Marcus Valerius. A famous Roman scholar and critic, born at Berytus, in Syria. He flourished in the second half of the first century A.D. He devoted almost all his attention to the archaic and classical literature of Rome, which had been previously neglected, and to the critical revision of the most important Roman poets, as Lucretius, Vergil, and Horace, after the manner of the Alexandrian scholars. Some of his criticisms on Vergil may possibly be preserved to us in a commentary to the Eclogues and Georgics, which bears his name. From a commentary, or criticism, on Persius we have his biography of that poet; and from his work *De Notis* we have an extract containing the abbreviations used for legal terms. Other grammatical writings bearing his name are the work of a grammarian of the fourth century. Probus ranks as the greatest of the Roman philologists. See Suet. *Frag.* ed. Reifferscheid, p. 138; Kübler, *De Probi Comment. Verg.* (Berlin, 1881); and Steub, *De Probis Grammaticis* (Jena, 1871). The treatise of the second Probus is printed in Keil's *Grammatici Latini.*

Procas. A mythical king of Alba Longa, succeeding Aventinus. He was the father of Numitor and Amulius (Livy, i. 3).

Prochȳta. Now Procida; an island off the coast of Campania near the promontory Misenum, is said to have been torn away by an earthquake either from this promontory or from the neighbouring island of Pithecusa or Aenaria (Pliny, *H. N.* ii. 203).

Proclus (Πρόκλος). The most important representative of the later Neo-Platonic School, born A.D. 412 at Byzantium. He received his first instruction at Xanthus, in Lycia, and betook himself to Alexandria to complete his education. There he attached himself chiefly to Heron, the mathematician, and to the Aristotelian Olympiodorus. Before the age of twenty, he removed to Athens to attend the lectures of the most celebrated Platonists of the time, Syrianus and Plutarchus. On the death of the latter he became head of the Platonic School until his own death in 485. His disciples were very numerous; and his learning and zeal for the education of the young, combined with his beneficence, his virtuous and strictly ascetic life, and his steadfastness in the faith of his fathers, gained him the enthusiastic devotion of his followers. We possess an account of his life, full of admiration for his character, by his pupil and successor, Marinus. The efforts of Proclus were directed to the support of paganism in its struggle with the now victorious Christianity, by reducing to a system all the philosophic and religious traditions of antiquity. His literary activity was very great, and extended over almost every department of knowledge; but Platonic philosophy was the centre of the whole. His philosophical works, now extant, are a commentary on a few dialogues of Plato (mainly on the *Timaeus*), also his chief work on the theology of Plato, as well as a summary of the theology of Plotinus, with writings treating several branches of philosophy from his own point of view. Some of his minor works have reached us only in a Latin translation. As specimens of his mathematical and astronomical works, we have a commentary on the first book of Euclid, a sketch of the astronomical teaching of Hipparchus, Ptolemy, and others, a slight treatise on the heavens, etc. One of his grammatical writings survives in his commentary on Hesiod's *Works and Days*. Lastly, we have two epigrams by him and six hymns. It is doubtful whether the *Grammatical Chrestomathy*, extracts from which, preserved by Photius, are the only source of our knowledge of the Greek cyclic poets, was really written by him, and not rather by a grammarian of the same name in the second century A.D. There is no complete edition of the works of Proclus. A partial edition is that of Cousin, 6 vols. (Paris, 1820). See Zeller, *Philos. der Griechen*, iii. 2, in the third edition.

Procné (Πρόκνη). A daughter of the Athenian king Pandion and Zeuxippé, sister of Philomela. She was given in marriage by her father to the Thracian prince Tereus, in Daulis near Parnassus, in return for assistance given him in war. Tereus became by her the father of Itys. Pretending that his wife Procné was dead, Tereus brought her sister Philomela from Athens, and ravished her on the way. He then cut out her tongue that she might be unable to inform against him, and concealed her in a grove on Parnassus; but the unfortunate girl contrived to inform her sister of what had happened by a robe, into which she ingeniously wove the story of her fate. Taking the opportunity of a feast of Dionysus in Parnassus, Procné went in quest of her sister, and agreed with her on a bloody revenge. They slew the boy Itys, and served him up to his father to eat. When Tereus learned the outrage, and was on the point of slaying the sisters, the gods changed him into a hoopoe or hawk, Procné into a nightingale, and Philomela into a swallow, or (according to another version) Procné into a swallow, and Philomela into a nightingale. See AËDON.

Procoeton (προκοιτών). An ante-room (Pliny, *Epist.* ii. 17, 10).

Proconnēsus (Προκόννησος). Now Marmora; an island of the Propontis, which takes from it its modern name (Sea of Marmora), off the northern coast of Mysia, northwest of the peninsula of Cyzicus or Dolionis. The island was celebrated for its marble, and hence its modern name.

Proconsul (ἀνθύπατος, *pro consule*, "deputy-consul"). A Roman officer to whom the consular power was intrusted for a specified district outside the city. The regular method of appointing the proconsul was to prolong the official power of the retiring consul (*prorogatio imperii*) on the conclusion of his year of office. In exceptional cases, however, others were appointed proconsuls, generally those who had already held the office of consul. This was especially done to increase the number of generals in command. The proconsuls were appointed for a definite or indefinite period; as a rule for a year, reckoned from the day on which they entered their province. This period might be prolonged by a new prorogation. In any case the proconsul continued in office till the appearance of his successor. With the growth of the provinces, the consuls as well as the praetors were employed to administer them as proconsuls on the expiration of their office. After Sulla this became the rule; indeed, the Senate decided which provinces were to be consular and which praetorian. The regulation, in B.C. 53, that past consuls should not govern a province till five years after their consulship broke down the immediate connection between the consulship and succession to a province, and the proconsuls thereby became in a more distinctive sense governors of provinces. After Augustus the title was given to governors of senatorial provinces, whether they had held the consulship before or not. As soon as the proconsul had been invested with his official power (*imperium*), he had to leave Rome forthwith, for there his *imperium* became extinct. Like the consuls, he had twelve lictors with bundles of rods and axes, whom he was bound to dismiss on reëntering Rome. In the province he combined military and judicial power over the subject peoples and the Roman citizens alike—only that in the case of the latter, on a capital charge, he had to allow them to appeal to Rome. To administer justice he travelled in the winter from town to town. In the case of war he might order out the Roman citizens as well as the provincials. His power was absolutely unlimited, so that he might be guilty of the greatest oppression and extortion, and was only liable to prosecution for these offences on the expiration of his office. He might advance a claim for a triumph or an *ovatio* (q. v.) for military services. When the senatorial provinces came generally to have no army under the Empire, the duties of the proconsuls became limited to administration, political and judicial. See Mommsen, *Röm. Staatsrecht*, ii. 90, 233, 238–246, 257; and the article PROVINCIA.

Procopius (Προκόπιος). A Greek historian of Caesarea in Palestine, a rhetorician and advocate by profession. In and after A.D. 526 he attended the general Belisarius as private secretary and adviser in nearly all his campaigns. He was afterwards made a senator, and in 562, when prefect of Constantinople, was deposed from his office by a conspiracy, and shortly afterwards died suddenly, more than seventy years old. He has left us a history of his own times down to 554 in eight books (Ἱστορίαι), dealing with the wars of Justinian against the Persians, Vandals, and East Goths; a book on the buildings of Justinian (Κτίσματα); and the *Anecdota* (Ἀνέκδοτα), or secret history, supplementing the first-mentioned work. It discloses the scandals of the court of the day, and, on account of its contents, was not published until after the death of the author. His information is partly derived from the oral testimony of others, but he prefers to record his own experiences. This, and his fresh treatment of his subject, together with his pure and, on the whole, simple style, make him one of the most eminent authors of his age. The collected works of Procopius, including orations, are edited by Dindorf in 3 vols. (Bonn, 1833–38). There is an old translation of Procopius into English by Henry Holcroft (London, 1653). See Renan, *Essais de Morale et de Critique* (3d ed. Paris, 1867).

Procŭlus, IULIUS. See ROMULUS.

Procŭlus, SEMPRONIUS. A Roman jurist, the founder of the school called after him the Proculiani. See ANTISTIUS LABEO; IURISPRUDENTIA.

Procurātor. Under the Roman Republic, the fully accredited agent of a private citizen; a steward; a *maître d'hôtel* (Sen. *Epist.* 14). (See PROMUS.) Under the Empire, the title was given to those who, as household officers of the emperor, were considered administrators of the imperial purse. The fiscal administration of the imperial provinces was in the hands of a procurator of equestrian rank, under whom were freedmen of the emperor, bearing the same title, and attending to particular departments of the administration. In the senatorial provinces, also, there was an imperial procurator, independent of the governor, to manage the domains and to collect the revenues belonging to the *fiscus*. Further, there were particular provinces which, before they were administered as actual provinces, were governed as domains by an administrator appointed by the emperor and personally responsible to him. He likewise was styled procurator, and in general had a position similar to that of the other governors. Such a procurator was Pontius Pilate in Judaea, which for a long time was under a procurator. The imperial chief treasury was administered by a *procurator a rationibus*, also called *procurator fisci*, at first an imperial freedman, but after the second century a knight (Suet. *Vitell.* 2). To administer the imperial privy purse, into which flowed the revenues from the crown lands and the private fortune of the emperor, there were special procurators. See FISCUS.

Prodĭcus (Πρόδικος). A Greek Sophist of Ceos, contemporary with Socrates. He repeatedly visited Athens as an ambassador from his native country. The applause which his speeches gained there induced him to come forward as a rhetorician. In his lectures on literary style he laid chief stress on the right use of words and the accurate discrimination between synonyms, and thereby paved the way for the dialectic discussions of Socrates (Plato, *Euthyd.* 277; *Cratyl.* 384; *Charmid.* 163). None of his lectures has come down to us in its original form. We have the substance only of his celebrated fable of the *Choice of Heracles* preserved by Xenophon (*Mem.* ii. 21–34).

Prodigium. The Latin term for an unnatural or, at any rate, unusual and inexplicable phenomenon, which was always treated as requiring expiation (*procuratio*). This was only done on behalf of the State, if the phenomenon had been observed on ground belonging to the State. The Senate, acting on the advice of the pontiffs, ordained either particular sacrifices, to specified deities, or a nine days' sacrifice, or a public intercession, and left the execution of the ordinance to the consuls (Livy, i. 20). If a prodigium caused so much alarm that the usual means of expiation seemed insufficient, the Senate had recourse to the Sibylline Books, or the Etruscan *haruspices*. (See HARUSPEX; SIBYLLA.) For the prodigium of a thunderbolt, see PUTEAL; and in general see Müller, *Die Etrusker*, ii. 191; Hartung, *Die Religion der Römer*, i. 96; Bouché-Leclercq, *Hist. de la Divination*, p. 181; and Mommsen, *Staatsverwaltung*, 2d ed. iii. pp. 259–264.

Prodosia (προδοσία). A general term of Greek law for treason, including any attempt to subvert the Constitution of the State. The trial was before the people and the punishment was death, the loss of the right of burial in Attic soil, and confiscation of property (Xen. *Hellen.* i. 7, 22). Lesser degrees of treason were, however, probably recognized and punished only by fines (Demosth. *c. Timocr.* p. 740 § 127).

Prodrŏmi. Greek skirmishers. See HIPPEIS.

Proedria (προεδρία). The right of occupying the front row of seats next the orchestra, at the dramatic performances in the Greek theatre. This distinction was enjoyed by the priests, the chief magistrates, distinguished citizens, the descendants of those who had fallen in battle for their country, and members of foreign States whom it was desired to honour, especially ambassadors. The term also denotes the presidency at the Council (see BOULÉ), and in the assemblies of the people. In the fifth century B.C. the *prytanes*, under their *epistates*, presided over the Council and the assemblies of the people; in the fourth, the *proedri* were instituted. The latter were appointed on each occasion from nine of the tribes, and the presidential duties were transferred to them and their *epistates* (a member of the tenth tribe). See Aristotle, *Athen. Polit.* xliv. p. 115, with Kenyon's note.

Proetĭdes. See PROETUS.

Proetus (Προῖτος). Son of Abas and Ocalé, and twin-brother of Acrisius. In the dispute between the two brothers for the kingdom of Argos Proetus was expelled, whereupon he fled to Iobatos, in Lycia, and married Antea or Stheneboea, the daughter of the latter. With the assistance of Iobates, Proetus was restored to his kingdom, and took Tiryns, which was now fortified by the Cyclopes. Acrisius then shared his kingdom with his brother, surrendering to him Tiryns, Midea, and the coast of Argolis. By his wife, Proetus became the father of three daughters, Lysippé, Iphinoë, and Iphianassa, who are often mentioned under the general name of PROETĬDES. When these daughters arrived at the age of maturity, they were stricken with madness, the cause of which is differently explained. Some say that it was a punishment inflicted upon them by Dionysus, because they had despised his worship; others relate that they were driven mad by Heré, because they presumed to consider themselves more handsome than the goddess, or because they had stolen some of the gold of her statue. The frenzy spread to the other women of Argos; till at length Proetus agreed to divide his kingdom between Melampus and his brother Bias, upon the former promising that he would cure the women of their madness. Melampus then chose the most robust among the young men, gave chase to the mad women, amid shouting and dancing, and drove them as far as Sicyon. During this pursuit, Iphinoë died, but the two other daughters were cured by Melampus by means of purifications, and were then married to Melampus and Bias. The place where the cure was effected upon his daughters is not the same in all traditions, some mentioning the well Anigros, others the fountain Clitor in Arcadia, or Lusi in Arcadia. Besides these daughters, Proetus had a son, Megapenthes. When Bellerophon came to Proetus to be purified of a murder which he had committed, the wife of Proetus fell in love with him; but, as Bellerophon declined her advances, she charged him before Proetus with having made improper proposals to her. Proetus then sent Bellerophon to Iobates in Lycia, with a letter desiring the latter to murder Bellerophon. (See BELLEROPHON.) According to Ovid (*Met.* v. 238) Acrisius was expelled from his kingdom by Proetus; and Perseus, the grandson of Acrisius, avenged his grandfather by turning Proetus into stone by means of the head of Medusa. See PERSEUS.

Professors. See EDUCATION.

Profesti Dies. See DIES.

Proletarii. The name in the Roman centuriate system (see COMITIA) of those citizens who were placed in the lowest of the five property classes, and who were exempt from military service and tribute. Their name owes its origin to the fact that they only benefited the State by their children (*proles*). Another name for them is *capite censi*—i. e. those who were classed in the list of citizens at the census solely in regard to their status as citizens (*caput*). Afterwards, the richer among them were taken to serve in the wars: these were then called *proletarii;* and those without any property at all, *capite censi.* In and after the time of Marius, when the levy of troops was no longer founded on the census, the Roman armies were recruited by preference from the last class. See Mommsen, *Staatsrecht*, iii. 238.

Prolŏgus (πρόλογος). A technical term applied to that part of a Greek drama which precedes the entrance of the first chorus. From the time of Euripides it came to mean a monologue containing a narrative of the facts introductory to the main action, and this is the meaning which the word possessed in the language of Roman comedy. It is thus opposed to ἐπίλογος, the concluding part of the play. Aristotle compares the prologue to the prelude in a piece of music (*Rhet.* iii. 14, 1). The word is also applied to the actor who speaks the Prologue. In some plays there are two speakers of this sort—e. g. in the *Alcestis* of Euripides and the *Trinummus* of Plautus. Terence uses the Prologue as a means of personal communication on the part of the author to the public and as a vehicle for replying to adverse criticism (e. g. in the *Andria*). (See Liebig, *De Prologis Terentianis et Plautinis* [Görlitz, 1859].) The tables of contents prefixed to the divisions of books are also called *prologi*, as those of the lost history of Pompeius Trogus. See Hallberg, *De Trogo Pompeio* (Paris, 1869).

Promăchus (πρόμαχος, "fighter in the front rank," "protector"). (1) An epithet of Athené (q. v.). (2) Son of Parthenopaeus and the nymph Clymené, one of the Epigoni (q. v.).

Promenade. See PORTICUS.

Prometheia (τὰ Προμήθεια). A festival in honour of Prometheus (q. v.). It was one of the five Attic feasts which were celebrated by a torch-race in the Ceramicus. See LAMPADEDROMIA.

Promētheus (Προμηθεύς, "forethought"). A son of the Titan Iapetus and the Ocean-nymph Clymené, brother of Atlas, Menoetius, and Epimetheus, father of Deucalion (q. v.). The most ancient account of him, as given by Hesiod (*Theog.* 521–616) is as follows: When the gods, after their conquest of the Titans, were negotiating with mankind about the honour to be paid them, Prometheus was charged with the duty of dividing a victim offered in sacrifice to the gods. He endeavoured to impose upon Zeus by dividing it in such a way as cleverly to conceal the half which consisted of flesh and the edible vitals under the skin of the animal, and to lay thereon the worst part, the stomach, while he heaped the bones together and covered them with fat.

Zeus divined the stratagem, but, out of enmity towards man, purposely chose the worst portion, and avenged himself by refusing mortals the use of fire. Thereupon Prometheus stole it from Olympus and brought it to men in a hollow reed (νάρθηξ). As a set-off to this great blessing, Zeus resolved to send them an equally great evil. He caused Hephaestus to make of clay a beautiful woman named Pandora—that is, the all-gifted; for the gods presented her with all manner of charms and adornments, coupled however with lies, flattering words, and a crafty mind. Hermes brought her, with a jar as her dowry, in which every evil was shut up, to the brother of Prometheus, named Epimetheus (i. e. the man of afterthought, for he never thought of what he did until it had brought him into trouble). In spite of his brother's warning not to receive any present from Zeus, he was ensnared by her charms and took her to wife. Pandora opened the jar, and out flew all manner of evils, troubles, and diseases, before unknown to man, and spread over all the earth. Only delusive Hope remained in the jar, since, before she could escape, Pandora put the lid on the jar again (Hes. *Op. et D.* 54–105). But Prometheus met with his punishment. Zeus had him bound in adamantine fetters to a pillar with an eagle to consume in the day-time his liver, which grew again in the night. At last Heracles, with the consent of Zeus, who desired to increase his son's renown, killed the eagle, and set the son of Iapetus free. According to this account, the guile of Prometheus, and his opposition to the will of Zeus, brought on man far more evil than good.

Aeschylus, on the other hand, taking the view suggested by the Attic cult of Prometheus, in which the fire-bringing god was honoured as the founder of human civilization, gave the myth an entirely different form in his trilogy of *Prometheus the Fire-bearer*, *Prometheus Bound*, and *Prometheus Released.* In these Prometheus is still, of course, the opponent of Zeus; but, at the same time, he is represented as full of the most devoted love for the human race. See AESCHYLUS.

Aeschylus makes him son of Themis, by whom he is put in possession of all the secrets of the future. In the war with the Titans, his advice assisted Zeus to victory. But when the god, after the partition of the world, resolved on destroying the rude human race, and to create other beings in their stead, Prometheus alone concerned himself with the fate of wretched mortals, and saved them from destruction. He brought them the fire he had stolen from Hephaestus at Lemnos, the fire that was to become the source of all discoveries and of mastery over nature; and raised them to a higher civilization by his inventive skill and by the arts which he taught mankind. For this he was punished by being chained on a rock beside the sea in the wilds of Scythia. Oceanus advised him to bend beneath the might of Zeus; but he consoled himself with the knowledge that, if the god begat a son by a certain goddess known to himself alone (Thetis), the son would dethrone his father. When no menaces could tear from him the secret, Zeus hurled him with a thunderbolt into Tartarus together with the rock to which he was chained. From this abode he first emerged into the light of day a long time after, to be fastened on Mount Caucasus and torn by the eagle until another immortal voluntarily entered Hades for him. At last Heracles, on his journey to the Hesperides, shot the eagle; the centaur Chiron (q. v.), suffering from his incurable wound, gladly renounced his immortality; and, after Prometheus had revealed the name of the goddess, he was set free. But, as a sign of his punishment, he ever after bore on his finger an iron ring and on his head a willow crown. He returned to Olympus, and once more became adviser and prophet of the gods. Legends related that he moulded men and animals of clay, and either animated these himself with the heavenly fire or induced Zeus or Athené to do so (Ovid, *Met.* i. 81; Hor. *Carm.* i. 16, 13). In Athens Prometheus shared with Hephaestus a common altar in the Academy, in the sacred precinct of Athené, and was honoured with a torch-race in a yearly festival called the Prometheia. There are monographs on the myth of Prometheus, by Weiske (1842); Lasaulx (1843); Holle (1879); and Milchhöfer (1882); see also Kuhn, *Die Herabkunft des Feuers* (1886); and E. B. Tylor, *Researches into the Early History of Mankind* (1865). The story of Prometheus has been made the subject of two fine poems by Shelley and Mrs. Browning.

Promĕtrae. See METRONOMI.

Promulsidārē. A tray for holding the dishes that contained the *promulsis* (q. v.).

Promulsis. Any relish taken before a meal, such as eggs, oysters, and radishes (Cic. *Ad Fam.* ix. 20). See CENA.

Promus. A steward or butler (Plaut. *Pseud.* ii. 2, 14).

Pronāos (*πρόναος*). In the Greek temple, the porch, portico, or entrance-hall to the temple proper, or *ναός*. See TEMPLUM.

Pronax (Πρῶναξ). The son of Talaüs and Lysimaché and brother of Adrastus and Eriphylé. By some the Nemean Games were said to have been founded in his honour.

Pronouns. See GRAMMATICA.

Pronŭba. A name given to Iuno as presiding over marriage. See IUNO.

Pronŭbae et Pronŭbi. See MATRIMONIUM, p. 1015.

Pronunciation of Greek. See GREEK, PRONUNCIATION OF.

Pronunciation of Latin. See LATIN, PRONUNCIATION OF.

Propertius, SEXTUS. A Roman elegiac poet born at Asisium (Assisi), in Umbria (Prop. i. 22, 9, 65–66, 121–126, and v. 1). The date of his birth is uncertain. He was somewhat older than Ovid, and was probably born about B.C. 50. He lost his parents at an early age; and, through the general confiscation of land in 42, was deprived of the greater part of his paternal estate. Still, he possessed enough to live a typical poet's life at Rome, whither he had proceeded soon after coming of age, about B.C. 34. He there associated with his patron Maecenas and with other poets, such as Vergil and Ovid. To complete his studies he afterwards went to Athens. When he was still quite young, the poet's spirit woke within him, and expanded through his attachment to the beautiful and witty Hostia. Under the name Cynthia, she henceforth was the subject of his love-poems. For five years (B.C. 28–23) this attachment lasted, though often disturbed by the jealousy of the sensitive poet and the capriciousness of his mistress. When it had come to an end, and even after Cynthia's death (probably before B.C. 18), the poet could not forget his old passion. He himself died young. He often expresses forebodings of an early death; there is no indication in his poems that any of them were written later than B.C. 16. They have come down to us in four books, but some scholars are of opinion that the poet himself had divided them into five, and that the original second and third books have been united, perhaps through the oversight of friends at the publication of the last. Propertius himself seems to have only published the first. In the first four books amatory poems preponderate. The fifth book, the confused order of which may well be referred to the poet's untimely death, deals mainly with subjects taken from Roman legends and history, in the same way as Ovid subsequently treated them in the *Fasti.*

Propertius possesses a poetical genius with which his talent is unable to keep pace. Endowed with a nature susceptible of passion as deep as it was strong, as ardent as it was easily evoked, and possessed of a rich fancy, he strives to express the fulness of his thoughts and feelings in a manner modelled closely on that of his Greek masters; and yet in his struggle with linguistic and metrical form, he fails to attain the agreeable in every instance. His expression is often peculiarly harsh and difficult, and his meaning is frequently obscured by far-fetched allusions to unfamiliar legends, or actual transcripts of them. Herein he follows the example of his models, the Alexandrian poets, Callimachus and Philetas. Nevertheless he is a great poet, and none of his countrymen has depicted the fire of passion so truly and so vividly as he. The personality of Propertius seems not to have been altogether agreeable, but to have been characterized by a certain conceit and youthful bumptiousness; and editors have argued with some probability that he is the person whom

Horace had in mind in depicting the famous bore in the ninth satire of the First Book, though there are some chronological difficulties in the way of this theory. See Palmer's notes on this satire.

The principal manuscript of Propertius is the Codex Neapolitanus, now at Wolfenbüttel, which dates from the fifteenth century, though long regarded as older. See the introduction to L. Müller's critical edition (Leipzig, 1880). The *editio princeps* of Propertius appeared at Venice in 1472. Propertius is edited by Hertzberg, with Latin notes, 3 vols. (1845); Keil (Leipzig, 1850); Palmer, with English notes (Dublin, 1880); Paley (1872); and Postgate (London, 1881). There is an English rendering by Cranstoun (1875). See Jacob, *Propertius* (Lübeck, 1847); on his style, the *Prolegomena* in Hertzberg's edition; and on his versification, Eschenburg, *Observationes Criticae in Propertium*, pp. 1–28 (Bonn, 1864); also Gruppe, *Die röm. Elegie*, i. pp. 274 foll.

Propylaeum, Propylaea (προπύλαιον, προπύλαια). (The singular and plural forms seem not to have differed in meaning. The gateway to the Athenian acropolis went almost invariably under the name Προπύλαια, but it is called Προπύλαιον in a contemporary official inscription (*C. I. A.* i. 314). The elder Pliny uses *propylon* for the same structure.) A gate-building, serving generally as an entrance to a sacred precinct. A city-gate is never so called.

The most important edifice of this kind, both architecturally and historically, and also the best preserved, is that designed by Mnesicles, and built in the years B.C. 437–432, as an entrance to the Athenian acropolis. The material is chiefly Pentelic marble; black Eleusinian marble is sparingly used for thresholds, wall-bases, etc.; the foundations are, in part, of Piraeus limestone (*poros*). The diagram shows the ground-plan both as originally designed and as actually carried out. (The unshaded parts were not built.) The central and essential part of the structure consists of two parallel lateral walls terminating in antae; a cross-wall, placed much nearer the eastern than the western front, and pierced by five doorways of three different widths; and two Doric hexastyle porticos, the greater or western one of which included six Ionic columns, placed three on each side of the central passage-way, and helping to support the flat ceiling. The whole was completely roofed over. The central and broadest of the five doorways was intended for processions, for animals, and perhaps also for wheeled vehicles; the other four, designed for ordinary pedestrians, were approached from the west by five steps. Each of the five doorways was provided originally with double doors. The central structure thus far described constituted the Propylaea proper. To this Mnesicles designed extensive wings, the like of which are not found with any other known Propylaea. Of these wings, only one, the northwestern, was carried out according to the design. This consists of a rectangular closed chamber and a Doric portico, whose three columns are much smaller than those of the central structure. The chamber was entered by a door in its south wall. On either

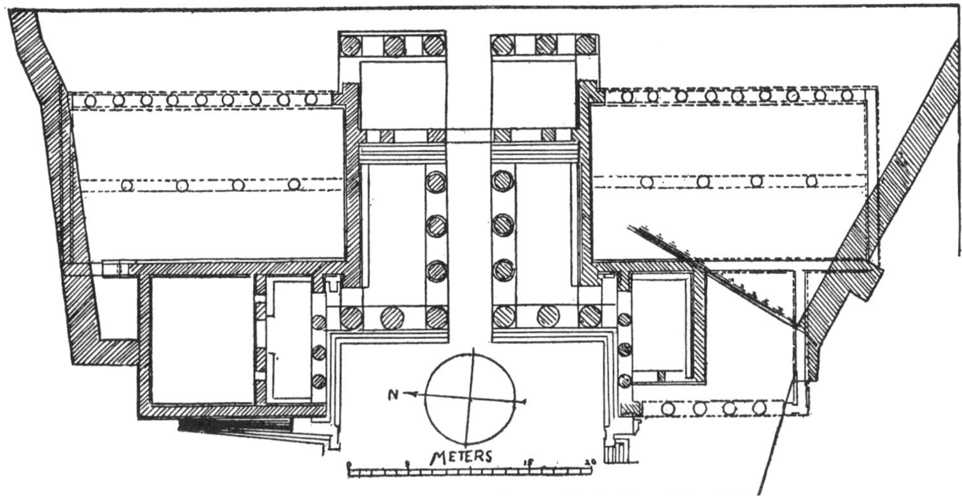

Ground-plan of the Athenian Propylaea. (Adapted from Dörpfeld.)

Propes. The lower end of the sheet (*pes*) attached to the clews of a square sail. See NAVIS.

Proplasma (πρόπλασμα). A model in clay or terra cotta made by a sculptor as a rough embodiment of his design for a statue (Cic. *Ad Att.* xii. 41).

Propnigēum (προπνιγεῖον). The mouth of a furnace (πνιγεύς); a term equivalent to the Latin *praefurnium* (Pliny, *Epist.* ii. 17, 11).

Propontis (Προποντίς). "The fore-sea." Now the Sea of Marmora; so called from its position with reference to the Pontus (Euxinus), being πρὸ τοῦ Πόντου, "before the Pontus." It is the small sea uniting the Euxine and the Aegaean, and dividing Europe (Thracia) from Asia (Mysia and Bithynia). See BOSPORUS.

Propraetor. A title given to a praetor who after discharging his judicial duties in Rome received the charge of a province. See PRAETOR; PROVINCIA.

Propugnacŭlum. (1) In general, any construction on land used for purposes of defence, as a barricade, rampart, etc. (2) The tower on a man-of-war from which the marines (*classiarii*) discharged missiles at the enemy (Hor. *Epod.* i. 2). See NAVIS.

side of the door was a window. Pausanias speaks of this northwestern wing as "a building to the left of the Propylaea containing pictures," whence it is often called the Pinacotheca by modern writers. The southwestern wing was to have been of the same dimensions as the northwestern, but of a different plan, with an open row of columns towards the west in place of a closed wall. This project had to be greatly changed; it is probable that unexpected opposition was raised to the destruction of a piece of venerable Pelasgic wall, and to encroachment on the precinct of Athena Nikê. As a result this wing became a shrunken and abnormal structure, with a free-standing double anta at the northwestern corner and a unique form of roof. Again, Mnesicles designed two great porticos flanking the Propylaea and fronting eastward. These were both given up, the one probably because it would have encroached upon the precinct of Artemis Brauronia, the other perhaps in consequence of the outbreak of the Peloponnesian War. Even those parts of the whole edifice which were actually erected did not everywhere receive the finishing touch. The most obvious evidence of this is the existence of numerous rough bosses on the exposed surfaces of the marble blocks. These bosses were for assistance in hoisting the blocks, and were intended to be subsequently worked off.

The Propylaeum of Mnesicles was a building of great originality and skill, and, though it lacks something of the perfect simplicity and harmony of a Doric temple of the same period, it must still be ranked as one of the greatest achievements of Greek architecture. The artistic forms are admirable, the Ionic capitals being especially noteworthy for combined vigour and refinement; the workmanship is of unsurpassed precision. The juxtaposition of different orders, necessitated by the greater height required for the interior columns, is by some considered unfortunate. There is a similar juxtaposition in the temple of Athenê Alea at Tegea, where the columns of the peristyle were Doric and those of the pronaos and opisthodomos Corinthian (probably). Owing to the width required for the principal entrance-way, the central intercolumniations on the east and west fronts are much greater than the others, with the result that there are two triglyphs instead of one over the central intercolumniations. This asymmetry would not be found in a temple. In consequence of the rise of the ground, the eastern pediment is nearly one and a half metres higher than the western. This superposition would have been very disagreeable if seen, but must have been invisible from most of the possible points of view. See ATHENAE, p. 155 (illustration).

The Propylaeum of Mnesicles was built on the site of an earlier and smaller structure of the same sort, of which slight traces can still be seen. Other remains of propylaea exist at Eleusis, Epidaurus, Olympia, Delos, and Prienê.

See Bohn, *Die Propyläen der Akropolis zu Athen* (1882); W. Dörpfeld in the *Mittheilungen des arch. Instituts in Athen*, x. 38–56, 131–144 (1885). From these sources most of the foregoing material has been derived. Also F. C. Penrose, *Principles of Athenian Architecture* (2d ed. 1888). L. Fenger's *Dorische Polychromie* (1886) devotes a plate to the polychromy of the Athenian Propylaea.

Proquaestor. See QUAESTOR.

Prora (*πρῷρα*). A ship's prow. See NAVIS.

Prorēta (*πρῳράτης*). The look-out on a ship, stationed upon the forecastle of the ship's prow. He was second in command to the *gubernator* (Plaut. *Rud.* iv. 3, 86).

Prorogatio. The Roman term for the extension either of a man's year of office (*prorogatio magistratus*), or of a supreme command (*prorogatio imperii*), or of a provincial administration (*prorogatio provinciae*).

Proscenium (*προσκήνιον*). See THEATRUM.

Proscriptio (from *proscribere*, "to advertise for sale"). From the time of Sulla (B.C. 82) it came to mean the sale of the property of those whom he had condemned to death and who were themselves styled *proscripti.* During the civil strife of the following fifty years, other leaders used the precedent thus established as a means of weakening the opposing party. A famous proscription is that of the Second Triumvirate (B.C. 43), under which Cicero was put to death. See CICERO; SULLA.

Prosecta. See ABLEGMINA.

Proserpĭna. See PERSEPHONÊ.

Prosodium (*προσῳδία*). A kind of song generally sung to the accompaniment of the flute at festal processions to the temple or the altar, chiefly in the worship of Apollo. It had a rhythm corresponding to the measure of the march.

Prospalta (*τὰ Πρόσπαλτα*). A deme of Attica belonging to the tribe Acamantis.

Prosper. A celebrated ecclesiastical writer. He was a native of Aquitania, and flourished during the first half of the fifth century A.D. He distinguished himself by his numerous writings in defence of the doctrines of Augustine against the attacks of the Semipelagians. Many of his theological works are extant; and there are also two chronicles bearing his name: (1) *Chronicon Consulare*, extending from A.D. 379, the date at which the chronicle of St. Jerome ends, down to 455, the events being arranged according to the years of the Roman consuls. We find short notices with regard to the Roman emperors, the Roman bishops, and political occurrences in general; but the troubles of the Church are especially dwelt upon, and, above all, the Pelagian heresy. (2) *Chronicon Imperiale*, comprehended within the same limits as the preceding (379–455), but the computations proceed according to the years of the Roman emperors, and not according to the consuls. While it agrees with the *Chronicon Consulare* in its general plan, it differs from it in many particulars, especially in the very brief allusions to the Pelagian controversy, and in the slight, almost disrespectful notices of Augustine. The second of these chronicles was probably not written by Prosper of Aquitania, and is assigned by most critics to Prosper Tiro, who, it is imagined, flourished in the sixth century. There are likewise several poems, which have come down to us under the name of Prosper. The best edition of Prosper's works is that of Lebrun and Maugeant (Paris, 1711).

Prostas (*προστάς*). The vestibule of a house.

Prostătes (*προστάτης*). The Greek name for the person who acted as patron to a former slave. See LIBERTUS; SERVUS.

Prostătes Tou Demou (προστάτης τοῦ δήμου). In Athens and other democratic States of Greece, a word denoting the person who by his character and ability was generally regarded as the most influential statesman of the day. Such, for example, was Pericles in his time. (Xen. *Mem.* i. 2, 40.) In most of the Doric States it was also the title of public officers of various kinds.

Prostitution. See MERETRIX.

Prostȳlos (πρόστυλος). Literally, "with columns in front," an epithet of a temple (ναός) with the columns in front of its portico standing completely free from the front wall of the temple itself. See TEMPLUM.

Protagonistes (πρωταγωνιστής). In the Greek drama the actor who played the leading part. See DRAMA; HISTRIO; TRAGOEDIA.

Protagŏras (Πρωταγόρας). A celebrated Sophist, born at Abdera, in Thrace, probably about B.C. 480, and died about 411, at the age of nearly seventy years. It is said that Protagoras was once a poor porter, and that the skill with which he had fastened together, and poised upon his shoulders, a large bundle of wood, attracted the attention of Democritus, who conceived a liking for him, took him under his care, and instructed him in philosophy (Diog. Laërt. ix. 53; x. 8; Gell. v. 3). This well-known story, however, appears to have arisen out of the statement of Aristotle that Protagoras invented a sort of porter's knot for the more convenient carrying of burdens. In addition to this, Protagoras was about twenty years older than Democritus. Protagoras was the first who called himself a Sophist, and taught for pay; and he practised his profession for the space of forty years. He must have come to Athens before B.C. 445, since he drew up a code of laws for the Thurians, who left Athens for the first time in that year. Whether he accompanied the colonists to Thurii, we are not informed; but at the time of the plague (430) we find him again in Athens. Between his first and second visit to Athens he had spent some time in Sicily, where he had acquired great fame; and he brought with him to Athens many admirers out of other Greek cities through which he had passed. His instructions were so highly valued that he sometimes received 100 minae from a pupil; and Plato says that Protagoras made more money than Phidias and ten other sculptors. In 411 he was accused of impiety by Pythodorus, one of the Four Hundred. His impeachment was founded on his book on the gods, which began with the statement, "Respecting the gods, I am unable to know whether they exist or do not exist" (Diog. Laërt. ix. 52). The impeachment was followed by his banishment, or, as others affirm, only by the burning of his book. His doctrine was, in fact, a sort of agnosticism based upon the impossibility of attaining any absolute criterion of truth. It is summed up in the sentence, "Man is the measure of all things" (πάντων ἄνθρωπος μέτρον, or, in Latin, *homo mensura omnium*), implying that each one must be his own final authority; for just as each thing appears to any individual, so it really is for him. This doctrine is therefore styled Individualism. Protagoras wrote a large number of works, of which the most important were entitled *Truth* (Ἀλήθεια) and *On the Gods* (Περὶ Θεῶν). The first contained the theory refuted by Plato in the *Theaetetus.* Plato gives a vivid picture of the teaching of Protagoras in the dialogue that bears his name. Protagoras was especially celebrated for his skill in the rhetorical art. By way of practice in the art he was accustomed to make his pupils discuss theses (*communes loci*), an exercise which is also recommended by Cicero. He also directed his attention to language, and endeavoured to explain difficult passages in the poets. He is said to have been the first to make the grammatical distinctions of moods in verbs and of genders in nouns.

See Geist, *De Protagora Sophista* (Giessen, 1827); Herbst, *Protagoras Leben und Sophistik* (Hamburg, 1832); Vitringa, *De Protagorae Vita* (Groningen, 1853); Blass, *Attische Beredsamkeit*, pp. 23–29; Ueberweg, *Hist. of Philosophy*, i. pp. 73–76 (Eng. trans. N. Y. 1872).

Protesilāus (Πρωτεσίλαος). The son of Iphiclus and Astyoché, dwelling in Phylacé in Thessaly. He is called Phylacius and Phylacides, either from his native place or from his being a grandson of Phylacus. He led the warriors of several Thessalian towns against Troy, and was the first of all the Greeks who was killed by the Trojans, being the first who leaped from the ships upon the Trojan coast. According to the common tradition he was slain by Hector. Protesilaüs is most celebrated in ancient story for the strong affection existing between him and his wife Laodamia, the daughter of Acastus. (See LAODAMIA.) His tomb was shown near Eleus, in the Thracian Chersonesus, where a magnificent temple was erected to him. There was a belief that nymphs had planted elm-trees around his grave, which died away when they had grown sufficiently high to see Troy, and that fresh shoots then sprang from the roots. There was also a sanctuary of Protesilaüs at Phylacé, at which funeral games were celebrated.

Proteus (Πρωτεύς). The prophetic old man of the sea, described in the earliest legends as a subject of Poseidon, whose flocks (the seals) he tended. According to Homer, he resided in the island of Pharos at a distance of one day's sail from the river Aegyptus (i. e. the Nile); whereas Vergil places his residence in the island of Carpathos between Crete and Rhodes. At mid-day Proteus rose from the sea, and slept in the shadow of the rocks of the coast, with the sea-monsters lying around him. Any one wishing to learn from him the future was obliged to catch hold of him at that time; as soon as he was seized he assumed every possible shape in order to escape the necessity of prophesying; but whenever he saw that his endeavours were of no avail he resumed his usual form, and told the truth. After finishing his prophecy he returned into the sea (*Odyss.* iv. 351). Homer ascribes to him a daughter Idothea. Another set of traditions describes Proteus as a son of Poseidon and as a king of Egypt, who had two sons—Telegonus and Polygonus or Tmolus. His Egyptian name is said to have been Cetes, for which the Greeks substituted that of Proteus. His wife is called Psamathé or Toroné, and, besides the above-mentioned sons, Theoclymenus and Theonoë are likewise called his children. He is said to have hospitably received Dionysus during his wanderings. Hermes brought to him Helen after her abduction; or, according to others, Proteus himself took her from Paris, gave to the lover a phantom, and restored the true Helen to

Menelaüs after his return from Troy (Herod. ii. 112, 118; Diod. i. 62).

Prothesmia (προθεσμία). The term in which actions and prosecutions could be brought in Athens. The προθεσμίας νόμος was a sort of statute of limitations, the time for bringing action for debt or for damages on account of injuries being apparently five years, but there were no doubt different periods assigned in the case of different actions.

Prothўrum (διάθυρον). The entrance-hall of a Roman house, being a small passage between the street-door (*ianua*) and the house-door (*ostium*). The Greek πρόθυρον is the Latin *vestibulum* (q. v.). See DOMUS.

Protogĕnes (Πρωτογένης). A celebrated Greek painter of Caunus, in Caria, who lived for the most part at Rhodes, in the time of Alexander the Great and his first successors. He died B.C. 300. His poverty seems to have prevented him from attending the school of any of the celebrated masters of his age, for no one is named as his instructor. He long remained poor, until the unselfish admiration which his contemporary and brother painter Apelles showed for his works raised him in riper years to great celebrity. His works, owing to the excessive care he bestowed on them, were few in number; but their perfect execution led to their being ranked by the unanimous voice of antiquity among the highest productions of art. His most celebrated works were a "Resting Satyr," and also a painting representing the Rhodian hero, Ialysus. On the latter he spent seven or, according to others, as many as eleven years. To insure its permanence he covered it with four distinct coats of paint, so that when the upper coating perished the lower might take its place (Pliny, *H. N.* xxxv. 101–105).

Proverbium (παροιμία). A proverb. Both the Greeks and Romans were fond of short, pithy sayings, embodying the accumulated experience of mankind, and they abound in the pages of the classic writers. Mere academic and philosophic sayings were styled γνῶμαι (*sententiae*), and writers in whom they abound are called "gnomic." (See EPOS.) The maxims of the Seven Sages were famous throughout Greece (see SEVEN SAGES), and among the Romans writers like Cato the Elder, Iulius Caesar, Tiro, and Suetonius made collections of apothegms. The mimes of Publilius Syrus were full of maxims, hundreds of which are still preserved. (See PUBLILIUS SYRUS.) For the literature of the subject, see Duplessis, *Bibliographie Parémiologique* (Paris, 1847); Rheinsberg-Düringsfeld, *Sprichwörter der Germanischen und Romanischen Sprachen* (1872–75), which is the ablest work on proverbs that has ever been written; and for convenient reference, the *Dictionary of Classical Quotations* in the Bohn Library (London, 1874).

Provincia. A word which, in Roman public law, designated primarily the sphere of action allotted to a particular magistrate. (See MAGISTRATUS.) When, in the third century B.C., Rome began to assume the permanent rule of territories outside of Italy, it became customary to intrust the government of each such territory to a single magistrate; and, by a natural transition, "province" became the technical term for conquered territory ruled by a Roman governor, and "provincials" the technical term for the inhabitants of such a territory—the subjects as distinguished from the citizens of Rome. Territories left under the sceptres of native princes, though practically controlled by Rome, were not provinces. Free and allied cities, though included within the boundaries of a province, were not parts of the province, nor were individuals who had received Roman citizenship properly numbered among the provincials. In the imperial period, however, with the gradual disappearance of the protected kingdoms and allied commonwealths and the gradual extension of Roman citizenship throughout the Roman world, the term province became purely territorial; the provinces were simply the great governmental districts outside of Italy. At the same time, in consequence of the growth of imperial absolutism, the distinction between Italy and the provinces lost all real importance. As early as the second century after Christ, the methods of provincial administration were introduced into Italy; and under Diocletian, at the close of the third century, the distinction disappeared even in name, Italy being divided into a number of provinces.

Provincial Officers.—Provision was made for the government of the first four provinces by increasing the number of praetors annually elected at Rome (so B.C. 227 and again B.C. 197). The praetors-elect drew lots to determine which should do duty in Rome and which should go to the provinces. With the increase in the number of provinces (B.C. 146–120) the Senate began to prolong (*prorogare*) the imperium of outgoing magistrates, who then ruled the provinces allotted them as *pro*consuls or *pro*praetors. The more important provinces—those in which military operations were in progress or in prospect—were commonly assigned to the outgoing consuls. A *lex Sempronia* (C. Gracchus) provided that the Senate should indicate annually, before the election of the consuls, which provinces were to be assigned to them. The consuls-elect then drew lots for these provinces. The system of governing the provinces through such promagistrates was made general by Sulla (about B.C. 80). The new criminal courts (*quaestiones*) established by him, together with the older civil courts, kept all the praetors (now eight in number) busy at Rome during their first year of office, and all the provinces (now ten in number) were allotted to proconsuls or propraetors. The consuls continued to draw lots for the consular provinces before taking office: the praetors drew lots during their year of office. With the further increase in the number of provinces (B.C. 64 there were fourteen or fifteen) recourse was had to various expedients. Two or more provinces were not infrequently assigned to a single proconsul, or a proconsul or propraetor was left in his province for two or more years. Exceptionally, an outgoing praetor or even a private citizen might be invested with proconsular powers, but only by a vote of the Comitia. Iulius Caesar restored the equilibrium between the urban magistracies and the provincial promagistracies by a further increase in the number of praetors.

Under Augustus a division of provinces was made between the emperor and the Senate. He reserved to himself those provinces in which it was necessary to maintain a considerable armed force, and assigned to the Senate those which

THE WESTERN PROVINCES OF THE ROMAN EMPIRE

were pacified. The senatorial provinces (ten in number) continued to be allotted to the ex-magistrates: Africa and Asia to ex-consuls, the rest to ex-praetors. All of the senatorial governors bore the title of proconsul, but those of consular rank had twelve fasces, those of praetorian rank but six. With the multiplication of the city magistracies and the decrease in the number of available provinces, governorships were no longer obtainable by the outgoing magistrates at the expiration of their regular terms, but only after a legal interval of five years, and then in the order of seniority. Under Tiberius the actual interval averaged about thirteen years.

Under the governors served: (1) *Legati*, lieutenants, usually nominated by the governor and appointed by the Senate. The governor assigned to them their duties, and had the power of dismissing them (see LEGATUS); (2) *comites* or *contubernales*, a staff of military and administrative assistants, appointed by the governor with the approval of the Senate, and removable at his pleasure; (3) *apparitores*, etc., secretaries, clerks, copyists, interpreters, attendants and messengers, engineers (*architecti*), physicians, and priests. All these (with the possible exception of the *medici*) were public employés, paid by the treasury. The governor might also take with him, at his own expense, as many clients and slaves as he saw fit; but until late in the republican period he was not permitted to take his wife.

The provincial quaestors, or treasury officials, were magistrates of subordinate rank, but of independent tenure and powers. They were elected, not appointed; and were responsible only to the treasury and the Senate. The number of quaestors annually elected at Rome had increased with the organization of new provinces, so that, even at the close of the republican period, the quaestors-elect drew lots for Italian or provincial duty, and proquaestors were rarely needed. Under the Empire these officials were gradually replaced by imperial procurators (q. v.).

The quaestors, legates, and *comites* constituted the governor's council. See *consilia*, under MAGISTRATUS.

In the provinces of Caesar the emperor himself was proconsul. The governors were his appointees and lieutenants, *legati Augusti pro praetore*. Their authority was as ample as that of a proconsul, but since it was a delegated authority they had but five fasces (*legati quinquefascales*). Their military aids (*legati legionis*) and their officers of justice (*legati iuridici*) were appointed by the emperor. The interests of the imperial fiscus were guarded by procurators.

Early in the imperial period there appears another type of imperial province, in which the emperor rules not as proconsul, but as sovereign proprietor, and not through a *legatus*, but through a viceroy (*praefectus*) or steward (*procurator*). Many of these provinces were ruled for a time by tributary kings or princes, and with the extinction or deposition of the original dynasty the resident procurator of Caesar becomes *procurator et praeses* or *procurator pro legato*. In nearly all of these provinces there was some obstacle, either in the temper of the inhabitants (as in Egypt and Iudaea) or in the topography (as in the Alps), or in the backward stage of civilization (as in Thrace and Mauretania) to the introduction of the ordinary provincial administration.

Organization and Government.—In the republican period the main lines of the provincial organization were fixed by the Senate, and the details were worked out in each province by a special committee of senatorial legates. The constitution thus framed was the *lex provinciae*. The normal unit of local government was the city or town. If there were no cities, local government districts were created by combining several villages or even, as in Spain and Gaul, by adopting the existing tribal districts. In such districts towns gradually grew up, sometimes about a market-place, sometimes about a Roman garrison. In other cases the nuclei of municipal organizations were furnished by Roman colonies. The effect of Roman rule was gradually to develop, where it did not previously exist, the Graeco-Latin municipal system. This development was largely due to the method of government instinctively adopted. It was always the Roman practice, while maintaining a strong central control, to leave the immediate management of local affairs to the local authorities, and to throw upon them as much of the provincial and even of the imperial business as they could manage—particularly the conscription of soldiers and the collection of taxes. Only where there were no trustworthy local authorities was a prefecture or local dictatorship established. In the imperial period municipal self-government was secured and enlarged, in proportion as the provinces were Romanized, by special charters and general laws. See MUNICIPIUM.

For the administration of justice the provinces were divided into much larger districts or dioceses (*conventus*). To the municipalities was left only a petty civil and criminal jurisdiction.

In the original demarkation of the municipal districts and judicial circuits the Romans retained the older native divisions only where the people submitted readily to the Roman rule. Where this was not the case the older political or racial connections were purposely severed; hostile communes were placed under the rule of those more friendly to Rome or under that of Roman colonies, and *connubium* and even *commercium* were suspended between different portions of the same province. But the Romans made no such innovations for the sake of innovation, or even for the sake of uniformity.

In the government of a province the governor was subject to no limitations except those expressly imposed by Roman legislation. In theory the provincials had no political or religious organization, no law, and no rights. They were conquered subjects of the Roman people (*dediticii*), holding their lives and their property at the pleasure of Rome. The authority of the governor was in principle absolute: he had *imperium militiae*. (See MAGISTRATUS.) Upon the exercise of his governmental power, however, certain restrictions were imposed, at first by Roman tradition and custom, and later, in many cases, by written law. In criminal matters he was sole judge of the law and the facts, but he was expected to administer criminal justice publicly and at stated places and times, to hear evidence and argument, and to consult his councillors. In the exercise of his civil jurisdiction he was expected, after hearing the pleadings and discovering the point at issue, to refer the decision to a *iudex* or *arbiter*.

In the absence of any provincial law (for the provincials had lost their own law and had no share in the civil law of Rome) he was obliged to lay down the rules which the *iudex* was to apply; but this he was expected (and ultimately required) to do in a general way, by a public edict, at the beginning of his term of office. He was bound to adhere to his own edict, and his successor generally reënacted it, with such emendations and additions as seemed advisable. These provincial edicts were, in general, admirably drawn, and they constituted an important element in the development of the *ius gentium*. See EDICTUM; IUS.

Such special laws as were passed at Rome for the protection of the provincials were intended primarily to safeguard the proprietary interest of the Roman people, to prevent the governors from so impairing the resources of the provinces as to lessen their value to Rome. By a series of laws the governors were forbidden to extort money or goods from the provincials, directly or indirectly. They were forbidden to accept gifts, and to purchase anything beyond current supplies. For oppression and maladministration they were liable to criminal indictment after their return to Rome. Such charges were originally tried by the Senate; then by a standing committee of the Senate; later by a regular court with a large bench of *iudices* (*quaestio repetundarum*). The governors were also expected to protect the provincials against the tax-farmers (*publicani*) and the speculators (*negotiatores*), but as a rule governors, publicans, and speculators acted in concert. When the provincials were unable to meet the exactions of the governor and the publicans, the speculators advanced the necessary sums at usurious interest; and if their loans were not repaid when due, troops were placed at their disposal for the collection of principal and interest. The transfer of the *iudicia* from the senatorial to the equestrian order (C. Gracchus) tended to force the governors into such a concert, because the publicans and speculators belonged to, and exercised a controlling influence in, the equestrian order. The short terms allotted to the provincial governors made their robberies more rapid, and the prospect of criminal prosecution forced them to steal on a larger scale that they might purchase their acquittal at Rome without sacrificing more than the moiety of their gains. That the governors should make their fortunes out of the provinces was so much a matter of course that the few honourable exceptions were matters of special note and record. Even the free and allied cities were not secure against robbery by the provincial ring. Some of them paid subsidies, which brought them into relations with the publicans and speculators: nearly all of them were bound to furnish recruits and, in case of need, to provide free quarters for the legions, which placed them at the mercy of the governor. The sale of protection against the quartering of troops was an important source of illegal revenue.

The establishment of the Empire greatly improved the position of the provincials. The theory that the provinces must not be so exploited as to lessen their productivity was now enforced, not only in the provinces of Caesar, but in those which were nominally under the control of the Senate. A careful census of the provinces and the abandonment of the wasteful and oppressive system of tax-farming made it possible to lessen the burden of the provincial taxes and yet increase the revenue. All the provincial governors, including the proconsuls, received not only their outfit and a liberal allowance for expenses, as in the Republican period, but a salary. The extension of municipal rights and of Roman citizenship gave the provincials much more effective protection against arbitrary and unjust treatment. The systematic organization of the cult of Rome and of the *divi Augusti* led to annual meetings of delegates from the localities, and to these assemblies (*communia*, *concilia*, *κοινά*), whose character and duties were at first purely religious, some representative functions were conceded, especially the right of petition. Under Tiberius they became something very like advisory administrative councils. Charges against the governors formulated by such bodies received serious consideration. Tacitus and Pliny mention twenty-seven trials of ex-governors, with but seven acquittals.

Public Works.—Even under the Republic much had been done to develop the resources of the provinces by the building of roads, the improvement of harbours, the establishment of colonies, etc. Under the Empire all these things were done on a larger scale and with more consistency of purpose. For an account of the imperial postal system, see CURSUS PUBLICUS.

Defence of the Frontiers.—With the pacification and gradual Romanization of the provinces the troops were gradually removed to the frontier. The frontier line (*limes*), even in those portions most exposed to barbarian inroads, was a road rather than a wall, and served primarily for the rapid concentration of troops. These were quartered in forts (*castella*). The road itself was protected, where it was deemed necessary, by ditches and palisades, and frequently by a broad zone of waste country, in which no settlements were tolerated. The movement of persons across the line was strictly controlled, as was also, for revenue purposes, the transit of goods.

General Development.—In judging the results of Roman conquest and rule, it must never be forgotten that the suppression of brigandage and piracy, and of the interminable wars which formerly raged between the petty States of the ancient world, gave to industry and commerce an unexampled security, which went far to balance the spoliation of the provinces even in the worst period of misgovernment. With the administrative reforms of the early Empire and the effective defence of the frontiers, the majority of the provinces grew rapidly in wealth, comfort, and civilization. The contributions of the ruder, non-Hellenic provinces to the art, literature, and science of the Roman world grew steadily in importance. Provincials played a prominent part in the government of the Empire: they gave it not only the bulk of its troops, but a constantly increasing number of military leaders, administrative officers, and jurists. In the end they furnished the majority of its emperors.

Later Empire.—In the course of the third century the military and the civil government of the provinces began to be assigned to different officers, the former to *duces*, the latter to *praesides* or *correctores*. Under Diocletian this separation of powers became general. At the same time the larger provinces were subdivided and grouped for administrative purposes into a dozen dioceses, each under a *vicarius*, and these, again, into four great prefectures—Gaul, Italy, Illyricum, and the Orient.

ROMAN PROVINCIAL ORGANIZATION.

Early Empire (to A.D. 117).				Later Empire (End of Fourth Century).			
	Date of Constitution.	Assigned to—(Ranking as—)	Title of Governor.		Title of Governor.	Diocese.	Praetorian Praefecture.
Sicilia.	B.C. 241	Senate (praetorian).	Proconsul.	Sicilia.	Consularis.	Italia (vicarius urbis).	Italia.
Sardinia and Corsica.	B.C. 231	B.C. 27 to A.D. 6 Senate (praetorian). Afterwards usually Caesar.	Proconsul. Procurator.	Sardinia. Corsica.	Praeses. Praeses.	Italia (vicarius urbis).	Italia.
Hispania Citerior (Tarraconensis).	B.C. 197	Caesar (consular).	Legatus propraetore.	Tarraconensis. Carthaginiensis. Insulae Baleares. Gallaecia et Asturia.	Praeses. Praeses. Praeses. Consularis.	Hispania.	Galliae.
Hispania Ulterior (Baetica).	B.C. 197	Senate (praetorian).	Proconsul.	Baetica (with which Tingitana is connected)	Consularis.	Hispania.	Galliae.
Lusitania.	B.C. 27	Caesar (praetorian).	Legatus propraetore.	Lusitania.	Consularis.		
Gallia Narbonensis.	B.C. 120	B.C. 27 to B.C. 22 Caesar. After B.C. 22 Senate (praetorian).	Legatus propraetore. Proconsul.	Narbonensis I., II. Viennensis.	Praesides. Consularis.	Gallia (Viennensis).	Galliae.
Aquitania.	B.C. 50 Separately organized B.C. 27 ?	Caesar (praetorian).	Legatus propraetore.	Novum populana. Aquitanica I., II.	Praeses. Praesides.	Gallia (Viennensis).	Galliae.
Lugdunensis.		Caesar (praetorian).	Legatus propraetore.	Lugdunensis I. Lugdunensis II., III., and IV. (Senonia).	Consularis. Praesides.	Gallia.	Galliae.
Belgica.		Caesar (praetorian).	Legatus propraetore.	Belgica I., II.	Consulares.	Gallia.	Galliae.
Germania Superior.	Separately organized A.D. 17?	Caesar (consular).	Legatus propraetore.	Maxima Sequanorum Germania I.	Praeses. Consularis.	Gallia.	Galliae.
Germania Inferior.		Caesar (consular).	Legatus propraetore.	Germania II.	Consularis.	Gallia.	Galliae.
Britannia.	A.D. 43	Caesar (consular).	Legatus propraetore.	Maxima Caesariensis. Valentia. Britannia I., II. Flavia Caesariensis.	Consularis. Consularis. Praesides. Praeses.	Britanniae.	Galliae.
Alpes Maritimae.	B.C. 14	Caesar.	Procurator.	Alpes Maritimae (including western slope of Cottian Alps).	Praeses.	Gallia (Viennensis).	Galliae.
Alpes Cottiae (Regnum Cottii).	Between A.D. 54 and 68	Caesar.	Procurator.	Alpes Cottiae.	Praeses.	Italia.	Italia.
Alpes Poeninae.	Second century.	Caesar.	Procurator.	Alpes Poeninae et Graiae.	Praeses.	Gallia.	Galliae.
Raetia.	B.C. 15	Caesar.	Procurator.	Raetia I., II.	Praesides.	Italia.	Italia.
Noricum.	B.C. 15	Caesar.	Procurator.	Noricum Mediterraneum. Noricum Ripense.	Praeses. Praeses.	Illyricum occidentale (Pannoniae).	Italia.
Pannonia Superior.	A.D. 10	Caesar (consular).	Legatus propraetore.	Pannonia I. Pannonia ripariensis or Savia. Pannonia II. Valeria.	Praeses. Corrector. Consularis. Praeses.	Illyricum occidentale (Pannoniae).	Italia.
Pannonia Inferior.	Divided betw. A.D. 102 and 107						
Illyricum, later Dalmatia.	Between B.C. 167 and 59	B.C. 27 to B.C. 11 Senate. After B.C. 11 Caesar (consular).	Proconsul. Legatus propraetore.	Dalmatia. Praevalitana.	Praeses. Praeses.	Illyricum occ.	Italia.
Moesia Superior.	Between B.C. 29 and A.D. 6	Caesar (consular).	Legatus propraetore.	Moesia I. Dardania. Dacia mediterranea. Dacia ripensis.	Praeses. Praeses. Consularis. Dux.	Dacia (under the direct administration of the praetorian prefect).	Illyricum.
Moesia Inferior (Ripa Thracia).	Divided betw. A.D. 81 and 96			Moesia II. Scythia.	Praeses. Praeses.	Thraciae.	Oriens.
Dacia.	A.D. 107	Caesar (consular).	Legatus propraetore.	Abandoned, A.D. 270–275			
Thracia.	A.D. 46	Caesar.	Procurator (under legatus Moesiae). Under Trajan, a legatus propraetore.	Thracia. Haemimontus. Rhodope. Europa.	Consularis. Praeses. Praeses. Consularis.	Thraciae.	Oriens.
Macedonia.	B.C. 146	Senate (praetorian). A.D. 15 to 44 Caesar.	Proconsul. Legatus propraetore.	Macedonia I. Macedonia II. Thessalia. Epirus nova.	Consularis. Praeses. Praeses. Praeses.	Macedonia.	Illyricum.
Epirus.	Separately organized towards end of first century.	Caesar.	Procurator.	Epirus vetus.	Praeses.	Macedonia.	Illyricum.
Achaia.	B.C. 27	Senate (praetorian).	Proconsul.	Achaia.	Proconsul, who stands directly under the praetorian prefect of Illyricum.		
Asia.	B.C. 133	Senate (consular).	Proconsul.	Asia proconsularis. Hellespontus. Lydia. Phrygia I. (pacatiana). Phrygia II. (salutaris). Caria. Insulae.	Proconsul, who stands directly under the Emperor. Consularis, who stands under the proconsul Asiae. Consularis. Praeses. Praeses. Praeses. Praeses, who stands under the proconsul Asiae.	Asia.	Oriens.

ROMAN PROVINCIAL ORGANIZATION—(*Continued*).

Early Empire (to A.D. 117).				Later Empire (End of Fourth Century).			
	Date of Constitution.	Assigned to— (Ranking as—)	Title of Governor.		Title of Governor.	Diocese.	Praetorian Praefecture.
Bithynia and Pontus.	B.C. 74 B.C. 65	Senate (praetorian).	Proconsul.	Bithynia. Honorias. Paphlagonia. Helenopontus.	Consularis. Praeses. Corrector. Praeses.	Pontus.	Oriens.
Galatia.	B.C. 25 Enlarged B.C. 7	Caesar (praetorian).	Legatus propraetore.	Pontus Polemoniacus. Galatia I. Galatia II. (salutaris). Lycaonia. Pisidia.	Praeses. Consularis. Praeses. Praeses. Praeses.	Pontus. Asia.	Oriens.
Cappadocia.	A.D. 17	Caesar (after A.D. 70 consular).	A.D. 18–70, procurator; afterwards, legatus propraetore.	Cappadocia I., II. Armenia I., II.	Praesides. Praesides.	Pontus.	Oriens.
Pamphylia and Lycia.	B.C. 25 A.D. 43	Caesar (praetorian).	Legatus propraetore.	Pamphylia. Lycia.	Consularis. Praeses.	Asia.	Oriens.
Cilicia.	B.C. 102? Fully organized B.C. 64	Caesar (praetorian).	Legatus propraetore.	Cilicia I. Cilicia II. Isauria.	Consularis. Praeses. Comes.	Oriens.	Oriens.
Cyprus.	B.C. 27	B.C. 27 to B.C. 22 Caesar; afterwards Senate (praetorian).	Proconsul.	Cyprus.	Consularis.	Oriens.	Oriens.
Syria.	B.C. 64	Caesar (consular).	Legatus propraetore.	Euphratensis. Syria I. Syria II. (salutaris). Phœnice I. Phœnice II.	Praeses. Consularis. Praeses. Consularis. Praeses.	Oriens.	Oriens.
Iudaea (Syria Palaestina).	Separately organized A.D. 6.	Caesar (after A.D. 70 praetorian.)	A.D. 6-41, 44-70 procurator; afterwards, legatus propraetore.	Palaestina I. Palaestina II.	Consularis. Praeses.	Oriens.	Oriens.
Arabia.	A.D. 105	Caesar (praetorian).	Legatus propraetore.	Palaestina III. Arabia.	Praeses. Dux.	Oriens.	Oriens.
Armenia.	A.D. 114	Caesar (praetorian).	Legatus propraetore.	Abandoned A.D. 117			
Mesopotamia (abandoned A.D. 117, reconquered......	A.D. 115 A.D. 165)	Caesar. (?)	— ? —	Osrhoëne. Mesopotamia.	Praeses. Praeses.	Oriens.	Oriens.
Assyria.	A.D. 115	Caesar.	— ? —	Abandoned A.D. 117			
Aegyptus.	B.C. 30	Caesar.	Praefectus (with consular rank).	Aegyptus. Augustamnica. Heptanomis (Arcadia). Thebais. Libya inferior.	Praeses. Corrector. Praeses. Praeses. Praeses.	Aegyptus.	Oriens.
Cyrene and Creta.	B.C. 74 B.C. 67 united B.C. 27	Senate (praetorian).	Proconsul.	Libya superior. Creta.	Praeses. Consularis.	Aegyptus. Macedonia.	Oriens. Illyricum.
Africa and Numidia.	B.C. 146 B.C. 46 united B.C. 25	Senate (consular).	Proconsul.	Tripolitana. Byzacena. Africa proconsularis. Numidia.	Praeses. Consularis. Proconsul, who stands directly under the Emperor. Consularis.	Africa.	Italia.
Mauretania Caesariensis.	A.D. 40	Caesar.	Procurator.	Mauretania I. (Sitifensis). Mauretania II. (Caesariensis).	Praeses. Praeses.	Africa.	Italia.
Mauretania Tingitana.	A.D. 40	Caesar.	Procurator.	Tingitana (connected with Baetica).	Praeses.	Hispania.	Galliae.

With the extension of the provincial organization to Italy proper, the following additional provinces were included (about 400) in the *praefectura Italiae:*

I. Under the *vicarius Italiae:* (1) Venetia et Histria, (2) Liguria, (3) Aemilia, (4) Flaminia et Picenum annonarium. II. Under the *vicarius urbis Romae:* (5) Tuscia et Umbria, (6) Picenum suburbicarium, (7) Valeria, (8) Samnium, (9) Campania, (10) Apulia et Calabria, (11) Lucania et Bruttii. Provinces 1–6 and 9 were governed by *consulares;* 10 and 11 by *correctores;* 7 and 8 by *praesides.*

Bibliography.—Marquardt, *Römische Verwaltung,* vol. i.; Person, *Les Provinces Romaines sous la République;* Arnold, *Roman Provincial Administration;* Mommsen, *Roman History,* vols. iii. and v.

Provocatio. The Roman term for the appeal from the verdict of the magistrate to the decision of the people.

Under the kings the court of appeal was the Comitia Curiata; after Servius Tullius, the Comitia Centuriata. While, under the arbitrary rule of the kings, the right of appeal was allowed, on the establishment of the Republic, in B.C. 509, this was imposed on the consuls as a duty, and was repeatedly enjoined by special enactments in all cases where it was a question of life and death, or of corporal punishment. The appeal was only valid within the city, and the Pomerium, but not in the camp. Moreover, no one could appeal against the dictator. When afterwards (B.C. 454), besides the consuls, the tribunes and aediles acquired the right of imposing a fine (*multa,* q. v.), a maximum limit was fixed for it, and if that was exceeded, there was an appeal to the Comitia Tributa.

As this appeal was expected in all legitimate cases, trials of this kind were held immediately before the Comitia concerned with such appeals; and after the verdict had been pronounced by the magistrate presiding, it was either confirmed or reversed by the votes of the people. About B.C. 195 the right of appeal was extended over the whole of Italy and the provinces. After permanent courts for certain offences had been established, the *quaestiones perpetuae* (see Quaestio), the jurisdiction of the people, and with it the appeal thereto, became more and more limited. For the provocatio under the Empire, see Appellatio.

Provocātōres. A class of gladiators whose special characteristics are not clearly defined in

THE EASTERN PROVINCES OF THE ROMAN EMPIRE.

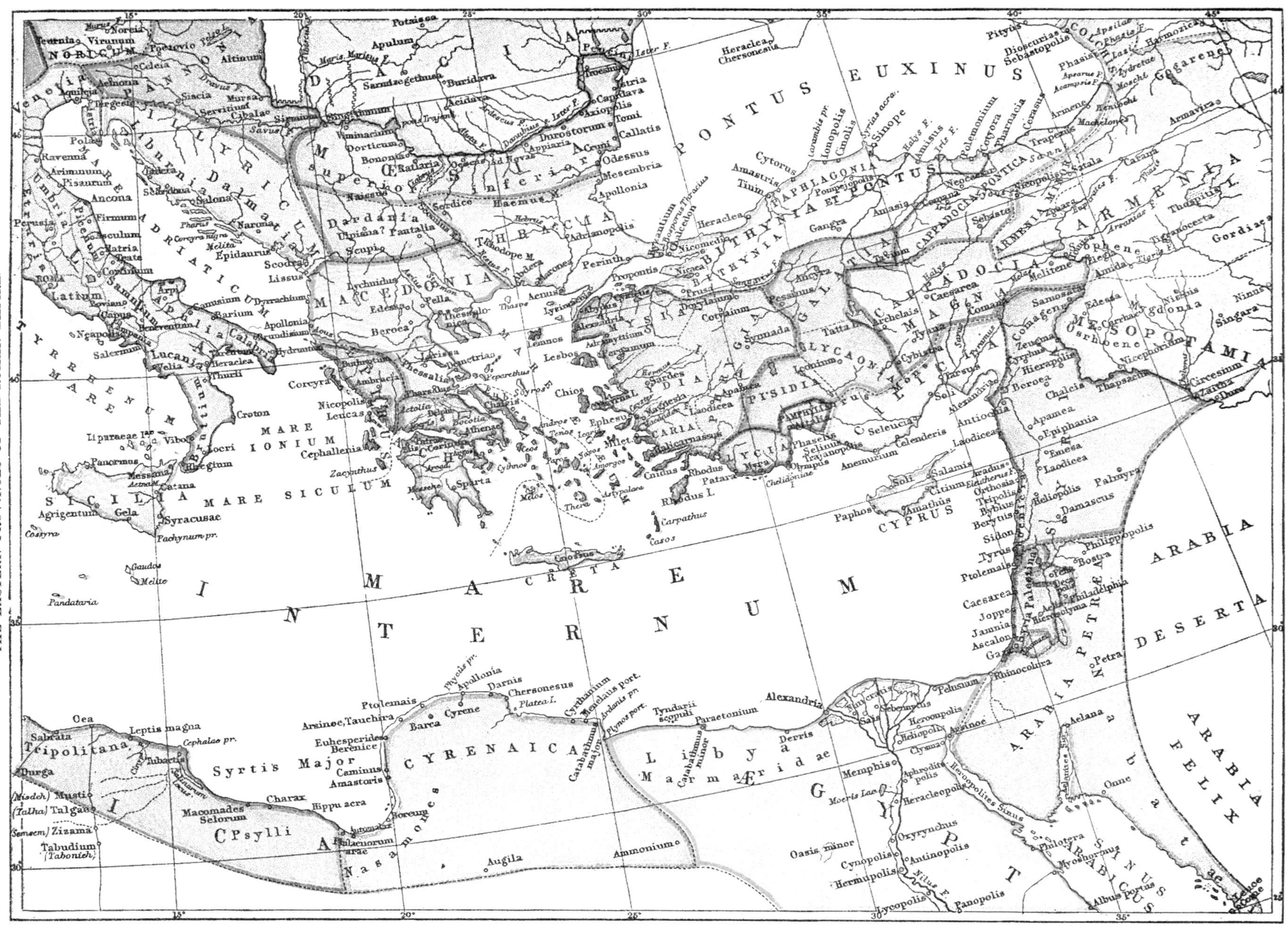

the passages where we find them mentioned (Cic. *Pro Sext.* 64).

Prow. See PRORA.

Proxĕnus (πρόξενος). The Greek term for the representative of a State who was appointed, from the citizens of another State, to attend to the interests of its citizens there resident, as often as they needed legal protection and assistance. In the interests of foreigners, many States appointed such representatives from among their own citizens. Their position may be compared with that of our consuls. The *proxenus* received many distinctions and honours from the State which he represented. To be nominated *proxenus* was in some cases only an honorary distinction, which the State conferred on such foreigners as resided in it as aliens (see METOECI), and were therefore unable to do any service abroad for the citizens of the State in which they resided. This distinction insured many privileges, such as freedom from taxation and from public burdens which otherwise fell on the resident aliens, and, in general, exemption from tolls and taxes; also the right to acquire property in land, free admission to the Senate and to the assemblies of the people, etc. See Monceaux, *Les Proxenies Grecques* (1886).

Proxĕnus (Πρόξενος). A Boeotian, the disciple of Gorgias, and friend of Xenophon. Being connected by the ties of hospitality with the younger Cyrus, the latter engaged him in his service. He was seized by Tissaphernes and put to death with the other Greek generals. It was at the invitation of Proxenus that Xenophon was induced to enter the service of Cyrus (Xen. *Anab.* i. 1, 11).

Prudentius, AURELIUS CLEMENS. The earliest of the Christian poets of any celebrity. He was a native of Spain, and was born A.D. 348. After practising as an advocate, and discharging the duties of a civil and criminal judge in two important cities, he received from the emperor Theodosius, or Honorius, a high military appointment at court; but as he advanced in years he became sensible of the emptiness of worldly honour and earnest in the exercises of religion. His poems are composed in a great variety of metres, and are brilliant in style and in the fervour of their Christian sentiment. The Latinity, for its period, is good; and his metrical skill surpasses that of his pagan contemporaries. The best editions of Prudentius are by Obbarius (Tübingen, 1845) and Dressel (Leipzig, 1860). See Faguet, *De Prudent. Carminibus Lyricis* (Paris, 1883); Rösler, *Der katholische Dichter Prudentius* (Freiburg, 1886); Puech, *Prudence* (Paris, 1888); and the monograph by Lease on the language and style (Baltimore, 1895). There is an English translation of selections from Prudentius by F. St. J. Thackeray, with good introduction and notes (1890).

Prusa or **Prusias** (Προῦσα). (1) P. AD OLYMPUM (ἡ ἐπὶ τῷ Ὀλύμπῳ), now Brusa. A great city of Bithynia, on the northern side of Mount Olympus, fifteen Roman miles from Cius and twenty-five from Nicaea. It was built by Prusias, king of Bithynia, or, according to some, by Hannibal. (2) Some writers distinguish from this a smaller city, called P. AD HYPIUM or HYPPIUM (πρὸς τῷ Ὑππίῳ ποταμῷ) which stood northwest of the former, and was originally called CIĔRUS (Κίερος), and belonged to the territory of Heraclea, but was conquered by Prusias, who named it after himself. It stood northwest of the former. Perhaps it is only another name for Cius.

Prusias (Προυσίας). (1) I. King of Bithynia from about B.C. 228 to 180, though the date neither of his accession nor of his death is exactly known. He was the son of Zielas, whom he succeeded. He appears to have been a monarch of vigour and ability, and raised his kingdom of Bithynia to a much higher pitch of power and prosperity than it had previously attained. It was at his court that Hannibal took refuge; and when the Romans demanded the surrender of the Carthaginian general, the king basely gave his consent, and Hannibal only escaped falling into the hands of his enemies by a voluntary death. (2) II. King of Bithynia, son and successor of the preceding, reigned from about B.C. 180 to 149. He courted assiduously the alliance of the Romans. He carried on war with Attalus, king of Pergamus, with whom, however, he was compelled by the Romans to conclude peace in 154. He was slain in 149 by order of his son Nicomedes, as is related in the life of the latter. (See NICOMEDES II.) Prusias is described to us as a man in whom personal deformity was combined with a character the most vicious and degraded. His passion for the chase is attested by the epithet of the "Huntsman" (Κυνηγός) given to him (Polyb. xxiv. 1).

Prymnēsia or **Prymnēsus** (Πρυμνησία). A city in the north of Phrygia, which appears, from its coins, to have been a chief seat of the worship of Midas as a hero (Ptol. v. 2, 24).

Prytaneia (πρυτανεία). (1) Any public office held by rotation for given periods; e. g. in Herodotus (vi. 110) the chief command for the day, held by each of the ten generals in turn. (2) The period of thirty-five or thirty-six days, i. e. about one-tenth of the year, during which each of the ten *phylae* presided in turn over the Boulé and Ecclesia. The order was determined by lot. The presiding tribe was represented by its *epistates*, who was appointed by lot to preside for the day, and could not hold this office more than once in each year (Aristot. *Athen. Polit.* 44). See BOULÉ.

Prytanēum (πρυτανεῖον). In many Greek towns, a public building consecrated to Hestia (q. v.), and containing the State hearth. At Athens, it was here that the State offered hospitable entertainment as a public compliment to foreign ambassadors, to Athenian envoys on their return from the successful discharge of their mission, also to citizens who had done good service to the State, especially to distinguished generals, and victors in the great Panhellenic Games, and sometimes even to their descendants. In the case of those who were Athenian citizens, this privilege was usually granted for life.

Prytănis (πρύτανις, "a president"). The name in various Greek free States for the highest officials. In many States, especially in early times, one, two, or five *prytaneis* ruled with almost kingly power. At Athens *prytanis* was the name for the member of a body of officials who presided over that body when it had any public business to transact. This title was also given to the presidents of the *naucrariae* and Senate (who, with their *epistates* at their head, presided over the Senate and Assembly during the fifth century B.C.). In the fourth century the presidential duties were transferred to the *proedri* and their *epistates*. See Aristot. *Athen. Polit.* 44, ed. Kenyon; and the articles BOULÉ; ECCLESIA; NAUCRARIA.

Psalterium (ψαλτήριον). A stringed instrument, something between the *cithara* and the *harpa* (Verg. *Ciris*, 179).

Psalteria. (1) From a painting at Thebes. (2) From an original in the British Museum.

Psaltria (ψάλτρια). A music-girl (Livy, xxxix. 6).

Psammenĭtus (Ψαμμήνιτος). Psamthek III., the last king of Egypt and a member of the Saïtic dynasty, the twenty-sixth of the royal lines that ruled in this country. Iulius Africanus calls him PSAMMECHERĪTES. He was the son and successor of Amasis, and ascended the throne at the very moment that Cambyses was marching against Egypt to dethrone the father. Psammenitus met Cambyses on the frontiers, near the Pelusiac branch of the Nile, with all his forces—Egyptians, Greeks, and Carians—but was totally defeated in a bloody battle. Shutting himself up in Memphis, he was besieged here by Cambyses, and, according to Ctesias, was finally betrayed and taken prisoner. All Egypt thereupon fell under the Persian power, and the reign of Psammenitus ended after a duration of only six months. The greatest outrages were heaped upon the unfortunate monarch and his family; but the firmness with which he endured them all touched at last even the ferocious Cambyses with compassion. Psammenitus was thereupon retained at court, treated with honour, and finally sent to Susa along with 6000 Egyptian captives. Having been accused, however, subsequently, of attempting to stir up a revolt, he was compelled to drink bull's blood, and ended his days (Herod. iii. 10 foll.).

Psammetĭchus (Ψαμμήτιχος). (1) The first king of Egypt who opened that country to strangers, and induced the Greeks to come and settle in it. He was the fourth in the Saïtic dynasty, and the son of Necos or Nechao, who had been put to death by the Aethiopians, at that time masters of Egypt. Psammetichus, being quite young at the time of his father's death, had been carried into Syria to avoid a similar fate, and, after the retreat of the conquerors, was recalled to his native country by the inhabitants of the Saïtic nome. It would seem that the Aethiopians, on their departure, had left Egypt a prey to trouble and dissension, and that the early princes of the Saïtic dynasty, also, had never enjoyed supreme control over the whole kingdom. When Psammetichus, therefore, ascended the throne, he was obliged to share his power with eleven other monarchs, and Egypt was thus divided into twelve independent sovereignties. This form of government was like what the Greeks called a "dyodecarchy" (δυοδεκαρχία). The twelve kings regulated in common, in a general council, all that related to the affairs of the kingdom considered as a whole. This state of things lasted for fifteen years, when it met with a singular termination. An oracle had declared that the whole kingdom would fall to the lot of that one of the twelve monarchs who should one day offer a libation with a brazen cup. It happened, then, one day, that the kings were all sacrificing in common in the temple of Hephaestus at Memphis, and that the high priest, who distributed the golden cups for libations, had brought with him, by some accident, only eleven. When it came, therefore, to the turn of Psammetichus, who was the last in order to pour out a libation, he unthinkingly employed for this purpose his brazen helmet. This incident occasioned great disquiet to his colleagues, who thought they saw in it the fulfilment of the oracle. Being unable, however, with any appearance of justice, to punish an unpremeditated act, they contented themselves with banishing him to his own kingdom, which lay on the coast, and with forbidding him to take any part thereafter in the general affairs of the country. Psammetichus, however, retaliated upon them by calling to his aid some Greek mercenaries who had landed on the Egyptian shore, and eventually conquered all his colleagues, and made himself master of the whole of Egypt (B.C. 652). The monarch now recompensed his Greek allies not only by paying them the sums of money which he had promised, but also in assigning them lands on the Syrian frontier, where they formed, in fact, a military colony. Psammetichus showed a great partiality for the Greeks on all occasions; and, in a Syrian expedition, gave them the place of honour on the right, while he assigned the left to the Egyptians. The discontent of the national troops was so great at this that a large number of the military caste, amounting, it is said, to 240,000 men, left Egypt and retired to Aethiopia. So strong was the preference of Psammetichus for everything Greek that he caused a number of children to be trained up after the Grecian manner, and with these he formed the body of interpreters, whom Herodotus found in his day existing in Egypt. Psammetichus also embellished his capital with several beautiful structures, and, among others, with the southern propylaea of the great temple of Hephaestus. He carried on a long war in Syria, and his forces are said to have remained twenty-nine years before the city of Azotus. It was during this period, probably, that he arrested by presents the victorious career of the Scythians, who had overrun Asia Minor, and were advancing upon Palestine and Egypt (B.C. 626). Psammetichus died after a reign of fifty-four years, leaving the crown to his son Necos.

Herodotus relates a curious story of Psammetichus, who, it seems, was desirous of ascertaining what nation was the most ancient in the world; or, in other words, what was the primitive language of men. In order to discover this, he took two newly born children, and, having caused them to be placed in a lonely hut, directed a shepherd to nourish them with the milk of goats, which animals were sent in to them at stated times, and to take care himself never to utter a word in their hearing. The object was to ascertain what words they would first utter of themselves. At length, on one occasion, when the shepherd went in to them as usual, both the children, running up to him, called out *bekos*. Psammetichus, on being informed of the circumstance, made inquiries about the word, and found that it was the Phrygian term for bread. He therefore concluded that the Phrygians were the most ancient of men (Herod. ii. 151 foll.).

(2) A descendant of the preceding, who came to the throne about B.C. 400, as a kind of subject-king to Persia.

Pselcis (Ψελκίς). A city in upper Aethopia (Dio Cass. liv. 5).

Psellus (Ψέλλος). (1) MICHAEL, a native of Andros in the ninth century A.D. He was probably the author of some of the works which are ascribed to the younger Psellus. (2) MICHAEL CONSTANTIUS, the younger, a far more celebrated person, flourished in the eleventh century of our era. He was born at Constantinople 1020, and lived at least till 1105. He taught philosophy, rhetoric, and dialectics at Constantinople, where he stood forth as almost the last upholder of the falling cause of learning. The emperors honoured him with the title of Prince of the Philosophers. His works are both in prose and poetry, on a vast variety of subjects, and distinguished by an eloquence and taste which are worthy of a better period. They are too numerous to be mentioned here. Edited by Migne (Paris, 1863).

Psephisma (ψήφισμα). The Greek, and especially the Athenian, term for a resolution of the people arrived at by voting. See BOULÉ; ECCLESIA.

Psephus (ψῆφος). A pebble or stone ball used by the Athenian dicasts in giving a verdict. Hence ψηφίζεσθαι is the regular term for voting, etc. See DICASTES.

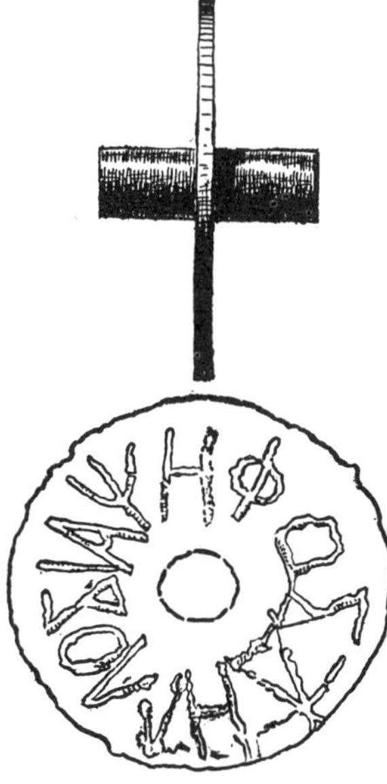
Greek Psephus. (Vischer.)

Pseudengrăphes Graphé (ψευδεγγραφῆς γραφή). An action to punish the false entry upon the official register at Athens of an item in reference to the existence or the collection of a debt. See Platner, *Klagen und Process*, ii. 117 foll.

Pseudisodŏmum (ψευδισόδομον). An early style of masonry used by the Greeks, in which the stones were regularly laid but were not of the same size (Vitruv. ii. 8, 6; Pliny, *N. H.* xxxvi. 51). (See ISODOMUS.) An example is found in the wall of the Lion Gate at Mycenae, for an illustration of which see MYCENAE.

Pseudodiptĕros (ψευδοδίπτερος, "falsely dipteral"). An epithet describing a temple which is surrounded on all four sides by only a single row of columns, placed at intervals which correspond to the position of the outer row of columns in a dipteral temple. See TEMPLUM.

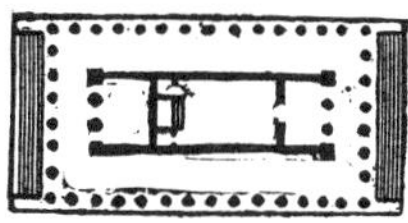
Pseudodipteral Arrangement.

Pseudoperiptĕros (ψευδοπερίπτερος, "falsely peripteral"). An epithet of a temple in which the side columns were "engaged" in the wall of the *cella*, instead of standing out at a distance from it. See TEMPLUM.

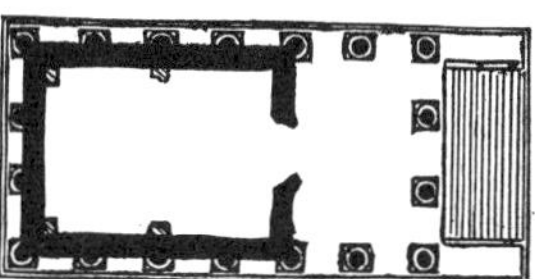
Pseudoperipteral Arrangement.

Pseudothȳrum (ψευδόθυρον). A secret door (Ammian. xiv. 1).

Pseudo-urbāna (sc. *aedificia*). The portions of a farm-house (*villa*) reserved for the owner and his family, separate from the tenements of the overseers and labourers (Vitruv. vi. 5, 3). In the case of a rich land-owner these portions would be as elegant as a house in town. See VILLA.

Psilōthrum (ψίλωθρον). A depilatory made from arsenic and lime, and used for removing hair from the surface of the skin (Mart. iii. 74).

Psophis (Ψωφίς). A town in the northwest of Arcadia, on the river Erymanthus, is said to have been originally called PHEGIA (Pausan. viii. 24, 2). It sided with the Aetolians against the Achaeans, but was taken B.C. 219 by Philip, king of Macedonia, who was then in alliance with the Achaeans.

Psychē (Ψυχή), "the soul," occurs, in the later times of antiquity, as a personification of the human soul. Psyché was the youngest of the three daughters of a king, and excited by her beauty the jealousy and envy of Venus. In order to avenge herself, the goddess ordered Cupid or Eros to inspire Psyché with a love for the most contemptible of all men; but Cupid was so stricken with her beauty that he himself fell in love with her. He accordingly conveyed her to a charming spot, where, unseen and unknown, he visited her every night, and left her as soon as the day began to dawn. Psyché might have continued to enjoy this state of happiness if she had attended to the advice of her lover, who told her never to give way to her curiosity, or to inquire who he was. But her jealous sisters made her believe that in the darkness of night she was embracing some hideous monster, and accordingly once, while Cupid was asleep, she drew near to him with a lamp, and, to her amazement, beheld the most handsome and lovely of the gods. In her excitement of joy and fear, a drop of hot oil fell from her lamp upon his shoulder. This awoke Cupid, who censured her for her mistrust, and escaped. Psyché's happiness was now gone, and after attempting in vain to throw herself into a river, she wandered about from temple to temple, inquiring after her lover, and at length came to the palace of Venus. There her real sufferings began, for Venus retained her, treated her as a slave, and imposed upon her the hardest and most humiliating labours. Psyché would have perished under the weight of her sufferings, had not Cupid, who still loved her in secret, invisibly comforted and assisted her in her toils. With his aid she at last succeeded in overcoming the jealousy and hatred of Venus: she became immortal, and was united to him forever. Many have tried to see in this lovely story an idea of which it is said to be the mythical embodiment; that Psyché is the human soul, which is purified by passions and misfortunes, and is thus prepared for the enjoyment of true and pure happiness. The story, however, is only a variation of an Indo-European folk-tale found among many peoples. See Zingow, *Psyche und Eros* (1881). It forms an episode in the *Metamorphoses* of Apuleius (iv. 28–vi. 24), and is borrowed by him from a Greek original. This episode is separately edited by Jahn and Michaelis (3d ed. Leipzig, 1883). See Jahn in his *Populäre Aufsätze* (Bonn, 1868); and the article APULEIUS. In works of art Psyche is represented as a maiden with the wings of a butterfly, along with Cupid in the different situations described in the allegory.

Psychomanteion (ψυχομαντεῖον). A Greek term for an oracle of the dead. See ORACULA.

Psychopompos (Ψυχοπομπός). "The guider of souls"; another name for Hermes (q. v.).

Psycter (ψυκτήρ). A vessel for cooling wine or water. It was of various shapes, but probably in general resembled the *calathus*. (See CALATHUS.) The name might be given to any vessel in which wine was cooled, even when the process was merely putting in snow, but the contrivance especially so called consisted of a smaller vessel placed within a larger one. Sometimes the wine or water to be iced was placed in the smaller and plunged into the larger vessel which contained snow; sometimes the snow was placed in the smaller vessel and let down into the larger vase of wine. When the wine was sufficiently iced, the smaller vessel was no doubt removed, and the wine ladled out with a *cyathus* (Athen. xi. 503): we have no reason to suppose that a tap was used, as seems to have been sometimes the case in the *Authepsa* for hot drinks. See AUTHEPSA.

Iced water, the *gelida* of Juv. v. 63 (*frigida*, Tac. *Ann.* xiii. 16), which, like the *calida*, was handed round to mix with the wine, or was used as a drink by itself (Athen. iii. p. 121 e, 122 f), was prepared in a ψυκτήρ as above described (in Mart. xiv. 116, *lagona nivaria*), and a special term *decocta* belongs to it, because it was boiled first in order that it might more readily be iced afterwards (Juv. v. 50, with Mayor's note). Pliny says that this *decocta* was an invention of Nero's (cf. Suet. *Ner.* 48), and that the water, which had sometime previously been boiled, was placed in a glass vessel and so plunged into a larger vessel of snow, that it might escape any impurities (*vitia*) of the snow.

The snow for this purpose, or for use in the *colus* or *saccus nivarius*, was kept through the summer in pits covered over with chaff and woollen cloths (Plut. *Symp.* vi. 6). Another method of Antiochus, whereby ὑδρίαι κεράμεαι were placed on straw on the top of the house at night, seems to have been the method of freezing by evaporation which is common in Persia at the present time. See Ussing in *Annal. d. Inst.* (1849); Beckmann, *Hist. of Inventions*, iii. 322; Becker-Göll, *Charikles*, ii. 346; *Gallus*, iii. 430; Marquardt, *Privatleben*, 333.

Psylli (Ψύλλοι). A Libyan people, the earliest known inhabitants of the district of North Africa called Cyrenaïca. Pliny (*H. N.* vii. 2, 13) speaks of them as able to heal wounds caused by serpents. Persons of this race are said to have been brought to the bedside of Cleopatra after she had been bitten by the asp (Suet. *Aug.* 17, with Peck's notes).

Psyttalēa (Ψυττάλεια). An island near Salamis (q. v.).

Pteleum (Πτελεόν). (1) An ancient seaport town of Thessaly in the district Phthiotis, at the southwestern extremity of the Sinus Pagasaeus, was destroyed by the Romans. (2) A town in Elis Triphylia, said to have been a colony from the preceding. (3) A fortress of Ionia, on the coast of Asia Minor, belonging to Erythrae.

Pterōma (πτέρωμα) and **Pteron** (πτερόν). An architectural term denoting a colonnade on the flank of a temple and projecting like a wing, whence the name (Pliny, *H. N.* xxxvi. 4, 9).

Ptolemaeus (Πτολεμαῖος), usually called **Ptolemy.** I. MINOR HISTORICAL PERSONS.—(1) The nephew of Antigonus, king of Asia. He carried on war in Greece on behalf of Antigonus, but in B.C. 310 he abandoned the cause of his uncle, and concluded a treaty with Cassander and Ptolemy the son of Lagus. He soon gave offence to the Egyptian king, and was, in consequence, compelled to put an end to his life by poison, B.C. 309. (2) The son of Lysimachus, king of Thrace. He was the eldest of the three sons of that monarch by his last wife Arsinoë, and the only one who escaped falling into the hands of Ptolemy Ceraunus. (3) The son of Pyrrhus, king of Epirus, by his wife Antigoné, the step-daughter of Ptolemy Lagi. When only fifteen years of age he was left by his father in charge of his hereditary dominions, when Pyrrhus himself set out on his expedition to Italy, 280. At a later time he fought under his father in Greece, and was slain in the course of Pyrrhus's campaign in the Peloponnesus, 272. (4) Surnamed PHILADELPHUS, son of M. Antony, the triumvir, by Cleopatra. After the death of Antony, B.C. 30, his life was spared by Augustus at the intercession of Iuba and Cleopatra, and he was brought up by Octavia with her own children.

II. KINGS OF EGYPT.—(1) Surnamed SOTER, the Preserver, but more commonly known as the son of Lagus, reigned B.C. 323–285. His father Lagus was a Macedonian of ignoble birth, but his mother Arsinoë had been a concubine of Philip of Macedon, on which account it seems to have been generally believed that Ptolemy was in reality the offspring of that monarch. Ptolemy is mentioned among the friends of the young Alexander before the death of Philip. He accompanied Alexander throughout his campaigns in Asia, and was always treated by the king with the greatest favour. On the division of the Empire which followed Alex-

Coin of Ptolemy Soter.

ander's death (323), Ptolemy obtained the government of Egypt. In 321 his dominions were invaded by Perdiccas, the regent; but the assassination of Perdiccas by his mutinous soldiers soon delivered Ptolemy from this danger. In the following year Ptolemy enlarged his dominions by seizing upon the important satrapy of Phœnicia and Coele-Syria. It was probably during this expedition that he made himself master of Jerusalem by attacking the city on the Sabbath. A few years afterwards (316) Ptolemy entered into an alliance with Cassander and Lysimachus against Antigonus, whose growing power had excited their common apprehensions. In the war which followed, Antigonus conquered Coele-Syria and Phœnicia (315–314); but Ptolemy recovered these provinces by the defeat of Demetrius, the son of Antigonus, in 312. In 311 hostilities were suspended by a general peace. This peace, however, was of short duration, and Ptolemy appears to have been the first to recommence the war. He crossed over to Greece, where he announced himself as the liberator of the Greeks, but effected little. In 306 Ptolemy was defeated by Demetrius in a great sea-fight off Salamis in Cyprus. In consequence of this defeat, Ptolemy lost the important island of Cyprus, which had previously been subject to him. Antigonus was so much elated by this victory as to assume the title of king, an example which Ptolemy, notwithstanding his defeat, immediately followed. Antigonus and Demetrius followed up their success by the invasion of Egypt, but were compelled to return to Syria without effecting anything. Next year (305) Ptolemy rendered the most important assistance to the Rhodians, who were besieged by Demetrius; and when Demetrius was at length compelled to raise the siege (304), the Rhodians paid divine honours to the Egyptian monarch as their saviour and preserver (Σωτήρ), a title which appears to have been now bestowed upon Ptolemy for the first time. Ptolemy took comparatively little part in the contest, which led to the decisive battle of Ipsus, in which Antigonus was defeated and slain (301). The latter years of Ptolemy's reign appear to have been devoted almost entirely to the arts of peace, and to promoting the internal prosperity of his dominions. In 285 Ptolemy abdicated in favour of his youngest son Ptolemy Philadelphus, the child of his latest and most beloved wife, Berenicé, excluding from the throne his two eldest sons Ptolemy Ceraunus and Meleager, the offspring of Eurydicé. The elder Ptolemy survived this event two years, and died in 283. His reign is variously estimated at thirty-eight or forty years, according as we include or not these two years which followed his abdication.

The character of Ptolemy has been generally represented in a very favourable light by historians, and there is no doubt that if we compare him with his contemporaries and rivals he appears to deserve the praises bestowed upon his mildness and moderation. But it is only with this important qualification that they can be admitted: for there are many evidences that he did not shrink from any measure that he deemed requisite in order to carry out the objects of his ambition. Yet as a ruler Ptolemy certainly deserves the highest praise. By his able and vigorous administration he laid the foundations of the wealth and prosperity which Egypt enjoyed for a long period. Under his fostering care Alexandria quickly rose to the place designed for it by its founder —that of the greatest commercial city of the world. Not less eminent were the services rendered by Ptolemy in the advancement of literature and science. In this department, indeed, it is not always easy to distinguish the portion of credit due to the father from that of his son: but it seems certain that to the elder monarch belongs the merit of having originated those literary institutions which assumed a more definite and regular form, as well as a more prominent place, under his successor. Such appears to have been the case with the two most celebrated of all—the Library and the Museum of Alexandria. The first suggestion of these important foundations is ascribed by some writers to Demetrius of Phalerus, who spent all the latter years of his life at the court of Ptolemy. But many other men of literary eminence were also gathered around the Egyptian king, among whom may be especially noticed the great geometrician Euclid, the philosophers Stilpo of Megara, Theodorus of Cyrené, and Diodorus surnamed Cronus, as well as the elegiac poet Philetas of Cos, and the grammarian Zenodotus. To the last two we are told Ptolemy confided the literary education of his son Philadelphus. Many anecdotes sufficiently attest the free intercourse which subsisted between the king and the men of letters by whom he was surrounded, and prove that the easy familiarity of his manners corresponded with his simple and unostentatious habits of life. We also find him maintaining a correspondence with Menander, whom he in vain endeavoured to attract to his court, and sending overtures probably of a similiar nature to Theophrastus. (See ALEXANDRIAN SCHOOL; BIBLIOTHECA.) Nor were the fine arts neglected: the rival painters Antiphilus and Apelles both exercised their talents at Alexandria, where some of their most celebrated pictures were produced. See Mahaffy, *The Empire of the Ptolemies* (1896).

Ptolemy was himself an author: he composed a history of the wars of Alexander, which is frequently cited by later writers, and is one of the chief authorities which Arrian made the groundwork of his own history.

(2) PHILADELPHUS (B.C. 285–247), the son of Ptolemy I. by his wife Berenicé, was born in the island of Cos, 309. His long reign was marked by few events of a striking character. He was engaged in war with his half-brother Magas, who had governed Cyrené as viceroy under Ptolemy Soter, but on the death of that monarch not only asserted his independence, but even attempted to invade Egypt. Magas was supported by Antiochus II., king of Syria; and the war was at length terminated by a treaty, which left Magas in undisputed possession of the Cyrenaïca, while his infant daughter Berenicé was betrothed to Ptolemy, the son of Philadelphus. Ptolemy also concluded a treaty with the Romans. He was frequently engaged in hostilities with Syria, which were terminated towards the close of his reign by a treaty of peace, by which Ptolemy gave his daughter Berenicé in marriage to Antiochus II. Ptolemy's chief care, however, was directed to the internal administration of his kingdom, and to the patronage of literature and science. The institutions of which the foundations had been laid by his father quickly rose un-

der his fostering care to the highest prosperity. The Museum of Alexandria became the resort and abode of all the most distinguished men of letters of the day, and in the library attached to it were accumulated all the treasures of ancient learning. Among the other illustrious names which adorned the reign of Ptolemy may be mentioned those of the poets Philetas and Theocritus, the philosophers Hegesias and Theodorus, the mathematician Euclid, and the astronomers Timocharis, Aristarchus of Samos, and Aratus. Nor was his patronage confined to the ordinary cycle of Hellenic literature. By his interest in natural history he gave a stimulus to the pursuit of that science, which gave birth to many important works, while he himself formed collections of rare animals within the precincts of the royal palace. It was during his reign also, and perhaps at his desire, that Manetho gave to the world in a Greek form the historical records of the Egyptians; and according to a well-known tradition it was by his express command that the Holy Scriptures of the Jews were translated into Greek. The new cities or colonies founded by Philadelphus in different parts of his dominions were extremely numerous. On the Red Sea alone we find at least two bearing the name of Arsinoë, one called after another of his sisters Philotera, and two cities named in honour of his mother Berenicé. The same names occur also in Cilicia and Syria: and in the latter country he founded the important fortress of Ptolemaïs in Palestine. All authorities concur in attesting the great power and wealth to which the Egyptian monarchy was raised under Philadelphus. He possessed at the close of his reign a standing army of 200,000 foot and 40,000 horse, besides war-chariots and elephants, a fleet of 1500 ships, and a sum of 740,000 talents in his treasury; while he derived from Egypt alone an annual revenue of 14,800 talents. His dominions comprised, besides Egypt itself, and portions of Aethiopia, Arabia, and Libya, the important provinces of Phœnicia and Coele-Syria, together with Cyprus, Lycia, Caria, and the Cyclades, and during a great part at least of his reign Cilicia and Pamphylia also. Before his death Cyrené was reunited to the monarchy by the marriage of his son Ptolemy with Berenicé, the daughter of Magas. The private life and relations of Philadelphus do not exhibit his character in as favourable a light as we might have inferred from the splendour of his administration. He put to death two of his brothers; and he banished his first wife Arsinoë, the daughter of Lysimachus, to Coptos in Upper Egypt on a charge of conspiracy. After her removal Ptolemy married his own sister Arsinoë, the widow of Lysimachus, a flagrant violation of the religious notions of the Greeks, but one which was frequently imitated by his successors. He evinced his affection for Arsinoë not only by bestowing her name upon many of his newly-founded colonies, but by assuming himself the surname of Philadelphus, a title which some writers referred in derision to his unnatural treatment of his two brothers. By this second marriage Ptolemy had no issue: but his first wife had borne him two sons—Ptolemy, who succeeded him on the throne, and Lysimachus; and a daughter, Berenicé, whose marriage to Antiochus II., king of Syria, has been already mentioned.

(3) Euergĕtes (B.C. 247–222), eldest son and successor of Philadelphus. Shortly after his accession he invaded Syria, in order to avenge the death of his sister Berenicé. (See Berenicé, No. 2.) He met with the most striking success. He advanced as far as Babylon and Susa, and after reducing Mesopotamia, Babylonia, and Susiana, received the submission of all the upper provinces of Asia as far as the confines of Bactria and India. From this career of conquest he was recalled by the news of seditions in Egypt, and returned to that country, carrying with him an immense booty, comprising, among other objects, all the statues of the Egyptian deities which had been carried off by Cambyses to Babylon or Persia. These he restored to their respective temples, an act by which he earned the greatest popularity with his native Egyptian subjects, who bestowed on him in consequence the title of Εὐεργέτης ("Benefactor"), by which he is generally known. While the arms of the king himself were thus successful in the East, his fleets reduced the maritime provinces of Asia, including Cilicia, Pamphylia, and Ionia, as far as the Hellespont, together with Lysimachia and other important places on the coast of Thrace which continued for a long period subject to the Egyptian rule. Concerning the events

Coin of Ptolemy Euergetes.

which followed the return of Euergetes to his own dominions (probably in 243) we are almost wholly in the dark; but it appears that the greater part of the eastern provinces speedily fell again into the hands of Seleucus, while Ptolemy retained possession of the maritime regions and a great part of Syria itself. He soon obtained a valuable ally in the person of Antiochus Hierax, the younger brother of Seleucus, whom he supported in his wars against his elder brother. We find Euergetes maintaining the same friendly relations as his father with Rome. During the latter years of his reign he subdued the Aethiopian tribes on his southern frontier, and advanced as far as Adule, a port on the Red Sea, where he established an emporium, and set up an inscription commemorating the exploits of his reign. To a copy of this, accidentally preserved to us by an Egyptian monk, Cosmas Indicopleustes, we are indebted for much of the scanty information we possess concerning his reign.

Ptolemy Euergetes is scarcely less celebrated than his father for his patronage of literature and science: he added so largely to the library at Alexandria that he has been sometimes erroneously deemed its founder. Eratosthenes, Apollonius Rhodius, and Aristophanes the grammarian flourished at Alexandria during his reign—sufficient to prove that the literature and learning of the Alexandrian school still retained their former eminence. By his wife Berenicé, who survived him, Euergetes left three children: (*a*) Ptolemy, his successor; (*b*) Magas; and (*c*) Arsinoë, afterwards married to her brother Ptolemy Philopator.

(4) PHILOPĂTOR (B.C. 222–205), eldest son and successor of Euergetes. He was very far from inheriting the virtues or abilities of his father, and his reign was the commencement of the decline of the Egyptian kingdom, which had been raised to such a height of power and prosperity by his three predecessors. Its beginning was stained with crimes of the darkest kind. He put to death his mother, Berenicé, and his brother, Magas, and his uncle Lysimachus, the brother of Euergetes. He then gave himself up without restraint to a life of indolence and luxury, while he abandoned to his minister Sosibius the care of all political affairs. The latter seems to have been as incapable as his master, and the kingdom was allowed to fall into a state of the utmost disorder, of which Antiochus the Great, king of Syria, was not slow to avail himself. In the first two campaigns (219, 218), Antiochus conquered the greater part of Coele-Syria and Palestine, but in the third year of the war (217), he was completely defeated by Ptolemy in person at the decisive battle of Raphia, and was glad to conclude a peace with the Egyptian monarch. On his return from his Syrian expedition, Ptolemy gave himself up more and more to every species of vice and debauchery. His mistress Agathoclea, and her brother Agathocles, divided with Sosibius the patronage and distribution of all places of honour or profit. Towards the close of his reign Ptolemy put to death his wife Arsinoë.

Coin of Ptolemy IV. Philopator.

His debaucheries shortened his life. He died in 205, leaving only one son, a child of five years old. We find Ptolemy following up the policy of his predecessors by cultivating the friendship of the Romans, to whom he furnished large supplies of corn during their struggle with Carthage. Plunged as he was in vice and debauchery, Philopator appears to have still inherited something of the love of letters for which his predecessors were so conspicuous. We find him associating on familiar terms with philosophers and men of letters, and especially patronizing the distinguished grammarian Aristarchus.

(5) EPIPHĂNES (B.C. 205–181), son and successor of Ptolemy IV. He was a child of five years old at the death of his father, 205. Philip, king of Macedonia, and Antiochus III. of Syria determined to take advantage of the minority of Ptolemy, and entered into a league to divide his dominions between them. In pursuance of this arrangement, Antiochus conquered Coele-Syria, while Philip reduced the Cyclades and the cities in Thrace which had still remained subject to Egypt. In this emergency the Egyptian ministers had recourse to the powerful intervention of the Romans, who commanded both monarchs to refrain from further hostilities, and restore all the conquered cities. In order to evade this demand without openly opposing the power of Rome, Antiochus concluded a treaty with Egypt, by which it was agreed that the young king should marry Cleopatra, the daughter of Antiochus, and receive back the Syrian provinces as her dower. This treaty took place in 199, but the marriage was not actually solemnized until six years after. The administration of Egypt was placed in the hands of Aristomenes, a man who was every way worthy of the charge. As early, however, as 196, the young king was declared of full age, and the ceremony of his anacleteria, or coronation, was solemnized with great magnificence. It was on this occasion that the decree was issued that has been preserved to us in the celebrated inscription known as the Rosetta Stone (q.v.). a monument of great interest in regard to the internal history of Egypt under the Ptolemies, independent of its importance as having afforded the key to the discovery of hieroglyphics. In 193 the marriage of Ptolemy with the Syrian princess Cleopatra was solemnized at Raphia. Ptolemy, however, refused to assist his father-in-law in the war against the Romans, which was at this time on the eve of breaking out, and he continued steadfast in his alliance with Rome. But he derived no advantage from the treaty which concluded it, and Antiochus still retained possession of Coele-Syria and Phœnicia. As long as Ptolemy continued under the guidance and influence of Aristomenes, his administration was equitable and popular. Gradually, however, he became estranged from his able and virtuous minister, and threw himself more and more into the power of flatterers and vicious companions, until at length he was induced to rid himself of Aristomenes, who was compelled to take poison. Towards the close of his reign Ptolemy conceived the project of recovering Coele-Syria from Seleucus, the successor of Antiochus, and had assembled a large mercenary force for that purpose; but having, by an unguarded expression, excited the apprehensions of some of his friends, he was cut off by poison in the twenty-fourth year of his reign and the twenty-ninth of his age (181). He left two sons, both named Ptolemy, who subsequently ascended the throne, under the names of Ptolemy Philometor and Euergetes II., and a daughter who bore her mother's name of Cleopatra. His reign was marked by the rapid decline of the Egyptian monarchy, for the provinces and cities wrested from it during his minority by Antiochus and Philip were never recovered, and at his death Cyprus and the Cyrenaïca were almost the only foreign possessions still attached to the crown of Egypt.

(6) PHILOMĒTOR (B.C. 181–146), eldest son and successor of Ptolemy V. He was a child at the death of his father in 181, and the regency was assumed during his minority by his mother Cleopatra, who, by her able administration, maintained the kingdom in a state of tranquillity. But after her death in 173, the chief power fell into the hands of Eulaeus and Lenaeus, ministers as corrupt as they were incapable, who had the rashness to engage in war with Antiochus Epiphanes, king of Syria, in the vain hope of recovering the provinces of Coele-Syria and Phœnicia. But their army was totally defeated by Antiochus near Pelusium, and Antiochus was able to advance without opposition as far as Memphis, 170. The young king himself fell into his hands, but was treated with kindness and distinction, as Antiochus hoped by his means to make himself the master of Egypt. On learning the captivity of his brother, the young

Ptolemy, who was then at Alexandria with his sister Cleopatra, assumed the title of king, under the name of Euergetes II., and prepared to defend the capital to the utmost. Antiochus hereupon laid siege to Alexandria, but he was unable to take the city, and withdrew into Syria, after establishing Philometor as king at Memphis, but retaining in his hands the frontier fortress of Pelusium. This last circumstance, together with the ravages committed by the Syrian troops, awakened Philometor, who had hitherto been a mere puppet in the hands of the Syrian king, to a sense of his true position, and he hastened to make overtures of peace to his brother and sister at Alexandria. It was agreed that the two brothers should reign together, and that Philometor should marry his sister Cleopatra. But this arrangement did not suit the views of Antiochus, who immediately renewed hostilities. The two brothers were unable to offer any effectual opposition, and he had advanced a second time to the walls of Alexandria, when he was met by a Roman embassy, headed by M. Popilius Laenas, who haughtily commanded him instantly to desist from hostilities. Antiochus did not venture to disobey, and withdrew to his own dominions in 168. Dissensions broke out between the brothers, and Euergetes expelled Philometor from Alexandria. Philometor repaired to Rome, and by the influence of the Roman Senate was reinstated in the sovereign power, Euergetes, however, receiving the territory of Cyrenē as a separate kingdom. To Cyprus also he soon laid claim, and war broke out once more, ending in the defeat of Euergetes, who from that time remained content with Cyrenē as a kingdom. The attention of Philometor appears to have been, from this time, principally directed to the side of Syria. Demetrius Soter having sought during the dissensions between the two brothers to make himself master of Cyprus, Ptolemy now supported the usurper Alexander Balas, to whom he gave his daughter Cleopatra in marriage (150). But when Ptolemy advanced with an army to the assistance of his son-in-law, Ammonius, the favourite and minister of Alexander, formed a plot against the life of Ptolemy; whereupon the latter took away his daughter Cleopatra from her faithless husband, and bestowed her hand on Demetrius Nicator, the son of Soter, whose cause he now espoused. In conjunction with Demetrius, Ptolemy carried on war against Alexander, whom he defeated in a decisive battle; but he died a few days afterwards in consequence of an injury which he had received from a fall from his horse in this battle (146). He had reigned thirty-five years from the period of his first accession, and eighteen from his restoration by the Romans. Philometor is praised for the mildness and humanity of his disposition. Polybius even tells us that not a single citizen of Alexandria was put to death by him for any political or private offence. On the whole, if not one of the greatest, he was at least one of the best of the race of the Ptolemies. He left three children: (*a*) A son, Ptolemy, who was proclaimed king after his father's death, under the name Ptolemy Eupator, but was put to death almost immediately after by his uncle Euergetes. (*b*) A daughter, Cleopatra, married first to Alexander Balas, then to Demetrius II. king of Syria; and (*c*) Another daughter, also named Cleopatra, who was afterwards married to her uncle Ptolemy Euergetes.

(7) Euergĕtes II. or Physcon (Φύσκων), "Big-Belly," reigned B.C. 146–117. His history down to the death of his brother has been already given. In order to secure undisputed possession of the throne, he married his sister Cleopatra, the widow of his brother Philometor, and put to death his nephew Ptolemy, who had been proclaimed king under the surname of Eupator. A reign thus commenced in blood was continued in a similar spirit. Many of the leading citizens of Alexandria, who had taken part against him on the death of his brother, were put to death, while the populace were given up to the cruelties of his mercenary troops, and the streets of the city were repeatedly deluged with blood. Thousands of the inhabitants fled from the scene of such horrors, and the population of Alexandria was so greatly thinned that the king found himself compelled to invite foreign settlers from all quarters to re-people his deserted capital. At the same time that he thus incurred the hatred of his subjects by his cruelties, he rendered himself an object of their aversion and contempt by abandoning himself to the most degrading vices. In consequence of these, he had become bloated and deformed in person, and enormously corpulent, whence the Alexandrians gave him the nickname of Physcon, by which he is more usually known. His union with Cleopatra was not of long duration. He became enamoured of his niece Cleopatra (the offspring of his wife by her former marriage with Philometor), and he did not hesitate to divorce the mother, and receive her daughter instead, as his wife and queen. By this proceeding he alienated still more the minds of his Greek subjects; and his vices and cruelties at length produced an insurrection at Alexandria. Thereupon he fled to Cyprus, and the Alexandrians declared his sister Cleopatra queen (130). Enraged at this, Ptolemy put to death Memphitis, his son by Cleopatra, and sent his head and hands to his unhappy mother. But Cleopatra having been shortly afterwards expelled from Alexandria in her turn, Ptolemy found himself unexpectedly reinstated on the throne (127). His sister Cleopatra fled to the court of her elder sister Cleopatra, the wife of Demetrius II., king of Syria, who espoused the cause of the fugitive. Ptolemy, in revenge, set up against him a pretender named Zabinas or Zebina, who assumed the title of Alexander II. But the usurper behaved with such haughtiness to Ptolemy that the latter suddenly changed his policy, became reconciled to his sister Cleopatra, whom he permitted to return to Egypt, and gave his daughter Tryphaena in marriage to Antiochus Grypus, the son of Demetrius. Ptolemy died after reigning twenty-nine years from the death of his brother Philometor; but he himself reckoned the years of his reign from the date of his first assumption of the regal title in 170. Although the character of Ptolemy Physcon was stained by the most infamous vices, and by the most sanguinary cruelty, he still retained that love of letters which appears to have been hereditary in the whole race of the Ptolemies. He had in his youth been a pupil of Aristarchus, and not only courted the society of learned men, but was himself the author of a work called Ὑπομνήματα, or memoirs, which extended to twenty-four books. He left two sons: Ptolemy, afterwards known as Soter II., and Alexander, both of whom subsequently ascended the throne of Egypt; and three daughters: (*a*) Cleopatra,

married to her brother Ptolemy Soter; (*b*) Tryphaena, the wife of Antiochus Grypus, king of Syria; and (*c*) Selenê, who was unmarried at her father's death. To his natural son Ptolemy, surnamed Apion, he bequeathed by his will the separate kingdom of Cyrenê.

(8) SOTER II., and also PHILOMĒTOR, but more commonly called LATHȲRUS or LATHŪRUS (Λάθουρος), reigned B.C. 117–107, and also 89–81. Although he was of full age at the time of his father's death (117), he was obliged to reign jointly with his mother, Cleopatra, who had been appointed by the will of her late husband to succeed him on the throne. She was indeed desirous of associating with herself her younger son, Ptolemy Alexander; but since Lathyrus was popular with the Alexandrians, she was obliged to give way, and sent Alexander to Cyprus. After declaring Lathyrus king, she compelled him to repudiate his sister Cleopatra, of whose influence she was jealous, and to marry his younger sister Selenê in her stead. After reigning ten years jointly with his mother, he was expelled from Alexandria by an insurrection of the people which she had excited against him (107). His brother Alexander now assumed the sovereignty of Egypt, in conjunction with his mother, while Lathyrus was able to establish himself in the possession of Cyprus. Cleopatra, indeed, attempted to dispossess him of that island also, but without success, and Ptolemy held it as an independent kingdom for the eighteen years during which Cleopatra and Alexander reigned in Egypt. After the death of Cleopatra and the expulsion of Alexander in 89, Ptolemy Lathyrus was recalled by the Alexandrians, and established anew on the throne of Egypt, which he occupied thenceforth without interruption till his death in 81. The most important event of this period was the revolt of Thebes, in Upper Egypt, which was still powerful enough to hold out for nearly three years against the arms of Ptolemy, but at the end of that time was taken and reduced to the state of ruin in which it has ever since remained. Lathyrus reigned in all thirty-five years and a half; ten in conjunction with his mother (117–107), eighteen in Cyprus (107–89), and seven and a half as sole ruler of Egypt. He left only one daughter, Berenicê, called also Cleopatra, who succeeded him on the throne; and two sons, both named Ptolemy, who, though illegitimate, became severally kings of Egypt and Cyprus.

(9) ALEXANDER I., youngest son of Ptolemy VII., reigned conjointly with his mother Cleopatra from the expulsion of his brother Lathyrus, B.C. 107 to 90. In this year he assassinated his mother; but he had not reigned alone a year, when he was compelled by a general sedition of the populace and military to quit Alexandria. He, however, raised fresh troops, but was totally defeated in a sea-fight by the rebels; whereupon Lathyrus was recalled by the Alexandrians to Egypt, as has been already related. Alexander now attempted to make himself master of Cyprus, and invaded that island, but was defeated and slain. He left a son, Alexander, who afterwards ascended the throne of Egypt.

(10) ALEXANDER II., son of the preceding, was at Rome at the death of Ptolemy Lathyrus in 81. Sulla, who was then dictator, nominated the young Alexander (who had obtained a high place in his favour) king of Egypt, and sent him to take possession of the crown. It was, however, agreed, in deference to the claims of Cleopatra Berenicê, the daughter of Lathyrus, whom the Alexandrians had already placed on the throne, that Alexander should marry her, and admit her to share the sovereign power. He complied with the letter of this treaty by marrying Cleopatra, but only nineteen days afterward caused her to be assassinated. The Alexandrians thereupon rose against their new monarch and put him to death.

(11) DIONȲSUS, but more commonly known by the appellation of AULĒTES, "the flute-player," was an illegitimate son of Ptolemy Lathyrus. When the assassination of Berenicê and the death of Alexander II. had completed the extinction of the legitimate race of the Lagidae, Ptolemy was proclaimed king by the Alexandrians, B.C. 80. He was anxious to obtain from the Roman Senate their ratification of his title to the crown, but it was not till the consulship of Caesar (59) that he was able to purchase by vast bribes the desired privilege. He had expended immense sums in the pursuit of this object, which he was compelled to raise by the imposition of fresh taxes, and the discontent thus excited combining with the contempt entertained for his character, led to his expulsion by the Alexandrians in 58. Thereupon he proceeded in person to Rome to procure from the Senate his restoration. His first reception was promising; and he procured a decree from the Senate commanding his restoration, and intrusting the charge of effecting it to P. Lentulus Spinther, then proconsul of Cilicia. Meanwhile, the Alexandrians sent an embassy of one hundred of their leading citizens to plead their cause with the Roman Senate; but Ptolemy had the audacity to cause the deputies, on their arrival in Italy, to be waylaid, and the greater part of them murdered. The indignation excited at Rome by this proceeding produced a reaction: the tribunes took up the matter against the nobility; and an oracle was produced from the Sibylline Books forbidding the restoration of the king by an armed force. The intrigues and disputes thus raised were protracted throughout the year 56, and at length Ptolemy, despairing of a favorable result, quitted Rome in disgust, and withdrew to Ephesus. But in 55, A. Gabinius, who was proconsul in Syria, was induced, by the influence of Pompey, aided by the enormous bribe of 10,000 talents from Ptolemy himself, to undertake his restoration. The Alexandrians had in the meantime placed on the throne of Egypt Berenicê, the eldest daughter of Ptolemy, who had married Archelaüs, the son of the general of Mithridates, and they opposed Gabinius with an army on the confines of the kingdom. They were, however, defeated in three successive battles, Archelaüs was slain, and Ptolemy once more established on the throne (55). One of his first acts was to put to death his daughter Berenicê, and many of the leading citizens of Alexandria. He survived his restoration only three years and a half, during which time he was supported by a large body of Roman soldiers who had been left behind by Gabinius for his protection. He died in 51, after a reign of twenty-nine years from the date of his first accession. He left two sons, both named Ptolemy, and two daughters, Cleopatra and Arsinoë.

(12) Eldest son of the preceding. By his father's will the sovereign power was left to himself and his sister Cleopatra jointly, and this arrangement was carried into effect without opposition (51). Auletes had also referred the execution of his will

to the Roman Senate, and the latter accepted the office, confirmed its provisions, and bestowed on Pompey the title of guardian of the young king. But the approach of the Civil War prevented them from taking any active part in the administration of affairs, which fell into the hands of a eunuch named Pothinus. It was not long before dissensions broke out between the latter and Cleopatra, which ended in the expulsion of the princess, after she had reigned in conjunction with her brother about three years (48). Hereupon she took refuge in Syria, and assembled an army, with which she invaded Egypt. The young king, accompanied by his guardians, met her at Pelusium, and it was while the two armies were here encamped opposite to one another that Pompey landed in Egypt, to throw himself as a suppliant on the protection of Ptolemy; but he was assassinated, by the orders of Pothinus, before he could obtain an interview with the king himself. Shortly after, Caesar arrived in Egypt, and took upon himself to settle the dispute between Ptolemy and his sister. But as Cleopatra's charms gained for her the support of Caesar, Pothinus determined to excite an insurrection against Caesar. Hence arose what is usually called the Alexandrian War. Ptolemy, who was at first in Caesar's hands, managed to escape, and put himself at the head of the insurgents; but he was defeated by Caesar, and was drowned in an attempt to escape by the river (47).

(13) The youngest son of Ptolemy Auletes. He was appointed by Caesar to reign jointly with Cleopatra after the death of his elder brother Ptolemy XII., 47; and although he was a mere boy, it was decreed that he should marry his sister, with whom he was thus to share the power. Both his marriage and his regal title were of course purely nominal; and in the year 43 Cleopatra put him to death.

III. Other Kings. — (1) Surnamed Alorītes, that is, of Alorus, regent, or, according to some authors, king of Macedonia. He obtained the supreme power by the assassination of Alexander II., the eldest son of Amyntas, B.C. 367, but was, in his turn, assassinated by Perdiccas III., 364. (2) Surnamed Apion, king of Cyrené (117-96), was an illegitimate son of Ptolemy Physcon, king of Egypt, who left him by his will the kingdom of the Cyrenaïca. At his death in 96, Apion bequeathed his kingdom by his will to the Roman people. The Senate, however, refused to accept the legacy, and declared the cities of the Cyrenaïca free. They were not reduced to the condition of a province till near thirty years afterwards. (3) Surnamed Ceraunus, king of Macedonia, the son of Ptolemy I., king of Egypt, by his second wife Eurydicé. When his father in B.C. 285 set aside the claim of Ceraunus to the throne and appointed his younger son Ptolemy Philadelphus his successor, Ceraunus repaired to the court of Lysimachus. After Lysimachus had perished in battle against Seleucus (281) Ptolemy Ceraunus was received by the latter in the most friendly manner; but shortly afterwards (280) he basely assassinated Seleucus, and took possession of the Macedonian throne. After reigning a few months he was defeated in battle by the Gauls, taken prisoner, and put to death. (4) Tetrarch of Chalcis in Syria, the son of Mennaeus. He appears to have held the cities of Heliopolis and Chalcis as well as the mountain district of Ituraea, from whence he was in the habit of infesting Damascus and the more wealthy parts of Coelé-Syria with predatory incursions. He reigned from about 70 to 40, when he was succeeded by his son Lysanias. (5) King of Cyprus, the younger brother of Ptolemy Auletes, king of Egypt, being like him an illegitimate son of Ptolemy Lathyrus. He was acknowledged as king of Cyprus at the same time that his brother Auletes obtained possession of the throne of Egypt (B.C. 80). He had offended P. Clodius by neglecting to ransom him when he had fallen into the hands of the Cilician pirates; and accordingly Clodius, when he became tribune (53), brought forward a law to deprive Ptolemy of his kingdom, and reduce Cyprus to a Roman province. Cato, who had to carry into execution this nefarious decree, sent to Ptolemy, advising him to submit, and offering him his personal safety, with the office of high-priest at Paphos, and a liberal maintenance. But the unhappy king refused these offers, and put an end to his own life (57). (6) King of Epirus, the second son of Alexander II., king of Epirus, and Olympias, and grandson of the great Pyrrhus. He succeeded to the throne on the death of his elder brother, Pyrrhus II., but reigned only a very short time. The date of his reign cannot be fixed with certainty, but as he was contemporary with Demetrius II., king of Macedonia, it may be placed between 239 and 229. (7) King of Mauretania, was the son and successor of Iuba II. By his mother Cleopatra he was descended from the kings of Egypt, whose name he bore. The period of his accession cannot be determined with certainty, but we know that he was on the throne in A.D. 18. He continued to reign without interruption till A.D. 40, when he was summoned to Rome by Caligula, and shortly after put to death, his great riches having excited the cupidity of the emperor.

IV. Claudius Ptolemaeus. A famous Greek mathematician, astronomer, and geographer. He came from Ptolemaïs Hermeiou (ruins at modern Menschie), in Upper Egypt, and lived and worked in the second century A.D. The most important of his writings which have been preserved are: (*a*) *Γεωγραφικὴ Ὑφήγησις* ("instructions for the drawing of maps"), a geographical work in eight books, the first of which contains the principles of mathematical geography, the drawing of maps, and the calculation of the longitudes and latitudes of places in the then known world; books ii.-vii. contain tables of names of places in the maps described, arranged according to degrees and their subdivisions; and book viii. contains an astronomical table of climates. This work is one of the chief sources of our knowledge of ancient geography. It is edited by Nobbe (Leipzig, 1845); and Müller (Paris, 1883). (*b*) *Μεγάλη Σύνταξις τῆς Ἀστρονομίας*, usually known by its Arabic name of *Almagest*. Since the *Tetrabiblus*, the work on astrology, was also entitled *σύνταξις*, the Arabs, to distinguish the two, probably called the greater work *μεγάλη*, and afterwards *μεγίστη*: the title *Almagest* (*Tabrir al Magesthi*) is a compound of this last adjective and the Arabic article. The *Almagest* is divided into thirteen books. It treats of the relations of the earth and heaven; the effect of position upon the earth; the theory of the sun and moon, without which that of the stars cannot be undertaken; the sphere of the fixed stars, and those of the five stars called *planets*. The seventh and eighth books are the most interesting to the modern astronomer, as they contain a catalogue of the stars. This catalogue gives the longitudes and latitudes of 1022 stars, described by their positions in the constellations. It seems that this catalogue is in the main really that of Hipparchus, altered to Ptolemy's own time by assuming the value of the precession of the equinoxes given by Hipparchus as the least which could be, some changes having also been made by Ptolemy's own observations. Indeed, the whole work of Ptolemy appears to have been based upon the observations of Hipparchus, whom he constantly cites as his authority. Ptolemy's system of the heavens, which made the earth the fixed centre, was not superseded till the time of Copernicus (A.D. 1473–1543). The best edition of the *Almagest* is by Halma, 2 vols. (Paris, 1813–16). (*c*) Τετράβιβλος Σύνταξις, generally called *Tetrabiblos*, or *Quadripartitum de Apotelesmatibus et Iudiciis Astrorum*. With this goes another small work, called Καρπός, or *Fructus Librorum Suorum*, often called *Centiloquium*, from its containing a hundred aphorisms. Both of these works are astrological, and it has been doubted by some whether they be genuine. But the doubt merely arises from the feeling that the contents are unworthy of Ptolemy. (*d*) Κανὼν Βασιλέων, a catalogue of Assyrian, Persian, Greek, and Roman sovereigns, with the length of their reigns, several times referred to by Syncellus. (*e*) *Φάσεις ἀπλανῶν ἀστέρων καὶ συναγωγὴ ἐπισημασειῶν*, *De Apparentiis et Significationibus inerrantium*, an annual list of sidereal phenomena. (*f*, *g*) *De Analemmate* and *Planisphaerium*. These works are obtained from the Arabic. The *Analemma* is a collection of graphical processes for facilitating the construction of sun-dials. The *Planisphere* is a description of the stereographic projection, in which the eye is at the pole of the circle on which the sphere is projected. (*h*) *Περὶ ὑποθέσεων τῶν πλανωμένων*, *De Planetarum Hypothesibus*. This is a brief statement of the principal hypotheses employed in the *Almagest* for the explanation of the heavenly motions. (*i*) *Ἁρμονικῶν βιβλία γ'.*, a treatise on the theory of the musical scale, and the most important ancient work on music next to that of Aristoxenus. Most of the works of Ptolemy are contained in the edition of Halma in 4 vols. (Paris, 1813–28). The principal MSS. are at Vienna, Venice, and Mount Athos. This last is photographed and published by Langlois (Paris, 1866).

Ptolemāïs (Πτολεμαΐς). (1) Also called ACĒ (Ἀκή) (in Old Test. Acco; Arab. Akka, Fr. St. Jean d'Acre, Eng. Acre), a celebrated city on the coast of Phœnicia, south of Tyre, and north of Mount Carmel, lies at the bottom of a bay surrounded by mountains, in a position marked out by nature as a key of the passage between Coele-Syria and Palestine. It is one of the oldest cities of Phœnicia, being mentioned in the Book of Judges (i. 31). (2) (At or near El-Lahum), a small town of Middle Egypt, in the Nomos Arsinoïtes. (3) P. HERMII (Menschie), a city of Upper Egypt, on the west bank of the Nile, below Abydos. (4) P. THERON, or EPITHĒRAS, a port on the Red Sea, on the coast of the Troglodytae. (5) Now Tolmeïta, or Tolometa, on the northwestern coast of Cyrenaïca, one of the five great cities of the Libyan Pentapolis.

Pubes, Pubertas. See CURATOR; IMPUBES; TUTOR.

Publicāni. A name given by the Romans to those who did business with the State, by becoming contractors for public buildings and for supplies, and to farmers of public lands (see AGER PUBLICUS), especially those who farmed the public taxes (*vectigalia*) for a certain time on payment of a fixed sum. In Rome, as indeed throughout the ancient world (see TELONES), the collection of taxes was not made by paid officials, but by farmers of taxes, who belonged to the equestrian order, as the senators were excluded from such business. The farmers of taxes, by the immense profits which they made, became a politically powerful class of capitalists. As the various taxes in the different provinces were let out as a whole by the censors, joint-stock companies were formed, *societates publicanorum*, whose members received a proportionate return for their invested capital. (See PROVINCIA.) One member, the *manceps*, made a tender at the public auction, concluded the contract with the censors, and gave the necessary security. The duration of the contract was a *lustrum*—i. e. the period between one censorship and another; in imperial times always five years. It began on the 15th of March.

The general superintendence was given to a *magister societatis* in Rome, who vacated office every year; the management of details was in the hands of numerous officials. According to the amount of the taxes farmed, the publicani received special names. The highest class, *decumani*, were the farmers of the *decuma*, the tenth part of the produce of the agricultural lands which had been taken from the old possessors. The *pecuarii* or *scripturarii* were the farmers of the *scriptura*, the tax levied for the use of the State pastures. The *conductores portoriorum* were the farmers of the *portoria*, the import and export dues, etc. In order to make the greatest possible gain, the publicani were guilty of the most grievous oppression of the provincials, whose only hope of relief lay in the governor, who was rarely able to help them for fear of these influential societies. Under the Empire the position of the provincials was improved; for the emperor, as the governor-in-chief of all the provinces, heard the final appeal in the case of any grievances In imperial times the *decumani* ceased to exist, and the letting out of taxes was intrusted to the official boards especially concerned with them. See VECTIGALIA.

Publications. See EDITIO PRINCEPS; LIBER.

Public Houses. See CAUPONA.

Publicŏla or **Poplicŏla**, PUBLIUS VALERIUS. A Roman who took a prominent part in the expulsion of the Tarquins, and who was therefore elected consul with Brutus (B.C. 509) and in three other years (B.C. 508, 507, 504). He did much to secure the rights of the plebeians, and secured the passage of a law giving to every citizen who was condemned by a magistrate the right of appeal to the people. He died in B.C. 503, and was mourned for ten days by the Roman matrons (Livy, i. 58; ii. 2–16; Dionys. iv. 67; v. 12, 40; Plut. *Publ.*).

Publilia. The second wife of Cicero the orator, whom he married in B.C. 46, when he was sixty years of age and she quite young. The marriage caused great scandal, as it was generally believed that Cicero was simply in love with her fortune. The marriage proved unhappy, and Publilia was divorced by her husband in B.C. 45 (Cic. *Ad Att.*

xii. 32; Dio Cass. xlvi. 18). See CICERO; TULLIA.

Publiliae Leges. Three laws carried B.C. 339 by the dictator Q. Publilius Philo: their substance is described by Livy (viii. 12). The first of them seems to stand in connection with one of the *leges Valeriae Horatiae* (B.C. 449) which enacted *ut quod tributim plebs iussisset populum teneret* (Livy, iii. 55)—i. e. it restored the Comitia Tributa after the second secession of the plebs, and perhaps also provided that plebiscita which had no constitutional import, or which related purely to matters of private law, should have the force of statute, even without subsequent confirmation or enactment by the centuries. In B.C. 339, the patricians having now brought themselves to take regular part in the business of the Comitia Tributa, confirmation by the centuries must have seemed a superfluity in any case; and accordingly the first Lex Publilia seems to have dispensed with it for all plebiscita whatsoever. They still, however, required to be sanctioned by the Senate before they acquired complete validity; but the necessity of this seems to have been abolished by the Lex Hortensia (B.C. 287), which enacted *ut eo iure, quod plebs statuisset, omnes Quirites tenerentur* (Gaius, i. 3; Dig. 1, 2, 2, 8; Laelius Felix in Gell. xv. 27; Pliny, *H. N.* xvi. § 37). There is, however, great difference of opinion as to the real import of, and the relation between, these three leges, which, if literally taken, seem all to have enacted the same thing. See Walter, *Geschichte des röm. Rechts*, § 65.

Publilius Syrus. A Roman writer of mimes (see MIMUS), a younger contemporary and rival of Laberius. He flourished about B.C. 43. Probably born at Antioch, in Syria, he came to Rome in early youth as a slave. On account of his wit he was liberated by his master, and received a careful education. As a writer of mimes and as an improviser, he was exceedingly popular, and, after the death of Laberius, held sole sway on the stage. His mimes contained, in addition to the farcical humour of this sort of writing, a great number of short, witty sayings. These were so much admired that they were excerpted at an early date, and used in schoosl, while the pieces themselves were soon forgotten.

In the Middle Ages these sayings were popular under the name of Seneca. We have an alphabetical collection of nearly seven hundred of these single-line apophthegms, bearing the title *Publilii Syri Mimi Sententiae*, though not all of them are certainly the work of their alleged author. Among them are many of much pungency and pith—e. g. *Necesse est multos timeat, quem multi timent; Beneficium accipere, libertatem est vendere;* (the motto of the *Edinburgh Review*) *Iudex damnatur cum nocens absolvitur;* and many others that find their parallels in the saws and maxims of modern times. They are collected by Ribbeck in his edition of the comic fragments (1873), and are separately edited by O. Friedrich (Berlin, 1880); and with English notes by Gray (1895).

Publilius, VOLĔRO. A tribune of the plebs, B.C. 472, and again 471, who effected an important change in the Roman constitution. In virtue of the laws which he proposed, the tribunes of the plebs and the aediles were elected by the Comitia Tributa, instead of by the Comitia Centuriata, as had previously been the case, and the tribes obtained the power of deliberating and determining in all matters affecting the whole nation, and not such only as concerned the plebs. Some say that the number of the tribunes was now for the first time raised to five, having been only two previously.

Publishers. See LIBER.

Pudicitia. The Roman goddess of modesty and chastity. She was at first worshipped in a chapel in Rome exclusively by the patrician matrons. When, in B.C. 296, the patrician Virginia was excluded from this worship by her marriage with the plebeian consul Volumnius, she erected in her own house a chapel to the goddess, so that the plebeian matrons might worship there. Afterwards this cult died out with the decay of morals. In imperial times altars were erected to Pudicitia in honour of the empresses. The goddess was represented as a draped matron, concealing her right hand in her garment. Pudicitia is the same as the Greek Αἰδώς, who had an altar at Athens.

Pugil (πύκτης). A boxer; one who fights with his fists (*pugni*). See ATHLETAE; CAESTUS; GYMNASIUM; PUGILATUS.

Pugilātus (πύξ, πυγμή, πυγμαχία, πυγμοσύνη). Boxing. The fist being the simplest and most natural weapon, it may be taken for granted that boxing was one of the earliest athletic games among the Greeks. Hence even gods and several of the earlier heroes are described either as victors in the πυγμή or as distinguished boxers, such as Apollo, Heracles, Tydeus, Polydeuces, and others (Theocrit. xxiv. 113; Apollod. iii. 6, § 4; Pausan. v. 8, 2). The Scholiast on Pindar (*Nem.* v. 89) says that Theseus was believed to have invented the art of boxing. The Homeric heroes are well acquainted with it (Hom. *Il.* xxiii. 691; cf. *Od.* viii. 103 foll.). Boxing for men was introduced at the Olympic Games in Ol. 23, and for boys in Ol. 37 (Pausan. v. 8, § 3). Contests in boxing for boys are also mentioned in the Nemea and Isthmia (Pausan. vi. 4, § 6).

In the earliest times boxers (*pugiles*, πύκται) fought naked, with the exception of a ζῶμα round their loins (Hom. *Il.* xxiii. 683; Verg. *Aen.* v. 421); but this was not used when boxing was introduced at Olympia, as the contests in wrestling and racing had been carried on here by persons entirely naked ever since Ol. 15. Respecting the leathern thongs with which pugilists surrounded their fists, see CAESTUS, where its various forms are illustrated by woodcuts.

The boxing of the ancients appears to have resembled the practice of modern times. It was a point of skill, we are told, not to attack the antagonist, but to remain on the defensive, and thus to wear out the opponent, until he was obliged to acknowledge himself to be conquered (Eustath. *ad Il.* p. 1322, 29). It was considered a merit in a boxer to conquer without receiving any wounds, so that the two great points in this game were to inflict blows, and at the same time not to expose one's self to any danger. As regards the position of the hands, no doubt it varied according to circumstances, then as now. In art-representations we see sometimes the right arm guarding and the left striking, sometimes the contrary: the blows were directed against the upper parts of the body, and

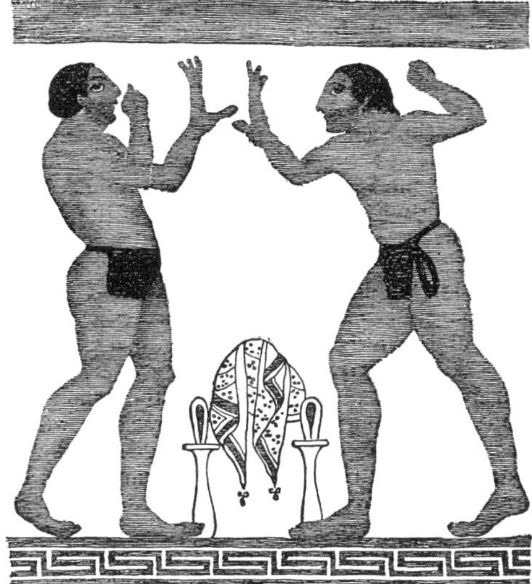

Pugilists, from a Tomb at Chiusi. (Dennis.)

the wounds inflicted on the head were often severe (Hom. *Od.* xviii. 96; Apollon. Rhod. ii. 785; Theocrit. ii. 126; Verg. *Aen.* v. 469; Aelian, *V. H.* x. 19). The ears especially were exposed to great danger, and with regular pugilists they were generally much mutilated and broken (Plato, *Gorg.* p. 516; *Protag.* p. 342; Martial, vii. 33, 5). Hence in works of art the ears of the pancratiasts always appear beaten flat, and, although swollen in some parts, are yet smaller than ears usually are. In order to protect the ears from severe blows, little covers, called ἀμφωτίδες, were invented (Poll. ii. 82). But these ear-covers were undoubtedly never used in the great public games, but only in the gymnasia and palaestrae, or at most in the public contests of boxing for boys; for they are never seen in any ancient work of art.

Two points of distinction between ancient and modern pugilists may be noticed: (1) that, as we gather from vase-pictures, the fist was not constantly doubled, as with us, but the fingers were often merely curved over, sometimes almost extended; in some representations, however, the fists are fairly clenched: probably the differences are due to the caestus; (2) the inarticulate sounds emitted by the boxers, instead of the modern silence: this, according to Cicero, was to add force to the blow (*Tusc.* ii. 23, 54).

The game of boxing, like all the other gymnastic and athletic games, was regulated by certain rules. Thus pugilists were not allowed to take hold of one another, or to use their feet for the purpose of making one another fall, as was the case in the pancratium. Cases of death, either during the fight itself or soon after, appear to have occurred rather frequently; but if a fighter wilfully killed his antagonist, he was severely punished (Pausan. vi. 9, § 3; viii. 40, § 3). If both the combatants were tired without wishing to give up the fight, they might pause a while to recover their strength; and in some cases they are described as resting on their knees (Apollon. Rhod. ii. 86). The contest did not end until one of the combatants was compelled by fatigue, wounds, or despair to declare himself conquered, which was generally done by lifting up one hand (Plut. *Lycurg.* 19).

The Ionians, especially those of Samos, were at all times more distinguished pugilists than the Dorians, and at Sparta boxing is said to have been forbidden by the laws of Lycurgus (Pausan. vi. 2, § 4; Plut. *Lycurg.* 19). But the ancients generally considered boxing as a useful training for military purposes, and a part of education no less important than any other gymnastic exercise. Even from a medical point of view, boxing was recommended (Aretaeus, *De Morb. Diut. Cur.* i. 2).

In Italy boxing appears likewise to have been practised from early times (Livy, i. 35). It continued as a popular game during the whole period of the Republic as well as of the Empire (Suet. *Aug.* 45; Cic. *De Leg.* ii. 15, 38; Suet. *Calig.* 18). Besides the *legitimi pugiles*, there was a peculiarly Italian institution of *catervarii pugiles*, who fought, not in pairs, but in a general mêlée (Suet. l. c.). See Krause, *Die Gymnastik und Agon. d. Hellenen*, pp. 497–534; Blümner in Baumeister, *Denkmäler*, p. 523; Grasberger, *Erziehung*, p. 205.

Pugillāres. Small tablets for writing. See Tabula; Writing and Writing Materials.

Pugio (μάχαιρα), dim. **Pugiuncŭlus** (ἐγχειρίδιον). A dagger with two edges (Suet. *Vitell.* 15).

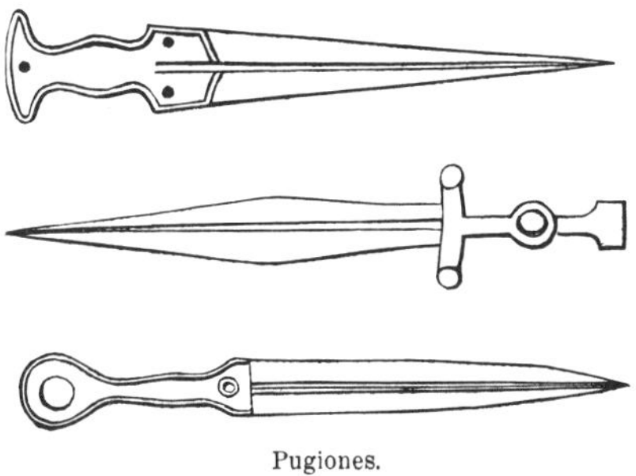

Pugiones.

Pulcher, Clodius. See Clodius.

Pulcheria. The eldest daughter of the Roman emperor Arcadius, born A.D. 399. In 414, when she was only fifteen years of age, she became the guardian of her brother Theodosius, and was declared Augusta or empress. She had the virtual government in her hands during the whole lifetime of her brother, who died in 450. On his death she remained at the head of affairs, and shortly afterwards she married Marcian, with whom she continued to reign in common till her death in 453. Pulcheria was a woman of ability, and was celebrated for her piety and her public and private virtues. See Theodosius II.

Pulchrum Promontorium. A promontory on the northern coast of the Carthaginian territory in North Africa, probably identical with the Apollinis Promontorium.

Pullarius. A person who had charge of the sacred chickens (*pulli*), and made predictions from the way in which they ate their food. See Augur, p. 167.

Pullus, L. Iunius. Consul B.C. 249, in the First Punic War. His fleet was destroyed by a storm, on account, it was said, of his neglecting the auspices. In despair he put an end to his own life (Cic. *N. D.* ii. 3).

Pulpĭtum (βῆμα). (1) The platform of a public speaker. (2) (λογεῖον). The stage of the Roman theatre. See THEATRUM.

Puls. A sort of porridge much eaten in Italy, so that it was regarded as a national dish. It was made of spelt (*far*, *odor*), and is to be distinguished from the other native dish *polenta*, which was a porridge of barley-meal (Pliny, *H. N.* xviii. 72).

Pulvīnar. A sort of pillow or cushion used on large couches (Petron. 135, 5), and especially associated with the feast of the Lectisternium, at which the images of the gods were laid upon cushions and had a banquet spread before them. See LECTISTERNIUM.

Punctuation. See PALAEOGRAPHY.

Punic Language. See CARTHAGO; PHŒNICÉ.

Punic Wars. A name given to the three wars fought between the Romans and the Carthaginians (*Poeni*).

THE FIRST PUNIC WAR (B.C. 264–241) began when the Romans allied themselves with the Mamertini (q. v.) of Messana, a people of Italian stock, who had appealed to Rome against the Syracusans under Hiero; and a little later against a Carthaginian force that had gained possession of the citadel of Messana. The Romans prevailed against Hiero, who made peace with them so that they could turn their whole attention to the Carthaginian armies. The principal events of this war are the siege and capture of Agrigentum by the Romans (B.C. 262), the defeat of the Roman naval force at Lipara (B.C. 260), the great naval victory of C. Duilius over the Carthaginians near Mylae (see COLUMNA ROSTRATA; DUILIUS); the still greater success of the Romans off Ecnomus (B.C. 256); the Roman invasion of Africa by Regulus, and his defeat and capture (B.C. 255); the Roman victory of L. Metellus at Panormus in Sicily (B.C. 250); the Roman naval defeat at Drepanum (B.C. 249); the decisive Roman victory off the Aegetes Islands (B.C. 242) when Catulus defeated Hanno; and the final treaty made by Hamilcar (B.C. 241) whereby the Romans secured Sicily and an indemnity of 3200 talents. See CARTHAGO; HAMILCAR; REGULUS; SICILIA.

THE SECOND PUNIC WAR (B.C. 218–201) began when Hannibal attacked the Spanish city of Saguntum, then in alliance with Rome (B.C. 219). The chief events were the invasion of Italy by Hannibal, the counter-invasion of Spain by Cn. Scipio, the Roman defeats on the Trebia and the Ticinus, near Lake Trasimenus (B.C. 217) and at Cannae (B.C. 216), the revolt of the Samnites, Apulians, Lucanians, and Bruttians to Hannibal, the war in Sicily ending in the capture of Syracuse by the Romans (B.C. 212), the war in Spain (Hasdrubal against the Scipios), the recovery of Tarentum by Fabius Maximus (B.C. 209), the defeat of Hasdrubal on the Metaurus by the Roman consul Nero, the expulsion of the Carthaginians from Spain by P. Scipio (B.C. 210–207) and his invasion of Africa, the recall of Hannibal to Carthage (B.C. 203), his final defeat by Scipio at Zama (B.C. 202), and the submission of Carthage (B.C. 201). See FABIUS; HANNIBAL; HASDRUBAL; SCIPIO.

THE THIRD PUNIC WAR (B.C. 149–146) began with the demand of the Romans for the destruction of the city of Carthage, a measure long advocated by Cato the Elder. (See CATO.) Although the Carthaginians had already surrendered all their arms to Rome, they resolved to perish rather than submit to the annihilation of their ancient and beautiful city. They slew all the resident Italians, manufactured new arms and military equipments, collected great stores of provisions, and even the women are said to have cut off their hair for use as strings for the catapults. The first attacks of the Roman soldiery were repulsed with great slaughter, and only the genius of the younger Scipio, who was present as a military tribune, saved the attacking army from total destruction. In B.C. 147, Scipio, though under the legal age, was unanimously elected consul, and at once took command of the forces operating against Carthage. He landed in Africa in the same year, restored both discipline and confidence to the demoralized troops, and, though his fleet of fifty ships was destroyed in a three days' naval engagement, he succeeded in carrying the city by storm after a desperate and bloody resistance which lasted nearly a week. Carthage was razed to the ground, and its territory divided between Utica and the new Roman province of Africa. See Neumann, *Geschichte Roms im Zeitalter der punischen Kriege* (Breslau, 1883) and the articles CARTHAGO; SCIPIO.

Punĭcum Bellum. See NAEVIUS.

Puns. The pun or play on words (*lusus verborum*) is common in both Greek and Latin as it is in the Oriental literatures. It was not merely an amusement or a trick of speech as it is to-day, but was based upon the generally prevalent notion that there is an intimate connection between things and their names, and that a likeness of name denotes a certain likeness of quality in the things named. (See PHILOLOGIA.) Hence a species of divination from names (Onomantia) existed, and omens were regularly sought in names. It is for this reason that we find the greatest writers systematically punning even in their most serious passages, as in the famous line of Aeschylus when he plays on the name of Helen (*Agamem.* 689):

Ἑλένη ἑλένας ἕλανδρας ἑλέπτολις.

(See also lines 1040, 1049 of the same play; and *Prom.* 718, 742, 875; Theocr. xxvi. 26, etc.) So the Romans enrolled in their military levies the names of good omen, such as Felix, Faustus, Victor, etc., at the head of the lists, and put such auspicious ones as Salvius Valerius first on the roll of the census. On one occasion the Roman troops mutinied because they were to be led into the field by one Atrius Umber (Livy, xxviii. 28). So Ausonius (*Epist.* xx.) says:

> Nam divinare est nomen componere, quod sit
> Fortunae, morum, vel necis iudicium.

Changes of name were often made on the principle of punning, as when the enemies of the Athenians (Ἀθηναῖοι) called them Κεχηναῖοι (Aristoph. *Eq.* 1262), when the Romans gave the drink-loving Tiberius Claudius Nero the expressive nickname of Biberius Caldius Mero, suggesting *bibo*, *calda*, and *merum* (see the article NOMEN at the end), and when Jerome called his adversary Vigilantius, "Dormitantius." Cicero was especially fond of puns, and a collection of these was made and published, which is mentioned by Quintilian (vi. 3, 5; cf. id. vi. 3, 3; Macrobius, *Sat.* ii. 2, 5, where some of them are quoted; Suet. *Iul.* 50; Plut. *Cic.* 38).

See the chapter of Quintilian, *De Risu* (vi. 3, 5); Lersch, *Sprachphilosophie*, iii. 11–17; Sturz, *Opus-*

cula, p. 78; Mervoyer, *Sur l'Association des Idées* (Paris, 1864); Farrar, *Chapters on Language*, pp. 235–250 (London, 1873); and Salverte, *History of Names*, pp. 8 foll. (London, 1862).

Pupa (κόρη). Literally, "a little girl"; and applied to a doll. Dolls were made by the Romans of rags, wood, wax, ivory, and terra-cotta. A wax-doll was called by the Greeks δάγυνον, δαγύς, and πλαγγών, and they often had movable limbs (Baumeister, *Denkm.* p. 778). At marriage the Greek girls dedicated their dolls to Artemis, the Roman girls to Venus (*Anth. Pal.* vi. 280; Pers. ii. 70); but if they died before marriage their dolls were buried with them. Dolls with movable limbs were called νευρόπαστα, and were worked by strings or wires. Marionettes were exhibited as in Italy to-day (Becq de Fouquières, *Les Jeux des Anciens*, pp. 27 foll.; Blümner, *Technologie*, ii. 123).

Roman Doll of Ivory. (Biscari, tav. v.)

Pupiēnus Maxĭmus, M. CLODIUS. A Roman who was elected emperor with Balbinus, in A.D. 238, when the Senate received intelligence of the death of the two Gordians in Africa; but the new emperors were slain by the soldiers at Rome in the same year. See BALBINUS.

Pupilla. An orphan girl; a ward, a minor. See INFANS; TUTELA.

Puppis (πρύμνα). The poop or stern of a ship. See NAVIS.

Purpŭra (πορφύρα). The finest and most costly dye of the ancients, a discovery of the Phœnicians, though known to the Greeks in the Homeric Age. This may be inferred from the frequent epithet πορφύρεος applied to robes, rugs, etc. It was also known to the Romans in the time of their kings. It was obtained from two kinds of shells in the Mediterranean Sea: (1) from the trumpet-shell (Gr. κῆρυξ; Lat. *bucinum, murex*); (2) from the true purple-shell (Gr. πορφύρα; Lat. *purpura, pelagia = murex brandaris* or *tribulus*). These shells respectively contained in a diminutive bladder a small quantity of (1) scarlet-coloured, (2) black-and-red-coloured juice. The juice collected from a number of these shells was placed in salt in the proportion of about one pint of salt to every seventy-five pounds avoirdupois of juice, and heated in metal vessels by the introduction of warm vapours; then the raw material, wool and silk, was dyed in it. The best and dearest purple was always the Phœnician, especially that of Tyre, although it was prepared by other inhabitants of the Mediterranean. As the colour of the *bucinum* was not lasting, it was not used by itself, but only in combination with the true purpura for producing certain varieties of purple dye. By mixing *bucinum* with black *pelagium*, the juice of the true purple-shell, the fashionable violet, called the "amethyst" purple, was produced; and, by a double process of dyeing, first in half-boiled *pelagium*, and then in *bucinum*, Tyrian purple was produced. This had the colour of clotted blood, and when looked at straight appeared black, but when held to the light it glowed with colour. A pound of violet wool cost in Caesar's time 100 *denarii* ($20), Tyrian purple wool above 1000 *denarii* ($200). By mixing *pelagium* with other matter—water, urine, and orchilla—the bright purple dyes—heliotrope-blue, mauve-blue, and violet-yellow—were obtained. Other colours were produced by the combination of the different methods of dyeing; first dyeing the material with violet colour, purple dye, and scarlet (produced from the *coccus ilicis*); then by using the Tyrian method they obtained the *tyrianthinum*, the Tyrian shell-purple, and the variety called the ὑσγινον, from ὕσγη, a variety of πρῖνος, or *quercus coccifera* (Pliny, *H. N.* ix. 124–141). The native dye was apparently not easily distinguished from the Tyrian when newly applied, except by the connoisseur (Hor. *Epist.* i. 10, 26–30). For further details, see Blümner's *Technologie*, i. 224–240.

Purple robes were used at an early date by the Greeks as a mark of dignity. Even the Athenian archons wore purple mantles officially. In Rome at one time broad, at another narrow, stripes of purple on the toga and tunic served as marks of distinction for senators, magistrates, and members of the equestrian order. The robes of the general were dyed in purple (see PALUDAMENTUM); so also was the gold-embroidered mantle worn by one who celebrated a triumph. For a long time home-purple was used; Tyrian purple was not introduced till the middle of the first century B.C., and from that time it became a luxury. In spite of repeated attempts to check by imperial decrees the use of real purple among private individuals, robes trimmed with purple, or altogether dyed with it, became more and more used. Only a complete robe of *blatta*, the finest kind of purple, of which there were five varieties, was reserved as an imperial privilege, and any private person who wore it was punished as being guilty of high-treason (*Cod. Theod.* iv. 40, 1). From the second century A.D. the emperors took part in this lucrative industry, and from the end of the fourth century A.D. the manufacture of the *blatta* became an imperial monopoly.

Purpurariae Insŭlae (probably the Madeira group). A group of islands in the Atlantic Ocean, off the northwestern coast of Africa.

Puteal. The Latin term for a circular stone enclosure, consisting of a dwarf wall, surrounding either (1) the mouth of a well (*puteus*) or (2) a spot struck by lightning. Italian superstition demanded that every flash of lightning which struck and was buried in the earth should have, as it were, a grave and a propitiatory offering, as in the case of a human being. According to the place where the flash fell, this offering was made, either by the State or by private individuals, in the earlier times according to the directions of the *pontifices*, at a later date after consultation with the Etruscan *haruspices*. The earth which was touched by the divine fire was carefully collected (Lucan, i. 606), and enclosed in a coffin constructed out of four side-pieces and without any bottom (this was the burying of the lightning). Then round the coffin a shaft, consisting of four walls and open at the top, was built up to the surface of the ground. A place which had thus been consecrated by the offering which the *haruspices* made of a sheep fully teethed (*bidens*) was especially called a *bidental*, and was not allowed to be desecrated. According to the pontifical rite introduced by Numa, the propitiatory offering consisted of onions, hair, and sardels. If a human being had been struck

Puteal. (Pompeii.)

by lightning, his body was not burnt, but buried on the spot (Pliny, *H. N.* ii. 145). Such a spot was called a *bidental*, and a propitiatory offering was made on his behalf (Fest. p. 27; Non. pp. 53, 26). See BIDENTAL.

Puteal enclosing a Tree. (From a Painting found at Herculaneum.)

The puteal, with bay wreaths, lyres, and a pair of pincers, may be seen on coins of the gens Scribonia. The ancient puteal in the Forum, near the Arcus Fabianus, was repaired by Scribonius Libo, whence it was called the Puteal Libonis or Puteal Scribonianum. In its neighbourhood he erected a tribunal for the praetor, which led to its becoming the resort of litigants, money-lenders, etc. (Hor. *Sat.* ii. 6, 35; *Ep.* i. 19, 8; Cic. *Pro Sestio*, 18).

Puteolānum. A country-house of Cicero, near Puteoli, where he wrote his *Quaestiones Academicae*, and where the emperor Hadrian was buried (Cic. *Ad Att.* xiv. 7; *Vit. Hadr.* 25).

Puteolānus Sinus. Now the Bay of Naples; a bay of the sea on the coast of Campania between the promontory Misenum and the promontory of Minerva. It was originally called Cumanus.

Puteŏli. Now Pozzuoli; originally named Dicaearchia. A celebrated seaport town of Campania, situated on a promontory on the eastern side of the Puteolanus Sinus, and a little to the east of Cumae, was founded by the Greeks of Cumae, B.C. 521, under the name of Dicaearchia. It obtained the name of Puteoli either from its numerous wells or from the stench arising from the mineral springs in its neighbourhood. The town was indebted for its importance to its excellent harbour, which was protected by an extensive mole to which Caligula attached a floating bridge, which extended as far as Baiae, a distance of two miles. Puteoli was the chief emporium for the commerce with Alexandria and with the greater part of Spain. The town was colonized by the Romans in B.C. 194, and also anew by Augustus, Nero, and Vespasian. It was destroyed by Alaric in A.D. 410, by Genseric in 455, and also by Totila in 545, but was on each occasion speedily rebuilt. There are still many ruins of the ancient town at the modern Pozzuoli.

Puteus (φρέαρ). (1) A well dug in the ground and supplied from its own spring. (2) The fountain in a Roman house. (See DOMUS.) (3) A pit for storing grain (Varro, *R. R.* i. 57).

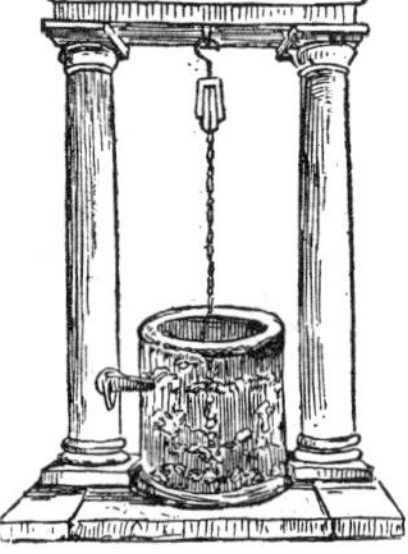

Roman Well. (From the Basilica of S. Giovanni Laterano, Rome.)

Putĭcŭlus and **Putĭcŭla.** A grave-pit used in the burial of the people of the lower classes and of slaves (Varro, *L. L.* v. 25). See SEPULCRUM.

Pyanepsia (τὰ πυανέψια, sc. ἱερά). A festival celebrated at Athens on the seventh day of the month PYANEPSION, the end of October, in honour of the departing god of summer, Apollo. The festival received its name from the cooked beans which were offered to the god as firstfruits of autumn. Another firstfruit offering of this festival was the *eiresioné* (εἰρεσιώνη), a branch of olive or bay, bound with purple and white wool, and hung about with all sorts of autumn fruits, pastry, and small vessels full of honey, wine, and oil. This branch was borne by a boy whose parents were both alive; a song, which bore the same name, *eiresioné*, was sung, while he was escorted by a procession to the temple of the god, where the wreath was deposited as a votive offering. Other branches were hung at the doors of the houses. In later times this festival was also kept as a mark of gratitude for the safe return of Theseus from Crete, which was supposed to have taken place on this day; and the cooking of the beans was regarded as commemorating the cooking of the scanty remains of the provisions of his ships. In the ancient calendar of the Attic festivals built into the wall of the metropolitan church at Athens, the festival of the Pyanepsia is represented by a youth carrying the *eiresioné*. Besides Apollo, the Horae were worshipped at the Pyanepsia with offerings and invocations, as the goddesses of the blessings of the year.

Pycnostȳlus (πυκνόστυλος). An architectural term applied to an arrangement of columns used only in the Ionic and Corinthian orders, and denoting the placing of columns very close to one another (Vitruv. iii. 2).

Pyctes (πύκτης). See PUGIL.

Pydna (Πύδνα). Now Kitron. A town of Macedonia in the district Pieria, was situated at a small distance west of the Thermaic Gulf, on which it had a harbour. It was originally a Greek colony, but it was subdued by the Macedonian kings, from whom, however, it frequently revolted. It was subdued by Philip, who enlarged and fortified the place. It is especially memorable on account of the victory gained under its walls by Aemilius Paulus over Perseus, the last king of Macedonia, 168. Under the Romans it was also called CITRUM or CITRUS.

Pygĕla (Πύγελα) or **Phygĕla** (Φύγελα). A small town of Ionia, on the coast of Lydia.

Pygmaei (Πυγμαῖοι, i. e. men of the height of a πυγμή, i. e. thirteen and a half inches). A fabulous people, first mentioned by Homer (*Il.* iii. 5) as dwelling on the shores of Ocean, and attacked by cranes in springtime. The fable is repeated by numerous writers in various forms, especially as to the locality, some placing them at the sources of the Nile (Aristot. *H. A.* viii. 12) in Aethiopia, others in India (Pliny, *H. N.* vi. 22), and others in the extreme north of the earth (Eustath. *ad* Hom. p. 372). Philostratus represents them as fighting with Heracles, one army of them attacking his right hand and one his left (*Icon.* ii. 21). Aristotle did not regard the stories of the Pygmies as wholly fabulous (*H. A.* viii. 14), and recent African explorers have discovered in that Continent two types of dwarfish people whose existence in ancient times coming vaguely to the knowledge of the Greeks and Romans doubtless gave rise to the various stories about them. Ctesias and Pomponius Mela also speak of Pygmies in Asia. See Tarver, *The Pygmies* (London, 1894); Quatrefages, *The Pygmies*, Eng. trans. (New York, 1895).

Battle of Pygmies and Cranes. (Pompeian Caricature.)

Pygmalion (Πυγμαλίων). (1) A king of Cyprus and father of Metharmé. He is said to have fallen in love with the ivory image of a maiden which he himself had made, and therefore to have prayed to Aphrodité to breathe life into it. When the request was granted, Pygmalion married the maiden, and became by her the father of Paphus (Ovid, *Met.* x. 243, etc.). (2) Son of Belus and brother of Dido, who murdered Sichaeus, Dido's husband. For details, see DIDO.

Pygmé (πυγμή). Boxing. See ATHLETAE; GYMNASIUM; PUGILATUS.

Pylădes (Πυλάδης). (1) The son of Strophius and Anaxibia, a sister of Agamemnon. His father was king of Phocis; and after the death of Agamemnon, Orestes was secretly carried to his father's court. Here Pylades contracted that friendship with Orestes which became proverbial. He assisted Orestes in murdering his mother Clytaemnestra, and also accompanied him to the Tauric Chersonesus; and he eventually married his sister Electra, by whom he became the father of Hellanicus, Medon, and Strophius. For details, see ORESTES. (2) A pantomime dancer in the reign of Augustus, spoken of in the article BATHYLLUS.

Pylae (Πύλαι). A general name for any narrow pass, such as Thermopylae, Pylae, Albaniae, Caspiae, etc.

Pylagŏrae (Πυλαγόραι) and **Pylagŏri** (Πυλαγόροι). See AMPHICTYONES.

Pylēné (Πυλήνη). An ancient town of Aetolia near the coast, mentioned by Homer. The Aeolians who took Pylené afterwards removed higher up into the country and founded Proschium.

Pylos (Πύλος). The name of three towns on the western coast of the Peloponnesus. (1) In Elis, at the foot of Mount Scollis, and about seventy or eighty stadia from the city of Elis on the road to Olympia, near the confluence of the Ladon and the Peneus. (2) In Triphylia, about thirty stadia from the coast, on the river Mamaüs, west of the mountain Minthé, and north of Lepreum. (3) In the southwest of Messenia, was situated at the foot of Mount Aegaleos on a promontory at the northern entrance of the basin, now called the Bay of Navarino, the largest and safest harbour in all Greece. This harbour was fronted and protected by the small island of Sphacteria (Sphagia), which stretched along the coast about $1\frac{3}{4}$ miles, leaving only two narrow entrances at each end. Pylos became memorable in the Peloponnesian War, when the Athenians under Demosthenes built a fort on the promontory Coryphasium a little south of the ancient city, and just within the northern entrance to the harbour (B.C. 425). The attempts of the Spartans to dislodge the Athenians proved unavailing; and the capture by Cleon of the Spartans who had landed on the island of Sphacteria was one of the most important events in the whole war (Thuc. iv. 3–13; 29–40).

Pyra (πυρά). A funeral pyre. See FUNUS; ROGUS.

Pyracmon. See CYCLOPES.

Pyrămis (πυραμίς). A pyramid; a form of structure which doubtless originated with the Egyptians, though it was adopted by the Etruscans and Romans, and is found in the so-called Cyclopean remains in Greece. (See CYCLOPES, p. 451.) The Romans used the pyramid as a design for sepulchral monuments (see illustration, p. 732), a fine existing specimen being the tomb of C. Cestius on the Appian Way just outside of Rome. The tomb of Augustus, remains of which are still to be seen, was pyramidal, rising to the height of some 328 feet. (See AUGUSTUS.) The pyramidal form is found in the Birs-Nimrûd or Tower of Belus (see pages 175, 176), and it occurred in the famous mausoleum at Halicarnassus. See illustration, p. 1018.

Pyramidal Tomb of Gaius Cestius. (From a photograph.)

Pyrămus (Πύραμος). See THISBÉ.

Pyrămus (Πύραμος). Now the Jihan; a large river in Asia Minor, rising in the Anti-Taurus range in Cappadocia, and flowing southwest through Cilicia until it falls into the sea near Mallus. It was also called LEUCOSȲRUS, from the Leucosyri, who lived on its banks.

Pyrēnê (Πυρήνη) or **Pyrenaei Montes** (*τὰ Πυρηναῖα ὄρη*). The Pyrenees; a range of mountains extending from the Atlantic to the Mediterranean, and forming the boundary between Gaul and Spain. The length of these mountains is about 270 miles in a straight line; their breadth varies from about 40 miles to 20; their greatest height is between 11,000 and 12,000 feet. The continuation of the mountains along the Maré Cantabricum was called Saltus Vasconum, and still farther west Mons Vindius or Vinnius.

Pyrēnes Promontorium or **Promontorium Venĕris.** Now C. Creus; the southeastern extremity of the Pyrenees in Spain, on the frontiers of Gaul, derived its second name from a temple of Venus on the promontory.

Pyrgi (Πύργοι). (1) The southernmost town of Triphylia, in Elis, near the Messenian frontier, said to have been founded by the Minyae. (2) Now Santa Severa; an ancient Pelasgic town on the coast of Etruria, was used as the port of Caeré or Agylla, and was a place of considerable importance as a commercial emporium.

Pyrgotĕles (Πυργοτέλης). A celebrated Greek engraver of gems who flourished in the fourth century B.C., in the reign of Alexander the Great, who admired him so much as to allow no other artist to engrave the royal seal-rings (Pliny, *H. N.* vii. 125; xxxvii. 8). See GEMMA.

Pyriphlegĕthon (Πυριφλεγέθων, "flaming with fire"). The name of one of the rivers in the lower world. See HADES; PHLEGETHON.

Pyromăchus (Πυρόμαχος) or **Phyromăchus** (Φυρόμαχος). (1) An Athenian sculptor who made the bas-reliefs on the frieze of the temple of Atheué Polias, about B.C. 408 (*C. I. A.* i. 324). (2) A Pergamene sculptor who with Antigonus, Isigonus, and Stratonicus produced a number of groups representing the battle of Attalus and Eumenes of Pergamum against the Gauls. The so-called "Dying Gladiator" (really a dying Gaul) in the Capitol at Rome is a copy from one of these groups. The date of Pyromachus is about B.C. 150.

Pyrrha (Πύρρα). See DEUCALION.

Pyrrha (Πύρρα). (1) A town on the west coast of the island of Lesbos, on the inner part of the deep bay named after it, and consequently on the narrowest part of the island. (2) A town and promontory of Phthiotis, in Thessaly, on the Pagasaean Gulf, and near the frontiers of Magnesia. Off this promontory there were two small islands named Pyrrha and Deucalion. See DEUCALION.

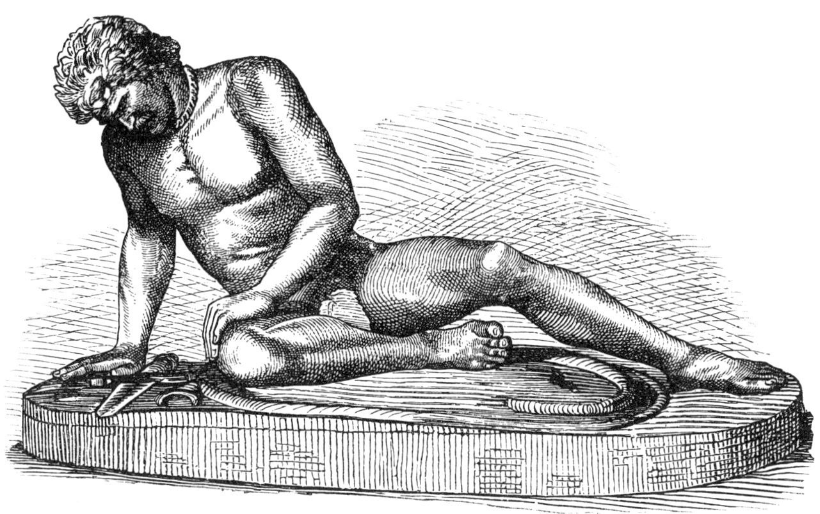

Dying Gaul copied from Pyromachus. (Capitoline Museum, Rome.)

Pyrrhĭca (*πυρρίχη*). A war-dance of Doric origin. It was danced to the sound of the flute in rapid measure by men dressed in armour, and illustrated the various positions of attack and defence. See SALTATIO.

Pyrrho (Πύρρων). The founder of the Sceptical or Pyrrhonian School of philosophy, a native of Elis in the Peloponnesus. He is said to have been poor, and to have followed at first the profession of a painter. He is then said to have been attracted to philosophy by the books of Democritus, to have attended the lectures of Bryson, a disciple of Stilpon, to have attached himself closely to Anaxarchus, and with him to have joined the expedition of Alexander the Great. During the greater part of his life he lived in retirement, and endeavoured to render himself independent of all external circumstances. His disciple Timon extolled with admiration his supreme repose of soul and his indifference to pleasure or pain. So highly was he valued by his fellow-citizens that they made him their high-priest, and erected a monument to him after his death. The Athenians conferred upon him the rights of citizenship. We know little respecting the principles of his sceptical philosophy, and the tales told about him by Diogenes Laërtius are probably the invention of his enemies. He asserted that certain knowledge on any subject was unattainable, and that the great object of man ought to be to lead a virtuous life. Pyrrho wrote no works, except a poem addressed to Alexander, which was rewarded by the latter in a royal manner. Pyrrho's philosophical system was first reduced to writing by his disciple Timon the Sillographer. (See TIMON.) He reached the age of ninety years, but his dates are uncertain.

Pyrrhus (Πύρρος). Mythological. See NEOPTOLEMUS.

Pyrrhus (Πύρρος). (1) I. A king of Epirus, son of Aeacides and Phthia, born B.C. 318. His ancestors claimed descent from Pyrrhus, the son of Achilles, who was said to have settled in Epirus after the Trojan War, and to have become the founder of the race of Molossian kings. On the deposition of his father by the Epirots (see AEACIDES), Pyrrhus, who was then a child only two years old, was saved from destruction by the faithful adherents of the king, who carried him to Glaucias, the king of the Taulantians, an Illyrian people. Glaucias took the child under his care and brought him up with his own children. He not only refused to surrender Pyrrhus to Cassander, but about ten years afterwards he marched into Epirus at the head of an army, and placed Pyrrhus on the throne, leaving him, however, under the care of guardians, as he was then only twelve years of age. In the course of four or five years, however, Cassander, who had gained his supremacy in Greece, prevailed upon the Epirots to expel their young king. Pyrrhus, who was then only seventeen years of age, joined Demetrius, who had married his sister Deïdamia, accompanied him to Asia, and was present at the battle of Ipsus (301), in which he gained great renown for his valour. Antigonus fell in the battle, and Demetrius became a fugitive; but Pyrrhus did not desert his brother-in-law in his misfortunes, and shortly afterwards went for him as a hostage into Egypt. Here he was fortunate enough to win the favour of Berenicé, the wife of Ptolemy, and received in marriage Antigoné, her daughter by her first husband. Ptolemy now supplied him with a fleet and forces, with which he returned to Epirus. Neoptolemus, who had reigned from the time that Pyrrhus had been driven from the kingdom, agreed to share the sovereignty with Pyrrhus. But such an arrangement could not last long, and Pyrrhus anticipated his own destruction by putting his rival to death. This appears to have happened in 295, in which year Pyrrhus is said to have begun to reign.

He was now twenty-three years old, and he soon became one of the most popular princes of his time. His daring courage made him a favourite with his troops, and his affability and generosity secured the love of his people. He seems at an early age to have taken Alexander as his model, and to have been fired with the ambition of imitating his exploits and treading in his footsteps. His eyes were first directed to the conquest of Macedonia. By assisting Alexander, the son of Cassander, against his brother Antipater, he obtained possession of the whole of the Macedonian dominions on the western side of Greece. But the Macedonian throne itself fell into the hands of Demetrius, greatly to the disappointment of Pyrrhus. The two former friends now became the most deadly enemies, and open war broke out between them in 291. After the war had been carried on with great vigour and various vicissitudes for four years, Pyrrhus joined the coalition formed in 287 by Seleucus, Ptolemy, and Lysimachus against Demetrius. Lysimachus and Pyrrhus invaded Macedonia; Demetrius was deserted by his troops and obliged to fly in disguise, and the kingdom was divided between Lysimachus and Pyrrhus. But the latter did not long retain his portion; the Macedonians preferred the rule of their old general Lysimachus, and Pyrrhus was accordingly driven out of the country after a reign of seven months (286).

For the next few years Pyrrhus reigned quietly in Epirus without embarking in any new enterprise. But a life of inactivity was insupportable to him, and accordingly he readily accepted the invitation of the Tarentines to assist them in their war against the Romans. He crossed over to Italy early in 280, in the thirty-eighth year of his age. He took with him 20,000 foot, 3000 horse, 2000 archers, 500 slingers, and either fifty or twenty elephants, having previously sent Milo, one of his generals, with a detachment of 3000 men. As soon as he arrived at Tarentum he began to make vigourous preparations for carrying on the war; and as the giddy and licentious inhabitants of Tarentum complained of the severity of his discipline, he forthwith treated them as their master rather than as their ally, shut up the theatre and all other public places, and compelled their young men to serve in his ranks. In the first campaign (280) the Roman consul M. Valerius Laevinus was defeated by Pyrrhus near Heraclea, on the bank of the river Siris. The battle was long and bravely contested, and it was not till Pyrrhus brought forward his elephants, which bore down everything before them, that the Romans took to flight. The loss of Pyrrhus, though inferior to that of the Romans, was still very considerable. A large proportion of his officers and best troops had fallen, and he said, as he viewed the field of battle, "Another such victory, and I must return to Epirus alone." He therefore availed himself of his success to send his minister Cineas to Rome with proposals of peace, while he himself marched slowly towards the city. His proposals, however, were rejected by the Senate. He accordingly continued his march, ravaging the Roman territory as he went along. He advanced within twenty-four miles of Rome; but as he found it impossible to compel the Romans to accept the peace, he retraced his steps and withdrew into winter-quarters at Tarentum. As soon as the armies were quartered for the winter, the Romans sent an embassy to Pyrrhus to endeavour to obtain the ransom of the Roman prisoners. The ambassadors were received by Pyrrhus in the most distinguished manner, and his interviews with C. Fabricius, who was at the head of the embassy, form one of the most celebrated stories in Roman history. See FABRICIUS.

In the second campaign (279) Pyrrhus gained another victory near Asculum over the Romans, who were commanded by the consuls P. Decius Mus and P. Sulpicius Saverrio. The battle, however, was followed by no decisive results, and the brunt of it had again fallen, as in the previous year, almost exclusively on the Greek troops of the king. He was therefore unwilling to hazard his surviving Greeks by another campaign with the Romans, and accordingly he lent a ready ear to the invitations of the Greeks in Sicily, who begged him to come to their assistance against the Carthaginians. The Romans were likewise anxious to get rid of so formidable an opponent, that they might complete the subjugation of Southern Italy without further interruption. When both parties had the same wishes, it was not difficult to find a fair pretext for bringing the war to a conclusion. This was afforded at the beginning of the following year (278) by one of the servants of Pyrrhus deserting to the Romans and proposing to the consuls to poison his master. The consuls Fabricius and Aemilius sent back the deserter to the king, stating that they abhorred a victory gained by treason. Thereupon Pyrrhus, to show his gratitude, sent Cineas to Rome with all the Roman prisoners without ransom and without conditions; and the Romans granted him a truce, though not a formal peace, as he had not consented to evacuate Italy.

Pyrrhus now crossed over into Sicily, where he remained upwards of two years, from the middle of 278 to the latter end of 276. At first he met with brilliant success, defeated the Carthaginians and took Eryx; but having failed in an attempt upon Lilybaeum, he lost his popularity with the Greeks, who began to form cabals and plots against him. This led to retaliation on the part of Pyrrhus, and to acts which were deemed both cruel and tyrannical by the Greeks. His position in Sicily at length became so uncomfortable and dangerous that he soon became anxious to abandon the island. Accordingly, when his Italian allies again begged him to come to their assistance, he gladly complied with their request. Pyrrhus returned to Italy in the autumn of 276. In the following year (275) the war was brought to a close. Pyrrhus was defeated with great loss near Beneventum by the Roman consul Curius Dentatus, and was obliged to leave Italy. He brought back with him to Epirus only 8000 foot and 500 horse, and had not money to maintain even these without undertaking new wars. Accordingly, in 273, he invaded Macedonia, of which Antigonus Gonatas, the son of Demetrius, was then king. His only object at first seems to have been plunder, but his success far exceeded his expectations. Antigonus was deserted by his own troops, and Pyrrhus thus became king of Macedonia a second time. But scarcely had he obtained possession of the kingdom before his restless spirit drove him into new enterprises. On the invitation of Cleonymus he turned his arms against Sparta, but was repulsed in an attack upon this city. From Sparta he marched towards Argos in order to support Aristeas, one of the leading citizens at Argos, against his rival Aristippus, whose cause was espoused by Antigonus. In the night-time Aristeas admitted Pyrrhus into the city, but the alarm having been given, the citadel and all the strong places were seized by the Argives of the opposite faction. On the dawn of day Pyrrhus saw that it would be necessary for him to retreat; and as he was fighting his way out of the city, an Argive woman hurled down from the housetop a ponderous tile, which struck Pyrrhus on the back of his neck. He fell from his horse stunned with the blow, and being recognized by some of the soldiers of Antigonus, was quickly despatched.

His head was cut off and carried to Antigonus, who turned away from the sight, and ordered the body to be interred with becoming honours. Pyrrhus perished in B.C. 272, in the forty-sixth year of his age and in the twenty-third of his reign.

He was the greatest warrior and one of the best princes of his time. With his daring courage, his military skill, and his kingly bearing, he might have become the most powerful monarch of his day if he had steadily pursued the immediate object before him. But he never rested satisfied with any acquisition, and was ever grasping at some fresh object: hence Antigonus compared him to a gambler, who made many good throws with the dice, but was unable to make the proper use of the game. Pyrrhus was regarded in subsequent times as one of the greatest generals that had ever lived. Hannibal said that of all generals Pyrrhus was the first, Scipio the second, and himself the third; or, according to another version of the story, Alexander was the first, Pyrrhus the second, and himself the third. Pyrrhus wrote a work on the art of war, which was read in the time of Cicero; and his commentaries are quoted both by Dionysius and Plutarch. Pyrrhus married four wives: (*a*) Antigoné, the daughter of Berenicé; (*b*) a daughter of Audoleon, king of the Paeonians; (*c*) Bircenna, a daughter of Bardylis, king of the Illyrians; (*d*) Lanassa, a daughter of Agathocles of Syracuse. His children were: (*a*) Ptolemy, born 295; killed in battle, 272; (*b*) Alexander, who succeeded his father as king of Epirus; (*c*) Helenus; (*d*) Nereis, who married Gelon of Syracuse; (*e*) Olympias, who married her own brother Alexander; (*f*) Deidamia or Laodamia. See the Life by Plutarch.

(2) II. A king of Epirus, son of Alexander II. and Olympias, and grandson of Pyrrhus I., was a child at the time of his father's death (between B.C. 262 and 258). During his minority the kingdom was governed by his mother, Olympias. According to one account Olympias survived Pyrrhus, who died soon after he had grown up to manhood; according to another account Olympias had poisoned a maiden to whom Pyrrhus was attached, and was herself poisoned by him in revenge.

Pythagŏras (Πυθαγόρας). (1) A celebrated Greek philosopher, a native of Samos, and the sŏn of Mnesarchus, who was either a merchant, or, according to others, an engraver of signets. The date of his birth is uncertain; but all authorities agree that he flourished in the times of Polycrates and Tarquinius Superbus (B.C. 540–510). He studied in his own country under Creophilus, Pherecydes of Syros, and others, and is said to have visited Egypt and many countries of the East for the purpose of acquiring knowledge. We have not much trustworthy evidence, either as to the kind and amount of knowledge which he acquired, or as to his definite philosophical views. It is certain, however, that he believed in the transmigration of souls; and he is said to have pretended that he had been Euphorbus, the son of Panthoüs, in the Trojan War, as well as various other characters. He is further said to have discovered the propositions that the triangle inscribed in a semicircle is right-angled; that the square on the hypotenuse of a right-angled triangle is equal to the sum of the squares on the sides. There is a celebrated story of his having discovered the arithmetical relations of the musical scale by observing accidentally the various sounds produced by hammers of different weights striking upon an anvil, and suspending by strings weights equal to those of the different hammers. The retailers of the story of course never took the trouble to verify the experiment, or they would have discovered that different hammers do not produce different sounds from the same anvil, any more than different clappers do from the same bell. Discoveries in astronomy are also attributed to Pythagoras. There can be little doubt that he paid great attention to arithmetic, and its application to weights, measures, and the theory of music. Apart from all direct testimony, however, it may safely be affirmed that the very remarkable influence exerted by Pythagoras, and even the fact that he was made the hero of so many marvellous stories, proves him to have been a man both of singular capabilities and of great acquirements. It may also be affirmed with safety that the religious element was the predominant one in the character of Pythagoras, and that religious ascendancy in connection with a certain mystic religious system was the object which he chiefly laboured to secure. It was this religious element which made the profoundest impression upon his contemporaries. They regarded him as standing in a peculiarly close connection with the gods. The Crotoniats even identified him with the Hyperborean Apollo. And, without viewing him as an impostor, we may easily believe that he himself, to some extent, shared the same views. He pretended to divination and prophecy; and he appears as the revealer of a mode of life calculated to raise his disciples above the level of mankind, and to recommend them to the favour of the gods. No certainty can be arrived at as to the length of time spent by Pythagoras in Egypt or the East, or as to his residence and efforts in Samos or other Grecian cities, before he settled at Crotona in Italy. He probably removed to Crotona because he found it impossible to realize his schemes in his native country while under the tyranny of Polycrates. The reason why he selected Crotona as the sphere of his operations it is impossible to ascertain; but soon after his arrival in that city he attained extensive influence, and gained over great numbers to enter into his views. His adherents were chiefly of the noble and wealthy classes. Three hundred of these were formed into a select brotherhood or club, bound by a sort of vow to Pythagoras and each other, for the purpose of cultivating the religious and ascetic observances enjoined by their master, and of studying his religious and philosophical theories. Everything that was done and taught among the members was kept a profound secret from all without its pale. It was an old Pythagorean maxim, that everything was not to be told to everybody. There were also gradations among the members themselves, as in the distinction of ἀκουσματικοί or "hearers" as contrasted with μαθηματικοί or esoteric students. In the admission of candidates Pythagoras is said to have placed great reliance on his physiognomical discernment. If admitted, they had to pass through a period of probation, in which their powers of maintaining silence were especially tested, as well as their general temper, disposition, and mental capacity. As regards the nature of the esoteric instruction to which only the most approved members of the fraternity were admitted, some have supposed that it had reference to the political views of Pythagoras. Others have maintained, with greater probability, that it related mainly to the *orgies*, or secret religious doctrines and usages, which undoubtedly formed a prominent feature in the Pythagorean system, and were peculiarly connected with the worship of Apollo. There were some outward peculiarities of an ascetic kind in the mode of life to which the members of the brotherhood were subjected. Some represent him as forbidding all animal food; but all the members cannot have been subjected to this prohibition, since the athletic Milo, for instance, could not possibly have dispensed with animal food. According to some ancient authorities, he allowed the use of all kinds of animal food except the flesh of oxen used for ploughing, and rams. There is a similar discrepancy as to the prohibition of fish and beans. But temperance of all kinds seems to have been strictly enjoined. It is also stated that they had common meals, resembling the Spartan syssitia, at which they met in companies of ten. Considerable importance seems to have been attached to music and gymnastics in the daily exercises of the disciples. Their whole discipline is represented as tending to produce a lofty serenity and self-possession, regarding the exhibition of which various anecdotes were current in antiquity. Among the best ascertained features of the brotherhood are the devoted attachment of the members to each other, and their sovereign contempt for those who did not belong to their ranks. It appears that they had some secret conventional symbols, by which members of the fraternity could recognize each other, even if they had never met before. Clubs similar to that at Crotona were established at Sybaris, Metapontum, Tarentum, and other cities of Magna Graecia. The institutions of Pythagoras were certainly not intended to withdraw those who adopted them from active exertion, that they might devote themselves exclusively to religious and philosophical contemplations. He rather aimed at the production of a calm bearing and elevated tone of character, through which those trained in the discipline of the Pythagorean life should exhibit in their personal and social capacities a reflection of the order and harmony of the universe. Whether he had any distinct political designs in the foundation of his brotherhood is doubtful; but it was perfectly natural, even without any express design on his part, that a club such as the Three Hundred of Crotona should gradually come to mingle political with other objects, and, by the facilities afforded by their secret and compact organization, should speedily gain extensive political influence. That this influence should be decisively on the side of aristocracy or oligarchy resulted naturally both from the nature of the Pythagorean institutions, and from the rank and social position of the members of the brotherhood. Through them, of course, Pythagoras himself exercised a large amount of indirect influence over the affairs both of Crotona and of other Italian cities. This Pythagorean brotherhood or order resembled in many respects the one founded by Loyola. It is easy to understand how this aristocratical and exclusive club would excite the jealousy and hostility not only of the democratical party in Crotona, but also of a considerable number of the opposite faction. The hatred which they had excited speedily led to their destruction. The populace of Crotona rose against them; and an attack was made upon them while assembled either in the house of Milo, or in some other place of meeting. The building was set on fire, and many of the assembled members perished; only the more active escaped. Similar commotions ensued in the other cities of Magna Graecia in which Pythagorean clubs had been formed. As an active and organized brotherhood, the Pythagorean Order was everywhere suppressed; but the Pythagoreans still continued to exist as a sect, the members of which kept up among themselves their religious observances and scientific pursuits, while individuals, as in the case of Archytas, acquired now and then great political influence.

Respecting the fate of Pythagoras himself, the accounts varied. Some say that he perished in the temple with his disciples, others that he fled first to Tarentum, and that, being driven thence, he escaped to Metapontum, and there starved himself to death. His tomb was shown at Metapontum in the time of Cicero. According to some accounts, Pythagoras married Theano, a lady of Crotona, and had a daughter Damo, and a son Telauges, or, according to others, two daughters, Damo and Myia; while other notices seem to imply that he had a wife and a daughter grown up when he came to Crotona. When we come to inquire what were the philosophical or religious opinions held by Pythagoras himself, we are met at the outset by the difficulty that even the authors from whom we have to draw possessed no authentic records bearing upon the age of Pythagoras himself. If Pythagoras ever wrote anything, his writings perished with him, or not long after. The probability is that he wrote nothing. Everything current under his name in antiquity is spurious. It is all but certain that Philolaüs was the first who *published* the Pythagorean doctrines, at any rate in a written form. (See PHILOLAÜS.) Still there was so marked a peculiarity running through the Pythagorean philosophy that there can be little question as to the germs of the system, at any rate, having been derived from Pythagoras himself. Pythagoras resembled the philosophers of the Ionic school, who undertook to solve, by means of a single primordial principle, the vague problem of the origin and constitution of the universe as a whole. His predilection for mathematical studies led him to trace the origin of all things to *number*, his theory being suggested, or at all events confirmed, by the observation of various numerical relations, or analogies to them, in the phenomena of the universe. Musical principles likewise played almost as important a part in the Pythagorean system as mathematical or numerical ideas. We find running through the entire system the idea that order, or harmony of relation, is the regulating principle of the whole universe. The intervals between the heavenly bodies were supposed to be determined according to the laws and relations of musical harmony. Hence arose the celebrated doctrine of the harmony of the spheres; for the heavenly bodies, in their motion, could not but occasion a certain sound or note, depending on their distances and velocities; and as these were determined by the laws of harmonical intervals, the notes altogether formed a regular musical scale or harmony. This harmony, however, we do not hear, either because we have been accustomed to it from the first, and have never had an opportunity of contrasting it with stillness, or because the sound is so powerful as to exceed our capacities for hearing. The ethics of the Pythagoreans consisted more in ascetic practice, and maxims for the restraint of the passions, especially of anger, and the cultivation of the power of endurance, than in scientific theory. What of the latter they had was, as might be expected, intimately connected with their number-theory. Happiness consisted in the science of the perfection of the virtues of the soul, or in the perfect science of numbers. Likeness to the Deity was to be the object of all our endeavours, man becoming better as he approaches the gods, who are the guardians and guides of men. Great importance was attached to the influence of music in controlling the force of the passions. Self-examination was strongly insisted on. The transmigration of souls was viewed apparently in the light of a process of purification. Souls under the dominion of sensuality either passed into the bodies of animals, or, if incurable, were thrust down into Tartarus to meet with expiation or condign punishment. The pure were exalted to higher modes of life, and at last attained to incorporeal existence. As regards the fruits of this system of training or belief, it is interesting to remark, that wherever we have notices of distinguished Pythagoreans, we usually hear of them as men of great uprightness, conscientiousness, and self-restraint, and as capable of devoted and enduring friendship. (See ARCHYTAS; DAMON; and PHINTIAS.) Existing works that bear the name of Pythagoras are spurious. See Günther, *Carmen Aureum* (Breslau, 1816); Schneeberger, *Die goldenen Sprüche des Pythagoras* (Münnerstadt, 1862). On the life of Pythagoras, see the Eng. version of the life by Iamblichus made by Taylor (London, 1818); and, in general, Ritter, *Geschichte der Pythagorischen Philosophie* (Hamburg, 1826); Brandis, *Ueber die Zahlenlehre der Pythagoreer und Platoniker* in the *Rheinisches Museum* for 1828; Gladisch, *Die Pythagoreer* (Posen, 1841); Grote, *History of Greece*, vol. iv. pp. 525–551; Langel, *Pythagore*, in the *Revue des Deux Mondes* for 1864, pp. 969–989; Rathgeber, *Grossgriechenland und Pythagoras* (Gotha, 1866); Baltzer, *Pythagoras der Weise von Samos* (Nordhausen, 1868); Chaignet, *Pythagore et la Philosophie Pythagorienne* (Paris, 1873); Gow, *Short History of Mathematics* (London, 1884); Zeller, *The Pre-Socratic Schools* (Eng. trans. 1882); and the article PHILOSOPHIA. (2) Of Rhegium, one of the most celebrated statuaries of Greece, probably flourished B.C. 480–430. His most important works appear to have been his statues of athletes.

Pytheas (Πυθέας). (1) An Athenian orator, distinguished by his unceasing animosity against Demosthenes. He had no political principles, made no pretensions to honesty, and changed sides as often as suited his convenience or his interest. Of the part that he took in political affairs only two or three facts are recorded. He opposed the honours which the Athenians proposed to confer upon Alexander, but he afterwards espoused the interests of the Macedonian party. He accused Demosthenes of having received bribes from Harpalus. In the Lamian War (B.C. 322) he joined Antipater, and had thus the satisfaction of surviving his great enemy Demosthenes. He is said to have been the author of the well-known saying that the orations of Demosthenes smelt of the lamp. (2) Of Massilia in Gaul, a celebrated Greek navigator, who sailed to the western and northern parts of Europe, and wrote a book containing the results of his discoveries. He probably lived in the time of Alexander the Great or shortly afterwards. He appears to have undertaken two voyages, one in which he visited Britain and Thulé, and of which he probably gave an account in his work on the Ocean; and a second, undertaken after his return from his first voyage, in which he coasted along the whole of Europe from Gadira (now Cadiz) to the Tanaïs (Don), and the description of which probably formed the subject of his *Periplus*. Pytheas made Thulé a six days' sail from Britain, and said that the day and the night were each six months long in Thulé; hence some modern writers have supposed that he must have reached Iceland, while others have maintained that he advanced as far as the Shetland Islands. But either supposition is very improbable, and neither is necessary; for reports of the great length of the day and night in the northern parts of Europe had already reached the Greeks before the time of Pytheas. There has been likewise much dispute as to what river we are to understand by the Tanaïs. The most probable conjecture is that, upon reaching the Elbe, Pytheas concluded that he had arrived at the Tanaïs, separating Europe from Asia. See Antichan, *Les Grands Voyages de Découvertes des Anciens* (Paris, 1891).

Pythia (τὰ Πύθια). The Pythian Games. Next to the Olympic Games, the most important of the four Greek national festivals. From B.C. 586 they were held on the Crissaean Plain below Delphi (originally called Pytho). They took place once in four years, in the third year of each Olympiad, in the Delphic month Bucatius, corresponding to a part of our middle of August. Before this time (B.C. 586) there used to take place at Delphi itself, once in eight years, a great festival in honour of Apollo, the traditional founder (Athen. xv. p. 701), in which the minstrels vied with one another in singing, to the accompaniment of the cithara, a paean in praise of the god, under the direction of the Delphic priests. After the first Sacred War, when the Crissaean Plain became the property of the priesthood, the Amphictyones introduced festivals once in four years, at which gymnastic contests and foot-races took place, as well as the customary musical contest. This contest also was further developed. Besides minstrels who sang to the cithara, players on the flute, and singers to accompaniment of the flute, took part in it, the last-named, however, for a short time only. The gymnastic and athletic contests, which were nearly the same as those held at Olympia, yielded in significance to the musical ceremonies, and of those the Pythian νόμος was the most important. It was a composition for the flute, worked out on a prescribed scheme, and celebrating the battle of Apollo with the dragon Python, and his triumph. (See DELPHI.) At first the prize for the victor was of some substantial value, but at the second festival it took the form of a wreath from the sacred bay tree in the Vale of Tempé. The victor also received, as in the other contests, a palm-branch. The judges were chosen by the Amphictyones. The Pythian, like the Olympic, Games were probably not discontinued till about A.D. 394. Minor Pythian Games were celebrated in other parts of the Greek world—e. g. at Ancyra in Galatia, at Aphrodisias in Caria, at Carthage, Delos, Miletus, Perinthus, Sicyon, etc. See Krause, *Die Pythien, Nemeen und Isthmien*, pp. 1–106.

Pythia (Πυθία). The priestess of Apollo at Delphi who pronounced the oracles. See DELPHI; ORACULUM.

Pythias (Πυθιάς). (1) The wife of Aristotle. (2) The daughter of Aristotle.

Pythius (Πύθιος). A Lydian, the son of Atys. He was a man of enormous wealth, which he derived from his gold mines in the neighbourhood of Celaenae in Phrygia. When Xerxes arrived at Celaenae, Pythius banqueted him and his whole army. His five sons accompanied Xerxes. Pythius, alarmed by an eclipse of the sun which happened, came to Xerxes, and begged that the eldest might be left behind. This request so enraged the king that he had the young man immediately killed and cut in two, and the two portions of his body placed on either side of the road, and then ordered the army to march between them (Herod. vii. 21).

Python (πύθων). A serpent sprung from the mud left by the deluge of Deucalion (q. v.). He was slain by Apollo. See APOLLO; DELPHI.

Pyxis (πυξίς). A small case made of box-wood (πύξος). It was used as a jewel-case or for the preservation of any small object of value (Petron. 110).

Pyxis. (Herculaneum.)

Pyxus (πυξοῦς). See BUXENTUM.

Q

Q, as a symbol.

IN LATIN.—Q = quaestiones, Quintus, quondam.

Q·Q = quicquid, quinquennalis, Quinti duo.

Q·A = quaestor aerarii, quotannis.

Q·D = quaestor designatus, quondam.

Q·M = qui militavit, quo minus.

Q·P = quaestoria potestate, quadrati pedes.

Q·V = qui vocatur.

Q·A·V(V·A) = qui annos(-is) vixit, qui vixit annos.

Q·C·A = quorum curam agebat.

Q·C·P = quinquennalis censoria potestate.

Q·C·R = quei cives Romani(erunt).

Q·E·D = quod eo die.

Q·M·C = qui militare coeperunt.

Q·P·F = qui primi fuerunt.

Q·B·F·F = quod bonum faustum felix(sit).

Q·D·R·A = qua de re agitur.

Q·E·C·F = (votum libens animo posuit) quoius eum compotem fecit.

Q·I·D·P = qui iure dicundo praeerit.

Q·P·A·P = quaestor pecuniae alimentorum publicorum.

Q·R·C·F = quando rex comitio fugit.

Q·V·P·Q = quoquoversus pedes quadratos.

Q·H·C·I·R = quo honore contentus impensam remisit.

Q·N·S·S·S = quorum nomina supra scripta sunt.

Q·S·P·P·S = qui sacris publicis praesto sunt.

Q·L·S·V·T·L = (dicite) qui legitis sit vobis terra levis.

Q·V·F·S·I·O = quod verba facta sunt in ordine.

Q·D·E·R·F·P·D·E·R·I·C = quid de ea re fieri placeret, de ea re ita censuerunt.

Quadi. A powerful German people of the Suevic race, who dwelt in the southeastern part of Germany, between Mount Gabreta, the Hercynian Forest, the Sarmatian Mountains, and the Danube. They were bounded on the west by the Marcomanni, with whom they were always closely united; on the north by the Gothini and Osi; on the east by the Iazyges Metanastae, from whom they were separated by the river Granuas (Gran); and on the south by the Pannonians, from whom they were divided by the Danube. In the reign of Tiberius the Quadi were taken under the protection of the Romans. In the reign of Marcus Aurelius, however, they joined the Marcomanni and other German tribes in the long and bloody war against the Empire, which lasted during the greater part of that emperor's reign. Their name is especially memorable in the history of this war by the victory which M. Aurelius gained over them in A.D. 174 (Dio Cass. lxxi. 8–20). Their independence was recognized by Commodus in A.D. 180. The Quadi disappear from history towards the end of the fourth century.

Quadra. (1) A square dining-table (Verg. *Aen.* vii. 115). See MENSA. (2) The plinth placed under the base of a column (Vitruv. iii. 4. 5). (3) Each of the narrow flat bands on a column forming respectively the upper and lower division between the hollow *scotia* and the swelling *torus* above and below it (Vitruv. iii. 5. 2). See COLUMNA.

Quadragesĭma. The fortieth part of imported goods (=2½ per cent.) collected in some of the Roman provinces as a customs tax. See Wilmanns, *Exempla Inscript. Lat.* 1397, 1398; and the article PORTORIUM.

Quadrans (= *teruncius*). A Roman copper coin, a quarter of an *as* = 3 *unciae*. (See AS; NUMISMATICS; UNCIA.) The quadrans was the usual price paid for a bath. It was equivalent to about a quarter of a cent. The quadrans bore three balls to indicate the number of *unciae*, accompanied by an open hand, a dolphin, a strigil, a star, a head of Hercules or of Ceres, or a ship. The Greek term is τετρᾶς.

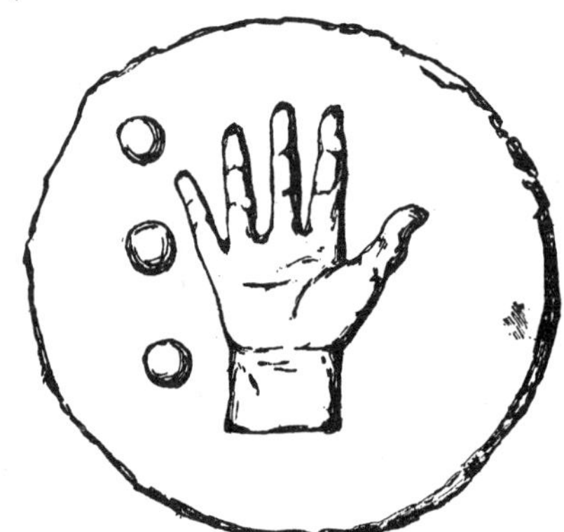

Quadrans. (Actual size.)

Quadrantal (also AMPHŎRA QUADRANTAL). A Roman measure of capacity, holding about twenty-four quarts (Fest. s. v. *publica pondera*, p. 24, ed. Müller). Half a quadrantal was an *urna;* one eighth, a *congius;* and one forty-eighth, a *sextarius.*

Quadrātae. Now Chiavasso; a Roman military station between Augusta Taurinorum (Turin) and Eporedia (Ivrea).

Quadrātus. (1) An early defender of the Christian religion, whose work (now lost) he dedicated to the emperor Hadrian in the year A.D. 126. Quadratus was in early life a resident of Asia Minor, and afterwards a bishop of the Church at Athens, but of the details of his career little is known. (2) ASINIUS. An author who wrote in Greek two historical works, one a history of Rome (Χιλιετηρίς) in the Ionic dialect, treating of the city from its foundation to the year A.D. 248, in which the Ludi Saeculares were celebrated; and a history of Parthia. Quadratus lived during the reigns of the emperors Philippus I. and Philippus II. (A.D. 244–249). (3) LUCIUS NINNIUS, a tribune of the plebs in B.C. 58, when he strongly sided with Cicero against his own colleague P. Clodius Pulcher (q. v.).

Quadrĭfrons. A surname of Ianus (q. v.). It is said that after the conquest of the Faliscans an image of Ianus was found with four foreheads (Serv. *ad* Verg. *Aen.* vii. 607). Hence a temple of Ianus Quadrifrons was afterwards built in the Forum Transitorium, which had four gates. The fact of the god being represented with four heads was considered by the ancients to be an indication of his being the divinity presiding over the year with its four seasons. See IANUS.

Ianus Quadrifrons in the Forum Transitorium at Rome.

Quadrīga (τέθριππον ἅρμα). A chariot drawn by four horses, used in battle and in athletic games. (See CIRCUS.) The illustration represents a quadriga as depicted on an ancient terra-cotta lamp. (See CURRUS.) The driver of a quadriga is called *quadrigarius.*

Quadriga. (Rich.)

Quadrigarius, Q. CLAUDIUS. A Roman annalist who flourished B.C. 120–78. His work, which contained at least twenty-three books, commenced immediately after the destruction of Rome by the Gauls, and must in all probability have come down to the death of Sulla, since the seventh consulship of Marius was commemorated in the nineteenth book. By Livy he is uniformly referred to simply as Claudius or Clodius. By other authors he is cited as Quintius, as Claudius, as Q. Claudius, as Claudius Quadrigarius, or as Quadrigarius. From the caution evinced by Livy in making use of him as an authority, especially in matters relating to numbers, it would appear that he was disposed to indulge, although in a less degree, in the same exaggerations as characterize his contemporary Valerius Antias. He is warmly praised by Gellius (x. 13; xiii. 29; xv. 1). See LIVIUS.

Quadrigātus (sc. *nummus*). A silver denarius having the device of a four-horse chariot (*quadriga*) on the reverse.

Quadrigatus. (Actual size.)

Quadrirēmis. A warship having four banks of oars. See NAVIS.

Quadrivium (τετραόδιον). (1) A place where four streets met (Juv. i. 64). (2) See LIBERALES ARTES.

Quadruplātor. A professional accuser in those cases under the Roman law which involved a pecuniary penalty (Cic. *Verr.* ii. 8. 22). The name probably owes its origin to the fact that the quadruplator professed to expose offences in which the fine was fixed at four times the damage, as, for example, a violation of the usury laws (Livy, vii. 28), and in which, therefore, his own reward would be large. See Geib, *Criminalprocess*, 106; and the article DELATOR.

Quaesītor. The Roman title of the president of an extraordinary or ordinary criminal court (*quaestio extraordinaria* or *perpetua*). According to Sulla's rules of procedure, six praetors chosen for criminal cases presided, and when this number was not sufficient additional judges, *iudices quaestionis*, were provided.

Quaestio. The Latin term for a court of inquiry, either *extraordinaria*, an extraordinary commission appointed by the Senate or people for special criminal cases, or *perpetua*, an ordinary criminal court for certain defined offences. The first court of this kind was held B.C. 149 to try a case of extortion.

In course of time, by the laws of Gaius Gracchus and of Sulla, the number of these tribunals was increased. In Cicero's time there were eight ordinary courts to try cases of extortion, high treason (*maiestas*), embezzlement (*peculatus*), unlawful canvassing for an office (*ambitus*), violence (*vis*), assassination, poisoning, and forgery. Every quaestio had a president (see QUAESITOR), either one of the praetors chosen by lot, or when the number of these was not sufficient, a *iudex quaestionis*, in addition to a certain number of sworn judges. See IUDEX.

It was open to any one except to women, infants, and those who were *infames*, to begin a criminal prosecution, even if he himself had not been the party injured. There was no public prosecutor; but the State, by means of pecuniary rewards and conferring of dignities, encouraged the prosecution of criminals. If, however, the accused party was found innocent, it was open to him to prosecute his accuser for chicanery. (See CALUMNIA.) The case was begun by the *postulatio*, a request, with a statement of the crime and name of the accused, for permission to prosecute, made to the praetor at an open sitting in the market-place. If several persons offered themselves as accusers, the choice was made by *divinatio* (q. v.). But besides the principal accuser, others were allowed, who signed the indictment, and were therefore called *subscriptores*. When permission had been obtained, there followed the *nominis delatio*, the handing in of the indictment; the *receptio* and *inscriptio*, the reception and entry of the same in the official list by the praetor; the *interrogatio*, the examination (also by the praetor) of the accused, who was now *reus* (q. v.). Unless he pleaded guilty or clearly proved his innocence, the *diei dictio*, or date of hearing the case, was fixed at the earliest in ten days, in special cases not till 100 days later. It was the duty of the complainant to collect in the meantime the necessary evidence and witnesses, and for this purpose he received an official authorization. At the sitting of the court, which was held publicly by the sworn judges (*cognitio*), after the judges and parties had been cited, the accuser delivered his accusation in a continuous speech, the *subscriptores* followed him, then the accused and his *patroni*. The duration of these speeches (*actiones*) was at first unlimited, but afterwards, to correct the abuse of this privilege, a water-clock was introduced, which limited the time of each speaker; the time allowed for the defence was about a third greater than that for the accusation. Then followed the proof (*probatio*) of the case. For this documents, circumstantial evidence, and declarations of witnesses were used. Next, unless the case was adjourned for the production of further proof (*ampliatio*), or for a new trial on the third day (*comperendinatio*), the votes of the judges on the question of guilt or innocence were taken. The voting was usually in secret. The judges received from the president wooden tablets covered with wax, on the one side inscribed with a C (*condemno*, "I condemn"), on the other with an A (*absolvo*, "I acquit"). They erased one of these letters and threw the tablets into an urn. In cases where they were unable to decide respecting the guilt or innocence of the accused, they could signify the same by writing on the tablet the letters N. L. (*non liquet*).

The result of the voting was then formally proclaimed by the president; and if a fine was inflicted, the amount (*litis aestimatio*) was then decided by the president and the sworn judges. A man once acquitted could not be retried for the same offence unless his acquittal had been procured by collusion (see PRAEVARICATIO) of the accuser. There was no way of altering the verdict of the sworn judges, and the punishment was exacted immediately after the sentence had been given. If it was one of degradation (*infamia*) or exile (*interdictio aquae et ignis;* see EXSILIUM), the man so punished could be reinstated in the rights he had forfeited (*restitutio in integrum*). This was done by a decree of the people; in later times, by the emperor's pardon. These courts of sworn judges lasted till the beginning of the third century A.D.

Quaestiōnes Naturāles. See SENECA.

Quaestiōnes Romānae. See PLUTARCHUS.

Quaestōres (from *quaero*, *quaesitor*, "the investigator," "searcher"). The Latin term originally given to two officials chosen by the king; they had to do with those suspected of capital offences. In the time of the Republic they performed the same duty under the consuls, by whom they were chosen every year. When the administration of justice in criminal cases came into the hands of the Comitia Centuriata, the quaestors received, in addition to their old privilege of pleading by the mandate of the consuls, which they lost later, the management of the State treasury (*aerarium*) in the temple of Saturn. They became recognized officials when they were elected at the Comitia Tributa under the presidency of the consuls (probably about B.C. 447). The quaestors had no regular badges of office. In 421 their number was doubled, and the plebeians received the right of appointing to the office of quaestor, though they did not exercise it till twelve years later. The four quaestors shared their duties, so that two of them acted as masters of the treasury (*quaestores aerarii*) and remained in the city (hence their name *quaestores urbani*), while the other two accompanied the consuls on campaigns, in order to administer the military chest.

It was part of the duty of the former two to collect the regular revenues of State (taxes and custom dues) and the extraordinary revenues (fines, levies for war, and money produced by the sale of booty); further, to make payments, which might not be made to the consuls except by special permission of the Senate; to control the accounts of income and expenditure, which were managed under their responsibility by a special class of officials (*scribae*); to make arrangements for public burials, for the erection of monuments, for the entertainment of foreign ambassadors, etc., at the expense of the treasury. Further, they preserved at their place of business—the temple of Saturn—the military standards, also the laws, the decrees of the Senate, and the plebiscita, and kept a register of the swearing in of the officials, which took place there.

After the subjection of Italy, four more quaestors were appointed in B.C. 267. They were stationed in different parts of Italy, at first at Ostia and Ariminum, probably to supervise the building of fleets. Sulla increased their number to twenty, ten of whom were appointed, in the place of the previous two, to accompany the proconsuls and propraetors to the provinces, two to help the consul who remained in the city, and two to help the other two original quaestors at their work in the city. The quaestors employed in the provinces (Sicily alone had two of these, stationed at Syracuse and Lilybaeum respectively) were principally occupied with finance; they managed the provincial treasury, and defrayed out of it the expenses of the army, the governor, and his retinue; any surplus they had to pay in to the State treasury at Rome, and to furnish an exact statement of accounts. The governor might appoint them his deputies, and if he died they assumed the command; in both of these cases they acted *pro praetore*—i. e. as propraetors. Caesar raised their number to forty, in order to be able to reward a greater number of his adherents; for the office gave admittance to the Senate, and the position of quaestor was looked upon as the first step in the official career. The age defined by law was from twenty-seven to thirty years. When the beginning of the magisterial year was fixed for January 1, the quaestors assumed office on December 5, on which day the quaestors in the *aerarium* decided by lot what the work of each should be.

Even under the Empire, when the normal number of quaestors was increased to twenty and the age reduced to twenty-five, the office of quaestor remained the first step to higher positions in the State. But the power of the quaestors grew more limited as the management of the treasury was intrusted to special *praefecti aerarii*, so that the city quaestors had only charge of the archives, to which the supervision of the paving of streets was added. After the division of the provinces between the emperor and the Senate, quaestors were only employed in the senatorial provinces, and were not abolished till the constitution of the provinces in general was altered by Diocletian. Four quaestors were told off for service to the consuls. The two *quaestores principis*, or *Augusti*, were a new creation: they were officers assigned to the emperors, if the latter were not consuls, in which case they would already be entitled to two quaestors. As secretaries to the emperor, they had to read his decrees to the Senate at its sittings. From these quaestors was developed, in the time of Constantine, the *quaestor Sacri Palatii*, the chancellor of the Empire.

Quail-fights. See VENATIONES.

Qualus (τάλαρος). A wicker basket. See CALATHUS.

Quariates. A people of Gallia Narbonensis on the river Druentia (Durance), below the modern Briançon (Pliny, *H. N.* iii. 35).

Quarries. See LAUTUMIAE.

Quartarius (τέταρτον). A measure of capacity, one fourth of the *sextarius* (pint).

Quasillus and **Quasillum** (τάλαρις). Diminutives of QUALUS and QUALUM.

Quaternio (τετράς, τετράδιον). A quire of four sheets (eight leaves) of paper; the origin of our word "quire."

Quattuorvĭri. The Roman term for an official body consisting of four men. See VIGINTISEXVIRI.

Quies. The Roman goddess of rest and tranquillity. She had a sanctuary on the Via Labicana, where travellers stopped to rest; and one outside the Porta Collina (Livy, iv. 41).

Quiētus, Q. LUSIUS. A Moorish chief who served with distinction under Trajan in both the Dacian and the Parthian Wars. Trajan made him governor of Iudaea, and raised him to the consulship in A.D. 116 or 117. After Trajan's death he returned to his native country, but he was suspected by Hadrian of fomenting the disturbances which then prevailed in Mauretania, and was shortly afterwards put to death by order of Hadrian (Dio Cass. lxviii. 8, 22, 30, 32; lxix. 2).

Quilt. See STRAGULUM.

Quinarius. A silver coin equal to a half-denarius, and worth about nine cents. See DENARIUS.

Quinarius. (Actual size.)

Quinctia (or **Quintia**) **Gens**. A Roman patrician gens, being one of the Alban houses that came to Rome with Tullus Hostilius. Its most distinguished branches bore the names Capitolinus, Cincinnatus, and Flaminius. See LUPERCALIA, p. 980.

Quinctilius Varus. See VARUS.

Quinctius Cincinnātus. See CINCINNATUS.

Quinctius Flaminīnus. See FLAMININUS.

Quincunx. (1) A copper Roman coin weighing five ounces (*quinque unciae*), whence the name. It was marked by five balls (cf. the illustration under QUADRANS), and was valued at five-twelfths of an *as*. It is extremely rare, there being no specimens even in the British Museum. (2) The name given to an arrangement of things by fives after the fashion of the points on a die, thus:

```
o   o
  o
o   o
```

and to a series arranged in this way:

```
o   o   o   o   o   o
  o       o       o
o   o   o   o   o   o
  o       o       o
o   o   o   o   o   o
```

It was a favourite method of arranging trees (Cic. *De Sen.* 17). The French use the same word in the phrase *en quinconce*.

Quincupĕdal. A Roman graduated measuring-rod, five feet long (Mart. xiv. 92).

Quindecimvĭri. The Roman term for an official body consisting of fifteen men, especially that appointed for the inspection of the Sibylline Books. See SIBYLLAE.

Quinquagesĭma, sc. *pars.* (1) A Roman tax of the fiftieth part, or two per cent. on the value of all slaves who were sold. It was instituted by Augustus (Dio Cass. lv. 31). (2) A similar tax at Athens (πεντηκοστή) levied on exports and imports. See PENTECOSTÉ.

Quinquātrus and **Quinquātria** (neut. pl.). A festival celebrated at Rome on the 19th of March, in honour of Mars and, in a greater degree, of Minerva, whose temple had been founded on that day on the Aventine. An incorrect explanation of the name *quinquatrus,* which means the fifth day after the Ides (Varro, *L. L.* vi. 14), led to the festival in honour of Minerva being afterwards prolonged to five days. It was celebrated by all whose employment was under the protection of the goddess, such as teachers and their pupils. The latter obtained a holiday during the festival, and began a new course of study when it was over. The former received at this time their yearly stipend —the *minerval.* (See LUDUS LITTERARIUS.) The festival was also celebrated by women and children (as being spinners and weavers), by artisans and artists of every kind, and by poets and painters. The first day of the festival was celebrated with sacrifices by the State in honour of the founding of the temple. On the following days the gladiators performed, and there were social gatherings in the houses. On June 13th the minor Quinquatrus (*Quinquatrus minusculae*) took place. This festival lasted three days. It was celebrated by the guild of the flute-players, an important and numerous body at Rome. They honoured the goddess as their special patroness by meeting at her temple, by masked processions through the city, and by a banquet in the temple of the Capitoline Iupiter. See Livy, lx. 30; Ovid, *Fast.* vi. 651; Juv. x. 115; and Marquardt, *Staatsverwaltung,* iii. 566 in the second edition.

Quinquennāles. The officials chosen every five years in the Italian municipalities (see MUNICIPIUM), corresponding to the Roman censors. See CENSOR.

Quinquennalia. Roman games instituted by Nero in A.D. 60, in imitation of the Greek festivals (πεντετηρίδες). They included contests in music, gymnastics, and equestrian feats, and were also known from their founder as NERONIA or the AGON NERONEUS (Suet. *Nero,* 12). See LUDI.

Quinquerēmis (τετρήρης). A Roman ship of war with five banks of oars. See NAVIS.

Quinquertium. A Roman athletic contest corresponding to the Greek πένταθλον. See PENTATHLON.

Quinquevĭri. A name given by the Romans to any board of five commissioners such as under the Republic were frequently appointed by the extraordinary magistrates to carry out any particular measure, as the Quinqueviri Mensarii or bankers authorized to manage public loans and other financial matters, something like a modern syndicate. Other functions that were sometimes assigned to such commissioners were the repairs of the city walls and towers (Livy, xxv. 7), the formation of colonies (usually, however, done by *triumviri*), etc. There was also a regular board of five (*Quinqueviri cis Tiberim*) to guard against fires, breaches of public order, etc. (Livy, xxxix. 14).

Quintāna Porta. See CASTRA.

Quintia Gens. See QUINCTIA GENS.

Quintiliānus, MARCUS FABIUS. A celebrated Roman rhetorician, born about A.D. 35 at Calagurris in Spain. After he had received his training as an orator at Rome, he returned home about A.D. 59, but again visited Rome in A.D. 68 in the suite of Galba. He there began to practise as an advocate, and also gave instruction in rhetoric. In this latter capacity he achieved such fame that he was able to open a school of rhetoric in the reign of Vespasian, and received a salary from the State. After twenty years' work he retired from his public duties in A.D. 90, and after some time devoted himself to the education of the grandchildren of Domitilla, Domitian's sister, for which he was rewarded by the emperor with the rank of consul. Though materially prosperous, his happiness was disturbed by the loss of his young wife and his two sons. He died between A.D. 97 and 100.

Of his works on rhetoric, composed in his later years, we possess the one that is more important, that on the training of an orator (*De Institutione Oratoria*) in twelve books. This he wrote in two years; but it was not until after repeated revision that he published it, just before the death of Domitian in the year 96. He dedicated it to his friend, the orator Victorius Marcellus, that he might use it for the education of his son Geta. This work gives a complete course of instruction in rhetoric, including all that is necessary for training in practical elocution, from the preliminary education of boyhood and earliest youth to the time of appearance in public. It describes a perfect orator, who, according to Quintilian, should be not only skilful in rhetoric, but also of good moral character, and concludes with practical advice. Especially interesting is the first book, which gives the principles of training and instruction, and the tenth book, for its criticisms on the Greek and Latin prose authors and poets recommended to the orator for special study. Many of these criticisms, however, are not original. Quintilian's special model, and his main authority, is Cicero, whose classical style, as opposed to the style of his own time exemplified in Seneca, he imitates successfully in his work. A collection of school exercises (*Declamationes*) which bears his name is probably not by him, but by one of his pupils, though Ritter accepts many of them as genuine.

The most important MS. of the *Institutiones* is the Codex Ambrosianus of the eleventh century. Other complete MSS. are much later—of the fifteenth century—and are full of interpolations. Early editions of Quintilian are those of Gibson (Oxford, 1693), Burmann (Leyden, 1720), and Gesner (Göttingen, 1738). A great edition is that of Spalding, 4 vols. (Leipzig, 1798–1816), to which a fifth volume was added by Zumpt (1829), and a sixth containing a lexicon and indices by Bonnell (1834). The chief edition is that of Halm (Leipzig, 1868), revised by Meister (Prague, 1886). Book X. has been separately edited by Herzog (3d ed., Leipzig, 1833), Schneidewin (Helmst., 1831); Bonnell and Meister (3d ed., Berlin, 1882); G. T. Krüger and G. Krüger (Leipzig, 1888), and J. E. B. Mayor (Pt. i., Camb., 1892). An excellent index is that in the Lemaire edition (Paris, 1821). There is a good German translation by Bossler and Baur, revised by Meister (Prague, 1886); and an English version by Watson, with notes based on Spalding, and may be found in the Bohn Classical Library. The *Declamationes* are edited by Ritter (1884).

Quintīlis Mensis. See CALENDARIUM.

Quintillus, M. AURELIUS. The brother of the emperor M. Aurelius Claudius, who was elevated to the throne by the troops whom he commanded at Aquileia, in A.D. 270. But as the army at Sirmium, where Claudius died, had proclaimed Aurelian emperor, Quintillus put an end to his own life, seeing himself deserted by his own soldiers, to whom the rigour of his discipline had given offence (Eutrop. ix. 12; Zos. i. 47).

Quintĭpor, i.e. *Quinti puer*. A slave name (Varro *ap.* Non. 448. 15).

Quintius Capitolīnus Barbātus, TITUS. A celebrated Roman general in the early history of the Republic, and equally distinguished in the internal history of the State. He frequently acted as mediator between the patricians and plebeians, with both of whom he was held in the highest esteem. He was six times consul—namely, in B.C. 471, 468, 465, 446, 443, 439. Several of his descendants held the consulship, but none of these require mention except T. QUINTIUS PENNUS CAPITOLĪNUS CRISPĪNUS, who was consul in B.C. 208, and was defeated by Hannibal (Polyb. x. 32).

Quintus. An eminent physician at Rome, in the former half of the second century after Christ. He was so much superior to his medical colleagues that they grew jealous of his eminence, and formed a sort of coalition against him, and forced him to quit the city by charging him with killing his patients. He died about A.D. 148 (Galen, *De Praenot*).

Quintus Curtius. See CURTIUS.

Quintus Smyrnaeus. See CALABER, QUINTUS.

Quirinalia. A festival celebrated on February 17th of each year at Rome in honour of Quirinus, that being the date on which Romulus was said to have been carried up to heaven (Ovid, *Fasti*, ii. 457). The day was also called STULTŌRUM FERIAE or "Feast of Fools," for which see FORNACALIA.

Quirinālis Flamen. See FLAMEN.

Quirinālis Mons. A hill at Rome, added to the city by Servius Tullius (Liv. i. 44). Numa, indeed, had a house upon this mountain, but it was not considered a part of the city until enclosed within the Tullian wall. The temple of Romulus Quirinus, from which it derived its name, was built by Numa, but afterward reconstructed with greater magnificence by Papirius Cursor, the dictator (Liv. x. 46). It was the centre of the district called Alta Semita under Augustus. See ROMA.

Quirīnus. The Sabine name of Mars, as the god who brandished the lance (from the Sabine *curis* = Latin *quiris*, the lance). The Sabines worshipped him under this name as the father of the founder of their old capital, Cures, just as the Romans honoured Mars as the father of Romulus. When the Sabines migrated to Rome, they took the cult and the name of the god of their race to their new home on the Quirinal Hill. In this way Quirinus, though identical with Mars, had a distinct and separate worship on the slope of the Quirinal. He possessed a temple with priests (see FLAMEN; SALII) and a special festival. When, in the course of time, their connection was forgotten, Quirinus was identified with the deified Romulus, the son of Mars. The name is also applied to the Ianus or something in the Forum, which it seems to designate as the "Ianus of the Roman people" (Suet. *Aug.* 22).

Quirīnus, P. SULPICIUS. A native of Lanuvium, of obscure origin, but raised to the highest honours by Augustus. He was consul B.C. 12, and subsequently carried on war against some of the robber tribes dwelling in the mountains of Cilicia. In B.C. 1 Augustus appointed him to direct the counsels of his grandson C. Caesar, then in Armenia. About A.D. 5 he was made governor of Syria, and as such took a census of the Jews. He died in A.D. 21 (Dio Cass. liv. 25; Suet. *Tib.* 49; Tac. *Ann.* iii. 48).

Quirītes. A word of uncertain derivation. Mommsen regards it as composed of the root of *curis* (*quiris*), "a spear," + the root of *ire*, and hence = "the spearmen," "warriors." It was the name of the oldest inhabitants of Rome, the Latin Ramnes and the Sabine Tities taken together. Afterwards it became the name of the Roman people (*populus Romanus Quiritium* or *populus Romanus Quirites*) in home affairs, while *Romani* was used in connection with foreign affairs. It was the proudest of the designations of the Romans. *Quirites* was also used to indicate peaceable citizens, or civilians, as opposed to soldiers (*milites*) (Tac. *Ann.* i. 42; Suet. *Iul.* 70; Lucan, v. 358). See CIVITAS.

Quiritium Ius. See IUS.

Quiver. See ARCUS; PHARETRA.

Quiza (Κούϊζα). Now Giza, near Oran; a municipium on the coast of Mauretania Caesariensis in the northern part of Africa (Pliny, *H. N.* v. 19).

Quoit. See DISCUS.

R

R (P), as a symbol.

IN GREEK.—Only as a numeral = 17 (old system) ρʹ = 100. ͵ρ = 100,000.

IN LATIN.—R = recessus, regnum, retro, revocatus, rubrica.

R·C = reficiendum curaverunt.
R·L = recte licet.
R·P = ratio privata.
R·T = ripa Tiberis.
R·P·C = rei publicae constituendae.
R·P·N = res publica nostra.
R·P·C·A = rei publicae causa abesse.
R·P·S·S = res publica supra scripta.
R·P·P·D·D = res publica Phnensium decreto decurionum.

Rabānus Maurus. A distinguished mediæval scholar, born at Mainz about A.D. 776, and educated at Fulda and at Tours under Alcuin. He taught with great success at Fulda, and in 847 was made archbishop of Mainz. His epitome of the Latin grammar of Priscianus (q. v.) was much used throughout the Middle Ages. See the Lives by his pupils Rudolphus and Trithemius prefixed to his collected works in Migne's *Patrologiae Cursus Completus*, vols. cvii.–cxii.; and the monographs by Spengler (1856), Köhler (1870), and Richter (1882). See LIBERALES ARTES.

Rabathmōba (Ῥαβαθμώβα). The Rabbath-Moab of the Old Testament; the ancient capital of the Moabites, on the eastern shore of the Dead Sea.

Rabbatamāna (Ῥαββατάμανα). The Rabbath-Ammon of the Old Testament; the ancient capital of the Ammonites in Peraea. Under Ptolemy II. (Philadelphus) it took the name PHILADELPHIA (Pliny, *H. N.* v. 74).

Rabirius. (1) GAIUS, an aged senator, accused in B.C. 63, by T. Labienus, tribune of the plebs, of having put to death the tribune L. Appuleius Saturninus in 100, nearly forty years before. (See SATURNINUS.) The accusation was set on foot at the instigation of Caesar, who judged it necessary to deter the Senate from resorting to arms against the popular party. The Duumviri Perduellionis (an obsolete tribunal) appointed to try Rabirius were C. Caesar himself and his relative L. Caesar. Rabirius was condemned, but appealed to the people in the Comitia Centuriata. The case excited the greatest interest, since it was not simply the life or death of Rabirius, but the power and authority of the Senate, which were at stake. Rabirius was defended by Cicero; but the eloquence of his advocate was of no avail, and the people would have ratified the decision of the duumvirs had not the meeting been broken up by the praetor, Q. Metellus Celer, who removed the military flag which floated on the Ianiculum. (2) Q. RABIRIUS POSTŬMUS was the son of the sister of the preceding. After the restoration of Ptolemy Auletes to his kingdom by means of Gabinius in B.C. 55, Rabirius repaired to Alexandria, and was invested by the king with the office of *dioecetes*, or chief treasurer. In this office his extortions were so terrible that Ptolemy had him apprehended; but Rabirius escaped from prison, probably through the connivance of the king, and returned to Rome. Here a trial awaited him. Gabinius had been sentenced to pay a heavy fine on account of his extortions in Egypt; and as he was unable to pay this fine, a suit was instituted against Rabirius, who was liable to make up the deficiency, if it could be proved that he had received any of the money of which Gabinius had illegally become possessed. Rabirius was defended by Cicero, and was probably condemned. (3) A Roman poet, who lived in the last years of the Republic, and wrote a poem on the Civil Wars. A portion of this, found at Herculaneum, has been edited by Kreyssig (Schneeberg, 1814); and by Bährens in his *Poetae Latini Minores* (1879).

Races and **Racing.** See CIRCUS; CURRUS; GYMNASIUM; HIPPODROMUS; OLYMPIA.

Racilius, LUCIUS. A friend of Cicero. He was tribune of the people in B.C. 56. He sided with Caesar in the Civil War and served in Spain in B.C. 48. Having conspired against Q. Cassius Longinus, the governor of that province, he was put to death (*Bell. Alex.* 52).

Rack. See ECULEUS; SUPPLICIUM.

Radagaisus. A Scythian who invaded Italy in the reign of the emperor Honorius, but was defeated by Stilicho near Florence (A.D. 408) and executed after his surrender, contrary to an express agreement (Oros. vii. 37).

Radius (ῥάβδος). (1) A pointed rod or wand, employed by professors of geometry, astronomy, or mathematics for describing diagrams in sand, etc. (Cic. *Tusc.* v. 23; Verg. *Ecl.* iii. 40). (2) (ἀκτίς). A ray of light, usually represented by artists as a sharp pointed spike; whence *corona radiis distincta* (Flor. iv. 2, 91), a crown ornamented with metal spikes to imitate the rays of the sun. (3) (ἀκτίς, κνήμη). The spoke of a wheel (Verg. *Georg.* ii. 444; Ovid, *Met.* ii. 318); so termed because it radiates from the nave, like a ray of light from a centre; hence *rota radiata* (Varro, *R. R.* iii. 5. 15), a wheel with spokes as contradistinguished from the solid wheel (*tympanum*), which had none.

Urania with Radius. (Pompeian painting.)

Raetia. See RHAETIA.

Raft. See RATIS.

Ragae. See RHAGAE.

Rags. See CENTO.

Rake. See PECTEN; RASTRUM.

Rallum (contracted from *radulum*). A scraper in the form of a spud, which a ploughman fixed on the butt end of his goad (*stimulus*), and used for scraping off the earth from the ploughshare (Pliny, *H. N.* xviii. 49, 2).

Radulum. (Rich.)

Ram. See ARIES.

Ramēses (RAAMSES), **Ramesses**, and **Ramses** (Egypt. *Ramessu*). The name of thirteen Egyptian kings belonging to the Eighteenth, Nineteenth, and Twentieth Dynasties. (See AEGYPTUS.) During their age most of the great monuments of Egypt were erected, and on the monumental inscriptions

Rameses II. (Head from Tanis.)

the name is of frequent occurrence under the form Ramessu. The second of the name, a famous warrior, is usually identified with the Pharaoh of the oppression, and Rameses III. with the Pharaoh of the Exodus, but the identification is not complete. Rameses III. is probably the same as Rhampsinitus (q. v.). In 1881 the mummy of Rameses II. was found at Deir-el-Bahari, and that of Rameses III. at Boulak in 1886. On the identification of Rameses II. with Sesostris, see SESOSTRIS. The reader is also referred to Edwards, *Pharaohs, Fellahs, and Explorers*, ch. iv. (N. Y. 1892).

Ramnes or **Ramnenses**. One of the three old patrician tribes at Rome (Varro, *L. L.* v. 55 and 81). See PATRICII; TRIBUS.

Rampart. See AGGER; VALLUM.

Ramses. See RAMESES.

Ranks. See ORDO.

Raphia (Ῥαφία) or **Raphēa** (Ῥάφεια). Now Repha; a seaport town in the extreme southwest of Palestine, beyond Gaza, on the edge of the desert.

Rapier. See GLADIUS.

Rapīna. See FURTUM.

Raptus Proserpĭnae. See CLAUDIANUS.

Rasĕnae. The Etruscans. See ETRURIA.

Rastrum, pl. RASTRI. (1) RASTRUM BIDENS (δίκελλα), a hoe or mattock. (2) RASTRUM QUADRIDENS (λίστρον?), a rake.

Ratiaria. Now Arcer; an important town in Moesia Superior on the Danube. It was the station for one of the Roman fleets (Ptol. iii. 9, 4).

Ratis (σχεδία). A raft; constructed as in modern times and used either for crossing rivers or for constructing pontoon-bridges (Livy, xxi. 27), or for short voyages from island to island (Thuc. vi. 2). The construction of a raft is described at length by Homer in the fifth book of the *Odyssey*.

Ratomăgus or **Rotomăgus**. Now Rouen; the chief town of the Vellocasses in Gallia Lugdunensis.

Rattle. See CREPUNDIA; SISTRUM.

Raudii Campi. See CAMPI RAUDII.

Raurăci. A people in Gallia Belgica, bounded on the south by the Helvetii, on the west by the Sequani, on the north by the Tribocci, and on the east by the Rhine. They must have been a people of considerable importance, as 23,000 of them are said to have emigrated with the Helvetii in B.C. 58, and they possessed several towns, of which the most important were Augusta (August) and Basilia (Basel or Bâle).

Rausia or **Rausium**. Now Ragusa; a town on the coast of Dalmatia whose importance begins only at a late period.

Ravenna. A town in Northern Italy, now Ravenna. An important place in Gallia Cisalpina, on the river Bedesis, and about a mile from the sea, though it is now about five miles in the interior, in consequence of the sea having receded all along this coast. Ravenna was situated in the midst of marshes, and was only accessible in one direction by land, probably by the road leading from Ariminum. It was said to have been founded by Thessalians (Pelasgians), and afterwards to have passed into the hands of the Umbrians, but it long remained an insignificant place, and its greatness does not begin till the time of the empire, when Augustus made it one of the two chief stations of the Roman fleet. Ravenna thus suddenly became one of the most important places in the north of Italy. When the Roman Empire was threatened by the barbarians, the emperors of the West took up their residence at Ravenna, which, on account of its situation and fortifications, was regarded as impregnable. After the downfall of the Western Empire, Theodoric also made it the capital of his kingdom; and after the overthrow of the Gothic dominion by Narses, it became the residence of the exarchs, or the governors of the Byzantine Empire in Italy, till the Lombards took the town, A.D. 752. Ravenna is remarkable for its possession of many fine specimens of early Christian art, which may be studied here to great advantage. See Finsler, *Ravenna in d. röm. Kaiserzeit* (Zürich, 1885).

Razor. See NOVACULA; TONSOR.

Readers. See ACROAMA; RECITATIONES.

Reaping-hook. See FALX.

Reātĕ. Now Rieti; an ancient town of the Sabines in Central Italy, said to have been founded by the Aborigines or Pelasgians, was situated on the Lacus Velinus and the Via Salaria. It was the chief place of assembly for the Sabines, and was subsequently a praefectura or a municipium. The valley in which Reaté was situated was so beautiful that it received the name of Tempé; and in its neighbourhood is the celebrated waterfall, which is now known under the name of the Fall of Terni or the Cascade delle Marmore.

Rebĭlus, C. CANINĬUS. One of Caesar's legates in Gaul and in the Civil War. On the last day of December in B.C. 45, on the sudden death of the consul Q. Fabius Maximus, Caesar made Rebilus consul for the few remaining hours of the day (Cic. *Ad Fam.* vii. 30; Suet. *Iul.* 76).

Recarănus. See HERACLES.

Recepta; **Actio de Recepto**. An action against the master of a ship, an innkeeper, or the keeper of a livery-stable (*stabularius*) for the recovery of property intrusted to him. These persons were liable for the value of such property even though no neglect or *dolus malus* could be proven against them (Pompon. in *Dig.* xiv. 1, 3, 1).

Recinium. See RICINIUM.

Recitatiōnes. At Rome books were sometimes read aloud before their publication—a custom introduced in the time of Augustus by Asinius Pollio. At first these readings took place only before friends especially invited; afterwards they were publicly announced, and were held before great assemblies, either in the theatre or at the public baths or in the Forum, admission being open to all. Introduced, in the first instance, with a view to obtaining the criticisms of the audience, to help the author in the final revision of his work, they soon became of such importance that they determined the success of the work so recited. At the same time second-rate talent was often blinded to its imperfections by the exaggerated applause of a clique. In the time of the younger Pliny these recitations were so much in fashion that (in the April of a particular year) hardly a day passed without one (*Ep.* i. 13, § 1; cf. iii. 7, § 5; 18, § 4; v. 17, § 4; vii. 7; Juv. i. 3; iii. 9; vii. 70, with Mayor's notes). They seem to have continued until the sixth century A.D.

Reckoning. See NUMERI.

Recognitio. See EQUITES.

Recta Tunĭca. See REGILLA.

Recuperatōres. The Roman term for a sworn committee, or board, of three to five members, convened by the praetor. Such a board had to adjudicate at Rome and in the provinces in money cases (more especially on claims for compensation and damages). At first only cases between Romans and foreigners were heard in this way, and were settled within ten days. Afterwards a board of this kind decided on all legal points which had to be settled promptly. See IUDEX.

Reda (or RAEDA, a word cognate with *rota*, and wrongly spelled *rheda*). The Roman travelling-carriage with four wheels, furnished with several seats, so as to be adapted for the transport of a large party, with their luggage and necessaries (Juv. iii. 10; Mart. iii. 47, 5). It appears to have been in very general use among the Romans, both for town and country (Cic. *Mil.* 20; *Ad Att.* vi. 1; v. 17; Suet. *Iul.* 57); and probably resembled the French *char-à-banc* with a cover overhead, for the carriage itself, as well as its name, was of Gallic original (Quint. i. 5. 68). The annexed illustration is from a drawing by Ginzrot (*Wagen und Fahrwerke*) after several models of carriages that appear on the columns of Trajan and M. Aurelius.

Reda. (Ginzrot.)

Redarius. (1) The driver of a *reda* (q. v.) (Cic. *Mil.* 10). (2) The maker of a *reda* (Capitol. *Max. et Balb.* 5).

Redemptor (ἐργολάβος). A contractor; like our own term, of general application for one who undertakes to perform any description of work, such as the building or repairing of a house, etc., for a stipulated amount (Cic. *Div.* ii. 21; Pliny, *H. N.* xxxvi. § 55).

Redhibitoria Actio. In Roman law an action to rescind a sale when the thing sold was found to possess a defect unknown to both buyer and seller (*Dig.* 21, 1).

Redicŭlus. A Roman deity who got his name from the belief that he induced Hannibal, when near the gates of Rome after his victory at Cannae, to return (*redire*) southward. On the Appian Way near the second mile-stone from the city was the Campus Rediculi; and the god had also a temple near the Porta Capena. He was probably one of the Lares of the city of Rome. See Festus, p. 282.

Redimicŭlum. A long lappet, or fillet attached to the *mitra* (Isidor. *Orig.* xix. 31, 5; Verg. *Aen.* ix. 616), or any other head-dress of similar character, for the purpose of fastening it under the chin; but the whole of which, when loose, would hang down over the shoulders and breast (Ovid, *Met.* x. 265). See MITRA.

Redimiculum. (Pompeian painting.)

Redŏnes. A people in the interior of Gallia Lugdunensis, whose chief town was Condaté (Rennes) (Caes. *B. G.* ii. 34; vii. 75).

Redux. An epithet of the goddess Fortuna (q. v.), as leading the traveller home in safety.

Regaliānus, Regalliānus, or **Regilliānus.** A Dacian who served with distinction under the emperors Claudius and Valerian. The Moesians, terrified by the cruelties inflicted by Gallienus on those who had taken part in the rebellion of Ingenuus, suddenly proclaimed Regalianus emperor, and quickly, with the consent of the soldiers, in a new fit of alarm, put him to death, A.D. 263. Hence he is enumerated among the Thirty Tyrants (q. v.).

Regia (τὸ βασίλειον, ῥηγία). Originally the building in which the king (*rex*), as the head of the State religion, performed the usual rites; and later, the one set apart for the Pontifex Maximus and perhaps for the Rex Sacrorum. (See PONTIFEX; REX SACRORUM.) The word is also the pure Latin equivalent of *basilica*. See BASILICA.

Regifugium. A Roman festival celebrated on February 24th perhaps to commemorate the expulsion of the kings (Ovid, *Fast.* ii. 685; Festus, s. h. v.). At this festival the Rex Sacrorum offered sacrifice on the Comitium, and then hastily fled. (See REX SACRORUM.) Probably in this case, as in many others, the sacrifice was originally regarded as a crime. The fact that the Salii were present is recorded by Festus (s. v. *Regifugium*); and possibly their presence had the same significance as the ceremony of leaping, etc., performed by them in March, presumably with a view to driving evil demons away from the city. See the *Classical Review*, v. 51 b; and Marquardt, *Staatsverwaltung*, iii. 324.

Regilla. The garment worn by the Roman bride on her wedding-day. It was woven in one piece in the old-fashioned way at the upright loom, and was also called *tunica recta*. See Festus, p. 286; and the article TELA.

Regilla or Tunica Recta.

Regillus, AEMILIUS. (1) MARCUS, a Roman, had been declared consul, with T. Otacilius, for B.C. 214, by the Centuria Praerogativa, and would have been elected, had not Q. Fabius Maximus, who presided at the Comitia, pointed out that there was need of generals of more experience to cope with Hannibal. Regillus died in B.C. 205, at which time he is spoken of as Flamen Martialis. (2) LUCIUS, son of the preceding, was praetor in B.C. 190, when he received the command of the fleet in the war against Antiochus.

Regillus Lacus. A lake in Latium, memorable for the victory gained on its banks by the Romans over the Latins, B.C. 498 (Livy, ii. 19). It was east of Rome, in the territory of Tusculum, and between Lavicum and Gabii; but it cannot be identified with certainty with any modern lake, though it was probably the same as the Lago di Cornufelle. Macaulay's stirring ballad on the battle is well known to English readers.

Regĭmen. See LEGIO; TURMA.

Regio (μοῖρα). A district or division of a country or city. See ITALIA; ROMA.

Register. See ALBUM (in Appendix); TABULA.

Regium Flumen. The Roman name for the canal Naarmalcha (q. v.).

Regium Lepĭdi, Regium Lepĭdum, or simply **Regium,** also **Forum Lepĭdi.** Now Reggio; a town of the Boii in Gallia Cisalpina, between Mutina and Tarentum.

Regni. A people on the southern coast of Britain in what is now Sussex.

Regŭla (κανών). A ruler for drawing straight lines on plane surfaces; as the *perpendiculum* (στάθμη) was used for a vertical direction (Vitruv. vii. 3, 5). The name *regula* is also applied to the thread of the screw (Blümner, *Technologie*, iv. 124).

Regŭlus, M. AQUILIUS. An informer under Nero and Domitian. He acquired an immense fortune, and was flattered by the poet Martial in his usual fulsome strain (Mart. i. 13, 83, 112).

Regŭlus, ATILIUS. (1) M., consul B.C. 335, carried on war against the Sidicini. (2) M., consul 294, carried on war against the Samnites. (3) M., consul 267, conquered the Sallentini, took the town of Brundusium, and obtained in consequence the honour of a triumph. In 256 he was consul a second time with L. Manlius Vulso Longus. The two consuls defeated the Carthaginian fleet, and afterwards landed in Africa with a large force. They met with great and striking success; and after Manlius returned to Rome with half of the army, Regulus remained in Africa with the other half and prosecuted the war with the utmost vigour. The Carthaginian generals Hasdrubal, Bostar, and Hamilcar avoided the plains, where their cavalry and elephants would have given them an advantage over the Roman army, and withdrew into the mountains. There they were attacked by Regulus, and defeated with great loss; 15,000 men are said to have been killed in battle, and 5000 men with 18 elephants to have been taken. The Carthaginian troops retired within the walls of the city, and Regulus now overran the country without opposition. Numerous towns fell into the power of the Romans, and among others Tunis, at the distance of only twenty miles from the capital. The Carthaginians, in despair, sent a herald to Regulus to solicit peace; but the Roman general would only grant it on such intolerable terms that the Carthaginians resolved to continue the war, and hold out to the last. In the midst of their distress and alarm, success came to them from an unexpected quarter. Among the Greek mercenaries who had lately arrived at Carthage was a Lacedaemonian of the name of Xanthippus. He pointed out to the Carthaginians that their defeat was owing to the incompetency of their generals, and not to the superiority of the Roman arms; and he inspired such confidence in the people that he was forthwith placed at the head of their troops. Relying on his 4000 cavalry and 100 elephants, Xanthippus boldly marched into the open country to meet the enemy. In the battle which ensued Regulus was totally defeated; 30,000 of his men were slain; scarcely 2000 escaped to Clypea; and Regulus himself was taken prisoner with 500 more (B.C. 255). Regulus remained in captivity for the next five years, till 250, when the Carthaginians, after their defeat by the proconsul Metellus, sent an embassy to Rome to solicit peace, or at least an exchange of prisoners. They allowed Regulus to accompany the ambassadors on the promise that he would return to Rome if their proposals were declined, thinking that he would persuade his countrymen to agree to an exchange of prisoners in order to obtain his own liberty. This mission of Regulus is one of the most celebrated stories in Roman history. The orators and poets related how Regulus at first refused to enter the city as a slave of the Carthaginians; how afterwards he would not give his opinion in the Senate, as he had ceased by his captivity to be a member of that illustrious body; how, at length, when he was allowed by the Romans to speak, he endeavoured to dissuade the Senate from assenting to a peace, or even to an exchange of prisoners, and when he saw them wavering, from their desire of redeeming him from captivity, how he told them that the Carthaginians had given him a slow poison, which would soon terminate his life; and how, finally, when the Senate through his influence refused the offers of the Carthaginians, he firmly resisted all the persuasions of his friends to remain in Rome, and returned to Carthage, where a martyr's death awaited him. On his arrival at Carthage he is said to have been put to death with the most excruciating tortures.

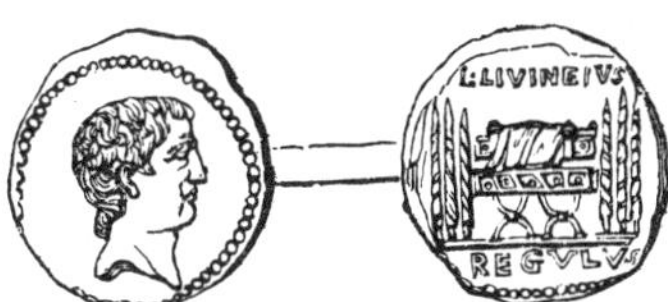

Coin of a Livineius, with Head of Regulus.

It was related that he was placed in a chest covered over in the inside with iron nails, and thus perished; and other writers stated in addition that after his eyelids had been cut off he was first thrown into a dark dungeon, and then suddenly exposed to the full rays of a burning sun. When the news of the barbarous death of Regulus reached Rome, the Senate is said to have given Hamilcar and Bostar, two of the noblest Carthaginian prisoners, to the family of Regulus, who revenged themselves by putting them to death with cruel torments.

This celebrated tale, however, has not been allowed to pass without question in modern times. Many writers supposed that it was invented in order to excuse the cruelties perpetrated by the family of Regulus on the Carthaginian prisoners committed to their custody. Regulus was one of the favourite characters of early Roman story. Not only was he celebrated on account of his heroism in giving the Senate advice which secured him a martyr's death, but also on account of his frugality and simplicity of life. Like Fabricius and Curius he lived on his hereditary farm, which he cultivated with his own hands; and subsequent ages loved to tell how he petitioned the Senate for his recall from Africa when he was in the full career of victory, as his farm was going to ruin in his absence and his family was suffering from want. See Wolff, *M. Atilii Reguli Vita* (1846); and Jäger, *M. Atilius Regulus* (1878).

(4) GAIUS, surnamed SERRĀNUS, consul B.C. 257, when he defeated the Carthaginian fleet off the Liparaean Islands, and obtained possession of the islands of Lipara and Melite. He was consul a second time in 250, with L. Manlius Vulso. The two consuls undertook the siege of Lilybaeum; but they were foiled in their attempts to carry the place by storm, and after losing a great number of men, were obliged to turn the siege into a blockade. This Regulus is the first Atilius who bears the surname *Serranus*. See SERRANUS.

Reii Apollināres. Now Riez; a Roman colony in Gallia Narbonensis, east of the Druentia (Durance).

Reins. See HABENA.

Reiske, JOHANN JAKOB. See article in Appendix.

Relatio. See SENATUS.

Relatiōnes. See SYMMACHUS.

Relegatio. Banishment from Rome; in imperial times a milder form of exile, which did not affect the rights as a citizen of the man sentenced to it. See DEPORTATIO; EXSILIUM.

Religio (RELLIGIO. The etymology of the word is doubtful. Cicero derived it from *relegere* [*N. D.* ii. 28, 72], which is supported by a passage in Gellius [iv. 9, 1]; but the probable base is that of the verb *ligare* [Serv. *ad* Verg. *Aen.* viii. 349; Lactant. iv. 28; Augustin. *Retract.* i. 13]; and the notion of binding seems to have been in the mind of Lucretius in using such expressions as *religionum nodis animos exsolvere* [i. 931; iv. 7]. See Munro on Lucret. i. 109; Mayor on Cic. *l. c.*; Corssen, *Aussprache*, i. 444 foll.; and for the spelling, Brambach, 131). The gods of the Greeks were originally personifications of the powers of nature, limited in their activity to that province of nature from the phenomena of which they are derived. As these phenomena were regarded as acts or sufferings of the gods in question, a cycle of myths was thus developed. In the minds of the people, the special significance of these myths necessarily vanished in proportion as the original connection of the gods with the phenomena of nature receded to the background, while greater prominence was given to the conception of the gods as personal beings holding sway, primarily in their own province of nature, and then beyond those limits, and no longer exclusively in connection with the powers of nature. In the oldest records of the intellectual life of Greece—the Homeric poems—this transition has already been carried out. The Homeric deities are exclusively occupied with the governing of mortals, whose whole life is represented as being under their influence; while traces of the old connection with the phenomena of nature are rarely found, and the old myths had long since become unintelligible tales, in which the actions of the gods appeared unreasonable and immoral, since their meaning was no longer clear. In regard to religion, as in other matters, the Homeric poems are of the utmost importance; for if in historical times a certain uniformity prevails in the representation of the deities, this may be traced in no small degree to the influence of Homer and of other poets (especially Hesiod) who were under his influence, and who gave distinct form to the vague representations of an earlier time. Nevertheless this uniformity only existed in a general way; in detail there was the greatest confusion, for the Greeks never attained to a uniform religious system and to fixed religious dogma. They possessed only a contradictory and ambiguous mythology. The only thing which was comparatively established was the traditional worship; but in this there was great diversity of place and time.

The common belief was that the gods were superhuman, though they were like mortals in form and in the ordinary necessities of life (food, drink, sleep); that they had power over nature and human beings; that all good and evil came from them; that their favour could be obtained by behaviour which was pleasing to them, and lost by that which displeased them. Among the Greek gods there was no representative of evil, neither in popular belief was there one of absolute perfection and holiness; and the deities were represented as being subject to moral weakness and deviation from right—a belief which was fostered by the traditional mythology. The gods possessed immortality, but did not exist from the beginning of all things.

I. In the opinion of the GREEKS, the ruling race of gods, the Olympians—so called from their abode, Olympus—were the third race of gods. The first ruler was Uranus (Heaven), who, by his mother Gaea (Earth), who bore him spontaneously, himself became the father of the Titans. He was expelled by his son Cronus, whose daughters, by his sister Rhea, were Hestia, Demeter, and Heré, and his sons, Hades (Pluto), Poseidon, and Zeus. He was himself expelled by his last-named son. When Zeus, by the aid of his brothers and sisters, had overcome the Titans, who rebelled against the new order of things, he divided the world with his brothers. The earth and Olympus remained common property; Hades obtained the nether world; Poseidon, the sea; Zeus, the heavens, and, as being the strongest and wisest, he also had authority over all the other gods, who worked his will, received from him their offices and spheres of action, and served him as helpers in the government of the universe. According to this division of province, the gods are divided into the divinities of heaven and earth and sea.

As in all religions founded on nature, so with the Greeks, the gods of heaven take the first place. They are specially called Olympians; and, in contrast to the gods of the earth and sea, are called the gods above, or the upper gods. The principal deities after Zeus are Heré, Athené, Apollo, Artemis, Aphrodité, Hephaestus, Ares, Hermes, and Hestia. Round them are grouped a number of minor deities, who either escort and serve the upper gods (as, for instance, Themis, and the Horae, the Graces, the Muses, Eros, Niké, Iris, Hebé, Ganymede), or else represent distinct phenomena of the heavens, as Helios (the sun), Selené (the moon), Eos (the dawn); or execute special services in the heaven-ordained government of the universe, as the goddess of birth, Eileithyia, the healing god Asclepius, and the goddesses of destiny (Moerae, Nemesis, Tyché). The gods of the sea, besides Poseidon and his spouse Amphitrité and his son Triton, are Oceanus and his offspring, Nereus and the Nereïds, Proteus, Ino (Leucothea), Melicertes (Palaemon), Glaucus (Pontius). The gods of the earth are Gaea herself, Rhea (Cybelé), Dionysus, Priapus, Pan, the Nymphs and Satyrs, Demeter and her daughter Persephoné, with her spouse Hades (Pluto). The last two are the rulers of the nether world, to which Hecaté and the Erinyes also belong.

The number of beings regarded as deities was never clearly defined. From the earliest times in Greece we find deities worshipped in one place who were not known in another. But some of these, as Dionysus and Pan, became common property in course of time; and the more lasting and more extensive the intercourse became with other peoples, more especially in the colonies, the introduction of foreign deities became greater. Some of these were identified with the gods already worshipped, while others preserved their original attributes, subject, of course, to modifications to suit the spirit of the Greeks. This aptitude for naturalizing foreign religions declined more and more as Greece ceased to flourish. On the other hand, some original deities lost their independence, and were merged into others, such as Helios and Apollo, Selené and Artemis. In the popular belief of the post-Homeric time, another numerous class of superhuman beings sprang up, which were regarded as being between gods and men, the demons (*δαίμονες*) and Heroes. See Heros.

As to their nature and their number, there was less uniformity than in the case of the real gods. The Heroes had only local importance. Even in the case of the gods universally worshipped, it was by no means all (not even the most important) that had a place everywhere in the public worship. In the case of certain gods, their worship was only exceptional; and those gods who by order of the State were worshipped in any particular place did not necessarily enjoy forever the position to which they were entitled. Even Zeus, who was universally regarded as the highest of the gods, and figured in the cult of most of the different States, was not himself worshipped as supreme; but those gods who had always had the first place in the cult of the respective States took precedence over him, and these were not always divinities of preëminent importance. In Athens, Pallas Athené was worshipped as the principal deity, Heré in Argos; among the Dorians, especially at Delphi, Apollo; among the Ionians, Poseidon; at Rhodes, Helios; at Naxos, Dionysus; at Thespiae, Eros; at Orchomenus, the Charites (or Graces). Even in the case of the same deities, the local customs often differed considerably in respect of the names that were given to them, their attributes, and the form of worship. These differences were due partly to local causes and local opinions, partly to foreign influence, and were occasionally so considerable that doubts arose whether different deities were not really represented under the same name, as, for instance, Aphrodité.

The deities were supposed to be specially gratified by the careful observance of the traditional ritual. This continued to be carried on according to ancient custom, so that the details of these ancient cults were often curious, and their connection with the religious ideas on which they rested was often unintelligible. However, with the development of morality the view began to prevail that the observance of duties towards the State and fellow-men was also favoured by the gods as guardians of the providential order of the world; but, in the eyes of the multitude, the principal meaning of *εὐσέβεια* (piety) was the performance of the ordained worship of the gods. Again, the care of the State was confined to the outward forms of religion and to the maintenance of the traditional legal ritual. Alterations in this ritual and the introduction of new cults were only made by authority of the legislative power, usually after an oracle had been consulted to determine the divine will. Besides the worship of the deities recognized by the State, private objects of devotion were found everywhere. For instance, in the case of foreign deities at Athens, where there were many strangers either passing through or permanently resident, foreign religions were tolerated so long as they did not endanger the traditional worship or excite public disturbance by their outward ritual. Many such cults were naturalized in this way, and became, in course of time, part of the State religion. Conquest, again, contributed largely towards the introduction of novelties, for the acquisition of new territory involved that of the religious rites held therein. And, lastly, old religions, which had been looked upon as supremely holy, even if they were not absolutely superseded in the course of time, became less important in comparison with others of later origin.

Shrines, and the statues of the gods preserved in them, were the central points of the worship of the different deities. As long as the gods were not represented as having human form, stones, especially those fallen from heaven, or blocks of wood, were the objects of worship. By various stages of progress the gods were at length represented by actual images. At first they were made of wood, then of stone and metal. Clay, and even wax, were generally used for private objects of devotion. Though the real purpose of these symbols and images was to represent the divinity to the worshippers by means of a visible sign, nevertheless, in the popular belief, it was generally presumed that the divinity was actively present in them. Accordingly, the welfare of the State was often supposed to be bound up with the possession of certain symbols and images of the gods.

The decline of the Greek religion began with the decline of the State after the Peloponnesian War. Although the philosophers had already directed their assault against the belief of the people, which, with its anthropomorphism and its inconsistency, exposed itself in many ways to the attacks of the critical spirit, yet the faith of the multitude in the old gods remained unshaken, for it had long attributed the deliverance from the perils of the Persian Wars to their mighty and merciful influence. But after the Peloponnesian War the notions of the philosophers gained ground among the people and undermined the old belief, without, however, supplying any alternative to the religious feeling, which could no longer be satisfied with the outward forms of worship which still survived. With unbelief superstition came in, which was fostered (especially after the Macedonian epoch) by the foreign and barbarous cults, and the degenerate forms of mysticism which were imported from Asia and Egypt.

II. The Italian tribes, from which the Roman people sprang, had a common origin with the Greeks and a common foundation of religious ideas; but on Italian soil these religious ideas received an essentially different direction. Like the Greeks, the Italians regarded the deities as persons separated as to sex and united in couples; but while the imaginative Greeks saw in their gods ideal forms full of individual life, the more sober mind of the Italian tribes, especially of the Romans, got no further than the abstract. Holding to the fundamental idea, they worshipped in the gods the abstract powers of nature, under whose influence man believed himself to be at every moment. The original Italian gods were grave and venerable, and, in a certain sense, more moral than those of the Greeks; but they lacked plastic form and poetic beauty. Accordingly, it is only with certain reservations that we can speak of a Roman mythology in a sense corresponding to that of the Greeks. The Romans lacked an Olympus and a Hades, and knew nothing of stories about the race and relationship and the love affairs of their deities. In this abstract nature of the Roman gods, it is intelligible that the Romans, during the first two hundred years from the foundation of Rome, possessed no images of their gods, but represented them by symbols—e. g. Iupiter by a flint-stone, Mars by a spear, Vesta by fire, which, even in later times, remained the symbol of the goddess. In the earliest Roman religion the deities of two Italian races, the Latins and the Sabines, were united, Rome having been originally peopled by the union of these tribes. The most important gods were the god of light and the god of all beginning, Ianus; the god of heaven, Iupiter, the greatest protector of the nation, with whom was joined the feminine element in Iuno, just as Iana (Diana) was connected with Ianus; Mars, originally the protector of agriculture, the ancestral god of the Latin race; Quirinus, originally the corresponding god of the Sabines; and Vesta, the goddess of the hearth of the State. Besides these principal deities, others were worshipped as patrons of the farmers and shepherds. Their activity extended over the earth, the fields, and the woods; they blessed the fruits of the field and garden, and gave prosperity to the cattle. Such were Tellus, Ceres, Saturnus and Ops, Liber and Libera, Faunus, Silvanus, Flora, Vertumnus, Pomona. The gods of the sea, however, who had such an important position in the Grecian mythology, had not nearly the same importance in Roman ideas as the gods of heaven and earth, for in the earliest times the sea was little regarded by the Romans. Another object of religious worship was the gods of the house and family, the Lares and Penates. But, besides these, there was an unlimited number of divine beings; for the Romans assumed that there were divine representatives of every inanimate or animate object, of every action and every event. Not only did every human being possess a special protector (*genius*, q. v.), but a number of deities watched over his development from conception to birth, and his further growth, mentally and bodily. See INDIGITAMENTA.

Again, there were manifold protecting gods for the different events of life, as Tutanus and Tutilina, who were invoked in times of trouble; Orbona, invoked by childless couples; and Febris, the goddess of fever. There were also separate gods for separate employments, and for the places where they were carried on. In this way the different institutions and phases of agriculture possessed special deities such as Robigus and Robigo, protectors of the crops against blight. So, also, with the different branches of cattle-breeding (Bubona, goddess of the breeding of horned cattle; Epona, goddess of the breeding of horses; Pales, of the breeding of sheep). Similarly with the separate parts of a house: Forculus, god of the door; Cardea, goddess of the hinge; Limentinus and Limentina, deities of the threshold. To these divine beings fresh ones were continually added, as the inclination of the Romans to recognize and trace divine influence in every single event led to the establishment of new cults after every new revelation of divine power. In this way the introduction of bronze coinage led to a *deus Aesculanus*, and later that of silver coinage to a *deus Argentinus*. Historical events gave an impulse to the personification of intellectual and moral qualities, such as Concordia, Honos, Virtus, Mens, etc. The same principle which recognized that there were some gods unknown, or, at any rate, not worshipped at Rome, led to the tolerance of private performance of foreign cults. Hence, also, it came about that the gods of conquered countries found a place in the Roman state religion, and occasionally were even introduced into the actual worship of Rome. In the latter case, however, the home deities preserved their rights in so far as the shrines of the newly imported deities were outside the limits of what was called the Pomerium (q. v.).

The religion of the Romans was gradually but completely altered by the influence of that of the Greeks. This influence made itself felt as early as the time of the latest kings. Shrines of the gods were first introduced under the elder Tarquin, and under the last Tarquin three supreme gods of the State were established—Iupiter, the representative of supreme power; Iuno, of supreme womanhood; Minerva, of supreme wisdom. These three deities received, as a token of their inseparability, a common temple on the Capitol, and were therefore called the Capitoline gods. This Greek influence was firmly established at the end of the time of the kings by the Sibylline Books, which originated among the Greeks of Asia Minor. (See SIBYLLAE.) By means of these a number of Greek and Asiatic gods were in course of time introduced into the Roman cult, partly as new deities, such as Apollo, Cybelé (*Magna Mater*), Aesculapius; partly under the names of native gods, with whom they were often identified in a very superficial way, as Demeter with Ceres, Dionysus with Liber, Persephoné with Libera, Aphrodité with Venus; and with them were introduced many innovations in the old established worship of the gods, especially the *Lectisternium* (q. v.). When, after the Second Punic War, Greek ideas irresistibly made their way in Rome, it became more and more common to identify the gods of Rome with those of Greece; and thus the original significance of many Roman deities was either obscured or even entirely lost. Divinities highly venerated of old were put into the background, and those of less importance came to be regarded as supreme, owing to their supposed analogy to Greek gods. In this way the following twelve were established by analogy to the Greek form of religion: Iupiter (Zeus), Iuno (Heré), Neptunus (Poseidon), Minerva (Athené), Mars (Ares), Venus (Aphrodité), Apollo, Diana (Artemis), Vulcanus (Hephaestus), Vesta (Hestia), Mercurius (Hermes), and Ceres (Demeter).

The Roman religion was from the beginning an affair of State. Religious, as well as political, institutions emanated from the kings, who, as high priests, organized the worship by law and laid the foundation of a law of ritual. The second king, Numa, was regarded as the real founder of the Roman cult, and of the priesthood charged with the carrying out of the same. After the kings had been abolished, religion was still controlled by the State, and the priests continued to be State officials, who were empowered by the State, on the one hand, to superintend the performance of the different cults, and, on the other (and this was the more important office), to give judgment in all matters of religion. They thus exercised considerable influence. Under the Republic, the royal prerogative of formulating decrees in all matters of religion was transferred to the Senate. As the Roman State in early times was exclusively composed of patricians, the public religion was originally their exclusive property; the plebs were not allowed to participate in that religion, and were only allowed to worship the Roman gods in private. Therefore, in the long struggle in which the plebs, with their ever-increasing power, endeavoured to secure their rights (a struggle that ended in B.C. 300), it was a question of religion as well as of politics. As regards the worship of the gods, according to Roman ideas, a pure and moral life was pleasing to them and gained their favour. This was, however, conditional on the exact performance of the outward ritual which the system of religion ordained for their cult. It consisted in a very prolonged ceremonial, performed according to the strictest injunctions and with painful minuteness of detail. This ceremonial was performed in public and private life, so that no community lacked its special shrines and sacrifices (see SACRA), and nothing of any importance was undertaken without religious sanction, which involved in particular the discovery of the divine will by means of certain signs (see AUGUR). The forms of outward worship were retained long after the decay of belief in the gods had set in. This decay was caused by the preponderance of the Greek element, and the contemporary introduction of Greek enlightenment; and it soon spread to the forms of worship. During the greater part of the republican period, the priests allowed religion to take a secondary place to politics, and, either from indifference or ignorance, neglected their official duties. Under the Empire, when the deification of deceased emperors was introduced (see APOTHEOSIS), an attempt was made to give an artificial life to the ancient forms of worship; but religious feeling could not be rekindled by forms which had long lost their meaning. When this feeling revived, it preferred, as in Greece, to find refuge in strange Oriental rites, especially those of Mithras and of Isis and Serapis, which, by means of their mysteries and their expiatory ceremonies, offered a certain degree of satisfaction, though, at the same time, they led the way to every conceivable kind of superstition.

The suppression of paganism began in the fourth century, from the time when Constantine decided in favour of Christianity, in A.D. 324. It commenced in the eastern half of the Roman Empire, while in the western half, and at Rome in particular, the Roman form of worship remained essentially undisturbed until the reign of Theodosius the Great (379–395), the resolute exterminator of paganism. In A.D. 394 the Olympic Games were held for the last time; in Rome the endowment of all public forms of worship out of the funds of the State was withdrawn, the priests were driven from the temples, and the temples closed. Nevertheless certain heathen customs long survived, such as the auguries of the consuls and some few festivals that admitted of being celebrated without offering sacrifice or entering a temple. Thus the Lupercalia were not abolished until 494, when they were transformed into a Christian festival.

BIBLIOGRAPHY.—See Hartung, *Religion und Mythologie der Griechen*, 4 vols. (Leipzig, 1865–73); Darmesteter, *Le Dieu Suprême des Indo-Européens* (Paris, 1885); Limbourg-Bronner, *Hist. de la Civilisation Morale et Religieuse des Grecs*, 8 vols. (Groningen, 1833–47); De la Saussaye, *Lehrbuch d. Religionsgeschichte*, 2 vols. (Freiburg, 1887); Girard, *Le Sentiment Religieux en Grèce d'Homère à Eschyle* (Paris, 1879); Nägelsbach, *Homerische Theologie* (Nürnberg, 1861); id. *Nachhomerische Theologie* (Nürnberg, 1857); Peterson, *Religion oder Mythologie*, etc. (Leipzig, 1870); Ploix, *La Nature des Dieux* (Paris, 1888); Lang, *Myth, Ritual, and Religion*, 2 vols. (London, 1887); Heffter, *Götterlehre der Griechen und Römer* (Hamburg, 1853); Hartung, *Die Religion der Römer*, 2 vols. (Erlangen, 1836); Jäkel, *De Diis Domesticis Priscorum Italorum* (Berlin, 1830); Jordan, *Symbolae ad Historiam Religionum Italicarum* (Königsberg, 1885); Boissier, *La Religion Romaine d'Auguste aux Antonins* (Paris, 1878); Granger, *The Worship of the Romans* (London, 1896); Babik, *De Deisideimonia Veterum* (Leipzig, 1891); Hild, *Étude sur les Démons dans la Littérature et la Religion des Grecs* (Paris, 1881); Cicero's treatise *De Natura Deorum* (best edition by J. B. Mayor, with introduction and English notes, Cambridge, 1884); and the works cited in the article MYTHOLOGIA, with the article itself.

Religiōsi Dies. See DIES.

Relish. See CENA; VICTUS.

Remancipatio. See EMANCIPATIO.

Remedia Amōris. See OVIDIUS.

Remi. One of the most powerful people in Gallia Belgica, inhabited the country through which the Axona flowed, and were bounded on the south by the Nervii, on the southeast by the Veromandui, on the east by the Suessiones and Bellovaci, and on the west by the Nervii. They formed an alliance with Caesar, when the rest of the Belgae made war against him, B.C. 57. Their chief town was Durocortorum, afterwards called Remi (Rheims) (Ptol. ii. 9, 12).

Remigium. A term used collectively of the oars of a ship; and also of the whole body of rowers (εἰρεσία).

Remmius Palaemon, QUINTUS. A Roman grammarian of the first century A.D., a native of Vicentia (Vicenza), and originally a slave. After receiving his freedom, he opened a school at Rome, where he taught with such success as to become the most noted grammarian of his age. His personal character is described as infamous (Juv. vi. 451; vii. 215; Sueton. *Gramm.* 23). He is said to have been the first to introduce the study of Vergil into the Roman schools as a text-book. The satirist Persius was one of his pupils. Several existing treatises are sometimes ascribed to him, but with no good reason. See Marschall, *De Remmii Palaemonis Libris Grammaticis* (Leipzig, 1887).

Remulcum (ῥῦμα). A rope for towing a ship.

Remuria. See LEMURIA.

Remus (ἐρετμός). An oar. See NAVIS.

Remus. See ROMULUS.

Renaissance. A name given to the great intellectual movement in the fourteenth and fifteenth centuries—a period which saw the transition from the Middle Ages to modern times. It began in the revolt of men of culture against the intellectual sterility and narrowness of the mediaeval spirit, and especially against scholasticism, whose pedantic and dogmatic narrowness had reached the extreme point of its development. The Renaissance began in Italy, and its first period (1300 to 1375) was marked by a universal revival of interest in classic literature and the classic ideals. It was a great revolt against bigotry and in favor of mental freedom, and its first sign was a passion for the largeness and richness of the pagan world. Traces of this feeling can be seen in Dante (1265–1321), who, although thoroughly mediaeval in his sympathies, chose Vergil as his model, and who, in the vigour and magnificence of his own verse, was a striking contrast to the dull formalists who had before his time written for the men of the Middle Age. Petrarch (1304–1374) is the first true son of the Renaissance. In his poem written in Latin hexameter on the subject of the Second Punic War and entitled *Africa*, he boldly followed the classic models, as he suggested the ancient Roman grace and freedom in his Italian *Rime*. He travelled in foreign countries and thus knew a larger world than his predecessors; and he may be said to have rediscovered Greek, which for some six centuries had been lost to the western world. His friend and disciple Boccaccio studied that language, and by his master's advice made a translation of Homer into Latin. Greeks were now encouraged to come from Constantinople to Italy, and in 1396 the learned Manuel Chysoloras began to teach in the chair of Greek founded at the instance of Salutato and Palla degli Strozzi at Florence. A Platonic academy was opened in the same city under the patronage of Cosimo de' Medici. Greek texts were brought from Constantinople, Europe was ransacked for copies of the long unused Latin classics, copyists multiplied them, libraries were founded, and schools for the study of both Greek and Latin in their classic forms were opened at Rome, Mantua, Verona, and many other towns. Pope Nicholas V. earnestly fostered the new movement, and laid the foundation of the great Vatican collection; Cardinal Bessarion greatly aided in the formation of the Library of St. Mark at Venice. Individual scholars went about looking for manuscripts of lost authors, for coins, medals, bronzes—anything that could give a better knowledge of classical antiquity. Among these men, the most famous were Poggio Bracciolini, who brought to light once more Quintilian, Lucretius, part of Cicero, Columella, Vitruvius, Silius Italicus and Asconius; and Cyriacus of Ancona, who sounded the key-note of the new movement in his famous saying, "I go to awake the dead." See BRACCIOLINI.

The second period of the Renaissance begins about 1375, and is marked by a continued zeal for classical study, and by the development of a broad learning and the new view of the intellectual life which is known as Humanism. By this time the movement had spread to Germany and France and the northern countries generally, where it developed into the wide scholarship and sound learning of men like Erasmus (q. v.), Melanchthon, Reuchlin (q. v.), the Scaligers, Muretus, and Casaubon. The movement had now gone far beyond the mere revival of classical studies, and was felt in every department of life. In philosophy it gradually replaced the purely formal methods of thought that scholasticism had fostered; in science it led to the great discoveries of Galileo and Copernicus; in architecture it brought about the revival of the classic style; in art it developed the new school of painting of which Michael Angelo and Raphael in Italy were the great names, and still another school in the Netherlands and Flanders; in religion its influence is seen in the revolt of Luther; and it indirectly inspired the passion for exploration that led to the discovery of the New World.

See Burckhardt, *Civilization of the Period of the Renaissance in Italy* (Eng. trans. last ed. 1890); Symonds, *The Renaissance in Italy*, 7 vols. (1875–86), especially vol. ii.; Pater, *The Renaissance* (last ed. 1888); Geiger, *Renaissance und Humanismus* (1881); Müntz, *La Renaissance en Italie et en France* (1886); Michelet, *Histoire de France*, vol. ix.; Voigt, *Die Wiederbelebung des klassischen Alterthums* (2d ed. 1881); and Villari, *Machiavelli* (Eng. trans. 1890), and *Savonarola* (Eng. trans. 1889). See also Nisard, *Les Gladiateurs de la République de Lettres* (Paris, 1854); and the articles BRACCIOLINI; SCALIGER; VALLA.

Rent. See VECTIGALIA.

Renuntiatio. The Roman term for the solemn and formal announcement of the names of the magistrates elected at the Comitia (q. v.) by the votes of the people. The announcement was made by the returning officer who presided at the election, and was necessary to give validity to the election.

Repagŭla. The bolt of a door. See IANUA.

Repast. See CENA.

Repetundārum Crimen (from *repetundae pecuniae*, "money which is ordered to be restored"). The name given by the Romans to the charge brought against officials for extorting money from Roman subjects or allies. Such charges were at first brought before the Senate, which heard the case itself, or else passed it on to a commission, or, again, caused it to be brought before the Comitia by the tribunes. At last, in B.C. 149, a standing court of justice (see QUAESTIO PERPETUA), in fact, the first in Rome, was instituted by the Lex Calpurnia, containing more precise definitions of acts liable to punishment, with forms of legal procedure, and determining the amount of the penalty. The increasing inclination of the officials to use the administration of the provinces as means of enriching themselves at the expense of the provincials led to repeated legislation with a view to increasing the penalty. The last law on the subject was Caesar's Lex Iulia, which was the basis of the procedure in such cases under the Empire. During that period, in consequence of the improved condition of provincial government, extortion on the part of officials became much rarer. Such extortion was generally punished by a fine of four times the amount extorted. It was also attended with a certain degree of disgrace (*infamia*), even if a still more severe punishment were not added for other offences committed at the same time and included in the indictment, e.g. the offence of *laesa maiestas*.

Repositorium. A piece of furniture employed by the Romans for bringing upon table the various dishes comprised in a course (Plin. *H. N.* xviii. § 90), and which was placed with its contents upon a table in the dining-room (Petron. 60, 4). It consisted of a large covered box or case (whence *theca repositorii*, Petron. 39, 3), either round or square, and sometimes made of choice woods inlaid with tortoise-shell, and enriched by ornaments of silver (Fenestella *ap.* Plin. *H. N.* xxxiii. § 52; Petron. 35, 2). The whole case was moreover divided into a number of stories, one above the other, each of which held a separate tray (*ferculum*) furnished with dishes like the dinner-baskets in which a French restaurateur sends out a dinner to his customers. This is clear from Petronius 36, 1 and 2. Compare also 35, 1 and 2, where a *repositorium* is placed upon the table, and, after the first division has been removed, another tray containing a different course of entrées is exposed to view—*superiorem partem repositorii abstulerunt. Quo facto, videmus infra, scilicet in altero ferculo, altilia*, etc.—which passage distinctly points out the difference between a *repositorium* and a *ferculum*.

Repotia. See MATRIMONIUM, p. 1016.

Repudium. See DIVORTIUM.

Res. See DOMINIUM.

Resaina (Ῥέσαινα), **Resaena, Resina** (Ῥέσινα). Now Ras-el-Ain. A city of Mesopotamia, near the sources of the Chaboras, on the road from Carrae to Nisibis. After its restoration and fortification by Theodosius, it was called THEODOSIOPŎLIS.

Rescriptum. See CONSTITUTIONES.

Reservoir. See AQUAE DUCTUS; FONS; LACUS.

Responsa. A name given to the official opinions given by those jurists who received from the Roman emperor the *ius respondendi*. See IUS.

Restitutio ("reinstating"). A term applied by the Romans to the cancelling of a legal decision, especially to the restoration of rights of citizenship forfeited by condemnation in a criminal court. Under the Republic this restoration could be legally obtained only by a vote of the people. Under the Empire, the emperor alone possessed the privilege of granting it.

Reté and **Retis**; dim. **Reticŭlum** (δίκτυον), a net. Nets were made most commonly of flax or hemp, whence they are sometimes called lina (λίνα). The meshes (*maculae*, βρόχοι, dim. βροχίδες) were great or small according to the purposes intended. By far the most important application of network was to the three kindred arts of fowling, hunting, and fishing. In fowling the use of nets was comparatively limited. In hunting it was usual to extend nets in a curved line of considerable length, so as in part to surround a space into which the beasts of chase, such as the hare, the boar, the deer, the lion, and the bear, were driven through the opening left on one side. This range of nets was flanked by cords, to which feathers dyed scarlet and of other bright colors were tied, so as to flare and flutter in the wind. The hunters then sallied forth with their dogs, dislodged the animals from their coverts, and by shouts and barking drove them first within the *formido*, as the apparatus of string and feathers was called, and then, as they were scared with this appearance, within the circuit of the nets. In the drawing below three servants with staves carry on their shoulders a large

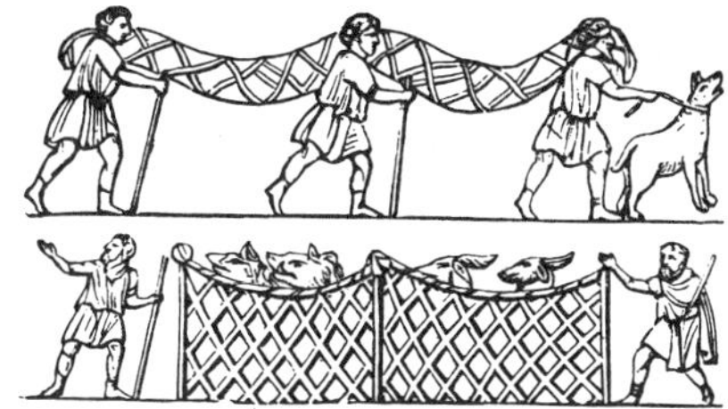

Hunting-nets. (Ince-Blundell Marbles.)

net, which is intended to be set up as already described. In the lower figure the net is set up. At each end of it stands a watchman holding a staff. Being intended to take such large quadrupeds as boars and deer (which are seen within it), the meshes are very wide (*retia rara*). The net is supported by three stakes (στάλικες, *ancones, vari*). To dispose the nets in this manner was called *retia ponere*, or *retia tendere*. The upper border of the net consists of a strong rope, which was called σαρδών. Fishing-nets (ἁλιευτικὰ δίκτυα) were of different kinds. Of these the most common were the ἀμφίβληστρον, or casting-net (*funda, iaculum, retinaculum*) and the σαγήνη—i. e. the drag-net, or seine (*tragum, tragula, verriculum*).

Retiarius. See GLADIATORES, p. 732.

Retractatiōnes. See AUGUSTINUS.

Reuchlin, JOHANN, also known by his Graecized name of CAPNIO. A distinguished scholar, born at Pforzheim, December 28, 1455. He was educated at Schlettstadt and at Paris, where he studied Greek under Hermonymus, a Spartan, and became exceedingly proficient in writing Latin. These pursuits he continued at Basel, where he wrote his Latin dictionary, entitled *Vocabularius Brevilioquus* in 1476. (See LEXICON.) After further travels he began lecturing at Tübingen (1481), whence he went to Heidelberg (1496). Reuchlin did much for the promotion of Greek studies in Germany, and himself edited a number of Greek texts (e. g. of Xenophon, Aeschines, Demosthenes), besides writing a Greek grammar. He became professor at Ingolstadt in 1520. His later years were given to the study of Hebrew and to semi-theological controversy. He died at Liebenzell, June 30, 1522. See the lives by Barham (London, 1843); Geiger (1871), and Horawitz (1877), and the critical monograph by Holstein (1888).

Reudigni. A people in the north of Germany, on the right bank of the Albis, north of the Langobardi (Tac. *Germ.* 40).

Reus. The term used by the Romans for the person accused, especially in a criminal trial. In such a case custom required the accused to appear in public in the garb of mourning, with beard and hair in an unkempt condition, in neglected attire, and stripped of every sign of rank. The mere accusation involved some suspension of legal rights, preventing the reus from standing for any office and from exercising the functions of a judge. The higher officials were exempt from criminal accusation while in office and when engaged in the discharge of public business. Lastly, lawsuits between two persons connected by ties of family or office, such as parents and children, patrons and clients, were regarded as inadmissible.

Revenues. See DECUMA; EISPHORA; PENTACOSTÉ; PORTORIUM; VECTIGALIA.

Rex (*βασιλεύς, ἄναξ*). A king. I. GREEK.—In the Heroic Age, as depicted in the poems of Homer, the kingly form of government was universal. The authority of these kings and its limitations were derived not from any definite scheme or written code, but from the force of traditionary usage and the natural influence of the circumstances in which the kings were placed, surrounded as they were by a body of chiefs and nobles, whose power was but little inferior to that of the kings themselves. Even the title *βασιλῆες* is applied to them as well as to the king. The maintenance of regal authority doubtless depended greatly on the possession of personal superiority in bravery, military prowess, wisdom in council, and eloquence in debate. When old age had blunted his powers and activity, a king ran a great chance of losing his influence. There was, however, an undefined notion of a sort of divine right connected with the kingly office, whence the epithet *διοτρεφής*, so commonly applied to kings in Homer. The characteristic emblem of the kingly office was the *σκῆπτρον*. (See SCEPTRUM.) Our information respecting the Grecian kings in the more historical age is not ample or minute enough to enable us to draw out a detailed scheme of their functions. Respecting the kings of Sparta the reader is referred to the article EPHORI. As an illustration of the gradual limitation of the prerogatives of the king or chief magistrate, the reader may consult the article ARCHON. The title basileus was sometimes applied to an officer who discharged the priestly functions of the more ancient kings, as in Athens. See ARCHON.

II. ROMAN.—Rome was originally governed by kings. All the ancient writers agree in representing the king as elected by the people for life, and as voluntarily intrusted by them with the supreme power in the State. No reference is made to the hereditary principle in the election of the first four kings; and it is not until the fifth king, Tarquinius Priscus, obtained the sovereignty that anything is said about the children of the deceased king. Since the people had conferred the regal power, it returned to them upon the death of the king. But as a new king could not be immediately appointed, an Interrex forthwith stepped into his place. (See INTERREGES.) The necessity for an immediate successor to the king arose from the circumstance that he alone had had the power of taking the *auspicia* on behalf of the State; and as the *auspicia* devolved upon the people at his death, it was imperative upon them to create a magistrate to whom they could delegate the *auspicia*, and who would thus possess the power of mediating between the gods and the State. Originally the peoples consisted only of the *patres* or *patricii;* and accordingly, on the death of the king, we read *res ad patres redit*, or, what is nearly the same thing, *auspicia ad patres redeunt*. The Interrex was elected by the whole body of the patricians, and he appointed (*prodebat*) his successor, as it was a rule that the first Interrex could not hold the Comitia for the election; but it frequently happened that the second Interrex appointed a third, the third a fourth, and so on, till the election took place. The Interrex presided over the Comitia Curiata, which were assembled for the election of the king. The person whom the Senate had selected was proposed by the Interrex to the people in a regular *rogatio*, which the people could only accept or reject, for they had not the initiative and could not themselves propose any name. If the people voted in favour of the rogation, they were said *creare regem*, and their acceptance of him was called *iussus populi*. But the king did not immediately enter upon his office. Two other acts had still to take place before he was invested with the full regal authority and power. First his *inauguratio* had to be performed, as it was necessary to obtain the divine will respecting his appointment by means of the *auspices*, since he was the high-priest of the people. The ceremony was performed by an augur, who conducted the newly-elected king to the Arx, or citadel, and there placed him on a stone seat with his face turned to the south, while the people waited below in anxious suspense until the augur announced that the gods had sent the favourable tokens confirming the king in his priestly character. The *inauguratio* did not confer upon him the *auspicia*, for these he obtained by his election to the royal office, as the Comitia were held *auspicato*. The second act which had to be performed was the conferring of the *imperium* upon the king. The *curiae* had only determined by their previous vote who was to be king, and had not by that act bestowed the necessary power upon him; they had, therefore, to grant him the *imperium* by a distinct vote. Accordingly the king himself proposed to the *curiae* a *lex curiata de imperio*, and the *curiae* by voting in favor of it gave him the *imperium*. Livy in his first book makes no mention of the *lex curiata de imperio*, but he uses the expressions *patres auctores fierunt*, *patres auctores facti;* and these expressions are equivalent to the *lex curiata de imperio* in the kingly period. The king possessed the supreme power in the earliest times, and the Senate and the Comitia Curiata were very slight checks upon its exercise. In the first place, the king alone possessed the right of taking the auspices on behalf of the State; and as no public business of any kind could be performed without the approbation of the gods expressed by the auspices, the king stood as mediator between the gods and the people, and in an early stage of society must necessarily have been regarded with religious awe. (See AUGUR.) Secondly, the people surrendered to the king the supreme military and judicial authority by conferring the *imperium* upon him. The king was not only the commander in war, but the supreme judge in peace. Seated on his throne in the Comitium, he administered justice to all comers, and decided in all cases which were brought before him, civil as well as criminal. Again, all the magistrates in the kingly period appear to have been appointed by the king and not elected by the *curiae*. Further, the king was not dependent upon the people for his support; but a large portion of the public land belonged to him, which was cultivated at the expense of the State on his behalf. He had also the absolute disposal of the booty taken in war and of the conquered lands. It must not, however, be supposed that the authority of the king was absolute. The Senate and the assembly of the people must have formed some check upon his power. But these were not independent bodies possessing the right of meeting at certain times and discussing questions of State. They could only be called together when the king chose, and, further, could only determine upon matters which the king submitted to them. The only public matter in which the king could not dispense with the coöperation of the Senate and the *curiae* was in declarations of war. There is no trace of the people having had anything to do with the conclusion of treaties of peace. The insignia of the king were the *fasces* with the axes (*secures*), which twelve lictors carried before him as often as he appeared in public, the *trabea*, the *sella curulis*, and the *toga praetexta* and *picta*. The *trabea* appears to have been the most ancient official dress, and is assigned especially to Romulus: it was of Latin origin, and is therefore represented by Vergil as worn by the Latin kings. The *toga praetexta* and *picta* were borrowed, together with the *sella curulis*, from the Etruscans, and their introduction is variously ascribed to Tullus Hostilius or Tarquinius Priscus.

See Mommsen, *Staatsrecht*, ii. pp. 1–17; id. *History of Rome*, i. ch. iv. pp. 66–70; Walter, *Geschichte des röm. Rechts*, § 17; and Seeley's introduction to his edition of the first book of Livy.

Rex Nemorensis. See ARICIA.

Rex Sacrōrum (or REX SACRIFICŬLUS), "the king of sacrifices." The name given by the Romans to a priest who, after the abolition of the royal power, had to perform certain religious rites connected with the name of king. He resembles the King Archon of the Athenian constitution. He was always a patrician, was chosen for life by the Pontifex Maximus with the assistance of the whole pontifical college (of which he became a member), and was inaugurated by the augurs. Although he was externally of high rank and, like the Pontifex Maximus, had an official residence in the Regia, the royal abode of Numa, and took the chair at the feasts and other festivities of the *pontifices*, yet in his religious authority he ranked below the Pontifex Maximus, and was not allowed to hold any public office, or even to address the people in public. His wife (like the wives of the flamens) participated in the priesthood. Our information as to the details of the office is imperfect. Before the knowledge of the calendar became public property, it was the duty of the Rex Sacrorum to summon the people to the Capitol on the Calends and Nones of each month, and to announce the festivals for the month. On the Calends he and the *regina* sacrificed, and at the same time invoked Ianus. Of the other sacrifices known to us we may mention the Regifugium on Feb. 24th, when the Rex Sacrorum sacrificed at the Comitium, and then fled in haste. This has been erroneously explained as a commemoration of the flight of Tarquinius Superbus, the last of the Roman kings; but it is much more probably one of the customs handed down from the time of the kings themselves, and perhaps connected with the purificatory sacrifice from which the month of February derived its name. At the end of the Republic the office, owing to the political disability attaching to the holder, proved unattractive, and was sometimes left unfilled; but under Augustus it appears to have been restored to fresh dignity, and in imperial times it continued to exist, at any rate, as late as the third century. See Mommsen, *Röm. Staatsrecht*, ii. 13–15 (3d ed.); Marquardt, *Staatsverwaltung*, iii. 321–324 (2d ed.).

Rex, MARCIUS. (1) QUINTUS, Roman praetor B.C. 144, built the aqueduct called Aqua Marcia. (2) QUINTUS, Roman consul in B.C. 118, founded in this year the colony of Narbo Martius in Gaul. (3) QUINTUS, Roman consul in 68, and proconsul in Cilicia in the following year. Being refused a triumph on his return to Rome, he remained outside the city till the Catilinarian conspiracy broke out in 63, when the Senate sent him to Faesulae to watch the movements of C. Mallius or Manlius, Catiline's general (Sulla, *Cat.* 32).

Rha (Ῥά). Now the Volga; a great river of Asia, first mentioned by Ptolemy, who describes it as rising in the north of Sarmatia, in two branches, Rha Occidentalis and Rha Orientalis (the Volga and the Kama), after the junction of which it flowed southwest, forming the boundary between Sarmatia Asiatica and Scythia, till near the Tanaïs (Don), where it suddenly turns to the southeast, and falls into the northwestern part of the Caspian (Ptol. v. 9; vi. 14).

Rhadamanthus (Ῥαδάμανθος) and **Rhadamanthys** (Ῥαδάμανθυς). The son of Zeus and Europa, and brother of King Minos of Crete. From fear of his brother he fled to Ocalea in Boeotia, and there married Alcmené (Pausan. viii. 53, 2). In consequence of his justice throughout life, he became, after his death, one of the judges in the lower world (Plato, *Min.* p. 320) or in the Islands of the Blessed (Pind. *Ol.* ii. 75), where he has for his associates Aeacus and Minos. The name points to an Egyptian origin of the myth.

Rhaetia and **Raetia** (the latter is preferable). A Roman province south of the Danube, was originally distinct from Vindelicia, and was bounded on the west by the Helvetii, on the east by Noricum, on the north by Vindelicia, and on the south by Cisalpine Gaul, thus corresponding to the Grisons in Switzerland, and to the greater part of the Tyrol. Towards the end of the first century, however, Vindelicia was added to the province of Rhaetia, whence Tacitus speaks of Augusta Vindelicorum as situated in Rhaetia. At a later time Rhaetia was subdivided into two provinces, Rhaetia Prima and Rhaetia Secunda, the former of which answered to the old province of Rhaetia, and the latter to Vindelicia. (See VINDELICIA.) Through Rhaetia runs the principal chain of the Alps called the Alpes Rhaeticae. In it rise some of the great rivers of Northern Italy—the Athesis (Adige) and the Addua (Adda)—besides the Oenus (Inn). The early inhabitants of Rhaetia were said to be Etruscans, and down to a late date a dialect of Etruscan was spoken in parts of the country. (See Strabo, pp. 204, 292, 313; Pliny, *H. N.* iii. 133; and Polybius, xxxiv. 10—the last being the earliest mention of the Rhaeti.) In the Roman period, the preponderant race were the Kelts, who were not subdued until the reign of Augustus. The chief towns were Tridentinum (Trent) and Augusta Vindelicorum (Augsburg). See Planta, *Die alte Rätien* (1872); and Oberziner, *I Reti* (1890).

Rhagae. An important city of ancient Media whose remains, mod. Persian *Raï*, are still pointed out about five miles southeast of Teheran. The city appears as Ῥάγαι in Arrian's *Anab.* iii. 20, 2. It is probable, moreover, that on the site of the original city destroyed by earthquake, Seleucos Nicator founded Ῥάγεια or Ῥάγα, called also Εὐρωπός (Strabo, pp. 514, 524; see also Ptolemy, 6, 5, 4). In the Old Persian Inscriptions (bk. ii. 72; iii. 2) RAGĀ is the name of a province; compare Ῥαγιανὴ Μηδία of Isidor of Charax. As a city, *Ragha* is twice mentioned in the Avesta, Vd. i. 16; Ys. xix. 18; and also several times by later Persian and Mohammedan writers, being specially connected with the name of Zoroaster (q. v.), apparently as his birthplace. There are a number of allusions to *Rages* in the Apocryphal Scriptures (Judith, i. 5, 15; Tobit, i. 14; v. 5; vi. 10). The fate of this once prosperous city, which was destroyed in the Parthian wars, rebuilt anew as Assacia under the Arsacid rulers, flourishing later as *Rai*, but finally in the twelfth century destroyed by the Tartars, and now lying in interesting ruins, affords an instructive lesson taught by the records of the past.

Rhamnus (Ῥαμνοῦς). Now Obrio Kastro; a demus in Attica, belonging to the tribe Aeantis, which derived its name from the ῥάμνος, a kind of prickly shrub. Rhamnus was situated on a small rocky peninsula on the east coast of Attica, sixty stadia from Marathon. It possessed a celebrated temple of Nemesis, who is hence called by the Latin poets *Rhamnusia dea* or *virgo* (Catull. lxvi. 71; Ovid, Trist. v. 819). A colossal statue of the goddess in this temple was the work of Agoracritus, the pupil of Phidias (Strabo, p. 396), or possibly by Phidias himself (Pausan. i. 33, 2). Remains of the temple still exist.

Rhampsinītus (Ῥαμψίνιτος). Rameses or Ramses III., one of the ancient kings of Egypt, who succeeded Proteus, and was himself succeeded by Cheops. Rhampsinitus belongs to the Twentieth Dynasty, and is known in inscriptions by the name of Ramessu-pa-neter. He is said to have stored up immense wealth in a stone treasury with a secret entrance, regarding the robbery of which Herodotus tells a very entertaining story (bk. ii. 121 foll.), resembling a similar tale narrated of the treasury built by Agamedes and Trophonius at Orchomenus, for which see TROPHONIUS. Rhampsinitus is said by Herodotus to have descended alive into Hades and to have won at dice from Persephoné (or Demeter) a golden napkin.

Rhapsōdus (ῥαψῳδός). A Greek term derived from ῥάβδω, originally designating the man who adapted the words to the epic song—i. e. the epic poet himself, who in the earlier time recited his own poetry. Afterwards the term especially denoted one who made the poems of others a subject of recitation.

At first such rhapsodists were generally poets themselves; but, with the gradual dying out of epic poetry, they came to hold the same position as was afterwards held by the actors, professionally declaiming the lays of the epic poets. Epic verses were originally sung to musical accompaniment, but after the time of Terpander, as lyric poetry became more independently cultivated, the accompaniment of stringed instruments fell into disuse; and then gradually, instead of a song-like recitation, a simple declamation, in which the rhapsodist held a branch of bay in his hand, came to be generally adopted. This had happened even before the time of Plato and Aristotle (see especially Plato's *Ion*). As in earlier times the singers moved from place to place, in order to get a hearing at the courts of princes or before festive gatherings, so the rhapsodists also led an unsettled and wandering life. At Athens (Lycurg. *Leocr.* § 102) and many other towns, as at Sicyon, before the time of the tyrant Clisthenes (Herod. v. 67), public recitations of the Homeric poems were appointed, at which the rhapsodists competed with one another for definite prizes, and thus found opportunity to display their art. It is true that other epic poems, and even the iambic poetry of Archilochus and Simonides of Amorgus, were also recited by rhapsodists; still at all times the labours of such reciters continued to be devoted in the first place to Homeric poetry (Pindar, *Nem.* ii. 2; Plato, *Ion*, 530 D; *Rep.* 599 E; *Phaedr.* 252 B). Hence they were also called Homeridae and Homeristae (Aristot. in *Athenaeus*, 620 B). It was to the older rhapsodists that the Homeric poems primarily owed their wide diffusion among the Greeks. In the course of time the high esteem in which the rhapsodists originally stood began to decline, because many practised their art as a matter of business and in a purely mechanical fashion. Still their employment survived long beyond the classical time, and not only did the public competition continue to exist, but it was also the custom to introduce rhapsodists at banquets and on other occasions. See EPOS; HOMERUS.

Rhapta (τὰ Ῥαπτά). A port on the eastern coast of Africa, the capital of Barbaria or Azania. It was the southernmost seaport known to the ancients, and was situated on the river RHAPTUS (Ptol. i. 9, 1).

Rhea (Ῥέα, Ep. and Ion. Ῥεία, Ῥείη, Ῥέη). A goddess whom the Greek legends identify as a representation of the fruitfulness of nature. She was the daughter of Uranus and Gaea, wife of her brother, the Titan Cronus, by whom she gave birth to the Olympian gods, Zeus, Hades, Poseidon, Heré, Hestia, Demeter. For this reason she was generally called the "mother of the gods." One of her oldest places of worship was Crete, where in a cave, near the town of Lyctus or else on Mounts Dircé or Ida, she was said to have given birth to Zeus (q. v.), and to have hidden him from the wiles of Cronus. The task of watching and nursing the new-born child she had intrusted to her devoted servants the Curetes, earth-born demons, armed with weapons of bronze, who drowned the cry of the child by the noise which they made by beating their spears against their shields. The name of Curetes was accordingly given to the priests of the Cretan Rhea and of the Idaean Zeus, who executed noisy war-dances at the festivals of those gods. In early times the Cretan Rhea was identified with the Asiatic CYBĔLÉ or CYBĒBÉ, "the Great Mother," a goddess of the powers of nature and the arts of cultivation, who was worshipped upon mountains in Mysia, Lydia, and Phrygia.

Turreted Head of Cybelé. (Caylus, *Recueil d'Antiq* v. pl. 3.)

In the former character she was a symbol of the procreative power of nature; in the latter, she originated the cultivation of the vine and agriculture, together with all forms of social progress and civilization, which depend upon these. Thus she was regarded as the founder of towns and cities, and therefore it is that art represents her as crowned with a diadem of towers.

The true home of this religion was the Phrygian Pessinus, on the river Sangarius, in the district afterwards known as Galatia, where the goddess was called Agdistis (Strabo, p. 567) or Angdistis, from a holy rock named Agdus upon Mount Dindymus above the town. Upon this mountain, after which the goddess derived her name of Dindymené, stood her earliest sanctuary as well as her oldest effigy (a stone that had fallen from heaven), and the grave of her beloved Attis (q. v.). Her priests, the emasculated Galli, here enjoyed almost royal

Rhea, or Cybelé. (From a Roman Lamp.)

honour. In Lydia she was worshipped, principally on Mount Tmolus, as the mother of Zeus and the foster-mother of Dionysus. There was also a temple of Cybelé at Sardis. Her mythical train was formed by the Corybantes, answering to the Curetes of the Cretan Rhea; these were said to accompany her over the wooded hills, with lighted torches and with wild dances, amid the resounding music of flutes and horns and drums and cymbals. After these the priests of Cybelé were also called Corybantes, and the festivals of the goddess were celebrated with similar orgies, in the frenzy of which the participators wounded each other or, like Attis, mutilated themselves. Besides these there were begging priests, called Metragyrtae and Cybebi, who roamed from place to place as inspired servants and prophets of the Great Mother. On the Hellespont and on the Propontis, Rhea-Cybelé was likewise the chief goddess; in particular in the Troad, where she was worshipped upon Mount Ida as "the Idaean Mother," and where the Idaean Dactyli (q. v.) formed her train. From Asia this religion advanced into Greece. After the Persian Wars it reached Athens, where in the Metroum, the temple of the Great Mother, which was used as a State record-office, there stood the ideal image of the goddess fashioned by Phidias (Pausan. i. 3, § 5). The worship of Cybelé did not, however, obtain public recognition here, any more than in the rest of Greece, on account of its orgiastic excesses and the offensive habits of its begging priests. It was cultivated only by particular associations and by the lower ranks of the people.

In ROME the worship of the Great Mother (*Magna Mater*) was introduced for political reasons in B.C. 204, at the command of a Sibylline Oracle, and for the purpose of driving Hannibal out of Italy. An embassy was sent to bring the holy stone from Pessinus; a festival was founded in honour of the goddess, to be held on April 2–4 (the Megalesia, from the Greek Μεγάλη Μήτηρ = *magna mater*); and in 217 a temple on the Palatine was dedicated to her. The service was performed by a Phrygian priest, a Phrygian priestess, and a number of Galli (emasculated priests of Cybelé), who were allowed to pass in procession through the city in accordance with their native rites. Roman citizens were forbidden to participate in this service, though the praetor on the Palatine and private persons among the patricians celebrated the feast by entertaining one another, the new cult being attached to that of Maia or Ops. The worship of Cybelé gained by degrees an ever-wider extension, so that under the early Empire a fresh festival was instituted, from March 15–27, with the observance of mourning, followed by the most extravagant joy. In this festival associations of women and men and the religious board of the Quindecimviri (q. v.) took part. In the first half of the second century A.D. the Taurobolia and Criobolia were added. In these ceremonies the person concerned went through a form of baptism with the blood of bulls and rams killed in sacrifice, with the object of cleansing him from pollutions and bringing about a new birth. The oak and pine were sacred to Rhea-Cybelé (see ATTIS), as also the lion. She was supposed to traverse the mountains riding on a lion, or in a chariot drawn by lions. In art she was usually represented enthroned between two lions, with the mural crown on her head and a small drum in her hand.

Rhea Silvia or **Ilia**. See ROMULUS.

Rhedŏnes. See REDONES.

Rhegium (Ῥήγιον). Now Reggio; a celebrated Greek town on the coast of Bruttium, in the south of Italy, was situated on the Fretum Siculum, or the strait which separates Italy and Sicily. Rhegium was founded about the beginning of the first Messenian War, B.C. 743, by Aeolian Chalcidians from Euboea and by Doric Messenians, who had quitted their native country on the commencement of hostilities between Sparta and Messenia. Even before the Persian Wars Rhegium was sufficiently powerful to send 3000 of its citizens to the assistance of the Tarentines, and in the time of the elder Dionysius it possessed a fleet of eighty ships of

Coin of Rhegium.

war. This monarch, having been offended by the inhabitants, took the city and treated it with the greatest severity. Rhegium never recovered its former greatness, though it still continued to be a place of considerable importance. The Rhegians having applied to Rome for assistance when Pyrrhus was in the south of Italy, the Romans placed in the town a garrison of 4000 soldiers, who had been levied among the Latin colonies in Campania.

These troops seized the town in B.C. 279, killed or expelled the male inhabitants, and took possession of their wives and children. The Romans were too much engaged at the time with their war against Pyrrhus to take notice of this outrage; but when Pyrrhus was driven out of Italy they took signal vengeance upon these Campanians, and restored the surviving Rhegians to their city. Rhegium was the place from which persons usually crossed over to Sicily, but the spot at which they embarked was called Columna Rhegina (Torre di Cavallo), and was 100 stadia north of the town See Axt, *Zur Topographie von Rhegion und Messana* (Grimma, 1887).

Rhenēa (Ῥήνεια), also **René** (Ῥήνη). Anciently called Ortygia and Celadussa, an island in the Aegaean Sea and one of the Cyclades, west of Delos, from which it was divided by a narrow strait only four stadia in width (Strabo, p. 486).

Rhenus (*Rhein* in German, *Rhine* in English). (1) One of the great rivers in Europe, forming in ancient times the boundary between Gaul and Germany, rises in Mount Adulas (St. Gothard), not far from the sources of the Rhone, and flows first in a westerly direction, passing through the Lacus Brigantinus (Lake of Constance) till it reaches Basilia (Basle), where it takes a northerly direction, and eventually flows into the ocean by several mouths. The ancients spoke of two main arms into which the Rhine was divided on entering the territory of the Batavi, of which the one on the east continued to bear the name of Rhenus, while that on the west, into which the Mosa (Maas or Meuse) flowed, was called Vahalis (Waal). After Drusus, in B.C. 12, had connected the Flevo Lacus (Zuyder Zee) with the Rhine by means of a canal (in making which he probably made use of the bed of the Yssel), we find mention of three mouths of the Rhine. Of these the names, as given by Pliny, are: on the west, Helium (the Vahalis of other writers); in the centre, Rhenus; and on the east, Flevum; but at a later time we again find mention of only two mouths. The Rhine is described by the ancients as a broad, rapid, and deep river. It receives many tributaries, of which the most important are the Mosella (Moselle) and Mosa (Maas or Meuse) on the left, and the Nicer (Neckar), Moenus (Main), and Luppia (Lippe) on the right. Its whole course amounts to about 950 miles. The inundations of the Rhine near its mouth are mentioned by the ancients. Caesar was the first Roman general who crossed the Rhine. He threw a bridge of boats across the river, probably in the neighbourhood of Cologne. (See PONS.) There is a history of the river Rhine from Keltic to modern times by Mehlis, 3 vols. (Berlin, 1876–79). (2) Reno, a tributary of the Padus (Po) in Gallia Cisalpina, near Bononia, on a small island in which Octavianus, Antony, and Lepidus formed the celebrated Second Triumvirate.

Rhesus (Ῥῆσος). (1) A river-god in Bithynia, one of the sons of Oceanus and Tethys. (2) Son of king Eïoneus in Thrace. He marched to the assistance of the Trojans in their war with the Greeks. An oracle had declared that Troy would never be taken if the snow-white horses of Rhesus should once drink the water of the Xanthus and feed upon the grass of the Trojan plain. But as soon as Rhesus had reached the Trojan territory, and had pitched his tents late at night, Odysseus and Diomedes penetrated into his camp, slew Rhesus himself, and carried off his horses. The story is the subject of a play ascribed to Euripides, but regarded by many as not genuine.

Rhetorĭca. I. GREEK. Among the Greeks ῥητορική (sc. τέχνη) comprised the practical as well as the theoretical art of speaking, and *rhetor* denoted an orator no less than a teacher of oratory. Among the Romans it denoted only the latter, the actual speaker being called *orator*. The first men who reduced oratory to a system capable of being taught appeared among the Sicilian Greeks, who, according to the testimony of the ancients, were distinguished for the keenness of their understanding and their love of disputation (Cic. *Brut.* 46). The Syracusan Corax (circ. B.C. 500) is said to have been the first who elaborated systematic rules for forensic speeches, and laid them down in writing in a manual on the art of rhetoric (τέχνη). His pupil Tisias (born circ. 480), and after him the Leontine Gorgias, further cultivated the art, and from about 427 carried it to Greece itself, and in particular to Athens, whither he went to ask for an alliance against Syracuse. So far as existing evidence shows, his rhetorical rules were of a highly artificial character, involving the use of studied antitheses and a multitude of tropes. He may, in fact, be regarded as the founder of the so-called Asiatic style of eloquence. In the judicial proceedings and the assemblies of the people the practice of oratory had long been familiar at Athens, though it had not been reduced to technical rules, and oratory had had a conspicuous representative in Pericles. At Athens the theory of oratory was further cultivated by the Sophists (σοφισταί, "men who professed knowledge or wisdom"). Their instruction in style and rhetoric was enjoyed by numerous Athenians, who desired, by the aid of study and practice, to attain to expertness in speaking. See SOPHISTAE.

The first Athenian who, besides imparting instruction in the new art, applied it practically to speaking in the assemblies of the people and before courts, and who published speeches as patterns for study, was Antiphon (died B.C. 411), the earliest of the so-called Ten Attic Orators. In his extant speeches the oratorical art is shown still in its beginnings. These, with the speeches interwoven in the historical work of his great pupil Thucydides, give an idea of the crude and harsh style of the technical oratory of the time; while the speeches of Andocides (who died about 399), the second of the Ten Orators, display a style that is still uninfluenced by the rhetorical teaching of the age. The first really classical orator is Lysias (died about 360), who, while in possession of all the technical rules of the time, handles with perfect mastery the common language of every-day life. Isocrates (436–338) is reckoned as the father of artistic oratory properly so called; he is a master in the careful choice of words, in the rounding off and rhythmical formation of periods, in the apt employment of figures of speech, and in everything which lends charm to language. By his mastery of style he has exercised the most far-reaching influence upon the oratorical diction of all succeeding time. Of the three kinds of speeches which were distinguished by the ancients —POLITICAL (OR DELIBERATIVE), FORENSIC, and SHOW-SPEECHES (OR DECLAMATIONS)—he specially cultivated the last. Among his numerous pupils is Isaeus (about 400–350), who, in his general method of oratory, closely follows Lysias, though he shows a more matured skill in the controversial use of oratorical resources. The highest point was attained by his pupil Demosthenes (q. v.), the greatest orator of antiquity (384–322); next to him comes his political opponent Aeschines (389–314). The number of the Ten Orators is completed by their contemporaries Hyperides, Lycurgus, and Dinarchus. In the last of these the beginning of the decline of oratorical art is already clearly apparent.

To the time of Demosthenes belongs the oldest manual of rhetoric which has been preserved to us—that of Anaximenes of Lampsacus. This is founded on the practice of oratory, and, being intended for immediate practical use, shows no trace of any philosophical groundwork or philosophical research. It is edited by Spengel (Zürich, 1844). Greek rhetoric owes to Aristotle its proper reduction into a scientific system. In contrast to Isocrates, who aims at perfection of form and style, Aristotle, in his *Rhetoric*, lays special stress on subject-matter, and mainly devotes himself to setting forth the means of producing conviction. In fact, Aristotle regards rhetoric as the counterpart of logic and closely allied with it. See the fine introduction and analysis by Cope in Cope and Sandys' edition of the treatise (3 vols. 1877). When Athens had lost her liberty, practical oratory was more and more reduced to silence; the productions of the last orators, such as Demetrius of Phalerum, were only a feeble echo of the past. Demetrius is said to have been the first to give to oratorical expression a tendency towards an elegant luxuriance. He was also the first to introduce the custom of making speeches upon imaginary subjects by way of practice for deliberative and forensic speaking.

In later times the home of oratory was transferred to the free Hellenic or hellenized communities of the coasts and islands of Asia Minor, especially Rhodes. On the soil of Asia a new style was developed, called the Asiatic. Its Asiatic originator is said to have been Hegesias of Magnesia near Mount Sipylus. He flourished in the latter half of the third century. In avowed opposition to the method of Demosthenes, who spoke in artistically formed periods, Hegesias not only went back to the simpler constructions of Lysias, but even endeavoured to outvie the latter in simplicity, breaking up all that he had to say into short sentences, and carefully avoiding periods of any length (Cic. *Orat.* 226). On the other hand, he sought to give a certain vividness to his speeches by an elaborately arranged order of words and by a far-fetched and often turgid phraseology. This was the prevailing fashion until the middle of the first century B.C. Even in Rome it had numerous followers, especially Hortensius, until by the influence of Cicero it was so utterly crushed out that Hegesias was soon forgotten, even among the Greeks. A peculiar kind of oratory (the so-called Rhodian) prevailed in Rhodes, where a closer approach was again made to the Attic models, and particularly to the representatives of the simple style, such as Hyperides. Conspicuous orators of this school were Apollonius and Molon, both of Alabanda in Caria, in the first half of the first century B.C. These two orators are expressly distinguished from one another by Strabo, p. 655; but they are confounded even by Quintilian, who erroneously speaks of Apollonius Molon (iii. 1, 16; xii. 6, 7).

The theory of oratory remained until about the end of the second century B.C. exclusively in the hands of the philosophers, and was little regarded by the Asiatic orators. After that time the orators and practical teachers of the art again applied themselves with eagerness to theoretical studies; the theorists adopted an eclectical method, seeking to combine the philosophical and more scientific proceeding of Aristotle with that of Isocrates, which addressed itself rather to the turns of phrase and the outward forms of oratory. The most noteworthy system was introduced by Hermagoras of Temnos (about B.C. 120), whose writings, which are no longer extant, supplied the chief foundation for the theoretical studies of the Romans at the beginning of the first century B.C. The system of rhetoric elaborated by him was afterwards further worked out and improved in detail. In the time of the Empire the rhetorical schools in general flourished, and we possess an extensive rhetorical literature of that age reaching as far as the fifth century A.D. It includes the works of authors who mainly treated of the literary and aesthetic side of rhetoric, especially those of Dionysius of Halicarnassus, the champion of Atticism and of refined taste, and the unknown author of the able treatise, Περὶ Ὕψους (see LONGINUS); also those of technical writers, such as Hermogenes, the most noteworthy representative of the scholastic rhetoric of the age, Apsines, Menander, Theon, Aphthonius, and others. On the revival of Greek oratory after the end of the first century, and particularly in the second century, see SOPHISTAE, and the works mentioned at the end of this article.

II. ROMAN. As among the Athenians, so also among the Romans, the institutions of the State early gave occasion for the practice of political and forensic oratory. Until the end of the third century B.C. this oratory was wholly spontaneous. The speech of the aged Appius Claudius Caecus, delivered in 280 against the peace with Pyrrhus, and afterwards published, was long preserved as the earliest written monument of Roman oratory. Numerous political speeches were published by the well-known Marcus Porcius Cato, the most noteworthy orator during the first half of the second century. After the Second Punic War, in spite of all the opposition of Cato and of those who thought with him, Greek culture forced its way irresistibly into Rome, and the Romans became eager to conform to the Greek theory of oratory also. Servius Sulpicius Galba (circ. B.C. 144) is spoken of as the first man who composed his speeches in accordance with the rules of Greek art, and not long afterwards the younger Gracchus, who died in 121, proved himself a consummate orator through the combination of natural gifts and art. Even at this time the publication of orations after delivery was a general custom, and men were already to be met with who actually wrote speeches for others. At the beginning of the first century B.C. the most noteworthy orators were Marcus Antonius and Lucius Licinius Crassus.

Rhetorical instruction was originally imparted by Greeks. In the first decade of the first century the freedman Plotius Gallus came forward as a teacher of rhetoric, and other Latin teachers followed him. These found a large number of hearers, but the censors interfered to stop the practice, as an innovation on the custom of their forefathers. It is true that this attempt to oppose the current, which had already set in, was in vain. Still it was only by freedmen that rhetorical instruction in Latin was given until the time of Augustus, when the Roman knight Blandus was the first free-born man who came forward as a public teacher of rhetoric. Even the Latin rhetoricians derived their theory exclusively from Greek sources, especially from Hermagoras, to whose influence the two earliest extant rhetorical writings of the Roman school are to be referred; these are the work of the pseudo-Cornificius, and the production of Cicero, *De Inventione.* Cicero (q. v.), the greatest orator of Rome and the only orator of the Republic of whom any complete speeches are extant, composed in his later years several other valuable writings upon rhetorical subjects, founded on his practice as an orator—viz. the *De Oratore*, the *Brutus*, and the *Orator*. Besides Cicero, the last age of the Republic possessed a series of other conspicuous orators, such as Hortensius (q. v.), Caelius, Brutus, and, above all, Caesar. A few more representatives of the oratory of the Republic survived to the time of Augustus. The most important of these is Asinius Pollio. But, with the old constitution, the occasions and materials for oratory also disappeared under the Monarchy, and the hindrances and limitations to its public exercise increased in the same proportion. Practice was gradually superseded by theory, orators by rhetoricians, speeches by declamations. The exercises of the rhetorical schools, which now became one of the chief centres of intellectual life, paid almost exclusive attention to the form, and dealt with imaginary subjects of political and forensic oratory, called *suasoriae* and *controversiae,* which were as far as possible removed from the practice of life. A vivid picture of these exercises is preserved in the reminiscences of the rhetorician Seneca, the father of the well-known philosopher. The manner of speaking contracted in the schools was adopted on the few occasions on which practical oratory could still be exercised, and these occasions were accordingly turned into exhibitions of theatrical declamation. It was in vain that men like Quintilian, in his work on the training of an orator (*Institutio Oratoria*), and Tacitus, in his *Dialogus,* pointed to the true classical patterns, and combated the fashion of their time, from which even they were not entirely free. Like these, the younger Pliny belongs to the end of the first century A.D.; his *Panegyricus,* addressed to Trajan, the only monument of Roman oratory after Cicero preserved in a complete form, became the model for the later panegyrists. In the second century A.D. Fronto, and the school named after him, sought to revive the old Roman spirit by a tasteless imitation of archaic expressions and forms of speech. The same style is practised, though with more ability, by the African Apuleius. After the end of the third century the oratorical art had its chief seat in the towns of Gaul, especially in Trèves (Treviri) and Bordeaux (Burdigala). Here a style of oratory was matured which possessed a certain smoothness and copiousness in words, but showed great lack of ideas. Upon the representatives of this style, the "Panegyrists," see PANEGYRICUS.

BIBLIOGRAPHY.—See Ballu, *Histoire Critique de l'Éloquence chez les Grecs* (1813); Gros, *Étude sur la Rhétorique chez les Grecs* (1835); Girard, *Études sur l'Éloquence Attique* (1874); Perrot, *Les Precurseurs de Démosthène* (1873); Blass, *Die Attische Beredsamkeit* (1877); the introduction to Cope and Sandys' edition of the *Rhetoric* of Aristotle (1877); the translation of the same treatise by Welldon (1886); Volkmann, *Die Rhetorik der Griechen und Römern* (1874); Berger and Cucheval, *Histoire de l'Éloquence Latine,* 2 vols. (1872); Westermann, *Geschichte der röm. Beredsamkeit* (1835); Demarteau, *L'Éloquence Républicaine de Rome* (1870); Tivier, *De Arte Declamandi apud Romanos* (1868); Poiret, *L'Éloquence Judiciaire à Rome* (1887); Ritter, *Die Quintilianische Declamationen* (1881); and Sears, *The History of Oratory* (Chicago, 1896). The Greek rhetorical writers are edited by Spengel (Stuttgart, 1828); and the minor Latin writers by Halm (Leipzig, 1863).

Rhetrae (*ῥῆτραι*). Specially the name of the ordinances of Lycurgus. The word *ῥήτρα* means a solemn compact, either originally emanating from or subsequently sanctioned by the gods, who are always parties to such agreements. The rhetrae of Lycurgus emanated from the Delphian god; but the kings, senators, and people all bound themselves, both to each other and to the gods, to obey them. Plutarch mentions four rhetrae (*Lyc.* 6 and 13), and describes them as relating to (*a*) the building of a temple to Zeus and Athenê; (*b*) the division of the people into *φυλαί* and *ὠβαί*; (*c*) the establishment of the Senate (*γερουσία*); and (*d*) the assemblage of the people at the time of the full moon.

Rhiānus (Ῥιανός) of Crete. A distinguished Alexandrian poet and grammarian, who flourished in B.C. 222. Some of his epigrams are present in the Greek Anthology. His remains are edited by Saal (Bonn, 1831).

Rhinocolūra (*τὰ Ῥινοκόλουρα*) or **Rhinocorūra** (*τὰ Ῥινοκόρουρα*). Now Kasr-el-Arish. The frontier town of Egypt and Palestine, lying in the midst of the desert, at the mouth of the brook (El-Arish) which was the boundary between the countries, and which is called in Scripture the River of Egypt. The name of it hence signifies "Cut-off-Noses," and is said to have been given it because it was the place to which criminals thus mutilated were banished under the Aethiopian dynasty of kings of Egypt (Strabo, p. 759).

Rhinthon (Ῥίνθων). A Greek comic poet, son of a potter of Tarentum, who lived about B.C. 300, and invented a style of composition of his own, which was much diffused in Magna Graecia, and is said to have been imitated even by the Romans. It was called the *Hilarotragoedia* (Ἱλαροτραγῳδία)—i. e. cheerful tragedy. It was a travesty of tragic myths by the intermixture of comic scenes. The scanty fragments of the thirty-eight plays of Rhinthon do not give us any adequate idea of this kind of composition. See PARODIA.

Rhinthonĭca Fabŭla. See RHINTHON.

Rhipaei Montes (*τὰ Ῥιπαῖα ὄρη*). The name of a lofty range of mountains in the northern part of the earth, respecting which there are diverse statements in the ancient writers. The name seems to have been given by the Greek poets quite indefinitely to all the mountains in the northern parts of Europe and Asia. Thus the Rhipaei Montes are sometimes called the Hyperborei Montes.

(See HYPERBOREI.) The later geographical writers place the Rhipaean Mountains northeast of Mount Alaunus on the frontiers of Asiatic Sarmatia, and state that the Tanaïs rises in these mountains. According to this account the Rhipaean Mountains may be regarded as a western branch of the Ural Mountains (Mela, i. 19, 18; Pliny, *H. N.* iv. 78).

Rhium (Ῥίον). Now Castello di Morea. A promontory in Achaia, opposite to the promontory of Antirrhium (Castello di Romelia), on the borders of Aetolia and Locris, with which it formed the narrow entrance to the Corinthian Gulf, which strait is now called the Little Dardanelles.

Rhizon (Ῥίζων) or **Rhizinium**. A town of Dalmatia. It was a stronghold of Queen Teuta (q. v.).

Rhizus (Ῥίζους). A town of Magnesia in Thessaly.

Rhoda (Ῥόδη) or **Rhodus** (Ῥόδος). Now Rozas. A Greek emporium on the coast of the Indigetae in Hispania Tarraconensis, founded by the Rhodians, and subsequently occupied by the inhabitants of Massilia (Livy, xxxiv. 8).

Rhodănus. Now the Rhône. One of the chief rivers of Gaul, which rises in Mount Adulas, on the Pennine Alps, not far from the sources of the Rhine, flows first in a westerly direction, and, after passing through the Lacus Lemanus, turns to the south, passes by the towns of Lugdunum, Vienna, Avenio, and Arelaté, receives several tributaries, and finally falls by several mouths into the Sinus Gallicus in the Mediterranean. The Rhône is a very rapid river, and its upward navigation is therefore difficult, though it is navigable for large vessels as high as Lugdunum (Lyons), and by means of the Arar still farther north.

Rhodé (Ῥόδη). See RHODOS.

Rhodius (Ῥόδιος). Probably the Brook of the Dardanelles. A small river of the Troad, mentioned both by Homer and Hesiod. It rose on the lower slopes of Mount Ida, and flowed northwest into the Hellespont, between Abydus and Dardanus, after receiving the Selleïs from the west.

Rhodŏpé (Ῥοδόπη). One of the highest mountain ranges in Thrace. It extends from Mount Scomius, east of the river Nestus and the boundaries of Macedonia, towards the coast, in a southeasterly direction. The river was sacred to Dionysus (Hor. *Carm.* iii. 25, 12).

Rhodōpis (Ῥοδῶπις). A celebrated Greek courtesan, of Thracian origin. She was a fellow-slave with the poet Aesop, both of them belonging to the Samian Iadmon. She afterwards became the property of Xanthus, another Samian, who carried her to Naucratis in Egypt, in the reign of Amasis, and at this great seaport she carried on the trade of an hetaera for the benefit of her master. While thus employed, Charaxus, the brother of the poetess Sappho, who had come to Naucratis as a merchant, fell in love with her, and ransomed her from slavery for a large sum of money. She was in consequence attacked by Sappho in a poem. She continued to live at Naucratis, and with the tenth part of her gains she dedicated at Delphi ten iron spits, which were seen by Herodotus. She is called Rhodopis by Herodotus, but Sappho in her poem spoke of her under the name of Doricha. It is therefore probable that Doricha was her real name, and that she received that of Rhodopis, which signifies the "rosy-cheeked," on account of her beauty. Cf. Herod. ii. 134, 135; Athen. p. 596; Suid. s. v.

Rhodos (Ῥόδος), sometimes called **Rhodé** (Ῥόδη). A daughter of Poseidon and Helia, or of Helios and Amphitrité, or of Poseidon and Aphrodité, or lastly of Oceanus. From her the island of Rhodes is said to have derived its name, and in this island she bore to Helios seven sons. (Pind. *Ol.* vii. 72.)

Rhodus (Ῥόδος). Now Rhodos, Rhodes; the most easterly island of the Aegaean, or, more specifically, of the Carpathian Sea, lying off the southern coast of Caria, due south of the promontory of Cynossema (Cape Aloupo), at the distance of about twelve geographical miles. Its length, from northeast to southwest, is about forty-five miles; its greatest breadth about twenty to twenty-five. In early times it was called Aethraea and Ophiussa, and several other names. There are various mythological stories about its origin and peopling. Its Hellenic colonization is ascribed to Tlepolemus, the son of Heracles, before the Trojan War, and after that war to Althaemenes. Homer mentions the three Dorian settlements in Rhodes—namely, Lindus, Ialysus, and Camirus; and these cities, with Cos, Cnidus, and Halicarnassus, formed the Dorian Hexapolis, which was established, from a period of unknown antiquity, in the southwest corner of Asia Minor. Rhodes soon became a great maritime State, or rather confederacy, the island being parcelled out between the three cities above mentioned. The Rhodians made distant voyages and founded numerous colonies.

Coin of Rhodes.

At the beginning of the Peloponnesian War, Rhodes was one of those Dorian maritime States which were subject to Athens; but in the twentieth year of the war, B.C. 412, it joined the Spartan alliance, and the oligarchical party, which had been depressed, and their leaders, the Eratidae, expelled, recovered their former power under Dorieus. In 408 the new capital, called RHODUS, was built, and peopled from the three ancient cities of Ialysus, Lindus, and Camirus. At the Macedonian conquest the Rhodians submitted to Alexander, but upon his death expelled the Macedonian garrison. In the ensuing wars they formed an alliance with Ptolemy, the son of Lagus, and their city, Rhodes, successfully endured a most famous siege by the forces of Demetrius Poliorcetes, who at length, in admiration of the valour of the besieged, presented them with the engines he had used against the city, from the sale of which they defrayed the cost of the celebrated Colossus (q. v.). At length they came into connection with the Romans, whose alliance they joined, with Attalus, king of Pergamus, in the war against Philip III. of Macedon. In the ensuing war with Antiochus the Rhodians gave the Romans great aid with their fleet; and in the subsequent partition of the Syrian possessions of Asia Minor, they were rewarded by the supremacy of Southern Caria, where they had had settlements from an early period. A temporary interruption of their alliance with Rome was caused by their espousing the cause of Perseus, for which they were severely punished (B.C. 168); but they recovered the favour of Rome by the important naval aid they rendered in the Mithridatic War. In the Civil Wars they took part with Caesar, and suffered in consequence from Cassius (42), but were afterwards compensated for their losses by the favour of Antonius. They were at length deprived of their independence by Claudius; and their prosperity received its final blow from an earthquake, which laid the city of Rhodes in ruins, in the reign of Antoninus Pius, A.D. 155. See Biliotti and Cottret, *L'Île de Rhodes* (1881); and Torr, *Rhodes in Ancient Times* (1885), which gives a good bibliography.

Rhoecus (Ῥοῖκος). (1) A Centaur, who, in conjunction with Hylaeus, pursued Atalanta in Arcadia, but was killed by her with an arrow. The Roman poets call him Rhoetus, and relate that he was wounded at the nuptials of Pirithoüs. (2) The son of Phileas or Philaeus, of Samos, an architect and statuary, who flourished about B.C. 640. He is said to have invented the art of casting statues in bronze and iron (Pausan. viii. 14. 5; x. 38. 3), and was the architect of the beautiful temple of Herê in his native island (Herod. iii. 60). It is known, however, that the casting of bronze had been known to the Phœnicians before his time, so that he merely introduced the art into Greece. See STATUARIA ARS.

Rhoetēum (τὸ Ῥοίτειον ἄκρον). Now Cape Intepeh or Barbieri; a promontory, or a strip of rocky coast, breaking into several promontories, in Mysia, on the Hellespont, near Aeantium, with a town of the same name.

Rhoetus (Ῥοῖτος). (1) A Centaur. See RHOECUS. (2) One of the giants who were slain by Dionysus; he is usually called Eurytus.

Rhombus. See TURBO.

Rhompaea, Romphaea (ῥομφαία), and **Rumpia**. A military weapon peculiar to the Thracians (Gell. x. 25); but whether belonging to the class of swords or of spears is a matter of doubt, though the latter seems the more probable. At all events, it was characterized by prodigious length (Livy, xxxi. 29), and by having, like the Roman *pilum*, a wooden shaft of the same dimensions as the iron head affixed to it (Val. Flacc. vi. 98).

Rhotacism. A technical term of scientific grammar, applied to the change of a voiced *s* (*z*) to *r* between two vowels. In Greek this change is rare, as in that language the intervocalic *s* regularly passed into *h* and then disappeared, leaving no trace of its existence, while in Latin it is regularly changed to *r*. (Cf. the Gk. μῦς, μυ-ός, Lat. *mus*, *mu-r-is*: Gk. νυός, Lat. *nu-r-us*.) In the dialect of Greek spoken in Elis, rhotacism occurred instead of loss of *s*, and so in some late Laconian words influenced by the usage of the neighbouring Elis. In Latin rhotacism is a regular law, for though there are many apparent exceptions to it, examination shows that in most of these cases the *s* was not originally intervocalic or else that the word is of (*a*) foreign or (*b*) late origin. For instance, in *causa* the *s* is not changed to *r* because it represents probably *ss*, Cicero having written it *caussa*. In many compounds *s* is not changed to *r* because it is to be regarded as an initial rather than as an intervocalic consonant—e. g. *desilio*, *positura*. In many other words the apparently intervocalic *s* represents a substitution for another original letter—e. g. *esuries* (√*ed* of *edo*), *prosa* (*provorsa*), *rosa* (cf. ῥόδον), *casa* (√*skad*, hence *cadta*). Such words as *basium*, *casium*, *gaesum*, *siser*, and probably *asinus* are non-Latin in their origin. The real exceptions to the operation of the regular change to *r* do not amount to more than a half dozen, such as *vasa*, *nasus*, *agaso*, *caseus*; and the exceptions are the basis of a special law known as CONWAY'S LAW, first set forth by Mr. R. S. Conway, in 1887, as a sort of corollary to Verner's Law. (See VERNER'S LAW.) Conway's Law is as follows: Medial *s* between words after an unaccented syllable became *r*, but after an accented syllable it was retained except when followed by *i* or *u* and preceded by *i* or *u* or a long vowel or diphthong; while medial *s* before nasals after an unaccented syllable was lost without compensation; after an accented syllable if arising before the period of rhotacism it was lost with compensatory lengthening of the preceding vowel (e. g. *aenus*, *primus*); if arising during the period of rhotacism it became *r* (e. g. *carmen*, *verna*).

Rhotacism in Latin is said to have been effected in the fourth century B. C., as Cicero says (*Ad Fam.* ix. 21) that L. Papirius, who was consul in B.C. 336, was the first of his family to give up the older spelling Papisius. But the change in general was probably effected earlier, for proper names are notoriously the last to suffer alterations of form.

Rhotacism occurs also in the Teutonic branches of the Indo-Germanic group of languages. (Cf. Germ. *eisen*, Engl. *iron*; Germ. *blasen*, Engl. *blare*; Engl. sing. *was*, plur. *were*.) The unvoiced *s* first passes into the voiced *s* (*z*) and thence to lingual *r*, for the position of the vocal organs in pronouncing *z* is substantially the same as that required for *r*.

See V. Henry, *Comparative Grammar of Greek and Latin*, pp. 74–76 (Engl. trans. New York, 1890); Roby, *Latin Grammar*, vol. i. pp. 98 foll.; Joret, *De Rhotacismo* (1875); Walter, *Rhotacism in the Italic Languages* (1877); and Conway, *Verner's Law in Italy* (London, 1887).

Rhoxolāni or **Roxolāni**. A warlike people in European Sarmatia, on the coast of the Palus Maeotis, and between the Borysthenes and the Tanaïs, usually supposed to be the ancestors of the modern Russians (Tac. *Hist.* i. 79).

Rhyme. The recurrence of similar sounds at the end of successive lines of verse was not formally recognized by the Greeks and Romans of classical times as a legitimate feature of poetical composition; and having a definite metrical system based upon the laws of syllabic quantity, the need was not especially felt of the added pleasure which the ear receives from rhyme. Nevertheless, rhyme is found in both Greek and Latin verse—in Greek probably as a sort of accident of composition which did, however, heighten the enjoyment of the listener, and in Latin sometimes as a consciously sought device. The two languages, therefore, stand on a different footing in this respect. (See Jahn's *Jahrbuch* for 1830, p. 256; Casaubon, *ad* Pers. i. 93, 94.) When the rhyme occurs in Homer, as in the following (*Il.* i. 225, 226),

Ἀτρείδην προσέειπε καὶ οὔπω λῆγε χόλοιο
Οἰνοβαρές, κυνὸς ὄμματ' ἔχων, κραδίην δ' ἐλάφοιο,

it has no especial significance, and simply occurs with probably no design on the poet's part. In Latin the function of rhyme is more important. The early (native) verse being accented like our own and rough in its structure, did undoubtedly introduce the element of rhyme to please the ear, so that when Ennius transplanted the metrical system of the Greeks and forced the Latin language to conform to its general requirements, he still retained some of the native peculiarities in his lines—especially alliteration and rhyme. (See ALLITERATION.) The following is a striking example of the conscious use of the latter:

Haec omnia vidi inflammari,
Priamo vi vitam evitari,
Iovis aram sanguine turpari.

And so in another of the older poets quoted by Cicero (*Tusc.* i. 28):

Caelum nitescere, arbores frondescere,
Vites laetificae pampinis pubescere,
Rami bacarum ubertate incurvescere.

As the system based on quantity became more and more definitely established, however, rhyme occurs less frequently, until in Vergil it appears to be almost studiously avoided except in rare instances where it heightens the effect by giving a sonorous swell to an impressive utterance, as is the case in the following (*Ecl.* iv. 50–51):

Aspice convexo nutantem pondere mundum
Terrasque tractusque maris caelique profundum!

See also *Georg.* ii. 500, 501; *Aen.* i. 319, 320; iii. 656, 657; iv. 256, 257; v. 385, 386; viii. 620, 621.

Ovid, partly because of his indolence and partly because his less severe taste probably enjoyed the richness of the melodic effect, uses rhyme with much greater frequency than Vergil; and he also admits the so-called Leonine rhyme, as in the following:

Quem mare carpentem, substrictaque crura gerentem,

and

Quot caelum stellas, tot habet tua Roma puellas,

and in the pentameter intentionally frequent:

Quaerebant flavos per nemus omne favos.

These Leonine rhymes became more and more frequent in the Silver Age of the language, and render easy the transitional reversion from the classic system to the popular one, as men's knowledge of the laws of quantity grew uncertain owing to the influx of foreign writers and a less careful training in the schools. See LEONINI VERSUS.

Ovid often uses the rhyme to point a climax precisely as Shakspeare does in many of the soliloquies and studied declamatory passages of his plays—e. g. at the end of Macbeth's famous soliloquy:

Hear it not, Duncan, for it is a knell
That summons thee to heaven or to hell!

and in the spirited address of Henry V. to his troops:

Cheerly to sea; the signs of war advance!
No king in England if not king in France!

The summing up of the whole matter is briefly as follows: rhyme was a subordinate element in the early popular poetry; it was suppressed during the Golden Age of literature, but as learning waned it again came to the front and resumed its place in the compositions of poets, so that in the Christian hymns it has practically supplanted the quantitative system, and appears as fully as in modern poetry.

The toleration and even fondness of the Romans for assonances may be seen even in their prose, as when they bring together such similar words—e. g. *florem et colorem* (Cic. *Brut.* 87), *veram et meram* (Pliny). For a full list of examples, see Näke in the *Rheinisches Museum* for 1829, pp. 392–401. When precisely the same syllables are repeated in successive words it is called PARECHĒSIS (παρήχησις)—e. g. *vi vitam* (in the first passages given above); *pleniore ore* (Cic. *De Offic.* i. 18); *pares res* (Hor. *Sat.* i. 3, 121). When successive words have the same ending, it is called HOMOEOTELEUTON (ὁμοιοτέλευτον).

See Bähr, *Geschichte der röm. Lit.* ii. p. 681; Schuch, *De Poësis Latinae Rhythmis et Rimis* (1856); Poggel, *Grundzüge einer Theorie des Reims* (1836); Grimm, *Zur Geschichte des Reims* (1855); two papers in *Gebaveri Anthologia Dissertatiorum*, pp. 265 foll. and 299 foll. (Leipzig, 1733); the introduction to Trench's *Sacred Latin Poetry*, 3d ed. (London, 1874); and the articles HYMNUS; LEONINI VERSUS.

Rhyndăcus (Ῥυνδακός). Now Edrenos; a considerable river of Asia Minor. Rising in Mount Dindymené, opposite to the sources of the Hermus, it flows north through Phrygia, then turns northwest, then west, and then north through Lake Apolloniatis, into the Propontis. From the point where it left Phrygia, it formed the boundary of Mysia and Bithynia.

Rhyparogrăphus (ῥυπαρογράφος). A painter of low, coarse, obscene, and trivial subjects, among which are enumerated scenes of ordinary life, interiors of barbers' shops, cobblers' stalls, animals, and objects of still-life (Pliny, *H. N.* xxxv. 37), such as those for which the Dutch and Flemish schools have become celebrated. It is clear from the adjective which gives the governing sense to the term (ῥυπαρός, "foul," "dirty"), that works of this description were held in low estimation by the talented and accomplished people of Greece; but the coarser-minded and more material Romans, whose love of art and taste was far less pure, being acquired or affected, not innate, set the highest value upon them, and bought them at prices oftentimes extravagant. See PICTURA.

Rhypes (Ῥύπες). One of the twelve cities of Achaia, situated between Aegium and Patrae. It was destroyed by Augustus, and its inhabitants removed to Patrae (Pausan. vii. 18. 7).

Rhytium (Ῥύτιον). A town in Crete, mentioned by Homer.

Rhyton (ῥυτόν) and **Rhytium**. A kind of drinking-horn. Originally it was probably made of an ox-horn (κέρας). Later, it had an opening at the bottom from which the person drank (Athen. xi. p. 497 e).

Rhyton from Pompeii. (*Museo Borbonico.*)

Ribbons. See FASCIA; INFULA; LEMNISCUS; VITTA.

Ricĭmer. The Roman "King-maker," was the son of a Suevian chief, and was brought up at the court of Valentinian III. He served with distinction under Aëtius, in the reign of Valentinian III. In A.D. 456 he commanded the fleet of the emperor Avitus, with which he gained a great victory over the Vandals, and in the same year he deposed Avitus; but as he was a barbarian by birth, he would not assume the title of emperor, but gave it to Majorian, intending to keep the real power in his own hands. But as Majorian proved more able and energetic than Ricimer had expected, he was put to death in 461 by order of Ricimer, who now raised Libius Severus to the throne. On the death of Severus in 465, Ricimer kept the government in his own hands for the next eighteen months; but in 467 Anthemius was appointed emperor of the West by Leo, emperor of the East. Ricimer acquiesced in the appointment, and received the daughter of Anthemius in marriage; but in 472 he made war against his father-in-law, and took Rome by storm. Anthemius perished in the assault, and Olybrius was proclaimed emperor by Ricimer, who died, however, forty days after the sack of Rome (Procop. *Vand.* i. 7, 57).

Ricina. One of the Ebudae Insulae (Hebrides). See Ptol. ii. 2, 11.

Ricinium and **Recīnus**. A covering for the head worn by the Roman women; probably a sort of mantle with a hood or cowl attached to it. It was worn by mime-players (Fest. s. v. *Rica*), by women before funerals, and by *camilli* at sacrifices.

Riddles. See AENIGMA.

Rings. See ANULUS.

Riscus (ῥίσκος). A wardrobe for feminine attire (Ter. *Eun.* iv. 6. 15).

Ritschl, FRIEDRICH WILHELM. See article in the Appendix.

Roads. See VIA.

Robbery. See FURTUM; LATRO.

Robigalia. See ROBIGUS.

Robīgo. See ROBIGUS.

Robīgus, the male, **Robīgo**, the female deity among the Romans (Tertull. *Spect.* 5), who protected the corn from blight (*robigo*) (Varro, *L. L.* vi. 16). On April 25th a festival called the Robigalia, supposed to have been instituted by Numa, was held in their honour in their grove, distant nearly five miles from Rome. The citizens marched to the spot in white festal attire, under the conduct of the *flamen Quirinalis*, Robigus having at first apparently represented only a particular function of Mars (or Quirinus), as protector of the arable land. After a prayer, accompanied by offerings of incense and wine, for the preservation of the ripening seed, the flamen offered sacrifice with the entrails of a young sorrel dog and a sheep. Certain races were also held.

Robur. See CARCER, p. 277.

Rogatio. A law proposed by the Roman magistrates. See LEX, p. 940; MAGISTRATUS.

Rogatōres. Officers appointed to act at the Roman Comitia (q. v.), whose duty it was to stand at the nearest end of the bridge (*pons suffragiorum*), which each citizen ascended in order to record his vote upon coming out from the enclosure (*ovile*) in which he had been previously mustered with the other members of his century, and to present a balloting token (*tabella*) to every one of them in turn, by whom it was taken and thrown into the box (*cista*) placed at the opposite extremity of the bridge. The illustration, from a coin, explains the entire process, showing at bottom the railing which enclosed the *ovile*, a voter ascending the bridge and receiving his ballot from the *rogator*, while another one at the opposite end is engaged in depositing his in the box. The term, however, originated before the practice of secret voting had obtained, when the poll-clerk had only to ask (*rogare*) the citizens how they intended to vote, and to register the result upon a waxed tablet containing a list of the candidates by making a mark or point (*punctum*) against the name of each one as a suffrage was recorded in his favour (Cic. *N. D.* ii. 4; id. *Div.* ii. 35; id. i. 17; id. *Sen.* 11; id. *Pis.* 15).

Rogator at the Ovilé.

Rogus. A funeral pyre. See FUNUS.

Roma (Ῥώμη). Rome. Rome lies on the river Tiber, about fourteen miles, in a straight line, from the sea. Its latitude (41° 53′ N.) is the same as that of Chicago; its longitude (12° 29′ E.) corresponds very nearly with that of Venice and of Leipzig. Its site forms a part of the gently rolling volcanic plain which lies between the sea and the Sabine and Alban Mountains, extending from Cape Linaro, on the north, as far south as Astura and the Pontine Marshes. The earlier city was confined to the left bank of the river, which here pursues a very winding course and, dividing, surrounds a small, flat island; but before the end of the Republic a considerable suburb had sprung up on the right bank, which became the fourteenth Regio in the division of the city under Augustus.

The oft-mentioned hills of Rome are low, and now, with some exceptions, of gentle slope. In ancient times they were more steep; for the intervening depressions (and to a less extent the lower parts of the hills themselves) have been covered, to the depth of nine, twelve, and in places even thirty feet, by the accumulation of débris. They are partly spurs, or irregular projections, from the line of bluffs which marks the descent from the general altitude of the Campagna into the valley of the Tiber, partly isolated masses nearer the river-bed. To the former class belong the Quirinal and Viminal hills, whose highest elevation above the surface of the Tiber (this being reckoned at 21.98 feet above sea-level) is about 158 feet; the Esquiline, with its two spurs Cispius (151 feet) and Oppius (161 feet); and the Caelian (141 feet), which is separated from both the Esquiline and the Aventine by valleys. The hills standing by themselves are the Capitoline (the two summits 141 feet, the depression between them 98 feet above the Tiber), which was originally connected with the Quirinal by a ridge; the Palatine (141 feet); and the Aventine (128 feet). To the north of the Quirinal, but not counted as one of the Seven Hills, was the Collis Hortorum, now the Pincio (164 feet). The small elevation southwest of the Aventine (Mons Testaceus, now Monte Testaccio, 115 feet) is entirely artificial, being composed chiefly of fragments of pottery. Along the right bank stretched the high ridge of the Ianiculum (253 feet), with its continuation, Mons Vaticanus.

Between the Quirinal and the Tiber was the level Campus Martius, at first a training-field outside the walls, in later times built upon and included within the city limits. The cattle-mart

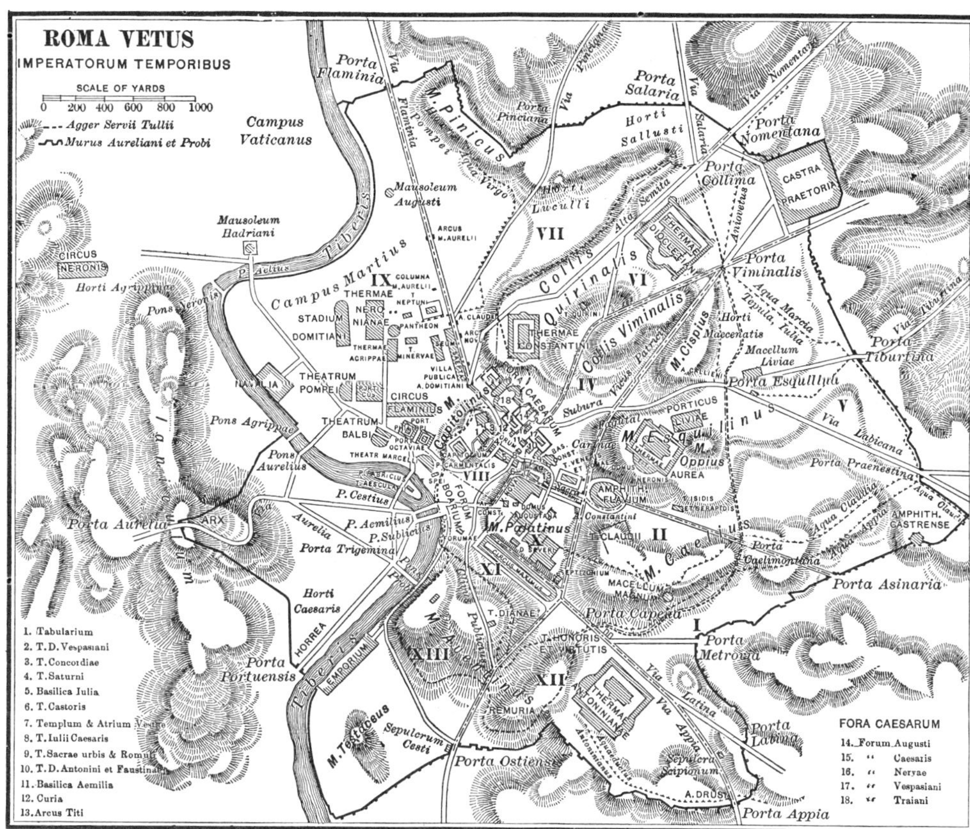

Plan of Rome.

(Forum Boarium) lay between the Palatine and the Tiber, the Circus Maximus between the Palatine and the Aventine. On the low ground north of the Palatine, stretching towards the Capitoline, was the Forum (often called Forum Romanum, or Forum Magnum, to distinguish it from the imperial forums), the spot in which the life of Rome centred; as it became too small for the congestion of business, relief was sought by building a series of extensions (Fora Caesarum) on the north side. The Colosseum (Amphitheatrum Flavium), the greatest monument of Roman architecture, stands in the depression between the Palatine, Esquiline, and Caelian Hills. See AMPHITHEATRUM.

In its development as a city Rome passed through several stages, some of which are clearly defined. Numerous indications point to the Palatine Hill as the seat of earliest settlement. At a remote period it was fortified by a strong wall of well-squared tufa blocks, laid without mortar; fragments of this wall have been discovered on the south and west sides. At least three gates gave access to the hill-top thus enclosed: the Porta Mugonia (*vetus porta Palatii*, cf. fig. 7) on the north side, the River-gate (Porta Romanula) on the west side, and a third, of which the name is uncertain, on the south side. To the latest times the Romans regarded the Palatine with especial reverence, and there cherished certain memorials associated with their oldest legends, such as the Hut of Romulus (Casa Romuli), which, though no doubt built of wood, and straw-thatched, was kept in repair, and was still standing in the fourth century A.D. See DOMUS, p. 536.

How long the Palatine city sufficed for the needs of the population cannot even be conjectured. After a time the limits seem to have been extended so as to include the Cispius, the Oppius, and the depression between them (Fagutal), together with the valley lying between these and the Palatine (Subura), as well as the small spur which the Palatine throws out towards the northeast (Velia), and a portion of its slope on the northwest side (Cermalus). To the city thus formed of seven parts (the original Palatine city being counted as one) the name Septimontium appears to have been given; but evidence regarding it is both meagre and unsatisfactory. More is known about the boundaries of Rome in the next stage of development, when enlarged by the addition of the Quirinal, Viminal, and Caelian Hills. It was now divided into four wards (*regiones;* cf. Varro, *L. L.* v. 45), the first (Regio Suburana) comprising the Caelian Hill and the Subura; the second (Esquilina), the Cispius, Oppius, and Fagutal; the third (Collina), the Quirinal and Viminal Hills; the fourth (Palatina) included the Palatine, Cermalus, and Velia. The Capitoline Hill was made a part of the city, but not set off as a separate ward; it was retained as a common sanctuary and fortress. Of the fortifications, by which this city of the four wards must have been protected, no trace has yet been found.

The bounds of Rome in the period with which the name of Servius Tullius is connected can be made out, for a large portion of the circuit, with exactness; for they were unchanged during the whole time of the Republic, and were marked by a line of imposing fortifications (*agger Servii Tullii*), remains of which have been discovered at many points. The Aventine Hill was now included within the limits, which were extended also further to the east on the Quirinal, Viminal, and Esquiline Hills. The wall of Servius was pierced by a number of gates, of which those most frequently mentioned are the Porta Carmentalis, at the foot of the Capitoline; the Porta Collina and Porta Esquilina, on the east side; and especially the Porta Capena, which opened into the Appian Way. The area bounded by the wall was about two square miles.

By the time of Augustus, Rome had extended beyond the Servian wall on every side. In B.C. 8 he divided the whole city, including the parts beyond the Servian limits, into fourteen wards (indicated on the Plan by Roman numerals). In each ward was afterwards placed a watch-house (*excubitorium*) for the *vigiles*, of whom there were seven cohorts (=about 7000 men), so distributed that each cohort looked after two wards; the duties of the *vigiles* were those of our policemen and firemen combined. The wards were subdivided into precincts (*vici;* the *vicus* as a subdivision is much older than the time of Augustus), each comprising a group, or block, of buildings; over the precincts were the precinct-masters (*magistri vicorum*), whose duties included not only the general oversight of other matters, but especially provision for the worship of the Lares Compitales (q. v.), to which the worship of the Genius of Augustus was added.

This larger Rome was finally fortified by a massive wall, commenced by Aurelian in A.D. 271, but not finished till the reign of Probus (A.D. 276–282). The Aurelian wall, as it is generally called (on the Plan, *Murus Aureliani et Probi*), was about 54 feet high on the outside, faced with brick, and strengthened (at any rate after the first restoration) by 381 square towers. It was repaired by Arcadius and Honorius in A.D. 403, afterwards by other rulers, and by several Popes; the greater part is still standing. It was constructed in great haste, as is shown by the large use of materials taken from other structures, and by the fact that walls previously erected for different purposes (e. g. see Plan, *Castra Praetoria* and *Amphitheatrum Castrense*), whose aggregate length amounted to about one sixth of the entire circuit, were incorporated in it as they stood. There were originally fourteen gates, vaulted, and flanked with round towers, besides the posterns, or small passages used for purposes of traffic in time of peace; the number was raised to fifteen by the enlargement of the Porta Pinciana from a postern to a gate of full size, probably by Honorius (*Bull. Com. Arch.* 1892, p. 102). The whole length of the wall was 11.7 miles (18837.50 m.); the area enclosed by it was 5.019 square miles, less than one-eighth the area of New York City.

The religious boundary of Rome, the Pomerium (q. v.), was not moved forward at the same time with the civil and military limits. The Pomerium of the city in the period when it comprised four wards and the Capitoline remained unchanged till the time of Sulla, who caused an extension to be made, but for some reason did not include the Aventine; this was outside the Pomerium till the reign of Claudius. Only he who had extended the territorial limits of Rome was entitled to the distinction of enlarging the Pomerium. After Sulla, at least Claudius, Nero, Vespasian, and Titus availed themselves of the privilege; and the line of Aurelian's wall for considerable distances seems to have coincided with a Pomerium previously fixed, perhaps also with an earlier limit of taxation for provisions brought into the city.

The population of Rome in the different periods cannot be estimated, even approximately; but, to judge from the area within the Aurelian wall, it can hardly at any time have exceeded 1,800,000.

The Tiber within the Aurelian wall was spanned by several bridges. The earliest was the Pons Sublicius, which was constructed of wood so that it could be cut down easily on the approach of an enemy; it was kept in repair, on religious grounds, even after bridges of stone stood above and below it. Next came the bridges connecting the island with the two banks, Pons Fabricius and Pons Cestius, both originally of wood, but renewed in stone in the first century B.C. The first stone bridge was the Pons Aemilius, also called Lapideus, dating from B.C. 142. The others were Pons Agrippae (reign of Augustus), Pons Aurelius (probably dating from the reign of Caracalla), and Pons Probi (reign of Probus). Frequently reckoned with these are two bridges outside the walls—the famous Mulvian Bridge (Pons Mulvius or Milvius, B.C. 109), two miles north on the Via Flaminia; and the Pons Aelius by the Campus Martius, built by Hadrian. Nero's bridge (Pons Neronis) was broken down, perhaps as early as the time of Hadrian. See PONS.

Along the Tiber were wharfs. The river-bed was skilfully adjusted—far more skilfully than under the system adopted some years ago and put into effect at enormous expense by the Italian engineers—to the great variation in the volume of water carried down, which at flood-height has been known to measure fourteen times the amount flowing when the river is at its ordinary level. The channel was graded at three elevations, so as to make three stages. Thus at the Pons Aelius the bottom division, for low water, was 218.2 feet wide; the middle division, for ordinary height, 319.9 feet wide; while to the upper division, designed to carry off the water in time of flood, a width of 442.9 feet was given (*Bull. Com. Arch.* 1893, p. 15). A complicated system of drains led into the Tiber through several large main sewers. Of the latter the Cloaca Maxima is justly celebrated as one of the best examples of early hydraulic construction. According to tradition it was built in the time of the Tarquins. Starting in the Subura, it followed a very irregular course, which was perhaps determined by the channel of a primitive brook (*Mitth.* 1891, p. 86). It passed beneath the Forum at the lowest point, under the east end of the Basilica Iulia, and emptied into the Tiber by the Forum Boarium. The channel of the Cloaca Maxima was paved with polygonal blocks of lava, and vaulted with large voussoirs of a hard kind of tufa (*lapis Gabinus*) laid without mortar; to give greater solidity at the mouth, the vaulting there for some distance was composed of voussoirs of peperino (*lapis Albanus*) arranged in three rings. The dimensions of the channel vary; where it is largest, at the opening into the Tiber, it is 14.75 feet wide and 18.96 feet high, measured from the pavement to the middle of the vault (*Ant. Demkm.* 1889, Taf. 37). See CLOACA.

The architecture of Rome in the early days was unpretentious. Even the temples, built after Etruscan patterns, were low and of common materials covered with stucco. The streets were narrow and crooked; as a large amount of wood was used in construction, it is not surprising that between the years B.C. 215 and 50 seven terrible conflagrations swept over the parts of the city along the Tiber and about the Forum; inundations of the river also at times caused great destruction. Not till near the end of the Republic did ambitious citizens direct their energies towards the erection of fine public buildings, such as Pompey's theatre;* some, in the same period, as Lucullus and Aemilius Scaurus, lavished money upon palatial residences, which they ornamented with costly marbles. Cicero, patriot that he was, found Rome inferior to Capua not only in general appearance, but particularly in the matter of streets; and he speaks contemptuously of the building materials—*in latere aut in caemento, ex quibus urbs effecta est* (*Div.* II. xlvii. 99; *Leg. Agr.* II. xxxv. 96). He himself had a house on the north slope of the Palatine which cost him 3,500,000 sesterces (about $144,000); the house of Aemilius Scaurus is said to have been sold to the infamous Clodius for the enormous sum of nearly 15,000,000 sesterces (about $615,000).

Iulius Caesar formed large plans for the beautifying of Rome, but in the midst of their accomplishment his life was cut short. Augustus completed the edifices which his adoptive father had left unfinished, and inaugurated a new epoch in the extent to which he carried not only the erection of buildings, but also the restoration of earlier structures (the temples restored by him numbered eighty-two) and the use of fine materials, especially marble and travertine (*lapis Tiburtinus*); his saying that he "found the city of brick and left it of marble" was no idle boast (Suet. *Aug.* 28; cf. Mommsen, *Res Gestae Divi Aug.* 19–21). His example was followed by other emperors, among whom the greatest builders were Vespasian, Titus, Trajan, and Hadrian; of lower rank than these as regards the architectural style, though not the size, of their buildings (chiefly *Thermae*), were Caracalla, Diocletian, and Constantine. Roman architecture was at its best in the period from Augustus to Hadrian.

The contributions of the Romans to the progress of the arts were greater in the field of architecture than in any other. From the time of Sulla they freely adopted the architectural forms of the Greeks; but with these they combined the extensive use of the round arch, and gradually worked out a system which enabled them to erect immense structures, such as lay within the range of neither the Greek nor the Etruscan architecture. Lacking the Greek sensitiveness to perfect proportion, they relied, for effect, more upon massiveness than upon symmetry, and indulged in greater richness of decoration than Greek taste would have allowed. Under the Empire they ransacked the known world for the choicest marbles, as well as for the hard stones, the granites, and porphyries; these they turned to account in every conceivable way, larger masses being used for columns and other architectural members, thin slabs for incrustation, and small fragments for mosaics. (See MUSIVUM OPUS.) Surfaces finished in stucco were decorated in brilliant colours, frequently with complicated designs, sometimes with paintings of high merit (see PICTURA); bas-reliefs also were painted. In their adaptation of the Greek orders of architecture the Romans made changes affecting alike the shaft, capital, and architrave. (See COLUMNA.) Borrowing also from the Greeks the plan of the oblong temple and that of the hill-side theatre, they altered both; at the same time, contrary to Greek practice, they raised their temples upon high foundations, and gave to their theatres a full elevation on the exterior. (See AEDES; THEATRUM.) But apart from these, they so developed several architectural types as to make them distinctively Roman; such were the circus (q. v.), the amphitheatre (see AMPHITHEATRUM), the basilica (q. v.), baths (see THERMAE), the triumphal arch (see ARCUS), the commemorative column (see COLUMNA COCHLIS), the round tomb (see MAUSOLEUM; SEPULCRUM), and the aqueduct, so far as this was constructed above ground on the principle of the arcade. The Roman roads also, though in the modern view belonging rather to the domain of engineering than to that of architecture, were equally characteristic (see VIA); and certain of their bridges, as that at Alcántara in Spain, command universal admiration. No other city has been able to boast of so great a number and variety of beautiful or impressive structures as Rome in the first half of the fourth century A.D. Accord-

Temple of Vesta. (Restoration.)

* Very little is known of the architectural character of the early basilicas about the Forum.

ing to a Catalogue dating from that period, the city contained 2 circuses, 2 amphitheatres, 3 theatres, 10 basilicas, 11 thermae, 36 arches of marble, 2 commemorative columns, 6 obelisks (imported from Egypt), 423 temples, 1790 *domus*—that is, extensive private residences, or palaces, of the wealthy—besides which there were reckoned 46,602 tenements (*insulae*); the open places were adorned with 2 *colossi* (probably those of Nero and Augustus), 22 "great horses" (presumably counting not merely the large equestrian statues, as that of Marcus Aurelius, now in the square of the Capitol, but also groups of which horses formed a part, as those of the Dioscuri on the Capitoline and the Quirinal), to which are added 80 gilded and 77 ivory statues of the gods, no mention being made of the countless lesser statues on every side.

The number of obelisks in Rome is known to have been about twice that given in the Catalogue. Of the 19 aqueducts by which, according to the Catalogue, the city was supplied with water, part were branches. The principal aqueducts were: Aqua Appia, built in B.C. 312; Anio Vetus, for the Esquiline Hill, B.C. 272; Aqua Marcia (B.C. 144) and Aqua Tepula (B.C. 125), extending to the Capitoline; three constructed in the reign of Augustus: Aqua Iulia (B.C. 33), in the line of the Marcia and Tepula; Aqua Virgo (B.C. 19), for the Campus Martius; and Aqua Alsietina (B.C. 2), for his *naumachia* on the right bank of the Tiber; Anio Novus, built by Caligula; Aqua Claudia, by Claudius; Aqua Traiana, by Trajan, the last on the right bank; Aqua Severiana and Aqua Alexandrina, constructed to supply baths, the former by Septimius, the latter by Alexander, Severus. According to Lanciani's calculations, the amount of water brought in daily by the aqueducts in the time of Nerva (before the last three named in the list were built) was about 23,839,793 cu. ft. (cu. m. 675,092; see his *I Comentarii di Frontino*, p. 362). Three of the aqueducts have been repaired and are in use—the Aqua Marcia, Aqua Virgo, and Aqua Traiana. See AQUAEDUCTUS.

The names and dates of the more noteworthy buildings will now be given in connection with a rapid survey of the City according to its main divisions, commencing with the Capitoline Hill.

On the northern summit of the Capitoline was the Stronghold (*Arx*) of the earlier city. Within

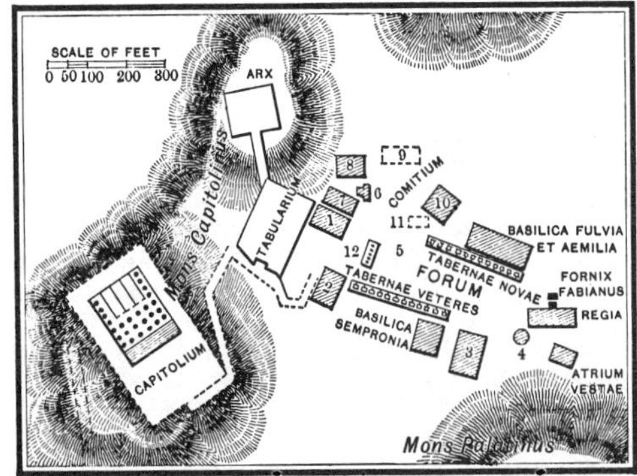

1. Temple of Concord.
2. Temple of Saturn.
3. Temple of Castor.
4. Temple of Vesta.
5. Probable location of the Temple of Ianus.
6. Prison—Carcer.
7. Probable location of the Basilica Opimia.
8. Probable location of the Basilica Porcia.
9. Probable location of the Curia Hostilia.
10. Curia Iulia.
11. Probable location of the Rostra before 44 B.C.
12. Rostra, after 44 B.C.
13. Probable location of the Temple of Iupiter Stator.

Plan of the Capitol and Forum in time of the Republic.

its walls were the Auguraculum, an open place where auspices were taken; the Temple of Iuno Moneta, with which the Mint was connected; and a Temple of Concord, built in B.C. 217; but their location is uncertain. On the southern summit was the most magnificent of all Roman temples, that of Iupiter Optimus Maximus, called the Capitolium. It stood in an *area*, on a high platform, and was nearly square, being Etruscan in plan and style; the sum of the four sides measured perhaps 760 feet. The front part was a triple colonnade; behind this were the three large *cellae*, the middle one for Iupiter, the other two for Minerva and Iuno. The original edifice is ascribed to the Tarquins, but it was not dedicated till the first year of the Republic, B.C. 509. It became a repository of the richest booty and votive offerings. In B.C. 83 it was burned to the ground; it was rebuilt, with richer adornment, the second temple being dedicated in B.C. 69. Again filled with treasures, it fell a prey to flames in A.D. 69. It was rebuilt a third time on the same plan, but as a Corinthian hexastyle, only to be burned again in A.D. 80. It was restored with great splendour, the fourth temple being dedicated by Domitian in A.D. 82. It was not again destroyed by fire, but remained to be dismantled by plunderers.

The Capitol was reached from the Forum by a graded road (*Clivus Capitolinus*, paved in B.C. 174), from which a branch led to the Arx. Of the open places, shrines, and private buildings on the Capitoline outside the Capitol and the Arx very little is known. The Tarpeian Rock was on the southeast side. On the slope of the Capitoline overlooking the Forum was the Tabularium, a depository for archives, erected in B.C. 78.

The northeast and southwest sides of the Forum in early times were lined with small shops (*tabernae*), which eventually were removed to make room for public buildings. The very ancient shrine of Ianus stood somewhere near the middle of the northwest side; the round Temple of Vesta at the southeast corner. The Palace of the Vestals (*Atrium Vestae*), southeast of the temple, was greatly changed by enlargements and restorations; near it was the official residence of the Pontifex Maximus (*Regia*). In the vaults of the Temple of Saturn (dedicated B.C. 497) the public treasure was kept (see AERARIUM); the eight Ionic columns remaining belong to a later restoration. The three beautiful Corinthian columns still standing on the foundation of the Temple of Castor (dedicated B.C. 484) date from a restoration in B.C. 6. The Temple of Concord was likewise of early date (dedicated B.C. 366); but the existing plan and fragments date from a remodelling of the edifice in B.C. 7. Under the Empire temples were erected in honour of Iulius Caesar (*Templum Divi Iulii*, marking the spot where his body was burned, dedicated B.C. 29); of Vespasian (three Corinthian columns remain); of Faustina, wife of Antoninus Pius, dedicated to him also after his death in A.D. 161 (now the Church of S. Lorenzo in Miranda); and of Romulus, the small son of Maxentius, who died in A.D. 309; this last building, of circular form (now incorporated in the Church of SS. Cosmas and Damian), lies just beyond the Temple of Faustina, northeast of the Forum. In A.D. 367 a series of twelve chapels, containing gilded statues of the Olympian divinities, was erected in the southwest corner (*Porticus Deorum Consentium*).

The oldest of the basilicas was the Basilica Porcia, built by the elder Cato in B.C. 184; this and the Basilica Opimia (B.C. 121) were removed, as the ground was needed for the extensions of the Forum. The Basilica Fulvia et Aemilia, built in B.C. 179, north of the shops, was extended afterwards to the edge of the Forum; as this side has not been excavated, its foundations cannot be traced. The Basilica Sempronia (B.C. 170) was erected on the site of the house of Scipio Africanus Maior, and was itself replaced by the magnificent Basilica Iulia, which was begun by Iulius Caesar in B.C. 54 and completed by Augustus. See BASILICA.

The open space of the Forum was paved with large blocks of stone. Along the south side passed the Holy Way (*Via Sacra*), the course of which varied somewhat in different periods. Across this, at the point where it entered the Forum (north of the *Regia*), was the Arch of the Fabii (*Fornix Fabianus*), erected in B.C. 121; south of the Temple of Iulius Caesar was the Arch of Augustus (B.C. 19), and at the upper end of the Basilica Iulia, the Arch of Tiberius (A.D. 16)—all these commemorating famous victories. The Arch of Septimius Severus (A.D. 203) is in a good state of preservation, though the six horses and the chariot which stood upon it, with Victory placing a crown upon the head of Severus, have long since disappeared. Several columns surmounted by statues stood in the Forum; the latest of them, the tasteless Column of Phocas (A.D. 608), is still in place, without the image.

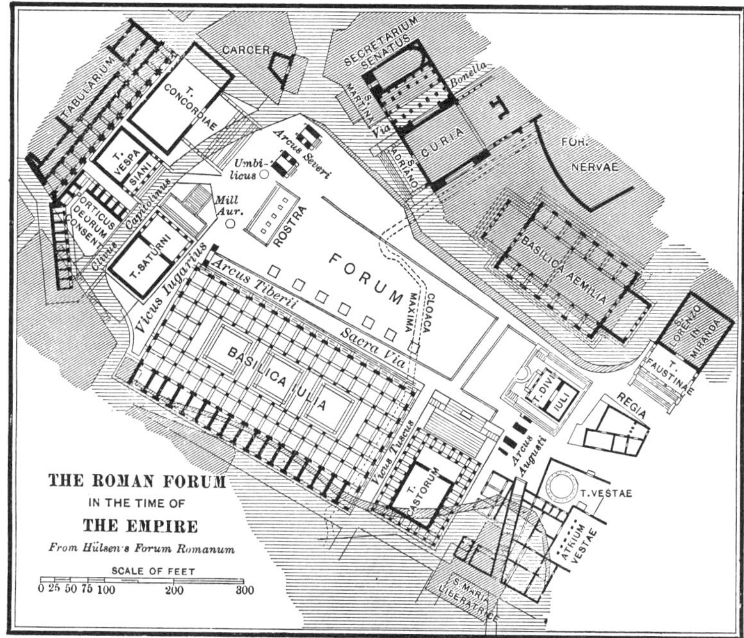

THE ROMAN FORUM
IN THE TIME OF
THE EMPIRE
From Hülsen's Forum Romanum
SCALE OF FEET
0 25 50 75 100 200 300

Near the northwest corner of the Forum was the only prison in Rome (*carcer*), comprising a large upper and smaller lower dungeon, the latter of very ancient construction. East of the prison was the open space of the Comitium (q. v.). Here were the ancient Senate-house (*Curia Hostilia*) and the Speakers' Platform, called Rostra, because ornamented with the beaks of the ships taken from the Antiates in B.C. 338. Both were removed by Caesar, who commenced the erection of a new Senate-house (*Curia Iulia*, finished by Augustus) and the rebuilding of the Rostra at the upper end of the Forum; when the Rostra began to be used in the new location is a matter of doubt. The Platform in its final form was about 78 feet long, 33 feet wide, and 10 feet high; the top was adorned with statues. A second Speakers' Platform (*Rostra Iulia*) was erected in front of the Temple of Iulius Caesar, forming part of the façade, and was ornamented with the beaks of ships taken at the battle of Actium. Near the southwest corner of the Rostra was the Golden Milestone (*Milliarium Aureum*), erected by Augustus, from which distances were calculated on the Roman roads; at the northwest corner Constantine set up the Umbilicus Romae, in the form of a cone, as the ideal centre of the city and the Roman world. There is much uncertainty in regard to the plan and location of several other structures about the Forum, as the Secretarium Senatus and Graecostasis. Somewhere near the middle of the open space was the Lacus Curtius, which appears to have become a dry *puteal* by the time of Augustus; near the Temple of Castor was the Lacus Iuturnae, which was still known in the Middle Ages.

The first extension of the Forum, made by Iulius Caesar (*Forum Caesaris* or *Forum Iulium*, see Map of Rome), was east of the Arx; in the centre was a Temple of Venus Genetrix, in front of which stood a bronze statue of Caesar's war-horse (Suet. *Caes.* 61). On the east side of this Augustus built a second extension (*Forum Augusti*), in which was the splendid Temple of Mars Ultor (dedicated B.C. 2), adorned with costly works of art. Nearer the Forum Romanum Vespasian laid off a similar area, and erected in it the magnificent Temple of Peace (*Templum Pacis*). This was connected with the forums of Caesar and Augustus by the Forum of Nerva, which was planned and almost finished by his predecessor Domitian; the boundary-wall

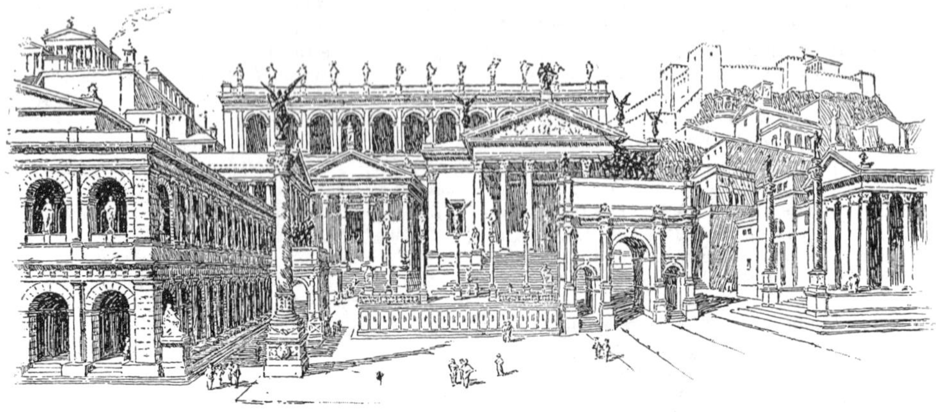

Restoration of the Forum.

was richly ornamented with Corinthian columns and reliefs, and in it was a prostyle hexastyle Temple of Minerva, also of the Corinthian order. The last and finest of the imperial forums was that of Trajan, who cut away the ridge between the Capitoline and Quirinal to make room for it. It was entered from the Forum of Augustus through a high triumphal arch. From this the visitor passed into an area with colonnades on either side, which opened out into two semicircular extensions; at the upper end of the latter was the great Basilica Ulpia. Beyond the Basilica was a small area in which rose the immense column of Trajan (without the base 97 feet, = 100 Roman feet, high), adorned with reliefs celebrating his campaigns against Decebalus. On either side of this were two buildings in which a large library was stored (*Bibliotheca Ulpia*); just beyond them Hadrian erected a temple in honour of Trajan and Plotina.

The greater part of the Palatine Hill in the Republican period was given up to the residences of wealthy citizens. There were, however, several temples the location of which, even now that a considerable portion of the hill has been excavated, has not been determined with exactness. Somewhere on the northern side was the very ancient Temple of Victory; farther down towards the Via Sacra lay the Temple of Iupiter Stator. Of later date were the Temple of the Magna Mater (dedicated B.C. 191), and the Temple of Iupiter Victor (see Plan), which seems to have been changed into a temple of the Sun by Elagabalus. But these temples were eclipsed in splendour by the Temple of Apollo, dedicated B.C. 28; the site of this, and of the library connected with it, has not yet been cleared.

Augustus, who was born on the Palatine, made it a place of imperial residence. His palace, enlarged by the additions of his successors (*Domus Augustana*), became the nucleus of a complex of palatial edifices to the magnificence of which the world has elsewhere afforded no parallel. (The arrangement in general, so far as the excavations have gone, may be made out from the Plan.) Ti-

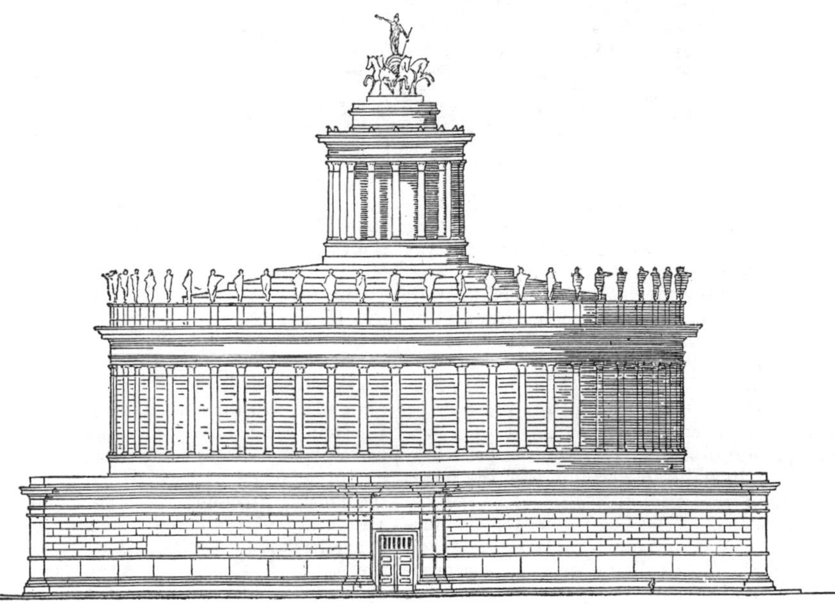

Restoration of Hadrian's Mausoleum.

berius seems to have had a separate palace before his father's death (*Domus Tiberiana*). Caligula added to this; and, utilizing the roofs of intermediate buildings, he made a bridge from the Palatine to the Capitoline. Nero, after the nine-days fire in July, A.D. 64, extended his Golden House (*Domus Aurea*) over the Velia and even to the Esquiline; together with the Palace on the Palatine it must have covered about a square mile, but the parts beyond the Palatine were removed by the following emperors. The Stadium was probably built by Hadrian. Septimius Severus extended the palace beyond the Stadium; at the southeast corner, overlooking the Via Appia, he erected the Septizonium, a beautiful marble balcony in at least three stories. On the slope of the Palatine at the middle of the south side was the Paedagogium, a school for the pages of the imperial household.

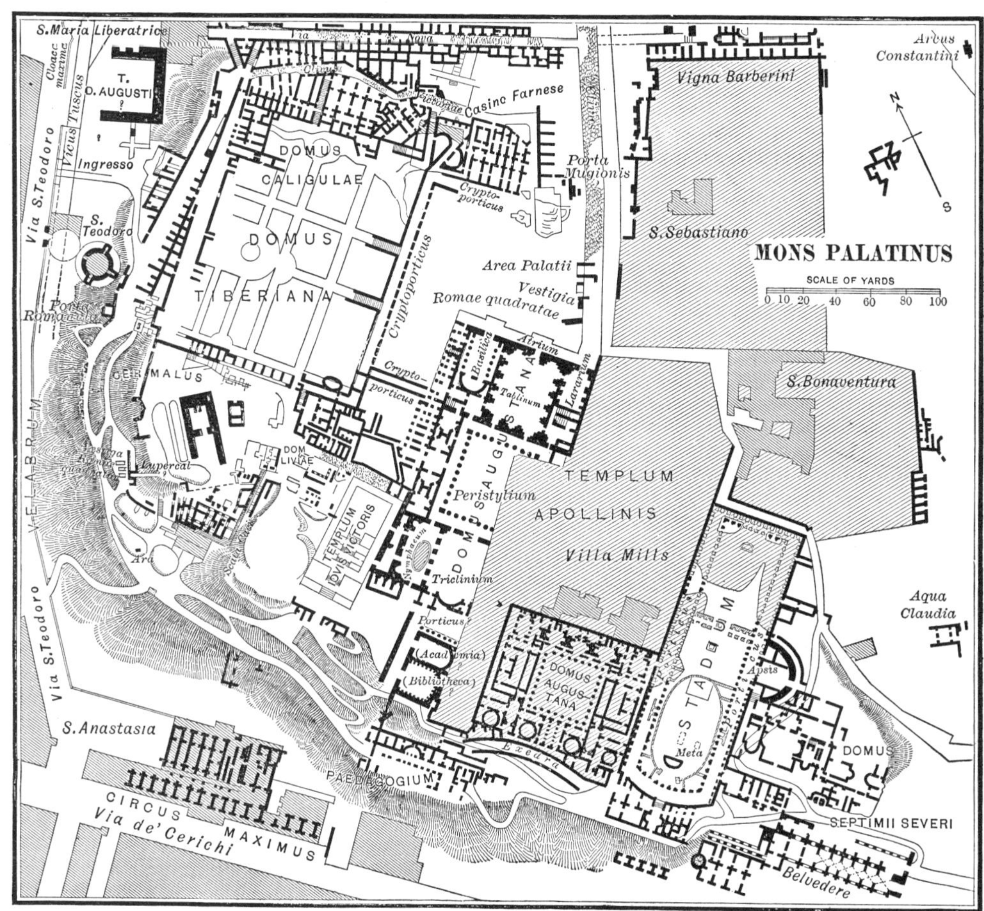

Plan of the Palatine.

North of the Palatine ran the Via Sacra, connecting at the east end with a street that skirted the southeast side and led into the Via Appia near the Porta Capena. Across the Via Sacra at the highest point of the Velia was the Arch of Titus, commemorating his victories over the Jews in A.D. 70 (dedicated in A.D. 81 by Domitian). Near this was the magnificent Temple of Venus and Rome, built by Hadrian, with two great apsidal niches facing in opposite directions (partly incorporated in the church of S. Francesca Romana). Further towards the Forum was the Basilica of Constantine, the main part of which was erected by Maxentius before B.C. 312; its remains are among the most impressive in Rome. At the end of the Via Sacra the triumphal Arch of Constantine is still standing, not far from the Colosseum. See ARCUS.

The Colosseum (probably so named from the colossus of Nero, more than 100 feet high, which stood near it) was commenced by Vespasian, and dedicated by Titus in A.D. 80, but it seems not to have been entirely finished till later. It is in the form of an ellipse, the circuit of which measures nearly one-third of a mile (1728 feet), the major axis 615 feet, the minor axis 510 feet; the area is about 5.7 acres. The four stories furnished seats for 87,000 spectators. More ample still was the Circus Maximus, which was first provided with a permanent structure by Caesar; his building was in three stories, the first of stone, the other two of wood, and was about 2130 feet long, seating 150,000 spectators. This Circus was several times burned, rebuilt, and enlarged; before A.D. 79 it accommodated 250,000 spectators, and at the beginning of the fourth century its capacity is said to have reached the incredible number of 485,000. See AMPHITHEATRUM.

The other great buildings in the eastern part of

Rome were the Thermae of Titus (Reg. III.), erected in A.D. 80 on a part of the site of the Golden House. The Thermae of Caracalla (*Thermae Antoninianae*, Reg. XII.) could accommodate at one time 1600 bathers, and were of unparalleled magnificence. The quadrangular enclosure (see Map of Rome) measures more than a fifth of a mile (1081 feet) on each side, and the ruins now have something of the appearance of a great fortress. On the Quirinal (Reg. VI.) were the immense Thermae of Diocletian (dedicated in A.D. 305), part of the remains of which have been turned to use in modern edifices, and the Thermae of Constantine, which, though restored as late as A.D. 443, have left few traces. See THERMAE.

The public edifices in the Campus Martius were numerous and important. Here was the Theatre of Pompey (erected B.C. 55); with this was connected the Porticus Pompei, together with the Exedra, in which stood the statue of Pompey mentioned in the narratives of the death of Caesar. Nearer the Capitoline and the Tiber were the Theatre of Marcellus, of which an imposing section of exterior wall is still to be seen, and the Theatre of Balbus, both dedicated in B.C. 11; among other buildings erected during the reign of Augustus were the Porticus of Octavia and Porticus of Philippus, both named after relatives of the emperor, the Thermae of Agrippa, and the original Pantheon. The Pantheon in its present form, dating from the reign of Hadrian (though the inscription of Agrippa is still on the front of the Portico), is not only in a better state of preservation than any other Roman edifice, but ranks high among remarkable buildings. Its plan has the form of a circle 140 feet in diameter on the inside, with a rectangular portico sustained by sixteen Corinthian columns of granite 39 feet high. Over the round structure, which is of brick, is a massive dome 140 feet at its highest point above the paved floor; the building is lighted by an aperture, 30 feet in diameter, at the centre of the dome. Near the Tiber, in the northern part of the Campus Martius, was the huge Mausoleum of Augustus, the chambers of which were used as burial-places for members of the imperial family down to Nerva. To his reign also belonged the completion of the new Saepta, commenced by Iulius Caesar; this, originally an open space marked off to facilitate voting by centuries, was now surrounded by marble porticos, and provided with elaborate barriers of division. The Stadium, built by the emperor Domitian for Greek games, had seats for 30,000 spectators; the Circus of Flaminius (B.C. 221) was probably still larger. In the Campus Martius were many temples, early and late, as those of Hope (*Templum Spei*), of Neptune (eleven columns remain), and of the Egyptian Isis. The Column of Marcus Aurelius, similar to that of Trajan, is well preserved; the triumphal arches across the Via Lata have disappeared.

The famous Temple of Aesculapius, founded in B.C. 291, was on the island in the Tiber. On the right bank of the river was a Circus, built for the most part by Caligula, but named after Nero. East of this Hadrian erected his massive Mausoleum (now Castello di S. Angelo), in the form of a drum of masonry, 240 feet in diameter, resting on a square base measuring 341 feet on the sides; the whole structure was about 165 feet high, and on the top was a gilded statue of the emperor. Near by he built a Circus.

The Palatine Hill as seen from the Capitoline (1893).

BIBLIOGRAPHY. — Indispensable for more than superficial study of the subject are the publications devoted to the presentation and discussion of new discoveries and the results of investigation: *Notizie degli Scavi*, a monthly report of all excavations and "finds" in Italian territory (from 1876); *Bullettino della Commissione Archeologica comunale di Roma* (from 1873); *Monumenti antichi pubblicati per cura della R. Accademia dei Lincei* (from 1891; vol. i., e. g., contains *L'Itinerario di Einsiedeln e l'Ordine di Benedetto Canonico*, by Lanciani, and Mommsen's *Commentarium Ludorum Saecularium Quintorum*). Of especial value are the publications of the German Archaeological Institute: *Mittheilungen des Kaiserlich Deutschen Archäologischen Instituts, Römische Abtheilung* (from 1886; following the *Annali* and *Bulletino*, 1829–85); *Jahrbuch des K. D. Arch. Inst.* (from 1886), with the *Archäologische Anzeiger* (from 1886; following the *Archäologische Zeitung*, 1843–85); and the *Antike Denkmäler* (from 1886; following the *Monumenti Inediti*, 1829–1885). The contributions of the French School at Rome appear in the *Mélanges d'Archéologie et d'Histoire* (from 1881).

Middleton's *Remains of Ancient Rome* (2 vols. London, 1892; enlarged edition of *Ancient Rome in 1885*) and Burn's *Rome and the Campagna* (London, 1876; small edition, with the title *Ancient Rome and its Neighbourhood*, London, 1895) are attractive in appearance, but untrustworthy in regard to details; of greater merit, so far as they go, are *The Roman Forum* (London, 1877) and *The Marvels of Rome* (edition of the *Mirabilia Urbis Romae*, London, 1889), by F. M. Nichols; Hülsen's *Forum Romanum* (English edition, Rome, 1893) contains two admirable reconstructions; worthy of recommendation also are the panorama by Bühlmann and Wagner, *Rom mit dem Triumphzug des Kaisers Constantin im Jahre 312*, with descriptive text by F. von Reber (Munich, 1890), and the reconstruction of the Baths of Diocletian by Paulin, *Les Thermes de Dioclétien* (Paris, 1890). There is a succinct but clear description of the ruins at Rome in Baedeker's *Central Italy and Rome* (11th edition, Leipzig, 1893). An interesting account of late discoveries is given by Lanciani in *Ancient Rome in the Light of Recent Discoveries* (Boston, 1888) and *Pagan and Christian Rome* (Boston, 1893). Prof. Lanciani is publishing a detail map of Rome, scale 1.1000; the 48 sheets appear in 8 *fasciculi* (Milan; fasc. 1–3, 1893–95). An excellent brief handbook is Otto Richter's *Topographie der Stadt Rom* (Nördlingen, 1889; reprinted from Müller's *Handbuch der klass. Alterthumswissenschaft*). Jordan's *Topographie der Stadt Rom im Alterthum* (Berlin, vol. i. pt. i. 1878, pt. ii. 1885, vol. ii. 1871) is of much value; Gilbert's *Geschichte und Topographie der Stadt Rom im Alterthum* (Leipzig, 3 pts. 1883, 1885, 1890) is less satisfactory. Among later works on Roman architecture, Choisy, *L'Art de Bâtir chez les Romains* (Paris, 1873), and Durm, *Die Baukunst der Römer* (in his *Handbuch der Architektur*, vol. ii. Darmstadt, 1885), are worthy of special mention. The inscriptions of the city of Rome are collected in vol. vi. of the *Corpus Inscriptionum Latinarum*. For the other ancient sources, and for fuller reference to modern works (including collections of engravings), the bibliographies at the beginning of the works by Richter, Burn, and Middleton, cited above, may be consulted; and a review of the literature since 1887 by Hülsen will be found in the *Mittheilungen*, vols. iv., vi., vii., and viii.

Romānae Quaestiōnes. See PLUTARCHUS.

Romances. See NOVELS AND ROMANCES.

Romulea. An ancient town of the Hirpini in Samnium, on the road from Beneventum to Tarentum.

Romulĭdae. A patronymic given to the Roman people from Romulus, their first king, and the founder of the city (Verg. *Aen.* viii. 638).

Romŭlus. The name of the mythical founder of Rome. According to the popular Roman tradition, recorded in the first book of Livy, he was the son of Mars and Ilia or Rhea Silvia, daughter of Numitor, and was born at the same birth with Remus. Amulius, who had usurped the throne of Alba, in defiance of the right of his elder brother Numitor, ordered the infants to be thrown into the Tiber, and their mother to be buried alive, the doom of a vestal virgin who violated her vow of chastity. The river happened at that time to have overflowed its banks, so that the two infants were not carried into the middle of the stream, but drifted along the margin, till the basket which contained them became entangled in the roots of a wild vine at the foot of the Palatine Hill. At this time a she-wolf, coming down to the river to drink, suckled the infants, and carried them to her den among the thickets hard by. Here they were found by Faustulus, the king's herdsman, who took them home to his wife Laurentia, by whom they were carefully nursed, and named Romulus and Remus. The two youths grew up, employed in the labours, the sports, and the perils of the pastoral occupation of their foster-father. But their royal blood could not be quite concealed. Their superior mien, courage, and abilities soon acquired for them a decided superiority over their young compeers, and they became leaders of the youthful herdsmen in their contests with robbers or with rivals. Having quarrelled with the herdsmen of Numitor, whose flocks were accustomed to graze on the neighbouring hill Aventinus, Remus fell into an ambuscade, and was dragged before Numitor to be punished. While Numitor, struck with the noble bearing of the youth, and influenced by the secret stirrings of nature within, was hesitating what punishment to inflict, Romulus, accompanied by Faustulus, hastened to the rescue of Remus. On their arrival at Alba, the secret of their origin was discovered, and a plan was speedily organized for the expulsion of Amulius and the restoration of their grandfather Numitor to his throne. This was soon accomplished; but the twin-brothers felt little disposition to remain in a subordinate position at Alba, after the enjoyment of the rude liberty and power to which they had been accustomed among their native hills. They therefore requested from their grandfather permission to build a city on the banks of the Tiber, where their lives had been so miraculously preserved. Scarcely had this permission been granted, when a contest arose between the two brothers respecting the site, the name, and the

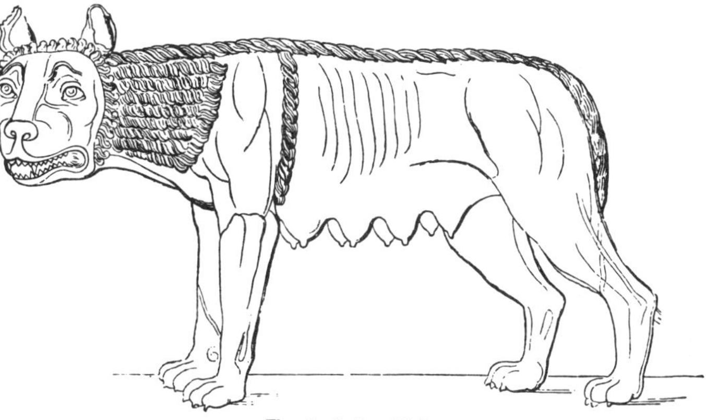

The Capitoline Wolf.

sovereignty of the city which they were about to found. Romulus wished it to be built on the Palatine Hill, and to be called by his name; Remus preferred the Aventine, and his own name. To terminate their dispute amicably, they agreed to refer it to the decision of the gods by augury. Romulus took his station on the Palatine Hill, Remus on the Aventine. At sunrise Remus saw six vultures, and immediately after Romulus saw twelve. The superiority was adjudged to Romulus, because he had seen the greater number; against which decision Remus remonstrated indignantly, on the ground that he had first received an omen. Romulus then proceeded to mark out the boundaries for the wall of the intended city. This was done by a plough with a brazen ploughshare, drawn by a bull and a heifer, and so directed that the furrow should fall inward. The plough was lifted and carried over the spaces intended to be left for gates; and in this manner a square space was marked out, including the Palatine Hill, and a small portion of the land at its base, termed Roma Quadrata. This took place on the 21st of April, on the day of the festival of Pales, the goddess of shepherds. While the wall was beginning to rise above the surface, Remus, whose mind was still rankling with his discomfiture, leaped over it, scornfully saying, "Shall such a wall as that keep your city?" Immediately Romulus, or, as others say, Celer, who had charge of erecting that part of the wall, struck him dead to the ground with the implement which he held in his hand, exclaiming, "So perish whosoever shall hereafter overleap these ramparts."

By this event Romulus was left the sole sovereign of the city; yet he felt deep remorse at his brother's fate, buried him honourably, and, when he sat to administer justice, placed an empty seat by his side, with a sceptre and crown, as if acknowledging the right of his brother to the possession of equal power. To augment as speedily as possible the number of his subjects, Romulus set apart, in his new city, a place of refuge, to which any man might flee, and be there protected from his pursuers. By this device the population increased rapidly in males, but there was a great deficiency in women; for the adjoining States, regarding the followers of Romulus as little better than a horde of brigands, refused to sanction intermarriages. But the schemes of Romulus were not to be so frustrated. In honour of the god Consus, he proclaimed games, to which he invited the neighbouring States. Great numbers came, accompanied by their families, and, at an appointed signal, the Roman youth, rushing suddenly into the midst of the spectators, snatched up the unmarried women in their arms, and carried them off by force. The outrage was immediately resented, and Romulus found himself involved in a war with all the neighbouring States. Fortunately for Rome, though those States had sustained a common injury, they did not unite their forces in the common cause. They fought singly, and were each in turn defeated; Caenina, Crustumerium, and Antemnae fell successively before the Roman arms. Romulus slew with his own hands Acron, king of Caenina, and bore off his spoils, dedicating them, as *spolia opima*, to Iupiter Feretrius. The third part of the lands of the conquered towns was seized by the victors, and such of the people of these towns as were willing to remove to Rome were received as free citizens. In the meantime, the Sabines, to avenge the insult which they had sustained, had collected together forces under Titus Tatius, king of the Quirites. The Romans were unable to meet so strong an army in the field, and withdrew within their walls. They had previously placed their flocks in what they thought a place of safety, on the Capitoline Hill, which, strong as it was by nature, they had still further secured by additional fortifications. Tarpeia, the daughter of the commander of that fortress, having fallen into the hands of the Sabines, agreed to betray the access to the hill for the ornaments they wore upon their arms. At their approach she opened the gate, and, as they entered, they crushed her to death beneath their shields. From her the cliff of the Capitoline Hill was called the Tarpeian Rock. The attempt of the Romans to regain this place of strength brought on a general engagement. The combat was long and doubtful. At one time the Romans were almost driven into the city, which the Sabines were on the point of entering along with them, when fresh courage was infused into the fugitives in consequence of Romulus vowing a temple to Iupiter Stator, and by a stream of water which rushed out of the Temple of Ianus and swept away the Sabines from the gate. The struggle was renewed during several successive days with various fortune and great mutual slaughter. At length the Sabine women who had been carried away, and who were now reconciled to their fate, rushed with loud outcries between the combatants, imploring their husbands and their fathers to spare on each side those who were now equally dear. Both parties paused; a conference began, a peace was concluded, and a treaty framed, by which the two nations were united into one, and Romulus and Tatius became the joint sovereigns of the united people. But, though united, each nation continued to be governed by its own king and Senate. During the double rule of Romulus and Tatius a war was undertaken against the Latin town of Cameria, which was reduced and made a Roman colony, and its people were admitted into the Roman State, as had been done with those whom Romulus previously subdued. Tatius was soon afterwards slain by the people of Laurentum, because he had refused to do them justice against his kinsmen, who had violated the laws of nations by insulting their ambassadors.

The death of Tatius left Romulus sole monarch of Rome. He was soon engaged in a war with Fidenae, a Tuscan settlement on the banks of the Tiber. This people he likewise overcame, and placed in the city a Roman colony. This war, extending the Roman frontier, led to a hostile collision with Veii, in which he was also successful, and deprived Veii, at that time one of the most powerful cities of Etruria, of a large portion of its territories, though he found that the city itself was too strong to be taken. The reign of Romulus now drew near its close. One day, while holding a review of his army, on a plain near Lake Capra, the sky was suddenly overcast with gloom and a tempest of thunder and lightning arose. The people fled in dismay; and when the storm abated, Romulus, over whose head it had raged most fiercely, was nowhere to be seen. A rumour was circulated that during the tempest he had been carried to heaven by his father, the god Mars. This opinion was speedily confirmed by the report of Iulius Proculus, who declared that, as he was returning by night from Alba to Rome, Romulus appeared before him in a form of more than mortal majesty, and bade him go and tell the Romans that Rome was destined by the gods to be the chief city of the earth; that human power should never be able to withstand her people; and that he himself would be their guardian god Quirinus (Plut. Romulus; Livy, i. 4). The traditional date of the translation of Romulus to heaven is B.C. 716. For a criticism of the legend and its relation to Roman history, see Lewis, *An Inquiry into the Credibility of Ancient Roman History* (1855); Ihne, *Early Rome*, Engl. trans. (N. Y. 1878); and Niebuhr's *History of Rome*, vol. i. Engl. edition (1859). In defence of the historical value of the legend, see Ampère, *Histoire Romaine à Rome* (Paris, 1871).

Romŭlus Augustŭlus. See AUGUSTULUS.

Romŭlus Silvius. See SILVIUS.

Rorarii. The name given in the old Roman legion to the citizens of the lowest property-class, who were armed only with a dart and a sling. These had to open the fighting in the capacity of skirmishers, and, when the close combat began, to withdraw behind the line. In later times their place was taken by the *velites* (q. v.). See EXERCITUS; LEGIO.

Rosciānum. Now Rossano; a fortress on the east coast of Bruttium between Thurii and Paternum.

Roscillus. A chief of the Allobroges who served Caesar in his Gallic campaigns, but sided with Pompey in the Civil War (B.C. 48).

Roscius. (1) LUCIUS, a Roman ambassador sent to Fidenae in B.C. 438. (2) SEXTIUS, of Ameria, a town in Umbria, accused of the murder of his father, and defended by Cicero (B.C. 80) in an oration which is still extant. (3) QUINTUS, the most celebrated comic actor at Rome, was a native of Solonium, a small place in the neighbourhood of Lanuvium. His histrionic powers procured him the favour of many of the Roman nobles, and, among others, of the dictator Sulla, who presented him with a gold ring, the symbol of equestrian rank. Roscius enjoyed the friendship of Cicero, who constantly speaks of him in terms both of admiration and affection. Roscius was considered by the Romans to have reached such perfection in his profession that it became the fashion to call every one who became particularly distinguished in the histrionic art by the name of Roscius. He realized an immense fortune by his profession, and died in B.C. 62. See HISTRIO. (4) OTHO. See OTHO.

Rosetta Stone. See HIEROGLYPHICS.

Rostra (properly "the ships' prows," from *rostrum*, the iron-bound prow [literally, "beak"] of a ship). The orators' platform in the Forum at Rome, so called because it was embellished with the bronze prows of the ships of the Latin fleet captured at Antium in B.C. 338 (Livy, viii. 14). Besides these it was also decorated with other monuments of the greatness of Rome, such as the Laws of the Twelve Tables, the Columna Rostrata (q. v.) of Duilius, and numerous statues of men of mark. Originally it stood between the part of the Forum called the Comitium and the Forum proper, opposite the Curia; but in B.C. 44 Caesar moved it to the north end of the Forum under the Capitol (Cic. *Phil.* ix. 2), and here built up part of it by the employment of the old materials. It was not completed until after his death, by Antonius. This new platform, which was afterwards repeatedly restored, appears by the existing remains to have consisted of an erection eleven feet higher than the pavement of the Forum, about seventy-eight feet in length, and thirty-three feet in depth. The front was decorated with two rows of ships' prows. The way up to the platform was at the back. This platform also was used down to the latest times of the Empire as a place for setting up honorary statues. The Rostra Iulia, so called to distinguish it from the other rostra, was the projecting *podium* of the Heroüm of Iulius Caesar, built by Augustus. Affixed to this were the prows of the vessels captured at Actium (Dio Cass. li. 19; Middleton, *Ancient Rome*, p. 179). See FORUM.

Rostrāta Columna. See COLUMNA ROSTRATA.

Rostrāta Corōna. See CORONA.

Rostrum. The beak of a ship. See NAVIS, p. 1078.

Rota. A wheel. See ANTLIA; CURRUS; MOLA; TYMPANUM.

Rotomăgus. See RATOMAGUS.

Roxāna (Ῥωξάνη). Daughter of Oxyartes the Bactrian. She fell into the hands of Alexander the Great on his capture of the hill-fort in Sogdiana named "the Rock," B.C. 327. Alexander was so captivated by her charms that he married her. Soon after Alexander's death (233) she gave birth to a son (Alexander Aegus), who was admitted to share the nominal sovereignty with Arrhidaeus, under the regency of Perdiccas. Roxana afterwards crossed over to Europe with her son, placed herself under the protection of Olympias, and threw herself into Pydna along with the latter. In 316 Pydna was taken by Cassander; Olympias was put to death; and Roxana and her son were placed in confinement in Amphipolis, where they were murdered by Cassander's orders in 311 (Plut. *Alex.*; Arrian, *Anab.* vii. 27; Diod. bks. xviii. and xix.).

Roxolāni. See RHOXOLANI.

Rubi. Now Ruvo; a town in Apulia, on the road from Canusium to Brundusium. Many vases have been found in the tombs on its site.

Rubĭco and **Rubĭcon**. A small river in Italy, falling into the Adriatic a little north of Ariminum, forming the boundary in the republican period between the province of Gallia Cisalpina and Italia proper. It is celebrated in history on account of Caesar's passage across it at the head of his army, by which act he declared war against the Senate. See Suet. *Iul.* 31; and the article CAESAR.

Rubra Saxa, called RUBRAE BREVES (sc. *petrae*) by Martial. A small place in Etruria, only a few miles from Rome, near the river Cremera, and on the Via Flaminia. Near this place Constantine won his great victory over Maxentius in A.D. 312.

Rubrēsus Lacus. A lake near Narbo in Gaul.

Rubrīca. Red ochre. The word is used of a law, because the titles of these were engrossed in red (Pers. v. 90).

Rubrum Maré. See ERYTHRAEUM MARÉ.

Ruby. See GEMMA.

Rudder. See GUBERNACULUM.

Rudens. "The Cable." A play of Plautus. See PLAUTUS.

Rudiae. Now Rotigliano or Rugge; a town of the Peucetii in Apulia, on the road from Brundusium to Venusia, was originally a Greek colony, and afterwards a Roman municipium. Rudiae is celebrated as the birthplace of Ennius (Sil. Ital. xii. 393).

Rudiarius. See GLADIATORES.

Rudicŭla (κύκηθρον). Diminutive of *rudis* (q. v.). A wooden spoon (Columell. xii. 46, 3) for beating up, stirring, or mixing together different ingredients while boiling, stewing, or making decoctions

Rudicula. (Pompeian painting.)

(Cato, *R. R.* 95, 1). The example, from a picture of still life at Pompeii, exhibits a plate of eggs, together with the vessel and spoon for beating them up.

Rudis. The wooden foil of the gladiators. On the discharge of a gladiator from further service, he was presented with a rudis marked with the letters SP (i. e. *spectatus*). Cf. Hor. *Epist.* i. 1, 2, with the commentators. See GLADIATORES.

Rufīnus. (1) P. CORNELIUS RUFĪNUS. A Roman who was consul in B.C. 290 with M' Curius Dentatus, and in conjunction with his colleague brought the Samnite War to a conclusion, and obtained a triumph in consequence. He was consul a second time in 277, and carried on the war against the Samnites and the Greeks in Southern Italy. The chief event of his second consulship was the capture of the important town of Croton. In 275 Rufinus was expelled from the Senate by the censors C. Fabricius and Q. Aemilius Papus, on account of his possessing ten pounds of silver plate. The dictator Sulla was descended from this Rufinus. His grandson was the first of the family who assumed the surname of Sulla. (2) LICINIUS RUFĪNUS. A jurist who lived under Alexander Severus. There are in the Digest seventeen excerpts from twelve books of *Regulae* by Rufinus. (3) The chief minister of state under Theodosius the Great, and an able but at the same time a treacherous and dangerous man. He instigated Theodosius to those cruel measures which brought ruin upon Antioch, A.D. 390. After the death of Theodosius in 395, Rufinus exercised paramount influence over the weak Arcadius; but towards the end of the year a conspiracy was formed against him by Eutropius and Stilicho, who induced Gainas, the Gothic ally of Arcadius, to join in the plot. Rufinus was in consequence slain by the troops of Gainas. (4) Surnamed TYRANNIUS or TURRANIUS, or TORĀNUS. A celebrated ecclesiastical writer, born probably about A.D. 345 in Italy. He was at first an inmate of the monastery at Aquileia, and he afterwards resided many years at a monastery in Palestine, where he became very intimate with St. Jerome. The two friends afterwards quarrelled, and Jerome attacked Rufinus with the utmost vehemence on account of his supporting the tenets of Origen. After remaining in the East for about twenty-six years, Rufinus returned to Italy in 397, where he published a Latin translation of the Apology for Origen by Pamphilus, and of the books of Origen, *De Principiis*, together with an original tract, *De Adulteratione Librorum Origenis.* In the preface to the *De Principiis* he quoted a panegyric which Jerome had at an earlier period pronounced upon Origen. This led to a bitter correspondence between the two former friends, which was crowned by the *Apologia* of the one *adversus Hieronymum*, and the *Apologia* of the other *adversus Rufinum.* Rufinus died in Sicily in 410, to which island he had fled upon the invasion of Italy by Alaric. Several of his works are extant, the chief edition being that of Vallarsi (Verona, 1745). (5) The author of a little poem in twenty-two lines, *Pasiphaës Fabula ex Omnibus Metris Horatianis*, which, as the name imports, contains an example of each of the different metres employed by Horace. His date is quite uncertain, but he may be the same person with the following. Edited by Bährens in the *Poet. Lat. Min.* vol. v. (6) A grammarian of Antioch, whose treatise *De Metris Comicis*, or rather extracts from it, is contained in the *Grammatici Latini* of Keil, vi. 569. (7) The author of thirty-eight epigrams in the Greek Anthology. His date is uncertain, but there can be no doubt that he was a Byzantine. His verses are of the same light amatory character as those of Agathias, Paulus, Macedonius, and others.

Rufius or **Rufus Festus Aviēnus.** See AVIENUS.

Rufus, L. CAECILIUS. The brother of P. Sulla by the same mother, but not by the same father. He was tribune of the plebs B.C. 63, when he rendered warm support to Cicero, and in particular opposed the agrarian law of Rullus. In his praetorship, B.C. 57, he joined most of the other magistrates in proposing the recall of Cicero from banishment.

Rufus, M. CAELIUS. A young Roman noble distinguished as an elegant writer and eloquent speaker, but equally conspicuous for his profligacy and extravagance. Notwithstanding his vices he lived on intimate terms with Cicero, who defended him in B.C. 56 in an oration still extant. The accusation was brought against him by Sempronius Atratinus, at the instigation of Clodia Quadrantaria, whom he had lately deserted. Clodia charged him with having borrowed money from her in order to murder Dion, the head of the embassy sent by Ptolemy Auletes to Rome, and with having made an attempt to poison her. In 52 Caelius was tribune of the plebs and in 50 aedile. During the years 51 and 50 he carried on an active correspondence with Cicero, who was then in Cilicia, and many of the letters which he wrote to Cicero at that time are preserved in the collection of Cicero's Letters. On the breaking out of the Civil War in 49 he espoused Caesar's side, and was rewarded for his services by the praetorship in 48. Being at this time overwhelmed with debt, he availed himself of Caesar's absence from Italy to bring forward a law for the abolition of debts. He was, however, resisted by the other magistrates and deprived of his office; whereupon he went into the south of Italy to join Milo (q. v.), whom he had secretly sent for from Massilia. Milo was killed near Thurii before Caelius could join him, and Caelius himself was put to death shortly afterwards at Thurii.

Rufus Ephesius. So called from Ephesus, the place of his birth. A celebrated Greek physician, who lived in the reign of Trajan (A.D. 98–117), and wrote several medical works, some of which are still extant.

Rufus, M. MINUCIUS. The colleague of Q. Fabius (B.C. 217) in the Second Punic War. See FABIUS.

Rufus, Q. CURTIUS. See CURTIUS.

Rufus, SEXTUS. See SEXTUS RUFUS.

Rufus, VALGIUS. See VALGIUS.

Ruga (ῥυτίς). Literally, a wrinkle; whence, the worm of a screw (Pliny, *H. N.* xviii. 74; and COCHLEA), and a small, irregular crease or fold in a piece of drapery, contradistinguished from *sinus*, a deep and loose one, and from *contabulatio*, a straight and regular one (Pliny, *H. N.* xxxv. 34; Macrob. *Sat.* ii. 9).

Rugii. An important people in Germany, who originally dwelt on the coast of the Baltic between the Viadus (Oder) and the Vistula. After disappearing a long time from history, they are found at a later time in Attila's army; and after Attila's death they founded a new kingdom on the northern bank of the Danube, in Austria and Hungary, the name of which is still preserved in the modern Rugiland. They have left traces of their name in the country which they originally inhabited, in the modern Rügen, Rügenwalde, Rega, Regenwalde (Tac. *Germ.* 43; Prop. *B. G.* ii. 14).

Rullus, P. SERVILIUS. Tribune of the plebs B.C. 63. He proposed an agrarian law, which Cicero attacked in three orations, which have come down to us. The law was in reality aimed against the power of the Senate and was instigated by Caesar, but it was presently withdrawn by Rullus himself.

Rumīna and **Rumīnus** (from *rumis* or *ruma*, "a teat"). Ancient Italian pastoral deities, who protected the suckling cattle and received offerings of milk (Varro, *R. R.* ii. 2, 5; ii. 11, 15). In Rome their sanctuary stood at the foot of the Palatine Hill, in the neighbourhood of the Lupercal; in the same place was the Ruminal fig-tree (probably a primitive emblem of the nurturing goddess; the *Rumina ficus* of Ovid, *Fasti*, ii. 412), under which Romulus and Remus were said to have been suckled by the wolf. (See ROMULUS.) The name Ruminus was also applied to Iupiter as the nourisher of all things (St. August. *De Civ. Dei*, vii. 11).

Runcīna (ῥυκάνη). A carpenter's plane, for smoothing and levelling surfaces in wood (Pliny, *H. N.* xvi. § 82), of which an example is afforded by a sepulchral marble at Rastadt, which is furnished with a handle, and shows the holes through which the shavings (*ramenta*) turned up.

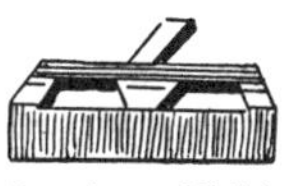

Runcina. (Rich.)

Rupilius, PUBLIUS. A Roman, consul in B.C. 132, who prosecuted with the utmost vehemence all the adherents of Tib. Gracchus, who had been slain in the preceding year. As proconsul in Sicily in the following year he made various regulations for the government of the province, which were known by the name of Leges Rupiliae. Rupilius was condemned in the tribunate of C. Gracchus, B.C. 123, on account of his illegal and cruel acts in the prosecution of the friends of Tib. Gracchus.

Ruscĭno. A town of the Sordones or Sordi, in the southeastern part of Gallia Narbonensis, at the foot of the Pyrenees. It is now Rousillon.

Rusellae. Now Grosseto; one of the most ancient cities of Etruria, situated on an eminence east of Lake Prelius and on the Via Aurelia. The walls of Rusellae still remain, and are some of the most ancient in Italy, being fine specimens of the so-called Cyclopean architecture. See CYCLOPS; MURUS.

Russātus. Literally "clothed in red"; a word especially applied to a charioteer (*auriga*) in the chariot races of the Circus who belonged to the Reds (*factio russata*). See Pliny, *H. N.* vii. § 54, and the article CIRCUS.

Rustĭcus, L. IUNIUS ARULĒNUS. A friend and pupil of Paetus Thrasea, and an ardent admirer of the Stoic philosophy. He was put to death by Domitian because he had written a panegyric upon Thrasea (Tac. *Ann.* xvi. 25; *Hist.* iii. 90). See THRASEA.

Rutabŭlum. (1) A fire-shovel, employed by bakers and smiths for throwing up the embers and ignitable matter in their ovens and forges (Festus, s. v.; Isidor. *Orig.* xx. 8, 6); whence it is commonly mentioned in conjunction with the tongs (*forceps*) (Suet. *Aug.* 75). The word is another form of *rutrum* (q. v.). (2) A wooden shovel, used for stirring together and amalgamating the new-made wine (*mustum*) with that which was boiled down (*defrutum*) and other ingredients infused into it.

Rutēni. A people in Gallia Aquitanica, on the frontiers of Gallia Narbonensis, in the modern Rovergne. Their chief town was Segodunum, later Civitas Rutenorum, now Rodez.

Rutilius Lupus. See LUPUS.

Rutilius Namatiānus, CLAUDIUS. A Latin poet of Gallic birth who in the fifth century of our era wrote an elegiac poem in several books, of which the first (644 lines) and a fragment of the second are extant. It describes his return from Rome to Gaul (*De Reditu*, also called *Itinerarium*). Rutilius was a pagan and attacked both the Jews and the Christian priests. Edited by L. Müller (Leipzig, 1870).

Rutilius Rufus, PUBLIUS. A Roman statesman and orator. He was military tribune under Scipio in the Numantine War, praetor B.C. 111, consul in 105, and legatus in 95 under Q. Mucius Scaevola, proconsul of Asia. While acting in this capacity he displayed so much honesty and firmness in repressing the extortions of the publicani that he became an object of fear and hatred to the whole body. Accordingly, on his return to Rome, he was impeached of malversation (*de repetundis*), found guilty, and compelled to withdraw into banishment, B.C. 92. He is said to have written a history of Rome in Greek (Livy, xxxix. 52; Gell. vi. 14).

Rutrum and dim. **Rutellum.** A sort of hoe which differed from the *rastrum* in having the handle fixed perpendicularly into the middle of the blade. It was used in breaking clods (Verg. *Georg.* i. 105).

Rutŭba. Now Roya; a river on the coast of Liguria, which flows into the sea near Album Intemelium.

Rutŭli. An ancient people in Italy, inhabiting

a narrow strip of country on the coast of Latium, a little to the south of the Tiber. Their chief town was Ardea, which was the residence of Turnus (q. v.). They were subdued at an early period by the Romans, and disappear from history (Livy, i. 56). See TURNUS.

Rutŭpae or **Rutupiae**. Now Richborough; a port of the Cantii, in the southeast of Britain, where there are still several Roman remains. The place was famous for the excellent oysters exported thence to Rome (Juv. iv. 141).

Rye Bread. See PISTOR.

S

S, as a symbol.

GREEK.—Σ = Σέξτος, Σέραπις, σεβαστῷ. As a numeral = 18 (old system). σ′ = 200, ͵σ = 200,000.

ROMAN.—S = Saeculum, salve, Saturnus, scriba, scripsit, secundae, Semis, sententia, sepultura, Servius, servus, sestertium, Severus, Sextus, si, Sicilia, Silvanus, singuli, situs, solvit, Spurius, stipendia, studiosus, suppurationes.

S·S = sancto sacrum, semper scriptus, senatus sententia, siti sunt, subscriptus, sumptu suo, susceptum solvit.

S·S·S = sicut (summa) supra scripti, supra scripti sunt.

S·A = Severiana Alexandrina (legio), Silvanus Augustus, somnus aeternalis.

S·C = sacra cognoscens, singularis consularis, scribendum curaverunt, sub cura.

S·D = sancta dea, Silvanus (Sol) deus, sinistra decumanum.

S·F = sacris faciundis.

S·H = semihora, summa honoraria.

S·I = stlitibus iudicandis.

S·M = sanctae memoriae, secundum municipium, Sol Mithras, solvit merito, submedicus.

S·N = sestertii nummi.

S·P = servus publicus, sub praefectus.

S·V = se vivo, spectavit victor.

S·C·C = senatus consulto curavit.

S·D·M = sacrum diis manibus, sine dolo malo.

S·F·S = sine fraude sua.

S·L·P = sibi liberis posterisque.

S·M·D = sacrum matri Deum.

SS·DD·NN = salvis dominis nostris (duobus).

S·V·Q = sine ulla querella.

S·C·F·C = senatus consulto faciendum curavit.

S·C·D·D = socii cultores domus divinae.

S·C·D·T = senatus consulto de thesauro.

S·L·L·M = solvit laetus libens merito.

S·P·Q·R = senatus populusque Romanus.

S·P·S·P = sibi posterisque suis posuit.

S·T(V)·T·L = sit tibi (vobis) terra levis.

S·D·L·S·D = sacerdos dei Liberi, sacerdos deae.

S·P·D·D·D = sua pecunia dono dedit dedicavit.

S·P·P·L·D·D·D = sua pecunia posuit loco dato decreto decurionum.

S·L·R·I·C·Q·O·O·R·E = siremps lex res ius causaque omnibus omnium rerum esto.

S·Q·H·A·P·E·S·S·A·V·D·F = si quis hanc arcam post excessum suprascriptorum aperire voluerit, dabit fisco.

Saba (O. T. Sheba). (1) The capital of the Sabaei (q. v.), in Arabia Felix, lay on a high woody mountain, and was pointed out by an Arabian tradition as the residence of the "Queen of Sheba," who visited King Solomon. (2) There was another city of the same name in the interior of Arabia Felix, where a place Sabea is still found, nearly in the centre of El-Yemen. (3) A seaport town of Aethiopia, on the Red Sea, south of Ptolemaïs Theron.

Sabăcon (Σαβακῶν, Shabaka). A king of Aethiopia, who invaded Egypt in the reign of the blind king Anysis, whom he dethroned and drove into the marshes. The Aethiopian conqueror then reigned over Egypt for fifty years, but at length quitted the country in consequence of a dream, whereupon Anysis regained his kingdom. This is the account which Herodotus received from the priests (ii. 137–140); but it appears from Manetho that there were three Aethiopian kings who reigned over Egypt, named Sabacon, Sebichus, and Taracus, whose collective reigns amount to forty or fifty years (B.C. 700–666), and who form the twenty-fifth dynasty of that writer. The account of Manetho is to be preferred to that of Herodotus.

Sabaei (Σαβαῖοι) or **Sabae** (Σάβαι) (O. T. Shebaiïm). One of the chief peoples of Arabia, dwelt in the southwest corner of the peninsula, in the most beautiful part of Arabia Felix, the north and centre of the province of El-Yemen. So at least Ptolemy places them (vi. 7, 23); but the fact seems to be that they are the chief representatives of a race which, at an early period, was widely spread on both sides of the southern part of the Red Sea, where Arabia and Aethiopia all but joined at the narrow strait of Bab-el-Mandeb; and hence, probably, the confusion often made between the Sheba and Seba of Scripture, or between the Shebaiim of Arabia and the Sebaiim of Aethiopia. Their country produced all the most precious spices and perfumes of Arabia. Their capital was Saba (Dio Cass. liii. 29).

Sabaria or **Savaria**. The modern Stein on the Auger. A town in Pannonia, where Severus was proclaimed emperor (Aurel. Vict. *Ep.* 19).

Sabătē. Now Trevignano; a town of Etruria on the lake called LACUS SABATĪNUS, now Lago di Bracciano.

Sabatīni. A people in Campania, who derived their name from the river Sabatus (Sabbato), a tributary of the Calor, which flows into the Vulturnus (Livy, xxvi. 33).

Sabazius (Σαβάζιος). A Thracian and Phrygian deity, whom the Greeks usually identified with Dionysus (Diod. iv. 4), and sometimes also with Zeus. His orgiastic worship was very closely connected with that of the Phrygian mother of the gods, Rhea-Cybelé, and of Attis. Along with this it was introduced into Athens in the fifth century B.C. (Aristoph. *Vespae*, 9; *Lysistr.* 388; Demos. *De Cor.* § 260). In later times it was widely spread in Rome and Italy, especially in the latter days of paganism. Like many of the Oriental deities, he represented the flourishing life of nature, which sinks in death, always to rise again. As an emblem of the yearly renovation of nature, the symbol specially appropriated to him was the snake. Accordingly, at the celebration of his mysteries, a golden snake was passed under the clothes and drawn over the bosom of the initiated (Clemens Alexandr. *Protrept.* p. 6). In the *Characteres* of Theophrastus, when the superstitious man "sees a serpent in his house, if it be the red snake, he will invoke Sabazius" (ch. 28, ed. Jebb).

Sabbath. See IUDAEI.

Sabelli. See SABINI.

Sabīna. The grand-niece of the Roman emperor Trajan. By the influence of Plotina, Trajan's wife, Sabina was married to Hadrian (A.D. 100), but the marriage proved to be an unhappy one, and she took her own life (about A.D. 138). It was reported that her husband had poisoned her, but this is unworthy of belief (Spart. *Hadr.* 1, 2, 11, 23; Oros. vii. 13).

Sabīna, POPPAEA. A woman of surpassing beauty, but licentious morals. She was the daughter of T. Ollius, but assumed the name of her maternal grandfather, Poppaeus Sabinus, who had been consul A.D. 9. She was first married to Rufius Crispinus, and afterwards to Otho, who was one of the boon companions of Nero. The latter soon became enamoured of her; and in order to get Otho out of the way, Nero sent him to govern the province of Lusitania (58). Poppaea now became the acknowledged mistress of Nero, over whom she exercised absolute sway. Anxious to become the wife of the emperor, she persuaded Nero first to murder his mother Agrippina (59), who was opposed to such a disgraceful union, and next to divorce and shortly afterwards put to death his innocent and virtuous wife Octavia (62). She then became the wife of Nero. In 65 Poppaea, being pregnant, was killed by a kick from her brutal husband (Suet. *Nero*, 35).

Poppaea Sabina.

Sabīni. See ITALIA; OSCI; ROMA; SAMNIUM.

Sabiniāni. See SABINUS.

Sabīnus, MASURIUS. One of the most celebrated Roman jurists, a pupil of Ateius Capito in the time of Tiberius, and founder of the school of jurists called after him, that of the *Sabiniani*. See ATEIUS CAPITO; IURISPRUDENTIA.

Sabis. (1) Now the Sambre. A broad and deep river in Gallia Belgica and in the territory of the Ambiani, falling into the river Mosa. (2) A small river on the coast of Carmania. (3) See SAPIS.

Sabrăta. Another name for Abrotonum (q. v.).

Sabre. See ACINACES.

Sabrīna, also called **Sabriāna**. Now the Severn. A river in the west of Britain, which flowed by Venta Silurum into the ocean (Tac. *Ann.* xii. 31).

Sacădas (Σακάδας). An eminent musician of Argos. He established at Sparta the second great school of Greek music, of which Thaletas was the real founder. See MUSICA.

Sacae (Σάκαι). One of the most numerous and most powerful of the Scythian nomadic tribes, who had their abodes east and northeast of the Massagetae, as far as Serica, in the steppes of Central Asia, which are now peopled by the Kirghiz Khasaks, in whose name that of their ancestors is traced by some geographers. They were very warlike, and excelled especially as cavalry and as archers both on horse and foot. The name of the Sacae is often used loosely for other Scythian tribes, and sometimes for the Scythians in general (Herod. iv. 6; v. 113). See SCYTHIA.

Saccus (σάκκος). Any kind of sack or bag. (1) A purse for holding money, especially a beggar's wallet. (2) A net for the hair. (See COMA.) (3) A sieve for straining wine (*saccus vinarius*); also called simply *linum* (Mart. xiv. 103) or *lintea* (id. xiv. 104).

Sacellum. The Latin name for a small sanctuary, which was a mere altar, or an enclosed uncovered place with an altar, or a little temple with either an altar or an image for purposes of worship. In Rome the greater part of these sanctuaries were among the oldest and holiest places of worship.

Sacellum at Pompeii.

Sacerdos (ἱερεύς). A priest; a person whose duty it was to perform certain rites associated with the relations existing between the State, or some organized body within the State, and the gods.

In GREECE, the word ἱερεύς (fem. ἱέρεια) is found as early as Homer, and denotes a person charged with definite and permanent religious duties—prayer, sacrifice, purification, or prophecy, or all of these combined. He was regularly associated with some special place of worship, as a temple or shrine, and was the minister of the god to whom the temple or shrine was dedicated (Pollux, i. 14). Priests, however, were not the only persons who exercised these functions, for we find them also performed by kings and magistrates, and also by heads of families and clans; so that it is evident that the priestly office had no exclusive right to the exercise of liturgical observances. They were, however, even in Homer's time, held in honour (*Il.*

v. 78), and even regarded as possessed of a species of divinity. Besides the name ἱερεύς, Homer also uses the terms ἀρητήρ and θυόσκοος.

In historic times, the priest was required to be a citizen of the State, so that in Athens no μέτοικος could act as such; and if the worship were one peculiar to a family or clan, he must be a full member of it. Priestesses enjoyed some of the rights granted to male citizens—e. g. the right of pleading before the council, and of signing documents. They were usually women of rank and family. For both priests and priestesses, bodily purity was a requisite, and this not only a moral but a physical purity. The priest must not touch a dead body, and a death in the family of the priest sometimes served to forfeit the office, and always acted as a temporary disqualification. Some priesthoods could only be filled by virgins (Pausan. ii. 33, 3), while the priests of the Ephesian Artemis were eunuchs, and boy priests are also mentioned (*C. I. G.* 6206). There was, however, no general regulation as to age, nor was marriage prohibited by any general law. Priests were appointed sometimes by hereditary descent, as in the case of the Eumolpidae at Athens (*C. I. A.* ii. 410), sometimes by election (*C. I. G.* 2270, 18), and sometimes by purchase (*C. I. G.* 2656).

The duties of a priest were partly administrative and partly liturgical. The first class of duties comprised the care of the temple, the regulation of the worshippers, and the management of the revenues. In keeping order he was assisted by officers like the modern vergers (ῥαβδοφόροι, κλειδοῦχοι, ζάκοροι, νεωκόροι). (For the chief liturgic duties, see SACRIFICIUM.) The privileges of a priest were special precedence, the use of a house, and a share of the perquisites arising from the sacrifices—e. g. specific portions of the victims (*C. I. A.* 610, 631), and fees, and also presents given by the worshippers (Aristoph. *Plut.* 676). The dress of a priest was not, in general, especially distinctive, except for the wreath worn on the head while sacrificing. The hair was also, in some cases, worn long. In some special rites, however, an ornamental dress was worn, as at the Eleusinia and in the cult of the dead (Aesh. *Eumen.* 982). See ELEUSINIA. On the frieze of the Parthenon, the priests appear in a long *chiton*.

For various classes of Greek priests, see the articles ELEUSINIA; EUMOLPIDAE; HIEROPOEI; SACRIFICIUM; and compare the articles MYSTERIA; ORACULA; RELIGIO.

At ROME, in comparison with the civil magistrates, all priests were regarded as *homines privati;* though all of them, as priests, were sacerdotes publici, in so far as their office (*sacerdotium*) was connected with any worship recognized by the State. The appellation of *sacerdos publicus* was, however, given principally to the chief pontiff and the Flamen Dialis, who were at the same time the only priests who were members of the Senate by virtue of their office. All priestly offices or *sacerdotia* were held for life, without responsibility to any civil magistrate. A priest was generally allowed to hold any other civil or military office besides his priestly dignity. Some priests, however, formed an exception, for the Duumviri, the Rex Sacrorum, and the Flamen Dialis were not allowed to hold any State office, and were also exempt from service in the armies. Their priestly character was, generally speaking, inseparable from their person as long as they lived; hence the augurs and Fratres Arvales retained their priestly character even when sent into exile, or when they were taken prisoners. It also occurs that one and the same person held two or three priestly offices at the same time. Thus we find the three dignities of Pontifex Maximus, augur, and Decemvir Sacrorum united in one individual. Bodily defects incapacitated a person at Rome, as among all ancient nations, from holding any priestly office. All priests were originally patricians, but from the year B.C. 367 the plebeians also began to take part in the sacerdotia (see PLEBES); and those priestly offices which down to the latest times remained in the hands of the patricians alone, such as that of the Rex Sacrorum, the Flamines, Salii, and others, had no influence upon the affairs of the State.

As regards the appointment of priests, the ancient writers unanimously state that at first they were appointed by the kings, but after the sacerdotia were once instituted, each college of priests —for nearly all priests constituted certain corporations called *collegia*—had the right of filling up, by *coöptatio*, the vacancies which occurred. (See PONTIFEX.) Other priests, on the contrary, such as the Vestal Virgins and the Flamines, were appointed (*capiebantur*) by the Pontifex Maximus, a rule which appears to have been observed down to the latest times; others again, such as the Duumviri Sacrorum, were elected by the people, or by the *curiae*, as, for example, the *curiones*. But in whatever manner they were appointed, all priests after their appointment required to be inaugurated by the pontiffs and the augurs, or by the latter alone. Those priests who formed colleges had originally, as we have already observed, the right of *coöptatio;* but in the course of time they were deprived of this right, or at least the coöptatio was reduced to a mere form, by several laws, called *leges de sacerdotiis*, such as the Lex Domitia, Lex Cornelia, and Lex Iulia; their nature is described in the article PONTIFEX, and what is there said in regard to the appointment of pontiffs applies equally to all the other colleges. All priests had some external distinction, as the *apex*, *tutulus*, or *galerus*, the *toga praetexta*, as well as honorary seats in the theatre, circus, and amphitheatre. Most of the priestly colleges possessed landed property, and some priests had also a regular annual salary (*stipendium*), which was paid to them from the public treasury. This is expressly stated in regard to the Vestal Virgins, the augurs, and the *curiones*, and may therefore be supposed to have been the case with other priests also. The Pontifex Maximus, the Rex Sacrorum, and the Vestal Virgins had moreover a *domus publica* as their place of residence.

See Martha, *Les Sacerdoces Athéniens;* Boissier, *La Religion Romaine;* and the articles AUGUR; AUGUSTALES; EPULONES; EXTISPEX; FLAMEN; HARUSPEX; PONTIFEX; SACRIFICIUM; SALII; SIBYLLINI LIBRI; TEMPLUM; VESTALES.

Sacerdos, MARIUS PLOTIUS. A Latin grammarian, perhaps of the end of the third century A.D., who wrote in Rome an *ars grammatica* in three books. The third treats of metre. See Keil, *Grammatici Latini*, vi. 417.

Sacer Mons. (1) An isolated hill in the country of the Sabines, on the right bank of the Anio and west of the Via Nomentana, three miles from

Rome, to which the plebeians repaired in their celebrated secessions (Livy, ii. 32; Dionys. vi. 45). (2) A mountain in Hispania Tarraconensis near the Minius.

Sacra. The Latin term for all transactions relating to the worship of the gods, especially sacrifice and prayer. They are either *sacra privata* or *publica*. The former were undertaken on behalf of the individual by himself, on behalf of the famly by the *pater familias*, or on behalf of the gens by the whole body of the gentiles. The centre of the domestic service of the gods is formed by the worship of the Penates and Lares. In particular cases recourse was also had to certain specified deities. Besides this, private sacra were attached to particular families; these passed to the heir with the succession and became a burden on him. Hence an inheritance without sacra (*hereditas sine sacris*) proverbially signified an unimpaired piece of good fortune (Plaut. *Capt.* 775; *Trin.* 483). As the family had sacra, so also had the gens (q. v.), which had arisen out of the family by expansion. These were performed by a sacrificial priest (*flamen*) appointed from among the gentiles, the celebration taking place in his own house or in a special sacellum in the presence of the assembled gentiles. The *sacra publica* were undertaken *pro populo* collectively (1) by the *curiae*, *pagi*, or *vici*, into which the community was divided, whence such sacrifices were called *sacra popularia;* or (2) by the individual gentes and societies (see SODALITAS), to which the superintendence of a particular cult had been committed by the State; or (3) by the magistrates and priests of the Roman State. The sacra of the gentes were with few exceptions performed in public, though the multitude present remained silent spectators; only in a few cases did they take part in the procession to the place of worship or in the sacrificial feast. See RELIGIO.

Sacramentum. The Roman term for the military oath of allegiance, originally the preliminary engagement entered upon with the general by newly enlisted troops (Cic. *De Off.* i. 11, § 36; Livy, xxii. 38, § 2). The oath was taken first by the legates and tribunes. These officers then administered it to the soldiers in the following manner: one soldier in each legion recited the formula of the oath, and the rest were called up by name, and, coming forward one by one, swore to the same oath with the words *idem in me*—i. e. "the same (holds good) for me." The oath remained in force only till the next campaign, and whenever there was a new general a new oath was taken. After the introduction of the twenty years' service by Marius (about B.C. 100), the men raised for service took the oath, not one by one, but all together and for the whole time of service, in the name of the State, afterwards in that of the emperor.

Sacramentum in the oldest and most general form of civil lawsuit, named after it *legis actio per sacramentum*, is a deposit made beforehand by the parties in the suit. It was originally five sheep or five oxen, according to the value of the object in dispute, afterwards a sum of money at the rate of ten *asses* for each sheep and one hundred for each ox. The deposit was given back to the successful party, while that of the loser was originally applied-to religious purposes; afterwards it went to the *aerarium*, or public treasury. See IUS IURANDUM.

Sacrarium. A place in which sacred things were kept (Suet. *Tib.* 51). In temples it probably

Sacrarium. (Pompeii.)

stood directly behind the wall of the *cella*. See Marquardt, *Staatsverwaltung*, iii. 168.

Sacra Via. The principal street in Rome. It ran from the valley between the Caelian and Esquiline Hills, through the arch of Titus, and past the Forum Romanum, to the Capitol. See ROMA; VIAE.

Sacred Chickens. See AUGUR.

Sacred Wars. A name given to three great struggles in the history of Greece in which the Amphictyonic Council was concerned. (1) The war waged at the behest of the Amphictyons against the Phocian city of Cirrha (B.C. 595–585), the accusation being that the Cirrhaeans had levied excessive tolls on pilgrims and had maltreated women on their return from the temple at Delphi. As the result of the war, the city was razed to the ground (Aesch. *c. Ctes.* p. 68; Strabo, ix. p. 418; Athen. xiii. p. 560). (2) and (3) See PHILIPPUS.

Sacrificium (*θυσία*). Sacrifices among the ancients formed the chief part of every religious act. According to the kind of sacrifice offered, they were divided into (1) bloodless offerings and (2) blood-offerings. The former consisted in first-fruits, viands, and cakes of various shape and make, which were some of them burned and some of them laid on the altars and sacrificial tables, and removed after a time; libations of wine, milk, water with honey or milk, and frankincense, for which in early times native products (wood and the berries of cedars, junipers, bay-trees, etc.) were used. Asiatic spices, such as incense and myrrh, scarcely came into use before the seventh century in Greece or until towards the end of the Republic at Rome.

For blood-offerings cattle, goats, sheep, and swine were used by preference. Other animals were only employed in special cults. Thus horses were offered in certain Greek regions to Poseidon and Helios, and at Rome on the occasion of the October feast to Mars; dogs to Hecaté and Robigus, asses to Priapus, cocks to Asclepius, and geese to Isis. Sheep and cattle, apparently, could be offered to any gods among the Greeks. As regards swine and goats, the regulations varied according to the different regions. Swine were sacrificed especially to Demeter and Dionysus, goats to the last-named divinity and to Apollo and Artemis as well as to Aphrodité, while they were excluded from the service of Athené, and it was only at Sparta that they were presented to Heré. At Epidaurus they might not be sacrificed to Asclepius, though elsewhere this was done without scruple. Part of the spoils of the chase—such as the antlers or fell of the stag, or the head and feet of the boar or the bear—was offered to Artemis Agrotera.

Sacrificial Attendant. (Roman relief.)

As regards the sex and colour of the victims, the Romans agreed in general with the Greeks in following the rule of sacrificing male creatures to gods, female to goddesses, and those of dark hue to the infernal powers. At Rome, however, there were special regulations respecting the victims appropriate to the different divinities. Thus the appropriate offering for Iupiter was a young steer of a white colour, or at least with a white spot on its forehead; for Mars, in the case of expiatory sacrifices, two bucks or a steer; the latter also for Neptune and Apollo; for Vulcan, a red calf and a boar; for Liber and Mercury, a he-goat; for Iuno, Minerva, and Diana, a heifer; for Iuno, as Lucina, a ewe lamb or (as also for Ceres and the Bona Dea) a sow; for Tellus, a pregnant, and for Proserpina a barren, heifer; and so on.

The regulations as regards the condition of the victims were not the same everywhere in Greece. Still, in general with them, as invariably with the Romans, the rule held good that only beasts which were without blemish, and had not yet been used for labour, should be employed. Similarly, there were definite rules, which were, however, not the same everywhere, concerning the age of the victims. Thus, by Athenian law, lambs could not be offered at all before their first shearing, and sheep only when they had borne lambs. The Romans distinguished victims by their ages as *lactantes*, sucklings, and *maiores*, full grown. The sacrifice of sucklings was subject to certain limitations: young pigs had to be five days old, lambs seven, and calves thirty. Animals were reckoned *maiores* if they were *bidentes*—i. e. if their upper and lower rows of teeth were complete. There were exact requirements for all cases as regards their sex and condition, and to transgress these was an offence that demanded expiation. If the victims could not be obtained as the regulations required, the pontifical law allowed their place to be taken by a representation in wax or dough, or by a different animal in substitution for the sort required. In many cults different creatures were combined for sacrifice—e. g. a bull, a sheep, and a pig (see SUOVETAURILIA), or a pig, a buck, and a ram, and the like. In State sacrifices victims were sometimes sacrificed in great numbers; e. g. at the Athenian festival in commemoration of the victory at Marathon 500 goats were slain. (See HECATOMBÉ.) Human sacrifices as a means of expiation were not unknown to the earliest Greek and Roman worship, and continued in certain cases (e. g. at the feast of the Lycaean Zeus and of Iupiter Latiaris) until the imperial period. Where, however, they continued to exist, criminals who were in any case doomed to death were selected, and in many places opportunity was further given them for escape. As a rule, these human sacrifices gave way to symbolical exercises in which the rite either merely suggested the original form, or else for human victims effigies or puppets were substituted. Of the former kind was the symbolical whipping of the Spartan boys at the altar of Artemis Orthia till blood was drawn (see DIAMASTIGOSIS); of the latter was the casting of puppets made of rushes into the Tiber in May (see ARGEI), and the use of *oscilla*. See Pausan. ix. 8, 1; vii. 19, 2; Macrob. i. 7, 34; and Mannhardt, *Wald- und Feldkülte*, pp. 265 foll.

In general, it was considered that purity in soul and body was an indispensable requirement for a sacrifice that was to be acceptable to a divinity. Accordingly, the celebrant washed at least his hands and feet, and appeared in clean (for the most part, white) robes. One who had incurred bloodguiltiness could not offer sacrifice at all; he who had polluted himself by touching anything unclean, particularly a corpse, needed special purification by fumigation. Precautions were also taken to insure the withdrawal of all persons who might be otherwise unpleasing to the divinity; from many sacrifices women were excluded; from others, men; from many, slaves and freedmen. At Rome, in early times, all plebeians were excluded by the patricians.

The victims were generally decked out with ribbons and wreaths (*infulae, vittae*), and sometimes the cattle had their horns gilded. If the creature voluntarily followed to the altar or even bowed its head, this was considered as a favourable sign; it was an unfavourable sign if it offered resistance or tried to escape. In that case, with the Romans, the object of the sacrifice was deemed to be frustrated. Among the Greeks those who took part in the sacrifice wore wreaths; a firebrand from the altar was dipped in water, and with the water thus consecrated they sprinkled themselves and the altar. They then strewed the head of the victim with baked barley-grains, and cast some hairs cut from its head into the sacrificial fire. After those present had been called upon to observe a devout silence, and avoid everything that might mar the solemnity of the occasion, the gods were invited, amid the sound of flutes or hymns sung to the lyre and dancing, to accept the sacrifice propitiously. The hands of the worshippers were raised, or extended, or pointed downwards, according as the prayer was made to a god of heaven, of the sea, or of the lower world respectively. The victim was then felled to the ground with a mace or a hatchet, and its throat cut with the sacrificial knife. During this operation the animal's head was held up if the sacrifice belonged to the upper gods, and bowed down if it belonged to those of the lower world or the dead. The blood caught from it was, in the former case, poured round the altar; in the latter, into a ditch. In the case just mentioned the sacrifice was entirely burned (and this was also the rule with animals that were not edible), and the ashes were poured into the ditch. In sacrifices to the gods of the upper world, only certain portions were burned to the gods, such as thigh-bones or chine-bones cut off the victim, some of the entrails, or some pieces of flesh with a layer of fat, rolled round the whole, together with libations of wine and oil, frankincense, and sacrificial cakes. The remainder, after removing the god's portion, as it was called, for the priests engaged in the sacrifice, was either roasted at once for the sacrificial banquet and so consumed, or taken home. Festal sacrifices at the public expense were often combined with a public meal. Sacrifice was made to the gods of the upper air in the morning; to those of the lower world in the evening.

Among the Romans, as among the Greeks, reverent silence prevailed during the sacrificial operations in case a careless word should become an evil omen, and to prevent any disturbance by external surroundings a flute-player played and the offerer of the sacrifice himself veiled his head during the rite. The prayer, formulated by the *pontifices*, and unintelligible to the priests themselves from its archaic language (Quint. i. 6, 40), was repeated by the votary after the priest, who read it from a written form, as any deviation from the exact words made the whole sacrifice of no avail. As a rule, the worshipper turned his face to the east, or, if the ceremony took place before the temple, to the image of the divinity, grasping the altar with his hands; and, when the prayer was ended, laid his hands on his lips, and turned himself from left to right (in many cults from right to left), or, again, walked round the altar and then seated himself. Then the victim (*victima* if a large one, *hostia* if a small one), selected as being without blemish, was consecrated, the priest sprinkling salted grains of dried and pounded spelt (*mola salsa*) and pouring wine from a cup upon its head, and also in certain sacrifices cutting some of the hairs off its head, and finally making a stroke with his knife along the back of the creature from its head to its tail. Cattle were killed with the mace, calves with the hammer, small animals with the knife, by the priest's attendants appointed for the purpose, to whom also the dissection of the victims was assigned. If the inspectors of sacrifice (see HARUSPEX) declared that the entrails (*exta*), cut out with the knife, were not normal, this was a sign that the offering was not pleasing to the divinity; and if it was a male animal which had been previously slaughtered, a female was now killed. If the entrails again proved unfavourable, the sacrifice was regarded as of no avail. On the other hand, in the case of prodigies, sacrifices were offered until favourable signs appeared. In other sin-offerings there was no inspection of entrails. Sin-offerings were either entirely burned or given to the priests. Otherwise the flesh was eaten by the offerers, and only the entrails, which were roasted on spits, or boiled, were offered up, together with particular portions of the meat, in the proper way, and placed in a dish upon the altar, after being sprinkled with *mola salsa* and wine. The slaughter of the victim took place in the morning, while the *exta* were offered at evening, the intervening time being taken up by the process of preparation. See A. Lang, *Myth, Ritual, and Religion*, 2 vols. (1887); Tylor, *Primitive Culture*, 2 vols. (1871); Frazer, *Totemism* (1887); Hartung, *Die Religion der Römer* (1836); the excellent accounts in Marquardt's *Privatleben der Römer*, pp. 183 foll., and in Gardner and Jevons, *Greek Antiquities*, bk. iii. ch. 6 (1895), and cf. the article RELIGIO.

Sacrilegium (*sacra*+*lego*, cf. Hor. *Sat.* i. 3, 117). The Roman name for the crime of stealing objects consecrated to some god or deposited in a consecrated place (Sen. *De Ben.* 7, 7). In Cicero's time the word was extended to cover also any damage or insult to sacred things (Cic. *N. D.* iii. 40, 94), and later still, to want of respect to the emperor. (See MAIESTAS.) A *Lex Iulia* punished sacrilege with *interdictio aqua et igni*, but for this *deportatio* was ultimately substituted; and under the Empire the heavier penalties of burning alive and *damnatio ad bestias* were inflicted (*Dig.* xlviii. 13, 6). Cf. HIEROSYLIAS GRAPHÉ.

Sacriportus. A small place in Latium, of uncertain site, memorable for the victory of Sulla over the younger Marius in B.C. 82.

Sacristan. See AEDITUUS.

Sacrum Promontorium. (1) Now Cape St. Vincent, on the western coast of Spain. (2) Cape Corsa, the northeastern point of Corsica. (3) Cape Iria, also Makri, Efta Kavi or Jedi Burum—i. e. "seven points," the extreme point of Mount Cragus, in Lycia, between Xanthus and Telmissus. (4) Cape Khelidoni, another promontory in Lycia, near the confines of Pamphylia, and opposite the Chelidonian islands, whence it is also called PROMONTORIUM CHELIDONIUM.

Saddle. See EPHIPPIUM; SAGMA.

Sadyattes (Σαδυάττης). A king of Lydia, succeeded his father Ardys, and reigned B.C. 629–617. He carried on war with the Milesians for six years, and at his death bequeathed the war to his son and successor, Alyattes. See ALYATTES.

Saeculāres Ludi. See LUDI, p. 972.

Saecŭlum. See LUDI, p. 972.

Saepīnum or **Sepīnum.** Now Sepino; a municipium in Samnium, on the road from Allifae to Beneventum.

Saetăbis. (1) Now Alcoy; a river on the southern coast of Hispania Tarraconensis, west of the Sucro. (2) Or SETĂBIS (Jativa), an important town of the Contestani, in Hispania Tarraconensis, and a Roman municipium, was situated on a hill south of the Sucro, and was celebrated for its manufacture of linen.

Saga ("a wise woman," cognate with *sagax*). A sorceress or fortune-teller, one deeply versed in occult lore (Hor. *Carm.* i. 27, 21), and with no malignity of disposition necessarily implied. For the ancient belief in witches, see the article STRIGA.

Roman Fortune-teller. (Pompeian painting.)

Sagalassus (Σαγαλασσός or Σελγησσός). Now Allahsun; a large fortified city of Pisidia, near the Phrygian border, a day's journey southeast of Apamea Cibotus. It lay, as its large ruins still show, in the form of an amphitheatre on the side of a hill, and had a citadel on a rock thirty feet high.

Sagarii. See SAGUM.

Sagăris. A river of European Sarmatia, falling into a bay in the northwest of the Euxine, which was called after it SAGARĬCUS SINUS, and which also received the river Axiaces.

Sagartii (Σαγάρτιοι). According to Herodotus, a nomad people of Persis. Afterwards they are found, on the authority of Ptolemy, in Media and the passes of Mount Zagros (Herod. i. 25).

Sagēna (σαγήνη). A seine or drag-net for taking fish. One end of it was floated by corks (*cortices*), and the other was sunk and extended by leaden weights. See Alciphron, *Epist.* i. 17; Manil. *Astron.* v. 678.

Sages, THE SEVEN. See SEVEN SAGES.

Sagitta (ὀϊστός, ἰός, τόξευμα). An arrow. Ancient arrows like those of modern times were feathered and tipped with metal (Hes. *Scut. Her.* 130–134). The point was called ἄρδις (Herod. i. 215). Flint arrow-heads have been found in Italy; and the Aethiopians in the army of Xerxes used

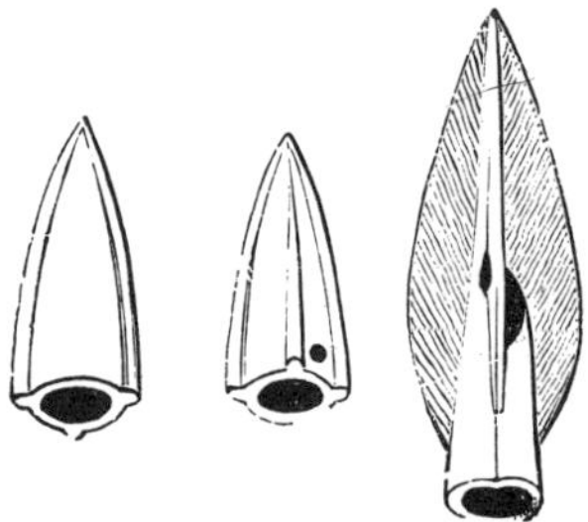

Greek Arrow-heads from Attica.

arrows tipped with a sharp stone (Herod. vii. 69); but Greek arrows were generally pointed with bronze, and this as early as Homer, who uses the epithet χαλκήρης of one (*Il.* xiii. 650, 662). The Homeric arrow-head, however, was three-tongued, and had barbs (ὄγκοι, *Il.* lv. 151). The Romans called barbed arrows *hamatae* and *aduncae;* and did not poison the ends (*venenatae sagittae*), as did the Getae, Scythae, and Mauri. Arrows were used

Ivory Arrow-head. (Schliemann.)

in warfare to carry fire. By this means Xerxes set the Athenian acropolis on fire (Herod. viii. 52), and Caesar used fire-arrows to set fire to Antony's ships (Pollux, i. 37). Archers were called *sagittarii* by the Romans, but in earlier times *arquites.* See ARCUS.

Sagittarii. The bowmen of the Roman armies. These were generally raised by levy or furnished by the allies. The Cretan, Balearic, and Asiatic bowmen were especially celebrated.

Sagma (σάγμα). A pack-saddle used on beasts of burden for loading goods, and opposed to the riding-saddle, for which see EPHIPPIUM.

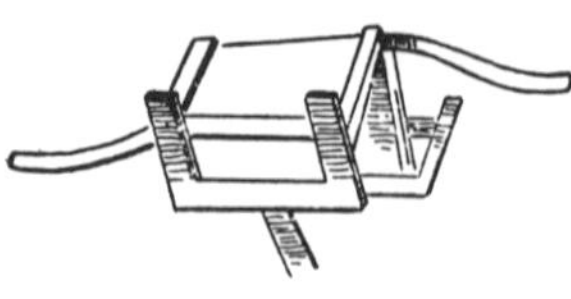

Sagma. (Pompeian painting.)

Sagmarius. A pack-animal. See SAGMA.

Sagmĭna. Another name for the sacred herbs (*verbenae*) given by the consul or praetor to the Fetiales whenever they went forth to demand reparation of a foreign people or to make a treaty. They were torn by the roots from the enclosure of the Capitol and carried by a person known as the *verbenarius.* For particulars, see FETIALES.

Sagra. A small river in Magna Graecia, on the southeastern coast of Bruttium, falling into the sea between Caulonia and Locri.

Sagrus. Now Sangro; a river of Samnium, flowing into the Adriatic (Ptol. iii. 1, 19).

Sagum. (1) A Keltic word. The military cloak of the Roman soldiers, which consisted of a four-cornered piece of cloth worn over the armour and

Lictor with Sagum. (Bas-relief in the Museum at Verona.)

fastened upon the shoulder by a clasp. It was a symbol of war, as the toga was a symbol of peace, so that *sagati* = *milites,* as opposed to *togati,* "civilians." (2) A saddle-cloth placed under a saddle of any sort (Veget. *Vet.* iii. 59, 2).

Saguntum, more rarely **Saguntus.** Now Murviedro, said to have been founded by the Zacynthians; a town of the Edetani or Sedetani, in Spain, south of the Iberus, on the river Palantias, about three miles from the coast. Although south of the Iberus, it had formed an alliance with the Romans; and its siege by Hannibal, B.C. 219, was the immediate cause of the Second Punic War (Livy, xxi. 14 foll.). The ruins of a theatre and a temple of Bacchus are extant at Murviedro, which is a corruption of *muri veteres.* The town was celebrated for its manufacture of beautiful cups. The name Saguntum is a phonetic corruption of Ζάκυνθος.

Sails. See NAVIS.

Saïs (Σαΐς). Now Sa-el-Hajjar; a great city of Egypt, in the Delta, on the eastern side of the Canopic branch of the Nile. It was the ancient capital of Lower Egypt, and contained the palace and burial-place of the Pharaohs as well as the tomb of Osiris. The city gave its name to the Saïtes Nomos. Here was the chief seat of the worship of Nit, who had a great temple, where every year a "Feast of Lamps" was celebrated by multitudes from all parts of Egypt. The place was also a famous centre of Egyptian learning, and to it many Greeks resorted for instruction. The story of the mysterious veiled statue at Saïs, of which Schiller has written a ballad, and which is the subject of a romance by Novalis, appears to be only a creation of Greek fancy.

Saïtis (Σαΐτις). A surname of Athenê, under which she had a sanctuary on Mount Pontinus, near Lerna, in Argolis. The name was traced by the Greeks to the Egyptians, among whom Athenê was said to have been called Saïs (Herod. ii. 75).

Sala. (1) Now the Saale; a river of Germany, between which and the Rhine Drusus died. It was a tributary of the Albis. (2) Now the Saale; also a river of Germany, and a tributary of the Moenus (Main), which formed the boundary between the Hermunduri and Chatti, with great salt springs in its neighbourhood.

Salacia. A Roman goddess of the salt water. She was identified with the Greek Amphitritê, and regarded as the wife of Neptune. See NEPTUNUS; POSEIDON.

Salamis (Σαλαμίς). (1) Now Koluri; an island off the west coast of Attica, and forming the southern boundary of the Bay of Eleusis. It is best known from the great naval victory of the Greeks

Salapia. Now Salpi. An ancient town of Apulia, in the district Daunia, was situated south of Sipontum, on a lake named after it. It is not mentioned till the Second Punic War when it revolted to Hannibal after the battle of Cannae; but it subsequently surrendered to the Romans, and delivered to the latter the Carthaginian garrison stationed in the town.

Salapīna Palus. Now the Lago di Salpi; a lake of Apulia, between the mouths of the Cerbalus and Aufidus.

Salaria. A town of the Bastetani, in Hispania Tarraconensis, and a Roman colony.

Salaria Via. A Roman road which ran from the Porta Salaria through Fidenae, Reate, and Asculum Picenum, to Castrum Truentinum, and thence along the coast to Ancona.

Salarium. A Roman term signifying properly the allowance of salt which the governor furnished for the magistrates and officers who formed his retinue; then the gratification in money which took the place of the salt. Under the Empire it was the pay (*stipendium*) of the imperial magistrates, as well as of the physicians and professors in the service of the State, though still used also in the early sense (Pliny, *H. N.* xxxi. 89; Hist. Aug. *Ant. P.* 11).

Salassi. A brave and warlike people in Gallia Transpadana, in the valley of the Duria (Val d'Aosta), at the foot of the Graian and Pennine Alps, whom some regarded as a branch of the Salyes or Salluvii, in Gaul. Their chief town was Augusta Praetoria (Aosta).

Saldae. Now Bougie; a large town of Northern Africa, originally belonging to the kingdom of Mauretania, and later to Mauretania Caesariensis. See Boissier, *L'Afrique Romaine* (1894).

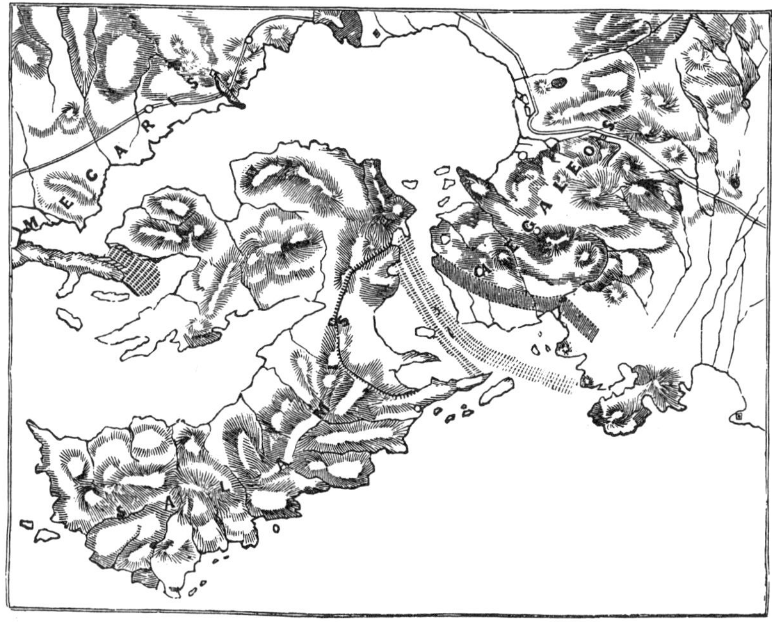

Salamis.

over the Persian fleet of Xerxes in B.C. 480. See XERXES. (2) A city in Cyprus said to have been founded by Teucer, son of Telamon. See TEUCER.

Salentīni or **Sallentīni.** A people in the southern part of Calabria, who dwelt around the promontory Iapygium, which is hence called **Salentī-**

num or **Salentīna**. They laid claim to a Greek origin, and pretended to have come from Crete into Italy under the guidance of Idomeneus (Verg. *Aen.* iii. 400). They were subdued by the Romans at the conclusion of their war with Pyrrhus, and having revolted in the Second Punic War were again easily reduced to subjection (Livy, *Epit.* 15).

Salernum. Now Salerno. An ancient town in Campania, at the innermost corner of the Sinus Paestanus, situated on a hill near the coast. It was made a Roman colony B.C. 194; but it attained its greatest prosperity in the Middle Ages, after it had been fortified by the Lombards.

Salgăma (*τὰ ἁρμαῖα*). Pickles. Roots, herbs, or fruits preserved in brine (Columell. x. 117; xii. 4).

Salganeus or **Salganea**. A small town of Boeotia, on the Euripus, and on the road from Anthedon to Chalcis.

Salientes. See FONS.

Salii (*Σαλίοι*, "dancers," from *salio*). An old Italian *collegium* of priests of Mars, said to have been introduced at Rome by Numa and doubled by Tullus Hostilius. The earlier college was called the SALII PALATĪNI and the later the SALII AGONĀLES or COLLĪNI. The former derived their name from their *curia* on the Palatine Hill; the latter, from the Colline Gate, near which stood their sanctuary on the Quirinal. Both colleges consisted of twelve life-members of patrician family, and recruited their numbers from young men, whose parents were required to be still living; at their head was a *magister*, a *praesul* (leader in the dance), and a *vates* (leader in the song). The cult of the Palatine Salii had to do with Mars, that of the Colline with Quirinus; but the chief connection of both was with the sacred shields, *ancilia*. (See illustration.) The chief ceremonial of the Salii was in March, the beginning of the campaigning season. On March 1st, they began a procession through the city, each of them dressed in an embroidered tunic, a bronze breastplate, and a peaked helmet, girt about with a sword, with one of the holy shields on the left arm, and in the right hand a staff, while trumpeters walked in front of them.

Salii with Ancilia. (Gruter.)

At all the altars and temples they made a halt, and, under the conduct of the two leaders, danced the war-dance in three measures, from which they take their name of Salii or "dancers," accompanying it by singing certain lays, beating their shields meanwhile with the staves. Every day the procession came to an end at certain appointed stations, where the shields were kept over the night in special houses, and the Salii themselves partook of a meal proverbial for its magnificence (Hor. *Carm.* i. 37, 2). Until March 24th the *ancilia* were in motion; within this time some special festivities were also held, in which the Salii took part. On March 11th there was a chariot-race in honour of Mars (*Equiria*) and a sacrificial feast in honour of the supposed fabricator of the shields, Mamurius Veturius; on the 19th was the ceremony of the cleansing of the shields, and on the 23d the cleansing of the holy trumpets (*tubae*) of the priests, called the *tubilustrium*. The days on which the *ancilia* were in motion were accounted solemn (*religiosi*), and on these days men avoided marching out to war, offering battle, and concluding a marriage. In October, the close of the campaigning season, the *ancilia* were once more brought out, in order to be cleansed in the Campus Martius. The lays of the Salii, called *axamenta* (from *axare*, "to repeat," a word found in Festus), were referred to Numa Pompilius, and were written in the archaic Saturnian verse, and in such primitive language, that they were scarcely intelligible even to the priests themselves, and as early as the beginning of the first century B.C. were the object of learned interpretation (Quint. i. 6, 40). Two or three connected bits of these lays have come down to us. The most intelligible is the following, reconstructed by Bergk, in a rude Saturnian measure:

|| *Cumé tonás, Leucésie,* | *práe tét tremónti,* ||
Quom tibeí cúneí | *déxtumúm tonáront;* ||

i. e. *Cum tonas, Lucetie* (thou god of light), *prae te tremunt, cum tibi cunei* (bolts of lightning) *a dextra tonuerunt.* (See Wordsworth, *Fragments and Specimens of Early Latin*, 564–566; Allen, *Early Latin*, p. 74). Besides Mars, other deities, such as Ianus, Iupiter, and Minerva, were invoked in them; the invocation of Mamurius Veturius formed the close (Ovid, *Fasti*, iii. 260 foll.). After the time of Augustus the names of individual emperors were also inserted in the lays.

Salīnae. Salt-works; the name of several towns which possessed salt-works in their vicinity. (1) A town in Britain, on the eastern coast, in the southern part of Lincolnshire. (2) A town of the Suetrii, in the Maritime Alps, in Gallia Narbonensis, east of Reii. (3) Torre delle Saline, a place on the coast of Apulia, near Salapia. (4) A place in Picenum, on the river Sannus (Salino). (5) Torda, a place in Dacia. (6) SALĪNAE HERCULEAE, near Herculaneum, in Campania.

Salinātor, Livius. (1) MARCUS, consul B.C. 219, with L. Aemilius Paulus, carried on war along with his colleague against the Illyrians. On their return to Rome, both consuls were brought to trial on the charge of having unfairly divided the booty among the soldiers. Paulus escaped with difficulty, but Livius was condemned. The sentence seems to have been an unjust one, and Livius took his disgrace so much to heart that he left the city and retired to his estate in the country, where he lived some years without taking any part in public affairs (Livy, xxii. 35). In 210 the consuls compelled him to return to the city, and in 207 he was elected consul a second time with C. Claudius Nero. He shared with his colleague in the glory of defeating Hasdrubal on the Metaurus. (For details, see CLAUDIUS NERO.) Next year (206) Livius was stationed in Etruria, as proconsul, with an army, and his imperium was prolonged for two successive years. In 204 he was censor with his former colleague in the consulship, Claudius Nero. The two censors had long been enemies; and their long-smothered resentment now burst forth, and occasioned a great scandal. Livius, in his censorship, imposed a tax upon salt, in consequence of which he received the surname of *Salinator*, which seems to have been given him in derision, but which became, notwithstanding, hereditary in his family (Livy, xxix. 37; Val. Max. ii. 9, 6; vii. 2, 6). (2) GAIUS, curule aedile B.C. 203, and praetor 202, in which year he obtained Bruttii as his province. In 193 he fought under the consul against the Boii, and in the same year was an unsuccessful candidate for the consulship. (3) GAIUS, praetor B.C. 191, when he had the command of the fleet in the war against Antiochus. He was consul 188, and obtained Gaul as his province (Livy, xxxvii. 9–25).

Salīnum, dim. **Salillum**. A salt-cellar; usually of silver, but among the poorer classes merely a shell (Hor. *Sat.* i. 3, 14). It was probably set in the middle of the table and had a sort of sanctity, inasmuch as salted meal (*mola salsa*) was offered to the Lares.

Sallentīni. See SALENTINI.

Sallustius or **Salustius** (Σαλούστιος). (1) The Praefectus Praetorio under the emperor Julian, with whom he was on terms of friendship. Sallustius was a heathen, but dissuaded the emperor from persecuting the Christians. He was perhaps the author of a treatise Περὶ θεῶν καὶ κόσμου, which is still extant. If so, he was attached to the doctrines of the Neo-Platonists. The best edition of this treatise is by Orelli (Zürich, 1821). (2) A Cynic philosopher of some note, who lived in the latter part of the fifth century after Christ. He was a native of Emesa in Syria, and studied successively at Emesa, Alexandria, and Athens. Sallustius was suspected of holding somewhat impious opinions regarding the gods. He seems at least to have been unsparing in his attacks upon the fanatical theology of the Neo-Platonists.

Sallustius Crispus, GAIUS. (1) A famous Roman historian, belonging to a plebeian family. He was born B.C. 86, at Amiternum, in the country of the Sabines. He was quaestor about 59, and tribune of the plebs in 52, the year in which Clodius was killed by Milo. In his tribunate he joined the popular party, and took an active part in opposing Milo. It is said that he had been caught by Milo in the act of adultery with his wife Fausta, the daughter of the dictator Sulla; that he had received a beating from the husband; and that he had been only let off on payment of a sum of money. In 50 Sallust was expelled from the Senate by the censors, probably because he belonged to Caesar's party, though some give as the ground of his ejection from the Senate the act of adultery already mentioned. In the Civil War he followed Caesar's fortunes. In 47 we find him praetor elect, by obtaining which dignity he was restored to his rank. He nearly lost his life in a mutiny of some of Caesar's troops in Campania, who had been led thither to pass over into Africa. He accompanied Caesar in his African war (46), and was left by Caesar as governor of Numidia, in which capacity he is charged with having oppressed the people, and enriched himself by unjust means. He was accused of maladministration before Caesar, but it does not appear that he was brought to trial. The charge is somewhat confirmed by the fact of his becoming immensely rich, as was shown by the expensive gardens which he formed (*horti Sallustiani*) on the Quirinalis. He retired into privacy after he returned from Africa, and he passed quietly through the troublesome period after Caesar's death. He died in the year 34, about four years before the battle of Actium. The story of his marrying Cicero's wife, Terentia, ought to be rejected.

It was probably not till after his return from Africa that Sallust wrote his historical works. (*a*) The *Catilina*, or *Bellum Catilinarium*, is a history of the conspiracy of Catiline during the consulship of Cicero, 63. The introduction to this history, which some critics admire, is only a feeble and rhetorical attempt to act the philosopher and moralist. The history, however, is valuable. Sallust was a living spectator of the events which he describes, and considering that he was not a friend of Cicero, and was a partisan of Caesar, he wrote with fairness. The speeches which he has inserted

Bust of Sallust. (St. Petersburg.)

in his history are certainly his own composition; but we may assume that Caesar's speech was extant, and that he gave the substance of it. (*b*) The *Iugurtha*, or *Bellum Iugurthinum*, contains the history of the war of the Romans against Iugurtha, king of Numidia, which began in 111, and continued until 106. It is probable that Sallust was led to write this work from having resided in Africa, and that he collected some materials there. He cites the Punic Books of King Hiempsal, as authority for his general geographical description (*Iug.* 17). The Jugurthine War has a philosophical introduction of the same stamp as that to the *Catilina*. As a history of the campaign, the Jugurthine War is of no value: there is a total neglect of geographical precision, and apparently not a very strict regard to chronology. (*c*) Sallustius also wrote *Historiarum Libri Quinque*, which were dedicated to Lucullus, a son of L. Licinius Lucullus. The work is supposed to have comprised the period from the consulship of M. Aemilius Lepidus and Q. Lutatius Catulus (78), the year of Sulla's death, to the consulship of L. Vulcatius Tullus and M. Aemilius Lepidus (66), the year in which Cicero was praetor. This work is lost, with the exception of fragments which have been collected and arranged. They contain, among other things, several orations and letters. Some fragments belonging to the third book, and relating to the war with Spartacus, have been published from a Vatican MS. in the present century, and a number of others were found in 1886 by Hauler in an Orleans palimpsest. (*d*) *Duae Epistolae de Re Publica Ordinanda,* which appear to be addressed to Caesar at the time when he was engaged in his Spanish campaign (49) against Petreius and Afranius, and are attributed to Sallust; but the opinions of critics on their authenticity are divided. (*e*) The *Declamatio in Sallustium,* which is attributed to Cicero, is generally admitted to be the work of some rhetorician, the matter of which is the well-known hostility between the orator and the historian. The same opinion is generally maintained as to the *Declamatio in Ciceronem,* which is attributed to Sallust.

Some of the Roman writers considered that Sallustius imitated the style of Thucydides (Quint. x. 1), and he has himself greatly influenced the style of Tacitus. His language is generally concise and perspicuous: perhaps his love of brevity may have caused the ambiguity that is sometimes found in his sentences. He also affected archaic words. Though he has considerable merit as a writer, his art is always apparent. He had no pretensions to great research or precision about facts. His reflections have often something of the same artificial and constrained character as his expressions. One may judge that his object was to obtain distinction as a writer; that style was what he thought of more than matter. He has, however, probably the merit of being the first Roman who wrote what is usually called history. He was not above his contemporaries as a politician; he was a party man, and there are no indications of any comprehensive views, which had a whole nation for their object. He hated the nobility, and depicted their vices in a spirit of bitter exaggeration.

There are many MSS. of Sallust, especially at Paris. These Codices Parisini, of the tenth and eleventh centuries (P, P^1, P^2), are the best, all being distinguished by a lengthy lacuna after *Iug.* 103, supplied from a second "family" of MSS. written later, and represented by several codices at Munich. Remains of the orations and letters of Sallust are preserved in two MSS. of the tenth century—one at Berne, and one in the Vatican. These give also annotations by an unknown grammarian.

There are separate editions of the *Catilina* by Cook (1884); Turner (1887); Eussner (1887), and Herbermann (New York, 1890); of the *Iugurtha* by Herzog (Leipzig, 1840); Schmalz (Gotha, 1866), and Brook (London, 1885). The fragments of his *Historiae* are given in Jordan's edition of the Sallust (1887); and separately edited by Maurenbrecher (fasc. i. and ii., Leipzig, 1891–93). Complete editions of Sallust are those of Gerlach (Basel, 1832), Kritz (1828, 1856), Dietsch (1859, 1864), Jordan (Berlin, 1876, 1887), and with English notes by Merivale (1852), Long (1860, revised by Frazer, 1890), and Capes (1884). There are lexicons to Sallust by Eichert (Hanover, 1864) and Mollweide (Strassburg, 1887). A good English translation is that of Pollard (1882). On the style, see Constans, *De Sermone Sallustiano* (Paris, 1880); and in general the monographs by Vogel (Mainz, 1857), Jäger (Salzburg, 1884), and Rambeau (Burg, 1879).

(2) The grandson of the historian's sister, adopted by Sallust and made his heir. He was the principal adviser of Augustus Caesar after the retirement of Maecenas. He died in A.D. 20 (Hor. *Carm.* ii. 2; Tac. *Ann.* i. 6; ii. 40; iii. 30).

Salmăcis. See HERMAPHRODITUS.

Salmantĭca. Now Salamanca, called HELMANTĬCA or HERMANDICA by Livy and ELMANTĬCA by Polybius (iii. 14). An important town of the Vettones in Lusitania, south of the Durius, on the road from Emerita to Caesaraugusta (Saragossa).

Salmasius, CLAUDIUS (Claude de Saumaise). A classical scholar, born at Semur in Burgundy, April 15th, 1588. His father, Bénigne de Saumaise, himself an accomplished scholar, gave him his first instruction, and at the age of ten the boy translated Pindar and wrote both Greek and Latin verse. He studied philosophy at Paris under the direction of Casaubon (q. v.), and later (1606) went to Heidelberg, where he took a course in jurisprudence, and studied so hard as greatly to injure his health, sitting at his desk through the whole of two nights out of every three, and adding to his linguistic resources a knowledge of Hebrew, Arabic, Coptic, and other languages. In 1631 he was called to Leyden to succeed Scaliger. He spent a year in Sweden (1650) at the solicitation of Queen Christina, but returned to Holland at the end of that time. In 1606 he discovered the Greek anthology of Kephalas at Heidelberg. (See ANTHOLOGY.) He died at Spa, September 6th, 1658.

Salmasius enjoyed a wide reputation for his great learning, which has been equalled by few. He was styled "the miracle of the world," "the most learned of all living men," but he lacked critical insight and system, so that he left nothing of lasting value to the world of learning. He is best remembered to-day for his abusive controversy with Milton over the question of the death of Charles I., and Milton's blindness was the result of excessive labour in the production of his answer to Salmasius.

Salmasius published *Plinianae Exercitationes* (1629); an edition of the *Augusta Historia* (1620); *Florus* (1629); *De Lingua Hellenistica* (1643); *De Re Militari Romanorum* (1657). See the eulogistic life of Salmasius prefixed to the collection of his letters (Leyden, 1656); L. Müller, *Geschichte der class. Philogie in den Niederlanden* (Leipzig, 1869); and for his controversy with Milton, Masson's *Life of Milton* (1876–79).

Salmōna (Σαλμώνη) or **Salmonia.** A town of Elis, in the district Pisatis, on the river Enipeus, said to have been founded by Salmoneus.

Salmōneus (Σαλμωνεύς). Son of Aeolus and Enareté and brother of Sisyphus. He originally lived in Thessaly, but emigrated to Elis, where he built the town of Salmoné. His presumption and arrogance were so great that he deemed himself equal to Zeus, and ordered sacrifices to be offered to himself; nay, he even imitated the thunder and lightning of Zeus, but the father of the gods killed him with his thunderbolt, destroyed his town, and punished him in the lower world (Verg. *Aen.* vi. 585). His daughter Tyro bore the patronymic Salmonis.

Salmydessus (Σαλμυδησσός), called HALMYDESSUS (Ἁλμυδησσός), also in later times Midja or Midjeh. A town of Thrace, on the coast of the Euxine, south of the promontory Thynias. The name was originally applied to the whole coast from this promontory to the entrance of the Bosporus; and it was from this coast that the Black Sea obtained the name of Pontus Axinos, or inhospitable.

Salo. Now the Xalon; a tributary of the Iberus, in Celtiberia, which flowed by Bilbilis, the birthplace of Martial, who frequently mentions it in his poems (i. 49; x. 20).

Salōna, Salōnae, or **Salon.** Now Salona; an important town of Illyria, and the capital of Dalmatia, was situated on a small bay of the sea. The emperor Diocletian was born at the small village of Dioclea, near Salona; and after his abdication he retired to the neighbourhood of this town, and here spent the rest of his days. The remains of his magnificent palace are still to be seen at the village of Spalatro, the ancient Spolatum, three miles south of Salona.

Court of the Palace of Diocletian at Spalatro.

Salonīnus, P. LICINIUS CORNELIUS VALERIĀNUS. The son of the Roman emperor Gallienus, and grandson of the emperor Valerian. He was put to death in Greece when Postumus captured Colonia Agrippina (Cologne) in A.D. 259, at which time Saloninus was about seventeen years of age (Trebell. Poll. *Salonin.*).

Salpensa. A Latin colony in Hispania Baetica, between Hispalis (Seville) and Gades (Cadiz). In 1851, an important inscription was discovered here containing part of a code of laws given to the place in the reign of Domitian (about A.D. 81–84). See the *C. I. L.* ii. 1963–64; Bruns, *Font.* 136.

Salpinx (σάλπιγξ). The Greek name for the long trumpet, like the Roman *tuba*, with which the signals were given in the army. It was also employed in religious ceremonies. See TUBA.

Salpinx.

Saltatio (ὄρχησις, χόρευσις). Dancing. The dancing of the Greeks and Romans had little in common with the exercise which goes by that name in modern times. It may be divided into two kinds, gymnastic and mimetic; that is, it was intended either to represent bodily activity, or to express by gestures, movements, and attitudes certain ideas or feelings, and also single events or a series of events, as in the modern ballet. All these movements, however, were accompanied by music; but the terms ὄρχησις and *saltatio* were used in so much wider a sense than our word dancing that they were applied to designate gestures even when the body did not move at all (*saltare solis oculis,* Apul. *Met.* x. p. 251).

We find dancing prevalent among the Greeks from the earliest times. It is frequently mentioned in the Homeric poems: the suitors of Penelopé delight themselves with music and dancing (*Odyss.* i. 152); and Odysseus is entertained at the court of Alcinoüs with the exhibitions of very skilful dancers, the rapid movements of whose feet excite his admiration (*Odyss.* viii. 265). Skilful dancers were at all times highly prized by the Greeks: we read of some who were presented with golden crowns, and had statues erected to their honour, and their memory celebrated by inscriptions.

The lively imagination and mimetic powers of the Greeks found abundant subjects for various kinds of dances, and, accordingly, the names of no less than two hundred different dances have come down to us. It would be inconsistent with the nature of this work to give a description of all that are known: only the most important can be mentioned, and such as will give a general idea of the dancing of the ancients.

Dancing was originally closely connected with religion. Plato thought all dancing should be based on religion, as it was, he says, among the Egyptians. It has been shown under CHORUS that the chorus in the oldest times consisted of the whole population of a city, who met in a public place to offer up thanksgivings to the god of their country by singing hymns and performing dances. These dances, which, like all others, were accompanied by music, were therefore of a strictly religious nature; and in all the public festivals, which were so numerous among the Greeks, dancing formed a very prominent part. We find, from the earliest times, that the worship of Apollo was connected with a religious dance called Hyporchema (q. v.). All the religious dances, with the exception of the Bacchic and the Corybantian, were very simple, and consisted of gentle movements of the body, with various turnings and windings around the altar: such a dance was the *γέρανος*, which Theseus is said to have performed at Delos on his return from Crete. The Dionysiac or Bacchic and the Corybantian were of a very different nature. In the former, the life and adventures of the god were represented by mimetic dancing (see DIONYSIA); the dance called Βακχική was a satyric dance, and chiefly prevailed in Ionia and Pontus; the most illustrious men in the State danced in it, representing Titans, Corybantians, satyrs, and husbandmen, and the spectators were so delighted with the exhibition that they remained sitting the whole day to witness it, forgetful of everything else. The Corybantian was of a very wild character: it was chiefly danced in Phrygia and in Crete: the dancers were armed, struck their swords against their shields, and displayed the most extravagant fury; it was accompanied chiefly by the flute. The following wood-cut, from the Museo Pio-Clementino, is supposed to represent a Corybantian dance. Respecting the dances in the theatre, see CHORUS.

Corybantian Dancers. (Krause.)

Dancing was applied to gymnastic purposes and to training for war, especially in the Doric States, and was believed to have contributed very much to the success of the Dorians in war, as it enabled them to perform their evolutions simultaneously and in order.

There were various dances in early times which served as a preparation for war; hence Homer calls the hoplitae *πρυλέες*, a war-dance having been called *πρύλις* by the Cretans. Of such dances the most celebrated was the Pyrrhic (*ἡ Πυρρίχη*), of which the *πρύλις* was probably only another name.

The invention of this dance is placed in the mythical age, and is usually assigned to one Pyrrhicos; but most of the accounts agree in assigning it a Cretan or Spartan origin, though others refer it to Pyrrhus or Neoptolemus, the son of Achilles, apparently misled by the name, for it was undoubtedly of Doric origin. It was danced to the sound of the flute, and its time was very quick and light, as is shown by the name of the Pyrrhic foot (˘˘), which must be connected with this dance: and from the same source came also the Proceleusmatic (˘˘˘˘), or challenging foot. The Pyrrhic dance was performed in different ways at various times and in various countries, for it was by no means confined to the Doric States. Plato describes it as representing, by rapid movements of the body, the way in which missiles and blows from weapons were avoided, and also the mode in which the enemy was attacked. In the non-Doric States it was probably not practised as a training for war, but only as a mimetic dance: thus we read of its being danced by women to entertain a company. It was also performed at Athens at the greater and lesser Panathenaea by Ephebi, who were called Pyrrhichists (*Πυρριχισταί*), and were trained at the expense of the choragus.

The following illustration, taken from Sir W. Hamilton's vases, represents three Pyrrhichists, two of whom, with sword and shield, are engaged in the dance, while the third is standing with a sword. Above them is a female balancing herself on the

Pyrrhic Dancers.

head of one, and apparently in the act of performing a somersault; she, no doubt, is taking part in the dance, and performing a very artistic kind of *κυβίστησις*, or tumbling, for the Greek performances of this kind surpass anything we can imagine in modern times. A woman spectator, sitting, looks on at the exhibition.

The Pyrrhic dance was introduced into the public games at Rome by Iulius Cæsar, when it was danced by the children of the leading men in Asia and Bithynia. It seems to have been much liked by the Romans; it was exhibited both by Caligula and Nero, and also frequently by Hadrian. Athenæus says that the Pyrrhic dance was still practised in his time (the third century A.D.) at Sparta.

Other kinds of dances were frequently performed at entertainments, in Rome as well as in Greece, by courtesans, many of which were of a very indecent and lascivious nature (Macrob. *Sat.* ii. 10;

Dancing-girl. (Pompeian painting.)

Plaut. *Stich.* v. 2, 11), resembling the *tango* of the modern Spaniards, and the *danse du ventre* of the Egyptian and Hindu dancing-girls. The dancers seem to have frequently represented Bacchanals; many such dancers appear in the paintings found at Herculaneum and Pompeii in a variety of graceful attitudes. (*Museo Borbonico*, vol. vii. tav. 34–40; vol. ix. tav. 17; vol. x. tav. 5, 6, 54.)

Among the dances performed without arms one of the most important was the ὅρμος, which was danced at Sparta by youths and maidens together: the youth danced first some movements suited to his age, and of a military nature; the maiden followed in measured steps and with feminine gestures. Another common dance at Sparta was the *Bibasis* (βίβασις), which was much practised both by men and women. The dance consisted in springing rapidly from the ground, and striking the feet behind; a feat of which a Spartan woman in Aristophanes (*Lysistr.* 28) prides herself. The number of successful strokes was counted, and the most skilful received prizes. We are told by a verse which has been preserved by Pollux (iv. 102), that a Laconian girl had danced the *bibasis* a thousand times, which was more than had ever been done before.

Acrobatic Dancer (Museo Borbonico.)

In many of the Greek States the art of dancing was carried to great perfection by females, who were frequently engaged to add to the pleasures and enjoyment of men at their symposia. These dancers always belonged to the courtesans. Xenophon (*Symp.* ix. 2–7) describes a mimetic dance which was represented at a symposium where Socrates was present. It was performed by a maiden and a youth, belonging to a Syracusan, who is called the ὀρχηστοδιδάσκαλος, and represented the loves of Dionysus and Ariadnê.

Dancing was common among the Romans in ancient times in connection with religious festivals and rites, and was practised, according to Servius (*ad* Verg. *Ecl.* v. 73), because the ancients thought that no part of the body should be free from the influence of religion. The dances of the Salii, which were performed by men of patrician families, are spoken of elsewhere. (See SALII.) There was another old Roman dance of a military nature, called *bellicrepa saltatio*, which is said to have been instituted by Romulus, after he had carried off the Sabine women, in order that a like misfortune might not befall his State (Festus, *s. v.*). Dancing, however, was not performed by any Roman citizen except in connection with religion; and it is only in reference to such dancing that we are to understand the statements that the ancient Romans did not consider dancing disgraceful, and that not only freemen but the sons of senators and noble matrons practised it (Quintil. *Inst. Orat.* i. 11, 18). In the later times of the Republic we know that it was considered highly disgraceful for a freeman to dance: Cicero reproaches Cato for calling Murena a dancer (*saltator*), and adds, "Nemo fere saltat sobrius, nisi forte insanit" (*Pro Muren.* 6, 13; *In Pison.* 10, 22). The professional dancing-girls at Rome came from foreign countries, oftenest from Spain; and those of Gades (Cadiz) were especially noted for the indecent suggestiveness of their performances.

The mimetic dances of the Romans, which were carried to such perfection under the Empire, are described under PANTOMIMUS. Respecting the dancers on the tight-rope, see FUNAMBULUS.

See Meursius, *Orchestra;* Burette, *De la Danse des Anciens;* Krause, *Gymnastik und Agon. d. Hell.* p. 807; Schömann, *Antiq.* p. 58; Becker-Göll, *Charikles*, i. 166; Blümner, *Privatleben*, p. 505; Marquardt, *Privatleben*, p. 109; Czerwinski, *Geschichte der Tanz-Kunst* (1862); and Voss, *Der Tanz und seine Geschichte* (1868).

Saltĭcae Fabŭlae. See PANTOMIMUS.

Salus. A Roman goddess, the personification of health, prosperity, and the public welfare. In the first of these three senses she answers closely to the Greek Hygeia (q. v.), and was accordingly represented in works of art with the same attributes as the Greek goddess. In the second sense she represents prosperity in general. In the third sense she is the goddess of the public welfare (Salus publica or Romana). In this capacity a temple was vowed to her in the year B.C. 307 by the censor C. Iunius Bubulcus, on the Quirinal Hill, which was afterwards decorated with paintings by C. Fabius Pictor. She was worshipped publicly on the 30th of April, in conjunction with Pax, Concordia, and Ianus. Salus was represented, like

Fortuna, with a rudder, a globe at her feet, and sometimes in a sitting posture, pouring from a patera a libation upon an altar, round which a serpent is winding. The goddess Strenia among the Sabines is the counterpart of the Roman Salus.

Salutatio. The morning greeting which Romans of rank were in the habit of receiving from clients, friends, and admirers in the *atrium* during the first two hours of the day; for this purpose the callers gathered in the vestibule even before sunrise (Mart. iv. 8; Pliny, *Ep.* iii. 12).

Salve. See COLLYRIUM; UNGUENTUM.

Salvīanus. A native of Colonia Agrippina (Cologne), one of the early fathers of the Christian Church. He led a religious life at Massilia during the greater part of the fifth century, and died in that city. Salvianus was the author of several works on devotional subjects, of which there are yet extant a treatise "on the Providence of God" (*De Gubernatione Dei*, etc.), in eight books; another in four books, written against avarice (*Adversus Avaritiam*), and nine pastoral letters. His works are edited by Halm (Berlin, 1877), and Paully (Vienna, 1883).

Salvius Iuliānus. See IULIĀNUS.

Salvius Otho. See OTHO.

Salyes or **Salluvii.** The most powerful and most celebrated of all the Ligurian tribes, inhabited the southern coast of Gaul from the Rhone to the Maritime Alps. They were troublesome neighbours to Massilia, with which city they frequently carried on war. They were subdued by the Romans, in B.C. 123, after a long and obstinate struggle, and the colony of Aquae Sextiae was founded in their territory by the consul Sextius.

Samăra. See SAMAROBRIVA.

Samarīa (Σαμάρεια; Hebr. *Shomron*). (1) A district of Palestine extending along the coast from near Caesarea to Joppa on the south. (See PALESTINA.) (2) An important city of Palestine on a line west of the Jordan River. It was founded by Omri, King of Israel, in the tenth century B.C., and was the capital of the Israelites until taken by Shalmaneser of Assyria, about B.C. 720. When the Jews returned from the Babylonian captivity, those of the Samaritans who worshipped Jehovah offered to assist them in rebuilding the temple at Jerusalem; but their aid was refused, and hence arose the lasting hatred between the Jews and the Samaritans. This religious animosity reached its height when, in the reign of Darius Nothus, the son of the Jewish high-priest, having married the daughter of Sanballat, governor of Samaria, went over to the Samaritans and became high-priest of a temple which his father-in-law built for him, on Mount Gerizim, near Sichem. The erection of this temple had also the effect of diminishing the importance of the city of Samaria. Under the Syrian kings and the Maccabean princes, we find the name of Samaria used distinctly as that of a province, which consisted of the district between Galilee on the north and Judaea on the south. Samaria was taken by Alexander the Great, by Ptolemy I. (B.C. 312), and by Demetrius Poliorcetes (B.C. 276). In the persecution of Antiochus Epiphanes, the Samaritans escaped by conforming to the king's edicts and dedicating the temple on Mount Gerizim to Zeus Hellenius (B.C. 167). As the power of the Asmonean princes increased, they attacked the Samaritans; and, about B.C. 110, the Jewish leader John Hyrcanus took and destroyed the temple on Mount Gerizim and the city of Samaria. The latter seems to have been soon rebuilt. Pompey assigned the district to the province of Syria, and Gabinius fortified the city anew. Augustus gave the district to Herod, who greatly renovated the city of Samaria, which he called Sebasté in honour of his patron. By the fourth century A.D. Samaria had ceased to be a place of any importance. There still exist remains of a basilica of the time of Herod, and of a Roman temple. See Appel, *De Reb. Samar. sub Imperio Romanorum* (1874).

Samarobrīva, afterwards AMBIĀNI. Now Amiens; the chief town of the Ambiani in Gallia Belgica, on the river Samara, whence its name, which signifies Samara Bridge.

Sambūca (σαμβύκη and σανδύκη). A triangular, stringed instrument resembling a harp, having a piercing tone (Pers. v. 95). When played, its pointed end stood downwards.

Egyptian Sambuca. (Wilkinson.)

Samé (Σάμη) or **Samos** (Σάμος). The ancient name of Cephallenia. (See CEPHALLENIA.) It was also the name of one of the four towns of Cephallenia. The town Samé or Samos was situated on the eastern coast, opposite Ithaca, and was taken and destroyed by the Romans, B.C. 189 (Livy, xxxviii. 28).

Samnītes. See GLADIATORES.

Samnium (*Sabnium* qs. *Sabinium*). A country in the centre of Italy, bounded on the north by the Marsi, Peligni, and Marrucini, on the west by Latium and Campania, on the south by Lucania, and on the east by the Frentani and Apulia. The Samnites were an offshoot of the Sabines, who emigrated from their country between the Nar, the Tiber, and the Anio, before the foundation of Rome, and settled in the country afterwards called Samnium. This country was at the time of their migration inhabited by Opicans, whom the Samnites conquered, and whose language they adopted; for we find at a later time that the Samnites spoke Opican or Oscan. See OSCI.

Samnium is a country marked by striking physical features. The greater part of it is occupied by a huge mass of mountains, called at the present day the Matese, which stands out from the central line of the Apennines. The circumference of the Matese is between seventy and eighty miles, and its greatest height is 6000 feet. The most important tribes of the Samnites were the Caudini and Pentri, of whom the former occupied the south side and the latter the north side of the Matese. To the Caudini belonged the towns of Allifae, Telesia, and Beneventum; to the Pentri, those of Aesernia, Bovianum, and Sepinum. Besides these chief tribes, we find mention of the Caraceni, who dwelt north of the Pentri, and to whom the town of Aufidena belonged; and of the Hirpini, who dwelt southeast of the Caudini, but who are sometimes mentioned as distinct from the Samnites.

The Samnites were distinguished for their bravery and love of freedom. Issuing from their mountain fastnesses, they overran a great part of Campania; and it was in consequence of Capua applying to the Romans for assistance against the Samnites that war broke out between the two peoples in B.C. 343. The Romans found the Samnites the most warlike and formidable enemies whom they had yet encountered in Italy; and the war, which commenced in B.C. 343, was continued with few interruptions for the space of fifty-three years. It was not till B.C. 290, when all their bravest troops had fallen, and their country had been repeatedly ravaged in every direction by the Roman legions, that the Samnites sued for peace and submitted to the supremacy of Rome. They never, however, lost their love of freedom; and accordingly they not only joined the other Italian allies in the war against Rome in B.C. 90, but, even after the other allies had submitted, they continued in arms. The Civil War between Marius and Sulla gave them hopes of recovering their independence; but they were defeated by Sulla before the gates of Rome (82) the greater part of their troops fell in battle, and the remainder were put to death. Their towns were laid waste, the inhabitants sold as slaves, and their place supplied by Roman colonists. See ITALIA; OSCI; UMBRIA.

Samos (Σάμος). Now Samo, Turk. Susam Adassi; one of the principal islands of the Aegaean Sea, lying in that portion of it called the Icarian Sea, off the coast of Ionia, from which it is separated only by a narrow strait formed by the overlapping of its eastern promontory Posidium (now Cape Colonna) with the westernmost spur of Mount Mycalé, Promontorium Trogilium (now Cape S. Maria). This strait, which is little more than three-fourths of a mile wide, was the scene of the battle of Mycalé. The island is formed by a range of mountains extending from east to west, whence it derived its name; for Σάμος was an old Greek word signifying a mountain: and the same root is seen in Samé, the old name of Cephallenia, and Samothracé—i. e. the Thracian Samos. The circumference of the island is about eighty miles. It was and is very fertile; and some of its products are indicated by its ancient names, Dryusa, Anthemura, Melamphyllus, and Cyparissia. According to the earliest traditions, it was a chief seat of the Carians and Leleges, and the residence of their first king, Ancaeus; and was afterwards colonized by Aeolians from Lesbos, and by Ionians from Epidaurus.

In the earliest historical records, we find Samos decidedly Ionian, and a powerful member of the Ionic Confederacy. Thucydides tells us that the Samians were the first of the Greeks, after the Corinthians, who paid great attention to naval affairs. They early acquired such power at sea, that, besides obtaining possession of parts of the opposite coast of Asia, they founded many colonies; among which were Bisanthé and Perinthus, in Thrace; Celenderis and Nagidus, in Cilicia; Cydonia, in Crete; Dicaearchia (Puteoli), in Italy; and Zanclé (Messana), in Sicily. After a transition from the state of a monarchy, through an aristocracy, to a democracy, the island became subject to the most famous of the so-called "tyrants," Polycrates (B.C. 532), under whom its power and splendour reached their highest pitch, and Samos would probably have become the mistress of the Aegaean but for the murder of Polycrates. At this period the Samians had extensive commercial relations

Coin of Samos.

with Egypt, and they obtained from Amasis the privilege of a separate temple at Naucratis. Their commerce extended into the interior of Africa, partly through their relations with Cyrené, and also by means of a settlement which they effected in one of the Oases, seven days' journey from Thebes. The Samians now became subject to the Persian Empire, under which they were governed by tyrants, with a brief interval at the time of the Ionian revolt, until the battle of Mycalé, which made them independent, B.C. 479. They now joined the Athenian Confederacy, of which they continued independent members until B.C. 440, when an opportunity arose for reducing them to entire subjection and depriving them of their fleet, which was effected by Pericles after an obstinate resistance of nine months' duration. In the Peloponnesian War (q. v.), Samos held firm to Athens to the last; and in the history of the latter part of that war, the island becomes extremely important as the headquarters of the exiled democratical party of the Athenians. Transferred to Sparta after the battle of Aegospotami (405), it was soon restored to Athens by that of Cnidus (394), but went over to Sparta again in 390. Soon after, it fell into the hands of the Persians, being conquered by the satrap Tigranes; but it was recovered by Timotheus for Athens. In the Social War, the Athenians successfully defended it against the attacks of the confederated Chians, Rhodians, and Byzantines, and placed in it a body of two thousand *cleruchi* (B.C. 352). After Alexander's death, it was taken from the Athenians by Perdiccas (323), but restored to them by Polysperchon (319). In the subsequent period, it seems to have been rather nominally than really a part of the Graeco-Syrian kingdom: we find it engaged in a long contest with Priené on a question of boundary, which was referred to Antiochus II., and afterwards to the Roman Senate. In the Macedonian War, Samos was taken by the Rhodians again, B.C. 200. In the Syrian War, the Samians took part with Antiochus the Great against Rome.

Little further mention is made of Samos till the time of Mithridates, with whom it took part in his first war against Rome, on the conclusion of which it was finally united to the province of Asia, B.C.

84. Meanwhile it had greatly declined, and during the war it had been wasted by the incursions of pirates. Its prosperity was partially restored under the propraetorship of Q. Cicero, B.C. 62, but still more by the residence in it of Antony and Cleopatra (32), and afterwards of Octavianus, who made Samos a free State. It was favoured by Caligula, but was deprived of its freedom by Vespasian, and it sank into insignificance as early as the second century, although its departed glory is found still recorded, under the emperor Decius, by the inscription on its coins, Σαμίων πρώτων Ἰωνίας.

Samos may be regarded as almost the chief centre of Ionian manners, energies, luxury, science, and art. In very early times there was a native school of statuary, at the head of which was Rhoecus, to whom tradition ascribed the invention of casting in metal. (See STATUARIA ARS.) In the hands of the same school architecture flourished greatly; the Heraeum, one of the finest of Greek temples, was erected in a marsh, on the western side of the city of Samos; and the city itself, especially under the government of Polycrates, was furnished with other splendid works, among which was an aqueduct pierced through a mountain. Samian architects became famous also beyond their own island; as, for example, Mandrocles, who constructed Darius's bridge over the Bosporus. Samian pottery was well known, and was in vogue in Greece and Italy in the second century B.C., and was imitated by the potters of Gaul and Britain. It was of a reddish colour, with reliefs. The island was the birthplace of Pythagoras (Herod. iv. 95), and of several minor poets and historians.

The capital of the island was the city SAMOS, on the southeastern coast. It had a magnificent harbour, and was adorned with many fine buildings, especially a temple of Heré (Heraeum), which in the time of Herodotus was the largest temple in existence (Herod. iii. 60; Pausan. vii. 4). It was of the Ionic order. Excavations made in 1880 show that its façade was one of some 150 feet.

See Guérin, *Patmos et Samos* (Paris, 1856); Tozer, *Islands of the Aegean* (1890); Curtius, *Geschichte von Samos* (1877); Bürchner, *Das Ionische Samos* (1892).

Samosăta (τὰ Σαμόσατα). Now Samisat, the capital of the province, and afterwards kingdom, of Commagené, in the north of Syria, stood on the right bank of the Euphrates, northwest of Edessa. It is celebrated in literary history as the birthplace of Lucian, and in church history as that of the heretic Paul, bishop of Antioch, in the third century. Nothing remains of it but a heap of ruins.

Samothrăcé (Σαμοθρᾴκη), **Samothrăca**, and **Samothracia** (Σαμοθρᾳκία). A small island in the north of the Aegaean Sea, opposite the mouth of the Hebrus in Thrace. It was the chief seat of the mysterious worship of the Cabiri. (See CABEIRIA.) The political history of Samothrace is of little importance. The Samothracians fought on the side of Xerxes at the battle of Salamis; and at this time they possessed on the Thracian mainland a few places, such as Salé, Serrhion, Mesambria, and Tempyra. In the time of the Macedonian kings, Samothracé appears to have been regarded as a kind of asylum, and Perseus accordingly fled thither after his defeat by the Romans at the battle of Pydna.

Sampsicerămus. The name of a petty prince of Emesa in Syria; a nickname given by Cicero to Cn. Pompeius (*Ad Att.* ii. 14, 16, 17, 23).

Sanchuniăthon (Σαγχουνιάθων). Said to have been an ancient Phœnician writer, whose works were translated into Greek by Philo Byblius, who lived in the latter half of the first century of the Christian era. A considerable fragment of the translation of Philo is preserved by Eusebius in the first book of his *Praeparatio Evangelica;* but it is now generally agreed among modern scholars that the work was a forgery of Philo. The fragments are published separately by Orelli (Leipzig, 1823). In 1835 a MS. purporting to be the entire version by Philo was said to have been found in the Portuguese convent of Sta. Maria de Merinhão. The Greek text of this was edited by Wagenfeld (Bremen, 1837) and translated into German (Lübeck, 1837). It was soon found to be a forgery, and the story of its discovery to be a falsehood. See Renan, *Mémoire sur Sanchoniathon* (1858).

Sancus. Usually called SEMO SANCUS. (See SEMONES.) A genius worshipped by the Sabines, Umbrians, and Romans, representing holiness and good faith in human life. In Rome he was principally worshipped under the name DEUS FIDIUS (from *fides*, "faith") as god of oaths, god of the public laws of hospitality and of nations, also of international intercourse and of the safety of the roads, which were placed under his protection. An oath in his name could be taken only under the open sky; therefore even his temple had a hole in the roof, and, when an oath by him was taken at home, the man swearing went into the uncovered court. On account of many points of resemblance he was identified with Hercules. He had a temple on the Quirinal (the foundation of which was celebrated June 5th), and another on the island in the Tiber (Ovid, *Fasti*, vi. 213–218).

Sandalium (σανδάλιον and σάνδαλιν). A Greek covering for the foot, worn principally by women, consisting of a thick sole of wood, cork, or leather, with a strap carried over the foot in front of the socket of the great toe, passed between this and the second toe, and tied to the other bands fastened to the edge of the sole before and behind. The back was supported by strap-work, which was often very neatly intertwined above the ankles.

Soles of the more simple kind were bound underneath the foot by a strap running crosswise over the instep, or by two straps fastened to the side-edges and tied together in a knot or by a clasp. Soles were also worn, which were provided with a close-fitting piece of leather at the heel and with a piece of leather, sometimes broad, at the sides. These last were so laced together by straps round the ankles that the toes and the flat of the foot remained uncovered. See SOLEA.

Woman's Sandal. (*Museo Borbonico*, vii. 39.)

Sandrocottus (Σανδρόκοττος). An Indian king in the time of Seleucus Nicator, who ruled over the powerful nation of the Gangaridae and Prasii on the banks of the Ganges (Plut. *Alex.* 62; Arr. *Anab.* v. 6, 2).

Sangallenses Sortes. A book of oracles found in a fragmentary condition at St. Gallen in Switzerland in a MS. of Merobaudes. They are derived from a Greek source and are written in popular Latin. Edited by Winnefeld (Bonn, 1887).

Sangarius (Σαγγάριος), **Sangăris** (Σάγγαρις), or **Sagăris** (Σάγαρις). Now Sakariyeh. The largest river of Asia Minor after the Halys; it had its source in a mountain called Adoreus, near the little town of Sangia, on the borders of Galatia and Phrygia, whence it flowed first north through Galatia, then west and northwest through the northeastern part of Phrygia, and then north through Bithynia, of which it originally formed the eastern boundary. It fell at last into the Euxine, about half way between the Bosporus and Heraclea (Strabo, p. 543).

Sangia. See SANGARIUS.

Sanguicŭlus. A sort of blood-pudding made by the Romans from the blood of a kid (Pliny, *H. N.* xxviii. 58).

Sannio. A name of the buffoon in the Roman mimes, derived from *sanna* ("a grimace"), whence come the Italian *Zanni* and our Zany (Cic. *De Orat.* ii. 61).

Sannio. (From an engraved gem.)

Sannyrion (Σαννυρίων). An Athenian comic poet who flourished about B.C. 407. His excessive leanness was ridiculed by Strattis and Aristophanes (Athen. p. 551).

Santŏnes or **Santŏni.** A powerful people in Gallia Aquitanica, dwelling on the coast of the ocean, north of the Garumna (Garonne). Under the Romans they were a free people. Their chief town was Mediolanum, afterwards Santones (Saintes) (Caes. *B. G.* i. 10).

Santra. A Roman writer on grammar and literature of the first century B.C. (Suet. *Gramm.* 14). Mercklin (*Phil.* iii. 344) thinks him an African.

Saocŏras (Σαόκορας). A river of Mesopotamia emptying into the Euphrates (Ptol. v. 18). It has not been satisfactorily identified.

Sapa (ἕψημα). The must of new wine, boiled down and used for strengthening other wine. See VINUM.

Sapaei (Σαπαῖοι). A people in Thrace, dwelling on Mount Pangaeus, between Lake Bistonis and the coast (Herod. vii. 110).

Sapaudia. A district in Gaul south of Lake Geneva (Ammian. Marc. xv. 11). Its name is the origin of the modern Savoy.

Saphar (Σάφαρ), **Sapphar** (Σάπφαρ), and **Taphar** (Τάφαρον). Now Dhafar; a city of Arabia on the southern coast of Arabia Felix. It was the capital of the Homeritae to whom the Sapharitae belonged (Ptol. vi. 6, 25).

Sapis. Now the Savio. A small river in Gallia Cisalpina, rising in the Apennines, and flowing into the Adriatic south of Ravenna, betweer the Po and the Aternus (Lucan, ii. 406).

Sapo (σάπων). A Keltic word, the original of our "soap," though it denoted not a detergent, but a sort of pomade used for colouring the hair a light brown. It was made with goat's tallow and ashes, and was sold in balls, in which form it was imported by the Romans from Germany and Gaul, and used to bleach the hair (Pliny, *H. N.* xviii. 191; Mart. viii. 33, 20; xiv. 26); Beckmann, *History of Inventions*, ii. p. 92 (London, 1846); and Blümner, *Technologie*, i. 161.

Sapor. See PERSIA.

Sapphire. See GEMMA.

Sappho (Σαπφώ; Aeolic, Ψάπφα). One of the two great leaders of the Aeolian school of lyric poetry, Alcaeus being the other. She was a native of Mitylené, or, as some said, of Eresos in Lesbos, and flourished towards the end of the seventh century B.C. Her father's name was Scamandronymus, who died when she was only six years old. She had three brothers, Charaxus, Larichus, and Eurigius. Charaxus was violently upbraided by his sister in a poem, because he became so enamoured of the courtesan Rhodopis at Naucratis in Egypt as to ransom her from slavery at an immense price. Sappho was contemporary with Alcaeus, Stesichorus, and Pittacus. That she was not only contemporary, but lived in friendly intercourse, with Alcaeus is shown by existing fragments of the poetry of both. Of the events of her life we have no other information than an obscure allusion in the Parian Marble and in Ovid (*Her.* xv. 51) to her flight from Mitylené to Sicily to escape some un-

Sappho. (From the painting by Alma-Tadema.)

known danger, between B.C. 604 and 592; and the common story that being in love with Phaon, and finding her love unrequited, she leaped down from the Leucadian Rock. This story, however, seems to have been an invention of later times. The name of Phaon does not occur in one of Sappho's fragments, and there is no evidence that he was mentioned in her poems. As for the leap from the Leucadian Rock, it is a mere metaphor, taken from an expiatory rite connected with the worship of Apollo, which seems to have been a frequent poetical image. At Mitylenê Sappho appears to have been the leader of a feminine literary set, most of the members of which were her pupils in poetry, fashion, and gallantry, so that from this association later writers have attempted to prove that the moral character of Sappho was not free from all reproach; and it is difficult to read the fragments which remain of her verse without being forced to come to the conclusion that a woman who could write such poetry could not be the pure woman that her modern apologists would have her. (See the defence of Sappho by Welcker [1816] and the various papers in the *Rheinisches Museum* for 1857–58.) Of her poetical genius, however, there cannot be a question. The ancient writers agree in expressing the most unbounded admiration for the passion, sincerity, and grace of her poetry. Already in her own age the recitation of one of her poems so affected Solon that he expressed an earnest desire to learn it before he died. Her lyric poems formed nine books, but of these only fragments have come down to us. The most important is a splendid ode to Aphroditê, of which we perhaps possess the whole. The best editions of the fragments is by Neue (Berlin, 1827), and that in Bergk's *Poet. Lyrici Graeci*, vol. iii. (4th ed. 1882). The fragments are all collected and translated into English by Wharton with a full bibliography in his *Sappho* (Chicago, 1895). See Arnold, *Sappho* (Berlin, 1871); Schöne, *Untersuchungen über das Leben der Sappho* (Leipzig, 1867); and Poestion, *Griechische Dichterinnen* (Vienna, 1876). There is a metrical translation of the fragments by Gasby-Smith (Washington, 1891).

Saraballa (Σαράβαλλα) and **Sarabāra** (Σαράβαρα). A name given to the loose trousers worn by the Asiatics and also by the Northern peoples. See BRACAE.

Sarancae, Sarangae (Σαράγγαι). A people of Sogdiana (Herod. iii. 93).

Sarāpis. See SERAPIS.

Sarāpis (σάραπις). A tunic whose use was restricted to the kings of Persia. It was of a purplish colour with a stripe of white down the front (Plaut. *Poen.* v. 5, 33).

Sarăvus. Now the Saar; a river of Gaul flowing into the Mosella on the right (Auson. *Mosell.* 367).

Sarcĭna. A pack or bundle, especially the "kit" of a Roman soldier carried by him on the march and comprising his arms, clothing, and rations (Caes. *B. G.* i. 24).

Sarcinātor. See SARTOR.

Sarcinātrix (ἀκέστρια). The feminine of *sarcinator*. See SARTOR.

Sarcophăgus (σαρκοφάγος). Literally, "flesh-devouring." A name given to a kind of limestone quarried at Assos in Troas, and remarkable for possessing the peculiar power of consuming or eating away the flesh and bones, with the exception of the teeth, of a body enclosed within it, in the short period of forty days (Pliny, *H. N.* xxxvi. 27). On account of this property it was extensively employed for making coffins, when the corpse was buried entire without burning; and

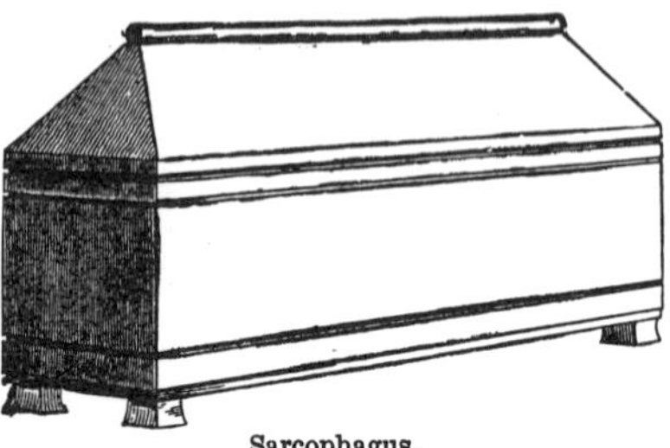

Sarcophagus.

thence the term came to be used in a general sense for any kind of coffin or tomb, without regard to the materials of which it was made (Juv. x. 172). See SEPULCRUM.

Sarcŭlum and **Sarcŭlus** (σκαλίς). A light hoe, smaller than the *ligo* (q. v.), used in weeding gardens, etc. (Pliny, *H. N.* xix. 33).

Sarculum. (Roman bas-relief.)

Sardanapālus (Σαρδανάπαλος). The last king who reigned over the Assyrian Empire of Nineveh. The account given of him by Ctesias asserts that he passed his time in his palace unseen by any of his subjects, dressed in woman's apparel, and surrounded by concubines. At length Arbaces, satrap of Media, and Beletys, the noblest of the Chaldaean priests, resolved to renounce allegiance to such a monarch, and advanced at the head of a formidable army against Nineveh. But all of a sudden the effeminate prince threw off his luxurious habits and appeared an undaunted warrior. Placing himself at the head of his troops, he twice defeated the rebels, but was at length worsted and obliged to shut himself up in Nineveh. Here he sustained a siege for two years, until at length, finding it impossible to hold out any longer, he collected all his treasures, wives, and concubines, and placing them on an immense pile which he had constructed, set it on fire, and thus destroyed both himself and them. The enemies then obtained possession of the city. This is the account of Ctesias, which has been preserved by Diodorus Siculus and which has been followed by most subsequent writers and chronologists (see Diod. ii. 21; Syncell. p. 359; August. *C. D.* xviii. 21), and has been taken as the subject of a very spirited dramatic fragment by Lord Byron entitled *Sardanapalus*. The death of Sardanapalus and the fall of the Assyrian Empire were placed B.C. 876. Modern writers however have shown that the whole narrative of Ctesias is mythical, and must not be received as genuine history. It is contradicted by the statements in Herodotus and the Christian writers. Sardanapalus is to be identified with the King Ashurbanipal, of whom many cuneiform records survive, and who made two successful expeditions against Egypt

(B.C. 670–650); but was defeated in B.C. 646, when Cyaxares, King of Media, and the governor of Babylon took Nineveh and destroyed it, Sardanapalus perishing in the flames. See Bezold's *Catalogue of the Cuneiform Tablets in the Kouyunjik Collection in the British Museum*, 3 vols. (1889–93); and the article ASSYRIA.

Sardemisus. A branch of Mount Taurus on the borders of Pisidia and Pamphylia, as far as Phaselis in Lycia (Pliny, *H. N.* v. 96).

Sardes. See SARDIS.

Sardi. See SARDINIA.

Sardinia (ἡ Σαρδώ or Σαρδών; later Σαρδανία or Σαρδηνία). Sardinia, a large island in the Mediterranean, is in the shape of a parallelogram, upwards of 140 miles in length from north to south, with an average breadth of 60. It was regarded by the ancients as the largest of the Mediterranean islands, and this opinion, though usually considered an error, is now found to be correct; since it appears by actual measurement that Sardinia is a little larger than Sicily. Sardinia lies in almost a central position between Spain, Gaul, Italy, and Africa. A chain of mountains runs along the whole of the eastern side of the island from north to south, occupying about one third of its surface. These mountains were called by the ancients Insani Montes, a name which they probably derived from their wild and savage appearance, and from their being the haunt of numerous robbers. Sardinia was very fertile, but was not extensively cultivated, in consequence of the uncivilized character of its inhabitants. Still the plains in the western and southern parts of the island produced a great quantity of corn, of which much was exported to Rome every year. Among the products of the island one of the most celebrated was the *Sardonica herba*, a poisonous plant, which was said to produce fatal convulsions in the person who ate of it. These convulsions agitated and distorted the mouth so that the person appeared to laugh, though in excruciating pain; hence the well-known *risus Sardonicus* (Σαρδώνιος γέλως, see Suidas, s. h. v.). Sardinia contained a large quantity of the precious metals, especially silver, the mines of which were worked in antiquity to a great extent. There were likewise numerous mineral springs; and large quantities of salt were manufactured on the western and southern coasts. The Greeks called the island ICHNŪSA (Ἰχνοῦσα), from its shape, which suggested a footprint, and SANDALIŌTIS as resembling a sandal (Pausan. x. 17, 2; Sil. Ital. xii. 358; Pliny, *H. N.* iii. 85).

The population of Sardinia was of a very mixed kind. To what race the original inhabitants belonged we are not informed; but it appears that Phœnicians, Tyrrhenians, and Carthaginians settled in the island at different periods. The Greeks are also said to have planted colonies in the island, but this account is very suspicious. Sardinia was known to the Greeks as early as B.C. 500, since we find that Histiaeus of Miletus promised Darius that he would render the island of Sardo tributary to his power. It was conquered by the Carthaginians at an early period, and continued in their possession until the end of the First Punic War. Shortly after this event the Romans availed themselves of the dangerous war which the Carthaginians were carrying on against their mercenaries in Africa to take possession of Sardinia, B.C. 238. It was now formed into a Roman province under the government of a praetor; but a large portion of it was only nominally subject to the Romans; and it was not till after many years and numerous revolts that the inhabitants submitted to the Roman dominion. Sardinia continued to belong to the Roman Empire till the fifth century, when it was taken possession of by the Vandals. See La Marmora, *Voyage en Sardaigne*, 5 vols. (2d ed. Paris, 1837–57); Edwardes, *Sardinia and the Sardes* (London, 1889); and the history by Manno, 4 vols. (Turin, 1825, and Florence, 1858).

Sardīs or **Sardes** (αἱ Σάρδεις, Ion. Σάρδιες, contracted Σάρδῑς). One of the most ancient and famous cities of Asia Minor, and the capital of the great Lydian monarchy, stood on the southern edge of the rich valley of the Hermus, at the northern foot of Mount Tmolus, on the little river Pactolus, 30 stadia (three geographical miles) south of the junction of that river with the Hermus (Herod. v. 101). On a lofty precipitous rock, forming an outpost of the range of Tmolus, was the almost impregnable citadel, which some suppose to be the Hydé of Homer, who, though he never mentions the Lydians or Sardis by name, speaks of Mount

Valley of the Hermus with Acropolis of Sardis.

Tmolus and the Lake of Gyges (*Il.* xx. 385). The erection of this citadel was ascribed to Meles, an ancient king of Lydia. It was surrounded by a triple wall, and contained the palace and treasury of the Lydian kings. At the downfall of the Lydian Empire, it resisted all the attacks of Cyrus, and was only taken by surprise. The story is told by Herodotus, who relates other legends of the fortress. The rest of the city, which stood in the plain on both sides of the Pactolus, was very slightly built, and was repeatedly burned down, first by

Coin of Sardis.

the Cimmerian Gauls in the seventh century B.C., then by the Greeks in the great Ionic revolt, and again, in part at least, by Antiochus the Great (B.C. 215); but on each occasion it was restored. Under the Persian and Greco-Syrian Empires, it was the residence of the satrap of Lydia. The rise of Pergamum greatly diminished its importance; but under the Romans it was still a considerable city, and the seat of a *conventus iuridicus* (Pliny, *H. N.* v. 111). In the reign of Tiberius, it was almost entirely destroyed by an earthquake, but was restored by the aid of that emperor (Tac. *Ann.* ii. 47). It was one of the seven Christian Churches of the province of Asia. In 1402 it was totally demolished by Tamerlane; but the triple wall of its acropolis can still be traced, and there are remains of the temple of Cybelé, a theatre, the stadium, and other structures, together with some vestiges of the necropolis, four miles distant from the city across the river Hermus. The site of the city is still called Sart. See LYDIA.

Sardōum Maré or **Sardonĭcum Maré** (τὸ Σαρδῷον πέλαγος). That part of the Mediterranean Sea which lies to the west and south of the island of Sardinia (Herod. i. 166; Pliny, *H. N.* iii. 75).

Sarissa (σάρισσα). A long lance used by the Macedonian hoplites for thrusting, and by the light cavalry. In the time of Philip and Alexander the Great it was eighteen feet in length, but was afterwards reduced to fourteen feet. Because of this weapon, the light cavalry were called σαρισσοφόροι. See Livy, ix. 19; xxxviii. 7; Polyb. xviii. 12; and the articles ARMA; EXERCITUS; PHALANX.

Alexander with Sarissa. (Pompeian mosaic.)

Sarmătae (Σαρμάται) or **Sauromătae** (Σαυρομάται). A people of Asia, dwelling on the northeast of the Palus Maeotis (Sea of Azov), east of the river Tanaïs (Don), which separated them from the Scythians of Europe. See SARMATIA.

Sarmatia (Σαρματία). The eastern part of Poland and southern part of Russia in Europe. A name first used by Mela for the part of northern Europe and Asia extending from the Vistula (Wisla) and the SARMATĬCI MONTES on the west, which divided it from Germany, to the Rha (Volga) on the east, which divided it from Scythia; bounded on the southwest and south by the rivers Ister (Danube), Tibiscus (Theiss), and Tyras (Dniester), which divided it from Pannonia and Dacia, and, farther, by the Euxine, and beyond it by Mount Caucasus, which divided it from Colchis, Iberia, and Albania; and extending on the north as far as the Baltic and the unknown regions of northern Europe. The people from whom the name of Sarmatia was derived inhabited only a small portion of the country. The greater part of it was peopled by Scythian tribes; but some of the inhabitants of its western part seem to have been of German origin, as the Venedi on the Baltic, and Iazyges, Rhoxolani, and Hamaxobii in southern Russia; the chief of the other tribes west of the Tanaïs were the Alauni or Alani Scythae, a Scythian people who came out of Asia and settled in the central part of Russia. The whole country was divided by the river Tanaïs (Don) into two parts, called respectively SARMATIA EUROPAEA and SARMATIA ASIATICA; but it should be observed that, according to the modern division of the continent, the whole of Sarmatia belongs to Europe. It should also be noticed that the Chersonesus Taurica (Crimea), though falling within the specified limits, was not considered as a part of Sarmatia, but as a separate country.

In a general way the name Sarmatia is often used very indefinitely of the whole of northeastern Europe. The historical sources of our knowledge of Sarmatia in ancient times are collected and discussed by Kalina, *De Fontibus*, etc. (1872).

Sarmatĭcae Portae (Σαρματικαὶ Πύλαι). The pass of Dariel. The central pass of the Caucasus, leading from Iberia to Sarmatia. It was also called Caucasiae Portae. See CAUCASUS.

Sarmatĭci Montes (τὰ Σαρματικὰ ὄρη). A range of mountains in Central Europe, extending from the sources of the Vistula to the Danube, between Germany on the west and Sarmatia on the east. They form a part of the Carpathian range.

Sarmatĭcus Oceănus (Σαρματικὸς Ὠκεανός) and PONTUS, SARMATĬCUM MARÉ. The Baltic. A great sea, washing the northern coast of European Sarmatia. The same name is sometimes given by the Roman poets to the Black Sea (Ovid, *Pont.* iv. 10, 38).

Sarmizegethūsa. The chief town of Dacia, near the modern Vachely or Gradischte, on the river Sargetia (Stral). It was the residence of the Dacian kings, and after Trajan's conquest of the country was made a Roman colony (Dio Cass. lv. 23).

Sarnus. Now the Sarno; a river in Campania, flowing by Nuceria, and falling into the Sinus Puteolanus near Pompeii (Strabo, p. 247).

Saron (Σάρων). The Sharon of the Old Testament; a plain in Palestine extending along the coast of Joppa towards Caesarea.

Saronĭcus Sinus (Σαρωνικὸς Κόλπος). The Gulf of Aegina. A bay of the Aegaean Sea lying between Attica and Argolis, and commencing between the promontory of Sunium in Attica and that of Scyllaeum in Argolis. It contains the islands of Aegina and Salamis.

Sarpēdon (Σαρπήδων). (1) The son of Zeus and Europa, and brother of Minos and Rhadamanthus. Being involved in a quarrel with Minos about Miletus, he took refuge with Cilix, whom he assisted against the Lycians. He afterwards became king of the Lycians, and Zeus granted him the privilege of living three generations (Herod. i. 173; Apollod. iii. 1, 2). (2) Son of Zeus and Laodamia, or, according to others, of Evander and Deïdamia, and a brother of Clarus and Themon. He was a Lycian prince, and a grandson of the preceding. In the Trojan War he was an ally of the Trojans, and distinguished himself by his valour, but was slain by Patroclus (*Il.* v. 475; xii. 292; xvi. 480). Apollo, by the command of Zeus, cleansed Sarpedon's body from blood and dust, covered it with ambrosia, and gave it to Sleep and Death to carry into Lycia, there to be honourably buried (*Il.* xvi. 667).

Sarpedonium Promontorium (ἡ Σαρπηδονίη ἄκρα). A promontory of Thrace, between the mouths of the rivers Melus and Erginus, opposite the island of Imbros (Herod. vii. 58).

Sarrācum. A wagon or cart used in ancient Italy, and resembling the *plaustrum* (q. v.). It

Supposed form of Sarracum. (Herculanean painting.)

was used for heavy carting, especially by farmers (Cic. *ap.* Quint. viii. 3. 21).

Sars. The Sar; a river on the western coast of Spain (Mela, iii. 1).

Sarsĭna. Now Sarsina; an ancient town of Umbria, on the river Sapis, southwest of Ariminum, and subsequently a Roman municipium, celebrated as the birthplace of the comic poet Plautus.

Sarta (Σάρτη). Now Sykia; a town on the eastern coast of the Sithonian promontory of Chalcidicé (Herod. vii. 122).

Sartāgo (τήγανον). The name of a kitchen utensil, usually translated "frying-pan" (Juv. x. 64).

Sartago. (Naples Museum.)

Sartor and **Sarcinātor** (ἀκεστής). A tailor; but not in the modern sense of the word, as ancient garments did not need to be cut out and fitted. The word, therefore, means one who patches and repairs clothes (Alciphr. *Epist.* iii. 27; Plaut. *Aul.* iii. 5, 41).

Sarus (Σάρος). Now Seihan; a considerable river in the southeast of Asia Minor. Rising in the Anti-Taurus, in the centre of Cappadocia, it flows south past Comana to the borders of Cilicia, where it receives a western branch that has run nearly parallel to it; and thence, flowing through Cilicia Campestris in a winding course, it falls into the sea a little east of the mouth of the Cydnus and southeast of Tarsus (Xen. *Anab.* i. 4, 1).

Saso or **Sasōnis Insŭla.** Now Saseno, Sassono, Sassa. A small rocky island off the coast of Illyria, north of the Acroceraunian promontory, much frequented by pirates (Pliny, *H. N.* iii. 152).

Saspīres or **Sapīres** (Σάσπειρες, Σάπειρες). A Scythian people in Asia, south of Colchis and north of Media, according to Herodotus (i. 104; iv. 37); but placed by Apollonius Rhodius (ii. 397) on the shores of the Euxine.

Sassanĭdae. The name of a Persian dynasty that reigned from A.D. 226 to 651. See PERSIA.

Sassŭla. A town in Latium, belonging to the territory of Tibur (Livy, vii. 19).

Satăla (τὰ Σάταλα and ἡ Σάταλα). (1) A town in the northeast of Armenia Minor, important as the key of the mountain passes into Pontus. It stood at the junction of four roads leading to places on the Euxine, a little north of the Euphrates, in a valley surrounded by mountains, 325 Roman miles from Caesarea in Cappadocia, and 135 from Trapezus. (2) A town in Lydia near the Hermus.

Satchel. See BULGA; PERA.

Saticŭla. A town of Samnium, situated upon a mountain on the frontiers of Campania (Livy, ix. 21, 22).

Satĭra (earlier form *satura*, from *satur*). A name which the Romans applied to a species of literature which they believed peculiarly their own (*Graecis intacti carminis*, Hor. *S.* i. 10, 66; *satura quidem tota nostra est*, Quint. x. 1, 93). The names of all other kinds of poetry indicate their Greek origin. It is probable that *satura* originally expressed the idea of fulness, abundance, which by special application was extended to mean variety, miscellany, promiscuity, without order. This secondary meaning occurs occasionally in all periods of the literature in the phrase *per saturam* or *in saturam: Sei quid in saturam feretur* (*Lex Repetund.* 72, *C. I. L.* i. p. 62); *per saturam aedilem factum* (Lucil. 1, 18 M); *non secundum edicti perpetui ordinationem, sed passim et quasi per saturam collectum, et utile cum inutilibus mixtum* (Justin. Praef. Dig. p. xv.). The term *satura* was applied to a statute with separate provisions, a bill with "riders" (Fest. 314 M; Gloss. Philox.); to a kind of poetry treating of various subjects (Paulus, *Excerpt.* 315 M); to an intermingling of prose and verse (Quint. x. 1, 95); to a mixture of dried grapes, pearled barley and nuts, sprinkled with a preparation of wine (*mulsum*); to a kind of sausage (Varro *ap.* Diom. p. 486 K); and to a dish of various kinds of fruit offered to Ceres (Acro, on Hor. *S.* 1, 1). It is also mentioned by the grammarians as coming from *satyri* (Diom. 485 K). The idea of medley pervades the entire use of the word in the literature, and fittingly describes one of the chief characteristics of the satura in the various stages of development.

Keller and others ignore this, and meet with many difficulties in attempting to connect the dramatic satura with σάτυροι, satyrs, and the literary satura with σάτυροι, the works of a certain Timon of Phlius. Mommsen and Ribbeck would derive *satura* from *satur*, but explain the latter as coming from σάτυροι in a very roundabout way.

According to Livy's condensed and somewhat confused account of the old dramatic satura (vii. 2), it would seem that the Romans were indebted to Etruria for certain of its elements. At the celebration of the harvest-home and other rural festivals, the light-hearted, merry people of Latium had long been accustomed to the jovial banter of the Fescennine verses, an entertainment consisting of dialogues of coarse jokes and personal abuse in metrical form, perhaps enlivened by the exhilarating tones of the pipe, or by the beating of time with the feet. In B.C. 364 the magistrates invited a band of Etrurian actors to Rome in the hope of staying the ravages of a terrible pestilence. These actors danced a sort of pantomime to the accompaniment of regularly composed music, and so pleased the people with their performance that the Roman youths — the same ones, no doubt, whose quick wit and dramatic power had made them the leaders in the merriment of their native entertainments — began to imitate the Etruscan actors and to combine the elements of the musical pantomime with the metrical dialogues of the Fescennine raillery, to which they applied the name *satura*, "medley," from its composite nature. (Cf. Ital. *farsa*, Fr. *farce*, Arabic *Quassîde* as applied to poetry, and Juvenal's term *farrago* for his Satires.) As the *satura* developed under the control of the Roman youths and the acting became more and more an art, it finally passed into the hands of professional actors, and the young Romans contented themselves with the less exacting performances of afterplays (*exodia*), to which the Atellanae also were reduced after the introduction of the regular drama. Livy's account covers a wide sweep in the development of the native drama.

If, as Mommsen and Wilamowitz (*Hermes*, ix. 331) maintain, the *fabula Atellana*, with its stock characters and rudimentary plot, developed in Latium long before the introduction of the regular drama under Greek influence, then the old dramatic satura was the intermediate step in the growth of the native Italian drama. As the *Versus Fescennini* were superseded by the satura as a dramatic entertainment, but lived on in the scurrilous verses of the marriage celebration and triumphal songs; so the satura, supplanted by the *fabula Atellana* and the regular drama, passed into that branch of poetry known as the literary satire.

Not a few recent scholars have questioned the very existence of an early dramatic satura, and, with Leo and Hendrickson, have regarded it a mere fiction of Livy in his attempt to construct for Roman literature what he learned from Aristotle (*Poet.* 4–5) to have existed in Greece. Leo attempts to prove it a fictitious parallel to the Greek satyr-drama, and Hendrickson to the old Attic comedy. To agree with them, one must believe that the Roman genius was unequal to the task of perfecting the native drama beyond the stage of the rude Fescennine verses, though we know that it sprang up and thrived independently in various parts of Greece and under various conditions. The chief reason for questioning the account of Livy—repeated with slight additions by Valerius Maximus (xi. 4, 4)—is the resemblance to Aristotle's description of the origin of comedy. The obscure reference in Euanthius, *De Com.* (ante med.) to satire as *alind genus fabulae* and *quod genus comoediae* shows that the dramatic satura was in his time a mere name, and its place in the growth of literature forgotten.

It is a fair inference from Livy (vii. 2, 8), that Andronicus, *qui ab saturis ausus est primus argumento fabulum serere*, had been in the habit of writing saturae before he turned to the regular drama; and in all probability the satura of Naevius, mentioned by Festus, 257 (M), is one of the last examples of the old dramatic satura rather than the beginning of the new literary satire. The conservative spirit of Naevius, his plebeian sympathies, and his adherence to the old Saturnian verse, in which the early saturae were probably written (the verse from Naevius's satura is apparently Saturnian), render this all the more probable.

With Ennius, an originator in so many lines, satura took on a new form. The success of the new drama with regular plot killed the demand for the old dramatic medley. The new plays, however, were moulded on the type of the New Attic Comedy, the comedy of manners, and gave little opportunity for the display of satire and ridicule which were so characteristic a part of the Roman genius, and which formerly found free play in the old-time burlesques. Ennius, therefore, remodelled the old satura, retaining the name, the spirit, and the essential features. The whole body of literary satire exhibits in varying degrees certain definite characteristics. The language does not rise to the height of the other styles of poetry; Horace speaks of his Satires as *sermones*, "conversations," and his muse as *pedestris*. It exhibits everywhere the peculiarities of the *sermo familiaris*. There is a strong tendency to dramatic form. Dialogue is an important feature in all satura down to Juvenal, and traces occur even in his bold declamatory style. Unusual laxity in structural arrangement, easy change of topic, and variety of metres are noticeable in the early writers. In some authors—e. g. Varro, Petronius, and Seneca—a mixture of prose and verse appears; and in all there is a great deal of obscenity, characteristic of its peculiar origin. The satirical spirit, in the modern sense of the word, varies in different authors according to their natural disposition, and to their political, social, and moral environment. The Romans recognized two kinds of satire: *Satira dicitur carmen apud Romanos nunc quidem maledictum et ad carpenda hominum vitia archeae comoediae charactere compositum, quale scripserunt Lucilius et Horatius et Persius, et olim carmen quod ex variis poematibus constabat satira vocabatur, quale scripserunt Pacuvius et Ennius*, Diom. (Suet.), i. 485 (K). This classification has been accepted too literally by modern scholars. Ennius was preëminently an epic poet, tragedian, and scholar, but the subjects of some of his saturae, the Greek writers who influenced him (the Sillographi, etc.), and his own known rationalistic tendencies, assure us that there was at least subtle satire lurking in many of his poems, if there were not also open ridicule. He was more influential perhaps than any other writer in moulding Roman thought on Greek lines, in introducing Greek culture, in awakening scepticism in religion, and in dispelling superstition. It is more than probable that this was accomplished somewhat by the spirit of satire and ridicule in his poem *Epicharmus*, which apparently reduced the gods of mythology to the elements of nature, and in the rationalistic poem, *Euhemerus*, or *Sacra Historia*. The indecencies of Sotades were, no doubt, ridiculed in the *Sota;* and the only reason for supposing that the *Heduphagetica* was not a parody of epic grandeur on the subject of high living was that Ennius is said to have died of the gout. The *Scipio* can be shown to be a part of his saturae, and it is probable that the *Ambracia* celebrated the deeds of his patron Fulvius Nobilior in the east, as the Scipio did those of Africanus in Africa. All the minor poems were perhaps collected under the title *Saturae*, and formed four and perhaps six or more books. See ENNIUS.

Lucilius, a Roman knight of influence, living at a time of great social and political unrest, that of the Gracchi, narrowed the scope of satire and stamped it so deeply with the spirit of invective that he was sometimes spoken of as its very founder (Hor. *S.* i. 10, 48). His criticism of men and affairs, instead of being vindictive and personal, like the lampoons of the Greek iambic writers, was ethical and partisan in tone, and animated by the spirit of the Old Attic Comedy (Hor. *S.* i. 4, 6), or of the editorial page of the modern newspaper. His "Miscellanies" included the greatest variety of subjects: avarice, gluttony, literature, grammar, friendship, philosophy, religion, superstition, public men, a journey to Sicily, a country dinner, his mistress, contentment with his own lot, his fame, etc., and gave, no doubt, a faithful picture of his times. He employed fables, tales, and dialogue, as did Ennius before him, and spoke either in his own person or in the words of another, as best suited his purpose. We have but fragments of his thirty books, some 1100 in number, too brief to discover the "keen wit and great versatility," the "wonderful learning and freedom" attributed to him by ancient critics. He began writing in trochaic septenarii, essayed other metres, and finally decided upon hexameters, which comprised twenty-one out of the thirty books, and became the usual form for later satire. See LUCILIUS.

The next important writer of saturae was Marcus Terentius Varro, a man of good social standing, prominent in affairs of state, a prolific writer, and the greatest of Roman scholars (Quintil. x. 1, 95). He wrote 150 books of satire like those of Ennius in form, except that prose was intermingled with a great variety of metres—more than twenty different kinds of verse occur in the 591 fragments. He was an old-fashioned man, with a strong sense of humour and real poetic genius. Thoroughly familiar with the spirit of the good old times and conscious of the rapid degeneration about him, he attempted to attract and instruct the young and unlearned with his mass of wise and good-humoured sketches, which treat of almost every conceivable subject, from philosophy down to the common-places of daily life (Cic. *Acad.* i. 2, 8). He imitated Menippus, the Cynic philosopher and satirist, whose style and manner may be seen in the works of Lucian; and no doubt the same gentle irony and mild satire pervaded the *Saturae Menippeae.* See VARRO.

Horace admired the rough vigour and caustic wit of Lucilius's satires, and made them the models of his own; but his humble social position and his former republican alliance prevented him from attacking, in a direct personal way, the evils of society and the State. The less personal subjects of Lucilius's verse—avarice, luxury, philosophy, superstition, the follies of men, etc.—he reviewed in a spirit of gentle irony or mild satire. It would appear from some of his satires—so close is the resemblance, even in details—that the only merit he claimed in his earlier poems was to reproduce his master's thoughts in a more polished and refined style. See HORATIUS.

Persius, a young Stoic of noble birth and high ideals, wrote six satires in strained and obscure language. On every page there are reminiscences of Horace, though there was little in common between the circumspect man of society and the callow, unsophisticated philosopher. In form and spirit his satires conform to the standard type. See PERSIUS.

The *Satira* of Petronius resembles Varro's in the medley of prose and various kinds of verse, but it is in reality a sort of satirical romance written in a masterly manner. Only about 100 pages from the fifteenth and sixteenth books remain, full of realistic pictures of society, literary criticism, ghost stories, anecdotes, adventures, all rich in wit and humour, but exceedingly obscene. The fine biographical details are, of course, all fiction. See PETRONIUS.

Juvenal is the last of the well-known satirists whose works are extant, and his writings exhibit in a more limited degree than any others the characteristic features of the literary satire. Dialogue has almost vanished; the dramatic element is nearly supplanted by the rhetorical; fables, tales, and anecdotes are lacking; the personal, autobiographical feature is not to be found; the peculiarities of the *sermo familiaris* are chiefly limited to the choice of words; the thought often rises to the heights of true poetry; the structure of the individual satires shows an advance in the more artistic relation of unity and variety; hexameter is the only metre. On the other hand, the remaining characteristics are unusually intensified. The spirit of raillery and mild satire of the preceding poets has become bitter invective. The inordinate amount of obscenity is somewhat mitigated in effect by the tone of denunciation, but he so parades this in some satires that we question whether he was not really infatuated by it. His pictures of later Rome are drawn in the terribly realistic manner of Hogarth. See IUVENALIS.

The history of satire presents a regular and organic structural development, while the spirit varies with the character of the author and his environment. Its scope is narrowed in its descent from writer to writer, but broadened when its growth is considered by periods. At all times it was one of the most effective instruments of reform; and our knowledge of Roman civilization would be vastly enriched if we had the works of all the twenty-eight or thirty writers who we know cultivated this branch of literature.

Some of the more important articles on the general subject of satire are: Casaubon, *De Satyr. Graec. Poesi et Rom. Sat.* (Paris, 1605, and Halle, 1774); Scheibe, *De Sat. Rom. Orig. et Progressu* (Zittau, 1849); O. Jahn, *Satura*, in *Hermes*, 2, p. 225; Nettleship, *The Roman Satura* (Oxford, 1878, reprinted in his *Lectures and Essays*, ii.); Grubel, *De Sat. Rom. Orig. et Progressu* (Posen, 1883); Keller,

Ueber d. Wort Satura, in *Philol.* 45, p. 389; Funck, *Satur u. die davon abgeleiteten Wörter* (Kiel, 1888); ibid., Wölfflin's *Archiv*, v. p. 32; Leo, *Varro und die Satira*, in *Hermes*, 24, p. 67; Hendrickson, *The Dramatic Satura and the Old Comedy at Rome*, in the *American Journal of Philology*, xv. 1, p. 1.

Satisdatio. See ACTIO in the Appendix.

Satniŏīs (Σατνιόεις). Now Tuzla; a river in the southern part of the Troad, flowing into the Aegaean Sea (*Il.* vi. 34).

Satrae (Σάτραι). A Thracian people on the Strymon (Herod. vii. 110).

Satrĭcum. Now Casale di Conca; a town in Latium, near Antium (Livy, ii. 39).

Satŭra. See SATIRA.

Satŭrae Palus. Now Lago di Paola; a lake or marsh in Latium, formed by the river Nymphaeus, and near the promontory Circeium. See POMPTINAE PALUDES.

Saturium or **Saturēium.** Now Saturo; a town in the south of Italy, near Tarentum, celebrated for its horses (Hor. *Sat.* i. 6, 59).

Saturnalia. A Roman festival in honour of Saturnus (q. v.). It was held late in December at the end of the vintage and harvesting, and was in early times the prototype of the English Harvest Home and the American Thanksgiving Day. At all periods it was a season of absolute relaxation, of merriment, and even license. While it continued, no business could be transacted, the law courts were closed, the schools kept holiday, to commence a war was impious, and even to punish a malefactor involved pollution (Macrob. *Sat.* i. 10, 16; Pliny, *Epist.* viii. 7). Special indulgences were granted to the slaves of each domestic establishment; they were relieved from all ordinary toils, were permitted to wear the *pilleus*, the badge of freedom, received full license of speech, and partook of a banquet attired in the clothes of their masters, and were waited upon by them at table (Macrob. *Sat.* i. 7; Dio Cass. lx. 19; Athen. xiv. 44). All classes devoted themselves to feasting and mirth, presents were interchanged among friends, wax tapers (*cerei*) being the common offering of the more humble to their superiors, and crowds thronged the streets, shouting *Io Saturnalia!* (hence *clamare Saturnalia*), while sacrifices were offered with uncovered head, from a conviction that no ill-omened sight should interrupt the rites of such a happy day. Many of the peculiar customs of this festival exhibit a remarkable resemblance to the sports of our own Christmas and of the Italian Carnival. Thus on the Saturnalia public gambling was allowed by the aediles, just as in the days of our ancestors the most rigid were wont to countenance card-playing on Christmas-eve; the whole population threw off the toga, wore a loose gown, called *synthesis* (q. v.), and walked about with the *pilleus* on their heads, which reminds us of the dominos, the peaked caps, and other disguises worn by masques and mummers; the *cerei* were probably employed as the *moccoli* now are on the last night of the Carnival; and lastly, one of the amusements in private society was the election of a mock king (Tac. *Ann.* xiii. 15; Lucian, *Saturn.* 4), which at once calls to recollection the characteristic ceremony of Twelfth Night.

During the Republic, although the whole month of December was considered as dedicated to Saturn, only one day, the XIV. Kal. Ian., was set apart for the sacred rites of the divinity. When the month was lengthened by the addition of two days upon the adoption of the Julian Calendar, the Saturnalia fell on the XVI. Kal. Ian., which gave rise to confusion and mistakes among the more ignorant portion of the people. To obviate this inconvenience, and allay all religious scruples, Augustus enacted that three whole days, the 17th, 18th, and 19th of December, should in all time coming be hallowed, thus embracing both the old and new style (Macrob. i. 10). Under the Empire the merry-making lasted for seven days, and three different festivals were celebrated during this period. First came the Saturnalia proper, commencing on XVI. Kal. Dec., followed by the Opalia (from Ops, the wife of Saturnus), anciently coincident with the Saturnalia, on XIV. Kal. Ian.; these two together lasted for five days, and the sixth and seventh were occupied with the Sigillaria (Sen. *Epist.* xii. 3), so called from the little earthenware figures (*sigilla, oscilla*) exposed for sale at this season, and given as toys to children. See Marquardt, *Staatsverwaltung*, iii. 586 foll.; Preller, *Röm. Myth.* p. 413.

Saturnia. (1) An ancient name of Italy. (See ITALIA; SATURNUS.) (2) Now Saturnia, formerly called Aurinia; an ancient town of Etruria, said to have been founded by the Pelasgians, was situated in the territory of Caletra, on the road from Rome to Cosa, about twenty miles from the sea (Pliny, *H. N.* iii. 52). (3) See SATURNIUS.

Saturnii Versus. See SATURNIUS VERSUS.

Saturnīnus. (1) One of the Thirty Tyrants (q. v.). He was a general of Valerian, by whom he was much beloved. Disgusted by the debauchery of Gallienus, he accepted from the soldiers the title of emperor, but was put to death by the troops, who could not endure the sternness of his discipline (Trebell. Poll. *Trig. Tyr.* 22). (2) A native of Gaul and an able officer, appointed by Aurelian commander of the Eastern frontier, and proclaimed emperor at Alexandria during the reign of Probus, by whose soldiers he was eventually slain (Vopisc. *Saturn.*).

Saturnīnus. (1) L. APULĒIUS, a Roman who was quaestor in B.C. 104 and tribune of the people in B.C. 102. He was closely allied with Marius and his party, and was very popular with the commons. He became a candidate for the tribuneship for the second time in B.C. 100. At the same time Glaucia, who next to Saturninus was the greatest demagogue of the day, offered himself as a candidate for the praetorship, and Marius for the consulship. Marius and Glaucia carried their elections; but A. Nonius, a partisan of the aristocracy, was chosen tribune instead of Saturninus. Nonius, however, was murdered on the same evening by the emissaries of Glaucia and Saturninus; and early the following morning Saturninus was chosen to fill the vacancy. As soon as he had entered upon his tribunate, he brought forward an agrarian law, which led to the banishment of Metellus Numidicus, as is related elsewhere. (See METELLUS, 10.) Saturninus proposed other popular measures, such as a *lex frumentaria*, and a law for founding new colonies in Sicily, Achaia, and Macedonia. In the Comitia for the election of the magistrates for the following year, Saturninus obtained the tribunate for the third time, and along with him there was chosen a certain Equitius, a runaway slave, who pretended to be a son of Tiberius Gracchus. Glaucia was at the same time a candidate for the consulship; the two other candidates were M. Antonius and C. Memmius. The election of M. Antonius was certain, and the struggle lay between Glaucia and Memmius. As the latter seemed likely to carry his election, Saturninus and Glaucia hired some ruffians who murdered him openly in the comitia. This last act produced a complete reaction against Saturninus and his associates. The Senate declared them public enemies, and ordered the consuls to put them down by force. Marius was unwilling to act against his friends, but he had no alternative, and his backwardness was compensated by the zeal of others. Driven out of the Forum, Saturninus, Glaucia, and the quaestor Saufeius took refuge in the Capitol, but the partisans of the Senate cut off the pipes which supplied the Capitol with water. Unable to hold out any longer, they surrendered to Marius. The latter did all he could to save their lives: as soon as they descended from the Capitol, he placed them for security in the Curia Hostilia, but the mob pulled off the tiles of the Senate-House, and pelted them with the tiles till they died. The Senate gave their sanction to these proceedings by rewarding with the citizenship a slave of the name of Scaeva, who claimed the honour of having killed Saturninus. Nearly forty years after these events, the tribune T. Labienus accused an aged senator, Rabirius, of having been the murderer of Saturninus. See Rabirius.

(2) Claudius, a jurist from whose *Liber Singularis de Poenis Paganorum* there is a single excerpt in the Digest. He was praetor under Antoninus Pius. (3) Pompēius, a contemporary of the younger Pliny, is praised by the latter as a distinguished orator, historian, and poet. Several of Pliny's letters are addressed to him. (4) C. Sentius, one of the persons of distinguished rank who deserted Sex. Pompeius in B.C. 35, and passed over to Octavian. He was consul in 19, and was afterwards appointed to the government of Syria. Three sons of Saturninus accompanied him as legati to Syria, and were present with their father at the trial of Herod's sons at Berytus in B.C. 6. (5) Venulēius, a Roman jurist, is said to have been a pupil of Papinianus, and a *consiliarius* of Alexander Severus. There are seventy-one excerpts from his writings in the Digest.

Saturnius. That is, "son of Saturnus," a term used as a surname of Iupiter, Neptune, and Pluto. For the same reason the name of Saturnia is given both to Iuno and Vesta.

Saturnius Versus. "Saturnian verse." The earliest (native) verse of the ancient Italians, of which at the present time only fragments exist in the shape of religious songs and ritualistic formulas, is accentual rather than quantitative in its metrical character, and is hardly to be reduced to a definite system. The verse, however, in general (*numerus Italicus*) seems to be based upon a series of four *theses*, sometimes separate but usually combined in twos and threes. The following prayer to Mars (Cato, *R. R.* 141) is an example:

Márs páter té précor | quáesóque úti síes | vólens própitiús.

Of these early rhythms, the so-called "Saturnian verse" is the most regular, as it is the one of which we have the greatest number of existing examples. It consists of two parts, each containing three *theses*. As to its exact character there are three theories: (*a*) the Accentual Theory; (*b*) the Quantitative Theory; and (*c*) the Modified Accentual Theory.

(*a*) Accentual Theory.—This regards the Saturnian line as divided into two halves, the first having three *theses* and the second either three or two. If only two, the second half of the line usually has an introductory unaccented syllable (Anacrusis). The quantity of the syllables plays no part in the scansion of the verse. Examples are the following:

Quóius fórma virtútei ‖ parísuma fúit

and

Dábunt málum Metélli ‖ Naévió poétae.

(*b*) Quantitative Theory.—This regards the Saturnian as a trochaic senarius with Anacrusis and a caesura after the third *arsis* or (rarely) after the third *thesis*. Short syllables may be lengthened by the *ictus* or metrical accent, and hiatus is allowed everywhere, being most common in the caesura. Examples are the following:

Eorúm sectám sequóntur ‖ múlti mórtáles

and

Cornéliús Lucius ‖ Scípió Barbátus

and

Quoīus fórma virtutei ‖ parisumá fúit.

Scholars differ greatly in their explanation of the verse in applying the quantitative theory, some using protraction freely, others rejecting the *diastolé* or lengthening of short vowels. The former regard the normal number of feet in each hemistich as four, e. g.

Dabúnt malúm Metélli ‖ Naévió poétae—

thus assimilating this scheme to that of the *numerus Italicus* in general as described above.

(*c*) Modified Accentual Theory.—This regards the number of *theses* in the first hemistich as three, and that in the second hemistich as two, with the accent falling at the beginning of each line. The number of syllables in the first hemistich is normally seven, in the second six, admitting, however, an extra short syllable where the ordinary pronunciation would suppress or slur it. A final short vowel is elided; otherwise partial (semi-) hiatus is allowed, and at the caesura a full hiatus. After the first two feet there is an alternation between words accented on the first and those accented on the second syllable. Examples are:

Dábunt málum Metélli | Naévio poétae

and

Prima incédit Céreris | Prosérpina púer.

The name "Saturnian" is applied to the verse either because much used in the early harvest songs in honour of Saturn or from the general meaning of "ancient" attached to the adjective *Saturnius*. (Cf. Verg. *Ecl.* iv. 6; and Nettleship, *Lectures and Essays*, i. pp. 55-57). Bentley regarded the verse as Greek in its origin, but the general opinion now held makes it indigenous to Italy; Hermann viewing it as Etruscan rather than Italian, but with no good reason. It is, in fact, a measure that finds its counterpart in the early literature of other Indo-European peoples, in the Spanish epic of the *Cid*, and in the *Nibelungenlied;* while every one is familiar with Macaulay's identification of it with the nursery line—

The queen was in her parlour ‖ eating bread and honey.

The Saturnian verse was used by the poet Naevius in writing his epic on the Punic War (*Bellum Punicum*), and by Livius Andronicus in his Latin version of the *Odyssey*. See LIVIUS; NAEVIUS.

Reference may be made to the following works: Hermann, *Doctrina Metr.* iii. 9; Bernhardy, *Röm. Lit.* pp. 70 foll.; Klotz, *Altrömische Metrik* (1890); Lindsay, *The Latin Language*, pp. 128 (note), 132, 159 (1894); id. in the *American Journal of Philology*, vol. xiv.; Teuffel in *Jahn's Jahrbücher*, lxvii. pp. 281 foll.; Westphal, *Allgemeine Metrik*, pp. 251–256 (1865); Spengel in *Philologus*, xxiii. pp. 81–113; Bücheler in *Jahn's Jahrbücher*, lxxvii. p. 61; Streuber, *De Inscriptionibus Quae ad Numerum Saturnium Referuntur* (Zürich, 1845); Ritschl, *Saturniae Poeseos Reliquiae* (Bonn, 1854); Allen, *Early Latin*, pp. 12, 13 (1880); and Gildersleeve and Lodge, *Lat. Grammar*, pp. 462, 463 (1894). Weise in a treatise published at Quedlinburg (1839) tries to show traces of the Saturnian in Plautus. For the identity between the Saturnian and the Old German epic line, see the monograph by Bartsch (Leipzig, 1867).

Saturnus. A mythical king of Italy, to whom was ascribed the introduction of agriculture and the habits of civilized life in general. The name is connected with the verb *sero*, sup. *satum*. The

Bust of Saturnus. (Vatican.)

Romans invariably identified Saturnus with the Greek Cronos, and hence made the former the father of Iupiter, Neptune, Pluto, Iuno, etc. (see CRONOS); but there is, in reality, no resemblance between the attributes of the two deities, except that both were regarded as the most ancient divinities in their respective countries. The resemblance is much stronger between Demeter and Saturn, for all that the Greeks ascribe to their Demeter is ascribed by the Italians to Saturn. Saturnus, then, deriving his name from sowing, is called the introducer of civilization and social order, both of which are inseparably connected with agriculture. His reign is conceived for the same reason to have been the Golden Age of Italy, and more especially of the Aborigines, his subjects (Varro, *R. R.* iii. 1, 5). As agricultural industry is the source of wealth and plenty, his wife was Ops, the representative of plenty (Varro, *L. L.* v. 57). By a confusion of Saturn with Cronos and this with the word Χρόνος, he is also spoken of as the god of time (Cic. *N. D.* ii. 25, 64); and Curtius identifies him with the Sun god of the Phœnicians, i. e. Baal (iv. 3, 15).

The legend ran that the god came to Italy in the reign of Ianus, by whom he was hospitably received, and that he formed a settlement on the Capitoline Hill, which was hence called the Saturnian Hill. At the foot of that hill, on the road leading up to the Capitol, there stood in after-times the temple of Saturn. Saturn then taught the people agriculture, suppressed their savage mode of life, and introduced among them civilization and morality. The result was that the whole country was called Saturnia, or the land of plenty. Saturn was suddenly removed from earth to the abodes of the gods, whereupon Ianus erected an altar to him in the Forum. It is further related that Latium received its name (from *lateo*) from this disappearance of Saturn, who for the same reason was regarded by some as a divinity of the nether world. The statue of Saturnus was hollow and filled with oil, probably to denote the fertility of Latium in olives; in his hand he held a crooked pruning-knife, and his feet were surrounded with a woollen ribbon. In the pediment of the temple of Saturn were seen two figures resembling Tritons with horns, and whose lower extremities grew out of the ground; the temple itself was used as the treasury of the State, and many records also were deposited in it. On the Saturnalia or feast held in honour of Saturn at Rome, see SATURNALIA.

Satȳri (Σάτυροι) and Doric **Titȳri** (Τίτυροι). The name of a class of beings in Greek mythology, who are inseparably connected with the worship of Dionysus, and represent the luxuriant vital powers of Nature. They are commonly said to be the sons of Hermes and Iphthima, or of the Naïades. The Satyrs are represented with bristly hair, the nose blunt and somewhat turned upward, the ears pointed at the top, like those of animals, with two small horns growing out of the top of the forehead, with a tail like that of a horse or goat, and with teat-like protuberances (φῆρεα) on the neck. In works of art they are represented at different stages of life; the older ones were commonly called

Satyr's Head. (Glyptothek, Munich.)

Sileni, and the younger ones are termed Satyrisci. The Satyrs are always described as fond of wine (whence they often appear either with a cup or a *thyrsus* in their hand), and of every kind of sensual pleasure, whence they are seen sleeping, playing musical instruments, or engaged in voluptuous dances with nymphs. Vase-painters represent them as resembling also the Bacchantes and (rarely) Iris. They are dressed with the skins of animals, and wear wreaths of vine, ivy, or fir. Like all the gods dwelling in forests and fields, they were greatly dreaded by mortals. Later writers, especially the Roman poets, confound the Satyrs with the Italian Fauni, and accordingly represent them with larger horns and goats' feet, although originally they were quite distinct kinds of beings. They are also incorrectly identified with the Panes. See FAUNUS; PAN; SILENUS.

Satyric Drama. One of the three varieties of the Attic drama. Its origin may be traced back to Pratinas of Phlius (about B.C. 500). It is probable that, after settling in Athens, he adapted the old dithyramb with its chorus of Satyrs, which was customary in his native place, to the form of tragedy which had been recently invented in Athens. This new kind of drama met with so much approval and was so much developed by Pratinas himself as well as by his son Aristeas, by Choerilus, by Aeschylus, and the dramatists who succeeded him, that it became the custom to act a satyric drama after a set of three tragedies. The intensity of the preceding plays was thus relieved, while the chorus of Satyrs and Sileni, the companions of Dionysus, served to indicate the original connection between that divinity and the drama. The material for a satyric drama, like that for a tragedy, was taken from an epic or legendary story, and the action, which took place under an open sky, in a lonely wood, the haunt of the Satyrs, had generally an element of tragedy; but the characteristic solemnity and stateliness of tragedies was somewhat diminished, without in any way impairing the splendour of the tragic costume and the dignity of the heroes introduced. The amusing effect of the play did not depend so much on the action itself, as was the case in comedy, but rather on the relation of the chorus to that action. That relation was in keeping with the wanton, saucy, and insolent, and at the same time cowardly, nature of the Satyrs. The number of persons in the chorus is not known; probably there were either twelve or fifteen, as in tragedy. In accordance with the popular notions about the Satyrs, their costume consisted of the skin of a goat, deer, or panther, thrown over the naked body, and besides this a hideous mask and bristling hair. The dance of the chorus in the satyric drama was called σίκιννις or σίκιννον, and consisted of a fantastic kind of skipping and jumping. The only satyric play now extant is the *Cyclops* of Euripides (translated into English by Shelley), though the *Alcestis* of the same poet has some satyric features. The Romans did not imitate this kind of drama in their literature (Marius Victor, in *Gram. Lat.* vi. 82), although, like the Greeks, they composed amusing afterpieces following their serious plays. See Welcker, *Griech. Tragödie,* 1361; and EXODIUM.

Satyrĭcon or (better) **Satirĭcon.** See PETRONIUS.

Satȳrus (Σάτυρος). (1) A king of Bosporus, son of Spartacus I. He reigned B.C. 407 or 406–393. He maintained friendly relations with Athens. He was slain at the siege of Theudosia in 393, and was succeeded by his son Leucon. (2) A king of Bosporus, who was the eldest of the sons of Paerisades I., whom he succeeded in B.C. 311, but reigned only nine months. (3) A distinguished comic actor at Athens, who is said to have given instructions to Demosthenes in the art of giving full effect to his speeches by appropriate action. (See DEMOSTHENES.) (4) A distinguished Peripatetic philosopher and historian, who lived in the time of Ptolemy Philopator, if not later. He wrote a collection of biographies, among which were lives of Philip and Demosthenes, and which is frequently cited by ancient writers.

Sauconna. A late name of the Gallic river Arar, whence comes its modern name Saône (Amm. Marcel. xv. 11).

Saufēius. (1) GAIUS, a Roman quaestor, B.C. 100. He was a follower of L. Saturninus (q. v.), and, taking refuge with him in the Capitol, was slain with his leader (Cic. *Pro Rab.* 7). (2) LUCIUS, a Roman knight who was a friend of Atticus. His valuable property in Italy was confiscated by the triumvirs, but restored to him at the intercession of Atticus (Nepos, *Att.* 12).

Sauroctŏnos (σαυροκτόνος, "lizard slayer"). A special name of Apollo (q. v.) as represented in a famous statue by Praxiteles (Pliny, *H. N.* xxxiv. 19).

Sauromătae. See SARMATAE.

Sauromătes (Σαυρομάτης). The name of several kings of Bosporus who are known for the most part only from their coins, which are of the period from Augustus to Constantine.

Saverrio, P. SULPICIUS. (1) A Roman consul (B.C. 304) who waged war with the Samnites, and in whose consulship (B.C. 229) two new tribes—the Aniensis and Terentina—were formed (Livy, ix. 49; x. 9). (2) A son of the preceding, consul in B.C. 279 with P. Decius Mus in the war against Pyrrhus (Val. Max. ix. 1).

Savo. Now the Savone; a river in Campania, which flows into the sea south of Sinuessa.

Savus. Now the Save or Sau; a navigable tributary of the Danube, which rises in the Carnic Alps, forms first the boundary between Noricum and Italy, afterwards between Pannonia and Illyria, and falls into the Danube near Singidunum (Pliny, *H. N.* iii. 139).

Saxa, DECIDIUS. A native of Celtiberia, and originally one of Caesar's common soldiers (Caes. *B. C.* i. 66). He eventually accompanied Antony to the East, and was made by him governor of Syria. Here he was defeated by the younger Labienus and the Parthians, and was slain in the flight after the battle (B.C. 40) (Dio Cass. xlvii. 35; xlviii. 24).

Saxa, Q. VOCONIUS. A tribune of the plebs, B.C. 169, who proposed the *lex Voconia.* See VOCONIA LEX.

Saxa Rubra. See RUBRA SAXA.

Saxŏnes. A German people originally dwelling in the southern part of the Cimbria Chersonesus between the rivers Albis (Elbe) and Chalusus (Trave), in what is now Holstein. They are not mentioned in history before A.D. 282, when they are described as bold and skilful sailors, engaging in piratical raids upon the coast of Gaul (Eutrop. vii. 13). They afterwards headed a powerful league which took their name, and at last occupied the country between the Elbe, the Rhine, the Lippe, and the German Ocean (Ptol. ii. 11, 11) With the Jutes and Angles they invaded Britain in the fifth century A.D.

Saxum Quadrātum. A rock of volcanic formation, so called from the rectangular masses into which its native fissures divide themselves. The earlier buildings at Rome are made of this material—e. g. the so-called Mamertine Prison, the Cloaca Maxima, and the substructure of the Capitol (Livy, vi. 4, 12).

Saxum Sacrum. The rock on the Aventine Hill at Rome, near which Remus took the auspices. See Cic. *Dom.* 53, 136; and ROMULUS.

Scabbard. See VAGINA.

Scabellum. A small square stool with a single step or a single height. The word is a diminutive of *scamnum* (q. v.). Cf. Quint. i. 4, 12.

Scaeva, CASSIUS. A centurion in Caesar's army, who distinguished himself by his extraordinary feats of valor at the battle of Dyrrhachium (Suet. *Iul.* 68; Val. Max. iii. 2, 23).

Scaevŏla. The name of a distinguished family of the Mucian gens. (1) GAIUS MUCIUS SCAEVŎLA. When King Porsena was besieging Rome, G. Mucius went out of the city with the intention of killing him, but by mistake stabbed the king's secretary instead of Porsena himself. The king in his passion and alarm ordered him to be burned alive, upon which Mucius thrust his right hand into a fire which was already lighted for a sacrifice, and held it there without flinching. The king, amazed at his firmness, ordered him to be removed from the altar, and bade him go away free and uninjured. To make some return for his generous behaviour, Mucius told him that there were three hundred of the first youths of Rome who had agreed with one another to kill the king; that the lot fell on him to make the first attempt, and that the rest would do the same when their turn came. Porsena being alarmed for his life, which he could not secure against so many desperate men, made proposals of peace to the Romans, and evacuated the territory. Mucius received the name of Scaevola, or "left-handed," from the loss of his right hand (Livy, ii. 12 and 13). (2) P. MUCIUS SCAEVŎLA, tribune of the plebs in B.C. 141, praetor in 136, and consul in 133, the year in which Tib. Gracchus lost his life. In 131 he succeeded his brother Mucianus as Pontifex Maximus. Scaevola was distinguished for his knowledge of the *ius pontificium.* His fame as a lawyer is recorded by Cicero in several passages. (3) Q. MUCIUS SCAEVŎLA, the augur, married the daughter of C. Laelius, the friend of Scipio Africanus the younger. He was tribune of the plebs in B.C. 128, plebeian aedile in 125, and as praetor was governor of the province of Asia in 121, the year in which C. Gracchus lost his life. He was prosecuted after his return from his province for the offence of *repetundae,* in 120, by T. Albucius, but was acquitted. He was consul in 117. He lived at least to the tribunate of P. Sulpicius Rufus, 88. Cicero, who was born in 106, informs us that after he had put on the *toga virilis,* his father took him to Scaevola, who was then an old man, and that he kept as close to him as he could, in order to profit by his remarks. After his death Cicero became a hearer of Q. Mucius Scaevola, the Pontifex. The augur was distinguished for his knowledge of the law; but none of his writings are recorded. He is one of the speakers in the treatise *De Oratore,* in the *Laelius,* and in the *De Republica* (i. 12). (4) Q. MUCIUS SCAEVŎLA, Pontifex Maximus, was tribune of the plebs in B.C. 106, curule aedile in 104, and consul in 95, with Licinius Crassus, the orator, as his colleague. After his consulship Scaevola was proconsul of Asia, in which capacity he gained the esteem of the people under his government. Subsequently he was made Pontifex Maximus. He lost his life in the consulship of C. Marius the younger and Cn. Papirius Carbo (82), having been proscribed by the Marian party. The virtues of Scaevola are recorded by Cicero, who, after the death of the augur, became an attendant (*auditor*) of the Pontifex. The purity of his moral character, his exalted notions of equity and fair dealing, his abilities as an administrator, an orator, and a jurist, place him among the first of the illustrious men of all ages and countries. He is the first Roman to whom we can attribute a scientific and systematic handling of the *ius civile,* which he accomplished in a work in eighteen books. He also wrote a book on legal definitions, which is the oldest work quoted in the Digest.

Scaffolding. See SCANSORIA MACHINA.

Scalae (κλῖμαξ). (1) A ladder or any contrivance for making an ascent. The usual form of ancient ladder was identical with our own, as shown in the annexed illustration. (2) A ship's ladder, let down the side of a vessel, as shown below. (3) The staircase in a house, usually constructed like our own (Livy, xxxix. 14). Sometimes they were enclosed by side-walls, so that the person using the stair was concealed. These were called "Greek stairs" (*scalae Graecae,* Vitruv. ix. *Praef.* 7), and were often used as hiding-places (Cic. *Mil.* 15; Hor. *Epist.* iii. 15). (4) In very late Latin, the word is used of stirrups.

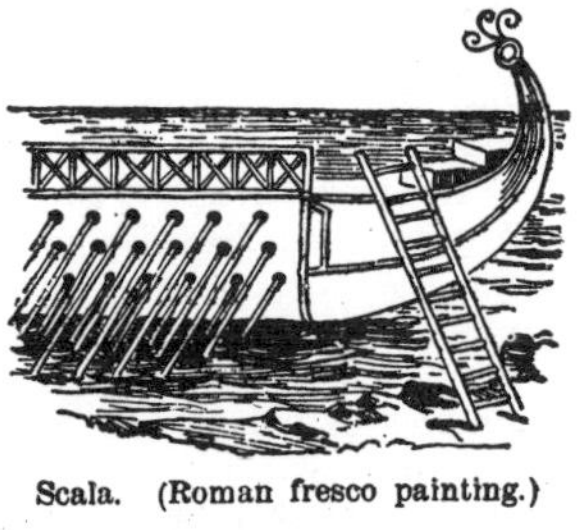

Scalae. (Column of Trajan.)

Scala. (Roman fresco painting.)

Scaldis. Now the Scheldt. An important river in the north of Gallia Belgica, flowing into the ocean, but which Caesar erroneously makes a tributary of the Mosa (*B. G.* vi. 33).

Scale. See LIBRA; TRUTINA.

Scalĭger. The Latinized form of a family name originally Italian (della Scala) and afterwards French (de l'Escale), made famous as that of two great classical scholars. (1) IULIUS CAESAR SCALĬGER, born in 1484 and claiming descent from an illustrious family of Verona, but by his enemies said to be the son of a sign-painter. After serving in the army under the emperor Maximilian, he entered the University of Bologna, where he remained a short time, and then took service in the French armies in Italy, winning the approval of King Francis for gallantry and remarkable feats of strength. He became naturalized as a French subject in 1528, when he settled at Agen and began practice as a physician. He had learned some Greek and prided himself on his Latin style, so that he felt called upon to attack Erasmus with bitter invectives for his satire on the stylists of Italy entitled *Ciceronianus*, a satire which Scaliger interpreted as an attack on Cicero himself. Scaliger died in 1558. His chief works were a grammar, *De Causis Linguae Latinae*, in thirteen books and of much value; a commentary on Theophrastus; an edition of Aristotle, *De Animalibus*, with notes; commentaries on Hippocrates, *De Insomniis;* and some Latin poems of considerable merit. Scaliger was a man of fine natural gifts but of a coarse and jealous nature, and with an education too unsystematic to enable his powers to appear in their true greatness. See Nisard, *Les Gladiateurs de la République des Lettres* (Paris, 1860); Bourousse de Laffore, *Jules César de l'Escale* (Agen, 1860); Magen, *Documents sur Julius Caesar Scaliger et sa Famille* (Agen, 1873).

(2) Joseph Justus Scaliger. The tenth child of Julius Caesar Scaliger, born at Agen in 1540. He studied as a boy at the Collège de Guyenne in Bordeaux, and was also trained by his father, who made him copy from eighty to two hundred lines of Latin verse every day, besides writing an original Latin theme. After his father's death, the young man went to Paris, where he studied at the University under Adrian Turnebus, from whom he learned Greek, reading all Homer in twenty-one days and the whole body of Greek poetry in four months. His linguistic studies advanced, until at last he boasted of being able to speak thirteen languages, ancient and modern. After travelling in Italy, England, and even Scotland, he settled at Valence in France (1570), and pursued a course of study under the jurist Cujacius; and from 1572 to 1574 was professor in the academy at Geneva founded by Calvin. About this time he began producing the great works that secured him the primacy among the classical scholars of Europe. Among these productions are to be mentioned his *Coniectanea* to Varro's *Lingua Latina* (1565); his *Catalecta Vergilii*, etc. (1572); his editions of Festus (1575), Catullus, Tibullus, and Propertius (1577); Manilius (1579); and especially a remarkable treatise on the Eusebian chronology, *De Emendatione Temporum* (1583); a *Thesaurus Temporum* (1606); twenty-four indices to Gruter's *Thesaurus Inscriptionum Latinarum* (1601); a numismatical treatise, *De Re Nummaria* (1616); besides *Opuscula* (1610), and *De Arte Critica* (1619).

In 1583 Scaliger was called to Leyden to succeed Justus Lipsius (q. v.), and at this university he spent the rest of his life. To his influence and example Holland owes the long line of illustrious scholars that follow one another so closely in the seventeenth century and whose memory is still cherished. His later years were made unhappy by the numerous controversies in which he became engaged, and whose motives sprang largely from the *odium theologicum*. An outrageous but immensely able attack made upon him by the Jesuit scholar Gaspar Scioppius is believed to have actually hastened Scaliger's death. This attack was contained in a treatise styled *Scaliger Hypobolimaeus*, and ridiculed Scaliger's pretensions to aristocratic descent, holding him up to the scorn of all Europe as a base-born impostor and an atheist. Scaliger died in 1609. His great learning, keen critical faculty, and rare achievements have led men to regard him as, on the whole, the first scholar of all time. Niebuhr spoke of him as standing "on the summit of real and universal knowledge, as no one after him has done." Pattison calls his "the most richly stored intellect that ever spent itself in acquiring knowledge."

See Bernays, *Joseph Justus Scaliger* (Berlin, 1855); Nisard, *Les Gladiateurs de la République des Lettres* (Paris, 1860); id. *Juste Lipse, Joseph Scaliger, et Isaac Casaubon* (Paris, 1852); and Pattison, *Essays*, vol. i. (Oxford, 1889). A bibliography of the writings of Scaliger in their different editions is given by Bernays.

Scalmus (σκαλμός). The thole—a strong wooden stay on the inside of a vessel to which the oar was attached by means of a strip (*struppus*) in order to hold it firmly in place (Cic. *Brut.* 53).

Scalpellum (σμιλίον). A scalpel; a small surgeon's knife used in cutting away flesh or in opening a vein (Cic. *Pro Sest.* 65; Celsus, ii. 10).

Scalprum (σμίλη, κολαπτήρ). A sharp instrument for cutting, varying in form and use from a common chisel (*scalprum fabrile*) driven by a mallet (Livy, xxvii. 49), to a penknife. The word is also applied to a pruning-hook (see Falx), to a cobbler's knife (Pollux, vii. 83), and a surgical instrument (see Scalpellum).

Scalptor. See Scalptura.

Scalptorium. An instrument in the shape of a human hand used for scratching parts of the body that were not otherwise easily accessible (Mart. xiv. 83).

Scalptūra or **Sculptūra**, originally signified cutting figures out of a solid material, but was more particularly applied to (1) the art of cutting figures into the material (intaglios), which was chiefly applied to producing seals and matrices for the mints; and (2) the art of producing raised figures (cameos), which served for the most part as ornaments. Sculpture in our sense of the word was usually designated by the term *statuaria* (*ars*). The first artist who is mentioned as an engraver (*scălptor*) of stones is Theodorus, the son of Telecles, the Samian, who engraved the stone in the ring of Polycrates (q. v.). The most celebrated among them was Pyrgoteles, who engraved the seal-rings for Alexander the Great. Several of the successors of Alexander and other wealthy persons adopted the custom of adorning their gold and silver vessels, *crateres*, candelabra, and the like, with precious stones on which raised figures (cameos) were worked. The art was in a particularly flourishing state at Rome under Augustus and his successors, in the hands of Dioscurides and other artists, many of whose works are still preserved. Numerous specimens of intaglios and cameos are still preserved in the various museums of Europe. See Gemma.

Scamander (Σκάμανδρος). (1) A river in the western part of the north coast of Sicily, falling into the sea near Segesta. (2) The celebrated river of the Troad. (See Troas.) As a mythological personage, the river-god was called Xanthus by the gods. His contest with Achilles is described by Homer (*Il.* xxi. 136 foll.).

Scamandrius. Son of Hector and Andromaché, whom the people of Troy called Astyanax, because his father was the protector of the city of Troy. See ASTYANAX.

Scambonĭdae (Σκαμβωνίδαι). A demus in Attica, between Athens and Eleusis, belonging to the tribe Leontis.

Scamnum. A stool or step placed by the side of a bed. It was larger than the *scabellum* and smaller than the *gradus* (q. v.). The word is also applied to any small footstool, especially to one with a double step.

Scandēa (Σκάνδεια). The harbour of Cythera. See CYTHERA.

Scandia, Scandinavia, or **Scatinavia.** The name given vaguely by the ancients to Norway, Sweden, and the surrounding islands, such as Fünen, Zealand, and Laaland. The Scandinavian peninsula was very imperfectly known even to the later Romans, who regarded it as an island or rather as a collection of islands which Ptolemy calls SCANDIAE. The geographers speak of a lofty mountain which they call Sevo, and of a Sinus Codanus, which is possibly the Cattegat. (See Ptol. ii. 11, 33; Pliny, *H. N.* iv. 96; and Mela, iii. 3, 6). The people inhabiting the country were called by Pliny and Tacitus, Hilleviones (Tac. *Germ.* 44).

Scandĭla. Now Scandole. A small island in the northeast of the Aegaean Sea, between Peparethos and Scyros.

Scandŭla (σχίδαξ). A shingle, used in early times for covering houses in place of the tiles (see TEGULA) that were afterward commonly employed. Shingles were used in Rome until about the third century B.C. (Pliny, *H. N.* xvi. 15).

Scansoria Machĭna (ἀκροβατικὴ μηχανή). A scaffolding for working on plans at an elevation from the ground (Vitruv. x. 1, 1).

Scantia Silva. A wood in Campania (Pliny, *H. N.* ii. 240).

Scapha (σκάφη). A skiff or cutter carried on large vessels to be lowered for use as required (Caes. *B. C.* iii. 24). They were rowed with from one to three pairs of oars.

Scapha. (Pompeian painting.)

Scapté Hylé (Σκαπτὴ Ὕλη). Also called, but less correctly, SCAPTESYLÉ, a small town on the coast of Thrace, opposite the island of Thasos. It contained celebrated gold mines, which were originally worked by the Thracians. Thucydides here arranged the materials for his history (Plut. *Cim.* 4; Marcell. *Thucyd.* 19).

Scaptia. A town in Latium from which one of the Roman tribes derived its name (Livy, viii. 17).

Scaptius, PUBLIUS. A Roman who traded in Cilicia, lending money to the people of Salamis in Cyprus, and using the troops of Appius Claudius to enforce his usurious terms. Cicero deprived him of the prefecture of Salamis which Claudius had given him, and refused him any further military aid (Cic. *Ad Att.* v. 21; vi. 1–3; xv. 13).

Scapŭla. (1) P. OSTORIUS. A Roman governor of Britain about A.D. 50, who defeated the powerful tribe of the Silures, took prisoner their king, Caractacus, and sent him in chains to Rome (Tac. *Ann.* xii. 31–39). (2) A son of the preceding, condemned for treason by Nero.

Scapus (σκᾶπος). (1) The shaft of a column; that which supports the capital, and rests upon the base (Vitruv. iii. 5). (2) The shaft of a pillar which supports one end of a stair in a staircase. (3) (καυλός). The shaft or stem of a lamp-stand (*candelabrum*). (4) The "yarn-beam" of a weaver's loom (Lucret. v. 1352).

Scarbantia or **Scarabantia.** Now Oedenburg. A town in Pannonia Superior (Pliny, *H. N.* iii. 146).

Scardus or **Scordus Mons** (τὸ Σκάρδον ὄρος). A range of lofty mountains, forming the boundary between Illyria and Dardania.

Scarphé (Σκάρφη), **Scarphēa** (Σκάρφεια) or **Scarphia** (Σκαρφία). A town of the Epicnemidii Locri, at which the roads leading through Thermopylae united (Livy, xxxiii. 3).

Scarpōna or **Scarponna.** Now Charpeigne; a town in Gallia Belgica.

Scato or **Cato,** VETTIUS. An Italian general in the Marsic War (B.C. 90) who defeated the Roman consuls in two successive battles. Being taken prisoner, he was stabbed to death by his own slave, to escape the disgrace of being punished by his captors (App. *B. C.* i. 40–43).

Scaurus, AEMILIUS. (1) MARCUS, a Roman who raised his family from obscurity to the highest rank among the Roman nobles. He was born in B.C. 163. His father, notwithstanding his patrician descent, had been obliged, through poverty, to carry on the trade of a coal merchant, and left his son a very slender patrimony. The latter had thought at first of carrying on the trade of a money-lender; but he finally resolved to devote himself to the study of eloquence, with the hope of rising to the honors of the State. He likewise served in the army, where he appears to have gained some distinction. He was curule aedile in 123, and obtained the consulship in 115, when he carried on war with success against several of the Alpine tribes. In 112 he was sent at the head of an embassy to Iugurtha; and in 111 he accompanied the consul, L. Calpurnius Bestia, as one of his legates, in the war against Iugurtha. The Numidian king bestowed large sums of money upon both Bestia and Scaurus, in consequence of which the consul granted the king most favourable terms of peace. This disgraceful transaction excited the greatest indignation at Rome; and C. Mamilius, the tribune of the people (110) brought forward a bill by which an inquiry was to be instituted against all those who had received bribes from Iugurtha. Although Scaurus had been one of the most guilty, such was his influence in the State that he contrived to be appointed one of the three quaesitores who were elected under the bill for the purpose of prosecuting the criminals. But, though he thus secured himself, he was unable to save any of his accomplices. Bestia and many others were condemned. In 109, Scaurus was censor with M. Livius Drusus. In his consulship he restored the Milvian Bridge, and constructed the Aemilian Way, which ran by Pisae and Luna as far as Dertona. In 107 he was elected consul a second time, in place of L. Cassius Longinus, who had fallen in battle against the Tigurini. In the struggles between the aristocratical and popular parties, Scaurus was always a warm supporter of the former. He was several times accused of different offences, chiefly by his private enemies; but such was his influence in the State, that he was always acquitted. He died about B.C. 89. By his wife Caecilia Scaurus had three children, two sons mentioned below, and a daughter Aemilia, first married to M'. Glabrio, and next to Cn. Pompey, subsequently the triumvir. (2) MARCUS, eldest son of the preceding, and stepson of the dictator Sulla, whom his mother Caecilia married after the death of his father. In the Third Mithridatic War he served under Pompey as quaestor. The latter sent him to Damascus with an army, and from thence he marched into Iudaea, to settle the disputes between the brothers Hyrcanus and Aristobulus. Scaurus was left by Pompey in the command of Syria with two legions. During his government of Syria he made a predatory incursion into Arabia Petraea, but withdrew on the payment of 300 talents by Aretas, the king of the country. He was curule aedile in B.C. 58, when he celebrated the public games with extraordinary splendour. The temporary theatre which he built accommodated 80,000 spectators, and was adorned in the most magnificent manner. Three hundred and sixty pillars decorated the stage, arranged in three stories, of which the lowest was made of white marble, the middle one of glass, and the highest of gilt wood. The combats of wild beasts were equally astonishing. One hundred and fifty panthers were exhibited in the circus, and five crocodiles and a hippopotamus were seen for the first time at Rome. In the year 56 he was praetor, and in the following year governed the province of Sardinia, which he plundered without mercy. On his return to Rome he was accused of the crime of *repetundae*. He was defended by Cicero, Hortensius, and others, and was acquitted, notwithstanding his guilt. He was accused again in 52, under Pompey's new law against bribery, and was condemned. He married Mucia, who had been previously the wife of Pompey, and by her he had one son. (3) Younger son of No. 1, fought under the proconsul, Q. Catulus, against the Cimbri at the Athesis, and having fled from the field, was indignantly commanded by his father not to come into his presence; whereupon the youth put an end to his life. (4) MARCUS, son of No. 2, and Mucia, the former wife of Pompey the triumvir, and consequently the half-brother of Sex. Pompey. He accompanied the latter into Asia, after the defeat of his fleet in Sicily, but betrayed him into the hands of the generals of M. Antonius, in 35. After the battle of Actium, he fell into the power of Octavian, and escaped death, to which he had been sentenced, only through the intercession of his mother, Mucia. (5) MAMERCUS, son of No. 5, was a distinguished orator and poet, but of a dissolute character. He was a member of the Senate at the time of the accession of Tiberius, A.D. 14, when he offended that suspicious emperor by some remarks which he made in the Senate. Being accused of *maiestas* in 34, he put an end to his own life.

Scaurus, M. AURELIUS, consul suffectus B.C. 103, was three years afterwards consular legate in Gaul, where he was defeated by the Cimbri, taken prisoner, and put to death (Vell. Pat. ii. 12).

Scaurus, Q. TERENTIUS. A well-known Roman grammarian who lived in the reign of Hadrian (Gell. xi. 15, 3). His son was lictor to the emperor Verus. Scaurus wrote a work on grammar (*Ars Grammatica*), besides commentaries on Plautus, Vergil, and the *Ars Poetica* of Horace. There still exists an abridgment of a treatise by him, *De Orthographia*, of some importance for the history of the Latin language; and another of a treatise on adverbs, prepositions, etc. Scaurus draws largely from Varro, and takes some account of the early Latin. The abridgments are given by Keil in his *Grammatici Latini* (vii. 11, 1–29; vii. 29, 3–33). See Bücheler in the *Rheinisches Museum*, xxxiv. 384.

Scelerātus Campus. A place in Rome, close to the Porta Collina, where Vestals who had broken their vows were entombed alive. See VESTALES.

Scena. The old Latin name for a hatchet with two edges (Fest. s. h. v.).

Scena. See THEATRUM.

Scenae (Σκηναί). "The tents"; a town of Mesopotamia near the border of Babylonia. Here dwelt the Scenitae.

Scenītae (Σκηνῖται, "dwellers in tents"). The general name used by the Greeks for the Bedawee (Bedouin) tribes of Arabia Deserta.

Scepsis (Σκῆψις, probably Eski-Upshi, or Eski-Shupshe). An ancient city in the interior of the Troad, southeast of Alexandria, in the mountains of Ida. Here the manuscripts of Aristotle and Theophrastus were buried to prevent their transference to Pergamum. (See Strabo, p. 608, and the article ARISTOTELES.) At Scepsis, Metrodorus, the philosopher, and Demetrius, the grammarian, were born.

Scepticism. A philosophical school founded by Pyrrho of Elis (about B.C. 365–275), which refused to acknowledge that truth was obtainable by the perception of the senses and the cognizance of the mind. In existing literature it is chiefly represented by the physician Sextus Empiricus. See PHILOSOPHIA.

Sceptrum (σκῆπτρον). Originally a long staff like the shaft of a spear (Justin. xliii. 3) used as a support in walking and to give dignity to the bearer. Later it became a badge of royal office. See BACULUM.

Scerdilaidas (Σκερδιλαίδας) or **Scerdilaedus** (Σκερδίλαιδος). A king of Illyria, who was in all probability a son of Pleuratus, and younger brother of Agron, both of them kings of that country. After the defeat and abdication of Teuta (B.C. 229), he probably succeeded to a portion of her dominions, but did not assume the title of king till after the death of his nephew Pinnes. He carried on war for some years against Philip, king of Macedonia, and thus appears as an ally of the Romans. He probably died about 205, and was succeeded by his son Pleuratus.

Scheda and **Schida** (σχίδη). See PAPYRUS.

Schedia (Σχεδιά). A town of Lower Egypt (Strabo, p. 800).

Schema Alcmanĭcum (σχῆμα Ἀλκμανικόν). A name given to the use of a verb in the plural (or dual) number with a noun in the singular when there follows another noun to which the verb has also reference—e. g. in Homer (*Il.* v. 774):

ἧχι ῥοὰς Σιμόεις συμβάλλετον ἠδὲ Σκάμανδρος.

So also *Od.* xi. 513; *Il.* xx. 138. The grammarians say that the construction was frequent in the poems of Alcman, whence the name.

Schema Pindaricum (σχῆμα Πινδαρικόν) or **Schema Boeoticum** (σχῆμα Βοιωτικόν). A name given to the use of a masculine or feminine subject in the plural joined with a verb in the singular —e. g. in Pindar (*Olymp.* xi. [x.]):

ὕμνοι ὑστέρων ἀρχαὶ λόγων τέλλεται.

Other instances (the construction is a rare one) are found in Herod. vi. 86 (in an oracle); Hom. *Hymn. in Cer.* 279; Pind. *Pyth.* x. 71; Hesiod, *Theog.* 321; and with the noun in the dual number in *Il.* xxiii. 477. In Attic writers the construction is usually limited to ἔστι and ἦν placed at the beginning of the sentence, so that the subject follows the verb and the expression is somewhat impersonal in its form, as in the French *Il est des hommes*, etc. Cf. Soph. *Trach.* 520; Eurip. *Ion*, 1146; Plato, *Euthyd.* p. 302 C; and for further instances, see Jelf, *Greek Grammar*, 386.

Scheria. See PHAEACES.

Schoenobătes (σχοινοβάτης). A rope-dancer. See FUNAMBULUS.

Schoenus (Σχοῖνος). A town of Boeotia on a river of the same name (Strabo, p. 408).

Schoenūs (Σχοινοῦς). A harbour of Corinth at the narrowest part of the Isthmus (Strabo, pp. 369, 380).

Scholium (σχόλιον). A note or comment. The name is especially applied to the short marginal notes made upon the MSS. of the Greek and Latin classics by grammarians and others, who are hence called Scholiasts. See GLOSSA.

Schools. See EDUCATION; LUDUS LITTERARIUS.

Schools of Medicine. See MEDICINA.

Schools of Philology. See PHILOLOGIA.

Schools of Philosophy. See PHILOSOPHIA.

Sciadephoria (σκιαδηφορία). A service performed at Athens by the daughters of the resident aliens (μέτοικοι), who at the Panathenaea carried the parasols of the Athenian maidens (Pollux, vii. 134). The wives of the *metoeci* on the same occasion carried a water-vessel (see HYDRIAPHORIA), and the aliens themselves vessels full of cakes and other offerings (σκαφηφορία) to the goddess. The duties thus imposed upon the resident aliens and their families were intended to mark them out as a class inferior in dignity to the citizens. See Schömann, *Ant. Iuris Publici*, p. 190; Hermann, *Staatsalterth.*, § 115, n. 10.

Sciăthus (Σκίαθος). Now Skiatho; a small island in the Aegaean Sea, north of Euboea and east of the Magnesian coast of Thessaly, with a town of the same name upon it. Near it both the Greek and the Persian fleets were stationed at the time of the invasion by Xerxes (Herod. vii. 176; viii. 7).

Scillūs (Σκιλλοῦς). A town of Elis in the district Triphylia, on the river Selinus, twenty stadia south of Olympia. Here Xenophon, when banished from Athens, lived for more than twenty years, and built a sanctuary to Artemis (Xen. *Anab.* v. 3, 7; Pausan. v. 6, 5; Strabo, p. 344).

Scimpodium (σκιμπόδιον). A couch or sofa, resembling a modern invalid's chair (Gell. xix. 10, 1).

Sciōnē (Σκιώνη). The chief town in the Macedonian peninsula of Pallené, on the western coast. It revolted from Athens in the Peloponnesian War, and being taken by Cleon, the male inhabitants were put to death and the women and children sold as slaves (Thuc. iv. 120, 133).

Scioppius, KASPAR (KASPAR SCHOPPE). A classical scholar and famous controversialist, who was born at Neumark, May 27, 1576. He studied at Heidelberg, Altorf, and Ingolstadt, and after visiting Rome in 1598 and being converted to Roman Catholicism, became widely known as the able and unsparing critic of the great Protestant scholars, publishing many pamphlets and controversial tracts. He was a man of great learning and possessed a style of unusual power and precision, and all of these qualities are exhibited in the well-known diatribe which he launched against Joseph Scaliger and which hastened the death of that great scholar. (See SCALIGER.) Scioppius died at Padua, November 19, 1649. His principal works are a grammar (*Grammatica Philosophica*), published in 1628; *Verisimilium Libri Quatuor* (1596); *Suspectae Lectiones* (1597); *De Arte Critica* (1597); *Paradoxa Litteraria* (1628); and a treatise *De Scholarum et Studiorum Ratione* (1636). See Nisard, *Les Gladiateurs de la République des Lettres* (Paris, 1860).

Scipio (σκίπων). A staff or sceptre, etymologically the same as *sceptrum* (q. v.).

Scipio. The name of an illustrious patrician family of the Cornelian gens. This name, which signifies a stick or staff, is said to have been given to the founder of the family, because he served as a staff in directing his blind father. This family produced some of the greatest men in Rome, and to them she was more indebted than to any others for the empire of the world. The family tomb of the Scipios was discovered in 1780, on the left of the Appia Via, about four hundred paces within the modern Porta S. Sebastiano. The inscriptions and other curiosities are now deposited in the Museo Pio-Clementino at Rome.

(1) P. CORNELIUS SCIPIO, *magister equitum* B.C. 396, and consular tribune 395 and 394. (2) L. CORNELIUS SCIPIO, consul 350. (3) P. CORNELIUS SCIPIO BARBĀTUS, consul 328, and dictator 306. He was also Pontifex Maximus. (4) L. CORNELIUS SCIPIO BARBĀTUS, consul 298, when he carried on war against the Etruscans, and defeated them near Volaterrae. He also served under the consuls in 297, 295, and 293 against the Samnites. This Scipio was the great-grandfather of the conqueror of Hannibal. The genealogy of the family can be traced with more certainty from this time. (5) CN. CORNELIUS SCIPIO ASĪNA, son of No. 4, was consul 260, in the First Punic War. In an attempt upon the Liparaean Islands, he was taken prisoner with seventeen ships. He probably recovered his liberty when Regulus invaded Africa, for he was consul a second time in 254. In this year he and his colleague, A. Atilius Calatinus, crossed over into Sicily and took the town of Panormus. (6) L. CORNELIUS SCIPIO, also son of No. 4, was consul 259. He drove the Carthaginians out of Sardinia and Corsica, defeating Hanno, the Carthaginian commander. He was censor in 258. (7) P. CORNELIUS SCIPIO ASĪNA, son of No. 5, was consul 221, and carried on war, with his colleague M. Minucius

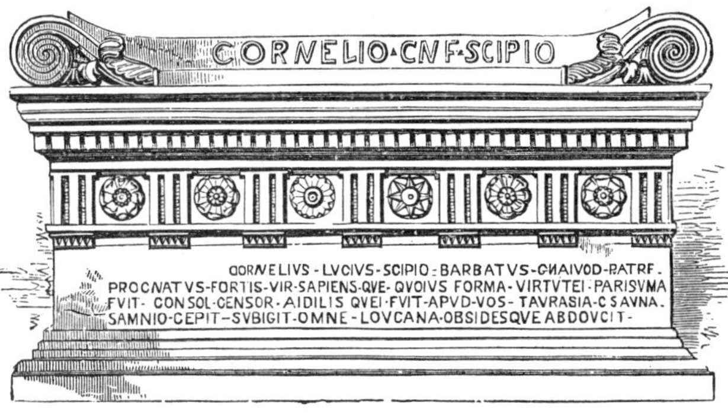

CORNELIO·CN·F·SCIPIO
CORNELIVS-LVCIVS-SCIPIO-BARBATVS-GNAIVOD-PATRE.
PROGNATVS-FORTIS-VIR-SAPIENS-QVE-QVOIVS FORMA-VIRTVTEI-PARISVMA
FVIT-CONSOL-CENSOR-AIDILIS QVEI-FVIT-APVD-VOS-TAVRASIA-CISAVNA.
SAMNIO-CEPIT-SVBIGIT-OMNE-LOVCANA-OBSIDESQVE ABDOVCIT-

Sarcophagus of L. Cornelius Scipio Barbatus.

Rufus, against the Istri, who were subdued by the consuls. He is mentioned again in 211, when he recommended that the Senate should recall all the generals and armies from Italy for the defence of the capital, because Hannibal was marching upon the city. (8) P. Cornelius Scipio, son of No. 6, was consul, with Ti. Sempronius Longus, in 218, the first year of the Second Punic War. He sailed with an army to Gaul, in order to encounter Hannibal before crossing the Alps; but, finding that Hannibal had crossed the Rhône, and had got the start of him by a three days' march, he resolved to sail back to Italy and await Hannibal's arrival in Cisalpine Gaul. But as the Romans had an army of twenty-five thousand men in Cisalpine Gaul, under the command of two praetors, Scipio sent into Spain the army which he had brought with him, under the command of his brother, Cn. Scipio. On his return to Italy, Scipio took the command of the army in Cisalpine Gaul, and hastened to meet Hannibal. An engagement took place between the cavalry and light-armed troops of the two armies. The Romans were defeated; the consul himself received a severe wound, and was only saved from death by the courage of his young son Publius, the future conqueror of Hannibal. Scipio now retreated across the Ticinus, crossed the Po also, first took up his quarters at Placentia, and subsequently withdrew to the hills on the left bank of the Trebia, where he was joined by the other consul, Sempronius Longus. The latter resolved upon a battle, in opposition to the advice of his colleague. The result was the complete defeat of the Roman army, which was obliged to take refuge within the walls of Placentia. In the following year (217), Scipio, whose imperium had been prolonged, crossed over into Spain. He and his brother Gneius continued in Spain until their death in 211, and did the most important service for their country by preventing reinforcements being sent to Hannibal from Spain. In 215 they transferred the war from the Ebro to the Guadalquivir and won two great victories at Illiturgis and Intibilis. They fortified an important harbour at Tarraco and regained Saguntum, and by adroit policy induced Syphax to turn against the Carthaginians in Africa; but in 212, having to confront three armies under Hasdrubal Barca, Hasdrubal Gisgo, and Mago, they enlisted 20,000 Celtiberians and divided their armies. This was a fatal step. The Spaniards were untrustworthy, and the armies of the Scipios were defeated separately and both the brothers were slain by the Carthaginians (Polyb. iii.; Livy, xii.–xxv.; App. *Annib.* 5–8; *Hisp.* 14–16). (9) Cn. Cornelius Scipio Calvus, son of No. 6, and brother of No. 8, was consul 222, with M. Claudius Marcellus. In conjunction with his colleague he carried on war against the Insubrians. In 218 he carried on war as the legate of his brother Publius for eight years in Spain, as has been related above (Polyb. ii. 34; Plut. *Marcell.* 6, 7).

(10) P. Cornelius Scipio Africānus Maior, son of No. 8, was born in B.C. 237. (According to Livy, xxvi. 18, and Val. Max. iii. 7, 1, he was born in 234, but the authority of Polybius should be followed, who says that he was twenty-seven when he went to Spain.) He was unquestionably one of the greatest men of Rome, and he acquired at an early age the confidence and admiration of his countrymen. His enthusiastic mind led him to believe that he was a special favourite of the gods; and he never engaged in any public or private business without first going to the Capitol, where he sat some time alone, enjoying communication with the gods. For all he proposed or executed he alleged the divine approval; and the Roman people gave credit to his assertions and regarded him as a being almost superior to the common race of men (Livy, xxvi. 19). There can be no doubt that Scipio himself believed in the divine revelations which he asserted to have been vouchsafed to him; and the extraordinary success which attended all his enterprises must have deepened this belief. He is first mentioned in 218 at the battle of the Ticinus, when he saved the life of his father as has been already related. He fought at Cannae two years afterwards (216), when he was already a tribune of the soldiers, and was one of the few Roman officers who survived that fatal day. He was chosen along with Appius Claudius to command the remains of the army, which had taken refuge at Canusium; and it was owing to his youthful heroism and presence of mind that the Roman nobles, who had thought of leaving Italy in despair, were prevented from carrying their rash project into effect. He had already gained the favour of the people to such an extent that he was elected aedile in 212, although he had not yet reached the legal age. In 210, after the death of his father and uncle in Spain, the Romans resolved to increase their army in that country, and to place it under the command of a proconsul. But when the people assembled to elect a proconsul, none of the generals of experience ventured to sue for so dangerous a command. At length Scipio, who was then barely twenty-four, offered himself as a candidate, and was chosen with enthusiasm to take the command. His success in Spain was striking and rapid. In the first campaign (210) he took the important city of Carthago Nova, and in the course of the next three years he drove the Carthaginians entirely out of Spain, and became master of that country. He returned to Rome in 206, and was elected consul for the following year (205), although he had not yet filled the office of praetor, and was only thirty years of age. He was anxious to cross over at once to Africa, and bring the contest to an end at the gates of Carthage; but the oldest members of the Senate, and among them Q. Fabius Max-

imus, opposed his project, partly through timidity and partly through jealousy of the youthful conqueror. All that Scipio could obtain was the province of Sicily, with permission to cross over to Africa; but the Senate refused him an army, thus making the permission of no practical use. But the allies had a truer view of the interests of Italy than the Roman Senate, and from all the towns of Italy volunteers flocked to join the standard of the youthful hero. The Senate could not refuse to allow him to enlist volunteers; and such was the enthusiasm in his favour that he was able to cross over to Sicily with an army and a fleet contrary to the expectations and even the wishes of the Senate. After spending the winter in Sicily, and completing all his preparations for the invasion of Africa, he crossed over to the latter country in the course of the following year. Success again attended his arms. The Carthaginians and their ally Syphax were defeated with great slaughter, and the former were compelled to recall Hannibal from Italy as the only hope of saving their country. The long struggle between the two peoples was at length brought to a close by the battle fought near the city of Zama on the 19th of October, 202, in which Scipio gained a decisive and brilliant victory over Hannibal. Carthage had no alternative but submission, but the final treaty was not concluded till the following year (201). Scipio returned to Italy in 201, and entered Rome in triumph. He was received with universal enthusiasm, and the surname of Africanus was conferred upon him. The people wished to make him consul and dictator for life, and to erect his statue in the Comitia, the Rostra, the Curia, and even in the Capitol, but he prudently declined all these invidious distinctions. As he did not choose to usurp the supreme power, and as he was an object of suspicion and dislike to the majority of the Senate, he took no prominent part in public affairs during the next few years. He was censor in 199 with P. Aelius Paetus, and consul a second time in 194 with Ti. Sempronius Longus. In 193 he was one of the three commissioners who were sent to Africa to mediate between Masinissa and the Carthaginians; and in the same year he was one of the ambassadors sent to Antiochus at Ephesus, at whose court Hannibal was then residing. The tale runs that he had there an interview with the great Carthaginian, who declared him the greatest general that ever lived. The compliment was paid in a manner the most flattering to Scipio. The latter had asked, "Who was the greatest general?" "Alexander the Great," was Hannibal's reply. "Who was the second?" "Pyrrhus." "Who the third?" "Myself," replied the Carthaginian. "What would you have said, then, if you had conquered me?" asked Scipio, in astonishment. "I should then have placed myself before Alexander, before Pyrrhus, and before all other generals." In 190 Africanus served as legate under his brother Lucius in the war against Antiochus the Great. Shortly after his return, he and his brother Lucius were accused of having received bribes from Antiochus to let the monarch off too leniently, and of having appropriated to their own use part of the money which had been paid by Antiochus to the Roman State. The details of the accusation are related with such discrepancies by the ancient authorities that it is impossible to determine with certainty the true history of the affair, or the year in which it occurred. It appears, however, that there were two distinct prosecutions, and the following is perhaps the most probable history of the transaction. In 187, two tribunes of the people of the name of Petillii, instigated by Cato and the other enemies of the Scipios, required L. Scipio to render an account of all the sums of money which he had received from Antiochus. L. Scipio accordingly prepared his accounts, but as he was in the act of delivering them up, the proud conqueror of Hannibal indignantly snatched them out of his hands, and tore them into pieces before the Senate. But this haughty conduct appears to have produced an unfavourable impression, and his brother, when brought to trial in the course of the same year, was declared guilty, and sentenced to pay a heavy fine. The tribune C. Minucius Augurinus ordered him to be dragged to prison and there detained till the money was paid; whereupon Africanus rescued his brother from the hands of the tribune's officer. The contest would probably have been attended with fatal results had not Tiberius Gracchus, the father of the celebrated tribune, and then tribune himself, had the prudence to release Lucius from the sentence of imprisonment. The successful issue of the prosecution of Lucius emboldened his enemies to bring the great Africanus himself before the people. His accuser was M. Naevius, the tribune of the people, and the accusation was brought in 185. When the trial came on, and Africanus was summoned, he proudly reminded the people that this was the anniversary of the day on which he had defeated Hannibal at Zama, and called upon them to follow him to the Capitol, in order there to return thanks to the immortal gods, and to pray that they would grant the Roman State other citizens like himself. Scipio struck a chord which vibrated in every heart, and he was immediately followed by crowds to the Capitol. Having thus set all the laws at defiance, Scipio immediately quitted Rome, and retired to his country seat at Liternum. The tribunes wished to renew the prosecution, but Gracchus wisely persuaded them to let it drop. Scipio never returned to Rome. He passed his remaining days in the cultivation of his estate at Liternum; and at his death is said to have requested that his body might be buried there, and not in his ungrateful country. The year of his death is equally uncertain; but he probably died in 183. Scipio married Aemilia, the daughter of L. Aemilius Paulus, who fell at the battle of Cannae, and by her he had four children, two sons (Nos. 12, 13), and two daughters, the elder of whom married P. Scipio Nasica Corcu-

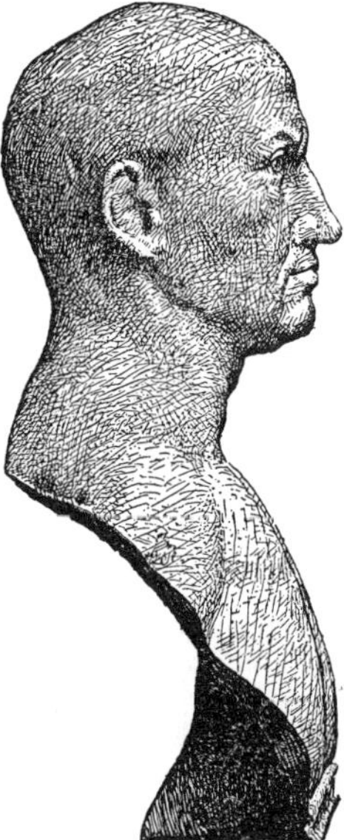
Scipio Africanus Maior. (Capitol.)

lum (No. 17), and the younger Tiberius Gracchus, and thus became the mother of the two celebrated tribunes. (See CORNELIA.) (11) L. CORNELIUS SCIPIO ASIATĬCUS, also called ASIAGĔNES or ASIAGĔNUS, was the son of No. 8, and the brother of the great Africanus. He served under his brother in Spain; was praetor in B.C. 193, when he obtained the province of Sicily; and consul in 190, with C. Laelius. The Senate had not much confidence in his abilities, and it was only through the offer of his brother Africanus to accompany him as a legate that he obtained the province of Greece and the conduct of the war against Antiochus. He defeated Antiochus at Mount Sipylus, in 190, entered Rome in triumph in the following year, and assumed the surname of Asiaticus. The history of his accusation and condemnation has been already related in the life of his brother. He was a candidate for the censorship in 184, but was defeated by the old enemy of his family, M. Porcius Cato, who deprived Asiaticus of his horse at the review of the *equites*. It appears, therefore, that even as late as this time an *eques* did not forfeit his horse by becoming a senator. (12) P. CORNELIUS SCIPIO AFRICĀNUS, elder son of the great Africanus, was prevented by his weak health from taking any part in public affairs. Cicero praises his oratiunculae and his Greek history, and remarks that, with the greatness of his father's mind he possessed a larger amount of learning. He had no son of his own, but adopted the son of L. Aemilius Paulus (see below, No. 15). (13) L. or CN. CORNELIUS SCIPIO AFRICĀNUS, younger son of the great Africanus. He accompanied his father into Asia in B.C. 190, and was taken prisoner by Antiochus. This Scipio was a degenerate son of an illustrious father, and only obtained the praetorship, in B.C. 174, through Cicereius, who had been a secretary of his father, giving way to him. In the same year he was expelled from the Senate by the censors. (14) L. CORNELIUS SCIPIO ASIATĬCUS, a descendant of No. 11, belonged to the Marian party, and was consul B.C. 83 with C. Norbanus. In this year Sulla returned to Italy: Scipio was deserted by his troops, and taken prisoner in his camp along with his son Lucius, but was dismissed by Sulla uninjured. He was, however, included in the proscription in the following year (82), whereupon he fled to Massilia, and passed there the remainder of his life. His daughter was married to P. Sestius.

(15) P. CORNELIUS SCIPIO AEMILIĀNUS AFRICANUS MINOR, was the younger son of L. Aemilius Paulus, the conqueror of Macedonia, and was adopted by P. Scipio (No. 12), the son of the conqueror of Hannibal. He was born about B.C. 185. In his seventeenth year he accompanied his father Paulus to Greece, and fought under him at the battle of Pydna, 168. Scipio devoted himself with ardour to the study of literature, and formed an intimate friendship with Polybius, when the latter came to Rome along with the other Achaean exiles in 167. (See POLYBIUS.) At a later period he also cultivated the acquaintance of the philosopher Panaetius, and he likewise admitted the poets Lucilius and Terence to his intimacy, and is said to have assisted the latter in the composition of his comedies. (See TERENTIUS.) His friendship with Laelius, whose tastes and pursuits were so congenial to his own, has been immortalized by Cicero's celebrated treatise entitled *Laelius sive de Amicitia*. Although thus devoted to the study of polite literature, Scipio is said to have cultivated the virtues which distinguished the older Romans, and to have made Cato the model of his conduct. If we may believe his panegyrists, he possessed all the simple virtues of an old Roman, mellowed by the refining influences of Greek civilization. Scipio first served in Spain with great distinction as military tribune under the consul L. Lucullus in 151. On the breaking out of the Third Punic War in 149 he accompanied the Roman army to Africa, again with the rank of military tribune. Here he gained still more renown. By his personal bravery and military skill he repaired, to a great extent, the mistakes of the consul Manilius, whose army on one occasion he saved from destruction. He returned to Rome in 148, and had already gained such popularity that when he became a candidate for the aedileship for the following year (147) he was elected consul, although he was only thirty-seven, and had not therefore attained the legal age. The Senate assigned to him Africa as his province, to which he forthwith sailed, accompanied by his friends Polybius and Laelius. He prosecuted the siege of Carthage with the utmost vigour. The Carthaginians defended themselves with the courage of despair, and the Romans were unable to force their way into the city till the spring of the following year (146). The inhabitants fought from street to street, and from house to house, and the work of destruction and butchery went on for days. The fate of this once magnificent city moved Scipio to tears, and anticipating that a similar catastrophe might one day befall Rome, he repeated the lines of the *Iliad* (vi. 448), in which Hector bewails the approaching fall of Troy. After reducing Africa to the form of a Roman province, Scipio returned to Rome in the same year, and celebrated a splendid triumph on account of his victory. The surname of Africanus, which he had inherited by adoption from the conqueror of Hannibal, had been now acquired by him by his own exploits. In 142 Scipio was censor, and in the administration of the duties of his office he attempted to repress the growing luxury and immorality of his contemporaries. His efforts, however, were thwarted by his colleague Mummius, who had himself acquired a love for Greek and Asiatic luxuries. In 139 Scipio was accused by Ti. Claudius Asellus of *maiestas*. Asellus attacked him out of private animosity, because he had been deprived of his horse, and reduced to the condition of an *aerarius* by Scipio in his censorship. Scipio was acquitted, and the speeches which he delivered on the occasion obtained great celebrity. It appears to have been after this event that Scipio was sent on an embassy to Egypt and Asia to attend to the Roman interests in those countries. The long continuance of the war in Spain again called Scipio to the consulship. He was appointed consul in his absence, and had the province of Spain assigned to him in 134. His operations were attended with success; and in 133 he brought the war to a conclusion by the capture of the city of Numantia after a long siege. He now received the surname of NUMANTĪNUS in addition to that of Africanus. During his absence in Spain Tiberius Gracchus had been put to death. Scipio was married to Sempronia, the sister of the fallen tribune, but he had no sympathy with his reforms, and no sorrow for his fate. Upon his return to Rome in 132, he did not disguise his sentiments, and when asked

in the assembly of the tribes by C. Papirius Carbo, the tribune, what he thought of the death of Tiberius Gracchus, he boldly replied that he was justly slain (*iure caesum*). The people loudly expressed their disapprobation; whereupon Scipio proudly bade them to be silent. He now took the lead in opposing the popular party, and endeavoured to prevent the agrarian law of Tiberius Gracchus from being carried into effect. In order to accomplish this object, he proposed in the Senate (129) that all disputes respecting the lands of the allies should be taken out of the hands of the commissioners appointed under the law of Tiberius Gracchus, and should be committed to other persons. This would have been equivalent to an abrogation of the law; and accordingly Fulvius Flaccus, Papirius Carbo, and C. Gracchus, the three commissioners, offered the most vehement opposition to his proposal. In the Forum he was accused by Carbo with the bitterest invectives as the enemy of the people, and upon his again expressing his approval of the death of Tiberius Gracchus, the people shouted out, "Down with the tyrant!" In the evening he went home with the intention of composing a speech for the following day; but next day he was found dead in his room. The most contradictory rumours were circulated respecting his death, but it was generally believed that he was murdered. Suspicion fell upon various persons; his wife Sempronia and her mother Cornelia were suspected by some; Carbo, Fulvius, and C. Gracchus by others. Of all these, Carbo was most generally believed to have been guilty, and is expressly mentioned as the murderer by Cicero. The general opinion entertained by the Romans of a subsequent age respecting Scipio is given by Cicero in his work on the Republic, in which Scipio is introduced as the principal speaker. (16) P. Cornelius Scipio Nasīca, that is, "Scipio with the pointed nose," was the son of Cn. Scipio Calvus, who fell in Spain in B.C. 211. He is first mentioned in 204 as a young man who was judged by the Senate to be the best citizen in the State, and was therefore sent to Ostia along with the Roman matrons to receive the statue of the Idaean Mother, which had been brought from Pessinus. He was curule aedile in 196; praetor in 194, when he fought with success in Further Spain; and consul 191, when he defeated the Boii, and triumphed over them on his return to Rome. Scipio Nasica was a celebrated jurist, and a house was given him by the state in the Via Sacra, in order that he might be more easily consulted. (17) P. Cornelius Scipio Nasīca Corcŭlum, son of No. 16, inherited from his father a love of jurisprudence, and became so celebrated for his discernment and for his knowledge of the pontifical and civil law, that he received his surname of Corculum. He married a daughter of Scipio Africanus the elder. He was consul for the first time in 162, but abdicated, together with his colleague, almost immediately after they had entered upon their office, on account of some fault in the auspices. He was censor in 159 with M. Popilius Laenas, and was consul a second time in 155, when he subdued the Dalmatians. He was a firm upholder of the old Roman habits and manners, and in his second consulship he induced the Senate to order the demolition of a theatre, which was near completion, as injurious to public morals. When Cato repeatedly expressed his desire for the destruction of Carthage, Scipio, on the other hand, declared that he wished for its preservation, since the existence of such a rival would prove a useful check upon the licentiousness of the multitude. He was elected Pontifex Maximus in 150. (18) P. Cornelius Scipio Nasīca Serapio, son of No. 17, is chiefly known as the leader of the Senate in the murder of Tiberius Gracchus. He was consul in 138, and in consequence of the severity with which he and his colleague conducted the levy of troops, they were thrown into prison by C. Curiatius, the tribune of the plebs. It was this Curiatius who gave Nasica the nickname of Serapio, from his resemblance to a person of low rank of this name; but, though given him in derision, it afterward became his distinguishing surname. In 133, when the tribes met to re-elect Tiberius Gracchus to the tribunate, and the utmost confusion prevailed in the Forum, Nasica called upon the consuls to save the Republic; but as they refused to have recourse to violence, he exclaimed, "As the consul betrays the State, do you who wish to obey the laws follow me;" and, so saying, he rushed forth from the temple of Fides, where the Senate was sitting, followed by the greater number of the senators. The people gave way before them, and Gracchus was assassinated as he attempted to escape. In consequence of his conduct on this occasion, Nasica became an object of such detestation to the people, that the Senate found it advisable to send him on a pretended mission to Asia, although he was Pontifex Maximus, and ought not, therefore, to have quitted Italy. He did not venture to return to Rome, and after wandering about from place to place, died soon afterwards at Pergamum. (19) P. Cornelius Scipio Nasīca, son of No. 18, was consul 111, and died during his consulship. (20) P. Cornelius Scipio Nasīca, son of No. 19, praetor in 94, is mentioned by Cicero as one of the advocates of Sextus Roscius of Ameria. He married Licinia, the second daughter of L. Crassus, the orator. He had two sons, both of whom were adopted, one by his maternal grandfather, L. Crassus, in his testament, and is therefore called L. Licinius Crassus Scipio, and the other by Q. Caecilius Metellus Pius, consul 80, and is therefore called Q. Caecilius Metellus Pius Scipio. This Scipio became the father-in-law of Cn. Pompey the triumvir, and fell in Africa in 46. His life is given under Metellus, No. 15. (21) Cn. Cornelius Scipio Hispallus, son of L. Scipio, who is only known as a brother of the two Scipios who fell in Spain. Hispallus was praetor 179, and consul 171. (22) Cn. Cornelius Scipio Hispallus, son of No. 21, was praetor 139, when he published an edict that all Chaldaeans (i. e. astrologers) should leave Rome and Italy within ten days.

See Capellmann, *De Scipionibus* (1841).

Sciras or **Sclerias**. A follower and imitator of Rhinthon. See Rhinthon.

Sciras (Σκίρας). A surname of Athené given from a temple in the Attic port of Phalerum, built by a soothsayer, Scirus, of Dodona (Pausan. i. 1, 4; ii. 36, 3).

Sciritae. A body of light infantry in the Spartan army, consisting of the περίοικοι (q. v.) of the district Sciritis.

Scirītis (Σκιρῖτις). A wild and mountainous district in the north of Laconia, on the borders of Arcadia, with a town called Scirus.

Sciron (Σκῖρων, also Σκείρων). A famous robber who infested the frontier between Attica and Megaris. He not only robbed the travellers who passed through the country, but compelled them on the Scironian Rock to wash his feet, and then kicked them into the sea while they were thus employed. At the foot of the rock there was a tortoise, which devoured the bodies of the robber's victims. He was slain by Theseus (Plut. *Thes.* 10). See THESEUS.

Scironia Saxa (Σκιρωνίδες πέτραι). Now Derveni Bouno. Large rocks on the eastern coast of Megaris, between which and the sea there was only a narrow, dangerous pass, called the Scironian Road. The name of the rocks was derived from that of the celebrated robber Sciron.

Scironĭdes (Σκιρωνίδης). An Athenian general who served at the siege of Miletus and against Chios in B.C. 412–411 (Thuc. viii. 25, 30, 54).

Scirophoria (τὰ Σκιροφόρια). An Athenian festival celebrated on the 12th of the month Scirophorion (June–July), called after it. It was in honour of Athené (or, according to some, Demeter and Koré), who was worshipped under the name of Sciras near Sciron, a spot on the Sacred Way leading from Athens to Eleusis. It had its name from the large white sunshade (σκίρον) beneath which the priestess of Athené (the patron goddess of the city), the priest of Erechtheus, and the priest of Helios went to Sciron to sacrifice. The sunshade was a symbol of heavenly protection against the rays of the sun, which began to burn more intensely during the month of the festival. This protection was invoked with special reason, for the dry limestone rock was thinly covered by a meagre surface of soil in the neighbourhood of Athens, and particularly near Sciron itself. In this, as in other festivals of invocation, there were also expiatory offerings; and hence they carried in the procession the hide of a ram that had been sacrificed to Zeus as the mild and gracious deity. See A. Mommsen, *Heortologie*, pp. 440 foll.

Scirpea. A wagon-body of basket-work. See PLAUSTRUM.

Scirpicŭlus. A sort of wicker basket. See CALATHUS.

Scirri or **Sciri**. A people variously described as Sarmatian (Pliny, *H. N.* iv. 97) and Scythian (Iornand. *R. G.* 49). To them belonged Odoacer (q. v.).

Scissor. A carver. See CENA, p. 313.

Scissors. See FORFEX.

Scobīna. A rasp for scraping wood (Pliny, *H. N.* xi. 68).

Scobis. Sawdust, which was used by the Romans for sprinkling upon the floor of rooms, especially of dining-rooms, as on the *terrasses* of modern French cafés and the floors of bar-rooms (Hor. *Sat.* ii. 4, 81; Juv. xiv. 67). In the houses of the wealthy, this sawdust was often coloured red or a bright yellow (Petron. 68). Elagabalus used gold-dust for the same purpose (Lamprid. *Elagab.* 31). The name is also used of filings of metals (cf. Blümner, *Technologie*, iv. 256).

Scodra. Now Scodar or Scutari; one of the most important towns in Illyricum, on the left bank of the river Barbana, at the southeast corner of the Lacus Labeatis, and about seventeen miles from the coast.

Scodrus. See SCARDUS.

Scolion (σκόλιον, sc. μέλος). A short lyrical poem, usually consisting of a single strophe, and intended to be sung after dinner over the wine. The ancients ascribed its invention to Terpander, and it received its first development among the Lesbians, and was written by such masters of song as Alcaeus, Sappho, Praxilla, Timocreon, Simonides, and Pindar. The last mentioned, however, gave it a more artistic form, with several strophes, in accordance with the rules of Dorian lyric verse. This class of poetry found a congenial home in the brilliant and lively city of Athens, where, to the very end of the Peloponnesian War, it was the regular custom at banquets, after all had joined in the paean, to pass round a lyre with a twig of myrtle, and to request all guests who had the requisite skill to sing such a song on the spur of the moment. To judge from the specimens that have been preserved, their contents were extremely varied: invocations of the gods, gnomic sayings, frequently with allusions to common proverbs and fables, and the praises of the blessings and pleasures of life. The most famous scolion was that by a certain Callistratus on Harmodius and Aristogiton, who had killed the tyrant Hipparchus, son of Pisistratus. It consists of four strophes, but the last three are only variations of the first. See HARMODIUS.

Scolŏti. See SCYTHIA.

Scolus (Σκῶλος). (1) A town in Boeotia, on the north slope of Mount Cithaeron (Herod. ix. 15). (2) A hamlet in Macedonia near Olynthus (Thuc. v. 18).

Scombraria. Now Islote; an island on the southeastern coast of Spain off Carthago Nova (Carthagena). It got its name from the mackerel (*scombri*) caught near by, from which the Romans prepared a sort of fish sauce (*garum*) resembling caviare (Strabo, p. 159).

Scomius Mons (τὸ Σκόμιον ὄρος). A mountain in Macedonia, which runs east of Mount Scardus, in the direction of north to south towards Mount Haemus.

Scopae (κάλλυντρον). A broom; usually made of twigs or rushes bound together (*scopae virgeae*, Cato, *R. R.* 156), and also of butcher's-broom (*ruscus*), palms, tamarisks, and myrtle. See Becker-Göll, *Gallus*, i. 35.

Scopas (Σκόπας). (1) An Aetolian, who held a leading position among his countrymen at the period of the outbreak of the war with Philip and the Achaeans (B.C. 220). He commanded the Aetolian army in the first year of the war; and he is mentioned again as general of the Aetolians, when the latter people concluded an alliance with the Romans to assist them against Philip (211) (Livy, xxxvi. 24). After the close of the war with Philip, Scopas and Dorimachus were appointed to reform the Aetolian constitution (204). Scopas had only undertaken the charge from motives of personal ambition; on finding himself disappointed in this object, he withdrew to Alexandria. Here he was received with the utmost favour by the ministers of the young king, Ptolemy V., and appointed to the chief command of the army against Antiochus the Great. At first he was successful, but was afterwards defeated by Antiochus at Panium, and reduced to shut himself up within the walls of Sidon, where he was ultimately compelled by famine to surrender (Joseph. *Ant.* xii. 3, 3). Notwithstanding this ill success he continued in high favour at the Egyptian court; but having formed a plot in 296 to obtain by force the chief administration of the kingdom, he was arrested and put to death (Polyb. xiii. 1; xvi. 18, 39).

(2) A distinguished sculptor, a native of Paros, who appears to have belonged to a family of artists in that island. He flourished from B.C. 395 to 350. He was probably somewhat older than Praxiteles, with whom he stands at the head of that second period of perfected art which is called the Later Attic School (in contradistinction to the Earlier Attic School of Phidias), and which arose at Athens after the Peloponnesian War. Scopas was an architect and a statuary as well as a sculptor. He was the architect of the Temple of Athené Alea at Tegea, in Arcadia, which was commenced soon after B.C. 394. He was one of the artists employed in executing the bas-reliefs that decorated the frieze of the Mausoleum at Halicarnassus in Caria. A portion of these bas-reliefs are now deposited in the British Museum. Among the single statues and groups of Scopas, the best known in modern times is his group of figures representing the destruction of the sons and daughters of Niobé. In Pliny's time the statues stood in the Temple of Apollo Sosianus (Pliny, xxxvi. 28). The remaining statues of this group, or copies of them, are all in the Florence Gallery, with the exception of the so-called Ilioneus at Munich, which some suppose to have belonged to the group. There is a head of Niobé in the collection of Lord Yarborough, which has some claim to be considered as the original. But the most esteemed of all the works of Scopas, in antiquity, was his group which stood in the shrine of Cn. Domitius in the Flaminian Circus, representing Achilles conducted to the island of Leucé by the divinities of the sea. It consisted of figures of Poseidon, Thetis, and Achilles, surrounded by Nereids, and attended by Tritons, and by an assemblage of sea monsters. See the monograph by Urlichs (1863); Perry, *Greek and Roman Sculpture*, pp. 378 foll. (1882); and the article STATUARIA ARS.

Scopas (Σκόπας). Now the Aladan; a river of Galatia, falling into the Sangarius, from the east, at Iuliopolis.

Scopŭla. A wisp-broom or hand-broom, used for cleaning the inside of jars (Cato, *R. R.* 26).

Scordisci. A people in Pannonia Superior, are sometimes classed among the Illyrians, but were the remains of an ancient and powerful Celtic tribe. They dwelt between the Savus and Dravus.

Scordiscus. A saddle. See EPHIPPIUM.

Scorpio. A kind of engine for projectiles, in earlier times identical with the catapult, and in later times with the *onager*. See TORMENTUM.

Scoti. A people mentioned, together with the Picti, by the later Roman writers as one of the chief tribes of the ancient Caledonians (Oros. i. 2; Amm. Marc. xxvii. 8, 4; Isid. *Orig.* xiv. 6). They dwelt in the south of Scotland and in Ireland; and from them the former country has derived its name. See Innes, *Ancient Inhabitants of Scotland* (1729); Skene, *Celtic Scotland* (last ed. 1886); and CALEDONIA.

Scotĭtas (Σκοτίτας). A district in the north of Laconia (Paus. iii. 10, 6).

Scotland. See BRITANNIA; CALEDONIA; SCOTI.

Scotussa (Σκότουσσα). A very ancient town of Thessaly, in the district Pelasgiotis, near the source of the Onchestus.

Scourge. See FLAGELLUM.

Screw. See COCHLEA.

Scribae ("writers," from *scribere*). The highest class among the inferior paid officials at Rome. (See APPARITOR.) They did not perform ordinary writers' services, which were usually assigned to slaves, but occupied the position of clerks, registrars, accountants, and secretaries. Of special importance were the *scribae quaestorii* attached to the *tribuni aerarii.* They formed three commissions of ten members each, and kept the accounts of the treasury. Two of their number were also attached to each provincial quaestor as accountants. The scribae also of the different aediles and tribunes appear to have formed a commission of ten members, while those taken from among them by the consuls, praetors, and censors seem to have been employed only during their term of office. The *pontifices* also had their scribae. See Mommsen, *Röm. Staatsrecht*, i. 331–339 (3d ed.); and for the Greek scribes, see GRAMMATEUS; NOTAE.

Scribilīta or **Scriblīta.** A sort of cake made of cheese and flour and eaten hot from the oven, with honey poured over the top (Cato, *R. R.* 78; Petron. 35; Mart. iii. 17).

Scribonia. Wife of Octavianus, afterwards the emperor Augustus, had been married twice before. By one of her former husbands, P. Scipio, she had two children—P. Scipio, who was consul in B.C. 16, and a daughter, Cornelia, who was married to Paulus Aemilius Lepidus, censor in B.C. 22. Scribonia was the sister of L. Scribonius Libo, who was the father-in-law of Sex. Pompey. Augustus married her in B.C. 40, on the advice of Maecenas, because he was then afraid that Sex. Pompey would form an alliance with Antony to crush him; but having renewed his alliance with Antony, Octavian divorced her in the following year (B.C. 39), on the very day on which she had borne him a daughter, Iulia, in order to marry Livia. Scribonia long survived her separation from Octavian. In A.D. 2 she accompanied, of her own accord, her daughter Iulia into exile to the island of Pandataria.

Scribonius Curio. See CURIO.

Scribonius Largus. A Roman physician who accompanied the emperor Claudius to Britain in A.D. 43. Between that year and A.D. 48 he compiled a treatise on medical prescriptions (*Compositiones Medicamentorum*), which we possess in a somewhat imperfect form. It contains 271 prescriptions tested by himself, and arranged according to the parts of the body, from the head downwards. The *editio princeps* is that of Ruellius (Paris, 1528), and it was subsequently edited by Rhodius (with a lexicon, Padua, 1655), and Bernhold (Strassburg, 1786). The standard edition is now that of Helmreich (Leipzig, 1887).

Scribonius Libo. See LIBO.

Scribonius Procŭlus. See PROCULUS.

Scrinium. A circular box or case for holding books, papers, etc. It must have closely resembled the *capsa*, yet Pliny (*H. N.* xvi. 84) distinguishes between them; whence it has been surmised that the scrinium was a *capsa* divided into compartments. See CAPSA.

Scriptōres Historiae Augustae. See AUGUSTAE HISTORIAE SCRIPTORES.

Scriptūra. A part of the revenue of the Roman Republic derived from the lease of such parts of the *ager publicus* as could be used for pasture (*pascua publica*). They were let by the censors to the publicans. (See PUBLICANI.) Those who grazed cattle on these lands were called *pecuarii* and paid for their use. Such cattle were registered (*scripti*), whence the name *scriptura*. When the pasture-lands were assigned to individual owners this tax disappeared. Cf. Pliny, *H. N.* xviii. 11; Cic. *Pro Flacco*, 8, 18.

Scrupŭlum. The smallest gold coin of the Romans, now very rare. It was in weight one-third of the *denarius*.

Sculponea. The wooden shoe of the Roman peasants and slaves. It was really little more than a thick sole of wood bound to the foot, as in the accompanying illustration.

Sculponea.

Sculptor. One who works in marble (Pliny, *H. N.* xxxvi. 5). See SCALPTURA; STATUARIA ARS.

Sculptūra. See STATUARIA ARS.

Scultenna. Now the Panaro. A river in Gallia Cispadana, rising in the Apennines, and flowing to the east of Mutina into the Padus (Po).

Scurra. A buffoon; a hanger-on of rich men. See PARASITUS.

Scutĭca. A whip with a thong of leather (Mart. x. 62). See FLAGELLUM.

Scutum (θυρεός). The large oblong shield generally adopted by the Roman infantry instead of the round buckler (*clipeus*), at the period when the military ceased to serve without pay. It was about four feet long by two and a half wide; formed out of boards, like a door (whence the Greek terms θύρα and θυρεός), firmly joined together and covered over with coarse cloth, under an outer coating of raw-hide, attached and strengthened round

Roman Soldiers with Shields. (Bartoli.)

the edges by a metal rim. The men of each legion had their shields painted of a different colour and charged with distinctive symbols (Livy, i. 43; viii. 8; Pliny, *H. N.* xvi. 77; Verg. *Aen* viii. 662; Veg. *Mil.* ii. 18; Polyb. ii. 30, 3; vi. 23, 2). See ARMA; CLIPEUS.

Scylăcē (Σκυλάκη) or **Scylaceïon.** An ancient city on the coast of Mysia Minor, at the foot of Mount Olympus, said to have been founded by the Pelasgians; and Herodotus (i. 57) speaks of the peculiar dialect spoken here in his time as "Pelasgian." See PELASGI.

Scylacium (Σκυλάκιον), also **Scylacēum** (Σκυλακεῖον), or **Scylletium** (Σκυλλήτιον). Now Squillace. A Greek town on the east coast of Bruttium, situated on the two adjoining hills at a short distance from the Coast, between the rivers Caecinus and Carcines. From this town the SCYLACIUS or SCYLLETĬCUS SINUS (Σκυλλητικὸς κόλπος) derived its name. It was at one time a dependency of Crotona, but was colonized by the Romans in B.C. 124, and again under Nerva.

Scylax (Σκύλαξ). (1) A native of Caryanda, in Caria, who was sent by Darius Hystaspis on a voyage of discovery down the Indus. Setting out from the city of Caspatyrus and the Pactyican district, Scylax reached the sea, and then sailed west through the Indian Ocean to the Red Sea, performing the whole voyage in thirty months (Herod. iv. 44). There is still extant a *Periplus* bearing the name of Scylax, but which could not have been written by the subject either of this or of the following article. The work is edited by C. Müller in the *Geographi Graeci Minores* (1861); and by Fabricius (1878). See Antichan, *Les Grands Voyages de Découvertes des Anciens* (Paris, 1890). (2) Of Halicarnassus, a friend of Panaetius, distinguished for his knowledge of the stars, and for his political influence in his own State (Cic. *Div.* ii. 42).

Scylax (Σκύλαξ). A river of Pontus emptying into the Iris.

Scylitzes or **Scylitza**, IOANNES. A Byzantine historian who flourished A.D. 1081. His works cover the period from A. D. 811 to 1801. Edited with Cedrenus by Bekker (Bonn, 1838).

Scylla (Σκύλλα) and **Charybdis** (Χαρυβδίς). The names of two rocks between Italy and Sicily. In the one nearest to Italy was a cave, in which dwelt Scylla, a daughter of Crataeis, a fearful monster, barking like a dog, with twelve feet, and six long necks and heads, each of which contained three rows of sharp teeth. The opposite rock, which was much lower, contained an immense fig-tree, under which dwelt Charybdis, who thrice every day swallowed down the waters of the sea, and thrice threw them up again (Hom. *Od.* xii. 73–110; 235–259; 430–444). This is the Homeric account; but later traditions give different accounts of Scylla's parentage. Heracles is said to have killed her, because she stole some of the oxen of Geryon; but Phorcys is said to have restored her to life. Vergil (*Aen.* vi. 286) speaks of several Scyllae, and places them in the lower world. Charybdis is de-

Scylla. (From a coin of Agrigentum.)

scribed as a daughter of Poseidon and Gaea, and as a voracious woman, who stole oxen from Heracles, and was hurled by the thunderbolt of Zeus into the sea. See Tzetz. *ad* Lycophr. 650; Eustath. p. 1719; Serv. *ad* Verg. *Aen.* iii. 420.

Scylla. See NISUS.

Scyllaeum (Σκύλλαιον). (1) Now Sciglio. A promontory on the coast of Bruttium, at the northern entrance to the Sicilian Strait, where the monster Scylla was supposed to live. See SCYLLA. (2) Now Scilla or Sciglio. A town in Bruttium, on the above-named promontory. There are still remains of the ancient citadel. (3) A promontory in Argolis, on the coast of Troezen, forming, with the promontory of Sunium in Attica, the entrance to the Saronic Gulf.

Scylletĭcus Sinus. See SCYLACIUM.

Scylletium. See SCYLACIUM.

Scyllis. See DIPOENUS.

Scymnus (Σκύμνος). A native of Chios, who wrote a *Periegesis*, or description of the earth, in prose, and which is therefore different from a Periegesis in iambic trimeter which has come down to us, and which describes the coast of Europe from the Pillars of Hercules to Apollonia in Pontus. This latter work is dedicated to King Nicomedes, probably Nicomedes III. (B.C. 91–96) of Bithynia. It is edited by Meineke (Berlin, 1846); and by C. Müller in the *Geographi Graeci Minores* (Paris, 1841).

Scyphus (σκύφος). A bowl-shaped cup.

Scyros (Σκῦρος). Now Scyro. An island in the Aegaean Sea, east of Euboea, and one of the Sporades. Here Thetis concealed her son Achilles in woman's attire among the daughters of Lycomedes, and here also Pyrrhus, the son of Achilles by Deidamia, was brought up. According to another tradition the island was conquered by Achilles, in order to revenge the death of Theseus, who is said to have been treacherously destroyed in Scyros by Lycomedes. The bones of Theseus were discovered by Cimon in Scyros, after his conquest of the island, B.C. 476, and were conveyed to Athens, where they were preserved in the Theseum (Thuc. i. 98; Diod. Sic. xi. 60). From this time Scyros continued subject to Athens till the period of the Macedonian supremacy; but the Romans compelled the last Philip to restore it to Athens, B.C. 196 (Livy, xxxiii. 30).

Scytălē (σκυτάλη). A staff, used especially in Sparta by the ephors for their secret despatches to officials, particularly to commanders, in foreign countries (Plut. *Lysand.* 19; Gell. xvii. 9, 3; Suid. s. h. v.). A narrow strip of white leather was wound about a round staff so that the edges came exactly together; it was then written on crosswise, and sent to its destination after being unrolled again. What had been written could only be read when the strip was again wound round an exactly similar staff, such as was given to every official when going abroad on public service. See NOTAE.

Scythae (Σκύθαι). A corps of archers among the Athenians, formed of State slaves, who performed the duties of police and were also employed in war. See DEMOSII.

Scythe. See FALX.

Scythia (Σκυθιά, and Σκυθική sc. γῆ). A name variously used by the ancients at different periods of history. The Scythia of Herodotus comprises, to speak generally, the southeastern parts of Europe, between the Carpathian Mountains and the river Tanaïs (Don). The Greeks became acquainted with this country through their settlements on the Euxine; and Herodotus, who had himself visited the coasts of the Euxine, collected all the information he could obtain about the Scythians and their country, and embodied the results in a most interesting digression, which forms the first part of his fourth book. He describes the country as a square of 4000 stadia (400 geographical miles) each way, the western boundary being the Ister (Danube) and the mountains of the Agathyrsi; the southern the shores of the Euxine and Palus Maeotis, from the mouth of the Ister to that of the Tanaïs, this side being divided into two equal parts, of 2000 stadia each, by the mouth of the Borysthenes (Dnieper); the eastern boundary was the Tanaïs, and on the north Scythia was divided by deserts from the Melanchlaeni, Androphagi, and Budini. It corresponded to the southern part of Russia in Europe. The people who inhabited this region were called by the Greeks Σκύθαι, a word of doubtful origin, which first occurs in Hesiod; but, in their own language, Σκόλοτοι, i. e. Slavonians. They were believed by Herodotus to be of Asiatic origin; and his account of them, taken in connection with the description given by Hippocrates of their physical peculiarities, has been regarded as proof that they were a part of the great Mongol race, who wandered, from unknown antiquity, over the steppes of Central Asia; yet the general drift of opinion at the present time is toward assigning to them Aryan affinities. Herodotus says further that they were driven out of their abodes in Asia, north of the Araxes, by the Massagetae; and that, migrating into Europe, they drove out the Cimmerians. If this account be true, it can hardly but have some connection with the irruption of the Cimmerians into Asia Minor, in the reign of the Lydian king Ardys, about B.C. 640.

The Scythians were a nomadic people, that is, shepherds or herdsmen, who had no fixed habitations, but roamed over a vast tract of country at their pleasure, and according to the wants of their cattle. They lived in a kind of covered wagons, which Aeschylus describes as "lofty houses of wicker-work, on well-wheeled chariots" (*Prom. Vinc.* 710). They were filthy in their habits, never washing, fought on horseback, scalped their enemies, and drank out of their skulls when slain. They kept large troops of horses, and were most expert in cavalry exercises and archery; and hence, as the Persian king Darius found, when he invaded their country (B.C. 507), it was almost impossible for an invading army to act against them. They simply retreated, wagons and all, before the enemy, harassing him with their light cavalry, and leaving famine and exposure, in their bare steppes, to do the rest. Like all nomadic races, they were divided into several hordes, the chief of whom were called the Royal Scythians; and to these all the rest owned some degree of allegiance. Their government was a sort of patriarchal monarchy or chieftainship. An important modification of their habits had, however, taken place, to a certain extent, before Herodotus described them. The fertility of the plains on the north of the Euxine, and the influence of the Greek settlements at the mouth of the Borysthenes and along the coast, had led the inhabitants of this part of Scythia to settle down as cultivators of the soil, and had brought them into commercial and other relations with the Greeks. Accordingly, Herodotus mentions two classes or hordes of Scythians who had thus abandoned their nomad life; first, on the west of the Borysthenes, two tribes of Hellenized Scythians, called Callipidae and Alazones; then, beyond these, "the Scythians who are ploughers (Σκύθαι ἀροτῆρες), who do not grow their corn for food, but for sale"; these dwelt about the river Hypanis (Boug), in the region now called the Ukraine, which is still, as it was to the Greeks, a great corn-exporting country. Again, on the east of the Borysthenes were "the Scythians who are husbandmen" (Σκύθαι γεωργοί), i. e. who grew corn for their own consumption: these were called Borysthenitae by the Greeks; their country extended

Scythian Horseman. (Sculptures at Kertch).

three days' journey east of the Borysthenes to the river Panticapes. Beyond these, to the east, dwelt "the nomad Scythians (νομάδες Σκύθαι), who neither sow nor plough at all." Herodotus expressly states that the tribes east of the Borysthenes were not Scythian. Of the history of these Scythian tribes there is little to state, beyond the tradition already mentioned, that they migrated from Asia and expelled the Cimmerians; their invasion of Media, in the reign of Cyaxares, when they held the supremacy of Western Asia for twenty-eight years, and the disastrous expedition of Darius into their country. In later times they were gradually overpowered by the neighbouring people, especially the Sarmatians, who gave their name to the whole country. (See SARMATIA.) Meanwhile, the conquests of Alexander and his successors in Central Asia had made the Greeks acquainted with tribes beyond the Oxus and the Iaxartes, who resembled the Scythians, and belonged, in fact, to the same race, and to whom, accordingly, the same name was applied. Hence, in writers of the time of the Roman Empire, the name of Scythia denotes the whole of Northern Asia, from the river Rha (Volga) on the west, which divided it from Asiatic Sarmatia, to Serica on the east, extending to India on the south. It was divided by Mount Imaüs into two parts, called respectively SCYTHIA INTRA IMAŬM, i. e. on the northwestern side of the range, and SCYTHIA EXTRA IMAŬM, on its southeastern side. The later Scythians overran Parthia (B.C. 128), and also invaded Northern India, where they maintained themselves for several centuries. The Jats and Rajputs of modern India have by some scholars been regarded as the descendants of these Scythian invaders.

See the editions of Herodotus by Rawlinson and Sayce; Neumann, *Die Hellenen im Skythenland* (1855); Müllenhoff and Kuno, *Die Skythen* (1871); Fressl, *Skytho-Saken* (1886); and Krause, *Tuisko-Land* (1891).

Scythīni (Σκυθινοί). A people on the western border of Armenia, through whose country the Greeks under Xenophon marched four days' journey (*Anab.* iv. 7, 18).

Scythīnus (Σκυθῖνος). A native of Teos. He versified the philosophic treatise of Heraclitus (q. v.), of which a fragment is preserved in Stobaeus. Edited by Müller in his *Frag. Hist. Graec.*

Scythopŏlis (Σκυθόπολις). The Old Test. Bethshan, now Beisan. An important city of Palestine, in the southeast of Galilee, according to the usual division, but sometimes also reckoned to Samaria, sometimes to Decapolis, and sometimes to Coele-Syria. It is often mentioned in Old Testament history, in the time of the Maccabees, and under the Romans. It had a mixed population of Canaanites, Philistines, and Assyrian settlers (Pliny, *H. N.* v. 74). Under the late Roman Empire it became the seat of the archbishop of Palestina Secunda, and it continued a flourishing city to the time of the first Crusade.

Scythotauri, Tauri Scythae, or **Tauroscȳthae.** A people of European Sarmatia near the Crimea (Pliny, *H. N.* iv. 85).

Sea-captain. See NAVARCHUS.

Sealing-wax. See CERA.

Seals. See SIGILLUM.

Seats. See SELLA.

Sebasté; in Latin, AUGUSTA. (1) Now Ayash, a city on the coast of Cilicia Aspera. (2) Now Segikler, a city of Phrygia, northwest of Eumenia. (3) A city in Pontus, also called Cabira. (See CABIRA.) (4) See SAMARIA.

Sebennȳtus (Σεβέννυτος). Now Semennout. A considerable city of Lower Egypt, in the Delta, on the western side of the branch of the Nile, called after it the Sebennytic Mouth. It was the capital of the Nomos Sebennytes or Sebennyticus (Ptol. iv. 5, 50).

Sebēthus. Now the Maddalena. A small river in Campania, flowing around Vesuvius, and falling into the Sinus Puteolanus at the eastern side of Neapolis (Naples). See NEAPOLIS.

Sebīnus Lacus. Now the Lago Seo; a lake in Gallia Cisalpina (Pliny, *H. N.* ii. 224).

Secespĭta. A sort of sacrificial knife, made of iron, with an ivory handle (Fest. s. h. v.).

Secespita. (From a frieze at Rome.)

Secretary. See GRAMMATEUS; SCRIBAE.

Secret writing. See NOTAE; SCYTALÉ.

Secular Games. See LUDI, p. 974.

Secundus, P. POMPONIUS. (1) A distinguished Roman poet, who lived in the reigns of Tiberius, Caligula, and Claudius. He was one of the friends of Seianus, and on the fall of that minister in A.D. 31, was thrown into prison, where he remained till the accession of Caligula in 37, by whom he was released. He was consul in 41, and in the reign of Claudius commanded in Germany, when he defeated the Chatti (Tac. *Ann.* v. 8; xi. 13; xii. 28). Secundus was an intimate friend of the elder Pliny, who wrote his life in two books (Quint. x. 1, 98). His tragedies were the most celebrated of his literary compositions. (2) IULIUS, a Roman orator, and a friend of Quintilian, is one of the speakers in the *Dialogus de Oratoribus* of Tacitus.

Secūris (πέλεκυς). An axe or hatchet used for a variety of purposes, as for a weapon (Curt. iii. 4); for sacrificing victims (Hor. *Carm.* iii. 23, 12); or for felling trees (Ovid, *Trist.* iv. 2, 5). When it had a small second edge projecting at the back of the regular blade it was called *securis dolabrata* (see DOLABRA), and *securis simplex* to distinguish it from the two-edged axe (*bipennis;* cf. Pallad. *R. R.* i. 43). The name is also given to the symbolical axe carried by the lictor in the *fasces* (see FASCES), and indicating the power of death which the State possessed. A pickaxe is also sometimes called *securis* (Stat. *Silv.* ii. 2, 87).

Secūtor. See GLADIATORES, p. 734.

Sedan-chair. See LECTICA.

Sedecŭla (διφρίσκος). A low seat or stool; a settee (Cic. *Ad Att.* iv. 10).

Sedes (ἕδρα). The generic term for any seat. For special kinds of chairs, benches, etc., see CATHEDRA; SEDECULA; SEDILÉ; SELLA.

Sedetāni. See EDETANI.

Sedigĭtus, VOLCATIUS. A Roman writer, from whose work *De Poëtis* Gellius (xv. 24) has preserved thirteen iambic senarii, in which the principal Latin comic dramatists are enumerated in the order of merit. In this "Canon," as it has been termed, the first place is assigned to Caecilius Statius, the second to Plautus, the third to Naevius, the fourth to Licinius, the fifth to Attilius, the sixth to Terentius, the seventh to Turpilius, the eighth to Trabea, the ninth to Luscius, the tenth, *antiquitatis causa*, to Ennius.

Sedīlé. In the singular, a general name for a seat. In the plural (*sedilia*), a row of seats in the theatre (Pliny, *Epist.* v. 6).

Sedulius, CAELIUS. A Christian poet of the second half of the fifth century; he died when still young. At first he wrote secular poetry, but afterwards composed a poem in five books on the miracles of Christ (*Carmen Paschale*), a simple narrative following the gospels, in many points imitating Vergil. This was followed by a prose version (*Opus Paschale*), laboured and bombastic in style; also by an elaborate comparison of the Old and New Testaments in fifty-five couplets, and a hymn to Christ in twenty-three quatrains of iambic dimeters, remarkable for the partial employment of rhyme as a musical element. The verses commence with the successive letters of the alphabet. Portions of this hymn have always been in use in the Church of Rome. We quote the first two stanzas:

> A solis ortus cardine
> Ad usque terrae limitem,
> Christum canamus Principem,
> Ortum Maria Virgine.
>
> Beatus Auctor saeculi
> Servile corpus induit;
> Ut carne carnem liberans
> Ne perderet quos condidit.

Edited by Arevalus (Rome, 1794); and Hulmer (Vienna, 1885). See HYMNUS.

Sedūni. An Alpine people in Gallia Belgica, east of the Lake of Geneva, in the valley of the Rhone, in the modern Vallais (Caes. *B. G.* iii. 1, 7).

Sedusii. A German people, forming part of the army of Ariovistus, when he invaded Gaul in B.C. 58. Their site can not be determined (Caes. *B. G.* i. 51).

Segesta. One of the Dii Indigetes; a god of sowing. See INDIGETES.

Segesta. Now Alcamo; the later Roman form of the town called by the Greeks EGESTA (Ἔγεστα) or AEGESTA (Αἴγεστα), in Vergil ACESTA; situated in the northwest of Sicily, near the coast between Panormus and Drepanum. It is said to have been founded by the Trojans on two small rivers, to which they gave the names of Simoïs and Scamander; hence the Romans called it a colony of Aeneas (Thucyd. vi. 2; Dionys. i. 52). Its ruins are still very beautiful, and include the remains of a Doric temple of the sixth century B.C.

Segestes. A Cheruscan chieftain, the opponent of Arminius. He warned the Roman general, Varus, of the movements of Arminius, but the warning was disregarded. (See ARMINIUS; VARUS.) In B.C. 14, Segestes was forced by his followers into a war with the Romans, but afterwards made peace with them and was allowed to live at Narbonne for the rest of his life (Tac. *Ann.* i. 55–59; Flor. iv. 12).

Segestré or **Segestrium** (στέγαστρον). A covering or wrapper of any material, as straw (Varro, *L. L.* v. 166), or fur (Fest. s. h. v.).

Segmentum. An ornament attached to women's dresses, in the shape of strips of gold tissue or other rich material, sewed upon the skirts in parallel lines and running around it like tucks (Isidor. *Orig.* xix. 22, 18).

Segni. A German people in Gallia Belgica, between the Treveri and Eburones, the name of whom is still preserved in the town of Sinei or Signei (Caes. *B. G.* vi. 32).

Segobrīga. The chief town of the Celtiberi, in Hispania Tarraconensis, southwest of Caesaraugusta (Saragossa), near the modern Priego.

Segontia or **Seguntia.** A town of the Celtiberi, in Hispania Tarraconensis, sixteen miles from Caesaraugusta (Saragossa).

Segovia. (1) Now Segovia; a town of the Arevaci, on the road from Emerita to Caesaraugusta. A magnificent Roman aqueduct is still extant at Segovia. (2) A town in Hispania Baetica on the Flumen Silicensé, near Sacili.

Segusiāni. One of the most important peoples in Gallia Lugdunensis, bounded by the Allobroges on the south, by the Sequani on the east, by the Aedui on the north, and by the Arverni on the west. In their territory was the town of Lugdunum (q.v.), the capital of the modern province (Caes. *B. G.* i. 10; vii. 64).

Segusio. Now Susa; the capital of Segusini and the residence of King Cottius, was situated in Gallia Transpadana, at the foot of the Cottian Alps. The triumphal arch erected at this place by the Gallic leader Cottius in honour of Augustus is still extant.

Seiānus, AELIUS. A Roman statesman, born at Vulsinii in Etruria. He was the son of Seius Strabo, who was commander of the praetorian troops at the close of the reign of Augustus, A.D. 14 (Tac. *Ann.* iv. 1). In the same year Seianus was made the colleague of his father in the command of the praetorian bands; and upon his father being sent as governor to Egypt, he obtained the sole command of these troops. He ultimately gained such influence over Tiberius that this suspicious man, who was close and reserved to all mankind, opened his bosom to Seianus, and made him his confidant. For many years he governed Tiberius; but, not content with this high position, he formed the design of obtaining the imperial power. With this view he sought to make himself popular with the soldiers, and gave posts of honour and emolument to his creatures and favourites. With the same object he resolved to get rid of all the members of the imperial family. He debauched Livia, the wife of Drusus, the son of Tiberius; and by promising her marriage and a participation in the imperial power, he was enabled to poison Drusus with her connivance and assistance (A.D. 23). An accident increased the credit of Seianus, and confirmed the confidence of Tiberius. The emperor, with Seianus and others, was feasting in a natural cave, between Amyclae, which was on the seacoast, and the hills of Fundi. The entrance of the cave suddenly fell in and crushed some of the slaves; and all the guests, in alarm, tried to make their escape. Seianus, resting his knees on the couch of Tiberius, and placing his shoulders under the falling rock, protected his master, and was discovered in this posture by the soldiers who came to their relief. After Tiberius had shut himself up in the island of Capreae, Seianus had full scope for his machinations; and the death of Livia, the mother of Tiberius (A.D. 29), was followed by the banishment of Agrippina and her sons Nero and Drusus. Tiberius at last began to suspect the designs of Seianus, and felt that it was time to rid himself of a man who was almost more than a rival. To cover his schemes and remove Seianus from about him, Tiberius made him joint consul with himself in A.D. 31. He then sent Sertorius Macro to Rome with a commission to take the command of the praetorian cohorts. Macro, after assuring himself of the troops, and depriving Seianus of his usual guard, produced a letter from Tiberius to the Senate, in which the emperor expressed his apprehensions of Seianus. The consul Regulus conducted him to prison, and the people loaded him with insult and outrage. The Senate on the same day decreed his death, and he was immediately executed. His body was dragged about the streets and finally thrown into the Tiber. Many of the friends of Seianus perished at the same time, and his son and daughter shared his fate (Tac. *Ann.* iv. 41–59, 74; v. 6–9; Suet. *Tib.*; Dio Cass. lvii., lviii.; Juv. x. 65–86). The story of Seianus is the subject of a play by Ben Jonson, entitled *Sejanus*, produced in 1603. See TIBERIUS.

Seisachtheia (σεισάχθεια, "a shaking off of burdens"). A term used for the removal of the burden of debt effected by Solon. All debts were cancelled, and the securing of debts upon the person of the debtor was made illegal, as in the Roman *tabulae novae*. See Aristot. *Polit. Ath.* 6; and SOLON.

Seiŭgis. A chariot drawn by six horses harnessed abreast of one another (Livy, xxxviii. 35).

Seius Strabo. See SEIANUS.

Selēnē (Σελήνη). The Greek goddess of the moon, daughter of the Titan Hyperion and Theia, sister of Helios and Eos. She was described as a beautiful woman with long wings and golden diadem, from which she shed a mild light (Homer, *Hymns*, xxxii. 7), riding in a car drawn by two white horses or mules or cows. The horns of the latter symbolized the crescent moon. In later times she was identified with Artemis (or else with Hecaté and Persephoné), as was Helios with Phoebus Apollo, and therefore was herself called Phoebé. After this she was also regarded as a huntress and archer, recognizable by her crescent as the goddess of the moon. She was worshipped on the days of the new and full moon. She bore to Zeus a daughter, Pandia, worshipped at Athens with her father at the festival of Pandia (Demosth. *Or.* 21, § 9). On her love for Endymion, see ENDYMION. The Romans called her LUNA, and had two temples to her at Rome—one on the Aventine and one on the Palatine.

Seleucīa, and rarely **Seleucēa** (Σελεύκεια). The name of several cities in Asia, built by Seleucus I., king of Syria. (1) SELEUCIA AD TIGRIN (ἡ ἐπὶ τοῦ Τίγρητος ποταμοῦ, πρὸς Τίγρει, ἀπὸ Τίγριος), also called SELEUCIA BABYLONIA (Σ. ἡ ἐν Βαβυλῶνι), SELEUCIA ASSYRIAE, and SELEUCIA PARTHŌRUM. A great city on the confines of Assyria and Babylonia, and for a long time the capital of Western Asia, until it was eclipsed by Ctesiphon. Its exact site has been disputed; but the most probable opinion is that it stood on the western bank of the Tigris, north of its junction with the Royal Canal, opposite to the mouth of the river Delas or Silla (Diala), and to the spot where Ctesiphon was afterwards built by the Parthians. It was a little to the south of the modern city of Bagdad. Perhaps a better site could not be found in Western Asia. It commanded the navigation of the Tigris and Euphrates, and the whole plain of those two rivers; and it stood at the junction of all the chief caravan roads by which the traffic between Eastern and Western Asia was carried on. In addition to these advantages, its people had, by the gift of Seleucus, the government of their own affairs. It was built in the form of an eagle with expanded wings, and was peopled by settlers from Assyria, Mesopotamia, Babylonia, Syria, and Iudaea. It rapidly rose, and eclipsed Babylon in wealth and splendour. Even after the Parthian kings had become masters of the banks of the Tigris, and had fixed their residence at Ctesiphon, Seleucia, though deprived of much of its importance, remained a very considerable city. In the reign of Titus, it had, according to Pliny, 600,000 inhabitants. It was burned by Trajan in his Parthian expedition, and again by L. Verus, the colleague of M. Aurelius Antoninus, when its population is given by different authorities as 300,000 or 400,000. It was again taken by Severus, and from this blow it never recovered. In Julian's expedition it was found entirely deserted. See Fabian, *De Seleucia Babylonia* (1869); and Schneiderwirth, *Seleucia am Tigris* (1874). (2) SELEUCIA PIERIA (Σ. Πιερία, ἡ ἐν Πιερίᾳ, ἡ πρὸς Ἀντιοχείᾳ, ἡ πρὸς θαλάσσᾳ, ἡ ἐπιθαλλασσία, called Seleukeh or Kepse, near Suadeiah). A great city and fortress of Syria, founded by Seleucus in April, B.C. 300, one month before the foundation of Antioch. It stood on the site of an ancient fortress, on the rocks overhanging the sea, at the foot of Mount Pieria, about four miles north of the

Orontes, and twelve miles west of Antioch. Its natural strength was improved by every known art of fortification, to which were added all the works of architecture and engineering required to make it a splendid city and a great seaport, while it obtained abundant supplies from the fertile plain between the city and Antioch. The remains of Seleucus I. were interred at Seleucia, in a mausoleum surrounded by a grove. In the war with Egypt, which ensued upon the murder of Antiochus II., Seleucia surrendered to Ptolemy III. Euergetes (B.C. 246). It was afterwards recovered by Antiochus the Great (219). In the war between Antiochus VIII. and IX. the people of Seleucia made themselves independent (109 or 108). Afterwards, having successfully resisted the attacks of Tigranes for fourteen years (84–70), they were confirmed in their freedom by Pompey. The city had fallen entirely into decay by the sixth century of our era. There are considerable ruins of the harbour and mole, of the walls of the city, and of its necropolis. The surrounding district was called Seleucis.

(3) SELEUCIA AD BELUM, a city of Syria, in the valley of the Orontes, near Apamea. Its site is doubtful. (4) SELEUCIA TRACHEŌTIS (Selefkeh), an important city of Cilicia Aspera, built by Seleucus I. on the western bank of the river Calycadnus, about four miles from its mouth, and peopled with the inhabitants of several neighbouring cities. It had an oracle of Apollo, and annual games in honour of Zeus Olympius. It vied with Tarsus in power and splendour, and was a free city under the Romans. It has remarkable claims to renown both in political and literary history—in the former as the place where Trajan and Frederick Barbarossa died; in the latter as the birthplace of the philosophers Athenaeus and Xenarchus, of the sophist Alexander, the secretary of M. Aurelius Antoninus, and of other learned men. On its site are still seen the ruins of temples, porticoes, aqueducts, and tombs. (5) SELEUCIA IN MESOPOTAMIA (Bir), on the left bank of the Euphrates, opposite to the ford of Zeugma, was a fortress of considerable importance in ancient military history. (6) A considerable city of Margiana, built by Alexander the Great, in a beautiful situation, and called Alexandria. It was destroyed by the barbarians and rebuilt by Antiochus I., who named it Seleucia after his father Seleucus I. The Roman prisoners taken at the defeat of Crassus by the Parthians were settled here by king Orodes. (7) SELEUCIA IN CARIA. See TRALLES.

There were other cities of the name of less importance in Pisidia, Pamphylia, Palestine, and Elymaïs.

Seleucĭdae. See SELEUCUS.

Seleucis (Σελευκίς). The most beautiful and fertile district of Syria, containing the northwestern part of the country between Mount Amanus on the north, the Mediterranean on the west, the districts of Cyrrhesticé and Chalybonitis on the northeast, the desert on the east, and Coele-Syria and the mountains of Lebanon on the south.

Seleucus (Σέλευκος). The name of several kings of Syria. (1) Surnamed NICĀTOR, the founder of the Syrian monarchy, reigned B.C. 312–280. He was the son of Antiochus, a Macedonian of distinction among the officers of Philip II., and was born about B.C. 358. He accompanied Alexander on his expedition to Asia, and distinguished himself particularly in the Indian campaigns. After the death of Alexander (323) he espoused the side of Perdiccas, whom he accompanied on his expedition against Egypt; but he took a leading part in the mutiny of the soldiers, which ended in the death of Perdiccas (321). In the second partition of the provinces which followed, Seleucus obtained the wealthy and important satrapy of Babylonia. In the war between Antigonus and Eumenes, Seleucus afforded efficient support to the former; but after the death of Eumenes (316), Antigonus began to treat the other satraps as his subjects. Thereupon Seleucus fled to Egypt, where he induced Ptolemy to unite with Lysimachus and Cassander in a league against their common enemy. In the war that ensued Seleucus took an active part. At length, in 312, he recovered Babylon; and it is from this period that the Syrian monarchy is commonly reckoned to commence. This era of the Seleucidae, as it is termed, has been determined by chronologists to the 1st of October, 312. Soon afterwards Seleucus defeated Nicanor, the satrap of Media, and followed up his victory by the conquest of Susiana, Media, and some adjacent districts. For the next few years he gradually extended his power over all the eastern provinces which had formed part of the empire of Alexander, from the Euphrates to the banks of the Oxus and

Coin of Seleucus Nicator.

the Indus. In 306 Seleucus followed the example of Antigonus and Ptolemy, by formally assuming the royal title and diadem. In 302 he joined the league formed for the second time by Ptolemy, Lysimachus, and Cassander, against their common enemy Antigonus. The united forces of Seleucus and Lysimachus gained a decisive victory over Antigonus at Ipsus (301), in which Antigonus himself was slain. In the division of the spoil, Seleucus obtained the largest share, being rewarded for his services with a great part of Asia Minor (which was divided between him and Lysimachus) as well as with the whole of Syria, from the Euphrates to the Mediterranean.

The empire of Seleucus was now by far the most extensive and powerful of those which had been formed out of the dominions of Alexander. It comprised the whole of Asia, from the remote provinces of Bactria and Sogdiana to the coasts of Phœnicia, and from the Paropamisus to the central plains of Phrygia, where the boundary which separated him from Lysimachus is not clearly defined. Seleucus appears to have felt the difficulty of exercising a vigilant control over so extensive an empire, and accordingly, in 293, he consigned the government of all the provinces beyond the Euphrates to his son Antiochus, upon whom he bestowed the title of king, as well as the hand of his own youthful wife, Stratonicé, for whom the prince had conceived a violent attachment. In

288, the ambitious designs of Demetrius (now become king of Macedonia) once more aroused the common jealousy of his old adversaries, and led Seleucus again to unite in a league with Ptolemy and Lysimachus against him. After Demetrius had been driven from his kingdom by Lysimachus, he transported the seat of war into Asia Minor, but he was compelled to surrender to Seleucus in 286. The Syrian king kept Demetrius in confinement till three years afterwards, but during the whole of that time treated him in a friendly and liberal manner. For some time jealousies had existed between Seleucus and Lysimachus; but the immediate cause of the war between the two monarchs, which terminated in the defeat and death of Lysimachus (281), is related in the life of the latter. Seleucus now crossed the Hellespont in order to take possession of the throne of Macedonia, which had been left vacant by the death of Lysimachus; but he had advanced no farther than Lysimachia, when he was assassinated by Ptolemy Ceraunus, to whom, as the son of his old friend and ally, he had extended a friendly protection. His death took place in the beginning of 280, only seven months after that of Lysimachus, and in the thirty-second year of his reign. He was in his seventy-eighth year. Seleucus appears to have carried out, with great energy and perseverance, the projects originally formed by Alexander himself for the Hellenization of his Asiatic empire; and we find him founding, in almost every province, Greek or Macedonian colonies, which became so many centres of civilization and refinement. Of these no less than sixteen are mentioned as bearing the name of Antiochia, after his father; five that of Laodicea, from his mother; seven were called after himself Seleucia; three from the name of his first wife, Apamea; and one Stratonicea, from his second wife, the daughter of Demetrius. Numerous other cities, whose names attest their Macedonian origin—Beroea, Edessa, Pella, etc.—likewise owed their first foundation to Seleucus.

(2) Surnamed CALLINĬCUS (246–226), the eldest son of Antiochus II. by his first wife Laodicé. The first measure of his administration, or rather that of his mother, was to put to death his stepmother Berenicé, together with her infant son. This act of cruelty produced the most disastrous effects. In order to avenge his sister, Ptolemy Euergetes, king of Egypt, invaded the dominions of Seleucus, and not only made himself master of Antioch and the whole of Syria, but carried his arms unopposed beyond the Euphrates and the Tigris. During these operations Seleucus kept wholly aloof; but when Ptolemy had been recalled to his own dominions by domestic disturbances, he recovered possession of the greater part of the provinces which he had lost. Soon afterward Seleucus became involved in a dangerous war with his brother Antiochus Hierax, who attempted to obtain Asia Minor as an independent kingdom for himself. This war lasted several years, but was at length terminated by the decisive defeat of Antiochus, who was obliged to abandon Asia Minor and take refuge in Egypt. Seleucus undertook an expedition to the East, with the view of reducing the revolted provinces of Parthia and Bactria, which had availed themselves of the disordered state of the Syrian Empire to throw off its yoke. He was, however, defeated by Arsaces, king of Parthia, in a great battle, which was long after celebrated by the Parthians as the foundation of their independence. After the expulsion of Antiochus, Attalus, king of Pergamus, extended his dominions over the greater part of Asia Minor; and Seleucus appears to have been engaged in an expedition for the recovery of these provinces, when he was accidentally killed by a fall from his horse, in the twenty-first year of his reign, 226. He left two sons, who successively ascended the throne, Seleucus Ceraunus and Antiochus, afterward surnamed the Great. His own surname of Callinicus was probably assumed after his recovery of the provinces that had been overrun by Ptolemy.

(3) Surnamed CERAUNUS (226–223), eldest son and successor of Seleucus II. The surname of Ceraunus ("Thunderbolt") was given him by the soldiery, apparently in derision, as he appears to have been feeble both in mind and body. He was assassinated by two of his officers, after a reign of only three years, and was succeeded by his brother, Antiochus the Great. (4) Surnamed PHILOPĀTOR (187–175), was the son and successor of Antiochus the Great. The defeat of his father by the Romans, and the ignominious peace which followed it, had greatly diminished the power of the Syrian monarchy, and the reign of Seleucus was, in consequence, feeble and inglorious, and was marked by no striking events. He was assassinated in 175 by one of his own ministers. He left two children: Demetrius, who subsequently ascended the throne; and Laodicé, married to Perseus, king of Macedonia. (5) Eldest son of Demetrius II., assumed the royal diadem on learning the death of his father, 125; but his mother, Cleopatra, who had herself put Demetrius to death, was indignant at hearing that her son had ventured to take such a step without her authority, and caused Seleucus also to be assassinated. (6) Surnamed EPIPHĂNES, and also NICĀTOR (95–93), was the eldest of the five sons of Antiochus VIII. (Grypus). His uncle, who laid claim to the kingdom, was defeated and slain by him. Presently, however, Seleucus was himself expelled from Syria by Antiochus Eusebus. He retired to Cilicia, where he made himself master of the city of Mopsuestia, whose citizens presently revolted against him and burned the palace, in whose flames Seleucus himself perished.

Selgé (Σέλγη). One of the chief of the independent mountain cities of Pisidia, stood on the south side of Mount Taurus, on the Eurymedon, just where the river breaks through the mountain chain. Its people were the most warlike of all the Pisidians, and claimed descent from the Lacedemonians, even inscribing the name *Λακεδαίμων* on their coins (Strabo, p. 570). Ruins of the ancient city still exist.

Selīnūs (Σελινοῦς). (1) A small river on the southwestern coast of Sicily, flowing by the town of the same name. (2) Now Crestena, a river of Elis, in the district Triphylia, near Scillus, flowing into the Alpheus west of Olympia. (3) Now Vostitza, a river of Achaia, rising in Mount Erymanthus. (4) A tributary of the Caicus, in Mysia, flowing by the town of Pergamum. (5) Now Castel Vetrano, one of the most important towns in Sicily, situated upon a hill on the southwestern coast and upon a river of the same name. It was founded by the Dorians from Megara Hyblaea, on the eastern coast of Sicily, B.C. 628. It soon attained great prosperity; but it was taken by the

Carthaginians in 409, when most of its inhabitants were slain or sold as slaves and the greater part of the city destroyed. The ruins of the ancient city are of great extent and magnificence, the temple of Zeus being one of the largest of which remains still exist. (6) Now Selenti, a town in Cilicia, situated on the coast.

Sella (δίφρος). The generic term for a seat. Chairs of every variety of shape were used by the ancients. (See CATHEDRA; LECTICA; SEDECULA; SOLIUM; THRONUS; TRIPUS.) A camp-chair was

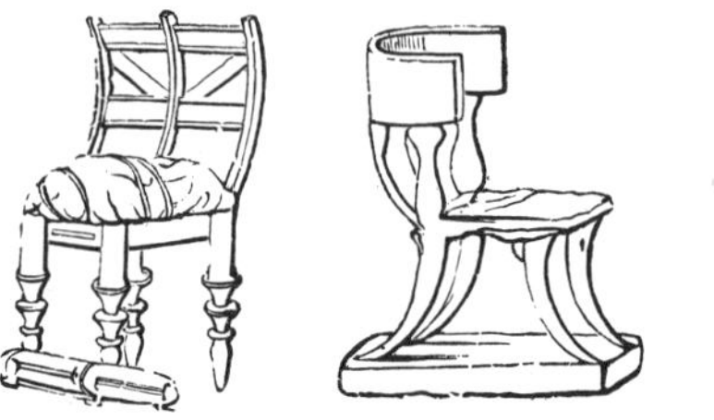

Sellae. (The first from a Pompeian painting; the second from a bronze original in the Vatican.)

called *sella castrensis* (Nero, *Galba*, 18). A night-stool was called *sella familiarica* (Varro, *R. R.* i. 13, 4).

Sella Curūlis. The Latin term for the chair of office belonging to the curule magistrates (consuls, praetors, curule aediles, dictator, *magister equitum*, and *flamen Dialis*), and also to the emperors. It was of ivory, without a back, and with curved legs, like those of a camp-stool, so arranged that

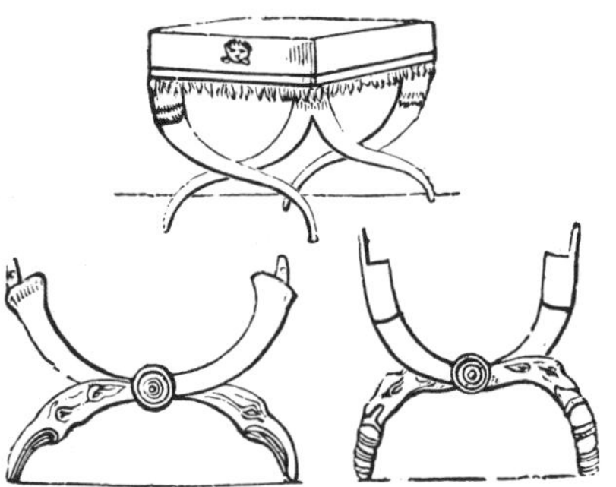

Forms of Sella Curulis. (Naples, and the Vatican.)

it could be folded up. The seat was of plaited leather straps. The curule magistrates sat on this seat while engaged in all official business, and also took it with them in war.

Sella Equestris. A saddle. See EPHIPPIUM.

Sellaria. A room furnished with benches or chairs (*sellae*). Cf. Pliny, *H. N.* xxxiv. 8, 19.

Sellasia (Σελλασία). A town in Laconia, north of Sparta, near the river Oenus. Here was fought a great battle between Cleomenes III. and Antigonus Doson in B.C. 221, resulting in the defeat of the former (Polyb. ii. 65–70).

Sellēis (Σελλήεις). (1) A river in Elis, on which the Homeric Ephyra stood, rising in Mount Pholoë, and falling into the sea south of the Peneus. (2) A river near Sicyon. (3) A river in Troas, near Arisbé, and a tributary of the Rhodius.

Selli or **Helli.** See DODONA.

Sellisternium. A religious celebration offered to the Roman female deities, resembling the *lectisternium* (q. v.), the main difference being that their images were ranged on seats or benches (*sellae*), and not on couches (*lecti*). See Val. Max. ii. 1, 2; Tac. *Ann.* xv. 44.

Selymbria (Σηλυμβρία) or **Selybria** (Σηλυβρία, Doric, Σαλαμβρία). Now Selivria. An important town in Thrace situated on the Propontis. It was a colony of the Megarians, and was founded earlier than Byzantium.

Sembella. A Roman coin equal to half of a *libella* or the twentieth part of a *denarius* (Varro, *L. L.* v. 174). No specimen is now preserved.

Semĕlé. See DIONYSUS.

Sementīvae Feriae. A festival of seed-time, celebrated in honour of Tellus (q. v.). See FERIAE.

Semiobŏlus (ἡμιόβολος). Half an obol; the Attic = nearly two cents, and the Aeginetan = nearly three cents.

Semirămis (Σεμίραμις) and **Ninus** (Νῖνος). The mythical founders of the Assyrian Empire of Ninus or Nineveh. Ninus (the Greek name for Rimmon Mirari) was a great warrior, who built the town of Ninus or Nineveh about B.C. 2182, and subdued the greater part of Asia. Semiramis was the daughter of the fish-goddess Derceto of Ascalon in Syria by a Syrian youth; but, being ashamed of her frailty, she made away with the youth, and exposed her infant daughter. But the child was miraculously preserved by doves, who fed her till she was discovered by the shepherds of the neighbourhood. She was then brought up by the chief shepherd of the royal herds, whose name was Simmas, and from whom she derived the name of Semiramis. Her surpassing beauty attracted the notice of Onnes, one of the king's friends and generals, who married her. He subsequently sent for his wife to the army, where the Assyrians were engaged in the siege of Bactra, which they had long endeavoured in vain to take. Upon her arrival in the camp she planned an attack upon the citadel of the town, mounted the walls with a few brave followers, and obtained possession of the place. Ninus was so charmed by her bravery and beauty that he resolved to make her his wife, whereupon her unfortunate husband put an end to his life. By Ninus Semiramis had a son, Ninyas, and on the death of Ninus she succeeded him on the throne. According to another account, Semiramis had obtained from her husband permission to rule over Asia for five days, and availed herself of this opportunity to cast the king into a dungeon, or, as is also related, to put him to death, and thus obtained the sovereign power. Her fame threw into the shade that of Ninus; and later ages loved to tell of her marvellous deeds and her heroic achievements. She built numerous cities, and erected many wonderful buildings; and several of the most extraordinary works in the East, which were extant in a later age, and the authors of which were unknown, were ascribed by popular tradition to this queen. In Nineveh she erected a tomb for her husband, nine stadia high and ten wide; she built the city of Babylon, with all its wonders; and she constructed the hanging gardens of Media, of which later writers give us such strange accounts (cf. Herod. i. 184). Besides conquering many nations of Asia, she subdued Egypt and a great part of Aethiopia, but was unsuccessful in an attack which she made upon India. After a reign of forty-two years she resigned the sovereignty to her son Ninyas, and disappeared from the earth, taking her flight to heaven in the form of a dove. The fabulous nature of this narrative is apparent. It is probable that Semiramis was originally a Syrian goddess, perhaps the same who was worshipped at Ascalon under the name of Astartê, or the Oriental Aphroditê, to whom the dove was sacred. Hence the stories of her voluptuousness, which were current even in the time of Augustus (Ov. *Am.* i. 5, 11). The stories that were current about Semiramis and Ninus are told by Diodorus Siculus, who drew largely upon Ctesias (q. v.). See Diod. bk. ii.; Ael. *Var. Hist.* vii. 1; and Lenormant, *La Légende de Sémiramis* (Brussels, 1873). See NINUS.

Semissis. Half an *as.* It bore the same device as the *as*, but with the letter S. See AS.

Semnae (σεμναί, "the dread ones"). A name of the Erinyes (q. v.).

Semnŏnes, more rarely **Sennŏnes.** A German people, described by Tacitus as the most powerful tribe of the Suevic race, dwelt between the rivers Viadus (Oder) and Albis (Elbe), from the Riesengebirge in the south as far as the country around Frankfort on the Oder and Potsdam in the north (Tac. *Germ.* 39; Ptol. ii. 11, 15).

Semōnes. The Latin name for certain supernatural beings. They appear to have been, like the Lares, a kind of Genii, or demigods, and guardian deities of the State. The word has often been connected with *se-*, to sow (cf. *se-men*); and would thus mean "sowers." Others would make it *sehomōnes*, demigods. On the Semones and Semo Sancus, see SANCUS.

Semo Sancus. See SANCUS.

Sempronia. (1) The daughter of Tib. Gracchus, censor in B.C. 169, and sister of the two celebrated tribunes, married Scipio Africanus Minor. (2) Wife of D. Iunius Brutus, consul in B.C. 77, was a woman of great personal attractions and literary accomplishments, but of a profligate character. She took part in Catiline's conspiracy, though her husband was not privy to it (Sall. *Cat.* 25, 40).

Sempronia Gens. A Roman gens of great antiquity, one of whose members was consul in B.C. 497, only twelve years after the expulsion of the kings. Of the many families in this gens, the Atratini were patricians, and the Aselliones, Blaesi, Gracchi, Sophi, Tuditani, and others, plebeians.

Sempronius Gracchus. See GRACCHUS.

Semuncia. See UNCIA.

Sena. (1) Now Senigaglia, styled GALLĬCA, and sometimes called SENOGALLIA; a town on the coast of Umbria, at the mouth of the small river Sena, founded by the Senones. (2) Now Siena, a town in Etruria, and a Roman colony, on the road from Clusium to Florentia (Tac. *Hist.* iv. 45).

Sena Insŭla. An island off the western part of Brittany, where there was an oracle of a Keltic goddess in charge of nine maidens, who professed to raise or lull the sea by their songs (Mela, iii. 6).

Senātus. The Roman Senate, or council of elders (*senes*), seems to have been, originally, an assembly of the chiefs of the different clans or houses (*gentes*), such as we find among nearly all Aryan peoples. Before the independent powers of these clans had been seriously diminished by the development of the royal prerogative, this assembly was probably the highest authority in the community. In the earliest Roman tradition, however, its normal function is to advise the king, and, in certain cases, to approve or disapprove his propositions. Its members, the "fathers," were chosen (*lecti*) by the reigning king; but the latter was bound by custom to choose them from the *gentes*, one representative of ripe age (*maior natu*) from each *gens*. The number of Senators therefore corresponded with the number of *gentes*, and it was only by the creation of new *gentes* that new elements could be introduced into the Senate (*patres minorum gentium*). Tarquin the Elder is said to have brought the Senate in this way to the strength which was subsequently regarded as normal—viz. three hundred. Upon the death of the king, and until his successor was chosen, the Senate assumed (or resumed) the government of the city, which it conducted through a series of senatorial *interreges*. See INTERREGES.

With the establishment of the Republic the Senate became the council of the chief magistrates. Its members were selected at first by the consuls, later by the censors. For a century and a half it remained, essentially at least, a patrician body, and served as the chief bulwark of the patrician power. The tradition that plebeians were summoned to the Senate by the later kings is scarcely credible; the statement that the earlier consuls admitted them is almost equally questionable.* It seems certain, at all events, that they were not regularly admitted, or admitted in any considerable number, until the middle or latter part of the fourth century B.C., when it was provided by a *lex Ovinia* that the censors should select *ex omni ordine optimum quemque.* The "best men" were interpreted, by usage, to be those who had been elected by the people to the higher magistracies; and ultimately the fact of election seems to have given the magistrate-elect seat and voice in the Senate. It was only when the list of ex-magistrates had been exhausted that others were appointed, preference being then given to citizens who had distinguished themselves in war. It was customary, at each census, to reappoint all surviving members of the Senate. The censors might indeed pass over (*praeterire*) the name of a senator, and thus exclude him, but only for cause stated. The Senate of the later Republic was accordingly a body of ex-magistrates, with what amounted to a life tenure.

ORGANIZATION AND PROCEDURE.—As an advisory body, the Senate met only when its advice was required—i. e. upon the call of a magistrate. Meetings were usually (but not necessarily) held in the Curia Hostilia, and on the Kalends or the Ides. A *lex Pupia* forbade meetings of the Senate at times when the Comitia were assembled, and a *lex Gabinia* ordered daily meetings through the

* It is stated that there were but 136 *gentes* in existence when the Republic was established, and that the Senate was brought up to its normal strength (300) by the free selection of the balance. It is also stated that all, or at least a portion, of the senators thus selected were plebeians; but this seems merely an inference from the other statement, and is, of course, in no sense a necessary inference. Among modern writers the dispute turns largely on the interpretation of the phrase *patres conscripti.* Many hold that the *patres* were patricians, the *conscripti* plebeians. Others assert that the *patres* were those who sat as representatives of the *gentes*, and that the rest, whether patricians or plebeians, were *conscripti.* Others again deny that there was any distinction between *patres* and *conscripti*, and translate the phrase, "enrolled senators."

month of February for the transaction of foreign and diplomatic business. The quorum required seems to have varied with the nature of the business before the house; for dispensation from a law it was fixed at 200. Penalties were imposed for unexcused failure to attend.

The magistrate who seeks the advice of the Senate (*senatum consulit*) acts as its chairman. He may lay before its members a distinctly formulated proposition which they are to approve or disapprove, or may submit (*referre*) a question on which their several opinions (*singulae sententiae*) are desired. In the latter case he calls upon the senators *nominatim*, in the order of their official rank—the *princeps* or dean of the Senate first, then the ex-censors, then the *consulares*, and so on down to the *quaestorii*, observing within each rank the order of seniority. Each senator sets forth his opinion at such length as he sees fit. The speeches may be interrupted by questions or corrections, and these may give rise to a running debate (*altercatio*). If the opinion of the Senate is clear, no vote need be taken; if not, the magistrate formulates the question (*verba facit*) and takes the sense of the Senate by a division (*discessio*). Senators who had held no elective office had the right of voting only, not the right of speech; hence they were termed "foot-senators" (*pedarii*). A number of questions might, of course, be submitted to the Senate at a single session. The order of business depended upon the pleasure of the magistrate, with one exception—*res divinae* took precedence of *res publicae*.

The Senate had neither secretaries nor, until the time of Iulius Caesar, records. The decision reached was written out by the presiding magistrate with the aid of a committee of senators. Except during the struggle between the orders, when the *senatus consulta* were kept in the temple of Ceres, the place of deposit was the *aerarium*.

Powers.—The advice of the Senate had to be obtained on certain matters of especial gravity, and might be obtained whenever it was desired. In theory, the advice that it gave was not binding, either upon the king or the republican magistrates. In fact, however, a resolution of the Senate, if less than a command, was much more than a counsel. Under the kings the Senate represented organizations older than the monarchy or the State itself. In its later republican form it included all the political experience and nearly all the political influence of the commonwealth. In the royal and early republican periods it was the guardian of the sacred traditions of the people. In the later Republic it represented, as against the magistrates with their brief terms and division of functions, as against the people with their varying impulses, the permanency and the unity of the policy of the State. In those matters in which custom accorded to its opinion the highest authority—in matters of religion, for example, and in questions of war and peace—it was practically a revolutionary act for the king or the magistrates to proceed in a course which the Senate discountenanced. Both in the royal period, therefore, and under the Republic, the Senate exercised an important restraining influence. In the later republican period its influence became more positive. It had, indeed, no organs for the enforcement of its will except the magistrates in office; but these seldom dared to refuse their aid. Most of them were members of senatorial families and had obtained office through family influence. To cross the will of the Senate was to imperil their own careers and those of their sons. During the conflict between the orders, the Senate had lost much of its authority; but when, at the close of this conflict, it was so reorganized as to include the leading representatives of all the great families, plebeian as well as patrician, it became more powerful than ever before. In the last two centuries of the Republic, in consequence of the increasing importance of Rome's foreign relations, which it had always directed, and the multiplication of subject-provinces which were under its special supervision, the Senate became the supreme power in the State. The selfish use of this power provoked the democratic reaction which established the Empire.

Among the rights attributed to the Senate, at one time or another, were the preliminary discussion of bills (*rogationes*) before their submission to the people; the examination and approval of the list of candidates for election; the quashing of popular resolves and of elections because the proper forms (particularly those required by religion) had not been observed; dispensation from laws in special cases, and the granting of privileges (especially corporate privileges); and, finally, the suspension of the ordinary laws in periods of stress and peril. In the early Republican period, the Senate claimed the right of ultimate approval or disapproval of laws and elections, but these claims were negatived by the *lex Publia* (B.C. 339) and the *lex Maenia* (B.C. 287). As regarded the provincial subjects of Rome, *senatus consulta* had the force of laws.

For a time the Senate exercised a sort of criminal jurisdiction, especially in the case of religious and political offences, through investigating committees (*quaestiones*); but these "questions" were ultimately transformed into permanent courts and made independent of the Senate.

In the field of administration the Senate exercised full control over the public finances. It fixed the taxes to be collected and the manner of their collection, voted appropriations, examined and verified the accounts of the treasury officials. It controlled the entire provincial administration. In the field of foreign relations nothing was done without its authorization. It sent and received ambassadors (*legati*), and conducted or controlled all diplomatic negotiations. It heard and acted upon the complaints of the allied cities and adjusted their differences. In the later Republican period wars were declared and treaties of peace and of alliance were ratified by the Comitia; but it was regarded as unconstitutional to bring these matters before the people without the previous authorization of the Senate.

In the republican, as in the royal, period the Senate carried on the government in case of *interregnum*. An *interregnum* existed, according to the republican theory, when both consuls died or resigned.

Finally, the Senate claimed an indefinite right of watching over and providing for the weal of the State (*salus rei publicae*), and it exercised an undisputed supremacy in strictly religious matters, except where these fell within the competence of the special priestly colleges.

The Senate of the Empire.—With the establishment of the Empire the powers of war and of peace and the control of Rome's foreign relations passed from the Senate to the emperor. Half of the provinces were ruled by the emperor's legates, and over the government of the rest he exercised an effective control. An imperial *fiscus* and an imperial war-treasury (*aerarium militare*) were established, and under Nero imperial praefects took the place of the senatorial quaestors in the old *aerarium*. On the other hand, the Senate gained new powers at the cost of the popular assembly: it passed laws and elected the magistrates. It also obtained a criminal jurisdiction concurrent with that of the ordinary courts. Some of these powers were afterwards withdrawn; but the bestowal and the withdrawal were alike matters of form. The substance of power was with the emperor: the magistrates from whom the Senate was still recruited were his nominees, and their election by the Senate was simply a ratification of the imperial choice. By virtue of his censorial powers, moreover, he could purge and reconstruct the Senate as he pleased. Senators were appointed more and more frequently without the form of election to any magistracy, and the number of provincials in the Senate steadily increased. The title *princeps senatus*, which the emperor assumed, obtained a new meaning: it indicated that he was the permanent president of the Senate.

The transfer of legislative power to the Senate carried with it one prerogative of great apparent importance—that of appointing the new emperor when the office became vacant, or at least of clothing him with imperial power. This right also proved unsubstantial: the succession was regularly determined either by the will of the deceased emperor or by the will of the army. The passing of the *lex de imperio* became as purely formal as the other acts of the Senate.

Sulla had raised the number of senators to 400; Iulius Caesar to 900. Augustus fixed it at 600. Regular meetings were held on the Kalends and Ides of each month. At first an attendance of 400 was required. It soon became necessary to increase the penalty of unexcused absence and also to reduce the legal quorum.

Ordo Senatorius.—The fact that the Senate was regularly recruited from a limited number of families had given to these families, even in the republican period, something of the character of a class. The formal distinctions accorded to the senators themselves (*latus clavus*, reserved seats at spectacles, etc.); their exclusion, not only from revenue-farming and other contracts with the government, but also from trade, and the extension of these prohibitions to the sons of senators, were steps towards the legal recognition of a senatorial order. In the imperial period this movement was completed. The senatorial census or property qualification was fixed at one million sesterces. The formal and ceremonial distinctions of the senators were multiplied, and were extended to their families. Class privileges were accorded them. Marriages between children of senators and persons of servile origin (*libertini*), previously regarded as unsuitable, were made illegal.

Municipal Senates.—In the self-governing cities of Italy and of the provinces, the whole municipal government was modelled on that of Rome, and the constitutions and functions of their city senates, or municipal councils in particular (*decuriones*, *curiae*), were closely analogous to those of the Roman Senate.

See P. Willems, *Le Sénat de la République Romaine* (1883); Hoffmann, *Der römische Senat;* Mommsen, *Römisches Staatsrecht* (3d ed. 1887); Karlowa, *Römische Rechtsgeschichte*, §§ 4, 50–52, 68.

Senātus Consultum. See Senatus.

Senātus Consultum de Bacchanalĭbus. See Bacchanalia.

Senĕca. (1) Marcus or Lucius Annaeus (the praenomen being uncertain), usually called Seneca Rhetor to distinguish him from his more celebrated son, was a native of Corduba in Spain. His birth may be placed about B.C. 60 and his death shortly after that of Tiberius (A.D. 37). His family was of equestrian rank and in good circumstances: his character, as revealed in his writings and described by his son, was marked by sobriety, industry, and sternness. We know little of his life, except that he resided on two occasions at least and for several years at Rome, where he is usually supposed, though on insufficient evidence, to have practised as a speaker and professor of rhetoric, without, however, attaining any very high distinction. He informs us that, except Cicero, he had listened to all the great masters of Roman eloquence; and Cicero he might have heard had he been willing to brave the risks of a visit to Rome while the Civil Wars were raging. But then, as for the greater part of his long life, he preferred the quiet dignity of his estate in Spain; and it was there that, when well advanced in middle age, he married Helvia, a lady of good lineage and ancient virtue, by whom he had three sons, all of whom attained distinction—Novatus, better known as the Gallio of the Acts of the Apostles; Seneca the philosopher; and Mela, father of the brilliant poet Lucan.

Seneca was the author of a Roman history extending from the commencement of the Civil Wars to the close of the reign of Tiberius. To this work two allusions—one in Lactantius (*Inst.* vii. 15, § 14) and one in Suetonius (*Tib.* 73)—must be referred. From the former we gather that, like Tacitus, he commenced his history by a brief generalizing retrospect of Rome's entire past, in which he compared the various epochs of her development to those of a human life. Lucius Seneca, in a fragment of a lost biography of his father, claims for it a place among the literary monuments of the age; but with some diffidence, as if conscious that his filial piety overpowered his critical judgment. At all events, we hear nothing of it from any other source. His other work, a series of reminiscences of contemporary rhetoricians, written in his old age, has, to a great extent, survived. It consists of ten books of *Controversiae*, or discussions of legal cases, and one book of *Suasoriae*, or themes for rhetorical declamation. The *Suasoriae* were written last, but come first in order of publication from grounds of educational convenience. The commencement is lost. The first, second, ninth, and tenth books of *Controversiae*, with their prefaces, are almost perfect. The gaps in the other books are partially filled up by an abridgment (*excerpta*) of the fourth or fifth century, the prefaces to books v., vi., and viii., however, being lost. These prefaces are by far the most interesting portion of the work. They are written by Seneca in his own person, and contain, besides pleasant commonplaces and sallies of genial humour, many valuable criticisms of the different speakers quoted, expressed in a pure and classical Latin. The *Controversiae*, which are almost entirely made up of quotations, are for the most part treated under three heads: first, the *Sententiae*, or opinions of the rhetoricians as to the applicability of the law to the question proposed; second, the *Divisio*, or distribution of the legal argument into its various points or subdivisions, each of which is considered separately; and thirdly, the *Colores*, or pleas for consideration, which, while admitting the fact, extenuate its gravity or alter its legal complexion.

It is evident that a considerable proportion of the rhetorical quotations was in Greek, declamatory exercises being indifferently undertaken in either language; but as the book was used exclusively in the Western Empire, the Greek portions were to a great extent discarded, and but few are now preserved. It is remarkable that Seneca himself displays a purer taste and literary style than any of the rhetoricians he quotes, in most of whom the characteristics of the Silver Age are already prominent.

The subjects of the *Suasoriae* are of the kind ridiculed by Juvenal: "Shall Alexander cross the ocean to find a new world to conquer?" "Shall Cicero plead with Antony for his life?" "Shall Leonidas withdraw from Thermopylae?" etc. They are mere school exercises, and, though ingenious and often eloquent, can hardly be called profitable reading.

BIBLIOGRAPHY.—In the earliest editions the above writings are mixed up with those of Seneca the philosopher, and were not separated before the editions of N. Faber (Paris, 1587–98) and A. Schott (Heidelberg, 1603–4; Paris, 1607–13). An edition was issued by Gronovius (Leiden, 1649; Amsterdam, 1672). Modern critical editions are those of C. Bursian (Leipzig, 1857); A. Kiessling (Leipzig, 1872); H. J. Müller (Prague, 1887). The following critical notices are mostly from Teuffel: H. Höfig, *De Sen. Rhet. IV. Codd. MSS. Schottianis* (Görlitz, 1858); J. Vahlen, *Rhein. Mus.* 13, 546; A. Kiessling, ib. 16, 50; *Beitr. z. Krit. lat. Prosaiker*, 32 (Basle and Geneva, 1864); *Neue Beitr. zur Kr. des Rh. S.* (Hamburg, 1871); Cl. Konitzer, *Quaest. in Sen. Crit.* (Breslau, 1864); *Beitr. z. Krit. des Rh. Sen.* (Breslau, 1866); R. Wachsmuth, *Quaest. in Sen.* (Posen, 1867); O. Rebling, *Obss. Crit. in Sen. Patrem.* (Göttingen, 1868); C. Bursian, *Spicilegium Crit. in Sen.* (Zürich, 1869); H. T. Karsten, *Spicil. Crit.* 33 (Leiden, 1881); *Elocutio Rhetorica Sen. Rhet.* (Rotterdam, 1881). Also J. Körber, *Ueber den Rhetor Sen.* (pp. 1–23, 58–66) *und die röm. Rhet. seiner Zeit* (pp. 23–58) (Marburg, 1864); O. Gruppe, *Quaestiones Annaeanae* (pp. 24–47) (Stettin, 1873); M. Sander, *Quaest. Syntacticae in Sen. Rhet.* (Greifswald, 1872); *D. Sprachgebrauch des Rhet. Sen.* (Waren, 1877–80); A. Ahlheim, *De Sen. Rhet. usu Dicendi* (Giessen, 1886); *L. A. Senecae Oratorum et Rhetorum Sententiae Divisiones Colores*, ed. H. J. Müller (*Bibl. Script. Gr. et Rom.* ed. Carl Schenkl) (Vienna, 1887).

(2) L. ANNAEUS, second son of the preceding, was born at Corduba about B.C. 3. He was from infancy of a delicate constitution, and liable to serious illnesses, in one of which he owed his life to the devoted care of his maternal aunt, in whose company, he tells us, he was brought to Rome. His instructors there were the eminent philosophers Fabianus, Attalus, and Sotion, under whom he studied with unremitting ardour, carrying his zeal for their precepts so far as to cultivate a somewhat ostentatious asceticism. His prudent father, alive to the jealousy of the court, recommended less perilous forms of virtue. Caligula, who affected to be a severe critic of Seneca's style, unquestionably envied his talent, and had marked him out for destruction, but was induced to spare his feeble health, which seemed to threaten an early grave. Under Claudius, Seneca rapidly rose to eminence. As quaestor he had the promise of a political career opened to him. He was also a successful pleader, a skilful professor of eloquence, and a leader in the world of fashion. But he had made powerful enemies. An intimacy was known to exist between him and Iulia Livilla, youngest daughter of Germanicus, which was liable to an unfavourable construction; so that when Messalina by her intrigues effected the exile of the princess, she was able to involve Seneca in a similar fate (A.D. 41). He was banished to Corsica, where he spent eight years, a fretful and helpless spectator of events. With the downfall of Messalina his fortunes revived. Agrippina, wishing to use him as the instrument of her ambitious projects, and perhaps, as Dio insinuates, captivated by his engaging person, contrived to secure his appointment as tutor to her son, the young Nero, then eleven years of age, and already destined for the throne. This was a position exactly suited to Seneca's genius. There is every reason to believe that he endeavoured to imbue his pupil's mind with maxims of wisdom and clemency; and the early part of Nero's reign, the "golden *quinquennium*" of justice and mercy, was long remembered as due to the influence of Seneca and Durrus, who jointly administered the State. It soon became evident, however, that Nero could not be controlled. The tutor tried to retain his influence by dangerous and unworthy concessions to the vices of the pupil, but without success. It was Nero who held Seneca bound by the magnetism of fear, of a more violent will, and of imperial splendours. The minister was compelled to follow the downward course of Nero's policy, giving such colour as his practised rhetoric afforded to its odious features till Agrippina's murder—the motive of which he was called upon to embody in a state-paper—brought the climax to a long series of inconsistencies between profession and practice, and showed him at once the moral hollowness and the actual insecurity of his position. From this time Nero seems to have turned against him; and although the long-foreseen blow did not descend until A.D. 65, when Piso's conspiracy gave a decent pretext for accusing him, yet for several years Seneca had been prepared for death, and had made generous, but ineffectual, attempts to disarm the emperor's malice. Bidden to effect his own death, the philosopher, with his high-born and beautiful wife Paulina, who insisted on dying with him, opened his veins. Paulina was restored by her friends to life, though with difficulty: he, after suffering excruciating agony, which he endured with cheerfulness, discoursing to his friends on the glorious realities to which he was about to pass, was at length suffocated by the vapour of a stove.

Seneca is undoubtedly the most brilliant figure of his time, and, except Tacitus, the most impor-

So-called Bust of Seneca the Philosopher. (Naples Museum.)

tant thinker and writer of the post-Augustan Empire. He embodied all the leading characteristics of the age, with which, unlike the majority of Roman citizens, he was in thorough harmony; and consequently he has been judged with more prejudice even by posterity than might have been expected.

That he was a truly great or good man can scarcely be maintained; that he was even a great thinker is open to question; but the inconsistencies of a life passed amid such overpowering temptations must not blind us to his real earnestness of purpose, or to the merit of exercising, under constant risk, a restraining influence on perhaps the vilest character known to history. It is impossible to doubt Seneca's love for virtue. Amid exaggerations, conceits, paradoxes, follies, the moral end is always held out as the only one worthy of being consistently followed, to which every kind of speculative knowledge is subordinate. His death, though not without a conscious study of effect, was a truly noble one; and we must believe him sincere when, on comparing himself with others and reconsidering his actions and omissions, he declares that he can look back with satisfaction upon his life. His opinion, thrice expressed, to the effect that true wisdom will not seek for an impracticable standard of purity in a hopelessly corrupt age, must be referred to the lower level of moral excellence, which Stoicism considered alone compatible with public life, and not to the ideal of the unencumbered, untempted sage.

Of Seneca's poetical writings, some few epigrams are preserved in the *Anthologia Latina*. We possess also nine tragedies correctly ascribed to him, viz.: *Hercules Furens*, *Troades* (or *Hecuba*), *Phoenissae* (not all genuine), *Medea*, *Phaedra* (or *Hippolytus*), *Oedipus*, *Agamemnon*, *Thyestes*, and *Hercules Oetaeus*, and one *praetexta*, the *Octavia*, incorrectly ascribed. Doubts have been thrown on the identity of the tragedian with the philosopher, but they are quite unfounded. The tragedies no doubt belong to his earlier life, and probably were written, partly during his exile, partly after his return to Rome, to assist the poetic proclivities of Nero. They are free imitations of Greek originals, which have in most cases survived so as to admit of a comparison. Both in dramatic power and loftiness of tragic feeling the Latin plays are immeasurably inferior. They abound, however, in brilliant declamation, philosophic contemplation, and witty aphorisms. They can hardly have been intended for the stage, to which they are wholly unsuited; but they are admirably fitted for declamatory reading, though even for this purpose overloaded with rhetoric.

Seneca's prose works were numerous and important; a considerable portion are lost, but the larger and more valuable part remains. Among the former are his speeches, written to be delivered by Nero, a treatise *De Situ Indiae*, another *De Situ et Sacris Aegypti*, another *De Motu Terrarum;* several treatises on moral philosophy, viz.: *Exhortationes*, *De Officiis*, *De Immatura Morte*, *De Superstitione*, *De Matrimonio*, *Quo Modo Amicitia Continenda Sit*, *De Paupertate*, *De Misericordia*, *De Remediis Fortuitorum*, and *De Verborum Copia;* a biography of his father, a panegyric on Messalina, and several books of letters. His extant works comprise (*a*) the twelve so-called dialogues, viz.: *Ad Lucilium de Providentia*, *Ad Serenum de Animi Tranquillitate*, *Ad S. de Otio*, *Ad S. de Constantia Sapientis*, *Ad Novatum de Ira Libri III.*, *Consolatio ad Marciam*, *Consolatio ad Polybium*, *Consolatio ad Helviam Matrem*, *De Vita Beata ad Gallionem*, *De Brevitate Vitae ad Paulinum;* (*b*) three books, *Ad Neronem de Clementia;* (*c*) seven books, *De Beneficiis ad Aebutium Liberalem;* (*d*) twenty books of moral letters, *Ad Lucilium* (but the collection is incomplete); (*e*) seven books, *Naturales Quaestiones*, addressed to Lucilius; (*f*) a political satire on the death and apotheosis of Claudius, called by Dio ἀποκολοκύντωσις, which is of interest as the only remaining example of the Satura Menippea; (*g*) fourteen spurious letters of a correspondence with St. Paul, which seem to have imposed upon St. Jerome (*De Vir. Illust.* 12). See EPISTOLA.

From this catalogue it will be seen how wide was the field embraced by Seneca's genius. Little need be said about his scientific works, except that they show no mean acuteness of conjecture and considerable knowledge of physical theories, though these are often subordinated to an ethical purpose. His views of nature are in the main Stoic, and his examples are probably drawn from Greek sources.

It is on his moral treatises that Seneca's fame rests. In the particular department that he selected, viz., the application of certain leading principles to practical life, he excels all other writers of antiquity. Nominally a Stoic, he belonged really to the Eclectic School, culling precepts from every form of doctrine with impartial appreciation. "The remedies of the soul," he says, "have been discovered long ago: it is for us to learn how to apply them." On this text his system is a comment. It requires, above all else, a thorough knowledge of the human heart, and in this Seneca is preëminent. In that dark and perilous period, when universal mistrust prevailed, the moralist must be able to dive into the secret recesses of the soul, drawing to light its hidden disquiet, and fortifying it against the blows of circumstance or the deeper thrusts of human turpitude. No writer, ancient or modern, shows a more complete mastery of the pathology of mind. Many of his letters are of the nature of sermons; others are spiritual meditations; others, brilliant attacks on the falsehood and vice of the time. In all these is the same incisiveness of style, the same fertility of illustration, the same varied experience, the same emphatic and reiterated pressing home of his point. This last feature is apt to weary the reader; and Seneca, well aware of the danger, endeavours, by every artifice of rhetorical ingenuity, to maintain the interest of his theme. "To impress the dull conscience, reiteration is a necessity: to knock once at the door when night is come is never enough: you must knock frequently and hard." This leads him to use a tone of exaggeration which, by its seeming insincerity, does injustice to the writer's heart, and has caused him to be too severely judged. His religious and moral maxims so often approximate to those of Christianity that the fathers of the church adopted the view that he had adopted their faith, to which the fictitious correspondence with St. Paul seemed to lend support. The coincidences, however, though sufficiently remarkable, are accidental only, and arise from the character of his mind, which was essentially that of a "seeker after God."

BIBLIOGRAPHY.—(1) *Editions of the Tragedies:* Delrio (Antwerp, 1576; Paris, 1620); Lipsius (Leiden, 1588); Gruter (Heidelberg, 1604); Scriverius (Leyden, 1621–51); Gronovius (Leyden, 1661; Amsterdam, 1682); Schröder (Delft, 1728). More modern editions are those of F. H. Bothe (Leipzig, 1819); T. Baden, 2 vols. (Leipzig, 1821); Peiper and Richter (Leipzig, 1867); Holtze in Tauchnitz series (Leipzig, 1872); and Leo, 2 vols. (Berlin, 1878–79).

(2) *Editions of Complete Prose Works:* Erasmus (Basle, 1515–20); Muretus (Rome, 1585); Gruter (Heidelberg, 1593); Lipsius (Antwerp, 1605); Variorum edition with Gronovius's notes in 2 vols. (Leiden, 1649; Amsterdam, 1672), enlarged and illustrated by Ruhkopf (Leipzig, 1797–1811); F. Haase in the Teubner series, 3 vols. (1852, 1872–1874); Holtze in Tauchnitz series in 5 vols. (Leipzig, 1832, 1873–78); *Œuvres Complètes de Sénèque, avec la traduction française de la collection Panckoucke par Charpentier et F. Lemaistre, précédes d'une notice sur Sénèque et d'une préface par Charpentier,* 4 vols. (Paris, 1860–61, 1867–73) (Garnier); *Œuvres complètes de Sénèque, avec traduction en Français,* being part of Nisard's collection of Latin authors in Didot's Latin classics (Paris, 1877). *The Workes of L. A. Senecæ, both Morall and Naturall, translated by Thos. Lodge, D. in Physicke* (London, 1614), contains all but the *Apocolocyntosis* and the (spurious) epistles to St. Paul.

(3) *Editions of Separate Works: De Providentia,* by Nauta (Leiden, 1825); *Ad Marciam,* by Michaelis (Haarlem, 1840); *Lib. de Beneficiis et Clementia,* by M. C. Gertz (Berlin, 1876); *Dialogorum Lib. XII, ex Recensione et cum Apparatu Critico,* H. A. Koch, revised by Vahlen (Jena, 1879). These dialogues are also edited by Gertz (Copenhagen, 1886); the *Epistolae Morales,* by Schweighäuser (Strassburg, 1809); *Selectae Epist.,* with arguments and French translation by Sommer (Paris, 1872); *Epistolae Aliquot,* by Bücheler (Bonn, 1879); *Nat. Quaestiones,* by Köler (Göttingen, 1819); the *Apocolocyntosis,* by Schusler (Utrecht, 1844), and by Bücheler in the *Symbola Philol.* p. 31 (Bonn) and in his smaller edition of Petronius (Berlin, 1882).

(4) *General Criticism.* A full list of the authorities for Seneca will be found in Teuffel's *History of Roman Literature,* vol. ii., translated by Warr (London, 1892). Biographical notices in Merivale, *Romans under the Empire,* chs. 52–54. On his philosophical and religious ideas, see Zeller, *Gk. Phil.,* English translation under "Eclecticism." Also his *Stoics, Epicureans, and Sceptics,* translated by Reichel; Farrar, *Seekers after God* (London, 1869); Martha, *Les Moralistes sous l'Empire Romain* (Paris, 1872); Dörgens, *Senecae Disciplinae Moralis cum Antoniniana Comparatio* (Leipzig, 1857); Gelpke, *De Senecae Vita et Moribus* (Berne, 1848).

Senia. Now Segna; a Roman colony in Liburnia in Illyricum.

Senio. The six-spot in dice. See TALUS; TESSERA.

Senŏnes. A powerful people in Gallia Lugdunensis, dwelling along the upper course of the Sequana (Seine). Their chief town was Agendicum, afterwards called Senones (Sens) (Caes. *B. G.* ii. 2). A portion of this people crossed the Alps about B.C. 400, in order to settle in Italy, and took up their abode on the Adriatic Sea between the rivers Utis and Aesis (between Ravenna and Ancona), after expelling the Umbrians. In this country they founded the town of Sena. They not only extended their ravages into Etruria, but marched against Rome and took the city, B.C. 390. From this time we find them engaged in constant hostilities with the Romans, till they were at length completely subdued, and the greater part of them destroyed by the consul Dolabella in B.C. 283. See GALLIA.

Sentinel. See EXCUBIAE; VIGILES.

Sentīnum. Now Sassoferrato; a fortified town in Umbria, not far from the river Aesis. In the third Samnite War (B.C. 295), Quintus Fabius here defeated the Gauls and Samnites (Livy, x. 27). See DECIUS.

Sentius Saturnīnus. See SATURNINUS.

Sepias (Σηπιάς). Now St. George. A promontory in the southeast of Thessaly, in the district Magnesia, on which a great part of the fleet of Xerxes was wrecked.

Seplasia. One of the principal streets in Capua, where perfumes and luxuries of a similar kind were sold (Cic. *In Pis.* 11, 24). See UNGUENTUM.

Sepphōris (Σεπφωρίς). Now Sefurieh; a city of Palestine, in the middle of Galilee. It was an insignificant place until Herod Antipas fortified it, and made it the capital of Galilee, under the name of DIOCAESARĒA.

Septem Aquae. A place in the territory of the Sabini, near Reaté.

Septem Fratres (Ἑπτὰ Ἀδελφοί). A mountain on the north coast of Mauretania Tingitana at the Fretum Gaditanum (Strait of Gibraltar).

Septem Maria. The lagoons at the mouth of the river Padus (Po). See Pliny, *H. N.* iii. 120.

Septempĕda. Now San Severino; a municipium in the interior of Picenum, on the road from Auximum to Urbs Salvia (Pliny, *H. N.* iii. 111).

Septerion (Σεπτήριον). A festival celebrated every nine years at Delphi, in memory of the slaying of the serpent Python by Apollo. See Plut. *Quaestiones Gr.* 12, and *Def. Orac.* 15.

Septimius Geta. See GETA.

Septimius Serēnus. See SERĒNUS.

Septimius Sevērus. See SEVERUS.

Septizonium. See the Appendix.

Sepulcrum. A tomb. Sepulchres cut in the rock were in common use among both the Greeks and the Romans, and in many places, especially in Lycia and in Asia Minor, they are found in vast numbers, some of them being highly ornate and elaborate. In Lycia they are generally built in imitation of a wooden building, and reproduce in stone the minutest details of wood-construction. The interior consists of a low chamber with stone couches, upon which the bodies were placed. Tombs in form like a sarcophagus (see SARCOPHAGUS) are also found, some of them with an arch as in the annexed example. Others are in the shape of a high square column or pedestal with a projecting cornice, as in the so-called Harpy Monument now in the British Museum. Temple-tombs or heroa (ἡρῷα) also occur in Asia Minor, these having a central chamber on a high base (*podium*), surrounded by a colonnade. The highest development of this sepulchral type is seen in the famous Mausoleum at Halicarnassus in Caria, a restoration of which is shown in the illustration on p. 1018. For elaborate rock-cut tombs, see the illustration in the article MYRA, p. 1069. An early form of tomb apparently much favored in Greece was the domed or "bee-hive" tomb, in which a large chamber is built in a circular form of courses of stone which gradually overlap so as to form a dome-shaped building, though not a true dome. The space for this chamber is excavated in the side of a hill and is approached by a stone-lined passage (δρόμος) cut into the slope of the hill. The best example of such a tomb is the so-called Treasury of Atreus at Mycenae, shown on p. 452.

Lycian Tomb. (Fellows.)

The tombs of the Etruscans were nearly always subterranean, consisting of chambers hewn out of the rock either below the surface of the earth or projecting horizontally into a cliff. The earliest Etruscan tombs date from the sixth century B.C. Temple-tombs also occur of which the following illustration gives an example.

The Etruscan tombs generally imitated the

Etruscan Temple-tomb at Norchia.

abode of the living; they are frequently adorned with paintings, and the bodies recline upon stone couches accompanied by vases and other objects, as shown in the illustration on the following page.

The Roman tombs were usually placed by the side of the roads leading out of the city, many of which are still preserved, among them the pyramidal tomb of C. Cestius, near the Porta Ostiensis (see illustration, p. 1346), the tomb of Caecilia Metella (see illustration, p. 1037) on the Appian Way, and the tomb of the Scipios, also on the Appian Way. The most splendid of the Roman sepulchral edifices that still remain is the Mausoleum of Hadrian, shown in the illustration on p. 1018.

Another style of Roman tomb built to contain a large number of bodies was the *columbarium*, consisting of a building containing a large number of niches, flat at the bottom and arched at the top, each niche as a rule being intended to hold two urns (*ollae*). The *columbarium* used for the burial of the servants and freedmen of the emperor Augustus, and especially of the empress Livia, on the Appian Way, contained room for upwards of 3000 *ollae*. See Lanciani, *Ancient Rome*, pp. 129, 130; and the article COLUMBARIUM.

Bodies were also interred in graves. The normal form of the Greek grave was that familiar to us—a hole or trench dug in the ground. In Attica in early times the dead were buried in their own houses (Plut. *Minos*, 315 D), but the later rule was for the interment to take place outside of the city walls, frequently by the side of the roads as at Rome. The Roman laws of the Twelve Tables forbade burial within the city, though exceptions were made in the case of distinguished persons—e. g. C. Fabricius (Cic. *De Leg.* ii. 23, 58). The Vestal Virgins and the emperors were also buried within the city. The Romans used besides trenches deep pits like wells (hence the name *puticuli*, from *puteus*, a well). Etruscan graves were frequently lined with stone. Gravestones were of various sorts both in Greece and Italy: (*a*) κόνισκοι, or

Interior of Etruscan Tomb at Veii.

The bodies, if burned, were placed in urns or in earthenware coffins, such as are shown in the following illustration. Within the tombs were always placed objects of all kinds, often of considerable value, and these are an extremely important source of knowledge regarding ancient arts, such as pottery, vase-painting, jewelry, gem-engraving, terracotta work, etc. The contents of tombs have also included strigils, swords, perfume-bottles, lamps, needles, pins, mirrors, rings, brooches, wreaths, diadems, and vessels for food, in some of which bits of food are still actually preserved.

round columns with a moulding at the top, beneath which was the inscription; (*b*) πλάκες, rectangular slabs lying upon the ground; (*c*) στῆλαι (see STELA); (*d*) *aediculae* or shrine-shaped stones, the top being supported by pilasters; (*e*) *mensae*, large rectangular blocks of stone; (*f*) *hydriae* or vases of marble; (*g*) θῆκαι, round or square stone receptacles which held the ashes; (*h*) *sarcophagi* (see SARCOPHAGUS).

D · M
COSSVTIAE
PRIMAE
MATRI
PIENTISSIME
BENEMERENTI
FECIT

Roman Mortuary Inscription. (British Museum.)

The following illustration shows the plan of the street at Pompeii usually called the Street of Tombs. See POMPEII.

Earthenware Coffins. (Stackelberg.)

BIBLIOGRAPHY.—See Baumeister, *Denkmäler*, s. v. "Gräber"; Dennis, *Cities and Cemeteries of Etruria* (1878); Stackelberg, *Die Gräber der Hellenen;* Becker-Göll, *Charicles*, iii. 114–167; Hermann-Blümner, *Privatalt.* pp. 373–387; Marquardt, *Privatleben*, pp. 340–385; Becker-Göll, *Gallus*, iii. 481–547; Overback-Mau, *Pompeii*, pp. 396–422; and the articles CATACUMBAE; CIPPUS; COLUMBARIUM; FUNUS; OLLA; SARCOPHAGUS; URNA.

Urn for Ashes of the Dead. (Pompeii.)

Sequăna (Σηκοάνας). Now the Seine; one of the principal rivers of Gaul, rising in the central parts of that country, and flowing through the province of Gallia Lugdunensis into the ocean opposite Britain. It is 346 miles in length. Its principal affluents are the Matrona (Marne), Esia (Oise), with its tributary the Axona (Aisne), and Incaunus (Yonne). This river has a slow current, and is navigable beyond Lutetia Parisiorum (Paris) (Caes. *B. G.* i. 1; Ptol. ii. 8, 2).

Sequăni. A powerful Celtic people in Gallia Belgica, inhabiting the country since called Franche Comté and Burgundy. In the later division of the provinces of the Empire the country of the

Street of Tombs. (Pompeii.)

Sequani formed a special province under the name of Maxima Sequanorum. They derived their name from the river Sequana, which had its source in the northwestern frontiers of their territory. Their chief town was Vesontio (Besançon) (Caes. *B. G.* i. 1, 3, 10–12; Lucan, i. 425).

Sequester, Vibius. The name attached to a glossary which professes to give an account of the geographical names contained in the Roman poets. It is in seven sections, to which in some MSS. is added a chapter giving an account of the seven wonders of the world. It has been edited by Bursian (Zürich, 1867).

Sera. A bolt or bar. See Ianua.

Sera. See Serica.

Serapēum. See Alexandria; Serapis.

Serapio. A surname of P. Cornelius Scipio Nasica (B.C. 138). See Scipio.

Serapion (Σεραπίων). A physician of Alexandria, who lived in the third century B.C., and belonged to the Empirical school of medicine. He was an opponent of the teachings of Hippocrates, but none of his works is now extant.

Serāpis or **Sarāpis** (Σάραπις; Egyptian, *Asarhapi = Osiris - Apis*). The Egyptian god Osiris (q. v.), in the character of god of the lower world; his corresponding incarnation as the god of the upper world was the bull Apis. (See Apis.) His worship was first independently developed in the time of the Ptolemies in Alexandria, the most beautiful ornament of which city was the magnificent temple of Serapis, the Serapeum. By the elimination of foreign elements, the conception of the god was so widely extended as to include the Egyptian Osiris, the Greek Pluto, the Greek god of healing, Asclepius, and Zeus-Iupiter. This new worship (together with the cult of Isis) rapidly spread from Egypt over the Asiatic coast, the Greek islands, and Greece itself, and found a firm footing even in Rome and Italy, in spite of repeated interference on the part of the State. Under the Empire, particularly in the time of Hadrian, it extended throughout the Roman world. (See Isis.) There was a fine temple to Serapis at Puteoli, of which remains still exist.

Serapis. (Vatican.)

Serapis was especially worshipped as a god of healing, and with his temples were connected dream-oracles that were much resorted to. He was represented, like Pluto, with an animal by his side, having the head of a dog, lion, or wolf, and a serpent coiled round its body. As Zeus-Serapis he is to be seen in the colossal bust in the Vatican, with a *modius*, or corn-measure, the symbol of the lower world, upon his head.

Serbōnis Lacus. See Sirbonis Lacus.

Serdĭca or **Sardĭca.** Now Sofia; an important town in Upper Moesia, and the capital of Dacia Interior, derived its name from the Thracian people Serdi. It bore in the Middle Ages the name of Triaditza (Eutrop. ix. 14, 22; Amm. Marc. xxx. 16).

Serēnus Annaeus. A friend of the philosopher Seneca, who dedicated to him his treatises *De Tranquillitate* and *De Constantia* (Sen. *Epist.* 63).

Serēnus, Aulus Septimius. A Roman lyric poet of the time of Hadrian, who wrote of the country and of rural scenes in artificial style. Only fragments of his works remain, and those are edited by Bährens in his *Frag. Poët. Rom.* 384 (1888).

Serēnus Sammonĭcus. A Roman physician and author who lived in the time of Severus and Caracalla. The latter caused him to be put to death in A.D. 212. To him, or more probably to his son Quintus Serenus, the instructor of the second Gordianus, must be attributed a didactic poem on medicine (*De Medicina Praecepta*), in 115 well-written hexameters, a collection of domestic prescriptions much used in the Middle Ages. It mostly follows Pliny. It is edited by Bährens in his *Poetae Lat. Min.* (Leipzig, 1886). On the diction and prosody, see Baur, *Quaestiones Sammoniceae* (Giessen, 1886).

Seres. See Serica.

Serf. See Servus.

Sergia Gens. A patrician gens tracing its descent from the Trojan Sergestus (Verg. *Aen.* v. 121). Catiline was a member of this gens.

Sergius. (1) See Catilina. (2) A Roman grammarian of uncertain date, though later than the fourth century A.D. Two small treatises of his are printed in Keil's *Grammatici Latini*, iv. 486–565.

Seria. A kind of cask used by the Romans.

Serĭca (ἡ Σηρική). A country in the extreme east of Asia, famous as the native region of the silkworm, which was also called σήρ; and hence the adjective *sericus* for "silken." The name was known to the Western nations at a very early period, through the use of silk, first in Western Asia, and afterwards in Greece. It is clear, however, that until some time after the commencement of our era the name had no distinct geographical signification. The Serica of Ptolemy corresponds to the northwestern part of China and the adjacent portions of Thibet and Chinese Tartary. The capital, Sera, is supposed by most to be Singan, on the Hoang-ho, but by some Peking. The Great Wall of China is mentioned by Ammianus Marcellinus (xxiii. 6, 64) under the name of *Aggeres Serium.* See Sericum.

Serĭca Vestis. See Sericum.

Serĭcum (σηρικόν, βομβύκια). Silk. Silk was known to the Greeks and Romans, who generally supposed that it grew upon leaves and was scraped off them (Strabo, xv. p. 693). It was imported overland from China through Samarcand and the Persian Gulf, and thence to Phœnicia (or Egypt) and Rome (Procop. *Anecd.* 25), probably in woven pieces. Silk soon became popular, and was worn even by men (Tac. *Ann.* ii. 33), so that its use became the subject of legislative enactment, as by Tiberius, who discouraged it, and Caligula, who approved of it (Suet. *Cal.* 52). It was always very expensive, and at one time, at least, sold for its weight in gold (Vopisc. *Aurel.* 45). It was frequently mixed with flax or wool (*subserica* and *tramoserica*), from which a garment of pure silk was distinguished by the name *holoserica*. Raw silk began to be produced in Europe in the reign of Justinian (A.D. 530), silkworms having then been brought to Constantinople by monks, and the production of silk was long a flourishing industry, though it was a government monopoly. See Pariset, *Histoire de la Soie*, i. pp. 1–90; Wardle, *Silk* (1888); and Blümner, *Technologie*, i. 192.

Serīphus (Σέριφος). Now Serpho; an island in the Aegaean Sea, and one of the Cyclades. It is celebrated in mythology as the island where Danaë and Perseus landed after they had been exposed by Acrisius, where Perseus was brought up, and where he afterwards turned the inhabitants into stone with the Gorgon's head. Seriphus was colonized by Ionians from Athens, and it was one of the few islands which refused submission to Xerxes. The island was employed by the Roman emperors as a place of banishment for State criminals (Tac. *Ann.* ii. 85; iv. 21; Juv. x. 170).

Sermo Plebēius. A term used, in contradistinction to the classic Latinity of Cicero or Caesar, to designate the speech of the common people, at Rome and in the provinces, which later became the basis of the modern Romance languages. Its relation to literary Latin has been subject to frequent misconception: thus, the two are not separate languages, although too often erroneously so termed; nor, on the other hand, is the Sermo Plebeius in any sense either the parent or the offspring of the classic speech. They are rather two kindred dialects, which, while steadily diverging, trace their origin to a common source in the speech of early Rome, the *prisca Latinitas*.

The differentiation between the popular and cultured speech begins properly with the early Roman poets; for, prior to the birth of a national literature, the language lacked the stability essential to a linguistic standard. It is noteworthy that Livius Andronicus, Naevius, and Ennius were all of them natives of Magna Graecia, and that accordingly Rome owes her first impulse in literature, as in the other arts, to external sources. These literary pioneers naturally regarded their native Greek as the highest criterion of excellence, and strove successively to impart something of its ease and grace to the rather unwieldy forms and heavy quantities of archaic Latin. The process of refining and polishing the language in accordance with Greek rules was continued by the famous literary circle which centred in the younger Scipio, to an extent best realized by a comparison of the plays of Terence, whose style is all but Ciceronian, with those of Plautus, which remain the best surviving specimens of early plebeian Latin.

Classic Latin, thus carefully fostered, culminated at length in the cadenced prose of Cicero and the harmonious rhythm of the Augustan poets — a proud achievement for the grammarians, but gained at the expense of the vitality of the language. Its growth had been checked before its natural resources were developed. Its vocabulary remained deficient; its rules for accent and quantity were borrowed; its later development was so largely artificial as to be necessarily unstable. Even in Livy and Tacitus there are seen the beginnings of the decadence which was destined to blight the later literature, and which was hastened by the steady encroachment of the Sermo Plebeius.

The latter, rude and untrammelled, was free to enlarge its vocabulary and modify its constructions to meet the needs of the people's slowly broadening horizon. It was essentially the language of the shops and streets, of the soldier and camp-follower, the slave and rustic—in short, of all but the privileged literary class. In the early period, the reciprocal influence exerted by the two diverging branches of the language was slight, for the literary circle was strictly limited, while the great mass of the people lived and died untouched by the new culture. Gradually, however, as knowledge became more general, and facilities for learning increased, the influence of the cultured language filtered slowly downward through the different grades of society, until all except the remoter rural districts must have felt the leaven of its influence. Conversely, the Sermo Plebeius, with its expressive slang phrases and hardy neologisms, became a more and more convenient source to draw upon, so that with each generation a larger proportion of plebeian forms and constructions found their way upward into the cultured speech. Hence arose a compromise, in the shape of the *sermo cotidianus*, the free-and-easy medium of every-day life, which facilitated communication between the classes, and into which the most cultured speakers were apt to relapse when conversing with their family and friends. Below this, down to the *lingua rustica*, the rudest form of the country districts, the language shaded off through numerous gradations, all possessing the same essential characteristics, and differing only in degree. The furthest division of the language which, with our present knowledge, it is safe to make is threefold—into *sermo urbanus*, *sermo cotidianus*, and *sermo plebeius*.

I. Provincial Latin.—The history of the Sermo Plebeius in the provinces presents certain peculiar features, which are noteworthy because they go far towards explaining the origin of those dialectic differences which resulted in the separate Romance languages. It was always the policy of Rome to force her speech, as well as her customs, upon the nations that she subjugated, and to that end Latin was made the official language of the provinces. The standard of Latinity, however, was not so easily regulated, the conquered people naturally acquiring it from the Romans with whom they earliest came in immediate contact—the common soldiers, petty officials, itinerant merchants, the rank and file that followed in the track of the successful armies. Accordingly, while provincial Latin is far from being synonymous with the Sermo Plebeius, and while many of the leading families must have spoken as pure a Latin as any heard at Rome, yet the plebeian element was more marked, more universal, extending higher in the social ranks, and even giving a distinctive local colour to provincial literature. The important point, however, is that, while the different provinces were acquired at long intervals, the Sermo Plebeius, which thus formed successively the basis of African, Spanish, and Gallic Latin, was itself undergoing a slow but constant evolution, and the form which Caesar's legions introduced into Gaul was very different from the speech of the soldiers who, a century earlier, had followed the younger Scipio to Carthage. It would be absurd to claim that the language, once established in a province, became crystallized, never to change again. On the contrary, and notably in the case of the African Latin, the later development is most striking; but, owing to its comparative isolation from the influence of the classic speech, plebeian Latin in the provinces tended to preserve certain archaic features much longer than at Rome, a condition quite analogous to that observed in the French of Quebec, or the English of the New England colonies. Accordingly, the Latin of the several provinces represents a varying degree of archaism, in the order of their dates of conquest; and one may search in vain in the Gallic writer Marcellus Empiricus for many of the archaisms prevalent in the works of the Africans Tertullian, Arnobius, and Caelius Aurelianus. The dialectic differences thus established played a far larger part than did any of the rapidly supplanted native tongues, in the ultimate separation of the Romance languages. Thus, Spanish, Portuguese, Catalonian, Provençal, French, and Roumanian show, in the order given, successive stages of the Sermo Plebeius, while Italian, representing the vulgar speech in its native land, where its ultimate development was reached, is the most advanced of all, excepting in the dialectic forms spoken in the island of Sardinia, Rome's earliest external conquest, which retain to this day many characteristics, such as accented ĭ and ŭ, and the *k*-sound after *e* and *i*, which must have been lost from the plebeian Latin at an early date, as they are wanting in the other Romance languages.

II. Sources.—The sources for our knowledge of the Sermo Plebeius are fairly abundant, but of very diverse degrees of importance. No one deliberately wrote in vulgar Latin, but only when, through carelessness or ignorance, he failed to attain the classic standard. Even the language of Plautus's slaves, and the realistic dialogue of Trimalchio and his *colliberti* in the *Satira* of Petronius, are softened to meet the exigencies of literature. Accordingly, the characteristics of plebeian speech must be gleaned from isolated statements of Roman grammarians, errors of orthography and syntax found in inscriptions, or in writers of inferior Latinity, and lastly from the corroborative evidence of the Romance languages. The testimony of Roman writers, however, although of the first importance, is extremely meagre, dealing largely with anomalies of vocabulary and style. The only ancient work bearing directly upon the subject, of which we have knowledge, that of T. Lavinius *De Verbis Sordidis*, has unfortunately perished. The most important existing document of this class is the curious grammatical fragment, the *Appendix Probi* (contained in the *Grammatici Latini*, ed. Keil), but whether of general, or merely local, authority is uncertain, for although some authorities regard it as an African production, its source is still problematic.

Among inscriptions the most important are the Pompeian wall inscriptions (in the *Corpus Inscriptionum Latinarum*, vol. iv.), comprising the careless scribblings of schoolboys, slaves, etc., on houses and public buildings, and containing many important clues to popular Latin in Southern Italy. The inscriptions from Gaul, Spain, and Africa are also useful in tracing dialectic changes. But the chief value of inscriptions, wherever found, is for the light they throw upon plebeian pronunciation, since the ignorant stone-cutters often spelled as they pronounced, and, unlike the equally ignorant scribes, left their errors recorded in an enduring form.

Turning to literature, we find a mass of material, which needs, however, careful discrimination. The scanty remnants of the early writers are all valuable, for plebeian Latin preserved many features of the *prisca Latinitas* long after they had been discarded by the classic speech; and in the Augustan age archaism was to a large extent synonymous with vulgarism. Plautus and the other early comic poets are of especial value, since their works were intended for the people and are accordingly written down to their level. Even Terence contains a certain plebeian element which had probably become traditional on the comic stage. Cato, famous as the opponent of Greek culture, naturally favoured the earlier and ruder form of speech, and his *De Agricultura* forms our unique source for the early *sermo rusticus*.

For the classic and Silver Latin period, material is more abundant. The *Bellum Hispaniense* and other supplements to Caesar's *Commentarii* are probably mild specimens of the *sermo militaris*. Cicero, elsewhere the standard of Latinity, assumes in his letters, as he himself confesses, a more colloquial tone: *Quid tibi ego in epistolis uideor? Nonne plebeio sermone agere tecum?* (*Ad Fam.* ix. 21); and they remain our best example of the *sermo cotidianus* of the upper classes. Satire, from its very nature and origin, required a less elevated style than other forms of poetry, and the satires of Horace, Persius, and Juvenal all afford a fruitful source for vulgarisms. There are also numerous writers on technical subjects, skilful in their several provinces, but weak in point of grammar: thus the architect Vitruvius, who would write correctly if he could, apologizes for his ignorance and begs that *si quid parum ad regulam artis grammaticae fuerit explicatum ignoscatur* (i. 1, 17). The elder Pliny, whose *Historia Naturalis* is confessedly a literary mosaic, is a treasure-house of plebeian vocabulary. The chief source, however, in ante-Hadrian Latin is and must remain the *Cena Trimalchionis* of Petronius, the narrative of which is told in the easy colloquial language of the upper classes, while the conversation of Trimalchio's circle is fairly redolent with vulgarisms, popular proverbs, and the current slang of the streets. See Petronius.

For post-classical Latin the entire range of literature is useful: for although departures from the classic norm must not be indiscriminately stigmatized as plebeian, few writers of the decadence escaped some taint of popular Latin. Of especial interest are Fronto, Gellius, and Apuleius, whose numerous archaisms are due as much to the *sermo Africus* as to the retrogressive movement begun under the emperor Hadrian. The later African writers are also of great importance, notably Tertullian, Arnobius, Commodian, and Augustine; for although African Latin has left no modern representative, it was the great vitality of that idiom which imprinted upon ecclesiastical Latin its distinctive character, and thus indirectly imparted a tinge, especially in vocabulary and syntax, to the modern Romance languages.

As specimens of very late Latin, where the language is on the verge of disintegration, Anthimus, the historians Fredegarius and Gregory of Tours, and the *Regula Monachorum* of St. Benedict, recently edited by Wölfflin (Leipzig, 1895), are very instructive.

III. Characteristics of Plebeian Latin.—(*a*) *Phonetics.*—The main changes occur in the vowel-system. Latin originally possessed five vowels—*a, e, i, o, u*—which might be long or short. Plebeian Latin, however, gives early proof of a growing qualitative difference, long vowels tending to become close, short vowels open. That all qualitative difference was eventually lost appears from the Romance languages, and is further evidenced by the growing frequency of false quantities in Christian poets after the third century (Commodian, Ausonius, Dracontius, etc.), and by the substitution of stress accent for metrical accent in late popular songs. Owing to such changes, ĭ tended early to merge in ē, and ŭ in ō soon after: see Varr. *R. R.* 1, 2, 14, *rustici viam veham appellant*, and the admonitions of Prob. *App.* 197, 25, *columna, non "colomna"*; id. 198, 23, *puella, non "poella"* (compare the Italian, *penna, pera; pollo, torre* = Latin *pinna, pira, pullus, turris*). Similarly the diphthongs *ae, au*, tended to weaken to *e, o*: see Varro, *L. L.* v. 97, *in Latio rure "edus"; qui in urbe, ut in multis, a addito, aedus;* Fest. 202, 13, *orata, genus piscis, appellatur a colore auri quod rustici "orum" dicebant, ut auriculas "oriculas"* (compare the Ital. *povero, toro;* Span. *pobre, toro*=Lat. *pauper, taurus*). Unaccented *au*, closely followed by *u*, weakened to *a*: see Caper, 108, 6, *ausculta, non "asculta"* (compare the Ital. *Agosto*, Fr. *Août*=Lat. *Augustus*). A result of the stress accent was frequent syncope of unaccented vowels, notably between liquids and mutes: see Prob. *App.* 198, 3, *calida, non "calda," frigida, non "frigda"* (compare *domnus* = *dominus* [Plaut.], *mattus* = *maditus* [Petr.], and Ital. *caldo, freddo*, Fr. *chaud, froid*). From the second century, a prosthetic *i* became frequent before *st, sc, sp*, etc., mainly in inscriptions, and has survived to some extent in the Romance languages (compare Fr. *étude, écrire* = Lat. *studium, scribere*).

The majority of Latin consonants have passed unaltered into the Romance language and exhibit few distinctly plebeian features. The most important changes, the assibilation of *ti* before a vowel and of *c* and *g* before *e* and *i*, belong to the latest period of Latinity. In post-Hadrian Latin *b* became confounded with *v* (comp. forms like *Berecundus, inbicto, berbeces*, from the second-century inscriptions; Prob. *App.* 198, 7, *alveus, non "albeus"*; Ital. *avere, inverno;* Fr. *avoir, hiver*=Lat. *habere, hibernum*). The aspirate was frequently misapplied, as to-day in Cockney English: Catullus (*Carm.* 84) ridicules forms like *chommoda, hinsidias* as a vulgar affectation (cf. Nigid. *ap.* Gell. xiii. 6, 3, *rusticus fit sermo si aspires perperam;* Caper, vii. 102, 12, *alica, non "halica"*). Final consonants were often neglected. Thus final *m*, lightly sounded even in classic Latin, was disregarded in the popular speech (cf. Prob. *App.* 199, 14, *passim, non "passi"*; *numquam, non "numqua"*; *pridem, non "pride"*; *olim, non "oli"*). The failure of final *s* to make position, a usage common in early poetry, had become "*subrusticum*" in Cicero's day (*Orator*, 48, 161): its omission becomes frequent in the second-century inscriptions. In Pompeian wall inscriptions final *t* is sometimes wanting (comp. forms like *ama, valia, peria*). The Sermo Plebeius carried assimilation much further than the classic speech: *nn* for *nd* was probably due to Osco-Umbrian influence. Comp. Prob. *App.* 197, 24, "*candela,*" *non* "*cannela,*" and forms like *dispennite* (Plaut.), *verecunnus* (*Inscrr. Pomp.*), with Oscan *upsannam* = Lat. *operandum.* Such forms are now common in the Neapolitan dialect. *tt* for *ct* is found in the fourth century inscriptions—e. g. *lattucae, ottobris* (cf. Prob. *App.* 198, 30: *auctor, non "auttor,"* and Ital. *notte, ottavo, pittore* = Lat. *noctem, octavus, pictor. tt* for *pt* is seen in inscriptional forms, such as *Settembris, scritus* (cf. Ital. *Settembre, scritto*); *ss* for *sp*, or *ps*. Comp. also the vulgar form *issa* for *ipsa* in Martial (i. 1 [9]): *scriserunt* (*Inscr.*); Ital. *scrissi.*

(*b*) *Word-Formation.*—The contrast between the Romance languages and classic Latin is nowhere sharper than in vocabulary. Many familiar classic words have vanished, plebeian forms surviving in their place; so the vulgar *bucca, caballus*, have replaced *os* (gen. *oris*), *equus* (cf. the French *bouche, cheval;* Ital. *bocca, cavallo*). Still oftener the simple Latin word has survived only in a derivative form, a condition due to the plebeian fondness for ponderous derivatives and compounds. The popular language was burdened with substantives in *-bulum, -mentum*, and *-monium*, and adjectives in *-bundus, -lentus*, and *-osus;* frequentative, inchoative, and desiderative verbs, diminutives, and prepositional compounds all abounded. Everywhere the effort was apparent to compensate by volume of sound for native poverty of thought. Such derivatives often differed but slightly, if at all, in meaning from the simple word, as the Romance languages testify (cf. the French *abeille, corbeille*, from Lat. diminutives *apicula, corbicula; chanter, jeter*, from frequentatives *cantare, iactare*). Through such misuse, words tended to wear out quickly, and it became necessary to reinforce them. Hence arose double diminutives, like *homullulus, lapillulus;* double frequentatives, like *cantitare, ductitare;* verbs with reduplicated prepositions, as *con-colligere, per-per-ire*, etc. The same fondness for lengthened forms is seen in the numerous compound suffixes resulting from secondary derivation, such as *-bili-tas, -osi-tas, -tor-ius, -ill-are*, or by deliberate compounding of separate endings, as *-ast-ellus, -ul-aster, -idini-tas, -eli-tas.* Furthermore, the two processes of composition and derivation are used in combination; a growing proportion of derivative verbs are compounded with prepositions, while the growing tendency to derive substantives and adjectives from compound verbs by preference gave rise to such forms as *stultiloquentia, vaniloquentia* (Plaut.), *circumspicientia* (Gell.), *disconvenientia, impraescientia, subtililoquentia* (Tert.), *suffumigatorius, superinunctorius* (Cass. Fel.); and such were often further compounded, notably with *in-* privative. Comp. *inrecogitatio* (Tert.), *incoinquinabilitas* (Fulg. Rusp.).

(*c*) *Inflection.*—The radical process by which case-forms and tense-endings were largely replaced in the Romance languages by prepositions and periphrastic conjugations belongs under the head of syntax. The following are the principal anomalies of plebeian inflection: transfers from the fourth declension to the second, and from the fifth to the first, even in Plautine Latin, thus anticipating the loss of the fourth and fifth in Romance languages. Comp. *senatus, -i, tumultus, -i, ecfigia* for *effigies* (Plaut.); transfers from the third declension to second: cf. *vasum, ossum* (Plaut.), *pauper, a, um* (Plaut., Petr.), and Ital. *vaso, osso, povero.* Substitutions of nominal endings in pronominal declension: *ipsus, istus;* gen. sing. *isti, ulli;* dat. sing. fem. *aliae, totae* (all in Plaut.). Numerous irregular comparatives and superlatives, made from superlative forms, as *postremior, extremior* (Apul.), *extremissimus* (Tert.), *minissimus* (Arnob.), or from other words not usually compared in classic Latin, as *ipsissimus, geminissimus, patruissimus* (Plaut.), *pathicissimus* (Mart.), *caenidior* (Catull.). Adverbs in *-ter*, formed irregularly from adjectives in *-us: avariter, firmiter, largiter* (Plaut.), *improbiter* (Petr.). The use of active forms, in place of deponent verbs: cf. *laeto, opitulo* (Liv. Andr.), *ioco, nicto* (Plaut.), *aemulo* (Apul.), *carnifico, vesco* (Tert.). Transfers from the third to the fourth conjugation (so frequent in the Romance languages): cf. *aggrediri, moriri* (Plaut.), Ital. *morire.* The formation of the fourth declension future in *-ibo*, by analogy with *-abo, -ebo:* cf. *nescibo, audibis, scibimus* (Plaut.). The unusual formation of certain perfects with the normal ending *-ivi:* cf. *posivi, institivi, potivi,* etc. Similarly the use of the normal imperatives *face, duce,* etc., for usual *fac, duc.*

(*d*) *Syntax.*—Neuter nouns tended to become masculine, more rarely feminine: cf. *caelus, fatus, vinus, triclinia* (Petr.), and the loss of the neuter in Ital., Span., etc. From the Romance standpoint, great importance attaches to the tendency to develop syntax at the expense of inflectional forms. Thus case-constructions were gradually replaced by prepositions: the partitive genitive by *de*, the dative of indirect object by *ad*, the instrumental ablative by *cum*. From early times the accusative tended to assume the functions of other cases—e. g. of the ablative after *utor, fruor, fungor,* etc., or of the dative after verbs of pleasing, trusting, etc. Gradually a confusion arose between the cases, and we find *in* construed indifferently with accusative or ablative; later *cum, de, ex* occur with the accusative; *ante, per,* etc., with the ablative. Adjectives were compared with the help of adverbs, such as *bene, magis, plus:* cf. Fr. *bien joli*, Span. *mas grande*, Ital. *più forte.* There was a tendency to use the verbs *esse, habere* as auxiliaries to form periphrastic tenses. The uses of the subjunctive mood were gradually curtailed: from the time of Plautus the indicative occurs in indirect questions, and in later Latin purpose is often expressed by the infinitive. Conversely, the infinitive with *verba sentiendi et declarandi* is constantly replaced by the indicative (more rarely the subjunctive) with *quod, quia, quoniam* in post-classic Latin: cf. *dixi quod mustella comedit* (Petr.), Fr. *j'ai dit que*... Finally, plebeian Latin is partial to double negatives: *nemini nihil satis est* (Petr.); cf. Ital. *non fa niente*, Fr. *je n'ai point.*

IV. Bibliography.—Most of the literature concerning the Sermo Plebeius is embodied in monographs, dealing either with special grammatical points or with the style of the individual writers. There exists as yet no comprehensive treatise covering the subject as a whole, although the results of modern scholarship have been to some extent embodied in such recent works as Stolz and Schmalz's *Lateinische Grammatik*, in Müller's *Handbuch der klassischen Alterthumswissenschaft*, vol. ii. (2d ed. Munich, 1890); Lindsay's *The Latin Language* (Oxford, 1894); and the new *Historische Grammatik der lateinischen Sprache*, of which only the first volume, by Prof. Stolz (*Einleitung, Lautlehre, Stammbildungslehre*), has yet appeared (Leipzig, 1894–95). The following list includes the more important works bearing upon this subject: Wölfflin, *Zum Vulgärlatein*, in the *Philologus*, vol. xxxiv. pp. 137–165; O. Rebling, *Versuch einer Charakteristik der römischen Umgangssprache* (2d ed. Kiel, 1882); Herm. Rönsch, *Itala und Vulgata* (Marburg and Leipzig, 1869); A. von Guericke, *De Linguae Vulgaris Reliquiis apud Petronium et in Inscriptionibus Parietariis Pompeianis* (Gumbinnen, 1875); E. Ludwig, *Bericht über die in den Jahren 1873–76 erschienenen Schriften über Vulgärlatein und spätere Latinität*, in Bursian's *Jahresbericht*, vol. vi. pp. 238 foll., and the same author's *De Petronii Sermone Plebeio* (Marburg, 1869); G. Koffmane, *Geschichte des Kirchenlateins*, pts. i. and ii. (Breslau, 1879–81); Ott, *Die neueren Forschungen im Gebiete des Bibel-Latein*, in the *Neue Jahrbuch für Philologie* (1874), pp. 757–792, 833–867; Storm, *Romance Languages*, in the *Encyclopaedia Britannica* (9th ed.), vol. xx. pp. 661–668; Paul Monceaux, *Le Latin Vulgaire d'après les Dernières Publications*, in the *Revue des Deux Mondes* (July 15, 1891), pp. 429–448; Budinsky, *Die Ausbreitung der lateinischen Sprache* (Berlin, 1881); A. Koehler, *De Auctoris Belli Africani et Belli hispaniensis Latinitate* (Erlangen, 1877); Kraut, *Ueber das vulgäre Element in der Sprache des Salustius* (Blaubeuren, 1881); Stinner, *De eo quo Cicero in Epistolis Usus est Sermone* (Oppeln, 1879); Cooper, *Word Formation in the Roman Sermo Plebeius* (Boston, 1895); and the list of authorities there cited. See also the list given by Schmalz in Müller's *Handbuch*, and many articles contained in the *Archiv für lateinische Lexicographie*, vols. i.–viii. (Leipzig, 1884–94). The following treatises are important for African Latin: Sittl, *Die lokalen Verschiedenheiten der lateinischen Sprache* (Erlangen, 1882); H. Kretschmann, *De Latinitate L. Apulei Madaurensis* (Königsberg, 1865); Wölfflin, *Ueber die Latinität des Afrikaners Cassius Felix*, in *Sittungsber. d. k. b. Akademie der Wissenschaften z.* Munchen, *Philos.-Histos. Cl.* (1880), pp. 381–432; three important articles in the eighth volume of the *Archiv f. Lat. Lex.:* Kübler, *Die lateinische Sprache auf afrikanischen Inschriften*, pp. 161–202; and Thielmann, *Die Lateinische Uebersetzung des Buches der Weisheit*, and *Die Lateinische Uebersetzung des Buches Sirach*, pp. 235–277, 501–561; Paul Monceaux, *Les Africains* (Paris, 1894); and Gaston Boissier, *L'Afrique Romaine* (Paris, 1895).

Sermȳla (Σερμύλη). A town in Macedonia on the peninsula Sithonia or its isthmus (Herod. vii. 122).

Serpentīni Versus. See Echoici Versus.

Serra (πρίων). A saw. The ancient forms of the saw were identical with those found in our own time, as the accompanying representations show, taken from a Pompeian painting, Gruter, and an Egyptian source respectively. The blade of the saw was called *lamina*. St. Jerome (*In Is.* xxviii. 27) is thought to refer to the circular saw; and Pliny (*H. N.* xxxvi. 9) speaks of a saw for cutting stone, but toothless, the place of teeth being supplied by emery or very fine sand. The word *serrarius* denotes a saw-maker, while *prista* is used of a person who saws.

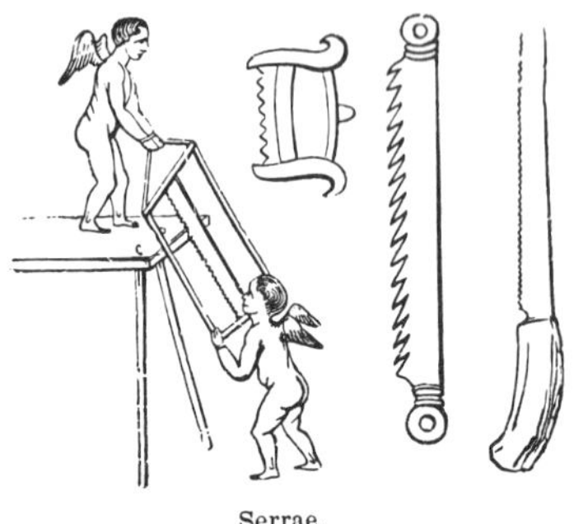

Serrae.

Serrānus, Atilius. Serranus was originally an agnomen of C. Atilius Regulus, consul B.C. 257 (see REGULUS), but afterwards became the name of a distinct family of the Atilia gens. Most of the ancient writers derive the name from *serere*, and relate that Regulus received the surname of Serranus because he was engaged in sowing when the news was brought him of his elevation to the consulship (Verg. *Aen.* vi. 845). It appears, however, from coins that *Saranus* is the proper form of the name, and some modern writers think that it is derived from Saranum, a town of Umbria. (1) GAIUS, consul B.C. 106 with Q. Servilius Caepio, the year in which Cicero and Pompey were born. Although a *stultissimus homo*, according to Cicero, he was elected in preference to Q. Catulus. He was one of the senators who took up arms against Saturninus in 100. (2) SEXTIUS, surnamed GAVIĀNUS, because he originally belonged to the Gavia gens. He was quaestor in 63 in the consulship of Cicero, who treated him with distinguished favour; but in his tribunate of the plebs (57) he took an active part in opposing Cicero's recall from banishment. After Cicero's return to Rome he put his veto upon the decree of the Senate restoring to Cicero the site on which his house had stood, but found it advisable to withdraw his opposition (Cic. *Pro Sest.* 33–43; *Post Red.* 5; *Ad Att.* iv. 2).

Serrātus. A Roman denarius having a serrated edge, struck under the Republic (Tac. *Germ.* 5; cf. Mommsen, *Röm. Münzwesen*, p. 771).

Serta. A wreath or garland. See CORONA.

Sertorius, QUINTUS. One of the most extraordinary men in the later times of the Roman Republic. He was a native of Nursia, a Sabine village, and was born of obscure but respectable parents. He served under Marius in the war against the Teutones; and before the battle of Aquae Sextiae (Aix), in B.C. 102, he entered the camp of the Teutones in disguise as a spy, for which hazardous undertaking his intrepid character and some knowledge of the Keltic language well qualified him. He also served as *tribunus militum* in Spain under T. Didius (97). He was quaestor in 91, and had before this time lost an eye in battle. On the outbreak of the Civil War in 88 he declared himself against the party of the nobles, and commanded one of the four armies which besieged Rome under Marius and Cinna (App. *B. C.* i. 67). He was, however, opposed to the bloody massacre which ensued after Marius and Cinna entered Rome.

In 83 Sertorius was praetor, and either in this year or the following he went into Spain, whence he crossed over to Mauretania, and gained a victory over Paccianus, one of Sulla's generals. After this, at the request of the Lusitanians, he became their leader, and for some years successfully resisted all the power of Rome. He availed himself of the superstitious character of that people to strengthen his authority over them. A fawn was brought to him by one of the natives as a present, which soon became so tame as to accompany him in his walks and attend him on all occasions. After Sulla had become master of Italy, Sertorius was joined by many Romans, and among the rest by M. Perperna, with fifty-three cohorts. (See PERPERNA.) To give some show of form to his formidable power, Sertorius established a Senate of 300, into which no provincial was admitted. The continued want of success on the part of Metellus, who had been sent against Sertorius in 79, induced the Romans to send Pompey to his assistance, but with an independent command. Pompey arrived in Spain in 76 with a large force (30,000 infantry and 1000 cavalry), but was unable to gain any decisive advantages. For the next five years Sertorius kept both Metellus and Pompey at bay, and cut to pieces a large number of their forces. Sertorius was at length assassinated at a banquet in 72 by Perperna and some other Roman officers, who had long been jealous of his authority. See his life by Plutarch and the dissertation by Smits, *De Quinto Sertorio* (1867).

Servilia. (1) The daughter of Q. Servilius Caepio and the daughter of Livia, the sister of the celebrated M. Livius Drusus, tribune of the plebs in B.C. 91. Servilia was married twice: first to M. Iunius Brutus, by whom she became the mother of the murderer of Caesar, and secondly to D. Iunius Silanus, consul in 62. (2) Sister of the preceding, was the second wife of L. Lucullus, consul in 74.

Servilia Gens. One of the Alban houses removed to Rome by Tullius Hostilius. Its more important families bore the names of AHALA, CAEPIO, CASCA, GLAUCIA, RULLUS, VATIA.

Servilius Ahăla. See AHALA.

Servilius Caepio. See CAEPIO.

Servilius Casca. See CASCA.

Servilius Rullus. See RULLUS.

Servĭtus. See SERVUS.

Servitūtes. Where one person has a right over property of another, which he can assert by legal remedy against any one who interferes with its exercise, and not merely against the owner of the property, he is said to have a *ius in re aliena*, and his right belongs to those which are "real" or *in rem*. By the existence of such a right the legal position of the owner is diminished in value: his ownership, which otherwise would be unrestricted, is curtailed, not in duration, but in extension. The presumption of law was in favour of the freedom of property, and the burden of proving his right over it lay on the other party: hence, when a thing was sold as *optima maxima*, this was legally understood to mean that it was warranted free from any real rights in persons other than the owner (Dig. 50, 16, 90, and 169). Two classes of such rights are known to Roman law: one recognized by the old Ius Civile, and termed *servitutes;* the other of praetorian origin, and known by specific names—viz. *Emphyteusis*, *Pignus*, and *Superficies*. See the articles under these heads. Servitutes are either personal or praedial. Of the first class are *habitatio* or the right of living in another person's house; and *operae servorum* or *animalium*, the right of using his slaves or animals. Among praedial servitutes are that *oneris ferendi*, the right to use a wall or edifice of his neighbour as a support for his own; *proiciendi*, the right to allow one's balcony to project over his neighbour's land; *cloacae immitendae*, the right of running a drain through a neighbour's premises, etc. The modern term for *servitutes* is "easements." See Schonemann, *Die Servituten* (1866); Molitor, *La Possession et les Servitutes en Droit Romain* (1851).

Servius Marius (or **Maurus**) **Honorātus.** A Roman grammarian, who lived towards the end of the fourth century A.D. He taught grammar and rhetoric at Rome, and composed, besides a commentary on the grammar of Donatus and some short treatises on grammar, a commentary on Vergil remarkable for its copious historical, mythological, and antiquarian notes, most of which are probably derived from the writings of much earlier scholars. It has not, however, reached us in its original form. Servius appears as one of the characters in the *Saturnalia* of Macrobius (q. v.). The commentary on Vergil is edited by Thilo and Hagen (Leipzig, 1878).

Servius Tullius. See TULLIUS.

Servus (δοῦλος). I. In GREECE, besides a class of serfs like the Penestae of Thessaly and the Helots of Sparta, who had come to this condition through being conquered in war, we find, even in Homeric times, actual slaves not differing greatly from freemen. They seem to have been possessed in large numbers only by princes and chieftains, who either obtained them as booty on expeditions (δοριάλωτοι), or bought them from such predatory adventurers as the Phœnicians (*Odyss.* xv. 483). In historic times the institution of slavery was very much developed, so that there is scarcely a State in which even the poorer citizens did not own a male or female slave to do the rough work considered unworthy of a free man (Aristoph. *Plut.* init.). In Attica, when the State was in its most flourishing condition, there were some 400,000 slaves, or about four times the number of the free citizens (Ctesicles *ap.* Athen. vi. p. 272 *c*). The Greeks justified slavery, much as did our antebellum teachers, by alleging that there were certain barbarians who had been intended by nature to be slaves. As a matter of fact, the slaves in Greece were for the most part barbarians by race. In exceptional cases, Greeks also were captured in war, and were thus reduced to permanent slavery; but, as a rule, they were exchanged or freed on the payment of a ransom. The countries of Asia Minor, Thrace, and the northern regions comprehended under the name of Scythia sent the greatest numbers to the slave-markets, of which the most important were at Delos, Chios, and Byzantium. Athens also had a slave-market, especially used by citizens who wished to expose undesirable slaves for sale. Most of the slaves in Attica were such as had been born from female slaves. The wealthy sometimes possessed several hundreds of them, of whom, naturally, only a part would be kept in the house. Some of the remainder worked on farms in the country, while others served on the merchantmen as rowers or sailors, others in the mines at Laurium, while others again, either singly or in numbers in a manufactory and under a superintendent, were engaged in some trade on their master's account. The owners also sometimes let out slaves to others, as in our Southern States before the war. Domestic slaves were employed in every conceivable kind of occupation in the house, and were also intrusted with the education of the boys, whom they had to accompany everywhere, especially to the school and to the palaestra; such slaves were called παιδαγωγοί. Indeed, as a rule, even the commonest Greek, if he could possibly manage it, never went out unescorted by a slave; while, if he was rich, a number of slaves followed him. At the same time, no Greek seems to have had the vast collection of slaves that many Romans had under the Empire. Fifty was regarded as a large number, though Nicias owned as many as 1000 or more (Xen. *De Vect.* 4). The chief difference, however, between the Greek and Roman view of slavery is that the Greeks regarded the slave as a labourer and an industrial necessity, while the Romans used him chiefly as a minister to their personal pleasures. See the remarks at the end of the present article, and cf. Athen. vi. p. 272 *e*.

Their treatment differed according to the character and the pecuniary position of the owner, and also depended upon their own good qualities and usefulness. In general, the Athenians were noted for showing more kindness to their slaves than did the rest of the Greeks. There were laws also that referred to them, and protected them against excessive caprice and harshness. But they had no legal rights; they could neither bring a charge nor appear as witnesses. It was only when they were put to the torture (βασανίζειν) that their evidence had any weight attached to it. But the master could not kill a slave unless the latter had been condemned in a law-court; otherwise he had to pay a penalty to some divinity. If cruelly treated, a slave could seek protection, usually in the temple of Theseus, and claim to be sold to another master. In case of maltreatment by a stranger, the master could bring a legal action, and obtain heavy damages. Slaves had no particular dress prescribed for them by law; but they were not allowed to let their hair grow long. They were not prohibited from entering temples and sanctuaries or from taking part in the public religious festivals; but they were excluded from the use of the gymnasia and from the assemblies of the people. Manumissions were not rare, especially such as were made by a clause in the owner's will, or if slaves bought their freedom with the savings made by permission of the master. Sometimes manumission was a reward for giving information about grave crimes, or for distinguished service in war; for slaves were not unfrequently employed in military service, especially in the fleet as rowers and sailors, or as marines. (See NAVIS.) (For the position of the liberated slaves, see LIBERTUS.) At Athens there was also a special class of public slaves (δημόσιοι). Chief among them were those called Scythae or archers, at first 300, then 600, and finally as many as 1200; the name Speusinii was also given them from a certain Speusinus, who is said to have established this institution (Pollux, viii. 132, and the *Etymologicum Magnum*). They served as police, and their duties were at first confined to the market-place, but afterwards were extended to the Areopagus. They were further employed for military purposes, like the similar corps, also consisting of public slaves, of 200 mounted archers (ἱπποτοξόται). The lower servants of the State officials, such as criers, scribes, jail-keepers, and hangmen, were mostly (the last-mentioned always) public slaves, and so were the workmen at the mint. Their position was one of much greater freedom than that of the private slaves, and did not differ greatly from that of the μέτοικοι. See DEMOSII.

II. The ROMANS, like the Greeks, possessed slaves from the earliest times; but their number was at first trifling, on account of the small households of the old Romans and their simple manner of life. But great estates gradually became frequent, and slaves were used by preference for agricultural work, because they were not subject to levy for military service. Luxury became more general, and a number of wants, previously unknown, were created by it; and in course of time the custom of employing slaves for industrial purposes was borrowed from the Greeks. All this caused a continual increase in the number of slaves, until in some cases they were collected in several thousands. Some of these were born in the house, and were called *vernae;* they were regarded as particularly faithful and trustworthy, and enjoyed certain liberties accordingly. The remainder were for the most part acquired among the spoils of war, or were introduced from other countries where slaves were kept. Those taken in war were sold by the quaestor either on the spot immediately or at the nearest market-place, or, according to the technical terms, either *sub hasta* ("under the lance") or *sub corona* ("under the wreath," which was placed on the head of captives in war to show that they were for sale). For this purpose slave-dealers (*mangones*), whose profitable trade was regarded with contempt, were always represented in the train of Roman armies. They also bought slaves in great numbers at the principal slave-marts, as at Rome and Delos. At Rome, the aediles superintended this kind of business, on which the government levied a tax for import and a further tax on the sale. The slave was placed on a platform (*catasta*), with his feet whitened with chalk or gypsum, if he had just come across the sea (Juv. i. 111), and with a label (*titulus*) round his neck, showing his home, age, abilities, and bodily defects, if any, the vendor being responsible for the correctness of these statements; if he would not bind himself in any such way, this was shown by placing a cap (*pilleus*) on the slave's head. (See PILLEUS.) Slaves distinguished for their beauty, their skill, or their literary or musical accomplishments, were not exhibited publicly, but in special places, and to such as were able to pay the prices for them, which frequently ran very high. Those born in the house were also sold by private agreement, without being exposed. There were slaves of every nationality, and on this depended in general the names by which they were called and the work which was assigned them. The *familia* (a designation including all the slaves, or *famuli*, belonging to the same master) was generally divided into that of the country (*familia rustica*) and that of the town (*familia urbana*).

The work done by the slaves was of the most varied character, and the great diversity of their occupations is partly explained by the fact that almost every kind of work required a special slave, and it was considered not consistent with good breeding, and a sign of poverty, if the same slave was intrusted with several different duties. Thus there were in the country special slaves for the various branches of agriculture, horticulture, and the tending of cattle, the cultivation of olives and vines, the keeping of bees and of poultry, and for the preserves and fishponds. These slaves were under the supervision of the *vilicus* (farm-bailiff) or *actor* (steward), who had to render the accounts to the master or his representative.

The number of town-slaves was not due to actual requirements, but depended upon the luxurious fashions which became more and more prevalent in the last two centuries of the Republic. In older times the house and everything belonging to it was in charge of the *aedituus* ("major domo," "steward"), who managed all household affairs, received and spent money, negotiated sales and purchases, and disposed of the stores. When the extension of the household made it necessary to keep a special person to control the expenditure, the steward's functions were limited to seeing that the house and furniture were properly cleaned and in a good state. Besides him there were subordinate servants for the various dwellings, the spare rooms for visitors, the shrine of the household gods, the images of the ancestors, the various kinds of furniture, the art collections, and the wardrobe; and there was also a porter (*ianitor* or *ostiarius*), who, according to an old custom, was chained like a dog (Suet. *De Rhet.* 3; Columel. 1 pr. § 10; Ovid, *Amores*, i. 6, 1).

The kitchen was in charge of a special slave, an even more expensive one than the *vilicus;* and under him were a host of assistants, wood-carriers, market-men, pastry-cooks, etc. The service at table also necessitated a numerous attendance of dressers, servers, carvers, fore-tasters, cup-bearers, table-clearers and others, who similarly were under a special foreman, the *tricliniarcha*, who saw to the general arrangements and to the lighting. The master and mistress of the house were served by special valets (*cubicularii*), who also had to announce visitors (*nomenclatores*), and pages and chambermaids and special servants for the bath and the toilet. It was considered of especial importance that, when the master or mistress of the house left it on foot or in a litter, the slaves following them should be numerous and richly attired. Some slaves went before their master (*anteambulones*), especially the *nomenclator*, who informed his master of the names of the persons they met; others followed (*pedisequi*); others, again, were told off for attending their master with torches and lanterns on leaving parties in the evening. The litter of each member of the family was carried by from six to eight *lecticarii*, particularly strong men, and by preference Cappadocians. For travelling across country there was always a large escort, consisting of crowds of equerries, outriders, grooms, etc. The most important position among the servants was occupied by those whom the master himself chose to assist him in his business or his recreations, as, for instance, those who attended to money matters and to the supervision of the slaves, secretaries, physicians, readers at meals or during the bath or before going to sleep, literary men (*litterati*), librarians, and transcribers of books. For other kinds of recreation there were also slaves who had received a musical training, *pantomimi*, fools, and jesters. See NANUS.

The various classes of slaves had each its special foreman, with a substitute whom he either received from his master or bought with his savings (*peculium*). These formed the class of the *ordinarii*, who enjoyed the special confidence of their master; this class included such servants as looked after the food, clothing, and medical attendance of the slaves, the maintenance and watching of the various buildings, the accounts of the household (*cellarius*), and the expenses of the master (*dispensator*). Young slaves were trained for the various requirements of the household; according to their abilities, they were taught some trade or art, or had practice given them either in keeping accounts or in learned studies. Under the Empire, those who were destined to be pages received their education in special *paedagogia* or establishments, kept not only by the emperor, but also by private citizens. As in Greece, trained slaves were established in some trade by themselves, or let out on hire; such was the case even with slaves who were artists or men of learning. Even posts of independence, such as the administration of an estate in the country, or of a bank, or the command of a ship, were intrusted to slaves, who received a share in the profits, or paid interest on the capital invested, or a fixed sum of money when the capital was their own. For the slaves were allowed to acquire a private fortune (*peculium*) from what they saved on their allowances and from the regular profits of their service. The masters regarded this arrangement with favour, especially as it represented a kind of caution money in case any damage was done. See PECULIUM.

The Roman slave was, in the eyes of the law, a mere chattel (Varro even styles him "a speaking tool" [*instrumentum vocale*]), and hence absolutely without any rights and completely exposed to the caprice of his master. The latter could compel him to do the meanest and most shameful things, could torture or kill him, or cast him out when he was old or weakly; and as this treatment was legally permitted, it was carried out in practice when occasion offered. Especial cruelty was experienced by the country-slaves, who worked in chains in the greater part of Italy, and were kept in a guarded work-house (*ergastulum*) at night; some of them were branded, or had half of their heads shaven. It was therefore a severe punishment for a town-slave to be sent into the country.

When the slaves were less numerous and were restricted to the drudgery of farm life, and when the consul himself had but one or two personal attendants, their treatment was, as has been said, the treatment accorded to animals. "Let the slave sleep or work," says Cato in his terse book of rules, implying that his working hours must all be devoted to toil. "Speak to slaves in monosyllables," says another writer (Seneca). "Treat them like wild beasts and subdue them by lashing. You will have as many enemies as you have slaves." And throughout the whole period of Roman history, the mere labourers fared as might have been expected among a people who followed out these harsh measures. A slave's life was long a matter of no concern to the State. It belonged wholly to his master. The elder Cato used not infrequently to put one of his slaves to death in the presence of his fellows to cow them into absolute subservience. There was no feeling of humanity visible in the treatment accorded to them. Pollio, the friend of Augustus, used a slave to feed the eels in his artificial lake. Augustus himself crucified a slave for killing a favourite quail. For worse offences worse punishments were devised. Men were lashed to death, crushed between two millstones; had their hands, feet, nose, lips, and eyes cut out and were then flung upon the bare ground to die; or they were suspended by hooks of iron to be devoured by the birds of prey. If a slave killed his master, not only he but all his companions were tortured and put to death; yet the killing of masters was not infrequent. Pliny in one of his letters gives one instance (iii. 14): "Largius Macedo, a man of praetorian rank, has suffered a dreadful fate at the hands of his slaves; a harsh master he was, too. While he was taking a bath at his Formian villa his slaves of a sudden surrounded him. One seized him by the throat, another struck him in the face; another bruised his breast and stomach, and when they thought him dead flung him on the heated marble to see whether he still lived." So Tacitus (*Ann.* xiv. 42) describes the murder of the city praefect, Pedianus Secundus, by his slaves, on which occasion four hundred innocent slaves were put to death with the guilty. Often the slaves, driven to desperation by their masters, banded together in a frantic struggle for vengeance. On one occasion several hundred broke out into the city, and rushing through the streets slew without discrimination every one they met, until they were themselves cut to pieces by a detachment of the Guards.

It was not until the influence of Christianity began to be felt that the Roman conception of humanity became sufficiently enlarged to embrace the slave as well as the freeman. Gradually the way to emancipation was made more and more easy. Gradually, too, the law began to throw some safeguards around the person of the slave, forbidding excessive cruelty on the master's part. At last, under Justinian, any slave could gain his freedom by becoming a monk or "spiritual person" (*Nov.* v. 2, 1; cxxiii. 7, 35).

The usual mode of killing slaves was crucifixion (see CRUX), which was put down by the Christian emperors. If a slave dared to wreak vengeance on his master, every slave who was under the same roof at the time was put to death with him. This cruelty of treatment, which grew continually in the last centuries of the Republic, brought on repeated and terrible insurrections of the slaves. Under the Empire they received some legal protection; in its very beginning, the master's right to condemn his slaves to fight with wild beasts was taken away from him and transferred to a regular judge—the praefect of the city at Rome and the procurator in the provinces. These officials were also empowered by Antoninus Pius to receive the complaints of slaves about cruel treatment, and to sell the slaves to another master, in case their complaints were found to rest on truth. Hadrian deprived the owners of the right of killing and torturing slaves at their pleasure, or of selling them to keepers of gladiatorial schools or to procurers; and, finally, Constantine placed the intentional killing of a slave on a level with murder. A kind of married relation between slaves, called *contubernium*, was permitted at an early time. Under the Empire, it became a rule to regard it as lasting and indissoluble, and even to celebrate the marriage of slaves by wedding festivities. Having no legal rights, the slave could not give evidence in a law court, and, as in Greece, only what he said when under torture was deemed worthy of credit. The Roman, like the Athenian, government had public slaves (*servi publici*), who, on the whole, had the same legal position as the private slaves. They lived in public buildings assigned to them by the censors, and received from the public chest a yearly sum to pay for their board (*cibaria*). They were partly employed as custodians of temples and public buildings (*aeditui*), partly as servants to the various priesthoods and to those magistrates who had duties relating to the police—namely, the censors and aediles who under Augustus had under their control a body of 600 *servi publici* for the prevention of fires (see VIGILES), the overseers of the water supply and of the prisons, and those who had to see capital offences carried out. The slaves of the latter included the hangman (*carnifex*), who was intrusted with the special duty of executing slaves, and who had to live outside the Esquiline Gate.

There was no distinctive dress for Roman slaves. It was once proposed in the Senate to give them a distinctive costume, but it was rejected since it was considered dangerous to show them how numerous they were (Sen. *De Clem.* i. 24). Male slaves were not allowed to wear the toga or bulla, nor females the stola; but otherwise they were dressed in nearly the same way as the poorer people, in tunics and cloaks of a dark colour (*pullati*) and slippers (*crepidae*), or in the country *sculponeae* or clogs (*vestis servilis*, Cic. *In Pis.* 38, 93).

The prices of ordinary slaves was low by reason of the great number of them on sale at Rome. The struggles of Rome with Pyrrhus, with Perseus, with Hannibal, with the Sicilians, with the Gauls, the Cimbri, and the Germans, all ending in the success of the Roman arms, turned the metropolis into a great slave-market whither the prisoners fresh from the field of battle, and representing every country, civilized and barbarian, poured in one continuous throng. Scipio Aemilianus is said to have sold nearly 60,000 Carthaginians into slavery. Marius made serfs of 140,000 Cimbri. Aemilius Paullus handed over 150,000 men, women, and children to the military quaestors who accompanied his army, and who acted as the fiscal agents of the government. Cicero received a sum of money equivalent to $500,000 from the sale of his prisoners of war. Gracchus is said to have enslaved so many Sardinians that the very name Sardus became a synonym for "slave." Popilius Laenas carried off 20,000 Statielli (Liguria) at once. Pompey and Caesar are roughly estimated to have sold at various times a million of human beings into slavery. The whole world was laid under contribution to supply the market for human chattels. "Long lines of chained prisoners from Germany, Gaul, and even Britain," says Duruy, "were led to Rome. Utica and Egypt furnished blacks; Numidia, swift runners; Alexandria, grammarians; Sidoné and Cyprus, those intelligent, docile, and corrupt Asiatics so highly prized as house servants; Greece, her handsome boys and girls; Epirus and Illyria, the most experienced shepherds; Germany, Gaul, and Thrace, the most savage gladiators; Cappadocia, the most patient labourers. Slave-dealers (*mangones*) accompanied every army, and the clash of arms had hardly ceased when the battle-field resounded with the sharp cries and sordid bustle of an auction-room."

How cheaply these newly-made slaves were rated is seen from the fact that Lucullus once sold a large number of prisoners at an average price of four drachmae—eighty cents—apiece. At Rome, the slave-market, as already stated, was under the supervision of the aediles; and the sales were usually at public auction, though slaves of great beauty or remarkable accomplishments were sometimes reserved for private sale, as we learn from Martial (ix. 60). The chief points of inquiry regarding an ordinary male slave were as to whether he was given to thievery, subject to epilepsy, of a suicidal tendency, and whether he had ever tried to escape. The slaves when on exhibition were often obliged to strip naked, and to jump, run, and move about to show their paces for the information of the intending purchasers. Medical experts were sometimes called in to give their opinion of the soundness of the slave.

In certain cases the law allowed a free person to be sold as a slave—e. g. those who attempted to evade public burdens by not having their names entered on the census (*incensi*), or who shirked military service, and the insolvent debtor under the old law of execution by *manus iniectio*. According to the old law, a thief caught in the act (*fur manifestus*) was adjudged (*addictus*) to the person whose property he had stolen. A free man over twenty years of age who collusively allowed himself to be sold as a slave in order to secretly share the purchase-money with the vendor was as early as the time of Mucius Scaevola refused his *proclamatio in libertatem* by the praetor, and so in effect adjudged a slave. By an enactment of Claudius also (Suet. *Claud.* 25), a freedman who had misconducted himself towards his patron might be again enslaved. Under the emperors it was established that a free man who was condemned to death, to penal servitude in the mines, or to fight with gladiators or wild beasts, became and died a slave.

The prices at which slaves sold at Rome varied, of course, very much with the time, the characteristics of the slave, and the requirements of the purchaser. In the time of Horace, an ordinary male slave cost about $90; somewhat later, $125. This was the price of a day labourer. More valuable were those who possessed some special accomplishment, who had a knowledge of medicine, or who were literary men.

Thus M. Scaurus bought a grammarian named Natius for 700,000 sesterces, or $28,000; boys sold for 100,000 sesterces ($4000) to 200,000 sesterces ($8000). A fool (*morio*) brought an average of 20,000 sesterces ($800) (Mart. viii. 13).

Good-looking girls were sold for immoral purposes for an average price of $1000; but if they were known to have already lost their virtue $25 was considered a fair price. Of all slaves, negroes and eunuchs were the most costly, the latter being largely sold for immoral purposes; so that Pliny records that Seianus, the minister of Tiberius, sold a eunuch named Paezon to Lutorius for the extraordinary sum of 50,000,000 sesterces, or $2,000,000. In later times some attempt was made to pass a sumptuary law regulating the prices of slaves.

Justinian fixed a regular tariff, eunuchs running from $150 to $350.

It is obvious that between the ordinary slave and his master there existed no ties of affection, and no feelings of gratitude that could lead to closer intimacy. This, however, was not true of the class of slaves who were sold as house-slaves, as personal attendants, as *paedagogi*, actors, teachers, and artists. These, coming often from the most polished communities of Greece, or often from the luxurious cities of Asia Minor, were infinitely the superiors of the Romans in intellectual training and accomplishments; and they could not fail to make themselves influential, and if not respected, at least felt. We can scarcely conceive of the ascendency which they attained at Rome. Everything was in their hands. They managed the estates, they kept the accounts, they arranged their masters' pleasures and kept them amused; they wrote their books, they painted their pictures, they controlled their fashions, they taught them music—and, more potent than all, they reared and trained their children. They swarmed in every household, and being keen-witted, intelligent, pliable, plausible, utterly shameless, and morally corrupt, they became a great plague spot in the heart of a community that had once been self-respecting, pure-minded, and devout. It is quite impossible to conceive of anything more demoralizing than such an influence, so widely exerted and so powerful for evil. It is not surprising to find a single century converting the Romans into a semi-Asiatic people living like Eastern voluptuaries, their houses glittering with gold and silver and jewels; their tables loaded with luxuries and crowded with sycophants; their halls swarming with human beings who won favour only by pandering to the most revolting vice and by stimulating jaded desire; their lives given over to gluttony and lust; their old ambition, their once strong intellects, their national pride, and their personal honour all flung away and turned to rottenness by the taint of that system which degrades and blights its victim by forcing him to be the unwilling instrument for the ruin of his fellow-men.

See Becker-Göll, *Gallus*, ii. 99–154; *Charikles*, iii. pp. 1–47; Lehmann, *De Publica Romanorum Servitute* (Leipzig, 1889); Wallon, *Histoire de l'Esclavage*, 3 vols. (2d ed. Paris, 1879); Gurowski, *Slavery in History* (New York, 1860); Lecky, *Hist. of European Morals*, i. 102 (note), 235, 262, 300–306 (Amer. ed. New York, 1884); Ingram, *Hist. of Slavery* (London, 1895); and the articles LIBERTUS; MANCIPIUM; MANUMISSIO; MEDIASTINUS.

Sesostris (Σέσωστρις). The name given by the Greeks to the great king of Egypt who is called in Manetho Ramses or Ramesses. Ramses (Egypt. Ra-messu Meri-Amen) is a name common to several kings of the eighteenth, nineteenth, and twentieth dynasties; but Sesostris may perhaps be identified with Ramses, the third king of the nineteenth dynasty, the son of Seti and the father of Menephthah II. (about B.C. 1333). Sesostris was a great conqueror. He is said to have subdued Ethiopia, the greater part of Asia, and the Thracians in Europe (Herod. ii. 102–111; Diod. i. 53–59). He returned to Egypt after an absence of nine years, and the countless captives whom he brought back with him were employed in the erection of numerous public works, such as those of which ruins still exist at Karnak, Luxor, Abu-Simbel, Memphis, and Thebes. Memorials of Ramses-Sesostris still exist throughout the whole of Egypt, from the mouth of the Nile to the south of Nubia, as also in the rock-tablets at Beyrut. An epic poem of one Pentaur, found on the monuments, celebrates his victories over the Kheta (i. e. Hittites). By some he has been identified with the Pharaoh of Exodus, but Lepsius thinks that the accounts of him confuse reminiscences of Sethos I. and Rameses II. See AEGYPTUS.

Sesostris or Ramses II. (Tanis.)

Sestertius (contracted from *semis tertius*—i. e. $2\frac{1}{2}$, expressed by the Roman symbol usually printed HS—i. e. II+S(*emis*), two units and a half). A coin, during the Republic, of silver; under the Empire, of copper, or more usually brass$=\frac{1}{4}$ *denarius*, originally $2\frac{1}{2}$ *asses* (whence the name); later, i. e. after B.C. 217, six *asses*. It was then worth $0.04. Under the early Empire it was worth about $0.05. After B.C. 209, when the Romans instituted a silver coinage, the copper *as* was suddenly reduced to 4 oz., and the *sestertius* ($2\frac{1}{2}\times 4$ oz.) became equivalent to one old *as* of 10 oz., instead of the original pound of 12 oz. It long continued to be used as the ordinary monetary unit. During the Republic and the first 300 years of the Empire amounts were reckoned in sesterces. Owing to the common use of *milia sestertiûm* (for *milia sestertiorum*), it became customary to treat *sestertium* as a neuter singular, and to omit *milia*. *Sestertium* thus denotes a sum of 1000 sesterces = (at $0.05 per sesterce) $50. A million sesterces ($50,000) was called originally *decies centena* (lit. "ten times one hundred thousand") *sestertium*, which was shortened to *decies sestertium*. 100,000 sesterces had thus

Sestertius of Nero in Brass.

become a customary unit for reckoning large sums of money. See NUMISMATICS, p. 1112.

Sestiānae Arae. The most westerly promontory of the northern coast of Hispania Tarraconensis, now Cape Villano. It had three altars dedicated to Augustus.

Sestīnum. Now Sestino; a town in Umbria on the Apennines, near the sources of the Pisaurus.

Sestius. See SEXTIUS.

Sestus (Σηστός). Now Ialova; a town in Thrace, situated at the narrowest part of the Hellespont, opposite Abydos in Asia, from which it was only seven stadia distant. It was founded by the Aeolians (Herod. vii. 33). It was celebrated in Grecian poetry on account of the loves of Leander and Hero (see LEANDER), and in history on account of the bridge of boats which Xerxes here built across the Hellespont. It was taken by the Romans in B.C. 190.

Set. An Egyptian god, identified by the Greeks with Typhon. See AEGYPTUS, p. 27; OSIRIS; TYPHON.

Setăbis. See SAETABIS.

Sethon (Σεθών). A priest of Hephaestus (Ptah), who made himself master of Egypt after the expulsion of Sabacon, king of the Ethiopians, and was succeeded by the Dodecarchia, or government of the twelve chiefs, which ended in the sole sovereignty of Psammetichus. Herodotus relates (ii. 141) that in Sethon's reign Sanacharibus, king of the Arabians and Assyrians, advanced against Egypt, at which Sethon was in great alarm, as he had insulted the warrior class, and deprived them of their lands, and they now refused to follow him to the war. But the god Hephaestus came to his assistance; for while the two armies were encamped near Pelusium, the field-mice in the night gnawed to pieces the bow-strings, the quivers, and the shield-handles of the Assyrians, who fled on the following day with great loss. The recollection of this miracle was perpetuated by a statue of the king in the temple of Hephaestus, holding a mouse in his hand, and saying, "Let every one look at me and be pious." This Sanacharibus is the Sennacherib of the Scriptures, and the destruction of the Assyrians at Pelusium is evidently only another version of the miraculous destruction of the Assyrians by the angel of the Lord, when they had advanced against Jerusalem in the reign of Hezekiah. According to the Jewish records, this event happened in B.C. 711.

Setia. Now Sezza or Sesse; an ancient town of Latium in the east of the Pomtine Marshes. It was celebrated for the excellent wine grown in its neighbourhood, which was reckoned in the time of Augustus the finest wine in Italy (Mart. x. 36; Juv. x. 27), and was called *vinum Setinum*. See VINUM.

Seven against Thebes, THE. Oedipus, king of Thebes, had pronounced a curse upon his sons Eteocles and Polynices that they should die at one another's hand. (See OEDIPUS.) In order to make the fulfilment of the curse impossible by separating himself from his brother, Polynices left Thebes while his father was still alive, and at Argos married Argea, the daughter of Adrastus (q. v.). On the death of his father he was recalled, and given by Eteocles, who was the elder of the two (Eurip. *Phoen.* 71), the choice between the kingdom and the treasures of Oedipus; but, on account of a quarrel that arose over the division, he departed a second time, and induced his father-in-law to undertake a war against his native city. According to another legend, the brothers deprived their father of the kingdom, and agreed to rule alternately, and to quit the city for a year at a time. Polynices, as the younger, first went into voluntary banishment; but when, after the expiration of a year, Eteocles denied him his right, and drove him out by violence, he fled to Argos, where Adrastus made him his son-in-law, and undertook to restore him with an armed force. Adrastus was the leader of the army; besides Polynices and Tydeus of Calydon, the other son-in-law of the king, there also took part in the expedition the king's brothers Hippomedon and Parthenopaeus (q. v.), Capaneus, a descendant of Proetus, and Amphiaraüs (q. v.), the latter against his will, and foreseeing his own death. The Atridae were invited to join in the expedition, but were withheld by evil omens from Zeus.

When the Seven reached Nemea on their march, a fresh warning befell them. Hypsipylé, the nurse of Opheltes, the son of King Lycurgus, laid her charge down on the grass in order to lead the thirsty warriors to a spring; during her absence the child was killed by a snake. They gave him solemn burial, and instituted the Nemean Games in his honour; but Amphiaraüs interpreted the occurrence as an omen of his own fate, and accordingly gave the boy the name of Archemorus (i. e. "leader to death"). When they arrived at the river Asopus in Boeotia, they sent Tydeus (q. v.) to Thebes in the hope of coming to terms. He was refused a hearing, and the Thebans laid an ambush for him on his return. The Seven now advanced to the walls of the city, and posted themselves with their troops one at each of its seven gates. Against them were posted seven chosen Thebans, among them Melanippus and Periclymenus. Menoeceus (q. v.) devoted himself to death to insure the victory for the Thebans. In the battle at the sanctuary of the Ismenian Apollo they were driven right back to their gates; the giant Capaneus had already climbed the wall by a scaling-ladder, and was presumptuously boasting that even the lightning of Zeus should not drive him back, when the flaming bolt of the god smote him down, and dashed him to atoms. The beautiful Parthenopaeus also fell, with his skull shattered by a rock that was hurled at him. Adrastus desisted from the assault, and the armies, which had suffered severely, agreed that the originators of the quarrel, Eteocles and Polynices, should fight out their difference in single combat. Both brothers fell, and a fresh battle arose over their bodies. In this all of the assailants met their death, except Adrastus, who was saved by the speed of his black-maned charger. According to the older legends, his eloquence persuaded the Thebans to give the fallen due burial. When the bodies of the hostile brothers were placed on the pyre, the flames, which were meant to destroy them together, parted into two portions. According to the version of the story invented by the Attic tragedians, the Thebans refused to bury their foes, but at the prayer of Adrastus were compelled to do so by Theseus; according to another version, he conquered the Thebans and buried the dead bodies at Eleusis in Attica. For the burial of Polynices, see ANTIGONÉ; and also EPIGONI. The story forms the subject of one of the extant plays of Aeschylus. See AESCHYLUS.

Seven Sages, THE. Under this name were included in antiquity seven men living in the period from B.C. 620–550. They were distinguished for practical wisdom, and conducted the affairs of their country as rulers, lawgivers, and councillors, and were reputed to be the authors of certain short maxims in common use, which were variously assigned among them; the names also of the seven were differently given. Those usually mentioned are: CLEOBŪLUS, tyrant of Lindus in Rhodes ("Moderation is the chief good"); PERIANDER, tyrant of Corinth, 668–584 ("Forethought in all things"); PITTĂCUS of Mitylenē, born about 650, deliverer and *aesymnetes* of his native city ("Know thine opportunity"); BIAS of Prienē in Caria, about B.C. 570 ("Too many workers spoil the work"); THALES of Miletus, 639–536 ("To be surety brings ruin"); CHILON of Sparta ("Know thyself"); SOLON of Athens ("Nothing in excess," i. e. observe moderation).

Seven Sleepers of Ephĕsus, THE. Seven Christians of Ephesus who, according to the story related by Gregory of Tours (*Mirac. Lib.* ch. 92), fled to a cave at the time of the persecution under the emperor Decius in the third century, and there fell into a sleep that lasted for nearly two hundred years. Returning to the city, they experienced the surprise that Rip Van Winkle felt on his famous return, and at last discovered the truth regarding their sleep. Having had an interview with the emperor and convinced him of the life beyond the grave, they sank into a second sleep that is to last until the Resurrection. Their names as usually given are Maximianus, Malchus, Martinianus, Dionysius, Johannes, Serapion, and Constantius. Gregory states that the story is of Syrian origin. The Seven are commemorated by the Roman Catholic Church on June 27th. See Koch, *Die Siebenschläfer-Legende* (Leipzig, 1882).

Seven Wonders of the World, THE. Seven ancient buildings or works of art, distinguished either for size or splendour, viz.: (1) the Egyptian pyramids; (2) the hanging gardens of Semiramis at Babylon; (3) the temple of Artemis, at Ephesus; (4) the statue of Zeus by Phidias (q. v.), at Olympia; (5) the Mausoleum (q. v.) at Halicarnassus; (6) the Colossus of Rhodes (see COLOSSUS); and (7) the lighthouse on the island of Pharos, off Alexandria in Egypt. (See PHAROS.) These wonders were thus classified and celebrated by one of the Alexandrian scholars, Philo of Byzantium, in a work entitled Περὶ τῶν Ἑπτὰ Θεαμάτων, which is edited by Orelli (Leipzig, 1816).

Sevērus, A. CAECINA. See CAECINA.

Sevērus, ARCH OF. See ARCUS TRIUMPHALIS.

Sevērus, CASSIUS. A celebrated orator and satirical writer in the time of Augustus and Tiberius, was born about B.C. 50 at Longula, in Latium. He was a man of low origin and dissolute character, but was much feared for the severity of his attacks upon the Roman nobles. He must have commenced his career as a public slanderer very early, if he is the person against whom the sixth Epode of Horace is directed, as is supposed by many ancient and modern commentators. Towards the latter end of the reign of Augustus, Severus was banished by Augustus to the island of Crete on account of his libellous verses; but as he still continued to write libels, he was removed by Tiberius in A.D. 24 to the desert island of Seriphus, where he died in great poverty in the twenty-fifth year of his exile, A.D. 33.

Sevērus, CORNELIUS, the author of a poem entitled *Bellum Siculum*. He was contemporary with Ovid, by whom he is addressed in one of the Epistles written from Pontus.

Sevērus, FLAVIUS VALERIUS. A Roman emperor (A.D. 306–307). He was proclaimed Caesar by Galerius in 306, and was soon afterwards sent against Maxentius, who had assumed the imperial title at Rome. The expedition, however, was unsuccessful; and Severus, having surrendered at Ravenna, was taken as a prisoner to Rome, and compelled to put an end to his life. See MAXENTIUS.

Sevērus, LIBIUS. A Roman emperor (A.D. 461–465). He was a Lucanian by birth, and owed his accession to Ricimer, who placed him on the throne after the assassination of Majorian. During his reign the real government was in the hands of Ricimer. Severus died a natural death (Iornand. *De Rebus Goth.* 45).

Sevērus, LUCIUS SEPTIMIUS. A Roman emperor (A.D. 193–211), who was born 146, near Leptis in Africa. After holding various important military commands under M. Aurelius and Commodus, he was at length appointed commander-in-chief of the army in Pannonia and Illyria. By this army he was proclaimed emperor after the death of Pertinax (193). He forthwith marched upon Rome, where Iulianus had been made emperor by the Praetorian troops. Iulianus was put to death upon his arrival before the city. (See IULIANUS.) Severus then turned his arms against Pescennius Niger, who had been saluted emperor by the Eastern legions. The struggle was brought to a close by a decisive battle near Issus, in which Niger was defeated by Severus, and, having been shortly afterwards taken prisoner, was put to death by order of the latter (194). Severus then laid siege to Byzantium, which refused to submit to him even after the death of Niger, and which was not taken till 196. The city was treated with great severity by Severus. Its walls were levelled with the earth, its soldiers and magistrates put to death, and the town itself, deprived of all its political privileges, made over to the Perinthians. During the continuance of this siege, Severus had crossed the Euphrates (195) and subdued the Mesopotamian Arabians. He returned to Italy in 196, and in the same year proceeded to Gaul to oppose Albinus, who had been proclaimed emperor by the troops in that country. Albinus was defeated and slain in a terrible battle fought near Lyons on the 19th of February, 197. Severus returned to Rome in the same year; but after remaining a short time in the capital, he set out for the East in order to repel the invasion of the Parthians, who were ravaging Mesopotamia. He crossed the Euphrates early in 198, and commenced a series of operations which were attended with brilliant results. Seleucia and Babylon were evacuated by the enemy, and Ctesiphon was taken and plundered after a short siege. After spending three years in the East, and visiting Arabia, Palestine, and Egypt, Severus returned to Rome in 202. For the next seven years he remained tranquilly at Rome, but in 208 he went to Britain with his sons Caracalla and Geta. Here he carried on war against the

L. Septimius Severus. (Bust in the Capitoline Museum.)

Caledonians, and erected the celebrated wall, which bore his name, from the Solway to the mouth of the Tyne. After remaining two years in Britain, he died at Eboracum (York) on the 4th of February, 211, in the sixty-fifth year of his age and the eighteenth of his reign. His life is written by Spartianus. See Duruy, *Septime-Sévère* (Paris, 1878); and Hassebrank, *Kaiser Septimius Severus*, 2 pts. (1890–91).

Sevērus, Marcus Aurelius Alexander, usually called **Alexander Sevērus**. A Roman emperor (A.D. 222–235), the son of Gessius Marcianus and Iulia Mamaea, and first cousin of Elagabalus. He was born at Arcé, in Phœnicia, in the temple of Alexander the Great, to which his parents had repaired for the celebration of a festival, on the 1st of October, A.D. 205. His original name appears to have been Alexianus Bassiānus, the latter appellation having been derived from his maternal grandfather. Upon the elevation of Elagabalus, he accompanied his mother and the court to Rome, a report having been spread abroad that he also, as well as the emperor, was the son of Caracalla. In 221 he was adopted by Elagabalus and created Caesar. The names Alexianus and Bassianus were laid aside, and those of M. Aurelius Alexander substituted; M. Aurelius in virtue of his adoption; Alexander in consequence, as was asserted, of a direct revelation on the part of the Syrian god. On the death of Elagabalus, on the 11th of March, A.D. 222, Alexander ascended the throne, adding Severus to his other designations, in order to mark more explicitly the descent which he claimed from the father of Caracalla. After reigning in peace some years, during which he reformed many abuses in the State, he was involved in a war with Artaxerxes, king of Persia, who had lately founded the new Empire of the Sassanidae on the ruins of the Parthian monarchy. Alexander gained a great victory over Artaxerxes in 232; but he was unable to prosecute his advantage in consequence of intelligence having reached him of a great movement among the German tribes. He celebrated a triumph at Rome in 233, and in the following year (234) set out for Gaul, which the Germans were devastating; but before he had made any progress in the campaign, he was waylaid by a small band of mutinous soldiers, instigated, it is said, by Maximinus, and slain, along with his mother, in the early part of 235, in the thirtieth year of his age and the fourteenth of his reign. Alexander Severus was distinguished by justice, wisdom, and clemency in all public transactions, and by the simplicity and purity of his private life. His life is written by Lampridius. See Porrath, *Der Kaiser Alexander Severus* (1876).

Alexander Severus.

Sevērus, Sulpicius. A writer chiefly celebrated as an ecclesiastical historian. He was a native of Aquitania, and flourished towards the close of the fourth century under Arcadius and Honorius. He was descended from a noble family, and was originally an advocate; but he eventually became a presbyter of the church, and attached himself closely to St. Martin of Tours. The extant works of Severus are: (*a*) *Historia Sacra*, an epitome of sacred history, extending from the creation of the world to the consulship of Stilicho and Aurelianus, A.D. 400; (*b*) *Vita S. Martini Turonensis;* (*c*) *Tres Epistolae;* (*d*) *Dialogi duo*, containing a review of the dissensions which had arisen among ecclesiastics in the East regarding the works of Origen; (*e*) *Epistolae Sex*. The best edition of the complete works of Severus is by Hahn (Vienna, 1886).

Sewers. See Cloaca.

Sextans. A Roman copper coin weighing two ounces (*unciae*), and equal to the sixth part of the *as*. It bore the effigy of a caduceus and a strigil.

Sextans, actual size.

Sextarius. A Roman measure, both liquid and dry, $= \frac{1}{6}$ *congius* or $\frac{1}{4}$ *modius* or about an English pint (Columell. ii. 9). See Mensura.

Sextiae Aquae. See Aquae.

Sextia Gens. A plebeian gens at Rome, one of whose members, L. Sextius Sextinus Lateranus, was the first plebeian to obtain the consulship (B.C. 366).

Sextius or **Sestius.** (1) PUBLIUS. A Roman who was quaestor in B.C. 63, and tribune of the plebs in 57. Like Milo, he kept a band of armed retainers to oppose P. Clodius and his partisans; and in the following year (56) he was accused of *vis* on account of his violent acts during his tribunate. He was defended by Cicero in an oration still extant, and was acquitted on the 14th of March, chiefly in consequence of the powerful influence of Pompey. On the breaking out of the Civil War in 49, Sextius first espoused Pompey's party, but he afterwards joined Caesar. See Cic. *Pro Sext.; Ad Att.* iii. 19, 20, 22; iv. 3, etc. (2) TITUS. One of Caesar's *legati* in Gaul, and afterwards the governor of the province of Numidia at the time of Caesar's death (B.C. 44). Here he waged war against Q. Cornificius, whom he defeated and slew in battle (Caes. *B. G.* vi. 1; App. *B. C.* iv. 53, 75).

Sextius Calvīnus. See CALVINUS.

Sextius Niger, QUINTUS. A Roman who lived during the last years of the Republic and under Augustus. He was the founder of a philosophical system, which aimed at the improvement of morals on the principles of the Stoics and Pythagoreans. Like his son, who bore the same name, he wrote in Greek. He is the author of a collection of Greek maxims of a monotheistic and ascetic character, a Christianized Latin translation of which, written in the second half of the fourth century by the presbyter Rufinus, is still extant.

Sextŭla. The smallest denomination found in the Roman monetary system. It was equal to one sixth of an ounce (*uncia*) (Varro, *L. L.* v. 171).

Sextus Empirĭcus. A physician who was a contemporary of Galen, and lived in the first half of the third century of the Christian era. Two of his works are extant—Πυρρώνιαι Ὑποτυπώσεις, dealing with the skeptical learning of Pyrrho (q. v.), in three books; and Πρὸς τοὺς Μαθηματικοὺς Ἀντιρρητικοί, in eleven books, against all positive philosophy. The first six books strive to show the falsity of the sciences of grammar, rhetoric, geometry, arithmetic, astrology, and music; the last five attack logic, physics, and ethics. Edited by Fabricius (Leipzig, 1718). See Haas, *Leben des Sextus Emp.* (1882); id. *Ueber die Schriften des Sextus Emp.* (1883); and the monographs by Jourdain (1858) and Pappenheim (1878).

Sextus Rufus (or **Rufius**) **Festus.** (1) The name prefixed to a work entitled *De Regionibus Urbis Romae.* (2) SEXTUS RUFUS is also the name prefixed to an abridgment of Roman history in twenty-eight short chapters, entitled *Breviarium de Victoriis et Provinciis Populi Romani,* and executed by command of the emperor Valens, to whom it is dedicated.

Shackles. See CATENA; COMPES; MANICAE; PEDICAE; VINCULA.

Shaving. See TONSOR.

Shields. See ARMA; CLIPEUS; SCUTUM.

Ships AND Shipping. See NAVIS.

Shirt. See SUBUCULA.

Shoes. See CALCEUS.

Shop. See TABERNA.

Shorthand. See NOTAE.

Shovel. See BATILLUM; PALA.

Sibae (Σίβαι) or **Sibi** (Σίβοι). An Indian people in the Punjab (Arrian, *Ind.* v.).

Sibīna or **Sibȳna** (σιβύνη). A boar-spear (Athen. ii. 5).

Sibyllae (in the sing., Lat. *Sibylla;* Gr. Σίβυλλα, from Doric σιο-βόλλα = θεοῦ βουλή, "the will of God"). The name given in antiquity to inspired prophetesses of some deity, in particular Apollo. They were usually regarded as maidens dwelling in lonely caves or by inspiring springs, who were possessed with a spirit of divination, and gave forth prophetic utterances while under the influence of enthusiastic frenzy. They were described sometimes as priestesses of Apollo, sometimes as his favourite wives or daughters. We have no certain information as to their number, names, country, or date. Though Plato (*Phaedr.* 294 B) knew of only one, others mention two, three, four (the Erythraean, the Samian, the Egyptian, and the Sardian), and even ten or twelve: the Babylonian, the Libyan, the (elder and younger) Delphian, the Cimmerian, the (elder and younger) Erythraean, the Samian, the Cumaean, the Hellespontine, the Phrygian, and the Tiburtine.

In the earliest times they are mentioned as dwelling in the neighbourhood of the Trojan Ida in Asia Minor, later at Erythrae in Ionia, in Samos, at Delphi, and at Cumae in Italy. The most famous was the Erythraean Sibyl, Herophilé, who is usually considered identical with the Cumaean, as she is represented as journeying by manifold wanderings from her home to Cumae. Here she is said to have lived for many generations in the crypts beneath the temple of Apollo, where she had even prophesied to Aeneas. In later times the designation of Sibyl was also given to the prophetic nymph Albunea near Tibur (Lactant. i. 6, 12).

The SIBYLLINE BOOKS, so often met with in Roman history, had their origin in a collection of oracular utterances in Greek hexameters, composed in the time of Solon and Cyrus at Gergis on Mount Ida, and ascribed to the Hellespontic Sibyl, buried in the temple of Apollo at Gergis. This collection was brought by way of Erythrae to Cumae, and finally, in the time of the last king, to Rome. According to the legend, the Cumaean Sibyl offered to Tarquinius Superbus nine books of prophecies; and as the king declined to purchase them, owing to the exorbitant price she demanded, she burned all but three of them, which the king purchased for the original price, and had them preserved in a vault beneath the Capitoline temple of Iupiter (Varro, *ap.* Lactant. *Inst. Div.* i. 6; Dionys. iv. 62; Isid. *Orig.* viii. 815). When they were destroyed in the burning of the Capitol in B.C. 83, the Senate sent envoys to make a collection of similar oracular sayings distributed over various places, in particular Ilium, Erythrae, and Samos. This new collection was deposited in the restored temple, together with similar sayings of native origin—e. g. those of the Sibyl at Tibur, of the brothers Marcius, and others. From the Capitol they were transferred by Augustus as pontifex, in B.C. 12, to the temple of Apollo on the Palatine, after they had been examined and copied; here they remained until about A.D. 405. They are said to have been burned by Stilicho. The use of these oracles was from the outset reserved for the State, and they were not consulted for the foretelling of future events, but on the occasion of remarkable calamities, such as pestilence, earthquake, and as a means of expiating portents. It was only the rites of expiation prescribed by the Sibylline Books that were communicated to the public, and not the oracles themselves. As these books recognized the gods worshipped and the rites observed in the neighbourhood of Troy, they were the principal cause of the introduction of a series of foreign deities and religious rites into the Roman State worship, of the amalgamation of national deities with the corresponding deities of Greece, and a general modification of the Roman religion after the Greek type.

Tarquinius is said to have intrusted the care of the books to a special *collegium* of two men of patrician rank. After B.C. 367 their number was increased to ten, half patrician and half plebeian; and in the first century B.C., probably in the time of Sulla, five more were added. These officials were entitled respectively *duumviri, decemviri,* and *quindecimviri sacris faciundis.* They were usually ex-consuls or ex-praetors. They held office for life, and were exempt from all other public duties. They had the responsibility of keeping the books in safety and secrecy, of consulting them at the order of the Senate, of interpreting the utterances they found therein, and of causing the measures thus enjoined to be carried out; in particular they had the superintendence of the worship of Apollo, the Magna Mater, and Ceres, which had been introduced by the Sibylline Books. See Marquardt, iii. 358 foll.; and Bouché-Leclercq, *Hist. de la Divination*, ii. pp. 133 foll.

These Sibylline Books have no connection with a collection of SIBYLLINE ORACLES in twelve books, written in Greek hexameters, which have come down to us. The latter contain a medley of pretended prophecies by various authors and of very various dates, from the middle of the second century B.C. to the fifth century A.D. They were composed partly by Alexandrian Jews, partly by Christians, in the interests of their respective religions; and in part they refer to events of the later Empire. They are edited by Alexandre (Paris, 1841–56); Friedlieb (Leipzig, 1852); Rzach (Vienna, 1891); and Diels (Berlin, 1891). See Dechent in the *Zeitschrift für Kirchengeschichte* (1878); and an article in the *Edinburgh Review* for July, 1877.

Sibyllīni Libri. See SIBYLLAE.

Sica. A knife or dagger shaped like the tusk of a wild boar (Pliny, *H. N.* xviii. 1). It was the national weapon of the Thracians (Val. Max. iii. 2, 12), and was used by the gladiators known as *Thraeces* (Suet. *Calig.* 32). In Rome it was carried by the lower classes, criminals, ruffians, and bullies, and was regarded as fit for such persons only (Cic. *Cat.* ii. 10; Quint. *Decl.* 321).

Sica. (Column of Antoninus.)

Sicambri. See SUGAMBRI.

Sicāni, Sicĕli, Siceliōtae. See SICILIA.

Sicarius. (1) An assassin, ruffian. See SICA. (2) A gladiator of the class called *Thraeces* who were armed with the *sica* (Cic. *Rosc. Amer.* 3).

Sicca Veneria. A considerable city of North Africa, on the frontier of Numidia and Zeugitana, built on a hill near the river Bagradas (Sall. *Iug.* 56).

Sichaeus, also called Acerbas. See DIDO.

Sicilia (Σικελία). Sicily; a large island in the Mediterranean Sea, off the southern coast of Italy. It was anciently identified with the Thrinacia (Θρινακία) of Homer, and is styled TRINACRIA and TRINĀCRIS, names supposed to mean "three-cornered," whence the Romans likewise styled the island TRIQUETRA (cf. Lucret. i. 717). The names Sicilia and Sicania come from that of its early inhabitants—the SICĔLI or SICĀNI. It is separated from Italy by the narrow channel called FRETUM SICŬLUM or simply FRETUM (Πορθμός), also SCYLLAEUM FRETUM, now the Strait of Messina. The part of the Mediterranean lying to the east and south of the island was called MARÉ SICŬLUM. Sicily is in the shape of a triangle, the north and south sides of which are about 175 miles long exclusive of the windings of the coast; the eastern side has a length of 115 miles. The northwestern point was the Promontorium Lilybaeum; the northeastern point, Promontorium Pelorus, and the southeastern point, Promontorium Pachynus. Sicily was originally a part of Italy, and was torn from it by some great convulsion of nature. A mountain range (Nebrodi Montes) extends through it as a continuation of the Apennines. Of this range the most important offshoots are Mount Aetna on the east of the island, Mount Eryx (S. Giuliano) on the west, and the Heraei Montes (Monti Sori) in the south. A number of small rivers have their sources in the mountains, but most of them are dry, or nearly so, in the summer. The soil of Sicily was very fertile, and produced in antiquity an immense quantity of wheat, on which the population of Rome relied to a great extent for their subsistence. So celebrated was it even in early times on account of its corn that it was represented as sacred to Demeter, and as the favourite abode of this goddess. Hence it was in this island that her daughter Persephoné was carried away by Pluto. Besides corn, the island produced excellent wine, saffron, honey, almonds, and the other Southern fruits.

The earliest inhabitants of Sicily are said to have been the savage Cyclopes and Laestrygones; but these are fabulous beings, and the first inhabitants mentioned in history are the Sicani (Σικανοί) or Siculi (Σικελοί), who crossed over into the island from Italy. Some writers, indeed, regard the Sicani and Siculi as two distinct tribes, supposing the latter only to have migrated from Italy, and the former to have been the aboriginal inhabitants of the country; but there is no good reason for making any distinction between them. They appear to have been a Keltic people. According to Thucydides, their original settlement was on the river Sicanus in Iberia; but as Thucydides extends Iberia as far as the Rhône, it is probable that Sicanus was a river of Gaul, and it may have been the Sequana, as some modern writers suppose. The ancient writers relate that these Sicani, being hard pressed by the Ligyes (Ligures), crossed the Alps and settled in Latium; that, being driven out of this country by the Aborigines with the help of Pelasgians, they migrated to the south of the peninsula, where they lived for a considerable time along with the Oenotrians, but finally crossed over into Sicily, to which they gave their name. They soon spread over the greater part of the island, but in later times were found chiefly in the interior and in the northern part; some of the most important towns belonging to them were Herbita, Agyrium, Adranum, and Enna. The next immigrants into the island were Cretans, who are said to have come to Sicily under their king, Minos, in pursuit of Daedalus, and to have settled on the southern coast in the neighbourhood of Agrigentum, where they founded Minoa (afterwards Heraclea Minoa). Then came the Elymaei, a small band of fugitive Trojans, who are said to have built Entella, Eryx, and Egesta. These Cretans and Elymaei, however, if indeed they ever visited Sicily, soon became incorporated with the Siculi. The Phœnicians likewise at an early period formed settlements, for the purposes of commerce, on all the coasts of Sicily, but more especially on the northern and northwestern parts. They were subsequently obliged to retire from the greater part of their settlements before the increasing power of the Greeks, and to

Siceliote Coin. (Third century B.C.)

confine themselves to Motya, Solūs, and Panormus. But the most important of all the immigrants into Sicily were the Greeks. The first body of Greeks who landed in the island were Chalcidians from Euboea, and Megarians led by the Athenian Thucles. These Greek colonists built the town of Naxos, B.C. 735. They were soon followed by other Greeks, who founded a number of very flourishing cities, such as Syracuse in 734, Leontini and Catana in 730, Megara Hybla in 726, Gela in 690, Selinus in 626, Agrigentum in 579, etc. The Greeks soon became the ruling race in the island, and received the name of SICELIŌTAE (Σικελιῶται) to distinguish them from the earlier inhabitants.

At a later time the Carthaginians obtained a firm footing in Sicily. Their first attempt was made in 480; but they were defeated by Gelon of Syracuse, and obliged to retire with great loss. Their second invasion in 409 was more successful. They took Selinus in this year, and four years afterwards (405) the powerful city of Agrigentum. They now became the permanent masters of the western part of the island, and were engaged in frequent wars with Syracuse and the other Greek cities. (For the Athenian invasion of Sicily, see SYRACUSAE.) The struggle between the Carthaginians and Greeks continued, with a few interruptions, down to the First Punic War; at the close of which (241) the Carthaginians were obliged to evacuate the island, the western part of which now passed into the hands of the Romans, and was made a Roman province. The eastern part still continued under the rule of Hieron of Syracuse as an ally of Rome; but after the revolt of Syracuse in the Second Punic War, and the conquest of that city by Marcellus, the whole island was made a Roman province, and was administered by a praetor. Under the Roman dominion more attention was paid to agriculture than to commerce; and consequently the Greek cities on the coast gradually declined in prosperity and wealth. The inhabitants of the province received the *ius Latii* from Iulius Caesar; and Antony conferred upon them, in accordance, as it was said, with Caesar's will, the full Roman franchise. Augustus, after his conquest of Sextus Pompey, who had held the island for several years, founded colonies at Messana, Tauromenium, Catana, Syracuse, Thermae, and Panormus. On the downfall of the Roman Empire, Sicily formed part of the kingdom of the Ostrogoths; but it was taken from them by Belisarius in A.D. 536, and annexed to the Byzantine Empire. It continued a province of this Empire till 828, when it was conquered by the Saracens.

Literature and the arts were cultivated with great success in the Greek cities of Sicily, especially at the time of the first Hiero (q. v.) of Syracuse (B.C. 478–467), and of Dionysius the elder, the friend of Plato. Sicily was the birthplace of the philosophers Empedocles, Epicharmus, and Dicaearchus; of the mathematician Archimedes; of the physicians Herodicus and Acron; of the historians Diodorus, Antiochus, Philistus, and Timaeus; of the rhetorician Gorgias; and of the poets Stesichorus, Theocritus, and Moschus.

Good histories of ancient Sicily are those of Holm, 2 vols. (Leipzig, 1870–74); Lloyd (1872); Freeman, vols. i.–iii. (1891–92); id. a short history in the "Story of the Nations Series" (1892). On the earliest inhabitants of Sicily, see the monograph by Costanzi, *De Siciliae Gentibus Antiquissimis* (1893); and on the Greek colonies that of Frömter (1886), and of Brunet de Presle, *Les Établissements des Grecs en Sicile* (Paris, 1845). See also Hoffweiler, *Sicilien in Wort und Bild* (Leipzig, 1870), and the articles AGRIGENTUM; CARTHAGO; DIONYSIUS; GELON; LEONTINI; PUNIC WARS; SELINUS; SYRACUSAE. For a map of Sicily, see ITALIA.

Sicilian Expedition. See PELOPONNESIAN WAR; SYRACUSAE.

Sicilĭcus. A mark of the form ɔ, placed in Roman inscriptions over consonants to denote doubling, like the Arabic *tashdîd.* The character is of rare occurrence in existing inscriptions, being most frequently found in those of the early Augustan period (*C. I. L.* v. 1361; x. 3743). It is mentioned by the grammarians Marius Victorinus (p. 2456) and Isidorus (*Orig.* i. 26).

Sicīlis. A spear-head (Pliny, *H. N.* vi. 15).

Sicĭma. See NEAPOLIS (5), p. 1084.

Sicinius. (1) L. SICINIUS BELLŪTUS, the leader of the plebeians in their secession to the Sacred Mount in B.C. 494. He was chosen one of the first tribunes. (2) L. SICINIUS DENTĀTUS, called by some writers the Roman Achilles, from his personal prowess. He was tribune of the plebs in 454. He was put to death by the decemvirs in 450, because he endeavoured to persuade the plebeians to secede to the Sacred Mount. The persons, nearly a hundred in number, sent to assassinate him fell upon him in a lonely spot, but he killed most of them before they succeeded in despatching him. Valerius Maximus (iii. 2, 24) enumerates the military honours won by Sicinius during the forty years of his service in the army. He had seen 120 battles, received 14 civic crowns, 3 mural crowns, 8 gold crowns, 180 gold chains (*torques*), 160 bracelets (*armillae*), 18 spears (*hastae purae*), 25 sets of horse-trappings, and bore the scars of 40 wounds on his breast.

Sicinnis. See SATYRIC DRAMA.

Sicinnium. A Greek dance. See SATYRIC DRAMA.

Sicĭnus (Σίκινος). Now Sikino; a small island in the Aegaean Sea, one of the Sporades, between Pholegandrus and Ios, with a town of the same name. It was originally called Oenoë (Apoll. Rh. i. 623).

Sicŏris. Now Segre; a river in Hispania Tarraconensis, which had its source in the territory of the Cerretani, and fell into the Iberus near Octogesa (Caes. *B. C.* i. 40, 48).

Sicŭli. See SICILIA.

Sicŭlum Fretum, Sicŭlum Maré. See SICILIA.

Sicŭlus Flaccus. See FLACCUS, SICULUS.

Sicyonia (Σικυωνία). A small district in the northeast of the Peloponnesus, whose area was probably somewhat less than one hundred square miles. It consisted of a plain near the sea with mountains in the interior. Its rivers, which ran in a northeasterly direction, were Sythas on the frontier of Achaia, Helisson, Selleïs, and Asopus in the interior, and Nemea on the frontier of the territory of Corinth. The land was fertile, and produced excellent oil. Its almonds and its fish were also much prized.

Its chief town was SICȲON (Σικυών, "cucumber-town"), which was situated a little to the west of the river Asopus. The ancient city, which was situated in the plain, was destroyed by Demetrius Poliorcetes, and a new city, which bore for a short time the name of Demetrius, was built by him on the high ground close to the Acropolis. The harbour, which, according to some, was connected with the city by means of long walls, was well fortified, and formed a town of itself. Sicyon was one of the most ancient cities of Greece. It is said to have been originally called AEGIALĒA or AEGIĂLI (Αἰγιάλεια, Αἰγιαλοί), after an ancient king, Aegialeus; to have been subsequently named MECŌNÉ (Μηκώνη, "poppy-town"), and to have been finally called Sicyon from an Athenian of that name. Sicyon is represented by Homer as forming part of the empire of Agamemnon; but on the invasion of Peloponnesus it became subject to Phalces, the son of Temenus, and was henceforward a Dorian State. The ancient inhabitants, however, were formed into a fourth tribe called Aegialeis, which possessed equal rights with the three tribes of the Hylleis, Pamphyli, and Dymanatae, into which the Dorian conquerors were divided. (See DORIS.) Sicyon, on account of the small extent of its territory, never attained much political importance, and was generally dependent either on Argos or Sparta. At the time of the Second Messenian War it became subject to a succession of tyrants, who administered their power with moderation and justice for a hundred years. The first of these tyrants was Andreas, who began to rule B.C. 676. He was followed in succession by Myron, Aristonymus, and Clisthenes, on whose death, about 576, a republican form of government was established. Clisthenes had no male children, but only a daughter, Agaristé, who was married to the Athenian Megacles. In the Persian Wars the Sicyonians sent fifteen ships to the battle of Salamis, and three hundred hoplites to the battle of Plataea. In the interval between the Persian and the Peloponnesian Wars the Sicyonians were twice defeated and their country laid waste by the Athenians, first under Tolmides in 456, and again under Pericles in 454. In the Peloponnesian War they took part with the Spartans. From this time till the Macedonian supremacy their history requires no special mention; but in the middle of the third century Sicyon took an active part in public affairs in consequence of its being the native town of Aratus, who united it to the Achaean League in 251. Under the Romans it gradually declined; and in the time of Pausanias, in the second century of the Christian era, many of its public buildings were in ruins. These ruins have been of late carefully studied by the members of the American School at Athens, who have excavated the tiers of seats and supports of the stage of a theatre. The position of the Acropolis, the temple of the Dioscuri, and the Stadium can also still be traced. (See the reports of the American School in *Papers of the American School at Athens*, vol. v.

Sicyon was for a long time the chief seat of Grecian art. It gave its name to one of the great schools of painting, which was founded by Eupompus, and which produced Pamphilus and Apelles. It is also said to have been the earliest school of statuary in Greece, which was introduced into Sicyon by Dipoenus and Scyllis from Crete about 560; but its earliest native artist of celebrity was Canachus. Lysippus was also a native of Sicyon.

Sida, Sidé (Σίδη). (1) Now Eski Adalia; a city of Pamphylia, on the coast, a little west of the river Melas. It was an Aeolian colony from Cyme in Aeolis, and was a chief seat of the worship of Athené, who is represented on its coins holding a pomegranate (σίδη) as the emblem of the city. (2) The old name of Polemonium (q. v.).

Sidareus (σιδάρεος). A small iron coin current at Byzantium (Poll. ix. 78). No specimens are known to exist.

Sidēnus. See POLEMONIUM.

Sidicīni. An Ausonian people in the northwest of Campania and on the borders of Samnium, who, being hard pressed by the Samnites, united themselves to the Campanians (Livy, vii. 29). Their chief town was Teanum.

Sidon (Σιδών, Old Test. Zidon). Now Saida; a city of Phœnicia, long the most powerful of that country's towns. It stood in a plain about a mile from the Mediterranean Sea, and some twenty miles north of Tyre, and with a double harbour of considerable extent, now filled with sand. Until Tyre wrested from it the maritime supremacy, it was the greatest commercial city of the Phœnicians. When Xerxes invaded Greece, the people of Sidon furnished his expedition with the best ships in the whole fleet, so that the king of Sidon had the chief place in the council of the Persian king. The city was burned at the time of its revolt against Artaxerxes III. (B.C. 351), but was rebuilt, and later fell with the whole of Phœnicia under the control of the Romans. See PHŒNICÉ.

Sidonius Apollināris, GAIUS SOLLIUS MODESTUS. An orator born at Lugdunum (Lyons) about A.D. 431. He was raised to the senatorial dignity by the emperor Avitus, whose daughter he had married. After the downfall of Avitus he lived some time in retirement, but in 467 appeared again in Rome as ambassador from the Arverni to Anthemius. He gained the favour of that prince by a panegyric; was made a patrician, and praefect of the city; and soon afterwards, though not a priest, bishop of Clermont in Auvergne. His extant works are some poems (*Carmina*) and nine books of letters (147 in number) in imitation of Pliny and Symmachus. These are edited by Lütjohann (Berlin, 1887).

Sidūs (Σιδοῦς). A fortified place in the territory of Corinth (Xen. *Hellen.* iv. 4, 13; iv. 5, 19).

Sidȳma (τὰ Σίδυμα). A town in Lycia, north of the mouth of the Xanthus. Remains of it still exist, with interesting inscriptions.

Siga (Σίγα). A considerable seaport town of Mauretania Caesariensis (Ptol. iv. 2, 2).

Sigēum. Now Yenisheri; the northwest promontory of the Troad, and the southern headland at the entrance of the Hellespont. It is here that Homer places the Grecian fleet and camp during the Trojan War. Near it was a seaport town of the same name (Herod. v. 95).

Sigillaria. See SATURNALIA.

Sigillum. (1) A small statue, figure, or image embossed in metal or cast in terra-cotta for architectural decoration (Ovid, *A. A.* i. 407; Cic. *Verr.* ii. 4, 22; Pliny, *H. N.* xxxvi. 59). (2) The impression made by a signet-ring (Cic. *Acad.* iv. 26). (3) A figure worked in embroidery (Ovid, *Met.* vi. 86).

Sigma. A couch made in a semicircular form for use at a round dining-table (*orbis*). Its name was given it from the old form of the Greek letter *sigma*, which was C (Mart. ix. 60).

Signa Militaria. See SIGNUM.

Signia. Now Segni. A town in Latium on the east side of the Volscian Mountains, founded by Tarquinius Priscus. It was celebrated for its temple of Iupiter Urius, for its astringent wine (Mart. xiii. 116), for its pears, and for a particular kind of tessellated pavement for the floors of houses, called *opus Signinum.* There still remains a gate of cyclopean structure, besides parts of the polygonal walls of the ancient city.

Signīnum Opus. A flooring made of tiles broken up into very small pieces, mixed with mortar, and then beaten down with a rammer (Pliny, *H. N.* xxxv. 46). See PAVIMENTUM; SIGNIA.

Signum (σημεῖον). The Roman name for a military standard, usually consisting of a badge (*insigne*) on a staff, carried by legions, maniples, and cohorts, as distinct from the *vexillum* (q. v.). The latter was a square flag fastened on a cross-bar carried by the cavalry and allied infantry detachments. The earliest Roman standard is said to have been a bundle of hay (*manipulus*) on a staff (Plut. *Rom.* 8). In the time of the manipular arrangement (see LEGIO; MANIPULUS), each maniple had its peculiar *insigne*, the eagle (the sign of the first *manipulus*), the wolf, the Minotaur, the horse, or the boar. After Marius had made the eagle (q. v.) the standard representing the signum of the whole legion, the forms of other animals were no longer employed. Instead of them the maniples had a spear with an outstretched hand upon the point. Afterwards the signa were also furnished with a *vexillum* and with various ornaments on the pole, especially round plates, often with representations of gods, emperors, and generals. The cohorts, probably as early as the time of Caesar, had particular signa; after Trajan they borrowed from the Parthians the *draco.* This was the image of a large dragon fixed upon a lance, with gaping jaws of silver, and with the rest of its body formed of coloured silk. When the wind blew down the open jaws, the body was inflated (Veget. *De Re Militari*, ii. 13; Ammian. Marcell. xvi. 10, 7). This last is to be seen on monuments among the standards of foreign nations, who also had a standard resembling a mediæval banner. On the march and in an attack with close columns, the signa were carried in the first line; in a pitched battle, behind the front rank. See Domazewski, *Die Fahnen im römischen Heere* (1885).

The Greeks carried no regular standard, but a scarlet flag (φοινικίς) was sometimes raised as a signal for joining battle both on land and sea (Polyaen. iii. 9, 27; Thucyd. i. 49). The Persians carried a golden eagle as a royal standard (Xen. *Anab.* i. 10, 12), and the Parthians had banners of silk. See VEXILLUM.

Silanion (Σιλανίων). An Athenian, a distinguished statuary in bronze, was a contemporary of Lysippus, and flourished B.C. 324. His statue of Sappho, which stood in the prytaneum at Syracuse in the time of Verres, is alluded to by Cicero in terms of the highest praise (Cic. *Verr.* iv. 57, 125).

Silărus. Now Silaro; a river in Lower Italy, forming the boundary between Lucania and Campania, which rises in the Apennines, and falls into the Sinus Paestanus a little to the north of Paestum.

Roman Standards. (Guhl and Koner.)

Sila Silva. Now Aspromonte; a large forest in Bruttium on the Apennines, extending south of Consentia to the Sicilian Strait.

Silēnus (Σειληνός). A sort of Satyr who in mythic legends accompanies the god Bacchus, and who is said to have brought up and instructed him. Like the other Satyrs, he is called a son of Hermes; but others make him a son of Pan by a nymph, or of Gaea. Being the constant companion of Bacchus, he is said, like the god, to have been born at Nysa. Moreover, he took part in the contest with the Giants, and slew Enceladus. He is described as a jovial old man, with a bald head, a blunt nose, fat and round like the wine bag that he always carried with him, and generally intoxicated. As he could not trust his own legs, he is generally represented riding on an ass or supported by other Satyrs (Ovid, *A. A.* i. 543). In every other respect he is described as resembling his brethren in their love of sleep, wine, and music. He is mentioned, along with Marsyas and Olympus, as the inventor of the flute, which he is often seen playing; and a special kind of dance was called after him "Silenus," while he himself is designated as the dancer. But it is a peculiar feature in his character that he was conceived also as an inspired prophet, who knew all the past and the most distant future, and as a sage who despised all the gifts of fortune. When he was drunk and asleep, he was in the power of mortals, who might compel him to prophesy and sing by surrounding him with chains of flowers. Silenus was probably at first a deity presiding over springs and running streams, and so the wine-skin with which he is frequently represented was doubtless originally a water-skin (Lucian, *Deor. Conc.* 4).

Silenus Astride of a Wine-skin. (Bronze found at Herculaneum.)

Silicernium. See Funus, p. 699.

Silĭqua (κεράτιον). The smallest Roman weight, the sixth part of a scruple (*scripulum*) or the $\frac{1}{144}$ part of an ounce. It was also the name of a small coin (*siliqua auri*), on which see Mommsen, *Röm. Münzwesen*, p. 791.

Silius Italĭcus, Gaius Catius (for the name, see *C. I. L.* vi. 1984). A Roman poet, born about A.D. 25. He acquired great reputation as an advocate, and was afterwards one of the centumviri. He was consul in 68, the year in which Nero perished; he was admitted to familiar intercourse with Vitellius, and was subsequently proconsul of Asia. In his seventy-fifth year, in consequence of the pain caused by an incurable disease, he starved himself to death in the house once occupied by Vergil (Pliny, *Epist.* iii. 7). The great work of Silius Italicus was a heroic poem in seventeen books, entitled *Punica,* which has descended to us entire, having been discovered by Poggio Bracciolini (q. v.) in 1416. The poem contains about 14,000 lines. Its opposing heroes are Scipio and Hannibal, and it deals with the Second Punic War in a spirit slavishly imitative of Vergil, to whom, by the way, he owed his estate at Naples. He also draws many ideas from the Homeric poems. The *editio princeps* appeared in 1471. Silius is edited by Ernesti (Leipzig, 1701); Ruperti, reprinted by Lemaire (Paris, 1823); and Bauer (Leipzig, 1890). See Heynacher, *Die Quellen des Silius,* 2 pts. (Ilfeld, 1874–77); Franke, *De Silii Punicorum Tropis* (Münster, 1889); Occioni, *Silio Italico e il suo Poema* (2d ed. Florence, 1871); and Groesst, *Quatenus Silius Italicus a Vergilio Pendere Videatur* (Halle, 1887). Silius is now regarded as also the author of the metrical abridgment of the *Iliad,* usually cited under the name of "Homerus Latinus" or "Pindarus Thebanus." See Pindarus, in the Appendix.

Silk. See Sericum.

Silli (σίλλοι). A peculiar kind of Greek lampoons in an epic form, such as Xenophanes of Colophon was the first to level against poets and philosophers. The principal representative of this class was Timon of Phlius. See Parodia; Timon.

Sillographers. See Parodia.

Silo (Σιλώ). The Old Test. Shiloh; a city of Palestine in the mountains of Ephraim.

Silo, Q. Pompaedius. The leader of the Marsi in the Social War. He fell in battle against Q. Metellus Pius (B.C. 88), and his death led to the end of the war (App. *B. C.* i. 40–53; Vell. Paterc. ii. 16).

Silsĭlis (Σίλσιλις). A fortified port in Upper Egypt on the west bank of the Nile.

Silŭres (Σίλυρες). A powerful people in Britain, inhabiting South Wales, who long offered a formidable resistance to the Romans, and afterwards to the Saxons (Tac. *Ann.* xii. 32). Caractacus (q. v.) was of this nation.

Silvae. See Statius.

Silvānus. A Latin divinity of the fields and forests, suggesting somewhat the early Italian conception of the agricultural Mars and also Faunus. He is likewise called the protector of the boundaries of fields (Hor. *Epod.* 2, 22). In connection with woods (*silvestris deus*), he especially presided over plantations, and delighted in trees growing wild, whence he is represented as carrying the trunk of a cypress. Silvanus is further described as the divinity protecting herds of cattle, promoting their fertility and driving away wolves. Later writers identified Silvanus with Pan, Faunus, Inuus, and Aegipan. In the Latin poets, as well as in works of art, he always appears as an old man, but cheerful and in love with Pomona. The sacrifices offered to him consisted of grapes, ears of corn, milk,

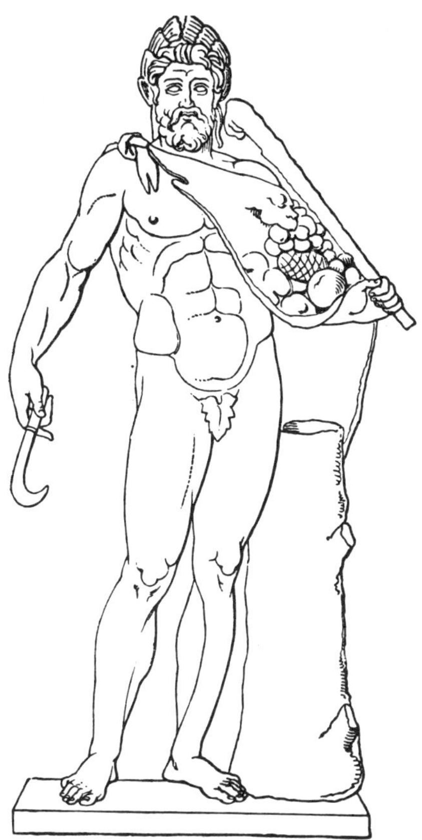

Silvanus. (Statue in Berlin Museum.)

meat, wine, and pigs. He was associated with the cypress (Serv. *ad* Verg. *Georg.* i. 20) and the pine, whence he is styled Silvanus Dendrophorus (*C. I. L.* vi. 241).

Silver. See ARGENTUM; NUMISMATICS.

Silver Shields, BEARERS OF. A corps of guards in the army of Alexander the Great. See ARGYRASPIDES.

Silvium. A town of the Peucetii in Apulia, on the borders of Lucania, twenty miles southeast of Venusia (Diod. xx. 80).

Silvius. The son of Ascanius. He is said to have been so called because he was born in a wood (*silva*). All the succeeding kings of Alba bore the cognomen Silvius. See Livy, i. 3.

Sima (κῦμα). A "sima" or "ogee." An architectural term denoting a moulding shaped like the nose of a goat (*simus* = "snub-nosed"), used for the uppermost part of a cornice (Vitruv. iii. 5, 12).

Sima.

Simmias (Σιμμίας). (1) Of Thebes, first the disciple of the Pythagorean philosopher Philolaüs, and afterwards the friend and disciple of Socrates, at whose death he was present. Simmias wrote twenty-three dialogues on philosophical subjects, all of which are lost. (2) Of Rhodes. A poet and grammarian of the Alexandrian School, who flourished about B.C. 300. The Greek Anthology contains six epigrams ascribed to Simmias, besides three short poems of that fantastic species called *griphi* or *carmina figurata*—that is, pieces in which the lines are so arranged as to make the whole poem resemble the form of some object; those of Simmias are entitled, from their forms, the *Wings* (πτέρυγες), the *Egg* (ᾠόν), and the *Hatchet* (πέλεκυς).

Simoïs. A river near Troy. (See TROIAS.) As a mythological personage, the river-god Simoïs is the son of Oceanus and Tethys, and the father of Astyochus and Hieromnemé (Hes. *Theog.* 342).

Simon (Σίμων). (1) One of the disciples of Socrates, and by trade a leather-cutter. Socrates used to visit his shop and chat with him on various subjects, and these conversations were afterwards written down and published, making in all thirty-three dialogues. They are now wholly lost (Diog. Laërt. ii. 122). (2) An artist of Aegina, famous for his works in bronze. He flourished in the fifth century B.C.

Simonĭdes (Σιμωνίδης). (1) Of Amorgos, the second, both in time and in reputation, of the three principal iambic poets of the early period of Greek literature—namely, Archilochus, Simonides, and Hipponax. He was a native of Samos, whence he led a colony to the neighbouring island of Amorgos, where he founded three cities—Minoa, Aegialus, and Arcesiné—in the first of which he fixed his own abode. He flourished about B.C. 664. Simonides was most celebrated for his iambic poems, which were of two species, gnomic and satirical. The most important of his extant fragments is a satire upon women, in which he derives the various, though generally bad, qualities of women from the variety of their origin: thus, the uncleanly woman is formed from the swine; the cunning woman, from the fox; the talkative woman, from the dog, and so on. The best editions of the fragments of Simonides of Amorgos are by Welcker (Bonn, 1835) and Bergk (1878).

(2) Of Ceos, one of the most celebrated lyric poets of Greece. He was the perfecter of the Elegy and Epigram, and the rival of Lasus and Pindar in the Dithyramb and the Epinician Ode. He was born at Iulis, in Ceos, B.C. 556, and was the son of Leoprepes. He appears to have been brought up to music and poetry as a profession. From his native island he proceeded to Athens, probably on the invitation of Hipparchus, who attached him to his society by great rewards. After remaining at Athens some time, probably even after the expulsion of Hippias, he went to Thessaly, where he lived under the patronage of the Aleuads and Scopads. He afterwards returned to Athens, and soon had the noblest opportunity of employing his poetic powers in the celebration of the great events of the Persian Wars. In 489 he conquered Aeschylus in the contest for the prize which the Athenians offered for an elegy on those who fell at Marathon. Ten years later he composed the epigrams which were inscribed upon the tomb of the Spartans who fell at Thermopylae, as well as an encomium on the same heroes; and he also celebrated the battles of Artemisium and Salamis, and the great men who commanded in them (Pausan. iii. 8, 2; Thucyd. i. 132). He had completed his eightieth year, when his long poetical career at Athens was crowned by the victory which he gained with the dithyrambic chorus (477), being the fifty-sixth prize which he had carried off. Shortly after this he was invited to Syracuse by Hiero, at whose court he lived till his death in 467.

Simonides was a great favourite with Hiero, and was treated by the tyrant with the greatest munificence. He still continued, when at Syracuse, to employ his talents occasionally in the service of other Grecian States. Simonides is said to have been the inventor of the mnemonic art and of the long vowels and double letters in the Greek alphabet (Cic. *De Orat.* ii. 86, 352). He made literature a profession, and is said to have been the first who took money for his poems; and the reproach of avarice is too often brought against him by his contemporary and rival, Pindar, as well as by subsequent writers, to be altogether discredited. The chief characteristics of the poetry of Simonides were sweetness (whence his surname of *Melicertes*) and elaborate finish, combined with the truest poetic conception and perfect power of expression; though in originality and fervour he was far inferior, not only to the early lyric poets, such as Sappho and Alcaeus, but also to his contemporary Pindar. He was probably both the most prolific and the most universally popular of all the Grecian lyric poets. The general character of his dialect is the Epic, mingled with Doric and Aeolic forms. Editions of his fragments are those by Schneidewin (Brunswick, 1835); and Bergk, *Poët. Lyr. Graec.* (1878). On his language, see Schaumburg, *De Dialecto Simonidis* (1878); and Mucke, *De Dialecto Simonidis cum Pind. Comparata* (1879).

Simplicius. A Peripatetic philosopher of the sixth century after Christ, and a native of Cilicia. When Justinian in A.D. 529 closed the school of philosophy in which he taught at Athens, he and six other philosophers emigrated to the court of the Persian king Chosroës. When he made peace with Justinian in 533, and obtained from him leave for the philosophers to return unmolested, Simplicius went to Alexandria, where he died in 549. We still possess some excellent commentaries of his on several writings of Aristotle (*Categories, Physics, De Caelo, De Anima*), edited by Karsten (1865), and on the *Enchiridion* of Epictetus, edited by Enk (Vienna, 1866). His complete works are edited by Schweighäuser (Leipzig, 1800).

Simpŭlum and **Simpuvium.** A ladle-shaped vessel like a *cyathus*, but of more primitive form (Varro, *L. L. V.* 124). It was used both at table and in the sacrifices. It was made of earthenware (Pliny, *H. N.* xxxv. 158). See CYATHUS.

Simpulum and Malleus.

Sinae (Σῖναι) (a name probably derived from the Chinese district or kingdom of Tsin). The easternmost people of Asia. Ptolemy describes their country as bounded on the north by Serica, and on the south and west by India extra Gangem. It corresponded to the southern part of China and the eastern part of the Burmese peninsula.

Sinaï or **Sina** (Σινᾶ). Now Jebel-et-Tur. A cluster of dark, lofty, rocky mountains in the southern angle of the triangular peninsula enclosed between the two heads of the Red Sea, and bounded on the north by the deserts on the borders of Egypt and Palestine. The name, which signifies "a region of broken and cleft rocks," is used in a wider sense for the whole peninsula, which formed a part of Arabia Petraea, and was peopled, at the time of the Exodus, by the Amalekites and Midianites, and afterwards by the Nabathaean Arabs. Sinaï and Horeb in the Old Testament are both general names for the whole group, the former being used in the first four books of Moses, and the latter in Deuteronomy. The summit on which the Law was given was probably that on the north, or the one usually called Horeb. There are a good many Nabathaean inscriptions dating from the early centuries of our era carved on the rocks of Sinaï. See Hull, *Mount Seir, Sinai, and West Palestine* (London, 1885); and Euting, *Sinaitische Inschriften* (1892).

Sindi (Σινδοί). (1) A people of Asiatic Sarmatia, on the eastern coast of the Euxinè, and at the foot of the Caucasus (Herod. iv. 28). They are also mentioned by the names of SINDONES and SINDIĀNI. (2) A people on the eastern coast of India extra Gangem (in Cochin China), also called SINDAE, and with a capital city, SINDA.

Sindiāna. See SINDI.

Sindĭcé. The land of the Sindi (q. v.).

Sindon (σινδών). A fine linen or muslin made in India and Egypt, and used in Greece and Italy for summer clothing (Mart. ii. 6; Diog. Laërt. vi. 90).

Singăra (τὰ Σίγγαρα). Now Sinjar (?). A strongly fortified city and Roman colony in the interior of Mesopotamia, eighty-four Roman miles south of Nisibis. Here Constantius was defeated by Sapor (Dio Cass. xviii. 22; Ammian. Marc. xviii. 5).

Singidūnum. Now Belgrade; a town in Moesia Superior at the union of the Savus (Save) and the Danubius. It was strongly fortified and was the headquarters of a legion (Ptol. iii. 9, 3; Procop. *Aed.* iv. 6).

Singing. See MUSICA.

Singitĭcus Sinus. See SINGUS.

Singus (Σίγγος). A town in Macedonia on the eastern coast of the peninsula Sithonia, which gave its name to the Sinus Singiticus (Thucyd. v. 18).

Sinis (Σίνις) or **Sinnis** (Σίννις). Son of Polypemon, Pemon, or Poseidon, by Sylea, the daughter of Corinthus. He was a robber, who frequented the Isthmus of Corinth, and killed the travellers whom he captured by fastening them to the top of a fir-tree, which he bent, and then let spring up again. He himself was killed in this manner by Theseus. See Apollod. iii. 16, 2; Pausan. ii. 1, 3; and THESEUS.

Sinon (Σίνον). A Greek, who accompanied his countrymen to the Trojan War. When the Greeks had fabricated the famous wooden horse, Sinon went to Troy, at the instigation of Odysseus, with his hands bound behind his back, and by the most solemn protestations assured Priam that the Greeks were gone from Asia, and that they had been ordered to sacrifice one of their soldiers to render the wind favourable to their return; and that, because the lot had fallen upon him, he had fled away from their camp, not to be cruelly sacrificed. These false assertions were immediately credited by the Trojans, and Sinon advised Priam to bring into his city the wooden horse which the Greeks had left behind them, and to consecrate it to Athenè. His advice was followed, and Sinon, in the night, to complete his perfidy, opened the side of the horse, from which issued a number of armed Greeks, who surprised the Trojans and pillaged their city (Hom. *Od.* viii. 492; Verg. *Aen.* ii. 79, etc.; Pausan. x. 20). See TROJAN WAR.

Sinōpé (Σινώπη). Now Sinope, Sinoub; the most important of all the Greek colonies on the shores of the Euxine, stood on the northern coast of Asia Minor, on the western headland of the great bay of which the delta of the river Halys forms the eastern headland, and a little east of the northernmost promontory of Asia Minor. It appears in

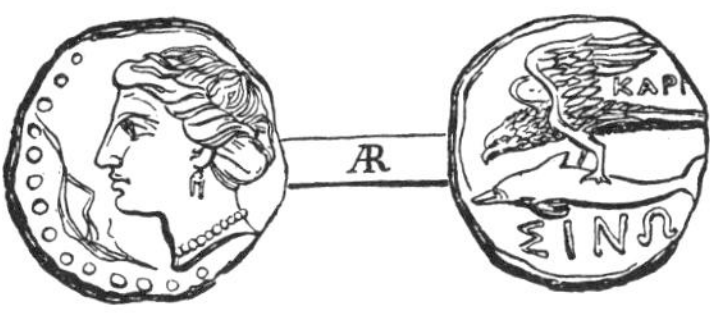

Coin of Sinopé.

history as a very early colony of the Milesians. Having been destroyed in the invasion of Asia by the Cimmerians, it was restored by a new colony from Miletus in B.C. 632, and soon became the greatest commercial city on the Euxine. Its territory, called Sinopis, extended to the banks of the Halys. It was the birthplace and residence of Mithridates the Great, who enlarged and beautified it. Shortly before the murder of Iulius Caesar it was colonized by the name of Iulia Caesarea Felix Sinopé, and remained a flourishing city, though it never recovered its former importance. At the time of Constantine it had declined so much as to be ranked second to Amasia. It was the native city of the renowned cynic philosopher Diogenes, of the comic poet Diphilus, and of the historian Baton.

Sintĭca. A district in Macedonia, inhabited by the Thracian people Sinti, extended east of Crestonia and north of Bisaltia as far as the Strymon and the lake Prasias. Its chief town was Heraclea Sintica (Thuc. ii. 98).

Sinuessa. Now Rocca di Mandragone; the last city of Latium on the confines of Campania, to which it originally belonged, was situated on the sea-coast and on the Via Appia. It was colonized by the Romans, together with the neighbouring town of Minturnae, in B.C. 296. It possessed a good harbour, and was a place of considerable commercial importance. In its neighbourhood were celebrated warm baths, called Aquae Sinuessanae (Tac. *Ann.* xii. 66).

Sinum or **Sinus** (δῖνος). A bowl used for wine or milk. It was large and deep and round in shape (Varro, *L. L.* v. 123; Verg. *Ecl.* vii. 33).

Sinus (κόλπος). Literally any surface bent into a hollow or semicircular form. Hence (1) a loose fold in a garment, usually made so as to lie across the breast (hence *sinus*, also meaning the breast), and used as a pocket for carrying any small object, as a letter, a purse, etc. (Cic. *Verr.* i. 5, 57); (2) the bosom of a sail; (3) a bay or gulf on a coast; (4) a round vessel for wine or milk. See SINUM.

Sion. See HIEROSOLYMA.

Siparium. The smaller curtain on the Roman stage about half-way between the front and the back. It was drawn up between the scenes. See AULAEUM; THEATRUM.

Siphnus (Σίφνος). Now Siphno; an island in the Aegaean Sea, forming one of the Cyclades, southeast of Seriphus. It is of an oblong form, and about forty miles in circumference. Its original name was Meropé, and it was colonized by Ionians from Athens. In consequence of their gold and silver mines, of which the remains are still visible, the Siphnians attained great prosperity, and were regarded in the time of Herodotus as the wealthiest of the islanders. Siphnus was one of the few islands which refused tribute to Xerxes; and one of its ships fought on the side of the Greeks at Salamis. The moral character of the Siphnians stood low, and hence to act like a Siphnian (Σιφνιάζειν) became a term of reproach (Aristoph. *ap.* Suid. s. h. v.).

Sipho or **Sipo** (σίφων). (1) A siphon; a pipe through which the water is made to rise by its own pressure. The principle of the siphon was used for fountains and for drawing liquids from casks (Pliny, *H. N.* ii. 66; Pollux, vi. 2). The siphon is of great antiquity, having been used by the ancient Egyptians, as is seen by paintings on the monuments. (See illustration under AEGYPTUS, p. 26.) (2) The name was also applied to a sort of fire-engine constructed on the principle of the siphon, as elaborated by Ctesibius of Alexandria, and which is described and illustrated in the article CTESIBICA MACHINA. See also Pliny, *Epist.* x. 35; Isidor. *Orig.* xx. 6; Ulp. *Dig.* 32, 7, 12.

Siphonarii or **Siponarii.** "Squirts." The slang name given at Rome to such of the *vigiles* as acted in the capacity of firemen. See SIPHO; VIGILES.

Sipo. See SIPHO.

Sipontum or **Sipuntum.** Now Siponto, called by the Greeks SIPUS (Σιποῦς). An ancient town in Apulia, in the district of Daunia, on the southern slope of Mount Garganus, and on the coast. It is said to have been founded by Diomedes, and was of Greek origin. It was colonized by the Romans, under whom it became a place of some commercial importance (Livy, xxxiv. 25).

Sipȳlus (Σίπυλος). A mountain of Lydia in Asia Minor, a branch of the Tmolus (Hom. *Il.* xxiv. 16). Here were a number of rich mines (Pausan. vii. 24, 7).

Sirbōnis Lacus (Σιρβώνιδος Λίμνη). A large and deep lake on the coast of Lower Egypt, east of Mount Casius. Its circuit was 1000 stadia. It was strongly impregnated with asphalt.

Sirēnes (Σειρῆνες). The daughters of Phorcys, according to later legend of Acheloüs, and one of the Muses. In Homer there are two, in later writers, three, called Ligea, Leucosia, and Parthenopé, or Aglaophemé, Molpé, and Thelxiepea. Homer describes them as dwelling between Circé's isle and Scylla, on an island, where they sit in a flowery meadow, surrounded by the mouldering bones of men, and with their sweet song allure and infatuate those that sail by. Whoever listens to their song and draws near them never again beholds wife and child. They know everything that happens on earth. When Odysseus sailed past, he had stopped up the ears of his companions with wax, while he had made them bind him to the mast, that he might hear their song without danger (*Od.* xii. 41–54; 153–300). Orpheus protected the Argonauts from their spell by his own singing (Apollon. Rh. iv. 903). As they were only to live till some one had sailed past unmoved by their song, they cast themselves into the sea, on account either of Odysseus or of Orpheus, and were changed to sunken rocks. When the adventures of Odysseus came to be localized on the Italian and Sicilian shore, the seat of the Sirens was transferred to the neighbourhood of Naples and Sorrento, to the three rocky and uninhabited islets called the SIRENŪSAE, the *Sirenum scopuli* of Vergil (*Aen.* v. 864; cf. Stat. *Silv.* ii. 2, 1), or to Capri, or to the Sicilian promontory of Pelorum. There they were said to have settled, after vainly searching the whole earth for the lost Persephoné, their former playmate in the meadows by the Acheloüs; and later legend also assigned this at the time when they in part assumed a winged shape. They were represented as great birds with the heads of women, or with the upper part of the body like that of a woman, with the legs of birds, and with or without wings. At a later period they were sometimes regarded as retaining their original character of fair and cruel tempters and deceivers. But they are more generally represented as singers of the dirge for the dead, and they were hence frequently placed as an ornament on tombs; or as symbols of the magic of beauty, eloquence, and song, on which account their sculptured forms were seen on the funeral monuments of fair women and girls, and of orators and poets—for instance, on those of Isocrates and Sophocles. The National Museum at Athens contains several examples of stone Sirens, not as reliefs, but as separate figures; and a funeral monument of this type may be noticed on a vase in the British Museum, where the Siren is standing on a pillar and playing the lyre. Cf. Eurip. *Hel.* 169; the *Anthologia Palatina*, vii. 710, 481; with Miss Harrison's *Myths of the Odyssey*, pp. 146–182, and *Mythology and Monuments of Athens*, pp. 582–5.

Sirenūsae. Called by Vergil (*Aen.* v. 864) SIRĒNUM SCOPŬLI. Three small uninhabited and rocky islands near the south side of the Promontory Misenum, off the coast of Campania, which were, according to tradition, the abode of the Sirens. See SIRENES.

Siris. (1) Now Sinno; a river in Lucania flowing into the Tarentine Gulf. (2) Now Torre di Senna, an ancient Greek town in Lucania at the mouth of the preceding river.

Sirius (Σείριος). The dog-star (Hes. *Op. et D.* 417). See CANICULOSI DIES.

Sirmio. Now Sirmione; a beautiful promontory on the southern shore of the Lacus Benacus (Lago di Garda), on which Catullus had an estate.

Sirmium. Now Mitrovitz; an important city in Pannonia Inferior, situated on the left bank of the Savus. It was founded by the Taurisci, and under the Romans became the capital of Pannonia, and the headquarters of all their operations in their wars against the Dacians and the neighbouring barbarians (Amm. Marc. xvii. 13; xix. 11).

Sirocco. See AUSTER.

Sisăpon. Now Almaden; a town in Hispania Baetica famous for its silver mines and cinnabar (Strabo, p. 142).

Siscia. Now Sissek, called SEGESTA by Appian. An important town in Pannonia Superior, situated upon an island formed by the rivers Savus, Colapis, and Odra, and on the road from Aemona to Sirmium (Dio Cass. xlix. 37).

Sisenna, L. CORNELIUS. A Roman annalist who was praetor in the year when Sulla died (B.C. 78), and probably obtained Sicily for his province in 77. From the local knowledge thus acquired he was enabled to render good service to Verres, whose cause he espoused. During the war against the pirates (67) he acted as the legate of Pompey, and, having been despatched to Crete in command of an army, died in that island at the age of about 52. His great work, entitled *Historiae*, extended to at least fourteen or nineteen books, which contained the history of his own time (Gell. xii. 15, 2). Cicero pronounces Sisenna superior as an historian to any of his predecessors (Brut. 64, 228). The fragments are given in Peter's *Hist. Reliq.* 297. In addition to his *Historiae*, Sisenna translated the Milesian tales of Aristides (printed by Bücheler in his small edition of Petronius [Berlin, 1882]), but is probably not the person of the same name who composed a commentary upon Plautus. See Schneider, *De Sisennae Historiae Reliquiis* (Jena, 1882).

Sistrum (σεῖστρον). A kind of rattle used in the mystical worship of Isis, and borrowed, at the same time with it, from the Egyptians. It consisted of a thin oval band of metal (bronze, silver,

Sistra.

or gold) fastened to a handle, and crossed by a number of little metal rods, bent at either end, and loosely inserted in the band. It was held in the hand and shaken (Tibull. i. 3, 24). The same word is sometimes applied to a child's rattle (Mart. xiv. 54; Pollux, ix. 127). See ISIS.

Sisygambis (Σισύγαμβις). The mother of Darius Codomannus, the last king of Persia, fell into the hands of Alexander after the battle of Issus, B.C. 333, together with the wife and daughter of Darius. Alexander treated these captives with the greatest generosity and kindness, and displayed towards Sisygambis, in particular, a reverence and delicacy of conduct which is one of the brighest ornaments of his character. After his death she put an end to her life by voluntary starvation (Plut. *Alex.* 21; Q. Curt. x. 5, 19).

Sisȳphus (Σίσυφος). The son of Aeolus and Enareté, whence he is called AEOLĪDES. He was married to Meropé, a daughter of Atlas or a Pleiad, and became by her the father of Glaucus, Ornytion (or Porphyrion), Thersander, and Halmus. In later accounts he is also called a son of Autolycus, and the father of Odysseus by Anticlea (see ANTICLEA); whence we find Odysseus sometimes called *Sisyphides* (Soph. *Philoct.* 417). He is said to have built the town of Ephyra, afterwards Corinth. As king of Corinth he promoted navigation and commerce, but he was fraudulent, avaricious, and deceitful. His wickedness during life was severely punished in the lower world, where he had to roll up hill a huge marble block, which as soon as it reached the top always rolled down again. The special reasons for this punishment are not the same in all authors: some relate that it was because he had betrayed the designs of the gods; others because he attacked travellers, and killed them with a huge block of stone; and others again because he had betrayed to Asopus that Zeus had carried off Aegina, the daughter of the latter. The more usual tradition related that Sisyphus requested his wife not to bury him, and that, when she complied with his request, Sisyphus in the lower world complained of this seeming neglect, and obtained from Pluto or Persephonê permission to return to the upper world to punish his wife. He then refused to return to the lower world, until Hermes carried him off by force; and this piece of treachery is said to have been the cause of his punishment (Theog. 703; Eustath. *ad* Hom. pp. 631, 1702).

Sităcê (Σιτάκη) or **Sittăcê** (Σιττάκη). A great and populous city of Babylonia, near but not on the Tigris, and eight parasangs within the Median Wall. Its probable site is marked by a ruin called the Tower of Nimrod. It gave the name of SITTACÊNÊ to the district on the lower course of the Tigris, east of Babylonia and northwest of Susiana.

Sitalces (Σιτάλκης). A king of the Thracian tribe of the Odrysians. He was the son of Teres, whom he succeeded on the throne. He increased his dominions by successful wars, so that they ultimately comprised the whole territory from Abdera to the mouths of the Danube, and from Byzantium to the sources of the Strymon (Thuc. ii. 29, 97). At the commencement of the Peloponnesian War he entered into an alliance with the Athenians, and in B.C. 429 he invaded Macedonia with a vast army, but was obliged to retire through failure of provisions, and was killed in B.C. 424 by the Triballi (Thuc. iv. 101).

Sitella. See SITULA.

Sithonia (Σιθωνία). The central one of the three peninsulas running out from Chalcidicê in Macedonia, between the Toronaic and Singitic gulfs. The Thracians were originally spread over the greater part of Macedonia; and the ancients derived the name of Sithonia from a Thracian king, Sithon. We also find mention of a Thracian people, Sithonii, on the shores of the Pontus Euxinus; and the poets frequently use *Sithonis* and *Sithonius* in the general sense of *Thracicus* (Herod. vii. 123).

Sitĭcen (τυμβαύλης). A musician who performed at funerals upon a kind of horn or trumpet (*tuba*). See Capito *ap.* Gell. xx. 2.

Sitĭfis (Σίτιφα). Now Setif; a town in Mauretania on the borders of Numidia. It was a colony under the Romans, and when Mauretania Caesariensis was divided, Sitifis became the capital of the eastern province which was called after it Mauretania Sitifensis (Ptol. iv. 2, 34).

Sitŏnes. A German tribe in Scandinavia, belonging to the race of the Suevi (Tac. *Germ.* 45).

Sitophylăces (σιτοφύλακες). At Athens, a board originally consisting of ten members, five in the city itself and five in the Piraeus, which superintended the trade in grain (σῖτος), and prevented prices becoming exorbitant. See Aristot. *Ath. Pol.* 51, and the article COMMERCE, p. 395.

Sitopōlae (σιτοπῶλαι). Middlemen at Athens who sold grain and who were carefully watched by the citizens as well as by the importers lest they should "corner the market" (συνωνεῖσθαι) and put up the price of cereals (συνιστάναι τὰς τιμάς), an offence legally punishable with death; nor was any bail allowed to them before trial. This law, however, was systematically evaded (Lys. *Or.* 22). See SITOPHYLACES.

Sitos (σῖτος). See SITOPHYLACES; SITOPOLAE.

Sittius or **Sitius**, PUBLIUS. A native of Nuceria in Campania, who was connected with Catiline, and went to Spain in B.C. 64, from which country he crossed over into Mauretania in the following year. He joined Caesar when the latter came to Africa, in 46, to prosecute the war against the Pompeian party. He was of great service to Caesar in this war, and at its conclusion was rewarded by him with the western part of Numidia, where he settled, distributing the land among his soldiers. After the death of Caesar, Arabio, the son of Masinissa, returned to Africa, and killed Sittius by stratagem (Sall. *Cat.* 21; *Bell. Afr.* 25, 93–96; App. *B. C.* iv. 54).

Sitŭla, dim. **Sitella** (ὑδρία). A bucket for drawing water from a well, or for carrying it (Plaut. *Amph.* ii. 2, 30). It was sometimes of pottery and sometimes of bronze (Marquardt, *Privatleben*, p. 656). The word is also applied to a voting-urn (Plaut. *Cas.* ii. 6, 11), and to an urn for drawing lots (Plaut. l. c.). See CISTA.

Skepticism. See PHILOSOPHIA; PYRRHO.

Skiff. See CYMBA; SCAPHA.

Skirmisher. See VELITES.

Slate. See TABULA.

Slave. See SERVUS.

Slaver. See SERVUS.

Slavi. A Sarmatian tribe dwelling between the Borysthenes (Dniester) and the Tanaïs (Don), and also called ANTES.

Sleep, GOD OF. See SOMNUS.

Sleeve. See MANICA.

Sling. See FUNDA.

Slipper. See CREPIDA; SOCCUS; SOLEA.

Slug. See GLANS.

Smaragdus Mons (Σμάραγδον ὄρος). Now Jebel Zaburah; a mountain of Upper Egypt, near the coast of the Red Sea, north of Berenicê. It obtained its name from its extensive mines for emeralds (*smaragdi*) (Pliny, *H. N.* xxxvii. 65).

Smerdis (Σμέρδις). The son of the Cyrus who was murdered by order of his brother Cambyses. (See CAMBYSES.) His real name was BARDES. The death of Smerdis was kept a profound secret; and accordingly, when the Persians became weary of the tyranny of Cambyses, one of the Magians, called by Herodotus Patizithes, who had been left by Cambyses in charge of his palace and treasures, availed himself of the likeness of his brother Gaumates to the deceased Smerdis to proclaim this brother as king, representing him as the younger son of Cyrus. Cambyses heard of the revolt in Syria, but he died of an accidental wound in the thigh as he was mounting his horse to march against the usurper. The false Smerdis was acknowledged as king by the Persians, and reigned for seven months without opposition. The leading Persian nobles, however, were not quite free from suspicion; and this suspicion was increased by the king never inviting any of them to the palace, and never appearing in public. Among the nobles who entertained these suspicions was Otanes, whose daughter Phaedima had been one of the wives of Cambyses, and had been transferred to his successor. The new king had some years before been deprived of his ears by Cyrus for some offence; and Otanes persuaded his daughter to ascertain whether her master had really lost his ears. Phaedima found out that such was the fact, and communicated the decisive information to her father. Otanes thereupon formed a conspiracy, and, in conjunction with six other noble Persians, succeeded in forcing his way into the palace, where they slew the false Smerdis and his brother Patizithes in the eighth month of their reign, B.C. 521 (Herod. iii. 30, 61–79). The usurpation of the false Smerdis was an attempt on the part of the Medes, to whom the Magians belonged, to obtain the supremacy, of which they had been deprived by Cyrus. The assassination of Gaumates and the accession of Darius Hystaspis again gave the ascendency to the Persians; and the anniversary of the day on which the Magians were massacred was commemorated among the Persians by a festival, called Magophonia, on which no Magian was allowed to show himself in public. The real nature of the transaction is also shown by the revolt of the Medes after the accession of Darius. See Hutecker, *Ueber d. falschen Smerdis* (1885); and the article PERSIA.

Smilis (Σμῖλις). The son of Euclides, of Aegina, a sculptor of the legendary period in Greece, whose name appears to be derived from σμίλη, a knife for carving wood, and afterwards a sculptor's chisel. Smilis is the legendary head of the Aeginetan School of sculpture, just as Daedalus is the legendary head of the Attic and Cretan Schools (Pausan. vii. 4, 4).

Smintheus (Σμινθεύς). A surname of Apollo, which is derived by some from σμίνθος, "a mouse," and by others from the town of Sminthé in Troas. The mouse was regarded by the ancients as inspired by the vapours arising from the earth, and as the symbol of prophetic power. This festival, which was celebrated at Rhodes, was called SMINTHIA (τὰ Σμίνθια). On the origin and significance of the name, see A. Lang, *Custom and Myth*, pp. 103 foll. (2d ed. London, 1885).

Smiths. See FABER.

Smugglers. See PORTORIUM.

Smyrna (Σμύρνα) or **Myrrha**. The mother of Adonis by her own father, Cinyras. See ADONIS.

Smyrna (Σμύρνα), and in some manuscripts **Zmyrna**. Now Smyrna (Turkish, Izmir); an ancient city of Asia Minor, the only one of the great cities on the coast that still remains of importance as a commercial port. It lay on the river Meles at the eastern end of the Sinus Smyrnaeus, whose depth allowed the largest ships to anchor at the very walls of the city. From it stretched back the great valley of the Hermus, in which lay the rich city of Sardis (q. v.), of which Smyrna served as the principal seaport. It was probably Aeolian in its origin, founded by colonists from Cymé (Herod. i. 150; Pausan. vii. 5, 1), but became a possession of the Ionians of Colophon, and from that time was politically classed with the Ionian cities. As to the time when it became a member of the Panionic Confederacy, we have only a very untrustworthy account, which refers its admission to the reign of Attalus, king of Pergamum. Its early history is also very obscure. There is an account in Strabo (p. 646) that it was destroyed by the Lydian king Sadyattes, and that its inhabitants were compelled to live in scattered villages until after the Macedonian conquest, when the city was rebuilt, twenty stadia from its former site, by Antigonus; but this is inconsistent with Pindar's mention of Smyrna as a beautiful city (*Fr.* 155). Thus much is clear, however, that at some period the old city of Smyrna, which stood on the northeastern side of the Hermaean Gulf, was abandoned, and that it was succeeded by a new city on the southeastern side of the same gulf (the present site), which is said to have been built by Antigonus, and which was enlarged and beautified by Lysimachus. This new city stood partly on the sea-shore and partly on a hill called Mastusia. The streets were paved with stone, and crossed one another at right angles. The city soon became one of the greatest and most prosperous in the world. It was especially favoured by the Romans on account of the aid it rendered them in the Syrian and Mithridatic Wars. It was the seat of a *conventus iuridicus*. In the Civil Wars it was taken

Coin of Smyrna. (Second century B.C.)

and partly destroyed by Dolabella, but it soon recovered. It occupies a distinguished place in the early history of Christianity, as one of the only two among the Seven Churches of Asia which St. John addresses in the Apocalypse without any admixture of rebuke, and as the scene of the labours and martyrdom of Polycarp. In the years A.D. 178–180 a succession of earthquakes, to which the city has always been much exposed, reduced it almost to ruins; but it was restored by the emperor M. Antoninus. In the successive wars under the Eastern Empire it was frequently much injured, but always recovered; and, under the Turks, who took it in A.D. 1424, it has survived repeated attacks of earthquake, fire, and plague, and still remains the great commercial city of the Levant. There are but few ruins of the ancient city. In addition to her other sources of renown, Smyrna stood at the head of the seven cities which claimed the birth of Homer. The poet was worshipped as a hero in a magnificent building called the Homereum (Ὁμήρειον). Near the sea-shore there stood a magnificent temple of Cybelé, whose head decorated the coins of the city.

Smyrna Trachēa. An early name of Ephesus (q. v.).

Smyrnaeus Sinus (Σμυρναϊκὸς κόλπος). Now the Gulf of Izmir or Smyrna. The great gulf on the western coast of Asia Minor, at the bottom of which Smyrna stands. See SMYRNA.

Soaemias. See SOEMIS.

Soccus. A loose slipper, or light, low shoe, fitting either foot, which the Romans adopted from the Greeks, among whom it was worn by both sexes. It was the characteristic of comedy, as the *cothurnus* (q. v.) was of tragedy (Hor. *A. P.* 80). To wear the soccus off the stage was regarded as un-Roman (Pliny, *H.N.* xxxvii. 6).

Comic Actor with Socci. (De l'Aulnaye, *Salt. Theatr.* pl. iv.)

Social War. (1) In Greek history a name given to the war between Athens and her allies (B.C. 357–355), which was caused by the exactions imposed by the Athenian generals upon the allied States. Artaxerxes, the Persian king, threatened to support the allied forces with a fleet of three hundred ships, so that Athens was obliged to consent to a peace by which her most important allies became practically independent of her. It was this war that forced Athens to remain quiet while Philip of Macedon was initiating some of his far-reaching measures of aggrandizement.

(2) In Roman history a name given to the war between Rome and the eight Sabellian nations (B.C. 90–89)—the Marsi, Paeligni, Marrucini, and Vestiniani, with the Picentines, Samnites, Apulians, and Lucanians. The war is also known as the MARSIC WAR. After several defeats, the Romans under Pompeius Strabo and L. Porcius Cato defeated the allies, whose general was Papius Mutilus, and the war ended with the surrender of the Sabellian forces; but Rome by a Lex Plautia Papiria granted nearly everything that the allies had demanded, especially an easy access to the Roman franchise. In this war 300,000 men are said to have perished.

Coin of the Eight Sabellian Nations.

Socii. Among the Romans the socii, as distinguished in constitutional law from Roman subjects, were the allies who, while their independence was recognized, stood in a more or less dependent relation to the Roman State. Under the Republic, up to the time when the right of citizenship was conferred on all the free inhabitants of Italy (B.C. 89), the Latins, and the Italian communities on the same footing with them, enjoyed a privileged position among the other allies. In the military organization of the Roman Republic the contingents which they furnished were called *socii* in contradistinction to the legions and the non-Italian auxiliaries. (See EXERCITUS; and cf. LEGIO.) SOCII NAVĀLES are the crews, furnished by the allied towns, of the ships of war. See Mommsen, *Staatsrecht*, iii. pp. 645–718; and the article FOEDERATAE CIVITATES.

Socrătes (Σωκράτης). (1) An Athenian philosopher, whose teaching revolutionized the whole drift of subsequent philosophical speculation. He was born in the deme Alopecé, near Athens, B.C. 469. His father, Sophroniscus, was a sculptor, and his mother, Phaenareté, was a midwife. In his youth Socrates for a time followed his father's occupation, and a group of sculptured Graces, preserved in the Acropolis, was exhibited as his work down to the time of Pausanias; but there is reason to believe that this arose from a confusion of names. It is thought by some that the relief of draped Graces in the Museo Chiaramonte in Rome represents the Athenian group, in which case it must have belonged to an earlier period of art than the century in which Socrates lived.

The personal qualities of Socrates were marked, and such as would readily attract attention. He enjoyed vigorous health, and was so robust as to be capable of enduring fatigue and hardship to a degree that astonished all who knew him. He went barefooted at all seasons of the year; and this not merely at Athens, but when serving as a soldier in the much colder climate of Thrace; and he wore the same clothing in winter as in summer. His features were of remarkable ugliness; and his flat nose, thick lips, and bulging eyes led to his being compared to a satyr.

As to the particulars of his life, there is no connected account. It is known that he served as a heavy-armed soldier at Potidaea, Delium, and Amphipolis; but he seems not to have filled any public office until B.C. 406, when he was a member of the Senate of Five Hundred, and as such refused, in spite of all personal risk, to put an unconstitutional question to vote. He displayed the same moral courage in refusing to obey the order of the Thirty Tyrants for the arrest of Leon of Salamis.

From the period of his middle life, at any rate, he devoted his time wholly to the self-imposed task of teaching, giving up all other business, both public and private, and neglecting all means of acquiring a fortune. It was probably his remissness in this respect which was responsible for the ill-temper and fretfulness of his wife Xanthippé, whose name has passed into all modern tongues as the type of a shrew. Socrates never opened a school and never lectured publicly, nor did he receive any money for his teaching, but went about in the most public parts of the city, such as the market-place, the gymnasia, and the work-shops, seeking opportunities for awakening in the young and old alike moral consciousness and an impulse towards self-knowledge with respect to the end and value of human action. His object, however, was only to aid those with whom he talked in developing such germs of knowledge as were already present in them, and not to communicate to them dog-

Socrates. (Vatican.)

So-called Prison of Socrates at Athens.

matically any knowledge of his own. He was especially severe upon false pretences and intellectual conceit; and, consequently, to many persons he became exceedingly obnoxious, and was the object of much dislike and misrepresentation. This is probably the reason why Aristophanes, in *The Clouds*, selected Socrates as the type of men engaged in philosophical and rhetorical teaching; the more so, as his grotesque physiognomy admitted so well of being imitated in the mask which the actor wore. The audience at the theatre would more readily recognize the peculiar figure which they were accustomed to see every day in the market-place than if Prodicus or Protagoras, whom most of them did not know by sight, had been brought on the stage; nor was it of much importance either to them or to Aristophanes whether Socrates was represented as teaching what he did really teach, or something utterly different.

Attached to none of the prevailing parties, Socrates found in each of them his friends and his enemies. Hated and persecuted by Critias, Charicles, and others among the Thirty Tyrants, who had a special reference to him in the decree which they issued, forbidding the teaching of the art of oratory, he was impeached after their banishment and by their opponents. An orator named Lycon, and a poet (a friend of Thrasybulus) named Meletus, had united in the impeachment with the powerful demagogue Anytus, an embittered antagonist of the Sophists and their system, and one of the leaders of the band which, setting out from Phylé, forced their way into the Piraeus, and drove out the Thirty Tyrants. The judges also are described as persons who had been banished, and who had returned with Thrasybulus. The chief articles of impeachment were that Socrates was guilty of corrupting the youth and of despising the tutelary deities of the State, putting in their place other new divinities. At the same time it had been made a matter of accusation against him that Critias, the most ruthless of the Tyrants, had come forth from his school. Some expressions of his, in which he had found fault with the democratic mode of electing by lot, had also been brought up against him; and there can be little doubt that use was made of his friendly relations with Theramenes, one of the most influential of the Thirty, with Plato's uncle Charmides, who fell by the side of Critias in the struggle with the popular party, and with other aristocrats, in order to irritate against him the party which at that time was dominant. The substance of the speech which Socrates delivered in his defence is probably preserved by Plato in the discourse which goes under the name of the "Apology of Socrates." Being condemned by a majority of only six votes, he expresses the conviction that he deserved to be maintained at the public cost in the Prytaneum, and refuses to acquiesce in the adjudication of imprisonment or a large fine or banishment. He will assent to nothing more than a fine of sixty minae, on the security of Plato, Crito, and other friends. Condemned to death by the judges, who were incensed by this speech, by a majority of eighty votes, he departs from them with the protestation that he would rather die after such a defence than live after one in which he should have endeavoured to excite their pity. The sentence of death could not be carried into execution until after the return of the vessel which had been sent to Delos on the periodical Theoric mission. The thirty days which intervened between its return and the condemnation of Socrates were devoted by him in prison to poetic attempts (the first he had made in his life) and to his usual conversation with his friends. One of these conversations, on the duty of obedience to the laws, Plato has reported in the *Crito*, so called after the faithful follower of Socrates, who had endeavoured without success to persuade him to make his escape. In another, imitated or worked up by Plato in the *Phaedo*, Socrates immediately before he drank the cup of hemlock developed the grounds of his immovable conviction of the immortality of the soul. He died with composure and cheerfulness in his seventieth year, B.C. 399.

Three peculiarities distinguished Socrates: (*a*) His long life passed in contented poverty and in public dialectics, of which we have already spoken. (*b*) His persuasion of a special religious mission. He had been accustomed constantly to hear, even from his childhood, a divine voice—interfering, at moments when he was about to act, in the way of restraint, but never in the way of instigation. Such prohibitory warning was wont to come upon him very frequently, not merely on great but even on small occasions, intercepting what he was about to do or to say. Though later writers speak of this as the Daemon or Genius of Socrates, he himself did not personify it, but treated it merely as a "divine sign, a prophetic or supernatural voice." He was accustomed not only to obey it implicitly, but to speak of it publicly and familiarly to others, so that the fact was well known both to his friends and to his enemies. See a paper by H. Jackson in the

English *Journal of Philology*, vol. v., and Freymüller, *De Socratis Daemonio* (1864). (*c*) His great intellectual originality, both of subject and of method, and his power of stirring and forcing the germ of inquiry and ratiocination in others. He was the first who turned his thoughts and discussions distinctly to the subject of ethics, and was the first to proclaim that "the proper study of mankind is man." With the philosophers who preceded him, the subject of examination had been Nature, or the Cosmos as one undistinguishable whole, blending together cosmogony, astronomy, geometry, physics, metaphysics, etc. In discussing ethical subjects Socrates employed the dialectic method, and thus laid the foundation of formal logic, which was afterwards expanded by Plato and systematized by Aristotle.

The originality of Socrates is shown by the results he achieved. Out of his intellectual school sprang not merely Plato, himself a host, but all the other leaders of Grecian speculation for the next half century, and all those who continued the great line of speculative philosophy down to later times. Euclid and the Megaric School of philosophers—Aristippus and the Cyrenaic Antisthenes and Diogenes, the first of those called the Cynics—all emanated more or less directly from the stimulus imparted by Socrates, and so, for that matter, did the Stoics and Epicureans, though each followed a different vein of thought. Ethics continued to be what Socrates had first made them—a distinct branch of philosophy—alongside of which politics, rhetoric, logic, and other speculations relating to man and society gradually arranged themselves; all of them more popular, as well as more keenly controverted, than physics, which at that time presented comparatively little charm, and still less of attainable certainty. There can be no doubt that the individual influence of Socrates permanently enlarged the horizon, improved the method, and multiplied the ascendant minds, of the Grecian speculative world, in a manner never since paralleled. Subsequent philosophers had a more elaborate doctrine and a larger number of disciples who imbibed their ideas; but none of them applied the same stimulating method with the same efficacy, and none of them so struck out of other minds that fire which sets light to original thought.

See Zeller, *Socrates and the Socratic Schools*, Engl. trans. (1877); Alberti, *Sokrates* (1869); Bertram, *Der Sokrates d. Xenoph. und Aristoph.* (1865); Carran, *La Sophistique de Socrate* (1886); Guttmann, *Ueber den wissenschaftlichen Standpunkt des Sokrates* (1881). The best ancient sources are Xenophon's *Memorabilia* and *Symposium*, with Plato's *Crito*, *Symposium*, *Apologia*, and *Phaedo*. See PHILOSOPHIA.

(2) An ecclesiastical historian, born at Constantinople about A.D. 379. He was a pupil of Ammonius and Helladius, and followed the profession of an advocate in his native city, whence he is surnamed Scholasticus. The *Ecclesiastical History* (Ἐκκλησιαστικὴ Ἱστορία) of Socrates extends from the reign of Constantine the Great, 306, to that of the younger Theodosius, 439. He appears to have been a man of less bigotry than most of his contemporaries, and the very difficulty of determining from internal evidence some points of his religious belief may be considered as arguing his comparative liberality. His history is divided into seven books. His work is edited by Hussey (1853) and Bright, with an introduction (1878); and is translated into English in Schaff's Library of Nicene and Post-Nicene Fathers, 2d series, vol. ii. (New York, 1891).

Sodalĭtas. The word properly means an association or club, and was especially applied to the religious brotherhoods among the Romans. By order of the State, they attended to the cult of some particular object of worship by jointly celebrating certain sacrifices and feasts, especially on the anniversary of the foundation of that cult.

The members, called *sodales*, stood in a legally recognized position of mutual obligation, which did not allow any one of them to appear against another as a prosecutor in a criminal case, or to become *patronus* of the prosecutor of a *sodalis*, or to officiate as judge upon a *sodalis*. Such a brotherhood were the Sodales Augustales, appointed A.D. 14 by the Senate for the cult of the deified Augustus, a college of twenty-one, and afterwards of twenty-eight members of senatorial rank, which also took upon itself the cult of Claudius after his deification, and bore, after that, the official title Sodales Augustales Claudiales. Besides these, there were the Sodales Flaviales Titiales for the cult of Vespasian and Titus, the Hadrianales for that of Hadrian, Antoniniani for that of Antoninus Pius and of the successively deified emperors (cp. Collegium).

The secular clubs, *sodalitates* or *collegia sodalicia*, were, in the later Republican age, much turned to account for political objects, and their organization used for purposes of bribery. (See Cicero's speech *Pro Plancio*.)

Sodalitium and **Sodalicium**. See AMBITUS.

Sodŏma (τὰ Σόδομα). A very ancient city of Canaan, in the beautiful valley of Siddim, closely connected with Gomorrha, over which and the other three "cities of the plain" the king of Sodom seems to have had a sort of supremacy. In the book of Genesis we find these cities as subject, in the time of Abraham, to the king of Elam and his allies (an indication of the early supremacy in western Asia of the masters of the Tigris and Euphrates Valley), and their attempt to cast off the yoke was the occasion of the first war recorded in history (Gen. xiv).

Soēmis or **Soaemias**, IULIA. The daughter of Iulia Maesa, and mother of Elagabalus, became the chosen counsellor of her son, and encouraged and shared his follies and enormities. She took a seat in the Roman Senate, into which a woman then for the first time entered, and also established a sort of Senate of Women in which she presided and promulgated edicts for regulating all matters connected with the morals, etiquette, and dress of Roman ladies. She was slain by the Praetorians on the 11th of March, A.D. 222 (Lamprid. *Elagab.* 2; Dio Cass. lxxviii. 30, 38).

Sogdiāna (Σογδιανή: Persian, Sogd). Comprising parts of Turkestan and Bokhara. The northeast province of the ancient Persian Empire, separated on the south from Bactriana and Margiana by the upper course of the Oxus (Jihoun); on the east and north from Scythia by the Sogdii Comedarum and Oscii Mountains (Kara-Dagh, Alatau, and Ak Tagh) and by the upper course of the Iaxartes (Sihoun), and bounded on the northwest by the great deserts east of the Sea of Aral. The natives of the country were of the Aryan race, resembling the Bactrians in their customs (Arrian, *Anab.* iii. 30; iv. 16, 18).

Sogdiānus (Σογδιανός). One of the illegitimate sons of Artaxerxes I. Longimanus. He acquired the throne on the death of his father (B.C. 425) by the murder of his legitimate brother Xerxes II. Sogdianus, however, was murdered in his turn, after a reign of seven months, by his brother Ochus. See PERSIA.

Sogdii Montes. See SOGDIANA.

Sol. The sun. See HELIOS.

Solarium (σκιάθηρον). A sundial (see GNOMON); also the flat roof of the Roman dwelling-house. See DOMUS, p. 546.

Soldurii (εὐχωλιμαῖοι). A Gallic word denoting the armed retainers of a military chief (Caes. *B. C.* iii. 22).

Solea. (1) A sandal, consisting of a sole bound by a strap across the instep (Festus, s. h. v.). (2) SOLEA SPARTEA, a shoe or boot of Spanish brown (*sparta*) used for protecting the diseased feet of cattle (Columell. vi. 12, 3). (3) SOLEA FERREA, a shoe for horses and mules made of metal (Sueton. *Nero*, 30; *Vesp.* 23), but bound on the hoof and not fastened with nails.

Soli or **Soloe** (Σόλοι). (1) A city on the coast of Cilicia, between the rivers Lamus and Cydnus, said to have been colonized by Argives and Lydians from Rhodes. Pompey restored the city, which had been destroyed by Tigranes, and peopled it with the survivors of the defeated bands of pirates; and from this time forth it was called POMPEIOPŎLIS. It was celebrated in literary history as the birthplace of the Stoic philosopher Chrysippus, of the comic poet Philemon, and of the astronomer and poet Aratus. Its name survives in the linguistic term "solecism" (*soloecismus*), which is said to have been first used because of the bad Greek spoken by the people of this city. (See Diog. Laërt. i. 2, 4; Strabo, p. 683; Suid. s. v. Σόλοι; Gell. i. 7, 3). (2) Now Aligora, in the valley of Solea, a considerable seaport town in the western part of the north coast of Cyprus. Here were temples of Isis and Aphroditē.

Solĭdus (νόμισμα). A Roman gold coin, introduced by the emperor Constantine about A.D. 312, which remained in use until the downfall of the Byzantine Empire; its weight was $\frac{1}{72}$ lb., its value about $3. The word is preserved in the modern Italian *soldo* and the French *sou*. See NUMISMATICS, page 1115.

Solīnus, GAIUS IULIUS. A Roman writer who composed, probably in the second half of the third century A.D., a collection of *Memorabilia* (*Collectanea Rerum Memorabilium*, better known by its later title, in the sixth century, *Polyhistor*). The most important portion (the geographical) is an abstract of a treatise on geography compiled from Pliny's *Natural History*. There is a critical edition by Mommsen (Berlin, 1864).

Solis Fons. See OASIS.

Solis Mons. See SOLOÏS.

Solitaurilia. See SUOVETAURILIA.

Solium (θρόνος). (1) Any high-backed chair with closed sides for arms (Serv. *ad* Verg. *Aen.* i. 506). (2) A chair of state, or throne, cushioned, and with the back covered with drapery (Verg. *Aen.* x. 116). (3) A seat at the bottom of a circular bath on which the bathers sat while washing (Suet. *Aug.* 82; Festus, s. h. v.).

Solium. (From the Vatican Vergil.)

Soloe. See SOLI.

Soloïs (Σολόεις). Now C. Cantin. A promontory running far out into the sea, in the southern part of the west coast of Mauretania. Upon it was a Phœnician temple to the god of the sea. The Romans called it SOLIS MONS.

Solōn (Σόλων). A celebrated Athenian legislator, born about B.C. 638. His father Execestides was a descendant of Codrus, and his mother was a cousin of the mother of Pisistratus. Execestides had seriously crippled his resources by a too prodigal expenditure; and Solon consequently found it either necessary or convenient in his youth to betake himself to the life of a foreign trader. It is likely enough that while necessity compelled him to seek a livelihood in some mode or other, his active and inquiring spirit led him to select that pursuit which would furnish the amplest means for its gratification. Solon early distinguished himself by his poetical abilities. His first effusions were in a somewhat light and amatory strain, which afterwards gave way to the more dignified and earnest purpose of inculcating profound reflections or sage advice. So widely indeed did his reputation spread that he was ranked as one of the famous Seven Sages (q. v.), and his name appears in all the lists of the seven. The occasion which first brought Solon prominently forward as an actor on the political stage was the contest between Athens and Megara respecting the possession of Salamis. The ill success of the attempts of the Athenians to make themselves masters of the island had led to the enactment of a law forbidding the writing or saying anything to urge the Athenians to renew the attempt. Soon after these events (about 595) Solon took a leading part in promoting hostilities on behalf of Delphi against Cirrha, and was the mover of the decree of the Amphictyons by which war was declared. It does not appear, however, what active part he took in the war. According to a common story, which, however, rests only on the authority of a late writer, Solon hastened the surrender of the town by causing the waters of the Plistus to be poisoned. It was about the time of the outbreak of this war that, in consequence of the distracted condition of Attica, which was rent by civil commotions, Solon was called upon by all parties to mediate between them, and alleviate the miseries that prevailed. He was chosen archon in 594, and under that legal title was invested with unlimited power for adopting such measures as the exigencies of the State demanded.

In fulfilment of the task intrusted to him, Solon addressed himself to the relief of the existing distress. This he effected with the greatest discretion and success by his celebrated "disburdening ordinance" (σεισάχθεια), a measure consisting of various distinct provisions, calculated to relieve the debtors with as little infringement as possible on the claims of the wealthy creditors. He also changed the standard of the monetary system from the Phidonian to the Euboic, which was the one generally in use in the great centres of commerce, Chalcis and Eretria, so that Athenian trade might be simplified in its exchanges (Aristotle, *Ath. Pol.* 10). A limit was also set to the rate of interest and to the accumulation of land (Aristotle, *Ath. Pol.* 6). The success of the Seisachtheia procured for Solon such confidence and popularity that he was further charged with the task of entirely remodelling the constitution. As a preliminary step, he repealed all the laws of Draco (q. v.), except those relating to bloodshed. The principal features of the Solonian Constitution may be briefly summarized for the benefit of the reader. The State as he left it was a timocracy (*τιμοκρατία*), that is to say, a form of oligarchy (*ὀλιγαρχία*) in which the possession of a certain amount of property is requisite for admission to the ruling class. (See OLIGARCHIA.) Solon established a sort of timocratic scale, so that those who did not belong to the nobility received the rights of citizens in a proportion determined partly by their property and their corresponding services to the State. For this purpose he divided the population into four classes, founded on the possession of land. (1) Pentacosiomedimni (*Πεντακοσιομέδιμνοι*), who had at least 500 *medimni* (750 bushels) of corn or *metretae* of wine or oil as yearly income. (2) Hippeis (*Ἱππεῖς*, *Ἱππῆς*), or knights, with at least 300 *medimni.* (3) Zeugitae (*Ζευγῖται*) (possessors of a yoke of oxen), with at least 150 *medimni.* (4) Thetes (*Θῆτες*) (workers for wages), with less than 150 *medimni* of yearly income. Solon's legislation only granted to the first three of these four classes a vote in the election of responsible officers, and only to the first class the power of election to the highest offices; as, for instance, that of archon. The fourth class was excluded from all official positions, but possessed the right of voting in the general public assemblies which chose officials and passed laws. They had also the right of taking part in the trials by jury which Solon had instituted. The first three classes were bound to serve as hoplites; the cavalry was raised out of the first two, while the fourth class was only employed as light-armed troops or on the fleet, and apparently for pay. The others served without pay. The first three classes alone were subject to direct taxation. The holders of office in the State were also unpaid. Solon established as the chief consultative body the Council of the Four Hundred (see BOULÉ), in which only the first three classes took part, and as chief administrative body the Areopagus (q. v.), which was to be filled up by those who had been archons. A Council of 401 members is said to have been part of Draco's constitution (about B.C. 621), the members being selected by lot from the whole body of citizens. Solon reduced the Council to 400, one hundred from each of the four tribes; and extended in some particulars the powers already possessed by the Areopagus (Aristotle, *Ath. Pol.* 4, 8). Besides this, he promulgated a code of laws embracing the whole of public and private life, the salutary effects of which lasted long after the end of his constitution. He also rectified the calendar, and regulated the system of weights and measures. He forbade the exportation of Attic products, except olive oil. Among his other regulations were those giving to childless persons the power of disposing of their property by will, punishing idleness, inflicting *ἀτιμία* on those citizens who in the time of any sedition remained neutral, and giving great rewards to the victors in the Olympian and Isthmian Games.

The laws of Solon were inscribed on wooden cylinders (*ἄξονες*) and triangular tablets (*κύρβεις*), and set up in the Acropolis, and later in the Prytaneum. Solon himself spoke of them as being not the best laws conceivable, but the best that the Athenians could be induced to accept. His Constitution was, in fact, a compromise between democracy proper and oligarchy, and it gives to Solon a title to rank with the great constructive statesmen of all time.

The great lawgiver's later history must be regarded as more legendary than authentic. After completing his task of legislation he left Athens for ten years, after exacting from the people a promise that they would leave his laws unaltered for that space of time (Aristotle, *Ath. Pol.* 11; Herod. i. 29; Plut. *Sol.* 25). After visiting Egypt, he is said to have gone to Cyprus, where he was received by the king of the little town of Aepea. Solon persuaded the king, Philocyprus, to remove from the old site and build a new town on the plain. The new settlement was called Soli, in honour of the illustrious visitor (Herod. v. 113). He is further said to have visited Lydia; and his interview with Croesus was one of the most celebrated stories in antiquity. "Who is the happiest man you have ever seen?" asked the magnificent king, fishing for a compliment. "I can speak of no one as happy until I have seen how his life has ended," replied the philosopher, thus giving deep offence to the monarch (Herod. i. 32). See CROESUS.

During the absence of Solon the old dissensions were renewed, and shortly after his arrival at Athens the supreme power was seized by Pisistratus. The tyrant, after his usurpation, is said to have paid considerable court to Solon, and on various occasions to have solicited his advice, which Solon did not withhold. Solon probably died about 558, two years after the overthrow of the Constitution, at the age of eighty. There was a story current in antiquity that, by his own directions, his ashes were collected and scattered round the island of Salamis. Of the poems of Solon several fragments remain. They do not indicate any great degree of imaginative power, but their style is vigorous and simple; and those that were called forth by special emergencies appear to have been marked by no small degree of energy.

See the histories of Greece by Thirlwall, Grote, Curtius, Cox, and Abbot; and the editions of Aristotle's *Constitution of Athens* by Kenyon (1891), Kaibel and Wilamowitz-Moellendorf (1891), with the translation by Poste (1891). See also Jonas, *De Solone Atheniensi* (1884). The remains of Solon's poetry are collected by Bergk in his *Poetae Lyrici Graeci* (4th ed. 1878) and discussed by Mettauer in his *Solon als Dichter* (1884) and Laeger, *De Veterum Epicorum Studio in Solonis Reliquiis* (1885). His life was written by Plutarch.

Solonian Constitution. See SOLON.

Solūs (*Σολοῦς*), also called **Soluntum** by the Romans. An ancient town on the northern coast of Sicily, between Panormus and Thermae. It was first colonized by the Phœnicians (Thucyd. vi. 2).

Solўma (τὰ Σόλυμα). (1) The mountain range which runs parallel to the east coast of Lycia, and is a southern continuation of Mount Climax. (2) Another name for HIEROSOLЎMA (q. v.).

Solўmi. See LYCIA.

Somnium Scipiōnis. "Scipio's Dream"; the title given to a portion of the sixth book of Cicero's treatise *De Republica*. The greater part of the treatise itself is lost, but the episode of Scipio's dream is preserved in the commentary of Macrobius (*Commentariorum in Somnium Scipionis Libri Duo*). It tells how the younger Scipio while in Africa was visited by the spirit of the great Africanus, who revealed to him in part his future career, and taught him that there is in the life to come a reward reserved for those who serve their country loyally and well.

Somnus (Ὕπνος). The god of sleep; the son of Nyx (q. v.) and twin-brother of Thanatos or Mors (*Il.* xiv. 231; xvi. 672). With his brother, according to Hesiod, he dwelt in the eternal darkness of the farthest West (*Theog.* 759). Thence he swept over land and sea, bringing sleep to men and gods, since he had power over all alike, and could lull to sleep even Zeus himself. On the chest of Cypselus at Olympia, both brothers were depicted as boys sleeping in the arms of their mother, Death being painted in black and Sleep in white (Pausan. v. 18, 1). Sleep was represented in art in various forms and situations, and frequently with the wings of an eagle or a butterfly on his forehead, and a poppy-stalk and a horn, from which he dropped slumber upon those whom he lulled to rest. The earlier conception made Dreams the sisters of Sleep, but in later times the dream-god figures as his son. Hermes was also a god of sleep.

Sontius. Now the Isonzo; a river in Venetia, in the north of Italy, rising in the Carnic Alps, and falling into the Sinus Tergestinus, east of Aquileia.

Sopăter (Σώπατρος). (1) Of Paphos, a writer of parody and burlesque (φλυαρογράφος), who flourished from B.C. 323 to 283. (2) Of Apamea, a distinguished Sophist, the head for some time of the school of Plotinus. He was a disciple of Iamblichus, after whose death (before A.D. 330) he went to Constantinople. Here he enjoyed the favour and personal friendship of Constantine, who afterwards, however, put him to death (between A.D. 330 and 337) from the motive, as was alleged, of giving a proof of the sincerity of his own conversion to Christianity. There are several grammatical and rhetorical works extant under the name of Sopater, but the best critics ascribe these to a younger Sopater, mentioned below. (3) The younger Sophist, of Apamea, or of Alexandria, is supposed to have lived about two hundred years later than the former. Besides his extant works already alluded to, Photius has preserved an extract of a work, entitled the *Historical Selections* (ἐκλογή), which contained a vast variety of facts and figments, collected from a great number of authors. The remains of his rhetorical works are contained in Walz's *Rhetores Graeci*.

Sophēnē (Σωφηνή). A district of Armenia Maior, lying between the ranges of Antitaurus and Masius; separated from Melitené, in Armenia Minor, by the Euphrates, from Mesopotamia by the Antitaurus, and from the eastern part of Armenia Maior by the river Nymphius. It fell to the Romans in the time of Pompey (cf. Tac. *Ann.* xiii. 7).

Sophistae (σοφισταί). Strictly a name given by the Greeks to all those who professed knowledge, or a particular knowledge or a particular art. Hence the Seven Sages are often thus called; but the name was especially applied to the educated men of ready speech, who, from about the year B.C. 450, used to travel through Greece from place to place, and impart what they knew for money. These were the University Extension lecturers of antiquity, and they have the merit of having popularized the interest in knowledge which had up to that time been confined within narrow circles, and especially of having contributed to the formation of eloquence; for they were the first to make style an object of study, and to institute serious investigations into the art of rhetorical expression. Their teaching was chiefly intended to give their pupils versatility in the use of speech, and thus to fit them for taking part in public life. As the subject of their discourses, they chose by preference questions of public interest to persons of general education. The expression, however, always remained the important thing, while positive knowledge fell more and more into the background. Some of them even started from the position that virtue and knowledge were only subjective notions. Protagoras of Abdera, who appeared about B.C. 445, is named as the first Sophist; after him the most important is Gorgias of Leontini; Prodicus of Ceos and Hippias of Elis are contemporaries of the other two. Wherever they appeared, especially in Athens, they were received with the greatest enthusiasm, and many flocked to hear them. Even such men as Pericles, Euripides, and Socrates sought their society; and Socrates owed to them much that was suggestive in his own pursuit of practical philosophy, though, on the other hand, he persistently attacked the principles underlying their public teaching. These principles became further exaggerated under their successors, who did not think they needed even knowledge of fact to talk as they pleased about everything. Accordingly the skill of the Sophists degenerated into mere technicalities and complete absence of reason, and became absolutely contemptible. (See Grote, *History of Greece*, ch. lxvii., and Sidgwick's essay in the (English) *Journal of Philology*, iv. 288.)

With the revival of Greek eloquence, from about the beginning of the second century A.D., the name of Sophist attained a new distinction. At that time the name was given to the professional orators, who appeared in public with great pomp and delivered declamations either prepared beforehand or improvised on the spot. Like the earlier Sophists, they went generally from place to place, and were overwhelmed with applause and with marks of distinction by their contemporaries, including even the Roman emperors. Dion Chrysostom, Herodes Atticus, Aristides, Lucian, and Philostratus the Elder belong to the flourishing period of this second school of Sophists, a period which extends over the whole of the second century. They appear afresh about the middle of the fourth century, devoting their philosophic culture to the zealous but unavailing defence of paganism. Among them was the emperor Julian and his contemporaries Libanius, Himerius, and Themistius.

Synesius may be considered as the last Sophist of importance. See A. W. Benn, *Greek Philosophers,* ch. ii. (London, 1883).

Sophŏcles (Σοφοκλῆς). (1) The second of the three great Greek tragedians, son of Sophilus or Sophillus, the wealthy owner of a manufactory of arms. He was born about B.C. 495 in the deme Colonus near Athens. He received a careful education in music, gymnastics, and dancing, and as a boy of fifteen was chosen to lead the paean sung by the chorus of boys after the victory of Salamis (Athen. p. 20). He afterwards showed his musical skill in public, when he represented the blind singer Thamyris in his drama of the same name, and played the cithara with such success that he was painted as Thamyris with the cithara in the Stoa Poicilé. Again, in the play called the *Nausicaa,* he won for himself general admiration in acting the part of the Phaeacian princess, by the dexterity and grace with which he struck the ball (Athen. p. 20 E). In all things his external appearance and demeanour were the reflex of a lofty mind. At his very first appearance as a tragic poet in 468, when twenty-seven years old, at the Great Dionysia, he gained a victory over Aeschylus, who was thirty years older, and from that time to extreme old age he kept the first place in tragedy. Unlike Aeschylus and Euripides, he never accepted the invitations of foreign princes. Though possessing no special inclination or fitness for political affairs, as his friend, the poet Ion of Chios, declares, he yet took his place in public life. Thus, in B.C. 440, he was one of the ten generals who, with Pericles, were in command of the fleet sent against Samos. Owing to his practical skill he was also employed in negotiations with the allies of Chios and Samos. During the Peloponnesian War he was again one of the generals, together with Nicias. In 435, as Hellenotamias, he was at the head of the management of the treasure of the allies, which was kept on the Acropolis; and, when the question arose in 413, of giving to the State an oligarchical constitution, he was on the commission of preliminary investigation (*C. I. A.* i. 237).

Sophocles. (Lateran Museum, Rome.)

The charm and refinement of his character seem to have won him many friends. Among them was the historian Herodotus, who much resembled him in taste and temperament. He was also deemed by the ancients a man specially beloved by the gods, especially by Asclepius, whose priest he probably was, and who was said to have granted him health and vigour of mind to extreme old age. By the Athenian Nicostraté he had a son, Iophon, who won some repute as a tragic poet, and by Theoris of Sicyon another son, Ariston, father of the Sophocles who gained fame for himself by tragedies of his own, and afterwards by the production of his grandfather's dramas. There was a story that a quarrel arose between Sophocles and his son Iophon, on account of his preference for this grandson, and that, when summoned by Iophon before the court as weak in mind and unable to manage his affairs, he obtained his own absolute acquittal by reading the *parodos* on his native place in the *Oedipus Coloneus,* just written, but not yet produced (Plutarch, *Moral.* p. 775 B). But this appears to be a legend founded on a misunderstood pleasantry of a comic poet. The tales of his death, which happened in B.C. 405, are also mythical. According to one account, he was choked by a grape; according to others, he died either when publicly reciting the *Antigoné,* or from excessive joy at some dramatic victory. The only fact unanimously attested by his contemporaries is, that his death was as dignified as his life. A singular story is connected even with his funeral. We are told that Dionysus, by repeated apparitions in dreams, prompted the general of the Spartans, who were then investing Athens, to grant a truce for the burial of the poet in the family grave outside the city. On his tomb stood a Siren as a symbol of the charm of poetry. After his death the Athenians worshipped him as a hero and offered an annual sacrifice in his memory. In later times, on the proposal of the orator Lycurgus, a bronze statue was erected to him, together with Aeschylus and Euripides, in the theatre; and of his dramas, as of theirs, an authorized and standard copy was made, in order to protect them against arbitrary alterations.

Sophocles was a very prolific poet. The number of his plays is given as between 123 and 130, of which above 100 are known to us by their titles and by fragments; but only seven have been preserved complete: the *Trachiniae* (so named from the chorus, and treating of the death of Heracles), the *Ajax,* the *Philoctetes,* the *Electra,* the *Oedipus Tyrannus,* the *Oedipus at Colonus,* and the *Antigoné.* The last-mentioned play was produced in the spring of 440; the *Philoctetes* in 410; the *Oedipus at Colonus* was not put on the stage until 401, after his death, by his grandson Sophocles. Besides tragedies, Sophocles composed paeans, elegies, epigrams, and a work in prose on the chorus. With his tragedies he gained the first prize more than twenty times, and still more often the second, but never the third. Even in his lifetime, and indeed through the whole of antiquity, he was held to be the most perfect of tragedians; one of the ancient writers calls him the "pupil of Homer."

If Aeschylus is the creator of Greek tragedy, it was Sophocles who brought it to perfection. He extended the dramatic action (1) by the introduction of a third actor, while in his last pieces he even added a fourth; and (2) by a due subordination of the chorus, to which, however, he gave a more artistic development, while he increased its numbers from twelve to fifteen persons. (See Reissenmayer, *De Choro Sophocleo* [1878]). He also perfected the costumes and decoration. Rejecting the plan of Aeschylus, by which one story was carried through three successive plays, he made every tragedy into a complete work of art, with a separate and complete action, the motives for every detail being most skilfully devised. His art was especially shown in the way in which the action is developed from the character of the *dramatis personae.* Sophocles' great mastery of his art appears, above all, in the clearness with which he portrays his characters, which are developed with a scrupulous attention to details, and in which he does not content himself, like Aeschylus, with mere outlines, nor, as Euripides often did, with copies from common life. His heroes, too, are ideal figures, like those of Aeschylus (Aristot. *Poët.* 25). While they lack the superhuman loftiness of the earlier poet's creations, they have a certain ideal truth of their own. Sophocles succeeded in doing what was impossible for Aeschylus and Euripides with their peculiar temperaments, in expressing the nobility of the female character, in its gentleness as well as in its heroic courage. In contrast to Euripides, Sophocles, like Aeschylus, is profoundly religious; and the attitude which he adopts towards the popular religion is marked by an instinctive reverence. The grace peculiar to Sophocles' nature makes itself felt even in his language, the charm of which was universally praised by the ancients. With his noble simplicity he takes in this respect also a middle place between the weightiness and boldness of the language of Aeschylus and the smoothness and rhetorical embellishment which distinguish that of Euripides.

The seven existing plays of Sophocles are all found in the same Codex Laurentianus in Florence that contains the plays of Aeschylus. Cobet regards all the other extant MSS. of the plays as derived from this. Few of them have the whole seven. Of these, two (a Codex Parisinus of the thirteenth century and a Codex Venetus of the fourteenth) are the best. See Meifert, *De Sophoclis Codicibus* (1891).

The *editio princeps* of Sophocles appeared at Venice in 1502. The chief editions of the entire seven plays are those of Brunck, 4 vols. (1786–89); G. Herrmann (1830–41); Wunder (1847–1878); Dindorf (Leipzig, 1825); Schneidewin, rev. by Nauck (Berlin, 1877–82); and Wolff (Leipzig, 1858–65). Annotated English editions are those of Blaydes and Paley, 2 vols. (1859–80); L. Campbell, 2 vols. (1871–81); and Jebb, vols. i.–v. (Cambridge, 1884–95). There are editions of separate plays with English notes by various scholars, among them the *Oedipus Tyrannus* by Jebb (1884), and by White (1890); the *Oedipus Coloneus* by Paley (1881), the *Antigoné* by Paley (1881), and by D'Ooge (1890); of the *Philoctetes* by Graves (1893); of the *Electra* by Jebb (1870); of the *Ajax* by Jebb (1869); and of the *Trachiniae* by Pretor (1877).

There is a lexicon to Sophocles by Ellendt (2d ed. revised by Genthe, Berlin, 1867–72), with a supplementary *Index Commentationum* (1874). There is a good translation of Sophocles into English verse by Plumptre (1871), and one by Campbell (1873). For general criticism, etc., see Hense, *Studien zu Sophocles* (1880); Patin, *Études sur les Tragiques Grecs*, vol. ii. (last ed. 1877); Campbell, *Sophocles* (1879); id. *A Guide to Greek Tragedy* (1891); Schlegel's *Lectures;* Kennedy's *Studia Sophoclea* (1874); and Ribbeck, *Sophokles und Seine Tragödien* (1869). On his language, style, etc., see the following monographs: Altum, *Similitudines Homeri cum Sophoclis* (1855); Borschke, *Aeschylus und Sophocles* (1872); Lichtenstein, *Shakspeare and Sophocles* (1850); Fleischmann, *Kunst der Characteristik bei Sophokles* (1875); Harmsen, *De Collocatione Verborum apud Sophoclem* (1880); Hartz, *De Anacoluthis apud Sophoclem* (1856); Jacobi, *De Usu Alliterationis apud Sophoclem* (1872); Juris, *De Sophoclis Verbis Singularibus* (1876); Maenss, *Die Präpositionen bei Sophokles* (1883); Schindler, *De Sophocle Verborum Inventore* (1877); Struve, *De Dictione Sophoclis* (1854); Schlegel, *Die tragische Ironie bei Sophokles* (1869); Fittbogen, *De Sophoclis Sententiis Ethicis* (1842); and Koch, *De Proverbiis apud Sophoclem* (1892).

(2) Son of Ariston and grandson of the elder Sophocles, was also an Athenian tragic poet. The love of his grandfather towards him has been already mentioned. In B.C. 401 he had brought out the *Oedipus at Colonus* of his grandfather; but he did not begin to exhibit his own dramas till 396.

Sophonisba (*Σοφόνισβα*). The daughter of the Carthaginian general Hasdrubal, the son of Gisco. She had been betrothed by her father, at a very early age, to the Numidian prince Masinissa, but at a subsequent period Hasdrubal, being desirous to gain over Syphax, the rival ruler of Numidia, to the Carthaginian alliance, gave her in marriage to that prince. After the defeat of Syphax, and the capture of his capital city of Cirta by Masinissa, Sophonisba fell into the hands of the conqueror, upon whom her beauty exercised so powerful an influence that he determined to marry her himself. Their wedding was accordingly celebrated without delay; but Scipio (who was apprehensive lest she should exercise the same influence over Masinissa which she had previously done over Syphax) refused to ratify this arrangement, and, upbraiding Masinissa with his weakness, insisted on the immediate surrender of the princess. Unable to resist this command, the Numidian king spared her the humiliation of captivity by sending her a bowl of poison, which she drank without hesitation, and thus put an end to her own life (Livy, xxix. 23; xxx. 3–15; Polyb. xiv. 1, 7; Zonar. ix. 11–13). The story of Sophonisba is the subject of a drama in English by Thomson, produced in 1729.

Sophron (*Σώφρων*). A native of Syracuse. He was a writer in Greek of mimes, and an elder contemporary of Euripides (about B.C. 460–420). He composed in the Dorian dialect prose dialogues, partly serious, partly comic, which faithfully represented scenes of actual life, mostly in the lower classes, interspersed with numerous proverbs and colloquial forms of speech. In spite of their prose form, Sophron's mimes were regarded as poems by the ancients. In Athens they are said to have become known through Plato, who thought very highly of them, and made use of them for the dramatic form of his dialogues (Quint. i. 10, 17; Diog. Laërt. iii. 13). After his death it is said that they were found under his pillow, together with the comedies of Aristophanes. In the Alexandrian Age, Theocritus took them for a pattern in his idylls (especially in the *Adoniazusae, Idyl.* 15). The Greek grammarians also paid particular attention to them on account of the popular idioms they contained. The fragments preserved are so scanty that they give no notion of the contents and form of the pieces; in any case they cannot have been intended for public representation. Sophron's son, Xenarchus, who lived during the reign of Dionysius I., also wrote mimes. See MIMUS.

Sophroniscus. See SOCRATES.

Sophronistae. See GYMNASIUM.

Sopiānae. Now Fünfkirchen; a town in Pannonia Inferior, the birthplace of the emperor Maximinus (Amm. Marc. xxviii. 1).

Sora. (1) Now Sora; a town in Latium, on the right bank of the river Liris and north of Arpinum, with a strongly fortified citadel. (2) A town in Paphlagonia, now Zora.

Soractê. Now Monte di S. Oreste; a celebrated mountain in Etruria, in the territory of the Falisci, near the Tiber, about twenty-four miles from Rome, but the summit of which, frequently covered with snow, was clearly visible from the city (Hor. *Carm.* i. 9); whence some have assumed that the climate of Italy was more rigorous in classical times than now. The whole mountain was sacred to Apollo Soranus, and on its summit was a temple of this god.

Sorānus. A Sabine deity worshipped on Mount Soractê, and in later times identified with Apollo (Verg. *Aen.* vii. 785–790; Pliny, *H. N.* vii. 19).

Sorānus. A Greek physician from Ephesus, who lived in the first half of the second century A.D., under Trajan and Hadrian. His writings are now represented by a work of considerable extent on the diseases of women, and a surgical treatise on fractures. The writings of Caelius Aurelianus (q. v.) on acute and chronic diseases are translated from him. See Scheele, *De Sorano Medico* (1884).

Sorānus, BAREA. A Roman of great integrity, consul suffectus in A.D. 52. He was accused of treason under Nero, and his daughter Servilia was charged with magic. Both were put to death, the chief witness against Soranus being his former teacher P. Egnatius Celer (Tac. *Ann.* xvi. 30; Juv. iii. 16).

Sortes (properly "lots"). Small tablets used for augury in different parts of Italy, especially in the temple of Fortuna at Praenestê (Cicero, *De Div.* ii. 41, 86). They were of oak or bronze, with some saying engraved upon them, and were shuffled and drawn by a boy. Seventeen such sayings (four in the original bronze, and the rest copies) are still preserved (*C. I. L.* i. pp. 268–270). They are known as the SORTES PRAENESTĪNAE, but they appear to have really belonged to the oracle of Geryon at Patavium (Padua). SORTES CONVIVIĀLES were sealed tablets sold at entertainments. When opened they entitled the holder to a prize of greater or less value (Sueton. *Aug.* 75; Lamprid. *Elagab.* 22).

The name *sortes* was given (1) to passages of some book used to foretell events, the method being to open the book at random, for which purpose Christians used the Bible; or (2) to lines of poetry, especially of Vergil, written on leaves, and drawn at haphazard. SORTES VERGILIĀNAE are mentioned in Spartianus (*Hadrian* 2), and alluded to by Lampridius (*Alex. Severus* 14). This use of Vergil continued to modern times. An historic instance of it is found in the life of Charles I. of England, who experimented once in the Bodleian Library at Oxford, and opened at the passage of the *Aeneid* (iv. 615–620) where Dido's imprecations against Aeneas foretold rebellion, defeat, and death. The story is told by Wellwood. See ORACULA.

Sortes Sangallenses. Fragments of a book of oracles found in a MS. at St. Gallen in Switzerland. Edited by Winnefeld (Bonn, 1887).

Sosibius (Σωσίβιος). A Lacedaemonian grammarian who flourished at Alexandria under Ptolemy II. (Athen. p. 493).

Sosigĕnes (Σωσιγένης). The Peripatetic philosopher, was the astronomer employed by Iulius Caesar to superintend the correction of the calendar (B.C. 46). See CALENDARIUM.

Sosiphănes (Σωσιφάνης). Of Syracuse; a Greek tragedian of the Alexandrian Pleiad, who lived about B.C. 300. Of his plays only a few lines have been preserved (Suidas, s. v.). See PLEIAS.

Sositheus (Σωσίθεος). A native of Alexandria in the Troad; a Greek tragedian, one of the Alexandrian Pleiad. He lived in the first half of the third century B.C. in Athens and in Alexandria in Egypt. In an epigram of the Greek Anthology (vii. 707) he is celebrated as the restorer of the satyric drama. We still possess an interesting fragment of his satyric plays, the *Daphnis* (twenty-one lines in Nauck's *Tragicorum Gr. Fragm.* 822, ed. 1889).

Sosius. (1) GAIUS, a Roman quaestor B.C. 66, and praetor in 49. He was afterwards one of Antony's principal lieutenants in the East, and in 37 placed Herod upon the throne of Jerusalem. (2) The name of two brothers (Sosii), booksellers at Rome in the time of Horace (*Epist.* i. 20, 2; *A. P.* 345).

Sospĭta, that is, "the saving goddess." A surname of Iuno at Lanuvium and at Rome, in both of which places she had a temple. See IUNO.

Sosthĕnes (Σωσθένης). A Macedonian soldier who defeated the Gauls at the time of their invasion of Greece in B.C. 280 (Just. xxiv. 5, 6). See GALLIA.

Sostrătus (Σώστρατος). The son of Dexiphanes, of Cnidus. He was one of the great architects who flourished during and after the life of Alexander the Great. He built for Ptolemy I. of Egypt the great Pharos or light-house at Alexandria, which was one of the Seven Wonders of the World, and also erected at Cnidus a portico supporting a terrace (Pliny, *H. N.* xxxvi. 83).

Sosus (Σῶσος). A celebrated artist in mosaic, who was working apparently at the time of the Attalidae in Pergamon. It was there that he executed his famous work, "The Unswept House" (ἀσάρωτος οἶκος), so called because remnants of food, and all that is usually swept away, were represented as strewn about in the most careless way upon the floor. "Much to be admired in this work" (says Pliny, *H. N.* xxxvi. 184) "is a dove drinking, and darkening the water by the shadow of its head; while other doves are sunning and pluming themselves on the rim of the vessel." This is copied in the mosaic (found in Hadrian's Villa at Tivoli), now in the Capitoline Museum at Rome. See illustration under MUSIVUM OPUS, p. 1065; and PICTURA.

Sotadēan Verse. See SOTADES.

Sotădes (Σωτάδης). A Greek poet from Maroneia in Thrace, who lived at Alexandria under Ptolemy Philadelphus about B.C. 276. He is said to have been drowned in the sea in a leaden chest for some sarcastic remark about the marriage of the king with his own sister Arsinoë. He composed in Ionic dialect and in a peculiar metre named after him (*Sotadeus* or *Sotadicus versus*, Σωτάδεια ᾄσματα) poems called κίναιδοι or φλύακες, malicious satires partly on indelicate subjects, which were intended for recitation accompanied by a mimic dance, and also travesties of mythological subjects, such as the

Iliad of Homer. He found numerous imitators (Athen. p. 620; Plut. *Op. Moral.* p. 11).

Soter (Σωτήρ, i. e. "the saviour"; Lat. SERVĀTOR or SOSPES). A title, occurs as the surname of several divinities, especially of Zeus. It was also a surname of Ptolemaeus I., king of Egypt, as well as of several of the other later Greek kings. See PTOLEMAEUS.

Sotion (Σωτίων). (1) An Alexandrian philosopher of the third century B.C., who wrote a work called *Διαδοχαί* on the different teachers of the schools of philosophy (Diog. Laërt. v. 86). (2) The teacher of the Roman philosopher Seneca (Sen. *Epist.* 108).

Sottiātes or **Sotiātes**. A powerful and warlike people in Gallia Aquitanica, on the frontiers of Gallia Narbonensis, who were subdued by P. Crassus, Caesar's legate (Caes. *B. G.* iii. 120).

Sozomĕnus (Σωζόμενος), usually called SOZOMEN in English, was a Greek ecclesiastical historian of the fifth century. He was probably a native of Bethelia or Bethel, a village near Gaza in Palestine. His parents were Christians. He practised as an advocate at Constantinople, whence he is styled *Scholasticus;* and he was still engaged in his profession when he wrote his history. This ecclesiastical history, which is extant, is in nine books, and is dedicated to the emperor Theodosius II. It commences with the reign of Constantine, and comes down a little later than the death of Honorius, A.D. 423. The work is incomplete, and breaks off in the middle of a chapter. The author, we know, had proposed to bring it down to 439, the year in which the history of Socrates ends. See SOCRATES (2).

Sparta (Σπάρτη, Dor. Σπάρτα), also called **Lacedaemon** (Λακεδαίμων). The capital of Laconica and the chief city of the Peloponnesus, was situated on the right bank of the Eurotas (Iri), about twenty miles from the sea. It stood on a plain which contained within it several rising grounds and hills. It was bounded on the east by the Eurotas, on the northwest by the small river Oenus (Kelesina), and on the southeast by the small river Tisia (Magula), both of which streams fell into the Eurotas. The plain in which Sparta stood was shut in on the east by Mount Menelaïeum, and on the west by Mount Taÿgetus; whence the city is called by Homer "the hollow Lacedaemon." It was of a circular form, about six miles in circumference, and consisted of several distinct quarters, which were originally separate villages, and which were never united into one regular town. Its site is occupied by the modern villages of Magula and Psykhiko; and the principal modern town in the neighbourhood is Mistra, which lies about two miles to the west on Mount Taÿgetus.

During the flourishing times of Greek independence, Sparta was never surrounded by walls, since the bravery of its citizens, and the difficulty of access to it, were supposed to render such defences needless. It was first fortified by the tyrant Nabis; but it did not possess regular walls until the time of the Romans. Sparta, unlike most Greek cities, had no proper Acropolis, but this name was given to one of the steepest hills of the town, on the summit of which stood the Temple of Athené Poliuchus, or Chalcioecus.

Five distinct quarters of the city are mentioned: (1) PITĂNÉ (Πιτάνη), which appears to have been the most important part of the city, and in which was situated the Agora, containing the council-house of the Senate, and the offices of the public magistrates. It was also surrounded by various temples and other public buildings. Of these, the most splendid was the Persian Stoa or portico, originally built of the spoils taken in the Persian War, and enlarged and adorned at later times. A part of the Agora was called the Chorus or dancing-place, in which the Spartan youths performed dances in honour of Apollo. (2) LIMNAE (Λίμναι), a suburb of the city, on the banks of the Eurotas, northeast of Pitané, was originally a hollow spot covered with water. (3) MESOA or MESSOA (Μεσόα, Μεσσόα), also by the side of the Eurotas, southeast of the preceding, containing the Dromus and the Platanistas, which was a spot nearly surrounded with water, and so called from the plane-trees growing there. (4) CYNOSŪRA (Κυνόσουρα), in the southwest of the city, and south of Pitané. (5) AEGĪDAE (Αἰγεῖδαι), in the northwest of the city, and west of Pitané.

The two principal streets of Sparta ran from the Agora to the extreme end of the city: these were, (1) Aphetae or Aphetais (Ἀφέται, Ἀφεταΐς sc. ὁδός), extending in a southeasterly direction, past the temple of Dictynna and the tombs of the Eurypontidae; and (2) Skias (Σκιάς), running nearly parallel to the preceding one, but farther to the east, and which derived its name from an ancient place of assembly, of a circular form, called Skias. The most important remains of ancient Sparta are the ruins of the theatre, which was near the Agora. On the topography of Sparta see a paper by N. E. Crosby in the *American Journal of Archaeology* for 1893 (pp. 335 foll.); and Stein, *Topographie des alten Sparta* (1890).

Sparta is said to have been founded by Lacedaemon, a son of Zeus and Taÿgeté, who married Sparta, the daughter of Eurotas, and called the city after the name of his wife. His son Amyclas is said to have been the founder of Amyclae, which was for a long time a more important town than Sparta itself. In the mythical period, Argos was the chief city in Peloponnesus, and Sparta is represented as subject to it. Here reigned Menelaüs, the younger brother of Agamemnon; and by the marriage of Orestes, the son of Agamemnon, with Hermioné, the daughter of Menelaüs, the two kingdoms of Argos and Sparta became united. The Dorian conquest of the Peloponnesus, which, according to tradition, took place thirty years after the Trojan War, made Sparta the capital of the country. Laconica fell to the share of the two sons of Aristodemus, Eurysthenes and Procles, who took up their residence at Sparta, and ruled over the kingdom conjointly. The old inhabitants of the country maintained themselves at Amyclae, which was not conquered for a long time. After the complete subjugation of the country we find three distinct classes in the population: the Dorian conquerors, who resided in the capital, and who were called Spartiatae or Spartans (see SPARTIATAE); the Perioeci or old Achaean inhabitants, who became tributary to the Spartans, and possessed no political rights; and the Helots, who were also a portion of the old Achaean inhabitants, but were reduced to a state of slavery. (See HELOTAE.) From various causes the Spartans became distracted by intestine quarrels, till at length Lycurgus, who belonged to the royal family, was

The Dromos at Sparta. (Restoration by Hoffmann.)

selected by all parties to give a new constitution to the State. The date of Lycurgus is uncertain; but it is impossible to place it later than B.C. 825.

The constitution of Lycurgus laid the foundation of Sparta's greatness; yet this constitution, traditionally ascribed to Lycurgus, is not to be regarded as wholly due to him. It represents the union of three distinct principles: the monarchical principle was represented by the kings, the aristocracy by the Senate, and the democratical element by the assembly of the people, and subsequently by their representatives, the ephors. The kings had originally to perform the common functions of the kings of the Heroic Age. They were high-priests, judges, and leaders in war; but in all of these departments they were in course of time superseded more or less. As judges they retained only a particular branch of jurisdiction, that referring to the succession of property. As military commanders they were to some extent restricted and watched by commissioners sent by the Senate; the functions of high-priest were curtailed least, perhaps because least obnoxious. In compensation for the loss of power, the kings enjoyed great honours, both during their life and after their death. The Senate (γερουσία) consisted of thirty members, one from each *obé* (ὠβά), all elected except the two kings, who were *ex officio* members, and represented each his own *obé*. In their functions they replaced the old council of the nobles as a sort of privy council to the kings, but their power was greater, since the votes of the kings were of no greater weight than those of other senators; they had the right of originating and discussing all measures before they could be submitted to the decision of the popular assembly; they had, in conjunction (later) with the ephors, to watch over the due observance of the laws and institutions; and they were judges in all criminal cases, without being bound by any written code. For all this they were not responsible, holding their office for life.

But with all these powers the elders formed no real aristocracy. They were not chosen either for property qualification or for noble birth. The Senate was open to the poorest citizen, who during sixty years had been obedient to the laws and zealous in the performance of his duties. The mass of the people—that is, the Spartans of pure Doric descent (see SPARTIATAE)—formed the sovereign power of the State. The popular assembly consisted of every Spartan of thirty years of age, and of unblemished character; only those were excluded who had not the means of contributing their portion to the *syssitia* (q. v.). They met at stated times to decide on all important questions brought before them, after a previous discussion in the Senate. They had no right of amendment, but only that of simple approval or rejection, which was given in the rudest form possible, by shouting. The popular assembly, however, had neither frequent nor very important occasions for directly exerting their sovereign power. Their chief activity consisted in delegating it; hence arose the importance of the ephors, who were the representatives of the popular element of the constitution. The five ephors answer in many points to the Roman tribunes of the people. Their appointment is included by Herodotus among the institutions of Lycurgus, but it is probable that Aristotle is right in dating these later, from the reign of Theopompus. (See EPHORI.) Their appointment was perhaps a concession to the people, at first as overseers of the markets and as magistrates who might check illegal oppression by kings or great men. Subsequently they absorbed most of the power in the State. To Lycurgus was ascribed also a prohibition to use written laws, or to have any coinage but iron: but these traditions must refer to later customs, since there were neither coins nor written laws in Greece as early as Lycurgus.

With reference to their subjects, the few Spartans formed a most decided aristocracy. On the conquest of Peloponnesus by the Dorians, part of the ancient inhabitants of the country, under name of the Perioeci (Περίοικοι), were allowed indeed to retain their personal liberty, but lost all civil rights, and were obliged to pay to the State a rent for the land that was left them. But a great part of the old inhabitants were reduced to a state of perfect slavery, different from that of the slaves of Athens and Rome, and more similar to the villanage of the feudal ages. These were called Helots (εἱλῶται). They were allotted, with patches of land, to individual members of the ruling class. They tilled the land, and paid a fixed rent to their masters, not, as Perioeci, to the State. The Spartans formed, as it were, an army of invaders in an enemy's country; their city was a camp, and every man a soldier. At Sparta the citizen only existed for the State; he had no interest but the State's, and no property but what belonged to the State. It was a fundamental principle of the constitution that all citizens were entitled to the enjoyment of an equal portion of the common property. This was done in order to secure to the commonwealth a large number of citizens and soldiers free from labour for their sustenance, and able to devote their whole time to warlike exercises, in order thus to keep up the ascendency of Sparta over her Perioeci and Helots. (See HELOTAE.) The Spartans were to be warriors, and nothing but warriors. Therefore, not only all mechanical labour was thought to degrade them; not only was husbandry despised and neglected, and commerce prevented, or at least impeded, by prohibitive laws and by the use of iron money; but also the nobler arts and sciences were so effectually stifled that Sparta is a blank in the history of the arts and literature of Greece. The State took care of a Spartan from his cradle to his grave, and superintended his education in the minutest points; and this was not confined to his youth, but extended throughout his whole life. The *syssitia*, or, as they were called at Sparta, *phiditia*, the common meals, may be regarded as an educational institution; for at these meals subjects of general interest were discussed and political questions debated. The youths and boys used to eat separately from the men, in their own divisions. See Jannet, *Les Institutions Sociales et le Droit Civil à Sparte* (2d ed. Paris, 1880).

Sparta gradually extended her sway over the greater part of the Peloponnesus. In B.C. 743 the Spartans attacked Messenia, and after a war of twenty years subdued this country, 723. In 685 the Messenians again took up arms, but at the end of seventeen years were again completely subdued; and their country from this time forward became an integral portion of Laconia. (See MESSENIA.) After the close of the Second Messenian War the Spartans continued their conquests in Peloponnesus. They defeated the Tegeans, and wrested the district of Thyreae from the Argives. At the time of the Persian invasion they were confessedly the first people in Greece, and to them was granted by unanimous consent the chief command in the war. But after the final defeat of the Persians the haughtiness of Pausanias disgusted most of the Greek States, particularly the Ionians, and led them to transfer the supremacy to Athens (477). From this time the power of Athens steadily increased, and Sparta possessed little influence outside of the Peloponnesus. The Spartans, however, made several attempts to check the rising greatness of Athens, and their jealousy of the latter led at length to the Peloponnesian War (431). (See PELOPONNESIAN WAR.) This war ended in the overthrow of Athens, and the restoration of the supremacy of Sparta over the rest of Greece (404). But the Spartans did not retain this supremacy more than thirty years. Their decisive defeat by the Thebans under Epaminondas at the battle of Leuctra (371) gave the Spartan power a shock from which it never recovered; and the restoration of the Messenians to their country two years afterwards completed the humiliation of Sparta. Thrice was the Spartan territory invaded by the Thebans, and the Spartan women saw for the first time the watch-fires of an enemy's camp. The Spartans now finally lost their supremacy over Greece, but no other Greek state succeeded to their power; and about thirty years afterwards the greater part of Greece was obliged to yield to Philip of Macedon. The Spartans, however, kept aloof from the Macedonian conqueror, and refused to take part in the Asiatic expedition of his son, Alexander the Great.

Under this later Macedonian king the power of Sparta declined still further. The simple institutions of Lycurgus were abandoned, and little by little luxury crept into the State. The number of citizens diminished, and the landed property became vested in a few families. Agis endeavoured to restore the ancient institutions of Lycurgus, but he perished in the attempt (240). Cleomenes III., who began to reign 236, was more successful. He succeeded in putting the ephors to death, and overthrowing the existing government (225); and he then made a redistribution of the landed property, and augmented the number of the Spartan citizens by admitting some of the Perioeci to this honour. His reforms infused new blood into the State, and for a short time he carried on war with success against the Achaeans. But Aratus, the general of the Achaeans, called in the assistance of Antigonus Doson, the king of Macedonia, who defeated Cleomenes at the decisive battle of Sellasia (221), and followed up his success by the capture of Sparta. Sparta now sank into insignificance, and was ruled by a succession of native tyrants, till at length it was compelled to abolish its peculiar institutions, and to join the Achaean League (q. v.). Shortly afterwards it fell, with the rest of Greece, under the Roman power.

See Müller, *The History and Antiquities of the Doric Race*, Eng. trans. 2 vols. (Oxford, 1830); Cox, *The Greeks and the Persians*, (New York, 1876); Jowett's translation of Thucydides (on the Peloponnesian War), with introduction, notes, and analysis, 2 vols. (New York, 1881); and the standard histories of Greece.

Spartăcus. The name of several kings of the Cimmerian Bosporus. (1) Succeeded the dynasty of the Archeanactidae in B.C. 438, and reigned until 431. He was succeeded by his son Seleucus. (2) Began to reign in B.C. 427, and reigned twenty years. He was succeeded in 407 by his son Satyrus. (3) Succeeded his father, Leucon, in B.C. 353, and died, leaving his kingdom to his son Parysades in 348. (4) Son of Eumelus, began to reign in B.C. 304, and reigned twenty years.

Spartăcus. A famous fighter, by birth a Thracian, and successively a shepherd, a soldier, and a chief of banditti. On one of his predatory expeditions he was taken prisoner, and sold to a trainer of gladiators. In B.C. 73 he was a member of the gladiatorial company of Lentulus, and was detained in his school at Capua, in readiness for the games at Rome. He persuaded his fellow-prisoners to make an attempt to gain their freedom. About seventy of them broke out of the training-school of Lentulus, and took refuge in the crater of Vesuvius. Spartacus was chosen leader, and was soon joined by a number of runaway slaves. These were blockaded by C. Claudius Pulcher at the head of three thousand men, but Spartacus attacked the besiegers and put them to flight. His numbers rapidly increased, and for two years (B.C. 73–71) he defeated one Roman army after another, and laid waste Italy, from the foot of the Alps to the southernmost corner of the peninsula. After both the consuls of the year 72 had been defeated by Spartacus, M. Licinius Crassus, the praetor, was appointed to the command of the war. Crassus carried on the contest with vigour and success; and, after gaining several advantages over the enemy, at length defeated them on the River Silarus in a decisive battle, in which Spartacus was slain. The character of Spartacus has been maligned by the Roman writers. Cicero compares the vilest of his contemporaries to him: Horace speaks of him (*Carm.* iii. 14, 19) as a common robber; none recognize his greatness, but the terror of his name survived to a late period of the Empire. Accident made Spartacus a shepherd, a freebooter, and a gladiator; nature formed him a hero. The excesses of his followers he could not always repress, and his efforts to restrain them often cost him his popularity. But he was in himself not less mild and just than he was able and valiant.

Spartea. See SOLEA (2).

Sparti (*σπαρτοί*, "the men sown"). The men in full armour who sprang up from the teeth of the dragon of Ares when sown by Cadmus. On their birth they immediately fought with one another, till only five remained. The survivors helped Cadmus to found Thebes, and were the ancestors of the Theban nobility. See CADMUS; THEBAE.

Spartiānus, Aelius. One of the *Scriptores Historiae Augustae,* lived in the time of Diocletian and Constantine, and wrote the biographies of several emperors. See AUGUSTAE HISTORIAE SCRIPTORES.

Spartiātae (*σπαρτιάται*). In Sparta the ruling class of those who had the full rights of citizens, as distinguished from the subject Perioeci (see PERIOECI) and Helots (see HELOTAE). They were the descendants of the Dorians, who had formerly conquered the land under the leadership of Aristodemus. As to the manner in which they were divided, see PHYLÉ. Their number is said never to have exceeded 10,000, and, as they were utterly opposed to the admission of foreign elements, it was constantly decreasing. At the time of the Persian Wars it still amounted to 8000, about B.C. 320 to little more than 1000.

They were called *ὅμοιοι* (men sharing equal rights), with reference to the equality established among them by the legislation of Lycurgus, (*a*) in their education, which was exclusively directed towards fitting them for service in war; (*b*) in their way of living, especially in the meals which they had in common (see SYSSITIA); (*c*) in their property; (*d*) and in their political rights.

To every family of Spartiatae an equal portion of land was assigned by Lycurgus, with a number of Helots who had settled upon it, who had to cultivate the property and deliver the produce to its possessor. The Spartiatae themselves were not allowed to engage in a handicraft, or in trade, or in agriculture; their whole life had to be devoted to the service of the State, and therefore they had their abode in Sparta itself. The allotted land and the Helots were accounted State property, and the possessors had no kind of right to dispose of them. Families which were dying out were preserved by adopting sons of families related to them, and similarly heiresses were married to men without inheritance of their own. If a family consisted of several male members, then the eldest was considered as head of the family, and had to support his brothers. The original equality of property came to an end, partly through the extinction of many families and the transference of their lot of ground, partly by the silent abrogation of the old law, which did not allow the Spartiatae to possess silver or gold, but chiefly after the law of Epitadeus, by which the free disposal of land was allowed, if not by sale, at least by gift during lifetime and by will. But the principle of aristocratic equality long continued in form; and only those who did not fulfil the conditions attached to the equality of rights, or who did not obey the injunctions of Lycurgus as to the education of the young, and as to the life of adult citizens, or who did not contribute to the common meals, suffered a diminution of their political rights. This involved exclusion from the government and administration of the State, as well as from the right of electing or being elected to office; but the punishment affected the individual only, and not his children, nor his position in personal law. See SPARTA.

Sparum. A spear used by the peasants as a weapon (Verg. *Aen.* xi. 682) and for hunting.

Specŭla. See article in the Appendix.

Speculātor. A scout or spy, of whom a special division was attached to each legion in the Roman army (Tac. *Hist.* i. 25). Under the Empire the *speculatores* were a body-guard or corps of adjutants attached to the person of the emperor (Tac. *Hist.* ii. 73; Sueton. *Calig.* 44).

Specŭlum (*ἔνοπτρον, κάτοπτρον*). For mirrors the ancients used round or oval, also square, plates of polished metal, generally of copper, mixed with tin, zinc, and other materials, and often silvered and gilded. In later times they were also made of massive silver, the finest being the work of Praxiteles in B.C. 328. They were often provided with a decorated handle and ornamented on the back with engravings, mostly of mythological objects. To keep them bright, a sponge with powdered pumice-stone was usually fastened to them (Plato, *Tim.*

Roman Mirror. (Caylus, *Recueil d'Antiq.* v. pl. 62.)

72 C). The best metallic mirrors were produced at Brundisium.

Glass mirrors were probably known in antiquity, consisting of a glass plate covered with a thin leaf of metal at the back (Pliny, *H. N.* xxxvi. 26). As thus prepared, however, they were not so good as the others, the modern backing of tinfoil and quicksilver being yet unknown.

The Etruscan mirrors are in some respects remarkably fine, the finest of all being represented below. Besides these hand-mirrors, there were also in the time of the emperors mirrors as high as a man (Sen. *Q. N.* i. 17; cf. Quintil. xi. 3, 68), which were either permanently fixed in the wall or (as in Vitruv. ix. 8, 2) let up and down like a sash.

Back of Etruscan Mirror. (Berlin Museum.)

Greek mirrors were unknown to archaeologists until 1867, when the first specimen was discovered at Corinth. In design they are even more beautiful than those of Etruria. They are of two kinds: (*a*) disc mirrors, like the Etruscan mirrors, and generally round, consisting of a single disc with a polished convex front, to reflect the face, and a concave back, ornamented with figures traced with the engraver's burin. This variety had a handle in the form of a statuette resting on a pedestal. (*b*) Another variety ("box-mirrors"), especially frequent in Greece, consists of two metallic discs, one enclosed within the other, and sometimes held together by a hinge. The cover was externally ornamented with figures in low-relief, and was internally polished and silvered to reflect the face. The second disc, forming the body of the case, was decorated internally with figures engraved with a sharp point. In the British Museum is a mirror from Corinth, representing Pan playing at the game of "Five Stones" with a Nymph attended by Eros. There is no mention of mirrors in Homer; and the oldest Greek mirrors now extant do not antedate the sixth century B.C. See Blümner, *Technologie*, iv. pp. 192, 194, 265 foll., 403; E. Gerhard, *Etruskische Spiegel* (Berlin, 1843); and De Witte, *Les Miroirs chez les Anciens* (Brussels, 1873).

Speos Artemĭdos. See PEOS ARTEMIDOS.

Spercheūs (Σπερχειός). Now Elladha; a river in the south of Thessaly, which rises in Mount Tymphrestus, runs in an easterly direction through the territory of the Aenianes and through the district Malis, and falls into the innermost corner of the Sinus Maliacus. As a river-god, Spercheus is a son of Oceanus and Gaea, and the father of Menesthius by Polydora, the daughter of Peleus (*Il.* xvi. 174; xxiii. 142; Pausan. i. 37, 2).

Spes. The Roman personification of hope, especially of hope for a good harvest, and (in later times) for the blessing of children. There were several temples to Spes in Rome, the oldest dating from B.C. 354 (Livy, xxiv. 47). She was represented as a youthful figure, moving along lightly in a long robe, which was raised a little in her left hand, while her right bore a bud, either closed or just about to open, denoting especially her tutelage of gardens. In the course of time she came to be usually considered as a goddess of the future, invoked at births and marriages, and on similar occasions. On the legend of the Greek goddess of Hope (Ἐλπίς), see PANDORA.

Speusippus (Σπεύσιππος). An Athenian philosopher, son of Eurymedon and Potoné, a sister of Plato. He accompanied his uncle, Plato, on his third journey to Syracuse, where he displayed considerable ability and prudence. He succeeded Plato as president of the Academy, but was at the head of the School for only eight years (B.C. 347–339). He wrote several works, all of which are lost, in which he developed the doctrines of his great master.

Sphacteria. See PYLOS.

Sphaera (σφαῖρα). A ball. See PILA.

Sphaeria (Σφαιρία). Now Poros; an island off the coast of Troezen, in Argolis, and between it and the island of Calauria (Pausan. ii. 33, 1).

Sphaeristerium (σφαιριστήριον). A court for the game of ball in the gymnasia and thermae. Σφαιριστική was the name of the art of playing at ball. See PILA.

Sphaeromachia (σφαιρομαχία). See PILA.

Sphaerus (Σφαῖρος). A Stoic philosopher, who studied first under Zeno of Citium, and afterwards under Cleanthes. He lived at Alexandria during the reigns of the first two Ptolemies. He also taught at Lacedaemon, and was believed to have had considerable influence in moulding the character of Cleomenes. He was in repute among the Stoics for the accuracy of his definitions. He was the author of several works, all of which are lost.

Sphendălé (Σφενδάλη). A deme of Attica belonging to the tribe Hippothoöntis. It was on the frontier of Boeotia.

Sphendŏné (σφενδόνη). A fastening for the hair of the Greek women. See COMA, p. 388.

Sphettus (Σφηττός). A deme of Attica near the silver-mines of Sunium. It belonged to the tribe Acamantis.

Sphinx (Σφίγξ, "the throttler"). A monster borrowed from Egyptian religion and symbolism, originally represented with the body of a winged lion and the breast and head of a human being, and subsequently in still more wonderful forms, as a man or woman with the breast, feet, and claws of a lion, the tail of a serpent, and the wings of a bird; or as a lion in front and a human being behind, with vulture's claws and eagle's wings. The Egyptian sphinxes are oftener male rather than female, and the Great Sphinx was intended to represent the god Hor-em-

Winged Sphinx of Greek Art. (From a fragment of pottery found at Daphnae. Drawing by Petrie.)

The Great Egyptian Sphinx. (From a photograph by Flinders Petrie.)

khu or Horus. It is older than the Fourth Dynasty, which began about B.C. 3700.

According to Hesiod, Sphinx was the daughter of the Chimaera and Orthrus; according to others, of Echidna and Typhon. Heré (or, according to others, Ares or Dionysus), in anger at the crimes of Laïus, sent her to Thebes from Ethiopia. She took up her abode on a rock near the city and gave every passer-by the well-known riddle, "What walks on four legs in the morning, on two at noon, and on three in the evening?" She flung from the rock all who could not answer it. When Oedipus explained the riddle rightly, as referring to man in the successive stages of infancy, the prime of life, and old age, she flung herself down from the rock. See OEDIPUS.

Spike. See CLAVUS.

Spina. (1) Now Spinazzino; a town in Gallia Cispadana, in the territory of the Lingones, on the most southerly of the mouths of the Padus (Po), which was called after it Ostium Spineticum. (2) Now Spino; a town in Gallia Transpadana, on the river Addua.

Spinning. See TELA.

Spinther (σφιγκτήρ). A coil bracelet worn by women on the left arm (Festus, s.h.v.). It was made of gold (Plaut. *Men.* iii. 3, 7).

Spira (σπεῖρα), dim. SPIRŬLA. (1) The base of a column, a member not existing in the Doric order, but always present in the Ionic and Corinthian. A special kind of base was called the Attic (Ἀττικουργές), it being really a variety of the Ionic. (2) A kind of cracker or cake made in a spiral form, like a sort of cruller (Cato, *R. R.* 77).

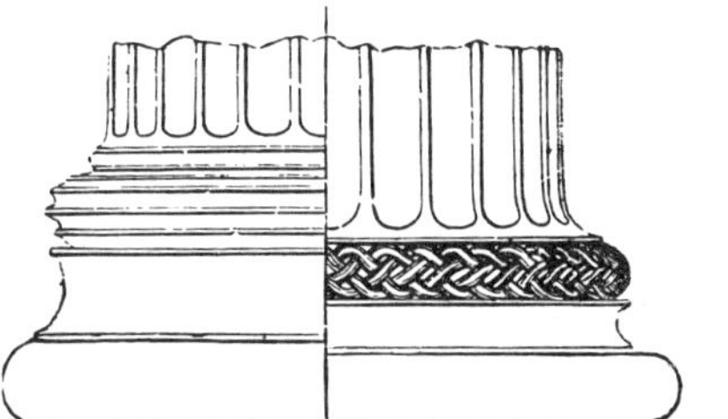

Spirae of Two Columns. (Left-hand figure from the Temple of Panops [Ionic] on the Ilissus; right-hand figure from the Temple of Athené Polias at Athens.)

Spit. See VERU.

Spithămé (σπιθαμή). A span; in Greek measurement, three quarters of a foot.

Splenium (σπλήνιον). A sort of court-plaster made of white linen or leather, and worn in patches on the face to conceal any defect or scar; and perhaps, as in modern times, to heighten the fairness of the complexion (Mart. ii. 29, 10; viii. 33).

Spoils of War. See SPOLIA.

Spolātum. See SALONA.

Spoletium or **Spolētum.** Now Spoleto; a town in Umbria, on the Via Flaminia, colonized by the Romans B.C. 242. It suffered severely in the wars between Marius and Sulla.

Spolia. The Roman term for the arms taken from an enemy defeated in single combat, and also for those portions of the captured armour which were promised by the general to soldiers who distinguished themselves. The word is not greatly different in meaning from *exuviae*, while *praeda* covers all kinds of booty, and *manubiae* is properly the part that falls to the commanding general. They were hung up in a temple, with a dedicatory inscription (Verg. *Aen.* iii. 288), or in the vestibule of the house, where they remained, even if the house passed into other hands. SPOLIA OPĪMA were the arms taken from the hostile general by a Roman leader commanding under his own auspices, and were consecrated to Iupiter Feretrius on the Capitol. This is said to have been first done by Romulus, who is the traditional founder of the sanctuary of Feretrius (Livy, i. 10). They were legitimately won on only two subsequent occasions by Aulus Cornelius Cossus from the king of Veii, and by M. Claudius Marcellus from the king of the Gaesatae (Plut. *Marc.* 8).

Sponda (ἐνήλατον). Any one of the four bars of the frame of a bedstead (*lectus*) to which the

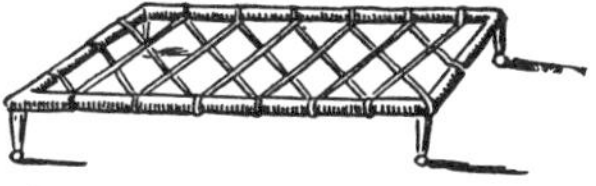

Lectus, showing Spondae. (Rich.)

cords supporting the mattress were affixed (Petron. *Sat.* 97).

Sponsa, Sponsus, and **Sponsalia.** See MATRIMONIUM.

Spoons. See COCLEAR.

Sporădes (Σποράδες). A group of scattered islands in the Aegaean Sea, off the island of Crete and the western coast of Asia Minor, so called in opposition to the Cyclades, which lay in a circle around Delos. See Tozer, *Islands of the Aegean* (1890).

Sport. See Ludi; Venationes.

Sporta (σπυρίς). A basket, plaited, and with a small flat bottom. See Sportula.

Sporta. (Naples Museum.)

Sportella (σπυρίδιον), dim. of *sporta.* A small basket in which cakes and other dainties were passed at table (Suet. *Domit.* 4).

Sportŭla, dim. of *sporta,* "a basket." Originally the portion of food given in a basket by the Roman patron to his clients who paid a ceremonial call (*salutatio*) in the morning. This was the equivalent of the invitation to a regular dinner (*cena recta*), which, under the Republic, the clients used from time to time to receive. Later, instead of giving food, a sum of money was substituted, generally a hundred *quadrantes* (about a dollar). Hence the word *sportula* ultimately came to mean this dole of money. For a lively picture of the scene at one of these distributions, see Juv. iii. 294 foll., with Mayor's note; cf. also the articles Clientes; Salutatio.

Spuma. A sort of pomade used by the Germans and Gauls, and imported into Rome. It was made of goat's tallow and beech-wood ashes, and was supposed to give a brownish tinge to the hair (Mart. xiv. 26; viii. 33, 20). See Sapo.

Spur. See Calcar.

Spurinna Vestritius. The haruspex who on the day of Caesar's assassination warned him to beware of the Ides of March (Sueton. *Iul.* 81). See Caesar.

Spurīnus, Q. Petillius. A Roman who was Praetor Urbanus in B.C. 181, in which year the books of King Numa Pompilius are said to have been discovered upon the estate of one L. Petillius. Spurinus obtained possession of the books, and upon his representation to the Senate that they ought not to be read and preserved, the Senate ordered them to be burned. (See Numa.) Spurinus was consul in B.C. 176, and fell in battle against the Ligurians.

Spy. See Speculator.

Squib. See Libellus.

Stabiae. Now Castellamare di Stabia; an ancient town in Campania, between Pompeii and Surrentum, which was destroyed by Sulla in the Social War, but which continued to exist down to the great eruption of Vesuvius in A.D. 79, when it was overwhelmed along with Pompeii and Herculaneum. It was at Stabiae that the elder Pliny perished. See Pompeii.

Stable. See Stabulum.

Stabŭlum (σταθμός). (1) A halting-place or posting-station. (2) A stable for horses, whence *stabularius* is a livery-stable keeper (Apul. *Met.* i. p. 13). (3) A pen for sheep or goats. (4) An aviary. (5) A stock-pond for fish (Columell. viii. 17, 7). See Piscina. (6) =πανδοκεῖον. A low inn (Petron. 6). See Caupona.

Stadium (στάδιον). The course for foot-races among the Greeks; the usual length of it was 600 Greek feet (625 Roman feet or 606 ft. 9 in. English), a measure which Heracles, according to the myth, had appointed for the course at Olympia (see Olympia). Subsequently this became the standard unit for measuring distances; and when doubled formed the δίαυλος, when quadrupled the ἱππικόν, and when multiplied by 6, 7, 8, 12, 20, or 24, the δόλιχος. On both of the longer sides of the course were natural or artificial elevations with terraced seats for the spectators. At one end there was generally a semicircular space especially intended for wrestling, and this was the place for the umpires. Near this was the pillar which marked the goal. The starting-point was also sometimes indicated by a pillar at the other end, which was originally straight, and in later times curved like the end near the goal. For the different kind of races, see Circus; Hippodromus.

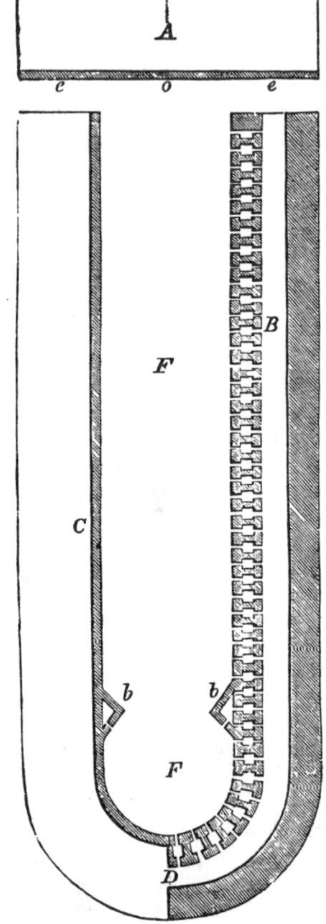

Stadium at Ephesus. (Krause.)

(A, boundary wall; B C, the sides; F F, the area; *b b*, pieces of masonry; *e e*, the entrances; from *o* to *p* is the length of an Olympic stadium.)

Staff. See Baculum; Sceptrum; Scipio.

Stage. See Theatrum.

Stagīrus (Στάγειρος), subsequently **Stagīra** (τὰ Στάγειρα). Now Stavro; a town of Macedonia, in Chalcidicé, on the Strymonic Gulf, and a little north of the isthmus which unites the promontory of Athos to Chalcidicé. It was a colony of Andros, was founded B.C. 656, and was originally called Orthagoria. It is celebrated as the birthplace of Aristotle, who in English literature is often spoken of as "the Stagirite."

Stair. See Gradus; Scalae.

Stalagmium. An ear-ring with one or more drops (σταλάγματα) of gold, beads, or precious stones (Festus, s. h. v.). See Inauris.

Stall. See STABULUM.

Stamen (στήμων). A spun thread. See TELA.

Standards, MILITARY. See LABARUM; SIGNUM; VEXILLUM.

Stannum. See METALLUM.

Stasīnus (Στασῖνος). Of Cyprus; an epic poet, to whom some of the ancient writers attributed the poem of the Epic Cycle, entitled *Cypria*, and embracing the period antecedent to the *Iliad*. See CYCLICI POETAE; HOMERUS.

Stata Mater. An Italian goddess who gave protection in cases of fires and conflagrations (see VULCANUS; Cicero, *De Leg.* ii. 28; *C. I. L.* vi. 763–766); she is sometimes identified with Vesta.

Stater (στατήρ, from ἵστημι, lit. "a standard" coin). (1) The principal gold coin of Greece. The Attic stater of gold, a gold piece of two gold *drachmae* = twenty silver *drachmae* = $3.25 in intrinsic value of silver. To the same standard of currency belonged the Macedonian gold stater first struck by Philip II. and Alexander the Great. (2) The silver stater is a term applied in later times to the Athenian tetradrachm, of four silver *drachmae* (= $0.60 in intrinsic value). See NUMISMATICS.

Macedonian Stater. (British Museum.)

Statēra. A steelyard, an instrument of later invention than the balance (*libra*). Its parts were the yard (*scapus*), divided into fractional parts by points (*puncta*), and suspended by a hook or chain (*ansa*). The sliding weight was called *aequipondium*. See Vitruv. x. 3, 4; and LANCULA; LIBRA.

Statielli, Statiellātes, or Statiellenses. A small tribe in Liguria, south of the Padus (Po), whose chief town was Statiellae Aquae (Acqui) on the road from Genua to Placentia.

Statilia Messalīna. See MESSALINA.

Statilius Taurus. See TAURUS.

Stationery. See CHARTA; PALAEOGRAPHY; PAPYRUS; WRITING AND WRITING MATERIALS.

Statiōnes. See CASTRA.

Statīra (Στάτειρα). (1) The wife of Artaxerxes II., king of Persia. She was poisoned by Parysatis, the mother of the king. (2) The sister and wife of Darius III., celebrated as the most beautiful woman of her time. She was taken prisoner by Alexander, together with her mother-in-law Sisygambis, and her daughters, after the battle of Issus, B.C. 333. They were all treated with the utmost respect by the conqueror; but Statira died shortly before the battle of Arbela, B.C. 331. (3) Also called Barsiné, elder daughter of Darius III. See BARSINÉ.

Statius Murcus. See MURCUS.

Statius, P. PAPINIUS. A Roman poet born at Neapolis about A.D. 61. He was the son of a distinguished grammarian, and accompanied his father to Rome, where the latter acted as the preceptor of Domitian, who held him in high honour. Under the skilful tuition of his father, the young Statius speedily rose to fame, and became peculiarly renowned for the brilliancy of his extemporaneous effusions, so that he gained the prize three times in the Alban contests; but having, after a long career of popularity, been vanquished in the quinquennial games, he retired to Neapolis, the place of his nativity, along with his wife Claudia, whose virtues he frequently commemorates. He died about A.D. 96. His chief work is the *Thebaïs*, an heroic poem, in twelve books, on the expedition of the Seven against Thebes. On the composition of this poem Statius spent twelve years. There is also extant a collection of his miscellaneous poems (thirty-two in number, mostly in hexameters) in five books, under the title of *Silvae;* and an unfinished poem called the *Achilleïs*. Statius may justly claim the praise of standing in the foremost rank among the heroic poets of the Silver Age; and in the Middle Ages he was much read (cf. Dante, *Purg.* xxi.). The *editio princeps* of the epics appeared in 1470; that of the *Silvae* in 1472. The best editions of the *Thebaïs* are those of Kohlmann (1844) and O. Müller (bks. i.–vi., 1870); of the *Achilleïs* by Kohlmann (Leipzig, 1884); of the *Silvae* by Markland (1728), Hand (Leipzig, 1817), and Bährens (Leipzig, 1876).

Statonia. A town in Etruria, and a Roman praefectura, on the river Albinia, and on the Lacus Statoniensis.

Stator. A public official who attended the Roman magistrates in the provinces. They seem to have been employed chiefly as messengers (Cic. *Ad Fam.* ii. 17; x. 21).

Stator (from *stare*). A Roman surname of Iupiter, describing him as staying the Romans in their flight from an enemy, and generally as preserving the existing order of things.

Statua (ἀνδριάς). A statue of a man, as distinguished from *signum*, the statue of a deity (Plaut. *Bacch.* iv. 3, 1; Cic. *In Pis.* 38).

Statuaria Ars; Sculptūra. The origin of painting as an art in Greece is connected with definite historical personages; but that of sculpture is lost in the mists of legend. Its authentic history does not begin until about the year B.C. 600. It was regarded as an art imparted to men by the gods; for such is the thought expressed in the assertion that the earliest statues fell from heaven. Some early application of taste and skill to plastic art may be indicated in the mythical stories respecting the Idaei Dactyli (q. v.) and the Telchines of Rhodes (Ovid, *Met.* vii. 365), who were reported to have worked in iron and bronze. (See TELCHINES.) The first artist spoken of by name, Daedalus (q. v.), who is mentioned as early as Homer, is merely a personification of the most ancient variety of art, that which was employed solely in the construction of wooden images of the gods. (See DAEDALA; DOKANA.) This is clearly proved by his name (= δαίδαλος, "the cunning artificer"). To him were attributed a series of inventions certainly separated far from each other in respect of time and place, and embracing important steps in the development of wood-carving and in the representation of the human form. Thus he is said to have invented the saw, the axe, the plummet, the gimlet, and glue (Pliny, *H. N.* vii. 198), to have been the first to open the eyes in the statues of the gods, to separate the legs, and to give freer motion to the arms, which before had hung close to the body (Diod. iv. 76). After him the early school of sculptors at Athens, his reputed native city, is sometimes called the school of Daedalus (Pausan. v. 25, 13). During a long residence in Crete he is said to have instructed the Cretans in the art of making wooden images (ξόανα) of the gods (ib. viii. 53, 8).

The invention of modelling figures in clay, from which sculpture in bronze originated, is assigned to the Sicyonian potter Butades at Corinth (Pliny, *H. N.* xxxv. 151). The art of working in metals must have been known early in Greece, as appears from the Homeric poems (e. g. *Il.* xviii. 468–608). An important step in this direction was due to Glaucus of Chios, who, in the seventh century B.C., invented the soldering of iron (σιδήρου κόλλησις, Herod. i. 25; Pausan. x. 16, 1) and the softening and hardening of metal by fire and water (Plut. *De Def. Or.* 47). The discovery of bronze-founding is attributed to Rhoecus and Theodorus of Samos about 580 (Pausan. viii. 14, 8). The high antiquity of Greek sculpture in stone may be inferred from a work of the very earliest period of Greek civilization—the powerful relief of two upright lions over the gate of the castle at Mycenae. See MYCENAE, p. 1068.

Archaic Relief from Sparta. (Reber.)

Sculpture in marble, as well as in gold and ivory, was much advanced by two famous pupils of Daedalus, Dipoenus and Scyllis of Crete, who were working in Argos and Sicyon about B.C. 550 (Pliny, *H. N.* xxxvi. 9, 14; Pausan. ii. 15, 22), and founded an influential school of art in the Peloponnesus, which included Hegylus and Theocles, Dontas and Doryclidas, Clearchus of Rhegium, Tectaeus and Angelion. Among their works are recorded not only statues of gods, but also of heroes, often united in large groups. Some conception of the artistic productions of this period may be formed from scattered monuments still extant, originating in different parts of the Greek world: e. g. the rude and more primitive metopes of Selinus in Sicily; the statues of Apollo from the island of Thera and from Tenea, near Corinth; and the reliefs on the Harpy Monument (q. v.) from the acropolis of Xanthus in Lycia. These works, in spite of their archaic stiffness, show an effort after individual and natural expression, though the position of the foot in striding, with the sole completely touching the ground, and the unemotional and stony smile on the mask-like face, are common to all. Even after Greek sculpture had mastered the representation of the human body, not only at rest, but also in the most violent movement, it still continued unable to overcome the lifeless rigidity of facial expression. This is seen in the Trojan battle-scenes (about B.C. 480) on the Aeginetan pediments. Here the figures are represented in every variety of position in the fight, and depicted, not indeed with any ideality, but with perfect mastery, even to the smallest detail; whereas the faces are entirely destitute of any expression appropriate to their situation. The athletic forms in which the Aeginetan heroes are represented indicate another important extension of the sphere of artistic representation. From about B.C. 544 it had become usual to erect statues of the victors in the athletic contests, Olympia especially abounding in these (Pausan. vi. 18, 7); the statues there mentioned are of wood. By this innovation the art was freed from the narrow limits to which it had been confined by the traditions of religion, and led on to a truer imitation of nature. In this department the school of Aegina was specially active, attaining its highest perfection in the bronze statuary of Glaucias, Callon, and, above all, Onatas (B.C. 500–460).

Metope Relief from the Acropolis at Selinus. (Athenê, Perseus, Medusa, Pegasus.)

Sculpture in bronze flourished simultaneously in the Peloponnesus at Sicyon under Canachus (for a supposed copy of his Apollo, see CANACHUS) and his brother, Aristocles, the founder of a school which lasted long after, and at Argos under Ageladas, the teacher of Phidias, Myron, and Polyclitus. The transition to the period of the finest art is represented by Calamis of Athens, Pythagoras of Rhegium, and especially Myron, another Athenian, in whom the art attained the highest truth to nature, with perfect freedom in the representation of the human body, and was thus prepared for the development of ideal forms.

Central Figures of the West Gable, Aegina.

This last step was taken at Athens, in the time of Pericles, by Phidias. In his creations, particularly in his statues of the gods, whether in bronze or in ivory and gold, he succeeded in combining perfect beauty of form with the most profound ideality, fixing forever the ideal type for Zeus and Athené, the two deities who were pre-eminently characterized by intellectual dignity. See Waldstein, *The Art of Pheidias* (1880); and the articles ATHENÉ; PARTHENON; PHIDIAS; ZEUS.

Of the pupils of Phidias the two who worked most nearly in the same spirit were Agoracritus and Alcamenes, the author of the sculpture of the western pediment of the Temple of Zeus at Olympia, part of which still remains. The perfection of Attic art at this time can be realized when we consider that, with all their beauty of execution, the extant marble sculptures of the Parthenon, Theseum, Erechtheum, and the Temple of Niké Apteros must be regarded as mere productions of the ordinary workshop when compared with the lost masterpieces of Phidias. The school of Phidias had rivals in the naturalistic school which followed Myron, including his son, Lycius, and Cresilas of Cydonia. Independent of both schools stood Paeonius of Mendé, whose Niké, as well as part of his sculptures on the eastern pediment of the Temple of Zeus at Olympia, is still extant (see OLYMPIA), and Callimachus, the

Copy of the Athené Parthenos. (Marble statuette at Athens.)

so-called inventor of the Corinthian order of architecture (Vitruv. iv. 1, 10) and of the application of the auger to working in marble (Pausan. i. 26, 6). Another school of sculpture in opposition to that of Athens was founded at Argos by Phidias's younger contemporary, Polyclitus, whose colossal gold and ivory statue of the Argive Heré directly challenged comparison with the works of Phidias in its materials, its ideality, and its artistic form, and established the ideal type of that goddess. He mainly devoted himself, however, to work in bronze, the department in which Argos had long been pre-eminent; and made it his aim to exhibit the perfection of beauty in the youthful form. He also established a *κανών* or scheme of the normal proportions of the body. Of his pupils the chief was Naucydes of Argos. See POLYCLITUS.

As in the first period of Greek sculpture, represented by Myron, Phidias, and Polyclitus, the schools of Athens and Argos held the first rank beyond dispute, so it was also in the second period, which embraces the fourth century down to the death of Alexander the Great. Athens, moreover, during this period remained true to the traditions of Phidias, and still occupied itself mainly with the ideal forms of gods and heroes, though in a spirit essentially altered. The more powerful emotions, the more deeply stirred passions of the period after the Peloponnesian War, were not without their influence on art. The sculptors of the time abandoned the representation of the dignified divinities of the earlier school, and turned to the forms of those deities whose nature gave room for softer or more emotional expression, especially Aphrodité and Dionysus and the circle of gods and dæmons who surrounded them. The highest aim of their art was to portray the profound pathos of the soul, to give expression to the play of the emotions. With this is connected the preference of this school for marble over bronze, as more suited for rendering the softer and finer shades of form or expression. The art of executing work in gold and ivory was almost lost, the resources of the States no longer sufficing, as a rule, for this purpose. The most eminent of the New Attic School were Scopas of Paros and Praxiteles of Athens. Scopas, also famous as an architect, was a master of the most elevated pathos. Praxiteles was no less masterly in regard to the softer graces in female or youthful forms, and in the representation of sweet moods of dreamy reverie. In his statues of Aphrodité at Cnidus and Eros at Thespiae he established ideal types for those divinities. The Hermes with the infant Dionysus, found at Olympia, remains as a memorial of his art. Of the productions of this school (in which the names of Bryaeus, Leochares, and Timotheus, who was joined with Scopas in his work on the Mausoleum at Halicarnassus, ought also to be mentioned) an opinion may be formed from the spirited reliefs on the Choragic Monument of Lysicrates (q. v.) at Athens. We have also extant, in a copy, the Niobid group (see NIOBÉ), concerning the original of which it was much disputed, even in ancient times, whether the author were Scopas or Praxiteles (Pliny, *H. N.* xxxvi. 28). In contrast to the ideal aims of Attic art, the Sicyonian School still remained true to its early naturalistic tendencies and to the art of sculpture in bronze, of which Argos had so long been the home. At the head of the school stood one of the most influential and prolific artists of antiquity, Lysippus of Sicyon. His efforts were directed to represent beauty and powerful development in the human body. Hence Heracles, as the impersonation of human physical strength, was portrayed by him oftener, and with more success, than any other deity, and his type fully established. Lysippus was most prolific as a portrait sculptor, a branch of art which had been much advanced in the invention by his brother Lysistratus of the method of taking plaster casts of the features (Pliny, *H. N.* xxxv. 153).

After Alexander the Great the practice of the art, which had thus developed to perfect mastery of technique, began to deteriorate with the general decay of the countries of Greece proper, and to give place to the flourishing artistic schools of Asia Minor and the neighbouring islands. The characteristic of this period is the rise of a method of treatment which strives after effect. Instead of the simplicity of earlier times we get a certain deliberate calculation of a theatrical type, a tendency to make the exhibition of technical skill an end in itself. The most productive school was that of Rhodes, at the head of which stood a pupil of Lysippus, Chares of Lindus, who designed the famous Colossus of Rhodes, the largest statue of ancient times. Two well-known extant works in marble proceeded from this school, the group of Laocoön (q. v.) and his sons, by Agesander, Athenodorus, and Polydorus, found at Rome in 1506, now one of the chief treasures of the Vatican Museum, and the Farnese Bull at Naples. This last group, by

Apollonius and Tauriscus of Tralles, represents the revenge of Zethus and Amphion on Dircé (see illustration, p. 86), and is the largest extant antique work which consists of a single block of marble. Both these are admirable in skill and technique, embodying with the greatest vividness the wild passions of a moment of horror; but the theatrical effect and the exhibition of technical skill are unduly exaggerated. To the Rhodian School is conjecturally assigned the fine group representing Menelaüs bearing the body of Patroclus, several imperfect copies of which are still extant. It is sometimes, however, regarded as one of the later products of the same school as the group of Niobé, and assigned to the early part of the third century B.C.

Hermes of Praxiteles. (From the Heraeum at Olympia.)

The second in rank of the schools of this period was that at Pergamum, where the sculptors Isogonus, Phyromachus, Stratonicus, and Antigonus celebrated in a series of bronze statues the victories of the kings Eumenes I. (263–241) and Attalus I. (241–197) over the Gauls. There are still extant, at Venice, Rome, and Naples, single figures from a magnificent offering of Attalus, which stood on the Acropolis at Athens, and consisted of groups of figures illustrating the conflict between the gods and the Giants, the battle of the Athenians and Amazons, the fight at Marathon, and the destruction of the Gauls by Attalus. Other masterpieces of the school are the work popularly called the "Dying Gladiator," now identified as a Gallic warrior, who has just stabbed himself after a defeat, and the group in the Villa Ludovisi, called "Pætus and Arria," which really represents a Gaul killing his wife and himself. But the most brilliant proof of their powers is furnished by the reliefs of the battle of the Giants from the acropolis at Pergamum.

Ancient Sculptor Modelling a Bust. (From a gem.)

This work, brought to light by Humann in 1878, and now at Berlin, is among the most important artistic products of antiquity. (See PERGAMENE SCULPTURES.) To this period may also be referred with certainty the original of the celebrated Belvedere Apollo, which probably had reference to the rescue of the Temple of Delphi from the Gallic army in B.C. 280, which was supposed to be the work of the god (see illustration, p. 99).

To Greek art in Egypt belong the types of Isis and Harpocrates, and the fine reclining figure of the river-god Nilus, with sixteen boys playing round him (see illustration, p. 1098).

The artistic activity of the kingdom of the Seleucidae in Syria is represented by Eutychides, a pupil of Lysippus, and his famous "Tyché," a work in bronze representing the presiding destiny of the city of Antioch on the Orontes (Pausan. vi. 2, 6).

After the subjugation of Greece by the Romans in the middle of the second century, Rome became the headquarters of Greek artists, whose work, though without novelty in invention, had many excellences, especially in perfect mastery of technique. Of the artists of the first century B.C. and the early imperial times the following are worthy of mention: Apollonius of Athens (Belvedere torso of Hercules at Rome), Glycon (Farnese Hercules at Naples [see illustration, p. 793]), and Cleomenes (the "Venus de' Medici" at Florence [see p. 367]), though the works of all these are more or less free reproductions of the creations of earlier masters; also Agasias of Ephesus, sculptor of the so-called "Borghese Gladiator" (really an athlete) in the Louvre at Paris, a very fine work in the spirit of the Pergamene School. (See illustration, p. 734.)

In the same period Pasiteles, an Italian Greek of great versatility, attempted a regeneration of art on the basis of careful study of nature and of earlier productions. This movement in favour of an academic eclecticism was continued by Pasiteles' pupil, Stephanus, who has left us a youthful figure (in the Villa Albani), and Stephanus's pupil, Menelaüs, the artist of the fine group called "Orestes and Electra." There was a revival of Greek art in the first half of the second century A.D. under Hadrian, when a new ideal type of youthful beauty was created in the numerous representations of the imperial favourite Antinoüs.

The artistic work of the Romans before the introduction of Greek culture was under Etruscan influence. The art of that people was chiefly displayed in pottery and the closely connected craft

Antinous. (Bust in the British Museum.)

of bronze-founding, which they developed with great technical skill and for which they had a special predilection. They not only filled their towns with quantities of bronze statues, Volsinii alone containing about 2000 at the time of its conquest by the Romans in B.C. 265 (Pliny, *H. N.* xxxiv. 34), but provided Rome also for a long time with works of the kind. Judging from the extant monuments, such as the "Mars of Todi" in the Vatican, the "Boy with a Goose under his Arm" at Leyden, and the "Robed Statue of Aulus Metellus" at Florence, the character of their art seems wanting in freedom of treatment and in genuine inspiration. After the conquest of Greece, Greek art took the place of Etruscan at Rome; and, thanks to the continually increasing love of magnificence among the Romans, which was not content with the adornment of public buildings and squares, but sought artistic decoration for private dwellings, a great activity in art was developed, whereof numberless extant works give evidence. Besides the Greek influence, to which we owe many copies of the masterpieces of Greek art gradually accumulated in Rome, a peculiarly Roman art arose. This was especially active in portrait sculpture.

Portrait statues were divided, according as they were in civil or military costume, into *togatae* and *loricatae* or *thoracatae* (*lorica* = θώραξ, a coat of mail). To these were added in later times the so-called *Achilleae*, idealized in costume and pose (Pliny, *H. N.* xxxiv. 8, 118). It was customary to depict emperors in the form of Iupiter or other gods, and their wives with the attributes of Iuno or Venus. Of the innumerable monuments of this description special mention is due to the statue of Augustus in the Vatican (see illustration, p. 170); the marble equestrian statues of Balbus and his son at Naples, found at Herculaneum; the bronze equestrian statue of M. Aurelius on the square of the Capitol at Rome; the seated statues of Agrippina the Elder in the Capitoline Museum, and the younger Agrippina at Naples.

Hand in hand with portrait sculpture went the art of historical reliefs. In accordance with the realistic spirit of Rome, as opposed to the Greek custom of idealizing persons and events, this department strove to secure the greatest possible accuracy and truth. The most important works of the kind are the reliefs on the Arch of Titus; those on the Arch of Constantine, taken from the Arch of Trajan (see ARCUS TRIUMPHALIS); and those on the columns of Trajan and M. Aurelius.

Marble Equestrian Statue of the Younger Balbus. (Naples Museum.)

(See illustration under ARCHITECTURA.) Roman historical sculpture is seen already on its decline in the reliefs of the Arch of Septimius Severus (A.D. 203), and the decline is complete in those of the Arch of Constantine. A subordinate branch of relief sculpture was employed on the *sarcophagi* common from the second century A.D. The subjects of these reliefs are rarely taken from events in the man's actual life; they are most usually scenes from legends of Greek gods or heroes, often after compositions of an earlier period, and accordingly showing a Greek character in their treatment.

White marble was the material chiefly employed in statuary: in the earlier times of Greek art, the local kinds, in Attica particularly the Pentelic, which is "fine in grain and of a pure white." From the fourth century on that of Paros was preferred. This is a very beautiful marble, though of a strongly crystalline grain; it is slightly translucent. It was used in Roman times in preference to the similar marble of Luna (Carrara), a "marble of many qualities, from the purest white and a fine sparkling grain, like loaf-sugar, to the coarser sorts disfigured with bluish-gray streaks." It was sometimes used for columns in Rome. The marble of Hymettus "appears to have been the first foreign marble introduced into Rome. It resembles the inferior kind of Luna marble, being rather coarse in grain and frequently stained with gray striations." Coloured marble first became popular under the emperors—e. g. black for Egyptian subjects (statues of Isis), red for Dionysus, Satyrs, and others in his train. To the same period belongs the use of striped and spotted kinds of marble, coloured alabaster, porphyry, and granite. Different colours of stone were also combined—e. g. the drapery of black marble or porphyry.

A noteworthy peculiarity of ancient sculpture, as also of architecture, is the habit of embellishing all kinds of marble work by the application of colours (Polychromy), which is known from references in ancient writers. Plato (*Rep.* 420 C) speaks of "painting statues." Plutarch (*De Gloria Athen.* 348 F) mentions "dyers" of statues side by side with gilders and encaustic painters. Lastly, Pliny (*H. N.* xxxv. 133) states that Praxiteles owned he was much indebted to the *circumlitio*, or touching-up, of his works by the painter Nicias. It is also attested by traces still present on many works. Thus the statues at Pompeii, especially those of late date, are in many cases coloured, especially certain parts of the drapery. A painting found at Pompeii introduces us into the studio of a female artist engaged in embellishing with paint a terminal statue of Hermes. The original sketch in colours lies on the ground, and she is pausing to examine her work, which is also watched with interest by two bystanders. Wood and pottery were always painted. Even sculptures intended for the adornment of buildings—e. g. metopes and friezes—not only had painted backgrounds (generally blue or red), but were themselves richly adorned with colouring. It is also held that originally even the bare parts of stone figures were painted; afterwards a coating of wax was thought enough (Vitruv. vii. 9). In particular statues, many artists coloured only the characteristic parts, fringes of garments, sandals, armour, weapons, snoods or head wrappings, and of the parts of the body, the lips, eyes, hair, beard, and nipples. Probably the cheeks, too, received a light reddish tinge; but all was done with discretion. The colours chiefly used were red, blue, and yellow, or gilding. The employment of different materials for the extremities and for the drapery also produced the effect of colouring. Similarly metal-

Relief from Column of Trajan.

sculpture secured variety of colour by the application of gold, silver, and copper to the bronze. The sparkle of the eyes was often represented by inlaid precious stones or enamel. Particular parts in marble statues, such as attributes, weapons, implements, were also made of metal. There are examples of this in the pediments of Aegina and in the frieze of the Parthenon. Under the Empire metal was sometimes used for the drapery. Thus the Braschi Antinoüs in the Vatican was formerly draped in bronze. On ancient stone-cutting, see GEMMA; on terra-cottas, see FICTILÉ; on working in metal, see CAELATURA.

BIBLIOGRAPHY.—See, for the general history of ancient sculpture, Lübke, *History of Sculpture*, Eng. trans. vol. i. (London, 1872); Upcott, *An Introduction to Greek Sculpture* (Oxford, 1887); Perry, *Greek and Roman Sculpture* (London, 1882); Mitchell, *A History of Ancient Sculpture* (New York, 1883); Overbeck, *Geschichte der griechischen Plastik* (Leipzig, 1882); Murray, *History of Greek Sculpture* (London, 1884); Brunn, *Geschichte der griechischen Künstler* (2d ed. Stuttgart, 1889); Collignon, *Greek Archaeology* (Eng. trans. 1886); Paris, *La Sculpture Antique* (Paris, 1888; Eng. trans. London, 1890); Loewy, *Inschriften griechischen Bildhauer* (Leipzig, 1885); Detlefsen, *De Arte Romana Antiquissima* (Glückst. 1888); St. Lami, *Dictionnaire des Sculpteurs de l'Antiquité* (Paris, 1884); Treu, *Sollen Wir unsre Statuen bemalen?* (Berlin, 1884); Böckel, *Die Polychromie in d. Antiken Sculptur* (1882); and Gardner, *Handbook of Greek Sculpture* (New York, 1896).

The technical part of sculpture is described in Blümner's *Technologie und Terminologie der Gewerbe und Künste bei Griechen und Römern*, 4 vols. (Leipzig, 1875–87). Beautiful reproductions of ancient plastic works are given in Furtwängler's *Masterpieces of Greek Sculpture* (N. Y. 1895); and in Brunn's *Denkmäler griechischer und römischer Sculptur*, published in parts. For the ancient sources of our information regarding Greek sculpture, etc., see Overbeck's *Schriftquellen zur Geschichte der bildenden Künste* (Leipzig, 1868); and H. S. Jones, *Ancient Writers on Greek Sculpture* (London, 1895).

Stelé. (Street of the Dead, Athens.)

Statute. See LEX.

Steam-Engine. See HERO.

Steel. See CHALYBES; METALLUM.

Stega (στέγη). Properly a Greek word signifying the deck of a ship, which the Romans called *constratum navis* (Plaut. *Bacch.* ii. 3, 44).

Stelé (στήλη). An upright tablet or slab of stone. At Athens such tablets were set up in a public place, especially on the Acropolis. Laws, decrees, treaties, etc., as well as sentences of punishment against defaulters were engraved upon them, and thus made publicly known. The use of stelae for funeral monuments was common in all Greek countries. In earlier times they are narrow and thin slabs of stone, slightly tapering towards the top, which is crowned either with *anthemia* (decorations of flowers and leaves), or with a small triangular pediment ornamented with rosettes. The shorter but broader stelé, crowned with a pediment, is later than the other kind. Many such stelae resemble small shrines or chapels. Besides the inscription referring to the dead, they often bear representations of them in relief, as in the famous monument to Dexileos, B.C. 390, near the Dipylum at Athens. From the stelae, many important Greek inscriptions have been recovered, on which see EPIGRAPHY.

Stelé from the Acropolis of Mycenae. (Reber.)

Stemma (στέμμα). (1) Properly a garland or wreath bound with fillets of wool and worn as a chaplet. (See CORONA; INFULA.) (2) A long scroll decorated with garlands and bearing a list of the family names. It was hung upon the ancestral busts that stood in their cases or niches (*aediculae*) in the *atrium* of the Roman house. (See IMAGINES.) Whence (3) a pedigree or family tree (Juv. viii. 1).

Stenography. See NOTAE.

Stentor (Στέντωρ). A herald of the Greeks in the Trojan War, whose voice was as loud as that of fifty other men together, so that his name has become proverbial for any loud-voiced person (*Il.* v. 783; Juv. xiii. 112).

Stentŏris Lacus. See HEBRUS.

Stenyclārus (Στενύκληρος). A town in the north of Messenia, which was the residence of the Dorian kings of the country (Herod. ix. 64).

Step. See GRADUS.

Stephănos (στέφανος). (1) A garland. (See

CORONA). (2) A metal band for the forehead, like a diadem. See COMA.

Stephănus, the Latinized form of ESTIENNE, in English sometimes absurdly called STEPHENS. The name of a celebrated family of printers, publishers, and classical scholars (descended from a noble Provençal family), found settled at Paris towards 1500 in the person of HENRY, who is supposed to have been born about 1470, and died in 1520. In Paris Henry carried on the business of printer and bookseller for upwards of twenty years. In 1526 ROBERT, his second son, born 1503, is found in possession of the business. Every year of Robert's life is marked by the issue from his printing-press of several volumes, many of them masterpieces of art, and all of them surpassing anything of the kind previously seen in France. He was at once printer, publisher, commentator, and author. In 1532 he published a Latin dictionary (*Thesaurus Linguae Latinae*) which for two centuries remained the standard work. He also published editions of several classical authors and numerous Latin grammars. His Bible of 1545, and his Greek Testament of 1549, each drew down upon him a religious prosecution; and though the prosecutions failed legally, they were disastrous to his private fortune. Having first sent his family to Geneva, he followed them there in 1549. Robert, his second son, shortly afterwards returned to Paris, where he resumed his father's business.

The second HENRY, born at Paris in 1528, succeeded his father, Robert, on his death in 1559. Though Henry possessed the same literary industry and ability as his father, he was unfortunately deficient in his father's practical turn of mind. Devoted to his art and to his calling, he seems to have been utterly wanting in worldly prudence. In two years we find that he had revised and published more than 4000 pages of Greek text, including some twenty *editiones principes;* while at the same time he was writing his *Apologia pro Herodoto* (1566)—a work of formidable length and learning. Rendered nervous and irritable by an overworked brain, and by pecuniary difficulties, travelling, originally undertaken from literary curiosity, grew into a necessity of his life, and he visited England, the Netherlands, and Italy, examining classical manuscripts and making the acquaintance of distinguished scholars. In 1572 appeared his great Greek lexicon (*Thesaurus Linguae Graecae*), in five folio volumes, on which he spent nearly his whole fortune (last reprint by Didot, 9 vols. [Paris, 1831–65]). In 1578 he visited Paris, where for several years he became a hanger-on of the court of Henry III., who bestowed upon him a pension, which the state of the royal exchequer rendered merely nominal. Quitting Paris, he wandered in poverty over Europe, his own family often ignorant of where he was to be found. He died at Lyons in 1598. Great as a publisher and commentator, Henry Estienne does not seem to have possessed much power as an original thinker, but his mastery of Greek seems to have been almost complete, and as a critic of the French language he is still esteemed in France. The traditions of the family were kept up by PAUL (1566–1627) and ANTOINE (1592–1674). See Feugère, *Caractères et Portraits Littéraires du XVI. Siècle* (Paris, 1864); also article in *Quarterly Review* (London, April, 1865); Bernard, *Les Estiennes* (Paris, 1856); Renouard, *L'Imprimerie des Étiennes* (Paris, 1843); and the paper in Pattison's *Essays* (Oxford, 1889).

Stephănus (Στέφανος). (1) An Athenian comic poet of the New Comedy, probably the son of Antiphanes, some of whose plays he is said to have exhibited. (2) Of Byzantium, the author of the geographical lexicon entitled *Ethnica* (Ἐθνικά), of which unfortunately we only possess an epitome. Stephanus was a grammarian at Constantinople, and lived after the time of Arcadius and Honorius, and before that of Justinian II. His work was reduced to an epitome by a certain Hermolaüs, who dedicated his abridgment to the emperor Justinian II. According to the title, the chief object of the work was to specify the gentile names derived from the several names of places and countries in the ancient world. But, while this is done in every article, the amount of information given went far beyond this. Nearly every article in the epitome contains a reference to some ancient writer, as an authority for the name of the place; but in the original, as we see from the extant fragments, there were considerable quotations from the ancient authors, besides a number of very interesting particulars, topographical, historical, mythological, and others. Thus the work was not merely what it professed to be, a lexicon of a special branch of technical grammar, but a valuable dictionary of geography. How great would have been its value to us, if it had come down to us unmutilated, may be seen by any one who compares the extant fragments of the original with the corresponding articles in the epitome. These fragments, however, are unfortunately very scanty. The best editions of the epitome of Stephanus are by Dindorf, 4 vols. (Leipzig, 1825); Westermann (Leipzig, 1839); and Meineke (Berlin, 1849). See Geffcken, *De Stephano Byzantio* (1886).

Sterculius, Stercutius, or **Sterquilīnus.** A Roman deity presiding over the manuring of fields. (See INDIGITAMENTA). He is by some identified with Picumnus (Serv. *ad* Verg. *Aen.* ix. 4; Isidor. *Orig.* iv. 11).

Stern of a Ship. See PUPPIS.

Sterŏpé (Στερόπη). One of the Pleiads, wife of Oenomaüs and daughter of Hippodamia. See PLEIAS.

Sterŏpes. See CYCLOPES.

Stesichŏrus (Στησίχορος). A celebrated Greek poet of Himera in Sicily, contemporary with Sappho, Alcaeus, Pittacus, and Phalaris. He is said to have been born B.C. 632, to have flourished about 608, and to have died in 552 at the age of eighty. Of the events of his life we have only a few obscure accounts. As with other great poets, his birth is fabled to have been attended by an omen; a nightingale sat upon the babe's lips, and sang a sweet strain. He is said to have been carefully educated at Catana, and afterwards to have enjoyed the friendship of Phalaris, the tyrant of Agrigentum. Many writers relate the fable of his being miraculously struck with blindness after writing an attack upon Helen, and recovering his sight when he had composed a Palinodia or recantation. He is said to have been buried at Catana by a gate of the city, which was called after him the Stesichorean Gate. Stesichorus was one of the nine chiefs of lyric poetry recognized by the ancients. He stands, with Alcman, at the head of one branch of the lyric art, the choral poetry of the Dorians. He was the first to break the monotony of the strophe and antistrophe by the introduction of the epode, and his metres were much more varied, and the structure of his strophes more elaborate, than those of Alcman. His odes contained all the essential elements of the perfect choral poetry of Pindar and the tragedians. The subjects of his poems were chiefly heroic; and he transferred the subjects of the old epic poetry to the lyric form, dropping, of course, the continuous narrative, and dwelling on isolated adventures of his heroes. He also composed poems on other subjects, and fables, among the latter the well-known one of the horse, the stag, and the man (Arist. *Rhet.* ii. 20). His extant remains may be classified under the following heads: (1) mythical poems; (2) hymns, encomia, epithalamia, paeans; (3) erotic poems, and scolia; (4) a pastoral poem, entitled *Daphnis;* (5) fables; (6) elegies. The dialect of Stesichorus was Dorian, with an intermixture of the epic. The best editions of his fragments are those by Kleine (Berlin, 1828), and by Bergk in his *Poetae Lyrici Graeci* (4th ed. 1878). On the dialect, see Holsten, *De Stesichori Dialecto* (1884); and Mucke, *De Dialecto Stesichori cum Pindar. Comparata* (1879).

Stesimbrŏtus (Στησίμβροτος), of Thasos, a rhapsodist and historian in the time of Cimon and Pericles, who is mentioned with praise by Plato and Xenophon (Plato, *Ion*, p. 550; Xen. *Mem.* iv. 2, 10). He wrote a work on Homer, the character of which is not known. See Heuer, *De Stesimbroto Thasio* (1863).

Steward. See DISPENSATOR; PROCURATOR; VILICUS.

Stheneboea (Σθενέβοια), called **Antēa** by many writers, was a daughter of the Lycian king Iobates, and the wife of Proetus. See BELLEROPHONTES.

Sthenĕlus (Σθένελος). (1) The son of Perseus and Andromeda, king of Mycenae, and husband of Nicippe, by whom he became the father of Alcinoë, Medusa, and Eurystheus. (2) The son of Androgeos, and grandson of Minos. He accompanied Heracles from Paros on his expedition against the Amazons, and, together with his brother Alcaeus, he was appointed by Heracles ruler of Thasos. (3) The son of Actor, likewise a companion of Heracles in his expedition against the Amazons. (4) The son of Capaneus and Evadnê, was one of the Epigoni, by whom Thebes was taken, and commanded the Argives under Diomedes in the Trojan War, being the faithful friend and companion of Diomedes. (5) The father of Cycnus, who was metamorphosed into a swan. Hence we find the swan called by Ovid *Stheneleïa volucris* and *Stheneleïa proles.* (6) A tragic poet, contemporary with Aristophanes, who attacked him in the *Wasps.*

Stheno. See GORGONES.

Stibadium. A circular dining-couch adapted to a round table (*orbis*). The same as the *sigma* (q. v.). (See Mart. xiv. 87.)

Stigma (στίγμα). Literally a mark made by puncturing (from στίζω). In general a brand or mark pricked or stamped upon an object, as on the forehead of a slave (Petron. 103). For theft the letter F (*fur*) was the usual brand, but sometimes the whole word was branded on, or even a sentence descriptive of the offence (Petron. l. c.). The name was also given to a mark pricked into the arm of conscripts for the army (Veget. *Mil.* i. 8; ii. 5) after they had been received and passed, the object being identification. The same thing was done to labourers employed in the State's factories (Imp. Zeno, *Cod.* xlii. 10).

Stigma. An old character of the Greek alphabet. See ALPHABET.

Stilĭcho. The son of a Vandal leader, who became one of the most distinguished generals of Theodosius I., on whose death (A.D. 395) he became the real ruler of the West under the emperor Honorius. It was he who defeated Alaric at the battle of Pollentia (403) and thus saved the Western Empire from the Visigoths. In 405 he won a great victory over Radagaisus, who had led a host of barbarians into Italy. His importance as a soldier is seen in the fact that only three months after his death, Alaric and his hosts were thundering at the gates of Rome. He was put to death at Ravenna in 408 (Zosim. bks. iv., v.).

Stillicidium. One of the SERVITUTES (q. v.).

Stilo, LUCIUS AELIUS PRAECONĪNUS. A celebrated Roman grammarian, one of the teachers of Varro and Cicero. He was one of the aristocratic party, and accompanied Q. Metellus Numidius into exile in B.C. 100. He was the author of commentaries on the *Axamenta* or songs of the Salian priests (see SALII), on the Twelve Tables, and of a work called *De Proloquiis.* To him has also by some been ascribed the pseudo-Ciceronian treatise *Ad Herennium.* From his eminence as a grammarian he was styled *philologus.* See PHILOLOGIA.

Stilpo (Στίλπων). A celebrated philosopher, who was a native of Megara, and taught philosophy in his native town. He is said to have surpassed his contemporaries in inventive power and dialectic art, and to have inspired almost all Greece with a devotion to the ethical Megarian philosophy, dwelling especially upon the conception of virtue and its consideration (Diog. Laërt. ii. 113–118; Sen. *Epist.* 9).

Stilts. See GRALLAE.

Stilus and (incorrectly) **Stylus** (γραφίς, γραφεῖον). (1) An iron, bronze, bone, or ivory instrument, the shape and size of a modern pencil, used by the ancients for writing upon wax tablets. One end was made sharp for this purpose, while the other was blunt and round for obliterating what had been written. Hence *vertere stilum* means "to erase" and "to correct." Another name for the stilus was *graphium,* and the case in which it was carried was called *graphiarium.* See illustration under GRAPHIUM. (2) A sharp stake or spike placed in pitfalls in front of an intrenchment to embarrass the approach of an enemy. See MUREX.

Stimŭla. The Latin name of Semelé, according to the pronunciation of the Romans; but probably also a native deity, one of the Indigetes, presiding over the incitements to love and passion (August. *De Civ. Dei,* iv. 11).

Stimŭlus (κέντρον). A goad or prick used in driving cattle, etc. It consisted of a stick with a sharp iron point in one end (Columell. ii. 2, 26).

Stipendiarii. See STIPENDIUM.

Stipendium (from *stips* and *pendo*). The pay of a Roman soldier. Originally each tribe had to contribute the necessary means to provide for its contingent. It was only at the beginning of the war against Veii in B.C. 404 that payment of a sum by the State was introduced. This was given to the soldiers, either before or after the campaign, as compensation for the cost of their living during its continuance. When this had gradually become a regular payment, it grew customary, in making it, to deduct everything which the State had provided for the army in the way of clothing, arms, and food; but under the Empire maintenance was given free. In the time of Polybius the pay of legionaries was 120 *denarii* ($20); of centurions twice, and of knights three times that amount. Caesar increased it to 225 *denarii* ($37.50) for a legionary, Domitian to 300 ($50). The praetorians received under Tiberius 720 *denarii* ($120). See EXERCITUS; PRAETORIANI.

Stipendium is also the name of the fixed normal tax imposed on conquered provinces, which might consist of money, or produce, or both (see PROVINCIA). During the Republic, when a country was conquered, this was usually fixed according to the amount of the existing taxes, and the country divided into fiscal districts, and the officials of the chief places in each compelled to pay in the portion which fell to them. Under Augustus the taxes were for the first time fixed upon the basis of a measurement of the ground occupied, and of a computation of property (*census*). The stipendium was either a ground-tax (*tributum soli*) or a personal tax (*tributum capitis*), which was partly a poll-tax, partly a property-tax, partly a tax on the trade carried on by the individual. In exceptional cases special taxes were also imposed. Those bound to pay the *stipendium* were called *stipendiarii*.

See Mommsen, *Staatsverwaltung*, v. pp. 90 foll.; Dureau de la Malle, *Économie Politique des Romains*, i. pp. 134 foll.; and Mommsen, *Die römische Tribus*, pp. 131 foll.

Stipes (στύπος). A round stake driven into the ground as a landmark (Ovid, *Fast.* ii. 642), or as a convenient place for hanging things upon, as the helmets of soldiers, etc., in camp (Suet. *Nero*, 29). The word was also used as a term of reproach, like our "blockhead."

Stiva (ἐχέτλη). The handle of a plough. See ARATRUM.

Stoa (στοά). The Greek term for a colonnade, such as those built outside or inside temples, around dwelling-houses, gymnasia, and market-places. They were also set up separately as ornaments of the streets and open places. The simplest form is that of a roofed colonnade, with a wall on one side, which was often decorated with paintings. Thus in the market-place at Athens the στοὰ ποικίλη (Painted Colonnade) was decorated with Polygnotus's representations of the destruction of Troy, the fight of the Athenians with the Amazons, and the battles of Marathon and Oenoe. The στοὰ βασίλειος, also in the market-place, in which the Archon Basileus sat as judge, was probably divided longitudinally into three parts by two rows of columns, and was the pattern for the Roman *basilica* (q. v.). Zeno of Citium taught in the στοὰ ποικίλη, and his adherents accordingly obtained the name of Stoics. See STOICI.

Among the Romans similar colonnades attached to other buildings, or built out in the open, were called *porticus*. They were named from the neighbouring edifices (e.g. *porticus Concordiae*, close to the Temple of Concord); from their builders (e.g. *porticus Pompeia*); also from the pictures set up in them (e.g. *porticus Argonautarum*); and from the business chiefly carried on in them, as *porticus Argentaria*, the hall of the money-changers. These halls were the chief places for public intercourse among the ancients. See PORTICUS.

Stobaeus, IOANNES (Ἰωάννης ὁ Στοβαῖος). A Greek writer of uncertain date (probably about A.D. 500), who derived his surname apparently from being a native of Stobi in Macedonia. Of his personal history we know nothing. Stobaeus was a man of extensive reading, in the course of which he noted down the most interesting passages; and to him we are indebted for a large proportion of the fragments that remain of the lost works of the early Greek poets and prose-writers to the number of 500. His work, which was a sort of anthology, was originally a single one, but in course of time was divided into two, each having two subdivisions—*Eclogae Physicae et Ethicae*, which is edited by Gaisford (1850) and Meineke (1860–64); and the *Anthologion* or *Florilegium*, edited by Gaisford (1822–25), Meineke (1856–57), and Wachsmuth and Hense, 3 vols. (Berlin, 1884–94).

Stobi (Στόβοι). A town of Macedonia, and the most important place in the district Paeonia, was probably situated on the river Erigon, north of Thessalonica, and northeast of Heraclea. It was made a Roman colony and a municipium, and under the later emperors was the capital of the province Macedonia II. or Salutaris.

Stockade. See VALLUM.

Stocking. See FASCIAE.

Stoechădes Insulae (Στοιχάδες Νῆσοι). Now Îles d'Hyères. A group of five small islands in the Mediterranean, off the coast of Gallia Narbonensis, and east of Massilia.

Stoeni. A Ligurian people, in the Maritime Alps, conquered by Q. Marcius Rex in B.C. 118.

Stoïci (Στοικοί). The adherents of a school of philosophy (Stoicism) founded by Zeno of Citium about A.D. 310. They derived their name from the Painted Stoa (στοὰ ποικίλη) in Athens, in which Zeno lectured. The Stoic teaching was one of stern morality, the principle being "a life in accordance with nature and controlled by virtue." It was an ascetic system, teaching perfect indifference (ἀπάθεια) to everything external, for nothing external could be either good or evil. Hence to the Stoics both pain and pleasure, poverty and riches, sickness and health, were supposed to be equally unimportant (see STOA). For further details, see Zeller, *Stoics, Epicureans, and Skeptics* (London, 1869); Ravisson, *Essai sur le Stoicisme* (Paris, 1852); Capes, *Stoicism* (London, 1880); and the articles PHILOSOPHIA; ZENO.

Stola. (From a painting in the Thermae of Titus.)

Stola. The outer garment worn by Roman matrons above the *tunica intima* or chemise (Petron. 81). It was longer than the body, slit open at the top on either side and fastened together by clasps, while below it was provided with a border (*instita*) woven on to it, and was gathered up below the breast by a girdle so as to form broad falling folds (*rugae*). It had either no sleeves or half-sleeves, according as the under-tunic had or had not half-sleeves. For the garb of women unmarried or in disgrace, see TOGA. Under the Empire the stola fell gradually out of use. After the fourth century A.D. there appears in its stead the *dalmatica* (q.v.), worn by men and women, which was a kind of tunic with sleeves. In Greek, the corresponding term *στολή* is used as a general word for any kind of robe, whether for men or for women.

Stool. See SCABELLUM.

Stores. See TABERNA.

Storia and **Storea.** A mat made of rushes, used for a covering (Caes. *B. C.* ii. 9).

Stove. See CAMINUS; FOCUS.

Strabo. A cognomen in many Roman *gentes*, signifying a person who squinted, and accordingly classed with the name Paetus (q.v.), though the latter word did not indicate such a complete distortion of vision as Strabo.

Strabo (*Στράβων*). A celebrated geographer, a native of Amasia in Pontus. The date of his birth is unknown, but may perhaps be placed about B.C. 63. He lived during the whole of the reign of Augustus, and during the early part, at least, of the reign of Tiberius. He is supposed to have died after A.D. 21. He received a careful education. He studied grammar under Aristodemus at Nysa in Caria, and philosophy under Xenarchus of Seleucia in Cilicia and Boethus of Sidon. He lived some years at Rome, and also travelled much in various countries. We learn from his own work that he was with his friend Ælius Gallus in Egypt in B.C. 24. He wrote an historical work (Ἱστορικὰ Ὑπομνήματα) in forty-three books, which is lost. It began where the history of Polybius ended, and was probably continued to the battle of Actium. He also wrote the work on Geography (Γεωγραφικά), in seventeen books, which has come down to us entire, with the exception of the seventh, of which we have only a meagre epitome.

Strabo's work, according to his own expression, was not intended for the use of all persons. It was designed for all who had had a good education, and particularly for those who were engaged in the higher departments of administration. Consistently with this view, his plan does not comprehend minute description, except when the place or the object is of great interest or importance; nor is his description limited to the physical characteristics of each country; it comprehends the important political events of which each country has been the theatre, a notice of the chief cities and the great men who made them illustrious; in short, whatever was most characteristic and interesting in every country. His work forms a striking contrast with the geography of Ptolemy, and the dry list of names, occasionally relieved by something added to them, in the geographical portion of the *Historia Naturalis* of Pliny. It is, in short, a book intended for reading, and it may be read; a kind of historical geography. Strabo's language is generally clear, except in very technical passages and in those where the text has been corrupted; it is appropriate to the matter, simple, and without affectation. The first two books of Strabo are an introduction to his Geography, and contain his views on the form and magnitude of the earth, and other subjects connected with mathematical geography. In the third book he begins his description: he devotes eight books to Europe, six to Asia, and the seventeenth and last to Egypt and Libya.

The *editio princeps* appeared at Venice in 1516. The best editions of Strabo are by Casaubon (Geneva, 1587), reprinted by Falconer (Oxford, 1807); by Koray (Paris, 1815); by Kramer, 3 vols. (Berlin, 1844–52); by Müller and Dübner (1853–56); and by Meineke (1866–77). There is a fine translation into French in 5 vols. made by command of Napoleon I. (Paris, 1805–19), with valuable notes. An English version is that of Hamilton and Falconer, 3 vols. (1854–57). Tozer's English edition of selections from Strabo (Oxford, 1893) has an excellent introduction. See also Bunbury's *History of Ancient Geography*, ii. pp. 209 foll., and Dubois, *Examen de la Géographie de Strabo* (Paris, 1891).

Strabo, Fannius. (1) GAIUS, consul B.C. 161 with M. Valerius Messala. In their consulship the rhetoricians were expelled from Rome. (2) GAIUS, son of the preceding, consul 122. He owed his election to the consulship chiefly to the influence of C. Gracchus, who was anxious to prevent his enemy Opimius from obtaining the office. But in his consulship Fannius supported the aristocracy, and took an active part in opposing the measures of Gracchus. He spoke against the proposal of Gracchus, who wished to give the Roman franchise to the Latins, in a speech which was regarded as a masterpiece in the time of Cicero. (3) GAIUS, son-in-law of Laelius, and frequently confounded with the preceding. He served in Africa, under Scipio Africanus, in B.C. 146, and in Spain under Fabius Maximus in 142. He is introduced by Cicero as one of the speakers both in his work *De Republica* and in his treatise *De Amicitia*. He owed his celebrity in literature to his History, which was written in Latin, and of which Brutus made an abridgment.

Strabo, SEIUS. See SEIANUS.

Stragŭlum (*στρῶμα*). A general term for a covering; but usually a blanket or coverlet for a bed (Cic. *Tusc.* v. 21). The word also means the horse-blanket or saddle-cloth on a horse or pack-animal (Mart. xiv. 86).

Stratēgus (*στρατηγός*). A general; an office and title most common in the democratic States of Greece, such as Athens, Tarentum, Syracuse, Argos, and Thurii. When the tyrants of the Ionic cities in Asia Minor were deposed by Aristagoras, he established *στρατηγοί* in their places as chief magistrates. At Athens they were instituted by Clisthenes when he remodelled the constitution (see CLISTHENES), and they assumed the duties previously discharged by the king or the Archon Polemarchus. They were ten in number, and were chosen by the vote (*χειροτονία*) of the people, one from each tribe. Before entering on their duties they passed an examination (*δοκιμασία*) as to their character; and no one was eligible for the office unless he had legitimate children and landed property in Attica. They had command of military expeditions and in general the direction of all that related to the conduct of wars, including the equipment of the forces. In levying the troops they were aided by the taxiarchs. (See TAXIARCHI.) They even collected the taxes levied for warlike purposes and managed the funds set apart for such objects. In lawsuits arising from these questions the strategi presided. They appointed each year the persons who were to serve as trierarchs (see TRIERARCHIA); and in cases of emergency they could summon special assemblies of the whole people. In the field it was usual for only three of them to be sent out at one time, but at Marathon all ten of them held command in turn. With them was associated the Archon Polemarchus (see ARCHON), and in the council of war his vote was equal to that of any of the strategi.

The name στρατηγός was also given to the chief of the Achaean League (see ACHAEAN LEAGUE), and to those of the Aetolian League (see AETOLICUM FOEDUS).

See Gilbert, *Greek Constitutional Antiquities*, pp. 230 foll., Eng. trans. (1895); a paper by Droysen in *Hermes*, vol. ix. (1875); K. F. Hermann, *Lehrbuch der griechischen Antiquitäten*, i. §§ 123, 129, 148, 152, 166; and the article EXERCITUS, p. 649.

Stratŏcles (Στρατοκλῆς). An Athenian orator, and a friend of the orator Lycurgus. He was a virulent opponent of Demosthenes, whom he charged with having accepted bribes from Harpalus. Stratocles especially distinguished himself by his extravagant flattery of Demetrius.

Straton (Στράτων). The son of Arcesilaüs of Lampsacus. He was a distinguished Peripatetic philosopher, and the tutor of Ptolemy Philadelphus. He succeeded Theophrastus as head of the school in B.C. 288, and, after presiding over it eighteen years, was succeeded by Lycon. He devoted himself especially to the study of natural science, whence he obtained the appellation of *Physicus* (Diog. Laërt. v. 58).

Stratonīcé (Στρατονίκη). The daughter of Demetrius Poliorcetes and Phila, the daughter of Antipater. In B.C. 300, at which time she could not have been more than seventeen years of age, she was married to Seleucus, king of Syria. Notwithstanding the disparity of their ages, she lived in harmony with the old king for some years, when it was discovered that her stepson Antiochus was deeply enamoured of her, and Seleucus, in order to save the life of his son, which was endangered by the violence of his passion, gave up Stratonicé in marriage to the young prince (Plut. *Demetr.* 31, 32, 38).

Stratonicēa (Στρατονίκεια). Now Eski-Hisar; one of the chief inland cities of Caria, built by Antiochus I. Soter, who fortified it strongly, and named it in honour of his wife Stratonicé. It stood east of Mylasa and south of Alabanda, near the river Marsyas, a southern tributary of the Maeander. Under the Romans it was a free city.

Stratōnis Turris. See CAESAREA.

Strator (ἀναβολεύς). An equerry who attended the consul or praetor in time of war, and under the Empire was attached to the person of the emperor. The office is the historical original of the position of Master of Horse in modern courts (Ulp. *Dig.* i. 16, 4).

Stratus (Στράτος). Now Lepenu or Lepanon, the chief town in Acarnania, ten stadia west of the Acheloüs. Its territory was called STRATĬCÉ.

Streets. See PLATEA; VIA.

Strenae. Gifts which it was customary for the Romans to make at the new year with accompanying good wishes. The word is connected with the name of a Sabine tutelary goddess, Strenia, who corresponds to the Roman Salus, and from whose precinct beside the Via Sacra at Rome consecrated branches were carried up to the Capitoline at the new year. The strenae consisted of branches of bay and of palm, sweetmeats made of honey, and figs or dates, as a good omen that the year might bring only joy and happiness (Ovid, *Fasti*, i. 185–190). The fruits were gilded (Martial, viii. 33, 11) as they are now in Germany; and the word, as well as the custom, survives in the French *étrennes.* Pieces of money, especially the ancient *as*, with the image of Ianus, who was especially honoured on this day, were also sent as presents, as well as small lamps of terra-cotta or bronze stamped with a motto and with minute representations of the usual gifts. Clients in particular were in the habit of complimenting their patrons with such presents; and, during and after the time of Augustus, the emperors benefited considerably by this custom, which lasted till the fifth century, although abolished several times by special edict (Sueton. *Aug.* 57 and 91; *Calig.* 42). It was discouraged by the Christian Fathers as being connected with the worship of a heathen goddess.

Striga (στρίγλα). A witch; a sorceress. The word is derived from *strix* (στρίξ), "a screech-owl," a creature believed by the ancients to suck the blood of young children (Plaut. *Pseud.* iii. 2, 31; Pliny, *H. N.* xi. 39, 95). There are many passages in classical literature that show the belief in witches to have been widespread. The most famous of ancient witch-stories are those in Petronius 63, where night-hags carry off a young boy and leave a manikin in his place; and in the *Metamorphoses* of Apuleius (bk. i. ad init.), where is an extremely gruesome tale, of considerable length, put into the mouth of a commercial traveller whose friend Socrates had been bled to death by witches. Horace (*Sat.* i. 8) relates the incantations of a number of sorceresses who dig up the bones of the dead in the cemetery on the Esquiline, and recall by their weird rites the famous scene in *Macbeth.* In the Fifth Epode is a still longer and very dramatic picture of witches burying a boy alive, so as to use his heart and liver in the preparation of magic potions. Cf. also Tibullus, i. 5; Ovid, *Fast.* vi. 133 foll.; and Fest. p. 314 Müll. The word VENEFĬCA (γυνὴ φαρμακίς) is also used of a witch; SAGA (q. v.) means a fortune-teller, not necessarily malignant.

Strigil. A flesh-scraper. See BALNEAE, pp. 193, 194.

Stringed Instruments. See CITHARA; LYRA; SAMBUCA.

Stroma. See STRAGULUM.

Stromăta. See CLEMENS ALEXANDRINUS.

Strombichĭdes (Στρομβιχίδης). An Athenian admiral in the Peloponnesian War (Thucyd. viii. 15, 30–40, 60–79).

Strongўle. See NAXOS.

Strongylion (Στρογγυλίων). A distinguished Greek statuary who flourished during the last thirty or forty years of the fifth century B.C. and was famous for his statues of horses and oxen (Pausan. ix. 30, 1).

Strophădes (Στροφάδες) **Insŭlae**, formerly called PLOTAE. Now Strofadia and Strivali. Two islands in the Ionian Sea, off the coast of Messenia and south of Zacynthus. The Harpies were pursued to these islands by the sons of Boreas; and it was from the circumstance of the latter *returning* from these islands after the pursuit that mythology derived the name (*στρέφω*, "to turn").

Strophium (*ταινία, ταινίδιον, ἀπόδεσμος*). (1) A wreath of flowers (Verg. *Copa*, 31). (See CORONA.) (2) (*στρόφιον*). A sash or scarf worn across the breast by women. See FASCIAE.

Strophius (*Στρόφιος*). A king of Phocis, son of Crissus and Antiphatia, and husband of Cydragora, Anaxibia, or Astyochia, by whom he became the father of Astydamia and Pylades. See ORESTES.

Structor (*τραπεζοποιός*). A servant whose duty it was to arrange the dishes of each course upon the tray (*ferculum*) and place them in proper order. He sometimes carved, though that was properly the function of the *scissor* (Mart. x. 48; Lamprid. *Elag.* 27). See CENA; TRICLINIUM.

Struppus (*τροπός*). (1) A leathern thong used in fastening the oar to its thowl (Vitruv. x. 3, 6). (2) The strap through which the poles (*asseres*) of a litter (*lectica*) were passed. See LECTICA.

Strymon (*Στρυμών*). Now Struma, called by the Turks Karasu; an important river in Macedonia, forming the boundary between that country and Thrace down to the time of Philip. It rose in Mount Scomius, flowed first south and then southeast, passed through the lake Prasias, and, immediately south of Amphipolis, fell into a bay of the Aegaean Sea, called after it STRYMONĬCUS SINUS.

Stuprum. See ADULTERIUM.

Stylobăta (*στυλοβάτης*). A stylobate or pedestal on which a column or row of columns rests to give them an additional elevation (Vitruv. iv. 3. 3).

Stylus. See STILUS.

Stymphalĭdes. See STYMPHALUS.

Stymphălis. See STYMPHALUS.

Stymphălus (*Στύμφαλος*). A town in the northeast of Arcadia, the territory of which was bounded on the north by Achaia, on the east by Sicyonia and Phliasia, on the south by the territory of Mantinea, and on the west by that of Orchomenus and Pheneus. The town itself was situated on a mountain of the same name, and on the north side of Lake STYMPHĂLIS (Zaraka), on which dwelt, according to tradition, the celebrated birds, called STYMPHALĬDES, destroyed by Heracles. See HERACLES.

Styra (*Τὰ Στύρα*). Now Stura; a town in Euboea on the southwest coast, not far from Carystus, and nearly opposite Marathon in Attica.

Styx (*Στύξ*). A name connected with the verb *στυγέω*, to hate or abhor, and applied to the principal river in the nether world, around which it flows seven times. (*Il.* ii. 755; Verg. *Aen.* vi. 439.) Styx is described as a daughter of Oceanus and Tethys. As a nymph she dwelt at the entrance of Hades, in a lofty grotto which was supported by silver columns. As a river, Styx is described as a branch of Oceanus, flowing from its tenth source; and the river Cocytus again is a branch of the Styx. By Pallas, Styx became the mother of Zelus, Niké, Bia, and Cratos. She was the first of all the immortals who took her children to Zeus, to assist him against the Titans; and, in return for this, her children were allowed forever to live with Zeus, and Styx herself became the divinity by whom the most solemn oaths were sworn. When one of the gods had to take an oath by Styx, Iris brought a cup full of water from the Styx, and the god, while taking the oath, poured out the water.

Suada. The Roman personification of persuasion, the Greek Pitho (*Πειθώ*), also called by the diminutive name SUADĒLA.

Suasoriae. See SENECA (1).

Suavillum or **Savillum**. A sweet cake made with honey, flour, eggs, and cheese (Cato, *R. R.* 84).

Subgrundarium or **Suggrundarium**. A place for the burial of children who died before cutting their teeth; for such children were not cremated. See Fulgent. s. h. v.; and cf. Pliny, *H. N.* vii. 15.

Sublaqueum. Now Subiaco, a small town of the Aequi in Latium, on the Anio, near its source.

Sublicius Pons. See PONS.

Subligacŭlum (*περίζωμα*). The linen bandage worn by the Roman gymnasts while performing their exercises. It was passed round the waist and between the legs. It was originally a loin-cloth and one of the most primitive articles of attire; and afterwards had different forms corresponding with our belt, apron, and drawers respectively. It was also called *campestre* (Hor. *Epist.* i. 11, 18).

Subscriptio. In the later days of the Roman Empire the Roman grammarians devoted themselves largely to editing the Latin classics, as the Alexandrian grammarians edited the great classical works of Greek literature. In the fourth and fifth centuries many men of eminence were numbered among these editors, who attached their names to their work. A signature of this sort is called *subscriptio*, and subsequent copyists carefully repeated the names at the head of the works which they copied side by side with those of subsequent revisers. Among the *subscriptiones* are found those of men like Symmachus (q. v.), Asterius (consul 494 A.D.), Mavortius (consul 527 A.D.), and many other important personages. These attestations are collected and discussed by Jahn in a monograph that is published in the *Abh. der sächs. Gesellschaft d. Wissensch.* for 1851.

Subsellium. A bench upon legs and without any back (Varro, *L. L.* v. 128).

Subsignāni. Soldiers who under the Empire had special privileges, and fought under a special standard instead of forming part of the legion. They are probably to be identified with the *vexillarii* (q. v.).

Subucŭla. A shirt; worn next to the skin, and made of wool (Sueton. *Aug.* 82). It had long sleeves and was probably worn by both sexes.

Subūra and **Suburra**. The Bowery of ancient Rome, comprehending the valley between the Esquiline, Quirinal, and Viminal, densely populated and rather disreputable in its character. Martial speaks of its noise (*clamosa Subura*, xii. 18, 2), and both Persius (v. 32) and Martial (xi. 78, 11) mention it as the resort of prostitutes. See ROMA.

Sucro. (1) Now Xucar; a river in Hispania Tarraconensis, rising in a southern branch of Mount Idubeda in the territory of the Celtiberi, and falling south of Valentia into a gulf of the Mediterranean called after it Sinus Sucronensis (Gulf of Valencia). (2) Now Cullera; a town of the Edetani in Hispania Tarraconensis, on the preceding river, and between the Iberus and Carthago Nova.

Sucŭlae. See HYADES.

Sudarium (καψιδρώτιον). A handkerchief for wiping away the perspiration from the face (Quint. vi. 3. 60). See MUCINUM.

Sudatorium. See BALNEAE.

Suēbi. See SUEVI.

Suessa Aurunca. Now Sessa; a town of the Aurunci in Latium, east of the Via Appia, between Minturnae and Teanum, on the western slope of Mount Massĭcus. It was the birthplace of the poet Lucilius, hence called by Juvenal (i. 20) *alumnus Auruncae.*

Suessa Pometia, also called **Pometia** simply. An ancient and important town of the Volsci in Latium, south of Forum Appii, taken by Tarquinius Priscus. It was one of the twenty-three cities situated in the plain afterwards covered by the Pomptine Marshes, which are said indeed to have derived their name from this town.

Suessetāni. A people in Hispania Tarraconensis, mentioned in connection with the Edetani.

Suessiōnes or **Suessōnes.** A powerful people in Gallia Belgica, who were reckoned the bravest of all the Belgic Gauls after the Bellovaci, and who could bring 50,000 men into the field in Caesar's time. The Suessiones dwelt in an extensive and fertile country east of the Bellovaci, south of the Veromandui, and west of the Remi. They possessed twelve towns, of which the capital was Noviodunum, subsequently Augusta Suessonum or Suessones (Soissons) (Caes. *B. G.* ii. 3, 12; vii. 75).

Suessŭla. Now Torre di Sessola; a town in Samnium, on the southern slope of Mount Tifata.

Suetonius Paulīnus. See PAULINUS.

Suetonius Tranquillus, GAIUS. A Roman historian and scholar, who was born about the beginning of the reign of Vespasian, and practised as an advocate at Rome in the reign of Trajan. He lived on intimate terms with the younger Pliny, several of whose letters are addressed to him. At the request of Pliny, Trajan granted to Suetonius the *ius trium liberorum;* for, though he was married, he had not three children, which number was necessary to relieve him from various legal disabilities. Suetonius was afterwards appointed private secretary (*magister epistolarum*) to Hadrian, but was deprived of this office by the emperor, along with Septicius Clarus, the praefect of the Praetorians, on the ground of his offensive familiarity with Sabina, the emperor's wife. His chief work is his lives of the first twelve emperors of Rome (*Vitae Duodecim Caesarum*) from Iulius to Domitian. Suetonius does not follow the chronological order in his *Lives,* but groups together his facts according to their nature. His language is very brief and precise, sometimes obscure, without any affectation of ornament; and his works abound in scandalous anecdotes. The existing treatise *De Illustribus Grammaticis et de Claris Rhetoribus* is perhaps only part of a larger work, the *Pratum,* which seems to have been a sort of encyclopaedia, as many fragments show, dealing with a great number of subjects. (See Schanz, *Röm. Litt.* iii. 42–54.) The only other productions of Suetonius still extant are a few lives of Roman authors.

The standard text of Suetonius is that of Roth (Leipzig, 1886), and of the fragments that of Reifferscheid (2d ed. Leipzig, 1890). A good annotated edition (Latin notes) is that of Baumgarten-Crusius and Hase in the Lemaire collection, 2 vols. (Paris, 1828). The first two books (Iulius and Augustus) are edited with an introduction and English notes by H. T. Peck (2d ed. New York, 1893). The *Lives* and the remains of the *Viri Illustres* are translated by Thomson and Forester (London, 1881). See Regent, *De Suetonii Vita et Scriptis* (Breslau, 1856); Thimm, *De Usu atque Elocutione C. Suetonii Tranquil.* (Königsberg, 1867); and Bagge, *De Elocutione Suetonii* (Upsala, 1875).

Suēvi and **Suēbi.** One of the greatest and most powerful peoples of Germany; or, more properly speaking, the collective name of a great number of German tribes, who were grouped together on account of their migratory mode of life, and spoken of in opposition to the more settled tribes, who went under the general name of Ingaevones. The Suevi are described by all the ancient writers as occupying the greater half of all Germany; but the accounts vary respecting the part of the country which they inhabited. The name survives in the modern Suabia (Schwaben). See Lehmann, *Das Volk d. Sueben* (1883); and article GERMANIA.

Sufes and **Suffes** (Phœn. *shōfēth,* "a judge"), pl. SUFFĒTES. The name of the higher magistrates among the Carthaginians. See CARTHAGO, p. 285.

Suffectus. A word applied to a Roman magistrate elected in place of one who vacated office before the end of the year for which he was elected. The substitute continued in office for the rest of the year. See CONSUL.

Sufflāmen (ἐποχεύς). A drag-chain used as a brake upon a wheel (Juv. viii. 148), and employed to relieve the pressure upon the horses when going down hill.

Suffragia Sex. The six patrician centuries of Roman *equites* in the kingly period. See EQUITES.

Suffragium. A vote. At Athens the popular vote in the assemblies was taken by a show of hands (χειροτονία) or by ballot (ψῆφος). For the Roman usages in voting, see COMITIA; and LEGES TABELLARIAE.

Sugambri, Sygambri, Sigambri, Sycambri, or **Sicambri.** One of the most powerful peoples of Germany at an early time, belonging to the Istaevones, and dwelling originally north of the Ubii on the Rhine, whence they spread towards the north as far as the Lippe. They were conquered by Tiberius in the reign of Augustus. Shortly afterwards they disappear from history, and are not mentioned again till the time of Ptolemy, who places them much farther north, close to the Bructeri and the Langobardi, somewhere between the Vecht and the Yssel. At a still later period we find them forming an important part of the confederacy known under the name of Franci.

Suggestus. A Latin word denoting any elevated place made by heaping up materials (*suggero*): (1) the platform from which orators addressed the people at the Comitia; (2) the place from which a general harangued his troops (see CONTIO); and (3) the seat (also called *cubiculum*) from which the emperor beheld the public games.

Suggrundarium. See SUBGRUNDARIUM.

Suĭdas (Σουΐδας). A Greek lexicographer, of whose personality nothing is known, but who lived about A.D. 970, and compiled, from the lexicographical, grammatical, and explanatory works of his predecessors, a lexicon which contains explanations of words, and accounts, mainly biographical, of earlier writers. The work is put together in alphabetical order hastily, and without skill or discrimination. It is also marred by numerous mistakes. Nevertheless, it is very valuable, owing to the wealth of information on literary history contained in it, much of this not being found elsewhere. The first edition appeared at Milan in 1499. The best editions are those of Küster, 3 vols. (1705); Gaisford, 3 vols. (Oxford, 1834); Bernhardy, 2 vols. (Halle, 1834); and Bekker (Berlin, 1854). See LEXICON.

Suiŏnes. The general name of all the German tribes inhabiting Scandinavia (Tac. *Germ.* 44). See SCANDIA.

Sulla, CORNELIUS. The name of a patrician family; in many very old-fashioned texts incorrectly written **Sylla**. This family was originally called Rufinus (see RUFINUS), and the first member of it who obtained the name of Sulla was P. Cornelius Sulla, mentioned below (No. 1). The origin of the name is uncertain.

(1) PUBLIUS, great-grandfather of the dictator Sulla, and grandson of P. Cornelius Rufinus, who was twice consul in the Samnite Wars. His father is not mentioned. He was Flamen Dialis, and likewise Praetor Urbanus and Praetor Peregrinus in B.C. 212, when he presided over the first celebration of the Ludi Apollinares.

(2) LUCIUS, surnamed FELIX, the dictator, was born in B.C. 138. Although his father left him only a small property, his means were sufficient to secure for him a good education. He studied Greek and Roman literature with diligence and success, and appears early to have imbibed that love for literature and art by which he was distinguished throughout life. At the same time he prosecuted pleasure with equal ardour, and his youth as well as his manhood was disgraced by the most sensual vices. Still his love of pleasure did not absorb all his time, nor did it emasculate his mind; for no Roman during the latter days of the Republic, with the exception of Iulius Caesar, had a clearer judgment, a keener discrimination of character, or a firmer will. The slender property of Sulla was increased by the liberality of his step-mother and of a courtesan named Nicopolis, both of whom left him all their fortune. His means, though still scanty for a Roman noble, now enabled him to aspire to the honours of the State. He was quaestor in 107, when he served under Marius in Africa. Hitherto he had only been known for his profligacy; but he displayed both zeal and ability in the discharge of his duties, and soon gained the approbation of his commander and the affections of the soldiers. It was to Sulla that Iugurtha was delivered by Bocchus; and the quaestor thus shared with the consul the glory of bringing this war to a conclusion. Sulla himself was so proud of his share in the success that he had a seal ring engraved, representing the surrender of Iugurtha, which he continued to wear till the day of his death. Sulla continued to serve under Marius with great distinction in the campaigns against the Cimbri and Teutones; but Marius becoming jealous of the rising fame of his officer, Sulla left Marius in 102, and took a command under the colleague of Marius, Q. Catulus, who intrusted the chief management of the war to Sulla. Sulla now returned to Rome, where he appears to have lived quietly for some years. He was praetor in 93, and in the following year (92) was sent as propraetor into Cilicia, with special orders from the Senate to restore Ariobarzanes to his kingdom of Cappadocia, from which he had been expelled by Mithridates. Sulla met with complete success. He defeated Gordius, the general of Mithridates, in Cappadocia, and placed Ariobarzanes on the throne.

The enmity between Marius and Sulla now assumed a more deadly form. Sulla's ability and increasing reputation had already led the aristocratic party to look up to him as one of their leaders; and thus political animosity was added to private hatred. In addition to this, Marius and Sulla were both anxious to obtain the command of the impending war against Mithridates; and the success which attended Sulla's recent operations in the East had increased his popularity, and pointed him out as the most suitable person for this important command. About this time Bocchus erected in the Capitol gilded figures, representing the surrender of Iugurtha to Sulla, at which Marius was so enraged that he could scarcely be prevented from removing them by force. The exasperation of both parties became so violent that they nearly had recourse to arms against each other; but the breaking out of the Social War hushed all private quarrels for the time. Marius and Sulla both took an active part in the war against the common foe. But Marius was now advanced in years; and he had the deep mortification of finding that his achievements were thrown into the shade by the superior energy of his rival. Sulla gained some brilliant victories over the enemy, and took Bovianum, the chief town of the Samnites. He was elected consul for 88, and received from the Senate the command of the Mithridatic War. The events which followed—his expulsion from Rome by Marius, his return to the city at the head of his legions, and the proscription of Marius and his leading adherents—are related in the article MARIUS.

Sulla remained at Rome till the end of the year, and set out for Greece at the beginning of 87, in order to carry on the war against Mithridates. He landed at Dyrrhachium, and forthwith marched against Athens, which had become the headquarters of the Mithridatic cause in Greece. After a long and obstinate siege, Athens was taken by storm on the first of March in 86, and was given up to rapine and plunder. Sulla then marched against Archelaüs, the general of Mithridates, whom he defeated in the neighbourhood of Chaeronea in Boeotia; and in the following year he again gained a decisive victory over the same general near Orchomenus. But while Sulla was carrying on the war with such success in Greece, his enemies had obtained the upper hand in Italy. The consul Cinna, who had been driven out of Rome by his colleague Octavius soon after Sulla's departure from Italy, had entered it again with Marius at the close of the year. Both Cinna and Marius were appointed consuls 86, and all the regulations of Sulla were swept away. Sulla, however, would not return to Italy till he had brought the war against Mithridates to a conclusion. After driving the generals of Mithridates out of Greece, Sulla crossed the Hellespont, and early in

84 concluded a peace with the king of Pontus. He now turned his arms against Fimbria, who had been appointed by the Marian party as his successor in the command. But the troops of Fimbria deserted their general, who put an end to his own life.

Sulla now prepared to return to Italy. After leaving his legate, L. Licinius Murena, in command of the province of Asia, with two legions, he set sail with his own army to Athens. While preparing for his deadly struggle in Italy, he did not lose his interest in literature. He carried with him from Athens to Rome the valuable library of Apellicon of Teos, which contained most of the works of Aristotle and Theophrastus. (See APELLICON.) He landed at Brundisium in the spring of 83. The Marian party far outnumbered him in troops, and had every prospect of victory. By bribery and promises, however, Sulla gained over a large number of the Marian soldiers, and he persuaded many of the Italian towns to espouse his cause. In the field his efforts were crowned with equal success; and he was ably supported by several of the Roman nobles, who espoused his cause in different parts of Italy. Of these one of the most distinguished was the young Cn. Pompey, who was at the time only twenty-three years of age. (See POMPEIUS, No. 10.) In the following year (82) the struggle was brought to a close by the decisive battle gained by Sulla over the Samnites and Lucanians under Pontius Telesinus before the Colline Gate of Rome. This victory was followed by the surrender of Praenesté and the death of the younger Marius, who had taken refuge in this town.

Sulla. (Bust in the Capitoline Museum.)

Sulla was now master of Rome and Italy; and he resolved to take the most ample vengeance upon his enemies, and to extirpate the popular party. One of his first acts was to draw up a list of his enemies who were to be put to death, called a *proscriptio*. It was the first instance of the kind in Roman history. All persons in this list were outlaws who might be killed by any one with impunity, even by slaves; their property was confiscated to the State, and was to be sold by public auction; their children and grandchildren lost their votes in the Comitia, and were excluded from all public offices. Further, all who killed a proscribed person received two talents as a reward, and whoever sheltered such a person was punished with death. Terror now reigned not only at Rome, but throughout Italy. Fresh lists of the proscribed constantly appeared. No one was safe; for Sulla gratified his friends by placing in the fatal lists their personal enemies, or persons whose property was coveted by his adherents. The confiscated property, it is true, belonged to the State, and had to be sold by public auction; but the friends and dependants of Sulla purchased it at a nominal price, as no one dared to bid against them. The number of persons who perished by the proscriptions is stated differently, but it appears to have amounted to many thousands. At the commencement of these horrors Sulla had been appointed dictator for as long a time as he judged it to be necessary. This was towards the close of 81. Sulla's chief object in being invested with the dictatorship was to carry into execution, in a legal manner, the great changes which he meditated in the constitution and the administration of justice. He had no intention of abolishing the Republic; and, consequently, he caused consuls to be elected for the following year, and was elected to the office himself in 80, while he continued to hold the dictatorship. The general object of Sulla's reforms was to restore, as far as possible, the ancient Roman constitution, and to give back to the Senate and the aristocracy the power which they had lost. Thus he deprived the tribunes of the plebs of all real power, and abolished altogether the legislative and judicial functions of the Comitia Tributa. At the beginning of 81 he celebrated a splendid triumph on account of his victory over Mithridates. In a speech which he delivered to the people at the close of the ceremony, he claimed for himself the surname of *Felix*, as he attributed his success in life to the favour of the gods. In order to strengthen his power, Sulla established military colonies throughout Italy. The inhabitants of the Italian towns which had fought against Sulla were deprived of the full Roman franchise, and were only allowed to retain the *commercium:* their land was confiscated and given to the soldiers who had fought under him. Twenty-three legions, or, according to another statement, forty-seven legions, received grants of land in various parts of Italy. A great number of these colonies was settled in Etruria, the population of which was thus almost entirely changed. These colonies had the strongest interest in upholding the institutions of Sulla, since any attempt to invalidate the latter would have endangered their newly acquired possessions. Sulla likewise created at Rome a kind of body-guard for his protection by giving the citizenship to a great number of slaves who had belonged to persons proscribed by him. The slaves thus rewarded are said to have been as many as ten thousand, and were called Cornelii after him as their patron.

After holding the dictatorship till the beginning of 79, Sulla resigned this office, to the surprise of all classes. He retired to his estate at Puteoli, and there, surrounded by the beauties of nature and art, he passed the remainder of his life in those literary and sensual enjoyments in which he had always taken so much pleasure. His dissolute mode of life hastened his death, but the immediate cause was the rupture of a blood-vessel; though some time before he had been suffering from the disgusting disease which is known in modern times by the name of *morbus pediculo-*

sus, or phthiriasis. He died in 78, in the sixtieth year of his age. He was honoured with a public funeral, and a monument was erected to him in the Campus Martius, the inscription on which had been composed by himself. It stated that none of his friends ever did him a kindness, and none of his enemies a wrong, without being fully repaid. Sulla was married five times: (*a*) To Ilia or Iulia, who bore him a daughter, married to Q. Pompeius Rufus, the son of Sulla's colleague in the consulship in 88; (*b*) to Aelia; (*c*) to Caelia; (*d*) to Caecilia Metella, who bore him a son, who died before Sulla, and likewise twins, a son and a daughter; (*e*) to Valeria, who bore him a daughter after his death.

Sulla wrote a history of his own life and times, called *Memorabilia* (Ὑπομνήματα). It was dedicated to L. Lucullus, and extended to twenty-two books, the last of which was finished by Sulla a few days before his death. He also wrote Fabulae Atellanae, and the Greek Anthology contains a short epigram which is ascribed to him. See Gerlach, *Marius und Sulla* (1856); and Beesly, *The Gracchi, Marius, and Sulla* (New York, 1878).

(3) FAUSTUS, son of the dictator by his fourth wife, Caecilia Metella, and a twin brother of Fausta, was born not long before B.C. 88, the year in which his father obtained the first consulship. He and his sister received the names of Faustus and Fausta respectively on account of the good fortune of their father. At the death of his father in 78 Faustus and his sister were left under the guardianship of L. Lucullus. Faustus accompanied Pompey into Asia, and was the first who mounted the walls of the Temple of Jerusalem in 63. In 60 he exhibited the gladiatorial games which his father, in his last will, had enjoined upon him. In 54 he was quaestor. In 52 he received from the Senate the commission to rebuild the Curia Hostilia, which had been burned down in the tumults following the murder of Clodius, and which was henceforward called the Curia Cornelia, in honour of Faustus and his father. He married Pompey's daughter, and sided with his father-in-law in the Civil War. He was present at the battle of Pharsalia, and subsequently joined the leaders of his party in Africa. After the battle of Thapsus in 46 he attempted to escape into Mauretania, but was taken prisoner by P. Sittius, and carried to Caesar. Upon his arrival in Caesar's camp he was murdered by the soldiers in a tumult. Faustus seems to have resembled his father only in his extravagance, for we know from Cicero that he was overwhelmed with debt at the breaking out of the Civil War.

(4) PUBLIUS, nephew of the dictator, elected consul along with P Autronius Paetus for the year B.C. 65; but neither he nor his colleague entered upon the office, as they were accused of bribery by L. Torquatus the younger, and were condemned. It was currently believed that Sulla was privy to both of Catiline's conspiracies, and he was accordingly charged with this crime by his former accuser, L. Torquatus, and by C. Cornelius. He was defended by Hortensius and Cicero, and the speech of the latter on his behalf is still extant. He was acquitted; but, independent of the testimony of Sallust (*Cat.* 17), his guilt may almost be inferred from the embarrassment of his advocate. In the Civil War, Sulla espoused Caesar's cause. He served under him as legate in Greece, and commanded with Caesar himself the right wing at the battle of Pharsalia (48). He died in 45.

(5) SERVIUS, brother of the preceding, took part in both of Catiline's conspiracies. His guilt was so evident that no one was willing to defend him; but we do not read that he was put to death along with the other conspirators (Sall. *Cat.* 17, 47).

Sulmo. (1) Now Sulmona; a town of the Peligni in the country of the Sabines, celebrated as the birthplace of Ovid. (2) Now Sermoneta; an ancient town of the Volsci in Latium, on the Ufens.

Sulphur Matches. See IGNIARIA.

Sulpicia. A Roman poetess who flourished towards the close of the first century A.D. She is celebrated for sundry amatory effusions, addressed to her husband Calenus. There is extant a satirical poem, in seventy hexameters, on the edict of Domitian by which philosophers were banished from Rome and from Italy, which is ascribed to Sulpicia by many modern critics, but is undoubtedly of very late origin, and perhaps is merely the elaboration of a school theme. It was found in the monastery at Bobbio in Italy in 1493. See Ellis in the (English) *Journal of Philology*, v. 265; id. in the *Academy*, i. 87; and Bährens, *De Sulpicia Quae Vocatur Satira* (Jena, 1873). It is generally appended to the editions of Juvenal and Persius.

Sulpicia Gens. One of the most ancient Roman gentes, producing a succession of distinguished men, from the foundation of the Republic to the imperial period. The chief families of the Sulpicii during the republican period bore the names of CAMERĪNUS, GALBA, GALLUS, RUFUS, and SAVERRIO.

Sulpicius Apollinăris. A contemporary of A. Gellius, and a learned grammarian. There are two poems in the Latin Anthology purporting to be written by Sulpicius of Carthage, whom some identify with the above-named Sulpicius Apollinaris. One of these poems consists of seventy-two lines, giving the argument of the twelve books of Vergil's *Aeneid*, six lines being devoted to each book. Sulpicius also wrote the metrical arguments prefixed to the plays of Plautus (?) and Terence. (See PERIOCHA.) His arguments to the *Aeneid* are printed in the *Poët. Lat. Min.* of Bährens, iv. 169. See Beck, *De Sulpicio Apollinari* (Groningen, 1884).

Sulpicius Galba. See GALBA.

Sulpicius Rufus. (1) PUBLIUS, one of the most distinguished orators of his time, born B.C. 124. He commenced public life as a supporter of the aristocratic party, and acquired great influence in the State by his splendid talents, while he was still young. In 93 he was quaestor, and in 89 he served as legate of the consul Cn. Pompeius Strabo in the Marsic War. In 88, he was elected to the tribunate; but he deserted the aristocratic party, and joined Marius. The causes of this sudden change are not expressly stated; but we are told that he was overwhelmed with debt; and there can be little doubt that he was bought by Marius. When Sulla marched upon Rome at the head of his army, Marius and Sulpicius took to flight. Marius succeeded in making his escape to Africa, but Sulpicius was discovered in a villa, and put to death. (2) PUBLIUS, probably son or grandson of the last, was one of Caesar's legates in Gaul and in the Civil War. He was praetor in B.C. 48. Cicero addresses him in 45 as imperator. It appears that he was at that time in Illyricum, along with Vatinius. (3) SERVIUS, with the surname LEMONIA, indicating the tribe to which he belonged, was a contemporary and friend of Cicero, and of about the same age. He first devoted himself to oratory, and he studied this art with Cicero in his youth. He afterwards studied law; and he became one of the best jurists as well as most eloquent orators of his age. He was quaestor of the district of Ostia in B.C. 74; curule aedile, 69; praetor, 65; and consul 51 with M. Claudius Marcellus. He appears to have espoused Caesar's side in the Civil War, and was appointed by Caesar proconsul of Achaia (46 or 45). He died in 43 in the camp of M. Antony, having been sent by the Senate on a mission to Antony, who was besieging Dec. Brutus in Mutina. Sulpicius wrote a great number of legal works. He is often cited by the jurists whose writings are excerpted in the Digest; but there is no excerpt directly from him in the Digest. He had numerous pupils, the most distinguished of whom were A. Ofilius and Alfenus Varus. There are extant in the collection of Cicero's Epistles (*Ad Fam.* iv.) two letters from Sulpicius to Cicero, one of which is the well-known letter of consolation on the death of Tullia, the daughter of the orator. The same book contains several letters from Cicero to Sulpicius. He is also said to have written some erotic poetry. Sulpicius left a son Servius, who is frequently mentioned in Caesar's correspondence.

Sulpurāta (sc. *ramenta*). See IGNIARIA.

Sumen. The udder of a sow, which was regarded as a great dainty by Roman *gourmets*, especially when taken from an animal that had just littered and before the teats had been sucked (Pliny, *H. N.* xi. 84; Mart. xiii. 44).

Summānus. An ancient Etruscan deity of the nocturnal heavens, to whom was ascribed thunder by night, as that by day was ascribed to Iupiter. He had a chapel on the Capitol, and his image in terra-cotta stood on the pediment of the great temple. Besides this, he had a temple near the Circus Maximus, where on the 20th of June an annual sacrifice was offered to him. His true significance became in later times so obscure that his name was falsely explained as meaning the highest of the Manes (*summus Manium*) and equivalent to Dis pater, or the Greek Pluto (Varro, *L. L.* v. 74; Cic. *De Div.* i. 10; Pliny, *H. N.* xxix. 57).

Sumptuariae Leges. Laws intended to limit and control the expenditure of the individual citizen.

The sumptuary legislation of GREECE was contained for the most part in the codes of the great lawgivers. A *rhetra* of Lycurgus is said to have forbidden the Spartans to have their houses made by any more elaborate implements than the axe and the saw; simplicity of food and clothing was enjoined on the male members of the population; iron money was originally the only coinage in use (Plut. *Apophth. Lac. Lys.* 3), and private possession of gold and silver was forbidden even after these metals were employed for public purposes (Plut. *Lys.* 17). By the laws of Zaleucus of Locri, we are told, the citizens of that State were forbidden to drink undiluted wine, except on the order of a physician, under pain of death (Athen. p. 429); while simplicity of dress and a limitation of the number of personal attendants were also enjoined. The Solonian legislation at Athens contained enactments against expensive feminine apparel and ornaments, particularly those given in the dowry (φερνή) of a bride, and against expensive funerals; there were also laws in force at Athens which limited the number of guests at entertainments (Athen. p. 245). Funeral regulations similar to those of Solon, we are told by Plutarch, existed in his native town of Chaeronea (Plut. *Sol.* 21).

ROMAN sumptuary legislation was progressive; it did not originate until a comparatively late period in the history of the State, and each law aimed at eradicating some definite and growing evil. The inefficiency of these laws and the extreme difficulty of enforcing them are amply attested (Tac. *Ann.* ii. 55; Gell. ii. 24, 3; Tertull. *Apol.* 6), but, even when recognized, were not sufficient to check further attempts in this direction. The fact that most of these laws dealt with the same subject—namely, the expenses of the table—and enjoined very similar restrictions, shows how quickly each of them must have sunk into desuetude.

The earliest sumptuary regulations were those contained in the Twelve Tables limiting the expenses of funerals (Cic. *De Leg.* ii. 23). They were possibly copied from the similar regulations of Solon.

The LEX OPPIA, passed in B.C. 215, provided that no woman should possess more than half an ounce of gold, or wear a dress of different colours, or ride in a carriage in the city or within a mile of it except during public religious ceremonies. This law, which was dictated by the necessities of the Second Punic War, was repealed twenty years later, in B.C. 195 (Livy, xxxiv. 1–8).

The LEX ORCHIA, passed three years after Cato's censorship, and therefore in B.C. 181, was the first law that restricted the expenses of the table. It prescribed a limit to the number of guests that might be invited to entertainments. Cato is said to have opposed its introduction.

Next followed the LEX FANNIA, whose date is fixed by Pliny (*H. N.* x. 71) as B.C. 161. It grew out of a *senatusconsultum*, which enjoined that the *principes civitatis* should swear before the consuls that they would not exceed a certain limit of expense in the banquets given at the Ludi Megalenses. Afterwards a consular law was promulgated, which went further than the Lex Orchia, in that it prescribed the nature and value of the eatables which were allowed to be consumed. It permitted the expenditure of 100 *asses* on the Ludi Romani, the Ludi Plebeii, and the Saturnalia, and of thirty on some other festival occasions; but on all other days of the year it allowed only ten *asses* to be spent. It further forbade the serving of any fowl but a single hen, and that not fattened. One of its clauses was of a protective character, since it enjoined that only native wines should be consumed (Gell. ii. 24; Macrob. iii. 17; Plin. *H. N.* x. § 71; Tertull. *Apol.* vi.).

The LEX DIDIA was passed eighteen years later, in B.C. 143. It was practically a re-enactment of the Lex Fannia.

The LEX LICINIA, of uncertain date, marks the next attempt at sumptuary legislation. It allowed 100 *asses* to be spent on the table on certain days, 200 on marriage feasts, and on certain other festivals (such as the Kalends, Nones, and Nundinae) thirty *asses;* it fixed a limit to the amount of meat and fish that was to be consumed on ordinary days, and encouraged the consumption of garden-produce.

The general neglect of the preceding laws caused the LEGES CORNELIAE of the dictator Sulla to be passed in B.C. 81, restricting the expenses on sepulchral monuments, and regulating the cost of funerals, which he himself violated on the death of his wife Metella (Plut. *Sulla,* 35). Another law restricted the luxury of the table, allowing thirty sesterces to be spent on the Kalends, Ides, Nones, the *dies ludorum,* and certain *feriae,* and three on all other days.

A LEX AEMILIA, which probably belongs to B.C. 78, did not fix a fresh limit to expenses, but laid down regulations as to the kinds and quantities of food.

The LEX ANTIA, which was subsequent to the last-named law but cannot be dated precisely, besides limiting the expenditure on banquets, also limited the class of persons with whom a magistrate might dine out during his time of office.

Next came the LEGES IULIAE. The dictator Caesar enforced the former sumptuary laws respecting entertainments, which had fallen into disuse (Dio Cass. xliii. 25). They were not attended to during his absence, but during his presence in Rome the enforcement of them was rigorous; guards were placed round the market to seize forbidden luxuries, and sometimes dishes were taken from the tables of private individuals (Suet. *Iul.* 43). He also passed a law prohibiting the use of litters, of purple garments, and of pearls, except in the case of persons of a certain rank or age, or on certain days (Suet. l. c.).

The emperor Augustus, in B.C. 22, passed laws regulating the expenses to be incurred on ordinary and festal days (Suet. *Aug.* 34). On the former an expenditure of 200 sesterces was permitted, on the latter an expenditure of 300, and on marriage festivals of 1000 sesterces; an edict of Augustus or Tiberius allowed expenses on various festivals to range from 300 to 2000 sesterces, the increase in the permitted expenditure being allowed in the hope that this concession would secure obedience to the law.

Tiberius, in spite of his distrust of the efficacy of sumptuary legislation (Tac. *Ann.* iii. 53, 54), was forced into making regulations to check the inordinate expenses on banquets (Suet. *Tib.* 34). To his reign also belongs a *senatusconsultum* prohibiting the use of gold plate except in sacred rites, and preventing men from wearing silk. Further sumptuary regulations checking the expenditure on food were made by Nero; among later emperors Antoninus Pius and Marcus Aurelius regulated the expenses of gladiatorial shows; and the emperor Tacitus again prohibited men from wearing silk, and forbade the wearing of gold-embroidered garments. It was during the later Republic and the early Empire that luxury especially flourished, although the studied simplicity of the courts of Augustus and Tiberius must have had some influence in restraining it. After Galba, began a new era of moderation, an effect which Tacitus traces to the decline of private fortunes, to the dangers attending the display of wealth, to the introduction of *novi homines* into the Senate and into the best society of Rome, but principally to the influence of Vespasian, a prince *antiquo cultu victuque* (Tac. *Ann.* iii. 55). Other emperors whose simplicity of life exercised an influence on the society of their times were Alexander Severus and Aurelian.

See Platner, *De Legibus Sumptuariis Romanis* (Leipzig, 1752); and Baudrillart, *Histoire du Luxe Privé et Public,* 4 vols. (Paris, 1878–80).

Sun-god. See HELIOS.

Sunium (Σούνιον). Now C. Colonni; a celebrated promontory forming the southern extremity of Attica, with a town of the same name upon it. Here was a splendid temple of Athené, elevated 300 feet above the sea, the columns of which are still extant, and have given the modern name to the promontory.

Suovetaurilia. A Roman sacrifice, consisting of a boar (*sus*), a ram (*ovis*), and a bullock (*taurus*), which was offered in nearly all cases of lustration.

Suovetaurilia. (Bartoli.)

For female deities the female animal, and on certain occasions young animals, were selected. See LUSTRATIO; LUSTRUM; SACRIFICIUM.

Superbus, TARQUINIUS. See TARQUINIUS.

Superstitio (δεισιδαιμονία). A word used by the ancients in a somewhat different sense from that in which we employ it, inasmuch as it denoted an excessive, unreasonable fear (*timor inanis*) of the gods as opposed to a proper and becoming reverence (*religio*). See Cicero, *N. D.* i. 42, 117, with Mayor's note; and the paper by Dr. Ernest Riess in the *Transactions of the American Philological Assoc.* (1895). For the ancient beliefs regarding sorcery, ghosts, etc., see AMULETUM; ASTROLOGIA; DAEMON; FASCINUM; LAMIA; UMBRA; VERSIPELLIS; and the article OCULUS MALUS in the Appendix.

Supĕrum Maré. See HADRIATICUM MARÉ.

Suppărum. An Oscan word (in Greek σίφαρος) denoting a small topsail of a vessel (Lucan, v. 428).

Supper. See CENA.

Supplicatio. The Roman fast day, or day of humiliation, celebrated originally in times of great distress, after the Sibylline Books had been duly consulted. The whole population, both of the towns and surrounding country, free-born and emancipated, men, women, and children, took part in the solemnity. The whole ceremony had a

Greek rather than a Roman colour. From the Temple of Apollo, priests and laymen, crowned with wreaths of bay, marched in procession to the sound of singing and the notes of the lyre, visiting all the holy places, especially those where *lectisternia* were held. According to the rite introduced from the Oriental Greeks of Asia Minor, the Romans touched with their faces the threshold of the sanctuaries, prostrated themselves before the statues of the gods, clasping their knees and kissing their hands and feet. While the prayers were being said, incense and wine were offered, the prayers being rehearsed by the members of the *collegium* intrusted with the care of the Sibylline Books (see SIBYLLAE), and the performance of the holy rites prescribed by them. On such days the temples ordinarily closed to the public, or only accessible under certain restrictions, were, so far as practicable, thrown open to all. The thanksgivings decreed by the Senate after great victories were celebrated in a similar manner. These originally lasted only one day, but in the course of time were lengthened (e. g. for Pompey's victory over Mithridates, one of ten days; for Caesar's conquest of the Belgae, one of fifteen days; and for his defeat of Vercingetorix, one of twenty days), until, at the end of the Republic, they sometimes extended over forty or fifty days, and were often united with a public feasting of the people.

Supplicium. See CRUX; ECULEUS; TORMENTUM (2).

Suppositicii. Gladiators substituted in place of those who had been defeated or killed (Mart. v. 24).

Sura (Σοῦρα). (1) Now Surie; a town of Syria, in the district Chalybonitis, on the Euphrates, a little west of Thapsacus. (2) Now Sour; a branch of the Mosella, above Treves (Auson. *Mosell.* 354).

Sura, Lentŭlus. See LENTULUS (1).

Sura, L. Licinius. An intimate friend of Trajan, and three times consul, in A.D. 98, 102, and 107. On the death of Sura, Trajan honoured him with a public funeral, and erected baths to perpetuate his memory. Two of Pliny's letters are addressed to him (Dio Cass. lxviii. 9, 15; Pliny, *Epist.* iv. 30; vii. 27).

Surēnas. The general of the Parthians, who defeated Crassus in B.C. 54. The word is probably not a proper name, but a title like "Vizier." See CRASSUS.

Surgeons and Surgery. See CHIRURGIA; MEDICINA; MEDICUS.

Surnames. See NOMEN.

Surrentum. Now Sorrento; an ancient town of Campania, opposite Capreae, and situated on the promontory (Prom. Minervae) separating the Sinus Paestanus from the Sinus Puteolanus. It was subsequently a Roman colony; and on the hills (Surrentini Colles) in its neighbourhood was grown one of the best wines in Italy, which was strongly recommended to convalescents, on account of its thinness and wholesomeness.

Susa (τὰ Σοῦσα; Old Test. Shushan; Pers. Shus). The winter residence of the Persian kings. It stood in the district Cissia of the province Susiana, on the eastern bank of the river Choaspes. Its name in old Persian signifies "Lily," and that flower is said to abound in the plain in which the city stood. Susa was of a quadrangular form, 120 (or, according to others, 200) stadia in circuit, and without fortifications; but it had a strongly fortified citadel, containing the palace and treasury of the Persian kings. The Greek name of this citadel, Memnonicé or Memnonium, is perhaps a corruption of the Aramaic *Maaninon*, "a fortress;" and this easy confusion of terms gave rise to the fable that the city was founded by Tithonus, the father of Memnon. An historical tradition ascribes its erection to Darius, the son of Hystaspes, but it existed already in the time of Daniel (Dan. viii. 2). There is, however, a difficulty as to the identification of the Shushan of Daniel with the Susa of the Greeks. The climate of Susa was very hot, and hence the choice of it for the winter palace. It was here that Alexander and his generals celebrated their marriage with the Persian princesses in B.C. 325, but the city declined after Babylon became the capital of Alexander and his successors. In B.C. 315 it was taken by Antiochus, who found in it a vast amount of treasure. The site of Susa is now marked by extensive mounds, on which are found fragments of bricks and broken pottery, with cuneiform inscriptions. The ruins of the ancient city cover a space of nearly three square miles, and they have been carefully explored by Loftus, Churchill, Dieulafoy, and others. The principal remains that still exist are four vast platforms like those at Persepolis (q. v.), with traces of a gigantic colonnade with a frontage of over 340 feet and a depth of 240 feet. The palace of Darius Hystaspis has also been excavated, and from it many artistic treasures taken to the Louvre. See Jane Dieulafoy, *La Perse, la Chaldée, et la Susiane* (Paris, 1887); id. *À Suse* (Paris, 1888); Marcel Dieulafoy, *L'Acropole de Suse* (Paris, 1890–92).

Susarion (Σουσαρίων). A Greek to whom the origin of the Attic Comedy is ascribed. He was a native of Megara, whence he removed into Attica to the village of Icaria, a place celebrated as a seat of the worship of Dionysus. The Megaric Comedy appears to have flourished, in its full development, about B.C. 600 and onwards, and it was introduced by Susarion into Attica between 580–564. See COMOEDIA.

Susiāna (Σουσιανή) or **Susis** (Σουσίς) (nearly corresponding to Khuzistan). One of the chief provinces of the ancient Persian Empire, lay between Babylonia and Persis, and between Mount Parachoatras and the head of the Persian Gulf. In this last direction its coast extended from the junction of the Euphrates with the Tigris to about the mouth of the river Oroatis (Tab). It was divided from Persis on the southeast and east by a mountainous tract, inhabited by independent tribes, who made even the kings of Persia pay them for a safe passage. On the north it was separated from Great Media by Mount Charbanus; on the west from Assyria by an imaginary line drawn south from near the Median pass in Mount Zagros to the Tigris; and from Babylonia by the Tigris itself. See the works cited under SUSA.

Sutĭlis Corōna. See CORONA.

Sutor (ῥάπτης). A cobbler. The ancient cobbler sewed leather with an awl (*subula*) and a bristle (*seta*). His shop was called *sutrina* (σκυτεῖον). See Pliny, *H. N.* x. 60.

Sutrium. Now Sutri; an ancient town of Etruria on the east side of the Saltus Ciminius, and on the road from Vulsinii to Rome, made a Roman colony in B.C. 383.

Swaddling-clothes. See FASCIAE.

Swing. See AEORA; OSCILLATIO.

Sybăris (Σύβαρις). (1) Now Coscile or Sibari; a river in Lucania, flowing by the city of the same name, and falling into the Crathis. (2) A celebrated Greek town in Lucania, situated between the rivers Sybaris and Crathis, at a short distance from the Tarentine Gulf, and near the confines of Bruttium. It was founded B.C. 720 by Achaeans and Troezenians, and soon attained an extraordinary degree of prosperity and wealth. Its inhabitants became so notorious for their love of luxury and pleasure that their name was employed to indicate any voluptuary. At the time of their highest prosperity their city was fifty stadia, or upwards of six miles, in circumference, and they exercised dominion over twenty-five towns, so that we are told they were able to bring into the field 300,000 men, a number, however, which appears incredible. But their prosperity was of short duration. The Achaeans having expelled the Troezenian part of the population, the latter took refuge at the neighbouring city of Croton, the inhabitants of which espoused their cause. In the war which ensued between the two States, the Sybarites were completely conquered by the Crotoniates, who followed up their victory by the capture of Sybaris, which they destroyed by turning the waters of the river Crathis against the town (B.C. 510) (Herod. v. 44; Diod. xii. 9; Athen. p. 521). The greater number of the surviving Sybarites took refuge in other Greek cities in Italy; but a few remained near their ancient town, and their descendants formed part of the town of Thurii founded in B.C. 443 near Sybaris. See THURII.

Sybŏta (τὰ Σύβοτα). Now Syvota; a number of small islands off the coast of Epirus, and opposite the promontory Leucimnê in Corcyra, with a harbor of the same name on the mainland.

Sychaeus. See DIDO; SICHAEUS.

Sychar, Sychem. See NEAPOLIS.

Sycophantes (συκοφάντης). A word which originally signified, according to the popular derivation, one who brought into notice cases of the prohibited export of figs from Attica. The term was afterwards applied to a professional informer and accuser. There were many such persons who carried on a lucrative business in Athens at the time of the decay of the democracy, in spite of the fact that the authors of false accusations were punished most severely. In later times the word denoted a person whose character combined the traits of a busybody, scandalmonger, sharper, and buffoon, and in this sense it is used in the Latin plays of Plautus. See Büchsenschütz, *Besitz und Erwerb*, pp. 568 foll.

Syēnê (Συήνη). Now Assouan; a city of Upper Egypt on the east bank of the Nile, just below the First Cataract. It was an important point in the astronomy and geography of the ancients, as it lay just under the tropic of Cancer, and was therefore chosen as the place through which they drew their chief parallel of latitude.

Syennĕsis (Συέννεσις). A common name of the kings of Cilicia. Of these the most important are: (1) A king of Cilicia, who joined with Labynetus (Nebuchadnezzar) in mediating between Cyaxares and Alyattes, the kings respectively of Media and Lydia, probably in B.C. 610. (2) Contemporary with Darius Hystaspis, to whom he was tributary. His daughter was married to Pixodorus. (3) Contemporary with Artaxerxes II. (Mnemon), ruled over Cilicia when the younger Cyrus marched through his country in his expedition against his brother Artaxerxes (Xen. *Anab.* i. 2, 21).

Sygambri. See SUGAMBRI.

Sylae (σῦλαι). The Greek equivalent of the modern "letters of marque and reprisal." When a Greek State had been insulted or injured by citizens of some other State, yet was unable or unwilling formally to declare war, it often gave a sort of license or commission to individuals to make reprisals upon the property and citizens of the offending nation. This was called σύλας or σῦλα διδόναι.

Sylla. See SULLA.

Syllogeis (συλλογεῖς). Also συλλογεῖς τοῦ δήμου, "the people's collectors"; special commissioners at Athens who made out a list of the property of the oligarchs prior to its confiscation.

Sylvānus. See SILVANUS.

Sylvius. See SILVIUS.

Symaethus (Σύμαιθος). Now Giaretta; a river on the east coast of Sicily and at the foot of Mount Aetna, forming the boundary between Leontini and Catana.

Symbŏla (συμβολή). The Greek term for a treaty between two States, determining the procedure in the event of lawsuits taking place between their respective subjects. A common provision of these contracts was that a party who lost his cause, when tried by the laws of the foreign State, could appeal to those of his own; and similarly the party who had been worsted in his own State was allowed to appeal to the law in his opponent's State. Such treaties were made chiefly to facilitate commercial communications between different States.

Symbolaeon (συμβόλαιον), **Synallagma** (συνάλλαγμα) and **Synthēkê** (συνθήκη). Words all denoting a contract, but with different ideas attached to each. The first denotes bargains between private persons; the second denotes any matter arranged between two individuals, whether it is a contract or not; the third means a solemn and important engagement, such as treaties and agreements between kings and States.

Symê (Σύμη). A small island off the southwest coast of Caria, lay in the mouth of the Sinus Doirdis to the west of the promontory of Cynossema.

Symmăchus, Q. AURELIUS. A distinguished scholar, statesman, and orator in the latter half of the fourth century of the Christian era, remarkable for his zeal in upholding the ancient pagan religion of Rome. He was educated in Gaul, and was proconsul of Africa in 373; and in 391 Theodosius raised him to the consulship. He died about 402. Of his works there are still extant ten books of epistles, three panegyrics on Valentinian I. and Gratian, a number of *relationes* or official reports of Symmachus as *praefectus urbi* to the emperor (A.D. 384–385), and fragments of six senatorial orations. These last were discovered in a palimpsest, part of which was in the Vatican Library and part at Milan (1815–1825). The complete works of Symmachus are edited by Seeck (Berlin, 1884). See the *Étude* by Morin (Paris, 1847).

Symmoria (συμμορία). A copartnership, or company. (1) A term used at Athens to denote a company formed to raise the property tax instituted in the year B.C. 428, to defray war expenses. (See EISPHORA.) Each of the ten *phylae* appointed 120 of its wealthier citizens, and these were divided into two symmoriae of sixty members each, so that the number of members in the twenty symmoriae amounted to 1200 (called συμμορίται). Out of each of the twenty symmoriae, fifteen of the wealthier citizens were chosen, making 300 in all, whose duty it was to pay the taxes in advance on behalf of the rest. This sum had to be refunded to them by the rest in conjunction with the poorer taxable citizens, who were likewise apportioned off to various symmoriae, but without becoming actual members of them, and were drawn upon by the real *symmoritae* to an extent proportional to their means. (2) After 358, this method was applied to the duty of equipping the war vessels, known as the *trierarchia*. (See LITURGIA.) Each of the twenty symmoriae had a certain number of ships assigned to it; the real *symmoritae* (not including the poorer citizens) divided the expense among themselves, and a varying number (at the most sixteen) of the richest had to raise the money advanced for a ship. To manage its affairs, each symmoria had its superintendents, curators, and assessors. The magisterial control was in both cases in the hands of the *strategi*, being connected with the military supplies. Though, by arrangement, the raising of taxes and fitting out of the ships were accelerated, yet it was open to abuse if the *symmoritae* unduly burdened the poor by an unjust distribution. In the disputes which thus arose, the decision rested with the *strategi*. If any one thought that another ought to have been taxed instead of himself, he could avail himself of *antidosis* (q. v.). Even the *metoeci*, who (like the citizens) had to pay war taxes, were divided into symmoriae. Aristotle (*Athen. Pol.* 61) describes one of the *strategi* as individually responsible for superintending the symmoriae for building triremes. See Thumser, *De Civium Atheniensium Muneribus* (Vienna, 1880).

Symphonia (συμφωνία). A species of musical entertainment at Greek and Roman banquets, but of a character not clearly defined in the existing passages in which the word occurs. In most cases the expressions used apply equally well to either vocal or instrumental music, and in no case is it possible to accept the reference as applicable to only one of them to the necessary exclusion of the other. An individual member of the band or chorus who rendered the music was called *symphoniacus* (Cic. *Pro Mil.* 21, 55) and *choraules* (Mart. ix. 77). Cf. Gell. xix. 3; Livy, xxxix. 6; and Marquardt, *Privatleben*, 181.

Symphoniăci. Musicians who played or sang together, usually for the entertainment of a company at dinner (Cic. *Pro Mil.* 21). See SYMPHONIA.

Symposium (συμπόσιον). A Greek term for a drinking-party. The symposium must be distinguished from the *deipnon* (δεῖπνον); for though drinking almost always followed a dinner-party, yet the former was regarded as entirely distinct from the latter, was regulated by different customs, and frequently received the addition of many guests who were not present at the dinner. For the Greeks did not usually drink at their dinner, and it was not till the conclusion of the meal that wine was introduced. Symposia were very frequent at Athens. Their enjoyment was heightened by agreeable conversation, by the introduction of music and dancing, and by games and amusements of various kinds; sometimes, too, philosophical subjects were discussed at them. The *Symposia* of Plato and Xenophon give us a lively idea of such entertainments at Athens. The name itself shows that the enjoyment of drinking was the main object of the symposia: wine from the juice of the grape (οἶνος ἀμπέλινος) was the only drink partaken of by the Greeks, with the exception of water. The wine was almost invariably mixed with water, and to drink it unmixed (ἄκρατον) was considered a characteristic of barbarians. The mixture was made in a large vessel called the *crater* (q. v.), from which it was

Symposium. (From the painting by Alma-Tadema.)

conveyed into the drinking-cups. The guests at a symposium reclined on couches, and were crowned with garlands of flowers. A master of the revels (ἄρχων τῆς πόσεως, συμποσίαρχος, or βασιλεύς) was usually chosen to conduct the symposium, whose commands the whole company had to obey, and who regulated the whole order of the entertainment and proposed the amusements. The same practice prevailed among the Romans, and their symposiarch was called *magister*, or *rex convivii*, or *arbiter bibendi*. The choice was generally determined by the throwing of *astragali* or *tali*. (See TALUS.) The proportion in which the wine and water were mixed was fixed by him, and also how much each of the company was to drink, for it was not usually left to the option of each person present to drink as much or as little as he pleased. The cups were always carried around from right to left (ἐπὶ δεξιά), and the same order was observed in the conversation and in everything that took place in the entertainment. The company frequently drank to the health of one another (προπίνειν, *propinare*), and each did it especially to the one to whom he handed the same cup. Respecting the games and amusements by which the symposia were enlivened, it is unnecessary to say much here, as most of them are described in separate articles in this work. Enigmas or riddles (*αἰνίγματα* or *γρῖφοι*) were among the most usual and favourite modes of diversion. Each of the company proposed one in turn to his right-hand neighbour; if he solved it, he was rewarded with a crown, a garland, a cake, or something of a similar kind, and sometimes with a kiss; if he failed, he had to drink a cup of unmixed wine, or of wine mixed with salt water, at one draught. The *cottabos* was also another favourite game at symposia, and was played at in various ways. (See COTTABOS.) Representations of symposia are very common on ancient vases. Two guests usually reclined on each couch (*κλίνη*), as is explained under CENA; TRICLINIUM; but sometimes there were five persons on one couch. A drinking-party among the Romans was sometimes called *convivium*, but the word *comissatio* (cognate with *κωμάζω*) more nearly corresponds to the Greek symposium. The Romans, however, usually drank during their dinner (*cena*), which they frequently prolonged during many hours, in the later times of the Republic and under the Empire. Their customs connected with drinking differed little from those of the Greeks, and have been incidentally noticed above.

See Becker-Göll, *Charikles*, ii. 335 foll.; Mahaffy, *Social Life in Greece*, ch. xi.; Becker-Göll, *Gallus*, i. 203–211; Marquardt, *Privatleben der Römer*, pp. 331–340; Valpy, *History of Toasting* (1881); Mew and Astion, *The Drinks of the World* (1892); and the articles CALDA; CERVESIA; PSYCTER; VINUM.

Syndĭcus (*σύνδικος*). A term meaning literally an advocate, but used in Athens to describe various magistrates. Thus the name is applied (1) to the five men who were appointed to defend, before the *nomothetae*, any law which it was proposed to abrogate (Dem. *Adv. Lept.* 501, Timocr. 707); (2) to men chosen to speak for the people in cases where the *δῆμος* was the complainant (Dem. *Adv. Lept.* 503, Hermann, *Lehrb. griech. Staatsalt.* 133); (3) to orators appointed to plead the cause of Athens before courts or councils abroad (Dem. *De Cor.* 271); (4) after the overthrow of the Thirty Tyrants, special officers called *σύνδικοι* were appointed to deal with cases involving confiscated property (Lys. *De Bon. Aristoph.* 32; Harpocr. s. v.).

Synĕdri (*σύνεδροι*). A general name given by the Greeks to the members of any council or deliberative body (*συνέδριον*), as the congress of the Greeks at Salamis and the court of the Areopagus. *Synedrion* also denotes the council-room in which the synedri regularly met.

Synegŏrus (*συνήγορος*). Literally "an advocate," but applied to Athenian officers of various functions. Litigants were theoretically required to conduct their cases in person, but the practice early arose of employing a friend, or later a hired expert, to act as *συνήγορος*. Such an advocate, after a short speech by his principal, would assume the leading part in the trial. An example of this is the defence of Ctesiphon by Demosthenes, against the accusation of Aeschines, though in this case Demosthenes was himself indirectly involved. The terms *συνήγορος* and *σύνδικος* seem to have been used indiscriminately in many cases. Thus the officers referred to under SYNDICUS (1, 2, 3) were known also as *συνήγοροι*. The term was also applied to magistrates chosen by lot to assist the *λογισταί* in the scrutiny of the accounts of a retiring magistrate (Arist. *Pol. Ath.* 54; Schol. Aristoph. *Vesp.* 689).

Synesius (*Συνέσιος*). A native of Cyrené. He was one of the most remarkable of the literary men of the fifth century. He was born A.D. 378, of a distinguished family, and studied at Alexandria under Hypatia and other celebrated instructors. So rapid was the progress he made, that, at the age of nineteen years, he was chosen by the inhabitants of Cyrené to present to the Emperor Arcadius a golden crown which had been voted him. The oration which he delivered on this occasion, and which is still preserved, has been much admired. At this period he was still a pagan; subsequently, however, he was persuaded by Theophilus, Bishop of Alexandria, to embrace Christianity. He was for a long time, however, very unsettled in his theological notions, and it was this very uncertainty which induced him for a considerable time to withstand the solicitations of Theophilus and not accept a bishopric. He yielded, however, in A.D. 410, and, separating from a wife for whom he cherished a deep affection, he was consecrated bishop of Ptolemaïs in Cyrenaïca. He died about 430. The works of Synesius are rather philosophical and literary than theological. They are written with elegance. When the subject admits, his diction is elevated, and sometimes even sublime. He possesses the art of rendering abstract subjects agreeable, by intermingling with them mythological and historical or else poetical passages. His letters, which are 154 in number, afford varied, amusing, and instructive reading. His hymns, in iambics of four or five feet, present a singular mixture of poetic images, Christian truths, and Platonic reveries, for it was to the school of Plato that he always continued to be more or less attached. The most complete edition of his works is that of Petau or Petavius (Paris, 1612; reprinted 1631–40), with additions by Morel. See Volkmann, *Synesius von Cyrene* (Berlin, 1869).

Syngrăphé (*συγγραφή*). A written contract as distinguished from *συνθήκη* and *συμβόλαιον*, which may be verbal, and from *ὁμολογία*, which is regularly verbal in its nature. At Athens all important contracts were made in writing (e. g. leases, loans, and agreements involving specific conditions), and the tablet containing them (*βιβλίον*, *γραμματεῖον*, or if double, *δίπτυχον*) was deposited with a third person mutually agreed upon as its custodian.

Synnăda (*τὰ Σύνναδα*), also **Synnas**. A city in the north of Phrygia Salutaris, at first inconsiderable, but afterwards a place of much importance, and from the time of Constantine the capital of Phrygia Salutaris.

Synoecia (*τὰ συνοίκια*) or **Synoecesia** (*τὰ συνοικέσια*). The eve of the Athenian festival of the Panathenaea (q. v.).

Synoecia (*συνοικία*). The Greek name for a lodging-house which held several families, and therefore corresponding to the Latin *insula*. See DOMUS.

Syntax. See GRAMMATICA.

Syntaxis (*σύνταξις*). The tribute paid by the allies of Athens into the treasury of the League was originally called φόρος (see DELOS). But after the downfall of the Athenian supremacy, and the establishment of the second confederacy in B.C. 378–7, the old name was dropped, as it had grown hateful to the allies with the general unpopularity of the rule of Athens, and the new assessment was known as σύνταξις (Harpocr. s. v. 169; Dem. *De Cor.* 305; *De Pace*, 60). See TELOS.

Synthĕsis. The Romans found the toga an inconvenient garment to wear while reclining at meals, and as the tunic alone was not considered suitable, they devised the *synthesis*, or *vestis cenatoria*, for use at such times. We know nothing of its form or appearance, except that it was a short and easy garment, of various colors, and was changed often during a feast by men of fashion (Mart. v. 79, 2). The same garment was usually worn at the Saturnalia (Mart. xiv. 11). The word is also applied to a collection of similar articles of dress of any kind, as a *synthesis tunicarum* (Mart. iv. 46). See CENA.

Syphax (Σύφαξ). A king of the Massaesylians, the westernmost tribe of the Numidians. His history is related in the life of his contemporary and rival, MASINISSA. Syphax was taken prisoner by Masinissa, B.C. 203, and was sent by Scipio, under the charge of Laelius, to Rome, where he died shortly after.

Syrăco. See SYRACUSAE.

Syracūsae (Συράκουσαι or Συράκοσσαι, Ion. Συρήκουσαι, also Συρακοῦσαι, Συρακούση). Now Siracusa in Italian; Syracuse in English: the wealthiest and most populous town in Sicily. It was situated on the south part of the east coast, 400 stadia north of the promontory Plemmyrium, and ten stadia northeast of the mouth of the river Anapus, near the lake or marsh called Syraco (Συρακώ), from which it derived its name. It was founded B.C. 734, one year after the foundation of Naxos, by a colony of Corinthians and other Dorians, led by Archias the Corinthian. The town was originally confined to the island Ortygia lying immediately off the coast; but it afterwards spread over the neighbouring mainland, and at the time of its greatest extension under the elder Dionysius it consisted of five distinct towns, each surrounded by separate walls. Some writers indeed describe Syracuse as consisting of four towns, but this simply arises from the fact that Epipolae was frequently not reckoned a portion of the city. These five towns were: (1) ORTYGIA (Ὀρτυγία), frequently called simply the ISLAND (Νᾶσος or Νῆσος), an island of an oblong shape, about two miles in circumference, lying between the Great Harbour on the west and the Little Harbour on the east. It was, as has been already remarked, the portion of the city first built, and it contained the citadel or Acropolis, surrounded by double walls, which Timoleon caused to be destroyed. In this island also was the celebrated fountain of Arethusa. It was originally separated from the mainland by a narrow channel, which was subsequently filled up by a causeway; but this causeway must at a still later time have been swept away, since we find in the Roman period that the island was connected with the mainland by means of a bridge. (2) ACHRADĪNA (Ἀχραδίνη) occupied originally the high ground of the peninsula north of Ortygia, and was surrounded on the north and east by the sea. The lower ground between Achradina and Ortygia was at first not included in the fortifications of either, but was

Fountain of Arethusa at Syracuse. (From a photograph.)

employed partly for religious processions and partly for the burial of the dead. At the time of the siege of Syracuse by the Athenians in the Peloponnesian War (415), the city consisted only of the two parts already mentioned, Ortygia forming the inner and Achradina the outer city, but separated, as explained above, by the low ground between the two. (3) TYCHÉ (Τύχη), named after the temple of Tyché or Fortune, and situated northwest of Achradina, in the direction of the port called Trogilus. At the time of the Athenian siege of Syracuse it was only an unfortified suburb, but it afterwards became the most populous part of the city. In this quarter stood the Gymnasium. (4) NEAPŎLIS (Νέα πόλις), nearly southwest of Achradina, was also, at the time of the Athenian siege of Syracuse, merely a suburb, and called TEMENĪTES, from having within it the statue and consecrated ground of Apollo Temenites. Neapolis contained the chief theatre of Syracuse, which was the largest in all Sicily, and many temples. (5) EPIPŎLAE (αἱ Ἐπιπολαί), a space of ground rising above the three quarters of Achradina, Tyché, and Neapolis, which gradually diminished in breadth as it rose higher, until it ended in a small conical mound. This rising ground was surrounded with strong walls by the elder Dionysius, and was thus included in Syracuse, which now became one of the most strongly fortified cities of the ancient world. The highest point of Epipolae was called Eurўēlus (Εὐρύηλος), on which stood the fort Labdalum (Λάβδαλον). After Epipolae had been added to the city, the circumference of Syracuse was one hundred and eighty stadia, or upward of twenty-two English miles; and the entire population of the city is supposed to have amounted to five hundred thousand souls at the time of its greatest prosperity.

Syracuse had two harbours. The Great Harbour, still called Porto Maggiore, is a splendid bay about five miles in circumference, formed by the island Ortygia and the promontory Plemmyrium. The Small Harbour, also called Laccius (Λάκκιος), lying between Ortygia and Achradina, was capacious enough to receive a large fleet of ships of war. There were several stone quarries (*lautumiae*) in Syracuse, which are frequently mentioned by ancient writers, and in which the unfortunate Athenian prisoners were confined. These quarries were partly in Achradina, on the descent from the higher ground to the lower level towards Ortygia, and partly in Neapolis, under the southern cliff of Epipolae. From these was taken the stone of which the city was built (Thucyd. vii. 86). The so-called "Ear of Dionysius," in which the tyrant was supposed to overhear the conversation of his captives, is probably an invention of a mediæval writer. The city was supplied with water from an aqueduct, which was constructed by Gelon and improved by Hieron. It was brought through Epipolae and Neapolis to Achradina and Ortygia. The modern city of Syracuse is confined to the island. The remaining quarters of the ancient city are now uninhabited, and their position marked only by a few ruins. Of these the most important are the remains of the great theatre, and of an amphitheatre of the Roman period. See THEATRUM.

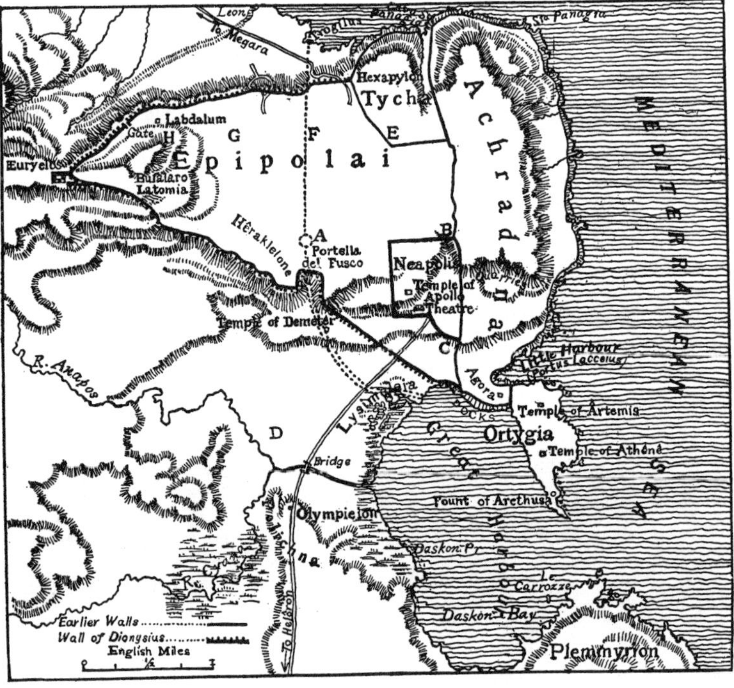

Plan of Ancient Syracuse. (After Freeman.)

The government of Syracuse was originally an aristocracy; and the political power was in the hands of the landed proprietors, called Geomori or Gamori. In course of time the people, having increased in numbers and wealth, expelled the Geomori and established a democracy. But this form of government did not last long. Gelon espoused the cause of the aristocratic party, and proceeded to restore them by force of arms; but on his approach the people opened the gates to him, and he was acknowledged without opposition tyrant or sovereign of Syracuse, B.C. 485. Under his rule and that of his brother Hieron, Syracuse was raised to an unexampled degree of wealth and prosperity. Hieron died in 467, and was succeeded by his brother Thrasybulus; but the rapacity and cruelty of the latter soon provoked a revolt among his subjects, which led to his deposition and the establishment of a democratic form of government. The next most important event in the history of Syracuse was the siege of the city by the Athenians, which ended in the total destruction of the great Athenian armament in 413. This affair, known in history as the Sicilian Expedition, was the turning-point in the Peloponnesian War (q. v.). The expedition set out from Athens in B.C. 415 under Alcibiades (q. v.), Nicias (q. v.), and Lamachus, and at first won a number of successes, so that Nicias, in 414, had seized Epipolae and begun the complete investment of Syracuse. The arrival of Gylippus, the Spartan general, turned the tide. The Syracusans defeated the Athenians, annihilated the invading army, and took Nicias and his later colleague Demosthenes prisoners. See GYLIPPUS.

The democracy continued to exist in Syracuse till B.C. 406, when the elder Dionysius made himself tyrant of the city. After a long and prosperous reign, he was succeeded in 367 by his son, the younger Dionysius, who was finally expelled by Timoleon in 343. A republican form of government was again established; but it did not last long; and in 317 Syracuse fell under the sway of Agathocles. This tyrant died in 289; and the city being distracted by factions, the Syracusans voluntarily conferred the supreme power upon Hieron II., with the title of king, in 270. Hieron cultivated friendly relations with the Romans; but on his death in 216, at the advanced age of ninety-two, his grandson Hieronymus, who succeeded him, espoused the side of the Carthaginians. A Roman army under Marcellus was sent against Syracuse; and after a siege of two years, during which Archimedes assisted his fellow-citizens by the construction of various engines of war (see ARCHIMEDES), the city was taken by Marcellus in 212. From this time Syracuse became a town of the Roman province of Sicily. See Lupus, *Die Stadt Syrakus im Alterthum* (Strassburg, 1887), and the works cited under SICILIA.

Syracusānus Portus (Συρακόσιος λίμην). Now Porto Vecchio; a harbour on the eastern coast of Corsica, where the Syracusans had probably established a factory for their trade: according to Diodorus, it was the best harbour in the island.

Syria (ἡ Συρία, in Aramaean Surja; now Soristan, Arab. Esh-Sham, i. e. "the land on the left," Syria), a country of western Asia, lying along the eastern end of the Mediterranean Sea, between Asia Minor and Egypt. In a wider sense the word was used for the whole tract of country bounded by the Tigris on the east, the mountains of Armenia and Cilicia on the north, the Mediterranean on the west, and the Arabian Desert on the south; the whole of which was peopled by the Aramaean branch of the great Semitic (or Syro-Arabian) race, and is included in the Old Testament under the name of Aram. The people were of the same races, and those of the north of the Taurus in Cappadocia and Pontus are called White Syrians (Λευκόσυροι), in contradistinction to the people of darker complexion in Syria Proper, who are sometimes even called Black Syrians (Σύροι μέλανες). Even when the name of Syria is used in its ordinary narrower sense, it is often confounded with Assyria, which only differs from Syria by having the definite article prefixed. Again, in the narrower sense of the name, Syria still includes two districts which are often considered as not belonging to it, namely, PHOENĪCĒ and PALAESTĪNA, and a third which is likewise often considered separate, namely, COELE-SYRIA; but this last is generally reckoned a part of Syria. In this narrower sense, then, Syria was bounded on the west (beginning from the south) by Mount Hermon, at the southern end of Antilibanus, which separated it from Palestine, by the range of Libanus, dividing it from Phoenicé, by the Mediterranean, and by Mount Amanus, which divided it from Cilicia; on the north (where it bordered on Cappadocia) by the main chain of Mount Taurus, and striking the Euphrates just below Iuliopolis, and considerably above Samosata; hence the Euphrates forms the eastern boundary. The western part of the country was intersected by a series of mountains, running south from the Taurus, under the names of Amanus, Pieria, Casius, Bargylus, and Libanus and Antilibanus; and the northern part, between the Amanus and the Euphrates, was also mountainous. The chief river of Syria was the Orontes, and the smaller rivers Chalus and Chrysorrhoas were also of importance. The valleys among the mountains were fertile, especially in the northern part; even the east, which is now merged in the great desert of Arabia, appears to have had more numerous and more extensive spaces capable of cultivation, and supported great cities, the ruins of which now stand in the midst of sandy wastes.

In the earliest historical period Syria contained a number of independent kingdoms, of which Damascus was the most powerful. These were subdued by David, but became again independent at the end of Solomon's reign; from which time we find the kings of Damascus sometimes at war with the kings of Israel, and sometimes in alliance with them against the kings of Judah, till the reign of Tiglath-Pileser, king of Assyria, who, having been invited by Ahaz, king of Judah, to assist him against the united forces of Rezin, king of Syria, and Pekah, king of Israel, took Damascus, and probably conquered all Syria, about B.C. 740. Having been a part successively of the Assyrian, Babylonian, Persian, and Macedonian Empires, it fell, after the battle of Ipsus (B.C. 301), to the share of Seleucus Nicator, and formed a part of the great kingdom of the Seleucidae, whose history is given

Typical Syrian of Egyptian Art. (Photograph by Flinders Petrie.)

in the articles ANTIOCHUS; DEMETRIUS; SELEUCUS. In this partition, however, Coelesyria and Palestine went, not to Syria, but to Egypt, and the possession of those provinces became the great source of contention between the Ptolemies and the Seleucids. By the irruptions of the Parthians on the east, and the unsuccessful war of Antiochus the Great with the Romans on the west, the Greek-Syrian kingdom was reduced to the limits of Syria itself, and became weaker and weaker, until it was overthrown by Tigranes, king of Armenia, B.C. 79. Soon afterwards, when the Romans had conquered Tigranes as well as Mithridates, Syria was quietly added by Pompey to the empire of the Republic, and was constituted a province B.C. 54; but its northern district, COMMAGĒNĒ, was not included in this arrangement. As the eastern province of the Roman Empire, and with its great desert frontier, Syria was constantly exposed to the irruptions of the Parthians, and, after them, of the Persians; but it long remained one of the most flourishing of the provinces. The attempt of Zenobia to make it the seat of empire is noticed under ZENOBIA. While the Roman emperors defended this precious possession against the attacks of the Persian kings with various success, a new danger arose, as early as the fourth century, from the Arabians of the Desert, who began to be known under the name of Saracens; and, when the rise of Mohammed had given to the Arabs that great religious impulse which revolutionized the Eastern world, Syria was the first great conquest that they made from the Eastern Empire, A.D. 632–638. In the time immediately succeeding the Macedonian conquest, Syria was regarded as consisting of two parts—the north, including the whole country down to the beginning of the Lebanon range, and the south, consisting of Coelesyria in its more extended sense. The former, which was called Syria Proper, or Upper Syria (ἡ ἄνω Συρία, Syria Superior), was divided into four districts or tetrarchies, which were named after their respective capitals, Seleucis, Antiochené, Laodicené, and Apamené.

The Roman province of SYRIA, as originally constituted by Pompey in B.C. 64, was by no means a single homogeneous region. Owing to the different nationalities and interests which Syria properly so called comprised, it was at first parcelled out between the Roman jurisdiction and a number of independent territories which were allowed to remain within it. Under the Roman proconsul of Syria were at first Upper Syria (with the chief towns Antioch, Seleucia, Apamea, Laodicea, Cyrrhus, Hieropolis, and Beroea), and the land of Phoenicia, including Tripolis, Byblus, Tyre, and Sidon; but Iudea was left for a time nominally independent, except for a short time when Gabinius broke it up into five districts. Caesar made Iudea a client State under its own princes, and it did not become a Roman province (of the second rank, under a procurator) until A.D. 6. Similarly Commagené was left under its own princes until A.D. 17, and again from 38 till 72, when it was finally joined to the province of Syria; Chalcis retained its own princes till 92, when Domitian added it to the province; Abilené till 49; Arethusa and Emesa till 78; Damascus was not included in the province of Syria till 106. The province of Syria under the Empire was governed by an imperial legate residing at Antioch: it was eventually divided into ten districts, named (mostly after their capital cities) Commagené, Cyrrhesticé, Pieria, Seleucis, Chalcidicé, Chalybonitis, Palmyrené, Apamené, Cassiotis, and Laodicené; but the last is sometimes included under Cassiotis. (See the several articles.) From A.D. 66 Iudea or Syria Palaestina was recognized as a separate province, and at the end of the second century Syria was divided into two provinces, Syria Magna or Coelesyria, and Syria Phoenicé. Constantine the Great separated the two northern districts—namely, Commagené and Cyrrhesticé—and erected them into a distinct province, called EUPHRATENSIS or EUPHRATESIA; and the rest of Syria was afterwards divided by Theodosius II. into the two provinces of SYRIA PRIMA, including the sea-coast and the country north of Antioch, and having that city for its capital; and SYRIA SECUNDA, the district along the Orontes, with Apamea for its capital; while the eastern districts were now a part of Persia.

Syria Dea (ἡ Συρίη Θεός). A deity of generation and fecundity worshipped in Syrian Hierapolis under the name Ἀτάργατις, whom the later Greeks and the Romans simply called "the Syrian goddess." From the time of the sovereignty of the Seleucidae, when the ancient paganism was highly honoured in Hierapolis, the worship of this goddess spread among the Greeks, and from them found its way to Rome, where she had a temple in the days of the Empire, and to other parts of Italy, and still farther west. The old idea of her attributes had so widened in the course of time that she shared those of Iuno, Venus, Rhea, Cybelé, Minerva, Diana, the Parcae, and other goddesses. She is represented on Roman monuments, seated on a throne between two lions. Her priests were generally eunuchs. They were in the habit of making excursions into Greece and Italy to extend the worship of the goddess by means of ecstatic dances and prophecies, and to collect pious alms for her sanctuary. See Apul. *Met.* viii. 24; Lucian, *De Dea Syria;* and the *C. I. L.* vi. 115, 116.

Syriae Portae (αἱ Συρίαι Πύλαι). Now the Pass of Beilan; a most important pass between Cilicia and Syria, lying between the shore of the Gulf of Issus on the west and Mount Amanus on the east.

Syriānus (Συριανός). A Greek philosopher of the Neo-Platonic School. He was a native of Alexandria, and studied at Athens under Plutarchus, whom he succeeded as head of the Neo-Platonic School in the early part of the fifth century A.D. The most distinguished of his disciples was Proclus, who regarded him with the greatest veneration, and gave directions that at his death he should be buried in the same tomb with Syrianus. Syrianus wrote several works, some of which are extant. Of these the most valuable are the commentaries on the *Metaphysics* of Aristotle.

Syrinx (σύριγξ). A Pan's pipe, called by the Romans *harundo* or *fistula.*

Syrinx (Σύριγξ). A powerful city of Hyrcania, the capital of that province under the Greek kings of Syria.

Syrinx (Σύριγξ). An Arcadian nymph, who, being pursued by Pan, fled into the river Ladon, and at her own prayer was metamorphosed into a reed, of which Pan then made his flute. See PAN.

Syrma (σύρμα). A long robe worn by tragic actors on the stage (Juv. viii. 229).

Syros (Σῦρος) or **Syrus**. Now Syra; an island

in the Aegaean Sea, and one of the Cyclades, lying between Rhenea and Cythnus.

Syrtes. See SYRTIS.

Syrtĭca Regio (ἡ Συρτική). Now the western part of Tripoli; the special name of that part of the northern coast of Africa which lay between the two Syrtes, from the river Triton, at the bottom of the Syrtis Minor, on the west, to the Philaenorum Arae, at the bottom of the Syrtis Maior, on the east. It was for the most part a very narrow strip of sand, interspersed with salt marshes, between the sea and a range of mountains forming the edge of the Great Desert (Sahara), with only here and there a few spots capable of cultivation, especially about the river Cinyps. It was peopled by Libyan tribes. Under the Romans it formed a part of the province of Africa. It was often called TRIPOLITĀNA, from its three chief cities, Abrotonum, Oea, and Leptis Magna; and this became its usual name under the Later Empire, and has been handed down to our own time in the modern name of the regency of Tripoli.

Syrtis (Σύρτις) and **Syrtes.** The two great gulfs in the eastern half of the northern coast of Africa. The name is derived by the ancients from σύρω, "to draw" or "to suck," but is possibly cognate with the Arabic *sert*, "a desert," a term at present applied to the whole coast as bordering upon the Great Desert. Both gulfs were proverbially dangerous, the Greater Syrtis from its sandbanks and quicksands, and its unbroken exposure to the north winds, the Less from its shelving rocky shores, its exposure to the northeast winds, and the consequent variableness of the tides in it. (1) **Syrtis Maior** (ἡ μεγάλη Σύρτις, Gulf of Sidra), the easternmost of the two, a wide and deep gulf on the shores of Tripolitana and Cyrenaïca, exactly opposite to the Ionic Sea. The Great Desert comes down close to its shores, forming a sandy coast, called by the ancients SYRTĬCA REGIO. The terror of being driven on shore in it is referred to in the narrative of St. Paul's voyage to Italy (Acts, xxvii. 17, "fearing lest they should fall into the Syrtis"); and the dangers of a march through the loose sand on its shores, sometimes of a burning heat, and sometimes saturated with sea-water, were scarcely less formidable. (2) **Syrtis Minor** (ἡ μικρὰ Σύρτις, Gulf of Khabs) lies in the southwestern angle of the great bend formed by the northern coast of Africa as it drops down to the south from the neighbourhood of Carthage, and then bears again to the east; in other words, in the angle between the eastern coast of Zeugitana and Byzacena (Tunis) and the northern coast of Tripolitana (Tripoli). In its mouth, near the northern extremity, lie the islands of Cercina and Cercinitis. In Herodotus, the word Syrtis occurs in a few passages, without any distinction between the Greater and the Less. It seems most probable that he means to denote by this term the Greater Syrtis, and that he included the Less in the lake Tritonis.

Syrus, PUBLILIUS. See PUBLILIUS SYRUS.

Syssitia (τὰ συσσίτια). The meals taken in public and in common among the Dorians in Sparta and Crete, and confined to men and youths only. In Sparta all the Spartiatae, or citizens over twenty years of age, were obliged to attend these meals, which were there called φειδίτια. No one was allowed to absent himself except for some satisfactory reason. The table was provided for by fixed monthly contributions of barley, wine, cheese, figs, and money to buy meat; the State only paid for the maintenance of the two kings, each of whom received a double portion. The places where the syssitia were held were called tents, and the guests were divided into messes of about fifteen members, vacancies in which were filled up by ballot, unanimous consent being necessary for election. The principal dish at the syssitia was a black broth (μέλας ζωμός) with pork, served with mixed wine. The tables were superintended by a woman of free birth, who had several men to assist her. She gave the best fare to those present who were most eminent in the service of the State. See Hoeck, *Kreta*, iii. 120–139; Bielchowsky, *De Spartanorum Syssitiis* (Breslau, 1869); and Gilbert, *Gk. Const. Ant.* p. 67 (1895).

Systȳlus (σύστυλος). Close-columned. A word denoting an intercolumniation of only two diameters apart (Vitruv. iii. 2). See TEMPLUM.

Sythas (Σύθας). A river on the frontiers of Achaia and Sicyonia.

T

T, as a symbol.

IN GREEK.—T=τῆς, τῶν, etc. Τίτος, Τιβέριος. As a numeral=19 (old system). τ′=300, ͵τ=300,000.

IN LATIN.—T=tabula, te, tergum, terra, tesserarius, tiro, Titus, tribunus, tumulus, teruncius ($\frac{1}{40}$ of a sestertius).

T·B·Q=tu bene quiescas.

T·C=titulum curavit.

T·F·C(R)=testamento faciendum (fieri) curavit (rogavit).

T·K=tabularium castrense.

T·L·H·F·C=testamento legavit; heres faciundum curavit.

T·O·B·Q=tibi ossa bene quiescant.

T·P=tanta pecunia, tribunicia potestate.

T·P·I(M)=testamentum (titulo) poni iussit (posuit memoriae).

T·R·P·D·S·T·T·L=te rogo praeteriens dicas sit tibi terra levis.

T·S·T·L(T·T·L·S)=terra sit tibi levis (tibi terra levis sit).

T·V·F=ture vino fecerunt.

Tabella. A tablet used as a ballot in voting either at the elections of the Comitia or in the courts of justice. See COMITIA; IUDEX; JUDICIAL PROCEDURE; TABELLARIAE LEGES.

Tabellariae Leges. Laws by which, for the purpose of weakening the power of the Optimates, the practice of voting by secret ballot was introduced at Rome. There were four of these laws: (1) the LEX GABINIA (B.C. 139), prescribing the use of the ballot in the election of magistrates; (2) the LEX CASSIA (B.C. 137), prescribing the ballot in the *iudicium populi* except in cases of treason (*perduellio*); (3) the LEX PAPIRIA (B.C. 131), introducing the ballot in voting on the enactment and repeal of laws; and (4) the LEX CAELIA (B.C. 107), extending the use of the ballot to questions even of *perduellio*. All these laws are mentioned by Cicero (*De Leg.* iii. 16, 35). See COMITIA.

Tabellarius. A letter-carrier or courier, employed by private persons to carry letters and messages (Cic. *Ad Fam.* xii. 12; xiv. 22). Ship captains often carried foreign letters and the tabellarii of the provincial governors and of the *publicani* (q. v.); also, as a favour, they often served private individuals (Cic. *Ad Att.* v. 15; id. 19). See also CURSUS PUBLICUS; EPISTOLA.

Tabellio. A sort of notary in the Imperial Age employed in drawing up legal documents. They had stands in the market-places (Capitol. *Macrin.* 4). See SCRIBAE.

Taberna (σκηναί, γέρρα). (1) A shop. It was so named because in Rome the shops consisted for the most part of boarded stalls projecting from the houses or raised under the colonnades which surrounded the market-places. Subsequently, however, as wealth and commerce increased, the ground-story of the rows of houses, and even palaces, in a street were appropriated for shops and let out to separate tradesmen, as in many of the great mansions in Continental towns. In the majority of cases the shop had no communication with the rest of the house, the tenant merely occupying it for the purpose of his business and dwelling himself elsewhere; but some few houses of a respectable class have been discovered at Pompeii in which the shop has an entrance from its back into the habitable parts of the mansion, and these are reasonably believed to have been in the occupancy of the persons who dwelt on the premises, and who

Roman Shop. (Pompeian painting.)

are, in consequence, supposed to have been wealthy tradesmen. The general appearance of a Roman shop, as uniformly exhibited by the numerous examples remaining at Pompeii, resembled those of our butchers and fish-dealers, being entirely open in front with the exception of a low wall forming the counter, and were closed by wooden shutters at night. They are mostly comprised in a single room, without any other convenience; though in some instances a small back parlour and other appurtenances are added. The annexed illustration represents an elevation restored of six shop-

Shop-fronts at Pompeii. (Restoration.)

fronts at Pompeii. Various signs on the fronts of shops denoted the especial business carried on. Thus a wooden goat indicated a milk-dealer's; an amphora, a wine-shop; a snake (the symbol of Aesculapius), an apothecary's; a row of hams, an eating-house, etc. (See DOMUS, pp. 548, 549.) (2) A tavern. See CAUPONA.

Sign from Baker's Shop. (Pompeii.)

Tabernacŭlum, Tentorium (κλισίη, σκηνή). (1) A tent. The first of these words was originally a hut made of boards (*tabulae*). Tents were regularly made of skins stretched on wooden supports, like our canvas tents; whence the name *tentorium*. In summer the soldiers slept in tents (*sub pellibus durare*, Livy, v. 2), but in winter they were lodged either in towns or, if in camp, in huts of stone or turf. To give them only tents in winter was regarded as very severe (Tac. *Ann.* xiii. 35). The κλισίαι of Homer were not really tents at all, but only wooden or walled huts. See Buchholz, *Hom. Realien*, ii. 340. (2) See AUGURES; DIVINATIO; TEMPLUM.

Tabernae. See TRES TABERNAE.

Tables, THE TWELVE. See TWELVE TABLES.

Tablīnum. A room in a Roman dwelling-house. See DOMUS, p. 545.

Tabŭla Bantīna. A bronze tablet found near Bantia, on the borders of Lucania and Apulia, in 1793, and now in the Naples Museum. It contains on one side thirty-three lines in Oscan, more or less complete, and on the other an inscription in Latin. The Oscan portion relates to the local affairs of Bantia (as to fines, oaths, penalties, etc.), and the Latin portion gives part of a local law. It is the most important source in existence for knowledge of the Oscan language. The Latin text will be found in Allen's *Early Latin* (Boston, 1880); the Oscan is printed in Mommsen's *Oskische Studien* (Berlin, 1845) and in Zvetaieff's *Sylloge Inscriptionum Oscarum* (St. Petersburg, 1878). See also the article OSCI.

Tabŭla Cebētis. See CEBES.

Tabŭla Iliăca. A marble slab covered with figures in low-relief and inscriptions, ten inches high and eleven and a half inches wide, now in the Capitoline Museum at Rome. It was found in 1683 near the site of the ancient Bovillae, and gives scenes from the Ἰλίου Πέρσις of Stesichorus, the *Iliad* of Homer, the *Aethiopis* of Arctinus of Miletus, and the *Little Iliad* (Ἰλιὰς Μικρά) of Lesches of Pyrrha. Jahn supposes it to have been intended for use in schools, but it was more probably an ornamental panel forming part of a receptacle for books. It is reproduced in its actual state and also in a restoration in Schreiber's *Atlas of Classical Antiquities* (Engl. edition by Anderson), plates xcii. A and xciii., with a full description (London, 1895).

Tabŭla Lusoria (πίναξ). A board for playing games. See DUODECIM SCRIPTA; LATRUNCULI.

Tabŭla Peutingeriāna. See ITINERARIA.

Tabŭlae or **Pugillāres** (πίνακες, δέλτοι, πινάκια). Tablets for writing. See WRITING AND WRITING MATERIALS.

Tabŭlae Duodĕcim. See TWELVE TABLES.

Tabŭlae Iguvīnae and **Eugubīnae.** See UMBRIA.

Tabŭlae Publĭcae. See TABULARIUM.

Tabularii. Notaries or accountants either public or private (see SCRIBA; TABELLIO). Public tabularii had the custody of public documents (Cod. Theod. viii. 2).

Tabularium. The place in Rome where the public archives (*tabulae publicae*) were preserved. These archives comprised the rogations, the *senatus consulta* and *plebiscita,* financial records, public contracts, censorial registers (*tabulae censoriae*), the records of the courts, registers of vital statistics, jury lists, and election returns. These were kept in different places, as in the Temple of Saturn, the Aerarium, and the Temple of Ceres. The officers charged with the care of public documents were the quaestors, the plebeian aediles, the tribunes, the praetors, and (under Tiberius) special *curatores tabulariorum publici* (Dio Cass. lxxvi. 16). See Mommsen, *Röm. Staatsrecht,* ii. 557-560. At Athens the public archives were kept in the Metroum (μητρῷον).

Taburnus. Now Taburno; a mountain belonging half to Campania and half to Samnium. It shut in the Caudine Pass on its southern side.

Tacăpē (Τακάπη). Now Khabs or Gabes; a city of North Africa, in the Regio Syrtica, at the innermost angle of the Syrtis Minor, to which the modern town gives its name.

Tacfarinas. A Numidian, and Roman auxiliary, who deserted, and became the leader of the Musulamii, a people bordering on Mauretania. He was at length defeated and slain in battle by Dolabella, A.D. 24 (Tac. *Ann.* ii. 52; iii. 73; iv. 24).

Tachompso (Ταχομψώ), also **Tacompsos** and **Metacompso** (Μετακομψώ). A city in the Dodecaschoenus—that is, the part of Aethiopia immediately above Egypt.

Tachos (Ταχώς). A king of Egypt who succeeded Acoris, and maintained the independence of his country for a short time during the latter end of the reign of Artaxerxes II. (B.C. 364-361). He was, however, overthrown by Nectanabis, who succeeded him as king of Egypt (Diod. xv. 92; Nep. *Chabr.* 2).

Tacĭtus. (1) PUBLIUS CORNELIUS. (The praenomen, Publius, is given in the best MS. [Med. I.]; and in an inscription.) One of the greatest of the Roman writers of history. The time and place of his birth are unknown. He was a little older than the younger Pliny, who was born A.D. 61. His father was probably Cornelius Tacitus, a Roman *eques,* who is mentioned as a procurator in Gallia Belgica, and who died in 79 (Pliny, *Epist.* vii. 76). Tacitus was first promoted by the emperor Vespasian, and he received other favours from both Titus and Domitian (*Hist.* i. 1). The most probable account is that Tacitus was appointed *tribunus militum laticlavius* by Vespasian, quaestor by Titus, and praetor by Domitian. In 78 he married the daughter of the famous general, C. Iulius Agricola, to whom he had been betrothed in the preceding year, while Agricola was consul. In the reign of Domitian, and in 88, Tacitus was praetor, and he assisted as one of the quindecimviri at the Ludi Saeculares which were celebrated in that year (*Ann.* xi. 11). Agricola died at Rome in 93, but neither Tacitus nor the daughter of Agricola was then with him. It is not known where Tacitus was during the last illness of Agricola. In the reign of Nerva, 97, Tacitus was appointed consul suffectus, in the place of T. Virginius Rufus, who had died in that year, and whose funeral oration he delivered. We know that Tacitus had attained oratorical distinction when the younger Pliny was commencing his career. He and Tacitus were appointed in the reign of Nerva (99) to conduct the prosecution of Marius, proconsul of Africa. Tacitus and Pliny were most intimate friends. In the collection of the letters of Pliny there are eleven letters addressed to Tacitus. The time of the death of Tacitus is unknown, but he appears to have survived Trajan, who died 117. Nothing is recorded of any children of his, though the Emperor Tacitus claimed a descent from the historian, and ordered his works to be placed in all public libraries. The following are the extant works of Tacitus: (*a*) *Vita Agricolae,* the life of Agricola, which was written after the death of Domitian (96), as we may probably conclude from the introduction, which was certainly written after Trajan's accession. This life is justly admired as a specimen of biography. It is a monument to the memory of a noble man and an able commander and administrator, by an affectionate son-in-law, who has portrayed, in his peculiar manner and with many masterly touches, the virtues of one of the most illustrious of the Romans. (*b*) *Historiae,* which were written after the death of Nerva (98) and before the *Annales.* They comprehended the period from the second consulship of Galba (68) to the death of Domitian (96), and the author designed to add the reigns of Nerva and Trajan. The first four books alone are extant in a complete form, and they comprehend only the events of about one year. The fifth book is imperfect, and goes no further than the commencement of the siege of Jerusalem by Titus, and the war of Civilis in Germany. It is not known how many books of the *Historiae* there were, but it must have been a large work if it was all written on the same scale as the first five books. (*c*) *Annales,* which commence with the death of Augustus (14), hence *ab excessu divi Augusti,* and comprise the period to the death of Nero (68)—a space of fifty-four years. The greater part of the fifth book is lost, and also the seventh, eighth, ninth, tenth, the beginning of the eleventh, and the end of the sixteenth, which is the last book. These lost parts comprised the whole of Caligula's reign, the first five years of Claudius, and the last two of Nero. (*d*) *De Moribus et Populis Germaniae,* usually called the *Germania,* a treatise describing the Germanic nations. It is of little value as a geographical description; the first few chapters contain as much of the geography of Germany as Tacitus knew. The main subject is the description of the political institutions, the religion, and the habits of the various tribes included under the name Germani. The value of the information contained in this treatise has often been discussed, and its credibility attacked; but we may estimate its true character by observing the precision of the writer as to those Germans who were best known to the Romans from being near the Rhine. That the hearsay accounts of more remote tribes must partake of the defects of all such evidence is obvious; and we cannot easily tell whether Tacitus embellished that which he had heard obscurely told. But to consider the Germany as a fiction, or as a purely political tract, is one of those absurdities which need only be recorded, not refuted. (*e*) *Dialogus de Oratoribus.* If this dialogue is the work of Tacitus, and it probably is, it must be his earliest work, for it was written in the sixth year of Vespasian. The style is more easy than that of the *Annales*—more diffuse, less condensed; but there is an obvious difference between the style of the *Dialogus* and the *Historiae*—nothing so striking as to make us contend for a different authorship. Besides this, it is nothing unusual for works of the same author, which are written at different times, to vary greatly in style, especially if they treat of different matters. The oldest MSS. also attribute the *Dialogus* to Tacitus. (See Gudeman's introduction to his edition of the work.) The treatise is an essay, in the form of a dialogue, giving an account of the decay of oratory under the Empire.

The *Annales* of Tacitus, the work of a mature age, contain the chief events of the period which they embrace, arranged under their several years. There seems no peculiar propriety in giving the name of *Annales* to this work, simply because the events are arranged in the order of time. In the *Annales* of Tacitus, the Princeps or Emperor is the centre about which events are grouped. Yet the most important public events, both in Italy and the provinces, are not omitted, though everything is treated as subordinate to the exhibition of imperial power. The *Historiae*, which were written before the *Annales*, are in a more diffuse style, and the treatment of the extant part is different from that of the *Annales.* Tacitus wrote the *Historiae* as a contemporary; the *Annales* as not a contemporary. They are two distinct works, not parts of one, which is clearly shown by the very different proportions of the two works: the first four books of the *Historiae* comprise about a year, and the first four books of the *Annales* comprise fourteen years.

The moral dignity of Tacitus is impressed upon his works; the consciousness of a love of truth, of the integrity of his purpose. His great power is in the knowledge of the human mind, his insight into the motives of human conduct; and he found materials for its exercise in the history of the emperors, and particularly Tiberius, whose strange career and enigmatical personality fascinated him. The *Annales* are filled with dramatic scenes and striking catastrophes. He laboured to produce effect by the exhibition of great personages on the stage; but as to the mass of the people we learn little from Tacitus. The style of Tacitus is peculiar, though it bears some resemblance to Sallust. In the *Annales* it is concise, vigorous, and pregnant with meaning; laboured, but elaborated with art, and stripped of every superfluity. A single word sometimes gives effect to a sentence; and if the meaning of the word is missed, the sense of the writer is not reached. Such a work is probably the result of many transcriptions by the author. Tacitus is generally brief and rapid in his sketches; but he is sometimes almost too minute when he comes to work out a dramatic scene; and he displays all the conscious rhetoric of his age. The condensed style of Tacitus sometimes makes him obscure, but it is a kind of obscurity that is dispelled by careful reading. Yet a man must read carefully and often, in order to understand him; and it cannot be supposed that Tacitus was ever a popular writer. He is often intensely epigrammatic, and exhibits the qualities of style that are found in the typical writers of the Silver Age. Many of his pregnant phrases have passed into the world's anthology of quotations, such as *Omne ignotum pro magnifico* and *Solitudinem faciunt, pacem appellant.* In his view of the condition of Roman society he is thoroughly pessimistic, and by contemplating only one section of it he is led into an unconscious exaggeration which the reader should correct by the reading of the contemporary and friend of Tacitus, Pliny the Younger, whose more pleasing picture of the time is a wholesome check upon any too sweeping condemnation of the imperial period of Rome's social history.

The manuscripts of Tacitus are few and unsatisfactory. For the first six books of the *Annales* only one source exists—the Codex Mediceus (I.) of the ninth century, and found about 1520. From this bks. vii.–ix. are lost, as are *Historiae* v.–xiv. For what remains of these, a second Codex Mediceus (II.) of the eleventh or twelfth century is the only authority. The *Germania* and *Dialogus* are found in two manuscripts—one at Leyden (Codex Leidensis [Perizonianus]), and the other in the Vatican. The *Agricola* is found in two transcriptions of an earlier MS. Both of these are in the Vatican. On the codices of Tacitus, see the introduction to the edition of the *Dialogus* by Michaelis (1868), and Gudeman (1894), and in Ritter's edition (1864).

Editions of the complete works of Tacitus are the *editio princeps* by Puteolanus (Milan, c. 1476); Lipsius (Antwerp, 1574); Gronovius (Amsterdam, 1672); Bekker, with variorum notes, 2 vols. (Leipzig, 1831); Ritter (last ed. Bonn, 1864); Döderlein, 2 vols. (Halle, 1841–47); Orelli, 2 vols. (Zürich, 1846, variously revised and republished, 1859, 1877); and texts by Halm (1884); and Müller (Prague, 1885).

Separate editions with English notes are those of the *Annales* by Furneaux, 2 vols. (Oxford, 1891–92); Allen (Boston, 1890); of the *Historiae* by Simcox (London, 1876), Godley (London, 1887–90), and Spooner (London, 1891); of the *Agricola* and *Germania* by Frost (London, 1861), Church and Brodribb (London, 1889), by Haverfield (announced), and by Hopkins (New York and Boston, 1893); of the *Dialogus* by Peterson (Oxford, 1893), and especially by Gudeman (New York and Boston, 1894), a most exhaustive and elaborate work, with extremely valuable prolegomena; also a compact and convenient edition by Bennett (New York and Boston, 1894). There are English translations of Tacitus by Gordon (London, 1728–31), Murphy (London, 1793), and by Church and Brodribb (London, 1876–77). There is a fine lexicon to Tacitus by Gerber and Greef, still appearing in parts. An older lexicon (complete) is that of Boetticher (1832).

On Tacitus, see Urlichs, *De Taciti Vita* (Würzburg, 1879); J. Müller, *Philos. und relig. Anschau-*

ungen des Tacitus (Feldkirch, 1874); and Schiller, *Geschichte d. röm. Kaiserzeit*, i. 586 (Gotha, 1883). On his diction, etc., see Dräger, *Ueber Syntax und Stil des Tacitus* (3d ed. Leipzig, 1882); Wolff, *Die Sprache des Tacitus* (Frankfurt, 1879); Gericke, *De Abundanti Dicendi Genere Tacitino* (Berlin, 1882), and the numerous monographs cited in Teuffel-Schwabe-Warr, ii. § 333, 16. See also the short studies by Donne (1873) and Church and Brodribb (1881).

(2) M. CLAUDIUS. A Roman emperor, who ruled from the 25th September, A.D. 275, until April, A.D. 276. He was elected by the Senate after the death of Aurelian, the army having requested the Senate to nominate a successor to the imperial throne. Tacitus was at the time seventy years of age, and was with difficulty persuaded to accept the purple. The high character which he had borne before his elevation to the throne he amply sustained during his brief reign. He endeavoured to repress the luxury and licentiousness of the age by various sumptuary laws, and he himself set an example to all around by the abstemiousness, simplicity, and frugality of his own habits. The only military achievement of this reign was the defeat and expulsion from Asia Minor of a party of Goths who had carried their devastation across the peninsula to the confines of Cilicia. He died either at Tarsus or at Tyana, about the 9th of April, 276. His life is given in the *Historia Augusta*.

Taeda (δαΐς, δᾷς, dim. δᾳδίον). A torch of firwood. See CANDELA; FAX; FUNALÉ; LUCERNA.

Taenărum (Ταίναρον). Now Cape Matapan; a promontory in Laconia, forming the southerly point of the Peloponnesus, on which stood a celebrated temple of Poseidon, possessing an inviolable asylum. A little to the north of the temple and the harbour of Achilleus was a town also called TAENĂRUM or TAENĂRUS, and at a later time CAENEPŎLIS. On the promontory was a cave, through which Heracles is said to have dragged Cerberus to the upper world. Here also was a statue of Arion seated on a dolphin, since he is said to have landed at this spot after his miraculous preservation by a dolphin (Herod. i. 23; Thuc. i. 128, 133; Pausan. iii. 25, 4). In the time of the Romans there were celebrated marble quarries on the promontory.

Taenia (ταινία). See INFULA; STROPHIUM; VITTA.

Tagasté. Now Tagilt; a city of Numidia, the birthplace of St. Augustine.

Tages. The son of a Genius Iovialis, and grandson of Iupiter, said to be a boy with the wisdom of an old man, who, at Tarquinii, in Etruria, suddenly rose out of a freshly ploughed field. He taught the chiefs (*lucumones*) of the twelve Etruscan tribes, who were summoned by the ploughman Tarchon, how to interpret the sacrifices, together with the lore of thunder and lightning and other kinds of divination which in later times were practised by the *haruspices*. Having done this, he disappeared again as suddenly as he had appeared. The lore of Tages was at first transmitted orally from generation to generation in the chief families, but was afterwards handed down in a comprehensive literature (Cicero, *De Div.* ii. 50, 51; Ovid, *Met.* xv. 558 foll.; Lucan, i. 637).

Tagus (ταγός). In general the commander of a district, but more especially the chief magistrate of Thessaly, or of any Thessalian town.

Tagus (Spanish Tajo, Portuguese Tejo, English Tagus). One of the chief rivers in Spain, rising in the land of the Celtiberians, between the mountains Orospeda and Idubeda, and, after flowing in a westerly direction, falling into the Atlantic. At its mouth stood Olisipo (Lisbon) (Pliny, *H. N.* iv. 115).

Talaria (πτερόεντα πέδιλα). Sandals with small wings attached. They usually appear on statues of Hermes, as in the annexed illustration.

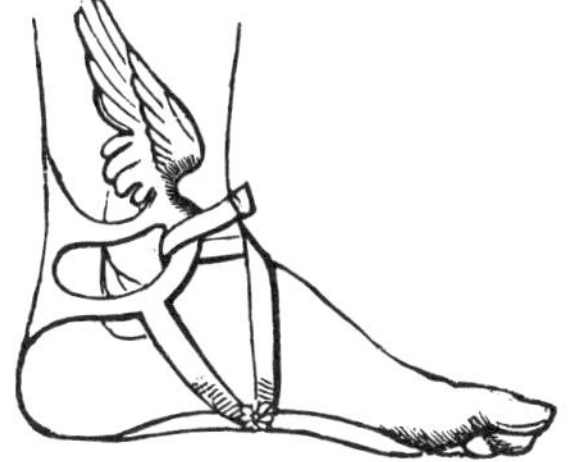

Talarium. (Naples Museum.)

Talassio, Talassius, Thalassius. A primitive Sabine deity invoked in the priestly books (*indigitamenta*) as the god of marriage. Varro regarded the noun as derived from τάλαρος, a wool-basket, as symbolizing the household work most typical of the Roman matron (Plut. *Quaest. Rom.* 31). See MATRIMONIUM, p. 1016.

Talaüs (Τάλαος). The son of Bias and Pero, and king of Argos. He was married to Lysimaché (Eurynomé, or Lysianassa), and was father of Adrastus, Parthenopaeus, Pronax, Mecisteus, Aristomachus, and Eriphylé. The patronymic *Talaïonides* is given to his sons Adrastus and Mecisteus (*Il.* ii. 566).

Talentum (τάλαντον; literally "a balance," and "the thing weighed"). The Greek term for (1) the heaviest unit of weight; (2) the designation of a sum of money consisting of a number of coins originally equal to it in legal weight and value. It was divided into 60 *minae* or 6000 *drachmae*. Among the different talents in use in Greece the most widely spread was the Attic, of which $\frac{1}{6000}$ part (*drachma*) weighed 57½ lbs. The intrinsic value of the metal contained in this sum of money was about $1180. The Aeginetan talent was worth about $1515. See MENSURA; NUMISMATICS.

Talna, IUVENTIUS. See THALNA.

Talos (Τάλως). (1) (See PERDIX.) (2) A brazen man, the work of Hephaestus, and given by Zeus to Minos, king of Crete, to watch that island, which he did by walking about it three times every day. When strangers approached he heated himself red hot and then embraced them, or, according to another version, threw showers of stones upon them. He had one vein in his body through which his blood ran and was stopped by a nail or plug in his foot. This plug Medea drew out by magic, and he bled to death (Apollod. i. 9, 26; Ap. Rh. iv. 1638; Schol. *ad* Plat. *Rep.* 425).

Talthybius (Ταλθύβιος). The herald of Agamemnon at Troy. He was worshipped as a hero at Sparta and Argos, where sacrifices also were offered to him.

Talus (ἀστράγαλος). A die used in gambling. The name of a bone in the hind-leg of cloven-footed animals which articulates with the tibia and helps to form the ankle-joint. In the language of anatomists it is still called *astragalus*; the English name is sometimes "huckle-bone," but more commonly "knuckle-bone." The astragali of sheep and goats, from their peculiar squareness and smoothness, have been used as playthings from the earliest times, and have often been found in Greek and Roman tombs, both natural and imitated in ivory, bronze, glass, and agate (Propert. iii. 24, 13; Mart. xiv. 14). They were used to play with, principally by women and children (Plu. *Alcib.* 2), occasionally by old men (Cic. *de Sen.* 16, § 58).

Girl Playing with Tali. (Herculanean painting.)

To play at this game was sometimes called πεντελιθίζειν, because five bones or other objects of a similar kind were employed (Hermipp. *Fr.* 33 M.); and this number is retained among ourselves. This game was entirely one of skill; and in ancient no less than in modern times it consisted not merely in catching the five bones on the back of the hand, as shown in the woodcut, but in a great variety of exercises requiring quickness, agility, and accuracy of sight.

The name was also given to dice (cf. our slang term "the bones") for playing games of chance (see ALEA). The length was greater than the breadth, so that they had four long sides and two pointed ends, one of them called κεραία, the other without a name. Of the four long sides, which alone were marked, two were broader, the others narrower. One of the broad sides was convex (πρηνής or πρανής, the other concave (ὑπτία); while of the narrow sides one was flat and called χῖον, the other indented. This was called κῷον, and, as the rarest was also the luckiest throw, marked 6: the χῖον was marked 1, the broader sides 3 and 4, so that the numbers 2 and 5 were wanting. From the difference of their shapes they did not absolutely require to be marked, and sometimes the pips were dispensed with. It was the under side of the die, not the upper, that counted, as must be inferred from the fact of the narrowest side giving the highest throw (Marquardt, *Privatl.* 828).

Roman Dice-box. (Rich.)

The Greek and Latin names of the numbers were as follows:—1. Μονάς, εἷς, κύων, Χῖος: *Unio, Volturius, canis;* 3. Τριάς: *Ternio;* 4. Τετράς: *Quaternio;* 6. Ἑξάς, ἑξίτης, Κῷος: *Senio.*

As the bone is broader in one direction than in the other, it was said to fall upright or prone (ὀρθὸς ἢ πρηνής, *rectus aut pronus*), according as it rested on a narrow or a broad side.

Two persons played together at this game, using four bones, which they threw up into the air, or emptied out of a dice-box (φιμός, *fritillus*). The numbers on the four sides of the four bones admitted of thirty-five different combinations. The lowest throw of all was four aces. But the value of a throw (βόλος, *iactus*) was not in all cases the sum of the four numbers turned up. The highest in value was that called *Venus, or iactus Venereus,* in which the numbers cast up were all different (Mart. xiv. 14), the sum of them being only fourteen. It was by obtaining this throw that the master of revels (*arbiter bibendi*) was chosen at the drinking-bouts. See Becq de Fouquières, *Les Jeux des Anciens,* 325 foll., and the article SYMPOSIUM. Cf. also TESSERA.

Tamassus (Ταμασσός) or **Tamăsus** (Τάμασος), probably the same as the Homeric **Temĕsé**. A town in the middle of Cyprus, northwest of Olympus, and twenty-nine miles southeast of Soloë (Ptol. v. 14, 6).

Tambrax (Τάμβραξ). A large city of Hyrcania (Polyb. x. 31).

Tamĕsis or **Tamĕsa**. Now the Thames; a river in Britain, on which stood Londinium, flowing into the sea on the eastern coast. Caesar crossed the Thames at the distance of eighty-six Roman miles from the sea, probably at Cowey Stakes, near Oatlands and the confluence of the Wey (Caes. *B. G.* v. 11; Tac. *Ann.* xiv. 32).

Tamias (ταμίας). In general, a person in charge of money, stock, or property, as a butler, steward, housekeeper, or treasurer. In the latter sense it was a title borne by several officials in Athens. (1) The most important of these was the treasurer (ἐπιμελητής) of the revenue, elected by show of hands every four years. He received from the ἀποδέκται or general collectors all the money which was to be disbursed for public expenses, and he paid away into the treasuries of the several authorities what was necessary for purposes of administration in their respective departments. He also provided the funds voted by the people for extraordinary purposes. (2) The same name was also borne by the ten treasurers of the goddess Athené, who had the care of the treasure of the goddess which was kept in the inner chamber of the Parthenon, besides the State treasure which (according to the ordinary account) was kept in the same place. They were elected annually by lot, one from each of the *phylae.* (3) Similarly, we have a board of ten regularly constituted treasurers to the rest of the gods. Their duty was to manage the sacred treasures, which in earlier times were kept in the separate temples, but in B.C. 418 were transferred to the Parthenon. (4) Under the title of ταμίας τῶν στρατιωτικῶν, we read of a financial officer of the war department. He was probably appointed after the Peloponnesian War in place of the Hellenotamiae (q. v.). Besides his duties in connection with the war department, he had a share in the management of the Panathenaic festival (Aristot. *Pol. Ath.* 49).

Tamna (Ταμνά) or **Thomna**. A mercantile city of Arabia Felix, where caravans dealt in spices and other Arabian products (Pliny, *H. N.* xvi. 153).

Tamos (Ταμώς). A native of Memphis in Egypt. He was lieutenant-governor of Ionia under Tissaphernes, and afterwards attached himself to the service of the younger Cyrus. When Cyrus died, he sailed to Egypt with a number of ships and a great treasure, and sought refuge with King Psammetichus, who treacherously put him to death in order to get possession of the ships and money (Xen. *Anab.* i. 2, 21; id. *Hellen.* iii. 1, 1; Diod. xiv. 19, 35).

Tamy̆nae (Ταμύναι). Now Aliveri; a city of Euboia with a temple of Apollo said to have been built by Admetus. Here the Athenians under Phocion gained a great victory over Callias of Chalcis in B.C. 354 (Plut. *Phoc.* 12).

Tanăger. Now the Negro or Tanagro; a river of Lucania, rising in the Apennines, which, after flowing in a northeasterly direction, loses itself under the earth near Polla for a space of about two miles, and finally falls into the Silarus near Forum Popilii.

Tanagra (Τάναγρα). Now Grimadha or Grimala; a celebrated town of Boeotia, situated on a steep ascent on the left bank of the Asopus, thirteen stadia from Oropus, and 200 stadia from Plataeae, in the district Tanagraea, which was also called Poemandris. Tanagra was supposed to be the same town as the Homeric Graea. Being near the frontiers of Attica, it was frequently exposed to the attacks of the Athenians; and near it the Athenians sustained a celebrated defeat, B.C. 457. Here was a temple to Dionysus, and minor temples erected to Themis, Aphroditê, Hermes Criophorus, and Hermes Promachus. Recent excavations at Tanagra have discovered the line of the walls, the site of many of the towers, and of the theatre. In 1873 the Necropolis was explored and yielded many terra-cotta statuettes and "figurines." See Kekulé, *Griechische Thonfiguren aus Tanagra* (Stuttgart, 1877); Murray's *Greek Archaeol.* (London, 1890); and the article TERRA-COTTAS.

Tanaïs (Τάναϊς). (1) Now the Don, i.e. "water"; a great river, which rises in the north of Sarmatia Europaea (about the centre of Russia), and flows to the southeast till it comes near the Volga, when it turns to the southwest, and falls into the northeast angle of the Palus Maeotis (Sea of Azof). It was usually considered the boundary between Europe and Asia. (2) A city of Sarmatia Asiatica, on the north side of the southern mouth of the Tanaïs, at a little distance from the sea.

Tanăquil. See TARQUINIUS.

Tanărus. Now the Tanaro; a river of Liguria emptying into the Po near Forum Fulvii (Valenza).

Tanētum. Now Taneto; a town of the Boii, in Gallia Cispadana, between Mutina and Parma.

Tanis (Τάνις; Egypt. Ta-au; O. T. Zoan). A very ancient city of Lower Egypt, in the eastern part of the Delta, on the right bank of the arm of the Nile, which was called after it the Tanitic, and on the southwest side of the great lake between this and the Pelusiac branch of the Nile, which was also called, after the city, Tanis (Lake of Menzaleh). It was one of the capitals of Lower Egypt under the Hyksos kings (B.C. 2100), and the chief city of the Tanites Nomos. In 1883–84 its ruins were explored by Flinders Petrie, whose monograph (1885) gives an account of his discoveries. See also Edwards, *Pharaohs, Fellahs, and Explorers* (New York, 1892), which is lavishly supplied with illustrations from photographs taken by Mr. Petrie.

Tantălus (Τάνταλος). (1) The son of Zeus and Pluto. His wife is called by some Euryanassa, by others Taÿgetê or Dionê, and by others Clytia or Eupryto. He was the father of Pelops, Broteas, and Niobê. All traditions agree in stating that he was a wealthy king, but while some call him king of Lydia, others describe him as king of Argos or Corinth. Tantalus is particularly celebrated in ancient story for the terrible punishment inflicted upon him after his death in the lower world, the causes of which are differently stated by the ancient writers. According to the common account Zeus invited him to his table, and communicated his divine counsels to him. Tantalus divulged the secrets thus intrusted to him; and he was punished in the lower world by being afflicted with a raging thirst, and at the same time placed in the midst of a lake, the waters of which always receded from him as soon as he attempted to drink them. Over his head, moreover, hung branches of fruit, which receded in like manner when he stretched out his hand to reach them. (Ovid. *Met.* iv. 457; Hor. *Sat.* i. 1, 68; Hygin. *Fab.* 82). Another account says that there was suspended over his head a huge rock, ever threatening to crush him (Pind. *Olymp.* i. 56). Another tradition relates that, wishing to test the gods, he cut his son Pelops in pieces, boiled them and set them before the gods at a repast. (See PELOPS.) A third account states that Tantalus stole nectar and ambrosia from the table of the gods and gave them to his friends (Pind. *Olymp.* i. 60); and a fourth relates the following story: Rhea caused the infant Zeus and his nurse to be guarded in Crete by a golden dog, whom Zeus afterwards appointed guardian of his temple in Crete. Pandareus stole this dog, and, carrying him to Mount Sipylus in Lydia, gave him to Tantalus to take care of. But when Pandareus demanded the dog back, Tantalus took an oath that he had never received it. Zeus thereupon changed Pandareus into a stone, and threw Tantalus down from Mount Sipylus. Others, again, relate that Hermes demanded the dog of Tantalus, and that the perjury was committed before Hermes. Zeus buried Tantalus under Mount Sipylus as a punishment; and there his tomb was shown in later times. The punishment of Tantalus was proverbial in ancient times, and from it the English language has borrowed

Shrine of Rameses II. at Tanis. (Photograph by Flinders Petrie.)

the verb "to tantalize," that is, to hold out hopes or prospects which cannot be realized. The patronymic Tantalides is frequently given to the descendants of Tantalus. Hence we find not only his son Pelops, but also Atreus, Thyestes, Agamemnon, Menelaüs, and Orestes called by this name. (2) Son of Thyestes, who was killed by Atreus. Others call him a son of Broteas. He was married to Clytaemnestra before Agamemnon, and is said by some to have been killed by Agamemnon. (3) Son of Amphion and Niobé.

Taŏchi (Τάοχοι). A people of Pontus, on the borders of Armenia (Xen. *Anab.* iv. 4, 18).

Tapētē (τάπης, τάπις). Tapestry; a carpet. Tapestry was known to the Greeks as early as Homer's time, being used for coverlets and pillows, and was also spread, in later ages, upon thrones, chairs, couches, etc. Carpets were made especially at Babylon, Tyre, Sardes, Carthage, and Alexandria. The most expensive kinds (μαλλωτοί) were like our baize or drugget, and had sometimes a nap on both sides (ἀμφίταποι) or on only one side (ἑτερόμαλλοι). They were beautifully dyed and often worked in figures of hunting scenes, etc. The Roman *toral* (q. v.) was a sort of tapestry.

Taphiae Insŭlae. A number of small islands in the Ionian Sea, lying between the coasts of Leucadia and Acarnania. They were also called the islands of the Teleboae, and their inhabitants were in like manner named TAPHII (Τάφιοι) or TELEBOAE (Τηλεβόαι). The largest of these islands is called TAPHUS by Homer, but TAPHIŪS (Ταφιοῦς) or TAPHIŪSA (Ταφιοῦσα) by later writers.

Taphus. See TAPHIAE.

Tappŭla Lex. A sort of drinking formulary drawn up as a burlesque of legal forms, written by a Roman humourist named Valerius Valentinus (Fest. 363; Val. Max. viii. 1, 8). A similar pot-house formula was found at Vercelli in 1882 on a bronze tablet (a fragment only). It is given in fac-simile in the *Bull. Arch.* for 1882 (186). Cf. Mommsen in the *Arch. Zeit.* xl. 176. Still another *lex convivialis* will be found printed in Bücheler's edition of Petronius, p. 239 (Berlin, 1882).

Taprobănē (Ταπροβάνη). Now Ceylon; a great island of the Indian Ocean, opposite to the southern extremity of India intra Gangem. The Gauls got their first knowledge of it from the explorations of Megasthenes and Onesicritus in the time of Alexander the Great. In the time of the emperor Claudius an embassy from Rome actually visited it (Ptol. vi. 10, 2; Curt. vi. 4, 24; Pliny, *H. N.* vi. 81).

Taras. See TARENTUM.

Taraxippus (Ταράξιππος). A demon who caused horses to shy. See HIPPODROMUS, p. 825.

Tarbelli. One of the most important people in Gallia Aquitanica between the ocean and the Pyrenees. Their chief town was Aquae Tarbellicae or Augustae (Dacqs) on the Aturus (Adour).

Tarchon. The son of Tyrrhenus, who is said to have built the town of Tarquinii. (See TARQUINII.) Vergil represents him as coming to the assistance of Aeneas against Turnus (*Aen.* iii. 506).

Tarentīni Ludi. See LUDI SAECULARES, p. 974.

Tarentīnus Sinus (Ταραντῖνος κόλπος). Now the Gulf of Tarentum; a great gulf in the south of Italy, between Bruttium, Lucania, and Calabria, beginning west near the Promontorium Lacinium and ending east near the Promontorium Iapygium, and named after the town of Tarentum.

Tarentum (Τάρας). Now Taranto; a Greek city on the western coast of Calabria in Italy with an excellent harbour, which formed a part of the Sinus Tarentinus. The surrounding country was both fertile and picturesque. Tarentum was traditionally said to have been built by the Iapygians, mingled with colonists from Crete, and to have derived its name from Taras, a son of Poseidon (Pausan. x. 10, 6). Its importance dates from the year B.C. 708, when it was captured by a body of Lacedaemonians under Phalanthus (see the article PARTHENIAE), after which it became a flourishing place, holding a sort of suzerainty over the rest of the cities of Magna Graecia. Its commerce was extensive; it had a powerful fleet; and could bring into the field an army of 30,000 infantry and 3000 cavalry, including the forces of its allies; its own troops numbered 22,000 men.

Coin of Tarentum (third century B.C.).

Its government was different at different periods of its history. At the time of Darius Hystaspis it was ruled by kings; but later it became a democracy. Its later law-code was the work of Archytas, who flourished about B.C. 400. As its wealth increased, its people became luxurious and effeminate; and being attacked by the neighbouring Lucanians, it appealed to Sparta for help. In answer to this appeal Archidamus, son of Agesilaüs, came to their assistance in B.C. 338; and he fell in battle fighting on their behalf. The next prince whom they invited to succour them was Alexander, king of Epirus, and uncle to Alexander the Great. At first he met with considerable success, but was eventually defeated and slain by the Bruttii in 326 near Pandosia on the banks of the Acheron. Shortly afterwards the Tarentines had to encounter a still more formidable enemy. Having attacked some Roman ships, and then grossly insulted the Roman ambassadors who had been sent to demand reparation, war was declared against the city by the powerful Republic. The Tarentines were saved for a time by Pyrrhus, king of Epirus (see PYRRHUS), who came to their help in 281; but two years after the defeat of this monarch and his withdrawal from Italy, the city was taken by the Romans (272). In the Second Punic War Tarentum revolted from Rome to Hannibal (212); but it was retaken by the Romans in 207. and was treated by them with great severity, From this time Tarentum declined in prosperity and wealth. It was subsequently made a Roman colony, and it still continued to be a place of considerable importance in the time of Augustus (Tac. *Ann.* i. 10). Its inhabitants retained their love of luxury and ease; and it is described by Horace as *molle Tarentum* and *imbelle Tarentum.* Even after the downfall of the Western Empire the Greek language was still spoken at Tarentum; and it was long one of the chief strongholds of the Byzantine Empire in the south of Italy.

The town of Tarentum consisted of two parts, viz.: a peninsula or island at the entrance of the harbour, and a town on the mainland, which was connected with the island by means of a bridge. On the northwest corner of the island, close to the entrance of the harbour, was the citadel: the principal part of the town was situated southwest of the isthmus. The modern town is confined to the island or peninsula on which the citadel stood. The neighbourhood of Tarentum produced the best wool in all Italy, and was also celebrated for its excellent wine, figs, pears, and other fruits. Its purple dye was also much valued in antiquity. On the history of the place, see the works by Döhle (1877) and De Vincentis (1878 foll.); and on the topography, that by Gagliardo (Taranto, 1886).

Tarichēa (Ταρίχεια). Now El-Kereh; a town of Galilee at the southern end of the Lake of Tiberias.

Tariff. See PENTECOSTÉ; PORTORIUM.

Tarné (Τάρνη). A city of Lydia, on Mount Tmolus, mentioned by Homer (*Il.* v. 44).

Tarpa, SP. MAECIUS. A Roman of literary taste, who selected the plays given at the celebration of Pompey's games in B.C. 55; and who afterwards was made censor over the public readings of the poets in the Collegium Poetarum under Augustus (Cic. *Ad Fam.* vii. 1; Hor. *A. P.* 287).

Tarpēia. Daughter of Sp. Tarpeius, the governor of the Roman citadel on the Saturnian Hill, afterwards called the Capitoline. She was tempted by the gold on the Sabine bracelets and collars to open a gate of the fortress to T. Tatius and his Sabines. As they entered, they threw upon her their shields, and thus crushed her to death. She was buried on the hill, and her memory was preserved by the name of the Tarpeian Rock, which was given to a part of the Capitoline (Livy, i. 11). A legend still exists at Rome to the effect that Tarpeia still sits in the heart of the hill covered with gold and jewels, and bound by a spell.

Tarpeian Rock. A rock on the Capitoline Hill in Rome, from which in early times State criminals were hurled. See ROMA; TARPEIA.

Tarquinia. See TARQUINIUS.

Tarquinii (Etrusc. *Turchina*). Now Corneto; a city of Etruria, situated on the river Marta. It was one of the twelve cities of the Etruscan League (see ETRURIA, p. 625), and was said to have been founded by one Tarchon, the brother of Tyrrhenus, who led the Lydian colony from Asia to Italy (Strabo, p. 219; Serv. *ad* Verg. *Aen.* x. 179, 198). Near this place the seer Tages (q. v.) first appeared. After Tarquinius Superbus was driven from Rome the people of Tarquinii gave him aid against the Romans, but were defeated by them (Livy, ii. 6; Dionys. v. 14). Some very interesting Etruscan paintings exist in the numerous caves on the hill at Corneto, which was the cemetery of the ancient city.

Tarquinius (Etrusc. *Tarcho*). The name of a family in early Roman tradition to which the fifth and seventh kings of Rome belonged. The legend of the Tarquins ran as follows: Demaratus, their ancestor, belonged to the noble family of the Bacchiadae at Corinth, and fled from his native city when the power of his order was overthrown by Cypselus. He settled at Tarquinii in Etruria, where he had mercantile connections. He married an Etruscan wife, by whom he had two sons, Lucumo and Aruns. The latter died in the lifetime of his father, leaving his wife pregnant; but as Demaratus was ignorant of this circumstance, he bequeathed all his property to Lucumo, and died himself shortly afterwards. But, although Lucumo was thus one of the most wealthy persons at Tarquinii, and had married Tanaquil, who belonged to a family of the highest rank, he was excluded, as a stranger, from all power and influence in the State. Discontented with this inferior position, and urged on by his wife, he resolved to leave Tarquinii and remove to Rome. He accordingly set out for Rome, riding in a chariot with his wife, and accompanied by a large train of followers. When they had reached the Ianiculum, an eagle seized his cap, and after carrying it away to a great height placed it again upon his head. Tanaquil, who was skilled in the Etruscan science of augury, bade her husband hope for the highest honour from this omen. Her predictions were soon verified. The stranger was received with welcome, and he and his followers were admitted to the rights of Roman citizens. He took the name of L. TARQUINIUS, to which Livy adds PRISCUS. His wealth, his courage, and his wisdom gained him the love both of Ancus Marcius and of the people. The former appointed him guardian of his children; and, when he died, the Senate and the people unanimously elected Tarquinius to the vacant throne. The reign of Tarquinius was distinguished by great exploits in war and by great works in peace. He defeated the Latins and Sabines; and the latter people ceded to him the town of Collatia, where he placed a garrison under the command of Egerius, the son of his deceased brother Aruns, who took the surname of Collatinus. Some traditions relate that Tarquinius defeated the Etruscans also. Among the important works which Tarquinius executed in peace, the most celebrated are the vast sewers by which the lower parts of the city were drained, and which still remain, with not a stone displaced, to bear witness to his power and wealth. He is also said in some traditions to have laid out the Circus Maximus in the valley which had been redeemed from water by the sewers, and also to have instituted the Great or Roman Games, which were henceforth performed in the Circus. The Forum, with its porticoes and rows of shops, was also his work, and he likewise began to surround the city with a stone wall, a work which was finished by his successor, Servius Tullius. The building of the Capitoline Temple is, moreover, attributed to the elder Tarquinius, though most traditions ascribe this work to his son, and only the vow to the father. Tarquinius also made some changes in the constitution of the State. He added one hundred new members to the Senate, who were called *patres minorum gentium*, to distinguish them from the old senators, who were now called *patres maiorum gentium.* He wished to add to the three centuries of equites established by Romulus three new centuries, and to call them after himself and two of his friends. His plan was opposed by the augur Attus Navius, who gave a convincing proof that the gods were opposed to his purpose. (See NAVIUS.) Accordingly, he gave up his design of establishing new centuries, but to each of the for-

Tomb of the Tarquins.

mer centuries he associated another under the same name, so that henceforth there were the first and second Ramnes, Tities, and Luceres. He increased the number of Vestal Virgins from four to six. Tarquinius was murdered, after a reign of thirty-eight years, at the instigation of the sons of Ancus Marcius. But the latter did not secure the reward of their crime, for Servius Tullius, with the assistance of Tanaquil, succeeded to the vacant throne (Livy, i. 34–41). Tarquinius left two sons and two daughters. His two sons, L. Tarquinius and Aruns, were subsequently married to the two daughters of Servius Tullius. One of his daughters was married to Servius Tullius, and the other to M. Brutus, by whom she became the mother of the celebrated L. Brutus, the first consul at Rome. Servius Tullius, whose life is given under TULLIUS, was murdered, after a reign of forty-four years, by his son-in-law, L. Tarquinius, who ascended the vacant throne.

L. TARQUINIUS SUPERBUS commenced his reign without any of the forms of election. One of the first acts of his reign was to abolish the rights which had been conferred upon the plebeians by Servius; and at the same time all the senators and patricians whom he mistrusted or whose wealth he coveted were put to death or driven into exile. He surrounded himself by a body-guard, by means of which he was enabled to do what he liked. His cruelty and tyranny obtained for him the surname of *Superbus*. But although a tyrant at home, he raised Rome to great influence and power among the surrounding nations. He gave his daughter in marriage to Octavius Mamilius of Tusculum, the most powerful of the Latin chiefs; and under his sway Rome became the head of the Latin Confederacy. He defeated the Volscians, and took the wealthy town of Suessa Pometia, with the spoils of which he commenced the erection of the Capitol which his father had vowed. In the vaults of this temple he deposited the Sibylline Books, which the king purchased from a Sibyl or prophetess. She had offered to sell him nine books for 300 pieces of gold. The king refused the offer with scorn. Therefore she went away and burned three, and then demanded the same price for the six. The king still refused. She again went away and burned three more, and still demanded the same price for the remaining three. The king now purchased the three books, and the Sibyl disappeared. (See SIBYLLA.) He next engaged in war with Gabii, one of the Latin cities, which refused to enter into the league. Unable to take the city by force of arms, Tarquinius had recourse to stratagem. His son, Sextus, pretending to be ill-treated by his father, and covered with the bloody marks of stripes, fled to Gabii. The infatuated inhabitants intrusted him with the command of their troops; whereupon he sent a messenger to his father to inquire how he should deliver the city into his hands. The king, who was walking in his garden when the messenger arrived, made no reply, but kept striking off the heads of the tallest poppies with his stick. Sextus took the hint. He put to death or banished all the leading men of the place, and then had no difficulty in compelling it to submit to his father.

In the midst of his prosperity, Tarquinius fell through a shameful outrage committed by one of his sons. Tarquinius and his sons were engaged in besieging Ardea, a city of the Rutulians. Here, as the king's sons, and their cousin, Tarquinius Collatinus, the son of Egerius, were feasting together, a dispute arose about the virtue of their wives. As nothing was doing in the field, they mounted their horses to visit their homes by surprise. They first went to Rome, where they surprised the king's daughters at a splendid banquet. They then hastened to Collatia, and there, though it was late in the night, they found Lucretia, the wife of Collatinus, spinning amid her handmaids. The beauty and virtue of Lucretia had fired the evil passions of Sextus. A few days afterwards he returned to Collatia, where he was hospitably received by Lucretia as her husband's kinsman. In the dead of night he entered the chamber with a drawn sword: by threatening to lay a slave with his throat cut beside her, whom he would pretend to have killed in order to avenge her husband's honour, he forced her to yield to his wishes. As soon as Sextus had departed, Lucretia sent for her husband and father. Collatinus came, accompanied by L. Brutus; Lucretius, with P. Valerius, who afterwards gained the surname of Publicola. They found her in an agony of sorrow. She told them what had happened, enjoined them to avenge her dishonour, and then stabbed herself to death. They all swore to avenge her. Brutus threw off his assumed stupidity, and placed himself at their head. They carried the corpse to Rome. Brutus, who was *tribunus celerum*, summoned the people, and related the deed of shame. All classes were inflamed with the same indignation. A decree was passed deposing the king, and banishing him and his family from the city. The army, encamped before Ardea, likewise renounced their allegiance to the tyrant. Tarquinius, with his two sons, Titus and Aruns, took refuge at Caeré in Etruria. Sextus repaired to Gabii, his own principality, where he was shortly after murdered by the friends of those whom he had put to death. Tarquinius reigned twenty-four years. He was banished B.C. 510. The people of Tarquinii and Veii espoused the cause of the exiled tyrant, and marched against Rome. The two consuls advanced to meet them. A bloody battle was fought, in which Brutus and Aruns, the son of Tarquinius, slew each other. Tarquinius next repaired to Lars Porsena, the powerful king of Clusium, who marched against Rome at the head of a vast army. The history of this expedition is related under PORSENA. After Porsena quitted Rome, Tarquinius took refuge with his son-in-law, Mamilius Octavius of Tusculum. Under the guidance of the latter, the Latin States espoused the cause of the exiled king, and declared war against Rome. The contest was decided by the celebrated battle of Lake Regillus, in which the Romans gained the victory by the help of Castor and Pollux. Tarquinius himself was wounded, but escaped with his life; his son Sextus is said to have fallen in this battle, though, according to another tradition, as we have already seen, he was slain by the inhabitants of Gabii. Tarquinius Superbus had now no other State to whom he could apply for assistance. He had already survived all his family; and he now fled to Aristobulus at Cumae, where he died a wretched and remorseful old man (Livy, ii. 121).

Such is the story of the Tarquins according to the ancient writers; but this story must not be received as a real history. It is the attempt to assign a definite origin to certain Roman institutions, to some features in the military organization, and to some ancient public works in the city, of which the history had been obscured by lapse of time. There can be no real doubt that it indicates as the time when these things were carried out a period during which a family of Etruscan origin held the chief power at Rome; and there is at least much probability (though this is denied by some writers of great authority) that this rule was imposed upon Rome by the dominant power of the Etruscans. See Mommsen, *History of Rome* (Amer. ed.), i. pp. 174, 321 foll., 590; Ihne, *Early Rome* (New York, 1878).

Tarracīna. Now Terracina, more anciently called **Anxur**, an ancient town of Latium, situated fifty-eight miles southeast of Rome, on the Via Appia and upon the coast, with a strongly fortified citadel upon a high hill, on which stood the Temple of Iupiter Anxurus. Remains of the ancient citadel are still visible.

Tarracina.

Tarrăco. Now Tarragona; an ancient town on the eastern coast of Spain, situated on a rock 760 feet high, between the river Iberus and the Pyrenees, on the river Tulcis. It was founded by the Massilians, and was made the headquarters of the two brothers P. and Cn. Scipio in their campaigns against the Carthaginians in the Second Punic War. It subsequently became a populous and flourishing town; and Augustus, who wintered here (B.C. 26) after his Cantabrian campaign, made it the capital of one of the three Spanish provinces (Hispania Tarraconensis), and also a Roman colony. See HISPANIA.

Tarrutēnus Paternus. See PATERNUS.

Tarsius (Τάρσιος). Now the Tarza or Karadere; a river of Mysia, rising in Mount Temnus, and flowing northeast, through the Miletopolites Lacus, into the Macestus.

Tarsus, Tarsos (Ταρσός). Now Terso; the chief city of Cilicia, standing near the centre of Cilicia Campestris, on the river Cydnus, about twelve miles above its mouth. All that can be determined with certainty as to its origin seems to be that it was a very ancient city of the Syrians, who were the earliest known inhabitants of this part of Asia Minor, and that it received Greek settlers at an early period. At the time of the Macedonian invasion it was held by the Persian troops, who were about to burn it, when they were prevented by Alexander's arrival. After playing an important part as a military post in the wars of the successors of Alexander, and under the Syrian kings, it became, by the peace between the Romans and Antiochus the Great, the frontier city of the Syrian kingdom on the northwest, and still flourishes, having a population estimated at 100,000. As the power of the Seleucidae declined it suffered much from the oppression of its governors, and from the wars between the members of the royal family. At the time of the Mithridatic War, it suffered, on the one hand, from Tigranes, who overran Cilicia, and, on the other, from the pirates, who had their strongholds in the mountains of Cilicia Aspera, and made frequent incursions into the level country. From both these enemies it was rescued by Pompey, who made it the capital of the new Roman province of Cilicia, B.C. 66. Under Augustus, the city obtained immunity from taxes, through the influence of the emperor's tutor, the Stoic Athenodorus, who was a native of the place. It enjoyed the favour and was called by the names of several of the later emperors. It was the scene of important events in the wars with the Persians, the Arabs, and the Turks, and also in the Crusades. Tarsus was the birthplace of many distinguished men, among them the Apostle Paul.

Tartărus (Τάρταρος). Son of Aether and Gaea, and by his mother Gaea the father of the Gigantes, Typhoeus, and Echidna. In the *Iliad*, Tartarus is a place beneath the earth, as far below Hades as Heaven is above the earth, and closed by iron gates. Later poets use the name as synonymous with Hades. See HADES.

Tartessus (Ταρτησσός). An ancient town in Spain, and one of the chief settlements of the Phœnicians, probably the same as the Tarshish of Scripture. The whole country west of Gibraltar was called TARTESSIS.

Taruscon or **Tarascon**. Now Tarascon. A town of the Salyes in Gaul, on the eastern bank of the Rhône, north of Arelaté (Arles) and east of Nemausus (Nîmes).

Tarvisium. Now Treviso; a town of Venetia in the north of Italy, on the river Silis, which became the seat of a bishopric, and a place of importance in the Middle Ages.

Task. See PENSUM.

Tatius, ACHILLES. See ACHILLES, p. 11.

Tatius, TITUS. A king of the Sabines. See ROMULUS.

Tatta (Τάττα). Now Tuz-Göl; a great salt lake in the centre of Asia Minor.

Tauchīra or **Teuchīra** (Ταύχειρα, Τεύχειρα). A colony of Cyrené, on the northwestern coast of Cyrenaïca, in Northern Africa. Under the Ptolemies it was called ARSINOË. It was a chief seat of the worship of Cybelé, who had here a great temple and an annual festival (Herod. iv. 171; Procop. *De Aed.* vi. 3).

Taulantii (Ταυλάντιοι). A people of Illyria, in the neighbourhood of Epidamnus (Thuc. i. 24).

Taunus. Now Taunus; a range of mountains in Germany, at no great distance from the confluence of the Moenus (Main) and the Rhine.

Taurasia. (1) See TAURINI. (2) A city of Samnium on the river Calor.

Taurentum and **Tauroïs**. A fortress belonging to Massilia, and near the latter city.

Tauri (Ταῦροι). A wild and savage people in European Sarmatia, who sacrificed all strangers to a goddess whom the Greeks identified with Artemis. The Tauri dwelt in the peninsula which was called after them Chersonesus Taurica (Crimea). See IPHIGENIA.

Taurii Ludi. See LUDI, p. 975.

Taurīni. A people of Liguria dwelling on the upper course of the Po, at the foot of the Alps. Their chief town was Taurasia, afterwards colonized by Augustus, and called Augusta Taurinorum (Turin).

Taurisci. A Keltic people in Noricum, and probably the old Keltic name of the entire population of the country.

Tauriscus (Ταυρισκός). A Greek artist of Tralles, belonging to the school of Rhodes. He and his fellow-countryman Apollonius were the sculptors of the celebrated group of Dircé, known as "the Farnese Bull," which is shown in the illustration under DIRCÉ.

Taurobolium. A rite celebrated at Rome after the Syrian cults began to be in vogue. (See Gibbon, *Decline and Fall*, ii. 265.) The ceremony was a sort of baptism in blood, and is described as follows by Prudentius (*Peristeph.* x. 1011–1050): The persons who were to be consecrated to regeneration, wearing the *mitra* with a golden circlet and the *cinctus Gabinus*, were placed beneath a platform upon which a bull or ram decked with garlands and having gilded horns was slain: the blood flowing through the chinks in the platform streamed over those beneath, each of whom was supposed to return home *taurobolio in aeternum renatus* (*C. I. L.* vi. 510). Cf. AEGOBOLIUM.

Tauroïs. A colony of the people of Massilia (Marseilles).

Tauromenium (Ταυρομένιον). Now Taormina; a city on the eastern coast of Sicily, situated on Mount Taurus, from which it derived its name,

Coin of Tauromenium.

and founded B.C. 358 by Andromachus with the remains of the inhabitants of Naxos. For the remains of the great stone theatre at this place, see THEATRUM.

Tauroscȳthae. See SCYTHOTAURI.

Taurus (from the Aramaean *Tur*, "a high mountain"). Now Taurus, Ala-Dagh, and other special names. A great mountain-chain of Asia. In its widest extent, the name was applied, by the later geographers, to the whole of the great chain which runs through Asia from west to east; but in its usual signification it denotes the mountain-chain in the south of Asia Minor, which begins at the Sacrum or Chelidonium Promontory at the southeast angle of Lycia, surrounds the Gulf of Pamphylia, passing through the middle of Pisidia; then along the southern frontier of Lycaonia and Cappadocia, which it divides from Cilicia and Commagené; thence, after being broken through by the Euphrates, it proceeds almost due east through the south of Armenia, forming the water-shed between the sources of the Tigris on the south and the streams which feed the upper Euphrates and the Araxes on the north; thus it continues as far as the southern margin of the lake Arsissa, where it ceases to bear the name of Taurus, and is continued in the chain which, under the names of Niphates, Zagros, etc., forms the northeast margin of the Tigris and Euphrates valley. Of this main range the branches Antitaurus and Amanus are important chains.

Taurus, STATILIUS. A distinguished general of Octavianus (Augustus) commanding his land forces at the battle of Actium (B.C. 31). Two years later he routed the Cantabri, Astures, and Vaccaei in Spain. He was consul in B.C. 26, and *praefectus urbi* in 16, during the absence of Augustus from Rome. An amphitheatre of stone was built by him in the year 30. (See App. *B. C.* v. 97–118; Tac. *Ann.* vi. 11; Dio Cass. xlix. 14; li. 20; liv. 19.)

Tavern. See CAUPONA.

Tavium (Ταουίον). The capital of the Trocmi, in Galatia, stood on the eastern side of the river Halys, but at some distance from the river, and formed the centre of meeting for roads leading to all parts of Asia Minor.

Tax. See EISPHORA; PORTORIUM; TELOS; TRIBUTUM; VECTIGALIA.

Taxiarchi (ταξίαρχοι). The Greek term for the commanders of τάξεις, which contained a variable number of men. In Athens the ten commanders of the ten τάξεις were so called. They were elected annually by show of hands, one for each tribe. They also had to look after the levying and distribution of recruits, and they were thus concerned in the drawing up of the register of those citizens who were liable to serve. On the Macedonian τάξις, see PHALANX.

Taxĭla (τὰ Τάξιλα) or **Taxiăla** (Ταξίαλα). An important city of India intra Gangem, stood in a large and fertile plain between the Indus and the Hydaspes, and was the capital of the Indian king Taxiles.

Taxĭles (Ταξίλης). (1) An Indian prince or king, who reigned over the tract between the Indus and the Hydaspes at the period of the expedition of Alexander, B.C. 327. His real name was Mophis or Omphis, and the Greeks appear to have called him Taxiles or Taxilas, from the name of his capital city of Taxila. (2) A general in the service of Mithridates the Great (Plut. *Sulla*, 15).

Taxis (τάξις). The principal division of the hoplites in the Athenian army, each of the ten tribes (φυλή) forming a τάξις. Among the other Greeks the word denotes a smaller division of troops. See PHALANX.

Taÿgĕtê (Ταϋγέτη). The daughter of Atlas and Pleionê, one of the Pleiades, from whom Mount Taÿgetus in Laconia is said to have derived its name. By Zeus she became the mother of Lacedaemon and of Eurotas (Pausan. iii. 1, 2).

Taÿgĕtus (Ταΰγετος) or **Taygĕtum** (Ταΰγετον) or **Taygĕta** (τὰ Ταΰγετα). A lofty range of mountains, of a wild and savage character, separating Laconia and Messenia, and extending from the frontiers of Arcadia down to the Promontorium Taenarum.

Teānum. (1) APŬLUM (now Ponte Rotto). A town of Apulia, on the river Frento and the confines of the Frentani, eighteen miles from Larinum. (2) SIDICĪNUM (now Teano), an important town of Campania, and the capital of the Sidicini, situated on the northern slope of Mount Massicus and on the Via Praenestina, six miles west of Cales.

Teărus (Τέαρος). Now Teara, Deara, or Dere; a brook in Thrace, the waters of which were useful in curing cutaneous diseases (Herod. iv. 90).

Teātê. Now Chieti; the capital of the Marrucini, situated on a steep hill on the river Aternus, and on the road from Aternum to Corfinium.

Tecmessa (Τέκμησσα). The daughter of the Phrygian king Teleutas, whose territory was ravaged by the Greeks during a predatory excursion from Troy. Tecmessa was taken prisoner, and was given to Aiax, the son of Telamon, by whom she had a son, Eurysaces.

Tectaeus (Τεκταῖος) and **Angelion** (Ἀγγελίων). Two early Greek sculptors before B.C. 550. They were the instructors of Callon of Aegina. A statue of Apollo at Delos was their work (Pausan. ii. 32, 5; ix. 35, 3).

Tectosăges. (1) In Gallia. See VOLCAE. (2) In Asia Minor. See GALATIA.

Tegea (Τεγέα). (1) Now Piali; an important city of Arcadia, the capital of the district TEGEĀTIS, which was bounded on the east by Argolis and Laconica, on the south by Laconia, on the west by Maenalia, and on the north by the territory of Mantinea. It was one of the most ancient towns of Arcadia, and is said to have been founded by Tegeates, the son of Lycaon. The Tegeatae sent 3000 men to the battle of Plataea, in which they were distinguished for their bravery (Herod. ix. 26). They remained faithful to Sparta in the Peloponnesian War; but after the battle of Leuctra they joined the rest of the Arcadians in establishing their independence. During the wars of the Achaean League, Tegea was taken both by Cleomenes, king of Sparta, and Antigonus Doson, king of Macedonia, and the ally of the Achaeans. (2) A town in Crete, said to have been founded by Agamemnon (Vell. Paterc. i. 1).

Tegillum. A coarse hood or cowl worn by Roman fishermen, peasants, etc., in wet weather (Plaut. *Rud.* ii. 7, 18).

Tegŭla (κέραμος, κεραμίς). A tile of baked clay. The name is applied as a generic term to (*a*) *testae* or wall-tiles; (*b*) *tubi, tegulae mammatae*, flue-tiles; and (*c*) tiles for roofing. In early Rome shingles (*scandulae*) were generally used for covering houses, but from the third century on tiles replaced them (Pliny, *H. N.* xvi. 36). Tiles were originally flat, but afterwards were made with a rustic flange on each side, as shown below. See more fully under FICTILÉ.

Ancient Tiles.

(1) Section of tiles from Pompeii. (2) Ornamental fronts of tiles. (3) Frontons of tiled roofs.

Teichopoei (τειχοποιοί). Public officials at Athens whose duty it was to build and keep in repair the public walls. They were probably ten in number, elected for the term of a year (Aeschin. *c. Ctes.* 14, 17, 24).

Tela (ἱστός), a loom. Although weaving was among the Greeks and Romans a distinct trade, carried on by a separate class of persons (ὑφάνται, *textores*, and *textrices, linteones*), yet every considerable domestic establishment, especially in the country, contained a loom (Cato, *R. R.* 10, 14) together with the whole apparatus necessary for the working of wool (ταλασία, ταλασιουργία, *lanificium*). (See CALATHUS.) These occupations were all supposed to be carried on under the protection of Athenê or Minerva, specially denominated Erganê (Ἐργάνη). When the farm or the palace was sufficiently large to admit of it, a portion of it called the *histon* (ἱστῶν) (Varro, *R. R.* i. 2) or *textrinum* was devoted to this purpose. The work was there principally carried on by female slaves (ἔριθοι, *quasillariae*), under the superintendence of the mistress of the house (Theocr. xv. 80). Everything woven consists of two essential parts, the warp and the woof, called in Latin *stamen* and *subtegmen, subtemen*, or *trama;* in Greek στημών and κροκή. The warp was called *stamen* in Latin (from *stare*) on account of its erect posture in the loom. The corresponding Greek term στημών, and likewise ἱστός, have evidently the same derivation. For the same reason, the very first operation in weaving was to set up the loom (ἱστὸν στήσασθαι); and the web or cloth, before it was cut down or "descended" from the loom, was called *pendens* or *pendula tela*, because it hung from the transverse beam, or *iugum*. These particulars are all clearly exhibited in the picture of Circé's loom given in the annexed illustration. We observe there, at about the middle of the apparatus, a transverse rod passing through the warp. A straight cane was well adapted to be so used, and its application is clearly expressed by Ovid in the words *stamen secernit harundo*. In plain weaving it was inserted between the threads of the warp so as to divide them into two portions, the threads on one side of the rod alternating with those on the other side throughout the whole breadth of the warp. In a very ancient form of the loom there was a roller underneath the *iugum*, turned by a handle, and on which the web was wound as the work advanced. The threads of the warp, besides being separated by a transverse rod or plank, were divided into thirty or forty parcels, to each of which a stone was suspended for the purpose of keeping the warp in a perpendicular position, and allowing the necessary play to the strokes of the *spatha*. While the comparatively coarse, strong, and much-twisted thread designed for the warp was thus arranged in parallel lines, the woof remained upon the spindle (*fusus*), forming a spool, bobbin, or pen (πήνη). This was either conveyed through the warp without any additional contrivance, or it was made to revolve in a shuttle (*radius*). This was made of box-wood, brought from the shores of the Euxine, and was pointed at its extremities that it might easily force its way through the warp. All that is effected by the shuttle is the conveyance of the woof across the warp. To keep every thread of the woof in its proper place it is necessary that the threads of the warp should be decussated. This was done by the leashes, called in Latin *licia*, in Greek μίτοι. By a leash we are to understand a thread having at one end a loop, through which a thread of the warp was passed, the other end being fastened to a straight rod called *liciatorium*, and in Greek κανών. The warp, having been divided by the *harundo*, as already mentioned, into two sets of threads, all those of the same set were passed through the loops of the corresponding set of leashes, and all these leashes were fastened at their other end to the same wooden rod. At least one set of leashes was necessary to decussate the warp, even in the plainest and simplest weaving. The number of sets was increased according to the complexity of the pattern, which was called *bilix* or *trilix* (δίμιτος, τρίμιτος or πολύμιτος) according as the number was two, three, or more. The process of annexing the leashes to the warp was called *ordiri telam*, also *licia telae addere*, or *adnectere*. It occupied two women at the same time, one of whom took in regular succession each separate thread of the warp and handed it over to the other (παραφέρειν, παραδίδοναι, προσφωρεῖσθαι); the other, as she received each thread, passed it through the loop in proper order; an act which is now called "entering," in Greek διάζεσθαι. Supposing the warp to have been thus adjusted, and the pen or the shuttle to have been carried through it, it was then decussated by drawing forwards the proper rod so as to carry one set of the threads of the warp across the rest, after which the woof was shot back again, and by the continual repetition of this process the warp and woof were interlaced. Two staves were occasionally used to fix the rods in such a position as was most convenient to assist the weaver in drawing her woof across her warp. After the woof had been conveyed by the shuttle through the warp, it was driven sometimes downwards, as is represented in the woodcut, but more commonly upwards. Two different instruments were used in this part of the process. The simplest, and probably the most ancient, was in the form of a large wooden sword (*spatha*, σπάθη). The *spatha* was, however, in a great degree superseded by the comb (*pecten*, κερκίς), the teeth of which were inserted between the threads of the warp, and thus made by a forcible impulse to drive the threads of the woof close together.

Ancient Loom. (Vatican Vergil.)

The lyre, the favorite musical instrument of the Greeks, was only known to the Romans as a foreign invention. Hence they appear to have described its parts by a comparison with the loom, with which they were familiar. The terms *iugum* and *stamina* were transferred by an obvious resemblance from the latter to the former object; and although they adopted into their own language the Greek word *plectrum* (πλῆκτρον) they used the Latin *pecten* to denote the same thing, not because the instrument used in striking the lyre was at all like a comb in shape and appearance, but because it was held in the right hand and inserted between the stamina of the lyre, as the comb was between the stamina of the loom. See Blümner, *Technologie*, i. pp. 120–157; Marquardt, *Privatleben der Römer*, 519–527; and a paper by Ahrens in *Philologus*, xxxv. pp. 385 foll.

Telămon. Now Telamone; a town and harbour of Etruria, a few miles south of the river Umbro, said to have been founded by Telamon on his return from the Argonautic expedition (Diod. iv. 56). Here the Romans defeated the Greeks in B.C. 225 (Polyb. i. 27–31).

Telămon (Τελαμών). The son of Aeacus and Endeïs, and brother of Peleus. Having assisted Peleus in slaying their half-brother Phocus (see PELEUS), Telamon was expelled from Aegina, and came to Salamis. Here he was first married to Glaucé, daughter of Cychreus, king of the island, on whose death Telamon became king of Salamis. He afterwards married Periboea or Eriboea, daughter of Alcathoüs, by whom he became the father of Aiax, who is hence frequently called *Telamoniades* and *Telamonius heros*. Telamon himself was one of the Calydonian hunters and one of the Argonauts. He was also a warm friend of Heracles, whom he joined in his expedition against Laomedon of Troy, which city he was the first to enter, and also against the Amazons (Pind. *Nem.* iii. 65). Heracles, in return, gave to him Theanira or Hesioné, a daughter of Laomedon, by whom he became the father of Teucer and Trambelus.

Telamōnes. See ATLANTES.

Telchīnes (Τελχῖνες). A family or a tribe said to have been descended from Thalassa or Poseidon, whence Eustathius gives them fins instead of feet (*ad* Hom. p. 771). They are represented in three different aspects: (1) As cultivators of the soil and ministers of the gods, in which capacity they came from Crete to Cyprus, and from thence to Rhodes, where they founded Camirus, Ialysus, and Lindus. Rhodes, which was named after them Telchinis, was abandoned by them because they foresaw that the island would be inundated. Poseidon was intrusted to them by Rhea, and they brought him up in conjunction with Caphira, a daughter of Oceanus. Rhea, Apollo, and Zeus, however, are also described as hostile to the Telchines. Apollo is said to have assumed the shape of a wolf, and to have thus destroyed the Telchines, and Zeus to have overwhelmed them by an inundation (Ovid, *Met.* vii. 367). (2) As sorcerers and envious daemons, their very eyes and aspect are said to have been destructive. They had it in their power to bring on hail, rain, and snow, and to assume any form they pleased; they, further, mixed Stygian water with sulphur, in order thereby to destroy animals and plants. (3) As artists they are said to have invented useful arts and institutions, and to have made images of the gods. They worked in brass and iron, and made the sickle of Cronos and the trident of Poseidon (Diod. v. 55; Pausan. ix. 19, 1; Strabo, pp. 472, 653; Tzetz. *Chil.* vii. 124). They seem in general to suggest the gnomes of the Northern mythology and the genii of Oriental folklore. They may be compared also with the Idaei Dactyli. See Dactyli.

Teleboae. See Taphiae.

Teleclīdes (Τηλεκλείδης). A Greek poet of the Old Comedy, a violent opponent of Pericles and supporter of Nicias (Plut. *Per.* 3, 16; *Nic.* 4). He is said to have written only six pieces, of which a few fragments are still extant, printed in Meineke's collection.

Telegŏnus (Τηλέγονος). The son of Odysseus and Circé. At his mother's command he set out to find his father. Landing on the coast of Ithaca, he began to plunder the fields, and Odysseus came out armed against him. Telegonus did not recognize his father, and mortally wounded him with the spine of a sting-ray which Circé had given him to serve as the barb of his lance. When he learned that the wounded man was his father, he took the body home with him, accompanied by Telemachus and Penelopé, and subsequently married the latter. He was supposed to be the founder of Tusculum (Hor. *Carm.* iii. 29, 8) and Praenesté, near Rome (Plut. *Parall. Min.* 41; Propert. ii. 32, 4). The legend of Telegonus was the theme of the *Telegonea* by the Cyclic poet Eugammon of Cyrené. The strange manner in which Odysseus met his death is also mentioned in Oppian (*Halieut.* ii. 497). Roman tradition ascribed to Telegonus a daughter Mamilia, the legendary ancestor of the Mamilii.

Telemăchus (Τηλέμαχος). The son of Odysseus and Penelopé. He was still an infant when the Trojan War began, and when his father had been absent from home nearly twenty years, Telemachus went to Pylos and Sparta to gather information concerning him. He was hospitably received by Nestor, who sent his own son to conduct Telemachus to Sparta. Menelaüs also received him kindly, and communicated to him the prophecy of Proteus concerning Odysseus. From Sparta Telemachus returned home; and on his arrival there he found his father, whom he assisted in slaying the suitors. (See Odysseus.) According to some accounts, Telemachus became the father of Persepolis either by Polycasté, the daughter of Nestor, or by Nausicaa, the daughter of Alcinoüs (Eustath. *ad* Hom. p. 1796; Dict. Cret. vi. 6). Others relate that he was induced by Athené to marry Circé, and became by her the father of Latinus (see Circé); or that he married Cassiphoné, a daughter of Circé, but in a quarrel with his mother-in-law slew her, for which he was in his turn killed by Cassiphoné (Tzetz. *ad* Lyc. 808). The story of Telemachus was taken as a basis for a famous romance by the great French Archbishop Fénelon, entitled *Télémaque*, which Louis XIV. regarded as a satire on his court, but which was long popular in France as a school-book.

Telĕmus. The son of Eurymus, and celebrated as a soothsayer (*Odyss.* ix. 509).

Telĕphus (Τήλεφος). The son of Heracles and Augé, the daughter of King Aleus of Tegea, and priestess of Athené. As soon as he was born he was exposed by his grandfather, who was angry because his daughter had broken the vows of her office. In some accounts she was set adrift, like Danaë, with her child and cast on the Mysian coast. In other versions of the story Telephus was reared by a hind (ἔλαφος), and educated by King Corythus in Arcadia. On reaching manhood, he consulted the Delphic Oracle to learn his parentage, and was ordered to go to King Teuthras in Mysia (Apollod. iii. 9, 1; Diod. iv. 33; Hyg. *Fab.* 100). He there found his mother, and succeeded Teuthras on the throne of Mysia. He married Laodicé or Astyoché, a daughter of Priam; and he attempted to prevent the Greeks from landing on the coast of Mysia. Dionysus, however, caused him to stumble over a vine, whereupon he was wounded by Achilles (Pind. *Ol.* ix. 112; *Isth.* v. 52; viii. 109; Pausan. x. 28; Dict. Cret. ii. 3). Being informed by an oracle that the wound could only be cured by "the wounder," Telephus repaired to the Grecian camp; and as the Greeks had likewise learned from an oracle that without the aid of Telephus they could not reach Troy, Achilles cured Telephus by means of the rust of the spear by which he had been wounded (Dict. Cret. ii. 10; Hor. *Epod.* xvii. 8; Ov. *Met.* xii. 112; *Rem. Am.* 47). Telephus, in return, pointed out to the Greeks the road which they ought to take. According to one story, Telephus, in order to induce the Greeks to help him, went to Argos, and snatching Orestes from his cradle threatened to kill him unless Agamemnon would persuade Achilles to heal the wound.

Telesia. Now Telese; a town in Samnium, on the road from Allifae to Beneventum.

Telesilla (Τελέσιλλα). A celebrated Argive lyric poetess and heroine, who flourished about B.C. 510. She led a band of her countrywomen in the war with the Spartans and took part in their victory, so that her statue was erected in the Temple of Aphrodité at Argos (Pausan. ii. 20, 7). Some fragments of her verse are printed in Bergk's *Poet. Lyr. Graeci* (1878). See Neue, *De Telesillae Reliquiis* (1843).

Telesīnus, Pontius. See Pontius.

Telĕtae (τελέται). See Mysteria.

Tellēnae. A town in Latium, between the later Via Ostiensis and the Via Appia.

Tellus. See Gaea.

Telo Martius. Now Toulon; a port-town of Gallia Narbonensis on the Mediterranean. It was of little account until the later Empire.

Telōnes, Telōnae (τελῶναι, from τέλος, "a tax"). Among the Athenians, the name telonae was given to the farmers of the taxes and imposts, which were not collected by State officers, but were sold at certain times by auction to the highest bidder. Smaller taxes were taken up by single persons who collected the money themselves. For larger taxes demanding a large capital, companies were often formed, represented by one person called the τελωνάρχης, who concluded the contract with the State. Sureties had also to be produced on this occasion. Such companies employed subordinate officers to collect the taxes. The payments were made by the farmers at certain periods at the senate-house, or βουλευτήριον, and one payment was usually made in advance when the contract was made. In default of payment, the farmer became ἄτιμος, and in certain circumstances might be imprisoned. If the debt was not paid by the expiration of the ninth *prytaneia*, it was doubled, and the property of the debtor and his sureties confiscated. The ἀτιμία descended to the children until the debt was paid. On the other hand, the farmer was protected by the State against fraud by severe laws. He was also exempt from military service, so that he might not be hindered in performing his duties. For the similar institution among the Romans, see PUBLICANI.

Telos (Τῆλος). A small island of the Carpathian Sea, one of the Sporades.

Telos (τέλος). A tax. The taxes imposed by the Athenians and collected at home were either ordinary or extraordinary. The former constituted a regular or permanent source of income; the latter were only raised in time of war or other emergency. The ordinary taxes were held mostly upon property, and upon citizens indirectly, in the shape of toll or customs; though the resident aliens paid a poll-tax (called μετοίκιον) for the liberty of residing at Athens under the protection of the State. There was a duty of two per cent. (πεντηκοστή) levied upon all exports and imports. An excise was paid on all sales in the market (called ἐπωνία), though it is not known what the amount was. Slave-owners paid a duty of three oboli for every slave they kept; and slaves who had been emancipated paid the same. This was for a long time a very productive tax before the fortification of Decelea by the Lacedaemonians. The justice fees (πρυτανεῖα, παράστασις) were a lucrative tax in time of peace. The extraordinary taxes were the property-tax, and the compulsory services called "liturgies" (λειτουργίαι). Some of these last were regular, and recurred annually; the most important, the *trierarchia*, was a war-service, and performed as occasion required. As these services were all performed, wholly or partly, at the expense of the individual, they may be regarded as a species of tax. (See EISPHORA; LITURGIA; TRIERARCHIA.) The tribute (φόρος) paid by the allied States to the Athenians formed, in the flourishing period of the Republic, a regular and most important source of revenue. In Olymp. 91–2, the Athenians substituted for the tribute a duty of five per cent. (εἰκοστή) on all commodities exported or imported by the subject States, thinking to raise by this means a larger income than by direct taxation. This was terminated by the issue of the Peloponnesian War, though the tribute was afterwards revived, on more equitable principles, under the name of σύνταξις. Other sources of revenue were derived by the Athenians from their mines (μέταλλα), and public lands, fines, and confiscations. The public demesne lands, whether pasture or arable, houses or other buildings, were usually let by auction to private persons. The conditions of the lease were engraved on stone. The rent was payable by prytaneias. These various sources of revenue produced, according to Aristophanes, an annual income of two thousand talents in the most flourishing period of Athenian hegemony. Though τέλος may signify any payment in the nature of a tax or duty, it is more commonly used of the ordinary taxes, as customs, etc. Ἰσοτέλεια signifies the right of being taxed on the same footing and having other privileges the same as citizens—a right sometimes granted to resident aliens; ἀτέλεια signifies an exemption from taxes, or other duties and services—an honour very rarely granted by the Athenians. As to the farming of taxes, see TELONES. See also Gilbert, *Greek Constitutional Antiquities*, pp. 351 foll., Eng. trans. (1895).

Telphussa. See THELPUSA.

Temenĭdae. See TEMENUS.

Temenītes. See SYRACUSAE.

Temĕnus (Τήμενος). The son of Aristomachus. He was one of the Heraclidae who invaded the Peloponnesus. (See HERACLIDAE.) After the conquest of the peninsula, he received Argos as his share. His descendants, the Temenidae, being expelled from Argos, are said to have founded the kingdom of Macedonia, whence the kings of Macedonia called themselves Temenidae (Herod. viii. 138; Thucyd. ii. 99).

Temĕsa or **Tempsa.** Now Torre del Piano del Casale; a town in Bruttium on the Sinus Terinaeus, was one of the most ancient Ausonian towns in the south of Italy; famous for its copper mines (Ov. *Met.* xv. 707; Stat. *Silv.* i. 1, 42).

Temnus. (1) (τὸ Τῆμνον ὄρος). Now Demirdji-Dagh; a mountain of Mysia, extending eastward from Ida to the borders of Phrygia, and dividing Mysia into two parts. It contains the sources of the Macestus, Mysius, Caïcus, and Evenus (Strabo, p. 616). (2) Now Kayajik; a city of Aeolis, in the northwest of Lydia, thirty miles south of Cymé. It was nearly destroyed by an earthquake in the reign of Tiberius, and is not noticed by Pliny. Under the Byzantine Empire it was called ARCHANGĔLUS (Strabo, p. 621; Xen. *Hell.* iv. 8, 5; Herod. i. 149; Pol. v. 77; Tac. *Ann.* ii. 47).

Tempé (Τέμπη, contr. of Τέμπεα). A beautiful and romantic valley in the north of Thessaly, between Mounts Olympus and Ossa, through which the Peneus escapes into the sea. The scenery of this glen is frequently praised by poets; and it was also celebrated as one of the favourite haunts of Apollo, who had transplanted his laurel from this spot to Delphi. The whole valley is rather less than five miles in length, and opens gradually to the east into a wide plain. Tempé is also of great importance in history, as it is the only pass through which an army can invade Thessaly from the north. In some parts the rocks on each side of the Peneus approach so close to each other as only to leave room between them for the stream, and the road is cut out of the rock in the narrowest point. Tempé is the only channel through which the waters of the Thessalian plain descend into the sea; and it was the common opinion in antiquity that these waters had once covered the country with a vast lake, till an outlet was formed for them by some great convulsion in nature which rent the rocks of Tempé asunder (Herod. vii. 129; Strabo, p. 430; Caesar, *B. C.* iii. 34; Catull. lxiv. 285; Ovid, *Met.* i. 568; Verg. *Georg.* ii. 469; Hor. *Od.* iii. 1, 24). So celebrated was the scenery of Tempé that its name was given to any beautiful valley. Cicero so calls a valley in the land of the Sabines near Reaté, through which the river Velinus flowed (Cic. *Ad Att.* iv. 15); and there was a Tempé in Sicily, through which the river Helorus flowed, hence called by Ovid *Tempe Heloria* (*Fast.* iv. 477).

Templum (the Greek τέμενος). Originally a space marked out with the *lituus* (q. v.) by the augur (see AUGURES) according to a certain fixed procedure when he pitched his tent (*tabernaculum capere*). It was then regarded as separate from any other land (*locus liberatus et effatus*). Its ground-plan was a square or rectangle, having its four sides turned to the different points of the compass; its front, however, according to strict Roman custom, faced towards the west, so that any one entering the temple had his face turned towards the east. It was not until later that the front was frequently made to face the east. The building erected on this space, and corresponding to it in plan, did not become a *fanum*, or sanctuary of the gods, until it had been consecrated by the *pontifices*. See DEDICATIO.

As, however, there were *fana* which were not templa—e. g., all circular buildings—so there were templa which were not *fana*. Of this sort were the places where public affairs were transacted, such as the Rostra in the Forum, the places where the Comitia met or the Senate assembled, and even the city of Rome itself. The sanctuaries of the gods were designed as templa if they were intended to serve for meetings of the Senate, and if the form of worship prescribed for such sanctuaries were appropriate to the definition of a templum. For the word as used to designate a building, see the next article.

Templum (ναός, Att. νεώς: ἱερόν). A temple, the word containing the root of the Greek τέμενος. (See the preceding article.) In ancient times temples were regarded as the dwelling-places and treasuries of the gods to whom they were dedicated. They might contain an image or not, but the latter case was exceptional. As they were not houses of worship intended for the devotion of a great multitude, they were usually of very limited extent. There were, however, temples of considerable size, among which was that of Artemis in Ephesus (see EPHESUS), 438 feet long by 226 broad; that of Heré in Samos; that begun by Pisistratus and finished by Hadrian, and dedicated to Zeus Olympius in Athens (see ATHENAE; OLYMPIEUM); and the temple of Zeus at Agrigentum, which was never wholly completed. All of these were nearly as large as the first mentioned. Only temples like that at Eleusis, in which the celebration of the Mysteries took place, were intended to accommodate a larger number of people. (See MYSTERIA.) The great sacrifices and banquets shared by all the people were celebrated in the court of the temple (περίβολος), which included the altars for sacrifice, and was itself surrounded by a wall with only one place of entrance. It was a feature common to all temples that they were not built directly on the surface of the ground, but were raised on a substructure which was mounted by means of an uneven number of steps, so that people were able as a good omen to put their right foot on the first and last step (Vitruv. iii. 4, 8; cf. Petron. 30).

The usual shape of GREEK temples was an oblong about twice as long as wide, at the front and back of which was a pediment or gable-roof (ἀετός, ἀέτωμα, *fastigium*). Round temples with dome-shaped roofs were the exception. The principal part of the temple was the chamber containing the image of the god. This stood upon a pedestal which was often placed in a small niche (*aedicula*) and usually stood facing the east, opposite folding-doors which always opened outwards. Before the image stood an altar used for bloodless sacrifices. This chamber, called in Greek ναός, and in Latin *cella*, generally received its light through the open door alone, but sometimes there was also an opening in the roof. There were also temples designated *hypaethral* (from ὕπαιθρος, "in the open air"); in these there was no roof to the middle chamber of the *cella*, which was separated from the lateral portions by one or more rows of pillars on each side.

Generally each temple belonged to only one god; but sometimes a temple was regarded as the dwelling-place of several deities, either those who were worshipped in groups, as the Muses, or those who were supposed to stand in close alliance or other relationship to each other, such as the twins Apollo and Artemis, and Apollo, as leader of the Muses, together with the Muses themselves. Frequently only one god had an image and altar in the chief *cella*, while others were worshipped in adjoining chapels. Lastly, there were double temples, with two *cellae* built in opposite directions. Many temples had, besides the *cella*, a kind of Holy of Holies (ἄδυτον, μέγαρον) which was entered only by the priests, and by them only at certain times, and which was sometimes under the ground. Usually an open porch or vestibule (πρόναος), with pillars in front, stood before the *cella*, and in it were exposed the dedicatory offerings. There was often also an inner chamber behind the image (ὀπισθόδομος) which served for various purposes, the valuables and money belonging to the temple being often kept there. It was surrounded by a wall, and the door was well secured by locks.

The various kinds of temples are usually distinguished according to the number and arrangement of the pillars. Thus:

(1) A temple *in antis* (ἐν παράσταστι) is one in which the *pronaos* (sometimes also the *opisthodomos*) was formed by the prolongation of the side walls of the temple (παράσταδες, *antae*) and by two columns placed between the terminal pilasters of the *antae* (q.v.).

(2) *Prostylos* (πρόστυλος), with the columns in front (fig. 1), is an epithet descriptive of a temple, the front of whose *pronaos* was formed in all its breadth by a row of columns quite separate from the walls, and with the columns at the extremities standing in front of the *antae*.

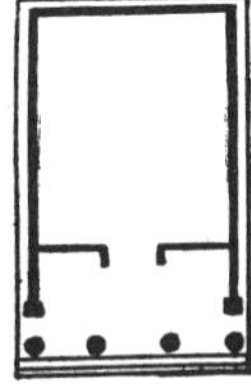

Fig. 1.

(3) *Amphiprostylos* (ἀμφιπρόστυ-

λος) describes a temple (fig. 2) with the columns arranged at the back as well as in the front.

(4) *Peripteros* (περίπτερος) describes a temple (fig. 3) surrounded on all sides by a colonnade sup-

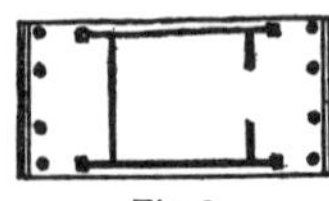

Fig. 2.

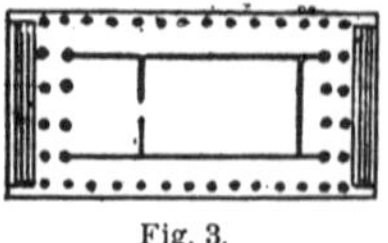

Fig. 3.

porting the architrave. This is the type most frequently employed by the Greeks.

(5) *Pseudoperipteros* (ψευδοπερίπτερος, "falsely *peripteros*") is an epithet of a temple in which the architrave appears to be carried by pilasters or by "engaged" columns in the walls of the *cella*. This form is seldom used by the Greeks, but often by the Romans.

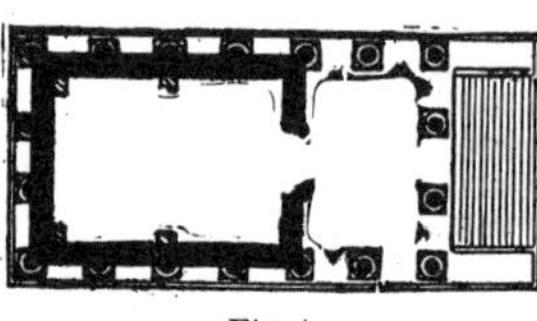

Fig. 4.

(6) *Dipteros* (δίπτερος) describes a temple (fig. 5) surrounded by two ranges of columns.

(7) *Pseudodipteros* (ψευδοδίπτερος, "falsely *dipteros*," fig. 6). A temple surrounded with only a sin-

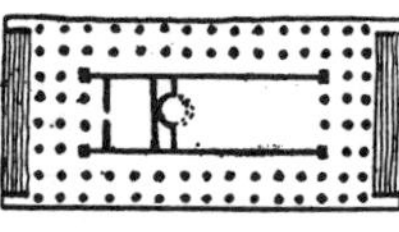

Fig. 5.

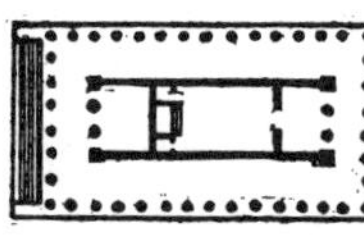

Fig. 6.

gle range of columns, but at such a distance that they correspond in position to the exterior range of the dipteral temple.

According to the number of columns in front, which must always be an even number, since the entrance was in the middle, it is usual to distinguish temples as *tetra-*, *hexa-*, *octa-*, *deca-*, or *dodecastylos* (with four, six, eight, ten, or twelve columns). The number of columns along each side was usually one more than twice the number along the front, but this was not the invariable rule. (For the architrave and for the columns of the different orders, see ARCHITECTURA; COLUMNA.) The frieze resting on the architrave, and (in the Doric order) the metopes (μέτοπαι) in particular (q. v.), as well as the two pediments (τύμπανα), were decorated with sculptures, and these sculptures, as well as the walls of the temple, often had more life-like and more varied appearance given to them by appropriate colouring. The coping of the roof, as well as the angles of the pediment, was ornamented by ἀκρωτήρια, which consisted of statues, vases, or ἀνθέμια, groups of flowers and leaves.

In the plan of their temples the ROMANS originally followed the Etruscans. The ground-plan of the Etruscan temple was nearly a square, the ratio of the depth to frontage being as six to five. Half of the space was taken up by the *cella* and the rest by the columns. The architrave was of wood, and without any special frieze. The great temple with three *cellae* on the Roman Capitol was built in the Etruscan style, the middle and largest *cella* being sacred to Iupiter, and the smaller ones on either side to Minerva and Iuno. Under Greek influence the different forms of the Greek temple began to be imitated at Rome, the most prevalent type being that described as *prostylos*, which lent itself most easily to the requirements of a templum in the strict sense of the term. An important alteration in the Greek form of temple was brought about by the introduction of vaulted arches or groined ceilings, which were seldom used by the Greeks, and never on a large scale, but were brought to great perfection by the Romans. They took the form of a cylindrical vaulting in the case of a quadrangular *cella* and a dome in the case of the round temples, which were frequent with the Romans. The two principal forms of the latter are (1) the *monopteros*, which consisted of a single circle of columns standing on a platform mounted by steps and supporting the columns which bore a dome on a circular architrave. (2) The *peripteros*, with the same arrangement of columns, but with a circular *cella* in the middle which was covered by a dome rising from the surrounding colonnade. In a third variety, of which we have an example in the Pantheon (q. v.), the circular body of the building is not surrounded by columns externally, but only provided on one side with an advanced portico.

The following are the principal Greek temples of which some remains still exist:

A. DORIC.

Syracuse, island of Ortygia, Temple of Artemis, hexastyle, very archaic, scanty remains. Seventh century B.C., or even earlier.

Selinus, Sicily, three temples on the Acropolis, all hexastyle, with nineteen, fourteen, and thirteen columns respectively on the flanks, of local limestone, very early in style. Seventh century.

Syracuse, Ortygia, Temple of Athené, hexastyle, now built into the cathedral. Late seventh century.

Selinus, great Temple of Zeus in the Agora, octastyle, with seventeen columns on the flanks: never finished. Seventh century.

Corinth, hexastyle, with fifteen columns on the flanks; only seven columns now remain. Late seventh century.

Segesta, Sicily, hexastyle, the peristyle perfect, but the *cella* wholly gone, probably unfinished. Sixth century.

Agrigentum, Sicily, the great Temple of Zeus, heptastyle, with fourteen columns on the flanks, pseudoperipteral, slight remains. Sixth century.

Aegina, hexastyle, with twelve columns on the flanks; very perfect. Sixth century.

Paestum (Lucania), the so-called Temple of Poseidon, hexastyle, with fourteen columns on the flanks; very perfect. Sixth century. See illustration under PAESTUM.

Delphi, Temple of the Pythian Apollo, hexastyle, peripteral; designed by Spintharus of Corinth soon after the burning of the previous temple (the fourth on that site) in the year B.C. 548. Second half of the sixth century.

Agrigentum, Sicily, three hexastyle temples, two of them very perfect. Late sixth or early fifth century.

Selinus, the middle temple on the Agora. About B.C. 500.

Assos, Asia Minor, hexastyle, with sculpture on the architrave, very rude in style, scanty remains. About B.C. 480.

Temple at Agrigentum. (From a photograph.)

Athens, so-called Temple of Theseus, hexastyle, with thirteen columns on the flanks, very perfect. About B.C. 465. See illustration on p. 151.

Olympia, Temple of Zeus, built by Libon of Elis, hexastyle, with thirteen columns on the flanks; slight remains standing. B.C. 469–457.

Olympia, the Heraeum, a mixture of many dates, mostly destroyed, hexastyle, with sixteen columns on the flanks.

Athens, the Parthenon, octastyle, with seventeen columns on the flanks, still fairly perfect, built by Ictinus. B.C. 450–438. See PARTHENON.

Selinus, hexastyle temple in the Agora. Middle of fifth century.

Sunium, Attica, hexastyle, a few columns only remaining. Middle of fifth century.

Bassae, Temple of Apollo Epicurius, hexastyle, with fifteen columns on the flanks, built by Ictinus, still fairly perfect. About B.C. 440.

Rhamnus, Attica, Temple of Nemesis, hexastyle, peripteral; and Temple of Themis, cella with portico *in antis*, and walls of polygonal masonry, a late survival of this early method of building. Middle of the fifth century.

View of the Athenian Acropolis and Parthenon from the Rear.

Eleusis, the Hall of the Mysteries, with a dodecastyle portico, which is a later addition. About B.C. 440–220.

Tegea, Temple of Athené Alea, built by Scopas, hexastyle, with thirteen columns on the flanks; date soon after B.C. 393.

Paestum, enneastyle temple, and a small hexastyle temple, probably built by native Lucanian architects in the fourth century B.C.

B. Ionic.

Athens, the temple of Niké Apteros and the Erechtheum on the Acropolis.

Temple of Niké Apteros. (Athens.)

Olympia, the circular Philippeum with eighteen Ionic columns outside, and, inside the cella, engaged columns of the Corinthian order: similar in plan to the Roman Temple of Vesta. See ROMA, p. 1381.

In Asia Minor.

Sardis, Temple of Cybelé, octastyle, with columns sixty feet high, of which only three remain, date about B.C. 500.

Xanthus in Lycia, Heroon of unknown dedication, a small tetrastyle, peripteral building on a lofty *podium*. Its sculpture is now in the British Museum. The date is doubtful, but it is probably not earlier than about B.C. 400.

The Troad, Temple of Apollo Smintheus, octastyle, pseudo-dipteral, with very close (pycnostyle) intercolumniation. Most of the existing building seems to date from a period probably about B.C. 400 to 350.

Samos, Temple of Heré, decastyle, dipteral. The existing temple is of the fourth century B.C. An earlier temple on the same site was built in the seventh century B.C. by Rhoecus of Samos.

Magnesia ad Maeandrum, Temple of Artemis Leucophryne, hexastyle, pseudo-dipteral, built by Hermogenes about B.C. 350.

Teos, Temple of Dionysus, hexastyle, also built by Hermogenes about B.C. 350.

Priené, Temple of Athené Polias, hexastyle, very similar to the temple at Teos; it was built in the second half of the fourth century B.C. and was dedicated by Alexander the Great.

Branchidae near Miletus, Temple of Apollo Didymaeus; decastyle, dipteral. This and the temple at Samos were the only two Greek decastyle temples.

Ephesus, Temple of Artemis (Artemision), octastyle, dipteral, built during the reign of Alexander the Great, B.C. 356–323. In many respects the most celebrated and magnificent temple of all Greece. See EPHESUS.

The following are the principal temples at ROME of which some remains still exist:

The Temple of Vesta, at the south of the Forum. Part of the very early tufa foundations and some fallen fragments of columns and entablatures remain. See ROMA, p. 1381.

The Pantheon, the most perfectly preserved of all. See PANTHEON.

The Temple of Castor, at the south angle of the Forum. A fine octastyle, peripteral building of the Corinthian order. Built in the reign of Augustus on the site of an older structure.

The Temple of Divus Iulius, near that of Castor, built by Augustus. Very scanty remains exist.

The Temple of Concord, near the Tabularium of the Capitol. Rebuilt by Augustus. Little but the *podium* remains.

The Temple of Vespasian, near that of Concord. A prostyle, hexastyle building of the Corinthian order. Built by Titus and Domitian. Three marble columns remain.

The Temple of Faustina, at the eastern angle of the Forum. A prostyle, hexastyle building of the Corinthian order, built by Antoninus Pius in memory of his wife Faustina. Except for the back wall of the *cella*, the temple is still fairly well preserved.

The Temple of Mars Ultor, in the Forum of Augustus, built by him to commemorate the vengeance inflicted on the murderers of Iulius Caesar. A good part of it still exists.

Temple of Roma Aeterna and Venus Felix, built by Hadrian and Antoninus Pius. It was a deca-

Ruins of the Temple of Roma and Venus.

style dipteral temple of the Corinthian order, and remains of its concrete *podium* exist to-day on the north side of the Via Sacra.

There are well-preserved ruins of Roman temples at Ancyra in Galatia and elsewhere in Asia Minor, in Northern Africa, at Nîmes in France (see NEMAUSUS), and in England.

See Nissen, *Das Templum* (Berlin, 1869); Michaelis, *Der Parthenon* (1875); Fergusson, *History of Architecture*, 4 vols. (London and New York, 1865–1876; new ed. 1891); Falkener, *Ephesus and the Temple of Diana* (London, 1862); Fergusson, *The Parthenon* (on the lighting of temples) (London, 1883); Norton, *The Temple of Zeus at Olympia* (Philadelphia, 1877); and the article ARCHITECTURA.

Ten Attic Orators. The ten orators included in the Alexandrian Canon. (See CANON ALEXANDRINUS.) They were Antiphon, Andocides, Lysias, Isocrates, Isaeus, Aeschines, Lycurgus, Demosthenes, Hyperides, and Dinarchus. See Quintil. x. 1, 76; Sears, *History of Oratory*, pp. 51 foll. (Boston, 1896); and Blass, *Attische Beredsamkeit.*

Tenctĕri or **Tenchtĕri.** A people of Germany dwelling on the Rhine between the Ruhr and the Sieg, south of the Usipetes, in conjunction with whom their name usually occurs (Caes. *B. G.* iv. 1, 4–16; Tac. *Germ.* 32).

Tenĕdos or **Tenĕdus** (Τένεδος). A small island of the Aegaean Sea, off the coast of Troas, of an importance very disproportionate to its size, on account of its position near the mouth of the Hellespont, from which it is about twelve miles distant. It appears in the legend of the Trojan War as the station to which the Greeks withdrew their fleet, in order to induce the Trojans to think that they had departed, and to receive the wooden horse (Verg. *Aen.* ii. 21). In the Persian War it was used by Xerxes as a naval station (Herod. vi. 31). It afterwards became a tributary ally of Athens, and adhered to her during the whole of the Peloponnesian War, and down to the peace of Antalcidas, by which it was surrendered to the Persians. At the Macedonian conquest the Tenedians regained their liberty. The women of the island were noted for their beauty (Athen. p. 609).

Tenes or **Tennes** (Τήννης). Son of Cycnus and Proclea, and brother of Hemithea. Cycnus was king of Colonae in Troas. His second wife was Philonomé, who fell in love with her step-son; but as he repulsed her advances she accused him to his father, who put both his son and daughter into a chest and threw them into the sea. But the chest was driven on the coast of the island of Leucophrys, of which the inhabitants elected Tenes king, and which he called Tenedos, after his own name (Pausan. x. 14, 2; Diod. v. 83).

Tennis. See PĬLA

Tenos (Τῆνος). Now Tino; a small island in the Aegaean Sea, southeast of Andros and north of Delos. Here was a celebrated temple of Poseidon (Herod. viii. 82).

Tensa and **Thensa.** The chariot used for processions, or for the gods at the Circensian Games at Rome (Cic. *Verr.* ii. 7, 72). The thensa was highly ornamented and drawn usually by horses. The chief senators in their official robes escorted it with the *pueri patrimi* (see PATRIMI), all laying hold of the bridles and traces or perhaps thongs attached to the vehicle. When the thensa was used for carrying the statues of the emperors it was sometimes drawn by elephants, as is seen from an existing medal of Nero.

Tent. See CONTUBERNALES; PAPILIO; PRAETORIUM; TENTORIUM.

Tentorium (σκηνή). A tent stretched upon cords and distinguished from *tabernaculum*, which was formed on a framework of wood. But the distinction is not strictly observed (Hirt. *B. G.* viii. 5; Suet. *Tib.* 18; Verg. *Aen.* i. 472).

Tentўra (τὰ Τέντυρα). Now Denderah; a city of Upper Egypt, on the western bank of the Nile, between Abydos and Coptos, with celebrated temples of Hathor (the Egyptian Aphrodité), Isis, and Typhon (Ptol. iv. 5, 6). There are still magnificent remains of the temples of Hathor and of Isis: in the latter was found the celebrated Zodiac, which is now preserved at Paris.

Teos (Τέως). Now Sighajik; one of the Ionian cities on the coast of Asia Minor, renowned as the birthplace of the lyric poet Anacreon. It stood at the end of the bay, between the promontories of Coryceum and Myonnesus. Here was a celebrated temple of Dionysus and a theatre, of which remains still exist.

Tepidarium. See BALNEAE, p. 192.

Terĕbra. (1) (τρύπανον). Any instrument used for boring holes in wood, stone, or metal. Of these there were several varieties—e. g., the *terebra antiqua*, a drill-borer; *terebra gallica*, a large gimlet, etc. See Blümner, *Technologie*, ii. pp. 223–226. (2) A military engine for boring into the walls of a besieged town. See ARIES.

Terentia. (1) The first wife of M. Cicero, the orator, to whom she bore two children, a son (Marcus) and a daughter (Tullia). She was a woman of sound sense and great resolution; and her firmness of character was of no small service to her weak and vacillating husband in some important periods of his life. During the Civil War, however, Cicero was offended with her extravagance (*Ad Att.* xi. 16, 24; Plut. *Cic.* 41), and divorced her in B.C. 46. (See PUBLILIA.) Terentia is said to have attained the age of 103. (2) Also called TERENTILLA, the wife of Maecenas, and said to have been one of the mistresses of Augustus. See Suet. *Aug.* 69, with Peck's note; and the article MAECENAS.

Terentiānus Maurus. A Roman writer on metres who probably lived in the second century A.D. A poem of his, entitled *De Litteris, Syllabis, Pedibus, Metris*, is extant. It shows considerable skill in handling the various metres, and regards all metres as based originally upon the hexameter and the iambic trimeter. It is in three parts or books, and is printed in Keil's *Grammatici Latini*, vi. 313; and separately by Santen and Van Lennep, with a commentary (Utrecht, 1828), Lachmann (Berlin, 1836), and Gaisford (Oxford, 1855).

Terentīni Ludi. See LUDI, p. 975.

Terentius Afer, PUBLIUS, usually called in English TERENCE. Our principal source of information regarding the life of P. Terentius Afer is an extract from Suetonius's work *De Viris Illustribus*, preserved by Donatus in the introduction to his commentary on Terence (see Suet. p. 291, Roth). Some of the statements contained in this life are confirmed by later writers, and light is thrown on the literary and personal relations of the poet by the prologues to the different plays. From these sources, chiefly, the facts of his life, so far as they are known, have been gleaned, and are in brief as follows: Terence was a native of Carthage (though his cognomen, Afer, suggests that he was of African [Libyan], not Phœnician, parentage). He came to Rome as a slave, where he became the property of the senator Terentius Lucanus, who, impressed by the natural gifts of the young African, had him educated, and afterwards gave him his freedom. How he came to Rome is uncertain. The suggestion that he was a captive taken in war is discredited by the fact that he lived within the period beginning with the close of the Second Punic War (B.C. 201), and ending with the commencement of the Third (B.C. 149)—a fact noted by Fenestella (Suet. p. 292, Roth). It is possible, however, that he was purchased by Lucanus from a slave-dealer who either caught him or bought him in Africa (see Teuffel-Schwabe, *Rom. Lit.* § 102, 3). According to the custom of the day he took the *nomen* of his former master; but his *praenomen* may have been received from another patron, who, it has been thought, was Scipio Africanus the Younger. He is described as of medium stature, graceful in person, and of dark complexion (Suet. p. 294, Roth). His personal attractions and the fact of his African birth won for him the esteem and confidence of Scipio Aemilianus, through whom and the comic poet Caecilius he became intimate with Gaius Laelius, Furius Philus, and other members of the younger circle of literary men at Rome—men who loved Greek literature for its own sake and lent the weight of their influence against the sentiment, prevalent at Rome since the days of Cato, that the pursuit of Greek culture and learning tended to luxury and the corruption of morals. Sulpicius Gallus, Quintus Fabius Labeo, and Marcus Popilius, men of consular rank, and distinguished for their literary attainments, were also among his friends and admirers.

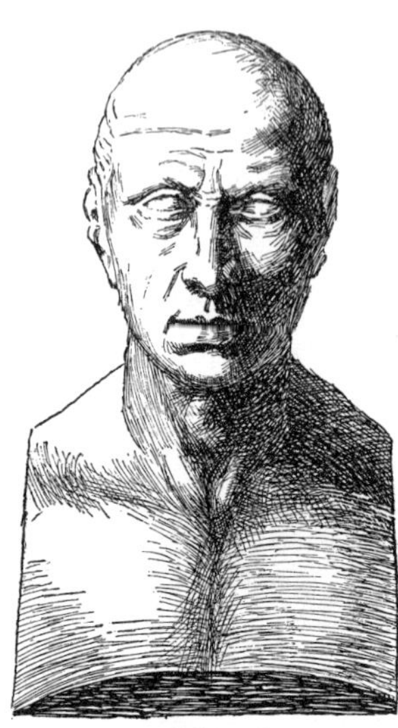

P. Terentius Afer.

A pretty but apocryphal story is told by Suetonius (p. 292, Roth) in reference to his first play, the *Andria*, or "Maid of Andros." On presenting it to the aediles for acceptance he was bidden by them to take it for judgment to Caecilius, then an old man. Terence entered the presence of Caecilius when the latter was at dinner, and being in mean attire was not received with very marked demonstrations of respect. Accordingly he proceeded to read his play, seated on a *subsellium* or stool placed at the foot of the festal couch, but had not gone far with his recitation when he was invited by the literary veteran to "recline" with him at table. The reading continued until the play was finished, when Caecilius again expressed his approval and delight. As Caecilius died in 168, and the *Andria* was first exhibited in 166, this story is regarded by some critics as doubtful; but the substance of it is given in the Eusebian Chronicle, and it may easily have happened that the *Andria* was ready for representation two years before its actual appearance on the stage. Now it was more particularly to please such men as Caecilius and Scipio, and others already named, who favoured a strict adherence to Greek models, that Terence wrote his comedies, and it would have been natural that before publishing his compositions he should read them in the presence of his noble friends and avail himself of their observations and suggestions. Such a practice would account in part for the genuine Roman character of Terence's style and language. But that his plays were actually written for him by Scipio and Laelius—a charge brought against him by his rivals—is not fully sustained by anything that we know. The charge was asserted by one Luscius Lanuvinus, who is referred to in Terence's prologues as *malivolus vetus poeta*. This "malignant old poet" was at the head of the opposite party, which contended vigorously for a close imitation of the earlier Latin comedians, and resented the innovations of what may be called the Greek school. His enmity, however, was largely ignored by Terence, who refused either to confirm or deny the charge of plagiarism (see Prol. to *Adel.* 15 foll.). This reticence has had the effect of lending an air of probability to the charge. It was no doubt owing, however, to a disinclination openly to avow that which might give offence to men whose good will he could not afford to lose; or else to an unwillingness to make public denial of what he considered to be unworthy of serious notice. Another sin laid at the door of our poet by his enemies was the practice of *contaminatio.* "Contamination" was the process of combining parts of two or more plays in one. It afforded opportunity to work up a more elaborate plot, and to introduce greater variety of incident and character, than a strict adherence to a single original would have done; but the practice was a dangerous one, as it often led to accidental contradictions and inconsistencies in the plot. Terence readily admits the charge, and defends it in his prologues.

After producing six comedies, between B.C. 166 and 160, Terence went to Greece, in order, we are told, to escape suspicion of plagiarism, or, as is more credible, to study Greek life and institutions, with the object of representing them more accurately on the Roman stage (see Suet. pp. 293–294, Roth). The best manuscripts state that he set out in his twenty-fifth year; inferior manuscripts say in his thirty-fifth. If the former are to be relied on, Terence must have been born in B.C. 185, which was also the year of Scipio's birth. This would make Terence only nineteen years old in B.C. 166, the year in which his first play was brought out. Now it is highly improbable that a composition so finished in style, and so true in its delineation of human character, as the *Andria* should have been the work of so youthful a writer. It is extremely natural, on the other hand, that his well-known intimacy with Scipio should have led to the supposition that the two men were contemporaries, and Suetonius quotes Cornelius Nepos as affirming that Terence, Scipio, and Laelius were of the same age (Suet. p. 292, Roth). On the contrary, Fenestella (an antiquarian of the Augustan period) is also cited by Suetonius as contending that the poet was older than his two friends. Everything considered, we are inclined to place the year of Terence's birth considerably earlier than B.C. 185, and it is not unlikely that the number XXXV, already alluded to as possibly representing his age at the time of the journey to Greece, gives the real clue to the situation, in spite of the fact that it occurs only in interpolated manuscripts. Terence never returned to Italy; but died abroad in B.C. 159. Accounts vary as to the place and manner of his death. Quintus Cosconius is authority for the statement that he perished at sea on his way back from Greece, and that his translations of one hundred and eight of Menander's comedies perished with him. This is in part confirmed by Vulcatius, whose lines on the death of Terence are given by Suetonius. Another account relates that he died at Stymphalus in Arcadia (or at Leucadia) from an illness induced by grief at the loss of his baggage and MSS., which he had sent on before him to the ship in which he was to sail for Italy. He died possessed, says Suetonius, of twenty *iugera* of cultivated land on the Appian Way, and his daughter subsequently was married to a Roman knight; but according to Porcius, whom also our biographer cites, he had not even a hired house whither a slave might report the news of his master's death; of so little profit to him had been his intimacy with Furius, Laelius, and Scipio.

The six comedies written and exhibited at Rome by Terence have been transmitted to us. The following enumeration gives them in the supposed order of their composition according to the Codex Bembinus:

I. The *Andria*, or Maid of Andros, based on the Ἀνδρία and Περινθία of Menander; first exhibited at the Ludi Megalenses, in B.C. 166.

II. The *Eunuchus*, based on the Εὐνοῦχος and Κόλαξ of Menander; first performed at the Ludi Megalenses, in B.C. 161.

III. The *Heauton Timorumenos*, or Self-tormentor, based on the Ἑαυτὸν Τιμορούμενος of Menander; first performed at the Ludi Megalenses, in B.C. 163.

IV. The *Phormio* (name of the parasite in the play), based on the Ἐπιδικαζόμενος of Apollodorus; first performed at the Ludi Romani, in B.C. 161.

V. The *Hecyra*, or Mother-in-law, based on the Ἑκυρά of Apollodorus, and (possibly) the Ἐπιτρέποντες of Menander; first brought out at the Ludi Megalenses, in B.C. 165.

VI. The *Adelphoe*, or Brothers, taken from the Ἀδελφοί of Menander, with one scene added from the Συναποθνήσκοντες of Diphilus; first performed at the funeral games of Aemilius Paulus, in B.C. 160.

The first performance of the *Hecyra* was interrupted by the greater attractions of a rope-dancer, as we learn from the prologues to the play (1. 4 and 2. 26). A second attempt at exhibition was made, but without success, at the funeral games of Lucius Aemilius Paulus—the occasion on which the *Adelphoe* was presented; but it was not until it had been brought before the public for the third time—at the Ludi Romani of the same year—that the *Hecyra* met with the desired recognition. (See Dziatzko, *Rhein. Mus.* 20, 576; 21, 72; Ritschl, *Op.* ii. 237; Teuffel, 110, 5, 3.)

The external history, so to speak, of the several plays was given in the *didascaliae* (διδασκαλίαι). These were prefatory notices inserted in the MSS., probably by Roman grammarians of the Augustan age, and when complete were indicative of the following particulars: (1) The name of the play and of the Latin poet; (2) the name of the public games or festival at which the play was first brought out; (3) the names of the managers or directors of the games; (4) the name of the chief actor and director of the troop or *grex;* (5) the name of the musical composer; (6) the species of flute employed; (7) the title of the Greek original, and the name of its author; (8) the number indicating the place of the play in the order of composition of the works of the poet; (9) the names of the consuls for the year in which the play was first exhibited. In examining the *didascaliae* of Terence we notice particularly that the principal actor and director of the troop for all the plays is Lucius Ambivius Turpio; that the composer of the flute-music is in every instance Flaccus, the slave of Claudius, and that two Greek poets only, Menander and Apollodorus, have been selected by Terence for imitation—if we except the small part played by Diphilus in contributing to the *Adelphoe.*

It is evident that Terence selected as his models the most refined of the writers of the New Comedy of Athens. A comparison of the plays with the fragments of the Greek comic poets (ed. Meineke) sustains this view; and his efforts at refinement of speech and manners, together with his fondness in general for things Greek, are especially noticeable in reference to certain peculiarities of treatment. Of all the titles of his plays not one is a purely Latin name; and the same may be said of his *dramatis personae*—of those at least who speak on the stage. His allusions to Roman customs and institutions are rare as compared with those in Plautus; and his personages, whether rich or poor, slaves or free, speak much alike, their style being that in vogue in the cultivated circles at Athens. Where Plautus uses the language of the street Terence continues to employ that of the *salon* and the drawing-room. Exaggerated puns and plays on words, newly made forms and forced expressions, coarse humour and obscene talk—which abounded in the plays of Plautus and rendered them highly acceptable to the Roman populace, whom Plautus wrote to please—these found slight favour with Terence, whose most appreciative audience, as has been already remarked, was of a different stamp. All six comedies are remarkable for their smoothness and moderate tone, as well as for the art with which the plot is unfolded, through the natural sequence of incidents and play of motives. Striking effects, sharp contrasts and incongruities, extravagance of speech and even creative fancy, which characterize the writings of the elder poet, are almost wholly absent. Terence did not aim at originality. His purpose was to present a true picture of Greek life and manners in the purest Latin at his command; and although the attempt was made with a loss to himself of the popularity enjoyed by Plautus, yet if the judgment of succeeding generations is a fair criterion he must be credited with having fully attained his object. The language which he received from Plautus he improved and rendered more artistic by shaping it carefully to the graceful rhythm and diction of the Greek dramatists, notably Menander. This is his great gift to Roman literature—a gift not wholly appreciated until the cultivation of letters, and in particular the study of Terence, had become fashionable in the time of Cicero.

Yet Terence had the faults of his qualities, and his defects are noticed by the literary critics of the century succeeding his own. He is called by Caesar a Menander cut-in-two (*O dimidiate Menander*, Suet. p. 294, Roth), since he reflects the refinement and finish of the Greek poet, but lacks his force and comic vigour; and Cicero in similar fashion credits him with having given Menander to the Romans, but in subdued tones (*sedatis vocibus*, Suet. p. 294, Roth). And in accordance with these criticisms we find the manners, habits, and customs of men correctly portrayed in his comedies, but their passions and desires suppressed and moderated. There is much ἦθος, but little πάθος. The lyrical element is much thrust into the background, and the whole metrical structure of the drama is less complex than in the comedies of Plautus. In short, while Plautus wrote always for the people, Terence never failed to keep in view the circle of noblemen and *literati*, whose encouragement and patronage were his mainstay, and whose culture and learning and breadth of view afforded him a standard and a guide.

While the comedies of Terence were occasionally exhibited after his death (see Dziatzko, *Ueber die Terenz. Didaskalien* in the *Rh. Mus.* xx. 570; xxi. 64), they became also a special subject for study with the learned. Suetonius's Life has transmitted to us the names of not a few historians, biographers, and antiquarians, who busied themselves with his writings. Such were Fenestella, Cornelius Nepos, Porcius Licinus, Volcacius Sedigitus, Varro, Santra, Q. Cosconius, Cicero, and Caesar. In the so-called *Auctorium Aeli Donati* also are the names of the critic Maecius (Tarpa) and the poet Vallegius or Vagellius. The first is reported as saying that there were two poets bearing the name of Terence, the other being a native of Fregellae and distinguished as Terentius Libo. The second is of interest to us as repeating the charge that Terence merely "brought out the plays of Scipio." Cicero quotes Terence in his letters and orations (cf. *Ad Fam.* i. 9, 19; Phil. ii. 6, 15), and Horace in his Satires and Epistles exhibits decided traces of the comic poet's influence and happy expression. This influence was not confined, however, to literature, but extended to the thought and speech of everyday life. Many of Terence's sayings became proverbs, and the oft-quoted verse *homo sum; humani nihil a me alienum puto* (*Heaut.* i. 1, 77) voices a spirit of tolerance and sympathy with human nature which was foreign to the old Roman austerity of character, and may be set down as the lesson taught the Romans by the comedy of Menander.

In later times also the writings of Terence have been pointed to as models of good style and poetic finish. Petrarch speaks of both him and Plautus in terms of unlimited eulogy. The great Latin writers of the Renaissance, such as Erasmus and Melanchthon, made a careful study of his works; and in modern literature the French especially have been his ardent admirers and most frequent imitators. He is described by Montaigne (in the words of Horace) as *liquidus puroque simillimus amni*, and the same writer adds, "he does so possess the soul with his graces that we forget those of his fable" (*Essays of Montaigne*, trans. by Ch. Cotton, chap. lxvii.). He is praised by Fénelon above Molière, while Sainte-Beuve accords him unstinted eulogy in his *Nouveaux Lundis;* and M. Joubert says of Terence: "Le miel attique est sur ses lèvres; on croirait aisément qu'il naquit sur le mont Hymette." (See *Histoire de la Littérature Latine*, by E. Neqrette; and Sellar, *Roman Poets of the Republic*, p. 220.) Michael Baron's *L'Andrienne* is a reflection of the *Andria;* Bruey's *Le Muet* and La Fontaine's *L'Eunuque* are based on the *Eunuchus*, and Molière's *Le Mariage Forcé* and *Les Fourberies de Scapin* remind us of the *Phormio*. Baron's *L'École des Pères*, and Fagan's *La Pupille* are more than suggested by the *Adelphoe*, which has also contributed largely to the *École des Maris* of Molière. In England the *Andria* has been imitated in Steele's *Conscious Lovers*, the *Adelphoe* in Garrick's *Guardian*, and the *Eunuchus* in Sir Charles Sedley's *Bellamira;* and the *Adelphoe* has furnished the leading characters in Cumberland's *Choleric Man*, and Shadwell's *Squire of Alsatia*. Indeed, dramatic literature in general owes much to Terence, and his influence upon the literary style of later ages has been both marked and extensive.

The farther the language of Terence became removed through time from the speech of everyday life the greater became the demand for exegetical commentaries on the text. Among the names of early commentators is that of M. Valerius Probus of Berytus, who is known to have revised and annotated editions of Lucretius, Vergil, Horace, Persius, and Terence in the first century of the Christian era. The commentary of Aelius Donatus, who taught at Rome about the middle of the fourth century A.D., relates to all the plays except the *Heauton Timorumenos*, and consists in reality of his own work united with that of an elder contemporary named Euanthius. That part which related to the *Heauton Timorumenos* has been lost, but its place is indifferently supplied by J. Calphurnius, who wrote in the fifteenth century. The commentary of Eugraphius, who is believed to have lived in the sixth century A.D., is of less value to us than that of Donatus. Its main purpose was to lay down for school children the laws of rhetoric as they applied to the study of Terence. The grammarians Servius (who wrote at Rome in the fourth century A.D.) and Priscianus (who wrote in Latin at Constantinople in the latter part of the fifth or the beginning of the sixth century) furnish important information. Other commentators were Aemilius Asper, Helenius Acro, and perhaps Arruntius Celsus the grammarian. Under the head of commentary should fall also the *periochae* of Sulpicius Apollinaris of the second century A.D., one of which is prefixed to each play and consists of twelve verses—each verse being an iambic senarius. The *periochae* contain brief summaries of the plots, and, like the *didascaliae* and the *praefationes* of Donatus (or Euanthius) connected with them, are of value in determining the meaning of the text.

To our list of early commentaries should be added the scholia of the Codex Bembinus. These are accessible in the special articles of Umpfenbach in *Hermes*, ii., and Studemund in *Neue Jahrb.* 97. The scholia of the other manuscripts were thought by Umpfenbach to be unworthy of particular study, but their importance has been demonstrated by Frid. Schlee, whose edition of the "*Scholia Terentiana* existing in MSS. other than the Bembine" was published at Leipzig in 1893. See an analysis of the same by S. G. Ashmore in the *Class. Rev.* vol. viii. No. 8.

The manuscripts of Terence have been separated into three classes. The Codex Bembinus (A) constitutes in itself Class I. The remaining codices have been divided by Umpfenbach into two groups, according to their supposed merit. To the first group, or Class II., belong the Victorianus (D), the Decurtatus (G), and Fragmentum Vindobonense (V). This is the D family. The second group, or Class III., contains the Parisinus (P), Vaticanus (C), Basilicanus (B), Ambrosianus (F), and Riccardianus (E). These are known as the P family. These nine codices are all that were considered by Umpfenbach to be worthy of collation. The most ancient of them is the Bembinus, so called from its owner, Cardinal Pietro Bembo, who lived from A.D. 1470 to 1547. It is also the most trustworthy, because it is the only MS. certainly free from the arbitrary alterations of the unknown grammarian Calliopius, who made an effort to settle the text of Terence in the fourth or fifth century A.D. The MSS. of Class III. contain marginal paintings or miniatures illustrating the scenes in the different plays. Those of the Codex Vaticanus are especially notable (see Frid. Leo, *Rh. Mus.* xxviii. 335). Twenty-six of them, comprising the complete set for the *Phormio,* have been reproduced in this country from photographs taken in the Vatican library expressly for the Classical Department of Harvard University, and with the permission of the Cardinal Librarian and the Pope. They are said never before (1893) to have been accurately reproduced. The illustrations in the Codex Parisinus are also very fine, and for this reason the MS. is kept on exhibition in the *Salle d'Exposition des Imprimés et des Manuscrits* in the Bibliothèque Nationale at Paris. A description of it is given by Umpfenbach in his preface. As to which of the two groups, Class II. or Class III., is the more authoritative, there is much dispute. For a discussion of the question see Ashmore's review of Schlee's work on the scholia, cited above, and an article by Professor E. M. Pease in the *Transactions of the American Philological Association* for 1887, vol. xviii. (See also Ashmore's edition of the *Adelphoe,* pp. li. and lii., Macmillan & Co.) On the whole, it is most probable that the Parisinus (P) and Vaticanus (C) have suffered less from errors creeping into the individual MSS. than the Victorianus (D) and the Decurtatus (G), and that more changes have been made in the archetype of the D family than in the archetype of the P family.

For references to special monographs and articles on the Terentian MSS. see Teuffel-Schwabe, *Rom. Lit.* § 109, 2.

Among modern editors of Terence, Gabriel Faernus (Florence, 1565) is well known for his careful examination of the Bembine Codex, and Guyet (Strassburg, 1657) for his scholarship and readiness to condemn as spurious difficult passages in the text. Richard Bentley is famous for the excellence of his critical commentary, and for the attention he gave to the metres. His editions (London, 1726; Amsterdam, 1727) mark an era in Terentian criticism. Bentley's English manuscripts of Terence are discussed by Umpfenbach (*Phil.* xxxii. 442), and by Minton Warren (*Amer. Jour. of Philol.* iii. 59). For more than a century after Bentley no edition of Terence appeared which could be mentioned as presenting a decided improvement of the text. That by E. St. John Parry (London, 1857) is lacking in critical discernment. That of Fleckeisen (Leipzig, 1857) presents a text which is in advance of that of Parry, for Fleckeisen made good use of a collation of the Bembine Codex by Petrus Victorius, now in the Royal Library at Munich. The critical value of Wagner's edition (London, 1869) is somewhat impaired by carelessness; but the text contains some improvements upon that of Fleckeisen. The edition of Umpfenbach (Berlin, 1870) was far in advance of all that had gone before it, and is based almost exclusively on the text of the Codex Bembinus. But the latest and most trustworthy text of the six plays is that of Dziatzko (Leipzig, 1884). In this the editor makes full recognition of the labours of Umpfenbach, and attaches due importance to the readings of the Bembine manuscript. Separate annotated editions of the *Phormio* (1874, revised 1884) and the *Adelphoe* (1881) have been published by the same scholar; and A. Spengel has edited the *Adelphoe* and *Andria* (Berlin, 1879 and 1888 respectively) with considerable critical acumen. Other (collective) editions are the *editio princeps* (Strassburg, 1470), and those of Muretus (Venice, 1555), F. Lindenbrog (c. Donati et Eugraphii Comm., Paris, 1602; Frankfort, 1623), Pareus (Neap. 1619), Boecler (Strassburg, 1657), Westerhovius (Haag. 1732; reprint by G. Stallbaum, Leipzig, 1830), Lemaire (Paris, 1827), Klotz

(c. Schol. Donati et Eugraphii, Leipzig, 1838). The editions of Westerhovius and Stallbaum contain also the commentaries of Donatus and Calphurnius.

See Hayley, *The Metres of Terence* (New York and Boston, 1895); and for references to works on Terentian metres, see Bond and Walpole's ed. of the *Phormio*, p. xxx., and Ashmore's *Adelphoe*, p. lvi., besides Teuffel-Schwabe, § 111, 7.

Terentius Varro. See VARRO.

Terentum or **Tarentum** (from *terere*, "to bore"). A volcanic cleft in the Campus Martius which gives the name to the Ludi Tarentini, then passing afterwards into the Ludi Saeculares. See LUDI, p. 974.

Teres (Τήρης). King of the Odrysae and father of Sitalces. He was the founder of the great Odrysian monarchy (Herod. iv. 80; vii. 137; Thuc. ii. 29). See ODRYSAE; SITALCES.

Tereus (Τηρεύς). A son of Ares and king of the Thracians in Daulis. He afterwards reigned in Phocis (Thuc. ii. 29). Pandion, king of Attica, who had two daughters, Philomela and Procné, called in the assistance of Tereus against some enemy, and gave him his daughter Procné in marriage. Tereus became by her the father of Itys, and then concealed her in the country, that he might dishonour her sister Philomela, whom he deceived by saying that Procné was dead. At the same time he deprived Philomela of her tongue. (For a different version of the story, cf. Ovid, *Met.* vi. 565.) Philomela, however, soon learned the truth, and made it known to her sister by a few words which she wove into a peplus. Procné thereupon killed her own son Itys, and served up the flesh of the child in a dish before Tereus. She then fled with her sister. Tereus pursued them with an axe, and when the sisters were overtaken they prayed to the gods to change them into birds. Procné, accordingly, became a nightingale, Philomela a swallow, and Tereus a hoopoe (Apollod. iii. 14, 8; Tzetz. *Chil.* vii. 142, 459; Ovid, *Met.* vi. 424–675; Serv. *ad Ecl.* vi. 78). According to some, Procné became a swallow, Philomela a nightingale, and Tereus a hawk (Hyg. *Fab.* 45). It is clear that this story is a development of the older myth about Aedon (q. v.), daughter of Pandareus (*Od.* xix. 58), and that the plaintive song of the nightingale had much to do with its origin.

Tergesté. Now Trieste; a town of Istria, on a bay in the northeast of the Adriatic Gulf, called after it Tergestinus Sinus. It was made a Roman colony by Vespasian (Pliny, *H. N.* iii. 127). For its use in a proverbial saying, see THEVESTÉ.

Tergīnum. A thong used in flogging slaves (Plaut. *Pseud.* i. 2, 22).

Tergiversatio. The Roman term for the dereliction of duty involved in a legal prosecution being dropped by the prosecutor. Under Nero this offence was punished by fines and disgrace (*infamia*).

Teridātes. See TIRIDATES.

Terīna. Now S. Eufemia; a town on the west coast of Bruttium, from which the Sinus Terinaeus derived its name (Pliny, *H. N.* iii. 72).

Teriŏlis or **Teriŏla Castra.** A fortress in Rhaetia, which has given its name to the country of the Tyrol.

Termessus (Τερμησσός). A city of Pisidia, high up on the Taurus in the pass through which the river Catarrhactes flowed, and regarded as so impregnable that even Alexander the Great made no attempt to take it (Polyb. xxii. 18).

Terminalia. See TERMINUS.

Termĭnus. The Roman god of boundaries and frontiers, under whose special protection were the stones (*termini*) which marked territorial limits. The regulations respecting these stones and the religious customs and institutions connected with them went back to the time of Numa Pompilius. At the setting of such a stone all those living near the boundary assembled, and in their presence the hole prepared for the reception of the stone was watered with the blood of a sacrificial animal; incense, field-produce, honey, and wine were sprinkled over it, and a victim sacrificed. The stone, anointed and decked with garlands and ribbons, was then placed upon the smouldering bones and pressed into the earth. Whoever pulled up the stone was cursed, together with his draught-cattle, and any one might kill him with impunity and without being defiled by his blood. In later times the punishment of fines was instituted instead.

The festival of the TERMINALIA was celebrated in Rome and in the country on the 23d of February (Dionys. ii. 74). The neighbours on either side of any boundary gathered round the landmark, with their wives, children, and servants, and crowned it, each on his own side, with garlands, and offered cakes and bloodless sacrifices. In later times, however, a lamb or sucking-pig was sometimes slain, and the stone sprinkled with the blood. Lastly, the whole neighbourhood joined in a general feast. A lamb was also sacrificed in the grove of Terminus, which was six Roman miles from Rome, near the ancient border of the town of Laurentum (Ovid, *Fasti*, ii. 639; Hor. *Epod.* ii. 59). On the Capitol there was a stone dedicated to Terminus, which had originally stood in the open air, but when the Temple of Iupiter was founded by the last king, Tarquinius Superbus, it was enclosed within the building, as the augurs would not allow it to be removed (Livy, i. 55; Varro, *L. L.* v. 74).

Terpander (Τέρπανδρος). The father of Greek music, and through it of lyric poetry. He was a native of Antissa in Lesbos, and flourished between B.C. 700 and 650 (Plut. *De Mus.* 30, p. 1141). He established the first musical school or system that existed in Greece, and added three strings to the lyre, which before his time had only four. The few remains of his verse are printed by Bergk in his lyrical collections. See MUSICA.

Terpsichŏrē (Τερψιχόρα). One of the nine Muses, who presided over the choral song and dancing. See MUSAE.

Terra. See GAEA.

Terracīna. See TARRACINA.

Terra-cottas (ἀγάλματα ὀπτῆς γῆς, *signa fictilia*). Apart from its use for vases, the Greeks first employed terra-cotta for the roofs and cornices of temples (see ANTEFIXA; ECTYPUS), an innovation ascribed to the Corinthian Butades of uncertain date; and the Etruscans and the Romans made the same use of it. These decorations consist of masks or reliefs. Later, statuary was made of the same material. Thus the statue of Iupiter, which one of the Tarquins set in the Capitol, was of terra-cotta (Pliny, *H. N.* xxxv. 157), and in the front pediment of the same temple was a *quadriga*

Figurine from Tanagra. (Drawn by Gudin.)

of terra-cotta. The greater part of the ancient terra-cottas now remaining consist of "figurines" or statuettes representing domestic deities, and also a great variety of models in various colours—white, green, and brown. Great quantities of these have been found in tombs and elsewhere, as at Tanagra, Pompeii, Camirus, Gela, Athens, and Corinth. See Rohden, *Terracotten von Pompeii* (1880); Henzy, *Catalogues des Figures en Terre-Cuite du Louvre* (1883); Kekulé, *Griech. Terracotten aus Tanagra* (1878); Martha, *Catalogues des Figurines des Museés d'Athènes* (1880); and the article FICTILÉ.

Tertulliānus, Q. SEPTIMIUS FLORENS, usually called TERTULLIAN, the most ancient of the Latin Christian Fathers now extant. Notwithstanding the celebrity which he has always enjoyed, our knowledge of his personal history is extremely limited, and is derived almost exclusively from a succinct notice by St. Jerome. From this we learn that Tertullian was a native of Carthage, the son of a proconsular centurion (a sort of aide-de-camp to provincial governors); that he wrote chiefly during the reigns of Septimius Severus and of Caracalla; that he became a presbyter, and remained orthodox until he had reached the term of middle life, when, in consequence of the envy and ill-treatment which he experienced on the part of the Roman clergy, he went over to the sect of the Montanists (see MONTANUS), and wrote several books in defence of these heretics; that he lived to a great age, and was the author of many works. His birth may be placed about A.D. 160, and his death about 240. The most interesting of his numerous works is his *Apologeticum*, or defence of Christianity. It was written at Carthage, probably about A.D. 200. Other treatises of his that are of especial value as throwing light on the history of his times and upon questions of antiquities are the *Ad Nationes*, the *De Idololatria*, the *De Spectaculis*, and the *Adversus Iudaeos*.

Tertullian is an interesting figure—a Puritan of the early Church—stern, uncompromising, and filled with a passionate religious fervour which makes some of his declamatory passages read like the exhortations of a Mucklewrath or a Macbriar. His Latinity is also worthy of careful study, as being a good specimen of the literary African, strongly tinged with an Hebraic colouring. It is he who first coined the Latin ecclesiastical terminology to which St. Augustine gave currency a little later. He quotes the Bible freely from a current translation into Latin now lost, and known as the *Itala*. See HIERONYMUS; ITALA; SERMO PLEBEIUS.

The best complete edition of his works is that of Oehler in 3 vols. (Leipzig, 1853–55); but a more critical edition is now in course of publication in the *Corpus Scriptorum Ecclesiast. Lat.* (pt. i. Vienna, 1890). See Harnack, *Dogmengeschichte*, 2d ed. in 3 vols. (Freiburg, 1888–90). The contents of the separate treatises are summarized by Fuller in Smith and Wace's *Dictionary of Christian Biography*, vol. iv. (London, 1887). There is an edition with English notes of the *De Spectaculis*, *De Idololatria*, and *De Corona Militis* by Currey (Cambridge, 1883). For an English translation of Tertullian, see Clark's *Ante-Nicene Christian Library*.

Teruncius, sc. *nummus*. A silver coin (Varro, *L. L.* v. 174), or perhaps only a convenient designation for a sum equal to one-fourth of the Roman *as*, and hence the same as the copper *quadrans*. See AS; QUADRANS.

Tessĕra. A square or cube; a die; a token. (1) For the tessera used in making pavements, see PAVIMENTUM. (2) As dice the tesserae were used in gambling. (See ALEA.) These were of the same form, and were commonly made of ivory, bone, or some close-grained wood. They were numbered on all the six sides like the dice now in use (Ovid, *Trist.* ii. 473 foll.); and in this respect as well as in their form they differed from the *tali*, which are often distinguished from tesserae by classical writers (See TALUS.) Whilst four *tali* were used in playing, only three tesserae were anciently employed. Hence arose the proverb, ἢ τρὶς ἕξ, ἢ τρεῖς κύβοι, i. e. "either three sixes or three aces," meaning all or none (Plat. *Legg.* xii. 968 E). Three sixes are mentioned as the highest throw in the *Agamemnon* of Aeschylus (33). The die used for gambling was called *tessera lusoria*.

Tessera Lusoria. (From Herculaneum.)

(3) *Tessera hospitalis* (σύμβολον). A token of mutual hospitality and friendship; consisting of a small die, which was given by a host to his guest at the time of departure, when it was broken into two parts, each party retaining one-half, in order that if either of them or their descendants should again meet, they might

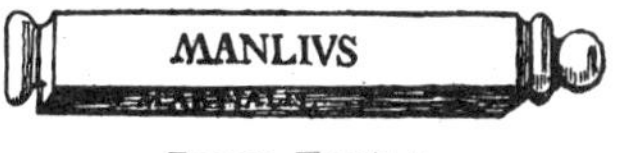

Tessera Hospitalis.

recognize each other, and renew or repay their ancient family obligations (Plaut. *Poen.* v. 2, 86–93).

(4) *Tessera frumentaria* and *nummaria*. A voucher or ticket given upon certain occasions by the magistrates to the poor, in exchange for which they received the quantities of bread, corn, wine, and oil, or sums of money inscribed upon it (Suet. *Nero*, 11; *Aug.* 40, 41); or sometimes scattered in a bounty (*congiarium*) amongst the crowd by the emperors, or wealthy personages, for the purpose of courting popular favour (Suet. *Dom.* 4). See FRUMENTARIAE LEGES.

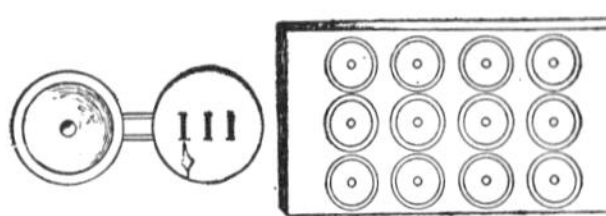

Tesserae Frumentariae. (Rich.)

(5) *Tessera theatralis*. A ticket of admission to the theatre, or other place of public amusement (Mart. viii. 78), distributed by the *duumvir* and entitling the holder to a place at the representation. On it were inscribed the number of the seat, the division and row in which it was situate, and in some cases the title of the play performed. See THEATRUM.

(6) *Tessera militaris* (σύνθημα). A billet or wooden tablet (Polyb. vi. 34) with the watchword inscribed upon it, which was given out by the officers to their soldiers, in order that they might have a test for distinguishing friends from foes; it was also employed as a means by which the orders of the commander were distributed through the different divisions of an army (Livy, vii. 35; xxvii. 46; Veg. *Mil.* ii. 7; Verg. *Aen.* vii. 637).

Tesseracontēres. A ship with forty banks of oars. See NAVIS.

Testa, C. TREBATIUS. A Roman jurist, and a contemporary and friend of Cicero. Trebatius enjoyed considerable reputation under Augustus as a lawyer. Horace addressed to him the First Satire of the Second Book; and Cicero's *Topica* is dedicated to him.

Testamentum. A will. In order to be able to make a valid Roman will, the testator had to have the *testamentifactio*, a term expressing the legal capacity to make a valid will. The *testamentifactio* was the privilege only of Roman citizens who were *patresfamilias*. The following persons consequently had not the *testamentifactio:* those who were in the *potestas* or *manus* of another, or in *mancipii causa*, as sons and daughters, wives *in manu*, and slaves; Latini Iuniani and Dediticii; Peregrini who could not dispose of their property according to the form of a Roman will; and an *impubes* or minor could not dispose of his property by will even with the consent of his tutor. When a male was fourteen years of age, he obtained the *testamentifactio*, and a female obtained the power, subject to certain restraints, on the completion of her twelfth year: deaf and dumb persons and lunatics (*muti, surdi, furiosi*, and *prodigi*) had not the *testamentifactio*. In order to constitute a valid will, it was necessary that an heir (*heres*) should be instituted, which might be done in such terms as follows: *Titius heres esto; Titium heredem esse iubeo.* Originally there were two modes of making wills; either at the Comitia Calata, which were appointed twice a year for that purpose, or *in procinctu*—that is, when a man was going to battle. A third mode of making wills was introduced which was effected *per aes et libram*, whence the name of *testamentum per aes et libram*. If a man had neither made his will at the Comitia Calata nor *in procinctu*, and was in imminent danger of death, he would mancipate (*mancipio dabat*) his *familia*—that is, his patrimonium—to a friend, and would tell him what he wished to be given to each person after his death. There seems to have been no rule of law that a testament must be written. The heir might either be made by oral declaration (*nuncupatio*) or by writing. Written wills, however, were the common form among the Romans, at least in the later republican and in the imperial periods. They were written on tablets of wood or wax, whence the word *cera* is often used as equivalent to *tabella;* and the expressions *prima, secunda cera* are equivalent to *prima, secunda pagina*. The will must have been in some way so marked as to be recognized, and the practice of the witnesses (*testes*) sealing and signing the will at last became common. It was necessary for the witnesses both to seal (*signare*)—that is, to make a mark with a ring (*anulus*) or something else on the wax— and to add their names (*adscribere*). Wills were to be tied with a triple thread (*linum*) on the upper part of the margin, which was to be perforated at the middle part, and the wax was to be put over the thread and sealed. Tablets which were produced in any other way had no validity. A man might make several copies of his will, which was often done for the sake of caution. When sealed, it was deposited with some friend, or in a temple, or with the Vestal Virgins; and after the testator's death it was opened (*resignare*) in due form. The witnesses or the major part were present, and after they had acknowledged their seals, the thread (*linum*) was broken and the will was opened and read, and a copy was made; the original was then sealed with the public seal and placed in the *archium*, whence a fresh copy might be had, if the first copy should ever be lost. See Gans, *Das Erbrecht;* and the articles HERES; LEGATUM.

Testamentum Porcelli. "The last will of a little pig." The title of a *jeu d'esprit* in Latin written before the fourth century A.D. and found in a MS. of the ninth century. It purports to be the will of a young pig who is about to be killed by the cook and who formally bequeathes the parts of his body to his friends and relatives. The document is attested in due form by seven pigs. It is evidently intended for children, for it has the real nursery ring, though some have supposed it to be written as a burlesque of legal forms. St. Jerome (*Comment. in Is.* xii. init.) says that it was repeated by boys at school exhibitions as an amusing bit of fun. It is edited with Latin notes by Moritz Haupt in his *Opuscula* (ii. 178 foll.), and with English notes by H. T. Peck in Peck and Arrowsmith's *Roman Life in Latin Prose and Verse* (New York, 1894). Bücheler prints the text in his smaller edition of Petronius (Berlin, 1882).

Testis. A witness. See DIKÉ; IUSIURANDUM; JUDICIAL PROCEDURE; MARTYRIA.

Testūdo (χελώνη). Literally "a tortoise (shell)". (1) The general designation for different kinds of sheds for the protection of soldiers engaged in a siege. (2) The name testudo was also applied to the covering made by a close body of soldiers, who placed their shields over their heads to secure themselves against the darts of the enemy. The shields fitted so closely together as to present one

Testudo made of Shields. (Antonine Column.)

unbroken surface without any interstices between them, and were also so firm that men could walk upon them, and even horses and chariots be driven over them. A testudo was formed (*testudinem facere*) either in battle to ward off the arrows and other missiles of the enemy, or, which was more frequently the case, to form a protection to the soldiers when they advanced to the walls or gates of a town for the purpose of attacking them. Sometimes the shields were disposed in such a way as to make the testudo slope. The soldiers in the first line stood upright, those in the second stooped a little, and each line successively was a little lower than the preceding down to the last, where the soldiers rested on one knee. Such a disposition of the shields was called *fastigata testudo*, on account of their sloping like the roof of a building. The advantages of this plan were obvious: the stones and missiles thrown upon the shields rolled off them like water from a roof; besides which, other soldiers frequently advanced upon them to attack the enemy upon the walls. The Romans were accustomed to form this kind of testudo, as an exercise, in the games of the Circus (Livy, xliv. 9).

Tethys (Τηθύς). The daughter of Uranus and Gaea, and wife of Oceanus, by whom she became the mother of the Oceanides and of the numerous river-gods (Hes. *Theog.* 136, 337).

Tetrachordon (*τετράχορδον*). A word meaning literally "four-stringed," and hence "having four notes." A scale comprising two tones and a half, which formed the old Greek musical system. The word does not mean any special instrument of music. Vitruvius applies the term to a water-organ (*hydraulus*) when it had only four barrels (x. 8, 2). See HYDRAULUS.

Tetradrachmon (*τετράδραχμων*). A Greek silver coin equivalent to four *drachmae*. See NUMISMATICS, p. 1114.

Tetralogia (*τετραλογία*). A Greek term given to the group of four plays which the poets produced in rivalry with each other at the dramatic contests held at the feast of Dionysus. After the introduction of the Satyric Drama (q. v.), this, or a drama of a comparatively cheerful character (such as the *Alcestis* of Euripides), formed the fourth piece of three tragedies or of a trilogy. By a tetralogy is more particularly meant such a group of four dramas as had belonged to the same cycle of myths, and had thus formed a connected whole. Of such a kind were the tetralogies of Aeschylus. It is doubtful, however, whether he found this type of connected tetralogy already in use or was the first to introduce it. Sophocles abolished the connection between the several pieces, and Euripides followed his example. A complete tetralogy is not extant, although a trilogy exists in the *Oresteia* of Aeschylus, consisting of the tragedies *Agamemnon, Choëphorae,* and *Eumenides;* the satyric play appended to it was the *Proteus.* See DRAMA; TRILOGIA.

Tetrarches (*τετράρχης*). Properly the ruler of one of the four parts of a district divided into four governments. Also the title of any petty prince, such as the rulers in those provinces of Asia which were allowed by Rome to retain a certain independence (Marquardt, *Staatsverw.* i. 401).

Tetrastȳlus. See TEMPLUM.

Tetrĭca. A mountain on the frontiers of Picenum and the land of the Sabines, belonging to the great chain of the Apennines (Varro, *R. R.* ii. 1, 5).

Tetrĭcus, C. PESUVIUS. One of the Thirty Tyrants, and the last of the pretenders who ruled Gaul during its separation from the Empire under Gallienus and his successor, A.D. 267–274. He was defeated by Aurelian at the battle of Châlons (274), and was treated by his conqueror with so much consideration as to give rise to the report that he had himself connived at the result (Eutrop. ix. 9; Trebell. Poll. *Tr. Tyr.* 23).

Tettarakonta (*οἱ τετταράκοντα*). "The Forty." Certain officers chosen by lot, who made regular circuits through the demes of Attica, whence they are called *δικασταὶ κατὰ δήμους*, to decide all cases of *αἰκία* and *τὰ περὶ τῶν βιαίων*; and also all other private causes where the matter in dispute was not above the value of ten drachmae. Their number was originally thirty, but was increased to forty after the expulsion of the Thirty Tyrants and the restoration of the democracy by Thrasybulus, in consequence, it is said, of the hatred of the Athenians to the number of thirty (Pollux, viii. 100). See Schömann, *Ant. Jur. Publ.* p. 267; and *Att. Process*, pp. 88–93 (ed. Lipsius).

Teucer (Τεῦκρος). (1) The son of the river-god Scamander by the nymph Idaea. He was the first king of Troy, whence the Trojans are sometimes called *Teucri.* (2) Son of Telamon and Hesionê, was a step-brother of Aiax, and the best archer among the Greeks at Troy. He founded the town of Salamis in Cyprus, and married Eunê, the daughter of Cyprus, by whom he became the father of Asteria. See AIAX; SALAMIS.

Teucri. See MYSIA; TEUCER; TROIA.

Teumessus (Τευμησσός). A mountain in Boeotia, near Hypatus, and close to Thebes, on the road from the latter place to Chalcis (Pausan. ix. 9, 1).

Teuta (Τεῦτα). The wife of Agron, king of the Illyrians. She assumed the sovereign power on the death of her husband, B.C. 231. In consequence of the injuries inflicted by the piratical expeditions of her subjects upon the Italian merchants, the Romans sent two ambassadors to demand satisfaction, but she not only refused to comply with their demands, but caused the younger of the two brothers to be assassinated on his way home. War was now declared against her by the Romans. The greater part of her territory was soon conquered, and she was obliged to sue for peace, which was granted to her (B.C. 228), on condition of her giving up the greater part of her dominions (Polyb. ii. 9–12).

Teuthrania. See MYSIA.

Teuthras (Τεύθρας). A mountain in the Mysian district of Teuthrania, a southwestern branch of Temnus.

Teuthras (Τεύθρας). An ancient king of Mysia. He was succeeded in the kingdom of Mysia by Telephus. (See TELEPHUS.) The fifty daughters of Teuthras, given as a reward to Heracles, are called by Ovid *Teuthrantia turba.*

Teutoburgiensis Saltus. A range of hills in Germany, extending from Osnabrück to Paderborn (the Teutoburger Wald or Lippische Wald). It is celebrated on account of the defeat and destruction there of Varus and three Roman legions by the Germans under Arminius, A.D. 9. See ARMINIUS; GERMANIA; VARUS.

Teutŏnes or **Teutŏni.** A powerful people in Germany, who invaded Gaul and the Roman dominions along with the Cimbri, at the latter end of the second century B.C. The name Teutones is not a collective name of the whole people of Germany, as some writers have supposed, but only of one particular tribe, who probably dwelt on the coast of the Baltic, near the Cimbri. See CIMBRI; GERMANIA.

Textile Fabrics. See TELA.

Textor, fem. **Textrix** (ὑφάντης, ὑφάντρια). A weaver. (See TELA.) The weavers at Rome were proverbial for their bad language, like the London fishwives, so that Petronius (ch. 32) uses *textorum dicta* in the sense of our "Billingsgate."

Textual Criticism. The criticism of a classical author with a view to establish a sound and defensible text is of two kinds, each of which supplements and aids the other. The first is DIPLOMATIC CRITICISM, which has to do with the age, authenticity, and value of the existing manuscripts (*diplomata*); and the second is VERBAL or GRAMMATICAL CRITICISM, which alters the text in order to make it conform to good sense or to the laws of the language, or to the critic's conception of what the author meant to say. The former is based upon Palaeography; the second in part upon the science of Philology and in part upon æsthetic principles. Wolff and Boeckh classified the former as "Superior" criticism, and the latter as "Inferior," but this terminology is not generally accepted. The best text-critic is he who can bring to bear upon his task a minute palaeographical knowledge and at the same time linguistic training and a sound literary sense.

Textual criticism in Greece originated in the necessity that was felt of a unification and collation of the various versions of the Homeric poems. Homer was to the Greeks much more than a poet; he was long regarded as a great teacher of practical and also of ethical wisdom, and he was read and studied in the schools in much the same spirit as a Christian would study the Bible, or a Mohammedan the Korân. Owing to the fact that the Homeric poems were largely transmitted orally and to the additional fact that the rhapsodists who recited them in public frequently altered the text to suit the special occasion or their own notion of an effective arrangement, there were many versions current even in very early times. It has been inferred that Solon took some steps toward the establishing of an Homeric canon (Plato, *Hipparch.* 228 B; Diog. Laërt. i. 57), and Pisistratus and his son Hipparchus are said to have intrusted a recension of the text to a commission of four scholars who were to edit and unify the poems. (See Flach, *Pisistratos und seine litterarische Thätigkeit* [Tübingen, 1885], and the article HOMERUS.) This recension is thought to have formed the basis of the famous "City Editions" (q. v.) which in turn were worked over by the Alexandrian scholars. Other special texts were made by Theagenes of Rhegium, Stesimbrotus of Thasos (c. 450 B.C.), and by Aristotle, who prepared a version for the use of his pupil Alexander the Great, usually called ἡ ἐκ νάρθηκος from the case in which it was kept (Plut. *Alex.* 8; cf. Cope's introduction to Aristotle's *Rhetoric*). Demetrius Phalereus also edited the *Iliad* and the *Odyssey*, while the Sophists spent considerable time in the critical study of Homer. (See Friedel, *De Sophistarum Studiis Homericis* [Halle, 1873]). At about this time criticism was also applied to the texts of other great writers—to those of Aeschylus, Sophocles, and Euripides—of whom an authentic text was promulgated by the orator and statesman Lycurgus, about B.C. 350, which was the only one allowed to be used by the actors. (See Korn, *De Aeschyli, Sophoclis, Euripidis Fabularum Exemplari Lycurgo Auctore Confecto* [Bonn, 1863].) Commentaries were also written on special points by the Stoics and by the Cynics.

A more definite and scientific criticism was that undertaken by the philological section of the School at Alexandria (see ALEXANDRIAN SCHOOL), and in connection with the great Alexandrian Library (see BIBLIOTHECA), for which great quantities of manuscripts were purchased by King Ptolemy at the advice of Demetrius Phalereus. All of the early heads of the School worked at text-recension. Zenodotus of Ephesus (B.C. 325–260) published a collection of Homeric glosses (see GLOSSA), and about B.C. 274 put forth a διόρθωσις or recension of both the *Iliad* and the *Odyssey*, also called the ἔκδοσις Ὁμήρου. In this, four kinds of corrections appear: (*a*) Elimination or the omission of lines known to be spurious; (*b*) Query or the indication of doubtful lines; (*c*) Transposition or a change in the order of the lines; and (*d*) Emendation or the substitution of new readings for the old. See Düntzer, *De Zenodoti Studiis Homericis* (Göttingen, 1848).

The existing texts were classified and characterized in the Πίνακες of Callimachus, the first great bibliographical work ever written; and Eratosthenes of Cyrené (c. 276–196 B.C.) wrote a critical treatise on the poets of the Old Comedy. He was succeeded by Aristophanes of Byzantium (c. 257–180 B.C.), perhaps the greatest philologist of antiquity. His criticism was partly diplomatic and partly verbal; and was guided always by the *sentiment critique.* He did much for both text-criticism and for language-study in general. To him is ascribed the invention of diacritical marks and symbols (σημεῖα κριτικά), all of great palaeographic importance. Ten of these are known as the δέκα προσῳδίαι: (*a*) the rough breathing (πνεῦμα δασύ); (*b*) the smooth breathing (πνεῦμα ψιλόν); (*c*) the grave accent (βαρεῖα); (*d*) the acute accent (ὀξεῖα); (*e*) the circumflex accent (τόνος ὀξυβαρεῖα or περισπωμένη); (*f* and *g*) the long and short marks (χρόνοι); (*h*) the διαστολή or comma (*virgule*); (*i*) the hyphen (ὑφέν); (*j*) the apostrophe (ἀπόστροφος). The Greek marks of punctuation are also ascribed to Aristophanes. His critical work included an edition of Homer (a second διόρθωσις), and also editions of Hesiod (the *Theogony*), Alcaeus, Anacreon, Pindar, Euripides, Aristophanes, and perhaps Simonides and Menander. The famous Alexandrian Canon was in part his work. See CANON ALEXANDRINUS.

His great pupil Aristarchus of Samothrace (c. 217–143 B.C.) did much for the study of formal grammar (see GRAMMATICA), and also edited Archilochus, Alcaeus, Hesiod, Pindar, Aeschylus, Sophocles, Aristophanes, and especially the Homeric poems, of which he put forth two separate recensions, writing συγγράμματα or special monographs, besides the ἐκδόσεις (texts) and ὑπομνήματα (commentaries). Aristarchus approached his task in a skeptical spirit, and employed five processes: (*a*) διόρθωσις or arrangement of the text; (*b*) ἀνάγνωσις or determination of accents; (*c*) τέχνη, determination of forms and questions of syntax; (*d*) ἐξήγησις or explanation of words, allusions, etc.; and (*e*) κρίσις, the determination of all questions respecting authenticity or integrity of the text, and the final judgment of the author as a whole. Aristarchus used a number of critical symbols in his work. Among them were the ὀβελός or spit (—) to mark a spurious line; the διπλῆ (⸖) to call attention to some special point; the dotted διπλῆ (⸖) to denote a variant from the reading of Zenodotus; and the ἀστερίσκος (✳) to denote a "formulaic" line. Of the 15,600 lines of the *Iliad* and *Odyssey*, Aristarchus "athetized," i. e. struck out as spurious, 1160. See Gardthausen, *Palaeographie*, pp. 288 foll. (Leipzig, 1879); and on Aristarchus in general Lehrs, *De Aristarchi Studiis Homericis* (Königsberg, 1833; 2d ed. 1882); Ludwich, *Aristarch's homer. Textkritik* (1884–85); and Jebb, *Homer* (Glasgow, 1887). Cf. also Mahaffy's *Gk. Lit.* i. pp. 35–39 (New York, 1880).

The later Alexandrians did also much careful work in the recension of texts, and so did the rival School of Pergamus, headed by Crates of Mallos, the "Anomalist" (see CRATES; PHILOLOGIA), who flourished in B.C. 168. (See Wagener, *De Aula Attalica* [1836].) Didymus Chalcenteros (B.C. 65–A.D. 10) is the last of the important Greek text critics. See DIDYMUS.

From the Greeks the Romans received the principles of textual criticism, and early began to apply these principles to the study of Latin works. Lucius Aelius Stilo investigated the text of the *Carmina Saliaria;* M. Antonius Griphus wrote commentaries on the *Annales* of Ennius. Cicero is said to have prepared an edition of Lucretius. (See LUCRETIUS.) To Varro we owe the establishment of a Plautine Canon. (See PLAUTUS; VARRO.) The greatest of the Roman text-critics was M. Valerius Probus Berytus (c. 80 A.D.), who edited, with critical signs, Vergil, Horace, Lucretius, and Terence, and wrote a treatise on the σημεῖα κριτικά. (See Suet. *Reliq.* p. 138, Reifferscheid; and the introduction to Conington's Vergil, i. pp. lxv. foll.) Glossography also flourished greatly among the Romans. See GLOSSA; SCHOLIA; SUBSCRIPTIO.

In the first period of the Renaissance in Italy the study of texts revived during the corruption of existing manuscripts. (See RENAISSANCE.) Among these early critics are Laurentius Valla (q. v.) and Politianus (q. v.). The critical acumen of scholars was much sharpened by the immense number of forged texts that began to appear. A single forger, Annius of Viterbo, alone put forth seventeen volumes of spurious works ascribed by him to the classical writers. (See Wachler in Ersch and Gruber's *Encyclopädie.*) Gradually a scientific basis for textual criticism was established, the great names in this process being those belonging to the so-called French or Polyhistorical School, the Scaligers, Lambinus, Salmasius, and Casaubon; and to the Anglo-Dutch or Critical School, Gronovius, Burmann, Hemsterhuys, and especially Richard Bentley. In more recent times, the important names are those of A. I. Bekker, Boeckh, Lachmann, Ritschl, Madvig, Cobet, Porson, Munro, Wilamowitz-Moellendorf, and Vahlen. See especially the articles BENTLEY; LACHMANN; SCALIGER.

Text-critics are generally to be classified according to the relative importance which they give to the subjective element in their criticism. Bentley, who is the father of the subjective method, in his later work largely disregarded the evidence of manuscripts in his determination of the proper lections, depending largely upon his own instinctive feeling as to what an author must have said. He has expressed this principle in a formal phrase —*Nobis et ratio et res ipsa centum codicibus potiores sunt*—and in following this out he did much that was rash and indefensible as well as much that is brilliant and convincing. The *reductio ad absurdum* of this subjective method will be found in Bentley's edition of Milton's *Paradise Lost,* in which he rewrote whole passages, because of reasons based on his own conception of what Milton must in reality have said. See Jebb's *Bentley* (New York, 1882).

The school that represents the antithesis of the Bentleian principle is that of which the Jesuit scholars of France stand as a type. These held to what they called *la tradition classique,* and studied to avoid any radical changes in a text whatever, going so far as to force an explanation of passages that evidently violate the laws of the ancient languages, history, and good sense. The Bentleians rewrite everything; the other school explains everything; and each set must be regarded as often equally unreasonable.

For an explanation of the methods and principles of modern text-criticism, the reader is referred to Cobet, *De Arte Interpretandi* (Leyden, 1847); Madvig, *Adversaria Critica,* especially vol. i. (1870); Tournier, *Exercices Critiques de l'École des Hautes Études* (Paris, 1875); and the Prolegomena to Lachmann's Lucretius (1850, last ed. 1866); Munro's Lucretius (last ed. 1886); Ellis's Catullus (last ed. 1889); and for a simple and interesting statement of more obvious matters, Gow's *Companion to School Classics,* pp. 47–66 (London and New York, 1888).

Thabor, Tabor, or **Atabyrium** (Ἀταβύριον). Now an isolated mountain at the eastern end of the plain of Esdraelon in Galilee.

Thabrăca (Θάβρακα) or **Tabrăca** (Τάβρακα). A city of Numidia at the mouth of the river Tusca (Ptol. vi. 3, 5).

Thaïs (Θαΐς). A celebrated Athenian courtesan, who accompanied Alexander the Great on his expedition into Asia. After the death of Alexander,

Thaïs attached herself to Ptolemy Lagi, by whom she became the mother of two sons, Leontiscus and Lagus, and of a daughter, Irené. She is said to have urged Alexander on to firing the palace of Darius during a revel—a story which suggested the most striking lines of Dryden's *Ode on St. Cecilia's Day*. The tradition is probably false (Athen. p. 576; Diod. xvii. 72; Plut. *Alex.* 38; Q. Curt. v. 7, 3).

Thala (Θάλα). A great city of Numidia, mentioned by Sallust and other writers, and probably identical with TELEPTÉ or THELEPTÉ, a city in the south of Numidia, seventy-one Roman miles northwest of Capsa.

Thalamēgus (θαλάμηγος). A sort of barge used by the kings and princes of Egypt for their trips on the Nile. Cleopatra's famous barge was a thalamegus (Suet. *Iul.* 52). The craft was fitted up with much luxury, and was named from the fact that it had cabins (*thalami*) for a numerous company. The pure Latin name is *navis cubiculata* (Sen. *De Ben.* vii. 70).

Thalămus (θάλαμος). The Greek term for a commodious room in a house, and especially the nuptial chamber. See DOMUS.

Thalassius, Talassius, or **Talassio.** See MATRIMONIUM, p. 1016; TALASSIO.

Thales (Θαλῆς). An Ionian, the founder of Greek philosophy. He was a contemporary of Solon and Croesus, and one of the Seven Sages, and was born at Miletus about B.C. 636, and died about 546, at the age of ninety, though the exact dates of his birth and death are not known. He is said to have predicted the eclipse of the sun which happened in the reign of the Lydian king Alyattes; to have diverted the course of the Halys in the time of Croesus; and later, in order to unite the Ionians when threatened by the Persians, to have instituted a federal council in Teos. Aristotle preserves a story of his knowledge of meteorology which was turned to a practical use (Polyb. i. 11, p. 1259). In the lists of the Seven Sages his name seems to have stood at the head, and he displayed his wisdom both by political sagacity and by prudence in acquiring wealth. In mathematics we find attributed to him only proofs of propositions which belong to the first elements of geometry, and which could not possibly have enabled him to calculate the eclipses of the sun and the course of the heavenly bodies. He may, however, have obtained a knowledge of the higher branches of mathematics from Egypt, which country he is said to have visited. In the annals of Greek philosophy he was probably the first who looked for a physical origin of the world instead of resting upon mythology. Thales maintained that water is the origin (ἀρχή) of things, meaning thereby that it is water out of which everything arises and into which everything resolves itself, and that the earth floated upon the water. Thales left no works behind him (Herod. i. 74, 170; Diog. Laërt. i. 25; Aristot. *Metaph.* i. 3, p. 983). See IONIAN SCHOOL OF PHILOSOPHY; PHILOSOPHIA.

Thalēs (Θαλῆς) or **Thalētas** (Θαλήτας). A celebrated musician and lyric poet. He was a native of Gortyna in Crete, and probably flourished shortly after Terpander (Pausan. i. 14, 4; Plut. *De Mus.* 9, p. 1135).

Thalīa (Θαλία and Θαλεία). (1) One of the nine Muses, and, at least in later times, the Muse of Comedy. (See MUSAE.) (2) One of the Nereïdes. (3) One of the Charites or Graces.

Thallo. See HORAE.

Thallophŏri (θαλλοφόροι). See PANATHENAEA.

Thamўris (Θάμυρις) or **Thamўras.** An ancient Thracian bard, son of Philammon and the nymph Argiopé. In his presumption he challenged the Muses to a trial of skill, and, being overcome in the contest, was deprived by them of his sight and of the power of singing. He was represented with a broken lyre in his hand (Pausan. iv. 33, 4; ix. 30, 2; x. 7, 2).

Thanătos (Θάνατος). The Greek god of death identified by the Romans with Mors. Homer describes him as the brother of Sleep, and Hesiod calls him the son of Night (Hes. *Theog.* 211, 756) and says that he dwells in the lower world. In the best period of Greek art, both Death and Sleep were represented as youths either asleep or with inverted torches (Verg. *Aen.* vi. 224). See SOMNUS.

Thapsăcus (Θάψακος). Old Test. Thipsach. An Aramean word, signified "a ford"; now Dibsi. A city of Syria, in the province of Chalybonitis, on the left bank of the Euphrates, 2000 stadia south of Zeugma, and fifteen parasangs from the mouth of the river Chaboras, the Araxes of Xenophon.

Thapsus (Θάψος). (1) A city on the eastern coast of Sicily, on a peninsula of the same name (Isola degli Magnisi). (2) A city on the eastern coast of Byzacena, in Africa Propria. Here Caesar finally defeated the army of Pompey and ended the Civil War. See CAESAR; POMPEIUS.

Thargelia (θαργήλια). The principal feast of Apollo in Athens, held on the seventh day of the month Thargelion (May–June), the birthday of the god. Originally it was connected with the ripening of the field-produce. A procession was formed, and the first-fruits of the year were offered to Apollo, together with Artemis and the Horae. It was at the same time an expiatory feast, at which a peculiar propitiatory sacrifice was offered, which was to purify the State from all guilt, and avert the wrath of the god, lest he should exercise his avenging and destroying power in burning up the harvest with parching heat, and in visiting the people with pestilence. Two persons, condemned to death, a man and a woman, as representatives of the male and female population, were led about with a garland of figs round their necks to the sound of flutes and singing, and scourged with seaweed and with the branches of a fig-tree. They were then sacrificed at a certain spot on the seashore, their bodies burned, and the ashes cast into the sea. In later times they seem to have been contented with throwing the victims (φαρμακοί) from a height into the sea, catching them as they fell, and banishing them from the country. Besides these sacrifices, festal processions and choral contests between men and boys took place. At the same time the great feast of Apollo was probably held at Delos, to which the Athenians sent a sacred embassy in the ancient ship in which Theseus is said to have sailed to Crete, and which was always kept in repair. See Preller, *Griechische Mythologie*, i. 209; and A. Mommsen, *Heortologie*, 50, 53, 414–425.

Thargelion (Θαργηλιών). The eleventh month in the Attic calendar, corresponding roughly to our May–June. See CALENDARIUM.

Thasos (Θάσος) or **Thasus.** Now Thaso or Tasso. An island in the north of the Aegaean Sea, off the coast of Thrace, and opposite the mouth of the river Nestus. It was at a very early period taken possession of by the Phœnicians, on account of its valuable gold-mines. According to tradition the Phœnicians were led by Thasus, son of Poseidon or Agenor, who came from the East in search of Europa, and from whom the island derived its name. Thasos was afterwards colonized by the Parians, B.C. 708, and among the colonists was the poet Archilochus. The Thracians once possessed a considerable territory on the coast of Thrace, and were one of the richest and most powerful peoples in the north of the Aegaean. They were subdued by the Persians under Mardonius, and subsequently became part of the Athenian maritime empire. They revolted, however, from Athens in B.C. 465, and, after sustaining a siege of three years, were subdued by Cimon in 463. They again revolted from Athens in 411, and called in the Spartans; but the island was again restored to the Athenians by Thrasybulus in 407. Some remains of the ancient town still exist, among them the Agora and a triumphal arch. See Hasselbach, *De Insula Thaso* (1838).

Thaumas (Θαύμας). The son of Pontus and Gé, and, by the Oceanid Electra, the father of Iris and the Harpies (Hes. *Theog.* 237). Hence Iris is called *Thaumantias, Thaumantis,* and *Thaumantea virgo.* See IRIS.

Theaetētus (Θεαίτητος). An Athenian, the son of Euphronius of Sunium, introduced as one of the speakers in Plato's *Theaetetus* and *Sophistes,* in which he is spoken of as a noble youth, ardent in the pursuit of knowledge, and especially in the study of geometry.

Theagĕnes (Θεαγένης). (1) A tyrant of Megara, who obtained his power about B.C. 630, having espoused the part of the commonalty against the nobles. He was driven out before his death. He gave his daughter in marriage to Cylon (q. v.). (2) A Thasian, the son of Timosthenes, renowned for his extraordinary strength and swiftness. He gained numerous victories at the Olympian, Pythian, Nemean, and Isthmian Games, and is said to have won 1400 crowns. He lived about B.C. 480 (Pausan. vi. 6, 5; id. 11, 2).

Theāno (Θεανώ). (1) The daughter of Cisseus, wife of Antenor, and priestess of Athené at Ilium. (2) A celebrated female philosopher of the Pythagorean School, appears to have been the wife of Pythagoras, and the mother by him of Telauges, Mnesarchus, Myia, and Arignoté; but the accounts respecting her were various (Diog. Laërt. viii. 42; Suidas, s. h. v.). Letters ascribed to her, but not genuine, exist, and are edited by Hercher (1873).

Theātrum (θέατρον). The architectural form of the Greek theatre was developed from the circular dancing-place, the ὀρχήστρα, used by the Bacchic dancers. At first there was no Chorus distinct from the general body of worshippers, all of whom were free to join in the dance. As soon, however, as a regular Chorus was instituted, it became necessary to reserve a circular space of ground for it. A ring of stones sufficed to mark off this circle. The altar of Dionysus was placed at its centre. The spectators stood around it and watched the dance. So long as the dramatic element was limited to a dialogue between the Chorus and one actor, that person could stand on a raised place in the middle of the Chorus and address himself to various points of the circle in turn; but when Aeschylus added a second actor, it became necessary that the actors should play towards some one side. It was then no longer possible that the spectators should form a complete circle, but they were now arranged in a semicircle, or something like it, though the whole circle of the dancing-place was still, as of old, kept clear for the Chorus. The actors stood facing the spectators, not within the circle of the dancing-place, but on the farther side of it. Behind them was the tent or booth (σκηνή) in which they dressed. It was an easy improvement to conceal this tent from the spectators by a modern screen which could represent the front of a house or anything else that suited the requirements of the play. This screen was the *proscaenium* (προσκήνιον) i. e. that which masked the σκηνή. The term was retained in the later history of the theatre, though its primitive sense was lost. The *proscaenium* was the background visible to the spectators, whether it was a temporary screen or a permanent wall. Then σκηνή came to denote that part of the theatre which belonged to the actors, as distinguished from ὀρχήστρα, the place of the Chorus. Aristotle (*Poet.* 24) uses the phrase ἐπὶ σκηνῆς where we should say "on the stage."

The oldest theatre of which we have any knowledge is the Dionysiac Theatre at Athens. It has generally been supposed that a permanent stone theatre existed in the Λήναιον, or precinct of Dionysus, from the early years of the fifth century B.C., a belief resting on a passage in Suidas (s. v. Πρατίνας). But the history of the Dionysiac Theatre has been placed in a new light by the recent researches of the German Archaeological Institute at Athens. Its excavations, begun in 1886, have yielded the following results: (1) In the fifth century B.C., and down to about B.C. 330, the precinct contained no permanent building for scenic purposes, but there was near it a circular ὀρχήστρα, about seventy-eight feet in diameter, of which traces have been found under the buildings erected by Lycurgus. This ὀρχήστρα was then the only permanent provision for drama. All scenery, therefore, was temporary, and the spectators sat on wooden benches. (2) The first permanent building for the drama in the Λήναιον was that completed by Lycurgus, about B.C. 330. It consisted of a stone wall with two small wings, like towers, projecting from it on right and left (A, A); the length of the wall between them was about sixty-five feet seven inches. The temporary decorations (of wood, with linen hangings) were erected in front of this wall, and supported by the wings. Behind the wall was an oblong room, extending somewhat beyond the wings, and serving for the use of the actors. A portico (C, C), opening on the precinct of Dionysus, ran along the south side of it. The new orchestra was to the north of this building. Dr. Dörpfeld supposes that it formed, like the older one, a complete circle, and that there was no raised stage; the actors stood on the same level with the Chorus. Rows of stone seats for the spectators were now constructed. After the time of Lycurgus no change, except of detail, took place in the auditorium. (3) At some later date, which cannot be fixed, a permanent stone proscenium (B), adorned with columns, and about ten or twelve feet high, was built in front of the wall with projecting wings

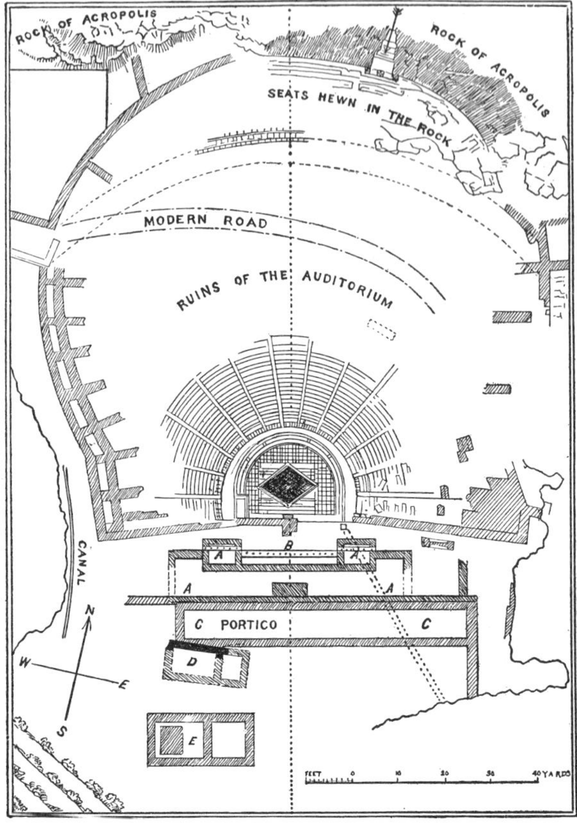

Dionysiac Theatre at Athens.

which Lycurgus had erected. As the wings no longer served a practical purpose (in supporting the temporary scenery), they were annexed to the new proscenium, a part being cut off the front of each, so as to bring them more nearly into line with it. (4) An architrave-inscription found in the theatre shows that it was modified and embellished in the reign of "Claudius," by whom Nero seems to be meant. It was probably at this time that the orchestra received its present pavement of Pentelic and Hymettus marble. To this period also is referred the erection of a raised stage, supported in front by a sculptured wall. (5) The latest recorded changes in the Dionysiac Theatre are associated with the name of a certain Phaedrus, and took place probably in the third century (*C. I. A.* iii. 239). To these belong the existing front wall of the stage, adorned with sculpture of an earlier period; also the balustrade which now separates the auditorium from the orchestra, and the partial covering of the orchestra-canal with marble flags.

It is maintained by Dr. Dörpfeld that, not only in the Dionysiac Theatre, but in all theatres of the Greek type, the actors stood on the same level with the Chorus; a stage raised above the orchestra was a Roman invention; and where such a stage occurs in a theatre of Greek origin, it is a later addition, made under Roman influence. The Roman raised stage, he thinks, was developed, when a Chorus was no longer used, by depressing the level of the circular orchestra in that part of it—the part farthest from the actors—where the Chorus formerly stood. This startling theory is based chiefly on the nature of the proscenium as it appears in the remains of some Greek theatres. The theatre of Epidaurus, built about the middle of the fourth century B.C., is the best-preserved example of the Greek type; excavations were made in it by the Greek Archaeological Society in 1883.

The orchestra forms a complete circle, defined by a ring of flat stones. Beyond this circle, on the side farthest from the audience, are remains of a wall, about twelve feet high, adorned with Ionic half-columns, and flanked by slightly projecting wings; there was one door in it, at the middle point. This wall must have been either the background of the scene, or the front of a raised stage. It is argued that it must have been the background, because (*a*) twelve feet would be too great a height for a stage; (*b*) the width of the stage — about eight feet — would have been too small; (*c*) there is no trace of steps leading from the top of the wall to the orchestra. A similar wall occurs in the theatre at Oropus, and is identified as the proscenium by an inscription which it bears. The theatre in the Piraeus affords another example.

On the other hand, several considerations tell in favour of the received view, that Greek actors, at every period, had a raised stage. (1) The statement of the architect Vitruvius, who wrote about A.D. 20, is decisive, so far as the Roman period is concerned. He states that the Greek theatre had a raised stage, about ten or twelve feet high, but narrower than the Roman; the Greeks, he says, called it λογεῖον. Vitruvius uses the word *proscaenium* to describe this stage; and the same use of the term occurs in other writers, both Roman and Greek. Dr. Dörpfeld is therefore reduced to assuming that Vitruvius has made a mistake—confusing the background of the scene in a Greek theatre with the front of a raised stage. But it is absurd to suppose that Vitruvius should have made such a blunder about the Greek theatres of his

Marble Sculptures on Front Wall of Stage, Dionysiac Theatre.

own day; and that, having accurately described a raised stage which did not exist, he should also have invented a name for it, λογεῖον. (2) The theatre at Megalopolis in Arcadia has lately been excavated by members of the British School at Athens (see the report of the School for 1890). The date of this theatre may be placed in the second half of the fourth century B.C. Here there is a raised stage, of which the height was originally about six feet, and the width about eighteen feet. A flight of steps, extending from end to end of it, led down to the orchestra. That it was a stage, and not a background, is proved (*a*) by these steps, (*b*) by the fact that access was given to it by three doors in the wall behind it. There is no reason to doubt that this stage is of the same date as the auditorium. A later Roman stage has been found in front of it. By this example, then, the existence of a raised stage in a Greek theatre of the fourth century B.C. is placed beyond doubt. (3) With regard to the fifth century B.C., it was not to be expected that any remains of a raised stage should be found; temporary wooden structures would leave no trace. The Greek plays do not supply any literary evidence which can be deemed conclusive. There are some passages which indicate that the place where the actors stood was accessible to the Chorus (e.g. Soph. *Oed. Col.* 836 foll.); as would be the case if we supposed a stage with steps leading up to it, as at Megalopolis. Among the passages which seem to imply a raised stage, we may notice Aristoph. *Vesp.* 1514, where Philocleon says, ἀτὰρ καταβατέον γ' ἐπ' αὐτούς. This may, indeed, be rendered, "I must *enter the lists* against them"; but it also implies some change of position, more marked than such as would consist in moving merely from one spot in the orchestra to another, and would be most naturally explained by a descent into the orchestra from the stage. Some vases of Lower Italy, referable to the period B.C. 300–100, depict scenes from the Old Attic Comedy acted on a raised λογεῖον (cf. Baumeister, *Denkmäler*, pp. 1750 foll.). Plato (*Symp.* p. 194 A) speaks of the tragic poet Agathon as ἀναβαίνοντος ἐπὶ ὀκρίβαντα μετὰ τῶν ὑποκριτῶν. This shows that the idea of placing actors on a raised platform was familiar to Athenians of the fifth century B.C. Even in the days before Thespis, when one member of the Chorus held a dialogue with the rest, he was mounted, we are told, on a kind of table (ἐλεός). A recent writer suggests that the source of this story may have been a Comedy in which the beginnings of Tragedy were burlesqued (Hiller, *Rhein. Museum*, xxxix. p. 329). If this were so, it would only show that some sort of raised stage was conceived as necessary for even the most primitive form of drama. Lastly, there is a strong *a priori* objection to the theory that actors and Chorus stood on the same level. The Chorus was usually drawn up in ranks facing the actors. With his *cothurnus* and mask, a tragic actor would still not overtop the Chorus by more than a head. Hence, a view of the actors would have almost been wholly denied to spectators whose seats were in the middle part of the lowest row. But those were the seats assigned to the most distinguished persons. This argument cannot be met by saying, as Dr. Dörpfeld does, that the Chorus was "usually" divided into ἡμιχόρια (leaving the actors visible between the two groups). Such an arrangement was not usual, but very exceptional. It may be allowed that, when the stage came to be as high as twelve feet, permanent means of communication between stage and orchestra cannot have existed, though temporary wooden steps might be employed at need. But before stages of that height came into use, such communication had ceased to be requisite, since the Chorus had no longer an active part in drama.

Vitruvius gives the ground-plan of a Greek theatre as follows: describe a circle for the orchestra, and in it inscribe three squares. One side of one of these squares will represent the front line of the stage (a b). A parallel tangent to the circle will be the back wall of the stage (c d). The stage (*pulpitum*, λογεῖον) must be not less than ten or more than twelve feet high. Next, parallel with a b, draw a diameter of the circle, e f. It will be seen in the diagram that at e and f the semicircle is so continued as to make a horseshoe, ending at g h. The curves which thus continue it are segments of circles described from e and f as respective centres, with e f as radius. This is known as "the construction from three centres," viz., e, f, and the centre of the orchestra. The auditorium is shut in by lines which bisect the right angles at i and k. The space between g h and c d is a raised stage.

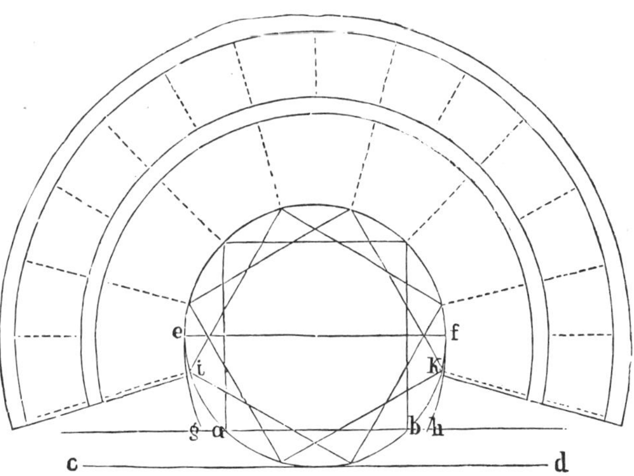

Greek Theatre, after Vitruvius.

The fourth century B.C. was the period at which stone theatres became usual in Greece. We may now proceed to consider their characteristics more in detail.

The Orchestra.—It has been seen that, even in the matured theatre, the "dancing-place" was still a complete circle, as in the old days of the Cyclic Choruses. Its central point was sometimes marked, either by a small pit (as at the Piraeus), or by a stone (as at Epidaurus). Such marks probably indicate the spot on which the altar of Dionysus was to be placed. The word θυμέλη, "a place of sacrifice," means in classical poetry either "a shrine," or, more specifically, "an altar." The most probable conclusion is that the θυμέλη was the altar of Dionysus, in the centre of the orchestra. Another view is that the name θυμέλη was transferred from the altar to a platform in the orchestra on which the altar was placed, and that this platform was the station of the Chorus—connected by steps with the lower level of the orchestra (κονίστρα) and with the higher level of the stage (λογεῖον). It is true that the use of θυμέλη to denote a kind of stage was current in later times, when *thymelici*, "music-hall artists," were distinguished from actors proper (Isidore, *Orig.* xviii. 47). But this use arose under Roman influences, and cannot be assumed for the Greece of the fifth or fourth century B.C. A channel, to carry off rain-water, often surrounded the orchestra, being bridged by stones at the points from which the stairways led up to the seats.

THE AUDITORIUM.—In default of a special term like *cavea*, this is sometimes called θέατρον: though that word, when it does not mean the whole building, more often denotes the spectators, as we speak of "the house." In the older Greek theatres the public entered by the side-passages (πάροδοι) between the proscenium and the orchestra—the same which the Chorus used. Sometimes, indeed, we find an alternative mode of access, viz. by a path traversing high ground, and leading directly to one of the upper tiers: this was the case at Athens. but it was exceptional. A crowd entering by the πάροδοι would find the pressure greatest at the mouths of the semicircular passage between the orchestra and the lowest row of seats—before the spectators had distributed themselves to the several parts of the house. This fact helps to explain a peculiarity of construction. The lowest row of seats is not, as a rule, completely concentric with the orchestra, but is usually so contrived as to leave a wider space at the points just mentioned. A further advantage of this arrangement was that it afforded a better view to those who sat at each end of the semicircle.

Flights of steps ascending from the orchestra to the highest tier of seats divided the auditorium into wedge-like segments. The Greek word for such a segment was κερκίς, which properly meant "radius"; the Latin term was *cuneus*. A further division into upper and lower zones was effected by passages called διαζώματα, "girdles" (*praecinctiones*), which ran completely round the semicircle. The word διάζωμα can denote, not only the passage itself, but the zone which it marks off (*C. I. G.* 4283). Above the highest tier, another open passage ran round the house. The term ἴκρια properly denoted the wooden benches on which, in the earlier times, the spectators sat. When stone seats were introduced (cir. B.C. 330), such seats were founded, where it was possible, on the natural rock of the slope. At Athens, as at Megalopolis, artificial substructions were required in several parts, and this must almost everywhere have been the case, more or less. The material used for the seats varied much. Sometimes it is marble, as at Iassus in Caria and Perga in Pamphylia; at Athens and in the Piraeus, it is a white limestone, finely wrought; while the smaller provincial theatres were often content with coarser stone and workmanship. The tiers of seats were called βάθρα or ἀναβαθμοί. At Athens the space allotted to one person was indicated merely by a line engraved on the stone: it is described as ἕδρα, τόπος, χώρα, χωρίον, or simply θέα.

The privilege of free seats (προεδρία) in the theatre was given chiefly to four classes of persons: (1) certain priests and priestesses, among whom the priest of Dionysus was foremost; (2) certain magistrates; (3) foreigners who were honoured in an official character, as πρέσβεις or θεωροί: (4) citizens or foreigners who were honoured in their personal capacity, as benefactors of the State. For such persons special seats were provided, like armchairs, called θρόνοι or καθέδραι. At Athens these chairs, made of Pentelic marble, occupy the whole of the lowest row, while others are placed in different parts of the house, though in no case higher up than the twenty-fourth row; those assigned to priests or officials bear their titles. At Epidaurus several rows of seats with backs and arms were assigned to those who enjoyed προεδρία.

The acoustic properties of a Greek theatre would be naturally good, since the actors had a high wall behind them and a rising slope in front. Vitruvius, indeed, says that artificial aid was sought from "brazen vessels," "which the Greeks call ἠχεῖα," so placed in the auditorium as to reverberate the voices of the actors. He even speaks of these "resonators" as being nicely adapted to the required musical pitch (ii. 1, 9). The theatre at Aizani in Cilicia has a series of niches above the διάζωμα: and similar niches exist elsewhere. According to one view, these niches held the ἠχεῖα, while another connects them merely with the substructions of seats.

The outer wall enclosing the auditorium ordinarily followed the curve of the semicircle, unless the nature of the ground caused some deviation. At Athens the auditorium was partly bounded on the north by the steep rock of the Acropolis, while the rest of its boundary was formed by strong walls of conglomerate. Where the external appearance of these walls became important, viz., in the south and southwestern portions, they were cased with finely wrought limestone. Examples occur in which the walls enclosing the auditorium were rectangular, as at Cnidus, and in the smaller theatre at Pompeii. The walls flanking the seats at each end of the semicircle were either carried in a single sloping line from the topmost tier to the orchestra, or built in a series of steps corresponding with the tiers. In the best Greek period such walls were not exactly parallel with the line of the proscenium, but started inwards a little, towards the centre of the orchestra. This was the case at Athens and Epidaurus.

SCENIC DECORATION.—The testimonies on this subject are of two classes. (1) Notices in writers chiefly belonging to the Roman age, especially lexicographers and scholiasts. Among these the most important is the grammarian Iulius Pollux (flour. A.D. 170), in his *Onomasticon*, book iv. §§ 128–132. As has lately been shown by Rohde, the source principally used by Pollux was a work by Iuba, a writer of the later Alexandrian Age, entitled Θεατρικὴ Ἱστορία, in at least seventeen books; while Iuba, in his turn, had sources going back to Aristophanes of Byzantium (B.C. 200), but not further. The besetting fault of Pollux, in abridging from this ample material, seems to have been an omission to distinguish between the normal and the occasional resources of the stage. (2) The second kind of evidence is that derived from the Greek dramatic texts themselves. This source, scanty as it is, is the principal one on which we have to rely in regard to the practice of the fifth and fourth centuries B.C. Not long ago it was the custom to treat the notices in Pollux and the other late authorities as if they could be applied without reserve to the great age of Athenian Tragedy and Comedy, but a more critical study has shown the need of greater caution in this respect.

In the extant plays of Aeschylus, Sophocles, Euripides, and Aristophanes, the action most often takes place in front of a house with a "practicable" door; sometimes in front of a temple, a cottage, a tent, a cave, or a rock. Painted linen hangings, erected on a wooden frame, would have sufficed for such a background. Aristotle, in sketching the growth of Tragedy, says that Aeschylus added the second actor, and made the dialogue predominate over the choral part, while Sophocles introduced the third actor and the use of scene-painting (σκηνογραφία). Now, this last fact must have stood out clearly in Athenian tradition, which Aristotle had every means of knowing, when he thus coupled it with the other novelty as an invention distinctive of Sophocles. It is usually assumed, even by recent writers, that Aristotle is here irreconcilable with Vitruvius, who ascribes the introduction of scene-painting to Aeschylus. Such an assumption is not, we think, necessary. The words of Vitruvius (vii. *praef.* 11) are: "primum Agatharchus Athenis, *Aeschylo docente tragoediam*, scaenam fecit et de ea commentarium reliquit"; and he then goes on to say how the stimulus given by Agatharchus led Democritus and Anaxagoras to develop principles of perspective. The phrase "while Aeschylus was exhibiting tragedy" merely describes Aeschylus as contemporary with the innovation. Sophocles first exhibited in B.C. 468, twelve years before the death of Aeschylus. Aristotle and Vitruvius are reconciled if we suppose that Sophocles introduced σκηνογραφία in the early days of his career; a fact which will also help us to understand why that improvement was peculiarly associated with his name. Even before Agatharchus had made a beginning of artistic σκηνογραφία, some ruder kind of drawing may have been used. Thus in the *Persae* of Aeschylus (B.C. 472) the palace was probably indicated. In the *Ion* of Euripides (cir. B.C. 421), where the scene is laid at Delphi, the Chorus of Athenian maidens point with admiration to the sculptures which adorn the front of the temple.

Remains of Greek Theatre at Tauromenium. (From a photograph.)

With regard to "massive" decoration, as distinguished from a painted background, the objects required by the texts are simple, such as altars, statues of gods or heroes, rocks, and seats. But the texts further prove that certain mechanical appliances were available at need. (1) The ἐκκύκλημα was a small movable stage on wheels, which could be rolled forward through the door in the proscenium. There was room on it for three or four persons, and it was low enough to allow of an actor stepping off it with ease. The most frequent use of the ἐκκύκλημα was when the corpse of a person slain within the house was to be shown to the audience—sometimes with the murderer standing beside it. The moment at which the ἐκκύκλημα was pushed forward is often, though not always, marked in the text by a reference to the opening of the door. But this was not the only case in which the appliance was used: it could also be employed for any tableau in the interior of a house. Thus in Aesch.

Eumen. the Pythia speaks the prologue in front of the temple, and then the ἐκκύκλημα is used to show Orestes at the omphalos within. Similarly in Soph. *Aiax*, when Tecmessa opens the tent, this machine serves to display Aiax prostrate amidst the slaughtered cattle. As appears from some passages, the ἐκκύκλημα could be pushed far enough forward to admit of an actor entering, or making his exit, at the door behind it. It should be noted that the use of the ἐκκύκλημα is not merely an inference from later writers and from hints in Tragedy, but is proved by the two parodies in Aristophanes, where Euripides and Agathon are wheeled out, and are thence once more withdrawn from view (*Ach.* 408 foll., ἐκκυκλήθητ' . . . ἐκκυκλήσομαι: *Thesm.* 265, ἐσκυκλησάτω). The exact nature of the ἐξώστρα is uncertain, but it was evidently akin to the ἐκκύκλημα, differing from it, possibly, only in the mode of propulsion. (2) Machinery for showing persons in the air was required by the appearances of the gods, and in some other cases — as when Medea is seen above the palace in the chariot given to her by the Sun (Eur. *Med.* 1319), or when Trygaeus soars aloft on his beetle (Aristoph. *Pax*, 80). Two different contrivances seem to have been used: both were, of course, concealed by the proscenium. One was an apparatus worked by a wheel (τροχός) and ropes (αἰῶραι), and called αἰώρημα, which was used when the person was to be seen gradually rising into the air, or descending from above. The other device was a sort of platform, projecting from the wings at the back of the proscenium, close to its upper edge. This was the so-called θεολογεῖον, used when the apparition of a god or hero was to be sudden. The κρεμάθρα in which Socrates is suspended (Aristoph. *Nub.* 218) is a burlesque of the tragic appliances. (3) Akin to the θεολογεῖον must have been the contrivance used when a person is to appear on the roof of a palace (as the watcher in Aesch. *Ag.*; Antigoné and the paedagogus in Eur. *Phoen.* etc.). A wooden platform, high up behind the proscenium, would have sufficed: according to Pollux, it was called a διστεγία.

These seem to be the only forms of decoration or mechanism which can certainly be inferred from the texts of the tragedians and of Aristophanes. They are all compatible with a temporary wooden structure and with a comparatively simple phase of scenic art. When, in the course of the fourth century B.C., permanent stone theatres became usual in Greek lands, the general character of scenic decoration was perhaps not at first affected thereby. Behind the proscenium there was now a permanent wall, forming the front of the building assigned to the actors. But the proscenium itself probably continued, for a time, to be temporary—a wooden structure, with painted hangings.

It may have been at this period that περίακτοι were first introduced. These were triangular wooden prisms, revolving on a pivot (whence the name), with scenery painted on each of their three faces. One περίακτος was placed at the left wing and another at the right. They took the place of modern side-scenes, and also served to indicate changes of scene, according to a regular conventional method. The περίακτος on the spectator's right hand represented the locality in which the action was taking place. The περίακτος on his left hand represented a region outside of that locality. If, for instance, the scene of the play was laid at Delphi, the right-hand περίακτος would illustrate that place, while the other might represent the road leading to Athens. The same rule governed entrances and exits: a Delphian would come on from the right, a stranger from the left. If the scene was to be changed from one spot near Delphi to another in the same vicinity, the left-hand περίακτος would be turned so as to present a new face, but the right-hand one would be left unaltered. If the scene was shifted from Delphi to Athens, both περίακτοι would be turned.

There are only two Greek plays in which it is necessary to assume a change of scene. In the *Eumenides* the action is transferred from Delphi to Athens; in the *Aiax*, from the front of the hero's tent to a lonely place on the sea-shore. It is probable that in the first of these examples the change was merely symbolized by substituting the βρέτας of Athené for a statue of Apollo, while the building painted on the background was identified, first with the Delphian temple, and then with the Erechtheum. In the second example, if the background was a landscape, nothing was required but to remove the hangings which represented the tent. The use of περίακτοι in the fifth century B.C. cannot be proved from the dramatic literature. On the other hand, they would have been found peculiarly convenient when the old wooden proscenia, with painted hangings, were replaced by stone proscenia adorned with sculpture. There is no evidence that, in addition to revolving scenery, the Greek theatre had scenes which could be shifted on grooves; though the Roman stage, as Servius tells us, had both (*ad* Verg. *Georg.* iii. 24).

Entrances for the Actors. — Pollux speaks of three doors in the proscenium, the central one being called θύρα βασίλειος, because the chief persons of the play used it. Vitruvius confirms this statement. Ruins of the Hellenistic or Roman Age show sometimes three doors, sometimes five. In the latter case, the two extreme doors may have opened, not on the stage, but on spaces at either side of it (παρασκήνια), used by actors waiting for their turns, or by officials. In the theatre at Megalopolis (fourth century B.C.) there were three entrances to the stage. Only one entrance is traceable in the remains at Epidaurus, Zea, and Oropus respectively. It is on a level with the orchestra; hence those who disbelieve in a raised stage regard it as the entrance for the actors. But it may have passed beneath a raised stage, serving to give the employés of the theatre a direct access to the orchestra. How many doors there may have been in the painted hangings of the old wooden proscenia, we cannot tell. The fifth-century texts show that, besides the door or doors in the proscenium, there were also entrances for the actors from the sides, right and left.

Pollux says that when ghosts appeared on the scene they came up either by ἀναπιέσματα (our "trap-doors") or by the χαρώνιοι κλίμακες. It has generally been supposed that these κλίμακες led from the orchestra to the stage. This is the case at Megalopolis. Another theory is that they connected the stage with a passage beneath it, invisible to the spectators.

No curtain was used in the Greek theatre. When a play opened with a group in position (such as the suppliants in the *Oed. Tyr.*), the actors must have simply walked on to the scene and assumed that position. When one play followed another and the background had to be changed, that change took place before the eyes of the spectators. In such matters we cannot judge the feelings of Athenians assembled at the Dionysia by the requirements of modern playgoers.

THE ADMINISTRATION OF THE THEATRE.—A Greek theatre was the property of the State, and the performances in it were acts of public worship under State control. At Athens, in the fifth and and fourth centuries B.C., drama accompanied two Dionysiac festivals—the Lenaea, in January, and the Great Dionysia, in March. At each festival both Tragedy and Comedy were produced; but the Lenaea were peculiarly associated with Comedy, and the Great Dionysia with Tragedy. The cost of the performances at each festival was defrayed from three sources: (1) The theatre was let by the State to a lessee, who received the money paid for admission, and in return undertook certain charges. One of these, as appears from an extant document (*C. I. A.* ii. 573), was the maintenance of the building in good repair. Hence the classical name for the lessee, ἀρχιτέκτων. He was also bound to provide a certain number of free seats (as for the persons entitled to προεδρία); but for these he was probably reimbursed by the treasury. The provision of scenery and of costume for the actors (excepting the *choreutae*) appears also to have devolved upon the lessee. He was certainly charged with the custody of the scenery and of all the theatrical dresses and properties. He also paid the cashiers, the persons who showed spectators to their places, and all other employés of the theatre. (2) The second source of contribution was the *choregia*. For each festival the Archon Eponymus appointed as many *choregi* as there were competing poets; at the Great Dionysia the number was usually three for Tragedy and three for Comedy. The *choregi* were chosen from men nominated by the ten Attic tribes in rotation. The duty of the *choregus* was to furnish one Chorus of fifteen persons for Tragedy, or of twenty-four for Comedy. He provided a suitable place for their training (χορηγεῖον), and maintained them till the festival was over. If the poet did not train them himself, the *choregus* had to find a χοροδιδάσκαλος. He had also to supply the flute-player (αὐλητής) who preceded the Chorus on entering or quitting the orchestra and played the occasional music. He purchased the costumes, masks, etc., for the Chorus. But his task was not finished when the Chorus was trained and equipped. He had also to supply any mute persons (κωφὰ πρόσωπα) that might be required for the piece. (3) The third contributor was the State. When a poet had applied to the archon for a Chorus and his application had been granted, the archon next assigned to him three actors, who were paid by the State. It did not rest with the poet to decide which of these three should be πρωταγωνιστής, etc.: he received them from the State already classified according to merit, as actors of first, second, and third parts. This classification rested ultimately on special ἀγῶνες in which actors were directly tried against each other, and which were distinct from the performances at the festivals. If a poet ever required a fourth actor (probably a very rare case), he could only go to the *choregus*, who might make an "extra grant" (παραχορήγημα). The State also paid the marshals (ῥαβδοῦχοι) who kept order in the theatre, and who were stationed in the orchestra. Lastly, a certain *honorarium*, distinct from the festival-prizes, was paid by the Treasury to each of the competing poets, according to the order in which they were placed by the judges.

The character of the dramatic contests as solemnities conducted by the State was strongly marked in the forms of procedure. A few days before the Great Dionysia, the ceremony called the προάγων ("prelude") was held in the old Odeion near the Enneacrunos. The competing poets, with their respective *choregi*, were then formally presented to the public; the actors and choruses were also present, in festal, but not in scenic, attire; and the titles of the plays to be produced at the approaching festival were officially announced. When the first day of the Great Dionysia arrived, the dramatic contests were preceded by the transaction of some public business in the theatre. It was then that crowns of honour were awarded for public services, and that the orphans of Athenians slain in war were presented to the citizens. In due course a public herald summoned the first on the list of competing poets. He entered the orchestra, attended by the *choregus* and Chorus, and poured a libation at the *thymelé* to Dionysus. His procession then withdrew; the orchestra was once more empty, and the play began. One prize for Tragedy and one for Comedy were awarded by ten judges, taken by lot from a large number of persons whom the Senate (with the *choregi*) had chosen from the tribes. At the close of the contests, five judges (taken from the ten by a second ballot) announced the awards. The successful poets were then crowned, before the audience, by the archon. Shortly after the festival, a public meeting, for business connected with it, was held in the theatre.

THE AUDIENCE.—According to a recent estimate, the Dionysiac Theatre was once capable of seating about 27,500 persons. It must be remembered that all the upper tiers have been destroyed, and that the ancient capacity was enormously greater than it would appear from the seats which still exist. Plato was using round numbers when he spoke of "more than 30,000 Greeks" as present in the Dionysiac Theatre at the tragic contests (*Symp.* 175 E), but it is quite conceivable that the number was sometimes nearer to 30,000 than to 20,000. The vast theatre at Megalopolis could hold, according to one modern computation, no fewer than 44,000 persons. Such numbers become intelligible when we consider that the Greek drama was essentially a popular festival, in which the entire civic body was invited to take part. Even young boys were present both at Comedy and at Tragedy. Women were certainly present at Tragedy; and a fragment of Alexis shows that, in the fourth century B.C., they were admitted to the performances of Comedy also. This, however, was the Middle Comedy—very different, in some respects, from the Old Comedy of Aristophanes. It would be a natural inference from the seclusion in which Athenian women lived that they were not admitted to the Old Comedy. But against this *a priori* argument may be set another—viz., that, at the Dionysia, Tragedy and Comedy were merely different sides of one ἀγών: those who could participate in one were entitled to share in the other. A line drawn on grounds of decorum would dissever elements which, in the Dionysiac idea, were inseparable. There is no conclusive literary evidence. At Ath-

Theatre at Segesta. (Restoration.)

ens the μέτοικοι were admitted to the theatre. Foreigners were also admitted, whether officials or private persons.

In the earliest days of Athenian drama, admission was doubtless free of charge; payment may have been introduced after the expulsion of the Pisistratidae, when the city began to find the cost too heavy. In the fifth and fourth centuries B.C. the price of admission for one day was two obols, or not quite $0.08. Pericles introduced the system by which the State paid two obols to each citizen for each day of the Dionysiac festivals, in order that he might attend the theatre. This θεωρικόν was partly defrayed from the tribute of the allies, and probably began about B.C. 454. It was distributed by the demarchs in the several demes; and, though it was first devised in the interests of the poor, the only condition of obtaining it seems to have been enrollment on the register of the deme. The number of persons receiving the θεωρικόν in B.C. 431 has been computed at 18,000. All seats were of the same class, except those reserved for persons who had the right of προεδρία, and who paid nothing. (Cf. Dem. *De Cor.* § 28.) The places of payment were probably in the πάροδοι leading to the orchestra. Specimens of ordinary Greek theatre-tickets are extant. These are small leaden coins, bearing on one side some emblem of the theatre, such as a Dionysus with a tripod, or an actor's mask; and on the obverse, the name of an Attic tribe, or a numeral. Many examples have been published by Benndorf (*Zeitschr. f. d. österr. Gymn.* xxvi.). Another kind of theatre-ticket also occurs. This is a small round mark of bone or ivory, bearing on one side some artistic device (such as the head of a deity), and on the other a number (never higher than 15), in both Greek and Roman figures. These were tickets, of the Imperial Age, for persons who had προεδρία. The numbers probably indicate divisions of the house. How far such division was carried is uncertain. The members of the Senate sat together in a definite part of the Dionysiac Theatre (τὸ βουλευτικόν). For youths between the ages of eighteen and twenty-one, a space was similarly reserved (τὸ ἐφηβικόν).

The performances began in the morning, and lasted till evening; but it is attested by the comic poet Pherecrates—who gained his first prize in B.C. 438—that the spectators had usually taken the morning meal (ἄριστον) before they came (Athen. x. 464 e). In the next century, however, we hear of performances beginning at daybreak (Aesch. *in Ctes.* § 76). The older Athenian custom was for all the spectators to wear wreaths (as at a sacrifice); but this had perhaps gone out before B.C. 350. As the whole day was spent in the theatre, the visitors brought light refreshments (τραγήματα) with them. *Choregi* sometimes courted popularity by a distribution of cakes and wine: and Aristophanes has pilloried those rival poets who employed slaves to throw nuts about the house. An Athenian audience was closely attentive—detecting the slightest fault of speech—and highly demonstrative. Loud clapping of hands and shouts of applause expressed their delight; disapproval found vent in stamping with the feet, hissing, and hooting (κλώζειν). Never, probably, has the ordeal for an actor been more se-

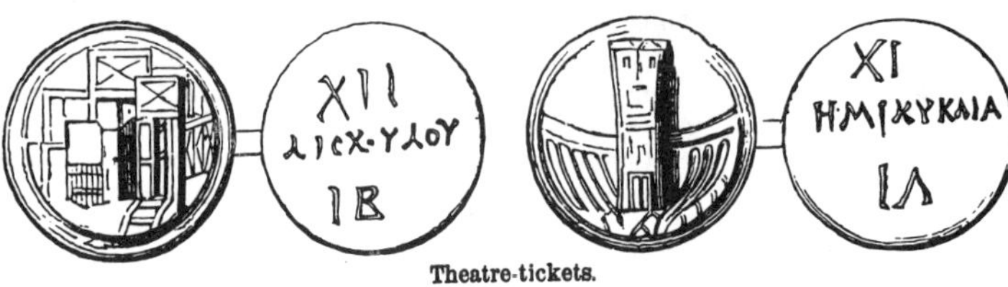

Theatre-tickets.

vere than it was at Athens. Persons of note who entered the house were recognized with frank favour, or the reverse. Indeed, the whole demeanour of Athenians at the Dionysia appears to have been marked by a certain sense of domestic ease, as if all the holiday-makers were members of one family.

From the latter part of the fourth century B.C. onwards, it became usual to produce drama, not merely at the Dionysia, but on any occasion of special rejoicing; a result partly due to the personal taste of Alexander the Great for theatrical shows of every kind. Hence the theatres gradually lost that sacred character which had been theirs so long as they were set apart for the worship of Dionysus. A further consequence was that they began to be used for various entertainments which had nothing to do with drama, such as the exhibitions of conjurers or acrobats, and, in the Roman age, gladiatorial shows, or combats with wild beasts. Even in the fifth century B.C., indeed, cock-fighting had been held on one day of the year in the Dionysiac Theatre.

Mention has been made of the meetings for public business held in the Dionysiac Theatre just before and after the Great Dionysia. In the latter part of the fifth century we hear of the citizens convening the ecclesia in the theatre at Munychia, and in the Dionysiac Theatre itself, when the Pnyx was not available (Thuc. viii. 93 foll.). By B.C. 250 it had become usual to hold ordinary meetings of the ecclesia in the Dionysiac Theatre; though the elections of magistrates (ἀρχαιρεσίαι) continued to be held on the Pnyx. From the fifth century B.C. the theatre had been the regular place for the bestowal of public honours, such as crowns. In later times a theatre was often also the scene of an exemplary punishment (Plut. *Timol.* 34). As statues of Themistocles and Miltiades stood in the Dionysiac Theatre, so, at every period of Greek antiquity, such places were adorned with monuments of statesmen and soldiers, no less than of poets, musicians, and actors. This was in accord with the true idea of the Greek theatre, which was not merely the home of an art, but also a centre of civic reunion.

Remains of Greek Theatre at Syracuse.

Rome possessed no theatre of stone till B.C. 55. Just a century earlier such an edifice had been in progress, when P. Cornelius Scipio Nasica procured a decree of the Senate for its destruction (Livy, *Epit.* 48). The spirit of the Roman veto on permanent theatres was one which refused to regard the drama except as a passing frivolity. Wooden theatres were erected, and pulled down when the occasion was over. But before the middle of the first century B.C. these temporary structures had already begun to show a high elaboration. The building put up by the aedile M. Aemilius Scaurus in B.C. 58 contained 80,000 seats; the proscenium was adorned with pillars of marble and statues of bronze; and the whole work seems to have possessed every element of grandeur except permanence. The old interdict had already lost its meaning; and three years later Pompeius was allowed to erect, near the Campus Martius, the first theatre of stone. The model is said to have been the theatre of Mitylené, and the number of seats 40,000. The theatre of Marcellus, built by Augustus, and named after his nephew, was also of stone, and could hold 20,500 persons. A third such building, with a capacity of 11,510, was completed in B.C. 13 by L. Cornelius Balbus. These are the *trina theatra* of Suetonius (*Aug.* 45). Meanwhile many provincial towns in Italy and elsewhere had long possessed stone theatres, built or altered under Roman influence.

The Roman type of theatre is simply the Greek type modified in certain particulars. The ground-

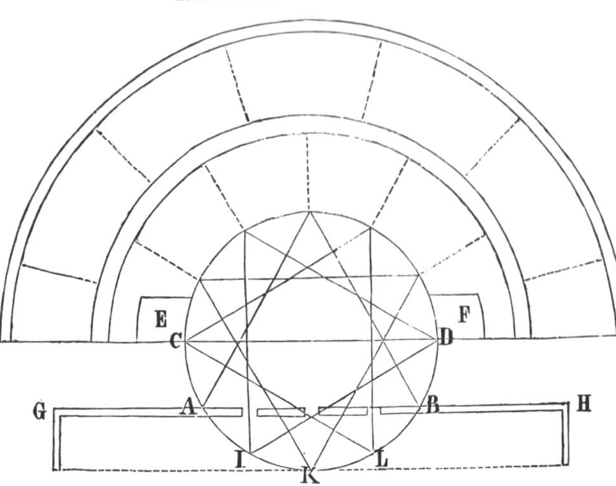

Roman Theatre, after Vitruvius.

plan is thus described by Vitruvius: In a circle of the same diameter which the orchestra is to have, inscribe three equilateral triangles. Take one side of any triangle, and let this be the back wall of the stage, *scaenae frons* (A B). A diameter of the circle, drawn parallel with A B, will represent the line dividing the stage from the orchestra (C D). The seats for the spectators are arranged round the orchestra in semicircles concentric with it. The five points above the line C D, where the angles touch the circumference, are the points from which five flights of steps lead up to the seats, dividing them into six *cunei*. Above the first zone, or semicircular passage (*praecinctio*), the seats are divided into twelve *cunei* by eleven stairways. Just above the points C and D, access is given to the orchestra by two vaulted passages which pass under the upper rows of seats (E, F). The platform of the stage is prolonged right and left, so that its total length (G H) is equal to twice the diameter of the orchestra. In the back wall of the stage there are to be three doors, the positions of which are marked by the points I, K, L. Thus the distinctive features of the Roman theatre are these two: (1) The orchestra is not, as in the Greek theatre, a circle (or the greater part of it), but only a semicircle. The diameter of the orchestra is now the front line of a raised stage. Consequently the auditorium, also, forms only a half-circle. The primary cause of this change was that the old Dionysiac Chorus had disappeared; the orchestra, therefore, had no longer a dramatic use. (2) In the Greek theatre the auditorium and the scene-buildings were not architecturally linked. The πάροδοι were open passages between them. In the Roman theatre the side-walls of the scene-building were carried forward till they met the side-walls of the auditorium. By this organic union of the two main parts the whole theatre was made a single compact building.

These two main differences explain the other points in which the Roman theatre varied from its Greek original. Thus: (*a*) Having closed the openings afforded by the πάροδοι, the Romans needed some other access to their semicircular orchestra. Here the arch served them. By cutting off a few seats in the lower rows at the angles right and left of the stage, they obtained height enough for vaulted passages, which ran under the auditorium into the orchestra. (*b*) The solid unity of the Roman theatres lent itself to the Roman taste for decoration of a monumental character. The permanent Greek proscenia, though usually adorned with columns, had been simple. But the richest embellishments of architecture and sculpture were lavished on the Roman proscenia, in which two or more stories were usually distinguished by carefully harmonized modes of treatment. (*c*) A similar magnificence was shown in the external façades. Greek theatres had usually been erected

Small Theatre at Pompeii. (Overbeck.)

on natural slopes. A Roman theatre was more often built on level ground. The auditorium rested on massive substructions, of which the walls were connected by arches. From the open spaces thus afforded, numerous wide staircases ascended, beneath the auditorium, to the several rows of seats. Corridors, opening on these staircases, ran along the inner side of the semicircular wall which enclosed the auditorium. The exterior of this wall was adorned with columns, having arcades between them, and rising in three or more successive stories, divided by architrave and cornice. Thus while the architectural significance of a Greek theatre depended wholly on the interior, a Roman theatre had also the external aspect of a stately public building.

With regard to the internal arrangements of the Roman theatre, the following points claim notice. (1) The raised stage (*pulpitum*, λογεῖον) is in some instances on a level with the lowest row of seats behind the orchestra. Sometimes, again, the stage is rather higher, but the (originally) lowest row of seats has been abolished, leaving the stage still level with those seats which are actually lowest. In a third class of examples, the stage is higher than the lowest row of seats—as it is at Orange in France. The Roman stage in the Dionysiac Theatre at Athens is of this class. (2) Awnings were spread over the theatre to protect the spectators from sun or rain. These were usually called *vela:* the term *velaria* occurs only in Juv. iv. 122. Pliny, who describes them as *carbasina vela* (of linen), says that they were introduced by Q. Catulus, in B.C. 78 (xix. 23). They were supported by masts (*mali*), fixed to the outer walls of the theatre by massive rings or sockets, which can still be seen at Orange and Pompeii. Between the masts were cross-beams (*trabes*), for greater convenience in unfurling the *vela*. Such awnings were of various colours, as yellow, red, dark-blue (Lucr. iv. 75 foll.). (3) Until the play began, the stage was concealed by a curtain, which was then lowered. The place into which it sank, just inside of the front line of the stage, can be seen in the larger theatre at Pompeii. At the end of the piece the curtain was drawn up. Hence, where we say "the curtain rises," the Romans said *aulaeum mittitur* or *subducitur;* "the curtain is up," *aulaeum premitur;* "the curtain falls," *aulaeum tollitur*. The word *siparium* (from the base of σίφαρος, topsail, *supparum*) meant a folding screen. Apuleius (A.D. 150) describes a kind of ballet as beginning "when the curtain had been lowered, and the screens folded up" (*sipariis complicitis* [*Met.* 10, p. 232]). If these screens were within the curtain, the reason for using them along with it may have been to heighten the effect of a tableau by disclosing it gradually. In the later parts of the piece, they may have served to conceal scene-shifting. Another use is also possible. Theatres of the Macedonian and Roman period sometimes had two stages, the higher being used by the regular actors, the lower by mimes or dancers; and the latter may have been concealed by the *siparium*, as the other by the *aulaeum*. The word *siparium* is regularly associated with comedy or mimes (Seneca, *De Tranq. An.* 11, § 8; Juv. viii. 186). (4) Assignment of seats. The orchestra was reserved for senators. As a special mark of distinction, foreigners (usually ambassadors) were occasionally admitted to it (see Tac. *Ann.* xiii. 54). The rest of the auditorium was called *cavea*. The Lex Roscia, proposed by the tribune L. Roscius Otho in B.C. 67, provided that the fourteen rows of seats in the *cavea* nearest to the orchestra should be reserved for the *equites*—excluding any who should have become bankrupt

Restoration of the Scena Stabilis at Herculaneum. (Overbeck.)

(Cic. *Phil.* ii. § 44). Owing to the large number of *equites* who had been ruined by the Civil Wars, Augustus decreed that the privilege given by the Lex Roscia should be enjoyed by any *eques* who had at any time possessed, or whose father had possessed, the amount of the *equester census*—viz., 400,000 sesterces (Suet. *Aug.* 40). This is probably the Lex Iulia Theatralis meant by Pliny (*H. N.* xxxiii. § 8). Augustus further assigned special portions of the *cavea* to (*a*) women; (*b*) *praetextati*—i. e. boys who had not yet assumed the toga virilis, and their paedagogi; (*c*) soldiers; (*d*) married men belonging to the plebs. This was a premium on marriage, like others provided in the Lex Iulia et Papia Poppaea. In some provincial theatres the town-councillors (*decuriones*) had seats of honour (*bisellia*) on the rows next the orchestra. Corresponding to the "royal box" in a European theatre was the *tribunal*, immediately over the stage on the spectator's left. This was occupied by the emperor, or by the president of the performance. A corresponding *tribunal* on the left side was assigned to the Vestals, among whom the empress sat. Thus, from the Augustan Age onwards, the contrast between a Greek and a Roman theatre was extended to the arrangements for the audience. Instead of the simple Greek distinction between those who had or had not προεδρία, the Roman auditorium exhibited an elaborate classification by sex, age, profession, and rank.

The Odeum.—The term ᾠδεῖον, denoting a species of theatre appropriated to musical performances, occurs first in a fragment of the comic poet Cratinus (cir. B.C. 450), with reference to the Odeum of Pericles, but it may have been in use from a much earlier time. The oldest recorded example is the Σκιάς at Sparta, which is said to have been round, and to have been named from the resemblance of its top to a sunshade (σκιάς or σκιάδειον: *Elym. Magn.*). Athens possessed three ᾠδεῖα: (1) that near the fountain Enneacrunus by the Ilissus, conjecturally referred to Pisistratus or Solon; (2) the Odeum of Pericles, a little to the northeast of the Dionysiac Theatre; (3) the Odeum built by Herodes Atticus in memory of his wife, on the south slope of the Acropolis. This was built later than A.D. 161. Considerable remains of it still exist. The Odeum may best be regarded as the supplement to the Greek theatre.

Bibliography.—Wieseler, *Theatergebäude* (Göttingen, 1881); Oemichen, *Griechischer Theaterbau* (Berlin, 1886); Höpken, *De Theatro Attico*, etc. (Berlin, 1884); Donaldson, *The Greek Theatre* (largely antiquated), 7th ed. (London, 1875); Haigh, *The Attic Theatre* (Cambridge, 1889); Müller, *Lehrbuch der griechischen Bühnenalterthümer* (Freiburg, 1886); Capps, *Vitruvius and the Gk. Stage* (Chicago, 1893); Marquardt, *Röm. Staatsalterthümer*, vol. iii. (2d ed. 1885); and papers by Wilamowitz-Möllendorf in *Hermes*, xxi. pp. 579 foll.; and by Kawerau and Arnold in Baumeister's *Denkmäler*, s. v. "Theatergebäude" and "Theatervorstellungen"; also Chorus; Comoedia; Drama; Tragoedia.

Thebae (Θῆβαι), in the poets sometimes **Thebé** (Θήβη; Dor. Θῆβα), later **Diospŏlis Magna** (Διόσπολις Μεγάλη, i. e. "Great City of Zeus"), in Egyptian Tuabu, in Scripture No or No Ammon. The capital of Thebaïs, or Upper Egypt, and, for a long time, of the whole country. It was reputed the oldest city of the world. It stood in about the centre of the Thebaïd, on both banks of the Nile, above Coptos, and in the Nomos Coptites. It is said to have been founded under the first dynasty by Menes; but this is unsupported by any evidence. Others ascribed its foundation to Osiris, who named it after his mother, and others to Busiris. It appears to have been at the height of its splendour, as the capital of Egypt, and as a chief seat of worship of Ammon, about B.C. 1330 under the Nineteenth Dynasty. The fame of its grandeur had reached the Greeks as early as the time of Homer, who describes it, with poetical exaggeration, as having a hundred gates, from each of which it could send out 200 war chariots fully armed (*Il.* ix. 381). Homer's epithet of "Hundred-Gated" (ἑκατόμπυλοι) is repeatedly applied to the city by later writers. Its real extent was calculated by the Greek writers at 140 stadia (fourteen geographical miles) in circuit; and in Strabo's time, when the long transference of the seat of power to Lower Egypt had caused it to decline greatly, it still had a circuit of eighty stadia (Diod. i. 50; xv. 45; Strabo, pp. 805, 815). That these computations are not exaggerated is proved by the existing ruins, which extend from side to side of the valley of the Nile, here about six miles wide; while the rocks which bound the valley are perforated with tombs. These ruins, which are perhaps the most magnificent in the world, enclose within their site the four modern villages of Karnak, Luxor (El Uksur), Medînet Habou, and Kurna—the two former on the eastern and the two latter on the western side of the river. They consist of temples, colossi, sphinxes, and obelisks, and, on the western side, of tombs, many of which are cut in the rock and adorned with paintings, which are still as fresh as if just finished. These ruins are remarkable alike for their great antiquity and for the purity of their style. It is most probable that the great buildings were all erected before the Persian invasion, when Thebes was taken by Cambyses, who secured treasure to the amount of some $10,000,000, and burned the wooden habitations, after which time it never regained the rank of a capital city; and thus its architectural monuments escaped that Greek influence which is so marked in the edifices of Lower Egypt. Among its chief buildings, the ancient writers mention the Memnonium, with the two colossi in front of it, the temple of Ammon, in which one of the three chief colleges of priests was established, and the tombs of the kings. See Memnon.

To describe the ruins in detail, and to discuss their identification, would far exceed the possible limits of this article. Suffice it to mention among the monuments on the western (Libyan) side the three temples of Seti I., Rameses II., and Rameses III. Near the second is the fallen colossus of Rameses II., the largest statue in Egypt. (See Rameses.) Beyond is the terraced temple of Queen Hatasu of the Eighteenth Dynasty, near which a remarkable series of mummies and papyri were found by Brugsch in 1881. At Medinet Habou is a great temple of Rameses III., with interesting sculptures describing his victories over the Philistines, and also a calendar. Northwest of this are the cemeteries of the sacred apes and the Valley of the Tombs of the Queens (seventeen sepulchres). On the eastern bank at Luxor is the beautiful temple of Amenoph III., with an obelisk whose fellow now stands in the Place de la Concorde at Paris. At Karnak is a splendid group of temples built under the Twelfth Dynasty. The finest portion of this maze of architectural magnificence is the Great Hall, 170 by 329 feet, with twelve imposing columns 62 feet in height and 12 feet in diameter,

Terraced Temple of Queen Hatasu. (Restoration by Brune.)

and 122 minor columns, and two obelisks, of which one is the tallest in Egypt, being 108 feet in height. On the walls are fine sculptures depicting the battles of Seti I. and Rameses II. against the Hittites, Arabs, Syrians, and Armenians. In one of the porticos is recorded the expedition of Shishak I. against Jerusalem in B.C. 971.

In classical times Thebes was a great show-place, and was visited by both Greek and Roman tourists, among the latter being the emperor Hadrian.

Thebae. (1) Θῆβαι, in poetry **Thebé** (Θήβη, Dor. Θήβα). Now Thion; the chief city in Boeotia. It was situated in a plain southeast of Lake Helicé and northeast of Plataeae. Its acropolis, which was an oval eminence of no great height, was called Cadmea (Καδμεία), because it was said to have been founded by Cadmus, the leader of a Phœnician colony. On each side of this acropolis is a small valley, running up from the Theban plain into the low ridge of hills by which it is separated from that of Plataeae. Of these valleys, the one to the west is watered by the Dircé, and the one to the east by the Ismenus, both of which, however, are insignificant little streams, though so celebrated in ancient story. The greater part of the city stood in these valleys, and was built some time after the acropolis. It is said that the fortifications of the city were constructed by Amphion and his brother Zethus; and that, when Amphion played his lyre, the stones moved of their own accord and formed the wall. The territory of Thebes was called THEBĀÏS (Θηβαΐς), and extended eastward as far as the Euboean Sea. No city is more celebrated in the mythical ages of Greece than Thebes. It was here that the use of letters was first introduced from Phœnicia into western Europe. It was the reputed birthplace of the two great divinities, Dionysus and Heracles. It was also the native city of the great seer Tiresias, as well as of the great musician Amphion. It was the scene of the tragic fate of Oedipus, and of one of the most celebrated wars in the mythical annals of Greece. Polynices, who had been expelled from Thebes by his brother Eteocles, induced six other heroes to espouse his cause, and marched against the city; but they were all defeated and slain by the Thebans, with the exception of Adrastus, Polynices, and Eteocles falling by each other's hands. This is usually called the war of the Seven against Thebes. A few years afterwards the Epigoni, or descendants of the seven heroes, marched against Thebes to avenge their fathers' death; they took the city and razed it to the ground. Thebes is not mentioned by Homer in the catalogue of the Greek cities which fought against Troy, as it was probably supposed not yet to have recovered from its devastation by the Epigoni. (See SEVEN AGAINST THEBES.) It appears, however, at the earliest historical period as a large and flourishing city; and it is represented as possessing seven gates (ἑπτάπυλος), the number assigned to it in the ancient legends. Its government, after the abolition of monarchy, was an aristocracy, or rather an oligarchy, which continued to be the prevailing form of government for a long time, although occasionally exchanged for that of a democracy. Towards the end of the Peloponnesian War, however, the oligarchy finally disappears; and Thebes appears under a democratical form of government from this time, till it became with the rest of Greece subject to the Romans.

The Thebans were from an early period inveterate enemies of their neighbours, the Athenians. Their hatred of the latter people was probably one

Coin of the Boeotian Thebes.

of the reasons which induced them to desert the cause of Grecian liberty in the great struggle against the Persian power. In the Peloponnesian War the Thebans naturally espoused the Spartan side, and contributed not a little to the downfall of Athens. But, in common with the other Greek States, they soon became disgusted with the Spartan supremacy, and joined the confederacy formed against Sparta in B.C. 394. The peace of Antalcidas in 387 put an end to hostilities in Greece; but the treacherous seizure of the Cadmea by the Lacedaemonian general Phoebidas in 382, and its recovery by the Theban exiles in 379, led to a war between Thebes and Sparta, in which the former not only recovered its independence, but forever destroyed the Lacedaemonian supremacy. This was the most glorious period in the Theban annals; and the decisive defeat of the Spartans at the battle of Leuctra in 371 made Thebes the first power in Greece. Her greatness, however, was mainly due to the preëminent abilities of her citizens, Epaminondas and Pelopidas; and with the death of the former at the battle of Mantinea in 362, she lost the supremacy which she had so recently gained. Soon afterwards Philip of Macedon began to exercise a paramount influence over the greater part of Greece. The Thebans were induced, by the eloquence of Demosthenes, to forget their old animosities against the Athenians, and to join the latter in protecting the liberties of Greece; but their united forces were defeated by Philip, at the battle of Chaeronea, in 338. Soon after the death of Philip and the accession of Alexander, the Thebans made a last attempt to recover their liberty, but were cruelly punished by the young king. The city was taken by Alexander in 336, and was entirely destroyed, with the exception of the temples, and the house of the poet Pindar; 6000 inhabitants were slain, and 30,000 sold as slaves. In 316 the city was rebuilt by Cassander, with the assistance of the Athenians. In 290 it was taken by Demetrius Poliorcetes, and again suffered greatly. Dicaearchus, who flourished about this time, has left us an interesting account of the city. He describes it as about seventy stadia (nearly nine miles) in circumference, in form nearly circular, and in appearance somewhat gloomy. He says that it is plentifully provided with water, and contains better gardens than any other city in Greece; that it is most agreeable in summer, on account of its plentiful supply of cool and fresh water, and its large gardens; but that in winter it is very unpleasant, being destitute of fuel, exposed to floods and cold winds, and frequently visited by heavy falls of snow. He further represents the people as proud and insolent, and always ready to settle disputes by fighting, rather than by the ordinary course of justice. It is supposed that the population of the city at this time may have been between 50,000 and 60,000 souls. See Sankey, *Spartan and Theban Supremacies* (1877).

After the Macedonian period Thebes rapidly declined in importance; and it received its last blow from Sulla, who gave half of its territory to the Delphians. Strabo describes it as only a village in his time; and Pausanias, who visited it in the second century of the Christian era, says that the Cadmea alone was then inhabited. The modern town is also confined to this spot, and the surrounding country is covered with a confused heap of ruins. See E. Fabricius, *Theben* (Heidelberg, 1891); and the articles EPAMINONDAS; PELOPIDAS.

(2) Called PHTHIOTĬCAE (*αἱ Φθιώτιδες*), an important city of Thessaly in the district Phthiotis, at a short distance from the coast, and with a good harbour (Polyb. v. 99). (3) A town in Lucania, rarely mentioned.

Thebāïs. (1) See AEGYPTUS. (2) See THEBAE.

Thebaïs. See STATIUS.

Thebānus, PINDĂRUS. See article in the Appendix.

Thebé (Θήβη Ὑποπλακίη). A city of Mysia, on the wooded slope of Mount Placus, destroyed by Achilles. It was said to have been the birthplace of Andromaché and Chryseïs (*Il.* i. 366; vi. 397).

Thebes, SEVEN AGAINST. See SEVEN AGAINST THEBES.

Thelepté. See THALA.

Thelpūsa (Θέλπουσα) and **Telphussa** (Τέλφουσσα). Now Vanena; a town in Arcadia on the river Ladon. It was a famous seat of the worship of Demeter-Erinnys, Persephoné, and Dionysus (Pausan. viii. 25, 2).

Themis (Θέμις). The daughter of Uranus and Gé. She was married to Zeus, by whom she became the mother of the Horae, Eunomia, Diké (Astraea), Irené, and of the Moerae. In the Homeric poems, Themis is the personification of the order of things established by law, custom, and equity, whence she is described as reigning in the assemblies of men, and as convening, by the command of Zeus, the assembly of the gods. She dwells in Olympus, and is on friendly terms with Hera. She is also described as a prophetic divinity, and is said to have been in possession of the Delphic Oracle as the successor of Gé, and predecessor of Apollo. Nymphs, believed to be daughters of Zeus and Themis, lived in a cave on the river Eridanus, and the Hesperides also are called daughters of Zeus and Themis. On coins she often bears a resemblance to the figure of Athené, and holds a cornucopia and a pair of scales.

Themiscȳra (Θεμίσκυρα). A plain on the coast of Pontus, extending east of the river Iris, beyond the Thermodon, celebrated from very ancient times as the country of the Amazons (Herod. iv. 86).

Themĭson (Θεμίσων). A Greek physician, the founder of the school of the Methodici.

Themistius (Θεμίστιος). A Greek rhetorician of Paphlagonia, who lived in the second half of the fourth century A.D., as teacher of philosophy and oratory at Constantinople. He was much honoured by his contemporaries for his noble disposition and his learning and eloquence, which gained for him the name of EUPHRĂDES, or eloquent speaker. He was honoured with various marks of distinction of the emperors. Constantius made him a senator; Julian described him as the first philosopher of his age; Theodosius selected him as tutor to his son Arcadius, and in 384 nominated him to the prefecture. He died about 388.

Thirty-four of his speeches (πολιτικοὶ λόγοι) have been preserved, one of them in a Latin translation only. They are partly philosophical and political, but principally eulogistic orations, either in compliment to or in memory of various emperors, composed in a clear, pleasant style, and valuable for the information they contain respecting contemporary history. Besides these, we possess four paraphrases by him of parts of Aristotle. The orations are edited by Dindorf (Leipzig, 1832).

Themisto (Θεμιστώ). The third wife of Athamas (q.v.), who married her under the impression that his wife Ino was dead. When he heard, however, that Ino was living as a votary of Dionysus, in the ravines of Parnassus, he secretly sent for her. Themisto, on hearing this, determined, in revenge, to kill Ino's children, and ordered a slave, who had lately come to the house, to dress her children in white and Ino's in black, so that she might be able to distinguish them in the night. But the slave, who was Ino herself, suspecting the evil intention, exchanged the clothes. Themisto, in consequence, killed her own children, and, on becoming aware of her mistake, slew herself also.

Themistŏcles (Θεμιστοκλῆς). A celebrated Athenian, the son of Neocles and Abrotonon, a Thracian woman, and born about B.C. 514. In his youth he had an impetuous character, and displayed great intellectual power combined with a lofty ambition and a desire for political distinction. He began his career by setting himself in opposition to those who had most power, among whom Aristides was the chief. The fame which Miltiades acquired by his generalship at Marathon made a deep impression on Themistocles; and he said that the trophy of Miltiades would not let him sleep. His rival Aristides was ostracized in B.C. 483, to which event Themistocles contributed; and from this time he was the political leader in Athens. In 481 he was Archon Eponymus. It was about this time that he persuaded the Athenians to employ the produce of the silver mines of Laurium in building ships, instead of distributing it among the Athenian citizens. His great object was to draw the Athenians to the sea, as he was convinced that it was only by their fleet that Athens could repel the Persians and obtain the supremacy in Greece. Upon the invasion of Greece by Xerxes, Themistocles was appointed to the command of the Athenian fleet; and to his energy, prudence, foresight, and courage the Greeks mainly owed their salvation from the Persian dominion. Upon the approach of Xerxes, the Athenians, on the advice of Themistocles, deserted their city, and removed their women, children, and infirm persons to Salamis, Aegina, and Troezen; but as soon as the Persians took possession of Athens, the Peloponnesians were anxious to retire to the Corinthian isthmus. Themistocles used all his influence in inducing the Greeks to remain and fight with the Persians at Salamis, and with the greatest difficulty persuaded the Spartan commander Eurybiades to stay at Salamis. But as soon as the fleet of Xerxes made its appearance, the Peloponnesians were again anxious to sail away; and when Themistocles saw that he should be unable to persuade them to remain, he sent a faithful slave to the Persian commanders, informing them that the Greeks intended to make their escape, and that the Persians had now the opportunity of accomplishing a noble enterprise, if they would only cut off the retreat of the Greeks. The Persians believed what they were told, and in the night their fleet occupied the whole of the channel between Salamis and the mainland. The Greeks were thus compelled to fight; and the result was the great and glorious victory, in which the greater part of the fleet of Xerxes was destroyed. This victory, which was due to Themistocles, established his reputation among the Greeks. On his visiting Sparta, he was received with extraordinary honours by the Spartans, who gave Eurybiades the palm of bravery and Themistocles the palm of wisdom and skill (Herod. viii. 124). The Athenians now began to restore their ruined city, and Themistocles urged them to rebuild the walls and make them stronger than before. The Spartans sent an embassy to Athens to dissuade them from fortifying their city, for which it is hard to assign any motive except national jealousy. Themistocles, who was at that time προστάτης τοῦ δήμου (i. e. one of the leaders of the popular party), went on an embassy to Sparta, where he amused the Spartans with lies, till the walls were far enough advanced to be in a state of defence. It was upon his advice also that the Athenians fortified the port of Piraeus. The influence of Themistocles does not appear to have survived the expulsion of the Persians from Greece and the fortification of the ports. He was probably justly accused of enriching himself by unfair means, for he had no scruples about the way of accomplishing an end. A story is told that, after the retreat of the fleet of Xerxes, when the Greek fleet was wintering at Pagasae, Themistocles told the Athenians in the public assembly that he had a scheme to propose which was beneficial to the State, but could not be divulged. Aristides was named to receive the secret, and to report upon it. His report was that nothing could be more profitable than the scheme of Themistocles, but nothing more unjust: the Athenians were guided by the report of Aristides. It is difficult, if not impossible, to reconcile the statement in Arist. *Ath. Pol.* 25, that Themistocles intrigued for the overthow of the Areopagus, with the date of his exile from Athens. The attack upon the Areopagus was in 463; but in 471, in consequence of the political strife between Themistocles and Aristides, the former was ostracized from Athens, and retired to Argos.

Themistocles.

After the discovery of the treasonable correspondence of Pausanias with the Persian king, the Lacedaemonians sent to Athens to accuse Themistocles of being privy to the design of Pausanias. Thereupon the Athenians sent off persons with the Lacedaemonians with instructions to arrest Themistocles (466). Themistocles, hearing of what was designed against him, first fled from Argos to Corcyra, and then to Epirus, where he took refuge in the house of Admetus, king of the Molossi, who happened to be from home. Admetus was no friend to Themistocles, but his wife told the fugitive that he would be protected if he would take their child in his arms and sit on the hearth. The king soon came in, and, respecting his suppliant attitude, raised him up, and refused to surrender him to the Lacedaemonian and Athenian agents. Themistocles finally reached the coast of Asia in safety. Xerxes was now dead (465), and Artaxerxes was on the throne (Thucyd. i. 235; Plut. *Them.* 23; Nep. *Them.* 4). Themistocles went up to visit the king at his royal residence; and on his arrival he sent the king a letter, in which he promised to do the king a good service, and prayed that he might be allowed to wait a year and then to explain personally what brought him there. In a year he made himself master of the Persian language and the Persian usages, and, being presented to the king, he obtained the greatest influence over him, and such as no Greek ever before enjoyed—partly owing to his high reputation and the hopes that he gave to the king of subjecting the Greeks to the Persians. The king gave him a handsome allowance, after the Persian fashion; Magnesia supplied him with bread nominally, but paid him annually fifty talents. Lampsacus supplied wine, and Myus the other provisions. Before he could accomplish anything he died; some say that he poisoned himself, finding that he could not perform his promise to the king. A monument was erected to his memory in the Agora of Magnesia, which place was within his government. It is said that his bones were secretly taken to Attica by his relations, and privately interred there.

Themistocles undoubtedly possessed great talents as a statesman, great political sagacity, a ready wit, and excellent judgment; but he was not an honest man, and, like many other clever men with little morality, he ended his career unhappily and ingloriously. Twenty-one letters attributed to Themistocles are spurious.

See Wolff, *De Vita Themistoclis* (1871); and Wecklein, *Ueber Themistokles*, etc. (1892).

Themistogĕnes (Θεμιστογένης). A native of Syracuse, supposed (on inadequate grounds) to be the author of the *Anabasis*, which has come down to us under the name of Xenophon (q. v.).

Theoclymĕnus (Θεοκλύμενος). Son of the soothsayer Polyphides, grandson of Melampus. When a fugitive from Argos, for a murder which he had committed, he met with Telemachus in Pylus, who succoured him and brought him to Ithaca. By means of his inherited gift of prophecy, he here made known to Penelopè the presence of Odysseus in the island, and warned the suitors of their fate.

Theocrĭtus (Θεόκριτος). The most famous of the Greek bucolic poets was a native of Syracuse, the son of Praxagoras and Philinna. He visited Alexandria towards the end of the reign of Ptolemy Soter, where he received the instruction of Philetas and Asclepiades, and began to distinguish himself as a poet. Other accounts make him a native of Cos, which would bring him more directly into connection with Philetas (Suidas, s. v. Θεόκριτος). His first efforts obtained for him the patronage of Ptolemy Philadelphus, who was associated in the kingdom with his father, Ptolemy Soter, in B.C. 285, and in whose praise, therefore, the poet wrote the fourteenth, fifteenth, and seventeenth Idyls. At Alexandria he became acquainted with the poet Aratus, to whom he addressed his sixth Idyl. Theocritus afterwards returned to Syracuse, and lived there under Hiero II. It appears from the sixteenth Idyl that Theocritus was dissatisfied, both with the want of liberality on the part of Hiero in rewarding him for his poems, and with the political state of his native country. It may therefore be supposed that he devoted the latter part of his life almost entirely to the contemplation of those scenes of nature and of country life on his representations of which his fame chiefly rests.

Theocritus was the creator of bucolic poetry in Greek, and, through imitators, such as Vergil, in Roman literature. (See VERGILIUS.) The bucolic *Idyls* of Theocritus are of a dramatic and mimetic character. They are *pictures* of the ordinary life of the common people of Sicily; whence their name εἴδη, εἰδύλλια. The pastoral poems and romances of later times are a totally different sort of composition from the bucolics of Theocritus, who knows nothing of the affected sentiment which has been ascribed to the imaginary shepherds of a fictitious Arcadia. He merely exhibits simple and faithful pictures of the common life of the Sicilian people, in a thoroughly objective, although truly poetical, spirit. Dramatic simplicity and truth are impressed upon the scenes exhibited in his poems, into the colouring of which he has thrown much of the natural comedy which is always seen in the common life of a free people. In his dramatic dialogue he is influenced by the mimes of Sophron (q. v.), as may be seen especially in the fifteenth Idyl (*Adoniazusae*). The poems of Theocritus of this class may be compared with those of Herondas, who belonged, like Theocritus, to the literary school of Philetas of Cos. In genius, however, Theocritus was greatly the superior. The collection which has come down to us under the name of Theocritus consists of thirty poems, called by the general title of *Idyls*, a fragment of a few lines from a poem entitled *Berenicé*, and twenty-two epigrams in the Greek Anthology. But these Idyls are not all bucolic, and were not all written by Theocritus. Those of which the genuineness is the most doubtful are the twelfth, twenty-third, twenty-sixth, twenty-seventh, and twenty-ninth; and Idyls xiii., xvi., xvii., xxii., xxiv., and xxvi. are in Epic style, and have more of Epic dialect, especially Idyl xvi. It is likely that these poems on Epic subjects were written early in the poet's life, and, as court poems, had some of the artificial and imitative character of the Alexandrians. In general the dialect of Theocritus is Doric, but two of the Idyls (xxviii. and xxix.) are in the Aeolic.

There are numerous manuscripts of Theocritus, especially in the Laurentian Library at Florence, in the Vatican, and at Paris; but none antedate the thirteenth century. Theocritus is edited by Valckenaer (1810); Wüstemann (Gotha, 1830); Meineke (1856); Fritzsche (Leipzig, 1869); Paley (London, 1863); Wordsworth (1877), and Kynaston (1873). There are translations into English verse by Chapman (1866) and Calverley (1869); and into English prose by Lang (1889), the last with an introduction. See Knapp, *Theokrit und die Idyllen-Dichtung* (1882); Bachelin, *Interprétation Littéraire et Philologique de la Première Idylle de Théocrite* (Paris, 1886); and Fritzsche, *Zu Theokrit und Virgil* (1860). There is a lexicon to Theocritus by Rumpel (1879).

Theodectes (Θεοδέκτης). Of Phaselis, in Lycia, a Greek rhetorician and tragic poet. He carried off the prize eight times, and in B.C. 351 his tragedy of *Mausolus* was victorious in the tragic contest instituted by Queen Artemisia in honour of her deceased husband Mausolus. In the rhetorical contest, held at the same time, he was defeated by Theopompus. Only unimportant fragments of his fifty tragedies are extant.

Theodōra (Θεοδώρα). The wife of the emperor Justinian I. Procopius, in his scandalous chronicle of the Byzantine court, describes her as the daughter of one Acacius, a showman, and as having been by turns an actress, a dancer, and a harlot of extraordinary shamelessness. She was at first Justinian's mistress, and in A.D. 527 became his wife, the emperor having secured the repeal of a law which forbade the marriage of a member of the Senate with an actress. From the time of her wedding, however, she lived a life of exemplary purity, and was to her husband a wise and trusty counsellor, and one whose courage saved the throne at the time of the riots that took place in 532. She was especially famous for her charity towards unfortunate women. She died at the age of forty in 548. The disgusting stories contained in the Ἀνέκδοτα of Procopius (q. v.) and repeated by Gibbon and Dahn are discredited by the fact that neither Evagrius nor Zonaras mentions them, and also by the self-confessed mendacity of Procopius himself. See Débedour, *L'Impératrice Théodora* (Paris, 1885); Dahn, *Prokopius* (Berlin, 1865); a paper by Mallet in the *English Historical Review*, vol. ii. (1887); and the article IUSTINIANUS. The story of Theodora is made the basis of a well-known drama by Victorien Sardou (1884).

Theodorīcus or **Theoderīcus**. (1) King of the Visigoths from A.D. 418 to 451. He was the successor of Wallia, but appears to have been the son of the great Alaric. He fell fighting on the side of Aëtius and the Romans at the great battle of Châlons, in which Attila was defeated, 451. (2) A king of the Visigoths A.D. 452–466, second son of Theodoric I. He succeeded to the throne by the murder of his brother Thorismond. He ruled over the greater part of Gaul and Spain. He was assassinated in 466 by his brother Euric, who succeeded him on the throne. Theodoric II. was a patron of letters and learned men. The poet Sidonius Apollinaris resided for some time at his court. (3) Surnamed THE GREAT, king of the Ostrogoths, succeeding his father Theodemir in 475. He was at first an ally of Zeno, the emperor of Constantinople, but was afterwards involved in hostilities with the emperor. In order to get rid of Theodoric, Zeno gave him permission to invade Italy, and expel the usurper Odoacer from the country. Theodoric entered Italy in 489, and, after defeating Odoacer in three great battles, laid siege to Ravenna, in which Odoacer took refuge. After a siege of three years Odoacer capitulated on condition that he and Theodoric should rule jointly over Italy; but Odoacer was soon afterwards murdered by his more fortunate rival (493). Theodoric thus became master of Italy, which he ruled for thirty-three years, till his death in 526. His long reign was prosperous and beneficent, and under his sway Italy recovered from the ravages to which it had been exposed for so many years. Theodoric was also a patron of literature: and among his ministers were Cassiodorus and Boëthius, the two last writers who can claim a place in the literature of ancient Rome. But prosperous as had been the reign of Theodoric, his last days were darkened by disputes with the Catholics, and by the condemnation and execution of Boëthius and Symmachus, whom he accused of a conspiracy to overthrow the Gothic dominion in Italy. His death is said to have been hastened by remorse. It his related that one evening, when a large fish was served on the table, he fancied that he beheld the head of Symmachus, and was so terrified that he took to his bed, and died three days afterwards. Theodoric was buried at Ravenna, and a monument was erected to his memory by his daughter Amalasuntha. His ashes were deposited in a porphyry vase, which is still to be seen at Ravenna. See Hodgkin, *Theodoric the Goth* (1891).

Theodōrus (Θεόδωρος). (1) Of Byzantium, a rhetorician, and a contemporary of Plato. (2) A philosopher of the Cyrenaic School, usually designated by ancient writers "the Atheist." He resided for some time at Athens; and being banished thence, went to Alexandria, where he entered the service of Ptolemy, son of Lagus. (3) An eminent rhetorician of the age of Augustus, was a native of Gadara. He settled at Rhodes, where Tiberius, afterwards emperor, during his retirement (B.C. 6–A.D. 2) to that island, was one of his hearers (Sueton. *Tib.* 57). He also taught at Rome. Theodorus was the founder of a school of rhetoricians called "Theodorei." (4) Of Samos, son of Rhoecus. In conjunction with his father, he erected the labyrinth of Lemnos (Pliny, *H. N.* xxxvi. 90), and advised the laying down of a layer of charcoal as part of the foundation of the Temple of Artemis at Ephesus (Diog. Laërt. ii. 103). He is said to have lived for a long time in Egypt, where he and his brother Telecles learned the Egyptian canon of proportion for the human figure. He was considered by the Greeks as one of the inventors of the art of casting in bronze (Pausan. viii. 14, 8). He wrote a work on the Temple of Heré at Samos, which was begun by his father (Vitruv. vii. pref. 12). (5) Son of Telecles, and nephew of the preceding. He flourished in the time of Croesus and Polycrates, whose ring he made (Herod. i. 51; iii. 41).

Theodosiānus Codex. See CODEX THEODOSIANUS; THEODOSIUS.

Theodosius (Θεοδόσιος). (1) Surnamed THE GREAT, Roman emperor of the East, A.D. 378–395. He was the son of the general Theodosius who restored Britain to the Empire, and was beheaded at Carthage in the reign of Valens (A.D. 376). The future emperor was born in Spain about A.D. 346. He received a good education; and he learned the art of war under his own father, whom he accompanied in his British campaigns. During his father's lifetime he was raised to the rank of Duke (*dux*) of Moesia, where he defeated the Sarmatians (374) and saved the province. On the death of his father he retired before court intrigues to his native country. He acquired a considerable military reputation in the lifetime of his father; and after the death of Valens, who fell in battle against the Goths, he was proclaimed emperor of the East by Gratian, who felt himself unable to sustain the burden of the Empire. The Roman Empire in the East was then in a critical position; for the Romans were disheartened by the bloody defeat which they had sustained, and the Goths were insolent in their victory. Theodosius, however, showed himself equal to the difficult position in which he was placed; he gained two signal victories over the Goths, and concluded a peace with the barbarians in 382.

In the following year (383) Maximus assumed the imperial purple in Britain, and invaded Gaul with a powerful army. In the war which followed Gratian was slain; and Theodosius, who did not consider it prudent to enter into a contest with Maximus, acknowledged the latter emperor of the countries of Spain, Gaul, and Britain, but he secured to Valentinian, the brother of Gratian, Italy, Africa, and western Illyricum. But when Maximus expelled Valentinian from Italy in 387, Theodosius espoused the cause of the latter, and marched into the West at the head of a powerful army. After defeating Maximus in Pannonia, Theodosius pursued him across the Alps to Aquileia. Here Maximus was surrendered by his own soldiers to Theodosius and was put to death. Theodosius spent the winter at Milan, and in the following year (389) he entered Rome in triumph, accompanied by Valentinian and his own son Honorius. Two events in the life of Theodosius about this time may be mentioned as evidence of his uncertain character and his savage temper. In 387 a riot took place at Antioch, in which the statues of the emperor, of his father, and of his wife were thrown down; but these idle demonstrations were quickly suppressed by an armed force. When Theodosius heard of these riots, he degraded Antioch from the rank of a city, stripped it of its possessions and privileges, and reduced it to the condition of a village dependent on Laodicea. But in consequence of the intercession of Antioch and the Senate of Constantinople, he pardoned the city, and all who had taken part in the riot. The other event is an eternal brand of infamy on the name of Theodosius. In 390, while the emperor was at Milan, a serious riot broke out at Thessalonica, in which the imperial officer and several of his troops were murdered. Theodosius resolved to take the most signal vengeance upon the whole city. An army of barbarians was sent to Thessalonica; the people were invited to the games of the Circus; and as soon as the place was full, the soldiers received the signal for massacre. For three hours the spectators were indiscriminately exposed to the fury of the soldiers, and 7000 of them, or, as some accounts say, more than twice that number, paid the penalty of the insurrection. St. Ambrose, Archbishop of Milan, represented to Theodosius his crime in a letter, and told him that penitence alone could efface his guilt. Accordingly, when the emperor proceeded to perform his devotions in the usual manner in the great church of Milan, the archbishop stopped him at the door, and demanded an acknowledgment of his guilt. The conscience-struck Theodosius humbled himself before the church, which has recorded his penance as one of its greatest victories. He laid aside the insignia of imperial power; in the posture of a suppliant in the church of Milan he asked pardon for his great sin before all the congregation; and, after eight months, the emperor was restored to communion with the Church.

Theodosius spent three years in Italy, during which he established Valentinian II. on the throne of the West. He returned to Constantinople towards the latter end of 391. Valentinian was slain in 392 by Arbogastes, who raised Eugenius to the Empire of the West. This involved Theodosius in a new war; but it ended in the defeat and death both of Eugenius and Arbogastes in 394. Theodosius died at Milan, four months after the defeat of Eugenius, on the 17th of January, 395. His two sons, Arcadius and Honorius, had already been elevated to the rank of Augusti, and it was arranged that the Empire should be divided between them, Arcadius having the East, and Honorius the West. Theodosius was a firm Catholic, and a fierce opponent and persecutor of the Arians and all heretics. It was in his reign also that the formal destruction of paganism took place; and we still possess a large number of the laws of Theodosius, prohibiting the exercise of the pagan religion, and forbidding the heathen worship under severe penalties, in some cases extending to death. (2) A Roman emperor of the East, A.D. 408–450. He was born in 401, and was only seven years of age at the death of his father Arcadius, whom he succeeded. Theodosius was a weak ruler; and his sister Pulcheria, who became his guardian in 414, possessed the virtual government of the Empire during the remainder of his long reign. The principal external events in the reign of Theodosius were the war with the Persians, which only lasted a short time (421–422), and was terminated by a peace for a hundred years; and the war with the Huns, who repeatedly defeated the armies of the emperor, and compelled him at length to conclude a disgraceful peace with them in 447 or 448. Theodosius died in 450, and was succeeded by his sister Pulcheria, who prudently took for her colleague in the Empire the senator Marcian, and made him her husband. Theodosius had been married in 421 to the accomplished Athenaïs, the daughter of the sophist Leontius, who received at her baptism the name of Eudocia. Their daughter Eudoxia was married to Valentinian III., the emperor of the West. In the reign of Theodosius, and that of Valentinian III., was made the compilation called the Codex Theodosianus. It was published in A.D. 438. It consists of sixteen books, which are divided into titles, with appropriate rubricae or headings; and the constitutions belonging to each title are arranged under it in chronological order. The first five books comprise the greater part of the constitution which relates to *ius privatum;* the sixth, seventh, and eighth books contain the law that relates to the constitution and administration; the ninth book treats of criminal law; the tenth and eleventh treat of the public revenue and some matters relating to procedure; the twelfth, thirteenth, fourteenth, and fifteenth books treat of the constitution and the administration of towns and other corporations; and the sixteenth contains the law relating to ecclesiastical matters.

LITERARY.—(1) Of Bithynia, a mathematician, mentioned by Strabo and by Vitruvius, the latter of whom speaks of him as the inventor of a universal sun-dial. (2) Of Tripolis, a mathematician and astronomer of some distinction, who appears to have flourished later than the reign of Trajan. He wrote several works, of which the three following are extant, and have been published: (*a*) Σφαιρικά, a treatise on the properties of the sphere, and of the circles described on its surface; (*b*) Περὶ Ἡμερῶν καὶ Νυκτῶν; and (*c*) Περὶ Οἰκήσεων.

Theodŏta (Θεοδότη). An Athenian courtesan, and one of the most celebrated persons of that class in Greece. She is introduced as a speaker in Xenophon's *Memorabilia* (iii. 11). She at last attached herself to Alcibiades, and, after his murder, she performed his funeral rites (Athen. pp. 220, 574). See ALCIBIADES.

Theognis (Θέογνις). Of Megara, an ancient elegiac and gnomic poet, said to have flourished B.C. 548 or 544. He may have been born about 570, and would therefore have been eighty at the commencement of the Persian Wars, 490, at which time we know from his own writings that he was alive. Theognis belonged to the oligarchical party in his native city, and in its fates he shared. He was a noble by birth, and all his sympathies were with the nobles. They are, in his poems, the ἀγαθοί and ἐσθλοί, and the commons the κακοί and δειλοί, terms which, in fact, at that period, were regularly used in this political signification, and not in their later ethical meaning. He was banished with the leaders of the oligarchical party, having previously been deprived of all his property; and most of his poems were composed while he was an exile. Most of his political verses are addressed to a certain Cyrnus, the son of Polypas. The other fragments of his poetry are of a social, most of them of a festive, character. They place us in the midst of a circle of friends who formed a kind of convivial society; all the members of this society belonged to the class whom the poet calls "the good." The collection of gnomic poetry which has come down to us under the name of Theognis contains, however, many additions from later poets. The genuine fragments of Theognis, with some passages which are poetical in thought, have much that helps us to understand his times.

The best editions are by Welcker (1826); Bekker (Leipzig, 1815 and 1827); Orelli (Zürich, 1840); Bergk (1878); Ziegler (2d ed. 1880); and Sitzler (1880). See Frere's *Theognis Restitutus* (Malta, 1842); Müller, *De Scriptis Theognidis* (1877); Sitzler, *Studien zum Elegiker Theognis* (1885); and Sittl, *Geschichte der griechischen Literatur*, i. pp. 261 foll.

Theogonia (*θεογονία*). A theogony, or genealogical account of the gods. The earliest of these is said to have been written by Musaeus (q. v.); but the most famous is that of Hesiod, which is still extant. See HESIODUS.

Theon (Θέων). (1) Of Samos. A Greek painter who flourished in the second half of the fourth century B.C. His pictures were celebrated for their powerful effect on the imagination, which caused those who looked at them to forget that they were only counterfeits of reality. The picture of a young hoplite charging the enemy was especially celebrated for this effect of illusion (Aelian, *V. H.* ii. 44).

(2) Of Smyrna. A Platonist living in the first half of the second century A.D. He was the author of a work of great value in connection with ancient Greek arithmetic: on the principles of mathematics, music, and astronomy required for the study of Plato. It is edited by Hiller (Leipzig, 1878).

(3) Of Alexandria. One of the last students at the Alexandrian Museum, born about A.D. 365. He is the author of a commentary on Euclid and on the astronomical tables of Ptolemaeus. He was the father of the celebrated Hypatia (q. v.). His works are edited by Halma (Paris, 1822).

(4) AELIUS. A rhetorician of Alexandria, who wrote, in the fifth century A.D., a book on rhetoric, to which were appended exercises on style, called Προγυμνάσματα, deserving of commendation both for their conciseness and lucidity of exposition, and for their criticisms on the style of the Attic orators. Edited by Finckh (Stuttgart, 1834).

Theonoë (Θεονόη). Daughter of Proetus and Psammathe, also called Idothea. See IDOTHEA.

Theophănes (Θεοφάνης). (1) CN. POMPĒIUS, of Mitylené in Lesbos. A learned Greek, who was one of the most intimate friends of Pompey, and wrote the history of his campaigns (Caes. *B. G.* iii. 18). (2) A Byzantine historian, who flourished most probably in the latter part of the sixth century of our era. He wrote, in ten books, the history of the Eastern Empire during the Persian war under Justin II., from A.D. 567 to 581. The work itself is lost, but some extracts from it are preserved by Photius. (3) Also a Byzantine historian, lived during the second half of the eighth century A.D. and the early part of the ninth. In consequence of his supporting the cause of image-worship, he was banished by Leo the Armenian to the island of Samothracé, where he died, in 818. Theophanes wrote a *Chronicon*, which is still extant, beginning at the accession of Diocletian, in 277, and coming down to 811. It consists, like the *Chronica* of Eusebius and of Syncellus, of two parts, a history arranged according to years, and a chronological table, of which the former is very superior to the latter. It is edited by De Boor (Leipzig, 1883).

Theophania (*θεοφάνια*). A Delphic festival celebrated in February on the alleged birthday of Apollo (Plut. *Quaest. Graec.* 9). In the Christian Greek writers, the name is used of Christmas Day.

Theophrastus (Θεόφραστος). The Greek philosopher. He was a native of Eresus in Lesbos, and studied philosophy at Athens, first under Plato and afterwards under Aristotle. He became the favourite pupil of Aristotle, who named Theophrastus his successor in the presidency of the Lyceum, and in his will bequeathed to him his library and the originals of his own writings. Theophrastus was a worthy successor of his great master, and nobly sustained the character of the school. He is said to have had two thousand disciples, and among them such men as the comic poet Menander. He was highly esteemed by the kings Philippus, Cassander, and Ptolemy, and was not the less the object of the regard of the Athenian people, as was decisively shown when he was impeached of impiety; for he was not only acquitted, but his accuser would have fallen a victim to his calumny had not Theophrastus generously interfered to save him. He died in B.C. 287, having presided over the Academy about thirty-five years. His age is variously stated. According to some accounts he lived 85 years, according to others 107 years. He is said to have closed his life with the complaint respecting the short duration of human existence, that it ended just when the insight into its problems was beginning. He wrote a great number of works, the great object of which was the development of the Aristotelian philosophy. His Ἠθικοὶ Χαρακτῆρες, in thirty chapters; his work on plants (Περὶ Φυτῶν Ἱστορίας), in ten books; his account of the causes of plants (Περὶ Φυτῶν Αἰτιῶν); and his treatise on stones (Περὶ Λίθων), are extant. These are edited together by Wimmer (Breslau, 1842–62). A separate edition of the *Characteres* is that of Jebb (London, 1870).

Theophylactus (Θεοφυλάκτος), surnamed **Simocatta**. A Byzantine historian, who lived at Constantinople, where he held some public offices under Heraclius, about A.D. 610–629. His chief work is a history of the reign of the emperor Maurice, in eight books, from the death of Tiberius II. and the accession of Maurice, in 582, down to the murder of Maurice and his children by Phocas in 602. (Edited by Bekker [Bonn, 1834].) There is also extant another work of Theophylactus, entitled *Quaestiones Physicae*, edited by Boissonade (Paris, 1835); and De Boor (1886). He was likewise the author of a collection of fictitious letters divided as *Morales* (twenty-eight), *Rusticae* (twenty-eight), and *Amatoriae* (twenty-eight).

Theopompus (Θεόπομπος). (1) A Greek poet of the Old Comedy, a younger contemporary of Aristophanes; he is known to have been engaged in composition as late as B.C. 370. Only fragments remain of his twenty-four dramas, which prepared the way for the transition to the Middle Comedy. See COMOEDIA.

(2) A Greek historian, born at Chios about B.C. 378. He left home, probably about 361, with his father, who was banished by the democratic party on account of his predilection for the Spartans, and, having been trained in oratory by Isocrates, spoke with great success in all the larger towns of Greece. He distinguished himself so greatly in the rhetorical contest instituted (351) by Queen Artemisia, wife of Mausolus, in honour of her deceased husband, that he obtained a brilliant victory over all competitors. He afterwards travelled, with the object of acquiring material for his historical works. The favour shown him by Alexander the Great induced him to return to Chios at the age of forty-five; but on the death of his patron he found himself again obliged to flee from his opponents, whose hatred he had incurred by his vehement adoption of the sentiments of the aristocracy. He took refuge with Ptolemy I., at Alexandria, about 305. Here he did not, however, meet with a favourable reception, and was compelled to withdraw, as his life was in danger. Of his subsequent career nothing is known.

Besides numerous orations (principally panegyrics) he composed two large histories, founded on the most careful and minute research: (*a*) *Hellenica* (Ἑλληνικαὶ Ἱστορίαι), in twelve books, a continuation of Thucydides, covering the period from 411–394; and (*b*) *Philippica* (Φιλιππικά), in fifty-eight books, treating of the life and times of Philip of Macedon. Of these works only fragments remain. The charge of malignity, which was brought against him by the ancients, seems to have originated in the reckless manner in which, on the testimony of Dionysius of Halicarnassus (*Ep. ad Cn. Pompeium*), he exposed the pettiness and baseness of the politics of those times, especially those of the Macedonian party. There seems to be better foundation for the charge brought against him of being too fond of digressions; for when, in later times, the digressions in the *Philippica* were omitted, the work was thereby reduced to sixteen books. Theopompus was the first Greek writer to make any definite mention of Rome, speaking of its capture by the Gauls (Pliny, *H. N.* iii. 57). His fragments are edited by C. and Th. Müller in the *Frag. Hist. Graec.* (Paris, 1841). See Stern, *Diodor und Theopompos* (1891).

(3) A king of Sparta who is said to have established the ephoralty (Pausan. iii. 7, 5).

Theōri (*θεωροί*). Persons sent by the Greek States on any special mission (*θεωρία*) associated with religion, such as the offering of sacrifice or the consultation of an oracle. Among some of the Doric States, such as the Messenians, Mantineans, and Troezenians, there were special officers called Theori, who consulted the oracles and interpreted their responses.

Theoria (*θεωρία*). See THEORI.

Theorĭcon (*τὸ θεωρικόν*, sc. *χρῆμα*, "theatre-money"). Money devoted by the State to the public shows and festivals, or given to the people as legacies. A distribution of two obols (about $0.08) a head, granted from the time of Pericles to the poorer Athenian citizens, from the common war-chest (see HELLENOTAMIAE), enabled them to attend the representations at the theatre, two obols being the entrance fee levied by the lessees of the theatre. By degrees this grant was distributed to citizens who laid claim to it in the case of other entertainments, such as festivals and sacrifices. For the contests and games at the Panathenaea, Dionysia, Eleusinia, Thargelia, money was set apart by the State, while some of the expense was borne by individuals. (See LITURGIA.) The public treasury also defrayed a portion of the cost of the Olympian, Pythian, Nemean, and Isthmian Games. It was abolished towards the end of the Peloponnesian War, but again introduced after the restoration of the democracy; and a special fund, to which, by a decree of the people, the whole surplus of the revenue was to be devoted, was set apart for this purpose, with a special treasurer, who had even for a time the management of the finances of the State. Demosthenes first succeeded, shortly before the battle of Chaeronea (B.C. 338), in putting an end to this system, which so severely taxed the resources of the State in time of war. See Fickelscherer, *De Theoricis Atheniensium Pecuniis* (Leipzig, 1877).

Theōris (*θεωρίς*). A trireme kept for sacred embassies. Three of these were kept at Athens. (Schömann, *Antiq.* Eng. trans. p. 441.) See THEORI.

Theoxenia (*θεοξένια*, also *θεοδαίσια*, "entertainments given to the gods"). A festival celebrated in many parts of Greece in honour, not only of the principal local divinity, but of many others who were considered as his guests. Such was the feast held at Delphi in honour of Apollo in the month hence called Theoxenius (August). Of the manner of its celebration nothing is known. Distinguished men, such as Pindar and his descendants, were also invited to the sacrificial feast. Elsewhere other gods appeared as hosts at the feast, as the Dioscuri, the patrons of hospitality, in Paros and Agrigentum. From these god-feasts the Romans probably derived the custom of their *lectisternia*. See LECTISTERNIUM.

Thera (Θήρα). Now Santorin; an island in the Aegaean Sea, and the chief of the Sporades, distant from Crete 700 stadia, and 25 Roman miles south of the Island of Ios. See Voswinckel, *De Theraeorum Insulis* (1856).

Theramĕnes (Θηραμένης). An Athenian, son of Hagnon. He was a leading member of the oligarchical government of the Four Hundred at Athens, in B.C. 411. Subsequently, however, he not only took a prominent part in the deposition of the Four Hundred, but came forward as the accuser of Antiphon and Archeptolemus, who had been his intimate friends, but whose death he was now the mean and cowardly instrument in procuring. After the capture of Athens by Lysander, Theramenes was chosen one of the Thirty Tyrants (404). But as from policy he endeavoured to check the tyrannical proceedings of his colleagues, Critias accused him before the council as a traitor, and procured his condemnation by violence. When he had drunk the hemlock, he dashed out the last drop from the cup, exclaiming, "This to the health of the handsome Critias!" (Xen. *Hell.* ii. 3, 2; Diod. xiv. 5). See Pöhlig, *Der Athener Theramenes* (Leipzig, 1877); and Wilamowitz, *Aristoteles und Athen.*

Therapeutics. See MEDICINA; MEDICUS.

Therapnae (Θεράπναι). (1) A town in Laconia, on the left bank of the Eurotas and a little above

Sparta, celebrated in mythology as the birthplace of Castor and Pollux. Menelaüs and Helen were said to be buried here (Pausan. iii. 19, 9). (2) A town in Boeotia.

Theras (Θήρας). A Spartan who colonized and gave name to the island of Thera (q. v.).

Therasia (Θηρασία). A small island west of Thera.

Therĭcles (Θηρικλῆς). A Corinthian potter, whose works obtained such celebrity that they became known throughout Greece by the name of *Θηρίκλεια* (sc. *ποτήρια*) or *κύλικες Θηρικλεῖαι* (or *-οι*), and these names were applied not only to cups of earthenware, but also to those of wood, glass, gold, and silver (Athen. pp. 470–472; Pliny, *H. N.* xvi. 205).

Therītas ("the savage one"). A name given at Sparta to Ares (q. v.).

Therma (Θέρμη). A town in Macedonia, afterwards called Thessalonica (see THESSALONICA), situated at the northeastern extremity of a great gulf of the Aegaean Sea, called THERMAÏCUS or THERMAEUS SINUS from the town at its head. This gulf was also called Macedonicus Sinus; its modern name is the Gulf of Salonica.

Thermae (*θέρμαι*, literally "hot-springs"). The name given by the Romans to the public buildings, founded in and after the time of Agrippa, which combined, with warm baths, the arrangements of a Greek gymnasium. These included open and covered colonnades for conversation, instruction, and different exercises, especially the game of ball. The most extensive and splendid establishments of the sort were to be found in Rome, and are still to be seen, though, for the greater part, in ruins. Of the existing remains the most important are those of the Thermae of Caracalla. These accommodated some 1600 bathers

Remains of the Thermae of Caracalla. (From a photograph.)

at once, but were inferior in size to the Thermae of Diocletian on the Quirinal Hill, which were built for the use of 3200 bathers. Of these there are extensive remains, including part of a theatre. The Thermae of Diocletian were dedicated in A.D. 350. See BALNEAE.

Thermae (Θέρμαι). A town in Sicily, built by the inhabitants of Himera after the destruction of the latter city by the Carthaginians. See HIMERA.

Thermaĭcus Sinus. See THERMA.

Thermōdon (Θερμώδων). Now Thermeh; a river of Pontus, in the district of Themiscyra, the reputed country of the Amazons, rises in a mountain called Amazonius Mountain, near Phanaroea, and falls into the sea about thirty miles east of the mouth of the Iris. At its mouth was the city of Themiscyra; and there is still, on the west side of the mouth of the Thermeh, a place of the same name, Thermeh.

Thermopolium (*θερμοπώλιον*). A shop where hot drink (*calda*) was sold. (Plaut. *Trin.* iv. 3, 6.) See CALDA; VINUM.

Thermopȳlae (Θερμοπύλαι), or simply **Pylae** (Πύλαι). "The Hot Gates," or "The Gates." A celebrated pass leading from Thessaly into Locris. It lay between Mount Oeta and an inaccessible morass, forming the edge of the Malic Gulf. At one end of the pass, close to Anthela, the mountain approaches so close to the morass as to leave room for only a single carriage between; this narrow entrance formed the western gate of Thermopylae. About a mile to the east the mountain again approached close to the sea, near the Locrian town of Alpeni, thus forming the eastern gate of Thermopylae. The space between these two gates was wider and more open, and was distinguished by its abundant flow of hot springs, which were sacred to Heracles: hence the name of the place. Thermopylae was the only pass by which an enemy could penetrate from northern into southern Greece; whence its great importance in Grecian history. It is especially celebrated on account of the heroic defence of Leonidas and the 300 Spartans against the mighty host of Xerxes in B.C. 480; and they only fell through the Persians having discovered a path over the mountains, and thus being enabled to attack the Greeks in the rear. This mountain path commenced from the neighbourhood of Trachis, ascended the gorge of the river Asopus and the hill called Anopaea, then crossed the crest of Oeta, and descended in the rear of Thermopylae near the town of Alpeni (Herod. vii. 207–228; Pausan. iv. 35, 9; x. 19–22). See Schliemann, *Untersuch. d. Thermopylen* (1883); and the article XERXES.

Thermum (Θέρμον) or **Therma** (τὸ Θέρμα). A town of the Aetolians near Stratus, with warm mineral springs, and regarded for some time as the capital of the country.

Theron (Θήρων). A tyrant of Agrigentum, in Sicily, who reigned from about B.C. 488 till his death in 472. He shared with Gelon in the great victory gained over the Carthaginians in 480. See Diod. xi. 20–25, 48, 53; Herod. vii. 165; and the article GELO.

Thersander (Θέρσανδρος). The son of Polynices and Argia, and one of the Epigoni (q. v.). He went with Agamemnon to Troy, and was slain in that expedition by Telephus (Herod. iv. 147; Verg. *Aen.* ii. 261).

Thersītes (Θερσίτης). The son of Agrius. He was the most deformed man and impudent talker among the Greeks at Troy (*Il.* ii. 212). According to the later poets he was killed by Achilles, because he had ridiculed him for lamenting the death of Penthesilea, queen of the Amazons (Tzetz. *ad* Lycophr. 999; Quint. Smyrn. i. 800).

Thesaurus (*θησαυρός*). The Greek term for a room in which all kinds of objects, provisions, jewels, etc., were stored; hence a treasury or treasure-house. In ordinary life the underground store-chambers, circular vaulted rooms with an opening above, similar to our cellars, were thus named. The same name was given to treasure-houses which each State maintained within the precincts of Panhellenic sanctuaries, as repositories for their offerings to the gods. Such were those at Olympia and Delphi. The subterranean tombs, shaped like beehives, and of a construction dating from remote Greek antiquity, which have been found in various places, have been wrongly described as "treasure-houses." The most celebrated of these are the so-called thesaurus of Atreus at Mycenae (see CYCLOPES; MYCENAE), and that of Minyas at Orchomenus (see TROPHONIUS). The latter is only partly, the former wholly, preserved. The ground-plan of these structures is circular, and consists of one enclosed room with a domed roof, constructed of horizontal layers of massive stone blocks, projecting one over the other. This circular chamber was used probably for service in honour of the dead. The actual resting-place of the body was a square room adjoining. The large room at Mycenae is fifty feet in diameter, and about the same in height. It consists of thirteen courses, the uppermost of which was only a single stone. It was decorated with hundreds of bronze plates, the holes for the nails being still visible.

Theseia (*Θήσεια*). A festival in honour of Theseus (q. v.), lasting for several days at Athens in the month Pyanepsion. See A. Mommsen, *Heortologie*, pp. 269–287.

Thēseus (*Θησεύς*). The great national hero of Attic legend. He was the son of Aegeus, king of Athens, and of Aethra, the daughter of Pittheus, king of Troezen. This, however, was the Attic tradition, which aimed at making Theseus a prince of Athenian descent. The older legend of Troezen itself made Theseus the son of Poseidon (Pausan. i. 17, 3; Diod. iv. 59; Plut. *Thes.* 6; Eur. *Hipp.* 887). Plutarch in his *Theseus* has gathered into a connected story various legends, some of Athenian origin, some from other countries: (1) his journey from Troezen to Athens, an Attic glorification of their hero; (2) the Cretan story of the Minotaur adapted to the Attic legends; (3) his later adventures, some of which are of Spartan origin. But the story may be related consecutively as Plutarch has given it.

Theseus was brought up at Troezen, and when he reached maturity he took, by his mother's directions, the sword and sandals, the tokens which had been left by Aegeus, and proceeded to Athens. Eager to emulate Heracles, he went by land, displaying his prowess by destroying the robbers and monsters that infested the country. Periphetes, Sinis, Phaea the Crommyonian sow, Sciron, Cercyon, and Procrustes fell before him. At Athens he was immediately recognized by Medea, who laid a plot for poisoning him at a banquet to which he was invited. By means of the sword which he carried, Theseus was recognized by Aegeus, acknowledged as his son, and declared his successor. The sons of Pallas, thus disappointed in their hopes of succeeding to the throne, attempted to secure the succession by violence, and declared war, but, being betrayed by the herald Leos, were destroyed. The capture of the Marathonian bull, which had long laid waste the surrounding country, was the next exploit of Theseus. After this Theseus went of his own accord as one of the seven youths whom the Athenians were obliged to send every year, with seven maidens, to Crete, to be devoured by the Minotaur. When they arrived at Crete, Ariadné, the daughter of Minos, became enamoured of Theseus, and provided him with a sword with which he slew the Minotaur, and a clue of thread by which he found his way out of the labyrinth. Having effected his object, Theseus sailed away, carrying off Ariadné. There were various legends about Ariadné; but according to the general account Theseus abandoned her in the island of Naxos on his way home. (See ARIADNÉ.) He was generally believed to have had by her two sons, Oenopion and Staphylus; yet this does not agree with the account in the *Odyssey*, which represents her as dying before her wedding with Theseus was brought about, and apparently after her union with Dionysus (*Od.* xi. 320). As the vessel in which Theseus sailed approached Attica, he neglected to hoist the white sail which was to have been the signal of the success of the expedition; whereupon Aegeus, thinking that his son had perished, threw himself into the sea. (See AEGEUS.) Theseus thus became king of Athens. Other adventures followed, again repeating those of Heracles. Theseus is said to have assailed the Amazons before they had recovered from the attack of Heracles, and to have carried off their queen Antiopé. The Amazons in their turn invaded Attica, and penetrated into Athens itself; and the final battle in which Theseus overcame them was fought in the very midst of the city. (See AMAZONES.) By Antiopé Theseus was said to have had a son named Hippolytus or Demophoön, and after her death to have married Phaedra. (See HIPPOLYTUS; PHAEDRA.)

Theseus figures in almost all the great heroic expeditions. He was one of the Argonauts (the anachronism of the attempt of Medea to poison him does not seem to have been noticed); he joined in the Calydonian hunt, and aided Adrastus in recovering the bodies of those slain before Thebes. He contracted a close friendship with Pirithoüs, and aided him and the Lapithae against the Centaurs. With the assistance of Pirithoüs he carried off Helen from Sparta while she was quite a girl, and placed her at Aphidnae, under the care of Aethra. In return he assisted Pirithoüs in his attempt to carry off Persephoné from the lower world. Pirithoüs perished in the enterprise, and Theseus was kept in hard durance until he was delivered by Heracles. Meantime Castor and Pollux invaded Attica, and carried off Helen and Aethra, Academus having informed the brothers where they were to be found. (See ACADEMUS.) Menestheus also endeavoured to incite the people against Theseus, who on his return found himself unable to re-establish his authority, and retired to Scyros, where he met with a treacherous death at the hands of Lycomedes. The departed hero was believed to have appeared to aid the Athenians at the battle of Marathon. In 469 the bones of Theseus were discovered by Cimon in Scyros, and brought to Athens, where they were deposited in a temple (the Theseum) erected in honour of the hero. A considerable part of this temple still remains, forming one of the most interesting monuments of Athens. A festival in honour of Theseus was celebrated on the eighth day of each month, especially in Pyanepsion. See p. 151.

There can be no doubt that Theseus is a purely legendary personage. Nevertheless, in later times the Athenians came to regard him as the author of a very important political revolution in Attica. Before his time Attica had been broken up into twelve petty independent States or townships, acknowledging no head, and connected only by a federal union. Theseus abolished the separate governments, and erected Athens into the capital of a single commonwealth. The festival of the Panathenaea (q. v.) was instituted to commemorate this important revolution. Theseus is said to have established a constitutional government, retaining in his own hands only certain definite powers and functions. He is further said to have distributed the Athenian citizens into the three classes of Eupatridae, Geomori, and Demiurgi. It would be a vain task to attempt to decide whether there is any historical basis for the legends about Theseus, and still more so to endeavour to separate the historical from the legendary in what has been preserved. The Theseus of the Athenians was a hero who fought the Amazons, and slew the Minotaur, and carried off Helen. A personage who should be nothing more than a wise king, consolidating the Athenian commonwealth, however possible his existence might be, would have no historical reality. The connection of Theseus with Poseidon, the national deity of the Ionic tribes, his coming from the Ionic town Troezen, forcing his way through the Isthmus into Attica, and establishing the Isthmia as an Ionic Panegyris, rather suggest that Theseus is, at least in part, the mythological representative of an Ionian immigration into Attica, which, adding perhaps to the strength and importance of Ionian settlers already in the country, might easily have led to that political aggregation of the disjointed elements of the State which is assigned to Theseus.

Thesmophoria (*θεσμοφόρια*). A festival to Demeter, as the founder of agriculture and of the civic rite of marriage, celebrated in many parts of Greece, but especially at Athens. It was held at Athens from the ninth to the thirteenth of the month Pyanepsion (the beginning of November), and only by married women of genuine Attic birth and of blameless reputation. Two of the wealthiest and most distinguished women were chosen out of every district to preside over the festivals; their duty was to perform the sacred functions in the name of the others, and to prepare the festal meal for the women of their own district. Even the priestess, who had the chief conduct of the whole festival, had to be a married woman. On the Stenia, the first day of the feast (Στήνια), the women went in procession, amid wanton jests and gibes, to the deme of Halimus, on the promontory of Colias, where nightly celebrations were held in the Temple of Demeter and her daughter Coré. After their return (*ἄνοδος*) in the early morning of the third day, a festival lasting for three days was held in Athens. No sacrifices were offered on the last day but one, which was spent amid fasting and mourning. On the last day, on which Demeter was invoked under the name of Calligeneia, "goddess of fair children," a feast (*ζημία*) was held amid mimic dances and games, which probably referred to the mythical stories of the goddess and her daughter. See Preller, *Demeter und Persephoné*, pp. 335–365; A. Mommsen, *Heortologie*, pp. 287–302.

Thesmothĕtae (*θεσμοθέται*). The six junior archons at Athens, on whom devolved, specially, the administration of certain branches of the law. For further details see ARCHON.

Thespĭae (Θεσπειαί and Θεσπιαί), or **Thespĭa** (Θεσπεία, Θεσπία). Now Eremo or Rimokastro; an ancient town in Boeotia on the southeastern slope of Mount Helicon, at no great distance from the Crissaean Gulf. It was burned to the ground by the Persians, but subsequently rebuilt. At Thespiae was preserved the celebrated marble statue of Eros by Praxiteles, who had given it to Phryné, by whom it was presented to her native town. (See PRAXITELES.) From the vicinity of Thespiae to Mount Helicon the Muses are called Thespiades, and Helicon itself is named the *Thespia rupes*. (Varro, *L. L.* vii. 2.)

Thespis (Θέσπις). The father of Greek Tragedy. He was a contemporary of Pisistratus, and a native of Icarus, one of the demes in Attica, where the worship of Dionysus had long prevailed. The alteration made by Thespis, which gave to the old Tragedy a new and dramatic character, was very simple but very important. Before his time the leader of the Chorus had recited the adventures of Dionysus and had been answered by the Chorus. Thespis introduced an actor (*ὑποκριτής*, or "answerer") to reply to the leader of the Chorus. It is clear that, though the performance still remained, as far as can be gathered, chiefly lyrical, and the dialogue was of comparatively small account, yet a decided step towards the drama had been made. Some modern scholars have credited Horace's statement that Thespis went about in a wagon as a strolling player (*A. P.* 276). It is suggested that the expressions for the freedom of jesting at the festival of the Lenaea (*τὰ ἐξ ἁμαξῶν, ἐξ ἁμάξης ὑβρίζειν*) may have given rise to the story. See TRAGOEDIA.

Thespius (Θέσπιος). Son of Erechtheus, who, according to some, founded the town of Thespiae in Boeotia (Pausan. ix. 26, 4). His descendants are called *Thespiadae*.

Thesprōti (Θεσπρωτοί). A people of Epirus, inhabiting the district called after them THESPROTIA or THESPRŌTIS (Θεσπρωτία), which extended along the coast from the Ambracian Gulf northwards as far as the river Thyamis, and inland as far as the territory of the Molossi. The Thesproti were the most ancient inhabitants of Epirus, and are said to have derived their name from Thesprotus, the son of Lycaon. They were Pelasgians, and in their country was the oracle of Dodona, the great centre of the Pelasgic worship. (See DODONA; ORACULA; PELASGI.) From Thesprotia issued the Thessalians, who took possession of the country afterwards called Thessaly.

Thessalia (Θεσσαλία). The largest division of Greece. It was bounded on the north by the Cambunian Mountains, which separated it from Macedonia; on the west by Mount Pindus, which separated it from Epirus; on the east by the Aegaean Sea; and on the south by the Maliac Gulf and Mount Oeta, which separated it from Locris, Phocis, and Aetolia. Thessaly proper is a vast plain, shut in on every side by mountain barriers, broken only at the northeastern corner by the valley and defile of Tempé, which separates Ossa from Olympus. This plain is drained by the river Peneus and its affluents, and is said to have been originally a vast lake, the waters of which were afterwards carried off through the vale of Tempé by some sudden convulsion which rent the rocks of this valley asunder. In addition to the plain already described, there were two other districts included under the general name of Thessaly: one called Magnesia, being a long, narrow strip of country extending along the coast of the Aegean Sea from Tempé to the Pagasaean Gulf, and bounded on the west by Mounts Ossa and Olympus; and the other being a long, narrow vale at the extreme south of the country, lying between Mounts Othrys and Oeta, and drained by the river Spercheus. Thessaly proper was divided in very early times into four districts or tetrarchies—a division which we still find existing in the Poloponnesian War. These districts were: (*a*) HESTIAEŌTIS (Ἑστιαιῶτις), the northwestern part of Thessaly, bounded on the north by Macedonia, on the west by Epirus, on the east by Pelasgiotis, and on the south by Thessaliotis; the Peneus may be said in general to have formed its southern limit. (*b*) PELASGIŌTIS (Πελασγιῶτις), the eastern part of the Thessalian plain, bounded on the north by Macedonia, on the west by Hestiaeotis, on the east by Magnesia, and on the south by the Sinus Pagasaeus and Phthiotis. (*c*) THESSALIŌTIS (Θεσσαλιῶτις), the southwestern part of the Thessalian plain, bounded on the north by Hestiaeotis, on the west by Epirus, on the east by Pelasgiotis, and on the south by Dolopia and Phthiotis. (*d*) PHTHIŌTIS (Φθιῶτις), the southeast of Thessaly, bounded on the north by Thessaliotis, on the west by Dolopia, on the south by the Sinus Maliacus, and on the east by the Pagasaean Gulf. It is in this district that Homer places Phthia and Hellas proper, and the dominions of Achilles. Besides these there were four other districts, viz.: (*e*) MAGNESIA. (See MAGNESIA.) (*f*) DOLOPIA (Δολοπία), a small district bounded on the east by Phthiotis, on the north by Thessaliotis, on the west by Athamania, and on the south by Oetaea. The Dolopes were an ancient people, for they are not only mentioned by Homer as fighting before Troy, but they also sent deputies to the Amphictyonic assembly. (*g*) OETAEA (Οἰταῖα), a district in the upper valley of the Spercheus, lying between Mounts Othrys and Oeta, and bounded on the north by Dolopia, on the south by Phocis, and on the east by Malis. (*h*) MALIS. (See MALIS.)

Thessalian Coin.

The Thessalians were a Thesprotian tribe, and, under the guidance of leaders who are said to have been descendants of Heracles, invaded the western part of the country, afterwards called Thessaliotis, whence they subsequently spread over the other parts of the country. For some time after the conquest, Thessaly was governed by kings of the race of Heracles; but the kingly power seems to have been abolished in early times, and the government in the separate cities became oligarchical, the power being chiefly in the hands of a few great families descended from the ancient kings. Of these, two of the most powerful were the Aleuadae and the Scopadae, the former of whom ruled at Larissa, and the latter at Cranon (or Crannon). At an early period the Thessalians were united into a confederate body. Each of the four districts into which the country was divided probably regulated its affairs by some kind of provincial council; and in case of war a chief magistrate was elected, under the name of Tagus (Ταγός), whose commands were obeyed by all the four districts. This confederacy, however, was not of much practical benefit to the Thessalian people, and appears to have been only used by the Thessalian nobles as a means of cementing and maintaining their power. The Thessalians never became of much importance in Grecian history. In B.C. 344 Philip completely subjected Thessaly to Macedonia, by placing at the head of the four divisions of the country governors devoted to his interests. The victory of T. Flamininus at Cynoscephalae, in 197, again gave the Thessalians a semblance of independence under the protection of the Romans.

Thessalonīca (Θεσσαλονίκη). Now Saloniki; more anciently THERMA (Θέρμη). An ancient city in Macedonia, situated at the northeastern extremity of the Sinus Thermaïcus. Under the name of Therma it was not a place of much importance. It was taken and occupied by the Athenians a short time before the commencement of the Peloponnesian War (B.C. 432), but was soon after restored by them to Perdiccas. It was made an important city by Cassander, who collected in this place the inhabitants of several adjacent towns (about B.C. 315), and who gave it the name of Thessalonica in honour of his wife, the daughter of Philip and sister of Alexander the Great. From this time it became a large and flourishing city. It was visited by the Apostle Paul about A.D. 53, and about two years afterwards he addressed from Corinth two epistles to his converts in the city.

Thessălus (Θεσσαλός). (1) A Greek physician, son of Hippocrates. He passed some of his time at the court of Archelaüs, king of Macedonia, who reigned B.C. 413–399. He was one of the founders of the sect of the Dogmatici, and is several times highly praised by Galen, who calls him the most eminent of the sons of Hippocrates. He was supposed by some of the ancient writers to be the author of several of the works that form part of the Hippocratic Collection, which he might have compiled from notes left by his father. (2) Also a Greek physician, a native of Tralles in Lydia, and one of the founders of the medical sect of the Methodici. He lived at Rome in the reign of the emperor Nero, A.D. 54–68, to whom he addressed one of his works; and he died and was buried, and his tomb was to be seen in Pliny's time, on the Via Appia. He considered himself superior to all his predecessors. He is frequently mentioned by Galen, but always in terms of contempt and ridicule. None of his works are extant.

Thestius (Θέστιος). The son of Ares and Demonicé or Androdicé, or, according to others, a son of Agenor and grandson of Pleuron, the king of Aetolia. He was the father of Iphiclus, Euippus, Plexippus, Eurypylus, Leda, Althaea, and Hypermnestra. The patronymic THESTIĂDES is given to his grandson Meleager, as well as to his sons; and the female patronymic THESTIAS to his daughter Althaea, the mother of Meleager.

Thestor (Θέστωρ). The son of Idmon and Laothoë, and father of Calchas, Theoclymenus, Leucippé, and Theonoë. The patronymic THESTORĬDES is frequently given to his son Calchas.

Thetes (Θῆτες). The lowest of the four property-classes instituted by Solon. See EISPHORA; SOLON.

Thetis (Θέτις). A daughter of Nereus and Doris. She was the wife of Peleus, by whom she became the mother of Achilles (*Il.* i. 538, xviii. 35; Hes. *Theog.* 244). As a goddess of the sea she dwelt, like her sisters the Nereids, below the waves with her father, Nereus. She there received Dionysus on his flight from Lycurgus, and the god, in his gratitude, presented her with a golden urn (*Il.* vi. 135; *Od.* xxiv. 75). When Hephaestus was thrown down from heaven, he was likewise received by Thetis. She had been brought up by Heré, and when she reached the age of maturity, Zeus and Heré gave her, against her will, in marriage to Peleus. Such was the Homeric story (*Il.* xviii. 85, 432); but later accounts add that Poseidon and Zeus himself first sued for her hand; but when Themis declared that the son of Thetis would be stronger than his father, both gods desisted from their suit, and desired her marriage with a mortal (Pind. *Isthm.* viii. 58). Chiron informed his friend Peleus how he might gain possession of her, even if she should metamorphose herself: for Thetis, like Proteus, had the power of assuming any form she pleased; and she had recourse to this means of escaping from Peleus, who, instructed by Chiron, held the goddess fast till she again assumed her proper form, and promised to marry him (Pind. *Nem.* iii. 60). This story, which appears first in Pindar, was a favourite subject in vase-painting of an early date. The wedding of Peleus was honoured with the presence of all the gods, with the exception of Eris or Discord, who was not invited, and who avenged herself by throwing among the assembled gods the apple which was the source of so much misery. (See PARIS.) For the action of Thetis in the story of her son, see ACHILLES.

Thevesté (Θεουέστη). Now Tebessa. A city of North Africa on the frontier of Numidia. A fine triumphal arch and the ruins of the ancient walls still exist. See Boissier, *L'Afrique Romaine* (1895). The Romans had a phrase *De Tebeste* (*Theveste*) *usque ad Tergeste*, like the Scripture "From Dan to Beersheba" (*Test. Porcell.*).

Thia (Θεία). A daughter of Uranus and Gê, one of the female Titans, became by Hyperion the mother of Helios, Eos (Aurora), and Selené (Luna)—that is, she was regarded as the deity from whom all light proceeded (Hes. *Theog.* 135, 171).

Thiăsus (*θίασος*). The Greek designation of a society which had selected some god for its patron, and held sacrifices, festal processions, and banquets at stated times in his honour. Frequently the members of such societies, which took their name either from their divine patron or else from the days of festal celebration, pursued other common ends, sometimes of business, sometimes of social life. The name *thiasus* was especially applied to the festivals in honour of Dionysus, and, in the representations of poetry and art, to the mythical retinue of the god, which consisted of Sileni, Satyrs, Nymphs, and Maenads.

Thinis. See THIS.

Thirlwall, CONNOP. An English scholar and historian, born at Stepney in 1797. He was educated at Charterhouse and Cambridge, where he took honours, and later studied law. In 1828 he began the publication of an English version of Niebuhr's *History of Rome*, and was one of the editors of the *Philological Museum* (1831–33). In 1835 he undertook a *History of Greece*, which was finished in eight volumes in 1847, and re-issued, with extensive revision, in 1847–52. In 1840 he was made Bishop of St. David's. He died July 27, 1875. His *History* has been called a Tory history of Greece, as Grote's has been styled a Whig history; and Thirlwall's sympathies are everywhere with aristocracy as against democracy; but his learning, sagacity, and candour are worthy of high commendation, and he is superior to Grote as a writer of English. A paper by Thirlwall, "On the Irony of Sophocles," which appeared in the *Philological Museum*, is a valuable contribution to Sophoclean study. See an article in the *Edinburgh Review* for April, 1876.

Thirty Tyrants. (1) The name usually given to the committee of thirty aristocrats who at the close of the Peloponnesian War (B.C. 404), and under the protection of the victorious Spartans, undertook the administration of the Athenian government. The chiefs of this body were Critias (q.v.) and Theramenes (q.v.). They secured a new Senate, put to death their chief political opponents, and installed a Spartan garrison in the Acropolis. A reign of terror ensued which led to a reaction; and presently a body of exiled citizens headed by Thrasybulus (q.v.) marched upon Athens, defeated the troops of the Thirty, and slew Critias. After some delay the Spartan government recognized the *status quo* and thus permitted the resumption of a democratic government (B.C. 403). See PELOPONNESIAN WAR.

(2) A name used to designate the crowd of usurpers who, in the reign of the Roman emperor Gallienus (253–268 A.D.), attempted to secure the imperial power. The name is hardly accurate, as there were in reality only some nineteen or twenty of those petty revolutionists. See GALLIENUS.

This (Θίς). A great city of Upper Egypt, capital of the Thinites Nomos, and the seat of the first two dynasties (B.C. 4400–4000). It is also called THINIS.

Thisbé (Θίσβη), afterwards **Thisbae** (Θίσβαι). Now Kakosia. A town of Boeotia, on the borders of Phocis, and between Mount Helicon and the Corinthian Gulf.

Thisbé (Θίσβη). A beautiful Babylonian maiden, beloved by Pyramus. The lovers, living in adjoining houses, often secretly conversed with each other through an opening in the wall, as their parents would not sanction their marriage. Once they agreed upon a rendezvous at the tomb of Ninus. Thisbé arrived first, and, while she was waiting for Pyramus, she perceived a lioness, which had just torn to pieces an ox, and took to flight. While running she lost her garment, which the lioness smeared with blood. In the meantime Pyramus arrived, and finding her garment covered with blood, he imagined that she had been murdered, and made away with himself under a mulberry-tree, the fruit of which henceforth was as red as blood. Thisbé, who afterwards found the body of her lover, likewise killed herself (Ovid, *Met.* iv. 55–465). The story is burlesqued by Shakespeare in a well-known episode in *A Midsummer-Night's Dream.*

Thoas (Θόας). (1) The son of Andraemon and Gorgé. He was king of Calydon and Pleuron, in Aetolia, and sailed with forty ships against Troy. (2) Son of Dionysus and Ariadné, king of Lemnos, and married to Myrina, by whom he became the father of Hypsipylé and Sicinus. When the Lemnian women killed all the men in the island, Hypsipylé saved and concealed her father, Thoas. The patronymic THOANTIAS is given to Hypsipylé, as the daughter of Thoas. (See HYPSIPYLÉ.) (3) Son of Borysthenes and king of Tauris, into whose dominions Iphigenia was carried by Artemis when she was to have been sacrificed. See IPHIGENIA.

Tholus (θόλος). A round structure, probably the earliest form of human habitation, and preserved by the Greeks in their houses and cities. Later this word is used of any circular building.

Thomas Magister. A rhetorician and grammarian, about A.D. 1310. He was a native of Thessalonica, and lived at the court of the emperor Andronicus Palaeologus I., where he held the offices of marshal (*magister officiorum*) and keeper of the archives (*chartophylax*); but he afterwards retired to a monastery, where he assumed the name of THEODŪLUS, and devoted himself to the study of the ancient Greek authors. His chief work, which has come down to us, is a lexicon of Attic words (Κατὰ Ἀλφάβητον Ὀνομάτων Ἀττικῶν Ἐκλογαί), compiled from the works of the elder grammarians, such as Phrynichus, Ammonius, Herodian, and Moeris. It is edited by Ritschl (Halle, 1831).

Thong. See LORICA.

Thorax (θώραξ). The Greek term for a cuirass, either of metal (usually bronze) or of leather. The metal cuirass consisted of two separate pieces, one covering the chest and stomach, and the other the back, attached to one another by means of clasps or buckles. They terminated with a curved edge just above the hip, and at this part were often covered with a leathern belt (ζωστήρ), fastened with buckles, to bind both pieces more firmly together. Another belt (μίτρα), lined with leather, was worn under the armour and above the chiton. This was fitted with a plate of metal growing broader towards the middle and serving to protect the belly. In later times the front plate of the cuirass was extended downwards, so as to cover the belly as far as the navel. As an additional protection to the belly and the upper part of the legs, there was on the inner side of the lower edge of the cuirass a series of short strips of leather or felt, covered with plates of metal, often in several layers. They resembled a kilt, and were called πτέρυγες ("feathers"). Smaller strips of the same kind were worn under the arms to protect the armpits.

The leather cuirass (σπολάς) was a kind of shirt reaching over the navel and hips, and fringed with

Thoraces. (From Greek vases.)

flexible strips along its lower edge. It was open either in front or on one side (usually the left), and was there fastened together by means of clasps or buckles. It was also provided with an upright piece protecting the neck, and with two shoulder-straps. It was frequently covered, either completely, or only under the arms, with metal, especially in the form of scales.

Linen cuirasses are also mentioned, even in ancient times. These were probably either thickly quilted or strongly woven corselets.

The Romans applied the name to a bust in marble or bronze (Vitruv. *Compend.* 2). See LORICA.

Thorĭcus (Θορικος). Now Theriko; one of the twelve ancient towns in Attica, and subsequently a demus belonging to the tribe Acamantis, was situated on the southeastern coast, a little above Sunium. Important ruins, especially those of an ancient theatre, still remain here.

Thoth. An Egyptian god identified by the Greeks with Hermes as presiding over human speech, letters, music, and astronomy, and as the inventor of the arts and sciences.

The God Thoth.

Thracia (Θρᾴκη, Ion. Θρῄκη). In earlier times the name of the vast space of country bounded on the north by the Danube, on the south by the Propontis and the Aegaean, on the east by the Pontus Euxinus, and on the west by the river Strymon and the easternmost of the Illyrian tribes. It was divided into two parts by Mount Haemus (the Balkan), running from west to east, and separating the plain of the lower Danube from the rivers which fall into the Aegaean. Its plains are drained by the Hebrus, the largest river in Thrace. At a later time the name Thrace was applied to a more limited extent of country. The district between the Strymon and the Nestus was added to Macedonia by Philip, and was usually called MACEDONIA ADIECTA. Under Augustus the part of the country north of the Haemus was made a separate Roman province under the name of Moesia (see MOESIA); but the district between the Strymon and the Nestus had been previously restored to Thrace by the Romans. The Roman province of Thrace was accordingly bounded on the west by the river Nestus; on the north by Mount Haemus, which divided it from Moesia; on the east by the Euxine, and on the south by the Propontis and Aegean.

Thrace, in its widest extent, was peopled in the times of Herodotus and Thucydides by a vast number of different tribes; but their customs and characters were marked by great uniformity. Herodotus says that, next to the Indians, the Thracians were the most numerous of all races, and if united under one head would have been irresistible. He describes them as a savage, cruel, and rapacious people, delighting in blood, but brave and warlike. According to his account, which is confirmed by other writers, the Thracian chiefs sold their children for exportation to the foreign merchant; they purchased their wives from their parents; they punctured or tattooed their bodies and those of the women belonging to them, as a sign of noble birth; they despised agriculture, and considered it most honourable to live by war and robbery. Deep drinking prevailed among them extensively (Hor. *Carm.* i. 27). They worshipped deities whom the Greeks assimilated to Ares, Dionysus, and Artemis: the great sanctuary and oracle of their god Dionysus was in one of the loftiest summits of Mount Rhodopé. The tribes on the southern coast attained to some degree of civilization, owing to the numerous Greek colonies which were founded in their vicinity; but the tribes in the interior seem to have retained their savage habits, with little mitigation, down to the time of the Roman Empire. In earlier times, however, some of the Thracian tribes must have been distinguished by a higher degree of civilization than prevailed among them at a later period. The earliest Greek poets, Orpheus, Linus, Musaeus, and others, are all represented as coming from Thrace. Eumolpus, likewise, who founded the Eleusinian Mysteries at Attica, is said to have been a Thracian, and to have fought against Erectheus, king of Athens. We also find mention of the Thracians in other parts of southern Greece: thus they are said to have once dwelt both in Phocis and Boeotia. They were also spread over a part of Asia: the Thynians and Bithynians, and perhaps also the Mysians, were members of the great Thracian race. Even Xenophon speaks of Thrace in Asia, which extended along the Asiatic side of the Bosporus, as far as Heraclea.

The principal Greek colonies along the coast, beginning at the Strymon and going eastwards, were Amphipolis, at the mouth of the Strymon; Abdera, a little to the west of the Nestus; Dicaea or Dicaepolis, a settlement of Maronea; Maronea itself, colonized by the Chians; Stryme, a colony of the Thasians; Mesembria, founded by the Samothracians; and Aenos, a Lesbian colony at the mouth of the Hebrus. The Thracian Chersonesus was probably colonized by the Greeks at an early period, but it did not contain any important Greek settlement till the migration of the first Miltiades to the country, during the reign of Pisistratus at Athens. On the Propontis the two chief Greek settlements were those of Perinthus and Selymbria; and on the Thracian Bosporus was the important town of Byzantium. There were only a few Greek settlements on the southwestern coast of the Euxine; the most important were those of Apollonia, Odessus, Callatis, Tomi, renowned as the place of Ovid's banishment, and Istria, near the southern mouth of the Danube.

The Thracians are said to have been conquered by Sesostris, king of Egypt, and subsequently to have been subdued by the Teucrians and Mysians; but the first really historical fact respecting them is their subjugation by Megabazus, the general of Darius. After the Persians had been driven out of Europe by the Greeks, the Thracians recovered their independence; and at the beginning of the Peloponnesian War, almost all the Thracian tribes were united under the dominion of Sitalces, king of the Odrysae, whose kingdom extended from Abdera to the Euxine and the mouth of the Danube. In the third year of the Peloponnesian War (B.C. 429), Sitalces, who had entered into an alliance with the Athenians, invaded Macedonia with a vast army of 150,000 men, but was compelled by the failure of provisions to return home, after remaining in Macedonia thirty days. Sitalces fell in battle against the Triballi in 424, and was succeeded by his nephew Seuthes, who during a long reign raised his kingdom to a height of power and prosperity which it had never previously attained, so that his regular revenues amounted to the annual sum of 400 talents, in addition to contributions of gold and silver in the form of presents, to a nearly equal amount. After the death of Seuthes, which appears to have happened a little before the close of the Peloponnesian War, we find his powerful kingdom split up into different parts; and when Xenophon, with the remains of the 10,000 Greeks, arrived on the opposite coast of Asia, another Seuthes applied to him for assistance to reinstate him in his dominions. Philip, the father of Alexander the Great, reduced the greater part of Thrace; and after the death of Alexander the country fell to the share of Lysimachus. It subsequently formed a part of the Macedonian dominions, but it continued to be governed by its native princes, and was only nominally subject to the Macedonian monarchs. Even under the Romans Thrace was for a long time governed by its own chiefs; and we do not know at what period it was made into a Roman province.

See Eben, *Die alten Thraker* (1877); and Kalopothakes, *De Thracia Provincia Romana* (1893).

Thrasea, P. PAETUS. A distinguished Roman senator and Stoic philosopher in the reign of Nero. He was a native of Patavium, and was probably born soon after the death of Augustus. He made the younger Cato his model, of whose life he wrote an account. He married Arria, the daughter of the heroic Arria who showed her husband, Caecina, how to die; and his wife was worthy of her mother and her husband. At a later period he gave his own daughter in marriage to Helvidius Priscus, who trod closely in the footsteps of his father-in-law. After incurring the hatred of Nero by the independence of his character and the freedom with which he expressed his opinions, he was condemned to death by the Senate by command of the emperor, A.D. 66. See Hoitsema, *De P. Thrasea Paeto* (1852).

Thrasybūlus (Θρασύβουλος). A celebrated Athenian, son of Lycus. He was zealously attached to the Athenian democracy, and took an active part in overthrowing the oligarchical government of the 400 in B.C. 403. See THIRTY TYRANTS.

Thrasyllus or **Thrasȳlus** (Θράσυλλος, Θράσυλος).

(1) An Athenian who actively assisted Thrasybulus in opposing the oligarchical revolution in B.C. 411, and, like him, was appointed as one of the generals at Samos. (See THRASYBULUS.) He was one of the commanders at the battle of Arginusae, and was among the six generals who returned to Athens and were put to death, 406. (See ARGINUSAE.) (2) An astrologer of Rhodes, with whom Tiberius became acquainted during his residence in that island, and whom he ever after held in the highest honour. In the scenes between him and the emperor, as described by Tacitus, Suetonius, and Dio, Thrasyllus is the prototype for Scott (in *Quentin Durward*) of Martius Galeotti, the astrologer of Louis XI. He confirmed the faith of Tiberius in his skill by casting his own horoscope as well as that of his master, and saying that he himself had reached a great crisis of danger, having suspected, as was the truth, that Tiberius was on the point of having him thrown over a precipice. This proof of prophetic power saved his life. He died in A.D. 36, the year before Tiberius, and is said to have saved the lives of many persons whom Tiberius would otherwise have put to death, by falsely predicting for this very purpose that the emperor would live a certain period longer than his intended victims. The son of this Thrasyllus succeeded to his father's skill, and he is said to have predicted the empire to Nero (Tac. *Ann.* vi. 20–22; Suet. *Aug.* 98; *Tib.* 14, 62; *Cal.* 19; Dio Cass. lv. 11; lvii. 15; lviii. 27).

Thrasymăchus (Θρασύμαχος). A native of Chalcedon, was a Sophist, and one of the earliest cultivators of the art of rhetoric. He was a contemporary of Gorgias. He is one of the speakers in Plato's *Republic*.

Thrasymēnus. See TRASIMENUS.

Thrax, also **Thraex** and **Threx**. See GLADIATORES, p. 734.

Thread. See TELA.

Threnos (θρῆνος). The Greek term for a dirge sung by a chorus to the accompaniment of flutes, either at the burial or at the funeral feast. See FUNUS; MUSICA.

Thrinacia (Θρινακία). A mythical island on which the herds of the Sun-god (Helios) grazed (*Od.* xi. 107; xii. 127; xix. 275), afterwards identified with Sicily (Trinacria). See HELIOS; SICILIA.

Thronium (Θρόνιον). Now Pikraki; the chief town of the Locri Epicnemidii, on the river Boagrius, at a short distance from the sea, with a harbour upon the coast.

Thronus (θρόνος). A throne; a Greek word equivalent to the Latin *solium* (q. v.). The general form of the throne was that of a chair (καθέδρα), but it was larger and more highly ornamented. Being high, it was always accompanied by a footstool (ὑποπόδιον, θρόνιον, *subsellium*). See illustration above.

Thucydĭdes (Θουκυδίδης). (1) An Athenian statesman, of the deme Alopecé, son of Melesias. After the death of Cimon in B.C. 449, Thucydides became the leader of the aristocratic party, which he concentrated and more thoroughly organized in opposition to Pericles. He left two sons, Melesias and Stephanus; and a son of the former of these, named Thucydides after his grandfather, was a pupil of Socrates. (2) The great Athenian historian, the

Heré Enthroned. (Vase in Naples Museum.)

son of Olorus or Orolus and Hegesipylé. He is said to have been connected with the family of Cimon; and we know that Miltiades, the conqueror of Marathon, married Hegesipylé, the daughter of a Thracian king called Olorus, by whom she became the mother of Cimon; and it has been conjectured with much probability that the mother of Thucydides was a granddaughter of Miltiades and Hegesipylé. According to a statement of Pamphila, Thucydides was forty years of age at the commencement of the Peloponnesian War (B.C. 431), and accordingly he was born in 471. There is a story in Lucian of Herodotus having read his History at the Olympic Games to the assembled Greeks; and Suidas adds that Thucydides, then a boy, was present, and shed tears of emulation—a presage of his own future historical distinction. But this celebrated story ought probably to be rejected as a fable. Thucydides is said to have been instructed in oratory by Antiphon, and in philosophy by Anaxagoras; but whether these statements are to be received cannot be determined. It is certain, however, that, being an Athenian of a good family, and living in a city which was the centre of Greek civilization, he must have had the best possible education; that he was a man of great ability and cultivated understanding his work clearly shows. He informs us that he possessed gold-mines in that part of Thrace which is opposite to the island of Thasos, and that he was a person of the greatest influence among those in that part of Thrace. This property, according to some accounts, he had from his ancestors; according to other accounts, he married a rich woman of Scaptesyle, and received it as a portion with her. Thucydides left a son called Timotheus; and a daughter also is mentioned, who is said by some to have written the eighth book of the History of Thucydides. Thucydides (ii. 48) was one of those who suffered from the great plague of Athens, and one of the few who recovered. We have no trustworthy evidence of Thucydides having distinguished himself as an orator, though it is not unlikely that he did, for his oratorical talent is shown by the speeches that he has inserted in his history. He was, however, employed in a military capacity, and he was in command of an Athenian squadron of seven ships, at Thasus, B.C. 424, when Eucles, who commanded in Amphipolis, sent for his assistance against Brasidas, who was before that town with an army. Brasidas, fearing the arrival of a superior force, offered favourable terms to Amphipolis, which were readily accepted, for there were few Athenians in the place, and the rest did not wish to make resistance. Thucydides arrived at Eion, at the mouth of the Strymon, on the evening of the same day on which Amphipolis surrendered; and though he was too late to save Amphipolis, he prevented Eion from falling into the hands of the enemy. In consequence of this failure, Thucydides became an exile, probably to avoid a severer punishment; for Cleon, who was at this time in great favour with the Athenians, appears to have excited popular suspicion against him. There are various untrustworthy accounts as to his places of residence during his exile; but we may conclude that he could not safely reside in any place which was under Athenian dominion, and as he kept his eye on the events of the war, he must have lived in those parts which belonged to the Spartan alliance. His own words certainly imply that, during his exile, he spent much of his time either in the Peloponnesus, or in places which were under Peloponnesian influence (v. 26); and his work was the result of his own experience and observations. His minute description of Syracuse and the neighbourhood leads to the probable conclusion that he was personally acquainted with the localities; and if he visited Sicily, it is probable that he also saw some parts of southern Italy. Thucydides says that he lived twenty years in exile (v. 26), and as his exile commenced in the beginning of 423, he may have returned to Athens in the beginning of 403, about the time when Thrasybulus liberated Athens. Thucydides is said to have been assassinated at Athens soon after his return; but other accounts place his death in Thrace. There is a general agreement, however, among the ancient authorities that he came to a violent end. His death cannot be placed later than 401.

The time when he composed his work has been a matter of dispute. He informs us himself that he was busy in collecting materials all through the war from the beginning to the end (i. 22), and of course he would register them as he got them. Plutarch says that he wrote the work in Thrace; but the work in the shape in which we have it was certainly not finished until after the close of the war, and he was probably engaged upon it at the time of his death. A question has been raised as to the authorship of the eighth and last book of Thucydides, which breaks off in the middle of the twenty-first year of the war (411). It differs from all the other books in containing no speeches, and it has also been supposed to be inferior to the rest as a piece of composition. Accordingly, several ancient critics supposed that the eighth book was not by Thucydides: some attributed it to his daughter, and some to Xenophon or Theopompus, because both of them continued the history. The words with which Xenophon's *Hellenica* commence (*μετὰ δὲ ταῦτα*) may chiefly have led to the supposition that he was the author, for his work is made to appear as a continuation of that of Thucydides. But this argument is in itself of little weight; and, besides, both the style of the eighth book is different from that of Xenophon, and the manner of treating the subject, for the division of the year into summers and winters, which Thucydides has observed in his first seven books, is continued in the eighth, but is not observed by Xenophon. The rhetorical style of Theopompus, which was the characteristic of his writing, renders it also improbable that he was the author of the eighth book. It seems the simplest supposition to consider Thucydides himself as the author of this book, since he names himself as the author twice (viii. 6, 60); though it is probable that he had not the opportunity of revising it with the same care as the first seven books. It is stated by an ancient writer that Xenophon made the work of Thucydides known, which may be true, as he wrote the first two books of his *Hellenica*, or the part which now ends with the second book, for the purpose of completing the history. The work of Thucydides, from the commencement of the second book, is chronologically divided into winters and summers, and each summer and winter make a year (ii. 1). His summer comprises the time from the vernal to

Thucydides. (Norfolk.)

the autumnal equinox, and the winter comprises the period from the autumnal to the vernal equinox. The division into books and chapters was probably made by the Alexandrian critics. The history of the Peloponnesian War opens the second book of Thucydides, and the first is introductory to the history.

He begins his first book by observing that the Peloponnesian War was the most important event in Grecian history, which he shows by a rapid review of the history of the Greeks from the earliest period to the commencement of the war (i. 1–21). After his introductory chapters he proceeds to explain the alleged grounds and causes of the war: the real causes were, he says, the Spartan jealousy of the Athenian power. His narrative is interrupted (chs. 89–118), after he has come to the time when the Lacedaemonians resolved on war, by a digression on the rise and progress of the power of Athens; a period which had been either omitted by other writers, or treated imperfectly, and with little regard to chronology, as by Hellanicus in his Attic history (ch. 97). He resumes his narrative (ch. 119) with the negotiations that preceded the war; but this leads to another digression of some length on the treason of Pausanias (chs. 128–134), and the exile of Themistocles (chs. 135–138). He concludes the book with the speech of Pericles, who advised the Athenians to refuse the demands of the Peloponnesians; and his subject, as already observed, begins with the second book.

A history which treats of so many events, which took place at remote spots, could only be written, in the time of Thucydides, by a man who took great pains to ascertain facts by personal inquiry. In modern times facts are made known by printing as soon as they occur; and the printed records of the time, such as newspapers, are often the only evidence of many facts which become history. When we know the careless way in which facts are now reported and recorded by incompetent persons, often upon very indifferent hearsay testimony, and compare with such records the pains that Thucydides took to ascertain the chief events of a war with which he was contemporary, in which he took a share as a commander, the opportunities which his means allowed, his great abilities, and serious, earnest character, it is a fair conclusion that we have as exact a history of a long eventful period by Thucydides as we have of any period in modern times.

The work of Thucydides shows the most scrupulous care and diligence in ascertaining facts; his strict attention to chronology, and the importance that he attaches to it, are additional proof of his historical accuracy. His narrative is brief and concise to a degree which makes the thought, or the crowd of thoughts, concentrated in a short and involved sentence often hard to understand; it generally contains bare facts expressed in the fewest possible words, but this stern and apparently passionless brevity is able to produce a pathos unsurpassed by any prose-writer. This is seen most notably in his account of the Athenian catastrophe at Syracuse. Few can read it (and there are other passages almost as moving in the history) without agreeing with the opinion of Macaulay, that nothing finer has been written in prose. But it is still more important to notice that Thucydides is the founder of philosophical history. He first showed that a great historian should not merely narrate events accurately, should not even content himself with a critical examination of his authorities, but should also try to trace the causes of events, and their consequences, their teaching in politics, and the light which they throw upon character. Many of his speeches are political essays, or materials for them; they are not mere imaginations of his own for rhetorical effect; they contain in many cases the general sense of what was actually delivered as nearly as he could ascertain, and in many instances he had good opportunities of knowing what was said, for he heard some speeches delivered (i. 22); but they are employed to show the motives and sentiments of the speakers and of their partisans or countrymen.

The number of existing manuscripts of Thucydides is about fifty, the oldest being the Codex Laurentianus (Florence) of the tenth century. Among the best are the Codex Cassellanus (Cassel), dated 1252, the Codex Augustanus (formerly at Augsburg, now in Munich), the Codex Cantabrigiensis (Cambridge), the Codex Palatinus (Heidelberg) of the eleventh century, and a Codex Vaticanus of somewhat later date. A manuscript (Codex Italus) collated by Bekker at Paris in 1812 is now lost.

The standard editions of Thucydides are those of Bekker, 4 vols. (1821); Poppo, 11 vols. (1821–40); the same abridged and revised by Stahl; Goeller, 2 vols. (1836); Didot, 3 vols. (1868); Arnold, 3 vols. (last ed. 1874); Bloomfield, 2 vols. (1842–43); Krüger, 2 vols. (1846–47); Steup (1893 foll.); Böhme-Widmann (5th ed. 1882). There are a number of excellent editions of parts of the history, of which may be mentioned those of Shilleto, bks. i. and ii.; Marchant, bk. ii.; Smith, bk. iii.; Graves, bks. iv. and v.; Fowler, bk. v.; Rutherford, bk. iv.; Lamberton, bks. vi. and vii.; Holden, bk. vii.; Smith, bk. vii.; Goodheart, bk. viii. See Forbes, *The Life and Method of Thucydides* (1895). There is an analysis of the history by Wheeler (1880).

There is a lexicon to Thucydides by Bétant, 2 vols. (1843–47), and a complete index by Von Essen (1887). There are translations into English by Bloomfield, 2 vols. (1843–47); Dale (1848); Crawley (1874); and especially by Jowett, with an introduction, 2 vols. (1881). The speeches contained in the history are translated by Wilkins (3d ed. 1881); on which see also Jebb in Abbott's *Hellenica* (1880).

Thulé (Θούλη). An island in the northern part of the German Ocean, regarded by the ancients as the most northerly point in the whole earth, and by some supposed to have been Iceland; by others, one of the Shetland group. It is first noticed by Pythius, the Greek navigator of Massilia (Marseilles), who says that it was six days' sail from Britain. (See PYTHIUS.) In literature it was accepted as the most northerly part of the earth (Verg. *Georg.* i. 30), whence the phrase "ultima Thulé."

Thurii (Θούριοι), more rarely **Thurium** (Θούριον). Now Terra Nuova; a Greek city in Lucania, founded B.C. 443, near the site of the ancient Sybaris, which had been destroyed more than sixty years before. (See SYBARIS.) It was built by the remains of the population of Sybaris, assisted by

Coin of Thurii. (Fourth century B.C.)

colonists from all parts of Greece, but especially from Athens. Among these colonists were the historian Herodotus and the orator Lysias. The new city, from which the remains of the Sybarites were soon expelled, rapidly attained great power and prosperity, and became one of the most important Greek towns in the south of Italy. See Pappritz, *Thurii* (1890).

Thyădes. See THYIA.

Thyămis (Θύαμις). Now Kalama; a river in Epirus, forming the boundary between Thesprotia and the district of Cestryna.

Thyestes (Θυέστης). The son of Pelops and Hippodamia, was the brother of Atreus and the father of Aegisthus. See ATREUS and AEGISTHUS.

Thyia (Θυία). A daughter of Castalius or Cephisseus, became by Apollo the mother of Delphus. She is said to have been the first to have sacrificed to Dionysus, and to have celebrated orgies in his honour. From her the Attic women, who went yearly to Mount Parnassus to celebrate the Dionysiac orgies with the Delphian Thyiades, received themselves the name of THYĬADES or THYĂDES. This word, however, comes from θύω, and properly signifies the raging or frantic women. See MAENAS.

Thymbra (Θύμβρη). (1) A city of the Troad, north of Ilium Vetus, with a celebrated temple of Apollo, who derived from this place the epithet Thymbraeus. (2) A wooded district in Phrygia, no doubt connected with THYMBRIUM.

Thymbrium (Θύμβριον). A small town of Phrygia, ten parasangs west of Tyriaeum, with the so-called fountain of Midas (Xen. *Anab.* i. 2).

Thymbrius (Θύμβριος). Now Thimbrek; a river of the Troad, falling into the Scamander.

Thymĕle (θυμέλη). The altar of Dionysus which stood in the centre of the orchestra in the Greek theatre. (See THEATRUM.) There was no thymelé in the Roman theatre, as the orchestra there was given up to the audience.

Thymĕlé. A celebrated *mīma* or female actress in the reign of Domitian, with whom she was a great favourite (Juv. i. 35; viii. 197).

Thymelĭci (θυμελικοί). The chorus in the Greek theatre, so called from the dance around the thymelé (q. v.). The word is opposed in meaning to σκηνικοί, the regular actors who performed on the stage (Vitruv. v. 7, 2).

Thymoetes (Θυμοίτης). One of the elders of Troy, whose son was killed by the order of Priam, because a soothsayer had predicted that Troy would be destroyed by a boy born on the day on which this child was born. See PARIS.

Thyni (Θυνοί). A Thracian people, whose original abodes were near Salmydessus, but who afterwards passed over into Bithynia (q. v.).

Thynia (Θυνία). (1) The land of the Thyni in Thrace. (2) Another name for Bithynia.

Thyōné (Θυώνη). The name of Semelé, under which Dionysus brought her from Hades, and introduced her among the immortals. Hence Dionysus is also called THYONEUS. See SEMELÉ.

Thyrea (Θυρέα). The chief town in Cynuria, the district on the borders of Laconia and Argolis, was situated upon a height on the bay of the sea called after it SINUS THYREĀTES. The territory of Thyrea was called THYREĀTIS.

Bacchic Worshipper carrying a Thyrsus. (Pompeian painting.)

Thyrsĭger. One who carries the *thyrsus* (q.v.). An epithet applied to Bacchus.

Thyrsus (θύρσος). A staff (originally a spear) carried by Dionysus and his attendants, and wreathed with ivy and vine-leaves, terminating at the top in a pine-cone.

Thyssagĕtae (Θυσσαγέται). A people of Sarmatia Asiatica, on the eastern shores of the Palus Maeotis (Sea of Azov) (Herod. iv. 122).

Tiāra (τιάρα) and **Tiāras** (τιάρας). A tiara; really a sort of cap or fez worn by the Persians, Armenians, Parthians, and other Asiatics. See MITRA.

Royal Tiara of an Armenian King. (Caylus, from a gem.)

Tibarēni (Τιβαρηνοί) or **Tibări** (Τίβαροι). A quiet agricultural people on the northern coast of Pontus, east of the river Iris.

Tiberias (Τιβεριάς). (1) A city of Galilee, on the southwestern shore of the Lake of Tiberias, and built by Herod Antipas in honour of the emperor Tiberius. (2) Or GENNESĂRET, also the Sea of Galilee, in the Old Test. Chinnereth, now Bahr Tubariyeh, the second of the three lakes in Palestine formed by the course of the Jordan. (See IORDANES.) Its length is eleven or twelve geographical miles, and its breadth from five to six. It lies deep among fertile hills, has very clear and sweet water, and is full of excellent fish.

Tiberīnus. One of the mythical kings of Alba, son of Capetus, and father of Agrippa, is said to have been drowned in crossing the river Albula, which was hence called Tiberis. The name is thus that of the personified Tiber who was solemnly invoked by the Romans (Cic. *N. D.* iii. 20, 52). He had a shrine on the Insula Tiberina.

Tibĕris also **Tibris, Tybris, Thybris, Amnis Tiberīnus** or simply **Tiberīnus.** Now the Tiber or Tevere; the chief river in Central Italy, on which stands the city of Rome. It is said to have been originally called ALBŬLA, and to have received the name of TIBĔRIS in consequence of Tiberinus, king of Alba, having been drowned in it. It has been supposed that Albula was the Latin and Tiberis the Etruscan name of the river. The Tiber rises in the Apennines, near Tifernum, and flows in a southwesterly direction, separating Etruria from Umbria, the land of the Sabines, and Latium. After flowing about 110 miles it receives the Nar (Nera), and from its confluence with this river its regular navigation begins. Three miles above Rome, at the distance of nearly seventy miles from the Nar, it receives the Anio (Teverone), and from this point becomes a river of considerable importance. Within the walls of Rome, the Tiber is about 300 feet wide and from twelve to eighteen feet deep. After heavy rains the river in ancient times, as at the present day, frequently overflowed its banks, and did considerable mischief to the lower parts of the city (Liv. xxiv. 9, xxx. 38, xxxv. 9, 21, xxxviii. 28; Dio Cass. xxxix. 61, liii. 20). To guard against these dangers Augustus instituted the *Curatores Alvei Tiberis* (Suet. *Aug.* 37). At Rome the maritime navigation of the river begins; and at eighteen miles from the city, and about four miles from the coast, it divides into two arms, forming an island, which was sacred to Venus and called Insula Sacra (Isola Sagra). The left branch of the river runs into the sea by Ostia, which was the ancient harbour of Rome; but in consequence of the accumulation of sand at the mouth of the left branch, the right branch was widened by Trajan, and was made the regular harbour of the city under the name of Portus Romanus, Portus Augusti, or simply Portus. (See OSTIA.) The whole length of the Tiber, with its windings, is about 200 miles. The waters of the river are muddy and yellowish, whence it is frequently called by the Roman poets *flavus Tiberis*. The poets also give it the epithets of *Tyrrhenus*, because it flowed past Etruria during the whole of its course, and of *Lydius*, because the Etruscans are said to have been of Lydian origin. See ETRURIA.

Tiberius. (1) An emperor of Rome from A. D. 14 to 37. His full name was TIBERIUS CLAUDIUS NERO CAESAR. He was the son of T. Claudius Nero and of Livia, and was born on the 16th of November, B.C. 42, before his mother married Augustus. Tiberius was tall and strongly made, and his health was good. His face was handsome, and his eyes large. He was carefully educated, and became well acquainted with Greek and Latin literature, his master in rhetoric being Theodorus of Gadara. Though not without military courage, as his life shows, he had a great timidity of character, and was of a jealous and suspicious temper; and these qualities rendered him cruel after he had acquired power. There can be little doubt that his morose reserve and his dissimulation had been increased, if not created, by his relations to Augustus. As emperor the difficulties of his position, and the influence of Livia and still more of Seianus, increased his tendency to jealousy and suspicion of all who seemed rivals or dangerous from their popularity. The system of espionage and delation (see DELATORES) once begun could only increase with each act of tyranny and cruelty, till his rule became a veritable reign of terror. Yet in reading his history, especially the tales of his monstrous and incredible licentiousness, it must be recollected that Tacitus and Suetonius both wrote with a strong bias against him and his rule, and were ready to accept as true the worst scandals which were handed down. If Velleius was prejudiced in the other direction, it is at least right to adopt some part of his less unfavourable portrait and to imagine that the old age of Tiberius was not so absolutely contradictory of his youth as it is sometimes made to appear. The cruelty of his rule applied only to Rome. The testimony of Iosephus and Philo shows that his provincial government was just and lenient.

In B.C. 11, Augustus compelled Tiberius, much against his will, to divorce his wife, Vipsania Agrippina, and to marry Iulia, the widow of Agrippa, and daughter of the emperor, with whom Tiberius, however, did not long live in harmony. Tiberius was thus brought into still closer contact with the imperial family; but as Gaius and Lucius Caesar, the grandsons of Augustus, were still living, the prospect of Tiberius succeeding to the imperial power seemed very remote. He was employed on various military services. In 20, he was sent by Augustus to restore Tigranes to the throne of Armenia. It was during this campaign that Horace addressed one of his epistles to Iulius Florus (i. 12), who was serving under Tiberius. In 15, Drusus and his brother Tiberius were engaged in warfare with the Raeti, and the exploits of the two brothers were sung by Horace (*Carm.* iv. 4, 14). In 13, Tiberius was consul with P. Quintilius Varus. In 11, while his brother Drusus was fighting against the Germans, Tiberius conducted the war against the Dalmatians and against the Pannonians. Drusus died in 9, owing to a fall from his horse. On the news of the accident, Tiberius was sent by Augustus to Drusus, whom he found just alive. Tiberius returned to the war in Germany, and crossed the Rhine. In 7 he was consul a second time. In 6 he obtained the *tribunicia potestas* for five years, but during this year he retired with the emperor's permission to Rhodes, where he spent the next seven years. Tacitus says that his chief reason for leaving Rome was to get away from his wife, who treated him with contempt, and whose licentious life was no secret to her husband; probably, too, he was unwilling to stay at Rome when the grandsons of Augustus were attaining years of maturity, for there was mutual jealousy between them and Tiberius. He returned to Rome A.D. 2. He was relieved from one trouble during his absence, for his wife Iulia had been banished to the island of Pandataria (B.C. 2), and he never saw her again. (See IULIA.) After the deaths of L. Caesar (A.D. 2) and C. Caesar (A.D. 4), Augustus adopted Tiberius, with the view of leaving to him the imperial power; and at the same time he required Tiberius to adopt Germanicus, the son of his brother Drusus, though Tiberius had a son Drusus by his wife Vipsania. From the year of his adoption to the death of Augustus, Tiberius was in command of the Roman armies, though he visited Rome several times. He was sent into Germany A.D. 4. He reduced all Illyricum to subjection A.D. 9; and in A.D. 12 he had the honour of a triumph at Rome for his German and Dalmatian victories.

Tiberius. (Vatican.)

On the death of Augustus at Nola, on the 19th of August, A.D. 14, Tiberius, who was on his way to Illyricum, was immediately summoned home by his mother, Livia. He assumed the imperial power without any opposition, affecting all the while a great reluctance. He began his reign by putting to death Postumus Agrippa, the surviving grandson of Augustus, and he alleged that it was done pursuant to the command of the late emperor. When he felt himself sure in his place, he began to strengthen the principate. He took from the popular assembly the election of the magistrates, and transferred it to the Senate. The news of the death of Augustus roused a mutiny among the legions in Pannonia, which was quelled by Drusus, the son of Tiberius. The armies on the Rhine under Germanicus showed a disposition to reject Tiberius, and if Germanicus had been inclined to try the fortune of a campaign, he might have had the assistance of the German armies against his uncle. But Germanicus restored discipline to the army by his firmness, and maintained his fidelity to the new emperor. The first year of his reign was marked by the death of Iulia, whom Augustus had removed from Pandataria to Rhegium. The death of Germanicus in the East, in A.D. 19, relieved Tiberius from all fear of a rival claimant to the throne; and it was believed by many that Germanicus had been poisoned by order of Tiberius. (See GERMANICUS.) From this time Tiberius began to indulge with less restraint in his love of tyranny, and many distinguished senators were soon put to death on the charge of treason against the emperor (*laesa maiestas*). Notwithstanding his suspicious nature, Tiberius gave his complete confidence to Seianus, who for many years possessed the real government of the State. This ambitious man aimed at the imperial power. In 23, Drusus, the son of Tiberius, was poisoned by the contrivance of Seianus. Three years afterwards (26) Tiberius left Rome, and withdrew into Campania. He never returned to the city. He left on the pretext of dedicating temples in Campania, but the real cause was probably his dislike to Rome, where he knew that he was unpopular; and Seianus was only too anxious to encourage any feeling which would keep the emperor at a distance from the city. That Tiberius went because he wished to hide his licentiousness in this place of retirement may be set down as a silly invention, for Rome was not a place where licentiousness was hated. He took up his residence (27) in the island of Capreae, at a short distance from the Campanian coast. The death of Livia (29), the emperor's mother, released Tiberius from one cause of anxiety. He had long been tired of her, because she wished to exercise authority, and one object in leaving Rome was to be out of her way. Livia's death gave Seianus and Tiberius free scope, for Tiberius never entirely released himself from a kind of subjection to his mother, and Seianus did not venture to attempt the overthrow of Livia's influence. The destruction of Agrippina and her children was now the chief purpose of Seianus; but he finally got from Tiberius (31) the reward that was his just desert, an ignominious death. (See SEIANUS.) The death of Seianus was followed by the execution of his friends; and for the remainder of the reign of Tiberius, Rome continued to be the scene of tragic occurrences. Tiberius died on the 16th of March, 37, at the villa of Lucullus, in Misenum. He was seventy-eight years of age, and had reigned twenty-two years. He was succeeded by Gaius (Caligula), the son of Germanicus, but, according to Tacitus, he had himself appointed no successor (Tac. *Ann.* vi. 46), though he had appointed Gaius the heir of his private property (Suet. *Tib.* 76) in conjunction with Tiberius Gemellus, whom Gaius afterwards put to death. On the other hand, Iosephus has a story of Tiberius committing the Empire to Gaius (*Ant.* xviii. 6, 9). Tiberius did not die a natural death. It was known that his end was rapidly approaching, and having had a fainting-fit, he was supposed to be dead. Thereupon Gaius came forth and was saluted as emperor; but he was alarmed by the intelligence that Tiberius had recovered and called for something to eat. Gaius was so frightened that he did not know what to do; but Macro, the prefect of the Praetorians, with more presence of mind, gave orders that a quantity of clothes should be thrown on Tiberius, and that he should be left alone (Tac. *Ann.* v. 50; Dio Cass. lviii. 28). Suetonius mentions a suspicion that Tiberius was poisoned at the last by Gaius (Suet. *Tib.* 73; *Cal.* 12). Tiberius wrote a brief commentary of his own life, the only book that the emperor Domitian studied (Suet. *Tib.* 67; *Dom.* 20), and also Greek poems, and a lyric poem on the death of L. Caesar (Suet. *Tib.* 70). Tiberius, both as a ruler and as a man, has not lacked defenders in modern times, among them Dean Merivale in his *Romans under the Empire* (1865); Beesly, *Catiline, Clodius, and Tiberius* (1878); and Baring-Gould, *The Tragedy of the Caesars*, vol. i. (1892). For the adverse view see Boissier, *L'Opposition sous les Césars* (1875). For the general history of his reign see Pasch, *Zur Kritik der Geschichte des Kaisers Tiberius* (Altenburg, 1866); Stahr, *Tiberius* (Berlin, 1873); H. Schiller, *Geschichte der römischen Kaiserzeit* (Gotha, 1883); and Freytag, *Tiberius und Tacitus* (Berlin, 1870). See also the essay prefixed to Furneaux's *Annales*, vol. i. (1884).

(2) TIBERIUS GEMELLUS, son of Drusus junior (DRUSUS, No. 5), twin with another son, who died early. He was therefore grandson of Tiberius and regarded as a dangerous rival by Caligula, who put him to death soon after his accession (Suet. *Tib.* 54; *Cal.* 14, 23). It is said that Tiberius doubted his legitimacy. This and his youth may have been reasons against his being named successor to the Empire (Suet. *Tib.* 62; Tac. *Ann.* vi. 46).

(3) A philosopher and sophist, of unknown time, the author of numerous works on grammar and rhetoric. One of his works, on the figures in the orations of Demosthenes (*Περὶ τῶν παρὰ Δημοσθένει Σχημάτων*), is still extant. It is edited by Spengel (1856).

Tibia (*αὐλός*). A pipe, the commonest musical instrument of the Greeks and Romans. It was very frequently a hollow cane, perforated with holes in the proper places. In other instances it was made of some kind of wood, especially box, and was bored with a gimlet. When a single pipe was used by itself, the performer upon it, as well as the instrument, was called *monaulos*. Among the varieties of the single pipe the most remarkable were the bagpipe, the performer upon which was called *utricularius* or *ἀσκαύλης*: and the *αὐλὸς πλάγιος* or *πλαγίαυλος*, which, as its name implies, had a mouth-piece inserted into it at right angles. Pan was the reputed inventor of this kind of tibia as well as of the *fistula* or *syrinx*. (See SYRINX.) But among the Greeks and Romans it was much more usual to play on two pipes at the same time. Hence a performance (*tibicinium*) on this instrument, even when executed by a single person, was called *canere* or *cantare tibiis*. This act is exhibited in very numerous works of ancient art, and often in such a way as to make it manifest that the two pipes were perfectly distinct, and not connected, as some have supposed, by a common mouth-piece. The mouth-pieces of the two pipes often passed through a *capistrum*. See. CAPISTRUM.

Three different kinds of pipes were originally used to produce music in the Dorian, Phrygian, and Lydian modes. It appears, also, that to produce the Phrygian mode the pipe had only two holes (τρυπήματα) above and that it terminated in a horn bending upwards. It thus approached to

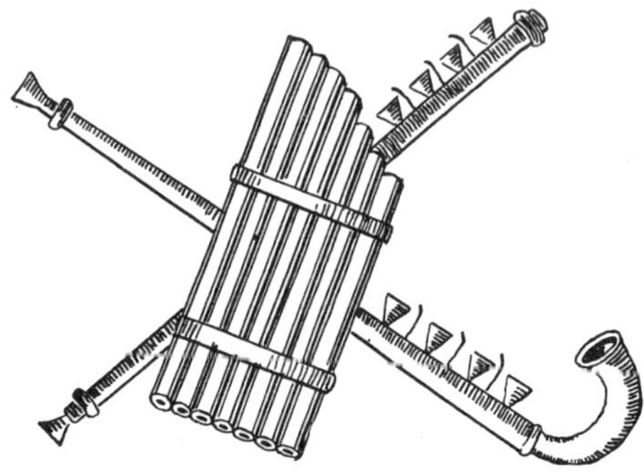

Tibiae and Syrinx

the nature of a trumpet, and produced slow, grave, and solemn tunes. The Lydian mode was much quicker, and more varied and animating. Horace mentions "Lydian pipes" as a proper accompaniment when he is celebrating the praise of ancient heroes. The Lydians themselves used this instrument in leading their troops to battle; and the pipes employed for the purpose are distinguished by Herodotus as "male and female"—i. e. probably bass and treble—corresponding to the ordinary sexual difference in the human voice. The corresponding Latin terms are *tibia dextra* and *sinistra:* the respective instruments are supposed to have been so called because the former was more properly held in the right hand and the latter in the left. The *tibia dextra* was used to lead or commence a piece of music, and the *sinistra* followed it as an accompaniment. The comedies of Terence having been accompanied by the pipe, the following notices are prefixed to explain the kind of music appropriate to each: *tibiis paribus*, i. e. with pipes in the same mode; *tibiis imparibus*, pipes in different modes; *tibiis duabus dextris*, two pipes of low pitch; *tibiis paribus dextris et sinistris*, pipes in the same mode, and of both low and high pitch. The use of the pipe among the Greeks and Romans was three-fold—viz. at sacrifices (*tibiae sacrificae*), entertainments (*ludicrae*), and funerals. (See FUNUS.) The pipe was not confined anciently to the male sex, but αὐλητρίδες, or female *tibicines*, were very common. See Gevaert, *Histoire et Théorie de la Musique dans l'Antiquité*, ii. pp. 270 foll. and 647 foll. (Ghent, 1881).

Tibiālē (περικνημίς). A sort of legging or gaiter encircling the shin (*tibia*) from the knee to the ankle, serving the purpose of modern stockings and drawers. It was worn by persons in delicate health, such as the emperor Augustus (Suet. *Aug.* 82), and by soldiers and huntsmen. Cf. FASCIA.

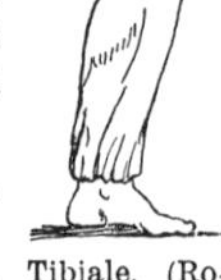

Tibiale. (Roman bas-relief.)

Tibīcen (αὐλητής). A flute-player. See TIBIA.

Tibiscus or **Tibissus**, probably the same as the **Parthiscus** or **Parthissus**. Now the Theiss. A river of Dacia, forming the western boundary of that country.

Tibullus, ALBIUS, a Roman elegiac poet of equestrian family. The date of his birth is uncertain, but he died young, soon after Vergil. His birth is therefore placed by conjecture B.C. 54, and his death B.C. 19. Of his youth and education absolutely nothing is known. The estate belonging to the equestrian ancestors of Tibullus was at Pedum, between Tibur and Praenesté. This property, like that of the other great poets of the day, Vergil and Horace, had been either entirely or partially confiscated during the Civil Wars; yet Tibullus retained or recovered part of it, perhaps through Messalla, and spent there the better portion of his short, but peaceful and happy, life (Tib. i. 1, 19; cf. Hor. *Ep.* i. 4, 7). When his friend and patron, Messalla, was going to his prefecture in Asia, B.C. 30, Tibullus, after first refusing, eventually agreed to accompany him, but fell ill on the way at Corcyra and returned thence to Rome (Tib. i. 1; i. 3). Afterwards, in 28, he went to Aquitania with Messalla, who had been sent by Augustus to suppress a formidable insurrection which had broken out in this province. Part of the glory of the Aquitanian campaign, which Tibullus celebrates in language of unwonted loftiness, redounds, according to the poet, to his own fame. He was present at the battle of Atax (Aude in Languedoc), which quelled the Aquitanian rebellion (Tib. i. 7). So ceased the active life of Tibullus; his remaining history is the chronicle of his poetry and of the loves which inspired it. The first object of his attachment is celebrated under the poetic name of Delia: according to Apuleius (*Apol.* 10) her real name was Plania. To Delia are addressed the first six elegies of the first book. The poet's attachment to Delia had begun before he left Rome for Aquitania. But Delia seems to have been faithless during his absence from Rome. On his return from Corcyra he found her ill, and attended her with affectionate solicitude (*Eleg.* i. 5), and hoped to induce her to retire with him into the country. But first a richer lover appears to have supplanted him with the inconstant Delia, and afterwards there appears a husband in his way. The second book of elegies is chiefly devoted to a new mistress named Nemesis (cf. Ovid, *Am.* iii. 9, 32; Mart. viii. 73, 7). It is probable, though not certain, that this Nemesis is the same as the Glycera mentioned only by Horace (*Carm.* i. 33, 2), who reproves him for dwelling so long in his plaintive elegies on the "pitiless Glycera."

The poetry of his contemporaries shows Tibullus to have been a gentle and singularly amiable man. To Horace especially he was an object of warm attachment. Besides the ode which alludes to his passion for Glycera (Hor. *Carm.* i. 33), the epistle to Tibullus gives the most full and pleasing view of his poetical retreat, and of his character; it is written by a kindred spirit. Horace does homage to that perfect purity of taste which distinguishes the poetry of Tibullus, and he takes pride in the candid but favourable judgment of his own Satires. The time of Tibullus he supposes to be shared between the finishing his exquisite small poems, which were to surpass even those of Cassius of Parma, up to that time the models of this kind of composition, and the enjoyment of the country. Tibullus possessed, according to his friend's notions, all the blessings of life—a competent fortune, favour with the great, fame, health; and he seemed to know how to enjoy all those blessings.

The first two books alone of the elegies under the name of Tibullus are of undoubted authenticity. The third is the work of another, a very inferior poet, whether Lygdamus be a real or fictitious name. This poet was much younger than Tibullus, for he was born in the year of the battle of Mutina, 43. It is probable that he was a less gifted member of Messalla's literary circle: this connection with the patron of Tibullus might account for his elegies being confused with the genuine poems of Tibullus. The hexameter poem on Messalla, which opens the fourth book, is so inferior that, although a successful elegiac poet may have failed when he attempted epic verse, it cannot readily be ascribed to a writer of the exquisite taste of Tibullus. If it is his, it must be regarded as an early poem written in an imitative manner, when he was under the full influence of the Alexandrian School. The smaller elegies of the fourth book have all the inimitable grace and simplicity of Tibullus. With the exception of the thirteenth (of which some lines are hardly surpassed by Tibullus himself) these poems relate to the love of a certain Sulpicia, a woman of noble birth, for Cerinthus, the real or fictitious name of a beautiful youth. Nor is there any improbability in supposing that Tibullus may have written elegies in the name or by the desire of Sulpicia. If Sulpicia was herself the poetess, she approached nearer to Tibullus than any other writer of elegies. The first book of elegies alone seems to have been published during the author's life, probably soon after the triumph of Messalla (27). The second book probably did not appear till after the death of Tibullus. With it may have been published the elegies of his imitator, perhaps his friend and associate in the society of Messalla, Lygdamus (if that be a real name), i. e. the third book and likewise the fourth, made up of poems belonging, as it were, to this intimate society of Messalla; the *Panegyricus Messallae* by some unnamed author, which, feeble as it is, seems to be of that age; the poems in the name of Sulpicia, with the concluding one, the thirteenth, a fragment of Tibullus himself. There are editions of Tibullus by Lachmann (Berlin, 1829); Dissen, 2 vols. (Göttingen, 1835); Bährens (Leipzig, 1878); Hiller, with a good index (Leipzig, 1885); selections by Ramsay. There is an English verse translation by Cranstoun, with notes (London, 1872). See Sellar's *Roman Poets of the Republic* for a good literary estimate of the poet.

Tibur. Now Tivoli; one of the most ancient towns of Latium, sixteen miles northeast of Rome, situated on the slope of a hill (hence called by Horace *supinum Tibur*), on the left bank of the Anio, which here forms a magnificent waterfall. It became subject to Rome with the other Latin cities on the final subjugation of Latium in B.C. 338. Under the Romans Tibur continued to be a large and flourishing town, since the salubrity and beautiful scenery of the place led many of the most distinguished Roman nobles to build here magnificent villas. Of these the most splendid was the villa of the emperor Hadrian, in the extensive remains of which many valuable specimens of ancient art have been discovered. Here also the celebrated Zenobia lived after adorning the triumph of her conqueror, Aurelian. Horace likewise had a country-house in the neighbourhood of Tibur, which he preferred to all his other residences. See Meyer, *Tibur* (1883).

Villa of Hadrian at Tibur. (Restoration by Bühlmann.)

Ticīnum. Now Pavia; a town of the Laevi, or, according to others, of the Insubres, in Gallia Cisalpina, on the left bank of the Ticinus. The Lombards called it Papia, whence its modern name.

Ticīnus. Now the Tessino; an important river in Gallia Cisalpina. It rises in Mons Adula, and after flowing through Lacus Verbanus (Lago Maggiore), falls into the Padus (Po) near Ticinum. It was upon the bank of this river that Hannibal gained his first victory over the Romans by the defeat of P. Scipio, B.C. 218.

Ticket. See TESSERA.

Tifāta. A mountain in Campania, east of Capua, where Sulla defeated the proconsul Norbanus (Vell. Pat. ii. 25).

Tifernum. (1) TIBERĪNUM. Now Città di Castello; a town of Umbria, near the sources of the river Tiber, whence its surname, and upon the confines of Etruria. (2) METAURENSĒ. Now S. Angelo in Vado; a town in Umbria, east of the preceding, on the river Metaurus. (3) A town in Samnium, on the river Tifernus.

Tifernus. Now the Biferno; a river of Samnium, rising in the Apennines, and flowing through the country of the Frentani into the Adriatic.

Tigellīnus, Sophonius. Son of a native of Agrigentum, the minister of Nero's worst passions, and of all his favourites the most obnoxious to the Roman people. On the accession of Otho, Tigellinus was compelled to put an end to his own life (Tac. *Ann.* bk. xv.; *Hist.* i. 72).

Tigellius Hermogĕnes. See Hermogenes.

Tight-rope Dancing. See Funambulus.

Tignarius, sc. *faber*. A carpenter and builder, or, more specifically, a roofer; one who puts together the beams (*tigna*) of a roof (Cic. *Brut.* 73).

Tigrānes (Τιγράνης). The name of several kings of Armenia. (1) Reigned B.C. 96–56 or 55. In 83 he made himself master of the whole Syrian monarchy, from the Euphrates to the sea. In 69, having refused to deliver up his son-in-law, Mithridates, to the Romans, Lucullus invaded Armenia, defeated the mighty host which Tigranes led against him, and followed up his victory by the capture of Tigranocerta. Subsequently Tigranes recovered his dominions; but on the approach of Pompey, in 66, he hastened to make overtures of submission, and laid his tiara at his feet, together with a sum of 6000 talents. Pompey left him in possession of Armenia proper, with the title of king. Tigranes died in 56 or 55. (2) Son of Artavasdes, and grandson of the preceding.

Tigranes.

Tigranocerta (τὰ Τιγρανόκερτα). The later capital of Armenia, built by Tigranes on a height by the river Nicephorius, in the valley between Mount Masius and Niphates.

Tigris (ὁ Τίγρις). A great river of western Asia, rises from several sources on the south side of that part of the Tauris chain called Niphates, in Armenia, and flows southeast, first through the narrow valley between Mount Masius and the prolongation of Mount Niphates, and then through the great plain which is bounded on the east by the last-named chain, till it falls into the head of the Persian Gulf, after receiving the Euphrates from the west.

Tigurīni. A tribe of the Helvetii, who joined the Cimbri in invading the country of the Allobroges in Gaul, where they defeated the consul L. Cassius Longinus, B.C. 107. They formed in the time of Caesar the most important of the four cantons (*pagi*) into which the Helvetii were divided. See Helvetii.

Tile. See Fictilé; Imbrex; Tegula.

Tilphusium (Τιλφούσιον). A town in Boeotia, situated upon a mountain of the same name south of Lake Copaïs, and between Coronea and Haliartus. It derived its name from the fountain Tilphusa, which was sacred to Apollo, and where Tiresias is said to have been buried (Pausan. ix. 33, 1).

Timaeus. (1) The historian, was the son of Andromachus, tyrant of Tauromenium in Sicily, and was born about B.C. 352. He was banished from Sicily by Agathocles, and passed his exile at Athens, where he had lived 50 years when he wrote the 34th book of his history. He probably died about 256. The great work of Timaeus was a history of Sicily from the earliest times to 264. The fragments are edited by C. and Th. Müller (Paris, 1841). Timaeus is said to have been the first to record events by Olympiads. (See Olympias.) (2) Of Locri, in Italy, a Pythagorean philosopher, is said to have been a teacher of Plato. He gives his name to a dialogue of Plato, in which is given the account of the mythical island Atlantis, lying in the Western Ocean, and supposed by many in modern times to have been suggested by vague stories of the American continent.

Timagĕnes. A rhetorician and an historian, who was a native of Alexandria, from which place he was carried as a prisoner to Rome, where he opened a school of rhetoric, and taught with great success. (Suid. s. h. v.)

Timanthes (Τιμάνθης). A celebrated Greek painter at Sicyon, contemporary with Zeuxis and Parrhasius, about B.C. 400. The masterpiece of Timanthes was his celebrated picture of the sacrifice of Iphigenia, in which Agamemnon was painted with his face hidden in his mantle (Pliny, *H. N.* xxxv. 73). See the illustration under Iphigenia.

Timāvus. A small river in the north of Italy, forming the boundary between Istria and Venetia, and falling into the Sinus Tergestinus in the Adriatic, between Tergesté and Aquileia. It is now the Timavo.

Time, Measurement of. See Calendarium; Horologium.

Timēma (τίμημα, "valuation," "assessment"). (1) The value at which an Athenian citizen's property was rated for taxation. (See Eisphora; Solon.) (2) In legal language, a fine. See Judicial Procedure.

Time-pieces. See Horologium.

Timocratia (τιμοκρατία, "government according to property-tax or valuation of property"). The name given among the Greeks to that form of government in which, while the citizens were equal in other respects, their share in the government was regulated by a certain gradation corresponding to the amount of their property. Thus those whose property entailed the greater expenditure in public services possessed proportionately greater privileges. The constitution established at Athens by Solon was founded on this principle. See Oligarchia; Solon.

Timocreon (Τιμοκρέων). A lyric poet of Rhodes, celebrated for the bitter and pugnacious spirit of his works, and especially for his attacks on Themistocles and Simonides (Athen. pp. 415, 416; Plut. *Them.* 21).

Timoleon (Τιμολέων). The son of Timodemus or Timaenetus and Demaristé. He belonged to one of the noblest families at Corinth. His early life was stained by a dreadful deed of blood. We are told that so ardent was his love of liberty that when his brother Timophanes endeavoured to make himself tyrant of their native city, Timoleon murdered him rather than allow him to destroy the liberty of the State. At the request of the Greek cities of Sicily, the Corinthians despatched Timoleon with a small force in B.C. 344 to repel the Carthaginians from that island. He obtained possession of Syracuse, and then proceeded to expel the tyrants from the other Greek cities of Sicily, but was interrupted in this undertaking by a formidable invasion of the Carthaginians, who landed at Lilybaeum, in 339, with an immense army, under the command of Hasdrubal and Hamilcar, consisting of 70,000 foot and 10,000 horse. Timoleon could only induce 12,000 men to march with him against the Carthaginians; but with this small force he gained a brilliant victory over the Carthaginians on the river Crimissus (339). The Carthaginians were glad to conclude a treaty with Timoleon in 338, by which the river Halycus was fixed as the boundary of the Carthaginian and Greek dominions in Sicily. Subsequently he expelled almost all the tyrants from the Greek cities in Sicily, and established democracies instead. Timoleon, however, was in reality the ruler of Sicily, for all the States consulted him on every matter of importance; and the wisdom of his rule is attested by the flourishing condition of the island for several years even after his death. He died in 337. His life was written by Plutarch.

Timomăchus (Τιμόμαχος). A distinguished Byzantine painter who lived in the time of Iulius Caesar. The latter purchased two of his pictures, the *Aiax* and *Medea*, for the immense sum of eighty Attic talents (nearly $90,000), and dedicated them in the Temple of Venus Genetrix (Pliny, *H. N.* vii. 126, xxxv. 136). It is held by many critics that Timomachus belonged to the Alexandrine Period of Greek art, and that Pliny was mistaken in supposing that the pictures which Caesar bought were painted in Caesar's time.

Timon (Τίμων). (1) The son of Timarchus of Phlius, a philosopher of the sect of the Skeptics, who flourished in the reign of Ptolemy Philadelphus, about B.C. 279 and onwards. He first studied philosophy at Megara, under Stilpo, and then returned home and married. He next went to Elis with his wife, and heard Pyrrho, whose tenets he adopted. Driven from Elis by straitened circumstances, he spent some time on the Hellespont and the Propontis, and taught at Chalcedon as a sophist with such success that he realized a fortune. He then removed to Athens, where he passed the remainder of his life, with the exception of a short residence at Thebes. He died at the age of almost ninety.

Timon appears to have been endowed by nature with a powerful and active mind, and with that quick perception of the follies of men which betrays its possessor into a spirit of universal distrust both of men and truths, so as to make him a skeptic in philosophy and a satirist in everything. His agnosticism (to use a modern term) is shown by his saying that man need only know three things—viz. what is the nature of things, how we are related to them, and what we can gain from them; but as our knowledge of things must always be subjective and unreal, we can only live in a state of suspended judgment. He wrote numerous works both in prose and poetry. The most celebrated of his poems were the satiric compositions called *silli* (σίλλοι), a word of somewhat doubtful etymology, but which undoubtedly describes metrical compositions of a character at once ludicrous and sarcastic. The invention of this species of poetry is ascribed to Xenophanes of Colophon. (See XENOPHANES.) The *Silli* of Timon were in three books, in the first of which he spoke in his own person, and the other two are in the form of a dialogue between the author and Xenophanes of Colophon, in which Timon proposed questions, to which Xenophanes replied at length. The subject was a sarcastic account of the tenets of all philosophers, living and dead—an unbounded field for skepticism and satire. They were in hexameter verse, and from the way in which they are mentioned by the ancient writers, as well as from the few fragments of them which have come down to us, it is evident that they were very admirable productions of their kind (Diog. Laërt. ix. 12, 109–115; Euseb. *Praep. Ev.* xiv. p. 761). The fragments of his poems are collected by Wölke, *De Graecorum Syllis* (Warsaw, 1820), and by Paul in his *Dissertatio de Sillis* (Berlin, 1821). See PARODIA.

(2) The Misanthrope (ὁ μισάνθρωπος), lived in the time of the Peloponnesian War. He was an Athenian, of the demus of Colyttus, and his father's name was Echecratides. In consequence of the ingratitude he experienced and the disappointments he suffered from his early friends and companions, he secluded himself entirely from the world, admitting no one to his society except Alcibiades, in whose reckless and variable disposition he probably found pleasure in tracing and studying an image of the world he had abandoned; and at last he is said to have died in consequence of refusing to suffer a surgeon to come to him and set a broken limb. One of Lucian's pieces bears his name (Aristoph. *Av.* 1548; *Lys.* 809; Plut. *Ant.* 70; Lucian, *Timon;* Suid. s. h. v.). See Binder, *Ueber Timon den Misanthropen* (1856). His name is embalmed in English literature in Shakspeare's play *Timon of Athens.*

Timotheus (Τιμόθεος). (1) A celebrated musician and poet of the later Athenian dithyramb. He was a native of Miletus, and the son of Thersander. He was born B.C. 446, and died in 357, in the ninetieth year of his age. He was at first unfortunate in his professional efforts. Even the Athenians, fond as they were of novelty, were offended at the bold innovations of Timotheus, and hissed his performance. On this occasion it is said that Euripides encouraged Timotheus by the prediction that he would soon have the theatres at his feet. This prediction appears to have been accomplished in the vast popularity which Timotheus afterwards enjoyed. He delighted in the most artificial and intricate forms of musical expression, and he used instrumental music, without a vocal accompaniment, to a greater extent than any previous composer. Perhaps the most important of his innovations, as the means of introducing all the others, was his addition to the number of the strings of the *cithara*, which he seems to have increased to eleven. (2) The son of Conon, the famous general. He was himself a distinguished Athenian soldier. He was first appointed to a public command in B.C. 378; and from this time his name frequently occurs as one of the Athenian generals down to 356. In this year he was associated with Iphicrates, Menestheus, and Chares in the command of the Athenian fleet. In consequence of his failure to relieve Samos he was arraigned in 354, and condemned to the crushing fine of 100 talents (more than $100,000). Being unable to pay the fine, he withdrew to Chalcis in Euboea, where he died shortly after. The Athenians subsequently remitted nine-tenths of the penalty, and allowed his son Conon to expend the remainder on the repair of the walls, which the famous Conon had restored. (His life is written by Nepos; see Diod. xv. 81, xvi. 7, 21; and the article IPHICRATES). (3) Son of Clearchus, the tyrant of Heraclea on the Euxine, whom he succeeded in the sovereignty, B.C. 353 (Diod. xvi. 36). There is extant a letter addressed to him by Isocrates. (4) A sculptor, whose country is not mentioned, but who belonged to the later Attic school of the time of Scopas and Praxiteles. He was one of the artists who executed the bas-reliefs which adorned the frieze of the Mausoleum. He is also mentioned as the author of a statue of Asclepius at Troezen and one of Artemis which was at Rome (Pausan. ii. 32, 3; Pliny, *H. N.* xxxvi. 32).

Tinder. See IGNIARIA.

Tingis (Τίγγις). Now Tangier; a city of Mauretania, on the southern coast of the Fretum Gaditanum (Strait of Gibraltar), and a place of very great antiquity. It was made by Augustus a free city, and by Claudius a colony, and the capital of Mauretania Tingitana.

Tinia. A small river in Umbria, rising near Spoletium, and falling into the Tiber.

Tintinnabŭlum (κώδων). A bell. Ancient bells were in shape and use much like those of modern times. Thus we find mention of a door-bell in Suetonius (*Aug.* 91), of bells for summoning servants in Seneca (*De Ira*, iii. 35), of a bell announcing a sacrifice, like our church bells, in Plautus (*Pseud.* i. 3, 98), and of bells for animals' necks, like our sheep-bells, in Sidonius (*Epist.* ii. 2). The word *campana* is used of a bell in late Latin, whence the Ital. *campanile.*

Ancient Bells.

Tiresias (Τειρεσίας). A Theban, was one of the most renowned soothsayers in all antiquity. He was blind from his seventh year, but lived to a very old age. The occasion of his blindness and of his prophetic power is variously related. In the war of the Seven against Thebes he declared that Thebes should be victorious if Menoeceus would sacrifice himself; and during the war of the Epigoni, when the Thebans had been defeated, he advised them to commence negotiations of peace, and to avail themselves of the opportunity that would thus be afforded them to take to flight. He himself fled with them (or, according to others, he was carried to Delphi as a captive), but on his way he drank from the well of Tilphusa, and died. Even in the lower world Tiresias was believed to retain the powers of perception, while the souls of other mortals were mere shades, and there also he continued to use his golden staff. The blind seer Tiresias acts so prominent a part in the mythical history of Greece that there is scarcely any event with which he is not connected in some way or other; and this introduction of the seer in so many occurrences, separated by long intervals of time, was facilitated by the belief in his long life. (See especially OEDIPUS.) Tiresias is the subject of a fine poem by Lord Tennyson (1885).

Tiribazus (Τιρίβαζος). A satrap of Armenia in 401, who dogged the retreat of the Ten Thousand Greeks, but without success (Xen. *Anab.* iv. 4, vii. 8; Diod. xiv. 27). He succeeded Tithraustes as satrap of Western Asia, and favoured the views of Antalcidas. In 386 he commanded the expedition against Evagoras. Some time afterwards he conspired against Artaxerxes II., and was put to death (Plut. *Artax.* 29).

Tiridātes or **Teridātes** (Τηριδάτης). (1) The second king of Parthia. (See ARSACES II.) (2) King of Armenia, and brother of Vologeses I. (Arsaces XXIII.), king of Parthia. He was made king of Armenia by his brother, but was driven out of the kingdom by Corbulo, the Roman general, and finally received the Armenian crown from Nero at Rome in A.D. 63.

Tiro. A recruit. See TIROCINIUM.

Tiro, M. TULLIUS. The freedman of Cicero, to whom he was an object of tender affection. He appears to have been a man of very amiable disposition and highly cultivated intellect. He was not only the amanuensis of the orator, and his assistant in literary labour, but was himself an author of no mean reputation, and notices of several works from his pen have been preserved by ancient writers. After the death of Cicero, Tiro purchased a farm in the neighbourhood of Puteoli, where he lived until he reached his one hundredth year. It is usually believed that Tiro was the inventor of the art of shorthand writing (*notae Tironianae*). (See NOTAE.) He also did much to preserve, arrange, and publish the literary work of his patron, especially his voluminous personal correspondence; and he was the author of a life and vindication of the great orator (Tac. *Dial.* 17; Gell. iv. 10, xv. 16). See Mitzschke, *Tullius Tiro* (Berlin, 1875).

Tirocinium ("a recruit's term of service"; from *tiro*, a "recruit"). The Roman term for the interval between the assumption of the *toga virilis* (in the sixteenth or seventeenth year) which marked the beginning of independence and of liability to compulsory military service, and the entrance on a military career or official activity in general. Under the Republic this time was fixed at a year. It was looked upon as the last stage of education, and in this a youth qualified himself either in the army for service in war or in the Forum for a political life.

In the latter instance the young man was handed over to the care of a man of proved experience in public affairs, whom he attended in the Forum and in the law-courts. In the former case he followed in the train (*cohors*) of a general, where, without performing the service of a common soldier, he fitted himself for the position of an officer.

Tiryns (Τίρυνς). A prehistoric citadel in the Argolic plain, about two and one-half miles north of Nauplia, and one mile from the sea. It occupies the summit of a low hill, about 980 feet long by 330 feet wide, and, in the southern half, 59 feet high above the surrounding plain, or 72 feet above sea level. Here, during a period probably not earlier than the fifteenth century B.C., nor later than the eleventh, was the stronghold of a powerful line of chieftains. Like Mycenae, Tiryns seems to have early fallen under the power of Argos, and in B.C. 468 it was annihilated by Argos, or at least reduced to absolute insignificance. Thorough excavations were carried on in the southern portion of the citadel by Dr. Schliemann and Dr. Dörpfeld in 1884 and 1885. The walls of fortification were cleared, and within them the remains of an extensive palace were revealed. The lower (northern) portion of the citadel remains unexcavated.

The citadel-wall of Tiryns is the classic example of "Cyclopian" masonry of the most primitive type. It is built of huge, irregular blocks of lime-

Citadel of Tiryns.

stone, many of them eight to ten feet long, three feet thick, and three feet high. These blocks were not fitted to one another, but the interstices were filled with clay and with small stones. In places there is a distinct approach toward an arrangement in horizontal courses. The thickness of the wall at the bottom varies from 16 feet to 28 feet, except in two places, where it is greatly increased in order to receive a system of store-chambers. The height of the existing remains is in places upward of 25 feet. The original height can only be guessed; it has been estimated at 50 feet, on the average, measured outside. The citadel had one, and only one, great entrance. This was on the east side. A broad ramp, so placed that the unshielded side of an attacking force would be exposed to the missiles of the defenders above, led to an opening, without gates, in the wall. What defence existed within this opening to the north is not known. To the south the passage was barred by a strong gate, whose threshold and related posts are still in their places. On the opposite (western) side of the citadel was a postern gate, from which ascended a narrow, winding stairway to the back of the palace; there were also two small gate apertures in the northern part of the citadel. On the east side, at the south end, was a gallery in the wall which furnished the means of communication with a series of rectangular store-chambers. The method of roofing by pushing the successive courses of stones farther and farther inward till they meet, should be noted (compare the "Treasury of Atreus" at Mycenae). This system of chambers with communicating gallery is repeated in the south wall, and there are here remains of the stairway by which access was obtained from the summit of the citadel.

The palace was contemporaneous with the fortification just described. Its walls, not needing especial strength, were built, in their lower portions, of moderate-sized stones laid in clay mixed with straw, with occasional beams of wood laid lengthwise. In many places the upper portions, beginning about three feet from the ground, consisted of unbaked bricks; in two places the bricks begin from the ground. These walls were protected by a plaster consisting of an undercoat of clay and an outer coat of pure lime. The latter was decorated with paintings, of which many fragmentary specimens have been found. Another sort of wall-decoration was found in the vestibule of a hall, extending across the western wall at the bottom. This was an alabaster frieze, sculptured with an elaborate pattern of palmettes, rosettes, etc., and studded with pieces of blue glass, supposed to be the κύανος of Homer. The floors throughout the palace were made of pure lime or of lime mixed with small pebbles. Thresholds were of wood or stone. Columns and antae were of wood. It is not certain whether there was a second story over any part of the building. The ground-plan was as follows: Through a large propylaeum, one passed into an irregular open court, and thence through a second and smaller propylaeum into a rectangular open court (αὐλή) having a floor of lime and pebbles and enclosed on three sides by colonnades. North of this came what was obviously the most important part of the house, consisting of a vestibule, an antechamber, and a rectangular roofed hall (μέγαρον). In the centre of this hall was a circular hearth, and around the hearth stood four wooden columns supporting the ceiling. As for the outlying rooms, most of them cannot be precisely designated. One, however, a square chamber approached by a passageway starting from the west side of the antechamber of the men's hall, was certainly a bathroom. Its floor was one gigantic stone, estimated to weigh over twenty tons. A fragment of a terracotta bath-tub was found here.

The palace of Tiryns corresponds in many important respects with the type of house or palace

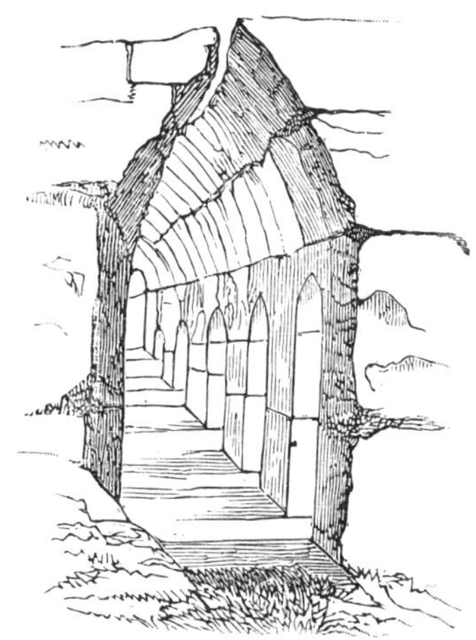

Arch at Tiryns.

presupposed in the Homeric poems (see DOMUS). There are, however, some differences, of which the most important concerns the communication between the men's and the women's apartments. This, in the Homeric house, was direct and easy; at Tiryns it was long and circuitous. This and the other differences may be due to difference of locality and date. It must not be forgotten that the fortifications and palace of Tiryns are pre-Homeric. See Schliemann, *Tiryns* (London, 1886); Gardner, *New Chapters in Greek History* (London, 1892).

Tisamĕnus (Τισαμενός). (1) A son of Orestes and Hermionē. He was king of Argos, but was deprived of his kingdom when the Heraclidae invaded the Peloponnesus. He was slain in a battle against them, and his tomb was afterwards shown at Helicé, from which place his remains were subsequently removed to Sparta by command of an oracle (Paus. ii. 18, 5; vii. 1, 3; Apollod. ii. 8, 2). (2) An Elean soothsayer, of the family of the Clytiadae. He was assured by the Delphic Oracle that he would be successful in five great conflicts. Supposing this to be a promise of distinction as an athlete, he devoted himself to gymnastic exercises; but the Spartans, understanding the oracle to refer, not to gymnastic, but to military victories, made great offers to Tisamenus to induce him to take with their kings the joint command of their armies. This he refused to do on any terms short of receiving the full franchise of their city, which the Spartans eventually granted. He was present with the Spartans at the battle of Plataea, B.C. 379, which was the first of the five conflicts referred to by the oracle. The second was with the Argives and Tegeans at Tegea; the third, with the Arcadians at Dipaea; the fourth was the Third Messenian War (465–455); and the last was the battle of Tanagra, with the Athenians and their allies, in 457 (Herod. ix. 33–36).

Tisiphŏné. See EUMENIDES.

Tissaphernes (Τισσαφέρνης). A famous Persian, who was appointed satrap of Lower Asia in B.C. 414. He espoused the cause of the Spartans in the Peloponnesian War, but he did not give them any effectual assistance, since his policy was not to allow either Spartans or Athenians to gain the supremacy, but to exhaust the strength of both parties by the continuance of the war. His plans, however, were thwarted by the arrival of Cyrus in Asia Minor in 407. This prince supplied the Lacedaemonians with effectual assistance. Tissaphernes and Cyrus were not on good terms; and after the death of Darius they were engaged in continual disputes about the cities in the satrapy of the latter, over which Cyrus claimed dominion. The ambitious views of Cyrus towards the throne at length became manifest to Tissaphernes, who lost no time in repairing to the king with information of the danger. At the battle of Cunaxa, in 401, he was one of the four generals who commanded the army of Artaxerxes, and his troops were the only portion of the left wing that was not put to flight by the Greeks. When the Ten Thousand had begun their retreat Tissaphernes professed his great anxiety to serve them, and promised to conduct them home in safety. In the course of the march he treacherously arrested Clearchus and four of the other generals, who were put to death. After this, Tissaphernes annoyed and harassed the Greeks in their march, without, however, seriously impeding it, till they reached the Carduchian Mountains, at which point he gave up the pursuit. Not long after, Tissaphernes, as a reward for his great services, was invested by the king, in addition to his own satrapy, with all the authority which Cyrus had enjoyed in Western Asia. On his arrival he claimed dominion over the Ionian cities, which applied to Sparta for aid. Their request was granted, and the Spartans carried on war against Tissaphernes with success for some years under the command successively of Thimbron, Dercyllidas, and Agesilaüs (400–395). The continued want of success on the part of Tissaphernes led to grievous complaints against him, and the charges were transmitted to court, where they were backed by all the influence of Parysatis, eager for the revenge on the enemy of Cyrus, her favourite son. The result was that Tithraustes was commissioned by the king to put Tissaphernes to death and to succeed him in his government, which was accordingly done (395) (Thucyd. viii.; Xen. *Hell.* i. 1, 2, 5; iii. 1, 2, 4; *Anab.*; Diod. xiii. 46; xiv. 23–27, 80).

Titānes (Τιτᾶνες, sing. Τιτάν). (1) The sons and daughters of Uranus and Gê or Gaea (Earth), originally dwelling in heaven, whence they are called Οὐρανίωνες or Οὐρανίδαι. They were twelve or thirteen in number who fall generally into pairs, viz., Oceanus and Tethys representing the sea; Hyperion and Theia (sun and moon); Coeus and Phoebe (light or star deities); Creios and Eurybia (deities of strength); Cronus and Rhea (heaven and earth); Themis and Mnemosyné, and Iapetus who was to produce mankind (Hes. *Th.* 133; Apollod. i. 1, 3). It is said that Uranus, the first ruler of the world, threw his sons, the Hecatoncheires (Hundred-Handed)—Briareus, Cottys, Gyes—and the Cyclopes—Arges, Steropes, and Brontes—into Tartarus. Gaea, indignant at this, produced iron, persuaded the Titans to rise against their father, and gave to Cronus an iron sickle. They did as their mother bade them, with the exception of Oceanus. Cronus, with his sickle, mutilated his father. (See URANUS.) From the drops of his blood there sprang the Erinnyes, Alecto, Tisiphoné, and Megaera. The Titans then deposed Uranus, liberated their brothers who had been cast into Tartarus, and raised Cronus to the throne. But Cronus hurled the Cyclopes back into Tartarus, and married his sister Rhea. Having been warned by Gaea and Uranus that he should be dethroned by one of his own children, he swallowed successively his children Hestia, Demeter, Heré, Pluto, and Poseidon. Rhea therefore, when she was pregnant with Zeus, went to Crete, and gave birth to the child in the Dictaean Cave, where he was brought up by the Curetes. When Zeus had grown up he availed himself of the assistance of Thetis, the daughter of Oceanus, who gave to Cronus a potion which caused him to bring up the stone and the children he had swallowed. (See CRONUS; ZEUS.) United with his brothers and sisters, Zeus now began the contest against Cronus and the ruling Titans. This contest (usually called the TITANOMACHIA) was carried on in Thessaly, Cronus and the Titans occupying Mount Othrys, and the sons of Cronus Mount Olympus. It lasted ten years, till at length Gaea promised victory to Zeus if he would deliver the Cyclopes and Hecatoncheires from Tartarus. Zeus accordingly slew Campé, who guarded the Cyclopes, and the latter furnished him with thunder and lightning. The Titans then were overcome, and hurled down into an abyss below Tartarus, and the Hecatoncheires were set to guard them (Hes. *Th.* 617, 697, 851; Apollod. i. 2, 1; Pausan. viii. 37, 3; cf. *Il.* xiv. 279). It must be observed that the fight of the Titans is sometimes confounded by ancient writers with the fight of the Gigantes. (See GIGANTES.)

The myth of the Titans grew out of an attempt to reconcile the Greek religion with that of other non-Greek nations who had occupied the Greek lands before them. Hence many of its features, especially the account of the wounding of Uranus, are not of a Greek character, and are ignored by Homer, but preserved by Hesiod. The Titan dynasties represent primitive alien supreme deities who have been brought into connection with the supreme Zeus of the Greeks and the other Olympian deities. In the Greek conception of the story, the Titans express the more terrible forces of nature, and also the struggle against the will of Zeus—*i. e.* against the lawful and orderly course of things (cf. *Il.* viii. 478, xiv. 200, xv. 224; Plat. *Leg.* iii. p. 701). See Meyer, *Die Giganten und Titanen* (Leipzig, 1887).

(2) The name Titanes is also given to those divine or semi-divine beings who were descended from the Titans, such as Prometheus, Hecaté, Latona, Pyrrha, and especially Helios (the Sun) and Selené (the Moon), as the children of Hyperion and Thia, and even the descendants of Helios, such as Circé.

Titanomachia. See TITANES.

Titaresius (Τιταρήσιος). Now Elassonitiko or Xeraghi; a river of Thessaly, also called Europus, rising in Mount Titarus, flowing through the country of the Perrhaebi, and falling into the Peneus, southeast of Phalanna.

Tithenidia (τιθηνίδια). A festival held by those Spartan nurses (τιτθαί) who had charge of the male children of citizens. During its celebration they carried the boys to the Temple of Artemis and sacrificed sucking-pigs in their honour (Athen. iv. p. 139; Plut. *Sympos.* iii. 9).

Tithōnus (Τιθωνός). The son of Laomedon and Strymo, and brother of Priam. By the prayers of Eos, who loved him, he obtained from the gods immortality, but not eternal youth, in consequence of which he completely shrank together in his old age; whence a decrepit old man was proverbially called Tithonus. Eos changed him into a cicada, or katydid (Hes. *Theog.* 984; Apollod. iii. 12, 4; Ovid, *Fast.* i. 461). The story suggested Lord Tennyson's fine poem *Tithonus*. See EOS.

Tithorea. See NEON.

Tithraustes. (Τιθραύστης). A Persian, who succeeded Tissaphernes in his satrapy, and put him to death by order of Artaxerxes Mnemon, B.C. 395. See TISSAPHERNES.

Tities. One of the three ancient patrician tribes at Rome. See PATRICII; TRIBUS.

Titinius. A Roman comic poet, the earliest representative of the *fabula togata.* (See COMOEDIA.) He flourished about B.C. 150. Owing to his skill in portraying character he was ranked next to Terence. Of his comedies we only possess fifteen titles and three fragments of a popular character, given in Ribbeck's collection (1872).

Titles. See INDEX; LIBER; TITULUS.

Titŭlus. (1) A sort of placard or sign attached to a pole and carried by soldiers in the triumphal processions with the record of their victories and captains inscribed upon it (Ovid, *Trist.* iv. 2, 20). (2) The lettering of a book's title. (See INDEX; LIBER.) (3) The advertisement or handbill displayed upon a house to announce it as for sale or to let (Pliny, *Epist.* vii. 27, 7), the latter, in the words EST LOCANDA, still used by the Romans of to-day. (4) In general, any epitaph (*titulus sepulcralis*) or other inscription.

Triumphal Titulus. (Arch of Titus.)

Titus Flavius Sabīnus Vespasiānus. A Roman emperor, A.D. 79–81, commonly called by his praenomen **Titus.** He was the son of the emperor Vespasianus and his wife Flavia Domitilla. He was born on the 30th of December, A.D. 40. When a young man, he served as military tribune in Britain and in Germany with great credit. After having been quaestor, he had the command of a legion, and served under his father in the Jewish Wars. Vespasian returned to Italy, after he had been proclaimed emperor on the first of July, A.D. 69; but Titus remained in Palestine to prosecute the siege of Jerusalem, during which he showed the talents of a general with the daring of a soldier. The siege of Jerusalem was concluded by the capture of the place on the 8th of September, 70. Titus returned to Italy in the following year (71), and triumphed at Rome with his father. He also received the title of Caesar, and became the associate of Vespasian in the government. His conduct at this time gave no good promise, and his attachment to Berenicé, the sister of Agrippa II., also made him unpopular; but he sent her away from Rome after he became emperor. Titus succeeded his father in 79, and his government proved an agreeable surprise to those who had anticipated a return of the times of Nero. During his whole reign Titus displayed a sincere desire for the happiness of the people, and he did all that he could to relieve them in times of distress. He assumed the office of Pontifex Maximus after the death of his father, and with the purpose, as he declared, of keeping his hands free from blood, a resolution which he kept. The first year of his reign is memorable for the great eruption of Vesuvius, which desolated a large part of the adjacent country, and buried with lava and ashes the towns of Herculaneum and Pompeii. Titus endeavoured to repair the ravages of this great eruption; and he was

Titus. (Bust in the British Museum.)

also at great care and expense in repairing the damage done by a great fire at Rome, which lasted three days and nights. He completed the Colosseum, and erected the baths which were called by his name. He died on the 13th of September, A.D. 81, after a reign of two years, two months, and twenty days. He was in the 41st year of his age; and there were suspicions that he was poisoned by his brother, Domitian. See Stange, *De Titi Vita* (1870); and Beulé, *Tite et sa Dynastie* (1872).

Tityus (Τιτυός). Son of Gaea, or of Zeus and Elara, the daughter of Orchomenus. He was a giant in Euboea. Instigated by Heré, he attempted to offer violence to Artemis when she passed through Panopaeus to Pytho, but he was killed by the arrows either of Artemis or Apollo; according to others, Zeus destroyed him with a flash of lightning. He was then cast into Tartarus, and there he lay outstretched on the ground, covering nine acres, while two vultures (others say snakes) devoured his liver. See GIGANTES.

Tlepolĕmus (Τληπόλεμος). A son of Heracles by Astyoché, daughter of Phylas, or by Astydamia, daughter of Amyntor. He was king of Argos, but, after slaying his uncle Licymnius, he was obliged to take to flight, and, in conformity with the command of an oracle, he settled in Rhodes, where he built the towns of Lindos, Ialysus, and Camirus. He joined the Greeks in the Trojan War with nine ships, but was slain by Sarpedon (*Il.* ii. 658; v. 627).

Tmolus (Τμῶλος). (1) The god of Mount Tmolus in Lydia is described as the husband of Pluto, the daughter of Himantes, (or Omphalé) and father of Tantalus, and is said to have decided the musical contest between Apollo and Pan. (2) Now Dagh, a celebrated mountain of Asia Minor, running east and west through the centre of Lydia, and dividing the plain of the Hermus on the north from that of the Caÿster on the south.

Toga (τήβεννα). The distinctive garb of the Roman citizen when appearing in public (see illustrations). Its use was forbidden to exiles and to foreigners; it was indispensable on all official occasions, even in imperial times, when more convenient garments had been adopted for ordinary use. It consisted of a white woollen cloth of semicircular cut, about five yards long by four wide, a certain portion of which was pressed by the fuller into long, narrow plaits. This cloth was doubled lengthwise, not down the centre, but so that one fold was deeper than the other. It was next thrown over the left shoulder in such a manner that the end in front reached to the ground, and the part behind was about twice a man's height in length. This end was then brought round under the right arm, and again thrown over the left shoulder so as to cover the whole of the right side from the arm-pit to the calf. The broad folds in which it hung over were thus gathered together on the left shoulder. The part which crossed the breast diagonally was known as the *sinus*, or bosom. It was deep enough to serve as a pocket for the reception of small articles.

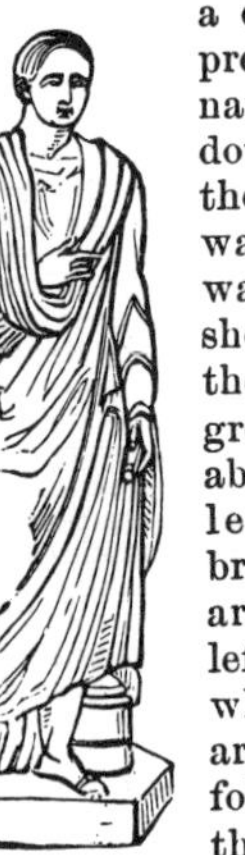
Ancient Mode of Wearing the Toga. (Dresden.)

In earlier times the Romans wore the *toga* even in warfare, although one of considerably less width. It was worn on such occasions in a peculiar mode called the *cinctus Gabinus*, or girding in the Gabian manner, after the town Gabii. In this, the end which, in the other mode, was thrown over the left shoulder, was drawn tightly round the body, so that in itself it formed a girdle, leaving both arms free and preventing the garment from falling off. This garb was subsequently retained only for certain ceremonial rites, as at the founding of towns, at the Ambarvalia, during incantations, at the opening of the Temple of Ianus, and at sacrificial observances of diverse kinds. After the *sagum* (q. v.) had been introduced as a military garment, the toga served as the exclusive garb and symbol of peace. Women also in olden times used to wear the toga: afterwards this was only the case with prostitutes; and disgraced wives were forbidden to wear the *stola*, the matron's dress of honour. The colour of the toga, as worn by men (*toga virilis*), was white: a dark-coloured toga (brown or black, *toga pulla* or *sordida*) was worn only by the lower classes, or in time of mourning, or by accused persons. A purple stripe woven in the garment was the distinctive mark of the curule magistrates and censors, of the State priests (but only when performing their functions), and afterwards of the emperors. This, which was called the *toga praetexta*, was also worn by boys until they attained manhood, and by girls until marriage. The *toga picta* was a robe adorned with golden stars; it was worn by a general on his triumph, by the magistrate who was giving public games, in imperial times by consuls on entering office, and by the emperor on festal occasions. (Cf. CLAVUS.) On the *toga candida*, see AMBITUS. The shoe appropriate to the toga was the *calceus* (q. v.).

Later Mode of Wearing the Toga. (*Museo Borbonico.*)

Togāta (sc. *fabula*). The general term for a play with an Italian plot and surroundings, including *praetextatae* (tragedies) and *tabernariae* (comedies). See Neukirch, *De Fabula Togata* (Leipzig, 1833); and the articles COMEDIA; PRAETEXTA.

Togāta Gallia. See GALLIA.

Toilet. See ACUS; BARBA; COMA; FUCUS; PECTEN; SAPO; UNGUENTUM.

Tokos. See FENUS.

Tolēnus or **Telonius.** Now the Turano; a river in the land of the Sabines, rising in the country of the Marsi and Aequi, and falling into the Velinus.

Tolētum. Now Toledo; the capital of the Carpetani in Hispania Tarraconensis, situated on the river Tagus, which nearly encompasses the town.

Tolistobogi, Tolistoboii. See GALATIA.

Tollēno. (1) A well-sweep (see ANTLIA). (2) A Roman siege-engine. See TORMENTUM.

Tolōsa. Now Toulouse; a town of Gallia Narbonensis, and the capital of the Tectosages. It was situated on the Garumna, near the frontiers of Aquitania. It was subsequently made a Roman colony, and was styled PALLADIA. Tolosa was a large and wealthy town, and contained a celebrated temple, in which is said to have been preserved a great part of the booty taken by Brennus from the Temple of Delphi. The town and temple were plundered by the consul Q. Servilius Caepio in B.C. 106.

Tolumnius, LAR. King of the Veientes, to whom Fidenae revolted in B.C. 438, and at whose instigation the inhabitants of Fidenae slew the four Roman ambassadors who had been sent to inquire into the reasons of their recent conduct. In the war which followed, Tolumnius was slain in single combat by Cornelius Cossus (Livy, iv. 17–19).

Tomacŭlum. A sort of sausage made of the intestines of a pig (Juv. x. 355), broiled and eaten hot (Petron. 31). It was sold about the streets of Rome in small tin ovens, like the modern Frankfürters.

Tomb. See SEPULCRUM.

Tomi or **Tomis.** Now Tomiswar or Jegni Pangola; a town of Thrace (subsequently Moesia), situated on the western shore of the Euxine, and at a later time the capital of Scythia Minor. It is renowned as the place of Ovid's banishment. See OVIDIUS.

Tomўris (Τόμυρις). A queen of the Massagetae, by whom the elder Cyrus was slain in battle, B.C. 529 (Herod. i. 205–214). See CYRUS.

Tongs. See FORCEPS.

Tonsa. A word used by the poets for the oar of a boat. The diminutive TONSILLA denotes a boat-hook (Att. *ap.* Fest. s. h. v.).

Tonsor (κουρεύς). A barber. The Greek and Roman barbers cut and dressed the hair and trimmed the beards of their customers, and also pared the nails and pulled out hairs with tweezers (*volsellae*). Persons of means were shaved and otherwise attended by valets of their own from among their slaves, but the common people frequented the barber-shop (κουρεῖον, *tonstrina*), which was with them a favourite lounging-place and famous for the gossip retailed there; for the ancient barbers were as fond of talk as those of modern times (Plaut. *Epid.* ii. 2, 16; *Asin.* ii. 2, 76; Polyb. iii. 20, 5; Hor. *Sat.* i. 7, 2). Female barbers (κουρεύτριαι, *tonstrices*) seem not to have been rare (Mart. ii. 17).

Ancient Barber at Work. (Baumeister, *Denkmäler*.)

The person who was to be operated on by the barber had a rough cloth (ὠμόλινον, *involucre*) laid on his shoulders, as now, to keep the hairs off his dress, etc. The second part of the business was shaving (*radere, rasitare*, ξυρεῖν). This was done with a ξυρόν, or *novacula*, a razor, which was kept in a razor-case (θήκη, ξυροθήκη, ξυροδόκης). Some, who would not submit to the operation of the razor, used instead some powerful depilatory ointments or plasters, as *psilothron, acida Creta, Venetum lutum, dropax*, etc. Stray hairs which escaped the razor were pulled out with small pincers or tweezers (*volsellae*, τριχολάβιον). The third part of the barber's work was, as stated above, to pare the nails of the hands, an operation which the Greeks expressed by the words ὀνυχίζειν and ἀπονυχίζειν. The instruments used for this purpose were called ὀνυχιστήρια, sc. μαχαίρια. See BARBA; COMA.

Tonstrīna. See TONSOR.

Toothpick. See DENTISCALPIUM.

Topia. Landscape paintings used to decorate the walls of a room. See PICTURA.

Topiarius. A landscape gardener. See HORTUS.

Toral, Torālē. A piece of cloth attached to the front of a dining-couch and extending from the mattress (*torus*) to the floor. It was usually of plain white cloth, so as to be readily washed (Hor. *Sat.* ii. 4, 84); but in the houses of the rich it was often of costly material, gold tissue or embroidery (Lamprid. *Elagab.* 19).

Torch. See FAX; TAEDA.

Torcŭlar (ληνός). A press used in making oil or wine. The earliest press was simply a block of stone raised by lever and allowed to descend on a basket (*fiscina*) of grapes or olives. The next development was a machine operated by the pressure of a beam (*prelum*) drawn down by ropes and worked by a sort of capstan (*sucula*). Still another press consisted of two uprights fixed in the earth and with crossbeams at the top and bottom. A number of boards (*tympana*) ran down each side of the uprights forced down upon the grapes by large blocks driven in as wedges by blows of a hammer or mallet. This last press is represented in the accompanying illustration. See OLIVUM; VINUM.

Torcular (Herculanean painting.)

Torcularium (ληνεών). A room in which olive oil was produced. See TORCULAR.

Toreutĭcē (τορευτική). A name derived from the graver's tool (τορεύς), and denoting the art of ornamental work in metal. It is treated under CAELATURA.

Tormentum (βάσανος). Torture. (1) GREEK.—By a decree of Scamandrius of uncertain date it was ordained that no free Athenian could be put to the torture (Andoc. *De Myst.* 43), and this appears to have been the general rule. The evidence of slaves was, however, always taken with torture, and their testimony was not otherwise received. From this circumstance their testimony appears to have been considered of more value than that of freemen. Any person might offer his own slave to be examined by torture, or demand that of his adversary, and the offer or demand was equally called πρόκλησις εἰς βάσανον, "challenge to torture." The parties interested either superintended the torture themselves, or chose certain persons for this purpose, hence called βασανισταί, who took the evidence of the slaves. The official torturer was called δήμιος or δημόκοινος. (2) ROMAN.—During the time of the Republic, freemen were never put to the torture, and slaves only were exposed to this punishment, which might be by scourging, laceration with hooks, or burning. Slaves, however, could not be tortured to prove the guilt of their own master, except in the case of *incestum*, which was a crime against the gods, or unless the Senate made an exception in some special instance. At a later time, slaves might be tortured to bear witness against their masters in cases of *maiestas* and adultery. (See ADULTERIUM.) Under the emperors even free persons were put to the torture to extract evidence from them in cases of *maiestas;* and although this indignity was confined for the most part to persons in humble circumstances, we read of cases in which even Roman senators and knights were exposed to it. The torture was inflicted by the public slaves known as *tortores* and *carnifices*.

See Becker-Göll, *Charikles*, pp. 37 foll.; Mahaffy, *Social Life in Greece*, 3d ed. pp. 240 foll.; Rein, *Criminalrecht der Römer*, p. 542; and the articles CRUX; ECULEUS; FIDICULA; FLAGRUM; MAIESTAS; SERVUS.

Tormentum. A military engine for hurling missiles of any kind. All the missiles used in war, except those thrown from the sling (see FUNDA), were projected either by the hand alone or with the aid of elastic substances. Of elastic instruments, the bow (see ARCUS) was used by all ancient nations. The *tormentum* was so called from the twisting (*torquendo*) of hairs, thongs, and vegetable fibres; and the word is often used by itself to denote engines of various kinds; often, also, these engines are specified separately under the names of *ballistae* and *catapultae*, which names, however, most commonly occur together in the accounts of sieges and other military operations, because the two kinds of engines denoted by them were almost always used in conjunction. (See HELEPOLIS.) The *ballista* (πετροβόλος) was used to shoot stones, the *catapulta* (καταπέλτης, καταπελτική) to project darts, especially the *falarica* (q. v.), and a kind of missile four and a half feet long, called *trifax*. While, in besieging a city, the ram (see ARIES) was employed in destroying the lower part of the wall, the *ballista* was used to overthrow the battlements (*propugnacula*), and the catapult to shoot any of the besieged who appeared between them. The forms of these machines being adapted to the objects which they were intended to throw, the catapult was long, the *ballista* nearly square, which explains the following humorous enumeration by Plautus (*Capt.* iv. 2, 16) of the three μηχαναί, the application of which has just been explained:

"Meus est ballista pugnus, cubitus catapulta est mihi,
Humerus aries."

In the same armament the number of catapults was commonly much greater than the number of *ballistae*. Also, these two classes of machines were both of them distinguished into the greater and the less, the number of "the less" being much more considerable than the number of "the greater." When Carthago Nova, which had served the Carthaginians for an arsenal, was taken by the Romans, the following were found in it: 120 large and 281 small catapults; 23 large and 52 small *ballistae*. Three sizes of the *ballista* are mentioned

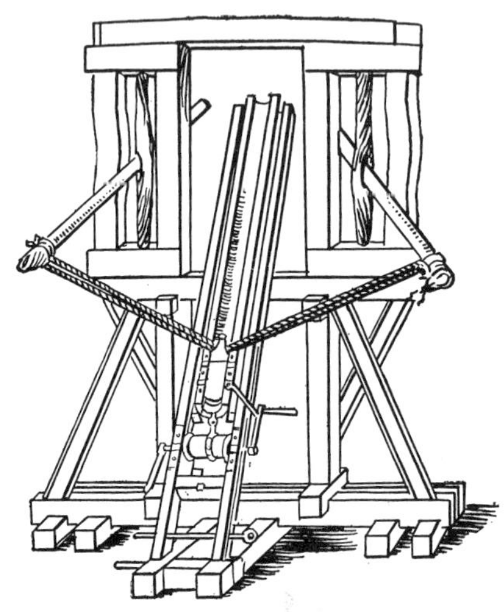

Ballista. (Baumeister.)

by historians, (*a*) that which threw stones weighing half a hundredweight (τριακονταμναίους λίθους), (*b*) a whole hundredweight (*ballista centenaria*, λιθοβόλος ταλαντιαῖος), and (*c*) three hundredweight (πετροβόλος τριτάλαντος). Besides these, Vitruvius (x. 11) mentions many other sizes, even down to the *ballista* which threw a stone of only two pounds' weight. In like manner, catapults were classified according to the length of the arrows shot from them. According to Iosephus, who gives some remarkable instances of the destructive force of the *ballista*, it threw stones to the distance of a quarter of a mile (*Bell. Iud.* iii. 7, 19–23). Neither from the best-known authors nor from the figures on the Column of Trajan are we able to form a very exact idea of the construction of these engines. Still less are we informed on the subject of the *scorpio* or *onager*, which was also a *tor-*

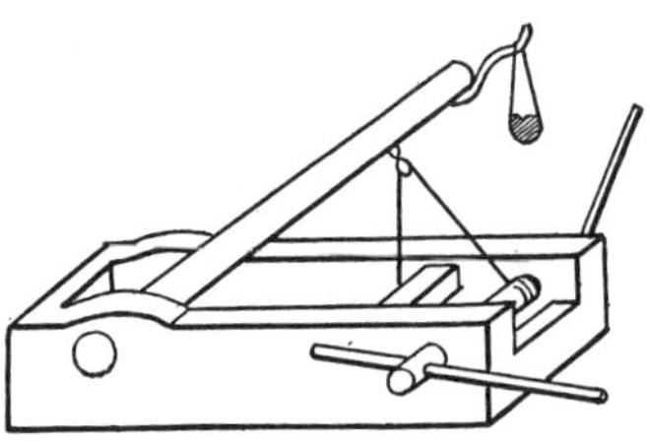

Onager or Scorpio. (Marquardt.)

mentum. The best notion of ancient artillery is to be gathered from the treatise of Hero (Βελοποιϊκά), and that of Philo (Περὶ Βελοποιϊκῶν), both written in the second or third century B.C.

The various kinds of *tormenta* appear to have been invented shortly before the time of Alexander the Great. When horsehair and other materials failed, the women in several instances cut off their own hair, and twisted it into ropes for the engines. (See PUNIC WARS.) These machines, with those who had the management of them, and who were called *ballistarii* and ἀφεταί, were drawn up in the rear of an advancing army, so as to throw over the heads of the front ranks. In order to attack a maritime city, they were carried on the decks of vessels constructed for the purpose (Diod. Sic. xx. 83–86).

Both of the chief varieties of *tormenta* were based upon the principle of the crossbow; but the elasticity of the bow was exchanged for elasticity in the twist of the cord. Consequently, as explained above, all pieces of heavy artillery were called by the Romans *tormenta*. The machine consisted of three parts: the stand, the groove for the shot, and the apparatus representing the bow. This consisted of a frame in three divisions, through the midmost of which passed the groove for the shot. In each of the lateral divisions was stretched, in a vertical direction, a set of strong elastic cords, made of the sinews of animals, or the long hair of animals or of women. These were stretched tight, and between each of them was fixed a straight unelastic arm of wood. The arms were joined by a cord, which was pulled back by a winch applied at the end of the groove. On letting this go, the arms, and with them the string and the object in front of it, were driven forward by the twisting of the vertical cords. The effectiveness of the engine thus depended on the

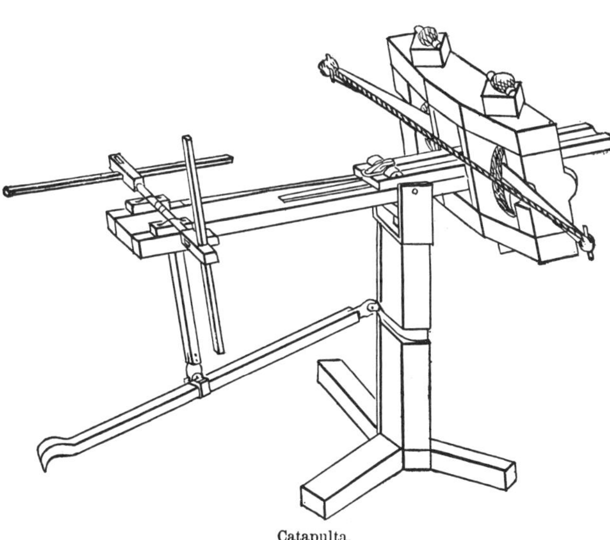

Catapulta.

power and twist of the cords, which may be said roughly to express its calibre. The engines were divided into two kinds, (1) *catapultae*, or *scorpiones*. In these the groove for the shot was horizontal, and they projected missiles of length and thickness varying according to the calibre; (2) *ballistae*, which shot stones, beams, or balls up to 162 lbs. weight, at an angle of 50 degrees. The calibre of the *ballista* was at least three times as great as that of the catapult. The average range of the catapult was about 383 yards, that of the *ballista* from about 295 to 503 yards.

After Constantine we hear no more of catapults, but only of *ballistae* and the *onager*. The *ballista* now shot arrows, and is described either as a huge cross-bow with an elastic bow of iron, or as virtually identical with the old catapult. The *onager*, also called *scorpio*, was a sling for stones, consisting of a frame in which was fastened a sort of wooden arm with a sling at one end.

As a rule, the heavy artillery was employed only in sieges; but artillery accompanied armies in the field for purposes of conquest or defence. The legions and the cohorts of the Praetorian Guard had their own artillery, and at the end of the fourth century every *centuria* in the legion had a *ballista* of the later kind drawn on wheels by mules (*carroballista*), and served by eleven men. Every cohort had an *onager*, carried on a cart drawn by two oxen. See the article by A. Müller in Baumeister's *Denkmäler*, s.v. "Festungskrieg und Belagerungswesen," i. pp. 525 foll.; Droysen, *Die griechischen Kriegsalterthümer*, pp. 187–204; Wescher, *Poliorcétique des Grecs* (1867); and Rüstow and Köchly, *Geschichte des griechischen Kriegswesens* (1852).

Torōnē (Τορώνη). A town of Macedonia, in the district of Chalcidicé, and on the southwest side of the peninsula Sithonia, from which the gulf between the peninsulas Sithonia and Pallené was called SINUS TORONAÏCUS.

Torquātus. The name of a patrician family of the Manlia gens. (1) T. MANLIUS IMPERIŌSUS TORQUĀTUS, the son of L. Manlius Capitolinus Imperiosus, dictator B.C. 363, was a favourite hero of Roman story. Manlius is said to have been dull of mind in his youth, and was brought up by his father in the closest retirement in the country. In 361 he served under the dictator T. Quintius Pennus in the war against the Gauls, and in this campaign earned immortal glory by slaying in single combat a gigantic Gaul. From the dead body of the barbarian he took the chain (*torques*) which had adorned him, and placed it around his own neck; and from this circumstance he obtained the surname of Torquatus. He was dictator in 353, and again in 349. He was also three times consul, namely, in 347, 344, and in 340. In the last of these years Torquatus and his colleague, P. Decius Mus, gained the great victory over the Latins at the foot of Vesuvius, which established forever the supremacy of Rome over Latium. Shortly before the battle, when the two armies were encamped opposite to one another, the consuls published a proclamation that no Roman should engage in single combat with a Latin on pain of death. This command was violated by young Manlius, the consul's son, who was in consequence executed by the lictor in presence of the assembled army. This severe sentence rendered Torquatus an object of detestation among the Roman youths as long as he lived; and the recollection of his severity was preserved in after-ages by the expression *Manliana imperia* (Livy, iv. 5, 19–28; id. viii. 3–12; Cic. *De Off.* iii. 31). (2) T. MANLIUS TORQUĀTUS, consul B.C. 235, when he conquered the Sardinians; censor in 231; and consul a second time in 224. He possessed the hereditary sternness and severity of his family; and we accordingly find him opposing in the Senate the ransom of those Romans who had been taken prisoners at the fatal battle of Cannae. He was dictator in 210. (3) L. MANLIUS TORQUĀTUS, consul B.C. 65 with L. Aurelius Cotta. He took an active part in suppressing the Catilinarian conspiracy in 63; and he also supported Cicero when he was banished in 58. (4) L. MANLIUS TORQUĀTUS, son of No. 3, belonged to the aristocratic party, and accordingly opposed Caesar on the breaking out of the Civil War in 49. He was praetor in that year, and was stationed at Alba with six cohorts. He subsequently joined Pompey in Greece, and in the following year (48) he had the command of Oricum intrusted to him; but was obliged to surrender both himself and the town to Caesar, who, however, dismissed Torquatus uninjured. After the battle of Pharsalia, Torquatus went to Africa, and upon the defeat of his party in that country in 46 he attempted to escape to Spain along with Scipio and others, but was taken prisoner by P. Sittius at Hippo Regius, and slain, together with his companions. Torquatus was well acquainted with Greek literature, and is praised by Cicero, with whom in early life he was closely connected, as a man well trained in every kind of learning. (5) A. MANLIUS TORQUĀTUS, praetor in B.C. 52, when he presided at the trial of Milo for bribery. On the breaking out of the Civil War he espoused the side of Pompey, and after the defeat of the latter retired to Athens, where he was living in exile in 45. He was an intimate friend of Cicero.

Torques and **Torquis** (στρεπτός). A twisted collar worn around the neck by the Persians, Gauls, and other foreign peoples; but on the breast

Roman Soldier with Torques. (From a bas-relief.)

by the Roman soldiers, to whom it was given as a decoration for valour (Juv. xvi. 60). TORQUIS BRACCHIĀLIS was a twisted bracelet. See ARMILLA.

Torus. A bed or couch.

Tower. See TURRIS.

Toys. See CREPUNDIA; NUCES; PUPA; TROCHUS; TURBO.

Trabea. The purple-striped cloak worn by Roman augurs and Roman *equites* (q. v.). See AUGUR; CLAVUS; EQUITES; TOGA.

Trabea, QUINTUS. A Roman comic dramatist, who occupies the eighth place in the canon of Volcatius Sedigitus. The period when he flourished is uncertain, but he has been placed about B.C. 130.

Trachis (Τραχίς) or **Trachin** (Τραχίν). (1) Also called HERACLĒA TRACHINIAE, or HERACLĒA PHTHIOTĬDIS, or simply HERACLĒA, a town of Thessaly in the district Malis, celebrated as the residence of Heracles for a time. (2) A town of Phocis, on the frontiers of Boeotia, and on the slope of Mount Helicon in the neighbourhood of Lebadea.

Trachonītis (Τραχωνῖτις) or **Trachon** (Τράχων). The northern district of Palestine beyond the Jordan, lying between Anti-Libanus and the mountains of Arabia, and bounded on the north by the territory of Damascus, on the east by Auranitis, on the south by Ituraea, and on the west by Gaulanitis.

Tractātor. A masseur; a slave who kneaded the body and limbs after the bath (Seneca, *Epist.* 66).

Trade. See COMMERCE; COMMERCIUM.

Traëns or **Traïs.** A river in Bruttium, now the Trionto, near which the Sybarites were defeated by the troops of Crotona in B.C. 510. See SYBARIS.

Tragoedia (τραγῳδία). I. Tragedy in GREECE originated in the lyric dithyramb; i. e. in the song of a chorus at the rites held in honour of Dionysus (see DIONYSIA). This song, in accordance with the cult of the god, expressed at one time exuberant joy, at another deep sorrow. The cult of Dionysus is also indicated by the very name of tragedy, signifying goat-song; i. e. (according to the usual explanation) the hymn sung by the chorus in their dance round the altar at the sacrifice of the goat (τράγος), dedicated to Dionysus. Others derive the name from the fact that, to represent Satyrs, the chorus were clad in goat-skins, and hence resembled goats. These choral songs seem to have received a certain dramatic form as early as the time of Arion, to whom the dithyramb owes its artistic development. The true drama, including tragic and satyric plays, was evolved subsequently in Athens.

Tradition ascribes the origin of tragedy to a contemporary of Solon named Thespis (q. v.), of Icaria, which was a chief seat of the cult of Dionysus. The date assigned to this is B.C. 540. Thespis was at the same time poet, leader of the chorus, and actor. According to the testimony of the ancients, his pieces consisted of a prologue, a series of choral songs standing in close connection with the action, and dramatic recitations introduced between the choruses. These recitations were delivered by the leader of the chorus, and were partly in the form of monologues, partly in that of short dialogues with the chorus, whereby the action of the play was advanced. The reciter was enabled to appear in different rôles by the aid of linen or wooden masks, which are also said to have been introduced by the poet himself. (See PERSONA.) The invention of Thespis, whose own pieces soon lapsed into oblivion, won the favour of Pisistratus and the approval of the Athenian public. Tragedy thus became an important element in the Attic festival of Dionysus. Thespis's immediate followers were Choerilus, Pratinas (the inventor of the Satyric Drāma), his son Aristias, and Phrynichus. Phrynichus especially did good service towards the development of tragedy by introducing an actor apart from the leader of the chorus, and so preparing the way for true dialogue. He further improved the chorus, which still, however, occupied a disproportionate space in comparison with the action of the play.

Tragedy was really brought into being by Aeschylus, when he added a second actor (called the δευτεραγωνιστής) to the first, or πρωταγωνιστής, and in this way rendered dialogue possible. He further subordinated the choruses to the dialogue. See AESCHYLUS.

Sophocles, in whom tragedy reaches its culminating-point, added to Aeschylus's two actors a third, or τριταγωνιστής: and Aeschylus accepted the innovation in his later plays. Thenceforward three actors were regularly granted by lot to each poet, at the public expense. Only rarely, and in exceptional cases, was a fourth employed. Sophocles also raised the number of the chorus from twelve to fifteen. The only other important innovation due to him was that he gave up the internal connection, preserved by Aeschylus, among the several plays of a tetralogy which were presented in competition by the tragic poets at the festival of Dionysus. See SOPHOCLES; TETRALOGIA; TRILOGIA.

The third great master of tragedy is Euripides, in whom, however, we already observe a decline in many respects from the severe standard of his predecessor (see EURIPIDES). During and after the age of these masters of the art, from whom alone have complete dramas come down to us, many other tragic poets were actively employed, whose works are known to us by name alone, or are only preserved in fragments.

It is remarkable that, in the case of the great tragic writers, the cultivation of tragic compositions seems to have been hereditary among their descendants, and among those of Aeschylus in particular, for many generations. His son Euphorion, his nephew Philocles, his grand-nephews Morsimus and Melanthius, his grandson Astydamas, and his great-grandsons Astydamas and Philocles, were poets of more or less note. In the family of Sophocles may be mentioned his son Iophon and his grandson Sophocles; and in that of Euripides, his son or nephew of the same name.

Among the other poets of the fifth century B.C., Ion, Achaeus, Aristarchus, and Neophron were accounted the most eminent. Agathon may also be included as the first who ventured to treat a subject of his own invention, whereas hitherto mythical history, especially that of Homer and the Cyclic Poets (q. v.), or, in rare instances, authentic history, had furnished the materials of the play. After the Peloponnesian War, tragedy shared the general and ever-increasing decline of political and religious vitality. In the fourth century, besides the descendants of Aeschylus, we must mention Theodectes, Aphareus, and Chaeremon, who partly wrote for readers only.

The number of tragedies produced at Athens is marvellous. According to the not altogether trustworthy records of the number of plays written by each poet, they amounted to 1400. The works of the foremost poets were represented over and over again, especially in the theatres of Asia Minor, under the successors of Alexander. During the first half of the third century Ptolemy Philadelphus built a great theatre in Alexandria, where he established competitions in exact imitation of those at Athens. This gave a new impetus to tragic poetry, and seven poets became conspicuous, who were known as the Alexandrian Pleiad, Alexander Aetolus, Philiscus, Sositheus, Homerus, Aeantides, Sosiphanes, and Lycophron. The taste of the Alexandrian critics deemed them worthy to occupy a place beside the five great tragic poets of Athens, Aeschylus, Sophocles, Euripides, Ion, and Achaeus. See CANON ALEXANDRINUS; PLEIAS.

Inasmuch as tragedy developed itself out of the chorus at the Dionysiac festivals, so, in spite of all the limitations which were introduced as a result of the evolution of the true drama, the chorus itself was always retained. Hence Greek tragedy consisted of two elements: the one truly dramatic, the prevailing metre of which was the iambic trimeter; the other consisting of song and dance (see CHORUS) in the numerous varieties of Dorian lyric poetry. The dramatic portion was generally made up of the following parts: the πρόλογος, from the beginning to the first entry of the chorus; the ἐπεισώδιον, the division between each choral song and the next; and the ἔξοδος, or concluding portion which followed the last chorus. The first important choral part was called the πάροδος: and the song following an *episodium*, a στάσιμον (sc. μέλος). There were further songs of lamentation by the chorus and actors together, which were called κόμμοι. A solo was sometimes sung by the actor alone; and this became especially common in the later tragedies.

II. ROMAN tragedy was founded entirely on that of the Greeks. In early times there existed crude dramatic productions (see SATIRA), which provided an opening for the translation from the Greek dramas brought on the stage by Livius Andronicus. He was a Greek by birth, but was brought to Rome as a captive about B.C. 200. It is to him that Roman tragedy owes its origin. His dramas and those of his successors were more or less free versions of Greek originals. Even the tragedies, or historical plays, drawn from national Roman materials, called *fabulae praetextae* or *praetextatae* (see PRAETEXTA), the first writer of which was his immediate successor Naevius (about B.C. 235), were entirely modelled on the Greek. The most noteworthy representatives of tragedy under the Republic were Ennius (B.C. 239–170), Pacuvius (220–130), and Attius (170–84), besides whom only a few other poets produced any works about this time. It is true that the scanty fragments we possess of these dramas admit of no positive judgment as to their merit, but there is no doubt that they rank far below the original creations of the Greeks. It may also be clearly inferred from the fragments that declamation and pathos formed a characteristic attribute of Roman tragedy, which was intensified by a studied archaism of expression. Moreover, the titles of their plays that have come down to us show that preference was given to subjects relating to the Trojan epic cycle; this is to be explained by the Trojan origin claimed by the Romans. (See TROJAN WAR.) Next to this the most popular were the myths of the Pelopidae, of the Theban cycle, and of the Argonauts. Euripides was the favourite model; after him Sophocles; rarely Aeschylus. Roman tragedy, like Greek, was made up of spoken dialogue in iambic trimeters and musical portions called *cantica*. See CANTICUM, and on the chorus in Roman tragedy see CHORUS (near the end).

In the time of Augustus the representatives of tragedy were Asinius Pollio, Varius, and Ovid; under Tiberius, Pomponius Secundus; under Nero and Vespasian, Curiatius Maternus, of whose works scarcely a line has been preserved. The only tragedies of Roman antiquity which we possess are those of the philosopher Seneca, which show great mastery of form and a fertile imagination, but suffer from an intolerable excess of rhetorical declamation. It is doubtful whether they were intended for the stage at all, and not rather for public recitation and for private reading. See SENECA (2).

See Schlegel, *Dramatic Literature*, Eng. trans. (London, 1844); Klein, *Griech. und röm. Drama*, 2 vols. (1865); Weissenfels, *Entwickelung der Tragödie der Griechen* (1892); Wecklein, *Ueber d. Stoff und Wirkung der griech. Tragödie* (1891); Günther, *Beiträge zur Geschichte und Aesthetik der antiken Tragödie* (1880); Kluge, *Die antike Tragödie in ihrem Verhältnisse zur modernen* (1880); Fritzsche, *De Origine Tragoediae* (1863); Armbruster, *Das Tragische und die Entwickelung der Tragödie* (1885); Walford, *Handbook of the Greek Drama* (London, 1856); Donaldson, *The Theatre of the Greeks* (8th ed. London, 1875); Bergk, *Griechische Litteraturgeschichte*, vol. iii. (Berlin, 1884); and the articles DRAMA; HISTRIO; SATYRIC DRAMA; THEATRUM.

Tragŭla. A sort of missile discharged by machinery (Varro, *L. L.* v. 115).

Traha. A sort of sledge or drag without wheels used by the ancients in threshing grain (Verg. *Georg.* i. 164).

Traianopŏlis. (1) A town in Mysia on the borders of Phrygia, refounded by Trajan in A.D. 117. (2) A town of Thrace on the Hebrus, founded by Trajan. (3) A town of Cilicia, otherwise called Selinus.

Traiānus, M. ULPIUS. A Roman emperor (A.D. 98–117), born at Italica, near Seville, in Spain, September 18th, A.D. 52 or 53. He was trained to arms, and, after ten years' service as military tribune, rose through the lower offices to the rank of praetor in 85, served with distinction in the East and in Germany, to which country he was sent from Spain by Domitian on the occasion of the revolt of Antonius Saturninus, legatus, with the Spanish legion Adiutrix under his command. He was consul in 91, and at the close of 97 he was adopted by the emperor Nerva, who gave him the rank of Caesar and the names of Nerva and Germanicus, and shortly after the title of Imperator, and the *tribunicia potestas*. His style and title after his elevation to the imperial dignity were IMPERĀTOR CAESAR NERVA TRAIĀNUS AUGUSTUS. He was the first Roman emperor who was born out of Italy. Nerva died in January, 98, and was succeeded by Trajan, who was then at Colonia (Cologne). His accession was hailed with joy, and he did not disappoint the expectations of the people. He was a great soldier both in the field and in military organization; and he was scarcely less great as an administrator. His finances were prosperous, partly from his good economy, though partly also from the good fortune of certain Dacian mining operations. Personally, he was strong and healthy, of a majestic appearance, laborious, and inured to fatigue. Though not a man of letters, he had good sense, a knowledge of the world, and a sound judgment. His mode of living was very simple, and in campaigns he shared all the sufferings and privations of the soldiers, by whom he was both loved and feared. He was a friend to justice, and had a sincere desire for the happiness of the people. His career led to a proverbial expression which after this time was formulated in a wish to each new emperor that in his reign he might be even "more fortunate than Augustus, and better than Trajan" (*Augusto felicior, melior Traiano*).

Trajan did not return to Rome for some months, being employed in settling the frontiers on the Rhine and the Danube. Especially, he completed the fortifications of the Rhine and of the Agri Decumates (q.v.), founded a new military station, Colonia Traiana, near Vetera, and constructed new roads by the Rhine and by the Danube, the latter work in preparation for the Dacian War. In 99 he proceeded to Rome, which he entered on foot, ac-

Trajan. (Bust in the British Museum.)

companied by his wife, Pompeia Plotina. In March, A.D. 101, Trajan left Rome for his campaign against the Daci. Decebalus, king of the Daci, had compelled Domitian to purchase peace by an annual payment of money; and Trajan determined on hostilities, which should settle matters so as to secure the peace of the frontier. This war employed Trajan between two and three years, but it ended with the defeat of Decebalus, who sued for peace at the feet of the Roman emperor. Trajan assumed the name of Dacius, and entered Rome in triumph (103). In the following year (104) Trajan commenced his second Dacian war against Decebalus, who had accepted the Roman terms merely to gain time, and now showed his intentions by building forts, collecting war material, and welcoming Ro-

Trajan giving a King to the Parthians. (Coin.)

man deserters. Decebalus was completely defeated, and put an end to his life (106). In the course of this war Trajan built (105) a permanent bridge across the Danube at the modern Turn Severin. The piers were of stone and of an enormous size, but the arches were of wood. (See PONS.) After the death of Decebalus, Dacia was reduced to the form of a Roman province, strong forts were built in various places, and Roman colonies were planted. (See DACIA.) The Column of Trajan at Rome was erected to commemorate his Dacian victories. In its sculptured illustrations of the campaign it has an historical value which has been well compared to that of the Bayeux Tapestry. (See COLUMNA.) On his return Trajan had a triumph, and he exhibited games to the people for 123 days. It is said that 11,000 animals were slaughtered during these amusements, and that 10,000 gladiators fought in the arena.

About this time Arabia Petraea was subjected to the Empire by A. Cornelius Palma, the governor of Syria, and an Indian embassy came to Rome. (See ARABIA.) The dominions of Agrippa II., who died A.D. 100, were also added to the province of Syria. In 114 Trajan left Rome to make war on the Armenians and the Parthians, the cause of the war being that the Parthian king, Chosroes, had deposed from the throne of Armenia Axidares, the Roman nominee. Trajan spent the winter of 114 at Antioch, and in the following year he invaded the Parthian dominions. The most striking and brilliant success attended his arms. In the course of two campaigns (115–116), he conquered the greater part of the Parthian Empire, and took the Parthian capital of Ctesiphon. In 116 he descended the Tigris and entered the Erythraean Sea (Persian Gulf). While he was thus engaged the Parthians rose against the Romans, but were again subdued by the generals of Trajan, Erucius Clarus, who reduced Babylonia and burned Seleucia, and Lucius Quietus, who reduced Mesopotamia. On his return to Ctesiphon, Trajan determined to give the Parthians a king, and placed the diadem on the head of Parthamaspates, son of Chosroes. In 117 Trajan fell ill, and as his complaint grew worse he set out for Italy. He lived to reach Selinus in Cilicia, afterwards called Traianopolis, where he died in August, 117, after a reign of nineteen years, six months, and fifteen days (*C. I. L.* vi. 1884). His ashes were taken to Rome in a golden urn, carried in triumphal procession, and deposited under the column which bears his name. He left no children, and he was succeeded by Hadrian. (See HADRIANUS.) Trajan constructed several great roads in the provinces and in Italy: among them was the road across the Pomptine Marshes, which he constructed with magnificent bridges over the streams. At Ostia he built a large new basin. At Rome he constructed the aqueduct called by his name, built a theatre in the Campus Martius, and, above all, made the Forum Traianum, with its basilicas and libraries, and his column in the centre. See the account of Trajan by Dierauer in vol. i. of Büdinger's *Untersuchungen* (1868), that by De la Berge (1877), and in Schiller's *Geschichte der röm. Kaiserzeit* (Gotha, 1883).

Traiectum. Now Utrecht; a town of the Batavi on the Rhine, later called TRAIECTUS RHENI, or TRAIECTUS AD RHENUM.

Tralles or **Trallis** (αἱ Τραλλεῖς, ἡ Τράλλις). A flourishing commercial city of Lydia, in Asia Minor. It stood on a plateau at the southern foot of Mount Messogis (with a citadel on a higher point), on the banks of the little river Eudon, a northern tributary of the Maeander, from which the city was distant eighty stadia (eight geographical miles). It was said to have been founded by Argives and Thracian settlers on the site of an older town called Anthea (Strab. p. 648; Diod. xvii. 65). Under the Seleucidae it bore the names of Seleucia and Antiochia.

Trama. See TELA.

Tranquillus, SUETONIUS. See SUETONIUS.

Transenna. A trap or gin for catching birds, made of network and shutting by a spring (Plaut. *Bacch.* iv. 5, 22).

Transtrum. A cross-beam; especially, in the plural, **Transtra** (τὰ σέλματα), the cross-benches upon which were seated the rowers in a ship. See NAVIS.

Transvectio. The festal parade of the Roman knights. See EQUITES.

Trapētum, Trapētus, and **Trapes.** A mill for bruising the olive and separating the fleshy part from the stone (Verg. *Georg.* ii. 519). It is described by Cato, *R. R.* xx.–xxii.

Trapeza (τράπεζα). A table. See MENSA.

Trapezītae (τραπεζῖται); in Latin ARGENTARII; MENSARII; NUMMULARII. Dealers in money; money-changers; usurers; bankers; so called from the "table" (τράπεζα, *mensa*) on which they did their business.

I. GREEK.—Bankers in Greece had their stands in the agora or other public places, and combined in their vocation a number of different pursuits. Thus, they gave change for coins of large denominations, as obols for drachmas; bought foreign money at a discount (καταλλάττω); furnished gold for export, lent money to merchants on the security of ships and cargoes, received money on deposit for which they paid interest, and acted as pawnbrokers, advancing cash on plate, jewels, and other personal property.

The notion of many Greeks that all taking of interest partook of the nature of usury was shared even by Aristotle (*Pol.* i. 10, 4); yet, while not altogether escaping the reproach which attached to their calling as such, the higher class of bankers in many instances acquired much personal respect, and a high reputation for ability combined with honesty (Dem. *Pro Phorm.* p. 957, § 44); their credit enabled them to raise money at a moment's notice in distant cities (id. *Contra Polycl.* p. 1224, § 56). Such confidence was placed in them that sometimes business was transacted with them without witnesses; money and contracts of debt were deposited with them, and agreements were concluded or cancelled in their presence (Dem. *Contra Callipp.* p. 1242, § 24; *Contra Dionysod.* p. 1287, § 15). They thus became a sort of unofficial notaries-public.

Before the rise of a banking system, the place of banks was to some extent supplied by the temples, which played no unimportant part in early Greek commerce. They were used as safe places for the deposit of treasure; and having large funds of their own, derived from the rent of their estates and from votive offerings, they employed productively both these and the sums confided to their care. Thus Clisthenes and the Alcmaeonidae borrowed from the Delphic sanctuary, with the consent of the Amphictyons, the funds with which the Pisistratidae were overthrown (Isocr. *Antid.* § 232); and at the outbreak of the Peloponnesian War the Corinthians proposed to equip a fleet with loans effected at Delphi and Olympia (Thuc. i. 121). It has been thought that the temples confined themselves to State loans, and did not lend money to individuals: Büchsenschütz, however, has shown from the Delian *Marmor Sandvicense* (see AMPHICTYONES) and other inscriptions that private persons enjoyed this accommodation. To the undoubted general rule that no banks were either worked or guaranteed by the State, an exception was imagined to exist at Byzantium on the strength of a passage in Aristotle (*Oecon.* ii. 4, 4); but all that is really stated is that an impoverished government, among other expedients, sold a monopoly of money-changing to a particular bank.

II. ROMAN.—Bankers are known to have existed in Rome as early as 309 B.C. (Livy, ix. 40, 16), and their functions were substantially the same as in Greece. Originally an *argentarius* was a private banker, and a *nummularius* a State officer, connected with the Mint (see MONETA); but in later Latin both terms as well as *mensarius, mensularius*, and *collectarius* are used indiscriminately of any one engaged in the business of lending or changing money.

The branches of a Roman banker's business were the following: (1) *Permutatio*, or the exchange of foreign coin for Roman coin, in which case a small commission (*collybus*) was paid to them (Cic. *Verr.* iii. 78, 180). In later times, when the Romans became acquainted with the Greek custom of using bills of exchange, the Roman bankers, e. g., received sums of money which had to be paid at Athens, and then drew a bill payable at Athens by some banker in that city (*permutare Athenas*, Cic. *Ad Att.* xv. 15, 4). This operation was also called *permutatio*. (2) The keeping of sums of money for other persons. Such money might be deposited by the owner merely to save himself the trouble of keeping it and making payments, and in this case it was called *depositum;* the *argentarius* then paid no interest, and the money was called *vacua pecunia*. When a payment was to be made, the owner drew a cheque (Plaut. *Curcul.* ii. 3, 66, etc.; iii. 66, etc.). Or the money was deposited on condition of the *argentarius* paying interest: in this case the money was called *creditum*, and the *argentarius* might of course employ the money himself in any lucrative manner (Suet. *Aug.* 39). In case of failure the law enacted that the claims of *depositarii* should be satisfied before those of creditors who had money at interest in the bank (*Dig.* xvi. 3, 7, 2). The *argentarius* thus did almost the same sort of business as a modern banker. Many persons intrusted all their capital to them (Cic. *Pro Caec.* 6, 16); and instances in which the *argentarii* made payments in the name of those whose money they had in hand are mentioned very frequently. A payment made through a banker was called *per mensam, de mensa*, or *per mensae scripturam*, while a payment made by the debtor in person was a payment *ex arca* or *de domo*. An *argentarius* never paid away any person's money without receiving a cheque (*perscriptio*), and the payment was then made either in cash, or, if the person who was to receive it kept an account with the same banker, he had it added in the banker's book to his own deposit. This was likewise called *perscribere* or simply *scribere* (Plaut. *Asin.* ii. 4, 34, etc.; *Curc.* v. 2, 20; Cic. *Ad Att.* iv. 18, § 2, ix. 12, 3, xii. 51, 3; Hor. *Sat.* ii. 3, 76). We also find that *argentarii* made payments for persons who had not deposited any money with them: this was equivalent to lending money, which in fact they often did for a certain percentage of interest. Of all this business, of the receipts as well as of the expenditure, the *argentarii* kept accurate accounts in books called *codices, tabulae*, or *rationes* (*Dig.* 2, 13, 1, 1), and there is every reason for believing that they were acquainted with what is called in book-keeping double entry. (3) A connection with commerce and public auctions. This branch of their business seems to have been one of the most ancient. In private sales and purchases they sometimes acted as agents for either party (*interpretes*), and sometimes they undertook to sell the whole estate of a person, as an inheritance. At public auctions they were almost invariably present, registering the articles sold, their prices and purchasers, and receiving the payment from the purchasers. At auctions, however, the *argentarii* might transact business through their clerks or servants, who were called *coactores* from their collecting the money. Horace's father and Vespasian's grandfather were *coactores*. This business, connected with auctions, seems to have belonged exclusively to *argentarii*.

Banking establishments were often owned by several partners (*socii*). Slaves were allowed to act as bankers on their own account with their *peculium*, and the master was liable for the amount of the *peculium* sunk in the business; but generally the slave was only the manager of the bank (*institor*) for his master. During imperial times the *argentarii*, like so many other branches of the community, organized themselves into a *collegium* (Orelli, 913, 995).

As regards the respectability of the *argentarii*, the passages of the ancients seem to contradict one another, for some writers speak of their occupation as respectable and honourable (Cic. *Pro Caec.* 4, 10); Aurel. Vict. 72; Suet. *Vesp.* 1; Acron. *ad* Hor. *Sat.* i. 6, 86), while others speak of them with contempt (Plaut. *Curc.* iv. 2, 20, *Casin.* Prol. 25, etc.); but this contradiction may be easily reconciled by distinguishing between a lower and a higher class of *argentarii*. A wealthy *argentarius* who carried on business on a large scale was undoubtedly as much a person of respectability as a banker in modern times; but others who did business only on a small scale, or degraded their calling by acting as usurers, cannot have been held in any esteem. It has already been observed that the *argentarii* had their shops round the Forum (Livy, ix. 40, xxvi. 11, 27); hence to become bankrupt was expressed by *foro cedere*, or *abire*, or *foro mergi*. The shops or booths were public property, and built by the censors, who sold the use of them to the *argentarii* (Livy, xxxix. 44, xl. 51).

BIBLIOGRAPHY.—On Greek banking, see Mahaffy's *Social Life in Greece*, ch. xiii. of the third edition; Hermann, *Privatalterth.* § 48; Becker-Göll, *Charikles*, sc. iv.; and Büchsenschütz, *Besitz und Erwerb*, pp. 500–510. On Roman banking, see Sieber, *De Argentariis* (Leipzig, 1737); Kraut, *De Argentariis* (Göttingen, 1826); Heimbach, *Die Lehre von dem Creditum* (Leipzig, 1849); Thomasset, *Des "Argentarii"* (Lyons, 1884); and Voigt, *Ueber die Bankiers . . . der Römer* (Leipzig, 1887). Cf. also the article FENUS.

Trapezophŏron (τραπεζοφόρον). A leg or other support for a table (τράπεζα), or for a sideboard. See ABACUS (6); MENSA.

Trapezūs (Τραπεζοῦς). (1) A city of Arcadia, on the Alpheus, the name of which was mythically derived from the τράπεζα, or altar, on which Lycaon was said to have offered human sacrifices to Zeus. At the time of the building of Megalopolis, the inhabitants of Trapezus, as was alleged, rather than be transferred to the new city, migrated to the shores of the Euxine, and their city fell to ruin (Paus. viii. 3, 2; Apollod. iii. 8, 1; Herod. vi. 127). (2) Now Tarabosan, Trabezun, or Trebizond); a colony of Sinopé, at almost the extreme east of the northern shore of Asia Minor. The city derived its name either from the table-like plateau on which it was built, or because emigrants from the Arcadian Trapezus took some part in its settlement (Paus. xiii. 27, 4). The former is the more likely statement, since there is no reason why the main body of colonists from Sinopé should have given it the name of another town. After Sinopé lost its independence, Trapezus belonged, first to Armenia Minor, and afterwards to the kingdom of Pontus. Under the Romans, it was made a free city, probably by Pompey, and, by Trajan, the capital of Pontus Cappadocius. Hadrian constructed a new harbour; and the city became a place of first-rate commercial importance. It was also strongly fortified. It was taken by the Goths in the reign of Valerian; but it had recovered, and was in a flourishing state at the time of Justinian, who repaired its fortifications (Procop. *Aed.* iii. 7). In the Middle Ages it was for some time the seat of a fragment of the Greek Empire, called the Empire of Trebizond.

Trasimēnus Lacus. Now Lago di Perugia; sometimes, but not correctly, written **Thrasymēnus.** A lake in Etruria, between Clusium and Perusia, memorable for the victory gained by Hannibal over the Romans under Flaminius, B.C. 217. See HANNIBAL.

Travesty. See PARODIA.

Treason. See MAIESTAS.

Treasury. See AERARIUM; THESAURUS; THOLUS.

Treba. Now Trevi; a town in Latium, near the sources of the Anio, northeast of Anagnia.

Trebatius Testa. See TESTA.

Trebellius Pollio. One of the six writers of the so-called *Augusta Historia*, flourished under Constantine. See AUGUSTAE HISTORIAE SCRIPTORES.

Trebia. Now the Trebbia; a small river in Gallia Cisalpina, falling into the Po near Placentia. It is memorable for the victory which Hannibal gained over the Romans, B.C. 218. See H. Müller, *Die Schlacht an der Trebia*, 2 pts. (1867–76); and the article HANNIBAL.

Trebonianus. See GALLUS.

Trebonius, GAIUS. A Roman who played a prominent part in the last days of the Republic. He commenced public life as a supporter of the aristocratic party, but changed sides soon afterwards, and in his tribunate of the plebs (B.C. 55) he proposed the *lex Trebonia*, by which Pompey obtained the two Spains, Crassus Syria, and Caesar the Gauls and Illyricum for another period of five years. (See CAESAR.) For this service he was rewarded by being appointed one of Caesar's legates in Gaul. In 48 Trebonius was city-praetor, and towards the end of 47 succeeded Q. Cassius Longinus as pro-praetor in the government of Farther Spain. Caesar raised him to the consulship in October, 45, and promised him the province of Asia. In return for all these honours and favours, Trebonius was one of the prime movers in the conspiracy to assassinate Caesar, and after the murder of his patron (44) he went as proconsul to the province of Asia. In the following year (43) Dolabella surprised Smyrna and put Trebonius to death.

Trebŭla. (1) Now Treglia; a town in Samnium situated in the southeastern part of the mountains of Cajazzo. (2) MUTUSCA, a town of the Sabines, of uncertain site.

Trechedipnum. A word of doubtful meaning (Juv. iii. 67). It may denote a kind of boot, or possibly a sort of coat. See Mayor *ad loc.*

Trendelenburg, FRIEDRICH ADOLF. A German scholar and student of philosophy, born at Eutin, November 30, 1802. He studied at Kiel and became Professor in the University of Berlin in 1833. He is best known for his exposition of Greek philosophy in relation to the modern schools of thought. He published *Elementa Logices Aristotelicae* (8th ed. 1878); and an edition of Aristotle's *De Anima* (2d ed. rev. by Belger, 1879); besides various works on the German philosophy, etc. He died January 24, 1872. See the memoir by Bratuschek (1873) and the work by Orphal (1891).

Trerus. Now the Sacco; a river in Latium, and a tributary of the Liris.

Tres Tabernae. (1) A station on the Via Appia in Latium, between Aricia and Forum Appii. It is mentioned in the account of St. Paul's journey to Rome. (2) Now Borghetto; a station in Gallia Cisalpina, on the road from Placentia to Mediolanum.

Tresvĭri. The Roman term for a board of three men. See TRESVIRI; and also VIGINTISEXVIRI.

Tresvĭri. Either ordinary magistrates or officers, or else extraordinary commissioners, who were frequently appointed at Rome to execute any public office. The form *triumvir* is quite legitimate, and the gen. plur. is often used as a predicate of a single individual; but it is doubtful whether there is any good authority for the nom. plur. *triumviri*, although it is often found in our texts: MSS. seem always to give *iiiviri.* The following is a list of the most important of both classes, arranged in alphabetical order:

(1) TRESVĬRI AGRO DIVIDUNDO. See TRESVIRI COLONIAE DEDUCENDAE below.

(2) TRESVĬRI CAPITĀLES appear to have been regularly appointed first in about B.C. 290 (Livy, *Epit.* 11). At first the tresviri were not chosen by the people, but nominated, probably by the Praetor Urbanus, who at a later time presided at their election.

In criminal cases their main duty was to look to the safer custody of the convicted, and to execute capital punishment. The usual form of execution was, for the upper classes and for women, strangling in prison (*triumvirale supplicium,* Tac. *Ann.* v. 10), a fate which befell the fellow-conspirators of Catiline (Sall. *Cat.* 55); slaves were crucified, also under their supervision. They had also the duty of receiving charges (Plaut. *Aul.* 413) and of arresting offenders; and generally of looking after the police of Rome, for which purpose they had a post in the Forum near the Columna Maenia (Cic. *Pro Cluent.* 13, 39). Their duty was to go the round of the streets by night, and to seize and punish disorderly characters (Plaut. *Amph.* ad init.), and, as being charged with the safety of the city, they were required to be present at once in cases of fire. There is no trace of any independent criminal jurisdiction; even a slave had to be condemned by a regular court; but this does not preclude the administration of such punishment as was necessary to keep order. They had further to exact and to pay into the treasury the *sacramenta* due in civil suits, and to decide upon the obligation to serve as *iudices* (Cic. *Brut.* 31, 117). Here, as in other cases, they appear as the assistants of the praetors. Under the Empire their functions were mainly discharged by the *praefectus vigilum.* See VIGILES.

(3) TRESVĬRI COLONIAE DEDUCENDAE were persons appointed to superintend the formation of a colony. Since they had besides to superintend the distribution of the land to the colonists, we find them also called *Tresviri Coloniae Deducendae Agroque Dividundo,* and sometimes simply *Tresviri Agro Dando.* The number three was the most usual one, but we also find commissions of five, seven, ten, fifteen, or twenty, as might be determined by the law instituting the colony.

(4) TRESVĬRI EPULŌNES. See EPULONES.

(5) TRESVĬRI EQUĬTUM TURMAS RECOGNOSCENDI, or LEGENDIS EQUĬTUM DECURIIS, were magistrates first appointed by Augustus to revise the lists of the *equites,* not at the census, but at the *transvectio equitum,* and to admit persons into the order, which was formerly part of the duties of the censors (Suet. *Aug.* 37).

(6) TRESVĬRI MONETĀLES. See MONETA.

(7) TRESVĬRI REFICIENDIS AEDĬBUS, elected in the Comitia Tributa in the time of the Second Punic War, a commission for the purpose of repairing and rebuilding certain temples (Livy, xxv. 7).

(8) TRESVĬRI REIPUBLĬCAE CONSTITUENDAE. We have no certain mention of officers or magistrates under this name till towards the close of the Republic, when the supreme power was shared between Lepidus, Antonius, and Caesar (Octavianus), who administered the affairs of the State under the title of *Tresviri Reipublicae Constituendae.* This office was conferred upon them in B.C. 43 by a law of P. Titius the tribune for five years (Livy, *Epit.* 120); and on the expiration of the term, in B.C. 38, was conferred upon them again, in B.C. 37, for five years more. The coalition between Iulius Caesar, Pompeius, and Crassus, in B.C. 60 (Vell. Pat. ii. 44; Livy, *Epit.* 103), is usually called the First Triumvirate, and that between Octavianus, Antony, and Lepidus, the Second; but it must be borne in mind that the former never bore the title of tresviri, nor were invested with any office under that name, whereas the latter were recognized as regular magistrates under the above-mentioned title.

(9) TRESVĬRI SACRIS CONQUIRENDIS DONISQUE PERSIGNANDIS, extraordinary officers elected in the Comitia Tributa in the time of the Second Punic War, to take care that all property given or consecrated to the gods was applied to that purpose (Livy, xxv. 7). See VOTA PUBLICA.

(10) TRESVĬRI SENATUS LEGENDI, officers appointed, whenever required by Augustus, to admit persons into the Senate, which had been the duty of the censors heretofore.

Tresvĭri Nocturni. See TRESVIRI CAPITALES under TRESVIRI.

Trevĭri or **Trevĕri.** A powerful people in Gallia Belgica, who were faithful allies of the Romans, and whose cavalry was the best in all Gaul. The river Mosella flowed through their territory, which extended westward from the Rhine as far as the Remi. Their chief town was made a Roman colony by Augustus, and was called AUGUSTA TREVIRŌRUM (Trier or Trèves). It stood on the right bank of the Mosella, and became under the later Empire one of the most flourishing Roman cities north of the Alps. It was the capital of Belgica Prima; and after the division of the Roman world by Diocletian (A.D. 292) into four districts it became the residence of the Caesar who had the government of Britain, Gaul, and Spain. The modern city still contains many interesting Roman remains, among them a famous arch or gate known as the Porta Nigra, baths, an amphitheatre, and a palace once occupied by the emperor Constantine. See the monographs by Wilmowski (1874–1876), Hettner (1880), Steinbach (1883), and Beissel (1888), and Freeman's *Historical and Architectural Studies* (1876).

Porta Nigra at Trèves.

Trials at Law. See DIKÉ; ACTIO (in the Appendix); JUDICIAL PROCEDURE.

Triarii. Heavily armed infantry soldiers in the Roman legions, of which they formed the third division, as the name implies. They were originally styled *pilani* from the heavy javelin (*pilum*) which they carried. See EXERCITUS; LEGIO; PILUM.

Triballi. A powerful people in Thrace, a branch of the Getae, dwelling along the Danube, who were defeated by Alexander the Great, B.C. 335 (Arrian, *Anab.* i. 2).

Tribocci. A German people, settled in Gallia Belgica, between Mount Vogesus and the Rhine, in the neighbourhood of Strasburg.

Tribon (τρίβων). A garment worn in Doric States by men and *ephebi*, generally in a double fold over the *chiton*. It was considerably shorter than the *himation* (q. v.). At Athens also there was a tendency to imitate Spartan simplicity, especially on the part of the philosophers, among whom this garment was worn chiefly by the Cynics (Auson. *Epist.* 53). Cf. ABOLLA.

Triboniānus. See CORPUS IURIS; IUSTINIANUS.

Tribŭla (τὰ τρίβολα) or **Tribŭlum.** A corn-drag, consisting of a thick and ponderous wooden board, which was armed underneath with pieces of iron or sharp flints, and drawn over the corn by a yoke of oxen, either the driver or a heavy weight being placed upon it, for the purpose of separating the grain and cutting the straw.

Tribŭlus (τρίβολος). A ball with sharp spikes, used to impede a charge of cavalry. It was also called *murex*. See illustration under MUREX.

Tribūnal (δικαστήριον). (1) A raised platform at one extremity of a law court, upon which the curule seats of the judges and other persons of distinction who wished to attend the proceedings were placed (Cic. *Verr.* ii. 38; Suet. *Tib.* 33).

(2) In a camp, the tribunal was an elevated platform upon which the general sat to administer justice (Tac. *Hist.* iv. 25); similar to the *suggestum* (q. v.).

(3) In a Roman theatre, the tribunal was an elevated seat in the pit (*orchestra*, Suet. *Claud.* 21), generally appropriated to the use of the praetor (id. *Aug.* 44).

Tribuni. See TRIBUNUS.

Tribūni Aerarii. The name given among the Romans in earlier times to the wealthy members of the several tribes who were intrusted with the levying of the war-tax (see TRIBUTUM) and the distribution of pay to the soldiers from the proceeds of it. What position they held after the payment of the troops was handed over to the quaestors is not clear, from want of information on the subject. In the first century B.C. they appear as a distinct class, from which, during the years B.C. 70–46, the third *decuria* of judges was appointed to represent the plebeians, the other two consisting of senators and knights.

Tribūni Milĭtum (χιλίαρχοι). Military tribunes; the superior officers of the Roman legions, six in number, two of whom always held the command for two months on alternate days. They were appointed before the levy took place, as they themselves had to be in office at that time. Originally they were nominated by the consuls; afterwards partly by them and partly by the people, inasmuch as the people elected twenty-four out of the number of candidates in the Comitia Tributa for the four legions which were levied regularly every year, while the consuls retained the appointment for the remaining legions. They were not as a rule taken from veteran centurions, but for the greater part from young men of senatorial or equestrian rank who had served their first campaign in the train or on the staff of a general, and then began their political career with this office. As a mark of distinction, all of them wore the gold ring of the equestrian order. They also wore a narrow or broad purple stripe on their *toga*, according as they were of equestrian or senatorial rank respectively. In the time of the Empire, they always led the legion on the march and in battle. They did not, however, as under the Republic, rank immediately below the commanders-in-chief, but under the *legatus legionis*, the commander of the legion and its auxiliary troops. See EXERCITUS; LEGIO.

Tribūnus, a tribune; a word that seems originally to have indicated an officer connected with a tribe (*tribus*), or who represented a tribe for certain purposes; and this is indeed the character of the officers who were designated by it in the earliest times of Rome, and may be traced also in the later officers of this name.

(1) TRIBUNES OF THE THREE ANCIENT TRIBES.—At the time when all the Roman citizens were contained in the three tribes of the Ramnes, Tities, and Luceres, each of these was headed by a tribune, and these three tribunes represented their respective tribes in all civil, religious, and military affairs; that is to say, they were in the city the magistrates of the tribes, and performed the sacra on their behalf, and in times of war they were their commanders. The TRIBUNUS CELĔRUM was the commander of the *Celeres*, the king's body-guard, and not the tribune of the tribe of the Ramnes, as is supposed by some modern writers. In what manner the Tribunus Celerum was appointed is uncertain, but it is probable that he was elected by the tribes; for we find that when the imperium was to be conferred upon the king, the Comitia were held under the presidency of the Tribunus Celerum; and in the absence of the king, to whom this officer was next in rank, he convoked the Comitia: it was in an assembly of this kind that Brutus proposed to deprive Tarquinius of the imperium. A law passed under the presidency of the Tribunus Celerum was called a *lex tribunicia*, to distinguish it from one passed under the presidency of the king. The tribunes of the three ancient tribes ceased to be appointed when these tribes themselves ceased to exist as political bodies, and when the patricians became incorporated in the local tribes of Servius Tullius. See TRIBUS.

(2) TRIBUNES OF THE SERVIAN TRIBES.—When Servius Tullius divided the commonalty into thirty local tribes, we again find a tribune at the head of these tribes. The duties of these tribunes, who were without doubt the most distinguished persons in their respective districts, appear to have consisted at first in keeping a register of the inhabitants in each district, and of their property, for purposes of taxation, and for levying the troops for the armies. When subsequently the Roman people became exempted from taxes, the main part of their business was taken from them, but they still continued to exist. The TRIBUNI AERARII, who occur down to the end of the Repub-

lic, were perhaps only the successors of the tribunes of the tribes. When (B.C. 406) the custom of giving pay (*stipendium*) to the soldiers was introduced, each of the Tribuni Aerarii had to collect the *tributum* (q. v.) in his own tribe, and with it to pay the soldiers; and in case they did not fulfil this duty, the soldiers had the right of *pignoris capio* against them. In later times their duties appear to have been confined to collecting the *tributum*, which they made over to the military quaestors who paid the soldiers. (See QUAESTOR.) The Lex Aurelia, B.C. 70, called the Tribuni Aerarii to the exercise of judicial functions along with the senators and equites, as these tribunes represented the body of the most respectable citizens. But of this distinction they were subsequently deprived by Iulius Caesar.

(3) TRIBŪNI PLEBIS (δήμαρχοι).—The ancient tribunes of the plebeian tribes had undoubtedly the right of convoking the meetings of their tribes, and of maintaining the privileges granted to them by King Servius, and subsequently by the Valerian laws. But this protection was very inadequate against the insatiable ambition and usurpations of the patricians. When the plebeians, impoverished by long wars, and cruelly oppressed by the patricians, at last seceded in B.C. 494 to the Mons Sacer, the patricians were obliged to grant to the plebeians the right of appointing tribunes (*tribuni plebis*) with more efficient powers to protect their own order than those which were possessed by the heads of the tribes. The purpose for which they were appointed was only to afford protection against any abuse on the part of the patrician magistrates; and that they might be able to afford such protection their persons were declared sacred and inviolable, and it was agreed that whoever invaded this inviolability should be an outlaw, and that his property should be forfeited to the Temple of Ceres. A subsequent law enacted that no one should oppose or interrupt a tribune while addressing the people, and that whoever should act contrary to this ordinance should give bail to the tribunes for the payment of whatever fine they should affix to his offence in arraigning him before the commonalty; if he refused to give bail, his life and property were forfeited. The tribunes were thus enabled to afford protection to any one who appealed to the assembly of the commonalty or required any other assistance. They were essentially the representatives and the organs of the plebeian order, and their sphere of action was the Comitia Tributa. With the patricians and their Comitia they had nothing to do. The tribunes themselves, however, were not judges, and could inflict no punishments, but could only propose the imposition of a fine to the commonalty (*multam irrogare*). The tribunes were thus in their origin only a protecting magistracy of the plebs, but in the course of time their power increased to such a degree that it surpassed that of all other magistrates, and the tribunes then became a magistracy for the whole Roman people, in opposition to the Senate and the oligarchical party in general, although they had nothing to do with the administration or the government. During the latter period of the Republic they became true tyrants, and may be compared to the National Convention of France during the first Revolution. At first the number of the tribunes was only two, but soon afterwards they were increased to five, one being taken from each of the five classes, and subsequently to ten, two being taken from each of the five classes. This last number appears to have remained unaltered down to the end of the Empire. The tribunes entered upon their office on the 10th of December, but were elected, at least in the time of Cicero, on the 17th of July. It is almost superfluous to state that none but plebeians were eligible to the office of tribune; hence when, towards the end of the Republic, patricians wished to obtain the office, they were obliged first to renounce their own order and to become plebeians; hence also, under the Empire, it was thought that the *princeps* (q. v.) should not be tribune because he was a patrician. But the influence which belonged to this office was too great for the emperors not to covet it. Hence Augustus was made tribune for life. During the Republic, however, the old regulation remained in force, even after the tribunes had ceased to be the protectors of the plebs alone. There is only one instance recorded in which patricians were elected to the tribuneship, and this was probably the consequence of an attempt to divide the tribuneship between the two orders. Although nothing appears to be more natural than that the tribunes should originally have been elected by that body of Roman citizens which they represented, yet the subject is involved in considerable obscurity. Some writers state that they were elected by the Comitia Curiata; others suppose that they were elected in the Comitia Centuriata; but whether they were elected in the latter or in the Comitia of the Tribes, it is certain that at first the sanction of the curies to the election was at all events necessary. But after the time of the Lex Publilia (B.C. 472) the sanction of the curies is not heard of, and the election of the tribunes was left entirely to the Comitia Tributa, which were convoked and held for this purpose by the old tribunes previous to the expiration of their office. One of the old tribunes was appointed by lot to preside at the election. As the meeting could not be prolonged after sunset, and the business was to be completed in one day, it sometimes happened that it was obliged to break up before the election was completed, and then those who were elected filled up the legitimate number of the college by *coöptatio*. But in order to prevent this irregularity, the tribune L. Trebonius, in B.C. 448, got an ordinance passed, according to which the college of the tribunes should never be completed by *coöptatio*, but the elections should be continued on the second day, if they were not completed on the first, till the number ten was made up. The place where the election of the tribunes was held was originally and lawfully the Forum, afterwards also the Campus Martius, and sometimes the area of the Capitol.

We now proceed to trace the gradual growth of the tribunitian power. Although its original character was merely protection (*auxilium* or βοήθεια) against patrician magistrates, the plebeians appear early to have regarded their tribunes also as mediators or arbitrators in matters among themselves. The whole power possessed by the college of tribunes was designated by the name *tribunicia potestas*, and extended at no time farther than one mile beyond the gates of the city; at a greater distance than this they came under the imperium of the magistrates, like every other citizen. As they were the public guardians, it was necessary that every one should have access to them at any time; hence the doors of their houses were open day and night for all who were in need of help and protection, which they were empowered to afford against any one, even against the highest magistrates. For the same reason a tribune was not allowed to be absent from the city for a whole day, except during the Feriae Latinae, when the whole people were assembled on the Alban Mount. In B.C. 456 the tribunes, in opposition to the consuls, assumed the right of convoking the Senate, in order to lay before it a rogation, and discuss the same; for until that time the consuls alone had had the right of laying *plebiscita* before the Senate for approbation. Some years after, B.C. 452, the tribunes demanded of the consuls to request the Senate to make a *senatusconsultum* for the appointment of persons to frame a new legislation; and during the discussions on this subject the tribunes themselves were present in the Senate. The written legislation which the tribunes then wished can only have related to their own order; but as such a legislation would only have widened the breach between the two orders, they afterwards gave way to the remonstrances of the patricians, and the new legislation was to embrace both orders. From the second decemvirate the tribuneship was suspended, but was restored after the legislation was completed, and now assumed a different character from the change that had taken place in the tribes. (See TRIBUS.) The tribunes now had the right to be present at the deliberations of the Senate; but they did not sit among the senators themselves, but upon benches before the opened doors of the senate-house. The inviolability of the tribunes, which had before only rested upon a contract between the two estates, was now sanctioned and confirmed by a law of M. Horatius. As the tribes now also included the patricians and their clients, the tribunes might naturally be asked to interpose on behalf of any citizen, whether patrician or plebeian. Hence the patrician ex-decemvir Appius Claudius implored the protection of the tribunes. About this time the tribunes also acquired the right of taking the auspices in the assemblies of the tribes. They also assumed again the right, which they had exercised before the time of the decemvirate, of bringing patricians who had violated the rights of the plebeians before the Comitia of the Tribes. By the Lex Valeria, passed in the Comitia Centuriata (B.C. 449), it was enacted that a plebiscitum, which had been voted by the tribes, should bind the patricians as well. While the college thus gained outwardly new strength every day, a change took place in its internal organization which to some extent paralyzed its powers. Before B.C. 394, everything had been decided in the college by a majority; but about this time, we do not know how, a change was introduced, which made the opposition (*intercessio*) of one tribune sufficient to render a resolution of his colleagues void. This new regulation does not appear in operation till 394 and 393 B.C.; the old one was still applied in B.C. 421 and 415. From their right of appearing in the Senate, and of taking part in its discussions, and from their being the representatives of the whole people, they gradually obtained the right of intercession against any action which a magistrate might undertake during the time of his office, and this even without giving any reason for it. Thus we find a tribune preventing a consul from convoking the Senate, and preventing the proposal of new laws or elections in the Comitia; they interceded against the official functions of the censors; and even against a command issued by the praetor. In the same manner a tribune might place his veto upon an ordinance of the Senate; and he could thus either compel the Senate to submit the subject to a fresh consideration, or could raise the session. In order to propose a measure to the Senate they might themselves convene a meeting, or when it had been convened by a consul they might make their proposal even in opposition to the consul, a right which no other magistrates had in the presence of the consuls. The Senate, on the other hand, had itself, in certain cases, recourse to the tribunes. Thus, in B.C. 431 it requested the tribunes to compel the consuls to appoint a dictator, in compliance with a decree of the Senate, and the tribunes compelled the consuls, by threatening them with imprisonment, to appoint A. Postumius Tubertus dictator. From this time forward we meet with several instances in which the tribunes compelled the consuls to comply with the decrees of the Senate, *si non essent in auctoritate senatus*, and to execute its commands. In their relation to the Senate a change was introduced by the *plebiscitum Atinium*, which ordained that a tribune, by virtue of his office, should be a senator. When this plebiscitum was made is uncertain; but we know that in B.C. 170 it was not yet in operation. It probably originated with C. Atinius, who was tribune in B.C. 132. But as the quaestorship, at least in later times, was the office which persons held previously to the tribuneship, and as the quaestorship itself conferred upon a person the right of a senator, the law of Atinius was in most cases superfluous.

In their relation to other magistrates we may observe, that the right of *intercessio* was not confined to stopping a magistrate in his proceedings, but they might even command their *viatores* to seize a consul or a censor, to imprison him, or to throw him from the Tarpeian Rock. When the tribunes brought an accusation against any one before the people, they had the right of *prehensio*, but not the right of *vocatio;* that is, they might command a person to be dragged by their *viatores* before the Comitia, but they could not summon him. They might, as in earlier times, propose a fine to be inflicted upon the person accused before the Comitia, but in some cases they dropped this proposal and treated the case as a capital one. The college of tribunes had also the power of making edicts. In cases in which one member of the college opposed a resolution of his colleagues nothing could be done, and the measure was dropped; but this useful check was removed by the example of Tiberius Gracchus, in which a precedent was given for proposing to the people that a tribune obstinately persisting in his veto should be deprived of his office. From the time of the Hortensian law the power of the tribunes had been gradually rising to such a height that at length it was superior to every other in the State. They had acquired the right of proposing to the Comitia Tributa or the Senate measures on nearly all the important affairs of the State, and it would be endless to enumerate the cases in which their power was manifested. Their proposals were indeed usually made *ex auctoritate senatus*, or had been communicated to and approved by it; but in cases in which the people itself had a direct interest, such as a general legal regulation, granting of the franchise, a change in the duties and powers of a magistrate, and others, might be brought before the people, without their having been previously communicated to the Senate, though there are also instances of the contrary. Subjects belonging to the administration could not be brought before the tribes without the tribunes having previously received through the consuls the *auctoritas* of the Senate. This, however, was done very frequently, and hence we have mention of a number of plebiscita on matters of administration. It sometimes even occurs that the tribunes brought the question concerning the conclusion of peace before the tribes, and then compelled the Senate to ratify the resolution, as expressing the wish of the whole people. Sulla, in his reform of the constitution on the early aristocratic principles, left to the tribunes only the *ius auxiliandi*, and deprived them of the right of making legislative or other proposals, either to the Senate or the Comitia, without having previously obtained the sanction of the Senate. But this arrangement did not last, for Pompey restored to them their former rights. During the latter period of the Republic, when the office of quaestor was in most cases held immediately before that of tribune, the tribunes were generally elected from among the senators, and this continued to be the case under the Empire. Sometimes, however, *equites* also obtained the office, and thereby became members of the Senate, where they were considered of equal rank with the quaestors. The tribunes of the people continued to exist down to the fifth century of our era, though their powers became naturally much limited, especially in the reign of Nero. They continued, however, to have the right of intercession against decrees of the Senate, and on behalf of injured individuals. See R. Müller, *Gesetz der zehn Tribunen* (Berlin, 1877); and the account in Bouché-Leclercq, *Institutions Romaines* (Paris, 1886); Mommsen, *Röm. Staatsrecht* (Leipzig, 1876); and for a simpler treatment, see Marlot, *Précis des Institutions Politiques de Rome* (Paris, 1886).

(4) TRIBŪNI MILĬTUM CUM CONSULĀRI POTESTATE.—When in B.C. 445 the tribune C. Canuleius brought forward the rogation that the consulship should not be confined to either order, the patricians evaded the attempt by a change in the constitution; the powers which had hitherto been united in the consulship were now divided between two magistrates—viz., the *tribuni militum cum consulari potestate* and the censors. Consequently, in B.C. 444, three military tribunes, with consular power, were appointed, and to this office the plebeians were to be equally eligible with the patricians. For the years following, however, the people were to be at liberty, on the proposal of the Senate, to decide whether consuls were to be elected according to the old customs, or consular tribunes. Henceforth, for many years, sometimes consuls and sometimes consular tribunes were appointed, and the number of the latter varied from three to four, until in B.C. 405 it was increased to six, and, as the censors were regarded as their colleagues, we have sometimes mention of eight tribunes. At last, however, in B.C. 367, the office of these tribunes was abolished by the Licinian law, and the consulship was restored. These consular tribunes were elected in the Comitia Centuriata, and undoubtedly with less solemn auspices than the consuls.

(5) TRIBŪNI MILITĀRES. See TRIBŪNI MILITUM, p. 1601.

Tribūnus Celĕrum. The designation, under the Roman Empire, of the commander of the cavalry, nominated by the emperor for the time being. See also under TRIBUNUS ad init.

Tribus (φῦλον, φυλή), a tribe. I. GREEK.—In the earliest times of Greek history mention is made of people being divided into tribes and clans. Homer speaks of such divisions in terms which seem to imply that they were elements that entered into the composition of every community. A person not included in any clan (ἀφρήτωρ) was regarded as a vagrant or outlaw. These divisions were rather natural than political, depending on family connection, and arising out of those times when each head of a family exercised a patriarchal sway over its members. The bond was cemented by religious communion, sacrifices, and festivals, which all the family or clansmen attended, and at which the chief usually presided.

Of the Dorian race there were originally three tribes, traces of which are found in all the countries which they colonized. Hence they are called by Homer Δωριέες τριχάϊκες. These tribes were the Hylleis (Ὑλλεῖς), Pamphyli (Πάμφυλοι), and Dymanatae or Dymanes (Δυμανάται or Δυμᾶνες). The first derived their name from Hyllus, son of Heracles, the two last from Pamphylus and Dymas, who are said to have fallen in the last expedition when the Dorians took possession of the Peloponnesus. The Hyllean tribe was perhaps the one of highest dignity; but at Sparta there does not appear to have been much distinction, for all the freemen there were by the constitution of Lycurgus on a footing of equality. To these three tribes others were added in different places, either when the Dorians were joined by other foreign allies, or when some of the old inhabitants were admitted to the rank of citizenship or equal privileges. Thus the Cadmean Aegeids are said by Herodotus to have been a great tribe at Sparta, descended (as he says) from Aegeus, grandson of Theras, though others have thought they were incorporated with the three Doric tribes. The subdivision of tribes into *phratriae* (φρατρίαι) or *patrae* (πάτραι), *gené* (γένη), *trittyes* (τρίττυες), etc., appears to have prevailed in various places. At Sparta each tribe contained ten *obae* (ὠβαί), a word denoting a local division or district; each *obé* contained ten *triacades* (τριακάδες), communities containing thirty families. But very little appears to be known of these divisions, how far they were local, or how far genealogical. After the time of Cleomenes the old system of tribes was changed; new ones were created corresponding to the different quarters of the town, and they seem to have been five in number. The first Attic tribes that we read of are said to have existed in the reign, or soon after the reign, of Cecrops, and were called Cecropis (Κεκροπίς), Autochthon (Αὐτόχθων), Actaea (Ἀκταία), and Paralia (Παραλία). In the reign of a subsequent king, Cranaüs, these names were changed to Cranaïs (Κραναΐς), Atthis (Ἀτθίς), Mesogaea (Μεσόγαια), and Diacris (Διακρίς). Afterwards we find a new set of names: Dias (Διάς), Athenaïs (Ἀθηναΐς), Poseidonias (Ποσειδωνιάς), and

Hephaestias (Ἡφαιστιάς), evidently derived from the deities who were worshipped in the country. Some of those secondly mentioned, if not all of them, seem to have been geographical divisions; and it is not improbable that, if not independent communities, they were at least connected by a very weak bond of union. But all these tribes were superseded by four others, which were probably founded soon after the Ionic settlement in Attica, and seem to have been adopted by other Ionic colonies out of Greece. The names Geleontes (Γελέοντες), Hopletes (Ὅπλητες), Argades (Ἀργάδεις), Aegicores (Αἰγικορεῖς), are said by Herodotus to have been derived from the sons of Ion, son of Xuthus. Upon this, however, many doubts have been thrown by modern writers. The etymology of the last three names would seem to suggest that the tribes were so called from the occupations which their respective members followed; the Hopletes being the armed men, or warriors; the Argades, labourers or husbandmen; the Aegicores, goatherds or shepherds. But whatever be the truth with respect to the origin of these tribes, one thing is certain, that before the time of Theseus, whom historians agree in representing as the great founder of the Attic commonwealth, the various people who inhabited the country continued to be disunited and split into factions. Theseus (q. v.) is said to have changed the relations of the tribes to each other, by introducing a gradation of ranks in each; dividing the people into Eupatridae (Εὐπατρίδαι), Geomori (Γεωμόροι), and Demiurgi (Δημιουργοί), of whom the first were nobles, the second agriculturists or yeomen, the third labourers and mechanics. At the same time, in order to consolidate the national unity, he enlarged the city of Athens, in which he incorporated several smaller towns, made it the seat of government, encouraged the nobles to reside there, and surrendered a part of the royal prerogative in their favour. The tribes or phylae were divided, either in the age of Theseus or soon after, each into three *phratriae* (φρατρίαι, a term equivalent to fraternities, and analogous in its political relation to the Roman *curiae*), and each *phratria* into thirty *gené* (γένη, equivalent to the Roman *gentes*), the members of a *genos* (γένος) being called *gennetae* (γεννῆται) or *homogalactes* (ὁμογαλάκτες). Each *genos* was distinguished by a particular name of a patronymic form, which was derived from some hero or mythic ancestor. These divisions, though the names seem to import family connection, were in fact artificial; which shows that some advance had now been made towards the establishment of a closer political union. The members of the *phratriae* and *gené* had their respective religious rites and festivals, which were preserved long after these communities had lost their political importance, and perhaps prevented them from being altogether dissolved. After the age of Theseus, the monarchy having been first limited and afterwards abolished, the whole power of the State fell into the hands of the Eupatridae or nobles, who held all civil offices, and had besides the management of religious affairs and the interpretation of the laws. Attica became agitated by feuds, and we find the people, shortly before the legislation of Solon, divided into three parties—Pediaei (Πεδιαῖοι) or lowlanders, Diacrii (Διάκριοι) or highlanders, and Parali (Πάραλοι) or people of the sea-coast. The first two remind one of the ancient division of tribes, Mesogaea and Diacris; and the three parties appear in some measure to represent the classes established by Theseus, the first being the nobles, whose property lay in the champaign and most fertile part of the country; the second, the smaller land-owners and shepherds; the third, the trading and mining class, who had by this time risen in wealth and importance. To appease their discords, Solon was called in; and thereupon framed his celebrated constitution and code of laws. Here we have only to notice that he retained the four tribes as he found them, but abolished the existing distinctions of rank, or at all events greatly diminished their importance, by introducing his property qualification, or division of the people into Pentacosiomedimni (Πεντακοσιομέδιμνοι), Hippeis (Ἱππεῖς), Zeugitae (Ζευγῖται), and Thetes (Θῆτες). (See SOLON.) The enactments of Solon continued to be the law at Athens, though in great measure suspended by the tyranny, until the democratic reform effected by Clisthenes. He abolished the old tribes, and created ten new ones, according to a geographical division of Attica, and named after ten of the ancient heroes: Erechtheïs, Aegeïs, Pandionis, Leontis, Acamantis, Oeneïs, Cecropis, Hippothoöntis, Aeantis, Antiochis. These tribes were divided each into ten *demi* (δῆμοι), the number of which was afterwards increased by subdivision; but the arrangement was so made that several demes not contiguous or near to one another were joined to make up a tribe. (See DEMUS.) The object of this arrangement was that, by the breaking of old associations, a perfect and lasting revolution might be effected in the habits and feelings as well as the political organization of the people. Solon allowed the ancient *phratriae* to exist, but they were deprived of all political importance. All foreigners admitted to the citizenship were registered in a phyle and demus, but not in a phratria or genos. The functions which had been discharged by the old tribes were now mostly transferred to the *demi*. Among others, we may notice that of the forty-eight *naucrariae* into which the old tribes had been divided for the purpose of taxation, but which now became useless, the taxes being collected on a different system. The reforms of Clisthenes (q. v.) were destined to be permanent. They continued to be in force (with some few interruptions) until the downfall of Athenian independence. The ten tribes were blended with the whole machinery of the constitution. Of the Senate of Five Hundred, fifty were chosen from each tribe. (See BOULÉ.) The allotment of dicasts was according to tribes; and the same system of election may be observed in most of the principal offices of State, judicial and magisterial, civil and military, etc. In B.C. 307, Demetrius Poliorcetes increased the number of tribes to twelve by creating two new ones—namely, Antigonias and Demetrias, which afterwards received the names of Ptolemaïs and Attalis; and a thirteenth was subsequently added by Hadrian, bearing his own name.

See Busolt, *Griechische Geschichte*, i. pp. 390 foll.; Schömann, *Antiq. of Greece*, Eng. trans. pt. ii. ch. 4; pt. iii. ch. 3; Fustel de Coulanges, *La Cité Antique*, pp. 131 foll., 10th ed. (1883); and Gilbert, *Greek Constitutional Antiq.* pp. 103 foll., Eng. trans. (1895).

II. ROMAN.—The three ancient Romulian tribes, the Ramnes, Tities, and Luceres, or the Ramnenses, Titienses, and Lucerenses, to which the patricians alone belonged, must be distinguished from the thirty plebeian tribes of Servius Tullius, which were entirely local—four for the city, and twenty-six for the country around Rome. The history and organization of the three ancient tribes are mentioned under PATRICII. They continued of political importance almost down to the period of the decemviral legislation; but after this time they no longer occur in the history of Rome, except as an obsolete institution. The institution and organization of the thirty plebeian tribes, and their subsequent reduction to twenty by the conquests of Porsena, are mentioned under PLEBES. The four city tribes were called by the same names as the regions which they occupied, viz., Suburana, Esquilina, Collina, and Palatina. The names of the sixteen country tribes which continued to belong to Rome after the conquest of Porsena are in their alphabetical order as follows: Aemilia, Camilia, Cornelia, Fabia, Galeria, Horatia, Lemonia, Menenia, Papiria, Pollia, Popillia, Pupinia, Romilia, Sergia, Veturia, and Voltinia. As Rome gradually acquired possession of more of the surrounding territory, the number of tribes also was gradually increased. When Appius Claudius, with his numerous train of clients, emigrated to Rome, lands were assigned to them in the district where the Anio flows into the Tiber, and a new tribe, the *tribus Claudia*, was formed. This tribe was subsequently enlarged, and was then designated by the name Crustumina or Clustumina. This name is the first instance of a country tribe being named after a place, for the sixteen older ones all derived their name from persons or heroes. In B.C. 387, the number of tribes was increased to twenty-five by the addition of four new ones—viz., the Stellatina, Tromentina, Sabatina, and Arniensis. In B.C. 358 two more, the Pomptina and Publilia, were formed of Volscians. In B.C. 332, the censors Q. Publilius Philo and Sp. Postumius increased the number of tribes to twenty-nine, by the addition of the Maecia and Scaptia. In B.C. 318 the Ufentina and Falerina were added. In B.C. 299 two others, the Aniensis and Terentina, were added by the censors, and at last, in B.C. 241, the number of tribes was augmented to thirty-five, by the addition of the Quirina and Velina. Eight new tribes were added upon the termination of the Social War, to include the Socii, who then obtained the Roman franchise; but they were afterwards incorporated among the old thirty-five tribes, which continued to be the number of the tribes to the end of the Republic. When the tribes, in their assemblies, transacted any business, a certain order (*ordo tribuum*) was observed, in which they were called upon to give their votes. The first in the order of succession was the Suburana, and the last the Arniensis. Any person belonging to a tribe had in important documents to add to his own name that of his tribe, in the ablative case. Whether the local tribes, as they were established by the constitution of Servius Tullius, contained only the plebeians, or included the patricians also, is a point on which the opinions of modern scholars are divided: but it appears most probable that down to the decemviral legislation the tribes and their assemblies were entirely plebeian. From the time of the decemviral legislation, the patricians and their clients were undoubtedly incorporated in the tribes. Respecting the assembly of the tribes, see COMITIA.

See Grotefend, *Imperium Romanum Tributim Descriptum* (1863); Kubitschek, *Imperium Romanum Tributim Descriptum* (1889); and Mommsen, *Die römischen Tribus* (Altona, 1844).

Tribūta Comitia. See COMITIA.

Tribūtum. Originally an extraordinary means of revenue among the Romans, levied on the burgesses in the proportion of one to three per thousand in times of war, when the means of the State treasury were of themselves not sufficient, and more especially after B.C. 406, when the State first took over the payment of the soldiers' wages. When the war was over, the money was generally repaid from contributions or from the booty. Subsequent to the conquest of Macedonia, B.C. 167, the income of the State from the provinces was so considerable that the burgesses, although not legally exempt, ceased any longer to be subject to this payment. The strictly regulated taxes of the provinces also went by the same name, *tributum soli*, the ground-tax, and *tributum capitis*, the personal tax. (See STIPENDIUM.) Italy, up to his time exempt, was also made liable to these taxes by Diocletian, towards the end of the third century A.D. Cf. PORTORIUM; VECTIGALIA.

Tricasses, Tricasii, or **Tricassīni.** A people in Gallia Lugdunensis, east of the Senones, whose chief town was Augustobona, afterwards Tricassae (Troyes).

Tricastīni. A people in Gallia Narbonensis, inhabiting a narrow slip of country between the Drome and the Isère. Their chief town was Augusta Tricastinorum, or simply Augusta (Aouste).

Tricca (Τρίκκη), subsequently **Tricăla** (Τρίκαλα). Now Trikkala; an ancient town of Thessaly in the district Hestiaeotis, situated on the Lethaeus, north of the Peneus. Homer represents it as governed by the sons of Asclepius; and it contained in later times a celebrated temple of this god.

Trichĭla, Trichĭlum, Tricla, and **Triclia.** A summer-house on the grounds of a villa or elsewhere. It was of wood or trellis-work and often entwined by ivy and other vines. Here the Romans often drank and took their meals in pleasant weather (Verg. *Copa*, 8).

Triciptīnus. See LUCRETIA GENS.

Tricliniarches and **Tricliniarcha.** The butler or major-domo who had the charge of the arrangements in the dining-room (*triclinium*). See TRICLINIUM.

Triclinium (τρίκλινον). The dining-room of a Roman house, as to the position of which, relatively to the other parts of the house, see DOMUS, pp. 547, 549, with the diagrams there given. It was of an oblong shape, and was twice as long as it was broad. The superintendence of the dining-room in a great house was intrusted to a slave called *tricliniarcha*, who, through other slaves, took care that everything was kept and proceeded in proper order. A triclinium generally contained three couches, and as the usual number of persons occupying each couch was three, the triclinium afforded accommodation for a party of nine. Sometimes, however, as many as four lay on each of the couches. Each man, in order to feed himself, lay flat upon his breast, or nearly so, and stretched out his hand towards the table; but afterwards, when his hunger was satisfied, he turned upon his left side, leaning on his elbow. To this Horace alludes in describing a sated person turning in order to repose upon his elbow (*Sat.* ii. 4, 39; but see Palmer *ad loc.*). We find the relative positions of two persons who lay next to one another commonly expressed in the prepositions *super* or *supra* and *infra*. A passage of Livy (xxxix. 43), in which he relates the cruel conduct of the consul L. Quintius Flamininus, shows that *infra aliquem cubare* was the same as *in sinu alicuius cubare*, and consequently that each person was considered as *below* him to whose breast his own head approached. On this principle we are enabled to explain the denominations both of the three couches, and of the three places on each couch. Supposing the annexed arrangement to represent the plan of a triclinium; it is evident that, as each guest re-

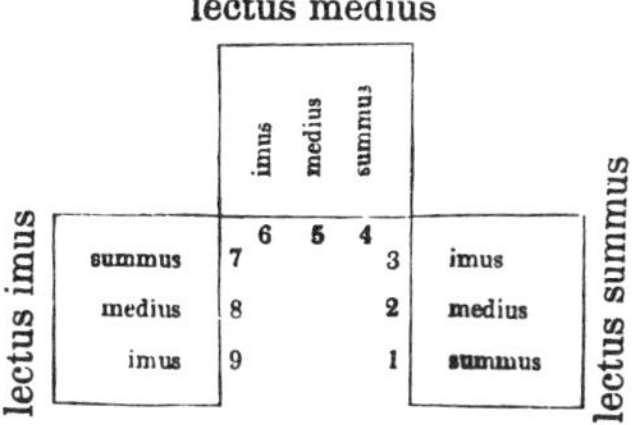

clined on his left side, the countenances of all when in this position were directed, first, from No. 1 towards No. 3, then from No. 4 towards No. 6, and lastly from No. 7 towards No. 9; that the guest No. 1 lay, in the sense explained, *above* No. 2, No. 3 *below* No. 2, and so of the rest; and that, going in the same direction, the couch to the right hand was *above* the others, and the couch to the left hand *below* the others. It will be found that in a passage of the Eighth Satire of the second book of Horace the guests are enumerated in the order of their reclining—an order exhibited in the annexed

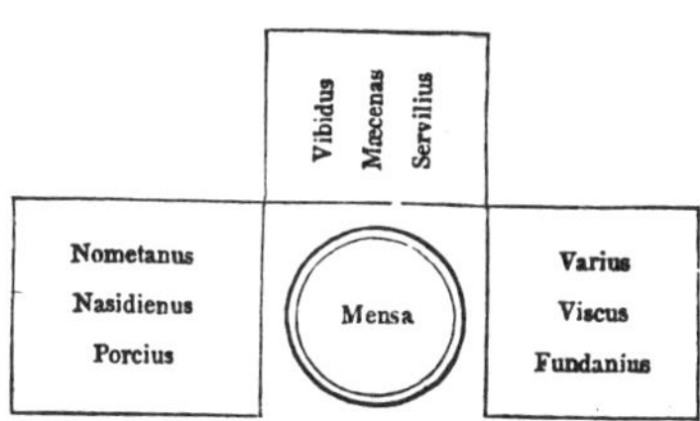

diagram. See CENA; MENSA. For the dinner dress, see SYNTHESIS.

Tricorii. A Ligurian people in Gallia Narbonensis, in the neighbourhood of Massilia (Marseilles) and Aquae Sextiae (Aix).

Tridens (τριόδους, τρίαινα). A trident. (1) A three-pronged fork for spearing fish. (2) A sort of pitchfork used by the class of gladiators called *retiarii*. (See GLADIATORES.) (3) The characteristic sign of Neptune, which in works of art he is depicted as carrying instead of a sceptre (Verg. *Aen.* ii. 610).

Tridentĭfer and **Tridentĭger.** "Trident-bearing"; adjectives often applied by the Latin poets to Neptune. See NEPTŪNUS.

Tridentum. Now Trent, in Italian Trento; the capital of the TRIDENTĪNI, and the chief town of Rhaetia, situated on the river Athesis (Adige) and on the pass of the Alps leading to Verona.

Triens. A Roman copper coin worth one third of an *as* and originally weighing four ounces (Pliny, *H. N.* xxxiii. 13). See AS; NUMISMATICS.

Triens.

Trierarches (τριηραρχής). Originally the commander of a trireme and afterwards of any large war-ship. See NAVIS.

Trierarchia (τριηραρχία). The superintendence of the equipment of a war-ship; one of the public burdens imposed on Athenian citizens. See LITURGIA.

Triēres (τριήρης). A Greek ship with three banks of oars. See NAVIS.

Trifax. A missile three and a half cubits long, discharged from a catapult (Gell. x. 25, 1). See TORMENTUM.

Triga. A three-horse chariot. See CURRUS.

Triglȳphus (τρίγλυφος, "three-channelled"). A name given in the Doric frieze to surfaces which, projecting over every column and between every two columns, are ornamented with three parallel channels, two complete ones in the middle and two halves at the corners. Between the triglyphs are the metopes. See ARCHITECTURA; PARTHENON.

Trigon. A kind of game played with a small hand-ball. See PILA.

Trigōnum (τρίγωνον). (1) A triangular piece of marble or tiling used in laying a mosaic pavement. (See PAVIMENTUM.) (2) A musical instrument, triangular in shape.

Trilogia (τριλογία). A set of three tragedies which, together with a satyric drama, formed a tetralogy. The several tragedies were generally, but not always, connected with each other in subject. The only surviving example is the *Oresteia* of Aeschylus, consisting of the *Agamemnon*, *Choephoroe*, and *Eumenides*. See Heimsoeth, *De Tragoediae Graecae Trilogiis* (1869); and the articles DRAMA; TETRALOGIA.

Trinacria. See SICILIA.

Trinobantes. One of the most powerful peoples of Britain, inhabiting the modern Essex. They offered a strong resistance to the Roman forces at the time of Claudius's invasion of the island (Tac. *Ann.* xiv. 31).

Triobŏlus (τριόβολος). A Greek silver coin worth three *oboli*, or half a drachma. The Attic triobol was worth about $0.08, and the Aeginetan about $0.12.

Triŏpas (Τριόπας and Τρίοψ). A son of Poseidon and Canacé, a daughter of Aeolus, or of Helios (the Sun) and Rhodos, and the father of Iphimedia and Erysichthon. Hence his son Erysichthon is called *Triopēïus*, and his granddaughter Mestra or Metra, the daughter of Erysichthon, *Triopēïs*. He is said to have expelled the Pelasgians from a part of Thessaly, but was himself at last obliged to leave the country, when he went to Caria in Asia Minor and founded Cnidus, hence called TRIOPIA (Herod. i. 1, 74; Apollod. i. 7, 4; Diod. v. 56). He or his son Erysichthon violated the sacred grove of Demeter, for which he was punished with endless hunger.

Triopia. See TRIOPAS.

Triopium (Τριόπιον). Now C. Krio; the promontory which terminates the peninsula of Cnidus, forming the southwestern headland of Caria and of Asia Minor.

Triops. See TRIOPAS.

Triphiodōrus. See TRYPHIODORUS.

Triphylia (Τριφυλία). The southern portion of Elis, lying between the Alpheus and the Neda, and said to have derived its name from the three different tribes by which it was peopled. Its chief town was Pylos. See ELIS.

Tripŏlis (Τρίπολις). Properly the name of a confederacy composed of three cities, or a district containing three cities; but it is also applied to single cities which had some such relation to others as to make the name appropriate. (1) Now Kash Yenjiji; a city on the Maeander, twelve miles west of Hierapolis, on the borders of Phrygia, Caria, and Lydia, to each of which it is assigned by different authorities. (2) Now Tireboli; a fortress on the coast of Pontus, on a river of the same name (Tireboli Su), ninety stadia east of the promontory Zephyrium (C. Zefreh). (3) Now Tripoli, Tarabulus; on the coast of Phœnicia, consisted of three distinct cities, one stadium (600 feet) apart, each having its own walls, but all united in a common constitution, having one place of assembly, and forming in reality one city. They were colonies of Tyre, Sidon, and Aradus respectively. (4) The district on the northern coast of Africa between the two Syrtes, comprising the three cities of Sabrata (or Abrotonum), Oea, and Leptis Magna, and also called TRIPOLITĀNA REGIO. See SYRTICA.

Triptolĕmus (Τριπτόλεμος). The son of Celeus, king of Eleusis, and Metanira or Polhymnia. Others describe him as a son of King Eleusis by Cothonea, or of Oceanus and Gaea, or of Trochilus by an Eleusinian woman. Triptolemus was the favourite of Demeter and the inventor of the plough and agriculture, and of civilization, which is the result of it. He was the great hero in the Eleusinian Mysteries. According to the common legend, he hospitably received Demeter at Eleusis, when she was wandering in search of her daughter. (See DEMETER; ELEUSINIA, p. 578.) The goddess, in return, wished to make his son Demophon immortal, and placed him in the fire in order to destroy his mortal parts; but Metanira screamed out at the sight, and the child was consumed by the flames. As a compensation for this bereavement, the goddess gave to Triptolemus a chariot with winged dragons and seeds of wheat. In this chariot Triptolemus rode over the earth, making man acquainted with the blessings of agriculture (Ovid, *Met.* v. 646; Pausan. i. 38, 6). On his return to Attica, Celeus endeavoured to kill him; but by the command of Demeter he was obliged to give up his country to Triptolemus, who now established the worship of Demeter, and instituted the Thesmophoria. (See THESMOPHORIA.) Triptolemus is represented in works of art as a youthful hero, sometimes with the *petasus*, on a chariot drawn by dragons, and holding in his hand a sceptre and corn ears.

Triptȳchon. See DIPTYCHON.

Tripudium. Literally a triple beat or stroke; but used in the language of Roman augury of the most favourable omen (*tripudium sollistimum*) given by the sacred chickens when they ate their food so greedily that some of it fell from their beaks to the ground (Cic. *De Div.* ii. 34). See AUGUR, p. 167.

Tripūs (τρίπους). A tripod; in general anything supported on three legs, as (1) a kettle or caldron which stood on three legs over the fire (Hom. *Il.* xxiii. 702; Isidor. *Orig.* xx. 8, 5). (2) A three-legged stool (Isidor. *Orig.* xx. 11, 12). (3) The seat of the Pythian priestess at Delphi. (See DELPHI; ORACULA.) (4) A sort of stand made of bronze or marble and either dedicated in a temple or used as an altar.

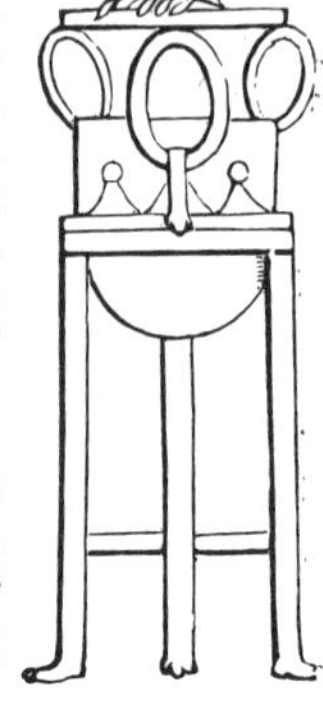

Tripod. (Fréjus.)

Trirēmis. See NAVIS.

Tritaea (Τρίταια). (1) A town of Phocis, northwest of Cleonae, on the left bank of the Cephissus and on the frontiers of Locris. (2) One of the twelve cities of Achaia, 120 stadia east of Pharae and near the frontiers of Arcadia.

Tritagonistes (τριταγωνιστής). The third actor in the Greek drama, who played in the least important parts. See DRAMA; HISTRIO; TRAGOEDIA.

Trito (Τριτώ) or **Tritogenīa** (Τριτογένεια). A surname of Athené, derived by some from Lake Tritonis in Libya, by others from the stream Triton near Alalcomenae in Boeotia; and by the grammarians from τριτώ, which, in the dialect of the Athamanians, is said to signify "head" (cf. *Il.* v. 875; Apollod. i. 3, 6). See ATHENÉ.

Triton (Τρίτων). The son of Poseidon and Amphitrité (or Celaeno), and described as living with them in a golden palace in the depths of the sea. The mythical Lake Tritonis, near the Mediterranean coast of Libya, was regarded as his peculiar abode, especially in the story of the Argonauts. He was represented as a man in his upper parts, terminating in a dolphin's tail; his special attribute is a twisted sea-shell, on which he blows, now violently, now gently, to raise or calm the billows. In the course of time there grew up the notion of a large number of Tritons, all represented as beings of double form and sometimes with the fore-feet of a horse as well as a human body and a fish's tail (called Centauro-tritones or Ichthyotauri). They were, however, always regarded as attendants on the other sea-gods while riding or driving over the waves; and they were represented accordingly in works of art. See Dressler, *Triton und die Tritonen* (Würzen, 1892).

Triton. (From a Roman lamp.)

Triton (Τρίτων), **Tritōnis** (Τριτωνίς), or **Tritonītis** (Τριτωνῖτις) **Palus.** A river and lake on the Mediterranean coast of Libya, which are mentioned in several old Greek legends, especially in the mythology of Athené, whom one account represented as born on Lake Tritonis. (See TRITO.) The lake is undoubtedly the great salt lake in the south of Tunis called El-Sibkah. Some of the ancient writers gave an altogether different locality to the legend, and identify the Triton with the river usually called Lathon in Cyrenaïca.

Triumphal Arches. See ARCUS TRIUMPHALIS.

Triumphalia. The insignia of a Roman general at his triumph. See TRIUMPHUS.

Triumphalia Carmina. Songs sung by the Roman soldiers as they marched through the city in a triumph. (See TRIUMPHUS.) On this occasion the greatest license was allowed them, and this license was reflected in their songs. Sometimes these were fierce and exultant, smacking of bloodshed and slaughter like the remarkable verses sung by the troops of Aurelian:

> Unus homo mille mille mille decollavimus!
> Mille mille mille mille bibat qui mille occidit;
> Tantum vini nemo habet quantum fudit sanguinis!

Sometimes they were full of ribaldry directed at their own commander, like the song sung by the soldiers of Iulius Caesar in his Gallic triumph:

> Urbani, servate uxores, moechum calvum adducimus.
> Aurum in Gallia effutuisti, hic sumpsisti mutuum.

(Vopisc. *Aurel.* 6; Suet. *Iul.* 51). This last recalls the ditties in which the British sailors used to celebrate Lord Nelson's too notorious amours.

Triumphus (θρίαμβος). A solemn procession in which a victorious Roman general entered the city in a chariot drawn by four horses. He was preceded by the captives and spoils taken in war, and was followed by his troops; and, after passing in state along the Via Sacra, ascended the Capitol to offer sacrifice in the Temple of Iupiter Capitolinus. From the early days of the Republic down to the extinction of liberty a regular triumph (*iustus triumphus*) was recognized as the climax of military glory, and was the cherished object of ambition to every Roman general. A triumph might be granted for successful achievements either by land or sea, but the latter were comparatively so rare that we may for the present defer the consideration of the naval triumph. After any decisive battle had been won, or a province subdued by a series of successful operations, the imperator forwarded to the Senate a laurel-wreathed despatch (*litterae laureatae*) containing an account of his exploits. If the intelligence proved satisfactory, the Senate decreed a public thanksgiving. (See SUPPLICATIO.) After the war had been concluded, the general with his army repaired to Rome, or ordered his army to meet him there on a given day, but did not enter the city. A meeting of the Senate was held without the walls, usually in the temple of either Bellona or Apollo, that he might have an opportunity of urging his pretensions in person, and these were then scrutinized and discussed with the most jealous care. The following rules were for the most part rigidly enforced, although the Senate assumed the discretionary power of relaxing them in special cases: (*a*) That no one could be permitted to triumph unless he had held the office of dictator, of consul, or of praetor. The honours granted to Pompey, who triumphed in his twenty-fourth year (B.C. 81), before he had held any of the great offices of the State, and again ten years afterwards, while still a simple knight, were altogether unprecedented. (*b*) That the magistrate should have been actually in office both when the victory was gained and when the triumph was to be celebrated. This regulation was insisted upon only during the earlier ages of the commonwealth. Its violation commenced with Q. Publilius Philo, the first person to whom the Senate ever granted a *prorogatio imperii* after the termination of a magistracy, and thenceforward proconsuls and propraetors were permitted to triumph without question. (*c*) That the war should have been prosecuted or the battle fought under the auspices and in the province and with the troops of the general seeking the triumph. Thus, if a victory was gained by the *legatus* of a general who was absent from the army, the honour of it did not belong to the former, but to the latter, inasmuch as he had the auspices. (*d*) That at least 5000 of the enemy should have been slain in a single battle, that the advantage should have been positive, and not merely a compensation for some previous disaster, and that the loss on the part of the Romans should have been small compared with that of their adversaries. Nevertheless, we find many instances of triumphs granted for general results, without reference to the numbers slain in any one engagement. (*e*) That the war should have been a legitimate contest against public foes, and not a civil contest. Hence Catulus celebrated no triumph over Lepidus, nor Antonius over Catiline, nor Cinna and Marius over their antagonists of the Sullan party, nor Caesar after Pharsalia; and when he did subsequently triumph after his victory over the sons of Pompey, it caused universal disgust. (*f*) That the dominion of the State should have been extended, and not merely something previously lost regained. The absolute acquisition of territory does not appear to have been essential. (*g*) That the war should have been brought to a conclusion and the province reduced to a state of peace, so as to permit of the army being withdrawn, the presence of the victorious soldiers being considered indispensable in a triumph.

The Senate claimed the exclusive right of deliberating upon all these points, and of giving or withholding the honour sought, and it for the most part exercised the privilege without question, except in times of great political excitement. The sovereignty of the people, however, in this matter was asserted at a very early date, and a triumph is said to have been voted by the tribes to Valerius and Horatius, the consuls of B.C. 446, in direct opposition to the resolution of the senators, and in a similar manner to C. Marcius Rutilus, the first plebeian dictator; while L. Postumius Megellus, consul B.C. 294, celebrated a triumph although resisted by the Senate and by seven out of the ten tribunes. Moreover, we read of a certain Appius Claudius, consul B.C. 143, who, having persisted in celebrating a triumph in defiance of both the Senate and the people, was accompanied by his daughter (or sister) Claudia, a Vestal Virgin, and by her interposition saved from being dragged from his chariot by a tribune. A disappointed general, however, seldom ventured to resort to such violent measures, but satisfied himself with going through the forms on the Alban Mount (*triumphus in Monte Albano*), a practice first introduced by C. Papirius Maso. If the Senate gave its consent, it at the same time voted a sum of money towards defraying the necessary expenses, and one of the tribunes *ex auctoritate Senatus* applied for a *plebiscitum* to permit the imperator to retain his imperium on the day when he entered the city. This last form could not be dispensed with either in an ovation or a triumph, because the imperium conferred by the Comitia

Curiata did not include the city itself; and when a general had once gone forth *paludatus*, his military power ceased as soon as he re-entered the gates, unless the general law had been previously suspended by a special enactment. In this manner the resolution of the Senate was, as it were, ratified by the plebs. For this reason, no one desiring a triumph ever entered the city until the question was decided, since by so doing he would *ipso facto* have forfeited all claim. We have a remarkable example of this in the case of Cicero, who, after his return from Cilicia, lingered in the vicinity of Rome day after day, and dragged about his lictors from one place to another, without entering the city, in the vain hope of a triumph.

In later times these pageants were marshalled with extraordinary pomp and splendour, and presented a most gorgeous spectacle. Minute details would necessarily be different according to circumstances, but the general arrangements were as follows: All the temples were thrown open, garlands of flowers decorated every shrine and image, and incense smoked on every altar. Meanwhile the imperator called an assembly of his soldiers, delivered an oration (*contio*) commending their valour, and concluded by distributing rewards to the most distinguished, and a sum of money to each individual, the amount depending on the value of the spoils. He then ascended his triumphal car and advanced to the Porta Triumpha-

Imperator in Triumphal Car. (From a marble in Seville.)

lis, where he was met by the whole body of the Senate, headed by the magistrates. The procession then defiled in the following order: (1) the Senate, headed by the magistrates; (2) a body of trumpeters; (3) a train of carriages and frames or litters loaded with spoils, those articles which were especially remarkable either on account of their beauty or rarity being disposed in such a manner as to be seen distinctly by the crowd. Boards were also borne aloft on *fercula*, on which were painted in large letters the names of vanquished nations and countries. Here, too, models were exhibited in ivory or wood of the cities and forts captured, and pictures of the mountains, rivers, and other great natural features of the subjugated region, with appropriate inscriptions, gold and silver in coin or bullion, arms, weapons, and cavalry trappings of every description, statues, pictures, vases, and other works of art, precious stones, elaborately wrought and richly embroidered stuffs, and every object which could be regarded as valuable or curious. (4) A body of flute-players. (5) The white bulls or oxen destined for sacrifice, with gilded horns, decorated with *infulae* and *serta*, attended by the slaughtering priests with their implements, and followed by the Camilli bearing in their hands *paterae* and other sacred vessels and instruments. (6) Elephants or any other strange animals peculiar to the conquered districts. (7) The arms and insignia of the leaders of the foe. (8) The enemy's leaders themselves, and such of their kindred as had been taken prisoners, followed by the whole band of inferior captives in fetters. (9) The crowns (*coronae*) and other tributes of respect and gratitude bestowed on the imperator by allied kings and States. (10) The lictors of the imperator in single file, their fasces wreathed with laurel. (11) The imperator himself in a circular chariot of a peculiar form, drawn by four horses, which were sometimes, though rarely, white. He was attired in a gold-embroidered robe (*toga picta*) and a flowered tunic (*tunica palmata*), and bore in his right hand a laurel bough, and in his left a sceptre. His brows were encircled with a wreath of Delphic laurel, in addition to which, in ancient times, his body was painted bright red. He was accompanied in his chariot by his children of tender years, and sometimes by very dear or highly honoured friends, while behind him stood a public slave, holding over his head a golden Etruscan crown ornamented with jewels. The presence of a slave in such a place at such a time seems to have been intended to avert *invidia* and the influence of the evil eye, and for the same purpose a *fascinum* (q. v.), a little bell, and a scourge were attached to the vehicle. Tertullian (*Apol.* 33) tells us that the slave ever and anon whispered in the ear of the imperator the warning words "*Respice post te, hominem memento te*," but this statement is not confirmed by early writers, though mentioned in Arrian. (12) Behind the chariot, or on the horses which drew it, rode the sons of the imperator, together with the *legati*, the *tribuni*, and the *equites*, all on horseback. (13) The rear was brought up by the whole body of the infantry in marching order, their spears adorned with laurel, some shouting "Io Triumphe!" and singing hymns to the gods, while others proclaimed the praises of their leader or indulged in keen sarcasms and coarse ribaldry at his expense, for the most perfect freedom of speech was granted and exercised. Just as the procession was ascending the Capitoline Hill, some of the hostile chiefs were led aside into the adjoining prison and put to death, a custom so barbarous that we could scarcely believe that it existed in a civilized age, were it not attested by the most unquestionable evidence. Pompey, indeed, refrained from perpetrating this atrocity in his third triumph, and Aurelian on a like occasion spared Zenobia (q. v.), but these are quoted as exceptions to the general rule. When it was announced that these murders had been completed, the victims were then sacrificed, an offering from the spoils was presented to Iupiter, the laurel wreath was deposited in the lap of the god, and the imperator was entertained at a public feast along with his friends in the temple. When he returned home in the evening he was preceded by torches and pipes, and escorted by a crowd of citizens. The whole of the proceedings, generally speaking, were brought to a close in one day; but when the quantity of spoil was very great, and the troops very numerous, a longer period was re-

Triumph of Marcus Aurelius. (Relief in the Palazzo dei Conservatori.)

quired for the exhibition, as when the triumph of Flaminius continued for three days in succession. But the glories of the imperator did not end with the show, nor even with his life. It was customary to provide him at the public expense with a site for a house, such mansions being styled *triumphales domus*. After death his kindred were permitted to deposit his ashes within the walls, and laurel-wreathed statues standing erect in triumphal cars, displayed in the vestibulum of the family mansion, transmitted his fame to posterity.

A TRIUMPHUS NAVĀLIS appears to have differed in no respect from an ordinary triumph, except that it must have been upon a smaller scale, and would be characterized by the exhibition of beaks of ships (*rostra*) and other nautical trophies. The earliest upon record was granted to C. Duilius, who laid the foundation of the supremacy of Rome by sea in the First Punic War; and who was so elated by his success that during the rest of his life, whenever he returned home at night from dinner, he caused flutes to sound and torches to be borne before him. A second naval triumph was celebrated by Lutatius Catulus for his victory off the Insulae Aegates (B.C. 241); a third by Q. Fabius Labeo (B.C. 189) over the Cretans; and a fourth by C. Octavius over Perseus, without captives and without spoils.

TRIUMPHUS CASTRENSIS was a procession of the soldiers through the camp in honour of a tribune or any officer inferior to the general, who had performed some brilliant exploit. After the extinction of freedom, the emperor being considered as the supreme commander of all the armies of the State, every military achievement was understood to be performed under his auspices, and hence, according to the forms of even the ancient constitution, he alone had a legitimate claim to a triumph. This principle was soon fully recognized and acted upon; for although Antonius had granted triumphs to his *legati*, and his example had been freely followed by Augustus in the early part of his career, yet after the year B.C. 14 he entirely discontinued the practice, and from that time forward triumphs were rarely, if ever, conceded to any except members of the imperial family. But to compensate in some degree for what was then taken away, the custom was introduced of bestowing what were termed *triumphalia ornamenta*—that is, permission to receive the titles bestowed upon the imperator of republican times and in the robes worn by him, with the right to bequeath triumphal statues to their descendants. See Peine, *De Ornamentis Triumphalibus* (Leipzig, 1885).

Triumvirates. See TRESVIRI.

Triumvĭri. See TRESVIRI.

Trivīcum. Now Trivico; a small town in Samnium, situated among the mountains separating Samnium from Apulia.

Trivium (τρίοδος). A place where three roads met (Cic. *Div.* i. 54).

Troas (Τρῳάς, sc. χῶρα). Now Chan; the territory of Ilium or Troy, forming the northwestern part of Mysia. It was bounded on the west by the Aegaean Sea, from the Promontorium Lectum to the Promontorium Sigeum at the entrance of the Hellespont; on the northwest by the Hellespont, as far as the river Rhodius, below Abydus; on the northeast and east by the mountains which border the valley of the Rhodius, and extend from its sources southwards to the main ridge of Mount Ida, and on the south by the northern coast of the Gulf of Adramyttium along the southern foot of Ida; but on the northeast and east the boundary is sometimes extended so far as to include the whole coast of the Hellespont and part of the Propontis, and the country as far as the river Granicus, thus embracing the district of Dardania, and somewhat more. Strabo extends the boundary still further east, to the river Aesopus, and also south to the Caïcus; but this clearly results from his including in the territory of Troy that of her neighbouring allies (*Il.* ix. 321, xxiv. 544; Herod. vii. 42; Strab. pp. 581–616). The Troad is for the most part mountainous, being intersected by Mount Ida and its branches: the largest plain is that in which Troy stood. The chief rivers were the Satnoïs on the south, the Rhodius on the north, and the Scamander (Mendere) with its affluent the Simoïs (Dombrek) in the centre.

Trochus (τροχός). A hoop for children. It was made of iron or bronze, and rolled by a sort of crooked stick or "key" (*clavis*). Sometimes, as with us, it had small bells fastened to it to jingle as the hoop rolled (Mart. xiv. 169).

Trochus. (From a gem.)

Trocmi and **Trocmii.** See GALATIA.

Troës. See TROIA.

Troezen (Τροιζήν). Now Dhamala; the capital of

Troezenia (Τροιζηνία), a district in the southeast of Argolis, on the Saronic Gulf, and opposite the island of Aegina. The town was situated at some little distance from the coast, on which it possessed a harbour called Pogon (Πώγων), opposite the island of Calauria. Troezen was a very ancient city, and is said to have been originally called Poseidonia, on account of its worship of Poseidon. It received the name of Troezen from Troezen, one of the sons of Pelops; and it is celebrated in mythology as the place where Pittheus, the maternal grandfather of Theseus, lived, and where Theseus himself was born. In the historical period it was a city of some importance. The Troezenians sent five ships of war to Salamis and 1000 heavy-armed men to Plataea. When the Persians entered Attica the Troezenians distinguished themselves by the kindness with which they received the Athenians, who were obliged to abandon their city (Herod. viii. 41; Plut. *Them.* 10). The friendship continued till the Peloponnesian War, when the Troezenians allied themselves with Sparta (Thuc. ii. 56).

Trogiliae. Three small islands lying off the promontory of Trogilium near Mycalé.

Trogītis Lacus. See Pisidia.

Troglodȳtae (Τρωγλοδύται, "dwellers in caves"). A name applied by the Greek geographers to various uncivilized people who had no abodes but caves, especially to the inhabitants of the western coast of the Red Sea, along the shores of Upper Egypt and Aethiopia (Herod. iv. 183). The Troglodytae of the west coast of the Red Sea are described by Agatharchides as a barbarous people, who wore little clothing, had wives in common, and put to death the aged and infirm. They lived on the produce of their flocks and herds. In the *Periplus* the Ethiopian Troglodytae are described as of a wild appearance and swifter than horses. This swiftness of foot is noticed also by Herodotus as characterizing the Ethiopian Troglodytae, and is said to be still a characteristic of the cave-dwellers in the same district. Herodotus adds that their language was like the twittering of bats, and that their food consisted of lizards and other reptiles. There were also Troglodytae in Moesia, on the banks of the Danube.

Trogus. See Iustinus; Pompeius Trogus.

Troia (Τροία). The name of the city of Troy or Ilium; also applied to the country. The mythical account of the kingdom of Troy is briefly as follows. Teucer, the first king, had a daughter who married Dardanus, the chieftain of the country northeast of the Troad (Dardania). Dardanus had two sons, Ilus and Ericthonius, and the latter was the father of Tros, from whom the country and people derived the names of Troas and Troes. Tros was the father of Ilus, who founded the city, which was called after him Ilium, and also, after his father, Troia. The next king was Laomedon, and after him Priam. (See Priamus.) In his reign the city was taken and destroyed by the confederated Greeks, after a ten years' siege. (For details see Achilles; Aeneas; Agamemnon; Aiax; Hector; Helena; Neoptolemus; Odysseus; Paris; and especially Trojan War.) As to the historical facts which may be regarded as established, there is evidence of a considerable city having been sacked and burned at a period which archæologists put not later than the twelfth century B.C. That this invasion may have been an enterprise of the Achaeans at that time is neither impossible nor unlikely. If the interpretation of recent Egyptian discoveries is right which makes Achaeans appear as assailants of Egypt in the reign of Rameses III., it would follow that the Achaeans of the twelfth or thirteenth century had power and spirit enough for such an enterprise; but in any case the history of Tiryns and Mycenae, as attested by their ruins, is evidence to the existence of their power at that time. There is therefore no reason why the traditions upon which the *Iliad* is based should not be regarded as true in their main outlines. It is probable enough that to avenge an act of piracy (which is a common and simple explanation of the rape of Helen) the Greeks of the "Achaean" period besieged and sacked Troy and thence returned to hold their own possessions undisturbed until the Dorian invasion. That there was no Greek settlement upon the site of Troy until a much later period is deduced from the remains of towns of a low state of civilization and of small importance which have been discovered above the ruins of the second city. On the literary use made of the legend of the Trojan War, see Cyclic Poets; Homerus; Vergilius.

Troiae Ludus (Τροία) (frequently called in Latin Troia, in the phrase *Troiam ludere*; in Suet. *Cal.* 18, *Troiae decursio*; in Tac. *Ann.* xi. 11, *ludicrum Troiae*). An equestrian sham-fight, performed in the Circus Maximus by boys of high rank. It was supposed to represent an exercise introduced by Aeneas and the Trojans after their landing in Italy, and celebrated afterwards by Ascanius at Alba (Verg. *Aen.* v. 597). The earliest mention in historical times is the celebration by Sulla in his dictatorship B.C. 81 (Plut. *Cat.* 3), and by Caesar when he dedicated the Temple of Venus (Dio Cass. xliii. 23). Augustus celebrated it certainly twice: first in B.C. 27 (Dio Cass. xlix. 43); on which occasion Tiberius at the age of fifteen was *ductor turmae puerorum maiorum* (Suet. *Tib.* 6); secondly, at the dedication of the Temple of Marcellus, B.C. 12, when his grandson Gaius took a chief part. He then discontinued the celebration because Asinius Pollio complained in the Senate that it was a dangerous sport, in which his grandson Aeserninus had broken his leg (Suet. *Aug.* 43). Caligula celebrated it in the first year of his reign, and again at the funeral games of Drusilla; and of Nero's boyhood we are told that he often *Troiam lusit* up to the age of eleven (Suet. *Ner.* 7).

The method of celebration may be gathered from Vergil (*Aen.* v. 553–603). In this account the Trojan boys are first marshalled in three squadrons of twelve each, under Ascanius, Priamus (son of Polites), and Atys. They come forward ceremoniously, much as the gladiators did, or as the performers in a modern bull-fight do now, to salute the spectators before the combat begins: then they break up their triple formation, and, forming into two equal bands, retire to opposite stations. After this, they charged and retired with evolutions so complicated that they seemed to Vergil comparable to nothing but the Cretan Labyrinth or troops of dolphins at play. It is hard to explain why Vergil introduces the difficulty of three leaders and three companies. In all historical accounts there were two. We can hardly doubt that Vergil, under cover of the story of Aeneas, is describing what he actually saw, and this must have been the celebration in B.C. 27. In that contest we know from Suetonius (*Tib.* 12) that Tiberius was one leader, and from the same chapter it may be inferred that Marcellus was another. We may surmise that Vergil introduced this elaborate account for the same reason which led him to bring in the touching allusion to Marcellus in *Aen.* vi. There may have been a third leader in the preliminary display on that occasion, to give distinction to Sextus Apuleius, the son of Augustus's colleague in the consulship, who, as appears from Tac. (*Ann.* ii. 50), afterwards married Marcella, daughter of Octavia. Assuming, then, that in the real celebration of B.C. 27 there were three leaders for the procession, and that for the combat two lines were formed, according to custom, under Tiberius and Marcellus, we may suppose that Vergil makes three corresponding leaders in his Troia—viz., Iulus and Atys out of compliment to Augustus, and a Priamus as appropriate to the Trojan game.

Troïlus (Τρωΐλος). The son of Priam and Hecuba, or, according to others, son of Apollo. He fell by the hands of Achilles.

Trojan War. The story of the Trojan War, like the story of the Argonauts, underwent, in the course of time, many changes and amplifications. The main portion of the story is contained in the two epic poems ascribed to Homer, the *Iliad* and the *Odyssey.* The incidents, either narrated or briefly touched upon in these, were elaborated or developed by the post-Homeric poets, partly by connecting them with other popular traditions, and partly by the addition of further details of their own invention. While in Homer it is simply the rape of Helen which is the occasion of the war, a later legend traced its origin to the marriage of Peleus and Thetis, when Eris threw down among the assembled gods the golden apple inscribed "For the fairest" (τῇ καλῇ). The quarrel that ensued between Heré, Athené, and Aphrodité for the prize of beauty was decided by Paris in favour of Aphrodité, who in return secured him the possession of Helen, while Heré and Athené became, from that time onward, the implacable enemies of the whole Trojan race.

According to Homer, after Helen had been carried off by Paris, Menelaüs and Agamemnon visited all the Greek chieftains in turn, and prevailed on them to take part in the expedition which they were preparing to avenge the wrong. According to the later account, the majority of the chieftains were already bound to follow the expedition by an oath, which they had sworn to Tyndareos. Agamemnon was the chosen commander-in-chief; next to him the most prominent Greek heroes are his brother Menelaüs, Achilles, and Patroclus, the two Aiaxes, Teucer, Nestor and his son Antilochus, Odysseus, Diomedes, Idomeneus, and Philoctetes, who, however, at the very outset of the expedition, had to be left behind, and does not appear on the scene of action until just before the fall of Troy. Later epics add the name of Palamedes.

The entire host of 100,000 men and 1186 ships assembled in the harbour of Aulis. Here, while they were sacrificing under a plane-tree, a snake darted out from under the altar and ascended the tree, and there, after devouring a brood of eight young sparrows and the mother-bird herself, was turned into stone. This omen Calchas, the seer of the host, interpreted to mean that the war would last nine years, and terminate in the tenth with the destruction of Troy (*Iliad*, ii. 299–332). Agamemnon had already received an oracle from the Delphian god that Troy would fall when the best of the Greeks quarrelled. In Homer the crossing to Troy follows immediately; but in the later story the Greeks at first land by mistake in Mysia, in the country of Telephus (q. v.), and, being dispersed by a storm and driven back to Greece, assemble afresh at Aulis, whence they are only permitted to set out after the sacrifice of Iphigenia (an incident entirely unknown to Homer). On the Greek side the first to fall is Protesilaüs, who is the first to land. The disembarkation cannot take place until Achilles has slain the mighty Cycnus. After pitching their camp, Odysseus and Menelaüs proceed as ambassadors to Troy, to demand the surrender of Helen. But this proposal, in spite of the inclination of Helen herself and the admonition of the Trojan Antenor, falls to the ground, owing to the opposition of Paris, and war is declared. The number of the Trojans, whose chief hero is Hector, scarcely amounts to the tenth part of that of the besiegers; and although they possess the aid of countless brave allies, such as Aeneas, Sarpedon, and Glaucus, in their fear of Achilles they dare not risk a general engagement. On the other hand, the Achaeans can do nothing against the well fortified and defended town, and see themselves confined to laying ambuscades and devastating the surrounding country, and compelled by lack of provisions to have recourse to foraging expeditions in the neighbourhood, undertaken by sea and by land under the generalship of Achilles. At length the decisive tenth year arrives. The Homeric *Iliad* narrates the events of this year, confining itself to the space of fifty-one days.

Chryses, priest of Apollo, comes in priestly garb into the camp of the Greeks to ransom his daughter Chryseïs from Agamemnon. He is rudely repulsed, and Apollo consequently visits the Greeks with a plague. In an assembly of the Greeks summoned by Achilles, Calchas declares the only means of appeasing the god to be the surrender of the girl without ransom. Agamemnon assents to the general wish; but, by way of compensation, takes from Achilles, whom he considers to be the instigator of the whole plot, his favourite slave Briseïs. Achilles withdraws in a rage to his tent, and implores his mother Thetis to obtain from Zeus a promise that the Greeks should meet with disaster in fighting the Trojans until Agamemnon should give her son complete satisfaction. The Trojans immediately take the open field, and Agamemnon is induced by a promise of victory, conveyed in a dream from Zeus, to appoint the following day for a battle. The hosts are already standing opposed to one another, prepared for fight, when they agree to a treaty that the conflict for Helen and the plundered treasures be decided by a duel between Paris and Menelaüs. Paris is overcome in the duel, and is only rescued from death by the intervention of Aphrodité. When Agamemnon presses for the fulfilment of the treaty, the Trojan Pandarus breaks the peace by shooting an arrow at Menelaüs, and the first open engagement in the war begins, in which, under the protection of Athené, Diomedes performs miracles of bravery and wounds even Aphrodité and Ares. Diomedes and the Lycian Glaucus are on the point of fighting, when they recognize one another as hereditary guest-friends. Hector goes from the battle to Troy, and the day ends with an indecisive duel between Hector and Aiax, son of Telamon. In the armistice ensuing, both sides bury their dead, and the Greeks, acting on the advice of Nestor, surround the camp with a wall and trench. When the fighting begins afresh, Zeus forbids the gods to take part in it, and ordains that the battle shall terminate with the discomfiture of the Greeks. On the following night Agamemnon already begins to meditate flight, but Nestor advises reconciliation with Achilles. The efforts of the ambassadors are, however, fruitless. Hereupon Odysseus and Diomedes go out to reconnoitre, capture Dolon, a Trojan spy, and surprise Rhesus, king of the Thracians, the newly arrived ally of the enemy. On the succeeding day Agamemnon's bravery drives the Trojans back to the walls of the town; but he himself, Diomedes, Odysseus, and other heroes leave the battle wounded; the Greeks retire behind the camp walls, to attack which the Trojans set out in five detachments. The opposition of the Greeks is brave; but Hector breaks the great gate with a rock, and the stream of enemies pours itself unimpeded into the camp. Once more the Greek heroes who are still capable of taking part in the fight, especially the two Aiaxes and Idomeneus, succeed, with the help of Poseidon, in repelling the Trojans, while Telamonian Aiax dashes Hector to the ground with a stone; but the latter soon reappears on the battle-field with fresh strength granted him by Apollo at the command of Zeus. Poseidon is obliged to leave the Greeks to their fate; they retire again to the ships, which Aiax in vain defends. The foremost ship is already burning, when Achilles gives way to the entreaties of his friend Patroclus, and sends him, clad in his own armour, with the Myrmidons to the help of the distressed Greeks. Supposing it to be Achilles himself, the Trojans in terror flee from the camp before Patroclus, who pursues them to the town, and lays low vast numbers of the enemy, including the brave Sarpedon, whose corpse is only rescued from the Greeks after a severe fight. At last Patroclus himself is slain by Hector with the help of Apollo; Achilles' arms are lost, and even the corpse is with difficulty saved. And now Achilles repents of his anger, reconciles himself to Agamemnon, and on the following day, furnished with new and splendid armour by Hephaestus at the request of Thetis, avenges the death of his friend on countless Trojans and finally on Hector himself. With the burial of Patroclus and the funeral games established in his honour, the restoration of Hector's corpse to Priam, and the burial of Hector, for which Achilles allows an armistice of eleven days, the *Iliad* concludes.

Immediately after the death of Hector the later legends bring the Amazons to the help of the Trojans, and their queen Penthesilea is slain by Achilles. Then appears Memnon, who is also mentioned by Homer; at the head of his Aethiopians he slays Antilochus son of Nestor, and is himself slain by Achilles. And now comes the fulfilment of the oracle given to Agamemnon at Delphi; for at a sacrificial banquet a violent quarrel arises between Achilles and Odysseus, the latter declaring craft and not valour to be the only means of capturing Troy. Soon after, in an attempt to force a way into the hostile town through the Scaean Gate, or, according to later legend, at the marriage of Priam's daughter Polyxena in the temple of the Thymbraean Apollo, Achilles falls slain by the arrow of Paris, directed by the god. After his burial, Thetis offers the arms of her son as a prize for the bravest of the Greek heroes, and they are adjudged to Odysseus. Thereupon his competitor, the Telamonian Aiax, slays himself. For these losses, however, the Greeks find some compensation. Acting on the admonition of Helenus, son of Priam, who had been captured by Odysseus, that Troy could not be conquered without the arrows of Heracles and the presence of a descendant of Aeacus, they fetch to the camp Philoctetes, the heir of Heracles, who had been abandoned on Lemnos, and Neoptolemus, the young son of Achilles, who had been brought up on Scyros. The latter, a worthy son of his father, slays the last ally of the Trojans, Eurypylus, the brave son of Telephus; and Philoctetes, with one of the arrows of Heracles, kills Paris. Even when the last condition of the capture of Troy (the removal of the Palladium from the temple of Athené on the citadel) has been successfully fulfilled by Diomedes and Odysseus, the town can only be taken by treachery. (See PALLADIUM.) On the advice of Athené, Epeius, son of Panopeus, builds a gigantic wooden horse, in the belly of which the bravest Greek warriors conceal themselves under the direction of Odysseus, while the rest of the Greeks burn the camp and embark on board ship, only, however, to anchor behind Tenedos. The Trojans, streaming out of the town, find the horse, and are in doubt what to do with it. According to the later legend they are deceived by the treacherous Sinon, a kinsman of Odysseus, who has of his own free will remained behind. He pretends that he has escaped from the death by sacrifice to which he had been doomed by the malice of Odysseus, and that the horse has been erected to expiate the robbery of the Palladium; to destroy it would be fatal to Troy, but should it be set on the citadel, Asia would conquer Europe. The fate of Laocoön removes the last doubt from the minds of the Trojans (see LAOCOÖN); the city gate being too small, they break down a portion of the wall and draw the horse up to the citadel as a dedicatory offering for Athené. While they are giving themselves up to transports of joy, Sinon in the night opens the door of the horse. The heroes descend and light the flames that give to the Greek fleet the preconcerted signal for its return. Thus Troy is captured; all the inhabitants are either slain or carried into slavery, and the city is destroyed. The only survivors of the royal house are Helenus, Cassandra, and Hector's wife Andromaché, besides Aeneas. For the fate of the rest see DEÏPHOBUS; HECUBA; POLYDORÙS; POLYXENA; PRIAMUS; TROÏLUS.

After Troy has been destroyed and plundered, Agamemnon and Menelaüs, contrary to custom, call the drunken Greeks to an assembly in the evening. A division ensues, half siding with Menelaüs in a desire to return home at once; while Agamemnon and the other half wish first to appease by sacrifice the deity of Athené, who has been offended by the outrage of the Locrian Aiax (see AIAX, 1). The army consequently sets out on its journey in two parts. Only Nestor, Diomedes, Neoptolemus, Philoctetes, and Idomeneus reach home in safety; while Menelaüs and Odysseus have first to undergo wanderings for many a long year.

Death overtakes the Locrian Aiax on the sea, and Agamemnon immediately after his arrival home. See CYCLIC POETS; EPOS; HOMERUS; ILIUM; TROIA; TRYPHIODORUS; TZETZES; VERGILIUS.

The Trojan legend appears in later literature, both mediæval and modern, and has inspired much that is interesting and beautiful in art as well. The spurious histories of Dares Phrygius and Dictys Cretensis (see DARES; DICTYS) supplied the material for the writers of the Middle Ages, who worked it up into many forms. The Arthurian legends and the Fabliaux both draw from it, and in A.D. 1160 it was elaborated in literary form by Benoît de Sainte-More, whose poem, *Le Roman de Troie*, in some 30,000 lines, is dedicated to Queen Eleanor of Poitiers and England. In this, the poet has apparently invented new episodes, such as the loves of Briseïda, daughter of Calchas, with Diomedes and Troïlus; whence Boccaccio's poem *Filostrato*, Chaucer's *Troïlus and Cryseyde*, and Shakspeare's *Troïlus and Cressida*, while Gower in his *Confessio Amantis* also alludes to it. Benoît's poem was translated into German in the twelfth century, into Latin by Guido della Colonna in the thirteenth century, and later into Italian. From it, again, Lydgate derived his *Troye Book* (first printed in 1513), Caxton his *Recuyell of the Historyes of Troye* (1474), the first book ever printed in English, and Thomas Heywood his *Life and Death of Hector* (1614). Geoffrey of Monmouth, Gaimar, Wace, and Layamon tell of a Trojan hero, Brut, who found his way to Britain. See Moland and D'Héricault, *Nouvelles Françaises en Prose du XIVe Siècle* (1858); Joly, *Benoît de Ste.-More et le Roman de Troie* (1870); Greif, *Die Mittelalterlichen Bearbeitungen der Trojanersage* (1886); Collilieux, *Dictys et Dares* (1886); and Gorra, *Testi Inediti di Storia Trojana* (Turin, 1887).

Tropaeum (*τρόπαιον*). The Greek term for a monument of victory, composed of the arms captured as booty, and set up on the spot where the conquered enemy had turned (*τρέπειν*) to flight. Representations of the stump of a tree, with cross-pieces and armour or weapons suspended from them, are often to be seen on coins. The Romans borrowed the custom from the Greeks, but generally erected as memorials of victory permanent monuments, with representations of the war carved in relief, and with trophies of arms suspended over the undecorated portions.

Trophies of Augustus Caesar. (Capitoline Museum.)

Trophonius (Τροφώνιος) and **Agamēdes** (Ἀγαμήδης). The sons of Erginus of Orchomenus, legendary heroes of architecture. Many important buildings were attributed to them, among others the Temple of Apollo at Delphi (Strabo, p. 421), that of Poseidon at Mantinea (Pausan. viii. 10, 2), the *thalamos* of Alcmené in Thebes (*ib.* ix. 11, 1), the treasuries of Augeas in Elis (Schol. *ad* Aristoph. *Nubes*, 508), and Hyrieus in Boeotian Hyria (Paus. ix. 37, 4). In the last named they inserted one stone so cleverly that it could be easily removed from the outside and the treasure stolen by night. But on one occasion, when Agamedes was caught in the trap laid by Hyrieus to discover the thief, Trophonius, to save himself from being betrayed as his brother's accomplice, cut off the head of Agamedes. Being pursued, however, by the king, he was swallowed up in the earth at Lebadea, and by the command of Apollo a cult and an oracle were dedicated to him as Zeus Trophonius.

The oracle was situated in a subterranean chamber, into which, after various preparatory rites, including the nocturnal sacrifice of a ram and the invocation of Agamedes, the inquirers descended to receive, under circumstances of a mysterious nature, a variety of revelations, which were afterwards taken down from their lips and duly interpreted. The descent into the cave, and the sights which there met the eye, were so awe-inspiring that the popular belief was that no one who visited the cave ever smiled again (Athenaeus, 614 A; cf. Aristoph. *Nubes*, 508); and it was proverbially said of persons of grave and serious aspect that they had been in the cave of Trophonius—a phrase that has passed into modern literature as a classic allusion.

According to another story the brothers, after the completion of the Delphic temple, asked Apollo for a reward, and he promised they should have on the seventh day the best thing that could be given to man; and on that day they both died a peaceful death (Cicero, *Tusc.* i. 114; Plut. *Consolatio ad Apoll.* 14).

Tros (Τρώς). The son of Erichthonius and Astyoché, and grandson of Dardanus. He was married to Callirrhoë, by whom he became the father of Ilus, Assaracus, and Ganymedes, and was king of Phrygia. The country and people of Troy derived their name from him. (See TROIA.) He gave up his son Ganymedes to Zeus for a present of horses. See GANYMEDES.

Trossŭlum. Now Trosso; a town in Etruria, nine miles from Volsinii, which is said to have been taken by some Roman *equites*, without the aid of foot-soldiers; whence the Roman knights obtained the name of TROSSŬLI (Pliny, *H. N.* xxxiii. 9).

Trousers. See BRACAE.

Trua (*τρυήλα*). A kind of ladle perforated with holes; also a perforated cap or plate in a sink, as in modern kitchens (Varro, *L. L.* v. 118). See TRULLA.

Trua. (From the House of Pansa, Pompeii.)

Truentum. A town of Picenum, on the river Truentus or Truentinus (Tronto).

Trulla (τρουλλίον). (1) A sort of ladle or dipper, practically the same as *trua*, of which this word is a diminutive. See TRUA.

(2) (τρύβλιον). Either used separately, or with the epithet *vinaria*. A drinking-cup, or utensil employed for taking the wine out of a larger recipient, which contained a quantity mixed with snow. It was a species of *cyathus* (q.v.), being furnished with an inner case perforated as a strainer, and fitting into the hollow bowl of the cup, so that when adjusted together the two would form but one body, which might be conveniently dipped into the large vessel, and filled; then, by removing the perforated case, any sediment or impurity deposited by the snow would be removed with it from the pure liquid left in the bowl (Cic. *Verr.* ii. 4, 27; Varro, *L. L.* v. 118; Pliny, *H. N.* xxxvii. 7).

Trulla, Fire-basket. (Rich.)

(3) The pan of a night-stool (Juv. iii. 118).

(4) A fire-basket of iron used for carrying hot coals from place to place (Livy, xxxvii. 11).

Trumpet. See SALPINX; TUBA.

Trutĭna (τρυτάνη.) See LANCULA; LIBRA; STATERA.

Trutulensis Portus. A harbour on the northeastern coast of Britain, near the estuary Taüs (Tay).

Tryphiodōrus (Τρυφιόδωρος). A Greek epic writer of Egypt, who composed at the beginning of the sixth century B.C. a poem on the capture of Troy (Ἰλίου Ἅλωσις) in 691 hexameters, a very indifferent poem, containing an account of the stratagem of the wooden horse and the sack of the city. It is edited by Northmore (London, 1804) and Köchly (Zürich, 1850).

Tryphon (Τρύφων). (1) DIODŎTUS, a usurper of the throne of Syria during the reign of Demetrius II. Nicator. After the death of Alexander Balas in B.C. 146, Tryphon first set up Antiochus, the infant son of Balas, as a pretender against Demetrius, but in 142 he murdered Antiochus and reigned as king himself. Tryphon was defeated and put to death by Antiochus Sidetes, the brother of Demetrius, in 139, after a reign of three years (see DEMETRIUS II.). (2) SALVIUS, one of the leaders of the revolted slaves in Sicily, was supposed to have a knowledge of divination, for which reason he was elected king by the slaves in 103. He displayed considerable abilities, and in a short time collected an army of 20,000 foot and 2000 horse, with which he defeated the propraetor P. Licinius Nerva. After this victory Salvius assumed all the pomp of royalty, and took the surname of Tryphon, probably because it had been borne by Diodotus, the usurper of the Syrian throne. He chose the strong fortress of Triocala as the seat of his new kingdom. Tryphon was defeated by L. Lucullus in 102, and was obliged to take refuge in Triocala. But Lucullus failed to take the place, and returned to Rome without effecting anything more. Lucullus was succeeded by C. Servilius; and on the death of Tryphon, about the same time, the kingdom devolved upon Athenion, who was not subdued till 101 (Flor. iii. 19).

Tub. See DOLIUM.

Tuba (σάλπιγξ). The Latin name for a straight wind-instrument of deep, clangorous sound, which was used at sacrifices, games, funerals, and in war among the infantry to give the signal for attack and retreat, and was blown by the *tubicen.* See LITUUS; SALPINX; and cf. CORNU.

Tubĕro, AELIUS. (1) QUINTUS, son-in-law of L. Aemilius Paulus, served under the latter in his war against Perseus, king of Macedonia. (2) Q., son of the preceding, was a pupil of Panaetius, and is called "the Stoic." He had a reputation for talent and legal knowledge. He was praetor in 123, and consul suffectus in 118. He was an opponent of Tib. Gracchus, as well as of C. Gracchus, and delivered some speeches against the latter, 123. Tubero is one of the speakers in Cicero's dialogue *De Republica.* (3) LUCIUS, an intimate friend of Cicero. On the breaking out of the Civil War, Tubero espoused the party of Pompey, under whom he served in Greece. He was afterwards pardoned by Caesar, and returned with his son Quintus to Rome. Tubero cultivated literature and philosophy. (4) Q., son of the preceding, obtained considerable reputation as a jurist, and is often quoted in the Digest.

Tubĭcen (σαλπιγκτής). A trumpeter. See SALPINX; TUBA.

Tubilustrium. A Roman festival in honour of Mars. See SALII.

Tucca, PLOTIUS. A friend of Horace and Vergil, to whom and Varius the latter bequeathed his unfinished works. See VERGILIUS.

Tucētum. A dish of potted pork or beef, larded (Schol. *ad* Pers. ii. 42).

Tuder. Now Todi; an ancient town of Umbria, situated on a hill near the Tiber, and on the road from Mevania to Rome.

Tudicŭla. A machine for bruising olives and removing the stones before putting the fleshy part in the oil-press. See TORCULAR.

Tuditānus, SEMPRONIUS. (1) PUBLIUS, tribune of the soldiers at the battle of Cannae in B.C. 216, and one of the few Roman officers who survived that fatal day. In 214 he was curule aedile; in 213 praetor, with Ariminum as his province, and was continued in the command for the two following years (212, 211). He was censor in 209 with M. Cornelius Cethegus, although neither he nor his colleague had yet held the consulship. In 205 he was sent into Greece with the title of proconsul, for the purpose of opposing Philip, with whom, however, he concluded a treaty, which was ratified by the Romans. Tuditanus was consul in 204, and received Bruttii as his province. He was at first defeated by Hannibal, but shortly afterwards he gained a decisive victory over the Carthaginian general (Livy, xxii. 50, 60, xxiv. 43–47, xxvii. 11, xxix. 11–13, xxxi. 2; App. *Annib.* 26). (2) GAIUS, plebeian aedile 198, and praetor 197, when he obtained Nearer Spain as his province. He was defeated by the Spaniards with great loss, and died shortly afterwards of a wound which he had received in the battle (Livy, xxxii. 27, xxxiii. 42; App. *Hisp.* 39). (3) MARCUS, tribune of the plebs 193; praetor 189, when he obtained Sicily as his province; and consul 185. In his consulship he carried on war in Liguria, and defeated the Apuani, while his colleague was equally successful against the Ingauni. He was carried off by the great pestilence which devastated Rome in 174 (Livy, xxxix. 40, 46, xli. 21). (4) GAIUS, praetor 132, and consul 129. In his consulship he carried on war against the Iapydes in Illyricum, over whom he gained a victory chiefly through the military skill of his legate, D. Iunius Brutus. Tuditanus was an orator and an historian, and in both obtained considerable distinction (Vell. Pat. ii. 4; App. *B. C.* i. 19, *Illyr.* 10; Cic. *Brut.* 25; Dionys. i. 11).

Tugurium. A hut; usually made of wood, with a bark or thatched roof (Pliny, *H. N.* xvi. 14). Cf. MAPALIA.

Tugurium. (Rich.)

Tullia. The name of the two daughters of Servius Tullius, the sixth king of Rome. See TULLIUS.

Tullia, frequently called by the endearing diminutive **Tulliŏla.** The daughter of Cicero and Terentia, born probably B.C. 79 or 78. She was betrothed in 67 to C. Calpurnius Piso Frugi, whom she married in 63, during the consulship of her father. During Cicero's banishment Tullia lost her first husband. She was married again in 56 to Furius Crassipes, a young man of rank and large property; but she did not live with him long, though the time and the reason of her divorce are alike unknown. In 50 she was married to her third husband, P. Cornelius Dolabella, who was a thorough profligate. The marriage took place during Cicero's absence in Cilicia, and, as might have been anticipated, was not a happy one. In 46 a divorce took place by mutual consent. At the beginning of 45 Tullia was delivered of a son, her second child by Dolabella. As soon as she was sufficiently recovered to bear the fatigues of a journey, she accompanied her father to Tusculum, but died there in February. To allay his grief at her death, Cicero wrote the treatise (now lost) *De Consolatione.* See CICERO.

Tullia Gens, patrician and plebeian. The patrician Tullii were one of the Alban families transplanted to Rome in the reign of Tullus Hostilius. The patrician branch of the gens appears to have become extinct at an early period, for after the early times of the Republic no one of the name occurs for some centuries, and the Tullii of a later age are not only plebeians, but, with the exception of their bearing the same name, cannot be regarded as having any connection with the ancient gens. The first plebeian Tullius who rose to the honours of the State was M. Tullius Decula, consul B.C. 81, and the next was the celebrated orator M. Tullius Cicero. See CICERO.

Tulliānum. See CARCER, p. 278.

Tullius Cicĕro. See CICERO.

Tullius, SERVIUS. According to the legends, the sixth king of Rome. The stories about his reign merely express the popular idea of the original growth of the Roman constitution; and as he embodies a great part of this growth, the history of which was lost, he is represented as a king with a peaceful reign, devoted to legislation and to public works in the city, but also to military organization. The legendary account states that his mother, Ocrisia, was one of the captives taken at Corniculum, and became a slave of Tanaquil, the wife of Tarquinius Priscus (Dionys. iv. 2; Ovid, *Fasti,* vi. 625). He was born in the king's palace, and notwithstanding his servile origin was brought up as the king's son, since Tanaquil by her powers of divination had foreseen the greatness of the child; and Tarquinius gave him his daughter in marriage, and intrusted him with the government. His rule was mild and beneficent, and so popular did he become that the sons of Ancus Marcius, fearing lest they should be deprived of their inheritance, procured the assassination of Tarquinius. (See TARQUINIUS.) They did not, however, reap the fruit of their crime, for Tanaquil, pretending that the king's wound was not mortal, told the people that Tarquinius had commanded Servius meantime to discharge the duties of the kingly office. Servius began to act as king; and when the death of Tarquinius could no longer be concealed, he was already in firm possession of the royal power. The great deeds of Servius were deeds of peace, and he was regarded by posterity as the author of all their civil rights and institutions, just as Numa was of their religious rites and ordinances. Three important events are assigned to Servius by tradition. First, he gave a new constitution to the Roman State. The two main objects of this constitution were to give the plebs political independence, and to assign to property that influence in the State which had previously belonged to birth exclusively. In order to carry his purpose into effect, Servius made a twofold division of the Roman people—one territorial, and the other according to property. (For details, see COMITIA.) Secondly, he was credited with the extension of the Pomerium, or boundary of Rome, and with the completion of the "Servian" city by incorporating with it the Quirinal, Viminal, and Esquiline Hills and its fortification. (See ROMA.) Thirdly, he established an important alliance with the Latins, by which Rome and the cities of Latium became the members of one great league. By his new constitution Servius incurred the hostility of the patricians, who conspired against him with L. Tarquinius. Servius, soon after his succession, had given his two daughters in marriage to the two sons of Tarquinius Priscus. L. Tarquinius the elder was married to a domestic wife; Aruns, the younger, to an aspiring and ambitious woman. On the other hand, Lucius was proud and haughty, but Aruns unambitious and quiet. The wife of Aruns, fearing that her husband would tamely resign the sovereignty to his elder brother, resolved to destroy both her father and her husband. She persuaded Lucius to murder his wife, and she murdered her own husband; and the survivors straightway married. Tullia now urged her husband to murder her father. A conspiracy was formed with the discontented patricians, and Tarquinius, having entered the Senate-house arrayed in the kingly robes, ordered the senators to be summoned to him as their king. At the first news of the commotion, Servius hastened to the Senate-house, and, standing at the doorway, ordered Tarquinius to come down from the throne. Tarquinius sprang forward, seized the old man and flung him down the steps. The king sought refuge in his house, but before he reached it he was overtaken by the servants of Tarquinius and murdered. Tullia drove to the Senate-house, and greeted her husband as king; and as she was returning, her charioteer pulled up, and showed her the corpse of her father lying across the road. She commanded him to drive on: the blood of her father spirted over the carriage and on her dress; and from that day forward the street bore the name of the Vicus Sceleratus—"Wicked Street." Servius had reigned forty-four years (Livy, i. 42–46; Dionys. iv. 2–12; Cic. *De Rep.* ii. 21; Ovid, *Fasti*, vi. 581).

Tullius Tiro. See TIRO.

Tullum. Now Toul; the capital of the Leuci in the southwestern part of Gallia Belgica (Ptol. ii. 9, 13).

Tumultuarii, sc. *milites*. Soldiers sworn in *en masse* in times of great danger to the State (*in tumultu*), *tumultus* being technically an Italic or Gallic war. The form by which these troops were sworn was called *coniuratio*, and differed from the *sacramentum* or regular military oath in that persons sworn by it were freed from its obligations as soon as the crisis was over. The first instance of this *coniuratio* that is recorded was in B.C. 216, in the Second Punic War (Livy, xxii. 38). See Mommsen in the *Eph. Epigraph.* v. 143; and cf. the articles DELECTUS; SACRAMENTUM.

Tumŭlus (τύμβος, κολώνη). A sort of cairn or rough mound of earth and stones piled up in a pyramidal shape over a grave. Sometimes it served as the base of a column (στήλη) erected as a monument. The word is also used in the general sense of a grave or tomb (Hom. *Il.* xxiv. 798; xi. 371; Verg. *Ecl.* v. 42). See the illustration in the article HORATIUS, p. 844.

Tunes or Tunis. Now Tunis; a strongly fortified city of Northern Africa, at the inner end of the Carthaginian Gulf, ten miles southwest of Carthage, at the mouth of the little river Catada.

Tungri. A German people, who crossed the Rhine, and settled in Gaul in the country formerly occupied by the Aduatici and the Eburones. Their chief town was called Tungri or ADUĂCA TONGRŌRUM (Tongern) (Tac. *Germ.* 2).

Tunĭca (χιτών). A garment for men and women worn next the person. With men it was a loose shirt of woollen stuff, consisting of pieces sewed together at the sides, and having either no sleeves or only short ones reaching half-way down the arm. Longer sleeves were considered effeminate, and first came into general use in the third and fourth centuries A.D. Ordinarily the tunica was girded up over the hip, and reached to the knees only. It was considered unbecoming to allow it to appear beneath the lower part of the *toga*. It was worn by the Roman at home and at work, and also by slaves and strangers. Senators and patricians were distinguished by a *tunica* with a broad purple stripe (*latus clavus*, hence *tunica laticlavia*)

Ordinary Tunic. (Column of Trajan.)

Slit Tunic. (Pompeian painting.)

extending from the neck to the under seam; the knights by a narrow one (*angustus clavus*, hence *tunica angusticlavia*). (See CLAVUS.) The purple *tunica*, adorned with golden palm-branches (*tunica palmata*), was, with the *toga picta* (see TOGA), the dress of a general on the occasion of a triumph. (See TRIUMPHUS.) It very early became the custom to wear beneath the tunic proper a *tunica interior*, which was of wool. Linen shirts did not come into use until the fourth century A.D. Women wore a double tunic, an under one, a chemise (*tunica intima*), consisting of a garment fitting closely to the body and reaching over the knee, and over this the *stola* (q. v.). See EXOMIS; SUBUCULA.

Woman with Stola and Inner Tunic. (From a marble.)

Tunica Intima or Chemise. (Roman bas-relief.)

Turban. See MITRA.

Turbo (βέμβιξ, ῥόμβος, στρόμβος). A humming-top used by Greek and Roman children, and made to revolve by whipping (Verg. *Aen.* vii. 378; Tibull. i. 5, 3). It appears to have resembled those used by children in modern times.

Turdetāni. The most numerous people in Hispania Baetica, dwelt in the south of the province, on both banks of the Baetis, as far as Lusitania. Their district was called Turdetania. See HISPANIA.

Turdŭli. A people in Hispania Baetica, situated to the east and south of the Turdetani (q. v.), with whom they were closely connected.

Turia or Turium. Now the Guadalaviar, a river on the eastern coast of Spain, flowing into the sea at Valentia, memorable for the battle fought on its banks between Pompey and Sertorius (Plut. *Pomp.* 18; *Sert.* 19).

Turibŭlum. See TUS.

Turma (ἴλη). A subdivision of the Roman cavalry. The 300 knights originally belonging to each legion were divided into ten turmae of thirty men: each of these had three *decuriones*, the first of whom commanded the whole *turma*, and three *optiones* (adjutants). The divisions of allied cavalry called *alae* (see ALA), each consisting of 300 men, contained five turmae of sixty men each. Under the Empire the independent divisions of cavalry of 500 or 1000 men, which were also called *alae*, consisted of sixteen or twenty-four turmae. The cavalry divisions of 120 horsemen in a cohort of 500 strong, which formed the unit in many cohorts, and of 240 horsemen in a cohort of 1000 strong, were divided into six and ten turmae respectively. See COHORS; EXERCITUS.

Turnēbus, ADRIĀNUS (ADRIEN TURNÈBE). A great French classical scholar of the sixteenth century, born at Andelys, near Rouen, in 1512, of Scottish descent, his family name having been originally Turnbull. He was educated at the University of Paris, in which he became Professor of Greek in 1547, and where J. J. Scaliger (q. v.) was one of his pupils. He was director of the royal press, in which capacity he did much for the dissemination of corrected classical texts, while winning a wide reputation for his own Hellenic scholarship. Montaigne, his personal friend, pronounced him the greatest man of letters whom Europe had seen for a thousand years. From the press which he directed came the *editio princeps* of Philo and of Synesius, and he himself edited Aeschylus, Aristotle's *Ethics*, Cicero *De Legibus*, and (with notes) Varro's treatise *De Lingua Latina* and Horace, with translations of Arrian, Oppian, Theophrastus, and portions of Plutarch. He died June 12th, 1565, greatly lamented. His miscellanies (*Opera*) were published in Strassburg in 1600 in 3 vols., containing, among other productions, his *Adversaria*, with critical emendations on many classical authors. See the account of Turnebus prefixed to that work, and also Maittaire's *Historia Typographorum Aliquot Parisiensium* (London, 1817).

Turnus (Τύρνος). (1) The son of Daunus and Venilia, brother of Iuturna (q. v.), king of the Rutulians at Ardea. He was induced by Amata, the sister of his mother, and wife of Latinus, to make war upon Aeneas for his bride Lavinia, who had already been betrothed to himself. After many hard fights he was slain in single combat by his rival (Verg. *Aen.* vii. 408; x. 76; xii. 408, 926; Livy, i. 2). His name is probably connected with Tyrrhenus, and in the legends is associated with that of Mezentius; so that the story is supposed by some to refer to a struggle of the Latins against the Etruscans. (See ETRURIA.) (2) A satirical poet who lived in the first and second centuries A.D. (Mart. vii. 97). Thirty hexameter lines that bear his name were written in the seventeenth century by J. L. G. Balzac. See Quicherat, *Mélanges de Philologie*, p. 259 (Paris, 1879).

Turŏnes, Turŏni, or **Turonii**. A people in the interior of Gallia Lugdunensis, between the Aulerci, Andes, and Pictones. Their chief town was Caesarodunum, subsequently TURŎNI (Tours), on the Liger (Loire) (Caes. *B. G.* ii. 35).

Turpilius, SEXTUS. A Roman writer of comedies, a younger contemporary of Terence. He died at Sinuessa in B.C. 103 or 101. We possess only some of the titles and a few fragments of his plays, printed in Ribbeck's collection (Leipzig, 1872). He was the last important writer of the *fabula palliata*.

Turpio, L. AMBIVIUS. A famous actor of the time of Terence (Cic. *De Sen.* 14).

Turris (τύρσις, πύργος). Any lofty building; a tower; a fort or fortified place. The regular tower of fortification was either round or square, several stories in height, with turrets (*pinnae*) surmounting them, loop-holes (*fenestrae*) in the walls, and an arched entrance (*fornix*) in the middle. A movable tower (*turris mobilis*) was used in sieges to protect the approach of the battering-ram to the walls. (See ARIES.) Such a tower was sometimes several stories in height, and could be raised or lowered in order to allow the troops in it to scale the walls (Livy, xxi. 11; Vitruv. x. 13). When elephants were used in battle, they carried a sort of tower on the back filled with soldiers (Livy, xxxvii. 40). For the towers on the decks of ships, see NAVIS.

Turris Hannibălis. Now Bourj Salektah; a castle on the coast of Byzacena, between Thapsus and Acholla, belonging to Hannibal, who embarked here when he fled to Antiochus the Great (Livy, xxxiii. 48).

Turris Stratōnis. See CAESAREA (3).

Tus and (incorrectly) **Thus** (λιβανωτός). Frankincense; a fragrant gum from a tree of Arabian growth, employed by the ancients at the sacrifice, in the service of the temples, and other ceremonials. It was carried to the altar by a boy (*camillus*) in a small square case (*acerra*), from which a few grains were taken out, and sprinkled over the burning altar (*ara turicrema*); or it was made up into pastilles, which were carried in a deep dish (*catinus*), and thence dropped upon a lighted brazier (*focus turicremus*); or, finally, it was kindled in a censer (*turibulum*), which was carried in the hand, and swung backwards and forwards to give out and diffuse its vapour, as in the ceremonies of the Roman Catholic Church (Hor. *Carm.* iii. 8, 2; Pers. v. 120). See the illustration from a Pompeian bronze original. Cf. ACERRA; SACRIFICIUM.

Turibulum. (Pompeian bronze.)

Tuscania. A town of Etruria on the river Marta (Pliny, *H. N.* iii. 52), in whose tombs many remains of the Etruscans have been found, including the inscribed dice that have given some clue to the Etruscan numerals. The town is now called Toscanella. See ETRURIA, p. 626.

Tusci, Tuscia. See ETRURIA.

Tuscŭlum. Now Frascati; an ancient town of Latium, situated about ten miles southeast of Rome, on a lofty summit of the mountains, which are called after the town, TUSCULĀNI MONTES. It is said to have been founded by Telegonus, the son of Odysseus; and it was always one of the most important of the Latin towns. Cato the Censor was a native of Tusculum. Its proximity to Rome, its salubrity, and the beauty of its situation made it a favourite residence of the Roman nobles during the summer (Strabo, p. 239). Cicero, among others, had a favourite villa at this place, which he frequently mentions under the name of TUSCULĀNUM.

Tutēla. The office of guardian among the Romans. It affected not only minors, but also widows and grown-up daughters until the time of their marriage, with the exception of the Vestals. In the case of *impuberes* or *pupilli*, ordinary minors, the guardian (*tutor*) managed their property until the time of their majority, which with girls began at twelve, with boys at fourteen. (See INFANS; IMPUBES.) At this age the guardianship ended, and girls became, like widows, possessed of independent power over their property, but still remained so far under guardianship that they were unable to take legal proceedings without the consent of their guardians.

Three kinds of *tutores* have been distinguished: (*a*) *tutor testamentarius*, who was named in the will. By a provision in the will women were sometimes allowed the choice of their guardian, who was then called *tutor optivus* ("chosen guardian"), to distinguish him from the *tutor dativus* (or "specified guardian"). If no guardian was named in the will, or the guardian named declined the office, or subsequently resigned it, the next of kin stepped in as (*b*) *tutor legitimus*. In the case of a widow, this was the son, if of age, or the husband's brother, and so on. In the case of a daughter, the brother, if of age, the uncle on the father's side, and so on. Among the patricians, if there were no kinsmen, the *gentiles* undertook the duties. If there was neither a *tutor testamentarius* nor a *tutor legitimus*, then the praetor appointed (*c*) a *tutor Atilianus*, so called because the *lex Atilia* (about B.C. 188) had introduced this kind of guardian. Under the Empire these guardians were named by the consuls, from the time of Marcus Aurelius by a regular *praetor tutelaris*. Women having three children were exempted by Augustus from all guardianship. Then Claudius abolished guardianship on the part of the *agnati* in the case of all women. Diocletian extended this abolition to the case of minors. After the time of Diocletian, guardianship over women fell into disuse, and afterwards women were themselves allowed to act as guardians. A guardian found guilty of betraying his trust was punished by *infamia* (q. v.). See CURATOR.

Among the Athenians the guardian (ἐπίτροπος), if not named by the father in the will, was generally appointed by the archon from the nearest relations. The archon was also the proper authority in suits relating to guardianship, which, during the minority of the ward, could be brought forward in the form of a public prosecution; and, after the ward had attained his majority, in that of a private lawsuit. See EPITROPUS.

Tutelary Deities. See DAEMON; GENIUS; RELIGIO.

Tuticānus. A Roman poet, and friend of Ovid (Ovid, *Pont.* iv. 12).

Tutor. A guardian. See TUTELA.

Tutŭlus. A kind of Roman head-dress, formed by plaiting the hair high above the forehead. It was characteristic of the *flamen* and his wife. See COMA; FLAMEN.

Tutulus. (Herculanean painting.)

Tweezers. See VOLSELLAE.

Twelve Tables (DUODĔCIM TABŬLAE). The Twelve Tables, the first code of Roman law,

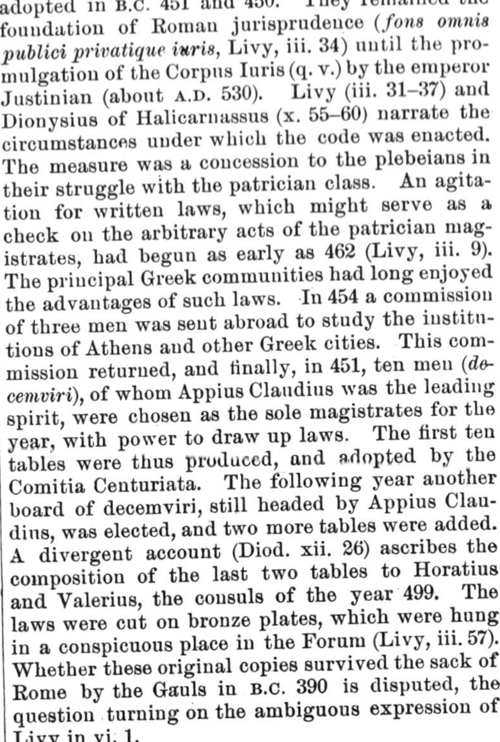

adopted in B.C. 451 and 450. They remained the foundation of Roman jurisprudence (*fons omnis publici privatique iuris*, Livy, iii. 34) until the promulgation of the Corpus Iuris (q. v.) by the emperor Justinian (about A.D. 530). Livy (iii. 31–37) and Dionysius of Halicarnassus (x. 55–60) narrate the circumstances under which the code was enacted. The measure was a concession to the plebeians in their struggle with the patrician class. An agitation for written laws, which might serve as a check on the arbitrary acts of the patrician magistrates, had begun as early as 462 (Livy, iii. 9). The principal Greek communities had long enjoyed the advantages of such laws. In 454 a commission of three men was sent abroad to study the institutions of Athens and other Greek cities. This commission returned, and finally, in 451, ten men (*decemviri*), of whom Appius Claudius was the leading spirit, were chosen as the sole magistrates for the year, with power to draw up laws. The first ten tables were thus produced, and adopted by the Comitia Centuriata. The following year another board of decemviri, still headed by Appius Claudius, was elected, and two more tables were added. A divergent account (Diod. xii. 26) ascribes the composition of the last two tables to Horatius and Valerius, the consuls of the year 499. The laws were cut on bronze plates, which were hung in a conspicuous place in the Forum (Livy, iii. 57). Whether these original copies survived the sack of Rome by the Gauls in B.C. 390 is disputed, the question turning on the ambiguous expression of Livy in vi. 1.

The authority of the Twelve Tables during the republican period was very great. Boys learned them by heart in the schools (Cic. *De Leg.* ii. 4, 9, and 23, 59). Later, this practice was discontinued. Though never repealed, the laws were gradually overlaid by praetorian decisions (*edicta*), which modified and supplemented them according to existing needs. These edicts came to be more important than the laws themselves (Cic. *De Leg.* i. 5, 17). There were several ancient commentaries on the Twelve Tables; the latest of these, by Gaius (second century A.D.), is often quoted in the Digests.

In general, the code of the Twelve Tables is spoken of by ancient writers in terms of admiration. The eleventh and twelfth tables, the work of the unpopular Second Decemvirate, are called by Cicero (*Rep.* ii. 37, 63) *duae tabulae iniquarum legum;* but the chief ground for this estimate of them appears to be the law, afterwards annulled, forbidding the intermarriage of patricians and plebeians. It must not be supposed that these two tables were an afterthought; it is clear from the language of Livy and Dionysius that the first ten tables, at the time of their adoption, were understood to be only a partial code, and that further legislation was expected. It is a noteworthy fact that the remarkable set of laws discovered in 1884 at Gortyna in Crete is cut upon a wall in twelve columns. See GORTYNA.

We cannot exactly define the relation of the Twelve Tables to preëxisting Roman law. But it is certain that they contained both new and old elements. There existed already a body of legal usages, and some of these had been formulated in maxims, known as *leges regiae*. Some of these maxims would seem from the language of Livy (vi. 1) to have existed in written form. The Twelve

Tables were based in part on this older law of custom (τὰ πάτρια ἔθη, Dionys. x. 55; οἱ παρὰ σφίσιν αὐτοῖς ἄγραφοι ἐθισμοί, *ibid.* 57). At least one of the *leges regiae*, relating to the *patria potestas*, was embodied in them (Dionys. ii. 27). On the other hand, they contained new features, and some of these were certainly derived from Greek sources. Thus we are told in particular by Cicero (*De Leg.* ii. 23, 59; 25, 64) that certain clauses restricting expense at funerals were taken almost word for word from the laws of Solon. Like statements are made by Gaius (*Dig.* x. 1, 13; xlvii. 22, 4) about two other laws. An Ephesian Greek named Hermodorus is said to have aided the decemviri in their work (Strab. p. 642; Pliny, *H. N.* xxxiv. 5, 11). The fact of Greek influence in the decemviral legislation is further brought out by striking resemblances between the Twelve Tables and the inscriptional code of Gortyna just mentioned—resemblances extending even to particular expressions (*se fraude esto*=ἄπατων ἥμην).

We possess about 100 fragments of the Twelve Tables, some containing quotations of their exact words, others only statements of content. The most important sources are Gellius (especially the interesting chapter xx. 1), Festus, Cicero, and Gaius. The arrangement of these fragments and their distribution among the Twelve Tables have been much discussed. The following is the system of Dirksen, which has obtained a considerable currency: Tables i. and ii., civil process; iii., procedure for debt; iv., *patria potestas;* v., guardianship and inheritance; vi., rights of property; vii., contracts; viii., *delicta* and *crimina;* ix., *ius publicum;* x., *ius sacrum* (including burial); xi. and xii., supplements and additions. This system is based on two things: (1) a few citations in which the number of the table is expressly stated; and (2) the citations from Gaius's commentary, the assumption being that the six books of that commentary corresponded to the twelve tablets of laws taken in pairs. But the validity of this assumption respecting Gaius's six books has been denied by many recent scholars, and even the hypothesis which underlies this and all previous attempts at arrangement—that the disposition of the code was strictly systematic, and that the contents of each tablet constituted a sort of unity, like a chapter—has been shown to be unsupported by analogies. (See, on all this, Schoell's *Prolegomena*, pp. 67, 68.) It may be added that the arrangement of the Gortynian Code, already mentioned, shows little system, and that its twelve columns are like pages of a book, and have nothing to do with the divisions of the subject-matter. It should therefore be borne in mind that all that we certainly know respecting the location of the different fragments is this: the law permitting the release of a son from *patria potestas* by three mancipations (sales) stood in the fourth table (Dionys. ii. 27); the sumptuary laws regulating funerals in the tenth (Cic. *De Leg.* ii. 25, 64); the prohibition of *conubium* between patricians and plebeians in one of the last two tables (Dionys. x. 60). Probably, also, the law defining proper causes of postponement for a suit was in the second table (Festus, p. 273, but the text is conjectural). Lastly, that the first table began with the words *si in ius vocat, ito* may be fairly inferred from Cic. *De Leg.* ii. 4, 9. It is the opinion of Mommsen that the *Fasti* or Calendar were contained in the Twelve Tables (cf. Cic. *Ad Att.* vi. 1, 8; Macrob. *Sat.* i. 13, 21), and Schoell assigns them to the eleventh table.

The language of the Twelve Tables abounds in archaisms. As examples may serve *im=eum, nox =noctu, endo=in* (*endo iacito inicito*), *escit=est, lessus=luctus, ast* as conditional particle, 'and if.' The condensation of expression is extreme: for instance, the subject is constantly omitted, even where there is a sudden change; as, *si nox furtum faxsit, si im occisit, iure caesus esto.* The laws contain some noteworthy provisions. Thus, gold must not be buried with a corpse, except that used to fasten teeth. The person of a debtor was forfeited to his creditors, who might divide his body among them. No actual occurrence of this, we are told, was on record in historical times.

The fragments of the Twelve Tables have been often edited, but the editions which mark a distinct advance are: J. Gothofredus, *Fragmenta XII Tabularum* (Heidelberg, 1616) (reprinted in Otto's *Thesaurus Iuris Romani*, vol. iii.); H. E. Dirksen, *Uebersicht der bisherigen Versuche zur Kritik und Herstellung des Textes der Zwölftafeln-Fragmente* (Leipzig, 1824); Rudolf Schoell, *Legis Duodecim Tabularum Reliquiae* (with valuable Prolegomena) (Leipzig, 1866).

Tyăna (Τύανα). Now Kiz Hisar; a city of Asia Minor, stood in the south of Cappadocia, at the northern foot of Mount Taurus. Tyana was the native place of Apollonius, the supposed worker of miracles. (See APOLLONIUS.) The southern district of Cappadocia, in which the city stood, was called Tyanitis. Near Tyana in Roman times was a great temple of Iupiter.

Tyché (Τύχη). (1) The Greek goddess of Fortune; also identified with Isis in one of her phases, and with the Roman goddess Fortuna. When identified with Isis she is represented with the lotus-flower, with erected feathers on her head, with the crescent and orb, and as holding a *sistrum.* See FORTUNA. (2) See SYRACUSAE.

Tydeus (Τυδεύς). The son of Oeneus, king of Calydon, and Periboea. He was obliged to leave Calydon in consequence of some murder which he had committed, but which is differently described by different authors. He fled to Adrastus at Argos, who purified him from the murder, and gave him his daughter Deïpylé in marriage, by whom he became the father of Diomedes, who is hence frequently called TYDĪDES. He accompanied Adrastus in the expedition against Thebes, where he was wounded by Melanippus, who, however, was slain by him (*Il.* xiv. 114–132). When Tydeus lay on the ground wounded, Athené appeared to him with a remedy which she had received from Zeus, and which was to make him immortal. This, however, was prevented by a stratagem of Amphiaraüs, who hated Tydeus, for he cut off the head of Melanippus and brought it to Tydeus, who divided it and ate the brain, or devoured some of the flesh. Athené, seeing this, shuddered, and left Tydeus to his fate. He consequently died, and was buried by Macon (Apollod. iii. 6, 8; Eustath. *ad* Hom. p. 1273).

Tymbres or **Tembrogius**. A river in Phrygia flowing into the Sangarius.

Tymnes (Τύμνης). A writer of epigrams, seven of whose productions are included in the Greek Anthology. Nothing is known of his death or personal history.

Tympănum (τύμπανον). (1) A tambourine, used more especially at the noisy revels of Dionysus and Cybelé; a broad rim of wood or metal covered with skin; sometimes also set round with a concave and semicircular sound-board. (2) A treadwheel for raising heavy weights and worked by man-power (Lucret. iv. 907).

Tymphaei (Τυμφαῖοι). A people of Epirus, on the borders of Thessaly, so called from Mount Tymphé. Their country was called TYMPHAEA (Τυμφαία).

Tymphrestus (Τυμφρηστός). Now Elladha; a mountain in Thessaly, in the country of the Dryopes, in which the river Spercheus rises.

Tyndareus, Tyndareōs (Τυνδάρεως). The son of Perieres and Gorgophoné, or, according to others, son of Oebalus, by the nymph Batia or by Gorgophoné. Tyndareus and his brother Icarius were expelled by their step-brother Hippocoön and his sons; whereupon Tyndareus fled to Thestius in Aetolia, and assisted him in his wars against his neighbours. In Aetolia Tyndareus married Leda, the daughter of Thestius, and was afterwards restored to Sparta by Heracles. By Leda, Tyndareus became the father of Timandra, Clytaemnestra, and Philopoë. One night Leda was embraced both by Zeus and by Tyndareus, and the result was the birth of Pollux and Helena, the children of Zeus, and of Castor and Clytaemnestra, the children of Tyndareus. The patronymic TYNDARĬDAE is frequently given to Castor and Pollux, and the female patronymic TYNDĂRIS to Helen and Clytaemnestra. When Castor and Pollux had been received among the immortals, Tyndareus invited Menelaüs to come to Sparta, and surrendered his kingdom to him. See DIOSCURI; HELENA; LEDA.

Tyndăris (Τυνδαρίς) or **Tyndarium** (Τυνδάριον). Now Tindaro; a town on the northern coast of Sicily, a little west of Messana, founded by the elder Dionysius, B.C. 396.

Typhon (Τυφάων) or **Typhōeus** (Τυφωεύς). A monster of the primitive world, who is described sometimes as a destructive hurricane, and sometimes as a fire-breathing giant. According to Homer, he was concealed in the earth in the country of the Arimi, which was lashed by Zeus with flashes of lightning (*Il.* ii. 782). In Hesiod, Typhaon and Typhoeus are two distinct beings. Typhaon is represented as a son of Typhoeus, and a fearful hurricane, and as having become by Echidna the father of the dog Orthus, Cerberus, the Lernaean hydra, Chimaera, and the Sphinx. Typhoeus, on the other hand, is called the youngest son of Tartarus and Gaea, or of Heré alone, because she was indignant at Zeus having given birth to Athené. He is described as a monster with 100 heads, fearful eyes, and terrible voices, who wanted to acquire the sovereignty of gods and men, but, after a fearful struggle, was subdued by Zeus with a thunderbolt. He begot the winds, whence he is also called the father of the Harpies; but the beneficent winds Notus, Boreas, Argestes, and Zephyrus were not his sons. He was buried in Tartarus, under Mount Aetna, the workshop of Hephaestus, whence it is called by the poets *Typhoïs Aetna* (Ovid, *Fasti*, iv. 491). Typhus was identified by the Greeks with the Egyptian god Set, who typified the power of darkness, and who slew Osiris. See Herod. ii. 156; iii. 5; and the article OSIRIS.

Tyrannion (Τυραννίων). (1) A Greek grammarian, a native of Amisus in Pontus, was taken captive by Lucullus, and carried to Rome, B.C. 72. He was given by Lucullus to Murena, who manumitted him. At Rome Tyrannion occupied himself in teaching. He was also employed in arranging the library of Apellicon, which Sulla brought to Rome, and which contained the writings of Aristotle. Cicero speaks in the highest terms of his learning and ability (*Ad Att.* ii. 6; iv. 4). See Planer, *De Tyrannione Grammatico* (1852). (2) A native of Phœnicia, the son of Artemidorus, and a pupil of the preceding. He was for some time a slave of Terentia, the wife of Cicero, who manumitted him. He taught at Rome and wrote a number of works now lost.

Tyrannus (τύραννος). In the Heroic Age all the governments in Greece were monarchical, the king uniting in himself the functions of the priest, the judge, and military chief. In the first two or three centuries following the Trojan War various causes were at work, which led to the abolition, or at least to the limitation, of the kingly power. Emigrations, extinctions of families, disasters in war, civil dissensions, may be reckoned among these causes. Hereditary monarchies became elective; the different functions of the king were distributed; he was called Archon (ἄρχων), Cosmus (κόσμος), or Prytanis (πρύτανις), instead of Basileus (βασιλεύς), and his character was changed no less than his name. Noble and wealthy families began to be considered on a footing of equality with royalty; and thus in process of time sprang up oligarchies or aristocracies, which most of the governments that succeeded the ancient monarchies were in point of fact, though not as yet called by such names. These oligarchies did not possess the elements of social happiness or stability. The principal families contended with each other for the greatest share of power, and were only unanimous in disregarding the rights of those whose station was beneath their own. The people, oppressed by the privileged classes, began to regret the loss of their old paternal form of government, and were ready to assist any one who would attempt to restore it. Thus were opportunities offered to ambitious and designing men to raise themselves by starting up as the champions of popular rights. Discontented nobles were soon found to prosecute schemes of this sort, and they had a greater chance of success if descended from the ancient royal family. An example is Pisistratus, who was the more acceptable to the people of Athens as being a descendant of the family of Codrus. Thus in many cities arose that species of monarchy which the Greeks called *tyrannis* (τυραννίς), which meant only a despotism, or the irresponsible dominion of one man. This very frequently was nothing more than a revival of the ancient government, and, though unaccompanied with any recognized hereditary title, or the reverence attached to old name and long prescription, was hailed by the lower orders of people as a good exchange, after suffering under the domination of the oligarchy. All "tyrannies," however, were not so acceptable to the majority; and sometimes we find the nobles concurring in the elevation of a despot, to further their own interests. Thus the Syracusan *Gamori*, who had been expelled by the populace, on receiving the protection of Gelon, sovereign of Gela and Camarina, enabled him to take possession of Syracuse, and establish his kingdom there. Sometimes the conflicting parties in the State, by mutual consent, chose some eminent man, in whom they had confidence, to reconcile their dissensions, investing him with a sort of dictatorial power for that purpose, either for a limited period or otherwise. Such a person they called *aesymnetes* (αἰσυμνήτης). The *tyrannus* must be distinguished, on the one hand, from the *aesymnetes*, inasmuch as he was not elected by general consent, but commonly owed his elevation to some violent movement or stratagem, such as the creation of a body-guard for him by the people, or the seizure of the citadel; and, on the other hand, from the ancient king, whose right depended, not on usurpation, but on inheritance and traditionary acknowledgment. The power of a king might be more absolute than that of a "tyrant," as Phidon of Argos is said to have made the royal prerogative greater than it was under his predecessors; yet he was still regarded as a king, for the difference between the two names depended upon title and origin, and not on the manner in which the power was exercised. The name "tyrant" was originally so far from denoting a person who abused his power, or treated his subjects with cruelty, that Pisistratus is praised for the moderation of his government. Afterwards, when "tyrants" themselves had become odious, the name also grew to be a word of reproach, just as *rex* did among the Romans. Among the early "tyrants" of Greece those most worthy of mention are: Clisthenes of Sicyon, grandfather of the Athenian Clisthenes, in whose family the government continued for a century from its establishment by Orthagoras, about B.C. 672; Cypselus of Corinth, who expelled the Bacchiadae, B.C. 656, and his son Periander, both remarkable for their cruelty; their dynasty lasted between seventy and eighty years; Procles of Epidaurus; Pantaleon of Pisa, who celebrated the thirty-fourth Olympiad, depriving the Eleans of the presidency; Theagenes of Megara, father-in-law to Cylon the Athenian; and Pisistratus, whose sons were the last of the early "tyrants" on the Grecian continent. In Sicily, where "tyranny" most flourished, the principal were Phalaris of Agrigentum, who established his power in B.C. 568; Theron of Agrigentum; Gelon, already mentioned, who, in conjunction with Theron, defeated Hamilcar the Carthaginian, on the same day on which the battle of Salamis was fought; and Hieron, his brother: the last three celebrated by Pindar. The following also are worthy of notice: Polycrates of Samos, Lygdamis of Naxos, Histiaeus and Aristagoras of Miletus. Perhaps the last mentioned can hardly be classed among the Greek "tyrants," as they were connected with the Persian monarchy.

The general characteristics of a "tyranny" were, that it was bound by no laws, and had no recognized limitation to its authority, however it might be restrained in practice by the good disposition of the "tyrant" himself, or by fear, or by the spirit of the age. It was commonly most odious to the wealthy and noble, whom the "tyrant" looked upon with jealousy as a check upon his power, and whom he often sought to get rid of by sending them into exile or putting them to death. The "tyrant" usually kept a body-guard of foreign mercenaries, by aid of whom he controlled the people at home; but he seldom ventured to make war, for fear of giving an opportunity to his subjects to revolt. The causes which led to the decline of "tyranny" among the Greeks were partly the degeneracy of the "tyrants" themselves, corrupted by power, indolence, flattery, and bad education; for even where the father set a good example, it was seldom followed by the son; partly the cruelties and excesses of particular men, which brought them all into disrepute; and partly the growing spirit of inquiry among the Greek people, who began to speculate upon political theories, and soon became discontented with a form of government which had nothing in theory, and little in practice, to recommend it. Few dynasties lasted beyond the third generation. Most of the tyrannies which flourished before the Persian War are said to have been overthrown by the exertions of Sparta, jealous, probably, of any innovation upon the old Doric constitution, especially of any tendency to ameliorate the condition of the Perioeci, and anxious to extend her own influence over the States of Greece by means of the benefits which she conferred. Upon the fall of "tyranny" the various republican forms of government were established, the Dorian States generally favouring oligarchy, the Ionian democracy. Of the "tyrants" of a later period, the most celebrated are the two Dionysii. The corruption of the Syracusans, their intestine discords, and the fear of the Carthaginian invaders, led to the appointment of Dionysius to the chief military command, with unlimited powers; by means of which he raised himself to the throne B.C. 406, and reigned for thirty-eight years, leaving his son to succeed him. The younger Dionysius, far inferior in every respect to his father, was expelled by Dion, afterwards regained the throne, and was again expelled by Timoleon, who restored liberty to the various States of Sicily.

See Plaes, *Die Tyrannis in ihren beiden Perioden bei den alten Griechen* (Bremen, 1852); Drumann, *De Tyrannis Graecorum* (Halle, 1812); Schömann, *Griech. Alterth.* i. pp. 169 foll.; Zeller in *Berichte der Berl. Acad.* (1885); and the articles OLIGARCHIA; TIMOCRATIA.

Tyras (Τύρας). Now the Dniester; subsequently called **Danastris**; a river in European Sarmatia, forming in the lower part of its course the boundary between Dacia and Sarmatia, and falling into the Pontus Euxinus north of the Danube. At its mouth was a town of the same name.

Tyriaeum (Τυριαῖον). Now Ilghin; a city of Lycaonia, twenty parasangs west of Iconium (Xen. *Anab.* i. 2, 24).

Tyro (Τυρώ). The daughter of Salmoneus and Alcidicé. She was the wife of Cretheus, and beloved by the river-god Enipeus in Thessaly, in whose form Poseidon appeared to her, and became by her the father of Pelias and Neleus. By Cretheus she was the mother of Aeson, Pheres, and Amythaon (*Od.* xi. 235; Apollod. i. 9, 8).

Tyros (τυρός). Cheese. See CASEUS.

Tyrrhēni, Tyrrhenia. See ETRURIA.

Tyrrhēnum Maré. See ETRURIA.

Tyrrhēnus (Τυρρηνός or Τυρσηνός). The son of the Lydian king Atys and Callithea, and brother of Lydus. He is said to have led a Pelasgian colony from Lydia into Italy, into the country of the Umbrians, and to have given to the colonists his name. Others call Tyrrhenus a son of Heracles by Omphalé, or of Telephus and Hiera, and a brother of Tarchon (Dionys. i. 28). The name Tarchon is perhaps only another form of Tyrrhenus. See ETRURIA.

Tyrtaeus (Τυρταῖος or Τύρταιος). A Greek described as the son of Archembrotus of Aphidnae in Attica. In the seventh century he introduced the Ionic elegy into Sparta. According to the older tradition, the Spartans during the Second Messenian War were commanded by an oracle to take a leader from among the Athenians, and thus to conquer their enemies, whereupon they chose Tyrtaeus as their leader (Plato, *De Leg.* i. p. 629; Lycurg. *c. Leoch.* p. 211; Diod. xv. 66). Later writers state that Tyrtaeus was a lame schoolmaster, of low family and reputation, whom the Athenians, when applied to by the Lacedaemonians in accordance with the oracle, purposely sent as the most inefficient leader they could select, being unwilling to assist the Lacedaemonians in extending their dominion in the Peloponnesus, and little thinking that the poetry of Tyrtaeus would achieve that victory to which his physical infirmity seemed to forbid his aspiring (Paus. iv. 15, 3; Just. iii. 5; Themist. xv. p. 242; Schol. *ad* Hor. *A. P.* 402). The poems of Tyrtaeus exercised an important influence upon the Spartans, quieting their dissensions at home, and animating their courage in the field. In order to appease their civil discords, he composed his celebrated elegy entitled *Legal Order* (Εὐνομία: Arist. *Pol.* v. 7, 1; Paus. iv. 18, 2). But still more celebrated were the poems by which he animated the courage of the Spartans in their conflict with the Messenians. These poems were of two kinds: namely, elegies, containing exhortations to constancy and courage, and descriptions of the glory of fighting bravely for one's native land; and more spirited compositions, in the anapaestic measure, which were intended as marching-songs (ἐμβατήρια), to be accompanied by the music of the flute (Paus. iv. 14, 1; Athen. p. 630; Plut. *Cleom.* 2; Hor. *A. P.* 402; Suid. *s. v.*). He lived, it is said, to see the success of his efforts in the entire conquest of the Messenians, and their reduction to the condition of Helots. His life therefore lasted down to B.C. 668, which was the last year of the Second Messenian War. It has been observed that Tyrtaeus in a fragment of the *Eunomia* seems to speak of himself as a Lacedaemonian, and though this might be explained by his having been made a citizen of Sparta, yet Herodotus (ix. 35) does not include him among the few foreigners who became Spartan citizens. Hence some (following Strab. p. 362) have doubted the truth of his Athenian origin. On the other hand, there is so strong a consensus of ancient authorities, including Plato (*l. c.*), for his Athenian origin that it can hardly be resisted.

The fragments of his poems are edited by Bach, with the remains of the elegiac poets Callinus and Asius (Leipzig, 1831), and in Bergk's *Poet. Lyr. Graec.* ii. pp. 8–22 (1878). See Carus, *De Tyrtaei Patria et Aetate* (1863); Hölbe, *De Tyrtaei Patria* (1864); and Hoffmann, *Ueber Tyrtaeus und seine Kriegslieder* (1877).

Tyrus (Τύρος: Aram. Tura: O. T. Tsōr). Now Sur; one of the greatest and most famous cities of the ancient world, standing on the coast of Phoenicé, about twenty miles south of Sidon. It was a colony of the Sidonians, but gradually eclipsed the mother city, and came to be the chief place of all Phoenicé for wealth, commerce, and colonizing activity. Respecting its colonies and maritime enterprise, see PHOENICÉ and CARTHAGO. The Assyrian king Shalmaneser laid siege to Tyre for five years, but without success. It was again besieged for thirteen years by Nebuchadnezzar, and there is a tradition that he took it, but the matter is not quite certain. At the period when the Greeks began to be well acquainted with the city, its old site had been abandoned, and a new city erected on a small island about half a mile from the shore and a mile in length, and a little north of the remains of the former city, which was now called Old Tyre (Παλαίτυρος). This island, which Pliny estimated at two and three-quarter miles in circumference, was separated from the mainland by a channel seven-tenths of a mile broad (Strab. p. 756), or according to Diodorus and Curtius, four stadia (Diod. xvii. 60; Q. Curt. iv. 2). At present the breadth is only one-third of a mile. With the additional advantage of its insular position, this new city soon rose to a prosperity scarcely less than that of its predecessor; though under the Persian kings (?) it seems to have ranked again below Sidon. (See SIDON.) There were two harbours: one on the north of the island, known as the Sidonian Harbour, and the other on the south side, known as the Egyptian Harbour (Arr. *An.* ii. 20; Strab. *l. c.*), the names expressing the direction in which they faced. In B.C. 322 the Tyrians refused to open their gates to Alexander, who laid siege to the city for seven months, and united the island on which it stood to the mainland by a mole constructed chiefly out of the ruins of Old Tyre. This mole has ever since formed a permanent connection between the island and the mainland (Arr. ii. 17–26; Q. Curt. iv. 4–27; Diod. xvii. 40–45). After its capture and sack by Alexander, Tyre never regained its former consequence, and its commerce was for the most part transferred to Alexandria. It was subject to the Syrian kings, but became a free city with its own coinage in B.C. 126, and till the time of Augustus, when it lost its independence (Dio Cass. liv. 7). Septimius Severus made it a Roman colony. It was the see of a Bishop, and St. Jerome calls it the most beautiful city of Phœnicia. It was a place of considerable importance in mediæval history, especially as one of the last points held by the Christians on the coast of Syria. See Jeremias, *Tyrus bis zur Zeit Nebukadnezar's* (1891).

Tzetzes. (1) IOANNES (Ιωάννης Τζέτζης). A Greek grammarian and poet of the second half of the twelfth century A.D. He lived in Constantinople, and though for his time he may be called learned, his erudition is wholly superficial, as is amply proved by his existing writings. Besides commentaries on Homer, Hesiod, Aristophanes, and other classical writers, which are valuable for the authorities quoted in them, he composed, in 1676 feeble hexameters, an epic poem entitled *Iliaca*, containing the legend of Troy from the birth of Paris till the opening of the *Iliad*, the incidents of the *Iliad* in detail, and the further course of the war up to the return of the Greeks. It is in three parts: (*a*) *Ante-Homerica;* (*b*) *Homerica;* (*c*) *Post-Homerica.* Besides this he wrote a book of histories in 12,661 "political verses"—i. e. verses based on accent rather than on syllabic quantity. (See POLITICI VERSUS.) These are commonly but wrongly called "chiliads" from an arbitrary division of the work into thirteen books of

1000 lines each. He is also the author of a collection of stories partly mythical, partly historical, worthless in themselves, but valuable as including numerous items of information which would otherwise have been unknown to us. The *Iliaca* is edited by Bekker (Berlin, 1816) and Lehrs (1840); the *Chiliades* by Kiessling (Leipzig, 1826).

(2) ISAAC TZETZES, brother of the preceding, was the author of a valuable commentary on Lycophron usually printed in editions of that author. See Hart, *De Tzetzarum Nomine, Vita, Scriptis* (1880).

U

U, as a symbol. See V.

Ubii. A German people, who originally dwelt on the right bank of the Rhine, but were transported across the river by Agrippa, in B.C. 37, at their own request, because they wished to escape the hostilities of the Suevi (Caes. *B. G.* iv. 3, 18; Tac. *Ann.* xii. 27; Suet. *Aug.* 21). They took the name of Agrippenses, from their town Colonia Agrippina (Cologne).

Ucalĕgon (Οὐκαλέγων). One of the elders at Troy, whose house was burned at the destruction of the city (*Il.* iii. 147; Verg. *Aen.* ii. 312). Hence Juvenal uses his name for a neighbour whose house is on fire (iii. 199).

Udo. A sort of sock or stocking made of goatskin (Mart. xiv. 140).

Ufens. Now the Uffente; a river in Latium, flowing from Setia, and falling into the Amasenus.

Uffŭgum. A town in Bruttium, between Scyllacium and Rhegium.

Ulpiānus, DOMITIUS. The most celebrated among Roman jurists next to Papinianus. Born at Tyre about A.D. 170, he began his career in Rome under Septimius Severus as colleague of Papinianus; and, under Elagabalus and Alexander Severus, whose preceptor and guardian he had been, he filled the office of a *praefectus praetorio.* During his tenure of this office he was murdered (228) before the eyes of the emperor by the Praetorians, whom he had exasperated by the strictness of his discipline. His two chief works, on the praetorian law (*Ad Edictum*), in eighty-three books, and on the civil law (*Ad Sabinum*), in fifty-one books, were held in high esteem, and formed the foundation of the Pandects of Justinian's *Corpus Iuris.* Of this portion the extracts from his writings form a full third. Besides these excerpts we have a small part of his *Regularum Liber Singularis* (ed. by Böcking [Bonn, 1855]), and of his *Institutiones*, included in Huschke's *Iurisprudentia Anteiustiniana*, 568, and edited by Vahlen (Bonn, 1856). See Schilling, *De Ulpiano* (Breslau, 1824); and Karlowa, *Röm. Rechtsgeschichte*, i. 743.

Ulpius Traiānus. See TRAIANUS.

Ultor. "The avenger;" a surname of Mars, to whom Augustus built a temple at Rome in the Forum, after taking vengeance upon the murderers of his great-uncle, Iulius Caesar.

Ulŭbrae. A small town in Latium, of uncertain site, but in the neighbourhood of the Pontine Marshes.

Ulysses. See ODYSSEUS.

Umbella. See UMBRACULUM.

Umbilīcus (ὀμφαλός). (1) See DELPHI, p. 481. (2) See LIBER, p. 951.

Umbo (ἄμβων). (1) A knob or boss projecting from the centre of a shield. (See CLIPEUS.) (2) A bunch or fold in a garment, especially that produced by drawing up a part of the toga and fastening it at the breast (Tertull. *Pall.* 5). (3) A curbstone; the raised margin of a sidewalk.

Umbra. (1) (εἴδωλον, *imago*). A ghost. The ancients believed that the spirit of the human body descended into subterranean regions after life was extinct, and there retained the same figure and appearance it had possessed during life, so as to be recognizable by the relatives and friends who followed it, but without any real corporeal substance; or, in other words, that it was visible but impalpable. Those who had passed a life of virtue were removed to Elysium (see ELYSII CAMPI), where they continued in the enjoyment of perpetual youth, and sharing in the intercourse of such friends and relatives as had obtained the same lot. Those, on the contrary, who had lived in vice were removed to Tartarus, where they wore out an existence of perpetual punishment (Serv. *ad* Verg. *Aen.* iv. 654; Tibull. iii. 2, 9; Lucret. i. 120; Hor. *Carm.* iv. 7, 14). Hence the poets and artists always invest the shades with a corporeal form, and with the same appearances which the body presented during life. Popular tradition held that the spirits of the dead could revisit the earth; so that there are many passages in ancient literature that are curiously suggestive of the modern "ghost-story." Several such are found in a letter of Pliny (vii. 27), where all the accessories of strange noises, clanking chains, etc., are introduced, and where the longest tale is the literary prototype of Washington Irving's ghost-story in *Dolph Heyliger.* See Tylor, *Primitive Culture* (1871); and the article LARVA. (2) A guest who comes to dinner on the invitation, not of the host, but of one whom the host has invited (Hor. *Epist.* i. 5, 28).

Umbracŭlum (σκιάδειον) and **Umbella.** A sunshade or parasol made like our own to open and shut (Aristoph. *Eq.* 1348). The ribs were called *virgae* (Ovid, *A. A.* ii. 209). It was usually carried

Lady with Maid carrying Umbraculum. (From a vase.)

by a female slave, who held it over the head of her mistress. The use of umbrellas was almost confined to women, for it was considered effeminate for men to use any protection against the sun except when travelling. Some luxurious men, however (Athen. xii. p. 534 *a*), occasionally braved public opinion and used them. In Hellenistic times a large straw hat came into fashion, doubtless as a substitute for the parasol. At Rome they were also taken to the amphitheatre as a protection against the sun. See Paciandi, *De Umbellae Gestatione* (Rome, 1752); Marquardt, *Privatleben*, p. 148. For the carrying of the parasol in processions, see SCIADEPHORIA.

Umbrella. See UMBRACULUM.

Umbria (Ὀμβρική). The portion of Central Italy between the rivers Sapis in the north and Nar in the south, the Apennines in the west, the Ager Gallicus near Ariminum and the Ager Picens near Hadria in the east; in Augustus's division, the sixth region of Italy, with about fifty important cities (Pliny, *H. N.* iii. 112 foll.), after B.C. 220, traversed by the Via Flaminia. It was able, at the time of the Second Punic War, to muster 20,000 warriors against the Keltic foe. The name Ὀμβρικοί (shorter Ὄμβροι) is first met in Herodotus as an undefined title for the Italic tribes in the region of the Po, of which the Etruscans took possession. The ancients derived the name from ὄμβρος, *imber*, making the people as old as the Deluge; the Umbrian-Roman comedian Plautus, with more probable correctness, in a joke (*Most.* 770) connects the word with *umbra*. The name probably designated the tribes of the western mountains from the standpoint of some of the Greeks.

Most nearly related to the Latins and the Sabellian tribes, the Umbrians were the ruling race of Northern Italy until the Romans, in the extension of their power, about B.C. 300, brought them also under their sway. The Sarsinates were the last to submit to the Roman *imperium* in the year 266, after a vain attempt to recover their freedom; the Sarsinate Plautus, who wrote for the Roman stage even before 200, is so completely Latinized that his ancient commentators had trouble to discover a single Umbrian word in his comedies. The historical importance of the Umbrians, therefore, belongs to an undefined period prior to the end of the fourth century B.C., when they formed a powerful barrier for the Italic peoples against the tribes of another race pushing on from the North. The elder Cato had placed the founding of the Umbrian city of Ameria in the year B.C. 1133, fifty years after the fall of Troy, as calculated by the Alexandrian scholars. Once subjugated by these strangers, or while still contending with them for supremacy in the plain of the Po and beyond the Apennines, the Umbrians had been more and more forced back, and at last confined to the above-named position in the valleys east of the Apennines. There they had been obliged to give place to the Kelts and Etruscans, who, to the last, were considered by the Umbrians the chief enemies of their own name. Various Keltic tribes had at different times pushed their way south through the plains of Lombardy into Umbrian territory (Livy, v. 34 foll.); the tomb of a Kelt, with Keltic and Roman inscriptions, was found at Tuder in the heart of Umbria. This race is represented in the ritual records of the Umbrians by the tribe of the Iapyds, which is not mentioned in the Roman annals until the second century B.C. The other hereditary enemy was the Etruscans. Not only did the Umbrians contend with Etruscans for the adjoining lands of the Po region, where many settlements were alternately Umbrian and Etruscan (Strabo, v. p. 216), but even in Etruria itself, many districts had been in the hands of the Umbrians before they were driven out by the Etruscans; and before the onsets of the Romans both nations made war against each other alternately to and fro across the Tiber, which formed the boundary between their territories. Thus the strongest barrier was set against the spread of the Umbrians to the north and west. It is no wonder, then, that the Umbrians, hemmed in by Kelts and Etruscans, were unable to offer any successful resistance to the conquering enemies of their own line pressing upon them from the Nar, since we see them without unity or centralized power, split up into a number of cities or States, which were just as hostile to each other as to the national enemy, as the Iguvini towards the Tadinates, the Sarsinates towards the rest of the Umbrians. The contrast to the political ideas and discipline of the Romans is apparent also in the contrasting application of an hereditary expression for their civil divisions. While the Romans subordinated the tribus as a fractional part to the *civitas*, with the Umbrians the *trifu*, i. e. the outlying country confederation belonging to the city, stood above the *tota*, as they called the city organization, as the essence of the State; e. g. the district of Iguvium or the tribus Sapinia on the northern boundary of the land (Livy, xxxi. 2). As in Rome, consuls, so at the head of Umbrian States we find *marones*, a word familiar through Vergil's cognomen.

The fact that we know a little more of the Umbrians, their language and civilization, than the scanty and inexact records of the ancient historians and geographers tell us, is due to the inscriptions on the monuments which the soil of the land has preserved for modern times. It is true that the smaller inscriptions from Asisium, Fulginia, Tuder, Ameria, including two dies for coinage, only seven in number, and of limited extent, give little information; but from the inscription of Assisi we may mention the mayor Propartis as the ancestor of the Umbrian Callimachus, who in the last verse of his elegy on Maecenas (iii. 9) evidently makes an allusion to the etymology, clearer in that form, of his name (*in partes*). Far richer and more valuable, in their extent almost unique in Italian epigraphy, are the seven bronze tablets excavated in 1444 in the theatre at Iguvium (now Gubbio) and still preserved at that place, written partly in the Umbrian, partly in the Latin alphabet, but all in the Umbrian dialect. They are the legacy of a religious brotherhood, which had at Iguvium nearly the same importance as the Pontifical Collegium at Rome, and at all events far surpassed the known Roman brotherhoods in weight and influence in the sacras of all the communities. The Temple of Iupiter Apenninus on the heights at Iguvium was famous in ancient times; but certain indications of the position of this temple and cult are lacking in the tablets.

These tablets (TABŬLAE IGUVĪNAE or EUGUBĪNAE) are the work of the Fratres Atiedii, who have here set down their ritual and in addition some decisions of their College. Of the ten great families for whose alliance a sacrifice of pigs and goats is offered twice a year, the *Atiedias familia* occupies the first place; the similarity of this name to the ethnic name of the Umbrian city Attidium is certainly not accidental. The most

One of the Eugubine Tablets. (Bréal.)

important tablets are I., VI., and VII., which describe the most essential sacrificial rites of the ancient communities, the lustration of the sacred citadel (*montem piare*), and the purification of the people (*circumferre populum*), from moment to moment and with all the ceremonies and prayers—Tablet I. briefly, VI. and VII. in greater detail, just as among the Roman *Fratres Arvales* the protocols of the rites are at first short, later more detailed and verbose. At the consecration of the citadel a procession went from gate to gate, and before and behind each gate a rich sacrifice was offered for the citadel and town of Iguvium. The celebration was concluded with sacrifices of bullocks at the Temple of Iupiter and a deity related to Iuno Curritis, which probably stood upon the citadel; the whole ceremony occupied the greater part of the day. "Then the citadel shall be purified; but if anything should be omitted, the officiating priest must observe the birds, turn back at the first gate, and begin the sacred rite anew." Tablet II. gives directions for a sacrifice improperly made and for the service of the dead, and on the other side for the half-yearly family reunions; III. and IV. add the ritual of the *ambarvalia* to the *amburbium* and *ambilustrium* described in I., VI., and VII.; V. contains decrees of the College as to what the officiating priest and the members of the society have to perform and to demand in regard to the expenses necessary for the *sacra*, the sacrificial feast, the distribution of the flesh, etc. As we possess no documents similar to these Umbrian remains concerning Roman religion and religious observances, and least of all from the time when the Roman cult was not yet permeated and adulterated by the Grecian, the great importance of these monuments for all investigation of Roman as well as of Italian ceremonial systems is self-evident. As the whole Roman literature, frequently as it refers to auspices and other kindred terms, does not tell us much of their nature, the arrangement of the temple, the methods and forms of auspices, etc., as the beginning of the sixth Umbrian tablet, its statements are necessarily the foundation for all scientific investigation of these questions. The significance of the *vacca honoraria* in contrast to the *hostiae piaculares* in the Roman Arval-rites had been shown in the Umbrian *vittu vufru*, before the recently discovered record of the Roman secular festival under Augustus had instructed even Roman antiquarians on the point (Mommsen, *Ephem. Epigraph.* viii. p. 270). See LUDI.

But infinitely greater in value than the information which these tablets contain is their linguistic importance, for we must not forget that some light is shed by the language upon those periods of the people on which history is silent, in so far as it interprets the origin of a race and its connection with or opposition to other peoples. Although in the last century, misled by the characters, scholars associated Umbrian and Etruscan, every one knows, from the language, that these two races had nothing in common. This, however, does not preclude the possibility that in consequence of centuries of proximity each one borrowed features from the other, or both from a third; as, e. g., the Umbrian-Italian words *maron* (city official) and *vinu* are found also in Etruscan. This much at least is sure, on the other hand, that the Umbrians received their writing and alphabet from the Etruscans. And this very point throws still further light on primitive times. For while their language unites the Umbrians with the Latins, Sabines, Samnites, and the smaller peoples of Central Italy, so that we roughly class them all as Italic, the writing separates the Umbrians from the Latins and Faliscans, and places them in a closer relation, produced probably by longer living together, with the Samnites (Oscans), who, together with the Umbrians, adopted the same Etruscan alphabet. In this alphabet, to which the sign 8 for the Italic fricative *f* is peculiar, the character for the vowel *o* was wanting (so in Umbrian *puplum* is written for *poplom*), as were also the characters for medial *g* (for which *Ikuvina* and *Ijuvina* are written), and *d*, which is supplied partly by *t* (*tekuries* for the Latin *decuries*). But the Umbrians compensated for this by incorporating two new characters in their alphabet, both modifications of an older *r*-sign, as the sound represented by the first letter had really relationship with the *r*-sound. The second letter was then arbitrarily formed in imitation of the first. The first is q, represented in Latin writing by *rs*, in general etymologically corresponding to the Greek δ—e.g., *persu*, for πόδα, *pedem;* sometimes to *l*, as in *karsitu* for καλέιτω, *calato*. The fact that the Latin transcription employed *r* as well as *s* indicates a dental sound, such as the rubbing of the tongue between the teeth produces. The other letter is d, rendered *s'* in the Latin writing, etymologically corresponding to *k* before *i* and *e*: *fas'ia* for Latin *faciat*, *pas'e* for Latin *pace*. This fact, that the Umbrian, in agreement with the Romance languages, changes the original guttural into the sibilant before light vowels, is the more remarkable since in related dialects no trace of this is found, nor in Latin before the time of Constantine. But this is one of many indications that important linguistic processes of the Romance languages have their beginning in the far-distant past of the Italic, but, pushed aside and restrained by the development and predominance of literary Latin, only with its decadence after the time of the Antonines come to the surface and into use again. The language of the Umbrians, as we know it from the monuments, embraces approximately the second century B.C. The inscriptions written in the Latin alphabet may be assigned on palaeographic and other grounds to the time of Sulla, roughly to B.C. 100; those written in Umbrian characters, therefore, tablets written from right to left as among the Etruscans, must be as much older as is required for certain changes in the language, shown in later tablets, to have become fixed. Among these changes the progress of rhotacism in place of an original *s* is especially prominent, as e.g. in the older tablets we find the genitive singular *totas* like σοφίας, *paterfamilias*, but in the later, *totar*. From this difference we distinguish Old Umbrian, written in the national alphabet, and New Umbrian, written in Latin; the former reaches scarcely beyond the war with Hannibal, but may perhaps, as appears from the older tablets (I. to V.), have been produced in different decades of the second century, since even in them slight differences in language appear.

On the whole, the Umbrian more nearly resembles the Oscan than the Latin, the reason for which has been already indicated in its phonology (Umbr.-Osc. *pantam*, Lat. *quantam*), in inflection (nominative plural Umbr.-Osc. *viros*, Lat. *viri;* Umbr.-Osc. *frateer*, Lat. *fratres;* fut. Umbr.-Osc. *fust*, Lat. *erit*, etc.), in vocabulary (Umbr.-Osc. *heriom*, Lat. *velle*). The discoveries of Oscan remains in recent years have confirmed the presumption of a very close agreement between Oscans and Umbrians in matter as well as in language (e.g. in the pentadic family order). But the Oscan gives the impression of a more vigorous plant, as though unfolded in the sunlight of Magna Graecia. It has more genuine, transparent, elegant forms, while with the Umbrians even their language reflects the pressure of their political relations, narrowing and stunted. All the diphthongs have disappeared (*oktur*, Lat. *auctor*, *kvestur*); the endings are mangled (*nome* for *nomen*, *emantu* for *emantur*, etc.); in composition four prepositions, appearing in Latin as *ab*, *ad*, *an*, and *in*, are reduced to the bare *a*-vowel.

If we bring Latin into comparison, the Umbrian has most similarity in its general structure with the Latin of two periods—the first, before it had been elaborated on literary lines, the second after the decline of the literature at its vulgarization and breaking up into provincial idioms. It is therefore not probable that a national literature preceded or accompanied the Umbrian which we know. Among the smaller tribes of Central Italy the Paeligni spoke a dialect occupying a place about midway between Umbrian and Oscan; but in spite of the greater separation in their positions, in historic times, the language of the Volsci comes near to the Umbrian. See ITALIA.

The principal authority is Aufrecht and Kirchhoff, *Die Umbrischen Sprachdenkmäler* (Berlin, 1849); Huschke, *Die Iguv. Tafeln* (Leipzig, 1859), chiefly for the facts; Bréal, *Les Tables Eugubines* (Paris, 1875, with photo-lithographic atlas), especially useful as an introduction to the language; Bücheler, *Umbrica* (Bonn, 1883); Von Planta, *Grammatik der Osk.-Umbr. Dialekte*, i. (Strassburg, 1893). For the history and geography, Nissen, *Italische Landeskunde*, i. p. 502 foll., and, above all, Borrmann in the *Corpus Inscript. Latinarum*, xi. 2, in which are collected the Latin inscriptions of Umbria. Cf. OSCI.

Umbro. Now the Ombrone; one of the largest rivers in Etruria, falling into the Tyrrhene Sea.

Uncia (οὐγκία). An ounce; the twelfth part of anything, especially of an *as*. It was the name of a small Roman copper coin (Varro, *L. L.* v. 171).

Roman Uncia (one-third of original size).

Uncials. See PALAEOGRAPHY.

Unctor. An anointer. See ALIPTAE; ATHLETAE; BALNEAE.

Undertaker. See FUNUS; USTOR.

Unelli. A people on the northern coast of Gaul, opposite Britain (Caes. *B. G.* ii. 34).

Unguentum (ἔλαιον, μύρον, σμῆγμα, σμῆμα). An ointment or perfume, both being extensively used by the ancients. The earliest and most common of unguents was olive-oil (see OLIVUM), used after the bath and in the preparation of the person for athletic contests. Other oils, more expensive and used partly for the skin and partly for the hair, are enumerated by Pliny (*H. N.* xiii. 4–18). They are usually named from the substance with which they were perfumed, as *irinum* (iris), *rosaceum* (rose), *narcissinum* (narcissus), *sesaminum* (sesame), *cardamomum* (cardamum), *cinnamomum* (cinnamon), *crocinum* (saffron), etc. Scented powders (διαπάσματα) were also popular (Theophr. *Odor.* 8). Luxurious persons carried oils and essences to the bath in little boxes (*narthecia*) or in scent-bottles (see ALABASTRUM). Perfumers were called μυρεψοί, μυροπῶλαι, *unguentarii*, and did a thriving business. In the effeminate city of Capua a whole street or square (the Seplasia) was given up to them (Cic. *In Pis.* ii. 24). See Boettiger, *Sabina*, last ed. rev. by Fischer (Munich, 1878); and for cosmetics the articles FUCUS; MELINUM. For soaps and powders see FULLO; SAPO; SPUMA.

Unio (οἴνη). (1) The one-spot on dice. See TALUS. (2) A solitaire pearl (Mart. viii. 81, 4).

Universities. See ALEXANDRIAN SCHOOL; EDUCATION.

Unlucky Days. See DIES.

Upis (Οὖπις). (1) A surname of Artemis as the goddess assisting women in childbirth. (2) The name of a mythical being, who is said to have reared Artemis, and who is mentioned by Vergil as one of the nymphs in her train (*Aen.* xi. 532). The masculine Upis is mentioned by Cicero as the father of Artemis.

Ur. See EDESSA.

Urania (Οὐρανία). (1) One of the Muses, a daughter of Zeus by Mnemosyné. The ancient bard Linus is called her son by Apollo, and Hymenaeus also is said to have been a son of Urania. She was regarded, as her name indicates, as the Muse of Astronomy, and was represented with a celestial globe, to which she points with a small staff. (2) Daughter of Oceanus and Tethys, who also occurs as a nymph in the train of Persephoné. (3) A surname of Aphrodité, describing her as "the heavenly," or spiritual, to distinguish her from Aphrodité Pandemos. Plato represents her as a daughter of Uranus, begotten without a mother. Wine was not used in the libations offered to her. See APHRODITÉ.

Urănus (Οὐρανός). Sometimes called a son and sometimes the husband of Gaea (Earth). By Gaea, Uranus became the father of Oceanus, Coeus, Crius, Hyperion, Iapetus, Thia, Rhea, Themis, Mnemosyné, Phoebe, Tethys, Cronos; of the Cyclopes —Brontes, Steropes, Arges; and of the Hecatoncheires—Cottus, Briareus, and Gyes. According to Cicero, Uranus was also the father of Mercury by Dia and of Venus by Hemera (Cic. *N. D.* iii. 22, 55–58). Uranus hated his children, and immediately after their birth he confined them in Tartarus, in consequence of which he was castrated and dethroned by Cronos at the instigation of Gaea. Out of the drops of his blood sprang the Gigantes, the Melian nymphs, and, according to some, Silenus; and from the foam gathering around his limbs in the sea sprang Aphrodité (Hes. *Th.* 126–193; Apollod. i. 1).

Urbigĕnus Pagus. See HELVETII.

Urbīnum. (1) HORTENSÉ. Now Urbino; a town in Umbria and a municipium. (2) METAURENSÉ. Now Urbania; a town in Umbria on the river Metaurus, and not far from its source.

Urceus, dim. **Urceŏlus** (πρόχοος). A one-handled jug used especially for pouring liquids from one vessel into another (Mart. xi. 56). It was a vessel in common use at the sacrifices. Its general shape was that shown in the illustration given under OENOCHOË.

Urcinium. Now Ajaccio; a town on the western coast of Corsica.

Uria. Called HYRIA by Herodotus; a town in Calabria, on the road from Brundusium to Tarentum, was the ancient capital of Iapygia, and is said to have been founded by the Cretans under Minos (Herod. vii. 170). It is now Oria.

Urinātor (ἀρνευτήρ, κολυμβητής). A trained diver (Livy, xliv. 10).

Urine as a detergent. See FULLO.

Urium. A small town in Apulia, from which the Sinus Urius took its name, being the bay on the northern side of Mount Garganus opposite the Diomedean Islands.

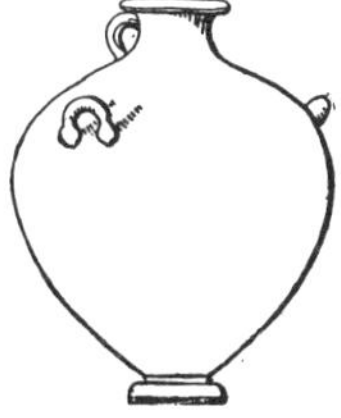
Urna.

Urna (κάλπις). (1) A Roman water-vessel of the shape shown in the accompanying illustration from an original. (2) A vessel of similar shape used for the ashes of the dead. (3) A vessel used for drawing lots at the Comitia, and as a ballot-box. See COMITIA.

Ursus. A contemporary of the emperor Domitian, whom he dissuaded from killing his wife Domitia. Statius addressed to him a poem of consolation on the death of a favourite slave (*Silv.* ii. 6), and he also mentions him in the preface to the second book of his *Silvae.*

Urvum or **Urbum.** The plough-tail, also called *bura.* See ARATRUM.

Usipĕtes or **Usipii.** A German people who, in the time of Caesar, took up their abode on the Lippe. At a later time they became lost under the general name of Alemanni (Caes. *B. G.* iv. 4; Tac. *Ann.* i. 50; xiii. 54).

Ustīca. A valley near the Sabine villa of Horace.

Ustor (νεκροκαύστης). The person who assisted the undertaker (*pollinctor, libitinarius*) in laying out a corpse upon the pyre for burning (Mart. iii. 93). The occupation was regarded as a low and somewhat degraded one (Lucan, viii. 731). See FUNUS.

Usucapio. A term of Roman law signifying the acquisition of full and complete ownership ("Quiritary") through undisputed possession for a prescribed period of time (*Dig.* xli. 3, 3). Only persons having *commercium* (q. v.) could exercise this right, and it did not, of course, apply to stolen property (*res furtivae*), and certain other things were exempted by law from acquisition through usucapio—e. g. property belonging to minors under guardianship, property belonging to towns, etc. (See also PIGNUS.) So sweeping, however, was the right of usucapio that if a man took possession of a piece of land or other property belonging to an inheritance, even though he knew that he had no title to it, and held it unchallenged for a year, it became his in full legal ownership (Gaius, ii. 54). See Schirmer, *Grundidee der Usucapion* (1855); Puchta, *Institutionen,* §§ 239, 240; and the article DOMINIUM.

Usūra. See FENUS.

Ususfructus. The so-called "real" right of using and taking the fruits of property, whether movable or immovable, whose use does not diminish its substance and value. It was one of the "servitudes," as to which see SERVITUTES.

Uter (ἀσκός). A bag made of the skin of an animal (an ox, pig, or goat), carefully stitched at the sides, and made tight by the application of pitch or wax. It was thus used (1) as a wine-skin (*uter vinarius*) chiefly for the transportation of wine from place to place (see VINUM); and (2) as a means of sport for the rustics, as shown in the article ASCOLIASMUS (q. v.) (Verg. *Georg.* ii. 384). Water was also carried in skin-bags by armies on the march. The persons in charge of the water-supply were therefore called UTRARII (Livy, xliv. 33).

Utĭca (Οὐτίκη and Ἰτυκή). Now Bou-Shater; the greatest city of ancient Africa next to Carthage. It was a Phœnician colony, much older, according to the ancient chronologists, than Carthage. Like others of the very ancient Phœnician colonies in the territory of Carthage, Utica maintained a comparative independence, even during the height of the Punic power, and was rather the ally of Carthage than her subject. It stood on the shore of the northern part of the Carthaginian Gulf, a little west of the mouth of the Bagradas, and twenty-seven Roman miles northwest of Carthage; but its site is now inland, in consequence of the changes effected by the Bagradas in the coast-line. In the Third Punic War, Utica took part with the Romans against Carthage, and was rewarded with the greatest part of the Carthaginian territory. It afterwards became renowned to all future time as the scene of the last stand made by the Pompeian party against Caesar, and of the self-sacrifice of the younger Cato, who is, in consequence, usually styled Cato Uticensis. See CATO.

Utrarii. Water-carriers who supplied the soldiers on the march with water from skins (*utres*) (Livy, xliv. 33.)

Uxantis. Now Ushant; an island off the western coast of Gaul.

Uxellodūnum. A town of the Cadurci in Gallia Aquitanica. It is now Issolu. It was besieged and taken by Iulius Caesar (*B. G.* viii. 32–44).

Uxentum. Now Ugento; a town in Calabria, northwest of the Iapygian promontory.

Uxii (Οὔξιοι). A warlike people, of predatory habits, who had their strongholds in Mount Parachoathras, on the northern border of Persis, in the district called Uxia, but who also occupied a considerable tract of country in Media.

Uxor. See MATRIMONIUM.

V

V (Υ), as a symbol.

IN GREEK.—Υ = υἱός (*C. I. G.* 5762). As a numeral = 20 (old system). υ′ = 300. ͵υ = 300,000.

IN LATIN.—V = veteranus, verna, via, Vibius, vicit, villa, Virtus, utere, uxor.

V·A·L = vices agens legati.

V·A·S·L·M = votum animo solvit libens merito.

V·B·D·R·P = vir bonus dignus re publica.

V·B·M·P = voto bene merenti posuit.

V·B·O·V·F = virum bonum ora vos faciatis.

V·B·S = vir bonus sanctus.

V·C (E·P)·A·V·P = vir clarissimus (egregius perfectissimus) agens vices praesidis.

V·C·L·M = voti compos libens merito.

V·C·P·P = vir clarissimus pater patrum.

V·C·Q·K = vir clarissimus quaestor candidatus.

V·C·R = voluntarii cives Romani.

V·D·P·R·L·P = unde de plano recte legi possit.

V·F = Viennae fecit.

V·F·S = verba facta sunt, vivus fecit sibi.

V·I (H, L, O, P, R) = vir illustris (honestus, laudabilis, optimus, perfectissimus, religiosus).

V·L = veteranus legionis.

V·L·L·M·S = votum libens laetus merito solvit.

V·M·F = vene (i. e. bene) merenti fecerunt.

V·P·A = vixit pius annis.

V·P·P·P·H (N, R) = vir perfectissimus praeses provinciae Hispaniae (Numidiae, Raetiae).

V·Q = viator quaestorius.

V·Q·R·F·E·V·S·D·M = uti quod recte factum esse volet sine dolo malo.

V·S = urbs sacra, vici situ.

V·S·F = votum solvit feliciter.

V·S·I = vice sacra iudicans.

V·S·L·A·F = votum solvit libens animo feliciter.

V·V = virgo Vestalis, uti voverat, Venus victrix.

V·V·S·L·M = ut voverat solvit, libens merito.

V·V·V = vale! vale! vale!

As a numeral = 5, as the half of X. See NUMERUS.

Vacca, Vaga, or **Vaba.** Now Beja. A city of Zeugitana in northern Africa, a day's journey south of Utica. It was destroyed by Metellus in the Jugurthine War, but was restored and colonized by the Romans. Justinian named it THEODORIAS in honour of his wife.

Vaccaei. A people in the interior of Hispania Tarraconensis, occupying the modern Toro, Palencia, Burgos, and Valladolid. Their chief towns were Palantia and Intercatia.

Vacūna. A Sabine goddess, worshipped especially in a sacred grove near the Lacus Velinus and Reaté (Pliny, *H. N.* iii. 109); and also in a temple near Horace's farm (Hor. *Epist.* i. 10, 49). Vacuna was particularly regarded as the goddess of victory, but was also a great national deity of the Sabines (Ovid, *Fasti*, vi. 307); she also presided over the works of the garden and field (hence identified both with Venus and with Ceres), and over the woods and hunting (hence identified with Diana). Moreover, as goddess of victory in war she is sometimes confused with Bellona and sometimes with Minerva (Dionys. i. 15; Schol. *ad* Hor. l. c.).

Vadimōnis Lacus. Now Lago di Bassano; a small lake of Etruria, of a circular form, with sulphureous waters, and renowned for its floating islands. It is celebrated in history for the defeat of the Etruscans in two great battles, first by the dictator Papirius Cursor, in B.C. 309; and again in 283, when the allied forces of the Etruscans and Gauls were routed by the consul Cornelius Dolabella.

Vadimonium. See ACTIO in the Appendix.

Vagienni. A petty people in Liguria, whose chief town was Augusta Vagiennorum.

Vagīna (κολεός, ξιφοθήκη). The scabbard of a sword, usually made of wood, but sometimes apparently of leather. See GLADIUS.

Vahălis. See RHENUS.

Valckenaer, LUDWIG CASPAR. A distinguished Dutch classical scholar, born at Leeuwarden in 1715. He was Professor at Franeker (1741) and in the University of Leyden (1766), and died in 1785. His best known works are an edition of Homer's *Iliad* with the scholia (1747); of the *Phoenissae* of Euripides (1755; 4th ed. Leipzig, 1824); of the *Hippolytus* of Euripides, with a remarkable discussion on the fragments of the lost plays of that dramatist (1768; new ed. Leipzig, 1823); of the Greek bucolic and didactic poets (1781); of the fragments of Callimachus (rev. by Luzac, 1799); and a *Diatribe de Aristobulo* (ed. by Luzac, 1806). See L. Müller, *Geschichte der classischen Philologie in den Niederlanden*, pp. 82 foll. (Leipzig, 1869).

Valens. An emperor of the East A.D. 364–378, born about A.D. 328, and made emperor by his brother Valentinian. (See VALENTINIANUS.) The greater part of Valens's reign was occupied by his wars with the Goths. At first he gained great advantages over the barbarians, and concluded a peace with them in 370, on the condition that they should not cross the Danube. In 376 the Goths were driven out of their country by the Huns, and were allowed by Valens to cross the Danube and settle in Thrace and the country on the borders of the Danube. Dissensions soon arose between the Romans and these dangerous neighbors, and in 377 the Goths took up arms under Fritigern. Valens collected a powerful army, and marched against the Goths, but he was defeated by them with immense slaughter, near Adrianople, on the 9th of August, 378. Valens was never seen after the battle: some say he died on the field; and others relate that he was burned to death in a peasant's house, to which he was carried, and which the barbarians set fire to without knowing who was in it (Amm. Marc. xxxi. 13). The reign of Valens is important in the history of the Empire on account of the admission of the Goths into the countries south of the Danube—the commencement of the decline of the Roman power. Furious contests between the rival creeds of the Catholics and the Arians also characterize this reign.

Valens, Fabius. One of the principal generals of the emperor Vitellius. In A.D. 69 he marched into Italy through Gaul, and, after forming a junction with the forces of Caecina, defeated Otho in the decisive battle of Bedriacum, which secured for Vitellius the sovereignty of Italy. Vitellius raised Valens and Caecina to the consulship, and left the whole government in their hands. Valens remained faithful to Vitellius when Antonius Primus, the general of Vespasian, marched into Italy; but as he had not sufficient force to oppose Antonius after the capture of Cremona, he resolved to sail to Gaul and rouse the Gallic provinces to support the cause of Vitellius. He was taken prisoner at the islands of the Stoechades (Hyères), off Massilia, and was shortly afterwards put to death at Urbinum (Urbino) (Tac. *Hist.* i. 7, 52–66; ii. 24–30, 56, 92, 99; iii. 40, 62; Plut. *Oth.* 6). See Vitellius.

Valentia. (1) Now Valencia; the chief town of the Edetani on the river Turia, three miles from the coast, and on the road from Carthago Nova to Castulo. (2) Now Valence; a town in Gallia Narbonensis on the Rhône, and a Roman colony. (3) A town of Sardinia of uncertain site. (4) Or Valentium, a town in Apulia, ten miles from Brundusium. (5) A province in the north of Britain, beyond the Roman wall. It existed for only a short time. See Britannia.

Valentiniānus. (1) A Roman emperor (A.D. 364–375), was the son of Gratianus, and was born A.D. 321, at Cibalis in Pannonia. His first wife was Valeria Severa, by whom he became the father of the emperor Gratianus. He held important military commands under Julian and Jovian; and on the death of the latter, in February, 364, Valentinian was elected emperor by the troops at Nicaea. A few weeks after his elevation Valentinian, by the desire of the soldiers, associated in the empire his brother Valens, and assigned to him the East, while he himself undertook the government of the West. Valentinian was a Catholic, though his brother Valens was an Arian; but he did not persecute either Arians or heathens. He possessed good abilities, prudence, and vigour of character. He had a capacity for military matters, and was a vigilant, impartial, and laborious administrator. The greater part of Valentinian's reign was occupied by the wars against the Alemanni and the other barbarians on the Roman frontier, in which his operations were attended with success. He not only drove the Alemanni out of Gaul, but on more than one occasion crossed the Rhine, and carried the war into the enemy's country. His usual residence was Treviri (Trèves). In 375 he went to Carnuntum on the Danube, in order to repel the Quadi and Sarmatians, who had invaded Pannonia. After an indecisive campaign he took up his winter-quarters at Bregetio. In this place, while giving an audience to the deputies of the Quadi, and speaking with great heat, he fell down in a fit and expired suddenly, on the 17th of November (Amm. Marc. xxviii.–xxx.; Zosim. iv. 17).

(2) A Roman emperor (A.D. 375–392), younger son of the preceding, proclaimed Augustus by the army after his father's death, though he was then only four or five years of age. His elder brother Gratianus, who had been proclaimed Augustus during the lifetime of their father, assented to the choice of the army, and a division of the West was made between the two brothers. Valentinian had Italy, Illyricum, and Africa; Gratian had the Gauls, Spain, and Britain. In 383 Gratian was defeated and slain by Maximus, who left Valentinian a precarious authority out of fear for Theodosius, the emperor of the East; but in 387 Valentinian was expelled from Italy by Maximus, and fled for refuge to Theodosius. In 388 Theodosius defeated Maximus, and restored Valentinian to his authority as emperor of the West. Theodosius returned to Constantinople in 391; and in the following year (392) Valentinian was murdered by the general Arbogastes, who raised Eugenius to the throne. Valentinian perished on the 15th of May, being only a few months above twenty years of age. His funeral oration was pronounced by St. Ambrose.

(3) Roman emperor A.D. 426–455, was born 419, and was the son of Constantius III. by Placidia, the sister of Honorius and the daughter of Theodosius I. He was declared Augustus in 425 by Theodosius II., and was placed over the West, but as he was only six years of age the government was intrusted to his mother Placidia. During his long reign the Empire was repeatedly exposed to the invasions of the barbarians; and it was only the military abilities of Aëtius which saved the Empire from ruin. In 429 the Vandals under Genseric crossed over into Africa, which they conquered, and of which they continued in possession till the reign of Justinian. The weakness of the Empire during this reign was shown also by the fact that the Britons (from whose country the Roman troops had been withdrawn forty years before), finding it vain to apply to Rome for aid against the incursions of the Picts, invited the Jutes under Hengest and Horsa to help them, in 449. The Goths likewise established themselves in Gaul; but Aëtius finally made peace with them (439), and with their assistance gained a great victory over Attila and the vast army of the Huns at Châlons in 451. (See Attila.) The power and influence of Aëtius excited the jealousy and fears of Valentinian, who murdered his faithful general in 454. (See Aëtius.) In the following year the emperor himself was slain by Petronius Maximus, whose wife he had violated.

Valeria. (1) A sister of P. Valerius Publicola, who advised the Roman matrons to ask Veturia, the mother of Coriolanus, to go to the camp of Coriolanus in order to deprecate his resentment. See CORIOLANUS. (2) The last wife of Sulla. She was the daughter of M. Valerius Messala, and bore a daughter soon after Sulla's death. (3) GALERIA VALERIA, daughter of Diocletian and Prisca. She was, upon the reconstruction of the Empire in A.D. 292, united to Galerius, one of the new Caesars. After the death of her husband in 311 Valeria rejected the proposals of his successor Maximinus, who in consequence stripped her of her possessions, and banished her along with her mother. After the death of Maximinus, Valeria and her mother were executed by order of Licinius, in A.D. 315. (4) MESSALĪNA. See MESSALINA.

Valeria Gens. One of the most ancient patrician houses at Rome. It was of Sabine origin, and the founder, Volesus or Volusus, is said to have settled at Rome with Titus Tatius. One of the descendants of this Volesus, P. Valerius, afterwards surnamed Publicola, plays a distinguished part in the story of the expulsion of the kings, and was elected consul in the first year of the Republic, B.C. 509. From this time down to the latest period of the Empire, for nearly 1000 years, the name occurs more or less frequently in the Fasti, and it was borne by several of the emperors. The Valeria gens enjoyed extraordinary honours and privileges at Rome. In early times they were always foremost in advocating the rights of the plebeians, and the laws which they proposed were the great charters of the liberties of the second order. (See LEX.) The Valeria gens was divided into various families under the Republic, the most important of which bore the name of CORVUS, FLACCUS, MESSALA, and PUBLICOLA.

Valeriānus. (1) P. LICINIUS, a Roman emperor, A.D. 253–260. He was entrapped into a conference by the Persians, taken prisoner (260) by Sapor, and passed the remainder of his life in captivity, subjected to every insult which Oriental cruelty could devise. His skin was stuffed after his death and hung in one of the Persian temples for many years. (2) A son of the preceding, who perished along with Gallienus at Milan in 268. See GALLIENUS.

Valerius. See VALERIA GENS.

Valerius. (1) ANTIAS. See ANTIAS.

(2) MAXĬMUS, a Roman historian. Of his life we know only that he accompanied the proconsul Sextus Pompeius to Asia in A.D. 27 (ii. 6, 8). On his return he composed, between A.D. 29 and 32, a collection of historical anecdotes in nine books, *Factorum et Dictorum Memorabilium Libri*, which he dedicated to the emperor Tiberius. The book consists of an uncritical collection of extracts taken mostly from Livy and Cicero, but also from Sallust and Pompeius Trogus. These are divided into domestic and foreign instances under different headings, mostly descriptive of moral qualities, sometimes grouped according to subjects and sometimes not. The style is bad, and full of rhetorical declamation; the character of the compiler reveals itself in his gross flattery of Tiberius. Nevertheless, owing to the convenient selection of anecdotes which the book offered to orators and authors, it was much quoted in the succeeding generations down to the Middle Ages. It has come down to us with two epitomes, drawn up in late Roman times, by Iulius Paris and Iannarius Nepotianus. The short dissertation *De Praenominibus*, appended to the work, has nothing to do with Valerius himself. It is an epitome drawn up by the above-mentioned Paris from the first portion of a work on Roman names by an unknown writer, who quotes old authorities on the subject, especially Varro. There are good text-editions of Valerius Maximus by Halm (Leipzig, 1865) and Kempf (2d ed. Leipzig, 1888); and with English notes on selected passages, by Smith (Boston, 1895).

(3) GAIUS VALERIUS FLACCUS BALBUS SETĪNUS, a Latin writer of epic verse, born at Setia, who flourished under Vespasian and Titus, and died before A.D. 90. We have an unfinished epic by him on the expedition of the Argonauts (*Argonautica*) in eight books, which was begun about the time of the destruction of Jerusalem (70), and was dedicated to Vespasian. The poem is a free paraphrase of the work of Apollonius Rhodius, with his characteristic style and manner, in language which, though careful and tastefully chosen, is sometimes difficult and obscure, and overladen with rhetorical adornment. Editions by Thilo (Halle, 1863); Schenkl (Berlin, 1871); and Bährens (Leipzig, 1875). See Peters, *De Valerii Flacci Vita et Carmine* (Königsberg, 1890).

(4) IULIUS VALERIUS, of Africa, who lived about the end of the third century A.D., and wrote a Latin translation of the Pseudo-Callisthenes. See CALLISTHENES.

(5) VALENTĪNUS. See TAPPULA LEX.

Valerius Volŭsus Maxĭmus, MARCUS or MANIUS. A Roman who was dictator in B.C. 494, when the dissensions *de nexis* between the burghers and commonalty of Rome were at the highest. (See NEXUM.) Valerius was popular with the plebs, and induced them to enlist for the Sabine and Aequian wars by promising that when the enemy was repulsed the condition of the debtors (*nexi*) should be alleviated. He defeated and triumphed over the Sabines; but, unable to fulfil his promise to the plebeians, resigned his dictatorship (Livy, ii. 30, 31).

Valetudinarium (νοσοκομεῖον). A room set apart for the reception and treatment of sick slaves—a sort of domestic hospital and infirmary (Col. xi. 1, 18; Sen. *De Ira*, i. 16). There were also military hospitals attached to the Roman camps; but there is no mention of public hospitals before the fourth century (Hieron. *Epist.* iii. 10). The nearest approach to a public hospital in Greece was the dispensary (ἰατρεῖον) of the physicians who treated the poor gratuitously and received a fixed salary from the State. See Daremberg, *Hist. de la Médecine*, ch. i.; and the articles MEDICINA; MEDICUS.

Valgius. See VARUS.

Valgius Rufus, GAIUS. A Roman poet, contemporary with Vergil and Horace.

Valla, LAURENTIUS. A celebrated Italian scholar of the period of the Renaissance. He was born at Rome in 1405, and studied at Florence, where, as also at Pavia, he taught the classics. His life was one of a vagrant indolence, interspersed by violent controversies with contemporary scholars; yet he was a remarkably gifted man, and his Latin style has always been justly admired. He edited and translated Herodotus, Xenophon, and Thucydides, and wrote a sort of manual of Latin usage (*Elegantiae Linguae Latinae*), which had an immense success and did much to expel the barbarisms of mediæval Latinity from the speech and the writings of the learned. See the elaborate monograph by Mancini (Florence, 1891); the chapter in Nisard, *Les Gladiateurs de la République des Lettres* (Paris, 1860); and the article RENAISSANCE.

Vallum (χαράκωμα). A palisade made of sharp stakes like *chevaux-de-frise*, and often placed by the ancient soldiers around the outer edge of the mound of earth (*agger*) thrown up about their camps (Polyb. xvii. 1, 1). The term often denotes both palisade and rampart. See the illustration under AGGER.

Vallus (χάραξ). A sharp stake used in making the *vallum* (q. v.).

Valvae (θύραι διάπριστοι). A folding door or shutter, i. e. one made of two or more leaves which fold back one behind the other. The house-doors were sometimes of this sort, as the marks on a threshold in Pompeii show (Pliny, *Epist.* ii. 17, 5; Isid. *Orig.* xv. 7, 4).

Van of an Army. See EXERCITUS.

Vandăli, Vandalii, or **Vindalii.** A confederacy of German peoples, who dwelt originally on the northern coast of Germany, but were afterwards settled north of the Marcomanni in the Riesengebirge, which are hence called VANDALICI MONTES. They subsequently appear for a short time in Dacia and Pannonia; but at the beginning of the fifth century (A.D. 409) they traversed Germany and Gaul, and invaded Spain. In that country they subjugated the Alani, and founded a powerful kingdom, the name of which is still preserved in Andalusia (Vandalusia). In A.D. 429 they crossed over into Africa, under their king Genseric (q. v.) and conquered all the Roman dominions in that country. Genseric subsequently invaded Italy, and took and plundered Rome in 455. The Vandals continued masters of Africa till 535, when their kingdom was destroyed by Belisarius, and annexed to the Byzantine Empire. See Papencordt, *Geschichte der vandalischen Herrschaft* (Berlin, 1837); Hodgkin, *Italy and her Invaders*, vols. ii. and iii.; and on their language, Wrede, *Ueber die Sprache der Wandalen* (Strassburg, 1886).

Vangiŏnes. A German people dwelling along the Rhine, in the neighbourhood of the modern Worms (Caes. *B. G.* i. 51).

Vannus (λίκνον). A large shallow basket used in winnowing. The basket in which the Bacchanals carried the sacrificial vessels and the offerings to Bacchus was styled VANNUS MYSTĬCA (Verg. *Georg.* i. 166).

Vaporarium. A sort of furnace for heating a room by means of flues (Cic. *Ad Q. Fratr.* iii. 1, 1). See BALNEAE; DOMUS.

Vappa. The dregs or lees of wine, or wine that had become flat (Hor. *Sat.* ii. 3, 144).

Vara (σταλίς). (1) The stake that supported a hunting-net. See illustration in the article RETIS. (2) An andiron on which logs of wood were laid and which supported the spit (*veru*). See VERU.

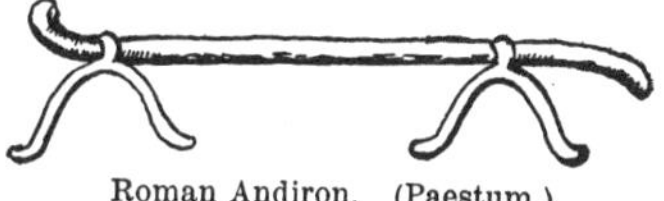

Roman Andiron. (Paestum.)

Varāgri. See VERAGRI.

Varguntēius. A Roman senator and one of Catiline's conspirators, who undertook, in conjunction with C. Cornelius, to murder Cicero in B.C. 63, but whose plan was frustrated by information conveyed to Cicero through Fulvia. He was afterwards brought to trial, but could find no one to defend him (Sall. *Cat.* 17, 47).

Varius Hybrĭda, QUINTUS. A tribune of the plebs, B.C. 90, who was a native of Sucro in Spain, and received the surname of Hybrida because his mother was a Spanish woman. In his tribuneship he carried a law *de maiestate*, in order to punish all those who had assisted or advised the *socii* to take up arms against the Roman people. Under this law many distinguished senators were condemned; but in the following year Varius himself was convicted under his own law, and was put to death (App. *B. C.* i. 57; Val. Max. viii. 6, 4; Cic. *De Or.* i. 25; *N. D.* iii. 33).

Varius Rufus, LUCIUS. A celebrated Roman poet whose poetical career began in the later days of the Republic. Like his younger friend Vergil, he was much honoured and appreciated by Augustus and Maecenas, to whom he also introduced his friend Horace. Vergil, at his death, in B.C. 19, left him and Plotius Tucca his literary remains, and Augustus intrusted to them the revision and publication. (See VERGILIUS.) He died before the year B.C. 12. At the opening of the Augustan era he was the most conspicuous of the Latin epic poets; but he obtained his greatest reputation by his tragedy *Thyestes*, which, with the *Medea* of Ovid, was considered the greatest effort of Roman literature in this department. The work was brought out at the games held in honour of the victory at Actium B.C. 29, and was rewarded by Augustus with an honorarium of a million sesterces ($40,000). Of this, as of his epic poems (on the death of Caesar and panegyric on Augustus), only a few verses survive.

Varro Atacīnus. See under VARRO.

Varro, TERENTIUS. (1) GAIUS, consul B.C. 216 with L. Aemilius Paulus. Varro is said to have been the son of a butcher, to have carried on business himself as a factor in his early years, and to have risen to eminence by pleading the causes of the lower classes against the opposition of the nobility (Livy, xxii. 25; Val. Max. iii. 4, 4). Notwithstanding the strong influence of the aristocracy, he was raised to the consulship by the people, who thought that it only needed a man of energy at the head of an overwhelming force to bring the war against Hannibal to a close, and who, moreover, had an excessive mistrust of the aims and motives of the Senate. His colleague was L. Aemilius Paulus, one of the leaders of the aristocratic party. The two consuls were defeated by Hannibal at the memorable battle of Cannae. (See HANNIBAL.) The battle was fought by Varro against the advice of Paulus. The Roman army was all but annihilated. Paulus and almost all the officers perished. Varro was one of the few who escaped and reached Venusia in safety, with about seventy horsemen. His conduct after the battle seems to have deserved praise. He proceeded to Canusium, where the remnant of the Roman army had taken refuge, and there adopted every precaution which the exigencies of the case required. His defeat was forgotten in the services he had lately rendered. On his return to the city all classes went out to meet him, and the Senate returned him thanks because he had not despaired of the commonwealth. This marked the determination of patricians and plebeians to work heartily together against the foreign enemy (Livy, xxii. 35–61; Polyb. iii. 106–116; Plut. *Fab.* 14–18; App. *Ann.* 17–26). Varro continued to be employed in Italy for several successive years in important military commands till nearly the close of the Punic War.

(2) M. TERENTIUS VARRO REATĪNUS, a celebrated writer, whose vast and varied erudition in almost every department of literature earned for him the title of the "most learned of the Romans" (Quint. x. i. 95; Dionys. ii. 21; August. *C. D.* vi. 2). He was born at Reatĕ B.C. 116, and was trained under L. Aelius Stilo Praeconinus, and afterwards by Antiochus, a philosopher of the Academy. Varro held a high naval command in the wars against the pirates and Mithridates, and afterwards served as the *legatus* of Pompeius in Spain in the Civil War, but was compelled to surrender his forces to Caesar (Flor. ii. 13, 29; Caes. *B.C.* i. 38, ii. 17–20). He then passed over into Greece, and shared the fortunes of the Pompeian party till after the battle of Pharsalia, when he obtained the forgiveness of Caesar, who employed him in superintending the collection and arrangement of the great library designed for public use (Suet. *Iul.* 44; Isid. *Orig.* vi. 5). For some years after this period Varro remained in literary seclusion, passing his time chiefly at his country seats near Cumae and Tusculum, occupied with study and composition. Caesar had forced Antony to restore to Varro an estate which he had seized (Cic. *Phil.* ii. 40, 103), and, perhaps in consequence, upon the formation of the Second Triumvirate his name appeared upon the list of the proscribed; but he succeeded in making his escape, and, after having remained for some time concealed, he obtained the protection of Octavian. His life is said to have been saved by Fufius Calenus (App. *B. C.* iv. 47), and it is probable that he recovered a great portion of his estates; but most of his magnificent library had been destroyed (Gell. iii. 10). The remainder of his career was passed in tranquillity, and he continued to labour in his favourite studies. His death took place B.C. 28, when he was in his eighty-ninth year.

Not only was Varro the most learned of Roman scholars, but he was likewise the most voluminous of Roman authors. Gellius (l. c.) states that Varro claimed to have written 490 books before he was seventy-seven: Ausonius gives in round numbers 600 as the total number of books written by Varro (*Prof. Burd.* xx. 10); and this agrees with a list given by St. Jerome which makes out the writings of Varro to consist of seventy-four different works, containing altogether 620 books. (Cf. also Augustin. *De Civ. Dei*, vi. 2; and Cic. *Acad.* i. 9.) Hence it would appear that 130 of the books were written in the last twelve years of his life. Of these works only two have survived: (*a*) *De Re Rustica Libri III*, still extant, written when the author was eighty years old, and the most important of all the treatises upon ancient agriculture now extant, being far superior to the more voluminous production of Columella, with which alone it can be compared. It is edited by Keil (Halle, 1884 foll.), and in the *Scriptores Rei Rusticae Veteres Latini*, by Schneider (Leipzig, 1764–1797). (2) *De Lingua Latina*, a grammatical treatise which extended to twenty-four books; but six only (v.–x.) have been preserved, and these in a mutilated condition. The remains of this treatise are particularly valuable, since they have been the means of preserving many terms and forms which would otherwise have been altogether lost, and much curious information is here treasured up connected with the ancient usages, both civil and religious, of the Romans. Editions by Spengel (Berlin, 1826, reëdited 1885); in Didot's collection (Paris, 1875); and by O. Müller (last ed. Leipzig, 1883). The remains of Varro's other grammatical treatises are discussed by Wilmanns (1864). The work entitled *Antiquitatum Libri* was divided into two sections: *Antiquitates Rerum Humanarum*, in twenty-five books, and *Antiquitates Rerum Divinarum*, in sixteen books. It described the political and religious institutions of Rome, and was Varro's greatest work, upon which chiefly his reputation for profound learning was based; but unfortunately only a few fragments of it have come down to us, printed in Merkel's edition of Ovid's *Fasti*, pp. cvi.–ccxlvii. (1841). With the second section of the work we are, comparatively speaking, familiar, since St. Augustine drew very largely from this source in his *De Civitate Dei.*

Varro wrote also a collection of biographies called *Imagines* or *Hebdomades* in fifteen books, which contain 700 lives or sketches of famous Greeks and Romans, arranged in groups of seven. It is said to have been illustrated with portraits and afterwards to have appeared in a cheaper edition without pictures. Another work, *Disciplinae*, in nine books, described the "liberal arts," viz., grammar, dialectic, rhetoric, geometry, arithmetic, astrology, music, medicine, and architecture (see LIBERALES ARTES); and he wrote other works on philosophy (*Logistorici* in seventy-six books), geography, and law. Among his poetical works were the *Saturae*, which were composed in a variety of metres and with an admixture of prose. Varro in these pieces copied to a certain extent the productions of Menippus the Gadarene (see MENIPPUS), and hence designated them as *Saturae Menippeae s. Cynicae.* They appear to have been a series of disquisitions on a vast variety of subjects, frequently, if not uniformly, couched in the shape of dialogue, the object proposed being the inculcation of moral lessons and serious truths in a familiar, playful, and even jocular style. The best editions of the fragments of these *Saturae* are by Riese (Leipzig, 1865), and Bücheler (with Petronius) (Berlin, 1882). The *Sententiae Varronis*, a collection of pithy sayings, may possibly have been gathered from the writings of Varro Reatinus, but this is wholly uncertain. They are edited by Devit (Padua, 1843). See Boissier, *Études sur M. T. Varron* (Paris, 1861); and Ritschl, *Die Schriftstellerei des Varro* in his *Opuscula*, iii. 419–505; id. *Parerga*, pp. 70 foll.

(3) P., a Latin poet of considerable celebrity, surnamed ATACĪNUS, from the Atax, a river of Gallia Narbonensis, his native province, was born B.C. 32. Of his personal history nothing further is known. He seems to have written, first, an epic on one of Caesar's Gallic wars, called *Bellum Sequanicum* (Prisc. *Gr. Lat.* ii. 497), and *Saturae* in imitation of Lucilius (Hor. *Sat.* i. 10, 46); and also at a later time to have written *Argonautica*, perhaps a free translation of the like work of Apollonius Rhodius; *Chorographia*, a sort of metrical system of geography and astronomy; and *Libri*

Navales, perhaps a poem on navigation. Only fragments of these productions have survived to the present time.

Varus. A cognomen in many Roman *gentes*, signifying a person who had his legs bent inward, and differed from VALGIUS, which signified a person having his legs turned outward.

Varus. A river in Gallia Narbonensis, forming the boundary between that province and Italy. It rises in Mount Cema in the Alps, and falls into the Mediterranean Sea between Antipolis and Nicaea. It is now the Var.

Varus, ALFĒNUS. (1) A Roman jurist, the *Alfenus vafer* of Horace, was a native of Cremona, where he carried on the trade of a barber or a cobbler. Having come to Rome, he became a pupil of Servius Sulpicius, attained the dignity of the consulship, and was honoured with a public funeral. (2) A general of Vitellius in the Civil War of A.D. 60.

Varus, QUINTILIUS. A Roman consul B.C. 13, and subsequently appointed to the government of Syria, where he acquired enormous wealth. Shortly after his return from Syria he was made governor of Germany (probably about A.D. 7), and was instructed by Augustus to introduce the Roman jurisdiction into that newly conquered country. The Germans, however, were not prepared to submit thus tamely to the Roman yoke, and found a leader in Arminius, a noble chief of the Cherusci, who organized a general revolt of all the German tribes between the Visurgis and the Weser. When he had fully matured his plans, he suddenly attacked Varus, at the head of a countless host of barbarians, as the Roman general was marching with his three legions through a pass of the Saltus Teutoburgiensis, a range of hills covered with wood, which extends north of the Lippe from Osnabrück to Paderborn, and is known in the present day by the name of the Teutoburgerwald or Lippische Wald. The battle lasted three days, and ended with the entire destruction of the Roman army. Varus put an end to his own life. His defeat was followed by the loss of all the Roman possessions between the Weser and the Rhine, and the latter river again became the boundary of the Roman dominions. When the news of this defeat reached Rome, the whole city was thrown into consternation; and Augustus, who was both weak and aged, gave way to the most violent grief, tearing his garments and calling upon Varus to give him back his legions—"Vare, Vare, redde legiones!" (Suet. *Aug.* 23; *Tib.* 16). See ARMINIUS; GERMANIA.

Vas. In law, a form of bail. See ACTIO (in the Appendix); JUDICIAL PROCEDURE; PRAES.

Vas. A vase; in the plural (*vasa*) a generic term for earthenware. In a technical sense it is also applied to the baggage of a Roman army in the field.

The shaping of baked clay into vessels was probably suggested and influenced by the use of gourds as vessels in primitive times; and the gourd-shape is that which predominates in the forms of Greek and Roman pottery. The earliest known types of Greek ceramic art are represented in the pottery exhumed by Schliemann at Hassarlik. This is rude in construction and clumsy in design, and in general falls under two classes—the first being shown in the two-handled vase represented below, and the so-called "owl-vase" exhibited in the second illustration. The first was identified by Schliemann with the Homeric δέπας ἀμφικύπελλον, and the second has an interest of its own in being a

Two-handled Vase from Hassarlik. (Schliemann.)

primitive attempt to give to a vase some of the attributes of a living model. These vases are made by hand, and have the dull, blackish colour produced by the smoke of the furnace.

Owl-vase from Hissarlik. (Schliemann.)

A more advanced type is found in the vases derived from the groves of Cyprus, especially at Alambra (Dali) and Larnaca (Kition), places colonized by the Phœnicians. These Cypriote vases are either (*a*) covered with a vitreous slip and baked to some shade of red, and occasionally decorated with slips of clay often in the shape of serpents; and (*b*) of fine clay delicately moulded, in colour gray or pale black. In shape they are either long and gourdlike or flat and broad like a shallow cup. Vases of the same general type have been found also on several of the Aegean Islands, such as Amorgos, Antiparos, Naxos, and Melos. Painted vases gave a new direction to the taste and ingenuity of the potter; and many such have been found at Thera (Santorin) whose ware is made entirely by the wheel, and are furnished with a foot so as to stand by themselves and not to be hung by a handle. In these, red, brown-black, and white are used on prepared grounds of gray, buff, and brownish red. It has been asserted by some, on the evidence of geology, that this ware dates back to the fifteenth or even to the twentieth century before Christ.

The next stage of development is represented by the "Mycenaean" ware, found, however, in many localities. It consists of vases painted either with opaque or with lustrous colours (violet-brown, red, or white) upon red or pale clay, and the ornamentation is derived largely from marine forms. A few specimens of early vases imitate in clay the Phœnician glass, painted in wavy lines of orange on red and highly polished. In both the Alambra and Mycenaean pottery are seen the beginnings of a new style of decoration known as the "geometric," influenced by the technique of metal-work, and exhibiting the ornamental designs of concentric arches, rosettes, spirals, etc. The finest specimens of this style after it is fully established come from Athens, which is regarded as the principal seat of its manufacture. The geometric style became the most popular of all, and it gave the artist sureness of hand and eye, and a sense of form and proportion that was very valuable.

A new feature is exemplified in vases found at Phalerum which employ new animal types, designed and grouped under the influence of Oriental models. A development of this style combined with the geometric is called by Conze the "Melian." From the production of this pottery, Oriental influence increases and adds much to the beauty and effectiveness of the painted vase.

Under the further influence of metal-work and embroidery, polychromy enters fully into the methods of the vase-painter. Light and shade, and discrimination of planes of surface, were made possible by the combination of silhouette and outline-drawing introduced by the potters of the island of Rhodes. The subjects chosen by this school are chiefly animals (goats, lions, bulls, boars, rams), and, later, the human figure. A definite scene (from the Epic) is first found depicted in clay on the Euphorbus Pinax, assigned by Kirchhoff to the seventh century B.C., and depicting the battle of Menelaüs and Hector over the body of Euphorbus. The polychromatic school reached its highest development at Naucratis. The Oriental style is found in its perfection in the ware of Corinth, which is crowded with ornament, so that at a little distance the separate figures cannot be distinguished, but the general effect is that of a rich Oriental brocade. Scenes from mythology and also from ordinary life now appear. (See DODWELL VASE.) This growing sense that human action is the true subject for the vase-painter's art led to the decline of Orientalism, which held to animals. After this change was thoroughly established, the great centre of fictile production was Athens (cir. 650–300 B.C.).

Oenochoë of quasi-Oriental type. (Birch.)

ATHENIAN pottery has two epochs—the "black-figure" and the "red-figure." A new discovery contributed to the rapid advance of Athenian ceramics—a deep-black varnish of the highest brilliancy, with a surface like polished metal, insensible to ordinary reagents, but not interfering with that porousness of the clay which under a Greek sun is so necessary for the coolness of water or wine. Its manufacture is still a secret; nor is it known where the invention first saw the light. So popular did it immediately become that the vase-painter covered the whole surface with it, leaving as field for the actual picture only a square panel of red ground-colour.

It is with the masters of black-figure style that the point first comes adequately to express the lines of musculature and bodily form. The rendering of drapery is a mark of relative date. At first the *chiton* is a straight daub of colour, as in Corinthian ware, and is often purple in hue with perhaps a black girdle; then patterns are scratched in, or elaborately painted on with white; folds begin to be marked, are outlined with the point, and dress gives some hint of the underlying contour of the body. An alternate use of purple and black for the folds is occasionally carried so far as to express light and shade. A like use of purple is to be seen in the treatment of muscles in animals, especially the horse. White is throughout a flesh-tint for female figures, but is also employed, on later vases, for the long *chiton* of a charioteer and the gray hair of old men.

Drawing is almost entirely in profile; full-face is rendered with little more adroitness than had been shown before. The eyes of men remain large and round; of women, oval and small. In more recent vases a trick grows up of crowding the field with long, purely conventional ivy sprays: equally conventional in rendering are the landscape features sometimes introduced, and no attempt is made at pictorial perspective.

The subjects of vases become now of less importance for their general history. In black-figure ware they are mainly mythological, sometimes *genre*. In mythology, the Dionysiac cycle and the feats of Heracles are by far most frequent; after them, the legends of Athenė and Hermes. Frequently as scenes from the Cyclic poets appear, scarcely any can be traced to the *Iliad* or *Odyssey*.

Ornament, as distinct from painted scenes, becomes stereotyped. Signed vases are now in vogue, and the *cylices* are especially fruitful in artists' signatures which have preserved their names. Ergotimos and Clitias, who made and painted the great François *crater*, were followed by Nearchus, whose sons Tleson and Ergoteles, with Ergotimos's son Euchirus, have signed many of the earlier *cylices*. Other names are Xenocles, Hermogenes, Archicles. In *amphorae* Exekias takes first place for spirited and careful drawing; Amasis carries nicety of detail almost to extravagance; Hischylos represents transition style. The most prolific and clever, as also the most popular, was Nicosthenes, who originated a new *cylix*, and is also known by a peculiar form of *amphora* introduced by him. On Nicosthenes, see Löschcke in the *Archäolog. Zeitung* for 1881, pp. 33 foll.

It is not known precisely where the making of red-figure ware originated; but its origin is assigned approximately to the year B.C. 500, and is said to have owed its development to high art. Hitherto, the ceramic art of the Greeks had been properly classed as "ornament"; hereafter it became a branch of painting. (See PICTURA.) It shows a great advance in drawing and is free from the conventionalism of the black-figure ware. In its development the influence of Polygnotus was very great. Contemporary with the red-figure vases is the polychromatic ware with a white ground. The great majority of this class are *lekythi*, though these are found also in red-figure.

Three classes of *lekythi* may be distinguished: (*a*) Figures generally in red or sienna; subjects entirely funereal; polychromy sober and restrained; style, fine. (*b*) Figures in black or brown; subjects generally funereal, but sometimes drawn from family life, the pantheon, or even mythology; polychromy brilliant and often directly pictorial; style fine. (*c*) Figures in yellow; painting almost always monochrome; style decadent, often careless. Still another type of ware is represented by vases simply covered with a lustrous black varnish, ornamented after the fourth century B.C. with gilding and an occasional figure in colours. Many are of great beauty. Vases in the shape of human heads and *rhyta* (see RHYTON) and others of terra-cotta modelled in the form of human busts are found.

From about the time of Alexander the Great (B.C. 325), the manufacture of red-figured vases was transferred to Italy, where there have always existed native schools of pottery. With the opening of the Hellenistic as opposed to the Hellenic Age, art became provincial. Sculpture and painting passed to Pergamum, Alexandria, and Rhodes, and in like manner pottery was chiefly cultivated in the cities of Magna Graecia.

No new world-wide trade, like that of Athens, no important novelty in technique, marked the transference. Although Apulia produced *amphorae* and *crateres* of great splendour, the decadence of style, which had already begun at Athens, is painfully apparent. Men sought to add fresh life to a waning industry by inventing giant vases and richer shapes, by bringing into play all the resources of polychromy, and even summoning plastic to their aid; but profuse ornament and gaudy colouring scarcely cloak bad drawing and bad taste. Yet the artists had a pride in their work, and signatures again occur, though in no great number. Two traits are characteristic: (*a*) The strict relation maintained on most examples between the use of the vase for service at the tomb and its decoration (either a scene of offerings at the tomb, or an appropriate myth); and—where the subject is not funereal—(*b*) the frequent borrowing from the stage (farces especially), and the rendering of other than dramatic scenes with dramatic accessories (cf. Heydemann, *Jahrbuch*, 1886, pp. 260 foll.).

Three separate South Italian fabrics may be distinguished, LUCANIAN, CAMPANIAN, APULIAN. The technique in all is that of red-figure ware. Each class exhibits a peculiarity in depicting the human figure, a peculiarity suggestive of difference of social type; each, too, introduces details of national costume.

Lucanian vases may be relatively somewhat older; at least their manufacture seems to have sooner come to an end. Though somewhat helpless in draughtmanship, their style is comparatively restrained; polychromy is little used, and the heavy, clumsy drapery seldom bears a trace of ornament. A favourite shape is the campaniform crater; another, a kind of amphora only found in Lucania.

Later examples show great fondness for polychromy, tints especially prominent being white and yellow—the latter, in most cases, a cheap substitute for gilding. Tendrils of vine, ivy, and other plants are often introduced, as also on Apulian ware, with a happy effect; and occasionally motifs are taken direct from nature, as, for instance, a bird singing on a spray. The most important class, and that of highest artistic merit, is the Apulian, a product probably of Tarentine activity. Characteristic are the giant *amphorae*, one blaze of ornament from head to foot; characteristic, too, the heavy Doric chin of the men, the slender neck and stout barrel of the horses, the zones of fishes and marine forms employed as ornament.

As regards colours in South Italian polychrome ware, the red ground-clay is often changed to brown, and white used as a flesh-tint for women, but also, with a dash of yellow, for men. Yellow is perhaps the favourite decorative colour. The South Italian (Greek) vase-making died out about B.C. 250, at which time LATIN painted vases begin to appear. Their ornamentation is quite simple and rude—a spray of vine or olive with perhaps an Eros in the centre (*Annali dell' Inst.* 1884). These are the last painted vases, and they are immediately succeeded by the Cales ware, black, metallic, and moulded (Gamurrini, *Gazette Archéol.* for 1879, pp. 47 foll.). Henceforth pottery, for so much life as is left to it, became a branch of plastic. On the Calene style followed the SAMIAN and ARETINE. Greek ceramic art had given place to Roman. The pottery of ROME is in itself of less importance, and is noted under FICTILÉ; but it has a value of its own, as the link by which the secrets of classical ceramic art were communicated to the Northern nations, among whom the Kelts rank first. Samian and Aretine vases were freely imitated in Gaul and England, where native fabrics grew up under Roman influence.

BIBLIOGRAPHY.—The literature of this subject is very extensive. The student may most conveniently refer to Jahn, *Einleitung zur Beschreibung der Vasensammlung zu München* (Munich, 1824);

Dumont and Chaplain, *Les Céramiques de la Grèce Propre* (Paris, 1881 foll.); Genick, *Griechische Keramik* (Berlin, 1883); Lau, *Griechische Vasen* (Munich, 1877); Birch, *Hist. of Ancient Pottery* (new ed. London, 1873); Jacquemart, *Hist. of the Ceramic Art*, Eng. trans. (London, 1873); Jännicke, *Grundriss der Keramik* (Stuttgart, 1879); Dennis, *Cities and Cemeteries of Etruria* (London, 1878); Heydemann, *Humoristische Vasenbilder* (Berlin, 1870); and, in general, Baumeister, *Denkmäler*, s. v. "Vasenkunde" (Munich, 1889), and Westropp's and Murray's manuals. Arndt's *Studien zur Vasenkunde* (Munich, 1887) is to be used with caution. Compare also the articles FICTILÉ; PICTURA; and TERRA-COTTAS.

Vascōnes. A powerful people on the northern coast of Hispania Tarraconensis, between the Iberus and the Pyrenees, in the modern Navarre and Guipuzco. Their chief towns were Pompelon and Calagurris. Their name is preserved in that of the Basques.

Vascŭla Dresseliāna. See EPIGRAPHY.

Vatia Isauricus, P. SERVILIUS. (1) A Roman consul in B.C. 79, who was sent in the following year as proconsul to Cilicia, in order to clear the seas of the pirates, whose ravages now spread far and wide. He carried on the war with great ability and success, and from his conquest of the Isauri he obtained the surname of Isauricus. After giving Cilicia the organization of a Roman province he entered Rome in triumph in 74. After his return Servilius took a leading part in public affairs. In 70 he was one of the *iudices* at the trial of Verres; in 66 he supported the rogation of Manilius for conferring upon Pompey the command of the war against the pirates; in 63 he was a candidate for the dignity of Pontifex Maximus, but was defeated by Iulius Caesar; in the same year he spoke in the Senate in favour of inflicting the extreme penalty upon the Catilinarian conspirators; in 57 he joined the other nobles in procuring Cicero's recall from banishment; in 56 he opposed the restoration of Ptolemy to his kingdom; and in 55 he was censor with M. Valerius Messala Niger. He took no part in the Civil Wars, probably on account of his advanced age, and died in 44. (2) A Roman praetor, in B.C. 54, who belonged originally to the aristocratic party, but espoused Caesar's side on the breaking out of the Civil War, and was consul with Caesar in 48. In 46 he governed the province of Asia as proconsul, during which time Cicero wrote to him several letters. After the death of Caesar in 44, he supported Cicero and the rest of the aristocratic party, in opposition to Antony; but became reconciled to Antony, and was again consul in 41.

Vatican Library. See LIBRARIES.

Vatican Museum. See MUSEUM.

Vaticānus Mons. A hill at Rome, forming the prolongation of the Ianiculum towards the north, and supposed to derive its name from the Latin word *vates*, "a soothsayer," or *vaticinium*, "divination," as it was once the seat of Etruscan divination (Fest. s. h. v.). The Campus Vaticanus included all the space between the foot of this range and the Tiber. According to Tacitus, the air of this part of Rome was considered very unwholesome (*Hist.* ii. 93). The ground now covered by St. Peter's, the papal palace, museum, and gardens, was anciently designated as *Vaticani loci*, "places belonging to the Vatican Hill" (Tacit. *Hist.* l. c.).

Vatinius. (1) PUBLIUS. A political adventurer in the last days of the Republic, who is described by Cicero as one of the greatest villains that ever lived. Vatinius was quaestor B.C. 63, and tribune of the plebs in 59, when he sold his services to Caesar, who was then consul along with Bibulus. In 56 he appeared as a witness against Milo and Sestius, two of Cicero's friends, in consequence of which the orator made a vehement attack upon the character of Vatinius, in the speech which has come down to us. Vatinius was praetor in 55, and in the following year (54) he was accused by C. Licinius Calvus of having gained the praetorship by bribery. He was defended on this occasion by Cicero, in order to please Caesar, whom Cicero had offended by his former attack upon Vatinius. During the Civil War Vatinius attached himself to the fortunes of Caesar. (2) Of Beneventum, one of the vilest and most hateful creatures of Nero's court, equally deformed in body and in mind, and who, after being a shoemaker's apprentice and a buffoon, ended by becoming a *delator*, or public informer (Tac. *Ann.* xv. 34). A variety of drinking-cup bore his name (Juv. v. 46).

Vectigalia. A Roman term originally denoting only the revenues flowing into the State chest from the State domains, and for the most part collected by contract. The domains consisted of cultivated grounds, the rent of which was paid in money or kind; of pastures and meadows, for the use of which a payment (*scriptura*) was made (see SCRIPTURA); of forests, from which revenue was derived mainly by the letting of pitch huts; of lakes and rivers let for fishing; and of mines and salt-works. With a view to protecting the citizens from exorbitant prices, the sale of salt had already been made a State monopoly in the earliest years of the Republic, and it remained such till late into the times of the Empire. In letting salt mines the price of the salt was fixed in the contract, as was also the case with many articles produced from mines (see METALLUM). The term *vectigal* also includes the rent paid for buildings, shops, booths, and baths erected on public sites; the payment for the use of bridges and roads, of public water-ways, and sewers in cases where private properties drained into them; export and import tolls (see PORTORIUM), as well as all other indirect taxes. Such was the tax which was introduced into Rome in B.C. 357, and under the emperors was levied throughout the whole Empire, the *vicesima libertatis* or *manumissionis*; a tax of five per cent. paid on every manumitted slave, either by himself or his master (see SERVUS). To these were added under Augustus the *centesima rerum venalium*, a tax of one per cent. on all articles sold at auctions; the *quinta et vicesima mancipiorum*, a tax of four per cent. on every slave sold; and the *vicesima hereditatum et legatorum*, a tax of five per cent. on all inheritances over 100,000 sesterces ($4000), and on all legacies not falling to the next of kin. This impost, with the increase of celibacy and the custom of leaving complimentary legacies to the whole circle of one's friends, proved exceedingly productive, and, though originally limited to Roman citizens, was, with the franchise, extended by Caracalla to all the inhabitants of the Empire, and at the same time raised to ten per cent. Plutarch states (*Pomp.* 45) that before Pompey's earlier conquests the vectigalia of the Roman State amounted to the annual sum of

200,000,000 sesterces ($8,000,000). See Naquet, *Les Impôts Indirects chez les Romains* (Paris, 1875); and the articles AERARIUM; PUBLICANI.

Vectis or **Vecta**. Now the Isle of Wight; an island off the southern coast of Britain. It was conquered by Vespasian in the reign of Claudius (Suet. *Vesp.* 4). Remains of Roman villas have been found at Carisbrook and Brading.

Vectis (μοχλός). A bar of wood or iron used for (1) a lever or handspike; (2) a crowbar; (3) the bar of a door (see IANUA); (4) a capstan-bar, etc.

Vediŏvis. See VEIOVIS.

Vedius Pollio. See POLLIO.

Vegetius, FLAVIUS RENĀTUS. The author of a treatise, *Rei Militaris Instituta*, or *Epitoma Rei Militaris*. The exact date is not established, but it was probably composed early in the fifth century A.D. It is a question whether its dedication to Theodosius is genuine, and some writers maintain that it was addressed to Valentinian III. The materials were derived, according to the declaration of the writer himself, from Cato the Censor *De Disciplina Militari*, from Cornelius Celsus, from Frontinus, from Paternus, and from the imperial constitutions of Augustus, Trajan, and Hadrian. The work is divided into four books. The first treats of the levying and training of recruits, including instructions for the fortification of a camp; the second, of the different classes into which soldiers are divided, and especially of the organization of the legion; the third, of the operations of an army in the field; the fourth, of the attack and defence of fortresses, and of marine warfare. Another division makes the number of books five, the fifth being the part relating to marine warfare. The value of this work, which is a somewhat uncritical compilation from different historians, is much diminished by the fact that the usages of periods the most remote from each other are mixed together into one confused mass, and not unfrequently, we have reason to suspect, are blended with arrangements which never existed except in the fancy of the author. It is probably right to ascribe to the same Vegetius the work on veterinary art called *Mulomedicina* (on the treatment of horses and mules), though it is written in a more popular style, as being intended for the use of less refined readers. The military work is edited by Oudendorp and Bessel (Strasburg, 1806); and the *Res Militaris* by Lang (Leipzig, 1885). The *Mulomedicina* is edited by Schneider (Leipzig, 1797).

Vehicŭlum (ὄχημα). A generic term for a vehicle or conveyance by water as well as by land (Cic. *Ad Att.* 10).

Veiento, FABRICIUS. A Roman praetor in A.D. 55, when he ran dogs instead of horses in the games. He was banished A.D. 62, in consequence of having published several libels. He afterwards returned to Rome, and became, in the reign of Domitian, one of the most infamous informers (*delatores*) and flatterers of that emperor. He also enjoyed the friendship of Nerva (Tac. *Ann.* xiv. 50; Dio Cass. lxi. 6; Pliny, *Ep.* iv. 22; Juv. iii. 185; iv. 113).

Veii. Now Isola Farnese; one of the most ancient and powerful cities of Etruria, situated on the river Cremera, about twelve miles from Rome. It was one of the twelve cities of the Etruscan Confederation, and apparently the largest of all. (See ETRURIA.) So far as we can judge from its present remains, it was about seven miles in circumference, which agrees with the statement of Dionysius that it was equal in size to Athens. Its territory (Ager Veiens) was extensive, and appears originally to have extended on the south and east to the Tiber; on the southwest to the sea, embracing the *salinae* or salt-works at the mouth of the river; and on the west to the territory of Caeré. The Ciminian forest appears to have been its northwestern boundary; on the east it must have embraced all the district south of Soracté and eastward to the Tiber. The cities of Capena and Fidenae were colonies of Veii. The Veientes were engaged in almost unceasing hostilities with Rome for more than three centuries and a half, and we have records of fourteen distinct wars between the two peoples. Veii was at length taken by the dictator Camillus, after a siege which is said to have lasted ten years. From this time Veii was abandoned; but after the lapse of ages it was colonized afresh by Augustus, and made a Roman municipium. The new colony, however, occupied scarcely a third of the ancient city, and had again sunk into decay in the reign of Hadrian.

Veil. See COA VESTIS; FLAMMEUM; RICINUM.

Veiŏvis (also **Vediŏvis**). An old Italian deity whose peculiar attributes were early forgotten. At Rome he had a famous shrine in the depression between the two peaks of the Capitoline Hill, the Capitol and the Arx (Ovid, *Fast.* iii. 430; Gell. v. 12). There lay his asylum and afterwards his temple between two sacred groves. His statue, by the side of which stood a goat as a symbol, had a youthful, beardless head, and carried a bundle of arrows in its right hand; it was therefore supposed that he was the same as the Greek Apollo. Others saw in him a youthful Iupiter; while at a later date he was identified with Dis, the god of the world below. He was probably a god of expiation, and hence at the same time the protector of runaway criminals. The goat, which was sacrificed to him annually on the 7th of March, appears elsewhere in the Roman cult as an expiatory sacrifice. Etymologists differ as to the composition of the name Veiovis. Some regard the prefix *ve-* as diminutive, hence "little Iupiter" (Ovid, *Fast.* iii. 445), i. e. youthful. Others make it intensive, as in *vepallidus*, and hence interpret "mighty" or "destructive" Iupiter. It is probably separative and negative in its nature, as in *vecors*, *vesanus*; and hence the name is really the "Anti-Iupiter," i. e. the antithesis of Iupiter, referring to Iupiter Inferus as the god of the lower world—Dis or Pluto, as noted above.

Velābrum. A district in Rome, originally a morass, on the western slope of the Palatine Hill, between the Vicus Tuscus and the Forum Boarium. See ROMA.

Velāmen. A general term for a loose covering for the person.

Velamenta (plural). Objects carried by suppliants as symbols of their condition, such as olive-branches, fillets of wool, *caducei*, etc. The Greek term is ἱκετήρια (Livy, xxiv. 30; Tac. *Hist.* i. 66).

Velarium. An awning which covered the unroofed part of the Roman theatres and amphitheatres (Juv. iv. 124). It was rolled and unrolled by means of ropes and pulleys fastened to masts set on the outer wall.

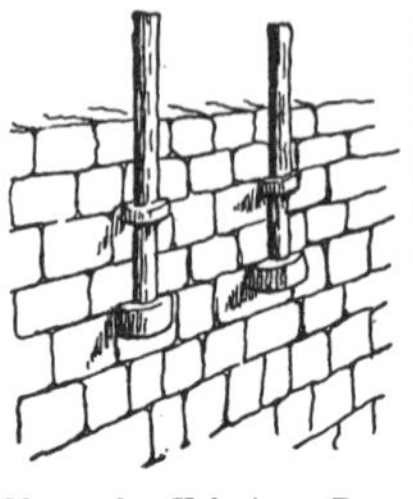
Masts for Velaria. (Pompeii.)

Velauni or **Vellāvi.** A people in Gallia Aquitanica, in the modern Velay, who were originally subject to the Arveni, but subsequently appear as an independent people.

Velĕda. A prophetic virgin, who by birth belonged to the Bructeri, and in the reign of Vespasian was regarded as a divine being by most of the nations in Central Germany. She lived in a tower near the river Luppia (Lippe). See Tac. *Germ.* 8; *Hist.* iv. 61, 65; v. 22, 24; Stat. *Silv.* i. 4, 90; Dio Cass. lxvii. 5.

Veles. See VELITES.

Velia or **Elea** (Ἐλέα), also called **Hyĕlē** (Ὑέλη). Now Castellamare; a Greek town of Lucania, on the western coast between Paestum and Buxentum, was founded by the Phocaeans, who had abandoned their native city to escape from the Persian sovereignty, about B.C. 543. It was situated about three miles east of the river Hales, and possessed a good harbour. It is celebrated as the birthplace of the philosophers Parmenides and Zeno, who founded a school of philosophy usually known under the name of the Eleatic. (See PHILOSOPHIA.) The different forms of the name of the town arise from the fact that the Romans preserve the original Aeolic digamma, representing it by their semi-consonantal V.

Velīnus. Now the Velino; a river in the territory of the Sabines, rising in the central Apennines and falling into the Nar. This river in the neighbourhood of Reaté overflowed its banks and formed several small lakes, the largest of which was called Lacus Velinus (Piè di Lago, also Lago delle Marmore).

Velĭtes (γροσφομάχοι, "skirmishers"). The name given in the old Roman legion to the 1200 citizens of the lowest class in the census, who were distributed among the sixty centuries; they differed from the other soldiers in having lighter armour. (See LEGIO.) When Marius introduced a uniform type of armour throughout all the ranks, this distinction disappeared.

Velĭtrae. Now Velletri; an ancient town of the Volscians in Latium, but subsequently belonging to the Latin League. It is chiefly celebrated as the birthplace of the emperor Augustus (Livy, iii. 41; Suet. *Aug.* 1).

Velius Longus. A Latin grammarian of the first half of the second century A.D. He was the composer of a work, *De Orthographia*, which is still extant, and is printed in Keil's *Grammatici Latini*.

Vellaunodūnum. Now Beaune; a town of the Senones in Gallia Lugdunensis (Caes. *B. G.* vii. 11).

Vellāvi. See VELAUNI.

Vellēius Patercŭlus. See PATERCULUS.

Vellocasses. A people in Gallia Lugdunensis, northwest of the Parisii, extending along the Sequana as far as the ocean. Their chief town was Rotomagus (Rouen) (Caes. *B. G.* ii. 4).

Velum. (1) (ἱστίον). A sail, especially the large square mainsail, as distinguished from the foresail (*dolon*) and the topsail (*supparum*). (See NAVIS.) (2) (παραπέτασμα). A curtain hung before the door of a house like a modern portière-curtain. The name is also applied to any other curtain, as a window-curtain or the curtain at a theatre. See THEATRUM.

Velum.

Venabŭlum. A hunting-spear. It had a long or broad head (Mart. xiv. 31), shaped like a lozenge.

Venāfrum. Now Venafro; a town in the north of Samnium, near the river Vulturnus, and on the confines of Latium, celebrated for the excellence of its olives (Juv. v. 86).

Venantius Fortunātus, HONORIUS CLEMENTIĀNUS. A Latin poet, born about A.D. 535 at Tarvisium (Treviso) in North Italy. After a learned education in Ravenna, he proceeded, about 560, to Gaul, where he became an ecclesiastic at Poitiers, and died as bishop about 600. Among his works we possess an epic poem on St. Martin, as well as a collection of three hundred poems in eleven books, of very various kinds, including panegyrics, epigrams, letters, elegies, hymns, and hence called *Miscellanea*. These poems, which are mostly elegiac, are not unsuccessful in form, and are of great value for the history of the time. One of the most interesting is the companion piece to the *Mosella* of Ausonius (q. v.), the description of a journey by the Moselle and Rhine from Metz to Andernach (*De Navigio Suo*). The prose works are edited by Krusch and the poems by Leo (Berlin, 1881–85).

Venatiōnes. The contests of beasts with one another, or of men with beasts, that formed part of the shows of which the Romans were passionately fond. They were first introduced at the games of Marcus Fulvius Nobilior, B.C. 186 (Livy, xxxix. 22). Those who took part in these contests were called *bestiarii*. They were either criminals and prisoners of war, who were poorly armed or completely unarmed, pitted against wild beasts which had previously been made furious by hunger, branding, and goading; or else hired fighters who, like gladiators, were trained in special schools and fully armed. Even in the last century of the Republic, and still more under the Empire, incredible expenses were incurred in the collection of the rarest animals from the remotest quarters of the globe and in the other arrangements for their baiting. Sulla first exhibited lions let loose in the Circus (Sen. *De Brev. Vit.* 13); Clodius Pulcher first gave an elephant fight; Scaurus first showed a hippopotamus and crocodiles in a pond or trench (Pliny, *H. N.* viii. 96). Pompey provided a show of 500 lions, 18 elephants, and 410 other African animals; and Caligula caused 400 bears and the same number of animals from Africa to tear each other to

Fight between Bear and Rhinoceros. (Rich, from a terra-cotta lamp.)

pieces. When the great amphitheatre of Titus was dedicated 9000 animals were killed; and at the Dacian celebration of Trajan, 11,000 (Suet. *Tit.* 7; Dio Cass. lxviii. 15). Occasionally at these combats with wild beasts the man condemned to death

Venatio. (Pompeian painting.)

was attired in an appropriate costume, so as to represent a sanguinary scene from mythology or history, as, for example, Orpheus being torn to pieces by bears. Down to the end of the Republic these shows took place in the Circus, and the greater exhibitions were held there even after that time, until the amphitheatres became the usual places of performance; and, indeed, when they were combined with the gladiatorial exhibitions, they took place in the early morning before them. They were continued down to the sixth century. See Friedländer, *Sittengeschichte Roms*, 5th ed. ii. pp. 348 foll.; Marquardt, *Staatsverwaltung*, iii. 565.

Among the Greeks, especially the Athenians, cock-fights and quail-fights were very popular. At Athens cock-fights were held once a year in the theatres at the public expense. The training of fighting-cocks was conducted with great care. Certain places, such as Tanagra in Boeotia, Rhodes, and Delos, had the reputation of producing the largest and strongest. To whet their eagerness for the combat, they were previously fed with garlic. Their legs were armed with brass spurs, and they were set opposite to each other on tables furnished with raised edges. Bets, often to an enormous amount, were laid on the fights by the gamesters as well as by the spectators.

Venĕdi or **Venĕdae**. A people in European Sarmatia, dwelling on the Baltic, east of the Vistula. The SINUS VENEDĬCUS (Gulf of Riga), and the VENEDĬCI MONTES, a range of mountains between Poland and East Prussia, were called after this people. The name is preserved in that of the curious people called the Wends, who in East Prussia still preserve many of the Slavonic traits of their ancestors.

Venefĭca. A witch, poisoner, sorceress. See SAGA.

Veneficium. The crime of poisoning which became common under the Empire, and even earlier, as is clear from the oration of Cicero for Cluentius. Several names of women have obtained an infamous immortality by reason of their skill as poisoners, among them Locusta, who poisoned Claudius at the desire of his wife Agrippina, and Britannicus, to please Nero. Poisoning was much resorted to by expectant heirs and by unfaithful wives. Mayor in his note on Juv. i. 70 has collected notices of the Roman *causes célèbres* that turn on charges of poisoning. By a law of Sulla, passed in B.C. 82 (*lex Cornelia de Sicariis et de Veneficis*), persons concerned in poisoning were punished by confiscation of property and *deportatio in insulam*. In later times, those of lower rank were thrown to wild beasts. On poisons for abortion, see ABORTIO.

Venĕris Pervigilium. See PERVIGILIUM.

Venĕti. See CIRCUS.

Venetia. (1) A district in the north of Italy, originally included under the general name of Gallia Cisalpina, but made by Augustus the tenth *regio* of Italy. It was bounded on the west by the river Athesis, which separated it from Gallia Cisalpina; on the north by the Carnic Alps; on the east by the river Timavus, which separated it from Istria; and on the south by the Adriatic Gulf. Its inhabitants, the Veneti, frequently called Heneti (Ἑνετοί) by the Greeks, were not an Italian race, but their real origin is doubtful, as their language was certainly not Keltic (Polyb. ii. 17). Herodotus speaks of them as an Illyrian race, and this is probably a correct view (Herod. i. 196; v. 9). In consequence of their hostility to the Keltic tribes in their neighbourhood, they formed at an early period an alliance with Rome; and their country was defended by the Romans against their dangerous enemies. On the conquest of the Cisalpine Gauls, the Veneti likewise became included under the Roman dominions. The Veneti continued to enjoy great prosperity down to the time of the Marcomannic wars, in the reign of the emperor Aurelius; but from this time their country was frequently devastated by the barbarians who invaded Italy; and at length, in the fifth century, many of its inhabitants, to escape the ravages of the Huns under Attila, took refuge in the islands off their coast, on which now stands the city of Venice. The chief towns of Venetia in ancient times were Patavium, Altinum, and Aquileia. (2) A district in the north-west of Gallia Lugdunensis, inhabited by the Veneti. Off their coast was a group of islands called INSŬLAE VENETĬCAE (Belle-Ile). The name is preserved in the modern Vannes.

Venĕtus Lacus. See BRIGANTINUS LACUS.

Venilia. A nymph, daughter of Pilumnus, sister of Amata, wife of King Latinus, and mother of Turnus and Iuturna by Daunus.

Vennŏnes. A people of Rhaetia, and according to Strabo the most savage of the Rhaetian tribes, inhabiting the Alps near the sources of the Athesis (Adige).

Venta. (1) BELGĀRUM. Now Winchester; the chief town of the Belgae in Britain. The modern city still contains several Roman remains. (2) ICENŌRUM. (See ICENI.) (3) SILŪRUM. Now Caerwent; a town of the Silures in Britain, in Monmouthshire.

Venti. See VENTUS.

Ventidius Bassus, PUBLIUS. A celebrated Roman general, who at first gained a poor living by letting mules and carriages to officials. Caesar, however, saw his abilities, and employed him in Gaul, and in the Civil War (Dio Cass. xliii. 51; Gell. xv. 4). After Caesar's death Ventidius sided with M. Antony, and in B.C. 43 was made consul suffectus. In 39 Antony sent Ventidius into Asia, where he defeated the Parthians and Labienus; and in the second campaign gained a still more brilliant victory over the Parthians, who had again invaded Syria. For these services he obtained a triumph in 38. His later history is unknown (Dio Cass. xliii. 51; Gell. xv. 4; Eutrop. vii. 3; Plut. *Ant.* 34; Juv. vii. 199).

Medal commemorating the Parthian Triumph of Ventidius.

Ventrālé (κοιλιόδεσμος). The ancient representation of the sash which in our time has begun to be worn by men in warm weather (Pliny, *H. N.* viii. 73). It was a square piece of cloth tied around the loins and over the abdomen, sometimes for medical purposes and sometimes for comfort. It was also arranged so as to be used for the purposes of a money-belt (Ulp. *Dig.* xlviii. 20, 6).

Ventus (ἄνεμος). Winds were regarded by Greeks and Romans alike as divine beings. In Homer, who mentions only the four chief winds, Boreas (North), Zephyrus (West), Eurus (East), and Notus (South), they are, according to one account (*Od.* x. 1–75), committed by Zeus to the charge of Aeolus (q. v.). But elsewhere they appear as independent personalities, who, dwelling in Thrace, display their activity at the command of Zeus and other gods, and are invoked by men with prayers and sacrifices (*Il.* xxiii. 195). Hesiod (*Theog.* 378) calls these winds children of Astraeus and Eos, and distinguishes them as beneficent beings from the destructive winds, the children of Typhoeus (*Theog.* 869). Some particular myths speak only of Boreas and Zephyrus, from whom, on account of their swiftness, famous horses were supposed to be descended. Thus (*Il.* xvi. 150) the horses of Achilles are called the children of Zephyrus and Podargé, one of the Harpies (see HARPYIAE). The latter, in accordance with their original nature, are also deities of the wind, or rather of the storm. In historical times the cult of the winds in general, or that of Boreas or Zephyrus in particular, flourished at special places in Greece. In Italy also the winds were held in much veneration, particularly the fructifying wind Favonius, which corresponded to Zephyrus. In Rome the tempests (*tempestates*) had a sanctuary of their own with regular sacrifices at the Porta Capena, which was founded in B.C. 259, in consequence of a vow made for the preservation of a Roman fleet in a storm at sea. Roman generals when embarking usually offered prayers to the winds and storms, as well as to the other gods, and cast offerings and bloody sacrifices into the waves to propitiate them. To the beneficent winds white animals were offered, and those of a dark colour to the malignant equinoctial and winter storms. The victims were generally rams and lambs.

In works of art the winds are usually represented with winged heads and shoulders, open mouth, and inflated cheeks. The most noteworthy monument, from an artistic point of view, is the Tower of the Winds, still standing in excellent preservation at Athens, on which eight winds are represented (Boreas, North; Kaikias, Northeast; Apeliotes, East; Eurus, Southeast; Notus, South; Lips, Southwest; Zephyrus, West; and Argestes or Sciron, Northwest).

Venus. An Italian goddess, who, after the Greek mythology influenced the Roman, was identified with Aphrodité, and in Latin literature has the same myths and characteristics (see under APHRODITÉ), though originally the Italian Venus was a goddess of gardens and of spring. Prior to her identification with Aphrodité she was one of the least important of the native deities; yet her cult was established at Rome at a very early date. A stone altar with an image of Venus MURTEA or MURCIA stood in the Circus near the place where the altar of Consus was concealed (see CIRCUS), and a sanctuary of the goddess below the Aventine had a myrtle-grove before it. Another ancient name of Venus was CLOACĪNA, which is said to have been derived from her image having been found in the great sewer (*cloaca*); but this tale is nothing but a *volksetymologie*, as the name, which is probably connected with *cluere*, rather marks her out as "the purifier." Under this title her statue was erected by Titus Tatius in a temple near the Forum. Venus was also styled CALVA ("the bald") and as such she had two temples near the Capitol. To explain this title the story was told that one of the temples was built by Ancus Marcius because his wife was in danger of losing her hair; others thought that it was a monument of a patriotic act of the Roman women, who, during the siege of the Gauls, cut off their hair and gave it to the men to make strings for their bows; and others again supposed it to refer to the fancies and caprices of lovers, *calvere* signifying "to tease." Very likely it refers to the fact that on her wedding-day the bride, either actually or symbolically, cut off a lock of hair to sacrifice it to Venus. (See MATRIMONIUM.) In these, the most ancient surnames of Venus, one can recognize her primitive character and attributes. She is also styled PAETA, as to which see PAETUS.

In later times, as her worship became much more extended, her identification with the Greek Aphrodité introduced various new attributes. At the beginning of the Second Punic War the worship of Venus Erycina was introduced from Sicily (see ERYX), and a temple was dedicated to her on the Capitol, to which subsequently another was added outside the Colline Gate. In the year B.C. 114, a Vestal Virgin was killed by lightning; and as the general moral corruption, especially among the Vestals, was believed to be the cause of this disaster, the Sibylline Books (see SIBYLLAE), upon being consulted, commanded that a temple should be built to Venus Verticordia (the goddess who turns the hearts of men) on the Via Salaria. After the close of the Samnite War, Fabius Gurges founded the worship of Venus Obsequens and Postvorta; Scipio Africanus the younger, that of Venus Genetrix, in which he was afterwards followed by Caesar, who added that of Venus Victrix. The worship of Venus was promoted by Caesar, who traced his descent from Aeneas, who was supposed to be the son of Mars and Venus. (See AENEAS.) The month of April, as the beginning of spring, was thought to be peculiarly sacred to the goddess of love, and recalled also the early Italian conception of her functions. Both ideas are beautifully blended in the magnificent apostrophe to Venus Genetrix with which Lucretius commences his poem *De Rerum Natura*, in which she is regarded as the creative, vivifying force of Nature, the source of life and strength in all things. Respecting the Greek goddess see APHRODITÉ.

Venus (Ἀφροδίτη). A name given to the best possible throw of the dice (*tesserae* or *tali*), which was the one in which the numbers all came up different (Suet. *Aug.* 71). See TALUS; TESSERA.

Venus de' Medici. See CLEOMENES.

Venus di Milo. See APHRODITÉ.

Venusia. Now Venosa; an ancient town of Apulia, south of the river Aufidus, and near Mount Vultur, situated in a romantic country, and memorable as the birthplace of the poet Horace. See HORATIUS.

Verāgri or **Varāgri.** A people in Gallia Belgica, on the Pennine Alps, near the confluence of the Dranse and the Rhône (Caes. *B. G.* iii. 1).

Verandah. See PORTICUS; STOA.

Verbānus Lacus. Now Lago Maggiore; a lake in Gallia Cisalpina, and the largest in all Italy, being about forty miles in length from north to south; its greatest breadth is eight miles.

Verbēna. Probably the vervain; an herb used by the Roman *fetiales* (q. v.) in their symbolical ceremonies. Cf. also SAGMINA.

Verber. The thong of a whip (see FLAGRUM); (2) the leathern part of a sling (Verg. *Georg.* i. 309). See FUNDA.

Vercellae. Now Vercelli; the chief town of the Libici in Gallia Cisalpina (Tac. *Hist.* i. 70).

Vercingetŏrix. A celebrated chieftain of the Arverni in Gaul, who carried on war with great ability against Caesar in B.C. 52. The history of this war occupies the seventh book of Caesar's commentaries on the Gallic War. Vercingetorix fell into Caesar's hands on the capture of Alesia, was subsequently taken to Rome, where he adorned the triumph of his conqueror in 45, and was afterwards put to death.

Verdict. See JUDICIAL PROCEDURE.

Veredarius. A government messenger among the Romans who carried official letters and despatches. The name is derived from that of the horses (*veredi*) that carried or drew him (Sidon. *Epist.* v. 7). See CURSUS PUBLICUS.

Verēdus. A fast horse used either as a hunter or a post-horse. See VEREDARIUS.

Verētum. Now Alessano; more anciently called Baris, a town in Calabria, on the road from Leuca to Tarentum, and 600 stadia southeast of the latter city.

Vergellus. A rivulet in Apulia, said to have been choked by the dead bodies of the Romans slain in the battle of Cannae (Flor. ii. 6, 18; Val. Max. ix. 2, 2).

Vergilius Maro, PUBLIUS. The most famous of the Roman poets, born on the 15th of October, B.C. 70, at Andes (Pietola), a small village near Mantua, in Cisalpine Gaul. There is no doubt that *Vergilius* is the more correct spelling, since inscriptions of the time of the Republic and the Early Empire where the name occurs give *Vergilius*, and never *Virgilius*. The same is true of the older MSS., as the Medicean; while the Greek authors write Βεργίλιος and Οὐεργίλιος. In the Middle Ages (from about the ninth century) the form *Virgilius* came into use by a fanciful derivation from *virga* "a rod," "a wand," Vergil being regarded as a great necromancer, as explained later in the present article. Even in the fifteenth century, however, Politian proved this form to be erroneous, and almost the only scholars to defend it in recent times are F. Schultz in his *Orthogr. Quaestiones* (Paderborn, 1855), and Oberdick in *Studien z. lat. Orthographie* (Münster, 1879). (See Hübner in *Jahn's Jahrbücher*, lxii. 360, and Ritschl, *Opuscula*, ii. 779.) The earliest known instance of the spelling *Virgilius* is in the fifth century A.D. (*C. I. L.* vi. 1710).

Vergil's father probably had a small estate which he cultivated, and he is said to have eked out his means by keeping bees. His mother's name was Magia Polla. He was educated at Cremona and Mediolanum (Milan), and assumed the *toga virilis* at Cremona on the day on which he began his sixteenth year, in 55. It is said that he subsequently studied at Neapolis (Naples) under Parthenius, a native of Bithynia, from whom he learned Greek. He was further instructed by Siron, an Epicurean, whose lectures were attended also by Alfenus Varus at Rome, where he also studied rhetoric under Epidius at the same time as did Octavianus. Vergil's writings prove that he received a learned education, and traces of Epicurean opinions are apparent in them (e. g. *Georg.* ii. 490). The health of Vergil was always feeble, and there is no evidence of his attempting to rise by those means through which many Romans gained distinction—oratory and arms.

After completing his education, Vergil appears to have retired to his paternal property. After the battle of Philippi (42) Octavian assigned to his soldiers lands in various parts of Italy. Octavius Musa, who was charged with this allotment in the Cremona district, extended the limits so as to include Mantua (cf. *Ecl.* ix. 28), and the farm belonging to Vergil's father was assigned to a centurion, whose name is given as Arrius. Asinius Pollio, the *legatus* of Transpadane Gaul, and Cornelius Gallus interested themselves in Vergil, who was probably already known to them as a poet, and advised him to apply to Octavian at Rome. Vergil did so, his father's farm was restored, and the First Eclogue expresses gratitude to Octavian. But there was a second spoliation when, after the war of Perusia, Alfenus Varus became *legatus* in Pollio's place. A primipilaris named Milienus Toro got possession of the farm, and Vergil himself was nearly killed by the violence of a certain Clodius. Vergil and his father took refuge in a country-house belonging to Siro (*Catal.* 10), and thence removed to Rome, where he wrote the Eclogues (*Eclogae*, *Bucolica*). Here Maecenas also became interested in Vergil, who was compensated by Augustus. He did not, indeed, recover his paternal estate, but land was given him elsewhere—possibly the estate which he had near Nola in Campania (Gell. vi. 20). His friendship with Maecenas was soon so firmly established that he was able to gain the same patronage for Horace (Hor. *Sat.* i. 6, 54). Horace, in one of his Satires (*Sat.* i. 5), in which he describes the journey from Rome to Brundusium, mentions Vergil as one of the party, and in language which shows that they were then in the closest intimacy. The most finished work of Vergil, his *Georgica*, an agricultural poem, was undertaken at the suggestion of Maecenas (*Georg.* iii. 41); the concluding lines were written at Naples (*Georg.* iv. 559); and the poem was completed after the battle of Actium, B.C. 31, while Octavian was in the East. Some of his pastoral poetry seems to have been written in the country about Tarentum (Prop. iii. 24, 67). His Eclogues had all been completed probably before the *Georgica* were begun.

The epic poem of Vergil, the *Aeneid*, was probably long contemplated by the poet. While Augustus was in Spain (27), he wrote to Vergil to express his wish for some great monument of his poetical talent. Vergil appears to have begun the *Aeneid* about this time. In 23 died Marcellus, the son of Octavia (Caesar's sister) by her first husband; and Vergil introduced into his sixth book of the *Aeneid* (883) the well-known allusion to the promise of this youth, who was cut off by a premature death. Octavia is said to have been present when the poet was reciting this allusion to her son, and to have fainted from her emotions. She rewarded the poet munificently for his excusable flattery.

Vergil Reading to Maecenas. (Painting by Jalabert.)

When Augustus was returning from Samos, where he had spent the winter of 20, he met Vergil at Athens. The poet, it is said, had intended to make a tour in Greece, but he accompanied the emperor to Megara and thence to Italy. His health, which had long been declining, was now completely broken, and he died soon after his arrival at Brundusium, on the 22d of September, B.C. 19, not having quite completed his fifty-first year. His remains were transferred to Naples, which had been his favourite residence, and on the road from Naples to Puteoli (Pozzuoli) a monument is still shown, supposed to be the tomb of the poet. The inscription said to have been placed on the tomb,

Mantua me genuit, Calabri rapuere, tenet nunc
Parthenope. Cecini pascua, rura, duces,

we cannot suppose to have been written by him. Vergil named as *heredes* in his testament his half-brother Valerius Proculus, to whom he left one-half of his property, and also Augustus, Maecenas, L. Varius, and Plotius Tucca. It is said that in his last illness he wished to burn the *Aeneid*, to which he had not given the finishing touches, but that his friends would not allow him. Whatever he may have wished to be done with the *Aeneid*, it was preserved and published by his friends Varius and Tucca. The poet had been enriched by the liberality of his patrons, and he left behind him a considerable property and a house on the Esquiline Hill near the gardens of Maecenas. He used his wealth liberally, and it is said that he supported his father, who had become blind, but did not die before his son had attained a mature age.

In his fortunes and his friends Vergil was a happy man. Munificent patronage gave him ample means of enjoyment and of leisure, and he had the friendship of all the most accomplished men of the day, among whom Horace especially entertained a strong affection for him. He was an amiable, good-tempered man, free from the mean passions of envy and jealousy; and in all but health he was prosperous. His fame, which was established in his lifetime, was cherished after his death as an inheritance in which every Roman had a share, and his works became school-books even before the death of Augustus. They were even consulted for chance oracles (*sortes Vergilianae*) under the Roman Empire (Capit. *Albin.* 5; Lamprid. *Alex. Sev.* 4; Spartian. *Hadr.* 2). (See SORTES.) The poems being full of learned and antiquarian allusions, soon gave employment to commentators and critics. Aulus Gellius has numerous remarks on Vergil; and Macrobius, in his *Saturnalia*, has filled four books (iii.–vi.) with his critical remarks on the poems. One of the most valuable commentaries on Vergil, in which a great amount of curious and instructive matter has been preserved, is that of Servius Maurus Honoratus. See SERVIUS.

The chief authority for the life of Vergil, apart from casual notices in his own poems or in those of contemporary poets, is the biography prefixed to the commentary written by Aelius Donatus in the fourth century A.D. This life was derived by Donatus from the biography composed by Suetonius in his *De Viris Illustribus*. (See DONATUS.) Suetonius is said to have derived this information from accounts by Varius, and by Melissus, who was a freedman of Maecenas (Gell. xvii. 10). Another life of Vergil was compiled from the commentary of Valerius Probus; a third, found in Jerome, is also derived from Suetonius; a fourth, of unknown authorship, is prefixed to the commentary of Servius on the *Aeneid;* and a fifth, also of unknown date, is found in the Bernese MS. of Vergil. The grammarian Phocas, in the fifth century, made a version in hexameters of Donatus's Life of Vergil. (See Nettleship's essay prefixed to Conington's edition of Vergil.) No authentic portrait of Vergil has been preserved.

The ten short poems called *Bucolica* were the earliest extant works of Vergil, and probably all written between 41 and 39. These *Bucolica* are not *Bucolica* in the same sense as the poems of Theocritus, which have the same title. They have all a pastoral form and colouring, but some of them have nothing more. They are also called *Eclogae* ("selections"), but there is no reason to suppose that this name originated with the poet. Their merit consists in their versification (which was smoother and more polished than any hexameters which the Romans had yet seen), and in their many natural and simple touches. But as an attempt to transfer the Syracusan style into Italy, they bear the stamp of imitation, and, however graceful and melodious, cannot be ranked with the more genuine pastorals of Theocritus. The Fourth Eclogue, entitled *Pollio*, which may have been written in 40, after the peace of Brundusium, has nothing of the pastoral character about it. It is half allegorical, half historical and prophetical—anything, in fact, but bucolic. The First Eclogue is bucolic in form and in treatment, with an historical basis. The Second Eclogue, the *Alexis*, is an amatory poem, with a bucolic colouring. The third, the fifth, the seventh, and the ninth are more clearly modelled on the form of the poems of his Sicilian prototype; and the eighth, the *Pharmaceutria* ("Incantation"), is a direct imitation of the original Greek. The tenth, entitled *Gallus*, perhaps written the last of all, is a love poem, which, if written in elegiac verse, would be more appropriately called an Elegy than a Bucolic.

The *Georgica*, or "Agricultural Poem," in four books, written B.C. 37–30, is a didactic poem, which Vergil dedicated to his patron Maecenas. He treats of the cultivation of the soil in the first book, of fruit-trees in the second, of horses and cattle in the third, and of bees in the fourth. This is generally regarded as his masterpiece, and it is unquestionably the most finished and perfect of his works, showing wonderful skill in treating the more prosaic subjects of practical daily life and embellishing them with magnificent bursts of poetry, yet so as still to present a complete and harmonious work. Its versification is the perfection of the Latin hexameter. Yet, great as are these merits, the *Aeneid* is the greater poem of the two. In grandeur, in poetical matter, and, to most readers, in interest, it is superior, and yields only to the *Georgics* in artistic completeness. The *Georgics* are, no doubt, based on the works of Hesiod and Aratus, but are so treated as to be rightly regarded as an original poem. In the first book he enumerates the subjects of his poem, among which is the treatment of bees; yet the management of bees seems but meagre material for one-fourth of the whole poem, and the author accordingly completed the fourth book with matter somewhat extraneous—the long story of Aristaeus.

The *Aeneid*, or adventures of Aeneas after the fall of Troy, is an epic poem on the model of the Homeric poems. It was founded upon an old Roman tradition that Aeneas and his Trojans settled in Italy, and were the founders of the Roman State. In the first book we have the story of Aeneas being driven by a storm on the coast of Africa, and being hospitably received by Dido, queen of Carthage, to whom he relates in the episode of the second and third books the fall of Troy and his own wanderings. In the fourth book the poet has elaborated the story of the love-affair of Dido and Aeneas, the departure of Aeneas in obedience to the will of the gods, and the suicide of the Carthaginian queen. The fifth book contains the visit to Sicily, and the sixth the landing of Aeneas at Cumae in Italy, and his descent to the infernal regions, where he sees his father Anchises, and has a prophetic vision of the glorious destinies of his race and of the future heroes of Rome. In the first six books the adventures of Odysseus in the *Odyssey* are the model, and these books contain more variety of incident and situation than those which follow. The last six books, the history of the struggles of Aeneas in Italy, are modelled after the battle-scenes of the *Iliad*. Latinus, the king of the Latini, offers the Trojan hero in marriage his daughter Lavinia, who had been betrothed to Turnus, the warlike king of the Rutuli. The contest is ended by the death of Turnus, who falls by the hand of Aeneas. The fortunes of Aeneas and his final settlement in Italy are the subject of the *Aeneid;* but it is the national epic of the Roman people, and its real object is to set forth the glories of Rome, and, less directly, of the Julian house, to which Augustus belonged, and to foster in the Romans a patriotic feeling, and, still more, a religious sentiment for the gods and heroes of their ancestors. In the first book, the foundation of Alba Longa is promised by Iupiter to Venus (*Aeneid*, i. 254), and the transfer of empire from Alba to Rome; from the line of Aeneas will descend the "Trojan Caesar," whose empire will be limited only by the ocean, and his glory by the heavens. The future rivalry between Rome and Carthage and the ultimate triumph of Rome are predicted. The poem abounds in allusions to the history of Rome; and the aim of the poet to confirm and embellish the popular tradition of the Trojan origin of the Roman State, and the descent of the Iulii from Venus, is apparent throughout. More interest is excited by Turnus than by Aeneas. It is true that it might be said of the *Iliad* that the character of Hector wins more admiration than that of Achilles; but the cases are not parallel, since Aeneas is in himself a weak and priggish person, and one unsuited to be the hero of an epic.

Vergil imitated other poets besides Homer, and he has occasionally borrowed from them, especially from Apollonius of Rhodes. The historical colouring which pervades it, and the great amount of antiquarian learning which he has scattered through it, make the *Aeneid* a study for the historian of Rome. In fact, Vergil's free use of all that his predecessors had written has been often misinterpreted both in ancient and in modern times so as to be made the basis of a charge of wholesale plagiarism. One Perellius Faustus even published a book on these alleged literary thefts (*furta*), while Octavius Aribius made an elaborate collection of the resemblances (ὁμοιότητες) between lines and expressions found in Vergil and those previously existing in the Greek. In fact these *obtrectatores* were so vehement and so numerous among his own countrymen that their assertions have found an echo in modern times. An English scholar has, however, well expressed the proper view of this phase of Vergilian criticism in the following sentences:

"A most interesting feature in the *Aeneid* is its incorporation of all that was best in preceding poetry. All Roman poets had imitated, but Vergil carried imitation to an extent hitherto unknown. Not only Greek but Latin writers are laid under contribution in every page. Some idea of his indebtedness to Homer may be formed from Conington's commentary. Sophocles and the other tragedians, Apollonius Rhodius and the Alexandrians are continually imitated, and almost always improved upon. And still more is this the case with his adaptations from Naevius, Ennius, Lucretius, Hostius, Furius, etc., whose works he had thoroughly mastered, and had stored in his memory their most striking rhythms or expressions. Massive lines from Ennius, which as a rule he has spared to touch, leaving them in all their rugged grandeur planted in the garden of his verse to point back like giant trees to the time when that garden was a forest, bear witness at once to his reverence for the old bard and to his own wondrous art. It is not merely for literary effect that the old poets are transferred into his pages. A nobler motive swayed him. The *Aeneid* was meant to be, above all things, a National Poem, carrying on the lines of thought, the style of speech, which national progress had chosen; it was not meant to eclipse so much as to do honour to the early literature. Thus those bards who like Naevius and Ennius had done good service to Rome by singing, however rudely, her history, find their *imagines* ranged in the gallery of the *Aeneid*. There they meet with the flamens and pontiffs unknown and unnamed, who drew up the ritual formularies, with the antiquarians and pious scholars who had sought to find a meaning in the immemorial names, whether of places or customs or persons; with the magistrates, moralists, and philosophers who had striven to ennoble or enlighten Roman virtue; with the Greek singers and sages, for they too had helped to rear the towering fabric of Roman greatness. All these meet together in the *Aeneid* as if in solemn conclave, to review their joint work, to acknowledge its final completion, and predict its impending fall. This is beyond question the explanation of the wholesale appropriation of others' thought and language, which otherwise would be sheer plagiarism. With that tenacious sense of national continuity which had given the Senate a policy for centuries, Vergil regards Roman literature as a gradually expanded whole; coming at the close of its first epoch, he sums up its results and enters into its labours. So far from hesitating whether to imitate, he rather hesitated whom not to include, if only by a single reference, in his mosaic of all that had entered into the history of Rome. His archaism is but another side of the same thing. Whether it takes the form of archaeological discussion, of antiquarian allusion, of a mode of narration which recalls the ancient source, or of obsolete expressions, forms of inflection, or poetical ornament, we feel that it is a sign of the poet's reverence for what was at once national and old. The structure of his verse, while full of music, often reminds us of the earlier writers. It certainly has more affinity with that of Lucretius than with that of Lucan. A learned Roman reading the *Aeneid* would feel his mind stirred by a thousand patriotic associations. The quaint old laws, the maxims and religious formulae he had learned in childhood would mingle with the richest poetry of Greece and Rome in a stream flowing evenly, and, as it would seem, from a single spring; and he who by his art had effected this wondrous union would seem to him the prophet as well as the poet of the era."

The larger editions of Vergil contain some short poems, which are attributed to him. The *Culex* ("Gnat") is a kind of bucolic poem in 413 hexameters, often very obscure. Vergil is known to have written a poem with this title (Donat. *Vit.;* Suet. *Vit. Lucan.;* Stat. *Silv.* ii. 7, 73); but it is on the whole probable that the poem which we have is by an imitator of Vergil. The *Ciris*, or the myth of Scylla, the daughter of Nisus, king of Megara, in 541 hexameters, borrows Vergil's forms, but was probably written by an imitator of Catullus, belonging to the literary circle of

Messala. The *Moretum* ("Hotchpotch") in 123 verses, the name of a dish of various ingredients, is a poem in hexameters, on the daily labour of a cultivator; but it contains only the description of the labours of the first part of the day, which consists in preparing the *moretum*. It is suggested, with probability, that this may be a translation or adaptation by Vergil of a Greek poem of Parthenius. The *Copa* ("Barmaid"), in 19 elegiac couplets, is an invitation by a barmaid or servant attached to a *caupona* to passers-by to come in and enjoy themselves. There is no good reason against accepting this as Vergil's work. There are also fourteen short pieces in various metres, classed under the general name of *Catalepton* (sometimes written as *Catalecta*). The name is derived from a title (κατὰ λεπτόν) which Aratus gave to a set of short poems (Strabo, p. 486). They were written in the period of Vergil, and it is probable that many are by Vergil—some the work of his earlier years.

Portion of the Schedae Vaticanae with *Aen.* vi. 45–48. (Written about the fourth century A. D.)

In the Middle Ages, Vergil was a great favourite, but was much misunderstood as regards his history and personality. Partly because of a vague remembrance by the people of the episode of the Descent into Hell which forms the subject of the Sixth Book of the *Aeneid*, and partly because his Fourth Eclogue was believed to be a heathen prophecy of the birth of Christ, Vergil came at last to be regarded as a great magician. His mother's name, Magia Polla (*magia*, "magic," *polla* as from *polleo*, "mighty"), appeared to confirm this notion, and his own name as finally derived from *virga*, "a wand," helped along the myth. In the strange mirage-like blending of fact and fancy that characterizes the legends of the mediævals, Vergil was finally described as a benevolent enchanter living at Rome under King Servius, or Darius, or Octavianus, the son of a king from "Campania in the Ardennes" and the daughter of a Roman Senator under the emperor Remus, who killed his uncle Romulus. Vergil was said to have studied at the University of Toledo, but to have spent most of his time at Rome and Naples. The latter city, in fact, he was said to have founded and to have buoyed it up in the sea on eggs. See Tunison, *Vergil in the Middle Age* (Cincinnati, 1889); Milberg, *Mirabilia Vergiliana* (Meissen, 1867), and especially Comparetti, *Vergil in the Middle Ages*, Eng. trans. (New York, 1896). The influence of Vergil on Dante is well known.

Manuscripts.—More than 150 manuscripts of Vergil, of all degrees of value, have been discovered and classified, among them some of a very early date. The most valuable are the Codex Vaticanus (3867), of the fourth or fifth century; the Codex Palatinus (Vatican), of the same age; and the Codex Mediceus or Laurentianus (Florence), which contains corrections made in the fifth century. Important fragments of manuscripts also exist, among them the Schedae Vaticanae, a set of sheets with illustrations, the Schedae Rescriptae Sangallenses (palimpsest), and the Schedae Rescriptae Veronenses (palimpsest). Another good source is the Codex Gudianus (Wolfenbüttel) of the ninth century. Three Codices in Berne of the ninth or tenth century also deserve mention. On the MSS. see Ribbeck's Prolegomena to his Vergil (1866); the fac-similes published by Wattenbach, Zangemeister, and Chatelain; and the paper by Nolhac, *Les Peintures des MSS. de Virgile* (*Mélanges de l'École Française à Rome*, 1884).

Bibliography.—The *editio princeps* of Vergil appeared at Rome about 1469. Early editions of the complete works are those of La Cerda (Madrid, 1608–17); D. Heinsius (Leyden, 1636; rev. by N. Heinsius, 1664, 1676); Delphin ed. (Paris, 1675); Burmann (Amsterdam, 1746). Later are those of Heyne, 4 vols. (Leipzig, 1767–75; third ed. in 6 vols. with glossary by Schlegel, 1798–1800); the same revised by Wagner with the minor poems (Leipzig, 1830–41) in 5 vols.; Forbiger, 4th ed. (Leipzig, 1872–75); Dübner (Paris, 1858); Ribbeck, with critical prolegomena, 5 vols. (Leipzig, 1859–68); Benoist, 3 vols. (2d ed. Paris, 1876); with English notes by Conington and Nettleship, 3 vols. (4th ed. London, 1881–83). More elementary are the editions by Wagner (3d ed. Leipzig, 1861); Ladewig and Schaffer (10th ed. Berlin, 1886); Kennedy (2d ed. London, 1879); Kappes, 4th ed. Leipzig, 1887); Papillon, 2 vols. (London, 1882); and Sidgwick (Cambridge, 1890). Good prose translations are those of Conington (3d ed. London, 1882); and Lonsdale and Lee (12th ed. London, 1890). Verse translations into English are those of Dryden, and of Bowen (incomplete). A good verse translation of the *Aeneid* is that of William Morris; of the *Eclogues* that of Calverley (1866) and Palmer (1883); of the *Georgics* that of Rhodes.

A good annotated edition of the *Bucolics* (Eclogues) and *Georgics* are those of Keightley (London, 1848); of the *Aeneid* by Papillon and Haigh (Oxford, 1890); of the *Copa* by Ilgen (Halle, 1820); of the *Ciris* by Unger (Halle, 1885); of the *Moretum* by Bährens in the *Poet. Latini Minores* (1886).

On Vergil's life and literary qualities see Nettleship's *Ancient Lives of Vergil* (London, 1879); Ste.-Beuve, *Étude sur Virgile* (Paris, 1870); Sellar, *Roman Poets of the Augustan Age* (1877); a paper by Myers in his *Classical Essays;* and the admirable chapters on Vergil in Tyrrell's *Latin Poetry* (Boston, 1895); and Mackail's *Latin Literature* (New York, 1895). See also the numerous monographs cited in the Teuffel-Schwabe-Warr *Hist. of Roman Lit.*, vol. i. pp. 425–450. On Vergil in the Middle Ages, see above.

Verginius. See Virginius.

Verna. A domestic slave born of a slave. See Servus.

Verner's Law, so named from the brilliant discoveries of Karl Verner, first published in *Kuhn's Zeitschrift*, xxiii. 97–130 (1875). It embodies an explanation of certain apparent exceptions to the laws for the first or Teutonic shifting of consonants (see Grimm's Law), affecting the representation in Teutonic of the Indo-European voiceless explosives (tenues) *k*, *t*, *p*, and the voiceless sibilant *s*; thus, while the *th* of Eng. *tooth* corresponds regularly to the *t* of Greek *ὀδόντος*, in Eng. *hard* it is a *d* which represents the *t* of Greek *κρατύς*: so Germ. *bruder* and *vater*, representing Gothic *brōþar* and *fadar*, correspond to Lat. *frāter* and *pater*, both having *t*. There is divergence even within the forms of the same word. The *c* (*k*) of Lat. *dūco* is represented in Germ. *ziehen: gezogen* both by *h* and *g*. It appears that Indo-European *k*, *t*, *p* produce not only Teutonic *h*, *þ*(*th*), *f*, as set forth in Grimm's law, but also *g*, *d*, *b*. The essential feature of Verner's discovery, which explained this diversity, was the recognition that it was connected with the diversity of the original word-accent in Indo-European. The syllable on which this accent fell varied in different words and in different forms of the same word. This method of accentuation is partially preserved in Sanskrit and Greek, as well as in the Balto-Slavic languages; cf. Gr. *δέκα*: Skr. *dáça*; Gr. *ὀκτώ*: Skr. *aṣṭá*; Gr. *πέντε*: Skr. *páñca*; Gr. *ἔτι*: Skr. *áti*; Gr. *ἐγώ*: Skr. *ahám*; Gr. *γένος*: Skr. *jánas*; Gr. *κλυτός*: Skr. *çrutá-s*; Gr. *νέος*: Skr. *náva-s*; Gr. *ἡδύς*: Skr. *svādú-s*; Gr. *μέθυ*: Skr. *mádhu*; Gr. *ζυγόν*: Skr. *yugá-m*; Gr. *πούς*, *ποδός*, *πόδα*: Skr. *pád*, *padás*, *pădam*.

The law is this: Indo-Europ. medial *k*, *t*, *p*, *s* become Teutonic *h*, *þ*(*th*), *ꝼ*, *s*, which then, if associated with voiced sounds, become voiced (ʒ, *đ*, *ƀ*, *z*), when the Indo-Europ. accent rested upon any other than the preceding syllable; or, to state it in another form, I.-E. *k*, *t*, *p*, *ṣ* appear as *h*, *th*, *f*, *s* when the I.-E. accent immediately preceded, otherwise (except before *s* or *t*) as *g*, *d*, *b*, *z*.

Examples: K. Gr. *δέκα*: Goth. *taíhun*, "ten"; Skr. *çváçura-s*: Germ. *Schwäher*, "father-in-law"; on the other hand, Skr. *çvaçrú*: Germ. *Schwieger* (*mutter*), mother-in-law; Gr. *δεκάς*: Goth. *tigus*, number 10.—T. Skr. *bhrā́tar-*, Gr. *φράτωρ*: Goth. *brōþar*, Eng. *brother*, but Gr. *κλυτός*: Eng. *loud*; Gr. *ἑκατόν*: Goth. *hund*, Eng. *hund-red*; Skr. *kētú-s*: Goth. *háidus*, Eng. *-hood*; Skr. *damitá-s*: Eng. *tamed*.—P. Skr. *limpā́mi*: Goth. *bileiban*.—S. (Teutonic *z* becomes in Germ. and Eng. *r*) Skr. *bhárasē* 2 sg. indic. pres. pass: Goth. *baíraza*. The I.-E. causatives were accented on the syllable following the root; hence I.-E. *noséyeti* appears as Germ. *nähren*, Goth. *nasjan*, "make healthy," causat. of root *nes-*, cf. Gr. *νέομαι*, *νόστος*, "return," Goth. *ganisan*, Germ. *genesen*; I.-E. *loiséyeti* appears as Germ. *ehren* (cf. Eng. *lore*), Goth. *laisjan* "make to know," causat. of root *leis-*, cf. Lat. *līra*, Germ. *geleise*; I.-E. *woséyeti*, Skr. *vāsáyati* appears as Goth. *wasjan*, cf. Eng. *wear*, causat. of root *wes-*, in Lat. *vestis*, etc.; so compare Goth. *reisan*, Eng. rise, with Goth. *urraisjan*, O. Eng. *rǣran*, Eng. *rear*, "make rise." For a parallel effect upon *t*-roots, cf. Skr. *vartáyati* (I.-E. *wortéyeti*), Goth. *frawardjan*, "spoil," from root *wert-* of Lat. *verto*, Goth. *waírþan*; I.-E. *sontéyeti*, Goth. *sandjan*, Eng. *send*, from root *sent-*, "go," in Goth. *sinþs*, "time," Lat. *sentis*, "path"; I.-E. *loitéyeti*, "cause to go," Eng. *lead*, Germ. *leiten*, causat. of root *leit-*, in Goth. *leiþan*, Germ. *leiden*.

The difference of the consonants in Eng. *was*: *were* is due to the fact that in Indo-Europ. the perfect was accented on the root in the singular and on the ending in the plural, cf. Skr. *vḗda* (=*οἶδα*), "I know," but *vidmá* (=*ἴδμεν* for *ἰδμέν*), "we know." To a similar variation in the I.-E. accent are due the phenomena of "grammatical interchange," such as: Germ. *ziehen: gezogen*; *leiden: gelitten*; *schneiden: geschnitten*; Eng. *lose: forlorn* (Germ. *verloren*); Eng. *seethe: sodden*.

References: Verner, *Kuhn's Zeitschrift*, xxiii. 97 foll.; Wilmanns, *Deutsche Grammatik*, §§ 22–24; Brugmann, *Compar. Grammar of the Indo-Germ. Languages*, i. §§ 530 foll., 581; Skeat, *Principles of English Etymology*, First Series, ch. ix; King and Cookson, *Sounds and Inflexions*, pp. 256 foll.; Brandt, *German Grammar*, §§ 411, 416; and Giles, *Manual of Comp. Phil.*, § 104 (Oxford, 1894).

Verolamium or **Verulamium**. Now Old Verulam, near St. Albans. The chief town of the Catuellani in Britain, probably the residence of King Cassivellaunus, conquered by Caesar.

Veromandui. A people in Gallia Belgica, between the Nervii and Suessiones, in the modern Vermandois. Their chief town was Augusta Veromanduorum (St. Quentin).

Verōna. Now Verona; an important town in Gallia Cisalpina, on the river Athesis. It was originally the capital of the Euganei, but subsequently belonged to the Cenomani. At a still later time it was made a Roman colony, with the surname Augusta; and under the Empire it was one of the largest and most flourishing towns in the north of Italy. It was the birthplace of Catullus; and, according to some accounts, of the elder Pliny. There are still many Roman remains at Verona, and among others an amphitheatre in a good state of preservation.

Roman Amphitheatre at Verona.

Verres, Gaius. A Roman quaestor in B.C. 82 to Cn. Papirius Carbo, and who therefore at that period belonged to the Marian party. He, however, deserted Carbo and went over to Sulla, who sent him to Beneventum, where he received a share of the confiscated estates. Verres next appears as the legate of Cn. Cornelius Dolabella, praetor of Cilicia from 80 to 79, one of the most rapacious of the provincial governors. On the death of the regular quaestor, C. Malleolus, Verres became the pro-quaestor of Dolabella. In Verres, Dolabella found an active and unscrupulous agent, and, in return, connived at his excesses. But the pro-quaestor proved as faithless to Dolabella as he had been to Carbo, and turned evidence against him on his prosecution by M. Scaurus in 78. Verres was Praetor Urbanus in 74, and afterwards propraetor in Sicily, where he remained nearly three years (73–71). The extortions and exactions of Verres in the island have become notorious through the celebrated orations of Cicero. No class of the inhabitants of Sicily was exempted from his avarice, his cruelty, or his insults. The wealthy had money or works of art to yield up; the middle classes might be made to pay heavier imposts; and the exports of the vineyards, the arable land, and the loom be saddled with heavier burdens. By capricious changes or violent abrogation of their compacts, Verres reduced to beggary both the producers and the farmers of the revenue. His three years' rule desolated the island more effectually than the two recent Servile Wars and than the old struggle between Carthage and Rome for the possession of the island. So diligently did he employ his opportunities that he boasted of having amassed enough for a life of opulence, even if he were compelled to disgorge two-thirds of his plunder in stifling inquiry or purchasing an acquittal.

As soon as he left Sicily the inhabitants resolved to bring him to trial. They committed the prosecution to Cicero, who had been Lilybaean quaestor in Sicily in 75, and had promised his good offices to the Sicilians whenever they might demand them. Cicero entered heartily into the cause of the Sicilians, and spared no pains to secure a conviction of the great criminal. Verres was defended by Hortensius (q. v.) and was supported by the whole power of the aristocracy. At first his partisans attempted to stop the prosecution by bribes, flatteries, and menaces; but finding this to be impossible, they endeavoured to substitute a sham prosecutor in the place of Cicero. Hortensius therefore offered as prosecutor Q. Caecilius Niger, who had been quaestor to the defendant, had quarrelled with him, and had consequently, it was alleged, the means of exposing officially his abuse of the public money. But the Sicilians rejected Caecilius altogether, not merely as no match for Hortensius, but as foisted into the cause by the defendant or his advocate. By a technical process of the Roman law called *divinatio*, the *iudices*, without hearing evidence, determined from the arguments of counsel alone who should be appointed prosecutor. They decided in Cicero's favour. The oration which Cicero delivered on this occasion was the *Divinatio in Q. Caecilium*. The pretensions of Caecilius were thus set aside. Yet hope did not forsake Verres and his friends. Evidence for the prosecution was to be collected in Sicily itself. Cicero was allowed 110 days for the purpose. Verres once again attempted to set up a sham prosecutor, who undertook to impeach him for his former extortions in Achaia, and to gather the evidence in 108 days. But the new prosecutor never went even so far as Brundisium in quest of evidence, and the design was abandoned. Instead of the 110 days allowed, Cicero, assisted by his cousin Lucius, completed his researches in fifty, and returned with a mass of evidence and a crowd of witnesses gathered from all parts of the island. Hortensius now grasped at his last chance of an acquittal, and it was not an unlikely one. Could the impeachment be put off to the next year, Verres was safe. Hortensius himself would then be consul, with Q. Metellus for his colleague, and M. Metellus would be Praetor Urbanus. For every firm and honest *iudex* whom the upright M'. Acilius Glabrio, then Praetor Urbanus, had named, a partial or venal substitute would be found. Glabrio himself would give place as *quaesitor* or president of the court to M. Metellus, a partisan, if not a kinsman, of the defendant. It was already the month of July. The games to be exhibited by Cn. Pompey were fixed for the middle of August, and would occupy a fortnight; the Roman games would immediately succeed them, and thus forty days intervene between Cicero's charge and the reply of Hortensius, who again, by dexterous adjournments, would delay the proceedings until the Games of Victory and the commencement of the new year. Cicero therefore abandoned all thought of eloquence or display, and, merely introducing his case in the first of the Verrine orations, rested all his hopes of success on the weight of testimony alone. Hortensius was quite unprepared with counter-evidence, and after the first day he abandoned the cause of Verres. Before the nine days occupied in hearing evidence were over, Verres quitted the city in despair, and was condemned in his absence. He retired to Marseilles, retaining so many of his treasures of art as to cause eventually his proscription by M. Antony in 43. Of the seven Verrine orations of Cicero, two only, the *Divinatio* and the *Actio Prima*, were spoken, while the remaining five were compiled from the depositions after the verdict. Cicero's own division of the impeachment is the following:

(*a*) Preliminary.	1. In Q. Caecilium or. Divinatio. 2. Prooemium—Actio Prima—Statement of the Case.

These alone were spoken.

(*b*) Orations founded on the depositions.	3. Verres's official life to B.C. 73. 4. Iurisdictio Siciliensis. 5. Oratio Frumentaria. 6. " De Signis. 7. " De Suppliciis.

These were circulated as documents or pamphlets after the flight of Verres. The result of the whole affair was to make Cicero the leader of the Roman bar in place of Hortensius.

See accounts of this very famous case given in the lives of Cicero by Brückner (1852); Forsyth (1869); and Trollope (1880); and cf. the articles Cicero; Hortensius.

Verrius Flaccus, Marcus. A Roman freedman, "who obtained renown chiefly by his method of teaching. To exercise the wits of his pupils, says Suetonius, he used to pit against each other those of the same age, give them a subject to write upon, and reward the winner with a prize, generally in the shape of a fine or rare copy of some ancient author" (Nettleship's *Essays*, p. 203). He educated the grandsons of Augustus and died under Tiberius. He devoted himself to literary and antiquarian studies resembling those of the learned Varro. Thus, he wrote *De Orthographia* and *Rerum Memoria Dignarum Libri;* but his most important work was entitled *De Verborum Significatu*, which may claim to be the first Latin lexicon ever written. It was arranged alphabetically; it gave interpretations of obsolete words, and explained the meaning of the oldest institutions of the State, including its religious customs, etc. We possess only fragments of an abridgment made by Festus, and a further abridgment of the latter, dedicated to Charlemagne, by Paulus. (See FESTUS; PAULUS.) A calendar of Roman festivals drawn by him was set up in marble at Praeneste, near Rome; of this there are some fragments still preserved containing the months of January to April inclusive and December. These fragments are known as the Fasti Praenestini (*C. I. L.* i. p. 311). See Nettleship's *Lectures and Essays*, pp. 201–247 (Oxford, 1885).

Ver Sacrum (ἔτος ἱερόν). "A sacred spring." A dedication practised by the Italian tribes, whereby, in times of severe hardship, all the products of the succeeding spring, i. e. the months of March and April, were consecrated to the gods. All the fruits and cattle were actually offered up in sacrifice; while the children that were then born, as soon as they were grown up, were driven out of the country as forfeited to heaven, and required to seek a new home. Originally both men and children were undoubtedly sacrificed, but expatriation was substituted for death as the sentiment of mercy grew more general. Whole generations in this way left their country, those of the Sabine stock being led by the animals sacred to Mars—a bull, a woodpecker, or a wolf. In Rome, whose origin is traced back by many to a Ver Sacrum, the *pontifices* superintended the vow and its fulfilment. The Ver Sacrum was vowed for the last time in the Second Punic War, B.C. 217, after the battle of Lake Trasimenus (Livy, xxii. 10). The vow was not fulfilled, however, until twenty-one years afterwards, B.C. 195 and 194 (Livy, xxxiii. 44; xxxiv. 44). See Marquardt, *Staatsverwaltung*, iii. 281; and Ihering, *Die Vorgeschichte der Indoeuropaeer*.

Versipellis. "Turn-skin." One who changes his skin; thence, one who transforms himself, or is transformed, into another person's figure, as of Iupiter into Amphitryon (Plaut. *Amphitr.* 121. Prol.); and so a wily, dissembling fellow who can assume any character (id. *Bacch.* iv. 4, 12). But the term designates more especially a man transformed into a wolf—a "were-wolf" (*loup-garou*). Thus, in an ancient legend of Arcadia, every member of a certain family was changed into a wolf for nine years, and after that period resumed his original shape (Pliny, *H. N.* viii. 22). Belief in were-wolves is very ancient. Herodotus (iv. 105) says that among the Neuri, a semi-Scythian people, each man became a wolf for a few days every year —a story repeated by Mela (ii. 1). Vergil in the Eighth Eclogue makes his enchanter, Moeris, do the same. It is supposed that the notion arose from the stories of the "wolf-boys" of India, of whom Mowgli, in Rudyard Kipling's *Jungle Book*, stands to the modern reader as a type. The best were-wolf story in ancient literature is that told by Petronius (ch. 62). See also Herz, *Der Werwolf* (1862); and Baring-Gould's *Book of Werewolves* (1866).

Versūra. See FENUS.

Versus Memoriāles. Verses written to aid the memory; e. g. containing the names of the Muses (*Poet. Lat. Min.* iii. 243), the names of the winds (id. v. 383), on the constellations (id. v. 349 foll.). They are in Latin, and do not in all probability antedate the fifth or sixth century A.D. Cf. Isidor. *De Re Nat.* 37.

Verticordia. See VENUS.

Vertumnus or **Vortumnus.** An alleged Etruscan divinity, but this origin seems to be refuted by his genuine Roman name (from *verto*). The Romans connected Vertumnus with all occurrences to which the verb *verto* applies, such as the change of seasons, purchase and sale, the return of rivers to their proper beds, etc. But in reality the god was connected only with the transformation of plants and their progress from blossom to fruit. Hence the story that when Vertumnus was in love

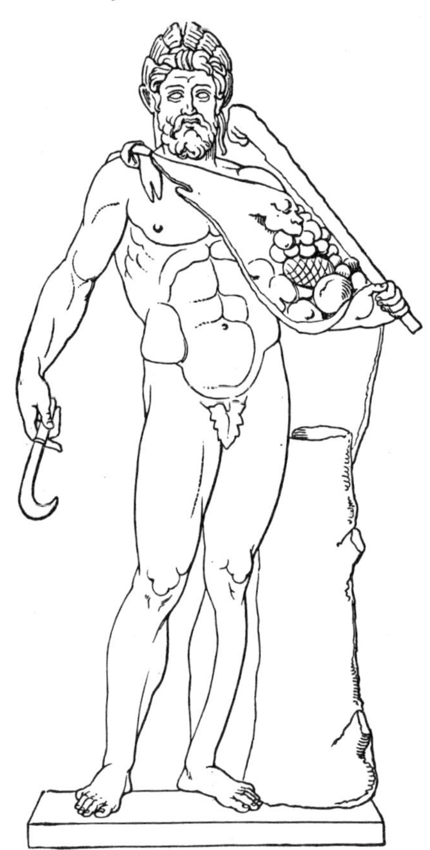

Vertumnus. (Berlin Museum.)

with Pomona he assumed all possible forms, until at last he gained his end by metamorphosing himself into a blooming youth. Gardeners accordingly offered to him the first produce of their gardens and garlands of budding flowers. The whole people celebrated a festival to Vertumnus on the 23d of August, under the name of the VORTUMNALIA, denoting the transition from the beautiful season of autumn to the less agreeable one. The importance of the worship of Vertumnus at Rome is evident from the fact that it was attended to by a special flamen (*flamen Vortumnalis*). See FLAMEN.

Veru (1) ὀβελός. A spit used for roasting meat (Varro, *L. L.* v. 127). It was often made of wood (Plin. *H. N.* xxx. 37; Verg. *Georg.* ii. 396; Ovid, *Fast.* ii. 363), sharpened at the point, so as to be driven through the meat (Sen. *Thyest.* 1063; Verg. *Aen.* i. 212), and placed over the fire (id. *Aen.* v. 103), and probably turned by the hand upon fire-dogs or andirons (*varae*). See VARA.

(2) (σαύνιον.) A missile weapon (Verg. *Aen.* vii. 665), adopted from the Samnites by the light infantry of the Romans. It had a sharp, round, iron point, like the spit after which it was named (Festus, s. v. "Samnites").

Verucŭlum and **Verictŭlum** (ὀβελίσκος). A small javelin carried by the Roman soldiers. It had an iron handle and was about three and a half feet long (Veget. *Mil.* ii. 15).

Verŭlae. Now Verdi; a town of the Hernici in Latium, southeast of Aletrium, and north of Frusino, subsequently a Roman colony.

Verulamium. See VEROLAMIUM.

Verus, L. AURELIUS. The colleague of M. Aurelius in the Empire, A.D. 161–169. He was born in 130, and his original name was L. Ceionius Commodus, was adopted by Hadrian in 136; and on the death of his father in 138, he was, in pursuance of the command of Hadrian, adopted, along with M. Aurelius, by M. Antoninus. On the death of Antoninus in 161, Verus succeeded him as emperor in conjunction with Marcus Aurelius. As to the events of his rule see AURELIUS. He died in A.D. 169.

Vescīnus Ager. A district of the Aurunci in Latium.

Vesēvus. See VESUVIUS.

Vesontio. Now Besançon; the chief town of the Sequani in Gallia Belgica, situated on the river Dubis (Doubs), which flowed around the town, with the exception of a space of 600 feet, on which stood a mountain, forming the citadel of the town. The place still has remains of a Roman aqueduct, an amphitheatre, and some other less important ruins.

Vespae Iudicium. A *jeu d'esprit* in Latin, probably written in the second or third century A.D. and consisting of 99 hexameters. It relates a contest between a cook and a baker with Vulcan for judge. The lines are neat and musical, and the sentiments show the writer to be a pagan in his faith and a rhetorician in his profession. A number of jokes and puns that are interspersed are rather academic in their tone. The poem is printed by Bährens in his *Poet. Lat. Min.* iv. 326. See Haupt, *Opuscula*, iii. 20.

Vespasiānus, TITUS FLAVIUS SABĪNUS. A Roman emperor from A.D. 70 to A.D. 79. He was born in the Sabine country on the 17th of November, A.D. 9. His father was a man of mean condition, of Reaté, in the country of the Sabini. His mother, Vespasia Polla, was the daughter of a *praefectus castrorum*, and the sister of a Roman senator. She was left a widow with two sons, Flavius Sabinus and Vespasian. Vespasian served as military tribune in Thrace, and was quaestor in Crete and Cyrenė. He was afterwards aedile and praetor. About this time he married Flavia Domitilla, the daughter of a Roman *eques*, by whom he had two sons, both of whom succeeded him. In the reign of Claudius he was sent into Germany as *legatus legionis*, and in 43 he held the same command in Britain, and reduced Vectis (Isle of Wight). He was consul in 51, and proconsul of Africa under Nero. He was at this time very poor, and was accused of getting money by dishonourable means; but he had a great military reputation, and was liked by the soldiers. Nero afterwards sent him to the East (66), to conduct the war against the Jews. His conduct of the Jewish War had raised his reputation, when the war broke out between Otho and Vitellius after the death of Galba. He was proclaimed emperor at Alexandria on the 1st of July, 69, and soon after all through the East. He reached Rome in the following year (70), leaving his son Titus to continue the war against the Jews. Titus took Jerusalem after a siege of five months; and a formidable insurrection of the Batavi, headed by Civilis, was put down about the same period. Vespasian, on his arrival at Rome, worked with great industry to restore order in the city and in the Empire. He disbanded some of the mutinous soldiers of Vitellius, and maintained discipline among his own. He co-operated in a friendly manner with the Senate in the public administration. The simplicity and frugality of his mode of life formed a striking contrast with the profusion and luxury of some of his predecessors,

Vespasian. (Naples Museum.)

and his example is said to have done more to reform the morals of Rome than all the laws which had ever been enacted. He lived more like a private person than a man who possessed supreme power: he was affable and easy of access to all persons. The personal anecdotes of such a man are some of the most instructive records of his reign. He was never ashamed of the meanness of his origin, and ridiculed all attempts to make out for him a distinguished genealogy. When Vologeses, the Parthian king, addressed to him a letter commencing in these terms, "Arsaces, king of kings, to Flavius Vespasianus," the answer began, "Flavius Vespasianus to Arsaces, king of kings."

If it be true, as it is recorded, that he was not annoyed at satire or ridicule, he exhibited an elevation of character almost unparalleled in one who filled so exalted a station. He knew the evil character of his son Domitian, and as long as he lived he kept him under proper restraint. The stories that are told of his avarice and of his modes of raising money, if true, detract from the dignity of his character; and it seems that he had a taste for petty saving and coarse humour. Yet it is admitted that he was liberal in all his expenditure for purposes of public utility. In 71 Titus returned to Rome, and both father and son triumphed together on account of the conquest of the Jews. The reign of Vespasian was marked by the conquest of North Wales and the island of Anglesey by Agricola, who was sent into Britain in 78. Vespasian also busied himself in securing the German frontier: he fortified the Agri Decumates and strengthened the defences of the Limes Germanicus. (See GERMANIA.) In Italy he reorganized the Praetorian Guard, forming one of nine cohorts composed of Italians only. His financial management was marked by great economy; but he was the author of some remarkable public works at Rome, the building of the magnificent Temple of Peace, and the rebuilding of the Temple of Iupiter Capitolinus. In the summer of 79, Vespasian, whose health was failing, went to spend some time at his paternal house in the mountains of the Sabini, but derived no benefit from treatment. He still attended to business, just as if he had been in perfect health, and, on feeling the approach of death, he said that an emperor should die standing; and in fact he did die in this attitude, on the 24th of June, 79, being sixty-nine years of age. His last words were characteristic of his somewhat cynical humour, "Methinks I am becoming a god" (*Ut puto, deus fio*) (Suet. *Vesp.*23; Dio Cass. cxvi.). See the account of Vespasian in Merivale's *History of the Romans under the Empire* (1865).

Vesta. An Italian goddess of the hearth, and more especially of the fire on the hearth, both in name and in nature akin to the Greek Hestia (q.v.), but worshipped by the Italian nations, particularly by the Latins, from ancient times independently of any connection with Greece. It has been shown that the worship of Vesta had its origin in the difficulty and the necessity of obtaining fire in primitive times. Hence, as even in the present time among savage tribes, arose the custom of keeping a fire always alight somewhere for the use of the community and of carrying fire thence for any new settlement. This custom was preserved by the conservatism of religion among civilized Greeks and Romans, after the necessity had ceased to exist, and the State-hearth was preserved in each Latin State, just as in Greece in the Prytanea; and in like fashion an outgoing settlement carried its sacred fire from the parent city. It was natural that from these observances the sacred flame itself should become personified as a goddess (Ovid, *Fast.* vi. 291) who presided over the hearth of each house, and in the State-hearth or sanctuary of Vesta over the whole commonwealth. Vesta was thus intimately connected with the Penates as deities of the household and of the State (see PENATES); and the fact that the sacred fire was brought from the parent city made the Romans trace back the origin of the cult to the more ancient Latin settlements, first to Lanuvium and Alba, and, after the idea of a Trojan origin prevailed, to Troy itself, whence it was supposed the sacred fire of Vesta as well as the Penates had come (Verg. *Aen.* ii. 296). To this cause belongs the ancient custom at Rome that praetors, consuls, and dictators, before they began their functions, sacrificed at Lanuvium, that town having been an ancient religious centre of the Latins. At Rome, as in other Latin cities, the sacred fire was tended and the service of Vesta maintained by a body of virgin priestesses, who lived together in a house (Atrium Vestae) to the southeast of the Forum, and under the northwest side of the Palatine, abutting on the Via Nova. This house, as rebuilt under Hadrian, was excavated in 1883, and from its character and the inscriptions (as late as the beginning of the fourth century A.D.) and sculptures found in it much additional light has been thrown on the Vestal service. See Jordan, *Das Tempel der Vesta und d. Haus der Vestalinnen* (Berlin, 1886); and Lanciani, in his *Ancient Rome*, ch. vi. (Boston, 1888).

It is no doubt right to assume that the Vestals represented the daughters of the chief in the primitive tribe, who maintained the State-fire in their father's hut. When Vesta was recognized as a personal deity it became necessary that the priestesses should dwell in a sort of nunnery, and that the goddess should have a separate temple; but this Aedes Vestae preserved the shape of the primitive chief's hut, and was a round building (see illustration under ROMA). The public worship of Vesta was maintained in this temple: her private worship belonged to every domestic hearth —in the earliest Roman houses in the *atrium*. In her aspect as a benign goddess of fire Vesta seems to have been akin to or identical with STATA MATER (q.v.). See Preuner, *Hestia-Vesta* (Tübingen, 1864); Maes, *Vesta e Vestali* (Rome, 1883); the discussion by Frazer in the (English) *Journal of Philology*, vol. xiv., and the articles LARES, PENATES, and VESTALES, in this Dictionary.

Vestālcs or Virgĭnes Vestāles. Vestal Virgins; the priestesses of Vesta. At Rome their number was at first four, but had already been increased to six during the last years of the kings. Every girl possessing the necessary qualification was liable to be called on to undertake the duty, and no exemption was granted, except upon very strict conditions. The office was confined to girls of not less than six and not more than ten years of age, without personal blemish, of free, respectable families, whose parents were still alive and resident in Italy. The choice was made by lot out of a number of twenty, nominated by the Pontifex. The virgin appointed to the priestly office immediately quitted her father's authority and entered that of the goddess. After her inauguration by the Pontifex, she was taken into the Atrium of Vesta, her future place of abode, was duly attired, and shorn of her hair. The time of service was by law thirty years, ten of which were set apart for learning, ten for performing, and ten for teaching the duties. At the end of this time leave was granted to the Vestals to lay aside their priesthood, return into private life, and marry. They seldom took advantage of this permission. They were under the control of the Pontifex, who, in the name of the goddess, exercised over them paternal authority. He administered corporal chastisement if they neglected their duties, more particularly if they allowed the sacred fire to go out;

and, if any one of them violated her vow of chastity, he had her carried on a bier to the Campus Sceleratus, near the Colline Gate, beaten with rods, and immured alive. Her seducer was scourged to death. In fact, it has been noted that the Vestals typified to the Romans womanly chastity, just as *flamen* and *flaminica* typified the purity of the marriage-relation.

No man was allowed to enter the apartments of the Vestals. Their service consisted in maintaining and keeping pure the eternal fire in the Temple of Vesta, watching the sacred shrines, performing the sacrifices, offering the daily and, when necessary, the special prayers for the welfare of the nation, and taking part in the feasts of Vesta, Tellus, and Bona Dea. They were dressed entirely in white, with a coronet-shaped head-band (*infula*), and ornamented with ribbons (*vittae*) suspended from it, and at a sacrifice covered with a white veil or hood (*suffibulum*) made of a piece of white woollen cloth with a purple border, rectangular in form. It was folded over the head and fastened in front below the throat by a *fibula* (Festus, p. 340, ed. Müller). The chief part in the sacrifices was taken by the eldest, the Virgo Vestalis Maxima.

Vestal Virgin.

The Vestal Virgins enjoyed various distinctions and privileges. When they went out, they were accompanied by a lictor, to whom even the consul gave place; at public games they had a place of honour; they were under a guardian, and were free to dispose of their property; they gave evidence without the customary oath; they were, on account of their incorruptible character, intrusted with important wills and public treaties; death was the penalty for injuring their person; those whom they escorted were thereby protected from any assault. To meet them by chance saved the criminal who was being led away to punishment; and to them, as to men of distinguished merit, was assigned the honour of burial in the Forum. See the works cited under VESTA.

Vestibŭlum. An entrance-court before a Roman house. See DOMUS.

Vestīni. A Sabellian people in Central Italy, lying between the Apennines and the Adriatic Sea, and separated from Picenum by the river Matrinus, and from the Marrucini by the river Aternus. They were conquered by the Romans in B.C. 328, and from this time appear as the allies of Rome (App. *B. C.* i. 39, 52).

Vestiplĭca. A lady's maid who had charge of her mistress's wardrobe (Quint. *Decl.* 363).

Vestis. The generic name for clothing. See, for the principal articles of wearing apparel, the articles ABOLLA; BRACAE; CALCEUS; CHITON; CHLAMYS; CREPIDA; FIMBRIAE; MANICA; PALLA; PALLIUM; PETASUS; PILLEUS; SAGUM; SERICUM; SOCCUS; STOLA; TOGA; TUNICA; and consult Weiss, *Kostümkunde* (1872); Köhler, *Trachten der Völker* (1872); Teirich, *Blätter für Kunstgewerbe*, vol. iv. (1875); Von Heyden, *Tracht der Kulturvölker Europas* (Leipzig, 1889); and the illustrations in Hope's *Costume of the Ancients* (2d ed. 1875); Moyn-Smith's *Ancient Greek Female Costume* (1882); and Racinet, *Le Costume Historique*, vol. ii. (Paris, 1887).

Vestispĭca. A lady's maid whose duty it was to look over her mistress's wardrobe and keep it in repair (Plaut. *Trinum.* ii. 1, 29).

Vesuvius, also called **Vesēvus**, **Vesbius**, and **Vesvius** (τὸ Βέσβιον ὄρος). A volcanic mountain in Campania, rising out of the plain southeast of Neapolis (Naples). There are no records of any eruption of Vesuvius before the Christian era, but the ancient writers were aware of its volcanic nature from the igneous appearance of its rocks. In A.D. 63 the volcano gave the first symptoms of agitation in an earthquake, which occasioned considerable damage to several towns in its vicinity; and on the 24th of August, A.D. 79, occurred the first great eruption of Vesuvius, which overwhelmed the cities of Stabiae, Herculaneum, and Pompeii. It was in this eruption that the elder Pliny lost his life. See HERCULANEUM; POMPEII.

Vetĕra Castra. The chief military station of the Roman troops on the Lower Rhine, near the modern Birten (Tac. *Ann.* i. 48).

Veterāni. During the later Republican period and under the Empire a term applied to those who at the end of their time of military service retired from the legion. They were kept with the army under the standard, under which they were taken to the military colonies appointed for them, and again served there for an indefinite period. See EVOCATI; EXERCITUS; LEGIO; and VEXILLARII.

Veterinarius. A veterinary; one who prescribed for cattle, horses, and dogs (Columel. vi. 8, 1; vii. 5, 14).

Vetranio. A Roman who commanded the legions in Illyria and Pannonia in A.D. 350, when Constans was treacherously destroyed, and was proclaimed emperor by his troops; but at the end of ten months resigned in favour of Constantius (Amm. Marcell. xv. 1; xxi. 8).

Vettius, LUCIUS. A Roman *eques*, in the pay of Cicero in B.C. 63, to whom he gave some valuable information respecting the Catilinarian conspiracy. In 59 he accused Curio, Cicero, L. Lucullus, and many other distinguished men, of having formed a conspiracy to assassinate Pompey. Cicero regarded this accusation as the work of Caesar, who used the tribune Vatinius as his instrument. On the day after he had given his evidence, Vettius was found strangled in prison (Suet. *Iul.* 17, 20; Cic. *In Vatin.* 10, 11; id. *Ad Att.* ii. 24). See CATILINA.

Vettōnes or **Vectōnes.** A people in the interior of Lusitania, east of the Lusitani and west of the Carpetani, extending from the Durius (Douro) to the Tagus.

Vetulonia, Vetulonium, or **Vetulonii.** An ancient city of Etruria, and one of the twelve cities of the Etruscan confederation. (See ETRURIA.) From this city the Romans are said to have borrowed the insignia of their magistrates—the fasces, sella curulis, and toga praetexta—as well as the use of the brazen trumpet in war (Dionys. iii. 51; Strabo, p. 220; Flor. i. 5; Sil. Ital. viii. 483). Its site has been discovered near a small village called Magliano, between the river Osa and the Albegna, and about eight miles inland.

Veturia Gens. A gens both patrician and plebeian, whose most distinguished families bore the names of CALVĪNUS, CICURĪNUS, and PHILO.

Veturius Mamurius. A mythical personage, said in Roman legend to have been the armourer who made the eleven *ancilia* exactly like the one that was sent from heaven in the reign of Numa (Plut. *Numa*, 13). His praises formed one of the chief subjects of the songs of the Salii. The name is really equivalent to Mars Vetus—the ancient Mars. This "Old Mars" was represented by a man clothed in skins who was driven out of the city (Lyd. iv. 36) to symbolize the old season of wintry darkness driven out before the new spring year. Similar ceremonies to represent the driving out of winter have been observed in the folklore of other countries. See SALII.

Vetus, ANTISTIUS. (1) Propraetor in Further Spain about B.C. 68, under whom Caesar served as quaestor (Plut. *Caes.* 5). (2) GAIUS, son of the preceding, quaestor in B.C. 61, and tribune of the plebs in 57, when he supported Cicero in opposition to Clodius. In the Civil War he espoused Caesar's party, and we find him in Syria in 45, fighting against Q. Caecilius Brassus. In 34 Vetus carried on war against the Salassi, and in 30 was consul suffectus. He accompanied Augustus to Spain in 25, and on the illness of the emperor continued the war against the Cantabri and Astures, whom he reduced to submission (Cic. *Ad Q. Fr.* ii. 1; Dio Cass. xlvii. 27, liii. 25; Flor. iv. 12, 21). (3) LUCIUS, Roman consul with the emperor Nero, A.D. 55. In 58 he commanded a Roman army in Germany, and formed the project of connecting the Mosella (Moselle) and the Arar (Saône) by a canal, and thus forming a communication between the Mediterranean and the Northern Ocean, as troops could be conveyed down the Rhone and the Saône into the Moselle through the canal, and down the Moselle into the Rhine, and so into the Ocean. Vetus put an end to his life in 65, in order to anticipate his sentence of death, which Nero had resolved upon (Tac. *Ann.* xiii. 11, 53; xiv. 57; xvi. 10).

Vexillarii. The oldest class of Roman veterans, who, at the end of their period of service, retired from the legion, but were kept together under a standard (*vexillum*) up to the time of their final dismissal. They formed, by the side of the legion, a select corps like the *evocati* of earlier times. They were exempt from ordinary service, and only bound to take part in actual fighting. See EVOCATI.

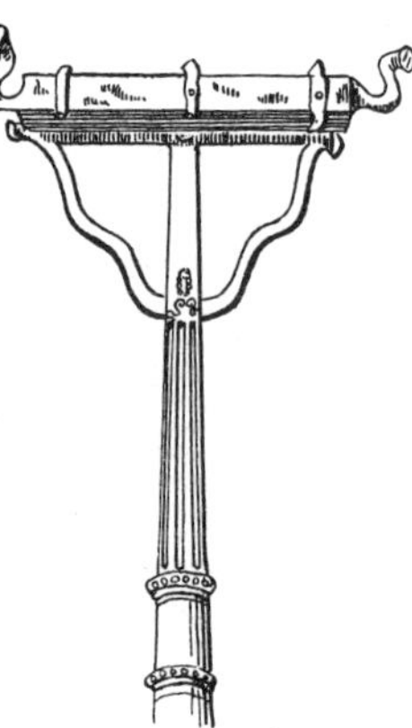

Staff for Vexillum. (From a bronze original, given by Rich.)

Vexillum. The Latin name for a four-cornered flag (Tertull. *Apol.* 16), attached to a cross-pole, and carried by the *vexillarius*. (See SIGNUM). Every squadron (*turma*), and probably every detachment of a body of troops which formed a separate command, had a red, white, or purple *vexillum* of this kind, and hence were themselves called a *vexillum*, or sometimes a *vexillatio*. The latter word, however, from the end of the third century A.D., signifies a squadron of cavalry. At Rome a red flag was displayed on the Capitol during the deliberations of the Comitia Centuriata, and was in time of war planted as the signal for battle on the general's tent or the admiral's ship. Vexilla served also as marks of distinction for the higher officers. See LABARUM; SIGNUM.

Via (ὁδός). A road. The earliest roads in Greece were the sacred ways, which led to the most important religious centres, where national festivals were celebrated, such festivals also serving the purpose of public markets or fairs. In general, the Greeks set a high value on well-levelled roads, which made travelling easy; but, in the best days of Greece, only unpaved roads were known, paved roads being of comparatively late origin.

The finest work in ancient road-making was that done by the Romans, who, mainly for military purposes, connected Rome with her newly acquired provinces by means of high-roads. They laid out their roads as far as possible in straight lines. The nature of the ground was almost entirely disregarded; where mountains intervened they were broken through, and interposing streams and valleys were spanned with bridges and viaducts.

The first Roman high-road, which, even in its present condition, is worthy of admiration, was the Via Appia, so called after the censor Appius

Via Appia, near Ariccia. (Canina.)

Claudius, who constructed it. It was made in B.C. 312 to join Rome to Capua, and was afterwards continued as far as Brundisium. This "queen of roads," *regina viarum* (Stat. *Silv.* ii. 2, 12), was a stone causeway, constructed, according to the nature of the country, with an embankment either beneath or beside it, and was of such a width that two broad wagons could easily pass each other. The surface was paved with polygonal blocks of hard stone, generally basalt, fitted closely together, and so laid down that the middle of the road was at a higher level than the sides, to allow the rain-water to run off. According to a subsequent method, the Roman roads first received a foundation of rubble or *breccia*, on which rested a layer of flat stones eight inches thick; above this was an equally thick layer of stones set in lime, which was covered by another layer of rubble about three inches deep. Above the rubble was laid down the pave-

Pavement of Via Appia. (Piranesi.)

ment proper, consisting of either hard stone (*silex*) or else irregular blocks of basaltic lava.

In the time of the emperor Hadrian, the cost of constructing such a road amounted to $4500 per Roman mile (about ⅘ English mile). From the end of the second century B.C. posts set up at a distance of 1000 paces from each other served to measure distances. See MILIARIUM.

The making and maintenance of the roads in Italy were provided for at the expense of the *aerarium*, or State treasury. During the republican age the roads were under the supervision of the censors. From the time of Augustus they were under imperial officials entitled *curatores viarum*. In the provinces, in general, the cost of the military roads, and indeed of all public works, was defrayed out of the provincial taxes. In the imperial provinces soldiers were also frequently employed in constructing roads. In a few cases toll was levied by special imperial permission. The following list of the great Roman roads that issued directly from the capital will be convenient for reference:

I. The VIA APPIA, the Great South Road. It was in perfect repair when Procopius wrote, long after the devastating inroads of the northern barbarians; and even to this day the cuttings through hills and masses of solid rock, the filling up of hollows, the bridging of ravines, the substructions to lessen the rapidity of steep descents, and the embankments over swamps, demonstrate the vast sums and the prodigious labour that must have been lavished on its construction. It issued from the Porta Capena, and, passing through Aricia, Tres Tabernae, Appii Forum, Tarracina, Fundi, Formiae, Minturnae, Sinuessa, and Casilinum, terminated at Capua, but was eventually extended through Calatia and Caudium to Beneventum, and finally from thence through Venusia, Tarentum, and Uria, to Brundisium.

The ramifications of the Via Appia most worthy of notice are:

(*a*) The VIA SETĪNA, which connected it with Setia.

(*b*) The VIA DOMITIĀNA struck off at Sinuessa, and, keeping close to the shore, passed through Liternum, Cumae, Puteoli, Neapolis, Herculaneum, Oplonti, Pompeii, and Stabiae to Surrentum, making the complete circuit of the Bay of Naples.

(*c*) The VIA CAMPĀNA or CONSULĀRIS, from Capua to Cumae, sending off a branch to Puteoli, and another through Atella to Neapolis.

(*d*) The VIA AQUILLIA began at Capua, and ran south through Nola and Nuceria to Salernum; from thence, after sending off a branch to Paestum, it took a wide sweep inland through Eburi and the region of the Mons Alburnus up the valley of the Tanager; it then struck south through the very heart of Lucania and Bruttium, and, passing Nerulum, Interamnia, and Consentia, returned to the sea at Vibo, and thence through Medma to Rhegium. This road sent off a branch near the sources of the Tanager, which ran down to the sea at Blanda or the Laus Sinus, and then continued along the whole line of the Bruttian coast through Laus and Terina to Vibo, where it joined the main stem.

(*e*) The VIA EGNATIA began at Beneventum, struck north through the country of the Hirpini to Equus Tuticus, entered Apulia at Aecae, and, passing through Herdonia, Canusium, and Rubi, reached the Adriatic at Barium, and followed the coast through Egnatia to Brundisium.

(*f*) The VIA TRAIĀNA began at Venusia and ran in a nearly straight line across Lucania to Heraclea on the Sinus Tarentinus; thence following, southward, the line of the east coast, it passed through Thurii, Crotona, and Scyllacium, and completed the circuit of Bruttium by meeting the Via Aquillia at Rhegium.

(*g*) A VIA MINUCIA is mentioned by Cicero, and a VIA NUMICIA by Horace, both of which seem to have passed through Samnium from north to south, connecting the Valerian and Aquillian, and cutting the Appian and Latin Ways. Their course is unknown. Some believe them to be one and the same.

II. The VIA LATĪNA, another great line leading to Beneventum, but keeping a course farther inland than the Via Appia. Soon after leaving the city, it sent off a short branch (VIA TUSCULĀNA) to Tusculum, and, passing through Compitum Anagninum, Ferentium, Frusino, Fregellae, Fabrateria, Aquinum, Casinum, Venafrum, Teanum, Allifae, and Telesia, joined the Via Appia at Beneventum.

A cross-road, called the VIA HADRIĀNA, running from Minturnae through Suessa Aurunca to Teanum, connected the Via Appia with the Via Latina.

III. From the Porta Esquilina issued the VIA LABICĀNA, which, passing Labicum, fell into the Via Latina at the station ad Bivium, thirty miles from Rome.

IV. The VIA PRAENESTĪNA, originally the VIA GABĪNA, issued from the same gate with the former. Passing through Gabii and Praenestĕ, it joined the Via Latina just below Anagnia.

V. Passing over the VIA COLLATĪNA as of little importance, we find the VIA TIBURTĪNA, which issued from the Porta Tiburtina, and, proceeding northeast to Tibur, a distance of about twenty miles, was continued from thence, in the same direction, under the name of the VIA VALERIA, and, traversing the country of the Sabines, passed through Carseoli and Corfinium to Aternum on the Adriatic, thence to Adria, and so along the coast to Castrum Truentinum, where it fell into the Via Salaria.

A branch of the Via Valeria led to Sublaqueum, and was called VIA SUBLACENSIS. Another branch extended from Adria along the coast southward through the country of Frentani to Larinum, being called, as some suppose, VIA FRENTĀNA APŬLA.

VI. The VIA NOMENTĀNA, anciently FICULNENSIS, ran from the Porta Collina, crossed the Anio to Nomentum, and, a little beyond, fell into the Via Salaria at Eretum.

VII. The VIA SALARIA, also from the Porta Collina (passing Fidenae and Crustumerium), ran north and east through Sabinum and Picenum to Reatĕ and Asculum Picenum. At Castrum Truentinum it reached the coast, which it followed until it joined the Via Flaminia at Ancona.

VIII. Next comes the VIA FLAMINIA, the Great North Road, commenced in the censorship of C. Flaminius, and carried ultimately to Ariminum. It issued from the Porta Flaminia, and proceeded nearly north to Ocriculum and Narnia in Umbria. Here a branch struck off, making a sweep to the east through Interamna and Spoletium, and fell again into the main trunk (which passed through Mevania) at Fulginia. It continued through Fa-

The Via Appia Restored. (Falke.)

num Flaminii and Nuceria, where it again divided, one line running nearly straight to Fanum Fortunae on the Adriatic, while the other, diverging to Ancona, continued from thence along the coast to Fanum Fortunae, where the two branches, uniting, passed on to Ariminum through Pisaurum. From thence the Via Flaminia was extended under the name of the VIA AEMILIA, and traversed the heart of Cisalpine Gaul through Bononia, Mutina, Parma, Placentia (where it crossed the Po), to Mediolanum. From this point branches were sent off through Bergomum, Brixia, Verona, Vicentia, Patavium, and Aquileia to Tergesté on the east, and through Novaria, Vercelli, Eporedia, and Augusta Praetoria to the Alpis Graia on the west, besides another branch in the same direction through Ticinum and Industria to Augusta Taurinorum. Nor must we omit the VIA POSTUMIA, which struck from Verona right down across the Apennines to Genoa, passing through Mantua and Cremona, crossing the Po at Placentia, and so through Iria, Dertona, and Libarna, sending off a branch from Dertona to Asta.

Of the roads leading out of the Via Flaminia in the immediate vicinity of Rome, the most important is the VIA CASSIA, which, diverging near the Pons Mulvius, and passing not far from Veii, traversed Etruria through Baccanae, Sutrium, Vulsinii, Clusium, Arretium, Florentia, Pistoria, and Luca, joining the Via Aurelia at Luna.

(*a*) The VIA AMERĪNA broke off from the Via Cassia near Baccanae, and held north through Falerii, Tuder, and Perusia, reuniting itself with the Via Cassia at Clusium.

(*b*) Not far from the Pons Mulvius the VIA CLODIA separated from the Via Cassia, and, proceeding to Sabaté on the Lacus Sabatinus, there divided into two, the principal branch passing through central Etruria to Rusellae, and thence due north to Florentia, the other passing through Tarquinii, and then falling into the Via Aurelia.

(*c*) Beyond Baccanae the VIA CIMĪNA branched off, crossing the Mons Ciminus, and rejoining the Via Cassia near Fanum Voltumnae.

IX. The VIA AURELIA, the Great Coast Road, issued originally from the Porta Ianiculensis, and subsequently from the Porta Aurelia. It reached the coast at Alsium, and followed the shore of the lower sea, along Etruria and Liguria, by Genua, as far as Forum Iulii in Gaul. In the first instance it extended no farther than Pisa.

X. The VIA PORTUENSIS kept the right bank of the Tiber to Portus Augusti.

XI. The VIA OSTIENSIS originally passed through the Porta Trigemina, afterwards through the Porta Ostiensis, and kept the left bank of the Tiber to Ostia. From thence it was continued, under the name of VIA SEVERIĀNA, along the coast southward through Laurentum, Antium, and Circaei, till it joined the Via Appia at Tarracina. The VIA LAURENTĪNA, leading direct to Laurentum, seems to have branched off from the Via Ostiensis at a short distance from Rome.

XII. Lastly, the VIA ARDEATĪNA, from Rome to Ardea. According to some, this branched off from the Via Appia.

Travelling on the public roads was facilitated by the establishment of (*a*) *mutationes* (ἀλλαγαί) or posting-houses, where horses were changed and vehicles were obtainable if required; and (*b*) *mansiones* (καταλύσεις), stations, caravansaries, or resting-places, where the journey could be conveniently broken. The towns and places where a halt on one ground or the other could be made are frequently detailed in the Antonine Itinerary. See CURSUS PUBLICUS; ITINERARIA.

The following illustration of a part of the Via Stabiana at Pompeii shows four stepping-stones.

Via Stabiana at Pompeii, with Stepping-stones. (From a photograph.)

They are to be found in nearly every street in the town, whatever its breadth. The narrower streets are practically blocked by single large stones in their centres; the broader streets are crossed by rows, containing from two to five stones. Their shape is, generally, a flat-topped oval: larger and smaller stones lying side by side. They measure, very commonly, about three feet by eighteen inches, and have their longer axis parallel to the footway on either side of the street. The height of the footway ranges from twelve to eighteen inches above the carriage-way, and the particular height is, in most cases, that of the stepping-stones also. The surface of the street being elliptical, the stone on the centre stands slightly higher than those at the sides. Many streets are marked with wheel-ruts, some of them deeply cut. They are found both in the interstices between the stepping-stones and elsewhere. The distance from rut to rut measures, as a rule, one yard, which was, accordingly, the gauge of the ordinary vehicles. Some special consideration of these stepping-stones is desirable.

Until the reign of Septimius Severus (A.D. 193–211) riding and driving, both in Rome and in the provincial towns, were closely restricted, and at times forbidden, by law (*C. I. L.* i. 206; Marquardt, *Privatleben*, ii. 727–738). Claudius (A.D. 41–54) forbade travellers to drive in carriages through provincial towns (Sueton. *Claud.* c. 25). Marcus Aurelius (A.D. 161–180) again forbade riding and driving in provincial towns. Under Severus carriages, in Rome at least, seem to have been more commonly used (Dio Cass. lxiv. 4).

Thus, the street-traffic of the ordinary Roman provincial town seems to have resembled that of the Tangier or Tetuan of to-day. Heavy burdens were carried on the backs of horses, mules, or cattle. Walking was the rule, riding on horseback or in a litter was the exception, driving almost unknown. Before the date of the edict of Claudius, and perhaps later, the law was probably indulgent to towns such as Baiae and Pompeii. Thither came the "carriage-company" of Rome to seek health and spend money. In the case of Pompeii carriages and horses were, beyond a doubt, confined to certain streets. An extant inscription shows that the station of the *cisiarii* was not even within the town walls. (See CISIUM.) Other streets were always reserved for foot-passengers, and possibly for litters. Others, again, once open to all traffic, and still bearing the marks of wheels, were afterwards closed to all but foot-passengers by huge stepping-stones or iron gratings.

The deep ruts already mentioned were the natural result of confining the traffic to a few streets. None of these were broad enough to allow of any considerable variation of the track, even had the fixed stepping-stones presented no additional difficulty. Moreover, there is evidence that some of the existing pavements bore traffic for at least 120 years. It is not surprising that even a small amount of wheeled traffic, unrelieved by the use of springs, and acting on the same stones for so many years, should have left deep traces behind.

The reasons for the erection of very large stepping-stones were, no doubt, at once local and practical. Pompeii occupies the summit and slopes of a small hill. Hence the lower streets, according to the drainage level of the ground, received the rain-water and refuse of the upper. In times of heavy rain the lower streets must have flowed like a torrent. No sewerage-system could have at once mastered the downward rush of the water. Indeed a similar sight may now be witnessed, during the winter rains, in the heavily paved streets of Florence, where stepping-stones of the largest size would not be out of place. At Pompeii, where the lie of the ground, together with the close-set stone surface and sides of the streets, provided a ready-made watercourse, sidewalks of substantial height were absolutely necessary to foot-passengers. The means of crossing from one sidewalk to another, in any weather, were therefore naturally provided by stepping-stones of corresponding size.

See Bergier, ***Histoire des Grands Chemins de l'Empire Romain*** (Brussels, 1736); Burn, ***Rome and the Campagna*** (London, 1870); and Middleton, ***Remains of Ancient Rome*** (1892).

Viădus. Now the Oder; a river of Germany, falling into the Baltic (Ptol. ii. 11, 2).

Viands. See VICTUS.

Viatĭcum (ἐφόδιον). Anything necessary as a preparation for a journey, as food, money, clothes, etc. (Pliny, *Epist.* vii. 12). It is also technically applied to the provision made by the State for an official when going upon a public mission (also called *legativum*), generally furnished by contractors (*redemptores*) for a fixed sum (Livy, xli. 1; Dio Cass. liii. 15). See Mommsen, *Röm. Staatsrecht*, i. 301.

Viātor ("roadster"). A subordinate official (see APPARITORES) employed by the Roman magistrates for sending a message or a summons, or for executing an arrest. The consuls and praetors had probably three *decuriae* of viatores; the tribunes had a special *decuria*, as also had the quaestors of the Treasury, and the officers who took their place under the Empire—i. e. the *praefecti aerarii;* also the aediles, the *tresviri capitales*, and the *quattuorviri viis purgandis*. They also appear in connection with provincial governors and sacerdotal bodies (Cic. *De Sen.* 16; Livy, vi. 15; Gell. xiii. 12).

Vibius Pansa. See PANSA.

Vibius Sequester. See SEQUESTER.

Vibo. Now Bivona; the Roman form of the Greek name HIPPONIUM, a town situated on the southwest coast of Bruttium, and on a gulf called after it SINUS VIBONENSIS, or HIPPONIĀTES. It is said to have been founded by the Locri Epizephyrii; but it was destroyed by the elder Dionysius, who transplanted its inhabitants to Syracuse. It was afterwards restored; and at a later time it fell into the hands of the Bruttii, together with the other Greek cities on this coast. It was taken from the Bruttii by the Romans, who colonized it B.C. 194, and called it VIBO VALENTIA. Cicero speaks of it as a municipium; and in the time of Augustus it was one of the most flourishing cities in the south of Italy.

Vicentia or **Vicetia**, less correctly **Vincentia.** Now Vicenza; a town on the river Togisonus in Venetia, in the north of Italy, and a Roman municipium.

Vicesĭma Hereditātum. See VECTIGALIA.

Vicesĭma Libertātis. See VECTIGALIA.

Victĭma (ἱερεῖον). See SACRIFICIUM.

Victor, SEX. AURELIUS. A Latin author who flourished in the middle of the fourth century under the emperor Constantius and his successors. He was born of humble parents, but rose to distinction by his zeal in the cultivation of literature. Having attracted the attention of Julian when at Sirmium, he was appointed by him governor of one division of Pannonia (Amm. Marc. xxi. 10, 6). At a subsequent period he was made city prefect by Theodosius, and is perhaps the same as the Sex. Aurelius Victor who was consul with Valentinian in A.D. 373. The following works, which present in a condensed form a continuous record of Roman affairs from the fabulous ages down to the death of the emperor Theodosius, have all been ascribed to this writer; but evidence upon which the determination of authorship depends is slender, and in all probability the third alone belongs to the Sex. Aurelius Victor whom we have noticed above. (*a*) *Origo Gentis Romanae*, in twenty-three chapters, containing the annals of the Roman race, from Ianus and Saturnus down to the era of Romulus. It is probably a production of some of the later grammarians who were desirous of prefixing a suitable introduction to the series. (*b*) *De Viris Illustribus Urbis Romae*, in eighty-six chapters, commencing with the birth of Romulus and Remus, and concluding with the death of Cleopatra, a work of merit, though of unknown authorship. (*c*) *De Caesaribus*, in forty-two chapters, exhibiting short biographies of the emperors, from Augustus to Constantius. There is no reason to doubt that this was a genuine work of Aurelius Victor. He uses Suetonius to a great extent in the earlier *Lives*. (*d*) *Epitome de Caesaribus*, in forty-eight chapters, beginning with Augustus and concluding with Theodosius. There are editions of these four works by Arntzen (1733) and by Schröter (1831). The *Origo* is edited separately by Sepp (Munich, 1879), and the *De Vir. Illustr.* by Keil (Breslau, 1872).

Victoria. The Roman goddess of Victory, said to be the daughter of Minerva, by whose command a temple to her was said to have been erected on the Palatine by Evander. In later times there were at least three sanctuaries in Rome that bore her name. For the Greek goddess of Victory, see NIKÉ.

Victoriātus. A Roman coin struck under the Republic, and named from its having borne as its "type" an image of Victory crowning a trophy. Its weight was about forty-five grains—i. e. three-fourths of the *denarius*, but was later reduced to equal half a *denarius*. The half victoriatus was also coined.

Victorīnus. One of the Thirty Tyrants, was the third of the usurpers who in succession ruled Gaul during the reign of Gallienus. He was assassinated at Agrippina by one of his own officers in A.D. 268, after reigning somewhat more than a year. See THIRTY TYRANTS.

Victorīnus Afer, GAIUS MARIUS. A scholar of African birth who taught rhetoric at Rome in the middle of the fourth century, with so much reputation that his statue was erected in the Forum of Trajan. In his old age he embraced Christianity; and when the edict of Julian prohibiting Christians from giving instruction in polite literature was promulgated, Victorinus chose to shut up his school rather than deny his religion. Besides his commentaries on the Scriptures, and other theological works, many of which are extant, Victorinus wrote: (*a*) *Commentarius* or *Expositio in Ciceronis Libros de Inventione*, the best edition of which is in the fifth volume of Orelli's edition of Cicero; (*b*) *Ars Grammatica de Orthographia et Ratione Metrorum*, a complete and voluminous treatise upon metres, in four books, printed in Keil's *Grammatici Latini*, vi. 1.

Victorius, PETRUS (PIETRO VETTORI). A great classical scholar and critic of the time of the Italian Renaissance, born in 1499 and died in 1584. He published editions of Cicero (with commentary), Sophocles (with commentary and scholia), Aeschylus, Aristotle's *Rhetoric*, *Ethics*, *Politics*, *Poetics*, *De Partibus Animalium* (translation and commentary), Xenophon's *Memorabilia*, Terence, Sallust, Varro *De Re Rustica*, Demetrius Phalereus *De Elocutione*, Dionysius, Isaeus, Dinarchus, Hipparchus (in part), Clemens Alexandrinus, and Porphyrius *De Abstinentia*, and thirty-eight books of readings (*Variae Lectiones*). See his life by Bandini (Florence, 1758); and Creuzer, *Opuscula*, pp. 21-36.

Victrix. An epithet of Venus (q. v.).

Victus; Cibus. Generic terms for food. Both the Greeks and the Romans gave much attention to gastronomy, the latter people, however, getting their knowledge of scientific cookery from the former. The chief sources of our information are, apart from the many casual allusions in the classic writers in general, Athenaeus (whose *Deipnosophistae* is full of curious lore regarding food, cookery, and the *ana* of distinguished epicures), Pliny the Elder, and the pseudo-Apicius. (See APICIUS; ATHENAEUS; PLINIUS.) As early as the second century B.C. there existed special dictionaries of terms employed in cookery. See LEXICON.

The articles of diet found in the ancient *menus* include most of the things that are eaten in modern times—the fish, flesh, and fowl at any rate. Of the fish, the mullet (*mullus*), turbot (*rhombus*), and carp (*cyprinus*) were especially prized. A sort of fish-sauce (*garum*), resembling anchovy-sauce or perhaps caviare, was also held in high esteem by gourmets. Oysters were dear in price and greatly liked, the best natives coming from Circeii. British oysters were imported from Rutupiae (Richborough), on the southern coast of Britain. Of meats, pork was held to be a dainty, whether as ham (*perna*) or in the form of *glandulae*, over which the parasite in the *Captivi* of Plautus grows so enthusiastic, or potted in the *tucetum* (q. v.). The breasts of a sow killed just after she had littered, but before she had given suck, were much sought, and the matrix (*vulva*) of the same animal, stuffed with onions, is often spoken of as extremely delectable. Sausages (*botuli*) were popular, but less the diet of the wealthy than of the poor, being hawked about the streets by itinerant venders. Beef and lamb were not very highly esteemed; nor was chicken a great dainty, capons excepted. Thrushes (*turdi*), pheasants (*phasiani*), fig-peckers (*ficedulae*), larks (*alaudae*), guinea-hens (*meleagrides*), and many other birds were sought as food. As in Italy and Southern France to-day, snails formed an esteemed article of diet. They were fattened on meal especially for the market, and sometimes attained to a huge size. The Romans served up dormice (*glires*) at expensive banquets. Maecenas introduced at Rome the flesh of young asses as a fashionable dish. The common people ate comparatively little meat, but made bread, fruit, salad, and the national dish *puls* (see PULS) their principal fare. Tripe (*omentum*) was also an especially plebeian dish. Oil was liberally used in the various dishes, as in Italy to-day. (See OLIVUM.) The most frequently mentioned condiments were salt (*sal*), pepper (*piper*), garlic (*allium*), leek (*porrum*), mustard (*sinapis*), and poppy-seeds. Asafoetida (*silphium*) was also used as a seasoning, its flavour being not unlike that of garlic. On vinegar, see ACETUM.

The ordinary fruits and vegetables were sold in the markets: grapes, apples, pears, peaches, plums, oranges, figs, quinces, melons, pomegranates, nuts, and pease, beets, cucumbers (which were also pickled), lettuce, beans, onions, turnips, cabbages, cauliflowers, and radishes.

The skill of the pastry-cook did much towards making a formal dinner successful. Pastry was set upon the table in the most varied forms, animal and vegetable, some idea of which may be gathered from the *Cena Trimalchionis*. Eggs of paste were served which, when broken, revealed young birds inside delicately cooked in sauce that counterfeited the appearance of a yolk. Cakes and sweetmeats were made in great quantities, honey being used for sweetening them. (See PLACENTA; SCRIBLITA.) Cheese entered largely into Roman cookery, especially into the manufacture of cakes, and the description of some of these as so made is very appetizing. (See CASEUS.) Butter was not largely used, its place being taken by oil. (See BUTYRUM.) For the methods of making bread and for the various kinds of bread, see the article PISTOR. Information regarding wines will be found under VINUM, and reference may also be made to the article SYMPOSIUM. For beer, see CERVESIA, and for other drinks, CALDA; POSCA. On the ancient notions regarding diet and the nutritive value of foods, see DIAETETICA, and cf. ATHLETAE; CENA.

On the whole general subject of food in antiquity, see Saalfeld, *Küche und Keller in Alt-Rom* (Berlin, 1883); Baudrillart, *Hist. du Luxe Privé*, etc., vol. ii. (Paris, 1880); and the special sections in Becker-Göll, *Charikles*; id. *Gallus*; and Friedländer's *Sittengeschichte Roms*. Prof. C. G. Herbermann has given an interesting table of the approximate cost of various articles of food in the Roman markets in his *Business Life in Ancient Rome* (New York, 1880). Cf. also the article SUMPTUARIAE LEGES.

Vicus (κώμη). Originally a habitation, taken in a collective sense, as a number of houses contiguous to each other; thence, a street with houses on each side, both in a country village or a city; and so a division or quarter of a town consisting of a certain number of dwellings.

Vienna. Now Vienne; the chief town of the Allobroges in Gallia Lugdunensis, situated on the Rhône, south of Lugdunum (Lyons).

Vigĭles. (1) Sentinels who were on duty about a camp at night. (See CASTRA.) (2) A name given to the police of Rome. Of these there were seven *cohortes* or battalions with fourteen station-houses (*excubitoria*). They were under the command of a superintendent (*praefectus vigilum*), who was responsible for the order of the city, it being his duty to protect the citizens from all forms of lawlessness. He was also charged with the duty of preventing and extinguishing fires, so that the vigiles were really a police and fire department combined. Policemen were regularly detailed for duty at the theatres, public baths, and other places of public resort; and had very considerable powers, resembling those exercised by the police in the Continental cities. As firemen they were provided with axes, ropes, buckets, and also operated a kind of hand fire-engine (*sipho, sipo*), whence they received the popular nickname of *siponarii*. Each of the seven cohorts was commanded by a captain (*tribunus*), and the whole force numbered 7000 men. In 1868, an *excubitorium* belonging to the seventh cohort was excavated at Rome, and on its walls were found many interesting inscriptions, scratched by the policemen when off duty, and giving a curious picture of the life and thought of the ancient vigiles, being of every possible description—humorous, complaining, serious, and obscene. See the account of this discovery and of the Roman police in general in Lanciani, *Ancient Rome in the Light of Recent Discoveries*, ch. viii. (Boston, 1888).

Vigiliae. See CASTRA.

Vigintisexvĭri (also, under the Empire, **Vigintivĭri**). A group of minor magistrates at Rome whose offices and functions were of different origin, but which as a rule must have been discharged by a person as a preliminary to his candidacy for the quaestorship. (See HONORES.) These magistrates were the *tresviri capitales*, the *tresviri monetales*, the *quattuorviri viis in urbe purgandis*, the *duoviri viis extra urbem purgandis*, the *decemviri litibus iudicandis*, and the *quattuor praefecti Capuam Cumas*. The fourth and sixth of these magistrates were abolished under Augustus. See Mommsen, *Röm. Staatsrecht*, ii. 578–595.

Vigintivĭri. See VIGINTISEXVĬRI.

Vilĭcus. A farm-bailiff; a slave who had the superintendence in chief of all the stock and business of a farm, the surveillance of the labouring slaves, the management and direction of the farming operations, and the duty of selling the produce of the estate. See VILLA.

Villa. A Roman farm or country-house, of which Roman writers mention two kinds—(*a*) the *villa rustica* or farm-house, and (*b*) the *villa urbana* or *pseudo-urbana*, a residence in the country or in the suburbs of a town. When both of these were attached to an estate, they were generally united in the same range of buildings, but sometimes they were placed at different parts of the estate. The part of the *villa rustica* in which the produce of the farm was kept was called *villa fructuaria.*

(*a*) The *villa rustica* is described by Varro (*R. R.* i. 11–13), Vitruvius (vi. 9), and Columella (i. 4, § 5 foll.).

The villa, which must be of size corresponding to that of the farm, is best placed at the foot of a wooded mountain, in a spot supplied with running water, and not exposed to severe winds nor to the effluvia of marshes, nor (by being close to a road) to a too frequent influx of visitors. If there was no running stream, tanks were constructed, one under cover for men, one in the open air for the beasts. The villa attached to a large farm had two courts (*cohortes, chortes, cortes*, Varro, i. 13). At the entrance to the outer court was the abode of the *vilicus* or steward, that he might observe who went in and out, and over the door was the room of the *procurator* (Colum. i. 6). Near this, in as warm a spot as possible, was the kitchen, which, besides being used for the preparation of food, was the place where the slaves (*familiae*) assembled after the labours of the day, and where they performed certain indoor work. Vitruvius places near the kitchen the baths and the press (*torcular*) for wine and oil. In the outer court were also the cellars for wine and oil (*cellae vinariae et oleariae*), which were placed on the level ground, and the granaries, which were in the upper stories of the farm-buildings, and carefully protected from damp.

heat, and insects. These store-rooms form the separate *villa fructuaria*.

In both courts were the chambers (*cellae*) of the slaves, fronting the south; but the *ergastulum* for those who were kept in chains (*vincti*) was underground, being lighted by several high and narrow windows. The inner court was occupied chiefly by the horses, cattle, and other live-stock, and here were the stables and stalls (*bubilia, equilia, ovilia*). A reservoir of water was made in the middle of each court—that in the outer court for soaking pulse and other vegetable produce, and that in the inner, which was supplied with fresh water by a spring, for the use of the cattle and poultry.

(*b*) The *villa urbana* or *pseudo-urbana* was so called because its interior arrangements corresponded for the most part to those of a town-house. (See DOMUS.) Vitruvius (vi. 8) merely states that the description of the latter will apply to the former also, except that in the town the *atrium* is placed close to the door, but in the country the peristyle comes first, and afterwards the *atrium*, surrounded by paved porticoes, looking upon the *palaestra* and *ambulatio*.

Hadrian's Villa at Tibur. (Restoration.)

A striking difference in the general aspect of a country-house from that of a town-house lay in the fact that the blank walls of the latter were replaced by long colonnades, broken by towers, apses, and the like.

The chief sources of information on this subject are two letters of Pliny, in one of which (ii. 17) he describes his Laurentine villa, in the other (v. 6) his Tuscan. The former of these, however, was not, strictly speaking, a *villa*, as it had no estate or farm-buildings attached to it; the latter was connected with a large estate. There are also a few allusions in one of Cicero's letters (*Ad Quint.* iii. 1) to the remains of a suburban villa at Pompeii, besides several Roman villas of which ruins exist in England.

See Becker-Göll, *Gallus*, iii. pp. 46–63; Overbeck, *Pompeii*, pp. 325 foll.; and for the remains of the Roman villas in England, Neville in the *Archæological Journal*, vols. ii., vi., vii., x. For Pliny's Laurentine villa, cf. Cowan's edition of Pliny, i.–ii. (with a plan); Burn's *Rome and the Campagna*, pp. 411–415 (with a plan); Aitchison in *The Builder* for Feb. 8th, 1890; and a paper by Dr. H. W. Magoun in the *Proceedings of the American Philological Association for* 1895.

Villius Annālis. See ANNALIS.

Viminālis Porta. A gate of Rome in the Servian walls, leading to the Via Tiburtina. See ROMA.

Vincŭlum. The generic term for a fetter of any kind. See CATENA; COMPES; MANICA.

Vindălum. A town of the Cavares in Gallia Narbonensis. It was situated at the junction of the Sulgas (Sorgue) and the Rhodanus (Rhône) (Strabo, p. 185).

Vindelĭci. See VINDELICIA.

Vindelicia. A Roman province, bounded on the north by the Danube, which separated it from Germany, on the west by the territory of the Helvetii in Gaul, on the south by Rhaetia, and on the east by the river Oenus (Inn), which separated it from Noricum, thus corresponding to the north-eastern part of Switzerland, the southeast of Baden, the south of Würtemberg and Bavaria, and the northern part of the Tyrol. It was originally a part of the province of Rhaetia, and was conquered by Tiberius in the reign of Augustus. At a later time Rhaetia was divided into two provinces, RHAETIA PRIMA and RHAETIA SECUNDA, the latter of which names was gradually supplanted by that of Vindelicia. It was drained by the tributaries of the Danube, of which the most important were the Licias, or Licus (Lech), with its tributary the Vindo, Vinda, or Virdo (Werlach), the Isarus (Isar), and Oenus (Inn). The eastern part of the Lacus Brigantinus (Lake of Constance) also belonged to Vindelicia. It derived its name from its chief inhabitants, the VINDELĬCI, a warlike people dwelling in the south of the country. The other tribes in Vindelicia were the Brigantii on the Lake of Constance, the Licatii or Licates on the Lech, and the Breuni (in the north of the Tyrol) on the Brenner. The chief town in the province was Augusta Vindelicorum (Augsburg), at the confluence of the Vindo and the Licus.

Vindemia (τρύγητος). Strictly a vintage or gathering of the grapes; then, by an extension of usage, applied to the harvesting of other produce, as olives, honey, etc. (Pliny, *H. N.* xv. 2; Columell. ix. 15, 1).

Vindex. See ACTIO in the Appendix.

Vindex, C. Iulius. A propraetor of Gallia Celtica in the reign of Nero, and the first of the Roman governors who disowned the authority of Nero (A.D. 68). He did not, however, aspire to the Empire himself, but offered it to Galba. Virginius Rufus, the governor of Upper Germany, marched with his army against Vindex. The two generals had a conference before Vesontio (Besançon), in which they appear to have come to some agreement; but as Vindex was about to enter the town, he was attacked by the soldiers of Virginius, and put an end to his own life.

Vindicatio. In Roman law, the name given to an action (*actio*) of the class known as "real" (*in rem*) or one relating to the title to ownership (*dominium*). The word is opposed to *condictio*, which is applied to a "personal" action (*in personam*) or actions for the enforcement of obligations arising from contract or debit (Gaius, iv. 2–5). See ACTIO in the Appendix.

Vindicius. A slave, who is said to have given information to the consuls of the conspiracy which was formed for the restoration of the Tarquins, and who was rewarded in consequence with liberty and the Roman franchise (Livy, ii. 5).

Vindicta. A rod with which the praetor, or the praetor's lictor, tapped the head of a slave as a sign that he was thus made free (Livy, ii. 5; Cic. *Top.* 2; Pers. v. 88.) See MANUMISSIO; SERVUS.

Vindobŏna. Now Vienna; the German Wien. A town in Pannonia, on the Danube, originally a Keltic place, and subsequently a Roman municipium. Under the Romans it became a town of importance; it was the chief station of the Roman fleet on the Danube, and the headquarters of a Roman legion. Here the emperor Marcus Aurelius died in A.D. 180. The place was taken and sacked by Attila (Ptol. ii. 15, 3; Iornand. *Get.* 50).

Vindonissa. Now Windisch; a town in Gallia Belgica, on the triangular tongue of land between the Aar and Reuss. It was an important Roman fortress in the country of the Helvetii (Tac. *Hist.* iv. 61, 70). Some Roman remains are still to be seen here, among them the traces of an amphitheatre, an aqueduct, and the foundations of walls.

Vinea. A shed employed by the Roman soldiers to protect themselves from the missiles of the enemy whilst occupied in undermining or breaching the walls of a fortress. It had a sloping roof of planks and wicker-work supported upon uprights, and was closed on three of its sides by similar materials, the whole frame being covered outside with raw hides or horse-hair cloth, to prevent its being set on fire. Each *vinea*, by itself, was about eight feet high and sixteen in length; but a number of them were joined together in a line and run up to the walls, so that the ram could be securely plied underneath them (Caes. *B. C.* ii. 2; Livy, xxxvii. 26; Veg. *Mil.* iv. 15).

Vinegar. See ACETUM.

Vinum (οἶνος). From the earliest times wine was the usual drink of the Greeks, and was made in every Hellenic country. The best was produced on the coasts and islands of the Aegean, such as Thasos, Rhodes, Cyprus, and, above all, Chios and Lesbos. The Greeks noted three colours in wines: (*a*) red (μέλας); (*b*) white or straw-coloured (λευκός); and brown or amber-coloured (κιρρός). The processes of making wine were substantially the same among both Greeks and Romans; but the more detailed information given by the ancient writers relates to the wines produced in Italy.

The cultivation of the vine was common in Lower Italy before its colonization by the Greeks, and the Romans had vineyards in very early times. In fact, one of the early names of Italy was Oenotria, or "land of the vine-pole." Wine was, however, long regarded as an article of luxury, and was limited in its use. The regular production of wine (the method of which was imported from Greece, together with the finer varieties of vines) first came in with the decline of the cultivation of cereals. The home-grown wines were of little esteem, as compared with the Greek, and especially the highly prized island wines, until the first century B.C. After this date the careful treatment of a number of Italian, and more particularly of Campanian, brands (such as the Falernian, Caecuban, and Massic) gained for them the reputation of being the first wines of the world. They formed an important article of export, not merely to the collective provinces of the Roman Empire, Greece herself not excepted, but also beyond the Roman frontier, so that even in India they were known (Arrian, *Peripl.* 6, 49). It was to protect the Italian wine-growers that, in the western provinces, down to the third century A.D., the cultivation of the vine was subject to certain limitations. No new vineyards could be added to those already existing, and the Italian vines could not be introduced, although Gaul produced many varieties of wine. Under the Empire, wine was the main article of produce and of trade in Italy, Greece, and Asia; and the wine merchants of Rome, who had, from the commencement of the second century, formed two corporations, one for the eastern and another for the western trade, held an important position. In the first century there were already eighty famous brands in the Roman market, of which number Italy supplied two-thirds. The finest wine made in Italy was the Setine (*vinum Setinum*), the chosen drink of Augustus, and made at Setia, near the Pontine Marshes. Next comes the Falernian, which required ten years to mature; then the Alban, both sweet and dry; the Massic, often mentioned by Horace; the Surrentine, which was not at its best until kept for twenty-five years; the Calene, a light wine; the Veliternian, and the Signine. The Mamertine, a light, sweet wine, was the favourite drink of Iulius Caesar (Mart. xiii. 117). Etruscan wines were generally bad, and so were the wines of Gaul, these being often "doctored" with aloes and other drugs. Good wine was imported from Asia Minor, especially from parts of Pontus, Paphlagonia, Bithynia, and Phœnicia. The Mareotic wine of Egypt was also much esteemed. It was a white wine, sweet and light, and with a delightful *bouquet*. Even more popular was the *vinum Taenioticum* from the Egyptian Delta.

The vine was grown partly on poles or espaliers, partly on trees, especially on elms, which, if the ground between were still used for agriculture, were planted at a distance of forty, sometimes of twenty, feet apart. The grapes intended for manufacture into wine were trodden with naked feet and then brought under the press. The must was then immediately poured into large pitched earthenware jars (πίθος, *dolium*). These were placed under ground in a wine-cellar, facing the north to keep them cool, and kept uncovered for a year in order to ferment thoroughly. The inferior wines which were of no great age were drunk immediately from the jar (Cic. *Brutus*, 228). The better kinds, which were meant for preservation, were poured into *amphorae.* (See AMPHORA.) These were closed with stone stoppers, sealed with pitch, clay, or gypsum, marked with a brand, furnished with a label (*tessera* or *nota*) giving their year and measure, and placed in the *apotheca.* This was a room in the upper story, built by preference over the bath-room in order to catch the smoke from the furnace, and thus to make the wine more mellow. Wine was also "improved" or its process of mellowing hastened by exposing the *amphorae* to the full glow of the sunlight, and sometimes by the use of chemicals. Sometimes, again, the vessels containing the must were sunk in the sea, the wine being then styled *thalassites* (Pliny, *H. N.* xiv. 78). By the Greeks, at least in the early period, wines were drunk mixed with various substances, as grated cheese and flour (*Il.* xi. 638), barley-meal and honey (*Od.* x. 234).

The most famous vintage year in Roman history was the year B.C. 121, when L. Opimius was consul. Great quantities of this year's wine were stored up, and some was in existence in Pliny's time, about two hundred years later (*H. N.* xiv. §§ 55, 94). It was known as *vinum Opimianum*, and is often mentioned in literature.

One method of improving the wine which was used in the East and in Greece was to keep the wine in goat-skins (ἀσκοί, *utres*), because the leather tended to cause evaporation of the water. In Italy the wine-skins appear to have been only used in transport. To produce flavour, strength, and bouquet, various means were employed, such as adding gypsum, clay, chalk, marble, resin, pitch, and even sea water, the last being especially in use in Greece and Asia Minor. Bad wines were improved by being mixed with fine brands and good lees; adulteration was extremely common. The number of artificial wines was very large; e. g. honey wine (*mulsum*), raisin wine (*passum*), and boiled must (the beverage of the common people and slaves), a poor drink prepared by pouring water on the remains of the pressed grapes, and called θάμνα, *lora*.

The place of our liqueurs was taken by flavoured wines, of which more than fifty kinds are mentioned. These were simply extracted from herbs, flowers, or sweet-smelling woods (thyme, myrtle, sweet rush, rose, heart's-ease, pine-cones and pine-wood, cypress, etc.), or mixed with oils, such as nard or myrrh. There were also wines made from fruits, such as apples, pomegranates, pears, dates, figs, or mulberries. In respect of colour three sorts of wine were distinguished: the black or dark red (*color sanguineus* and *niger*) which was considered the strongest; the white (*albus*), which was thought thin and weak; and the brown or amber-coloured (*fulvus*), which was considered particularly serviceable for promoting digestion. As in its ordinary treatment the wine often retained much sediment, it had to be made clear before it was drunk. This was done either with yolk of eggs or by straining the wine through a cloth or sieve, which was filled with snow to make it cool. Greeks and Romans alike generally drank their wine liberally mixed with water; and to drink it unmixed (*merum*, ἄκρατον) was regarded as a sign of great intemperance. See CENA; DIAETETICA; and cf. SYMPOSIUM.

For particulars regarding the production and use of wine by the ancients, the reader is referred to the following works: Barry, *The Wines of the Ancients* (London, 1775); Henderson, *History of Ancient and Modern Wines* (London, 1824); Becker-Göll, *Charikles*, ii. pp. 337–352; id. *Gallus*, iii. pp. 412–442; Marquardt, *Röm. Privatalterthümer*, ii. 54–84; and Mew and Astion, *The Drinks of the World* (London, 1892). For beer, see CERVESIA.

Vipsania Agrippīna. (1) The daughter of M. Vipsanius Agrippa by his first wife Pomponia. Augustus gave her in marriage to his step-son Tiberius, by whom she was much beloved; but after she had borne him a son, Drusus, Tiberius was compelled to divorce her by the command of the emperor, in order to marry Iulia, the daughter of the latter. Vipsania afterwards married Asinius Gallus. She died in A.D. 20. (2) Daughter of M. Vipsanius Agrippa by his second wife Iulia, better known by the name of Agrippina. See AGRIPPINA.

Vipsanius Agrippa, MARCUS. See AGRIPPA.

Virbius. A Latin divinity worshipped along with Diana in the grove at Aricia, at the foot of the Alban Mount. He is said to have been the same as Hippolytus, who was restored to life by Asclepius at the request of Artemis. It was told that Hippolytus was placed by this goddess under the care of the nymph Aricia, and received the name of Virbius. By this nymph he became the father of a son, who was also called Virbius, and whom his mother sent to the assistance of Turnus against Aeneas (Verg. *Aen.* vii. 761; Ovid, *Met.* xv. 545). This is a transference to Italy of the story of Hippolytus being devoted to the service of Artemis. It has been suggested with great probability that Virbius was originally a tree spirit of the sacred grove, to whom horses (as representatives of the spirit) were sacrificed. Hence they were in time represented as hostile to the deity Virbius, and therefore excluded from the grove. This was explained by making Virbius the same as Hippolytus, whose death was caused by his horses running away. See HIPPOLYTUS.

Virdo. See VINDELICIA.

Virdumărus. See VIRIDOMARUS.

Virga (ῥάβδος). A twig, bough, or switch cut from a tree. Hence (1) a riding-whip (Mart. ix. 23); (2) a switch for punishing school-boys (Juv. vii. 210) (see LUDUS LITTERARIUS); (3) a walking-stick (see BACULUM); (4) a wand of office carried by the Roman lictors (see FASCES; LICTOR); (5) a magic wand (Verg. *Aen.* iv. 242); and (6), in the plural, the ribs of an umbrella (Ovid, *A. A.* ii. 209).

Circé with Wand. (From a marble.)

Virgilius. See VERGILIUS.

Virgĭnes Vestāles. See VESTALES.

Virginia or **Verginia.** The daughter of L. Virginius, a Roman centurion. She was a beautiful and innocent girl, betrothed to L. Icilius. Her beauty excited the lust of the decemvir Appius Claudius, who instigated one of his clients to seize the maiden and claim her as his slave. Her father, who had come from the camp the morning on which Claudius gave judgment assigning Virginia to his client, seeing that all hope was gone, prayed the decemvir to be allowed to speak one word to the nurse in his daughter's hearing, in order to ascertain whether she was really his daughter. The request was granted; Virginius drew them both aside, and snatching up a butcher's knife from one of the stalls, plunged it into his daughter's breast, exclaiming, "There is no way but this to keep thee free"; then, holding his bloody knife on high, he rushed to the gate of the city, and hastened to the Roman camp. The result is known. Both camp and city rose against the decemvirs, who were deprived of their power, and the old form of government was restored. L. Virginius was the first who was elected tribune, and by his orders Appius was dragged to prison, where he put an end to his own life (Livy, iii. 44–58; Dionys. xi. 28–46). See CLAUDIUS.

Virginia or **Verginia Gens.** A gens both patrician and plebeian. The patrician Virginii frequently filled the highest honours of the State during the early years of the Republic. They all bore the name Tricostus.

Virginius or **Verginius,** LUCIUS. The father of Virginia, whose tragic fate occasioned the downfall of the decemvirs, B.C. 449. See VIRGINIA.

Virginius Rufus. A Roman consul A.D. 63, and governor of Upper Germany at the time of the revolt of Iulius Vindex in Gaul (68). The soldiers of Virginius wished to raise him to the Empire; but he refused the honour, and marched against Vindex, who perished before Vesontio. (See VINDEX.) After the death of Nero, Virginius supported the claims of Galba, and accompanied him to Rome. After Otho's death the soldiers again attempted to proclaim Virginius emperor, and in consequence of his refusal of the honour he narrowly escaped with his life. Virginius died in the reign of Nerva, in his third consulship, A.D. 97, at eighty-three years of age. He was honoured with a public funeral, and his panegyric was pronounced by the historian Tacitus, who was then consul. His epitaph, composed by himself, notices his refusal of the throne:

> *Hic situs est Rufus, pulso qui Vindice quondam*
> *Imperium adseruit non sibi sed patriae.*

The younger Pliny, of whom Virginius had been the tutor or guardian, also mentions him with praise (Tac. *Hist.* i. 8, 77; ii. 49, 68; Plut. *Galb.* 4, 6, 10; Dio Cass. lxiii. 24–27; lxiv. 4; lxviii. 2; Pliny, *Epist.* ii. 1; v. 3; vi. 10; ix. 19).

Viriāthus. A celebrated Lusitanian who is described by the Romans as originally a shepherd or huntsman, and afterwards a robber, or, as he would be called in Spain in the present day, a guerrilla chief. He was one of the Lusitanians who escaped the treacherous and savage massacre of the people by the proconsul Galba in B.C. 150. (See GALBA.) He collected a formidable force, and for several successive years defeated one Roman army after another. In 140 the proconsul Fabius Servilianus concluded a peace with Viriathus in order to save his army, which had been enclosed by the Lusitanians in a mountain pass. But Servilius Caepio, who succeeded to the command of Farther Spain in 140, renewed the war, and shortly afterwards procured the assassination of Viriathus by bribing three of his friends (Appian, *Hisp.* 60–75; Eutrop. iv. 16; Val. Max. ix. 6, 4).

Viridarium. A sort of conservatory in a Roman house. See DOMUS.

Viridomărus. (1) Or BRITOMARTUS. A leader of the Gauls, slain by Marcellus. (See MARCELLUS.) (2) Or VIRDUMĂRUS, a chieftain of the Aedui, whom Caesar had raised from a low rank to the highest honour, but who afterwards joined the Gauls in their great revolt in B.C. 52 (Caes. *B. G.* vii. 38, 54, 63).

Viriplāca. One of the Roman *dii indigetes,* a goddess who enabled wives to please their husbands. See INDIGETES.

Viroconium or **Urioconium.** Now Wroxeter; a town in Britain on the roads from Deva (Chester) to Londinum and to Glevum (Gloucester). It stood at the confluence of the Terne with the Severn, and here Ostorius Scapula fortified a camp for the Fourteenth Legion as a defence for the Welsh border (Tac. *Ann.* xii. 31; cf. Ptol. ii. 3, 19).

Virtus. The Roman personification of manly valour. She was represented with a short tunic, her right breast uncovered, a helmet on her head, a spear in her left hand, a sword in the right, and standing with her right foot on a helmet. A temple of Virtus was built by Marcellus close to the one of Honor. See HONOR.

Vis. The general term used in Roman law for criminal violence. The *lex Plotia* (B.C. 89) was the first regular statute punishing those who pillaged houses, occupied public places in arms, and assembled armed men for the purpose of overawing the Senate or the magistrates. Several *leges Iuliae* of Iulius Caesar and of Augustus were also passed to complete and consolidate previous enactments. Two kinds of vis are mentioned — *vis publica,* which probably meant violence immediately directed against the State, and *vis privata,* which would be violence primarily against an individual right, but criminal because it interfered with public order. The punishments assigned by the *leges Iuliae* ranged from death (house-pillaging, abduction, riot resulting in death) to exile. See Rein, *Criminalrecht der Römer,* pp. 732 foll.

Vistŭla. Now the Vistula (in German, Weichsel); an important river of Germany, forming the boundary between Germany and Sarmatia, rising in the Hercynia Silva and falling into the Maré Suevicum or the Baltic.

Visurgis. Now the Weser; an important river of Germany, falling into the German Ocean.

Vitellius. (1) LUCIUS, father of the Roman emperor. He was a consummate flatterer, and by his arts gained promotion. After being consul in A.D. 34, he had been appointed governor of Syria, and had made favourable terms of peace with Artabanus. But all this only excited Caligula's jealousy, so that he sent for Vitellius to put him to death. The governor saved himself by his abject humiliation and the gross flattery which pleased and softened the savage tyrant. He paid similar court to

Claudius and Messalina, and was rewarded by being twice consul with Claudius, and also censor (Dio Cass. lix. 27; Tac. *Ann.* xi. 1–3; xii. 42). (2) LUCIUS, son of the preceding, and brother of the emperor, was consul in 48. He was put to death by the party of Vespasian on his brother's fall (Tac. *Hist.* iv. 2; Dio Cass. lxv. 22). (3) AULUS, Roman emperor from January 2 to December 22, A.D. 69. He was the son of No. 1. He was consul during the first six months of 48, and his brother Lucius during the following six. He had some knowledge of letters and some eloquence. His vices made him a favourite of Tiberius, Gaius Caligula, Claudius, and Nero, who loaded him with

Vitellius. (Bust in Vienna.)

favours. It caused great surprise, however, when Galba chose such a man to command the legions in Lower Germany, for he had little military talent. Both Upper and Lower Germany had been attached to Virginius Rufus, and disliked the rule of Galba; the two legions at Moguntiacum (Mayence) had not taken the oath of allegiance to him. Accordingly, they had already been disposed to find a nominee of their own, and when the news of Galba's death arrived, the legions of both Germanies combined to acknowledge Vitellius as Imperator, and he was proclaimed at Colonia Agrippinensis (Cologne) on the 2d of January, 69. His generals Fabius Valens and Caecina marched into Italy, defeated Otho's troops at the decisive battle of Betriacum, or Bedriacum, and thus secured for Vitellius the undisputed command of Italy. The soldiers of Otho, after his death, took the oath of fidelity to Vitellius. (See OTHO.) Vitellius reached Rome in July. He disturbed no one in the enjoyment of what had been given by Nero, Galba, and Otho, nor did he confiscate any person's property; and though some of Otho's adherents were put to death, he let the next of kin take their possessions. Yet though he showed moderation in this part of his conduct, he showed none in his expenditure. He was a glutton and an epicure, and his chief amusement was the table, on which he spent enormous sums of money. Meantime Vespasian, who had at first taken the oath of allegiance to Vitellius, was proclaimed emperor at Alexandria on the 1st of July. Vespasian was speedily recognized by all the East; and the legions of Illyricum under Antonius Primus entered the north of Italy and declared for Vespasian. Vitellius despatched Caecina with a powerful force to oppose Primus; but Caecina was not faithful to his master. Primus defeated the Vitellians in two battles, and afterwards took and pillaged the city of Cremona. Primus then marched upon Rome, and forced his way into the city, after much fighting. Vitellius was seized in the palace, led through the streets with every circumstance of ignominy, and dragged to the Gemoniae Scalae, where he was killed with repeated blows. His head was carried about Rome, and his body was thrown into the Tiber; but it was afterwards buried by his wife, Galeria Fundana. A few days before the death of Vitellius, the Capitol had been burned in the assault made by his soldiers upon this building, where Flavius Sabinus, the brother of the emperor Vespasian, had taken refuge (Tac. *Hist.* ii., iii.; Suet. *Vitell.*; Dio Cass. lxv.).

Vitrum (ὕαλος). Glass. The Egyptians made glass at a very early period, the oldest existing specimen being a blue vase of opaque glass now in the British Museum, as old as the sixteenth century B.C. Cups and bottles of uncertain date have been taken in considerable numbers from the tombs and mummy-cases. In the paintings of Beni-Hassan (about 2300 B.C.) the process of glass-blowing is clearly depicted. The Assyrians likewise made admirable glass, the oldest existing specimen being a sort of bottle of green glass found at Nimroud, and dating from 719 B.C. It is now in the British Museum.

A story has been preserved by Pliny (*H. N.* xxxvi. § 191) that glass was first discovered accidentally by some merchants who, having landed on the Syrian coast at the mouth of the river Belus, and being unable to find stones to support their cooking-pots, brought for this purpose from their ship some of the lumps of nitre which composed the cargo. This being fused by the heat of the fire, united with the sand upon which it rested and formed a stream of vitrified matter. The Phœnicians probably learned the art of glass-making from the Egyptians; but the tale is no doubt connected with the fact recorded by Strabo (xvi. p. 758) and Iosephus (*Bell. Iud.* ii. 9), that the sand of the district in question was esteemed peculiarly suitable for glass-making, and exported in great quantities to the workshops of Sidon, long the most famous in the ancient world. Alexandria, another centre of the industry, sustained its reputation for many centuries; Rome derived thence a great portion of its supplies, and as late as the reign of Aurelian we find the manufacture still flourishing (Cic. *Pro Rabir. Post.* xiv. 40; Strabo, l. c.; Martial, xi. 11; xii. 74; xiv. 115; Vopisc. *Aurel.* 45).

Homer does not certainly mention glass, but at Mycenae and Tiryns glass beads and other ornaments have been found. The words ὕαλος and ὕελος in the early Greek writers (e. g. Herod. iii. 24) do not always refer to glass, but often to rock-crystal, rock-salt, amber, or alabaster; and it is not till Theophrastus, the pupil of Aristotle, that the word is surely to be rendered "glass." Of the Roman writers, Lucretius is the first to use the term *vitrum* (iv. 604; vi. 991), but it must have been known at Rome long before this time, as Cicero (l. c.) speaks of it as a common article of merchandise. Phœnician glass is found in the

Etruscan cemeteries at Tarquinii dating from the eighth century B.C. Scaurus in his temporary theatre, erected in B.C. 58, used glass freely in the interior decoration (see THEATRUM); and the Augustan poets often mention the substance (e. g. Verg. *Georg.* iv. 350; *Aen.* vii. 759; Ovid, *Amor.* i. 6, 55; Hor. *Carm.* iii. 13, 1). Pliny states that glass was made in Italy, Gaul, and Spain, and that drinking-cups of glass had superseded those of gold and silver (Pliny, *H. N.* xxxvi. §§ 192–199). Under Alexander Severus we find the glass-makers (*vitrearii*) enumerated in the tax-lists with other artisans. Strabo notes the cheapness of glass, and says that a glass drinking-cup sold in his time for half an *as*, or less than a cent.

The following are the chief uses to which glass was applied:

(*a*) Bottles, vases, cups, and urns for the ashes of the dead (*cineraria*). Of all of these great numbers exist, in a great variety of forms and colours, some having been blown into moulds so as to take the shape of—e. g. a bunch of grapes, a sea-shell, a negro's head, etc. (See illustration, s. v. DIATRETA.) The finest of all under this class is the celebrated Portland Vase in the British Museum, found in the sixteenth century near Rome. See PORTLAND VASE.

(*b*) Glass pastes giving fac-similes of engraved precious stones. These were worn by those who could not afford real gems (Pliny, *H. N.* xxxv. 48). Precious stones were also imitated in glass with very great skill, so that only experts could detect the imposition. The sapphire, amethyst, carbuncle, and especially the emerald, were the oftenest counterfeited (Pliny, *H. N.* xxxvii. 197; Trebell. Poll. *Gall.* 12; Seneca, *Epist.* 90; Isidor. *Orig.* xvi. 15, 27). See GEMMA.

(*c*) One very elegant application of glass deserves to be particularly noticed. A number of fine stalks of glass of different colours were placed vertically, and arranged in such a manner as to depict upon the upper surface some figure or pattern, upon the principle of a minute mosaic. The filaments thus combined were then subjected to such a degree of heat as would suffice to soften without melting them, and were thus cemented together into a solid mass. It is evident that the picture brought out upon the upper surface would extend down through the whole of the little column thus formed, and hence, if it was cut into thin slices at right angles to the direction of the fibres, each of these sections would upon both sides represent the design which would be multiplied to an extent in proportion to the total length of the glass threads. Further, if the column is heated and drawn out, the design becomes proportionately minute. When these sections have been again fused together side by side, the result is *millefiori* glass. Many mosaic pavements and pictures (*opus musivum*) belong to this head, since the cubes were frequently composed of opaque glass as well as marble. See MUSIVUM OPUS.

(*d*) One method of decoration employed by the ancients consisted in enclosing designs in gold-leaf between two layers of transparent glass. This is most common from the third century A.D., when small Christian subjects are thus represented.

(*e*) Thick sheets of glass of various colours appear to have been laid down for paving floors, and to have been attached as a lining to the walls and ceilings of apartments in dwelling-houses, just as *scagliola* is frequently employed in Italy. Rooms fitted up in this way were called *vitreae camerae*, and the panels *vitreae quadraturae*. Such was the kind of decoration introduced by Scaurus for the scene of his theatre, not columns nor pillars of glass as some, nor bas-reliefs as others, have imagined (Pliny, *H. N.* xxxvi. § 189; Stat. *Sil.* i. 5, 42; Seneca, *Ep.* 76; Vopisc. *Firm.* 3).

(*f*) The question whether glass windows were known to the ancients has, after much discussion, been set at rest by the excavations at Pompeii, for not only have many fragments of flat glass been disinterred from time to time, but in the *tepidarium* of the public baths a bronze lattice came to light with some of the panes still inserted in the frame, so as to determine at once not only their existence, but the mode in which they were secured and arranged (Mazois, *Ruines de Pompéi*, iii. p. 77).

For the use of glass in mirrors, see SPECULUM.

The numerous specimens existing prove that the ancients were well acquainted with the art of imparting a great variety of colours to their glass; they were probably less successful in their attempts to render it perfectly pure and free from all colour, since we are told by Pliny that it was considered most valuable in this state. It was wrought according to the different methods now practised, being fashioned into the required shape by the blowpipe; or cut, as we term it, although "ground" (*teritur*) is a more accurate phrase, upon a wheel; or engraved with a sharp tool, like silver (Pliny, *H. N.* xxxvi. § 193). The process was difficult, and accidents occurred frequently (Mart. xiv. 115). The art of etching upon glass, now so common, was entirely unknown to the ancients, since it depends upon the properties of fluoric acid, a chemical discovery of the last century.

Petronius and Dio Cassius assert that malleable glass was discovered in the reign of the emperor Tiberius. They tell a story of how a man demanded an interview with the emperor, and, on being admitted, showed him a glass vessel and then dashed it violently upon the ground. When taken up, it was neither broken nor cracked, but dinted like a piece of metal. The man then produced a mallet, and hammered it back into its original shape. The emperor inquired whether any one was acquainted with the secret, and was answered in the negative; upon which the order was given that the man should be instantly beheaded, lest the precious metals might lose their value, should such a composition become generally known.

See Nesbitt, *Notes on the History of Glass-making* (1871); Blümner, *Technologie*, iv. p. 379 (1887); Deville, *Histoire de l'Art de la Verrerie* (1873); Fröhner, *La Verrerie Antique* (1879); Beckmann, *History of Inventions* (1856); Marquardt and Mommsen, *Röm. Alterthümer*, vii. pp. 774 foll. (1886).

Vitruvius Pollio, MARCUS. A celebrated Roman writer on architecture, of whom nothing is known except a few facts contained in scattered passages of his own work. He appears to have served as a military engineer under Iulius Caesar, in the African War (B.C. 46), and he was broken down with age when he composed his work, which is dedicated to the emperor Augustus. Though he usually speaks of the emperor as "Imperator" or "Caesar," he employs also the title Augustus, which was adopted in B.C. 27, and he mentions (iii. 2, 7) the Temple of Quirinus, which was built

B.C. 16; but he knows only one stone theatre at Rome (iii. 2, 2): whence it is inferred that the work was completed between B.C. 16 and B.C. 13, in which year two more stone theatres were built. He professes his intention to furnish the emperor with a standard by which to judge of the buildings he had already erected, as well as those which he might afterwards erect; which can have no meaning, unless he wished to protest against the style of architecture which prevailed in the buildings already erected. That this was really his intention appears from several other arguments, and especially from his frequent references to the unworthy means by which architects obtained wealth and favour, with which he contrasts his own moderation and contentment in his more obscure position. In a word, having apparently few great buildings of his own to point to as embodying his views (the basilica at Fanum is the only work of his which is mentioned), he desired to lay before the world in writing his principles of architecture. His work is a valuable compendium of those written by numerous Greek architects, whom he mentions chiefly in the preface to his seventh book, and by some Roman writers on architecture. Its chief defects are its brevity, of which Vitruvius himself boasts, and which he often carries so far as to be unintelligible, and the obscurity of the style, arising in part from the natural difficulty of technical language, but in part also from the author's want of skill in writing, and sometimes from his imperfect comprehension of his Greek authorities. His work is entitled *De Architectura Libri X.* In the first book, after the dedication to the emperor and a general description of the science of architecture and an account of the proper education of an architect, he treats of a choice of a proper site for a city, the disposition of its plan, its fortifications, and the several buildings within it. The second book is on the materials used in building. The third and fourth books are devoted to temples and the four orders of architecture employed in them, namely: the Ionic, Corinthian, Doric, and Tuscan. The fifth book relates to public buildings, the sixth to private houses, and the seventh to interior decorations. The eighth is on the subject of water: the mode of finding it; its different kinds; and the various modes for conveying it for the supply of cities. The ninth book treats of various kinds of sundials and other instruments for measuring time; and the tenth of the machines used in building, and of military engines. Each book has a preface, upon some matter more or less connected with the subject; and these prefaces are the source of most of our information about the author. The best editions of Vitruvius are those of Schneider, 3 vols. (Leipzig, 1807–8); Stratico, 4 vols. (Udine, 1825–30), with plates and a lexicon; Marini, 4 vols. (Rome, 1836), recently revised by Lorentzen; and of Rose and Müller-Strübing (Leipzig, 1867). There is a German translation with a commentary by Reber (Stuttgart, 1864), and an English version by Gwilt (revised ed. London, 1874). There is an index by Nohl (1876). The language of Vitruvius belongs in a way to the *sermo plebeius*, being that of a professional engineer with no pretensions to general culture. See SERMO PLEBEIUS.

Vitta. A ribbon or band worn round the forehead and head by free-born ladies, both before and after marriage (Verg. *Aen.* ii. 168), to confine the hair, and to distinguish them from women of the town (Ovid, *Rem. Am.* 386). The name also designates the sacred fillet (*infula*) worn by the Vestals and other priestesses, though strictly it was the ribbon which held together the flock of wool. (See INFULA.) The word also denotes a ribbon used for any other purpose, as in garlands, festoons, etc.

Vitta. (From a medal.)

Vivarium (ζωγρεῖον). A general term for any place in which beasts, fowls, fish, or any kind of animals were kept alive, either for the purposes of gain or pleasure; a park for game, a rabbit-warren, fish-pond, decoy, preserve for oysters, etc. (Gell. ii. 20; Pliny, *H. N.* viii. 50, 78; id. ix. 81).

Viviscus. Now Vevey; a town on the eastern shore of Lacus Lemannus (Lake Geneva).

Vocatio in Ius. See ACTIO in the Appendix.

Voconia Lex. A law passed by Q. Voconius Saxa, tribune of the people (B.C. 169), and containing two provisions: (1) that no one enrolled as having a property of 100,000 *asses* ($1000) should make any woman his heir; and (2) that no such person should leave to another a sum greater than that which the regular heirs were to receive. The intention of this law was to curb the extravagance of women by limiting their pecuniary means (Gell. xvii. 6; xx. 1). It was evaded in various ways: (*a*) by a person avoiding enrollment in the census; and (*b*) by the creation of trusts (*fidei commissa*) for the benefit of women. See Vangerow, *Lex Voconia* (1863); and cf. the article SUMPTUARIAE LEGES.

Voconius Saxa. See SAXA.

Vocontii. A powerful and important people in Gallia Narbonensis, inhabiting the southeastern part of Dauphiné and a part of Provence between the Drac and the Durance, bounded on the north by the Allobroges, and on the south by the Salyes and Albioeci. They were allowed by the Romans to live under their own laws, and as the allies rather than the subjects of Rome.

Vogĕsus, Vosăgus, or **Vosgĕsus.** Now the Vosges; a range of mountains of Gaul, in the territory of the Lingones, running parallel to the Rhine, and separating its basin from that of the Mosella. The rivers Sequana (Seine), Arar (Saône), and Mosella (Moselle) rise in these mountains.

Volaterrae. Now Volaterra, called by the Etruscans **Velathri**; one of the twelve cities of the Etruscan confederation, built on a lofty and precipitous hill, about 1800 English feet above the level of the sea. It was the most northerly city of the confederation, and its dominions extended eastward as far as the territory of Arretium, which was fifty miles distant; westward as far as the Mediterranean, which was more than twenty miles off; and southward at least as far as Populonia, which was either a colony or an acquisition of Volaterrae. In consequence of possessing the two great ports of Luna and Populonia, Volaterrae, though so far inland, was reckoned as one of the powerful maritime cities of Etruria. We have no record of its conquest by the Romans. Like most of the Etruscan cities, it espoused the Marian party

Arch at Volaterrae.

against Sulla; and it was not till after a siege of two years that the city fell into Sulla's hands. After the fall of the Western Empire, it was for a time the residence of the Lombard kings. The modern town contains several interesting Etruscan remains.

Volaterrāna Vada. A small town in the territory of Volaterrae.

Volcae. A powerful Keltic people in Gallia Narbonensis, divided into the two tribes of the Volcae Tectosages and Volcae Arecomici, extending from the Pyrenees and the frontiers of Aquitania along the coast as far as the Rhône. They lived under their own laws, without being subject to the Roman governor of the province, and they also possessed the *ius Latii.* The Tectosages inhabited the western part of the country from the Pyrenees as far as Narbo, and the Arecomici the eastern part from Narbo to the Rhône, and even beyond the Rhône (Liv. xxi. 26; Strab. p. 203). The chief town of the Tectosages was Tolosa. A portion of the Tectosages left their native country under Brennus, and were one of the three great tribes into which the Galatians in Asia Minor were divided. See GALATIA.

Volcanalia. See VULCANUS.

Volcānus. See VULCANUS.

Volcatius Gallicānus. One of the writers of the *Augusta Historia.* See AUGUSTAE HISTORIAE SCRIPTORES.

Volcatius Sedigĭtus. See SEDIGITUS.

Volci or **Vulci.** (1) Now Vulci; an inland city of Etruria, about eighteen miles northwest of Tarquinii. Of the history of this city we know nothing; but its extensive sepulchres, and the vast treasures of ancient art which they contain, prove that Vulci must at one time have been a powerful and flourishing city. (2) Vallo, a town in Lucania, thirty-six miles southeast of Paestum on the road to Buxentum.

Volĕro Publilius. See PUBLILIUS.

Vologēses. The name of five kings of Parthia. See ARSACES XXIII., XXVII., XXVIII., XXIX., XXX.

Volsci. An ancient people in Latium, originally distinct from the Latins. They dwelt on both sides of the river Liris, and extended down to the Tyrrhene Sea. Their language was nearly allied to the Umbrian. (See UMBRIA.) They were from an early period engaged in almost unceasing hostilities with the Romans, and were not completely subdued by the latter till B.C. 338, after which time they disappear from history. See ITALIA.

Volsellae (τριχολαβίς). (1) A pair of tweezers for pulling out hair (Mart. ix. 28, 5). (2) A pair of forceps (Celsus, vi. 12, 1) used by surgeons and dentists. See CHIRURGIA.

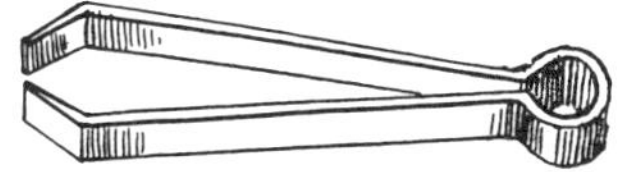

Volsellae, Tweezers. (Rich.)

Volsinii or **Vulsinii.** Now Bolsena; called **Velsĭna** or **Velsunna** by the Etruscans. One of the most ancient and most powerful of the twelve cities of the Etruscan Confederation, was situated on a lofty hill on the northeastern extremity of the lake called after it LACUS VOLSINIENSIS and VULSINIENSIS (Lago di Bolsena). The Volsinienses carried on war with the Romans in B.C. 392, 311, 294, and 280, but were on each occasion defeated, and in the last of these years appear to have been finally subdued. Their city was then razed to the ground by the Romans, and its inhabitants were compelled to settle on a less defensible site in the plain, that of the modern Bolsena.

Volturcius or **Vulturcius,** TITUS. One of Catiline's conspirators, who turned informer upon obtaining the promise of pardon. He was one of those who accompanied the ambassadors of the Allobroges and was arrested with them on the Pons Mulvius. See Cicero's third oration against Catiline.

Volūmen. See LIBER; PAPYRUS; WRITING AND WRITING MATERIALS.

Volumnia. The wife of Coriolanus. See CORIOLANUS.

Volupia or **Voluptas.** The personification of sensual pleasure among the Romans, and honoured with a temple near the Porta Romanula.

Volusius Maeciānus, LUCIUS. A Roman jurist who was in the consilium of Antoninus Pius, and was one of the teachers of Marcus Aurelius. Maecianus wrote several works; and there are forty-two excerpts from his writings in the Digest. A treatise *De Asse et Ponderibus* is attributed to him, but there is some doubt about the authorship. It is edited by Böcking (Bonn, 1831).

Volŭsus or **Volĕsus.** The reputed ancestor of the Valeria gens, who is said to have settled at Rome with Titus Tatius. See VALERIA GENS.

Vomānus. Now the Vomano; a small river in Picenum.

Vomitorium. See AMPHITHEATRUM.

Vonōnes. The name of two kings of Parthia. See ARSACES XVIII., XXII.

Vopiscus. A Roman praenomen, signifying a twin-child who was born safe, while the other twin died before birth (Pliny, *H. N.* vii. 47; Solin. 1). Like many other ancient Roman praenomens, it was afterwards used as a cognomen.

Vopiscus Flavius. A native of Syracuse, and one of the six *Scriptores Historiae Augustae.* He flourished about A.D. 300. See AUGUSTAE HISTORIAE SCRIPTORES.

Vortumnalia. See VERTUMNUS.

Vosăgus. See VOGESUS.

Vosgĕsus. See VOGESUS.

Vota Publĭca. Vows made by the State in great crises, as during war (Livy, v. 21) or pestilence (Livy, iv. 25). They were in the nature of promises to the gods of gifts or sacrifices in return for aid and favour. The vow was made on behalf of the State by a consul, praetor, or dictator, who was said *suscipere votum,* at the behest of the Senate. The announcement of the vow (*nuncupatio*) was publicly made in a set formula dictated by the Pontifex Maximus (Livy, xxxvi. 2), and it was entered in the public records. The vow was generally fulfilled by the magistrate who made it or by his regular successor, but it might devolve upon another (Livy, xxxvi. 2). Besides these extraordinary public vows, there was an annual *votum publicum* (of victims to be offered) made by the new consuls on January 1st, *pro rei publicae salute.* Under the Republic a special vow was added for the emperor's safety (Dio Cass. li. 9). See Marquardt, *Staatsverwaltung,* iii. pp. 265–268; Mommsen, *Röm. Staatsrecht,* i. 244; ii. 810; and for the most remarkable of all the public vows, see the article VER SACRUM.

Voting. See COMITIA; DIKÉ; OVILÉ; TABELLARIAE LEGES.

Votōrum Nuncupatio. See VOTA PUBLICA.

Vowels. See PHILOLOGIA.

Vulcaniae Insŭlae. See AEOLIAE INSULAE.

Vulcānus or **Volcānus** (which is the earlier form of the word). The Italian god of fire. Vulcanus differed originally from Vesta in being the god rather of destructive fire than of the kindly hearth-fire; and it is probable that the VULCĀNAL as one of the central sanctuaries in an Italian town (e.g. the altar and Area Vulcani in the Comitium at Rome) was originally a place for propitiatory offerings against destructive fire. In this way Vulcanus was connected with the goddess who stayed conflagrations (Stata Mater). That, however, in some places he was at one time also regarded as a god of the hearth-fire is indicated by the story of his son Caeculus (see CAECUS), and perhaps by that of Servius Tullius. But another primitive characteristic was his benign influence also as a god of summer heat, which led to his being paired with Maia, the goddess of spring or summer crops fostered by the sun (Gell. xiii. 23; Macrob. i. 12; Varr. *L. L.* v. 84); and in this aspect he may have been connected with the Italian Venus even before the Greek influence introduced this association from the analogy of Hephaestus and Aphroditē. As regards the connection of the Italian Vulcan with the smith's works of forging and melting, there is no clear evidence. It is asserted that MULCĬBER, a synonym of Vulcanus (and possibly once the name of another deity amalgamated or identified with him), represents this function of Vulcan, and is derived from *mulcere,* to soften metals; but this is by no means certain, and it is possible that the connection of Vulcanus (or Mulciber) with metal-work and the smithy is merely part of the transference to him of all the attributes of Hephaestus, with whom he is entirely identified in literature. For the myths thus transferred to Vulcanus, see HEPHAESTUS.

Vulci. See VOLCI.

Vulgāta. See HIERONYMUS; ITALA; SERMO PLEBEIUS.

Vulgientes. An Alpine people in Gallia Narbonensis, whose chief town was Apta Iulia (Apt).

Vulsinii. See VOLSINII.

Vulso, MANLIUS. (1) LUCIUS, consul B.C. 256 with M. Atilius Regulus. He invaded Africa with his colleague (see REGULUS No. 3). Vulso returned to Italy at the fall of the year with half of the army, and obtained the honour of a triumph. In 250 Vulso was consul a second time with T. Atilius Regulus Serranus, and with his colleague commenced the siege of Lilybaeum (Polyb. i. 39–48; Zonar. viii. 15). (2) GNAEUS, curule aedile B.C. 197, praetor with Sicily as his province 195, and consul 189. He was sent into Asia in order to conclude the peace which Scipio Asiaticus had made with Antiochus, and to arrange the affairs of Asia. He attacked and conquered the Gallograeci or Galatians in Asia Minor without waiting for any formal instructions from the Senate. His march is important in the discussion of the topography of Asia Minor, and has been carefully traced by Professor Ramsay. It was from Ephesus to Ancyra, in the country of the Tectosages, and as far as the banks of the Halys (Livy, xxxviii. 12–27; Polyb. xxii. 16). He set out on his return to Italy in 188, but in his march through Thrace he suffered much from the attacks of the Thracians, and lost a considerable part of the booty he had obtained in Asia. He reached Rome in 187. His triumph was a brilliant one, but his campaign in Asia had a pernicious influence upon the morals of his countrymen. He had allowed his army every kind of license, and his soldiers introduced into Rome the luxuries of the East (Livy, xxxviii. 37–50; xxxix. 6; Polyb. xxii. 24; App. *Syr.* 42).

Vultur. A mountain dividing Apulia and Lucania near Venusia, is a branch of the Apennines. It is celebrated by Horace as one of the haunts of his youth (*Od.* iii. 4, 9–16; Lucan, ix. 185). It attains an elevation of 4433 feet above the sea. From it the southeast wind was called Vulturnus by the Romans.

Vulturnum. Now Castel di Volturno; a town in Campania, at the mouth of the river Vulturnus, was originally a fortress erected by the Romans in the Second Punic War (Livy, xxv. 20, 22). At a later time it was made a colony (Livy, xxxiv. 45; Varr. *L. L.* v. 5).

Vulturnus. Now the Volturno; the chief river in Campania, rising in the Apennines in Samnium, and falling into the Tyrrhene Sea.

W

Wagons. See ARCUMA; BENNA; CARRUS; CARPENTUM; CISIUM; CURRUS; ESSEDUM; PETORRITUM; PILENTUM; PLAUSTRUM; REDA; SARRACUM; TENSA; VEHICULUM.

Wain. See PLAUSTRUM.

Waiters. See CENA; FAMULUS; SERVUS.

Wall. (1) Of a city. See MURUS. (2) Of a house. See DOMUS; PARIES.

Wallet. See BULGA; PERA; VENTRALE.

"**Walnut Tree,**" POEM OF THE. See NUX.

Wand. See VIRGA.

Warming of Houses. See BALNEAE; DOMUS; FOCULUS; FURNUS.

Warrant. See DIPLOMA.

Wars. See (1) LELANTINE WAR; (2) PELOPONNESIAN WAR; (3) PUNIC WARS; (4) SOCIAL WAR.

Washing. See FULLO.

Wasps of Aristophanes. See ARISTOPHANES.

Watch-house. See EXCUBITORIUM.

Watchman. See CASTRA; EXCUBITORES; VIGILES.

Watch-tower. See SPECULA in the Appendix.

Water-clock. See HOROLOGIUM.

Water-closets. See DOMUS; FORICAE; LATRINA.

Water-supply. See AQUAE DUCTUS; FONS.

Waterworks. See AQUAE DUCTUS.

Wax. See CERA; CEROMA.

Wax-candles. See CANDELA; CEREUS.

Weapons. See ARCUS; ARMA; FUNDA; GLADIUS; GLANS; HASTA; IACULUM; PILUM; SAGITTA; TORMENTUM.

Weaving. See TELA.

Wedding-cake. See MUSTACEUM.

Weddings. See MATRIMONIUM.

Wedding-veil. See FLAMMEUM; RICINIUM.

Wedge. See CUNEUS.

Week. The Greeks originally divided their month into three parts of ten days each, and the Romans had a sort of week of eight days—between the *nundinae* or market-days. (See NUNDINAE.) The Egyptians, however, like the Jews, had a week of seven days, named from the seven planets, and from Alexandria this seven-day week (*ἑβδομάς*, *hebdomas*, *septimana*) spread to Greece, and, at about the beginning of the Christian era, to Rome also. In the Codex Theodosianus (q.v.) the name *septimana* first appears in the sense of "week," and from it came the Italian *settimana*, the Spanish *semana*, and the French *semaine*.

Weeping Philosopher. See HERACLITUS.

Weights and Measures. See PONDUS; and the Tables in the Appendix.

Wells. See FONS; PUTEUS.

Were-wolves. See VERSIPELLIS.

West-wind. See ZEPHYRUS.

Wheel. See ROTA; TYMPANUM.

Wherry. See LINTER.

Whip. See FLAGELLUM; SCUTICA.

Whiskers. See BARBA; MUSTAX.

Wigs. See CALIENDRUM; COMA; GALERUM.

Wills. See HERES; TESTAMENTUM.

Winckelmann, JOHANN JOACHIM. A very distinguished German archæologist, born in Stendal, Prussia, December 9th, 1717, the son of a shoemaker. With great difficulty young Winckelmann gained a preparatory training in the schools of his native town, and at Berlin and Salzwedel, whence he went to the Universities of Halle and Jena, at which he showed a remarkable proficiency in the Greek and Latin languages, and a strong bent towards the study of archæology and ancient art. After teaching for several years at Seehausen, he was made librarian at Nöthnitz, near Dresden. The magnificent collections of the latter place filled him with a desire to visit Rome, learning of which the Papal Nuncio, Archinto, promised to provide him with the means on condition of his joining the Church—a condition which Winckelmann, after a long period of hesitation, accepted in 1755. In the same year he received from the Pope a small pension. He at once journeyed to Rome, where he formed the acquaintance of Raphael Mengs, who greatly aided him in his studies of classic art.

Winckelmann now entered upon a period of prosperity, becoming librarian to Cardinal Alessandro Albani, in whose palace and villa he was made at home; and in 1763, the Pope appointed him Professor of Antiquities, and Hellenist to the great Vatican Library. His improved circumstances allowed him to travel, so that he spent some time at Florence, Naples, Pompeii, and Herculaneum, declining an appointment at Berlin, in order to remain in Italy. In 1768, having visited Vienna, he received from the Empress Maria Theresa the gift of some exceedingly rare gold coins, whose value tempted the cupidity of an Italian thief, one Arcangeli, and led him to assassinate Winckelmann while returning to Rome (June 8th). He was buried in the cemetery adjoining the cathedral of Trieste, where he died.

Winckelmann was the founder of archæology as a science, and laid down the lines of antiquarian investigation and research that modern scholars have so successfully followed out. His influence was much more than a purely scholastic one, however. To his views of the beautiful and to his enthusiasm for classical antiquity may be traced much of the inspiration of Lessing and Heyne, and other writers of the Augustan Age of German literature. His greatest work is the *Geschichte der Kunst des Alterthums* (1764), with its supplementary work *Anmerkungen über die Geschichte der Kunst* (1767), both included in the Vienna edition of 1776 (Eng. trans. by Lodge, 2d ed. 4 vols. 1856–72). Other works are the *Gedanken über die Nachahmung der griechischen Werke in Malerei und Bildhauerkunst* (1755); *Description des Pierres Gravées du feu Baron de Stosch* (1760); *Monumenti Antichi Inediti*, 2 vols. (1767–68; 2d ed. 1821); *Versuch einer Allegorie* (1766, republished with additions from manuscripts, 1866); and several reports on Herculaneum, etc. His letters were edited and published by F. Forster, in 2 vols., *Winckelmann's Briefe* (Berlin, 1824); and his complete works have been published under the care of Fernow, H. Meyer, and Schultz, in 8 vols. (Dresden, 1808–1820).

On his literary influence the reader is referred to Goethe's *Winckelmann und sein Jahrhundert*, published in collaboration with H. Meyer and others (Tübingen, 1805). His life was written by Karl Justi, *Winckelmann, sein Leben, seine Werke und seine Zeitgenossen*, 3 vols. (Leipzig, 1866–72).

Windows. See DOMUS.

Ancient Window. (Baumeister.)

Winds. See VENTUS.

Wine. See VINUM.

Wisdom, GODDESS OF. See ATHENÉ; MINERVA.

Wise Men, THE SEVEN. See SEVEN SAGES.

Witch. See SAGA; STRIGA; VENEFICA.

Witness. See DIKÉ; JUDICIAL PROCEDURE; MARTYRIA; TESTIS.

Witticisms. See JESTS.

Wives. See MATRIMONIUM.

Wizards. See MAGUS; STRIGA.

Wolf, FRIEDRICH AUGUST. A great Homeric scholar, born in Hainrode, in Germany, on February 15th, 1759. He was educated in the University of Göttingen, where he also gave private lessons; and in 1779 removed to Ilfeld, where he became the teacher of a school. In 1782 he was made rector of the public school at Osterode, and in 1783 Professor of Philosophy at the University of Halle, where he remained until the university was closed in 1806, when he removed to Berlin and took an active part in the foundation of the new university in that city, being employed by the Minister of Public Instruction. Wolf had already won a commanding position among the scholars of Germany by his epoch-making *Prolegomena in Homerum*, prefixed to the second edition of his *Homeri et Homeridarum Opera*, which appeared in 1795. In it he set forth the so-called Wolfian theory of the origin of the Homeric poems, claiming that the *Iliad* is made up of a number of ballads and songs which at first existed separately in the verses of different rhapsodists, by whom they were handed down from generation to generation until they were united by Pisistratus in the singer's epic that was afterwards ascribed to Homer. This theory he based upon his assertion that writing was not known at the time of the composition of the poems, and also upon the contradictions and inconsistencies to be detected in the poems themselves. (See HOMERUS; RHAPSODUS.) The Wolfian hypothesis was not original with Wolf himself, having been advanced before his time by other scholars (Casaubon, Vico, Bentley, Hedelin, Perrault, and Wood); but Wolf was the first to present the arguments with sufficient acuteness, logic, and impressiveness to make a profound impression upon the scholarship of the day.

Other valuable works of Wolf are his *Demosthenis Leptinea*, with a most learned introduction (1789); editions of Plato's *Symposium;* of Hesiod's *Theogony;* of Cicero's *Tusculanae;* of several of the Ciceronian Orations (*Post Reditum in Senatu, Ad Quirites de Domo Sua, De Haruspicum Responsis*, and the *Oratio pro Marcello*, which Wolf regarded as spurious); of the *Clouds* of Aristophanes; and of Casaubon's Suetonius. His *Kleine Schriften*, edited by G. Bernhardy, appeared in 2 vols. in 1869. Wolf died at Marseilles, August 8th, 1824. See Körte, *Leben und Studien F. A. Wolf's*, 2 vols. (Essen, 1833); Arnoldt, *Wolf in seinem Verhältnisse zum Schulwesen und zur Pädagogik*, 2 vols. (Brunswick, 1861–62); Bursian, *Geschichte der class. Philologie* (Munich, 1883); and Jebb's *Homer* (Glasgow, 1877). Cf. the article TEXTUAL CRITICISM.

Wonders, THE SEVEN. See SEVEN WONDERS.

Wood-nymphs. See NYMPHAE.

Word-books. See LEXICON.

Worship. See RELIGIO; SACRIFICIUM; TEMPLUM.

Writing. See ALPHABET; PALAEOGRAPHY.

Writing and Writing Materials. Ancient writing was done on (*a*) leaves, as of the olive and bay; (*b*) bark, as of the lime-tree (φιλύρα); (*c*) linen cloth; (*d*) clay and pottery; (*e*) walls; (*f*) metals, rarely gold or silver, often lead plates and bronze; (*g*) wood, either coated with wax or some kind of glaze or not; (*h*) papyrus; (*i*) skins, especially parchment or vellum (διφθέραι, *membranae*). (See the articles CODEX; EPIGRAPHY; FICTILÉ; GRAFFITI; LIBER; OSCI; PALAEOGRAPHY; PAPYRUS; TABULA.) Paper was not found in Europe until its use was learned from the Arabs in the eighth century A.D.

The pen used in writing upon papyrus was a split reed (*calamus*), the best being supplied by Egypt and Cnidus in Caria. The ink (*atramentum*) employed was a preparation resembling India ink, made of soot and gum, or of the juice of the cuttle-fish. Both of these could be erased with a sponge (*spongia*), whereas ink made of oxide of iron and gall-nuts, which appears to have been introduced later, and to have been the only kind capable of being used for parchment, left more or less clear traces behind, even if rubbed out with pumice-stone. Red ink was also used in very early times. The ink-bottle was called μελανδόχον, *atramentarium*, and was a small cylindrical jar, or two such jars, one for black and one for red ink. In ordinary life people used for letters, notices, and despatches, as also in schools, wooden tablets (*tabellae*) with a

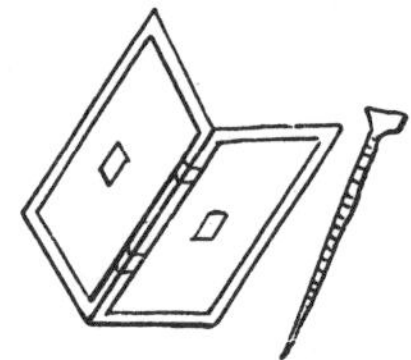

Wax Tablet and Stilus. (Perret, *Catacombes de Rome.*)

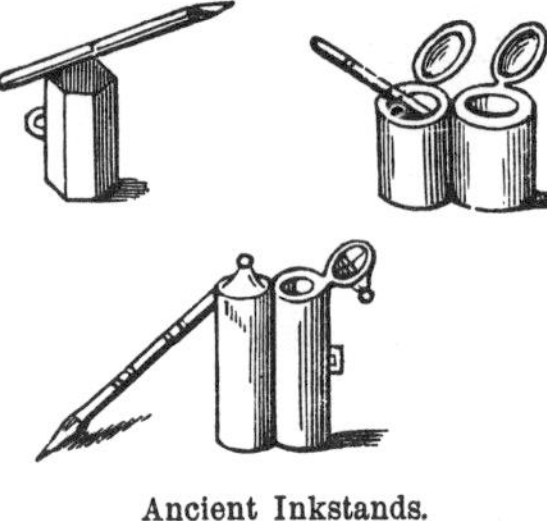

Ancient Inkstands.

raised rim, within which was spread a thin layer of wax. On this the characters were scratched with the point of a metal or ivory instrument called a *stilus;* they could be effaced with the other end of the instrument, which was bent or flattened out like a paper-folder (see STILUS). Two or more such tablets could be fastened together in the form of a book. (See DIPTYCHON.) See Thompson, *Greek and Latin Palaeography*, pp. 12–53 (New York, 1893); and the article PALAEOGRAPHY in this Dictionary.

Writing Case. See CAPSA.

X

X, as a symbol.

IN GREEK.—Ξ = ξένοι on Attic ephebic inscriptions. As a numeral = 14 (old system). ξ′ = 60; ͵ξ = 60,000.

IN LATIN.—X = 10. See NUMERUS.

Xanthippé (Ξανθίππη). The wife of the Athenian philosopher Socrates. Many anecdotes have come down in the pages of ancient writers regarding this famous woman, whose name has become proverbial in all languages as that of a typical shrew. It is likely, however, that many of these are apocryphal, and that, on the other hand, there was much in the unpractical ways of Socrates to provoke even a good-tempered woman who loved order and a reasonable degree of conventionality. It is fair to remember, also, that Socrates himself, in a conversation with his son Lamprocles (Xen. *Mem.* ii. 2), ascribes to Xanthippé numerous domestic virtues; while it is recorded that she showed great affection and solicitude for her husband during his imprisonment. See SOCRATES.

Xanthippus (Ξάνθιππος). (1) The son of Ariphron and father of Pericles. He succeeded Themistocles as commander of the Athenian fleet in B.C. 479, and commanded the Athenians at the decisive battle of Mycalé. (2) A Lacedaemonian, who commanded the Carthaginians against Regulus. See REGULUS.

Xanthus (Ξάνθος). (1) See SCAMANDER. (2) Now the Echen Chai; the chief river of Lycia, rises in Mount Taurus, and flows south through Lycia, between Mount Cragus and Mount Massicytus, falling at last into the Mediterranean Sea a little west of Patara. It is navigable for a considerable part of its course.

Xanthus (Ξάνθος). Now Gunik; the most famous city of Lycia, standing on the west bank of the river of the same name, sixty stadia from its mouth. Twice in the course of its history it sustained sieges, which terminated in the self-destruction of the inhabitants with their property, first against the Persians under Harpagus, and long afterwards against the Romans under Brutus. The city was never restored after its destruction on the latter occasion. Xanthus was rich in temples and tombs, and other monuments of a most interesting character, and several important remains of its works of art are now exhibited in the British Museum.

Xanthus (Ξάνθος). A Greek historian. See LOGOGRAPHI.

Xenāgus (ξεναγός). The Spartan commander of the several contingents in the Peloponnesian League (Thuc. ii. 75; Xen. *Hellen.* iv. 2, 19).

Xenarchus (Ξέναρχος). (1) The son of Sophron, and, like his father, a celebrated writer of mimes. He lived during the Rhegian War (B.C. 399–389), at the court of Dionysius (Arist. *Poët.* 2). (2) An Athenian comic poet of the Middle Comedy, who lived as late as the time of Alexander the Great (Suid. *s. v.*). Several fragments of his writings are collected in Meineke's *Fragm. Com. Graec.*

Xenelasia (ξενηλασία). The right possessed and exercised by the Lacedaemonian magistrates of expelling from Sparta any stranger whose presence was injurious to the public order or morals. This was an enactment of Lycurgus himself, and was intended to preserve the native character of the Spartans from any taint of foreign influence (Xen. *De Rep. Lac.* 14, 4). See Schömann, *Antiq. of Greece*, Eng. trans. p. 278.

Xeni (ξένοι). See MERCENARII.

Xenia (ξενία). See HOSPITIUM in the Appendix.

Xenia (ξένια). (1) Presents that it was customary among the Greeks and Romans for a host to give or send to his guests, as a mark of hospitality and friendship (Pliny, *Epist.* vi. 31, 14), consisting, for the most part, of delicacies for the table; as may be collected from the thirteenth book of Martial, which is inscribed with the title *Xenia*, and relates chiefly to articles of food.

(2) Pictures of still-life, such as dead game, poultry, fish, fruit, vegetables, etc. (Vitruv. vi. 7, 4; Philostrat. *Imag.* i. 31, ii. 25); so termed because they represented such objects as a host sent in presents to his guests. Many pictures of this kind have been found among the paintings of Pompeii, one of which is given under PICTURA.

Xenias Graphé (ξενίας γραφή). An action brought at Athens against any one who unlawfully exercised the rights of citizenship. If convicted, such a person was sold as a slave and his property was forfeited to the State.

Xenŏcles (Ξενοκλῆς). An Athenian tragic poet, ridiculed by Aristophanes, and yet the conqueror of Euripides on one occasion (B.C. 415). He was of dwarfish stature, and son of the tragic poet Carcinus. In the *Peace*, Aristophanes applies the term μηχανοδίφας to the family. From the scholiast it appears that Xenocles was celebrated for introducing stage machinery and spectacular effects, especially in the ascent or descent of his gods.

Xenocrătes (Ξενοκράτης). A philosopher, born at Chalcedon in B.C. 400. He first attached himself to Æschines, but afterwards became a disciple of Plato, who took much pains in cultivating his genius, which was naturally heavy. Plato, comparing him with Aristotle, who was also one of his pupils, called the former a dull ass who needed the spur, and the latter a mettlesome horse who required the curb. His temper was gloomy, his aspect stern, and his manners little tinctured with urbanity. These material defects his master took great pains to correct, frequently advising him to sacrifice to the Graces; and the pupil, patient of instruction, knew how to value the kindness of his preceptor. He compared himself to a vessel with a narrow orifice, which receives with difficulty, but firmly retains whatever is put into it. So attached was Xenocrates to his master that when Dionysius, in a violent fit of anger, threatened to find one who should cut off his head, he said, "Not before he has cut off this," pointing to his own. As long as Plato lived, Xenocrates was one of his most esteemed disciples; after his death he closely adhered to his doctrine; and in B.C. 339 he took the chair in the Academy as the successor of Speusippus. Aristotle, who, about this time, returned from Macedonia, in expectation, as it should seem, of filling the chair, was greatly disappointed and chagrined at this nomination, and immediately instituted a school in the Lyceum, in opposition to that of the Academy where Xenocrates continued to preside till his death. Xenocrates was celebrated among the Athenians, not only for his wisdom, but also for his virtues (Val. Max. ii. 10; Cic. *Ad Att.* ii. 16; Diog. Laërt. iv. 7).

So eminent was his reputation for integrity that when he was called upon to give evidence in a judicial transaction, in which an oath was usually required, the judges unanimously agreed that his simple asseveration should be taken, as a public testimony to his merit. Even Philip of Macedon found it impossible to corrupt him. When he was sent, with several others, upon an embassy to that king, he declined all private intercourse with him, that he might escape the temptations of a bribe. Philip afterwards said that of all those who had come to him on embassies from foreign States, Xenocrates was the only one whose friendship he had not been able to purchase (Diog. Laërt. iv. 8). During the time of the Lamiac War, being sent an ambassador to the court of Antipater for the redemption of several Athenian captives, he was invited by the prince to sit down with him at supper, but declined the invitation in the words of Odysseus to Circé (*Odyss.* x. 383). This pertinent and ingenious application of a passage in Homer, or, rather, the generous and patriotic spirit which it expressed, was so pleasing to Antipater that he immediately released the prisoners. It may be mentioned as another example of moderation in Xenocrates, that when Alexander, to mortify Aristotle, against whom he had an accidental pique, sent Xenocrates a magnificent present of fifty talents, he accepted only thirty minae, returning the rest to Alexander with this message: that the large sum which Alexander had sent was more than he should have been able to spend during his whole life. So abstemious was he with respect to food that his provision was frequently spoiled before it was consumed. His chastity was invincible, and Laïs, a celebrated Athenian courtesan, attempted, without success, to seduce him. He was an admirer of the mathematical sciences, and was so fully convinced of their utility that when a young man who was unacquainted with geometry and astronomy desired admission, he refused his request, saying that he was not yet possessed of the handles of philosophy. In fine, Xenocrates was eminent both for the purity of his morals and for his acquaintance with science, and supported the credit of the Platonic School by his lectures, his writings, and his conduct. He lived until B.C. 316, when he lost his life by accidentally falling, in the dark, into a reservoir of water.

The philosophical tenets of Xenocrates were truly Platonic, but in his method of teaching he made use of the language of the Pythagoreans. He made Unity and Diversity principles in nature, or gods; the former of whom he represented as the father, and the latter as the mother, of the universe. He taught that the heavens are divine, and the stars gods; and that, besides these divinities, there are terrestrial demons of a middle order, between the gods and man, which partake of the nature both of mind and body, and are therefore, like human beings, capable of passions and liable to diversity of character.

(2) A Greek physician of Aphrodisias, a work of whose is still remaining, on the food afforded by fishes. It is edited by Coray (Paris, 1814).

Xenophănes (*Ξενοφάνης*). The founder of the Eleatic school of philosophy was a native of Colophon, and born about B.C. 556. Xenophanes early left his own country and took refuge in Sicily, where he supported himself by reciting, at the court of Hiero, elegiac and iambic verses, which he had written in criticism of the Theogonies of Hesiod and Homer. From Sicily he passed over into Magna Graecia, where he took up the profession of philosophy, and became a celebrated preceptor in the Pythagorean school. Indulging, however, a greater freedom of thought than was usual among the disciples of Pythagoras, he ventured to introduce new opinions of his own, and in many particulars to oppose the doctrines of Epimenides, Thales, and Pythagoras. He held the Pythagorean chair of philosophy for about seventy years, and lived to the extreme age of a hundred. In metaphysics, Xenophanes taught that if there had ever been a time when nothing existed, nothing could ever have existed; that whatever is, always has been from eternity, without deriving its existence from any prior principles; that nature is one and without limit; that what is one is similar in all its parts, else it would be many; that the one infinite, eternal, and homogeneous universe is immutable and incapable of change; that God is one incorporeal eternal being, and, like the universe, spherical in form; that he is of the same nature with the universe, comprehending all things within himself; is intelligent, and pervades all things, but bears no resemblance to human nature either in body or mind. See V. Cousin, *Xénophane, Fondateur de l'École d'Élée*, in his *Nouveaux Fragments Philos.* (Paris, 1828); Bergk, *Commentatio de Arist. Libello de Xenophane, Zenone, et Gorgia* (Marburg, 1843); Reinhold, *De Genuina Xenophanis Disciplina* (Jena, 1847); Kern, *Quaestionum Xenophanearum Capita Duo* (Naumburg, 1864); Rüffer, *De Philosoph. Xenophanis Coloph. Parte Morali* (Leipzig, 1868); and Ueberweg's *Hist. of Philos.* i. pp. 49–54 (Eng. trans. N. Y. 1872). The fragments of his writings are collected in Karsten's *Philosophorum Graecorum Veterum Operum Reliquiae*, vol. i. (Amsterdam, 1835), and in Schneidewin's *Elegiaci Graeci* (1838).

Xenŏphon (*Ξενοφῶν*). (1) An Athenian, the son of one Gryllus, born about B.C. 444. In his early life he was a pupil of Socrates; but the turning-point in his career came when he decided to serve in the Greek contingent raised by Cyrus against Artaxerxes in 401. Xenophon himself mentions (*Anab.* iii. 1) the circumstances under which he joined this army. Proxenus, a friend of Xenophon, was already with Cyrus, and he invited Xenophon to come to Sardis, and promised to introduce him to the Persian prince. Xenophon consulted his master, Socrates, who advised him to consult the oracle of Delphi, as it was a hazardous matter for him to enter the service of Cyrus, who was considered to be the friend of the Lacedaemonians and the enemy of Athens. Xenophon went to Delphi, but he did not ask the god whether he should go or not: he probably had made up his mind. He merely inquired to what gods he should sacrifice in order that he might be successful in his intended enterprise. Socrates was not satisfied with his pupil's mode of consulting the oracle, but as he had got an answer, he told him to go; and Xenophon went to Sardis, which Cyrus was just about to leave. He accompanied Cyrus into Upper Asia. In the battle of Cunaxa (B.C. 401) Cyrus lost his life, his barbarian troops were dispersed, and the Greeks were left alone on the wide plains between the Tigris and the Euphrates. (See CYRUS.) It was after the treacherous massacre of Clearchus and others of the Greek commanders by the Persian satrap Tissaphernes (q.v.) that Xenophon came forward. He had held no command in the army of Cyrus, nor had he, in fact, served as a soldier, yet he was elected one of the generals, and took the principal part in conducting the Greeks in their memorable retreat along the Tigris over the high table-lands of Armenia to Trapezus (Trebizond) on the Black Sea. From Trapezus the troops were conducted to Chrysopolis, which is opposite to Byzantium. The Greeks were in great distress, and some of them under Xenophon entered the service of Seuthes, king of Thrace. As the Lacedaemonians under Thimbron, or Thibron, were now at war with Tissaphernes and Pharnabazus, Xenophon and his troops were invited to join the army of Thimbron, and Xenophon led them back out of Asia to join Thimbron (399). Xenophon, who was very poor, made an expedition into the plain of the Caïcus with his troops before they joined Thimbron, to plunder the house and property of a Persian named Asidates. The Persian, with his women, children, and all his movables, was seized, and Xenophon, by this robbery, replenished his empty pockets (*Anab.* vii. 8, 23). He tells the story himself, and is evidently not at all ashamed of it. In other ways also he showed himself the prototype of an adventurous leader of *condottieri*, with no ties of country or preference of nationality. He formed a scheme for establishing a town with the Ten Thousand on the shores of the Euxine; but it fell through. He joined the Spartans, as has been seen, and he continued in their service even when they were at war with Athens. Agesilaüs, the Spartan, was commanding the Lacedaemonian forces in Asia against the Persians in 396, and Xenophon was with him at least during part of the campaign. When Agesilaüs was recalled (394), Xenophon accompanied him, and he was on the side of the Lacedaemonians in the battle which they fought at Coronea (394) against the Athenians. As a natural consequence a decree of exile was passed against him at Athens. It seems that he went to Sparta with Agesilaüs after the battle of Coronea, and soon after he settled at Scillus in Elis, not far from Olympia, a spot of which he has given a description in the *Anabasis* (v. 3, 7). Here he was joined by his wife, Philesia, and his children. His children were educated in Sparta.

Xenophon was now a Lacedaemonian so far as he could become one. His time during his long residence at Scillus was employed in hunting, writing, and entertaining his friends; and perhaps the *Anabasis* and part of the *Hellenica* were composed here. The treatise on hunting and that on the horse were probably also written during this time, when amusement and exercise of this kind formed part of his occupation. On the downfall of the Spartan supremacy, at Leuctra in 371, Xenophon was at last expelled from his quiet retreat at Scillus by the Eleans, after remaining there about twenty years. The sentence of banishment from Athens was repealed on the motion of Eubulus, but it is uncertain in what year. There is no evidence that Xenophon ever returned to Athens. He is said to have retired to Corinth after his expulsion from Scillus, and as we know nothing more, we assume that he died there. In the battle of Mantinea (B.C. 362) the Spartans and the Athenians were opposed to the Thebans, and Xenophon's two sons, Gryllus and Diodorus, fought on the side of the allies. Gryllus fell in the same battle in which Epaminondas lost his life. The events alluded to in the epilogue to the *Cyropaedia* (viii. 8, 4) show that the epilogue at least was written after 362. The time of his death, for reasons given above, seems to have been later than 357.

The following is a list of Xenophon's works: (1) The *Anabasis* (Ἀνάβασις), a history of the expedition of the Younger Cyrus, and of the retreat of the Greeks who formed part of his army. It is divided into seven books. As regards the title it will be noticed that under the name "The March *Up*" (ἀνά, i. e. inland from the coast of Cunaxa) is included also the much longer account of the return march *down* to the Euxine. This work has immortalized Xenophon's name. It is a clear and fascinating narrative, written in a simple style, free from affectation, and giving a great deal of curious information on the country which was traversed by the retreating Greeks, and on the manners of the people. It was the first work which made the Greeks acquainted with some portions of the Persian Empire, and it showed the weakness of that extensive monarchy. The skirmishes of the retreating Greeks with their enemies, and the battles with some of the barbarian tribes, are not such events as elevate the work to the character of a military history, nor can it as such be compared with Caesar's *Commentarii.* There is no weight whatever in the argument that, because Xenophon (*Hellen.* iii. 1, 2) speaks of the expedition of Cyrus as having been related by Themistogenes, the *Anabasis* is therefore not Xenophon's work. The statement can be explained either on the theory that Xenophon speaks of his own work under a fictitious name (which was possibly the case also with the *Oeconomicus*), or, more simply, by supposing that another account was actually written by Themistogenes. It is known that a separate account was written by Sophaenetus, and there may have been others. If the latter theory be correct, it would be a natural inference that Xenophon's *Anabasis* was written after the third book of the *Hellenica.* (2) The *Hellenica* (Ἑλληνικά) of Xenophon is divided into seven books, and covers the forty-eight years from the time when the History of Thucydides ends (see THUCYDIDES) to the battle of Mantinea (B.C. 362). The *Hellenica* is generally a dry narrative of events, and there is nothing in the treatment of them which gives a special interest to the work. Some events of importance are briefly treated, but a few striking incidents are presented with some particularity. The *Hellenica* was not written at one time. Differences are traced between the first two and the later books as regards the arrangement, which in the earlier books is year by year, while, in the later, events growing out of one another are grouped together; and, as regards political sentiment, in the diminished admiration for Sparta which appears in the last three books. It is clear that book vi. was written after 357, since it mentions the death of Alexander of Pherae (vi. 4, 35); but the first four books were probably written a good deal earlier. (3) The *Cyropaedia* (Κυροπαιδεία), in eight books, is a kind of political romance, the basis of which is the history of the Elder Cyrus, the founder of the Persian monarchy. It shows how citizens are to be made virtuous and brave; and Cyrus is the model of a wise and good ruler. As a history it has no authority at all. Xenophon adopted the current stories as to Cyrus and the chief events of his reign, without any intention of subjecting them to a critical examination; nor have we any reason to suppose that his picture of Persian morals and Persian discipline is anything more than a fiction. Xenophon's object was to represent what a State might be, and he placed the scene of his fiction far enough off to give it the colour of possibility. His own philosophical notions and the usages of Sparta were the real materials out of which he constructed his political system. The *Cyropaedia* is evidence enough that Xenophon did not like the political constitution of his own country, and that a well-ordered monarchy or kingdom appeared to him preferable to a democracy like Athens. (4) The *Agesilaüs* (Ἀγησίλαος) is a panegyric on Agesilaüs II., king of Sparta, the friend of Xenophon. The genuineness is disputed, not without reason, and a recent critic holds it to be the work of a young rhetorician of the school of Isocrates. (5) The *Hipparchicus* (Ἱππαρχικός) is a treatise on the duties of a commander of cavalry, and it contains many military precepts. (6) The *De Re Equestri*, a treatise on the horse (Ἱππική), was written after the *Hipparchicus*, to which treatise he refers at the end of the treatise on the horse. This essay is not limited to horsemanship as regards the rider: it shows how a man is to avoid being cheated in buying a horse, how a horse is to be trained, and the like. (7) The *Cynegeticus* (Κυνηγετικός) is a treatise on hunting; and on the dog, and the breeding and training of dogs; on the various kinds of game, and the mode of taking them. It is a treatise written by a genuine sportsman who loved the exercise and excitement of the chase, and it may be read with pleasure by a sportsman of the present day. (8, 9) The *Respublica Lacedaemoniorum* and *Respublica Atheniensium*, the two treatises on the Spartan and Athenian States (Λακεδαιμονίων Πολιτεία and Ἀθηναίων Πολιτεία), were both ascribed to Xenophon, but the *Respublica Atheniensium* is certainly not by his hand. It was written by some one of the oligarchical party, and possibly it is right to date it as early as 420, and therefore to regard it as the earliest Attic prose work. On the other hand, a modern critic of Xenophon (Hartmann) believes it to be by a later writer compiling from Xenophon, Aristophanes, and other sources of information. The same critic denies the genuineness of the *Resp. Laced.*, which is more generally accepted. (10) The *De Vectigalibus*, a treatise on the Revenues of Athens (Πόροι ἢ περὶ Προσόδων), is designed to show how the public revenue of Athens may be improved. (11) The *Memorabilia of Socrates*, in four books (Ἀπομνημονεύματα Σωκράτους), was written by Xenophon to defend the memory of his master against the charge of irreligion and of corrupting the Athenian youth. Socrates is represented as holding a series of conversations, in which he develops and inculcates his moral doctrines. It is entirely a practical work, such as we might expect from the practical nature of Xenophon's mind, and it professes to exhibit Socrates as he taught. It is true that it may exhibit only one side of the Socratic argumentation, and that it does not deal in subtleties of philosophy. Xenophon was a hearer of Socrates, an admirer of his master, and anxious to defend his memory. The charges against Socrates for which he suffered were, that "Socrates was guilty of not believing in the gods which the State believed in, and introducing other new daemons (δαιμόνια): he was also guilty of corrupting the youth." Xenophon replies to these two charges specifically, and he then goes on to show what Socrates' mode of life was. The whole treatise is intended to be an answer to the charge for which Socrates was executed, and it is therefore, in its nature, not intended to be a complete exhibition of Socrates. That it is a genuine picture of the man is indisputable, and its value therefore is very great. (12) The *Apology of Socrates* (Ἀπολογία Σωκράτους πρὸς τοὺς Δικαστάς) is a short speech, containing the reasons which induced Socrates to prefer death to life. It is not one of the author's best works, and was possibly a rhetorical exercise much later than Xenophon. (13) The *Symposium* (Συμπόσιον), or Banquet of Philosophers, in which Xenophon delineates the character of Socrates. The speakers are supposed to meet at the house of Callias, a rich Athenian, at the celebration of the Great Panathenaea. Socrates and others are the speakers. The piece is interesting as a picture of an Athenian drinking-party, and of the amusement and conversation with which it was diversified. The nature of love and friendship is discussed. It is probable that Plato wrote his *Symposium* later, to some extent as a corrective. (14) The *Hiero* (Ἱέρων ἢ Τυραννικός) is a dialogue between King Hiero and Simonides, in which the king speaks of the dangers and difficulties incident to an exalted station, and the superior happiness of a private man. The poet, on the other hand, enumerates the advantages which the possession of power gives, and the means which it offers of obliging and doing services. (15) The *Oeconomicus* (Οἰκονομικός) is an excellent treatise in the form of a dialogue between Socrates and Critobulus, in which Socrates gives instruction in the art called economic, which relates to the administration of a household and of a man's property.

In language as well as in politics, Xenophon was a cosmopolitan. His long residence in other lands resulted in his losing or abandoning pure Attic: he admits words from all dialects; hence he cannot be adduced as an authority for strict Attic usage, and it has been well shown by abundant instances that his diction is in many respects an anticipation of the common dialect of the Macedonian period.

Of each of Xenophon's treatises there are from thirty to forty manuscripts. Of the *Anabasis*, the best is a Codex Parisinus (No. 1640), and dating from the fourteenth century. Of the *Cyropaedia*, the most esteemed is also in Paris (No. 1635), of the fifteenth century, though a copy at Wolfenbüttel (Codex Guelferbytanus) of about the twelfth century is also valuable. Of the twenty-one manuscripts of the *Hellenica*, the best are two Codices Parisini (Nos. 1642 and 1738) of the fourteenth and fifteenth centuries.

Editions of the whole of Xenophon are those of Dindorf, 5 vols. (1875), Henning (1863), and Sauppe (1867). The *editio princeps* was by Boninus, printed by P. Giunta at Florence in 1516. Good separate editions, with notes, are the following: of the *Anabasis* by Macmichael (1883), Cobet (1873), bks. i.–iv. by Goodwin and White (1886), Stone (1890); of the *Cyropaedia* by Holden (1887); of the *Hellenica* by Breitenbach (1873); Keller (1890); bks. i.–iv. by Manath (1888), bks. i.–ii. by Dowdall (1890); of the *Memorabilia* by Winans (1878), and Marshall (1891); of the *Hiero* by Holden (1885); of the *Oeconomicus* by Holden (1888); of the *De Re Equestri* by Morgan (1893); of the *Agesilaüs* by Güthling (1887); of the *Symposium* by Hug (1880). There is a good English translation of Xenophon by Dakyns, 2 vols. (New York, 1890–93). There is a good lexicon to Xenophon by Sturz (1801), and Sauppe's *Lexilogus Xenophonteus* (1865) is also recommended. There is a special *Wörterbuch zur Xenophon's Anabasis* by Vollbrecht (1876). See also Taylor's *Syntax to the Anabasis* (1880); and on Xenophon the studies by Roquette (1884) and Croiset (1873).

(2) Of Ephesus, a writer of prose fiction, as to whose date and personality nothing is known. His remaining work is entitled *Ephesiaca, or the Loves of Anthia and Abrocomas* (*Ἐφεσιακά, τὰ κατὰ Ἀνθίαν καὶ Ἀβροκόμην*). The style of the work is simple, and the story is conducted without confusion, notwithstanding the number of personages introduced; but the adventures are of a very improbable kind. Xenophon was possibly the oldest of the Greek romance writers. Editions of his work are those by Peerlkamp (Haarlem, 1818); and by Passow (Leipzig, 1833). See NOVELS AND ROMANCES.

Xerxes (*Ξέρξης*). (1) A king of Persia from B.C. 485 to 465. He was the son of Darius Hystaspis and Atossa. By the influence of Atossa, who was a daughter of Cyrus, Artabazanes, the son of Darius by his former wife, was set aside from the succession and Xerxes made him heir. Xerxes succeeded to the throne in B.C. 485, Darius having died in the midst of his warlike preparations against Greece, which had been delayed by a revolt of the Egyptians. Bred up in the luxury of the Persian court, among slaves and women, a mark for their flattery and intrigues, Xerxes had none of the experience which Darius had gained in early life. He was probably inferior to his father in ability; but the difference between them in fortune and education seems to have left more traces in their history than any disparity of nature. Ambition was not the prominent feature in the character of Xerxes; and, had he followed his unbiassed inclination, he would, perhaps, have been content to turn the preparations of Darius against the revolted Egyptians, and have abandoned the expedition against Greece, to which he was not urged on by any personal motives. But he was surrounded by men who were led by various passions and interests to desire that he should prosecute his father's plans of conquest and revenge. Mardonius was eager to renew an enterprise in which he had been foiled through unavoidable mischance, and not through his own incapacity. He had a reputation to retrieve, and might look forward to the possession of a great European satrapy, at such a distance from the court as would make him almost an absolute sovereign. He was warmly seconded by those Greeks who had been drawn to Susa by the report of the approaching invasion of their country, and who wanted foreign aid to accomplish their designs. The Thessalian house of the Aleuadae, either because they thought their power insecure, or expected to increase it by becoming vassals of the Persian king, sent their emissaries to invite him to the conquest of Greece. The exiled Pisistratidae had no other chance for the recovery of Athens. They had brought a man named Onomacritus with them to court, who was one of the first among the Greeks to practise the art of forging prophecies and oracles. While their family ruled at Athens he had been detected in fabricating verses, which he had interpolated in a work ascribed to the ancient seer Musaeus, and Hipparchus, previously his patron, had banished him from the city. But the exiles saw the use they might make of his talents, and had taken him into their service. They now recommended him to Xerxes as a man who possessed a treasure of prophetical knowledge, and the young king listened with unsuspecting confidence to the encouraging predictions which Onomacritus drew from his inexhaustible stores. These various devices at length prevailed. The imagination of Xerxes was inflamed with the prospect of rivalling or surpassing the achievements of his glorious predecessors, and of extending his dominion to the ends of the earth (Herod. vii. 8). He resolved on the invasion of Greece. First, however, in the second year of his reign, he led an army against Egypt, and brought it again under the Persian yoke, which was purposely made more burdensome and galling than before. He intrusted this conquest to the care of his brother Achaemenes, and then returned to Persia, and bent all his thoughts towards the West. Only one of his counsellors, his uncle Artabanus, is said to have been wise and honest enough to endeavour to divert him from the enterprise, and especially to dissuade him from risking his own person in it. If any reliance could be placed on the story told by Herodotus about the deliberations held on this question in the Persian cabinet, we might suspect that the influence and arts of the Magian priesthood, which we find in this reign rising in credit, had been set at work by the adversaries of Artabanus to counteract his influence over the mind of his nephew, and to confirm Xerxes in his martial mood. The vast preparations were continued with redoubled activity, to raise an armament worthy of the presence of the king. His aim was not merely to collect a force sufficient to insure the success of his undertaking and to scare away all opposition, but also, and perhaps principally, to set his whole enormous power in magnificent array, that he might enjoy the sight of it himself, and display it to the admiration of the world.

For four years longer Asia was still kept in restless turmoil; no less time was needed to provide the means of subsistence for the countless host that was about to be poured out upon Europe. Besides the stores that were to be carried in the fleet which was to accompany the army, it was necessary that magazines should be formed along the whole line of march as far as the confines of Greece. But, in addition to these prudent precautions, two works were begun, which scarcely served any other purpose than that of showing the power and majesty of Xerxes, and proving that he would suffer no obstacles to bar his progress. It would have been easy to transport his troops in ships over the Hellespont; but it was better suited to the dignity of the monarch, who was about to unite both continents under his dominion, to join them by a bridge laid upon the subject channel, and to march across as along a royal road. The storm that had destroyed the fleet which accompanied Mardonius in his unfortunate expedition had made the coast of Athos terrible to the Persians. The simplest mode of avoiding this formidable cape would have been to draw their ships over the narrow, low neck that connects the mountain with the mainland. But Xerxes preferred to leave a monument of his greatness and of his enterprise in a canal cut through the isthmus, a distance of about a mile and a half. This work employed a multitude of men for three years. The construction of the two bridges which were thrown across the Hellespont was intrusted to the skill of the Phœnicians and Egyptians.

When these preparations were drawing to a close, Xerxes set forth for Sardis, where he designed to spend the following winter, and to receive the reinforcements which he had appointed there to join the main army (B.C. 481). During his stay at Sardis the Phœnician and Egyptian engineers completed their bridges on the Hellespont; but the work was not strong enough to resist a violent storm, which broke it to pieces soon after it was finished. How far this disaster was owing to defects in its construction, which might have been avoided by ordinary skill and foresight, does not appear; but Xerxes is said to have been so much angered by the accident that he put the architects to death. Such a burst of passion would be credible enough in itself, and is only rendered doubtful by the extravagant fables that gained credit on the subject among the Greeks, who, in the bridging of the sacred Hellespont, saw the beginning of a long career of audacious impiety, and gradually transformed the fastenings with which the passage was finally secured into fetters and scourges with which the barbarian, in his madness, had thought to chastise the aggression of the rebellious stream. The construction of new bridges was committed to other engineers, perhaps to Greeks; but their names have not come down, like that of Mandrocles. By their skill two broad causeways were made to stretch from the neighbourhood of Abydus to a projecting point on the opposite shore of the Chersonesus, resting each on a row of ships, which were stayed against the strong current that bore upon them from the north by anchors and by cables fastened to both sides of the channel. The length was not far short of a mile. When all was in readiness the mighty armament was set in motion.

Early in the spring (B.C. 480) Xerxes began his march from Sardis, in all the pomp of a royal progress. The baggage led the way: it was followed by the first division of the armed crowd that had been brought together from the tributary nations; a motley throng, including many strange varieties of complexion, dress, and language, commanded by Thessalian generals, but retaining each tribe its national armour and mode of fighting. An interval was then left, after which came 1000 picked Persian cavalry, followed by an equal number of spearsmen, whose lances, which they carried with the points turned downward, ended in knobs of gold. Next, ten sacred horses, of the Nisaean breed, were led in gorgeous trappings, preceding the chariot of the Persian Zeus, drawn by eight white horses, the driver following on foot. Then came the royal chariot, also drawn by Nisaean horses, in which Xerxes sat in state; but from time to time he exchanged it for an easier carriage, which sheltered him from the sun and changes of the weather. He was followed by two bands of horse and foot, like those which went immediately before him, and by a body of 10,000 Persian infantry, the flower of the whole army, who were called the Immortals, because their number was kept constantly full. A thousand of them, who occupied the outer ranks, bore lances tipped with gold; those of the rest were similarly ornamented with silver. They were followed by an equal number of Persian cavalry. The remainder of the host brought up the rear. In this order the army reached Abydus, and Xerxes, from a lofty throne, surveyed the crowded sides and bosom of the Hellespont, and a sort of mimic sea-fight; a spectacle which Herodotus might well think sufficient to have moved him with a touch of human sympathy. The passage did not begin before the king had prayed to the rising sun, and had tried to propitiate the Hellespont itself by libations, and by casting into it golden vessels and a sword. After the bridges had been strewed with myrtle and purified with incense, the ten thousand Immortals, crowned with chaplets, led the way. The army crossed by one bridge, the baggage by the other; yet the living tide flowed without intermission for seven days and seven nights before the last man, as Herodotus heard, the king himself, the tallest and most majestic person in the host, had arrived on the European shore. In the great plain of Doriscus, on the banks of Hebrus, an attempt was made to number the land force. A space was enclosed large enough to contain 10,000 men; into this the myriads were successively poured and discharged, till the whole mass had been rudely counted. They were then drawn up according to their natural divisions, and Xerxes rode in his chariot along the ranks, while the royal scribes recorded the names, and most likely the equipments, of the different races. The real military strength of the armament was almost lost among the undisciplined hordes who could only impede its movements as well as consume its stores. The Persians were the core of both the land and the sea force; none of the other troops are said to have equalled them in discipline or in courage; and the 24,000 men who guarded the royal person were the flower of the whole nation. Yet these were much better fitted for show than for action; and of the rest, we hear that they were distinguished from the mass of the army, not only by their superior order and valour, but also by the abundance of gold they displayed, by the train of carriages, women, and servants that followed them, and by the provisions set apart for their use.

Marching through Thrace and Macedonia, Xerxes met no resistance until he reached the Pass of Thermopylae between Mount Oeta and the sea. This the Spartan king Leonidas, with about 7000 men, had occupied. For two days they beat back the huge masses of Persians who assailed the pass, but whose very numbers proved an impediment to their success. Even the Immortals were unsuccessful, and Xerxes, who was watching the battle, leaped thrice from his throne in his rage. Presently, however, by the treachery of a Malian named Ephialtes, a body of Persian troops was led by a secret path to the rear of the Greeks. Leonidas at once dismissed all his men except his immediate guard of 300 Spartans and a body of Thespians, and with these advanced into the plain and perished after an heroic struggle (B.C. 480). Meantime a storm had wrecked 400 of the Persian ships of war, and an indecisive naval battle had been fought off Artemisium. Xerxes occupied Athens, pillaged the Acropolis, but suffered a great naval defeat at Salamis, where 200 of his ships were sunk.

After this disastrous defeat at Salamis, Xerxes felt desirous of escaping from a state of things which was now becoming troublesome and dangerous, and Mardonius saw that he would gladly listen to any proposal that would facilitate his return. He was aware that, without a fleet, the war might probably be tedious, in which case the immense bulk of the present army would be only an encumbrance, from the difficulty of subsisting it. Besides, the ambition of Mardonius was flattered with the idea of his becoming the conqueror of Greece, while he feared that, if he now returned, he might be made answerable for the ill success of the expedition which he had advised. He therefore proposed to Xerxes to return into Asia with the body of the army, leaving himself, with 300,000 of the best troops, to complete the conquest of Greece. Xerxes assented, and, the army having retired into Boeotia, Mardonius made his selection, and then, accompanying the king into Thessaly, there parted from him, leaving him to pursue his march towards Asia, while he himself prepared to winter in Thessaly and Macedonia.

Widely different from the appearance of the glittering host, which a few months before had advanced over the plains of Macedonia and Thrace to the conquest of Greece, was the aspect of the crowd which was now hurrying back along the same road. The splendour, the pomp, the luxury, the waste, were exchanged for disaster and distress, want and disease. The magazines had been emptied by the careless profusion or peculation of those who had the charge of them; the granaries of the countries traversed by the retreating multitude were unable to supply its demands; ordinary food was often not to be found; and it was compelled to draw a scanty and unwholesome nourishment from the herbage of the plains, the bark and leaves of the trees. Sickness soon began to spread its ravages among them, and Xerxes was compelled to consign numbers to the care of the cities that lay on his road, already impoverished by the cost of his first visit, in the hope that they would tend their guests, and would not sell them into slavery if they recovered. The passage of the Strymon is said to have been peculiarly disastrous. The river had been frozen in the night hard enough to bear those who arrived first. But the ice suddenly gave way under the heat of the morning sun, and numbers perished in the waters. It is a little surprising that Herodotus, when he is describing the miseries of the retreat, does not notice this disaster, which is so prominent in the narrative of the Persian messenger in Aeschylus. There can, however, be no doubt as to the fact; and perhaps it may furnish a useful warning not to lay too much stress on the silence of Herodotus, as a ground for rejecting even important and interesting facts which are only mentioned by later writers, though such as he must have heard of, and might have been expected to relate. It seems possible that the story he mentions of Xerxes embarking at Eïon (viii. 118) may have arisen out of the tragical passage of the Strymon.

In forty-five days after he had left Mardonius in Thessaly, he reached the Hellespont; the bridges had been broken up by foul weather, but the fleet was there to carry the army over to Abydus. Here it rested from its fatigues, and found plentiful quarters; but intemperate indulgence rendered the sudden change from scarcity to abundance almost as deadly as the previous famine. The remnant that Xerxes brought back to Sardis was a wreck, a fragment, rather than a part of his huge host.

The history of Xerxes, after the termination of his Grecian campaign, may be comprised in a brief compass. He gave himself up to a life of dissolute pleasure, and was slain by Artabanus, a captain of the royal guards, B.C. 464.

(2) A son of Artaxerxes Mnemon, who succeeded his father, but was slain, after a reign of forty-five days, by his brother Sogdianus.

Xestes (ξέστης). The same as the Latin *sextarius*, from which the word is derived. See SEXTARIUS.

Xiphilīnus (Ξιφιλῖνος). A native of Trapezus, who was a monk at Constantinople, and made an abridgment of Dio Cassius, from the thirty-sixth to the eightieth book, at the command of the emperor Michael VII. Ducas (A.D. 1071 to 1078). The work is executed with carelessness, and is of value only as preserving the main facts of the original, the greater part of which is lost. It is printed in most of the editions of Dio Cassius (q. v.).

Xiphos (ξίφος). The straight, two-edged sword of the Greeks. See ARMA; GLADIUS.

Xoăna. See STATUARIA ARS.

Xoïs (Ξόϊς) or **Choïs** (Χόϊς). An ancient city of Lower Egypt, north of Leontopolis, on an island of the Nile, in the Nomos Sebennyticus, the seat, at one time, of a dynasty of Egyptian kings. Its site is very doubtful.

Xuthus (Ξοῦθος). Son of Hellen by the nymph Orseïs, and a brother of Dorus and Aeolus. He was king of Peloponnesus, and the husband of Creüsa, the daughter of Erechtheus, by whom he became the father of Achaeus and Ion (q. v.). Others state that after the death of his father, Hellen, Xuthus was expelled from Thessaly by his brothers, and went to Athens, where he married the daughter of Erechtheus. After the death of Erechtheus, Xuthus, being chosen arbitrator, adjudged the kingdom to his eldest brother-in-law, Cecrops, in consequence of which he was expelled by the other sons of Erechtheus, and settled in Aegialus, in the Peloponnesus.

Xyēlé (ξυήλη). The short, slightly curved, one-edged sword of the Spartans.

Xypĕté (Ξυπέτη). A deme of Attica belonging to the tribe Cecropis, to the west of Athens.

Xystarcha or **Xystarches** (ξυστάρχης). An officer who superintended the exercise of the *xystus* (Ammian. xxi. 1).

Xystĭcus (ξυστικός). An athlete who practised his exercise in a covered corridor or *xystus* (Suet. *Aug.* 45; *Galb.* 15).

Xystus or **Xystum** (ξυστός). (1) Among the Greeks, a covered corridor in the gymnasium (q. v.), where the athletes exercised in winter (Vitruv. v. 11, 4; vi. 7, 5). (2) Among the Romans, an open walk or terrace in a garden, amidst flower-beds edged with box (Suet. *Aug.* 72; Phaedr. ii. 5). See HORTUS.

Y

For the Greek Υ as a symbol, see under V.

Yard. See AREA.

Year, DIVISIONS OF THE. See CALENDARIUM.

Yoke. See IUGUM.

Z

Z, as a symbol.

IN GREEK.—Z = ζήσας, ζήσαντ. As a numeral ζ′ = 7; ͵ζ = 7000.

IN LATIN.—Z = centurio.

Zabătus (Ζάβατος). The Zab; a river of Assyria, rising on the south of Armenia and flowing southwest into the Tigris below Larissa (Xen. *Anab.* ii. 5, 1).

Zacynthus (Ζάκυνθος). Now Zanté; an island in the Ionian Sea, off the coast of Elis, about forty miles in circumference. It contained a large and flourishing town of the same name upon the eastern coast, the citadel of which was called Psophis. Zacynthus was inhabited by a Greek population at an early period. It is said to have derived its name from Zacynthus, a son of Dardanus, who colonized the island from Psophis in Arcadia. It was afterwards colonized by Achaeans from Peloponnesus. It formed part of the maritime empire of Athens, and continued faithful to the Athenians during the Peloponnesian War. At a later time it was subject to the Macedonian monarchs, and on the conquest of Macedonia by the Romans passed into the hands of the latter (Livy, xxxvi. 32). It was said to have colonized the Spanish city of Saguntum (q. v.). See Partsch, *Die Insel Zante* (Gotha, 1891).

Zagreus (Ζαγρεύς). A surname of the mystic Dionysus (Bacchus), whom Zeus, in the form of a serpent, is said to have begotten by Persephoné, before she was carried off by Pluto. He was torn to pieces by the Titans, after he had assumed various shapes to evade them. His mangled remains were buried at Delphi, and Athené brought his heart to Zeus, who swallowed it and thereupon brought forth a new Dionysus called Iacchus, who was nursed by nymphs and satyrs in a winnowing-basket (*vannus*), thenceforth a symbol of Dionysus. The story, nearly akin to the Egyptian myth of Osiris, whom the Greeks identified with Dionysus, is now regarded as a myth, in the first place, of the death in winter and renewal in spring of the vegetation; for the swinging of the basket was the ritual by which in early times it was sought to rouse the plant-life from its sleep; and, in the second place, it expressed the belief in a death and a resurrection: for both these reasons Iacchus (or Dionysus) was associated with Demeter and Coré (or Persephoné) in the Mysteries. The notoriety of the evils resulting from the worst festivals of Dionysus, and the evil repute of the Bacchanalia, have tended to obscure the purer and more elevating part of the religion, but it is important not to forget it. The rending of Dionysus-Zagreus cannot be dismissed as merely the crushing of the grape; it is rather the tearing of the victims in savage sacrifices, possibly in "totem" sacrifices; and in such sacrifices the deity, that is, sacred animal (at one time a human sacrifice), was often slain, and the eating of the slaughtered victim was supposed to give to the worshippers some of the strength and power of the deity. Out of some such ritual the story of the death of Zagreus probably arose. The rites spread westward from Crete through the islands, and so reached Athens (Diod. v. 74). Hence perhaps the savage worship of Dionysus ὠμηστής (eater of raw flesh) at Lesbos, Chios, and Tenedos, betokening human sacrifice to the god of vines in early times, though it may as probably have been derived from Thrace or Phrygia; for the frantic worship of the Thracian or the Boeotian *thiasus* had the same characteristics. At Naxos his rites were less barbarous, and that island, which claimed also to be the birthplace of the god, seems to have passed on some of the ritual, including the marriage of Dionysus, to Athens. Dionysus, or Bacchus, was introduced into the Roman worship through Magna Graecia and Etruria, and with all the worst features of the rites, and the name and story of Bacchus took the place of the native Italian deity of the vintage. See DIONYSIA; DIONYSUS; MYSTERIA.

Zagros (Ζάγρος). A range of mountains forming the southeastern continuation of the Taurus along the Tigris and Euphrates rivers.

Zaleucus (Ζάλευκος). The celebrated lawgiver of the Epizephyrian Locrians, is said by some to have been originally a slave, but is described by others as a man of good family. He could not, however, have been a disciple of Pythagoras, as some writers state, since he lived upwards of one hundred years before Pythagoras. The date of the legislation of Zaleucus is assigned to B.C. 660. His code, which was severe, is stated to have been the first collection of written laws that the Greeks possessed (Strabo, pp. 259, 398). Among other enactments we are told that the penalty of adultery was the loss of the eyes (Ael. *V. H.* xiii. 24; Val. Max. v. 5, 3). There is a celebrated story of the son of Zaleucus having become liable to this penalty, and the father himself suffering the loss of one eye, that his son might not be utterly blinded. It is further related that among his laws was one forbidding any citizen, under penalty of death, to enter the senate-house in arms. On one occasion, however, on a sudden emergency in time of war, Zaleucus transgressed his own law, which was remarked to him by one present; whereupon he fell upon his own sword, declaring that he would himself vindicate the law (Eustath. *ad Il.* p. 62). Other authors tell the same story of Charondas, and of Diocles (Diod. xii. 19; Val. Max. vi. 5, 4).

Zalmoxis (Ζάλμοξις) or **Zamolxis** (Ζάμολξις). Said to have been so called from the bear's skin (ζάλμος) in which he was clothed as soon as he was born. He was, according to the story current among the Greeks on the Hellespont, a Getan, who had been a slave to Pythagoras in Samos, but was manumitted, and acquired not only great wealth, but large stores of knowledge from Pythagoras, and from the Egyptians, whom he visited in the course of his travels. He returned among the Getae, introducing the civilization and the religious ideas which he had gained, especially regarding the immortality of the soul. Herodotus, however, suspects that he was an indigenous Getan divinity (Herod. iv. 95).

Zama Regia (Ζάμα). Now Zowarîn, southeast of Kaff. A strongly fortified city in the interior of Numidia, on the borders of the Carthaginian territory. It was the scene of one of the most important battles in the history of the world, that in which Hannibal was defeated by Scipio, and the Second Punic War was ended, B.C. 202. See Köhn, *De Pugna ad Zamam Commissa* (Halle, 1888); and the articles HANNIBAL; PUNIC WARS.

Zancha or **Zanga**. A high and close boot, made of soft black leather (Acron. *ad* Hor. *Sat.* i. 6, 27), worn by the Oriental races under their trousers (*bracae*) (Imp. Gall. *ap.* Treb. *Claud.* 17).

Zanclé. See MESSANA.

Zarangae. The same as the Drangae, or natives of Drangiana (q. v.).

Zela (τὰ Ζῆλα) or **Ziēla**. Now Zilleh; a city in the south of Pontus, not far south of Amasia. The surrounding district was called ZELETIS or ZELITIS. At Zela the Roman general Valerius Triarius was defeated by Mithridates; but the city is more celebrated for another great battle, that in which Iulius Caesar defeated Pharnaces, and of which he wrote his famous despatch to Rome—*Veni, vidi, vici* (Plut. *Caes.* 50; App. *Mithr.* 89; *Bell. Alex.* 73).

Zelēa (Ζέλεια). An ancient city of Mysia, at the foot of Mount Ida, and on the river Aesopus, eighty stadia from its mouth, belonging to the territory of Cyzicus. It was the headquarters of the Persian army at the time of Alexander's invasion (Arr. *Anab.* i. 13).

Zelus (Ζῆλος). The personification of zeal or strife, described as a son of Pallas and Styx, and a brother of Niké.

Zema (ζέμα). A vessel used for boiling (Apic. viii. 1).

Zeno (Ζήνων). (1) The founder of the School of the Stoics, born at Citium, in the island of Cyprus. His father was a merchant, but, noticing in his son a strong bent towards learning, he early devoted him to the study of philosophy. In his mercantile capacity, the father had frequent occasions to visit Athens, where he purchased for the young Zeno several of the writings of the most eminent Socratic philosophers. These he read with great avidity; and, when about thirty years of age, he determined to take a voyage to a city which was so celebrated. Upon his first arrival in Athens, going accidentally into the shop of a bookseller, he took up a volume of the commentaries of Xenophon, and, after reading a few passages, was so much delighted with the work, and formed so high an idea of its author, that he asked the bookseller where he might meet with such men. Crates, the Cynic philosopher, happening at that instant to be passing by, the bookseller pointed to him, and said, "Follow that man." Zeno soon found an opportunity of attending upon the instructions of Crates, and was so well pleased with his doctrine that he became one of his disciples. But, though he highly admired the general principles and spirit of the Cynic School, he could not easily reconcile himself to their peculiar manners. Besides, his inquisitive turn of mind would not allow him to adopt that indifference to every scientific inquiry which was one of the characteristic distinctions of the sect. He therefore attended upon other masters, who professed to instruct their disciples in the nature and causes of things. When Crates, displeased at his following other philosophers, attempted to drag him by force out of the school of Stilpo, the Megarian, Zeno said to him, "You may seize my body, but Stilpo has laid hold of my mind." After continuing to attend the lectures of Stilpo for several years, he passed over to other schools, particularly those of Xenocrates and Diodorus Chronus. By the latter he was instructed in dialectics. At last, after attending almost every other teacher, he offered himself as a disciple of Polemo. This philosopher appears to have been aware that Zeno's intention in thus passing from one school to another was to collect materials from various quarters for a new system of his own; for, when he came into Polemo's school, the latter said to him, "I am no stranger to your Phœnician arts, Zeno; I perceive that your design is to creep slyly into my garden and steal away my fruit." Polemo was not mistaken in his opinion. Having made himself master of the views of others, Zeno determined to become the founder of a new sect. The place which he made choice of for his school was called the Poecilé (Ποικίλη Στοά), or "Painted Porch," a public portico, so called from the pictures of Polygnotus and other eminent masters with which it was adorned. This portico, being the most famous in Athens, was called, by way of distinction, Στοά, "the Porch." It was from this circumstance that the followers of Zeno were called *Stoics* (Στωϊκοί), i. e. "men of the Porch."

Zeno excelled in that kind of subtle reasoning which was then popular. At the same time, he taught a strict system of moral doctrine, and exhibited a model of moral discipline in his own life. The Stoic School, in fact, was a branch of the Cynic, and, so far as respected morals, differed from it more in words than in reality. Its founder, while he avoided the eccentricities of the Cynics, retained the spirit of their moral teaching; and at the same time, from a diligent comparison of the tenets of other masters, he framed a new system of speculative philosophy. It is not at all surprising, therefore, that he obtained a considerable vogue, and even enjoyed the favour of the great. Antigonus Gonatas, king of Macedon, while residing at Athens, attended his lectures, and, upon his return, earnestly invited him to his court. Zeno, in fact, possessed so large a share of esteem among the Athenians that, on account of his approved integrity, they deposited the keys of their citadel in his hands. They also honoured him with a golden crown and a statue of bronze. Among his countrymen, the inhabitants of Cyprus, and with the Sidonians, from whom his family was derived, he was likewise highly esteemed.

In his person Zeno was tall and slender; his aspect was stern, and his brow contracted. His constitution was feeble, but he preserved his health by great abstemiousness. His food consisted only of figs, bread, and honey; yet his table was frequently honoured with the company of great men. He paid more attention to neatness in his personal appearance than did the Cynic philosophers. In his dress, indeed, he was plain, but this is not to be imputed to avarice, but to a contempt of external magnificence. He showed as much respect to the poor as to the rich, and conversed freely with persons of the meanest occupations. He had only one servant, or, according to Seneca, none. Although Zeno's sobriety and continence were even proverbial, he was not without enemies. Among his contemporaries, several philosophers of great ability and eloquence employed their talents against him. Arcesilaüs and Carneades, the founders of the Middle Academy, were his professed opponents. Towards the close of his life, also, he found another powerful antagonist in Epicurus (q. v.), whose temper and doctrines were alike inimical to the severe gravity and philosophical pride of the Stoic sect. Hence mutual invectives passed between the Stoics and other sects.

Zeno lived to the extreme age of ninety-eight, and at last, in consequence of an accident, put an end to his life. As he was walking out of his school he fell down, and in the fall broke one of his fingers. He was so affected by this with a consciousness of infirmity that, striking the earth, he exclaimed, Ἔρχομαι, τί μ' αὔεις; "I am coming, why do you call me?" and immediately went home and strangled himself. He died B.C. 264. The Athenians, at the request of Antigonus, erected a monument to his memory in the Ceramicus.

His writings, of which a list is given by Diogenes Laërtius (vii. 4), have all been lost. They treated of the State, and of the Life according to Nature. For his doctrines, see Zeller, *Stoics, Epicureans, and Skeptics* (1870), and the articles PHILOSOPHIA; STOÏCI.

(2) The Eleatic philosopher, a native of Elea (Velia) in Italy, son of Teleutagoras, and the favourite disciple of Parmenides. He was born about B.C. 488, and at the age of forty accompanied Parmenides to Athens. (See PARMENIDES.) He appears to have resided some time at Athens, and is said to have unfolded his doctrines to men like Pericles and Callias for the price of 100 minae. Zeno is said to have taken part in the legislation of Parmenides, to the maintenance of which the citizens of Elea had pledged themselves every year by an oath. His love of freedom is shown by the courage with which he exposed his life in order to deliver his native country from a tyrant. Whether he perished in the attempt or survived the fall of the tyrant is a point on which the authorities vary. They also state the name of the tyranny differently. Zeno devoted all his energies to explain and develop the philosophical system of Parmenides. See Zeller's *Pre-Socratic Schools* (1881).

(3) An Epicurean philosopher, a native of Sidon, and a contemporary of Cicero, who heard him when at Athens. He was sometimes termed *Coryphaeus Epicureorum.* He seems to have been noted for the disrespectful terms in which he spoke of other philosophers, calling, for instance, Socrates "the Attic buffoon." He was a disciple of Apollodorus, and is described as a clear-headed thinker and perspicacious expounder of his views.

Zenobia (*Ζηνοβία*). A celebrated princess, wife of Odenathus, and after his death queen of Palmyra (q. v.). With equal talents for jurisprudence, finance, and government, her agile and elastic frame enabled her to direct and share the toils of war. Disdaining the litter, she was continually on horseback, and could even keep pace on foot with the march of her soldiery. History has preserved some reminiscences of her personal appearance, her dress, and her habits, which represent her as a woman of engaging beauty, gifted with the graces of a court, and accomplished in intellectual endowments. In complexion a brunette, her teeth were of a pearly whiteness, and her eyes black and sparkling; her mien was animated, and her voice clear and powerful. With a helmet on her head, and wearing a purple mantle fringed with gems and clasped with a buckle at the waist, so as to leave one of her arms bare to the shoulder, she presented herself at the council of war; and adopting from policy a regal pomp, she was worshipped with Persian prostration. Pure in her manners to the utmost refinement of delicacy, and temperate in her habits, she would nevertheless challenge in their cups her Persian and Armenian guests, and retire the victor without drunkenness. Chiefly versed in the languages of Syria and Egypt, her diffidence restrained her from conversing freely in Latin; but she had read the Roman history in Greek, was herself an historian, and had compiled the annals of Alexandria and the East. Her authority was acknowledged by a large portion of Asia Minor when the Roman emperor Aurelian succeeded to the throne. Jealous of her power, and determined to dispossess her of some of the rich provinces comprehended in her dominions, he marched at the head of a powerful army to Asia. Having defeated the queen's general near Antioch, he compelled her to retreat to Emesa. Under the walls of this city another engagement was fought, in which the emperor was again victorious. The queen fled to Palmyra, determined to support a siege. Aurelian followed her, and, on making his approaches to the walls, found them mounted in every part with mural engines, which plied the besiegers with stones, darts, and fire-balls. To the summons for a surrender of the city and kingdom, on the condition of her life being spared, Zenobia replied in a proud and spirited letter, written in Greek by her secretary, the celebrated Longinus (q. v.). Her hopes of victory soon vanished; and, though she harassed the Romans night and day by continual sallies from her walls and the working of her military engines, she despaired of success when she heard that the armies which were marching to her relief from Armenia, Persia, and the East had either been intercepted or gained over by the foe. She fled from Palmyra in the night on her dromedaries, but was overtaken by the Roman cavalry while attempting to cross the Euphrates, and was brought into the presence of Aurelian, and tried before a tribunal at Emesa, Aurelian himself presiding. The soldiers were clamorous for her death, but she, in a manner unworthy of her former fame, saved her own life by throwing the blame on her counsellors, especially on Longinus, who was, in consequence, put to death. Zenobia was carried to Rome, to grace the emperor's triumph (A.D. 274), and was led along in chains of gold. She is said to have almost sunk beneath the weight of jewels with which she was adorned on that occasion. She was treated with great humanity, and Aurelian gave her large possessions near Tiber, where she was permitted to pass the remainder of her days. Her two sons afterwards married into distinguished families at Rome. See the life of Aurelian by Vopiscus; and Ware's historical romance, *Zenobia* (N. Y. 1837).

Zenobius (Ζηνόβιος). A Greek Sophist of Antioch, who lived at Rome as teacher of rhetoric in the first half of the second century B.C., and, availing himself of the works of earlier writers, made a collection of proverbs, still extant in an abridged form, arranged alphabetically and divided into hundreds. In all there are 552, the last division being incomplete. They are printed by Schott in his *Paroemiae Hellenicae* (Antwerp, 1612). See Jungblut, *De Zenobio* (1882).

Zenodōrus (Ζηνόδωρος). A Greek statuary, whose native country is uncertain. He practised his art in Cisalpine Gaul, and also in Rome during the reign of Nero. Pliny speaks of a Mercury of his, and also of a colossal statue of Nero 110 feet high, afterwards dedicated to the Sun on the downfall of that emperor. See COLOSSUS.

Zenodŏtus (Ζηνόδοτος). A celebrated grammarian of Ephesus, superintendent of the great library at Alexandria, who flourished under Ptolemy Philadelphus, about B.C. 308. Zenodotus was employed by Philadelphus, together with his two contemporaries, Alexander the Aetolian and Lycophron the Chalcidian, to collect and revise all the Greek poets. Alexander, we are told, undertook the task of collecting the tragedies, Lycophron the comedies, and Zenodotus the poems of Homer and of the other illustrious poets. Zenodotus, however, devoted his chief attention to the *Iliad* and *Odyssey*. Hence he is called the first reviser (διορθωτής) of Homer, and his recension (διόρθωσις) of the *Iliad* and *Odyssey* obtained the greatest celebrity. The corrections which Zenodotus applied to the text of Homer were of three kinds: (1) He expunged verses; (2) he marked some as spurious, but left them in his copy; (3) he introduced new readings and transposed or altered verses. The great attention which Zenodotus paid to the language of Homer caused a new epoch in the grammatical study of the Greek language. The results of his investigations respecting the meaning and the use of words were contained in two works which he published under the title of a glossary (Γλῶσσαι), and a dictionary of barbarous or foreign phrases. See Düntzer, *De Zenodoti Studiis Homericis* (Göttingen, 1848); Römer, *Ueber die Homerrecension des Zenod.* (Munich, 1885); and the article TEXTUAL CRITICISM.

Zephyrium (Ζεφύριον, sc. ἀκρωτήριον, i. e. "the western promontory"). The name of several promontories of the ancient world, not all of which, however, faced the west. The chief of them were: (1) Now C. di Brussano, a promontory in Bruttium, forming the southeastern extremity of the country, from which the Locri, who settled in the neighbourhood, are said to have obtained the name of Epizephyrii. (See LOCRI.) (2) A promontory on the west coast of Cyprus. (3) In Cilicia (prob. C. Cavaliere), a far-projecting promontory, west of Prom. Sarpedon.

Zephy̆rus (Ζέφυρος). The personification of the west wind, described by Hesiod as a son of Astraeus and Eos. Zephyrus and Boreas are frequently mentioned together by Homer, and both

Zephyrus. (From the Tower of the Winds at Athens.)

dwelt together in a palace in Thrace. By the Harpy Podargé, Zephyrus became the father of the horses Xanthus and Balius, which belonged to Achilles (*Il.* xvi. 150); but he was married to Chloris, whom he had carried off by force, and by whom he had a son, Carpus.

Zerynthus (Ζήρυνθος). A town of Thrace, in the territory of Aenos, with a temple of Apollo and a cave of Hecaté, who are hence called Zerynthius and Zerynthia respectively.

Zetes (Ζήτης) and **Calăis** (Κάλαϊς). The sons of Boreas and Orithyia, frequently called the BOREADAE, are mentioned among the Argonauts, and are described as winged beings (Pind. *Pyth.* iv. 325; Ap. Rh. i. 219). Their sister, Cleopatra, who was married to Phineus, king of Salmydessus, had been thrown with her sons into prison by Phineus at the instigation of his second wife. Here she was found by Zetes and Calaïs, when they arrived at Salmydessus in the Argonautic expedition. They liberated their sister and her children, gave the kingdom to the latter, and sent the second wife of Phineus to her own country, Scythia (Diod. iv. 44). Other accounts relate that the Boreadae delivered Phineus from the Harpies; for it had been foretold that the Harpies might be killed by the sons of Boreas, but that the sons of Boreas must die if they should not be able to overtake the Harpies (Apollod. i. 9, 21). Others, again, state that the Boreadae perished in their pursuit of the Harpies, or that Heracles killed them with his arrows near the island of Tenos (Hyg. *Fab.* 14). Their tombs were said to be in Tenos, adorned with sepulchral *stelae*, one of which moved whenever the wind blew from the north. Calaïs is also mentioned as the founder of the Campanian town of Cales (Sil. It. viii. 515). See HARPYIAE.

Zetētae (ζητηταί). Officials at Athens appointed on special occasions: (1) as investigators of crimes, to discover the authors and to bring them to punishment; and (2) to discover property confiscated to the State, and to receive information against persons who concealed property to which the State had a claim. See Schöll, *Quaestiones Fiscales Iuris Attici*, etc. (Berlin, 1893).

Zethus (Ζῆθος). Brother of Amphion. See AMPHION.

Zeugis, Zeugitāna Regio (ἡ Ζευγιτανή). The northern part of Tunis. The northern district of Africa Propria. See AFRICA.

Zeugītae (ζευγῖται). See SOLON.

Zeugma (Ζεῦγμα). Probably Rumkaleh; a city of Syria, on the borders of Commagené and Cyrrhesticé, built by Seleucus Nicator on the western bank of the Euphrates, at a point where the river was crossed by a bridge of boats, which had been constructed by Alexander the Great (Polyb. v. 43).

Zeus (Ζεύς). The supreme god in the Greek mythology; according to the common legend, the eldest son of Cronus and Rhea, hence called CRONIDES. According to a myth indigenous to Crete, he was the youngest son, and Rhea, in dread of Cronus, who had swallowed all his previous children, bore him secretly in a cave of the island, where he was suckled by the goat Amalthea (q. v.), while the Curetes (q. v.) drowned the cries of the child by the clash of their weapons; but Rhea outwitted Cronus by giving him a stone to swallow instead. When he was grown up, Zeus married Metis (q. v.), who, by means of a charm, compelled Cronus to disgorge the children he had swallowed. When, with the help of his brothers and sisters, Poseidon, Hades, Hestia, Demeter, and Heré, he had overthrown Cronus and the Titans, the world was divided into three parts, Zeus obtaining heaven,

Zeus of Otricoli. (Vatican.)

Poseidon the sea, and Hades the lower world; the earth and Olympus being appointed for the common possession of all the three. But the king of the gods is Zeus, whose power, as Homer says, is greater than that of all the other gods together.

Next to him, but in a subordinate position, stands, as queen of the gods, his sister and consort Heré, the mother of Ares, Hephaestus, and Hebé, who was regarded as preëminently his rightful wife. Not incompatible with this, however, was the idea that the marriage with Heré was the earliest of a series of marriages with other goddesses—first, according to Hesiod, with Metis, whom he swallowed, in order to bring forth Athené from his own head; then with Themis, the mother of the Hours and the Fates; afterwards with Eurynomé, the mother of the Graces; Demeter, the mother of Persephoné; Mnemosyné, the mother of the Muses; and Leto, the mother of Apollo and Artemis. The fact that still later, in Dodona, Dioné, the mother of Aphrodité, was also honoured as the wife of Zeus shows the origin of the legend. Originally different wives of Zeus were recognized in the different local cults. When the legend of the marriage with Heré had become the predominant one, an attempt was made to harmonize the different versions of the story by the supposition of successive marriages. In the same way the loves of Zeus with half-divine, half-mortal women, of whom Alcmené, the mother of Heracles, was said to be the last, were originally rural legends, which derived the descent of indigenous divinities, like Hermes and Dionysus, or of heroes and noble families, from the highest god; and not until they had become the common property of the whole Greek people, which was practically the case as early as the time of Homer, could the love affairs of the greatest of the gods become the theme of those mythical stories which are so repugnant to modern taste.

The very name of Zeus (Skt. *dyaus*, "the bright sky") identifies him as the god of the sky and its phenomena. As such he was everywhere worshipped on the highest mountains, on whose summits he was considered to be enthroned. Of all places the Thessalian mountain Olympus (q. v.), even in the earliest ages, met with the most general recognition as the abode of Zeus and of the gods who were associated with him. From Zeus come all changes in the sky or the winds; he is the gatherer of the clouds, which dispense the fertilizing rain, while he is also the thunderer, and the hurler of the irresistible lightning. As by the shaking of his aegis (q. v.) he causes sudden storm and tempest to break forth, so he calms the elements again, brightens the sky, and sends forth favouring winds. The changes of the seasons also proceed from him as the father of the Hours.

As the supreme lord of heaven, he was worshipped under the name of Olympian Zeus in many parts of Greece, but especially in Olympia, where the Olympian Games (q. v.) were celebrated in his honour. The cult of Zeus at the ancient seat of the oracle at Dodona recognized his character as dispenser of the fertilizing dew. Among the numerous mountain-cults in the Peloponnesus, the oldest and most original was that of the Lycaean Zeus, on Mount Lycaeus in Arcadia, where human beings were actually sacrificed to him in propitiation. (See LYCAEA.) In Attica, again, many festivals refer to the god as a personification of the powers of nature. Various rites of purification and expiation were observed in his honour as the god of wrath (Μαιμάκτης), in the month Maemacterion (Nov.–Dec.), at the beginning of the winter storms; while towards the end of winter he was worshipped as the gracious god (Μειλίχιος) at the festival of the Diasia (q. v.). Among the islands, Rhodes and Crete were the principal seats of the

Interior of the Temple of Zeus in Olympia. (Restoration by Bühlmann.)

worship of the sky-god; not only his birth but also his death was there celebrated, and even his grave was shown, in accordance with the widely spread notion that the annual death of Nature in winter was the death of the god. In Asia, the summit of Mount Ida in the Troad was especially and beyond all other places sacred to Zeus.

As he presides over the gods and the whole of nature, so also is he the ruler of men, who all stand in need of his help, and to whom, according to Homer, he weighs out their destinies on golden scales, and distributes good and evil out of the two jars which stand in his palace, filled the one with good and the other with evil gifts. But his natural attributes are goodness and love; hence Homer calls him "the father of gods and men." He gives to all things a good beginning and a good end: he is the saviour in all distress. To Zeus the Saviour (Σωτήρ) it was customary to drink the third cup at a meal, and in Athens to sacrifice on the last day of the year. From him comes everything good, noble, and strong, and also bodily vigour and valour, which were exhibited in his honour, particularly at the Olympian and Nemean Games. He is also the giver of victory; indeed, the goddess of victory (see NIKÉ), and her brothers and sister, Force, Might, and Strife (Βία, Κράτος, Ζῆλος), are his constant companions. From him, as ruler of the world, proceed those universal laws which regulate the course of all things, and he knows and sees everything, the future as well as the past. Hence all revelation comes in the first instance from him. At times he himself announces to mortals his hidden counsels by manifold signs, thunder and lightning and other portents in the sky; by birds, especially the eagle, which was sacred to him; by prophetic voices (see MANTIKÉ) and special oracles. (See AMMON; DODONA; ORACULA.) At times he makes use of other deities for this purpose, chiefly of his son Apollo, through whose mouth he speaks at Delphi in particular. Thus the course of the world is ordained by him; he is the author and preserver of all order in the life of men. In conjunction with Themis, Diké, and Nemesis, he watches over justice and truth, the foundations of human society; in particular he is the special god who guards the sanctity of the oath; he is also the avenger of perjury, the keeper of boundaries and of property, the defender of the laws of hospitality and the rights of the suppliant. But nevertheless to him who has offended against the laws of human life, Zeus, as the supreme god of atonement, offers the power of expiating his guilt by rites of purification. As he presides over the family and community of the gods, so also he is the chief patron of the family and of all communal life. In the former relation he was especially worshipped in all branches of the family as protector of house and home (Ἑρκεῖος), and defender of the domestic hearth (Ἐφέστιος): in the latter, as the shield of the State, e. g. in Athens at the Diipolia (q. v.); as director of the popular assembly and of the council; as the god of covenants; as the source of kingship, whose symbol, the sceptre, was traced back to him. From him also proceed both national and personal freedom; hence a sanctuary was dedicated at Athens by freedmen to Zeus the Liberator (Ἐλευθέριος); and after the battle of Plataea a thanksgiving festival, Eleutheria (q. v.), was instituted by the allied Greeks, which was still celebrated by the Plataeans in Roman times, and attended by deputies from the other States.

Zeus is to the Greeks—as Iupiter (q. v.), who in

his principal characteristics exactly corresponds to him, is to the Romans—the essence of all divine power. No deity received such widespread worship; all the others were, in the popular belief, subordinated to him at a greater or less distance. The active operations of most of the gods appear only as an outcome of his being, particularly those of his children, among whom the nearest to him are Atheně and Apollo, his favourites, who often seem to be joined with their father in the highest union.

The eagle and the oak were sacred to Zeus; the eagle, together with the sceptre and the lightning, is also one of his customary attributes. The most famous statue of Zeus in antiquity was that executed by Phidias in gold and ivory for the temple at Olympia. It represented the enthroned Olympian god with a divine expression of the highest dignity, and at the same time with the benevolent mildness of the deity who graciously listens to prayer. The figure of the seated god was about forty feet high; and since the base was as high as twelve feet, the statue almost touched with its crown the roof of the temple, so as to call forth in the spectator the feeling that no earthly dwelling would be adequate for such a divinity. The bearded head was ornamented with a wreath of olive leaves, the victor's prize at Olympia. The upper part of the body, made of ivory, was naked, the lower part was wrapped in a golden mantle falling from the hips to the feet, which, adorned with golden sandals, rested on a footstool. Beside this lay golden lions. The right hand bore the goddess of victory, the left the sceptre, surmounted by an eagle. Like the base, and the whole space around, the seat of the throne was decorated with various works of art. It was supported by figures of the goddess of victory; and on the back of the throne, which rose above the head of the god, were represented the hovering forms of the Hours and the Graces. This statue was the model for most of the later representatives of Zeus. Among those that are extant the well-known bust of Zeus found at Otricoli (Ocriculum in Umbria), and now in the Vatican Museum, is supposed to be an imitation of the great work of Phidias. In the most direct relation to the latter stand the figures of Zeus on the coins of Elis (see ELIS, p. 587). Among the standing statues of Zeus the most famous was the bronze colossus, forty cubits (or sixty feet) high, by Lysippus at Tarentum. See COLOSSUS. On the general relation of Zeus to the mythological system of the Greeks, see Preller, *Griechische Mythologie* (last ed. rev. by Robert, Berlin, 1887); and Welcker, *Griechische Götterlehre* (1857–63).

Zeuxis (Ζεῦξις). A celebrated Greek painter of the Ionic School, a contemporary of Parrhasius; he was a native of Heraclea in South Italy, and lived till about B.C. 400 at different places in Greece, at last, as it appears, settling in Ephesus. According to the accounts of his works which have been preserved, in contrast to the great mural painter, Polygnotus, he especially devoted himself to painting on panels. He endeavoured above all things to make his subjects attractive by investing them with the charm of novelty and grace. He also has the merit of having further improved the distribution of light and shade, introduced by his elder contemporaries. Especially celebrated was his picture of Helen, painted for the temple of Heré on the Lacinian promontory (Cic. *De Invent.* ii. 1, 1). He aimed at the highest degree of illusion. As is well known, he is said to have painted grapes so naturally that the birds flew to peck at them (Pliny, *H. N.* xxxv. 61–66). See PARRHASIUS; PICTURA.

Zodiăcus, sc. *circulus* (ζωδιακὸς κύκλος). The circle of the Zodiac (Aul. Gell. xiii. 9, 3).

Zoïlus (Ζωΐλος). A grammarian, a native of Amphipolis, who flourished in the time of Philip of Macedon. He was celebrated for the asperity with which he assailed Homer (Ὁμηρομάστιξ), and his name became proverbial for a captious and malignant critic (Ael. *V. H.* xi. 10). See Spindler, *De Zoïlo Homeromastige Qui Vocatur*, 2 pts. (1888–89).

Zona (ζώνη). (1) A flat and rather broad girdle worn by young unmarried women (ζώνη παρθενική) around their hips (Hom. *Od.* v. 231; Ov. *Fast.* ii. 231), as exemplified in the accompanying illustration; whereas the common girdle (*cingulum*) was placed immediately under the bosom. The zone was not laid aside until after the wedding, when the bridegroom had unfastened it with his own hands; whence the expression *zonam solvere* (Catull. ii. 13; Ovid, *Her.* ii. 115) means "to enter the married state." (2) A broad belt worn by men round their loins (Hom. *Il.* xi. 234; Plaut. *Merc.* v. 2, 84), and made double or hollow like our shot-belts, for the purpose of carrying money deposited in it about the person (C. Gracch. *ap.* Gell. xv. 12; Suet. *Vit.* 16); whence the expression *zonam perdere* (Hor. *Ep.* ii. 2, 40) means "to lose one's money." (3) The Greek writers also use the term for a soldier's belt, worn round the loins, to cover the juncture of the cuirass and the kilt of leather straps. See THORAX.

Flora, showing Zona. (National Museum, Naples.)

Zonăras, IOANNES (Ἰωάννης ὁ Ζωναράς). A Greek historian, who lived at Constantinople as chief of the imperial body-guard and first private secretary to the emperor under Alexius I. (Comnenus). He next became a monk, and composed a history of the world (Χρονικόν) down to A.D. 1118, divided into eighteen books. Its value consists in its exact quotations from lost works of earlier writers, especially from those of Dio Cassius, referring to the Empire. The history of his own time he recorded as an eye-witness. The work is edited by Du Cange (Paris, 1686), and Dindorf (Leipzig, 1868–75). A lexicon by Zonaras is edited by Tittmann (Leipzig, 1808).

Zoné (Ζώνη). A town of Thrace, where Orpheus is said to have sung (Herod. vii. 59).

Zophŏrus (ζῳφόρος). "Bearing animals"; a word applied to a panel or relief, and hence used of the continuous carved frieze of the Ionic and Corinthian architecture, which represents the triglyphs and metopes of the Doric buildings (Vitruv. iii. 5, 10).

Zophorus.

Zopy̆rus (Ζώπυρος). (1) A distinguished Persian, son of Megabyzus. After Darius Hystaspis had besieged Babylon for twenty months in vain, Zopyrus resolved to gain the place for his master by the most extraordinary self-sacrifice. Accordingly, one day he appeared before Darius with his body mutilated in the most horrible manner; both his ears and nose were cut off, and his person otherwise disfigured. After explaining to Darius his intentions, he fled to Babylon as a victim of the cruelty of the Persian king. The Babylonians gave him their confidence, and placed him at the head of their troops. He soon found means to betray the city to Darius, who severely punished the inhabitants for their revolt. Darius appointed Zopyrus satrap of Babylon for life, with the enjoyment of its entire revenues (Herod. iii. 153–160). (2) The Physiognomist, who attributed many vices to Socrates, which the latter admitted were his natural propensities, but said that they had been overcome by philosophy (Cic. *Tusc. Disp.* iv. 37; *De Fato*, 5).

Zoroaster or **Zoroastres** (Ζωροάστρης). The prophet of ancient Iran, and one of the great religious teachers of the East. He is commonly spoken of as a Magian (Μάγος, *Magus*), or as a reformer of the old faith of Persia; the religion which he founded is best designated as Zoroastrianism, after his own name, for the lessons of his teaching sank deep into the heart of Iran. There can be no question as to the fact that Zoroaster was an actual historical personage in spite of doubts that have been raised on the subject.

Considerable uncertainty has prevailed as to the exact date at which Zoroaster lived; so much, however, is certain, that his era must be placed at least six centuries before Christ; and although the historical origin of Zoroastrianism has not yet been cleared up, the religion presumably became the faith of the great Achaemenian kings, and entered upon its long history as one of the important early religions of the world. The national power of the creed was broken by the victorious invasion of Alexander the Great, but Zoroastrianism outlived the blow, and still lingered in Iran under the Seleucid government and the Parthian sway until the third century of our own era, when it once more rose to supremacy at the time of the Sassanidae (A.D. 226–651), and was restored to its pristine glory. (See Persia.) The final overthrow of the Zoroastrian belief, however, came in the seventh century with the rise of Islam; for the religion of Ormazd was almost blotted out in Iran by the Mohammedan conquest, although a few true followers of Zoroaster are still to be found scattered here and there in their old home. The small band, however, which preferred exile to conversion and sought refuge in India became the ancestors of the flourishing community of Parsis to-day in Bombay; these are the veritable Zoroastrian descendants of the persecuted faithful who found among the Hindus a place of safe retreat and of freedom to worship Ormazd. They are the chief conservators of what remains of the sacred literature, which has naturally suffered from the various vicissitudes and crises through which the religion has passed.

Respecting Zoroaster's life and teaching, our sources of information are either directly the Avesta, or Zend-Avesta, and the Pahlavi books, below mentioned, or they are indirectly the statements found in other Oriental writings or contained in allusions in the classics. Next to the ancient Avesta and the Pahlavi writings, which latter belong chiefly to Sassanian times (A.D. 226–651), the most important Oriental contributions to our knowledge come from the later Persian national epic Shāh-Nāmah, or "book of kings" (tenth century A.D.), and from the Zartusht Nāmah, a legendary sketch of Zoroaster's life (thirteenth century A.D.). Both of these, however, must be used with proper judgment. Considerable valuable information, moreover, is to be gathered from Arabic writings; though these statements are often tinged by a Mohammedan colouring.

All classical antiquity is agreed on the point of Zoroaster's being an historical personage, even if he was in the eyes of the authors of the time a more or less hazy figure. He was regarded by the writers of Greece and Rome as the arch-representative of the Magi, and was more famous sometimes perhaps on account of the magic arts attributed to him than for the depth of his philosophy or his legislation, his religious or moral teaching. The Magi were the reputed masters of learning in ancient times (Cic. *De Div.* 1, 23, et al.), but it is difficult to form a clear picture of their doctrines and teachings, except so far as we may believe them to be reflected in Zoroaster, making due allowance, however, for changes or reforms which he may have instituted. The tradition preserved to the effect that Pythagoras studied under these masters in Babylon, or that he may have caught some Zoroastrian ideas, may not be altogether without foundation (Cic. *De Fin.* v. 29; Val. Max. viii. 7; Pliny, *H. N.* xxx. 1, 2; Apul. *Florid.* p. 19; Porphyr. *Vita Pythag.* 41; Lactant. *Institut.* iv. 2; Iambl. *Vita Pythag.* c. 19; Clem. Alex. *Strom.* i. p. 357, et al.). Plato, moreover, according to tradition, was anxious to visit the Orient and to study with the Magi had he not been prevented by the Persian wars (Diog. Laërt. iii. 7; Apul. *De Habitud. Doctrin. Plat.* p. 569). The followers of the sophist Prodicus are reported as boasting of possessing secret writings of Zoroaster (Clem. Alex. *Strom.* i. p. 357), and even a Magian teacher named Gobryas has been claimed for

Socrates (cf. *Axiochos* attributed to Plato). Instances might be multiplied. Aristotle, Eudoxus of Cnidus, Deinon, and especially Theopompus, were familiar with Zoroastrian tenets (cf. Diog. Laërt. *Prooem.* 8; Pliny, *H. N.* xxx. 1, 20; Plut. *Is. et Os.* 47). An allusion is also found to a work bearing Zoroaster's name by Heracleidus Ponticus, a pupil of Plato and Aristotle (cf. Plut. *Adv. Colot.* p. 1115 A). Hermippus, moreover, made careful studies of Magism and of Zoroastrian writings (cf. Pliny, *H. N.* xxx. 1, 2); finally, there are common enough references to Zoroastrian ideas to be found in Plutarch, Strabo, Pliny, and others. A number of purported books by Zoroaster, such as Περὶ Λίθων Τιμίων, Περὶ Φύσεως, Λόγια, Βίβλιοι Ἀπόκρυφοι Ζωροάστρου, Ἀστεροσκοπικά (cf. Suidas and Pliny), or Gemistus Pletho's Μαγικὰ Λόγια τῶν ἀπὸ τοῦ Ζωροάστρου Μάγων, from which citations are quoted, are doubtless apocryphal; they nevertheless show the reputation which Zoroaster later enjoyed (for references cf. Fabricius, *Bibl. Graec.* vol. i. p. 304 seq.), although his name is not mentioned by Herodotus nor by Xenophon, and there are only doubtful grounds for assuming its presence in the fragments that happen to be preserved of Ctesias. The earliest authenticated allusion to Zoroaster by name in the classics seems to be that in the Platonic *Alcibiades*, i. 122; but according to Diogenes Laërtius (*Prooem.* 2) he is mentioned by the earlier Xanthus of Lydia. The Greek form Ζωροάστρης, under which the sage is known to fame, is a modified form of *Zarathushtra* (cf. Mod. Pers. *Zardusht*), which is the prophet's actual name in the Avesta; Diodorus Siculus (i. 94) once has Ζαθραύστης.

In regard to the date at which Zoroaster lived a wide diversity of opinion has prevailed. The statements of antiquity on the subject may conveniently be divided into three groups. First (1) may be considered those classical references that assign to him the extravagant age of B.C. 6000. These are confined simply to the classics, but they have the claim of being based upon information possessed by Aristotle, Eudoxus, and Hermippus (cf. Pliny, *H. N.* xxx. 1, 2; Plut. *Is. et Os.* 46; Schol. Plato's *Alcibiades*, i. 122; Diog. Laërt. *De Vita Philos. Prooem.* 2; Lactant. *Institut.* vii. 16; and cf. Suid. s. v. *Zoroastres*). Such extraordinary figures are presumably due to the Greeks' misunderstanding the statements of the Persians in regard to the position of Zoroaster's millennium in the great world-period of 12,000 years. Second (2) come those statements which connect the name of Zoroaster with that of the uncertain Semiramis and Ninus (Diod. Sic. ii. 6; Fragm. of Ceph. in Euseb. *Chron.* i. 43, and iv. 35; Syncel. *Chronograph.* i. p. 315; Theon, *Progymnasmata*, 9; Justin, *Hist. Philippic.* i. 1; Arnob. *Adv. Gent.* i. 5; compare also Suidas, s. v. *Zoroastres*, and the Armenian Moses of Khorni, i. 16). Third (3), the direct Zoroastrian tradition as found in the Pahlavi books *Bundahish*, xxxiv. 7–8; *Ardā-i Vīrāf*, i. 1–5, supported also by abundant Arabic allusions (Albīrūnī, Masūdī, etc.), is unanimous in placing the opening of Zoroaster's ministry at 258 years before the era of Alexander, or 272 years before the close of his dominion, which would give Zoroaster's date as falling between the latter half of the seventh century B.C. and the middle of the sixth century; in fact, in the period just preceding the Achaemenian dynasty. This is doubtless not far from the truth, and may be finally regarded as the best view to adopt. Tradition has it that Zoroaster was forty-two years old when he first converted King Vishtaspa, who became his patron; but there is no good ground for identifying this ruler with Hystaspes the father of Darius. Such identification is made by Ammianus Marcellinus (xxvi. 6, 32), and has met with considerable support, but the doubt which Agathias (ii. 24) raises on this subject is better founded.

Like Homer, Zoroaster's native place is debated ground, but the Oriental tradition cannot be far astray that assigns Atropatené in Media, or even more precisely the city of Oroomiah, as his native land, and places the field of his religious activity in Bactria, where the faith became the organized State religion and apparently spread back towards Media and Persia. Such a view, at least, finds support when the Avesta and the Pahlavi books, supplemented also by Arabic and Syriac writings, are combined with statements found in the classics (Diod. Sic. ii. 6; Fragm. Ceph. in Euseb. *Chron.* i. 43, and iv. 35; *Praeparatio Evang.* x. 9; Theon, *Progym.* 9; Justin, *Hist. Philippic.* i. 1; Arnob. *Adv. Gent.* i. 5; Ammian. Marcel. 23, 6, 32; Clem. Alex. *Strom.* i. p. 357; Pliny, *H. N.* xxx. 1, 2; Diog. Laërt. *Prooem.* 2; Suid. s. v. *Zoroastres;* cf. also the Armenian Moses of Khorni, i. 16).

Numerous legends and myths early gathered about the name of Zoroaster, and several of these are preserved in classical writers. The tradition, for example, about his laughing instead of crying when he was born, as told by Pliny (*H. N.* vii. 16, 15), is found also in the East; but the romantic story of his death by lightning (Suid. s. v. *Zoroastres;* Pseud.-Clem. *Recogn.* iv. 27–29, *Homil.* ix. 3; *Chronic. Pasch.* i. p. 67) is not in accordance with the prevailing Oriental testimony to the effect that he was massacred at the age of seventy-seven when Balkh was stormed by the Turanians. In his lifetime he is said to have performed a number of miracles; the report, moreover, that he lived in silence in the wilderness for a number of years is doubtless to be explained as alluding to a period of religious meditation and preparation (Pliny, *H. N.* xi. 42, 97; Schol. Plato's *Alcibiades*, i. 122; Plut. *Quaest. Sympos.* iv. 1, p. 660). The consistent Oriental tradition that he began his ministry at the age of thirty appears also in the Scholion to the *Alcibiades*. Furthermore, Pliny (*H. N.* xxx. 1, 2), Diogenes Laërtius (*Prooem.* 2), and Suidas (s. v. *Magoi*) are able to give the names of some of the Magi that succeeded him.

Zoroaster's religion may be characterized primarily as dualism in so far as it proclaims the incessant warfare that reigns on earth between the good principle, Ahura Mazda or Ormazd (Ὡρομάσδης), and the evil spirit, Anra Mainyu, Ahriman (Ἀρειμάνιος). At the end of the world the good will finally triumph, evil will be destroyed, and a general resurrection of the dead will take place (Plut. *Is. et Os.* 47). The doctrine of rewards and punishments for the immortal soul is a cardinal theme in Zoroaster's preaching; the principle, moreover, is inculcated of preserving the purity of the body and of the care of useful animals, especially the cow. The exercise of scrupulous caution is enjoined for preserving the elements, fire, water, and earth, from defilement, particularly from contact with dead matter; hence arose the strange custom of exposing corpses upon the *dakhmas*, or towers of silence, to be devoured by dogs and birds—a custom which has been commented upon from the days of Herodotus to the present (Herod. i. 140; Porphyr. *De Abstin.* iv. 21, etc.). The general spirituality of the Persian religious ideas was often remarked upon by the Greeks (Herod. i. 131; Deinon Fragm. 9; Diog. Laërt. *Prooem.* 6; Plut. *Is. et Os.* 46; Porphyr. *Vita Pythag.* 41); and owing to the more or less close relations between Iran on the one side and Greece and Rome upon the other, the figure of Zoroaster is one of considerable interest to the student of the classics; while, by way of criticism, it may be added that in classical writers there is hardly a statement regarding him or the Magian faith which does not find some support, corroboration, or parallel in the sacred texts themselves.

BIBLIOGRAPHY.—The most complete collection as yet of allusions in the classics to Zoroaster, the Magi, and the Persians is to be found in Kleuker, *Zend-Avesta*, Anhang ii. 3 (Leipzig and Riga, 1783); consult also Rapp in *Zeitschrift d. deutschen morgenländischen Gesellschaft*, xix. 1–89, xx. 49 seq., and Windischmann, *Zoroastrische Studien* (Berlin, 1863). The standard text of the Zoroastrian Scriptures is edited by Geldner, *Avesta* (Stuttgart, 1884–1895). Translations from the Avesta and the Pahlavi literature by Darmesteter, Mills, and West have appeared in the *Sacred Books of the East*, vol. iv. (Oxford, 1880 foll.); the most recent translation is in French by Darmesteter, *Annales du Musée Guimet* (Paris, 1892–93). For a complete list of works of reference consult the articles "Avesta," "Pahlavi," and "Religion of Iran" in Geiger and Kuhn's *Grundriss der iranischen Philologie* (Strasburg, 1895–96).

Zosĭmus (Ζώσιμος). A Greek historian who lived as a high officer of State at Constantinople in the second half of the fifth century A.D., and composed a work, distinguished for its intelligent and liberal views, on the fall of the Roman Empire. It is in six books: i. giving a sketch of the time from Augustus to Diocletian; ii.–iv. a fuller account of events down to the division of the Empire by Theodosius the Great; v. and vi. treat in greater detail of the period from 395 to 410; the conclusion of book vi. is probably wanting, as Zosimus had the intention of continuing the history up to his own time. He attributes the fall of the Empire in part to the overthrow of heathenism and the introduction of Christianity, with which, of course, he was not acquainted in its purest form, but only in the degenerate state into which it had sunk in some places in the fourth century. This history is edited by Bekker (1837) and by Mendelssohn (1887). See Martin, *De Fontibus Zosimi* (1866). A monograph on the various prodigies, oracles, etc., recorded by Zosimus was published by H. Piristi in 1893.

Zoster (Ζωστήρ). Now C. of Vari; a promontory on the west of Attica, between Phalerum and Sunium.

Zothēca. A small private room or study, adjoining a large one (Pliny, *Epist.* ii. 17, 21).

Zumpt. (1) KARL GOTTLIEB, a German classical scholar, born in Berlin March 20th, 1792. He pursued his studies under Kreuzer at Heidelberg, under Wolf and Böckh at Berlin, and on finishing his university course became in succession Professor of Classics at the Joachimsthal Gymnasium, of History at the Military School, Professor Extraordinary of Roman Literature at the University of Berlin, and Professor Ordinarius in the same university in 1838. He died at Karlsbad, June 25th, 1849. He published a very popular Latin Grammar (Berlin, 1818), which has gone through many editions (Eng. trans. by Schmitz, 3d ed. London, 1852), and which has been the basis of several other grammars in English. He also edited Quintilian (Leipzig, 1831); parts of Cicero; and Quintus Curtius (Brunswick, 1849); and was the author of the following treatises: *Annales Veterum Regnorum et Populorum imprimis Romanorum* (1819, 3d ed. 1862); *Ueber die bauliche Einrichtung des römischen Wohnhauses* (2d ed. 1851); *Die Religion der Römer* (1845). (2) AUGUST WILHELM, nephew of the preceding, was born in Königsberg Dec. 4th, 1815, and was educated at the University of Berlin. He became professor in the Friedrich-Wilhelm Gymnasium, and died April 22d, 1877. He wrote various works on Roman epigraphy and antiquities, and especially *Das Criminalrecht der römischen Republik*, 2 vols. (1869). See Padaletti, *A. W. Zumpt* (Leipzig, 1878).

Zythum and Zythus (ζῦθος). A kind of ale or beer made of barley or other grain, for which see the article CERVESIA.

APPENDIX

A

Actio. In the widest sense, *actio* means right of action, and is nearly equivalent to *ius* in the sense of a private right. In the narrower and original sense, it means proceedings taken to enforce a right.

(1) The LEGIS ACTIŌNES were the forms of procedure proper to the old civil law. They were not all suits in the modern sense, i. e. they did not all imply the submission of the case to the judgment of a court: *legis actio per pignoris capionem*, the enforcement of a claim by distress, was wholly extra-judicial, and *legis actio per manus iniectionem*, enforcement of a claim by the arrest of the debtor, involved merely a formal recognition by the magistrate that the arrest was technically justified (*addictio*). The action by distress was admissible only in certain special and peculiar cases where sacral or public interests were involved (see Gaius, *Inst.* iv. 26–29), but the action by arrest was admissible wherever the defendant's right was technically clear, not only when judgment had actually been rendered—*manus iniectio pro iudicato*—but in other cases, e. g. against the nexal debtor (cf. NEXUM). In such cases the arrested debtor could not himself dispute the creditor's right: a *vindex* must intervene in his behalf, who, if defeated, became liable for twice the amount of the debt (*duplum*). In the later Republic, however, the debtor, if not *iudicatus*, was regularly permitted to dispute the arrest and act as his own *vindex* (*lex Vallia*), so that arrest, except on a judgment-debt, became simply a method of opening a suit—*manus iniectio pura*. Cf. Gaius, *Inst.* iv. 21–25.

The *legis actio sacramento* (also *sacramenti* and *per sacramentum*), on the contrary, was from the outset a suit in the modern sense. It was the regular form of procedure (*actio generalis*) for obtaining a decision in a case of disputed right. (Cf. Gaius, *Inst.* iv. 13–17.) The plaintiff summoned the defendant to appear before the magistrate—*in ius vocatio*. If the latter refused to come he was treated as having confessed judgment, and the plaintiff might proceed to *manus iniectio*, a rule which insured prompt compliance with the plaintiff's summons. The litigants stated their case by the use of set and formal phrases, accompanied by ceremonial acts. The forms varied according to the nature of the suit. (*a*) If a property right is in dispute (*actio in rem*), the plaintiff asserted his right, and the defendant replied by a counter-assertion of right, the assertion in each case (and hence the action itself) being termed *vindicatio.* Cases of disputed right over wife or children, as over slaves, were treated as proceedings *in rem* (family rights not being distinguished from property rights); but here the *vindicatio* of one of the parties might be *in libertatem*, i. e. he might assert that the person claimed as slave or child or wife was really free from *potestas* or *manus*. In all these vindicatory proceedings each party held a staff (*fistuca*), which, according to Gaius, represented a spear (*quasi hastae loco*), and the entire ritual suggested an impending appeal to the ordeal of battle. But at this point the magistrate enjoined peace, and the antagonists challenged each other to wager a certain sum (*sacramentum*, 50 or 500 *asses*, according to the value of the object in dispute) on the truth of their respective assertions. Each party presented sureties (*praedes*) for the payment of the sum wagered. The magistrate then *dabat vindicias*—i. e. assigned the person or thing in dispute to the custody of one of the litigants, who presented sureties for its redelivery in case sentence should be rendered against him. Where a question of liberty was at stake, ancient usage, confirmed by the Twelve Tables, assigned the custody of the person *secundum libertatem*, i. e. to the party asserting liberty (cf. the case of Virginia, Livy, 3, 44; *Dig.* 1, 2, 2, § 24); and provided that in such cases the smaller *sacramentum* of 50 *asses* should always be employed. (*b*) It is probable that where *manus iniectio* had been initiated against a debtor and a *vindex* intervened, the latter used the forms of the *vindicatio in libertatem;* and Brinz conjectures that there was originally no other means of testing a question of debt by *actio sacramento* (Grünhut's *Zeitschr.* i. 23). But according to the ordinary opinion, based on Gaius, *Inst.* iv. 13–15, 20, and Valer. Prob. *De Iuris Not. Signif.* iv. 1, 2, the sacramental action ran *in personam*, for the recovery of a definite sum owed, whether on contract or by reason of tort, and without vindicatory forms, the plaintiff asserting and the defendant denying the debt, and each then challenging the other to the customary wager. In both cases, whether the action was *in rem* or *in personam*, the proceedings *in iure*, i. e. before the magistrate, closed up with *litis contestatio*, i. e. the calling in of witnesses to attest the issue raised by the pleadings; and the case was then sent for trial to a *iudex* or body of *iudices*. These had only to find that the *sacramentum* of the one party was *iustum*, that of the other *iniustum*. The sum wagered by the defeated party fell into the public treasury.

Another true suit was the *legis actio per iudicis arbitrive postulationem*, which opens with a direct request for the appointment of a *iudex* or referee. This was probably the form of action used whenever the direct averment of a definite right was impossible, e. g. when the sum in dispute was uncertain, or when it was necessary to draw the line between opposing rights, e. g. to determine boundaries or to divide an inheritance.

The latest of the *legis actiones*, established by a special statute (*lex Silia*) was that *per condictionem*, called also simply *condictio*. It was simpler in form than the *actio sacramento;* ran for the recovery of any definite sum of money (*certa pecunia*), and later (by a *lex Calpurnia*) of any definite object (*omnis certa res*); and provided roughly for the payment of damages to the victorious party, each antagonist promising the other at the beginning of the suit to pay a penalty of one-third of the amount in litigation in case the division went against him (*stipulatio et restipulatio tertiae partis*).

The *legis actiones* were so called, according to Gaius, either because they were introduced by *leges* or because the pleadings were based upon the language of the *leges*, and were observed like laws (*Inst.* iv. 11). The former explanation, at least, is untrue. All the *legis actiones*, except the *condictio*, are obviously older than the Twelve Tables. They were of customary origin, and the special forms employed were worked out by the *pontifices*. This is particularly clear in the case of the *actio sacramento*. *Sacramentum* is properly an oath, not a wager; and it is clear that in the original form of this action a religious issue was raised for priestly decision by the opposition of the oaths of the two parties. Even after the Twelve Tables, the *pontifices* controlled the forms of action, and all the details of procedure until A.U.C. 450, when a book of forms, drawn up by Appius Claudius Caecus, was published (*populo traditus*) by his client, the scribe Cn. Flavius. The law of civil pleadings then came to be known as *ius Flavianum* (Livy, ix. 46; *Dig.* 1, 2, 2, §§ 5, 6). A century later Sext. Aelius Paetus published, in his *Tripertita*, the text of the Twelve Tables, the established pontifical *interpretatio*, and a revised formulary of actions (*ius Aelianum*).

Procedure in Iudicio.—The *legis actiones* were really only forms of pleading. All that took place *in iure* before the magistrate served simply to define the issue. The actual trial of the suit took place before a special *iudex* selected by the parties or appointed by the magistrate, or before a standing body of elected *iudices*, where the case fell under the special competence of such a board (cf. Centumviri; Decemviri). Proceedings *in iudicio* were minutely regulated by the Twelve Tables. The parties were to appear before noon of the day set for trial. In case of the absence of either, sentence was rendered in favour of the party present. Both parties appearing, each briefly stated his case (*causae coiectio*), and then each submitted a fuller argument (*peroratio*) with evidence. The decision had to be reached by sunset.

Execution of Judgment.—The *iudices* were not magistrates, and they could issue no commands. They simply expressed an opinion (*sententia*) on the issue submitted to them. If the *sententia* sustained the plaintiff's claim and the defendant failed to satisfy judgment within 30 days, the plaintiff (his right being now clear) proceeded to arrest the debtor (*manus iniectio pro iudicato*). If no *vindex* intervened the creditor held the debtor in chains for 60 days, leading him out *in comitium* on three successive market-days (*trinis nundinis continuis*) and proclaiming the amount of the judgment. After this, judgment being still unsatisfied, the debtor was sold into foreign slavery (*trans Tiberim*). If there were several creditors they might cut him in pieces. This latter provision of the Twelve Tables, the ancients asserted, was never enforced; and some moderns have tried to explain it as referring to the estate, not the person, of the debtor. The right of selling the debtor was commuted, either by custom or law (*lex Poetilia ?*) into a right of holding him to work off the debt, and ultimately into a simple right of imprisonment.

All the *legis actiones* were *iuris civilis*, and could not be brought by or against foreigners. Where the private rights of the latter were guaranteed by treaty a special form of action was provided for their protection—the *recuperatio*. As in the case of the civil actions, the preliminary pleadings took place before a magistrate, and the decision was referred to special judges called *recuperatores*.

For full description of the *legis actiones*, see Muirhead, *Roman Law*, pp. 181–235.

(2) The Praetorian Formula.—Towards the end of the Republic the *legis actiones* were almost wholly superseded by a new and freer system of pleading worked out by the praetors—the procedure by *formula*. It probably originated in the courts established for non-citizen subjects of Rome (*peregrini dediticii*), who could not proceed according to the *ius civile* of Rome, for they had no share in it; nor by their own civil laws, for they had lost these by the overthrow of their *civitates;* nor by *recuperatio*, for they enjoyed no treaty rights.

In fact, there was for them no law save that which the Roman magistrates—the praetor of the Peregrini at Rome and the Roman governors in the provinces—saw fit to make for them. It therefore became usual for the magistrate, after hearing what the parties had to say, to send the case to a *iudex*, with instructions to investigate such and such allegations of the parties, and if the allegations of the plaintiff appeared true, and those of the defendant untrue, to condemn the defendant. The advantage of this freer form of procedure proved so great that it was extended by a *lex Aebutia* and two *leges Iuliae* (Gaius, *Inst.* iv. 30) to suits between Romans. It then became possible for the city praetor either to instruct the *iudex* to decide according to the old civil law (*formula in ius concepta*) or according to the freer principles of the *ius gentium* (cf. Ius), in which case the *formula* was in *factum concepta*. The *formula in factum concepta* was thus in reality a law-making formula; it was the instrument by which the praetor carried through the reforms which were embodied in the edict. In proportion as the praetorian law came to be recognized as *ius*, this distinction faded; and in the earlier Empire *actio in factum* came to mean a special action, outside of the established forms (cf. below, *actio utilis*). The formula was always addressed in writing to the *iudex*, and was cast in hypothetical form. The essential allegations of the plaintiff—his statement of facts (*demonstratio*) and his assertion of right (*intentio*)—were set forth as supposititious; if they proved true, the *iudex* was to condemn the defendant (*condemnatio*). If the defence consisted in a general denial, no mention of it was necessary in the formula; but if the defendant alleged special reasons why the plaintiff's claim could not be legally or equitably enforced, these were submitted to the *iudex* in an *exceptio*. Counter-allegations by the plaintiff might also require mention (*replicatio*), and so on, possibly, to a *triplicatio;* the allegations of the plaintiff appearing regularly in the positive form, *si*, *aut si, nec non*, etc., and those of the defendant in the negative, *nisi, nec*, etc. Where, as in partition suits, it was desirable that the referee should assign certain pieces of property to one or the other of the parties, a power to do this was inserted (*adiudicatio*). The praetorian formula was equally applicable to actions *in rem* and *in personam*. It always ran, indeed, for condemnation in money damages; but where the plaintiff was suing to recover property, the *iudex* was empowered to advise restitution (*arbitrium restituendi*), and to condemn in exemplary damages if his advice was not obeyed. The written formula did away with the necessity of *litis contestatio* in the old sense, but the term was retained to designate the conclusion of proceedings *in iure*.

Procedure *in iudicio* remained substantially unchanged. Argument by professional advocates (*oratores*) became usual in important cases, and hearings might be continued from day to day. Execution of judgment still took place by the arrest and imprisonment of the debtor. Levy on the entire estate was introduced in cases of bankruptcy, but the seizure of single articles to satisfy judgment did not appear until the Imperial period. By voluntary *cessio bonorum* a debtor might escape the infamy which attached itself to forced bankruptcy, and by an oath of poverty (*eiuratio bonae copiae*) he freed himself from imprisonment.

In spite of the development of the formula, the *legis actio sacramento* was employed in the Imperial period in two classes of cases: (*a*) where the decision was to be rendered according to the *ius civile* and by the centumviral court (Gaius, *Inst.* iv. 31); (*b*) where a sham suit was employed for purposes of emancipation, adoption, etc. In the later Imperial period the use of *legis actio* was confined to this second class of cases, and the term came to mean the authority of a magistrate to preside over and legalize such transactions, being thus equivalent to *iurisdictio voluntaria*.

For fuller account of procedure by the *formula*, see Muirhead, *Roman Law*, pp. 357–377; Sohm, *Institutes*, pp. 163–212.

(3) Iudicia Extraordinaria, characteristic of Roman precedence, both by *legis actio* and by *formula*, was the separation of *ius* and *iudicium*, i. e. of the pleadings and the actual trial. This *ordo iudiciorum* (*privatorum*), which took the decision of the case out of the hands of the magistrate and placed it in those of a free and independent citizen, was regarded by the Romans of the Republic as one of the chief bulwarks of personal liberty. In the Empire this *ordo iudiciorum* was first undermined and then swept away. Procedure *extra ordinem*, where an imperial official hears the evidence as well as the pleadings and himself renders the decision, appeared at the beginning of the Imperial period, both in special cases where new remedies were granted, and for the more speedy decision of all sorts of cases. Later it became usual, even in the ordinary courts, to select persons attached to the court (assessors or advocates) for services as *iudices*, private citizens being excused from this duty. The presiding magistrate and those subaltern *iudices* hear the entire case together, both the pleadings and the evidence, and the *iudices* retire *pro forma* to render the decision.

The *formula* thus became unnecessary, the *iudices* having heard the pleadings. In other cases the hearing of pleadings and evidence was delegated from the outset to a *iudex*. Constantine forbade such delegation when the magistrate was able to try the case himself. With this implied recognition of the power of the magistrate to render sentence, the distinction between *ius* and *iudicium* disappeared; and in the time of Justinian all *iudicia* were declared to be *extraordinaria*.

Execution of judgment took place in the later Empire—*manu militari*, i. e. by officers of the court, and was always directed primarily against the estate and only in second instance against the person.

(4) Classification of Actions.—Through all the periods of Roman procedure a sharp distinction was drawn between actions *in rem* or *petitiones*, which are based on some right in the thing and run against all who interfere with this right, and actions *in personam*, which run against a particular person and his legal successors by reason of something which he has done to bind himself (*se obligare*), e. g. his contract or tort (*delictum*)—actions which logically ran *in personam* only, but which were made to run *in rem* (e. g. *actio quod metus causa*)—were termed *actiones in rem scriptae*. *Actiones mixtae* were such as ran at the same time for recovery of property and of a penalty, or for the recovery of debt and penalty; but the same term was also applied to cases in which both parties might be regarded as being at once plaintiff and defendant, and in which either or both parties might be condemned (e. g. actions of partition). *Actio certa* (*condictio certi*) ran for the recovery of a definite object or sum; *incerta*, for unliquidated damages. *Actio directa* is the action which regularly arises from a contract or other legal act; possible counter-claims, growing out of the same transaction, are enforced by *actio contraria*. *Actio directa* was also used to designate an established and familiar form of action, in distinction from *actio utilis* or *in factum* (cf. the English "action on the case"), which is given where no established action lies—*ad exemplum actionis directae*. The relation of an adapted and widened action to the earlier and narrower remedy was often expressed by *quasi* (e. g. *actio Serviana, quasi-Serviana*); actions in which the *iudex* was instructed to decide what was due on grounds of general equity (*ex fide bona*) were called *bona fide actiones*, in distinction from *actiones strictae* or *stricti iuris*. *Actio civilis, legitima* was one that lay at *ius civili*; actions created by the praetors or aediles were termed *honorariae*. *Actiones temporales, temporariae*, were such as must be brought within a certain time after the right of action arose. All others were *perpetuae*. In the later Empire all actions were subject to limitation or prescription, but those which ran for thirty or more years were still termed *perpetuae*. *Actio popularis* was one in which any citizen might appear as plaintiff. Such actions were designed to secure some public interest. They resembled the ordinary (private) actions only in that the penalty recovered usually went in whole or in part to the plaintiff. *Actio praeiudicialis*, cf. Praeiudicium.

The best manual of Roman civil procedure is Von Keller's *Römischer Civilprocess* (6th ed. by Wach, Leipzig, 1883; French translation by Capmas, Paris, 1876).

Album (λεύκωμα). A space or patch covered with white plaster against the walls of a building, upon which public announcements or advertisements to the public were written; and thence the name is given to any sort of white tablet bearing an inscription, such as a list of the senators, the praetor's edicts, or things of a like nature (Paul. *Sentent.* i. t. 14; Seneca, *Ep.* 48; Cic. *Orat.* ii. 12). The annual edicts of the praetor were posted up in this way; and Cicero states that the *annales maximi* were posted on an album by the Pontifex Maximus (*De Orat.* ii. 12, 52).

ALBUM SENATORIUM is the official list of the senators (Tac. *Ann.* iv. 42); ALBUM IUDĬCUM is the panel of the *iudices*. See IUDEX.

Anthon, CHARLES. An American classical scholar born in New York in 1797. He was educated at Columbia College, where he became Adjunct Professor of Greek and Latin in 1820, and full Professor in 1825. He died in 1867. Dr. Anthon did a great deal towards disseminating a fuller and richer knowledge of the Greek and Latin literatures in the United States by his editions of the best known authors elaborately annotated, and was among the first of English-speaking scholars to draw largely upon the results of German research in his own work. His best known editions are those of Horace (1830), Homer, Livy, Tacitus, Caesar, and Euripides. He also wrote a number of text-books for the teaching of Greek and Latin, and was the author of a widely used *Classical Dictionary*, besides re-editing for American use some of Dr. William Smith's dictionaries relating to antiquities and ancient literature.

Asȳlum (*ἄσυλον*). Among the Greeks the right of sanctuary appertained to those who took refuge in temples, altars, sacred groves, and at statues of the gods, and these were resorted to by debtors, slaves, and criminals as places of refuge. Only certain definite places, however, gave absolute protection, and we read of persons being forced from the sanctuary by the application of fire, while others were starved out, as in the well-known case of Pausanias (q. v.). In Roman times the *ius asyli* was so frequently an obstruction to the course of justice that the Senate limited it to a few cities (Tac. *Ann.* iii. 60).

The Roman law did not recognize the right of sanctuary in general, and Livy speaks of it as a Greek custom (xxxv. 51). Yet by special enactment the Temple of Divus Iulius was made an asylum of refuge (Dio Cass. xlvii. 19), and slaves in the provinces, if ill-treated by their masters, could take refuge before a statue of the emperor (Gaius, i. 53; cf. SERVUS).

On the general subject, see Förster, *De Asylis Graecorum* (Berlin, 1847); Neu, *De Asylis* (Göttingen, 1837); Bringer, *De Asylorum Origine, Usu,* etc. (Leyden, 1828); and Rein, *Criminalrecht der Römer*, p. 896.

B

Brunck, RICHARD FRANÇOIS PHILIPPE. A classical scholar, born at Strassburg, December 30th, 1729. He was educated in Paris, and took up the study of Greek, in which he won a sound reputation for keen criticism of texts. He was noted for his great skepticism as to the accuracy of copyists. He died June 12th, 1803. His chief works are *Analecta Veterum Poetarum Graecorum* (1772–76); and editions of Anacreon (1778); Apollonius Rhodius (1780); Aristophanes (1781–83); the Gnomic Poets (1784); Vergil (1785); and Sophocles (1786).

C

Calgăcus and **Galgăcus.** A British chieftain who fought against the Romans at the time when Agricola was in command in Britain. A spirited oration is put into his mouth by Tacitus (*Agric.* 29 foll.).

Canon Porsoniānus. A rule laid down by Richard Porson (q. v.), in his preface to the *Hecuba* of Euripides, to the effect that in the tragic (iambic) trimeter of the Greeks the fifth foot should not commence with a long syllable when it is itself the end of a word of several syllables and is followed by a word of three syllables; e. g. that *εἰκὸς σ' εἰδέναι* could not finish an iambic trimeter line.

Culpa. Any wrongful act or omission, whether due to intent or not. Taken generally, it includes what the Romans term *dolus malus*, but properly the latter is distinguished from culpa when this term is used accurately; *dolus malus* being an intentional and deliberate violation, whether by act or omission, of another's rights, and culpa an unintentional violation, consisting apparently always in the omission or neglect of some legal duty. It is true that *damnum* under the Lex Aquilia is often the consequence of some act; but the act usually derives its culpable character rather from the omission of some duty than from the positive act which is done; the latter, in itself, does not entail legal liability, but because it is done wilfully, heedlessly, or rashly. See Hasse, *Die "Culpa" des römischen Rechts* (1838); and Mommsen, in his *Obligationenrecht*, iii. pp. 345 foll.

Cumae (Κύμη). A town of Campania, the most ancient of the Greek colonies in Italy and Sicily. It was founded from Cymé in Aeolis, in conjunction with Chalcis and Eretria in Euboea (Strab. p. 243; Verg. *Aen.* vi. 2). Its foundation is placed in B.C. 1050, but the date must be regarded as uncertain. It was situated on a steep hill of Mount Gaurus, a little north of the promontory Misenum. It became in early times a great and flourishing city; its commerce was extensive; its territory included a great part of the rich Campanian plain; its population was at least 60,000; and its power is attested by its colonies in Italy and Sicily—Puteoli, Palaeopolis (afterwards Neapolis), Zanclé (afterwards Messana). But it had powerful enemies to encounter in the Etruscans and the Italian nations. It was also weakened by internal dissensions, and one of its citizens, Aristodemus, made himself tyrant of the place. Its power became so much reduced that it was only saved from the attacks of the Etruscans by the assistance of Hiero, who annihilated the Etruscan fleet, 474. It maintained its independence till 417, when it was taken by the Campanians and most of its inhabitants sold as slaves (Diod. xii. 76). From this time Capua became the chief city of Campania; and although Cumae was subsequently a Roman municipium and a colony, it continued to decline in importance. At last the Acropolis was the only part of the town that remained, and this was eventually destroyed by Narses in his wars with the Goths. Cumae was celebrated as the residence of the earliest Sibyl, and as the place where Tarquinius Superbus died. See SIBYLLAE

D

Decurtātum Bosii. See DŬBOIS, SIMÉON.

Dino (Δείνων and Δίνων). The father of the historian Clitarchus (q. v.), and himself the author of a history of Persia, frequently referred to by the ancient writers—e. g. Nepos (*Con.* 5), Plutarch (*Alex.* 36, et saep.), Aelian (*H. A.* xvii. 10), and Diogenes Laërtius (i. 8). He flourished about 275 B.C. Only fragments of his history survive.

Dubois, SIMÉON. A French classical scholar (1535–80), better known by his Latinized name BOSIUS, who forged a number of variant readings to Cicero's letters in an edition which he published at Limoges in 1580. This edition he pretended to have based on a MS. which he had obtained from a private soldier, and from readings said to have been furnished by one Crusellius. The MS. is usually styled the *Decurtatum Bosii*, and the readings *Lectiones Crusellianae*. The fraud of Dubois was not thoroughly proven until Haupt and Mommsen, in 1855, instituted an elaborate criticism of his readings and showed their spurious nature.

F

Figurines. See TANAGRA; TERRA-COTTAS.

G

Genealogical Theory of Language. See INDO-EUROPEAN LANGUAGES.

H

Hospitium. (1) An inn. See CAUPONA. (2) (ξενία, προξενία). Hospitality was one of the characteristic features of almost all nations in the primitive period. In civilized countries the necessity of general hospitality is not so much felt; but at a time when the State or the laws of nations afforded scarcely any security, and when the traveller on his journey did not meet with any places destined for his reception and accommodation, the exercise of hospitality was absolutely necessary. Among the nations of antiquity, with whom the right of hospitality was sanctified by religion, it was to some degree observed to the latest period of their existence, and acquired a political importance which it has never had in any other age. It was in Greece, as well as at Rome, of a twofold nature, either private or public, in as far as it was either established between individuals (*hospitium privatum*, ξενία) or between two States (*hospitium publicum*, προξενία).

The stranger who appeared with no hostile object was regarded in the light of a suppliant and under the especial protection of Zeus Xenios. Hence he was kindly received, and on his departure broke a die (ἀστράγαλος, *tessera*) with the host, each keeping a half for mutual recognition by themselves or by their descendants in future times. The ties of hospitality thus formed were hereditary in families. At Rome a stranger (*hospes*) was equally protected by custom and law, and the *tessera hospitalis* was equally a pledge and a symbol of this relation of host and guest. A formal hospitality when once declared could only be broken off in an equally formal way by a solemn *renuntiatio*. Public, as opposed to private, hospitality was a like relation between nations and cities, who were bound to show especial kindness to each other's citizens. See CIVITAS; FOEDERATAE CIVITATES; POLITEIA; PROXENUS; TESSERA.

I

Ius Anŭli Aurei. The right to wear a gold ring was originally a military distinction (Cic. *Verr.* iii. 80, 187), and was ultimately the prerogative of the knights (*equites*) of the military tribune (App. *Pun.* 104), and also of such senators as were *nobiles* or had served as *legati*. The right was also granted as a special privilege to individuals by the military commanders and provincial governors, and carried with it all the dignities of knighthood. Thus Sulla gave the *anulus aureus* to the actor Roscius (Macrob. *Sat.* ii. 10). Under the Empire, the emperor bestowed the *ius anuli* at will. See Lange, *Röm. Alterth.* ii. 8, 163; Marquardt, *Privatleben*, 680 foll., and Herbert Spencer's *Ceremonial Institutions*, ch. ix.

L

Libri Lintei. A name given to such of the Roman *libri magistratum* or early lists of the annual magistrates as were written on linen (*linteum*). They were kept in the Capitol, and are frequently mentioned by Livy as one of his sources of information (Livy, iv. 20, 8; cf. Pliny, *H. N.* xiii. 69). See H. Peter, *Hist. Rom. Reliq.* i. cccxlv.

Linteum (ὀθόνη). Generally any cloth made of linen; but Pliny (*H. N.* xii. 22) applies the same term to cotton fabrics. Especially a towel, napkin, or handkerchief (Plaut. *Most.* i. 3, 110), the same as *sudarium* (q. v.); a curtain to close the sides of a *lectica*, or palanquin (Mart. ii. 57); the sail of a ship, which was made of strips of cloth sewed together (Verg. *Aen.* iii. 686).

Linum (λίνον). Flax; thence anything made with flax; as, a sewing-thread; a fishing-line; a string of pearls; a string bound round the tablets (*tabellae*) upon which letters or any other documents were written, and then tied in a knot, over which the seal was affixed (Cic. *Cat.* iii. 5; Plaut. *Bacch.* iv. 3, 79–111; cf. EPISTOLA); a net, the meshes of which were made of string.

Lyons Mosaic. See CIRCUS, p. 355.

M

Madvig, JOHAN NIKOLAI. A Danish statesman, educator, and classical scholar, born at Svaneke, August 7th, 1804. He was educated at Frederiksborg and Copenhagen, and in 1829 was called to the chair of Latin in the University at the latter place. He twice held the ministerial portfolio of Religion and Education, and was several times presiding officer of the Danish Parliament. As a scholar and especially as a text critic Madvig had a world-wide reputation, and in his work upon the texts of Cicero and Livy he won especial distinction. His most valuable works are *Emendationes in Ciceronis Libros Philosophicos* (1828); *Emendationes Livianae* (1860; 2d ed. 1876); *Adversaria Critica* (3 vols. 1871–84); *Opuscula Academica* (2 vols. 1834–42; last ed. 1887); editions of Cicero, *De Finibus* (1839; 3d ed. 1876); Cicero, *De Senectute* and *De Amicitia* (1835; 2d ed. 1869); of Livy (4 vols. 1861–66); and two grammatical works, a *Latin Grammar* (1841; 7th ed. 1881); and a *Greek Syntax*

(1846), both having been widely used in England and the United States in English translations and revisions. He also wrote a work on the constitution and administration of the Roman State, intended to correct and supplement Mommsen's *History* (2 vols. 1881–82). See his *Autobiography* (1887).

Maemacterion (Μαιμακτηριών). The fifth month in the Attic year, corresponding roughly to our November. See CALENDARIUM.

Maemactes (Μαιμάκτης). See ZEUS.

Malus Ocŭlus (ὀφθαλμὸς βάσκανος). The superstition of the "evil eye" is mentioned by Aristotle (*Probl.* xx. 34), and seems to have been very general among both the Greeks and Romans, as it is in Italy to-day under the name of *jettatura*. Amulets were worn as charms against it, and Theocritus speaks of "spitting thrice" to avert it (vi. 39). The evil eye was supposed to injure children particularly, but sometimes cattle also; whence Vergil (*Ecl.* iii. 103) says:

> Nescio quis teneros oculus mihi fascinat agnos.

Various amulets were used to avert the influence of the evil eye. The most common of these appears to have been the *phallus* (q. v.), called by the Romans *fascinum*, which was hung round the necks of children (Varr. *L. L.* vii. 97, ed. Müller). Pliny (*H. N.* xix. § 50) also says that *Satyrica signa*, by which he means the phallus, were placed in gardens and on hearths as a protection against the fascinations of the envious; and we learn from Pollux (viii. 118) that blacksmiths were accustomed to place the same figures before their forges with the same design. Sometimes other objects were employed for this purpose. Pisistratus is said to have hung the figure of a kind of grasshopper before the Acropolis as a preservative against fascination (Hesych. s. v. Καταχήνη). To point the middle finger (*digitus infamis, digitus impudicus*) at a person was a way of averting his evil influence, and this gesture is still common in Southern Italy, especially Naples, to-day. Cf. Wachsmuth in the Berlin *Athenaeum*, ii. pp. 209 foll.; Jahn, *Ueber den Aberglauben des bösen Blicks* (1855); and on various charms used against the evil eye, see the articles AMULETUM; BULLA; FASCINUM; PHALLUS; and cf. SUPERSTITIO.

O

Ocŭlus Malus. See MALUS OCULUS.

P

Pindărus Thebānus. The name given to the metrical abridgment of the *Iliad* of Homer in Latin, now generally regarded as a youthful production of Silius Italicus. (See SILIUS.) It consists of 1070 hexameters, of which 537 are based upon bks. i.–v. of the *Iliad*. The Catalogue of the Ships is reproduced with much care, but many other more interesting details are omitted. The name HOMĔRUS LATĪNUS is also found in the MSS. Edited by Weytingh (Leyden, 1809); and Plessis (Paris, 1885). See the treatise by Müller (Berlin, 1857).

Poseideon (Ποσειδεών). The sixth month of the Attic year, corresponding roughly to our December. See CALENDARIUM.

R

Reciprŏci Versus. See ECHOÏCI VERSUS.

Reiske, JOHANN JACOB. A celebrated Greek scholar, born at Zörbig, in Saxony, on Christmas Day, 1716. He was educated at Leipzig, where he gave much attention to the study of the Semitic languages, especially Arabic, but also took up medicine, graduating as a physician in 1746. In 1758, after living in great indigence, he secured the rectorship of the Nikolai Gymnasium, an office which he held till his death, August 14th, 1774. As rector he devoted his attention chiefly to Hellenic literature, in which he became a recognized authority. His most important published works are editions of Plutarch (including notes and translation), in 12 vols. (1782); Dionysius of Halicarnassus, 6 vols. (1777); of the Greek orators, in 12 vols. (1770–75); and of Dio Chrysostom, Libanius, Theŏcritus, and Tyrius Maximus; besides his *Animadversiones in Graecos Auctores*, in 5 vols. (1757–66). Some of these works, as the dates show, were published after his death by his wife, Ernestine Christine Reiske. See his *Autobiography* (1783); and Haupt, *Opuscula*, iii. pp. 137 foll.

Ritschl, FRIEDRICH WILHELM. One of the most eminent classical philologists of modern times, born at Grossvargula, in Thuringia, April 6th, 1806. He studied at Leipzig under Hermann, and from 1826 to 1829 at Halle, where he eagerly availed himself of the lectures and society of Reissig. In 1832 he was called to Breslau as Extraordinary Professor, receiving at the same time a joint directorship of the philological seminary. Two years aftewards he became Ordinary Professor, and spent the winter and spring of 1836–37 on a tour through Italy. In 1839 he accepted an invitation to Bonn as Professor of Classical Literature and Rhetoric. The Prussian government conferred on him the rank of Privy-Councillor in 1856. His first literary works were devoted to the Greek grammarians, as the edition of Thomas Magister (Halle, 1832), the acute and penetrating treatise *De Oro et Orione* (Breslau, 1834), and the richly elucidatory *Die alexandrin. Bibliotheken und die Sammlung der Homerischen Gedichte durch Peisistratus* (Breslau, 1838), sufficiently prove; but his greatest work is his edition of Plautus (Bonn, 1848–53), executed with the richest critical apparatus, and accompanied by comprehensive prolegomena on the Plautine metres. This work secured for him a splendid reputation among his countrymen. Among the numerous productions of Ritschl which may be regarded as preparatory to this *chef-d'œuvre*, the most important is his *Parerga Plautina et Terentiana* (Leipzig, 1848). Subsequently his literary activity took another direction — a systematic treatment of Latin inscriptions, with the view of illustrating the history of the Latin language. His labours in this department were crowned with success, for Ritschl has thrown more light upon the successive phases of the language than almost any other single individual. To this field belong his *Lex Rubria* (Bonn, 1851); *Titulus Mummianus* (Berlin, 1852); *Monumenta Epigraphica Tria* (Berlin, 1852); *Inscriptio Columnae Rostratae* (Berlin, 1852); *Anthologiae Latinae Corollarium* (Berlin, 1853); *De Sepulcro Furiorum* (Berlin, 1853); *De Fictilibus Litteratis*, etc. (Berlin, 1853); *Poesis Saturninae Spicelegium* (Bonn, 1854); *De Titulo Metri-*

co *Lambacsensi* (1855); *De Varronis Hebdomadum Libris* (1856); *In Leges Viselliam, Antoniam, Corneliam Observationes Epigraphicae* (1860); and *Prooemiorum Bonnensium Decas* (1862). Besides these works, Ritschl contributed a large number of learned dissertations to the programmes of the University of Bonn, to the transactions of the Archæological Institute of Rome, and to the *Rheinisches Museum für Philologie*. On the twenty-fifth anniversary of his appointment to Bonn, there began to be published *Symbola Philologorum Bonnensium in Honorem Frid. Ritschelii* (1864–67). He died November 8th, 1876. See L. Müller, *Friedrich Wilhelm Ritschl* (Berlin, 1877); and Ribbeck, *F. W. Ritschl* (Leipzig, 1881).

Ruhnken, David. A classical scholar, born January 2d, 1723, at Stolpe, in Pomerania. He was educated at the Königsberg Gymnasium and at Wittenberg University, where he spent two years in the assiduous study of ancient literature, history, and jurisprudence. Afterwards he went to Leyden, where for six years he prosecuted his classical studies under the guidance of Hemsterhuis, and bestowed particular attention on the Greek writers. He planned a new edition of Plato, collected the scholia of that author, and published an edition of Timaeus's *Lexicon Vocum Platonicarum* (Leyden, 1754; reëdited in a much improved form, 1833). He went in 1755 to Paris, where, for a whole year, he examined the MSS. of the Royal Library and of the Library of Saint-Germain. Hemsterhuis had him appointed as *lector* (reader) in the University of Leyden, in which capacity he was the assistant and colleague of his great master. In October, 1757, he introduced his series of lectures by a discourse, *De Graecia Artium et Doctrinarum Inventrice* (Leyden, 1757). For four years he discharged the duties of his office with skill and success, and in 1761 succeeded Oudendorp in the chair of Eloquence and History. In 1774 he succeeded Gronovius as librarian to the University, which he enriched with a multitude of valuable books and MSS. He died May 14th, 1798, and in gratitude to his memory the city of Leyden purchased his great library, and gave his widow an annuity of 500 florins.

Ruhnken will long be remembered as one of the best scholars and critics of the eighteenth century. His fine taste and sagacity, aided by an astonishing memory and vast learning, enabled him to illustrate the authors of antiquity with wonderful success. He was also a brilliant lecturer, for which he was, no doubt, indebted to the extreme lucidity and grace of his Latin style. In addition to the works already noted, he published editions of vol. ii. of Alberti's *Hesychius;* of Rutilius Lupus; of Velleius Paterculus; of Muretus; of the Homeric Hymns; and wrote a history of the Greek orators (1768; last ed. Leipzig, 1841). He contributed to the editions of the classics by Ernesti and Schweighäuser. His life has been written by his famous pupil Wyttenbach (Leyden, 1799; new ed. Leipzig, 1824; Freiburg, 1846).

S

Sal Attĭcum. See Acetum.

Schliemann, Heinrich. An archæologist born at Neubuckow, in Germany, January 6th, 1822. He was the son of a Lutheran pastor, who inspired him at an early age with an enthusiastic admiration of the heroes of ancient Greece. His mother died when he was nine years old, and he then lived for two years with his uncle at Kalkhorst. At fourteen he was compelled to enter a grocer's shop as a clerk at Fürstenberg to support himself. He remained in that humble position for over five years, when he obtained a position as clerk to an Amsterdam firm, and in 1846 was sent to St. Petersburg by the firm as their local agent; and a year later established there a business of his own. In the course of a busy life he travelled extensively in Europe and America, and acquired many languages. After he had amassed wealth he commenced his archæological investigations and excavations in the East. In 1874 he obtained permission from the Greek government to excavate Mycenae, where, in 1877, he made the marvellous discovery of the five royal tombs which local tradition had pointed out to Pausanius as those of Agamemnon and his companions, who had been murdered by Aegisthus. His later excavations are well known. He published *Ithaka, der Peloponnes und Troja; Trojanische Alterthümer* (1874); *Reise in der Troas* (1881); *Mykenae* (1877); *Orchomenos* (1881); *Troja* (1883); *Tiryns* (1886); and *Bericht über die Ausgrabungen ins Troja im Jahre 1890* (1891). He died December 27th, 1890. See Schuchardt's *Schliemann's Excavations* (Eng. trans., 1891).

Scirophorion (Σκιροφοριών). The twelfth month in the Attic year, corresponding roughly to our June. See Calendarium.

Septimontium. The fortified group of the seven hills at Rome. See Roma.

Septizonium. A particular kind of edifice, of great magnificence, consisting of seven stories of columns, one above the other, supporting seven distinct entablatures or zones, from which it received the name. Two such structures are specially recorded in the city of Rome—one in the Twelfth Region, which existed before the time of the emperor Titus (Suet. *Tit.* 2; Ammian. xv. 6, 3); and the other in the Tenth Region, under the Palatine Hill, and near the Circus Maximus, which was built by Septimius Severus (Spart. *Sev.* 19). Three stories of this last structure remained standing during the pontificate of Sixtus V., but were taken down by him for the purpose of employing the columns in building the Vatican. See Middleton, *Remains of Ancient Rome*, i. 218; 219 (note).

Spanish Period of Latinity. A name given to the first century A.D., in which period so many of the leading writers of Latin literature were men of Spanish birth, the most conspicuous being the younger Seneca, Quintilian, Lucan, and Martial.

Specŭla (σκοπιά, σκοπή). A watch-tower whence signals were transmitted, and where they were received by the guards stationed there.

T

Tetrapŏlis (Τετράπολις). One of the twelve districts into which Attica was divided before the time of Theseus. See Marathon; Theseus.

V

Viermänner Scholien. "Scholia of the Four Men." A name given by German scholars to an epitome, made about 200 A.D., of four works relating to the *Iliad* of Homer, and written by four men (Didymus, Aristonicus, Herodian, and Nicanor). See Homerus, p. 838.

GREEK AND ROMAN TABLES OF WEIGHTS AND MEASURES.

TABLE I.

GRECIAN MEASURES OF LENGTH. (Attic Standard.)

I. SMALLER MEASURES.												Decimals of a Metre.	Decimals of a Foot.	Feet.	Inches.
Δάκτυλος												.0185	.0607	..	.7281
2	Κόνδυλος											.037	.1213	..	1.4562
4	2	Παλαστή, Δῶρον, Δοχμή, or Δακτυλοδοχμή										.074	.2427	..	2.9124
8	4	2	Διχάς, or Λιχάς									.148	.4852	..	5.8248
11	$5\frac{1}{2}$	$2\frac{3}{4}$	$1\frac{3}{8}$	Ὀρθοδῶρον								.203	.6673	..	8.0091
12	6	3	$1\frac{1}{2}$	$1\frac{1}{11}$	Σπιθαμή							.222	.7281	..	8.7372
16	8	4	2	$1\frac{5}{11}$	$1\frac{1}{3}$	ΠΟΥ'Σ						.296	.9708	..	11.6496
18	9	$4\frac{1}{2}$	$2\frac{1}{4}$	$1\frac{7}{11}$	$1\frac{1}{2}$	$1\frac{1}{8}$	Πυγμή					.333	1.0921	1	1.1058
20	10	5	$2\frac{1}{2}$	$1\frac{9}{11}$	$1\frac{2}{3}$	$1\frac{1}{4}$	$1\frac{1}{9}$	Πυγών				.370	1.2135	1	2.562
24	12	6	3	$2\frac{2}{11}$	2	$1\frac{1}{2}$	$1\frac{1}{3}$	$1\frac{1}{5}$	ΠΗ͂ΧΥΣ			.444	1.4562	1	5.4744
72	36	18	9	$6\frac{6}{11}$	6	$4\frac{1}{2}$	4	$3\frac{3}{5}$	3	Ξύλον		1.332	4.3686	4	4.4232
96	48	24	12	$8\frac{8}{11}$	8	6	$5\frac{1}{3}$	$4\frac{4}{5}$	4	$1\frac{1}{3}$	'ΟΡΓΥΙΑ'.	1.776	5.8248	5	9.8976

Note.—For other Standards, see Notes to Table II.

TABLE II.

ROMAN MEASURES OF LENGTH.

I. SMALLER MEASURES.							Decimals of a Metre.	Decimals of a Foot.	Feet.	Inches.
Digitus							.0185	.060675	..	.7281
$1\frac{1}{3}$	Uncia or Pollex						.0247	.0809	..	.9708
4	3	Palmus					.074	.2427	..	2.9124
12	9	3	Palmus Maior (of late times)				.222	.7281	..	8.7372
16	12	4	$1\frac{1}{3}$	Pes			.296	.9708	..	11.6496
20	15	5	$1\frac{2}{3}$	$1\frac{1}{4}$	Palmipes		.370	1.2135	1	2.562
24	18	6	2	$1\frac{1}{2}$	$1\frac{1}{5}$	Cubitus	.444	1.4562	1	5.4744

NOTES TO TABLES I. AND II.

A metre is 39.37 English inches; an English foot is .3048 metre.

It is not thought necessary to give the whole scale of the Uncial divisions of the foot. They can easily be calculated from the Uncia.

Other Standards.—The *relations* of the measures to one another were always, with hardly any exception, those above given; but the *standards* varied in different places and at different times. Thus the Attic *πούς* being .296 m., the Aeginetan was .333 m., the Olympic .3205 m., the Philetaerean 333 m., the Ionic .350 m., the Phrygian .2775 m.

In the West, though the Roman foot was .296 m., the same as the Attic, the older Italian foot was only .275 m., and the Drusian foot, used in Gaul and Germany, was .333 m.

In Egypt, under the Pharaohs, the Royal ell was .525 m., the smaller ell .425 m.; under the Ptolemies the Royal ell was .533 m., the greater foot .355 m., and the smaller foot .303 m.

The Great Babylonian ell was .550 m., the Royal or Persian ell .495 m., the Phœnician ell .4435 m.

Compared with one another, the Attic, Roman, and Phœnician feet are the same; the Aeginetan, Philetaerean, and Drusian are the same; the Italian and Phrygian are the same; the Ionic and Royal (or Greater) Egyptian are the same—either exactly or very nearly indeed.

TABLE III.

GRECIAN MEASURES OF LENGTH. (Attic Standard.)

II. LARGER MEASURES.—LAND AND ITINERARY.											Decimals of a Metre.	Decimals of a Mile.	Miles.	Feet.	Inches.
ΠΟΥ'Σ											0.296	.0001838	..	..	11.6496
$1\frac{1}{2}$	ΠΗ͂ΧΥΣ										0.444	.0002757	..	1	5.4744
$2\frac{1}{2}$	$1\frac{2}{3}$	Βῆμα									0.739	.0004596	..	2	5.124
6	4	$2\frac{2}{5}$	'ΟΡΓΥΙΑ'								1.774	.001103	..	5	9.8976
10	$6\frac{2}{3}$	4	$1\frac{2}{3}$	Κάλαμος, Ἄκαινα, or Δεκάπους							2.957	.001838	..	9	8.496
100	$66\frac{2}{3}$	40	$16\frac{2}{3}$	10	Πλέθρον						29.57	.01838	..	97	0.96
600	400	240	100	60	6	ΣΤΑ'ΔΙΟΝ or ΣΤΑ'ΔΙΟΣ					177.4	.11028	..	582	5.76
1200	800	480	200	120	12	2	Δίαυλος				354.8	.22056	..	1164	11.52
2400	1600	960	400	240	24	4	2	Ἱππικόν				.44112	..	2329	11.04
18,000	12,000	7200	3000	1800	180	30	15	$7\frac{1}{2}$	Παρασάγγης			3.3084	3	1634	4.8
36,000	24,000	14,400	6000	3600	360	60	30	15	2	Σχοῖνος		6.6168	6	3268	9.6

Note.—The *σχοῖνος*, above given, is that of Herodotus, but the measure seems to have varied in different reaches of the Nile, and the Romans reckoned it about 4 Roman miles. On the parasang, see note to next Table.

TABLE IV.

ROMAN MEASURES OF LENGTH.

II. LARGER MEASURES.—LAND AND ITINERARY.							Decimals of a Metre.	Decimals of a Mile.	Miles.	Feet.	Inches.
PES							0.296	.0001838	..	..	11.6496
$1\frac{1}{2}$	Cubitus						0.444	.0002757	..	1	5.4744
$2\frac{1}{2}$	$1\frac{2}{3}$	Gradus, or Pes Sestertius					0.740	.0004596	..	2	5.124
5	$3\frac{1}{3}$	2	PASSUS				1.48	.0009193	..	4	10.248
10	$6\frac{2}{3}$	4	2	Decempeda, or Pertica			2.96	.001838	..	9	8.496
120	80	48	24	12	Actus (in length)		35.52	.2206	..	116	5.952
5000	$3333\frac{1}{3}$	2000	1000	500	$41\frac{2}{3}$	MILLE PASSUUM	1480	.9193	..	4854	..

NOTES TO TABLES III. AND IV.

N. B.—The Roman mile only differs from the English by less than $^{1}/_{10}$.

Ancient Road Measures.—As in Tables I. and II., so here, the relations of the measures to one another are correctly given, but the standards varied. It is proper, therefore, to add the length of various road measures according to the standards in use in different parts of the ancient world.

The Attic *stadium* being 177 m., the Olympic was 192 m., the Ptolemaic 185 m., the Ionic 210 m. (A metre is 39.37 English inches.)

The Romans, using round numbers, reckoned 8 stadia to the mile. According to this relation, the Roman stadium would be 185 m., and the old Italian 165 m.

Similarly the Greeks reckoned 30 stadia to the parasang, but the parasang was really 30 *Persian* stadia, which were longer than the Greek, being 196.8 m. The true parasang was therefore 5904 m., or 3 miles 1180 yards. (So Oppert, but Hultsch reckons it as 5670 m.)

The Gallic *leuga* was 2220 m.; the German *rasta* 4440 m.

TABLE V.

GRECIAN MEASURES OF SURFACE. (ATTIC STANDARD.)

ORDINARY LAND MEASURES.			Square Metres.	Square Feet.	Perches.	Square Feet.
ΠΟΥ'Σ τετράγωνος (Square Foot)			0.087	.94245	..	.94245
100	Ἄκαινα (Square of the κάλαμος)		8.74	94.245	..	94.245
10,000	100	ΠΛΕ'ΘΡΟΝ	8740	9424.5	34	167.5

NOTES.

The English acre being 160 perches or 4840 sq. yds., the πλέθρον is obviously less than ¼ of an acre.

The Egyptian ἄρουρα (Herod. ii. 168) was a square of 50 Egyptian ells each way. The ell being taken at 0.524 m., or about 21 English inches, this gives a value of about 820 sq. yds. for the ἄρουρα.

TABLE VI.

ROMAN MEASURES OF SURFACE.

ORDINARY LAND MEASURES.										Square Feet.	Acres.	Roods.	Perches.	Square Feet.
PES QUADRATUS										.94245	..	..	..	.9425
100	Scrupulum, or Decempeda Quadrata*									94.245	..	..	..	94.245
480	$4\frac{4}{5}$	ACTUS SIMPLEX								452.377	..	.	1	180.127
2400	24	5	UNCIA†							2261.89	..	..	8	83.885
3600	36	$7\frac{1}{2}$	$1\frac{1}{2}$	Clima						3392.83	..	..	12	125.83
14,400	144	30	6	4	ACTUS QUADRATUS					13,571.318	..	1	9	231.07
28,800	288	60	12	8	2	IUGERUM				27,142.636	..	2	19	189.89‡
57,600	576	120	24	16	4	2	Heredium			54,285.272	1	0	39	107.53
5,760,000	57,600	12,000	2400	1600	400	200	100	Centuria.		5,428,527.2	124	2	19	135.25
23,040,000	230,400	48,000	9600	6400	1600	800	400	4	Saltus	21,714,108.8	498	1	37	268.75

* This was the square of the *pertica* or standard 10-foot measuring-rod.

† The *As* to which this *Uncia* and the above *Scrupulum* belong is the *Iugerum*. The other uncial divisions of the *Iugerum* may easily be calculated from the *Uncia*. The *Semissis* is, of course, the *Actus Quadratus*.

‡ i. e. almost ⅝ of an acre. The Italian *Vorsus* was about $^{3}/_{10}$ of a *Iugerum*, or nearly 18 perches.

TABLE VII.

GRECIAN MEASURES OF CAPACITY.

I. ATTIC LIQUID MEASURES. (SOLONIAN.)												Gallons.	Pints.	Approximate.	
														Gallons.	Pints.
Κοχλιάριον												..	.008	..	$\frac{1}{120}$
2	Χήμη											..	.016	..	$\frac{1}{60}$
2½	1¼	Μύστρον										..	.02	.	$\frac{1}{48}$
5	2½	2	Κόγχη									..	.04	.	$\frac{1}{24}$
10	5	4	2	ΚΥ'ΑΘΟΣ								..	.08	..	$\frac{1}{12}$
15	7½	6	3	1½	'Οξύβαφον							..	.12	..	$\frac{1}{8}$
30	15	12	6	3	2	Τέταρτον						..	.24	..	$\frac{1}{4}$
60	30	24	12	6	4	2	Κοτύλη, Τρυβλίον, or Ἡμίνα					..	.48	..	$\frac{1}{2}$
120	60	48	24	12	8	4	2	ΞΕ'ΣΤΗΣ (Sextarius)				..	.96	..	1
720	360	288	144	72	48	24	12	6	ΧΟΥ͂Σ			..	5.76	..	6
5760	2880	2304	1152	576	384	192	96	48	8	ROMAN AMPHORA (κεράμιον)		5	6.08	6	..
8640	4320	3456	1728	864	576	288	144	72	12	1½	ΑΜΦΟΡΕΥ'Σ ΜΕΤΡΗΤΗ'Σ	8	5.12	9	..

NOTE.—The above table is calculated from the κύαθος, as estimated above. If it is estimated at .045 litre, the μετρητής will be determined at about 1 pint less.

TABLE VIII.

ROMAN MEASURES OF CAPACITY.

I. LIQUID MEASURES.											Gallons.	Pints.	Approximate.	
													Gallons.	Pints.
Ligula											..	.02	..	$\frac{1}{48}$
4	CYATHUS*										..	.08	..	$\frac{1}{12}$
6	1½	Acetabulum									..	.12	..	$\frac{1}{8}$
12	3	2	Quartarius, i. e. ¼ of the *Sextarius*								..	.24	..	$\frac{1}{4}$
24	6	4	2	Hemina or Cotyla							..	.48	..	$\frac{1}{2}$
48	12	8	4	2	SEXTARIUS, i. e. $\frac{1}{6}$ of the *Congius*						..	.96	..	1
288	72	48	24	12	6	CONGIUS					..	5.76	..	6
1152	288	192	96	48	24	4	Urna				2	7.04	3	..
2304	576	384	192	96	48	8	2	AMPHORA QUADRANTAL			5	6.08	6	..
46,080	11,520	7680	3840	1920	960	160	40	20	Culeus		115	1.6	120	..

* According to the uncial division, the *Sextarius* was the *As*, and the *Cyathus* the *Uncia*.

NOTE.—The above table is also calculated from the *Cyathus*, determined at .08 pint, and here also a calculation from the *Cyathus* = .045 litre would make a trifling difference in the *Amphora*.

TABLE IX.

GRECIAN MEASURES OF CAPACITY.

II. ATTIC DRY MEASURES. (SOLONIAN.)								Gallons.	Pints.	Approximate.	
										Gallons.	Pints.
ΚΥ'ΑΘΟΣ								..	.08	..	$\frac{1}{12}$
1½	'Οξύβαφον							..	.12	..	$\frac{1}{8}$
6	4	ΚΟΤΥ'ΛΗ, or Ἡμίνα						..	.48	..	$\frac{1}{2}$
12	8	2	ΞΕ'ΣΤΗΣ (*Sextarius*)					..	.96	..	1
24	16	4	2	ΧΟΙ͂ΝΙΞ				..	1.92	..	2
96	64	16	8	4	Ἡμίεκτον			..	7.68	1	..
192	128	32	16	8	2	Ἑκτεύς (equal to the Roman *Modius*)		1	7.36	2	..
1152	768	192	96	48	12	6	ΜΕ'ΔΙΜΝΟΣ	11	4.16	12	..

TABLE X.

ROMAN MEASURES OF CAPACITY.

II. DRY MEASURES.								Gallons.	Pints.	Approximate. Gallons.	Approximate. Pints.
Ligula								..	.02	..	$\frac{1}{48}$
4	CYATHUS*							..	.08	..	$\frac{1}{12}$
6	$1\frac{1}{2}$	Acetabulum						..	.12	..	$\frac{1}{8}$
12	3	2	Quartarius, i. e. $\frac{1}{4}$ of the *Sextarius*					..	.24	..	$\frac{1}{4}$
24	6	4	2	Hemina or Cotyla				..	.48	..	$\frac{1}{2}$
48	12	8	4	2	SEXTARIUS, i. e. $\frac{1}{6}$ of the *Congius*			..	.96	..	1
384	96	64	32	16	8	Semimodius		..	7.68	1	..
768	192	128	64	32	16	2	MODIUS	1	7.36	2	..

* See also Table VIII. and Note.

TABLE XI.

N. B.—One pound avoirdupois is exactly 7000 grains; one ounce avoirdupois is $437\frac{1}{2}$ grains. 1 gramme is 15.43234 grains.

(A.) Aeginetan and Attic Commercial Weights.

					Grammes.	Grains.
Obol					1.05	16
6	Drachm				6.30	97
12	2	Didrachm (στατήρ)			12.60	195
600	100	50	Mina		630	9,750
36,000	6000	3000	60	Talent	37,800	585,000

(B.) Euboic Weights.

				Grammes.	Grains.
Drachm				4.20	65
2	Stater			8.40	130
100	50	Mina		420	6,500
6000	3000	60	Talent	25,200	390,000

N.B.—Just as the Euboic drachm is $\frac{1}{3}$ of the Aeginetan stater, so the Corinthian drachm is $\frac{1}{3}$ of the Euboic stater.

(C.) Attic Weights (Solonian Coinage).

				Grammes.	Grains.
Drachm				4.40	67.5
2	Didrachm or Stater.			8.80	135
100	50	Mina		440	6,750
6000	3000	60	Talent	26,400	405,000

N.B.—It will be seen that the ratio of the Aeginetan stater (195 gr.) to the Attic (135 gr.) is a good deal larger than 100:73 or 138:100 or $83\frac{1}{3}$:60, which are the ratios ascribed to Solon's reduction of the Attic coinage.

(D.) Various Oriental Weights.

			Grammes. (Approximate.)	Grains. (Approximate.)	Avoirdupois. (Approximate.)
1. Egyptian.					
Kat			9	140	$\frac{1}{3}$ oz.
10	Outen or Ten		90	1400	$3\frac{1}{5}$ oz.
2. Babylonian Heavy Gold.					
Shekel			16.83	260	$\frac{3}{5}$ oz.
50	Mina		841.5	13,000	1 lb. $13\frac{5}{7}$ oz.
3000	60	Talent.	50,490	780,000	$111\frac{3}{7}$ lbs.

(D.) Various Oriental Weights.—(*Continued.*)

			Grammes. (Approximate.)	Grains. (Approximate.)	Avoirdupois. (Approximate.)
3. Babylonian Heavy Silver.					
Shekel			22.4	344	4/5 oz.
50	Mina		1,122	17,200	2 lbs. 7 1/3 oz.
3000	60	Talent	67,320	1,032,000	147 3/7 lbs.
4. Babylonian Light Gold and Light Silver Standards were exactly half the heavy gold and heavy silver respectively, so that:					
Light Gold Shekel			8.41	130	3/10 oz.
Light Silver Shekel			11.2	172	2/5 oz.
5. Phœnician Silver.					
Shekel			14.9	230	6/11 oz.
50	Mina		745	11,500	1 lb. 10 2/7 oz.
3000	60	Talent	44,700	690,000	98 4/7 lbs.

TABLE XII.

ROMAN WEIGHTS.

I. THE UNCIAL DIVISIONS OF THE POUND.												Grammes.	Avoirdupois Weight. Oz.	Grs.
UNCIA												27.288	..	430.83 1/3*
1 1/2	Sescuncia, or Sescunx											40.932	1	203.75
2	1 1/3	Sextans										54.576	1	404.16 2/3
3	2	1 1/2	Quadrans, or Teruncius									81.864	2	168.7500
4	2 1/3	2	1 1/3	Triens								109.152	3	270.83 1/3
5	3 1/3	2 1/2	1 2/3	1 1/4	Quincunx							136.440	4	354.16 2/3
6	4	3	2	1 1/2	1 1/5	SEMIS, or Semissis						163.728	5	337.5
7	4 1/3	3 1/2	2 1/3	1 3/4	1 2/5	1 1/6	Septunx					191.016	6	320.33 1/3
8	5 1/3	4	2 2/3	2	1 3/5	1 1/3	1 1/7	Bes, or Bessis				218.304	7	104.16 2/3
9	6	4 1/2	3	2 1/4	1 4/5	1 1/2	1 2/7	1 1/8	Dodrans			245.592	8	277.5
10	6 1/3	5	3 1/3	2 1/2	2	1 2/3	1 3/7	1 1/4	1 1/9	Dextans		272.880	9	270.83 1/3
11	7 1/3	5 1/2	3 2/3	2 3/4	2 1/5	1 5/6	1 4/7	1 3/8	1 2/9	1 1/10	Deunx	300.168	10	260.83 1/3
12	8	6	4	3	2 2/5	2	1 5/7	1 1/2	1 1/3	1 1/5	1 1/11 As, or LIBRA	327.456	11†	237.5†

* This differs from the ounce avoirdupois (437.5 grains) by less than 7 grains. † The *as* is taken at 5050 grains, instead of 5052.55.

TABLE XIII.

ROMAN WEIGHTS.

II. SUBDIVISIONS OF THE UNCIA.										Grains.
Siliqua										2.9224
3	Obolus									8.767361
6	2	SCRUPULUM								17.53472
12	4	2	Semisextula							35.0694
24	8	4	2	SEXTULA						70.138
36	12	6	3	1 1/2	Sicilicus					105.2083
48	16	8	4	2	1 1/3	Duella				140.277
72	24	12	6	3	2	1 1/2	Semuncia			120.416
144	48	24	12	6	4	3	2	UNCIA		420.833
1728	576	288	144	72	48	36	24	12	As, or LIBRA	5050

TABLE XIV.

NORMAL WEIGHTS OF ROMAN COINS IN ENGLISH GRAINS.

	B.C. 350.	B.C. 269.*	B.C. 210.†	B.C. 89.	Augustus.‡	Nero.	Caracalla.§
GOLD.							
Aureus	..	..	52.5	..	126	112	101
SILVER.							
Denarius	..	70	60	60	60	52	..
Quinarius	..	35	30	..	30	26	..
Sestertius	..	17.5	15	..	15	..	..
Victoriatus	..	..	..	45	..	..	..
Antoninianus	..	..	..	..	..	..	84
COPPER.							
Sestertius (brass)	..	..	..	..	420	420	
Dupondius (brass)	..	..	..	..	210	210	
As (*libella*)	5050	1750	421	210	200 ?	200	
Semis	2525	875	210	105	100 ?		

* In B.C 269 1 *denarius* = 4 *sestertii* = 10 *asses* or *libellae*.
† In B.C. 210 1 *denarius* = 1 Attic drachma = 4 *sestertii* = 16 *asses*. (1 *aureus* = 15 *denarii*.)
‡ Temp. Augusti, 1 *aureus* = 26 *denarii* = 100 *sestertii* = 400 *asses*.
§ Temp. Caracallae, 1 *aureus* = 20 *Antoniniani* = 100 *sestertii* = 400 *asses*.

The gold *solidus* of Constantine and his successors weighed a little over 80 grains.

FINIS

70
71
72
74
75
79
81
83
88